# SCRABBLE®
*BRAND Crossword Game*

# DICTIONARY

D1342412

William Collins' dream of knowledge for all began with the publication of his first book in 1819. A self-educated mill worker, he not only enriched millions of lives, but also founded a flourishing publishing house. Today, staying true to this spirit, Collins books are packed with inspiration, innovation, and practical expertise. They place you at the centre of a world of possibility and give you exactly what you need to explore it.

Language is the key to this exploration, and at the heart of Collins Dictionaries is language as it is really used. New words, phrases, and meanings spring up every day, and all of them are captured and analysed by the Collins Word Web. Constantly updated, and with over 2.5 billion entries, this living language resource is unique to our dictionaries.

Words are tools for life. And a Collins Dictionary makes them work for you.

**Collins. Do more.**

# SCRABBLE®
BRAND Crossword Game

# DICTIONARY

Collins

**HarperCollins Publishers**
Westerhill Road
Bishopbriggs
Glasgow
G64 2QT
Great Britain

First edition 2006

Reprint 10 9 8 7 6 5

© HarperCollins Publishers 2006

ISBN 978-0-00-721359-7

www.collins.co.uk

A catalogue record for this book is
available from the British Library

Typeset by Wordcraft, Glasgow

Printed in Great Britain by
Clays Ltd, St Ives plc

**Acknowledgements**
We would like to thank those authors ar
publishers who kindly gave permission :
copyright material to be used in the Coll
Word Web. We would also like to thank
Times Newspapers Ltd for providing
valuable data.

# Contents

vi
Editorial staff and contributors

vii
Introduction

ix
Using the SCRABBLE® Dictionary

xi
Addendum

1–882
SCRABBLE® Dictionary

# Introduction

Collins **SCRABBLE® Dictionary** is an invaluable tool for any competitive or club player, as well as for those who play with their friends and family.

This dictionary contains every word of between two and nine letters, with either a definition or a cross-reference to a defined root word.

It allows every **SCRABBLE®** player, whether a beginner or veteran, access to the definitions of all the most useful words in **SCRABBLE®**, enabling them to learn words by meaning rather than simply as combinations of letters. For many players definitions are the key to remembering words, and to using them in **SCRABBLE®**, and the ability to check meanings, inflections, and variant spellings will add interest to most social games.

The definitions are succinct and practical. In many cases, only a single definition is given, and in general only those parts of speech necessary for existing inflections are included. Cross-referred words include noun plurals, verb inflections, the comparative and superlative forms of adjectives, and variant spellings. Adjectives formed with obvious suffixes, such as *-like* and *-less*, are also cross-referred to the root word when the meaning is easily deduced.

In any **SCRABBLE®** game, most words will be between two and nine letters in length. Therefore, this book contains only those words, and does not include words between 10 and 15 letters in length. This accounts for the omission of some plurals and inflected forms of words that are themselves in the dictionary.

Unlike a conventional dictionary, every word in each section is listed in strict alphabetical order, regardless of the relationship between words. Thus there may be several, or many, words between the singular form of a noun and its plural. This strict alphabetization allows rapid checking of words – which is particularly important during **SCRABBLE®** tournaments.

Collins would like to give warm thanks to Darryl Francis and Allan Simmons for their enormous contribution to the wordlist in this dictionary. They worked tirelessly with the editorial team to get this right. Any errors – and all the definitions in this book – are the responsibility of the publisher.

## Using the Official SCRABBLE® Dictionary

This book includes all playable words of two to nine letters in length, in one straight alphabetical list. These words are either defined or cross-referred. Cross-referred words include noun plurals, verb inflections, the comparative and superlative forms of adjectives, and variant spellings. Adjectives formed with obvious suffixes, such as -*like* and -*less* are also cross-referred to the root word.

In **Collins SCRABBLE® Dictionary**, only a single definition is given for each part of speech, and in general only those parts of speech necessary for existing inflections are included. Some definitions have been sourced from **Collins English Dictionary, Complete and Unabridged**, and other definitions have been written specially for this dictionary. While we have shortened many of the **Collins English Dictionary** definitions for the purpose of this book, they are fuller than the others.

| | |
|---|---|
| **Word order** | **Collins SCRABBLE® Dictionary** is in strict alphabetical order. |
| **Offensive terms** | there may be words in **Collins SCRABBLE® Dictionary** that most or some players might consider derogatory, offensive, or even taboo. |
| **Accents** | as English language SCRABBLE® tiles are not accented, no accents are shown in **Collins SCRABBLE® Dictionary.** |
| **Main entry words** | printed in bold capitals, eg: |

**AA**

All entry words,
in one alphabetical
sequence, eg:

**AA**
**AAH**
**AAHED**
**AAL**
**AALI**

| | |
|---|---|
| **Parts of Speech** | shown in italics as an abbreviation, eg: |

**AA** *n*

When more than one part
of speech is given, the
change of part of speech is
shown after an arrow, eg:

**ABANDON** *vb* desert or leave
▷ *n* lack of inhibition

| Cross-references | noun plurals, verb inflections, comparatives and superlatives, and derivatives are all cross-referred to their root form: |
|---|---|

**ABASH** *vb* cause or feel ill at ease, embarrassed, or confused

...

**ABASHES** > ABASH
**ABASHING** > ABASH
**ABASHLESS** > ABASH
**ABASHMENT** > ABASH

| Variant forms | variant forms and synonyms are cross-referred to the most commonly-used form of a word, eg: |
|---|---|

**CAFTAN** *same as* > KAFTAN

noun plurals, verb inflections, comparitives, superlatives, and derivatives of the variant form are all cross-referred to the root form of that particular variant, eg

**CAFTAN** *same as* > KAFTAN
...

**CAFTANS** > CAFTAN

| Phrases | when a word is most comonly used in a phrase, the phrase is given in italics and defined, eg: |
|---|---|

**BANGALORE** as in *bangalore torpedo* explosive device in a long metal tube, used to blow gaps in barbed-wire barriers

The following words are also eligible for SCRABBLE®:

ARCHEAN
ASHRAF
CANAPES
COURIERED
EDITIONED
GRICED
HUNNISH
JAMMINGS
JONGS
KLETT
KLETTS
LINELESS
LIPAEMIAS
MAASES
MATCHPLAY
MIRANDISE
NATIS
OUS
PEEKABO
PEEKABOS
PEREGALS
PERFINGS
PERIBOLI
PEROXO
PHILAMOT
PHILAMOTS
PHYCOCYAN
PINKERS
PINKIER
PINKIEST

PINTADAS
PIRNIES
PISCINES
PLANARIAS
PLATONICS
PLINKINGS
PLUMPIE
PODAL
PODDIER
PODDIEST
POLTFEET
PONCEAUX
PONKED
PONKING
PONTIE
PONTILES
POSTALS
POUFF
POWTERED
POWTERING
PRACTICS
PRAEDIALS
PRAIRIED
PRATFELL
PRATTED
PRATTING
PRATTS
PRAYINGLY
PREADOPT
PREADOPTS

PRECIEUX
PREDIALS
PREDIED
PREDIES
PREDYING
PREFARD
PREHIRING
PREJUDIZE
PRELIVES
PREMIXT
PRESSFULS
PRESSORS
PREZES
PRIMATALS
PRINCESSE
PROPINE
PROPINED
PROPINES
PROPINING
PROWESSED
PROYNED
PROYNING
PRYSED
PRYSES
PRYSING
PSHAWED
PSHAWING
PSOASES
PTYXISES
PUBISES

PUDDENING
PULVINULE
PUZEL
PUZELS
PYEING
PYGALS
PYONERS
PYONINGS
PYROSISES
RANCOURED
RECLADDED
RECLADS
RHEOPHILE
SADDOES
SENSI
SENSIS
SMUDGINGS
SNIDED
SNIDING
SPOOFINGS
STETSON
STETSONS
TAPUED
TAPUING
TEXTED
TEXTING
TOGGERED
TOGGERING
UNCOES

# Aa

**AA** *n* volcanic rock consisting of angular blocks of lava with a very rough surface

**AAH** *vb* exclaim in pleasure or surprise

**AAHED** > AAH

**AAHING** > AAH

**AAHS** > AAH

**AAL** *n* Asian shrub or tree

**AALII** *n* bushy sapindaceous shrub, *Dodonaea viscosa*, of Australia, Hawaii, Africa, and tropical America, having small greenish flowers and sticky foliage

**AALIIS** > AALII

**AALS** > AAL

**AARDVARK** *n* S African anteater with long ears and snout

**AARDVARKS** > AARDVARK

**AARDWOLF** *n* nocturnal mammal, *Proteles cristatus*, that inhabits the plains of southern Africa and feeds on termites and insect larvae: family *Hyaenidae* (hyenas), order *Carnivora* (carnivores)

**AARGH** *interj* cry of pain

**AARRGH** *interj* cry of pain

**AARRGHH** *interj* cry of pain

**AARTI** *n* Hindu ceremony in which lights with wicks soaked in ghee are lit and offered up to one or more deities

**AARTIS** > AARTI

**AAS** > AA

**AASVOGEL** *n* South African bird of prey

**AASVOGELS** > AASVOGEL

**AB** *n* abdominal muscle

**ABA** *n* type of cloth from Syria, made of goat hair or camel hair

**ABAC** *n* mathematical diagram

**ABACA** *n* Philippine plant, *Musa textilis*, related to the banana: family *Musaceae*. Its leafstalks are the source of Manila hemp

**ABACAS** > ABACA

**ABACI** > ABACUS

**ABACK** *adv* towards the back; backwards

**ABACS** > ABAC

**ABACTINAL** *adj* (of organisms showing radial symmetry) situated away from or opposite to the mouth

**ABACTOR** *n* cattle thief

**ABACTORS** > ABACTOR

**ABACUS** *n* beads on a wire frame, used for doing calculations

**ABACUSES** > ABACUS

**ABAFT** *adv* closer to the rear of (a ship) ▷ *adj* closer to the stern of a ship

**ABAKA** *n* abaca

**ABAKAS** > ABAKA

**ABALONE** *n* edible sea creature with a shell lined with mother of pearl

**ABALONES** > ABALONE

**ABAMP** same as > ABAMPERE

**ABAMPERE** *n* cgs unit of current in the electromagnetic system

**ABAMPERES** > ABAMPERE

**ABAMPS** > ABAMP

**ABAND** *vb* abandon

**ABANDED** > ABAND

**ABANDING** > ABAND

**ABANDON** *vb* desert or leave (one's wife, children, etc) ▷ *n* lack of inhibition

**ABANDONED** *adj* deserted

**ABANDONEE** *n* person to whom something is formally relinquished, esp an insurer having the right to salvage a wreck

**ABANDONER** > ABANDON

**ABANDONS** > ABANDON

**ABANDS** > ABAND

**ABAPICAL** *adj* away from or opposite the apex

**ABAS** > ABA

**ABASE** *vb* humiliate or degrade (oneself)

**ABASED** > ABASE

**ABASEDLY** > ABASE

**ABASEMENT** > ABASE

**ABASER** > ABASE

**ABASERS** > ABASE

**ABASES** > ABASE

**ABASH** *vb* cause to feel ill at ease, embarrassed, or confused

**ABASHED** *adj* embarrassed and ashamed

**ABASHEDLY** > ABASHED

**ABASHES** > ABASH

**ABASHING** > ABASH

**ABASHLESS** > ABASH

**ABASHMENT** > ABASH

**ABASIA** *n* disorder affecting ability to walk

**ABASIAS** > ABASIA

**ABASING** > ABASE

**ABASK** *adv* in pleasant warmth

**ABATABLE** > ABATE

**ABATE** *vb* make or become less strong

**ABATED** > ABATE

**ABATEMENT** *n* diminution or alleviation

**ABATER** > ABATE

**ABATERS** > ABATE

**ABATES** > ABATE

**ABATING** > ABATE

**ABATIS** *n* rampart of felled trees bound together, placed with their branches outwards

**ABATISES** > ABATIS

**ABATOR** *n* person who effects an abatement

**ABATORS** > ABATOR

**ABATTIS** same as > ABATIS

**ABATTISES** > ABATTIS

**ABATTOIR** *n* place where animals are killed for food

**ABATTOIRS** > ABATTOIR

**ABATTU** *adj* dejected

**ABATURE** *n* trail left by hunted stag

**ABATURES** > ABATURE

**ABAXIAL** *adj* facing away from the axis, as the surface of a leaf

**ABAXILE** *adj* away from the axis

**ABAYA** *n* Arab outer garment

**ABAYAS** > ABAYA

**ABB** *n* yarn used in weaving

**ABBA** *n* title for a bishop in the Coptic Church

**ABBACIES** > ABBACY

**ABBACY** *n* office or jurisdiction of an abbot or abbess

**ABBAS** > ABBA

**ABBATIAL** *adj* of or relating

1

to an abbot, abbess, or abbey

**ABBE** *n* French abbot

**ABBED** *adj* displaying well-developed abdominal muscles

**ABBES** > ABBE

**ABBESS** *n* nun in charge of a convent

**ABBESSES** > ABBESS

**ABBEY** *n* dwelling place of, or a church belonging to, a community of monks or nuns

**ABBEYS** > ABBEY

**ABBOT** *n* head of an abbey of monks

**ABBOTCIES** > ABBOT

**ABBOTCY** > ABBOT

**ABBOTS** > ABBOT

**ABBOTSHIP** > ABBOT

**ABBS** > ABB

**ABCEE** *n* alphabet

**ABCEES** > ABCEE

**ABCOULOMB** *n* cgs unit of electric charge in the electromagnetic system

**ABDABS** *n* highly nervous state

**ABDICABLE** > ABDICATE

**ABDICANT** > ABDICATE

**ABDICATE** *vb* give up (the throne or a responsibility)

**ABDICATED** > ABDICATE

**ABDICATES** > ABDICATE

**ABDICATOR** > ABDICATE

**ABDOMEN** *n* part of the body containing the stomach and intestines

**ABDOMENS** > ABDOMEN

**ABDOMINA** > ABDOMEN

**ABDOMINAL** > ABDOMEN

**ABDUCE** *vb* abduct

**ABDUCED** > ABDUCE

**ABDUCENS** as in *abducens nerve* either of the sixth pair of cranial nerves, which supply the lateral rectus muscle of the eye

**ABDUCENT** *adj* (of a muscle) abducting

**ABDUCES** > ABDUCE

**ABDUCING** > ABDUCE

**ABDUCT** *vb* carry off, kidnap

**ABDUCTED** > ABDUCT

**ABDUCTEE** > ABDUCT

**ABDUCTEES** > ABDUCT

**ABDUCTING** > ABDUCT

**ABDUCTION** *n* act of taking someone away by force or cunning

**ABDUCTOR** > ABDUCT

**ABDUCTORS** > ABDUCT

**ABDUCTS** > ABDUCT

**ABEAM** *adj* at right angles to the length of a ship or aircraft

**ABEAR** *vb* bear or behave

**ABEARING** > ABEAR

**ABEARS** > ABEAR

**ABED** *adv* in bed

**ABEGGING** *adj* in the act of begging for money etc

**ABEIGH** *adv* aloof

**ABELE** *n* white poplar tree

**ABELES** > ABELE

**ABELIA** *n* garden plant with pink or white flowers

**ABELIAN** > ABELIA

**ABELIAS** > ABELIA

**ABELMOSK** *n* tropical bushy malvaceous plant, *Hibiscus abelmoschus*, cultivated for its yellow-and-crimson flowers and for its musk-scented seeds, which yield an oil used in perfumery

**ABELMOSKS** > ABELMOSK

**ABERNETHY** *n* crisp unleavened biscuit

**ABERRANCE** > ABERRANT

**ABERRANCY** > ABERRANT

**ABERRANT** *adj* showing aberration ▷ *n* person whose behaviour is considered to be aberrant

**ABERRANTS** > ABERRANT

**ABERRATE** *vb* deviate from what is normal or correct

**ABERRATED** > ABERRATE

**ABERRATES** > ABERRATE

**ABESSIVE** *n* grammatical case indicating absence

**ABESSIVES** > ABESSIVE

**ABET** *vb* help or encourage in wrongdoing

**ABETMENT** > ABET

**ABETMENTS** > ABET

**ABETS** > ABET

**ABETTAL** > ABET

**ABETTALS** > ABET

**ABETTED** > ABET

**ABETTER** > ABET

**ABETTERS** > ABET

**ABETTING** > ABET

**ABETTOR** > ABET

**ABETTORS** > ABET

**ABEYANCE** *n* state of being suspended or put aside temporarily

**ABEYANCES** > ABEYANCE

**ABEYANCY** *n* abeyance

**ABEYANT** > ABEYANCE

**ABFARAD** *n* cgs unit of capacitance in the electromagnetic system

**ABFARADS** > ABFARAD

**ABHENRIES** > ABHENRY

**ABHENRY** *n* cgs unit of inductance in the electromagnetic system

**ABHENRYS** > ABHENRY

**ABHOR** *vb* detest utterly

**ABHORRED** > ABHOR

**ABHORRENT** *adj* hateful, loathsome

**ABHORRER** > ABHOR

**ABHORRERS** > ABHOR

**ABHORRING** > ABHOR

**ABHORS** > ABHOR

**ABID** > ABIDE

**ABIDANCE** > ABIDE

**ABIDANCES** > ABIDE

**ABIDDEN** > ABIDE

**ABIDE** *vb* endure, put up with

**ABIDED** > ABIDE

**ABIDER** > ABIDE

**ABIDERS** > ABIDE

**ABIDES** > ABIDE

**ABIDING** *adj* lasting ▷ *n* action of one who abides

**ABIDINGLY** > ABIDING

**ABIDINGS** > ABIDING

**ABIES** *n* fir tree

**ABIETIC** *adj* pertaining to fir trees

**ABIGAIL** *n* maid for a lady

**ABIGAILS** > ABIGAIL

**ABILITIES** > ABILITY

**ABILITY** *n* competence, power

**ABIOGENIC** *adj* abiogenetic

**ABIOSES** > ABIOSIS

**ABIOSIS** *n* absence of life

**ABIOTIC** > ABIOSIS

**ABJECT** *adj* utterly miserable ▷ *vb* throw down

**ABJECTED** > ABJECT

**ABJECTING** > ABJECT

**ABJECTION** > ABJECT

**ABJECTLY** > ABJECT

**ABJECTS** > ABJECT

**ABJOINT** *vb* cut off

**ABJOINTED** > ABJOINT

**ABJOINTS** > ABJOINT

**ABJURE** *vb* deny or renounce on oath

**ABJURED** > ABJURE

**ABJURER** > ABJURE

**ABJURERS** > ABJURE

**ABJURES** > ABJURE

**ABJURING** > ABJURE

**ABLATE** *vb* remove by ablation

**ABLATED** > ABLATE

**ABLATES** > ABLATE

**ABLATING** > ABLATE

**ABLATION** *n* surgical removal of an organ or part

**ABLATIONS** > ABLATION

**ABLATIVAL** > ABLATIVE

**ABLATIVE** *n* case of nouns in Latin and other languages, indicating source, agent, or instrument of action ▷ *adj* (in certain inflected languages such as Latin) denoting a case of nouns, pronouns, and adjectives indicating the agent in passive sentences or the instrument, manner, or place of the action described by the verb

**ABLATIVES** > ABLATIVE

**ABLATOR** *n* heat shield of a space vehicle, which melts or wears away during re-entry into the earth's atmosphere

**ABLATORS** > ABLATOR

**ABLAUT** *n* vowel gradation, esp in Indo-European languages

**ABLAUTS** > ABLAUT

**ABLAZE** *adj* burning fiercely ▷ *adv* on fire

**ABLE** *adj* capable, competent ▷ *vb* enable

**ABLED** *adj* having a range of physical powers as specified

**ABLEGATE** *n* papal envoy

**ABLEGATES** > ABLEGATE

**ABLEISM** *n* discrimination against disabled or handicapped people

**ABLEISMS** > ABLEISM

**ABLEIST** > ABLEISM

**ABLEISTS** > ABLEISM

**ABLER** > ABLE

**ABLES** > ABLE

**ABLEST** > ABLE

**ABLET** *n* freshwater fish

**ABLETS** > ABLET

**ABLING** > ABLE

**ABLINGS** *adv* possibly

**ABLINS** *adv* Scots word meaning perhaps

**ABLOOM** *adj* in flower

**ABLOW** *adj* blooming

**ABLUENT** *n* substance used for cleansing

**ABLUENTS** > ABLUENT

**ABLUSH** *adj* blushing

**ABLUTED** *adj* washed thoroughly

**ABLUTION** *n* ritual washing of a priest's hands or of sacred vessels

**ABLUTIONS** > ABLUTION

**ABLY** *adv* competently or skilfully

**ABMHO** *n* unit of electrical conductance

**ABMHOS** > ABMHO

**ABNEGATE** *vb* deny to oneself

**ABNEGATED** > ABNEGATE

**ABNEGATES** > ABNEGATE

**ABNEGATOR** > ABNEGATE

**ABNORMAL** *adj* not normal or usual ▷ *n* abnormal person or thing

**ABNORMALS** > ABNORMAL

**ABNORMITY** > ABNORMAL

**ABNORMOUS** > ABNORMAL

**ABO** *offensive name for* > ABORIGINE

**ABOARD** *adv* on, in, onto, or into (a ship, train, or plane) ▷ *prep* on, in, onto, or into (a ship, plane, or train)

**ABODE** *n* home, dwelling ▷ *vb* forebode

**ABODED** > ABODE

**ABODEMENT** > ABODE

**ABODES** > ABODE

**ABODING** > ABODE

**ABOHM** *n* cgs unit of resistance in the electromagnetic system: equivalent to $10^{-9}$ ohm

**ABOHMS** > ABOHM

**ABOIDEAU** *n* dyke with a sluicegate that allows flood water to drain but keeps the sea water out

**ABOIDEAUS** > ABOIDEAU

**ABOIDEAUX** > ABOIDEAU

**ABOIL** *adj* boiling

**ABOITEAU** *same as* > ABOIDEAU

**ABOITEAUS** >ABOITEAU
**ABOITEAUX** >ABOITEAU
**ABOLISH** vb do away with
**ABOLISHED** >ABOLISH
**ABOLISHER** >ABOLISH
**ABOLISHES** >ABOLISH
**ABOLITION** n act of
abolishing or the state of
being abolished
**ABOLLA** n Roman cloak
**ABOLLAE** >ABOLLA
**ABOLLAS** >ABOLLA
**ABOMA** n South American
snake
**ABOMAS** >ABOMA
**ABOMASA** >ABOMASUM
**ABOMASAL** >ABOMASUM
**ABOMASI** >ABOMASUM
**ABOMASUM** n fourth and
last compartment of the
stomach of ruminants,
which receives and digests
food from the psalterium
and passes it on to the
small intestine
**ABOMASUS** n abomasum
**ABOMINATE** vb dislike
intensely
**ABONDANCE** same
as >ABUNDANCE
**ABOON** Scots word
for >ABOVE
**ABORAL** adj away from or
opposite the mouth
**ABORALLY** >ABORAL
**ABORD** vb accost
**ABORDED** >ABORD
**ABORDING** >ABORD
**ABORDS** >ABORD
**ABORE** >ABEAR
**ABORIGEN** n aborigine
**ABORIGENS** >ABORIGEN
**ABORIGIN** n aborigine
**ABORIGINE** n original
inhabitant of a country or
region, esp Australia
**ABORIGINS** >ABORIGIN
**ABORNE** adj Shakespearean
form of auburn
**ABORNING** >ABEAR
**ABORT** vb have an abortion
or perform an abortion
on ▷ n premature
termination or failure of
(a space flight, military
operation, etc)
**ABORTED** >ABORT
**ABORTEE** n woman having
an abortion
**ABORTEES** >ABORTEE
**ABORTER** >ABORT
**ABORTERS** >ABORT
**ABORTING** >ABORT
**ABORTION** n operation to
end a pregnancy
**ABORTIONS** >ABORTION
**ABORTIVE** adj unsuccessful
**ABORTS** >ABORT
**ABORTUARY** n place where
abortions are carried out
**ABORTUS** n aborted fetus
**ABORTUSES** >ABORTUS
**ABOS** >ABO
**ABOUGHT** >ABY

**ABOULIA** same as >ABULIA
**ABOULIAS** >ABOULIA
**ABOULIC** >ABOULIA
**ABOUND** vb be plentiful
**ABOUNDED** >ABOUND
**ABOUNDING** >ABOUND
**ABOUNDS** >ABOUND
**ABOUT** adv nearly,
approximately
**ABOUTS** prep about
**ABOVE** adv over or higher
(than) ▷ n something that
is or appears above
**ABOVES** >ABOVE
**ABRACHIA** n condition of
having no arms
**ABRACHIAS** >ABRACHIA
**ABRADABLE** >ABRADE
**ABRADANT** >ABRADE
**ABRADANTS** >ABRADE
**ABRADE** vb scrape away or
wear down by friction
**ABRADED** >ABRADE
**ABRADER** >ABRADE
**ABRADERS** >ABRADE
**ABRADES** >ABRADE
**ABRADING** >ABRADE
**ABRAID** vb awake
**ABRAIDED** >ABRAID
**ABRAIDING** >ABRAID
**ABRAIDS** >ABRAID
**ABRAM** adj auburn
**ABRASAX** same as >ABRAXAS
**ABRASAXES** >ABRASAX
**ABRASION** n scraped area
on the skin
**ABRASIONS** >ABRASION
**ABRASIVE** adj harsh and
unpleasant in manner ▷ n
substance for cleaning or
polishing by rubbing
**ABRASIVES** >ABRASIVE
**ABRAXAS** n ancient charm
composed of Greek letters:
originally believed to
have magical powers and
inscribed on amulets,
etc, but from the second
century AD personified
by Gnostics as a deity,
the source of divine
emanations
**ABRAXASES** >ABRAXAS
**ABRAY** vb awake
**ABRAYED** >ABRAY
**ABRAYING** >ABRAY
**ABRAYS** >ABRAY
**ABRAZO** n embrace
**ABRAZOS** >ABRAZO
**ABREACT** vb alleviate
(emotional tension)
through abreaction
**ABREACTED** >ABREACT
**ABREACTS** >ABREACT
**ABREAST** adj side by side
**ABREGE** n abridgment
**ABREGES** >ABREGE
**ABRI** n shelter or place of
refuge, esp in wartime
**ABRICOCK** n apricot
**ABRICOCKS** >ABRICOCK
**ABRIDGE** vb shorten by
using fewer words
**ABRIDGED** >ABRIDGE

**ABRIDGER** >ABRIDGE
**ABRIDGERS** >ABRIDGE
**ABRIDGES** >ABRIDGE
**ABRIDGING** >ABRIDGE
**ABRIM** adj full to the brim
**ABRIN** n poisonous
compound
**ABRINS** >ABRIN
**ABRIS** >ABRI
**ABROACH** adj (of a cask,
barrel, etc) tapped
**ABROAD** adv in a foreign
country ▷ adj (of news,
rumours, etc) in general
circulation ▷ n foreign
place
**ABROADS** >ABROAD
**ABROGABLE** adj able to be
abrogated
**ABROGATE** vb cancel (a law
or agreement) formally
**ABROGATED** >ABROGATE
**ABROGATES** >ABROGATE
**ABROGATOR** >ABROGATE
**ABROOKE** vb bear or tolerate
**ABROOKED** >ABROOKE
**ABROOKES** >ABROOKE
**ABROOKING** >ABROOKE
**ABROSIA** n condition
involving refusal to eat
**ABROSIAS** >ABROSIA
**ABRUPT** adj sudden,
unexpected ▷ n abyss
**ABRUPTER** >ABRUPT
**ABRUPTEST** >ABRUPT
**ABRUPTION** n breaking off
of a part or parts from a
mass
**ABRUPTLY** >ABRUPT
**ABRUPTS** >ABRUPT
**ABS** >AB
**ABSCESS** n inflamed
swelling containing
pus ▷ vb form a swelling
containing pus
**ABSCESSED** >ABSCESS
**ABSCESSES** >ABSCESS
**ABSCIND** vb cut off
**ABSCINDED** >ABSCIND
**ABSCINDS** >ABSCIND
**ABSCISE** vb separate or be
separated by abscission
**ABSCISED** >ABSCISE
**ABSCISES** >ABSCISE
**ABSCISIN** n plant hormone
**ABSCISING** >ABSCISE
**ABSCISINS** >ABSCISIN
**ABSCISS** n cutting off
**ABSCISSA** n cutting off
**ABSCISSAE** >ABSCISSA
**ABSCISSAS** >ABSCISSA
**ABSCISSE** n cutting off
**ABSCISSES** >ABSCISSE
**ABSCISSIN** n plant
hormone
**ABSCOND** vb leave secretly
**ABSCONDED** >ABSCOND
**ABSCONDER** >ABSCOND
**ABSCONDS** >ABSCOND
**ABSEIL** vb go down a steep
drop by a rope fastened at
the top and tied around
one's body ▷ n instance of
abseiling

**ABSEILED** >ABSEIL
**ABSEILING** >ABSEIL
**ABSEILS** >ABSEIL
**ABSENCE** n being away
**ABSENCES** >ABSENCE
**ABSENT** adj not present
▷ vb stay away
**ABSENTED** >ABSENT
**ABSENTEE** n person who
should be present but is
not
**ABSENTEES** >ABSENTEE
**ABSENTER** >ABSENT
**ABSENTERS** >ABSENT
**ABSENTING** >ABSENT
**ABSENTLY** adv in an absent-
minded or preoccupied
manner
**ABSENTS** >ABSENT
**ABSEY** n alphabet
**ABSEYS** >ABSEY
**ABSINTH** same
as >ABSINTHE
**ABSINTHE** n strong green
aniseed-flavoured liqueur
**ABSINTHES** >ABSINTHE
**ABSINTHS** >ABSINTH
**ABSIT** n overnight leave
from college
**ABSITS** >ABSIT
**ABSOLUTE** adj complete,
perfect ▷ n something
that is absolute
**ABSOLUTER** >ABSOLUTE
**ABSOLUTES** >ABSOLUTE
**ABSOLVE** vb declare to be
free from blame or sin
**ABSOLVED** >ABSOLVE
**ABSOLVENT** n something
that absolves
**ABSOLVER** >ABSOLVE
**ABSOLVERS** >ABSOLVE
**ABSOLVES** >ABSOLVE
**ABSOLVING** >ABSOLVE
**ABSONANT** adj unnatural
and unreasonable
**ABSORB** vb soak up (a
liquid)
**ABSORBANT** n absorbent
substance
**ABSORBATE** n absorbed
substance
**ABSORBED** adj engrossed
**ABSORBENT** adj able
to absorb liquid ▷ n
substance that absorbs
**ABSORBER** n person or
thing that absorbs
**ABSORBERS** >ABSORBER
**ABSORBING** adj occupying
one's interest or attention
**ABSORBS** >ABSORB
**ABSTAIN** vb choose not to
do something
**ABSTAINED** >ABSTAIN
**ABSTAINER** >ABSTAIN
**ABSTAINS** >ABSTAIN
**ABSTERGE** vb cleanse
**ABSTERGED** >ABSTERGE
**ABSTERGES** >ABSTERGE
**ABSTINENT** adj refraining
from a certain activity
**ABSTRACT** adj existing as
a quality or idea rather

3

than a material object ▷ *n* summary ▷ *vb* summarize

**ABSTRACTS** >ABSTRACT

**ABSTRICT** *vb* release

**ABSTRICTS** >ABSTRICT

**ABSTRUSE** *adj* not easy to understand

**ABSTRUSER** >ABSTRUSE

**ABSURD** *adj* incongruous or ridiculous ▷ *n* conception of the world, esp in Existentialist thought, as neither designed nor predictable but irrational and meaningless

**ABSURDER** >ABSURD

**ABSURDEST** >ABSURD

**ABSURDISM** *n* belief that life is meaningless

**ABSURDIST** >ABSURDISM

**ABSURDITY** >ABSURD

**ABSURDLY** >ABSURD

**ABSURDS** >ABSURD

**ABTHANE** *n* ancient Scottish church territory

**ABTHANES** >ABTHANE

**ABUBBLE** *adj* bubbling

**ABUILDING** *adj* being built

**ABULIA** *n* pathological inability to take decisions

**ABULIAS** >ABULIA

**ABULIC** >ABULIA

**ABUNA** *n* male head of Ethiopian family

**ABUNAS** >ABUNA

**ABUNDANCE** *n* copious supply

**ABUNDANCY** *n* abundance

**ABUNDANT** *adj* plentiful

**ABUNE** *Scots word for* >ABOVE

**ABURST** *adj* bursting

**ABUSABLE** >ABUSE

**ABUSAGE** *n* wrong use

**ABUSAGES** >ABUSAGE

**ABUSE** *vb* use wrongly ▷ *n* prolonged ill-treatment

**ABUSED** >ABUSE

**ABUSER** >ABUSE

**ABUSERS** >ABUSE

**ABUSES** >ABUSE

**ABUSING** >ABUSE

**ABUSION** *n* wrong use or deception

**ABUSIONS** >ABUSION

**ABUSIVE** *adj* rude or insulting

**ABUSIVELY** >ABUSIVE

**ABUT** *vb* be next to or touching

**ABUTILON** *n* any shrub or herbaceous plant of the malvaceous genus *Abutilon*, such as the flowering maple, that have showy white, yellow, or red flowers

**ABUTILONS** >ABUTILON

**ABUTMENT** *n* construction that supports the end of a bridge

**ABUTMENTS** >ABUTMENT

**ABUTS** >ABUT

**ABUTTAL** *same*

*as* >ABUTMENT

**ABUTTALS** >ABUTTAL

**ABUTTED** >ABUT

**ABUTTER** *n* owner of adjoining property

**ABUTTERS** >ABUTTER

**ABUTTING** >ABUT

**ABUZZ** *adj* noisy, busy with activity etc

**ABVOLT** *n* cgs unit of potential difference in the electromagnetic system

**ABVOLTS** >ABVOLT

**ABWATT** *n* cgs unit of power in the electromagnetic system, equal to the power dissipated when a current of 1 abampere flows across a potential difference of 1 abvolt: equivalent to 10⁻⁷ watt

**ABWATTS** >ABWATT

**ABY** *vb* pay the penalty for

**ABYE** *same as* >ABY

**ABYEING** >ABYE

**ABYES** >ABYE

**ABYING** >ABY

**ABYS** >ABY

**ABYSM** *archaic word for* >ABYSS

**ABYSMAL** *adj* extremely bad, awful

**ABYSMALLY** >ABYSMAL

**ABYSMS** >ABYSM

**ABYSS** *n* very deep hole or chasm

**ABYSSAL** *adj* of or belonging to the ocean depths, esp below 2000 metres (6500 feet)

**ABYSSES** >ABYSS

**ACACIA** *n* tree or shrub with yellow or white flowers

**ACACIAS** >ACACIA

**ACADEME** *n* place of learning

**ACADEMES** >ACADEME

**ACADEMIA** *n* academic world

**ACADEMIAS** >ACADEMIA

**ACADEMIC** *adj* of an academy or university ▷ *n* lecturer or researcher at a university

**ACADEMICS** >ACADEMIC

**ACADEMIES** >ACADEMY

**ACADEMISM** *n* adherence to rules and traditions in art, literature, etc

**ACADEMIST** >ACADEMY

**ACADEMY** *n* society to advance arts or sciences

**ACAI** *n* berry found in Brazilian rainforest

**ACAIS** >ACAI

**ACAJOU** *n* type of mahogany used by cabinet-makers in France

**ACAJOUS** >ACAJOU

**ACALCULIA** *n* inability to make simple mathematical calculations

**ACALEPH** *n* any of the coelenterates of the former taxonomic group *Acalephae*, which included the jellyfishes

**ACALEPHAE** >ACALEPH

**ACALEPHAN** >ACALEPH

**ACALEPHE** *n* acaleph

**ACALEPHES** >ACALEPHE

**ACALEPHS** >ACALEPH

**ACANTH** *n* acanthus

**ACANTHA** *n* thorn or prickle

**ACANTHAE** >ACANTHA

**ACANTHAS** >ACANTHA

**ACANTHI** >ACANTHUS

**ACANTHIN** *n* organic chemical used in medicine

**ACANTHINE** *adj* of or resembling an acanthus

**ACANTHINS** >ACANTHIN

**ACANTHOID** *adj* resembling a spine

**ACANTHOUS** *adj* of an acanthus

**ACANTHS** >ACANTH

**ACANTHUS** *n* prickly plant

**ACAPNIA** *n* lack of carbon dioxide

**ACAPNIAS** >ACAPNIA

**ACARBOSE** *n* diabetes medicine

**ACARBOSES** >ACARBOSE

**ACARI** >ACARUS

**ACARIAN** >ACARUS

**ACARIASES** >ACARIASIS

**ACARIASIS** *n* infestation of the hair follicles and skin with acarids, esp mites

**ACARICIDE** *n* any drug or formulation for killing acarids

**ACARID** *n* any of the small arachnids of the order *Acarina* (or *Acari*), which includes the ticks and mites ▷ *adj* of or relating to the order *Acarina*

**ACARIDAN** *same as* >ACARID

**ACARIDANS** >ACARIDAN

**ACARIDEAN** >ACARID

**ACARIDIAN** >ACARID

**ACARIDS** >ACARID

**ACARINE** *n* acarid

**ACARINES** >ACARINE

**ACAROID** *adj* resembling a mite or tick

**ACAROLOGY** *n* study of mites and ticks

**ACARPOUS** *adj* (of plants) producing no fruit

**ACARUS** *n* any of the free-living mites of the widely distributed genus *Acarus*, several of which, esp *A. siro*, are serious pests of stored flour, grain, etc

**ACATER** *n* buyer of provisions

**ACATERS** >ACATER

**ACATES** *n* provisions

**ACATOUR** *n* buyer of provisions

**ACATOURS** >ACATOUR

**ACAUDAL** *adj* having no tail

**ACAUDATE** *same as* >ACAUDAL

**ACAULINE** *adj* having no stem

**ACAULOSE** *same as* >ACAULINE

**ACAULOUS** *adj* having a short stem or no stem

**ACCA** *n* academic

**ACCABLE** *adj* dejected or beaten

**ACCAS** >ACCA

**ACCEDE** *vb* consent or agree (to)

**ACCEDED** >ACCEDE

**ACCEDENCE** >ACCEDE

**ACCEDER** >ACCEDE

**ACCEDERS** >ACCEDE

**ACCEDES** >ACCEDE

**ACCEDING** >ACCEDE

**ACCEND** *vb* set alight

**ACCENDED** >ACCEND

**ACCENDING** >ACCEND

**ACCENDS** >ACCEND

**ACCENSION** >ACCEND

**ACCENT** *n* distinctive style of pronunciation of a local, national, or social group ▷ *vb* place emphasis on

**ACCENTED** >ACCENT

**ACCENTING** >ACCENT

**ACCENTOR** *n* any small sparrow-like songbird of the genus *Prunella*, family *Prunellidae*, which inhabit mainly mountainous regions of Europe and Asia

**ACCENTORS** >ACCENTOR

**ACCENTS** >ACCENT

**ACCENTUAL** *adj* of, relating to, or having accents

**ACCEPT** *vb* receive willingly

**ACCEPTANT** *adj* receiving willingly

**ACCEPTED** *adj* generally approved

**ACCEPTEE** *n* person who has been accepted

**ACCEPTEES** >ACCEPTEE

**ACCEPTER** >ACCEPT

**ACCEPTERS** >ACCEPT

**ACCEPTING** >ACCEPT

**ACCEPTIVE** *adj* ready to accept

**ACCEPTOR** *n* person or organization on which a draft or bill of exchange is drawn after liability has been accepted, usually by signature

**ACCEPTORS** >ACCEPTOR

**ACCEPTS** >ACCEPT

**ACCESS** *n* means of or right to approach or enter ▷ *vb* obtain (data) from a computer

**ACCESSARY** *same as* >ACCESSORY

**ACCESSED** >ACCESS

**ACCESSES** >ACCESS

**ACCESSING** >ACCESS

**ACCESSION** *n* taking up of an office or position ▷ *vb* make a record of

(additions to a collection)

**ACCESSORY** n supplementary part or object ▷ adj supplementary

**ACCIDENCE** n inflectional morphology

**ACCIDENT** n mishap, often causing injury

**ACCIDENTS** > ACCIDENT

**ACCIDIA** same as > ACCIDIE

**ACCIDIAS** > ACCIDIA

**ACCIDIE** n spiritual sloth

**ACCIDIES** > ACCIDIE

**ACCINGE** vb put a belt around

**ACCINGED** > ACCINGE

**ACCINGES** > ACCINGE

**ACCINGING** > ACCINGE

**ACCIPITER** n any hawk of the genus Accipiter, typically having short rounded wings and a long tail

**ACCITE** vb summon

**ACCITED** > ACCITE

**ACCITES** > ACCITE

**ACCITING** > ACCITE

**ACCLAIM** vb applaud, praise ▷ n enthusiastic approval

**ACCLAIMED** > ACCLAIM

**ACCLAIMER** > ACCLAIM

**ACCLAIMS** > ACCLAIM

**ACCLIMATE** vb adapt or become accustomed to a new climate or environment

**ACCLIVITY** n upward slope, esp of the ground

**ACCLIVOUS** > ACCLIVITY

**ACCLOY** vb choke or clog

**ACCLOYED** > ACCLOY

**ACCLOYING** > ACCLOY

**ACCLOYS** > ACCLOY

**ACCOAST** vb accost

**ACCOASTED** > ACCOAST

**ACCOASTS** > ACCOAST

**ACCOIED** > ACCOY

**ACCOIL** n welcome ▷ vb gather together

**ACCOILS** > ACCOIL

**ACCOLADE** n award or praise ▷ vb give an award or praise

**ACCOLADED** > ACCOLADE

**ACCOLADES** > ACCOLADE

**ACCOMPANY** vb go along with

**ACCOMPT** vb account

**ACCOMPTED** > ACCOMPT

**ACCOMPTS** > ACCOMPT

**ACCORAGE** vb encourage

**ACCORAGED** > ACCORAGE

**ACCORAGES** > ACCORAGE

**ACCORD** n agreement, harmony ▷ vb fit in with

**ACCORDANT** adj in conformity or harmony

**ACCORDED** > ACCORD

**ACCORDER** > ACCORD

**ACCORDERS** > ACCORD

**ACCORDING** adj in proportion

**ACCORDION** n portable musical instrument played by moving the two sides apart and together, and pressing a keyboard or buttons to produce the notes

**ACCORDS** > ACCORD

**ACCOST** vb approach and speak to, often aggressively ▷ n greeting

**ACCOSTED** > ACCOST

**ACCOSTING** > ACCOST

**ACCOSTS** > ACCOST

**ACCOUNT** n report, description ▷ vb judge to be

**ACCOUNTED** > ACCOUNT

**ACCOUNTS** > ACCOUNT

**ACCOURAGE** vb encourage

**ACCOURT** vb entertain

**ACCOURTED** > ACCOURT

**ACCOURTS** > ACCOURT

**ACCOUTER** same as > ACCOUTRE

**ACCOUTERS** > ACCOUTER

**ACCOUTRE** vb provide with equipment or dress, esp military

**ACCOUTRED** > ACCOUTRE

**ACCOUTRES** > ACCOUTRE

**ACCOY** vb soothe

**ACCOYED** > ACCOY

**ACCOYING** > ACCOY

**ACCOYLD** > ACCOIL

**ACCOYS** > ACCOY

**ACCREDIT** vb give official recognition to

**ACCREDITS** > ACCREDIT

**ACCRETE** vb grow or cause to grow together

**ACCRETED** > ACCRETE

**ACCRETES** > ACCRETE

**ACCRETING** > ACCRETE

**ACCRETION** n gradual growth

**ACCRETIVE** > ACCRETION

**ACCREW** vb accrue

**ACCREWED** > ACCREW

**ACCREWING** > ACCREW

**ACCREWS** > ACCREW

**ACCROIDES** n red alcohol-soluble resin

**ACCRUABLE** > ACCRUE

**ACCRUAL** n act of accruing

**ACCRUALS** > ACCRUAL

**ACCRUE** vb increase gradually

**ACCRUED** > ACCRUE

**ACCRUES** > ACCRUE

**ACCRUING** > ACCRUE

**ACCUMBENT** adj (of plant parts and plants) lying against some other part or thing

**ACCURACY** n faithful representation of the truth

**ACCURATE** adj exact, correct

**ACCURSE** vb curse

**ACCURSED** adj under a curse

**ACCURSES** > ACCURSE

**ACCURSING** > ACCURSE

**ACCURST** same

as > ACCURSED

**ACCUSABLE** > ACCUSE

**ACCUSABLY** > ACCUSE

**ACCUSAL** n accusation

**ACCUSALS** > ACCUSAL

**ACCUSANT** n person who accuses

**ACCUSANTS** > ACCUSANT

**ACCUSE** vb charge with wrongdoing

**ACCUSED** n person or people accused of a crime in a court

**ACCUSER** > ACCUSE

**ACCUSERS** > ACCUSE

**ACCUSES** > ACCUSE

**ACCUSING** > ACCUSE

**ACCUSTOM** vb make used to

**ACCUSTOMS** > ACCUSTOM

**ACE** n playing card with one symbol on it ▷ adj excellent ▷ vb serve an ace in racquet sports

**ACED** > ACE

**ACEDIA** same as > ACCIDIE

**ACEDIAS** > ACEDIA

**ACELDAMA** n place with ill feeling

**ACELDAMAS** > ACELDAMA

**ACELLULAR** adj not made up of or containing cells

**ACENTRIC** adj without a centre ▷ n acentric chromosome or fragment

**ACEPHALIC** n having no head or one that is reduced and indistinct, as certain insect larvae

**ACEQUIA** n irrigation ditch

**ACEQUIAS** > ACEQUIA

**ACER** n any tree or shrub of the genus Acer, often cultivated for their brightly coloured foliage

**ACERATE** same as > ACERATED

**ACERATED** adj having sharp points

**ACERB** adj bitter

**ACERBATE** vb embitter or exasperate

**ACERBATED** > ACERBATE

**ACERBATES** > ACERBATE

**ACERBER** > ACERB

**ACERBEST** > ACERB

**ACERBIC** adj harsh or bitter

**ACERBITY** n bitter speech or temper

**ACEROLA** n cherry-like fruit

**ACEROLAS** > ACEROLA

**ACEROSE** adj shaped like a needle, as pine leaves

**ACEROUS** same as > ACEROSE

**ACERS** > ACER

**ACERVATE** adj growing in heaps or clusters

**ACERVULI** > ACERVULUS

**ACERVULUS** n spore-producing part of plant

**ACES** > ACE

**ACESCENCE** > ACESCENT

**ACESCENCY** > ACESCENT

**ACESCENT** adj slightly sour or turning sour ▷ n

something that is turning sour

**ACESCENTS** > ACESCENT

**ACETA** > ACETUM

**ACETABULA** n deep cuplike cavities on the side of the hipbones that receive the head of the thighbone

**ACETAL** n 1,1-diethoxyethane

**ACETALS** > ACETAL

**ACETAMID** same as > ACETAMIDE

**ACETAMIDE** n white or colourless soluble deliquescent crystalline compound

**ACETAMIDS** > ACETAMID

**ACETATE** n salt or ester of acetic acid

**ACETATED** adj combined with acetic acid

**ACETATES** > ACETATE

**ACETIC** adj of or involving vinegar

**ACETIFIED** > ACETIFY

**ACETIFIER** > ACETIFY

**ACETIFIES** > ACETIFY

**ACETIFY** vb become or cause to become acetic acid or vinegar

**ACETIN** n type of acetate

**ACETINS** > ACETIN

**ACETONE** n colourless liquid used as a solvent

**ACETONES** > ACETONE

**ACETONIC** > ACETONE

**ACETOSE** same as > ACETOUS

**ACETOUS** adj containing, producing, or resembling acetic acid or vinegar

**ACETOXYL** n medicine used to treat acne

**ACETOXYLS** > ACETOXYL

**ACETUM** n solution that has dilute acetic acid as solvent

**ACETYL** n of, consisting of, or containing the monovalent group $CH_3CO$-

**ACETYLATE** vb introduce an acetyl group into (a chemical compound)

**ACETYLENE** n colourless flammable gas used in welding metals

**ACETYLIC** > ACETYL

**ACETYLIDE** n any of a class of carbides in which the carbon is present as a diatomic divalent ion $(C_2^{2-})$. They are formally derivatives of acetylene

**ACETYLS** > ACETYL

**ACH** interj Scots expression of surprise

**ACHAENIA** > ACHAENIUM

**ACHAENIUM** n achene

**ACHAGE** n pain

**ACHAGES** > ACHAGE

**ACHALASIA** n failure of the cardiac sphincter of the oesophagus to relax, resulting in difficulty in swallowing

**ACHARNE** *adj* furiously violent

**ACHARYA** *n* prominent religious teacher and spiritual guide

**ACHARYAS** >ACHARYA

**ACHATES** *same as* >ACATES

**ACHE** *n* dull continuous pain ▷ *vb* be in or cause continuous dull pain

**ACHED** >ACHE

**ACHENE** *n* dry one-seeded indehiscent fruit with the seed distinct from the fruit wall. It may be smooth, as in the buttercup, or feathery, as in clematis

**ACHENES** >ACHENE

**ACHENIA** >ACHENIUM

**ACHENIAL** >ACHENE

**ACHENIUM** *n* achene

**ACHENIUMS** >ACHENIUM

**ACHES** >ACHE

**ACHIER** >ACHY

**ACHIEST** >ACHY

**ACHIEVE** *vb* gain by hard work or ability

**ACHIEVED** >ACHIEVE

**ACHIEVER** >ACHIEVE

**ACHIEVERS** >ACHIEVE

**ACHIEVES** >ACHIEVE

**ACHIEVING** >ACHIEVE

**ACHILLEA** *n* any plant of the N temperate genus *Achillea*, with white, yellow, or purple flowers, some species of which are widely grown as garden plants: family *Asteraceae* (composites)

**ACHILLEAS** >ACHILLEA

**ACHIMENES** *n* any plant of the tropical S American tuberous-rooted perennial genus *Achimenes*, with showy red, blue, or white tubular flowers, some of which are grown as greenhouse plants: family *Gesneriaceae*

**ACHINESS** >ACHY

**ACHING** >ACHE

**ACHINGLY** >ACHE

**ACHINGS** >ACHE

**ACHIOTE** *n* annatto

**ACHIOTES** >ACHIOTE

**ACHIRAL** *adj* of a tuber producing arrowroot

**ACHKAN** *n* man's coat in India

**ACHKANS** >ACHKAN

**ACHOLIA** *n* condition involving lack of bile secretion

**ACHOLIAS** >ACHOLIA

**ACHOO** *interj* sound of a sneeze

**ACHROMAT** *n* lens designed to bring light of two chosen wavelengths to the same focal point, thus reducing chromatic aberration

**ACHROMATS** >ACHROMAT

**ACHROMIC** *adj* colourless

**ACHROMOUS** *same as* >ACHROMIC

**ACHY** *adj* affected by a continuous dull pain

**ACICULA** *n* needle-shaped part, such as a spine, prickle, or crystal

**ACICULAE** >ACICULA

**ACICULAR** >ACICULA

**ACICULAS** >ACICULA

**ACICULATE** *adj* having aciculae

**ACICULUM** *n* needle-like bristle that provides internal support for the appendages (chaetae) of some polychaete worms

**ACICULUMS** >ACICULUM

**ACID** *n* one of a class of compounds, corrosive and sour when dissolved in water, that combine with a base to form a salt ▷ *adj* containing acid

**ACIDEMIA** *n* abnormally high level of acid in blood

**ACIDEMIAS** >ACIDEMIA

**ACIDER** >ACID

**ACIDEST** >ACID

**ACIDFREAK** *n* person taking LSD regularly

**ACIDHEAD** *n* person who uses LSD

**ACIDHEADS** >ACIDHEAD

**ACIDIC** *adj* containing acid

**ACIDIER** >ACID

**ACIDIEST** >ACID

**ACIDIFIED** >ACIDIFY

**ACIDIFIER** >ACIDIFY

**ACIDIFIES** >ACIDIFY

**ACIDIFY** *vb* convert into acid

**ACIDITIES** >ACIDITY

**ACIDITY** *n* quality of being acid

**ACIDLY** >ACID

**ACIDNESS** >ACID

**ACIDOPHIL** *adj* (of cells or cell contents) easily stained by acid dyes ▷ *n* acidophil organism

**ACIDOSES** >ACIDOSIS

**ACIDOSIS** *n* condition characterized by an abnormal increase in the acidity of the blood and extracellular fluids

**ACIDOTIC** >ACIDOSIS

**ACIDS** >ACID

**ACIDULATE** *vb* make slightly acid or sour

**ACIDULENT** *same as* >ACIDULOUS

**ACIDULOUS** *adj* rather sour

**ACIDURIA** *n* abnormally high level of acid in urine

**ACIDURIAS** >ACIDURIA

**ACIDY** >ACID

**ACIERAGE** *n* iron-plating of metal

**ACIERAGES** >ACIERAGE

**ACIERATE** *vb* change (iron)

into steel

**ACIERATED** >ACIERATE

**ACIERATES** >ACIERATE

**ACIFORM** *adj* shaped like a needle

**ACINAR** *adj* of small sacs

**ACING** >ACE

**ACINI** >ACINUS

**ACINIC** >ACINUS

**ACINIFORM** *adj* shaped like a bunch of grapes

**ACINOSE** >ACINUS

**ACINOUS** >ACINUS

**ACINUS** *n* any of the terminal saclike portions of a compound gland

**ACKEE** *n* sapindaceous tree, *Blighia sapida*, native to tropical Africa and cultivated in the Caribbean for its fruit, edible when cooked

**ACKEES** >ACKEE

**ACKER** *same as* >ACCA

**ACKERS** >ACKER

**ACKNEW** >ACKNOW

**ACKNOW** *vb* recognize

**ACKNOWING** >ACKNOW

**ACKNOWNE** *adj* aware

**ACKNOWS** >ACKNOW

**ACLINIC** *adj* unbending

**ACMATIC** *adj* highest or ultimate

**ACME** *n* highest point of achievement or excellence

**ACMES** >ACME

**ACMIC** *same as* >ACMATIC

**ACMITE** *n* chemical with pyramid-shaped crystals

**ACMITES** >ACMITE

**ACNE** *n* pimply skin disease

**ACNED** *adj* marked by acne

**ACNES** >ACNE

**ACNODAL** >ACNODE

**ACNODE** *n* point whose coordinates satisfy the equation of a curve although it does not lie on the curve

**ACNODES** >ACNODE

**ACOCK** *adv* cocked

**ACOELOUS** *adj* not having a stomach

**ACOEMETI** *n* order of monks

**ACOLD** *adj* feeling cold

**ACOLUTHIC** *adj* of an afterimage

**ACOLYTE** *n* follower or attendant

**ACOLYTES** >ACOLYTE

**ACOLYTH** *n* acolyte

**ACOLYTHS** >ACOLYTH

**ACONITE** *n* poisonous plant with hoodlike flowers

**ACONITES** >ACONITE

**ACONITIC** >ACONITE

**ACONITINE** *n* poison made from aconite

**ACONITUM** *same as* >ACONITE

**ACONITUMS** >ACONITUM

**ACORN** *n* nut of the oak tree

**ACORNED** *adj* covered with

acorns

**ACORNS** >ACORN

**ACOSMISM** *n* belief that no world exists outside the mind

**ACOSMISMS** >ACOSMISM

**ACOSMIST** >ACOSMISM

**ACOSMISTS** >ACOSMISM

**ACOUCHI** *n* any of several South American rodents of the genus *Myoprocta*, closely related to the agoutis but much smaller, with a white-tipped tail: family *Dasyproctidae*

**ACOUCHIES** >ACOUCHY

**ACOUCHIS** >ACOUCHY

**ACOUCHY** *same as* >ACOUCHI

**ACOUSTIC** *adj* of sound and hearing

**ACOUSTICS** *n* science of sounds

**ACQUAINT** *vb* make familiar, inform

**ACQUAINTS** >ACQUAINT

**ACQUEST** *n* something acquired

**ACQUESTS** >ACQUEST

**ACQUIESCE** *vb* agree to what someone wants

**ACQUIGHT** *vb* acquit

**ACQUIGHTS** >ACQUIGHT

**ACQUIRAL** >ACQUIRE

**ACQUIRALS** >ACQUIRE

**ACQUIRE** *vb* gain, get

**ACQUIRED** >ACQUIRE

**ACQUIREE** *n* one who acquires

**ACQUIREES** >ACQUIREE

**ACQUIRER** >ACQUIRE

**ACQUIRERS** >ACQUIRE

**ACQUIRES** >ACQUIRE

**ACQUIRING** >ACQUIRE

**ACQUIST** *n* acquisition

**ACQUISTS** >ACQUIST

**ACQUIT** *vb* pronounce (someone) innocent

**ACQUITE** *vb* acquit

**ACQUITES** >ACQUITE

**ACQUITING** >ACQUITE

**ACQUITS** >ACQUIT

**ACQUITTAL** *n* deliverance and release of a person appearing before a court on a charge of crime, as by a finding of not guilty

**ACQUITTED** >ACQUIT

**ACQUITTER** >ACQUIT

**ACRASIA** *n* lack of willpower

**ACRASIAS** >ACRASIA

**ACRASIN** *n* chemical produced by slime moulds

**ACRASINS** >ACRASIN

**ACRATIC** >ACRASIA

**ACRAWL** *adv* crawling

**ACRE** *n* measure of land, 4840 square yards (4046.86 square metres)

**ACREAGE** *n* land area in acres ▷ *adj* of or relating to a large allotment of land, esp in a rural area

**ACREAGES** >ACREAGE

**ACRED** *adj* having acres of land

**ACRES** >ACRE

**ACRID** *adj* pungent, bitter

**ACRIDER** >ACRID

**ACRIDEST** >ACRID

**ACRIDIN** *n* acridine

**ACRIDINE** *n* colourless crystalline solid

**ACRIDINES** >ACRIDINE

**ACRIDINS** >ACRIDIN

**ACRIDITY** >ACRID

**ACRIDLY** >ACRID

**ACRIDNESS** >ACRID

**ACRIMONY** *n* bitterness and resentment felt about something

**ACRITARCH** *n* type of fossil

**ACRITICAL** *adj* not critical

**ACROBAT** *n* person skilled in gymnastic feats requiring agility and balance

**ACROBATIC** >ACROBAT

**ACROBATS** >ACROBAT

**ACRODONT** *adj* (of the teeth of some reptiles) having no roots and being fused at the base to the margin of the jawbones ▷ *n* acrodont reptile

**ACRODONTS** >ACRODONT

**ACRODROME** *adj* (of the veins of a leaf) running parallel to the edges of the leaf and fusing at the tip

**ACROGEN** *n* any flowerless plant, such as a fern or moss, in which growth occurs from the tip of the main stem

**ACROGENIC** >ACROGEN

**ACROGENS** >ACROGEN

**ACROLECT** *n* most correct form of language

**ACROLECTS** >ACROLECT

**ACROLEIN** *n* colourless or yellowish flammable poisonous pungent liquid

**ACROLEINS** >ACROLEIN

**ACROLITH** *n* (esp in ancient Greek sculpture) a wooden, often draped figure with only the head, hands, and feet in stone

**ACROLITHS** >ACROLITH

**ACROMIA** >ACROMION

**ACROMIAL** >ACROMION

**ACROMION** *n* outermost edge of the spine of the shoulder blade

**ACRONIC** *adj* acronical

**ACRONICAL** *adj* occurring at sunset

**ACRONYCAL** *same as* >ACRONICAL

**ACRONYM** *n* word formed from the initial letters of other words, such as NASA

**ACRONYMIC** >ACRONYM

**ACRONYMS** >ACRONYM

**ACROPETAL** *adj* (of leaves and flowers) produced in order from the base upwards so that the

youngest are at the apex

**ACROPHOBE** *n* person afraid of heights

**ACROPHONY** *n* use of symbols to represent sounds

**ACROPOLIS** *n* citadel of an ancient Greek city

**ACROSOMAL** >ACROSOME

**ACROSOME** *n* structure at the tip of a sperm cell

**ACROSOMES** >ACROSOME

**ACROSPIRE** *n* first shoot developing from the plumule of a germinating grain seed

**ACROSS** *adv* from side to side (of)

**ACROSTIC** *n* lines of writing in which the first or last letters of each line spell a word or saying

**ACROSTICS** >ACROSTIC

**ACROTER** *n* plinth bearing a statue, etc, at either end or at the apex of a pediment

**ACROTERIA** *n* acroters

**ACROTERS** >ACROTER

**ACROTIC** *adj* of a surface

**ACROTISM** *n* absence of pulse

**ACROTISMS** >ACROTISM

**ACRYLATE** *n* chemical compound in plastics and resins

**ACRYLATES** >ACRYLATE

**ACRYLIC** *adj* (synthetic fibre, paint, etc) made from acrylic acid ▷ *n* man-made fibre used for clothes and blankets

**ACRYLICS** >ACRYLIC

**ACRYLYL** *n* type of monovalent group

**ACRYLYLS** >ACRYLYL

**ACT** *n* thing done ▷ *vb* do something

**ACTA** *n* minutes of meeting

**ACTABLE** >ACT

**ACTANT** *n* (in valency grammar) a noun phrase functioning as the agent of the main verb of a sentence

**ACTANTS** >ACTANT

**ACTED** >ACT

**ACTIN** *n* protein that participates in many kinds of cell movement, including muscle contraction, during which it interacts with filaments of a second protein, myosin

**ACTINAL** *adj* of or denoting the oral part of a radiate animal, such as a jellyfish, sea anemone, or sponge, from which the rays, tentacles, or arms grow

**ACTINALLY** >ACTINAL

**ACTING** *n* art of an actor ▷ *adj* temporarily performing the duties of

**ACTINGS** >ACTING

**ACTINIA** *n* any sea anemone of the genus *Actinia*, which are common in rock pools

**ACTINIAE** >ACTINIA

**ACTINIAN** *n* sea-anemone

**ACTINIANS** >ACTINIAN

**ACTINIAS** >ACTINIA

**ACTINIC** *adj* (of radiation) producing a photochemical effect

**ACTINIDE** *n* member of the actinide series

**ACTINIDES** >ACTINIDE

**ACTINISM** >ACTINIC

**ACTINISMS** >ACTINIC

**ACTINIUM** *n* radioactive chemical element

**ACTINIUMS** >ACTINIUM

**ACTINOID** *adj* having a radiate form, as a sea anemone or starfish ▷ *n* member of the actinide series

**ACTINOIDS** >ACTINOID

**ACTINON** *same as* >ACTINIDE

**ACTINONS** >ACTINON

**ACTINOPOD** *n* any protozoan of the phylum *Actinopoda*, such as a radiolarian or a heliozoan, having stiff radiating cytoplasmic projections

**ACTINS** >ACTIN

**ACTION** *n* process of doing something ▷ *vb* put into effect

**ACTIONED** >ACTION

**ACTIONER** *n* film with a fast-moving plot, usually containing scenes of violence

**ACTIONERS** >ACTIONER

**ACTIONING** >ACTION

**ACTIONIST** *n* activist

**ACTIONS** >ACTION

**ACTIVATE** *vb* make active

**ACTIVATED** >ACTIVATE

**ACTIVATES** >ACTIVATE

**ACTIVATOR** >ACTIVATE

**ACTIVE** *adj* moving, working ▷ *n* active form of a verb

**ACTIVELY** >ACTIVE

**ACTIVES** >ACTIVE

**ACTIVISE** *same as* >ACTIVIZE

**ACTIVISED** >ACTIVISE

**ACTIVISES** >ACTIVISE

**ACTIVISM** *n* policy of taking direct and often militant action to achieve an end, esp a political or social one

**ACTIVISMS** >ACTIVISM

**ACTIVIST** >ACTIVISM

**ACTIVISTS** >ACTIVISM

**ACTIVITY** *n* state of being active

**ACTIVIZE** *vb* make active

**ACTIVIZED** >ACTIVIZE

**ACTIVIZES** >ACTIVIZE

**ACTON** *n* jacket or jerkin,

originally of quilted cotton, worn under a coat of mail

**ACTONS** >ACTON

**ACTOR** *n* person who acts in a play, film, etc

**ACTORISH** >ACTOR

**ACTORLY** *adj* of or relating to an actor

**ACTORS** >ACTOR

**ACTRESS** *n* woman who acts in a play, film, broadcast, etc

**ACTRESSES** >ACTRESS

**ACTRESSY** *adj* exaggerated and affected in manner

**ACTS** >ACT

**ACTUAL** *adj* existing in reality

**ACTUALISE** *same as* >ACTUALIZE

**ACTUALIST** *n* person dealing in hard fact

**ACTUALITE** *n* humorous word for truth

**ACTUALITY** *n* reality

**ACTUALIZE** *vb* make actual or real

**ACTUALLY** *adv* really, indeed

**ACTUALS** *pl n* commercial commodities that can be bought and used

**ACTUARIAL** >ACTUARY

**ACTUARIES** >ACTUARY

**ACTUARY** *n* statistician who calculates insurance risks

**ACTUATE** *vb* start up (a device)

**ACTUATED** >ACTUATE

**ACTUATES** >ACTUATE

**ACTUATING** >ACTUATE

**ACTUATION** >ACTUATE

**ACTUATOR** >ACTUATE

**ACTUATORS** >ACTUATE

**ACTURE** *n* action

**ACTURES** >ACTURE

**ACUATE** *adj* sharply pointed

**ACUITIES** >ACUITY

**ACUITY** *n* keenness of vision or thought

**ACULEATE** *adj* cutting

**ACULEATED** *same as* >ACULEATE

**ACULEI** >ACULEUS

**ACULEUS** *n* prickle or spine, such as the thorn of a rose

**ACUMEN** *n* ability to make good judgments

**ACUMENS** >ACUMEN

**ACUMINATE** *adj* narrowing to a sharp point, as some types of leaf ▷ *vb* make pointed or sharp

**ACUMINOUS** >ACUMEN

**ACUPOINT** *n* any of the specific points on the body where a needle is inserted in acupuncture or pressure is applied in acupressure

**ACUPOINTS** >ACUPOINT

**ACUSHLA** *n* Irish endearment

**ACUSHLAS** > ACUSHLA
**ACUTANCE** *n* physical rather than subjective measure of the sharpness of a photographic image
**ACUTANCES** > ACUTANCE
**ACUTE** *adj* severe ▷ *n* accent (´) over a letter to indicate the quality or length of its sound, as in café
**ACUTELY** > ACUTE
**ACUTENESS** > ACUTE
**ACUTER** > ACUTE
**ACUTES** > ACUTE
**ACUTEST** > ACUTE
**ACYCLIC** *adj* not cyclic
**ACYCLOVIR** *n* drug used against herpes
**ACYL** *n* member of the monovalent group of atoms RCO-
**ACYLATE** *vb* introduce an acyl group into a compound
**ACYLATED** > ACYLATE
**ACYLATES** > ACYLATE
**ACYLATING** > ACYLATE
**ACYLATION** *n* introduction into a chemical compound of an acyl group
**ACYLOIN** *n* organic chemical compound
**ACYLOINS** > ACYLOIN
**ACYLS** > ACYL
**AD** *n* advertisement
**ADAGE** *n* wise saying, proverb
**ADAGES** > ADAGE
**ADAGIAL** > ADAGE
**ADAGIO** *adv* (piece to be played) slowly and gracefully ▷ *n* movement or piece to be performed slowly
**ADAGIOS** > ADAGIO
**ADAMANCE** *n* being adamant
**ADAMANCES** > ADAMANCE
**ADAMANCY** *n* being adamant
**ADAMANT** *adj* unshakable in determination or purpose ▷ *n* any extremely hard or apparently unbreakable substance
**ADAMANTLY** > ADAMANT
**ADAMANTS** > ADAMANT
**ADAMSITE** *n* yellow poisonous crystalline solid that readily sublimes
**ADAMSITES** > ADAMSITE
**ADAPT** *vb* alter for new use or new conditions
**ADAPTABLE** > ADAPT
**ADAPTED** > ADAPT
**ADAPTER** *same as* > ADAPTOR
**ADAPTERS** > ADAPTER
**ADAPTING** > ADAPT
**ADAPTION** *n* adaptation
**ADAPTIONS** > ADAPTION
**ADAPTIVE** > ADAPT
**ADAPTOGEN** *n* any of various natural substances

used in herbal medicine to normalize and regulate the systems of the body
**ADAPTOR** *n* device for connecting several electrical appliances to a single socket
**ADAPTORS** > ADAPTOR
**ADAPTS** > ADAPT
**ADAW** *vb* subdue
**ADAWED** > ADAW
**ADAWING** > ADAW
**ADAWS** > ADAW
**ADAXIAL** *adj* facing towards the axis, as the surface of a leaf that faces the stem
**ADAYS** *adv* daily
**ADD** *vb* combine (numbers or quantities)
**ADDABLE** > ADD
**ADDAX** *n* large light-coloured antelope, *Addax nasomaculatus*, having ribbed loosely spiralled horns and inhabiting desert regions in N Africa: family *Bovidae*, order *Artiodactyla*
**ADDAXES** > ADDAX
**ADDEBTED** *adj* indebted
**ADDED** > ADD
**ADDEDLY** > ADD
**ADDEEM** *vb* adjudge
**ADDEEMED** > ADDEEM
**ADDEEMING** > ADDEEM
**ADDEEMS** > ADDEEM
**ADDEND** *n* any of a set of numbers that is to be added
**ADDENDA** > ADDENDUM
**ADDENDS** > ADDEND
**ADDENDUM** *n* addition
**ADDENDUMS** > ADDENDUM
**ADDER** *n* small poisonous snake
**ADDERS** > ADDER
**ADDERWORT** *n* plant of the dock family
**ADDIBLE** *adj* addable
**ADDICT** *n* person who is unable to stop taking drugs ▷ *vb* cause (someone or oneself) to become dependent (on something, esp a narcotic drug)
**ADDICTED** > ADDICT
**ADDICTING** > ADDICT
**ADDICTION** *n* condition of being abnormally dependent on some habit, esp compulsive dependency on narcotic drugs
**ADDICTIVE** *adj* causing addiction
**ADDICTS** > ADDICT
**ADDIES** > ADDY
**ADDING** *n* act or instance of addition ▷ *adj* of, for, or relating to addition
**ADDIO** *interj* farewell ▷ *n* cry of addio

**ADDIOS** > ADDIO
**ADDITION** *n* adding
**ADDITIONS** > ADDITION
**ADDITIVE** *n* something added, esp to a foodstuff, to improve it or prevent deterioration ▷ *adj* characterized or produced by addition
**ADDITIVES** > ADDITIVE
**ADDITORY** *adj* adding to something
**ADDLE** *vb* make or become confused or muddled ▷ *adj* indicating a confused or muddled state
**ADDLED** > ADDLE
**ADDLEMENT** > ADDLE
**ADDLES** > ADDLE
**ADDLING** > ADDLE
**ADDOOM** *vb* adjudge
**ADDOOMED** > ADDOOM
**ADDOOMING** > ADDOOM
**ADDOOMS** > ADDOOM
**ADDORSED** *adj* back to back
**ADDRESS** *n* place where a person lives ▷ *vb* mark the destination, as on an envelope
**ADDRESSED** > ADDRESS
**ADDRESSEE** *n* person addressed
**ADDRESSER** > ADDRESS
**ADDRESSES** > ADDRESS
**ADDRESSOR** > ADDRESS
**ADDREST** > ADDRESS
**ADDS** > ADD
**ADDUCE** *vb* mention something as evidence or proof
**ADDUCED** > ADDUCE
**ADDUCENT** > ADDUCE
**ADDUCER** > ADDUCE
**ADDUCERS** > ADDUCE
**ADDUCES** > ADDUCE
**ADDUCIBLE** > ADDUCE
**ADDUCING** > ADDUCE
**ADDUCT** *vb* (of a muscle) to draw or pull (a leg, arm, etc) towards the median axis of the body ▷ *n* compound formed by direct combination of two or more different compounds or elements
**ADDUCTED** > ADDUCT
**ADDUCTING** > ADDUCT
**ADDUCTION** > ADDUCT
**ADDUCTIVE** > ADDUCE
**ADDUCTOR** *n* muscle that adducts
**ADDUCTORS** > ADDUCTOR
**ADDUCTS** > ADDUCT
**ADDY** *n* e-mail address
**ADEEM** *vb* cancel
**ADEEMED** > ADEEM
**ADEEMING** > ADEEM
**ADEEMS** > ADEEM
**ADEMPTION** *n* failure of a specific legacy, as by a testator disposing of the subject matter in his lifetime
**ADENINE** *n* purine base

present in tissues of all living organisms as a constituent of the nucleic acids DNA and RNA and of certain coenzymes
**ADENINES** > ADENINE
**ADENITIS** *n* inflammation of a gland or lymph node
**ADENOID** *adj* of or resembling a gland
**ADENOIDAL** *adj* having a nasal voice caused by swollen adenoids
**ADENOIDS** *pl n* tissue at the back of the throat
**ADENOMA** *n* tumour, usually benign, occurring in glandular tissue
**ADENOMAS** > ADENOMA
**ADENOMATA** > ADENOMA
**ADENOSES** > ADENOSIS
**ADENOSINE** *n* nucleoside formed by the condensation of adenine and ribose
**ADENOSIS** *n* disease of glands
**ADENYL** *n* enzyme
**ADENYLIC** as in *adenylic acid* nucleotide consisting of adenine, ribose or deoxyribose, and a phosphate group
**ADENYLS** > ADENYL
**ADEPT** *n* very skilful (person) ▷ *adj* proficient in something requiring skill
**ADEPTER** > ADEPT
**ADEPTEST** > ADEPT
**ADEPTLY** > ADEPT
**ADEPTNESS** > ADEPT
**ADEPTS** > ADEPT
**ADEQUACY** > ADEQUATE
**ADEQUATE** *adj* sufficient, enough
**ADERMIN** *n* vitamin
**ADERMINS** > ADERMIN
**ADESPOTA** *n* anonymous writings
**ADESSIVE** *n* grammatical case denoting place
**ADESSIVES** > ADESSIVE
**ADHAN** *n* call to prayer
**ADHANS** > ADHAN
**ADHARMA** *n* wickedness
**ADHARMAS** > ADHARMA
**ADHERABLE** > ADHERE
**ADHERE** *vb* stick (to)
**ADHERED** > ADHERE
**ADHERENCE** > ADHERE
**ADHEREND** *n* something attached by adhesive
**ADHERENDS** > ADHEREND
**ADHERENT** *n* devotee, follower ▷ *adj* sticking or attached
**ADHERENTS** > ADHERENT
**ADHERER** > ADHERE
**ADHERERS** > ADHERE
**ADHERES** > ADHERE
**ADHERING** > ADHERE
**ADHESION** *n* sticking (to)
**ADHESIONS** > ADHESION

**ADHESIVE** n substance used to stick things together ▷ adj able to stick to things
**ADHESIVES** >ADHESIVE
**ADHIBIT** vb administer or apply
**ADHIBITED** >ADHIBIT
**ADHIBITS** >ADHIBIT
**ADHOCRACY** n management that responds to urgent problems rather than planning to avoid them
**ADIABATIC** adj (of a thermodynamic process) taking place without loss or gain of heat ▷ n curve or surface on a graph representing the changes in two or more characteristics (such as pressure and volume) of a system undergoing an adiabatic process
**ADIAPHORA** n matters of indifference
**ADIEU** n goodbye
**ADIEUS** >ADIEU
**ADIEUX** >ADIEU
**ADIOS** sentence substitute Spanish for goodbye
**ADIPIC** as in adipic acid colourless crystalline solid used in the preparation of nylon
**ADIPOCERE** n waxlike fatty substance formed during the decomposition of corpses
**ADIPOCYTE** n fat cell that accumulates and stores fats
**ADIPOSE** adj of or containing fat ▷ n animal fat
**ADIPOSES** >ADIPOSIS
**ADIPOSIS** n obesity
**ADIPOSITY** >ADIPOSE
**ADIPOUS** adj made of fat
**ADIPSIA** n complete lack of thirst
**ADIPSIAS** >ADIPSIA
**ADIT** n almost horizontal shaft into a mine, for access or drainage
**ADITS** >ADIT
**ADJACENCE** >ADJACENT
**ADJACENCY** >ADJACENT
**ADJACENT** adj near or next (to) ▷ n side lying between a specified angle and a right angle in a right-angled triangle
**ADJACENTS** >ADJACENT
**ADJECTIVE** n word that adds information about a noun or pronoun ▷ adj additional or dependent
**ADJIGO** n yam plant, Dioscorea hastifolia, native to SW Australia that has edible tubers
**ADJIGOS** >ADJIGO
**ADJOIN** vb be next to

**ADJOINED** >ADJOIN
**ADJOINING** adj being in contact
**ADJOINS** >ADJOIN
**ADJOINT** n type of mathematical matrix
**ADJOINTS** >ADJOINT
**ADJOURN** vb close (a court) at the end of a session
**ADJOURNED** >ADJOURN
**ADJOURNS** >ADJOURN
**ADJUDGE** vb declare (to be)
**ADJUDGED** >ADJUDGE
**ADJUDGES** >ADJUDGE
**ADJUDGING** >ADJUDGE
**ADJUNCT** n something incidental added to something else
**ADJUNCTLY** >ADJUNCT
**ADJUNCTS** >ADJUNCT
**ADJURE** vb command (to do)
**ADJURED** >ADJURE
**ADJURER** >ADJURE
**ADJURERS** >ADJURE
**ADJURES** >ADJURE
**ADJURING** >ADJURE
**ADJUROR** >ADJURE
**ADJURORS** >ADJURE
**ADJUST** vb adapt to new conditions
**ADJUSTED** >ADJUST
**ADJUSTER** >ADJUST
**ADJUSTERS** >ADJUST
**ADJUSTING** >ADJUST
**ADJUSTIVE** >ADJUST
**ADJUSTOR** >ADJUST
**ADJUSTORS** >ADJUST
**ADJUSTS** >ADJUST
**ADJUTAGE** n nozzle
**ADJUTAGES** >ADJUTAGE
**ADJUTANCY** >ADJUTANT
**ADJUTANT** n army officer in charge of routine administration
**ADJUTANTS** >ADJUTANT
**ADJUVANCY** >ADJUVANT
**ADJUVANT** adj aiding or assisting ▷ n something that aids or assists
**ADJUVANTS** >ADJUVANT
**ADLAND** n advertising industry and the people who work in it
**ADLANDS** >ADLAND
**ADMAN** n man who works in advertising
**ADMASS** n mass advertising
**ADMASSES** >ADMASS
**ADMEASURE** vb measure out (land, etc) as a share
**ADMEN** >ADMAN
**ADMIN** n administration
**ADMINICLE** n something contributing to prove a point without itself being complete proof
**ADMINS** >ADMIN
**ADMIRABLE** adj deserving or inspiring admiration
**ADMIRABLY** >ADMIRABLE
**ADMIRAL** n highest naval rank
**ADMIRALS** >ADMIRAL

**ADMIRALTY** n office or jurisdiction of an admiral
**ADMIRANCE** n admiration
**ADMIRE** vb regard with esteem and approval
**ADMIRED** >ADMIRE
**ADMIRER** >ADMIRE
**ADMIRERS** >ADMIRE
**ADMIRES** >ADMIRE
**ADMIRING** >ADMIRE
**ADMISSION** n permission to enter
**ADMISSIVE** >ADMISSION
**ADMIT** vb confess, acknowledge
**ADMITS** >ADMIT
**ADMITTED** >ADMIT
**ADMITTEE** n one who admits
**ADMITTEES** >ADMITTEE
**ADMITTER** >ADMIT
**ADMITTERS** >ADMIT
**ADMITTING** >ADMIT
**ADMIX** vb mix or blend
**ADMIXED** >ADMIX
**ADMIXES** >ADMIX
**ADMIXING** >ADMIX
**ADMIXT** >ADMIX
**ADMIXTURE** n mixture
**ADMONISH** vb reprove sternly
**ADMONITOR** >ADMONISH
**ADNASCENT** adj growing with something else
**ADNATE** adj growing closely attached to an adjacent part or organ
**ADNATION** >ADNATE
**ADNATIONS** >ADNATE
**ADNEXA** pl n organs adjoining the uterus
**ADNEXAL** >ADNEXA
**ADNOMINAL** n word modifying a noun ▷ adj of or relating to an adnoun
**ADNOUN** n adjective used as a noun
**ADNOUNS** >ADNOUN
**ADO** n fuss, trouble
**ADOBE** n sun-dried brick
**ADOBELIKE** >ADOBE
**ADOBES** >ADOBE
**ADOBO** n Philippine dish
**ADOBOS** >ADOBO
**ADONIS** n beautiful young man
**ADONISE** vb adorn
**ADONISED** >ADONISE
**ADONISES** >ADONISE
**ADONISING** >ADONISE
**ADONIZE** vb adorn
**ADONIZED** >ADONIZE
**ADONIZES** >ADONIZE
**ADONIZING** >ADONIZE
**ADOORS** adv at the door
**ADOPT** vb take (someone else's child) as one's own
**ADOPTABLE** >ADOPT
**ADOPTED** adj having been adopted
**ADOPTEE** n one who has been adopted
**ADOPTEES** >ADOPTEE
**ADOPTER** n person who

adopts
**ADOPTERS** >ADOPTER
**ADOPTING** >ADOPT
**ADOPTION** >ADOPT
**ADOPTIONS** >ADOPT
**ADOPTIOUS** adj adopted
**ADOPTIVE** adj related by adoption
**ADOPTS** >ADOPT
**ADORABLE** adj very attractive
**ADORABLY** >ADORABLE
**ADORATION** n deep love or esteem
**ADORE** vb love intensely
**ADORED** >ADORE
**ADORER** >ADORE
**ADORERS** >ADORE
**ADORES** >ADORE
**ADORING** >ADORE
**ADORINGLY** >ADORE
**ADORN** vb decorate, embellish
**ADORNED** >ADORN
**ADORNER** >ADORN
**ADORNERS** >ADORN
**ADORNING** >ADORN
**ADORNMENT** >ADORN
**ADORNS** >ADORN
**ADOS** >ADO
**ADOWN** adv down
**ADOZE** adv asleep
**ADPRESS** vb press together
**ADPRESSED** >ADPRESS
**ADPRESSES** >ADPRESS
**ADRAD** adj afraid
**ADREAD** vb dread
**ADREADED** >ADREAD
**ADREADING** >ADREAD
**ADREADS** >ADREAD
**ADRED** adj filled with dread
**ADRENAL** adj near the kidneys ▷ n adrenal gland
**ADRENALIN** n hormone secreted by the adrenal glands in response to stress
**ADRENALLY** >ADRENAL
**ADRENALS** >ADRENAL
**ADRIFT** adv drifting
**ADROIT** adj quick and skilful
**ADROITER** >ADROIT
**ADROITEST** >ADROIT
**ADROITLY** >ADROIT
**ADRY** adj dry
**ADS** >AD
**ADSCRIPT** n serf
**ADSCRIPTS** >ADSCRIPT
**ADSORB** vb (of a gas or vapour) condense and form a thin film on a surface
**ADSORBATE** n substance that has been or is to be adsorbed on a surface
**ADSORBED** >ADSORB
**ADSORBENT** adj capable of adsorption ▷ n material, such as activated charcoal, on which adsorption can occur
**ADSORBER** >ADSORB
**ADSORBERS** >ADSORB

**ADSORBING** >ADSORB
**ADSORBS** >ADSORB
**ADSUKI** *same as* >ADZUKI
**ADSUKIS** >ADSUKI
**ADSUM** *sentence substitute* I
am present
**ADUKI** *same as* >ADZUKI
**ADUKIS** >ADUKI
**ADULARIA** *n* white or
colourless glassy variety of
orthoclase
**ADULARIAS** >ADULARIA
**ADULATE** *vb* flatter or praise
obsequiously
**ADULATED** >ADULATE
**ADULATES** >ADULATE
**ADULATING** >ADULATE
**ADULATION** *n* uncritical
admiration
**ADULATOR** >ADULATE
**ADULATORS** >ADULATE
**ADULATORY** *adj* expressing
praise, esp obsequiously
**ADULT** *adj* fully grown,
mature ⊳ *n* adult person
or animal
**ADULTERER** *n* person who
has committed adultery
**ADULTERY** *n* sexual
unfaithfulness of a
husband or wife
**ADULTESE** *n* language
spoken by adults
**ADULTESES** >ADULTESE
**ADULTHOOD** >ADULT
**ADULTLIKE** >ADULT
**ADULTLY** >ADULT
**ADULTNESS** >ADULT
**ADULTRESS** *n* US word for a
female adulterer
**ADULTS** >ADULT
**ADUMBRAL** *adj* shadowy
**ADUMBRATE** *vb* outline
**ADUNC** *adj* hooked
**ADUNCATE** *adj* hooked
**ADUNCATED** *adj* hooked
**ADUNCITY** *n* quality of
being hooked
**ADUNCOUS** *adj* hooked
**ADUST** *vb* dry up or darken
by heat
**ADUSTED** >ADUST
**ADUSTING** >ADUST
**ADUSTS** >ADUST
**ADVANCE** *vb* go or bring
forward ⊳ *n* forward
movement ⊳ *adj* done or
happening before an event
**ADVANCED** *adj* at a late
stage in development
**ADVANCER** >ADVANCE
**ADVANCERS** >ADVANCE
**ADVANCES** >ADVANCE
**ADVANCING** >ADVANCE
**ADVANTAGE** *n* more
favourable position or
state
**ADVECT** *vb* move
horizontally in air
**ADVECTED** >ADVECT
**ADVECTING** >ADVECT
**ADVECTION** *n* transferring
of heat in a horizontal
stream of gas

**ADVECTIVE** >ADVECTION
**ADVECTS** >ADVECT
**ADVENE** *vb* add as extra
**ADVENED** >ADVENE
**ADVENES** >ADVENE
**ADVENING** >ADVENE
**ADVENT** *n* arrival
**ADVENTIVE** *adj* (of a
species) introduced to
a new area and not yet
established there ⊳ *n*
such a plant or animal
**ADVENTS** >ADVENT
**ADVENTURE** *n* exciting
and risky undertaking or
exploit ⊳ *vb* take a risk or
put at risk
**ADVERB** *n* word that adds
information about a verb,
adjective, or other adverb
**ADVERBIAL** *n* word or
group of words playing
the grammatical role of
an adverb, such as in *the
rain* in the sentence *I'm
singing in the rain* ⊳ *adj* of
or relating to an adverb or
adverbial
**ADVERBS** >ADVERB
**ADVERSARY** *n* opponent or
enemy
**ADVERSE** *adj* unfavourable
**ADVERSELY** >ADVERSE
**ADVERSER** >ADVERSE
**ADVERSEST** >ADVERSE
**ADVERSITY** *n* very difficult
or hard circumstances
**ADVERT** *n* advertisement
⊳ *vb* draw attention (to)
**ADVERTED** >ADVERT
**ADVERTENT** *adj* heedful
**ADVERTING** >ADVERT
**ADVERTISE** *vb* present or
praise (goods or services)
to the public in order to
encourage sales
**ADVERTIZE** *same
as* >ADVERTISE
**ADVERTS** >ADVERT
**ADVEW** *vb* look at
**ADVEWED** >ADVEW
**ADVEWING** >ADVEW
**ADVEWS** >ADVEW
**ADVICE** *n* recommendation
as to what to do
**ADVICEFUL** >ADVICE
**ADVICES** >ADVICE
**ADVISABLE** *adj* prudent,
sensible
**ADVISABLY** >ADVISABLE
**ADVISE** *vb* offer advice to
**ADVISED** *adj* considered,
thought-out
**ADVISEDLY** >ADVISED
**ADVISEE** *n* person
receiving advice
**ADVISEES** >ADVISEE
**ADVISER** *n* person who
offers advice, e.g. on
careers to students or
school pupils
**ADVISERS** >ADVISER
**ADVISES** >ADVISE
**ADVISING** >ADVISE

**ADVISINGS** >ADVISE
**ADVISOR** *same as* >ADVISER
**ADVISORS** >ADVISOR
**ADVISORY** *adj* giving advice
⊳ *n* statement giving
advice or a warning
**ADVOCAAT** *n* liqueur with a
raw egg base
**ADVOCAATS** >ADVOCAAT
**ADVOCACY** *n* active support
of a cause or course of
action
**ADVOCATE** *vb* propose or
recommend ⊳ *n* person
who publicly supports a
cause
**ADVOCATED** >ADVOCATE
**ADVOCATES** >ADVOCATE
**ADVOCATOR** *n* person who
advocates
**ADVOUTRER** *n* adulterer
**ADVOUTRY** *n* adultery
**ADVOWSON** *n* right of
presentation to a vacant
benefice
**ADVOWSONS** >ADVOWSON
**ADWARD** *vb* award
**ADWARDED** >ADWARD
**ADWARDING** >ADWARD
**ADWARDS** >ADWARD
**ADWARE** *n* type of computer
software that collects
information about a user's
browsing patterns in
order to display relevant
advertisements in his or
her Web browser
**ADWARES** >ADWARE
**ADWOMAN** *n* woman
working in advertising
**ADWOMEN** >ADWOMAN
**ADYNAMIA** *n* loss of vital
power or strength, esp as
the result of illness
**ADYNAMIAS** >ADYNAMIA
**ADYNAMIC** >ADYNAMIA
**ADYTA** >ADYTUM
**ADYTUM** *n* most sacred
place of worship in an
ancient temple from
which the laity was
prohibited
**ADZ** *same as* >ADZE
**ADZE** *n* tool with an arched
blade at right angles to the
handle ⊳ *vb* use an adze
**ADZED** >ADZE
**ADZES** >ADZE
**ADZING** >ADZE
**ADZUKI** *n* leguminous
plant, *Phaseolus angularis*,
that has yellow flowers
and pods containing
edible brown seeds and is
widely cultivated as a food
crop in China and Japan
**ADZUKIS** >ADZUKI
**AE** *determiner* one
**AECIA** >AECIUM
**AECIAL** >AECIUM
**AECIDIA** >AECIDIUM
**AECIDIAL** >AECIDIUM
**AECIDIUM** *same as* >AECIUM
**AECIUM** *n* globular or

cup-shaped structure in
some rust fungi in which
aeciospores are produced
**AEDES** *n* any mosquito of
the genus *Aedes* (formerly
*Stegomyia*) of tropical and
subtropical regions, esp *A.
aegypti*, which transmits
yellow fever and dengue
**AEDICULE** *n* opening such
as a door or a window,
framed by columns
on either side, and a
pediment above
**AEDICULES** >AEDICULE
**AEDILE** *n* magistrate of
ancient Rome in charge
of public works, games,
buildings, and roads
**AEDILES** >AEDILE
**AEDINE** *adj* of a species of
mosquito
**AEFALD** *adj* single
**AEFAULD** *adj* single
**AEGIRINE** *n* green mineral
**AEGIRINES** >AEGIRINE
**AEGIRITE** *n* green mineral
**AEGIRITES** >AEGIRITE
**AEGIS** *n* sponsorship,
protection
**AEGISES** >AEGIS
**AEGLOGUE** *n* eclogue
**AEGLOGUES** >AEGLOGUE
**AEGROTAT** *n* (in British and
certain other universities,
and, sometimes, schools)
a certificate allowing
a candidate to pass an
examination although he
has missed all or part of it
through illness
**AEGROTATS** >AEGROTAT
**AEMULE** *vb* emulate
**AEMULED** >AEMULE
**AEMULES** >AEMULE
**AEMULING** >AEMULE
**AENEOUS** *adj* brass-
coloured or greenish-gold
**AENEUS** *n* aquarium fish
**AEOLIAN** *adj* of or relating
to the wind
**AEOLIPILE** *n* device
illustrating the reactive
forces of a gas jet: usually a
spherical vessel mounted
so as to rotate and
equipped with angled exit
pipes from which steam
within it escapes
**AEOLIPYLE** >AEOLIPILE
**AEON** *n* immeasurably long
period of time
**AEONIAN** *adj* everlasting
**AEONIC** >AEON
**AEONS** >AEON
**AEPYORNIS** *n* any of the
large extinct flightless
birds of the genus
*Aepyornis*, remains of
which have been found in
Madagascar
**AEQUORIN** *n* type of protein
**AEQUORINS** >AEQUORIN
**AERATE** *vb* put gas into (a

liquid), as when making a fizzy drink
**AERATED** >AERATE
**AERATES** >AERATE
**AERATING** >AERATE
**AERATION** >AERATE
**AERATIONS** >AERATE
**AERATOR** >AERATE
**AERATORS** >AERATE
**AERIAL** *adj* in, from, or operating in the air ▷ *n* metal pole, wire, etc, for receiving or transmitting radio or TV signals
**AERIALIST** *n* trapeze artist or tightrope walker
**AERIALITY** >AERIAL
**AERIALLY** >AERIAL
**AERIALS** >AERIAL
**AERIE** *a variant spelling (esp US) of* > EYRIE
**AERIED** *adj* in a very high place
**AERIER** >AERY
**AERIES** >AERIE
**AERIEST** >AERY
**AERIFIED** >AERIFY
**AERIFIES** >AERIFY
**AERIFORM** *adj* having the form of air
**AERIFY** *vb* change or cause to change into a gas
**AERIFYING** >AERIFY
**AERILY** >AERY
**AERO** *n* of or relating to aircraft or aeronautics
**AEROBAT** *n* person who does stunt flying
**AEROBATIC** *adj* pertaining to stunt flying
**AEROBATS** >AEROBAT
**AEROBE** *n* organism that requires oxygen to survive
**AEROBES** >AEROBE
**AEROBIA** >AEROBIUM
**AEROBIC** *adj* designed for or relating to aerobics
**AEROBICS** *n* exercises designed to increase the amount of oxygen in the blood
**AEROBIONT** *n* organism needing oxygen to live
**AEROBIUM** *same as* > AEROBE
**AEROBOMB** *n* bomb dropped from aircraft
**AEROBOMBS** >AEROBOMB
**AEROBRAKE** *vb* use airbrakes to slow aircraft
**AEROBUS** *n* type of monorail
**AEROBUSES** >AEROBUS
**AERODART** *n* metal arrow dropped from an aircraft as a weapon
**AERODARTS** >AERODART
**AERODROME** *n* small airport
**AERODUCT** *n* air duct
**AERODUCTS** >AERODUCT
**AERODYNE** *n* any heavier-than-air machine, such as an aircraft, that derives the greater part of its lift from aerodynamic forces

**AERODYNES** >AERODYNE
**AEROFOIL** *n* part of an aircraft, such as the wing, designed to give lift
**AEROFOILS** >AEROFOIL
**AEROGEL** *n* colloid that has a continuous solid phase containing dispersed gas
**AEROGELS** >AEROGEL
**AEROGRAM** *n* airmail letter on a single sheet of paper that seals to form an envelope
**AEROGRAMS** >AEROGRAM
**AEROGRAPH** *n* airborne instrument recording meteorological conditions
**AEROLITE** *n* stony meteorite consisting of silicate minerals
**AEROLITES** >AEROLITE
**AEROLITH** *n* meteorite
**AEROLITHS** >AEROLITH
**AEROLITIC** >AEROLITE
**AEROLOGIC** >AEROLOGY
**AEROLOGY** *n* study of the atmosphere, particularly its upper layers
**AEROMANCY** *n* using weather observation to foretell the future
**AEROMETER** *n* instrument for determining the mass or density of a gas, esp air
**AEROMETRY** *n* branch of physics concerned with the mechanical properties of gases, esp air
**AEROMOTOR** *n* aircraft engine
**AERONAUT** *n* person who flies in a lighter-than-air craft, esp the pilot or navigator
**AERONAUTS** >AERONAUT
**AERONOMER** *n* scientist studying atmosphere
**AERONOMIC** >AERONOMY
**AERONOMY** *n* science of the earth's upper atmosphere
**AEROPAUSE** *n* region of the upper atmosphere above which aircraft cannot fly
**AEROPHAGY** *n* spasmodic swallowing of air
**AEROPHOBE** *n* person suffering from aerophobia
**AEROPHONE** *n* wind instrument
**AEROPHORE** *n* device for playing a wind instrument
**AEROPHYTE** *another name for* > EPIPHYTE
**AEROPLANE** *n* powered flying vehicle with fixed wings
**AEROPULSE** *n* type of jet engine
**AEROS** >AERO
**AEROSAT** *n* communications satellite
**AEROSATS** >AEROSAT
**AEROSCOPE** *n* device for observing the atmosphere

**AEROSHELL** *n* parachute used to slow spacecraft
**AEROSOL** *n* pressurized can from which a substance can be dispensed as a fine spray
**AEROSOLS** >AEROSOL
**AEROSPACE** *n* earth's atmosphere and space beyond ▷ *adj* of rockets or space vehicles
**AEROSTAT** *n* lighter-than-air craft, such as a balloon
**AEROSTATS** >AEROSTAT
**AEROTAXES** >AEROTAXIS
**AEROTAXIS** *n* movement away from or towards oxygen
**AEROTONE** *n* bath incorporating air jets for massage
**AEROTONES** >AEROTONE
**AEROTRAIN** *n* train driven by a jet engine
**AERUGO** *(esp of old bronze) another name for* > VERDIGRIS
**AERUGOS** >AERUGO
**AERY** *adj* lofty, insubstantial, or visionary
**AESC** *n* rune
**AESCES** >AESC
**AESCULIN** *n* chemical in horse-chestnut bark
**AESCULINS** >AESCULIN
**AESIR** *n* chief of the Norse gods
**AESTHESES** >AESTHESIS
**AESTHESIA** *n* normal ability to experience sensation, perception, or sensitivity
**AESTHESIS** *variant of* > ESTHESIS
**AESTHETE** *n* person who has or affects an extravagant love of art
**AESTHETES** >AESTHETE
**AESTHETIC** *adj* relating to the appreciation of art and beauty ▷ *n* principle or set of principles relating to the appreciation of art and beauty
**AESTIVAL** *adj* of or occurring in summer
**AESTIVATE** *vb* pass the summer
**AETHER** *same as* > ETHER
**AETHEREAL** *a variant spelling of* > ETHEREAL
**AETHERIC** >AETHER
**AETHERS** >AETHER
**AETIOLOGY** *n* philosophy or study of causation
**AFALD** *adj* single
**AFAR** *adv* at, from, or to a great distance ▷ *n* great distance
**AFARA** *n* African tree
**AFARAS** >AFARA
**AFARS** >AFAR
**AFAWLD** *adj* single
**AFEAR** *vb* frighten

**AFEARD** *an archaic or dialect word for* > AFRAID
**AFEARED** *same as* > AFEARD
**AFEARING** >AFEAR
**AFEARS** >AFEAR
**AFEBRILE** *adj* without fever
**AFF** *adv* off
**AFFABLE** *adj* friendly and easy to talk to
**AFFABLY** >AFFABLE
**AFFAIR** *n* event or happening
**AFFAIRE** *n* love affair
**AFFAIRES** >AFFAIRE
**AFFAIRS** *pl n* personal or business interests
**AFFEAR** *vb* frighten
**AFFEARD** >AFFEAR
**AFFEARE** *vb* frighten
**AFFEARED** >AFFEAR
**AFFEARES** >AFFEARE
**AFFEARING** >AFFEAR
**AFFEARS** >AFFEAR
**AFFECT** *vb* act on, influence ▷ *n* emotion associated with an idea or set of ideas
**AFFECTED** *adj* displaying affectation
**AFFECTER** >AFFECT
**AFFECTERS** >AFFECT
**AFFECTING** *adj* arousing feelings of pity
**AFFECTION** *n* fondness or love
**AFFECTIVE** *adj* relating to affects
**AFFECTS** >AFFECT
**AFFEER** *vb* assess
**AFFEERED** >AFFEER
**AFFEERING** >AFFEER
**AFFEERS** >AFFEER
**AFFERENT** *adj* bringing or directing inwards to a part or an organ of the body, esp towards the brain or spinal cord ▷ *n* nerve that conveys impulses towards an organ of the body
**AFFERENTS** >AFFERENT
**AFFIANCE** *vb* bind (a person or oneself) in a promise of marriage ▷ *n* solemn pledge, esp a marriage contract
**AFFIANCED** >AFFIANCE
**AFFIANCES** >AFFIANCE
**AFFIANT** *n* person who makes an affidavit
**AFFIANTS** >AFFIANT
**AFFICHE** *n* poster or advertisement, esp one drawn by an artist, as for the opening of an exhibition
**AFFICHES** >AFFICHE
**AFFIDAVIT** *n* written statement made on oath
**AFFIED** >AFFY
**AFFIES** >AFFY
**AFFILIATE** *vb* (of a group) link up with a larger group ▷ *n* person or organization that is affiliated with

another
**AFFINAL** > AFFINE
**AFFINE** adj of, characterizing, or involving transformations which preserve collinearity, esp in classical geometry, those of translation, rotation and reflection in an axis ▷ n relation by marriage
**AFFINED** adj closely related
**AFFINELY** > AFFINE
**AFFINES** > AFFINE
**AFFINITY** n close connection or liking
**AFFIRM** vb declare to be true
**AFFIRMANT** > AFFIRM
**AFFIRMED** > AFFIRM
**AFFIRMER** > AFFIRM
**AFFIRMERS** > AFFIRM
**AFFIRMING** > AFFIRM
**AFFIRMS** > AFFIRM
**AFFIX** vb attach or fasten ▷ n word or syllable added to a word to change its meaning
**AFFIXABLE** > AFFIRM
**AFFIXAL** > AFFIX
**AFFIXED** > AFFIX
**AFFIXER** > AFFIX
**AFFIXERS** > AFFIX
**AFFIXES** > AFFIX
**AFFIXIAL** > AFFIX
**AFFIXING** > AFFIX
**AFFIXMENT** > AFFIX
**AFFIXTURE** > AFFIX
**AFFLATED** adj inspired
**AFFLATION** n inspiration
**AFFLATUS** n impulse of creative power or inspiration, esp in poetry, considered to be of divine origin
**AFFLICT** vb give pain or grief to
**AFFLICTED** > AFFLICT
**AFFLICTER** n one who afflicts
**AFFLICTS** > AFFLICT
**AFFLUENCE** n wealth
**AFFLUENCY** n affluence
**AFFLUENT** adj having plenty of money ▷ n tributary stream
**AFFLUENTS** > AFFLUENT
**AFFLUENZA** n guilt or lack of motivation experienced by people who have made or inherited large amounts of money
**AFFLUX** n flowing towards a point
**AFFLUXES** > AFFLUX
**AFFLUXION** n flow towards something
**AFFOORD** vb consent
**AFFOORDED** > AFFOORD
**AFFOORDS** > AFFOORD
**AFFORCE** vb strengthen
**AFFORCED** > AFFORCE
**AFFORCES** > AFFORCE
**AFFORCING** > AFFORCE

**AFFORD** vb have enough money to buy
**AFFORDED** > AFFORD
**AFFORDING** > AFFORD
**AFFORDS** > AFFORD
**AFFOREST** vb plant trees on
**AFFORESTS** > AFFOREST
**AFFRAP** vb strike
**AFFRAPPED** > AFFRAP
**AFFRAPS** > AFFRAP
**AFFRAY** n noisy fight, brawl ▷ vb frighten
**AFFRAYED** > AFFRAY
**AFFRAYER** > AFFRAY
**AFFRAYERS** > AFFRAY
**AFFRAYING** > AFFRAY
**AFFRAYS** > AFFRAY
**AFFRENDED** adj brought back into friendship
**AFFRET** n furious attack
**AFFRETS** > AFFRET
**AFFRICATE** n composite speech sound consisting of a stop and a fricative articulated at the same point, such as the sound written ch, as in chair.
**AFFRIGHT** vb frighten ▷ n sudden terror
**AFFRIGHTS** > AFFRIGHT
**AFFRONT** n insult ▷ vb hurt someone's pride or dignity
**AFFRONTE** adj facing
**AFFRONTED** > AFFRONT
**AFFRONTEE** adj facing
**AFFRONTS** > AFFRONT
**AFFUSION** n baptizing of a person by pouring water onto his head
**AFFUSIONS** > AFFUSION
**AFFY** vb trust
**AFFYDE** > AFFY
**AFFYING** > AFFY
**AFGHAN** n type of biscuit
**AFGHANI** n standard monetary unit of Afghanistan, divided into 100 puli
**AFGHANIS** > AFGHANI
**AFGHANS** > AFGHAN
**AFIELD** adj away from one's usual surroundings or home
**AFIRE** adj on fire
**AFLAJ** n Arabian irrigation channel
**AFLAME** adj burning
**AFLATOXIN** n toxin produced by the fungus Aspergillus flavus growing on peanuts, maize, etc, causing liver disease (esp cancer) in man
**AFLOAT** adj floating ▷ adv floating
**AFLUTTER** adv in or into a state nervous or excited state
**AFOOT** adj happening, in operation ▷ adv happening
**AFORE** adv before
**AFOREHAND** adv beforehand
**AFORESAID** adj referred to previously

**AFORETIME** adv formerly
**AFOUL** adj in or into a state of difficulty, confusion, or conflict (with)
**AFRAID** adj frightened
**AFREET** n powerful evil demon or giant monster
**AFREETS** > AFREET
**AFRESH** adv again, anew
**AFRIT** same as > AFREET
**AFRITS** > AFRIT
**AFRO** n bush-like frizzy hairstyle
**AFRONT** adv in front
**AFROS** > AFRO
**AFT** adv at or towards the rear of a ship or aircraft ▷ adj at or towards the rear of a ship or aircraft
**AFTER** adv at a later time
**AFTERBODY** n any discarded part that continues to trail a satellite, rocket, etc, in orbit
**AFTERCARE** n support given to a person discharged from a hospital or prison
**AFTERCLAP** n unexpected consequence
**AFTERDAMP** n poisonous gas formed after the explosion of firedamp in a coal mine
**AFTERDECK** n unprotected deck behind the bridge of a ship
**AFTEREYE** vb gaze at someone or something that has passed
**AFTEREYED** > AFTEREYE
**AFTEREYES** > AFTEREYE
**AFTERGAME** n second game that follows another
**AFTERGLOW** n glow left after a source of light has gone
**AFTERHEAT** n heat generated in a nuclear reactor after it has been shut down, produced by residual radioactivity in the fuel elements
**AFTERINGS** n last of the milk drawn in milking
**AFTERLIFE** n life after death
**AFTERMATH** n results of an event considered together
**AFTERMOST** adj closer or closest to the rear or (in a vessel) the stern
**AFTERNOON** n time between noon and evening
**AFTERPAIN** n pain that comes after a while
**AFTERPEAK** n space behind the aftermost bulkhead, often used for storage
**AFTERS** n sweet course of a meal
**AFTERSHOW** n party held after a public performance

of a play or film
**AFTERSUN** n moisturizing lotion applied to the skin to soothe sunburn and avoid peeling
**AFTERSUNS** > AFTERSUN
**AFTERTAX** adj after tax has been paid
**AFTERTIME** n later period
**AFTERWARD** adv after an earlier event or time
**AFTERWORD** n epilogue or postscript in a book, etc
**AFTMOST** adj furthest towards rear
**AFTOSA** n foot-and-mouth disease
**AFTOSAS** > AFTOSA
**AG** n agriculture
**AGA** n title of respect, often used with the title of a senior position
**AGACANT** adj irritating
**AGACANTE** adj irritating
**AGACERIE** n coquetry
**AGACERIES** > AGACERIE
**AGAIN** adv once more
**AGAINST** prep in opposition or contrast to
**AGALACTIA** n absence or failure of secretion of milk
**AGALLOCH** another name for > EAGLEWOOD
**AGALLOCHS** > AGALLOCH
**AGALWOOD** n eaglewood
**AGALWOODS** > AGALWOOD
**AGAMA** n any small terrestrial lizard of the genus Agama, which inhabit warm regions of the Old World: family Agamidae
**AGAMAS** > AGAMA
**AGAMETE** n reproductive cell, such as the merozoite of some protozoans, that develops into a new form without fertilization
**AGAMETES** > AGAMETE
**AGAMI** n South American bird
**AGAMIC** adj asexual
**AGAMID** same as > AGAMA
**AGAMIDS** > AGAMID
**AGAMIS** > AGAMI
**AGAMOGONY** n asexual reproduction in protozoans that is characterized by multiple fission
**AGAMOID** n lizard of the agamid type
**AGAMOIDS** > AGAMOID
**AGAMONT** another name for > SCHIZONT
**AGAMONTS** > AGAMONT
**AGAMOUS** adj without sex
**AGAPAE** > AGAPE
**AGAPAI** > AGAPE
**AGAPE** adj (of the mouth) wide open ▷ n love feast among the early Christians
**AGAPEIC** > AGAPE
**AGAPES** > AGAPE

**AGAR** n jelly-like substance obtained from seaweed and used as a thickener in food

**AGARIC** n fungus with gills on the underside of the cap, such as a mushroom

**AGARICS** >AGARIC

**AGAROSE** n gel used in chemistry

**AGAROSES** >AGAROSE

**AGARS** >AGAR

**AGAS** >AGA

**AGAST** adj aghast

**AGATE** n semiprecious form of quartz with striped colouring ▷ adv on the way

**AGATES** >AGATE

**AGATEWARE** n ceramic ware made to resemble agate or marble

**AGATISE** same as >AGATIZE

**AGATISED** >AGATISE

**AGATISES** >AGATISE

**AGATISING** >AGATISE

**AGATIZE** vb turn into agate

**AGATIZED** >AGATIZE

**AGATIZES** >AGATIZE

**AGATIZING** >AGATIZE

**AGATOID** adj like agate

**AGAVE** n tropical American plant with tall flower stalks and thick leaves

**AGAVES** >AGAVE

**AGAZE** adj gazing at something

**AGAZED** adj amazed

**AGE** n length of time a person or thing has existed ▷ vb make or grow old

**AGED** adj old

**AGEDLY** >AGED

**AGEDNESS** >AGED

**AGEE** adj awry, crooked, or ajar ▷ adv awry

**AGEING** n fact or process of growing old ▷ adj becoming or appearing older

**AGEINGS** >AGEING

**AGEISM** n discrimination against people on the grounds of age

**AGEISMS** >AGEISM

**AGEIST** >AGEISM

**AGEISTS** >AGEISM

**AGELAST** n someone who never laughs

**AGELASTIC** >AGELAST

**AGELASTS** >AGELAST

**AGELESS** adj apparently never growing old

**AGELESSLY** >AGELESS

**AGELONG** adj lasting for a very long time

**AGEMATE** n person the same age as another person

**AGEMATES** >AGEMATE

**AGEN** archaic form of >AGAIN

**AGENCIES** >AGENCY

**AGENCY** n organization providing a service

**AGENDA** n list of things to be dealt with, esp at a meeting

**AGENDAS** >AGENDA

**AGENDUM** >AGENDA

**AGENDUMS** same as >AGENDA

**AGENE** n chemical used to whiten flour

**AGENES** >AGENE

**AGENESES** >AGENESIS

**AGENESIA** n imperfect development

**AGENESIAS** >AGENESIA

**AGENESIS** n (of an animal or plant) imperfect development

**AGENETIC** >AGENESIS

**AGENISE** same as >AGENIZE

**AGENISED** >AGENISE

**AGENISES** >AGENISE

**AGENISING** >AGENISE

**AGENIZE** vb whiten using agene

**AGENIZED** >AGENIZE

**AGENIZES** >AGENIZE

**AGENIZING** >AGENIZE

**AGENT** n person acting on behalf of another ▷ vb act as an agent

**AGENTED** >AGENT

**AGENTIAL** >AGENT

**AGENTING** >AGENT

**AGENTINGS** >AGENT

**AGENTIVAL** adj of the performer of an action

**AGENTIVE** adj (in some inflected languages) denoting a case of nouns, etc, indicating the agent described by the verb ▷ n agentive case

**AGENTIVES** >AGENTIVE

**AGENTRIES** >AGENTRY

**AGENTRY** n acting as agent

**AGENTS** >AGENT

**AGER** n something that ages

**AGERATUM** n any tropical American plant of the genus *Ageratum*, such as *A. houstonianum* and *A. conyzoides*, which have thick clusters of purplish-blue flowers

**AGERATUMS** >AGERATUM

**AGERS** >AGER

**AGES** >AGE

**AGEUSIA** n lack of the sense of taste

**AGEUSIAS** >AGEUSIA

**AGGADA** n explanation in Jewish literature

**AGGADAH** same as >AGGADA

**AGGADAHS** >AGGADAH

**AGGADAS** >AGGADA

**AGGADIC** adj of aggada

**AGGADOT** >AGGADA

**AGGADOTH** >AGGADA

**AGGER** n earthwork or mound forming a rampart, esp in a Roman military camp

**AGGERS** adj aggressive

**AGGIE** n American agricultural student

**AGGIES** >AGGIE

**AGGRACE** vb add grace to

**AGGRACED** >AGGRACE

**AGGRACES** >AGGRACE

**AGGRACING** >AGGRACE

**AGGRADE** vb build up the level of (any land surface) by the deposition of sediment

**AGGRADED** >AGGRADE

**AGGRADES** >AGGRADE

**AGGRADING** >AGGRADE

**AGGRATE** vb gratify

**AGGRATED** >AGGRATE

**AGGRATES** >AGGRATE

**AGGRATING** >AGGRATE

**AGGRAVATE** vb make worse

**AGGREGATE** n total ▷ adj gathered into a mass ▷ vb combine into a whole

**AGGRESS** vb attack first or begin a quarrel

**AGGRESSED** >AGGRESS

**AGGRESSES** >AGGRESS

**AGGRESSOR** n person or body that engages in aggressive behaviour

**AGGRI** adj of African beads

**AGGRIEVE** vb grieve

**AGGRIEVED** adj upset and angry

**AGGRIEVES** >AGGRIEVE

**AGGRO** n aggressive behaviour

**AGGROS** >AGGRO

**AGGRY** adj of African beads

**AGHA** same as >AGA

**AGHAS** >AGHA

**AGHAST** adj overcome with amazement or horror

**AGILA** n eaglewood

**AGILAS** >AGILA

**AGILE** adj nimble, quick-moving

**AGILELY** >AGILE

**AGILENESS** >AGILE

**AGILER** >AGILE

**AGILEST** >AGILE

**AGILITIES** >AGILE

**AGILITY** >AGILE

**AGIN** prep against, opposed to

**AGING** same as >AGEING

**AGINGS** >AGING

**AGINNER** n someone who is against something

**AGINNERS** >AGINNER

**AGIO** n difference between the nominal and actual values of a currency

**AGIOS** >AGIO

**AGIOTAGE** n business of exchanging currencies

**AGIOTAGES** >AGIOTAGE

**AGISM** same as >AGEISM

**AGISMS** >AGISM

**AGIST** vb care for and feed (cattle or horses) for payment

**AGISTED** >AGIST

**AGISTER** n person who grazes cattle for money

**AGISTERS** >AGISTER

**AGISTING** >AGIST

**AGISTMENT** >AGEISM

**AGISTOR** n person who grazes cattle for money

**AGISTORS** >AGISTOR

**AGISTS** >AGIST

**AGITA** n acid indigestion

**AGITABLE** >AGITATE

**AGITANS** as in *paralysis agitans* Parkinson's disease

**AGITAS** >AGITA

**AGITATE** vb disturb or excite

**AGITATED** adj anxious or worried >AGITATE

**AGITATES** >AGITATE

**AGITATING** >AGITATE

**AGITATION** n state of excitement, disturbance, or worry

**AGITATIVE** >AGITATE

**AGITATO** adv (to be performed) in an agitated manner

**AGITATOR** n person who agitates for or against a cause, etc

**AGITATORS** >AGITATOR

**AGITPOP** n use of pop music to promote political propaganda

**AGITPOPS** >AGITPOP

**AGITPROP** n political agitation and propaganda

**AGITPROPS** >AGITPROP

**AGLARE** adj glaring

**AGLEAM** adj glowing

**AGLEE** same as >AGLEY

**AGLET** n metal sheath or tag at the end of a shoelace, ribbon, etc

**AGLETS** >AGLET

**AGLEY** adj awry

**AGLIMMER** adj glimmering

**AGLITTER** adj sparkling, glittering

**AGLOO** same as >AGLU

**AGLOOS** >AGLOO

**AGLOSSAL** >AGLOSSIA

**AGLOSSATE** >AGLOSSIA

**AGLOSSIA** n congenital absence of the tongue

**AGLOSSIAS** >AGLOSSIA

**AGLOW** adj glowing

**AGLU** n breathing hole made in ice by a seal

**AGLUS** >AGLU

**AGLY** Scots word for >WRONG

**AGLYCON** n chemical compound

**AGLYCONE** n chemical compound

**AGLYCONES** >AGLYCONE

**AGLYCONS** >AGLYCON

**AGMA** n symbol used to represent a velar nasal consonant

**AGMAS** >AGMA

**AGMINATE** adj gathered or clustered together

**AGNAIL** another name for >HANGNAIL

**AGNAILS** >AGNAIL

13

**AGNAME** n name additional to first name and surname
**AGNAMED** adj having an agname
**AGNAMES** > AGNAME
**AGNATE** adj related by descent from a common male ancestor ▷ n male or female descendant by male links from a common male ancestor
**AGNATES** > AGNATE
**AGNATHAN** n any jawless eel-like aquatic vertebrate of the superclass Agnatha, which includes the lampreys and hagfishes ▷ adj of, relating to, or belonging to the superclass Agnatha
**AGNATHANS** > AGNATHAN
**AGNATHOUS** adj (esp of lampreys and hagfishes) lacking jaws
**AGNATIC** > AGNATE
**AGNATICAL** > AGNATE
**AGNATION** > AGNATE
**AGNATIONS** > AGNATE
**AGNISE** vb acknowledge
**AGNISED** > AGNISE
**AGNISES** > AGNISE
**AGNISING** > AGNISE
**AGNIZE** vb acknowledge
**AGNIZED** > AGNIZE
**AGNIZES** > AGNIZE
**AGNIZING** > AGNIZE
**AGNOMEN** n fourth name or second cognomen occasionally acquired by an ancient Roman
**AGNOMENS** > AGNOMEN
**AGNOMINA** > AGNOMEN
**AGNOMINAL** > AGNOMEN
**AGNOSIA** n loss or diminution of the power to recognize familiar objects or people, usually as a result of brain damage
**AGNOSIAS** > AGNOSIA
**AGNOSIC** > AGNOSIA
**AGNOSTIC** n person who believes that it is impossible to know whether God exists ▷ adj of agnostics
**AGNOSTICS** > AGNOSTIC
**AGO** adv in the past
**AGOG** adj eager or curious
**AGOGE** n ancient Greek tempo
**AGOGES** > AGOGE
**AGOGIC** n musical accent
**AGOGICS** > AGOGIC
**AGOING** adj moving
**AGON** n (in ancient Greece) a festival at which competitors contended for prizes. Among the best known were the Olympic, Pythian, Nemean, and Isthmian Games
**AGONAL** adj of agony
**AGONE** an archaic word for > AGO

**AGONES** > AGON
**AGONIC** adj forming no angle
**AGONIES** > AGONY
**AGONISE** same as > AGONIZE
**AGONISED** > AGONISE
**AGONISES** > AGONISE
**AGONISING** > AGONISE
**AGONIST** n any muscle that is opposed in action by another muscle
**AGONISTES** n person suffering inner struggle
**AGONISTIC** adj striving for effect
**AGONISTS** > AGONIST
**AGONIZE** vb worry greatly
**AGONIZED** > AGONIZE
**AGONIZES** > AGONIZE
**AGONIZING** > AGONIZE
**AGONS** > AGON
**AGONY** n extreme physical or mental pain
**AGOOD** adv seriously or earnestly
**AGORA** n marketplace in Athens, used for popular meetings, or any similar place of assembly in ancient Greece
**AGORAE** > AGORA
**AGORAS** > AGORA
**AGOROT** > AGORA
**AGOROTH** n agorot
**AGOUTA** n Haitian rodent
**AGOUTAS** > AGOUTA
**AGOUTI** n any hystricomorph rodent of the genus Dasyprocta, of Central and South America and the Caribbean: family Dasyproctidae. Agoutis are agile and long-legged, with hooflike claws, and are valued for their meat
**AGOUTIES** > AGOUTI
**AGOUTIS** > AGOUTI
**AGOUTY** n agouti
**AGRAFE** same as > AGRAFFE
**AGRAFES** > AGRAFE
**AGRAFFE** n fastening consisting of a loop and hook, formerly used in armour and clothing
**AGRAFFES** > AGRAFFE
**AGRAPHA** > AGRAPHON
**AGRAPHIA** n loss of the ability to write, resulting from a brain lesion
**AGRAPHIAS** > AGRAPHIA
**AGRAPHIC** > AGRAPHIA
**AGRAPHON** n saying of Jesus not in Gospels
**AGRARIAN** adj of land or agriculture ▷ n person who favours the redistribution of landed property
**AGRARIANS** > AGRARIAN
**AGRASTE** > AGRACE
**AGRAVIC** adj of zero gravity
**AGREE** vb be of the same opinion
**AGREEABLE** adj pleasant

and enjoyable
**AGREEABLY** > AGREEABLE
**AGREED** adj determined by common consent
**AGREEING** > AGREE
**AGREEMENT** n agreeing
**AGREES** > AGREE
**AGREGE** n winner in examination for university teaching post
**AGREGES** > AGREGE
**AGREMENS** n amenities
**AGREMENT** n diplomatic approval of a country
**AGREMENTS** n amenities
**AGRESTAL** adj (of uncultivated plants such as weeds) growing on cultivated land
**AGRESTIAL** adj agrestal
**AGRESTIC** adj rural
**AGRIA** n appearance of pustules
**AGRIAS** > AGRIA
**AGRIMONY** n yellow-flowered plant with bitter-tasting fruits
**AGRIN** adv grinning
**AGRIOLOGY** n study of primitive peoples
**AGRISE** vb fill with fear
**AGRISED** > AGRISE
**AGRISES** > AGRISE
**AGRISING** > AGRISE
**AGRIZE** vb fill with fear
**AGRIZED** > AGRIZE
**AGRIZES** > AGRIZE
**AGRIZING** > AGRIZE
**AGRODOLCE** n Italian sweet-and-sour sauce
**AGROLOGIC** > AGROLOGY
**AGROLOGY** n scientific study of soils and their potential productivity
**AGRONOMIC** > AGRONOMY
**AGRONOMY** n science of soil management and crop production
**AGROUND** adv onto the bottom of shallow water ▷ adj on or onto the ground or bottom, as in shallow water
**AGRYPNIA** n inability to sleep
**AGRYPNIAS** > AGRYPNIA
**AGRYZE** vb fill with fear
**AGRYZED** > AGRYZE
**AGRYZES** > AGRYZE
**AGRYZING** > AGRYZE
**AGS** > AG
**AGTERSKOT** n final payment to a farmer for crops
**AGUACATE** n avocado
**AGUACATES** > AGUACATE
**AGUE** n periodic fever with shivering
**AGUED** adj suffering from fever
**AGUELIKE** > AGUE
**AGUES** > AGUE
**AGUEWEED** n North American gentianaceous

plant, Gentiana quinquefolia, that has clusters of pale blue-violet or white flowers
**AGUEWEEDS** > AGUEWEED
**AGUISE** vb dress
**AGUISED** > AGUISE
**AGUISES** > AGUISE
**AGUISH** > AGUE
**AGUISHLY** > AGUE
**AGUISING** > AGUISE
**AGUIZE** vb dress
**AGUIZED** > AGUIZE
**AGUIZES** > AGUIZE
**AGUIZING** > AGUIZE
**AGUTI** n agouti
**AGUTIS** > AGUTI
**AH** vb say ah
**AHA** interj exclamation expressing triumph, surprise, etc, according to the intonation of the speaker
**AHCHOO** interj sound made by someone sneezing
**AHEAD** adv in front
**AHEAP** adv in a heap
**AHED** > AH
**AHEIGHT** adv at height
**AHEM** interj clearing of the throat in order to attract attention
**AHEMERAL** adj not constituting a full 24-hour day
**AHENT** adv behind
**AHI** n yellowfin tuna
**AHIGH** adv at height
**AHIMSA** n (in Hindu, Buddhist, and Jainist philosophy) the law of reverence for, and nonviolence to, every form of life
**AHIMSAS** > AHIMSA
**AHIND** adv behind
**AHING** > AH
**AHINT** adv behind
**AHIS** > AHI
**AHISTORIC** adj not related to history; not historical
**AHOLD** n holding
**AHOLDS** > AHOLD
**AHORSE** adv on horseback
**AHOY** interj hail used to call a ship
**AHS** > AH
**AHULL** adv with sails furled
**AHUNGERED** adj very hungry
**AHUNGRY** adj very hungry
**AHURU** n small pink cod, Auchenoceros punctatus, of SW Pacific waters
**AHURUHURU** same as > AHURU
**AI** n shaggy-coated slow-moving animal of South America
**AIA** n female servant in East
**AIAS** > AIA
**AIBLINS** Scots word for > PERHAPS
**AID** n (give) assistance

or support ▷ vb help
financially or in other ways
AIDANCE n help
AIDANCES > AIDANCE
AIDANT adj helping
AIDE n assistant
AIDED > AID
AIDER > AID
AIDERS > AID
AIDES > AIDE
AIDFUL adj helpful
AIDING > AID
AIDLESS adj without help
AIDMAN n military medical
assistant
AIDMEN > AIDMAN
AIDOI adj of the genitals
AIDOS Greek word
for > SHAME
AIDS > AID
AIERIES > AIERY
AIERY n eyrie
AIGA n Māori word for
family
AIGAS > AIGA
AIGLET same as > AGLET
AIGLETS > AIGLET
AIGRET same as > AIGRETTE
AIGRETS > AIGRET
AIGRETTE n long plume
worn on hats or as a
headdress, esp one of long
egret feathers
AIGRETTES > AIGRETTE
AIGUILLE n rock mass or
mountain peak shaped
like a needle
AIGUILLES > AIGUILLE
AIKIDO n Japanese system
of self-defence employing
similar principles to judo,
but including blows from
the hands and feet
AIKIDOS > AIKIDO
AIKONA interj South African
expression meaning no
AIL vb trouble, afflict
AILANTHIC > AILANTHUS
AILANTHUS n E Asian
simaroubaceous
deciduous tree, Ailanthus
altissima, planted in Europe
and North America,
having pinnate leaves,
small greenish flowers,
and winged fruits
AILANTO n Asian tree
AILANTOS > AILANTO
AILED > AIL
AILERON n movable flap
on an aircraft wing which
controls rolling
AILERONS > AILERON
AILETTE n shoulder
armour
AILETTES > AILETTE
AILING adj sickly
AILMENT n illness
AILMENTS > AILMENT
AILS > AIL
AIM vb point (a weapon or
missile) or direct (a blow
or remark) at a target ▷ n
aiming

AIMED > AIM
AIMER > AIM
AIMERS > AIM
AIMFUL adj with purpose or
intention
AIMFULLY > AIMFUL
AIMING > AIM
AIMLESS adj having no
purpose
AIMLESSLY > AIMLESS
AIMS > AIM
AIN variant of > AVIN
AINE adj French word for
elder (male)
AINEE adj French word for
elder (female)
AINGA n Māori word for
village
AINGAS > AINGA
AINS > AIN
AINSELL n Scots word
meaning own self
AINSELLS > AINSELL
AIOLI n garlic mayonnaise
AIOLIS > AIOLI
AIR n mixture of gases
forming the earth's
atmosphere ▷ vb make
known publicly
AIRBAG n safety device in
a car, consisting of a bag
that inflates automatically
in an accident to protect
the driver or passenger
AIRBAGS > AIRBAG
AIRBASE n centre from
which military aircraft
operate
AIRBASES > AIRBASE
AIRBOAT n shallow-
draught boat powered by
an aeroplane engine on a
raised structure for use in
swamps
AIRBOATS > AIRBOAT
AIRBORNE adj carried by air
AIRBOUND adj heading into
the air
AIRBRICK n brick with
holes in it, put into the
wall of a building for
ventilation
AIRBRICKS > AIRBRICK
AIRBRUSH n atomizer
that sprays paint by
compressed air ▷ vb paint
using an airbrush
AIRBURST n explosion of a
bomb, shell, etc, in the air
AIRBURSTS > AIRBURST
AIRBUS n commercial
passenger aircraft
AIRBUSES > AIRBUS
AIRBUSSES > AIRBUS
AIRCHECK n recording of a
radio broadcast
AIRCHECKS > AIRCHECK
AIRCOACH n bus travelling
to and from an airport
AIRCRAFT n any machine
that flies, such as an
aeroplane
AIRCREW n crew of an
aircraft

AIRCREWS > AIRCREW
AIRDATE n date of a
programme broadcast
AIRDATES > AIRDATE
AIRDRAWN adj imaginary
AIRDROME same
as > AERODROME
AIRDROMES > AIRDROME
AIRDROP n delivery of
supplies, troops, etc, from
an aircraft by parachute
▷ vb deliver (supplies, etc)
by an airdrop
AIRDROPS > AIRDROP
AIRED > AIR
AIRER n device on which
clothes are hung to dry
AIRERS > AIRER
AIREST > AIR
AIRFARE n money for an
aircraft ticket
AIRFARES > AIRFARE
AIRFIELD n place where
aircraft can land and take
off
AIRFIELDS > AIRFIELD
AIRFLOW n flow of air in
a wind tunnel or past a
moving aircraft, car, train,
etc
AIRFLOWS > AIRFLOW
AIRFOIL same
as > AEROFOIL
AIRFOILS > AIRFOIL
AIRFRAME n body of an
aircraft, excluding its
engines
AIRFRAMES > AIRFRAME
AIRGAP n gap between
parts in an electrical
machine
AIRGAPS > AIRGAP
AIRGLOW n faint light from
the upper atmosphere in
the night sky, esp in low
latitudes
AIRGLOWS > AIRGLOW
AIRGRAPH n photographic
reduction of a letter for
sending airmail
AIRGRAPHS > AIRGRAPH
AIRHEAD n person who
is stupid or incapable of
serious thought
AIRHEADED > AIRHEAD
AIRHEADS > AIRHEAD
AIRHOLE n hole that allows
the passage of air
AIRHOLES > AIRHOLE
AIRIER > AIRY
AIRIEST > AIRY
AIRILY adv in a light-
hearted and casual
manner
AIRINESS n quality or
condition of being fresh,
light, or breezy
AIRING n exposure to air
for drying or ventilation
AIRINGS > AIRING
AIRLESS adj stuffy
AIRLIFT n transport of
troops or cargo by aircraft
when other routes are

blocked ▷ vb transport by
airlift
AIRLIFTED > AIRLIFT
AIRLIFTS > AIRLIFT
AIRLIKE > AIR
AIRLINE n company
providing scheduled
flights for passengers and
cargo
AIRLINER n large
passenger aircraft
AIRLINERS > AIRLINER
AIRLINES > AIRLINE
AIRLOCK n air bubble
blocking the flow of liquid
in a pipe
AIRLOCKS > AIRLOCK
AIRMAIL n system of
sending mail by aircraft
▷ adj of, used for, or
concerned with airmail
▷ vb send by airmail
AIRMAILED > AIRMAIL
AIRMAILS > AIRMAIL
AIRMAN n member of the
air force
AIRMEN > AIRMAN
AIRMOBILE adj using
aircraft as transport
AIRN Scots word for > IRON
AIRNED > AIRN
AIRNING > AIRN
AIRNS > AIRN
AIRPARK n car park at
airport
AIRPARKS > AIRPARK
AIRPLANE same
as > AEROPLANE
AIRPLANES > AIRPLANE
AIRPLAY n broadcast
performances of a record
on radio
AIRPLAYS > AIRPLAY
AIRPORT n airfield for
civilian aircraft, with
facilities for aircraft
maintenance and
passengers
AIRPORTS > AIRPORT
AIRPOST n system of
delivering mail by air
AIRPOSTS > AIRPOST
AIRPOWER n strength of a
nation's air force
AIRPOWERS > AIRPOWER
AIRPROOF vb make
something airtight
AIRPROOFS > AIRPROOF
AIRS pl n manners put on
to impress people
AIRSCAPE n picture or view
of sky
AIRSCAPES > AIRSCAPE
AIRSCREW n aircraft
propeller
AIRSCREWS > AIRSCREW
AIRSHAFT n shaft for
ventilation
AIRSHAFTS > AIRSHAFT
AIRSHED n air over a
particular geographical
area
AIRSHEDS > AIRSHED
AIRSHIP n lighter-than-air

self-propelled aircraft
**AIRSHIPS** >AIRSHIP
**AIRSHOT** n (in golf) shot that misses the ball completely, but counts as a stroke
**AIRSHOTS** >AIRSHOT
**AIRSHOW** n occasion when an air base is open to the public and a flying display and, usually, static exhibitions are held
**AIRSHOWS** >AIRSHOW
**AIRSICK** adj nauseated from travelling in an aircraft
**AIRSIDE** n part of an airport nearest the aircraft
**AIRSIDES** >AIRSIDE
**AIRSPACE** n atmosphere above a country, regarded as its territory
**AIRSPACES** >AIRSPACE
**AIRSPEED** n speed of an aircraft relative to the air in which it moves
**AIRSPEEDS** >AIRSPEED
**AIRSTOP** n helicopter landing-place
**AIRSTOPS** >AIRSTOP
**AIRSTREAM** n wind, esp at a high altitude
**AIRSTRIKE** n attack by military aircraft
**AIRSTRIP** n cleared area where aircraft can take off and land
**AIRSTRIPS** >AIRSTRIP
**AIRT** n direction or point of the compass, esp the direction of the wind ▷ vb direct
**AIRTED** >AIRT
**AIRTH** same as >AIRT
**AIRTHED** >AIRTH
**AIRTHING** >AIRTH
**AIRTHS** >AIRTH
**AIRTIGHT** adj sealed so that air cannot enter
**AIRTIME** n time allocated to a particular programme, topic, or type of material on radio or television
**AIRTIMES** >AIRTIME
**AIRTING** >AIRT
**AIRTS** >AIRT
**AIRWARD** adj into air
**AIRWARDS** adv into air
**AIRWAVE** n radio wave used in radio and television broadcasting
**AIRWAVES** >AIRWAVE
**AIRWAY** n air route used regularly by aircraft
**AIRWAYS** >AIRWAY
**AIRWISE** adv towards the air
**AIRWOMAN** >AIRMAN
**AIRWOMEN** >AIRMAN
**AIRWORTHY** adj (of aircraft) fit to fly
**AIRY** adj well-ventilated
**AIS** >AI

**AISLE** n passageway separating seating areas in a church, theatre, etc, or row of shelves in a supermarket
**AISLED** >AISLE
**AISLELESS** >AISLE
**AISLES** >AISLE
**AISLEWAY** n aisle
**AISLEWAYS** >AISLEWAY
**AISLING** Irish word for >DREAM
**AISLINGS** >AISLING
**AIT** n islet, esp in a river
**AITCH** n letter h or the sound represented by it
**AITCHBONE** n cut of beef from the rump bone
**AITCHES** >AITCH
**AITS** >AIT
**AITU** n half-human half-divine being
**AITUS** >AITU
**AIVER** n a working horse
**AIVERS** >AIVER
**AIZLE** n Scots word for hot ashes
**AIZLES** >AIZLE
**AJAR** adv (of a door) partly open ▷ adj not in harmony
**AJEE** same as >AGEE
**AJIVA** n Jainist term for non-living thing
**AJIVAS** >AJIVA
**AJOWAN** n plant related to caraway
**AJOWANS** >AJOWAN
**AJUGA** n garden plant
**AJUGAS** >AJUGA
**AJUTAGE** n nozzle
**AJUTAGES** >AJUTAGE
**AJWAN** n plant related to caraway
**AJWANS** >AJWAN
**AKA** n vine, Metrosideros scandens, found in New Zealand
**AKARYOTE** n cell without a nucleus
**AKARYOTES** >AKARYOTE
**AKARYOTIC** >AKARYOTE
**AKATEA** n vine with white flowers, Metrosideros diffusa, found in New Zealand
**AKATHISIA** n inability to sit still because of uncontrollable movement caused by reaction to drugs
**AKE** vb old spelling of ache
**AKEAKE** n New Zealand tree
**AKEAKES** >AKEAKE
**AKED** >AKE
**AKEDAH** n binding of Isaac in Bible
**AKEDAHS** >AKEDAH
**AKEE** same as >ACKEE
**AKEES** >AKEE
**AKELA** n adult leader of a pack of Cub Scouts
**AKELAS** >AKELA
**AKENE** same as >ACHENE

**AKENES** >AKENE
**AKENIAL** >ACHENE
**AKES** >AKE
**AKHARA** n (in India) gymnasium
**AKHARAS** >AKHARA
**AKIMBO** adj with arms akimbo with hands on hips and elbows projecting outwards
**AKIN** adj related by blood
**AKINESES** >AKINESIS
**AKINESIA** n loss of power to move
**AKINESIAS** >AKINESIA
**AKINESIS** n loss of power to move
**AKINETIC** >AKINESIA
**AKING** >AKE
**AKIRAHO** n small New Zealand shrub, Olearia paniculata, with white flowers
**AKITA** n large powerfully-built dog of a Japanese breed with erect ears, a typically white coat, and a large full tail carried curled over its back
**AKITAS** >AKITA
**AKKAS** slang word for >MONEY
**AKOLUTHOS** n leader of Byzantine Varangian Guard
**AKRASIA** n weakness of will
**AKRASIAS** >AKRASIA
**AKRATIC** >AKRASIA
**AKVAVIT** same as >AQUAVIT
**AKVAVITS** >AKVAVIT
**AL** same as >AAL
**ALA** n wing or flat winglike process or structure, such as a part of some bones and cartilages
**ALAAP** n part of raga in Indian music
**ALAAPS** >ALAAP
**ALABAMINE** old name for >ASTATINE
**ALABASTER** n soft white translucent stone ▷ adj of or resembling alabaster
**ALACHLOR** n type of herbicide
**ALACHLORS** >ALACHLOR
**ALACK** archaic or poetic word for >ALAS
**ALACKADAY** same as >ALACK
**ALACRITY** n speed, eagerness
**ALAE** >ALA
**ALAIMENT** old spelling of >ALLAYMENT
**ALAIMENTS** >ALAIMENT
**ALALAGMOI** >ALALAGMOS
**ALALAGMOS** n ancient Greek war cry
**ALALIA** n complete inability to speak
**ALALIAS** >ALALIA
**ALAMEDA** n public walk or promenade lined with

trees, often poplars
**ALAMEDAS** >ALAMEDA
**ALAMO** n poplar tree
**ALAMODE** n soft light silk used for shawls and dresses, esp in the 19th century
**ALAMODES** >ALAMODE
**ALAMORT** adj exhausted and downcast
**ALAMOS** >ALAMO
**ALAN** n member of ancient European nomadic people
**ALAND** vb come onto land
**ALANDS** >ALAND
**ALANE** Scots word for >ALONE
**ALANG** n type of grass in Malaysia
**ALANGS** >ALANG
**ALANIN** n alanine
**ALANINE** n nonessential aliphatic amino acid that occurs in many proteins
**ALANINES** >ALANINE
**ALANINS** >ALANIN
**ALANNAH** interj my child: used as a term of address or endearment ▷ n cry of alannah
**ALANNAHS** >ALANNAH
**ALANS** >ALAN
**ALANT** n flowering plant used in herbal medicine
**ALANTS** >ALANT
**ALANYL** n chemical found in proteins
**ALANYLS** >ALANYL
**ALAP** n Indian vocal music without words
**ALAPA** n part of raga in Indian music
**ALAPAS** >ALAPA
**ALAPS** >ALAP
**ALAR** adj relating to, resembling, or having wings or alae
**ALARM** n sudden fear caused by awareness of danger ▷ vb fill with fear
**ALARMABLE** >ALARMABLE
**ALARMED** >ALARM
**ALARMEDLY** >ALARM
**ALARMING** >ALARM
**ALARMISM** >ALARMIST
**ALARMISMS** >ALARMIST
**ALARMIST** n person who alarms others needlessly ▷ adj causing needless alarm
**ALARMISTS** >ALARMIST
**ALARMS** >ALARM
**ALARUM** n alarm, esp a call to arms ▷ vb raise the alarm
**ALARUMED** >ALARUM
**ALARUMING** >ALARUM
**ALARUMS** >ALARUM
**ALARY** adj of, relating to, or shaped like wings
**ALAS** adv unfortunately, regrettably
**ALASKA** n dessert made of cake and ice cream

**ALASKAS** >ALASKA
**ALASTOR** *n* avenging demon
**ALASTORS** >ALASTOR
**ALASTRIM** *n* form of smallpox
**ALASTRIMS** >ALASTRIM
**ALATE** *adj* having wings or winglike extensions ▷ *n* winged insect
**ALATED** *adj* having wings
**ALATES** >ALATE
**ALATION** *n* state of having wings
**ALATIONS** >ALATION
**ALAY** *vb* allay
**ALAYED** >ALAY
**ALAYING** >ALAY
**ALAYS** >ALAY
**ALB** *n* long white robe worn by a Christian priest
**ALBA** *n* song of lament
**ALBACORE** *n* tuna found in warm seas, eaten for food
**ALBACORES** >ALBACORE
**ALBARELLI** >ALBARELLO
**ALBARELLO** *n* jar for drugs
**ALBAS** >ALBA
**ALBATA** *n* variety of German silver consisting of nickel, copper, and zinc
**ALBATAS** >ALBATA
**ALBATROSS** *n* large sea bird with very long wings
**ALBE** *old word for* >ALBEIT
**ALBEDO** *n* ratio of the intensity of light reflected from an object, such as a planet, to that of the light it receives from the sun
**ALBEDOES** >ALBEDO
**ALBEDOS** >ALBEDO
**ALBEE** *archaic form of* >ALBEIT
**ALBEIT** *conj* even though
**ALBERGHI** >ALBERGO
**ALBERGO** *n* Italian word for inn
**ALBERT** *n* kind of watch chain usually attached to a waistcoat
**ALBERTITE** *n* black solid variety of bitumen that has a conchoidal fracture and occurs in veins in oil-bearing strata
**ALBERTS** >ALBERT
**ALBESCENT** *adj* shading into, growing, or becoming white
**ALBESPINE** *old name for* >HAWTHORN
**ALBESPYNE** *old name for* >HAWTHORN
**ALBICORE** *n* species of tunny
**ALBICORES** >ALBICORE
**ALBINAL** >ALBINO
**ALBINESS** *n* female albino
**ALBINIC** >ALBINO
**ALBINISM** >ALBINO
**ALBINISMS** >ALBINO
**ALBINO** *n* person or animal with white skin and hair

and pink eyes
**ALBINOISM** >ALBINO
**ALBINOS** >ALBINO
**ALBINOTIC** >ALBINO
**ALBITE** *n* colourless, milky-white, yellow, pink, green, or black mineral
**ALBITES** >ALBITE
**ALBITIC** >ALBITE
**ALBITICAL** >ALBITE
**ALBITISE** *vb* turn into albite
**ALBITISED** >ALBITISE
**ALBITISES** >ALBITISE
**ALBITIZE** *vb* turn into albite
**ALBITIZED** >ALBITIZE
**ALBITIZES** >ALBITIZE
**ALBIZIA** *n* mimosa
**ALBIZIAS** >ALBIZIA
**ALBIZZIA** *n* mimosa
**ALBIZZIAS** >ALBIZZIA
**ALBRICIAS** *interj* Spanish expression of welcome
**ALBS** >ALB
**ALBUGO** *n* opacity of the cornea
**ALBUGOS** >ALBUGO
**ALBUM** *n* book with blank pages for keeping photographs or stamps in
**ALBUMEN** *same as* >ALBUMIN *n* egg white
**ALBUMENS** >ALBUMEN
**ALBUMIN** *n* protein found in blood plasma, egg white, milk, and muscle
**ALBUMINS** >ALBUMIN
**ALBUMOSE** *the US name for* >PROTEOSE
**ALBUMOSES** >ALBUMOSE
**ALBUMS** >ALBUM
**ALBURNOUS** >ALBURNUM
**ALBURNUM** *former name for* >SAPWOOD
**ALBURNUMS** >ALBURNUM
**ALBUTEROL** *n* drug used to treat lung diseases
**ALCADE** *same as* >ALCALDE
**ALCADES** >ALCADE
**ALCAHEST** *same as* >ALKAHEST
**ALCAHESTS** >ALCAHEST
**ALCAIC** *n* verse consisting of strophes with four tetrametric lines
**ALCAICS** >ALCAIC
**ALCAIDE** *n* commander of a fortress or castle
**ALCAIDES** >ALCAIDE
**ALCALDE** *n* (in Spain and Spanish America) the mayor or chief magistrate in a town
**ALCALDES** >ALCALDE
**ALCARRAZA** *n* Spanish water container
**ALCATRAS** *n* pelican
**ALCAYDE** *n* alcaide
**ALCAYDES** >ALCAYDE
**ALCAZAR** *n* any of various palaces or fortresses built in Spain by the Moors
**ALCAZARS** >ALCAZAR

**ALCHEMIC** >ALCHEMY
**ALCHEMIES** >ALCHEMY
**ALCHEMISE** *same as* >ALCHEMIZE
**ALCHEMIST** *n* person who practises alchemy
**ALCHEMIZE** *vb* alter (an element, metal, etc) by alchemy
**ALCHEMY** *n* medieval form of chemistry concerned with trying to turn base metals into gold and to find the elixir of life
**ALCHERA** *n* (in the mythology of Australian Aboriginal peoples) mythical Golden Age of the past
**ALCHERAS** >ALCHERA
**ALCHYMIES** >ALCHYMY
**ALCHYMY** *old spelling of* >ALCHEMY
**ALCID** *n* bird of the auk family
**ALCIDINE** *adj* of, relating to, or belonging to the *Alcidae*, a family of sea birds including the auks, guillemots, puffins, and related forms
**ALCIDS** >ALCID
**ALCO** *same as* >ALKO
**ALCOHOL** *n* colourless flammable liquid present in intoxicating drinks
**ALCOHOLIC** *adj* of alcohol ▷ *n* person addicted to alcohol
**ALCOHOLS** >ALCOHOL
**ALCOLOCK** *n* breath-alcohol ignition-interlock device, which is fitted to the ignition in certain motor vehicles. The driver must blow into a tube and, if his or her breath contains too much alcohol, a lock is activated to prevent the vehicle starting
**ALCOLOCKS** >ALCOLOCK
**ALCOOL** *n* form of pure grain spirit distilled in Quebec
**ALCOOLS** >ALCOOL
**ALCOPOP** *n* alcoholic drink that tastes like a soft drink
**ALCOPOPS** >ALCOPOP
**ALCORZA** *n* Spanish sweet
**ALCORZAS** >ALCORZA
**ALCOS** >ALCO
**ALCOVE** *n* recess in the wall of a room
**ALCOVED** *adj* with or in an alcove
**ALCOVES** >ALCOVE
**ALDEA** *n* Spanish village
**ALDEAS** >ALDEA
**ALDEHYDE** *n* one of a group of chemical compounds derived from alcohol by oxidation
**ALDEHYDES** >ALDEHYDE
**ALDEHYDIC** >ALDEHYDE

**ALDER** *n* tree related to the birch
**ALDERFLY** *n* insect with large broad-based hind wings, which produces aquatic larvae
**ALDERMAN** *n* formerly, senior member of a local council
**ALDERMEN** >ALDERMAN
**ALDERN** *adj* made of alder wood
**ALDERS** >ALDER
**ALDICARB** *n* crystalline compound used as a pesticide
**ALDICARBS** >ALDICARB
**ALDOL** *n* colourless or yellowish oily liquid
**ALDOLASE** *n* enzyme present in the body
**ALDOLASES** >ALDOLASE
**ALDOLS** >ALDOL
**ALDOSE** *n* sugar that contains the aldehyde group or is a hemiacetal
**ALDOSES** >ALDOSE
**ALDOXIME** *n* oxime formed by reaction between hydroxylamine and an aldehyde
**ALDOXIMES** >ALDOXIME
**ALDRIN** *n* brown to white poisonous crystalline solid
**ALDRINS** >ALDRIN
**ALE** *n* kind of beer
**ALEATORIC** *same as* >ALEATORY
**ALEATORY** *adj* dependent on chance
**ALEBENCH** *n* bench at alehouse
**ALEC** *same as* >ALECK
**ALECITHAL** *adj* (of an ovum) having little or no yolk
**ALECK** *n* irritatingly oversmart person
**ALECKS** >ALECK
**ALECOST** *another name for* >COSTMARY
**ALECOSTS** >ALECOST
**ALECS** >ALEC
**ALECTRYON** *n* New Zealand tree
**ALEE** *adj* on or towards the lee
**ALEF** *n* first letter of Hebrew alphabet
**ALEFS** >ALEF
**ALEFT** *adv* at or to left
**ALEGAR** *n* malt vinegar
**ALEGARS** >ALEGAR
**ALEGGE** *vb* alleviate
**ALEGGED** >ALEGGE
**ALEGGES** >ALEGGE
**ALEGGING** >ALEGGE
**ALEHOUSE** *n* public house
**ALEHOUSES** >ALEHOUSE
**ALEMBIC** *n* anything that distils or purifies, esp an obsolete vessel used for distillation
**ALEMBICS** >ALEMBIC

ALEMBROTH n mercury compound in alchemy

ALENCON n elaborate lace worked on a hexagonal mesh

ALENCONS > ALENCON

ALENGTH adv at length

ALEPH n first letter in the Hebrew alphabet

ALEPHS > ALEPH

ALEPINE n type of cloth

ALEPINES > ALEPINE

ALERCE n wood of the sandarac tree

ALERCES > ALERCE

ALERION n eagle in heraldry

ALERIONS > ALERION

ALERT adj watchful, attentive ▷ n warning of danger ▷ vb warn of danger

ALERTED > ALERT

ALERTER > ALERT

ALERTEST > ALERT

ALERTING > ALERT

ALERTLY > ALERT

ALERTNESS > ALERT

ALERTS > ALERT

ALES > ALE

ALETHIC adj of or relating to such philosophical concepts as truth, necessity, possibility, contingency, etc

ALEURON n outer protein-rich layer of certain seeds, esp of cereal grains

ALEURONE same as > ALEURON

ALEURONES > ALEURONE

ALEURONIC > ALEURON

ALEURONS > ALEURON

ALEVIN n young fish, esp a young salmon or trout

ALEVINS > ALEVIN

ALEW n cry to call hunting hounds

ALEWASHED adj showing effects of beer drinking

ALEWIFE n North American fish

ALEWIVES > ALEWIFE

ALEWS > ALEW

ALEXANDER n cocktail made with creme de cacao

ALEXIA n disorder of the central nervous system characterized by impaired ability to read

ALEXIAS > ALEXIA

ALEXIC > ALEXIA

ALEXIN n complement

ALEXINE same as > ALEXIN

ALEXINES > ALEXINE

ALEXINIC > ALEXIN

ALEXINS > ALEXIN

ALEYE vb allay

ALEYED > ALEYE

ALEYES > ALEYE

ALEYING > ALEYE

ALF n uncultivated Australian

ALFA n type of grass

ALFAKI n expert in Muslim law

ALFAKIS > ALFAKI

ALFALFA n kind of plant used to feed livestock

ALFALFAS > ALFALFA

ALFAQUI n expert in Muslim law

ALFAQUIN n expert in Muslim law

ALFAQUINS > ALFAQUIN

ALFAQUIS > ALFAQUI

ALFAS > ALFA

ALFERECES > ALFEREZ

ALFEREZ n Spanish standard-bearer

ALFILARIA n plant with finely divided leaves and small pink or purplish flowers

ALFILERIA same as > ALFILARIA

ALFORJA n saddlebag made of leather or canvas

ALFORJAS > ALFORJA

ALFREDO adj cooked with a cheese and egg sauce

ALFRESCO adj in the open air ▷ adv in the open air

ALFS > ALF

ALGA n unicellular or multicellular organism formerly classified as a plant

ALGAE > ALGA

ALGAECIDE n substance for killing algae

ALGAL > ALGA

ALGAROBA same as > ALGARROBA

ALGAROBAS > ALGAROBA

ALGARROBA n edible pod of these trees

ALGARROBO n carob

ALGAS > ALGA

ALGATE adv anyway

ALGATES adv anyway

ALGEBRA n branch of mathematics using symbols to represent numbers

ALGEBRAIC adj of or relating to algebra

ALGEBRAS > ALGEBRA

ALGERINE n soft striped woollen cloth

ALGERINES > ALGERINE

ALGESES > ALGESIS

ALGESIA n capacity to feel pain

ALGESIAS > ALGESIA

ALGESIC > ALGESIA

ALGESIS n feeling of pain

ALGETIC > ALGESIA

ALGICIDAL > ALGICIDE

ALGICIDE n any substance that kills algae

ALGICIDES > ALGICIDE

ALGID adj chilly or cold

ALGIDITY > ALGID

ALGIDNESS > ALGID

ALGIN n gelatinous solution obtained as a by-product in the extraction

of iodine from seaweed

ALGINATE n salt or ester of alginic acid

ALGINATES > ALGINATE

ALGINIC as in alginic acid powdery substance extracted from kelp

ALGINS > ALGIN

ALGOID adj resembling or relating to algae

ALGOLOGY n branch of biology concerned with the study of algae

ALGOMETER n instrument for measuring sensitivity to pressure or to pain

ALGOMETRY > ALGOMETER

ALGOR n chill

ALGORISM n Arabic or decimal system of counting

ALGORISMS > ALGORISM

ALGORITHM n logical arithmetical or computational procedure for solving a problem

ALGORS > ALGOR

ALGUACIL n Spanish law officer

ALGUACILS > ALGUACIL

ALGUAZIL n Spanish law officer

ALGUAZILS > ALGUAZIL

ALGUM n type of wood mentioned in Bible

ALGUMS > ALGUM

ALIAS adv also known as ▷ n false name

ALIASES > ALIAS

ALIASING n error in a vision or sound signal arising from limitations in the system that generates or processes the signal

ALIASINGS > ALIASING

ALIBI n plea of being somewhere else when a crime was committed ▷ vb provide someone with an alibi

ALIBIED > ALIBI

ALIBIES > ALIBI

ALIBIING > ALIBI

ALIBIS > ALIBI

ALIBLE adj nourishing

ALICANT n wine from Alicante in Spain

ALICANTS > ALICANT

ALICYCLIC adj (of an organic compound) having aliphatic properties, in spite of the presence of a ring of carbon atoms

ALIDAD same as > ALIDADE

ALIDADE n surveying instrument used in plane-tabling for drawing lines of sight on a distant object and taking angular measurements

ALIDADES > ALIDADE

ALIDADS > ALIDAD

ALIEN adj foreign ▷ n

foreigner ▷ vb transfer (property, etc) to another

ALIENABLE adj able to be transferred to another owner

ALIENAGE > ALIEN

ALIENAGES > ALIEN

ALIENATE vb cause to become hostile

ALIENATED > ALIENATE

ALIENATES > ALIENATE

ALIENATOR > ALIENATE

ALIENED > ALIEN

ALIENEE n person to whom a transfer of property is made

ALIENEES > ALIENEE

ALIENER > ALIEN

ALIENERS > ALIEN

ALIENING > ALIEN

ALIENISM n study and treatment of mental illness

ALIENISMS > ALIENISM

ALIENIST n psychiatrist who specializes in the legal aspects of mental illness

ALIENISTS > ALIENIST

ALIENLY > ALIEN

ALIENNESS > ALIEN

ALIENOR n person who transfers property to another

ALIENORS > ALIENOR

ALIENS > ALIEN

ALIF n first letter of Arabic alphabet

ALIFORM adj wing-shaped

ALIFS > ALIF

ALIGARTA n alligator

ALIGARTAS > ALIGARTA

ALIGHT vb step out of (a vehicle) ▷ adj on fire ▷ adv on fire

ALIGHTED > ALIGHT

ALIGHTING > ALIGHT

ALIGHTS > ALIGHT

ALIGN vb bring (a person or group) into agreement with the policy of another

ALIGNED > ALIGN

ALIGNER > ALIGN

ALIGNERS > ALIGN

ALIGNING > ALIGN

ALIGNMENT n arrangement in a straight line

ALIGNS > ALIGN

ALIKE adj like, similar ▷ adv in the same way

ALIKENESS > ALIKE

ALIMENT n something that nourishes or sustains the body or mind ▷ vb support or sustain

ALIMENTAL > ALIMENT

ALIMENTED > ALIMENT

ALIMENTS > ALIMENT

ALIMONIED adj provided with alimony

ALIMONIES > ALIMONY

ALIMONY n allowance paid under a court order to a separated or divorced spouse

**ALINE** *a rare spelling of* >ALIGN

**ALINED** >ALINE

**ALINEMENT** >ALINE

**ALINER** >ALINE

**ALINERS** >ALINE

**ALINES** >ALINE

**ALINING** >ALINE

**ALIPED** *n* animal, like the bat, whose toes are joined by a membrane that serves as a wing ▷ *adj* (of bats and similar animals) having the digits connected by a winglike membrane

**ALIPEDS** >ALIPED

**ALIPHATIC** *adj* (of an organic compound) having an open chain structure

**ALIQUANT** *adj* denoting or belonging to a number that is not an exact divisor of a given number

**ALIQUOT** *adj* of or denoting an exact divisor of a number ▷ *n* exact divisor

**ALIQUOTS** >ALIQUOT

**ALISMA** *n* marsh plant

**ALISMAS** >ALISMA

**ALISON** *same as* >ALYSSUM

**ALISONS** >ALISON

**ALIST** *adj* leaning over

**ALIT** *rare past tense and past participle of* >ALIGHT

**ALITERACY** >ALITERATE

**ALITERATE** *n* person who is able to read but disinclined to do so ▷ *adj* of or relating to aliterates

**ALIUNDE** *adj* from a source extrinsic to the matter, document, or instrument under consideration

**ALIVE** *adj* living, in existence

**ALIVENESS** >ALIVE

**ALIYA** *n* immigration to Holy Land

**ALIYAH** *n* immigration to the Holy Land

**ALIYAHS** >ALIYAH

**ALIYAS** >ALIYA

**ALIYOS** *n* remission of sin in Jewish faith

**ALIYOT** >ALIYAH

**ALIYOTH** >ALIYAH

**ALIZARI** *n* madder from Middle East

**ALIZARIN** *n* brownish-yellow powder or orange-red crystalline solid

**ALIZARINE** *n* alizarin

**ALIZARINS** >ALIZARIN

**ALIZARIS** >ALIZARI

**ALKAHEST** *n* hypothetical universal solvent sought by alchemists

**ALKAHESTS** >ALKAHEST

**ALKALI** *n* substance which combines with acid and neutralizes it to form a salt

**ALKALIC** *adj* (of igneous rocks) containing large amounts of alkalis, esp sodium and potassium

**ALKALIES** >ALKALI

**ALKALIFY** *vb* make or become alkaline

**ALKALIN** *adj* leaning over

**ALKALINE** *adj* having the properties of or containing an alkali

**ALKALIS** >ALKALI

**ALKALISE** *same as* >ALKALIZE

**ALKALISED** >ALKALISE

**ALKALISER** >ALKALISE

**ALKALISES** >ALKALISE

**ALKALIZE** *vb* make alkaline

**ALKALIZED** >ALKALIZE

**ALKALIZER** >ALKALIZE

**ALKALIZES** >ALKALIZE

**ALKALOID** *n* any of a group of organic compounds containing nitrogen

**ALKALOIDS** >ALKALOID

**ALKALOSES** >ALKALOSIS

**ALKALOSIS** *n* abnormal increase in the alkalinity of the blood and extracellular fluids

**ALKALOTIC** >ALKALOSIS

**ALKANE** *n* any saturated hydrocarbon with the general formula $CnH_2n+2$

**ALKANES** >ALKANE

**ALKANET** *n* European boraginaceous plant, *Alkanna tinctoria*, the roots of which yield a red dye

**ALKANETS** >ALKANET

**ALKANNIN** *same as* >ALKANET

**ALKANNINS** >ALKANNIN

**ALKENE** *n* type of unsaturated hydrocarbon

**ALKENES** >ALKENE

**ALKIE** *same as* >ALKY

**ALKIES** >ALKY

**ALKINE** *n* alkyne

**ALKINES** >ALKINE

**ALKO** *n* heavy drinker or alcoholic

**ALKOS** >ALKO

**ALKOXIDE** *n* chemical compound containing oxygen

**ALKOXIDES** >ALKOXIDE

**ALKOXY** *adj* of type of chemical compound containing oxygen

**ALKY** *n* heavy drinker or alcoholic

**ALKYD** *n* synthetic resin

**ALKYDS** >ALKYD

**ALKYL** *n* of, consisting of, or containing the monovalent group $CnH_2n+1$

**ALKYLATE** *vb* add alkyl group to a compound

**ALKYLATED** >ALKYLATE

**ALKYLATES** >ALKYLATE

**ALKYLIC** >ALKYL

**ALKYLS** >ALKYL

**ALKYNE** *n* any unsaturated

aliphatic hydrocarbon

**ALKYNES** >ALKYNE

**ALL** *adj* whole quantity or number (of) ▷ *adv* wholly, entirely ▷ *n* entire being, effort, or property

**ALLANITE** *n* rare black or brown mineral

**ALLANITES** >ALLANITE

**ALLANTOIC** >ALLANTOIS

**ALLANTOID** *adj* relating to or resembling the allantois

**ALLANTOIN** *n* chemical used in cosmetics

**ALLANTOIS** *n* membranous sac growing out of the ventral surface of the hind gut of embryonic reptiles, birds, and mammals. It combines with the chorion to form the mammalian placenta

**ALLATIVE** *n* word in grammatical case denoting movement towards

**ALLATIVES** >ALLATIVE

**ALLAY** *vb* reduce (fear or anger)

**ALLAYED** >ALLAY

**ALLAYER** >ALLAY

**ALLAYERS** >ALLAY

**ALLAYING** >ALLAY

**ALLAYINGS** >ALLAY

**ALLAYMENT** *n* mitigation

**ALLAYS** >ALLAY

**ALLCOMERS** *n* everyone who comes

**ALLEDGE** *vb* allege

**ALLEDGED** >ALLEDGE

**ALLEDGES** >ALLEDGE

**ALLEDGING** >ALLEDGE

**ALLEE** *n* avenue

**ALLEES** >ALLEE

**ALLEGE** *vb* state without proof

**ALLEGED** *adj* stated but not proved

**ALLEGEDLY** *adv* reportedly

**ALLEGER** >ALLEGE

**ALLEGERS** >ALLEGE

**ALLEGES** >ALLEGE

**ALLEGGE** *vb* alleviate

**ALLEGGED** >ALLEGGE

**ALLEGGES** >ALLEGGE

**ALLEGGING** >ALLEGGE

**ALLEGIANT** *n* loyalty

**ALLEGING** >ALLEGE

**ALLEGORIC** *adj* used in, containing, or characteristic of allegory

**ALLEGORY** *n* story with an underlying meaning as well as the literal one

**ALLEGRO** *adv* (piece to be played) in a brisk lively manner ▷ *n* piece or passage to be performed in a brisk lively manner

**ALLEGROS** >ALLEGRO

**ALLEL** *n* form of gene

**ALLELE** *n* any of two or more genes that are responsible for alternative

characteristics, such as smooth or wrinkled seeds in peas

**ALLELES** >ALLELE

**ALLELIC** >ALLELE

**ALLELISM** >ALLELE

**ALLELISMS** >ALLELE

**ALLELS** >ALLEL

**ALLELUIA** *n* song of praise to God

**ALLELUIAH** *interj* alleluia

**ALLELUIAS** >ALLELUIA

**ALLEMANDE** *n* first movement of the classical suite, composed in a moderate tempo in a time signature of four-four

**ALLENARLY** *adv* solely

**ALLERGEN** *n* substance capable of causing an allergic reaction

**ALLERGENS** >ALLERGEN

**ALLERGIC** *adj* having or caused by an allergy ▷ *n* person suffering from an allergy

**ALLERGICS** >ALLERGIC

**ALLERGIES** >ALLERGY

**ALLERGIN** *n* allergen

**ALLERGINS** >ALLERGIN

**ALLERGIST** *n* physician skilled in the diagnosis and treatment of diseases or conditions caused by allergy

**ALLERGY** *n* extreme sensitivity to a substance, which causes the body to react to it

**ALLERION** *n* eagle in heraldry

**ALLERIONS** >ALLERION

**ALLETHRIN** *n* clear viscous amber-coloured liquid

**ALLEVIANT** *n* medical treatment that reduces pain but does not cure the underlying problem

**ALLEVIATE** *vb* lessen (pain or suffering)

**ALLEY** *n* narrow street or path

**ALLEYCAT** *n* homeless cat that roams in back streets

**ALLEYCATS** >ALLEYCAT

**ALLEYED** *adj* having alleys

**ALLEYS** >ALLEY

**ALLEYWAY** *n* narrow passage with buildings or walls on both sides

**ALLEYWAYS** >ALLEYWAY

**ALLHEAL** *n* any of several plants reputed to have healing powers, such as selfheal and valerian

**ALLHEALS** >ALLHEAL

**ALLIABLE** *adj* able to form an alliance

**ALLIANCE** *n* state of being allied

**ALLIANCES** >ALLIANCE

**ALLICE** *n* species of fish

**ALLICES** >ALLICE

**ALLICHOLY** *n* melancholy

ALLICIN n chemical found in garlic

ALLICINS >ALLICIN

ALLIED adj joined, as by treaty, agreement, or marriage

ALLIES >ALLY

ALLIGARTA n alligator

ALLIGATE vb join together

ALLIGATED >ALLIGATE

ALLIGATES >ALLIGATE

ALLIGATOR n reptile of the crocodile family, found in the southern US and China

ALLIS n species of fish

ALLISES >ALLIS

ALLIUM n any plant of the genus Allium, such as the onion, garlic, shallot, leek, or chive: family Alliaceae

ALLIUMS >ALLIUM

ALLNESS n being all

ALLNESSES >ALLNESS

ALLNIGHT adj lasting all night

ALLOBAR n form of element

ALLOBARS >ALLOBAR

ALLOCABLE >ALLOCATE

ALLOCARPY n production of fruit through cross-fertilization

ALLOCATE vb assign to someone or for a particular purpose

ALLOCATED >ALLOCATE

ALLOCATES >ALLOCATE

ALLOCATOR >ALLOCATE

ALLOD same as >ALLODIUM

ALLODIA >ALLODIUM

ALLODIAL adj (of land) held as an allodium

ALLODIUM n lands held in absolute ownership, free from such obligations as rent or services due to an overlord

ALLODIUMS >ALLODIUM

ALLODS >ALLOD

ALLOGAMY n cross-fertilization in flowering plants

ALLOGENIC adj having different genes

ALLOGRAFT n tissue graft from a donor genetically unrelated to the recipient

ALLOGRAPH n document written by a person who is not a party to it

ALLOMERIC adj of similar crystalline structure

ALLOMETRY n study of the growth of part of an organism in relation to the growth of the entire organism

ALLOMONE n chemical substance secreted externally by certain animals, such as insects, affecting the behaviour or physiology of another species detrimentally

ALLOMONES >ALLOMONE

ALLOMORPH n any of the phonological representations of a single morpheme

ALLONGE n paper extension to bill of exchange

ALLONGES >ALLONGE

ALLONS interj French word meaning let's go

ALLONYM n name, often one of historical significance or that of another person, assumed by a person, esp an author

ALLONYMS >ALLONYM

ALLOPATH n person who practises or is skilled in allopathy

ALLOPATHS >ALLOPATH

ALLOPATHY n orthodox method of treating disease, by using drugs that produce an effect opposite to the effect of the disease being treated, as contrasted with homeopathy

ALLOPATRY n condition of taking place or existing in areas that are geographically separated from one another

ALLOPHANE n variously coloured amorphous mineral consisting of hydrated aluminium silicate and occurring in cracks in some sedimentary rocks

ALLOPHONE n any of several speech sounds that are regarded as contextual or environmental variants of the same phoneme

ALLOPLASM n part of the cytoplasm that is specialized to form cilia, flagella, and similar structures

ALLOSAUR n any large carnivorous bipedal dinosaur common in the North America in late Jurassic times

ALLOSAURS >ALLOSAUR

ALLOSTERY n condition of an enzyme in which the structure and activity of the enzyme are modified by the binding of a metabolic molecule

ALLOT vb assign as a share or for a particular purpose

ALLOTMENT n distribution

ALLOTROPE n any of two or more physical forms in which an element can exist

ALLOTROPY n existence of an element in two or more physical forms

ALLOTS >ALLOT

ALLOTTED >ALLOT

ALLOTTEE n person to whom something is allotted

ALLOTTEES >ALLOTTEE

ALLOTTER n person who allots

ALLOTTERS >ALLOTTER

ALLOTTERY n something allotted

ALLOTTING >ALLOT

ALLOTYPE n additional type specimen selected because of differences from the original type specimen, such as opposite sex or morphological details

ALLOTYPES >ALLOTYPE

ALLOTYPIC >ALLOTYPE

ALLOTYPY n existence of allotypes

ALLOVER n fabric completely covered with a pattern

ALLOVERS >ALLOVER

ALLOW vb permit

ALLOWABLE adj permissible

ALLOWABLY >ALLOWABLE

ALLOWANCE n amount of money given at regular intervals

ALLOWED >ALLOW

ALLOWEDLY adv by general admission or agreement

ALLOWING >ALLOW

ALLOWS >ALLOW

ALLOXAN n chemical found in uric acid

ALLOXANS >ALLOXAN

ALLOY n mixture of two or more metals ▷ vb mix (metals)

ALLOYED >ALLOY

ALLOYING >ALLOY

ALLOYS >ALLOY

ALLOZYME n any one of a number of different structural forms of the same enzyme encoded by a different allele

ALLOZYMES >ALLOZYME

ALLS >ALL

ALLSEED n any of several plants that produce many seeds, such as knotgrass

ALLSEEDS >ALLSEED

ALLSORTS n assorted sweets

ALLSPICE n spice made from the berries of a tropical American tree

ALLSPICES >ALLSPICE

ALLUDE vb refer indirectly to

ALLUDED >ALLUDE

ALLUDES >ALLUDE

ALLUDING >ALLUDE

ALLURE n attractiveness ▷ vb entice or attract

ALLURED >ALLURE

ALLURER >ALLURE

ALLURERS >ALLURE

ALLURES >ALLURE

ALLURING adj extremely attractive

ALLUSION n indirect reference

ALLUSIONS >ALLUSION

ALLUSIVE adj containing or full of allusions

ALLUVIA >ALLUVIUM

ALLUVIAL adj of or relating to alluvium ▷ n soil consisting of alluvium

ALLUVIALS >ALLUVIAL

ALLUVION n wash of the sea or of a river

ALLUVIONS >ALLUVION

ALLUVIUM n fertile soil deposited by flowing water

ALLUVIUMS >ALLUVIUM

ALLY vb unite or be united, esp formally, as by treaty, confederation, or marriage ▷ n country, person, or group allied with another

ALLYING >ALLY

ALLYL n of, consisting of, or containing the monovalent group $CH_2$: $CHCH_2$

ALLYLIC >ALLYL

ALLYLS >ALLYL

ALLYOU pron all of you

ALMA n Egyptian dancing girl

ALMAGEST n medieval treatise concerning alchemy or astrology

ALMAGESTS >ALMAGEST

ALMAH n Egyptian dancing girl

ALMAHS >ALMAH

ALMAIN n German dance

ALMAINS >ALMAIN

ALMANAC n yearly calendar with detailed information on anniversaries, phases of the moon, etc

ALMANACK same as >ALMANAC

ALMANACKS >ALMANACK

ALMANACS >ALMANAC

ALMANDINE n deep violet-red garnet

ALMANDITE n form of garnet

ALMAS >ALMA

ALME n Egyptian dancing girl

ALMEH n Egyptian dancing girl

ALMEHS >ALMEH

ALMEMAR n (in Ashkenazic usage) the raised platform in a synagogue on which the reading desk stands

ALMEMARS >ALMEMAR

ALMERIES >ALMERY

ALMERY n cupboard for church vessels

ALMES >ALME

ALMIGHTY adj all-powerful ▷ adv extremely

ALMIRAH n cupboard

ALMIRAHS >ALMIRAH

ALMNER n almoner

ALMNERS >ALMONER
ALMOND n edible oval-shaped nut which grows on a small tree
ALMONDS >ALMOND
ALMONDY >ALMOND
ALMONER n formerly, a hospital social worker
ALMONERS >ALMONER
ALMONRIES >ALMONRY
ALMONRY n house of an almoner, usually the place where alms were given
ALMOST adv very nearly
ALMOUS Scots word for >ALMS
ALMS pl n gifts to the poor
ALMSGIVER n one who gives alms
ALMSHOUSE n (formerly) a house, financed by charity, which offered accommodation to the poor
ALMSMAN n person who gives or receives alms
ALMSMEN >ALMSMAN
ALMSWOMAN n woman who gives or receives alms
ALMSWOMEN >ALMSWOMAN
ALMUCE n fur-lined hood or cape formerly worn by members of certain religious orders, more recently by canons of France
ALMUCES >ALMUCE
ALMUD n Spanish unit of measure
ALMUDE n Spanish unit of measure
ALMUDES >ALMUDE
ALMUDS >ALMUD
ALMUG n type of wood mentioned in Bible
ALMUGS >ALMUG
ALNAGE n measurement in ells
ALNAGER n inspector of cloth
ALNAGERS >ALNAGER
ALNAGES >ALNAGE
ALNICO n alloy of various metals including iron, nickel, and cobalt
ALNICOS >ALNICO
ALOCASIA n any of various tropical plants of the genus Alocasia
ALOCASIAS >ALOCASIA
ALOD n feudal estate with no superior
ALODIA >ALODIUM
ALODIAL >ALODIUM
ALODIUM same as >ALLODIUM
ALODIUMS >ALODIUM
ALODS >ALOD
ALOE n plant with fleshy spiny leaves
ALOED adj containing aloes
ALOES another name for >EAGLEWOOD
ALOETIC >ALOE

ALOETICS >ALOE
ALOFT adv in the air ▷ adj in or into a high or higher place
ALOGIA n inability to speak
ALOGIAS >ALOGIA
ALOGICAL adj without logic
ALOHA a Hawaiian word for >HELLO
ALOHAS >ALOHA
ALOIN n bitter crystalline compound derived from various species of aloe: used as a laxative and flavouring agent
ALOINS >ALOIN
ALONE adv without anyone or anything else
ALONELY >ALONE
ALONENESS >ALONE
ALONG adv forward
ALONGSIDE adv beside (something)
ALONGST adv along
ALOOF adj distant or haughty in manner
ALOOFLY >ALOOF
ALOOFNESS >ALOOF
ALOPECIA n loss of hair
ALOPECIAS >ALOPECIA
ALOPECIC >ALOPECIA
ALOPECOID >ALOPECIA
ALOUD adv in an audible voice ▷ adj in a normal voice
ALOW adj in or into the lower rigging of a vessel, near the deck
ALOWE Scots word for >ABLAZE
ALP n high mountain
ALPACA n Peruvian llama
ALPACAS >ALPACA
ALPACCA same as >ALPACA
ALPACCAS >ALPACCA
ALPARGATA n Spanish sandal
ALPEEN n Irish cudgel
ALPEENS >ALPEEN
ALPENGLOW n reddish light on the summits of snow-covered mountain peaks at sunset or sunrise
ALPENHORN same as >ALPHORN
ALPHA n first letter in the Greek alphabet
ALPHABET n set of letters used in writing a language
ALPHABETS >ALPHABET
ALPHAS >ALPHA
ALPHASORT vb arrange in alphabetical order
ALPHORN n wind instrument used in the Swiss Alps, consisting of a very long tube of wood or bark with a cornet-like mouthpiece
ALPHORNS >ALPHORN
ALPHOSIS n absence of skin pigmentation, as in albinism

ALPHYL n univalent radical
ALPHYLS >ALPHYL
ALPINE adj of high mountains ▷ n mountain plant
ALPINELY >ALPINE
ALPINES >ALPINE
ALPINISM >ALPINIST
ALPINISMS >ALPINIST
ALPINIST n mountain climber
ALPINISTS >ALPINIST
ALPS >ALP
ALREADY adv before the present time
ALRIGHT adj all right
ALS >AL
ALSIKE n clover native to Europe and Asia
ALSIKES >ALSIKE
ALSO adv in addition, too
ALSOON same as >ALSOONE
ALSOONE adv as soon
ALT n octave directly above the treble staff
ALTAR n table used for Communion in Christian churches
ALTARAGE n donations placed on altar for priest
ALTARAGES >ALTARAGE
ALTARS >ALTAR
ALTARWISE adv in the position of an altar
ALTER vb make or become different
ALTERABLE >ALTER
ALTERABLY >ALTER
ALTERANT n alternative
ALTERANTS >ALTERANT
ALTERCATE vb argue, esp heatedly
ALTERED >ALTER
ALTERER >ALTER
ALTERERS >ALTER
ALTERING >ALTER
ALTERITY n quality of being different
ALTERN adj alternate
ALTERNANT adj alternating
ALTERNAT n practice of deciding precedence by lot
ALTERNATE vb (cause to) occur by turns ▷ adj occurring by turns ▷ n person who substitutes for another in his absence
ALTERNATS >ALTERNAT
ALTERNE n neighbouring but different plant group
ALTERNES >ALTERNE
ALTERS >ALTER
ALTESSE n French word for highness
ALTESSES >ALTESSE
ALTEZA n Spanish word for highness
ALTEZAS >ALTEZA
ALTEZZA n Italian word for highness
ALTEZZAS >ALTEZZA
ALTHAEA n plant such as the hollyhock, having tall spikes of showy white,

yellow, or red flowers
ALTHAEAS >ALTHAEA
ALTHEA same as >ALTHAEA
ALTHEAS >ALTHEA
ALTHO conj short form of although
ALTHORN n valved brass musical instrument belonging to the saxhorn or flügelhorn families
ALTHORNS >ALTHORN
ALTHOUGH conj despite the fact that; even though
ALTIGRAPH n instrument that measures altitude
ALTIMETER n instrument that measures altitude
ALTIMETRY n science of measuring altitudes, as with an altimeter
ALTIPLANO n high plateau
ALTISSIMO adj (of music) very high in pitch
ALTITUDE n height above sea level
ALTITUDES >ALTITUDE
ALTO n (singer with) the highest adult male voice ▷ adj denoting such an instrument, singer, or voice
ALTOIST n person who plays the alto saxophone
ALTOISTS >ALTOIST
ALTOS >ALTO
ALTRICES pl n altricial birds
ALTRICIAL adj (of the young of some species of birds after hatching) naked, blind, and dependent on the parents for food ▷ n altricial bird, such as a pigeon
ALTRUISM n unselfish concern for the welfare of others
ALTRUISMS >ALTRUISM
ALTRUIST >ALTRUISM
ALTRUISTS >ALTRUISM
ALTS >ALT
ALUDEL n pear-shaped vessel, open at both ends, formerly used with similar vessels for collecting condensates, esp of subliming mercury
ALUDELS >ALUDEL
ALULA n tuft of feathers attached to the first digit of a bird
ALULAE >ALULA
ALULAR >ALULA
ALUM n double sulphate of aluminium and potassium
ALUMIN n aluminium oxide
ALUMINA n aluminium oxide
ALUMINAS >ALUMINA
ALUMINATE n salt of the ortho or meta acid forms of aluminium hydroxide
ALUMINE n French word for alumina

ALUMINES >ALUMINE
ALUMINIC adj of
aluminium
ALUMINISE same
as >ALUMINIZE
ALUMINIUM n light silvery-
white metal that does not
rust
ALUMINIZE vb cover with
aluminium
ALUMINOUS adj resembling
aluminium
ALUMINS >ALUMIN
ALUMINUM same
as >ALUMINIUM
ALUMINUMS >ALUMINUM
ALUMISH adj like alum
ALUMIUM old name
for >ALUMINIUM
ALUMIUMS >ALUMIUM
ALUMNA n female graduate
of a school, college, etc
ALUMNAE >ALUMNA
ALUMNI >ALUMNUS
ALUMNUS n graduate of a
college
ALUMROOT n North
American plants having
small white, reddish, or
green bell-shaped flowers
and astringent roots
ALUMROOTS >ALUMROOT
ALUMS >ALUM
ALUMSTONE same
as >ALUNITE
ALUNITE n white, grey, or
reddish mineral
ALUNITES >ALUNITE
ALURE n area behind
battlements
ALURES >ALURE
ALVEARIES >ALVEARY
ALVEARY n beehive
ALVEATED adj with vaults
like beehive
ALVEOLAR adj of, relating
to, or resembling an
alveolus ▷ n alveolar
consonant, such as the
speech sounds written t, d,
and s in English
ALVEOLARS >ALVEOLAR
ALVEOLATE adj having
many alveoli
ALVEOLE n alveolus
ALVEOLES >ALVEOLE
ALVEOLI >ALVEOLUS
ALVEOLUS n any small pit,
cavity, or saclike dilation,
such as a honeycomb cell,
a tooth socket, or the tiny
air sacs in the lungs
ALVINE adj of or relating to
the intestines or belly
ALWAY same as >ALWAYS
ALWAYS adv at all times
ALYSSUM n garden plant
with small yellow or white
flowers
ALYSSUMS >ALYSSUM
AM see >BE
AMA n vessel for water
AMABILE adj sweet
AMADAVAT same

as >AVADAVAT
AMADAVATS >AMADAVAT
AMADODA pl n grown men
AMADOU n spongy
substance made from
certain fungi, such as
Polyporus (or Fomes)
fomentarius and related
species, used as tinder to
light fires, in medicine to
stop bleeding, and, esp
formerly, by anglers to dry
off dry flies between casts
AMADOUS >AMADOU
AMAH n (in the East,
formerly) a nurse or
maidservant
AMAHS >AMAH
AMAIN adv with great
strength, speed, or haste
AMALGAM n blend or
combination
AMALGAMS >AMALGAM
AMANDINE n protein found
in almonds
AMANDINES >AMANDINE
AMANDLA n political slogan
calling for power to the
Black population
AMANDLAS >AMANDLA
AMANITA n type of fungus
AMANITAS >AMANITA
AMANITIN n poison from
amanita
AMANITINS >AMANITIN
AMARACUS n marjoram
AMARANT n amaranth
AMARANTH n imaginary
flower that never fades
AMARANTHS >AMARANTH
AMARANTIN n protein
AMARANTS >AMARANT
AMARELLE n variety of sour
cherry that has pale red
fruit and colourless juice
AMARELLES >AMARELLE
AMARETTI >AMARETTO
AMARETTO n Italian liqueur
with a flavour of almonds
AMARETTOS >AMARETTO
AMARNA adj pertaining to
the reign of the Pharaoh
Akhenaton
AMARONE n strong dry red
Italian wine
AMARONES >AMARONE
AMARYLLID n plant of the
amaryllis family
AMARYLLIS n lily-like plant
with large red, pink, or
white flowers
AMAS >AMA
AMASS vb collect or
accumulate
AMASSABLE >AMASS
AMASSED >AMASS
AMASSER >AMASS
AMASSERS >AMASS
AMASSES >AMASS
AMASSING >AMASS
AMASSMENT >AMASS
AMATE vb match
AMATED >AMATE
AMATES >AMATE

AMATEUR n person who
engages in a sport or
activity as a pastime
rather than as a profession
▷ adj not professional
AMATEURS >AMATEUR
AMATING >AMATE
AMATION n lovemaking
AMATIONS >AMATION
AMATIVE a rare word
for >AMOROUS
AMATIVELY >AMATIVE
AMATOL n explosive
mixture of ammonium
nitrate and TNT, used in
shells and bombs
AMATOLS >AMATOL
AMATORIAL same
as >AMATORY
AMATORIAN >AMATORY
AMATORY adj relating to
romantic or sexual love
AMAUROSES >AMAUROSIS
AMAUROSIS n blindness,
esp when occurring
without observable
damage to the eye
AMAUROTIC >AMAUROSIS
AMAUT n hood on an
Inuit woman's parka for
carrying a child
AMAUTS >AMAUT
AMAZE vb surprise greatly,
astound
AMAZED >AMAZE
AMAZEDLY >AMAZE
AMAZEMENT n incredulity or
great astonishment
AMAZES >AMAZE
AMAZING adj causing
wonder or astonishment
AMAZINGLY >AMAZING
AMAZON n any tall, strong,
or aggressive woman
AMAZONIAN >AMAZON
AMAZONITE n green variety
of microcline used as a
gemstone
AMAZONS >AMAZON
AMBACH same as >AMBATCH
AMBACHES >AMBACH
AMBAGE n ambiguity
AMBAGES >AMBAGE
AMBAGIOUS >AMBAGE
AMBAN n Chinese official
AMBANS >AMBAN
AMBARI same as >AMBARY
AMBARIES >AMBARY
AMBARIS >AMBARI
AMBARY n tropical Asian
malvaceous plant, Hibiscus
cannabinus, that yields a
fibre similar to jute
AMBASSAGE n embassy
AMBASSIES >AMBASSY
AMBASSY n embassy
AMBATCH n tree or
shrub of the Nile Valley,
Aeschynomene elaphroxylon,
valued for its light-
coloured pithlike wood
AMBATCHES >AMBATCH
AMBEER n saliva coloured
by tobacco juice

AMBEERS >AMBEER
AMBER n clear yellowish
fossil resin ▷ adj
brownish-yellow
AMBERED adj fixed in amber
AMBERGRIS n waxy
substance secreted by
the sperm whale, used in
making perfumes
AMBERIES >AMBERY
AMBERINA n type of
glassware
AMBERINAS >AMBERINA
AMBERITE n powder like
amber
AMBERITES >AMBERITE
AMBERJACK n any of several
large carangid fishes of
the genus Seriola, esp
S. dumerili, with golden
markings when young,
occurring in tropical
and subtropical Atlantic
waters
AMBEROID n synthetic
amber made by
compressing pieces of
amber and other resins
together at a high
temperature
AMBEROIDS >AMBEROID
AMBEROUS adj like amber
AMBERS >AMBER
AMBERY adj like amber
AMBIANCE same
as >AMBIENCE
AMBIANCES >AMBIANCE
AMBIENCE n atmosphere of
a place
AMBIENCES >AMBIENCE
AMBIENT adj surrounding
▷ n ambient music
AMBIENTS >AMBIENT
AMBIGUITY n possibility of
interpreting an expression
in more than one way
AMBIGUOUS adj having
more than one possible
meaning
AMBIPOLAR adj (of plasmas
and semiconductors)
involving both positive
and negative charge
carriers
AMBIT n limits or boundary
AMBITION n desire for
success
AMBITIONS >AMBITION
AMBITIOUS adj having a
strong desire for success
AMBITS >AMBIT
AMBITTY adj crystalline
and brittle
AMBIVERT n person who is
intermediate between an
extrovert and an introvert
AMBIVERTS >AMBIVERT
AMBLE vb walk at a leisurely
pace ▷ n leisurely walk
or pace
AMBLED >AMBLE
AMBLER >AMBLE
AMBLERS >AMBLE
AMBLES >AMBLE

**AMBLING** *n* walking at a leisurely pace

**AMBLINGS** >AMBLING

**AMBLYOPIA** *n* impaired vision with no discernible damage to the eye or optic nerve

**AMBLYOPIC** >AMBLYOPIA

**AMBO** *n* either of two raised pulpits from which the gospels and epistles were read in early Christian churches

**AMBOINA** same as >AMBOYNA

**AMBOINAS** >AMBOINA

**AMBONES** >AMBO

**AMBOS** >AMBO

**AMBOYNA** *n* mottled curly-grained wood of an Indonesian leguminous tree, *Pterocarpus indicus*, used in making furniture

**AMBOYNAS** >AMBOYNA

**AMBRIES** >AMBRY

**AMBROID** same as >AMBEROID

**AMBROIDS** >AMBROID

**AMBROSIA** *n* anything delightful to taste or smell

**AMBROSIAL** >AMBROSIA

**AMBROSIAN** >AMBROSIA

**AMBROSIAS** >AMBROSIA

**AMBROTYPE** *n* early type of glass negative that could be made to appear as a positive by backing it with black varnish or paper

**AMBRY** *n* recessed cupboard in the wall of a church near the altar, used to store sacred vessels, etc

**AMBSACE** *n* double ace, the lowest throw at dice

**AMBSACES** >AMBSACE

**AMBULACRA** *n* radial bands on the ventral surface of echinoderms, such as the starfish and sea urchin, on which the tube feet are situated

**AMBULANCE** *n* motor vehicle designed to carry sick or injured people

**AMBULANT** *adj* moving about from place to place

**AMBULANTS** >AMBULANT

**AMBULATE** *vb* wander about or move from one place to another

**AMBULATED** >AMBULATE

**AMBULATES** >AMBULATE

**AMBULATOR** *n* person who walks

**AMBULETTE** *n* motor vehicle designed for transporting ill or handicapped people

**AMBUSCADE** *n* ambush ▷ *vb* ambush or lie in ambush

**AMBUSCADO** *n* ambuscade

**AMBUSH** *n* act of waiting in a concealed position to make a surprise attack ▷ *vb* attack from a concealed position

**AMBUSHED** >AMBUSH

**AMBUSHER** >AMBUSH

**AMBUSHERS** >AMBUSH

**AMBUSHES** >AMBUSH

**AMBUSHING** >AMBUSH

**AMEARST** old form of >AMERCE

**AMEBA** same as >AMOEBA

**AMEBAE** >AMEBA

**AMEBAN** >AMEBA

**AMEBAS** >AMEBA

**AMEBEAN** same as >AMOEBEAN

**AMEBIASES** >AMEBIASIS

**AMEBIASIS** *n* disease caused by amoeba

**AMEBIC** >AMEBA

**AMEBOCYTE** *n* any cell having properties similar to an amoeba, such as shape, mobility, and ability to engulf particles

**AMEBOID** same as >AMOEBOID

**AMEER** *n* (formerly) the ruler of Afghanistan

**AMEERATE** *n* country ruled by an ameer

**AMEERATES** >AMEERATE

**AMEERS** >AMEER

**AMEIOSES** >AMEIOSIS

**AMEIOSIS** *n* absence of pairing of chromosomes during meiosis

**AMELCORN** *n* variety of wheat

**AMELCORNS** >AMELCORN

**AMELIA** *n* congenital absence of arms or legs

**AMELIAS** >AMELIA

**AMEN** *n* term used at the end of a prayer or religious statement ▷ *vb* say amen

**AMENABLE** *adj* likely or willing to cooperate

**AMENABLY** >AMENABLE

**AMENAGE** *vb* tame

**AMENAGED** >AMENAGE

**AMENAGES** >AMENAGE

**AMENAGING** >AMENAGE

**AMENAUNCE** *n* person's bearing

**AMEND** *vb* make small changes to correct or improve (something)

**AMENDABLE** >AMEND

**AMENDE** *n* public apology and reparation made to satisfy the honour of the person wronged

**AMENDED** >AMEND

**AMENDER** >AMEND

**AMENDERS** >AMEND

**AMENDES** >AMENDE

**AMENDING** >AMEND

**AMENDMENT** *n* improvement or correction

**AMENDS** *n* recompense or compensation given or gained for some injury, insult, etc

**AMENE** *adj* pleasant

**AMENED** >AMEN

**AMENING** >AMEN

**AMENITIES** >AMENITY

**AMENITY** *n* useful or enjoyable feature

**AMENS** >AMEN

**AMENT** *n* mentally deficient person

**AMENTA** >AMENTUM

**AMENTAL** >AMENTUM

**AMENTIA** *n* severe mental deficiency, usually congenital

**AMENTIAS** >AMENTIA

**AMENTS** >AMENT

**AMENTUM** same as >AMENT

**AMERCE** *vb* punish by a fine

**AMERCED** >AMERCE

**AMERCER** >AMERCE

**AMERCERS** >AMERCE

**AMERCES** >AMERCE

**AMERCING** >AMERCE

**AMERICIUM** *n* white metallic element artificially produced from plutonium

**AMESACE** same as >AMBSACE

**AMESACES** >AMESACE

**AMETHYST** *n* bluish-violet variety of quartz used as a gemstone ▷ *adj* purple or violet

**AMETHYSTS** >AMETHYST

**AMETROPIA** *n* loss of ability to focus images on the retina, caused by an imperfection in the refractive function of the eye

**AMETROPIC** >AMETROPIA

**AMI** *n* male friend

**AMIA** *n* species of fish

**AMIABLE** *adj* friendly, pleasant-natured

**AMIABLY** >AMIABLE

**AMIANTHUS** *n* any of the fine silky varieties of asbestos

**AMIANTUS** *n* amianthus

**AMIAS** >AMIA

**AMICABLE** *adj* friendly

**AMICABLY** >AMICABLE

**AMICE** *n* rectangular piece of white linen worn by priests around the neck and shoulders under the alb or, formerly, on the head

**AMICES** >AMICE

**AMICI** >AMICUS

**AMICUS** *n* Latin for friend

**AMID** *prep* in the middle of, among ▷ *n* same as >AMIDE

**AMIDASE** *n* enzyme

**AMIDASES** >AMIDASE

**AMIDE** *n* any organic compound containing the group –$CONH_2$

**AMIDES** >AMIDE

**AMIDIC** >AMIDE

**AMIDIN** *n* form of starch

**AMIDINE** *n* crystalline compound

**AMIDINES** >AMIDINE

**AMIDINS** >AMIDIN

**AMIDMOST** *adv* in the middle

**AMIDO** *adj* containing amide

**AMIDOGEN** *n* chemical compound derived from ammonia

**AMIDOGENS** >AMIDOGEN

**AMIDOL** *n* chemical used in developing photographs

**AMIDOLS** >AMIDOL

**AMIDONE** *n* pain-killing drug

**AMIDONES** >AMIDONE

**AMIDS** same as >AMID

**AMIDSHIP** *adj* in the middle of a ship

**AMIDSHIPS** *adv* at or towards the middle of a ship ▷ *adj* at, near, or towards the centre of a vessel

**AMIDST** same as >AMID

**AMIE** *n* female friend

**AMIES** >AMIE

**AMIGA** *n* Spanish female friend

**AMIGAS** >AMIGA

**AMIGO** *n* friend

**AMIGOS** >AMIGO

**AMILDAR** *n* manager in India

**AMILDARS** >AMILDAR

**AMIN** same as >AMINE

**AMINE** *n* organic base formed by replacing one or more of the hydrogen atoms of ammonia by organic groups

**AMINES** >AMINE

**AMINIC** >AMINE

**AMINITIES** >AMINITY

**AMINITY** *n* amenity

**AMINO** *n* of, consisting of, or containing the group of atoms –$NH_2$

**AMINS** >AMIN

**AMIR** *n* (formerly) the ruler of Afghanistan

**AMIRATE** >AMIR

**AMIRATES** >AMIR

**AMIRS** >AMIR

**AMIS** >AMI

**AMISES** >AMI

**AMISS** *adv* wrongly, badly ▷ *adj* wrong, faulty ▷ *n* evil deed

**AMISSES** >AMISS

**AMISSIBLE** *adj* likely to be lost

**AMISSING** *adj* missing

**AMITIES** >AMITY

**AMITOSES** >AMITOSIS

**AMITOSIS** *n* unusual form of cell division in which the nucleus and cytoplasm divide by constriction without the formation of chromosomes

**AMITOTIC** >AMITOSIS

**AMITROLE** *n* pesticide

**AMITROLES** > AMITROLE
**AMITY** n friendship
**AMLA** n species of Indian tree
**AMLAS** > AMLA
**AMMAN** same as > AMTMAN
**AMMANS** > AMMAN
**AMMETER** n instrument for measuring electric current
**AMMETERS** > AMMETER
**AMMINE** n compound that has molecules containing one or more ammonia molecules bound to another molecule, group, or atom by coordinate bonds
**AMMINES** > AMMINE
**AMMINO** adj containing ammonia molecules
**AMMIRAL** old word for > ADMIRAL
**AMMIRALS** > AMMIRAL
**AMMO** n ammunition
**AMMOCETE** n ammocoete
**AMMOCETES** > AMMOCETE
**AMMOCOETE** n larva of primitive jawless vertebrates, such as the lamprey, that lives buried in mud and feeds on microorganisms
**AMMON** n Asian wild sheep
**AMMONAL** n explosive made by mixing TNT, ammonium nitrate, and aluminium powder
**AMMONALS** > AMMONAL
**AMMONATE** same as > AMMINE
**AMMONATES** > AMMONATE
**AMMONIA** n strong-smelling alkaline gas containing hydrogen and nitrogen
**AMMONIAC** n strong-smelling gum resin obtained from the stems of the N Asian umbelliferous plant Dorema ammoniacum and formerly used as an expectorant, stimulant, perfume, and in porcelain cement
**AMMONIACS** > AMMONIAC
**AMMONIAS** > AMMONIA
**AMMONIATE** vb unite or treat with ammonia
**AMMONIC** adj of or concerned with ammonia or ammonium compounds
**AMMONICAL** > AMMONIC
**AMMONIFY** vb treat or impregnate with ammonia or a compound of ammonia
**AMMONITE** n fossilized spiral shell of an extinct sea creature
**AMMONITES** > AMMONITE
**AMMONITIC** > AMMONITE
**AMMONIUM** n type of monovalent chemical group
**AMMONIUMS** > AMMONIUM

**AMMONO** adj using ammonia
**AMMONOID** n type of fossil
**AMMONOIDS** > AMMONOID
**AMMONS** > AMMON
**AMMOS** > AMMO
**AMNESIA** n loss of memory
**AMNESIAC** > AMNESIA
**AMNESIACS** > AMNESIA
**AMNESIAS** > AMNESIA
**AMNESIC** > AMNESIA
**AMNESICS** > AMNESIA
**AMNESTIC** adj relating to amnesia
**AMNESTIED** > AMNESTY
**AMNESTIES** > AMNESTY
**AMNESTY** n general pardon for offences against a government ▷ vb overlook or forget (an offence)
**AMNIA** > AMNION
**AMNIC** adj relating to amnion
**AMNIO** n amniocentesis
**AMNION** n innermost of two membranes enclosing an embryo
**AMNIONIC** > AMNION
**AMNIONS** > AMNION
**AMNIOS** > AMNIO
**AMNIOTE** n any vertebrate animal, such as a reptile, bird, or mammal, that possesses an amnion, chorion, and allantois during embryonic development
**AMNIOTES** > AMNIOTE
**AMNIOTIC** adj of or relating to the amnion
**AMNIOTOMY** n breaking of the membrane surrounding a fetus to induce labour
**AMOEBA** n microscopic single-celled animal able to change its shape
**AMOEBAE** > AMOEBA
**AMOEBAEAN** adj of or relating to lines of verse dialogue that answer each other alternately
**AMOEBAN** > AMOEBA
**AMOEBAS** > AMOEBA
**AMOEBEAN** same as > AMOEBAEAN
**AMOEBIC** > AMOEBA
**AMOEBOID** adj of, related to, or resembling amoebae
**AMOK** n state of murderous frenzy, originally observed among Malays
**AMOKS** > AMOK
**AMOKURA** n white pelagian bird, Paethon rubricauda, of tropical latitudes in the Indian and Pacific oceans, with a red beak and long red tail feathers
**AMOLE** n American plant
**AMOLES** > AMOLE
**AMOMUM** n plant of ginger family
**AMOMUMS** > AMOMUM

**AMONG** prep in the midst of
**AMONGST** same as > AMONG
**AMOOVE** vb stir someone's emotions
**AMOOVED** > AMOOVE
**AMOOVES** > AMOOVE
**AMOOVING** > AMOOVE
**AMORAL** adj without moral standards
**AMORALISM** > AMORAL
**AMORALIST** > AMORAL
**AMORALITY** > AMORAL
**AMORALLY** > AMORAL
**AMORANCE** n condition of being in love
**AMORANCES** > AMORANCE
**AMORANT** > AMORANCE
**AMORCE** n small percussion cap
**AMORCES** > AMORCE
**AMORET** n sweetheart
**AMORETS** > AMORET
**AMORETTI** > AMORETTO
**AMORETTO** n (esp in painting) a small chubby naked boy representing a cupid
**AMORETTOS** > AMORETTO
**AMORINI** > AMORINO
**AMORINO** same as > AMORETTO
**AMORISM** > AMORIST
**AMORISMS** > AMORIST
**AMORIST** n lover or a writer about love
**AMORISTIC** > AMORIST
**AMORISTS** > AMORIST
**AMORNINGS** adv each morning
**AMOROSA** n lover
**AMOROSAS** > AMOROSA
**AMOROSITY** n quality of being amorous
**AMOROSO** adv (to be played) lovingly ▷ n rich sweetened sherry of a dark colour
**AMOROSOS** > AMOROSO
**AMOROUS** adj feeling, showing, or relating to sexual love
**AMOROUSLY** > AMOROUS
**AMORPHISM** > AMORPHOUS
**AMORPHOUS** adj without distinct shape
**AMORT** adj in low spirits
**AMORTISE** same as > AMORTIZE
**AMORTISED** > AMORTISE
**AMORTISES** > AMORTISE
**AMORTIZE** vb pay off (a debt) gradually by periodic transfers to a sinking fund
**AMORTIZED** > AMORTIZE
**AMORTIZES** > AMORTIZE
**AMOSITE** n form of asbestos
**AMOSITES** > AMOSITE
**AMOTION** n act of removing
**AMOTIONS** > AMOTION
**AMOUNT** n extent or quantity ▷ vb be equal or add up to
**AMOUNTED** > AMOUNT

**AMOUNTING** > AMOUNT
**AMOUNTS** > AMOUNT
**AMOUR** n (secret) love affair
**AMOURETTE** n minor love affair
**AMOURS** > AMOUR
**AMOVE** vb stir someone's emotions
**AMOVED** > AMOVE
**AMOVES** > AMOVE
**AMOVING** > AMOVE
**AMOWT** same as > AMAUT
**AMOWTS** > AMOWT
**AMP** n ampere ▷ vb excite or become excited
**AMPASSIES** > AMPASSY
**AMPASSY** n ampersand
**AMPED** > AMP
**AMPERAGE** n strength of an electric current measured in amperes
**AMPERAGES** > AMPERAGE
**AMPERE** n basic unit of electric current
**AMPERES** > AMPERE
**AMPERSAND** n character (&), meaning and
**AMPERZAND** n ampersand
**AMPHIBIA** n class of amphibians
**AMPHIBIAN** n animal that lives on land but breeds in water ▷ adj of, relating to, or belonging to the class Amphibia
**AMPHIBOLE** n any of a large group of minerals consisting of the silicates of calcium, iron, magnesium, sodium, and aluminium
**AMPHIBOLY** n ambiguity of expression, esp where due to a grammatical construction
**AMPHIGORY** n piece of nonsensical writing in verse or, less commonly, prose
**AMPHIOXI** > AMPHIOXUS
**AMPHIOXUS** another name for the > LANCELET
**AMPHIPATH** adj of or relating to a molecule that possesses both hydrophobic and hydrophilic elements
**AMPHIPOD** n any marine or freshwater crustacean of the order Amphipoda, such as the sand hoppers, in which the body is laterally compressed: subclass Malacostraca ▷ adj of, relating to, or belonging to the Amphipoda
**AMPHIPODS** > AMPHIPOD
**AMPHOLYTE** n electrolyte that can be acid or base
**AMPHORA** n two-handled ancient Greek or Roman jar
**AMPHORAE** > AMPHORA
**AMPHORAL** > AMPHORA

**AMPHORAS** > AMPHORA

**AMPHORIC** *adj* resembling the sound produced by blowing into a bottle. Amphoric breath sounds are heard through a stethoscope placed over a cavity in the lung

**AMPING** > AMP

**AMPLE** *adj* more than sufficient

**AMPLENESS** > AMPLE

**AMPLER** > AMPLE

**AMPLEST** > AMPLE

**AMPLEXUS** *n* mating in amphibians

**AMPLIDYNE** *n* magnetic amplifier

**AMPLIFIED** > AMPLIFY

**AMPLIFIER** *n* device used to amplify a current or sound signal

**AMPLIFIES** > AMPLIFY

**AMPLIFY** *vb* increase the strength of (a current or sound signal)

**AMPLITUDE** *n* greatness of extent

**AMPLOSOME** *n* stocky body type

**AMPLY** *adv* fully or generously

**AMPOULE** *n* small sealed glass vessel containing liquid for injection

**AMPOULES** > AMPOULE

**AMPS** > AMP

**AMPUL** *n* ampoule

**AMPULE** *same as* > AMPOULE

**AMPULES** > AMPULE

**AMPULLA** *n* dilated end part of certain tubes in the body

**AMPULLAE** > AMPULLA

**AMPULLAR** > AMPULLA

**AMPULLARY** > AMPULLA

**AMPULS** > AMPUL

**AMPUTATE** *vb* cut off (a limb or part of a limb) for medical reasons

**AMPUTATED** > AMPUTATE

**AMPUTATES** > AMPUTATE

**AMPUTATOR** > AMPUTATE

**AMPUTEE** *n* person who has had a limb amputated

**AMPUTEES** > AMPUTEE

**AMREETA** *same as* > AMRITA

**AMREETAS** > AMREETA

**AMRIT** *n* sanctified solution of sugar and water used in the Amrit Ceremony

**AMRITA** *n* ambrosia of the gods that bestows immortality

**AMRITAS** > AMRITA

**AMRITS** > AMRIT

**AMSINCKIA** *n* Californian herb

**AMTMAN** *n* magistrate in parts of Europe

**AMTMANS** > AMTMAN

**AMTRAC** *n* amphibious tracked vehicle

**AMTRACK** *n* amphibious tracked vehicle

**AMTRACKS** > AMTRACK

**AMTRACS** > AMTRAC

**AMU** *n* unit of mass

**AMUCK** *same as* > AMOK

**AMUCKS** > AMUCK

**AMULET** *n* something carried or worn as a protection against evil

**AMULETIC** > AMULET

**AMULETS** > AMULET

**AMUS** > AMU

**AMUSABLE** *adj* capable of being amused

**AMUSE** *vb* cause to laugh or smile

**AMUSEABLE** *same as* > AMUSABLE

**AMUSED** > AMUSE

**AMUSEDLY** > AMUSE

**AMUSEMENT** *n* state of being amused

**AMUSER** > AMUSE

**AMUSERS** > AMUSE

**AMUSES** > AMUSE

**AMUSETTE** *n* type of light cannon

**AMUSETTES** > AMUSETTE

**AMUSIA** *n* inability to recognize musical tones

**AMUSIAS** > AMUSIA

**AMUSING** *adj* mildly entertaining

**AMUSINGLY** > AMUSING

**AMUSIVE** *adj* deceptive

**AMYGDAL** *n* almond

**AMYGDALA** *n* almond-shaped part, such as a tonsil or a lobe of the cerebellum

**AMYGDALAE** > AMYGDALA

**AMYGDALAS** > AMYGDALA

**AMYGDALE** *n* vesicle in a volcanic rock, formed from a bubble of escaping gas, that has become filled with light-coloured minerals, such as quartz and calcite

**AMYGDALES** > AMYGDALE

**AMYGDALIN** *n* white soluble bitter-tasting crystalline glycoside extracted from bitter almonds

**AMYGDALS** > AMYGDAL

**AMYGDULE** *same as* > AMYGDALE

**AMYGDULES** > AMYGDULE

**AMYL** *n* of, consisting of, or containing any of eight isomeric forms of the monovalent group $C_5H_{11}$-

**AMYLASE** *n* enzyme, present in saliva, that helps to change starch into sugar

**AMYLASES** > AMYLASE

**AMYLENE** *another name (no longer in technical usage) for* > PENTENE

**AMYLENES** > AMYLENE

**AMYLIC** *adj* of or derived from amyl

**AMYLOGEN** *n* soluble part of starch

**AMYLOGENS** > AMYLOGEN

**AMYLOID** *n* complex protein resembling starch, deposited in tissues in some degenerative diseases ▷ *adj* starchlike

**AMYLOIDAL** > AMYLOID

**AMYLOIDS** > AMYLOID

**AMYLOPSIN** *n* enzyme of the pancreatic juice that converts starch into sugar

**AMYLOSE** *n* minor component (about 20 per cent) of starch, consisting of long unbranched chains of glucose units. It is soluble in water and gives an intense blue colour with iodine

**AMYLOSES** > AMYLOSE

**AMYLS** > AMYL

**AMYLUM** *another name for* > STARCH

**AMYLUMS** > AMYLUM

**AMYOTONIA** *another name for* > MYOTONIA

**AMYTAL** *n* barbiturate

**AMYTALS** > AMYTAL

**AN** *adj* form of **a** used before vowels, and sometimes before 'h'

**ANA** *adv* (of ingredients in a prescription) in equal quantities ▷ *n* collection of reminiscences, sketches, etc, of or about a person or place

**ANABAENA** *n* any freshwater alga of the genus *Anabaena*, sometimes occurring in drinking water, giving it a fishy taste and smell

**ANABAENAS** > ANABAENA

**ANABANTID** *n* any of various spiny-finned fishes constituting the family *Anabantidae* and including the fighting fish, climbing perch, and gourami ▷ *adj* of, relating to, or belonging to the family *Anabantidae*

**ANABAS** *n* type of fish

**ANABASES** > ANABASIS

**ANABASIS** *n* march of Cyrus the Younger and his Greek mercenaries from Sardis to Cunaxa in Babylonia in 401 BC

**ANABATIC** *adj* (of air currents) rising upwards, esp up slopes

**ANABIOSES** > ANABIOSIS

**ANABIOSIS** *n* ability to return to life after apparent death

**ANABIOTIC** > ANABIOSIS

**ANABLEPS** *n* any of various cyprinodont fishes constituting the genus *Anableps*, which includes the four-eyed fishes

**ANABOLIC** *adj* of or relating to anabolism

**ANABOLISM** *n* metabolic process in which body tissues are synthesized from food

**ANABOLITE** *n* product of anabolism

**ANABRANCH** *n* stream that leaves a river and enters it again further downstream

**ANACHARIS** *n* water plant

**ANACLINAL** *adj* (of valleys and similar formations) progressing in a direction opposite to the dip of the surrounding rock strata

**ANACLISES** > ANACLITIC

**ANACLISIS** > ANACLITIC

**ANACLITIC** *adj* of or relating to relationships that are characterized by the strong dependence of one person on others or another

**ANACONDA** *n* large S American snake which kills by constriction

**ANACONDAS** > ANACONDA

**ANACRUSES** > ANACRUSIS

**ANACRUSIS** *n* one or more unstressed syllables at the beginning of a line of verse

**ANADEM** *n* garland for the head

**ANADEMS** > ANADEM

**ANAEMIA** *n* deficiency in the number of red blood cells

**ANAEMIAS** > ANAEMIA

**ANAEMIC** *adj* having anaemia

**ANAEROBE** *n* organism that does not require oxygen

**ANAEROBES** > ANAEROBE

**ANAEROBIA** *same as* > ANAEROBES

**ANAEROBIC** *adj* not requiring oxygen

**ANAGLYPH** *n* stereoscopic picture consisting of two images of the same object, taken from slightly different angles

**ANAGLYPHS** > ANAGLYPH

**ANAGLYPHY** > ANAGLYPH

**ANAGOGE** *n* allegorical or spiritual interpretation, esp of sacred works such as the Bible

**ANAGOGES** > ANAGOGE

**ANAGOGIC** > ANAGOGE

**ANAGOGIES** > ANAGOGY

**ANAGOGY** *same as* > ANAGOGE

**ANAGRAM** *n* word or phrase made by rearranging the letters of another word or phrase

**ANAGRAMS** > ANAGRAM

**ANAL** *adj* of the anus

**ANALCIME** *same as* > ANALCITE

**ANALCIMES** > ANALCIME

**ANALCIMIC** > ANALCIME

**ANALCITE** *n* white, grey, or

colourless zeolite mineral
**ANALCITES** >ANALCITE
**ANALECTA** same
  as >ANALECTS
**ANALECTIC** >ANALECTS
**ANALECTS** pl n selected
  literary passages from one
  or more works
**ANALEMMA** n graduated
  scale shaped like a figure
  of eight that indicates
  the daily declination of
  the sun
**ANALEMMAS** >ANALEMMA
**ANALEPTIC** adj (of a drug,
  etc) stimulating the
  central nervous system
  ▷ n any drug, such as
  doxapram, that stimulates
  the central nervous system
**ANALGESIA** n absence of
  pain
**ANALGESIC** adj (drug)
  relieving pain ▷ n drug
  that relieves pain
**ANALGETIC** n painkilling
  drug
**ANALGIA** same
  as >ANALGESIA
**ANALGIAS** >ANALGIA
**ANALITIES** >ANALITY
**ANALITY** n quality of being
  psychologically anal
**ANALLY** >ANAL
**ANALOG** same as >ANALOGUE
**ANALOGA** >ANALOGON
**ANALOGIC** >ANALOGY
**ANALOGIES** >ANALOGY
**ANALOGISE** same
  as >ANALOGIZE
**ANALOGISM** >ANALOGIZE
**ANALOGIST** >ANALOGY
**ANALOGIZE** vb use analogy
**ANALOGON** n analogue
**ANALOGONS** >ANALOGON
**ANALOGOUS** adj similar in
  some respects
**ANALOGS** >ANALOG
**ANALOGUE** n something
  that is similar in some
  respects to something
  else ▷ adj displaying
  information by means of
  a dial
**ANALOGUES** >ANALOGUE
**ANALOGY** n similarity in
  some respects
**ANALYSAND** n any person
  who is undergoing
  psychoanalysis
**ANALYSE** vb make an
  analysis of (something)
**ANALYSED** >ANALYSE
**ANALYSER** >ANALYSE
**ANALYSERS** >ANALYSE
**ANALYSES** >ANALYSIS
**ANALYSING** >ANALYSE
**ANALYSIS** n separation of
  a whole into its parts for
  study and interpretation
**ANALYST** n person skilled in
  analysis
**ANALYSTS** >ANALYST
**ANALYTE** n substance that

is being analyzed
**ANALYTES** >ANALYTE
**ANALYTIC** adj relating to
  analysis ▷ n analytical
  logic
**ANALYTICS** >ANALYTIC
**ANALYZE** same as >ANALYSE
**ANALYZED** >ANALYZE
**ANALYZER** >ANALYZE
**ANALYZERS** >ANALYZE
**ANALYZES** >ANALYZE
**ANALYZING** >ANALYZE
**ANAMNESES** >ANAMNESIS
**ANAMNESIS** n ability to
  recall past events
**ANAMNIOTE** n any
  vertebrate animal, such as
  a fish or amphibian, that
  lacks an amnion, chorion,
  and allantois during
  embryonic development
**ANAN** interj expression of
  failure to understand
**ANANA** n pineapple
**ANANAS** n plant related to
  the pineapple
**ANANASES** >ANANAS
**ANANDROUS** adj (of flowers)
  having no stamens
**ANANKE** n unalterable
  necessity
**ANANKES** >ANANKE
**ANANTHOUS** adj (of higher
  plants) having no flowers
**ANAPAEST** n metrical foot
  of three syllables, the first
  two short, the last long
**ANAPAESTS** >ANAPAEST
**ANAPEST** same
  as >ANAPAEST
**ANAPESTIC** >ANAPEST
**ANAPESTS** >ANAPEST
**ANAPHASE** n third stage of
  mitosis, during which the
  chromatids separate and
  migrate towards opposite
  ends of the spindle
**ANAPHASES** >ANAPHASE
**ANAPHASIC** >ANAPHASE
**ANAPHOR** n word referring
  back to a previous word
**ANAPHORA** n use of a word
  such as a pronoun that
  has the same reference as
  a word previously used in
  the same discourse
**ANAPHORAL** >ANAPHORA
**ANAPHORAS** >ANAPHORA
**ANAPHORIC** adj of or
  relating to anaphorism
**ANAPHORS** >ANAPHOR
**ANAPLASIA** n reversion of
  plant or animal cells to a
  simpler less differentiated
  form
**ANAPLASTY** n plastic
  surgery
**ANAPTYXES** >ANAPTYXIS
**ANAPTYXIS** n insertion
  of a short vowel between
  consonants in order to
  make a word more easily
  pronounceable
**ANARCH** n instigator or

personification of anarchy
**ANARCHAL** >ANARCHY
**ANARCHIAL** >ANARCHY
**ANARCHIC** >ANARCHY
**ANARCHIES** >ANARCHY
**ANARCHISE** vb make
  anarchic
**ANARCHISM** n doctrine
  advocating the abolition
  of government
**ANARCHIST** n person who
  advocates the abolition of
  government
**ANARCHIZE** vb make
  anarchic
**ANARCHS** >ANARCH
**ANARCHY** n lawlessness and
  disorder
**ANARTHRIA** n loss of the
  ability to speak coherently
**ANARTHRIC** >ANARTHRIA
**ANAS** >ANA
**ANASARCA** n generalized
  accumulation of
  serous fluid within the
  subcutaneous connective
  tissue, resulting in
  oedema
**ANASARCAS** >ANASARCA
**ANASTASES** >ANASTASIS
**ANASTASIS** n Christ's
  harrowing of hell
**ANASTATIC** >ANASTASIS
**ANATA** n (in Theravada
  Buddhism) the belief
  that since all things are
  constantly changing,
  there can be no such
  thing as a permanent,
  unchanging self
**ANATAS** >ANATA
**ANATASE** n rare blue or
  black mineral
**ANATASES** >ANATASE
**ANATHEMA** n detested
  person or thing
**ANATHEMAS** >ANATHEMA
**ANATMAN** same as >ANATA
**ANATMANS** >ANATMAN
**ANATOMIC** >ANATOMY
**ANATOMIES** >ANATOMY
**ANATOMISE** same
  as >ANATOMIZE
**ANATOMIST** n expert in
  anatomy
**ANATOMIZE** vb dissect (an
  animal or plant)
**ANATOMY** n science of the
  structure of the body
**ANATOXIN** n bacterial toxin
  used in inoculation
**ANATOXINS** >ANATOXIN
**ANATROPY** n (of a plant
  ovule) condition of
  being inverted during
  development by a bending
  of the stalk (funicle)
  attaching it to the carpule
**ANATTA** n annatto
**ANATTAS** >ANATTA
**ANATTO** same as >ANNATTO
**ANATTOS** >ANATTO
**ANAXIAL** adj asymmetrical
**ANBURIES** >ANBURY

**ANBURY** n soft spongy
  tumour occurring in
  horses and oxen
**ANCE** dialect form of >ONCE
**ANCESTOR** n person from
  whom one is descended
**ANCESTORS** >ANCESTOR
**ANCESTRAL** adj of or
  inherited from ancestors
  ▷ n relation that holds
  between x and y if there
  is a chain of instances of
  a given relation leading
  from x to y
**ANCESTRY** n lineage or
  descent
**ANCHO** n chili pepper
**ANCHOR** n heavy hooked
  device attached to a boat
  by a cable and dropped
  overboard to fasten the
  ship to the sea bottom
  ▷ vb fasten with or as if
  with an anchor
**ANCHORAGE** n place where
  boats can be anchored
**ANCHORED** >ANCHOR
**ANCHORESS** >ANCHORITE
**ANCHORET** n achorite
**ANCHORETS** >ANCHORET
**ANCHORING** >ANCHOR
**ANCHORITE** n religious
  recluse
**ANCHORMAN** n broadcaster
  in a central studio who
  links up and presents
  items from outside camera
  units and other studios
**ANCHORMEN** >ANCHORMAN
**ANCHORS** pl n brakes of a
  motor vehicle
**ANCHOS** >ANCHOS
**ANCHOVETA** n small
  anchovy, Cetengraulis
  mysticetus, of the American
  Pacific, used as bait by
  tuna fishermen
**ANCHOVIES** >ANCHOVY
**ANCHOVY** n small strong-
  tasting fish
**ANCHUSA** n any Eurasian
  plant of the boraginaceous
  genus Anchusa, having
  rough hairy stems and
  leaves and blue flowers
**ANCHUSAS** >ANCHUSA
**ANCHUSIN** same
  as >ALKANET
**ANCHUSINS** >ANCHUSIN
**ANCHYLOSE** same
  as >ANKYLOSE
**ANCIENT** adj dating from
  very long ago ▷ n member
  of a civilized nation in the
  ancient world, esp a Greek,
  Roman, or Hebrew
**ANCIENTER** >ANCIENT
**ANCIENTLY** adv in ancient
  times
**ANCIENTRY** n quality of
  being ancient
**ANCIENTS** >ANCIENT
**ANCILE** n mythical Roman
  shield

**ANCILIA** > ANCILE
**ANCILLA** *n* Latin word for servant
**ANCILLAE** > ANCILLA
**ANCILLARY** *adj* supporting the main work of an organization ▷ *n* subsidiary or auxiliary thing or person
**ANCILLAS** > ANCILLA
**ANCIPITAL** *adj* flattened and having two edges
**ANCLE** *old spelling of* > ANKLE
**ANCLES** > ANCLE
**ANCOME** *n* inflammation
**ANCOMES** > ANCOME
**ANCON** *n* projecting bracket or console supporting a cornice
**ANCONAL** > ANCON
**ANCONE** *same as* > ANCON
**ANCONEAL** > ANCON
**ANCONES** > ANCONE
**ANCONOID** > ANCON
**ANCORA** *adv* Italian for encore
**ANCRESS** *n* female anchorite
**ANCRESSES** > ANCRESS
**AND** *n* additional matter or problem
**ANDANTE** *adv* (piece to be played) moderately slowly ▷ *n* passage or piece to be performed moderately slowly
**ANDANTES** > ANDANTE
**ANDANTINI** > ANDANTINO
**ANDANTINO** *adv* slightly faster or slower than andante ▷ *n* passage or piece to be performed in this way
**ANDESINE** *n* feldspar mineral of the plagioclase series
**ANDESINES** > ANDESINE
**ANDESITE** *n* fine-grained tan or grey volcanic rock
**ANDESITES** > ANDESITE
**ANDESITIC** > ANDESITE
**ANDESYTE** *n* andesite
**ANDESYTES** > ANDESYTE
**ANDIRON** *n* iron stand for supporting logs in a fireplace
**ANDIRONS** > ANDIRON
**ANDOUILLE** *n* spicy smoked pork sausage with a blackish skin
**ANDRADITE** *n* yellow, green, or brownish-black garnet
**ANDRO** *n* type of sex hormone
**ANDROECIA** *n* stamens of flowering plants collectively
**ANDROGEN** *n* any of several steroids, produced as hormones by the testes or made synthetically, that promote development of male sexual organs and

male secondary sexual characteristics
**ANDROGENS** > ANDROGEN
**ANDROGYNE** *n* person having both male and female sexual characteristics and genital tissues
**ANDROGYNY** *n* condition of having male and female characteristics
**ANDROID** *n* robot resembling a human ▷ *adj* resembling a human being
**ANDROIDS** > ANDROID
**ANDROLOGY** *n* branch of medicine concerned with diseases and conditions specific to men
**ANDROMEDA** *n* type of shrub
**ANDROS** > ANDRO
**ANDS** > AND
**ANDVILE** *old form of* > ANVIL
**ANDVILES** > ANDVILE
**ANE** *Scots word for* > ONE
**ANEAR** *adv* nearly ▷ *vb* approach
**ANEARED** > ANEAR
**ANEARING** > ANEAR
**ANEARS** > ANEAR
**ANEATH** *Scots word for* > BENEATH
**ANECDOTA** *n* unpublished writings
**ANECDOTAL** *adj* containing or consisting exclusively of anecdotes rather than connected discourse or research conducted under controlled conditions
**ANECDOTE** *n* short amusing account of an incident
**ANECDOTES** > ANECDOTE
**ANECDOTIC** > ANECDOTE
**ANECDYSES** > ANECDYSIS
**ANECDYSIS** *n* period between moults in arthropods
**ANECHOIC** *adj* having a low degree of reverberation of sound
**ANELACE** *same as* > ANLACE
**ANELACES** > ANELACE
**ANELASTIC** *adj* not elastic
**ANELE** *vb* anoint, esp to give extreme unction to
**ANELED** > ANELE
**ANELES** > ANELE
**ANELING** > ANELE
**ANEMIA** *n* anaemia
**ANEMIAS** > ANEMIA
**ANEMIC** *same as* > ANAEMIC
**ANEMOGRAM** *n* record produced by anemograph
**ANEMOLOGY** *n* study of winds
**ANEMONE** *n* plant with white, purple, or red flowers
**ANEMONES** > ANEMONE
**ANEMOSES** > ANEMOSIS
**ANEMOSIS** *n* cracking in timber caused by wind affecting growing tree

**ANENST** *dialect word for* > AGAINST
**ANENT** *prep* lying against
**ANERGIA** *n* anergy
**ANERGIAS** > ANERGIA
**ANERGIC** > ANERGY
**ANERGIES** > ANERGY
**ANERGY** *n* lack of energy
**ANERLY** *Scots word for* > ONLY
**ANEROID** *adj* not containing a liquid ▷ *n* barometer that does not contain liquid
**ANEROIDS** > ANEROID
**ANES** > ANE
**ANESTRA** > ANESTRUS
**ANESTRI** > ANESTRUS
**ANESTROUS** > ANESTRUS
**ANESTRUM** *n* anestrus
**ANESTRUS** *same as* > ANOESTRUS
**ANETHOL** *n* substance derived from oil of anise
**ANETHOLE** *n* white water-soluble crystalline substance with a liquorice-like odour
**ANETHOLES** > ANETHOLE
**ANETHOLS** > ANETHOL
**ANETIC** *adj* medically soothing
**ANEUPLOID** *adj* (of polyploid cells or organisms) having a chromosome number that is not an exact multiple of the haploid number ▷ *n* cell or individual of this type
**ANEURIN** *a less common name for* > THIAMINE
**ANEURINS** > ANEURIN
**ANEURISM** *same as* > ANEURYSM
**ANEURISMS** > ANEURISM
**ANEURYSM** *n* permanent swelling of a blood vessel
**ANEURYSMS** > ANEURYSM
**ANEW** *adv* once more
**ANGA** *n* a part in Indian music
**ANGAKOK** *n* Inuit shaman
**ANGAKOKS** > ANGAKOK
**ANGARIA** *n* species of shellfish
**ANGARIAS** > ANGARIA
**ANGARIES** > ANGARY
**ANGARY** *n* right of a belligerent state to use the property of a neutral state or to destroy it if necessary, subject to payment of full compensation to the owners
**ANGAS** > ANGA
**ANGASHORE** *n* miserable person given to complaining
**ANGEKKOK** *n* Inuit shaman
**ANGEKKOKS** > ANGEKKOK
**ANGEKOK** *n* Inuit shaman
**ANGEKOKS** > ANGEKOK
**ANGEL** *n* spiritual being

believed to be an attendant or messenger of God ▷ *vb* provide financial support for
**ANGELED** > ANGEL
**ANGELFISH** *n* South American aquarium fish with large fins
**ANGELHOOD** *n* state of being an angel
**ANGELIC** *adj* very kind, pure, or beautiful
**ANGELICA** *n* aromatic plant
**ANGELICAL** *same as* > ANGELIC
**ANGELICAS** > ANGELICA
**ANGELING** > ANGEL
**ANGELS** > ANGEL
**ANGELUS** *n* series of prayers recited in the morning, at midday, and in the evening, commemorating the Annunciation and Incarnation
**ANGELUSES** > ANGELUS
**ANGER** *n* fierce displeasure or extreme annoyance ▷ *vb* make (someone) angry
**ANGERED** > ANGER
**ANGERING** > ANGER
**ANGERLESS** > ANGER
**ANGERLY** *adv* old form of angrily
**ANGERS** > ANGER
**ANGICO** *n* South American tree
**ANGICOS** > ANGICO
**ANGINA** *n* heart disorder causing sudden severe chest pains
**ANGINAL** > ANGINA
**ANGINAS** > ANGINA
**ANGINOSE** > ANGINA
**ANGINOUS** > ANGINA
**ANGIOGRAM** *n* X-ray picture obtained by angiography
**ANGIOLOGY** *n* branch of medical science concerned with the blood vessels and the lymphatic system
**ANGIOMA** *n* tumour consisting of a mass of blood vessels or lymphatic vessels
**ANGIOMAS** > ANGIOMA
**ANGIOMATA** > ANGIOMA
**ANGKLUNG** *n* Asian musical instrument
**ANGKLUNGS** > ANGKLUNG
**ANGLE** *n* space between or shape formed by two lines or surfaces that meet ▷ *vb* bend or place (something) at an angle
**ANGLED** > ANGLE
**ANGLEDUG** *n* earthworm
**ANGLEDUGS** > ANGLEDUG
**ANGLEPOD** *n* American wild flower
**ANGLEPODS** > ANGLEPOD
**ANGLER** *n* person who fishes with a hook and line
**ANGLERS** > ANGLER

ANGLES >ANGLE

ANGLESITE n white or grey secondary mineral

ANGLEWISE >ANGLE

ANGLEWORM n earthworm used as bait by anglers

ANGLICE adv in English

ANGLICISE same as >ANGLICIZE

ANGLICISM n word, phrase, or idiom peculiar to the English language, esp as spoken in England

ANGLICIST n expert in or student of English literature or language

ANGLICIZE vb make or become English in outlook, form, etc

ANGLIFIED >ANGLIFY

ANGLIFIES >ANGLIFY

ANGLIFY same as >ANGLICIZE

ANGLING n art or sport of fishing with a hook and line

ANGLINGS >ANGLING

ANGLIST same as >ANGLICIST

ANGLISTS >ANGLIST

ANGLO n White inhabitant of the US not of Latin extraction

ANGLOPHIL n person having admiration for England or the English

ANGLOS >ANGLO

ANGOLA same as >ANGORA

ANGOPHORA n Australian tree related to the eucalyptus

ANGORA n variety of goat, cat, or rabbit with long silky hair

ANGORAS >ANGORA

ANGOSTURA n bitter aromatic bark

ANGRIER >ANGRY

ANGRIES >ANGRY

ANGRIEST >ANGRY

ANGRILY >ANGRY

ANGRINESS >ANGRY

ANGRY adj full of anger ▷ n angry person

ANGST n feeling of anxiety

ANGSTIER >ANGSTY

ANGSTIEST >ANGSTY

ANGSTROM n unit of length used to measure wavelengths

ANGSTROMS >ANGSTROM

ANGSTS >ANGST

ANGSTY adj displaying or feeling angst, esp in a self-conscious manner

ANGUIFORM adj shaped like a snake

ANGUINE adj of, relating to, or similar to a snake

ANGUIPED adj having snakes for legs

ANGUIPEDE adj having snakes for legs

ANGUISH n great mental pain ▷ vb afflict or be afflicted with anguish

ANGUISHED adj feeling or showing great mental pain

ANGUISHES >ANGUISH

ANGULAR adj (of a person) lean and bony

ANGULARLY >ANGULAR

ANGULATE adj having angles or an angular shape ▷ vb make or become angular

ANGULATED >ANGULATE

ANGULATES >ANGULATE

ANGULOSE adj having angles

ANGULOUS adj having angles

ANHEDONIA n inability to feel pleasure

ANHEDONIC >ANHEDONIA

ANHEDRAL n downward inclination of an aircraft wing in relation to the lateral axis

ANHINGA n type of bird

ANHINGAS >ANHINGA

ANHUNGRED adj very hungry

ANHYDRASE n enzyme that catalyzes the removal of water

ANHYDRIDE n substance that combines with water to form an acid

ANHYDRITE n colourless or greyish-white mineral found in sedimentary rocks

ANHYDROUS adj containing no water

ANI n any of several gregarious tropical American birds of the genus *Crotophaga*: family *Cuculidae* (cuckoos). They have a black plumage, long square-tipped tail, and heavily hooked bill

ANICCA n (in Theravada Buddhism) the belief that all things, including the self, are impermanent and constantly changing: the first of the three basic characteristics of existence

ANICCAS >ANICCA

ANICONIC adj (of images of deities, symbols, etc) not portrayed in a human or animal form

ANICONISM >ANICONIC

ANICONIST >ANICONIC

ANICUT n dam in India

ANICUTS >ANICUT

ANIDROSES >ANIDROSIS

ANIDROSIS n absence of sweating

ANIGH adv near

ANIGHT adv at night

ANIL n West Indian shrub, from which indigo is obtained

ANILE adj of or like a feeble old woman

ANILIN n aniline

ANILINE n colourless oily liquid obtained from coal tar and used for making dyes, plastics, and explosives

ANILINES >ANILINE

ANILINGUS n sexual stimulation involving oral contact with the anus

ANILINS >ANILIN

ANILITIES >ANILE

ANILITY >ANILE

ANILS >ANIL

ANIMA n feminine principle as present in the male unconscious

ANIMACIES >ANIMACY

ANIMACY n state of being animate

ANIMAL n living creature with specialized sense organs and capable of voluntary motion, esp one other than a human being ▷ adj of animals

ANIMALIAN >ANIMAL

ANIMALIC >ANIMAL

ANIMALIER n painter or sculptor of animal subjects, esp a member of a group of early 19th-century French sculptors who specialized in realistic figures of animals, usually in bronze

ANIMALISE same as >ANIMALIZE

ANIMALISM n preoccupation with physical matters

ANIMALIST >ANIMALISM

ANIMALITY n animal instincts of human beings

ANIMALIZE vb make (a person) brutal or sensual

ANIMALLY adv physically

ANIMALS >ANIMAL

ANIMAS >ANIMA

ANIMATE vb give life to ▷ adj having life

ANIMATED adj interesting and lively

ANIMATELY >ANIMATE

ANIMATER same as >ANIMATOR

ANIMATERS >ANIMATER

ANIMATES >ANIMATE

ANIMATIC n animated film sequence

ANIMATICS >ANIMATIC

ANIMATING >ANIMATE

ANIMATION n technique of making cartoon films

ANIMATISM n belief that inanimate objects have consciousness

ANIMATIST >ANIMATISM

ANIMATO adv (to be performed) in a lively manner

ANIMATOR n person who makes animated cartoons

ANIMATORS >ANIMATOR

ANIME n type of Japanese animated film with themes and styles similar to manga comics

ANIMES >ANIME

ANIMI >ANIMUS

ANIMIS >ANIMI

ANIMISM n belief that natural objects possess souls

ANIMISMS >ANIMISM

ANIMIST >ANIMISM

ANIMISTIC >ANIMISM

ANIMISTS >ANIMISM

ANIMOSITY n hostility, hatred

ANIMUS n hatred, animosity

ANIMUSES >ANIMUS

ANION n ion with negative charge

ANIONIC >ANION

ANIONS >ANION

ANIS >ANI

ANISE n plant with liquorice-flavoured seeds

ANISEED n liquorice-flavoured seeds of the anise plant

ANISEEDS >ANISEED

ANISES >ANISE

ANISETTE n liquorice-flavoured liqueur made from aniseed

ANISETTES >ANISETTE

ANISIC >ANISE

ANISOGAMY n type of sexual reproduction in which the gametes are dissimilar, either in size alone or in size and form

ANISOLE n colourless pleasant-smelling liquid used as a solvent

ANISOLES >ANISOLE

ANKER n old liquid measure for wine

ANKERITE n greyish to brown mineral that resembles dolomite

ANKERITES >ANKERITE

ANKERS >ANKER

ANKH n T-shaped cross with a loop on the top, which symbolized eternal life in ancient Egypt

ANKHS >ANKH

ANKLE n joint between the foot and leg ▷ vb move

ANKLEBONE the nontechnical name for >TALUS

ANKLED >ANKLE

ANKLES >ANKLE

ANKLET n ornamental chain worn round the ankle

ANKLETS >ANKLET

ANKLING >ANKLE

ANKLONG n Asian musical instrument

ANKLONGS >ANKLONG

ANKLUNG n Asian musical instrument

ANKLUNGS >ANKLUNG
ANKUS n stick used, esp in India, for goading elephants
ANKUSES >ANKUS
ANKUSH n Indian weapon
ANKUSHES >ANKUSH
ANKYLOSE vb (of bones in a joint, etc) to fuse or stiffen by ankylosis
ANKYLOSED >ANKYLOSE
ANKYLOSES >ANKYLOSE
ANKYLOSIS n abnormal immobility of a joint, caused by a fibrous growth
ANKYLOTIC >ANKYLOSIS
ANLACE n medieval short dagger with a broad tapering blade
ANLACES >ANLACE
ANLAGE n organ or part in the earliest stage of development
ANLAGEN >ANLAGE
ANLAGES >ANLAGE
ANLAS same as >ANLACE
ANLASES >ANLAS
ANN n old Scots word for a widow's pension
ANNA n former Indian coin worth one sixteenth of a rupee
ANNAL n recorded events of one year
ANNALISE vb record in annals
ANNALISED >ANNALISE
ANNALISES >ANNALISE
ANNALIST >ANNAL
ANNALISTS >ANNAL
ANNALIZE vb record in annals
ANNALIZED >ANNALIZE
ANNALIZES >ANNALIZE
ANNALS >ANNAL
ANNAS >ANNA
ANNAT n singular of annates
ANNATES pl n first year's revenue of a see, an abbacy, or a minor benefice, paid to the pope
ANNATS >ANNAT
ANNATTA n annatto
ANNATTAS >ANNATTA
ANNATTO n small tropical American tree, Bixa orellana, having red or pinkish flowers and pulpy seeds that yield a dye
ANNATTOS >ANNATTO
ANNEAL vb toughen (metal or glass) by heating and slow cooling ▷ n act of annealing
ANNEALED >ANNEAL
ANNEALER >ANNEAL
ANNEALERS >ANNEAL
ANNEALING >ANNEAL
ANNEALS >ANNEAL
ANNECTENT adj connecting
ANNELID n worm with a segmented body, such as an earthworm ▷ adj of,

relating to, or belonging to the Annelida
ANNELIDAN >ANNELID
ANNELIDS >ANNELID
ANNEX vb seize (territory)
ANNEXABLE >ANNEX
ANNEXE n extension to a building
ANNEXED >ANNEX
ANNEXES >ANNEXE
ANNEXING >ANNEX
ANNEXION n old form of annexation
ANNEXIONS >ANNEXION
ANNEXMENT >ANNEX
ANNEXURE n something that is added
ANNEXURES >ANNEXURE
ANNICUT n dam in India
ANNICUTS >ANNICUT
ANNO adv Latin for in the year
ANNONA n American tree or shrub
ANNONAS >ANNONA
ANNOTATE vb add notes to (a written work)
ANNOTATED >ANNOTATE
ANNOTATES >ANNOTATE
ANNOTATOR >ANNOTATE
ANNOUNCE vb make known publicly
ANNOUNCED >ANNOUNCE
ANNOUNCER n person who introduces radio or television programmes
ANNOUNCES >ANNOUNCE
ANNOY vb irritate or displease
ANNOYANCE n feeling of being annoyed
ANNOYED >ANNOY
ANNOYER >ANNOY
ANNOYERS >ANNOY
ANNOYING adj causing irritation or displeasure
ANNOYS >ANNOY
ANNS >ANN
ANNUAL adj happening once a year ▷ n plant that completes its life cycle in a year
ANNUALISE same as >ANNUALIZE
ANNUALIZE vb calculate (a rate) for or as if for a year
ANNUALLY >ANNUAL
ANNUALS >ANNUAL
ANNUITANT n person in receipt of or entitled to an annuity
ANNUITIES >ANNUITY
ANNUITY n fixed sum paid every year
ANNUL vb declare (something, esp a marriage) invalid
ANNULAR adj ring-shaped ▷ n ring finger
ANNULARLY >ANNULAR
ANNULARS >ANNULAR
ANNULATE adj having, composed of, or marked with rings ▷ n annelid

ANNULATED >ANNULATE
ANNULATES >ANNULATE
ANNULET n moulding in the form of a ring, as at the top of a column adjoining the capital
ANNULETS >ANNULET
ANNULI >ANNULUS
ANNULLED >ANNUL
ANNULLING >ANNUL
ANNULMENT n formal declaration that a contract or marriage is invalid
ANNULOSE adj (of earthworms, crustaceans, and similar animals) having a body formed of a series of rings
ANNULS >ANNUL
ANNULUS n area between two concentric circles
ANNULUSES >ANNULUS
ANOA n type of small cattle
ANOAS >ANOA
ANOBIID n any type of beetle
ANOBIIDS >ANOBIID
ANODAL >ANODE
ANODALLY >ANODE
ANODE n positive electrode in a battery, valve, etc
ANODES >ANODE
ANODIC >ANODE
ANODISE same as >ANODIZE
ANODISED >ANODISE
ANODISES >ANODISE
ANODISING >ANODISE
ANODIZE vb coat (metal) with a protective oxide film by electrolysis
ANODIZED >ANODIZE
ANODIZES >ANODIZE
ANODIZING >ANODIZE
ANODONTIA n congenital absence of teeth
ANODYNE n something that relieves pain or distress ▷ adj relieving pain or distress
ANODYNES >ANODYNE
ANODYNIC >ANODYNE
ANOESES >ANOESIS
ANOESIS n feeling without understanding
ANOESTRA >ANOESTRUS
ANOESTRI >ANOESTRUS
ANOESTRUM >ANOESTRUS
ANOESTRUS n period of sexual inactivity between two periods of oestrus in many mammals
ANOETIC >ANOESIS
ANOINT vb smear with oil as a sign of consecration
ANOINTED >ANOINT
ANOINTER >ANOINT
ANOINTERS >ANOINT
ANOINTING >ANOINT
ANOINTS >ANOINT
ANOLE n type of lizard
ANOLES >ANOLE
ANOLYTE n part of electrolyte around anode
ANOLYTES >ANOLYTE

ANOMALIES >ANOMALY
ANOMALOUS adj different from the normal or usual order or type
ANOMALY n something that deviates from the normal, irregularity
ANOMIC >ANOMIE
ANOMIE n lack of social or moral standards
ANOMIES >ANOMIE
ANOMY same as >ANOMIE
ANON adv in a short time, soon
ANONYM n anonymous person or publication
ANONYMA n promiscuous woman
ANONYMAS >ANONYMA
ANONYMISE same as >ANONYMIZE
ANONYMITY >ANONYMOUS
ANONYMIZE vb organize in a way that preserves anonymity
ANONYMOUS adj by someone whose name is unknown or withheld
ANONYMS >ANONYM
ANOOPSIA n squint in which the eye turns upwards
ANOOPSIAS >ANOOPSIA
ANOPHELES n any of various mosquitoes constituting the genus Anopheles, some species of which transmit the malaria parasite to man
ANOPIA n inability to see
ANOPIAS >ANOPIA
ANOPSIA n squint in which the eye turns upwards
ANOPSIAS >ANOPSIA
ANORAK n light waterproof hooded jacket
ANORAKS >ANORAK
ANORECTAL adj of the anus and rectum
ANORECTIC >ANOREXIA
ANORETIC n anorectic
ANORETICS >ANORETIC
ANOREXIA n psychological disorder characterized by fear of becoming fat and refusal to eat
ANOREXIAS >ANOREXIA
ANOREXIC >ANOREXIA
ANOREXICS >ANOREXIA
ANOREXIES >ANOREXY
ANOREXY old name for >ANOREXIA
ANORTHIC another word for >TRICLINIC
ANORTHITE n white to greyish-white or reddish-white mineral
ANOSMATIC >ANOSMIA
ANOSMIA n loss of the sense of smell, usually as the result of a lesion of the olfactory nerve, disease in another organ or part, or obstruction of the nasal

passages
**ANOSMIAS** > ANOSMIA
**ANOSMIC** > ANOSMIA
**ANOTHER** adj one more
**ANOUGH** adj enough
**ANOUROUS** adj having no tail
**ANOVULANT** n drug preventing ovulation
**ANOVULAR** adj without ovulation
**ANOW** adj old form of enough
**ANOXAEMIA** n deficiency in the amount of oxygen in the arterial blood
**ANOXAEMIC** > ANOXAEMIA
**ANOXEMIA** same as > ANOXAEMIA
**ANOXEMIAS** > ANOXEMIA
**ANOXEMIC** > ANOXEMIA
**ANOXIA** n lack or absence of oxygen
**ANOXIAS** > ANOXIA
**ANOXIC** > ANOXIA
**ANSA** n either end of Saturn's rings
**ANSAE** > ANSA
**ANSATE** adj having a handle or handle-like part
**ANSATED** adj ansate
**ANSERINE** adj of or resembling a goose ▷ n chemical compound
**ANSERINES** > ANSERINE
**ANSEROUS** same as > ANSERINE
**ANSWER** n reply to a question, request, letter, etc ▷ vb give an answer (to)
**ANSWERED** > ANSWER
**ANSWERER** > ANSWER
**ANSWERERS** > ANSWER
**ANSWERING** > ANSWER
**ANSWERS** > ANSWER
**ANT** n small insect living in highly-organized colonies
**ANTA** n pilaster attached to the end of a side wall or sometimes to the side of a doorway
**ANTACID** n substance that counteracts acidity, esp in the stomach ▷ adj having the properties of this substance
**ANTACIDS** > ANTACID
**ANTAE** > ANTA
**ANTALGIC** n pain-relieving drug
**ANTALGICS** > ANTALGIC
**ANTALKALI** n substance that neutralizes alkalis
**ANTAR** old word for > CAVE
**ANTARA** n South American panpipes
**ANTARAS** > ANTARA
**ANTARCTIC** adj relating to Antarctica
**ANTARS** > ANTAR
**ANTAS** > ANTA
**ANTBEAR** n aardvark
**ANTBEARS** > ANTBEAR

**ANTBIRD** n any of various dull-coloured South American passerine birds that typically feed on ants
**ANTBIRDS** > ANTBIRD
**ANTE** n player's stake in poker ▷ vb place (one's stake) in poker
**ANTEATER** n mammal which feeds on ants by means of a long snout
**ANTEATERS** > ANTEATER
**ANTECEDE** vb go before, as in time, order, etc
**ANTECEDED** > ANTECEDE
**ANTECEDES** > ANTECEDE
**ANTECHOIR** n part of a church in front of the choir, usually enclosed by screens, tombs, etc
**ANTED** > ANTE
**ANTEDATE** vb precede in time ▷ n earlier date
**ANTEDATED** > ANTEDATE
**ANTEDATES** > ANTEDATE
**ANTEED** > ANTE
**ANTEFIX** n carved ornament at the eaves of a roof to hide the joint between the tiles
**ANTEFIXA** > ANTEFIX
**ANTEFIXAE** > ANTEFIX
**ANTEFIXAL** > ANTEFIX
**ANTEFIXES** > ANTEFIX
**ANTEING** > ANTE
**ANTELOPE** n deerlike mammal with long legs and horns
**ANTELOPES** > ANTELOPE
**ANTELUCAN** adj before daylight
**ANTENATAL** adj during pregnancy, before birth ▷ n examination during pregnancy
**ANTENATI** n people born before certain date
**ANTENNA** n insect's feeler
**ANTENNAE** > ANTENNA
**ANTENNAL** > ANTENNA
**ANTENNARY** > ANTENNA
**ANTENNAS** > ANTENNA
**ANTENNULE** n one of a pair of small mobile appendages on the heads of crustaceans in front of the antennae, usually having a sensory function
**ANTEPAST** n appetizer
**ANTEPASTS** > ANTEPAST
**ANTERIOR** adj the front
**ANTEROOM** n small room leading into a larger one, often used as a waiting room
**ANTEROOMS** > ANTEROOM
**ANTES** > ANTE
**ANTETYPE** n earlier form
**ANTETYPES** > ANTETYPE
**ANTEVERT** vb displace (an organ or part) by tilting it forward
**ANTEVERTS** > ANTEVERT
**ANTHELIA** > ANTHELION

**ANTHELION** n faint halo sometimes seen in polar or high altitude regions around the shadow of an object cast onto a thick cloud bank or fog
**ANTHELIX** n prominent curved fold of cartilage just inside the outer rim of the external ear
**ANTHEM** n song of loyalty, esp to a country ▷ vb provide with an anthem
**ANTHEMED** > ANTHEM
**ANTHEMIA** > ANTHEMION
**ANTHEMIC** > ANTHEM
**ANTHEMING** > ANTHEM
**ANTHEMION** n floral design, used esp in ancient Greek and Roman architecture and decoration, usually consisting of honeysuckle, lotus, or palmette leaf motifs
**ANTHEMS** > ANTHEM
**ANTHER** n part of a flower's stamen containing pollen
**ANTHERAL** > ANTHER
**ANTHERID** n antheridium
**ANTHERIDS** > ANTHERID
**ANTHERS** > ANTHER
**ANTHESES** > ANTHESIS
**ANTHESIS** n time when a flower becomes sexually functional
**ANTHILL** n mound of soil, leaves, etc, near the entrance of an ants' nest, carried and deposited there by the ants while constructing the nest
**ANTHILLS** > ANTHILL
**ANTHOCARP** n fruit developing from many flowers
**ANTHOCYAN** n any of a class of water-soluble glycosidic pigments
**ANTHODIA** > ANTHODIUM
**ANTHODIUM** another name for > CAPITULUM
**ANTHOID** adj resembling a flower
**ANTHOLOGY** n collection of poems or other literary pieces by various authors
**ANTHOTAXY** n arrangement of flowers on a stem or parts on a flower
**ANTHOZOAN** n any of the solitary or colonial sessile marine coelenterates of the class Anthozoa, including the corals, sea anemones, and sea pens, in which the body is in the form of a polyp ▷ adj of or relating to the class Anthozoa
**ANTHOZOIC** > ANTHOZOAN
**ANTHRACES** > ANTHRAX
**ANTHRACIC** adj of anthrax
**ANTHRAX** n dangerous disease of cattle and

sheep, communicable to humans
**ANTHRAXES** > ANTHRAX
**ANTHROPIC** adj of or relating to human beings
**ANTHURIUM** n any of various tropical American aroid plants constituting the genus Anthurium, many of which are cultivated as house plants for their showy foliage and their flowers, which are borne in a long-stalked spike surrounded by a flaring heart-shaped white or red bract
**ANTI** adj opposed (to) ▷ n opponent of a party, policy, or attitude
**ANTIABUSE** adj designed to prevent abuse
**ANTIACNE** adj inhibiting the development of acne
**ANTIAGING** adj resisting the effects of ageing
**ANTIAIR** adj countering attack by aircraft or missile
**ANTIALIEN** adj designed to prevent foreign animal or plant species from becoming established
**ANTIAR** another name for > UPAS
**ANTIARIN** n poison derived from antiar
**ANTIARINS** > ANTIARIN
**ANTIARMOR** adj designed or equipped to combat armoured vehicles
**ANTIARS** > ANTIAR
**ANTIATOM** n atom composed of antiparticles, in which the nucleus contains antiprotons with orbiting positrons
**ANTIATOMS** > ANTIATOM
**ANTIAUXIN** n substance acting against auxin
**ANTIBIAS** adj countering bias
**ANTIBLACK** adj hostile to black people
**ANTIBODY** n protein produced in the blood, which destroys bacteria
**ANTIBOSS** adj acting against bosses
**ANTIBUG** adj acting against computer bugs
**ANTIBUSER** n person who opposes the policy of transporting students to faraway schools to achieve racial balance
**ANTIC** n actor in a ludicrous or grotesque part ▷ adj fantastic
**ANTICAL** adj (of the position of plant parts) in front of or above another part
**ANTICALLY** > ANTICAL

**ANTICAR** n opposed to cars

**ANTICHLOR** n substance used to remove chlorine from a material after bleaching or to neutralize the chlorine present

**ANTICISE** same as > ANTICIZE

**ANTICISED** > ANTICISE

**ANTICISES** > ANTICISE

**ANTICITY** adj opposed to cities

**ANTICIVIC** adj opposed to citizenship

**ANTICIZE** vb play absurdly

**ANTICIZED** > ANTICIZE

**ANTICIZES** > ANTICIZE

**ANTICK** vb perform antics

**ANTICKE** adj old form of antique

**ANTICKED** > ANTICK

**ANTICKING** > ANTICK

**ANTICKS** > ANTICK

**ANTICLINE** n fold of rock raised up into a broad arch so that the strata slope down on both sides

**ANTICLING** adj acting against clinging

**ANTICLY** adv grotesquely

**ANTICODON** n element of RNA

**ANTICOLD** adj preventing or fighting the common cold

**ANTICOUS** adj on the part of a flower furthest from the stem

**ANTICRACK** adj protecting a computer against unauthorized access

**ANTICRIME** adj preventing or fighting crime

**ANTICS** pl n absurd acts or postures

**ANTICULT** n organisation that is opposed to religious cults

**ANTICULTS** > ANTICULT

**ANTIDORA** n bread used in Russian Orthodox Communion

**ANTIDOTAL** > ANTIDOTE

**ANTIDOTE** n substance that counteracts a poison ▷ vb counteract with an antidote

**ANTIDOTED** > ANTIDOTE

**ANTIDOTES** > ANTIDOTE

**ANTIDRAFT** adj opposed to conscription

**ANTIDRUG** adj intended to discourage illegal drug use

**ANTIDUNE** n sand hill or inclined bedding plane that forms a steep slope against the direction of a fast-flowing current

**ANTIDUNES** > ANTIDUNE

**ANTIELITE** adj opposed to elitism

**ANTIENT** old spelling of > ANCIENT

**ANTIENTS** > ANTIENT

**ANTIFAT** adj acting to remove or prevent fat

**ANTIFLU** adj acting against influenza

**ANTIFOAM** adj allowing gas to escape rather than form foam

**ANTIFOG** adj preventing the buildup of moisture on a surface

**ANTIFRAUD** adj acting against fraud

**ANTIFUR** adj opposed to the wearing of fur garments

**ANTIGANG** adj designed to restrict the activities of criminal gangs

**ANTIGAY** adj hostile to homosexuals

**ANTIGEN** n substance causing the blood to produce antibodies

**ANTIGENE** n antigen

**ANTIGENES** > ANTIGENE

**ANTIGENIC** > ANTIGEN

**ANTIGENS** > ANTIGEN

**ANTIGLARE** adj cutting down glare

**ANTIGRAFT** adj designed to reduce corruption

**ANTIGUN** adj opposed to the possession of guns

**ANTIHELIX** same as > ANTHELIX

**ANTIHERO** n central character in a book, film, etc, who lacks the traditional heroic virtues

**ANTIHUMAN** adj inhuman

**ANTIJAM** adj preventing jamming

**ANTIKING** n rival to an established king

**ANTIKINGS** > ANTIKING

**ANTIKNOCK** n substance added to motor fuel to reduce knocking in the engine caused by too rapid combustion

**ANTILABOR** adj opposed to labor interests

**ANTILEAK** adj preventing leaks

**ANTILEFT** adj opposed to the left wing in politics

**ANTILIFE** adj in favour of abortion

**ANTILIFER** n person in favour of abortion

**ANTILOCK** adj designed to prevent overbraking

**ANTILOG** n number whose logarithm to a given base is a given number

**ANTILOGS** > ANTILOG

**ANTILOGY** n contradiction in terms

**ANTIMACHO** adj opposed to macho attitudes

**ANTIMALE** adj opposed to men

**ANTIMAN** adj opposed to men

**ANTIMASK** n interlude in a masque

**ANTIMASKS** > ANTIMASK

**ANTIMERE** n part or organ of a bilaterally or radially symmetrical organism that corresponds to a similar structure on the other side of the axis, such as the right or left limb of a four-legged animal

**ANTIMERES** > ANTIMERE

**ANTIMERIC** > ANTIMERE

**ANTIMINE** adj designed to counteract landmines

**ANTIMONIC** adj of or containing antimony in the pentavalent state

**ANTIMONY** n brittle silvery-white metallic element

**ANTIMONYL** n of, consisting of, or containing the monovalent group SbO-

**ANTIMUON** n antiparticle of a muon

**ANTIMUONS** > ANTIMUON

**ANTIMUSIC** n music intended to overthrow traditional conventions and expectations

**ANTIMYCIN** n antibiotic drug

**ANTING** n placing or rubbing of ants by birds on their feathers. The body fluids of the ants are thought to repel parasites

**ANTINGS** > ANTING

**ANTINODAL** > ANTINODE

**ANTINODE** n point at which the amplitude of one of the two kinds of displacement in a standing wave has maximum value. Generally the other kind of displacement has its minimum value at this point

**ANTINODES** > ANTINODE

**ANTINOISE** n sound generated so that it is out of phase with a noise, such as that made by an engine, in order to reduce the noise level by interference

**ANTINOME** n opposite

**ANTINOMES** > ANTINOME

**ANTINOMIC** > ANTINOMY

**ANTINOMY** n contradiction between two laws or principles that are reasonable in themselves

**ANTINOVEL** n type of prose fiction in which conventional elements of the novel are rejected

**ANTINUKE** same as > ANTINUKER

**ANTINUKER** n person who is opposed to nuclear weapons or energy

**ANTINUKES** > ANTINUKE

**ANTIPAPAL** adj opposed to the pope

**ANTIPARTY** adj opposed to a political party

**ANTIPASTI** > ANTIPASTO

**ANTIPASTO** n appetizer in an Italian meal

**ANTIPATHY** n dislike, hostility

**ANTIPHON** n hymn sung in alternate parts by two groups of singers

**ANTIPHONS** > ANTIPHON

**ANTIPHONY** n antiphonal singing of a musical composition by two choirs

**ANTIPILL** adj opposed to the use of the contraceptive pill

**ANTIPODAL** adj of or relating to diametrically opposite points on the earth's surface

**ANTIPODE** n exact or direct opposite

**ANTIPODES** pl n any two places diametrically opposite one another on the earth's surface

**ANTIPOLAR** > ANTIPOLE

**ANTIPOLE** n opposite pole

**ANTIPOLES** > ANTIPOLE

**ANTIPOPE** n pope set up in opposition to the one chosen by church laws

**ANTIPOPES** > ANTIPOPE

**ANTIPORN** adj opposed to pornography

**ANTIPOT** adj opposed to illegal use of marijuana

**ANTIPRESS** adj hostile to the news media

**ANTIPYIC** n drug acting against suppuration

**ANTIPYICS** > ANTIPYIC

**ANTIQUARK** n antiparticle of a quark

**ANTIQUARY** n student or collector of antiques or ancient works of art

**ANTIQUATE** vb make obsolete or old-fashioned

**ANTIQUE** n object of an earlier period, valued for its beauty, workmanship, or age ▷ adj made in an earlier period ▷ vb give an antique appearance to

**ANTIQUED** > ANTIQUE

**ANTIQUELY** > ANTIQUE

**ANTIQUER** n collector of antiques

**ANTIQUERS** > ANTIQUE

**ANTIQUES** > ANTIQUE

**ANTIQUEY** adj having the appearance of an antique

**ANTIQUING** > ANTIQUE

**ANTIQUITY** n great age

**ANTIRADAR** adj preventing detection by radar

**ANTIRAPE** adj protecting against rape

**ANTIRED** adj of a particular colour of antiquark

**ANTIRIOT** adj (of police officers, equipment,

measures, etc) designed for or engaged in the control of crowds

**ANTIROCK** *adj* designed to prevent a vehicle from rocking

**ANTIROLL** *adj* designed to prevent a vehicle from tilting

**ANTIROYAL** *adj* opposed to the monarchy

**ANTIRUST** *adj* (of a product or procedure) effective against rust ▷ *n* substance or device that prevents rust

**ANTIRUSTS** > ANTIRUST

**ANTIS** > ANTI

**ANTISAG** *adj* preventing sagging

**ANTISCIAN** *n* person living on other side of equator

**ANTISENSE** *adj* acting in opposite way to RNA

**ANTISERA** > ANTISERUM

**ANTISERUM** *n* blood serum containing antibodies used to treat or provide immunity to a disease

**ANTISEX** *adj* opposed to sexual activity

**ANTISHARK** *adj* protecting against sharks

**ANTISHIP** *adj* designed for attacking ships

**ANTISHOCK** *n* one of a pair of walking poles designed to reduce stress on the knees

**ANTISKID** *adj* intended to prevent skidding

**ANTISLEEP** *adj* acting to prevent sleep

**ANTISLIP** *adj* acting to prevent slipping

**ANTISMOG** *adj* reducing smog

**ANTISMOKE** *adj* preventing smoke

**ANTISMUT** *adj* opposed to obscene material

**ANTISNOB** *n* person opposed to snobbery

**ANTISNOBS** > ANTISNOB

**ANTISOLAR** *adj* opposite to the sun

**ANTISPAM** *adj* intended to prevent spam

**ANTISPAST** *n* group of four syllables in poetic metre

**ANTISTAT** *n* substance preventing static electricity

**ANTISTATE** *adj* opposed to state authority

**ANTISTATS** > ANTISTAT

**ANTISTICK** *adj* preventing things from sticking to a surface

**ANTISTORY** *n* story without a plot

**ANTISTYLE** *n* style that rejects traditional aesthetics

**ANTITANK** *adj* (of weapons) designed to destroy military tanks

**ANTITAX** *adj* opposed to taxation

**ANTITHEFT** *adj* (of a device, campaign, system, etc) designed to prevent theft

**ANTITHET** *n* example of antithesis

**ANTITHETS** > ANTITHET

**ANTITOXIC** > ANTITOXIN

**ANTITOXIN** *n* (serum containing) an antibody that acts against a toxin

**ANTITRADE** *n* wind blowing in the opposite direction to a trade wind

**ANTITRAGI** *n* cartilaginous projections of the external ear opposite the tragus

**ANTITRUST** *adj* (of laws) opposing business monopolies ▷ *n* regulating or opposing trusts, monopolies, cartels, or similar organizations, esp in order to prevent unfair competition

**ANTITUMOR** *adj* acting against tumours

**ANTITYPAL** > ANTITYPE

**ANTITYPE** *n* person or thing that is foreshadowed or represented by a type or symbol, esp a character or event in the New Testament prefigured in the Old Testament

**ANTITYPES** > ANTITYPE

**ANTITYPIC** > ANTITYPE

**ANTIULCER** *adj* used to treat ulcers

**ANTIUNION** *adj* opposed to union

**ANTIURBAN** *adj* opposed to city life

**ANTIVENIN** *n* antitoxin that counteracts a specific venom, esp snake venom

**ANTIVENOM** *n* venom antidote

**ANTIVIRAL** *adj* inhibiting the growth of viruses ▷ *n* any antiviral drug: used to treat diseases caused by viruses, such as herpes infections and AIDS

**ANTIVIRUS** *adj* relating to software designed to protect computer files from viruses ▷ *n* such a piece of software

**ANTIWAR** *adj* opposed to war

**ANTIWEAR** *adj* preventing wear

**ANTIWEED** *adj* killing or preventing weeds

**ANTIWHITE** *adj* hostile to white people

**ANTIWOMAN** *adj* hostile to

women

**ANTIWORLD** *n* hypothetical or supposed world or universe composed of antimatter

**ANTLER** *n* branched horn of a male deer

**ANTLERED** *adj* having antlers

**ANTLERS** > ANTLER

**ANTLIA** *n* butterfly proboscis

**ANTLIAE** > ANTLIA

**ANTLIATE** *adj* relating to antlia

**ANTLIKE** *adj* of or like an ant or ants

**ANTLION** *n* any of various neuropterous insects of the family *Myrmeleontidae*, which typically resemble dragonflies and are most common in tropical regions

**ANTLIONS** > ANTLION

**ANTONYM** *n* word that means the opposite of another

**ANTONYMIC** > ANTONYM

**ANTONYMS** > ANTONYM

**ANTONYMY** *n* use of antonyms

**ANTRA** > ANTRUM

**ANTRAL** > ANTRUM

**ANTRE** *n* cavern or cave

**ANTRES** > ANTRE

**ANTRORSE** *adj* directed or pointing upwards or forwards

**ANTRUM** *n* natural cavity, esp in a bone

**ANTRUMS** > ANTRUM

**ANTS** > ANT

**ANTSIER** > ANTSY

**ANTSIEST** > ANTSY

**ANTSINESS** > ANTSY

**ANTSY** *adj* restless, nervous, and impatient

**ANTWACKIE** *adj* old-fashioned

**ANUCLEATE** *adj* without a nucleus

**ANURAL** *adj* without a tail

**ANURAN** *n* any of the vertebrates of the order *Anura* (or *Salientia*), characterized by absence of a tail and very long hind legs specialized for hopping: class *Amphibia* (amphibians). The group includes the frogs and toads ▷ *adj* of, relating to, or belonging to the order *Anura*

**ANURANS** > ANURAN

**ANURESES** > ANURESIS

**ANURESIS** *n* inability to urinate even though urine is formed by the kidneys and retained in the urinary bladder

**ANURETIC** > ANURESIS

**ANURIA** *n* complete

suppression of urine formation, often as the result of a kidney disorder

**ANURIAS** > ANURIA

**ANURIC** > ANURIA

**ANUROUS** *adj* lacking a tail

**ANUS** *n* opening at the end of the alimentary canal, through which faeces are discharged

**ANUSES** > ANUS

**ANVIL** *n* heavy iron block on which metals are hammered into particular shapes ▷ *vb* forge on an anvil

**ANVILED** > ANVIL

**ANVILING** > ANVIL

**ANVILLED** > ANVIL

**ANVILLING** > ANVIL

**ANVILS** > ANVIL

**ANVILTOP** *n* type of stormcloud formation

**ANVILTOPS** > ANVILTOP

**ANXIETIES** > ANXIETY

**ANXIETY** *n* state of being anxious

**ANXIOUS** *adj* worried and tense

**ANXIOUSLY** > ANXIOUS

**ANY** *adj* one or some, no matter which ▷ *adv* at all

**ANYBODIES** > ANYBODY

**ANYBODY** *n* any person at random

**ANYHOW** *adv* anyway

**ANYMORE** *adv* at present

**ANYON** *n* (in mathematics) projective representation of a Lie group

**ANYONE** *pron* any person ▷ *n* any person at random

**ANYONES** > ANYONE

**ANYONS** > ANYON

**ANYPLACE** *adv* in, at, or to any unspecified place

**ANYROAD** *a northern English dialect word for* > ANYWAY

**ANYTHING** *pron* any object, event, or action whatever ▷ *n* any thing at random

**ANYTHINGS** > ANYTHING

**ANYTIME** *adv* at any time

**ANYWAY** *adv* at any rate, nevertheless

**ANYWAYS** *nonstandard word for* > ANYWAY

**ANYWHEN** *adv* at any time

**ANYWHERE** *adv* in, at, or to any place

**ANYWHERES** *nonstandard word for* > ANYWHERE

**ANYWISE** *adv* in any way or manner

**ANZIANI** *n* Italian word for councillors

**AORIST** *n* tense of the verb in classical Greek and in certain other inflected languages, indicating past action without reference to whether the action involved was momentary or continuous

**AORISTIC** > AORIST
**AORISTS** > AORIST
**AORTA** *n* main artery of the body, carrying oxygen-rich blood from the heart
**AORTAE** > AORTA
**AORTAL** > AORTA
**AORTAS** > AORTA
**AORTIC** > AORTA
**AORTITIS** *n* inflammation of the aorta
**AOUDAD** *n* wild mountain sheep, *Ammotragus lervia*, of N Africa, having horns curved in a semicircle and long hair covering the neck and forelegs
**AOUDADS** > AOUDAD
**APACE** *adv* swiftly
**APACHE** *n* Parisian gangster or ruffian
**APACHES** > APACHE
**APADANA** *n* ancient Persian palace hall
**APADANAS** > APADANA
**APAGE** *interj* Greek word meaning go away
**APAGOGE** *n* reduction to absurdity
**APAGOGES** > APAGOGE
**APAGOGIC** > APAGOGE
**APAID** > APAY
**APANAGE** *same as* > APPANAGE
**APANAGED** *adj* having apanage
**APANAGES** > APANAGE
**APAREJO** *n* kind of packsaddle made of stuffed leather cushions
**APAREJOS** > APAREJO
**APART** *adv* to pieces or in pieces
**APARTHEID** *n* former official government policy of racial segregation in S Africa
**APARTMENT** *n* room in a building
**APARTNESS** > APART
**APATETIC** *adj* of or relating to coloration that disguises and protects an animal
**APATHATON** *old word for* > EPITHET
**APATHETIC** *adj* having or showing little or no emotion
**APATHIES** > APATHY
**APATHY** *n* lack of interest or enthusiasm
**APATITE** *n* pale green to purple mineral, found in igneous rocks
**APATITES** > APATITE
**APATOSAUR** *n* long-necked dinosaur
**APAY** *vb* old word meaning satisfy
**APAYD** > APAY
**APAYING** > APAY
**APAYS** > APAY
**APE** *n* tailless monkey such

as the chimpanzee or gorilla ▷ *vb* imitate
**APEAK** *adj* in a vertical or almost vertical position
**APED** > APE
**APEDOM** *n* state of being an ape
**APEDOMS** > APEDOM
**APEEK** *adv* nautical word meaning vertically
**APEHOOD** *n* state of being ape
**APEHOODS** > APEHOOD
**APELIKE** > APE
**APEMAN** *n* extinct primate thought to have been the forerunner of true humans
**APEMEN** > APEMAN
**APEPSIA** *n* digestive disorder
**APEPSIAS** > APEPSIA
**APEPSIES** > APEPSY
**APEPSY** *n* apepsia
**APER** *n* person who apes
**APERCU** *n* outline
**APERCUS** > APERCU
**APERIENT** *adj* having a mild laxative effect ▷ *n* mild laxative
**APERIENTS** > APERIENT
**APERIES** > APERY
**APERIODIC** *adj* not periodic
**APERITIF** *n* alcoholic drink taken before a meal
**APERITIFS** > APERITIF
**APERITIVE** *n* laxative
**APERS** > APER
**APERT** *adj* open
**APERTNESS** > APERT
**APERTURAL** > APERTURE
**APERTURE** *n* opening or hole
**APERTURED** *adj* having an aperture
**APERTURES** > APERTURE
**APERY** *n* imitative behaviour
**APES** > APE
**APETALIES** > APETALOUS
**APETALOUS** *adj* (of flowering plants) having no petals
**APETALY** > APETALOUS
**APEX** *n* highest point
**APEXES** > APEX
**APGAR** as in *apgar score* system for determining the condition of an infant at birth
**APHAGIA** *n* refusal or inability to swallow
**APHAGIAS** > APHAGIA
**APHAKIA** *n* absence of the lens of an eye, congenital or otherwise
**APHAKIAS** > APHAKIA
**APHANITE** *n* any fine-grained rock, such as a basalt, containing minerals that cannot be distinguished with the naked eye
**APHANITES** > APHANITE

**APHANITIC** > APHANITE
**APHASIA** *n* disorder of the central nervous system that affects the ability to speak and understand words
**APHASIAC** > APHASIA
**APHASIACS** > APHASIA
**APHASIAS** > APHASIA
**APHASIC** > APHASIA
**APHASICS** > APHASIA
**APHELIA** > APHELION
**APHELIAN** > APHELION
**APHELION** *n* point of a planet's orbit that is farthest from the sun
**APHELIONS** > APHELION
**APHERESES** > APHERESIS
**APHERESIS** *n* omission of a letter or syllable at the beginning of a word
**APHERETIC** > APHERESIS
**APHESES** > APHESIS
**APHESIS** *n* gradual disappearance of an unstressed vowel at the beginning of a word, as in *squire* from *esquire*
**APHETIC** > APHESIS
**APHETISE** *vb* lose a vowel at the beginning of a word
**APHETISED** > APHETISE
**APHETISES** > APHETISE
**APHETIZE** *vb* lose a vowel at the beginning of a word
**APHETIZED** > APHETIZE
**APHETIZES** > APHETIZE
**APHICIDE** *n* substance for killing aphids
**APHICIDES** > APHICIDE
**APHID** *n* small insect which sucks the sap from plants
**APHIDES** > APHIS
**APHIDIAN** > APHID
**APHIDIANS** > APHID
**APHIDIOUS** > APHID
**APHIDS** > APHID
**APHIS** *n* any of various aphids constituting the genus *Aphis*, such as the blackfly
**APHOLATE** *n* type of pesticide
**APHOLATES** > APHOLATE
**APHONIA** *n* loss of the voice caused by damage to the vocal tract
**APHONIAS** > APHONIA
**APHONIC** *adj* affected with aphonia ▷ *n* person affected with aphonia
**APHONICS** > APHONIC
**APHONIES** > APHONY
**APHONOUS** > APHONIA
**APHONY** *same as* > APHONIA
**APHORISE** *same as* > APHORIZE
**APHORISED** > APHORISE
**APHORISER** > APHORISE
**APHORISES** > APHORISE
**APHORISM** *n* short clever saying expressing a general truth
**APHORISMS** > APHORISM

**APHORIST** > APHORISM
**APHORISTS** > APHORISM
**APHORIZE** *vb* write or speak in aphorisms
**APHORIZED** > APHORIZE
**APHORIZER** > APHORIZE
**APHORIZES** > APHORIZE
**APHOTIC** *adj* characterized by or growing in the absence of light
**APHRODITE** *n* North American butterfly
**APHTHA** *n* small ulceration on a mucous membrane, as in thrush, caused by a fungal infection
**APHTHAE** > APHTHA
**APHTHOUS** > APHTHA
**APHYLLIES** > APHYLLOUS
**APHYLLOUS** *adj* (of plants) having no leaves
**APHYLLY** > APHYLLOUS
**APIACEOUS** *adj* parsley-like
**APIAN** *adj* of, relating to, or resembling bees
**APIARIAN** *adj* of or relating to the breeding and care of bees ▷ *n* apiarist
**APIARIANS** > APIARIAN
**APIARIES** > APIARY
**APIARIST** *n* beekeeper
**APIARISTS** > APIARIST
**APIARY** *n* place where bees are kept
**APICAL** *adj* of, at, or being an apex ▷ *n* sound made with the tip of the tongue
**APICALLY** > APICAL
**APICALS** > APICAL
**APICES** *plural of* > APEX
**APICIAN** *adj* of fine or dainty food
**APICULATE** *adj* (of leaves) ending in a short sharp point
**APICULI** > APICULUS
**APICULUS** *n* short sharp point
**APIECE** *adv* each
**APIMANIA** *n* extreme enthusiasm for bees
**APIMANIAS** > APIMANIA
**APING** > APE
**APIOL** *n* substance formerly used to assist menstruation
**APIOLOGY** *n* study of bees
**APIOLS** > APIOL
**APISH** *adj* stupid or foolish
**APISHLY** > APISH
**APISHNESS** > APISH
**APISM** *n* behaviour like an ape
**APISMS** > APISM
**APIVOROUS** *adj* eating bees
**APLANAT** *n* aplanatic lens
**APLANATIC** *adj* (of a lens or mirror) free from spherical aberration
**APLANATS** > APLANAT
**APLANETIC** *adj* (esp of some algal and fungal spores) nonmotile or lacking a motile stage

APLASIA n congenital absence or abnormal development of an organ or part

APLASIAS > APLASIA

APLASTIC adj relating to or characterized by aplasia

APLENTY adv in plenty

APLITE n light-coloured fine-grained acid igneous rock with a sugary texture, consisting of quartz and feldspars

APLITES > APLITE

APLITIC > APLITE

APLOMB n calm self-possession

APLOMBS > APLOMB

APLUSTRE n stern ornament on an ancient Greek ship

APLUSTRES > APLUSTRE

APNEA same as > APNOEA

APNEAL > APNEA

APNEAS > APNEA

APNEIC > APNEA

APNEUSES > APNEUSIS

APNEUSIS n protracted gasping inhalation followed by short inefficient exhalation, which can cause asphyxia

APNEUSTIC adj of or relating to apneusis

APNOEA n temporary inability to breathe

APNOEAL > APNOEA

APNOEAS > APNOEA

APNOEIC > APNOEA

APO n type of protein

APOAPSES > APOAPSIS

APOAPSIS n point in an orbit furthest from the object orbited

APOCARP n apocarpous gynoecium or fruit

APOCARPS > APOCARP

APOCARPY n presence of many carpels

APOCOPATE vb omit the final sound or sounds of (a word)

APOCOPE n omission of the final sound or sounds of a word

APOCOPES > APOCOPE

APOCOPIC > APOCOPE

APOCRINE adj denoting a type of glandular secretion in which part of the secreting cell is lost with the secretion, as in mammary glands

APOCRYPHA n writings or statements of uncertain authority

APOD n animal without feet

APODAL adj (of snakes, eels, etc) without feet

APODE n animal without feet

APODES > APODE

APODICTIC adj unquestionably true by virtue of demonstration

APODOSES > APODOSIS

APODOSIS n consequent of a conditional statement, as the game will be cancelled in if it rains the game will be cancelled

APODOUS same as > APODAL

APODS > APOD

APOENZYME n protein component that together with a coenzyme forms an enzyme

APOGAEIC > APOGEE

APOGAMIC > APOGAMY

APOGAMIES > APOGAMY

APOGAMOUS > APOGAMY

APOGAMY n type of reproduction, occurring in some ferns, in which the sporophyte develops from the gametophyte without fusion of gametes

APOGEAL > APOGEE

APOGEAN > APOGEE

APOGEE n point of the moon's or a satellite's orbit that is farthest from the earth

APOGEES > APOGEE

APOGEIC > APOGEE

APOGRAPH n exact copy

APOGRAPHS > APOGRAPH

APOLLO n strikingly handsome youth

APOLLOS > APOLLO

APOLOG same as > APOLOGUE

APOLOGAL > APOLOGUE

APOLOGIA n formal written defence of a cause

APOLOGIAE > APOLOGIA

APOLOGIAS > APOLOGIA

APOLOGIES > APOLOGY

APOLOGISE same as > APOLOGIZE

APOLOGIST n person who formally defends a cause

APOLOGIZE vb make an apology

APOLOGS > APOLOG

APOLOGUE n allegory or moral fable

APOLOGUES > APOLOGUE

APOLOGY n expression of regret for wrongdoing

APOLUNE n point in a lunar orbit when a spacecraft is at its greatest distance from the moon

APOLUNES > APOLUNE

APOMICT n organism, esp a plant, produced by apomixis

APOMICTIC > APOMIXIS

APOMICTS > APOMICT

APOMIXES > APOMIXIS

APOMIXIS n (esp in plants) any of several types of asexual reproduction, such as parthenogenesis and apogamy, in which fertilization does not take place

APOOP adv on the poop deck

APOPHASES > APOPHASIS

APOPHASIS n device of mentioning a subject by stating that it will not be mentioned

APOPHATIC adj of theology that says God is indescribable

APOPHONY n change in the quality of vowels

APOPHYGE n outward curve at each end of the shaft of a column, adjoining the base or capital

APOPHYGES > APOPHYGE

APOPHYSES > APOPHYSIS

APOPHYSIS n process, outgrowth, or swelling from part of an animal or plant

APOPLAST n nonprotoplasmic component of a plant, including the cell walls and intercellular material

APOPLASTS > APOPLAST

APOPLEX vb afflict with apoplexy

APOPLEXED > APOPLEX

APOPLEXES > APOPLEX

APOPLEXY n stroke

APOPTOSES > APOPTOSIS

APOPTOSIS n programmed death of some of an organism's cells as part of its natural growth and development

APOPTOTIC > APOPTOSIS

APORETIC > APORIA

APORIA n doubt, real or professed, about what to do or say

APORIAS > APORIA

APORT adj on or towards the port side

APOS > APO

APOSITIA n unwillingness to eat

APOSITIAS > APOSITIA

APOSITIC > APOSITIA

APOSPORIC > APOSPORY

APOSPORY n development of the gametophyte from the sporophyte without the formation of spores

APOSTACY same as > APOSTASY

APOSTASY n abandonment of one's religious faith or other belief

APOSTATE n person who has abandoned his or her religion, political party, or cause ▷ adj guilty of apostasy

APOSTATES > APOSTATE

APOSTATIC > APOSTATE

APOSTIL n marginal note

APOSTILLE n apostil

APOSTILS > APOSTIL

APOSTLE n one of the twelve disciples chosen by Christ to preach his gospel

APOSTLES > APOSTLE

APOSTOLIC adj of or relating to the Apostles or their teachings

APOTHECE n obsolete word for shop

APOTHECES > APOTHECE

APOTHECIA n cup-shaped structures that contain the asci, esp in lichens

APOTHEGM n short cryptic remark containing some general or generally accepted truth; maxim

APOTHEGMS > APOTHEGM

APOTHEM n perpendicular line or distance from the centre of a regular polygon to any of its sides

APOTHEMS > APOTHEM

APOZEM n medicine dissolved in water

APOZEMS > APOZEM

APP n application program

APPAID > APPAY

APPAIR vb old form of impair

APPAIRED > APPAIR

APPAIRING > APPAIR

APPAIRS > APPAIR

APPAL vb dismay, terrify

APPALL same as > APPAL

APPALLED > APPALL

APPALLING adj dreadful, terrible

APPALLS > APPALL

APPALOOSA n North American horse breed

APPALS > APPAL

APPALTI > APPALTO

APPALTO n Italian word for contact

APPANAGE n land or other provision granted by a king for the support of a member of the royal family, esp a younger son

APPANAGED adj having appanage

APPANAGES > APPANAGE

APPARAT n Communist Party organization in the former Soviet Union and other states

APPARATS > APPARAT

APPARATUS n equipment for a particular purpose

APPAREL n clothing ▷ vb clothe, adorn, etc

APPARELED > APPAREL

APPARELS > APPAREL

APPARENCY old word for > APPARENT

APPARENT adj readily seen, obvious ▷ n heir apparent

APPARENTS > APPARENT

APPARITOR n officer who summons witnesses and executes the orders of an ecclesiastical and (formerly) a civil court

APPAY old word for > SATISFY

APPAYD > APPAY

APPAYING > APPAY

**APPAYS** >APPAY
**APPEACH** old word for >ACCUSE
**APPEACHES** >APPEACH
**APPEACHES** >APPEACH
**APPEAL** vb make an earnest request ▷ n earnest request
**APPEALED** >APPEAL
**APPEALER** >APPEAL
**APPEALERS** >APPEAL
**APPEALING** adj attractive or pleasing
**APPEALS** >APPEAL
**APPEAR** vb become visible or present
**APPEARED** >APPEAR
**APPEARER** >APPEAR
**APPEARERS** >APPEAR
**APPEARING** >APPEAR
**APPEARS** >APPEAR
**APPEASE** vb pacify (a person) by yielding to his or her demands
**APPEASED** >APPEASE
**APPEASER** >APPEASE
**APPEASERS** >APPEASE
**APPEASES** >APPEASE
**APPEASING** >APPEASE
**APPEL** n stamp of the foot, used to warn of one's intent to attack
**APPELLANT** n person who makes an appeal to a higher court
**APPELLATE** adj of appeals
**APPELLEE** n person who is accused or appealed against
**APPELLEES** >APPELLEE
**APPELLOR** n person initiating a law case
**APPELLORS** >APPELLOR
**APPELS** >APPEL
**APPEND** vb join on, add
**APPENDAGE** n thing joined on or added
**APPENDANT** adj attached, affixed, or added ▷ n person or thing attached or added
**APPENDED** >APPEND
**APPENDENT** same as >APPENDANT
**APPENDING** >APPEND
**APPENDIX** n separate additional material at the end of a book
**APPENDS** >APPEND
**APPERIL** old word for >PERIL
**APPERILL** old word for >PERIL
**APPERILLS** >APPERILL
**APPERILS** >APPERIL
**APPERTAIN** vb belong to
**APPESTAT** n neural control centre within the hypothalamus of the brain that regulates the sense of hunger and satiety
**APPESTATS** >APPESTAT
**APPETENCE** n craving or desire
**APPETENCY** same

as >APPETENCE
**APPETENT** adj eager
**APPETIBLE** adj old word meaning desirable
**APPETISE** vb stimulate the appetite
**APPETISED** >APPETISE
**APPETISER** same as >APPETIZER
**APPETISES** >APPETISE
**APPETITE** n desire for food or drink
**APPETITES** >APPETITE
**APPETIZE** vb stimulate the appetite
**APPETIZED** >APPETIZE
**APPETIZER** n thing eaten or drunk to stimulate the appetite
**APPETIZES** >APPETIZE
**APPLAUD** vb show approval of by clapping one's hands
**APPLAUDED** >APPLAUD
**APPLAUDER** >APPLAUD
**APPLAUDS** >APPLAUD
**APPLAUSE** n approval shown by clapping one's hands
**APPLAUSES** >APPLAUSE
**APPLE** n round firm fleshy fruit that grows on trees
**APPLECART** n cart used to carry apples
**APPLEJACK** n brandy made from apples
**APPLES** >APPLE
**APPLET** n computing program that runs within a page on the World Wide Web
**APPLETS** >APPLET
**APPLEY** adj resembling or tasting like an apple
**APPLIABLE** adj applicable
**APPLIANCE** n device with a specific function
**APPLICANT** n person who applies for something
**APPLICATE** adj applied practicably
**APPLIED** adj (of a skill, science, etc) put to practical use
**APPLIER** >APPLY
**APPLIERS** >APPLY
**APPLIES** >APPLY
**APPLIQUE** n decoration or trimming of one material sewn or otherwise fixed onto another ▷ vb sew or fix (a decoration) on as an appliqué
**APPLIQUED** >APPLIQUE
**APPLIQUES** >APPLIQUE
**APPLY** vb make a formal request
**APPLYING** >APPLY
**APPOINT** vb assign to a job or position
**APPOINTED** >APPOINT
**APPOINTEE** n person who is appointed
**APPOINTER** >APPOINT
**APPOINTOR** n person

to whom a power to nominate persons to take property is given by deed or will
**APPOINTS** >APPOINT
**APPORT** n production of objects by apparently supernatural means at a spiritualists' seance
**APPORTION** vb divide out in shares
**APPORTS** >APPORT
**APPOSABLE** adj capable of being apposed or brought into apposition
**APPOSE** vb place side by side or near to each other
**APPOSED** >APPOSE
**APPOSER** >APPOSE
**APPOSERS** >APPOSE
**APPOSES** >APPOSE
**APPOSING** >APPOSE
**APPOSITE** adj suitable, apt
**APPRAISAL** n assessment of the worth or quality of a person or thing
**APPRAISE** vb estimate the value or quality of
**APPRAISED** >APPRAISE
**APPRAISEE** n person being appraised
**APPRAISER** >APPRAISE
**APPRAISES** >APPRAISE
**APPREHEND** vb arrest and take into custody
**APPRESS** vb press together
**APPRESSED** >APPRESS
**APPRESSES** >APPRESS
**APPRISE** vb make aware (of)
**APPRISED** >APPRISE
**APPRISER** >APPRISE
**APPRISERS** >APPRISE
**APPRISES** >APPRISE
**APPRISING** >APPRISE
**APPRIZE** same as >APPRISE
**APPRIZED** >APPRIZE
**APPRIZER** >APPRIZE
**APPRIZERS** >APPRIZE
**APPRIZES** >APPRIZE
**APPRIZING** >APPRIZE
**APPRO** n approval
**APPROACH** vb come near or nearer (to) ▷ n approaching or means of approaching
**APPROBATE** vb accept as valid
**APPROOF** old word for >TRIAL
**APPROOFS** >APPROOF
**APPROS** >APPRO
**APPROVAL** n consent
**APPROVALS** >APPROVAL
**APPROVE** vb consider good or right
**APPROVED** >APPROVE
**APPROVER** >APPROVE
**APPROVERS** >APPROVE
**APPROVES** >APPROVE
**APPROVING** >APPROVE
**APPS** >APP
**APPUI** n support
**APPUIED** >APPUY
**APPUIS** >APPUI

**APPULSE** n very close approach of two celestial bodies so that they are in conjunction but no eclipse or occultation occurs
**APPULSES** >APPULSE
**APPULSIVE** >APPULSE
**APPUY** vb support
**APPUYED** >APPUY
**APPUYING** >APPUY
**APPUYS** >APPUY
**APRACTIC** >APRAXIA
**APRAXIA** n disorder of the central nervous system caused by brain damage and characterized by impaired ability to carry out purposeful muscular movements
**APRAXIAS** >APRAXIA
**APRAXIC** >APRAXIA
**APRES** prep French word for after
**APRICATE** vb bask in sun
**APRICATED** >APRICATE
**APRICATES** >APRICATE
**APRICOCK** old word for >APRICOT
**APRICOCKS** >APRICOT
**APRICOT** n yellowish-orange juicy fruit like a small peach ▷ adj yellowish-orange
**APRICOTS** >APRICOT
**APRIORISM** n philosophical doctrine that there may be genuine knowledge independent of experience
**APRIORIST** >APRIORISM
**APRIORITY** n condition of being innate in the mind
**APRON** n garment worn over the front of the body to protect the clothes ▷ vb equip with an apron
**APRONED** >APRON
**APRONFUL** n amount held in an apron
**APRONFULS** >APRONFUL
**APRONING** >APRON
**APRONLIKE** >APRON
**APRONS** >APRON
**APROPOS** adv appropriate(ly)
**APROTIC** adj (of solvents) neither accepting nor donating hydrogen ions
**APSARAS** n Hindu water sprite
**APSARASES** >APSARAS
**APSE** n arched or domed recess, esp in a church
**APSES** >APSE
**APSIDAL** >APSIS
**APSIDES** >APSIS
**APSIDIOLE** n small arch
**APSIS** n either of two points lying at the extremities of the elliptical orbit of a planet or satellite
**APSO** n Tibetan terrier
**APSOS** >APSO
**APT** adj having a specified tendency ▷ vb be fitting

**APTED** > APT
**APTER** > APT
**APTERAL** adj (esp of a classical temple) not having columns at the sides
**APTERIA** > APTERIUM
**APTERISM** > APTEROUS
**APTERISMS** > APTEROUS
**APTERIUM** n bare patch on the skin of a bird
**APTEROUS** adj (of insects) without wings, as silverfish and springtails
**APTERYX** n kiwi (the bird)
**APTERYXES** > APTERYX
**APTEST** > APT
**APTING** > APT
**APTITUDE** n natural ability
**APTITUDES** > APTITUDE
**APTLY** > APT
**APTNESS** > APT
**APTNESSES** > APT
**APTOTE** n noun without inflections
**APTOTES** > APTOTE
**APTOTIC** > APTOTE
**APTS** > APT
**APYRASE** n enzyme
**APYRASES** > APYRASE
**APYRETIC** > APYREXIA
**APYREXIA** n absence of fever
**APYREXIAS** > APYREXIA
**AQUA** n water
**AQUABATIC** adj of gymnastic feats in water
**AQUABOARD** n board used to ride on water
**AQUACADE** same as > AQUASHOW
**AQUACADES** > AQUACADE
**AQUADROME** n venue for water sports
**AQUAE** > AQUA
**AQUAFARM** vb cultivate fish or shellfish
**AQUAFARMS** > AQUAFARM
**AQUAFER** n aquifer
**AQUAFERS** > AQUAFER
**AQUALUNG** n mouthpiece attached to air cylinders, worn for underwater swimming
**AQUALUNGS** > AQUALUNG
**AQUANAUT** n person who lives and works underwater
**AQUANAUTS** > AQUANAUT
**AQUAPHOBE** n person afraid of water
**AQUAPLANE** n board on which a person stands to be towed by a motorboat ▷ vb ride on an aquaplane
**AQUAPORIN** n any one of a group of proteins in cell membranes that allow the passage of water across the membrane
**AQUARELLE** n method of watercolour painting in transparent washes
**AQUARIA** > AQUARIUM

**AQUARIAL** adj > AQUARIUM
**AQUARIAN** n person who keeps an aquarium
**AQUARIANS** > AQUARIAN
**AQUARIIST** n old form of AQUARIST
**AQUARIST** n curator of an aquarium
**AQUARISTS** > AQUARIST
**AQUARIUM** n tank in which fish and other underwater creatures are kept
**AQUARIUMS** > AQUARIUM
**AQUAROBIC** adj pertaining to exercises performed standing up in a swimming pool
**AQUAS** > AQUA
**AQUASHOW** n exhibition of swimming and diving, often accompanied by music
**AQUASHOWS** > AQUASHOW
**AQUATIC** adj living in or near water ▷ n marine or freshwater animal or plant
**AQUATICS** pl n water sports
**AQUATINT** n print like a watercolour, produced by etching copper ▷ vb etch (a block, etc) in aquatint
**AQUATINTA** n aquatint
**AQUATINTS** > AQUATINT
**AQUATONE** n fitness exercise in water
**AQUATONES** > AQUATONE
**AQUAVIT** n grain- or potato-based spirit from the Scandinavian countries, flavoured with aromatic seeds and spices, esp caraway
**AQUAVITS** > AQUAVIT
**AQUEDUCT** n structure carrying water across a valley or river
**AQUEDUCTS** > AQUEDUCT
**AQUEOUS** adj of, like, or containing water
**AQUEOUSLY** > AQUEOUS
**AQUIFER** n deposit of rock, such as sandstone, containing water that can be used to supply wells
**AQUIFERS** > AQUIFER
**AQUILEGIA** another name for > COLUMBINE
**AQUILINE** adj (of a nose) curved like an eagle's beak
**AQUILON** n name for the north wind
**AQUILONS** > AQUILON
**AQUIVER** adv quivering
**AR** n letter R
**ARAARA** another name for > TREVALLY
**ARAARAS** > ARAARA
**ARABA** n Asian carriage
**ARABAS** > ARABA
**ARABESK** same as > ARABESQUE
**ARABESKS** > ARABESK
**ARABESQUE** n ballet position in which one

leg is raised behind and the arms are extended ▷ adj designating, of, or decorated in this style
**ARABIC** as in gum arabic gum exuded by certain acacia trees
**ARABICA** n high-quality coffee bean
**ARABICAS** > ARABICA
**ARABICISE** same as > ARABICIZE
**ARABICIZE** vb make or become Arabic
**ARABILITY** n suitability of land for growing crops
**ARABIN** n essence of gum arabic
**ARABINOSE** n pentose sugar in plant gums
**ARABINS** > ARABIN
**ARABIS** n any plant of the annual or perennial genus Arabis, some of which form low-growing mats with downy grey foliage and white flowers: family Brassicaceae (crucifers)
**ARABISE** vb make or become Arab
**ARABISED** > ARABISE
**ARABISES** > ARABISE
**ARABISING** > ARABISE
**ARABIZE** vb make or become Arab
**ARABIZED** > ARABIZE
**ARABIZES** > ARABIZE
**ARABIZING** > ARABIZE
**ARABLE** adj suitable for growing crops on ▷ n arable land or farming
**ARABLES** > ARABLE
**ARACEOUS** same as > AROID
**ARACHIS** n Brazilian plant
**ARACHISES** > ARACHIS
**ARACHNID** n eight-legged invertebrate, such as a spider, scorpion, tick, or mite
**ARACHNIDS** > ARACHNID
**ARACHNOID** n middle of the three membranes that cover the brain and spinal cord ▷ adj of or relating to the middle of the three meninges
**ARAGONITE** n generally white or grey mineral, found in sedimentary rocks
**ARAISE** vb old form of raise
**ARAISED** > ARAISE
**ARAISES** > ARAISE
**ARAISING** > ARAISE
**ARAK** same as > ARRACK
**ARAKS** > ARAK
**ARALIA** n any plant of the genus Aralia of trees, shrubs, and herbaceous plants. The greenhouse and house plant generally known as aralia is Schefflera elegantissima of a related genus, grown for its

decorative evergreen foliage: family Araliaceae
**ARALIAS** > ARALIA
**ARAME** n Japanese edible seaweed
**ARAMES** > ARAME
**ARAMID** n synthetic fibre
**ARAMIDS** > ARAMID
**ARANEID** n any of numerous arachnids constituting the order Araneae (or Araneida), which comprises the spiders
**ARANEIDAN** > ARANEID
**ARANEIDS** > ARANEID
**ARANEOUS** adj like a spider's web
**ARAPAIMA** n very large primitive freshwater teleost fish that occurs in tropical S America
**ARAPAIMAS** > ARAPAIMA
**ARAPONGA** n South American bird with a bell-like call
**ARAPONGAS** > ARAPONGA
**ARAPUNGA** n South American bird with a bell-like call
**ARAPUNGAS** > ARAPUNGA
**ARAR** n African tree
**ARAROBA** n Brazilian leguminous tree, Andira araroba
**ARAROBAS** > ARAROBA
**ARARS** > ARAR
**ARAUCARIA** n any tree of the coniferous genus Araucaria of South America, Australia, and Polynesia, such as the monkey puzzle and bunya-bunya
**ARAYSE** vb old form of raise
**ARAYSED** > ARAYSE
**ARAYSES** > ARAYSE
**ARAYSING** > ARAYSE
**ARB** short for > ARBITRAGE
**ARBA** n Asian carriage
**ARBALEST** n large medieval crossbow, usually cocked by mechanical means
**ARBALESTS** > ARBALEST
**ARBALIST** same as > ARBALEST
**ARBALISTS** > ARBALIST
**ARBAS** > ARBA
**ARBELEST** n arbalest
**ARBELESTS** > ARBELEST
**ARBITER** n person empowered to judge in a dispute
**ARBITERS** > ARBITER
**ARBITRAGE** n purchase of currencies, securities, or commodities in one market for immediate resale in others in order to profit from unequal prices
**ARBITRAL** adj of or relating to arbitration
**ARBITRARY** adj based on personal choice or chance, rather than reason

**ARBITRATE** vb settle (a dispute) by arbitration
**ARBITRESS** n female arbitrator
**ARBITRIUM** n power to decide
**ARBLAST** n arbalest
**ARBLASTER** > ARBLAST
**ARBLASTS** > ARBLAST
**ARBOR** n revolving shaft or axle in a machine
**ARBOREAL** adj of or living in trees
**ARBORED** n having arbors
**ARBOREOUS** adj thickly wooded
**ARBORES** > ARBOR
**ARBORET** n old name for an area planted with shrubs
**ARBORETA** > ARBORETUM
**ARBORETS** > ARBORET
**ARBORETUM** n place where rare trees or shrubs are cultivated
**ARBORIO** as in arborio rice variety of round-grain rice used for making risotto
**ARBORISE** same as > ARBORIZE
**ARBORISED** > ARBORISE
**ARBORISES** > ARBORISE
**ARBORIST** n specialist in the cultivation of trees
**ARBORISTS** > ARBORIST
**ARBORIZE** vb give or take on a treelike branched appearance
**ARBORIZED** > ARBORIZE
**ARBORIZES** > ARBORIZE
**ARBOROUS** adj of trees
**ARBORS** > ARBOR
**ARBOUR** n glade sheltered by trees
**ARBOURED** adj having arbours
**ARBOURS** > ARBOUR
**ARBOVIRAL** > ARBOVIRUS
**ARBOVIRUS** n any one of a group of viruses that cause such diseases as encephalitis and dengue and are transmitted to humans by arthropods, esp insects and ticks
**ARBS** > ARB
**ARBUSCLE** n small tree
**ARBUSCLES** > ARBUSCLE
**ARBUTE** old name for > ARBUTUS
**ARBUTEAN** > ARBUTUS
**ARBUTES** > ARBUTE
**ARBUTUS** n evergreen shrub with strawberry-like berries
**ARBUTUSES** > ARBUTUS
**ARC** n part of a circle or other curve ▷ vb form an arc
**ARCADE** n covered passageway lined with shops ▷ vb provide with an arcade
**ARCADED** > ARCADE
**ARCADES** > ARCADE

**ARCADIA** n traditional idealized rural setting
**ARCADIAN** n person who leads a rural life
**ARCADIANS** > ARCADIAN
**ARCADIAS** > ARCADIA
**ARCADING** > ARCADE
**ARCADINGS** > ARCADE
**ARCANA** n either of the two divisions of a pack of tarot cards
**ARCANAS** > ARCANA
**ARCANE** adj mysterious and secret
**ARCANELY** > ARCANE
**ARCANIST** n person with secret knowledge
**ARCANISTS** > ARCANIST
**ARCANUM** n profound secret or mystery known only to initiates
**ARCANUMS** > ARCANUM
**ARCATURE** n small-scale arcade
**ARCATURES** > ARCATURE
**ARCCOS** same as > ARCCOSINE
**ARCCOSES** > ARCCOS
**ARCCOSINE** n trigonometric function
**ARCED** > ARC
**ARCH** n curved structure supporting a bridge or roof ▷ vb (cause to) form an arch ▷ adj superior, knowing
**ARCHAEA** n order of prokaryotic microorganisms
**ARCHAEAL** > ARCHAEAN
**ARCHAEAN** n type of microorganism
**ARCHAEANS** > ARCHAEAN
**ARCHAEI** > ARCHAEUS
**ARCHAEON** variant of > ARCHAEAN
**ARCHAEUS** n spirit believed to inhabit a living thing
**ARCHAIC** adj ancient
**ARCHAICAL** same as > ARCHAIC
**ARCHAISE** same as > ARCHAIZE
**ARCHAISED** > ARCHAISE
**ARCHAISER** > ARCHAISE
**ARCHAISES** > ARCHAISE
**ARCHAISM** n archaic word or phrase
**ARCHAISMS** > ARCHAISM
**ARCHAIST** > ARCHAISM
**ARCHAISTS** > ARCHAISM
**ARCHAIZE** vb give an archaic appearance or character to, as by the use of archaisms
**ARCHAIZED** > ARCHAIZE
**ARCHAIZER** > ARCHAIZE
**ARCHAIZES** > ARCHAIZE
**ARCHANGEL** n chief angel
**ARCHDUCAL** adj of or relating to an archduke, archduchess, or archduchy
**ARCHDUCHY** n territory of an archduke or

archduchess
**ARCHDUKE** n duke of specially high rank
**ARCHDUKES** > ARCHDUKE
**ARCHED** adj provided with or spanned by an arch or arches
**ARCHEI** > ARCHEUS
**ARCHENEMY** n chief enemy
**ARCHER** n person who shoots with a bow and arrow
**ARCHERESS** n female archer
**ARCHERIES** > ARCHERY
**ARCHERS** > ARCHER
**ARCHERY** n art or sport of shooting with a bow and arrow
**ARCHES** > ARCH
**ARCHEST** > ARCH
**ARCHETYPE** n perfect specimen
**ARCHEUS** n spirit believed to inhabit a living thing
**ARCHFIEND** n the. the chief of fiends or devils
**ARCHFOE** n chief enemy
**ARCHFOES** > ARCHFOE
**ARCHICARP** n female reproductive structure in ascomycetous fungi that consists of a cell or hypha and develops into the ascogonium
**ARCHIL** a variant spelling of > ORCHIL
**ARCHILOWE** n treat given in return
**ARCHILS** > ARCHIL
**ARCHIMAGE** n great magician or wizard
**ARCHINE** n Russian unit of length equal to about 71 cm
**ARCHINES** > ARCHINE
**ARCHING** > ARCH
**ARCHINGS** > ARCH
**ARCHITECT** n person qualified to design and supervise the construction of buildings
**ARCHITYPE** n primitive original from which others derive
**ARCHIVAL** > ARCHIVE
**ARCHIVE** n collection of records or documents ▷ vb store (documents, data, etc) in an archive or other repository
**ARCHIVED** > ARCHIVE
**ARCHIVES** > ARCHIVE
**ARCHIVING** > ARCHIVE
**ARCHIVIST** n person in charge of archives
**ARCHIVOLT** n moulding around an arch, sometimes decorated
**ARCHLET** n small arch
**ARCHLETS** > ARCHLET
**ARCHLUTE** n old bass lute
**ARCHLUTES** > ARCHLUTE
**ARCHLY** > ARCH
**ARCHNESS** > ARCH
**ARCHOLOGY** n study of the

origins of things
**ARCHON** n (in ancient Athens) one of the nine chief magistrates
**ARCHONS** > ARCHON
**ARCHONTIC** > ARCHON
**ARCHOSAUR** n early type of dinosaur
**ARCHRIVAL** n chief rival
**ARCHWAY** n passageway under an arch
**ARCHWAYS** > ARCHWAY
**ARCHWISE** adv like an arch
**ARCIFORM** adj shaped like an arch
**ARCING** > ARC
**ARCINGS** > ARC
**ARCKED** > ARC
**ARCKING** > ARC
**ARCKINGS** > ARC
**ARCMIN** n 1/60 of a degree of an angle
**ARCMINS** > ARCMIN
**ARCO** adv musical direction meaning with bow
**ARCOGRAPH** n instrument used for drawing arcs without using a central point
**ARCOLOGY** n architecture blending buildings with the natural environment
**ARCS** > ARC
**ARCSEC** n 1/3600 of a degree of an angle
**ARCSECOND** n unit used in astronomy
**ARCSECS** > ARCSEC
**ARCSIN** same as > ARCSINE
**ARCSINE** n trigonometrical function
**ARCSINES** > ARCSINE
**ARCSINS** > ARCSIN
**ARCTAN** n trigonometrical function
**ARCTANS** > ARCTAN
**ARCTIC** adj very cold ▷ n high waterproof overshoe with buckles
**ARCTICS** > ARCTIC
**ARCTIID** n any moth of the family Arctiidae, which includes the footman, ermine, and tiger moths
**ARCTIIDS** > ARCTIID
**ARCTOID** adj like a bear
**ARCTOPHIL** n arctophile
**ARCUATE** adj shaped or bent like an arc or bow
**ARCUATED** same as > ARCUATE
**ARCUATELY** > ARCUATE
**ARCUATION** n use of arches or vaults in buildings
**ARCUS** n circle around the cornea of the eye
**ARCUSES** > ARCUS
**ARD** n primitive plough
**ARDEB** n unit of dry measure used in Egypt and other Middle Eastern countries. In Egypt it is approximately equal to 0.195 cubic metres

**ARDEBS** >ARDEB
**ARDENCIES** >ARDENT
**ARDENCY** >ARDENT
**ARDENT** adj passionate
**ARDENTLY** >ARDENT
**ARDOR** same as >ARDOUR
**ARDORS** >ARDOR
**ARDOUR** n passion
**ARDOURS** >ARDOUR
**ARDRI** n Irish high king
**ARDRIGH** n Irish high king
**ARDRIGHS** >ARDRIGH
**ARDRIS** >ARDRI
**ARDS** >ARD
**ARDUOUS** adj hard to
accomplish, strenuous
**ARDUOUSLY** >ARDUOUS
**ARE** n unit of measure, 100
square metres ▷ vb used
as the singular form with
you
**AREA** n part or region
**AREACH** vb old form of reach
**AREACHED** >AREACH
**AREACHES** >AREACH
**AREACHING** >AREACH
**AREAD** vb old word
meaning declare
**AREADING** >AREAD
**AREADS** >AREAD
**AREAE** >AREA
**AREAL** >AREA
**AREALLY** >AREA
**AREAR** n old form of arrear
**AREAS** >AREA
**AREAWAY** n passageway
between parts of a
building or between
different buildings
**AREAWAYS** >AREAWAY
**ARECA** n any of various tall
palms of the genus *Areca*,
which are native to SE Asia
and have white flowers
and orange or red egg-
shaped nuts
**ARECAS** >ARECA
**ARECOLINE** n drug derived
from betel nut
**ARED** >AREAD
**AREDD** >AREAD
**AREDE** vb old word
meaning declare
**AREDES** >AREDE
**AREDING** >AREDE
**AREFIED** >AREFY
**AREFIES** >AREFY
**AREFY** vb dry up
**AREFYING** >AREFY
**AREG** a plural of >ERG
**AREIC** adj relating to area
**ARENA** n seated enclosure
for sports events
**ARENAS** >ARENA
**ARENATION** n use of hot
sand as a medical poultice
**ARENE** n aromatic
hydrocarbon
**ARENES** >ARENE
**ARENITE** n any arenaceous
rock
**ARENITES** >ARENITE
**ARENITIC** >ARENITE
**ARENOSE** adj sandy

**ARENOUS** adj sandy
**AREOLA** n small circular
area, such as the coloured
ring around the human
nipple
**AREOLAE** >AREOLA
**AREOLAR** >AREOLA
**AREOLAS** >AREOLA
**AREOLATE** >AREOLA
**AREOLATED** adj areolate
**AREOLE** n space outlined
on a surface, such as an
area between veins on a
leaf or on an insect's wing
**AREOLES** >AREOLE
**AREOLOGY** n study of the
planet Mars
**AREOMETER** n instrument
for measuring the density
of liquids
**AREOSTYLE** n building with
widely-spaced columns
**AREPA** n Colombian
cornmeal cake
**AREPAS** >AREPA
**ARERE** adv old word
meaning backwards
**ARES** >ARE
**ARET** vb old word meaning
entrust
**ARETE** n sharp ridge
separating two cirques
or glacial valleys in
mountainous regions
**ARETES** >ARETE
**ARETHUSA** n North
American orchid, *Arethusa
bulbosa*, having one long
narrow leaf and one rose-
purple flower fringed with
yellow
**ARETHUSAS** >ARETHUSA
**ARETS** >ARET
**ARETT** vb old word
meaning entrust
**ARETTED** >ARETT
**ARETTING** >ARETT
**ARETTS** >ARETT
**AREW** adv old word meaning
in a row
**ARF** n barking sound
**ARFS** >ARF
**ARGAL** same as >ARGALI
**ARGALA** n Indian stork
**ARGALAS** >ARGALA
**ARGALI** n wild sheep,
*Ovis ammon*, inhabiting
semidesert regions
in central Asia: family
*Bovidae*, order *Artiodactyla*.
It is the largest of the
sheep, having massive
horns in the male, which
may almost form a circle
**ARGALIS** >ARGALI
**ARGALS** >ARGAL
**ARGAN** n Moroccan tree
**ARGAND** n lamp with a
hollow circular wick
**ARGANDS** >ARGAND
**ARGANS** >ARGAN
**ARGEMONE** n prickly poppy
**ARGEMONES** >ARGEMONE
**ARGENT** n silver

**ARGENTAL** adj of or
containing silver
**ARGENTIC** adj of or
containing silver in the
divalent or trivalent state
**ARGENTINE** adj of, relating
to, or resembling silver ▷ n
type of small silver fish
**ARGENTITE** n dark grey
mineral that consists of
silver sulphide, usually in
cubic crystalline forms,
and occurs in veins,
often with native silver.
It is found esp in Mexico,
Nevada, and Saxony and
is an important source of
silver. Formula: Ag$_2$S
**ARGENTOUS** adj of or
containing silver in the
monovalent state
**ARGENTS** >ARGENT
**ARGENTUM** an obsolete name
for >SILVER
**ARGENTUMS** >ARGENTUM
**ARGHAN** n agave plant
**ARGHANS** >ARGHAN
**ARGIL** n clay, esp potters'
clay
**ARGILLITE** n any
argillaceous rock, esp a
hardened mudstone
**ARGILS** >ARGIL
**ARGINASE** n type of enzyme
**ARGINASES** >ARGINASE
**ARGININE** n essential
amino acid of plant and
animal proteins, necessary
for nutrition and for the
production of excretory
urea
**ARGININES** >ARGININE
**ARGLE** vb quarrel
**ARGLED** >ARGLE
**ARGLES** >ARGLE
**ARGLING** >ARGLE
**ARGOL** n crude potassium
hydrogen tartrate,
deposited as a crust on the
sides of wine vats
**ARGOLS** >ARGOL
**ARGON** n inert gas found in
the air
**ARGONAUT** n paper nautilus
**ARGONAUTS** >ARGONAUT
**ARGONON** n inert gas
**ARGONS** >ARGON
**ARGOSIES** >ARGOSY
**ARGOSY** n large merchant
ship
**ARGOT** n slang or jargon
**ARGOTIC** >ARGOT
**ARGOTS** >ARGOT
**ARGUABLE** adj capable of
being disputed
**ARGUABLY** adv it can be
argued that
**ARGUE** vb try to prove by
giving reasons
**ARGUED** >ARGUE
**ARGUER** >ARGUE
**ARGUERS** >ARGUE
**ARGUES** >ARGUE

**ARGUFIED** >ARGUFY
**ARGUFIER** >ARGUFY
**ARGUFIERS** >ARGUFY
**ARGUFIES** >ARGUFY
**ARGUFY** vb argue or quarrel,
esp over something trivial
**ARGUFYING** >ARGUFY
**ARGUING** >ARGUE
**ARGULI** >ARGULUS
**ARGULUS** n parasite on fish
**ARGUMENT** n quarrel
**ARGUMENTA** n appeals to
reason
**ARGUMENTS** >ARGUMENT
**ARGUS** n any of various
brown butterflies
**ARGUSES** >ARGUS
**ARGUTE** adj shrill or keen
**ARGUTELY** >ARGUTE
**ARGYLE** adj made of knitted
or woven material with a
diamond-shaped pattern
of two or more colours ▷ n
sock made of this
**ARGYLES** >ARGYLE
**ARGYLL** n sock with
diamond pattern
**ARGYLLS** >ARGYLL
**ARGYRIA** n staining of skin
by exposure to silver
**ARGYRIAS** >ARGYRIA
**ARGYRITE** n mineral
containing silver sulphide
**ARGYRITES** >ARGYRITE
**ARHAT** n Buddhist, esp a
monk who has achieved
enlightenment and at
death passes to nirvana
**ARHATS** >ARHAT
**ARHATSHIP** >ARHAT
**ARHYTHMIA** n irregular
heartbeat
**ARHYTHMIC** >ARHYTHMIA
**ARIA** n elaborate song for
solo voice, esp one from
an opera
**ARIARY** n currency of
Madagascar
**ARIAS** >ARIA
**ARID** adj parched, dry
**ARIDER** >ARID
**ARIDEST** >ARID
**ARIDITIES** >ARID
**ARIDITY** >ARID
**ARIDLY** >ARID
**ARIDNESS** >ARID
**ARIEL** n Arabian gazelle,
*Gazella arabica* (or *dama*)
**ARIELS** >ARIEL
**ARIETTA** n short relatively
uncomplicated aria
**ARIETTAS** >ARIETTA
**ARIETTE** same as >ARIETTA
**ARIETTES** >ARIETTE
**ARIGHT** adv rightly
**ARIKI** n first-born male or
female in a notable family
**ARIL** n appendage on
certain seeds, such as
those of the yew and
nutmeg, developed from
or near the funicle of the
ovule and often brightly
coloured and fleshy

**ARILED** adj having an aril
**ARILLARY** adj having an aril
**ARILLATE** > ARILLATED
**ARILLATED** adj having an aril
**ARILLI** > ARILLUS
**ARILLODE** n structure in certain seeds that resembles an aril but is developed from the micropyle of the ovule
**ARILLODES** > ARILLODE
**ARILLOID** adj of or like an aril
**ARILLUS** n aril
**ARILS** > ARIL
**ARIOSE** adj songlike
**ARIOSI** > ARIOSO
**ARIOSO** n recitative with the lyrical quality of an aria
**ARIOSOS** > ARIOSO
**ARIOT** adv riotously
**ARIPPLE** adv in ripples
**ARIS** n Cockney slang for buttocks
**ARISE** vb come about
**ARISEN** > ARISE
**ARISES** > ARISE
**ARISH** n field that has been mown
**ARISHES** > ARISH
**ARISING** > ARISE
**ARISTA** n stiff bristle such as the awn of some grasses and cereals
**ARISTAE** > ARISTA
**ARISTAS** > ARISTA
**ARISTATE** > ARISTA
**ARISTO** n aristocrat
**ARISTOS** > ARISTO
**ARISTOTLE** n bottle
**ARK** n boat built by Noah, which survived the Flood ▷ vb place in an ark
**ARKED** > ARK
**ARKING** > ARK
**ARKITE** n passenger in ark
**ARKITES** > ARKITE
**ARKOSE** n sandstone consisting of grains of feldspar and quartz cemented by a mixture of quartz and clay minerals
**ARKOSES** > ARKOSE
**ARKOSIC** > ARKOSE
**ARKS** > ARK
**ARLE** vb make downpayment
**ARLED** > ARLE
**ARLES** > ARLE
**ARLING** > ARLE
**ARM** n either of the upper limbs from the shoulder to the wrist ▷ vb supply with weapons
**ARMADA** n large number of warships
**ARMADAS** > ARMADA
**ARMADILLO** n small S American mammal covered in strong bony plates
**ARMAGNAC** n dry brown brandy

**ARMAGNACS** > ARMAGNAC
**ARMAMENT** n military weapons
**ARMAMENTS** > ARMAMENT
**ARMATURE** n revolving structure in an electric motor or generator, wound with coils carrying the current
**ARMATURED** > ARMATURE
**ARMATURES** > ARMATURE
**ARMBAND** n band of material worn round the arm, such as one bearing an identifying mark, etc, or a black one indicating mourning
**ARMBANDS** > ARMBAND
**ARMCHAIR** n upholstered chair with side supports for the arms ▷ adj taking no active part
**ARMCHAIRS** > ARMCHAIR
**ARMED** adj equipped with or supported by arms, armour, etc
**ARMER** > ARM
**ARMERS** > ARM
**ARMET** n close-fitting medieval visored helmet with a neck guard
**ARMETS** > ARMET
**ARMFUL** n as much as can be held in the arms
**ARMFULS** > ARMFUL
**ARMGAUNT** adj word in Shakespeare of uncertain meaning
**ARMHOLE** n opening in a garment through which the arm passes
**ARMHOLES** > ARMHOLE
**ARMIES** > ARMY
**ARMIGER** n person entitled to bear heraldic arms, such as a sovereign or nobleman
**ARMIGERAL** > ARMIGER
**ARMIGERO** n armiger
**ARMIGEROS** > ARMIGERO
**ARMIGERS** > ARMIGER
**ARMIL** n bracelet
**ARMILLA** n bracelet
**ARMILLAE** > ARMILLA
**ARMILLARY** adj of or relating to bracelets
**ARMILLAS** > ARMILLA
**ARMILS** > ARMIL
**ARMING** n act of taking arms or providing with arms
**ARMINGS** > ARMING
**ARMISTICE** n agreed suspension of fighting
**ARMLESS** > ARM
**ARMLET** n band worn round the arm
**ARMLETS** > ARMLET
**ARMLIKE** > ARM
**ARMLOAD** n amount carried in the arms
**ARMLOADS** > ARMLOAD
**ARMLOCK** vb grip someone's

arms
**ARMLOCKED** > ARMLOCK
**ARMLOCKS** > ARMLOCK
**ARMOIRE** n large cabinet, originally used for storing weapons
**ARMOIRES** > ARMOIRE
**ARMONICA** n glass harmonica
**ARMONICAS** > ARMONICA
**ARMOR** same as > ARMOUR
**ARMORED** same as > ARMOURED
**ARMORER** same as > ARMOURER
**ARMORERS** > ARMORER
**ARMORIAL** adj of or relating to heraldry or heraldic arms ▷ n book of coats of arms
**ARMORIALS** > ARMORIAL
**ARMORIES** > ARMORY
**ARMORING** > ARMOR
**ARMORIST** n heraldry expert
**ARMORISTS** > ARMORIST
**ARMORLESS** > ARMOR
**ARMORS** > ARMOR
**ARMORY** same as > ARMOURY
**ARMOUR** n metal clothing formerly worn to protect the body in battle ▷ vb equip or cover with armour
**ARMOURED** adj having a protective covering
**ARMOURER** n maker, repairer, or keeper of arms or armour
**ARMOURERS** > ARMOURER
**ARMOURIES** > ARMOURY
**ARMOURING** > ARMOUR
**ARMOURS** > ARMOUR
**ARMOURY** n place where weapons are stored
**ARMOZEEN** n material used for clerical gowns
**ARMOZEENS** > ARMOZEEN
**ARMOZINE** n material used for clerical gowns
**ARMOZINES** > ARMOZINE
**ARMPIT** n hollow under the arm at the shoulder
**ARMPITS** > ARMPIT
**ARMREST** n part of a chair or sofa that supports the arm
**ARMRESTS** > ARMREST
**ARMS** > ARM
**ARMSFUL** > ARMFUL
**ARMURE** n silk or wool fabric with a small cobbled pattern
**ARMURES** > ARMURE
**ARMY** n military land forces of a nation
**ARMYWORM** n caterpillar of a widely distributed noctuid moth
**ARMYWORMS** > ARMYWORM
**ARNA** n Indian water buffalo
**ARNAS** > ARNA
**ARNATTO** n annatto
**ARNATTOS** > ARNATTO

**ARNICA** n any N temperate or arctic plant of the genus *Arnica*, typically having yellow flowers: family *Asteraceae* (composites)
**ARNICAS** > ARNICA
**ARNOTTO** n annatto
**ARNOTTOS** > ARNOTTO
**ARNUT** n plant with edible tubers
**ARNUTS** > ARNUT
**AROBA** n Asian carriage
**AROBAS** > AROBA
**AROHA** n love, compassion, or affection
**AROHAS** > AROHA
**AROID** adj of, relating to, or belonging to the *Araceae*, a family of plants having small flowers massed on a spadix surrounded by a large petaloid spathe. The family includes arum, calla, and anthurium ▷ n any plant of the *Araceae*
**AROIDS** > AROID
**AROINT** vb drive away
**AROINTED** > AROINT
**AROINTING** > AROINT
**AROINTS** > AROINT
**AROLLA** n European pine tree
**AROLLAS** > AROLLA
**AROMA** n pleasant smell
**AROMAS** > AROMA
**AROMATASE** n enzyme involved in the production of oestrogen
**AROMATIC** adj having a distinctive pleasant smell ▷ n something, such as a plant or drug, that gives off a fragrant smell
**AROMATICS** > AROMATIC
**AROMATISE** same as > AROMATIZE
**AROMATIZE** vb make aromatic
**AROSE** past tense of > ARISE
**AROUND** adv on all sides (of)
**AROUSABLE** > AROUSE
**AROUSAL** > AROUSE
**AROUSALS** > AROUSE
**AROUSE** vb stimulate, make active
**AROUSED** > AROUSE
**AROUSER** > AROUSE
**AROUSERS** > AROUSE
**AROUSES** > AROUSE
**AROUSING** > AROUSE
**AROW** adv in a row
**AROYNT** vb old word meaning to drive away
**AROYNTED** > AROYNT
**AROYNTING** > AROYNT
**AROYNTS** > AROYNT
**ARPEGGIO** n notes of a chord played or sung in quick succession
**ARPEGGIOS** > ARPEGGIO
**ARPEN** n old French measure of land
**ARPENS** > ARPEN
**ARPENT** n former French

unit of length equal to 190 feet (approximately 58 metres)
**ARPENTS** >ARPENT
**ARPILLERA** n Peruvian wall-hanging
**ARQUEBUS** n portable long-barrelled gun dating from the 15th century
**ARRACACHA** n S American plant
**ARRACK** n alcoholic drink distilled from grain or rice
**ARRACKS** >ARRACK
**ARRAH** interj Irish exclamation
**ARRAIGN** vb bring (a prisoner) before a court to answer a charge
**ARRAIGNED** >ARRAIGN
**ARRAIGNER** >ARRAIGN
**ARRAIGNS** >ARRAIGN
**ARRANGE** vb plan
**ARRANGED** >ARRANGE
**ARRANGER** >ARRANGE
**ARRANGERS** >ARRANGE
**ARRANGES** >ARRANGE
**ARRANGING** >ARRANGE
**ARRANT** adj utter, downright
**ARRANTLY** >ARRANT
**ARRAS** n tapestry wall-hanging
**ARRASED** adj having an arras
**ARRASENE** n material used in embroidery
**ARRASENES** >ARRASENE
**ARRASES** >ARRAS
**ARRAUGHT** >AREACH
**ARRAY** n impressive display or collection ▷ vb arrange in order
**ARRAYAL** >ARRAY
**ARRAYALS** >ARRAY
**ARRAYED** >ARRAY
**ARRAYER** >ARRAY
**ARRAYERS** >ARRAY
**ARRAYING** >ARRAY
**ARRAYMENT** n act of arraying
**ARRAYS** >ARRAY
**ARREAR** n singular of arrears
**ARREARAGE** same as >ARREARS
**ARREARS** pl n money owed used in some Spanish-speaking countries
**ARRECT** adj pricked up
**ARREEDE** vb old word meaning declare
**ARREEDES** >ARREEDE
**ARREEDING** >ARREEDE
**ARREST** vb take (a person) into custody ▷ n act of taking a person into custody
**ARRESTANT** n substance that stops a chemical reaction
**ARRESTED** >ARREST
**ARRESTEE** n arrested person
**ARRESTEES** >ARRESTEE
**ARRESTER** n person who

arrests
**ARRESTERS** >ARRESTER
**ARRESTING** adj attracting attention, striking
**ARRESTIVE** adj making something stop
**ARRESTOR** n person or thing that arrests
**ARRESTORS** >ARRESTOR
**ARRESTS** >ARREST
**ARRET** n judicial decision
**ARRETS** >ARRET
**ARRHIZAL** adj without roots
**ARRIAGE** n Scottish feudal service
**ARRIAGES** >ARRIAGE
**ARRIBA** interj exclamation of pleasure or approval
**ARRIDE** vb old word meaning gratify
**ARRIDED** >ARRIDE
**ARRIDES** >ARRIDE
**ARRIDING** >ARRIDE
**ARRIERE** adj French word meaning old-fashioned
**ARRIERO** n Spanish word for mule driver
**ARRIEROS** >ARRIERO
**ARRIS** n sharp edge at the meeting of two surfaces at an angle with one another, as at two adjacent sides of a stone block
**ARRISES** >ARRIS
**ARRISH** n corn stubble
**ARRISHES** >ARRISH
**ARRIVAL** n arriving
**ARRIVALS** >ARRIVAL
**ARRIVANCE** n old word meaning people who have arrived
**ARRIVANCY** n arrivance
**ARRIVE** vb reach a place or destination
**ARRIVED** >ARRIVE
**ARRIVER** >ARRIVE
**ARRIVERS** >ARRIVE
**ARRIVES** >ARRIVE
**ARRIVING** >ARRIVE
**ARRIVISME** n unscrupulous ambition
**ARRIVISTE** n person who is unscrupulously ambitious
**ARROBA** n unit of weight used in some Spanish-speaking countries
**ARROBAS** >ARROBA
**ARROGANCE** >ARROGANT
**ARROGANCY** >ARROGANT
**ARROGANT** adj proud and overbearing
**ARROGATE** vb claim or seize without justification
**ARROGATED** >ARROGATE
**ARROGATES** >ARROGATE
**ARROGATOR** >ARROGATE
**ARROW** n pointed shaft shot from a bow
**ARROWED** adj having an arrow pattern
**ARROWHEAD** n pointed tip of an arrow

**ARROWING** >ARROW
**ARROWLESS** >ARROW
**ARROWLIKE** >ARROW
**ARROWROOT** n nutritious starch obtained from the root of a W Indian plant
**ARROWS** >ARROW
**ARROWWOOD** n any of various trees or shrubs, esp certain viburnums, having long straight tough stems formerly used by N American Indians to make arrows
**ARROWWORM** n any small marine invertebrate of the genus Sagitta, having an elongated transparent body with fins and prehensile oral bristles
**ARROWY** adj like an arrow
**ARROYO** n steep-sided stream bed that is usually dry except after heavy rain
**ARROYOS** >ARROYO
**ARS** >AR
**ARSE** n buttocks or anus ▷ vb play the fool
**ARSED** >ARSE
**ARSEHOLE** n anus
**ARSEHOLES** >ARSEHOLE
**ARSENAL** n place where arms and ammunition are made or stored
**ARSENALS** >ARSENAL
**ARSENATE** n salt or ester of arsenic acid
**ARSENATES** >ARSENATE
**ARSENIATE** n arsenate
**ARSENIC** n toxic grey element ▷ adj of or containing arsenic
**ARSENICAL** adj of or containing arsenic ▷ n drug or insecticide containing arsenic
**ARSENICS** >ARSENIC
**ARSENIDE** n compound in which arsenic is the most electronegative element
**ARSENIDES** >ARSENIDE
**ARSENIOUS** adj of or containing arsenic in the trivalent state
**ARSENITE** n salt or ester of arsenous acid, esp a salt containing the ion $A_5O_3^{3-}$
**ARSENITES** >ARSENITE
**ARSENO** adj containing arsenic
**ARSENOUS** same as >ARSENIOUS
**ARSES** >ARSIS
**ARSEY** adj aggressive, irritable, or argumentative
**ARSHEEN** n old measure of length in Russia
**ARSHEENS** >ARSHEEN
**ARSHIN** n old measure of length in Russia
**ARSHINE** n old measure of length in Russia
**ARSHINES** >ARSHINE
**ARSHINS** >ARSHIN

**ARSIER** >ARSY
**ARSIEST** >ARSY
**ARSINE** n colourless poisonous gas used in the manufacture of organic compounds, to dope transistors, and as a military poisonous gas
**ARSINES** >ARSINE
**ARSING** >ARSE
**ARSINO** adj containing arsine
**ARSIS** n (in classical prosody) the long syllable or part on which the ictus falls in a metrical foot
**ARSON** n crime of intentionally setting property on fire
**ARSONIST** >ARSON
**ARSONISTS** >ARSON
**ARSONITE** n person committing arson
**ARSONITES** >ARSONITE
**ARSONOUS** adj of arson
**ARSONS** >ARSON
**ARSY** same as >ARSEY
**ART** n creation of works of beauty, esp paintings or sculpture
**ARTAL** a plural of >ROTL
**ARTEFACT** n something made by human beings
**ARTEFACTS** >ARTEFACT
**ARTEL** n (in the former Soviet Union) a cooperative union or organization, esp of producers, such as peasants
**ARTELS** >ARTEL
**ARTEMISIA** n any herbaceous perennial plant of the genus Artemisia, of the N hemisphere, such as mugwort, sagebrush, and wormwood: family Asteraceae (composites)
**ARTERIAL** adj of an artery ▷ n major road
**ARTERIALS** >ARTERIAL
**ARTERIES** >ARTERY
**ARTERIOLE** n any of the small subdivisions of an artery that form thin-walled vessels ending in capillaries
**ARTERITIS** n inflammation of an artery
**ARTERY** n one of the tubes carrying blood from the heart
**ARTESIAN** as in artesian well well sunk through impermeable strata receiving water from an area at a higher altitude than that of the well
**ARTFUL** adj cunning, wily
**ARTFULLY** >ARTFUL
**ARTHRITIC** >ARTHRITIS
**ARTHRITIS** n painful inflammation of a joint or

joints
**ARTHRODIA** n joint
**ARTHROPOD** n animal,
such as a spider or insect,
with jointed limbs and a
segmented body
**ARTHROSES** > ARTHROSIS
**ARTHROSIS** n disease of
joint
**ARTI** n ritual performed
in homes and temples in
which incense and light is
offered to a deity
**ARTIC** n articulated vehicle
**ARTICHOKE** n flower head
of a thistle-like plant,
cooked as a vegetable
**ARTICLE** n written piece in
a magazine or newspaper
▷ vb bind by a written
contract
**ARTICLED** > ARTICLE
**ARTICLES** > ARTICLE
**ARTICLING** > ARTICLE
**ARTICS** > ARTIC
**ARTICULAR** adj of or
relating to joints
**ARTIER** > ARTY
**ARTIES** > ARTY
**ARTIEST** > ARTY
**ARTIFACT** same
as > ARTEFACT
**ARTIFACTS** > ARTIFACT
**ARTIFICE** n clever trick
**ARTIFICER** n craftsman
**ARTIFICES** > ARTIFICE
**ARTILLERY** n large-calibre
guns
**ARTILY** > ARTY
**ARTINESS** > ARTY
**ARTIS** > ARTI
**ARTISAN** n skilled worker,
craftsman
**ARTISANAL** > ARTISAN
**ARTISANS** > ARTISAN
**ARTIST** n person who
produces works of art, esp
paintings or sculpture
**ARTISTE** n professional
entertainer such as a
singer or dancer
**ARTISTES** > ARTISTE
**ARTISTIC** adj of or
characteristic of art or
artists
**ARTISTRY** n artistic skill
**ARTISTS** > ARTIST
**ARTLESS** adj free from
deceit or cunning
**ARTLESSLY** > ARTLESS
**ARTS** > ART
**ARTSIER** > ARTSY
**ARTSIES** > ARTSY
**ARTSIEST** > ARTSY
**ARTSINESS** > ARTSY
**ARTSMAN** old word
for > CRAFTSMAN
**ARTSMEN** > ARTSMAN
**ARTSY** adj interested in the
arts ▷ n person interested
in the arts
**ARTWORK** n all the
photographs and
illustrations in a

publication
**ARTWORKS** > ARTWORK
**ARTY** adj having an affected
interest in art ▷ n person
interested in art
**ARUGOLA** n salad plant
**ARUGOLAS** > ARUGOLA
**ARUGULA** another name
for > ROCKET
**ARUGULAS** > ARUGULA
**ARUHE** n edible root of a
fern
**ARUM** n any plant of the
ariod genus Arum
**ARUMS** > ARUM
**ARUSPEX** variant spelling
of > HARUSPEX
**ARUSPICES** > ARUSPEX
**ARVAL** adj of ploughed land
**ARVICOLE** n water rat
**ARVICOLES** > ARVICOLE
**ARVO** n afternoon
**ARVOS** > ARVO
**ARY** dialect form of > ANY
**ARYBALLOS** n ancient
Greek flask
**ARYL** n of, consisting of, or
containing an aromatic
group
**ARYLS** > ARYL
**ARYTENOID** adj denoting
either of two small
cartilages of the larynx
that are attached to the
vocal cords ▷ n arytenoid
cartilage or muscle
**ARYTHMIA** n any variation
**ARYTHMIAS** > ARYTHMIA
**ARYTHMIC** > ARYTHMIA
**AS** adv used to indicate
amount or extent in
comparisons ▷ n ancient
Roman unit of weight
**ASAFETIDA** n bitter resin
with an unpleasant onion-
like smell
**ASANA** n any of various
postures in yoga
**ASANAS** > ASANA
**ASAR** > AS
**ASARUM** n dried strong-
scented root of the wild
ginger plant: a flavouring
agent and source of an
aromatic oil used in
perfumery, formerly used
in medicine
**ASARUMS** > ASARUM
**ASBESTIC** > ASBESTOS
**ASBESTINE** > ASBESTOS
**ASBESTOS** n fibrous
mineral which does not
burn
**ASBESTOUS** > ASBESTOS
**ASBESTUS** n asbestos
**ASCARED** adj afraid
**ASCARID** n any parasitic
nematode worm of the
family Ascaridae, such as
the common roundworm
of man and pigs
**ASCARIDES** > ASCARID
**ASCARIDS** > ASCARID
**ASCARIS** n ascarid

**ASCAUNT** adv old word
meaning slantwise
**ASCEND** vb go or move up
**ASCENDANT** adj dominant
or influential
**ASCENDED** > ASCEND
**ASCENDENT** same
as > ASCENDANT
**ASCENDER** n part of certain
lower-case letters, such as
b or h, that extends above
the body of the letter
**ASCENDERS** > ASCENDER
**ASCENDEUR** n metal grip
that is threaded on a rope
and can be alternately
tightened and slackened
as an aid to climbing the
rope: used attached to
slings for the feet and
waist
**ASCENDING** adj moving
upwards
**ASCENDS** > ASCEND
**ASCENSION** n act of
ascending
**ASCENSIVE** adj moving
upwards
**ASCENT** n ascending
**ASCENTS** > ASCENT
**ASCERTAIN** vb find out
definitely
**ASCESES** > ASCESIS
**ASCESIS** n exercise of self-
discipline
**ASCETIC** adj (person)
abstaining from worldly
pleasures and comforts
▷ n person who abstains
from worldly comforts and
pleasures
**ASCETICAL** ascetic
**ASCETICS** > ASCETIC
**ASCI** > ASCUS
**ASCIAN** n person living in
the tropics
**ASCIANS** > ASCIAN
**ASCIDIA** > ASCIDIUM
**ASCIDIAN** n any minute
marine invertebrate
animal of the class
Ascidiacea, such as the
sea squirt, the adults of
which are degenerate and
sedentary
**ASCIDIANS** > ASCIDIAN
**ASCIDIATE** > ASCIDIUM
**ASCIDIUM** n part of a
plant that is shaped
like a pitcher, such as
the modified leaf of the
pitcher plant
**ASCITES** n accumulation
of serous fluid in the
peritoneal cavity
**ASCITIC** > ASCITES
**ASCITICAL** > ASCITES
**ASCLEPIAD** n Greek verse
form
**ASCLEPIAS** n any plant
of the perennial mostly
tuberous genus Asclepias;
some are grown as garden
or greenhouse plants

for their showy orange-
scarlet or purple flowers:
family Asclepiadaceae
**ASCOCARP** n (in some
ascomycetous fungi)
a globular structure
containing the asci
**ASCOCARPS** > ASCOCARP
**ASCOGONIA** n female
reproductive bodies in
some fungi
**ASCONCE** adv old form of
askance
**ASCORBATE** n salt of
ascorbic acid
**ASCORBIC** as in ascorbic
acid white crystalline
vitamin present in plants,
esp citrus fruits, tomatoes,
and green vegetables
**ASCOSPORE** n one of the
spores (usually eight in
number) that are produced
in an ascus
**ASCOT** n cravat with
wide square ends,
usually secured with an
ornamental stud
**ASCOTS** > ASCOT
**ASCRIBE** vb attribute, as to
a particular origin
**ASCRIBED** > ASCRIBE
**ASCRIBES** > ASCRIBE
**ASCRIBING** > ASCRIBE
**ASCUS** n saclike structure
that produces (usually)
eight ascospores during
sexual reproduction in
ascomyceteous fungi such
as yeasts and mildews
**ASDIC** an early form
of > SONAR
**ASDICS** > ASDIC
**ASEA** adv towards the sea
**ASEISMIC** adj denoting a
region free of earthquakes
**ASEITIES** > ASEITY
**ASEITY** n existence derived
from itself, having no
other source
**ASEPALOUS** adj (of a plant
or flower) having no sepals
**ASEPSES** > ASEPSIS
**ASEPSIS** n aseptic
condition
**ASEPTATE** adj not divided
into cells or sections by
septa
**ASEPTIC** adj free from
harmful bacteria ▷ n
aseptic substance
**ASEPTICS** > ASEPTIC
**ASEXUAL** adj without sex
**ASEXUALLY** > ASEXUAL
**ASH** n powdery substance
left when something is
burnt ▷ vb reduce to
ashes
**ASHAKE** adv shaking
**ASHAME** vb make ashamed
**ASHAMED** adj feeling shame
**ASHAMEDLY** > ASHAMED
**ASHAMES** > ASHAME
**ASHAMING** > ASHAME

ASHCAKE *n* cornmeal bread
ASHCAKES > ASHCAKE
ASHCAN *n* large metal dustbin
ASHCANS > ASHCAN
ASHED > ASH
ASHEN *adj* pale with shock
ASHERIES > ASHERY
ASHERY *n* place where ashes are made
ASHES > ASH
ASHET *n* shallow oval dish or large plate
ASHETS > ASHET
ASHFALL *n* dropping of ash from a volcano
ASHFALLS > ASHFALL
ASHIER > ASHY
ASHIEST > ASHY
ASHINE *adv* old word meaning shining
ASHINESS > ASHY
ASHING > ASH
ASHIVER *adv* shivering
ASHKEY *n* winged fruit of the ash
ASHKEYS > ASHKEY
ASHLAR *n* square block of hewn stone used in building ▷ *vb* build with ashlars
ASHLARED > ASHLAR
ASHLARING > ASHLAR
ASHLARS > ASHLAR
ASHLER *same as* > ASHLAR
ASHLERED > ASHLER
ASHLERING > ASHLER
ASHLERS > ASHLER
ASHLESS > ASH
ASHMAN *n* man who shovels ashes
ASHMEN > ASHMAN
ASHORE *adv* towards or on land ▷ *adj* on land, having come from the water
ASHPLANT *n* walking stick made from an ash sapling
ASHPLANTS > ASHPLANT
ASHRAM *n* religious retreat where a Hindu holy man lives
ASHRAMA *n* stage in Hindu spiritual life
ASHRAMAS > ASHRAMA
ASHRAMITE *n* person living in an ashram
ASHRAMS > ASHRAM
ASHTRAY *n* receptacle for tobacco ash and cigarette butts
ASHTRAYS > ASHTRAY
ASHY *adj* pale greyish
ASIAGO *n* either of two varieties (ripened or fresh) of a cow's-milk cheese produced in NE Italy
ASIAGOS > ASIAGO
ASIDE *adv* one side ▷ *n* remark not meant to be heard by everyone present
ASIDES > ASIDE
ASINICO *n* old Spanish word for fool
ASINICOS > ASINICO

ASININE *adj* stupid, idiotic
ASININELY > ASININE
ASININITY > ASININE
ASK *vb* say or write (something) in a form that requires an answer
ASKANCE *adv* with an oblique glance ▷ *vb* turn aside
ASKANCED > ASKANCE
ASKANCES > ASKANCE
ASKANCING > ASKANCE
ASKANT *same as* > ASKANCE
ASKANTED > ASKANT
ASKANTING > ASKANT
ASKANTS > ASKANT
ASKARI *n* (in East Africa) a soldier or policeman
ASKARIS > ASKARI
ASKED > ASK
ASKER > ASK
ASKERS > ASK
ASKESES > ASKESIS
ASKESIS *n* practice of self-discipline
ASKEW *adj* one side, crooked
ASKEWNESS > ASKEW
ASKING > ASK
ASKINGS > ASK
ASKLENT *Scots word for* > ASLANT
ASKOI > ASKOS
ASKOS *n* ancient Greek vase
ASKS > ASK
ASLAKE *vb* slake
ASLAKED > ASLAKE
ASLAKES > ASLAKE
ASLAKING > ASLAKE
ASLANT *adv* at a slant (to), slanting (across)
ASLEEP *adj* sleeping
ASLOPE *adj* sloping
ASLOSH *adj* awash
ASMEAR *adj* smeared
ASMOULDER *adv* old word meaning smouldering
ASOCIAL *n* person who avoids social contact
ASOCIALS > ASOCIAL
ASP *n* small poisonous snake
ASPARAGUS *n* plant whose shoots are cooked as a vegetable
ASPARKLE *adv* sparkling
ASPARTAME *n* artificial sweetener
ASPARTATE *n* enzyme found in blood
ASPARTIC *as in aspartic acid* nonessential amino acid that is a component of proteins and acts as a neurotransmitter
ASPECT *n* feature or element ▷ *vb* look at
ASPECTED > ASPECT
ASPECTING > ASPECT
ASPECTS > ASPECT
ASPECTUAL *adj* of or relating to grammatical aspect
ASPEN *n* kind of poplar tree ▷ *adj* trembling

ASPENS > ASPEN
ASPER *n* former Turkish monetary unit, a silver coin, worth 1/120 of a piastre
ASPERATE *adj* (of plant parts) having a rough surface due to a covering of short stiff hairs ▷ *vb* make rough
ASPERATED > ASPERATE
ASPERATES > ASPERATE
ASPERGE *vb* sprinkle
ASPERGED > ASPERGE
ASPERGER > ASPERGE
ASPERGERS > ASPERGE
ASPERGES > ASPERGE
ASPERGILL *n* perforated instrument used to sprinkle holy water
ASPERGING > ASPERGE
ASPERITY *n* roughness of temper
ASPERMIA *n* failure to form or emit semen
ASPERMIAS > ASPERMIA
ASPEROUS *same as* > ASPERATE
ASPERS > ASPER
ASPERSE *vb* spread false rumours about
ASPERSED > ASPERSE
ASPERSER > ASPERSE
ASPERSERS > ASPERSE
ASPERSES > ASPERSE
ASPERSING > ASPERSE
ASPERSION *n* disparaging or malicious remark
ASPERSIVE > ASPERSE
ASPERSOIR *n* sprinkler for holy water
ASPERSOR > ASPERSE
ASPERSORS > ASPERSE
ASPERSORY *n* sprinkler for holy water
ASPHALT *n* black hard tarlike substance used for road surfaces etc ▷ *vb* cover with asphalt
ASPHALTED > ASPHALT
ASPHALTER *n* person who lays asphalt
ASPHALTIC > ASPHALT
ASPHALTS > ASPHALT
ASPHALTUM *n* asphalt
ASPHERIC *adj* not spherical
ASPHODEL *n* plant with clusters of yellow or white flowers
ASPHODELS > ASPHODEL
ASPHYXIA *n* suffocation
ASPHYXIAL > ASPHYXIA
ASPHYXIAS > ASPHYXIA
ASPHYXIES > ASPHYXY
ASPHYXY *n* old form of > ASPHYXIA
ASPIC *n* savoury jelly used to coat meat, eggs, fish, etc
ASPICK *old word for* > ASP
ASPICKS > ASPICK
ASPICS > ASPIC
ASPIDIA > ASPIDIUM
ASPIDIOID > ASPIDIUM

ASPIDIUM *n* variety of fern
ASPINE *old word for* > ASPEN
ASPINES > ASPINE
ASPIRANT *n* person who aspires ▷ *adj* aspiring or striving
ASPIRANTS > ASPIRANT
ASPIRATA *n* rough stop
ASPIRATAE > ASPIRATA
ASPIRATE *vb* pronounce with an *h* sound ▷ *n* *h* sound ▷ *adj* (of a stop) pronounced with a forceful and audible expulsion of breath
ASPIRATED > ASPIRATE
ASPIRATES > ASPIRATE
ASPIRATOR *n* device for removing fluids from a body cavity by suction
ASPIRE *vb* yearn (for), hope (to do or be)
ASPIRED > ASPIRE
ASPIRER > ASPIRE
ASPIRERS > ASPIRE
ASPIRES > ASPIRE
ASPIRIN *n* drug used to relieve pain and fever
ASPIRING > ASPIRE
ASPIRINS > ASPIRIN
ASPIS *n* horned viper
ASPISES > ASPIS
ASPISH *adj* like an asp
ASPLENIUM *n* type of fern
ASPORT *vb* old word meaning take away
ASPORTED > ASPORT
ASPORTING > ASPORT
ASPORTS > ASPORT
ASPOUT *adv* spouting
ASPRAWL *adv* sprawling
ASPREAD *adv* spreading
ASPRO *n* associate professor at an academic institution
ASPROS > ASPRO
ASPROUT *adv* sprouting
ASPS > ASP
ASQUAT *adv* squatting
ASQUINT *adj* with a glance from the corner of the eye, esp a furtive one
ASRAMA *n* stage in Hindu spiritual life
ASRAMAS > ASRAMA
ASS *n* donkey
ASSAGAI *same as* > ASSEGAI
ASSAGAIED > ASSAGAI
ASSAGAIS > ASSAGAI
ASSAI *adv* (usually preceded by a musical direction) very ▷ *n* any of several Brazilian palm trees of the genus *Euterpe*, esp *E. edulis*, that have small dark purple fleshy edible fruit
ASSAIL *vb* attack violently
ASSAILANT *n* person who attacks another, either physically or verbally
ASSAILED > ASSAIL
ASSAILER > ASSAIL
ASSAILERS > ASSAIL

ASSAILING >ASSAIL
ASSAILS >ASSAIL
ASSAIS >ASSAI
ASSAM n (in Malaysia) tamarind as used in cooking
ASSAMS >ASSAM
ASSART vb clear ground for cultivation
ASSARTED >ASSART
ASSARTING >ASSART
ASSARTS >ASSART
ASSASSIN n person who murders a prominent person
ASSASSINS >ASSASSIN
ASSAULT n violent attack ▷ vb attack violently
ASSAULTED >ASSAULT
ASSAULTER >ASSAULT
ASSAULTS >ASSAULT
ASSAY n analysis of a substance, esp a metal, to ascertain its purity ▷ vb make such an analysis
ASSAYABLE >ASSAY
ASSAYED >ASSAY
ASSAYER >ASSAY
ASSAYERS >ASSAY
ASSAYING >ASSAY
ASSAYINGS >ASSAY
ASSAYS >ASSAY
ASSED adj motivated
ASSEGAAI same as >ASSEGAI
ASSEGAAIS >ASSEGAI
ASSEGAI n slender spear used in S Africa ▷ vb spear with an assegai
ASSEGAIED >ASSEGAI
ASSEGAIS >ASSEGAI
ASSEMBLE vb collect or congregate
ASSEMBLED >ASSEMBLE
ASSEMBLER n person or thing that assembles
ASSEMBLES >ASSEMBLE
ASSEMBLY n assembled group
ASSENT n agreement or consent ▷ vb agree or consent
ASSENTED >ASSENT
ASSENTER n person supporting another's nomination
ASSENTERS >ASSENTER
ASSENTING >ASSENT
ASSENTIVE >ASSENT
ASSENTOR n any of the eight voters legally required to endorse the nomination of a candidate in a parliamentary or local election in addition to the nominator and seconder
ASSENTORS >ASSENTOR
ASSENTS >ASSENT
ASSERT vb declare forcefully
ASSERTED >ASSERT
ASSERTER >ASSERT
ASSERTERS >ASSERT
ASSERTING >ASSERT

ASSERTION n positive statement, usu. made without evidence
ASSERTIVE adj confident and direct in dealing with others
ASSERTOR >ASSERT
ASSERTORS >ASSERT
ASSERTORY adj making affirmation
ASSERTS >ASSERT
ASSES >ASS
ASSESS vb judge the worth or importance of
ASSESSED >ASSESS
ASSESSES >ASSESS
ASSESSING >ASSESS
ASSESSOR n person who values property for taxation or insurance purposes
ASSESSORS >ASSESSOR
ASSET n valuable or useful person or thing
ASSETLESS >ASSET
ASSETS >ASSET
ASSEVER vb old form of asseverate
ASSEVERED >ASSEVER
ASSEVERS >ASSEVER
ASSEZ adv (as part of a musical direction) fairly
ASSHOLE same as >ARSEHOLE
ASSHOLES >ASSHOLE
ASSIDUITY n constant and close application
ASSIDUOUS adj hard-working
ASSIEGE vb old form of besiege
ASSIEGED >ASSIEGE
ASSIEGES >ASSIEGE
ASSIEGING >ASSIEGE
ASSIENTO n slave trade treaty between Britain and Spain
ASSIENTOS >ASSIENTO
ASSIGN vb appoint (someone) to a job or task ▷ n person to whom property is assigned
ASSIGNAT n paper money issued by the Constituent Assembly in 1789, backed by the confiscated land of the Church and the émigrés
ASSIGNATS >ASSIGNAT
ASSIGNED >ASSIGN
ASSIGNEE n person to whom some right, interest, or property is transferred
ASSIGNEES >ASSIGNEE
ASSIGNER >ASSIGN
ASSIGNERS >ASSIGN
ASSIGNING >ASSIGN
ASSIGNOR n person who transfers or assigns property
ASSIGNORS >ASSIGNOR
ASSIGNS >ASSIGN
ASSIST vb give help or

support ▷ n pass by a player which enables another player to score a goal
ASSISTANT n helper ▷ adj junior or deputy
ASSISTED >ASSIST
ASSISTER >ASSIST
ASSISTERS >ASSIST
ASSISTING >ASSIST
ASSISTIVE adj providing a means of reducing a physical impairment
ASSISTOR >ASSIST
ASSISTORS >ASSIST
ASSISTS >ASSIST
ASSIZE n sitting of a legislative assembly or administrative body
ASSIZED >ASSIZE
ASSIZER n weights and measures official
ASSIZERS >ASSIZER
ASSIZES >ASSIZE
ASSIZING >ASSIZE
ASSLIKE >ASS
ASSOCIATE vb connect in the mind ▷ n partner in business ▷ adj having partial rights or subordinate status
ASSOIL vb absolve
ASSOILED >ASSOIL
ASSOILING >ASSOIL
ASSOILS >ASSOIL
ASSOILZIE vb old Scots word meaning absolve
ASSONANCE n rhyming of vowel sounds but not consonants
ASSONANT >ASSONANCE
ASSONANTS >ASSONANCE
ASSONATE vb show assonance
ASSONATED >ASSONATE
ASSONATES >ASSONATE
ASSORT vb arrange or distribute into groups of the same type
ASSORTED adj consisting of various types mixed together
ASSORTER >ASSORT
ASSORTERS >ASSORT
ASSORTING >ASSORT
ASSORTIVE >ASSORT
ASSORTS >ASSORT
ASSOT vb old word meaning make infatuated
ASSOTS >ASSOT
ASSOTT vb besot
ASSOTTED >ASSOT
ASSOTTING >ASSOT
ASSUAGE vb relieve (pain, grief, thirst, etc)
ASSUAGED >ASSUAGE
ASSUAGER >ASSUAGE
ASSUAGERS >ASSUAGE
ASSUAGES >ASSUAGE
ASSUAGING >ASSUAGE
ASSUASIVE >ASSUAGE
ASSUETUDE n state of being accustomed
ASSUMABLE >ASSUME

ASSUMABLY >ASSUME
ASSUME vb take to be true without proof
ASSUMED adj false
ASSUMEDLY >ASSUME
ASSUMER >ASSUME
ASSUMERS >ASSUME
ASSUMES >ASSUME
ASSUMING adj expecting too much ▷ n action of one who assumes
ASSUMINGS >ASSUMING
ASSUMPSIT n (before 1875) an action to recover damages for breach of an express or implied contract or agreement that was not under seal
ASSURABLE >ASSURE
ASSURANCE n assuring or being assured
ASSURE vb promise or guarantee
ASSURED adj confident ▷ n beneficiary under a life assurance policy
ASSUREDLY >ASSURED
ASSUREDS >ASSURED
ASSURER >ASSURE
ASSURERS >ASSURE
ASSURES >ASSURE
ASSURGENT adj (of leaves, stems, etc) curving or growing upwards
ASSURING >ASSURE
ASSUROR >ASSURE
ASSURORS >ASSURE
ASSWAGE old spelling of >ASSUAGE
ASSWAGED >ASSWAGE
ASSWAGES >ASSWAGE
ASSWAGING >ASSWAGE
ASTABLE adj not stable
ASTARE adv staring
ASTART old word for >START
ASTARTED >ASTART
ASTARTING >ASTART
ASTARTS >ASTART
ASTASIA n inability to stand
ASTASIAS >ASTASIA
ASTATIC adj not static
ASTATIDE n binary compound of astatine with a more electropositive element
ASTATIDES >ASTATIDE
ASTATINE n radioactive nonmetallic element
ASTATINES >ASTATINE
ASTATKI n fuel derived from petroleum
ASTATKIS >ASTATKI
ASTEISM n use of irony
ASTEISMS >ASTEISM
ASTELIC >ASTELY
ASTELIES >ASTELY
ASTELY n lack of central cylinder in plants
ASTER n plant with daisy-like flowers
ASTERIA n gemstone with starlike light effect
ASTERIAS >ASTERIA

ASTERID *n* variety of flowering plant
ASTERIDS > ASTERID
ASTERISK *n* star-shaped symbol (°) used in printing or writing to indicate a footnote, etc ▷ *vb* mark with an asterisk
ASTERISKS > ASTERISK
ASTERISM *n* three asterisks arranged in a triangle to draw attention to the text that follows
ASTERISMS > ASTERISM
ASTERN *adv* at or towards the stern of a ship ▷ *adj* at or towards the stern of a ship
ASTERNAL *adj* not connected or joined to the sternum
ASTEROID *n* any of the small planets that orbit the sun between Mars and Jupiter ▷ *adj* of, relating to, or belonging to the class *Asteroidea*
ASTEROIDS > ASTEROID
ASTERS > ASTER
ASTERT *vb* start
ASTERTED > ASTERT
ASTERTING > ASTERT
ASTERTS > ASTERT
ASTHENIA *n* abnormal loss of strength
ASTHENIAS > ASTHENIA
ASTHENIC *adj* of, relating to, or having asthenia ▷ *n* person having long limbs and a small trunk
ASTHENICS > ASTHENIC
ASTHENIES > ASTHENY
ASTHENY *same as* > ASTHENIA
ASTHMA *n* illness causing difficulty in breathing
ASTHMAS > ASTHMA
ASTHMATIC *adj* of, relating to, or having asthma ▷ *n* person who has asthma
ASTHORE *n* Irish endearment
ASTHORES > ASTHORE
ASTICHOUS *adj* not arranged in rows
ASTIGMIA *n* defect of a lens resulting in the formation of distorted images
ASTIGMIAS > ASTIGMIA
ASTILBE *n* any perennial saxifragaceous plant of the genus *Astilbe* of E Asia and N America: cultivated for their ornamental spikes or panicles of pink or white flowers
ASTILBES > ASTILBE
ASTIR *adj* out of bed
ASTOMATAL *adj* having no stomata
ASTOMOUS *adj* having no mouth
ASTONE *vb old form of* > ASTONISH

ASTONED > ASTONE
ASTONES > ASTONE
ASTONIED *adj* stunned
ASTONIES > ASTONY
ASTONING > ASTONE
ASTONISH *vb* surprise greatly
ASTONY *vb old form of* > ASTONISH
ASTONYING > ASTONY
ASTOOP *adv* stooping
ASTOUND *vb* overwhelm with amazement
ASTOUNDED > ASTOUND
ASTOUNDS > ASTOUND
ASTRACHAN *same as* > ASTRAKHAN
ASTRADDLE *adj* with a leg on either side of something
ASTRAGAL *n* small convex moulding, usually with a semicircular cross section
ASTRAGALI *n* bones of the ankles that articulate with the leg bones to form ankle joints
ASTRAGALS > ASTRAGAL
ASTRAKHAN *n* dark curly fleece of lambs from Astrakhan in Russia
ASTRAL *adj* of stars ▷ *n* oil lamp
ASTRALLY > ASTRAL
ASTRALS > ASTRAL
ASTRAND *adv* on shore
ASTRANTIA *n* flowering plant
ASTRAY *adv* off the right path
ASTRICT *vb* bind, confine, or constrict
ASTRICTED > ASTRICT
ASTRICTS > ASTRICT
ASTRIDE *adv* with a leg on either side (of) ▷ *adj* with a leg on either side
ASTRINGE *vb* cause contraction
ASTRINGED > ASTRINGE
ASTRINGER *n* person who keeps goshawks
ASTRINGES > ASTRINGE
ASTROCYTE *n* any of the star-shaped cells in the tissue supporting the brain and spinal cord (neuroglia)
ASTRODOME *n* transparent dome on the top of an aircraft, through which observations can be made, esp of the stars
ASTROFELL *n* plant in Spenser's poetry
ASTROID *n* hypocycloid having four cusps
ASTROIDS > ASTROID
ASTROLABE *n* instrument formerly used to measure the altitude of stars and planets
ASTROLOGY *n* study of the alleged influence of the

stars, planets, and moon on human affairs
ASTRONAUT *n* person trained for travelling in space
ASTRONOMY *n* scientific study of heavenly bodies
ASTROPHEL *n* plant in Spenser's poetry
ASTRUT *adv* old word meaning in a protruding way
ASTUCIOUS *adj* old form of astute
ASTUCITY *n* quality of being astute
ASTUN *vb* old form of astonish
ASTUNNED > ASTUN
ASTUNNING > ASTUN
ASTUNS > ASTUN
ASTUTE *adj* perceptive or shrewd
ASTUTELY > ASTUTE
ASTUTER > ASTUTE
ASTUTEST > ASTUTE
ASTYLAR *adj* without columns or pilasters
ASUDDEN *adv* old form of suddenly
ASUNDER *adv* into parts or pieces ▷ *adj* into parts or pieces
ASWARM *adj* filled, esp with moving things
ASWAY *adv* swaying
ASWIM *adv* floating
ASWING *adv* swinging
ASWIRL *adv* swirling
ASWOON *adv* swooning
ASYLA > ASYLUM
ASYLLABIC *adj* not functioning in the manner of a syllable
ASYLUM *n* refuge or sanctuary
ASYLUMS > ASYLUM
ASYMMETRY *n* lack of symmetry
ASYMPTOTE *n* straight line closely approached but never met by a curve
ASYNAPSES > ASYNAPSIS
ASYNAPSIS *n* failure of pairing of chromosomes at meiosis
ASYNDETA > ASYNDETON
ASYNDETIC *adj* (of a catalogue or index) without cross references
ASYNDETON *n* omission of a conjunction between the parts of a sentence
ASYNERGIA *n* lack of coordination between muscles or parts, as occurs in cerebellar disease
ASYNERGY *same as* > ASYNERGIA
ASYSTOLE *n* absence of heartbeat
ASYSTOLES > ASYSTOLE
ASYSTOLIC > ASYSTOLE
AT *n* Laotian monetary unit

worth one hundredth of a kip
ATAATA *n* grazing marine gastropod
ATAATAS > ATAATA
ATABAL *n* N African drum
ATABALS > ATABAL
ATABEG *n* Turkish ruler
ATABEGS > ATABEG
ATABEK *n* Turkish ruler
ATABEKS > ATABEK
ATABRIN *n* drug formerly used for treating malaria
ATABRINE *same as* > ATABRIN
ATABRINES > ATABRINE
ATABRINS > ATABRIN
ATACAMITE *n* mineral containing copper
ATACTIC *adj* (of a polymer) having a random sequence of the stereochemical arrangement of groups on carbon atoms in the chain
ATAGHAN *a variant of* > YATAGHAN
ATAGHANS > ATAGHAN
ATALAYA *n* watchtower in Spain
ATALAYAS > ATALAYA
ATAMAN *n* elected leader of the Cossacks
ATAMANS > ATAMAN
ATAMASCO *n* N American lily
ATAMASCOS > ATAMASCO
ATAP *n* palm tree of S Asia
ATAPS > ATAP
ATARACTIC *adj* able to calm or tranquillize ▷ *n* ataractic drug
ATARAXIA *n* calmness or peace of mind
ATARAXIAS > ATARAXIA
ATARAXIC *same as* > ATARACTIC
ATARAXICS > ATARAXIC
ATARAXIES > ATARAXY
ATARAXY *same as* > ATARAXIA
ATAVIC > ATAVISM
ATAVISM *n* recurrence of a trait present in distant ancestors
ATAVISMS > ATAVISM
ATAVIST > ATAVISM
ATAVISTIC *adj* of or relating to reversion to a former or more primitive type
ATAVISTS > ATAVISM
ATAXIA *n* lack of muscular coordination
ATAXIAS > ATAXIA
ATAXIC > ATAXIA
ATAXICS > ATAXIA
ATAXIES > ATAXY
ATAXY *same as* > ATAXIA
ATCHIEVE *vb* old form of > ACHIEVE
ATCHIEVED > ATCHIEVE
ATCHIEVES > ATCHIEVE
ATE *past tense of* > EAT
ATEBRIN *n* drug formerly used to treat malaria

ATEBRINS >ATEBRIN
ATECHNIC *adj* without technical ability
ATELIC *adj* of action without end
ATELIER *n* workshop, artist's studio
ATELIERS >ATELIER
ATEMOYA *n* tropical fruit tree
ATEMOYAS >ATEMOYA
ATEMPORAL *adj* not governed by time
ATENOLOL *n* type of beta-blocker
ATENOLOLS >ATENOLOL
ATES *n* shop selling confectionery
ATHAME *n* (in Wicca) witch's ceremonial knife, usually with a black handle, used in rituals rather than for cutting or carving
ATHAMES >ATHAME
ATHANASY *n* absence of death
ATHANOR *n* alchemist's furnace
ATHANORS >ATHANOR
ATHEISE *vb* speak atheistically
ATHEISED >ATHEISE
ATHEISES >ATHEISE
ATHEISING >ATHEISE
ATHEISM *n* belief that there is no God
ATHEISMS >ATHEISM
ATHEIST >ATHEISM
ATHEISTIC >ATHEISM
ATHEISTS >ATHEISM
ATHEIZE *vb* speak atheistically
ATHEIZED >ATHEIZE
ATHEIZES >ATHEIZE
ATHEIZING >ATHEIZE
ATHELING *n* (in Anglo-Saxon England) a prince of any of the royal dynasties
ATHELINGS >ATHELING
ATHEMATIC *adj* not based on themes
ATHENAEUM *n* institution for the promotion of learning
ATHENEUM *same as* >ATHENAEUM
ATHENEUMS >ATHENEUM
ATHEOLOGY *n* opposition to theology
ATHEOUS *adj* without a belief in god
ATHERINE *n* small fish
ATHERINES >ATHERINE
ATHEROMA *n* fatty deposit on or within the inner lining of an artery, often causing an obstruction to the blood flow
ATHEROMAS >ATHEROMA
ATHETESES >ATHETESIS
ATHETESIS *n* dismissal of a text as not genuine
ATHETISE *vb* reject as not genuine

ATHETISED >ATHETISE
ATHETISES >ATHETISE
ATHETIZE *vb* reject as not genuine
ATHETIZED >ATHETIZE
ATHETIZES >ATHETIZE
ATHETOID >ATHETOSIS
ATHETOSES >ATHETOSIS
ATHETOSIC >ATHETOSIS
ATHETOSIS *n* condition characterized by uncontrolled rhythmic writhing movement, esp of fingers, hands, head, and tongue, caused by cerebral lesion
ATHETOTIC >ATHETOSIS
ATHIRST *adj* having an eager desire
ATHLETA *n old form of* >ATHLETE
ATHLETAS >ATHLETA
ATHLETE *n* person trained in or good at athletics
ATHLETES >ATHLETE
ATHLETIC *adj* physically fit or strong
ATHLETICS *n* track and field events
ATHODYD *another name for* >RAMJET
ATHODYDS >ATHODYD
ATHRILL *adv* feeling thrills
ATHROB *adv* throbbing
ATHROCYTE *n* cell able to store matter
ATHWART *adv* transversely
ATIGI *n* type of parka worn by the Inuit in Canada
ATIGIS >ATIGI
ATILT *adj* in a tilted or inclined position
ATIMIES >ATIMY
ATIMY *n* loss of honour
ATINGLE *adv* tingling
ATISHOO *n* sound of a sneeze
ATISHOOS >ATISHOO
ATLANTES >ATLAS
ATLAS *n* book of maps
ATLASES >ATLAS
ATLATL *n* Native American throwing stick
ATLATLS >ATLATL
ATMA *same as* >ATMAN
ATMAN *n* personal soul or self
ATMANS >ATMAN
ATMAS >ATMA
ATMOLOGY *n* study of aqueous vapour
ATMOLYSE *vb* separate gases by filtering
ATMOLYSED >ATMOLYSE
ATMOLYSES >ATMOLYSIS
ATMOLYSIS *n* method of separating gases that depends on their differential rates of diffusion through a porous substance
ATMOLYZE *vb* separate gases by filtering
ATMOLYZED >ATMOLYZE

ATMOLYZES >ATMOLYZE
ATMOMETER *n* instrument for measuring the rate of evaporation of water into the atmosphere
ATMOMETRY >ATMOMETER
ATOC *n* skunk
ATOCIA *n* inability to have children
ATOCIAS >ATOCIA
ATOCS >ATOC
ATOK *n* skunk
ATOKAL *adj* having no children
ATOKE *n* part of a worm
ATOKES >ATOKE
ATOKOUS *adj* having no children
ATOKS >ATOK
ATOLL *n* ring-shaped coral reef enclosing a lagoon
ATOLLS >ATOLL
ATOM *n* smallest unit of matter which can take part in a chemical reaction
ATOMIC *adj* of or using atomic bombs or atomic energy
ATOMICAL >ATOMIC
ATOMICITY *n* state of being made up of atoms
ATOMICS *n* science of atoms
ATOMIES >ATOMY
ATOMISE *same as* >ATOMIZE
ATOMISED >ATOMISE
ATOMISER *same as* >ATOMIZER
ATOMISERS >ATOMISER
ATOMISES >ATOMISE
ATOMISING >ATOMISE
ATOMISM *n* ancient philosophical theory that the ultimate constituents of the universe are atoms
ATOMISMS >ATOMISM
ATOMIST >ATOMISM
ATOMISTIC >ATOMISM
ATOMISTS >ATOMISM
ATOMIZE *vb* reduce to atoms or small particles
ATOMIZED >ATOMIZE
ATOMIZER *n* device for discharging a liquid in a fine spray
ATOMIZERS >ATOMIZER
ATOMIZES >ATOMIZE
ATOMIZING >ATOMIZE
ATOMS >ATOM
ATOMY *n* atom or minute particle
ATONABLE >ATONE
ATONAL *adj* (of music) not written in an established key
ATONALISM >ATONAL
ATONALIST >ATONAL
ATONALITY *n* absence of or disregard for an established musical key in a composition
ATONALLY >ATONAL
ATONE *vb* make amends (for sin or wrongdoing)

ATONEABLE >ATONE
ATONED >ATONE
ATONEMENT *n* something done to make amends for wrongdoing
ATONER >ATONE
ATONERS >ATONE
ATONES >ATONE
ATONIA *n* lack of normal muscle tone
ATONIAS >ATONIA
ATONIC *adj* (of a syllable, word, etc) carrying no stress ▷ *n* unaccented or unstressed syllable, word, etc, such as *for* in *food for thought*
ATONICITY >ATONIC
ATONICS >ATONIC
ATONIES >ATONY
ATONING >ATONE
ATONINGLY >ATONE
ATONY *n* lack of normal tone or tension, as in muscles
ATOP *adv* on top
ATOPIC *adj* of or relating to hereditary hypersensitivity to certain allergens
ATOPIES >ATOPY
ATOPY *n* hereditary tendency to be hypersensitive to certain allergens
ATRAMENT *n* old word meaning black liquid
ATRAMENTS >ATRAMENT
ATRAZINE *n* white crystalline compound
ATRAZINES >ATRAZINE
ATREMBLE *adv* trembling
ATRESIA *n* absence of or unnatural narrowing of a body channel
ATRESIAS >ATRESIA
ATRESIC >ATRESIA
ATRETIC >ATRESIA
ATRIA >ATRIUM
ATRIAL >ATRIUM
ATRIP *adj* (of an anchor) no longer caught at the bottom
ATRIUM *n* upper chamber of either half of the heart
ATRIUMS >ATRIUM
ATROCIOUS *adj* extremely cruel or wicked
ATROCITY *n* wickedness
ATROPHIA *n* wasting disease
ATROPHIAS >ATROPHIA
ATROPHIC >ATROPHY
ATROPHIED >ATROPHY
ATROPHIES >ATROPHY
ATROPHY *n* wasting away of an organ or part ▷ *vb* (cause to) waste away
ATROPIA *n* atropine
ATROPIAS >ATROPIA
ATROPIN *same as* >ATROPINE
ATROPINE *n* poisonous alkaloid obtained from

45

deadly nightshade
**ATROPINES** >ATROPINE
**ATROPINS** >ATROPIN
**ATROPISM** n condition caused by using belladonna
**ATROPISMS** >ATROPISM
**ATROPOUS** adj growing straight
**ATT** n old Siamese coin
**ATTABOY** sentence substitute expression of approval or exhortation
**ATTACH** vb join, fasten, or connect
**ATTACHE** n a specialist attached to a diplomatic mission
**ATTACHED** adj fond of
**ATTACHER** >ATTACH
**ATTACHERS** >ATTACH
**ATTACHES** >ATTACH
**ATTACHING** >ATTACH
**ATTACK** vb launch a physical assault (against) ▷ n act of attacking
**ATTACKED** >ATTACK
**ATTACKER** >ATTACK
**ATTACKERS** >ATTACK
**ATTACKING** >ATTACK
**ATTACKMAN** n attacking player in sport
**ATTACKMEN** >ATTACKMAN
**ATTACKS** >ATTACK
**ATTAGIRL** humorous feminine version of >ATTABOY
**ATTAIN** vb achieve or accomplish (a task or aim)
**ATTAINDER** n (formerly) the extinction of a person's civil rights resulting from a sentence of death or outlawry on conviction for treason or felony
**ATTAINED** >ATTAIN
**ATTAINER** >ATTAIN
**ATTAINERS** >ATTAIN
**ATTAINING** >ATTAIN
**ATTAINS** >ATTAIN
**ATTAINT** vb pass judgment of death or outlawry upon (a person) ▷ n dishonour
**ATTAINTED** >ATTAINT
**ATTAINTS** >ATTAINT
**ATTAP** n palm tree of South Asia
**ATTAPS** >ATTAP
**ATTAR** n fragrant oil made from roses
**ATTARS** >ATTAR
**ATTASK** old word for >CRITICIZE
**ATTASKED** >ATTASK
**ATTASKING** >ATTASK
**ATTASKS** >ATTASK
**ATTASKT** >ATTASK
**ATTEMPER** vb modify by blending
**ATTEMPERS** >ATTEMPER
**ATTEMPT** vb try, make an effort ▷ n effort or endeavour
**ATTEMPTED** >ATTEMPT

**ATTEMPTER** >ATTEMPT
**ATTEMPTS** >ATTEMPT
**ATTEND** vb be present at
**ATTENDANT** n person who assists, guides, or provides a service ▷ adj accompanying
**ATTENDED** >ATTEND
**ATTENDEE** n person who is present at a specified event
**ATTENDEES** >ATTENDEE
**ATTENDER** >ATTEND
**ATTENDERS** >ATTEND
**ATTENDING** >ATTEND
**ATTENDS** >ATTEND
**ATTENT** old word for >ATTENTION
**ATTENTAT** n attempt
**ATTENTATS** >ATTENTAT
**ATTENTION** n concentrated direction of the mind
**ATTENTIVE** adj giving attention
**ATTENTS** >ATTENT
**ATTENUANT** adj causing dilution or thinness, esp of the blood ▷ n attenuant drug or agent
**ATTENUATE** vb weaken or become weak ▷ adj diluted, weakened, slender, or reduced
**ATTERCOP** n spider
**ATTERCOPS** >ATTERCOP
**ATTEST** vb affirm the truth of, be proof of
**ATTESTANT** >ATTEST
**ATTESTED** adj (of cattle) certified to be free from a disease, such as tuberculosis
**ATTESTER** >ATTEST
**ATTESTERS** >ATTEST
**ATTESTING** >ATTEST
**ATTESTOR** >ATTEST
**ATTESTORS** >ATTEST
**ATTESTS** >ATTEST
**ATTIC** n space or room within the roof of a house
**ATTICISE** same as >ATTICIZE
**ATTICISED** >ATTICISE
**ATTICISES** >ATTICISE
**ATTICISM** n elegant, simple, and clear expression
**ATTICISMS** >ATTICISM
**ATTICIST** >ATTICISM
**ATTICISTS** >ATTICISM
**ATTICIZE** vb conform or adapt to the norms of Attica
**ATTICIZED** >ATTICIZE
**ATTICIZES** >ATTICIZE
**ATTICS** >ATTIC
**ATTIRE** n fine or formal clothes ▷ vb dress, esp in fine elegant clothes
**ATTIRED** >ATTIRE
**ATTIRES** >ATTIRE
**ATTIRING** >ATTIRE
**ATTIRINGS** >ATTIRE
**ATTITUDE** n way of

thinking and behaving
**ATTITUDES** >ATTITUDE
**ATTOLASER** n high-power laser capable of producing pulses with a duration measured in attoseconds
**ATTOLLENS** adj (of muscle) used to lift
**ATTOLLENT** adj muscle used in lifting
**ATTONCE** adv old word for at once
**ATTONE** vb old word meaning appease
**ATTONES** >ATTONE
**ATTORN** vb acknowledge a new owner of land as one's landlord
**ATTORNED** >ATTORN
**ATTORNEY** n person legally appointed to act for another
**ATTORNEYS** >ATTORNEY
**ATTORNING** >ATTORN
**ATTORNS** >ATTORN
**ATTRACT** vb arouse the interest or admiration of
**ATTRACTED** >ATTRACT
**ATTRACTER** >ATTRACT
**ATTRACTOR** >ATTRACT
**ATTRACTS** >ATTRACT
**ATTRAHENS** adj (of muscle) drawing towards
**ATTRAHENT** adj something that attracts
**ATTRAP** vb adorn
**ATTRAPPED** >ATTRAP
**ATTRAPS** >ATTRAP
**ATTRIBUTE** vb regard as belonging to or produced by ▷ n quality or feature representative of a person or thing
**ATTRIST** vb old word meaning to sadden
**ATTRISTED** >ATTRIST
**ATTRISTS** >ATTRIST
**ATTRIT** vb wear down or dispose of gradually
**ATTRITE** vb wear down
**ATTRITED** >ATTRITE
**ATTRITES** >ATTRITE
**ATTRITING** >ATTRITE
**ATTRITION** n constant wearing down to weaken or destroy
**ATTRITIVE** >ATTRITION
**ATTRITS** >ATTRIT
**ATTRITTED** >ATTRIT
**ATTUENT** adj carrying out attuition
**ATTUITE** vb perceive by attuition
**ATTUITED** >ATTUITE
**ATTUITES** >ATTUITE
**ATTUITING** >ATTUITE
**ATTUITION** n way of mentally perceiving something
**ATTUITIVE** >ATTUITION
**ATTUNE** vb adjust or accustom (a person or thing)
**ATTUNED** >ATTUNE

**ATTUNES** >ATTUNE
**ATTUNING** >ATTUNE
**ATUA** n spirit or demon
**ATUAS** >ATUA
**ATWAIN** adv old word meaning into two parts
**ATWEEL** Scots word for >WELL
**ATWEEN** an archaic or Scots word for >BETWEEN
**ATWITTER** adv twittering
**ATWIXT** old word for >BETWEEN
**ATYPIC** adj not typical
**ATYPICAL** adj not typical
**AUA** n yellow-eye mullet
**AUBADE** n song or poem appropriate to or greeting the dawn
**AUBADES** >AUBADE
**AUBERGE** n inn or tavern
**AUBERGES** >AUBERGE
**AUBERGINE** n dark purple tropical fruit, cooked and eaten as a vegetable
**AUBRETIA** same as >AUBRIETIA
**AUBRETIAS** >AUBRETIA
**AUBRIETA** same as >AUBRIETIA
**AUBRIETAS** >AUBRIETA
**AUBRIETIA** n trailing plant with purple flowers
**AUBURN** adj (of hair) reddish-brown ▷ n moderate reddish-brown colour
**AUBURNS** >AUBURN
**AUCEPS** n old word meaning person who catches hawks
**AUCEPSES** >AUCEPS
**AUCTION** n public sale in which articles are sold to the highest bidder ▷ vb sell by auction
**AUCTIONED** >AUCTION
**AUCTIONS** >AUCTION
**AUCTORIAL** adj of or relating to an author
**AUCUBA** n Japanese laurel
**AUCUBAS** >AUCUBA
**AUDACIOUS** adj recklessly bold or daring
**AUDACITY** >AUDACIOUS
**AUDAD** n wild African sheep
**AUDADS** >AUDAD
**AUDIAL** adj of sound
**AUDIBLE** adj loud enough to be heard ▷ n change of playing tactics called by the quarterback when the offence is lined up at the line of scrimmage ▷ vb call an audible
**AUDIBLED** >AUDIBLE
**AUDIBLES** >AUDIBLE
**AUDIBLING** >AUDIBLE
**AUDIBLY** >AUDIBLE
**AUDIENCE** n group of spectators or listeners
**AUDIENCES** >AUDIENCE
**AUDIENCIA** n court in S America

AUDIENT n person who hears

AUDIENTS >AUDIENT

AUDILE n person who possesses a faculty for auditory imagery that is more distinct than his visual or other imagery ▷ adj of or relating to such a person

AUDILES >AUDILE

AUDING n practice of listening to try to understand

AUDINGS >AUDING

AUDIO adj of sound or hearing ▷ n of or relating to sound or hearing

AUDIOBOOK n recorded reading of a book

AUDIOGRAM n graphic record of the acuity of hearing of a person obtained by means of an audiometer

AUDIOLOGY n scientific study of hearing, often including the treatment of persons with hearing defects

AUDIOPHIL n audiophile

AUDIOS >AUDIO

AUDIOTAPE n tape for recording sound

AUDIPHONE n type of hearing aid consisting of a diaphragm that, when placed against the upper teeth, conveys sound vibrations to the inner ear

AUDIT n official examination of business accounts ▷ vb examine (business accounts) officially

AUDITABLE >AUDIT

AUDITED >AUDIT

AUDITEE n one who is audited

AUDITEES >AUDITEE

AUDITING >AUDIT

AUDITION n test of a performer's ability for a particular role or job ▷ vb test or be tested in an audition

AUDITIONS >AUDITION

AUDITIVE n person who learns primarily by listening

AUDITIVES >AUDITIVE

AUDITOR n person qualified to audit accounts

AUDITORIA n areas of concert halls, theatres, schools, etc, in which audiences sit

AUDITORS >AUDITOR

AUDITORY adj of or relating to hearing

AUDITRESS n female auditor

AUDITS >AUDIT

AUE interj Māori

exclamation

AUF old word for >OAF

AUFGABE n word used in psychology to mean task

AUFGABES >AUFGABE

AUFS >AUF

AUGEND n number to which another number, the addend, is added

AUGENDS >AUGEND

AUGER n tool for boring holes

AUGERS >AUGER

AUGHT adv in any least part ▷ n less common word for NOUGHT (zero)

AUGHTS >AUGHT

AUGITE n black or greenish-black mineral

AUGITES >AUGITE

AUGITIC >AUGITE

AUGMENT vb increase or enlarge ▷ n (in Greek and Sanskrit grammar) a vowel or diphthong prefixed to a verb to form a past tense

AUGMENTED >AUGMENT

AUGMENTER >AUGMENT

AUGMENTOR >AUGMENT

AUGMENTS >AUGMENT

AUGUR vb be a sign of (future events) ▷ n (in ancient Rome) a religious official who observed and interpreted omens and signs to help guide the making of public decisions

AUGURAL >AUGUR

AUGURED >AUGUR

AUGURER old word for >AUGUR

AUGURERS >AUGURER

AUGURIES >AUGURY

AUGURING >AUGUR

AUGURS >AUGUR

AUGURSHIP >AUGUR

AUGURY n foretelling of the future

AUGUST same as >AUGUSTE adj dignified and imposing

AUGUSTE n type of circus clown who usually wears battered ordinary clothes and is habitually maladroit or unlucky

AUGUSTER >AUGUST

AUGUSTES >AUGUSTE

AUGUSTEST >AUGUST

AUGUSTLY >AUGUST

AUGUSTS >AUGUST

AUK n northern sea bird with short wings and black-and-white plumage

AUKLET n any of various small auks of the genera Aethia and Ptychoramphus

AUKLETS >AUKLET

AUKS >AUK

AULA n hall

AULARIAN n Oxford University student belonging to hall

AULARIANS >AULARIAN

AULAS >AULA

AULD a Scots word for >OLD

AULDER >AULD

AULDEST >AULD

AULIC adj relating to a royal court

AULNAGE n measurement in ells

AULNAGER n inspector of cloth

AULNAGERS >AULNAGER

AULNAGES >AULNAGE

AULOI >AULOS

AULOS n ancient Greek pipes

AUMAIL old word for >ENAMEL

AUMAILED >AUMAIL

AUMAILING >AUMAIL

AUMAILS >AUMAIL

AUMBRIES >AUMBRY

AUMBRY same as >AMBRY

AUMIL n manager in India

AUMILS >AUMIL

AUNE n old French measure of length

AUNES >AUNE

AUNT n father's or mother's sister

AUNTER old word for >ADVENTURE

AUNTERS >AUNTER

AUNTHOOD >AUNT

AUNTHOODS >AUNT

AUNTIE n aunt

AUNTIES >AUNTY

AUNTLIER >AUNTLY

AUNTLIEST >AUNTLY

AUNTLIKE >AUNT

AUNTLY adj of or like an aunt

AUNTS >AUNT

AUNTY same as >AUNTIE

AURA n distinctive air or quality of a person or thing

AURAE >AURA

AURAL adj of or using the ears or hearing

AURALITY >AURAL

AURALLY >AURAL

AURAR plural of >EYRIR

AURAS >AURA

AURATE n salt of auric acid

AURATED adj combined with auric acid

AURATES >AURATE

AUREATE adj covered with gold, gilded

AUREATELY >AUREATE

AUREI >AUREUS

AUREITIES >AUREITY

AUREITY n attributes of gold

AURELIA n large jellyfish

AURELIAN n person who studies butterflies and moths

AURELIANS >AURELIAN

AURELIAS >AURELIA

AUREOLA same as >AUREOLE

AUREOLAE >AUREOLA

AUREOLAS >AUREOLA

AUREOLE n halo

AUREOLED >AUREOLE

AUREOLES >AUREOLE

AUREOLING >AUREOLE

AURES >AURIS

AUREUS n gold coin of the Roman Empire

AURIC adj of or containing gold in the trivalent state

AURICLE n upper chamber of the heart

AURICLED >AURICLE

AURICLES >AURICLE

AURICULA n alpine primrose with leaves shaped like a bear's ear

AURICULAE >AURICULA

AURICULAR adj of, relating to, or received by the sense or organs of hearing ▷ n auricular feather

AURICULAS >AURICULA

AURIFIED >AURIFY

AURIFIES >AURIFY

AURIFORM adj shaped like an ear

AURIFY vb turn into gold

AURIFYING >AURIFY

AURIS n medical word for ear

AURISCOPE n medical instrument for examinig the external ear

AURIST a former name for >AUDIOLOGY

AURISTS >AURIST

AUROCHS n recently extinct European wild ox

AUROCHSES >AUROCHS

AURORA n bands of light sometimes seen in the sky in polar regions

AURORAE >AURORA

AURORAL >AURORA

AURORALLY >AURORA

AURORAS >AURORA

AUROREAN adj of dawn

AUROUS adj of or containing gold, esp in the monovalent state

AURUM n gold

AURUMS >AURUM

AUSFORM vb temper steel

AUSFORMED >AUSFORM

AUSFORMS >AUSFORM

AUSLANDER n German word meaning foreigner

AUSPEX same as >AUGUR

AUSPICATE vb inaugurate with a ceremony intended to bring good fortune

AUSPICE n patronage or guidance

AUSPICES >AUSPICE

AUSTENITE n solid solution of carbon in face-centred-cubic gamma iron, usually existing above 723°C

AUSTERE adj stern or severe

AUSTERELY >AUSTERE

AUSTERER >AUSTERE

AUSTEREST >AUSTERE

AUSTERITY n state of being austere

AUSTRAL adj southern ▷ n former monetary unit of

47

Argentina equal to 100 centavos, replaced by the peso
**AUSTRALES** > AUSTRAL
**AUSTRALIS** *adj* Australian
**AUSTRALS** > AUSTRAL
**AUSUBO** *n* tropical tree
**AUSUBOS** > AUSUBO
**AUTACOID** *n* any natural internal secretion, esp one that exerts an effect similar to a drug
**AUTACOIDS** > AUTACOID
**AUTARCH** *n* absolute ruler
**AUTARCHIC** > AUTARCHY
**AUTARCHS** > AUTARCH
**AUTARCHY** *n* absolute power or autocracy
**AUTARKIC** > AUTARKY
**AUTARKIES** > AUTARKY
**AUTARKIST** > AUTARKY
**AUTARKY** *n* policy of economic self-sufficiency
**AUTECIOUS** *adj* (of parasites, esp the rust fungi) completing the entire life cycle on a single species of host
**AUTECISM** > AUTECIOUS
**AUTECISMS** > AUTECIOUS
**AUTEUR** *n* director whose creative influence on a film is so great as to be considered its author
**AUTEURISM** > AUTEUR
**AUTEURIST** > AUTEUR
**AUTEURS** > AUTEUR
**AUTHENTIC** *adj* known to be real, genuine
**AUTHOR** *n* writer of a book etc ▷ *vb* write or originate
**AUTHORED** > AUTHOR
**AUTHORESS** *n* female author
**AUTHORIAL** > AUTHOR
**AUTHORING** *n* creation of documents, esp multimedia documents
**AUTHORISE** *same as* > AUTHORIZE
**AUTHORISH** > AUTHOR
**AUTHORISM** *n* condition of being author
**AUTHORITY** *n* power to command or control others
**AUTHORIZE** *vb* give authority to
**AUTHORS** > AUTHOR
**AUTISM** *n* disorder characterized by lack of response to people and limited ability to communicate
**AUTISMS** > AUTISM
**AUTIST** *n* autistic person
**AUTISTIC** > AUTISM
**AUTISTICS** > AUTISM
**AUTISTS** > AUTIST
**AUTO** *n* automobile ▷ *vb* travel in an automobile
**AUTOBAHN** *n* German motorway
**AUTOBAHNS** > AUTOBAHN

**AUTOBUS** *n* motor bus
**AUTOBUSES** > AUTOBUS
**AUTOCADE** *another name for* > MOTORCADE
**AUTOCADES** > AUTOCADE
**AUTOCAR** *n* motor car
**AUTOCARP** *n* fruit produced through self-fertilization
**AUTOCARPS** > AUTOCARP
**AUTOCARS** > AUTOCAR
**AUTOCIDAL** *adj* (of insect pest control) effected by the introduction of sterile or genetically altered individuals into the wild population
**AUTOCLAVE** *n* apparatus for sterilizing objects by steam under pressure ▷ *vb* put in or subject to the action of an autoclave
**AUTOCOID** *n* hormone
**AUTOCOIDS** > AUTOCOID
**AUTOCRACY** *n* government by an autocrat
**AUTOCRAT** *n* ruler with absolute authority
**AUTOCRATS** > AUTOCRAT
**AUTOCRIME** *n* crime of stealing a car
**AUTOCRINE** *adj* relating to self-stimulation through production of a factor and its receptor
**AUTOCROSS** *n* motor-racing over a rough course
**AUTOCUE** *n* electronic television prompting device
**AUTOCUES** > AUTOCUE
**AUTOCUTIE** *n* young and attractive but inexperienced female television presenter
**AUTOCYCLE** *n* bicycle powered or assisted by a small engine
**AUTODYNE** *adj* denoting or relating to an electrical circuit in which the same elements and valves are used as oscillator and detector ▷ *n* autodyne circuit
**AUTODYNES** > AUTODYNE
**AUTOECISM** *n* (of a parasite) completion of an entire lifecycle on a single species of host
**AUTOED** > AUTO
**AUTOFLARE** *n* automatic landing systen in aircraft
**AUTOFOCUS** *n* camera system in which the lens is focused automatically
**AUTOGAMIC** > AUTOGAMY
**AUTOGAMY** *n* self-fertilization in flowering plants
**AUTOGENIC** *adj* produced from within
**AUTOGENY** *n* hypothetical process by which living organisms first arose

on earth from nonliving matter
**AUTOGIRO** *n* self-propelled aircraft resembling a helicopter but with an unpowered rotor
**AUTOGIROS** > AUTOGIRO
**AUTOGRAFT** *n* tissue graft obtained from one part of a patient's body for use on another part
**AUTOGRAPH** *n* handwritten signature of a (famous) person ▷ *vb* write one's signature on or in
**AUTOGUIDE** *n* traffic information transmission system
**AUTOGYRO** *same as* > AUTOGIRO
**AUTOGYROS** > AUTOGYRO
**AUTOHARP** *n* zither-like musical instrument
**AUTOHARPS** > AUTOHARP
**AUTOICOUS** *adj* (of plants, esp mosses) having male and female reproductive organs on the same plant
**AUTOING** > AUTO
**AUTOLATRY** *n* self-worship
**AUTOLOGY** *n* study of oneself
**AUTOLYSE** *vb* undergo or cause to undergo autolysis
**AUTOLYSED** > AUTOLYSE
**AUTOLYSES** > AUTOLYSE
**AUTOLYSIN** *n* any agent that produces autolysis
**AUTOLYSIS** *n* destruction of cells and tissues of an organism by enzymes produced by the cells themselves
**AUTOLYTIC** > AUTOLYSIS
**AUTOLYZE** *same as* > AUTOLYSE
**AUTOLYZED** > AUTOLYZE
**AUTOLYZES** > AUTOLYZE
**AUTOMAKER** *n* car manufacturer
**AUTOMAN** *n* car manufacturer
**AUTOMAT** *n* vending machine
**AUTOMATA** > AUTOMATON
**AUTOMATE** *vb* make (a manufacturing process) automatic
**AUTOMATED** > AUTOMATE
**AUTOMATES** > AUTOMATE
**AUTOMATIC** *adj* (of a device) operating mechanically by itself ▷ *n* self-loading firearm
**AUTOMATON** *n* robot
**AUTOMATS** > AUTOMAT
**AUTOMEN** > AUTOMAN
**AUTOMETER** *n* small device inserted in a photocopier to enable the process of copying to begin and to record the number of copies made
**AUTONOMIC** *adj* occurring

involuntarily or spontaneously
**AUTONOMY** *n* self-government
**AUTONYM** *n* writing published under the real name of an author
**AUTONYMS** > AUTONYM
**AUTOPEN** *n* mechanical device used to produce imitation signatures
**AUTOPENS** > AUTOPEN
**AUTOPHAGY** *n* consumption of one's own tissue
**AUTOPHOBY** *n* reluctance to refer to oneself
**AUTOPHONY** *n* medical diagnosis by listening to vibration of one's own voice in patient
**AUTOPHYTE** *n* autotrophic plant, such as any green plant
**AUTOPILOT** *n* automatic pilot
**AUTOPISTA** *n* Spanish motorway
**AUTOPOINT** *n* point-to-point race in cars
**AUTOPSIA** *n* autopsy
**AUTOPSIAS** > AUTOPSIA
**AUTOPSIC** > AUTOPSY
**AUTOPSIED** > AUTOPSY
**AUTOPSIES** > AUTOPSY
**AUTOPSIST** > AUTOPSY
**AUTOPSY** *n* examination of a corpse to determine the cause of death
**AUTOPTIC** > AUTOPSY
**AUTOPUT** *n* motorway in the former Yugoslavia
**AUTOPUTS** > AUTOPUT
**AUTOROUTE** *n* French motorway
**AUTOS** > AUTO
**AUTOSCOPY** *n* hallucination in which one sees oneself
**AUTOSOMAL** > AUTOSOME
**AUTOSOME** *n* any chromosome that is not a sex chromosome
**AUTOSOMES** > AUTOSOME
**AUTOSPORE** *n* nonmotile algal spore that develops adult characteristics before being released
**AUTOTELIC** *adj* justifying itself
**AUTOTIMER** *n* device for turning a system on and off automatically at times predetermined by advance setting
**AUTOTOMIC** > AUTOTOMY
**AUTOTOMY** *n* casting off by an animal of a part of its body, to facilitate escape when attacked
**AUTOTOXIC** > AUTOTOXIN
**AUTOTOXIN** *n* any poison or toxin formed in the organism upon which it acts
**AUTOTROPH** *n* organism

capable of manufacturing complex organic nutritive compounds from simple inorganic substances

**AUTOTUNE** n software package that automatically manipulates a recording of a vocal track until it is in tune regardless of whether or not the original performance was in tune

**AUTOTUNES** > AUTOTUNE

**AUTOTYPE** n photographic process for producing prints in black and white, using a carbon pigment ▷ vb process using autotype

**AUTOTYPED** > AUTOTYPE

**AUTOTYPES** > AUTOTYPE

**AUTOTYPIC** > AUTOTYPE

**AUTOTYPY** > AUTOTYPE

**AUTOVAC** n vacuum pump in a car petrol tank

**AUTOVACS** > AUTOVAC

**AUTUMN** n season between summer and winter

**AUTUMNAL** adj of, occurring in, or characteristic of autumn

**AUTUMNS** > AUTUMN

**AUTUMNY** adj like autumn

**AUTUNITE** n yellowish fluorescent radioactive mineral

**AUTUNITES** > AUTUNITE

**AUXESES** > AUXESIS

**AUXESIS** n growth in animal or plant tissues resulting from an increase in cell size without cell division

**AUXETIC** n something that promotes growth

**AUXETICS** > AUXETIC

**AUXILIAR** old word for > AUXILIARY

**AUXILIARS** > AUXILIAR

**AUXILIARY** adj secondary or supplementary ▷ n person or thing that supplements or supports

**AUXIN** n any of various plant hormones, such as indoleacetic acid, that promote growth and control fruit and flower development. Synthetic auxins are widely used in agriculture and horticulture

**AUXINIC** > AUXIN

**AUXINS** > AUXIN

**AUXOCYTE** n any cell undergoing meiosis, esp an oocyte or spermatocyte

**AUXOCYTES** > AUXOCYTE

**AUXOMETER** n instrument for measuring magnification

**AUXOSPORE** n diatom cell before its silicaceous cell wall is formed

**AUXOTONIC** adj (of muscle contraction) occurring against increasing force

**AUXOTROPH** n mutant strain of microorganism having nutritional requirements additional to those of the normal organism

**AVA** adv at all ▷ n Polynesian shrub

**AVADAVAT** n either of two Asian weaverbirds of the genus Estrilda, esp E. amandava, having a red plumage: often kept as cagebirds

**AVADAVATS** > AVADAVAT

**AVAIL** vb be of use or advantage (to) ▷ n use or advantage

**AVAILABLE** adj obtainable or accessible

**AVAILABLY** > AVAILABLE

**AVAILE** old word for > LOWER

**AVAILED** > AVAIL

**AVAILES** > AVAILE

**AVAILFUL** old word for > USEFUL

**AVAILING** > AVAIL

**AVAILS** > AVAIL

**AVAL** adj of a grandparent

**AVALANCHE** n mass of snow or ice falling down a mountain ▷ vb come down overwhelmingly (upon)

**AVALE** old word for > LOWER

**AVALED** > AVALE

**AVALES** > AVALE

**AVALING** > AVALE

**AVANT** prep before

**AVANTI** interj forward!

**AVANTIST** n proponent of the avant-garde

**AVANTISTS** > AVANTIST

**AVARICE** n greed for wealth

**AVARICES** > AVARICE

**AVAS** > AVA

**AVASCULAR** adj (of certain tissues, such as cartilage) lacking blood vessels

**AVAST** sentence substitute stop! cease!

**AVATAR** n appearance of a god in animal or human form

**AVATARS** > AVATAR

**AVAUNT** sentence substitute go away! depart! ▷ vb go away; depart

**AVAUNTED** > AVAUNT

**AVAUNTING** > AVAUNT

**AVAUNTS** > AVAUNT

**AVE** n expression of welcome or farewell

**AVEL** a variant of > OVEL

**AVELLAN** adj of hazelnuts

**AVELLANE** adj of hazelnuts

**AVELS** > AVEL

**AVENGE** vb take revenge in retaliation for (harm done) or on behalf of (a person harmed)

**AVENGED** > AVENGE

**AVENGEFUL** > AVENGE

**AVENGER** > AVENGE

**AVENGERS** > AVENGE

**AVENGES** > AVENGE

**AVENGING** > AVENGE

**AVENIR** n future

**AVENIRS** > AVENIR

**AVENS** n any of several temperate or arctic rosaceous plants

**AVENSES** > AVENS

**AVENTAIL** n front flap of a helmet

**AVENTAILE** n avantail

**AVENTAILS** > AVENTAIL

**AVENTRE** old word for > THRUST

**AVENTRED** > AVENTRE

**AVENTRES** > AVENTRE

**AVENTRING** > AVENTRE

**AVENTURE** old form of > ADVENTURE

**AVENTURES** > AVENTURE

**AVENTURIN** n dark-coloured glass, usually green or brown, spangled with fine particles of gold, copper, or some other metal

**AVENUE** n wide street

**AVENUES** > AVENUE

**AVER** vb state to be true

**AVERAGE** n typical or normal amount or quality ▷ adj usual or typical ▷ vb calculate the average of

**AVERAGED** > AVERAGE

**AVERAGELY** > AVERAGE

**AVERAGES** > AVERAGE

**AVERAGING** > AVERAGE

**AVERMENT** > AVER

**AVERMENTS** > AVER

**AVERRABLE** > AVER

**AVERRED** > AVER

**AVERRING** > AVER

**AVERS** > AVER

**AVERSE** adj disinclined or unwilling

**AVERSELY** > AVERSE

**AVERSION** n strong dislike

**AVERSIONS** > AVERSION

**AVERSIVE** n tool or technique intended to repel animals etc

**AVERSIVES** > AVERSIVE

**AVERT** vb turn away

**AVERTABLE** > AVERT

**AVERTED** > AVERT

**AVERTEDLY** > AVERT

**AVERTER** > AVERT

**AVERTERS** > AVERT

**AVERTIBLE** > AVERT

**AVERTING** > AVERT

**AVERTS** > AVERT

**AVES** > AVE

**AVGAS** n aviation fuel

**AVGASES** > AVGAS

**AVGASSES** > AVGAS

**AVIAN** adj of or like a bird ▷ n bird

**AVIANISE** same as > AVIANIZE

**AVIANISED** > AVIANISE

**AVIANISES** > AVIANISE

**AVIANIZE** vb modify microorganisms in a chicken embryo

**AVIANIZED** > AVIANIZE

**AVIANIZES** > AVIANIZE

**AVIANS** > AVIAN

**AVIARIES** > AVIARY

**AVIARIST** n person who keeps an aviary

**AVIARISTS** > AVIARIST

**AVIARY** n large cage or enclosure for birds

**AVIATE** vb pilot or fly in an aircraft

**AVIATED** > AVIATE

**AVIATES** > AVIATE

**AVIATIC** adj pertaining to aviation

**AVIATING** > AVIATE

**AVIATION** n art of flying aircraft

**AVIATIONS** > AVIATION

**AVIATOR** n pilot of an aircraft

**AVIATORS** > AVIATOR

**AVIATRESS** > AVIATOR

**AVIATRICE** > AVIATOR

**AVIATRIX** > AVIATOR

**AVICULAR** adj of small birds

**AVID** adj keen or enthusiastic

**AVIDER** > AVID

**AVIDEST** > AVID

**AVIDIN** n protein, found in egg-white, that combines with biotin to form a stable compound that cannot be absorbed, leading to a biotin deficiency in the consumer

**AVIDINS** > AVIDIN

**AVIDITIES** > AVIDITY

**AVIDITY** n quality or state of being avid

**AVIDLY** > AVID

**AVIDNESS** > AVID

**AVIETTE** n aeroplane driven by human strength

**AVIETTES** > AVIETTE

**AVIFAUNA** n all the birds in a particular region

**AVIFAUNAE** > AVIFAUNA

**AVIFAUNAL** > AVIFAUNA

**AVIFAUNAS** > AVIFAUNA

**AVIFORM** adj like a bird

**AVIGATOR** another word for > AVIATOR

**AVIGATORS** > AVIGATOR

**AVINE** adj of birds

**AVION** n aeroplane

**AVIONIC** > AVIONICS

**AVIONICS** n science and technology of electronics applied to aeronautics and astronautics

**AVIONS** > AVION

**AVIRULENT** adj (esp of bacteria) not virulent

**AVISANDUM** n consideration of a law case by a judge

**AVISE** old word for > ADVISE

**AVISED** > AVISE

AVISEMENT > AVISE
AVISES > AVISE
AVISING > AVISE
AVISO n boat carrying messages
AVISOS > AVISO
AVITAL adj of a grandfather
AVIZANDUM n judge's or court's decision to consider a case privately before giving judgment
AVIZE old word for > ADVISE
AVIZED > AVIZE
AVIZEFULL > AVIZE
AVIZES > AVIZE
AVIZING > AVIZE
AVO n Macao currency unit
AVOCADO n pear-shaped tropical fruit with a leathery green skin and yellowish-green flesh
AVOCADOES > AVOCADO
AVOCADOS > AVOCADO
AVOCATION n occupation
AVOCET n long-legged wading bird with a long slender upward-curving bill
AVOCETS > AVOCET
AVODIRE n African tree
AVODIRES > AVODIRE
AVOID vb prevent from happening
AVOIDABLE > AVOID
AVOIDABLY > AVOID
AVOIDANCE n act of keeping away from or preventing from happening
AVOIDANT adj (of behaviour) demonstrating a tendency to avoid intimacy or interaction with others
AVOIDED > AVOID
AVOIDER > AVOID
AVOIDERS > AVOID
AVOIDING > AVOID
AVOIDS > AVOID
AVOISION n nonpayment of tax
AVOISIONS > AVOISION
AVOS > AVO
AVOSET n avocet
AVOSETS > AVOSET
AVOUCH vb vouch for
AVOUCHED > AVOUCH
AVOUCHER > AVOUCH
AVOUCHERS > AVOUCH
AVOUCHES > AVOUCH
AVOUCHING > AVOUCH
AVOURE old word for > AVOWAL
AVOURES > AVOURE
AVOUTERER old word for > ADULTERER
AVOUTRER old word for > ADULTERER
AVOUTRERS > AVOUTRER
AVOUTRIES > AVOUTRY
AVOUTRY old word for > ADULTERY
AVOW vb state or affirm
AVOWABLE > AVOW

AVOWABLY > AVOW
AVOWAL > AVOW
AVOWALS > AVOW
AVOWED > AVOW
AVOWEDLY > AVOW
AVOWER > AVOW
AVOWERS > AVOW
AVOWING > AVOW
AVOWRIES > AVOWRY
AVOWRY old word for > AVOWAL
AVOWS > AVOW
AVOYER n former Swiss magistrate
AVOYERS > AVOYER
AVRUGA n herring roe with a smoky flavour, sometimes used as a less expensive alternative to caviar
AVRUGAS > AVRUGA
AVULSE vb take away by force
AVULSED > AVULSE
AVULSES > AVULSE
AVULSING > AVULSE
AVULSION n forcible tearing away or separation of a bodily structure or part, either as the result of injury or as an intentional surgical procedure
AVULSIONS > AVULSION
AVUNCULAR adj (of a man) friendly, helpful, and caring towards someone younger
AVYZE old word for > ADVISE
AVYZED > AVYZE
AVYZES > AVYZE
AVYZING > AVYZE
AW variant of > ALL
AWA adv away
AWAIT vb wait for
AWAITED > AWAIT
AWAITER > AWAIT
AWAITERS > AWAIT
AWAITING > AWAIT
AWAITS > AWAIT
AWAKE vb emerge or rouse from sleep ▷ adj not sleeping
AWAKED > AWAKE
AWAKEN vb awake
AWAKENED > AWAKEN
AWAKENER > AWAKEN
AWAKENERS > AWAKEN
AWAKENING n start of a feeling or awareness in someone
AWAKENS > AWAKEN
AWAKES > AWAKE
AWAKING > AWAKE
AWAKINGS > AWAKE
AWANTING adj missing
AWARD vb give (something, such as a prize) formally ▷ n something awarded, such as a prize
AWARDABLE > AWARD
AWARDED > AWARD
AWARDEE > AWARD
AWARDEES > AWARD
AWARDER > AWARD

AWARDERS > AWARD
AWARDING > AWARD
AWARDS > AWARD
AWARE adj having knowledge, informed
AWARENESS > AWARE
AWARER > AWARE
AWAREST > AWARE
AWARN vb old form of warn
AWARNED > AWARN
AWARNING > AWARN
AWARNS > AWARN
AWASH adv washed over by water ▷ adj washed over by water
AWATCH adv watching
AWATO n New Zealand caterpillar
AWAVE adv in waves
AWAY adv from a place ▷ adj not present ▷ n game played or won at an opponent's ground
AWAYDAY n day trip taken for pleasure
AWAYDAYS > AWAYDAY
AWAYES old word for > AWAY
AWAYNESS > AWAY
AWAYS > AWAY
AWDL n traditional Welsh poem
AWDLS > AWDL
AWE n wonder and respect mixed with dread ▷ vb fill with awe
AWEARIED old word for > WEARY
AWEARY old form of > WEARY
AWEATHER adj towards the weather
AWED > AWE
AWEE adv for a short time
AWEEL interj Scots word meaning well
AWEIGH adj (of an anchor) no longer hooked onto the bottom
AWEING > AWE
AWELESS > AWE
AWES > AWE
AWESOME adj inspiring awe
AWESOMELY > AWESOME
AWESTRIKE vb inspire awe in
AWESTRUCK adj filled with awe
AWETO n New Zealand caterpillar
AWETOS > AWETO
AWFUL adj very bad or unpleasant ▷ adv very
AWFULLER > AWFUL
AWFULLEST > AWFUL
AWFULLY adv in an unpleasant way
AWFULNESS > AWFUL
AWHAPE old word for > AMAZE
AWHAPED > AWHAPE
AWHAPES > AWHAPE
AWHAPING > AWHAPE
AWHATO n New Zealand caterpillar
AWHEEL adv on wheels
AWHEELS same as > AWHEEL

AWHETO n New Zealand caterpillar
AWHILE adv for a brief time
AWHIRL adv whirling
AWING > AWE
AWKWARD adj clumsy or ungainly
AWKWARDER > AWKWARD
AWKWARDLY > AWKWARD
AWL n pointed tool for piercing wood, leather, etc
AWLBIRD n woodpecker
AWLBIRDS > AWLBIRD
AWLESS > AWE
AWLS > AWL
AWLWORT n small stemless aquatic plant, Subularia aquatica, of the N hemisphere, having slender sharp-pointed leaves and minute, often submerged, white flowers: family Brassicaceae (crucifers)
AWLWORTS > AWLWORT
AWMOUS Scots word for > ALMS
AWMRIE n cupboard for church vessels
AWMRIES > AWMRIE
AWMRY n cupboard for church vessels
AWN n any of the bristles growing from the flowering parts of certain grasses and cereals
AWNED > AWN
AWNER n machine for removing awns
AWNERS > AWNER
AWNIER > AWNY
AWNIEST > AWNY
AWNING n canvas roof supported by a frame to give protection against the weather
AWNINGED adj sheltered with awning
AWNINGS > AWNING
AWNLESS > AWN
AWNS > AWN
AWNY adj having awns
AWOKE past tense of > AWAKE
AWOKEN > AWAKE
AWOL n person who is absent without leave
AWOLS > AWOL
AWORK adv old word meaning at work
AWRACK adv in wrecked condition
AWRONG adv old word meaning wrongly
AWRY adj with a twist to one side, askew
AWSOME adj old form of awesome
AX same as > AXE
AXAL adj of an axis
AXE n tool with a sharp blade for felling trees or chopping wood ▷ vb dismiss (employees), restrict (expenditure), or

terminate (a project)
**AXEBIRD** n nightjar of northern Queensland and New Guinea with a cry that sounds like a chopping axe
**AXEBIRDS** > AXEBIRD
**AXED** > AXE
**AXEL** n jump in which the skater takes off from the forward outside edge of one skate, makes one and a half, two and a half, or three and a half turns in the air, and lands on the backward outside edge of the other skate
**AXELS** > AXEL
**AXEMAN** n man who wields an axe, esp to cut down trees
**AXEMEN** > AXEMAN
**AXENIC** adj (of a biological culture or culture medium) free from other microorganisms
**AXES** > AXIS
**AXIAL** adj forming or of an axis
**AXIALITY** > AXIAL
**AXIALLY** > AXIAL
**AXIL** n angle where the stalk of a leaf joins a stem
**AXILE** adj of, relating to, or attached to the axis
**AXILEMMA** same as > AXOLEMMA
**AXILEMMAS** > AXILEMMA
**AXILLA** n area on the undersurface of a bird's wing corresponding to the armpit
**AXILLAE** > AXILLA
**AXILLAR** same as > AXILLARY
**AXILLARS** > AXILLAR
**AXILLARY** adj of, relating to, or near the armpit ▷ n one of the feathers growing from the axilla of a bird's wing
**AXILLAS** > AXILLA
**AXILS** > AXIL
**AXING** > AXE
**AXINITE** n crystalline substance
**AXINITES** > AXINITE
**AXIOLOGY** n theory of values, moral or aesthetic
**AXIOM** n generally accepted principle
**AXIOMATIC** adj containing axioms
**AXIOMS** > AXIOM
**AXION** n type of hypothetical elementary particle
**AXIONS** > AXION
**AXIS** n (imaginary) line round which a body can rotate or about which an object or geometrical figure is symmetrical
**AXISED** adj having an axis
**AXISES** > AXIS

**AXITE** n type of gunpowder
**AXITES** > AXITE
**AXLE** n shaft on which a wheel or pair of wheels turns
**AXLED** adj having axle
**AXLES** > AXLE
**AXLETREE** n bar fixed across the underpart of a wagon or carriage that has rounded ends on which the wheels revolve
**AXLETREES** > AXLETREE
**AXLIKE** > AX
**AXMAN** same as > AXEMAN
**AXMEN** > AXMAN
**AXOID** n type of curve
**AXOIDS** > AXOID
**AXOLEMMA** n membrane that encloses the axon of a nerve cell
**AXOLEMMAS** > AXOLEMMA
**AXOLOTL** n aquatic salamander of central America
**AXOLOTLS** > AXOLOTL
**AXON** n long threadlike extension of a nerve cell that conducts nerve impulses from the cell body
**AXONAL** > AXON
**AXONE** same as > AXON
**AXONEMAL** > AXONEME
**AXONEME** n part of cell consisting of proteins
**AXONEMES** > AXONEME
**AXONES** > AXONE
**AXONIC** > AXON
**AXONS** > AXON
**AXOPLASM** n part of cell
**AXOPLASMS** > AXOPLASM
**AXSEED** n crown vetch
**AXSEEDS** > AXSEED
**AY** adv ever ▷ n expression of agreement
**AYAH** n (in parts of the former British Empire) a native maidservant or nursemaid
**AYAHS** > AYAH
**AYAHUASCA** n type of Brazilian plant
**AYAHUASCO** n South American vine
**AYATOLLAH** n Islamic religious leader in Iran
**AYE** n affirmative vote or voter ▷ adv always
**AYELP** adv yelping
**AYENBITE** old word for > REMORSE
**AYENBITES** > AYENBITE
**AYES** > AYE
**AYGRE** old word for > EAGER
**AYIN** n 16th letter in the Hebrew alphabet
**AYINS** > AYIN
**AYONT** adv beyond
**AYRE** old word for > AIR
**AYRES** > AYRE
**AYRIE** old word for > EYRIE
**AYRIES** > AYRIE
**AYS** > AY

**AYU** n small Japanese fish
**AYURVEDA** n ancient medical treatise on the art of healing and prolonging life
**AYURVEDAS** > AYURVEDA
**AYURVEDIC** > AYURVEDA
**AYUS** > AYU
**AYWORD** n old word meaning byword
**AYWORDS** > AYWORD
**AZALEA** n garden shrub grown for its showy flowers
**AZALEAS** > AZALEA
**AZAN** n call to prayer five times a day, usually by a muezzin from a minaret
**AZANS** > AZAN
**AZEDARACH** n astringent bark of the chinaberry tree, formerly used as an emetic and cathartic
**AZEOTROPE** n mixture of liquids that boils at a constant temperature, at a given pressure, without a change in composition
**AZEOTROPY** > AZEOTROPE
**AZERTY** n common European version of typewriter keyboard layout with the characters a, z, e, r, t, and y positioned on the top row of alphabetic characters at the left side of the keyboard
**AZIDE** n type of chemical compound
**AZIDES** > AZIDE
**AZIDO** adj containing an azide
**AZIMUTH** n arc of the sky between the zenith and the horizon
**AZIMUTHAL** > AZIMUTH
**AZIMUTHS** > AZIMUTH
**AZINE** n any organic compound having a six-membered ring containing at least one nitrogen atom
**AZINES** > AZINE
**AZIONE** n musical drama
**AZIONES** > AZIONE
**AZLON** n fibre made from protein
**AZLONS** > AZLON
**AZO** adj of, consisting of, or containing the divalent group -N:N-
**AZOIC** adj without life
**AZOLE** n organic five-membered ring compound containing one or more atoms in the ring, the number usually being specified by a prefix
**AZOLES** > AZOLE
**AZOLLA** n tropical water fern
**AZOLLAS** > AZOLLA
**AZON** n type of drawing

paper
**AZONAL** adj not divided into zones
**AZONIC** adj not confined to a zone
**AZONS** > AZON
**AZOTAEMIA** a less common name for > URAEMIA
**AZOTAEMIC** > AZOTAEMIA
**AZOTE** an obsolete name for > NITROGEN
**AZOTED** > AZOTE
**AZOTEMIA** same as > AZOTAEMIA
**AZOTEMIAS** > AZOTEMIA
**AZOTEMIC** > AZOTAEMIA
**AZOTES** > AZOTE
**AZOTH** n panacea postulated by Paracelsus
**AZOTHS** > AZOTH
**AZOTIC** adj of, containing, or concerned with nitrogen
**AZOTISE** same as > AZOTIZE
**AZOTISED** > AZOTISE
**AZOTISES** > AZOTISE
**AZOTISING** > AZOTISE
**AZOTIZE** vb combine or treat with nitrogen or a nitrogen compound
**AZOTIZED** > AZOTIZE
**AZOTIZES** > AZOTIZE
**AZOTIZING** > AZOTIZE
**AZOTOUS** adj containing nitrogen
**AZOTURIA** n presence of excess nitrogen in urine
**AZOTURIAS** > AZOTURIA
**AZUKI** same as > ADZUKI
**AZUKIS** > AZUKI
**AZULEJO** n Spanish porcelain tile
**AZULEJOS** > AZULEJO
**AZURE** n (of) the colour of a clear blue sky ▷ adj deep blue
**AZUREAN** adj azure
**AZURES** > AZURE
**AZURINE** n blue dye
**AZURINES** > AZURINE
**AZURITE** n azure-blue mineral associated with copper deposits
**AZURITES** > AZURITE
**AZURN** old word for > AZURE
**AZURY** adj bluish
**AZYGIES** > AZYGY
**AZYGOS** n biological structure not in a pair
**AZYGOSES** > AZYGOS
**AZYGOUS** adj developing or occurring singly
**AZYGY** n state of not being joined in pair
**AZYM** n unleavened bread
**AZYME** n unleavened bread
**AZYMES** > AZYME
**AZYMITE** n member of a church using unleavened bread in the Eucharist
**AZYMITES** > AZYMITE
**AZYMOUS** adj unleavened
**AZYMS** > AZYM

# Bb

**BA** n symbol for the soul in Ancient Egyptian religion

**BAA** vb make the characteristic bleating sound of a sheep ▷ n cry made by a sheep

**BAAED** > BAA

**BAAING** > BAA

**BAAINGS** > BAA

**BAAL** n any false god or idol

**BAALEBOS** n master of the house

**BAALIM** > BAAL

**BAALISM** > BAAL

**BAALISMS** > BAAL

**BAALS** > BAAL

**BAAS** South African word for > BOSS

**BAASES** > BAAS

**BAASKAAPS** > BAASKAAP

**BAASKAAP** n (in South Africa) control by Whites of non-Whites

**BAASKAPS** > BAASKAP

**BAASSKAP** same as > BAASKAP

**BAASSKAPS** > BAASSKAP

**BABA** n small cake of leavened dough, sometimes mixed with currants and usually soaked in rum

**BABACO** n greenish-yellow egg-shaped fruit

**BABACOOTE** n large lemur

**BABACOS** > BABACO

**BABALAS** adj drunk

**BABAS** > BABA

**BABASSU** n Brazilian palm tree, Orbignya martiana (or O. speciosa), having hard

---

edible nuts that yield an oil used in making soap, margarine, etc

**BABASSUS** > BABASSU

**BABBELAS** same as > BABALAS

**BABBITRY** > BABBITT

**BABBITT** vb line (a bearing) or face (a surface) with Babbitt metal or a similar soft alloy

**BABBITTED** > BABBITT

**BABBITTRY** > BABBITT

**BABBITTS** > BABBITT

**BABBLE** vb talk excitedly or foolishly ▷ n muddled or foolish speech

**BABBLED** > BABBLE

**BABBLER** n person who babbles

**BABBLERS** > BABBLER

**BABBLES** > BABBLE

**BABBLIER** > BABBLE

**BABBLIEST** > BABBLE

**BABBLING** > BABBLE

**BABBLINGS** > BABBLE

**BABBLY** > BABBLE

**BABE** n baby

**BABEL** n confused mixture of noises or voices

**BABELDOM** > BABEL

**BABELDOMS** > BABEL

**BABELISH** > BABEL

**BABELISM** > BABEL

**BABELISMS** > BABEL

**BABELS** > BABEL

**BABES** > BABE

**BABESIA** n parasite causing infection in cattle

**BABESIAS** > BABESIA

**BABICHE** n thongs or lacings of rawhide

**BABICHES** > BABICHE

---

**BABIED** > BABY

**BABIER** > BABY

**BABIES** > BABY

**BABIEST** > BABY

**BABIRUSA** n wild pig, Babyrousa babyrussa, inhabiting marshy forests in Indonesia. It has an almost hairless wrinkled skin and enormous curved canine teeth

**BABIRUSAS** > BABIRUSA

**BABIRUSSA** same as > BABIRUSA

**BABKA** n cake

**BABKAS** > BABKA

**BABLAH** n type of acacia

**BABLAHS** > BABLAH

**BABOO** same as > BABU

**BABOOL** n type of acacia

**BABOOLS** > BABOOL

**BABOON** n large monkey with a pointed face and a long tail

**BABOONERY** n uncouth behaviour

**BABOONISH** adj uncouth

**BABOONS** > BABOON

**BABOOS** > BABOO

**BABOOSH** same as > BABOUCHE

**BABOOSHES** > BABOOSH

**BABOUCHE** n Middle-Eastern slipper

**BABOUCHES** > BABOUCHE

**BABU** n (in India) a title or form of address more or less equivalent to Mr, placed before a person's full name or after his first name

**BABUCHE** same as > BABOUCHE

---

**BABUCHES** > BABUCHE

**BABUDOM** > BABU

**BABUDOMS** > BABU

**BABUISM** > BABU

**BABUISMS** > BABU

**BABUL** n any of several leguminous trees of the genus Acacia, esp A. arabica of N Africa and India, which bear small yellow flowers and are a source of gum arabic, tannin, and hardwood

**BABULS** > BABUL

**BABUS** > BABU

**BABUSHKA** n headscarf tied under the chin, worn by Russian peasant women

**BABUSHKAS** > BABUSHKA

**BABY** n very young child or animal ▷ adj comparatively small of its type ▷ vb treat as a baby

**BABYDOLL** n woman's short nightdress

**BABYDOLLS** > BABYDOLL

**BABYFOOD** n puréed food for babies

**BABYFOODS** > BABYFOOD

**BABYHOOD** > BABY

**BABYHOODS** > BABY

**BABYING** > BABY

**BABYISH** > BABY

**BABYISHLY** > BABY

**BABYPROOF** adj safe for babies to handle ▷ vb make babyproof

**BABYSAT** > BABYSIT

**BABYSIT** vb look after a child in its parents' absence

**BABYSITS** > BABYSIT

**BAC** n baccalaureate

**BACALAO** *n* dried salt cod
**BACALAOS** > BACALAO
**BACCA** *n* berry
**BACCAE** > BACCA
**BACCARA** *same as* > BACCARAT
**BACCARAS** > BACCARA
**BACCARAT** *n* card game involving gambling
**BACCARATS** > BACCARAT
**BACCARE** *same as* > BACKARE
**BACCAS** > BACCA
**BACCATE** *adj* like a berry in form, texture, etc
**BACCATED** > BACCATE
**BACCHANAL** *n* follower of Bacchus ▷ *adj* of or relating to Bacchus
**BACCHANT** *n* priest or votary of Bacchus
**BACCHANTE** *n* priestess or female votary of Bacchus
**BACCHANTS** > BACCHANT
**BACCHIAC** > BACCHIUS
**BACCHIAN** *same as* > BACCHIC
**BACCHIC** *adj* riotously drunk
**BACCHII** > BACCHIUS
**BACCHIUS** *n* metrical foot of one short syllable followed by two long ones
**BACCIES** > BACCY
**BACCIFORM** *adj* shaped like a berry
**BACCO** *n* tobacco
**BACCOES** > BACCO
**BACCOS** > BACCO
**BACCY** *n* tobacco
**BACH** *same as* > BATCH
**BACHA** *n* Indian English word for young child
**BACHARACH** *n* German wine
**BACHAS** > BACHA
**BACHCHA** *n* Indian English word for young child
**BACHCHAS** > BACHCHA
**BACHED** > BACH
**BACHELOR** *n* unmarried man
**BACHELORS** > BACHELOR
**BACHES** > BACH
**BACHING** > BACH
**BACHS** > BACH
**BACILLAR** *same as* > BACILLARY
**BACILLARY** *adj* of or caused by bacilli
**BACILLI** > BACILLUS
**BACILLUS** *n* rod-shaped bacterium
**BACK** *n* rear part of the human body, from the neck to the pelvis ▷ *vb* (cause to) move backwards ▷ *adj* situated behind ▷ *adv* at, to, or towards the rear
**BACKACHE** *n* ache or pain in one's back
**BACKACHES** > BACKACHE
**BACKARE** *interj* instruction to keep one's distance; back off

**BACKBAND** *n* back support
**BACKBANDS** > BACKBAND
**BACKBEAT** *n* second and fourth beats in music written in even time or, in more complex time signatures, the last beat of the bar
**BACKBEATS** > BACKBEAT
**BACKBENCH** *n* lower-ranking seats in Parliament
**BACKBEND** *n* gymnastic exercise in which the trunk is bent backwards until the hands touch the floor
**BACKBENDS** > BACKBEND
**BACKBIT** > BACKBITE
**BACKBITE** *vb* talk spitefully about an absent person
**BACKBITER** > BACKBITE
**BACKBITES** > BACKBITE
**BACKBLOCK** *n* singular of backblock: bush or remote farming area
**BACKBOARD** *n* board that is placed behind something to form or support its back
**BACKBOND** *n* legal document
**BACKBONDS** > BACKBOND
**BACKBONE** *n* spinal column
**BACKBONED** > BACKBONE
**BACKBONES** > BACKBONE
**BACKBURN** *vb* clear (an area of bush) by creating a fire that burns in the opposite direction from the wind ▷ *n* act or result of backburning
**BACKBURNS** > BACKBURN
**BACKCAST** *n* backward casting of fishing rod
**BACKCASTS** > BACKCAST
**BACKCHAT** *n* impudent replies
**BACKCHATS** > BACKCHAT
**BACKCHECK** *vb* (in ice hockey) return from attack to defence
**BACKCLOTH** *n* painted curtain at the back of a stage set
**BACKCOMB** *vb* comb (the hair) towards the roots to give more bulk to a hairstyle
**BACKCOMBS** > BACKCOMB
**BACKCOURT** *n* part of the court between the service line and the baseline
**BACKCROSS** *vb* mate (a hybrid of the first generation) with one of its parents ▷ *n* offspring so produced
**BACKDATE** *vb* make (a document) effective from a date earlier than its completion
**BACKDATED** > BACKDATE
**BACKDATES** > BACKDATE
**BACKDOOR** *adj* secret,

underhand, or obtained through influence
**BACKDOWN** *n* abandonment of an earlier claim
**BACKDOWNS** > BACKDOWN
**BACKDRAFT** *n* reverse movement of air
**BACKDROP** *vb* provide a backdrop to (something)
**BACKDROPS** > BACKDROP
**BACKDROPT** > BACKDROP
**BACKED** *adj* having a back or backing
**BACKER** *n* person who gives financial support
**BACKERS** > BACKER
**BACKET** *n* shallow box
**BACKETS** > BACKET
**BACKFALL** *n* fall onto the back
**BACKFALLS** > BACKFALL
**BACKFIELD** *n* quarterback and running backs in a team
**BACKFILE** *n* archives of a newspaper or magazine
**BACKFILES** > BACKFILE
**BACKFILL** *vb* refill an excavated trench, esp (in archaeology) at the end of an investigation ▷ *n* soil used to do this
**BACKFILLS** > BACKFILL
**BACKFIRE** *vb* (of a plan) fail to have the desired effect ▷ *n* (in an engine) explosion of unburnt gases in the exhaust system
**BACKFIRED** > BACKFIRE
**BACKFIRES** > BACKFIRE
**BACKFISCH** *n* young girl
**BACKFIT** *vb* overhaul nuclear power plant
**BACKFITS** > BACKFIT
**BACKFLIP** *n* backwards somersault
**BACKFLIPS** > BACKFLIP
**BACKFLOW** *n* reverse flow
**BACKFLOWS** > BACKFLOW
**BACKHAND** *n* stroke played with the back of the hand facing the direction of the stroke ▷ *adv* with a backhand stroke ▷ *vb* play (a shot) backhand
**BACKHANDS** > BACKHAND
**BACKHAUL** *vb* transmit data
**BACKHAULS** > BACKHAUL
**BACKHOE** *n* digger ▷ *vb* dig with a backhoe
**BACKHOED** > BACKHOE
**BACKHOES** > BACKHOE
**BACKHOUSE** *n* toilet
**BACKIE** *n* ride on the back of someone's bicycle
**BACKIES** > BACKIE
**BACKING** *n* support
**BACKINGS** > BACKING
**BACKLAND** *n* undeveloped land behind a property
**BACKLANDS** > BACKLAND
**BACKLASH** *n* sudden and adverse reaction ▷ *vb* create a sudden and

adverse reaction
**BACKLESS** *adj* (of a dress) low-cut at the back
**BACKLIFT** *n* backward movement of bat
**BACKLIFTS** > BACKLIFT
**BACKLIGHT** *vb* illuminate (something) from behind
**BACKLIST** *n* publisher's previously published books that are still available ▷ *vb* put on a backlist
**BACKLISTS** > BACKLIST
**BACKLIT** *adj* illuminated from behind
**BACKLOAD** *n* load for lorry on return journey ▷ *vb* load a lorry for a return journey
**BACKLOADS** > BACKLOAD
**BACKLOG** *n* accumulation of things to be dealt with
**BACKLOGS** > BACKLOG
**BACKLOT** *n* area outside a film or television studio used for outdoor filming
**BACKLOTS** > BACKLOT
**BACKMOST** *adj* furthest back
**BACKOUT** *n* instance of withdrawing (from an agreement, etc)
**BACKOUTS** > BACKOUT
**BACKPACK** *n* large pack carried on the back ▷ *vb* go hiking with a backpack
**BACKPACKS** > BACKPACK
**BACKPAY** *n* pay received by an employee from an increase awarded retrospectively
**BACKPAYS** > BACKPAY
**BACKPEDAL** *vb* retract or modify a previous opinion, principle, etc
**BACKPIECE** *n* tattoo on the back
**BACKRA** *n* white person
**BACKRAS** > BACKRA
**BACKREST** *n* support for the back of something
**BACKRESTS** > BACKREST
**BACKROOM** *n* place where research or planning is done, esp secret research in wartime
**BACKROOMS** > BACKROOM
**BACKRUSH** *n* seaward return of wave
**BACKS** > BACK
**BACKSAW** *n* small handsaw stiffened along its upper edge by a metal section
**BACKSAWS** > BACKSAW
**BACKSEAT** *n* seat at the back, esp of a vehicle
**BACKSEATS** > BACKSEAT
**BACKSET** *n* reversal
**BACKSETS** > BACKSET
**BACKSEY** *n* sirloin
**BACKSEYS** > BACKSEY
**BACKSHISH** *same as* > BAKSHEESH
**BACKSHORE** *n* area of beach

above high tide mark
**BACKSIDE** *n* buttocks
**BACKSIDES** > BACKSIDE
**BACKSIGHT** *n* sight of a rifle nearer the stock
**BACKSLAP** *vb* demonstrate effusive joviality
**BACKSLAPS** > BACKSLAP
**BACKSLASH** *n* slash which slopes to the left
**BACKSLID** > BACKSLIDE
**BACKSLIDE** *vb* relapse into former bad habits
**BACKSPACE** *vb* move a typewriter carriage or computer cursor backwards ▷ *n* typewriter key that effects such a movements
**BACKSPEER** *same as* > BACKSPEIR
**BACKSPEIR** *vb* interrogate
**BACKSPIN** *n* backward spin given to a ball to reduce its speed at impact
**BACKSPINS** > BACKSPIN
**BACKSTAB** *vb* attack deceitfully
**BACKSTABS** > BACKSTAB
**BACKSTAGE** *adj* behind the stage in a theatre ▷ *adv* behind the stage in a theatre ▷ *n* area behind the stage in a theatre
**BACKSTAIR** *adj* underhand
**BACKSTALL** *n* backward flight of a kite
**BACKSTAMP** *n* mark stamped on the back of an envelope ▷ *vb* mark with a backstamp
**BACKSTAY** *n* stay leading aft from the upper part of a mast to the deck or stern
**BACKSTAYS** > BACKSTAY
**BACKSTOP** *n* screen or fence to prevent balls leaving the playing area ▷ *vb* provide with backing or support
**BACKSTOPS** > BACKSTOP
**BACKSTORY** *n* events assumed before a story begins
**BACKSWEPT** *adj* slanting backwards
**BACKSWING** *n* backward movement of a bat, etc
**BACKSWORD** *same as* a broad-bladed sword
**BACKTRACK** *vb* return by the same route by which one has come
**BACKUP** *n* support or reinforcement
**BACKUPS** > BACKUP
**BACKVELD** *n* (in South Africa) remote sparsely populated area
**BACKVELDS** > BACKVELD
**BACKWARD** *same as* > BACKWARDS
**BACKWARDS** *adv* towards the rear
**BACKWASH** *n* water washed

backwards by the motion of a boat ▷ *vb* remove oil from (combed wool)
**BACKWATER** *n* isolated or backward place or condition ▷ *vb* reverse the direction of a boat, esp to push the oars of a rowing boat
**BACKWOOD** > BACKWOODS
**BACKWOODS** *pl n* remote sparsely populated area
**BACKWORD** *n* act or an instance of failing to keep a promise or commitment
**BACKWORDS** > BACKWORD
**BACKWORK** *n* work carried out under the ground
**BACKWORKS** > BACKWORK
**BACKWRAP** *n* back support
**BACKWRAPS** > BACKWRAP
**BACKYARD** *n* yard at the back of a house, etc
**BACKYARDS** > BACKYARD
**BACLAVA** *same as* > BAKLAVA
**BACLAVAS** > BACLAVA
**BACLOFEN** *n* drug used to treat stroke victims
**BACLOFENS** > BACLOFEN
**BACON** *n* salted or smoked pig meat
**BACONER** *n* pig that weighs between 83 and 101 kg, from which bacon is cut
**BACONERS** > BACONER
**BACONS** > BACON
**BACS** > BAC
**BACTERIA** *pl n* large group of microorganisms
**BACTERIAL** > BACTERIA
**BACTERIAN** > BACTERIA
**BACTERIAS** > BACTERIA
**BACTERIC** > BACTERIA
**BACTERIN** *n* vaccine prepared from bacteria
**BACTERINS** > BACTERIN
**BACTERISE** *same as* > BACTERIZE
**BACTERIUM** singular form of > BACTERIA
**BACTERIZE** *vb* subject to bacterial action
**BACTEROID** *adj* resembling a bacterium ▷ *n* any rodlike bacterium of the genus *Bacteroides*, occurring in the gut of man and animals
**BACULA** > BACULUM
**BACULINE** *adj* relating to flogging
**BACULITE** *n* fossil
**BACULITES** > BACULITE
**BACULUM** *n* bony support in the penis of certain mammals, esp the carnivores
**BACULUMS** > BACULUM
**BAD** *adj* not good ▷ *n* unfortunate or unpleasant events collectively ▷ *adv* badly
**BADASS** *n* tough or aggressive person ▷ *adj*

tough or aggressive
**BADASSED** > BADASS
**BADASSES** > BADASS
**BADDER** > BAD
**BADDEST** > BAD
**BADDIE** *n* bad character in a story, film, etc, esp an opponent of the hero
**BADDIES** > BADDY
**BADDISH** > BAD
**BADDY** *same as* > BADDIE
**BADE** > BID
**BADGE** *n* emblem worn to show membership, rank, etc ▷ *vb* put a badge on
**BADGED** > BADGE
**BADGELESS** > BADGE
**BADGER** *n* nocturnal burrowing mammal of Europe, Asia, and N America with a black and white head ▷ *vb* pester or harass
**BADGERED** > BADGER
**BADGERING** > BADGER
**BADGERLY** > BADGER
**BADGERS** > BADGER
**BADGES** > BADGE
**BADGING** > BADGE
**BADINAGE** *n* playful and witty conversation ▷ *vb* engage in badinage
**BADINAGED** > BADINAGE
**BADINAGES** > BADINAGE
**BADINERIE** *n* name given in the 18th century to a type of quick, light movement in a suite
**BADIOUS** *adj* chestnut; brownish-red
**BADLAND** > BADLANDS
**BADLANDS** *pl n* any deeply eroded barren area
**BADLY** *adv* poorly
**BADMAN** *n* hired gunman, outlaw, or criminal
**BADMASH** *n* evil-doer ▷ *adj* naughty or bad ▷ *n* hooligan
**BADMASHES** > BADMASH
**BADMEN** > BADMAN
**BADMINTON** *n* game played with rackets and a shuttlecock, which is hit back and forth over a high net
**BADMOUTH** *vb* speak unfavourably about (someone or something)
**BADMOUTHS** > BADMOUTH
**BADNESS** > BAD
**BADNESSES** > BAD
**BADS** > BAD
**BAEL** *n* spiny Indian rutaceous tree, *Aegle marmelos*
**BAELS** > BAEL
**BAETYL** *n* magical meteoric stone
**BAETYLS** > BAETYL
**BAFF** *vb* strike ground with golf club
**BAFFED** > BAFF
**BAFFIES** *pl n* slippers

**BAFFING** > BAFF
**BAFFLE** *vb* perplex or puzzle ▷ *n* device to limit or regulate the flow of fluid, light, or sound
**BAFFLED** > BAFFLE
**BAFFLEGAB** *n* insincere speech
**BAFFLER** > BAFFLE
**BAFFLERS** > BAFFLE
**BAFFLES** > BAFFLE
**BAFFLING** *adj* impossible to understand
**BAFFS** > BAFF
**BAFFY** *n* golf club
**BAFT** *n* coarse fabric
**BAFTS** > BAFT
**BAG** *n* flexible container with an opening at one end ▷ *vb* put into a bag
**BAGARRE** *n* brawl
**BAGARRES** > BAGARRE
**BAGASS** *same as* > BAGASSE
**BAGASSE** *n* pulp remaining after the extraction of juice from sugar cane or similar plants: used as fuel and for making paper, etc
**BAGASSES** > BAGASSE
**BAGATELLE** *n* something of little value
**BAGEL** *n* hard ring-shaped bread roll
**BAGELS** > BAGEL
**BAGFUL** *n* amount (of something) that can be held in a bag
**BAGFULS** > BAGFUL
**BAGGAGE** *n* suitcases packed for a journey
**BAGGAGES** > BAGGAGE
**BAGGED** > BAG
**BAGGER** *n* person who packs groceries
**BAGGERS** > BAGGER
**BAGGIE** *n* plastic bag
**BAGGIER** > BAGGY
**BAGGIES** > BAGGY
**BAGGIEST** > BAGGY
**BAGGILY** > BAGGY
**BAGGINESS** > BAGGY
**BAGGING** > BAG
**BAGGINGS** > BAG
**BAGGIT** *n* unspawned salmon
**BAGGITS** > BAGGIT
**BAGGY** *same as* > BAGIE
**BAGH** *n* (in India and Pakistan) a garden
**BAGHOUSE** *n* dust-filtering chamber
**BAGHOUSES** > BAGHOUSE
**BAGHS** > BAGH
**BAGIE** *n* turnip
**BAGIES** > BAGIE
**BAGLESS** *adj* (esp of a vacuum cleaner) not containing a bag
**BAGLIKE** > BAG
**BAGMAN** *n* travelling salesman
**BAGMEN** > BAGMAN
**BAGNETTE** *variant of* > BAGUETTE

BAGNETTES > BAGNETTE
BAGNIO n brothel
BAGNIOS > BAGNIO
BAGPIPE vb play the bagpipes
BAGPIPED > BAGPIPE
BAGPIPER > BAGPIPES
BAGPIPERS > BAGPIPES
BAGPIPES pl n musical wind instrument with reed pipes and an inflatable bag
BAGPIPING > BAGPIPE
BAGS > BAG
BAGSFUL > BAGFUL
BAGUET same as > BAGUETTE
BAGUETS > BAGUET
BAGUETTE n narrow French stick loaf
BAGUETTES > BAGUETTE
BAGUIO n hurricane
BAGUIOS > BAGUIO
BAGWASH n laundry that washes clothes without drying or pressing them
BAGWASHES > BAGWASH
BAGWIG n 18th-century wig with hair pushed back into a bag
BAGWIGS > BAGWIG
BAGWORM n type of moth
BAGWORMS > BAGWORM
BAH interj expression of contempt or disgust
BAHADA same as > BAJADA
BAHADAS > BAHADA
BAHADUR n title formerly conferred by the British on distinguished Indians
BAHADURS > BAHADUR
BAHT n standard monetary unit of Thailand, divided into 100 satang
BAHTS > BAHT
BAHUT n decorative cabinet
BAHUTS > BAHUT
BAHUVRIHI n class of compound words consisting of two elements the first of which is a specific feature of the second
BAIDARKA n narrow hunting boat
BAIDARKAS > BAIDARKA
BAIGNOIRE n low-level theatre box
BAIL n money deposited with a court as security for a person's reappearance in court ▷ vb pay bail for (a person)
BAILABLE adj eligible for release on bail
BAILBOND n document in which a prisoner and one or more sureties guarantee that the prisoner will attend the court hearing of the charges against him if he is released on bail
BAILBONDS > BAILBOND
BAILED > BAIL

BAILEE n person to whom the possession of goods is transferred under a bailment
BAILEES > BAILEE
BAILER > BAIL
BAILERS > BAIL
BAILEY n outermost wall or court of a castle
BAILEYS > BAILEY
BAILIE n (in Scotland) a municipal magistrate
BAILIES > BAILIE
BAILIFF n sheriff's officer who serves writs and summonses
BAILIFFS > BAILIFF
BAILING > BAIL
BAILIWICK n area a person is interested in or operates in
BAILLI n magistrate
BAILLIAGE n magistrate's area of authority
BAILLIE variant of > BAILIE
BAILLIES > BAILLIE
BAILLIS > BAILLI
BAILMENT n contractual delivery of goods in trust to a person for a specific purpose
BAILMENTS > BAILMENT
BAILOR n person who retains ownership of goods but entrusts possession of them to another under a bailment
BAILORS > BAILOR
BAILOUT n instance of helping (a person, organization, etc) out of a predicament
BAILOUTS > BAILOUT
BAILS > BAIL
BAILSMAN n one standing bail for another
BAILSMEN > BAILSMAN
BAININ n Irish collarless jacket made of white wool
BAININS > BAININ
BAINITE n mixture of iron and iron carbide found in incompletely hardened steels, produced when austenite is transformed at temperatures between the pearlite and martensite ranges
BAINITES > BAINITE
BAIRN n child
BAIRNISH > BAIRN
BAIRNLIER > BAIRN
BAIRNLIKE > BAIRN
BAIRNLY > BAIRN
BAIRNS > BAIRN
BAISEMAIN n kissing of the hand
BAIT n piece of food on a hook or in a trap to attract fish or animals ▷ vb put a piece of food on or in (a hook or trap)
BAITED > BAIT
BAITER > BAIT

BAITERS > BAIT
BAITFISH n small fish used as bait
BAITH adj both
BAITING > BAIT
BAITINGS > BAIT
BAITS > BAIT
BAIZA n Omani unit of currency
BAIZAS > BAIZA
BAIZE n woollen fabric used to cover billiard and card tables ▷ vb line or cover with such fabric
BAIZED > BAIZE
BAIZES > BAIZE
BAIZING > BAIZE
BAJADA n sloping surface formed from rock deposits
BAJADAS > BAJADA
BAJAN n freshman at Aberdeen University
BAJANS > BAJAN
BAJRA n Indian millet
BAJRAS > BAJRA
BAJREE variant of > BAJRA
BAJREES > BAJREE
BAJRI variant of > BAJRA
BAJRIS > BAJRI
BAJU n Malay jacket
BAJUS > BAJU
BAKE vb cook by dry heat as in an oven ▷ n party at which the main dish is baked
BAKEAPPLE n cloudberry
BAKEBOARD n board for bread-making
BAKED > BAKE
BAKEHOUSE same as > BAKERY
BAKELITE n tradename for any one of a class of thermosetting resins used as electric insulators and for making plastic ware, telephone receivers, etc
BAKELITES > BAKELITE
BAKEMEAT n pie
BAKEMEATS > BAKEMEAT
BAKEN > BAKE
BAKER n person whose business is to make or sell bread, cakes, etc
BAKERIES > BAKERY
BAKERS > BAKER
BAKERY n place where bread, cakes, etc are baked or sold
BAKES > BAKE
BAKESHOP n bakery
BAKESHOPS > BAKESHOP
BAKESTONE n flat stone in an oven
BAKEWARE n dishes for baking
BAKEWARES > BAKEWARE
BAKHSHISH same as > BAKSHEESH
BAKING n process of cooking bread, cakes, etc ▷ adj (esp of weather) very hot and dry
BAKINGS > BAKING

BAKKIE n small truck
BAKKIES > BAKKIE
BAKLAVA n rich cake of Middle Eastern origin consisting of thin layers of pastry filled with nuts and honey
BAKLAVAS > BAKLAVA
BAKLAWA same as > BAKLAVA
BAKLAWAS > BAKLAWA
BAKRA n White person, esp one from Britain ▷ adj (of people) White, esp British
BAKRAS > BAKRA
BAKSHEESH n (in some Eastern countries) money given as a tip ▷ vb give such money to (a person)
BAKSHISH same as > BAKSHEESH
BAL n balmoral
BALACLAVA n close-fitting woollen hood that covers the ears and neck, as originally worn by soldiers in the Crimean War
BALADIN n dancer
BALADINE n female dancer
BALADINES > BALADINE
BALADINS > BALADIN
BALALAIKA n guitar-like musical instrument with a triangular body
BALANCE n stability of mind or body ▷ vb weigh in a balance
BALANCED adj having weight equally distributed
BALANCER n person or thing that balances
BALANCERS > BALANCER
BALANCES > BALANCE
BALANCING > BALANCE
BALANITIS n inflammation of the glans penis, usually due to infection
BALAS n red variety of spinel, used as a gemstone
BALASES > BALAS
BALATA n tropical American sapotaceous tree, Manilkara bidentata, yielding a latex-like sap
BALATAS > BALATA
BALBOA n standard currency unit of Panama, divided into 100 centesimos
BALBOAS > BALBOA
BALCONET n small balcony
BALCONETS > BALCONET
BALCONIED > BALCONY
BALCONIES > BALCONY
BALCONY n platform on the outside of a building with a rail along the outer edge
BALD adj having little or no hair on the scalp ▷ vb make bald
BALDACHIN n richly ornamented silk and gold brocade
BALDAQUIN same

*as* > BALDACHIN
**BALDED** > BALD
**BALDER** > BALD
**BALDEST** > BALD
**BALDFACED** *same as* > BALD
**BALDHEAD** *n* person with a bald head
**BALDHEADS** > BALDHEAD
**BALDICOOT** *another name for* > COOT
**BALDIER** > BALDY
**BALDIES** > BALDY
**BALDIEST** > BALDY
**BALDING** *adj* becoming bald
**BALDISH** > BALD
**BALDLY** > BALD
**BALDMONEY** *another name for* > SPIGNEL
**BALDNESS** > BALD
**BALDPATE** *n* person with a bald head
**BALDPATED** > BALDPATE
**BALDPATES** > BALDPATE
**BALDRIC** *n* wide silk sash or leather belt worn over the right shoulder to the left hip for carrying a sword, etc
**BALDRICK** *same as* > BALDRIC
**BALDRICKS** > BALDRICK
**BALDRICS** > BALDRIC
**BALDS** > BALD
**BALDY** *adj* bald ▷ *n* bald person
**BALE** *same as* > BAIL
**BALECTION** *same as* > BOLECTION
**BALED** > BALE
**BALEEN** *n* whalebone
**BALEENS** > BALEEN
**BALEFIRE** *n* bonfire
**BALEFIRES** > BALEFIRE
**BALEFUL** *adj* vindictive or menacing
**BALEFULLY** > BALEFUL
**BALER** > BAIL
**BALERS** > BAIL
**BALES** > BALE
**BALING** > BALE
**BALISAUR** *n* badger-like animal
**BALISAURS** > BALISAUR
**BALISTA** *same as* > BALLISTA
**BALISTAE** > BALISTA
**BALISTAS** > BALISTA
**BALK** *vb* stop short, esp suddenly or unexpectedly ▷ *n* roughly squared heavy timber beam
**BALKANISE** *variant of* > BALKANIZE
**BALKANIZE** *vb* divide (a territory) into small warring states
**BALKED** > BALK
**BALKER** > BALK
**BALKERS** > BALK
**BALKIER** > BALKY
**BALKIEST** > BALKY
**BALKILY** > BALKY
**BALKINESS** > BALKY
**BALKING** > BALK

**BALKINGLY** > BALK
**BALKINGS** > BALK
**BALKLINE** *n* line delimiting the balk area on a snooker table
**BALKLINES** > BALKLINE
**BALKS** > BALK
**BALKY** *adj* inclined to stop abruptly and unexpectedly
**BALL** *n* round or nearly round object, esp one used in games ▷ *vb* form into a ball
**BALLABILE** *n* part of ballet where all dancers perform
**BALLABILI** > BALLABILE
**BALLAD** *n* narrative poem or song ▷ *vb* sing or write a ballad
**BALLADE** *n* verse form consisting of three stanzas and an envoy, all ending with the same line
**BALLADED** > BALLAD
**BALLADEER** *n* singer of ballads ▷ *vb* perform as a balladeer
**BALLADES** > BALLADE
**BALLADIC** > BALLAD
**BALLADIN** *same as* > BALADIN
**BALLADINE** *same as* > BALADINE
**BALLADING** > BALLAD
**BALLADINS** > BALLADIN
**BALLADIST** > BALLAD
**BALLADRY** *n* ballad poetry or songs
**BALLADS** > BALLAD
**BALLAN** *n* species of fish
**BALLANS** > BALLAN
**BALLANT** *vb* write a ballad
**BALLANTED** > BALLANT
**BALLANTS** > BALLANT
**BALLAST** *n* substance, such as sand, used to stabilize a ship when it is not carrying cargo ▷ *vb* give stability or weight to
**BALLASTED** > BALLAST
**BALLASTER** > BALLAST
**BALLASTS** > BALLAST
**BALLAT** *vb* write a ballad
**BALLATED** > BALLAT
**BALLATING** > BALLAT
**BALLATS** > BALLAT
**BALLCLAY** *n* clay suitable for ceramics
**BALLCLAYS** > BALLCLAY
**BALLCOCK** *n* device for regulating the flow of a liquid into a tank, cistern, etc, consisting of a floating ball mounted at one end of an arm and a valve on the other end that opens and closes as the ball falls and rises
**BALLCOCKS** > BALLCOCK
**BALLED** > BALL
**BALLER** *n* ball-game player
**BALLERINA** *n* female ballet dancer
**BALLERINE** > BALLERINA

**BALLERS** > BALLER
**BALLET** *n* classical style of expressive dancing based on conventional steps
**BALLETED** > BALLAD
**BALLETIC** > BALLET
**BALLETING** > BALLAD
**BALLETS** > BALLET
**BALLGAME** *n* any game played with a ball
**BALLGAMES** > BALLGAME
**BALLHAWK** *n* skilled baseball player
**BALLHAWKS** > BALLHAWK
**BALLIES** > BALLY
**BALLING** > BALL
**BALLINGS** > BALL
**BALLISTA** *n* ancient catapult for hurling stones, etc
**BALLISTAE** > BALLISTA
**BALLISTAS** > BALLISTA
**BALLISTIC** *adj* of or relating to ballistics ▷ *n* the study of the flight of projectiles
**BALLIUM** *same as* > BAILEY
**BALLIUMS** > BALLIUM
**BALLOCKS** *same as* > BOLLOCKS
**BALLON** *n* light, graceful quality
**BALLONET** *n* air or gas compartment in a balloon or nonrigid airship, used to control buoyancy and shape
**BALLONETS** > BALLONET
**BALLONNE** *n* bouncing step
**BALLONNES** > BALLONNE
**BALLONS** > BALLON
**BALLOON** *n* inflatable rubber bag used as a plaything or decoration ▷ *vb* fly in a balloon
**BALLOONED** > BALLOON
**BALLOONS** > BALLOON
**BALLOT** *n* method of voting ▷ *vb* vote or ask for a vote from
**BALLOTED** > BALLOT
**BALLOTEE** > BALLOT
**BALLOTEES** > BALLOT
**BALLOTER** > BALLOT
**BALLOTERS** > BALLOT
**BALLOTING** > BALLOT
**BALLOTINI** *n* small glass beads
**BALLOTS** > BALLOT
**BALLOW** *n* heavy club
**BALLOWS** > BALLOW
**BALLPARK** *n* stadium used for baseball games
**BALLPARKS** > BALLPARK
**BALLPOINT** *n* pen with a tiny ball bearing as a writing point
**BALLROOM** *n* large hall for dancing
**BALLROOMS** > BALLROOM
**BALLS** *pl n* testicles
**BALLSIER** > BALLSY
**BALLSIEST** > BALLSY
**BALLSY** *adj* courageous

and spirited
**BALLUP** *n* something botched or muddled
**BALLUPS** > BALLUP
**BALLUTE** *n* inflatable balloon parachute
**BALLUTES** > BALLUTE
**BALLY** *another word for* > BALLYHOO
**BALLYARD** *n* baseball ground
**BALLYARDS** > BALLYARD
**BALLYHOO** *n* exaggerated fuss ▷ *vb* advertise or publicize by sensational or blatant methods
**BALLYHOOS** > BALLYHOO
**BALLYRAG** *same as* > BULLYRAG
**BALLYRAGS** > BALLYRAG
**BALM** *n* aromatic substance used for healing and soothing ▷ *vb* apply balm to
**BALMACAAN** *n* man's knee-length loose flaring overcoat with raglan sleeves
**BALMED** > BALM
**BALMIER** > BALMY
**BALMIEST** > BALMY
**BALMILY** > BALMY
**BALMINESS** > BALMY
**BALMING** > BALM
**BALMLIKE** > BALM
**BALMORAL** *n* laced walking shoe
**BALMORALS** > BALMORAL
**BALMS** > BALM
**BALMY** *adj* (of weather) mild and pleasant
**BALNEAL** *adj* of or relating to baths or bathing
**BALNEARY** *same as* > BALNEAL
**BALONEY** *n* foolish talk; nonsense
**BALONEYS** > BALONEY
**BALOO** *n* bear
**BALOOS** > BALOO
**BALS** > BAL
**BALSA** *n* very light wood from a tropical American tree
**BALSAM** *n* type of fragrant balm ▷ *vb* embalm
**BALSAMED** > BALSAM
**BALSAMIC** > BALSAM
**BALSAMING** > BALSAM
**BALSAMS** > BALSAM
**BALSAMY** > BALSAM
**BALSAS** > BALSA
**BALSAWOOD** *same as* > BALSA
**BALTHASAR** *same as* > BALTHAZAR
**BALTHAZAR** *n* wine bottle holding the equivalent of sixteen normal bottles (approximately 12 litres)
**BALTI** *n* spicy Indian dish served in a metal dish
**BALTIS** > BALTI
**BALU** *same as* > BALOO
**BALUN** *n* device for coupling

two electrical circuit
elements, such as an aerial
and its feeder cable, where
one is balanced and the
other is unbalanced
**BALUNS** > BALUN
**BALUS** > BALU
**BALUSTER** n set of posts
supporting a rail ▷ adj
(of a shape) swelling at
the base and rising in a
concave curve to a narrow
stem or neck
**BALUSTERS** > BALUSTER
**BALZARINE** n light fabric
**BAM** vb cheat
**BAMBI** n born-again
middle-aged biker: an
affluent middle-aged
man who rides a powerful
motorbike
**BAMBINI** > BAMBINO
**BAMBINO** n young child, esp
an Italian one
**BAMBINOS** > BAMBINO
**BAMBIS** > BAMBI
**BAMBOO** n tall treelike
tropical grass with hollow
stems
**BAMBOOS** > BAMBOO
**BAMBOOZLE** vb cheat or
mislead
**BAMMED** > BAM
**BAMMER** > BAM
**BAMMERS** > BAM
**BAMMING** > BAM
**BAMPOT** n fool
**BAMPOTS** > BAMPOT
**BAMS** > BAM
**BAN** vb prohibit or forbid
officially ▷ n official
prohibition
**BANAK** n tree of the genus
Virola, of Central America:
family Myristicaceae
**BANAKS** > BANAK
**BANAL** adj ordinary and
unoriginal
**BANALER** > BANAL
**BANALEST** > BANAL
**BANALISE** > BANAL
**BANALISED** > BANAL
**BANALISES** > BANAL
**BANALITY** > BANAL
**BANALIZE** > BANAL
**BANALIZED** > BANAL
**BANALIZES** > BANAL
**BANALLY** > BANAL
**BANANA** n yellow crescent-
shaped fruit
**BANANAS** adj crazy
**BANAUSIAN** > BANAUSIC
**BANAUSIC** adj merely
mechanical
**BANC** n in banc sitting as a
full court
**BANCO** n call made in
gambling games
**BANCOS** > BANCO
**BANCS** > BANC
**BAND** n group of musicians
playing together ▷ vb
unite
**BANDA** n African thatched

hut
**BANDAGE** n piece of
material used to cover a
wound or wrap an injured
limb ▷ vb cover with a
bandage
**BANDAGED** > BANDAGE
**BANDAGER** > BANDAGE
**BANDAGERS** > BANDAGE
**BANDAGES** > BANDAGE
**BANDAGING** > BANDAGE
**BANDAID** n tradename for
an adhesive plaster for cut
**BANDALORE** n old-
fashioned type of yo-yo
**BANDANA** same
as > BANDANNA
**BANDANAS** > BANDANA
**BANDANNA** n large brightly
coloured handkerchief or
neckerchief
**BANDANNAS** > BANDANNA
**BANDAR** n species of
monkey
**BANDARI** n Indian English
word for female monkey
**BANDARIS** > BANDARI
**BANDARS** > BANDAR
**BANDAS** > BANDA
**BANDBOX** n lightweight
usually cylindrical box for
hats
**BANDBOXES** > BANDBOX
**BANDBRAKE** n type of brake
**BANDEAU** n narrow ribbon
worn round the head
**BANDEAUS** > BANDEAU
**BANDEAUX** > BANDEAU
**BANDED** > BAND
**BANDELET** n moulding
round top of column
**BANDELETS** > BANDELET
**BANDELIER** same
as > BANDOLEER
**BANDER** > BAND
**BANDEROL** same
as > BANDEROLE
**BANDEROLE** n narrow flag
usually with forked ends
**BANDEROLS** > BANDEROL
**BANDERS** > BAND
**BANDH** n (in India) a general
strike
**BANDHS** > BANDH
**BANDICOOT** n ratlike
Australian marsupial
**BANDIED** > BANDY
**BANDIER** > BANDY
**BANDIES** > BANDY
**BANDIEST** > BANDY
**BANDINESS** > BANDY
**BANDING** n practice of
grouping schoolchildren
according to ability to
ensure a balanced intake
at different levels of ability
to secondary school
**BANDINGS** > BANDING
**BANDIT** n robber, esp a
member of an armed gang
**BANDITO** n Mexican bandit
**BANDITOS** > BANDITO
**BANDITRY** > BANDIT
**BANDITS** > BANDIT

**BANDITTI** > BANDIT
**BANDITTIS** > BANDIT
**BANDMATE** n fellow
member of band
**BANDMATES** > BANDMATE
**BANDOBAST** same
as > BANDOBUST
**BANDOBUST** n (in India and
Pakistan) an arrangement
**BANDOG** n ferocious dog
**BANDOGS** > BANDOG
**BANDOLEER** same
as > BANDOLIER
**BANDOLEON** same
as > BANDONEON
**BANDOLERO** n highwayman
**BANDOLIER** n shoulder belt
for holding cartridges
**BANDOLINE** n glutinous
hair dressing, used (esp
formerly) to keep the hair
in place
**BANDONEON** n type of
square concertina, esp
used in Argentina
**BANDONION** same
as > BANDONEON
**BANDOOK** same
as > BUNDOOK
**BANDOOKS** > BANDOOK
**BANDORA** same
as > BANDORE
**BANDORAS** > BANDORA
**BANDORE** n 16th-century
plucked musical
instrument resembling a
lute but larger and fitted
with seven pairs of metal
strings
**BANDORES** > BANDORE
**BANDROL** same
as > BANDEROLE
**BANDROLS** > BANDROL
**BANDS** > BAND
**BANDSAW** n power saw with
continuous blade
**BANDSAWS** > BANDSAW
**BANDSHELL** n bandstand
concave at back
**BANDSMAN** n player in a
musical band
**BANDSMEN** > BANDSMAN
**BANDSTAND** n roofed
outdoor platform for a
band
**BANDSTER** n binder of
wheat sheaves
**BANDSTERS** > BANDSTER
**BANDURA** n type of lute
**BANDURAS** > BANDURA
**BANDWAGON** n type of
wagon
**BANDWIDTH** n range of
frequencies within a
given waveband used for a
particular transmission
**BANDY** adj having legs
curved outwards at the
knees ▷ vb exchange
(words) in a heated
manner
**BANDYING** > BANDY
**BANDYINGS** > BANDY
**BANDYMAN** n carriage or

cart
**BANDYMEN** > BANDYMAN
**BANE** n person or thing
that causes misery or
distress ▷ vb cause harm
or distress to (someone)
**BANEBERRY** n any
ranunculaceous plant of
the genus Actaea, esp A.
spicata, which has small
white flowers and red or
white poisonous berries
**BANED** > BANE
**BANEFUL** adj destructive,
poisonous, or fatal
**BANEFULLY** > BANEFUL
**BANES** > BANE
**BANG** vb make a short
explosive noise
**BANGALAY** n myrtaceous
Australian tree, Eucalyptus
botryoides, valued for its
hard red wood
**BANGALAYS** > BANGALAY
**BANGALORE** as in bangalore
torpedo explosive device in
a long metal tube, used to
blow gaps in barbed-wire
barriers
**BANGALOW** n Australian
palm, Archontophoenix
cunninghamiana, native
to New South Wales and
Queensland
**BANGALOWS** > BANGALOW
**BANGED** > BANG
**BANGER** n old decrepit car
**BANGERS** > BANGER
**BANGING** > BANG
**BANGINGS** > BANG
**BANGKOK** n type of straw
hat
**BANGKOKS** > BANGKOK
**BANGLE** n bracelet worn
round the arm or the ankle
**BANGLED** > BANGLE
**BANGLES** > BANGLE
**BANGS** > BANG
**BANGSRING** same
as > BANXRING
**BANGSTER** n ruffian
**BANGSTERS** > BANGSTER
**BANGTAIL** n horse's tail cut
straight across but not
through the bone
**BANGTAILS** > BANGTAIL
**BANI** > BAN
**BANIA** same as > BANYAN
**BANIAN** same as > BANYAN
**BANIANS** > BANYAN
**BANIAS** > BANIA
**BANING** > BANE
**BANISH** vb send (someone)
into exile
**BANISHED** > BANISH
**BANISHER** > BANISH
**BANISHERS** > BANISH
**BANISHES** > BANISH
**BANISHING** > BANISH
**BANISTER** same
as > BANNISTER
**BANISTERS** pl n railing
supported by posts on a
staircase

**BANJAX** vb ruin; destroy
**BANJAXED** > BANJAX
**BANJAXES** > BANJAX
**BANJAXING** > BANJAX
**BANJO** n guitar-like musical instrument with a circular body
**BANJOES** > BANJO
**BANJOIST** > BANJO
**BANJOISTS** > BANJO
**BANJOS** > BANJO
**BANJULELE** n small banjo
**BANK** n institution offering services such as the safekeeping and lending of money ▷ vb deposit (cash or cheques) in a bank
**BANKABLE** adj likely to ensure financial success
**BANKBOOK** n book held by depositors at certain banks, in which the bank enters a record of deposits, withdrawals, and earned interest
**BANKBOOKS** > BANKBOOK
**BANKCARD** n card guaranteeing payment of cheque
**BANKCARDS** > BANKCARD
**BANKED** > BANK
**BANKER** n manager or owner of a bank
**BANKERLY** > BANKER
**BANKERS** > BANKER
**BANKET** n gold-bearing conglomerate found in South Africa
**BANKETS** > BANKET
**BANKING** > BANK
**BANKINGS** > BANK
**BANKIT** same as > BANQUETTE
**BANKITS** > BANKIT
**BANKNOTE** n piece of paper money
**BANKNOTES** > BANKNOTE
**BANKROLL** n roll of currency notes ▷ vb provide the capital for
**BANKROLLS** > BANKROLL
**BANKRUPT** n person declared by a court to be unable to pay his or her debts ▷ adj financially ruined ▷ vb make bankrupt
**BANKRUPTS** > BANKRUPT
**BANKS** > BANK
**BANKSIA** n Australian evergreen tree or shrub
**BANKSIAS** > BANKSIA
**BANKSIDE** n riverside
**BANKSIDES** > BANKSIDE
**BANKSMAN** n crane driver's helper, who signals instructions to the driver for the movement of the crane and its jib
**BANKSMEN** > BANKSMAN
**BANLIEUE** n suburb of a city
**BANLIEUES** > BANLIEUE
**BANNABLE** > BAN

**BANNED** > BAN
**BANNER** n long strip of cloth displaying a slogan, advertisement, etc ▷ vb (of a newspaper headline) to display (a story) prominently ▷ adj outstandingly successful
**BANNERALL** same as > BANDEROLE
**BANNERED** > BANNER
**BANNERET** n small banner
**BANNERETS** > BANNERET
**BANNERING** > BANNER
**BANNEROL** same as > BANDEROLE
**BANNEROLS** > BANNEROL
**BANNERS** > BANNER
**BANNET** n bonnet
**BANNETS** > BANNET
**BANNING** > BAN
**BANNISTER** same as > BANISTERS
**BANNOCK** n round flat cake made from oatmeal or barley
**BANNOCKS** > BANNOCK
**BANNS** pl n public declaration, esp in a church, of an intended marriage
**BANOFFEE** n filling for a pie, consisting of toffee and banana
**BANOFFEES** > BANOFFEE
**BANOFFI** same as > BANOFFEE
**BANOFFIS** > BANOFFI
**BANQUET** n elaborate formal dinner ▷ vb hold or take part in a banquet
**BANQUETED** > BANQUET
**BANQUETER** > BANQUET
**BANQUETS** > BANQUET
**BANQUETTE** n upholstered bench
**BANS** same as > BANNS
**BANSELA** same as > BONSELA
**BANSELAS** > BANSELA
**BANSHEE** n (in Irish folklore) female spirit whose wailing warns of a coming death
**BANSHEES** > BANSHEE
**BANSHIE** same as > BANSHEE
**BANSHIES** > BANSHIE
**BANT** n string ▷ vb tie with string
**BANTAM** n small breed of chicken
**BANTAMS** > BANTAM
**BANTED** > BANT
**BANTENG** n wild ox
**BANTENGS** > BANTENG
**BANTER** vb tease jokingly ▷ n teasing or joking conversation
**BANTERED** > BANTER
**BANTERER** > BANTER
**BANTERERS** > BANTER
**BANTERING** > BANTER
**BANTERS** > BANTER
**BANTIES** > BANTY
**BANTING** > BANT

**BANTINGS** > BANT
**BANTLING** n young child
**BANTLINGS** > BANTLING
**BANTS** > BANT
**BANTU** n offensive name for a person who speaks a Bantu language
**BANTUS** > BANTU
**BANTY** n bantam
**BANXRING** n tree-shrew
**BANXRINGS** > BANXRING
**BANYAN** n Indian tree whose branches grow down into the soil forming additional trunks
**BANYANS** > BANYAN
**BANZAI** interj patriotic cheer, battle cry, or salutation
**BANZAIS** > BANZAI
**BAOBAB** n African tree with a thick trunk and angular branches
**BAOBABS** > BAOBAB
**BAP** n large soft bread roll
**BAPS** > BAP
**BAPTISE** same as > BAPTIZE
**BAPTISED** > BAPTISE
**BAPTISER** > BAPTISE
**BAPTISERS** > BAPTISE
**BAPTISES** > BAPTISE
**BAPTISIA** n species of wild flower
**BAPTISIAS** > BAPTISIA
**BAPTISING** > BAPTISE
**BAPTISM** n Christian religious ceremony in which a person is immersed in or sprinkled with water as a sign of being cleansed from sin and accepted into the Church
**BAPTISMAL** > BAPTISM
**BAPTISMS** > BAPTISM
**BAPTIST** n one who baptizes
**BAPTISTRY** n part of a Christian church in which baptisms are carried out
**BAPTISTS** > BAPTIST
**BAPTIZE** vb perform baptism on
**BAPTIZED** > BAPTIZE
**BAPTIZER** > BAPTIZE
**BAPTIZERS** > BAPTIZE
**BAPTIZES** > BAPTIZE
**BAPTIZING** > BAPTIZE
**BAPU** n spiritual father
**BAPUS** > BAPU
**BAR** n rigid usually straight length of metal, wood, etc, that is longer than it is wide or thick, used esp as a barrier or as a structural or mechanical part ▷ vb fasten or secure with a bar
**BARACAN** same as > BARRACAN
**BARACANS** > BARACAN
**BARACHOIS** n (in the Atlantic Provinces of Canada) a shallow lagoon formed by a sand bar

**BARAGOUIN** n incomprehensible language
**BARASINGA** n type of deer
**BARATHEA** n fabric made of silk and wool or cotton and rayon, used esp for coats
**BARATHEAS** > BARATHEA
**BARATHRUM** n abyss
**BARAZA** n place where public meetings are held
**BARAZAS** > BARAZA
**BARB** n cutting remark ▷ vb provide with a barb or barbs
**BARBAL** adj of a beard
**BARBARIAN** n member of a primitive or uncivilized people ▷ adj uncivilized or brutal
**BARBARIC** adj cruel or brutal
**BARBARISE** same as > BARBARIZE
**BARBARISM** n condition of being backward or ignorant
**BARBARITY** n state of being barbaric or barbarous
**BARBARIZE** vb make or become barbarous
**BARBAROUS** adj uncivilized
**BARBASCO** n S American plant
**BARBASCOS** > BARBASCO
**BARBASTEL** n insectivorous forest bat
**BARBATE** adj having tufts of long hairs
**BARBATED** > BARBATE
**BARBE** n Waldensian missionary
**BARBECUE** n grill on which food is cooked over hot charcoal, usu. outdoors ▷ vb cook (food) on a barbecue
**BARBECUED** > BARBECUE
**BARBECUER** > BARBECUE
**BARBECUES** > BARBECUE
**BARBED** > BARB
**BARBEL** n long thin growth that hangs from the jaws of certain fishes, such as the carp
**BARBELL** n long metal rod to which heavy discs are attached at each end for weightlifting
**BARBELLS** > BARBELL
**BARBELS** > BARBEL
**BARBEQUE** same as > BARBECUE
**BARBEQUED** > BARBEQUE
**BARBEQUES** > BARBEQUE
**BARBER** n person who cuts men's hair and shaves beards ▷ vb cut the hair of
**BARBERED** > BARBER
**BARBERING** > BARBER
**BARBERRY** n shrub with orange or red berries
**BARBERS** > BARBER
**BARBES** > BARBE

**BARBET** n any small tropical brightly coloured bird of the family *Capitonidae*, having short weak wings and a sharp stout bill with tuftlike feathers at its base: order *Piciformes* (woodpeckers, etc)
**BARBETS** > BARBET
**BARBETTE** n (formerly) an earthen platform inside a parapet, from which heavy guns could fire over the top
**BARBETTES** > BARBETTE
**BARBICAN** n walled defence to protect a gate or drawbridge of a fortification
**BARBICANS** > BARBICAN
**BARBICEL** n any of the minute hooks on the barbules of feathers that interlock with those of adjacent barbules
**BARBICELS** > BARBICEL
**BARBIE** short for > BARBECUE
**BARBIES** > BARBIE
**BARBING** > BARB
**BARBITAL** same as > BARBITONE
**BARBITALS** > BARBITAL
**BARBITONE** n long-acting barbiturate used medicinally, usually in the form of the sodium salt, as a sedative or hypnotic
**BARBLESS** > BARB
**BARBOLA** n small models of flowers, etc made from plastic paste
**BARBOLAS** > BARBOLA
**BARBOTINE** n clay used in making decorated pottery
**BARBS** > BARB
**BARBULE** n very small barb
**BARBULES** > BARBULE
**BARBUT** n open-faced helmet
**BARBUTS** > BARBUT
**BARBWIRE** n barbed wire
**BARBWIRES** > BARBWIRE
**BARBY** > BARBECUE
**BARCA** n boat
**BARCAROLE** n Venetian boat song
**BARCAS** > BARCA
**BARCHAN** n crescent-shaped shifting sand dune, convex on the windward side and steeper and concave on the leeward
**BARCHANE** same as > BARCHAN
**BARCHANES** > BARCHANE
**BARCHANS** > BARCHAN
**BARD** n poet ▷ vb place a piece of pork fat on
**BARDASH** n kept boy in a homosexual relationship
**BARDASHES** > BARDASH
**BARDE** same as > BARD
**BARDED** > BARDE
**BARDES** > BARDE

**BARDIC** > BARD
**BARDIE** n type of Australian grub
**BARDIER** > BARD
**BARDIES** > BARDIE
**BARDIEST** > BARD
**BARDING** > BARD
**BARDISM** > BARD
**BARDISMS** > BARD
**BARDLING** n inferior poet
**BARDLINGS** > BARDLING
**BARDO** n (in Tibetan Buddhism) the state of the soul between its death and its rebirth
**BARDOS** > BARDO
**BARDS** > BARD
**BARDSHIP** > BARD
**BARDSHIPS** > BARD
**BARDY** > BARD
**BARE** adj unclothed, naked ▷ vb uncover
**BAREBACK** adv (of horse-riding) without a saddle
**BAREBOAT** n boat chartered without crew, provisions, etc
**BAREBOATS** > BAREBOAT
**BAREBONE** n computer casing containing bare essentials
**BAREBONED** adj short of resources
**BAREBONES** > BAREBONE
**BARED** > BARE
**BAREFACED** adj shameless or obvious
**BAREFIT** > BAREFOOT
**BAREFOOT** adv with the feet uncovered
**BAREGE** n light silky gauze fabric made of wool ▷ adj made of such a fabric
**BAREGES** > BAREGE
**BAREGINE** n curative ingredient in thermal waters
**BAREGINES** > BAREGINE
**BAREHAND** vb handle with bare hands
**BAREHANDS** > BAREHAND
**BAREHEAD** adv with head unvovered
**BARELY** adv only just
**BARENESS** > BARE
**BARER** > BARE
**BARES** > BARE
**BARESARK** another word for > BERSERK
**BARESARKS** > BARESARK
**BAREST** > BARE
**BARF** vb vomit ▷ n act of vomiting
**BARFED** > BARF
**BARFING** > BARF
**BARFLIES** > BARFLY
**BARFLY** n person who frequents bars
**BARFS** > BARF
**BARFUL** adj presenting difficulties
**BARGAIN** n agreement establishing what each party will give, receive, or

perform in a transaction ▷ vb negotiate the terms of an agreement
**BARGAINED** > BARGAIN
**BARGAINER** > BARGAIN
**BARGAINS** > BARGAIN
**BARGANDER** same as > BERGANDER
**BARGE** n flat-bottomed boat used to transport freight ▷ vb push violently
**BARGED** > BARGE
**BARGEE** n person in charge of a barge
**BARGEES** > BARGEE
**BARGEESE** > BARGOOSE
**BARGELLO** n zigzag tapestry stitch
**BARGELLOS** > BARGELLO
**BARGEMAN** same as > BARGEE
**BARGEMEN** > BARGEMAN
**BARGEPOLE** n long pole used to propel a barge
**BARGES** > BARGE
**BARGEST** same as > BARGHEST
**BARGESTS** > BARGEST
**BARGHEST** n mythical goblin in the shape of a dog
**BARGHESTS** > BARGHEST
**BARGING** > BARGE
**BARGOON** Canadian word for > BARGAIN
**BARGOONS** > BARGOON
**BARGOOSE** n type of goose; sheldrake
**BARGUEST** same as > BARGHEST
**BARGUESTS** > BARGUEST
**BARHOP** vb visit several bars in succession
**BARHOPPED** > BARHOP
**BARHOPS** > BARHOP
**BARIATRIC** adj of the treatment of obesity
**BARIC** adj of or containing barium
**BARILLA** n impure mixture of sodium carbonate and sodium sulphate obtained from the ashes of certain plants, such as the saltworts
**BARILLAS** > BARILLA
**BARING** > BARE
**BARISH** adj quite thinly covered
**BARISTA** n person who makes and sells coffee in a coffee bar
**BARISTAS** > BARISTA
**BARITE** n colourless or white mineral consisting of barium sulphate in orthorhombic crystalline form, occurring in sedimentary rocks and with sulphide ores: a source of barium.
**BARITES** > BARITE
**BARITONAL** > BARITONE
**BARITONE** n (singer with) the second lowest adult

male voice ▷ adj relating to or denoting a baritone
**BARITONES** > BARITONE
**BARIUM** n soft white metallic element
**BARIUMS** > BARIUM
**BARK** vb (of a dog) make its typical loud abrupt cry
**BARKAN** same as > BARCHAN
**BARKANS** > BARKAN
**BARKED** > BARK
**BARKEEP** n barkeeper
**BARKEEPER** another name (esp US) for > BARTENDER
**BARKEEPS** > BARKEEP
**BARKEN** vb become dry with a bark-like outer layer
**BARKENED** > BARKEN
**BARKENING** > BARKEN
**BARKENS** > BARKEN
**BARKER** n person at a fairground who calls loudly to passers-by in order to attract customers
**BARKERS** > BARKER
**BARKHAN** same as > BARCHAN
**BARKHANS** > BARKHAN
**BARKIER** > BARKY
**BARKIEST** > BARKY
**BARKING** adj mad ▷ adv extremely
**BARKLESS** > BARK
**BARKS** > BARK
**BARKY** adj having the texture or appearance of bark
**BARLEDUC** n French preserve made of currants
**BARLEDUCS** > BARLEDUC
**BARLESS** > BAR
**BARLEY** n tall grasslike plant cultivated for grain ▷ sentence substitute cry for truce or respite from the rules of a game
**BARLEYS** > BARLEY
**BARLOW** n type of strong knife
**BARLOWS** > BARLOW
**BARM** n yeasty froth on fermenting malt liquors
**BARMAID** n woman who serves in a pub
**BARMAIDS** > BARMAID
**BARMAN** same as > BARTENDER
**BARMBRACK** n loaf of bread with currants in it
**BARMEN** > BARMAN
**BARMIE** same as > BARMY
**BARMIER** > BARMY
**BARMIEST** > BARMY
**BARMINESS** > BARMY
**BARMKIN** n protective wall around castle
**BARMKINS** > BARMKIN
**BARMS** > BARM
**BARMY** adj insane
**BARN** n large building on a farm used for storing grain ▷ vb keep in a barn
**BARNACLE** n shellfish that lives attached to rocks, ship bottoms, etc

BARNACLED > BARNACLE
BARNACLES > BARNACLE
BARNBRACK same
as > BARMBRACK
BARNED > BARN
BARNET n hair
BARNETS > BARNET
BARNEY n noisy fight or
argument ▷ vb argue or
quarrel
BARNEYED > BARNEY
BARNEYING > BARNEY
BARNEYS > BARNEY
BARNIER > BARNY
BARNIEST > BARNY
BARNING > BARN
BARNLIKE > BARN
BARNS > BARN
BARNSTORM vb tour rural
districts putting on shows
or making speeches in a
political campaign
BARNY adj reminiscent of
a barn
BARNYARD n yard adjoining
a barn
BARNYARDS > BARNYARD
BAROCCO same
as > BAROQUE
BAROCCOS > BAROCCO
BAROCK same as > BAROQUE
BAROCKS > BAROCK
BAROGRAM n record of
atmospheric pressure
traced by a barograph or
similar instrument
BAROGRAMS > BAROGRAM
BAROGRAPH n barometer
that automatically keeps
a record of changes in
atmospheric pressure
BAROLO n red Italian wine
BAROLOS > BAROLO
BAROMETER n instrument
for measuring
atmospheric pressure
BAROMETRY > BAROMETER
BAROMETZ n fern whose
woolly rhizoma resemble
a lamb
BARON n member of the
lowest rank of nobility
BARONAGE n barons
collectively
BARONAGES > BARONAGE
BARONESS n woman
holding the rank of baron
BARONET n commoner
who holds the lowest
hereditary British title
BARONETCY n rank,
position, or patent of a
baronet
BARONETS > BARONET
BARONG n broad-bladed
cleaver-like knife used in
the Philippines
BARONGS > BARONG
BARONIAL adj of, relating
to, or befitting a baron or
barons
BARONIES > BARONY
BARONNE n baroness
BARONNES > BARONNE

BARONS > BARON
BARONY n domain or rank
of a baron
BAROPHILE > BAROPHILIC
BAROQUE n highly ornate
style of art, architecture,
or music from the late 16th
to the early 18th century
▷ adj ornate in style
BAROQUELY > BAROQUE
BAROQUES > BAROQUE
BAROSAUR n large dinosaur
BAROSAURS > BAROSAUR
BAROSCOPE n any
instrument for measuring
atmospheric pressure,
esp a manometer with
one side open to the
atmosphere
BAROSTAT n device for
maintaining constant
pressure, such as one used
in an aircraft cabin
BAROSTATS > BAROSTAT
BAROUCHE n four-
wheeled horse-drawn
carriage, popular in the
19th century, having a
retractable hood over the
rear half, seats inside for
two couples facing each
other, and a driver's seat
outside at the front
BAROUCHES > BAROUCHE
BARP n hillock or bank of
stones
BARPERSON n person who
serves in a pub: used esp in
advertisements
BARPS > BARP
BARQUE n sailing ship, esp
one with three masts
BARQUES > BARQUE
BARQUETTE n boat-shaped
pastry shell
BARRA n barramundi
BARRABLE > BAR
BARRACAN n thick, strong
fabric
BARRACANS > BARRACAN
BARRACE n record of teams
entering a sports contest
BARRACES > BARRACE
BARRACK vb criticize loudly
or shout against (a team or
speaker)
BARRACKED > BARRACK
BARRACKER > BARRACK
BARRACKS pl n building
used to accommodate
military personnel
BARRACOON n (formerly)
a temporary place of
confinement for slaves
or convicts, esp those
awaiting transportation
BARRACUDA n tropical sea
fish
BARRAGE n continuous
delivery of questions,
complaints, etc ▷ vb
attack or confront with a
barrage
BARRAGED > BARRAGE

BARRAGES > BARRAGE
BARRAGING > BARRAGE
BARRANCA n ravine or
precipice
BARRANCAS > BARRANCA
BARRANCO same
as > BARRANCA
BARRANCOS > BARRANCO
BARRAS > BARRA
BARRAT n fraudulent
dealings
BARRATER same
as > BARRATOR
BARRATERS > BARRATER
BARRATOR n person guilty
of barratry
BARRATORS > BARRATOR
BARRATRY n (formerly)
the vexatious stirring up
of quarrels or bringing of
lawsuits
BARRATS > BARRAT
BARRE n rail at hip height
used for ballet practice
▷ vb execute guitar chords
by laying the index finger
over some or all of the
strings so that the pitch
of each stopped string is
simultaneously raised
▷ adv by using the barré
BARRED > BAR
BARREED > BARRE
BARREFULL same
as > BARFUL
BARREING > BARRE
BARREL n cylindrical
container with rounded
sides and flat ends ▷ vb
put in a barrel
BARRELAGE > BARREL
BARRELED > BARREL
BARRELFUL same
as > BARREL
BARRELING > BARREL
BARRELLED > BARREL
BARRELS > BARREL
BARREN adj (of a woman or
female animal) incapable
of producing offspring
BARRENER > BARREN
BARRENEST > BARREN
BARRENLY > BARREN
BARRENS pl n (in North
America) a stretch of
usually level land that
is sparsely vegetated or
barren
BARRES > BARRE
BARRET n small flat cap
resembling a biretta
BARRETOR n quarrelsome
person
BARRETORS > BARRETOR
BARRETRY same
as > BARRATRY
BARRETS > BARRET
BARRETTE n clasp or pin
for holding women's hair
in place
BARRETTER same
as > BARRETOR
BARRETTES > BARRETTE
BARRICADE n barrier,

esp one erected hastily
for defence ▷ vb erect
a barricade across (an
entrance)
BARRICADO same
as > BARRICADE
BARRICO n small container
for liquids
BARRICOES > BARRICO
BARRICOS > BARRICO
BARRIE adj very good
BARRIER n anything that
prevents access, progress,
or union ▷ vb create or
form a barrier
BARRIERED > BARRIER
BARRIERS > BARRIER
BARRIES > BARRY
BARRIEST > BARRY
BARRING > BAR
BARRINGS > BAR
BARRIO n Spanish-
speaking quarter in a town
or city, esp in the US
BARRIOS > BARRIO
BARRISTER n lawyer
qualified to plead in a
higher court
BARRO adj embarrassing
BARROOM n room or
building where alcoholic
drinks are served over a
counter
BARROOMS > BARROOM
BARROW n wheelbarrow
BARROWFUL same
as > BARROW
BARROWS > BARROW
BARRULET n narrow band
across heraldic shield
BARRULETS > BARRULET
BARRY n mistake or blunder
BARS > BAR
BARSTOOL n high stool in
bar
BARSTOOLS > BARSTOOL
BARTEND vb serve drinks
from a bar
BARTENDED > BARTEND
BARTENDER n man who
serves in a bar
BARTENDS > BARTEND
BARTER vb trade (goods) in
exchange for other goods
▷ n trade by the exchange
of goods
BARTERED > BARTER
BARTERER > BARTER
BARTERERS > BARTER
BARTERING > BARTER
BARTERS > BARTER
BARTISAN same
as > BARTIZAN
BARTISANS > BARTISAN
BARTIZAN n small turret
projecting from a wall,
parapet, or tower
BARTIZANS > BARTIZAN
BARTON n farmyard
BARTONS > BARTON
BARTSIA n type of
semiparasitic plant
BARTSIAS > BARTSIA
BARWARE n glasses, etc

used in a bar
**BARWARES** > BARWARE
**BARWOOD** n red wood from small African tree
**BARWOODS** > BARWOOD
**BARYE** n unit of pressure in the cgs system equal to one dyne per square centimetre. 1 barye is equivalent to 1 microbar
**BARYES** > BARYE
**BARYON** n elementary particle that has a mass greater than or equal to that of the proton
**BARYONIC** adj of or relating to a baryon
**BARYONS** > BARYON
**BARYTA** same as > BARITE
**BARYTAS** > BARYTA
**BARYTE** same as > BARYTA
**BARYTES** > BARYTE
**BARYTIC** > BARYTA
**BARYTON** n bass viol with sympathetic strings as well as its six main strings
**BARYTONE** adj having the last syllable unaccented ▷ n word in which the last syllable is unaccented
**BARYTONES** > BARYTONE
**BARYTONS** > BARYTON
**BAS** > BA
**BASAL** adj of, at, or constituting a base
**BASALLY** > BASAL
**BASALT** n dark volcanic rock
**BASALTES** n unglazed black stoneware
**BASALTIC** > BASALT
**BASALTINE** n type of mineral
**BASALTS** > BASALT
**BASAN** n sheepskin tanned in bark
**BASANITE** n black basaltic rock containing plagioclase, augite, olivine, and nepheline, leucite, or analcite, formerly used as a touchstone
**BASANITES** > BASANITE
**BASANS** > BASAN
**BASCINET** same as > BASINET
**BASCINETS** > BASCINET
**BASCULE** n drawbridge that operates by a counterbalanced weight
**BASCULES** > BASCULE
**BASE** n bottom or supporting part of anything ▷ vb use as a basis (for) ▷ adj dishonourable or immoral
**BASEBALL** n team game in which runs are scored by hitting a ball with a bat then running round four bases
**BASEBALLS** > BASEBALL
**BASEBAND** n transmission

technique using a narrow range of frequencies that allows only one message to be telecommunicated at a time
**BASEBANDS** > BASEBAND
**BASEBOARD** n board functioning as the base of anything
**BASEBORN** adj born of humble parents
**BASED** > BASE
**BASELARD** n short sword
**BASELARDS** > BASELARD
**BASELESS** adj not based on fact
**BASELINE** n value or starting point on an imaginary scale with which other things are compared
**BASELINER** n tennis player who plays most of his or her shots from the back of the court
**BASELINES** > BASELINE
**BASELY** > BASE
**BASEMAN** n fielder positioned near a base
**BASEMEN** > BASEMAN
**BASEMENT** n partly or wholly underground storey of a building
**BASEMENTS** > BASEMENT
**BASENESS** > BASE
**BASENJI** n small smooth-haired breed of dog of African origin having a tightly curled tail and an inability to bark
**BASENJIS** > BASENJI
**BASEPLATE** n flat supporting plate or frame
**BASER** > BASE
**BASES** > BASIS
**BASEST** > BASE
**BASH** vb hit violently or forcefully ▷ n heavy blow
**BASHAW** n important or pompous person
**BASHAWISM** > BASHAW
**BASHAWS** > BASHAW
**BASHED** > BASH
**BASHER** > BASH
**BASHERS** > BASH
**BASHES** > BASH
**BASHFUL** adj shy or modest
**BASHFULLY** > BASHFUL
**BASHING** > BASH
**BASHINGS** > BASH
**BASHLESS** adj not ashamed
**BASHLIK** n Caucasian hood
**BASHLIKS** > BASHLIK
**BASHLYK** same as > BASHLIK
**BASHLYKS** > BASHLYK
**BASHO** n grand tournament in sumo wrestling
**BASIC** adj of or forming a base or basis ▷ n fundamental principle, fact, etc
**BASICALLY** adv in a fundamental or elementary manner

**BASICITY** n state of being a base
**BASICS** > BASIC
**BASIDIA** > BASIDIUM
**BASIDIAL** > BASIDIUM
**BASIDIUM** n structure, produced by basidiomycetous fungi after sexual reproduction, in which spores are formed at the tips of projecting slender stalks
**BASIFIED** > BASIFY
**BASIFIER** > BASIFY
**BASIFIERS** > BASIFY
**BASIFIES** > BASIFY
**BASIFIXED** adj (of an anther) attached to the filament by its base
**BASIFUGAL** a less common word for > ACROPETAL
**BASIFY** vb make basic
**BASIFYING** > BASIFY
**BASIL** n aromatic herb used in cooking
**BASILAR** adj of or situated at a base
**BASILARY** same as > BASILAR
**BASILECT** n debased dialect
**BASILECTS** > BASILECT
**BASILIC** > BASILICA
**BASILICA** n rectangular church with a rounded end and two aisles
**BASILICAE** > BASILICA
**BASILICAL** > BASILICA
**BASILICAN** > BASILICA
**BASILICAS** > BASILICA
**BASILICON** n healing ointment
**BASILISK** n legendary serpent said to kill by its breath or glance
**BASILISKS** > BASILISK
**BASILS** > BASIL
**BASIN** n round open container
**BASINAL** > BASIN
**BASINED** > BASIN
**BASINET** n close-fitting medieval helmet of light steel usually with a visor
**BASINETS** > BASINET
**BASINFUL** n amount a basin will hold
**BASINFULS** > BASINFUL
**BASING** > BASE
**BASINLIKE** > BASIN
**BASINS** > BASIN
**BASION** n (in anatomy) midpoint on the forward border of the foramen magnum
**BASIONS** > BASION
**BASIPETAL** adj (of leaves and flowers) produced in order from the apex downwards so that the youngest are at the base
**BASIS** n fundamental principles etc from which something is started or developed

**BASK** vb lie in or be exposed to something, esp pleasant warmth
**BASKED** > BASK
**BASKET** n container made of interwoven strips of wood or cane
**BASKETFUL** n as much as a basket will hold
**BASKETRY** n art or practice of making baskets
**BASKETS** > BASKET
**BASKING** > BASK
**BASKS** > BASK
**BASMATI** n variety of long-grain rice with slender aromatic grains, used for savoury dishes
**BASMATIS** > BASMATI
**BASNET** same as > BASINET
**BASNETS** > BASNET
**BASOCHE** n society of medieval French lawyers who performed comic plays
**BASOCHES** > BASOCHE
**BASON** same as > BASIN
**BASONS** > BASON
**BASOPHIL** adj (of cells or cell contents) easily stained by basic dyes ▷ n basophil cell, esp a leucocyte
**BASOPHILE** same as > BASOPHIL
**BASOPHILS** > BASOPHIL
**BASQUE** n tight-fitting bodice for women
**BASQUED** > BASQUE
**BASQUES** > BASQUE
**BASQUINE** n tight-fitting bodice
**BASQUINES** > BASQUINE
**BASS** vb speak or sing in a low pitch
**BASSE** same as > BASS
**BASSED** > BASS
**BASSER** > BASS
**BASSES** > BASS
**BASSEST** > BASS
**BASSET** n long low smooth-haired breed of hound with short strong legs and long ears ▷ vb outcrop
**BASSETED** > BASSET
**BASSETING** > BASSET
**BASSETS** > BASSET
**BASSETT** same as > BASSET
**BASSETTED** > BASSET
**BASSETTS** > BASSET
**BASSI** > BASSO
**BASSIER** > BASSY
**BASSIEST** > BASSY
**BASSINET** n wickerwork or wooden cradle or pram, usually hooded
**BASSINETS** > BASSINET
**BASSING** > BASS
**BASSIST** n player of a double bass, esp in a jazz band
**BASSISTS** > BASSIST
**BASSLY** > BASS
**BASSNESS** > BASS

**BASSO** n singer with a bass voice

**BASSOON** n low-pitched woodwind instrument

**BASSOONS** > BASSOON

**BASSOS** > BASSO

**BASSWOOD** n any of several North American linden trees, esp Tilia americana

**BASSWOODS** > BASSWOOD

**BASSY** adj manifesting strong bass tones

**BAST** n fibrous material obtained from the phloem of jute, hemp, flax, lime, etc, used for making rope, matting, etc

**BASTA** interj enough; stop

**BASTARD** n offensive term for an obnoxious or despicable person ▷ adj offensive term for an illegitimate by birth

**BASTARDLY** > BASTARD

**BASTARDRY** n malicious or cruel behaviour

**BASTARDS** > BASTARD

**BASTARDY** n condition of being a bastard

**BASTE** vb moisten (meat) during cooking with hot fat

**BASTED** > BASTE

**BASTER** > BASTE

**BASTERS** > BASTE

**BASTES** > BASTE

**BASTI** n (in India) a slum inhabited by poor people

**BASTIDE** n small isolated house in France

**BASTIDES** > BASTIDE

**BASTILE** same as > BASTILLE

**BASTILES** > BASTILE

**BASTILLE** n prison

**BASTILLES** > BASTILLE

**BASTINADE** same as > BASTINADO

**BASTINADO** n punishment or torture by beating on the soles of the feet with a stick ▷ vb beat (a person) in this way

**BASTING** n loose temporary stitches

**BASTINGS** > BASTING

**BASTION** n projecting part of a fortification

**BASTIONED** > BASTION

**BASTIONS** > BASTION

**BASTIS** > BASTI

**BASTLE** n fortified house

**BASTLES** > BASTLE

**BASTO** n ace of clubs in certain card games

**BASTOS** > BASTO

**BASTS** > BAST

**BASUCO** n cocaine-based drug

**BASUCOS** > BASUCO

**BAT** n any of various types of club used to hit the ball in certain sports ▷ vb strike with or as if with a bat

**BATABLE** > BAT

**BATATA** n sweet potato

**BATATAS** > BATATA

**BATAVIA** n variety of lettuce with smooth pale green leaves

**BATAVIAS** > BATAVIA

**BATBOY** n boy who works at baseball game

**BATBOYS** > BATBOY

**BATCH** n group of people or things dealt with at the same time ▷ vb group (items) for efficient processing

**BATCHED** > BATCH

**BATCHER** > BATCH

**BATCHERS** > BATCH

**BATCHES** > BATCH

**BATCHING** > BATCH

**BATCHINGS** > BATCH

**BATE** vb (of hawks) to jump violently from a perch or the falconer's fist, often hanging from the leash while struggling to escape

**BATEAU** n light flat-bottomed boat used on rivers in Canada and the northern US

**BATEAUX** > BATEAU

**BATED** > BATE

**BATELESS** > BATE

**BATELEUR** n African crested bird of prey, Terathopius ecaudatus, with a short tail and long wings: subfamily Circaetinae, family Accipitridae (hawks, etc)

**BATELEURS** > BATELEUR

**BATEMENT** n reduction

**BATEMENTS** > BATEMENT

**BATES** > BATE

**BATFISH** n any angler of the family Ogcocephalidae, having a flattened scaleless body and moving on the sea floor by means of fleshy pectoral and pelvic fins

**BATFISHES** > BATFISH

**BATFOWL** vb catch birds by temporarily blinding them with light

**BATFOWLED** > BATFOWL

**BATFOWLER** > BATFOWL

**BATFOWLS** > BATFOWL

**BATGIRL** n girl who works at baseball games

**BATGIRLS** > BATGIRL

**BATH** n large container in which to wash the body ▷ vb wash in a bath

**BATHCUBE** n cube of soluble scented material for use in a bath

**BATHCUBES** > BATHCUBE

**BATHE** vb swim in open water for pleasure

**BATHED** > BATHE

**BATHER** > BATHE

**BATHERS** pl n swimming costume

**BATHES** > BATHE

**BATHETIC** adj containing or displaying bathos

**BATHHOUSE** n building containing baths, esp for public use

**BATHING** > BATHE

**BATHLESS** > BATH

**BATHMAT** n mat to stand on after a bath

**BATHMATS** > BATHMAT

**BATHMIC** > BATHMISM

**BATHMISM** n growth-force

**BATHMISMS** > BATHMISM

**BATHOLITE** same as > BATHOLITH

**BATHOLITH** n very large irregular-shaped mass of igneous rock, esp granite, formed from an intrusion of magma at great depth, esp one exposed after erosion of less resistant overlying rocks

**BATHORSE** n officer's packhorse

**BATHORSES** > BATHORSE

**BATHOS** n sudden ludicrous change in speech or writing from a serious subject to a trivial one

**BATHOSES** > BATHOS

**BATHROBE** n loose-fitting garment for wear before or after a bath or swimming

**BATHROBES** > BATHROBE

**BATHROOM** n room with a bath, sink, and usu. a toilet

**BATHROOMS** > BATHROOM

**BATHS** > BATH

**BATHTUB** n bath, esp one not permanently fixed

**BATHTUBS** > BATHTUB

**BATHWATER** n used or unused water in a bathtub

**BATHYAL** adj denoting or relating to an ocean depth of between 200 and 2000 metres (about 100 and 1000 fathoms), corresponding to the continental slope

**BATHYBIUS** n gelatinous substance on seabed

**BATHYLITE** same as > BATHOLITH

**BATHYLITH** same as > BATHOLITH

**BATIK** n process of printing fabric using wax to cover areas not to be dyed ▷ vb treat material with this process

**BATIKED** > BATIK

**BATIKING** > BATIK

**BATIKS** > BATIK

**BATING** > BATE

**BATISTE** n fine plain-weave cotton fabric: used esp for shirts and dresses

**BATISTES** > BATISTE

**BATLER** n flat piece of wood for beating clothes, etc before washing

**BATLERS** > BATLER

**BATLET** same as > BATLER

**BATLETS** > BATLER

**BATLIKE** > BAT

**BATMAN** n officer's servant in the armed forces

**BATMEN** > BATMAN

**BATOLOGY** n study of brambles

**BATON** n thin stick used by the conductor of an orchestra ▷ vb carry or wave a baton

**BATONED** > BATON

**BATONING** > BATON

**BATONS** > BATON

**BATOON** same as > BATON

**BATOONED** > BATOON

**BATOONING** > BATOON

**BATOONS** > BATOON

**BATRACHIA** n group of amphibians including frogs and toads

**BATS** > BAT

**BATSMAN** n person who bats or specializes in batting

**BATSMEN** > BATSMAN

**BATSWING** adj in the form of the wing of a bat

**BATSWOMAN** > BATSMAN

**BATSWOMEN** > BATSMAN

**BATT** same as > BAT

**BATTA** n soldier's allowance

**BATTALIA** n arrangement of army prepared for battle

**BATTALIAS** > BATTALIA

**BATTALION** n army unit consisting of three or more companies

**BATTAS** > BATTA

**BATTEAU** same as > BATEAU

**BATTEAUX** > BATTEAU

**BATTED** > BAT

**BATTEL** vb make fertile

**BATTELED** > BATTEL

**BATTELER** > BATTEL

**BATTELERS** > BATTEL

**BATTELING** > BATTEL

**BATTELLED** > BATTEL

**BATTELS** > BATTEL

**BATTEMENT** n extension of one leg forwards, sideways, or backwards, either once or repeatedly

**BATTEN** n strip of wood fixed to something, esp to hold it in place ▷ vb strengthen or fasten with battens

**BATTENED** > BATTEN

**BATTENER** > BATTEN

**BATTENERS** > BATTEN

**BATTENING** > BATTEN

**BATTENS** > BATTEN

**BATTER** vb hit repeatedly ▷ n mixture of flour, eggs, and milk, used in cooking

**BATTERED** adj subjected to persistent physical violence, esp by a close relative living in the same house

**BATTERER** n person who batters someone

BATTERERS > BATTERER

BATTERIE n movement in ballet involving the legs beating together

BATTERIES > BATTERY

BATTERING n act or practice of battering someone

BATTERO n heavy club

BATTEROS > BATTERO

BATTERS > BATTER

BATTERY n device that produces electricity in a torch, radio, etc ▷ adj kept in series of cages for intensive rearing

BATTIER > BATTY

BATTIEST > BATTY

BATTIK same as > BATIK

BATTIKS > BATTIK

BATTILL old spelling of > BATTLE

BATTILLED > BATTILL

BATTILLS > BATTILL

BATTINESS > BATTY

BATTING > BAT

BATTINGS > BAT

BATTLE n fight between large armed forces ▷ vb struggle

BATTLEBUS n coach that transports politicians and their advisers round the country during an election campaign

BATTLED > BATTLE

BATTLER > BATTLE

BATTLERS > BATTLE

BATTLES > BATTLE

BATTLING > BATTLE

BATTOLOGY n unnecessary repetition of words

BATTS > BATT

BATTU adj (in ballet) involving a beating movement

BATTUE n beating of woodland or cover to force game to flee in the direction of hunters

BATTUES > BATTUE

BATTUTA n (in music) a beat

BATTUTAS > BATTUTA

BATTY adj eccentric or crazy

BATWING adj shaped like the wings of a bat, as a black tie, collar, etc

BATWOMAN n female servant in any of the armed forces

BATWOMEN > BATWOMAN

BAUBEE same as > BAWBEE

BAUBEES > BAUBEE

BAUBLE n trinket of little value

BAUBLES > BAUBLE

BAUBLING > BAUBLE

BAUCHLE vb shuffle along

BAUCHLED > BAUCHLE

BAUCHLES > BAUCHLE

BAUCHLING > BAUCHLE

BAUD n unit used to measure the speed of transmission of electronic data

BAUDEKIN old variant of > BALDACHIN

BAUDEKINS > BAUDEKIN

BAUDRIC same as > BALDRIC

BAUDRICK same as > BALDRIC

BAUDRICKE same as > BALDRIC

BAUDRICKS > BAUDRICK

BAUDRICS > BAUDRIC

BAUDRONS n name for a cat

BAUDS > BAUD

BAUERA n small evergreen Australian shrub

BAUERAS > BAUERA

BAUHINIA n any climbing or shrubby leguminous plant of the genus Bauhinia, of tropical and warm regions, widely cultivated for ornament

BAUHINIAS > BAUHINIA

BAUK same as > BALK

BAUKED > BAUK

BAUKING > BAUK

BAUKS > BAUK

BAULK > BALK

BAULKED > BALK

BAULKER > BALK

BAULKERS > BALK

BAULKIER > BAULKY

BAULKIEST > BAULKY

BAULKILY > BALKY

BAULKING > BALK

BAULKS > BALK

BAULKY same as > BALKY

BAUR n humorous anecdote; joke

BAURS > BAUR

BAUSOND adj (of animal) dappled with white spots

BAUXITE n claylike substance that is the chief source of aluminium

BAUXITES > BAUXITE

BAUXITIC > BAUXITE

BAVARDAGE n chattering

BAVAROIS n cold dessert consisting of a rich custard set with gelatine and flavoured in various ways

BAVIN n impure limestone

BAVINS > BAVIN

BAWBEE n former Scottish silver coin

BAWBEES > BAWBEE

BAWBLE same as > BAUBLE

BAWBLES > BAWBLE

BAWCOCK n fine fellow

BAWCOCKS > BAWCOCK

BAWD n person who runs a brothel, esp a woman

BAWDIER > BAWDY

BAWDIES > BAWDY

BAWDIEST > BAWDY

BAWDILY > BAWDY

BAWDINESS > BAWDY

BAWDKIN same as > BALDACHIN

BAWDKINS > BAWDKIN

BAWDRIC n heavy belt to support sword

BAWDRICS > BAWDRIC

BAWDRIES > BAWDRY

BAWDRY n obscene talk or language

BAWDS > BAWD

BAWDY adj (of writing etc) containing humorous references to sex ▷ n obscenity or eroticism, esp in writing or drama

BAWL vb shout or weep noisily ▷ n loud shout or cry

BAWLED > BAWL

BAWLER > BAWL

BAWLERS > BAWL

BAWLEY n small fishing boat

BAWLEYS > BAWLEY

BAWLING > BAWL

BAWLINGS > BAWL

BAWLS > BAWL

BAWN n fortified enclosure

BAWNEEN same as > BAININ

BAWNEENS > BAWNEEN

BAWNS > BAWN

BAWR same as > BAUR

BAWRS > BAWR

BAWSUNT adj black and white in colour

BAWTIE n name for a dog

BAWTIES > BAWTIE

BAWTY same as > BAWTIE

BAXTER old variant of > BAKER

BAXTERS > BAXTER

BAY n wide semicircular indentation of a shoreline ▷ vb howl in deep tones

BAYADEER same as > BAYADERE

BAYADEERS > BAYADEER

BAYADERE n dancing girl, esp one serving in a Hindu temple ▷ adj (of fabric, etc) having horizontal stripes

BAYADERES > BAYADERE

BAYAMO n Cuban strong wind

BAYAMOS > BAYAMO

BAYARD n bay horse

BAYARDS > BAYARD

BAYBERRY n tropical American tree that yields an oil used in making bay rum

BAYE vb bathe

BAYED > BAY

BAYES > BAYE

BAYING > BAY

BAYLE n barrier

BAYLES > BAYLE

BAYMAN n fisherman

BAYMEN > BAYMAN

BAYONET n sharp blade that can be fixed to the end of a rifle ▷ vb stab with a bayonet

BAYONETED > BAYONET

BAYONETS > BAYONET

BAYOU n (in the southern US) a sluggish marshy tributary of a lake or river

BAYOUS > BAYOU

BAYS > BAY

BAYT same as > BATE

BAYTED > BAYT

BAYTING > BAYT

BAYTS > BAYT

BAYWOOD n light soft wood of a tropical American mahogany tree, Swietenia macrophylla, of the bay region of SE Mexico

BAYWOODS > BAYWOOD

BAYYAN n Islamic declaration

BAYYANS > BAYYAN

BAZAAR n sale in aid of charity

BAZAARS > BAZAAR

BAZAR same as > BAZAAR

BAZARS > BAZAR

BAZAZZ same as > PIZZAZZ

BAZAZZES > BAZAZZ

BAZILLION same as > GAZILLION

BAZOO a US slang word for > MOUTH

BAZOOKA n portable rocket launcher that fires an armour-piercing projectile

BAZOOKAS > BAZOOKA

BAZOOMS pl n woman's breasts

BAZOOS > BAZOO

BAZOUKI same as > BOUZOUKI

BAZOUKIS > BAZOUKI

BDELLIUM n any of several African or W Asian trees of the burseraceous genus Commiphora that yield a gum resin

BDELLIUMS > BDELLIUM

BE vb exist or live

BEACH n area of sand or pebbles on a shore ▷ vb run or haul (a boat) onto a beach

BEACHBALL n light ball for playing on beach

BEACHBOY n male lifeguard on beach

BEACHBOYS > BEACHBOY

BEACHCOMB vb collect objects, seashells, etc on seashore

BEACHED > BEACH

BEACHES > BEACH

BEACHGOER n person who goes to the beach

BEACHHEAD n beach captured by an attacking army on which troops can be landed

BEACHIER > BEACHY

BEACHIEST > BEACHY

BEACHING > BEACH

BEACHSIDE adj situated near a beach

BEACHWEAR n clothes suitable for the beach

BEACHY adj with gentle sandy slopes

BEACON n fire or light on a hill or tower, used as a

warning ▷ vb guide or warn
**BEACONED** > BEACON
**BEACONING** > BEACON
**BEACONS** > BEACON
**BEAD** n small piece of plastic, wood, etc, pierced for threading on a string to form a necklace etc ▷ vb decorate with beads
**BEADBLAST** n jet of small glass beads blown from a nozzle under air or steam pressure ▷ vb clean or treat (a surface) with a beadblast
**BEADED** > BEAD
**BEADER** n person making things with beads
**BEADERS** > BEADER
**BEADHOUSE** n chapel
**BEADIER** > BEADY
**BEADIEST** > BEADY
**BEADILY** > BEADY
**BEADINESS** > BEADY
**BEADING** n strip of moulding used for edging furniture
**BEADINGS** > BEADING
**BEADLE** n (formerly) a minor parish official who acted as an usher
**BEADLEDOM** n petty officialdom
**BEADLES** > BEADLE
**BEADLIKE** > BEAD
**BEADMAN** same as > BEADSMAN
**BEADMEN** > BEADMAN
**BEADROLL** n list of persons for whom prayers are to be offered
**BEADROLLS** > BEADROLL
**BEADS** > BEAD
**BEADSMAN** n person who prays for another's soul, esp one paid or fed for doing so
**BEADSMEN** > BEADSMAN
**BEADWORK** same as > BEADING
**BEADWORKS** > BEADWORK
**BEADY** adj small, round, and glittering
**BEAGLE** n small hound with short legs and drooping ears ▷ vb hunt with beagles, normally on foot
**BEAGLED** > BEAGLE
**BEAGLER** n person who hunts with beagles
**BEAGLERS** > BEAGLER
**BEAGLES** > BEAGLE
**BEAGLING** > BEAGLE
**BEAGLINGS** > BEAGLE
**BEAK** n projecting horny jaws of a bird ▷ vb strike with the beak
**BEAKED** > BEAK
**BEAKER** n large drinking cup
**BEAKERS** > BEAKER
**BEAKIER** > BEAK
**BEAKIEST** > BEAK

**BEAKLESS** > BEAK
**BEAKLIKE** > BEAK
**BEAKS** > BEAK
**BEAKY** > BEAK
**BEAM** n broad smile ▷ vb smile broadly
**BEAMED** > BEAM
**BEAMER** n full-pitched ball bowled at the batsman's head
**BEAMERS** > BEAMER
**BEAMIER** > BEAM
**BEAMIEST** > BEAM
**BEAMILY** > BEAM
**BEAMINESS** > BEAM
**BEAMING** > BEAM
**BEAMINGLY** > BEAM
**BEAMINGS** > BEAM
**BEAMISH** adj smiling
**BEAMISHLY** > BEAMISH
**BEAMLESS** > BEAM
**BEAMLET** n small beam
**BEAMLETS** > BEAMLET
**BEAMLIKE** > BEAM
**BEAMS** > BEAM
**BEAMY** > BEAM
**BEAN** n seed or pod of various plants, eaten as a vegetable or used to make coffee etc ▷ vb strike on the head
**BEANBAG** n small cloth bag filled with dried beans and thrown in games
**BEANBAGS** > BEANBAG
**BEANBALL** n baseball intended to hit batter's head
**BEANBALLS** > BEANBALL
**BEANED** > BEAN
**BEANERIES** > BEANERY
**BEANERY** n cheap restaurant
**BEANFEAST** n any festive or merry occasion
**BEANIE** n close-fitting woollen hat
**BEANIES** > BEANY
**BEANING** > BEAN
**BEANLIKE** > BEAN
**BEANO** n celebration or party
**BEANOS** > BEANO
**BEANPOLE** n tall thin person
**BEANPOLES** > BEANPOLE
**BEANS** > BEAN
**BEANSTALK** n stem of a bean plant
**BEANY** same as > BEANIE
**BEAR** vb support or hold up (something) ▷ n any plantigrade mammal of the family Ursidae
**BEARABLE** adj endurable
**BEARABLY** > BEARABLE
**BEARBERRY** n type of shrub
**BEARBINE** n type of bindweed
**BEARBINES** > BEARBINE
**BEARCAT** n lesser panda
**BEARCATS** > BEARCAT
**BEARD** n hair growing on the lower parts of a man's

face ▷ vb oppose boldly
**BEARDED** > BEARD
**BEARDIE** n another name for bearded loach
**BEARDIER** > BEARDY
**BEARDIES** > BEARDIE
**BEARDIEST** > BEARDY
**BEARDING** > BEARD
**BEARDLESS** adj without a beard
**BEARDS** > BEARD
**BEARDY** adj having a beard
**BEARE** same as > BEAR
**BEARED** > BEAR
**BEARER** n person who carries, presents, or upholds something
**BEARERS** > BEARER
**BEARES** > BEARE
**BEARGRASS** n North American plant
**BEARHUG** n wrestling hold in which the arms are locked tightly round an opponent's chest and arms
**BEARHUGS** > BEARHUG
**BEARING** > BEAR
**BEARINGS** > BEAR
**BEARISH** adj like a bear
**BEARISHLY** > BEARISH
**BEARLIKE** > BEAR
**BEARNAISE** n rich sauce made from egg yolks, lemon juice or wine vinegar, butter, shallots, herbs, and seasoning
**BEARS** > BEAR
**BEARSKIN** n tall fur helmet worn by some British soldiers
**BEARSKINS** > BEARSKIN
**BEARWARD** n bear keeper
**BEARWARDS** > BEARWARD
**BEARWOOD** another name for > CASCARA
**BEARWOODS** > BEARWOOD
**BEAST** n large wild animal
**BEASTHOOD** > BEAST
**BEASTIE** n small animal
**BEASTIES** > BEASTIE
**BEASTILY** > BESTIAL
**BEASTINGS** same as > BEESTINGS
**BEASTLIER** > BEASTLY
**BEASTLIKE** > BEAST
**BEASTLY** adj unpleasant or disagreeable ▷ adv extremely
**BEASTOID** n autonomous robot that can perform some of the tasks of animals
**BEASTOIDS** > BEASTOID
**BEASTS** > BEAST
**BEAT** vb strike with or as if with a series of violent blows; dash or pound repeatedly (against) ▷ n stroke or blow ▷ adj totally exhausted
**BEATABLE** > BEAT
**BEATBOX** n drum machine
**BEATBOXES** > BEATBOX
**BEATEN** > BEAT

**BEATER** n device used for beating
**BEATERS** > BEATER
**BEATH** vb dry; heat
**BEATHED** > BEATH
**BEATHING** > BEATH
**BEATHS** > BEATH
**BEATIER** > BEATY
**BEATIEST** > BEATY
**BEATIFIC** adj displaying great happiness
**BEATIFIED** > BEATIFY
**BEATIFIES** > BEATIFY
**BEATIFY** vb declare (a dead person) to be among the blessed in heaven: the first step towards canonization
**BEATING** > BEAT
**BEATINGS** > BEAT
**BEATITUDE** n any of the blessings on the poor, meek, etc, in the Sermon on the Mount
**BEATLESS** > BEAT
**BEATNIK** n young person in the late 1950s who rebelled against conventional attitudes etc
**BEATNIKS** > BEATNIK
**BEATS** > BEAT
**BEATY** adj (of music) having a strong rhythm
**BEAU** n boyfriend or admirer
**BEAUCOUP** n large amount
**BEAUCOUPS** > BEAUCOUP
**BEAUFET** same as > BUFFET
**BEAUFETS** > BEAUFET
**BEAUFFET** same as > BUFFET
**BEAUFFETS** > BEAUFFET
**BEAUFIN** same as > BIFFIN
**BEAUFINS** > BEAUFIN
**BEAUISH** adj vain and showy
**BEAUS** > BEAU
**BEAUT** n person or thing that is outstanding or distinctive ▷ adj good or excellent ▷ interj exclamation of joy or pleasure
**BEAUTEOUS** adj beautiful
**BEAUTIED** > BEAUTY
**BEAUTIES** > BEAUTY
**BEAUTIFUL** adj very attractive to look at
**BEAUTIFY** vb make beautiful
**BEAUTS** > BEAUT
**BEAUTY** n combination of all the qualities of a person or thing that delight the senses and mind ▷ interj expression of approval or agreement ▷ vb make beautiful
**BEAUTYING** > BEAUTY
**BEAUX** > BEAU
**BEAUXITE** same as > BAUXITE
**BEAUXITES** > BEAUXITE
**BEAVER** n amphibious rodent with a big flat tail ▷ vb work steadily or

assiduously
**BEAVERED** > BEAVER
**BEAVERIES** > BEAVERY
**BEAVERING** > BEAVER
**BEAVERS** > BEAVER
**BEAVERY** n place for keeping beavers
**BEBEERINE** n alkaloid, resembling quinine, obtained from the bark of the greenheart and other plants
**BEBEERU** n tropical American tree
**BEBEERUS** > BEBEERU
**BEBLOOD** vb stain with blood
**BEBLOODED** > BEBLOOD
**BEBLOODS** > BEBLOOD
**BEBOP** same as > BOP
**BEBOPPED** > BEBOP
**BEBOPPER** > BEBOP
**BEBOPPERS** > BEBOP
**BEBOPPING** > BEBOP
**BEBOPS** > BEBOP
**BEBUNG** n vibrato effect on clavichord
**BEBUNGS** > BEBUNG
**BECALL** vb use insulting words about someone
**BECALLED** > BECALL
**BECALLING** > BECALL
**BECALLS** > BECALL
**BECALM** vb make calm
**BECALMED** adj (of a sailing ship) motionless through lack of wind
**BECALMING** > BECALM
**BECALMS** > BECALM
**BECAME** > BECOME
**BECAP** vb put cap on
**BECAPPED** > BECAP
**BECAPPING** > BECAP
**BECAPS** > BECAP
**BECARPET** vb lay carpet on
**BECARPETS** > BECARPET
**BECASSE** n woodcock
**BECASSES** > BECASSE
**BECAUSE** conj on account of the fact that; on account of being; since
**BECCACCIA** n woodcock
**BECCAFICO** n any of various European songbirds, esp warblers of the genus Sylvia, eaten as a delicacy in Italy and other countries
**BECHALK** vb mark with chalk
**BECHALKED** > BECHALK
**BECHALKS** > BECHALK
**BECHAMEL** n thick white sauce flavoured with onion and seasoning
**BECHAMELS** > BECHAMEL
**BECHANCE** vb happen (to)
**BECHANCED** > BECHANCE
**BECHANCES** > BECHANCE
**BECHARM** vb delight
**BECHARMED** > BECHARM
**BECHARMS** > BECHARM
**BECK** n stream ▷ vb attract someone's attention by

nodding or gesturing
**BECKE** same as > BEAK
**BECKED** > BECK
**BECKES** > BECK
**BECKET** n clevis forming part of one end of a sheave, used for securing standing lines by means of a thimble
**BECKETS** > BECKET
**BECKING** > BECK
**BECKON** vb summon with a gesture ▷ n summoning gesture
**BECKONED** > BECKON
**BECKONER** > BECKON
**BECKONERS** > BECKON
**BECKONING** > BECKON
**BECKONS** > BECKON
**BECKS** > BECK
**BECLAMOR** vb clamour excessively
**BECLAMORS** > BECLAMOR
**BECLASP** vb embrace
**BECLASPED** > BECLASP
**BECLASPS** > BECLASP
**BECLOAK** vb dress in cloak
**BECLOAKED** > BECLOAK
**BECLOAKS** > BECLOAK
**BECLOG** vb put clogs on
**BECLOGGED** > BECLOG
**BECLOGS** > BECLOG
**BECLOTHE** vb put clothes on
**BECLOTHED** > BECLOTHE
**BECLOTHES** > BECLOTHE
**BECLOUD** vb cover or obscure with a cloud
**BECLOUDED** > BECLOUD
**BECLOUDS** > BECLOUD
**BECLOWN** vb clown around
**BECLOWNED** > BECLOWN
**BECLOWNS** > BECLOWN
**BECOME** vb come to be
**BECOMES** > BECOME
**BECOMING** adj attractive or pleasing ▷ n any process of change
**BECOMINGS** > BECOMING
**BECOWARD** vb make cowardly
**BECOWARDS** > BECOWARD
**BECQUEREL** n SI unit of activity of a radioactive source
**BECRAWL** vb crawl all over
**BECRAWLED** > BECRAWL
**BECRAWLS** > BECRAWL
**BECRIME** vb make someone guilty of a crime
**BECRIMED** > BECRIME
**BECRIMES** > BECRIME
**BECRIMING** > BECRIME
**BECROWD** vb crowd with something
**BECROWDED** > BECROWD
**BECROWDS** > BECROWD
**BECRUST** vb cover with crust
**BECRUSTED** > BECRUST
**BECRUSTS** > BECRUST
**BECUDGEL** vb arm with cudgel
**BECUDGELS** > BECUDGEL
**BECURL** vb curl

**BECURLED** > BECURL
**BECURLING** > BECURL
**BECURLS** > BECURL
**BECURSE** vb curse
**BECURSED** > BECURSE
**BECURSES** > BECURSE
**BECURSING** > BECURSE
**BECURST** > BECURSE
**BED** n piece of furniture on which to sleep ▷ vb plant in a bed
**BEDABBLE** vb dabble; moisten
**BEDABBLED** > BEDABBLE
**BEDABBLES** > BEDABBLE
**BEDAD** interj by God (oath)
**BEDAGGLE** vb soil by trailing through dirt
**BEDAGGLED** > BEDAGGLE
**BEDAGGLES** > BEDAGGLE
**BEDAMN** vb damn
**BEDAMNED** > BEDAMN
**BEDAMNING** > BEDAMN
**BEDAMNS** > BEDAMN
**BEDARKEN** vb make dark
**BEDARKENS** > BEDARKEN
**BEDASH** vb sprinkle with liquid
**BEDASHED** > BEDASH
**BEDASHES** > BEDASH
**BEDASHING** > BEDASH
**BEDAUB** vb smear with something sticky or dirty
**BEDAUBED** > BEDAUB
**BEDAUBING** > BEDAUB
**BEDAUBS** > BEDAUB
**BEDAWIN** same as > BEDOUIN
**BEDAWINS** > BEDAWIN
**BEDAZE** vb daze
**BEDAZED** > BEDAZE
**BEDAZES** > BEDAZE
**BEDAZING** > BEDAZE
**BEDAZZLE** vb dazzle or confuse, as with brilliance
**BEDAZZLED** > BEDAZZLE
**BEDAZZLES** > BEDAZZLE
**BEDBOARD** n base of bed
**BEDBOARDS** > BEDBOARD
**BEDBUG** n small blood-sucking wingless insect that infests dirty houses
**BEDBUGS** > BEDBUG
**BEDCHAIR** n adjustable chair to support invalid in bed
**BEDCHAIRS** > BEDCHAIR
**BEDCOVER** n cover for bed
**BEDCOVERS** > BEDCOVER
**BEDDABLE** adj sexually attractive
**BEDDED** > BED
**BEDDER** n (at some universities) a college servant employed to keep students' rooms in order
**BEDDERS** > BEDDER
**BEDDING** > BED
**BEDDINGS** > BED
**BEDE** n prayer
**BEDEAFEN** vb deafen
**BEDEAFENS** > BEDEAFEN
**BEDECK** vb cover with decorations
**BEDECKED** > BEDECK

**BEDECKING** > BEDECK
**BEDECKS** > BEDECK
**BEDEGUAR** n growth found on rosebushes
**BEDEGUARS** > BEDEGUAR
**BEDEHOUSE** same as > BEADHOUSE
**BEDEL** archaic spellings of > BEADLE
**BEDELL** same as > BEADLE
**BEDELLS** > BEDELL
**BEDELS** > BEDEL
**BEDELSHIP** > BEDEL
**BEDEMAN** same as > BEADSMAN
**BEDEMEN** > BEADSMAN
**BEDERAL** same as > BEDRAL
**BEDERALS** > BEDERAL
**BEDES** > BEDE
**BEDESMAN** same as > BEADSMAN
**BEDESMEN** > BEDESMAN
**BEDEVIL** vb harass, confuse, or torment
**BEDEVILED** > BEDEVIL
**BEDEVILS** > BEDEVIL
**BEDEW** vb wet or cover with or as if with drops of dew
**BEDEWED** > BEDEW
**BEDEWING** > BEDEW
**BEDEWS** > BEDEW
**BEDFAST** an archaic word for > BEDRIDDEN
**BEDFELLOW** n temporary associate
**BEDFRAME** n framework of bed
**BEDFRAMES** > BEDFRAME
**BEDGOWN** n night dress
**BEDGOWNS** > BEDGOWN
**BEDIAPER** vb put a nappy on
**BEDIAPERS** > BEDIAPER
**BEDIDE** > BEDYE
**BEDIGHT** vb array or adorn ▷ adj adorned or bedecked
**BEDIGHTED** > BEDIGHT
**BEDIGHTS** > BEDIGHT
**BEDIM** vb make dim or obscure
**BEDIMMED** > BEDIM
**BEDIMMING** > BEDIM
**BEDIMPLE** vb form dimples in
**BEDIMPLED** > BEDIMPLE
**BEDIMPLES** > BEDIMPLE
**BEDIMS** > BEDIM
**BEDIRTIED** > BEDIRTY
**BEDIRTIES** > BEDIRTY
**BEDIRTY** vb make dirty
**BEDIZEN** vb dress or decorate gaudily or tastelessly
**BEDIZENED** > BEDIZEN
**BEDIZENS** > BEDIZEN
**BEDLAM** n noisy confused situation
**BEDLAMISM** > BEDLAM
**BEDLAMITE** n lunatic
**BEDLAMP** n bedside light
**BEDLAMPS** > BEDLAMP
**BEDLAMS** > BEDLAM
**BEDLESS** > BED
**BEDLIKE** adj like a bed

**BEDMAKER** *n* person who makes beds

**BEDMAKERS** > BEDMAKER

**BEDMATE** *n* person who shares a bed

**BEDMATES** > BEDMATE

**BEDOTTED** *adj* scattered; strewn

**BEDOUIN** *n* member of any of the nomadic tribes of Arabs inhabiting the deserts of Arabia, Jordan, and Syria, as well as parts of the Sahara

**BEDOUINS** > BEDOUIN

**BEDPAN** *n* shallow bowl used as a toilet by bedridden people

**BEDPANS** > BEDPAN

**BEDPLATE** *n* heavy metal platform or frame to which an engine or machine is attached

**BEDPLATES** > BEDPLATE

**BEDPOST** *n* vertical support on a bedstead

**BEDPOSTS** > BEDPOST

**BEDQUILT** *n* padded bed cover

**BEDQUILTS** > BEDQUILT

**BEDRAGGLE** *vb* make (hair, clothing, etc) limp, untidy, or dirty, as with rain or mud

**BEDRAIL** *n* rail or board along the side of a bed that connects the headboard with the footboard

**BEDRAILS** > BEDRAIL

**BEDRAL** *n* minor church official

**BEDRALS** > BEDRAL

**BEDRAPE** *vb* adorn

**BEDRAPED** > BEDRAPE

**BEDRAPES** > BEDRAPE

**BEDRAPING** > BEDRAPE

**BEDRENCH** *vb* drench

**BEDRID** *same as* > BEDRIDDEN

**BEDRIDDEN** *adj* confined to bed because of illness or old age

**BEDRIGHT** *n* rights expected in the marital bed

**BEDRIGHTS** > BEDRIGHT

**BEDRIVEL** *vb* drivel around

**BEDRIVELS** > BEDRIVEL

**BEDROCK** *n* solid rock beneath the surface soil

**BEDROCKS** > BEDROCK

**BEDROLL** *n* portable roll of bedding, such as a sleeping bag, used esp for sleeping in the open

**BEDROLLS** > BEDROLL

**BEDROOM** *n* room used for sleeping ▷ *adj* containing references to sex

**BEDROOMED** *adj* containing specified number of bedrooms

**BEDROOMS** > BEDROOM

**BEDROP** *vb* drop on

**BEDROPPED** > BEDROP

**BEDROPS** > BEDROP

**BEDROPT** > BEDROP

**BEDRUG** *vb* drug excessively

**BEDRUGGED** > BEDRUG

**BEDRUGS** > BEDRUG

**BEDS** > BED

**BEDSHEET** *n* sheet for bed

**BEDSHEETS** > BEDSHEET

**BEDSIDE** *n* area beside a bed ▷ *adj* placed at or near the side of the bed

**BEDSIDES** > BEDSIDE

**BEDSIT** *n* furnished sitting room with a bed

**BEDSITS** > BEDSIT

**BEDSITTER** *same as* > BEDSIT

**BEDSOCKS** *n* socks worn in bed

**BEDSONIA** *n* bacterium causing diseases such as trachoma

**BEDSONIAS** > BEDSONIA

**BEDSORE** *n* ulcer on the skin, caused by a lengthy period of lying in bed due to illness

**BEDSORES** > BEDSORE

**BEDSPREAD** *n* top cover on a bed

**BEDSPRING** *vb* spring supporting mattress on bed

**BEDSTAND** *n* bedside table

**BEDSTANDS** > BEDSTAND

**BEDSTEAD** *n* framework of a bed

**BEDSTEADS** > BEDSTEAD

**BEDSTRAW** *n* plant with small white or yellow flowers

**BEDSTRAWS** > BEDSTRAW

**BEDTICK** *n* case containing stuffing in mattress

**BEDTICKS** > BEDTICK

**BEDTIME** *n* time when one usually goes to bed

**BEDTIMES** > BEDTIME

**BEDU** *adj* relating to beduins

**BEDUCK** *vb* duck under water

**BEDUCKED** > BEDUCK

**BEDUCKING** > BEDUCK

**BEDUCKS** > BEDUCK

**BEDUIN** *variant of* > BEDOUIN

**BEDUINS** > BEDUIN

**BEDUMB** *vb* make dumb

**BEDUMBED** > BEDUMB

**BEDUMBING** > BEDUMB

**BEDUMBS** > BEDUMB

**BEDUNCE** *vb* cause to look or feel foolish

**BEDUNCED** > BEDUNCE

**BEDUNCES** > BEDUNCE

**BEDUNCING** > BEDUNCE

**BEDUNG** *vb* spread with dung

**BEDUNGED** > BEDUNG

**BEDUNGING** > BEDUNG

**BEDUNGS** > BEDUNG

**BEDUST** *vb* cover with dust

**BEDUSTED** > BEDUST

**BEDUSTING** > BEDUST

**BEDUSTS** > BEDUST

**BEDWARD** *adj* towards bed

**BEDWARDS** *adv* towards bed

**BEDWARF** *vb* hamper growth of

**BEDWARFED** > BEDWARF

**BEDWARFS** > BEDWARF

**BEDWARMER** *n* metal pan containing hot coals, formerly used to warm a bed

**BEDWETTER** *n* person who urinates in bed

**BEDYDE** > BEDYE

**BEDYE** *vb* dye

**BEDYED** > BEDYE

**BEDYEING** > BEDYE

**BEDYES** > BEDYE

**BEE** *n* insect that makes wax and honey

**BEEBEE** *n* air rifle

**BEEBEES** > BEEBEE

**BEEBREAD** *n* mixture of pollen and nectar prepared by worker bees and fed to the larvae

**BEEBREADS** > BEEBREAD

**BEECH** *n* tree with a smooth greyish bark

**BEECHEN** > BEECH

**BEECHES** > BEECH

**BEECHIER** > BEECH

**BEECHIEST** > BEECH

**BEECHMAST** *n* nuts of beech tree

**BEECHNUT** *n* small brown triangular edible nut of the beech tree

**BEECHNUTS** > BEECHNUT

**BEECHWOOD** *n* wood of beech tree

**BEECHY** > BEECH

**BEEDI** *n* Indian cigarette

**BEEDIES** > BEEDI

**BEEF** *n* flesh of a cow, bull, or ox ▷ *vb* complain

**BEEFALO** *n* cross between cow and buffalo

**BEEFALOES** > BEEFALO

**BEEFALOS** > BEEFALO

**BEEFCAKE** *n* musclemen as displayed in photographs

**BEEFCAKES** > BEEFCAKE

**BEEFEATER** *n* yeoman warder at the Tower of London

**BEEFED** > BEEF

**BEEFIER** > BEEFY

**BEEFIEST** > BEEFY

**BEEFILY** > BEEFY

**BEEFINESS** > BEEFY

**BEEFING** > BEEF

**BEEFLESS** > BEEF

**BEEFS** > BEEF

**BEEFSTEAK** *n* piece of beef that can be grilled, fried, etc, cut from any lean part of the animal

**BEEFWOOD** *n* any of various trees that produce very hard wood

**BEEFWOODS** > BEEFWOOD

**BEEFY** *adj* like beef

**BEEGAH** *same as* > BIGHA

**BEEGAHS** > BEEGAH

**BEEHIVE** *n* structure in which bees live

**BEEHIVES** > BEEHIVE

**BEEKEEPER** *n* person who keeps bees for their honey

**BEELIKE** > BEE

**BEELINE** *n* most direct route between two places ▷ *adj* make a beeline for (something)

**BEELINED** > BEELINE

**BEELINES** > BEELINE

**BEELINING** > BEELINE

**BEEN** > BE

**BEENAH** *n* understanding; insight

**BEENAHS** > BEENAH

**BEENTO** *n* person who has resided in Britain, esp during part of his education ▷ *adj* of, relating to, or characteristic of such a person

**BEENTOS** > BEENTO

**BEEP** *n* high-pitched sound, like that of a car horn ▷ *vb* (cause to) make this noise

**BEEPED** > BEEP

**BEEPER** > BEEP

**BEEPERS** > BEEP

**BEEPING** > BEEP

**BEEPS** > BEEP

**BEER** *n* alcoholic drink brewed from malt and hops

**BEERAGE** *n* brewing industry

**BEERAGES** > BEERAGE

**BEERHALL** *n* large public room where beer is consumed

**BEERHALLS** > BEERHALL

**BEERIER** > BEERY

**BEERIEST** > BEERY

**BEERILY** > BEERY

**BEERINESS** > BEERY

**BEERS** > BEER

**BEERY** *adj* smelling or tasting of beer

**BEES** > BEE

**BEESOME** *same as* > BISSON

**BEESTINGS** *n* first milk secreted by the mammary glands of a cow or similar animal immediately after giving birth

**BEESWAX** *n* wax secreted by bees, used in polishes etc ▷ *vb* polish with such wax

**BEESWAXED** > BEESWAX

**BEESWAXES** > BEESWAX

**BEESWING** *n* light filmy crust of tartar that forms in port and some other wines after long keeping in the bottle

**BEESWINGS** > BEESWING

**BEET** *n* plant with an edible root and leaves ▷ *vb*

improve or make better

BEETED > BEET

BEETFLIES > BEETFLY

BEETFLY n muscid fly, *Pegomyia hyoscyami*: a common pest of beets and mangel-wurzels

BEETING > BEET

BEETLE n insect with a hard wing cover on its back ▷ adj overhang or jut ▷ vb scuttle or scurry

BEETLED > BEETLE

BEETLER n one who operates a beetling machine

BEETLERS > BEETLER

BEETLES > BEETLE

BEETLING > BEETLE

BEETROOT n type of beet plant with a dark red root

BEETROOTS > BEETROOT

BEETS > BEET

BEEVES > BEEF

BEEYARD n place where bees are kept

BEEYARDS > BEEYARD

BEEZER n person or chap ▷ adj excellent

BEEZERS > BEEZER

BEFALL vb happen to (someone)

BEFALLEN > BEFALL

BEFALLING > BEFALL

BEFALLS > BEFALL

BEFANA n Italian gift-bearing good fairy

BEFANAS > BEFANA

BEFELD > BEFALL

BEFELL > BEFALL

BEFFANA same as > BEFANA

BEFFANAS > BEFFANA

BEFINGER vb mark by handling

BEFINGERS > BEFINGER

BEFINNED adj with fins

BEFIT vb be appropriate or suitable for

BEFITS > BEFIT

BEFITTED > BEFIT

BEFITTING > BEFIT

BEFLAG vb decorate with flags

BEFLAGGED > BEFLAG

BEFLAGS > BEFLAG

BEFLEA vb infect with fleas

BEFLEAED > BEFLEA

BEFLEAING > BEFLEA

BEFLEAS > BEFLEA

BEFLECK vb fleck

BEFLECKED > BEFLECK

BEFLECKS > BEFLECK

BEFLOWER vb decorate with flowers

BEFLOWERS > BEFLOWER

BEFLUM vb fool; deceive

BEFLUMMED > BEFLUM

BEFLUMS > BEFLUM

BEFOAM vb cover with foam

BEFOAMED > BEFOAM

BEFOAMING > BEFOAM

BEFOAMS > BEFOAM

BEFOG vb surround with fog

BEFOGGED > BEFOG

BEFOGGING > BEFOG

BEFOGS > BEFOG

BEFOOL vb make a fool of

BEFOOLED > BEFOOL

BEFOOLING > BEFOOL

BEFOOLS > BEFOOL

BEFORE adv indicating something earlier in time, in front of, or preferred to ▷ prep preceding in space or time

BEFORTUNE vb happen to

BEFOUL vb make dirty or foul

BEFOULED > BEFOUL

BEFOULER > BEFOUL

BEFOULERS > BEFOUL

BEFOULING > BEFOUL

BEFOULS > BEFOUL

BEFRET vb fret about something

BEFRETS > BEFRET

BEFRETTED > BEFRET

BEFRIEND vb become friends with

BEFRIENDS > BEFRIEND

BEFRINGE vb decorate with fringe

BEFRINGED > BEFRINGE

BEFRINGES > BEFRINGE

BEFUDDLE vb confuse, muddle, or perplex

BEFUDDLED > BEFUDDLE

BEFUDDLES > BEFUDDLE

BEG vb solicit (money, food, etc), esp in the street

BEGAD interj emphatic exclamation

BEGALL vb make sore by rubbing

BEGALLED > BEGALL

BEGALLING > BEGALL

BEGALLS > BEGALL

BEGAN > BEGIN

BEGAR n compulsory labour

BEGARS > BEGAR

BEGAT > BEGET

BEGAZE vb gaze about or around

BEGAZED > BEGAZE

BEGAZES > BEGAZE

BEGAZING > BEGAZE

BEGEM vb decorate with gems

BEGEMMED > BEGEM

BEGEMMING > BEGEM

BEGEMS > BEGEM

BEGET vb cause or create

BEGETS > BEGET

BEGETTER > BEGET

BEGETTERS > BEGET

BEGETTING > BEGET

BEGGAR n person who begs, esp one who lives by begging ▷ vb be beyond the resources of

BEGGARDOM > BEGGAR

BEGGARED > BEGGAR

BEGGARIES > BEGGARY

BEGGARING > BEGGAR

BEGGARLY adj meanly inadequate

BEGGARS > BEGGAR

BEGGARY n extreme poverty or need

BEGGED > BEG

BEGGING > BEG

BEGGINGLY > BEG

BEGGINGS > BEG

BEGHARD n member of a Christian brotherhood that was founded in Flanders in the 13th century and followed a life based on that of the Beguines

BEGHARDS > BEGHARD

BEGIFT vb give gift or gifts to

BEGIFTED > BEGIFT

BEGIFTING > BEGIFT

BEGIFTS > BEGIFT

BEGILD vb gild

BEGILDED > BEGILD

BEGILDING > BEGILD

BEGILDS > BEGILD

BEGILT > BEGILD

BEGIN vb start

BEGINNE same as > BEGINNING

BEGINNER n person who has just started learning to do something

BEGINNERS > BEGINNER

BEGINNES > BEGINNE

BEGINNING n start

BEGINS > BEGIN

BEGIRD vb surround

BEGIRDED > BEGIRD

BEGIRDING > BEGIRD

BEGIRDLE vb surround with girdle

BEGIRDLED > BEGIRDLE

BEGIRDLES > BEGIRDLE

BEGIRDS > BEGIRD

BEGIRT > BEGIRD

BEGLAD vb make glad

BEGLADDED > BEGLAD

BEGLADS > BEGLAD

BEGLAMOR same as > BEGLAMOUR

BEGLAMORS > BEGLAMOR

BEGLAMOUR vb glamourize

BEGLERBEG n governor in the Ottoman empire

BEGLOOM vb make gloomy

BEGLOOMED > BEGLOOM

BEGLOOMS > BEGLOOM

BEGNAW vb gnaw at

BEGNAWED > BEGNAW

BEGNAWING > BEGNAW

BEGNAWS > BEGNAW

BEGO vb harrass; beset

BEGOES > BEGO

BEGOGGLED adj wearing goggles

BEGOING > BEGO

BEGONE > BEGO

BEGONIA n tropical plant with waxy flowers

BEGONIAS > BEGONIA

BEGORAH same as > BEGORRA

BEGORED adj smear with gore

BEGORRA interj emphatic exclamation, regarded as a characteristic utterance of

Irishmen

BEGORRAH same as > BEGORRA

BEGOT past participle of > BEGET

BEGOTTEN past participle of > BEGET

BEGRIM same as > BEGRIME

BEGRIME vb make dirty

BEGRIMED > BEGRIME

BEGRIMES > BEGRIME

BEGRIMING > BEGRIME

BEGRIMMED > BEGRIM

BEGRIMS > BEGRIM

BEGROAN vb groan at

BEGROANED > BEGROAN

BEGROANS > BEGROAN

BEGRUDGE vb envy (someone) the possession of something

BEGRUDGED > BEGRUDGE

BEGRUDGER > BEGRUDGE

BEGRUDGES > BEGRUDGE

BEGS > BEG

BEGUILE vb cheat or mislead

BEGUILED > BEGUILE

BEGUILER > BEGUILE

BEGUILERS > BEGUILE

BEGUILES > BEGUILE

BEGUILING adj charming, often in a deceptive way

BEGUIN another name for > BEGHARD

BEGUINAGE n convent for members of beguine sisterhood

BEGUINE n S American dance

BEGUINES > BEGUINE

BEGUINS > BEGUIN

BEGULF vb overwhelm

BEGULFED > BEGULF

BEGULFING > BEGULF

BEGULFS > BEGULF

BEGUM n Muslim woman of high rank

BEGUMS > BEGUM

BEGUN past participle of > BEGIN

BEGUNK vb delude; trick

BEGUNKED > BEGUNK

BEGUNKING > BEGUNK

BEGUNKS > BEGUNK

BEHALF n interest, part, benefit, or respect

BEHALVES > BEHALF

BEHAPPEN vb befall

BEHAPPENS > BEHAPPEN

BEHATTED adj wearing a hat

BEHAVE vb act or function in a particular way

BEHAVED > BEHAVE

BEHAVER > BEHAVE

BEHAVERS > BEHAVE

BEHAVES > BEHAVE

BEHAVING > BEHAVE

BEHAVIOR same as > BEHAVIOUR

BEHAVIORS > BEHAVIOR

BEHAVIOUR n manner of behaving

BEHEAD vb remove the head

**from**
**BEHEADAL** > BEHEAD
**BEHEADALS** > BEHEAD
**BEHEADED** > BEHEAD
**BEHEADER** > BEHEAD
**BEHEADERS** > BEHEAD
**BEHEADING** > BEHEAD
**BEHEADS** > BEHEAD
**BEHELD** > BEHOLD
**BEHEMOTH** *n* huge person or thing
**BEHEMOTHS** > BEHEMOTH
**BEHEST** *n* order or earnest request
**BEHESTS** > BEHEST
**BEHIGHT** *vb* entrust
**BEHIGHTS** > BEHIGHT
**BEHIND** *adv* indicating position to the rear, lateness, responsibility, etc ▷ *n* buttocks ▷ *prep* in or to a position further back than ▷ *adj* in a position further back
**BEHINDS** > BEHIND
**BEHOLD** *vb* look (at)
**BEHOLDEN** *adj* indebted or obliged
**BEHOLDER** > BEHOLD
**BEHOLDERS** > BEHOLD
**BEHOLDING** > BEHOLD
**BEHOLDS** > BEHOLD
**BEHOOF** *n* advantage or profit
**BEHOOFS** > BEHOOF
**BEHOOVE** *same as* > BEHOVE
**BEHOOVED** > BEHOOVE
**BEHOOVES** > BEHOOVE
**BEHOOVING** > BEHOOVE
**BEHOTE** *same as* > BEHIGHT
**BEHOTES** > BEHOTE
**BEHOTING** > BEHOTE
**BEHOVE** *vb* be necessary or fitting for
**BEHOVED** > BEHOVE
**BEHOVEFUL** *adj* useful; of benefit
**BEHOVELY** *adj* useful
**BEHOVES** > BEHOVE
**BEHOVING** > BEHOVE
**BEHOWL** *vb* howl at
**BEHOWLED** > BEHOWL
**BEHOWLING** > BEHOWL
**BEHOWLS** > BEHOWL
**BEIGE** *adj* pale brown ▷ *n* very light brown, sometimes with a yellowish tinge, similar to the colour of undyed wool
**BEIGEL** *same as* > BAGEL
**BEIGELS** > BEIGEL
**BEIGES** > BEIGE
**BEIGNE** *variant of* > BEIGNET
**BEIGNES** > BEIGNE
**BEIGNET** *n* square deep-fried pastry served hot and sprinkled with icing sugar
**BEIGNETS** > BEIGNET
**BEIGY** > BEIGE
**BEIN** *adj* financially comfortable
**BEING** > BE
**BEINGLESS** > BE
**BEINGNESS** > BE

**BEINGS** > BE
**BEINKED** *adj* daubed with ink
**BEINNESS** > BEIN
**BEJABBERS** *same as* > BEJABERS
**BEJABERS** *interj* by Jesus!
**BEJADE** *vb* jade; tire
**BEJADED** > BEJADE
**BEJADES** > BEJADE
**BEJADING** > BEJADE
**BEJANT** *same as* > BAJAN
**BEJANTS** > BEJANT
**BEJEEBERS** *same as* > BEJABERS
**BEJEEZUS** *same as* > BEJESUS
**BEJESUIT** *vb* convert to Jesuitism
**BEJESUITS** > BEJESUIT
**BEJESUS** *interj* exclamation of surprise
**BEJEWEL** *vb* decorate with or as if with jewels
**BEJEWELED** > BEJEWEL
**BEJEWELS** > BEJEWEL
**BEJUMBLE** *vb* jumble up
**BEJUMBLED** > BEJUMBLE
**BEJUMBLES** > BEJUMBLE
**BEKAH** *n* half shekel
**BEKAHS** > BEKAH
**BEKISS** *vb* smother with kisses
**BEKISSED** > BEKISS
**BEKISSES** > BEKISS
**BEKISSING** > BEKISS
**BEKNAVE** *vb* treat as knave
**BEKNAVED** > BEKNAVE
**BEKNAVES** > BEKNAVE
**BEKNAVING** > BEKNAVE
**BEKNIGHT** *vb* esteem
**BEKNIGHTS** > BEKNIGHT
**BEKNOT** *vb* tie knot or knots in
**BEKNOTS** > BEKNOT
**BEKNOTTED** > BEKNOT
**BEKNOWN** *adj* known about
**BEL** *n* unit for comparing two power levels or measuring the intensity of a sound, equal to 10 decibels
**BELABOR** *same as* > BELABOUR
**BELABORED** > BELABOR
**BELABORS** > BELABOR
**BELABOUR** *vb* attack verbally or physically
**BELABOURS** > BELABOUR
**BELACE** *vb* decorate with lace
**BELACED** > BELACE
**BELACES** > BELACE
**BELACING** > BELACE
**BELADIED** > BELADY
**BELADIES** > BELADY
**BELADY** *vb* call a lady
**BELADYING** > BELADY
**BELAH** *n* Australian casuarina tree, *Casuarina glauca*, yielding a useful timber
**BELAHS** > BELAH
**BELAMIES** > BELAMY

**BELAMOURE** *n* loved one
**BELAMY** *n* close friend
**BELAR** *same as* > BELAH
**BELARS** > BELAR
**BELATE** *vb* cause to be late
**BELATED** *adj* late or too late
**BELATEDLY** > BELATED
**BELATES** > BELATE
**BELATING** > BELATE
**BELAUD** *vb* praise highly
**BELAUDED** > BELAUD
**BELAUDING** > BELAUD
**BELAUDS** > BELAUD
**BELAY** *vb* secure a line to a pin or cleat ▷ *n* attachment (of a climber) to a mountain by tying the rope off round a rock spike, piton, nut, etc, to safeguard the party in the event of a fall
**BELAYED** > BELAY
**BELAYER** > BELAY
**BELAYERS** > BELAY
**BELAYING** > BELAY
**BELAYS** > BELAY
**BELCH** *vb* expel wind from the stomach noisily through the mouth ▷ *n* act of belching
**BELCHED** > BELCH
**BELCHER** > BELCH
**BELCHERS** > BELCH
**BELCHES** > BELCH
**BELCHING** > BELCH
**BELDAM** *n* old woman, esp an ugly or malicious one
**BELDAME** *same as* > BELDAM
**BELDAMES** > BELDAME
**BELDAMS** > BELDAM
**BELEAGUER** *vb* trouble persistently
**BELEAP** *vb* leap over
**BELEAPED** > BELEAP
**BELEAPING** > BELEAP
**BELEAPS** > BELEAP
**BELEAPT** > BELEAP
**BELEE** *vb* put on sheltered side
**BELEED** > BELEE
**BELEEING** > BELEE
**BELEES** > BELEE
**BELEMNITE** *n* any extinct marine cephalopod mollusc of the order *Belemnoidea*, related to the cuttlefish
**BELEMNOID** *adj* shaped like a dart
**BELFRIED** *adj* with a belfry
**BELFRIES** > BELFRY
**BELFRY** *n* part of a tower where bells are hung
**BELGA** *n* former Belgian monetary unit worth five francs
**BELGARD** *n* kind gaze
**BELGARDS** > BELGARD
**BELGAS** > BELGA
**BELIE** *vb* show to be untrue
**BELIED** > BELIE
**BELIEF** *n* faith or confidence

**BELIEFS** > BELIEF
**BELIER** > BELIE
**BELIERS** > BELIE
**BELIES** > BELIE
**BELIEVE** *vb* accept as true or real
**BELIEVED** > BELIEVE
**BELIEVER** > BELIEVE
**BELIEVERS** > BELIEVE
**BELIEVES** > BELIEVE
**BELIEVING** > BELIEVE
**BELIKE** *adv* perhaps
**BELIQUOR** *vb* cause to be drunk
**BELIQUORS** > BELIQUOR
**BELITTLE** *vb* treat as having little value or importance
**BELITTLED** > BELITTLE
**BELITTLER** > BELITTLE
**BELITTLES** > BELITTLE
**BELIVE** *adv* speedily
**BELL** *n* hollow, usu. metal, cup-shaped instrument that emits a ringing sound when struck ▷ *vb* utter (such a cry)
**BELLBIND** *n* bindweed-type climber
**BELLBINDS** > BELLBIND
**BELLBIRD** *n* Australasian bird with bell-like call
**BELLBIRDS** > BELLBIRD
**BELLBOY** *n* man or boy employed in a hotel, club, etc, to carry luggage and answer calls for service
**BELLBOYS** > BELLBOY
**BELLCOTE** *n* small roofed structure for bell
**BELLCOTES** > BELLCOTE
**BELLE** *n* beautiful woman, esp the most attractive woman at a function
**BELLED** > BELL
**BELLEEK** *n* kind of thin fragile porcelain with a lustrous glaze
**BELLEEKS** > BELLEEK
**BELLES** > BELLE
**BELLETER** *n* person who makes bells
**BELLETERS** > BELLETER
**BELLHOP** *same as* > BELLBOY
**BELLHOPS** > BELLHOP
**BELLIBONE** *n* beautiful and good woman
**BELLICOSE** *adj* warlike and aggressive
**BELLIED** > BELLY
**BELLIES** > BELLY
**BELLING** > BELL
**BELLINGS** > BELL
**BELLMAN** *n* man who rings a bell, esp (formerly) a town crier
**BELLMEN** > BELLMAN
**BELLOCK** *vb* shout
**BELLOCKED** > BELLOCK
**BELLOCKS** > BELLOCK
**BELLOW** *vb* make a low deep cry like that of a bull ▷ *n* loud deep roar
**BELLOWED** > BELLOW

BELLOWER > BELLOW
BELLOWERS > BELLOW
BELLOWING > BELLOW
BELLOWS pl n instrument for pumping a stream of air into something
BELLPULL n handle, rope, or cord pulled to operate a doorbell or servant's bell
BELLPULLS > BELLPULL
BELLPUSH n button pressed to operate an electric bell
BELLS > BELL
BELLWORT n any plant of the North American liliaceous genus Uvularia, having slender bell-shaped yellow flowers
BELLWORTS > BELLWORT
BELLY n part of the body of a vertebrate which contains the intestines ▷ vb (cause to) swell out
BELLYACHE n pain in the abdomen ▷ vb complain repeatedly
BELLYBAND n strap around the belly of a draught animal, holding the shafts of a vehicle
BELLYFUL n more than one can tolerate
BELLYFULS > BELLYFUL
BELLYING > BELLY
BELLYINGS > BELLY
BELLYLIKE > BELLY
BELOMANCY n art of divination using arrows
BELON n type of oyster
BELONG vb be the property of
BELONGED > BELONG
BELONGER n native-born Caribbean
BELONGERS > BELONGER
BELONGING n secure relationship
BELONGS > BELONG
BELONS > BELON
BELOVE vb love
BELOVED adj dearly loved ▷ n person dearly loved
BELOVEDS > BELOVED
BELOVES > BELOVE
BELOVING > BELOVE
BELOW adv at or to a position lower than, under ▷ prep at or to a position lower than
BELOWS same as > BELLOWS
BELS > BEL
BELT n band of cloth, leather, etc, worn usu. around the waist ▷ vb fasten with a belt
BELTED > BELT
BELTER n outstanding person or event
BELTERS > BELTER
BELTING n material used to make a belt or belts ▷ adj excellent
BELTINGS > BELTING

BELTLESS > BELT
BELTLINE n line separating car's windows from main body
BELTLINES > BELTLINE
BELTMAN n (formerly) the member of a beach life-saving team who swam out with a line attached to his belt
BELTMEN > BELTMAN
BELTS > BELT
BELTWAY n people and institutions located in the area bounded by the Washington Beltway, taken to be politically and socially out of touch with the rest of America and much given to political intrigue
BELTWAYS > BELTWAY
BELUGA n large white sturgeon of the Black and Caspian Seas, from which caviar and isinglass are obtained
BELUGAS > BELUGA
BELVEDERE n building designed and situated to look out on pleasant scenery
BELYING > BELIE
BEMA n speaker's platform in the assembly in ancient Athens
BEMAD vb cause to become mad
BEMADAM vb call a person madam
BEMADAMED > BEMADAM
BEMADAMS > BEMADAM
BEMADDED > BEMAD
BEMADDEN vb cause to become mad
BEMADDENS > BEMADDEN
BEMADDING > BEMAD
BEMADS > BEMAD
BEMAS > BEMA
BEMATA > BEMA
BEMAUL vb maul
BEMAULED > BEMAUL
BEMAULING > BEMAUL
BEMAULS > BEMAUL
BEMAZED adj amazed
BEMBEX n type of wasp
BEMBEXES > BEMBEX
BEMBIX same as > BEMBEX
BEMBIXES > BEMBIX
BEMEAN a less common word for > DEMEAN
BEMEANED > BEMEAN
BEMEANING > BEMEAN
BEMEANS > BEMEAN
BEMEANT > BEMEAN
BEMEDAL vb decorate with medals
BEMEDALED > BEMEDAL
BEMEDALS > BEMEDAL
BEMETE vb measure
BEMETED > BEMETE
BEMETES > BEMETE
BEMETING > BEMETE
BEMINGLE vb mingle

BEMINGLED > BEMINGLE
BEMINGLES > BEMINGLE
BEMIRE vb soil with or as if with mire
BEMIRED > BEMIRE
BEMIRES > BEMIRE
BEMIRING > BEMIRE
BEMIST vb cloud with mist
BEMISTED > BEMIST
BEMISTING > BEMIST
BEMISTS > BEMIST
BEMIX vb mix thoroughly
BEMIXED > BEMIX
BEMIXES > BEMIX
BEMIXING > BEMIX
BEMIXT > BEMIX
BEMOAN vb express sorrow or dissatisfaction about
BEMOANED > BEMOAN
BEMOANER > BEMOAN
BEMOANERS > BEMOAN
BEMOANING > BEMOAN
BEMOANS > BEMOAN
BEMOCK vb mock
BEMOCKED > BEMOCK
BEMOCKING > BEMOCK
BEMOCKS > BEMOCK
BEMOIL vb soil with mud
BEMOILED > BEMOIL
BEMOILING > BEMOIL
BEMOILS > BEMOIL
BEMONSTER vb treat as monster
BEMOUTH vb endow with mouth
BEMOUTHED > BEMOUTH
BEMOUTHS > BEMOUTH
BEMUD vb cover with mud
BEMUDDED > BEMUD
BEMUDDING > BEMUD
BEMUDDLE vb confound
BEMUDDLED > BEMUDDLE
BEMUDDLES > BEMUDDLE
BEMUDS > BEMUD
BEMUFFLE vb muffle up
BEMUFFLED > BEMUFFLE
BEMUFFLES > BEMUFFLE
BEMURMUR vb murmur at
BEMURMURS > BEMURMUR
BEMUSE vb confuse
BEMUSED adj puzzled or confused
BEMUSEDLY > BEMUSED
BEMUSES > BEMUSE
BEMUSING > BEMUSE
BEMUZZLE vb put muzzle on
BEMUZZLED > BEMUZZLE
BEMUZZLES > BEMUZZLE
BEN n mountain peak ▷ adv in ▷ adj inner
BENADRYL n tradename of an antihistamine drug used in sleeping tablets
BENADRYLS > BENADRYL
BENAME an archaic word for > NAME
BENAMED > BENAME
BENAMES > BENAME
BENAMING > BENAME
BENCH n long seat ▷ vb put a person on a bench
BENCHED > BENCH
BENCHER n member of the

governing body of one of the Inns of Court, usually a judge or a Queen's Counsel
BENCHERS > BENCHER
BENCHES > BENCH
BENCHIER > BENCHY
BENCHIEST > BENCHY
BENCHING > BENCH
BENCHLAND n level ground at foot of mountains
BENCHLESS > BENCH
BENCHMARK n criterion by which to measure something ▷ vb measure or test against a benchmark
BENCHTOP adj for use at bench
BENCHY adj (of a hillside) hollowed out in benches
BEND vb (cause to) form a curve ▷ n curved part
BENDABLE > BEND
BENDAY vb (printing) reproduce using Benday technique
BENDAYED > BENDAY
BENDAYING > BENDAY
BENDAYS > BENDAY
BENDED > BEND
BENDEE same as > BENDY
BENDEES > BENDY
BENDER n drinking bout
BENDERS > BENDER
BENDIER > BENDY
BENDIEST > BENDY
BENDING > BEND
BENDINGLY > BEND
BENDINGS > BEND
BENDLET n narrow diagonal stripe on heraldic shield
BENDLETS > BENDLET
BENDS > BEND
BENDWAYS same as > BENDWISE
BENDWISE adv diagonally
BENDY adj flexible or pliable ▷ n same as > OKRA
BENDYS > BENDY
BENE n blessing
BENEATH prep below ▷ adv below
BENEDICK n recently-married man
BENEDICKS > BENEDICK
BENEDICT n newly married man
BENEDICTS > BENEDICT
BENEDIGHT adj blessed
BENEFACT vb be benefactor to
BENEFACTS > BENEFACT
BENEFIC adj a rare word for beneficent
BENEFICE n church office providing its holder with an income ▷ vb provide with a benefice
BENEFICED > BENEFICE
BENEFICES > BENEFICE
BENEFIT n something that improves or promotes ▷ vb do or receive good

BENEFITED > BENEFIT
BENEFITER > BENEFIT
BENEFITS > BENEFIT
BENEMPT *a past participle of* > NAME
BENEMPTED > BENEMPT
BENES > BENE
BENET *vb* trap (something) in a net
BENETS > BENET
BENETTED > BENET
BENETTING > BENET
BENGALINE *n* heavy corded fabric, esp silk with woollen or cotton cord
BENI *n* sesame plant
BENIGHT *vb* shroud in darkness
BENIGHTED *adj* ignorant or uncultured
BENIGHTEN *same as* > BENIGHT
BENIGHTER > BENIGHT
BENIGHTS > BENIGHT
BENIGN *adj* showing kindliness
BENIGNANT *adj* kind or gracious
BENIGNER > BENIGN
BENIGNEST > BENIGN
BENIGNITY *n* kindliness
BENIGNLY > BENIGN
BENIS > BENI
BENISEED *n* sesame
BENISEEDS > BENISEED
BENISON *n* blessing, esp a spoken one
BENISONS > BENISON
BENITIER *n* basin for holy water
BENITIERS > BENITIER
BENJ *another word for* > BHANG
BENJAMIN *same as* > BENZOIN
BENJAMINS > BENJAMIN
BENJES > BENJ
BENNE *another name for* > SESAME
BENNES > BENNE
BENNET *n* Eurasian and N African rosaceous plant, *Geum urbanum*, with yellow flowers
BENNETS > BENNET
BENNI *n* sesame
BENNIES > BENNY
BENNIS > BENNI
BENNY *n* amphetamine tablet, esp benzedrine: a stimulant
BENOMYL *n* fungicide, derived from imidazole, used on cereal and fruit crops: suspected of being carcinogenic
BENOMYLS > BENOMYL
BENS > BEN
BENT *adj* not straight ▷ *n* personal inclination, propensity, or aptitude
BENTGRASS *n* variety of grass
BENTHAL > BENTHOS

BENTHIC > BENTHOS
BENTHOAL > BENTHON
BENTHON *same as* > BENTHOS
BENTHONIC > BENTHOS
BENTHONS > BENTHON
BENTHOS *n* animals and plants living at the bottom of a sea or lake
BENTHOSES > BENTHOS
BENTIER > BENTY
BENTIEST > BENTY
BENTO *n* thin lightweight box divided into compartments, which contain small separate dishes comprising a Japanese meal
BENTONITE *n* valuable clay, formed by the decomposition of volcanic ash, that swells as it absorbs water: used as a filler in the building, paper, and pharmaceutical industries
BENTOS > BENTO
BENTS > BENT
BENTWOOD *n* wood bent in moulds, used mainly for furniture ▷ *adj* made from such wood
BENTWOODS > BENTWOOD
BENTY *adj* covered with bentgrass
BENUMB *vb* make numb or powerless
BENUMBED > BENUMB
BENUMBING > BENUMB
BENUMBS > BENUMB
BENZAL *n* transparent crystalline substance
BENZALS > BENZAL
BENZENE *n* flammable poisonous liquid used as a solvent, insecticide, etc
BENZENES > BENZENE
BENZENOID *adj* similar to benzene
BENZIDIN *same as* > BENZIDINE
BENZIDINE *n* grey or reddish poisonous crystalline powder
BENZIDINS > BENZIDINE
BENZIL *n* yellow compound radical
BENZILS > BENZIL
BENZIN *same as* > BENZINE
BENZINE *n* volatile liquid used as a solvent
BENZINES > BENZINE
BENZINS > BENZIN
BENZOATE *n* any salt or ester of benzoic acid, containing the group $C_6H_5COO-$ or the ion $C_6H_5COO^-$
BENZOATES > BENZOATE
BENZOIC *adj* of, containing, or derived from benzoic acid or benzoin
BENZOIN *n* gum resin containing benzoic acid,

obtained from various trees of the genus *Styrax*, esp *S. benzoin* of Java and Sumatra, and used in ointments, perfume, etc
BENZOINS > BENZOIN
BENZOL *n* crude form of benzene, containing toluene, xylene, and other hydrocarbons, obtained from coal tar or coal gas and used as a fuel
BENZOLE *same as* > BENZOL
BENZOLES > BENZOLE
BENZOLINE *n* unpurified benzene
BENZOLS > BENZOL
BENZOYL *n* of, consisting of, or containing the monovalent group $C_6H_5CO-$
BENZOYLS > BENZOYL
BENZYL *n* of, consisting of, or containing the monovalent group $C_6H_5CH_2-$
BENZYLIC > BENZYL
BENZYLS > BENZYL
BEPAINT *vb* dye; paint
BEPAINTED > BEPAINT
BEPAINTS > BEPAINT
BEPAT *vb* pat
BEPATCHED *adj* mended with or covered in patches
BEPATS > BEPAT
BEPATTED > BEPAT
BEPATTING > BEPAT
BEPEARL *vb* decorate with pearls
BEPEARLED > BEPEARL
BEPEARLS > BEPEARL
BEPELT *vb* pelt energetically
BEPELTED > BEPELT
BEPELTING > BEPELT
BEPELTS > BEPELT
BEPEPPER *vb* shower with small missiles
BEPEPPERS > BEPEPPER
BEPESTER *vb* pester persistently
BEPESTERS > BEPESTER
BEPIMPLE *vb* form pimples on
BEPIMPLED > BEPIMPLE
BEPIMPLES > BEPIMPLE
BEPITIED > BEPITY
BEPITIES > BEPITY
BEPITY *vb* feel great pity for
BEPITYING > BEPITY
BEPLASTER *vb* cover in thick plaster
BEPLUMED *adj* decorated with feathers
BEPOMMEL *vb* beat vigorously
BEPOMMELS > BEPOMMEL
BEPOWDER *vb* cover with powder
BEPOWDERS > BEPOWDER
BEPRAISE *vb* praise highly
BEPRAISED > BEPRAISE
BEPRAISES > BEPRAISE

BEPROSE *vb* (of poetry) reduce to prose
BEPROSED > BEPROSE
BEPROSES > BEPROSE
BEPROSING > BEPROSE
BEPUFF *vb* puff up
BEPUFFED > BEPUFF
BEPUFFING > BEPUFF
BEPUFFS > BEPUFF
BEQUEATH *vb* dispose of (property) as in a will
BEQUEATHS > BEQUEATH
BEQUEST *n* legal gift of money or property by someone who has died
BEQUESTS > BEQUEST
BERAKE *vb* rake thoroughly
BERAKED > BERAKE
BERAKES > BERAKE
BERAKING > BERAKE
BERASCAL *vb* accuse of being rascal
BERASCALS > BERASCAL
BERATE *vb* scold harshly
BERATED > BERATE
BERATES > BERATE
BERATING > BERATE
BERAY *vb* soil; defile
BERAYED > BERAY
BERAYING > BERAY
BERAYS > BERAY
BERBERE *n* hot-tasting Ethiopian paste made from garlic, cayenne pepper, coriander, and other spices, often used in stews
BERBERES > BERBERE
BERBERIN *same as* > BERBERINE
BERBERINE *n* yellow bitter-tasting alkaloid obtained from barberry
BERBERINS > BERBERIN
BERBERIS *n* shrub with red berries
BERBICE *as in berbice chair* large armchair with long arms that can be folded inwards to act as leg rests
BERCEAU *n* arched trellis for climbing plants
BERCEAUX > BERCEAU
BERCEUSE *n* lullaby
BERCEUSES > BERCEUSE
BERDACHE *n* Native American transvestite
BERDACHES > BERDACHE
BERDASH *same as* > BERDACHE
BERDASHES > BERDASH
BERE *n* barley
BEREAVE *vb* deprive (of) something or someone valued, esp through death
BEREAVED *adj* having recently lost a close friend or relative through death
BEREAVEN > BEREAVE
BEREAVER > BEREAVE
BEREAVERS > BEREAVE
BEREAVES > BEREAVE
BEREAVING > BEREAVE
BEREFT *adj* deprived

BERES > BERE

BERET n round flat close-fitting brimless cap

BERETS > BERET

BERETTA n type of pistol

BERETTAS > BERETTA

BERG n iceberg

BERGAMA n type of Turkish rug

BERGAMAS > BERGAMA

BERGAMASK n person from Bergamo

BERGAMOT n small Asian tree, the fruit of which yields an oil used in perfumery

BERGAMOTS > BERGAMOT

BERGANDER n species of duck

BERGEN n large rucksack with a capacity of over 50 litres

BERGENIA n evergreen ground-covering plant

BERGENIAS > BERGENIA

BERGENS > BERGEN

BERGERE n type of French armchair

BERGERES > BERGERE

BERGFALL n avalanche

BERGFALLS > BERGFALL

BERGHAAN same as > BERGMEHL

BERGHAANS > BERGHAAN

BERGMEHL n light powdery variety of calcite

BERGMEHLS > BERGMEHL

BERGOMASK same as > BERGAMASK

BERGS > BERG

BERGYLT n large northern marine food fish

BERGYLTS > BERGYLT

BERHYME vb mention in poetry

BERHYMED > BERHYME

BERHYMES > BERHYME

BERHYMING > BERHYME

BERIBERI n disease, endemic in E and S Asia, caused by dietary deficiency of thiamine (vitamin B₁). It affects the nerves to the limbs, producing pain, paralysis, and swelling

BERIBERIS > BERIBERI

BERIMBAU n Brazilian single-stringed bowed instrument, used to accompany capoeira

BERIMBAUS > BERIMBAU

BERIME same as > BERHYME

BERIMED > BERIME

BERIMES > BERIME

BERIMING > BERIME

BERINGED adj wearing a ring or rings

BERK n stupid person

BERKELIUM n radioactive element

BERKO adj berserk

BERKS > BERK

BERLEY n bait scattered on

water to attract fish ▷ vb scatter (bait) on water

BERLEYED > BERLEY

BERLEYING > BERLEY

BERLEYS > BERLEY

BERLIN n fine wool yarn used for tapestry work, etc

BERLINE same as > BERLIN

BERLINES > BERLINE

BERLINS > BERLIN

BERM n narrow grass strip between the road and the footpath in a residential area ▷ vb create a berm

BERME same as > BERM

BERMED > BERM

BERMES > BERME

BERMING > BERM

BERMS > BERM

BERMUDAS pl n close-fitting shorts that come down to the knees

BERNICLE n barnacle goose: a N European goose that has a black-and-white head and body and grey wings

BERNICLES > BERNICLE

BEROB vb rob

BEROBBED > BEROB

BEROBBING > BEROB

BEROBED adj wearing a robe

BEROBS > BEROB

BEROUGED adj wearing rouge

BERRET same as > BERET

BERRETS > BERRET

BERRETTA same as > BIRETTA

BERRETTAS > BERRETTA

BERRIED > BERRY

BERRIES > BERRY

BERRIGAN n Australian tree, Pittosporum phylliraeoides, with hanging branches

BERRIGANS > BERRIGAN

BERRY n small soft stoneless fruit ▷ vb bear or produce berries

BERRYING > BERRY

BERRYINGS > BERRY

BERRYLESS > BERRY

BERRYLIKE > BERRY

BERSEEM n Mediterranean clover, Trifolium alexandrinum, grown as a forage crop and to improve the soil in the southwestern US and the Nile valley

BERSEEMS > BERSEEM

BERSERK adj frenziedly violent or destructive ▷ n member of a class of ancient Norse warriors who worked themselves into a frenzy before battle and fought with insane fury and courage

BERSERKER same as > BERSERK

BERSERKLY > BERSERK

BERSERKS > BERSERK

BERTH n bunk in a ship or train ▷ vb dock (a ship)

BERTHA n wide deep capelike collar, often of lace, usually to cover up a low neckline

BERTHAGE n place for mooring boats

BERTHAGES > BERTHAGE

BERTHAS > BERTHA

BERTHE n type of lace collar

BERTHED > BERTH

BERTHES > BERTHE

BERTHING > BERTH

BERTHS > BERTH

BERYL n hard transparent mineral

BERYLINE > BERYL

BERYLLIA n beryllium oxide

BERYLLIAS > BERYLLIA

BERYLLIUM n toxic silvery-white metallic element

BERYLS > BERYL

BES variant of > BETH

BESAINT vb give saint status to

BESAINTED > BESAINT

BESAINTS > BESAINT

BESANG > BESING

BESAT > BESIT

BESAW > BESEE

BESCATTER vb strew

BESCORCH vb scorch badly

BESCOUR vb scour thoroughly

BESCOURED > BESCOUR

BESCOURS > BESCOUR

BESCRAWL vb cover with scrawls

BESCRAWLS > BESCRAWL

BESCREEN vb conceal with screen

BESCREENS > BESCREEN

BESEE vb provide for; mind

BESEECH vb ask earnestly

BESEECHED > BESEECH

BESEECHER > BESEECH

BESEECHES > BESEECH

BESEEING > BESEE

BESEEKE same as > BESEECH

BESEEKES > BESEEKE

BESEEKING > BESEEKE

BESEEM vb be suitable for

BESEEMED > BESEEM

BESEEMING > BESEEM

BESEEMLY > BESEEM

BESEEMS > BESEEM

BESEEN > BESEE

BESEES > BESEE

BESES > BES

BESET vb trouble or harass constantly

BESETMENT > BESET

BESETS > BESET

BESETTER > BESET

BESETTERS > BESET

BESETTING adj tempting, harassing, or assailing

BESHADOW vb darken with shadow

BESHADOWS > BESHADOW

BESHAME vb cause to feel

shame

BESHAMED > BESHAME

BESHAMES > BESHAME

BESHAMING > BESHAME

BESHINE vb illuminate

BESHINES > BESHINE

BESHINING > BESHINE

BESHIVER vb shatter

BESHIVERS > BESHIVER

BESHONE > BESHINE

BESHOUT vb shout about

BESHOUTED > BESHOUT

BESHOUTS > BESHOUT

BESHREW vb wish evil on

BESHREWED > BESHREW

BESHREWS > BESHREW

BESHROUD vb cover with a shroud

BESHROUDS > BESHROUD

BESIDE prep at, by, or to the side of

BESIDES prep in addition ▷ adv in addition

BESIEGE vb surround with military forces

BESIEGED > BESIEGE

BESIEGER > BESIEGE

BESIEGERS > BESIEGE

BESIEGES > BESIEGE

BESIEGING > BESIEGE

BESIGH vb sigh for

BESIGHED > BESIGH

BESIGHING > BESIGH

BESIGHS > BESIGH

BESING vb sing about joyfully

BESINGING > BESING

BESINGS > BESING

BESIT vb suit; fit

BESITS > BESIT

BESITTING > BESIT

BESLAVE vb treat as slave

BESLAVED > BESLAVE

BESLAVER vb fawn over

BESLAVERS > BESLAVER

BESLAVES > BESLAVE

BESLAVING > BESLAVE

BESLIME vb cover with slime

BESLIMED > BESLIME

BESLIMES > BESLIME

BESLIMING > BESLIME

BESLOBBER vb slobber over

BESLUBBER same as > BESLOBBER

BESMEAR vb smear over

BESMEARED > BESMEAR

BESMEARER > BESMEAR

BESMEARS > BESMEAR

BESMILE vb smile on

BESMILED > BESMILE

BESMILES > BESMILE

BESMILING > BESMILE

BESMIRCH vb tarnish (someone's name or reputation)

BESMOKE vb blacken with smoke

BESMOKED > BESMOKE

BESMOKES > BESMOKE

BESMOKING > BESMOKE

BESMOOTH vb smooth

BESMOOTHS > BESMOOTH

BESMUDGE vb blacken

BESMUDGED > BESMUDGE
BESMUDGES > BESMUDGE
BESMUT vb blacken with
smut
BESMUTCH same
as > BESMIRCH
BESMUTS > BESMUT
BESMUTTED > BESMUT
BESNOW vb cover with snow
BESNOWED > BESNOW
BESNOWING > BESNOW
BESNOWS > BESNOW
BESOGNIO n worthless
person
BESOGNIOS > BESOGNIO
BESOIN n need
BESOINS > BESOIN
BESOM n broom made of
twigs ▷ vb sweep with a
besom
BESOMED > BESOM
BESOMING > BESOM
BESOMS > BESOM
BESONIAN same
as > BEZONIAN
BESONIANS > BESONIAN
BESOOTHE vb soothe
BESOOTHED > BESOOTHE
BESOOTHES > BESOOTHE
BESORT vb fit
BESORTED > BESORT
BESORTING > BESORT
BESORTS > BESORT
BESOT vb make stupid or
muddled
BESOTS > BESOT
BESOTTED adj infatuated
BESOTTING > BESOT
BESOUGHT a past participle
of > BESEECH
BESOULED adj having a soul
BESPAKE same as > BESPOKE
BESPANGLE vb cover or
adorn with or as if with
spangles
BESPAT > BESPIT
BESPATE > BESPIT
BESPATTER vb splash, e.g.
with dirty water
BESPEAK vb indicate or
suggest
BESPEAKS > BESPEAK
BESPECKLE vb mark with
speckles
BESPED > BESPEED
BESPEED vb get on with
(doing something)
BESPEEDS > BESPEED
BESPICE vb flavour with
spices
BESPICED > BESPICE
BESPICES > BESPICE
BESPICING > BESPICE
BESPIT vb cover with
spittle
BESPITS > BESPIT
BESPOKE adj (esp of a suit)
made to the customer's
specifications
BESPOKEN > BESPEAK
BESPORT vb amuse oneself
BESPORTED > BESPORT
BESPORTS > BESPORT
BESPOT vb mark with spots

BESPOTS > BESPOT
BESPOTTED > BESPOT
BESPOUSE vb marry
BESPOUSED > BESPOUSE
BESPOUSES > BESPOUSE
BESPOUT vb speak
pretentiously
BESPOUTED > BESPOUT
BESPOUTS > BESPOUT
BESPREAD vb cover (a
surface) with something
BESPREADS > BESPREAD
BESPRENT adj sprinkled
over
BEST adj most excellent of a
particular group etc ▷ adv
in a manner surpassing all
others ▷ n utmost effort
▷ vb defeat
BESTAD same as > BESTEAD
BESTADDE same
as > BESTEAD
BESTAIN vb stain
BESTAINED > BESTAIN
BESTAINS > BESTAIN
BESTAR vb decorate with
stars
BESTARRED > BESTAR
BESTARS > BESTAR
BESTEAD vb serve; assist
BESTEADED > BESTEAD
BESTEADS > BESTEAD
BESTED > BEST
BESTI Indian English word
for > SHAME
BESTIAL adj brutal or
savage
BESTIALLY > BESTIAL
BESTIALS > BESTIAL
BESTIARY n medieval
collection of descriptions
of animals
BESTICK vb cover with
sharp points
BESTICKS > BESTICK
BESTILL vb cause to be still
BESTILLED > BESTILL
BESTILLS > BESTILL
BESTING > BEST
BESTIR vb cause (oneself)
to become active
BESTIRRED > BESTIR
BESTIRS > BESTIR
BESTIS > BESTI
BESTORM vb assault
BESTORMED > BESTORM
BESTORMS > BESTORM
BESTOW vb present (a gift)
or confer (an honour)
BESTOWAL > BESTOW
BESTOWALS > BESTOW
BESTOWED > BESTOW
BESTOWER > BESTOW
BESTOWERS > BESTOW
BESTOWING > BESTOW
BESTOWS > BESTOW
BESTREAK vb streak
BESTREAKS > BESTREAK
BESTREW vb scatter or lie
scattered over (a surface)
BESTREWED > BESTREW
BESTREWN > BESTREW
BESTREWS > BESTREW
BESTRID > BESTRIDE

BESTRIDE vb have or put a
leg on either side of
BESTRIDES > BESTRIDE
BESTRODE > BESTRIDE
BESTROW same as > BESTREW
BESTROWED > BESTROW
BESTROWN > BESTROW
BESTROWS > BESTROW
BESTS > BEST
BESTUCK > BESTICK
BESTUD vb set with, or as
with studs
BESTUDDED > BESTUD
BESTUDS > BESTUD
BESUITED adj wearing a
suit
BESUNG > BESING
BESWARM vb swarm over
BESWARMED > BESWARM
BESWARMS > BESWARM
BET n agreement between
two parties that a sum
of money or other stake
will be paid by the loser to
the party who correctly
predicts the outcome of an
event ▷ vb make or place
a bet with (a person or
persons)
BETA n second letter in
the Greek alphabet, a
consonant, transliterated
as b
BETACISM vb type of
speech impediment
BETACISMS > BETACISM
BETAINE n sweet-tasting
alkaloid that occurs in the
sugar beet
BETAINES > BETAINE
BETAKE vb betake oneself go
BETAKEN > BETAKE
BETAKES > BETAKE
BETAKING > BETAKE
BETAS > BETA
BETATOPIC adj (of atoms)
differing in proton number
by one, theoretically as a
result of emission of a beta
particle
BETATRON n type of particle
accelerator for producing
high-energy beams of
electrons
BETATRONS > BETATRON
BETATTER vb make ragged
BETATTERS > BETATTER
BETAXED adj burdened
with taxes
BETE same as > BEET
BETED > BETE
BETEEM vb accord
BETEEME same as > BETEEM
BETEEMED > BETEEM
BETEEMES > BETEEME
BETEEMING > BETEEM
BETEEMS > BETEEM
BETEL n Asian climbing
plant, the leaves and nuts
of which can be chewed
BETELNUT n seed of the
betel palm, chewed with
betel leaves and lime by
people in S and SE Asia as

a digestive stimulant and
narcotic
BETELNUTS > BETELNUT
BETELS > BETEL
BETES > BETE
BETH n second letter of
the Hebrew alphabet
transliterated as b
BETHANK vb thank
BETHANKED > BETHANK
BETHANKIT n grace spoken
before meal
BETHANKS > BETHANK
BETHEL n seaman's chapel
BETHELS > BETHEL
BETHESDA n church
building of certain
Christian denomintaions
BETHESDAS > BETHESDA
BETHINK vb cause (oneself)
to consider or meditate
BETHINKS > BETHINK
BETHORN vb cover with
thorns
BETHORNED > BETHORN
BETHORNS > BETHORN
BETHOUGHT > BETHINK
BETHRALL vb make slave of
BETHRALLS > BETHRALL
BETHS > BETH
BETHUMB vb (of books) wear
by handling
BETHUMBED > BETHUMB
BETHUMBS > BETHUMB
BETHUMP vb thump hard
BETHUMPED > BETHUMP
BETHUMPS > BETHUMP
BETHWACK vb strike hard
with flat object
BETHWACKS > BETHWACK
BETID > BETIDE
BETIDE vb happen (to)
BETIDED > BETIDE
BETIDES > BETIDE
BETIDING > BETIDE
BETIGHT > BETIDE
BETIME vb befall
BETIMED > BETIME
BETIMES > BETIME
BETIMING > BETIME
BETING > BETE
BETISE n folly or lack of
perception
BETISES > BETISE
BETITLE vb give title to
BETITLED > BETITLE
BETITLES > BETITLE
BETITLING > BETITLE
BETOIL vb tire through
hard work
BETOILED > BETOIL
BETOILING > BETOIL
BETOILS > BETOIL
BETOKEN vb indicate or
signify
BETOKENED > BETOKEN
BETOKENS > BETOKEN
BETON n concrete
BETONIES > BETONY
BETONS > BETON
BETONY n North American
plant
BETOOK the past tense
of > BETAKE

**BETOSS** *vb* toss about
**BETOSSED** > BETOSS
**BETOSSES** > BETOSS
**BETOSSING** > BETOSS
**BETRAY** *vb* hand over or expose (one's nation, friend, etc) treacherously to an enemy
**BETRAYAL** > BETRAY
**BETRAYALS** > BETRAY
**BETRAYED** > BETRAY
**BETRAYER** > BETRAY
**BETRAYERS** > BETRAY
**BETRAYING** > BETRAY
**BETRAYS** > BETRAY
**BETREAD** *vb* tread over
**BETREADS** > BETREAD
**BETRIM** *vb* decorate
**BETRIMMED** > BETRIM
**BETRIMS** > BETRIM
**BETROD** > BETREAD
**BETRODDEN** > BETREAD
**BETROTH** *vb* promise to marry or to give in marriage
**BETROTHAL** *n* engagement to be married
**BETROTHED** *adj* engaged to be married ▷ *n* person to whom one is engaged
**BETROTHS** > BETROTH
**BETS** > BET
**BETTA** *n* fighting fish
**BETTAS** > BETTA
**BETTED** > BET
**BETTER** *adj* more excellent than others ▷ *adv* in a more excellent manner ▷ *pl n* one's superiors ▷ *vb* improve upon
**BETTERED** > BETTER
**BETTERING** > BETTER
**BETTERS** > BETTER
**BETTIES** > BETTY
**BETTING** > BET
**BETTINGS** > BET
**BETTONG** *n* short-nosed rat kangaroo
**BETTONGS** > BETTONG
**BETTOR** *n* person who bets
**BETTORS** > BETTOR
**BETTY** *n* type of short crowbar
**BETUMBLED** *adj* thrown into disorder
**BETWEEN** *adv* indicating position in the middle, alternatives, etc ▷ *prep* at a point intermediate to two other points in space, time, etc
**BETWEENS** > BETWEEN
**BETWIXT** *adv* between
**BEUNCLED** *adj* having many uncles
**BEURRE** *n* butter
**BEURRES** > BEURRE
**BEVATRON** *n* proton synchrotron at the University of California
**BEVATRONS** > BEVATRON
**BEVEL** *n* slanting edge ▷ *vb* slope
**BEVELED** > BEVEL

**BEVELER** > BEVEL
**BEVELERS** > BEVEL
**BEVELING** > BEVEL
**BEVELLED** > BEVEL
**BEVELLER** > BEVEL
**BEVELLERS** > BEVEL
**BEVELLING** > BEVEL
**BEVELMENT** > BEVEL
**BEVELS** > BEVEL
**BEVER** *n* snack
**BEVERAGE** *n* drink
**BEVERAGES** > BEVERAGE
**BEVERS** > BEVER
**BEVIES** > BEVY
**BEVOMIT** *vb* vomit over
**BEVOMITED** > BEVOMIT
**BEVOMITS** > BEVOMIT
**BEVOR** *n* armour protecting lower part of face
**BEVORS** > BEVOR
**BEVUE** *n* careless error
**BEVUES** > BEVUE
**BEVVIED** > BEVVY
**BEVVIES** > BEVVY
**BEVVY** *n* alcoholic drink ▷ *vb* drink alcohol
**BEVVYING** > BEVVY
**BEVY** *n* flock or group
**BEWAIL** *vb* express great sorrow over
**BEWAILED** > BEWAIL
**BEWAILER** > BEWAIL
**BEWAILERS** > BEWAIL
**BEWAILING** > BEWAIL
**BEWAILS** > BEWAIL
**BEWARE** *vb* be on one's guard (against)
**BEWARED** > BEWARE
**BEWARES** > BEWARE
**BEWARING** > BEWARE
**BEWEARIED** > BEWEARY
**BEWEARIES** > BEWEARY
**BEWEARY** *vb* cause to be weary
**BEWEEP** *vb* express grief through weeping
**BEWEEPING** > BEWEEP
**BEWEEPS** > BEWEEP
**BEWENT** > BEGO
**BEWEPT** > BEWEEP
**BEWET** *vb* make wet
**BEWETS** > BEWET
**BEWETTED** > BEWET
**BEWETTING** > BEWET
**BEWHORE** *vb* treat as whore
**BEWHORED** > BEWHORE
**BEWHORES** > BEWHORE
**BEWHORING** > BEWHORE
**BEWIG** *vb* adorn with wig
**BEWIGGED** > BEWIG
**BEWIGGING** > BEWIG
**BEWIGS** > BEWIG
**BEWILDER** *vb* confuse utterly
**BEWILDERS** > BEWILDER
**BEWINGED** *adj* having wings
**BEWITCH** *vb* attract and fascinate
**BEWITCHED** > BEWITCH
**BEWITCHER** > BEWITCH
**BEWITCHES** > BEWITCH
**BEWORM** *vb* fill with worms
**BEWORMED** > BEWORM

**BEWORMING** > BEWORM
**BEWORMS** > BEWORM
**BEWORRIED** > BEWORRY
**BEWORRIES** > BEWORRY
**BEWORRY** *vb* beset with worry
**BEWRAP** *vb* wrap up
**BEWRAPPED** > BEWRAP
**BEWRAPS** > BEWRAP
**BEWRAPT** > BEWRAP
**BEWRAY** *an obsolete word for* > BETRAY
**BEWRAYED** > BEWRAY
**BEWRAYER** > BEWRAY
**BEWRAYERS** > BEWRAY
**BEWRAYING** > BEWRAY
**BEWRAYS** > BEWRAY
**BEY** *n* (in the Ottoman empire) a title given to senior officers, provincial governors, and certain other officials
**BEYLIC** *n* province ruled over by bey
**BEYLICS** > BEYLIC
**BEYLIK** *same as* > BEYLIC
**BEYLIKS** > BEYLIK
**BEYOND** *prep* at or to a point on the other side of ▷ *adv* at or to the far side of something ▷ *n* unknown, esp life after death
**BEYONDS** > BEYOND
**BEYS** > BEY
**BEZ** *n* part of deer's horn
**BEZANT** *n* medieval Byzantine gold coin
**BEZANTS** > BEZANT
**BEZAZZ** *another word for* > PIZZAZZ
**BEZAZZES** > BEZAZZ
**BEZEL** *n* sloping edge of a cutting tool
**BEZELS** > BEZEL
**BEZES** > BEZ
**BEZIL** *archaic word for* > ALCOHOLIC
**BEZILS** > BEZIL
**BEZIQUE** *n* card game for two or more players
**BEZIQUES** > BEZIQUE
**BEZOAR** *n* hard mass, such as a stone or hairball, in the stomach and intestines of animals, esp ruminants, and man: formerly thought to be an antidote to poisons
**BEZOARDIC** *adj* relating to bezoar
**BEZOARS** > BEZOAR
**BEZONIAN** *n* knave or rascal
**BEZONIANS** > BEZONIAN
**BEZZANT** *same as* > BEZANT
**BEZZANTS** > BEZZANT
**BEZZLE** *vb* drink to excess
**BEZZLED** > BEZZLE
**BEZZLES** > BEZZLE
**BEZZLING** > BEZZLE
**BHAGEE** *same as* > BHAJI
**BHAGEES** > BHAGEE
**BHAJAN** *n* singing of devotional songs and hymns

**BHAJANS** > BHAJAN
**BHAJEE** *same as* > BHAJI
**BHAJEES** > BHAJEE
**BHAJI** *n* Indian deep-fried savoury of chopped vegetables in spiced batter
**BHAJIS** > BHAJI
**BHAKTA** *n* Hindu term for devotee of God
**BHAKTAS** > BHAKTA
**BHAKTI** *n* loving devotion to God leading to nirvana
**BHAKTIS** > BHAKTI
**BHANG** *n* preparation of Indian hemp used as a narcotic and intoxicant
**BHANGRA** *n* type of traditional Punjabi folk music combined with elements of Western pop music
**BHANGRAS** > BHANGRA
**BHANGS** > BHANG
**BHARAL** *n* wild Himalayan sheep, *Pseudois nayaur*, with a bluish-grey coat and round backward-curving horns
**BHARALS** > BHARAL
**BHAT** *n* currency of Thailand
**BHAVAN** *n* (in India) a large house or building
**BHAVANS** > BHAVAN
**BHAWAN** *same as* > BHAVAN
**BHAWANS** > BHAWAN
**BHEESTIE** *same as* > BHEESTY
**BHEESTIES** > BHEESTY
**BHEESTY** *same as* > BUISHTI
**BHEL** *same as* > BAEL
**BHELS** > BHEL
**BHIKHU** *n* fully ordained Buddhist monk
**BHIKHUS** > BHIKHU
**BHIKKHUNI** *n* fully ordained Buddhist nun
**BHINDI** *same as* > BINDHI
**BHINDIS** > BHINDI
**BHISHTI** *n* (formerly in India) a water-carrier
**BHISHTIS** > BHISHTI
**BHISTEE** *same as* > BHISHTI
**BHISTEES** > BHISTEE
**BHISTI** *same as* > BHISHTI
**BHISTIE** *same as* > BHISHTI
**BHISTIES** > BHISTIE
**BHISTIS** > BHISTI
**BHOOT** *same as* > BHUT
**BHOOTS** > BHOOT
**BHUNA** *n* Indian sauce
**BHUNAS** > BHUNA
**BHUT** *n* Hindu term for type of ghost
**BHUTS** > BHUT
**BI** *short for* > BISEXUAL
**BIACETYL** *adj* liquid with strong odour
**BIACETYLS** > BIACETYL
**BIALI** *same as* > BIALY
**BIALIES** > BIALY
**BIALIS** > BIALI
**BIALY** *n* type of bagel
**BIALYS** > BIALY
**BIANNUAL** *adj* occurring

twice a year ▷ *n*
something that happens
biannually
**BIANNUALS** > BIANNUAL
**BIAS** *n* mental tendency,
esp prejudice ▷ *vb* cause
to have a bias ▷ *adj*
slanting obliquely ▷ *adv*
obliquely
**BIASED** > BIAS
**BIASEDLY** > BIAS
**BIASES** > BIAS
**BIASING** > BIAS
**BIASINGS** > BIAS
**BIASNESS** > BIAS
**BIASSED** > BIAS
**BIASSEDLY** > BIAS
**BIASSES** > BIAS
**BIASSING** > BIAS
**BIATHLETE** *n* athlete
taking part in biathlon
**BIATHLON** *n* contest in
which skiers with rifles
shoot at four targets along
a 20-kilometre (12.5-mile)
cross-country course
**BIATHLONS** > BIATHLON
**BIAXAL** *same as* > BIAXIAL
**BIAXIAL** *adj* (esp of a
crystal) having two axes
**BIAXIALLY** > BIAXIAL
**BIB** *same as* > BIBCOCK
**BIBACIOUS** *adj* tending to
drink to excess
**BIBASIC** *adj* with two
bases
**BIBATION** *n* drinking to
excess
**BIBATIONS** > BIBATION
**BIBB** *n* wooden support on
a mast for the trestletrees
**BIBBED** > BIB
**BIBBER** *n* drinker
**BIBBERIES** > BIBBERY
**BIBBERS** > BIBBER
**BIBBERY** *n* drinking to
excess
**BIBBING** > BIB
**BIBBLE** *n* pebble
**BIBBLES** > BIBBLE
**BIBBS** > BIBB
**BIBCOCK** *n* tap with a
nozzle bent downwards
**BIBCOCKS** > BIBCOCK
**BIBELOT** *n* attractive or
curious trinket
**BIBELOTS** > BIBELOT
**BIBLE** *n* any book
containing the sacred
writings of a religion
**BIBLES** > BIBLE
**BIBLESS** > BIB
**BIBLICAL** *adj* of, occurring
in, or referring to the Bible
**BIBLICISM** *n* bible-
learning
**BIBLICIST** > BIBLICISM
**BIBLIKE** > BIB
**BIBLIOTIC** *n* study of
books
**BIBLIST** *same*
*as* > BIBLICIST
**BIBLISTS** > BIBLIST
**BIBS** > BIB

**BIBULOUS** *adj* addicted to
alcohol
**BICAMERAL** *adj* (of a
legislature) consisting of
two chambers
**BICARB** *n* bicarbonate of
soda
**BICARBS** > BICARB
**BICAUDAL** *adj* having two
tails
**BICCIES** > BICCY
**BICCY** *n* biscuit
**BICE** *n* medium blue colour
**BICENTRIC** *adj* having two
centres
**BICEP** *same as* > BICEPS
**BICEPS** *n* muscle with two
origins, esp the muscle
that flexes the forearm
**BICEPSES** > BICEPS
**BICES** > BICE
**BICHORD** *adj* having two
strings for each note
**BICHROME** *adj* having two
colours
**BICIPITAL** *adj* having two
heads
**BICKER** *vb* argue over
petty matters ▷ *n* petty
squabble
**BICKERED** > BICKER
**BICKERER** > BICKER
**BICKERERS** > BICKER
**BICKERING** > BICKER
**BICKERS** > BICKER
**BICKIE** *short for* > BISCUIT
**BICKIES** > BICKIE
**BICOASTAL** *adj* relating
to both the east and west
coasts of the US
**BICOLOR** *same*
*as* > BICOLOUR
**BICOLORED** *same*
*as* > BICOLOUR
**BICOLORS** > BICOLOR
**BICOLOUR** *adj* two-
coloured
**BICOLOURS** > BICOLOUR
**BICONCAVE** *adj* (of a lens)
having concave faces on
both sides
**BICONVEX** *adj* (of a lens)
having convex faces on
both sides
**BICORN** *adj* having two
horns or hornlike parts
**BICORNATE** *same*
*as* > BICORN
**BICORNE** *same as* > BICORN
**BICORNES** > BICORNE
**BICORNS** > BICORN
**BICRON** *n* billionth part of
a metre
**BICRONS** > BICRON
**BICUSPID** *adj* having two
points ▷ *n* bicuspid tooth
**BICUSPIDS** > BICUSPID
**BICYCLE** *n* vehicle with
two wheels, one behind
the other, pedalled by the
rider ▷ *vb* ride a bicycle
**BICYCLED** > BICYCLE
**BICYCLER** > BICYCLE
**BICYCLERS** > BICYCLE

**BICYCLES** > BICYCLE
**BICYCLIC** *adj* of, forming,
or formed by two circles,
cycles, etc
**BICYCLING** > BICYCLE
**BICYCLIST** > BICYCLE
**BID** *vb* offer (an amount)
in attempting to buy
something, esp in
competition with others
as at an auction ▷ *n* offer
of a specified amount, as
at an auction
**BIDARKA** *n* canoe covered
in animal skins, esp
sealskin, used by the Inuit
of Alaska
**BIDARKAS** > BIDARKA
**BIDARKEE** *same*
*as* > BIDARKA
**BIDARKEES** > BIDARKEE
**BIDDABLE** *adj* obedient
**BIDDABLY** > BIDDABLE
**BIDDEN** > BID
**BIDDER** > BID
**BIDDERS** > BID
**BIDDIES** > BIDDY
**BIDDING** > BID
**BIDDINGS** > BID
**BIDDY** *n* woman, esp an old
gossipy one
**BIDE** *vb* stay or continue
**BIDED** > BIDE
**BIDENT** *n* instrument with
two prongs
**BIDENTAL** *n* sacred place
where lightning has struck
**BIDENTALS** > BIDENTAL
**BIDENTATE** > BIDENT
**BIDENTS** > BIDENT
**BIDER** > BIDE
**BIDERS** > BIDE
**BIDES** > BIDE
**BIDET** *n* low basin for
washing the genital area
**BIDETS** > BIDET
**BIDI** *same as* > BEEDI
**BIDING** > BIDE
**BIDINGS** > BIDE
**BIDIS** > BIDI
**BIDON** *n* oil drum
**BIDONS** > BIDON
**BIDS** > BID
**BIELD** *n* shelter ▷ *vb*
shelter or take shelter
**BIELDED** > BIELD
**BIELDIER** > BIELDY
**BIELDIEST** > BIELDY
**BIELDING** > BIELD
**BIELDS** > BIELD
**BIELDY** *adj* sheltered
**BIEN** *adv* well
**BIENNALE** *n* event
occurring every two years
**BIENNALES** > BIENNALE
**BIENNIA** > BIENNIUM
**BIENNIAL** *adj* occurring
every two years ▷ *n* plant
that completes its life
cycle in two years
**BIENNIALS** > BIENNIAL
**BIENNIUM** *n* period of two
years
**BIENNIUMS** > BIENNIUM

**BIER** *n* stand on which
a corpse or coffin rests
before burial
**BIERS** > BIER
**BIESTINGS** *same*
*as* > BEESTINGS
**BIFACE** *n* prehistoric stone
tool
**BIFACES** > BIFACE
**BIFACIAL** *adj* having two
faces or surfaces
**BIFARIOUS** *adj* having
parts arranged in two
rows on either side of a
central axis
**BIFF** *n* blow with the fist
▷ *vb* give (someone) such
a blow
**BIFFED** > BIFF
**BIFFER** *n* someone, such as
a sportsperson, who has a
reputation for hitting hard
**BIFFERS** > BIFFER
**BIFFIES** > BIFFY
**BIFFIN** *n* variety of red
cooking apple
**BIFFING** > BIFF
**BIFFINS** > BIFFIN
**BIFFO** *n* fighting or
aggressive behaviour ▷ *adj*
aggressive
**BIFFOS** > BIFFO
**BIFFS** > BIFF
**BIFFY** *n* outdoor toilet
**BIFID** *adj* divided into two
by a cleft in the middle
**BIFIDITY** > BIFID
**BIFIDLY** > BIFID
**BIFILAR** *adj* having two
parallel threads, as in the
suspension of certain
measuring instruments
**BIFILARLY** > BIFILAR
**BIFLEX** *adj* bent or flexed in
two places
**BIFOCAL** *adj* having two
different focuses
**BIFOCALED** *adj* wearing
bifocals
**BIFOCALS** *pl n* spectacles
with lenses permitting
near and distant vision
**BIFOLD** *adj* that can be
folded in two places
**BIFOLIATE** *adj* having only
two leaves
**BIFORATE** *adj* having
two openings, pores, or
perforations
**BIFORKED** *adj* two-pronged
**BIFORM** *adj* having
or combining the
characteristics of two
forms, as a centaur
**BIFORMED** *same as* > BIFORM
**BIFTER** *n* cannabis
cigarette
**BIFTERS** > BIFTER
**BIFURCATE** *vb* fork into
two branches ▷ *adj* forked
into two branches
**BIG** *adj* of considerable
size, height, number, or
capacity ▷ *adv* on a grand

scale ▷ vb build
**BIGA** n chariot drawn by two horses
**BIGAE** > BIGA
**BIGAMIES** > BIGAMY
**BIGAMIST** > BIGAMY
**BIGAMISTS** > BIGAMY
**BIGAMOUS** > BIGAMY
**BIGAMY** n crime of marrying a person while still legally married to someone else
**BIGARADE** n Seville orange
**BIGARADES** > BIGARADE
**BIGAROON** same as > BIGARREAU
**BIGAROONS** > BIGAROON
**BIGARREAU** n any of several heart-shaped varieties of sweet cherry that have firm flesh
**BIGEMINAL** adj double; twinned
**BIGEMINY** n heart complaint
**BIGENER** n hybrid between individuals of different genera
**BIGENERIC** adj (of a hybrid plant) derived from parents of two different genera
**BIGENERS** > BIGENER
**BIGEYE** n any tropical or subtropical red marine percoid fish of the family Priacanthidae, having very large eyes and rough scales
**BIGEYES** > BIGEYE
**BIGFEET** > BIGFOOT
**BIGFOOT** n yeti ▷ vb throw one's weight around
**BIGFOOTED** > BIGFOOT
**BIGFOOTS** > BIGFOOT
**BIGG** n type of barley
**BIGGED** > BIG
**BIGGER** > BIG
**BIGGEST** > BIG
**BIGGETY** same as > BIGGITY
**BIGGIE** n something big or important
**BIGGIES** > BIGGIE
**BIGGIN** n plain close-fitting cap, often tying under the chin, worn in the Middle Ages and by children in the 17th century
**BIGGING** > BIG
**BIGGINGS** > BIG
**BIGGINS** > BIGGIN
**BIGGISH** > BIG
**BIGGITY** adj conceited
**BIGGON** same as > BIGGIN
**BIGGONS** > BIGGON
**BIGGS** > BIGG
**BIGGY** same as > BIGGIE
**BIGHA** n in India, unit for measuring land
**BIGHAS** > BIGHA
**BIGHEAD** n conceited person
**BIGHEADED** > BIGHEAD
**BIGHEADS** > BIGHEAD
**BIGHORN** n large wild

sheep, Ovis canadensis, inhabiting mountainous regions in North America and NE Asia: family Bovidae, order Artiodactyla. The male has massive curved horns, and the species is well adapted for climbing and leaping
**BIGHORNS** > BIGHORN
**BIGHT** n long curved shoreline ▷ vb fasten or bind with a bight
**BIGHTED** > BIGHT
**BIGHTING** > BIGHT
**BIGHTS** > BIGHT
**BIGLY** > BIG
**BIGMOUTH** n noisy, indiscreet, or boastful person
**BIGMOUTHS** > BIGMOUTH
**BIGNESS** > BIG
**BIGNESSES** > BIG
**BIGNONIA** n any tropical American bignoniaceous climbing shrub of the genus Bignonia (or Doxantha), cultivated for their trumpet-shaped yellow or reddish flowers
**BIGNONIAS** > BIGNONIA
**BIGOS** n Polish stew
**BIGOSES** > BIGOS
**BIGOT** n person who is intolerant, esp regarding religion or race
**BIGOTED** > BIGOT
**BIGOTEDLY** > BIGOT
**BIGOTRIES** > BIGOTRY
**BIGOTRY** n attitudes, behaviour, or way of thinking of a bigot
**BIGOTS** > BIGOT
**BIGS** > BIG
**BIGSTICK** adj of or relating to irresistible military strength
**BIGTIME** adj important
**BIGUANIDE** n any of a class of compounds some of which are used in the treatment of certain forms of diabetes
**BIGWIG** n important person
**BIGWIGS** > BIGWIG
**BIHOURLY** adj occurring every two hours
**BIJECTION** n mathematical function or mapping that is both an injection and a surjection and therefore has an inverse
**BIJECTIVE** adj (of a function, relation, etc) associating two sets in such a way that every member of each set is uniquely paired with a member of the other
**BIJOU** adj (of a house) small but elegant ▷ n something small and

delicately worked
**BIJOUS** > BIJOU
**BIJOUX** > BIJOU
**BIJUGATE** adj (of compound leaves) having two pairs of leaflets
**BIJUGOUS** same as > BIJUGATE
**BIJWONER** same as > BYWONER
**BIJWONERS** > BIJWONER
**BIKE** same as > BICYCLE
**BIKED** > BIKE
**BIKER** n person who rides a motorcycle
**BIKERS** > BIKER
**BIKES** > BIKE
**BIKEWAY** n cycle lane
**BIKEWAYS** > BIKEWAY
**BIKIE** n member of a motorcycle gang
**BIKIES** > BIKIE
**BIKING** > BIKE
**BIKINGS** > BIKE
**BIKINI** n woman's brief two-piece swimming costume
**BIKINIED** > BIKINI
**BIKINIS** > BIKINI
**BIKKIE** slang word for > BISCUIT
**BIKKIES** > BIKKIE
**BILABIAL** adj of, relating to, or denoting a speech sound articulated using both lips ▷ n bilabial speech sound
**BILABIALS** > BILABIAL
**BILABIATE** adj divided into two lips
**BILANDER** n small two-masted cargo ship
**BILANDERS** > BILANDER
**BILATERAL** adj affecting or undertaken by two parties
**BILAYER** n part of cell membrane
**BILAYERS** > BILAYER
**BILBERRY** n bluish-black edible berry
**BILBIES** > BILBY
**BILBO** n (formerly) a sword with a marked temper and elasticity
**BILBOA** same as > BILBO
**BILBOAS** > BILBOA
**BILBOES** > BILBO
**BILBOS** > BILBO
**BILBY** n Australian marsupial with long pointed ears and grey fur
**BILE** n bitter yellow fluid secreted by the liver ▷ vb Scots word for BOIL
**BILECTION** same as > BOLECTION
**BILED** > BILE
**BILES** > BILE
**BILESTONE** another name for > GALLSTONE
**BILEVEL** n hairstyle with two different lengths
**BILEVELS** > BILEVEL
**BILGE** n nonsense ▷ vb (of

a vessel) to take in water at the bilge
**BILGED** > BILGE
**BILGES** > BILGE
**BILGIER** > BILGE
**BILGIEST** > BILGE
**BILGING** > BILGE
**BILGY** > BILGE
**BILHARZIA** n disease caused by infestation of the body with blood flukes
**BILIAN** n type of tree used for its wood
**BILIANS** > BILIAN
**BILIARIES** > BILIARY
**BILIARY** adj of bile, the ducts that convey bile, or the gall bladder ▷ n disease found in dogs
**BILIMBI** n type of fruit-bearing tree
**BILIMBING** same as > BILIMBI
**BILIMBIS** > BILIMBI
**BILINEAR** adj of or referring to two lines
**BILING** > BILE
**BILINGUAL** adj involving or using two languages ▷ n bilingual person
**BILIOUS** adj sick, nauseous
**BILIOUSLY** > BILIOUS
**BILIRUBIN** n orange-yellow pigment in the bile
**BILITERAL** adj relating to two letters
**BILK** vb cheat, esp by not paying ▷ n swindle or cheat
**BILKED** > BILK
**BILKER** > BILK
**BILKERS** > BILK
**BILKING** > BILK
**BILKS** > BILK
**BILL** n n money owed for goods or services supplied ▷ vb to send or present an account for payment to (a person)
**BILLABLE** adj that can be charged to a client
**BILLABONG** n stagnant pool in an intermittent stream
**BILLBOARD** n large outdoor board for displaying advertisements
**BILLBOOK** n business record of bills received, paid, etc
**BILLBOOKS** > BILLBOOK
**BILLBUG** n type of weevil
**BILLBUGS** > BILLBUG
**BILLED** > BILL
**BILLER** n stem of a plant
**BILLERS** > BILLER
**BILLET** vb assign a lodging to (a soldier) ▷ n accommodation for a soldier in civil lodgings
**BILLETED** > BILLET
**BILLETEE** > BILLET
**BILLETEES** > BILLET
**BILLETER** > BILLET

**BILLETERS** > BILLET
**BILLETING** > BILLET
**BILLETS** > BILLET
**BILLFISH** n any of various fishes having elongated jaws, esp any fish of the family *Istiophoridae*, such as the spearfish and marlin
**BILLFOLD** n small folding case, usually of leather, for holding paper money, documents, etc
**BILLFOLDS** > BILLFOLD
**BILLHEAD** n printed form for making out bills
**BILLHEADS** > BILLHEAD
**BILLHOOK** n tool with a hooked blade, used for chopping etc
**BILLHOOKS** > BILLHOOK
**BILLIARD** n (modifier) of or relating to billiards
**BILLIARDS** n game played on a table with balls and a cue
**BILLIE** same as > BILLY
**BILLIES** > BILLY
**BILLING** n relative importance of a performer or act as reflected in the prominence given in programmes, advertisements, etc
**BILLINGS** > BILLING
**BILLION** n one thousand million ▷ *determiner* amounting to a billion
**BILLIONS** > BILLION
**BILLIONTH** > BILLION
**BILLMAN** n person who uses a billhook
**BILLMEN** > BILLMAN
**BILLON** n alloy consisting of gold or silver and a base metal, usually copper, used esp for coinage
**BILLONS** > BILLON
**BILLOW** n large sea wave ▷ *vb* rise up or swell out
**BILLOWED** > BILLOW
**BILLOWIER** > BILLOWY
**BILLOWING** > BILLOW
**BILLOWS** > BILLOW
**BILLOWY** adj full of or forming billows
**BILLS** > BILL
**BILLY** n metal can or pot for cooking on a camp fire
**BILLYBOY** n type of river barge
**BILLYBOYS** > BILLYBOY
**BILLYCAN** same as > BILLY
**BILLYCANS** > BILLYCAN
**BILLYCOCK** n any of several round-crowned brimmed hats of felt, such as the bowler
**BILLYO** n like billyo phrase used to emphasize or intensify something
**BILLYOH** same as > BILLYO
**BILLYOHS** > BILLYOH
**BILLYOS** > BILLYO
**BILOBAR** same

*as* > BILOBATE
**BILOBATE** adj divided into or having two lobes
**BILOBATED** same *as* > BILOBATE
**BILOBED** same *as* > BILOBATE
**BILOBULAR** adj having two lobules
**BILOCULAR** adj divided into two chambers or cavities
**BILSTED** n American gum tree
**BILSTEDS** > BILSTED
**BILTONG** n strips of dried meat
**BILTONGS** > BILTONG
**BIMA** same as > BEMA
**BIMAH** same as > BEMA
**BIMAHS** > BIMAH
**BIMANAL** same *as* > BIMANOUS
**BIMANOUS** adj (of man and the higher primates) having two hands distinct in form and function from the feet
**BIMANUAL** adj using or requiring both hands
**BIMAS** > BIMA
**BIMBASHI** n Turkish military official
**BIMBASHIS** > BIMBASHI
**BIMBETTE** n particularly unintelligent bimbo
**BIMBETTES** > BIMBETTE
**BIMBLE** as in *bimble box* type of dense Australian tree
**BIMBO** n attractive but empty-headed young person, esp a woman
**BIMBOES** > BIMBO
**BIMBOS** > BIMBO
**BIMENSAL** adj occurring every two months
**BIMESTER** n period of two months
**BIMESTERS** > BIMESTER
**BIMETAL** n material made from two sheets of metal
**BIMETALS** > BIMETAL
**BIMETHYL** another word *for* > ETHANE
**BIMETHYLS** > BIMETHYL
**BIMODAL** adj having two modes
**BIMONTHLY** adj every two months ▷ *adv* every two months ▷ *n* periodical published every two months
**BIMORPH** n assembly of two piezoelectric crystals cemented together so that an applied voltage causes one to expand and the other to contract, converting electrical signals into mechanical energy. Conversely, bending can generate a voltage:

used in loudspeakers, gramophone pick-ups, etc
**BIMORPHS** > BIMORPH
**BIN** n container for rubbish or for storing grain, coal, etc ▷ *vb* put in a rubbish bin
**BINAL** adj twofold
**BINARIES** > BINARY
**BINARISM** n state of being binary
**BINARISMS** > BINARISM
**BINARY** adj composed of, relating to, or involving two ▷ *n* something composed of two parts or things
**BINATE** adj occurring in two parts or in pairs
**BINATELY** > BINATE
**BINAURAL** adj relating to, having, or hearing with both ears
**BIND** vb make secure with or as if with a rope ▷ *n* annoying situation
**BINDABLE** > BIND
**BINDER** n firm cover for holding loose sheets of paper together
**BINDERIES** > BINDERY
**BINDERS** > BINDER
**BINDERY** n bookbindery
**BINDHI** same as > BINDI
**BINDHIS** > BINDHI
**BINDI** n decorative dot worn in the middle of the forehead, esp by Hindu women
**BINDING** > BIND
**BINDINGLY** > BIND
**BINDINGS** > BIND
**BINDIS** > BINDI
**BINDLE** n small packet
**BINDLES** > BINDLE
**BINDS** > BIND
**BINDWEED** n plant that twines around a support
**BINDWEEDS** > BINDWEED
**BINE** n climbing or twining stem of any of various plants, such as the woodbine or bindweed
**BINER** n clip used by climbers
**BINERS** > BINER
**BINERVATE** adj having two nerves
**BINES** > BINE
**BING** n heap or pile, esp of spoil from a mine
**BINGE** n bout of excessive indulgence, esp in drink ▷ *vb* indulge in a binge (esp of eating or drinking)
**BINGED** > BINGE
**BINGEING** > BINGE
**BINGER** n person who is addicted to crack cocaine
**BINGERS** > BINGER
**BINGES** > BINGE
**BINGHI** n Australian derogatory slang for an Aboriginal person

**BINGHIS** > BINGHI
**BINGIES** > BINGY
**BINGING** > BINGE
**BINGLE** n minor crash or upset, as in a car or on a surfboard ▷ *vb* layer (hair)
**BINGLED** > BINGLE
**BINGLES** > BINGLE
**BINGLING** > BINGLE
**BINGO** n gambling game in which numbers are called out and covered by the players on their individual cards ▷ *sentence substitute* cry by the winner of a game of bingo
**BINGOES** > BINGO
**BINGOS** > BINGO
**BINGS** > BING
**BINGY** Australian slang *for* > STOMACH
**BINIOU** n small high-pitched Breton bagpipe
**BINIOUS** > BINIOU
**BINIT** n (computing) early form of bit
**BINITS** > BINIT
**BINK** n ledge
**BINKS** > BINK
**BINMAN** another name *for* > DUSTMAN
**BINMEN** > BINMAN
**BINNACLE** n box holding a ship's compass
**BINNACLES** > BINNACLE
**BINNED** > BIN
**BINNING** > BIN
**BINOCLE** n binocular-style telescope
**BINOCLES** > BINOCLE
**BINOCS** > BINOCULAR
**BINOCULAR** adj involving both eyes
**BINOMIAL** adj consisting of two terms ▷ *n* mathematical expression consisting of two terms, such as $3x + 2y$
**BINOMIALS** > BINOMIAL
**BINOMINAL** adj of or denoting the binomial nomenclature ▷ *n* two-part taxonomic name
**BINOVULAR** adj relating to or derived from two different ova
**BINS** > BIN
**BINT** n derogatory term for a girl
**BINTS** > BINT
**BINTURONG** n arboreal SE Asian viverrine mammal, *Arctictis binturong*, closely related to the palm civets but larger and having long shaggy black hair
**BINUCLEAR** adj having two nuclei
**BIO** short for > BIOGRAPHY
**BIOACTIVE** adj able to interact with living system
**BIOASSAY** n method of determining the concentration, activity,

or effect of a change to substance by testing its effect on a living organism and comparing this with the activity of an agreed standard ▷ *vb* subject to a bioassay

**BIOASSAYS** > BIOASSAY

**BIOBLAST** *same as* > BIOPLAST

**BIOBLASTS** > BIOBLAST

**BIOCENOSE** *adj* living together in mutual dependence

**BIOCHEMIC** *adj* of or relating to chemical compounds, reactions, etc, occurring in living organisms

**BIOCHIP** *n* small glass or silicon plate containing an array of biochemical molecules or structures, used as a biosensor or in gene sequencing

**BIOCHIPS** > BIOCHIP

**BIOCIDAL** > BIOCIDE

**BIOCIDE** *n* substance used to destroy living things

**BIOCIDES** > BIOCIDE

**BIOCLEAN** *adj* free from harmful bacteria

**BIOCYCLE** *n* cycling of chemicals through the biosphere

**BIOCYCLES** > BIOCYCLE

**BIODATA** *n* information regarding an individual's education and work history, esp in the context of a selection process

**BIODIESEL** *n* biofuel intended for use in diesel engines

**BIODOT** *n* temperature-sensitive device stuck to the skin in order to monitor stress

**BIODOTS** > BIODOT

**BIOETHIC** > BIOETHICS

**BIOETHICS** *n* study of ethical problems arising from biological research and its applications in such fields as organ transplantation, genetic engineering, or artificial insemination

**BIOFACT** *n* item of biological information

**BIOFACTS** > BIOFACT

**BIOFILM** *n* thin layer of living organisms

**BIOFILMS** > BIOFILM

**BIOFOULER** *n* animal that obstructs or pollutes the environment

**BIOFUEL** *n* gaseous, liquid, or solid substance of biological origin that is used as a fuel

**BIOFUELED** *adj* running on biofuel

**BIOFUELS** > BIOFUEL

**BIOG** *short form of* > BIOGRAPHY

**BIOGAS** *n* gaseous fuel produced by the fermentation of organic waste

**BIOGASES** > BIOGAS

**BIOGASSES** > BIOGAS

**BIOGEN** *n* hypothetical protein assumed to be the basis of the formation and functioning of body cells and tissues

**BIOGENIC** *adj* originating from a living organism

**BIOGENIES** > BIOGENY

**BIOGENOUS** > BIOGENY

**BIOGENS** > BIOGEN

**BIOGENY** *n* principle that a living organism must originate from a parent form similar to itself

**BIOGRAPH** *vb* write biography of

**BIOGRAPHS** > BIOGRAPH

**BIOGRAPHY** *n* account of a person's life by another person

**BIOGS** > BIOG

**BIOHAZARD** *n* material of biological origin that is hazardous to humans

**BIOHERM** *n* mound of material laid down by sedentary marine organisms, esp a coral reef

**BIOHERMS** > BIOHERM

**BIOLOGIC** *adj* of or relating to biology ▷ *n* drug, such as a vaccine, that is derived from a living organism

**BIOLOGICS** > BIOLOGIC

**BIOLOGIES** > BIOLOGY

**BIOLOGISM** *n* explaining human behaviour through biology

**BIOLOGIST** > BIOLOGY

**BIOLOGY** *n* study of living organisms

**BIOLYSES** > BIOLYSIS

**BIOLYSIS** *n* death and dissolution of a living organism

**BIOLYTIC** > BIOLYSIS

**BIOMARKER** *n* substance, physiological characteristic, gene, etc that indicates, or may indicate, the presence of disease, a physiological abnormality, or a psychological condition

**BIOMASS** *n* total number of living organisms in a given area

**BIOMASSES** > BIOMASS

**BIOME** *n* major ecological community, extending over a large area and usually characterized by a dominant vegetation

**BIOMES** > BIOME

**BIOMETER** *n* device for

measuring natural radiation

**BIOMETERS** > BIOMETER

**BIOMETRIC** *adj* of any automated system using physiological or behavioural traits as a means of identification.

**BIOMETRY** *n* analysis of biological data using mathematical and statistical methods, especially for purposes of identification

**BIOMINING** *n* using plants, etc to collect precious metals for extraction

**BIOMORPH** *n* form or pattern resembling living thing

**BIOMORPHS** > BIOMORPH

**BIONIC** *adj* having a part of the body that is operated electronically

**BIONICS** *n* study of biological functions in order to develop electronic equipment that operates similarly

**BIONOMIC** > BIONOMICS

**BIONOMICS** *a less common name for* > ECOLOGY

**BIONOMIES** > BIONOMY

**BIONOMIST** > BIONOMICS

**BIONOMY** *n* laws of life

**BIONT** *n* living thing

**BIONTIC** > BIONT

**BIONTS** > BIONT

**BIOPARENT** *n* biological parent

**BIOPHILIA** *n* innate love for the natural world, supposed to be felt universally by humankind

**BIOPHOR** *n* hypothetical material particle

**BIOPHORE** *same as* > BIOPHOR

**BIOPHORES** > BIOPHORE

**BIOPHORS** > BIOPHOR

**BIOPIC** *n* film based on the life of a famous person

**BIOPICS** > BIOPIC

**BIOPIRACY** *n* use of wild plants by international companies to develop medicines, without recompensing the countries from which they are taken

**BIOPIRATE** > BIOPIRACY

**BIOPLASM** *n* living matter

**BIOPLASMS** > BIOPLASM

**BIOPLAST** *n* very small unit of bioplasm

**BIOPLASTS** > BIOPLAST

**BIOPSIC** > BIOPSY

**BIOPSIED** > BIOPSY

**BIOPSIES** > BIOPSY

**BIOPSY** *n* examination of tissue from a living body ▷ *vb* perform a biopsy on

**BIOPSYING** > BIOPSY

**BIOPTIC** > BIOPSY

**BIOREGION** *n* area in which climate and environment are consistent

**BIORHYTHM** *n* complex recurring pattern of physiological states, believed to affect physical, emotional, and mental states

**BIOS** > BIO

**BIOSAFETY** *n* precautions taken to control the cultivation and distribution of genetically modified crops and products

**BIOSCOPE** *n* kind of early film projector

**BIOSCOPES** > BIOSCOPE

**BIOSCOPY** *n* examination of a body to determine whether it is alive

**BIOSENSOR** *n* device used to monitor living systems

**BIOSOCIAL** *adj* relating to the interaction of biological and social elements

**BIOSOLID** *n* residue from treated sewage

**BIOSOLIDS** > BIOSOLID

**BIOSPHERE** *n* part of the earth's surface and atmosphere inhabited by living things

**BIOSTABLE** *adj* resistant to the effects of microorganisms

**BIOSTATIC** *adj* of or relating to the branch of biology that deals with the structure of organisms in relation to their function

**BIOSTROME** *n* rock layer consisting of a deposit of organic material, such as fossils

**BIOTA** *n* plant and animal life of a particular region or period

**BIOTAS** > BIOTA

**BIOTECH** *n* biotechnology

**BIOTECHS** > BIOTECH

**BIOTERROR** *n* use of biological weapons by terrorists

**BIOTIC** *adj* of or relating to living organisms ▷ *n* living organism

**BIOTICAL** *same as* > BIOTIC

**BIOTICS** > BIOTIC

**BIOTIN** *n* vitamin of the B complex, abundant in egg yolk and liver

**BIOTINS** > BIOTIN

**BIOTITE** *n* black or dark green mineral of the mica group

**BIOTITES** > BIOTITE

**BIOTITIC** > BIOTITE

**BIOTOPE** *n* small area, such as the bark of a tree, that supports its own distinctive community

**BIOTOPES** > BIOTOPE
**BIOTOXIN** n toxic substance produced by a living organism
**BIOTOXINS** > BIOTOXIN
**BIOTRON** n climate-control chamber
**BIOTRONS** > BIOTRON
**BIOTROPH** n parasitic organism, esp a fungus
**BIOTROPHS** > BIOTROPH
**BIOTURBED** adj stirred by organisms
**BIOTYPE** n group of genetically identical plants within a species, produced by apomixis
**BIOTYPES** > BIOTYPE
**BIOTYPIC** > BIOTYPE
**BIOVULAR** adj (of twins) from two separate eggs
**BIOWEAPON** n living organism or a toxic product manufactured from it, used to kill or incapacitate
**BIPACK** n obsolete filming process
**BIPACKS** > BIPACK
**BIPAROUS** adj producing offspring in pairs
**BIPARTED** adj divided into two parts
**BIPARTITE** adj consisting of two parts
**BIPARTY** adj involving two parties
**BIPED** n animal with two feet ▷ adj having two feet
**BIPEDAL** adj having two feet
**BIPEDALLY** > BIPEDAL
**BIPEDS** > BIPED
**BIPHASIC** adj having two phases
**BIPHENYL** n white or colourless crystalline solid used as a heat-transfer agent
**BIPHENYLS** > BIPHENYL
**BIPINNATE** adj (of pinnate leaves) having the leaflets themselves divided into smaller leaflets
**BIPLANE** n aeroplane with two sets of wings, one above the other
**BIPLANES** > BIPLANE
**BIPOD** n two-legged support or stand
**BIPODS** > BIPOD
**BIPOLAR** adj having two poles
**BIPRISM** n prism having a highly obtuse angle to facilitate beam splitting
**BIPRISMS** > BIPRISM
**BIPYRAMID** n geometrical form consisting of two pyramids with a common polygonal base
**BIRACIAL** adj for, representing, or including members of two races, esp

White and Black
**BIRADIAL** adj showing both bilateral and radial symmetry, as certain sea anemones
**BIRADICAL** n molecule with two centres
**BIRAMOSE** same as > BIRAMOUS
**BIRAMOUS** adj divided into two parts, as the appendages of crustaceans
**BIRCH** n tree with thin peeling bark ▷ vb flog with a birch
**BIRCHBARK** as in birchbark biting Native Canadian craft in which designs are bitten onto bark from birch trees
**BIRCHED** > BIRCH
**BIRCHEN** > BIRCH
**BIRCHES** > BIRCH
**BIRCHING** > BIRCH
**BIRD** n creature with feathers and wings, most types of which can fly ▷ vb hunt for birds
**BIRDBATH** n small basin or trough for birds to bathe in, usually in a garden
**BIRDBATHS** > BIRDBATH
**BIRDBRAIN** n stupid person
**BIRDCAGE** n wire or wicker cage in which captive birds are kept
**BIRDCAGES** > BIRDCAGE
**BIRDCALL** n characteristic call or song of a bird
**BIRDCALLS** > BIRDCALL
**BIRDDOG** n dog used or trained to retrieve game birds
**BIRDDOGS** > BIRDDOG
**BIRDED** > BIRD
**BIRDER** n birdwatcher
**BIRDERS** > BIRDER
**BIRDFARM** n place where birds are kept
**BIRDFARMS** > BIRDFARM
**BIRDFEED** n food for birds
**BIRDFEEDS** > BIRDFEED
**BIRDHOUSE** n small shelter or box for birds to nest in
**BIRDIE** n score of one stroke under par for a hole ▷ vb play (a hole) in one stroke under par
**BIRDIED** > BIRDIE
**BIRDIEING** > BIRDIE
**BIRDIES** > BIRDIE
**BIRDING** > BIRD
**BIRDINGS** > BIRD
**BIRDLIFE** n birds collectively
**BIRDLIKE** > BIRD
**BIRDLIME** n sticky substance smeared on twigs to catch small birds ▷ vb smear (twigs) with birdlime to catch (small birds)

**BIRDLIMED** > BIRDLIME
**BIRDLIMES** > BIRDLIME
**BIRDMAN** n man concerned with birds, such as a fowler or ornithologist
**BIRDMEN** > BIRDMAN
**BIRDS** > BIRD
**BIRDSEED** n mixture of various kinds of seeds for feeding cage birds
**BIRDSEEDS** > BIRDSEED
**BIRDSEYE** n type of primrose
**BIRDSEYES** > BIRDSEYE
**BIRDSHOT** n small pellets designed for shooting birds
**BIRDSHOTS** > BIRDSHOT
**BIRDSONG** n musical call of a bird or birds
**BIRDSONGS** > BIRDSONG
**BIRDWATCH** vb watch birds
**BIRDWING** n type of butterfly
**BIRDWINGS** > BIRDWING
**BIREME** n ancient galley having two banks of oars
**BIREMES** > BIREME
**BIRETTA** n stiff square cap worn by the Catholic clergy
**BIRETTAS** > BIRETTA
**BIRIANI** same as > BIRYANI
**BIRIANIS** > BIRIANI
**BIRIYANI** same as > BIRIANI
**BIRIYANIS** > BIRIYANI
**BIRK** n birch tree ▷ adj consisting of or made of birch
**BIRKEN** adj relating to the birch tree
**BIRKIE** n spirited or lively person ▷ adj lively
**BIRKIER** > BIRKIE
**BIRKIES** > BIRKIE
**BIRKIEST** > BIRKIE
**BIRKS** > BIRK
**BIRL** same as > BURL
**BIRLE** same as > BURL
**BIRLED** > BIRL
**BIRLER** > BIRL
**BIRLERS** > BIRL
**BIRLES** > BIRLE
**BIRLIEMAN** n judge dealing with local law
**BIRLIEMEN** > BIRLIEMAN
**BIRLING** > BIRL
**BIRLINGS** > BIRL
**BIRLINN** n small Scottish book
**BIRLINNS** > BIRLINN
**BIRLS** > BIRL
**BIRO** n tradename of a kind of ballpoint pen
**BIROS** > BIRO
**BIRR** vb make or cause to make a whirring sound ▷ n whirring sound
**BIRRED** > BIRR
**BIRRETTA** same as > BIRETTA
**BIRRETTAS** > BIRRETTA
**BIRRING** > BIRR
**BIRROTCH** n Ethiopian

monetary unit
**BIRRS** > BIRR
**BIRSE** n bristle
**BIRSES** > BIRSE
**BIRSIER** > BIRSY
**BIRSIEST** > BIRSY
**BIRSLE** vb roast
**BIRSLED** > BIRSLE
**BIRSLES** > BIRSLE
**BIRSLING** > BIRSLE
**BIRSY** adj bristly
**BIRTH** n process of bearing young ▷ vb give birth to
**BIRTHDAY** n anniversary of the day of one's birth
**BIRTHDAYS** > BIRTHDAY
**BIRTHDOM** n birthright
**BIRTHDOMS** > BIRTHDOM
**BIRTHED** > BIRTH
**BIRTHING** > BIRTH
**BIRTHINGS** > BIRTH
**BIRTHMARK** n blemish on the skin formed before birth
**BIRTHNAME** n name person was born with
**BIRTHRATE** n ratio of live births in a specified area, group, etc, to the population of that area, etc, usually expressed per 1000 population per year
**BIRTHROOT** n any of several North American plants of the genus Trillium, esp T. erectum, whose tuber-like roots were formerly used by the American Indians as an aid in childbirth: family Trilliaceae
**BIRTHS** > BIRTH
**BIRTHWORT** n any of several climbing plants of the genus Aristolochia, esp A. clematitis of Europe, once believed to ease childbirth: family Aristolochiaceae
**BIRYANI** n any of a variety of Indian dishes made with rice, highly flavoured and coloured with saffron or turmeric, mixed with meat or fish
**BIRYANIS** > BIRYANI
**BIS** adv twice ▷ sentence substitute encore! again!
**BISCACHA** same as > VISCACHA
**BISCACHAS** > BISCACHA
**BISCOTTI** > BISCOTTO
**BISCOTTO** n small Italian biscuit
**BISCUIT** n small flat dry sweet or plain cake ▷ adj pale brown
**BISCUITS** > BISCUIT
**BISCUITY** adj reminiscent of biscuit
**BISE** n cold dry northerly wind in Switzerland and the neighbouring parts of France and Italy, usually in the spring

**BISECT** *vb* divide into two equal parts
**BISECTED** > BISECT
**BISECTING** > BISECT
**BISECTION** > BISECT
**BISECTOR** *n* straight line or plane that bisects an angle
**BISECTORS** > BISECTOR
**BISECTRIX** *n* bisector of the angle between the optic axes of a crystal
**BISECTS** > BISECT
**BISERIAL** *adj* in two rows
**BISERIATE** *adj* (of plant parts, such as petals) arranged in two whorls, cycles, rows, or series
**BISERRATE** *adj* (of leaf margins, etc) having serrations that are themselves serrate
**BISES** > BISE
**BISEXUAL** *adj* sexually attracted to both men and women ▷ *n* bisexual person
**BISEXUALS** > BISEXUAL
**BISH** *n* mistake
**BISHES** > BISH
**BISHOP** *n* clergyman who governs a diocese ▷ *vb* make a bishop
**BISHOPDOM** *n* jurisdiction of bishop
**BISHOPED** > BISHOP
**BISHOPESS** > BISHOP
**BISHOPING** > BISHOP
**BISHOPRIC** *n* diocese or office of a bishop
**BISHOPS** > BISHOP
**BISK** *a less common spelling of* > BISQUE
**BISKS** > BISK
**BISMAR** *n* type of weighing scale
**BISMARS** > BISMAR
**BISMILLAH** *interj* in the name of Allah, a preface to all except one of the surahs of the Koran, used by Muslims as a blessing before eating or some other action
**BISMUTH** *n* pinkish-white metallic element
**BISMUTHAL** > BISMUTH
**BISMUTHIC** *adj* of or containing bismuth in the pentavalent state
**BISMUTHS** > BISMUTH
**BISNAGA** *n* type of cactus
**BISNAGAS** > BISNAGA
**BISON** *same as* > BUFFALO
**BISONS** > BISON
**BISONTINE** *adj* relating to bison
**BISQUE** *n* thick rich soup made from shellfish
**BISQUES** > BISQUE
**BISSON** *adj* blind
**BIST** *a form of the second person singular of* > BE
**BISTABLE** *adj* (of an electronic system) having two stable states ▷ *n* bistable system
**BISTABLES** > BISTABLE
**BISTATE** *adj* involving two states
**BISTER** *same as* > BESTIR
**BISTERED** > BISTER
**BISTERS** > BISTER
**BISTORT** *n* Eurasian polygonaceous plant, *Polygonum bistorta*, having leaf stipules fused to form a tube around the stem and a spike of small pink flowers
**BISTORTS** > BISTORT
**BISTOURY** *n* long surgical knife with a narrow blade
**BISTRE** *n* transparent water-soluble brownish-yellow pigment made by boiling the soot of wood, used for pen and wash drawings
**BISTRED** > BISTRE
**BISTRES** > BISTRE
**BISTRO** *n* small restaurant
**BISTROIC** > BISTRO
**BISTROS** > BISTRO
**BISULCATE** *adj* marked by two grooves
**BISULFATE** *n* bisulphate
**BISULFIDE** *n* bisulphide
**BISULFITE** *n* bisulphite
**BIT** *n* small piece, portion, or quantity
**BITABLE** > BITE
**BITCH** *n* female dog, fox, or wolf ▷ *vb* complain or grumble
**BITCHED** > BITCH
**BITCHEN** *same as* > BITCHING
**BITCHERY** *n* spiteful talk
**BITCHES** > BITCH
**BITCHFEST** *n* malicious and spiteful discussion of people, events, etc
**BITCHIER** > BITCHY
**BITCHIEST** > BITCHY
**BITCHILY** > BITCHY
**BITCHING** *adj* wonderful or excellent
**BITCHY** *adj* spiteful or malicious
**BITE** *vb* grip, tear, or puncture the skin, as with the teeth or jaws ▷ *n* act of biting
**BITEABLE** > BITE
**BITEPLATE** *n* device used by dentists
**BITER** > BITE
**BITERS** > BITE
**BITES** > BITE
**BITESIZE** *adj* small enough to put in the mouth whole
**BITEWING** *n* dental x-ray film
**BITEWINGS** > BITEWING
**BITING** > BITE
**BITINGLY** > BITE
**BITINGS** > BITE

**BITLESS** *adj* without a bit
**BITMAP** *n* picture created by colour or shading on a visual display unit ▷ *vb* create a bitmap of
**BITMAPPED** > BITMAP
**BITMAPS** > BITMAP
**BITO** *n* African and Asian tree
**BITONAL** *adj* consisting of black and white tones
**BITOS** > BITO
**BITOU** *bitou bush* type of sprawling woody shrub
**BITS** > BIT
**BITSER** *n* mongrel dog
**BITSERS** > BITSER
**BITSIER** > BITSY
**BITSIEST** > BITSY
**BITSTOCK** *n* handle or stock of a tool into which a drilling bit is fixed
**BITSTOCKS** > BITSTOCK
**BITSTREAM** *n* sequence of digital data
**BITSY** *adj* very small
**BITT** *n* one of a pair of strong posts on the deck of a ship for securing mooring and other lines ▷ *vb* secure (a line) by means of a bitt
**BITTACLE** *same as* > BINNACLE
**BITTACLES** > BITTACLE
**BITTE** *interj* you're welcome
**BITTED** > BITT
**BITTEN** > BITE
**BITTER** *adj* having a sharp unpleasant taste ▷ *n* beer with a slightly bitter taste ▷ *adv* very ▷ *vb* make or become bitter
**BITTERED** > BITTER
**BITTERER** > BITTER
**BITTEREST** > BITTER
**BITTERING** > BITTER
**BITTERISH** > BITTER
**BITTERLY** > BITTER
**BITTERN** *n* wading marsh bird with a booming call
**BITTERNS** > BITTERN
**BITTERNUT** *n* E North American hickory tree, *Carya cordiformis*, with thin-shelled nuts and bitter kernels
**BITTERS** *pl n* bitter-tasting spirits flavoured with plant extracts
**BITTIE** *n* small piece
**BITTIER** > BITTY
**BITTIES** > BITTIE
**BITTIEST** > BITTY
**BITTINESS** > BITTY
**BITTING** > BITT
**BITTINGS** > BITT
**BITTOCK** *n* small amount
**BITTOCKS** > BITTOCK
**BITTOR** *n* bittern
**BITTORS** > BITTOR
**BITTOUR** *same as* > BITTOR
**BITTOURS** > BITTOUR

**BITTS** > BITT
**BITTUR** *same as* > BITTOR
**BITTURS** > BITTOR
**BITTY** *adj* lacking unity, disjointed
**BITUMED** *adj* covered with bitumen
**BITUMEN** *n* black sticky substance obtained from tar or petrol
**BITUMENS** > BITUMEN
**BIUNIQUE** *adj* one-to-one correspondence
**BIVALENCE** *n* semantic principle that there are exactly two truth values, so that every meaningful statement is either true or false
**BIVALENCY** > BIVALENT
**BIVALENT** *adj* (of homologous chromosomes) associated together in pairs ▷ *n* structure formed during meiosis consisting of two homologous chromosomes associated together
**BIVALENTS** > BIVALENT
**BIVALVATE** *same as* > BIVALVE
**BIVALVE** *adj* (marine mollusc) with two hinged segments to its shell ▷ *n* sea creature, such as an oyster or mussel, that has a shell consisting of two hinged valves and breathes through gills
**BIVALVED** > BIVALVE
**BIVALVES** > BIVALVE
**BIVARIANT** *same as* > BIVARIATE
**BIVARIATE** *adj* (of a distribution) involving two random variables, not necessarily independent of one another
**BIVIA** > BIVIUM
**BIVINYL** *another word for* > BUTADIENE
**BIVINYLS** > BIVINYL
**BIVIOUS** *adj* offering a choice of two different ways
**BIVIUM** *n* parting of ways
**BIVOUAC** *n* temporary camp in the open air ▷ *vb* camp in a bivouac
**BIVOUACKS** > BIVOUAC
**BIVOUACS** > BIVOUAC
**BIVVIED** > BIVVY
**BIVVIES** > BIVVY
**BIVVY** *n* small tent or shelter ▷ *vb* camp in a bivouac
**BIVVYING** > BIVVY
**BIWEEKLY** *adv* every two weeks ▷ *n* periodical published every two weeks
**BIYEARLY** *adv* every two years
**BIZ** *n* business

BIZARRE *adj* odd or unusual ▷ *n* bizarre thing
BIZARRELY > BIZARRE
BIZARRES > BIZARRE
BIZARRO *n* bizarre person
BIZARROS > BIZARRO
BIZAZZ *same as* > PIZAZZ
BIZAZZES > BIZAZZ
BIZCACHA *same as* > VISCACHA
BIZCACHAS > BIZCACHA
BIZE *n* dry, cold wind in France
BIZES > BIZE
BIZNAGA *same as* > BISNAGA
BIZNAGAS > BIZNAGA
BIZONAL > BIZONE
BIZONE *n* place comprising two zones
BIZONES > BIZONE
BIZZES > BIZ
BIZZIES > BIZZY
BIZZO *n* empty and irrelevant talk or ideas
BIZZOS > BIZZO
BIZZY *n* policeman
BLAB *vb* reveal (secrets) indiscreetly
BLABBED > BLAB
BLABBER *vb* talk without thinking ▷ *n* person who blabs
BLABBERED > BLABBER
BLABBERS > BLABBER
BLABBING > BLAB
BLABBINGS > BLAB
BLABBY *adj* talking too much; indiscreet
BLABS > BLAB
BLACK *adj* of the darkest colour, like coal ▷ *n* darkest colour ▷ *vb* make black
BLACKBALL *vb* exclude from a group ▷ *n* hard boiled sweet with black-and-white stripes
BLACKBAND *n* type of iron ore
BLACKBIRD *n* common European thrush ▷ *vb* (formerly) to kidnap and sell into slavery
BLACKBODY *n* hypothetical body that would be capable of absorbing all the electromagnetic radiation falling on it
BLACKBOY *n* grass tree
BLACKBOYS > BLACKBOY
BLACKBUCK *n* Indian antelope, *Antilope cervicapra*, the male of which has spiral horns, a dark back, and a white belly
BLACKBUTT *n* Australian eucalyptus tree with hard wood used as timber
BLACKCAP *n* brownish-grey warbler, the male of which has a black crown
BLACKCAPS > BLACKCAP
BLACKCOCK *n* male of the black grouse

BLACKDAMP *n* air that is low in oxygen content and high in carbon dioxide as a result of an explosion in a mine
BLACKED > BLACK
BLACKEN *vb* make or become black
BLACKENED > BLACKEN
BLACKENER > BLACKEN
BLACKENS > BLACKEN
BLACKER > BLACK
BLACKEST > BLACK
BLACKFACE *n* performer made up to imitate a Black person
BLACKFIN *n* type of tuna
BLACKFINS > BLACKFIN
BLACKFISH *n* small dark Australian estuary fish
BLACKFLY *n* black aphid, *Aphis fabae*, that infests beans, sugar beet, and other plants
BLACKGAME *n* large N European grouse
BLACKGUM *n* US tree
BLACKGUMS > BLACKGUM
BLACKHEAD *n* black-tipped plug of fatty matter clogging a skin pore
BLACKING *n* preparation for giving a black finish to shoes, metals, etc
BLACKINGS > BLACKING
BLACKISH > BLACK
BLACKJACK *n* pontoon or a similar card game ▷ *vb* hit with or as if with a kind of truncheon
BLACKLAND *n* dark soil
BLACKLEAD *another name for* > GRAPHITE
BLACKLEG *n* person who continues to work during a strike ▷ *vb* refuse to join a strike
BLACKLEGS > BLACKLEG
BLACKLIST *n* list of people or organizations considered untrustworthy etc ▷ *vb* put on a blacklist
BLACKLY > BLACK
BLACKMAIL *n* act of attempting to extort money by threats ▷ *vb* (attempt to) obtain money by blackmail
BLACKNESS > BLACK
BLACKOUT *n* extinguishing of all light as a precaution against an air attack
BLACKOUTS > BLACKOUT
BLACKPOLL *n* North American warbler, *Dendroica striata*, the male of which has a black-and-white head
BLACKS > BLACK
BLACKTAIL *n* variety of mule deer having a black tail
BLACKTOP *n* bituminous

mixture used for paving
BLACKTOPS > BLACKTOP
BLACKWASH *n* wash for colouring a surface black
BLACKWOOD *n* tall Australian acacia tree, *A. melanoxylon*, having small clusters of flowers and curved pods and yielding highly valued black timber
BLAD *same as* > BLAUD
BLADDED > BLAD
BLADDER *n* sac in the body where urine is held
BLADDERED *adj* intoxicated
BLADDERS > BLADDER
BLADDERY > BLADDER
BLADDING > BLAD
BLADE *n* cutting edge of a weapon or tool
BLADED > BLADE
BLADELESS > BLADE
BLADELIKE > BLADE
BLADER *n* person skating with in-line skates
BLADERS > BLADER
BLADES > BLADE
BLADEWORK *n* rowing technique
BLADING *n* act or instance of skating with in-line skates
BLADINGS > BLADING
BLADS > BLAD
BLADY as in *blady grass* coarse leafy Australasian grass
BLAE *adj* bluish-grey
BLAEBERRY *another name for* > BILBERRY
BLAER > BLAE
BLAES *n* hardened clay or shale, esp when crushed and used to form the top layer of a sports pitch: bluish-grey or reddish in colour
BLAEST > BLAE
BLAFF *n* West Indian stew
BLAFFS > BLAFF
BLAG *vb* obtain by wheedling or cadging ▷ *n* robbery, esp with violence
BLAGGED > BLAG
BLAGGER > BLAG
BLAGGERS > BLAG
BLAGGING > BLAG
BLAGGINGS > BLAG
BLAGS > BLAG
BLAGUE *n* pretentious but empty talk
BLAGUER > BLAGUE
BLAGUERS > BLAGUE
BLAGUES > BLAGUE
BLAGUEUR *n* bluffer
BLAGUEURS > BLAGUEUR
BLAH *n* worthless or silly talk ▷ *adj* uninteresting ▷ *vb* talk nonsense or boringly
BLAHED > BLAH
BLAHING > BLAH
BLAHS > BLAH
BLAIN *n* blister, blotch, or

sore on the skin
BLAINS > BLAIN
BLAISE *same as* > BLAES
BLAIZE *same as* > BLAES
BLAM *n* representation of the sound of a bullet being fired
BLAMABLE > BLAME
BLAMABLY > BLAME
BLAME *vb* consider (someone) responsible ▷ *n* responsibility for something that is wrong
BLAMEABLE > BLAME
BLAMEABLY > BLAME
BLAMED *euphemistic word for* > DAMNED
BLAMEFUL *adj* deserving blame
BLAMELESS *adj* free from blame
BLAMER > BLAME
BLAMERS > BLAME
BLAMES > BLAME
BLAMING > BLAME
BLAMS > BLAM
BLANCH *vb* become white or pale
BLANCHED > BLANCH
BLANCHER > BLANCH
BLANCHERS > BLANCH
BLANCHES > BLANCH
BLANCHING > BLANCH
BLANCO *n* whitening substance ▷ *vb* whiten (something) with blanco
BLANCOED > BLANCO
BLANCOING > BLANCO
BLANCOS > BLANCO
BLAND *adj* dull and uninteresting ▷ *n* bland thing
BLANDER > BLAND
BLANDEST > BLAND
BLANDISH *vb* persuade by mild flattery
BLANDLY > BLAND
BLANDNESS > BLAND
BLANDS > BLAND
BLANK *adj* not written on ▷ *n* empty space ▷ *vb* cross out, blot, or obscure
BLANKED > BLANK
BLANKER > BLANK
BLANKEST > BLANK
BLANKET *n* large thick cloth used as covering for a bed ▷ *adj* applying to a wide group of people, situations, conditions, etc ▷ *vb* cover as with a blanket
BLANKETED > BLANKET
BLANKETS > BLANKET
BLANKETY *adv* euphemism for any taboo word
BLANKIES > BLANKY
BLANKING > BLANK
BLANKINGS > BLANK
BLANKLY > BLANK
BLANKNESS > BLANK
BLANKS > BLANK
BLANKY *n* comfort blanket
BLANQUET *n* variety of pear

BLANQUETS > BLANQUET
BLARE vb sound loudly and harshly ▷ n loud harsh noise
BLARED > BLARE
BLARES > BLARE
BLARING > BLARE
BLARNEY n flattering talk ▷ vb cajole with flattery
BLARNEYED > BLARNEY
BLARNEYS > BLARNEY
BLART vb sound loudly and harshly
BLARTED > BLART
BLARTING > BLART
BLARTS > BLART
BLASE adj indifferent or bored through familiarity
BLASH n splash
BLASHES > BLASH
BLASHIER > BLASHY
BLASHIEST > BLASHY
BLASHY adj windy and rainy
BLASPHEME vb speak disrespectfully of (God or sacred things)
BLASPHEMY n behaviour or language that shows disrespect for God or sacred things
BLAST n explosion ▷ vb blow up (a rock etc) with explosives ▷ interj expression of annoyance
BLASTED adv extreme or extremely ▷ adj blighted or withered
BLASTEMA n mass of undifferentiated animal cells that will develop into an organ or tissue: present at the site of regeneration of a lost part
BLASTEMAL > BLASTEMA
BLASTEMAS > BLASTEMA
BLASTEMIC > BLASTEMA
BLASTER > BLAST
BLASTERS > BLAST
BLASTIE n ugly creature
BLASTIER > BLASTY
BLASTIES > BLASTIE
BLASTIEST > BLASTY
BLASTING n distortion of sound caused by overloading certain components of a radio system
BLASTINGS > BLASTING
BLASTMENT n something that frustrates one's plans
BLASTOFF n launching of a rocket
BLASTOFFS > BLASTOFF
BLASTOID n extinct echinoderm found in fossil form
BLASTOIDS > BLASTOID
BLASTOMA n tumour composed of embryonic tissue that has not yet developed a specialized function
BLASTOMAS > BLASTOMA
BLASTOPOR n opening of

the archenteron in the gastrula that develops into the anus of some animals
BLASTS > BLAST
BLASTULA n early form of an animal embryo that develops from a morula, consisting of a sphere of cells with a central cavity
BLASTULAE > BLASTULA
BLASTULAR > BLASTULA
BLASTULAS > BLASTULA
BLASTY adj gusty
BLAT vb cry out or bleat like a sheep
BLATANCY > BLATANT
BLATANT adj glaringly obvious
BLATANTLY > BLATANT
BLATE adj shy; ill at ease
BLATER > BLATE
BLATEST > BLATE
BLATHER vb speak foolishly ▷ n foolish talk
BLATHERED > BLATHER
BLATHERER > BLATHER
BLATHERS > BLATHER
BLATS > BLAT
BLATT n newspaper
BLATTANT same as > BLATANT
BLATTED > BLAT
BLATTER n, vb prattle
BLATTERED > BLATTER
BLATTERS > BLATTER
BLATTING > BLAT
BLATTS > BLATT
BLAUBOK n South African antelope
BLAUBOKS > BLAUBOK
BLAUD vb slap
BLAUDED > BLAUD
BLAUDING > BLAUD
BLAUDS > BLAUD
BLAW vb blow
BLAWED > BLAW
BLAWING > BLAW
BLAWN > BLAW
BLAWORT n harebell
BLAWORTS > BLAWORT
BLAWS > BLAW
BLAY n small river fish
BLAYS > BLAY
BLAZE n strong fire or flame ▷ vb burn or shine brightly
BLAZED > BLAZE
BLAZER n lightweight jacket, often in the colours of a school etc
BLAZERED > BLAZER
BLAZERS > BLAZER
BLAZES pl n hell
BLAZING > BLAZE
BLAZINGLY > BLAZING
BLAZON vb proclaim publicly ▷ n coat of arms
BLAZONED > BLAZON
BLAZONER > BLAZON
BLAZONERS > BLAZON
BLAZONING > BLAZON
BLAZONRY n art or process of describing heraldic arms in proper form
BLAZONS > BLAZON

BLEACH vb make or become white or colourless ▷ n bleaching agent
BLEACHED > BLEACH
BLEACHER > BLEACH
BLEACHERS pl n tier of seats in a sports stadium, etc, that are unroofed and inexpensive
BLEACHERY n place where bleaching is carried out
BLEACHES > BLEACH
BLEACHING > BLEACH
BLEAK adj exposed and barren ▷ n any slender silvery European cyprinid fish of the genus Alburnus, esp A. lucidus, occurring in slow-flowing rivers
BLEAKER > BLEAK
BLEAKEST > BLEAK
BLEAKISH > BLEAK
BLEAKLY > BLEAK
BLEAKNESS > BLEAK
BLEAKS > BLEAK
BLEAKY same as > BLEAK
BLEAR vb make (eyes or sight) dim with or as if with tears ▷ adj bleary
BLEARED > BLEAR
BLEARER > BLEAR
BLEAREST > BLEAR
BLEAREYED adj with eyes blurred, as with old age or after waking
BLEARIER > BLEARY
BLEARIEST > BLEARY
BLEARILY > BLEARY
BLEARING > BLEAR
BLEARS > BLEAR
BLEARY adj with eyes dimmed, as by tears or tiredness
BLEAT vb (of a sheep, goat, or calf) utter its plaintive cry ▷ n cry of sheep, goats, and calves
BLEATED > BLEAT
BLEATER > BLEAT
BLEATERS > BLEAT
BLEATING > BLEAT
BLEATINGS > BLEAT
BLEATS > BLEAT
BLEB n fluid-filled blister on the skin
BLEBBING n formation of bleb
BLEBBINGS > BLEB
BLEBBY > BLEB
BLEBS > BLEB
BLED > BLEED
BLEE n complexion; hue
BLEED vb lose or emit blood
BLEEDER n despicable person
BLEEDERS > BLEEDER
BLEEDING > BLEED
BLEEDINGS > BLEED
BLEEDS > BLEED
BLEEP n high-pitched signal or beep ▷ vb make such a noise
BLEEPED > BLEEP
BLEEPER n small portable

radio receiver that makes a bleeping signal
BLEEPERS > BLEEPER
BLEEPING > BLEEP
BLEEPS > BLEEP
BLEES > BLEE
BLELLUM n babbler; blusterer
BLELLUMS > BLELLUM
BLEMISH n defect or stain ▷ vb spoil or tarnish
BLEMISHED > BLEMISH
BLEMISHER > BLEMISH
BLEMISHES > BLEMISH
BLENCH vb shy away, as in fear
BLENCHED > BLENCH
BLENCHER > BLENCH
BLENCHERS > BLENCH
BLENCHES > BLENCH
BLENCHING > BLENCH
BLEND vb mix or mingle (components or ingredients) ▷ n mixture
BLENDE n mineral consisting mainly of zinc sulphide
BLENDED > BLEND
BLENDER n electrical appliance for puréeing vegetables etc
BLENDERS > BLENDER
BLENDES > BLENDE
BLENDING > BLEND
BLENDINGS > BLEND
BLENDS > BLEND
BLENNIES > BLENNY
BLENNIOID adj of, relating to, or belonging to the Blennioidea, a large suborder of small mainly marine spiny-finned fishes having an elongated body with reduced pelvic fins. The group includes the blennies, butterfish, and gunnel ▷ n any fish belonging to the Blennioidea
BLENNY n small fish with a tapering scaleless body
BLENT a past participle of > BLEND
BLERT n foolish person
BLERTS > BLERT
BLESBOK n antelope, Damaliscus dorcas (or albifrons), of southern Africa. The coat is a deep reddish-brown with a white blaze between the eyes
BLESBOKS > BLESBOK
BLESBUCK same as > BLESBOK
BLESBUCKS > BLESBUCK
BLESS vb make holy by means of a religious rite
BLESSED > BLESS
BLESSEDER > BLESS
BLESSEDLY > BLESS
BLESSER > BLESS
BLESSERS > BLESS
BLESSES > BLESS

BLESSING > BLESS
BLESSINGS > BLESS
BLEST > BLESS
BLET n state of softness or decay in certain fruits, such as the medlar, brought about by overripening ▷ vb go soft
BLETHER same as > BLATHER
BLETHERED > BLETHER
BLETHERER > BLETHER
BLETHERS > BLETHER
BLETS > BLET
BLETTED > BLET
BLETTING > BLET
BLEUATRE adj blueish
BLEW > BLOW
BLEWART same as > BLAWORT
BLEWARTS > BLEWART
BLEWITS n edible saprotroph agaricaceous fungus, Tricholoma saevum, having a pale brown cap and bluish stalk
BLEWITSES > BLEWITS
BLEY same as > BLAY
BLEYS > BLEY
BLIGHT n person or thing that spoils or prevents growth ▷ vb cause to suffer a blight
BLIGHTED > BLIGHT
BLIGHTER n irritating person
BLIGHTERS > BLIGHTER
BLIGHTIES > BLIGHTY
BLIGHTING > BLIGHT
BLIGHTS > BLIGHT
BLIGHTY n home country; home leave
BLIKSEM interj South African expression of surprise
BLIMBING same as > BILIMBI
BLIMBINGS > BLIMBING
BLIMEY interj exclamation of surprise or annoyance
BLIMP n small airship
BLIMPISH adj complacent and reactionary
BLIMPS > BLIMP
BLIMY same as > BLIMEY
BLIN Scots word for > BLIND
BLIND adj unable to see ▷ vb deprive of sight ▷ n covering for a window
BLINDAGE n (esp formerly) a protective screen or structure, as over a trench
BLINDAGES > BLINDAGE
BLINDED > BLIND
BLINDER > BLIND
BLINDERS > BLIND
BLINDEST > BLIND
BLINDFISH n any of various small fishes, esp the cavefish, that have rudimentary or functionless eyes and occur in subterranean streams
BLINDFOLD vb prevent (a person) from seeing by covering the eyes ▷ n

piece of cloth used to cover the eyes ▷ adv with the eyes covered by a cloth
BLINDGUT same as > CAECUM
BLINDGUTS > BLINDGUT
BLINDING n sand or grit spread over a road surface to fill up cracks ▷ adj making one blind or as if blind
BLINDINGS > BLINDING
BLINDLESS > BLIND
BLINDLY > BLIND
BLINDNESS > BLIND
BLINDS > BLIND
BLINDSIDE vb take (someone) by surprise
BLINDWORM same as > SLOWWORM
BLING adj flashy ▷ n ostentatious jewellery
BLINGER > BLING
BLINGEST > BLING
BLINGING adj flashy and expensive
BLINGLISH n spoken English mixed with Black slang
BLINGS > BLING
BLINI pl n Russian pancakes made of buckwheat flour and yeast
BLINIS same as > BLINI
BLINK vb close and immediately reopen (the eyes) ▷ n act of blinking
BLINKARD n something that twinkles
BLINKARDS > BLINKARD
BLINKED > BLINK
BLINKER vb provide (a horse) with blinkers ▷ n flashing light for sending messages, as a warning device, etc, such as a direction indicator on a road vehicle
BLINKERED adj considering only a narrow point of view
BLINKERS > BLIND
BLINKING adv extreme or extremely
BLINKS > BLINK
BLINNED > BLIN
BLINNING > BLIN
BLINS > BLIN
BLINTZ n thin pancake folded over a filling usually of apple, cream cheese, or meat
BLINTZE same as > BLINTZ
BLINTZES > BLINTZE
BLINY same as > BLINI
BLIP n spot of light on a radar screen indicating the position of an object ▷ vb produce such a noise
BLIPPED > BLIP
BLIPPING > BLIP
BLIPS > BLIP
BLIPVERT n very short television advertisement

BLIPVERTS > BLIPVERT
BLISS n perfect happiness ▷ vb make or become perfectly happy
BLISSED > BLISS
BLISSES > BLISS
BLISSFUL adj serenely joyful or glad
BLISSING > BLISS
BLISSLESS > BLISS
BLIST archaic form of > BLESSED
BLISTER n small bubble on the skin ▷ vb (cause to) have blisters
BLISTERED > BLISTER
BLISTERS > BLISTER
BLISTERY > BLISTER
BLITE n type of herb
BLITES > BLITE
BLITHE adj casual and indifferent
BLITHEFUL same as > BLITHE
BLITHELY > BLITHE
BLITHER same as > BLETHER
BLITHERED > BLITHER
BLITHERS > BLITHER
BLITHEST > BLITHE
BLITZ n violent and sustained attack by aircraft ▷ vb attack suddenly and intensively
BLITZED > BLITZ
BLITZER > BLITZ
BLITZERS > BLITZ
BLITZES > BLITZ
BLITZING > BLITZ
BLIVE same as > BELIVE
BLIZZARD n blinding storm of wind and snow
BLIZZARDS > BLIZZARD
BLIZZARDY > BLIZZARD
BLOAT vb cause to swell, as with liquid or air ▷ n abnormal distention of the abdomen in cattle, sheep, etc, caused by accumulation of gas in the stomach
BLOATED adj swollen, as with a liquid, air, or wind
BLOATER n salted smoked herring
BLOATERS > BLOATER
BLOATING > BLOAT
BLOATINGS > BLOAT
BLOATS > BLOAT
BLOATWARE n software with more features than necessary
BLOB n soft mass or drop ▷ vb put blobs, as of ink or paint, on
BLOBBED > BLOB
BLOBBIER > BLOB
BLOBBIEST > BLOB
BLOBBING > BLOB
BLOBBY > BLOB
BLOBS > BLOB
BLOC n people or countries combined by a common interest
BLOCK n large solid piece

of wood, stone, etc ▷ vb obstruct or impede by introducing an obstacle
BLOCKABLE > BLOCK
BLOCKADE n sealing off of a place to prevent the passage of goods ▷ vb impose a blockade on
BLOCKADED > BLOCKADE
BLOCKADER > BLOCKADE
BLOCKADES > BLOCKADE
BLOCKAGE n act of blocking or state of being blocked
BLOCKAGES > BLOCKAGE
BLOCKBUST vb (try to) bring about the sale of property at a bargain price by stirring up fears of racial change in an area
BLOCKED adj functionally impeded by amphetamine
BLOCKER n person or thing that blocks
BLOCKERS > BLOCKER
BLOCKHEAD n stupid person
BLOCKHOLE n lines marked near stumps on cricket pitch
BLOCKIE n owner of a small property, esp a farm
BLOCKIER > BLOCKY
BLOCKIES > BLOCKIE
BLOCKIEST > BLOCKY
BLOCKING n interruption of anode current in a valve because of the application of a high negative voltage to the grid
BLOCKINGS > BLOCKING
BLOCKISH adj lacking vivacity or imagination
BLOCKS > BLOCK
BLOCKWORK n wall-building style
BLOCKY adj like a block, esp in shape and solidity
BLOCS > BLOC
BLOG n journal written on-line and accessible to users of the internet
BLOGGER > BLOG
BLOGGERS > BLOG
BLOGGING > BLOG
BLOGGINGS > BLOG
BLOGS > BLOG
BLOKE n man
BLOKEDOM n state of being a bloke
BLOKEDOMS > BLOKEDOM
BLOKEISH adj denoting or exhibiting the characteristics believed typical of an ordinary man
BLOKES > BLOKE
BLOKEY same as > BLOKEISH
BLOKIER > BLOKEY
BLOKIEST > BLOKEY
BLOKISH same as > BLOKEISH
BLONCKET adj blue-grey
BLOND adj (of men's hair) of a light colour ▷ n person, esp a man, having light-

coloured hair and skin
**BLONDE** *n* fair-haired
(person) ▷ *adj* (of hair) fair
**BLONDER** > BLONDE
**BLONDES** > BLONDE
**BLONDEST** > BLONDE
**BLONDINE** *vb* dye hair
blonde
**BLONDINED** > BLONDINE
**BLONDINES** > BLONDINE
**BLONDING** *n* act or an
instance of dyeing hair
blonde
**BLONDINGS** > BLONDING
**BLONDISH** > BLOND
**BLONDNESS** > BLOND
**BLONDS** > BLOND
**BLOOD** *n* red fluid that flows
around the body ▷ *vb*
initiate (a person) to war
or hunting
**BLOODBATH** *n* massacre
**BLOODED** *adj* (of horses,
cattle, etc) of good
breeding
**BLOODFIN** *n* silvery
red-finned South
American freshwater fish,
*Aphyocharax rubripinnis*:
a popular aquarium
fish: family *Characidae*
(characins)
**BLOODFINS** > BLOODFIN
**BLOODHEAT** *n* normal
human body temperature
**BLOODIED** > BLOODY
**BLOODIER** > BLOODY
**BLOODIES** > BLOODY
**BLOODIEST** > BLOODY
**BLOODILY** > BLOODY
**BLOODING** > BLOOD
**BLOODINGS** > BLOOD
**BLOODLESS** *adj* without
blood or bloodshed
**BLOODLIKE** > BLOOD
**BLOODLINE** *n* all the
members of a family group
over generations, esp
regarding characteristics
common to that group
**BLOODLUST** *n* desire to see
bloodshed
**BLOODRED** *adj* having a
deep red colour
**BLOODROOT** *n* North
American papaveraceous
plant, *Sanguinaria
canadensis*, having a single
whitish flower and a fleshy
red root that yields a red
dye
**BLOODS** > BLOOD
**BLOODSHED** *n* slaughter or
killing
**BLOODSHOT** *adj* (of an eye)
inflamed
**BLOODWOOD** *n* any of several
species of Australian
eucalyptus that exude a
red sap
**BLOODWORM** *n* red wormlike
aquatic larva of the midge,
*Chironomus plumosus*,
which lives at the bottom

of stagnant pools and
ditches
**BLOODWORT** *n* plant with
red dye in roots
**BLOODY** *adj* covered with
blood ▷ *adv* extreme or
extremely ▷ *vb* stain with
blood
**BLOODYING** > BLOODY
**BLOOEY** *adj* out of order;
faulty
**BLOOIE** *same as* > BLOOEY
**BLOOM** *n* blossom on a
flowering plant ▷ *vb* (of
flowers) open
**BLOOMED** *adj* (of a lens)
coated with a thin film of
magnesium fluoride or
some other substance to
reduce the amount of light
lost by reflection
**BLOOMER** *n* stupid mistake
**BLOOMERS** *pl n* woman's
baggy knickers
**BLOOMERY** *n* place in which
malleable iron is produced
directly from iron ore
**BLOOMIER** > BLOOMY
**BLOOMIEST** > BLOOMY
**BLOOMING** *adj* extreme or
extremely
**BLOOMLESS** > BLOOM
**BLOOMS** > BLOOM
**BLOOMY** *adj* having a fine
whitish coating on the
surface, such as on the rind
of a cheese
**BLOOP** *vb* (baseball) hit a
ball into air beyond infield
**BLOOPED** > BLOOP
**BLOOPER** *n* stupid mistake
**BLOOPERS** > BLOOPER
**BLOOPING** > BLOOP
**BLOOPS** > BLOOP
**BLOOSME** *same
as* > BLOSSOM
**BLOOSMED** > BLOOSME
**BLOOSMES** > BLOOSME
**BLOOSMING** > BLOOSME
**BLOQUISTE** *n* supporter of
autonomy for Quebec
**BLORE** *n* strong blast of
wind
**BLORES** > BLORE
**BLOSSOM** *n* flowers of a
plant ▷ *vb* (of plants)
flower
**BLOSSOMED** > BLOSSOM
**BLOSSOMS** > BLOSSOM
**BLOSSOMY** > BLOSSOM
**BLOT** *n* spot or stain ▷ *vb*
cause a blemish in or on
**BLOTCH** *n* discoloured area
or stain ▷ *vb* become or
cause to become marked
by such discoloration
**BLOTCHED** > BLOTCH
**BLOTCHES** > BLOTCH
**BLOTCHIER** > BLOTCHY
**BLOTCHILY** > BLOTCHY
**BLOTCHING** > BLOTCH
**BLOTCHY** *adj* covered in or
marked by blotches
**BLOTLESS** > BLOT

**BLOTS** > BLOT
**BLOTTED** > BLOT
**BLOTTER** *n* sheet of
blotting paper
**BLOTTERS** > BLOTTER
**BLOTTIER** > BLOTTY
**BLOTTIEST** > BLOTTY
**BLOTTING** *n* blot analysis
**BLOTTINGS** > BLOTTING
**BLOTTO** *adj* extremely
drunk
**BLOTTY** *adj* covered in blots
**BLOUBOK** *same as* > BLAUBOK
**BLOUBOKS** > BLOUBOK
**BLOUSE** *n* woman's
shirtlike garment ▷ *vb*
hang or cause to hang in
full loose folds
**BLOUSED** > BLOUSE
**BLOUSES** > BLOUSE
**BLOUSIER** > BLOUSY
**BLOUSIEST** > BLOUSY
**BLOUSILY** > BLOUSY
**BLOUSING** > BLOUSE
**BLOUSON** *n* short loose
jacket with a tight waist
**BLOUSONS** > BLOUSON
**BLOUSY** *adj* loose; blouse-
like
**BLOVIATE** *vb* discourse at
length
**BLOVIATED** > BLOVIATE
**BLOVIATES** > BLOVIATE
**BLOW** *vb* (of air, the wind,
etc) move ▷ *n* hard hit
**BLOWBACK** *n* escape to
the rear of gases formed
during the firing of a
weapon or in a boiler,
internal-combustion
engine, etc
**BLOWBACKS** > BLOWBACK
**BLOWBALL** *n* dandelion
seed head
**BLOWBALLS** > BLOWBALL
**BLOWBY** *n* leakage of gas
past the piston of an
engine at maximum
pressure
**BLOWBYS** > BLOWBY
**BLOWDOWN** *n* accident
in a nuclear reactor in
which a cooling pipe
bursts causing the loss
of essential coolant
▷ *vb* open a valve in a
steam boiler to eject
any sediment that has
collected
**BLOWDOWNS** > BLOWDOWN
**BLOWED** > BLOW
**BLOWER** *n* mechanical
device, such as a fan, that
blows
**BLOWERS** > BLOWER
**BLOWFISH** *a popular name
for* > PUFFER
**BLOWFLIES** > BLOWFLY
**BLOWFLY** *n* fly that lays its
eggs in meat
**BLOWGUN** *same
as* > BLOWPIPE
**BLOWGUNS** > BLOWGUN
**BLOWHARD** *n* boastful

person ▷ *adj* blustering or
boastful
**BLOWHARDS** > BLOWHARD
**BLOWHOLE** *n* nostril of a
whale
**BLOWHOLES** > BLOWHOLE
**BLOWIE** *n* bluebottle
**BLOWIER** > BLOWY
**BLOWIES** > BLOWIE
**BLOWIEST** > BLOWY
**BLOWINESS** > BLOWY
**BLOWING** > BLOW
**BLOWJOB** *slang term
for* > FELLATIO
**BLOWJOBS** > BLOWJOB
**BLOWKART** *n* land vehicle
with a sail
**BLOWKARTS** > BLOWKART
**BLOWLAMP** *another name
for* > BLOWTORCH
**BLOWLAMPS** > BLOWLAMP
**BLOWN** > BLOW
**BLOWOFF** *n* discharge of a
surplus fluid
**BLOWOFFS** > BLOWOFF
**BLOWOUT** *n* sudden loss of
air in a tyre
**BLOWOUTS** > BLOWOUT
**BLOWPIPE** *n* long tube from
which darts etc are shot by
blowing
**BLOWPIPES** > BLOWPIPE
**BLOWS** > BLOW
**BLOWSE** *n* large, red-faced
woman
**BLOWSED** *same as* > BLOWSY
**BLOWSES** > BLOWSE
**BLOWSIER** > BLOWSY
**BLOWSIEST** > BLOWSY
**BLOWSILY** > BLOWSY
**BLOWSY** *adj* fat, untidy, and
red-faced
**BLOWTORCH** *n* small burner
producing a very hot flame
**BLOWTUBE** *n* tube for
blowing air or oxygen
into a flame to intensify
its heat
**BLOWTUBES** > BLOWTUBE
**BLOWUP** *n* fit of temper
**BLOWUPS** > BLOWUP
**BLOWY** *adj* windy
**BLOWZE** *variant of* > BLOWSE
**BLOWZED** *same as* > BLOWSY
**BLOWZES** > BLOWZE
**BLOWZIER** > BLOWZY
**BLOWZIEST** > BLOWZY
**BLOWZILY** > BLOWZY
**BLOWZY** *same as* > BLOWSY
**BLUB** *a slang word
for* > BLUBBER
**BLUBBED** > BLUB
**BLUBBER** *n vb* sob without
restraint ▷ *adj* swollen or
fleshy ▷ *n* fat of whales,
seals, etc
**BLUBBERED** > BLUBBER
**BLUBBERER** > BLUBBER
**BLUBBERS** > BLUBBER
**BLUBBERY** *adj* of,
containing, or like blubber
**BLUBBING** > BLUB
**BLUBS** > BLUB
**BLUCHER** *n* high shoe with

laces over the tongue
**BLUCHERS** > BLUCHER
**BLUDE** *Scots form of* > BLOOD
**BLUDES** > BLUDE
**BLUDGE** *vb* evade work ▷ *n*
easy task
**BLUDGED** > BLUDGE
**BLUDGEON** *n* short thick
club ▷ *vb* hit with a
bludgeon
**BLUDGEONS** > BLUDGEON
**BLUDGER** *n* person who
scrounges
**BLUDGERS** > BLUDGER
**BLUDGES** > BLUDGE
**BLUDGING** > BLUDGE
**BLUDIE** *Scots form*
*of* > BLOODY
**BLUDIER** > BLUDIE
**BLUDIEST** > BLUDIE
**BLUDY** *same as* > BLUDIE
**BLUE** *n* colour of a clear
unclouded sky ▷ *adj* of the
colour blue ▷ *vb* make or
become blue
**BLUEBACK** *n* type of salmon
**BLUEBACKS** > BLUEBACK
**BLUEBALL** *n* type of
European herb
**BLUEBALLS** > BLUEBALL
**BLUEBEARD** *n* any man who
murders his wife or wives
**BLUEBEAT** *n* type of West
Indian pop music of the
1960s
**BLUEBEATS** > BLUEBEAT
**BLUEBELL** *n* flower with
blue bell-shaped flowers
**BLUEBELLS** > BLUEBELL
**BLUEBERRY** *n* very small
blackish edible fruit
that grows on a North
American shrub
**BLUEBILL** *another name*
*for* > SCAUP
**BLUEBILLS** > BLUEBILL
**BLUEBIRD** *n* North
American songbird with a
blue plumage
**BLUEBIRDS** > BLUEBIRD
**BLUEBLOOD** *n* royal or
aristocratic person
**BLUEBOOK** *n* (in Britain) a
government publication,
usually the report of a
commission
**BLUEBOOKS** > BLUEBOOK
**BLUEBUCK** *same*
*as* > BLAUBOK
**BLUEBUCKS** > BLUEBUCK
**BLUEBUSH** *n* any of various
blue-grey herbaceous
Australian shrubs of the
genus *Maireana*
**BLUECAP** *another name*
*for* > BLUETIT
**BLUECAPS** > BLUECAP
**BLUECOAT** *n* person who
wears blue uniform
**BLUECOATS** > BLUECOAT
**BLUECURLS** *n* North
American plant
**BLUED** > BLUE
**BLUEFIN** *another name*

*for* > TUNNY
**BLUEFINS** > BLUEFIN
**BLUEFISH** *n* bluish
marine percoid food and
game fish, *Pomatomus*
*saltatrix*, related to the
horse mackerel: family
*Pomatomidae*
**BLUEGILL** *n* common
North American
freshwater sunfish,
*Lepomis macrochirus*: an
important food and game
fish
**BLUEGILLS** > BLUEGILL
**BLUEGOWN** *n* in past,
pauper, recipient of blue
gown on King's birthday
**BLUEGOWNS** > BLUEGOWN
**BLUEGRASS** *n* any of several
North American bluish-
green grasses
**BLUEGUM** *n* tall fast-
growing widely cultivated
Australian myrtaceous
tree, *Eucalyptus globulus*,
having aromatic leaves
containing a medicinal
oil, bark that peels off in
shreds, and hard timber
**BLUEGUMS** > BLUEGUM
**BLUEHEAD** *n* type of fish
**BLUEHEADS** > BLUEHEAD
**BLUEING** > BLUE
**BLUEINGS** > BLUE
**BLUEISH** *same as* > BLUISH
**BLUEJACK** *n* type of oak
tree
**BLUEJACKS** > BLUEJACK
**BLUEJAY** *n* common North
American jay, *Cyanocitta*
*cristata*, having bright blue
plumage with greyish-
white underparts
**BLUEJAYS** > BLUEJAY
**BLUEJEANS** *n* blue denim
jeans
**BLUELINE** *n* blue-toned
photographic proof
**BLUELINER** *n* machine for
making blueprints
**BLUELINES** > BLUELINE
**BLUELY** > BLUE
**BLUENESS** > BLUE
**BLUENOSE** *n* puritanical or
prudish person
**BLUENOSED** > BLUENOSE
**BLUENOSES** > BLUENOSE
**BLUEPOINT** *n* type of small
oyster
**BLUEPRINT** *n*
photographic print
of a plan ▷ *vb* make a
blueprint of (a plan)
**BLUER** > BLUE
**BLUES** *pl n* type of music
**BLUESHIFT** *n* shift in the
spectral lines of a stellar
spectrum
**BLUESIER** > BLUES
**BLUESIEST** > BLUES
**BLUESMAN** *n* blues
musician
**BLUESMEN** > BLUESMAN

**BLUEST** > BLUE
**BLUESTEM** *n* type of tall
grass
**BLUESTEMS** > BLUESTEM
**BLUESTONE** *n* blue-grey
sandstone containing
much clay, used for
building and paving
**BLUESY** > BLUES
**BLUET** *n* North American
rubiaceous plant,
*Houstonia caerulea*, with
small four-petalled blue
flowers
**BLUETICK** *n* fast-running
dog
**BLUETICKS** > BLUETICK
**BLUETIT** *n* small European
bird with a blue crown,
wings, and tail and yellow
underparts
**BLUETITS** > BLUETIT
**BLUETS** > BLUET
**BLUETTE** *n* short, brilliant
piece of music
**BLUETTES** > BLUETTE
**BLUEWEED** *n* Eurasian
boraginaceous weed,
*Echium vulgare*, having blue
flowers and pink buds
**BLUEWEEDS** > BLUEWEED
**BLUEWING** *n* type of duck
**BLUEWINGS** > BLUEWING
**BLUEWOOD** *n* type of
Mexican shrub
**BLUEWOODS** > BLUEWOOD
**BLUEY** *adj* bluish ▷ *n*
informal Australian word
meaning blanket
**BLUEYS** > BLUEY
**BLUFF** *vb* pretend to be
confident in order to
influence (someone) ▷ *n*
act of bluffing ▷ *adj* good-
naturedly frank and hearty
**BLUFFABLE** > BLUFF
**BLUFFED** > BLUFF
**BLUFFER** > BLUFF
**BLUFFERS** > BLUFF
**BLUFFEST** > BLUFF
**BLUFFING** > BLUFF
**BLUFFLY** > BLUFF
**BLUFFNESS** > BLUFF
**BLUFFS** > BLUFF
**BLUGGIER** > BLUGGY
**BLUGGIEST** > BLUGGY
**BLUGGY** *same as* > BLOODY
**BLUID** *Scots word*
*for* > BLOOD
**BLUIDIER** > BLUID
**BLUIDIEST** > BLUID
**BLUIDS** > BLUID
**BLUIDY** > BLUID
**BLUIER** > BLUEY
**BLUIEST** > BLUEY
**BLUING** > BLUE
**BLUINGS** > BLUE
**BLUISH** *adj* slightly blue
**BLUME** *Scots word*
*for* > BLOOM
**BLUMED** > BLUME
**BLUMES** > BLUME
**BLUMING** > BLUME
**BLUNDER** *n* clumsy mistake

▷ *vb* make a blunder
**BLUNDERED** > BLUNDER
**BLUNDERER** > BLUNDER
**BLUNDERS** > BLUNDER
**BLUNGE** *vb* mix (clay or a
similar substance) with
water in order to form
a suspension for use in
ceramics
**BLUNGED** > BLUNGE
**BLUNGER** *n* large vat in
which the contents, esp
clay and water, are mixed
by rotating arms
**BLUNGERS** > BLUNGER
**BLUNGES** > BLUNGE
**BLUNGING** > BLUNGE
**BLUNK** *vb* ruin; botch
**BLUNKED** > BLUNK
**BLUNKER** > BLUNK
**BLUNKERS** > BLUNK
**BLUNKING** > BLUNK
**BLUNKS** > BLUNK
**BLUNT** *adj* not having a
sharp edge or point ▷ *vb*
make less sharp ▷ *n*
cannabis cigarette
**BLUNTED** > BLUNT
**BLUNTER** > BLUNT
**BLUNTEST** > BLUNT
**BLUNTHEAD** *n* frequent user
of marijuana
**BLUNTING** > BLUNT
**BLUNTISH** > BLUNT
**BLUNTLY** > BLUNT
**BLUNTNESS** > BLUNT
**BLUNTS** > BLUNT
**BLUR** *vb* make or become
vague or less distinct ▷ *n*
something vague, hazy, or
indistinct
**BLURB** *n* promotional
description, as on the
jacket of a book ▷ *vb*
describe or recommend in
a blurb
**BLURBED** > BLURB
**BLURBING** > BLURB
**BLURBIST** *n* writer of
blurbs
**BLURBISTS** > BLURBIST
**BLURBS** > BLURB
**BLURRED** > BLUR
**BLURREDLY** > BLUR
**BLURRIER** > BLUR
**BLURRIEST** > BLUR
**BLURRILY** > BLUR
**BLURRING** > BLUR
**BLURRY** > BLUR
**BLURS** > BLUR
**BLURT** *vb* utter suddenly
and involuntarily
**BLURTED** > BLURT
**BLURTER** > BLURT
**BLURTERS** > BLURT
**BLURTING** > BLURT
**BLURTINGS** > BLURT
**BLURTS** > BLURT
**BLUSH** *vb* become red
in the face, esp from
embarrassment or shame
▷ *n* reddening of the face
**BLUSHED** > BLUSH
**BLUSHER** *n* cosmetic for

giving the cheeks a rosy colour

**BLUSHERS** > BLUSHER

**BLUSHES** > BLUSH

**BLUSHET** n modest young woman

**BLUSHETS** > BLUSHET

**BLUSHFUL** > BLUSH

**BLUSHING** > BLUSH

**BLUSHINGS** > BLUSH

**BLUSHLESS** > BLUSH

**BLUSTER** vb speak loudly or in a bullying way ▷ n empty threats or protests

**BLUSTERED** > BLUSTER

**BLUSTERER** > BLUSTER

**BLUSTERS** > BLUSTER

**BLUSTERY** > BLUSTER

**BLUSTROUS** adj inclined to bluster

**BLUTWURST** n blood sausage

**BLYPE** n piece of skin peeled off after sunburn

**BLYPES** > BLYPE

**BO** interj, n exclamation uttered to startle or surprise someone, esp a child in a game

**BOA** n large nonvenomous snake

**BOAB** short for > BAOBAB

**BOABS** > BOAB

**BOAK** same as > BOKE

**BOAKED** > BOAK

**BOAKING** > BOAK

**BOAKS** > BOAK

**BOAR** n uncastrated male pig

**BOARD** n long flat piece of sawn timber ▷ vb go aboard (a train, aeroplane, etc)

**BOARDABLE** > BOARD

**BOARDED** > BOARD

**BOARDER** n person who pays rent in return for accommodation in someone else's home

**BOARDERS** > BOARDER

**BOARDING** n act of embarking on an aircraft, train, ship, etc

**BOARDINGS** > BOARDING

**BOARDLIKE** > BOARD

**BOARDMAN** n man who carries a sandwich board

**BOARDMEN** > BOARDMAN

**BOARDROOM** n room where the board of a company meets

**BOARDS** > BOARD

**BOARDWALK** n promenade, esp along a beach, usually made of planks

**BOARFISH** n any of various spiny-finned marine teleost fishes of the genera Capros, Antigonia, etc, related to the dories, having a deep compressed body, a long snout, and large eyes

**BOARHOUND** n dog used to hunt boar

**BOARISH** adj coarse, cruel, or sensual

**BOARISHLY** > BOARISH

**BOARS** > BOAR

**BOART** same as > BORT

**BOARTS** > BOART

**BOAS** > BOA

**BOAST** vb speak too proudly about one's talents etc ▷ n bragging statement

**BOASTED** > BOAST

**BOASTER** > BOAST

**BOASTERS** > BOAST

**BOASTFUL** adj tending to boast

**BOASTING** > BOAST

**BOASTINGS** > BOAST

**BOASTLESS** > BOAST

**BOASTS** > BOAST

**BOAT** n small vehicle for travelling across water ▷ vb travel in a boat

**BOATABLE** adj able to be carried by boat

**BOATBILL** n nocturnal tropical American wading bird, Cochlearius cochlearius, similar to the night herons but with a broad flattened bill: family Ardeidae, order Ciconiiformes

**BOATBILLS** > BOATBILL

**BOATED** > BOAT

**BOATEL** n waterside hotel catering for boating people

**BOATELS** > BOATEL

**BOATER** n flat straw hat

**BOATERS** > BOATER

**BOATFUL** > BOAT

**BOATFULS** > BOAT

**BOATHOOK** n pole with a hook at one end, used aboard a vessel for fending off other vessels or obstacles or for catching a line or mooring buoy

**BOATHOOKS** > BOATHOOK

**BOATHOUSE** n shelter by the edge of a river, lake, etc, for housing boats

**BOATIE** n boating enthusiast

**BOATIES** > BOATIE

**BOATING** n rowing, sailing, or cruising in boats as a form of recreation

**BOATINGS** > BOATING

**BOATLIFT** n evacuation by boat

**BOATLIFTS** > BOATLIFT

**BOATLIKE** > BOAT

**BOATLOAD** n amount of cargo or number of people held by a boat or ship

**BOATLOADS** > BOATLOAD

**BOATMAN** n man who works on, hires out, or repairs boats

**BOATMEN** > BOATMAN

**BOATNECK** n wide open neck on garment

**BOATNECKS** > BOATNECK

**BOATS** > BOAT

**BOATSMAN** same as > BOATMAN

**BOATSMEN** > BOATSMAN

**BOATSWAIN** n petty officer on a merchant ship or a warrant officer on a warship who is responsible for the maintenance of the ship and its equipment

**BOATTAIL** n type of blackbird

**BOATTAILS** > BOATTAIL

**BOATYARD** n place where boats are kept, repaired, etc

**BOATYARDS** > BOATYARD

**BOB** vb move or cause to move up and down repeatedly, as while floating in water ▷ n short abrupt movement, as of the head

**BOBA** n type of Chinese tea

**BOBAC** same as > BOBAK

**BOBACS** > BOBAC

**BOBAK** n type of marmot

**BOBAKS** > BOBAK

**BOBAS** > BOBA

**BOBBED** > BOB

**BOBBEJAAN** n baboon

**BOBBER** n type of float for fishing

**BOBBERIES** > BOBBERY

**BOBBERS** > BOBBER

**BOBBERY** n mixed pack of hunting dogs, often not belonging to any of the hound breeds ▷ adj noisy or excitable

**BOBBIES** > BOBBY

**BOBBIN** n reel on which thread is wound

**BOBBINET** n netted fabric of hexagonal mesh, made on a lace machine

**BOBBINETS** > BOBBINET

**BOBBING** > BOB

**BOBBINS** > BOBBIN

**BOBBISH** > CHEERY

**BOBBITT** vb sever the penis of

**BOBBITTED** > BOBBITT

**BOBBITTS** > BOBBITT

**BOBBLE** n small ball of material, usu for decoration ▷ vb (of a ball) to bounce erratically because of an uneven playing surface

**BOBBLED** > BOBBLE

**BOBBLES** > BOBBLE

**BOBBLIER** > BOBBLY

**BOBBLIEST** > BOBBLY

**BOBBLING** > BOBBLE

**BOBBLY** adj (of fabric) covered in small balls; worn

**BOBBY** n policeman

**BOBBYSOCK** n ankle-length sock worn esp by teenage girls

**BOBBYSOX** pl n bobbysocks

**BOATSMAN** same as > BOATMAN

**BOBCAT** n North American feline mammal, Lynx rufus, closely related to but smaller than the lynx, having reddish-brown fur with dark spots or stripes, tufted ears, and a short tail

**BOBCATS** > BOBCAT

**BOBECHE** n candle drip-catcher

**BOBECHES** > BOBECHE

**BOBFLOAT** n small buoyant float, usually consisting of a quill stuck through a piece of cork

**BOBFLOATS** > BOBFLOAT

**BOBLET** n two-man bobsleigh

**BOBLETS** > BOBLET

**BOBOL** n fraud carried out by one or more persons with access to public funds in collusion with someone in a position of authority ▷ vb commit a bobol

**BOBOLINK** n American songbird, Dolichonyx oryzivorus, the male of which has a white back and black underparts in the breeding season: family Icteridae (American orioles)

**BOBOLINKS** > BOBOLINK

**BOBOLLED** > BOBOL

**BOBOLLING** > BOBOL

**BOBOLS** > BOBOL

**BOBOTIE** n dish of curried mince

**BOBOTIES** > BOBOTIE

**BOBOWLER** n large moth

**BOBOWLERS** > BOBOWLER

**BOBS** > BOB

**BOBSLED** same as > BOBSLEIGH

**BOBSLEDS** > BOBSLED

**BOBSLEIGH** n sledge for racing down an icy track ▷ vb ride on a bobsleigh

**BOBSTAY** n strong stay between a bowsprit and the stem of a vessel for holding down the bowsprit

**BOBSTAYS** > BOBSTAY

**BOBTAIL** n docked tail ▷ adj having the tail cut short ▷ vb dock the tail of

**BOBTAILED** > BOBTAIL

**BOBTAILS** > BOBTAIL

**BOBWEIGHT** n balance weight

**BOBWHEEL** n poetic device

**BOBWHEELS** > BOBWHEEL

**BOBWHITE** n brown North American quail, Colinus virginianus, the male of which has white markings on the head: a popular game bird

**BOBWHITES** > BOBWHITE

**BOBWIG** n type of short wig

**BOBWIGS** > BOBWIG

**BOCACCIO** n edible

American fish

**BOCACCIOS** > BOCACCIO

**BOCAGE** n wooded countryside characteristic of northern France, with small irregular-shaped fields and many hedges and copses

**BOCAGES** > BOCAGE

**BOCCA** n mouth

**BOCCAS** > BOCCA

**BOCCE** same as > BOCCIE

**BOCCES** > BOCCE

**BOCCI** same as > BOCCIE

**BOCCIA** same as > BOCCIE

**BOCCIAS** > BOCCIA

**BOCCIE** n Italian version of bowls played on a lawn smaller than a bowling green

**BOCCIES** > BOCCIE

**BOCCIS** > BOCCI

**BOCHE** n derogatory slang for a German soldier

**BOCHES** > BOCHE

**BOCK** a variant spelling of > BOKE

**BOCKED** > BOCK

**BOCKEDY** adj (of a structure, piece of furniture, etc) unsteady

**BOCKING** > BOCK

**BOCKS** > BOCK

**BOCONCINI** pl n small pieces of mozzarella

**BOD** n person

**BODACH** n old man

**BODACHS** > BODACH

**BODACIOUS** adj impressive or remarkable

**BODDLE** same as > BODLE

**BODDLES** > BODDLE

**BODE** vb portend or presage

**BODED** > BODE

**BODEFUL** adj portentous

**BODEGA** n shop in a Spanish-speaking country that sells wine

**BODEGAS** > BODEGA

**BODEGUERO** n wine seller or grocer

**BODEMENT** > BODE

**BODEMENTS** > BODE

**BODES** > BODE

**BODGE** vb make a mess of

**BODGED** > BODGE

**BODGER** adj worthless or second-rate

**BODGERS** > BODGER

**BODGES** > BODGE

**BODGIE** n unruly or uncouth young man, esp in the 1950s ▷ adj inferior

**BODGIER** > BODGIE

**BODGIES** > BODGIE

**BODGIEST** > BODGIE

**BODGING** > BODGE

**BODHRAN** n shallow one-sided drum popular in Irish and Scottish folk music

**BODHRANS** > BODHRAN

**BODICE** n upper part of a dress

**BODICES** > BODICE

**BODIED** > BODY

**BODIES** > BODY

**BODIKIN** n little body

**BODIKINS** > BODIKIN

**BODILESS** adj having no body or substance

**BODILY** adj relating to the body ▷ adv by taking hold of the body

**BODING** > BODE

**BODINGLY** > BODE

**BODINGS** > BODE

**BODKIN** n blunt large-eyed needle

**BODKINS** > BODKIN

**BODLE** n small obsolete Scottish coin

**BODLES** > BODLE

**BODRAG** n enemy attack

**BODRAGS** > BODRAG

**BODS** > BOD

**BODY** n entire physical structure of an animal or human

**BODYBOARD** n surfboard that is shorter and blunter than the standard board and on which the surfer lies rather than stands

**BODYCHECK** n obstruction of another player ▷ vb deliver a bodycheck to (an opponent)

**BODYGUARD** n person or group of people employed to protect someone

**BODYING** > BODY

**BODYLINE** n (in cricket) fast bowling aimed at the batsman's body

**BODYLINES** > BODYLINE

**BODYSHELL** n external shell of a motor vehicle

**BODYSUIT** n one-piece undergarment for a baby

**BODYSUITS** > BODYSUIT

**BODYSURF** vb ride a wave by lying on it without a surfboard

**BODYSURFS** > BODYSURF

**BODYWORK** n outer shell of a motor vehicle

**BODYWORKS** > BODYWORK

**BOEHMITE** n grey, red, or brown mineral that consists of alumina in rhombic crystalline form and occurs in bauxite

**BOEHMITES** > BOEHMITE

**BOEP** n South African word for a big belly

**BOEPS** > BOEP

**BOERBUL** n crossbred mastiff used esp as a watchdog

**BOERBULS** > BOERBUL

**BOEREWORS** n spiced sausage

**BOERTJIE** South African word for > FRIEND

**BOERTJIES** > BOERTJIE

**BOET** n brother

**BOETS** > BOET

**BOEUF** boeuf bourgignon

casserole of beef, vegetables, herbs, etc, cooked in red wine

**BOFF** n boffin ▷ vb hit

**BOFFED** > BOFF

**BOFFIN** n scientist or expert

**BOFFING** > BOFF

**BOFFINS** > BOFFIN

**BOFFO** adj very good

**BOFFOLA** n great success

**BOFFOLAS** > BOFFOLA

**BOFFOS** > BOFFO

**BOFFS** > BOFF

**BOG** n wet spongy ground ▷ vb mire or delay

**BOGAN** n youth who dresses and behaves rebelliously

**BOGANS** > BOGAN

**BOGART** vb monopolize or keep (something, esp a marijuana cigarette) to oneself selfishly

**BOGARTED** > BOGART

**BOGARTING** > BOGART

**BOGARTS** > BOGART

**BOGBEAN** same as > BUCKBEAN

**BOGBEANS** > BOGBEAN

**BOGEY** n evil or mischievous spirit ▷ vb play (a hole) in one stroke over par

**BOGEYED** > BOGEY

**BOGEYING** > BOGEY

**BOGEYISM** n demonization

**BOGEYISMS** > BOGEYISM

**BOGEYMAN** n frightening person, real or imaginary, used as a threat, esp to children

**BOGEYMEN** > BOGEYMAN

**BOGEYS** > BOGEY

**BOGGARD** same as > BOGGART

**BOGGARDS** > BOGGARD

**BOGGART** n ghost or poltergeist

**BOGGARTS** > BOGGART

**BOGGED** > BOG

**BOGGER** n lavatory

**BOGGERS** > BOGGER

**BOGGIER** > BOG

**BOGGIEST** > BOG

**BOGGINESS** > BOG

**BOGGING** > BOG

**BOGGISH** > BOG

**BOGGLE** vb be surprised, confused, or alarmed

**BOGGLED** > BOGGLE

**BOGGLER** > BOGGLE

**BOGGLERS** > BOGGLE

**BOGGLES** > BOGGLE

**BOGGLING** > BOGGLE

**BOGGY** > BOG

**BOGIE** same as > BOGEY

**BOGIED** > BOGIE

**BOGIEING** > BOGIE

**BOGIES** > BOGY

**BOGLAND** n area of wetland

**BOGLANDS** > BOGLAND

**BOGLE** n rhythmic dance performed to ragga music

**BOGLES** > BOGLE

**BOGMAN** n body of a person

found preserved in a peat bog

**BOGMEN** > BOGMAN

**BOGOAK** n oak or other wood found preserved in peat bogs; bogwood

**BOGOAKS** > BOGOAK

**BOGONG** n large nocturnal Australian moth

**BOGONGS** > BOGONG

**BOGS** > BOG

**BOGUS** adj not genuine

**BOGUSLY** > BOGUS

**BOGUSNESS** > BOGUS

**BOGWOOD** same as > BOGOAK

**BOGWOODS** > BOGWOOD

**BOGY** same as > BOGEY

**BOGYISM** same as > BOGEYISM

**BOGYISMS** > BOGYISM

**BOGYMAN** same as > BOGEYMAN

**BOGYMEN** > BOGYMAN

**BOH** same as > BO

**BOHEA** n black Chinese tea, once regarded as the choicest, but now as an inferior grade

**BOHEAS** > BOHEA

**BOHEMIA** n area frequented by unconventional (esp creative) people

**BOHEMIAN** adj unconventional in lifestyle or appearance ▷ n person, esp an artist or writer, who lives an unconventional life

**BOHEMIANS** > BOHEMIAN

**BOHEMIAS** > BOHEMIA

**BOHO** short for > BOHEMIAN

**BOHOS** > BOHO

**BOHRIUM** n element artificially produced in minute quantities

**BOHRIUMS** > BOHRIUM

**BOHS** > BOH

**BOHUNK** n derogatory name for a labourer from east or central Europe

**BOHUNKS** > BOHUNK

**BOI** n lesbian who dresses like a boy

**BOIL** vb (cause to) change from a liquid to a vapour so quickly that bubbles are formed ▷ n state or action of boiling

**BOILABLE** > BOIL

**BOILED** > BOIL

**BOILER** n piece of equipment which provides hot water

**BOILERIES** > BOILERY

**BOILERS** > BOILER

**BOILERY** n place where water is boiled to extract salt

**BOILING** adj very hot ▷ n sweet

**BOILINGLY** > BOILING

**BOILINGS** > BOILING

**BOILOFF** n quantity of liquified gases lost in

evaporation
**BOILOFFS** > BOILOFF
**BOILOVER** n surprising result in a sporting event, esp in a horse race
**BOILOVERS** > BOILOVER
**BOILS** > BOIL
**BOING** vb rebound making a noise
**BOINGED** > BOING
**BOINGING** > BOING
**BOINGS** > BOING
**BOINK** same as > BOING
**BOINKED** > BOINK
**BOINKING** > BOINK
**BOINKS** > BOINK
**BOIS** > BOI
**BOISERIE** n finely crafted wood-carving
**BOISERIES** > BOISERIE
**BOITE** n artist's portfolio
**BOITES** > BOITE
**BOK** n S African antelope
**BOKE** vb retch or vomit ▷ n retch
**BOKED** > BOKE
**BOKES** > BOKE
**BOKING** > BOKE
**BOKO** slang word for > NOSE
**BOKOS** > BOKO
**BOKS** > BOK
**BOLA** n missile used by gauchos and Indians of South America, consisting of two or more heavy balls on a cord. It is hurled at a running quarry, such as an ox or rhea, so as to entangle its legs
**BOLAR** adj relating to clay
**BOLAS** same as > BOLA
**BOLASES** > BOLAS
**BOLD** adj confident and fearless ▷ n boldface
**BOLDEN** vb make bold
**BOLDENED** > BOLDEN
**BOLDENING** > BOLDEN
**BOLDENS** > BOLDEN
**BOLDER** > BOLD
**BOLDEST** > BOLD
**BOLDFACE** n weight of type characterized by thick heavy lines ▷ vb print in boldface
**BOLDFACED** > BOLDFACE
**BOLDFACES** > BOLDFACE
**BOLDLY** > BOLD
**BOLDNESS** > BOLD
**BOLDS** > BOLD
**BOLE** n tree trunk
**BOLECTION** n stepped moulding covering and projecting beyond the joint between two members having surfaces at different levels
**BOLERO** n (music for) traditional Spanish dance
**BOLEROS** > BOLERO
**BOLES** > BOLE
**BOLETE** n type of fungus
**BOLETES** > BOLETE
**BOLETI** > BOLETUS
**BOLETUS** n any saprotroph

basidiomycetous fungus of the genus Boletus, having a brownish umbrella-shaped cap with spore-bearing tubes in the underside: family Boletaceae. Many species are edible
**BOLETUSES** > BOLETUS
**BOLIDE** n large exceptionally bright meteor that often explodes
**BOLIDES** > BOLIDE
**BOLINE** n (in Wicca) a knife, usually sickle-shaped and with a white handle, used for gathering herbs and carving symbols
**BOLINES** > BOLINE
**BOLIVAR** n standard monetary unit of Venezuela, equal to 100 céntimos
**BOLIVARES** > BOLIVAR
**BOLIVARS** > BOLIVAR
**BOLIVIA** n type of woollen fabric
**BOLIVIANO** n (until 1963 and from 1987) the standard monetary unit of Bolivia, equal to 100 centavos
**BOLIVIAS** > BOLIVIA
**BOLIX** same as > BOLLOCKS
**BOLIXED** > BOLIX
**BOLIXES** > BOLIX
**BOLIXING** > BOLIX
**BOLL** n rounded seed capsule of cotton, flax, etc ▷ vb form into a boll
**BOLLARD** n short thick post used to prevent the passage of motor vehicles
**BOLLARDS** > BOLLARD
**BOLLED** > BOLL
**BOLLEN** > BOLL
**BOLLETRIE** n type of W Indian tree
**BOLLING** > BOLL
**BOLLIX** same as > BOLLOCKS
**BOLLIXED** > BOLLIX
**BOLLIXES** > BOLLIX
**BOLLIXING** > BOLLIX
**BOLLOCK** vb rebuke severely
**BOLLOCKED** > BOLLOCK
**BOLLOCKS** pl n testicles ▷ interj exclamation of annoyance, disbelief, etc ▷ vb rebuke severely
**BOLLOX** same as > BOLLOCKS
**BOLLOXED** > BOLLOX
**BOLLOXES** > BOLLOX
**BOLLOXING** > BOLLOX
**BOLLS** > BOLL
**BOLLWORM** n any of various moth caterpillars that feed on and destroy cotton bolls
**BOLLWORMS** > BOLLWORM
**BOLO** n large single-edged knife, originating in the Philippines

**BOLOGNA** n type of sausage
**BOLOGNAS** > BOLOGNA
**BOLOGRAPH** n record made by a bolometer
**BOLOMETER** n sensitive instrument for measuring radiant energy by the increase in the resistance of an electrical conductor
**BOLOMETRY** > BOLOMETER
**BOLONEY** a variant spelling of > BALONEY
**BOLONEYS** > BOLONEY
**BOLOS** > BOLO
**BOLSHEVIK** n any political radical
**BOLSHIE** adj difficult or rebellious ▷ n any political radical
**BOLSHIER** > BOLSHIE
**BOLSHIES** > BOLSHY
**BOLSHIEST** > BOLSHIE
**BOLSHY** same as > BOLSHIE
**BOLSON** n desert valley surrounded by mountains, with a shallow lake at the centre
**BOLSONS** > BOLSON
**BOLSTER** vb support or strengthen ▷ n long narrow pillow
**BOLSTERED** > BOLSTER
**BOLSTERER** > BOLSTER
**BOLSTERS** > BOLSTER
**BOLT** n sliding metal bar for fastening a door etc ▷ vb run away suddenly
**BOLTED** > BOLT
**BOLTER** > BOLT
**BOLTERS** > BOLT
**BOLTHEAD** n glass receptacle used in chemistry
**BOLTHEADS** > BOLTHEAD
**BOLTHOLE** n place of escape from danger
**BOLTHOLES** > BOLTHOLE
**BOLTING** > BOLT
**BOLTINGS** > BOLT
**BOLTLESS** > BOLT
**BOLTLIKE** > BOLT
**BOLTONIA** n any North American plant of the genus Boltonia, having daisy-like flowers with white, violet, or pinkish rays: family Compositae (composites)
**BOLTONIAS** > BOLTONIA
**BOLTROPE** n rope sewn to the foot or luff of a sail to strengthen it
**BOLTROPES** > BOLTROPE
**BOLTS** > BOLT
**BOLUS** same as > BOLE
**BOLUSES** > BOLUS
**BOMA** n enclosure, esp a palisade or fence of thorn bush, set up to protect a camp, herd of animals, etc
**BOMAS** > BOMA
**BOMB** n container fitted with explosive material ▷ vb attack with bombs

**BOMBABLE** > BOMB
**BOMBARD** vb attack with heavy gunfire or bombs ▷ n ancient type of cannon that threw stone balls
**BOMBARDE** n alto wind instrument similar to the oboe or medieval shawm, used mainly in Breton traditional music
**BOMBARDED** > BOMBARD
**BOMBARDER** > BOMBARD
**BOMBARDES** > BOMBARDE
**BOMBARDON** n brass instrument of the tuba type, similar to a sousaphone
**BOMBARDS** > BOMBARD
**BOMBASINE** same as > BOMBAZINE
**BOMBAST** n pompous language ▷ vb speak pompous language
**BOMBASTED** > BOMBAST
**BOMBASTER** > BOMBAST
**BOMBASTIC** > BOMBAST
**BOMBASTS** > BOMBAST
**BOMBAX** n type of S American tree
**BOMBAXES** > BOMBAX
**BOMBAZINE** n twill fabric, usually of silk and worsted, formerly worn dyed black for mourning
**BOMBE** n dessert of ice cream lined or filled with custard, cake crumbs, etc ▷ adj (of furniture) having a projecting swollen shape
**BOMBED** > BOMB
**BOMBER** n aircraft that drops bombs
**BOMBERS** > BOMBER
**BOMBES** > BOMBE
**BOMBESIN** n hormone found in brain
**BOMBESINS** > BOMBESIN
**BOMBILATE** same as > BOMBINATE
**BOMBINATE** vb make a buzzing noise
**BOMBING** > BOMB
**BOMBINGS** > BOMB
**BOMBLET** n small bomb
**BOMBLETS** > BOMBLET
**BOMBLOAD** n quantity of bombs carried at one time
**BOMBLOADS** > BOMBLOAD
**BOMBO** n inferior wine
**BOMBORA** n submerged reef
**BOMBORAS** > BOMBORA
**BOMBOS** > BOMBO
**BOMBPROOF** adj able to withstand the impact of a bomb
**BOMBS** > BOMB
**BOMBSHELL** n shocking or unwelcome surprise
**BOMBSIGHT** n mechanical or electronic device in an aircraft for aiming bombs
**BOMBSITE** n area where the buildings have been destroyed by bombs

BOMBSITES > BOMBSITE
BOMBYCID *n* any moth, including the silkworm moth, of the family *Bombycidae*, most of which occur in Africa and SE Asia ▷ *adj* of, relating to, or belonging to the *Bombycidae* .
BOMBYCIDS > BOMBYCID
BOMBYCOID *adj* of or like bombycids
BOMBYX *n* type of moth
BOMBYXES > BOMBYX
BOMMIE *n* outcrop of coral reef
BOMMIES > BOMMIE
BON *adj* good
BONA *n* goods
BONACI *n* type of fish
BONACIS > BONACI
BONAMANI > BONAMANO
BONAMANO *n* gratuity
BONAMIA *n* parasite
BONAMIAS > BONAMIA
BONANZA *n* sudden good luck or wealth
BONANZAS > BONANZA
BONASSUS *same as* > BONASUS
BONASUS *n* European bison
BONASUSES > BONASUS
BONBON *n* sweet
BONBONS > BONBON
BONCE *n* head
BONCES > BONCE
BOND *n* something that binds, fastens or holds together ▷ *vb* bind
BONDABLE > BOND
BONDAGE *n* slavery
BONDAGER > BONDAGE
BONDAGERS > BONDAGE
BONDAGES > BONDAGE
BONDED *adj* consisting of, secured by, or operating under a bond or bonds
BONDER *same as* > BONDSTONE
BONDERS > BONDER
BONDING *n* process by which individuals become emotionally attached to one another
BONDINGS > BONDING
BONDLESS > BOND
BONDMAID *n* unmarried female serf or slave
BONDMAIDS > BONDMAID
BONDMAN *same as* > BONDSMAN
BONDMEN > BONDMAN
BONDS > BOND
BONDSMAN *n* person bound by bond to act as surety for another
BONDSMEN > BONDSMAN
BONDSTONE *n* long stone or brick laid in a wall as a header
BONDUC *n* type of N American tree
BONDUCS > BONDUC
BONDWOMAN *n* female slave

BONDWOMEN > BONDWOMAN
BONE *n* any of the hard parts in the body that form the skeleton ▷ *vb* remove the bones from (meat for cooking etc)
BONEBLACK *n* black residue from the destructive distillation of bones, containing about 10 per cent carbon and 80 per cent calcium phosphate, used as a decolorizing agent and pigment
BONED > BONE
BONEFISH *n* silvery marine clupeoid game fish, *Albula vulpes*, occurring in warm shallow waters: family *Albulidae*
BONEHEAD *n* stupid or obstinate person
BONEHEADS > BONEHEAD
BONELESS > BONE
BONEMEAL *n* product of dried and ground animal bones, used as a fertilizer or in stock feeds
BONEMEALS > BONEMEAL
BONER *n* blunder
BONERS > BONER
BONES > BONE
BONESET *n* any of various North American plants of the genus *Eupatorium*, esp *E. perfoliatum*, which has flat clusters of small white flowers: family *Asteraceae* (composites)
BONESETS > BONESET
BONEY *same as* > BONY
BONEYARD *an informal name for a* > CEMETERY
BONEYARDS > BONEYARD
BONEYER > BONEY
BONEYEST > BONEY
BONFIRE *n* large outdoor fire
BONFIRES > BONFIRE
BONG *n* deep reverberating sound, as of a large bell ▷ *vb* make a deep reverberating sound
BONGED > BONG
BONGING > BONG
BONGO *n* small drum played with the fingers
BONGOES > BONGO
BONGOIST *n* bongo player
BONGOISTS > BONGOIST
BONGOS > BONGO
BONGRACE *n* shade for face
BONGRACES > BONGRACE
BONGS > BONG
BONHAM *n* piglet
BONHAMS > BONHAM
BONHOMIE *n* cheerful friendliness
BONHOMIES > BONHOMIE
BONHOMMIE *same as* > BONHOMIE
BONHOMOUS *adj* exhibiting bonhomie
BONIATO *n* sweet potato

BONIATOS > BONIATO
BONIBELL *same as* > BONNIBELL
BONIBELLS > BONIBELL
BONIE *same as* > BONNY
BONIER > BONY
BONIEST > BONY
BONIFACE *n* pub landlord
BONIFACES > BONIFACE
BONILASSE *n* an attractive young woman
BONINESS > BONY
BONING > BONE
BONINGS > BONE
BONISM *n* doctrine that the world is good, although not the best of all possible worlds
BONISMS > BONISM
BONIST > BONISM
BONISTS > BONISM
BONITA *slang term for* > HEROIN
BONITAS > BONITA
BONITO *n* small tunny-like marine food fish
BONITOES > BONITO
BONITOS > BONITO
BONJOUR *interj* hello
BONK *vb* have sex with
BONKED > BONK
BONKERS *adj* crazy
BONKING > BONK
BONKINGS > BONK
BONKS > BONK
BONNE *n* housemaid or female servant
BONNES > BONNE
BONNET *n* metal cover over a vehicle's engine ▷ *vb* place a bonnet on
BONNETED > BONNET
BONNETING > BONNET
BONNETS > BONNET
BONNIBELL *n* beautiful girl
BONNIE *same as* > BONNY
BONNIER > BONNY
BONNIES > BONNY
BONNIEST > BONNY
BONNILY > BONNY
BONNINESS > BONNY
BONNOCK *n* thick oatmeal cake
BONNOCKS > BONNOCK
BONNY *adj* beautiful ▷ *adv* agreeably or well
BONOBO *n* anthropoid ape, *Pan paniscus*, of central W Africa: similar to the chimpanzee but much smaller and having a black face.
BONOBOS > BONOBO
BONSAI *n* ornamental miniature tree or shrub
BONSAIS > BONSAI
BONSELA *n* small gift of money
BONSELAS > BONSELA
BONSELLA *same as* > BONSELA
BONSELLAS > BONSELLA
BONSOIR *interj* good evening

BONSPELL *same as* > BONSPIEL
BONSPELLS > BONSPIEL
BONSPIEL *n* curling match
BONSPIELS > BONSPIEL
BONTEBOK *n* antelope, *Damaliscus pygargus* (or *dorcas*), of southern Africa, having a deep reddish-brown coat with a white blaze, tail, and rump patch
BONTEBOKS > BONTEBOK
BONUS *n* something given, paid, or received above what is due or expected
BONUSES > BONUS
BONXIE *n* great skua
BONXIES > BONXIE
BONY *adj* having many bones
BONZA *same as* > BONZER
BONZE *n* Chinese or Japanese Buddhist priest or monk
BONZER *adj* excellent
BONZES > BONZE
BOO *interj* shout of disapproval ▷ *vb* shout 'boo' to show disapproval
BOOB *n* foolish mistake ▷ *vb* make a foolish mistake ▷ *adj* of poor quality, similar to that provided in prison
BOOBED > BOOB
BOOBHEAD *n* repeat offender in a prison
BOOBHEADS > BOOBHEAD
BOOBIALLA *n* any of various trees or shrubs of the genus *Myoporum*, esp *M. insulare*
BOOBIE *same as* > BOOBY
BOOBIES > BOOBY
BOOBING > BOOB
BOOBIRD *n* person who boos
BOOBIRDS > BOOBIRD
BOOBISH > BOOBY
BOOBOISIE *n* group of people considered as stupid
BOOBOO *n* blunder
BOOBOOK *n* small spotted Australian brown owl
BOOBOOKS > BOOBOOK
BOOBOOS > BOOBOO
BOOBS > BOOB
BOOBY *n* foolish person
BOOBYISH > BOOBY
BOOBYISM > BOOBY
BOOBYISMS > BOOBY
BOOCOO *same as* > BEAUCOUP
BOOCOOS > BOOCOO
BOODIE *n* type of kangaroo
BOODIED > BOODY
BOODIES > BOODY
BOODLE *n* money or valuables, esp when stolen, counterfeit, or used as a bribe ▷ *vb* give or receive money corruptly or illegally
BOODLED > BOODLE

**BOODLER** > BOODLE
**BOODLERS** > BOODLE
**BOODLES** > BOODLE
**BOODLING** > BOODLE
**BOODY** vb sulk
**BOODYING** > BOODY
**BOOED** > BOO
**BOOFHEAD** n stupid person
**BOOFHEADS** > BOOFHEAD
**BOOFIER** > BOOFY
**BOOFIEST** > BOOFY
**BOOFY** adj muscular and strong but stupid
**BOOGER** n dried mucous from the nose
**BOOGERMAN** American form of > BOGEYMAN
**BOOGERMEN** > BOOGERMAN
**BOOGERS** > BOOGER
**BOOGEY** same as > BOOGIE
**BOOGEYED** > BOOGEY
**BOOGEYING** > BOOGEY
**BOOGEYMAN** same as > BOGEYMAN
**BOOGEYMEN** > BOOGEYMAN
**BOOGEYS** > BOOGEY
**BOOGIE** vb dance to fast pop music ▷ n session of dancing to pop music
**BOOGIED** > BOOGIE
**BOOGIEING** > BOOGIE
**BOOGIEMAN** same as > BOGEYMAN
**BOOGIEMEN** > BOOGIEMAN
**BOOGIES** > BOOGIE
**BOOGY** same as > BOOGIE
**BOOGYING** > BOOGY
**BOOGYMAN** same as > BOGEYMAN
**BOOGYMEN** > BOOGYMAN
**BOOH** same as > BOO
**BOOHAI** n up the boohai thoroughly lost
**BOOHAIS** > BOOHAI
**BOOHED** > BOOH
**BOOHING** > BOOH
**BOOHOO** vb sob or pretend to sob noisily ▷ n distressed or pretended sobbing
**BOOHOOED** > BOOHOO
**BOOHOOING** > BOOHOO
**BOOHOOS** > BOOHOO
**BOOHS** > BOOH
**BOOING** > BOO
**BOOJUM** n American tree
**BOOJUMS** > BOOJUM
**BOOK** n number of pages bound together between covers ▷ vb reserve (a place, passage, etc) in advance
**BOOKABLE** > BOOK
**BOOKCASE** n piece of furniture containing shelves for books
**BOOKCASES** > BOOKCASE
**BOOKED** > BOOK
**BOOKEND** n one of a pair of usually ornamental supports for holding a row of books upright
**BOOKENDS** > BOOKEND
**BOOKER** > BOOK

**BOOKERS** > BOOK
**BOOKFUL** > BOOK
**BOOKFULS** > BOOK
**BOOKIE** short for > BOOKMAKER
**BOOKIER** > BOOKY
**BOOKIES** > BOOKIE
**BOOKIEST** > BOOKY
**BOOKING** n reservation, as of a table or seat
**BOOKINGS** > BOOKING
**BOOKISH** adj fond of reading
**BOOKISHLY** > BOOKISH
**BOOKLAND** n common land given to private owner
**BOOKLANDS** > BOOKLAND
**BOOKLESS** > BOOK
**BOOKLET** n thin book with paper covers
**BOOKLETS** > BOOKLET
**BOOKLICE** > BOOKLOUSE
**BOOKLIGHT** n small light that can be clipped onto a book for reading by
**BOOKLORE** n knowledge or beliefs gleaned from books
**BOOKLORES** > BOOKLORE
**BOOKLOUSE** n wingless insect that feeds on bookbinding paste, etc
**BOOKMAKER** n person whose occupation is taking bets
**BOOKMAN** n learned person
**BOOKMARK** n person whose occupation is taking bets ▷ vb identify and store (a website) so that one can return to it quickly and easily
**BOOKMARKS** > BOOKMARK
**BOOKMEN** > BOOKMAN
**BOOKOO** same as > BOOCOO
**BOOKOOS** > BOOKOO
**BOOKPLATE** n label bearing the owner's name and an individual design or coat of arms, pasted into a book
**BOOKRACK** n rack for holding books
**BOOKRACKS** > BOOKRACK
**BOOKREST** n stand for supporting open book
**BOOKRESTS** > BOOKREST
**BOOKS** > BOOK
**BOOKSHELF** n shelf for books
**BOOKSHOP** n shop where books are sold
**BOOKSHOPS** > BOOKSHOP
**BOOKSIE** same as > BOOKSY
**BOOKSIER** > BOOKSY
**BOOKSIEST** > BOOKSY
**BOOKSTALL** n stall or stand where periodicals, newspapers, or books are sold
**BOOKSTAND** n support for open book
**BOOKSTORE** same as > BOOKSHOP
**BOOKSY** adj inclined to be bookish or literary

**BOOKWORK** n academic study
**BOOKWORKS** > BOOKWORK
**BOOKWORM** n person devoted to reading
**BOOKWORMS** > BOOKWORM
**BOOKY** adj bookish
**BOOL** n bowling bowl ▷ vb play bowls
**BOOLED** > BOOL
**BOOLING** > BOOL
**BOOLS** > BOOL
**BOOM** vb make a loud deep echoing sound ▷ n loud deep echoing sound
**BOOMBOX** n portable stereo system
**BOOMBOXES** > BOOMBOX
**BOOMED** > BOOM
**BOOMER** n large male kangaroo
**BOOMERANG** n curved wooden missile which can be made to return to the thrower ▷ vb (of a plan) recoil unexpectedly
**BOOMERS** > BOOMER
**BOOMIER** > BOOMY
**BOOMIEST** > BOOMY
**BOOMING** > BOOM
**BOOMINGLY** > BOOM
**BOOMINGS** > BOOM
**BOOMKIN** n short boom projecting from the deck of a ship, used to secure the main-brace blocks or to extend the lower edge of the foresail
**BOOMKINS** > BOOMKIN
**BOOMLET** n small boom in business, birth rate, etc
**BOOMLETS** > BOOMLET
**BOOMS** > BOOM
**BOOMSLANG** n large greenish venomous tree-living snake of southern Africa
**BOOMTOWN** n town that is enjoying sudden prosperity or has grown rapidly
**BOOMTOWNS** > BOOMTOWN
**BOOMY** adj characterized by heavy bass sound
**BOON** n something extremely useful, helpful, or beneficial
**BOONDOCK** > BOONDOCKS
**BOONDOCKS** n remote rural area
**BOONER** n young working-class person from Canberra
**BOONERS** > BOONER
**BOONG** n offensive term for a Black person
**BOONGA** n offensive term for a Pacific Islander
**BOONGARY** n tree kangaroo of NE Queensland, Australia
**BOONGAS** > BOONG
**BOONGS** > BOONG
**BOONIES** short form

of > BOONDOCKS
**BOONLESS** > BOON
**BOONS** > BOON
**BOOR** n rude or insensitive person
**BOORD** obsolete spelling of > BOARD
**BOORDE** obsolete spelling of > BOARD
**BOORDES** > BOORDE
**BOORDS** > BOORD
**BOORISH** adj ill-mannered, clumsy, or insensitive
**BOORISHLY** > BOORISH
**BOORKA** same as > BURKA
**BOORKAS** > BOORKA
**BOORS** > BOOR
**BOORTREE** same as > BOURTREE
**BOORTREES** > BOORTREE
**BOOS** > BOO
**BOOSE** same as > BOOZE
**BOOSED** > BOOSE
**BOOSES** > BOOSE
**BOOSHIT** adj very good
**BOOSING** > BOOSE
**BOOST** n encouragement or help ▷ vb improve
**BOOSTED** > BOOST
**BOOSTER** n small additional injection of a vaccine
**BOOSTERS** > BOOSTER
**BOOSTING** > BOOST
**BOOSTS** > BOOST
**BOOT** n outer covering for the foot that extends above the ankle ▷ vb kick
**BOOTABLE** > BOOT
**BOOTBLACK** another word for > SHOEBLACK
**BOOTED** adj wearing boots
**BOOTEE** n baby's soft shoe
**BOOTEES** > BOOTEE
**BOOTERIES** > BOOTERY
**BOOTERY** n shop where boots and shoes are sold
**BOOTH** n small partly enclosed cubicle
**BOOTHOSE** n stocking worn with boots
**BOOTHS** > BOOTH
**BOOTIE** n Royal Marine
**BOOTIES** > BOOTY
**BOOTIKIN** n small boot
**BOOTIKINS** > BOOTIKIN
**BOOTING** > BOOT
**BOOTJACK** n device that grips the heel of a boot to enable the foot to be withdrawn easily
**BOOTJACKS** > BOOTJACK
**BOOTLACE** n strong lace for fastening a boot
**BOOTLACES** > BOOTLACE
**BOOTLAST** n foot shape placed in boots or shoes to keep their shape
**BOOTLASTS** > BOOTLAST
**BOOTLEG** adj produced, distributed, or sold illicitly ▷ vb make, carry, or sell (illicit goods) ▷ n something made or sold illicitly, such as alcohol

during Prohibition in the US

**BOOTLEGS** > BOOTLEG

**BOOTLESS** adj of little or no use

**BOOTLICK** vb seek favour by servile or ingratiating behaviour towards (someone, esp someone in authority)

**BOOTLICKS** > BOOTLICK

**BOOTMAKER** n person who makes boots and shoes

**BOOTS** > BOOT

**BOOTSTRAP** n leather or fabric loop on the back or side of a boot

**BOOTY** n valuable articles obtained as plunder

**BOOZE** n (consume) alcoholic drink ▷ vb drink alcohol, esp in excess

**BOOZED** > BOOZE

**BOOZER** n person who is fond of drinking

**BOOZERS** > BOOZER

**BOOZES** > BOOZE

**BOOZEY** same as > BOOZY

**BOOZIER** > BOOZY

**BOOZIEST** > BOOZY

**BOOZILY** > BOOZY

**BOOZINESS** > BOOZY

**BOOZING** > BOOZE

**BOOZY** adj inclined to or involving excessive drinking of alcohol

**BOP** vb dance to pop music ▷ n form of jazz with complex rhythms and harmonies

**BOPEEP** n quick look; peek

**BOPEEPS** > BOPEEP

**BOPPED** > BOP

**BOPPER** > BOP

**BOPPERS** > BOP

**BOPPING** > BOP

**BOPS** > BOP

**BOR** n neighbour

**BORA** n Aboriginal ceremony

**BORACES** > BORAX

**BORACHIO** n pig's skin wine carrier

**BORACHIOS** > BORACHIO

**BORACIC** same as > BORIC

**BORACITE** n white mineral that forms salt deposits of magnesium borate

**BORACITES** > BORACITE

**BORAGE** n Mediterranean plant with star-shaped blue flowers

**BORAGES** > BORAGE

**BORAK** n rubbish

**BORAKS** > BORAK

**BORAL** n type of fine powder

**BORALS** > BORAL

**BORANE** n any compound of boron and hydrogen, used in the synthesis of other boron compounds and as high-energy fuels

**BORANES** > BORANE

**BORAS** > BORA

**BORATE** n salt or ester of boric acid. Salts of boric acid consist of $BO_3$ and $BO_4$ units linked together ▷ vb treat with borax, boric acid, or borate

**BORATED** > BORATE

**BORATES** > BORATE

**BORATING** > BORATE

**BORAX** n soluble white mineral occurring in alkaline soils and salt deposits

**BORAXES** > BORAX

**BORAZON** n extremely hard form of boron nitride

**BORAZONS** > BORAZON

**BORD** obsolete spelling of > BOARD

**BORDAR** n smallholder who held cottage in return for menial work

**BORDARS** > BORDAR

**BORDE** obsolete spelling of > BOARD

**BORDEAUX** adj any of several wines produced around Bordeaux

**BORDEL** same as > BORDELLO

**BORDELLO** n brothel

**BORDELLOS** > BORDELLO

**BORDELS** > BORDEL

**BORDER** n dividing line between political or geographical regions ▷ vb provide with a border

**BORDEREAU** n memorandum or invoice prepared for a company by an underwriter, containing a list of reinsured risks

**BORDERED** > BORDER

**BORDERER** n person who lives in a border area, esp the border between England and Scotland

**BORDERERS** > BORDERER

**BORDERING** > BORDER

**BORDERS** > BORDER

**BORDES** > BORDE

**BORDS** > BORD

**BORDURE** n outer edge of a shield, esp when decorated distinctively

**BORDURES** > BORDURE

**BORE** vb make (someone) weary by being dull

**BOREAL** adj of or relating to the north or the north wind

**BOREALIS** aurora borealis lights seen around the North Pole

**BOREAS** n name for the north wind

**BOREASES** > BOREAS

**BORECOLE** another name for > KALE

**BORECOLES** > BORECOLE

**BORED** > BORE

**BOREDOM** n state of being bored

**BOREDOMS** > BOREDOM

**BOREE** same as > MYALL

**BOREEN** n country lane or narrow road

**BOREENS** > BOREEN

**BOREES** > BOREE

**BOREHOLE** n hole driven into the ground to obtain geological information, release water, etc

**BOREHOLES** > BOREHOLE

**BOREL** adj unlearned

**BORER** n machine or hand tool for boring holes

**BORERS** > BORER

**BORES** > BEAR

**BORESCOPE** n long narrow device for inspection of, e.g. bore

**BORESOME** adj boring

**BORGHETTO** n settlement outside city walls

**BORGO** n small attractive medieval village

**BORGOS** > BORGO

**BORIC** adj of or containing boron

**BORIDE** n compound in which boron is the most electronegative element, esp a compound of boron and a metal

**BORIDES** > BORIDE

**BORING** n act or process of making or enlarging a hole ▷ adj dull

**BORINGLY** > BORING

**BORINGS** > BORING

**BORK** vb dismiss from job unfairly

**BORKED** > BORK

**BORKING** > BORK

**BORKS** > BORK

**BORLOTTI** as in borlotti bean variety of kidney bean

**BORM** vb smear with paint, oil, etc

**BORMED** > BORM

**BORMING** > BORM

**BORMS** > BORM

**BORN** adj possessing certain qualities from birth

**BORNA** as in borna disease viral disease found in mammals, esp horses

**BORNE** > BEAR

**BORNEOL** n white solid terpene alcohol

**BORNEOLS** > BORNEOL

**BORNITE** n mineral consisting of a sulphide of copper and iron that tarnishes to purple

**BORNITES** > BORNITE

**BORNITIC** > BORNITE

**BORNYL** as in bornyl alcohol white solid alcohol from a Malaysian tree

**BORNYLS** > BORNYL

**BORON** n element used in hardening steel

**BORONIA** n Australian aromatic flowering shrub

**BORONIAS** > BORONIA

**BORONIC** > BORON

**BORONS** > BORON

**BOROUGH** n town or district with its own council

**BOROUGHS** > BOROUGH

**BORREL** adj ignorant

**BORRELIA** n type of bacterium

**BORRELIAS** > BORRELIA

**BORRELL** same as > BORREL

**BORROW** vb obtain (something) temporarily

**BORROWED** > BORROW

**BORROWER** > BORROW

**BORROWERS** > BORROW

**BORROWING** > BORROW

**BORROWS** > BORROW

**BORS** > BORS

**BORSCH** same as > BORSCHT

**BORSCHES** > BORSCH

**BORSCHT** n Russian soup based on beetroot

**BORSCHTS** > BORSCHT

**BORSHCH** same as > BORSCHT

**BORSHCHES** > BORSHCH

**BORSHT** same as > BORSCHT

**BORSHTS** > BORSHT

**BORSIC** n strong light composite material of boron fibre and silicon carbide used in aviation

**BORSICS** > BORSIC

**BORSTAL** n (formerly in Britain) prison for young criminals

**BORSTALL** same as > BORSTAL

**BORSTALLS** > BORSTAL

**BORSTALS** > BORSTAL

**BORT** n inferior grade of diamond used for cutting and drilling or, in powdered form, as an industrial abrasive

**BORTIER** > BORT

**BORTIEST** > BORT

**BORTS** > BORT

**BORTSCH** same as > BORSCHT

**BORTSCHES** > BORTSCH

**BORTY** > BORT

**BORTZ** same as > BORT

**BORTZES** > BORTZ

**BORZOI** n tall dog with a long silky coat

**BORZOIS** > BORZOI

**BOS** > BO

**BOSBERAAD** n meeting in an isolated venue to break a political deadlock

**BOSBOK** same as > BUSHBUCK

**BOSBOKS** > BOSBOK

**BOSCAGE** n mass of trees and shrubs

**BOSCAGES** > BOSCAGE

**BOSCHBOK** same as > BUSHBUCK

**BOSCHBOKS** > BOSCHBOK

**BOSCHE** same as > BOCHE

**BOSCHES** > BOSCHE

**BOSCHVARK** same as > BUSHPIG

**BOSCHVELD** same as > BUSHVELD

**BOSH** *n* empty talk, nonsense
**BOSHBOK** *same as* > BUSHBUCK
**BOSHBOKS** > BOSHBOK
**BOSHES** > BOSH
**BOSHTA** *same as* > BOSHTER
**BOSHTER** *adj* excellent
**BOSHVARK** *same as* > BOSCHVARK
**BOSHVARKS** > BOSHVARK
**BOSK** *n* small wood of bushes and small trees
**BOSKAGE** *same as* > BOSCAGE
**BOSKAGES** > BOSKAGE
**BOSKER** *adj* excellent
**BOSKET** *n* clump of small trees or bushes
**BOSKETS** > BOSKET
**BOSKIER** > BOSKY
**BOSKIEST** > BOSKY
**BOSKINESS** > BOSKY
**BOSKS** > BOSK
**BOSKY** *adj* containing or consisting of bushes or thickets
**BOSOM** *n* chest of a person, esp the female breasts ▷ *adj* very dear ▷ *vb* embrace
**BOSOMED** > BOSOM
**BOSOMIER** > BOSOMY
**BOSOMIEST** > BOSOMY
**BOSOMING** > BOSOM
**BOSOMS** > BOSOM
**BOSOMY** *adj* (of a woman) having large breasts
**BOSON** *n* any of a group of elementary particles, such as a photon or pion, that has zero or integral spin and obeys the rules of Bose-Einstein statistics
**BOSONIC** > BOSON
**BOSONS** > BOSON
**BOSQUE** *same as* > BOSK
**BOSQUES** > BOSQUE
**BOSQUET** *same as* > BOSKET
**BOSQUETS** > BOSQUET
**BOSS** *n* raised knob or stud ▷ *vb* employ, supervise, or be in charge of ▷ *adj* excellent
**BOSSBOY** *n* Black African foreman of a gang of workers
**BOSSBOYS** > BOSSBOY
**BOSSDOM** *n* bosses collectively
**BOSSDOMS** > BOSSDOM
**BOSSED** > BOSS
**BOSSER** > BOSS
**BOSSES** > BOSS
**BOSSEST** > BOSS
**BOSSET** *n* either of the rudimentary antlers found in young deer
**BOSSETS** > BOSSET
**BOSSIER** > BOSSY
**BOSSIES** > BOSSY
**BOSSIEST** > BOSSY
**BOSSILY** > BOSSY
**BOSSINESS** > BOSSY
**BOSSING** *n* act of shaping malleable metal, such as lead cladding, with mallets to fit a surface
**BOSSISM** *n* domination or the system of domination of political organizations by bosses
**BOSSISMS** > BOSSISM
**BOSSY** *same as* > BOSS
**BOSTANGI** *n* imperial Turkish guard
**BOSTANGIS** > BOSTANGI
**BOSTHOON** *n* boor
**BOSTHOONS** > BOSTHOON
**BOSTON** *n* card game for four, played with two packs
**BOSTONS** > BOSTON
**BOSTRYX** *n* phenomenon in which flowers develop on one side only
**BOSTRYXES** > BOSTRYX
**BOSUN** *same as* > BOATSWAIN
**BOSUNS** > BOSUN
**BOT** *n* larva of a botfly, which typically develops inside the body of a horse, sheep, or man
**BOTA** *n* leather container
**BOTANIC** *same as* > BOTANICAL
**BOTANICA** *n* botany
**BOTANICAL** *adj* of or relating to botany or plants ▷ *n* any drug or pesticide that is made from parts of a plant
**BOTANICAS** > BOTANICA
**BOTANICS** > BOTANIC
**BOTANIES** > BOTANY
**BOTANISE** *same as* > BOTANIZE
**BOTANISED** > BOTANISE
**BOTANISER** > BOTANISE
**BOTANISES** > BOTANISE
**BOTANIST** > BOTANY
**BOTANISTS** > BOTANY
**BOTANIZE** *vb* collect or study plants
**BOTANIZED** > BOTANIZE
**BOTANIZER** > BOTANIZE
**BOTANIZES** > BOTANIZE
**BOTANY** *n* study of plants
**BOTARGO** *n* relish consisting of the roe of mullet or tunny, salted and pressed into rolls
**BOTARGOES** > BOTARGO
**BOTARGOS** > BOTARGO
**BOTAS** > BOTA
**BOTCH** *vb* spoil through clumsiness ▷ *n* badly done piece of work or repair
**BOTCHED** > BOTCH
**BOTCHEDLY** > BOTCH
**BOTCHER** > BOTCH
**BOTCHERS** > BOTCH
**BOTCHERY** *n* instance of botching
**BOTCHES** > BOTCH
**BOTCHIER** > BOTCHY
**BOTCHIEST** > BOTCHY
**BOTCHILY** > BOTCHY

**BOTCHING** > BOTCH
**BOTCHINGS** > BOTCH
**BOTCHY** *adj* clumsily done or made
**BOTEL** *same as* > BOATEL
**BOTELS** > BOTEL
**BOTFLIES** > BOTFLY
**BOTFLY** *n* any of various stout-bodied hairy dipterous flies of the families Oestridae and Gasterophilidae, the larvae of which are parasites of man, sheep, and horses
**BOTH** *pron* two considered together ▷ *adj* two considered together ▷ *determiner* two
**BOTHAN** *n* unlicensed drinking house
**BOTHANS** > BOTHAN
**BOTHER** *vb* take the time or trouble ▷ *n* trouble, fuss, or difficulty ▷ *interj* exclamation of slight annoyance
**BOTHERED** > BOTHER
**BOTHERING** > BOTHER
**BOTHERS** > BOTHER
**BOTHIE** *same as* > BOTHY
**BOTHIES** > BOTHY
**BOTHOLE** *n* hole made by the larva of the botfly
**BOTHOLES** > BOTHOLE
**BOTHRIA** > BOTHRIUM
**BOTHRIUM** *n* groove-shaped sucker on tapeworm
**BOTHRIUMS** > BOTHRIUM
**BOTHY** *n* hut used for temporary shelter
**BOTHYMAN** *n* man who lives in bothy
**BOTHYMEN** > BOTHYMAN
**BOTNET** *n* network of infected computers
**BOTNETS** > BOTNET
**BOTONE** *adj* having lobes at the ends
**BOTONEE** *same as* > BOTONE
**BOTONNEE** *same as* > BOTONE
**BOTRYOID** *adj* shaped like a bunch of grapes
**BOTRYOSE** *same as* > BOTRYOID
**BOTRYTIS** *n* any of a group of fungi of the genus Botrytis, several of which cause plant diseases
**BOTS** *n* digestive disease of horses and some other animals caused by the presence of botfly larvae in the stomach
**BOTT** *same as* > BOT
**BOTTE** *n* thrust or hit
**BOTTED** > BOT
**BOTTEGA** *n* workshop; studio
**BOTTEGAS** > BOTTEGA
**BOTTES** > BOTTE
**BOTTIES** > BOTTY
**BOTTINE** *n* light boot for

women or children
**BOTTINES** > BOTTINE
**BOTTING** > BOT
**BOTTLE** *n* container for holding liquids ▷ *vb* put in a bottle
**BOTTLED** > BOTTLE
**BOTTLEFUL** > BOTTLE
**BOTTLER** *n* exceptional person or thing
**BOTTLERS** > BOTTLER
**BOTTLES** > BOTTLE
**BOTTLING** > BOTTLE
**BOTTLINGS** > BOTTLE
**BOTTOM** *n* lowest, deepest, or farthest removed part of a thing ▷ *adj* lowest or last ▷ *vb* provide with a bottom
**BOTTOMED** > BOTTOM
**BOTTOMER** *n* pit worker
**BOTTOMERS** > BOTTOMER
**BOTTOMING** *n* lowest level of foundation material for a road or other structure
**BOTTOMRY** *n* contract whereby the body owner of a ship borrows money to enable the vessel to complete the voyage and pledges the ship as security for the loan
**BOTTOMS** > BOTTOM
**BOTTOMSET** as in *bottomset bed* fine sediment deposited at the front of a growing delta
**BOTTONY** *same as* > BOTONE
**BOTTS** > BOTT
**BOTTY** *n* diminutive for bottom
**BOTULIN** *n* potent toxin produced by the bacterium Clostridium botulinum in imperfectly preserved food, etc, causing botulism
**BOTULINAL** > BOTULIN
**BOTULINS** > BOTULIN
**BOTULINUM** *n* botulin-secreting bacterium
**BOTULINUS** *n* anaerobic bacterium, Clostridium botulinum, whose toxins (botulins) cause botulism: family Bacillaceae
**BOTULISM** *n* severe food poisoning
**BOTULISMS** > BOTULISM
**BOUBOU** *n* long flowing garment worn by men and women in Mali, Nigeria, Senegal, and some other parts of Africa
**BOUBOUS** > BOUBOU
**BOUCHE** *n* notch cut in top corner of shield
**BOUCHEE** *n* small pastry case filled with a savoury mixture, served hot with cocktails or as an hors d'oeuvre
**BOUCHEES** > BOUCHEE
**BOUCHES** > BOUCHE

**BOUCLE** n looped yarn giving a knobbly effect ▷ adj of or designating such a yarn or fabric
**BOUCLEE** n support for a cue in billiards formed by doubling the first finger so that its tip is aligned with the thumb at its second joint, to form a loop through which the cue may slide
**BOUCLEES** > BOUCLEE
**BOUCLES** > BOUCLE
**BOUDERIE** n sulkiness
**BOUDERIES** > BOUDERIE
**BOUDIN** n French version of a black pudding
**BOUDINS** > BOUDIN
**BOUDOIR** n woman's bedroom or private sitting room
**BOUDOIRS** > BOUDOIR
**BOUFFANT** adj (of a hairstyle) having extra height through backcombing ▷ n bouffant hair style
**BOUFFANTS** > BOUFFANT
**BOUFFE** n type of light or satirical opera common in France during the 19th century
**BOUFFES** > BOUFFE
**BOUGE** vb move
**BOUGED** > BOUGE
**BOUGES** > BOUGE
**BOUGET** n budget
**BOUGETS** > BOUGET
**BOUGH** n large branch of a tree
**BOUGHED** > BOUGH
**BOUGHLESS** > BOUGH
**BOUGHPOT** n container for displaying boughs
**BOUGHPOTS** > BOUGHPOT
**BOUGHS** > BOUGH
**BOUGHT** > BUY
**BOUGHTEN** a dialect word for > BUY
**BOUGHTS** > BUY
**BOUGIE** n long slender semiflexible cylindrical instrument for inserting into body passages, such as the rectum or urethra, to dilate structures, introduce medication, etc
**BOUGIES** > BOUGIE
**BOUGING** > BOUGE
**BOUILLI** n stew
**BOUILLIS** > BOUILLI
**BOUILLON** n thin clear broth or stock
**BOUILLONS** > BOUILLON
**BOUK** n bulk; volume
**BOUKS** > BOUK
**BOULDER** n large rounded rock ▷ vb convert into boulders
**BOULDERED** > BOULDER
**BOULDERER** > BOULDER
**BOULDERS** > BOULDER
**BOULDERY** > BOULDER

**BOULE** same as > BOULLE
**BOULES** n game, popular in France, in which metal bowls are thrown to land as close as possible to a target ball
**BOULEVARD** n wide, usu. tree-lined, street
**BOULLE** adj denoting or relating to a type of marquetry of patterned inlays of brass and tortoiseshell, occasionally with other metals such as pewter, much used on French furniture from the 17th century ▷ n something ornamented with such marquetry
**BOULLES** > BOULLE
**BOULT** same as > BOLT
**BOULTED** > BOULT
**BOULTER** > BOLT
**BOULTERS** > BOLT
**BOULTING** > BOULT
**BOULTINGS** > BOULT
**BOULTS** > BOULT
**BOUN** vb prepare to go out
**BOUNCE** vb (of a ball etc) rebound from an impact ▷ n act of rebounding
**BOUNCED** > BOUNCE
**BOUNCER** n person employed at a disco etc to remove unwanted people
**BOUNCERS** > BOUNCER
**BOUNCES** > BOUNCE
**BOUNCIER** > BOUNCY
**BOUNCIEST** > BOUNCY
**BOUNCILY** > BOUNCY
**BOUNCING** adj vigorous and robust
**BOUNCY** adj lively, exuberant, or self-confident
**BOUND** > BIND
**BOUNDABLE** > BIND
**BOUNDARY** n dividing line that indicates the farthest limit
**BOUNDED** adj (of a set) having a bound, esp where a measure is defined in terms of which all the elements of the set, or the differences between all pairs of members, are less than some value, or else all its members lie within some other well-defined set
**BOUNDEN** adj morally obligatory
**BOUNDER** n morally reprehensible person
**BOUNDERS** > BOUNDER
**BOUNDING** > BIND
**BOUNDLESS** adj unlimited
**BOUNDNESS** > BIND
**BOUNDS** pl n limit
**BOUNED** > BOUN
**BOUNING** > BOUN
**BOUNS** > BOUN
**BOUNTEOUS** adj giving

freely
**BOUNTIED** > BOUNTY
**BOUNTIES** > BOUNTY
**BOUNTIFUL** adj plentiful
**BOUNTREE** another name for > BOUNTREE
**BOUNTREES** > BOUNTREE
**BOUNTY** n generosity
**BOUNTYHED** n generosity
**BOUQUET** n bunch of flowers
**BOUQUETS** > BOUQUET
**BOURASQUE** n violent storm
**BOURBON** n whiskey made from maize
**BOURBONS** > BOURBON
**BOURD** n prank
**BOURDER** n prankster
**BOURDERS** > BOURDER
**BOURDON** n 16-foot organ stop of the stopped diapason type
**BOURDONS** > BOURDON
**BOURDS** > BOURD
**BOURG** n French market town, esp one beside a castle
**BOURGEOIS** n middle-class (person) ▷ adj characteristic of or comprising the middle class
**BOURGEON** same as > BURGEON
**BOURGEONS** > BOURGEON
**BOURGS** > BOURG
**BOURKHA** same as > BURKA
**BOURKHAS** same as > BOURKHA
**BOURLAW** same as > BYRLAW
**BOURLAWS** > BOURLAW
**BOURN** n (in S Britain) stream
**BOURNE** same as > BOURN
**BOURNES** > BOURNE
**BOURNS** > BOURN
**BOURREE** n traditional French dance in fast duple time
**BOURREES** > BOURREE
**BOURRIDE** n Mediterranean fish soup
**BOURRIDES** > BOURRIDE
**BOURSE** n stock exchange of continental Europe, esp Paris
**BOURSES** > BOURSE
**BOURSIER** n stock-exchange worker
**BOURSIERS** > BOURSIER
**BOURSIN** n tradename of a smooth white creamy cheese, often flavoured with garlic
**BOURSINS** > BOURSIN
**BOURTREE** n elder tree
**BOURTREES** > BOURTREE
**BOUSE** vb raise or haul with a tackle
**BOUSED** > BOUSE
**BOUSES** > BOUSE
**BOUSIER** > BOUSY
**BOUSIEST** > BOUSY
**BOUSING** > BOUSE

**BOUSOUKI** same as > BOUZOUKI
**BOUSOUKIA** > BOUSOUKI
**BOUSOUKIS** > BOUSOUKI
**BOUSY** adj drunken; boozy
**BOUT** n period of activity or illness
**BOUTADE** n outburst
**BOUTADES** > BOUTADE
**BOUTIQUE** n small clothes shop
**BOUTIQUES** > BOUTIQUE
**BOUTIQUEY** adj typical of boutiques
**BOUTON** n knob-shaped contact between nerve fibres
**BOUTONNE** adj reserved or inhibited
**BOUTONNEE** same as > BOUTONNE
**BOUTONS** > BOUTON
**BOUTS** > BOUT
**BOUVARDIA** n flowering plant
**BOUVIER** n large powerful dog of a Belgian breed, having a rough shaggy coat: used esp for cattle herding and guarding
**BOUVIERS** > BOUVIER
**BOUZOUKI** n Greek stringed musical instrument
**BOUZOUKIA** > BOUZOUKI
**BOUZOUKIS** > BOUZOUKI
**BOVATE** n obsolete measure of land
**BOVATES** > BOVATE
**BOVID** adj of, relating to, or belonging to the Bovidae, a family of ruminant artiodactyl hollow-horned mammals including sheep, goats, cattle, antelopes, and buffalo ▷ n any bovid animal
**BOVIDS** > BOVID
**BOVINE** adj relating to cattle ▷ n any animal belonging to the Bovini
**BOVINELY** > BOVINE
**BOVINES** > BOVINE
**BOVINITY** > BOVINE
**BOVVER** n rowdiness, esp caused by gangs of teenage youths
**BOVVERS** > BOVVER
**BOW** vb lower (one's head) or bend (one's knee or body) as a sign of respect or shame ▷ n movement made when bowing
**BOWAT** n lamp
**BOWATS** > BOWAT
**BOWBENT** adj bent; bow-like
**BOWED** adj lowered, bent forward, or curved
**BOWEL** n intestine, esp the large intestine ▷ vb remove the bowels
**BOWELED** > BOWEL
**BOWELING** > BOWEL
**BOWELLED** > BOWEL
**BOWELLESS** > BOWEL

BOWELLING > BOWEL

BOWELS > BOWEL

BOWER n shady leafy shelter ▷ vb surround as with a bower

BOWERBIRD n songbird of Australia and New Guinea, the males of which build bower-like display grounds to attract females

BOWERED > BOWER

BOWERIES > BOWER

BOWERING > BOWER

BOWERS > BOWER

BOWERY > BOWER

BOWES same as > BOUGH

BOWET same as > BOWAT

BOWETS > BOWET

BOWFIN n primitive North American freshwater bony fish, Amia calva, with an elongated body and a very long dorsal fin: family Amiidae

BOWFINS > BOWFIN

BOWFRONT adj having a front that curves outwards

BOWGET obsolete variant of > BUDGET

BOWGETS > BOWGET

BOWHEAD n large-mouthed arctic whale, Balaena mysticetus, that has become rare through overfishing but is now a protected species

BOWHEADS > BOWHEAD

BOWHUNTER n person hunting with bow and arrows

BOWIE as in Bowie knife type of hunting knife

BOWING n technique of using the bow in playing a violin, viola, cello, or related instrument

BOWINGLY > BOWING

BOWINGS > BOWING

BOWKNOT n decorative knot usually having two loops and two loose ends

BOWKNOTS > BOWKNOT

BOWL n round container with an open top ▷ vb roll smoothly along the ground

BOWLDER same as > BOULDER

BOWLDERS > BOWLDER

BOWLED > BOWL

BOWLEG > BOWLEGS

BOWLEGGED adj having legs that curve outwards like a bow

BOWLEGS

BOWLER n player who sends (a ball) towards the batsman

BOWLERS > BOWLER

BOWLESS > BOW

BOWLFUL same as > BOWL

BOWLFULS > BOWLFUL

BOWLIKE > BOW

BOWLINE n line used to keep the sail taut against the wind

BOWLINES > BOWLINE

BOWLING n game in which bowls are rolled at a group of pins

BOWLINGS > BLOW

BOWLLIKE > BOWL

BOWLS n game played on a very smooth area of grass in which opponents roll biased wooden bowls as near a small bowl (the jack) as possible

BOWMAN n archer

BOWMEN > BOWMAN

BOWNE same as > BOUN

BOWNED > BOWNE

BOWNES > BOWNE

BOWNING > BOWNE

BOWPOT same as > BOUGHPOT

BOWPOTS > BOWPOT

BOWR n muscle

BOWRS > BOWR

BOWS > BOW

BOWSAW n saw with a thin blade in a bow-shaped frame

BOWSAWS > BOWSAW

BOWSE same as > BOUSE

BOWSED > BOWSE

BOWSER n tanker containing fuel for aircraft, military vehicles, etc

BOWSERS > BOWSER

BOWSES > BOWSE

BOWSEY n Irish word for mean person

BOWSEYS > BOWSEY

BOWSHOT n distance an arrow travels from the bow

BOWSHOTS > BOWSHOT

BOWSIE n low-class mean or obstreperous person

BOWSIES > BOWSIE

BOWSING > BOWSE

BOWSPRIT n spar projecting from the bow of a sailing ship

BOWSPRITS > BOWSPRIT

BOWSTRING n string of an archer's bow

BOWSTRUNG > BOWSTRING

BOWWOW n imitation of the bark of a dog ▷ vb make a noise like a dog

BOWWOWED > BOWWOW

BOWWOWING > BOWWOW

BOWWOWS > BOWWOW

BOWYANG n band worn round trouser leg below knee

BOWYANGS > BOWYANG

BOWYER n person who makes or sells archery bows

BOWYERS > BOWYER

BOX n container with a firm flat base and sides ▷ vb put into a box

BOXBALL n street ball game

BOXBALLS > BOXBALL

BOXBERRY n fruit of the partridgeberry or wintergreen

BOXBOARD n tough paperboard made from wood and wastepaper pulp: used for making boxes, etc

BOXBOARDS > BOXBOARD

BOXCAR n closed railway freight van

BOXCARS > BOXCAR

BOXED > BOX

BOXEN > BOX

BOXER n person who participates in the sport of boxing

BOXERCISE n system of sustained exercises combining boxing movements with aerobic activities

BOXERS > BOXER

BOXES > BOX

BOXFISH another name for > TRUNKFISH

BOXFISHES > BOXFISH

BOXFUL > BOX

BOXFULS > BOX

BOXHAUL vb bring (a square-rigger) onto a new tack by backwinding the foresails and steering hard round

BOXHAULED > BOXHAUL

BOXHAULS > BOXHAUL

BOXIER > BOXY

BOXIEST > BOXY

BOXILY > BOXY

BOXINESS > BOXY

BOXING n sport of fighting with the fists

BOXINGS > BOXING

BOXKEEPER n person responsible for theatre boxes

BOXLIKE > BOX

BOXROOM n small room in which boxes, cases, etc may be stored

BOXROOMS > BOXROOM

BOXTHORN n matrimony vine

BOXTHORNS > BOXTHORN

BOXWALLAH n salesman

BOXWOOD n hard yellow wood of the box tree, used to make tool handles, etc

BOXWOODS > BOXWOOD

BOXY adj squarish or chunky

BOY n male child ▷ vb act the part of a boy in a play

BOYAR n member of an old order of Russian nobility, ranking immediately below the princes: abolished by Peter the Great

BOYARD same as > BOYAR

BOYARDS > BOYARD

BOYARISM > BOYAR

BOYARISMS > BOYAR

BOYARS > BOYAR

BOYAU n connecting trench

BOYAUX > BOYAU

BOYCHICK same as > BOYCHIK

BOYCHICKS > BOYCHICK

BOYCHIK n young boy

BOYCHIKS > BOYCHIK

BOYCOTT vb refuse to deal with (an organization or country) ▷ n instance of boycotting

BOYCOTTED > BOYCOTT

BOYCOTTER > BOYCOTT

BOYCOTTS > BOYCOTT

BOYED > BOY

BOYF n boyfriend

BOYFRIEND n male friend with whom a person is romantically or sexually involved

BOYFS > BOYF

BOYG n troll-like mythical creature

BOYGS > BOYG

BOYHOOD n state or time of being a boy

BOYHOODS > BOYHOOD

BOYING > BOY

BOYISH adj of or like a boy in looks, behaviour, or character, esp when regarded as attractive or endearing

BOYISHLY > BOYISH

BOYLA n Australian Aboriginal word for magician

BOYLAS > BOYLA

BOYO n boy or young man: often used in direct address

BOYOS > BOYO

BOYS > BOY

BOYSIER > BOYSY

BOYSIEST > BOYSY

BOYSY adj suited to or typical of boys or young men

BOZO n man, esp a stupid one

BOZOS > BOZO

BOZZETTI > BOZZETTO

BOZZETTO n small sketch of planned work

BRA same as > BRASSIERE

BRAAI vb grill or roast (meat) over open coals

BRAAIED > BRAAI

BRAAIING > BRAAI

BRAAIS > BRAAI

BRAATA n small portion added to a purchase of food by a market vendor, to encourage the customer to return

BRAATAS same as > BRAATA

BRAATASES > BRAATA

BRABBLE rare word for > SQUABBLE

BRABBLED > BRABBLE

BRABBLER > BRABBLE

BRABBLERS > BRABBLE

BRABBLES > BRABBLE

BRABBLING > BRABBLE

BRACCATE adj (of birds) having feathered legs

**BRACCIA** > BRACCIO
**BRACCIO** n former unit of measurement; length of man's arm
**BRACE** n object fastened to something to straighten or support it ▷ vb steady or prepare (oneself) for something unpleasant
**BRACED** > BRACE
**BRACELET** n ornamental chain or band for the wrist
**BRACELETS** pl n handcuffs
**BRACER** n person or thing that braces
**BRACERO** n Mexican World War II labourer
**BRACEROS** > BRACERO
**BRACERS** > BRACER
**BRACES** pl n pair of straps worn over the shoulders for holding up the trousers
**BRACH** n bitch hound
**BRACHAH** n blessing
**BRACHAHS** > BRACHAH
**BRACHES** > BRACH
**BRACHET** same as > BRACH
**BRACHETS** > BRACHET
**BRACHIA** > BRACHIUM
**BRACHIAL** adj of or relating to the arm or to an armlike part or structure ▷ n brachial part or structure
**BRACHIALS** > BRACHIAL
**BRACHIATE** adj having widely divergent paired branches ▷ vb (of some arboreal apes and monkeys) swing by the arms from one hold to the next
**BRACHIUM** n arm, esp the upper part
**BRACHS** > BRACH
**BRACING** adj refreshing and invigorating ▷ n system of braces used to strengthen or support
**BRACINGLY** > BRACING
**BRACINGS** > BRACING
**BRACIOLA** n Italian meat roulade
**BRACIOLAS** > BRACIOLA
**BRACIOLE** same as > BRACIOLA
**BRACIOLES** > BRACIOLE
**BRACK** same as > BARMBRACK
**BRACKEN** n large fern
**BRACKENS** > BRACKEN
**BRACKET** n pair of characters used to enclose a section of writing ▷ vb put in brackets
**BRACKETED** > BRACKET
**BRACKETS** > BRACKET
**BRACKISH** adj (of water) slightly salty
**BRACKS** > BRACK
**BRACONID** n type of fly with parasitic larva
**BRACONIDS** > BRACONID
**BRACT** n leaf at the base of a flower
**BRACTEAL** > BRACT

**BRACTEATE** adj (of a plant) having bracts ▷ n fine decorated dish or plate of precious metal
**BRACTED** > BRACT
**BRACTEOLE** n secondary bract subtending a flower within an inflorescence
**BRACTLESS** > BRACT
**BRACTLET** variant of > BRACTEOLE
**BRACTLETS** > BRACTLET
**BRACTS** > BRACT
**BRAD** n small tapered nail with a small head
**BRADAWL** n small boring tool
**BRADAWLS** > BRADAWL
**BRADDED** > BRAD
**BRADDING** > BRAD
**BRADOON** same as > BRIDOON
**BRADOONS** > BRADOON
**BRADS** > BRAD
**BRAE** n hill or slope
**BRAEHEID** n summit of a hill or slope
**BRAEHEIDS** > BRAEHEID
**BRAES** > BRAE
**BRAG** vb speak arrogantly and boastfully ▷ n boastful talk or behaviour
**BRAGGART** n person who boasts loudly ▷ adj boastful
**BRAGGARTS** > BRAGGART
**BRAGGED** > BRAG
**BRAGGER** > BRAG
**BRAGGERS** > BRAG
**BRAGGEST** > BRAG
**BRAGGIER** > BRAGGY
**BRAGGIEST** > BRAGGY
**BRAGGING** > BRAG
**BRAGGINGS** > BRAG
**BRAGGY** adj boastful
**BRAGLY** > BRAG
**BRAGS** > BRAG
**BRAHMA** n heavy breed of domestic fowl with profusely feathered legs and feet
**BRAHMAN** n member of highest Hindu caste
**BRAHMANI** n woman of the highest Hindu caste
**BRAHMANIS** > BRAHMANI
**BRAHMANS** > BRAHMAN
**BRAHMAS** > BRAHMA
**BRAHMIN** same as > BRAHMAN
**BRAHMINS** > BRAHMIN
**BRAID** vb interweave (hair, thread, etc) ▷ n length of hair etc that has been braided ▷ adj broad ▷ adv broadly
**BRAIDE** adj given to deceit
**BRAIDED** adj (of a river or stream) flowing in several shallow interconnected channels separated by banks of deposited material
**BRAIDER** > BRAID
**BRAIDERS** > BRAID

**BRAIDEST** > BRAID
**BRAIDING** n braids collectively
**BRAIDINGS** > BRAIDING
**BRAIDS** > BRAID
**BRAIL** n one of several lines fastened to the leech of a fore-and-aft sail to aid in furling it ▷ vb furl (a fore-and-aft sail) using brails
**BRAILED** > BRAIL
**BRAILING** > BRAIL
**BRAILLE** n system of writing for the blind consisting of raised dots that can be interpreted by touch ▷ vb print or write using this method
**BRAILLED** > BRAILLE
**BRAILLER** n device for producing text in braille
**BRAILLERS** > BRAILLER
**BRAILLES** > BRAILLE
**BRAILLING** > BRAILLE
**BRAILLIST** n braille transcriber
**BRAILS** > BRAIL
**BRAIN** n soft mass of nervous tissue in the head ▷ vb hit (someone) hard on the head
**BRAINBOX** n skull
**BRAINCASE** n part of cranium that covers brain
**BRAINDEAD** adj having suffered irreversible stoppage of breathing due to brain damage
**BRAINED** > BRAIN
**BRAINFART** n idea expressed without much previous thought
**BRAINIAC** n highly intelligent person
**BRAINIACS** > BRAINIAC
**BRAINIER** > BRAINY
**BRAINIEST** > BRAINY
**BRAINILY** > BRAINY
**BRAINING** > BRAIN
**BRAINISH** adj impulsive
**BRAINLESS** adj stupid
**BRAINPAN** n skull
**BRAINPANS** > BRAINPAN
**BRAINS** > BRAIN
**BRAINSICK** adj relating to or caused by insanity
**BRAINSTEM** n stalklike part of the brain consisting of the medulla oblongata, the midbrain, and the pons Varolii
**BRAINWASH** vb cause (a person) to alter his or her beliefs, esp by methods based on isolation, sleeplessness, etc
**BRAINWAVE** n sudden idea
**BRAINY** adj clever
**BRAIRD** vb appear as shoots
**BRAIRDED** > BRAIRD
**BRAIRDING** > BRAIRD
**BRAIRDS** > BRAIRD
**BRAISE** vb cook slowly in

a covered pan with a little liquid
**BRAISED** > BRAISE
**BRAISES** > BRAISE
**BRAISING** > BRAISE
**BRAIZE** same as > BRAISE
**BRAIZES** > BRAIZE
**BRAK** n crossbred dog ▷ adj (of water) slightly salty
**BRAKE** same as > BRACKEN
**BRAKEAGE** > BRAKE
**BRAKEAGES** > BRAKE
**BRAKED** > BRAKE
**BRAKELESS** > BRAKE
**BRAKEMAN** n crew member of a goods or passenger train. His duties include controlling auxiliary braking power and inspecting the train
**BRAKEMEN** > BRAKEMAN
**BRAKES** > BRAKE
**BRAKESMAN** n pithead winch operator
**BRAKESMEN** > BRAKESMAN
**BRAKIER** > BRAKY
**BRAKIEST** > BRAKY
**BRAKING** > BRAKE
**BRAKS** > BRAK
**BRAKY** adj brambly
**BRALESS** > BRA
**BRAMBLE** n Scots word for blackberry
**BRAMBLED** > BRAMBLE
**BRAMBLES** > BRAMBLE
**BRAMBLIER** > BRAMBLE
**BRAMBLING** n Eurasian finch, *Fringilla montifringilla*, with a speckled head and back and, in the male, a reddish brown breast and darker wings and tail
**BRAMBLY** > BRAMBLE
**BRAME** n powerful feeling of emotion
**BRAMES** > BRAME
**BRAN** n husks of cereal grain
**BRANCARD** n couch on shafts, carried between two horses
**BRANCARDS** > BRANCARD
**BRANCH** n secondary stem of a tree ▷ vb (of stems, roots, etc) divide, then develop in different directions
**BRANCHED** > BRANCH
**BRANCHER** n young bird learning to fly
**BRANCHERS** > BRANCHER
**BRANCHERY** n branches
**BRANCHES** > BRANCH
**BRANCHIA** n gill in aquatic animals
**BRANCHIAE** > BRANCHIA
**BRANCHIAL** adj of or relating to the gills of an aquatic animal, esp a fish
**BRANCHIER** > BRANCH
**BRANCHING** > BRANCH
**BRANCHLET** n small branch
**BRANCHY** > BRANCH
**BRAND** n particular product

▷ vb mark with a brand
BRANDADE n French puréed fish dish
BRANDADES > BRANDADE
BRANDED adj identifiable as being the product of a particular manufacturer or marketing company
BRANDER > BRAND
BRANDERED > BRAND
BRANDERS > BRAND
BRANDIED > BRANDY
BRANDIES > BRANDY
BRANDING > BRAND
BRANDINGS > BRAND
BRANDISE n three-legged metal stand for cooking pots
BRANDISES > BRANDISE
BRANDISH vb wave (a weapon etc) in a threatening way ▷ n threatening or defiant flourish
BRANDLESS > BRAND
BRANDLING n small red earthworm, Eisenia foetida (or Helodrilus foetidus), found in manure and used as bait by anglers
BRANDRETH n framework of bars used for cooking meat over fire
BRANDS > BRAND
BRANDY n alcoholic spirit distilled from wine ▷ vb give brandy to
BRANDYING > BRANDY
BRANGLE vb quarrel noisily
BRANGLED > BRANGLE
BRANGLES > BRANGLE
BRANGLING > BRANGLE
BRANK vb walk with swaggering gait
BRANKED > BRANK
BRANKIER > BRANKY
BRANKIEST > BRANKY
BRANKING > BRANK
BRANKS pl n (formerly) iron bridle used to restrain scolding women
BRANKY adj ostentatious
BRANLE n old French country dance performed in a linked circle
BRANLES > BRANLE
BRANNED > BRAN
BRANNER n person or machine that treats metal with bran
BRANNERS > BRANNER
BRANNIER > BRANNY
BRANNIEST > BRANNY
BRANNIGAN n noisy quarrrel
BRANNING > BRAN
BRANNY adj having the appearance or texture of bran
BRANS > BRAN
BRANSLE another word for > BRANTLE
BRANSLES > BRANSLE
BRANT n small goose,

Branta bernicla, that has a dark grey plumage and short neck and occurs in most northern coastal regions
BRANTAIL n singing bird with red tail
BRANTAILS > BRANTAIL
BRANTLE n French country dance
BRANTLES > BRANTLE
BRANTS > BRANT
BRAS > BRA
BRASCO n lavatory
BRASCOS > BRASCO
BRASERO n metal grid for burning coals
BRASEROS > BRASERO
BRASES > BRA
BRASH adj offensively loud, showy, or self-confident ▷ n loose rubbish, such as broken rock, hedge clippings, etc ▷ vb assault
BRASHED > BRASH
BRASHER > BRASH
BRASHES > BRASH
BRASHEST > BRASH
BRASHIER > BRASHY
BRASHIEST > BRASHY
BRASHING > BRASH
BRASHLY > BRASH
BRASHNESS > BRASH
BRASHY adj loosely fragmented
BRASIER same as > BRAZIER
BRASIERS > BRASIER
BRASIL same as > BRAZIL
BRASILEIN same as > BRAZILEIN
BRASILIN same as > BRAZILIN
BRASILINS > BRASILIN
BRASILS > BRASIL
BRASS n alloy of copper and zinc ▷ vb make irritated or annoyed
BRASSAGE n amount charged by government for making coins
BRASSAGES > BRASSAGE
BRASSARD n identifying armband or badge
BRASSARDS > BRASSARD
BRASSART same as > BRASSARD
BRASSARTS > BRASSART
BRASSED > BRASS
BRASSERIE n restaurant serving drinks and cheap meals
BRASSES > BRASS
BRASSET same as > BRASSART
BRASSETS > BRASSET
BRASSICA n any plant of the cabbage and turnip family
BRASSICAS > BRASSICA
BRASSIE n former name for a club, a No. 2 wood, originally having a brass-plated sole and with a shallower face than a

driver to give more loft
BRASSIER > BRASSY
BRASSIERE n bra
BRASSIES > BRASSIE
BRASSIEST > BRASSY
BRASSILY > BRASSY
BRASSING > BRASS
BRASSISH > BRASS
BRASSWARE n items made of brass
BRASSY same as > BRASSIE
BRAST same as > BURST
BRASTING > BRAST
BRASTS > BRAST
BRAT n unruly child
BRATCHET n hunting dog
BRATCHETS > BRATCHET
BRATLING n small badly-behaved child
BRATLINGS > BRATLING
BRATPACK n group of precocious and successful young actors, writers, etc
BRATPACKS > BRATPACK
BRATS > BRAT
BRATTICE n partition of wood or treated cloth used to control ventilation in a mine ▷ vb fit with a brattice
BRATTICED > BRATTICE
BRATTICES > BRATTICE
BRATTIER > BRAT
BRATTIEST > BRAT
BRATTISH same as > BRATTICE
BRATTLE vb make a rattling sound
BRATTLED > BRATTLE
BRATTLES > BRATTLE
BRATTLING > BRATTLE
BRATTY > BRAT
BRATWURST n type of small pork sausage
BRAUNCH old variant of > BRANCH
BRAUNCHED > BRAUNCH
BRAUNCHES > BRAUNCH
BRAUNITE n brown or black mineral
BRAUNITES > BRAUNITE
BRAVA n professional assassin
BRAVADO n showy display of self-confidence ▷ vb behave with bravado
BRAVADOED > BRAVADO
BRAVADOES > BRAVADO
BRAVADOS > BRAVADO
BRAVAS > BRAVA
BRAVE adj having or showing courage, resolution, and daring ▷ n Native American warrior ▷ vb confront with resolution or courage
BRAVED > BRAVE
BRAVELY > BRAVE
BRAVENESS > BRAVE
BRAVER > BRAVE
BRAVERIES > BRAVE
BRAVERS > BRAVE
BRAVERY > BRAVE
BRAVES > BRAVE

BRAVEST > BRAVE
BRAVI > BRAVO
BRAVING > BRAVE
BRAVO interj well done! ▷ n cry of 'bravo' ▷ vb cry or shout 'bravo'
BRAVOED > BRAVO
BRAVOES > BRAVO
BRAVOING > BRAVO
BRAVOS > BRAVO
BRAVURA n display of boldness or daring
BRAVURAS > BRAVURA
BRAVURE > BRAVURA
BRAW adj fine or excellent, esp in appearance or dress ▷ pl n best clothes
BRAWER > BRAW
BRAWEST > BRAW
BRAWL n noisy fight ▷ vb fight noisily
BRAWLED > BRAWL
BRAWLER > BRAWL
BRAWLERS > BRAWL
BRAWLIE adj in good health
BRAWLIER > BRAWLIE
BRAWLIEST > BRAWLIE
BRAWLING > BRAWL
BRAWLINGS > BRAWL
BRAWLS > BRAWL
BRAWLY > BRAW
BRAWN n physical strength
BRAWNED > BRAWN
BRAWNIER > BRAWNY
BRAWNIEST > BRAWNY
BRAWNILY > BRAWNY
BRAWNS > BRAWN
BRAWNY adj muscular and strong
BRAWS n fine apparel
BRAXIES > BRAXY
BRAXY n acute and usually fatal bacterial disease of sheep characterized by high fever, coma, and inflammation of the fourth stomach, caused by infection with Clostridium septicum
BRAY vb (of a donkey) utter its loud harsh sound ▷ n donkey's loud harsh sound
BRAYED > BRAY
BRAYER > BRAY
BRAYERS > BRAY
BRAYING > BRAY
BRAYS > BRAY
BRAZA n Spanish unit of measurement
BRAZAS > BRAZA
BRAZE vb join (two metal surfaces) with brass ▷ n high-melting solder or alloy used in brazing
BRAZED > BRAZE
BRAZELESS > BRAZE
BRAZEN adj shameless and bold ▷ vb face and overcome boldly or shamelessly
BRAZENED > BRAZEN
BRAZENING > BRAZEN
BRAZENLY > BRAZEN
BRAZENRY adj audacity

BRAZENS > BRAZEN
BRAZER > BRAZE
BRAZERS > BRAZE
BRAZES > BRAZE
BRAZIER n portable
container for burning
charcoal or coal
BRAZIERS > BRAZIER
BRAZIERY > BRAZIER
BRAZIL n red wood
obtained from various
tropical leguminous trees
of the genus *Caesalpinia*,
such as *C. echinata*
of America: used for
cabinetwork
BRAZILEIN n red
crystalline solid
BRAZILIN n pale yellow
soluble crystalline solid
BRAZILINS > BRAZILIN
BRAZILS > BRAZIL
BRAZING > BRAZE
BREACH n breaking of a
promise, obligation, etc
▷ vb break (a promise,
law, etc)
BREACHED > BREACH
BREACHER > BREACH
BREACHERS > BREACH
BREACHES > BREACH
BREACHING > BREACH
BREAD n food made by
baking a mixture of
flour and water or milk
▷ vb cover (food) with
breadcrumbs before
cooking
BREADBOX n airtight
container for bread, cakes,
etc
BREADED > BREAD
BREADHEAD n person solely
concerned with money
BREADING > BREAD
BREADLESS > BREAD
BREADLINE n queue of
people waiting for free
food given as charity
BREADNUT n moraceous
tree, *Brosimum alicastrum*,
of Central America and the
Caribbean
BREADNUTS > BREADNUT
BREADROOM n place where
bread is kept on ship
BREADROOT n leguminous
plant, *Psoralea esculenta*,
of central North America,
having an edible starchy
root
BREADS > BREAD
BREADTH n extent of
something from side to
side
BREADTHS > BREADTH
BREADY adj having the
appearance or texture of
bread
BREAK > BRACKEN
BREAKABLE adj capable of
being broken ▷ n fragile
easily broken article
BREAKAGE n act or result of

breaking
BREAKAGES > BREAKAGE
BREAKAWAY n (consisting
of) a dissenting group who
have left a larger unit ▷ adj
dissenting ▷ vb leave
hastily or escape
BREAKBACK adj
backbreaking; arduous
BREAKBEAT n type of
electronic dance music
BREAKBONE as in *breakbone
fever* dengue
BREAKDOWN n act or
instance of breaking down
BREAKER n large wave
BREAKERS > BREAKER
BREAKEVEN n the level of
commercial activity at
which the total cost and
total revenue of a business
enterprise are equal
BREAKFAST n first meal of
the day ▷ vb eat breakfast
BREAKING > BRACKEN
BREAKINGS > BRACKEN
BREAKNECK adj fast and
dangerous
BREAKOFF n act or an
instance of breaking off or
stopping
BREAKOFFS > BREAKOFF
BREAKOUT n escape,
esp from prison or
confinement
BREAKOUTS > BREAKOUT
BREAKS > BRACKEN
BREAKTIME n period of rest
or recreation, esp at school
BREAKUP n separation or
disintegration
BREAKUPS > BREAKUP
BREAKWALL n breakwater
BREAM n any of several
Eurasian freshwater
cyprinid fishes of the
genus *Abramis*, esp *A.
brama*, having a deep
compressed body covered
with silvery scales ▷ vb
clean debris (from the
bottom of a vessel)
BREAMED > BREAM
BREAMING > BREAM
BREAMS > BREAM
BREARE same as > BRIER
BREARES > BREARE
BREASKIT same
as > BRISKET
BREASKITS > BREASKIT
BREAST n either of the
two soft fleshy milk-
secreting glands on a
woman's chest ▷ vb reach
the summit of
BREASTED > BREAST
BREASTFED adj fed at
mother's breast
BREASTING > BREAST
BREASTPIN n brooch worn
on the breast, esp to close
a garment
BREASTS > BREAST
BREATH n taking in and

letting out of air during
breathing
BREATHE vb take in oxygen
and give out carbon
dioxide
BREATHED adj relating to or
denoting a speech sound
for whose articulation the
vocal cords are not made
to vibrate
BREATHER n short rest
BREATHERS > BREATHER
BREATHES > BREATHE
BREATHFUL > BREATH
BREATHIER > BREATHY
BREATHILY > BREATHY
BREATHING n passage of air
into and out of the lungs
to supply the body with
oxygen
BREATHS > BREATH
BREATHY adj (of the
speaking voice)
accompanied by an
audible emission of breath
BRECCIA n rock consisting
of angular fragments
embedded in a finer
matrix, formed by erosion,
impact, volcanic activity,
etc
BRECCIAL > BRECCIA
BRECCIAS > BRECCIA
BRECCIATE > BRECCIA
BRECHAM n straw horse-
collar
BRECHAMS > BRECHAM
BRECHAN same
as > BRECHAM
BRECHANS > BRECHAN
BRED > BREED
BREDE archaic spelling
of > BRAID
BREDED > BREDE
BREDES > BREDE
BREDIE n meat and
vegetable stew
BREDIES > BREDIE
BREDING > BREDE
BREE n broth, stock, or
juice
BREECH n buttocks ▷ vb fit
(a gun) with a breech
BREECHED > BREECH
BREECHES pl n trousers
extending to just below
the knee
BREECHING n strap of
a harness that passes
behind a horse's haunches
BREED vb produce new
or improved strains of
(domestic animals or
plants) ▷ n group of
animals etc within a
species that have
certain clearly defined
characteristics
BREEDER n person who
breeds plants or animals
BREEDERS > BREEDER
BREEDING > BREED
BREEDINGS > BREED
BREEDS > BREED

BREEKS pl n trousers
BREEM same as > BREME
BREENGE vb lunge forward
▷ n violent movement
BREENGED > BREENGE
BREENGES > BREENGE
BREENGING > BREENGE
BREER another word
for > BRAIRD
BREERED > BREER
BREERING > BREER
BREERS > BREER
BREES > BREE
BREESE same as > BREEZE
BREESES > BREESE
BREEST > BREAST
BREESTS > BREAST
BREEZE n gentle wind ▷ vb
move quickly or casually
BREEZED > BREEZE
BREEZES > BREEZE
BREEZEWAY n roofed
passageway connecting
two buildings, sometimes
with the sides enclosed
BREEZIER > BREEZY
BREEZIEST > BREEZY
BREEZILY > BREEZY
BREEZING > BREEZE
BREEZY adj windy
BREGMA n point on the top
of the skull where the
coronal and sagittal
sutures meet: in infants
this corresponds to the
anterior fontanelle
BREGMATA > BREGMA
BREGMATE > BREGMA
BREGMATIC > BREGMA
BREHON n (formerly) judge
in Ireland
BREHONS > BREHON
BREI vb speak with a
uvular r, esp in Afrikaans
BREID n bread
BREIDS > BREID
BREIING > BREI
BREINGE same as > BREENGE
BREINGED > BREINGE
BREINGES > BREINGE
BREINGING > BREINGE
BREIS > BREI
BREIST Scot word
for > BREAST
BREISTS > BREIST
BREKKIES > BREKKY
BREKKY slang word
for > BREAKFAST
BRELOQUE n charm
attached to watch chain
BRELOQUES > BRELOQUE
BREME adj well-known
BREN n type of machine
gun
BRENNE vb burn
BRENNES > BRENNE
BRENNING > BREN
BRENS > BREN
BRENT n type of goose ▷ adj
steep
BRENTER > BRENT
BRENTEST > BRENT
BRENTS > BRENT
BRER n brother: usually

prefixed to a name
**BRERE** *same as* > BRIER
**BRERES** > BRERE
**BRERS** > BRER
**BRETASCHE** *another word for* > BRATTICE
**BRETESSE** *another word for* > BRATTICE
**BRETESSES** > BRETESSE
**BRETHREN** > BROTHER
**BRETON** n hat with an upturned brim and a rounded crown
**BRETONS** > BRETON
**BRETTICE** *same as* > BRATTICE
**BRETTICED** > BRETTICE
**BRETTICES** > BRETTICE
**BREVE** n accent (˘), placed over a vowel to indicate that it is short or is pronounced in a specified way
**BREVES** > BREVE
**BREVET** n document entitling a commissioned officer to hold temporarily a higher military rank without the appropriate pay and allowances ▷ vb promote by brevet
**BREVETCY** > BREVET
**BREVETE** *adj* patented
**BREVETED** > BREVET
**BREVETING** > BREVET
**BREVETS** > BREVET
**BREVETTED** > BREVET
**BREVIARY** n book of prayers to be recited daily by a Roman Catholic priest
**BREVIATE** n summary
**BREVIATES** > BREVIATE
**BREVIER** n (formerly) size of printer's type approximately equal to 8 point
**BREVIERS** > BREVIER
**BREVIS** *same as* > BREWIS
**BREVISES** > BREVIS
**BREVITIES** > BREVITY
**BREVITY** n shortness
**BREW** vb make (beer etc) by steeping, boiling, and fermentation ▷ n beverage produced by brewing
**BREWAGE** n product of brewing
**BREWAGES** > BREWAGE
**BREWED** > BREW
**BREWER** > BREW
**BREWERIES** > BREWERY
**BREWERS** > BREW
**BREWERY** n place where beer etc is brewed
**BREWING** n quantity of a beverage brewed at one time
**BREWINGS** > BREWING
**BREWIS** n bread soaked in broth, gravy, etc
**BREWISES** > BREWIS
**BREWPUB** n pub that incorporates a brewery on

its premises
**BREWPUBS** > BREWPUB
**BREWS** > BREW
**BREWSKI** n beer
**BREWSKIES** > BREWSKI
**BREWSKIS** > BREWSKI
**BREWSTER** n person, particularly a woman, who brews
**BREWSTERS** > BREWSTER
**BREY** *same as* > BREI
**BREYED** > BREY
**BREYING** > BREY
**BREYS** > BREY
**BRIAR** n ericaceous shrub, *Erica arborea*, of S Europe, having a hard woody root (briarroot)
**BRIARD** n medium-sized dog of an ancient French sheep-herding breed having a long rough coat of a single colour
**BRIARDS** > BRIARD
**BRIARED** > BRIAR
**BRIARROOT** n hard woody root of the briar, used for making tobacco pipes
**BRIARS** > BRIAR
**BRIARWOOD** *same as* > BRIARROOT
**BRIARY** > BRIAR
**BRIBABLE** > BRIBE
**BRIBE** vb offer or give something to someone to gain favour, influence, etc ▷ n something given or offered as a bribe
**BRIBEABLE** > BRIBE
**BRIBED** > BRIBE
**BRIBEE** n one who is bribed
**BRIBEES** > BRIBEE
**BRIBER** > BRIBE
**BRIBERIES** > BRIBERY
**BRIBERS** > BRIBE
**BRIBERY** n process of giving or taking bribes
**BRIBES** > BRIBE
**BRIBING** > BRIBE
**BRICABRAC** n miscellaneous small objects, esp furniture and curios, kept because they are ornamental or rare
**BRICHT** *Scot word for* > BRIGHT
**BRICHTER** > BRICHT
**BRICHTEST** > BRICHT
**BRICK** n (rectangular block of) baked clay used in building ▷ vb build, enclose, or fill with bricks
**BRICKBAT** n blunt criticism
**BRICKBATS** > BRICKBAT
**BRICKCLAY** n clay for making bricks
**BRICKED** > BRICK
**BRICKEN** *adj* made of brick
**BRICKIE** n bricklayer
**BRICKIER** > BRICKY
**BRICKIES** > BRICKIE
**BRICKIEST** > BRICKY
**BRICKING** > BRICK
**BRICKINGS** > BRICK

**BRICKKILN** n kiln for making bricks
**BRICKLE** *variant of* > BRITTLE
**BRICKLES** > BRICKLE
**BRICKLIKE** > BRICK
**BRICKS** > BRICK
**BRICKWALL** *same as* > BRICOLE
**BRICKWORK** n structure, such as a wall, built of bricks
**BRICKY** *same as* > BRICKIE
**BRICKYARD** n place in which bricks are made, stored, or sold
**BRICOLAGE** n jumbled effect produced by the close proximity of buildings from different periods and in different architectural styles
**BRICOLE** n shot in which the cue ball touches a cushion after striking the object ball and before touching another ball
**BRICOLES** > BRICOLE
**BRIDAL** *adj* of a bride or a wedding ▷ n wedding or wedding feast
**BRIDALLY** > BRIDAL
**BRIDALS** > BRIDAL
**BRIDE** n woman who has just been or is about to be married
**BRIDECAKE** n wedding cake
**BRIDED** > BRIDE
**BRIDEMAID** n old form of bridesmaid
**BRIDEMAN** n bridegroom's attendant
**BRIDEMEN** > BRIDEMAN
**BRIDES** > BRIDE
**BRIDESMAN** *same as* > BRIDEMAN
**BRIDESMEN** > BRIDESMAN
**BRIDEWELL** n house of correction
**BRIDGABLE** > BRIDGE
**BRIDGE** n structure for crossing a river etc ▷ vb build a bridge over (something)
**BRIDGED** > BRIDGE
**BRIDGES** > BRIDGE
**BRIDGING** n one or more timber struts fixed between floor or roof joists to stiffen the construction and distribute the loads
**BRIDGINGS** > BRIDGING
**BRIDIE** n semicircular pie containing meat and onions
**BRIDIES** > BRIDIE
**BRIDING** > BRIDE
**BRIDLE** n headgear for controlling a horse ▷ vb show anger or indignation
**BRIDLED** > BRIDLE
**BRIDLER** > BRIDLE
**BRIDLERS** > BRIDLE

**BRIDLES** > BRIDLE
**BRIDLEWAY** n path for riding horses
**BRIDLING** > BRIDLE
**BRIDOON** n horse's bit: small snaffle used in double bridles
**BRIDOONS** > BRIDOON
**BRIE** *same as* > BREE
**BRIEF** *adj* short in duration ▷ n condensed statement or written synopsis ▷ vb give information and instructions to (a person)
**BRIEFCASE** n small flat case for carrying papers, books, etc
**BRIEFED** > BRIEF
**BRIEFER** > BRIEF
**BRIEFERS** > BRIEF
**BRIEFEST** > BRIEF
**BRIEFING** n meeting at which detailed information or instructions are given, as for military operations, etc
**BRIEFINGS** > BRIEFING
**BRIEFLESS** *adj* (said of a barrister) without clients
**BRIEFLY** > BRIEF
**BRIEFNESS** > BRIEF
**BRIEFS** *pl n* men's or women's underpants without legs
**BRIER** *same as* > BRIAR
**BRIERED** > BRIER
**BRIERIER** > BRIER
**BRIERIEST** > BRIER
**BRIERROOT** *same as* > BRIARROOT
**BRIERS** > BRIER
**BRIERWOOD** *same as* > BRIARROOT
**BRIERY** > BRIER
**BRIES** > BRIE
**BRIG** n two-masted square-rigged ship
**BRIGADE** n army unit smaller than a division ▷ vb organize into a brigade
**BRIGADED** > BRIGADE
**BRIGADES** > BRIGADE
**BRIGADIER** n high-ranking army officer
**BRIGADING** > BRIGADE
**BRIGALOW** n type of acacia tree
**BRIGALOWS** > BRIGALOW
**BRIGAND** n bandit
**BRIGANDRY** > BRIGAND
**BRIGANDS** > BRIGAND
**BRIGHT** *adj* emitting or reflecting much light ▷ *adv* brightly
**BRIGHTEN** vb make or become bright or brighter
**BRIGHTENS** > BRIGHTEN
**BRIGHTER** > BRIGHT
**BRIGHTEST** > BRIGHT
**BRIGHTISH** > BRIGHT
**BRIGHTLY** > BRIGHT
**BRIGHTS** *pl n* high beam of the headlights of a motor

vehicle
**BRIGS** > BRIG
**BRIGUE** vb solicit
**BRIGUED** > BRIGUE
**BRIGUES** > BRIGUE
**BRIGUING** > BRIGUE
**BRIGUINGS** > BRIGUE
**BRIK** n Tunisian deep-fried spicy pastry filled with fish or meat and sometimes an egg
**BRIKS** > BRIK
**BRILL** n European food fish, *Scophthalmus rhombus*, a flatfish similar to the turbot but lacking tubercles on the body: family *Bothidae*
**BRILLER** > BRILL
**BRILLEST** > BRILL
**BRILLIANT** adj shining with light ▷ n popular circular cut for diamonds and other gemstones in the form of two many-faceted pyramids (the top one truncated) joined at their bases
**BRILLO** n tradename for a type of scouring pad impregnated with a detergent
**BRILLOS** > BRILLO
**BRILLS** > BRILL
**BRIM** n upper rim of a vessel ▷ vb fill or be full to the brim
**BRIMFUL** adj completely filled with
**BRIMFULL** same as > BRIMFUL
**BRIMFULLY** > BRIMFUL
**BRIMING** n phosphorescence of sea
**BRIMINGS** > BRIMING
**BRIMLESS** > BRIM
**BRIMMED** > BRIM
**BRIMMER** n vessel, such as a glass or bowl, filled to the brim
**BRIMMERS** > BRIMMER
**BRIMMING** > BRIM
**BRIMS** > BRIM
**BRIMSTONE** n sulphur
**BRIMSTONY** > BRIMSTONE
**BRIN** n thread of silk from silkworm
**BRINDED** adj streaky or patchy
**BRINDISI** n song sung in celebration
**BRINDISIS** > BRINDISI
**BRINDLE** n brindled animal
**BRINDLED** adj brown or grey streaked with a darker colour
**BRINDLES** > BRINDLE
**BRINE** n salt water ▷ vb soak in or treat with brine
**BRINED** > BRINE
**BRINELESS** > BRINE
**BRINER** > BRINE
**BRINERS** > BRINE
**BRINES** > BRINE

**BRING** vb carry, convey, or take to a designated place or person
**BRINGDOWN** n cause to be elated and then suddenly depressed, as from using drugs
**BRINGER** > BRING
**BRINGERS** > BRING
**BRINGING** > BRING
**BRINGINGS** > BRING
**BRINGS** > BRING
**BRINIER** > BRINY
**BRINIES** > BRINY
**BRINIEST** > BRINY
**BRININESS** > BRINY
**BRINING** > BRINE
**BRINISH** > BRINE
**BRINJAL** n dark purple tropical fruit, cooked and eaten as a vegetable
**BRINJALS** > BRINJAL
**BRINJARRY** n grain trader
**BRINK** n edge of a steep place
**BRINKMAN** n one who goes in for brinkmanship
**BRINKMEN** > BRINKMAN
**BRINKS** > BRINK
**BRINNIES** > BRINNY
**BRINNY** n stone, esp when thrown
**BRINS** > BRIN
**BRINY** adj very salty
**BRIO** n liveliness
**BRIOCHE** n soft roll or loaf made from a very light yeast dough, sometimes mixed with currants
**BRIOCHES** > BRIOCHE
**BRIOLETTE** n pear-shaped gem cut with long triangular facets
**BRIONIES** > BRIONY
**BRIONY** same as > BRYONY
**BRIOS** > BRIO
**BRIQUET** same as > BRIQUETTE
**BRIQUETED** > BRIQUET
**BRIQUETS** > BRIQUET
**BRIQUETTE** n block of compressed coal dust ▷ vb make into the form of a brick or bricks
**BRIS** n ritual circumcision of male babies, usually at eight days old, regarded as the formal entry of the child to the Jewish community
**BRISANCE** n shattering effect or power of an explosion or explosive
**BRISANCES** > BRISANCE
**BRISANT** > BRISANCE
**BRISE** n type of jump
**BRISES** > BRIS
**BRISK** adj lively and quick ▷ vb enliven
**BRISKED** > BRISK
**BRISKEN** vb make or become more lively or brisk
**BRISKENED** > BRISKEN

**BRISKENS** > BRISKEN
**BRISKER** > BRISK
**BRISKEST** > BRISK
**BRISKET** n beef from the breast of a cow
**BRISKETS** > BRISKET
**BRISKING** > BRISK
**BRISKISH** > BRISK
**BRISKLY** > BRISK
**BRISKNESS** > BRISK
**BRISKS** > BRISK
**BRISKY** another word for > BRISK
**BRISLING** same as > SPRAT
**BRISLINGS** > BRISLING
**BRISS** same as > BRIS
**BRISSES** > BRIS
**BRISTLE** n short stiff hair ▷ vb (cause to) stand up like bristles
**BRISTLED** > BRISTLE
**BRISTLES** > BRISTLE
**BRISTLIER** > BRISTLE
**BRISTLING** > BRISTLE
**BRISTLY** > BRISTLE
**BRISTOL** n bristol board type of heavy cardboard
**BRISTOLS** pl n woman's breasts
**BRISURE** n mark of cadency in heraldry
**BRISURES** > BRISURE
**BRIT** n young of a herring, sprat, or similar fish
**BRITANNIA** n coin bearing figure of Britannia
**BRITCHES** same as > BREECHES
**BRITH** same as > BRIS
**BRITHS** > BRITH
**BRITS** > BRIT
**BRITSCHKA** n light open carriage
**BRITSKA** same as > BRITZKA
**BRITSKAS** > BRITSKA
**BRITT** n young herring or sprat
**BRITTANIA** variant spelling of > BRITANNIA
**BRITTLE** adj hard but easily broken ▷ n crunchy sweet made with treacle and nuts
**BRITTLED** > BRITTLE
**BRITTLELY** > BRITTLE
**BRITTLER** > BRITTLE
**BRITTLES** > BRITTLE
**BRITTLEST** > BRITTLE
**BRITTLING** > BRITTLE
**BRITTLY** > BRITTLE
**BRITTS** > BRITT
**BRITZKA** n long horse-drawn carriage with a folding top over the rear seat and a rear-facing front seat
**BRITZKAS** > BRITZKA
**BRITZSKA** same as > BRITZKA
**BRITZSKAS** > BRITZSKAS
**BRIZE** same as > BREEZE
**BRIZES** > BRIZE
**BRO** n family member
**BROACH** vb introduce (a

topic) for discussion ▷ n spit for roasting meat
**BROACHED** > BROACH
**BROACHER** > BROACH
**BROACHERS** > BROACH
**BROACHES** > BROACH
**BROACHING** > BROACH
**BROAD** adj having great breadth or width ▷ n woman
**BROADAX** same as > BROADAXE
**BROADAXE** n broad-bladed axe
**BROADAXES** > BROADAXE
**BROADBAND** n telecommunication transmission technique using a wide range of frequencies
**BROADBEAN** n variety of bean
**BROADBILL** n any passerine bird of the family *Eurylaimidae*, of tropical Africa and Asia, having bright plumage and a short wide bill
**BROADBRIM** n broad-brimmed hat, esp one worn by the Quakers in the 17th century
**BROADCAST** n programme or announcement on radio or television ▷ vb transmit (a programme or announcement) on radio or television ▷ adj dispersed over a wide area ▷ adv far and wide
**BROADEN** vb make or become broad or broader
**BROADENED** > BROADEN
**BROADENER** > BROADEN
**BROADENS** > BROADEN
**BROADER** > BROAD
**BROADEST** > BROAD
**BROADISH** > BROAD
**BROADLEAF** n any tobacco plant having broad leaves, used esp in making cigars
**BROADLINE** n company dealing in large volumes of cheap products
**BROADLOOM** adj of or designating carpets woven on a wide loom ▷ n of or designating carpets or carpeting woven on a wide loom to obviate the need for seams
**BROADLY** > BROAD
**BROADNESS** > BROAD
**BROADS** > BROAD
**BROADSIDE** n strong verbal or written attack ▷ adv with a broader side facing an object
**BROADTAIL** n highly valued black wavy fur obtained from the skins of newly born karakul lambs
**BROADWAY** n wide road
**BROADWAYS** > BROADWAY

**BROADWISE** *adv* rare form of breadthwise

**BROCADE** *n* rich fabric woven with a raised design ▷ *vb* weave with such a design

**BROCADED** > BROCADE

**BROCADES** > BROCADE

**BROCADING** > BROCADE

**BROCAGE** *another word for* > BROKERAGE

**BROCAGES** > BROCAGE

**BROCARD** *n* basic principle of civil law

**BROCARDS** > BROCARD

**BROCATEL** *n* heavy upholstery brocade

**BROCATELS** > BROCATEL

**BROCCOLI** *n* type of cabbage with greenish flower heads

**BROCCOLIS** > BROCCOLI

**BROCH** *n* (in Scotland) a circular dry-stone tower large enough to serve as a fortified home

**BROCHAN** *n* type of thin porridge

**BROCHANS** > BROCHAN

**BROCHE** *adj* woven with a raised design, as brocade

**BROCHED** > BROCHE

**BROCHES** > BROCHE

**BROCHETTE** *n* skewer used for holding pieces of meat or vegetables while grilling

**BROCHING** > BROCHE

**BROCHO** *same as* > BRACHAH

**BROCHOS** > BROCHO

**BROCHS** > BROCH

**BROCHURE** *n* booklet that contains information about a product or service

**BROCHURES** > BROCHURE

**BROCK** *n* badger

**BROCKAGE** *same as* > BROKERAGE

**BROCKAGES** > BROCKAGE

**BROCKED** *adj* having different colours

**BROCKET** *n* any small deer of the genus *Mazama*, of tropical America, having small unbranched antlers

**BROCKETS** > BROCKET

**BROCKIT** *same as* > BROCKED

**BROCKRAM** *another word for* > BRECCIA

**BROCKRAMS** > BROCKRAM

**BROCKS** > BROCK

**BROCOLI** *same as* > BROCCOLI

**BROCOLIS** > BROCOLI

**BROD** *vb* prod

**BRODDED** > BROD

**BRODDING** > BROD

**BRODDLE** *vb* poke or pierce (something)

**BRODDLED** > BRODDLE

**BRODDLES** > BRODDLE

**BRODDLING** > BRODDLE

**BRODEKIN** *another word for* > BUSKIN

**BRODEKINS** > BRODEKIN

**BRODKIN** *same as* > BRODEKIN

**BRODKINS** > BRODKIN

**BRODS** > BROD

**BROEKIES** *pl n* underpants

**BROG** *n* bradawl

**BROGAN** *n* heavy laced, usually ankle-high, work boot

**BROGANS** > BROGAN

**BROGGED** > BROG

**BROGGING** > BROG

**BROGH** *same as* > BROCH

**BROGHS** > BROGH

**BROGS** > BROG

**BROGUE** *n* sturdy walking shoe

**BROGUEISH** > BROGUE

**BROGUERY** > BROGUE

**BROGUES** > BROGUE

**BROGUISH** > BROGUE

**BROIDER** *archaic word for* > EMBROIDER

**BROIDERED** > BROIDER

**BROIDERER** > BROIDER

**BROIDERS** > BROIDER

**BROIDERY** *n* old form of embroidery

**BROIL** *vb* cook by direct heat under a grill ▷ *n* process of broiling

**BROILED** > BROIL

**BROILER** *n* young tender chicken for roasting

**BROILERS** > BROILER

**BROILING** > BROIL

**BROILS** > BROIL

**BROKAGE** *another word for* > BROKERAGE

**BROKAGES** > BROKAGE

**BROKE** *vb* negotiate or deal

**BROKED** > BROKE

**BROKEN** > BRACKEN

**BROKENLY** > BRACKEN

**BROKER** *n* agent who buys or sells goods, securities, etc ▷ *vb* act as a broker (in)

**BROKERAGE** *n* commission charged by a broker

**BROKERED** > BROKER

**BROKERIES** > BROKERY

**BROKERING** > BROKER

**BROKERS** > BROKER

**BROKERY** *n* work done by broker

**BROKES** > BROKE

**BROKING** > BROKE

**BROKINGS** > BROKE

**BROLGA** *n* large grey Australian crane with a trumpeting call

**BROLGAS** > BROLGA

**BROLLIES** > BROLLY

**BROLLY** *n* umbrella

**BROMAL** *n* yellowish oily synthetic liquid formerly used medicinally as a sedative and hypnotic

**BROMALS** > BROMAL

**BROMATE** *same as* > BROMINATE

**BROMATED** > BROMATE

**BROMATES** > BROMATE

**BROMATING** > BROMATE

**BROME** *n* type of grass

**BROMELAIN** *n* enzyme in pineapples

**BROMELIA** *n* type of plant

**BROMELIAD** *n* any plant of the tropical American family *Bromeliaceae*, typically epiphytes with a rosette of fleshy leaves. The family includes the pineapple and Spanish moss

**BROMELIAS** > BROMELIA

**BROMELIN** *n* protein-digesting enzyme found in pineapple and extracted for use in treating joint pain and inflammation, hay fever, and various other conditions

**BROMELINS** > BROMELIN

**BROMEOSIN** *another name for* > EOSIN

**BROMES** > BROME

**BROMIC** *adj* of or containing bromine in the trivalent or pentavalent state

**BROMID** *same as* > BROMIDE

**BROMIDE** *n* chemical compound used in medicine and photography

**BROMIDES** > BROMIDE

**BROMIDIC** *adj* ordinary

**BROMIDS** > BROMID

**BROMIN** *same as* > BROMINE

**BROMINATE** *vb* treat or react with bromine

**BROMINE** *n* dark red liquid element that gives off a pungent vapour

**BROMINES** > BROMINE

**BROMINISM** *same as* > BROMISM

**BROMINS** > BROMIN

**BROMISE** *same as* > BROMIZE

**BROMISED** > BROMIZE

**BROMISES** > BROMIZE

**BROMISING** > BROMIZE

**BROMISM** *n* poisoning caused by the excessive intake of bromine or compounds containing bromine

**BROMISMS** > BROMISM

**BROMIZE** *vb* treat with bromine

**BROMIZED** > BROMIZE

**BROMIZES** > BROMIZE

**BROMIZING** > BROMIZE

**BROMMER** *n* S African word for bluebottle

**BROMMERS** > BROMMER

**BROMO** *n* something that contains bromide

**BROMOFORM** *n* heavy colourless liquid substance with a sweetish taste

**BROMOS** > BROMO

**BRONC** *same as* > BRONCO

**BRONCHI** > BRONCHUS

**BRONCHIA** *pl n* bronchial tubes

**BRONCHIAL** *adj* of the bronchi

**BRONCHIUM** *n* medium-sized bronchial tube

**BRONCHO** *same as* > BRONCO

**BRONCHOS** > BRONCHO

**BRONCHUS** *n* either of the two branches of the windpipe

**BRONCO** *n* (in the US) wild or partially tamed pony

**BRONCOS** > BRONCO

**BRONCS** > BRONC

**BROND** *n* old form of brand

**BRONDS** > BROND

**BRONDYRON** *n* sword

**BRONZE** *n* alloy of copper and tin ▷ *adj* made of, or coloured like, bronze ▷ *vb* (esp of the skin) make or become brown

**BRONZED** > BRONZE

**BRONZEN** *adj* made of or the colour of bronze

**BRONZER** *n* cosmetic applied to the skin to simulate a sun tan

**BRONZERS** > BRONZER

**BRONZES** > BRONZE

**BRONZIER** > BRONZE

**BRONZIEST** > BRONZE

**BRONZIFY** *vb* cause to become colour of bronze

**BRONZING** *n* blue pigment producing a metallic lustre when ground into paint media at fairly high concentrations

**BRONZINGS** > BRONZING

**BRONZITE** *n* type of orthopyroxene often having a metallic or pearly sheen

**BRONZITES** > BRONZITE

**BRONZY** > BRONZE

**BROO** *n* brow of hill

**BROOCH** *n* ornament with a pin, worn fastened to clothes ▷ *vb* decorate with a brooch

**BROOCHED** > BROOCH

**BROOCHES** > BROOCH

**BROOCHING** > BROOCH

**BROOD** *n* number of birds produced at one hatching ▷ *vb* (of a bird) sit on or hatch eggs

**BROODED** > BROOD

**BROODER** *n* enclosure or other structure, usually heated, used for rearing young chickens or other fowl

**BROODERS** > BROODER

**BROODIER** > BROODY

**BROODIEST** > BROODY

**BROODILY** > BROODY

**BROODING** > BROOD

**BROODINGS** > BROOD

**BROODLESS** > BROOD

**BROODMARE** *n* mare for breeding

BROODS > BROOD

BROODY adj moody and sullen

BROOK n small stream ▷ vb bear or tolerate

BROOKABLE > BROOK

BROOKED > BROOK

BROOKIE n brook trout

BROOKIES > BROOKIE

BROOKING > BROOK

BROOKITE n reddish-brown to black mineral

BROOKITES > BROOKITE

BROOKLET n small brook

BROOKLETS > BROOKLET

BROOKLIKE > BROOK

BROOKLIME n either of two blue-flowered scrophulariaceous trailing plants, Veronica americana of North America or V. beccabunga of Europe and Asia, growing in moist places

BROOKS > BROOK

BROOKWEED n either of two white-flowered primulaceous plants, Samolus valerandi of Europe or S. floribundus of North America, growing in moist places

BROOL n low roar

BROOLS > BROOL

BROOM n long-handled sweeping brush ▷ vb sweep with a broom

BROOMBALL n type of ice hockey played with broom

BROOMCORN n variety of sorghum, Sorghum vulgare technicum, the long stiff flower stalks of which have been used for making brooms

BROOMED > BROOM

BROOMIER > BROOMY

BROOMIEST > BROOMY

BROOMING > BROOM

BROOMRAPE n any orobanchaceous plant of the genus Orobanche: brownish small-flowered leafless parasites on the roots of other plants, esp on legumes

BROOMS > BROOM

BROOMY adj covered with growth of broom

BROOS > BROO

BROOSE n race at country wedding

BROOSES > BROOSE

BROS > BRO

BROSE n oatmeal or pease porridge, sometimes with butter or fat added

BROSES > BROSE

BROSY adj smeared with porridge

BROTH n soup, usu. containing vegetables

BROTHEL n house where men pay to have sex with prostitutes

BROTHELS > BROTHEL

BROTHER n boy or man with the same parents as another person ▷ interj exclamation of amazement, disgust, surprise, disappointment, etc ▷ vb treat someone like a brother

BROTHERED > BROTHER

BROTHERLY adj of or like a brother, esp in showing loyalty and affection ▷ adv in a brotherly way

BROTHERS > BROTHER

BROTHS > BROTH

BROTHY adj having appearance or texture of broth

BROUGH same as > BROCH

BROUGHAM n horse-drawn closed carriage with a raised open driver's seat in front

BROUGHAMS > BROUGHAM

BROUGHS > BROUGH

BROUGHT > BRING

BROUGHTA same as > BRAATA

BROUGHTAS same as > BRAATA

BROUHAHA n loud confused noise

BROUHAHAS > BROUHAHA

BROUZE same as > BROOSE

BROUZES > BROUZE

BROW n part of the face from the eyes to the hairline

BROWALLIA n flowering plant

BROWBAND n strap of a horse's bridle that goes across the forehead

BROWBANDS > BROWBAND

BROWBEAT vb frighten (someone) with threats

BROWBEATS > BROWBEAT

BROWED adj having a brow

BROWLESS > BROW

BROWN n colour of earth or wood ▷ adj (of bread) made from wheatmeal or wholemeal flour ▷ vb make or become brown

BROWNED > BROWN

BROWNER > BROWN

BROWNEST > BROWN

BROWNIE n small square nutty chocolate cake

BROWNIER > BROWN

BROWNIES > BROWNIE

BROWNIEST > BROWN

BROWNING n substance used to darken gravies

BROWNINGS > BROWNING

BROWNISH > BROWN

BROWNNESS > BROWN

BROWNNOSE vb be abjectly subservient

BROWNOUT n dimming or reduction in the use of electric lights in a city, esp to conserve electric power or as a defensive precaution in wartime

BROWNOUTS > BROWNOUT

BROWNS > BROWN

BROWNY > BROWN

BROWRIDGE n ridge of bone over eyes

BROWS > BROW

BROWSABLE > BROWSE

BROWSE vb look through (a book or articles for sale) in a casual manner ▷ n instance of browsing

BROWSED > BROWSE

BROWSER n software package that enables a user to read hypertext, esp on the Internet

BROWSERS > BROWSER

BROWSES > BROWSE

BROWSIER > BROWSE

BROWSIEST > BROWSE

BROWSING > BROWSE

BROWSINGS > BROWSE

BROWST n brewing (of ale, tea)

BROWSTS > BROWST

BROWSY > BROWSE

BRR same as > BRRR

BRRR interj used to suggest shivering

BRU South African word for > FRIEND

BRUCELLA n type of bacterium

BRUCELLAE > BRUCELLA

BRUCELLAS > BRUCELLA

BRUCHID n type of beetle

BRUCHIDS > BRUCHID

BRUCIN same as > BRUCINE

BRUCINE n bitter poisonous alkaloid resembling strychnine

BRUCINES > BRUCINE

BRUCINS > BRUCIN

BRUCITE n white translucent mineral

BRUCITES > BRUCITE

BRUCKLE adj brittle

BRUGH n large house

BRUGHS > BRUGH

BRUHAHA same as > BROUHAHA

BRUHAHAS > BRUHAHA

BRUILZIE same as > BRULZIE

BRUILZIES > BRUILZIE

BRUIN n name for a bear, used in children's tales, fables, etc

BRUINS > BRUIN

BRUISE n discoloured area on the skin caused by an injury ▷ vb cause a bruise on

BRUISED > BRUISE

BRUISER n strong tough person

BRUISERS > BRUISER

BRUISES > BRUISE

BRUISING adj causing bruises, as by a blow ▷ n bruise or bruises

BRUISINGS > BRUISING

BRUIT vb report ▷ n abnormal sound heard within the body during auscultation, esp a heart murmur

BRUITED > BRUIT

BRUITER > BRUIT

BRUITERS > BRUIT

BRUITING > BRUIT

BRUITS > BRUIT

BRULE n shortened form of the archaic word for a mixed-race person of Canadian Indian and White (usually French-Canadian) ancestry

BRULES > BRULE

BRULOT n coffee-based alcoholic drink, served flaming

BRULOTS > BRULOT

BRULYIE same as > BRULYIE

BRULYIES > BRULYIE

BRULZIE n noisy dispute

BRULZIES > BRULZIE

BRUMAL adj of, characteristic of, or relating to winter

BRUMBIES > BRUMBY

BRUMBY n wild horse

BRUME n heavy mist or fog

BRUMES > BRUME

BRUMMAGEM n something that is cheap and flashy, esp imitation jewellery

BRUMMER same as > BROMMER

BRUMMERS > BRUMMER

BRUMOUS > BRUME

BRUNCH n breakfast and lunch combined ▷ vb eat brunch

BRUNCHED > BRUNCH

BRUNCHER > BRUNCH

BRUNCHERS > BRUNCH

BRUNCHES > BRUNCH

BRUNCHING > BRUNCH

BRUNET adj dark brown

BRUNETS > BRUNET

BRUNETTE n girl or woman with dark brown hair ▷ adj dark brown

BRUNETTES > BRUNETTE

BRUNG > BRING

BRUNIZEM n prairie soil

BRUNIZEMS > BRUNIZEM

BRUNT n main force or shock of a blow, attack, etc ▷ vb suffer the main force or shock of a blow, attack, etc

BRUNTED > BRUNT

BRUNTING > BRUNT

BRUNTS > BRUNT

BRUS > BRU

BRUSH n device made of bristles, wires, etc used for cleaning, painting, etc ▷ vb clean, scrub, or paint with a brush

BRUSHBACK n (baseball) ball intended to hit the batter

BRUSHED adj treated with a

BRUSHING process to raise the nap and give a softer and warmer finish
**BRUSHER** > BRUSH
**BRUSHERS** > BRUSH
**BRUSHES** > BRUSH
**BRUSHFIRE** n fire in bushes and scrub
**BRUSHIER** > BRUSHY
**BRUSHIEST** > BRUSHY
**BRUSHING** > BRUSH
**BRUSHINGS** > BRUSH
**BRUSHLAND** n land characterized by patchy shrubs
**BRUSHLESS** > BRUSH
**BRUSHLIKE** > BRUSH
**BRUSHMARK** n indented lines sometimes left by the bristles of a brush on a painted surface
**BRUSHOFF** n an abrupt dismissal or rejection
**BRUSHOFFS** > BRUSHOFF
**BRUSHUP** n the act or an instance of tidying one's appearance
**BRUSHUPS** > BRUSHUP
**BRUSHWOOD** n cut or broken-off tree branches and twigs
**BRUSHWORK** n characteristic manner of applying paint with a brush
**BRUSHY** adj like a brush
**BRUSK** same as > BRUSQUE
**BRUSKER** > BRUSK
**BRUSKEST** > BRUSK
**BRUSQUE** adj blunt or curt in manner or speech
**BRUSQUELY** > BRUSQUE
**BRUSQUER** > BRUSQUE
**BRUSQUEST** > BRUSQUE
**BRUSSEN** adj bold
**BRUST** same as > BURST
**BRUSTING** > BRUST
**BRUSTS** > BRUST
**BRUT** adj (of champagne or sparkling wine) very dry ▷ n very dry champagne
**BRUTAL** adj cruel and vicious
**BRUTALISE** same as > BRUTALIZE
**BRUTALISM** n austere architectural style of the 1950s on, characterized by the use of exposed concrete and angular shapes
**BRUTALIST** > BRUTALISM
**BRUTALITY** > BRUTAL
**BRUTALIZE** vb make or become brutal
**BRUTALLY** > BRUTAL
**BRUTE** n brutal person ▷ adj wholly instinctive or physical, like an animal
**BRUTED** > BRUTE
**BRUTELIKE** > BRUTE
**BRUTELY** > BRUTE
**BRUTENESS** > BRUTE
**BRUTER** n diamond cutter

**BRUTERS** > BRUTER
**BRUTES** > BRUTE
**BRUTIFIED** > BRUTIFY
**BRUTIFIES** > BRUTIFY
**BRUTIFY** less common word for > BRUTALIZE
**BRUTING** n diamond cutting
**BRUTINGS** > BRUTING
**BRUTISH** adj of or like an animal
**BRUTISHLY** > BRUTISH
**BRUTISM** n stupidity; vulgarity
**BRUTISMS** > BRUTISM
**BRUTS** > BRUT
**BRUX** vb grind one's teeth
**BRUXED** > BRUX
**BRUXES** > BRUX
**BRUXING** > BRUX
**BRUXISM** n habit of grinding the teeth, esp unconsciously
**BRUXISMS** > BRUXISM
**BRYOLOGY** n branch of botany concerned with the study of bryophytes
**BRYONIES** > BRYONY
**BRYONY** n wild climbing hedge plant
**BRYOPHYTE** n any plant of the phyla Bryophyta (mosses), Hepatophyta (liverworts), or Anthocerophyta (hornworts), having stems and leaves but lacking true vascular tissue and roots and reproducing by spores
**BRYOZOAN** n any aquatic invertebrate animal of the phylum Bryozoa, forming colonies of polyps each having a ciliated feeding organ (lophophore) ▷ adj of, relating to, or belonging to the Bryozoa
**BRYOZOANS** > BRYOZOA
**BUAT** same as > BOWAT
**BUATS** > BUAT
**BUAZE** n fibrous African plant
**BUAZES** > BUAZE
**BUB** n youngster
**BUBA** another name for > YAWS
**BUBAL** n any of various antelopes, esp an extinct N African variety of hartebeest
**BUBALE** n large antelope
**BUBALES** > BUBALE
**BUBALINE** adj (of antelopes) related to or resembling the bubal
**BUBALIS** same as > BUBAL
**BUBALISES** > BUBALIS
**BUBALS** > BUBAL
**BUBAS** > BUBA
**BUBBA** n ordinary American person
**BUBBAS** > BUBBA
**BUBBIES** > BUBBY
**BUBBLE** n ball of air in a

liquid or solid ▷ vb form bubbles
**BUBBLED** > BUBBLE
**BUBBLEGUM** n type of chewing gum that can be blown into large bubbles
**BUBBLER** n drinking fountain in which the water is forced in a stream from a small vertical nozzle
**BUBBLERS** > BUBBLER
**BUBBLES** > BUBBLE
**BUBBLIER** > BUBBLY
**BUBBLIES** > BUBBLY
**BUBBLIEST** > BUBBLY
**BUBBLING** > BUBBLE
**BUBBLY** adj excited and lively ▷ n champagne
**BUBBY** n old word for woman's breast
**BUBINGA** n reddish-brown wood from African tree
**BUBINGAS** > BUBINGA
**BUBKES** n very small amount
**BUBO** n inflammation and swelling of a lymph node, esp in the armpit or groin
**BUBOED** > BUBO
**BUBOES** > BUBO
**BUBONIC** > BUBO
**BUBS** > BUB
**BUBU** same as > BOUBOU
**BUBUKLE** n red spot on skin
**BUBUKLES** > BUBUKLE
**BUBUS** > BUBU
**BUCCAL** adj of or relating to the cheek
**BUCCALLY** > BUCCAL
**BUCCANEER** n pirate ▷ vb be or act like a buccaneer
**BUCCANIER** same as > BUCCANEER
**BUCCINA** n curved Roman horn
**BUCCINAS** > BUCCINA
**BUCELLAS** n type of Portuguese white wine
**BUCENTAUR** n state barge of Venice from which the doge and other officials dropped a ring into the sea on Ascension Day to symbolize the ceremonial marriage of the state with the Adriatic
**BUCHU** n any of several S. African rutaceous shrubs of the genus Barosma, esp B. betulina, whose leaves are used as an antiseptic and diuretic
**BUCHUS** > BUCHU
**BUCK** n male of the goat, hare, kangaroo, rabbit, and reindeer ▷ vb (of a horse etc) jump with legs stiff and back arched
**BUCKAROO** n cowboy
**BUCKAROOS** > BUCKAROO
**BUCKAYRO** same as > BUCKAROO
**BUCKAYROS** > BUCKAYRO

**BUCKBEAN** n marsh plant, Menyanthes trifoliata, with white or pink flowers: family Menyanthaceae
**BUCKBEANS** > BUCKBEAN
**BUCKBOARD** n open four-wheeled horse-drawn carriage with the seat attached to a flexible board between the front and rear axles
**BUCKBRUSH** n American shrub
**BUCKED** > BUCK
**BUCKEEN** n (in Ireland) poor young man who aspires to the habits and dress of the wealthy
**BUCKEENS** > BUCKEEN
**BUCKER** > BUCK
**BUCKEROO** same as > BUCKAROO
**BUCKEROOS** > BUCKEROO
**BUCKERS** > BUCK
**BUCKET** vb open-topped roughly cylindrical container ▷ vb rain heavily
**BUCKETED** > BUCKET
**BUCKETFUL** same as > BUCKET
**BUCKETING** > BUCKET
**BUCKETS** > BUCKET
**BUCKEYE** n any of several North American trees of the genus Aesculus, esp A. glabra (Ohio buckeye), having erect clusters of white or red flowers and prickly fruits: family Hippocastanaceae
**BUCKEYES** > BUCKEYE
**BUCKHORN** n horn from a buck, used for knife handles, etc
**BUCKHORNS** > BUCKHORN
**BUCKHOUND** n hound, smaller than a staghound, used for hunting the smaller breeds of deer, esp fallow deer
**BUCKIE** n whelk or its shell
**BUCKIES** > BUCKIE
**BUCKING** > BUCK
**BUCKISH** > BUCK
**BUCKISHLY** > BUCK
**BUCKLE** n clasp for fastening a belt or strap ▷ vb fasten or be fastened with a buckle
**BUCKLED** > BUCKLE
**BUCKLER** n small round shield worn on the forearm ▷ vb defend
**BUCKLERED** > BUCKLER
**BUCKLERS** > BUCKLER
**BUCKLES** > BUCKLE
**BUCKLING** another name for > BLOATER
**BUCKLINGS** > BUCKLING
**BUCKO** n lively young fellow: often a term of address

BUCKOES > BUCKO

BUCKOS > BUCKO

BUCKRA n (used contemptuously by Black people, esp in the US) White man

BUCKRAKE n large rake attached to tractor

BUCKRAKES > BUCKRAKE

BUCKRAM n cotton or linen cloth stiffened with size, etc, used in lining or stiffening clothes, bookbinding, etc ▷ vb stiffen with buckram

BUCKRAMED > BUCKRAM

BUCKRAMS > BUCKRAM

BUCKRAS > BUCKRA

BUCKS > BUCK

BUCKSAW n woodcutting saw having its blade set in a frame and tensioned by a turnbuckle across the back of the frame

BUCKSAWS > BUCKSAW

BUCKSHEE adj free

BUCKSHEES > BUCKSHEE

BUCKSHISH n tip, present or gift

BUCKSHOT n large lead pellets used for shooting game

BUCKSHOTS > BUCKSHOT

BUCKSKIN n skin of a male deer ▷ adj greyish-yellow

BUCKSKINS pl n (in the US and Canada) breeches, shoes, or a suit of buckskin

BUCKSOM same as > BUXOM

BUCKTAIL n in fishing, fly with appearance of minnow

BUCKTAILS > BUCKTAIL

BUCKTEETH > BUCKTOOTH

BUCKTHORN n thorny shrub whose berries were formerly used as a purgative

BUCKTOOTH n projecting upper front tooth

BUCKU same as > BUCHU

BUCKUS > BUCKU

BUCKWHEAT n small black grain used for making flour

BUCKYBALL n ball-like polyhedral carbon molecule of the type found in buckminsterfullerene and other fullerenes

BUCKYTUBE n tube of carbon atoms structurally similar to buckminsterfullerene

BUCOLIC adj of the countryside or country life ▷ n pastoral poem

BUCOLICAL > BUCOLIC

BUCOLICS > BUCOLIC

BUD n swelling on a plant that develops into a leaf or flower ▷ vb produce buds

BUDA n derogatory Indian English word for an old man

BUDAS > BUDA

BUDDED > BUD

BUDDER > BUD

BUDDERS > BUD

BUDDHA n person who has achieved a state of perfect enlightenment

BUDDHAS > BUDDHA

BUDDIED > BUDDY

BUDDIER > BUDDY

BUDDIES > BUDDY

BUDDIEST > BUDDY

BUDDING > BUDDY

BUDDINGS > BUDDY

BUDDLE n sloping trough in which ore is washed ▷ vb wash (ore) in a buddle

BUDDLED > BUDDLE

BUDDLEIA n shrub with long spikes of purple flowers

BUDDLEIAS > BUDDLEIA

BUDDLES > BUDDLE

BUDDLING > BUDDLE

BUDDY n friend ▷ vb act as a friend to ▷ adj friendly

BUDDYING > BUDDY

BUDGE vb move slightly ▷ n lambskin dressed for the fur to be worn on the outer side

BUDGED > BUDGE

BUDGER > BUDGE

BUDGEREE adj good

BUDGERO same as > BUDGEROW

BUDGEROS > BUDGERO

BUDGEROW n barge use on Ganges

BUDGEROWS > BUDGEROW

BUDGERS > BUDGE

BUDGES > BUDGE

BUDGET n financial plan for a period of time ▷ vb plan the expenditure of (money or time) ▷ adj cheap

BUDGETARY > BUDGET

BUDGETED > BUDGET

BUDGETEER > BUDGET

BUDGETER > BUDGET

BUDGETERS > BUDGET

BUDGETING > BUDGET

BUDGETS > BUDGET

BUDGIE n short form of budgerigar

BUDGIES > BUDGIE

BUDGING > BUDGE

BUDI n derogatory Indian English word an for old woman

BUDIS > BUDI

BUDLESS > BUD

BUDLIKE > BUD

BUDMASH same as > BADMASH

BUDMASHES > BUDMASH

BUDO n combat and spirit in martial arts

BUDOS > BUDO

BUDS > BUD

BUDWORM n pest that eats tree leaves and buds

BUDWORMS > BUDWORM

BUFF n soft flexible undyed leather ▷ adj dull yellowish-brown ▷ vb clean or polish with soft material

BUFFA > BUFFO

BUFFABLE > BUFF

BUFFALO n member of the cattle tribe, Syncerus caffer, mostly found in game reserves in southern and eastern Africa and having upward-curving horns ▷ vb confuse

BUFFALOED > BUFFALO

BUFFALOES > BUFFALO

BUFFALOS > BUFFALO

BUFFE > BUFFO

BUFFED > BUFF

BUFFEL as in buffel grass grass used for pasture in Africa, India, and Australia

BUFFER same as > BUFF

BUFFERED > BUFFER

BUFFERING > BUFFER

BUFFERS > BUFFER

BUFFEST > BUFF

BUFFET n counter where drinks and snacks are served ▷ vb knock against or about

BUFFETED > BUFFET

BUFFETER > BUFFET

BUFFETERS > BUFFET

BUFFETING n response of an aircraft structure to buffet, esp an irregular oscillation of the tail

BUFFETS > BUFFET

BUFFI > BUFFO

BUFFIER > BUFFY

BUFFIEST > BUFFY

BUFFING > BUFF

BUFFINGS > BUFFING

BUFFO n (in Italian opera of the 18th century) comic part, esp one for a bass

BUFFOON n clown or fool

BUFFOONS > BUFFOON

BUFFOS > BUFFO

BUFFS > BUFF

BUFFY adj having appearance or texture of buff

BUFO n type of toad

BUFOS > BUFO

BUFOTALIN n principal poisonous substance in the skin and saliva of the common European toad

BUG n insect ▷ vb irritate

BUGABOO n imaginary source of fear

BUGABOOS > BUGABOO

BUGBANE n any of several ranunculaceous plants of the genus Cimicifuga, esp C. foetida of Europe, whose flowers are reputed to repel insects

BUGBANES > BUGBANE

BUGBEAR n thing that causes obsessive anxiety

BUGBEARS > BUGBEAR

BUGEYE n oyster-dredging boat

BUGEYES > BUGEYE

BUGGAN n evil spirit

BUGGANE same as > BUGGAN

BUGGANES > BUGGANE

BUGGANS > BUGGAN

BUGGED > BUG

BUGGER n unpleasant or difficult person or thing ▷ vb tire ▷ interj exclamation of annoyance or disappointment

BUGGERED > BUGGER

BUGGERIES > BUGGERY

BUGGERING > BUGGER

BUGGERS > BUGGER

BUGGERY n anal intercourse

BUGGIER > BUGGY

BUGGIES > BUGGY

BUGGIEST > BUGGY

BUGGIN same as > BUGGAN

BUGGINESS > BUGGY

BUGGING > BUG

BUGGINGS > BUG

BUGGINS > BUGGIN

BUGGY n light horse-drawn carriage having two or four wheels ▷ adj infested with bugs

BUGHOUSE n offensive name for a mental hospital or asylum ▷ adj offensive word for insane

BUGHOUSES > BUGHOUSE

BUGLE n instrument like a small trumpet ▷ vb play or sound (on) a bugle

BUGLED > BUGLE

BUGLER > BUGLE

BUGLERS > BUGLE

BUGLES > BUGLE

BUGLET n small bugle

BUGLETS > BUGLET

BUGLEWEED same as > BUGLE

BUGLING > BUGLE

BUGLOSS n any of various hairy Eurasian boraginaceous plants of the genera Anchusa, Lycopsis, and Echium, esp L. arvensis, having clusters of blue flowers

BUGLOSSES > BUGLOSS

BUGONG same as > BOGONG

BUGONGS > BUGONG

BUGOUT n act of running away

BUGOUTS > BUGOUT

BUGS > BUG

BUGSEED n form of tumbleweed

BUGSEEDS > BUGSEED

BUGSHA same as > BUQSHA

BUGSHAS > BUGSHA

BUGWORT another name for > BUGBANE

BUGWORTS > BUGWORT

BUHL same as > BOULLE

BUHLS > BUHL

BUHLWORK n woodwork with decorative inlay

BUHLWORKS > BUHLWORK

BUHR > BURR

**BUHRS** >BURR
**BUHRSTONE** n hard tough rock containing silica, fossils, and cavities, formerly used as a grindstone
**BUHUND** n type of Norwegian dog
**BUHUNDS** >BUHUND
**BUIBUI** n piece of black cloth worn as a shawl by Muslim women, esp on the E African coast
**BUIBUIS** >BUIBUI
**BUIK** same as >BOOK
**BUIKS** >BUIK
**BUILD** vb make, construct, or form by joining parts or materials ▷ n shape of the body
**BUILDABLE** adj suitable for building on
**BUILDDOWN** n planned reduction
**BUILDED** >BUILD
**BUILDER** n person who constructs houses and other buildings
**BUILDERS** >BUILDER
**BUILDING** >BUILD
**BUILDINGS** >BUILD
**BUILDS** >BUILD
**BUILDUP** n gradual approach to a climax or critical point
**BUILDUPS** >BUILDUP
**BUILT** >BUILD
**BUIRDLIER** >BUIRDLY
**BUIRDLY** adj well-built
**BUIST** vb brand sheep with identification mark
**BUISTED** >BUIST
**BUISTING** >BUIST
**BUISTS** >BUIST
**BUKE** same as >BOOK
**BUKES** >BUKE
**BUKKAKE** n type of sexual practice
**BUKKAKES** >BUKKAKE
**BUKSHEE** n person in charge of paying wages
**BUKSHEES** >BUKSHEE
**BUKSHI** same as >BUKSHEE
**BUKSHIS** >BUKSHI
**BULB** n onion-shaped root which grows into a flower or plant ▷ vb form into the shape of a bulb
**BULBAR** adj of or relating to a bulb, esp the medulla oblongata
**BULBED** >BULB
**BULBEL** same as >BULBIL
**BULBELS** >BULBEL
**BULBIL** n small bulblike organ of vegetative reproduction growing in leaf axils or on flower stalks of plants such as the onion and tiger lily
**BULBILS** >BULBIL
**BULBING** >BULB
**BULBLET** n small bulb at base of main bulb

**BULBLETS** >BULBLET
**BULBOSITY** >BULBOUS
**BULBOUS** adj round and fat
**BULBOUSLY** >BULBOUS
**BULBS** >BULB
**BULBUL** n any songbird of the family Pycnonotidae of tropical Africa and Asia, having brown plumage and, in many species, a distinct crest
**BULBULS** >BULBUL
**BULGE** n swelling on a normally flat surface ▷ vb swell outwards
**BULGED** >BULGE
**BULGER** >BULGE
**BULGERS** >BULGE
**BULGES** >BULGE
**BULGHUR** same as >BULGUR
**BULGHURS** >BULGHUR
**BULGIER** >BULGE
**BULGIEST** >BULGE
**BULGINE** same as >BULLGINE
**BULGINES** >BULGINE
**BULGINESS** >BULGE
**BULGING** >BULGE
**BULGINGLY** >BULGE
**BULGUR** n kind of dried cracked wheat
**BULGURS** >BULGUR
**BULGY** >BULGE
**BULIMIA** n disorder characterized by compulsive overeating followed by vomiting
**BULIMIAC** >BULIMIA
**BULIMIAS** >BULIMIA
**BULIMIC** >BULIMIA
**BULIMICS** >BULIMIA
**BULIMIES** >BULIMIA
**BULIMUS** >BULIMIA
**BULIMUSES** >BULIMIA
**BULIMY** >BULIMIA
**BULK** n volume, size, or magnitude of something ▷ vb cohere or cause to cohere in a mass
**BULKAGE** >BULK
**BULKAGES** >BULK
**BULKED** >BULK
**BULKER** n ship that carries unpackaged cargo, usually consisting of a single dry commodity, such as coal or grain
**BULKERS** >BULKER
**BULKHEAD** n partition in a ship or aeroplane
**BULKHEADS** >BULKHEAD
**BULKIER** >BULKY
**BULKIEST** >BULKY
**BULKILY** >BULKY
**BULKINESS** >BULKY
**BULKING** n expansion of excavated material to a volume greater than that of the excavation from which it came
**BULKS** >BULK
**BULKY** adj very large and massive, esp so as to be unwieldy

**BULL** adj any male bovine animal, esp one that is sexually mature
**BULLA** n leaden seal affixed to a papal bull, having a representation of Saints Peter and Paul on one side and the name of the reigning pope on the other
**BULLACE** n small Eurasian rosaceous tree, Prunus domestica insititia (or P. insititia), of which the damson is the cultivated form
**BULLACES** >BULLACE
**BULLAE** >BULLA
**BULLARIES** >BULLARY
**BULLARY** n boilery for preparing salt
**BULLATE** adj puckered or blistered in appearance
**BULLBAR** singular form of >BULLBARS
**BULLBARS** n large protective metal grille on the front of some vehicles, esp four-wheel-drive vehicles
**BULLBAT** another name for >NIGHTHAWK
**BULLBATS** >BULLBAT
**BULLBRIER** n prickly American vine
**BULLDOG** n thickset dog with a broad head and a muscular body
**BULLDOGS** >BULLDOG
**BULLDOZE** vb demolish or flatten with a bulldozer
**BULLDOZED** >BULLDOZE
**BULLDOZER** n powerful tractor for moving earth
**BULLDOZES** >BULLDOZE
**BULLDUST** n fine dust
**BULLDUSTS** >BULLDUST
**BULLDYKE** n mannish lesbian
**BULLDYKES** >BULLDYKE
**BULLED** >BULL
**BULLER** vb make bubbling sound
**BULLERED** >BULLER
**BULLERING** >BULLER
**BULLERS** >BULLER
**BULLET** n small piece of metal fired from a gun ▷ vb move extremely quickly
**BULLETED** >BULLET
**BULLETIN** n short official report or announcement ▷ vb make known by bulletin
**BULLETING** >BULLET
**BULLETINS** >BULLETIN
**BULLETRIE** n W Indian fruit tree
**BULLETS** >BULLET
**BULLFIGHT** n public show in which a matador kills a bull
**BULLFINCH** n common European songbird
**BULLFROG** n large

American frog with a deep croak
**BULLFROGS** >BULLFROG
**BULLGINE** n steam locomotive
**BULLGINES** >BULLGINE
**BULLHEAD** n any of various small northern mainly marine scorpaenoid fishes of the family Cottidae that have a large head covered with bony plates and spines
**BULLHEADS** >BULLHEAD
**BULLHORN** n portable loudspeaker having a built-in amplifier and microphone
**BULLHORNS** >BULLHORN
**BULLIED** >BULLY
**BULLIER** >BULLY
**BULLIES** >BULLY
**BULLIEST** >BULLY
**BULLING** >BULL
**BULLINGS** >BULL
**BULLION** n gold or silver in the form of bars
**BULLIONS** >BULLION
**BULLISH** adj like a bull
**BULLISHLY** >BULLISH
**BULLNECK** n enlarged neck
**BULLNECKS** >BULLNECK
**BULLNOSE** n rounded exterior angle, as where two walls meet
**BULLNOSES** >BULLNOSE
**BULLOCK** n castrated bull ▷ vb work hard and long
**BULLOCKED** >BULLOCK
**BULLOCKS** >BULLOCK
**BULLOCKY** n driver of a team of bullocks
**BULLOSA** epidermolysis bullosa type of genetic skin disorder
**BULLOUS** adj blistered
**BULLPEN** n large cell where prisoners are confined together temporarily
**BULLPENS** >BULLPEN
**BULLPOUT** n type of fish
**BULLPOUTS** >BULLPOUT
**BULLRING** n arena for staging bullfights
**BULLRINGS** >BULLRING
**BULLRUSH** same as >BULRUSH
**BULLS** >BULL
**BULLSHAT** >BULLSHIT
**BULLSHIT** n exaggerated or foolish talk ▷ vb talk bullshit to
**BULLSHITS** >BULLSHIT
**BULLSHOT** n cocktail of vodka and beef stock
**BULLSHOTS** >BULLSHOT
**BULLSNAKE** n American burrowing snake
**BULLWADDY** n N Australian tree, Macropteranthes kekwickii, growing in dense thickets
**BULLWEED** n knapweed
**BULLWEEDS** >BULLWEED

103

**BULLWHACK** *vb* flog with short whip

**BULLWHIP** *n* long tapering heavy whip, esp one of plaited rawhide ▷ *vb* whip with a bullwhip

**BULLWHIPS** > BULLWHIP

**BULLY** *n* person who hurts, persecutes, or intimidates weaker people ▷ *vb* hurt, intimidate, or persecute (a weaker or smaller person), esp to make him do something ▷ *adj* dashing

**BULLYBOY** *n* ruffian or tough, esp a hired one

**BULLYBOYS** > BULLYBOY

**BULLYING** > BULLY

**BULLYISM** > BULLY

**BULLYISMS** > BULLY

**BULLYRAG** *vb* bully, esp by means of cruel practical jokes

**BULLYRAGS** > BULLYRAG

**BULNBULN** *another name for* > LYREBIRD

**BULNBULNS** > BULNBULN

**BULRUSH** *n* tall stiff reed

**BULRUSHES** > BULRUSH

**BULRUSHY** > BULRUSH

**BULSE** *n* purse or bag for diamonds

**BULSES** > BULSE

**BULWADDEE** > BULLWADDY

**BULWADDY** > BULLWADDY

**BULWARK** *n* wall used as a fortification ▷ *vb* defend or fortify with or as if with a bulwark

**BULWARKED** > BULWARK

**BULWARKS** > BULWARK

**BUM** *n* buttocks or anus ▷ *vb* get by begging ▷ *adj* of poor quality

**BUMALO** *same as* > BUMMALO

**BUMALOTI** *same as* > BUMALOTI

**BUMALOTIS** > BUMALOTI

**BUMBAG** *n* small bag attached to a belt and worn round the waist

**BUMBAGS** > BUMBAG

**BUMBAZE** *vb* confuse; bewilder

**BUMBAZED** > BUMBAZE

**BUMBAZES** > BUMBAZE

**BUMBAZING** > BUMBAZE

**BUMBLE** *vb* speak, do, or move in a clumsy way ▷ *n* blunder or botch

**BUMBLEBEE** *n* large hairy bee

**BUMBLED** > BUMBLE

**BUMBLEDOM** *n* self-importance in a minor office

**BUMBLER** > BUMBLE

**BUMBLERS** > BUMBLE

**BUMBLES** > BUMBLE

**BUMBLING** > BUMBLE

**BUMBLINGS** > BUMBLE

**BUMBO** *n* drink with gin or rum, nutmeg, lemon juice, etc

**BUMBOAT** *n* any small boat used for ferrying supplies or goods for sale to a ship at anchor or at a mooring

**BUMBOATS** > BUMBOAT

**BUMBOS** > BUMBO

**BUMELIA** *n* thorny shrub

**BUMELIAS** > BUMELIA

**BUMF** *n* official documents or forms

**BUMFLUFF** *n* soft and fluffy growth of hair on the chin of an adolescent

**BUMFLUFFS** > BUMFLUFF

**BUMFS** > BUMF

**BUMFUZZLE** *vb* confuse

**BUMKIN** *same as* > BUMPKIN

**BUMKINS** > BUMKIN

**BUMMALO** *n* Bombay duck

**BUMMALOS** > BUMMALO

**BUMMALOTI** *another word for* > BUMMALO

**BUMMAREE** *n* dealer at Billingsgate fish market

**BUMMAREES** > BUMMAREE

**BUMMED** > BUM

**BUMMEL** *n* stroll

**BUMMELS** > STROLL

**BUMMER** *n* unpleasant or disappointing experience

**BUMMERS** > BUMMER

**BUMMEST** > BUM

**BUMMING** > BUM

**BUMMLE** *Scots variant of* > BUMBLE

**BUMMLED** > BUMMLE

**BUMMLES** > BUMMLE

**BUMMLING** > BUMMLE

**BUMMOCK** *n* submerged mass of ice projecting downwards

**BUMMOCKS** > BUMMOCK

**BUMP** *vb* knock or strike with a jolt ▷ *n* dull thud from an impact or collision

**BUMPED** > BUMP

**BUMPER** *n* bar on the front and back of a vehicle to protect against damage ▷ *adj* unusually large or abundant ▷ *vb* toast with a bumper

**BUMPERED** > BUMPER

**BUMPERING** > BUMPER

**BUMPERS** > BUMPER

**BUMPH** *same as* > BUMF

**BUMPHS** > BUMPH

**BUMPIER** > BUMPY

**BUMPIEST** > BUMPY

**BUMPILY** > BUMPY

**BUMPINESS** > BUMPY

**BUMPING** > BUMP

**BUMPINGS** > BUMP

**BUMPKIN** *n* awkward simple country person

**BUMPKINLY** > BUMPKIN

**BUMPKINS** > BUMPKIN

**BUMPOLOGY** *n* humorous word for phrenology

**BUMPS** > BUMP

**BUMPTIOUS** *adj* offensively self-assertive

**BUMPY** *adj* having an uneven surface

**BUMS** > BUM

**BUMSTERS** *pl n* trousers cut so that the top lies just above the cleft of the buttocks

**BUMSUCKER** *n* toady

**BUN** *n* small sweet bread roll or cake

**BUNA** *n* synthetic rubber formed by polymerizing butadiene or by copolymerizing it with such compounds as acrylonitrile or styrene

**BUNAS** > BUNA

**BUNCE** *n* windfall; boom ▷ *vb* charge someone too much money

**BUNCED** > BUNCE

**BUNCES** > BUNCE

**BUNCH** *n* number of things growing, fastened, or grouped together ▷ *vb* group or be grouped together in a bunch

**BUNCHED** > BUNCH

**BUNCHES** *pl n* hairstyle in which hair is tied into two sections on either side of the head at the back

**BUNCHIER** > BUNCHY

**BUNCHIEST** > BUNCHY

**BUNCHILY** > BUNCHY

**BUNCHING** > BUNCH

**BUNCHINGS** > BUNCH

**BUNCHY** *adj* composed of or resembling bunches

**BUNCING** > BUNCE

**BUNCO** *n* swindle, esp one by confidence tricksters ▷ *vb* swindle

**BUNCOED** > BUNCO

**BUNCOING** > BUNCO

**BUNCOMBE** *same as* > BUNKUM

**BUNCOMBES** *ŝ* BUNCOMBE

**BUNCOS** > BUNCO

**BUND** *n* embankment or German federation ▷ *vb* form into an embankment

**BUNDE** > BUND

**BUNDED** > BUND

**BUNDH** *same as* > BANDH

**BUNDHS** > BUNDH

**BUNDIES** > BUNDY

**BUNDING** > BUND

**BUNDIST** > BUND

**BUNDISTS** > BUND

**BUNDLE** *n* number of things gathered loosely together ▷ *vb* cause to go roughly or unceremoniously

**BUNDLED** > BUNDLE

**BUNDLER** > BUNDLE

**BUNDLERS** > BUNDLE

**BUNDLES** > BUNDLE

**BUNDLING** > BUNDLE

**BUNDLINGS** > BUNDLE

**BUNDOBUST** *same as* > BANDOBUST

**BUNDOOK** *n* rifle

**BUNDOOKS** > BUNDOOK

**BUNDS** > BUND

**BUNDT** *n* type of sweet cake

**BUNDTS** > BUNDT

**BUNDU** *n* largely uninhabited wild region far from towns

**BUNDUS** > BUNDU

**BUNDWALL** *n* concrete or earth wall surrounding a storage tank containing crude oil or its refined product, designed to hold the contents of the tank in the event of a rupture or leak

**BUNDWALLS** > BUNDWALL

**BUNDY** *n* time clock at work

**BUNFIGHT** *n* tea party

**BUNFIGHTS** > BUNFIGHT

**BUNG** *n* stopper for a cask etc ▷ *vb* close with a bung

**BUNGALOID** *n* bungalow-type house

**BUNGALOW** *n* one-storey house

**BUNGALOWS** > BUNGALOW

**BUNGED** > BUNG

**BUNGEE** *n* strong elastic cable

**BUNGEES** > BUNGEE

**BUNGER** *n* firework

**BUNGERS** > BUNGER

**BUNGEY** *same as* > BUNGEE

**BUNGEYS** > BUNGEY

**BUNGHOLE** *n* hole in a cask or barrel through which liquid can be drained

**BUNGHOLES** > BUNGHOLE

**BUNGIE** *same as* > BUNGEE

**BUNGIES** > BUNGY

**BUNGING** > BUNG

**BUNGLE** *vb* spoil through incompetence ▷ *n* blunder or muddle

**BUNGLED** > BUNGLE

**BUNGLER** > BUNGLE

**BUNGLERS** > BUNGLE

**BUNGLES** > BUNGLE

**BUNGLING** > BUNGLE

**BUNGLINGS** > BUNGLE

**BUNGS** > BUNG

**BUNGWALL** *n* Australian fern, *Blechnum indicum*, having an edible rhizome

**BUNGWALLS** > BUNGWALL

**BUNGY** > BUNGEE

**BUNIA** *same as* > BUNNIA

**BUNIAS** > BUNIA

**BUNION** *n* inflamed swelling on the big toe

**BUNIONS** > BUNION

**BUNJE** *same as* > BUNGEE

**BUNJEE** *same as* > BUNGEE

**BUNJEES** > BUNJEE

**BUNJES** > BUNJE

**BUNJIE** *same as* > BUNGEE

**BUNJIES** > BUNJIE

**BUNJY** *same as* > BUNGEE

**BUNK** *n* narrow shelflike bed ▷ *vb* prepare to sleep

**BUNKED** > BUNK

**BUNKER** *n* sand-filled hollow forming an obstacle on a golf course ▷ *vb* drive (the ball) into a bunker

**BUNKERED** > BUNKER
**BUNKERING** > BUNKER
**BUNKERS** > BUNKER
**BUNKHOUSE** n (in the US and Canada) building containing the sleeping quarters of workers on a ranch
**BUNKING** > BUNK
**BUNKMATE** n person who sleeps in the same quarters as another
**BUNKMATES** > BUNKMATE
**BUNKO** same as > BUNCO
**BUNKOED** > BUNKO
**BUNKOING** > BUNKO
**BUNKOS** > BUNKO
**BUNKS** > BUNK
**BUNKUM** n nonsense
**BUNKUMS** > BUNKUM
**BUNN** same as > BUN
**BUNNET** same as > BONNET
**BUNNETS** > BUNNET
**BUNNIA** n Hindu shopkeeper
**BUNNIAS** > BUNNIA
**BUNNIES** > BUNNY
**BUNNS** > BUNN
**BUNNY** n child's word for a rabbit
**BUNODONT** adj (of the teeth of certain mammals) having cusps that are separate and rounded
**BUNRAKU** n Japanese form of puppet theatre in which the puppets are usually about four feet high, with moving features as well as limbs and each puppet is manipulated by up to three puppeteers who remain onstage
**BUNRAKUS** > BUNRAKU
**BUNS** pl n buttocks
**BUNSEN** as in bunsen burner gas burner used in scientific labs
**BUNSENS** > BUNSEN
**BUNT** vb (of an animal) butt (something) with the head or horns ▷ n act or an instance of bunting
**BUNTAL** n straw obtained from leaves of the talipot palm
**BUNTALS** > BUNTAL
**BUNTED** > BUNT
**BUNTER** n batter who deliberately taps ball lightly
**BUNTERS** > BUNTER
**BUNTIER** > BUNT
**BUNTIEST** > BUNT
**BUNTING** n decorative flags
**BUNTINGS** > BUNTING
**BUNTLINE** n one of several lines fastened to the foot of a square sail for hauling it up to the yard when furling
**BUNTLINES** > BUNTLINE
**BUNTS** > BUNT
**BUNTY** > BUNT

**BUNYA** n tall dome-shaped Australian coniferous tree
**BUNYAS** > BUNYA
**BUNYIP** n legendary monster said to live in swamps and lakes
**BUNYIPS** > BUNYIP
**BUOY** n floating marker anchored in the sea ▷ vb prevent from sinking
**BUOYAGE** n system of buoys
**BUOYAGES** > BUOYAGE
**BUOYANCE** same as > BUOYANCY
**BUOYANCES** > BUOYANCE
**BUOYANCY** n ability to float in a liquid or to rise in a fluid
**BUOYANT** adj able to float
**BUOYANTLY** > BUOYANT
**BUOYED** > BUOY
**BUOYING** > BUOY
**BUOYS** > BUOY
**BUPKES** same as > BUBKES
**BUPKUS** same as > BUBKES
**BUPLEVER** n type of plant
**BUPLEVERS** > BUPLEVER
**BUPPIE** n affluent young Black person
**BUPPIES** > BUPPY
**BUPPY** variant of > BUPPY
**BUPRESTID** n any beetle of the mainly tropical family Buprestidae, the adults of which are brilliantly coloured and the larvae of which bore into and cause damage to trees, roots, etc ▷ adj of, relating to, or belonging to the family Buprestidae
**BUQSHA** n former Yemeni coin
**BUQSHAS** > BUQSHA
**BUR** > BURR
**BURA** same as > BURAN
**BURAN** n blizzard, with the wind blowing from the north and reaching gale force
**BURANS** > BURAN
**BURAS** > BURA
**BURB** n suburb
**BURBLE** vb make a bubbling sound ▷ n bubbling or gurgling sound
**BURBLED** > BURBLE
**BURBLER** > BURBLE
**BURBLERS** > BURBLE
**BURBLES** > BURBLE
**BURBLIER** > BURBLY
**BURBLIEST** > BURBLY
**BURBLING** > BURBLE
**BURBLINGS** > BURBLE
**BURBLY** adj burbling
**BURBOT** n freshwater fish of the cod family that has barbels around its mouth
**BURBOTS** > BURBOT
**BURBS** > BURB
**BURD** Scots form of > BIRD
**BURDASH** n fringed sash worn over coat
**BURDASHES** > BURDASH

**BURDEN** n heavy load ▷ vb put a burden on
**BURDENED** > BURDEN
**BURDENER** > BURDEN
**BURDENERS** > BURDEN
**BURDENING** > BURDEN
**BURDENOUS** > BURDEN
**BURDENS** > BURDEN
**BURDIE** Scots form of > BIRDIE
**BURDIES** > BURDIE
**BURDIZZO** n surgical instrument used to castrate animals
**BURDIZZOS** > BURDIZZO
**BURDOCK** n weed with prickly burrs
**BURDOCKS** > BURDOCK
**BURDS** > BURD
**BUREAU** n office that provides a service
**BUREAUS** > BUREAU
**BUREAUX** > BUREAU
**BURET** same as > BURETTE
**BURETS** > BURET
**BURETTE** n glass tube for dispensing known volumes of fluids
**BURETTES** > BURETTE
**BURG** n fortified town
**BURGAGE** n (in England) tenure of land or tenement in a town or city, which originally involved a fixed money rent
**BURGAGES** > BURGAGE
**BURGANET** same as > BURGONET
**BURGANETS** > BURGANET
**BURGEE** n triangular or swallow-tailed flag flown from the mast of a merchant ship for identification and from the mast of a yacht to indicate its owner's membership of a particular yacht club
**BURGEES** > BURGEE
**BURGEON** vb develop or grow rapidly ▷ n bud of a plant
**BURGEONED** > BURGEON
**BURGEONS** > BURGEON
**BURGER** n hamburger
**BURGERS** > BURGER
**BURGESS** n (in England) citizen or freeman of a borough
**BURGESSES** > BURGESS
**BURGH** n Scottish borough
**BURGHAL** > BURGH
**BURGHER** n citizen
**BURGHERS** > BURGHER
**BURGHS** > BURGH
**BURGHUL** same as > BULGUR
**BURGHULS** > BURGHUL
**BURGLAR** n person who enters a building to commit a crime, esp theft ▷ vb burgle
**BURGLARED** > BURGLAR
**BURGLARS** > BURGLAR
**BURGLARY** n crime of

entering a building as a trespasser to commit theft or another offence
**BURGLE** vb break into (a house, shop, etc)
**BURGLED** > BURGLE
**BURGLES** > BURGLE
**BURGLING** > BURGLE
**BURGONET** n light 16th-century helmet, usually made of steel, with hinged cheekpieces
**BURGONETS** > BURGONET
**BURGOO** n porridge
**BURGOOS** > BURGOO
**BURGOUT** same as > BURGOO
**BURGOUTS** > BURGOUT
**BURGRAVE** n military governor of a German town or castle, esp in the 12th and 13th centuries
**BURGRAVES** > BURGRAVE
**BURGS** > BURG
**BURGUNDY** adj dark-purplish red
**BURHEL** same as > BHARAL
**BURHELS** > BURHEL
**BURIAL** n burying of a dead body
**BURIALS** > BURIAL
**BURIED** > BURY
**BURIER** n person or thing that buries
**BURIERS** > BURIER
**BURIES** > BURY
**BURIN** n steel chisel used for engraving metal, wood, or marble
**BURINIST** > BURIN
**BURINISTS** > BURIN
**BURINS** > BURIN
**BURITI** n type of palm tree
**BURITIS** > BURITI
**BURK** same as > BERK
**BURKA** same as > BURQA
**BURKAS** > BURKA
**BURKE** vb murder in such a way as to leave no marks on the body, usually by suffocation
**BURKED** > BURKE
**BURKER** > BURKE
**BURKERS** > BURKE
**BURKES** > BURKE
**BURKING** > BURKE
**BURKITE** > BURKE
**BURKITES** > BURKE
**BURKS** > BURK
**BURL** n small knot or lump in wool ▷ vb remove the burls from (cloth)
**BURLADERO** n safe area for bull-fighter in bull ring
**BURLAP** n coarse fabric woven from jute, hemp, or the like
**BURLAPS** > BURLAP
**BURLED** > BURL
**BURLER** > BURL
**BURLERS** > BURL
**BURLESK** same as > BURLESQUE
**BURLESKS** > BURLESK
**BURLESQUE** n artistic work

which satirizes a subject
by caricature ▷ adj of
or characteristic of a
burlesque ▷ vb represent
or imitate (a person or
thing) in a ludicrous way
BURLETTA n type of comic
opera
BURLETTAS > BURLETTA
BURLEY same as > BERLEY
BURLEYCUE same
as > BURLESQUE
BURLEYED > BURLEY
BURLEYING > BURLEY
BURLEYS > BURLEY
BURLIER > BURLY
BURLIEST > BURLY
BURLILY > BURLY
BURLINESS > BURLY
BURLING > BURL
BURLS > BURL
BURLY adj (of a person)
broad and strong
BURN vb be or set on fire ▷ n
injury or mark caused by
fire or exposure to heat
BURNABLE > BURN
BURNABLES > BURN
BURNED > BURN
BURNER n part of a stove
or lamp that produces the
flame
BURNERS > BURNER
BURNET n type of rose
BURNETS > BURNET
BURNIE n sideburn
BURNIES > BURNIE
BURNING > BURN
BURNINGLY > BURN
BURNINGS > BURN
BURNISH vb make smooth
and shiny by rubbing ▷ n
shiny finish
BURNISHED > BURNISH
BURNISHER > BURNISH
BURNISHES > BURNISH
BURNOOSE same
as > BURNOUS
BURNOOSED > BURNOUS
BURNOOSES > BURNOUSE
BURNOUS n long circular
cloak with a hood, worn
esp by Arabs
BURNOUSE same
as > BURNOUS
BURNOUSED > BURNOUS
BURNOUSES > BURNOUSE
BURNOUT n failure of a
mechanical device from
excessive heating
BURNOUTS > BURNOUT
BURNS > BURN
BURNSIDE n land alongside
of burn
BURNSIDES > BURNSIDE
BURNT > BURN
BUROO n government
office from which
unemployment benefit is
distributed
BUROOS > BUROO
BURP n belch ▷ vb belch
BURPED > BURP
BURPEE n type of physical

exercise movement
BURPEES > BURPEE
BURPING > BURP
BURPS > BURP
BURQA n long enveloping
garment worn by Muslim
women in public, covering
all but the wearer's eyes
BURQAS > BURQA
BURR n small power-driven
hand-operated rotary file,
esp for removing burrs or
for machining recesses
▷ vb form a rough edge on
(a workpiece)
BURRAMYS n very rare
mountain pigmy possum,
Burramys parvus, of
Australia. It is about the
size of a rat and restricted
in habitat to very high
altitudes, mainly Mt
Hotham, Victoria. Until
1966 it was known only as
a fossil
BURRAWANG n Australian
plant with fernlike leaves
and an edible nut
BURRED > BURR
BURREL same as > BHARAL
BURRELL variant
of > BHARAL
BURRELLS > BURRELL
BURRELS > BURREL
BURRER n person who
removes burrs
BURRERS > BURRER
BURRHEL same as > BURREL
BURRHELS > BURRHEL
BURRIER > BURRY
BURRIEST > BURRY
BURRING > BURR
BURRITO n tortilla folded
over a filling of minced
beef, chicken, cheese, or
beans
BURRITOS > BURRITO
BURRO n donkey, esp one
used as a pack animal
BURROS > BURRO
BURROW n hole dug in the
ground by a rabbit etc ▷ vb
dig holes in the ground
BURROWED > BURROW
BURROWER > BURROW
BURROWERS > BURROW
BURROWING > BURROW
BURROWS > BURROW
BURRS > BURR
BURRSTONE same
as > BUHRSTONE
BURRY adj full of or covered
in burs
BURS > BURR
BURSA n small fluid-filled
sac that reduces friction
between movable parts of
the body, esp at joints
BURSAE > BURSA
BURSAL > BURSA
BURSAR n treasurer of
a school, college, or
university
BURSARIAL adj of, relating

to, or paid by a bursar or
bursary
BURSARIES > BURSARY
BURSARS > BURSAR
BURSARY n scholarship
BURSAS > BURSA
BURSATE > BURSA
BURSE n flat case used at
Mass as a container for the
corporal
BURSEED n type of plant
BURSEEDS > BURSEED
BURSERA adj of a type of
gum tree
BURSES > BURSE
BURSICON n hormone,
produced by the insect
brain, that regulates
processes associated with
ecdysis, such as darkening
of the cuticle
BURSICONS > BURSICON
BURSIFORM adj shaped like
a pouch or sac
BURSITIS n inflammation
of a bursa, esp one in the
shoulder joint
BURST vb break or cause
to break open or apart
suddenly and noisily, esp
from internal pressure ▷ n
sudden breaking open or
apart ▷ adj broken apart
BURSTED > BURST
BURSTEN > BURST
BURSTER > BURST
BURSTERS > BURST
BURSTING > BURST
BURSTONE same
as > BUHRSTONE
BURSTONES > BURSTONE
BURSTS > BURST
BURTHEN archaic word
for > BURDEN
BURTHENED > BURTHEN
BURTHENS > BURTHEN
BURTON n type of hoisting
tackle
BURTONS > BURTON
BURWEED n any of various
plants that bear burs, such
as the burdock
BURWEEDS > BURWEED
BURY vb place in a grave
BURYING > BURY
BUS n large motor vehicle
for carrying passengers
between stops ▷ vb travel
by bus
BUSBAR n electrical
conductor, maintained
at a specific voltage
and capable of carrying
a high current, usually
used to make a common
connection between
several circuits in a system
BUSBARS > BUSBAR
BUSBIES > BUSBY
BUSBOY n waiter's
assistant
BUSBOYS > BUSBOY
BUSBY n tall fur hat worn by
some soldiers

BUSED > BUS
BUSERA n Ugandan
alcoholic drink made from
millet: sometimes mixed
with honey
BUSERAS > BUSERA
BUSES > BUS
BUSGIRL n waiter's
assistant
BUSGIRLS > BUSGIRL
BUSH n dense woody plant,
smaller than a tree ▷ vb
fit a bush to (a casing or
bearing)
BUSHBABY n small African
tree-living mammal with
large eyes
BUSHBUCK n small
nocturnal spiral-horned
antelope, Tragelaphus
scriptus, of the bush and
tropical forest of Africa.
Its coat is reddish-brown
with a few white markings
BUSHBUCKS > BUSHBUCK
BUSHCRAFT n ability and
experience in matters
concerned with living in
the bush
BUSHED adj extremely tired
BUSHEL n obsolete unit of
measure equal to 8 gallons
(36.4 litres) ▷ vb alter or
mend (a garment)
BUSHELED > BUSHEL
BUSHELER > BUSHEL
BUSHELERS > BUSHEL
BUSHELING > BUSHEL
BUSHELLED > BUSHEL
BUSHELLER > BUSHEL
BUSHELMAN > BUSHEL
BUSHELMEN > BUSHEL
BUSHELS > BUSHEL
BUSHER > BUSH
BUSHERS > BUSH
BUSHES > BUSH
BUSHFIRE n uncontrolled
fire in the bush
BUSHFIRES > BUSHFIRE
BUSHFLIES > BUSHFLY
BUSHFLY n any of various
small black dipterous flies
of Australia, esp Musca
vetustissima, that breed in
faeces and dung: family
Calliphoridae
BUSHGOAT n S African
antelope
BUSHGOATS > BUSHGOAT
BUSHIDO n feudal code of
the Japanese samurai,
stressing self-discipline,
courage and loyalty
BUSHIDOS > BUSHIDO
BUSHIE same as > BUSHY
BUSHIER > BUSHY
BUSHIES > BUSHY
BUSHIEST > BUSHY
BUSHILY > BUSHY
BUSHINESS > BUSHY
BUSHING same as > BUSH
BUSHINGS > BUSHING
BUSHLAND n land
characterized by natural

vegetation

**BUSHLANDS** > BUSHLAND

**BUSHLESS** > BUSH

**BUSHLIKE** > BUSH

**BUSHMAN** *n* person who lives or travels in the bush

**BUSHMEAT** *n* meat taken from any animal native to African forests, including species that may be endangered or not usually eaten outside Africa

**BUSHMEATS** > BUSHMEAT

**BUSHMEN** > BUSHMAN

**BUSHPIG** *n* wild pig, *Potamochoerus porcus*, inhabiting forests in tropical Africa and Madagascar. It is brown or black, with pale markings on the face

**BUSHPIGS** > BUSHPIG

**BUSHTIT** *n* small grey active North American songbird

**BUSHTITS** > BUSHTIT

**BUSHVELD** *n* bushy countryside

**BUSHVELDS** > BUSHVELD

**BUSHWA** *n* nonsense

**BUSHWAH** *same as* > BUSHWA

**BUSHWAHS** > BUSHWAH

**BUSHWALK** *vb* hike through bushland

**BUSHWALKS** > BUSHWALK

**BUSHWAS** > BUSHWA

**BUSHWHACK** *vb* ambush

**BUSHWOMAN** > BUSHWOMAN

**BUSHWOMEN** > BUSHMAN

**BUSHY** *adj* (of hair) thick and shaggy ▷ *n* person who lives in the bush

**BUSIED** > BUSY

**BUSIER** > BUSY

**BUSIES** > BUSY

**BUSIEST** > BUSY

**BUSILY** *adv* in a busy manner

**BUSINESS** *n* purchase and sale of goods and services

**BUSINESSY** *adj* of, relating to, typical of, or suitable for the world of commercial or industrial business

**BUSING** > BUS

**BUSINGS** > BUS

**BUSK** *vb* act as a busker ▷ *n* strip of whalebone, wood, steel, etc, inserted into the front of a corset to stiffen it

**BUSKED** > BUSK

**BUSKER** > BUSK

**BUSKERS** > BUSK

**BUSKET** *n* bouquet

**BUSKETS** > BUSKET

**BUSKIN** *n* (formerly) sandal-like covering for the foot and leg, reaching the calf and usually laced

**BUSKINED** *adj* relating to tragedy

**BUSKING** > BUSK

**BUSKINGS** > BUSK

**BUSKINS** > BUSKIN

**BUSKS** > BUSK

**BUSKY** *same as* > BOSKY

**BUSLOAD** *n* number of people bus carries

**BUSLOADS** > BUSLOAD

**BUSMAN** *n* person who drives a bus

**BUSMEN** > BUSMAN

**BUSS** *archaic or dialect word for* > KISS

**BUSSED** > BUS

**BUSSES** > BUS

**BUSSING** > BUS

**BUSSINGS** > BUS

**BUSSU** *n* type of palm tree

**BUSSUS** > BUSSU

**BUST** *n* chest of a human being, esp a woman's bosom ▷ *adj* broken ▷ *vb* burst or break

**BUSTARD** *n* bird with long strong legs, a heavy body, a long neck, and speckled plumage

**BUSTARDS** > BUSTARD

**BUSTED** > BUST

**BUSTEE** *same as* > BASTI

**BUSTEES** > BUSTEE

**BUSTER** *n* person or thing destroying something as specified

**BUSTERS** > BUSTER

**BUSTI** *same as* > BASTI

**BUSTIC** *n* type of small American tree

**BUSTICATE** *vb* break

**BUSTICS** > BUSTIC

**BUSTIER** *n* close-fitting strapless women's top

**BUSTIERS** > BUSTIER

**BUSTIEST** > BUSTY

**BUSTINESS** > BUSTY

**BUSTING** > BUST

**BUSTINGS** > BUST

**BUSTIS** > BUSTI

**BUSTLE** *vb* hurry with a show of activity or energy ▷ *n* energetic and noisy activity

**BUSTLED** > BUSTLE

**BUSTLER** > BUSTLE

**BUSTLERS** > BUSTLE

**BUSTLES** > BUSTLE

**BUSTLINE** *n* shape or size of woman's bust

**BUSTLINES** > BUSTLINE

**BUSTLING** > BUSTLE

**BUSTS** > BUST

**BUSTY** *adj* (of a woman) having a prominent bust

**BUSULFAN** *n* drug used to treat cancer

**BUSULFANS** > BUSULFAN

**BUSUUTI** *n* long garment with short sleeves and a square neckline, worn by Ugandan women, esp in S Uganda

**BUSUUTIS** > BUSUUTI

**BUSY** *adj* actively employed ▷ *vb* keep (someone, esp oneself) busy

**BUSYBODY** *n* meddlesome

or nosy person

**BUSYING** > BUSY

**BUSYNESS** > BUSY

**BUSYWORK** *n* unproductive work

**BUSYWORKS** > BUSYWORK

**BUT** *prep* except ▷ *adv* only ▷ *n* outer room of a two-roomed cottage: usually the kitchen

**BUTADIENE** *n* colourless easily liquefiable flammable gas

**BUTANE** *n* gas used for fuel

**BUTANES** > BUTANE

**BUTANOL** *n* colourless substance

**BUTANOLS** > BUTANOL

**BUTANONE** *n* colourless soluble flammable liquid used mainly as a solvent for resins

**BUTANONES** > BUTANONE

**BUTCH** *adj* markedly or aggressively masculine ▷ *n* lesbian who is noticeably masculine

**BUTCHER** *n* person who slaughters animals or sells their meat ▷ *vb* kill and prepare (animals) for meat

**BUTCHERED** > BUTCHER

**BUTCHERER** > BUTCHER

**BUTCHERLY** > BUTCHER

**BUTCHERS** > BUTCHER

**BUTCHERY** *n* senseless slaughter

**BUTCHES** > BUTCH

**BUTCHEST** > BUTCH

**BUTCHING** > BUTCH

**BUTCHINGS** > BUTCH

**BUTCHNESS** > BUTCH

**BUTE** *n* drug used illegally to dope horses

**BUTENE** *n* pungent colourless gas

**BUTENES** > BUTENE

**BUTEO** *n* type of American hawk

**BUTEONINE** *adj* of hawks

**BUTEOS** > BUTEO

**BUTES** > BUTE

**BUTLE** *vb* act as butler

**BUTLED** > BUTLE

**BUTLER** *n* chief male servant ▷ *vb* act as a butler

**BUTLERAGE** > BUTLER

**BUTLERED** > BUTLER

**BUTLERIES** > BUTLERY

**BUTLERING** > BUTLER

**BUTLERS** > BUTLER

**BUTLERY** *n* butler's room

**BUTLES** > BUTLE

**BUTLING** > BUTLE

**BUTMENT** *same as* > ABUTMENT

**BUTMENTS** > BUTMENT

**BUTS** > BUT

**BUTSUDAN** *n* (in Buddhism) small household altar

**BUTSUDANS** > BUTSUDAN

**BUTT** *n* thicker or blunt end of something, such as the

end of the stock of a rifle ▷ *vb* strike or push with the head or horns

**BUTTALS** *n* abuttal

**BUTTE** *n* isolated steep flat-topped hill

**BUTTED** > BUTT

**BUTTER** *n* edible fatty yellow solid made form cream ▷ *vb* put butter on

**BUTTERBUR** *n* plant of the Eurasian genus *Petasites* with fragrant whitish or purple flowers, woolly stems, and leaves formerly used to wrap butter: family *Asteraceae* (composites)

**BUTTERCUP** *n* small yellow flower

**BUTTERED** > BUTTER

**BUTTERFAT** *n* fatty substance of milk from which butter is made, consisting of a mixture of glycerides, mainly butyrin, olein, and palmitin

**BUTTERFLY** *n* insect with brightly coloured wings

**BUTTERIER** > BUTTERY

**BUTTERIES** > BUTTERY

**BUTTERINE** *n* artificial butter made partly from milk

**BUTTERING** > BUTTER

**BUTTERNUT** *n* walnut tree, *Juglans cinerea* of E North America

**BUTTERS** > BUTTER

**BUTTERY** *n* (in some universities) room in which food and drink are sold to students ▷ *adj* containing, like, or coated with butter

**BUTTES** > BUTTE

**BUTTHEAD** *n* stupid person

**BUTTHEADS** > BUTTHEAD

**BUTTIES** > BUTTY

**BUTTING** > BUTT

**BUTTINSKI** *same as* > BUTTINSKY

**BUTTINSKY** *n* busybody

**BUTTLE** *vb* act as butler

**BUTTLED** > BUTTLE

**BUTTLES** > BUTTLE

**BUTTLING** > BUTTLE

**BUTTOCK** *n* either of the two fleshy masses that form the human rump ▷ *vb* perform a kind of wrestling manoeuvre on a person

**BUTTOCKED** > BUTTOCK

**BUTTOCKS** > BUTTOCK

**BUTTON** *n* small disc or knob sewn to clothing, which can be passed through a slit in another piece of fabric to fasten them ▷ *vb* fasten with buttons

**BUTTONED** > BUTTON

**BUTTONER** > BUTTON

**BUTTONERS** > BUTTON
**BUTTONING** > BUTTON
**BUTTONS** n page boy
**BUTTONY** > BUTTON
**BUTTRESS** n structure to support a wall ▷ vb support with, or as if with, a buttress
**BUTTS** > BUTT
**BUTTSTOCK** n part of gun
**BUTTY** n sandwich
**BUTTYMAN** n offensive term for a homosexual
**BUTTYMEN** > BUTTYMAN
**BUTUT** n Gambian monetary unit worth one hundredth of a dalasi
**BUTUTS** > BUTUT
**BUTYL** adj of or containing any of four isomeric forms of the group $C_4H_9-$ ▷ n of, consisting of, or containing any of four isomeric forms of the group $C_4H_9-$
**BUTYLATE** vb introduce butyl into (compound)
**BUTYLATED** > BUTYLATE
**BUTYLATES** > BUTYLATE
**BUTYLENE** same as > BUTENE
**BUTYLENES** > BUTYLENE
**BUTYLS** > BUTYL
**BUTYRAL** n type of resin
**BUTYRALS** > BUTYRAL
**BUTYRATE** n any salt or ester of butyric acid
**BUTYRATES** > BUTYRATE
**BUTYRIC** as in butyric acid type of acid
**BUTYRIN** n colourless liquid ester or oil found in butter. It is formed from butyric acid and glycerine
**BUTYRINS** > BUTYRIN
**BUTYROUS** adj butyraceous
**BUTYRYL** n radical of butyric acid
**BUTYRYLS** > BUTYRYL
**BUVETTE** n roadside café
**BUVETTES** > BUVETTE
**BUXOM** adj (of a woman) healthily plump and full-bosomed
**BUXOMER** > BUXOM
**BUXOMEST** > BUXOM
**BUXOMLY** > BUXOM
**BUXOMNESS** > BUXOM
**BUY** vb acquire by paying money for ▷ n thing acquired through payment
**BUYABLE** > BUY
**BUYABLES** > BUY
**BUYBACK** n repurchase by a company of some or all of its shares from an investor, who acquired them by putting venture capital into the company when it was formed
**BUYBACKS** > BUYBACK
**BUYER** n customer
**BUYERS** > BUYER
**BUYING** > BUY
**BUYOFF** n purchase

**BUYOFFS** > BUYOFF
**BUYOUT** n purchase of a company, esp by its former management or staff
**BUYOUTS** > BUYOUT
**BUYS** > BUY
**BUZKASHI** n game played in Aghanistan, in which opposing teams of horsemen strive for possession of the headless carcass of a goat
**BUZKASHIS** > BUZKASHI
**BUZUKI** same as > BOUZOUKI
**BUZUKIA** > BUZUKI
**BUZUKIS** > BUZUKI
**BUZZ** n rapidly vibrating humming sound ▷ vb make a humming sound
**BUZZARD** n bird of prey of the hawk family
**BUZZARDS** > BUZZARD
**BUZZCUT** n very short haircut
**BUZZCUTS** > BUZZCUT
**BUZZED** > BUZZ
**BUZZER** n electronic device that produces a buzzing sound as a signal
**BUZZERS** > BUZZER
**BUZZES** > BUZZ
**BUZZIER** > BUZZY
**BUZZIEST** > BUZZY
**BUZZING** > BUZZ
**BUZZINGLY** > BUZZ
**BUZZINGS** > BUZZ
**BUZZWIG** n bushy wig
**BUZZWIGS** > BUZZWIG
**BUZZWORD** n word, often originating in a particular jargon, that becomes a vogue word in the community as a whole or among a particular group
**BUZZWORDS** > BUZZWORD
**BUZZY** adj making a buzzing sound
**BWANA** n (in E Africa) master, often used as a respectful form of address corresponding to sir
**BWANAS** > BWANA
**BWAZI** same as > BUAZE
**BWAZIS** > BWAZI
**BY** prep indicating the doer of an action, nearness, movement past, time before or during which, etc ▷ adv near ▷ n bye
**BYCATCH** n unwanted fish and other sea animals caught in a fishing net along with the desired kind of fish
**BYCATCHES** > BYCATCH
**BYCOKET** n former Italian high-crowned hat
**BYCOKETS** > BYCOKET
**BYDE** same as > BIDE
**BYDED** > BYDE
**BYDES** > BYDE
**BYDING** > BYDE
**BYE** n situation where a player or team wins

a round by having no opponent ▷ interj goodbye ▷ sentence substitute goodbye
**BYELAW** n rule made by a local authority for the regulation of its affairs or management of the area it governs
**BYELAWS** > BYELAW
**BYES** > BYE
**BYGONE** adj past
**BYGONES** > BYGONE
**BYKE** > BICYCLE
**BYKED** > BICYCLE
**BYKES** > BICYCLE
**BYKING** > BICYCLE
**BYLANDER** same as > BILANDER
**BYLANDERS** > BYLANDER
**BYLANE** n side lane or alley off a road
**BYLANES** > BYLANE
**BYLAW** n rule made by a local authority
**BYLAWS** > BYLAW
**BYLINE** n line under the title of a newspaper or magazine article giving the author's name ▷ vb give a byline to
**BYLINED** > BYLINE
**BYLINER** > BYLINE
**BYLINERS** > BYLINE
**BYLINES** > BYLINE
**BYLINING** > BYLINE
**BYLIVE** same as > BELIVE
**BYNAME** n nickname
**BYNAMES** > BYNAME
**BYNEMPT** > BENAME
**BYPASS** n main road built to avoid a city ▷ vb go round or avoid
**BYPASSED** > BYPASS
**BYPASSES** > BYPASS
**BYPASSING** > BYPASS
**BYPAST** > BYPASS
**BYPATH** n little-used path or track, esp in the country
**BYPATHS** > BYPATH
**BYPLACE** n private place
**BYPLACES** > BYPLACE
**BYPLAY** n secondary action or talking carried on apart while the main action proceeds, esp in a play
**BYPLAYS** > BYPLAY
**BYPRODUCT** n secondary product
**BYRE** n shelter for cows
**BYREMAN** n man who works in byre
**BYREMEN** > BYREMAN
**BYRES** > BYRE
**BYREWOMAN** n woman who works in byre
**BYREWOMEN** > BYREWOMAN
**BYRL** same as > BIRL
**BYRLADY** interj short for By Our Lady
**BYRLAKIN** interj By Our Ladykin
**BYRLAW** same as > BYLAW
**BYRLAWS** > BYRLAW

**BYRLED** > BYRL
**BYRLING** > BYRL
**BYRLS** > BYRL
**BYRNIE** n archaic word for coat of mail
**BYRNIES** > BYRNIE
**BYROAD** n secondary or side road
**BYROADS** > BYROAD
**BYROOM** n private room
**BYROOMS** > BYROOM
**BYS** > BY
**BYSSAL** adj of mollusc's byssus
**BYSSI** > BYSSUS
**BYSSINE** adj made from flax
**BYSSOID** adj consisting of fine fibres
**BYSSUS** n mass of strong threads secreted by a sea mussel or similar mollusc that attaches the animal to a hard fixed surface
**BYSSUSES** > BYSSUS
**BYSTANDER** n person present but not involved
**BYSTREET** n obscure or secondary street
**BYSTREETS** > BYSTREET
**BYTALK** n trivial conversation
**BYTALKS** > BYTALK
**BYTE** n group of bits processed as one unit of data
**BYTES** > BYTE
**BYTOWNITE** n rare mineral
**BYWAY** n minor road
**BYWAYS** > BYWAY
**BYWONER** n poor tenant-farmer
**BYWONERS** > BYWONER
**BYWORD** n person or thing regarded as a perfect example of something
**BYWORDS** > BYWORD
**BYWORK** n work done outside usual working hours
**BYWORKS** > BYWORK
**BYZANT** same as > BEZANT
**BYZANTINE** adj of, characteristic of, or relating to Byzantium or the Byzantine Empire
**BYZANTS** > BYZANT

# Cc

CAA *a Scot word for* > CALL
CAAED > CAA
CAAING > CAA
CAAS > CAA
CAATINGA *n* Brazilian semi-arid scrub forest
CAATINGAS > CAATINGA
CAB *n* taxi ▷ *vb* take a taxi
CABA *same as* > CABAS
CABAL *n* small group of political plotters ▷ *vb* form a cabal
CABALA *a variant spelling of* > KABBALAH
CABALAS > CABALA
CABALETTA *n* final section of an aria
CABALETTE > CABALETTA
CABALISM > CABALA
CABALISMS > CABALA
CABALIST > CABALA
CABALISTS > CABALA
CABALLED > CABAL
CABALLER > CABAL
CABALLERO *n* Spanish gentleman
CABALLERS > CABAL
CABALLINE *adj* pertaining to a horse
CABALLING > CABAL
CABALS > CABAL
CABANA *n* tent used as a dressing room by the sea
CABANAS > CABANA
CABARET *n* dancing and singing show in a nightclub
CABARETS > CABARET
CABAS *n* reticule
CABBAGE *n* vegetable with a large head of green leaves ▷ *vb* steal
CABBAGED > CABBAGE

CABBAGES > CABBAGE
CABBAGEY > CABBAGE
CABBAGING > CABBAGE
CABBAGY > CABBAGE
CABBALA *a variant spelling of* > KABBALAH
CABBALAH *same as* > CABBALA
CABBALAHS > CABBALA
CABBALAS > CABBALA
CABBALISM > CABBALA
CABBALIST > CABBALA
CABBED > CAB
CABBIE *n* taxi driver
CABBIES > CABBIE
CABBING > CAB
CABBY *same as* > CABBIE
CABDRIVER *n* taxi-driver
CABER *n* tree trunk tossed in competition at Highland games
CABERNET *n* type of grape, or the red wine made from it
CABERNETS > CABERNET
CABERS > CABER
CABESTRO *n* halter made from horsehair
CABESTROS > CABESTRO
CABEZON *n* large food fish, *Scorpaenichthys marmoratus,* of North American Pacific coastal waters, having greenish flesh: family *Cottidae* (bullheads and sea scorpions)
CABEZONE *same as* > CABEZON
CABEZONES > CABEZON
CABEZONS > CABEZON
CABILDO *n* Spanish municipal council
CABILDOS > CABILDO

CABIN *n* compartment in a ship or aircraft ▷ *vb* confine in a small space
CABINED > CABIN
CABINET *n* piece of furniture with drawers or shelves
CABINETRY *n* cabinetmaking
CABINETS > CABINET
CABINING > CABIN
CABINMATE *n* sharer of cabin
CABINS > CABIN
CABLE *n* strong thick rope; a wire or bundle of wires that conduct electricity ▷ *vb* send (someone) a message by cable
CABLECAST *n* broadcast on cable
CABLED > CABLE
CABLEGRAM *n* message sent by cable
CABLER *n* cable broadcasting company
CABLERS > CABLER
CABLES > CABLE
CABLET *n* small cable, esp a cable-laid rope that has a circumference of less than 25 centimetres (ten inches)
CABLETS > CABLET
CABLEWAY *n* system for moving people or bulk materials in which suspended cars, buckets, etc, run on cables that extend between terminal towers
CABLEWAYS > CABLEWAY
CABLING > CABLE
CABLINGS > CABLE

CABMAN *n* driver of a cab
CABMEN > CABMAN
CABOB *vb* roast on a skewer
CABOBBED > CABOB
CABOBBING > CABOB
CABOBS > CABOB
CABOC *n* type of Scottish cheese
CABOCEER *n* in African history, indigenous representative appointed by his leader to deal with European slave traders
CABOCEERS > CABOCEER
CABOCHED *adj* in heraldry, with the face exposed, but neck concealed
CABOCHON *n* smooth domed gem, polished but unfaceted
CABOCHONS > CABOCHON
CABOCS > CABOC
CABOMBA *n* type of aquatic plant
CABOMBAS > CABOMBA
CABOODLE *n* lot, bunch, or group
CABOODLES > CABOODLE
CABOOSE *n* guard's van on a train
CABOOSES > CABOOSE
CABOSHED *same as* > CABOCHED
CABOTAGE *n* coastal navigation or shipping, esp within the borders of one country
CABOTAGES > CABOTAGE
CABOVER *adj* of or denoting a truck or lorry in which the cab is over the engine
CABRE *adj* heraldic term designating an animal

rearing

**CABRESTA** variant of > CABESTRO

**CABRESTAS** > CABRESTA

**CABRESTO** variant of > CABESTRO

**CABRESTOS** > CABRESTO

**CABRETTA** n soft leather obtained from the skins of certain South American or African sheep

**CABRETTAS** > CABRETTA

**CABRIE** n pronghorn antelope

**CABRIES** > CABRIE

**CABRILLA** n any of various serranid food fishes, esp Epinephelus analogus, occurring in warm seas around Florida and the Caribbean

**CABRILLAS** > CABRILLA

**CABRIO** short for > CABRIOLET

**CABRIOLE** n type of furniture leg, popular in the first half of the 18th century, in which an upper convex curve descends tapering to a concave curve

**CABRIOLES** > CABRIOLE

**CABRIOLET** n small horse-drawn carriage with a folding hood

**CABRIOS** > CABRIO

**CABRIT** n pronghorn antelope

**CABRITS** > CABRIT

**CABS** > CAB

**CABSTAND** n taxi-rank

**CABSTANDS** > CABSTAND

**CACA** n heroin

**CACAFOGO** same as > CACAFUEGO

**CACAFOGOS** > CACAFUEGO

**CACAFUEGO** n spitfire

**CACAO** same as > COCOA

**CACAOS** > COCOA

**CACAS** > CACA

**CACHAEMIA** n poisoned condition of the blood

**CACHAEMIC** > CACHAEMIA

**CACHALOT** n sperm whale

**CACHALOTS** > CACHALOT

**CACHE** n hidden store of weapons or treasure ▷ vb store in a cache

**CACHECTIC** > CACHEXIA

**CACHED** > CACHE

**CACHEPOT** n ornamental container for a flowerpot

**CACHEPOTS** > CACHEPOT

**CACHES** > CACHE

**CACHET** n prestige, distinction ▷ vb apply a commemorative design to an envelope, as a first-day cover

**CACHETED** > CACHET

**CACHETING** > CACHET

**CACHETS** > CACHET

**CACHEXIA** n generally weakened condition of

body or mind resulting from any debilitating chronic disease

**CACHEXIAS** > CACHEXIA

**CACHEXIC** > CACHEXIA

**CACHEXIES** > CACHEXIA

**CACHEXY** same as > CACHEXIA

**CACHING** > CACHE

**CACHOLONG** n a type of opal

**CACHOLOT** same as > CACHALOT

**CACHOLOTS** > CACHALOT

**CACHOU** same as > CATECHU

**CACHOUS** > CATECHU

**CACHUCHA** n graceful Spanish solo dance in triple time

**CACHUCHAS** > CACHUCHA

**CACIQUE** n American Indian chief in a Spanish-speaking region

**CACIQUES** > CACIQUE

**CACIQUISM** n (esp in Spanish America) government by local political bosses

**CACKIER** > CACKY

**CACKIEST** > CACKY

**CACKLE** vb laugh shrilly ▷ n cackling noise

**CACKLED** > CACKLE

**CACKLER** > CACKLE

**CACKLERS** > CACKLE

**CACKLES** > CACKLE

**CACKLING** > CACKLE

**CACKY** adj of or like excrement

**CACODEMON** n evil spirit or devil

**CACODOXY** n heterodoxy

**CACODYL** n oily poisonous liquid with a strong garlic smell

**CACODYLIC** > CACODYL

**CACODYLS** > CACODYL

**CACOEPIES** > CACOEPY

**CACOEPY** n bad or mistaken pronunciation

**CACOETHES** n uncontrollable urge or desire, esp for something harmful

**CACOETHIC** > CACOETHES

**CACOGENIC** adj reducing the quality of a race

**CACOLET** n seat fitted to the back of a mule

**CACOLETS** > CACOLET

**CACOLOGY** n bad choice of words

**CACOMIXL** n carnivorous mammal

**CACOMIXLE** same as > CACOMIXL

**CACOMIXLS** > CACOMIXL

**CACONYM** n erroneous name

**CACONYMS** > CACONYM

**CACONYMY** > CACONYM

**CACOON** n large seed of the sword-bean

**CACOONS** > CACOON

**CACOPHONY** n harsh

discordant sound

**CACOTOPIA** n dystopia, the opposite of utopia

**CACTI** > CACTUS

**CACTIFORM** adj cactus-like

**CACTOID** adj resembling a cactus

**CACTUS** n fleshy desert plant with spines but no leaves

**CACTUSES** > CACTUS

**CACUMEN** n apex

**CACUMINA** > CACUMEN

**CACUMINAL** adj relating to or denoting a consonant articulated with the tip of the tongue turned back towards the hard palate ▷ n consonant articulated in this manner

**CAD** n dishonourable man

**CADAGA** n eucalyptus tree, E. torelliana, of tropical and subtropical Australia, having a smooth green trunk

**CADAGAS** > CADAGA

**CADAGI** same as > CADAGA

**CADAGIS** > CADAGI

**CADASTER** n official register showing details of ownership, boundaries, and value of real property in a district, made for taxation purposes

**CADASTERS** > CADASTER

**CADASTRAL** > CADASTER

**CADASTRE** same as > CADASTER

**CADASTRES** > CADASTER

**CADAVER** n corpse

**CADAVERIC** > CADAVER

**CADAVERS** > CADAVER

**CADDICE** same as > CADDIS

**CADDICES** > CADDIS

**CADDIE** n person who carries a golfer's clubs ▷ vb act as a caddie

**CADDIED** > CADDIE

**CADDIES** > CADDIE

**CADDIS** n type of coarse woollen yarn, braid, or fabric

**CADDISED** adj trimmed with a type of ribbon

**CADDISES** > CADDIS

**CADDISFLY** n small fly

**CADDISH** > CAD

**CADDISHLY** > CAD

**CADDY** same as > CADDIE

**CADDYING** > CADDIE

**CADDYSS** same as > CADDIS

**CADDYSSES** > CADDIS

**CADE** n juniper tree ▷ adj (of a young animal) left by its mother and reared by humans, usually as a pet

**CADEAU** n present

**CADEAUX** > CADEAU

**CADEE** old form of > CADET

**CADEES** > CADEE

**CADELLE** n widely distributed beetle, Tenebroides mauritanicus,

that feeds on flour, grain, and other stored foods: family Trogositidae

**CADELLES** > CADELLE

**CADENCE** n rise and fall in the pitch of the voice ▷ vb modulate musically

**CADENCED** > CADENCE

**CADENCES** > CADENCE

**CADENCIES** > CADENCY

**CADENCING** > CADENCE

**CADENCY** same as > CADENCE

**CADENT** adj having cadence

**CADENTIAL** > CADENT

**CADENZA** n complex solo passage in a piece of music

**CADENZAS** > CADENZA

**CADES** > CADE

**CADET** n young person training for the armed forces or police

**CADETS** > CADET

**CADETSHIP** > CADET

**CADGE** vb get (something) by taking advantage of someone's generosity

**CADGED** > CADGE

**CADGER** n person who cadges

**CADGERS** > CADGER

**CADGES** > CADGE

**CADGIER** > CADGY

**CADGIEST** > CADGY

**CADGING** > CADGE

**CADGY** adj cheerful

**CADI** n judge in a Muslim community

**CADIE** n messenger

**CADIES** > CADIE

**CADIS** > CADI

**CADMIC** > CADMIUM

**CADMIUM** n bluish-white metallic element used in alloys

**CADMIUMS** > CADMIUM

**CADRANS** n instrument used in gemcutting

**CADRANSES** > CADRANS

**CADRE** n small group of people selected and trained to form the core of a political organization or military unit

**CADRES** > CADRE

**CADS** > CAD

**CADUAC** n windfall

**CADUACS** > CADUAC

**CADUCEAN** > CADUCEUS

**CADUCEI** > CADUCEUS

**CADUCEUS** n staff entwined with two serpents and bearing a pair of wings at the top, carried by Hermes (Mercury) as messenger of the gods

**CADUCITY** n perishableness

**CADUCOUS** adj (of parts of a plant or animal) shed during the life of the organism

**CAECA** > CAECUM

**CAECAL** > CAECUM

**CAECALLY** > CAECUM

**CAECILIAN** n any tropical limbless cylindrical amphibian of the order Apoda (or Gymnophiona), resembling earthworms and inhabiting moist soil

**CAECITIS** n inflammation of the caecum

**CAECUM** n pouch at the beginning of the large intestine

**CAEOMA** n aecium in some rust fungi that has no surrounding membrane

**CAEOMAS** > CAEOMA

**CAERULE** same as > CERULE

**CAERULEAN** same as > CERULEAN

**CAESAR** n any emperor, autocrat, dictator, or other powerful ruler

**CAESAREAN** n surgical incision through the abdominal and uterine walls in order to deliver a baby

**CAESARIAN** variant spelling of > CAESAREAN

**CAESARISM** another word for > IMPERIALISM

**CAESARS** > CAESAR

**CAESE** interj Shakespearean interjection

**CAESIOUS** adj having a waxy bluish-grey coating

**CAESIUM** n silvery-white metallic element used in photocells

**CAESIUMS** > CAESIUM

**CAESTUS** same as > CESTUS

**CAESTUSES** > CAESTUS

**CAESURA** n pause in a line of verse

**CAESURAE** > CAESURA

**CAESURAL** > CAESURA

**CAESURAS** > CAESURA

**CAESURIC** > CAESURA

**CAFARD** n feeling of severe depression

**CAFARDS** > CAFARD

**CAFE** n small or inexpensive restaurant serving light refreshments

**CAFES** > CAFE

**CAFETORIA** n self-service restaurant

**CAFETIERE** n kind of coffeepot in which boiling water is poured onto ground coffee and a plunger fitted with a metal filter is pressed down, forcing the grounds to the bottom

**CAFETORIA** variant of > CAFETERIA

**CAFF** n café

**CAFFEIN** same as > CAFFEINE

**CAFFEINE** n stimulant found in tea and coffee

**CAFFEINES** > CAFFEINE

**CAFFEINIC** adj of or containing caffeine

**CAFFEINS** > CAFFEINE

**CAFFEISM** n addiction to caffeine

**CAFFEISMS** > CAFFEISM

**CAFFILA** n caravan train

**CAFFILAS** > CAFFILA

**CAFFS** > CAFF

**CAFILA** same as > CAFFILA

**CAFILAS** > CAFILA

**CAFTAN** same as > KAFTAN

**CAFTANED** adj wearing caftan

**CAFTANS** > CAFTAN

**CAG** same as > CAGOULE

**CAGANER** n figure of a squatting defecating person, a traditional character in Catalan Christmas crèche scenes

**CAGANERS** > CAGANER

**CAGE** n enclosure of bars or wires, for keeping animals or birds ▷ vb confine in a cage

**CAGEBIRD** n bird habitually kept caged

**CAGEBIRDS** > CAGEBIRD

**CAGED** > CAGE

**CAGEFUL** n amount which fills a cage to capacity

**CAGEFULS** > CAGEFUL

**CAGELIKE** > CAGE

**CAGELING** n bird kept in a cage

**CAGELINGS** > CAGELING

**CAGER** n basketball player

**CAGERS** > CAGER

**CAGES** > CAGE

**CAGEWORK** n something constructed as if from the bars of a cage

**CAGEWORKS** > CAGEWORK

**CAGEY** adj reluctant to go into details

**CAGEYNESS** > CAGEY

**CAGIER** > CAGEY

**CAGIEST** > CAGEY

**CAGILY** > CAGEY

**CAGINESS** > CAGY

**CAGING** > CAGE

**CAGMAG** adj done shoddily ▷ vb chat idly

**CAGMAGGED** > CAGMAG

**CAGMAGS** > CAGMAG

**CAGOT** n member of a class of French outcasts

**CAGOTS** > CAGOT

**CAGOUL** same as > CAGOULE

**CAGOULE** n lightweight hooded waterproof jacket

**CAGOULES** > CAGOULE

**CAGOULS** > CAGOUL

**CAGS** > CAG

**CAGY** same as > CAGEY

**CAGYNESS** > CAGY

**CAHIER** n notebook

**CAHIERS** > CAHIER

**CAHOOT** n partnership

**CAHOOTS** > CAHOOT

**CAHOW** n Bermuda petrel

**CAHOWS** > CAHOW

**CAID** n Moroccan district administrator

**CAIDS** > CAID

**CAILLACH** same as > CAILLEACH

**CAILLACHS** > CAILLACH

**CAILLE** n quail

**CAILLEACH** n old woman

**CAILLES** > CAILLE

**CAILLIACH** same as > CAILLEACH

**CAIMAC** same as > CAIMACAM

**CAIMACAM** n Turkish governor of a sanjak

**CAIMACAMS** > CAIMACAM

**CAIMACS** > CAIMAC

**CAIMAN** same as > CAYMAN

**CAIMANS** > CAIMAN

**CAIN** n (in Scotland and Ireland) payment in kind, usually farm produce paid as rent

**CAINS** > CAIN

**CAIQUE** n long narrow light rowing skiff used on the Bosporus

**CAIQUES** > CAIQUE

**CAIRD** n travelling tinker

**CAIRDS** > CAIRD

**CAIRN** n mound of stones erected as a memorial or marker

**CAIRNED** adj marked by a cairn

**CAIRNGORM** n yellow or brownish quartz gemstone

**CAIRNS** > CAIRN

**CAIRNY** adj covered with cairns

**CAISSON** same as > COFFERDAM

**CAISSONS** > CAISSON

**CAITIFF** n cowardly or base person ▷ adj cowardly

**CAITIFFS** > CAITIFF

**CAITIVE** n captive

**CAITIVES** > CAITIVE

**CAJAPUT** same as > CAJUPUT

**CAJAPUTS** > CAJAPUT

**CAJEPUT** same as > CAJUPUT

**CAJEPUTS** > CAJEPUT

**CAJOLE** vb persuade by flattery

**CAJOLED** > CAJOLE

**CAJOLER** > CAJOLE

**CAJOLERS** > CAJOLE

**CAJOLERY** > CAJOLE

**CAJOLES** > CAJOLE

**CAJOLING** > CAJOLE

**CAJON** n Peruvian wooden box used as a drum

**CAJONES** > CAJON

**CAJUN** n music of the Cajun people, combining blues and European folk music

**CAJUPUT** n small myrtaceous tree or shrub, Melaleuca leucadendron, native to the East Indies and Australia, with whitish flowers and leaves

**CAJUPUTS** > CAJUPUT

**CAKE** n sweet food baked from a mixture of flour, eggs, etc ▷ vb form into a

hardened mass or crust

**CAKED** > CAKE

**CAKES** > CAKE

**CAKEWALK** n dance based on a march with intricate steps, originally performed by African-Americans with the prize of a cake for the best performers ▷ vb perform the cakewalk

**CAKEWALKS** > CAKEWALK

**CAKEY** > CAKE

**CAKIER** > CAKE

**CAKIEST** > CAKE

**CAKINESS** > CAKE

**CAKING** > CAKE

**CAKINGS** > CAKE

**CAKY** > CAKE

**CALABASH** n type of large round gourd

**CALABAZA** n variety of squash

**CALABAZAS** > CALABAZA

**CALABOGUS** n mixed drink containing rum, spruce beer, and molasses

**CALABOOSE** n prison

**CALABRESE** n kind of green sprouting broccoli

**CALADIUM** n any of various tropical plants of the aroid genus Caladium, which are widely cultivated as potted plants for their colourful variegated foliage

**CALADIUMS** > CALADIUM

**CALALOO** same as > CALALU

**CALALOOS** > CALALOO

**CALALU** n edible leaves of various plants, used as greens or in making thick soups

**CALALUS** > CALALU

**CALAMANCO** n glossy woollen fabric woven with a checked design that shows on one side only

**CALAMAR** n any member of the squid family

**CALAMARI** n squid cooked for eating, esp cut into rings and fried in batter

**CALAMARIS** > CALAMARI

**CALAMARS** > CALAMAR

**CALAMARY** variant of > CALAMARI

**CALAMATA** same as > KALAMATA

**CALAMATAS** > CALAMATA

**CALAMI** > CALAMUS

**CALAMINE** n pink powder consisting chiefly of zinc oxide, used in skin lotions and ointments ▷ vb apply calamine

**CALAMINED** > CALAMINE

**CALAMINES** > CALAMINE

**CALAMINT** n any aromatic Eurasian plant of the genus Satureja (or Calamintha), having clusters of purple or pink flowers: family *Lamiaceae* (labiates)

**CALAMINTS** > CALAMINT

**CALAMITE** *n* any extinct treelike plant of the genus *Calamites*, of Carboniferous times, related to the horsetails

**CALAMITES** > CALAMITE

**CALAMITY** *n* disaster

**CALAMUS** *n* any tropical Asian palm of the genus *Calamus*, some species of which are a source of rattan and canes

**CALANDO** *adv* (to be performed) with gradually decreasing tone and speed

**CALANDRIA** *n* cylindrical vessel through which vertical tubes pass, esp one forming part of an evaporator, heat exchanger, or nuclear reactor

**CALANTHE** *n* type of orchid

**CALANTHES** > CALANTHE

**CALASH** *n* horse-drawn carriage with low wheels and a folding top

**CALASHES** > CALASH

**CALATHEA** *n* S American perennial plant, many species of which are grown as greenhouse or house plants for their decorative variegated leaves

**CALATHEAS** > CALATHEA

**CALATHI** > CALATHUS

**CALATHOS** *same as* > CALATHUS

**CALATHUS** *n* vase-shaped basket represented in ancient Greek art, used as a symbol of fruitfulness

**CALAVANCE** *n* type of pulse

**CALCANEA** > CALCANEUS

**CALCANEAL** > CALCANEUS

**CALCANEAN** > CALCANEUS

**CALCANEI** > CALCANEUS

**CALCANEUM** *same as* > CALCANEUS

**CALCANEUS** *n* largest tarsal bone, forming the heel in man

**CALCAR** *n* spur or spurlike process, as on the leg of a bird or the corolla of a flower

**CALCARATE** > CALCAR

**CALCARIA** > CALCAR

**CALCARINE** > CALCAR

**CALCARS** > CALCAR

**CALCEATE** *vb* to shoe

**CALCEATED** > CALCEATE

**CALCEATES** > CALCEATE

**CALCED** *adj* wearing shoes

**CALCEDONY** *n* a microcrystalline often greyish form of quartz with crystals arranged in parallel fibres: a gemstone.

**CALCES** > CALX

**CALCIC** *adj* of, containing,

or concerned with lime or calcium

**CALCICOLE** *n* any plant that thrives in lime-rich soils

**CALCIFIC** *adj* forming or causing to form lime or chalk

**CALCIFIED** > CALCIFY

**CALCIFIES** > CALCIFY

**CALCIFUGE** *n* any plant that thrives in acid soils but not in lime-rich soils

**CALCIFY** *vb* harden by the depositing of calcium salts

**CALCIMINE** *n* white or pale tinted wash for walls ▷ *vb* cover with calcimine

**CALCINE** *vb* oxidize (a substance) by heating

**CALCINED** > CALCINE

**CALCINES** > CALCINE

**CALCINING** > CALCINE

**CALCITE** *n* colourless or white form of calcium carbonate

**CALCITES** > CALCITE

**CALCITIC** > CALCITE

**CALCIUM** *n* silvery-white metallic element found in bones, teeth, limestone, and chalk

**CALCIUMS** > CALCIUM

**CALCRETE** *another name for* > CALICHE

**CALCRETES** > CALCRETE

**CALCSPAR** *another name for* > CALCITE

**CALCSPARS** > CALCSPAR

**CALCTUFA** *another name for* > TUFA

**CALCTUFAS** > CALCTUFA

**CALCTUFF** *another name for* > TUFA

**CALCTUFFS** > CALCTUFF

**CALCULAR** *adj* relating to calculus

**CALCULARY** *adj* relating to stone

**CALCULATE** *vb* solve or find out by a mathematical procedure or by reasoning

**CALCULI** > CALCULUS

**CALCULOSE** *adj* relating to calculi

**CALCULOUS** *adj* of or suffering from a stonelike accretion of minerals and salts found in ducts or hollow organs of the body

**CALCULUS** *n* branch of mathematics dealing with infinitesimal changes to a variable number or quantity

**CALDARIA** > CALDARIUM

**CALDARIUM** *n* (in ancient Rome) a room for taking hot baths

**CALDERA** *n* large basin-shaped crater at the top of a volcano, formed by the collapse or explosion of the cone

**CALDERAS** > CALDERA

**CALDRON** *same as* > CAULDRON

**CALDRONS** > CALDRON

**CALECHE** *a variant of* > CALASH

**CALECHES** > CALECHE

**CALEFIED** > CALEFY

**CALEFIES** > CALEFY

**CALEFY** *vb* to make warm

**CALEFYING** > CALEFY

**CALEMBOUR** *n* pun

**CALENDAL** > CALENDS

**CALENDAR** *n* chart showing a year divided up into months, weeks, and days ▷ *vb* enter in a calendar

**CALENDARS** > CALENDAR

**CALENDER** *n* machine in which paper or cloth is smoothed by passing it between rollers ▷ *vb* smooth in such a machine

**CALENDERS** > CALENDER

**CALENDRER** > CALENDER

**CALENDRIC** > CALENDAR

**CALENDRY** *n* place where calendering is carried out

**CALENDS** *pl n* first day of each month in the ancient Roman calendar

**CALENDULA** *n* marigold

**CALENTURE** *n* mild fever of tropical climates, similar in its symptoms to sunstroke

**CALESA** *n* horse-drawn buggy

**CALESAS** > CALESA

**CALESCENT** *adj* increasing in heat

**CALF** *n* young cow, bull, elephant, whale, or seal

**CALFDOZER** *n* small bulldozer

**CALFLESS** > CALF

**CALFLICK** *another word for* > COWLICK

**CALFLICKS** > CALFLICK

**CALFLIKE** > CALF

**CALFS** > CALF

**CALFSKIN** *n* fine leather made from the skin of a calf

**CALFSKINS** > CALFSKIN

**CALIATOUR** *n* red sandalwood

**CALIBER** *same as* > CALIBRE

**CALIBERED** > CALIBER

**CALIBERS** > CALIBER

**CALIBRATE** *vb* mark the scale or check the accuracy of (a measuring instrument)

**CALIBRE** *n* person's ability or worth

**CALIBRED** > CALIBRE

**CALIBRES** > CALIBRE

**CALICES** > CALIX

**CALICHE** *n* bed of sand or clay in arid regions cemented by calcium carbonate, sodium chloride, and other soluble

minerals

**CALICHES** > CALICHE

**CALICLE** *same as* > CALYCLE

**CALICLES** > CALICLE

**CALICO** *n* white cotton fabric

**CALICOES** > CALICO

**CALICOS** > CALICO

**CALICULAR** > CALYCLE

**CALID** *adj* warm

**CALIDITY** > CALID

**CALIF** *same as* > CALIPH

**CALIFATE** *same as* > CALIPHATE

**CALIFATES** > CALIFATE

**CALIFONT** *n* gas water heater

**CALIFONTS** > CALIFONT

**CALIFS** > CALIF

**CALIGO** *n* speck on the cornea causing poor vision

**CALIGOES** > CALIGO

**CALIGOS** > CALIGO

**CALIMA** *n* Saharan dust-storm

**CALIMAS** > CALIMA

**CALIOLOGY** *n* the study of birds' nests

**CALIPASH** *n* greenish glutinous edible part of the turtle found next to the upper shell, considered a delicacy

**CALIPEE** *n* yellow glutinous edible part of the turtle found next to the lower shell, considered a delicacy

**CALIPEES** > CALIPEE

**CALIPER** *same as* > CALLIPER

**CALIPERED** > CALLIPER

**CALIPERS** > CALIPER

**CALIPH** *n* Muslim ruler

**CALIPHAL** > CALIPH

**CALIPHATE** *n* office, jurisdiction, or reign of a caliph

**CALIPHS** > CALIPH

**CALISAYA** *n* bark of any of several tropical trees of the rubiaceous genus *Cinchona*, esp *C. calisaya*, from which quinine is extracted

**CALISAYAS** > CALISAYA

**CALIVER** *n* type of musket

**CALIVERS** > CALIVER

**CALIX** *n* cup

**CALK** *same as* > CAULK

**CALKED** > CALK

**CALKER** > CALK

**CALKERS** > CALK

**CALKIN** > CALK

**CALKING** > CALK

**CALKINGS** > CALK

**CALKINS** > CALK

**CALKS** > CALK

**CALL** *vb* name ▷ *n* cry, shout

**CALLA** *n* any southern African plant of the aroid genus *Zantedeschia*, esp *Z. aethiopica*, which has a white funnel-shaped spathe enclosing a yellow spadix

CALLABLE *adj* (of a security) subject to redemption before maturity

CALLAIDES > CALLAIS

CALLAIS *n* green stone found as beads and ornaments in the late Neolithic and early Bronze Age of W Europe

CALLALOO *n* leafy green vegetable

CALLALOOS > CALLALOO

CALLAN *same as* > CALLANT

CALLANS > CALLAN

CALLANT *n* youth

CALLANTS > CALLANT

CALLAS > CALLA

CALLBACK *n* telephone call made in response to an earlier call

CALLBACKS > CALLBACK

CALLBOARD *n* notice board listing opportunities for performers

CALLBOY *n* person who notifies actors when it is time to go on stage

CALLBOYS > CALLBOY

CALLED > CALL

CALLEE *n* computer function being used

CALLEES > CALLEE

CALLER *n* person or thing that calls, esp a person who makes a brief visit ▷ *adj* (of food, esp fish) fresh

CALLERS > CALLER

CALLET *n* scold

CALLETS > CALLET

CALLID *adj* cunning

CALLIDITY > CALLID

CALLIGRAM *n* poem in which words are positioned so as to create a visual image of the subject on the page

CALLING *n* vocation, profession

CALLINGS > CALLING

CALLIOPE *n* steam organ

CALLIOPES > CALLIOPE

CALLIPASH *same as* > CALIPASH

CALLIPEE *same as* > CALIPEE

CALLIPEES > CALLIPEE

CALLIPER *n* metal splint for supporting the leg ▷ *vb* measure the dimensions of (an object) with callipers

CALLIPERS > CALLIPER

CALLOP *n* edible freshwater fish, *Plectroplites ambiguus*, of Australia, often golden or pale yellow in colour

CALLOPS > CALLOP

CALLOSE *n* carbohydrate, a polymer of glucose, found in plants, esp in the sieve tubes

CALLOSES > CALLOSE

CALLOSITY *same as* > CALLUS

CALLOUS *adj* showing no concern for other people's feelings ▷ *vb* make or become callous

CALLOUSED > CALLOUS

CALLOUSES > CALLOUS

CALLOUSLY > CALLOUS

CALLOW *adj* young and inexperienced ▷ *n* someone young and inexperienced

CALLOWER > CALLOW

CALLOWEST > CALLOW

CALLOWS > CALLOW

CALLS > CALL

CALLUNA *n* type of heather

CALLUNAS > CALLUNA

CALLUS *n* area of thick hardened skin ▷ *vb* produce or cause to produce a callus

CALLUSED > CALLUS

CALLUSES > CALLUS

CALLUSING > CALLUS

CALM *adj* not agitated or excited ▷ *n* peaceful state ▷ *vb* make or become calm

CALMANT *n* sedative

CALMANTS > CALMANT

CALMATIVE *adj* (of a remedy or agent) sedative ▷ *n* sedative remedy or drug

CALMED > CALM

CALMER > CALM

CALMEST > CALM

CALMIER > CALMY

CALMIEST > CALMY

CALMING > CALM

CALMINGLY > CALM

CALMINGS > CALM

CALMLY > CALM

CALMNESS > CALM

CALMS > CALM

CALMSTONE *same as* > CAMSTONE

CALMY *adj* tranquil

CALO *n* military servant

CALOMEL *n* colourless tasteless powder

CALOMELS > CALOMEL

CALORIC *adj* of heat or calories ▷ *n* hypothetical elastic fluid formerly postulated as the embodiment of heat

CALORICS > CALORIC

CALORIE *n* unit of measurement for the energy value of food

CALORIES > CALORIE

CALORIFIC *adj* of calories or heat

CALORISE *same as* > CALORIZE

CALORISED > CALORISE

CALORISES > CALORISE

CALORIST *n* believer in caloric theory

CALORISTS > CALORIST

CALORIZE *vb* coat (a ferrous metal) by spraying

with aluminium powder and then heating

CALORIZED > CALORIZE

CALORIZES > CALORIZE

CALORY *same as* > CALORIE

CALOS > CALO

CALOTTE *n* skullcap worn by Roman Catholic clergy

CALOTTES > CALOTTE

CALOTYPE *n* early photographic process invented by W. H. Fox Talbot, in which the image was produced on paper treated with silver iodide and developed by sodium thiosulphite

CALOTYPES > CALOTYPE

CALOYER *n* monk of the Greek Orthodox Church, esp of the Basilian Order

CALOYERS > CALOYER

CALP *n* type of limestone

CALPA *n* Hindu unit of time

CALPAC *n* large black brimless hat made of sheepskin or felt, worn by men in parts of the Near East

CALPACK *same as* > CALPAC

CALPACKS > CALPACK

CALPACS > CALPAC

CALPAIN *n* type of enzyme

CALPAINS > CALPAIN

CALPAS > CALPA

CALPS > CALP

CALQUE *same as* > CAULK

CALQUED > CALQUE

CALQUES > CALQUE

CALQUING > CALQUE

CALTHA *n* marsh marigold

CALTHAS > CALTHA

CALTHROP *same as* > CALTHROP

CALTHROPS > CALTROP

CALTRAP *same as* > CALTROP

CALTRAPS > CALTRAP

CALTROP *n* floating Asian plant

CALTROPS > CALTROP

CALUMBA *n* Mozambiquan root used for medicinal purposes

CALUMBAS > CALUMBA

CALUMET *n* peace pipe

CALUMETS > CALUMET

CALUMNIES > CALUMNY

CALUMNY *n* false or malicious statement

CALUTRON *n* device used for the separation of isotopes

CALUTRONS > CALUTRON

CALVADOS *n* type of apple brandy

CALVARIA *n* top part of the skull of vertebrates

CALVARIAL > CALVARIUM

CALVARIAN > CALVARIUM

CALVARIAS > CALVARIA

CALVARIES > CALVARY

CALVARIUM *same as* > CALVARIA

CALVARY *n* representation of Christ's crucifixion,

usually sculptured and in the open air

CALVE *vb* give birth to a calf

CALVED > CALVE

CALVER *vb* prepare fish for cooking

CALVERED > CALVER

CALVERING > CALVER

CALVERS > CALVER

CALVES > CALF

CALVING > CALVE

CALVITIES *n* baldness

CALX *n* powdery metallic oxide formed when an ore or mineral is roasted

CALXES > CALX

CALYCATE > CALYX

CALYCEAL *adj* resembling a calyx

CALYCES > CALYX

CALYCINAL *same as* > CALYCINE

CALYCINE *adj* relating to, belonging to, or resembling a calyx

CALYCLE *n* cup-shaped structure, as in the coral skeleton

CALYCLED > CALYCLE

CALYCLES > CALYCLE

CALYCOID *adj* resembling a calyx

CALYCULAR > CALYCLE

CALYCULE *n* bracts surrounding the base of the calyx

CALYCULES > CALYCULE

CALYCULI > CALYCULUS

CALYCULUS *same as* > CALYCLE

CALYPSO *n* West Indian song with improvised topical lyrics

CALYPSOES > CALYPSO

CALYPSOS > CALYPSO

CALYPTER *n* alula

CALYPTERA *same as* > CALYPTRA

CALYPTERS > CALYPTER

CALYPTRA *n* membranous hood covering the spore-bearing capsule of mosses and liverworts

CALYPTRAS > CALYPTRA

CALYX *n* outer leaves that protect a flower bud

CALYXES > CALYX

CALZONE *n* folded pizza filled with cheese, tomatoes, etc

CALZONES > CALZONE

CALZONI > CALZONE

CAM *n* device that converts a circular motion to a to-and-fro motion ▷ *vb* furnish (a machine) with a cam

CAMA *n* hybrid offspring of a camel and a llama

CAMAIEU *n* cameo

CAMAIEUX > CAMAIEU

CAMAIL *n* neck and shoulders covering of mail worn with and laced to the basinet

**CAMAILED** >CAMAIL

**CAMAILS** >CAMAIL

**CAMAN** n wooden stick used to hit the ball in shinty

**CAMANACHD** n shinty

**CAMANS** >CAMAN

**CAMARILLA** n group of confidential advisers, esp formerly, to the Spanish kings

**CAMARON** n shrimp

**CAMARONS** >CAMARON

**CAMAS** same as >CAMASS

**CAMASES** >CAMAS

**CAMASH** same as >CAMASS

**CAMASHES** >CAMASH

**CAMASS** n type of North American plant

**CAMASSES** >CAMASS

**CAMBER** n slight upward curve to the centre of a surface ▷ vb form or be formed with a surface that curves upwards to its centre

**CAMBERED** >CAMBER

**CAMBERING** >CAMBER

**CAMBERS** >CAMBER

**CAMBIA** >CAMBIUM

**CAMBIAL** >CAMBIUM

**CAMBIFORM** >CAMBIUM

**CAMBISM** >CAMBIST

**CAMBISMS** >CAMBIST

**CAMBIST** n dealer or expert in foreign exchange

**CAMBISTRY** >CAMBIST

**CAMBISTS** >CAMBIST

**CAMBIUM** n meristem that increases the girth of stems and roots by producing additional xylem and phloem

**CAMBIUMS** >CAMBIUM

**CAMBOGE** n type of gum resin

**CAMBOGES** >CAMBOGE

**CAMBOGIA** another name for >GAMBOGE

**CAMBOGIAS** >CAMBOGIA

**CAMBOOSE** n cabin built as living quarters for a gang of lumbermen

**CAMBOOSES** >CAMBOOSE

**CAMBREL** a variant of >GAMBREL

**CAMBRELS** >CAMBREL

**CAMBRIC** n fine white linen fabric

**CAMBRICS** >CAMBRIC

**CAMCORDER** n combined portable video camera and recorder

**CAME** >COME

**CAMEL** n humped mammal that can survive long periods without food or water in desert regions

**CAMELBACK** n type of locomotive

**CAMELEER** n camel-driver

**CAMELEERS** >CAMELEER

**CAMELEON** same as >CHAMELEON

**CAMELEONS** >CAMELEON

**CAMELHAIR** n hair of camel

**CAMELIA** same as >CAMELLIA

**CAMELIAS** >CAMELIA

**CAMELID** adj of or relating to camels ▷ n any animal of the camel family

**CAMELIDS** >CAMELID

**CAMELINE** n material made from camel hair

**CAMELINES** >CAMELINE

**CAMELISH** >CAMEL

**CAMELLIA** n evergreen ornamental shrub with white, pink, or red flowers

**CAMELLIAS** >CAMELLIA

**CAMELLIKE** >CAMEL

**CAMELOID** n member of the camel family

**CAMELOIDS** >CAMELOID

**CAMELOT** n supposedly idyllic period or age

**CAMELOTS** >CAMELOT

**CAMELRIES** >CAMELRY

**CAMELRY** n troops mounted on camels

**CAMELS** >CAMEL

**CAMEO** n brooch or ring with a profile head carved in relief ▷ vb to appear in a brief role

**CAMEOED** >CAMEO

**CAMEOING** >CAMEO

**CAMEOS** >CAMEO

**CAMERA** n apparatus used for taking photographs or pictures for television or cinema

**CAMERAE** >CAMERA

**CAMERAL** adj of or relating to a judicial or legislative chamber

**CAMERAMAN** n man who operates a camera for television or cinema

**CAMERAMEN** >CAMERAMAN

**CAMERAS** >CAMERA

**CAMERATED** adj vaulted

**CAMES** obsolete form of >CANVAS

**CAMESE** same as >CAMISE

**CAMESES** >CAMESE

**CAMION** n lorry, or, esp formerly, a large dray

**CAMIONS** >CAMION

**CAMIS** n light robe

**CAMISA** n smock

**CAMISADE** same as >CAMISADO

**CAMISADES** >CAMISADE

**CAMISADO** n (formerly) an attack made under cover of darkness

**CAMISADOS** >CAMISADO

**CAMISAS** >CAMISA

**CAMISE** n loose light shirt, smock, or tunic originally worn in the Middle Ages

**CAMISES** >CAMISE

**CAMISIA** n surplice

**CAMISIAS** >CAMISIA

**CAMISOLE** n woman's bodice-like garment

**CAMISOLES** >CAMISOLE

**CAMLET** n tough waterproof cloth

**CAMLETS** >CAMLET

**CAMMED** >CAM

**CAMMIE** n webcam award

**CAMMIES** >CAMMIE

**CAMMING** >CAM

**CAMO** short for camouflage

**CAMOGIE** n form of hurling played by women

**CAMOGIES** >CAMOGIE

**CAMOMILE** n aromatic plant, used to make herbal tea

**CAMOMILES** >CAMOMILE

**CAMOODI** a Caribbean name for >ANACONDA

**CAMOODIS** >CAMOODI

**CAMORRA** n secret criminal group

**CAMORRAS** >CAMORRA

**CAMORRIST** >CAMORRA

**CAMOS** >CAMO

**CAMOTE** n type of sweet potato

**CAMOTES** >CAMOTE

**CAMOUFLET** n type of bomb used in a seige to collapse an enemy's tunnel

**CAMP** vb stay in a camp ▷ adj effeminate or homosexual ▷ adj (place for) temporary lodgings consisting of tents, huts, or cabins

**CAMPAGNA** same as >CHAMPAIGN

**CAMPAGNAS** >CAMPAGNA

**CAMPAGNE** >CAMPAGNA

**CAMPAIGN** n series of coordinated activities designed to achieve a goal ▷ vb take part in a campaign

**CAMPAIGNS** >CAMPAIGN

**CAMPANA** n bell or bell shape

**CAMPANAS** >CAMPANA

**CAMPANERO** n South American bellbird

**CAMPANILE** n bell tower, usu. one not attached to another building

**CAMPANILI** >CAMPANILE

**CAMPANIST** n expert on bells

**CAMPANULA** n plant with blue or white bell-shaped flowers

**CAMPCRAFT** n skills required when camping

**CAMPEADOR** n champion; term applied especially to El Cid

**CAMPED** >CAMP

**CAMPER** n person who lives or temporarily stays in a tent, cabin, etc

**CAMPERS** >CAMPER

**CAMPESINO** n Latin American rural peasant

**CAMPEST** >CAMP

**CAMPFIRE** n outdoor fire in

a camp, esp one used for cooking or as a focal point for community events

**CAMPFIRES** >CAMPFIRE

**CAMPHANE** n one of the terpene hydrocarbons

**CAMPHANES** >CAMPHANE

**CAMPHENE** n colourless crystalline insoluble terpene

**CAMPHENES** >CAMPHENE

**CAMPHINE** n type of solvent

**CAMPHINES** >CAMPHINE

**CAMPHIRE** an archaic name for >HENNA

**CAMPHIRES** >CAMPHIRE

**CAMPHOL** another word for >BORNEOL

**CAMPHOLS** >CAMPHOL

**CAMPHOR** n aromatic crystalline substance used medicinally and in mothballs

**CAMPHORIC** >CAMPHOR

**CAMPHORS** >CAMPHOR

**CAMPI** >CAMPO

**CAMPIER** >CAMPY

**CAMPIEST** >CAMPY

**CAMPILY** >CAMPY

**CAMPINESS** >CAMPY

**CAMPING** >CAMP

**CAMPINGS** >CAMP

**CAMPION** n red, pink, or white wild flower

**CAMPIONS** >CAMPION

**CAMPLE** vb to argue

**CAMPLED** >CAMPLE

**CAMPLES** >CAMPLE

**CAMPLING** >CAMPLE

**CAMPLY** >CAMP

**CAMPNESS** >CAMP

**CAMPO** n level or undulating savanna country, esp in the uplands of Brazil

**CAMPODEID** n member of the Campodea genus of bristle-tails

**CAMPONG** n in Malaysia, a village

**CAMPONGS** >CAMPONG

**CAMPOREE** n local meeting or assembly of Scouts

**CAMPOREES** >CAMPOREE

**CAMPOS** >CAMPO

**CAMPOUT** n camping trip

**CAMPOUTS** >CAMPOUT

**CAMPS** >CAMP

**CAMPSHIRT** n short-sleeved shirt

**CAMPSITE** n area on which holiday makers may pitch a tent

**CAMPSITES** >CAMPSITE

**CAMPSTOOL** n folding stool

**CAMPUS** n grounds of a university or college ▷ vb to restrict a student to campus, as a punishment

**CAMPUSED** >CAMPUS

**CAMPUSES** >CAMPUS

**CAMPUSING** >CAMPUS

**CAMPY** adj effeminate

**CAMS** >CAM

**CAMSHAFT** n part of an

engine consisting of a rod to which cams are fixed

**CAMSHAFTS** >CAMSHAFT

**CAMSHO** *adj* crooked

**CAMSHOCH** *same as* >CAMSHO

**CAMSTAIRY** *adj* perverse

**CAMSTANE** *same as* >CAMSTONE

**CAMSTANES** >CAMSTONE

**CAMSTEARY** *same as* >CAMSTAIRY

**CAMSTONE** *n* a limestone used for whitening stone doorsteps

**CAMSTONES** >CAMSTONE

**CAMUS** *n* type of loose robe

**CAMUSES** >CAMUS

**CAMWOOD** *n* W African leguminous tree, *Baphia nitida*, whose hard wood was formerly used in making a red dye

**CAMWOODS** >CAMWOOD

**CAN** *vb* be able to ▷*n* metal container for food or liquids

**CANADA** *n* canada goose

**CANADAS** >CANADA

**CANAIGRE** *n* dock, *Rumex hymenosepalus*, of the southern US, the root of which yields a substance used in tanning

**CANAIGRES** >CANAIGRE

**CANAILLE** *n* masses or rabble

**CANAILLES** >CANAILLE

**CANAKIN** *same as* >CANNIKIN

**CANAKINS** >CANAKIN

**CANAL** *n* artificial waterway ▷*vb* dig a canal through

**CANALBOAT** *n* boat made for canals

**CANALED** >CANAL

**CANALING** >CANAL

**CANALISE** *same as* >CANALIZE

**CANALISED** >CANALIZE

**CANALISES** >CANALIZE

**CANALIZE** *vb* give direction to

**CANALIZED** >CANALIZE

**CANALIZES** >CANALIZE

**CANALLED** >CANAL

**CANALLER** *n* canal boat worker

**CANALLERS** >CANALLER

**CANALLING** >CANAL

**CANALS** >CANAL

**CANAPE** *n* small piece of bread or toast with a savoury topping

**CANAPES** >CANAPE

**CANARD** *n* false report

**CANARDS** >CANARD

**CANARIED** >CANARY

**CANARIES** >CANARY

**CANARY** *n* small yellow songbird often kept as a pet ▷*vb* perform a dance called the canary

**CANARYING** >CANARY

**CANASTA** *n* card game like rummy, played with two packs

**CANASTAS** >CANASTA

**CANASTER** *n* coarsely broken dried tobacco leaves

**CANASTERS** >CANASTER

**CANBANK** *n* container for receiving cans for recycling

**CANBANKS** >CANBANK

**CANCAN** *n* lively high-kicking dance performed by a female group

**CANCANS** >CANCAN

**CANCEL** *vb* stop (something that has been arranged) from taking place ▷*n* new leaf or section of a book replacing a defective one, one containing errors, or one that has been omitted

**CANCELED** >CANCEL

**CANCELEER** *vb* (of a hawk) to turn in flight when a stoop fails, in order to re-attempt it

**CANCELER** >CANCEL

**CANCELERS** >CANCEL

**CANCELIER** *a variant of* >CANCELEER

**CANCELING** >CANCEL

**CANCELLED** >CANCEL

**CANCELLER** >CANCEL

**CANCELLI** *n* any lattice-like structures

**CANCELS** >CANCEL

**CANCER** *n* serious disease resulting from a malignant growth or tumour

**CANCERATE** *vb* to become cancerous

**CANCERED** *adj* affected by cancer

**CANCEROUS** >CANCER

**CANCERS** >CANCER

**CANCHA** *n* toasted maize

**CANCHAS** >CANCHA

**CANCRINE** *adj* crab-like

**CANCROID** *adj* resembling a cancerous growth ▷*n* skin cancer, esp one of only moderate malignancy

**CANCROIDS** >CANCROID

**CANDELA** *n* unit of luminous intensity

**CANDELAS** >CANDELA

**CANDENT** *adj* emitting light as a result of being heated to a high temperature

**CANDID** *adj* honest and straightforward ▷*n* unposed photograph

**CANDIDA** *n* yeastlike parasitic fungus which causes thrush

**CANDIDACY** >CANDIDATE

**CANDIDAL** >CANDIDA

**CANDIDAS** >CANDIDA

**CANDIDATE** *n* person seeking a job or position

**CANDIDER** >CANDID

**CANDIDEST** >CANDID

**CANDIDLY** >CANDID

**CANDIDS** >CANDID

**CANDIE** *n* South Indian unit of weight

**CANDIED** *adj* coated with sugar

**CANDIES** >CANDY

**CANDLE** *n* stick of wax enclosing a wick, which is burned to produce light ▷*vb* test by holding up to a candle

**CANDLED** >CANDLE

**CANDLELIT** *adj* lit by the light of candles

**CANDLENUT** *n* euphorbiaceous tree, *Aleurites mollucana*, of tropical Asia and Polynesia

**CANDLEPIN** *n* bowling pin, as used in skittles, tenpin bowling, candlepins, etc

**CANDLER** >CANDLE

**CANDLERS** >CANDLE

**CANDLES** >CANDLE

**CANDLING** >CANDLE

**CANDOCK** *n* type of water lily, or horsetail

**CANDOCKS** >CANDOCK

**CANDOR** *same as* >CANDOUR

**CANDORS** >CANDOR

**CANDOUR** *n* honesty and straightforwardness

**CANDOURS** >CANDOUR

**CANDY** *n* sweet or sweets ▷*vb* make sweet

**CANDYGRAM** *n* message accompanied by sweets

**CANDYING** >CANDY

**CANDYTUFT** *n* garden plant with clusters of white, pink, or purple flowers

**CANE** *n* stem of the bamboo or similar plant ▷*vb* beat with a cane

**CANEBRAKE** *n* thicket of canes

**CANED** >CANE

**CANEFRUIT** *n* fruit, like the raspberry, which grows on woody-stemmed plants

**CANEH** *n* Hebrew unit of length

**CANEHS** >CANEH

**CANELLA** *n* fragrant cinnamon-like inner bark of a West Indian tree, *Canella winterana* (family *Canellaceae*) used as a spice and in medicine

**CANELLAS** >CANELLA

**CANELLINI** *n* white kidney bean

**CANEPHOR** *n* sculpted figure carrying a basket on its head

**CANEPHORA** *same as* >CANEPHOR

**CANEPHORE** *same as* >CANEPHOR

**CANEPHORS** >CANEPHOR

**CANER** >CANE

**CANERS** >CANE

**CANES** >CANE

**CANESCENT** *adj* white or greyish due to the presence of numerous short white hairs

**CANEWARE** *n* type of unglazed stoneware

**CANEWARES** >CANEWARE

**CANFIELD** *n* gambling game adapted from a type of patience

**CANFIELDS** >CANFIELD

**CANFUL** *n* amount a can will hold

**CANFULS** >CANFUL

**CANG** *same as* >CANGUE

**CANGLE** *vb* to wrangle

**CANGLED** >CANGLE

**CANGLES** >CANGLE

**CANGLING** >CANGLE

**CANGS** >CANG

**CANGUE** *n* (formerly in China) a large wooden collar worn by petty criminals as a punishment

**CANGUES** >CANGUE

**CANICULAR** *adj* of or relating to the star Sirius or its rising

**CANID** *n* animal of the dog family

**CANIDS** >CANID

**CANIER** >CANY

**CANIEST** >CANY

**CANIKIN** *same as* >CANNIKIN

**CANIKINS** >CANIKIN

**CANINE** *adj* of or like a dog ▷*n* sharp pointed tooth between the incisors and the molars

**CANINES** >CANINE

**CANING** *n* beating with a cane as a punishment

**CANINGS** >CANING

**CANINITY** >CANINE

**CANISTEL** *n* Caribbean fruit

**CANISTELS** >CANISTEL

**CANISTER** *n* metal container ▷*vb* to put into canisters

**CANISTERS** >CANISTER

**CANITIES** *n* grey hair

**CANKER** *n* ulceration, ulcerous disease ▷*vb* infect or become infected with or as if with canker

**CANKERED** >CANKER

**CANKERING** >CANKER

**CANKEROUS** *adj* having cankers

**CANKERS** >CANKER

**CANKERY** *adj* like a canker

**CANN** *vb* direct a ship's steering

**CANNA** *n* any of various tropical plants constituting the genus *Canna*, having broad leaves and red or yellow showy flowers for which they are cultivated: family *Cannaceae*

**CANNABIC** > CANNABIS
**CANNABIN** n greenish-black poisonous resin obtained from the Indian hemp plant
**CANNABINS** > CANNABIN
**CANNABIS** n Asian plant with tough fibres
**CANNACH** n cotton grass
**CANNACHS** > CANNACH
**CANNAE** vb can not
**CANNAS** > CANNA
**CANNED** > CAN
**CANNEL** n type of dull coal
**CANNELON** n type of meat loaf
**CANNELONI** pl n pasta in the shape of tubes, which are usually stuffed
**CANNELONS** > CANNELON
**CANNELS** > CANNEL
**CANNELURE** n groove or fluting, esp one around the cylindrical part of a bullet
**CANNER** n person or organization whose job is to can foods
**CANNERIES** > CANNERY
**CANNERS** > CANNER
**CANNERY** n factory where food is canned
**CANNIBAL** n person who eats human flesh
**CANNIBALS** > CANNIBAL
**CANNIE** same as > CANNY
**CANNIER** > CANNY
**CANNIEST** > CANNY
**CANNIKIN** n small can, esp one used as a drinking vessel
**CANNIKINS** > CANNIKIN
**CANNILY** > CANNY
**CANNINESS** > CANNY
**CANNING** > CAN
**CANNINGS** > CAN
**CANNISTER** same as > CANISTER
**CANNOLI** n Sicilian pudding of pasta shells filled with sweetened ricotta
**CANNOLIS** > CANNOLI
**CANNON** n gun of large calibre ▷ vb to collide (with)
**CANNONADE** n continuous heavy gunfire ▷ vb attack (a target) with cannon
**CANNONED** > CANNON
**CANNONEER** n (formerly) a soldier who served and fired a cannon
**CANNONIER** same as > CANNONEER
**CANNONING** > CANNON
**CANNONRY** n volley of artillery fire
**CANNONS** > CANNON
**CANNOT** vb can not
**CANNS** > CANN
**CANNULA** n narrow tube for insertion into a bodily cavity, as for draining off fluid, introducing

medication, etc
**CANNULAE** > CANNULA
**CANNULAR** adj shaped like a cannula
**CANNULAS** > CANNULA
**CANNULATE** vb insert a cannula into ▷ adj shaped like a cannula
**CANNY** adj shrewd, cautious ▷ adv quite
**CANOE** n light narrow open boat propelled by a paddle or paddles ▷ vb use a canoe
**CANOEABLE** > CANOE
**CANOED** > CANOE
**CANOEING** > CANOE
**CANOEINGS** > CANOE
**CANOEIST** > CANOE
**CANOEISTS** > CANOE
**CANOER** > CANOE
**CANOERS** > CANOE
**CANOES** > CANOE
**CANOEWOOD** n type of tree
**CANOLA** n cooking oil extracted from a variety of rapeseed developed in Canada
**CANOLAS** > CANOLA
**CANON** n priest serving in a cathedral
**CANONESS** n woman belonging to any one of several religious orders and living under a rule but not under a vow
**CANONIC** same as > CANONICAL
**CANONICAL** adj conforming with canon law
**CANONISE** same as > CANONIZE
**CANONISED** > CANONISE
**CANONISER** > CANONISE
**CANONISES** > CANONISE
**CANONIST** n specialist in canon law
**CANONISTS** > CANONIST
**CANONIZE** vb declare (a person) officially to be a saint
**CANONIZED** > CANONIZE
**CANONIZER** > CANONIZE
**CANONIZES** > CANONIZE
**CANONRIES** > CANONRY
**CANONRY** n office, benefice, or status of a canon
**CANONS** > CANON
**CANOODLE** vb kiss and cuddle
**CANOODLED** > CANOODLE
**CANOODLER** > CANOODLE
**CANOODLES** > CANOODLE
**CANOPIC** adj of ancient Egyptian vase
**CANOPIED** > CANOPY
**CANOPIES** > CANOPY
**CANOPY** n covering above a bed, door, etc ▷ vb cover with or as if with a canopy
**CANOPYING** > CANOPY
**CANOROUS** adj tuneful
**CANS** > CAN
**CANSFUL** > CANFUL

**CANSO** n love song
**CANSOS** > CANSO
**CANST** vb form of CAN used with the pronoun thou or its relative form
**CANSTICK** n candlestick
**CANSTICKS** > CANSTICK
**CANT** n insincere talk ▷ vb use cant ▷ adj oblique
**CANTABANK** n itinerant singer
**CANTABILE** adv flowing and melodious ▷ n piece or passage performed in this way
**CANTAL** n French cheese
**CANTALA** n tropical American plant, Agave cantala, similar to the century plant: family Agavaceae (agaves)
**CANTALAS** > CANTALA
**CANTALOUP** n type of melon
**CANTALS** > CANTAL
**CANTAR** variant form of > KANTAR
**CANTARS** > CANTAR
**CANTATA** n musical work consisting of arias, duets, and choruses
**CANTATAS** > CANTATA
**CANTATE** n 98th psalm sung as a nonmetrical hymn
**CANTATES** > CANTATE
**CANTDOG** same as > CANTHOOK
**CANTDOGS** > CANTDOG
**CANTED** > CANT
**CANTEEN** n restaurant attached to a workplace or school
**CANTEENS** > CANTEEN
**CANTER** vb move at gait between trot and gallop
**CANTERED** > CANTER
**CANTERING** > CANTER
**CANTERS** > CANTER
**CANTEST** > CANT
**CANTHAL** > CANTHUS
**CANTHARI** > CANTHARUS
**CANTHARID** n any beetle of the family Cantharidae, having a soft elongated body
**CANTHARIS** n singular of plural noun, cantharides: a diuretic and urogenital stimulant or irritant prepared from the dried bodies of Spanish fly (family Meloidae, not Cantharidae), once thought to be an aphrodisiac
**CANTHARUS** n large two-handled pottery cup
**CANTHI** > CANTHUS
**CANTHITIS** n inflammation of canthus
**CANTHOOK** n wooden pole with a hook used for handling logs
**CANTHOOKS** > CANTHOOK
**CANTHUS** n inner or outer

corner or angle of the eye, formed by the natural junction of the eyelids
**CANTIC** > CANT
**CANTICLE** n short hymn with words from the Bible
**CANTICLES** > CANTICLE
**CANTICO** vb to dance as part of an act of worship
**CANTICOED** > CANTICO
**CANTICOS** > CANTICO
**CANTICOY** same as > CANTICO
**CANTICOYS** > CANTICOY
**CANTICUM** n canticle
**CANTICUMS** > CANTICUM
**CANTIER** > CANTY
**CANTIEST** > CANTY
**CANTILENA** n smooth flowing style in the writing of vocal music
**CANTILY** > CANTY
**CANTINA** n bar or wine shop, esp in a Spanish-speaking country
**CANTINAS** > CANTINA
**CANTINESS** > CANTY
**CANTING** > CANT
**CANTINGLY** > CANT
**CANTINGS** > CANT
**CANTION** n song
**CANTIONS** > CANTION
**CANTLE** n back part of a saddle that slopes upwards ▷ vb to set up, or stand, on high
**CANTLED** > CANTLE
**CANTLES** > CANTLE
**CANTLET** n piece
**CANTLETS** > CANTLET
**CANTLING** > CANTLE
**CANTO** same as > CANTUS
**CANTON** n political division of a country, esp Switzerland ▷ vb divide into cantons
**CANTONAL** > CANTON
**CANTONED** > CANTON
**CANTONING** > CANTON
**CANTONISE** vb to divide into cantons
**CANTONIZE** same as > CANTONISE
**CANTONS** > CANTON
**CANTOR** n man employed to lead services in a synagogue
**CANTORIAL** adj of or relating to a precentor
**CANTORIS** adj (in antiphonal music) to be sung by the cantorial side of a choir
**CANTORS** > CANTOR
**CANTOS** > CANTO
**CANTRAIP** n witch's spell or charm
**CANTRAIPS** > CANTRAIP
**CANTRAP** same as > CANTRAIP
**CANTRAPS** > CANTRAP
**CANTRED** n district comprising a hundred villages

CANTREDS > CANTRED

CANTREF *same as* > CANTRED

CANTREFS > CANTRED

CANTRIP *n* magic spell ▷ *adj* (of an effect) produced by black magic

CANTRIPS > CANTRIP

CANTS > CANT

CANTUS *n* medieval form of church singing

CANTY *adj* lively

CANULA *same as* > CANNULA

CANULAE > CANULA

CANULAR *adj* shaped like a cannula

CANULAS > CANULA

CANULATE *same as* > CANNULATE

CANULATED > CANULATE

CANULATES > CANULATE

CANVAS *n* heavy coarse cloth used for sails and tents, and for oil painting ▷ *vb* to cover with, or be applied to, canvas

CANVASED > CANVAS

CANVASER > CANVAS

CANVASERS > CANVAS

CANVASES > CANVAS

CANVASING > CANVAS

CANVASS *vb* try to get votes or support (from) ▷ *n* canvassing

CANVASSED > CANVASS

CANVASSER > CANVASS

CANVASSES > CANVASS

CANY *adj* cane-like

CANYON *n* deep narrow valley

CANYONEER *n* canyon explorer

CANYONING *n* sport of going down a canyon river by any of various means

CANYONS > CANYON

CANZONA *n* type of 16th- or 17th-century contrapuntal music, usually for keyboard, lute, or instrumental ensemble

CANZONAS > CANZONA

CANZONE *n* Provençal or Italian lyric, often in praise of love or beauty

CANZONES > CANZONE

CANZONET *n* short, cheery, or lively Italian song

CANZONETS > CANZONET

CANZONI > CANZONE

CAP *n* soft close-fitting covering for the head ▷ *vb* cover or top with something

CAPA *n* type of Spanish cloak

CAPABLE *adj* having the ability (for)

CAPABLER > CAPABLE

CAPABLEST > CAPABLE

CAPABLY > CAPABLE

CAPACIOUS *adj* roomy

CAPACITOR *n* device for storing electrical charge

CAPACITY *n* ability to

contain, absorb, or hold ▷ *adj* of the maximum amount or number possible

CAPARISON *n* decorated covering for a horse or other animal, esp (formerly) for a warhorse ▷ *vb* put a caparison on

CAPAS > CAPA

CAPE *n* short cloak ▷ *vb* to cut and remove the hide of an animal

CAPED > CAPE

CAPELAN *another word for* > CAPELIN

CAPELANS > CAPELAN

CAPELET *n* small cape

CAPELETS > CAPELET

CAPELIN *n* small marine food fish, *Mallotus villosus*, occurring in northern and Arctic seas: family Osmeridae (smelts)

CAPELINE *n* cap-shaped bandage to cover the head or an amputation stump

CAPELINES > CAPELINE

CAPELINS > CAPELIN

CAPELLET *n* wen-like swelling on a horse

CAPELLETS > CAPELLET

CAPELLINE *same as* > CAPELINE

CAPELLINI *n* type of pasta

CAPER *n* high-spirited prank ▷ *vb* skip about

CAPERED > CAPER

CAPERER > CAPER

CAPERERS > CAPER

CAPERING > CAPER

CAPERS *pl n* pickled flower buds of a Mediterranean shrub used in sauces

CAPES > CAPE

CAPESKIN *n* soft leather obtained from the skins of a type of lamb or sheep having hairlike wool ▷ *adj* made of this leather

CAPESKINS > CAPESKIN

CAPEWORK *n* use of the cape by the matador in bullfighting

CAPEWORKS > CAPEWORK

CAPFUL *n* quantity held by a (usually bottle) cap

CAPFULS > CAPFUL

CAPH *n* letter of the Hebrew alphabet

CAPHS > CAPH

CAPI > CAPO

CAPIAS *n* (formerly) a writ directing a sheriff or other officer to arrest a named person

CAPIASES > CAPIAS

CAPILLARY *n* very fine blood vessel ▷ *adj* (of a tube) having a fine bore

CAPING > CAPE

CAPITA > CAPUT

CAPITAL *n* chief city of a country ▷ *adj* involving or

punishable by death

CAPITALLY *adv* in an excellent manner

CAPITALS > CAPITAL

CAPITAN *another name for* > HOGFISH

CAPITANI > CAPITANO

CAPITANO *n* chief; captain

CAPITANOS > CAPITANO

CAPITANS > CAPITAN

CAPITATE *adj* shaped like a head, as certain flowers or inflorescences

CAPITATED *adj* having fixed upper limit

CAPITAYN *n* captain

CAPITAYNS > CAPITAYN

CAPITELLA *n* plural form of singular: capitellum, an enlarged knoblike structure at the end of a bone that forms an articulation with another bone

CAPITOL *n* (in America) building housing the state legislature

CAPITOLS > CAPITOL

CAPITULA > CAPITULUM

CAPITULAR *adj* of or associated with a cathedral chapter ▷ *n* member of a cathedral chapter

CAPITULUM *n* racemose inflorescence in the form of a disc of sessile flowers, the youngest at the centre. It occurs in the daisy and related plants

CAPIZ *n* bivalve shell of a mollusc (*Placuna placenta*) found esp in the Philippines and having a smooth translucent shiny interior: used in jewellery, ornaments, lampshades, etc

CAPIZES > CAPIZ

CAPLE *n* horse

CAPLES > CAPLE

CAPLESS > CAP

CAPLET *n* medicinal tablet, usually oval in shape, coated in a soluble substance

CAPLETS > CAPLET

CAPLIN *same as* > CAPELIN

CAPLINS > CAPLIN

CAPMAKER > CAP

CAPMAKERS > CAP

CAPO *n* device fitted across the strings of a guitar or similar instrument so as to raise the pitch

CAPOCCHIA *n* fool

CAPOEIRA *n* combination of martial art and dance, which originated among African slaves in 19th-century Brazil

CAPOEIRAS > CAPOEIRA

CAPON *n* castrated cock fowl fattened for eating

CAPONATA *n* Sicilian antipasto relish

CAPONATAS > CAPONATA

CAPONIER *n* covered passageway built across a ditch as a military defence

CAPONIERE *same as* > CAPONIER

CAPONIERS > CAPONIER

CAPONISE *same as* > CAPONIZE

CAPONISED > CAPONISE

CAPONISES > CAPONISE

CAPONIZE *vb* make (a cock) into a capon

CAPONIZED > CAPONIZE

CAPONIZES > CAPONIZE

CAPONS > CAPON

CAPORAL *n* strong coarse dark tobacco

CAPORALS > CAPORAL

CAPOS > CAPO

CAPOT *n* winning of all the tricks by one player ▷ *vb* score a capot (against)

CAPOTASTO *same as* > CAPO

CAPOTE *n* long cloak or soldier's coat, usually with a hood

CAPOTES > CAPOTE

CAPOTS > CAPOT

CAPOTTED > CAPOT

CAPOTTING > CAPOT

CAPOUCH *same as* > CAPUCHE

CAPOUCHES > CAPOUCHE

CAPPED > CAP

CAPPER > CAP

CAPPERS > CAP

CAPPING > CAP

CAPPINGS > CAP

CAPRATE *n* any salt of capric acid

CAPRATES > CAPRATE

CAPRIC *adj* (of a type of acid) smelling of goats

CAPRICCI > CAPRICCIO

CAPRICCIO *n* lively piece composed freely and without adhering to the rules for any specific musical form

CAPRICE *same as* > CAPRICCIO

CAPRICES > CAPRICE

CAPRID *n* any member of the goat family

CAPRIDS > CAPRID

CAPRIFIED > CAPRIFY

CAPRIFIES > CAPRIFY

CAPRIFIG *n* wild variety of fig, *Ficus carica sylvestris*, of S Europe and SW Asia, used in the caprification of the edible fig

CAPRIFIGS > CAPRIFIG

CAPRIFOIL *variant of* > CAPRIFOLE

CAPRIFOLE *n* honeysuckle

CAPRIFORM *adj* goatlike

CAPRIFY *vb* induce figs to ripen

CAPRINE *adj* of or resembling a goat

CAPRIOLE *n* upward but

117

not forward leap made by a horse ▷ *vb* perform a capriole

**CAPRIOLED** > CAPRIOLE

**CAPRIOLES** > CAPRIOLE

**CAPRIS** *pl n* women's tight-fitting trousers

**CAPROATE** *n* any salt of caproic acid

**CAPROATES** > CAPROATE

**CAPROCK** *n* layer of rock that overlies a salt dome

**CAPROCKS** > CAPROCK

**CAPROIC** as in *caproic acid* oily acid found in milk

**CAPRYLATE** *n* any salt of caprylic acid

**CAPRYLIC** *variant of* > CAPRIC

**CAPS** > CAP

**CAPSAICIN** *n* colourless crystalline bitter alkaloid

**CAPSICIN** *n* liquid or resin extracted from capsicum

**CAPSICINS** > CAPSICIN

**CAPSICUM** *n* kind of pepper used as a vegetable or as a spice

**CAPSICUMS** > CAPSICUM

**CAPSID** *n* outer protein coat of a mature virus

**CAPSIDAL** > CAPSID

**CAPSIDS** > CAPSID

**CAPSIZAL** > CAPSIZE

**CAPSIZALS** > CAPSIZE

**CAPSIZE** *vb* (of a boat) overturn accidentally

**CAPSIZED** > CAPSIZE

**CAPSIZES** > CAPSIZE

**CAPSIZING** > CAPSIZE

**CAPSOMER** *n* one of the units making up a viral capsid

**CAPSOMERE** *n* any of the protein units that together form the capsid of a virus

**CAPSOMERS** > CAPSOMER

**CAPSTAN** *n* rotating cylinder round which a ship's rope is wound

**CAPSTANS** > CAPSTAN

**CAPSTONE** *n* one of a set of slabs on the top of a wall, building, etc

**CAPSTONES** > CAPSTONE

**CAPSULAR** *adj* relating to a capsule

**CAPSULARY** *same as* > CAPSULAR

**CAPSULATE** *adj* within or formed into a capsule

**CAPSULE** *n* soluble gelatine case containing a dose of medicine ▷ *adj* very concise ▷ *vb* to contain within a capsule

**CAPSULED** > CAPSULE

**CAPSULES** > CAPSULE

**CAPSULING** > CAPSULE

**CAPSULISE** *same as* > CAPSULIZE

**CAPSULIZE** *vb* state (information) in a highly condensed form

**CAPTAIN** *n* commander of a ship or civil aircraft ▷ *vb* be captain of

**CAPTAINCY** > CAPTAIN

**CAPTAINED** > CAPTAIN

**CAPTAINRY** *n* condition or skill of being a captain

**CAPTAINS** > CAPTAIN

**CAPTAN** *n* type of fungicide

**CAPTANS** > CAPTAN

**CAPTION** *n* title or explanation accompanying an illustration ▷ *vb* provide with a caption

**CAPTIONED** > CAPTION

**CAPTIONS** > CAPTION

**CAPTIOUS** *adj* tending to make trivial criticisms

**CAPTIVATE** *vb* attract and hold the attention of

**CAPTIVE** *n* person kept in confinement ▷ *adj* kept in confinement ▷ *vb* to take prisoner

**CAPTIVED** > CAPTIVE

**CAPTIVES** > CAPTIVE

**CAPTIVING** > CAPTIVE

**CAPTIVITY** *n* state of being kept in confinement

**CAPTOPRIL** *n* drug used to treat high blood pressure and congestive heart failure

**CAPTOR** *n* person who captures a person or animal

**CAPTORS** > CAPTOR

**CAPTURE** *vb* take by force ▷ *n* capturing

**CAPTURED** > CAPTURE

**CAPTURER** > CAPTURE

**CAPTURERS** > CAPTURE

**CAPTURES** > CAPTURE

**CAPTURING** > CAPTURE

**CAPUCCIO** *n* hood

**CAPUCCIOS** > CAPUCCIO

**CAPUCHE** *n* large hood or cowl, esp that worn by Capuchin friars

**CAPUCHED** *adj* hooded

**CAPUCHES** > CAPUCHE

**CAPUCHIN** *n* S American monkey with thick hair on the top of its head

**CAPUCHINS** > CAPUCHIN

**CAPUERA** *variant of* > CAPOEIRA

**CAPUERAS** > CAPUERA

**CAPUL** *same as* > CAPLE

**CAPULS** > CAPUL

**CAPUT** *n* main or most prominent part of an organ or structure

**CAPYBARA** *n* very large S American rodent

**CAPYBARAS** > CAPYBARA

**CAR** *n* motor vehicle designed to carry a small number of people

**CARABAO** *n* water buffalo

**CARABAOS** > CARABAO

**CARABID** *n* any typically

dark-coloured beetle of the family *Carabidae*, including the bombardier and other ground beetles. ▷ *adj* of, relating to, or belonging to the *Carabidae*

**CARABIDS** > CARABID

**CARABIN** *same as* > CARBINE

**CARABINE** *same as* > CARBINE

**CARABINER** *a variant spelling of* > KARABINER

**CARABINES** > CARABINE

**CARABINS** > CARABIN

**CARACAL** *n* lynx with reddish fur, which inhabits deserts of N Africa and S Asia

**CARACALS** > CARACAL

**CARACARA** *n* any of various large carrion-eating diurnal birds of prey of the genera *Caracara, Polyborus*, etc, of S North, Central, and South America, having long legs and naked faces: family *Falconidae* (falcons)

**CARACARAS** > CARACARA

**CARACK** *same as* > CARRACK

**CARACKS** > CARACK

**CARACOL** *same as* > CARACOLE

**CARACOLE** *n* half turn to the right or left ▷ *vb* execute a half turn to the right or left

**CARACOLED** > CARACOLE

**CARACOLER** > CARACOLE

**CARACOLES** > CARACOLE

**CARACOLS** > CARACOL

**CARACT** *n* sign or symbol

**CARACTS** > CARACT

**CARACUL** *n* black loosely curled fur obtained from the skins of newly born lambs of the karakul sheep

**CARACULS** > CARACUL

**CARAFE** *n* glass bottle for serving water or wine

**CARAFES** > CARAFE

**CARAGANA** *n* pea tree

**CARAGANAS** > CARAGANA

**CARAGEEN** *same as* > CARRAGEEN

**CARAGEENS** > CARAGEEN

**CARAMBA** *n* Spanish interjection similar to 'wow!'

**CARAMBOLA** *n* yellow edible star-shaped fruit that grows on a Brazilian tree

**CARAMBOLE** *vb* make a carom or carambola (shot in billiards)

**CARAMEL** *n* chewy sweet made from sugar and milk ▷ *vb* to turn into caramel

**CARAMELS** > CARAMEL

**CARANGID** *n* any marine percoid fish of the family *Carangidae*, having a compressed body and deeply forked tail. The group includes the jacks, horse mackerel, pompano,

and pilot fish ▷ *adj* of, relating to, or belonging to the *Carangidae*

**CARANGIDS** > CARANGID

**CARANGOID** *same as* > CARANGID

**CARANNA** *n* gumlike substance

**CARANNAS** > CARANNA

**CARAP** *n* crabwood

**CARAPACE** *n* hard upper shell of tortoises and crustaceans

**CARAPACED** *adj* having carapace

**CARAPACES** > CARAPACE

**CARAPAX** *n* carapace

**CARAPAXES** > CARAPAX

**CARAPS** > CARAP

**CARASSOW** *same as* > CURASSOW

**CARASSOWS** > CARASSOW

**CARAT** *n* unit of weight of precious stones

**CARATE** *n* tropical disease

**CARATES** > CARATE

**CARATS** > CARAT

**CARAUNA** *same as* > CARANNA

**CARAUNAS** > CARAUNA

**CARAVAN** *n* large enclosed vehicle for living in, designed to be towed by a car or horse ▷ *vb* travel or have a holiday in a caravan

**CARAVANCE** *same as* > CALAVANCE

**CARAVANED** > CARAVAN

**CARAVANER** *n* person who holidays in a caravan

**CARAVANS** > CARAVAN

**CARAVEL** *n* two- or three-masted sailing ship, esp one with a broad beam, high poop deck, and lateen rig that was used by the Spanish and Portuguese in the 15th and 16th centuries

**CARAVELLE** *variant of* > CARAVEL

**CARAVELS** > CARAVEL

**CARAWAY** *n* plant whose seeds are used as a spice

**CARAWAYS** > CARAWAY

**CARB** *n* carbohydrate

**CARBACHOL** *n* carbamylcholine, a cholinergic agent

**CARBAMATE** *n* salt or ester of carbamic acid

**CARBAMIC** as in *carbamic acid* hypothetical compound known only in carbamate salts

**CARBAMIDE** *another name for* > UREA

**CARBAMINO** *adj* relating to the compound produced when carbon dioxide reacts with an amino group

**CARBAMOYL** *same as* > CARBAMYL

**CARBAMYL** *n* radical from carbamic acid

**CARBAMYLS** >CARBAMYL

**CARBANION** *n* negatively charged organic ion in which most of the negative charge is localized on a carbon atom

**CARBARN** *n* streetcar depot

**CARBARNS** >CARBARN

**CARBARYL** *n* organic compound of the carbamate group

**CARBARYLS** >CARBARYL

**CARBAZOLE** *n* colourless insoluble solid obtained from coal tar

**CARBEEN** *n* Australian eucalyptus tree, *E. tessellaris*, having drooping branches and grey bark

**CARBEENS** >CARBEEN

**CARBENE** *n* neutral divalent free radical, such as methylene: $CH_2$

**CARBENES** >CARBENE

**CARBIDE** *n* compound of carbon with a metal

**CARBIDES** >CARBIDE

**CARBIES** >CARBY

**CARBINE** *n* light automatic rifle

**CARBINEER** *n* (formerly) a soldier equipped with a carbine

**CARBINES** >CARBINE

**CARBINIER** *same as* >CARBINEER

**CARBINOL** *another word for* >CARABINOL

**CARBINOLS** >CARBINOL

**CARBO** *n* carbohydrate

**CARBOLIC** as in *carbolic acid* phenol, when it is used as a disinfectant

**CARBOLICS** >CARBOLIC

**CARBOLISE** *same as* >CARBOLIZE

**CARBOLIZE** *another word for* >PHENOLATE

**CARBON** *n* nonmetallic element occurring as charcoal, graphite, and diamond, found in all organic matter

**CARBONADE** *n* stew of beef and onions cooked in beer

**CARBONADO** *n* piece of meat, fish, etc, scored and grilled ▷ *vb* score and grill (meat, fish, etc)

**CARBONARA** *n* pasta sauce containing cream, bacon and cheese

**CARBONATE** *n* salt or ester of carbonic acid ▷ *vb* form or turn into a carbonate

**CARBONIC** *adj* containing carbon

**CARBONISE** *same as* >CARBONIZE

**CARBONIUM** as in *carbonium ion* type of positively charged organic ion

**CARBONIZE** *vb* turn into carbon as a result of

heating

**CARBONOUS** >CARBON

**CARBONS** >CARBON

**CARBONYL** *n* of, consisting of, or containing the divalent group =CO

**CARBONYLS** >CARBONYL

**CARBORA** *n* former name for the koala

**CARBORAS** >CARBORA

**CARBOS** >CARBO

**CARBOXYL** as in *carboxyl group* functional group in organic acids

**CARBOXYLS** >CARBOXYL

**CARBOY** *n* large bottle with a protective casing

**CARBOYED** >CARBOY

**CARBOYS** >CARBOY

**CARBS** >CARB

**CARBUNCLE** *n* inflamed boil

**CARBURATE** *same as* >CARBURET

**CARBURET** *vb* combine or mix (a gas) with carbon or carbon compounds ▷ *vb* to combine with carbon

**CARBURETS** >CARBURET

**CARBURISE** *same as* >CARBONIZE

**CARBURIZE** *same as* >CARBONIZE

**CARBY** *n* short for carburettor

**CARCAJOU** *a North American name for* >WOLVERINE

**CARCAJOUS** >CARCAJOU

**CARCAKE** *n* (formerly, in Scotland) a cake traditionally made for Shrove Tuesday

**CARCAKES** >CARCAKE

**CARCANET** *n* jewelled collar or necklace

**CARCANETS** >CARCANET

**CARCASE** *same as* >CARCASS *vb* to make a carcase of

**CARCASED** >CARCASE

**CARCASES** >CARCASE

**CARCASING** >CARCASE

**CARCASS** *n* dead body of an animal ▷ *vb* to make a carcass of

**CARCASSED** >CARCASS

**CARCASSES** >CARCASS

**CARCEL** *n* French unit of light

**CARCELS** >CARCEL

**CARCERAL** *adj* relating to prison

**CARCINOID** *n* small serotonin-secreting tumour

**CARCINOMA** *n* malignant tumour

**CARD** *n* piece of thick stiff paper or cardboard used for identification, reference, or sending greetings or messages ▷ *vb* comb out fibres of wool or cotton before spinning

**CARDAMINE** *n* bittercress

**CARDAMOM** *n* spice obtained from the seeds of a tropical plant

**CARDAMOMS** >CARDAMOM

**CARDAMON** *same as* >CARDAMOM

**CARDAMONS** >CARDAMON

**CARDAMUM** *same as* >CARDAMOM

**CARDAMUMS** >CARDAMUM

**CARDAN** as in *cardan joint* type of universal joint

**CARDBOARD** *n* thin stiff board made from paper pulp ▷ *adj* without substance

**CARDCASE** *n* small case for holding business cards

**CARDCASES** >CARDCASE

**CARDECU** *n* old French coin (a quarter of a crown)

**CARDECUE** *same as* >CARDECU

**CARDECUES** >CARDECUE

**CARDECUS** >CARDECU

**CARDED** >CARD

**CARDER** >CARD

**CARDERS** >CARD

**CARDI** *n* cardigan

**CARDIA** *n* lower oesophageal sphincter

**CARDIAC** *adj* of the heart ▷ *n* person with a heart disorder

**CARDIACAL** >CARDIAC

**CARDIACS** >CARDIAC

**CARDIAE** >CARDIA

**CARDIALGY** *n* pain in or near the heart

**CARDIAS** >CARDIA

**CARDIE** *short for* >CARDIGAN

**CARDIES** >CARDIE

**CARDIGAN** *n* knitted jacket

**CARDIGANS** >CARDIGAN

**CARDINAL** *n* any of the high-ranking clergymen of the RC Church who elect the Pope and act as his counsellors ▷ *adj* fundamentally important

**CARDINALS** >CARDINAL

**CARDING** >CARD

**CARDINGS** >CARD

**CARDIO** *adj* exercising heart

**CARDIOID** *n* heart-shaped curve generated by a fixed point on a circle as it rolls around another fixed circle of equal radius, *a*. Equation: $r = a(1 - \cos \_Gphi\_)$, where $r$ is the radius vector and $\_Gphi\_$ is the polar angle.

**CARDIOIDS** >CARDIOID

**CARDIS** >CARDI

**CARDITIC** >CARDITIS

**CARDITIS** *n* inflammation of the heart

**CARDON** *n* variety of cactus

**CARDONS** >CARDON

**CARDOON** *n* thistle-like S European plant, *Cynara cardunculus*, closely

related to the artichoke, with spiny leaves, purple flowers, and a leafstalk that may be blanched and eaten: family *Asteraceae* (composites)

**CARDOONS** >CARDOON

**CARDPHONE** *n* public telephone operated by the insertion of a phonecard instead of coins

**CARDPUNCH** *n* device for putting data from a CPU onto punched cards

**CARDS** >CARD

**CARDSHARP** *n* professional card player who cheats

**CARDUUS** *n* thistle

**CARDUUSES** >CARDUUS

**CARDY** *same as* >CARDIE

**CARE** *vb* be concerned ▷ *n* careful attention, caution

**CARED** >CARE

**CAREEN** *vb* tilt over to one side

**CAREENAGE** >CAREEN

**CAREENED** >CAREEN

**CAREENER** >CAREEN

**CAREENERS** >CAREEN

**CAREENING** >CAREEN

**CAREENS** >CAREEN

**CAREER** *n* series of jobs in a profession or occupation that a person has through their life ▷ *vb* rush in an uncontrolled way ▷ *adj* having chosen to dedicate his or her life to a particular occupation

**CAREERED** >CAREER

**CAREERER** >CAREER

**CAREERERS** >CAREER

**CAREERING** >CAREER

**CAREERISM** >CAREERIST

**CAREERIST** *n* person who seeks advancement by any possible means

**CAREERS** >CAREER

**CAREFREE** *adj* without worry or responsibility

**CAREFUL** *adj* cautious in attitude or action

**CAREFULLY** >CAREFUL

**CAREGIVER** *same as* >CARER

**CARELESS** *adj* done or acting with insufficient attention

**CARELINE** *n* telephone service set up by a company or other organization to provide its customers or clients with information about its products or services

**CARELINES** >CARELINE

**CAREME** *n* period of Lent

**CAREMES** >CAREME

**CARER** *n* person who looks after someone who is ill or old, often a relative

**CARERS** >CARER

**CARES** >CARE

**CARESS** *n* gentle affectionate touch or

embrace ▷ vb touch gently and affectionately

CARESSED > CARESS

CARESSER > CARESS

CARESSERS > CARESS

CARESSES > CARESS

CARESSING > CARESS

CARESSIVE adj caressing

CARET n symbol indicating a place in written or printed matter where something is to be inserted

CARETAKE vb to work as a caretaker

CARETAKEN > CARETAKE

CARETAKER n person employed to look after a place ▷ adj performing the duties of an office temporarily

CARETAKES > CARETAKE

CARETOOK > CARETAKE

CARETS > CARET

CAREWORN adj showing signs of worry

CAREX n any member of the sedge family

CARFARE n fare that a passenger is charged for a ride on a bus, etc

CARFARES > CARFARE

CARFAX n place where principal roads or streets intersect, esp a place in a town where four roads meet

CARFAXES > CARFAX

CARFOX same as > CARFAX

CARFOXES > CARFOX

CARFUFFLE a variant spelling of > KERFUFFLE

CARFUL n maximum number of people a car will hold

CARFULS > CARFUL

CARGEESE > CARGOOSE

CARGO n goods carried by a ship, aircraft, etc ▷ vb to load

CARGOED > CARGO

CARGOES > CARGO

CARGOING > CARGO

CARGOOSE n crested grebe

CARGOS > CARGO

CARHOP n waiter or waitress at a drive-in restaurant ▷ vb work as a carhop

CARHOPPED > CARHOP

CARHOPS > CARHOP

CARIACOU n type of deer

CARIACOUS > CARIACOU

CARIAMA another word for > SERIEMA

CARIAMAS > CARIAMA

CARIBE n piranha

CARIBES > CARIBE

CARIBOU n large N American reindeer

CARIBOUS > CARIBOU

CARICES > CAREX

CARIED adj (of teeth) decayed

CARIERE obsolete word for > CAREER

CARIERES > CARIERE

CARIES n tooth decay

CARILLON n set of bells played by keyboard or mechanically ▷ vb play a carillon

CARILLONS > CARILLON

CARINA n keel-like part or ridge, as in the breastbone of birds or the fused lower petals of a leguminous flower

CARINAE > CARINA

CARINAL adj keel-like

CARINAS > CARINA

CARINATE adj having a keel or ridge

CARINATED same as > CARINATE

CARING adj feeling or showing care and compassion for other people ▷ n practice or profession of providing social or medical care

CARIOCA n Brazilian dance similar to the samba

CARIOCAS > CARIOCA

CARIOLE n small open two-wheeled horse-drawn vehicle

CARIOLES > CARIOLE

CARIOSE same as > CARIOUS

CARIOSITY > CARIOUS

CARIOUS adj (of teeth or bone) affected with caries

CARITAS n divine love; charity

CARITASES > CARITAS

CARITATES > CARITAS

CARJACK vb attack (a car driver) to rob them or to steal the car ▷ vb to steal a car, by force, from a person who is present

CARJACKED > CARJACK

CARJACKER > CARJACK

CARJACKS > CARJACK

CARJACOU variation of > CARIACOU

CARJACOUS > CARJACOU

CARK vb break down

CARKED > CARK

CARKING > CARK

CARKS > CARK

CARL another word for > CHURL

CARLE same as > CARL

CARLES > CARLE

CARLESS > CAR

CARLIN same as > CARLING

CARLINE same as > CARLING

CARLINES > CARLINE

CARLING n fore-and-aft beam in a vessel, used for supporting the deck, esp around a hatchway or other opening

CARLINGS > CARLING

CARLINS > CARLIN

CARLISH adj churlish

CARLOAD n amount that can be carried by a car

CARLOADS > CARLOAD

CARLOCK n type of Russian isinglass

CARLOCKS > CARLOCK

CARLOT n boor

CARLOTS > CARLOT

CARLS > CARL

CARMAKER n car manufacturing company

CARMAKERS > CARMAKER

CARMAN n man who drives a car or cart

CARMELITE n member of an order of mendicant friars

CARMEN > CARMAN

CARMINE adj vivid red ▷ n vivid red colour, sometimes with a purplish tinge

CARMINES > CARMINE

CARN n cairn

CARNAGE n extensive slaughter of people

CARNAGES > CARNAGE

CARNAHUBA same as > CARNAUBA

CARNAL adj of a sexual or sensual nature ▷ vb act in a carnal manner

CARNALISE vb to sensualise

CARNALISM > CARNALISE

CARNALIST > CARNALISE

CARNALITY > CARNAL

CARNALIZE same as > CARNALISE

CARNALLED > CARNAL

CARNALLY > CARNAL

CARNALS > CARNAL

CARNAROLI n variety of short-grain rice used for risotto

CARNATION n cultivated plant with fragrant white, pink, or red flowers

CARNAUBA n Brazilian fan palm, Copernicia cerifera

CARNAUBAS > CARNAUBA

CARNELIAN n reddish-yellow gemstone

CARNEOUS adj fleshy

CARNET n customs licence permitting motorists to take their cars across certain frontiers

CARNETS > CARNET

CARNEY same as > CARNY

CARNEYED > CARNEY

CARNEYING > CARNEY

CARNEYS > CARNEY

CARNIE same as > CARNY

CARNIED > CARNY

CARNIER > CARNY

CARNIES > CARNY

CARNIEST > CARNY

CARNIFEX n executioner

CARNIFIED > CARNIFY

CARNIFIES > CARNIFY

CARNIFY vb (esp of lung tissue, as the result of pneumonia) to be altered so as to resemble skeletal muscle

CARNITINE n type of white betaine

CARNIVAL n festive period with processions, music, and dancing in the street

CARNIVALS > CARNIVAL

CARNIVORA n members of a group of carnivorous mammals

CARNIVORE n meat-eating animal

CARNIVORY n state of being carnivore

CARNOSAUR n meat-eating dinosaur

CARNOSE adj fleshy

CARNOSITY n fleshy protrusion

CARNOTITE n radioactive yellow mineral

CARNS > CARN

CARNY vb coax or cajole or act in a wheedling manner ▷ n person who works in a carnival ▷ adj sly

CARNYING > CARNY

CAROACH same as > CAROCHE

CAROACHES > CAROACH

CAROB n pod of a Mediterranean tree, used as a chocolate substitute

CAROBS > CAROB

CAROCH same as > CAROCHE

CAROCHE n stately ceremonial carriage used in the 16th and 17th centuries

CAROCHES > CAROCHE

CAROL n joyful Christmas hymn ▷ vb sing carols

CAROLED > CAROL

CAROLER > CAROL

CAROLERS > CAROL

CAROLI > CAROLUS

CAROLING > CAROL

CAROLINGS > CAROL

CAROLLED > CAROL

CAROLLER > CAROL

CAROLLERS > CAROL

CAROLLING > CAROL

CAROLS > CAROL

CAROLUS n any of several coins struck in the reign of a king called Charles, esp an English gold coin from the reign of Charles I

CAROLUSES > CAROLUS

CAROM n shot in which the cue ball is caused to contact one object ball after another ▷ vb to carambole

CAROMED > CAROM

CAROMEL vb to turn into caramel

CAROMELS > CAROMEL

CAROMING > CAROM

CAROMS > CAROM

CAROTENE n any of four orange-red hydrocarbons, found in many plants, converted to vitamin A in the liver

**CAROTENES** > CAROTENE
**CAROTID** *n* either of the two arteries supplying blood to the head ▷ *adj* of either of these arteries
**CAROTIDAL** > CAROTID
**CAROTIDS** > CAROTID
**CAROTIN** *same as* > CAROTENE
**CAROTINS** > CAROTIN
**CAROUSAL** *n* merry drinking party
**CAROUSALS** > CAROUSAL
**CAROUSE** *vb* have a merry drinking party
**CAROUSED** > CAROUSE
**CAROUSEL** *n* revolving conveyor belt for luggage or photographic slides
**CAROUSELS** > CAROUSEL
**CAROUSER** > CAROUSE
**CAROUSERS** > CAROUSE
**CAROUSES** > CAROUSE
**CAROUSING** > CAROUSE
**CARP** *n* large freshwater fish ▷ *vb* complain, find fault
**CARPACCIO** *n* Italian dish of thin slices of raw meat or fish
**CARPAL** *n* wrist bone
**CARPALE** *same as* > CARPAL
**CARPALES** > CARPAL
**CARPALIA** > CARPAL
**CARPALS** > CARPAL
**CARPARK** *n* area or building reserved for parking cars
**CARPARKS** > CARPARK
**CARPED** > CARP
**CARPEL** *n* female reproductive organ of a flowering plant
**CARPELS** > CARPEL
**CARPENTER** *n* person who makes or repairs wooden structures ▷ *vb* do the work of a carpenter
**CARPENTRY** *n* skill or work of a carpenter
**CARPER** > CARP
**CARPERS** > CARP
**CARPET** *n* heavy fabric for covering floors ▷ *vb* cover with a carpet
**CARPETBAG** *n* travelling bag made of carpeting
**CARPETED** > CARPET
**CARPETING** *n* carpet material or carpets in general
**CARPETS** > CARPET
**CARPI** > CARPUS
**CARPING** *adj* tending to make petty complaints ▷ *n* petty complaint
**CARPINGLY** > CARPING
**CARPINGS** > CARPING
**CARPOLOGY** *n* branch of botany concerned with the study of fruits and seeds
**CARPOOL** *vb* (of a group of people) to share the use of a single car to travel to

work or school
**CARPOOLED** > CARPOOL
**CARPOOLER** > CARPOOL
**CARPOOLS** > CARPOOL
**CARPORT** *n* shelter for a car, consisting of a roof supported by posts
**CARPORTS** > CARPORT
**CARPS** > CARP
**CARPUS** *n* set of eight bones of the wrist
**CARR** *n* area of bog or fen in which scrub, esp willow, has become established
**CARRACK** *n* galleon sailed in the Mediterranean as a merchantman in the 15th and 16th centuries
**CARRACKS** > CARRACK
**CARRACT** *same as* > CARRACK
**CARRACTS** > CARRACT
**CARRAGEEN** *n* edible red seaweed of North America and N Europe
**CARRAT** *same as* > CARAT
**CARRATS** > CARRAT
**CARRAWAY** *same as* > CARAWAY
**CARRAWAYS** > CARRAWAY
**CARRECT** *same as* > CARRACK
**CARRECTS** > CARRECT
**CARREFOUR** *n* public square, esp one at the intersection of several roads
**CARREL** *n* small individual study room or private desk, often in a library, where a student or researcher can work undisturbed
**CARRELL** *same as* > CARREL
**CARRELLS** > CARRELL
**CARRELS** > CARREL
**CARRIAGE** *n* one of the sections of a train for passengers
**CARRIAGES** > CARRIAGE
**CARRICK** as in *carrick bend* type of knot
**CARRIED** > CARRY
**CARRIER** *n* person or thing that carries something
**CARRIERS** > CARRIER
**CARRIES** > CARRY
**CARRIOLE** *same as* > CARIOLE
**CARRIOLES** > CARRIOLE
**CARRION** *n* dead and rotting flesh
**CARRIONS** > CARRION
**CARRITCH** *n* catechism
**CARROCH** *variant of* > CAROCHE
**CARROCHES** > CAROM
**CARROM** *same as* > CAROM
**CARROMED** > CARROM
**CARROMING** > CARROM
**CARROMS** > CARROM
**CARRON** as in *carron oil* ointment of limewater and linseed oil
**CARRONADE** *n* obsolete naval gun of short barrel

and large bore
**CARROT** *n* long tapering orange root vegetable
**CARROTIER** > CARROTY
**CARROTIN** *n* carotene
**CARROTINS** > CARROTIN
**CARROTS** > CARROT
**CARROTTOP** *n* facetious term for a person with red hair
**CARROTY** *adj* (of hair) reddish-orange
**CARROUSEL** *a variant spelling of* > CAROUSEL
**CARRS** > CARR
**CARRY** *vb* take from one place to another
**CARRYALL** *n* light four-wheeled horse-drawn carriage usually designed to carry four passengers
**CARRYALLS** > CARRYALL
**CARRYBACK** *n* amount carried back in accounting
**CARRYCOT** *n* light portable bed for a baby, with handles and a hood
**CARRYCOTS** > CARRYCOT
**CARRYING** > CARRY
**CARRYON** *n* fuss or commotion
**CARRYONS** > CARRYON
**CARRYOUT** *n* hot cooked food bought in a shop for consumption elsewhere
**CARRYOUTS** > CARRYOUT
**CARRYOVER** *n* sum or balance carried forward in accounting
**CARRYTALE** *n* gossip
**CARS** > CAR
**CARSE** *n* riverside area of flat fertile alluvium
**CARSES** > CARSE
**CARSEY** *slang word for* > TOILET
**CARSEYS** > CARSEY
**CARSICK** *adj* nauseated from riding in a car
**CART** *n* open two-wheeled horse-drawn vehicle for carrying goods or passengers ▷ *vb* carry, usu. with some effort
**CARTA** *n* charter
**CARTABLE** > CART
**CARTAGE** *n* process or cost of carting
**CARTAGES** > CARTAGE
**CARTAS** > CARTA
**CARTE** *n* fencing position
**CARTED** > CART
**CARTEL** *n* association of competing firms formed to fix prices
**CARTELISE** *same as* > CARTELIZE
**CARTELISM** > CARTEL
**CARTELIST** > CARTEL
**CARTELIZE** *vb* form or be formed into a cartel
**CARTELS** > CARTEL
**CARTER** > CART
**CARTERS** > CART

**CARTES** > CARTE
**CARTFUL** *n* amount a cart can hold
**CARTFULS** > CARTFUL
**CARTHORSE** *n* large heavily built horse
**CARTILAGE** *n* strong flexible tissue forming part of the skeleton
**CARTING** > CART
**CARTLOAD** *n* amount a cart can hold
**CARTLOADS** > CARTLOAD
**CARTOGRAM** *n* map showing statistical information in diagrammatic form
**CARTOLOGY** *n* theory of mapmaking
**CARTON** *n* container made of cardboard or waxed paper ▷ *vb* enclose (goods) in a carton
**CARTONAGE** *n* material from which mummy masks and coffins were made
**CARTONED** > CARTON
**CARTONING** > CARTON
**CARTONS** > CARTON
**CARTOON** *n* humorous or satirical drawing ▷ *vb* to depict in a cartoon
**CARTOONED** > CARTOON
**CARTOONS** > CARTOON
**CARTOONY** > CARTOON
**CARTOP** *adj* designed to be transported on top of a vehicle
**CARTOPPER** *n* anything designed to be transported on top of a vehicle
**CARTOUCH** *same as* > CARTOUCHE
**CARTOUCHE** *n* ornamental tablet or panel in the form of a scroll
**CARTRIDGE** *n* casing containing an explosive charge and bullet for a gun
**CARTROAD** *n* road for carts to drive on
**CARTROADS** > CARTROAD
**CARTS** > CART
**CARTULARY** *n* collection of charters or records, esp relating to the title to an estate or monastery
**CARTWAY** *n* way by which carts travel
**CARTWAYS** > CARTWAY
**CARTWHEEL** *n* sideways somersault supported by the hands with legs outstretched ▷ *vb* to perform a cartwheel movement
**CARUCAGE** *n* tax due on a carucate
**CARUCAGES** > CARUCAGE
**CARUCATE** *n* area of land an oxen team could plough in a year
**CARUCATES** > CARUCATE

CARUNCLE n fleshy outgrowth on the heads of certain birds, such as a cock's comb

CARUNCLES > CARUNCLE

CARVACROL n aromatic phenol found in oregano

CARVE vb cut to form an object

CARVED > CARVE

CARVEL same as > CARAVEL

CARVELS > CARVEL

CARVEN an archaic or literary past participle of > CARVE

CARVER n carving knife

CARVERIES > CARVERY

CARVERS > CARVER

CARVERY n restaurant where customers pay a set price for unrestricted helpings of carved meat and other food

CARVES > CARVE

CARVIES > CARVY

CARVING n figure or design produced by carving stone or wood

CARVINGS > CARVING

CARVY n caraway seed

CARWASH n drive-through structure containing automated equipment for washing cars

CARWASHES > CARWASH

CARYATIC same as > CARYATID

CARYATID n supporting column in the shape of a female figure

CARYATIDS > CARYATID

CARYOPSES > CARYOPSIS

CARYOPSIS n dry seedlike fruit having the pericarp fused to the seed coat of the single seed: produced by the grasses

CARYOTIN variant of > KARYOTIN

CARYOTINS > CARYOTIN

CASA n house

CASABA n kind of winter muskmelon having a yellow rind and sweet juicy flesh

CASABAS > CASABA

CASAS > CASA

CASAVA same as > CASSAVA

CASAVAS > CASAVA

CASBAH n citadel of a N African city

CASBAHS > CASBAH

CASCABEL n knoblike protrusion on the rear part of the breech of an obsolete muzzle-loading cannon

CASCABELS > CASCABEL

CASCABLE same as > CASCABEL

CASCABLES > CASCABLE

CASCADE n waterfall ▷ vb flow or fall in a cascade

CASCADED > CASCADE

CASCADES > CASCADE

CASCADING > CASCADE

CASCADURA n Trinidadian fish

CASCARA n bark of a N American shrub, used as a laxative

CASCARAS > CASCARA

CASCHROM n wooden hand-plough

CASCHROMS > CASCHROM

CASCO n Argentinian homestead

CASCOS > CASCO

CASE n instance, example ▷ vb inspect (a building) with the intention of burgling it

CASEASE n proteolytic enzyme formed by certain bacteria that activates the solution of albumin and casein in milk and cheese

CASEASES > CASEASE

CASEATE vb undergo caseation

CASEATED > CASEATE

CASEATES > CASEATE

CASEATING > CASEATE

CASEATION n formation of cheese from casein during the coagulation of milk

CASEBOOK n book in which records of legal or medical cases are kept

CASEBOOKS > CASEBOOK

CASEBOUND another word for > HARDBACK

CASED > CASE

CASEFIED > CASEFY

CASEFIES > CASEFY

CASEFY vb make or become similar to cheese

CASEFYING > CASEFY

CASEIC adj relating to cheese

CASEIN n a phosphoprotein, precipitated from milk by the action of rennin, forming the basis of cheese: used in the manufacture of plastics and adhesives

CASEINATE n protein found in milk

CASEINS > CASEIN

CASELOAD n number of cases that someone like a doctor or social worker deals with at any one time

CASELOADS > CASELOAD

CASEMAKER n in bookbinding, machine that makes stiff covers for hardbacks

CASEMAN n in printing, a person who sets and corrects type

CASEMATE n armoured compartment in a ship or fortification in which guns are mounted

CASEMATED > CASEMATE

CASEMATES > CASEMATE

CASEMEN > CASEMAN

CASEMENT n window that is hinged on one side

CASEMENTS > CASEMENT

CASEOSE n peptide produced by the peptic digestion of casein

CASEOSES > CASEOSE

CASEOUS adj of or like cheese

CASERN n (formerly) a billet or accommodation for soldiers in a town

CASERNE same as > CASERN

CASERNES > CASERNE

CASERNS > CASERN

CASES > CASE

CASETTE variant of > CASSETTE

CASETTES > CASETTE

CASEWORK n social work based on close study of the personal histories and circumstances of individuals and families

CASEWORKS > CASEWORK

CASEWORM n caddis worm

CASEWORMS > CASEWORM

CASH n banknotes and coins ▷ adj of, for, or paid in cash ▷ vb obtain cash for

CASHABLE > CASH

CASHAW n winter squash

CASHAWS > CASHAW

CASHBACK n discount offered in return for immediate payment

CASHBACKS > CASHBACK

CASHBOOK n journal in which cash receipts and payments are recorded

CASHBOOKS > CASHBOOK

CASHBOX n box for holding cash

CASHBOXES > CASHBOX

CASHED > CASH

CASHES > CASH

CASHEW n edible kidney-shaped nut

CASHEWS > CASHEW

CASHIER n person responsible for handling cash in a bank, shop, etc ▷ vb dismiss with dishonour from the armed forces

CASHIERED > CASHIER

CASHIERER > CASHIER

CASHIERS > CASHIER

CASHING > CASH

CASHLESS adj functioning, operated, or performed without using coins or banknotes for money transactions but instead using credit cards or electronic transfer of funds

CASHMERE n fine soft wool obtained from goats

CASHMERES > CASHMERE

CASHOO n catechu

CASHOOS > CASHOO

CASHPOINT n cash dispenser

CASIMERE same as > CASSIMERE

CASIMERES > CASIMERE

CASIMIRE variant of > CASSIMERE

CASIMIRES > CASIMIRE

CASING n protective case, covering

CASINGS > CASING

CASINI > CASINO

CASINO n public building or room where gambling games are played

CASINOS > CASINO

CASITA n small house

CASITAS > CASITA

CASK n barrel used to hold alcoholic drink ▷ vb to put into a cask

CASKED > CASK

CASKET n small box for valuables ▷ vb to put into a casket

CASKETED > CASKET

CASKETING > CASKET

CASKETS > CASKET

CASKING > CASK

CASKS > CASK

CASKSTAND n frame on which a cask rests

CASKY adj (of wine) having a musty smell due to resting too long in the cask

CASQUE n helmet or a helmet-like process or structure, as on the bill of most hornbills

CASQUED > CASQUE

CASQUES > CASQUE

CASSABA same as > CASABA

CASSABAS > CASABA

CASSAREEP n juice of the bitter cassava root, boiled down to a syrup and used as a flavouring, esp in West Indian cookery

CASSATA n ice cream, originating in Italy, usually containing nuts and candied fruit

CASSATAS > CASSATA

CASSATION n (esp in France) annulment, as of a judicial decision by a higher court

CASSAVA n starch obtained from the roots of a tropical American plant, used to make tapioca

CASSAVAS > CASSAVA

CASSENA same as > CASSINA

CASSENAS > CASSENA

CASSENE same as > CASSINA

CASSENES > CASSENE

CASSEROLE n covered dish in which food is cooked slowly, usu. in an oven ▷ vb cook in a casserole

CASSETTE n plastic container for magnetic tape

CASSETTES > CASSETTE

CASSIA n tropical plant

whose pods yield a mild
laxative
**CASSIAS** >CASSIA
**CASSIMERE** n woollen
suiting cloth of plain or
twill weave
**CASSINA** n American tree
**CASSINAS** >CASSINA
**CASSINE** same as >CASSINA
**CASSINES** >CASSINE
**CASSINGLE** n cassette
single
**CASSINO** n card game for
two to four players in
which players pair cards
from their hands with
others exposed on the
table
**CASSINOS** >CASSINO
**CASSIS** n blackcurrant
cordial
**CASSISES** >CASSIS
**CASSOCK** n long tunic, usu.
black, worn by priests
**CASSOCKED** >CASSOCK
**CASSOCKS** >CASSOCK
**CASSONADE** n raw sugar
**CASSONE** n highly-
decorated Italian dowry
chest
**CASSONES** >CASSONE
**CASSOULET** n stew
originating from France,
made from haricot beans
and goose, duck, pork, etc
**CASSOWARY** n large
flightless bird of Australia
and New Guinea
**CASSPIR** n armoured
military vehicle
**CASSPIRS** >CASSPIR
**CAST** n actors in a play
or film collectively ▷ vb
select (an actor) to play a
part in a play or film
**CASTABLE** adj able to be
cast
**CASTANET** >CASTANETS
**CASTANETS** pl n musical
instrument, used
by Spanish dancers,
consisting of curved pieces
of hollow wood clicked
together in the hand
**CASTAWAY** n shipwrecked
person ▷ adj shipwrecked
or put adrift ▷ vb cause
(a ship, person, etc)
to be shipwrecked or
abandoned
**CASTAWAYS** >CASTAWAY
**CASTE** n any of the
hereditary classes into
which Hindu society is
divided
**CASTED** adj having a caste
**CASTEISM** n belief in, and
adherence to, the caste
system
**CASTEISMS** >CASTEISM
**CASTELESS** adj having no
caste
**CASTELLA** >CASTELLUM
**CASTELLAN** n keeper or

governor of a castle
**CASTELLUM** n fort
**CASTER** n person or thing
that casts
**CASTERS** >CASTER
**CASTES** >CASTE
**CASTIGATE** vb reprimand
severely
**CASTING** >CAST
**CASTINGS** >CAST
**CASTLE** n large fortified
building, often built as a
ruler's residence ▷ vb (in
chess) move (the king)
two squares laterally on
the first rank and place the
nearest rook on the square
passed over by the king
**CASTLED** adj like a castle in
construction
**CASTLES** >CASTLE
**CASTLING** >CASTLE
**CASTOCK** n kale stalk
**CASTOCKS** >CASTOCK
**CASTOFF** n person or thing
that has been discarded or
abandoned
**CASTOFFS** >CASTOFF
**CASTOR** same as >CASTER
**CASTOREUM** n oil secreted
from the beaver, used as
bait by trappers
**CASTORIES** >CASTORY
**CASTORS** >CASTOR
**CASTORY** n dye derived
from beaver pelts
**CASTRAL** adj relating to
camps
**CASTRATE** vb remove the
testicles of
**CASTRATED** >CASTRATE
**CASTRATER** >CASTRATE
**CASTRATES** >CASTRATE
**CASTRATI** >CASTRATO
**CASTRATO** n (in 17th- and
18th-century opera) a male
singer whose testicles
were removed before
puberty, allowing the
retention of a soprano or
alto voice
**CASTRATOR** >CASTRATE
**CASTRATOS** >CASTRATO
**CASTS** >CAST
**CASUAL** adj careless,
nonchalant ▷ n
occasional worker
**CASUALISE** vb to make (a
regular employee) into a
casual worker
**CASUALISM** >CASUALISE
**CASUALIZE** same
as >CASUALISE
**CASUALLY** >CASUAL
**CASUALS** >CASUAL
**CASUALTY** n person killed
or injured in an accident
or war
**CASUARINA** n Australian
tree with jointed green
branches
**CASUIST** n person, esp a
theologian, who attempts
to resolve moral dilemmas

by the application of
general rules and the
careful distinction of
special cases
**CASUISTIC** >CASUIST
**CASUISTRY** n reasoning
that is misleading or
oversubtle
**CASUISTS** >CASUIST
**CASUS** n event
**CAT** n small domesticated
furry mammal ▷ vb flog
with a cat-'o-nine-tails
**CATABASES** >CATABASIS
**CATABASIS** n descent or
downward movement
**CATABATIC** >CATABASIS
**CATABOLIC** adj of a
metabolic process in
which complex molecules
are broken down into
simple ones with the
release of energy
**CATACLASM** n breaking
down
**CATACLYSM** n violent
upheaval
**CATACOMB** n underground
burial place, esp the
galleries at Rome,
consisting of tunnels with
vaults or niches leading off
them for tombs
**CATACOMBS** >CATACOMB
**CATAFALCO** n temporary
raised platform on which a
body lies in state before or
during a funeral
**CATALASE** n enzyme
that catalyses the
decomposition of
hydrogen peroxide
**CATALASES** >CATALASE
**CATALATIC** adj relating to
catalase
**CATALEPSY** n trancelike
state in which the body
is rigid
**CATALEXES** >CATALEXIS
**CATALEXIS** n the state of
lacking a syllable in the
last foot of a line of poetry
**CATALO** same as >CATTALO
**CATALOES** >CATALO
**CATALOG** same
as >CATALOGUE
**CATALOGED** >CATALOGUE
**CATALOGER** >CATALOGUE
**CATALOGIC** >CATALOG
**CATALOGS** >CATALOG
**CATALOGUE** n book
containing details of items
for sale ▷ vb enter (an
item) in a catalogue
**CATALOS** >CATALO
**CATALPA** n tree of N
America and Asia with
bell-shaped whitish
flowers
**CATALPAS** >CATALPA
**CATALYSE** vb speed up (a
chemical reaction) by a
catalyst
**CATALYSED** >CATALYSE

**CATALYSER** >CATALYSE
**CATALYSES** >CATALYSIS
**CATALYSIS** n acceleration
of a chemical reaction by
the action of a catalyst
**CATALYST** n substance
that speeds up a chemical
reaction without itself
changing
**CATALYSTS** >CATALYST
**CATALYTIC** adj of or
relating to catalysis
**CATALYZE** same
as >CATALYSE
**CATALYZED** >CATALYZE
**CATALYZER** >CATALYZE
**CATALYZES** >CATALYZE
**CATAMARAN** n boat with
twin parallel hulls
**CATAMENIA** another word
for >MENSES
**CATAMITE** n boy kept as a
homosexual partner
**CATAMITES** >CATAMITE
**CATAMOUNT** n any of
various medium-sized
felines, such as the puma
or lynx
**CATAPAN** n governor in the
Byzantine Empire
**CATAPANS** >CATAPAN
**CATAPHORA** n use of a word
such as a pronoun that has
the same reference as a
word used subsequently in
the same discourse
**CATAPHYLL** n simplified
form of plant leaf, such as a
scale leaf or cotyledon
**CATAPLASM** another name
for >POULTICE
**CATAPLEXY** n sudden
temporary paralysis,
brought on by severe
shock
**CATAPULT** n Y-shaped
device with a loop of
elastic, used by children
for firing stones ▷ vb
shoot forwards or upwards
violently
**CATAPULTS** >CATAPULT
**CATARACT** n eye disease in
which the lens becomes
opaque
**CATARACTS** >CATARACT
**CATARHINE** n having a thin
or narrow nose
**CATARRH** n excessive
mucus in the nose and
throat, during or following
a cold
**CATARRHAL** >CATARRH
**CATARRHS** >CATARRH
**CATASTA** n platform
on which slaves were
presented for sale
**CATASTAS** >CATASTA
**CATATONIA** n form
of schizophrenia
characterized by stupor,
with outbreaks of
excitement
**CATATONIC** >CATATONIA

**CATATONY** another word for > CATATONIA

**CATAWBA** n type of red North American grape

**CATAWBAS** > CATAWBA

**CATBIRD** n any of several North American songbirds of the family Mimidae (mockingbirds), esp Dumetella carolinensis, whose call resembles the mewing of a cat

**CATBIRDS** > CATBIRD

**CATBOAT** n sailing vessel with a single mast, set well forward and often unstayed, and a large sail, usually rigged with a gaff

**CATBOATS** > CATBOAT

**CATBRIER** n greenbrier

**CATBRIERS** > CATBRIER

**CATCALL** n derisive whistle or cry ▷ vb utter such a call (at)

**CATCALLED** > CATCALL

**CATCALLER** > CATCALL

**CATCALLS** > CATCALL

**CATCH** vb seize, capture ▷ n device for fastening a door, window, etc

**CATCHABLE** > CATCH

**CATCHALL** n something designed to cover a variety of situations

**CATCHALLS** > CATCHALL

**CATCHCRY** n well-known much-used phrase, perhaps associated with a particular group

**CATCHED** rarely used past tense of > CATCH

**CATCHEN** same as > CATCH

**CATCHER** n person or thing that catches, esp in a game or sport

**CATCHERS** > CATCHER

**CATCHES** > CATCH

**CATCHFLY** n any of several caryophyllaceous plants of the genus Silene that have sticky calyxes and stems on which insects are sometimes trapped

**CATCHIER** > CATCHY

**CATCHIEST** > CATCHY

**CATCHING** > CATCH

**CATCHINGS** > CATCH

**CATCHMENT** n structure in which water is collected

**CATCHPOLE** n (in medieval England) a sheriff's officer who arrested debtors

**CATCHPOLL** same as > CATCHPOLE

**CATCHT** same as > CATCHED

**CATCHUP** a variant spelling (esp US) of > KETCHUP

**CATCHUPS** > CATCHUP

**CATCHWEED** n goosegrass

**CATCHWORD** n well-known and frequently used phrase

**CATCHY** adj (of a tune) pleasant and easily remembered

**CATCLAW** n type of shrub; black bead

**CATCLAWS** > CATCLAW

**CATE** n delicacy

**CATECHIN** n soluble yellow solid substance found in mahogany wood

**CATECHINS** > CATECHIN

**CATECHISE** same as > CATECHIZE

**CATECHISM** n instruction on the doctrine of a Christian Church in a series of questions and answers

**CATECHIST** > CATECHIZE

**CATECHIZE** vb instruct by using a catechism

**CATECHOL** n colourless crystalline phenol found in resins and lignins

**CATECHOLS** > CATECHOL

**CATECHU** n water-soluble astringent resinous substance obtained from any of certain tropical plants, esp the leguminous tree Acacia catechu of S Asia, and used in medicine, tanning, and dyeing

**CATECHUS** > CATECHU

**CATEGORIC** adj unqualified

**CATEGORY** n class, group

**CATELOG** obsolete word for > CATALOGUE

**CATELOGS** > CATELOG

**CATENA** n connected series, esp of patristic comments on the Bible

**CATENAE** > CATENA

**CATENANE** n type of chemical compound in which the molecules have two or more rings that are interlocked like the links of a chain

**CATENANES** > CATENANE

**CATENARY** n curve assumed by a heavy uniform flexible cord hanging freely from two points. When symmetrical about the y-axis and intersecting it at $y = a$, the equation is $y = a \cosh x/a$ ▷ adj of, resembling, relating to, or constructed using a catenary or suspended chain

**CATENAS** > CATENA

**CATENATE** vb arrange or be arranged in a series of chains or rings

**CATENATED** > CATENATE

**CATENATES** > CATENATE

**CATENOID** n geometrical surface generated by rotating a catenary about its axis

**CATENOIDS** > CATENOID

**CATER** vb provide what is needed or wanted, esp food or services

**CATERAN** n (formerly) a member of a band of brigands and marauders in the Scottish highlands

**CATERANS** > CATERAN

**CATERED** > CATER

**CATERER** n person whose job is to provide food for social events such as parties and weddings

**CATERERS** > CATERER

**CATERESS** n female caterer

**CATERING** n supplying of food for a social event

**CATERINGS** > CATERING

**CATERS** > CATER

**CATERWAUL** n wail, yowl ▷ vb make a yowling noise like a cat

**CATES** pl n choice dainty food

**CATFACE** n deformity of the surface of a tree trunk, caused by fire or disease

**CATFACES** > CATFACE

**CATFACING** n disorder that affects tomatoes, causing scarring of the fruit

**CATFALL** n line used as a tackle for hoisting an anchor to the cathead

**CATFALLS** > CATFALL

**CATFIGHT** n fight between two women

**CATFIGHTS** > CATFIGHT

**CATFISH** n fish with whisker-like barbels round the mouth

**CATFISHES** > CATFISH

**CATGUT** n strong cord used to string musical instruments and sports rackets

**CATGUTS** > CATGUT

**CATHARISE** vb to purify

**CATHARIZE** same as > CATHARISE

**CATHARSES** > CATHARSIS

**CATHARSIS** n relief of strong suppressed emotions

**CATHARTIC** adj causing catharsis ▷ n drug that causes catharsis

**CATHEAD** n fitting at the bow of a vessel for securing the anchor when raised

**CATHEADS** > CATHEAD

**CATHECT** vb to invest mental or emotional energy in

**CATHECTED** > CATHECT

**CATHECTIC** adj of or relating to cathexis

**CATHECTS** > CATHECT

**CATHEDRA** n bishop's throne

**CATHEDRAE** > CATHEDRA

**CATHEDRAL** n principal church of a diocese

**CATHEDRAS** > CATHEDRA

**CATHEPSIN** n proteolytic enzyme responsible for the autolysis of cells after death

**CATHEPTIC** > CATHEPSIN

**CATHETER** n tube inserted into a body cavity to drain fluid

**CATHETERS** > CATHETER

**CATHETUS** n straight line or radius perpendicular to another line or radius

**CATHEXES** > CATHEXIS

**CATHEXIS** n concentration of psychic energy on a single goal

**CATHISMA** n short hymn used as a response

**CATHISMAS** > CATHISMA

**CATHODAL** > CATHODE

**CATHODE** n negative electrode, by which electrons leave a circuit

**CATHODES** > CATHODE

**CATHODIC** > CATHODE

**CATHOLE** n hole in a ship through which ropes are passed

**CATHOLES** > CATHOLE

**CATHOLIC** adj (of tastes or interests) covering a wide range ▷ n member of the Roman Catholic Church

**CATHOLICS** > CATHOLIC

**CATHOLYTE** same as > CATOLYTE

**CATHOOD** n state of being a cat

**CATHOODS** > CATHOOD

**CATHOUSE** a slang word for > BROTHEL

**CATHOUSES** > CATHOUSE

**CATION** n positively charged ion

**CATIONIC** > CATION

**CATIONS** > CATION

**CATJANG** n tropical shrub

**CATJANGS** > CATJANG

**CATKIN** n drooping flower spike of certain trees

**CATKINATE** adj like catkin

**CATKINS** > CATKIN

**CATLIKE** > CAT

**CATLIN** same as > CATLING

**CATLING** n long double-edged surgical knife for amputations

**CATLINGS** > CATLING

**CATLINS** > CATLIN

**CATMINT** n Eurasian plant with scented leaves that attract cats

**CATMINTS** > CATMINT

**CATNAP** vb doze ▷ n short sleep or doze

**CATNAPER** > CATNAP

**CATNAPERS** > CATNAP

**CATNAPPED** > CATNAP

**CATNAPPER** > CATNAP

**CATNAPS** > CATNAP

**CATNEP** same as > CATMINT

**CATNEPS** > CATNEP

**CATNIP** same as > CATMINT

**CATNIPS** > CATNIP

**CATOLYTE** n part of the electrolyte that surrounds the cathode in an

electrolytic cell
CATOLYTES > CATOLYTE
CATOPTRIC adj relating to reflection
CATRIGGED adj rigged like a catboat
CATS > CAT
CATSKIN n skin and/or fur of a cat
CATSKINS > CATSKIN
CATSPAW n person used by another as a tool
CATSPAWS > CATSPAW
CATSUIT n one-piece usually close-fitting trouser suit
CATSUITS > CATSUIT
CATSUP a variant (esp US) of > KETCHUP
CATSUPS > CATSUP
CATTABU n cross between common cattle and zebu
CATTABUS > CATTABU
CATTAIL n reed mace
CATTAILS > CATTAIL
CATTALO n hardy breed of cattle developed by crossing the American bison with domestic cattle
CATTALOES > CATTALO
CATTALOS > CATTALO
CATTED > CAT
CATTERIES > CATTERY
CATTERY n place where cats are bred or looked after
CATTIE same as > CATTY
CATTIER > CATTY
CATTIES > CATTY
CATTIEST > CATTY
CATTILY > CATTY
CATTINESS > CATTY
CATTING > CAT
CATTISH > CAT
CATTISHLY > CAT
CATTLE pl n domesticated cows and bulls
CATTLEMAN n person who breeds, rears, or tends cattle
CATTLEMEN > CATTLEMAN
CATTLEYA n any tropical American orchid of the genus Cattleya, cultivated for their purplish-pink or white showy flowers
CATTLEYAS > CATTLEYA
CATTY adj spiteful ▷ n unit of weight, used esp in China, equal to about one and a half pounds or about 0.67 kilogram
CATWALK n narrow pathway or platform
CATWALKS > CATWALK
CATWORKS n machinery on a drilling platform
CATWORM n active carnivorous polychaete worm, Nephtys hombergi, that is about 10cm (4in) long, having a pearly sheen to its body: often dug for bait

CATWORMS > CATWORM
CAUCHEMAR n nightmare
CAUCUS n local committee or faction of a political party ▷ vb hold a caucus
CAUCUSED > CAUCUS
CAUCUSES > CAUCUS
CAUCUSING > CAUCUS
CAUCUSSED > CAUCUS
CAUCUSSES > CAUCUS
CAUDA n area behind the anus of an animal
CAUDAD adv towards the tail or posterior part
CAUDAE > CAUDA
CAUDAL adj at or near an animal's tail
CAUDALLY > CAUDAL
CAUDATE adj having a tail or a tail-like appendage ▷ n lizard-like amphibian
CAUDATED same as > CAUDATE
CAUDATES > CAUDATE
CAUDATION > CAUDATE
CAUDEX n thickened persistent stem base of some herbaceous perennial plants
CAUDEXES > CAUDEX
CAUDICES > CAUDEX
CAUDICLE n stalk to which an orchid's pollen masses are attached
CAUDICLES > CAUDICLE
CAUDILLO n (in Spanish-speaking countries) a military or political leader
CAUDILLOS > CAUDILLO
CAUDLE n hot spiced wine drink made with gruel, formerly used medicinally ▷ vb make such a drink
CAUDLED > CAUDLE
CAUDLES > CAUDLE
CAUDLING > CAUDLE
CAUDRON Spenserian spelling of > CAULDRON
CAUDRONS > CAUDRON
CAUF n cage for holding live fish in the water
CAUGHT > CATCH
CAUK n type of barite
CAUKER n one who caulks
CAUKERS > CAUKER
CAUKS > CAUK
CAUL n membrane sometimes covering a child's head at birth
CAULD a Scot word for > COLD
CAULDER > CAULD
CAULDEST > CAULD
CAULDRIFE adj susceptible to cold
CAULDRON n large pot used for boiling
CAULDRONS > CAULDRON
CAULDS > CAULD
CAULES > CAULIS
CAULICLE n small stalk or stem
CAULICLES > CAULICLE
CAULICULI n plural form of singular cauliculus:

another word for caulicle
CAULIFORM adj resembling a caulis
CAULINARY another word for > CAULINE
CAULINE adj relating to or growing from a plant stem
CAULIS n main stem of a plant
CAULK vb fill in (cracks) with paste etc
CAULKED > CAULK
CAULKER > CAULK
CAULKERS > CAULK
CAULKING > CAULK
CAULKINGS > CAULK
CAULKS > CAULK
CAULOME n plant's stem structure, considered as a whole
CAULOMES > CAULOME
CAULS > CAUL
CAUM same as > CAM
CAUMED > CAUM
CAUMING > CAUM
CAUMS > CAUM
CAUMSTONE same as > CAMSTONE
CAUP n type of quaich
CAUPS > CAUP
CAUSA n reason or cause
CAUSABLE > CAUSE
CAUSAE > CAUSA
CAUSAL adj of or being a cause ▷ n something that suggests a cause
CAUSALGIA n burning sensation along the course of a peripheral nerve together with local changes in the appearance of the skin
CAUSALGIC > CAUSALGIA
CAUSALITY n relationship of cause and effect
CAUSALLY > CAUSAL
CAUSALS > CAUSAL
CAUSATION n relationship of cause and effect
CAUSATIVE adj producing an effect ▷ n causative form or class of verbs
CAUSE n something that produces a particular effect ▷ vb be the cause of
CAUSED > CAUSE
CAUSELESS > CAUSE
CAUSEN old infinitive of > CAUSE
CAUSER > CAUSE
CAUSERIE n informal talk or conversational piece of writing
CAUSERIES > CAUSERIE
CAUSERS > CAUSE
CAUSES > CAUSE
CAUSEWAY n raised path or road across water or marshland
CAUSEWAYS > CAUSEWAY
CAUSEY n cobbled street ▷ vb cobble
CAUSEYED > CAUSEY
CAUSEYS > CAUSEY

CAUSING > CAUSE
CAUSTIC adj capable of burning by chemical action ▷ n caustic substance
CAUSTICAL > CAUSTIC
CAUSTICS > CAUSTIC
CAUTEL n craftiness
CAUTELOUS > CAUTEL
CAUTELS > CAUTEL
CAUTER n cauterising instrument
CAUTERANT same as > CAUTERY
CAUTERIES > CAUTERY
CAUTERISE same as > CAUTERIZE
CAUTERISM > CAUTERIZE
CAUTERIZE vb burn (a wound) with heat or a caustic agent to prevent infection
CAUTERS > CAUTER
CAUTERY n coagulation of blood or destruction of body tissue by cauterizing
CAUTION n care, esp in the face of danger ▷ vb warn, advise
CAUTIONED > CAUTION
CAUTIONER > CAUTION
CAUTIONRY n in Scots law, standing surety
CAUTIONS > CAUTION
CAUTIOUS adj showing caution
CAUVES > CAUF
CAVA n Spanish sparkling wine produced by a method similar to that used for champagne
CAVALCADE n procession of people on horseback or in cars
CAVALERO n cavalier
CAVALEROS > CAVALERO
CAVALETTI n bars supported on low stands used in dressage and horse jumping
CAVALIER adj showing haughty disregard ▷ n gallant gentleman
CAVALIERS > CAVALIER
CAVALLA n any of various tropical carangid fishes, such as Gnathanodon speciosus (golden cavalla)
CAVALLAS > CAVALLA
CAVALLIES > CAVALLY
CAVALLY same as > CAVALLA
CAVALRIES > CAVALRY
CAVALRY n part of the army orig. on horseback, but now often using fast armoured vehicles
CAVAS > CAVA
CAVASS n Turkish armed police officer
CAVASSES > CAVASS
CAVATINA n solo song resembling a simple aria
CAVATINAS > CAVATINA
CAVATINE > CAVATINA

125

**CAVE** n hollow in the side of a hill or cliff ▷ vb hollow out

**CAVEAT** n warning ▷ vb to introduce a caveat

**CAVEATED** > CAVEAT

**CAVEATING** > CAVEAT

**CAVEATOR** n person who enters a caveat

**CAVEATORS** > CAVEATOR

**CAVEATS** > CAVEAT

**CAVED** > CAVE

**CAVEFISH** n any of various small freshwater cyprinodont fishes of the genera Amblyopsis, Chologaster, etc, living in subterranean and other waters in S North America

**CAVEL** n drawing of lots among miners for an easy and profitable place at the coalface

**CAVELIKE** adj resembling a cave

**CAVELS** > CAVEL

**CAVEMAN** n prehistoric cave dweller

**CAVEMEN** > CAVEMAN

**CAVENDISH** n tobacco that has been sweetened and pressed into moulds to form bars

**CAVER** > CAVING

**CAVERN** n large cave ▷ vb shut in or as if in a cavern

**CAVERNED** > CAVERN

**CAVERNING** > CAVERN

**CAVERNOUS** adj like a cavern in vastness, depth, or hollowness

**CAVERNS** > CAVERN

**CAVERS** > CAVING

**CAVES** > CAVE

**CAVESSON** n kind of hard noseband, used (esp formerly) in breaking a horse in

**CAVESSONS** > CAVESSON

**CAVETTI** > CAVETTO

**CAVETTO** n concave moulding, shaped to a quarter circle in cross section

**CAVETTOS** > CAVETTO

**CAVIAR** n salted sturgeon roe, regarded as a delicacy

**CAVIARE** same as > CAVIAR

**CAVIARES** > CAVIARE

**CAVIARIE** same as > CAVIAR

**CAVIARIES** > CAVIARY

**CAVIARS** > CAVIAR

**CAVICORN** adj (of sheep, goats, etc) having hollow horns as distinct from the solid antlers of deer ▷ n sheep, goats, etc with hollow horns as distinct from the solid antlers of deer

**CAVICORNS** > CAVICORN

**CAVIE** n hen coop

**CAVIER** same as > CAVIAR

**CAVIERS** > CAVIER

**CAVIES** > CAVY

**CAVIL** vb make petty objections ▷ n petty objection

**CAVILED** > CAVIL

**CAVILER** > CAVIL

**CAVILERS** > CAVIL

**CAVILING** > CAVIL

**CAVILLED** > CAVIL

**CAVILLER** > CAVIL

**CAVILLERS** > CAVIL

**CAVILLING** > CAVIL

**CAVILS** > CAVIL

**CAVING** n sport of exploring caves

**CAVINGS** > CAVING

**CAVITARY** adj containing cavities

**CAVITATE** vb to form cavities or bubbles

**CAVITATED** > CAVITATE

**CAVITATES** > CAVITATE

**CAVITIED** > CAVITY

**CAVITIES** > CAVITY

**CAVITY** n hollow space

**CAVORT** vb skip about

**CAVORTED** > CAVORT

**CAVORTER** > CAVORT

**CAVORTERS** > CAVORT

**CAVORTING** > CAVORT

**CAVORTS** > CAVORT

**CAVY** n any small South American hystricomorph rodent of the family Caviidae, esp any of the genus Cavia, having a thickset body and very small tail

**CAW** n cry of a crow, rook, or raven ▷ vb make this cry

**CAWED** > CAW

**CAWING** > CAW

**CAWINGS** > CAW

**CAWK** same as > CAUK

**CAWKER** n metal projection on a horse's shoe to prevent slipping

**CAWKERS** > CAWKER

**CAWKS** > CAWK

**CAWS** > CAW

**CAXON** n type of wig

**CAXONS** > CAXON

**CAY** n low island or bank composed of sand and coral fragments

**CAYENNE** n very hot condiment, bright red in colour, made from dried capsicums

**CAYENNED** adj seasoned with cayenne

**CAYENNES** > CAYENNE

**CAYMAN** n S American reptile similar to an alligator

**CAYMANS** > CAYMAN

**CAYS** > CAY

**CAYUSE** n small American Indian pony used by cowboys

**CAYUSES** > CAYUSE

**CAZ** short for > CASUAL

**CAZIQUE** same as > CACIQUE

**CAZIQUES** > CAZIQUE

**CEANOTHUS** n any shrub of the North American rhamnaceous genus Ceanothus: grown for their ornamental, often blue, flower clusters

**CEAS** same as > CAESE

**CEASE** vb bring or come to an end

**CEASED** > CEASE

**CEASEFIRE** n temporary truce

**CEASELESS** adj without stopping

**CEASES** > CEASE

**CEASING** > CEASE

**CEASINGS** > CEASE

**CEAZE** obsolete spelling of > SEIZE

**CEAZED** > CEAZE

**CEAZES** > CEAZE

**CEAZING** > CEAZE

**CEBADILLA** same as > SABADILLA

**CEBID** n any member of the Cebidae family of New World monkeys

**CEBIDS** > CEBID

**CEBOID** same as > CEBID

**CEBOIDS** > CEBOID

**CECA** > CECUM

**CECAL** > CECUM

**CECALLY** > CECUM

**CECILS** n fried meatballs

**CECITIES** > CECITY

**CECITIS** n inflammation of the c(a)ecum

**CECITISES** > CECITIS

**CECITY** n rare word for blindness

**CECROPIA** n large North American moth

**CECROPIAS** > CECROPIA

**CECUM** same as > CAECUM

**CEDAR** n evergreen coniferous tree ▷ adj made of the wood of a cedar tree

**CEDARBIRD** n type of waxwing

**CEDARED** adj covered with cedars

**CEDARN** adj relating to cedar

**CEDARS** > CEDAR

**CEDARWOOD** n wood of any of the cedar trees

**CEDARY** adj like cedar

**CEDE** vb surrender (territory or legal rights)

**CEDED** > CEDE

**CEDER** > CEDE

**CEDERS** > CEDE

**CEDES** > CEDE

**CEDI** n standard monetary unit of Ghana, divided into 100 pesewas

**CEDILLA** n character placed under a c in some languages, to show that it is pronounced s, not k

**CEDILLAS** > CEDILLA

**CEDING** > CEDE

**CEDIS** > CEDI

**CEDRATE** n citron

**CEDRATES** > CEDRATE

**CEDRINE** adj relating to cedar

**CEDULA** n form of identification in Spanish-speaking countries

**CEDULAS** > CEDULA

**CEE** n third letter of the alphabet

**CEES** > CEE

**CEIBA** n any bombacaceous tropical tree of the genus Ceiba, such as the silk-cotton tree

**CEIBAS** > CEIBA

**CEIL** vb line (a ceiling) with plaster, boarding, etc

**CEILED** > CEIL

**CEILER** > CEIL

**CEILERS** > CEIL

**CEILI** variant spelling of > CEILIDH

**CEILIDH** n informal social gathering for singing and dancing, esp in Scotland

**CEILIDHS** > CEILIDH

**CEILING** n inner upper surface of a room ▷ vb make a ceiling

**CEILINGED** > CEILING

**CEILINGS** > CEILING

**CEILIS** > CEILI

**CEILS** > CEIL

**CEINTURE** n belt

**CEINTURES** > CEINTURE

**CEL** short for > CELLULOID

**CELADON** n type of porcelain having a greyish-green glaze: mainly Chinese

**CELADONS** > CELADON

**CELANDINE** n wild plant with yellow flowers

**CELEB** n celebrity

**CELEBRANT** n person who performs a religious ceremony

**CELEBRATE** vb hold festivities to mark (a happy event, anniversary, etc)

**CELEBRITY** n famous person

**CELEBS** > CELEB

**CELERIAC** n variety of celery with a large turnip-like root

**CELERIACS** > CELERIAC

**CELERIES** > CELERY

**CELERITY** n swiftness

**CELERY** n vegetable with long green crisp edible stalks

**CELESTA** n instrument like a small piano in which key-operated hammers strike metal plates

**CELESTAS** > CELESTA

**CELESTE** same as > CELESTA

**CELESTES** > CELESTE

**CELESTIAL** adj heavenly, divine

**CELESTINE** same

*as* >CELESTITE
**CELESTITE** *n* white, red, or blue mineral
**CELIAC** *same as* >COELIAC
**CELIACS** >CELIAC
**CELIBACY** >CELIBATE
**CELIBATE** *adj* unmarried or abstaining from sex, esp because of a religious vow of chastity ▷ *n* celibate person
**CELIBATES** >CELIBATE
**CELIBATIC** *adj* celibate
**CELL** *n* smallest unit of an organism that is able to function independently
**CELLA** *n* inner room of a classical temple, esp the room housing the statue of a deity
**CELLAE** >CELLA
**CELLAR** *n* underground room for storage ▷ *vb* store in a cellar
**CELLARAGE** *n* area of a cellar
**CELLARED** >CELLAR
**CELLARER** *n* monastic official responsible for food, drink, etc
**CELLARERS** >CELLARER
**CELLARET** *n* case, cabinet, or sideboard with compartments for holding wine bottles
**CELLARETS** >CELLARET
**CELLARING** >CELLAR
**CELLARIST** *same as* >CELLARER
**CELLARMAN** *n* person in charge of a cellar
**CELLARMEN** >CELLARMAN
**CELLAROUS** *adj* relating to a cellar
**CELLARS** >CELLAR
**CELLARWAY** *n* way into cellar
**CELLBLOCK** *n* group of prison cells
**CELLED** *adj* cellular
**CELLI** >CELLO
**CELLING** *n* formation of cells
**CELLIST** >CELLO
**CELLISTS** >CELLO
**CELLMATE** *n* person with whom a prisoner shares a prison cell
**CELLMATES** >CELLMATE
**CELLO** *n* large low-pitched instrument of the violin family
**CELLOIDIN** *n* nitrocellulose compound derived from pyroxylin, used in a solution of alcohol and ether for embedding specimens before cutting sections for microscopy
**CELLOS** >CELLO
**CELLOSE** *n* a disaccharide obtained by the hydrolysis of cellulose by cellulase.

**CELLOSES** >CELLOSE
**CELLPHONE** *n* portable telephone operated by cellular radio
**CELLS** >CELL
**CELLULAR** *adj* of or consisting of cells ▷ *n* cellular phone
**CELLULARS** >CELLULAR
**CELLULASE** *n* any enzyme that converts cellulose to the disaccharide cellobiose
**CELLULE** *n* very small cell
**CELLULES** >CELLULE
**CELLULITE** *n* fat deposits under the skin alleged to resist dieting
**CELLULOID** *n* kind of plastic used to make toys and, formerly, photographic film
**CELLULOSE** *n* main constituent of plant cell walls, used in making paper, plastics, etc
**CELLULOUS** >CELLULOSE
**CELOM** *same as* >COELOM
**CELOMATA** >CELOM
**CELOMIC** >CELOM
**CELOMS** >CELOM
**CELOSIA** *same as* >COCKSCOMB
**CELOSIAS** >CELOSIA
**CELOTEX** *n* tradename for a type of insulation board
**CELOTEXES** >CELOTEX
**CELS** >CEL
**CELSITUDE** *n* loftiness
**CELT** *n* stone or metal axelike instrument with a bevelled edge
**CELTS** >CELT
**CEMBALI** >CEMBALO
**CEMBALIST** >CEMBALO
**CEMBALO** *n* harpsichord
**CEMBALOS** >CEMBALO
**CEMBRA** *n* Swiss pine
**CEMBRAS** >CEMBRA
**CEMENT** *n* fine grey powder mixed with water and sand to make mortar or concrete ▷ *vb* join, bind, or cover with cement
**CEMENTA** >CEMENTUM
**CEMENTED** >CEMENT
**CEMENTER** >CEMENT
**CEMENTERS** >CEMENT
**CEMENTING** >CEMENT
**CEMENTITE** *n* hard brittle compound of iron and carbon
**CEMENTS** >CEMENT
**CEMENTUM** *n* thin bonelike tissue that covers the dentine in the root of a tooth
**CEMENTUMS** >CEMENTUM
**CEMETERY** *n* place where dead people are buried
**CEMITARE** *obsolete spelling of* >SCIMITAR
**CEMITARES** >CEMITARE
**CENACLE** *n* supper room,

esp one on an upper floor
**CENACLES** >CENACLE
**CENDRE** *adj* ash-blond
**CENOBITE** *same as* >COENOBITE
**CENOBITES** >CENOBITE
**CENOBITIC** >CENOBITE
**CENOTAPH** *n* monument honouring soldiers who died in a war
**CENOTAPHS** >CENOTAPH
**CENOTE** *n* (esp in the Yucatán peninsula) a natural well formed by the collapse of an overlying limestone crust: often used as a sacrificial site by the Mayas
**CENOTES** >CENOTE
**CENOZOIC** *adj* of or relating to the most recent geologicl era, characterized by the development and increase of the mammals
**CENS** *n* type of annual property rent
**CENSE** *vb* burn incense near or before (an altar, shrine, etc)
**CENSED** >CENSE
**CENSER** *n* container for burning incense
**CENSERS** >CENSER
**CENSES** >CENSE
**CENSING** >CENSE
**CENSOR** *n* person authorized to examine films, books, etc, to ban or cut anything considered obscene or objectionable ▷ *vb* ban or cut parts of (a film, book, etc)
**CENSORED** >CENSOR
**CENSORIAL** >CENSOR
**CENSORIAN** >CENSOR
**CENSORING** >CENSOR
**CENSORS** >CENSOR
**CENSUAL** >CENSUS
**CENSURE** *n* severe disapproval ▷ *vb* criticize severely
**CENSURED** >CENSURE
**CENSURER** >CENSURE
**CENSURERS** >CENSURE
**CENSURES** >CENSURE
**CENSURING** >CENSURE
**CENSUS** *n* official count of a population ▷ *vb* to conduct a census
**CENSUSED** >CENSUS
**CENSUSES** >CENSUS
**CENSUSING** >CENSUS
**CENT** *n* hundredth part of a monetary unit such as the dollar or euro
**CENTAGE** *n* rate per hundred
**CENTAGES** >CENTAGE
**CENTAI** >CENTAS
**CENTAL** *n* unit of weight equal to 100 pounds (45.3 kilograms)
**CENTALS** >CENTAL

**CENTARE** *same as* >CENTIARE
**CENTARES** >CENTARE
**CENTAS** *n* monetary unit of Lithuania, worth one hundredth of a litas
**CENTAUR** *n* mythical creature with the head, arms, and torso of a man, and the lower body and legs of a horse
**CENTAUREA** *n* any plant of the genus *Centaurea*, which includes the cornflower and knapweed
**CENTAURIC** *adj* integrating mind and body
**CENTAURS** >CENTAUR
**CENTAURY** *n* any Eurasian plant of the genus *Centaurium*, esp C. *erythraea*, having purplish-pink flowers and formerly believed to have medicinal properties: family Gentianaceae
**CENTAVO** *n* monetary unit worth one hundredth of the main unit of currency in Portugal and many Latin American countries
**CENTAVOS** >CENTAVO
**CENTENARY** *n* 100th anniversary or its celebration ▷ *adj* of or relating to a period of 100 years
**CENTENIER** *n* in Jersey, a local police officer
**CENTER** *same as* >CENTRE
**CENTERED** >CENTER
**CENTERING** *same as* >CENTRING
**CENTERS** >CENTER
**CENTESES** >CENTESIS
**CENTESIMI** >CENTESIMO
**CENTESIMO** *n* former monetary unit of Italy, San Marino, and the Vatican City worth one hundredth of a lira
**CENTESIS** *n* surgical puncturing of part of the body with a hollow needle, to extract fluid
**CENTIARE** *n* unit of area equal to one square metre
**CENTIARES** >CENTIARE
**CENTIGRAM** *n* one hundredth of a gram
**CENTILE** *n* one of 99 actual or notional values of a variable dividing its distribution into 100 groups with equal frequencies
**CENTILES** >CENTILE
**CENTIME** *n* monetary unit worth one hundredth of a franc
**CENTIMES** >CENTIME
**CENTIMO** *n* monetary unit of Costa Rica, Paraguay, Peru, and Venezuela. It is

worth one hundredth of
their respective standard
currency units

**CENTIMOS** >CENTIMO

**CENTINEL** *obsolete variant
of* >SENTINEL

**CENTINELL** *obsolete variant
of* >SENTINEL

**CENTINELS** >CENTINEL

**CENTIPEDE** *n* small
wormlike creature with
many legs

**CENTNER** *n* unit of weight
equivalent to 100 pounds
(45.3 kilograms)

**CENTNERS** >CENTNER

**CENTO** *n* piece of writing,
esp a poem, composed
of quotations from other
authors

**CENTOIST** *n* one who
composes centos

**CENTOISTS** >CENTOIST

**CENTONATE** *adj* having
many patches

**CENTONEL** *obsolete variant
of* >SENTINEL

**CENTONELL** *obsolete variant
of* >SENTINEL

**CENTONELS** >CENTONEL

**CENTONES** >CENTO

**CENTONIST** *same
as* >CENTOIST

**CENTOS** >CENTO

**CENTRA** >CENTRUM

**CENTRAL** *adj* of, at, or
forming the centre ▷ *n*
workplace serving as a
telecommunications
facility

**CENTRALER** >CENTRAL

**CENTRALLY** >CENTRAL

**CENTRALS** >CENTRAL

**CENTRE** *n* middle point or
part ▷ *vb* put in the centre
of something

**CENTRED** *adj* mentally and
emotionally confident,
focused, and well-
balanced

**CENTREING** *same
as* >CENTRING

**CENTRES** >CENTRE

**CENTRIC** *adj* being central
or having a centre

**CENTRICAL** *same
as* >CENTRIC

**CENTRIES** >CENTRY

**CENTRING** *n* temporary
structure, esp one made of
timber, used to support an
arch during construction

**CENTRINGS** >CENTRING

**CENTRIOLE** *n* either of two
rodlike bodies in most
animal cells that form the
poles of the spindle during
mitosis

**CENTRISM** >CENTRIST

**CENTRISMS** >CENTRIST

**CENTRIST** *n* person
favouring political
moderation

**CENTRISTS** >CENTRIST

**CENTRODE** *n* locus
produced by plotting
course of the
instantaneous centre
of two bodies in relative
motion

**CENTRODES** >CENTRODE

**CENTROID** *n* centre of mass
of an object of uniform
density, esp of a geometric
figure

**CENTROIDS** >CENTROID

**CENTRUM** *n* main part or
body of a vertebra

**CENTRUMS** >CENTRUM

**CENTRY** *obsolete variant
of* >SENTRY

**CENTS** >CENT

**CENTU** *n* Lithuanian money
unit

**CENTUM** *adj* denoting or
belonging to the Indo-
European languages in
which original velar stops
(k) were not palatalized,
namely languages of the
Hellenic, Italic, Celtic,
Germanic, Anatolian, and
Tocharian branches ▷ *n*
hundred

**CENTUMS** >CENTUM

**CENTUMVIR** *n* one of the
Roman judges who sat in
civil cases

**CENTUPLE** *n* one
hundredfold

**CENTUPLED** >CENTUPLE

**CENTUPLES** >CENTUPLE

**CENTURIAL** *adj* of or
relating to a Roman
century

**CENTURIES** >CENTURY

**CENTURION** *n* (in
ancient Rome) officer
commanding 100 men

**CENTURY** *n* period of 100
years

**CEORL** *n* freeman of the
lowest class in Anglo-
Saxon England

**CEORLISH** >CEORL

**CEORLS** >CEORL

**CEP** *another name
for* >PORCINO

**CEPACEOUS** *adj* having an
onion-like smell or taste

**CEPE** *another spelling
of* >CEP

**CEPES** >CEPE

**CEPHALAD** *adv* towards the
head or anterior part

**CEPHALATE** *adj* possessing
a head

**CEPHALIC** *adj* of or relating
to the head ▷ *n* remedy for
pains in the head

**CEPHALICS** >CEPHALIC

**CEPHALIN** *n* phospholipid,
similar to lecithin, that
occurs in the nerve tissue
and brain

**CEPHALINS** >CEPHALIN

**CEPHALOUS** *adj* with a head

**CEPHEID** *n* type of variable

star with a regular cycle of
variations in luminosity

**CEPHEIDS** >CEPHEID

**CEPS** >CEP

**CERACEOUS** *adj* waxlike or
waxy

**CERAMAL** *same as* >CERMET

**CERAMALS** >CERAMAL

**CERAMIC** *n* hard brittle
material made by heating
clay to a very high
temperature ▷ *adj* made
of ceramic

**CERAMICS** *n* art of
producing ceramic objects

**CERAMIDE** *n* any of a class
of biologically important
compounds used as
moisturizers in skin-care
preparations

**CERAMIDES** >CERAMIDE

**CERAMIST** >CERAMICS

**CERAMISTS** >CERAMICS

**CERASIN** *n* meta-arabinic
acid

**CERASINS** >CERASIN

**CERASTES** *n* any venomous
snake of the genus
*Cerastes*, esp the horned
viper

**CERASTIUM** *n* mouse-eared
chickweed

**CERATE** *n* hard ointment
or medicated paste
consisting of lard or oil
mixed with wax or resin

**CERATED** *adj* (of certain
birds, such as the falcon)
having a cere

**CERATES** >CERATE

**CERATIN** *same as* >KERATIN

**CERATINS** >CERATIN

**CERATITIS** *same
as* >KERATITIS

**CERATODUS** *n* any of
various extinct lungfish
constituting the genus
*Ceratodus*, common in
Cretaceous and Triassic
times

**CERATOID** *adj* having the
shape or texture of animal
horn

**CERBEREAN** *adj* of or
resembling Cerberus, the
three-headed dog that
guarded the entrance to
Hades in Greek mythology

**CERBERIAN** *same
as* >CERBEREAN

**CERCAL** *adj* of or relating
to a tail

**CERCARIA** *n* one of the
larval forms of trematode
worms. It has a short
forked tail and resembles
an immature adult

**CERCARIAE** >CERCARIA

**CERCARIAL** >CERCARIA

**CERCARIAN** >CERCARIA

**CERCARIAS** >CERCARIA

**CERCI** >CERCUS

**CERCIS** *n* any tree or shrub
of the leguminous genus

*Cercis*, which includes the
redbud and Judas tree

**CERCISES** >CERCIS

**CERCUS** *n* one of a pair of
sensory appendages at
the tip of the abdomen of
some insects and other
arthropods

**CERE** *n* soft waxy swelling,
containing the nostrils, at
the base of the upper beak
of a parrot ▷ *vb* wrap (a
corpse) in a cerecloth

**CEREAL** *n* grass plant with
edible grain, such as oat or
wheat

**CEREALIST** *n* expert in
cereals

**CEREALS** >CEREAL

**CEREBELLA** *n* plural of
singular cerebellum: one
of the major divisions of
the vertebrate brain

**CEREBRA** >CEREBRUM

**CEREBRAL** *same
as* >CACUMINAL

**CEREBRALS** >CEREBRAL

**CEREBRATE** *vb* use the
mind

**CEREBRIC** >CEREBRUM

**CEREBROID** >CEREBRUM

**CEREBRUM** *n* main part of
the brain

**CEREBRUMS** >CEREBRUM

**CERECLOTH** *n* waxed
waterproof cloth of a kind
formerly used as a shroud

**CERED** >CERE

**CEREMENT** *n* any burial
clothes

**CEREMENTS** >CEREMENT

**CEREMONY** *n* formal act or
ritual

**CEREOUS** *adj* waxlike

**CERES** >CERE

**CERESIN** *n* white wax
extracted from ozocerite

**CERESINE** *same
as* >CERESIN

**CERESINES** >CERESINE

**CERESINS** >CERESINE

**CEREUS** *n* any tropical
American cactus of
the genus *Cereus*, esp *C.
jamacaru* of N Brazil, which
grows to a height of 13
metres (40 feet)

**CEREUSES** >CEREUS

**CERGE** *n* large altar candle

**CERGES** >CERGE

**CERIA** *n* ceric oxide

**CERIAS** >CERIA

**CERIC** *adj* of or containing
cerium in the tetravalent
state

**CERING** >CERE

**CERIPH** *same as* >SERIF

**CERIPHS** >CERIPH

**CERISE** *adj* cherry-red
▷ *n* moderate to dark red
colour

**CERISES** >CERISE

**CERITE** *n* hydrous silicate
of cerium

CERITES > CERITE

CERIUM n steel-grey metallic element

CERIUMS > CERIUM

CERMET n any of several materials consisting of a metal matrix with ceramic particles disseminated through it. They are hard and resistant to high temperatures

CERMETS > CERMET

CERNE obsolete variant of > ENCIRCLE

CERNED > CERNE

CERNES > CERNE

CERNING > CERNE

CERNUOUS adj (of some flowers or buds) drooping

CERO n large spiny-finned food fish, Scomberomorus regalis, of warm American coastal regions of the Atlantic: family Scombridae (mackerels, tunnies, etc)

CEROGRAPH n writing on wax

CEROMANCY n divination by interpreting significance of shapes formed when melted wax is dropped into water

CEROON n hide-covered bale

CEROONS > CEROON

CEROS > CERO

CEROTIC as in cerotic acid white insoluble odourless wax

CEROTYPE n process for preparing a printing plate by engraving a wax-coated copper plate and then using this as a mould for an electrotype

CEROTYPES > CEROTYPE

CEROUS adj of or containing cerium in the trivalent state

CERRIAL adj relating to the cerris

CERRIS n Turkey oak

CERRISES > CERRIS

CERT n certainty

CERTAIN adj positive and confident

CERTAINER > CERTAIN

CERTAINLY adv without doubt ▷ sentence substitute by all means

CERTAINTY n state of being sure

CERTES adv with certainty

CERTIFIED > CERTIFY

CERTIFIER > CERTIFY

CERTIFIES > CERTIFY

CERTIFY vb confirm, attest to

CERTITUDE n confidence, certainty

CERTS > CERT

CERULE adj sky-blue

CERULEAN n deep blue colour ▷ n light shade of blue

CERULEANS > CERULEAN

CERULEIN n type of dyestuff

CERULEINS > CERULEIN

CERULEOUS adj sky-blue

CERUMEN n soft brownish-yellow wax secreted by glands in the auditory canal of the external ear

CERUMENS > CERUMEN

CERUSE n white lead

CERUSES > CERUSE

CERUSITE same as > CERUSSITE

CERUSITES > CERUSITE

CERUSSITE n usually white mineral, found in veins

CERVELAS n French garlicky pork sausage

CERVELAT n smoked sausage made from pork and beef

CERVELATS > CERVELAT

CERVEZA n Spanish word for beer

CERVEZAS > CERVEZA

CERVICAL adj of or relating to the neck or cervix

CERVICES > CERVIX

CERVICUM n flexible region between the prothorax and head in insects

CERVICUMS > CERVICUM

CERVID n any ruminant mammal of the family Cervidae, including the deer, characterized by the presence of antlers ▷ adj of, relating to, or belonging to the Cervidae

CERVIDS > CERVID

CERVINE adj resembling or relating to a deer

CERVIX n narrow entrance of the womb

CERVIXES > CERVIX

CESAREAN variant of > CAESAREAN

CESAREANS > CESAREAN

CESAREVNA n wife of a Russian tsar's eldest son

CESARIAN US variant of > CAESAREAN

CESARIANS > CESARIAN

CESIOUS same as > CAESIOUS

CESIUM same as > CAESIUM

CESIUMS > CESIUM

CESPITOSE adj growing in dense tufts

CESS n any of several special taxes, such as a land tax in Scotland ▷ vb tax or assess for taxation

CESSATION n ceasing

CESSE obsolete variant of > CEASE

CESSED > CESS

CESSER n coming to an end of a term interest or annuity

CESSERS > CESSER

CESSES > CESS

CESSING > CESS

CESSION n ceding

CESSIONS > CESSION

CESSPIT same as > CESSPOOL

CESSPITS > CESSPIT

CESSPOOL n covered tank or pit for collecting and storing sewage or waste water

CESSPOOLS > CESSPOOL

CESTA n in jai alai, the basket used to throw and catch the pelota

CESTAS > CESTA

CESTI > CESTUS

CESTODE n any parasitic flatworm of the class Cestoda, which includes the tapeworms

CESTODES > CESTODE

CESTOI > CESTOS

CESTOID adj (esp of tapeworms and similar animals) ribbon-like in form ▷ n ribbon-like worm

CESTOIDS > CESTOID

CESTOS same as > CESTUS

CESTOSES > CESTOS

CESTUI n "the one (who)"; legal term, used in certain phrases, to designate a person

CESTUIS > CESTUI

CESTUS n girdle of Aphrodite (Venus) decorated to cause amorousness

CESTUSES > CESTUS

CESURA a variant spelling of > CAESURA

CESURAE > CESURA

CESURAL > CESURA

CESURAS > CESURA

CESURE same as > CAESURA

CESURES > CESURE

CETACEAN n fish-shaped sea mammal such as a whale or dolphin ▷ adj relating to these mammals

CETACEANS > CETACEAN

CETACEOUS same as > CETACEAN

CETANE n colourless liquid hydrocarbon, used as a solvent

CETANES > CETANE

CETE n group of badgers

CETERACH n scale-fern

CETERACHS > CETERACH

CETES > CETE

CETOLOGY n branch of zoology concerned with the study of whales (cetaceans)

CETRIMIDE n quaternary ammonium compound used as a detergent

CETYL n univalent alcohol radical

CETYLS > CETYL

CETYWALL n valerian

CETYWALLS > CETYWALL

CEVADILLA same as > SABADILLA

CEVAPCICI n sausages made with beef and paprika

CEVICHE n Peruvian seafood dish

CEVICHES > CEVICHE

CEYLANITE same as > CEYLONITE

CEYLONITE n pleonaste

CH variant of > ICH

CHA n tea

CHABAZITE n pink, white, or colourless zeolite mineral

CHABLIS n dry white French wine

CHABOUK n type of whip

CHABOUKS > CHABOUK

CHABUK same as > CHABOUK

CHABUKS > CHABUK

CHACE obsolete variant of > CHASE

CHACED > CHACE

CHACES > CHACE

CHACHKA n cheap trinket

CHACHKAS > CHACHKA

CHACING > CHACE

CHACK vb to bite

CHACKED > CHACK

CHACKING > CHACK

CHACKS > CHACK

CHACMA n baboon, Papio (or Chaeropithecus) ursinus, having coarse greyish hair and occurring in southern and eastern Africa

CHACMAS > CHACMA

CHACO same as > SHAKO

CHACOES > CHACO

CHACONNE n musical form consisting of a set of variations on a repeated melodic bass line

CHACONNES > CHACONNE

CHACOS > CHACO

CHAD n small pieces removed during the punching of holes in punch cards, printer paper, etc

CHADAR same as > CHUDDAR

CHADARIM > CHEDER

CHADARS > CHADAR

CHADDAR same as > CHUDDAR

CHADDARS > CHADDAR

CHADDOR same as > CHUDDAR

CHADDORS > CHADDOR

CHADLESS adj (of a keypunch) not producing chads

CHADO n Japanese tea ceremony

CHADOR same as > CHUDDAR

CHADORS > CHADOR

CHADOS > CHADO

CHADRI n shroud which covers the body from head to foot, usually worn by females in Islamic countries

CHADS > CHAD

**CHAEBOL** n large, usually family-owned, business group in South Korea

**CHAEBOLS** > CHAEBOL

**CHAETA** n any of the chitinous bristles on the body of such annelids as the earthworm and the lugworm: used in locomotion

**CHAETAE** > CHAETA

**CHAETAL** > CHAETA

**CHAETODON** n butterfly fish

**CHAETOPOD** n any annelid worm of the classes Oligochaeta or Polychaeta

**CHAFE** vb make sore or worn by rubbing

**CHAFED** > CHAFE

**CHAFER** n large beetle

**CHAFERS** > CHAFER

**CHAFES** > CHAFE

**CHAFF** n grain husks ▷ vb tease good-naturedly

**CHAFFED** > CHAFF

**CHAFFER** vb haggle

**CHAFFERED** > CHAFFER

**CHAFFERER** > CHAFFER

**CHAFFERS** > CHAFFER

**CHAFFERY** n bargaining

**CHAFFIER** > CHAFF

**CHAFFIEST** > CHAFF

**CHAFFINCH** n small European songbird

**CHAFFING** > CHAFF

**CHAFFINGS** > CHAFF

**CHAFFRON** same as > CHAMFRON

**CHAFFRONS** > CHAFFRON

**CHAFFS** > CHAFF

**CHAFFY** > CHAFF

**CHAFING** > CHAFE

**CHAFT** n jaw

**CHAFTS** > CHAFT

**CHAGAN** n Mongolian royal or imperial title

**CHAGANS** > CHAGAN

**CHAGRIN** n annoyance and disappointment ▷ vb embarrass and annoy

**CHAGRINED** > CHAGRIN

**CHAGRINS** > CHAGRIN

**CHAI** n tea, esp as made in India with added spices

**CHAIN** n flexible length of connected metal links ▷ vb restrict or fasten with or as if with a chain

**CHAINE** adj (of a dance turn) producing a full rotation for every two steps taken ▷ vb produce a full rotation for every two steps taken

**CHAINED** > CHAIN

**CHAINES** > CHAINE

**CHAINFALL** n type of hoist

**CHAINING** > CHAIN

**CHAINLESS** adj having no chain

**CHAINLET** n small chain

**CHAINLETS** > CHAINLET

**CHAINMAN** n person who does the chaining in a survey

**CHAINMEN** > CHAINMAN

**CHAINS** > CHAIN

**CHAINSAW** n motor-driven saw with teeth linked in a continuous chain ▷ vb operate a chainsaw

**CHAINSAWS** > CHAINSAW

**CHAINSHOT** n cannon shot of two balls joined by a chain

**CHAINWORK** n work linked or looped in the manner of a chain

**CHAIR** n seat with a back, for one person ▷ vb preside over (a meeting)

**CHAIRDAYS** n old age

**CHAIRED** > CHAIR

**CHAIRING** > CHAIR

**CHAIRLIFT** n series of chairs suspended from a moving cable for carrying people up a slope

**CHAIRMAN** n person in charge of a company's board of directors or a meeting ▷ vb to act as chairman of

**CHAIRMANS** > CHAIRMAN

**CHAIRMEN** > CHAIRMAN

**CHAIRS** > CHAIR

**CHAIS** > CHAI

**CHAISE** n light horse-drawn carriage

**CHAISES** > CHAISE

**CHAKALAKA** n relish made from tomatoes, onions, and spices

**CHAKRA** n (in yoga) any of the seven major energy centres in the body

**CHAKRAS** > CHAKRA

**CHAL** n in Romany, person or fellow

**CHALAH** same as > CHALLAH

**CHALAHS** > CHALAH

**CHALAN** vb (in India) to cause an accused person to appear before a magistrate

**CHALANED** > CHALAN

**CHALANING** > CHALAN

**CHALANS** > CHALAN

**CHALAZA** n one of a pair of spiral threads of albumen holding the yolk of a bird's egg in position

**CHALAZAE** > CHALAZA

**CHALAZAL** > CHALAZA

**CHALAZAS** > CHALAZA

**CHALAZIA** > CHALAZION

**CHALAZION** n small cyst on the eyelid resulting from chronic inflammation of a meibomian gland

**CHALCID** n any tiny hymenopterous insect of the family Chalcididae and related families, whose larvae are parasites of other insects

**CHALCIDS** > CHALCID

**CHALCOGEN** n any of the elements oxygen, sulphur, selenium, tellurium, or polonium, of group 6A of the periodic table

**CHALDER** n former Scottish dry measure

**CHALDERS** > CHALDER

**CHALDRON** n unit of capacity equal to 36 bushels. Formerly used in the US for the measurement of solids, being equivalent to 1.268 cubic metres. Used in Britain for both solids and liquids, it is equivalent to 1.309 cubic metres

**CHALDRONS** > CHALDRON

**CHALEH** same as > CHALLAH

**CHALEHS** > CHALEH

**CHALET** n kind of Swiss wooden house with a steeply sloping roof

**CHALETS** > CHALET

**CHALICE** n large goblet

**CHALICED** adj (of plants) having cup-shaped flowers

**CHALICES** > CHALICE

**CHALK** n soft white rock consisting of calcium carbonate ▷ vb draw or mark with chalk

**CHALKED** > CHALK

**CHALKFACE** n work or art of teaching in a school

**CHALKIER** > CHALK

**CHALKIEST** > CHALK

**CHALKING** > CHALK

**CHALKLIKE** > CHALK

**CHALKPIT** n quarry for chalk

**CHALKPITS** > CHALKPIT

**CHALKS** > CHALK

**CHALKY** > CHALK

**CHALLA** same as > CHALLAH

**CHALLAH** n bread, usually in the form of a plaited loaf, traditionally eaten by Jews to celebrate the Sabbath

**CHALLAHS** > CHALLAH

**CHALLAN** same as > CHALAN

**CHALLANED** > CHALLAN

**CHALLANS** > CHALLAN

**CHALLAS** > CHALLA

**CHALLENGE** n demanding or stimulating situation ▷ vb issue a challenge to

**CHALLIE** same as > CHALLIS

**CHALLIES** > CHALLIE

**CHALLIS** n lightweight plain-weave fabric of wool, cotton, etc, usually with a printed design

**CHALLISES** > CHALLIS

**CHALLOT** > CHALLAH

**CHALLOTH** > CHALLAH

**CHALLY** same as > CHALLIS

**CHALONE** n any internal secretion that inhibits a physiological process or function

**CHALONES** > CHALONE

**CHALONIC** > CHALONE

**CHALOT** > CHALAH

**CHALOTH** > CHALAH

**CHALS** > CHAL

**CHALUMEAU** n early type of reed instrument, precursor of the clarinet

**CHALUPA** n Mexican dish

**CHALUPAS** > CHALUPA

**CHALUTZ** n member of an organization of immigrants to Israeli agricultural settlements

**CHALUTZES** > CHALUTZ

**CHALUTZIM** > CHALUTZ

**CHALYBEAN** adj (of steel) of superior quality

**CHALYBITE** another name for > SIDERITE

**CHAM** an archaic word for > KHAN

**CHAMADE** n (formerly) a signal by drum or trumpet inviting an enemy to a parley

**CHAMADES** > CHAMADE

**CHAMBER** n hall used for formal meetings ▷ vb act lasciviously

**CHAMBERED** > CHAMBER

**CHAMBERER** n lascivious person

**CHAMBERS** pl n judge's room for hearing private cases not taken in open court

**CHAMBRAY** n smooth light fabric of cotton, linen, etc, with white weft and a coloured warp

**CHAMBRAYS** > CHAMBRAY

**CHAMBRE** adj (of wine) at room temperature

**CHAMELEON** n small lizard that changes colour to blend in with its surroundings

**CHAMELOT** same as > CAMLET

**CHAMELOTS** > CHAMELOT

**CHAMETZ** n leavened food which may not be eaten during Passover

**CHAMETZES** > CHAMETZ

**CHAMFER** same as > CHASE

**CHAMFERED** > CHAMFER

**CHAMFERER** > CHAMFER

**CHAMFERS** > CHAMFER

**CHAMFRAIN** same as > CHAMFRON

**CHAMFRON** n piece of armour for a horse's head

**CHAMFRONS** > CHAMFRON

**CHAMISA** n American shrub

**CHAMISAL** n place overgrown with chamiso

**CHAMISALS** > CHAMISAL

**CHAMISAS** > CHAMISA

**CHAMISE** same as > CHAMISO

**CHAMISES** > CHAMISE

**CHAMISO** n fourwing saltbush

**CHAMISOS** > CHAMISO

**CHAMLET** same as > CAMLET

**CHAMLETS** > CHAMLET

**CHAMMIED** > CHAMMY

**CHAMMIES** > CHAMMY

**CHAMMY** same as > CHAMOIS

**CHAMMYING** > CHAMMY

**CHAMOIS** n small mountain antelope or a pice of leather from its skin, used for polishing ▷ vb polish with a chamois

**CHAMOISED** > CHAMOIS

**CHAMOISES** > CHAMOIS

**CHAMOIX** same as > CHAMOIS

**CHAMOMILE** same as > CAMOMILE

**CHAMP** vb chew noisily

**CHAMPAC** n magnoliaceous tree, Michelia champaca, of India and the East Indies. Its fragrant yellow flowers yield an oil used in perfumes and its wood is used for furniture

**CHAMPACA** same as > CHAMPAC

**CHAMPACAS** > CHAMPACA

**CHAMPACS** > CHAMPAC

**CHAMPAGNE** n sparkling white French wine ▷ adj denoting a luxurious lifestyle

**CHAMPAIGN** n expanse of open level or gently undulating country

**CHAMPAK** same as > CHAMPAC

**CHAMPAKS** > CHAMPAK

**CHAMPART** n granting of land to a person, on condition that a portion of the crops will be given to the seller

**CHAMPARTS** > CHAMPART

**CHAMPED** > CHAMP

**CHAMPER** > CHAMP

**CHAMPERS** n champagne

**CHAMPERTY** n (formerly) an illegal bargain between a party to litigation and an outsider whereby the latter agrees to pay for the action and thereby share in any proceeds recovered

**CHAMPING** > CHAMP

**CHAMPION** n overall winner of a competition ▷ vb support ▷ adj excellent ▷ adv very well

**CHAMPIONS** > CHAMPION

**CHAMPLEVE** adj of or relating to a process of enamelling by which grooves are cut into a metal base and filled with enamel colours ▷ n object enamelled by this process

**CHAMPS** > CHAMP

**CHAMPY** adj (of earth) churned up (by cattle, for example)

**CHAMS** > CHAM

**CHANCE** n likelihood, probability ▷ vb risk, hazard

**CHANCED** > CHANCE

**CHANCEFUL** > CHANCE

**CHANCEL** n part of a church containing the altar and choir

**CHANCELS** > CHANCEL

**CHANCER** n unscrupulous or dishonest opportunist who is prepared to try any dubious scheme for making money or furthering his own ends

**CHANCERS** > CHANCER

**CHANCERY** n Lord Chancellor's court, now a division of the High Court of Justice

**CHANCES** > CHANCE

**CHANCEY** same as > CHANCY

**CHANCIER** > CHANCY

**CHANCIEST** > CHANCY

**CHANCILY** > CHANCY

**CHANCING** > CHANCE

**CHANCRE** n small hard growth which is the first sign of syphilis

**CHANCRES** > CHANCRE

**CHANCROID** n soft venereal ulcer, esp of the male genitals, caused by infection with the bacillus Haemophilus ducreyi ▷ adj relating to or resembling a chancroid or chancre

**CHANCROUS** > CHANCRE

**CHANCY** adj uncertain, risky

**CHANDELLE** n abrupt climbing turn almost to the point of stalling, in which an aircraft's momentum is used to increase its rate of climb ▷ vb carry out a chandelle

**CHANDLER** n dealer, esp in ships' supplies

**CHANDLERS** > CHANDLER

**CHANDLERY** n business, warehouse, or merchandise of a chandler

**CHANFRON** same as > CHAMFRON

**CHANFRONS** > CHANFRON

**CHANG** n loud discordant noise

**CHANGA** interj in Indian English, an expression of approval or agreement

**CHANGE** n becoming different ▷ vb make or become different

**CHANGED** > CHANGE

**CHANGEFUL** adj often changing

**CHANGER** > CHANGE

**CHANGERS** > CHANGE

**CHANGES** > CHANGE

**CHANGEUP** n type of baseball pitch

**CHANGEUPS** > CHANGEUP

**CHANGING** > CHANGE

**CHANGS** > CHANG

**CHANK** n shell of several types of sea conch, used to make bracelets

**CHANKS** > CHANK

**CHANNEL** n band of broadcasting frequencies ▷ vb direct or convey through a channel

**CHANNELED** > CHANNEL

**CHANNELER** > CHANNEL

**CHANNELS** > CHANNEL

**CHANNER** n gravel

**CHANNERS** > CHANNER

**CHANOYO** a variant of > CHADO

**CHANOYOS** > CHANOYO

**CHANOYU** same as > CHADO

**CHANOYUS** > CHADO

**CHANSON** n song

**CHANSONS** > CHANSON

**CHANT** vb utter or sing (a slogan or psalm) ▷ n rhythmic or repetitious slogan

**CHANTABLE** > CHANT

**CHANTAGE** n blackmail

**CHANTAGES** > CHANTAGE

**CHANTED** > CHANT

**CHANTER** n (on bagpipes) pipe on which the melody is played

**CHANTERS** > CHANTER

**CHANTEUSE** n female singer, esp in a nightclub or cabaret

**CHANTEY** the usual US spelling of > SHANTY

**CHANTEYS** > CHANTEY

**CHANTIE** n chamber pot

**CHANTIES** > CHANTY

**CHANTILLY** as in chantilly lace delicate ornamental lace

**CHANTING** > CHANT

**CHANTOR** same as > CHANTER

**CHANTORS** > CHANTOR

**CHANTRESS** n female chanter

**CHANTRIES** > CHANTRY

**CHANTRY** n endowment for the singing of Masses for the soul of the founder or others designated by him

**CHANTS** > CHANT

**CHANTY** same as > SHANTY

**CHANUKIAH** a variant spelling of > HANUKIAH

**CHAO** n Vietnamese rice porridge

**CHAOLOGY** n study of chaos theory

**CHAORDIC** adj combining elements of chaos and order

**CHAOS** n complete disorder or confusion

**CHAOSES** > CHAOS

**CHAOTIC** > CHAOS

**CHAP** n man or boy ▷ vb (of the skin) to make or become raw and cracked, esp by exposure to cold

**CHAPARRAL** n (in the southwestern US) a dense growth of shrubs and trees, esp evergreen oaks

**CHAPATI** n (in Indian cookery) flat thin unleavened bread

**CHAPATIES** > CHAPATI

**CHAPATIS** > CHAPATI

**CHAPATTI** same as > CHAPATI

**CHAPATTIS** > CHAPATTI

**CHAPBOOK** n book of popular ballads, stories, etc, formerly sold by chapmen or pedlars

**CHAPBOOKS** > CHAPBOOK

**CHAPE** n metal tip or trimming for a scabbard

**CHAPEAU** n hat

**CHAPEAUS** > CHAPEAU

**CHAPEAUX** > CHAPEAU

**CHAPEL** n place of worship with its own altar, within a church

**CHAPELESS** > CHAPE

**CHAPELRY** n district legally assigned to and served by an Anglican chapel

**CHAPELS** > CHAPEL

**CHAPERON** n (esp formerly) an older or married woman who accompanies or supervises a young unmarried woman on social occasions ▷ vb act as a chaperon to

**CHAPERONE** same as > CHAPERON

**CHAPERONS** > CHAPERON

**CHAPES** > CHAPE

**CHAPESS** n woman

**CHAPESSES** > CHAPESS

**CHAPITER** same as > CAPITAL

**CHAPITERS** > CHAPITER

**CHAPKA** same as > CZAPKA

**CHAPKAS** > CHAPKA

**CHAPLAIN** n clergyman attached to a chapel, military body, or institution

**CHAPLAINS** > CHAPLAIN

**CHAPLESS** adj lacking a lower jaw

**CHAPLET** n garland for the head ▷ vb create a garland

**CHAPLETED** > CHAPLET

**CHAPLETS** > CHAPLET

**CHAPMAN** n travelling pedlar

**CHAPMEN** > CHAPMAN

**CHAPPAL** n one of a pair of sandals, usually of leather, worn in India

**CHAPPALS** > CHAPPAL

**CHAPPATI** same as > CHAPATI

**CHAPPATIS** > CHAPPATI

**CHAPPED** > CHAP

**CHAPPESS** same as > CHAPESS

**CHAPPIE** n man or boy

**CHAPPIER** > CHAPPY

**CHAPPIES** > CHAPPIE

**CHAPPIEST** > CHAPPY

**CHAPPING** > CHAP

**CHAPPY** adj (of skin) chapped

**CHAPRASSI** n in India, during the British Empire, an office messenger

**CHAPS** > CHAP

**CHAPSTICK** n cylinder of a

substance for preventing
or soothing chapped lips
**CHAPT** *adj* chapped
**CHAPTER** *n* division of a
book ▷ *vb* divide into
chapters
**CHAPTERAL** >CHAPTER
**CHAPTERED** >CHAPTER
**CHAPTERS** >CHAPTER
**CHAPTREL** *n* capital of a
pillar supporting an arch
**CHAPTRELS** >CHAPTREL
**CHAQUETA** *n* South
American cowboy jacket
**CHAQUETAS** >CHAQUETA
**CHAR** *vb* blacken by partial
burning ▷ *n* charwoman
**CHARA** *n* type of green
freshwater algae
**CHARABANC** *n* coach for
sightseeing
**CHARACID** *same*
*as* >CHARACIN
**CHARACIDS** >CHARACIN
**CHARACIN** *n* any small
carnivorous freshwater
cyprinoid fish of the family
*Characidae*, of Central and
South America and Africa.
They are similar to the
carps but more brightly
coloured
**CHARACINS** >CHARACIN
**CHARACT** *n* distinctive
mark
**CHARACTER** *n* combination
of qualities distinguishing
a person, group, or place
**CHARACTS** >CHARACT
**CHARADE** *n* absurd pretence
**CHARADES** *n* game in
which one team acts out
each syllable of a word or
phrase, which the other
team has to guess
**CHARANGA** *n* type of
orchestra used in
performing traditional
Cuban music
**CHARANGAS** >CHARANGA
**CHARANGO** *n* Andean ten-
stringed mandolin
**CHARANGOS** >CHARANGO
**CHARAS** *another name*
*for* >HASHISH
**CHARASES** >CHARAS
**CHARBROIL** *vb* to grill over
charcoal
**CHARCOAL** *n* black
substance formed by
partially burning wood
▷ *adj* very dark grey ▷ *vb*
write, draw, or blacken
with charcoal
**CHARCOALS** >CHARCOAL
**CHARCOALY** >CHARCOAL
**CHARD** *n* variety of beet,
*Beta vulgaris cicla*, with
large succulent leaves
and thick stalks, used as a
vegetable
**CHARDS** >CHARD
**CHARE** *same as* >CHAR
**CHARED** >CHAR

**CHARES** >CHAR
**CHARET** *obsolete variant*
*of* >CHARIOT
**CHARETS** >CHARET
**CHARGE** *vb* ask as a price
▷ *n* price charged
**CHARGED** >CHARGE
**CHARGEFUL** *adj* expensive
**CHARGER** *n* device for
charging an accumulator
**CHARGERS** >CHARGER
**CHARGES** >CHARGE
**CHARGING** >CHARGE
**CHARGRILL** *vb* to grill over
charcoal
**CHARIDEE** *n* jocular
spelling of charity, as
pronounced in a mid-
Atlantic accent
**CHARIDEES** >CHARIDEE
**CHARIER** >CHARY
**CHARIEST** >CHARY
**CHARILY** *adv* cautiously
**CHARINESS** *n* state of being
chary
**CHARING** >CHAR
**CHARIOT** *n* two-wheeled
horse-drawn vehicle used
in ancient times in wars
and races ▷ *vb* to ride in a
chariot
**CHARIOTED** >CHARIOT
**CHARIOTS** >CHARIOT
**CHARISM** *same*
*as* >CHARISMA
**CHARISMA** *n* person's power
to attract or influence
people
**CHARISMAS** >CHARISMA
**CHARISMS** >CHARISM
**CHARITIES** >CHARITY
**CHARITY** *n* organization
that gives help, such as
money or food, to those
in need
**CHARIVARI** *n* discordant
mock serenade to
newlyweds, made with
pans, kettles, etc ▷ *vb*
make such a serenade
**CHARK** *vb* to char
**CHARKA** *same as* >CHARKHA
**CHARKAS** >CHARKA
**CHARKED** >CHARK
**CHARKHA** *n* (in India) a
spinning wheel, esp for
cotton
**CHARKHAS** >CHARKHA
**CHARKING** >CHARK
**CHARKS** >CHARK
**CHARLADY** *same*
*as* >CHARWOMAN
**CHARLATAN** *n* person who
claims expertise that he or
she does not have
**CHARLEY** *as in* *charley horse*
muscle stiffness after
strenuous exercise
**CHARLEYS** >CHARLEY
**CHARLIE** *n* fool
**CHARLIER** *as in* *charlier shoe*
special light horseshoe
**CHARLIES** >CHARLIE
**CHARLOCK** *n* weed with

hairy leaves and yellow
flowers
**CHARLOCKS** >CHARLOCK
**CHARLOTTE** *n* dessert made
with fruit and bread or
cake crumbs
**CHARM** *n* attractive quality
▷ *vb* attract, delight
**CHARMED** *adj* delighted or
fascinated
**CHARMER** *n* attractive
person
**CHARMERS** >CHARMER
**CHARMEUSE** *n* trademark
for a lightweight fabric
with a satin-like finish
**CHARMFUL** *adj* highly
charming or enchanting
**CHARMING** *adj* attractive
**CHARMLESS** *adj* devoid of
charm
**CHARMONIA** *pl n* elementary
particles containing an
antiquark and a charm
quark
**CHARMS** >CHARM
**CHARNECO** *n* type of sweet
wine
**CHARNECOS** >CHARNECO
**CHARNEL** *adj* ghastly ▷ *n*
ghastly thing
**CHARNELS** >CHARNEL
**CHAROSET** *n* dish of
chopped fruit, nuts and
wine, eaten at Passover
**CHAROSETH** *same*
*as* >CHAROSET
**CHAROSETS** >CHAROSET
**CHARPAI** *same as* >CHARPOY
**CHARPAIS** >CHARPAI
**CHARPIE** *n* lint pieces used
to make surgical dressings
**CHARPIES** >CHARPIE
**CHARPOY** *n* bedstead of
woven webbing or hemp
stretched on a wooden
frame on four legs,
common in India
**CHARPOYS** >CHARPOY
**CHARQUI** *n* meat, esp beef,
cut into strips and dried
**CHARQUID** >CHARQUI
**CHARQUIS** >CHARQUI
**CHARR** *same as* >CHAR
**CHARRED** >CHAR
**CHARRIER** >CHARRY
**CHARRIEST** >CHARRY
**CHARRING** >CHAR
**CHARRO** *n* Mexican cowboy
**CHARROS** >CHARRO
**CHARRS** >CHARR
**CHARRY** *adj* of or relating to
charcoal
**CHARS** >CHAR
**CHART** *n* graph, table,
or diagram showing
information ▷ *vb* plot the
course of
**CHARTA** *n* charter
**CHARTABLE** >CHART
**CHARTAS** >CHARTA
**CHARTED** >CHART
**CHARTER** *n* document
granting or demanding

certain rights ▷ *vb* hire by
charter
**CHARTERED** *adj* officially
qualified to practise a
profession
**CHARTERER** >CHARTER
**CHARTERS** >CHARTER
**CHARTING** >CHART
**CHARTISM** *n* historical
reform movement in
Britain
**CHARTISMS** >CHARTISM
**CHARTIST** *n* supporter of
chartism
**CHARTISTS** >CHARTIST
**CHARTLESS** *adj* not
mapped
**CHARTS** >CHART
**CHARVER** *n* derogatory
term for a young woman
**CHARVERS** >CHARVER
**CHARWOMAN** *n* woman
whose job is to clean other
people's homes
**CHARWOMEN** >CHARWOMAN
**CHARY** *adj* wary, careful
**CHAS** >CHA
**CHASE** *vb* run after quickly
in order to catch or drive
away ▷ *n* chasing, pursuit
**CHASEABLE** >CHASE
**CHASED** >CHASE
**CHASEPORT** *n* porthole
through which a chase
gun is fired
**CHASER** *n* milder drink
drunk after another
stronger one
**CHASERS** >CHASER
**CHASES** >CHASE
**CHASING** >CHASE
**CHASINGS** >CHASE
**CHASM** *n* deep crack in the
earth ▷ *vb* create a chasm
**CHASMAL** >CHASM
**CHASMED** >CHASM
**CHASMIC** >CHASM
**CHASMIER** >CHASMY
**CHASMIEST** >CHASMY
**CHASMS** >CHASM
**CHASMY** *adj* full of chasms
**CHASSE** *n* one of a series
of gliding steps in ballet
in which the same foot
always leads ▷ *vb* perform
either of these steps
**CHASSED** >CHASSE
**CHASSEED** >CHASSE
**CHASSEING** >CHASSE
**CHASSEPOT** *n* breech-
loading bolt-action rifle
formerly used by the
French Army
**CHASSES** >CHASSE
**CHASSEUR** *n* member of
a unit specially trained
and equipped for swift
deployment ▷ *adj*
designating or cooked in a
sauce consisting of white
wine and mushrooms
**CHASSEURS** >CHASSEUR
**CHASSIS** *n* frame, wheels,
and mechanical parts of a

vehicle

**CHASTE** adj abstaining from sex outside marriage or altogether

**CHASTELY** > CHASTE

**CHASTEN** vb subdue by criticism

**CHASTENED** > CHASTEN

**CHASTENER** > CHASTEN

**CHASTENS** > CHASTEN

**CHASTER** > CHASTE

**CHASTEST** > CHASTE

**CHASTISE** vb scold severely

**CHASTISED** > CHASTISE

**CHASTISER** > CHASTISE

**CHASTISES** > CHASTISE

**CHASTITY** n state of being chaste

**CHASUBLE** n long sleeveless robe worn by a priest when celebrating Mass

**CHASUBLES** > CHASUBLE

**CHAT** n informal conversation ▷ vb have an informal conversation

**CHATBOT** n computer program in the form of a virtual e-mail correspondent that can reply to messages from computer users

**CHATBOTS** > CHATBOT

**CHATCHKA** variant of > TCHOTCHKE

**CHATCHKAS** > CHATCHKA

**CHATCHKE** same as > TCHOTCHKE

**CHATCHKES** > CHATCHKE

**CHATEAU** n French castle

**CHATEAUS** > CHATEAU

**CHATEAUX** > CHATEAU

**CHATELAIN** same as > CASTELLAN

**CHATLINE** n telephone service enabling callers to join in general conversation with each other

**CHATLINES** > CHATLINE

**CHATON** n in jewellery, a stone with a reflective metal foil backing

**CHATONS** > CHATON

**CHATOYANT** adj having changeable lustre ▷ n gemstone with a changeable lustre

**CHATROOM** n site on the Internet where users have group discussions by e-mail

**CHATROOMS** > CHATROOM

**CHATS** > CHAT

**CHATTA** n umbrella

**CHATTAS** > CHATTA

**CHATTED** > CHAT

**CHATTEL** n item of movable personal property

**CHATTELS** > CHATTEL

**CHATTER** vb speak quickly and continuously about unimportant things ▷ n idle talk

**CHATTERED** > CHATTER

**CHATTERER** same as > COTINGA

**CHATTERS** > CHATTER

**CHATTERY** > CHATTER

**CHATTI** (in India) an earthenware pot

**CHATTIER** > CHATTY

**CHATTIES** > CHATTI

**CHATTIEST** > CHATTY

**CHATTILY** > CHATTY

**CHATTING** > CHAT

**CHATTIS** > CHATTI

**CHATTY** adj (of a person) fond of friendly, informal conversation

**CHAUFE** obsolete variant of > CHAFE

**CHAUFED** > CHAUFE

**CHAUFER** same as > CHAUFFER

**CHAUFERS** > CHAUFER

**CHAUFES** > CHAUFE

**CHAUFF** obsolete variant of > CHAFE

**CHAUFFED** > CHAUFF

**CHAUFFER** n small portable heater or stove

**CHAUFFERS** > CHAUFFER

**CHAUFFEUR** n person employed to drive a car for someone ▷ vb act as driver for (someone)

**CHAUFFING** > CHAUFF

**CHAUFFS** > CHAUFF

**CHAUFING** > CHAUFE

**CHAUMER** n chamber

**CHAUMERS** > CHAUMER

**CHAUNCE** archaic variant of > CHANCE

**CHAUNCED** > CHAUNCE

**CHAUNCES** > CHAUNCE

**CHAUNCING** > CHAUNCE

**CHAUNGE** archaic variant of > CHANGE

**CHAUNGED** > CHAUNGE

**CHAUNGES** > CHAUNGE

**CHAUNGING** > CHAUNGE

**CHAUNT** a less common variant of > CHANT

**CHAUNTED** > CHAUNT

**CHAUNTER** > CHAUNT

**CHAUNTERS** > CHAUNT

**CHAUNTING** > CHAUNT

**CHAUNTRY** same as > CHANTRY

**CHAUNTS** > CHAUNT

**CHAUSSES** n tight-fitting medieval garment covering the feet and legs, usually made of chain mail

**CHAUSSURE** n any type of footwear

**CHAUVIN** n chauvinist

**CHAUVINS** > CHAUVIN

**CHAV** n informal derogatory word for a young working-class person who wears casual sports clothes

**CHAVE** vb old dialect term for "I have"

**CHAVENDER** n chub

**CHAVETTE** n informal derogatory word for a young working-class

female who wears casual sports clothes

**CHAVETTES** > CHAVETTE

**CHAVISH** > CHAV

**CHAVS** > CHAV

**CHAW** vb chew (tobacco), esp without swallowing it ▷ n something chewed, esp a plug of tobacco

**CHAWBACON** n bumpkin

**CHAWDRON** n entrails

**CHAWDRONS** > CHAWDRON

**CHAWED** > CHAW

**CHAWER** > CHAW

**CHAWERS** > CHAW

**CHAWING** > CHAW

**CHAWK** n jackdaw

**CHAWKS** > CHAWK

**CHAWS** > CHAW

**CHAY** n plant of the madder family

**CHAYA** same as > CHAY

**CHAYAS** > CHAYA

**CHAYOTE** n tropical American cucurbitaceous climbing plant, Sechium edule, that has edible pear-shaped fruit enclosing a single enormous seed

**CHAYOTES** > CHAYOTE

**CHAYROOT** n root of the chay plant

**CHAYROOTS** > CHAYROOT

**CHAYS** > CHAY

**CHAZAN** same as > CANTOR

**CHAZANIM** > CHAZAN

**CHAZANS** > CHAZAN

**CHAZZAN** variant of > CHAZAN

**CHAZZANIM** > CHAZZAN

**CHAZZANS** > CHAZZAN

**CHAZZEN** same as > CHAZZAN

**CHAZZENIM** > CHAZZEN

**CHAZZENS** > CHAZZEN

**CHE** pron dialectal form meaning "I"

**CHEAP** adj costing relatively little ▷ adv at very little cost ▷ n bargain ▷ vb take the cheapest option

**CHEAPED** > CHEAP

**CHEAPEN** vb lower the reputation of

**CHEAPENED** > CHEAPEN

**CHEAPENER** > CHEAPEN

**CHEAPENS** > CHEAPEN

**CHEAPER** > CHEAP

**CHEAPEST** > CHEAP

**CHEAPIE** n something inexpensive

**CHEAPIES** > CHEAPIE

**CHEAPING** > CHEAP

**CHEAPISH** > CHEAP

**CHEAPJACK** n person who sells cheap and shoddy goods ▷ adj shoddy or inferior

**CHEAPLY** > CHEAP

**CHEAPNESS** > CHEAP

**CHEAPO** n very cheap and possibly shoddy thing

**CHEAPOS** > CHEAPO

**CHEAPS** > CHEAP

**CHEAPY** same as > CHEAPIE

**CHEAT** vb act dishonestly to gain profit or advantage ▷ n person who cheats

**CHEATABLE** > CHEAT

**CHEATED** > CHEAT

**CHEATER** > CHEAT

**CHEATERS** > CHEAT

**CHEATERY** n cheating

**CHEATING** > CHEAT

**CHEATINGS** > CHEAT

**CHEATS** > CHEAT

**CHEBEC** n type of boat

**CHEBECS** > CHEBEC

**CHECHAKO** same as > CHEECHAKO

**CHECHAKOS** > CHECHAKO

**CHECHAQUO** same as > CHEECHAKO

**CHECHIA** n Berber skullcap

**CHECHIAS** > CHECHIA

**CHECK** vb examine or investigate ▷ n control designed to ensure accuracy

**CHECKABLE** > CHECK

**CHECKBOOK** n American word for chequebook

**CHECKED** > CHECK

**CHECKER** same as > CHEQUER

**CHECKERED** same as > CHEQUERED

**CHECKERS** n game for two players using a checkerboard and 12 checkers each. The object is to jump over and capture the opponent's pieces

**CHECKING** > CHECK

**CHECKLESS** adj without check or restraint

**CHECKLIST** vb check items, facts, etc, against those in a list used for verification

**CHECKMARK** vb make a mark of approval or verification

**CHECKMATE** n winning position in which an opponent's king is under attack and unable to escape ▷ vb place the king of (one's opponent) in checkmate ▷ interj call made when placing an opponent's king in checkmate

**CHECKOFF** n procedure where an employer pays the employee's union dues straight from his or her salary

**CHECKOFFS** > CHECKOFF

**CHECKOUT** n counter in a supermarket, where customers pay

**CHECKOUTS** > CHECKOUT

**CHECKRAIL** another word for > GUARDRAIL

**CHECKREIN** n bearing rein

**CHECKROOM** n place at a railway station, airport, etc, where luggage may

be left for a small charge
with an attendant for
safekeeping

**CHECKROW** *n* row of plants,
esp corn, in which the
spaces between adjacent
plants are equal to those
between adjacent rows to
facilitate cultivation ▷ *vb*
plant in checkrows

**CHECKROWS** >CHECKROW

**CHECKS** >CHECK

**CHECKSUM** *n* digit
representing the number
of bits of information
transmitted, attached to
the end of a message, to
verify the integrity of data

**CHECKSUMS** >CHECKSUM

**CHECKUP** *n* thorough
medical examination ▷ *vb*
investigate or make an
inquiry into (a person's
character, evidence, etc),
esp when suspicions have
been aroused

**CHECKUPS** >CHECKUP

**CHECKY** *adj* having squares
of alternating tinctures
or furs

**CHEDDAR** *n* type of smooth
hard yellow or whitish
cheese

**CHEDDARS** >CHEDDAR

**CHEDDARY** >CHEDDAR

**CHEDDITE** *n* explosive
made by mixing a
powdered chlorate or
perchlorate with a fatty
substance, such as castor
oil

**CHEDDITES** >CHEDDITE

**CHEDER** *n* (in Western
countries) elementary
religious education
classes, usually outside
normal school hours

**CHEDERS** >CHEDER

**CHEDITE** *same
as* >CHEDDITE

**CHEDITES** >CHEDITE

**CHEECHAKO** *n* local name
for a newcomer to Alaska

**CHEEK** *n* either side of the
face below the eye ▷ *vb*
speak impudently to

**CHEEKBONE** *n* bone at
the top of the cheek, just
below the eye

**CHEEKED** >CHEEK

**CHEEKFUL** *n* quantity that
can be held in a cheek

**CHEEKFULS** >CHEEKFUL

**CHEEKIER** >CHEEKY

**CHEEKIEST** >CHEEKY

**CHEEKILY** >CHEEKY

**CHEEKING** >CHEEK

**CHEEKLESS** >CHEEK

**CHEEKS** >CHEEK

**CHEEKY** *adj* impudent,
disrespectful

**CHEEP** *n* young bird's high-
pitched cry ▷ *vb* utter a
cheep

**CHEEPED** >CHEEP

**CHEEPER** >CHEEP

**CHEEPERS** >CHEEP

**CHEEPING** >CHEEP

**CHEEPS** >CHEEP

**CHEER** *vb* applaud or
encourage with shouts
▷ *n* shout of applause or
encouragement

**CHEERED** >CHEER

**CHEERER** >CHEER

**CHEERERS** >CHEER

**CHEERFUL** *adj* having a
happy disposition

**CHEERIER** >CHEERY

**CHEERIEST** >CHEERY

**CHEERILY** >CHEERY

**CHEERING** >CHEER

**CHEERIO** *interj* goodbye ▷ *n*
small red cocktail sausage
▷ *sentence substitute*
farewell greeting

**CHEERIOS** >CHEERIO

**CHEERLEAD** *vb* to lead a
crowd in formal cheers at
sports events

**CHEERLED** >CHEERLEAD

**CHEERLESS** *adj* dreary,
gloomy

**CHEERLY** *adv* cheerful or
cheerfully

**CHEERO** *same as* >CHEERIO

**CHEEROS** >CHEERO

**CHEERS** *interj* drinking
toast ▷ *sentence substitute*
drinking toast

**CHEERY** *adj* cheerful

**CHEESE** *n* food made from
coagulated milk curd ▷ *vb*
stop

**CHEESED** >CHEESE

**CHEESES** >CHEESE

**CHEESEVAT** *n* in
cheesemaking, vat in
which curds are formed
and cut

**CHEESIER** >CHEESY

**CHEESIEST** >CHEESY

**CHEESILY** >CHEESY

**CHEESING** >CHEESE

**CHEESY** *adj* like cheese

**CHEETAH** *n* large fast-
running spotted African
wild cat

**CHEETAHS** >CHEETAH

**CHEEWINK** *same
as* >CHEWINK

**CHEEWINKS** >CHEEWINK

**CHEF** *n* cook in a restaurant
▷ *vb* to work as a chef

**CHEFDOM** *n* state or
condition of being a chef

**CHEFDOMS** >CHEFDOM

**CHEFED** >CHEF

**CHEFFED** >CHEF

**CHEFFING** >CHEF

**CHEFING** >CHEF

**CHEFS** >CHEF

**CHEGOE** *same as* >CHIGGER

**CHEGOES** >CHIGGER

**CHEILITIS** *n*
inflammation of the lip(s)

**CHEKA** *n* secret police set
up in Russia in 1917

**CHEKAS** >CHEKA

**CHEKIST** *n* member of the
cheka

**CHEKISTS** >CHEKIST

**CHELA** *n* disciple of a
religious teacher

**CHELAE** >CHELA

**CHELAS** >CHELA

**CHELASHIP** >CHELA

**CHELATE** *n* coordination
compound in which a
metal atom or ion is bound
to a ligand at two or more
points on the ligand, so as
to form a heterocyclic ring
containing a metal atom
▷ *adj* of or possessing
chelae ▷ *vb* form a chelate

**CHELATED** >CHELATE

**CHELATES** >CHELATE

**CHELATING** >CHELATE

**CHELATION** *n* process by
which a chelate is formed

**CHELATOR** >CHELATE

**CHELATORS** >CHELATE

**CHELICERA** *n* one of a pair
of appendages on the
head of spiders and other
arachnids: often modified
as food-catching claws

**CHELIFORM** *adj* shaped like
a chela

**CHELIPED** *n* (on a
arthropod) either of two
legs which each carry a
claw

**CHELIPEDS** >CHELIPED

**CHELLUP** *n* noise

**CHELLUPS** >CHELLUP

**CHELOID** *a variant spelling
of* >KELOID

**CHELOIDAL** >CHELOID

**CHELOIDS** >CHELOID

**CHELONE** *n* any plant of
the hardy N American
genus *Chelone*, grown for
its white, rose, or purple
flower spikes: family
*Scrophulariaceae*

**CHELONES** >CHELONE

**CHELONIAN** *n* any reptile
of the order *Chelonia*,
including the tortoises
and turtles, in which most
of the body is enclosed in
a protective bony capsule
▷ *adj* of, relating to, or
belonging to the *Chelonia*

**CHELP** *vb* (esp of women
or children) to chatter or
speak out of turn

**CHELPED** >CHELP

**CHELPING** >CHELP

**CHELPS** >CHELP

**CHEMIC** *vb* to bleach ▷ *n*
chemist

**CHEMICAL** *n* substance
used in or resulting from
a reaction involving
changes to atoms or
molecules ▷ *adj* of
chemistry or chemicals

**CHEMICALS** >CHEMICAL

**CHEMICKED** >CHEMIC

**CHEMICS** >CHEMIC

**CHEMISE** *n* woman's loose-
fitting slip

**CHEMISES** >CHEMISE

**CHEMISM** *n* chemical action

**CHEMISMS** >CHEMISM

**CHEMISORB** *vb* take
up (a substance) by
chemisorption

**CHEMIST** *n* shop selling
medicines and cosmetics

**CHEMISTRY** *n* science
of the composition,
properties, and reactions
of substances

**CHEMISTS** >CHEMIST

**CHEMITYPE** *n* process by
which a relief impression
is obtained from an
engraving

**CHEMITYPY** >CHEMITYPE

**CHEMMIES** >CHEMMY

**CHEMMY** *n* gambling card
game

**CHEMO** *n* short form of
chemotherapy

**CHEMOKINE** *n* type of
protein

**CHEMOS** >CHEMO

**CHEMOSORB** *same
as* >CHEMISORB

**CHEMOSTAT** *n* apparatus
for growing bacterial
cultures at a constant rate
by controlling the supply
of nutrient medium

**CHEMPADUK** *n* evergreen
moraceous tree, *Artocarpus
champeden* (or *A. integer*),
of Malaysia, similar to the
jackfruit

**CHEMURGIC** >CHEMURGY

**CHEMURGY** *n* branch of
chemistry concerned
with the industrial use of
organic raw materials, esp
materials of agricultural
origin

**CHENAR** *n* oriental plane
tree

**CHENARS** >CHENAR

**CHENET** *another word
for* >GENIP

**CHENETS** >CHENET

**CHENILLE** *n* (fabric of)
thick tufty yarn

**CHENILLES** >CHENILLE

**CHENIX** *n* ancient measure,
slightly more than a quart

**CHENIXES** >CHENIX

**CHENOPOD** *n* any flowering
plant of the family
*Chenopodiaceae*, which
includes the beet, mangel-
wurzel, spinach, and
goosefoot

**CHENOPODS** >CHENOPOD

**CHEONGSAM** *n* straight
dress, usually of silk or
cotton, with a stand-up
collar and a slit in one
side of the skirt, worn by
Chinese women

**CHEQUE** *n* written order to

one's bank to pay money from one's account

CHEQUER n piece used in Chinese chequers ▷ vb make irregular in colour or character

CHEQUERED adj marked by varied fortunes

CHEQUERS n game of draughts

CHEQUES > CHEQUE

CHEQUING as in chequing account (in Canada) account against which cheques can be drawn

CHEQUY same as > CHECKY

CHER adj dear or expensive

CHERALITE n rare phosphate-silicate of Thorium and Calcium

CHERE feminine variant of > CHER

CHERIMOYA n large tropical fruit with custardlike flesh

CHERISH vb cling to (an idea or feeling)

CHERISHED > CHERISH

CHERISHER > CHERISH

CHERISHES > CHERISH

CHERNOZEM n black soil, rich in humus and carbonates, in cool or temperate semiarid regions, as the grasslands of Russia

CHEROOT n cigar with both ends cut flat

CHEROOTS > CHEROOT

CHERRIED > CHERRY

CHERRIER > CHERRY

CHERRIES > CHERRY

CHERRIEST > CHERRY

CHERRY n small red or black fruit with a stone ▷ adj deep red ▷ vb to cheer

CHERRYING > CHERRY

CHERT n microcrystalline form of silica usually occurring as bands or layers of pebbles in sedimentary rock. Formula: $SiO_2$. Varieties include flint, lyddite (Lydian stone)

CHERTIER > CHERT

CHERTIEST > CHERT

CHERTS > CHERT

CHERTY > CHERT

CHERUB n angel, often represented as a winged child

CHERUBIC > CHERUB

CHERUBIM > CHERUB

CHERUBIMS > CHERUB

CHERUBIN n cherub ▷ adj cherubic

CHERUBINS > CHERUBIN

CHERUBS > CHERUB

CHERUP same as > CHIRRUP

CHERUPED > CHERUP

CHERUPING > CHERUP

CHERUPS > CHERUP

CHERVIL n aniseed-flavoured herb

CHERVILS > CHERVIL

CHESHIRE n breed of American pig

CHESHIRES > CHESHIRE

CHESIL n gravel or shingle

CHESILS > CHESIL

CHESNUT rare variant of > CHESTNUT

CHESNUTS > CHESNUT

CHESS n game for two players with 16 pieces each, played on a chequered board of 64 squares

CHESSEL n mould used in cheese-making

CHESSELS > CHESSEL

CHESSES > CHESS

CHESSMAN n piece used in chess

CHESSMEN > CHESSMAN

CHEST n front of the body, from neck to waist ▷ vb to hit with the chest, as with a ball in football

CHESTED > CHEST

CHESTFUL n amount a chest will hold

CHESTFULS > CHESTFUL

CHESTIER > CHESTY

CHESTIEST > CHESTY

CHESTILY > CHESTY

CHESTING > CHEST

CHESTNUT n reddish-brown edible nut ▷ adj (of hair or a horse) reddish-brown

CHESTNUTS > CHESTNUT

CHESTS > CHEST

CHESTY adj symptomatic of chest disease

CHETAH same as > CHEETAH

CHETAHS > CHETAH

CHETH same as > HETH

CHETHS > CHETH

CHETNIK n member of a Serbian nationalist paramilitary group

CHETNIKS > CHETNIK

CHETRUM n monetary unit in Bhutan

CHETRUMS > CHETRUM

CHEVAL as in cheval glass full-length mirror that can swivel

CHEVALET n bridge of a stringed musical instrument

CHEVALETS > CHEVALET

CHEVALIER n member of the French Legion of Honour

CHEVELURE n nebulous part of the tail of a comet

CHEVEN n chub

CHEVENS > CHEVEN

CHEVEREL n kid or goatskin leather

CHEVERELS > CHEVEREL

CHEVERIL same as > CHEVEREL

CHEVERILS > CHEVERIL

CHEVERON same as > CHEVRON

CHEVERONS > CHEVERON

CHEVERYE same as > CHIEFERY

CHEVERYES > CHEVERYE

CHEVET n semicircular or polygonal east end of a church, esp a French Gothic church, often with a number of attached apses

CHEVETS > CHEVET

CHEVIED > CHEVY

CHEVIES > CHEVY

CHEVILLE n peg of a stringed musical instrument

CHEVILLES > CHEVILLE

CHEVIN same as > CHEVEN

CHEVINS > CHEVIN

CHEVIOT n type of British sheep reared for its wool

CHEVIOTS > CHEVIOT

CHEVRE n any cheese made from goats' milk

CHEVRES > CHEVRE

CHEVRET n type of goats' cheese

CHEVRETS > CHEVRET

CHEVRETTE n skin of a young goat

CHEVRON n V-shaped pattern, esp on the sleeve of a military uniform to indicate rank ▷ vb make a chevron

CHEVRONED > CHEVRON

CHEVRONS > CHEVRON

CHEVRONY adj in heraldry, bearing chevrons

CHEVY same as > CHIVY

CHEVYING > CHEVY

CHEW vb grind (food) between the teeth ▷ n act of chewing

CHEWABLE > CHEW

CHEWED > CHEW

CHEWER > CHEW

CHEWERS > CHEW

CHEWET n type of meat pie

CHEWETS > CHEWET

CHEWIE n chewing gum

CHEWIER > CHEWY

CHEWIES > CHEWY

CHEWIEST > CHEWY

CHEWINESS > CHEWY

CHEWING > CHEW

CHEWINK n towhee

CHEWINKS > CHEWINK

CHEWS > CHEW

CHEWY adj requiring a lot of chewing ▷ n dog's rubber toy

CHEZ prep at the home of

CHI n 22nd letter of the Greek alphabet, a consonant, transliterated as ch or rarely kh

CHIA n plant of the mint family

CHIACK vb tease or banter ▷ n good-humoured banter

CHIACKED > CHIACK

CHIACKING > CHIACK

CHIACKS > CHIACK

CHIANTI n dry red Italian wine

CHIANTIS > CHIANT

CHIAO n Chinese coin equal to one tenth of one yuan

CHIAREZZA n (in music) clarity

CHIAREZZE > CHIAREZZA

CHIAS > CHIA

CHIASM same as > CHIASMA

CHIASMA n cross-shaped connection produced by the crossing over of pairing chromosomes during meiosis

CHIASMAL > CHIASMA

CHIASMAS > CHIASMA

CHIASMATA > CHIASMA

CHIASMI > CHIASMUS

CHIASMIC > CHIASMA

CHIASMS > CHIASMA

CHIASMUS n reversal of the order of words in the second of two parallel phrases

CHIASTIC > CHIASMUS

CHIAUS same as > CHOUSE

CHIAUSED > CHIAUS

CHIAUSES > CHIAUS

CHIAUSING > CHIAUS

CHIB vb in Scots English, stab or slash with a sharp weapon ▷ n sharp weapon

CHIBBED > CHIB

CHIBBING > CHIB

CHIBOL n spring onion

CHIBOLS > CHIBOL

CHIBOUK n Turkish tobacco pipe with an extremely long stem

CHIBOUKS > CHIBOUK

CHIBOUQUE same as > CHIBOUK

CHIBS > CHIB

CHIC adj stylish, elegant ▷ n stylishness, elegance

CHICA n Spanish young girl

CHICALOTE n poppy, Argemone platyceras, of the southwestern US and Mexico with prickly leaves and white or yellow flowers

CHICANA n female chicano

CHICANAS > CHICANA

CHICANE n obstacle in a motor-racing circuit ▷ vb deceive or trick by chicanery

CHICANED > CHICANE

CHICANER > CHICANE

CHICANERS > CHICANE

CHICANERY n trickery, deception

CHICANES > CHICANE

CHICANING > CHICANE

CHICANO n American citizen of Mexican origin

CHICANOS > CHICANO

CHICAS > CHICA

CHICCORY a variant spelling of > CHICORY

CHICER > CHIC

135

CHICEST > CHIC
CHICH another word for > CHICKPEA
CHICHA n Andean drink made from fermented maize
CHICHAS > CHICHA
CHICHES > CHICKPEA
CHICHI adj affectedly pretty or stylish ▷ n quality of being affectedly pretty or stylish
CHICHIER > CHICHI
CHICHIEST > CHICHI
CHICHIS > CHICHI
CHICK n baby bird
CHICKADEE n small N American songbird
CHICKAREE n American red squirrel
CHICKEE n opensided, thatched building on stilts
CHICKEES > CHICKEE
CHICKEN n domestic fowl ▷ adj cowardly ▷ vb to lose one's nerve
CHICKENED > CHICKEN
CHICKENS > CHICKEN
CHICKLING n small chick
CHICKORY same as > CHICORY
CHICKPEA n edible yellow pealike seed
CHICKPEAS > CHICKPEA
CHICKS > CHICK
CHICKWEED n weed with small white flowers
CHICLE n gumlike substance obtained from the sapodilla
CHICLES > CHICLE
CHICLY > CHIC
CHICNESS > CHIC
CHICO n spiny chenopodiaceous shrub
CHICON same as > CHICORY
CHICONS > CHICON
CHICORIES > CHICORY
CHICORY n plant whose leaves are used in salads
CHICOS > CHICO
CHICS > CHIC
CHID > CHIDE
CHIDDEN > CHIDE
CHIDE vb rebuke, scold
CHIDED > CHIDE
CHIDER > CHIDE
CHIDERS > CHIDE
CHIDES > CHIDE
CHIDING > CHIDE
CHIDINGLY > CHIDE
CHIDINGS > CHIDE
CHIDLINGS n intestines of a pig prepared as a dish
CHIEF n head of a group of people ▷ adj most important
CHIEFDOM n any tribal social group led by a chief
CHIEFDOMS > CHIEFDOM
CHIEFER > CHIEF
CHIEFERY n lands belonging to a chief
CHIEFESS n female chief

CHIEFEST > CHIEF
CHIEFLESS adj lacking a chief
CHIEFLING n petty chief
CHIEFLY adv especially ▷ adj of or relating to a chief or chieftain
CHIEFRIES > CHIEFRY
CHIEFRY same as > CHIEFERY
CHIEFS > CHIEF
CHIEFSHIP n state of being a chief
CHIEFTAIN n leader of a tribe
CHIEL n young man
CHIELD same as > CHIEL
CHIELDS > CHIEL
CHIELS > CHIEL
CHIFFON n fine see-through fabric ▷ adj made of chiffon
CHIFFONS > CHIFFON
CHIFFONY > CHIFFON
CHIGETAI n variety of the Asiatic wild ass, Equus hemionus, of Mongolia
CHIGETAIS > CHIGETAI
CHIGGA n informal Australian derogatory word for a young working-class person from Hobart, Tasmania
CHIGGAS > CHIGGA
CHIGGER n parasitic larva of any of various free-living mites of the family Trombidiidae, which causes intense itching of human skin
CHIGGERS > CHIGGER
CHIGNON n knot of hair pinned up at the back of the head ▷ vb make a chignon
CHIGNONED > CHIGNON
CHIGNONS > CHIGNON
CHIGOE same as > CHIGGER
CHIGOES > CHIGOE
CHIGRE same as > CHIGGER
CHIGRES > CHIGRE
CHIHUAHUA n tiny short-haired dog
CHIK n slatted blind
CHIKARA n Indian seven-stringed musical instrument
CHIKARAS > CHIKARA
CHIKHOR same as > CHUKAR
CHIKHORS > CHIKHOR
CHIKOR same as > CHUKAR
CHIKORS > CHIKOR
CHIKS > CHIK
CHILBLAIN n inflammation of the fingers or toes, caused by exposure to cold
CHILD n young human being, boy or girl ▷ vb to give birth
CHILDBED n condition of giving birth to a child
CHILDBEDS > CHILDBED
CHILDCARE n care provided

for children without homes (or with a seriously disturbed home life) by a local authority
CHILDE n young man of noble birth
CHILDED > CHILD
CHILDER dialect variant of > CHILDREN
CHILDES > CHILDE
CHILDHOOD n time or condition of being a child
CHILDING > CHILD
CHILDISH adj immature, silly
CHILDLESS > CHILD
CHILDLIER > CHILD
CHILDLIKE adj innocent, trustful
CHILDLY > CHILD
CHILDNESS n nature of a child
CHILDREN > CHILD
CHILDS > CHILD
CHILE a variant spelling of > CHILLI
CHILES > CHILE
CHILI same as > CHILLI
CHILIAD n group of one thousand
CHILIADAL > CHILIAD
CHILIADIC > CHILIAD
CHILIADS > CHILIAD
CHILIAGON n thousand-sided polygon
CHILIARCH n commander of a thousand men
CHILIASM n belief in the Second Coming of Christ
CHILIASMS > CHILIASM
CHILIAST > CHILIASM
CHILIASTS > CHILIASM
CHILIDOG n hot dog served with chilli sauce
CHILIDOGS > CHILIDOG
CHILIES > CHILI
CHILIOI n thousand
CHILIOIS > CHILIOI
CHILIS > CHILI
CHILL n feverish cold ▷ vb make (something) cool or cold ▷ adj unpleasantly cold
CHILLADA n spicy Mexican dish made of fried vegetables and pulses
CHILLADAS > CHILLADA
CHILLED > CHILL
CHILLER n cooling or refrigerating device
CHILLERS > CHILLER
CHILLEST > CHILL
CHILLI n small red or green hot-tasting capsicum pod, used in cooking
CHILLIER > CHILLY
CHILLIES > CHILLI
CHILLIEST > CHILLY
CHILLILY > CHILLY
CHILLING > CHILL
CHILLINGS > CHILL
CHILLIS > CHILLI
CHILLNESS > CHILL
CHILLS > CHILL

CHILLUM n short pipe, usually of clay, used esp for smoking cannabis
CHILLUMS > CHILLUM
CHILLY adj moderately cold
CHILOPOD n any arthropod of the class Chilopoda, which includes the centipedes
CHILOPODS > CHILOPOD
CHILTEPIN n variety of chilli pepper
CHIMAERA same as > CHIMERA
CHIMAERAS > CHIMAERA
CHIMAERIC > CHIMAERA
CHIMAR same as > CHIMERE
CHIMARS > CHIMAR
CHIMB same as > CHIME
CHIMBLEY same as > CHIMNEY
CHIMBLEYS > CHIMBLEY
CHIMBLIES > CHIMBLY
CHIMBLY same as > CHIMNEY
CHIMBS > CHIME
CHIME n musical ringing sound of a bell or clock ▷ vb make a musical ringing sound
CHIMED > CHIME
CHIMER > CHIME
CHIMERA n unrealistic hope or idea
CHIMERAS > CHIMERA
CHIMERE n sleeveless red or black gown, part of a bishop's formal dress though not a vestment
CHIMERES > CHIMERE
CHIMERIC > CHIMERA
CHIMERID n fish of the genus Chimaera
CHIMERIDS > CHIMERID
CHIMERISM n medical condition in which a person possesses two genetically distinct sets of cells
CHIMERS > CHIME
CHIMES > CHIME
CHIMING > CHIME
CHIMLA same as > CHIMNEY
CHIMLAS > CHIMLA
CHIMLEY same as > CHIMNEY
CHIMLEYS > CHIMLEY
CHIMNEY n hollow vertical structure for carrying away smoke from a fire ▷ vb to climb two vertical, parallel, chimney-like rock faces
CHIMNEYED > CHIMNEY
CHIMNEYS > CHIMNEY
CHIMO interj Inuit greeting and toast
CHIMP n chimpanzee
CHIMPS > CHIMP
CHIN n part of the face below the mouth ▷ vb hit someone in the chin
CHINA n fine earthenware or porcelain
CHINAMAN n in cricket, a

ball bowled by a left-handed bowler to a right-handed batsman that spins from off to leg

CHINAMEN > CHINAMAN

CHINAMPA n in Mesoamerican agriculture, an artificially created island used for growing crops

CHINAMPAS > CHINAMPA

CHINAR same as > CHINAR

CHINAROOT n bristly greenbrier

CHINARS > CHENAR

CHINAS > CHINA

CHINAWARE n articles made of china, esp those made for domestic use

CHINBONE n front part of the mandible which forms the chin

CHINBONES > CHINBONE

CHINCAPIN n dwarf chestnut tree

CHINCH another name for a > BEDBUG

CHINCHES > CHINCH

CHINCHIER > CHINCHY

CHINCHY adj tightfisted

CHINCOUGH n whooping cough

CHINDIT n Allied soldier fighting behind the Japanese lines in Burma during World War II

CHINDITS > CHINDIT

CHINE same as > CHIME

CHINED > CHINE

CHINES > CHINE

CHINESE adj of or relating to China

CHINING > CHINE

CHINK n small narrow opening ▷ vb make a light ringing sound

CHINKAPIN same as > CHINCAPIN

CHINKARA n Indian gazelle

CHINKARAS > CHINKARA

CHINKED > CHINK

CHINKIE n offensive term for a (takeaway) meal of Chinese food

CHINKIER > CHINK

CHINKIES > CHINKIE

CHINKIEST > CHINK

CHINKING > CHINK

CHINKS > CHINK

CHINKY > CHINK

CHINLESS adj having a receding chin

CHINNED > CHIN

CHINNING > CHIN

CHINO n durable cotton twill cloth

CHINONE n benzoquinone

CHINONES > CHINONE

CHINOOK n warm dry southwesterly wind blowing down the eastern slopes of the Rocky Mountains

CHINOOKS > CHINOOK

CHINOS pl n trousers made of a kind of hard-wearing cotton

CHINOVNIK n Russian official or bureaucrat

CHINS > CHIN

CHINSTRAP n strap on a helmet which fastens under the chin

CHINTS obsolete variant of > CHINTZ

CHINTSES > CHINTS

CHINTZ n printed cotton fabric with a glazed finish

CHINTZES > CHINTZ

CHINTZIER > CHINTZY

CHINTZY adj of or covered with chintz

CHINWAG n chat

CHINWAGS > CHINWAG

CHIP n strip of potato, fried in deep fat ▷ vb break small pieces from

CHIPBOARD n thin board made of compressed wood particles

CHIPMUCK another word for > CHIPMUCK

CHIPMUCKS > CHIPMUK

CHIPMUNK n small squirrel-like N American rodent with a striped back

CHIPMUNKS > CHIPMUNK

CHIPOCHIA same as > CAPOCCHIA

CHIPOLATA n small sausage

CHIPOTLE n dried chilli pepper

CHIPOTLES > CHIPOTLE

CHIPPABLE > CHIP

CHIPPED > CHIP

CHIPPER vb chirp or chatter

CHIPPERED > CHIPPER

CHIPPERS > CHIPPER

CHIPPIE same as > CHIPPY

CHIPPIER > CHIPPY

CHIPPIES > CHIPPY

CHIPPIEST > CHIPPY

CHIPPING > CHIP

CHIPPINGS > CHIP

CHIPPY n fish-and-chip shop ▷ adj resentful or oversensitive about being perceived as inferior

CHIPS > CHIP

CHIPSET n highly integrated circuit on the motherboard of a computer that controls many of its data transfer functions

CHIPSETS > CHIPSET

CHIRAGRA n gout occurring in the hands

CHIRAGRAS > CHIRAGRA

CHIRAGRIC > CHIRAGRA

CHIRAL > CHIRALITY

CHIRALITY n configuration or handedness (left or right) of an asymmetric, optically active chemical compound

CHIRIMOYA same as > CHERIMOYA

CHIRK vb to creak, like a door ▷ adj spritely; high-spirited

CHIRKED > CHIRK

CHIRKER > CHIRK

CHIRKEST > CHIRK

CHIRKING > CHIRK

CHIRKS > CHIRK

CHIRL vb to warble

CHIRLED > CHIRL

CHIRLING > CHIRL

CHIRLS > CHIRL

CHIRM n chirping of birds ▷ vb (esp of a bird) to chirp

CHIRMED > CHIRM

CHIRMING > CHIRM

CHIRMS > CHIRM

CHIRO n an informal name for chiropractor

CHIROLOGY n palmistry

CHIRONOMY n art of hand movement in oratory or theatrical performance

CHIROPODY n treatment of the feet, esp the treatment of corns, verrucas, etc

CHIROPTER n type of bat

CHIROS > CHIRO

CHIRP vb (of a bird or insect) make a short high-pitched sound ▷ n chirping sound

CHIRPED > CHIRP

CHIRPER > CHIRP

CHIRPERS > CHIRP

CHIRPIER > CHIRPY

CHIRPIEST > CHIRPY

CHIRPILY > CHIRPY

CHIRPING > CHIRP

CHIRPS > CHIRP

CHIRPY adj lively and cheerful

CHIRR vb (esp of certain insects, such as crickets) to make a shrill trilled sound ▷ n sound of chirring

CHIRRE same as > CHIRR

CHIRRED > CHIRR

CHIRREN n dialect form of children

CHIRRES > CHIRRE

CHIRRING > CHIRR

CHIRRS > CHIRR

CHIRRUP vb (of some birds) to chirp repeatedly ▷ n chirruping sound

CHIRRUPED > CHIRRUP

CHIRRUPER > CHIRRUP

CHIRRUPS > CHIRRUP

CHIRRUPY > CHIRRUP

CHIRT vb to squirt

CHIRTED > CHIRT

CHIRTING > CHIRT

CHIRTS > CHIRT

CHIRU n Tibetan antelope, Pantholops hodgsoni, having a dense woolly pinkish-brown fleece prized as the source of shahtoosh wool: now close to extinction

due to illegal slaughter for its fleece

CHIRUS > CHIRU

CHIS > CHI

CHISEL n metal tool with a sharp end for shaping wood or stone ▷ vb carve or form with a chisel

CHISELED same as > CHISELLED

CHISELER > CHISEL

CHISELERS > CHISEL

CHISELING > CHISEL

CHISELLED adj finely or sharply formed

CHISELLER n person who uses a chisel

CHISELS > CHISEL

CHIT n short official note, such as a receipt ▷ vb to sprout

CHITAL n type of deer

CHITALS > CHITAL

CHITCHAT n chat, gossip ▷ vb gossip

CHITCHATS > CHITCHAT

CHITIN n tough substance forming the outer layer of the bodies of arthropods

CHITINOID > CHITIN

CHITINOUS > CHITIN

CHITINS > CHITIN

CHITLIN > CHITLINS

CHITLING > CHITLINGS

CHITLINGS same as > CHIDLINGS

CHITLINS same as > CHITTERLINGS

CHITON n (in ancient Greece and Rome) a loose woollen tunic worn knee length by men and full length by women

CHITONS > CHITON

CHITOSAN n polysaccharide derived from chitin

CHITOSANS > CHITOSAN

CHITS > CHIT

CHITTED > CHIT

CHITTER vb twitter or chirp

CHITTERED > CHITTER

CHITTERS > CHITTER

CHITTIER > CHIT

CHITTIES > CHITTY

CHITTIEST > CHIT

CHITTING > CHIT

CHITTY same as > CHIT adj childish

CHIV n knife ▷ vb stab (someone)

CHIVALRIC > CHIVALRY

CHIVALRY n courteous behaviour, esp by men towards women

CHIVAREE same as > CHARIVARI vb to perform a chivaree

CHIVAREED > CHIVAREE

CHIVAREES > CHIVAREE

CHIVARI same as > CHARIVARI

CHIVARIED > CHIVARI

CHIVARIES > CHIVARI

CHIVE *n* small Eurasian purple-flowered alliaceous plant, *Allium schoenoprasum*, whose long slender hollow leaves are used in cooking to flavour soups, stews, etc ▷ *vb* file or cut off

CHIVED > CHIVE

CHIVES *same as* > CHIVE

CHIVIED > CHIVVY

CHIVIES > CHIVVY

CHIVING > CHIVE

CHIVS > CHIV

CHIVVED > CHIV

CHIVVIED > CHIVVY

CHIVVIES > CHIVVY

CHIVVING > CHIV

CHIVVY *same as* > CHIVVY

CHIVVYING > CHIVVY

CHIVVY *vb* harass or nag ▷ *n* hunt

CHIVYING > CHIVVY

CHIYOGAMI *n* type of highly decorated Japanese craft paper

CHIZ *n* cheat ▷ *vb* cheat

CHIZZ *same as* > CHIZ

CHIZZED > CHIZ

CHIZZES > CHIZ

CHIZZING > CHIZ

CHLAMYDES > CHLAMYS

CHLAMYDIA *n* any Gram-negative bacteria of the genus *Chlamydia*, responsible for some sexually transmitted diseases

CHLAMYS *n* woollen cloak worn by ancient Greek soldiers

CHLAMYSES > CHLAMYS

CHLOASMA *n* appearance on a person's skin, esp of the face, of patches of darker colour: associated with hormonal changes caused by liver disease or the use of oral contraceptives

CHLOASMAS > CHLOASMA

CHLORACNE *n* disfiguring skin disease that results from contact with or ingestion or inhalation of certain chlorinated aromatic hydrocarbons

CHLORAL *n* colourless oily liquid with a pungent odour, made from chlorine and acetaldehyde and used in preparing chloral hydrate and DDT

CHLORALS > CHLORAL

CHLORATE *n* type of chemical salt

CHLORATES > CHLORATE

CHLORDAN *same as* > CHLORDANE

CHLORDANE *n* white insoluble toxic solid

CHLORDANS > CHLORDAN

CHLORELLA *n* any microscopic unicellular green alga of the genus

*Chlorella*: some species are used in the preparation of human food

CHLORIC *adj* of or containing chlorine in the pentavalent state

CHLORID *n* type of chlorine compound

CHLORIDE *n* compound of chlorine and another substance

CHLORIDES > CHLORIDE

CHLORIDIC > CHLORIDE

CHLORIDS > CHLORID

CHLORIN *same as* > CHLORINE

CHLORINE *n* strong-smelling greenish-yellow gaseous element, used to disinfect water

CHLORINES > CHLORINE

CHLORINS > CHLORIN

CHLORITE *n* any of a group of green soft secondary minerals consisting of . the hydrated silicates of aluminium, iron, and magnesium in monoclinic crystalline form: common in metamorphic rocks

CHLORITES > CHLORITE

CHLORITIC > CHLORITE

CHLOROSES > CHLOROSIS

CHLOROSIS *n* disorder, formerly common in adolescent girls, characterized by pale greenish-yellow skin, weakness, and palpitation and caused by insufficient iron in the body

CHLOROTIC > CHLOROSIS

CHLOROUS *adj* of or containing chlorine in the trivalent state

CHOANA *n* posterior nasal aperture

CHOANAE > CHOANA

CHOBDAR *n* in India and Nepal, king's macebearer or attendant

CHOBDARS > CHOBDAR

CHOC *short form of* > CHOCOLATE

CHOCCIER > CHOCCY

CHOCCIES > CHOCCY

CHOCCIEST > CHOCCY

CHOCCY *n* chocolate ▷ *adj* made of, tasting of, smelling of, or resembling chocolate

CHOCHO *same as* > CHAYOTE

CHOCHOS > CHOCHO

CHOCK *n* block or wedge used to prevent a heavy object from moving ▷ *vb* secure by a chock ▷ *adv* as closely or tightly as possible

CHOCKED > CHOCK

CHOCKER *adj* full up

CHOCKFUL *adj* filled to capacity

CHOCKFULL *variant*

*of* > CHOCKFUL

CHOCKING > CHOCK

CHOCKO *same as* > CHOCO

CHOCKOS > CHOCKO

CHOCKS > CHOCK

CHOCO *n* member of the Australian army

CHOCOLATE *n* sweet food made from cacao seeds ▷ *adj* dark brown

CHOCOLATY > CHOCOLATE

CHOCOS > CHOCO

CHOCS > CHOC

CHOCTAW *n* turn from the inside edge of one skate to the outside edge of the other or vice versa

CHOCTAWS > CHOCTAW

CHODE > CHIDE

CHOENIX *same as* > CHENIX

CHOENIXES > CHOENIX

CHOG *n* core of a piece of fruit

CHOGS > CHOG

CHOICE *n* choosing ▷ *adj* of high quality

CHOICEFUL *adj* fickle

CHOICELY > CHOICE

CHOICER > CHOICE

CHOICES > CHOICE

CHOICEST > CHOICE

CHOIR *n* organized group of singers, esp in church ▷ *vb* to sing in chorus

CHOIRBOY *n* boy who sings in a church choir

CHOIRBOYS > CHOIRBOY

CHOIRED > CHOIR

CHOIRGIRL *n* girl who sings in a choir

CHOIRING > CHOIR

CHOIRLIKE > CHOIR

CHOIRMAN *n* man who sings in a choir

CHOIRMEN > CHOIRMAN

CHOIRS > CHOIR

CHOKE *vb* hinder or stop the breathing of (a person) by strangling or smothering ▷ *n* device controlling the amount of air that is mixed with the fuel in a petrol engine

CHOKEABLE > CHOKE

CHOKEBORE *n* shotgun bore that becomes narrower towards the muzzle so that the shot is not scattered

CHOKECOIL *n* type of electronic inductor

CHOKED *adj* disappointed or angry

CHOKEDAMP *another word for* > BLACKDAMP

CHOKEHOLD *n* act of holding a person's neck across the windpipe, esp from behind

CHOKER *n* tight-fitting necklace

CHOKERS > CHOKER

CHOKES > CHOKE

CHOKEY *n* a slang word for prison ▷ *adj* involving,

caused by, or causing choking

CHOKEYS > CHOKEY

CHOKIDAR *n* in India, a gatekeeper

CHOKIDARS > CHOKIDAR

CHOKIER > CHOKEY

CHOKIES > CHOKEY

CHOKIEST > CHOKEY

CHOKING > CHOKE

CHOKINGLY > CHOKE

CHOKO *n* pear-shaped fruit of a tropical American vine, eaten as a vegetable

CHOKOS > CHOKO

CHOKRA *n* in India, a boy or young man

CHOKRAS > CHOKRA

CHOKRI *n* in India, a girl or young woman

CHOKRIS > CHOKRI

CHOKY *same as* > CHOKEY

CHOLA *n* Hispanic girl

CHOLAEMIA *n* toxic medical condition indicated by the presence of bile in the blood

CHOLAEMIC > CHOLAEMIA

CHOLAS > CHOLA

CHOLATE *n* salt of cholic acid

CHOLATES > CHOLATE

CHOLECYST *n* gall bladder

CHOLELITH *n* gallstone

CHOLEMIA *same as* > CHOLAEMIA

CHOLEMIAS > CHOLEMIA

CHOLENT *n* meal usually consisting of a stew of meat, potatoes, and pulses prepared before the Sabbath on Friday and left to cook until eaten for Sabbath lunch

CHOLENTS > CHOLENT

CHOLER *n* bad temper

CHOLERA *n* serious infectious disease causing severe vomiting and diarrhoea

CHOLERAIC > CHOLERA

CHOLERAS > CHOLERA

CHOLERIC *adj* bad-tempered

CHOLEROID > CHOLERA

CHOLERS > CHOLER

CHOLI *n* short-sleeved bodice, as worn by Indian women

CHOLIAMB *n* imperfect iambic trimeter, with a spondee as the last foot

CHOLIAMBS > CHOLIAMB

CHOLIC *as in cholic acid* crystalline acid found in bile

CHOLINE *n* colourless viscous soluble alkaline substance present in animal tissues, esp as a constituent of lecithin: used as a supplement to the diet of poultry and in medicine for preventing the accumulation of fat in the liver

**CHOLINES** > CHOLINE

**CHOLIS** > CHOLI

**CHOLLA** *n* any of several spiny cacti of the genus *Opuntia* that grow in the southwestern US and Mexico and have cylindrical stem segments

**CHOLLAS** > CHOLLA

**CHOLLERS** *pl n* jowls or cheeks

**CHOLO** *n* chicano gangster

**CHOLOS** > CHOLO

**CHOLTRIES** > CHOLTRY

**CHOLTRY** *n* caravanserai

**CHOMA** *same as* > CHOMMIE

**CHOMAS** > CHOMA

**CHOMETZ** *same as* > CHAMETZ

**CHOMETZES** > CHOMETZ

**CHOMMIE** *n* (in informal South African English) friend

**CHOMMIES** > CHOMMIE

**CHOMP** *vb* chew noisily ▷ *n* act or sound of chewing in this manner

**CHOMPED** > CHOMP

**CHOMPER** > CHOMP

**CHOMPERS** > CHOMP

**CHOMPING** > CHOMP

**CHOMPS** > CHOMP

**CHON** *n* North and South Korean monetary unit worth one hundredth of a won

**CHONDRAL** *adj* of or relating to cartilage

**CHONDRE** *another word for* > CHONDRULE

**CHONDRES** > CHONDRE

**CHONDRI** > CHONDRUS

**CHONDRIFY** *vb* become or convert into cartilage

**CHONDRIN** *n* resilient translucent bluish-white substance that forms the matrix of cartilage

**CHONDRINS** > CHONDRIN

**CHONDRITE** *n* stony meteorite consisting mainly of silicate minerals in the form of chondrules

**CHONDROID** *adj* resembling cartilage

**CHONDROMA** *n* benign cartilaginous growth or neoplasm

**CHONDRULE** *n* one of the small spherical masses of mainly silicate minerals present in chondrites

**CHONDRUS** *n* cartilage

**CHONS** > CHON

**CHOOF** *vb* go away

**CHOOFED** > CHOOF

**CHOOFING** > CHOOF

**CHOOFS** > CHOOF

**CHOOK** *n* hen or chicken ▷ *vb* make the sound of a hen or chicken

**CHOOKED** > CHOOK

**CHOOKIE** *same as* > CHOOK

**CHOOKIES** > CHOOK

**CHOOKING** > CHOOK

**CHOOKS** > CHOOK

**CHOOM** *n* Englishman

**CHOOMS** > CHOOM

**CHOOSE** *vb* select from a number of alternatives

**CHOOSER** > CHOOSE

**CHOOSERS** > CHOOSE

**CHOOSES** > CHOOSE

**CHOOSEY** *same as* > CHOOSY

**CHOOSIER** > CHOOSY

**CHOOSIEST** > CHOOSY

**CHOOSING** > CHOOSE

**CHOOSY** *adj* fussy, hard to please

**CHOP** *vb* cut with a blow from an axe or knife ▷ *n* cutting or sharp blow

**CHOPHOUSE** *n* restaurant specializing in steaks, grills, chops, etc

**CHOPIN** *same as* > CHOPINE

**CHOPINE** *n* sandal-like shoe on tall wooden or cork bases popular in the 18th century

**CHOPINES** > CHOPINE

**CHOPINS** > CHOPIN

**CHOPLOGIC** *n* person who uses excessively subtle or involved logic

**CHOPPED** > CHOP

**CHOPPER** *n* helicopter ▷ *vb* travel by helicopter

**CHOPPERED** > CHOPPER

**CHOPPERS** > CHOPPER

**CHOPPIER** > CHOPPY

**CHOPPIEST** > CHOPPY

**CHOPPILY** > CHOPPY

**CHOPPING** > CHOP

**CHOPPINGS** > CHOP

**CHOPPY** *adj* (of the sea) fairly rough

**CHOPS** > CHOP

**CHOPSOCKY** *n* genre of martial arts film

**CHOPSTICK** *n* one of a pair of thin sticks used as eating utensils

**CHORAGI** > CHORAGUS

**CHORAGIC** > CHORAGUS

**CHORAGUS** *n* leader of a chorus

**CHORAL** *adj* of a choir

**CHORALE** *n* slow stately hymn tune

**CHORALES** > CHORALE

**CHORALIST** *n* singer or composer of chorals

**CHORALLY** > CHORAL

**CHORALS** > CHORAL

**CHORD** *n* straight line joining two points on a curve ▷ *vb* provide (a melodic line) with chords

**CHORDA** *n* in anatomy, a cord

**CHORDAE** > CHORDA

**CHORDAL** > CHORD

**CHORDATE** *n* any animal that has a long fibrous rod just above the gut to support the body, such as

the vertebrates ▷ *adj* of, relating to, or belonging to the *Chordata*

**CHORDATES** > CHORDATE

**CHORDED** > CHORD

**CHORDEE** *n* painful penile erection, a symptom of gonorrhoea

**CHORDEES** > CHORDEE

**CHORDING** *n* distribution of chords throughout a piece of harmony

**CHORDINGS** > CHORDING

**CHORDS** > CHORD

**CHORDWISE** *adv* in the direction of an aerofoil chord ▷ *adj* moving in this direction

**CHORE** *n* routine task ▷ *vb* to carry out chores

**CHOREA** *n* disorder of the nervous system characterized by uncontrollable brief jerky movements

**CHOREAL** > CHOREA

**CHOREAS** > CHOREA

**CHOREATIC** > CHOREA

**CHORED** > CHORE

**CHOREE** *n* trochee

**CHOREES** > CHOREE

**CHOREGI** > CHOREGUS

**CHOREGIC** > CHOREGUS

**CHOREGUS** *n* in ancient Greece, the producer/ financier of a dramatist's works

**CHOREIC** > CHOREA

**CHOREMAN** *n* handyman

**CHOREMEN** > CHOREMAN

**CHOREOID** *adj* resembling chorea

**CHORES** > CHORE

**CHOREUS** *same as* > CHOREE

**CHOREUSES** > CHOREUS

**CHORIA** > CHORION

**CHORIAL** > CHORION

**CHORIAMB** *n* metrical foot used in classical verse consisting of four syllables, two short ones between two long ones

**CHORIAMBI** > CHORIAMB

**CHORIAMBS** > CHORIAMB

**CHORIC** *adj* of, like, for, or in the manner of a chorus, esp of singing, dancing, or the speaking of verse

**CHORINE** *n* chorus girl

**CHORINES** > CHORINE

**CHORING** > CHORE

**CHORIOID** *same as* > CHOROID

**CHORIOIDS** > CHORIOID

**CHORION** *n* outer of two membranes that form a sac around the embryonic reptile, bird, or mammal

**CHORIONIC** > CHORION

**CHORIONS** > CHORION

**CHORISES** > CHORISIS

**CHORISIS** *n* multiplication of leaves etc by branching or splitting

**CHORISM** > CHORISIS

**CHORISMS** > CHORISIS

**CHORIST** *n* choir member

**CHORISTER** *n* singer in a choir

**CHORISTS** > CHORIST

**CHORIZO** *n* kind of highly seasoned pork sausage of Spain or Mexico

**CHORIZONT** *n* person who challenges the authorship of a work

**CHORIZOS** > CHORIZO

**CHOROID** *adj* resembling the chorion, esp in being vascular ▷ *n* brownish vascular membrane of the eyeball between the sclera and the retina

**CHOROIDAL** > CHOROID

**CHOROIDS** > CHOROID

**CHOROLOGY** *n* study of the causal relations between geographical phenomena occurring within a particular region

**CHORRIE** *n* dilapidated old car

**CHORRIES** > CHORRIE

**CHORTEN** *n* Buddhist shrine

**CHORTENS** > CHORTEN

**CHORTLE** *vb* chuckle in amusement ▷ *n* amused chuckle

**CHORTLED** > CHORTLE

**CHORTLER** > CHORTLE

**CHORTLERS** > CHORTLE

**CHORTLES** > CHORTLE

**CHORTLING** > CHORTLE

**CHORUS** *n* large choir ▷ *vb* sing or say together

**CHORUSED** > CHORUS

**CHORUSES** > CHORUS

**CHORUSING** > CHORUS

**CHORUSSED** > CHORUS

**CHORUSSES** > CHORUS

**CHOSE** > CHOOSE

**CHOSEN** > CHOOSE

**CHOSES** > CHOOSE

**CHOTA** *adj* (in British Empire Indian usage) small

**CHOTT** *a variant spelling of* > SHOTT

**CHOTTS** > CHOTT

**CHOU** *n* type of cabbage

**CHOUGH** *n* large black Eurasian and N African bird of the crow family

**CHOUGHS** > CHOUGH

**CHOULTRY** *same as* > CHOLTRY

**CHOUNTER** *same as* > CHUNTER

**CHOUNTERS** > CHOUNTER

**CHOUSE** *vb* to cheat

**CHOUSED** > CHOUSE

**CHOUSER** > CHOUSE

**CHOUSERS** > CHOUSE

**CHOUSES** > CHOUSE

**CHOUSH** *n* Turkish messenger

**CHOUSHES** > CHOUSH

**CHOUSING** > CHOUSE

**CHOUT** n blackmail

**CHOUTS** > CHOUT

**CHOUX** > CHOU

**CHOW** n thick-coated dog with a curled tail, orig. from China ▷ vb eat

**CHOWCHOW** same as > CHOW

**CHOWCHOWS** > CHOWCHOW

**CHOWDER** n thick soup containing clams or fish ▷ vb to make a chowder of

**CHOWDERED** > CHOWDER

**CHOWDERS** > CHOWDER

**CHOWED** > CHOW

**CHOWHOUND** n person who loves eating

**CHOWING** > CHOW

**CHOWK** n marketplace or market area

**CHOWKIDAR** same as > CHOKIDAR

**CHOWKS** > CHOWK

**CHOWRI** n fly-whisk

**CHOWRIES** > CHOWRI

**CHOWRIS** > CHOWRI

**CHOWRY** same as > CHOWRI

**CHOWS** > CHOW

**CHOWSE** same as > CHOUSE

**CHOWSED** > CHOWSE

**CHOWSES** > CHOWSE

**CHOWSING** > CHOWSE

**CHOWTIME** n mealtime

**CHOWTIMES** > CHOWTIME

**CHRESARD** n amount of water present in the soil that is available to plants

**CHRESARDS** > CHRESARD

**CHRISM** n consecrated oil used for anointing in some churches

**CHRISMA** > CHRISMON

**CHRISMAL** n chrism container

**CHRISMALS** > CHRISMAL

**CHRISMON** n monogram and symbol of Christ's name

**CHRISMONS** > CHRISMON

**CHRISMS** > CHRISM

**CHRISOM** same as > CHRISM

**CHRISOMS** > CHRISOM

**CHRISTEN** vb baptize

**CHRISTENS** > CHRISTEN

**CHRISTIAN** adj exhibiting kindness or goodness

**CHRISTIE** same as > CHRISTY

**CHRISTIES** > CHRISTIE

**CHRISTOM** same as > CHRISOM

**CHRISTOMS** > CHRISTOM

**CHRISTY** n skiing turn for stopping or changing direction quickly

**CHROMA** n attribute of a colour that enables an observer to judge how much chromatic colour it contains irrespective of achromatic colour present

**CHROMAKEY** n (in colour television) a special effect in which a coloured background can be eliminated and a different background substituted

**CHROMAS** > CHROMA

**CHROMATE** n any salt or ester of chromic acid

**CHROMATES** > CHROMATE

**CHROMATIC** adj of colour or colours

**CHROMATID** n either of the two strands into which a chromosome divides during mitosis. They separate to form daughter chromosomes at anaphase

**CHROMATIN** n part of the nucleus of a cell that forms the chromosomes and can easily be dyed

**CHROME** n anything plated with chromium ▷ vb plate with chromium ▷ vb to chromium-plate ▷ adj of or having the appearance of chrome

**CHROMED** > CHROME

**CHROMEL** n nickel-based alloy containing about 10 per cent chromium, used in heating elements

**CHROMELS** > CHROMEL

**CHROMENE** n chemical compound

**CHROMENES** > CHROMENE

**CHROMES** > CHROME

**CHROMIC** adj of or containing chromium in the trivalent state

**CHROMIDE** n any member of the cichlid family of fish

**CHROMIDES** > CHROMIDE

**CHROMIDIA** n chromatins in cell cytoplasm

**CHROMIER** > CHROME

**CHROMIEST** > CHROMY

**CHROMING** > CHROME

**CHROMINGS** > CHROME

**CHROMISE** same as > CHROMIZE

**CHROMISED** > CHROMISE

**CHROMISES** > CHROMISE

**CHROMITE** n brownish-black mineral which is the only commercial source of chromium

**CHROMITES** > CHROMITE

**CHROMIUM** n grey metallic element used in steel alloys and for electroplating

**CHROMIUMS** > CHROMIUM

**CHROMIZE** vb chrome-plate

**CHROMIZED** > CHROMIZE

**CHROMIZES** > CHROMIZE

**CHROMO** n picture produced by the process of making coloured prints by lithography

**CHROMOGEN** n compound that forms coloured compounds on oxidation

**CHROMOS** > CHROMO

**CHROMOUS** adj of or containing chromium in the divalent state

**CHROMY** > CHROME

**CHROMYL** n of, consisting of, or containing the divalent radical $CrO_2$

**CHROMYLS** > CHROMYL

**CHRONAXIE** n minimum time required for excitation of a nerve or muscle when the stimulus is double the minimum (threshold) necessary to elicit a basic response

**CHRONAXY** same as > CHRONAXIE

**CHRONIC** adj (of an illness) lasting a long time ▷ n chronically-ill patient

**CHRONICAL** > CHRONIC

**CHRONICLE** n record of events in order of occurrence ▷ vb record in or as if in a chronicle

**CHRONICS** > CHRONIC

**CHRONON** n unit of time equal to the time that a photon would take to traverse the diameter of an electron: about $10^{-24}$ seconds

**CHRONONS** > CHRONON

**CHRYSALID** adj of or relating to a chrysalis

**CHRYSALIS** n insect in the stage between larva and adult, when it is in a cocoon

**CHRYSANTH** n chrysanthemum

**CHTHONIAN** adj of or relating to the underworld

**CHTHONIC** same as > CHTHONIAN

**CHUB** n European freshwater fish of the carp family

**CHUBASCO** n in Mexico, a hurricane

**CHUBASCOS** > CHUBASCO

**CHUBBIER** > CHUBBY

**CHUBBIEST** > CHUBBY

**CHUBBILY** > CHUBBY

**CHUBBY** adj plump and round

**CHUBS** > CHUB

**CHUCK** vb throw ▷ n cut of beef from the neck to the shoulder

**CHUCKED** > CHUCK

**CHUCKER** n person who throws something

**CHUCKERS** > CHUCKER

**CHUCKHOLE** n pothole

**CHUCKIE** n small stone

**CHUCKIES** > CHUCKIE

**CHUCKING** > CHUCK

**CHUCKLE** vb laugh softly ▷ n soft laugh

**CHUCKLED** > CHUCKLE

**CHUCKLER** > CHUCKLE

**CHUCKLERS** > CHUCKLE

**CHUCKLES** > CHUCKLE

**CHUCKLING** > CHUCKLE

**CHUCKS** > CHUCK

**CHUCKY** same as > CHUCKIE

**CHUDDAH** same as > CHUDDAR

**CHUDDAHS** > CHUDDAH

**CHUDDAR** n large shawl or veil worn by Muslim or Hindu women that covers them from head to foot

**CHUDDARS** > CHUDDAR

**CHUDDER** same as > CHUDDAR

**CHUDDERS** > CHUDDER

**CHUDDIES** pl n underpants

**CHUDDY** n chewing gum

**CHUFA** n sedge, Cyperus esculentus, of warm regions of the Old World, with nutlike edible tubers

**CHUFAS** > CHUFA

**CHUFF** vb (of a steam engine) move while making a puffing sound ▷ n puffing sound of or as if of a steam engine ▷ adj boorish

**CHUFFED** adj very pleased

**CHUFFER** > CHUFF

**CHUFFEST** > CHUFF

**CHUFFIER** > CHUFFY

**CHUFFIEST** > CHUFFY

**CHUFFING** > CHUFF

**CHUFFS** > CHUFF

**CHUFFY** adj boorish and surly

**CHUG** n short dull sound like the noise of an engine ▷ vb operate or move with this sound

**CHUGALUG** vb to gulp down a drink in one go

**CHUGALUGS** > CHUGALUG

**CHUGGED** > CHUG

**CHUGGER** > CHUG

**CHUGGERS** > CHUG

**CHUGGING** > CHUG

**CHUGS** > CHUG

**CHUKAR** n common Indian partridge, Alectoris chukar (or graeca), having red legs and bill and a black-barred sandy plumage

**CHUKARS** > CHUKAR

**CHUKKA** n period of play in polo

**CHUKKAR** same as > CHUKKA

**CHUKKARS** > CHUKKAR

**CHUKKAS** > CHUKKA

**CHUKKER** same as > CHUKKA

**CHUKKERS** > CHUKKER

**CHUKOR** same as > CHUKAR

**CHUKORS** > CHUKOR

**CHUM** n close friend ▷ vb be or become an intimate friend (of)

**CHUMASH** n printed book containing one of the Five Books of Moses

**CHUMASHES** > CHUMASH

**CHUMLEY** same as > CHIMNEY

**CHUMLEYS** > CHUMLEY

**CHUMMAGE** n formerly, fee paid by a prisoner for sole occupancy of a cell

**CHUMMAGES** > CHUMMAGE

CHUMMED > CHUM
CHUMMIER > CHUMMY
CHUMMIES > CHUMMY
CHUMMIEST > CHUMMY
CHUMMILY > CHUMMY
CHUMMING > CHUM
CHUMMY adj friendly ▷ n chum
CHUMP n stupid person ▷ vb chew noisily
CHUMPED > CHUMP
CHUMPING n collecting wood for bonfires on Guy Fawkes Day
CHUMPINGS > CHUMPING
CHUMPS > CHUMP
CHUMS > CHUM
CHUMSHIP n friendship
CHUMSHIPS > CHUMSHIP
CHUNDER vb vomit ▷ n vomit
CHUNDERED > CHUNDER
CHUNDERS > CHUNDER
CHUNK n thick solid piece ▷ vb to break up into chunks
CHUNKED > CHUNK
CHUNKIER > CHUNKY
CHUNKIEST > CHUNKY
CHUNKILY > CHUNKY
CHUNKING n grouping together of a number of items by the mind, after which they can be remembered as a single item, such as a word or a musical phrase
CHUNKINGS > CHUNKING
CHUNKS > CHUNK
CHUNKY adj (of a person) broad and heavy
CHUNNEL n rail tunnel beneath the English Channel, linking England and France
CHUNNELS > CHUNNEL
CHUNNER same as > CHUNTER
CHUNNERED > CHUNNER
CHUNNERS > CHUNNER
CHUNTER vb mutter or grumble incessantly in a meaningless fashion
CHUNTERED > CHUNTER
CHUNTERS > CHUNTER
CHUPATI same as > CHUPATTI
CHUPATIS > CHUPATI
CHUPATTI variant spellings of > CHAPATI
CHUPATTIS > CHUPATTI
CHUPATTY same as > CHUPATTI
CHUPPA variant of > CHUPPAH
CHUPPAH n canopy under which a marriage is performed
CHUPPAHS > CHUPPAH
CHUPPAS > CHUPPA
CHUPRASSY same as > CHAPRASSI
CHURCH n building for public Christian worship

▷ vb bring (someone, esp a woman after childbirth) to church for special ceremonies
CHURCHED > CHURCH
CHURCHES > CHURCH
CHURCHIER > CHURCHY
CHURCHING > CHURCH
CHURCHISM n adherence to the principles of an established church
CHURCHLY adj appropriate to, associated with, or suggestive of church life and customs
CHURCHMAN n clergyman
CHURCHMEN > CHURCHMAN
CHURCHWAY n way or road that leads to a church
CHURCHY adj like a church, church service, etc
CHURIDAR as in churidar pyjamas long tight-fitting trousers, worn by Indian men and women
CHURIDARS > CHURIDAR
CHURINGA n sacred amulet of the native Australians
CHURINGAS > CHURINGA
CHURL n surly ill-bred person
CHURLISH adj surly and rude
CHURLS > CHURL
CHURN n machine in which cream is shaken to make butter ▷ vb stir (cream) vigorously to make butter
CHURNED > CHURN
CHURNER > CHURN
CHURNERS > CHURN
CHURNING n quantity of butter churned at any one time
CHURNINGS > CHURNING
CHURNMILK n buttermilk
CHURNS > CHURN
CHURR same as > CHIRR
CHURRED > CHURR
CHURRING > CHURR
CHURRO n Spanish dough stick snack
CHURROS > CHURRO
CHURRS > CHURR
CHURRUS n hemp resin
CHURRUSES > CHURRUS
CHUSE obsolete variant of > CHOOSE
CHUSES > CHUSE
CHUSING > CHUSE
CHUT interj expression of surprise or annoyance ▷ vb make such an expression
CHUTE n steep slope down which things may be slid ▷ vb to descend by a chute
CHUTED > CHUTE
CHUTES > CHUTE
CHUTING > CHUTE
CHUTIST > CHUTE
CHUTISTS > CHUTE
CHUTNEE same as > CHUTNEY

CHUTNEES > CHUTNEE
CHUTNEY n pickle made from fruit, vinegar, spices, and sugar
CHUTNEYS > CHUTNEY
CHUTZPA same as > CHUTZPAH
CHUTZPAH n unashamed self-confidence
CHUTZPAHS > CHUTZPAH
CHUTZPAS > CHUTZPA
CHYACK same as > CHIACK
CHYACKED > CHYACK
CHYACKING > CHYACK
CHYACKS > CHYACK
CHYLDE archaic word for > CHILD
CHYLE n milky fluid formed in the small intestine during digestion
CHYLES > CHYLE
CHYLIFIED > CHYLIFY
CHYLIFIES > CHYLIFY
CHYLIFY vb to be turned into chyle
CHYLOUS > CHYLE
CHYLURIA n presence of chyle in urine
CHYLURIAS > CHYLURIA
CHYME n thick fluid mass of partially digested food that leaves the stomach
CHYMES > CHYME
CHYMIC same as > CHEMIC
CHYMICS > CHYMIC
CHYMIFIED > CHYMIFY
CHYMIFIES > CHYMIFY
CHYMIFY vb to form into chyme
CHYMIST same as > CHEMIST
CHYMISTRY same as > CHEMISTRY
CHYMISTS > CHYMIST
CHYMOSIN another name for > RENNIN
CHYMOSINS > CHYMOSIN
CHYMOUS > CHYME
CHYND adj chined
CHYPRE n perfume made from sandalwood
CHYPRES > CHYPRE
CHYTRID n variety of fungus
CHYTRIDS > CHYTRID
CIABATTA n type of bread made with olive oil
CIABATTAS > CIABATTA
CIABATTE > CIABATTA
CIAO an informal word for > HELLO
CIAOS > CIAO
CIBATION n feeding
CIBATIONS > CIBATION
CIBOL same as > CHIBOL
CIBOLS > CIBOL
CIBORIA > CIBORIUM
CIBORIUM n goblet-shaped lidded vessel used to hold consecrated wafers in Holy Communion
CIBOULE same as > CHIBOL
CIBOULES > CIBOULE
CICADA n large insect that makes a high-pitched

drone
CICADAE > CICADA
CICADAS > CICADA
CICALA same as > CICADA
CICALAS > CICALA
CICALE > CICALA
CICATRICE n scar
CICATRISE same as > CICATRIZE
CICATRIX n scar
CICATRIZE vb (of a wound or defect in tissue) to close or be closed by scar formation
CICELIES > CICELY
CICELY n type of plant
CICERO n measure for type that is somewhat larger than the pica
CICERONE n person who guides and informs sightseers ▷ vb to act as a cicerone
CICERONED > CICERONE
CICERONES > CICERONE
CICERONI > CICERONE
CICEROS > CICERO
CICHLID n any tropical freshwater percoid fish of the family Cichlidae, which includes the mouthbrooders. Cichlids are popular aquarium fishes ▷ adj of, relating to, or belonging to the Cichlidae
CICHLIDAE n cichlids
CICHLIDS > CICHLID
CICHLOID > CICHLID
CICINNUS n scorpioid cyme
CICISBEI > CICISBEO
CICISBEO n escort or lover of a married woman, esp in 18th-century Italy
CICISBEOS > CICISBEO
CICLATON n rich material of silk and gold
CICLATONS > CICLATON
CICLATOUN same as > CICLATON
CICOREE same as > CHICORY
CICOREES > CICOREE
CICUTA n spotted hemlock
CICUTAS > CICUTA
CICUTINE same as > CONIINE
CICUTINES > CICUTINE
CID n leader
CIDARIS n sea urchin
CIDARISES > CIDARIS
CIDE Shakespearean variant of > DECIDE
CIDED > CIDE
CIDER n alcoholic drink made from fermented apple juice
CIDERKIN n weak type of cider
CIDERKINS > CIDERKIN
CIDERS > CIDER
CIDERY > CIDER
CIDES > CIDE
CIDING > CIDE

CIDS > CID
CIEL same as > CEIL
CIELED > CIEL
CIELING > CIEL
CIELINGS > CIEL
CIELS > CIEL
CIERGE same as > CERGE
CIERGES > CIERGE
CIG same as > CIGARETTE
CIGAR n roll of cured tobacco leaves for smoking
CIGARET same as > CIGARETTE
CIGARETS > CIGARET
CIGARETTE n thin roll of shredded tobacco in thin paper, for smoking
CIGARILLO n small cigar often only slightly larger than a cigarette
CIGARLIKE > CIGAR
CIGARS > CIGAR
CIGGIE same as > CIGARETTE
CIGGIES > CIGGIE
CIGGY same as > CIGARETTE
CIGS > CIG
CIGUATERA n food poisoning caused by a toxin in seafood
CILANTRO same as > CORIANDER
CILANTROS > CILANTRO
CILIA > CILIUM
CILIARY adj of or relating to cilia
CILIATE adj possessing or relating to cilia ▷ n protozoan of the phylum Ciliophora
CILIATED > CILIATE
CILIATELY > CILIATE
CILIATES > CILIATE
CILIATION > CILIATE
CILICE n haircloth fabric or garment
CILICES > CILICE
CILICIOUS adj made of hair
CILIOLATE adj covered with minute hairs, as some plants
CILIUM n short thread projecting from a cell, whose rhythmic beating causes movement
CILL a variant spelling (used in the building industry) for > SILL
CILLS > CILL
CIMAR same as > CYMAR
CIMARS > CIMAR
CIMBALOM n type of dulcimer, esp of Hungary
CIMBALOMS > CIMBALOM
CIMELIA n (especially, ecclesiastical) treasures
CIMEX n any of the heteropterous insects of the genus Cimex, esp the bedbug
CIMICES > CIMEX
CIMIER n crest of a helmet
CIMIERS > CIMIER

CIMINITE n type of igneous rock
CIMINITES > CIMINITE
CIMMERIAN adj very dark or gloomy
CIMOLITE n clayey, whitish mineral
CIMOLITES > CIMOLITE
CINCH n easy task ▷ vb fasten a girth around (a horse)
CINCHED > CINCH
CINCHES > CINCH
CINCHING > CINCH
CINCHINGS > CINCH
CINCHONA same as > CALISAYA
CINCHONAS > CINCHONA
CINCHONIC > CINCHONA
CINCINNUS same as > CICINNUS
CINCT adj encircled
CINCTURE n something, such as a belt or girdle, that goes around another thing ▷ vb to encircle
CINCTURED > CINCTURE
CINCTURES > CINCTURE
CINDER n piece of material that will not burn, left after burning coal ▷ vb burn to cinders
CINDERED > CINDER
CINDERING > CINDER
CINDEROUS > CINDER
CINDERS > CINDER
CINDERY > CINDER
CINE as in cine camera camera able to film moving pictures
CINEAST same as > CINEASTE
CINEASTE n enthusiast for films
CINEASTES > CINEASTE
CINEASTS > CINEAST
CINEMA n place for showing films
CINEMAS > CINEMA
CINEMATIC > CINEMA
CINEOL n colourless oily liquid with a camphor-like odour and a spicy taste
CINEOLE same as > CINEOL
CINEOLES > CINEOLE
CINEOLS > CINEOL
CINEPHILE n film enthusiast
CINEPLEX n (tradename for) a large cinema complex
CINERAMIC adj relating to a cinematic process producing widescreen images
CINERARIA n garden plant with daisy-like flowers
CINERARY adj of (someone's) ashes
CINERATOR same as > CREMATOR
CINEREA n grey matter of the brain and nervous system
CINEREAL adj ashy

CINEREAS > CINEREA
CINEREOUS adj of a greyish colour
CINERIN n either of two organic compounds used as insecticides
CINERINS > CINERIN
CINES > CINE
CINGULA > CINGULUM
CINGULAR adj ring-shaped
CINGULATE > CINGULUM
CINGULUM n girdle-like part, such as the ridge round the base of a tooth or the band of fibres connecting parts of the cerebrum
CINNABAR n heavy red mineral containing mercury
CINNABARS > CINNABAR
CINNAMIC > CINNAMON
CINNAMON n spice obtained from the bark of an Asian tree
CINNAMONS > CINNAMON
CINNAMONY > CINNAMON
CINNAMYL n univalent radical of cinnamic compounds
CINNAMYLS > CINNAMYL
CINQUAIN n stanza of five lines
CINQUAINS > CINQUAIN
CINQUE n number five in cards, dice, etc
CINQUES > CINQUE
CION same as > SCION
CIONS > CION
CIOPPINO n Italian rich fish stew
CIOPPINOS > CIOPPINO
CIPHER n system of secret writing ▷ vb put (a message) into secret writing
CIPHERED > CIPHER
CIPHERER > CIPHER
CIPHERERS > CIPHER
CIPHERING > CIPHER
CIPHERS > CIPHER
CIPHONIES > CIPHONY
CIPHONY n ciphered telephony; process of enciphering audio information, producing encrypted speech
CIPOLIN n Italian marble with alternating white and green streaks
CIPOLINS > CIPOLIN
CIPOLLINO same as > CIPOLIN
CIPPI > CIPPUS
CIPPUS n pillar bearing an inscription
CIRCA prep approximately, about
CIRCADIAN adj of biological processes that occur regularly at 24-hour intervals
CIRCAR n in India, part of a province

CIRCARS > CIRCAR
CIRCINATE adj (of part of a plant, such as a young fern) coiled so that the tip is at the centre
CIRCITER prep around, about
CIRCLE n perfectly round geometric figure, line, or shape ▷ vb move in a circle (round)
CIRCLED > CIRCLE
CIRCLER > CIRCLE
CIRCLERS > CIRCLE
CIRCLES > CIRCLE
CIRCLET n circular ornament worn on the head
CIRCLETS > CIRCLET
CIRCLING > CIRCLE
CIRCLINGS > CIRCLE
CIRCLIP n flat spring ring split at one point so that it can be sprung open, passed over a shaft or spindle, and allowed to close into a closely fitting annular recess to form a collar on the shaft. A similar design can be closed to pass into a bore and allowed to spring out into an annular recess to form a shoulder in the bore
CIRCLIPS > CIRCLIP
CIRCS pl n circumstances
CIRCUIT n complete route or course, esp a circular one ▷ vb make or travel in a circuit around (something)
CIRCUITAL > CIRCUIT
CIRCUITED > CIRCUIT
CIRCUITRY n electrical circuit(s)
CIRCUITS > CIRCUIT
CIRCUITY n (of speech, reasoning, etc) a roundabout or devious quality
CIRCULAR adj in the shape of a circle ▷ n letter for general distribution
CIRCULARS > CIRCULAR
CIRCULATE vb send, go, or pass from place to place or person to person
CIRCUS n (performance given by) a travelling company of acrobats, clowns, performing animals, etc
CIRCUSES > CIRCUS
CIRCUSSY > CIRCUS
CIRCUSY > CIRCUS
CIRE adj (of fabric) treated with a heat or wax process to make it smooth ▷ n such a surface on a fabric
CIRES > CIRE
CIRL n bird belonging to the bunting family
CIRLS > CIRL
CIRQUE n steep-sided

semicircular hollow found
in mountainous areas
**CIRQUES** >CIRQUE
**CIRRATE** *adj* bearing or
resembling cirri
**CIRRHOSED** >CIRRHOSIS
**CIRRHOSES** >CIRRHOSIS
**CIRRHOSIS** *n* serious liver
disease, often caused by
drinking too much alcohol·
**CIRRHOTIC** >CIRRHOSIS
**CIRRI** >CIRRUS
**CIRRIFORM** *adj* cirrus-like
**CIRRIPED** *same*
*as* >CIRRIPEDE
**CIRRIPEDE** *n* any marine
crustacean of the subclass
*Cirripedia*, including the
barnacles, the adults
of which are sessile or
parasitic ▷ *adj* of, relating
to, or belonging to the
*Cirripedia*
**CIRRIPEDS** >CIRRIPED
**CIRROSE** *same as* >CIRRATE
**CIRROUS** *same as* >CIRRATE
**CIRRUS** *n* high wispy cloud
**CIRSOID** *adj* resembling
a varix
**CIS** *adj* having two groups
of atoms on the same side
of a double bond
**CISALPINE** *adj* on this (the
southern) side of the Alps,
as viewed from Rome
**CISCO** *n* whitefish, esp the
lake herring of cold deep
lakes of North America
**CISCOES** >CISCO
**CISCOS** >CISCO
**CISELEUR** *n* person who is
expert in ciselure
**CISELEURS** >CISELEUR
**CISELURE** *n* art or process
of chasing metal
**CISELURES** >CISELURE
**CISLUNAR** *adj* of or relating
to the space between the
earth and the moon
**CISPADANE** *adj* on this (the
southern) side of the River
Po, as viewed from Rome
**CISPLATIN** *n* cytotoxic
drug that acts by
preventing DNA
replication and hence
cell division, used in the
treatment of tumours, esp
of the ovary and testis
**CISSIER** >CISSY
**CISSIES** >CISSY
**CISSIEST** >CISSY
**CISSIFIED** *another word*
*for* >SISSY
**CISSING** *n* appearance of
pinholes, craters, etc, in
paintwork due to poor
adhesion of the paint to
the surface
**CISSINGS** >CISSING
**CISSOID** *n* geometric curve
whose two branches meet
in a cusp at the origin and
are asymptotic to a line

parallel to the *y*-axis
**CISSOIDS** >CISSOID
**CISSUS** *n* any plant of the
climbing genus *Cissus*,
some species of which,
esp the kangaroo vine (*C.
antarctica*) from Australia,
are grown as greenhouse
or house plants for their
shiny green or mottled
leaves: family *Vitaceae*
**CISSUSES** >CISSUS
**CISSY** *same as* >SISSY
**CIST** *n* wooden box for
holding ritual objects
used in ancient Rome and
Greece ▷ *vb* make a cist
**CISTED** >CIST
**CISTERN** *n* water tank, esp
one that holds water for
flushing a toilet
**CISTERNA** *n* sac or partially
closed space containing
body fluid, esp lymph or
cerebrospinal fluid
**CISTERNAE** >CISTERNA
**CISTERNAL** >CISTERN
**CISTERNS** >CISTERN
**CISTIC** *adj* cist-like
**CISTRON** *n* section of a
chromosome that encodes
a single polypeptide chain
**CISTRONIC** >CISTRON
**CISTRONS** >CISTRON
**CISTS** >CIST
**CISTUS** *n* any plant of the
genus *Cistus*
**CISTUSES** >CISTUS
**CISTVAEN** *n* pre-Christian
stone coffin or burial
chamber
**CISTVAENS** >CISTVAEN
**CIT** *n* pejorative term for a
town dweller
**CITABLE** >CITE
**CITADEL** *n* fortress in a city
**CITADELS** >CITADEL
**CITAL** *n* court summons
**CITALS** >CITAL
**CITATION** *n*
commendation for bravery
**CITATIONS** >CITATION
**CITATOR** *n* legal
publication listing cases
and statutes, their history
and current status
**CITATORS** >CITATOR
**CITATORY** >CITATION
**CITE** *vb* quote, refer to
**CITEABLE** >CITE
**CITED** >CITE
**CITER** >CITE
**CITERS** >CITE
**CITES** >CITE
**CITESS** *n* female cit
**CITESSES** >CITESS
**CITHARA** *n* stringed
musical instrument
of ancient Greece and
elsewhere, similar to the
lyre and played with a
plectrum
**CITHARAS** >CITHARA
**CITHARIST** *n* player of the

cithara
**CITHER** *same as* >CITTERN
**CITHERN** *same as* >CITTERN
**CITHERNS** >CITHERN
**CITHERS** >CITHER
**CITHREN** *same as* >CITHARA
**CITHRENS** >CITHREN
**CITIED** *adj* having cities
**CITIES** >CITY
**CITIFIED** >CITIFY
**CITIFIES** >CITIFY
**CITIFY** *vb* cause to
conform to or adopt the
customs, habits, or dress
of city people
**CITIFYING** >CITIFY
**CITIGRADE** *adj* relating to
(fast-moving) wolf spiders
**CITING** >CITE
**CITIZEN** *n* native or
naturalized member of a
state or nation
**CITIZENLY** >CITIZEN
**CITIZENRY** *n* citizens
collectively
**CITIZENS** >CITIZEN
**CITO** *adv* swiftly
**CITOLA** *n* type of medieval
stringed instrument
**CITOLAS** >CITOLA
**CITOLE** *a rare word*
*for* >CITTERN
**CITOLES** >CITOLE
**CITRAL** *n* yellow volatile
liquid with a lemon-like
odour, found in oils of
lemon grass, orange,
and lemon and used in
perfumery
**CITRALS** >CITRAL
**CITRANGE** *n* type of acidic
and aromatic orange
**CITRANGES** >CITRANGE
**CITRATE** *n* any salt or ester
of citric acid
**CITRATED** *adj* treated with
a citrate
**CITRATES** >CITRATE
**CITREOUS** *adj* of a
greenish-yellow colour
**CITRIC** *adj* of or derived
from citrus fruits or citric
acid
**CITRIN** *n* vitamin P
**CITRINE** *n* brownish-
yellow variety of quartz: a
gemstone
**CITRINES** >CITRINE
**CITRININ** *n* a mycotoxin
**CITRININS** >CITRININ
**CITRINS** >CITRIN
**CITRON** *n* lemon-like fruit
of a small Asian tree
**CITRONS** >CITRON
**CITROUS** *same as* >CITRUS
**CITRUS** *n* any tree or
shrub of the tropical and
subtropical rutaceous
genus *Citrus*, which
includes the orange,
lemon, lime, grapefruit,
citron, and calamondin
▷ *adj* of, relating to, or
belonging to the genus

*Citrus* or to the fruits of
plants of this genus
**CITRUSES** >CITRUS
**CITRUSSY** *adj* having or
resembling the taste or
colour of a citrus fruit
**CITRUSY** *same as* >CITRUSSY
**CITS** >CIT
**CITTERN** *n* medieval
stringed instrument
resembling a lute but
having wire strings and a
flat back
**CITTERNS** >CITTERN
**CITY** *n* large or important
town
**CITYFIED** >CITYFY
**CITYFIES** >CITYFY
**CITYFY** *same as* >CITIFY
**CITYFYING** >CITYFY
**CITYSCAPE** *n* urban
landscape
**CITYWARD** *adv* towards a
city
**CITYWIDE** *adj* occurring
throughout a city
**CIVE** *same as* >CHIVE
**CIVES** >CIVE
**CIVET** *n* spotted catlike
African mammal
**CIVETLIKE** >CIVET
**CIVETS** >CIVET
**CIVIC** *adj* of a city or
citizens
**CIVICALLY** >CIVIC
**CIVICISM** *n* principle of
civil government
**CIVICISMS** >CIVICISM
**CIVICS** *n* study of the
rights and responsibilities
of citizenship
**CIVIE** *same as* >CIVVY
**CIVIES** >CIVIE
**CIVIL** *adj* relating to
the citizens of a state as
opposed to the armed
forces or the Church
**CIVILIAN** *adj* not
belonging to the armed
forces ▷ *n* person who
is not a member of the
armed forces or police
**CIVILIANS** >CIVILIAN
**CIVILISE** *same as* >CIVILIZE
**CIVILISED** *same*
*as* >CIVILIZED
**CIVILISER** >CIVILISE
**CIVILISES** >CIVILISE
**CIVILIST** *n* civilian
**CIVILISTS** >CIVILIST
**CIVILITY** *n* polite or
courteous behaviour
**CIVILIZE** *vb* refine or
educate (a person)
**CIVILIZED** *adj* having a
high state of culture and
social development
**CIVILIZER** >CIVILIZE
**CIVILIZES** >CIVILIZE
**CIVILLY** >CIVIL
**CIVILNESS** >CIVIL
**CIVISM** *n* good citizenship
**CIVISMS** >CIVISM
**CIVVIES** >CIVVY

CIVVY *n* civilian
CIZERS *archaic spelling of* > SCISSORS
CLABBER *vb* to cover with mud
CLABBERED > CLABBER
CLABBERS > CLABBER
CLACH *n* stone
CLACHAN *n* small village
CLACHANS > CLACHAN
CLACHS > CLACH
CLACK *n* sound made by two hard objects striking each other ▷ *vb* make this sound
CLACKBOX *n* casing enclosing a clack
CLACKDISH *n* formerly, a dish carried by a beggar
CLACKED > CLACK
CLACKER *n* object that makes a clacking sound
CLACKERS > CLACKER
CLACKING > CLACK
CLACKS > CLACK
CLAD *vb* bond a metal to (another metal), esp to form a protective coat
CLADDAGH *n* Irish ring
CLADDAGHS > CLADDAGH
CLADDED *adj* covered with cladding
CLADDER > CLAD
CLADDERS > CLAD
CLADDIE *another name for* > KORARI
CLADDIES > CLADDIE
CLADDING > CLOTHE
CLADDINGS > CLOTHE
CLADE *n* group of organisms considered as having evolved from a common ancestor
CLADES > CLADE
CLADISM > CLADIST
CLADISMS > CLADIST
CLADIST *n* proponent of cladistics: a method of grouping animals that makes use of lines of descent rather than structural similarities
CLADISTIC > CLADIST
CLADISTS > CLADIST
CLADODE *n* flattened stem resembling and functioning as a leaf, as in butcher's-broom
CLADODES > CLADODE
CLADODIAL > CLADODE
CLADOGRAM *n* treelike diagram illustrating the development of a clade
CLADS > CLAD
CLAES *Scots word for* > CLOTHES
CLAFOUTI *same as* > CLAFOUTIS
CLAFOUTIS *n* French baked pudding
CLAG *n* sticky mud ▷ *vb* stick, as mud
CLAGGED > CLAG
CLAGGIER > CLAGGY

CLAGGIEST > CLAGGY
CLAGGING > CLAG
CLAGGY *adj* stickily clinging, as mud
CLAGS > CLAG
CLAIM *vb* assert as a fact ▷ *n* assertion that something is true
CLAIMABLE > CLAIM
CLAIMANT *n* person who makes a claim
CLAIMANTS > CLAIMANT
CLAIMED > CLAIM
CLAIMER > CLAIM
CLAIMERS > CLAIM
CLAIMING > CLAIM
CLAIMS > CLAIM
CLAM *n* edible shellfish with a hinged shell ▷ *vb* gather clams
CLAMANCY *n* urgency
CLAMANT *adj* noisy
CLAMANTLY > CLAMANT
CLAMBAKE *n* picnic, often by the sea, at which clams, etc, are baked
CLAMBAKES > CLAMBAKE
CLAMBE *old variant of* > CLIMB
CLAMBER *vb* climb awkwardly ▷ *n* climb performed in this manner
CLAMBERED > CLAMBER
CLAMBERER > CLAMBER
CLAMBERS > CLAMBER
CLAME *archaic variant of* > CLAIM
CLAMES > CLAIM
CLAMLIKE > CLAM
CLAMMED > CLAM
CLAMMER *n* person who gathers clams
CLAMMERS > CLAMMER
CLAMMIER > CLAMMY
CLAMMIEST > CLAMMY
CLAMMILY > CLAMMY
CLAMMING > CLAM
CLAMMY *adj* unpleasantly moist and sticky
CLAMOR *same as* > CLAMOUR
CLAMORED > CLAMOR
CLAMORER > CLAMOR
CLAMORERS > CLAMOR
CLAMORING > CLAMOR
CLAMOROUS > CLAMOR
CLAMORS > CLAMOR
CLAMOUR *n* loud protest ▷ *vb* make a loud noise or outcry
CLAMOURED > CLAMOUR
CLAMOURER > CLAMOUR
CLAMOURS > CLAMOUR
CLAMP *n* tool with movable jaws for holding things together tightly ▷ *vb* fasten with a clamp
CLAMPDOWN *n* sudden restrictive measure
CLAMPED > CLAMP
CLAMPER *n* spiked metal frame fastened to the sole of a shoe to prevent slipping on ice ▷ *vb* to tread heavily

CLAMPERED > CLAMPER
CLAMPERS > CLAMPER
CLAMPING > CLAMP
CLAMPS > CLAMP
CLAMS > CLAM
CLAMSHELL *n* dredging bucket that is hinged like the shell of a clam
CLAMWORM *the US name for the* > RAGWORM
CLAMWORMS > CLAMWORM
CLAN *n* group of families with a common ancestor, esp among Scottish Highlanders
CLANG *vb* make a loud ringing metallic sound ▷ *n* ringing metallic sound
CLANGBOX *n* device fitted to a jet-engine to change the direction of thrust
CLANGED > CLANG
CLANGER *n* obvious mistake
CLANGERS > CLANGER
CLANGING > CLANG
CLANGINGS > CLANG
CLANGOR *same as* > CLANGOUR
CLANGORED > CLANGOR
CLANGORS > CLANGOR
CLANGOUR *n* loud continuous clanging sound ▷ *vb* make or produce a loud resonant noise
CLANGOURS > CLANGOUR
CLANGS > CLANG
CLANK *n* harsh metallic sound ▷ *vb* make such a sound
CLANKED > CLANK
CLANKIER > CLANKY
CLANKIEST > CLANKY
CLANKING > CLANK
CLANKINGS > CLANK
CLANKS > CLANK
CLANKY *adj* making clanking sounds
CLANNISH *adj* (of a group) tending to exclude outsiders
CLANS > CLAN
CLANSHIP *n* association of families under the leadership of a chieftain
CLANSHIPS > CLANSHIP
CLANSMAN *n* man belonging to a clan
CLANSMEN > CLANSMAN
CLAP *vb* applaud by hitting the palms of one's hands sharply together ▷ *n* act or sound of clapping
CLAPBOARD *n* long thin timber board with one edge thicker than the other, used esp in the US and Canada in wood-frame construction by lapping each board over the one below ▷ *vb* cover with such boards
CLAPBREAD *n* type of cake

made from oatmeal
CLAPDISH *same as* > CLACKDISH
CLAPNET *n* net that can be closed instantly by pulling a string
CLAPNETS > CLAPNET
CLAPPED > CLAP
CLAPPER *n* piece of metal inside a bell, which causes it to sound when struck against the side ▷ *vb* make a sound like a clapper
CLAPPERED > CLAPPER
CLAPPERS > CLAPPER
CLAPPING > CLAP
CLAPPINGS > CLAP
CLAPS > CLAP
CLAPT *old inflection* > CLAP
CLAPTRAP *n* foolish or pretentious talk
CLAPTRAPS > CLAPTRAP
CLAQUE *n* group of people hired to applaud
CLAQUER *same as* > CLAQUEUR
CLAQUERS > CLAQUER
CLAQUES > CLAQUE
CLAQUEUR *n* member of a claque
CLAQUEURS > CLAQUEUR
CLARAIN *n* one of the four major lithotypes of banded coal
CLARAINS > CLARAIN
CLARENCE *n* closed four-wheeled horse-drawn carriage, having a glass front
CLARENCES > CLARENCE
CLARENDON *n* style of boldface roman type
CLARET *n* dry red wine from Bordeaux ▷ *adj* purplish-red ▷ *vb* to drink claret
CLARETED > CLARET
CLARETING > CLARET
CLARETS > CLARET
CLARIES > CLARY
CLARIFIED > CLARIFY
CLARIFIER > CLARIFY
CLARIFIES > CLARIFY
CLARIFY *vb* make (a matter) clear and unambiguous
CLARINET *n* keyed woodwind instrument with a single reed
CLARINETS > CLARINET
CLARINI > CLARINO
CLARINO *adj* of or relating to a high passage for the trumpet in 18th-century music ▷ *n* high register of the trumpet
CLARINOS > CLARINO
CLARION *n* obsolete high-pitched trumpet ▷ *adj* clear and ringing ▷ *vb* proclaim loudly
CLARIONED > CLARION
CLARIONET *same as* > CLARINET

**CLARIONS** > CLARION
**CLARITIES** > CLARITY
**CLARITY** n clearness
**CLARKIA** n any North American onagraceous plant of the genus *Clarkia*: cultivated for their red, purple, or pink flowers
**CLARKIAS** > CLARKIA
**CLARO** n mild light-coloured cigar
**CLAROES** > CLARO
**CLAROS** > CLARO
**CLARSACH** n Celtic harp of Scotland and Ireland
**CLARSACHS** > CLARSACH
**CLART** vb to dirty
**CLARTED** > CLART
**CLARTHEAD** n slow-witted or stupid person
**CLARTIER** > CLARTY
**CLARTIEST** > CLARTY
**CLARTING** > CLART
**CLARTS** pl n lumps of mud, esp on shoes
**CLARTY** adj dirty, esp covered in mud
**CLARY** n any of several European plants of the genus *Salvia*, having aromatic leaves and blue flowers: family *Lamiaceae* (labiates)
**CLASH** vb come into conflict ▷ n fight, argument
**CLASHED** > CLASH
**CLASHER** > CLASH
**CLASHERS** > CLASH
**CLASHES** > CLASH
**CLASHING** > CLASH
**CLASHINGS** > CLASH
**CLASP** n device for fastening things ▷ vb grasp or embrace firmly
**CLASPED** > CLASP
**CLASPER** > CLASP
**CLASPERS** pl n paired organ of male insects, used to clasp the female during copulation
**CLASPING** > CLASP
**CLASPINGS** > CLASP
**CLASPS** > CLASP
**CLASPT** old inflection of > CLASP
**CLASS** n group of people sharing a similar social position ▷ vb place in a class
**CLASSABLE** > CLASS
**CLASSED** > CLASS
**CLASSER** > CLASS
**CLASSERS** > CLASS
**CLASSES** > CLASS
**CLASSIBLE** adj able to be classed
**CLASSIC** adj being a typical example of something ▷ n author, artist, or work of art of recognized excellence
**CLASSICAL** adj of or in a restrained conservative style
**CLASSICO** adj (of Italian wines) coming from the centre of a specific wine-growing region
**CLASSICS** pl n the.a body of literature regarded as great or lasting, esp that of ancient Greece or Rome
**CLASSIER** > CLASSY
**CLASSIEST** > CLASSY
**CLASSIFIC** adj relating to classification
**CLASSIFY** vb divide into groups with similar characteristics
**CLASSILY** > CLASSY
**CLASSING** > CLASS
**CLASSINGS** > CLASS
**CLASSIS** n governing body of elders or pastors
**CLASSISM** n belief that people from certain social or economic classes are superior to others
**CLASSISMS** > CLASSISM
**CLASSIST** > CLASSISM
**CLASSISTS** > CLASSISM
**CLASSLESS** adj not belonging to a class
**CLASSMAN** n graduate of Oxford University with a classed honours degree
**CLASSMATE** n friend or contemporary in the same class of a school
**CLASSMEN** > CLASSMAN
**CLASSON** n elementary atomic particle
**CLASSONS** > CLASSON
**CLASSROOM** n room in a school where lessons take place
**CLASSWORK** n school work done in class
**CLASSY** adj stylish and elegant
**CLAST** n fragment of a clastic rock
**CLASTIC** adj (of sedimentary rock, etc) composed of fragments of pre-existing rock that have been transported some distance from their points of origin ▷ n clast
**CLASTICS** > CLASTIC
**CLASTS** > CLAST
**CLAT** n irksome or troublesome task ▷ vb to scrape
**CLATCH** vb to move making a squelching sound
**CLATCHED** > CLATCH
**CLATCHES** > CLATCH
**CLATCHING** > CLATCH
**CLATHRATE** adj resembling a net or lattice ▷ n solid compound in which molecules of one substance are physically trapped in the crystal lattice of another
**CLATS** > CLAT

**CLATTED** > CLAT
**CLATTER** n (make) a rattling noise ▷ vb make a rattling noise, as when hard objects hit each other
**CLATTERED** > CLATTER
**CLATTERER** > CLATTER
**CLATTERS** > CLATTER
**CLATTERY** > CLATTER
**CLATTING** > CLAT
**CLAUCHT** vb to seize by force
**CLAUCHTED** > CLAUCHT
**CLAUCHTS** > CLAUCHT
**CLAUGHT** same as > CLAUCHT
**CLAUGHTED** > CLAUGHT
**CLAUGHTS** > CLAUGHT
**CLAUSAL** > CLAUSE
**CLAUSE** n section of a legal document
**CLAUSES** > CLAUSE
**CLAUSTRA** > CLAUSTRUM
**CLAUSTRAL** same as > CLOISTRAL
**CLAUSTRUM** n thin layer of gret matter in the brain
**CLAUSULA** n type of cadence in polyphony
**CLAUSULAE** > CLAUSULA
**CLAUSULAR** > CLAUSE
**CLAUT** same as > CLAT
**CLAUTED** > CLAUT
**CLAUTING** > CLAUT
**CLAUTS** > CLAUT
**CLAVATE** adj shaped like a club with the thicker end uppermost
**CLAVATED** same as > CLAVATE
**CLAVATELY** > CLAVATE
**CLAVATION** > CLAVATE
**CLAVE** n one of a pair of hardwood sticks struck together to make a hollow sound, esp to mark the beat of Latin-American dance music
**CLAVECIN** n harpsichord
**CLAVECINS** > CLAVECIN
**CLAVER** vb talk idly ▷ n idle talk
**CLAVERED** > CLAVER
**CLAVERING** > CLAVER
**CLAVERS** > CLAVER
**CLAVES** > CLAVE
**CLAVI** > CLAVUS
**CLAVICLE** n either of the two bones connecting the shoulder blades with the upper part of the breastbone
**CLAVICLES** > CLAVICLE
**CLAVICORN** n any beetle of the group *Clavicornia*, including the ladybirds, characterized by club-shaped antennae ▷ adj of, relating to, or belonging to the *Clavicornia*
**CLAVICULA** n clavicle
**CLAVIE** n tar-barrel traditionally set alight in Moray in Scotland on Hogmanay

**CLAVIER** n any keyboard instrument
**CLAVIERS** > CLAVIER
**CLAVIES** > CLAVIE
**CLAVIFORM** same as > CLAVATE
**CLAVIGER** n key- or club-bearer
**CLAVIGERS** > CLAVIGER
**CLAVIS** n key
**CLAVULATE** adj club-shaped
**CLAVUS** n corn on the toe
**CLAW** n sharp hooked nail of a bird or beast ▷ vb tear with claws or nails
**CLAWBACK** n recovery of a sum of money
**CLAWBACKS** > CLAWBACK
**CLAWED** > CLAW
**CLAWER** > CLAW
**CLAWERS** > CLAW
**CLAWING** > CLAW
**CLAWLESS** > CLAW
**CLAWLIKE** adj resembling a claw or claws
**CLAWS** > CLAW
**CLAXON** same as > KLAXON
**CLAXONS** > CLAXON
**CLAY** n fine-grained earth, soft when moist and hardening when baked, used to make bricks and pottery ▷ vb cover or mix with clay
**CLAYBANK** n dull brownish-orange colour
**CLAYBANKS** > CLAYBANK
**CLAYED** > CLAY
**CLAYEY** > CLAY
**CLAYIER** > CLAY
**CLAYIEST** > CLAY
**CLAYING** > CLAY
**CLAYISH** > CLAY
**CLAYLIKE** > CLAY
**CLAYMORE** n large two-edged sword formerly used by Scottish Highlanders
**CLAYMORES** > CLAYMORE
**CLAYPAN** n layer of stiff impervious clay situated just below the surface of the ground, which holds water after heavy rain
**CLAYPANS** > CLAYPAN
**CLAYS** > CLAY
**CLAYSTONE** n compact very fine-grained rock consisting of consolidated clay particles
**CLAYTONIA** n any low-growing North American succulent portulacaceous plant of the genus *Claytonia*
**CLAYWARE** n pottery
**CLAYWARES** > CLAYWARE
**CLEAN** adj free from dirt or impurities ▷ vb make (something) free from dirt ▷ adv completely
**CLEANABLE** > CLEAN
**CLEANED** > CLEAN
**CLEANER** n person or thing that removes dirt

**CLEANERS** >CLEANER

**CLEANEST** >CLEAN

**CLEANING** n act of cleaning something

**CLEANINGS** >CLEANING

**CLEANLIER** >CLEANLY

**CLEANLILY** >CLEANLY

**CLEANLY** adv easily or smoothly ▷ adj habitually clean or neat

**CLEANNESS** >CLEAN

**CLEANS** >CLEAN

**CLEANSE** vb make clean

**CLEANSED** >CLEANSE

**CLEANSER** n cleansing agent, such as a detergent

**CLEANSERS** >CLEANSER

**CLEANSES** >CLEANSE

**CLEANSING** >CLEANSE

**CLEANSKIN** n unbranded animal

**CLEANUP** n process of cleaning up or eliminating something

**CLEANUPS** >CLEANUP

**CLEAR** adj free from doubt or confusion ▷ adv in a clear or distinct manner ▷ vb make or become clear

**CLEARABLE** >CLEAR

**CLEARAGE** n clearance

**CLEARAGES** >CLEARAGE

**CLEARANCE** n clearing

**CLEARCOLE** n type of size containing whiting ▷ vb paint (a wall) with this size

**CLEARCUT** n act of felling all trees in area

**CLEARCUTS** >CLEARCUT

**CLEARED** >CLEAR

**CLEARER** >CLEAR

**CLEARERS** >CLEAR

**CLEAREST** >CLEAR

**CLEAREYED** adj having good judgment

**CLEARING** n treeless area in a wood

**CLEARINGS** >CLEARING

**CLEARLY** adv in a clear, distinct, or obvious manner

**CLEARNESS** >CLEAR

**CLEARS** >CLEAR

**CLEARSKIN** same as >CLEANSKIN

**CLEARWAY** n stretch of road on which motorists may stop in an emergency

**CLEARWAYS** >CLEARWAY

**CLEARWEED** n plant like nettle

**CLEARWING** n type of moth

**CLEAT** n wedge ▷ vb supply or support with a cleat or cleats

**CLEATED** >CLEAT

**CLEATING** >CLEAT

**CLEATS** >CLEAT

**CLEAVABLE** >CLEAVE

**CLEAVAGE** n space between a woman's breasts, as revealed by a low-cut dress

**CLEAVAGES** >CLEAVAGE

**CLEAVE** vb split apart ▷ n split

**CLEAVED** >CLEAVE

**CLEAVER** n butcher's heavy knife with a square blade

**CLEAVERS** n plant with small white flowers and sticky fruits

**CLEAVES** >CLEAVE

**CLEAVING** >CLEAVE

**CLEAVINGS** >CLEAVE

**CLECHE** adj (in heraldry) voided so that only a narrow border is visible

**CLECK** vb (of birds) to hatch ▷ n piece of gossip

**CLECKED** >CLECK

**CLECKIER** >CLECK

**CLECKIEST** >CLECK

**CLECKING** >CLECK

**CLECKINGS** >CLECK

**CLECKS** >CLECK

**CLECKY** >CLECK

**CLEEK** n large hook, such as one used to land fish ▷ vb to seize

**CLEEKED** >CLEEK

**CLEEKING** >CLEEK

**CLEEKIT** >CLEEK

**CLEEKS** >CLEEK

**CLEEP** same as >CLEPE

**CLEEPED** >CLEEP

**CLEEPING** >CLEEP

**CLEEPS** >CLEEP

**CLEEVE** n cliff

**CLEEVES** >CLEEVE

**CLEF** n symbol at the beginning of a stave to show the pitch

**CLEFS** >CLEF

**CLEFT** >CLEAVE

**CLEFTED** >CLEAVE

**CLEFTING** >CLEAVE

**CLEFTS** >CLEAVE

**CLEG** another name for a >HORSEFLY

**CLEGS** >CLEG

**CLEIDOIC** as in cleidoic egg egg of birds and insects

**CLEIK** same as >CLEEK

**CLEIKS** >CLEEK

**CLEITHRAL** adj covered with a roof

**CLEM** vb be hungry or cause to be hungry

**CLEMATIS** n climbing plant with large colourful flowers

**CLEMENCY** n kind or lenient treatment

**CLEMENT** adj (of weather) mild

**CLEMENTLY** >CLEMENT

**CLEMMED** >CLEM

**CLEMMING** >CLEM

**CLEMS** >CLEM

**CLENCH** vb close or squeeze (one's teeth or fist) tightly ▷ n firm grasp or grip

**CLENCHED** >CLENCH

**CLENCHER** >CLENCH

**CLENCHERS** >CLENCH

**CLENCHES** >CLENCH

**CLENCHING** >CLENCH

**CLEOME** n any herbaceous or shrubby plant of the mostly tropical capparidaceous genus Cleome, esp C. spinosa, cultivated for their clusters of white or purplish flowers with long stamens

**CLEOMES** >CLEOME

**CLEOPATRA** n yellow butterfly, Gonepteryx cleopatra, the male of which has its wings flushed with orange

**CLEPE** vb call by the name of

**CLEPED** >CLEPE

**CLEPES** >CLEPE

**CLEPING** >CLEPE

**CLEPSYDRA** n ancient device for measuring time by the flow of water or mercury through a small aperture

**CLEPT** >CLEPE

**CLERGIES** >CLERGY

**CLERGY** n priests and ministers as a group

**CLERGYMAN** n member of the clergy

**CLERGYMEN** >CLERGYMAN

**CLERIC** n member of the clergy

**CLERICAL** adj of clerks or office work

**CLERICALS** pl n distinctive dress of a clergyman

**CLERICATE** n clerical post

**CLERICITY** n condition of being a clergyman

**CLERICS** >CLERIC

**CLERID** n beetle that preys on other insects

**CLERIDS** >CLERID

**CLERIHEW** n form of comic or satiric verse, consisting of two couplets and containing the name of a well-known person

**CLERIHEWS** >CLERIHEW

**CLERISIES** >CLERISY

**CLERISY** n learned or educated people

**CLERK** n employee in an office, bank, or court who keeps records, files, and accounts ▷ vb work as a clerk

**CLERKDOM** >CLERK

**CLERKDOMS** >CLERK

**CLERKED** >CLERK

**CLERKESS** n female office clerk

**CLERKING** >CLERK

**CLERKISH** >CLERK

**CLERKLIER** >CLERKLY

**CLERKLIKE** adj acting in a scholarly manner

**CLERKLING** n young or inexperienced clerk

**CLERKLY** adj of or like a clerk ▷ adv in the manner of a clerk

**CLERKS** >CLERK

**CLERKSHIP** >CLERK

**CLERUCH** n settler in a cleruchy

**CLERUCHIA** same as >CLERUCHY

**CLERUCHS** >CLERUCH

**CLERUCHY** n (in the ancient world) a special type of Athenian colony, in which settlers retained their Athenian citizenship and the community remained a political dependency of Athens

**CLEUCH** same as >CLOUGH

**CLEUCHS** >CLEUCH

**CLEUGH** same as >CLOUGH

**CLEUGHS** >CLEUGH

**CLEVE** same as >CLEEVE

**CLEVEITE** n crystalline variety of the mineral uraninite

**CLEVEITES** >CLEVEITE

**CLEVER** adj intelligent, quick at learning

**CLEVERER** >CLEVER

**CLEVEREST** >CLEVER

**CLEVERISH** >CLEVER

**CLEVERLY** >CLEVER

**CLEVES** >CLEEVE

**CLEVIS** n U-shaped component of a shackle for attaching a drawbar to a plough or similar implement

**CLEVISES** >CLEVIS

**CLEW** n ball of thread, yarn, or twine ▷ vb coil or roll into a ball

**CLEWED** >CLEW

**CLEWING** >CLEW

**CLEWS** >CLEW

**CLIANTHUS** n Australian or NZ plant with slender scarlet flowers

**CLICHE** n expression or idea that is no longer effective because of overuse ▷ vb use a cliché (in speech or writing)

**CLICHED** >CLICHE

**CLICHEED** >CLICHE

**CLICHES** >CLICHE

**CLICK** n short sharp sound ▷ vb make this sound

**CLICKABLE** adj (of a website) having links that can be accessed by clicking a computer mouse

**CLICKED** >CLICK

**CLICKER** >CLICK

**CLICKERS** >CLICK

**CLICKET** vb make a click

**CLICKETED** >CLICKET

**CLICKETS** >CLICKET

**CLICKING** >CLICK

**CLICKINGS** >CLICK

**CLICKLESS** >CLICK

**CLICKS** >CLICK

**CLICKWRAP** adj (of agreement) consented to by user clicking computer button

**CLIED** >CLY

**CLIENT** n person who uses the services of a professional person or company

**CLIENTAGE** same as > CLIENTELE

**CLIENTAL** > CLIENT

**CLIENTELE** n clients collectively

**CLIENTS** > CLIENT

**CLIES** > CLY

**CLIFF** n steep rock face, esp along the sea shore ▷ vb scale a cliff

**CLIFFED** > CLIFF

**CLIFFHANG** vb (of a serial or film) to end on a note of suspense

**CLIFFHUNG** > CLIFFHANG

**CLIFFIER** > CLIFF

**CLIFFIEST** > CLIFF

**CLIFFLIKE** > CLIFF

**CLIFFS** > CLIFF

**CLIFFY** > CLIFF

**CLIFT** same as > CLIFF

**CLIFTED** > CLIFF

**CLIFTIER** > CLIFF

**CLIFTIEST** > CLIFF

**CLIFTS** > CLIFF

**CLIFTY** > CLIFF

**CLIMACTIC** adj consisting of, involving, or causing a climax

**CLIMATAL** > CLIMATE

**CLIMATE** n typical weather conditions of an area ▷ vb acclimatize

**CLIMATED** > CLIMATE

**CLIMATES** > CLIMATE

**CLIMATIC** > CLIMATE

**CLIMATING** > CLIMATE

**CLIMATISE** vb in Australia, adapt or become accustomed to a new climate or environment

**CLIMATIZE** same as > CLIMATISE

**CLIMATURE** n clime

**CLIMAX** n most intense point of an experience, series of events, or story ▷ vb reach a climax

**CLIMAXED** > CLIMAX

**CLIMAXES** > CLIMAX

**CLIMAXING** > CLIMAX

**CLIMB** vb go up, ascend ▷ n climbing

**CLIMBABLE** > CLIMB

**CLIMBDOWN** n act of backing down from opinion

**CLIMBED** > CLIMB

**CLIMBER** n person or thing that climbs

**CLIMBERS** > CLIMBER

**CLIMBING** > CLIMB

**CLIMBINGS** > CLIMB

**CLIMBS** > CLIMB

**CLIME** n place or its climate

**CLIMES** > CLIME

**CLINAL** > CLINE

**CLINALLY** > CLINE

**CLINAMEN** n bias

**CLINAMENS** > CLINAMEN

**CLINCH** vb settle (an argument or agreement) decisively ▷ n movement in which one competitor holds on to the other to avoid punches

**CLINCHED** > CLINCH

**CLINCHER** n something decisive

**CLINCHERS** > CLINCHER

**CLINCHES** > CLINCH

**CLINCHING** > CLINCH

**CLINE** n continuous variation in form between members of a species having a wide variable geographical or ecological range

**CLINES** > CLINE

**CLING** vb hold tightly or stick closely ▷ n tendency of cotton fibres in a sample to stick to each other

**CLINGED** > CLING

**CLINGER** > CLING

**CLINGERS** > CLING

**CLINGFILM** n thin polythene material for wrapping food

**CLINGFISH** n any small marine teleost fish of the family Gobiesocidae, having a flattened elongated body with a sucking disc beneath the head for clinging to rocks, etc

**CLINGIER** > CLING

**CLINGIEST** > CLING

**CLINGING** > CLING

**CLINGS** > CLING

**CLINGY** > CLING

**CLINIC** n building where outpatients receive medical treatment or advice

**CLINICAL** adj of a clinic

**CLINICIAN** n physician, psychiatrist, etc, who specializes in clinical work as opposed to one engaged in laboratory or experimental studies

**CLINICS** > CLINIC

**CLINIQUE** same as > CLINIC

**CLINIQUES** > CLINIC

**CLINK** n (make) a light sharp metallic sound ▷ vb make a light sharp metallic sound

**CLINKED** > CLINK

**CLINKER** n fused coal left over in a fire or furnace ▷ vb form clinker during burning

**CLINKERED** > CLINKER

**CLINKERS** > CLINKER

**CLINKING** > CLINK

**CLINKS** > CLINK

**CLINOAXES** > CLINOAXIS

**CLINOAXIS** n in a monoclinic crystal, the lateral axis which forms an oblique angle with the vertical axis

**CLINOSTAT** n apparatus for studying tropisms in plants, usually a rotating disc to which the plant is attached so that it receives an equal stimulus on all sides

**CLINQUANT** adj glittering, esp with tinsel ▷ n tinsel or imitation gold leaf

**CLINT** n section of a limestone pavement separated from adjacent sections by solution fissures

**CLINTONIA** n any temperate liliaceous plant of the genus Clintonia, having white, greenish-yellow, or purplish flowers, broad ribbed leaves, and blue berries

**CLINTS** > CLINT

**CLIP** vb cut with shears or scissors ▷ n short extract of a film

**CLIPART** n large collection of simple drawings stored in a computer

**CLIPARTS** > CLIPART

**CLIPBOARD** n portable writing board with a clip at the top for holding paper

**CLIPE** same as > CLYPE

**CLIPED** > CLIPE

**CLIPES** > CLIPE

**CLIPING** > CLIPE

**CLIPPABLE** > CLIP

**CLIPPED** > CLIP

**CLIPPER** n fast commercial sailing ship

**CLIPPERS** pl n tool for clipping

**CLIPPIE** n bus conductress

**CLIPPIES** > CLIPPIE

**CLIPPING** > CLIP

**CLIPPINGS** > CLIP

**CLIPS** > CLIP

**CLIPSHEAR** n earwig

**CLIPSHEET** n sheet of paper with text printed on one side only

**CLIPT** old inflection of > CLIP

**CLIQUE** n small exclusive group ▷ vb to form a clique

**CLIQUED** > CLIQUE

**CLIQUES** > CLIQUE

**CLIQUEY** adj exclusive, confined to a small group

**CLIQUIER** > CLIQUEY

**CLIQUIEST** > CLIQUEY

**CLIQUING** > CLIQUE

**CLIQUISH** > CLIQUE

**CLIQUISM** > CLIQUE

**CLIQUISMS** > CLIQUE

**CLIQUY** same as > CLIQUEY

**CLITELLA** > CLITELLUM

**CLITELLAR** > CLITELLUM

**CLITELLUM** n thickened saddle-like region of epidermis in earthworms and leeches whose

secretions bind copulating worms together and later form a cocoon around the eggs

**CLITHRAL** same as > CLEITHRAL

**CLITIC** adj (of a word) incapable of being stressed, usually pronounced as if part of the word that follows or precedes it: for example, in French, me, te, and le are clitic pronouns ▷ n clitic word

**CLITICISE** same as > CLITICIZE

**CLITICIZE** vb pronounce as part of following or preceding word

**CLITICS** > CLITIC

**CLITORAL** > CLITORIS

**CLITORIC** > CLITORIS

**CLITORIS** n small sexually sensitive organ at the front of the vulva

**CLITTER** vb to stridulate

**CLITTERED** > CLITTER

**CLITTERS** > CLITTER

**CLIVERS** same as > CLEAVERS

**CLIVIA** n plant belonging to the Amaryllid family

**CLIVIAS** > CLIVIA

**CLOACA** n cavity in most animals, except higher mammals, into which the alimentary canal and the genital and urinary ducts open

**CLOACAE** > CLOACA

**CLOACAL** > CLOACA

**CLOACAS** > CLOACA

**CLOACINAL** > CLOACA

**CLOACITIS** n inflammation of the cloaca in birds, including domestic fowl, and other animals with a common opening of the urinary and gastrointestinal tracts

**CLOAK** n loose sleeveless outer garment ▷ vb cover or conceal

**CLOAKED** > CLOAK

**CLOAKING** > CLOAK

**CLOAKROOM** n room where coats may be left temporarily

**CLOAKS** > CLOAK

**CLOAM** adj made of clay or earthenware ▷ n clay or earthenware pots, dishes, etc, collectively

**CLOAMS** > CLOAM

**CLOBBER** vb hit ▷ n belongings, esp clothes

**CLOBBERED** > CLOBBER

**CLOBBERS** > CLOBBER

**CLOCHARD** n tramp

**CLOCHARDS** > CLOCHARD

**CLOCHE** n cover to protect young plants

**CLOCHES** > CLOCHE

**CLOCK** n instrument for showing the time ▷ vb record (time) with a stopwatch
**CLOCKED** > CLOCK
**CLOCKER** > CLOCK
**CLOCKERS** > CLOCK
**CLOCKING** > CLOCK
**CLOCKINGS** > CLOCK
**CLOCKLIKE** > CLOCK
**CLOCKS** > CLOCK
**CLOCKWISE** adj in the direction in which the hands of a clock rotate
**CLOCKWORK** n mechanism similar to the kind in a clock, used in wind-up toys
**CLOD** n lump of earth ▷ vb pelt with clods
**CLODDED** > CLOD
**CLODDIER** > CLOD
**CLODDIEST** > CLOD
**CLODDING** > CLOD
**CLODDISH** > CLOD
**CLODDY** > CLOD
**CLODLY** > CLOD
**CLODPATE** n dull or stupid person
**CLODPATED** adj stupid
**CLODPATES** > CLODPATE
**CLODPOLE** same as > CLODPATE
**CLODPOLES** > CLODPOLE
**CLODPOLL** same as > CLODPATE
**CLODPOLLS** > CLODPOLL
**CLODS** > CLOD
**CLOFF** n cleft of a tree
**CLOFFS** > CLOFF
**CLOG** vb obstruct ▷ n wooden or wooden-soled shoe
**CLOGDANCE** n dance performed in clogs
**CLOGGED** > CLOG
**CLOGGER** n clogmaker
**CLOGGERS** > CLOGGER
**CLOGGIER** > CLOG
**CLOGGIEST** > CLOG
**CLOGGILY** > CLOG
**CLOGGING** > CLOG
**CLOGGY** > CLOG
**CLOGS** > CLOG
**CLOISON** n partition
**CLOISONNE** n design made by filling in a wire outline with coloured enamel ▷ adj of, relating to, or made by cloisonné
**CLOISONS** > CLOISON
**CLOISTER** n covered pillared arcade, usu. in a monastery ▷ vb confine or seclude in or as if in a monastery
**CLOISTERS** > CLOISTER
**CLOISTRAL** adj of, like, or characteristic of a cloister
**CLOKE** same as > CLOAK
**CLOKED** > CLOKE
**CLOKES** > CLOKE
**CLOKING** > CLOKE
**CLOMB** a past tense and past participle of > CLIMB

**CLOMP** same as > CLUMP
**CLOMPED** > CLOMP
**CLOMPING** > CLOMP
**CLOMPS** > CLOMP
**CLON** same as > CLONE
**CLONAL** > CLONE
**CLONALLY** > CLONE
**CLONE** n animal or plant produced artificially from the cells of another animal or plant, and identical to the original ▷ vb produce as a clone
**CLONED** > CLONE
**CLONER** > CLONE
**CLONERS** > CLONE
**CLONES** > CLONE
**CLONIC** > CLONUS
**CLONICITY** > CLONUS
**CLONIDINE** n antihypertensive drug
**CLONING** > CLONE
**CLONINGS** > CLONE
**CLONISM** n series of clonic spasms
**CLONISMS** > CLONISM
**CLONK** vb make a loud dull thud ▷ n loud thud
**CLONKED** > CLONK
**CLONKING** > CLONK
**CLONKS** > CLONK
**CLONS** > CLON
**CLONUS** n type of convulsion characterized by rapid contraction and relaxation of a muscle
**CLONUSES** > CLONUS
**CLOOP** n sound made when a cork is drawn from a bottle
**CLOOPS** > CLOOP
**CLOOT** n hoof
**CLOOTS** > CLOOT
**CLOP** vb make or move along with a sound as of a horse's hooves striking the ground ▷ n sound of this nature
**CLOPPED** > CLOP
**CLOPPING** > CLOP
**CLOPS** > CLOP
**CLOQUE** n fabric with an embossed surface
**CLOQUES** > CLOQUE
**CLOSABLE** > CLOSE
**CLOSE** vb shut ▷ n end, conclusion ▷ adj near ▷ adv closely, tightly ▷ n passageway leading to a tenement building
**CLOSEABLE** > CLOSE
**CLOSED** > CLOSE
**CLOSEDOWN** n closure or stoppage of operations
**CLOSEHEAD** n entrance to a close
**CLOSELY** > CLOSE
**CLOSENESS** > CLOSE
**CLOSEOUT** n termination of an account on which the margin is exhausted
**CLOSEOUTS** > CLOSEOUT
**CLOSER** > CLOSE
**CLOSERS** > CLOSE

**CLOSES** > CLOSE
**CLOSEST** > CLOSE
**CLOSET** n cupboard ▷ adj private, secret ▷ vb shut (oneself) away in private
**CLOSETED** > CLOSET
**CLOSETFUL** n quantity that may be contained in a closet
**CLOSETING** > CLOSET
**CLOSETS** > CLOSET
**CLOSEUP** n photo taken close to subject
**CLOSEUPS** > CLOSEUP
**CLOSING** > CLOSE
**CLOSINGS** > CLOSE
**CLOSURE** n closing ▷ vb (in a deliberative body) to end (debate) by closure
**CLOSURED** > CLOSURE
**CLOSURES** > CLOSURE
**CLOSURING** > CLOSURE
**CLOT** n soft thick lump formed from liquid ▷ vb form soft thick lumps
**CLOTBUR** n burdock
**CLOTBURS** > CLOTBUR
**CLOTE** n burdock
**CLOTES** > CLOTE
**CLOTH** n (piece of) woven fabric
**CLOTHE** vb put clothes on
**CLOTHED** > CLOTHE
**CLOTHES** n garments
**CLOTHIER** n maker or seller of clothes or cloth
**CLOTHIERS** > CLOTHIER
**CLOTHING** > CLOTHE
**CLOTHINGS** > CLOTHE
**CLOTHLIKE** > CLOTH
**CLOTHS** > CLOTH
**CLOTPOLL** same as > CLODPOLL
**CLOTPOLLS** > CLOTPOLL
**CLOTS** > CLOT
**CLOTTED** > CLOT
**CLOTTER** vb to clot
**CLOTTERED** > CLOTTER
**CLOTTERS** > CLOTTER
**CLOTTIER** > CLOTTY
**CLOTTIEST** > CLOTTY
**CLOTTING** > CLOT
**CLOTTINGS** > CLOT
**CLOTTISH** > CLOT
**CLOTTY** adj full of clots
**CLOTURE** n closure in the US Senate ▷ vb end (debate) in the US Senate by cloture
**CLOTURED** > CLOTURE
**CLOTURES** > CLOTURE
**CLOTURING** > CLOTURE
**CLOU** n crux; focus
**CLOUD** n mass of condensed water vapour floating in the sky ▷ vb become cloudy
**CLOUDAGE** n mass of clouds
**CLOUDAGES** > CLOUDAGE
**CLOUDED** > CLOUD
**CLOUDIER** > CLOUDY
**CLOUDIEST** > CLOUDY
**CLOUDILY** > CLOUDY
**CLOUDING** > CLOUD

**CLOUDINGS** > CLOUD
**CLOUDLAND** n realm or fantasy or impractical notions
**CLOUDLESS** > CLOUD
**CLOUDLET** n small cloud
**CLOUDLETS** > CLOUDLET
**CLOUDLIKE** > CLOUD
**CLOUDS** > CLOUD
**CLOUDTOWN** n cloudland
**CLOUDY** adj having a lot of clouds
**CLOUGH** n gorge or narrow ravine
**CLOUGHS** > CLOUGH
**CLOUR** vb to thump or dent
**CLOURED** > CLOUR
**CLOURING** > CLOUR
**CLOURS** > CLOUR
**CLOUS** > CLOU
**CLOUT** n hard blow ▷ vb hit hard
**CLOUTED** > CLOUT
**CLOUTER** > CLOUT
**CLOUTERLY** adj clumsy
**CLOUTERS** > CLOUT
**CLOUTING** > CLOUT
**CLOUTS** > CLOUT
**CLOVE** n tropical evergreen myrtaceous tree
**CLOVEN** > CLEAVE
**CLOVEPINK** n carnation
**CLOVER** n plant with three-lobed leaves
**CLOVERED** adj covered with clover
**CLOVERS** > CLOVER
**CLOVERY** > CLOVER
**CLOVES** > CLOVE
**CLOVIS** as in clovis point flint projectile dating from the 10th millennium BC
**CLOW** n clove
**CLOWDER** n collective terms for a group of cats
**CLOWDERS** > CLOWDER
**CLOWN** n comic entertainer in a circus ▷ vb behave foolishly
**CLOWNED** > CLOWN
**CLOWNERY** > CLOWN
**CLOWNING** > CLOWN
**CLOWNINGS** > CLOWN
**CLOWNISH** > CLOWN
**CLOWNS** > CLOWN
**CLOWS** > CLOW
**CLOY** vb make weary or cause weariness through an excess of something initially pleasurable or sweet
**CLOYE** vb to claw
**CLOYED** > CLOY
**CLOYES** > CLOVE
**CLOYING** adj sickeningly sweet
**CLOYINGLY** > CLOYING
**CLOYLESS** adj not cloying
**CLOYMENT** n satiety
**CLOYMENTS** > CLOYMENT
**CLOYS** > CLOY
**CLOYSOME** adj cloying
**CLOZAPINE** n drug used to treat mental illness

**CLOZE** as in *cloze test* test of the ability to understand text

**CLOZES** >CLOZE

**CLUB** *n* association of people with common interests ▷ *vb* hit with a club

**CLUBABLE** *same as* >CLUBBABLE

**CLUBBABLE** *adj* suitable to be a member of a club

**CLUBBED** >CLUB

**CLUBBER** *n* person who regularly frequents nightclubs and similar establishments

**CLUBBERS** >CLUBBER

**CLUBBIER** >CLUBBY

**CLUBBIEST** >CLUBBY

**CLUBBILY** >CLUBBY

**CLUBBING** >CLUB

**CLUBBINGS** >CLUB

**CLUBBISH** *adj* clubby

**CLUBBISM** *n* advantage gained through membership of a club or clubs

**CLUBBISMS** >CLUBBISM

**CLUBBIST** >CLUBBISM

**CLUBBISTS** >CLUBBISM

**CLUBBY** *adj* sociable, esp effusively so

**CLUBFACE** *n* face of golf club

**CLUBFACES** >CLUBFACE

**CLUBFEET** >CLUBFOOT

**CLUBFOOT** *n* congenital deformity of the foot

**CLUBHAND** *n* congenital deformity of the hand

**CLUBHANDS** >CLUBHAND

**CLUBHAUL** *vb* force (a sailing vessel) onto a new tack, esp in an emergency

**CLUBHAULS** >CLUBHAUL

**CLUBHEAD** *n* head of golf club

**CLUBHEADS** >CLUBHEAD

**CLUBHOUSE** *n* premises of a sports or other club, esp a golf club

**CLUBLAND** *n* (in Britain) the area of London around St. James's, which contains most of the famous London clubs

**CLUBLANDS** >CLUBLAND

**CLUBMAN** *n* man who is an enthusiastic member of a club or clubs

**CLUBMEN** >CLUBMAN

**CLUBROOM** *n* room in which a club meets

**CLUBROOMS** >CLUBROOM

**CLUBROOT** *n* disease of cabbages

**CLUBROOTS** >CLUBROOT

**CLUBRUSH** *n* any rush of the genus Scirpus

**CLUBS** >CLUB

**CLUBWOMAN** *n* woman who is an enthusiastic member of a club or clubs

**CLUBWOMEN** >CLUBWOMAN

**CLUCK** *n* low clicking noise made by a hen ▷ *vb* make this noise

**CLUCKED** >CLUCK

**CLUCKIER** >CLUCKY

**CLUCKIEST** >CLUCKY

**CLUCKING** >CLUCK

**CLUCKS** >CLUCK

**CLUCKY** *adj* wishing to have a baby

**CLUDGIE** *n* toilet

**CLUDGIES** >CLUDGIE

**CLUE** *n* something that helps to solve a mystery or puzzle ▷ *vb* help solve a mystery or puzzle

**CLUED** >CLUE

**CLUEING** >CLUE

**CLUELESS** *adj* stupid

**CLUES** >CLUE

**CLUING** >CLUE

**CLUMBER** *n* type of thickset spaniel

**CLUMBERS** >CLUMBER

**CLUMP** *n* small group of things or people ▷ *vb* walk heavily

**CLUMPED** >CLUMP

**CLUMPER** >CLUMP

**CLUMPERS** >CLUMP

**CLUMPIER** >CLUMP

**CLUMPIEST** >CLUMP

**CLUMPING** >CLUMP

**CLUMPISH** >CLUMP

**CLUMPLIKE** >CLUMP

**CLUMPS** >CLUMP

**CLUMPY** >CLUMP

**CLUMSIER** >CLUMSY

**CLUMSIEST** >CLUMSY

**CLUMSILY** >CLUMSY

**CLUMSY** *adj* lacking skill or physical coordination

**CLUNCH** *n* hardened clay

**CLUNCHES** >CLUNCH

**CLUNG** >CLING

**CLUNK** *n* dull metallic sound ▷ *vb* make such a sound

**CLUNKED** >CLUNK

**CLUNKER** *n* dilapidated old car or other machine

**CLUNKERS** >CLUNKER

**CLUNKIER** >CLUNKY

**CLUNKIEST** >CLUNKY

**CLUNKING** >CLUNK

**CLUNKS** >CLUNK

**CLUNKY** *adj* making a clunking noise

**CLUPEID** *n* any widely distributed soft-finned teleost fish of the family *Clupeidae*, typically having oily flesh, and including the herrings, sardines, shad, etc ▷ *adj* of, relating to, or belonging to the family *Clupeidae*

**CLUPEIDS** >CLUPEID

**CLUPEOID** *adj* of, relating to, or belonging to the *Isospondyli* (or *Clupeiformes*), a large order of soft-finned fishes, including the herrings, salmon, and tarpon ▷ *n* any fish belonging to the order *Isospondyli*

**CLUPEOIDS** >CLUPEOID

**CLUSIA** *n* tree of the tropical American genus Clusia

**CLUSIAS** >CLUSIA

**CLUSTER** *n* small close group ▷ *vb* gather in clusters

**CLUSTERED** >CLUSTER

**CLUSTERS** >CLUSTER

**CLUSTERY** >CLUSTER

**CLUTCH** *vb* grasp tightly ▷ *n* device enabling two revolving shafts to be connected and disconnected, esp in a motor vehicle

**CLUTCHED** >CLUTCH

**CLUTCHES** >CLUTCH

**CLUTCHING** >CLUTCH

**CLUTCHY** *adj* (of a person) tending to cling

**CLUTTER** *vb* scatter objects about (a place) untidily ▷ *n* untidy mess

**CLUTTERED** >CLUTTER

**CLUTTERS** >CLUTTER

**CLUTTERY** *adj* full of clutter

**CLY** *vb* to steal or seize

**CLYING** >CLY

**CLYPE** *vb* tell tales ▷ *n* person who tells tales

**CLYPEAL** >CLYPEUS

**CLYPEATE** >CLYPEUS

**CLYPED** >CLYPE

**CLYPEI** >CLYPEUS

**CLYPES** >CLYPE

**CLYPEUS** *n* cuticular plate on the head of some insects between the labrum and the frons

**CLYPING** >CLYPE

**CLYSTER** *a former name for an* >ENEMA

**CLYSTERS** >CLYSTER

**CNEMIAL** >CNEMIS

**CNEMIDES** >CNEMIS

**CNEMIS** *n* shin or tibia

**CNIDA** *n* nematocyst

**CNIDAE** >CNIDA

**CNIDARIAN** *n* any invertebrate of the phylum *Cnidaria*, which comprises the coelenterates ▷ *adj* of, relating to, or belonging to the *Cnidaria*

**COACH** *n* long-distance bus ▷ *vb* train, teach

**COACHABLE** *adj* capable of being coached

**COACHDOG** *n* Dalmatian dog

**COACHDOGS** >COACHDOG

**COACHED** >COACH

**COACHEE** *n* person who receives training from a coach, esp in business or office practice

**COACHEES** >COACHEE

**COACHER** >COACH

**COACHERS** >COACH

**COACHES** >COACH

**COACHIES** >COACHY

**COACHING** >COACH

**COACHINGS** >COACH

**COACHLINE** *n* decorative line on the bodywork of a vehicle

**COACHLOAD** *n* quantity that a coach can carry

**COACHMAN** *n* driver of a horse-drawn coach or carriage

**COACHMEN** >COACHMAN

**COACHWHIP** *n* whipsnake

**COACHWOOD** *n* Australian tree, *Ceratopetalum apetalum*, yielding light aromatic wood used for furniture, turnery, etc

**COACHWORK** *n* body of a car

**COACHY** *n* coachman

**COACT** *vb* to act together

**COACTED** >COACT

**COACTING** >COACT

**COACTION** *n* any relationship between organisms within a community

**COACTIONS** >COACTION

**COACTIVE** >COACTION

**COACTOR** >COACT

**COACTORS** >COACT

**COACTS** >COACT

**COADAPTED** *adj* adapted to one another

**COADJUTOR** *n* bishop appointed as assistant to a diocesan bishop

**COADMIRE** *vb* to admire together

**COADMIRED** >COADMIRE

**COADMIRES** >COADMIRE

**COADMIT** *vb* to admit together

**COADMITS** >COADMIT

**COADUNATE** *same as* >CONNATE

**COAEVAL** *n* contemporary

**COAEVALS** >COAEVAL

**COAGENCY** *n* joint agency

**COAGENT** >COAGENCY

**COAGENTS** >COAGENCY

**COAGULA** >COAGULUM

**COAGULANT** *n* substance causing coagulation

**COAGULASE** *n* any enzyme that causes coagulation of blood

**COAGULATE** *vb* change from a liquid to a semisolid mass ▷ *n* solid or semisolid substance produced by coagulation

**COAGULUM** *n* any coagulated mass

**COAGULUMS** >COAGULUM

**COAITA** *n* spider monkey

**COAITAS** >COAITA

**COAL** *n* black rock consisting mainly of carbon, used as fuel ▷ *vb* take in, or turn into coal

**COALA** *same as* >KOALA

**COALAS** >COALA
**COALBALL** *n* in coal, nodule containing petrified plant or animal remains
**COALBALLS** >COALBALL
**COALBIN** *n* bin for holding coal
**COALBINS** >COALBIN
**COALBOX** *n* box for holding coal
**COALBOXES** >COALBOX
**COALED** >COAL
**COALER** *n* ship, train, etc, used to carry or supply coal
**COALERS** >COALER
**COALESCE** *vb* come together, merge
**COALESCED** >COALESCE
**COALESCES** >COALESCE
**COALFACE** *n* exposed seam of coal in a mine
**COALFACES** >COALFACE
**COALFIELD** *n* area with coal under the ground
**COALFISH** *n* dark-coloured gadoid food fish, *Pollachius virens*, occurring in northern seas
**COALHOLE** *n* small coal cellar
**COALHOLES** >COALHOLE
**COALHOUSE** *n* shed or building for storing coal
**COALIER** >COAL
**COALIEST** >COAL
**COALIFIED** >COALIFY
**COALIFIES** >COALIFY
**COALIFY** *vb* to turn into coal
**COALING** >COAL
**COALISE** *vb* to form a coalition
**COALISED** >COALISE
**COALISES** >COALISE
**COALISING** >COALISE
**COALITION** *n* temporary alliance, esp between political parties
**COALIZE** *same as* >COALISE
**COALIZED** >COALIZE
**COALIZES** >COALIZE
**COALIZING** >COALIZE
**COALLESS** *adj* without coal
**COALMAN** *n* man who delivers coal
**COALMEN** >COALMAN
**COALMINE** *n* mine from which coal is extracted
**COALMINER** >COALMINE
**COALMINES** >COALMINE
**COALPIT** *n* pit from which coal is extracted
**COALPITS** >COALPIT
**COALS** >COAL
**COALSACK** *n* dark nebula near the constellation Cygnus
**COALSACKS** >COALSACK
**COALSHED** *n* shed in which coal is stored
**COALSHEDS** >COALSHED
**COALTAR** *n* black tar distilled from coal
**COALTARS** >COALTAR

**COALY** >COAL
**COALYARD** *n* yard in which coal is stored
**COALYARDS** >COALYARD
**COAMING** *n* raised frame round a ship's hatchway for keeping out water
**COAMINGS** >COAMING
**COANCHOR** *vb* to co-present a TV programme
**COANCHORS** >COANCHOR
**COANNEX** *vb* to annex with something else
**COANNEXED** >COANNEX
**COANNEXES** >COANNEX
**COAPPEAR** *vb* to appear jointly
**COAPPEARS** >COAPPEAR
**COAPT** *vb* to secure
**COAPTED** >COAPT
**COAPTING** >COAPT
**COAPTS** >COAPT
**COARB** *n* spiritual successor
**COARBS** >COARB
**COARCTATE** *adj* (of a pupa) enclosed in a hard barrel-shaped case (puparium), as in the housefly ▷ *vb* (esp of the aorta) to become narrower
**COARSE** *adj* rough in texture
**COARSELY** >COARSE
**COARSEN** *vb* make or become coarse
**COARSENED** >COARSEN
**COARSENS** >COARSEN
**COARSER** >COARSE
**COARSEST** >COARSE
**COARSISH** >COARSE
**COASSIST** *vb* to assist jointly
**COASSISTS** >COASSIST
**COASSUME** *vb* to assume jointly
**COASSUMED** >COASSUME
**COASSUMES** >COASSUME
**COAST** *n* place where the land meets the sea ▷ *vb* move by momentum, without the use of power
**COASTAL** >COAST
**COASTALLY** >COAST
**COASTED** >COAST
**COASTER** *n* small mat placed under a glass
**COASTERS** >COASTER
**COASTING** >COAST
**COASTINGS** >COAST
**COASTLAND** *n* land fringing a coast
**COASTLINE** *n* outline of a coast
**COASTS** >COAST
**COASTWARD** *adv* towards the coast
**COASTWISE** *adv* along the coast
**COAT** *n* outer garment with long sleeves ▷ *vb* cover with a layer
**COATDRESS** *n* garment that can be worn as a coat or a dress

**COATE** *same as* >QUOTE
**COATED** *adj* covered with an outer layer, film, etc
**COATEE** *n* short coat, esp for a baby
**COATEES** >COATEE
**COATER** *n* machine that applies a coating to something
**COATERS** >COATER
**COATES** >COATE
**COATI** *n* any omnivorous mammal of the genera *Nasua* and *Nasuella*, of Central and South America: family *Procyonidae*, order *Carnivora* (carnivores). They are related to but larger than the raccoons, having a long flexible snout and a brindled coat
**COATING** *n* covering layer
**COATINGS** >COATING
**COATIS** >COATI
**COATLESS** *adj* without a coat
**COATRACK** *n* rack for hanging coats on
**COATRACKS** >COATRACK
**COATROOM** *n* cloakroom
**COATROOMS** >COATROOM
**COATS** >COAT
**COATSTAND** *n* stand for hanging coats on
**COATTAIL** *n* long tapering tail at the back of a man's tailored coat
**COATTAILS** >COATTAIL
**COATTEND** *vb* to attend jointly
**COATTENDS** >COATTEND
**COATTEST** *vb* to attest jointly
**COATTESTS** >COATTEST
**COAUTHOR** *n* person who shares the writing of a book, article, etc, with another ▷ *vb* be the joint author of (a book, article, etc)
**COAUTHORS** >COAUTHOR
**COAX** *vb* persuade gently
**COAXAL** *same as* >COAXIAL
**COAXED** >COAX
**COAXER** >COAX
**COAXERS** >COAX
**COAXES** >COAX
**COAXIAL** *adj* (of a cable) transmitting by means of two concentric conductors separated by an insulator
**COAXIALLY** >COAXIAL
**COAXING** >COAX
**COAXINGLY** >COAX
**COB** *n* stalk of an ear of maize ▷ *vb* beat, esp on the buttocks
**COBAEA** *n* any climbing shrub of the tropical American genus *Cobaea*, esp *C. scandens*, grown for its large trumpet-shaped

purple or white flowers: family *Polemoniaceae*
**COBAEAS** >COBAEA
**COBALAMIN** *n* vitamin B12
**COBALT** *n* brittle silvery-white metallic element
**COBALTIC** *adj* of or containing cobalt, esp in the trivalent state
**COBALTINE** *same as* >COBALTITE
**COBALTITE** *n* rare silvery-white mineral
**COBALTOUS** *adj* of or containing cobalt in the divalent state
**COBALTS** >COBALT
**COBB** *same as* >COB
**COBBED** >COB
**COBBER** *n* friend
**COBBERS** >COBBER
**COBBIER** >COBBY
**COBBIEST** >COBBY
**COBBING** >COB
**COBBLE** *n* cobblestone ▷ *vb* pave (a road) with cobblestones
**COBBLED** >COBBLE
**COBBLER** *n* shoe mender
**COBBLERS** *pl n* nonsense ▷ *interj* exclamation of strong disagreement
**COBBLERY** *n* shoemaking or shoemending
**COBBLES** *pl n* coal in small rounded lumps
**COBBLING** >COBBLE
**COBBLINGS** >COBBLE
**COBBS** >COBB
**COBBY** *adj* short and stocky
**COBIA** *n* large dark-striped game fish of tropical and subtropical seas
**COBIAS** >COBIA
**COBLE** *n* small single-masted flat-bottomed fishing boat
**COBLES** >COBLE
**COBLOAF** *n* round loaf of bread
**COBLOAVES** >COBLOAF
**COBNUT** *another name for* >HAZELNUT
**COBNUTS** >COBNUT
**COBRA** *n* venomous hooded snake of Asia and Africa
**COBRAS** >COBRA
**COBRIC** >COBRA
**COBRIFORM** *adj* cobra-like
**COBS** >COB
**COBURG** *n* rounded loaf with a cross cut on the top
**COBURGS** >COBURG
**COBWEB** *n* spider's web
**COBWEBBED** >COBWEB
**COBWEBBY** >COBWEB
**COBWEBS** >COBWEB
**COBZA** *n* Romanian lute
**COBZAS** >COBZA
**COCA** *n* dried leaves of a S American shrub which contain cocaine
**COCAIN** *same as* >COCAINE
**COCAINE** *n* addictive drug

used as a narcotic and as
an anaesthetic
**COCAINES** > COCAINE
**COCAINISE** *same*
*as* > COCAINIZE
**COCAINISM** *n* use of
cocaine
**COCAINIST** *n* cocaine
addict
**COCAINIZE** *vb*
anaesthetize with cocaine
**COCAINS** > COCAIN
**COCAPTAIN** *vb* to captain
jointly
**COCAS** > COCA
**COCCAL** > COCCUS
**COCCI** > COCCUS
**COCCIC** > COCCUS
**COCCID** *n* any
homopterous insect of the
superfamily *Coccoidea*, esp
any of the family *Coccidae*,
which includes the scale
insects
**COCCIDIA** > COCCIDIUM
**COCCIDIUM** *n* any parasitic
protozoan of the order
Coccidia
**COCCIDS** > COCCID
**COCCO** *n* taro
**COCCOID** > COCCUS
**COCCOIDAL** > COCCUS
**COCCOIDS** > COCCUS
**COCCOLITE** *n* variety of
pyroxene
**COCCOLITH** *n* any of the
round calcareous plates
in chalk formations:
formed the outer layer of
unicellular plankton
**COCCOS** > COCCO
**COCCOUS** > COCCUS
**COCCUS** *n* any spherical
or nearly spherical
bacterium, such as a
staphylococcus
**COCCYGEAL** > COCCYX
**COCCYGES** > COCCYX
**COCCYGIAN** > COCCYX
**COCCYX** *n* bone at the base
of the spinal column
**COCCYXES** > COCCYX
**COCH** *obsolete variant*
*of* > COACH
**COCHAIR** *vb* to chair jointly
**COCHAIRED** > COCHAIR
**COCHAIRS** > COCHAIR
**COCHES** > COCH
**COCHIN** *n* large breed of
domestic fowl
**COCHINEAL** *n* red dye
obtained from a Mexican
insect, used for food
colouring
**COCHINS** > COCHIN
**COCHLEA** *n* spiral tube in
the internal ear, which
converts sound vibrations
into nerve impulses
**COCHLEAE** > COCHLEA
**COCHLEAR** *adj* of or
relating to the cochlea ▷ *n*
spoonful
**COCHLEARE** *variant*

*of* > COCHLEAR
**COCHLEARS** > COCHLEAR
**COCHLEAS** > COCHLEA
**COCHLEATE** *adj* shaped like
a snail's shell
**COCINERA** *n* in Mexico, a
female cook
**COCINERAS** > COCINERA
**COCK** *n* male bird, esp of
domestic fowl ▷ *vb* draw
back (the hammer of a
gun) to firing position
**COCKADE** *n* feather or
rosette worn on a hat as a
badge
**COCKADED** > COCKADE
**COCKADES** > COCKADE
**COCKAMAMY** *adj* ridiculous
or nonsensical
**COCKAPOO** *n* cross between
a cocker spaniel and a
poodle
**COCKAPOOS** > COCKAPOO
**COCKATEEL** *same*
*as* > COCKATIEL
**COCKATIEL** *n* crested
Australian parrot with a
greyish-brown and yellow
plumage
**COCKATOO** *n* crested parrot
of Australia or the East
Indies
**COCKATOOS** > COCKATOO
**COCKBILL** *vb* to tilt up one
end of
**COCKBILLS** > COCKBILL
**COCKBIRD** *n* male bird
**COCKBIRDS** > COCKBIRD
**COCKBOAT** *n* any small boat
**COCKBOATS** > COCKBOAT
**COCKCROW** *n* daybreak
**COCKCROWS** > COCKCROW
**COCKED** > COCK
**COCKER** *n* devotee of
cockfighting ▷ *vb* pamper
or spoil by indulgence
**COCKERED** > COCKER
**COCKEREL** *n* young
domestic cock
**COCKERELS** > COCKEREL
**COCKERING** > COCKER
**COCKERS** > COCKER
**COCKET** *n* document issued
by a customs officer
**COCKETS** > COCKET
**COCKEYE** *n* eye affected
with strabismus or one
that squints
**COCKEYED** *adj* crooked,
askew
**COCKEYES** > COCKEYE
**COCKFIGHT** *n* fight
between two gamecocks
fitted with sharp metal
spurs
**COCKHORSE** *n* rocking horse
**COCKIER** > COCKY
**COCKIES** > COCKY
**COCKIEST** > COCKY
**COCKILY** > COCKY
**COCKINESS** *n* conceited
self-assurance
**COCKING** > COCK
**COCKISH** *adj* wanton

**COCKLE** *n* edible shellfish
▷ *vb* fish for cockles
**COCKLEBUR** *n* any coarse
weed of the genus
*Xanthium*, having spiny
burs: family *Asteraceae*
(composites)
**COCKLED** > COCKLE
**COCKLEERT** *a Southwest
English dialect variant*
*of* > COCKCROW
**COCKLEMAN** *n* man who
collects cockles
**COCKLEMEN** > COCKLEMAN
**COCKLER** *n* person
employed to gather
cockles
**COCKLERS** > COCKLER
**COCKLES** > COCKLE
**COCKLIKE** *adj* resembling
a cock
**COCKLING** > COCKLE
**COCKLOFT** *n* small loft,
garret, or attic
**COCKLOFTS** > COCKLOFT
**COCKMATCH** *n* cockfight
**COCKNEY** *n* native of
London, esp of its East
End ▷ *adj* characteristic of
cockneys or their dialect
**COCKNEYFY** *vb* cause (one's
speech, manners, etc) to
fit the stereotyped idea of
a cockney
**COCKNEYS** > COCKNEY
**COCKNIFY** *same*
*as* > COCKNEYFY
**COCKPIT** *n* pilot's
compartment in an
aircraft
**COCKPITS** > COCKPIT
**COCKROACH** *n* beetle-
like insect which is a
household pest
**COCKS** > COCK
**COCKSCOMB** *n* comb of a
domestic cock
**COCKSFOOT** *n* perennial
Eurasian grass, *Dactylis
glomerata*, cultivated as
a pasture grass in North
America and South Africa
**COCKSHIES** > COCKSHY
**COCKSHOT** *another name
for* > COCKSHY
**COCKSHOTS** > COCKSHOT
**COCKSHUT** *n* dusk
**COCKSHUTS** > COCKSHUT
**COCKSHY** *n* target aimed at
in throwing games
**COCKSIER** > COCKSY
**COCKSIEST** > COCKSY
**COCKSPUR** *n* spur on the leg
of a cock
**COCKSPURS** > COCKSPUR
**COCKSURE** *adj*
overconfident, arrogant
**COCKSWAIN** *same*
*as* > COXSWAIN
**COCKSY** *adj* cocky
**COCKTAIL** *n* mixed
alcoholic drink
**COCKTAILS** > COCKTAIL
**COCKUP** *n* something done

badly ▷ *vb* ruin or spoil
**COCKUPS** > COCKUP
**COCKY** *adj* conceited and
overconfident ▷ *n* farmer
whose farm is regarded as
small or of little account
**COCO** *n* coconut palm
**COCOA** *n* powder made
from the seed of the cacao
tree
**COCOANUT** *same*
*as* > COCONUT
**COCOANUTS** > COCONUT
**COCOAS** > COCOA
**COCOBOLA** *n* type of
rosewood
**COCOBOLAS** > COCOBOLA
**COCOBOLO** *same*
*as* > COCOBOLA
**COCOBOLOS** > COCOBOLO
**COCOMAT** *n* mat made from
coconut fibre
**COCOMATS** > COCOMAT
**COCONUT** *n* large hard fruit
of a type of palm tree
**COCONUTS** > COCONUT
**COCOON** *n* silky protective
covering of a silkworm
▷ *vb* wrap up tightly for
protection
**COCOONED** > COCOON
**COCOONERY** *n* place where
silkworms feed and make
cocoons
**COCOONING** > COCOON
**COCOONS** > COCOON
**COCOPAN** *n* (in South Africa)
a small wagon running
on narrow-gauge railway
lines used in mines
**COCOPANS** > COCOPAN
**COCOPLUM** *n* tropical shrub,
also known as icaco, or
its fruit
**COCOPLUMS** > COCOPLUM
**COCOS** > COCO
**COCOTTE** *n* small fireproof
dish in which individual
portions of food are
cooked
**COCOTTES** > COCOTTE
**COCOUNSEL** *vb* to counsel
jointly
**COCOYAM** *n* either of two
food plants of West Africa,
the taro or the yantia,
both of which have edible
underground stems
**COCOYAMS** > COCOYAM
**COCOZELLE** *n* variety of
squash
**COCREATE** *vb* to create
jointly
**COCREATED** > COCREATE
**COCREATES** > COCREATE
**COCREATOR** > COCREATE
**COCTILE** *adj* made by
exposing to heat
**COCTION** *n* boiling
**COCTIONS** > COCTION
**COCULTURE** *vb* to culture
together
**COCURATOR** *n* joint curator
**COCUSWOOD** *n* wood from

the tropical American leguminous tree *Brya ebenus*, used for inlaying, turnery, musical instruments, etc

**COD** *n* large food fish of the North Atlantic ▷ *adj* having the character of an imitation or parody ▷ *vb* make fun of

**CODA** *n* final part of a musical composition

**CODABLE** *adj* capable of being coded

**CODAS** > CODA

**CODDED** > COD

**CODDER** *n* cod fisherman or his boat

**CODDERS** > CODDER

**CODDING** > COD

**CODDLE** *vb* pamper, overprotect ▷ *n* stew made from ham and bacon scraps

**CODDLED** > CODDLE

**CODDLER** > CODDLE

**CODDLERS** > CODDLE

**CODDLES** > CODDLE

**CODDLING** > CODDLE

**CODE** *n* system of letters, symbols, or prearranged signals by which messages can be communicated secretly or briefly ▷ *vb* put into code

**CODEBOOK** *n* book containing the means to decipher a code

**CODEBOOKS** > CODEBOOK

**CODEBTOR** *n* fellow debtor

**CODEBTORS** > CODEBTOR

**CODEC** *n* set of equipment that encodes an analogue speech or video signal into digital form for transmission purposes and at the receiving end decodes the digital signal into a form close to its original

**CODECS** > CODEC

**CODED** > CODE

**CODEIA** *n* codeine

**CODEIAS** > CODEIA

**CODEIN** *same as* > CODEINE

**CODEINA** *obsolete variant of* > CODEINE

**CODEINAS** > CODEINA

**CODEINE** *n* drug used as a painkiller

**CODEINES** > CODEINE

**CODEINS** > CODEIN

**CODELESS** *adj* lacking a code

**CODEN** *n* unique six-character code assigned to a publication for identification purposes

**CODENAME** *same as* > CODEWORD

**CODENAMES** > CODEWORD

**CODENS** > CODEN

**CODER** *n* person or thing that codes

**CODERIVE** *vb* to derive jointly

**CODERIVED** > CODERIVE

**CODERIVES** > CODERIVE

**CODERS** > CODER

**CODES** > CODE

**CODESIGN** *vb* to design jointly

**CODESIGNS** > CODESIGN

**CODETTA** *n* short coda

**CODETTAS** > CODETTA

**CODEVELOP** *vb* to develop jointly

**CODEWORD** *n* (esp in military use) a word used to identify a classified plan, operation, etc

**CODEWORDS** > CODEWORD

**CODEX** *n* volume of manuscripts of an ancient text

**CODFISH** *n* cod

**CODFISHES** > CODFISH

**CODGER** *n* old man

**CODGERS** > CODGER

**CODICES** > CODEX

**CODICIL** *n* addition to a will

**CODICILS** > CODICIL

**CODIFIED** > CODIFY

**CODIFIER** > CODIFY

**CODIFIERS** > CODIFY

**CODIFIES** > CODIFY

**CODIFY** *vb* organize (rules or procedures) systematically

**CODIFYING** > CODIFY

**CODILLA** *n* coarse tow of hemp and flax

**CODILLAS** > CODILLA

**CODILLE** *n* in the cardgame ombre, term indicating that the game is won

**CODILLES** > CODILLE

**CODING** > CODE

**CODINGS** > CODE

**CODIRECT** *vb* to direct jointly

**CODIRECTS** > CODIRECT

**CODIST** *n* codifier

**CODISTS** > CODIST

**CODLIN** *same as* > CODLING

**CODLING** *n* young cod

**CODLINGS** > CODLING

**CODLINS** > CODLIN

**CODOLOGY** *n* art or practice of bluffing or deception

**CODOMAIN** *n* set of values that a function is allowed to take

**CODOMAINS** > CODOMAIN

**CODON** *n* unit that consists of three adjacent bases on a DNA molecule and that determines the position of a specific amino acid in a protein molecule during protein synthesis

**CODONS** > CODON

**CODPIECE** *n* bag covering the male genitals, attached to the breeches

**CODPIECES** > CODPIECE

**CODRIVE** *vb* take alternate

turns driving a car with another person

**CODRIVEN** > CODRIVE

**CODRIVER** *n* one of two drivers who take turns to drive a car

**CODRIVERS** > CODRIVER

**CODRIVES** > CODRIVE

**CODRIVING** > CODRIVE

**CODROVE** > CODRIVE

**CODS** > COD

**COED** *adj* educating both sexes together ▷ *n* school or college that educates both sexes together

**COEDIT** *vb* edit (a book, newspaper, etc) jointly

**COEDITED** > COEDIT

**COEDITING** > COEDIT

**COEDITOR** > COEDIT

**COEDITORS** > COEDIT

**COEDITS** > COEDIT

**COEDS** > COED

**COEFFECT** *n* secondary effect

**COEFFECTS** > COEFFECT

**COEHORN** *n* type of small artillery mortar

**COEHORNS** > COEHORN

**COELIAC** *adj* of or relating to the abdomen ▷ *n* person who has coeliac disease

**COELIACS** > COELIAC

**COELOM** *n* body cavity of many multicellular animals, situated in the mesoderm and containing the digestive tract and other visceral organs

**COELOMATA** *n* animals possessing a coelom

**COELOMATE** *adj* possessing a coelom

**COELOME** *same as* > COELOM

**COELOMES** > COELOME

**COELOMIC** > COELOM

**COELOMS** > COELOM

**COELOSTAT** *n* astronomical instrument consisting of a plane mirror mounted parallel to the earth's axis and rotated about this axis once every two days so that light from a celestial body, esp the sun, is reflected onto a second mirror, which reflects the beam into a telescope

**COEMBODY** *vb* to embody jointly

**COEMPLOY** *vb* to employ together

**COEMPLOYS** > COEMPLOY

**COEMPT** *vb* buy up something in its entirety

**COEMPTED** > COEMPT

**COEMPTING** > COEMPT

**COEMPTION** *n* buying up of the complete supply of a commodity

**COEMPTS** > COEMPT

**COENACLE** *same as* > CENACLE

**COENACLES** > COENACLE

**COENACT** *vb* to enact jointly

**COENACTED** > COENACT

**COENACTS** > COENACT

**COENAMOR** *vb* enamour jointly

**COENAMORS** > COENAMOR

**COENDURE** *vb* to endure together

**COENDURED** > COENDURE

**COENDURES** > COENDURE

**COENOBIA** > COENOBIUM

**COENOBITE** *n* member of a religious order in a monastic community

**COENOBIUM** *n* monastery or convent

**COENOCYTE** *n* mass of protoplasm containing many nuclei and enclosed by a cell wall: occurs in many fungi and some algae

**COENOSARC** *n* system of protoplasmic branches connecting the polyps of colonial organisms such as corals

**COENURE** *variant form of* > COENURUS

**COENURES** > COENURE

**COENURI** > COENURUS

**COENURUS** *n* encysted larval form of the tapeworm *Multiceps*, containing many encapsulated heads. In sheep it can cause the gid, and when eaten by dogs it develops into several adult forms

**COENZYME** *n* nonprotein organic molecule that forms a complex with certain enzymes and is essential for their activity

**COENZYMES** > COENZYME

**COEQUAL** *n* equal ▷ *adj* of the same size, rank, etc

**COEQUALLY** > COEQUAL

**COEQUALS** > COEQUAL

**COEQUATE** *vb* to equate together

**COEQUATED** > COEQUATE

**COEQUATES** > COEQUATE

**COERCE** *vb* compel, force

**COERCED** > COERCE

**COERCER** > COERCE

**COERCERS** > COERCE

**COERCES** > COERCE

**COERCIBLE** > COERCE

**COERCIBLY** > COERCE

**COERCING** > COERCE

**COERCION** *n* act or power of coercing

**COERCIONS** > COERCION

**COERCIVE** > COERCE

**COERECT** *vb* to erect together

**COERECTED** > COERECT

**COERECTS** > COERECT

**COESITE** *n* polymorph of silicon dioxide

**COESITES** > COESITE

**COETERNAL** *adj* existing

together eternally
**COEVAL** *n* contemporary
  ▷ *adj* contemporary
**COEVALITY** > COEVAL
**COEVALLY** > COEVAL
**COEVALS** > COEVAL
**COEVOLVE** *vb* to evolve
together
**COEVOLVED** > COEVOLVE
**COEVOLVES** > COEVOLVE
**COEXERT** *vb* to exert
together
**COEXERTED** > COEXERT
**COEXERTS** > COEXERT
**COEXIST** *vb* exist together,
esp peacefully despite
differences
**COEXISTED** > COEXIST
**COEXISTS** > COEXIST
**COEXTEND** *vb* extend or
cause to extend equally in
space or time
**COEXTENDS** > COEXTEND
**COFACTOR** *n* number
associated with an
element in a square
matrix, equal to the
determinant of the matrix
formed by removing the
row and column in which
the element appears from
the given determinant
**COFACTORS** > COFACTOR
**COFEATURE** *vb* to feature
together
**COFF** *vb* buy
**COFFED** > COFF
**COFFEE** *n* drink made from
the roasted and ground
seeds of a tropical shrub
  ▷ *adj* medium-brown
**COFFEEPOT** *n* pot in which
coffee is brewed or served
**COFFEES** > COFFEE
**COFFER** *n* chest, esp for
storing valuables ▷ *vb*
store
**COFFERDAM** *n* watertight
enclosure pumped dry to
enable construction work
to be done
**COFFERED** > COFFERDAM
**COFFERING** > COFFERDAM
**COFFERS** > COFFERDAM
**COFFIN** *n* box in which
a corpse is buried or
cremated ▷ *vb* place in or
as in a coffin
**COFFINED** > COFFIN
**COFFING** > COFF
**COFFINING** > COFFIN
**COFFINITE** *n* uranium-
bearing silicate mineral
**COFFINS** > COFFIN
**COFFLE** *n* (esp formerly) a
line of slaves, beasts, etc,
fastened together ▷ *vb* to
fasten together in a coffle
**COFFLED** > COFFLE
**COFFLES** > COFFLE
**COFFLING** > COFFLE
**COFFRET** *n* small coffer
**COFFRETS** > COFFRET
**COFFS** > COFF

**COFINANCE** *vb* to finance
jointly
**COFOUND** *vb* to found
jointly
**COFOUNDED** > COFOUND
**COFOUNDER** > COFOUND
**COFOUNDS** > COFOUND
**COFT** > COFF
**COG** *n* one of the teeth on
the rim of a gearwheel
  ▷ *vb* roll (cast-steel ingots)
to convert them into
blooms
**COGENCE** > COGENT
**COGENCES** > COGENT
**COGENCIES** > COGENT
**COGENCY** > COGENT
**COGENER** *n* congener
**COGENERS** > COGENER
**COGENT** *adj* forcefully
convincing
**COGENTLY** > COGENT
**COGGED** > COG
**COGGER** *n* deceiver
**COGGERS** > COGGER
**COGGIE** *n* quaich or
drinking cup
**COGGIES** > COGGIE
**COGGING** > COG
**COGGINGS** > COG
**COGGLE** *vb* wobble or rock
**COGGLED** > COGGLE
**COGGLES** > COGGLE
**COGGLIER** > COGGLE
**COGGLIEST** > COGGLE
**COGGLING** > COGGLE
**COGGLY** > COGGLE
**COGIE** *same as* > COGGIE
**COGIES** > COGIE
**COGITABLE** *adj* conceivable
**COGITATE** *vb* think deeply
about
**COGITATED** > COGITATE
**COGITATES** > COGITATE
**COGITATOR** > COGITATE
**COGITO** *n* philosophical
theory that one must exist
because one is capable of
thought
**COGITOS** > COGITO
**COGNAC** *n* French brandy
**COGNACS** > COGNAC
**COGNATE** *adj* derived from a
common original form ▷ *n*
cognate word or language
**COGNATELY** > COGNATE
**COGNATES** > COGNATE
**COGNATION** > COGNATE
**COGNISANT** *same
as* > COGNIZANT
**COGNISE** *same as* > COGNIZE
**COGNISED** > COGNISE
**COGNISER** > COGNISE
**COGNISERS** > COGNISE
**COGNISES** > COGNISE
**COGNISING** > COGNISE
**COGNITION** *n* act or
experience of knowing or
acquiring knowledge
**COGNITIVE** *adj* of or
relating to cognition
**COGNIZANT** *adj* aware
**COGNIZE** *vb* perceive,
become aware of, or know

**COGNIZED** > COGNIZE
**COGNIZER** > COGNIZE
**COGNIZERS** > COGNIZE
**COGNIZES** > COGNIZE
**COGNIZING** > COGNIZE
**COGNOMEN** *n* nickname
**COGNOMENS** > COGNOMEN
**COGNOMINA** > COGNOMEN
**COGNOSCE** *vb* in Scots law,
to give judgment upon
**COGNOSCED** > COGNOSCE
**COGNOSCES** > COGNOSCE
**COGNOVIT** *n* in law, a
defendant's confession
that the case against him
is just
**COGNOVITS** > COGNOVIT
**COGON** *n* any of the coarse
tropical grasses of the
genus *Imperata*, esp *I.
cylindrica* and *I. exaltata* of
the Philippines, which are
used for thatching
**COGONS** > COGON
**COGS** > COG
**COGUE** *n* wooden pail or
drinking vessel
**COGUES** > COGUE
**COGWAY** *n* rack railway
**COGWAYS** > COGWAY
**COGWHEEL** *same
as* > GEARWHEEL
**COGWHEELS** > COGWHEEL
**COHAB** *n* cohabitor
**COHABIT** *vb* live together as
husband and wife without
being married
**COHABITED** > COHABIT
**COHABITEE** > COHABIT
**COHABITER** > COHABIT
**COHABITOR** > COHABIT
**COHABITS** > COHABIT
**COHABS** > COHAB
**COHEAD** *vb* to head jointly
**COHEADED** > COHEAD
**COHEADING** > COHEAD
**COHEADS** > COHEAD
**COHEIR** *n* person who
inherits jointly with
others
**COHEIRESS** > COHEIR
**COHEIRS** > COHEIR
**COHERE** *vb* hold or stick
together
**COHERED** > COHERE
**COHERENCE** *n* logical or
natural connection or
consistency
**COHERENCY** *same
as* > COHERENCE
**COHERENT** *adj* logical and
consistent
**COHERER** *n* electrical
component formerly used
to detect radio waves,
consisting of a tube
containing loosely packed
metal particles. The waves
caused the particles to
cohere, thereby changing
the current through the
circuit
**COHERERS** > COHERER
**COHERES** > COHERE

**COHERING** > COHERE
**COHERITOR** *n* coheir
**COHESIBLE** *adj* capable of
cohesion
**COHESION** *n* sticking
together
**COHESIONS** > COHESION
**COHESIVE** *adj* sticking
together to form a whole
**COHIBIT** *vb* to restrain
**COHIBITED** > COHIBIT
**COHIBITS** > COHIBIT
**COHO** *n* Pacific salmon,
*Oncorhynchus kisutch*
**COHOBATE** *vb* redistil (a
distillate), esp by allowing
it to mingle with the
remaining matter
**COHOBATED** > COHOBATE
**COHOBATES** > COHOBATE
**COHOE** *same as* > COHO
**COHOES** > COHO
**COHOG** *n* quahog, an edible
clam
**COHOGS** > COHOG
**COHOLDER** *n* joint holder
**COHOLDERS** > COHOLDER
**COHORN** *same as* > COEHORN
**COHORNS** > COEHORN
**COHORT** *n* band of
associates
**COHORTS** > COHORT
**COHOS** > COHO
**COHOSH** *n* type of
N American plant
**COHOSHES** > COHOSH
**COHOST** *vb* to host jointly
**COHOSTED** > COHOST
**COHOSTESS** *vb* (of a
woman) to host jointly
**COHOSTING** > COHOST
**COHOSTS** > COHOST
**COHOUSING** *n* type of
housing with some shared
facilities
**COHUNE** *n* tropical
American feather palm,
*Attalea* (or *Orbignya*) *cohune*,
whose large oily nuts yield
an oil similar to coconut
oil
**COHUNES** > COHUNE
**COHYPONYM** *n* word
which is one of multiple
hyponyms of another word
**COIF** *vb* arrange the hair of
  ▷ *n* close-fitting cap worn
in the Middle Ages
**COIFED** *adj* wearing a coif
**COIFFE** *vb* to coiffure
**COIFFED** > COIF
**COIFFES** > COIFFE
**COIFFEUR** *n* hairdresser
**COIFFEURS** > COIFFEUR
**COIFFEUSE** > COIFFEUR
**COIFFING** > COIF
**COIFFURE** *n* hairstyle ▷ *vb*
dress or arrange (the hair)
**COIFFURED** > COIFFURE
**COIFFURES** > COIFFURE
**COIFING** > COIF
**COIFS** > COIF
**COIGN** *variant spelling
of* > QUOIN *vb* wedge

153

COIGNE *same as* >COIGN
COIGNED >COIGN
COIGNES >COIGNE
COIGNING >COIGN
COIGNS >COIGN
COIL *vb* wind in loops ▷ *n* something coiled
COILED >COIL
COILER >COIL
COILERS >COIL
COILING >COIL
COILS >COIL
COIN *n* piece of metal money ▷ *vb* invent (a word or phrase)
COINABLE >COIN
COINAGE *n* coins collectively
COINAGES >COINAGE
COINCIDE *vb* happen at the same time
COINCIDED >COINCIDE
COINCIDES >COINCIDE
COINED >COIN
COINER >COIN
COINERS >COIN
COINFECT *vb* infect at same time as other infection
COINFECTS >COINFECT
COINFER *vb* infer jointly
COINFERS >COINFER
COINHERE *vb* to inhere together
COINHERED >COINHERE
COINHERES >COINHERE
COINING >COIN
COININGS >COIN
COINMATE *n* fellow inmate
COINMATES >COINMATE
COINS >COIN
COINSURE *vb* insure jointly
COINSURED >COINSURE
COINSURER >COINSURE
COINSURES >COINSURE
COINTER *vb* to inter together
COINTERS >COINTER
COINTREAU *n* tradename for a French orange liqueur
COINVENT *vb* to invent jointly
COINVENTS >COINVENT
COIR *n* coconut fibre, used for matting
COIRS >COIR
COISTREL *n* knave
COISTRELS >COISTREL
COISTRIL *same as* >COISTREL
COISTRILS >COISTRIL
COIT *n* buttocks
COITAL >COITUS
COITALLY >COITUS
COITION *same as* >COITUS
COITIONAL >COITION
COITIONS >COITION
COITS >COIT
COITUS *n* sexual intercourse
COITUSES >COITUS
COJOIN *vb* to conjoin
COJOINED >COJOIN
COJOINING >COJOIN
COJOINS >COJOIN

COJONES *pl n* testicles
COKE *n* solid fuel left after gas has been distilled from coal ▷ *vb* become or convert into coke
COKED >COKE
COKEHEAD *n* cocaine addict
COKEHEADS >COKEHEAD
COKELIKE >COKE
COKERNUT *same as* >COCONUT
COKERNUTS >COKERNUT
COKES *n* fool
COKESES >COKES
COKIER >COKY
COKIEST >COKY
COKING >COKE
COKULORIS *n* palette with irregular holes, placed between lighting and camera to prevent glare
COKY *adj* like coke
COL *n* high mountain pass
COLA *n* dark brown fizzy soft drink
COLANDER *n* perforated bowl for straining or rinsing foods
COLANDERS >COLANDER
COLAS >COLA
COLBIES >COLBY
COLBY *n* type of mild-tasting hard cheese
COLBYS >COLBY
COLCANNON *n* dish, originating in Ireland, of potatoes and cabbage or other greens boiled and mashed together
COLCHICA >COLCHICUM
COLCHICUM *n* any Eurasian liliaceous plant of the genus *Colchicum*, such as the autumn crocus
COLCOTHAR *n* finely powdered form of ferric oxide produced by heating ferric sulphate and used as a pigment and as jewellers' rouge
COLD *adj* lacking heat ▷ *n* lack of heat
COLDBLOOD *n* any heavy draught-horse
COLDCOCK *vb* to knock to the ground
COLDCOCKS >COLDCOCK
COLDER >COLD
COLDEST >COLD
COLDHOUSE *n* unheated greenhouse
COLDIE *n* cold can or bottle of beer
COLDIES >COLDIE
COLDISH >COLD
COLDLY >COLD
COLDNESS >COLD
COLDS >COLD
COLE *same as* >CABBAGE
COLEAD *vb* to lead together
COLEADER >COLEAD
COLEADERS >COLEAD
COLEADING >COLEAD
COLEADS >COLEAD

COLECTOMY *n* surgical removal of part or all of the colon
COLED >COLEAD
COLEOPTER *n* aircraft that has an annular wing with the fuselage and engine on the centre line
COLES >COLE
COLESEED *n* common rape or cole
COLESEEDS >COLESEED
COLESLAW *n* salad dish of shredded raw cabbage in a dressing
COLESLAWS >COLESLAW
COLESSEE *n* joint lessee
COLESSEES >COLESSEE
COLESSOR *n* joint lessor
COLESSORS >COLESSOR
COLETIT *n* coal tit
COLETITS >COLETIT
COLEUS *n* any plant of the Old World genus *Coleus*: cultivated for their variegated leaves, typically marked with red, yellow, or white
COLEUSES >COLEUS
COLEWORT >CABBAGE
COLEWORTS >CABBAGE
COLEY *same as* >COALFISH
COLEYS >COLEY
COLIBRI *n* hummingbird
COLIBRIS >COLIBRI
COLIC *n* severe pains in the stomach and bowels
COLICIN *n* bactericidal protein
COLICINE *n* antibacterial protein
COLICINES >COLICINE
COLICINS >COLICIN
COLICKIER >COLICKY
COLICKY *adj* relating to or suffering from colic
COLICROOT *n* either of two North American liliaceous plants, *Aletris farinosa* or *A. aurea*, having tubular white or yellow flowers and a bitter root formerly used to relieve colic
COLICS >COLIC
COLICWEED *n* any of several plants of the genera *Dicentra* or *Corydalis*, such as the squirrel corn and Dutchman's-breeches: family *Fumariaceae*
COLIES >COLY
COLIFORM *n* type of bacteria of the intestinal tract
COLIFORMS >COLIFORM
COLIN *n* quail
COLINEAR *same as* >COLLINEAR
COLINS >COLIN
COLIPHAGE *n* bacteriophage
COLISEUM *n* large building, such as a stadium or theatre, used for

entertainments, sports, etc
COLISEUMS >COLISEUM
COLISTIN *n* polymyxin antibiotic
COLISTINS >COLISTIN
COLITIC >COLITIS
COLITIS *n* inflammation of the colon
COLITISES >COLITIS
COLL *vb* to embrace
COLLAGE *n* art form in which various materials or objects are glued onto a surface ▷ *vb* to make a collage
COLLAGED >COLLAGE
COLLAGEN *n* protein found in cartilage and bone that yields gelatine when boiled
COLLAGENS >COLLAGEN
COLLAGES >COLLAGE
COLLAGING >COLLAGE
COLLAGIST >COLLAGE
COLLAPSAR *n* collapsed star, either a white dwarf, neutron star, or black hole
COLLAPSE *vb* fall down suddenly ▷ *n* collapsing
COLLAPSED >COLLAPSE
COLLAPSES >COLLAPSE
COLLAR *n* part of a garment round the neck ▷ *vb* seize, arrest
COLLARD *n* variety of the cabbage, *Brassica oleracea acephala*, having a crown of edible leaves
COLLARDS >COLLARD
COLLARED >COLLAR
COLLARET *n* small collar
COLLARETS >COLLARET
COLLARING >COLLAR
COLLARS >COLLAR
COLLATE *vb* gather together, examine, and put in order
COLLATED >COLLATE
COLLATES >COLLATE
COLLATING >COLLATE
COLLATION *n* collating
COLLATIVE *adj* involving collation
COLLATOR *n* person or machine that collates texts or manuscripts
COLLATORS >COLLATOR
COLLEAGUE *n* fellow worker, esp in a profession
COLLECT *vb* gather together ▷ *n* short prayer
COLLECTED *adj* calm and controlled
COLLECTOR *n* person who collects objects as a hobby
COLLECTS >COLLECT
COLLED >COLL
COLLEEN *n* girl
COLLEENS >COLLEEN
COLLEGE *n* place of higher education
COLLEGER *n* member of a college

COLLEGERS > COLLEGER
COLLEGES > COLLEGE
COLLEGIA > COLLEGIUM
COLLEGIAL adj of or relating to a college
COLLEGIAN n member of a college
COLLEGIUM n (in the former Soviet Union) a board in charge of a department
COLLET n (in a jewellery setting) a band or coronet-shaped claw that holds an individual stone ▷ vb mount in a collet
COLLETED > COLLET
COLLETING > COLLET
COLLETS > COLLET
COLLICULI n plural form of singular colliculus: small elevation, as on the surface of the optic lobe of the brain
COLLIDE vb crash together violently
COLLIDED > COLLIDE
COLLIDER n particle accelerator in which beams of particles are made to collide
COLLIDERS > COLLIDER
COLLIDES > COLLIDE
COLLIDING > COLLIDE
COLLIE n silky-haired sheepdog
COLLIED > COLLY
COLLIER n coal miner
COLLIERS > COLLIER
COLLIERY n coal mine
COLLIES > COLLY
COLLIGATE vb connect or link together
COLLIMATE vb adjust the line of sight of (an optical instrument)
COLLINEAR adj lying on the same straight line
COLLING n embrace
COLLINGS > COLLING
COLLINS n tall fizzy iced drink made with gin, vodka, rum, etc, mixed with fruit juice, soda water, and sugar
COLLINSES > COLLINS
COLLINSIA n North American plant of the scrophulariaceous genus Collinsia, having blue, white, or purple flowers
COLLISION n violent crash between moving objects
COLLOCATE vb (of words) occur together regularly
COLLODION n colourless or yellow syrupy liquid that consists of a solution of pyroxylin in ether and alcohol: used in medicine and in the manufacture of photographic plates, lacquers, etc
COLLODIUM same

as > COLLODION
COLLOGUE vb confer confidentially
COLLOGUED > COLLOGUE
COLLOGUES > COLLOGUE
COLLOID n suspension of particles in a solution ▷ adj of or relating to the gluelike translucent material found in certain degenerating tissues
COLLOIDAL adj of, denoting, or having the character of a colloid
COLLOIDS > COLLOID
COLLOP n small slice of meat
COLLOPS > COLLOP
COLLOQUE vb to converse
COLLOQUED > COLLOQUE
COLLOQUES > COLLOQUE
COLLOQUIA n plural form of singular colloquium: informal gathering
COLLOQUY n conversation or conference
COLLOTYPE n method of lithographic printing from a flat surface of hardened gelatine: used mainly for fine-detail reproduction in monochrome or colour
COLLOTYPY > COLLOTYPE
COLLS > COLL
COLLUDE vb act in collusion
COLLUDED > COLLUDE
COLLUDER > COLLUDE
COLLUDERS > COLLUDE
COLLUDES > COLLUDE
COLLUDING > COLLUDE
COLLUSION n secret or illegal cooperation
COLLUSIVE > COLLUSION
COLLUVIA > COLLUVIUM
COLLUVIAL > COLLUVIUM
COLLUVIES n offscourings
COLLUVIUM n mixture of rock fragments from the bases of cliffs
COLLY n soot or grime, such as coal dust ▷ vb begrime
COLLYING > COLLY
COLLYRIA > COLLYRIUM
COLLYRIUM a technical name for an > EYEWASH
COLOBI > COLOBUS
COLOBID > COLOBUS
COLOBOMA n structural defect of the eye, esp in the choroid, retina, or iris
COLOBOMAS > COLOBOMA
COLOBUS n any leaf-eating arboreal Old World monkey of the genus Colobus, of W and central Africa, having a slender body, long silky fur, long tail, and reduced or absent thumbs
COLOBUSES > COLOBUS
COLOCATE vb to locate together
COLOCATED > COLOCATE

COLOCATES > COLOCATE
COLOCYNTH n cucurbitaceous climbing plant, Citrullus colocynthis, of the Mediterranean region and Asia, having bitter-tasting fruit
COLOG n logarithm of the reciprocal of a number
COLOGNE n mild perfume
COLOGNED > COLOGNE
COLOGNES > COLOGNE
COLOGS > COLOG
COLOMBARD n grape used to make wine
COLON n punctuation mark (:); Costa Rican monetary unit
COLONE variant of > COLON
COLONEL n senior commissioned army or air-force officer
COLONELCY > COLONEL
COLONELS > COLONEL
COLONES > COLONE
COLONI > COLONUS
COLONIAL n inhabitant of a colony ▷ adj of or inhabiting a colony or colonies
COLONIALS > COLONIAL
COLONIC adj of or relating to the colon ▷ n irrigation of the colon by injecting large amounts of fluid high into the colon
COLONICS > COLONIC
COLONIES > COLONY
COLONISE same
as > COLONIZE
COLONISED > COLONISE
COLONISER > COLONISE
COLONISES > COLONISE
COLONIST n settler in a colony
COLONISTS > COLONIST
COLONITIS same
as > COLITIS
COLONIZE vb make into a colony
COLONIZED > COLONIZE
COLONIZER > COLONIZE
COLONIZES > COLONIZE
COLONNADE n row of columns
COLONS > COLON
COLONUS n ancient Roman farmer
COLONY n group of people who settle in a new country but remain under the rule of their homeland
COLOPHON n publisher's symbol on a book
COLOPHONS > COLOPHON
COLOPHONY another name for > ROSIN
COLOR same as > COLOUR
COLORABLE > COLOR
COLORABLY > COLOR
COLORADO adj (of a cigar) of middling colour and strength
COLORANT n any substance

that imparts colour, such as a pigment, dye, or ink
COLORANTS > COLORANT
COLORBRED adj (of animals) bred for their colour
COLORCAST vb broadcast in colour
COLORED US spelling of > COLOURED
COLOREDS > COLORED
COLORER > COLOR
COLORERS > COLOR
COLORFAST adj variant of colourfast: (of a fabric) having a colour that does not run when washed
COLORFUL > COLOR
COLORIFIC adj producing, imparting, or relating to colour
COLORING > COLOUR
COLORINGS > COLOUR
COLORISE same
as > COLOURIZE
COLORISED > COLORISE
COLORISER > COLORISE
COLORISES > COLORISE
COLORISM > COLOR
COLORISMS > COLOR
COLORIST > COLOR
COLORISTS > COLOR
COLORIZE same
as > COLOURIZE
COLORIZED > COLOURIZE
COLORIZER > COLORIZE
COLORIZES > COLORIZE
COLORLESS > COLOR
COLORMAN same
as > COLOURMAN
COLORMEN > COLOURMAN
COLORS > COLOR
COLORWAY variant
of > COLOURWAY
COLORWAYS > COLORWAY
COLORY same as > COLOURY
COLOSSAL adj very large
COLOSSEUM same
as > COLISEUM
COLOSSI > COLOSSUS
COLOSSUS n huge statue
COLOSTOMY n operation to form an opening from the colon onto the surface of the body, for emptying the bowel
COLOSTRAL > COLOSTRUM
COLOSTRIC > COLOSTRUM
COLOSTRUM n thin milky secretion from the nipples that precedes and follows true lactation. It consists largely of serum and white blood cells
COLOTOMY n colonic incision
COLOUR n appearance of things as a result of reflecting light ▷ vb apply colour to
COLOURANT same
as > COLORANT
COLOURED adj having colour ▷ n person who is not white

COLOUREDS > COLOURED

COLOURER > COLOUR

COLOURERS > COLOUR

COLOURFUL adj with bright or varied colours

COLOURING n application of colour

COLOURISE same as > COLOURIZE

COLOURIST n person who uses colour, esp an artist

COLOURIZE vb add colour electronically to (an old black-and-white film)

COLOURMAN n person who deals in paints

COLOURMEN > COLOURMAN

COLOURS > COLOUR

COLOURWAY n one of several different combinations of colours in which a given pattern is printed on fabrics, wallpapers, etc

COLOURY adj possessing colour

COLPITIS another name for > VAGINITIS

COLPOTOMY n surgical incision into the wall of the vagina

COLS > COL

COLT n young male horse ▷ vb to fool

COLTAN n metallic ore found esp in the E Congo, consisting of columbite and tantalite and used as a source of tantalum

COLTANS > COLTAN

COLTED > COLT

COLTER same as > COULTER

COLTERS > COULTER

COLTING > COLT

COLTISH adj inexperienced

COLTISHLY > COLTISH

COLTS > COLT

COLTSFOOT n weed with yellow flowers and heart-shaped leaves

COLTWOOD n plant mentioned in Spenser's Faerie Queene

COLTWOODS > COLTWOOD

COLUBRIAD n epic poem about a snake

COLUBRID n any snake of the family Colubridae, including many harmless snakes, such as the grass snake and whip snakes, and some venomous types ▷ adj of, relating to, or belonging to the Colubridae

COLUBRIDS > COLUBRID

COLUBRINE adj of or resembling a snake

COLUGO n flying lemur

COLUGOS > COLUGO

COLUMBARY n dovecote

COLUMBATE n niobate

COLUMBIC another word for > NIOBIC

COLUMBINE n garden flower with five petals

▷ adj of, relating to, or resembling a dove

COLUMBITE n black mineral occurring in coarse granite

COLUMBIUM the former name of > NIOBIUM

COLUMBOUS another word for > NIOBOUS

COLUMEL n in botany, the central column in a capsule

COLUMELLA n central part of the spore-producing body of some fungi and mosses

COLUMELS > COLUMEL

COLUMN n pillar ▷ vb create a column

COLUMNAL > COLUMN

COLUMNAR > COLUMN

COLUMNEA n flowering plant

COLUMNEAS > COLUMNEA

COLUMNED > COLUMN

COLUMNIST n journalist who writes a regular feature in a newspaper

COLUMNS > COLUMN

COLURE n either of two great circles on the celestial sphere, one of which passes through the celestial poles and the equinoxes and the other through the poles and the solstices

COLURES > COLURE

COLY n any of the arboreal birds of the genus Colius, family Coliidae, and order Coliiformes, of southern Africa. They have a soft hairlike plumage, crested head, and very long tail

COLZA n oilseed rape, a Eurasian plant with bright yellow flowers

COLZAS > COLZA

COMA n state of deep unconsciousness

COMADE > COMAKE

COMAE > COMA

COMAKE vb to make together

COMAKER > COMAKE

COMAKERS > COMAKE

COMAKES > COMAKE

COMAKING > COMAKE

COMAL > COMA

COMANAGE vb to manage jointly

COMANAGED > COMANAGE

COMANAGER > COMANAGE

COMANAGES > COMANAGE

COMARB same as > COARB

COMARBS > COMARB

COMART n covenant

COMARTS > COMART

COMAS > COMA

COMATE adj having tufts of hair ▷ n companion

COMATES > COMATE

COMATIC > COMA

COMATIK variant

of > KOMATIK

COMATIKS > COMATIK

COMATOSE adj in a coma

COMATULA same as > COMATULID

COMATULAE > COMATULID

COMATULID n any of a group of crinoid echinoderms, including the feather stars, in which the adults are free-swimming

COMB n toothed implement for arranging the hair ▷ vb use a comb on

COMBAT vb fight, struggle ▷ n fight or struggle

COMBATANT n fighter ▷ adj fighting

COMBATED > COMBAT

COMBATER > COMBAT

COMBATERS > COMBAT

COMBATING > COMBAT

COMBATIVE adj eager or ready to fight, argue, etc

COMBATS > COMBAT

COMBATTED > COMBAT

COMBE same as > COMB

COMBED > COMB

COMBER n long curling wave

COMBERS > COMBER

COMBES > COMBE

COMBI n combination boiler

COMBIER > COMBY

COMBIES > COMBY

COMBIEST > COMBY

COMBINATE adj betrothed

COMBINE vb join together ▷ n association of people or firms for a common purpose

COMBINED > COMBINE

COMBINEDS > COMBINE

COMBINER > COMBINE

COMBINERS > COMBINE

COMBINES > COMBINE

COMBING > COMB

COMBINGS pl n loose hair or fibres removed by combing, esp from animals

COMBINING > COMBINE

COMBIS > COMBI

COMBLE n apex; zenith

COMBLES > COMBLE

COMBLESS adj without a comb

COMBLIKE adj resembling a comb

COMBO n small group of jazz musicians

COMBOS > COMBO

COMBRETUM n any tree or shrub belonging to the genus Combretum

COMBS > COMB

COMBUST adj (of a star or planet) invisible for a period between 24 and 30 days each year due to its proximity to the sun ▷ vb burn

COMBUSTED > COMBUST

COMBUSTOR n combustion system of a jet engine or ramjet, comprising the combustion chamber, the fuel injection apparatus, and the igniter

COMBUSTS > COMBUST

COMBWISE adv in the manner of a comb

COMBY adj comb-like ▷ n combination boiler

COME vb move towards a place, arrive

COMEBACK n return to a former position ▷ vb return, esp to the memory

COMEBACKS > COMEBACK

COMEDDLE vb mix

COMEDDLED > COMEDDLE

COMEDDLES > COMEDDLE

COMEDIAN n entertainer who tells jokes

COMEDIANS > COMEDIAN

COMEDIC adj of or relating to comedy

COMEDIES > COMEDY

COMEDO the technical name for > BLACKHEAD

COMEDONES > COMEDO

COMEDOS > COMEDO

COMEDOWN n decline in status ▷ vb come to a place regarded as lower

COMEDOWNS > COMEDOWN

COMEDY n humorous play, film, or programme

COMELIER > COMELY

COMELIEST > COMELY

COMELILY > COMELY

COMELY adj nice-looking

COMEMBER n fellow member

COMEMBERS > COMEMBER

COMEOVER n person who has come from Britain to the Isle of Man to settle

COMEOVERS > COMEOVER

COMER n person who comes

COMERS > COMER

COMES > COME

COMET n heavenly body with a long luminous tail

COMETARY > COMET

COMETH > COME

COMETHER n coaxing; allure

COMETHERS > COMETHER

COMETIC > COMET

COMETS > COMET

COMFIER > COMFY

COMFIEST > COMFY

COMFINESS > COMFY

COMFIT n sugar-coated sweet

COMFITS > COMFIT

COMFITURE n confiture

COMFORT n physical ease or wellbeing ▷ vb soothe, console

COMFORTED > COMFORT

COMFORTER n person or thing that comforts

COMFORTS > COMFORT

COMFREY n tall plant with

bell-shaped flowers
**COMFREYS** > COMFREY
**COMFY** adj comfortable
**COMIC** adj humorous, funny ▷ n comedian
**COMICAL** adj amusing
**COMICALLY** > COMICAL
**COMICE** n kind of pear
**COMICES** > COMICE
**COMICS** > COMIC
**COMING** > COME
**COMINGLE** same as > COMMINGLE
**COMINGLED** > COMMINGLE
**COMINGLES** > COMINGLE
**COMINGS** > COME
**COMIQUE** n comic actor
**COMIQUES** > COMIQUE
**COMITADJI** n Balkan guerrilla fighter
**COMITAL** adj relating to a count or earl
**COMITATUS** n leader's retinue
**COMITIA** n ancient Roman assembly that elected officials and exercised judicial and legislative authority
**COMITIAL** > COMITIA
**COMITIAS** > COMITIA
**COMITIES** > COMITY
**COMITY** n friendly politeness, esp between different countries
**COMIX** n comic books in general
**COMM** as in comm badge small wearable badge-shaped radio transmitter and receiver
**COMMA** n punctuation mark (,)
**COMMAND** vb order ▷ n authoritative instruction that something must be done
**COMMANDED** > COMMAND
**COMMANDER** n military officer in command of a group or operation
**COMMANDO** n (member of) a military unit trained for swift raids in enemy territory
**COMMANDOS** > COMMANDO
**COMMANDS** > COMMAND
**COMMATA** > COMMA
**COMMENCE** vb begin
**COMMENCED** > COMMENCE
**COMMENCER** > COMMENCE
**COMMENCES** > COMMENCE
**COMMEND** vb praise
**COMMENDAM** n temporary holding of an ecclesiastical benefice
**COMMENDED** > COMMEND
**COMMENDER** > COMMEND
**COMMENDS** > COMMEND
**COMMENSAL** adj (of two different species of plant or animal) living in close association, such that one

species benefits without harming the other ▷ n commensal plant or animal
**COMMENT** n remark ▷ vb make a comment
**COMMENTED** > COMMENT
**COMMENTER** > COMMENT
**COMMENTOR** > COMMENT
**COMMENTS** > COMMENT
**COMMER** same as > COMER
**COMMERCE** n buying and selling, trade ▷ vb to trade
**COMMERCED** > COMMERCE
**COMMERCES** > COMMERCE
**COMMERE** n female compere
**COMMERES** > COMMERE
**COMMERGE** vb to merge together
**COMMERGED** > COMMERGE
**COMMERGES** > COMMERGE
**COMMERS** > COMMER
**COMMIE** adj communist
**COMMIES** > COMMIE
**COMMINATE** vb to anathematise
**COMMINGLE** vb mix or be mixed
**COMMINUTE** vb break (a bone) into several small fragments
**COMMIS** n apprentice waiter or chef ▷ adj (of a waiter or chef) apprentice
**COMMISSAR** n (formerly) official responsible for political education in Communist countries
**COMMIT** vb perform (a crime or error)
**COMMITS** > COMMIT
**COMMITTAL** n act of committing or pledging
**COMMITTED** > COMMIT
**COMMITTEE** n group of people appointed to perform a specified service or function
**COMMITTER** > COMMIT
**COMMIX** a rare word for > MIX
**COMMIXED** > COMMIX
**COMMIXES** > COMMIX
**COMMIXING** > COMMIX
**COMMIXT** > COMMIX
**COMMO** short for > COMMUNIST
**COMMODE** n seat with a hinged flap concealing a chamber pot
**COMMODES** > COMMODE
**COMMODIFY** vb to make into a commodity
**COMMODITY** n something that can be bought or sold
**COMMODO** same as > COMODO
**COMMODORE** n senior commissioned officer in the navy
**COMMON** adj occurring often ▷ n area of grassy land belonging to a community ▷ vb sit at table with strangers
**COMMONAGE** n use of

something, esp a pasture, in common with others
**COMMONED** > COMMON
**COMMONER** n person who does not belong to the nobility
**COMMONERS** > COMMONER
**COMMONEST** > COMMON
**COMMONEY** n playing marble of a common sort
**COMMONEYS** > COMMONEY
**COMMONING** > COMMON
**COMMONLY** adv usually
**COMMONS** n people not of noble birth viewed as forming a political order
**COMMORANT** n resident
**COMMOS** > COMMO
**COMMOT** n in medieval Wales, a division of land
**COMMOTE** same as > COMMOT
**COMMOTES** > COMMOTE
**COMMOTION** n noisy disturbance
**COMMOTS** > COMMOT
**COMMOVE** vb disturb
**COMMOVED** > COMMOVE
**COMMOVES** > COMMOVE
**COMMOVING** > COMMOVE
**COMMS** pl n communications
**COMMUNAL** adj shared
**COMMUNARD** n member of a commune
**COMMUNE** n group of people who live together and share everything ▷ vb feel very close (to)
**COMMUNED** > COMMUNE
**COMMUNER** > COMMUNE
**COMMUNERS** > COMMUNE
**COMMUNES** > COMMUNE
**COMMUNING** > COMMUNE
**COMMUNION** n sharing of thoughts or feelings
**COMMUNISE** same as > COMMUNIZE
**COMMUNISM** n belief that all property and means of production should be shared by the community
**COMMUNIST** n supporter of any form of communism ▷ adj of, characterized by, favouring, or relating to communism
**COMMUNITY** n all the people living in one district
**COMMUNIZE** vb make (property) public
**COMMUTATE** vb reverse the direction of (an electric current)
**COMMUTE** vb travel daily to and from work ▷ n journey made by commuting
**COMMUTED** > COMMUTE
**COMMUTER** n person who commutes to and from work
**COMMUTERS** > COMMUTER
**COMMUTES** > COMMUTE
**COMMUTING** > COMMUTE

**COMMUTUAL** adj mutual
**COMMY** same as > COMMIE
**COMODO** adv (to be performed) at a convenient relaxed speed
**COMONOMER** n monomer that, with another, constitutes a copolymer
**COMORBID** adj (of illness) happening at same time as other illness
**COMOSE** another word for > COMATE
**COMOUS** adj hairy
**COMP** n person who sets and corrects type ▷ vb set or correct type
**COMPACT** adj closely packed ▷ n small flat case containing a mirror and face powder ▷ vb pack closely together
**COMPACTED** > COMPACT
**COMPACTER** > COMPACT
**COMPACTLY** > COMPACT
**COMPACTOR** n machine which compresses waste material for easier disposal
**COMPACTS** > COMPACT
**COMPADRE** n masculine friend
**COMPADRES** > COMPADRE
**COMPAGE** obsolete form of > COMPAGES
**COMPAGES** n structure or framework
**COMPAND** vb (of a transmitter signal) to compress before, and expand after, transmission
**COMPANDED** > COMPAND
**COMPANDER** n system for improving the signal-to-noise ratio of a signal at a transmitter or recorder by first compressing the volume range of the signal and then restoring it to its original amplitude level at the receiving or reproducing apparatus
**COMPANDOR** same as > COMPANDER
**COMPANDS** > COMPAND
**COMPANIED** > COMPANY
**COMPANIES** > COMPANY
**COMPANING** > COMPANY
**COMPANION** n person who associates with or accompanies someone ▷ vb accompany or be a companion to
**COMPANY** n business organization ▷ vb associate or keep company with someone
**COMPARE** vb examine (things) and point out the resemblances or differences
**COMPARED** > COMPARE
**COMPARER** > COMPARE
**COMPARERS** > COMPARE

**COMPARES** >COMPARE
**COMPARING** >COMPARE
**COMPART** vb to divide into parts
**COMPARTED** >COMPART
**COMPARTS** >COMPART
**COMPAS** n rhythm in flamenco
**COMPASS** n instrument for showing direction, with a needle that points north ▷ vb encircle or surround
**COMPASSED** >COMPASS
**COMPASSES** >COMPASS
**COMPAST** adj rounded
**COMPEAR** vb in Scots law, to appear in court
**COMPEARED** >COMPEAR
**COMPEARS** >COMPEAR
**COMPED** >COMPOSITOR
**COMPEER** n person of equal rank, status, or ability ▷ vb to equal
**COMPEERED** >COMPEER
**COMPEERS** >COMPEER
**COMPEL** vb force (to be or do)
**COMPELLED** >COMPEL
**COMPELLER** >COMPEL
**COMPELS** >COMPEL
**COMPEND** n compendium
**COMPENDIA** n plural form of singular compendium: book containing a collection of useful hints
**COMPENDS** >COMPEND
**COMPER** n person who regularly enters competitions in newspapers, magazines, etc, esp competitions offering consumer goods as prizes
**COMPERE** n person who presents a stage, radio, or television show ▷ vb be the compere of
**COMPERED** >COMPERE
**COMPERES** >COMPERE
**COMPERING** >COMPERE
**COMPERS** >COMPER
**COMPESCE** vb to curb
**COMPESCED** >COMPESCE
**COMPESCES** >COMPESCE
**COMPETE** vb try to win or achieve (a prize, profit, etc)
**COMPETED** >COMPETE
**COMPETENT** adj having the skill or knowledge to do something well
**COMPETES** >COMPETE
**COMPETING** >COMPETE
**COMPILE** vb collect and arrange (information), esp to make a book
**COMPILED** >COMPILE
**COMPILER** n person who compiles information
**COMPILERS** >COMPILER
**COMPILES** >COMPILE
**COMPILING** >COMPILE
**COMPING** >COMP
**COMPINGS** >COMP
**COMPITAL** adj pertaining

to crossroads
**COMPLAIN** vb express resentment or displeasure
**COMPLAINS** >COMPLAIN
**COMPLAINT** n complaining
**COMPLEAT** an archaic spelling of >COMPLETE
**COMPLECT** vb interweave or entwine
**COMPLECTS** >COMPLECT
**COMPLETE** adj thorough, absolute ▷ vb finish
**COMPLETED** >COMPLETE
**COMPLETER** >COMPLETE
**COMPLETES** >COMPLETE
**COMPLEX** adj made up of parts ▷ n whole made up of parts ▷ vb to form a complex
**COMPLEXED** >COMPLEX
**COMPLEXER** >COMPLEX
**COMPLEXES** >COMPLEX
**COMPLEXLY** >COMPLEX
**COMPLEXUS** n complex
**COMPLIANT** adj complying, obliging, or yielding
**COMPLICE** n associate or accomplice
**COMPLICES** >COMPLICE
**COMPLICIT** adj involved in a crime or questionable act
**COMPLIED** >COMPLY
**COMPLIER** >COMPLY
**COMPLIERS** >COMPLY
**COMPLIES** >COMPLY
**COMPLIN** same as >COMPLINE
**COMPLINE** n last service of the day in the Roman Catholic Church
**COMPLINES** >COMPLINE
**COMPLINS** >COMPLIN
**COMPLISH** vb accomplish
**COMPLOT** n plot or conspiracy ▷ vb plot together
**COMPLOTS** >COMPLOT
**COMPLUVIA** n plural form of singular compluvium: an unroofed space over the atrium in a Roman house, though which rain fell and was collected
**COMPLY** vb act in accordance (with)
**COMPLYING** >COMPLY
**COMPO** n mixture of materials, such as mortar, plaster, etc ▷ adj intended to last for several days
**COMPONE** same as >COMPONY
**COMPONENT** adj (being) part of a whole ▷ n constituent part or feature of a whole
**COMPONY** adj made up of alternating metal and colour, colour and fur, or fur and metal
**COMPORT** vb behave (oneself) in a specified way
**COMPORTED** >COMPORT

**COMPORTS** >COMPORT
**COMPOS** >COMPO
**COMPOSE** vb put together
**COMPOSED** adj calm
**COMPOSER** n person who writes music
**COMPOSERS** >COMPOSER
**COMPOSES** >COMPOSE
**COMPOSING** >COMPOSE
**COMPOSITE** adj made up of separate parts ▷ n something composed of separate parts ▷ vb merge related motions from local branches of (a political party, trade union, etc) so as to produce a manageable number of proposals for discussion at national level
**COMPOST** n decayed plants used as a fertilizer ▷ vb make (vegetable matter) into compost
**COMPOSTED** >COMPOST
**COMPOSTER** n bin or other container used to turn garden waste into compost
**COMPOSTS** >COMPOST
**COMPOSURE** n calmness
**COMPOT** same as >COMPOTE
**COMPOTE** n fruit stewed with sugar
**COMPOTES** >COMPOTE
**COMPOTIER** n dish for holding compote
**COMPOTS** >COMPOT
**COMPOUND** adj (thing, esp chemical) made up of two or more combined parts or elements ▷ vb combine or make by combining ▷ n fenced enclosure containing buildings
**COMPOUNDS** >COMPOUND
**COMPRADOR** n (formerly in China and some other Asian countries) a native agent of a foreign enterprise
**COMPRESS** vb squeeze together ▷ n pad applied to stop bleeding or cool inflammation
**COMPRINT** vb to print jointly
**COMPRINTS** >COMPRINT
**COMPRISAL** >COMPRISE
**COMPRISE** vb be made up of or make up
**COMPRISED** >COMPRISE
**COMPRISES** >COMPRISE
**COMPRIZE** same as >COMPRISE
**COMPRIZED** >COMPRIZE
**COMPRIZES** >COMPRIZE
**COMPS** >COMP
**COMPT** obsolete variant of >COUNT
**COMPTABLE** n countable
**COMPTED** >COMPT
**COMPTER** n formerly, a prison

**COMPTERS** >COMPT
**COMPTIBLE** same as >COMPTABLE
**COMPTING** >COUNT
**COMPTROLL** obsolete variant of >CONTROL
**COMPTS** >COMPT
**COMPULSE** vb to compel
**COMPULSED** >COMPULSE
**COMPULSES** >COMPULSE
**COMPUTANT** n calculator
**COMPUTE** vb calculate, esp using a computer ▷ n calculation
**COMPUTED** >COMPUTE
**COMPUTER** n electronic machine that stores and processes data
**COMPUTERS** >COMPUTER
**COMPUTES** >COMPUTE
**COMPUTING** n activity of using computers and writing programs for them ▷ adj of or relating to computers
**COMPUTIST** n one who computes
**COMRADE** n fellow member of a union or socialist political party
**COMRADELY** >COMRADE
**COMRADERY** n comradeship
**COMRADES** >COMRADE
**COMS** pl n one-piece woollen undergarment with longs sleeves and legs
**COMSYMP** n Communist Party sympathizer
**COMSYMPS** >COMSYMP
**COMTE** n European nobleman
**COMTES** >COMTE
**COMUS** n wild party
**COMUSES** >COMUS
**CON** vb deceive, swindle ▷ n convict ▷ prep with
**CONACRE** n farming land let for a season or for eleven months ▷ vb to let conacre
**CONACRED** >CONACRE
**CONACRES** >CONACRE
**CONACRING** >CONACRE
**CONARIA** >CONARIUM
**CONARIAL** >CONARIUM
**CONARIUM** n pineal gland
**CONATION** n element in psychological processes that tends towards activity or change and appears as desire, volition, and striving
**CONATIONS** >CONATION
**CONATIVE** adj denoting an aspect of verbs in some languages used to indicate the effort of the agent in performing the activity described by the verb
**CONATUS** n effort or striving of natural impulse
**CONCAUSE** n shared cause
**CONCAUSES** >CONCAUSE
**CONCAVE** adj curving

inwards ▷ *vb* make concave
CONCAVED > CONCAVE
CONCAVELY > CONCAVE
CONCAVES > CONCAVE
CONCAVING > CONCAVE
CONCAVITY *n* state or quality of being concave
CONCEAL *vb* cover and hide
CONCEALED > CONCEAL
CONCEALER > CONCEAL
CONCEALS > CONCEAL
CONCEDE *vb* admit to be true
CONCEDED > CONCEDE
CONCEDER > CONCEDE
CONCEDERS > CONCEDE
CONCEDES > CONCEDE
CONCEDING > CONCEDE
CONCEDO *interj* I allow; I concede (a point)
CONCEIT *n* too high an opinion of oneself ▷ *vb* like or be able to bear (something, such as food or drink)
CONCEITED *adj* having an excessively high opinion of oneself
CONCEITS > CONCEIT
CONCEITY *adj* full of conceit
CONCEIVE *vb* imagine, think
CONCEIVED > CONCEIVE
CONCEIVER > CONCEIVE
CONCEIVES > CONCEIVE
CONCENT *n* concord, as of sounds, voices, etc
CONCENTER *same as* > CONCENTRE
CONCENTRE *vb* converge or cause to converge on a common centre
CONCENTS > CONCENT
CONCENTUS *n* vocal harmony
CONCEPT *n* abstract or general idea
CONCEPTI > CONCEPTUS
CONCEPTS > CONCEPT
CONCEPTUS *n* any product of conception, including the embryo, foetus and surrounding tissue
CONCERN *n* anxiety, worry ▷ *vb* worry (someone)
CONCERNED *adj* interested, involved
CONCERNS > CONCERN
CONCERT *n* musical entertainment
CONCERTED *adj* done together
CONCERTI > CONCERTO
CONCERTO *n* large-scale composition for a solo instrument and orchestra
CONCERTOS > CONCERTO
CONCERTS > CONCERT
CONCETTI > CONCETTO
CONCETTO *n* conceit, ingenious thought
CONCH *same as* > CONCHA

CONCHA *n* any bodily organ or part resembling a shell in shape, such as the external ear
CONCHAE > CONCHA
CONCHAL > CONCHA
CONCHAS > CONCHA
CONCHATE *adj* shell-shaped
CONCHE *vb* (in chocolate-making) to use a conche (machine which mixes and smooths the chocolate mass)
CONCHED > CONCHE
CONCHES > CONCHE
CONCHIE *n* conscientious objector
CONCHIES > CONCHIE
CONCHING > CONCHE
CONCHITIS *n* inflammation of the outer ear
CONCHO *n* American metal ornament
CONCHOID *n* type of plane curve
CONCHOIDS > CONCHOID
CONCHOS > CONCHO
CONCHS > CONCH
CONCHY *same as* > CONCHIE
CONCIERGE *n* (in France) caretaker in a block of flats
CONCILIAR *adj* of, from, or by means of a council, esp an ecclesiastical one
CONCISE *adj* brief and to the point ▷ *vb* mutilate
CONCISED > CONCISE
CONCISELY > CONCISE
CONCISER > CONCISE
CONCISES > CONCISE
CONCISEST > CONCISE
CONCISING > CONCISE
CONCISION *n* quality of being concise
CONCLAVE *n* secret meeting
CONCLAVES > CONCLAVE
CONCLUDE *vb* decide by reasoning
CONCLUDED > CONCLUDE
CONCLUDER > CONCLUDE
CONCLUDES > CONCLUDE
CONCOCT *vb* make up (a story or plan)
CONCOCTED > CONCOCT
CONCOCTER > CONCOCT
CONCOCTOR > CONCOCT
CONCOCTS > CONCOCT
CONCOLOR *adj* of a single colour
CONCORD *n* state of peaceful agreement, harmony ▷ *vb* to agree
CONCORDAL > CONCORD
CONCORDAT *n* pact or treaty
CONCORDED > CONCORD
CONCORDS > CONCORD
CONCOURS *n* contest
CONCOURSE *n* large open public place where people can gather
CONCREATE *vb* to create at the same time

CONCRETE *n* mixture of cement, sand, stone, and water, used in building ▷ *vb* cover with concrete ▷ *adj* made of concrete
CONCRETED > CONCRETE
CONCRETES > CONCRETE
CONCREW *vb* to grow together
CONCREWED > CONCREW
CONCREWS > CONCREW
CONCUBINE *n* woman living in a man's house but not married to him but kept for his sexual pleasure
CONCUPIES > CONCUPY
CONCUPY *n* concupiscence
CONCUR *vb* agree
CONCURRED > CONCUR
CONCURS > CONCUR
CONCUSS *vb* injure (the brain) by a fall or blow
CONCUSSED > CONCUSS
CONCUSSES > CONCUSS
CONCYCLIC *adj* (of a set of geometric points) lying on a common circle
COND *old inflection of* > CON
CONDEMN *vb* express disapproval of
CONDEMNED > CONDEMN
CONDEMNER > CONDEMN
CONDEMNOR > CONDEMN
CONDEMNS > CONDEMN
CONDENSE *vb* make shorter
CONDENSED *adj* (of printers' type) narrower than usual for a particular height
CONDENSER *same as* > CAPACITOR
CONDENSES > CONDENSE
CONDER *n* person who directs the steering of a vessel
CONDERS > CONDER
CONDIDDLE *vb* to steal
CONDIE *n* culvert; tunnel
CONDIES > CONDIE
CONDIGN *adj* (esp of a punishment) fitting
CONDIGNLY > CONDIGN
CONDIMENT *n* seasoning for food, such as salt or pepper
CONDITION *n* particular state of being ▷ *vb* train or influence to behave in a particular way
CONDO *n* condominium
CONDOES > CONDO
CONDOLE *vb* express sympathy with someone in grief, pain, etc
CONDOLED > CONDOLE
CONDOLENT *adj* expressing sympathy with someone in grief
CONDOLER > CONDOLE
CONDOLERS > CONDOLE
CONDOLES > CONDOLE
CONDOLING > CONDOLE
CONDOM *n* rubber sheath worn on the penis or in the vagina during sexual intercourse to prevent

conception or infection
CONDOMS > CONDOM
CONDONE *vb* overlook or forgive (wrongdoing)
CONDONED > CONDONE
CONDONER > CONDONE
CONDONERS > CONDONE
CONDONES > CONDONE
CONDONING > CONDONE
CONDOR *n* large vulture of S America
CONDORES > CONDOR
CONDORS > CONDOR
CONDOS > CONDO
CONDUCE *vb* lead or contribute (to a result)
CONDUCED > CONDUCE
CONDUCER > CONDUCE
CONDUCERS > CONDUCE
CONDUCES > CONDUCE
CONDUCING > CONDUCE
CONDUCIVE *adj* likely to lead (to)
CONDUCT *n* management of an activity ▷ *vb* carry out (a task)
CONDUCTED > CONDUCT
CONDUCTI > CONDUCTUS
CONDUCTOR *n* person who conducts musicians
CONDUCTS > CONDUCT
CONDUCTUS *n* medieval liturgical composition
CONDUIT *n* channel or tube for fluid or cables
CONDUITS > CONDUIT
CONDYLAR > CONDYLE
CONDYLE *n* rounded projection on the articulating end of a bone, such as the ball portion of a ball-and-socket joint
CONDYLES > CONDYLE
CONDYLOID *adj* of or resembling a condyle
CONDYLOMA *n* skin tumour near the anus or genital organs, esp as a result of syphilis
CONE *n* object with a circular base, tapering to a point ▷ *vb* shape like a cone or part of a cone
CONED > CONE
CONELRAD *n* US defence and information system for use in the event of air attack
CONELRADS > CONELRAD
CONENOSE *n* bloodsucking bug of the genus Triatoma
CONENOSES > CONENOSE
CONEPATE *same as* > CONEPATL
CONEPATES > CONEPATE
CONEPATL *n* skunk
CONEPATLS > CONEPATL
CONES > CONE
CONEY *same as* > CONY
CONEYS > CONEY
CONF *n* online forum
CONFAB *n* conversation ▷ *vb* converse
CONFABBED > CONFAB

**CONFABS** > CONFAB
**CONFECT** vb prepare by combining ingredients
**CONFECTED** > CONFECT
**CONFECTS** > CONFECT
**CONFER** vb discuss together
**CONFEREE** n person who takes part in a conference
**CONFEREES** > CONFEREE
**CONFERRAL** > CONFER
**CONFERRED** > CONFER
**CONFERREE** same as > CONFEREE
**CONFERRER** > CONFER
**CONFERS** > CONFER
**CONFERVA** n any of various threadlike green algae, esp any of the genus Tribonema, typically occurring in fresh water
**CONFERVAE** > CONFERVA
**CONFERVAL** > CONFERVA
**CONFERVAS** > CONFERVA
**CONFESS** vb admit (a fault or crime)
**CONFESSED** > CONFESS
**CONFESSES** > CONFESS
**CONFESSOR** n priest who hears confessions
**CONFEST** adj admitted
**CONFESTLY** adv confessedly
**CONFETTI** n small pieces of coloured paper thrown at weddings
**CONFETTO** n sweetmeat
**CONFIDANT** n person confided in
**CONFIDE** vb tell someone (a secret)
**CONFIDED** > CONFIDE
**CONFIDENT** adj sure, esp of oneself
**CONFIDER** > CONFIDE
**CONFIDERS** > CONFIDE
**CONFIDES** > CONFIDE
**CONFIDING** adj trusting
**CONFIGURE** vb to design or set up
**CONFINE** vb keep within bounds ▷ n limit
**CONFINED** adj enclosed or restricted
**CONFINER** > CONFINE
**CONFINERS** > CONFINE
**CONFINES** > CONFINE
**CONFINING** > CONFINE
**CONFIRM** vb prove to be true
**CONFIRMED** adj firmly established in a habit or condition
**CONFIRMEE** n person to whom a confirmation is made
**CONFIRMER** > CONFIRM
**CONFIRMOR** n person who makes a confirmation
**CONFIRMS** > CONFIRM
**CONFISEUR** n confectioner
**CONFIT** n preserve
**CONFITEOR** n Catholic prayer asking for forgiveness
**CONFITS** > CONFIT

**CONFITURE** n confection, preserve of fruit, etc
**CONFIX** vb to fasten
**CONFIXED** > CONFIX
**CONFIXES** > CONFIX
**CONFIXING** > CONFIX
**CONFLATE** vb combine or blend into a whole
**CONFLATED** > CONFLATE
**CONFLATES** > CONFLATE
**CONFLICT** n disagreement ▷ vb be incompatible
**CONFLICTS** > CONFLICT
**CONFLUENT** adj flowing together or merging ▷ n stream that flows into another, usually of approximately equal size
**CONFLUX** n merging or folowing togther, especially of rivers
**CONFLUXES** > CONFLUX
**CONFOCAL** adj having a common focus or common foci
**CONFORM** vb comply with accepted standards or customs
**CONFORMAL** adj (of a transformation) preserving the angles of the depicted surface
**CONFORMED** > CONFORM
**CONFORMER** > CONFORM
**CONFORMS** > CONFORM
**CONFOUND** vb astound, bewilder
**CONFOUNDS** > CONFOUND
**CONFRERE** n colleague
**CONFRERES** > CONFRERE
**CONFRERIE** n brotherhood
**CONFRONT** vb come face to face with
**CONFRONTE** adj in heraldry, (of two animals) face to face
**CONFRONTS** > CONFRONT
**CONFS** > CONF
**CONFUSE** vb mix up
**CONFUSED** adj lacking a clear understanding of something
**CONFUSES** > CONFUSE
**CONFUSING** adj causing bewilderment
**CONFUSION** n mistaking one person or thing for another
**CONFUTE** vb prove wrong
**CONFUTED** > CONFUTE
**CONFUTER** > CONFUTE
**CONFUTERS** > CONFUTE
**CONFUTES** > CONFUTE
**CONFUTING** > CONFUTE
**CONGA** n dance performed by a number of people in single file ▷ vb dance the conga
**CONGAED** > CONGA
**CONGAING** > CONGA
**CONGAS** > CONGA
**CONGE** n permission to depart or dismissal, esp when formal ▷ vb to take

one's leave
**CONGEAL** vb (of a liquid) become thick and sticky
**CONGEALED** > CONGEAL
**CONGEALER** > CONGEAL
**CONGEALS** > CONGEAL
**CONGED** > CONGE
**CONGEE** same as > CONGE
**CONGEED** > CONGEE
**CONGEEING** > CONGEE
**CONGEES** > CONGEE
**CONGEING** > CONGEE
**CONGENER** n member of a class, group, or other category, esp any animal of a specified genus
**CONGENERS** > CONGENER
**CONGENIAL** adj pleasant, agreeable
**CONGENIC** adj (of inbred animal cells) genetically identical except for a single gene locus
**CONGER** n large sea eel
**CONGERIES** n collection of objects or ideas
**CONGERS** > CONGER
**CONGES** > CONGE
**CONGEST** vb crowd or become crowded to excess
**CONGESTED** adj crowded to excess
**CONGESTS** > CONGEST
**CONGIARY** n Roman emperor's gift to the people or soldiers
**CONGII** > CONGIUS
**CONGIUS** n unit of liquid measure equal to 1 Imperial gallon
**CONGLOBE** vb to gather into a globe or ball
**CONGLOBED** > CONGLOBE
**CONGLOBES** > CONGLOBE
**CONGO** same as > CONGOU
**CONGOES** > CONGOU
**CONGOS** > CONGO
**CONGOU** n kind of black tea from China
**CONGOUS** > CONGOU
**CONGRATS** sentence substitute congratulations
**CONGREE** vb to agree
**CONGREED** > CONGREE
**CONGREES** > CONGREE
**CONGREET** vb (of two or more people) to greet one another
**CONGREETS** > CONGREET
**CONGRESS** n formal meeting for discussion
**CONGRUE** vb to agree
**CONGRUED** > CONGRUE
**CONGRUENT** adj similar, corresponding
**CONGRUES** > CONGRUE
**CONGRUING** > CONGRUE
**CONGRUITY** > CONGRUOUS
**CONGRUOUS** adj appropriate or in keeping
**CONI** > CONUS
**CONIA** same as > CONIINE
**CONIAS** > CONIINE
**CONIC** adj having the shape

of a cone
**CONICAL** adj cone-shaped
**CONICALLY** > CONIC
**CONICINE** same as > CONIINE
**CONICINES** > CONICINE
**CONICITY** > CONICAL
**CONICS** n branch of geometry concerned with the parabola, ellipse, and hyperbola
**CONIDIA** > CONIDIUM
**CONIDIAL** > CONIDIUM
**CONIDIAN** > CONIDIUM
**CONIDIUM** n asexual spore formed at the tip of a specialized hypha (conidiophore) in fungi such as Penicillium
**CONIES** > CONY
**CONIFER** n cone-bearing tree, such as the fir or pine
**CONIFERS** > CONIFER
**CONIFORM** adj cone-shaped
**CONIINE** n colourless poisonous soluble liquid alkaloid found in hemlock
**CONIINES** > CONIINE
**CONIMA** n gum resin from the conium hemlock tree
**CONIMAS** > CONIMA
**CONIN** same as > CONIINE
**CONINE** same as > CONIINE
**CONINES** > CONINE
**CONING** > CONE
**CONINS** > CONIN
**CONIOLOGY** a variant spelling of > KONIOLOGY
**CONIOSES** > CONIOSIS
**CONIOSIS** n any disease or condition caused by dust inhalation
**CONIUM** n either of the two N temperate plants of the umbelliferous genus Conium, esp hemlock
**CONIUMS** > CONIUM
**CONJECT** vb to conjecture
**CONJECTED** > CONJECT
**CONJECTS** > CONJECT
**CONJEE** vb prepare as, or in, a conjee (a gruel of boiled rice and water)
**CONJEED** > CONJEE
**CONJEEING** > CONJEE
**CONJEES** > CONJEE
**CONJOIN** vb join or become joined
**CONJOINED** > CONJOIN
**CONJOINER** > CONJOIN
**CONJOINS** > CONJOIN
**CONJOINT** adj united, joint, or associated
**CONJUGAL** adj of marriage
**CONJUGANT** n either of a pair of organisms or gametes undergoing conjugation
**CONJUGATE** vb inflect (a verb) systematically
**CONJUNCT** adj joined ▷ n one of the propositions or formulas in a conjunction
**CONJUNCTS** > CONJUNCT

CONJUNTO *n* style of Mexican music

CONJUNTOS >CONJUNTO

CONJURE *vb* perform tricks that appear to be magic

CONJURED >CONJURE

CONJURER *same as* >CONJUROR

CONJURERS >CONJUROR

CONJURES >CONJURE

CONJURIES >CONJURY

CONJURING *n* performance of tricks that appear to defy natural laws ▷ *adj* denoting or relating to such tricks or entertainment

CONJUROR *n* person who performs magic tricks for people's entertainment

CONJURORS >CONJUROR

CONJURY *n* magic

CONK *n* nose ▷ *vb* strike (someone) on the head or nose

CONKED >CONK

CONKER *n* nut of the horse chestnut

CONKERS *n* game played with conkers tied on strings

CONKIER >CONKY

CONKIEST >CONKY

CONKING >CONK

CONKS >CONK

CONKY *adj* affected by the timber disease, conk

CONN *same as* >CON

CONNATE *adj* existing in a person or thing from birth

CONNATELY >CONNATE

CONNATION *n* joining of similar parts or organs

CONNATURE *n* sharing a common nature or character

CONNE *same as* >CON

CONNECT *vb* join together

CONNECTED *adj* joined or linked together

CONNECTER >CONNECT

CONNECTOR >CONNECT

CONNECTS >CONNECT

CONNED >CON

CONNER *same as* >CONDER

CONNERS >CONNER

CONNES >CONNE

CONNEXION *n* act or state of connecting

CONNEXIVE *adj* connective

CONNING >CON

CONNINGS >CON

CONNIVE *vb* allow (wrongdoing) by ignoring it

CONNIVED >CONNIVE

CONNIVENT *adj* (of parts of plants and animals) touching without being fused, as some petals, insect wings, etc

CONNIVER >CONNIVE

CONNIVERS >CONNIVE

CONNIVERY *n* act of conniving

CONNIVES >CONNIVE

CONNIVING >CONNIVE

CONNOTATE *vb* to connote

CONNOTE *vb* (of a word, phrase, etc) to imply or suggest (associations or ideas) other than the literal meaning

CONNOTED >CONNOTE

CONNOTES >CONNOTE

CONNOTING >CONNOTE

CONNOTIVE *adj* act or state of connecting

CONNS >CONN

CONNUBIAL *adj* of marriage

CONODONT *n* any of various small Palaeozoic toothlike fossils derived from an extinct eel-like marine animal

CONODONTS >CONODONT

CONOID *n* geometric surface formed by rotating a parabola, ellipse, or hyperbola about one axis ▷ *adj* conical, cone-shaped

CONOIDAL *same as* >CONOID

CONOIDIC >CONOID

CONOIDS >CONOID

CONOMINEE *n* joint nominee

CONQUER *vb* defeat

CONQUERED >CONQUER

CONQUERER *variant of* >CONQUEROR

CONQUEROR >CONQUER

CONQUERS >CONQUER

CONQUEST *n* conquering

CONQUESTS >CONQUEST

CONQUIAN *same as* >COONCAN

CONQUIANS >COONCAN

CONS >CON

CONSCIENT *adj* conscious

CONSCIOUS *adj* alert and awake ▷ *n* conscious part of the mind

CONSCRIBE *vb* to enrol compulsorily

CONSCRIPT *n* person enrolled for compulsory military service ▷ *vb* enrol (someone) for compulsory military service

CONSEIL *n* advice

CONSEILS >CONSEIL

CONSENSUS *n* general agreement

CONSENT *n* agreement, permission ▷ *vb* permit, agree to

CONSENTED >CONSENT

CONSENTER >CONSENT

CONSENTS >CONSENT

CONSERVE *vb* protect from harm, decay, or loss ▷ *n* jam containing large pieces of fruit

CONSERVED >CONSERVE

CONSERVER >CONSERVE

CONSERVES >CONSERVE

CONSIDER *vb* regard as

CONSIDERS >CONSIDER

CONSIGN *vb* put somewhere

CONSIGNED >CONSIGN

CONSIGNEE *n* person, agent, organization, etc, to which merchandise is consigned

CONSIGNER *same as* >CONSIGNOR

CONSIGNOR *n* person, enterprise, etc, that consigns goods

CONSIGNS >CONSIGN

CONSIST *vb* be composed (of)

CONSISTED >CONSIST

CONSISTS >CONSIST

CONSOCIES *n* natural community with a single dominant species

CONSOL *n* consolidated annuity, a British government bond

CONSOLATE *vb* to console

CONSOLE *vb* comfort in distress ▷ *n* panel of controls for electronic equipment

CONSOLED >CONSOLE

CONSOLER >CONSOLE

CONSOLERS >CONSOLE

CONSOLES >CONSOLE

CONSOLING >CONSOLE

CONSOLS *pl n* irredeemable British government securities carrying annual interest rates of two and a half or four per cent

CONSOLUTE *adj* (of two or more liquids) mutually soluble in all proportions

CONSOMME *n* thin clear meat soup

CONSOMMES >CONSOMME

CONSONANT *n* speech sound made by partially or completely blocking the breath stream, such as b or f ▷ *adj* agreeing (with)

CONSONOUS *adj* harmonious

CONSORT *vb* keep company (with) ▷ *n* husband or wife of a monarch

CONSORTED >CONSORT

CONSORTER >CONSORT

CONSORTIA *n* plural form of singular consortium: association of financiers, companies etc

CONSORTS >CONSORT

CONSPIRE *vb* plan a crime together in secret

CONSPIRED >CONSPIRE

CONSPIRER >CONSPIRE

CONSPIRES >CONSPIRE

CONSTABLE *n* police officer of the lowest rank

CONSTANCY *n* quality of having a resolute mind, purpose, or affection

CONSTANT *adj* continuous ▷ *n* unvarying quantity

CONSTANTS >CONSTANT

CONSTATE *vb* to affirm

CONSTATED >CONSTATE

CONSTATES >CONSTATE

CONSTER *obsolete variant of* >CONSTRUE

CONSTERED >CONSTRUE

CONSTERS >CONSTRUE

CONSTRAIN *vb* compel, force

CONSTRICT *vb* make narrower by squeezing

CONSTRUAL *n* act of construing

CONSTRUCT *vb* build or put together ▷ *n* complex idea resulting from the combination of simpler ideas

CONSTRUE *vb* interpret ▷ *n* something that is construed, such as a piece of translation

CONSTRUED >CONSTRUE

CONSTRUER >CONSTRUE

CONSTRUES >CONSTRUE

CONSUL *n* official representing a state in a foreign country

CONSULAGE *n* duty paid by merchants for a consul's protection of their goods while abroad

CONSULAR *n* anyone of consular rank

CONSULARS >CONSULAR

CONSULATE *n* workplace or position of a consul

CONSULS >CONSUL

CONSULT *vb* go to for advice or information

CONSULTA *n* official planning meeting

CONSULTAS >CONSULTA

CONSULTED >CONSULT

CONSULTEE *n* person who is consulted

CONSULTER >CONSULT

CONSULTOR >CONSULT

CONSULTS >CONSULT

CONSUME *vb* eat or drink

CONSUMED >CONSUME

CONSUMER *n* person who buys goods or uses services

CONSUMERS >CONSUMER

CONSUMES >CONSUME

CONSUMING >CONSUME

CONSUMPT *n* quantity used up; consumption

CONSUMPTS >CONSUMPT

CONTACT *n* communicating ▷ *vb* get in touch with ▷ *interj* (formerly) a call made by the pilot to indicate that an aircraft's ignition is switched on and that the engine is ready for starting by swinging the propeller

CONTACTED >CONTACT

CONTACTEE *n* person contacted by aliens

CONTACTOR *n* type of

switch for repeatedly
opening and closing
an electric circuit.
Its operation can
be mechanical,
electromagnetic, or
pneumatic
**CONTACTS** > CONTACT
**CONTADINA** n female
Italian farmer
**CONTADINE** > CONTADINA
**CONTADINI** > CONTADINO
**CONTADINO** n Italian
farmer
**CONTAGIA** > CONTAGIUM
**CONTAGION** n passing on of
disease by contact
**CONTAGIUM** n specific virus
or other direct cause of any
infectious disease
**CONTAIN** vb hold or be
capable of holding
**CONTAINED** > CONTAIN
**CONTAINER** n object used
to hold or store things in
**CONTAINS** > CONTAIN
**CONTANGO** n (formerly,
on the London Stock
Exchange) postponement
of payment for and
delivery of stock from
one account day to the
next ▷ vb arrange such a
postponement of payment
(for)
**CONTANGOS** > CONTANGO
**CONTE** n tale or short story,
esp of adventure
**CONTECK** n contention
**CONTECKS** > CONTECK
**CONTEMN** vb regard with
contempt
**CONTEMNED** > CONTEMN
**CONTEMNER** > CONTEMN
**CONTEMNOR** > CONTEMN
**CONTEMNS** > CONTEMN
**CONTEMPER** vb to modify
**CONTEMPO** adj
contemporary
**CONTEMPT** n dislike and
disregard
**CONTEMPTS** > CONTEMPT
**CONTEND** vb deal with
**CONTENDED** > CONTEND
**CONTENDER** > CONTEND
**CONTENDS** > CONTEND
**CONTENT** n meaning or
substance of a piece of
writing ▷ adj satisfied
with things as they are
▷ vb make (someone)
content
**CONTENTED** adj satisfied
with one's situation or life
**CONTENTLY** > CONTENT
**CONTENTS** > CONTENT
**CONTES** > CONTE
**CONTESSA** n Italian
countess
**CONTESSAS** > CONTESSA
**CONTEST** n competition
or struggle ▷ vb dispute,
object to
**CONTESTED** > CONTEST

**CONTESTER** > CONTEST
**CONTESTS** > CONTEST
**CONTEXT** n circumstances
of an event or fact
**CONTEXTS** > CONTEXT
**CONTICENT** adj silent
**CONTINENT** n one of the
earth's large masses of
land ▷ adj able to control
one's bladder and bowels
**CONTINUA** > CONTINUUM
**CONTINUAL** adj constant
**CONTINUE** vb (cause to)
remain in a condition or
place
**CONTINUED** > CONTINUE
**CONTINUER** > CONTINUE
**CONTINUES** > CONTINUE
**CONTINUO** n continuous
bass part, usu. played on a
keyboard instrument
**CONTINUOS** > CONTINUO
**CONTINUUM** n continuous
series
**CONTLINE** n space between
the bilges of stowed casks
**CONTLINES** > CONTLINE
**CONTO** n former Portuguese
monetary unit worth 1000
escudos
**CONTORNO** n in Italy, side
dish of salad or vegetables
**CONTORNOS** > CONTORNO
**CONTORT** vb twist out of
shape
**CONTORTED** adj twisted out
of shape
**CONTORTS** > CONTORT
**CONTOS** > CONTO
**CONTOUR** n outline ▷ vb
shape so as to form or
follow the contour of
something
**CONTOURED** > CONTOUR
**CONTOURS** > CONTOUR
**CONTRA** n counter-
argument
**CONTRACT** n (document
setting out) a formal
agreement ▷ vb make a
formal agreement (to do
something)
**CONTRACTS** > CONTRACT
**CONTRAIL** n aeroplane's
vapour trail
**CONTRAILS** > CONTRAIL
**CONTRAIR** adj contrary
**CONTRALTI** > CONTRALTO
**CONTRALTO** n (singer with)
the lowest female voice
▷ adj of or denoting a
contralto
**CONTRARY** n complete
opposite ▷ adj opposed,
completely different ▷ adv
in opposition
**CONTRAS** > CONTRA
**CONTRAST** n obvious
difference ▷ vb compare
in order to show
differences
**CONTRASTS** > CONTRAST
**CONTRASTY** adj (of a
photograph or subject)

having sharp gradations
in tone, esp between light
and dark areas
**CONTRAT** old form
of > CONTRACT
**CONTRATE** adj (of gears)
having teeth set at a right
angle to the axis
**CONTRATS** > CONTRAT
**CONTRIST** vb to make sad
**CONTRISTS** > CONTRIST
**CONTRITE** adj sorry and
apologetic
**CONTRIVE** vb make happen
**CONTRIVED** adj planned or
artificial
**CONTRIVER** > CONTRIVE
**CONTRIVES** > CONTRIVE
**CONTROL** n power to direct
something ▷ vb have
power over
**CONTROLE** adj officially
registered
**CONTROLS** > CONTROL
**CONTROUL** obsolete variant
of > CONTROL
**CONTROULS** > CONTROUL
**CONTUMACY** n obstinate
disobedience
**CONTUMELY** n scornful or
insulting treatment
**CONTUND** vb to pummel
**CONTUNDED** > CONTUND
**CONTUNDS** > CONTUND
**CONTUSE** vb injure (the
body) without breaking
the skin
**CONTUSED** > CONTUSE
**CONTUSES** > CONTUSE
**CONTUSING** > CONTUSE
**CONTUSION** n bruise
**CONTUSIVE** > CONTUSE
**CONUNDRUM** n riddle
**CONURBAN** adj relating to
an urban region
**CONURBIA** n conurbations
considered collectively
**CONURBIAS** > CONURBIA
**CONURE** n any of various
small American parrots
of the genus Aratinga and
related genera
**CONURES** > CONURE
**CONUS** n any of several
cone-shaped structures,
such as the conus
medullaris, the lower end
of the spinal cord
**CONVECT** vb to circulate hot
air by convection
**CONVECTED** > CONVECT
**CONVECTOR** n heater that
gives out hot air
**CONVECTS** > CONVECT
**CONVENE** vb gather or
summon for a formal
meeting
**CONVENED** > CONVENE
**CONVENER** n person who
calls a meeting
**CONVENERS** > CONVENER
**CONVENES** > CONVENE
**CONVENING** > CONVENE
**CONVENOR** same

as > CONVENER
**CONVENORS** > CONVENOR
**CONVENT** n building where
nuns live ▷ vb to summon
**CONVENTED** > CONVENT
**CONVENTS** > CONVENT
**CONVERGE** vb meet or join
**CONVERGED** > CONVERGE
**CONVERGES** > CONVERGE
**CONVERSE** vb have
a conversation ▷ n
opposite or contrary ▷ adj
reversed or opposite
**CONVERSED** > CONVERSE
**CONVERSER** > CONVERSE
**CONVERSES** > CONVERSE
**CONVERSO** n medieval
Spanish Jew converting to
Catholicism
**CONVERSOS** > CONVERSO
**CONVERT** vb change
in form, character, or
function ▷ n person
who has converted to a
different belief or religion
**CONVERTED** > CONVERT
**CONVERTER** n person or
thing that converts
**CONVERTOR** same
as > CONVERTER
**CONVERTS** > CONVERT
**CONVEX** adj curving
outwards ▷ vb make
convex
**CONVEXED** > CONVEX
**CONVEXES** > CONVEX
**CONVEXING** > CONVEX
**CONVEXITY** n state or
quality of being convex
**CONVEXLY** > CONVEX
**CONVEY** vb communicate
(information)
**CONVEYAL** n act or means
of conveying
**CONVEYALS** > CONVEYAL
**CONVEYED** > CONVEY
**CONVEYER** same
as > CONVEYOR
**CONVEYERS** > CONVEYER
**CONVEYING** > CONVEY
**CONVEYOR** n person or
thing that conveys
**CONVEYORS** > CONVEYOR
**CONVEYS** > CONVEY
**CONVICT** vb declare guilty
▷ n person serving a
prison sentence ▷ adj
convicted
**CONVICTED** > CONVICT
**CONVICTS** > CONVICT
**CONVINCE** vb persuade by
argument or evidence
**CONVINCED** > CONVINCE
**CONVINCER** > CONVINCE
**CONVINCES** > CONVINCE
**CONVIVE** vb to feast
together
**CONVIVED** > CONVIVE
**CONVIVES** > CONVIVE
**CONVIVIAL** adj sociable,
lively
**CONVIVING** > CONVIVE
**CONVO** n conversation
**CONVOCATE** vb to call

together
**CONVOKE** *vb* call together
**CONVOKED** > CONVOKE
**CONVOKER** > CONVOKE
**CONVOKERS** > CONVOKE
**CONVOKES** > CONVOKE
**CONVOKING** > CONVOKE
**CONVOLUTE** *vb* form into a twisted, coiled, or rolled shape ▷ *adj* rolled longitudinally upon itself
**CONVOLVE** *vb* wind or roll together
**CONVOLVED** > CONVOLVE
**CONVOLVES** > CONVOLVE
**CONVOS** > CONVO
**CONVOY** *n* group of vehicles or ships travelling together ▷ *vb* escort while in transit
**CONVOYED** > CONVOY
**CONVOYING** > CONVOY
**CONVOYS** > CONVOY
**CONVULSE** *vb* (of part of the body) undergo violent spasms
**CONVULSED** > CONVULSE
**CONVULSES** > CONVULSE
**CONY** *n* rabbit
**COO** *vb* (of a dove or pigeon) make a soft murmuring sound ▷ *n* sound of cooing ▷ *interj* exclamation of surprise, awe, etc
**COOCH** *n* slang term for vagina
**COOCHES** > COOCH
**COOCOO** *old spelling of* > CUCKOO
**COOED** > COO
**COOEE** *interj* call to attract attention ▷ *vb* utter this call ▷ *n* calling distance
**COOEED** > COOEE
**COOEEING** > COOEE
**COOEES** > COOEE
**COOER** > COO
**COOERS** > COO
**COOEY** *same as* > COOEE
**COOEYED** > COOEY
**COOEYING** > COOEY
**COOEYS** > COOEY
**COOF** *n* simpleton
**COOFS** > COOF
**COOING** > COO
**COOINGLY** > COO
**COOINGS** > COO
**COOK** *vb* prepare (food) by heating ▷ *n* person who cooks food
**COOKABLE** > COOK
**COOKBOOK** *n* book containing recipes and instructions for cooking
**COOKBOOKS** > COOKBOOK
**COOKED** > COOK
**COOKER** *n* apparatus for cooking heated by gas or electricity
**COOKERIES** > COOKERY
**COOKERS** > COOKER
**COOKERY** *n* art of cooking
**COOKEY** *same as* > COOKIE

**COOKEYS** > COOKEY
**COOKHOUSE** *n* place for cooking, esp a camp kitchen
**COOKIE** *n* biscuit
**COOKIES** > COOKIE
**COOKING** > COOK
**COOKINGS** > COOK
**COOKLESS** *adj* devoid of a cook
**COOKMAID** *n* maid who assists a cook
**COOKMAIDS** > COOKMAID
**COOKOFF** *n* cookery competition
**COOKOFFS** > COOKOFF
**COOKOUT** *n* party where a meal is cooked and eaten out of doors
**COOKOUTS** > COOKOUT
**COOKROOM** *n* room in which food is cooked
**COOKROOMS** > COOKROOM
**COOKS** > COOK
**COOKSHACK** *n* makeshift building in which food is cooked
**COOKSHOP** *n* shop that sells cookery equipment
**COOKSHOPS** > COOKSHOP
**COOKSTOVE** *n* stove for cooking
**COOKTOP** *n* flat unit for cooking in saucepans or the top part of a stove
**COOKTOPS** > COOKTOP
**COOKWARE** *n* cooking utensils
**COOKWARES** > COOKWARE
**COOKY** *same as* > COOKIE
**COOL** *adj* moderately cold ▷ *vb* make or become cool ▷ *n* coolness
**COOLABAH** *n* Australian myrtaceous tree, *Eucalyptus microtheca*, that grows along rivers and has smooth bark and long narrow leaves
**COOLABAHS** > COOLABAH
**COOLAMON** *n* shallow dish of wood or bark, used for carrying water
**COOLAMONS** > COOLAMON
**COOLANT** *n* fluid used to cool machinery while it is working
**COOLANTS** > COOLANT
**COOLDOWN** *n* gentle stretching exercises after strenuous activity, to allow the heart rate gradually to return to normal
**COOLDOWNS** > COOLDOWN
**COOLED** > COOL
**COOLER** *n* container for making or keeping things cool
**COOLERS** > COOLER
**COOLEST** > COOL
**COOLHOUSE** *n* greenhouse in which a cool temperature is

maintained
**COOLIBAH** *same as* > COOLABAH
**COOLIBAHS** > COOLIBAH
**COOLIBAR** *same as* > COOLABAH
**COOLIBARS** > COOLIBAR
**COOLIE** *n* unskilled Oriental labourer
**COOLIES** > COOLIE
**COOLING** > COOL
**COOLINGLY** > COOL
**COOLISH** > COOL
**COOLLY** > COOL
**COOLNESS** > COOL
**COOLS** > COOL
**COOLTH** *n* coolness
**COOLTHS** > COOLTH
**COOLY** *same as* > COOLIE
**COOM** *n* waste material, such as dust from coal, grease from axles, etc ▷ *vb* to blacken
**COOMB** *same as* > COMB
**COOMBE** *same as* > COMB
**COOMBES** > COOMBE
**COOMBS** > COOMB
**COOMED** > COOM
**COOMIER** > COOMY
**COOMIEST** > COOMY
**COOMING** > COOM
**COOMS** > COOM
**COOMY** *adj* grimy
**COON** *n* raccoon
**COONCAN** *n* card game for two players, similar to rummy
**COONCANS** > COONCAN
**COONDOG** *n* dog trained to hunt raccoons
**COONDOGS** > COONDOG
**COONHOUND** *n* dog for hunting raccoons
**COONS** > COON
**COONSKIN** *n* pelt of a raccoon
**COONSKINS** > COONSKIN
**COONTIE** *n* evergreen plant, *Zamia floridana* of S Florida, related to the cycads and having large dark green leathery leaves: family *Zamiaceae*
**COONTIES** > COONTIE
**COONTY** *same as* > COONTIE
**COOP** *n* cage or pen for poultry ▷ *vb* confine in a restricted area
**COOPED** > COOP
**COOPER** *n* person who makes or repairs barrels ▷ *vb* make or mend (barrels, casks, etc)
**COOPERAGE** *n* craft, place of work, or products of a cooper
**COOPERATE** *vb* work or act together
**COOPERED** > COOPER
**COOPERIES** > COOPERY
**COOPERING** > COOPER
**COOPERS** > COOPER
**COOPERY** *same as* > COOPERAGE

**COOPING** > COOP
**COOPS** > COOP
**COOPT** *vb* add (someone) to a group by the agreement of the existing members
**COOPTED** > COOPT
**COOPTING** > COOPT
**COOPTION** > COOPT
**COOPTIONS** > COOPT
**COOPTS** > COOPT
**COORDINAL** *adj* (of animals or plants) belonging to the same order
**COORIE** *same as* > COURIE
**COORIED** > COORIE
**COORIEING** > COORIE
**COORIES** > COORIE
**COOS** > COO
**COOSEN** *same as* > COZEN
**COOSENED** > COOSEN
**COOSENING** > COOSEN
**COOSENS** > COOSEN
**COOSER** *n* stallion
**COOSERS** > COOSER
**COOSIN** *same as* > COZEN
**COOSINED** > COOSIN
**COOSINING** > COOSIN
**COOSINS** > COOSIN
**COOST** *Scots form of* > CAST
**COOT** *n* small black water bird
**COOTCH** *n* hiding place ▷ *vb* hide
**COOTCHED** > COOTCH
**COOTCHES** > COOTCH
**COOTCHING** > COOTCH
**COOTER** *n* type of freshwater turtle
**COOTERS** > COOTER
**COOTIE** *same as* > LOUSE
**COOTIES** > COOTIE
**COOTIKIN** *n* gaiter
**COOTIKINS** > COOTIKIN
**COOTS** > COOT
**COOZE** *n* US and Canadian taboo slang word for the female genitals
**COOZES** > COOZE
**COP** *same as* > COPPER
**COPACETIC** *adj* very good
**COPAIBA** *n* transparent yellowish viscous oleoresin obtained from certain tropical South American trees of the leguminous genus *Copaifera*: used in varnishes and ointments
**COPAIBAS** > COPAIBA
**COPAIVA** *same as* > COPAIBA
**COPAIVAS** > COPAIVA
**COPAL** *n* resin used in varnishes
**COPALM** *n* aromatic brown resin obtained from the sweet gum tree
**COPALMS** > COPALM
**COPALS** > COPAL
**COPARCENY** *n* form of joint ownership of property
**COPARENT** *n* fellow parent
**COPARENTS** > COPARENT
**COPARTNER** *n* partner or associate

COPASETIC same as > COPACETIC
COPASTOR n fellow pastor
COPASTORS > COPASTOR
COPATAINE adj (of a hat) high-crowned
COPATRIOT n fellow patriot
COPATRON n fellow patron
COPATRONS > COPATRON
COPAY n amount payable for treatment by person with medical insurance
COPAYMENT n fee paid for medical insurance
COPAYS > COPAY
COPE vb deal successfully (with) ▷ n large ceremonial cloak worn by some Christian priests
COPECK same as > KOPECK
COPECKS > COPECK
COPED > COPE
COPEMATE n partner
COPEMATES > COPEMATE
COPEN n shade of blue
COPENS > COPEN
COPEPOD n any minute free-living or parasitic crustacean of the subclass Copepoda of marine and fresh waters: an important constituent of plankton ▷ adj of, relating to, or belonging to the Copepoda
COPEPODS > COPEPOD
COPER n horse-dealer ▷ vb to smuggle liquor to deep-sea fishermen
COPERED > COPER
COPERING > COPER
COPERS > COPER
COPES > COPE
COPESETIC same as > COPACETIC
COPESTONE same as > CAPSTONE
COPIED > COPY
COPIER n machine that copies
COPIERS > COPIER
COPIES > COPY
COPIHUE n Chilean bellflower
COPIHUES > COPIHUE
COPILOT n second pilot of an aircraft
COPILOTS > COPILOT
COPING n sloping top row of a wall
COPINGS > COPING
COPIOUS adj abundant, plentiful
COPIOUSLY > COPIOUS
COPITA n tulip-shaped sherry glass
COPITAS > COPITA
COPLANAR adj lying in the same plane
COPLOT vb plot together
COPLOTS > COPLOT
COPLOTTED > COPLOT
COPOLYMER n chemical compound of high molecular weight formed

by uniting the molecules of two or more different compounds (monomers)
COPOUT n act of avoiding responsibility
COPOUTS > COPOUT
COPPED > COPPER
COPPER n soft reddish-brown metal ▷ adj reddish-brown ▷ vb coat or cover with copper
COPPERAH same as > COPRA
COPPERAHS > COPPERAH
COPPERAS n ferrous sulphate
COPPERED > COPPER
COPPERING > COPPER
COPPERISH adj copper-like
COPPERS > COPPER
COPPERY > COPPER
COPPICE n small group of trees growing close together ▷ vb trim back (trees or bushes) to form a coppice
COPPICED > COPPICE
COPPICES > COPPICE
COPPICING > COPPICE
COPPIES > COPPY
COPPIN n ball of thread
COPPING > COPPER
COPPINS > COPPIN
COPPLE n hill rising to a point
COPPLES > COPPLE
COPPRA same as > COPRA
COPPRAS > COPPRA
COPPY n small wooden stool
COPRA n dried oil-yielding kernel of the coconut
COPRAH same as > COPRA
COPRAHS > COPRAH
COPRAS > COPRA
COPREMIA n poisoning due to chronic constipation
COPREMIAS > COPREMIA
COPREMIC > COPREMIA
COPRESENT vb to present jointly
COPRINCE n fellow prince
COPRINCES > COPRINCE
COPRODUCE vb to produce jointly
COPRODUCT n joint product
COPROLITE n any of various rounded stony nodules thought to be the fossilized faeces of Palaeozoic-Cenozoic vertebrates
COPROLITH n hard stony mass of dried faeces
COPROLOGY n preoccupation with excrement
COPROSMA n any shrub of the Australasian rubiaceous genus Coprosma: sometimes planted for ornament
COPROSMAS > COPROSMA
COPROZOIC adj (of animals) living in dung

COPS > COPPER
COPSE same as > COPPICE vb to trim back (trees) to form a copse
COPSED > COPSE
COPSES > COPSE
COPSEWOOD n brushwood
COPSHOP n police station
COPSHOPS > COPSHOP
COPSIER > COPSY
COPSIEST > COPSY
COPSING > COPSE
COPSY adj having copses
COPTER n helicopter
COPTERS > COPTER
COPUBLISH vb to publish jointly
COPULA n verb used to link the subject and complement of a sentence, e.g. become in they become chums
COPULAE > COPULA
COPULAR > COPULA
COPULAS > COPULA
COPULATE vb have sexual intercourse
COPULATED > COPULATE
COPULATES > COPULATE
COPURIFY vb to purify together
COPY n thing made to look exactly like another ▷ vb make a copy of
COPYABLE > COPY
COPYBOOK n book of specimens for imitation
COPYBOOKS > COPYBOOK
COPYBOY n formerly, in journalism, boy who carried copy and ran errands
COPYBOYS > COPYBOY
COPYCAT n person who imitates or copies someone ▷ vb to imitate with great attention to detail
COPYCATS > COPYCAT
COPYDESK n desk where newspaper copy is edited
COPYDESKS > COPYDESK
COPYEDIT vb prepare text for printing by styling, correcting, etc
COPYEDITS > COPYEDIT
COPYGIRL n female copyboy
COPYGIRLS > COPYGIRL
COPYGRAPH n process for copying type
COPYHOLD n tenure less than freehold of land in England evidenced by a copy of the Court roll
COPYHOLDS > COPYHOLD
COPYING > COPY
COPYISM n slavish copying
COPYISMS > COPYISM
COPYIST n person who makes written copies
COPYISTS > COPYIST
COPYLEFT n permission to use something free of

charge
COPYLEFTS > COPYLEFT
COPYREAD vb subedit
COPYREADS > COPYREAD
COPYRIGHT n exclusive legal right to reproduce and control a book, work of art, etc ▷ vb take out a copyright on ▷ adj protected by copyright
COPYTAKER n (esp in a newspaper office) a person employed to type reports as journalists dictate them over the telephone
COQUET vb behave flirtatiously
COQUETRY n flirtation
COQUETS > COQUET
COQUETTE n woman who flirts
COQUETTED > COQUET
COQUETTES > COQUETTE
COQUILLA n type of South American nut
COQUILLAS > COQUILLA
COQUILLE n any dish, esp seafood, served in a scallop shell
COQUILLES > COQUILLE
COQUINA n soft limestone consisting of shells, corals, etc, that occurs in parts of the US
COQUINAS > COQUINA
COQUITO n Chilean palm tree, Jubaea spectabilis, yielding edible nuts and a syrup
COQUITOS > COQUITO
COR interj exclamation of surprise, amazement, or admiration
CORACLE n small round boat of wicker covered with skins
CORACLES > CORACLE
CORACOID n paired ventral bone of the pectoral girdle in vertebrates
CORACOIDS > CORACOID
CORAGGIO interj exhortation to hold one's nerve
CORAGGIOS > CORAGGIO
CORAL n hard substance formed from the skeletons of very small sea animals ▷ adj orange-pink
CORALLA > CORALLUM
CORALLINE adj of, relating to, or resembling coral ▷ n any of various red algae impregnated with calcium carbonate, esp any of the genus Corallina
CORALLITE n skeleton of a coral polyp
CORALLOID same as > CORALLINE
CORALLUM n skeleton of any zoophyte
CORALROOT n any N temperate leafless orchid

of the genus *Corallorhiza*, with small yellow-green or purple flowers and branched roots resembling coral

**CORALS** > CORAL

**CORALWORT** *n* coralroot or toothwort

**CORAM** *prep* before, in the presence of

**CORAMINE** *n* drug which is a circulatory stimulant

**CORAMINES** > CORAMINE

**CORANACH** *same as* > CORONACH

**CORANACHS** > CORANACH

**CORANTO** *same as* > COURANTE

**CORANTOES** > CORANTO

**CORANTOS** > CORANTO

**CORBAN** *n* gift to God

**CORBANS** > CORBAN

**CORBE** *obsolete variant of* > CORBEL

**CORBEAU** *n* blackish green colour

**CORBEAUS** > CORBEAU

**CORBEIL** *n* carved ornament in the form of a basket of fruit, flowers, etc

**CORBEILLE** *same as* > CORBEIL

**CORBEILS** > CORBEIL

**CORBEL** *n* stone or timber support sticking out of a wall ▷ *vb* lay (a stone or brick) so that it forms a corbel

**CORBELED** > CORBEL

**CORBELING** *n* set of corbels stepped outwards, one above another

**CORBELLED** > CORBEL

**CORBELS** > CORBEL

**CORBES** > CORBE

**CORBICULA** *n* pollen basket

**CORBIE** *n* raven or crow

**CORBIES** > CORBIE

**CORBINA** *n* type of North American whiting

**CORBINAS** > CORBINA

**CORBY** *same as* > CORBIE

**CORCASS** *n* in Ireland, marshland

**CORCASSES** > CORCASS

**CORD** *n* thin rope or thick string ▷ *adj* (of fabric) ribbed ▷ *vb* bind or furnish with a cord or cords

**CORDAGE** *n* lines and rigging of a vessel

**CORDAGES** > CORDAGE

**CORDATE** *adj* heart-shaped

**CORDATELY** > CORDATE

**CORDED** *adj* tied or fastened with cord

**CORDELLE** *vb* to tow

**CORDELLED** > CORDELLE

**CORDELLES** > CORDELLE

**CORDER** > CORD

**CORDERS** > CORD

**CORDGRASS** *n* type of coarse grass

**CORDIAL** *adj* warm and friendly ▷ *n* drink with a fruit base

**CORDIALLY** > CORDIAL

**CORDIALS** > CORDIAL

**CORDIFORM** *adj* heart-shaped

**CORDINER** *n* shoemaker

**CORDINERS** > CORDINER

**CORDING** > CORD

**CORDINGS** > CORD

**CORDITE** *n* explosive used in guns and bombs

**CORDITES** > CORDITE

**CORDLESS** *adj* (of an electrical appliance) powered by an internal battery, so that there is no cable connecting the appliance itself to the electrical mains

**CORDLIKE** > CORD

**CORDOBA** *n* standard monetary unit of Nicaragua, divided into 100 centavos

**CORDOBAS** > CORDOBA

**CORDON** *n* chain of police, soldiers, etc, guarding an area ▷ *vb* put or form a cordon (around)

**CORDONED** > CORDON

**CORDONING** > CORDON

**CORDONNET** *n* type of thread

**CORDONS** > CORDON

**CORDOTOMY** *n* method of pain relief in which nerves are cut > CHORDOTOMY

**CORDOVAN** *n* fine leather now made principally from horsehide, isolated from the skin layers above and below it and tanned

**CORDOVANS** > CORDOVAN

**CORDS** *pl n* trousers made of corduroy

**CORDUROY** *n* cotton fabric with a velvety ribbed surface

**CORDUROYS** *pl n* trousers made of corduroy

**CORDWAIN** *an archaic name for* > CORDOVAN

**CORDWAINS** > CORDWAIN

**CORDWOOD** *n* wood that has been cut into lengths of four feet so that it can be stacked in cords

**CORDWOODS** > CORDWOOD

**CORDYLINE** *n* any tree of the genus Cordyline

**CORE** *n* central part of certain fruits, containing the seeds ▷ *vb* remove the core from

**CORED** > CORE

**COREDEEM** *vb* to redeem together

**COREDEEMS** > COREDEEM

**COREGENT** *n* joint regent

**COREGENTS** > COREGENT

**COREIGN** *vb* to reign jointly

**COREIGNS** > COREIGN

**CORELATE** *same as* > CORRELATE

**CORELATED** > CORELATE

**CORELATES** > CORELATE

**CORELESS** > CORE

**CORELLA** *n* white Australian cockatoo

**CORELLAS** > CORELLA

**COREMIA** > COREMIUM

**COREMIUM** *n* spore-producing organ of certain fungi

**COREOPSIS** *n* any plant of the genus *Coreopsis*, of America and tropical Africa, cultivated for their yellow, brown, or yellow-and-red daisy-like flowers: family *Asteraceae* (composites)

**CORER** > CORE

**CORERS** > CORE

**CORES** > CORE

**COREY** *n* slang word for the penis

**COREYS** > COREY

**CORF** *n* wagon or basket used formerly in mines

**CORFHOUSE** *n* shed used for curing salmon and storing nets

**CORGI** *n* short-legged sturdy dog

**CORGIS** > CORGI

**CORIA** > CORIUM

**CORIANDER** *n* plant grown for its aromatic seeds and leaves

**CORIES** > CORY

**CORING** > CORE

**CORIOUS** *adj* leathery

**CORIUM** *n* deep inner layer of the skin, beneath the epidermis, containing connective tissue, blood vessels, and fat

**CORIUMS** > CORIUM

**CORIVAL** *same as* > CORRIVAL

**CORIVALRY** > CORIVAL

**CORIVALS** > CORIVAL

**CORIXID** *n* type of water bug

**CORIXIDS** > CORIXID

**CORK** *n* thick light bark of a Mediterranean oak ▷ *vb* seal with a cork ▷ *adj* made of cork

**CORKAGE** *n* restaurant's charge for serving wine bought elsewhere

**CORKAGES** > CORKAGE

**CORKBOARD** *n* thin slab made of granules of cork, used as a floor or wall finish and as an insulator

**CORKBORER** *n* tool for cutting a hole in a stopper to insert a glass tube

**CORKED** *adj* (of wine) spoiled through having a decayed cork

**CORKER** *n* splendid or outstanding person or thing

**CORKERS** > CORKER

**CORKIER** > CORKY

**CORKIEST** > CORKY

**CORKINESS** > CORKY

**CORKING** *adj* excellent

**CORKIR** *n* lichen from which red or purple dye is made

**CORKIRS** > CORKIR

**CORKLIKE** > CORK

**CORKS** > CORK

**CORKSCREW** *n* spiral metal tool for pulling corks from bottles ▷ *adj* like a corkscrew in shape ▷ *vb* move in a spiral or zigzag course

**CORKTREE** *n* type of evergreen oak tree

**CORKTREES** > CORKTREE

**CORKWING** *n* greenish or bluish European fish of the wrasse family, *Ctenolabrus melops*

**CORKWINGS** > CORKWING

**CORKWOOD** *n* small tree, *Leitneria floridana*, of the southeastern US, having very lightweight porous wood: family *Leitneriaceae*

**CORKWOODS** > CORKWOOD

**CORKY** *same as* > CORKED

**CORM** *n* bulblike underground stem of certain plants

**CORMEL** *n* new small corm arising from the base of a fully developed one

**CORMELS** > CORMEL

**CORMIDIA** > CORMIDIUM

**CORMIDIUM** *n* iteration of the repeating zooid pattern in a siphosome

**CORMLIKE** *adj* resembling a corm

**CORMOID** *adj* like a corm

**CORMORANT** *n* large dark-coloured long-necked sea bird

**CORMOUS** > CORM

**CORMS** > CORM

**CORMUS** *n* corm

**CORMUSES** > CORMUS

**CORN** *n* cereal plant such as wheat or oats ▷ *vb* feed (animals) with corn, esp oats

**CORNACRE** *same as* > CONACRE

**CORNACRES** > CORNACRE

**CORNAGE** *n* rent fixed according to the number of horned cattle pastured

**CORNAGES** > CORNAGE

**CORNBALL** *n* person given to mawkish or unsophisticated behaviour

**CORNBALLS** > CORNBALL

**CORNBORER** *n* larva of the pyralid moth

**CORNBRAID** *vb* braid hair in cornrows

**CORNBRASH** n type of limestone which produces good soil for growing corn
**CORNBREAD** n bread made from maize meal
**CORNCAKE** n kind of cornmeal flatbread
**CORNCAKES** > CORNCAKE
**CORNCOB** n core of an ear of maize, to which the kernels are attached
**CORNCOBS** > CORNCOB
**CORNCRAKE** n brown Eurasian bird with a harsh cry
**CORNCRIB** n ventilated building for the storage of unhusked maize
**CORNCRIBS** > CORNCRIB
**CORNEA** n transparent membrane covering the eyeball
**CORNEAE** > CORNEA
**CORNEAL** > CORNEA
**CORNEAS** > CORNEA
**CORNED** adj (esp of beef) cooked and then preserved or pickled in salt or brine, now often canned
**CORNEITIS** n inflammation of cornea
**CORNEL** n any cornaceous plant of the genus Cornus, such as the dogwood and dwarf cornel
**CORNELIAN** same as > CARNELIAN
**CORNELS** > CORNEL
**CORNEMUSE** n French bagpipe
**CORNEOUS** adj horny
**CORNER** n area or angle where two converging lines or surfaces meet ▷ vb force into a difficult or inescapable position
**CORNERED** > CORNER
**CORNERING** > CORNER
**CORNERMAN** n in baseball, first baseman
**CORNERMEN** > CORNERMAN
**CORNERS** > CORNER
**CORNET** same as > CORNETT
**CORNETCY** n commission or rank of a cornet
**CORNETIST** n person who plays the cornet
**CORNETS** > CORNET
**CORNETT** n musical instrument consisting of a straight or curved tube of wood or ivory having finger holes like a recorder and a cup-shaped mouthpiece like a trumpet
**CORNETTI** > CORNETTO
**CORNETTO** same as > CORNETT
**CORNETTS** > CORNETT
**CORNFED** adj fed on corn
**CORNFIELD** n field planted with cereal crops
**CORNFLAG** n gladiolus
**CORNFLAGS** > CORNFLAG

**CORNFLAKE** n singular form of plural cornflakes: toasted flakes made from cornmeal, sold as a breakfast cereal
**CORNFLIES** > CORNFLY
**CORNFLOUR** n fine maize flour
**CORNFLY** n small fly whose larvae cause swollen, gouty stems in cereal crops
**CORNHUSK** n outer protective covering of an ear of maize
**CORNHUSKS** > CORNHUSK
**CORNI** > CORNO
**CORNICE** n decorative moulding round the top of a wall ▷ vb furnish or decorate with or as if with a cornice
**CORNICED** > CORNICE
**CORNICES** > CORNICE
**CORNICHE** n coastal road, esp one built into the face of a cliff
**CORNICHES** > CORNICHE
**CORNICHON** n type of small gherkin
**CORNICING** > CORNICE
**CORNICLE** n wax-secreting organ on an aphid's abdomen
**CORNICLES** > CORNICLE
**CORNICULA** n plural form of singular corniculum: small horn
**CORNIER** > CORNY
**CORNIEST** > CORNY
**CORNIFIC** adj producing horns
**CORNIFIED** > CORNIFY
**CORNIFIES** > CORNIFY
**CORNIFORM** adj horn-shaped
**CORNIFY** vb turn soft tissue hard
**CORNILY** > CORNY
**CORNINESS** > CORNY
**CORNING** > CORN
**CORNIST** n horn-player
**CORNISTS** > CORNIST
**CORNLAND** n land suitable for growing corn or grain
**CORNLANDS** > CORNLAND
**CORNLOFT** n loft for storing corn
**CORNLOFTS** > CORNLOFT
**CORNMEAL** n meal made from maize
**CORNMEALS** > CORNMEAL
**CORNMILL** n flour mill
**CORNMILLS** > CORNMILL
**CORNMOTH** n moth whose larvae feed on grain
**CORNMOTHS** > CORNMOTH
**CORNO** n French horn
**CORNOPEAN** n cornet (the brass musical instrument)
**CORNPIPE** n musical instrument made from a stalk of corn etc
**CORNPIPES** > CORNPIPE
**CORNPONE** n American corn

bread
**CORNPONES** > CORNPONE
**CORNRENT** n rent paid in corn, rather than money
**CORNRENTS** > CORNRENT
**CORNROW** n hairstyle in which the hair is plaited in close parallel rows ▷ vb style the hair in a cornrow
**CORNROWED** > CORNROW
**CORNROWS** > CORNROW
**CORNS** > CORN
**CORNSTALK** n stalk or stem of corn
**CORNSTONE** n mottled green and red limestone
**CORNU** n part or structure resembling a horn or having a hornlike pattern, such as a cross section of the grey matter of the spinal cord
**CORNUA** > CORNU
**CORNUAL** > CORNU
**CORNUS** n any member of the genus Cornus, such as dogwood
**CORNUSES** > CORNUS
**CORNUTE** adj having or resembling cornua ▷ vb to make a cuckold of
**CORNUTED** same as > CORNUTE
**CORNUTES** > CORNUTE
**CORNUTING** > CORNUTE
**CORNUTO** n cuckold
**CORNUTOS** > CORNUTO
**CORNWORM** n cornmoth larva
**CORNWORMS** > CORNWORM
**CORNY** adj unoriginal or oversentimental
**COROCORE** same as > COROCORO
**COROCORES** > COROCORE
**COROCORO** n South Asian vessel fitted with outriggers
**COROCOROS** > COROCORO
**CORODIES** > CORODY
**CORODY** n (originally) the right of a lord to receive free quarters from his vassal
**COROLLA** n petals of a flower collectively
**COROLLARY** n idea, fact, or proposition which is the natural result of something else ▷ adj consequent or resultant
**COROLLAS** > COROLLA
**COROLLATE** adj having a corolla
**COROLLINE** adj relating to a corolla
**CORONA** n ring of light round the moon or sun
**CORONACH** n dirge or lamentation for the dead
**CORONACHS** > CORONACH
**CORONAE** > CORONA
**CORONAL** n circlet for the head ▷ adj of or relating to

a corona or coronal
**CORONALLY** > CORONAL
**CORONALS** > CORONAL
**CORONARY** adj of the arteries surrounding the heart ▷ n coronary thrombosis
**CORONAS** > CORONA
**CORONATE** vb to crown
**CORONATED** > CORONATE
**CORONATES** > CORONATE
**CORONEL** n iron head of a tilting spear
**CORONELS** > CORONEL
**CORONER** n official responsible for the investigation of violent, sudden, or suspicious deaths
**CORONERS** > CORONER
**CORONET** n small crown
**CORONETED** adj wearing a coronet
**CORONETS** > CORONET
**CORONIS** n in Greek grammar, symbol placed over a contracted syllable
**CORONISES** > CORONIS
**CORONIUM** n highly-ionized iron and nickel seen as a green line in the solar coronal spectrum
**CORONIUMS** > CORONIUM
**CORONOID** adj crown-shaped
**COROTATE** vb to rotate together
**COROTATED** > COROTATE
**COROTATES** > COROTATE
**COROZO** n tropical American palm, Corozo oleifera, whose seeds yield a useful oil
**COROZOS** > COROZO
**CORPORA** > CORPUS
**CORPORAL** n noncommissioned officer in an army ▷ adj of the body
**CORPORALE** same as > CORPORAL
**CORPORALS** > CORPORAL
**CORPORAS** n communion cloth
**CORPORATE** adj of business corporations
**CORPOREAL** adj physical or tangible
**CORPORIFY** vb to embody
**CORPOSANT** n Saint Elmo's fire
**CORPS** n military unit with a specific function
**CORPSE** n dead body ▷ vb laugh or cause to laugh involuntarily or inopportunely while on stage
**CORPSED** > CORPSE
**CORPSES** > CORPSE
**CORPSING** > CORPSE
**CORPSMAN** n medical orderly or stretcher-bearer
**CORPSMEN** > CORPSMAN

CORPULENT *adj* fat or plump

CORPUS *n* collection of writings, esp by a single author

CORPUSCLE *n* red or white blood cell

CORPUSES > CORPUS

CORRADE *vb* (of rivers, streams, etc) to erode (land) by the abrasive action of rock particles

CORRADED > CORRADE

CORRADES > CORRADE

CORRADING > CORRADE

CORRAL *n* enclosure for cattle or horses ▷ *vb* put in a corral

CORRALLED > CORRAL

CORRALS > CORRAL

CORRASION *n* erosion of rocks caused by fragments transported over them by water, wind, or ice

CORRASIVE > CORRASION

CORREA *n* Australian evergreen shrub of the genus *Correa*, with large showy tubular flowers

CORREAS > CORREA

CORRECT *adj* free from error, true ▷ *vb* put right

CORRECTED > CORRECT

CORRECTER > CORRECT

CORRECTLY > CORRECT

CORRECTOR > CORRECT

CORRECTS > CORRECT

CORRELATE *vb* place or be placed in a mutual relationship ▷ *n* either of two things mutually related ▷ *adj* having a mutual, complementary, or reciprocal relationship

CORRIDA *the Spanish word for* > BULLFIGHT

CORRIDAS > CORRIDA

CORRIDOR *n* passage in a building or train

CORRIDORS > CORRIDOR

CORRIE *same as* > CIRQUE

CORRIES > CORRIE

CORRIGENT *n* corrective

CORRIVAL *a rare word for* > RIVAL *vb* to vie

CORRIVALS > CORRIVAL

CORRODANT > CORRODE

CORRODE *vb* eat or be eaten away by chemical action or rust

CORRODED > CORRODE

CORRODENT > CORRODE

CORRODER > CORRODE

CORRODERS > CORRODE

CORRODES > CORRODE

CORRODIES > CORRODY

CORRODING > CORRODE

CORRODY *same as* > CORODY

CORROSION *n* process by which something, esp a metal, is corroded

CORROSIVE *adj* (esp of acids or alkalis) capable of destroying solid materials

▷ *n* corrosive substance, such as a strong acid or alkali

CORRUGATE *vb* fold into alternate grooves and ridges ▷ *adj* folded into furrows and ridges

CORRUPT *adj* open to or involving bribery ▷ *vb* make corrupt

CORRUPTED > CORRUPT

CORRUPTER > CORRUPT

CORRUPTLY > CORRUPT

CORRUPTOR > CORRUPT

CORRUPTS > CORRUPT

CORS > COR

CORSAC *n* fox, *Vulpes corsac*, of central Asia

CORSACS > CORSAC

CORSAGE *n* small bouquet worn on the bodice of a dress

CORSAGES > CORSAGE

CORSAIR *n* pirate

CORSAIRS > CORSAIR

CORSE *n* corpse

CORSELET *n* one-piece undergarment combining a corset and bra

CORSELETS > CORSELET

CORSES > CORSE

CORSET *n* women's close-fitting undergarment worn to shape the torso ▷ *vb* dress or enclose in, or as in, a corset

CORSETED > CORSET

CORSETIER *n* man who makes and fits corsets

CORSETING > CORSET

CORSETRY *n* making of or dealing in corsets

CORSETS > CORSET

CORSEY *n* pavement or pathway

CORSEYS > CORSEY

CORSIVE *n* corrodent

CORSIVES > CORSIVE

CORSLET *same as* > CORSELET

CORSLETED > CORSLET

CORSLETS > CORSLET

CORSNED *n* ordeal whereby an accused person had to eat a morsel of bread; swallowing it freely indicated innocence; choking, guilt

CORSNEDS > CORSNED

CORSO *n* promenade

CORSOS > CORSO

CORTEGE *n* funeral procession

CORTEGES > CORTEGE

CORTEX *n* outer layer of the brain or other internal organ

CORTEXES > CORTEX

CORTICAL > CORTEX

CORTICATE *adj* (of plants, seeds, etc) having a bark, husk, or rind

CORTICES > CORTEX

CORTICOID *n* steroid hormone

CORTICOSE *adj* consisting of or like bark

CORTILE *n* open, internal courtyard

CORTILI > CORTILE

CORTIN *n* adrenal cortex extract containing cortisone and other hormones

CORTINA *n* weblike part of certain mushrooms

CORTINAS > CORTINA

CORTINS > CORTIN

CORTISOL *n* principal glucocorticoid secreted by the adrenal cortex

CORTISOLS > CORTISOL

CORTISONE *n* steroid hormone used to treat various diseases

CORULER *n* joint ruler

CORULERS > CORULER

CORUNDUM *n* hard mineral used as an abrasive

CORUNDUMS > CORUNDUM

CORUSCANT *adj* giving off flashes of light

CORUSCATE *vb* sparkle

CORVEE *n* day's unpaid labour owed by a feudal vassal to his lord

CORVEES > CORVEE

CORVES > CORF

CORVET *same as* > CURVET

CORVETED > CORVET

CORVETING > CORVET

CORVETS > CORVET

CORVETTE *n* lightly armed escort warship ▷ *vb* to participate in social activities with fellow Corvette car enthusiasts

CORVETTED > CORVETTE

CORVETTES > CORVETTE

CORVID *n* any member of the crow family

CORVIDS > CORVID

CORVINA *same as* > CORBINA

CORVINAS > CORVINA

CORVINE *adj* of, relating to, or resembling a crow

CORVUS *n* type of ancient hook

CORVUSES > CORVUS

CORY *n* catfish belonging to the South American Corydoras genus

CORYBANT *n* wild attendant of the goddess Cybele

CORYBANTS > CORYBANT

CORYDALIS *n* any erect or climbing plant of the N temperate genus *Corydalis*, having finely-lobed leaves and spurred yellow or pinkish flowers: family Fumariaceae

CORYLUS *n* hazel genus

CORYLUSES > CORYLUS

CORYMB *n* flat-topped flower cluster with the stems growing progressively shorter

towards the centre ▷ *vb* be corymb-like

CORYMBED > CORYMB

CORYMBOSE > CORYMB

CORYMBOUS > CORYMB

CORYMBS > CORYMB

CORYPHAEI *n* plural form of singular coryphaeus: leader of the chorus

CORYPHE *n* coryphaeus

CORYPHEE *n* leading dancer of a corps de ballet

CORYPHEES > CORYPHEE

CORYPHENE *n* any fish of the genus Coryphaena

CORYPHES > CORYPHE

CORYZA *n* acute inflammation of the mucous membrane of the nose, with discharge of mucus

CORYZAL > CORYZA

CORYZAS > CORYZA

COS *same as* > COSINE

COSCRIPT *vb* to script jointly

COSCRIPTS > COSCRIPT

COSE *vb* get cosy

COSEC *same as* > COSECANT

COSECANT *n* (in trigonometry) the ratio of the length of the hypotenuse to that of the opposite side in a right-angled triangle

COSECANTS > COSECANT

COSECH *n* hyperbolic cosecant

COSECHS > COSECH

COSECS > COSEC

COSED > COSE

COSEISMAL *adj* of or designating points at which earthquake waves are felt at the same time ▷ *n* such a line on a map

COSEISMIC *same as* > COSEISMAL

COSES > COSE

COSET *n* mathematical set

COSETS > COSET

COSEY *n* tea cosy

COSEYS > COSEY

COSH *n* heavy blunt weapon ▷ *vb* hit with a cosh

COSHED > COSH

COSHER *vb* pamper or coddle

COSHERED > COSHER

COSHERER > COSHER

COSHERERS > COSHER

COSHERIES > COSHERY

COSHERING > COSHER

COSHERS > COSHER

COSHERY *n* Irish chief's right to lodge at his tenants' houses

COSHES > COSH

COSHING > COSH

COSIE *same as* > COSY

COSIED > COSY

COSIER *n* cobbler

COSIERS > COSIER

COSIES > COSY

**COSIEST** > COSY
**COSIGN** vb to sign jointly
**COSIGNED** > COSIGN
**COSIGNER** > COSIGN
**COSIGNERS** > COSIGN
**COSIGNING** > COSIGN
**COSIGNS** > COSIGN
**COSILY** > COSY
**COSINE** n (in trigonometry) ratio of the length of the adjacent side to that of the hypotenuse in a right-angled triangle
**COSINES** > COSINE
**COSINESS** > COSY
**COSING** > COSE
**COSMEA** n plant of the genus Cosmos
**COSMEAS** > COSMEA
**COSMESES** > COSMESIS
**COSMESIS** n aesthetic covering on a prosthesis to make it look more natural
**COSMETIC** n preparation used to improve the appearance of a person's skin ▷ adj improving the appearance only
**COSMETICS** > COSMETIC
**COSMIC** adj of the whole universe
**COSMICAL** > COSMIC
**COSMID** n segment of DNA
**COSMIDS** > COSMID
**COSMIN** same as > COSMINE
**COSMINE** n substance resembling dentine, forming the outer layer of cosmoid scales
**COSMINES** > COSMINE
**COSMINS** > COSMIN
**COSMISM** n Russian cultural and philosophical movement
**COSMISMS** > COSMISM
**COSMIST** > COSMISM
**COSMISTS** > COSMISM
**COSMOCRAT** n ruler of the world
**COSMOGENY** same as > COSMOGONY
**COSMOGONY** n study of the origin of the universe
**COSMOID** adj (of the scales of coelacanths and lungfish) consisting of two inner bony layers and an outer layer of cosmine
**COSMOLINE** n type of petroleum jelly
**COSMOLOGY** n study of the origin and nature of the universe
**COSMONAUT** n Russian name for an astronaut
**COSMORAMA** n lifelike display, using mirrors and lenses, which shows reflections of various views of parts of the world
**COSMOS** n universe
**COSMOSES** > COSMOS
**COSMOTRON** n large type of particle accelerator

**COSPHERED** adj sharing the same sphere
**COSPONSOR** vb to sponsor jointly
**COSS** another name for > KOS
**COSSACK** n Slavonic warrior-peasant who served in the Russian cavalry under the tsars
**COSSACKS** > COSSACK
**COSSES** > COSS
**COSSET** vb pamper ▷ n any pet animal, esp a lamb
**COSSETED** > COSSET
**COSSETING** > COSSET
**COSSETS** > COSSET
**COSSIE** n informal name for a swimming costume
**COSSIES** > COSSIE
**COST** n amount of money, time, labour, etc, required for something ▷ vb have as its cost
**COSTA** n riblike part, such as the midrib of a plant leaf
**COSTAE** > COSTA
**COSTAL** n strengthening rib of an insect's wing
**COSTALGIA** n pain in the ribs
**COSTALLY** > COSTAL
**COSTALS** > COSTAL
**COSTAR** n actor who shares the billing with another ▷ vb share the billing with another actor
**COSTARD** n English variety of apple tree
**COSTARDS** > COSTARD
**COSTARRED** > COSTAR
**COSTARS** > COSTAR
**COSTATE** adj having ribs
**COSTATED** same as > COSTATE
**COSTE** vb to draw near
**COSTEAN** vb to mine for lodes
**COSTEANED** > COSTEAN
**COSTEANS** > COSTEAN
**COSTED** > COST
**COSTER** n person who sells fruit, vegetables etc from a barrow
**COSTERS** > COSTER
**COSTES** > COSTE
**COSTING** > COST
**COSTIVE** adj having or causing constipation
**COSTIVELY** > COSTIVE
**COSTLESS** > COST
**COSTLIER** > COSTLY
**COSTLIEST** > COSTLY
**COSTLY** adj expensive
**COSTMARY** n herbaceous plant, Chrysanthemum balsamita, native to Asia. Its fragrant leaves were used as a seasoning and to flavour ale: family Asteraceae (composites)
**COSTOTOMY** n surgical incision into a rib
**COSTREL** n flask, usually of earthenware or leather

**COSTRELS** > COSTREL
**COSTS** > COST
**COSTUME** n style of dress of a particular place or time, or for a particular activity ▷ vb provide with a costume
**COSTUMED** > COSTUME
**COSTUMER** same as > COSTUMIER
**COSTUMERS** > COSTUMIER
**COSTUMERY** n collective term for costumes
**COSTUMES** > COSTUME
**COSTUMEY** adj (stage) costume-like; unrealistic
**COSTUMIER** n maker or seller of costumes
**COSTUMING** > COSTUME
**COSTUS** n Himalayan herb with an aromatic root
**COSTUSES** > COSTUS
**COSY** adj warm and snug ▷ n cover for keeping things warm ▷ vb to make oneself snug and warm
**COSYING** > COSY
**COT** n baby's bed with high sides ▷ vb entangle or become entangled
**COTAN** same as > COTANGENT
**COTANGENT** n (in trigonometry) the ratio of the length of the adjacent side to that of the opposite side in a right-angled triangle
**COTANS** > COTANGENT
**COTE** same as > COT
**COTEAU** n hillside
**COTEAUX** > COTEAU
**COTED** > COT
**COTELETTE** n cutlet
**COTELINE** n kind of muslin
**COTELINES** > COTELINE
**COTENANCY** > COTENANT
**COTENANT** n person who holds property jointly or in common with others
**COTENANTS** > COTENANT
**COTERIE** n exclusive group, clique
**COTERIES** > COTERIE
**COTES** > COTE
**COTH** n hyperbolic cotangent
**COTHS** > COTH
**COTHURN** same as > COTHURNUS
**COTHURNAL** > COTHURNUS
**COTHURNI** > COTHURNUS
**COTHURNS** > COTHURNUS
**COTHURNUS** n buskin worn in ancient Greek tragedy
**COTICULAR** adj relating to whetstones
**COTIDAL** adj (of a line on a tidal chart) joining points at which high tide occurs simultaneously
**COTILLION** n French formation dance of the 18th century
**COTILLON** same

as > COTILLION
**COTILLONS** > COTILLON
**COTING** > COT
**COTINGA** n any tropical American passerine bird of the family Cotingidae, such as the umbrella bird and the cock-of-the-rock, having a broad slightly hooked bill
**COTINGAS** > COTINGA
**COTININE** n substance used to indicate presence of nicotine
**COTININES** > COTININE
**COTISE** same as > COTTISE
**COTISED** > COTISE
**COTISES** > COTISE
**COTISING** > COTISE
**COTLAND** n grounds that belong to a cotter
**COTLANDS** > COTLAND
**COTQUEAN** n coarse woman
**COTQUEANS** > COTQUEAN
**COTRUSTEE** n fellow trustee
**COTS** > COT
**COTT** same as > COT
**COTTA** n short form of surplice
**COTTABUS** n ancient Greek game involving throwing wine into a vessel
**COTTAE** > COTTA
**COTTAGE** n small house in the country ▷ vb engage in homosexual activity in a public lavatory
**COTTAGED** > COTTAGE
**COTTAGER** n person who lives in a cottage
**COTTAGERS** > COTTAGER
**COTTAGES** > COTTAGE
**COTTAGEY** adj resembling a cottage
**COTTAGING** n homosexual activity between men in a public lavatory
**COTTAR** same as > COTTER
**COTTARS** > COTTAR
**COTTAS** > COTTA
**COTTED** > COT
**COTTER** n pin or wedge used to secure machine parts ▷ vb secure (two parts) with a cotter
**COTTERED** > COTTER
**COTTERING** > COTTER
**COTTERS** > COTTIER
**COTTID** n any fish of the scorpaenoid family Cottidae, typically possessing a large head, tapering body, and spiny fins, including the pogge, sea scorpion, bullhead, father lasher, and cottus
**COTTIDS** > COTTID
**COTTIER** same as > COTTER
**COTTIERS** > COTTIER
**COTTING** > COT
**COTTISE** n type of heraldic decoration ▷ vb (in heraldry) decorate with a

cottise
COTTISED >COTTISE
COTTISES >COTTISE
COTTISING >COTTISE
COTTOID *adj* resembling a fish of the genus Cottus
COTTON *n* white downy fibre covering the seeds of a tropical plant ▷ *vb* take a liking
COTTONADE *n* coarse fabric of cotton or mixed fibres, used for work clothes, etc
COTTONED >COTTON
COTTONING >COTTON
COTTONS >COTTON
COTTONY >COTTON
COTTOWN *Scots variant of* >COTTON
COTTOWNS >COTTON
COTTS >COTT
COTTUS *n* scorpaenoid fish of the family *Cottidae*; the type genus, having four yellowish knobs on its head
COTTUSES >COTTUS
COTURNIX *n* variety of quail
COTWAL *n* Indian police officer
COTWALS >COTWAL
COTYLAE >COTYLE
COTYLE *n* cuplike cavity
COTYLEDON *n* first leaf of a plant embryo
COTYLES >COTYLE
COTYLOID *adj* shaped like a cup ▷ *n* small bone forming part of the acetabular cavity in some mammals
COTYLOIDS >COTYLOID
COTYPE *n* additional type specimen from the same brood as the original type specimen
COTYPES >COTYPE
COUCAL *n* any ground-living bird of the genus *Centropus*, of Africa, S Asia, and Australia, having long strong legs: family *Cuculidae* (cuckoos)
COUCALS >COUCAL
COUCH *n* piece of upholstered furniture for seating more than one person ▷ *vb* express in a particular way
COUCHANT *adj* in a lying position
COUCHE *adj* in heraldry (of a shield), tilted
COUCHED >COUCH
COUCHEE *n* reception held late at night
COUCHEES >COUCHEE
COUCHER >COUCH
COUCHES >COUCH
COUCHETTE *n* bed converted from seats on a train or ship
COUCHING *n* method of

embroidery in which the thread is caught down at intervals by another thread passed through the material from beneath
COUCHINGS >COUCHING
COUDE *adj* (of a reflecting telescope) having plane mirrors positioned to reflect light from the primary mirror along the axis onto a detector
COUGAN *n* drunk and rowdy person
COUGANS >COUGAN
COUGAR *n* puma
COUGARS >COUGAR
COUGH *vb* expel air from the lungs abruptly and noisily ▷ *n* act or sound of coughing
COUGHED >COUGH
COUGHER >COUGH
COUGHERS >COUGH
COUGHING >COUGH
COUGHINGS >COUGH
COUGHS >COUGH
COUGUAR *same as* >COUGAR
COUGUARS >COUGUAR
COULD >CAN
COULDEST *same as* >COULDST
COULDST *vb* form of COULD used with the pronoun *thou* or its relative form
COULEE *n* flow of molten lava
COULEES >COULEE
COULIBIAC *n* Russian fish pie
COULIS *n* thin purée of vegetables or fruit, usually served as a sauce surrounding a dish
COULISSE *n* timber member grooved to take a sliding panel, such as a sluicegate, portcullis, or stage flat
COULISSES >COULISSE
COULOIR *n* deep gully on a mountain side, esp in the French Alps
COULOIRS >COULOIR
COULOMB *n* SI unit of electric charge
COULOMBIC >COULOMB
COULOMBS >COULOMB
COULTER *n* blade at the front of a ploughshare
COULTERS >COULTER
COUMARIC >COUMARIN
COUMARIN *n* white vanilla-scented crystalline ester, used in perfumes and flavourings and as an anticoagulant
COUMARINS >COUMARIN
COUMARONE *n* a colourless insoluble aromatic liquid obtained from coal tar and used in the manufacture of synthetic resins
COUMAROU *n* tonka bean

tree, or its seed
COUMAROUS >COUMAROU
COUNCIL *n* group meeting for discussion or consultation ▷ *adj* of or by a council
COUNCILOR *n* member of a council
COUNCILS >COUNCIL
COUNSEL *n* advice or guidance ▷ *vb* give guidance to
COUNSELED >COUNSEL
COUNSELEE *n* one who is counselled
COUNSELOR *n* person who gives counsel
COUNSELS >COUNSEL
COUNT *vb* say numbers in order ▷ *n* counting
COUNTABLE *adj* capable of being counted
COUNTABLY >COUNTABLE
COUNTBACK *n* system of deciding the winner of a tied competition by comparing earlier points or scores
COUNTDOWN *n* counting backwards to zero of the seconds before an event ▷ *vb* count numbers backwards towards zero, esp in timing such a critical operation
COUNTED >COUNT
COUNTER *n* long flat surface in a bank or shop, on which business is transacted ▷ *vb* oppose, retaliate against ▷ *adv* in the opposite direction
COUNTERED >COUNTER
COUNTERS >COUNTER
COUNTESS *n* woman holding the rank of count or earl
COUNTIAN *n* dweller in a given county
COUNTIANS >COUNTIAN
COUNTIES >COUNTY
COUNTING >COUNT
COUNTLESS *adj* too many to count
COUNTLINE *n* (in confectionery marketing) a chocolate-based bar
COUNTRIES >COUNTRY
COUNTROL *obsolete variant of* >CONTROL
COUNTROLS >COUNTROL
COUNTRY *n* nation
COUNTS >COUNT
COUNTSHIP >COUNT
COUNTY *n* (in some countries) division of a country ▷ *adj* upper-class
COUP *n* successful action ▷ *vb* turn or fall over
COUPE *n* sports car with two doors and a sloping fixed roof
COUPED >COUP
COUPEE *n* (in dance) a

forward movement on one leg, with the other slightly bent and raised
COUPEES >COUPEE
COUPER *n* dealer
COUPERS >COUPER
COUPES >COUPE
COUPING >COUP
COUPLE *n* two people who are married or romantically involved ▷ *vb* connect, associate
COUPLED >COUPLE
COUPLEDOM *n* state of living as a couple, esp when regarded as being interested in each other to the exclusion of the outside world
COUPLER *n* link or rod transmitting power between two rotating mechanisms or a rotating part and a reciprocating part
COUPLERS >COUPLER
COUPLES >COUPLE
COUPLET *n* two consecutive lines of verse, usu. rhyming and of the same metre
COUPLETS >COUPLET
COUPLING *n* device for connecting things, such as railway carriages
COUPLINGS >COUPLING
COUPON *n* piece of paper entitling the holder to a discount or gift
COUPONING *n* in marketing, distribution or redemption of promotional coupons
COUPONS >COUPON
COUPS >COUP
COUPURE *n* entrenchment made by beseiged forces behind a breach in their defences
COUPURES >COUPURE
COUR *obsolete variant of* >COVER
COURAGE *n* ability to face danger or pain without fear
COURAGES >COURAGE
COURANT *n* courante ▷ *adj* (of an animal) running
COURANTE *n* old dance in quick triple time
COURANTES >COURANTE
COURANTO *same as* >COURANTE
COURANTOS >COURANTO
COURANTS >COURANT
COURB *vb* to bend
COURBARIL *n* tropical American leguminous tree, *Hymenaea courbaril*. Its wood is a useful timber and its gum is a source of copal
COURBED >COURB
COURBETTE *same*

**as** > CURVET
**COURBING** > COURB
**COURBS** > COURB
**COURD** *obsolete variant of* > COVERED
**COURE** *obsolete variant of* > COVER
**COURED** > COURE
**COURES** > COURE
**COURGETTE** *n* type of small vegetable marrow
**COURIE** *vb* nestle or snuggle
**COURIED** > COURIE
**COURIEING** > COURIE
**COURIER** *n* person employed to look after holiday-makers ▷ *vb* send (a parcel, letter, etc) by courier
**COURIERS** > COURIER
**COURIES** > COURIE
**COURING** > COUR
**COURLAN** *another name for* > LIMPKIN
**COURLANS** > COURLAN
**COURS** > COUR
**COURSE** *n* series of lessons or medical treatment ▷ *vb* (of liquid) run swiftly
**COURSED** > COURSE
**COURSER** *n* swift horse
**COURSERS** > COURSER
**COURSES** *another word for* > MENSES
**COURSING** *n* hunting with hounds trained to hunt game by sight
**COURSINGS** > COURSING
**COURT** *n* body which decides legal cases ▷ *vb* try to gain the love of
**COURTED** > COURT
**COURTEOUS** *adj* polite
**COURTER** *n* suitor
**COURTERS** > COURTER
**COURTESAN** *n* mistress or high-class prostitute
**COURTESY** *n* politeness, good manners
**COURTEZAN** *same as* > COURTESAN
**COURTIER** *n* attendant at a royal court
**COURTIERS** > COURTIER
**COURTING** > COURT
**COURTINGS** > COURT
**COURTLET** *n* small court
**COURTLETS** > COURTLET
**COURTLIER** > COURTLY
**COURTLIKE** *adj* courtly
**COURTLING** *n* fawning courtier
**COURTLY** *adj* ceremoniously polite
**COURTROOM** *n* room in which the sittings of a law court are held
**COURTS** > COURT
**COURTSHIP** *n* courting of an intended spouse or mate
**COURTSIDE** *n* in sport, area closest to the court

**COURTYARD** *n* paved space enclosed by buildings or walls
**COUSCOUS** *n* type of semolina used in North African cookery
**COUSIN** *n* child of one's uncle or aunt
**COUSINAGE** *n* kinship
**COUSINLY** > COUSIN
**COUSINRY** *n* collective term for cousins
**COUSINS** > COUSIN
**COUTEAU** *n* large two-edged knife used formerly as a weapon
**COUTEAUX** > COUTEAU
**COUTER** *n* armour designed to protect the elbow
**COUTERS** > COUTER
**COUTH** *adj* refined ▷ *n* refinement
**COUTHER** > COUTH
**COUTHEST** > COUTH
**COUTHIE** *adj* sociable
**COUTHIER** > COUTHIE
**COUTHIEST** > COUTHIE
**COUTHS** > COUTH
**COUTHY** *same as* > COUTHIE
**COUTIL** *n* type of tightly-woven twill cloth
**COUTILLE** *same as* > COUTIL
**COUTILLES** > COUTILLE
**COUTILS** > COUTIL
**COUTURE** *n* high-fashion designing and dressmaking ▷ *adj* relating to high fashion design and dress-making
**COUTURES** > COUTURE
**COUTURIER** *n* person who designs women's fashion clothes
**COUVADE** *n* custom in certain cultures of treating the husband of a woman giving birth as if he were bearing the child
**COUVADES** > COUVADE
**COUVERT** *another word for* > COVER
**COUVERTS** > COUVERT
**COUZIN** *n* South African word for a friend
**COUZINS** > COUZIN
**COVALENCE** *same as* > COVALENCY
**COVALENCY** *n* ability to form a bond in which two atoms share a pair of electrons
**COVALENT** > COVALENCY
**COVARIANT** *n* variant that varies leaving certain mathematical relationships it has with another variant (its covariant) unchanged
**COVARIATE** *n* statistical variable
**COVARIED** > COVARY
**COVARIES** > COVARY
**COVARY** *vb* vary together maintaining a

certain mathematical relationship
**COVARYING** > COVARY
**COVE** *n* small bay or inlet ▷ *vb* form an architectural cove in
**COVED** > COVE
**COVELET** *n* small cove
**COVELETS** > COVELET
**COVELLINE** *same as* > COVELLITE
**COVELLITE** *n* indigo copper (blue sulphide of copper)
**COVEN** *n* meeting of witches
**COVENANT** *n* contract ▷ *vb* agree by a covenant
**COVENANTS** > COVENANT
**COVENS** > COVEN
**COVENT** *same as* > CONVENT
**COVENTS** > COVENT
**COVER** *vb* place something over, to protect or conceal ▷ *n* anything that covers
**COVERABLE** > COVER
**COVERAGE** *n* amount or extent covered
**COVERAGES** > COVERAGE
**COVERALL** *n* thing that covers something entirely
**COVERALLS** > COVERALL
**COVERED** > COVER
**COVERER** > COVER
**COVERERS** > COVER
**COVERING** *another word for* > COVER
**COVERINGS** > COVERING
**COVERLESS** > COVER
**COVERLET** *n* bed cover
**COVERLETS** > COVERLET
**COVERLID** *same as* > COVERLET
**COVERLIDS** > COVERLID
**COVERS** > COVER
**COVERSED** as in *coversed sine* obsolete function in trigonometry
**COVERSINE** *n* function in trigonometry
**COVERSLIP** *n* very thin piece of glass placed over a specimen on a glass slide
**COVERT** *adj* concealed, secret ▷ *n* thicket giving shelter to game birds or animals
**COVERTLY** > COVERT
**COVERTS** > COVERT
**COVERTURE** *n* condition or status of a married woman considered as being under the protection and influence of her husband
**COVERUP** *n* concealment of a mistake, crime, etc
**COVERUPS** > COVERUP
**COVES** > COVE
**COVET** *vb* long to possess (what belongs to someone else)
**COVETABLE** > COVET
**COVETED** > COVET
**COVETER** > COVET

**COVETERS** > COVET
**COVETING** > COVET
**COVETISE** *n* covetousness
**COVETISES** > COVETISE
**COVETOUS** *adj* jealously longing to possess something
**COVETS** > COVET
**COVEY** *n* small flock of grouse or partridge
**COVEYS** > COVEY
**COVIN** *n* conspiracy between two or more persons to act to the detriment or injury of another
**COVING** *same as* > COVE
**COVINGS** > COVING
**COVINOUS** *adj* deceitful
**COVINS** > COVIN
**COVYNE** *same as* > COVIN
**COVYNES** > COVYNE
**COW** *n* mature female of cattle and of certain other mammals, such as the elephant or seal ▷ *vb* intimidate, subdue
**COWAGE** *n* tropical climbing leguminous plant, *Stizolobium* (or *Mucuna*) *pruriens*, whose bristly pods cause severe itching and stinging
**COWAGES** > COWAGE
**COWAL** *n* shallow lake or swampy depression supporting vegetation
**COWALS** > COWAL
**COWAN** *n* drystone waller
**COWANS** > COWAN
**COWARD** *n* person who lacks courage ▷ *vb* show (someone) up to be a coward
**COWARDED** > COWARD
**COWARDICE** *n* lack of courage
**COWARDING** > COWARD
**COWARDLY** *adj* of or characteristic of a coward
**COWARDRY** *n* cowardice
**COWARDS** > COWARD
**COWBANE** *n* any of several N temperate poisonous umbelliferous marsh plants of the genus *Cicuta*, esp *C. virosa*, having clusters of small white flowers
**COWBANES** > COWBANE
**COWBELL** *n* bell hung around a cow's neck
**COWBELLS** > COWBELL
**COWBERRY** *n* creeping ericaceous evergreen shrub, *Vaccinium vitis-idaea*, of N temperate and arctic regions, with pink or red flowers and edible slightly acid berries
**COWBIND** *n* any of various bryony plants, esp the white bryony
**COWBINDS** > COWBIND

COWBIRD n any of various American orioles of the genera *Molothrus*, *Tangavius*, etc, esp *M. ater* (common or brown-headed cowbird). They have a dark plumage and short bill

COWBIRDS > COWBIRD

COWBOY n (in the US) ranch worker who herds and tends cattle, usu. on horseback ▷ vb work or behave as a cowboy

COWBOYED > COWBOY

COWBOYING > COWBOY

COWBOYS > COWBOY

COWED > COW

COWEDLY > COW

COWER vb cringe in fear

COWERED > COWER

COWERING > COWER

COWERS > COWER

COWFEEDER n dairyman

COWFISH n any trunkfish, such as *Lactophrys quadricornis*, having hornlike spines over the eyes

COWFISHES > COWFISH

COWFLAP n cow dung

COWFLAPS > COWFLAP

COWFLOP n foxglove

COWFLOPS > COWFLOP

COWGIRL n female cowboy

COWGIRLS > COWGIRL

COWGRASS n red clover

COWHAGE same as > COWAGE

COWHAGES > COWHAGE

COWHAND same as > COWBOY

COWHANDS > COWBOY

COWHEARD same as > COWHERD

COWHEARDS > COWHEARD

COWHEEL n heel of a cow, used as cooking ingredient

COWHEELS > COWHEEL

COWHERB n European caryophyllaceous plant, *Saponaria vaccaria*, having clusters of pink flowers: a weed in the US

COWHERBS > COWHERB

COWHERD n person employed to tend cattle

COWHERDS > COWHERD

COWHIDE n hide of a cow ▷ vb to lash with a cowhide whip

COWHIDED > COWHIDE

COWHIDES > COWHIDE

COWHIDING > COWHIDE

COWHOUSE n byre

COWHOUSES > COWHOUSE

COWIER > COWY

COWIEST > COWY

COWING > COW

COWINNER n joint winner

COWINNERS > COWINNER

COWISH adj cowardly

COWITCH another name for > COWAGE

COWITCHES > COWITCH

COWK vb retch or feel nauseated

COWKED > COWK

COWKING > COWK

COWKS > COWK

COWL same as > COWLING

COWLED adj wearing a cowl

COWLICK n tuft of hair over the forehead

COWLICKS > COWLICK

COWLING n cover on an engine

COWLINGS > COWLING

COWLS > COWL

COWLSTAFF n pole, used by two people, for carrying a vessel

COWMAN n man who owns cattle

COWMEN > COWMAN

COWORKER n fellow worker

COWORKERS > COWORKER

COWP same as > COUP

COWPAT n pool of cow dung

COWPATS > COWPAT

COWPEA n leguminous tropical climbing plant, *Vigna sinensis*, producing long pods containing edible pealike seeds: grown for animal fodder and sometimes as human food

COWPEAS > COWPEA

COWPED > COWP

COWPIE n cowpat

COWPIES > COWPIE

COWPING > COWP

COWPLOP n cow dung

COWPLOPS > COWPLOP

COWPOKE n cowboy

COWPOKES > COWPOKE

COWPOX n disease of cows, the virus of which is used in the smallpox vaccine

COWPOXES > COWPOX

COWPS > COWP

COWRIE n brightly-marked sea shell

COWRIES > COWRIE

COWRITE vb to write jointly

COWRITER > COWRITE

COWRITERS > COWRITE

COWRITES > COWRITE

COWRITING > COWRITE

COWRITTEN > COWRITE

COWROTE > COWRITE

COWRY same as > COWRIE

COWS > COW

COWSHED n byre

COWSHEDS > COWSHED

COWSKIN same as > COWHIDE

COWSKINS > COWSKIN

COWSLIP n small yellow wild European flower

COWSLIPS > COWSLIP

COWTREE n South American tree that produces latex

COWTREES > COWTREE

COWY adj cowlike

COX n coxswain ▷ vb act as cox of (a boat)

COXA n technical name for the hipbone or hip joint

COXAE > COXA

COXAL > COXA

COXALGIA n pain in the hip joint

COXALGIAS > COXALGIA

COXALGIC > COXALGIA

COXALGIES > COXALGIA

COXALGY same as > COXALGIA

COXCOMB same as > COCKSCOMB

COXCOMBIC > COXCOMB

COXCOMBRY n conceited arrogance or foppishness

COXCOMBS > COXCOMB

COXED > COX

COXES > COX

COXIER > COXY

COXIEST > COXY

COXINESS > COXY

COXING > COX

COXITIDES > COXITIS

COXITIS n inflammation of the hip joint

COXLESS > COX

COXSWAIN n person who steers a rowing boat

COXSWAINS > COXSWAIN

COXY adj cocky

COY adj affectedly shy or modest ▷ vb to caress

COYDOG n cross between a coyote and a dog

COYDOGS > COYDOG

COYED > COY

COYER > COY

COYEST > COY

COYING > COY

COYISH > COY

COYISHLY > COY

COYLY > COY

COYNESS > COY

COYNESSES > COY

COYOTE n prairie wolf of N America

COYOTES > COYOTE

COYOTILLO n thorny poisonous rhamnaceous shrub, *Karwinskia humboldtiana* of Mexico and the southwestern US, the berries of which cause paralysis

COYPOU same as > COYPU

COYPOUS > COYPOU

COYPU n beaver-like aquatic rodent native to S America, bred for its fur

COYPUS > COYPU

COYS > COY

COYSTREL same as > COISTREL

COYSTRELS > COYSTREL

COYSTRIL same as > COISTREL

COYSTRILS > COYSTRIL

COZ n archaic word for > COUSIN

COZE vb to chat

COZED > COZE

COZEN vb cheat, trick

COZENAGE > COZEN

COZENAGES > COZEN

COZENED > COZEN

COZENER > COZEN

COZENERS > COZEN

COZENING > COZEN

COZENS > COZEN

COZES > COZE

COZEY n tea cosy

COZEYS > COZEY

COZIE same as > COZEY

COZIED > COSY

COZIER n cobbler

COZIERS > COZIER

COZIES > COZEY

COZIEST > COZY

COZILY > COZY

COZINESS > COZY

COZING > COZE

COZY same as > COSY vb to make oneself snug and warm

COZYING > COZY

COZZES > COZ

CRAAL vb to enclose in a craal (or kraal)

CRAALED > CRAAL

CRAALING > CRAAL

CRAALS > CRAAL

CRAB n edible shellfish with ten legs, the first pair modified into pincers

CRABABBLE n tree bearing small sour apple-like fruit

CRABBED > CRAB

CRABBEDLY > CRAB

CRABBER n crab fisherman

CRABBERS > CRABBER

CRABBIER > CRABBY

CRABBIEST > CRABBY

CRABBILY > CRABBY

CRABBING > CRAB

CRABBY adj bad-tempered

CRABEATER n species of seal

CRABGRASS n type of coarse weedy grass

CRABLIKE adj resembling a crab

CRABMEAT n edible flesh of a crab

CRABMEATS > CRABMEAT

CRABS > CRAB

CRABSTICK n stick, cane, or cudgel made of crabapple wood

CRABWISE adv (of motion) sideways

CRABWOOD n tropical American meliaceous tree, *Carapa guianensis*

CRABWOODS > CRABWOOD

CRACK vb break or split partially ▷ n sudden sharp noise ▷ adj first-rate, excellent

CRACKA n US derogatory word for a poor White person

CRACKAS > CRACKA

CRACKBACK n in American football, illegal blocking of an opponent

CRACKDOWN n severe disciplinary measures

CRACKED adj damaged by cracking ▷ n sharp noise

CRACKER n thin dry biscuit

CRACKERS *adj* insane

CRACKET *n* low stool, often one with three legs

CRACKETS > CRACKET

CRACKHEAD *n* person addicted to the drug crack

CRACKING *adj* very fast

CRACKINGS > CRACKING

CRACKJAW *adj* difficult to pronounce ▷ *n* word or phrase that is difficult to pronounce

CRACKJAWS > CRACKJAW

CRACKLE *vb* make small sharp popping noises ▷ *n* crackling sound

CRACKLED > CRACKLE

CRACKLES > CRACKLE

CRACKLIER > CRACKLY

CRACKLING *n* crackle

CRACKLY *adj* making a cracking sound

CRACKNEL *n* type of hard plain biscuit

CRACKNELS > CRACKNEL

CRACKPOT *adj* eccentric ▷ *n* eccentric person

CRACKPOTS > CRACKPOT

CRACKS > CRACK

CRACKSMAN *n* burglar, esp a safe-breaker

CRACKSMEN > CRACKSMAN

CRACKUP *n* physical or mental breakdown

CRACKUPS > CRACKUP

CRACKY *adj* full of cracks

CRACOWE *n* medieval shoe with a sharply pointed toe

CRACOWES > CRACOWE

CRADLE *n* baby's bed on rockers ▷ *vb* hold gently as if in a cradle

CRADLED > CRADLE

CRADLER > CRADLE

CRADLERS > CRADLE

CRADLES > CRADLE

CRADLING *n* framework of iron or wood, esp as used in the construction of a ceiling

CRADLINGS > CRADLING

CRAFT *n* occupation requiring skill with the hands ▷ *vb* make skilfully

CRAFTED > CRAFT

CRAFTER *n* person doing craftwork

CRAFTERS > CRAFTER

CRAFTIER > CRAFTY

CRAFTIEST > CRAFTY

CRAFTILY > CRAFTY

CRAFTING > CRAFT

CRAFTLESS *adj* guileless

CRAFTS > CRAFT

CRAFTSMAN *n* skilled worker

CRAFTSMEN > CRAFTSMAN

CRAFTWORK *n* handicraft

CRAFTY *adj* skilled in deception

CRAG *n* steep rugged rock

CRAGFAST *adj* stranded on a crag

CRAGGED *same as* > CRAGGY

CRAGGIER > CRAGGY

CRAGGIEST > CRAGGY

CRAGGILY > CRAGGY

CRAGGY *adj* having many crags

CRAGS > CRAG

CRAGSMAN *n* rock climber

CRAGSMEN > CRAGSMAN

CRAIC *n* Irish word meaning fun

CRAICS > CRAIC

CRAIG *a Scot word for* > CRAG

CRAIGS > CRAIG

CRAKE *n* bird of the rail family, such as the corncrake ▷ *vb* to boast

CRAKED > CRAKE

CRAKES > CRAKE

CRAKING > CRAKE

CRAM *vb* force into too small a space ▷ *n* act or condition of cramming

CRAMBE *n* any plant of the genus Crambe

CRAMBES > CRAMBE

CRAMBO *n* word game in which one team says a rhyme or rhyming line for a word or line given by the other team

CRAMBOES > CRAMBO

CRAMBOS > CRAMBO

CRAME *n* merchant's booth or stall

CRAMES > CRAME

CRAMESIES > CRAMESY

CRAMESY *same as* > CRAMOISY

CRAMMABLE *adj* able to be crammed or filled

CRAMMED > CRAM

CRAMMER *n* person or school that prepares pupils for an examination

CRAMMERS > CRAMMER

CRAMMING > CRAM

CRAMOISIE *same as* > CRAMOISY

CRAMOISY *adj* of a crimson colour ▷ *n* crimson cloth

CRAMP *n* painful muscular contraction ▷ *vb* affect with a cramp

CRAMPBARK *n* guelder rose

CRAMPED *adj* closed in

CRAMPER *n* spiked metal plate used as a brace for the feet in throwing the stone

CRAMPERS > CRAMPER

CRAMPET *n* cramp iron

CRAMPETS > CRAMPET

CRAMPFISH *n* electric ray

CRAMPIER > CRAMPY

CRAMPIEST > CRAMPY

CRAMPING > CRAMP

CRAMPIT *same as* > CRAMPET

CRAMPITS > CRAMPIT

CRAMPON *n* spiked plate strapped to a boot for climbing on ice ▷ *vb* climb using crampons

CRAMPONED > CRAMPON

CRAMPONS > CRAMPON

CRAMPOON *same as* > CRAMPON

CRAMPOONS > CRAMPOON

CRAMPS > CRAMP

CRAMPY *adj* affected with cramp

CRAMS > CRAM

CRAN *n* unit of capacity used for measuring fresh herring, equal to 37.5 gallons

CRANAGE *n* use of a crane

CRANAGES > CRANAGE

CRANBERRY *n* sour edible red berry

CRANCH *vb* to crunch

CRANCHED > CRANCH

CRANCHES > CRANCH

CRANCHING > CRANCH

CRANE *n* machine for lifting and moving heavy weights ▷ *vb* stretch (one's neck) to see something

CRANED > CRANE

CRANEFLY *n* fly with long legs, slender wings, and a narrow body

CRANES > CRANE

CRANIA > CRANIUM

CRANIAL *adj* of or relating to the skull

CRANIALLY > CRANIAL

CRANIATE *adj* having a skull or cranium ▷ *n* vertebrate

CRANIATES > CRANIATE

CRANING > CRANE

CRANIUM *n* skull

CRANIUMS > CRANIUM

CRANK *n* arm projecting at right angles from a shaft, for transmitting or converting motion ▷ *vb* turn with a crank ▷ *adj* (of a sailing vessel) easily keeled over by the wind

CRANKCASE *n* metal case that encloses the crankshaft in an internal-combustion engine

CRANKED > CRANK

CRANKER > CRANK

CRANKEST > CRANK

CRANKIER > CRANK

CRANKIEST > CRANK

CRANKILY > CRANK

CRANKING > CRANK

CRANKISH *adj* somewhat eccentric or bad-tempered

CRANKLE *vb* to bend or wind

CRANKLED > CRANKLE

CRANKLES > CRANKLE

CRANKLING > CRANKLE

CRANKLY *adj* vigorously

CRANKNESS *n* (of a vessel) liability to capsize

CRANKOUS *adj* fretful

CRANKPIN *n* short cylindrical pin in a crankshaft, to which the connecting rod is attached

CRANKPINS > CRANKPIN

CRANKS > CRANK

CRANKY *same as* > CRANK

CRANNIED > CRANNY

CRANNIES > CRANNY

CRANNOG *n* ancient Celtic lake or bog dwelling dating from the late Bronze Age to the 16th century AD, often fortified and used as a refuge

CRANNOGE *same as* > CRANNOG

CRANNOGES > CRANNOGE

CRANNOGS > CRANNOG

CRANNY *n* narrow opening ▷ *vb* to become full of crannies

CRANNYING > CRANNY

CRANREUCH *n* hoarfrost

CRANS > CRAN

CRANTS *n* garland carried in front of a maiden's bier

CRANTSES > CRANTS

CRAP *n* rubbish, nonsense ▷ *vb* defecate

CRAPAUD *n* frog or toad

CRAPAUDS > CRAPAUD

CRAPE *same as* > CREPE

CRAPED > CRAPE

CRAPELIKE > CRAPE

CRAPES > CRAPE

CRAPIER > CRAPE

CRAPIEST > CRAPE

CRAPING > CRAPE

CRAPLE *same as* > GRAPPLE

CRAPLES > CRAPLE

CRAPOLA *n* rubbish

CRAPOLAS > CRAPOLA

CRAPPED > CRAP

CRAPPER *n* toilet

CRAPPERS > CRAPPER

CRAPPIE *n* N American freshwater fish

CRAPPIER > CRAPPY

CRAPPIES > CRAPPIE

CRAPPIEST > CRAPPY

CRAPPING > CRAP

CRAPPY *adj* worthless, lousy

CRAPS > CRAP

CRAPSHOOT *n* dice game

CRAPULENT *adj* given to or resulting from excessive eating or drinking

CRAPULOUS *same as* > CRAPULENT

CRAPY > CRAPE

CRARE *n* type of trading vessel

CRARES > CRARE

CRASES > CRASIS

CRASH *n* collision involving a vehicle or vehicles ▷ *vb* (cause to) collide violently with a vehicle, a stationary object, or the ground ▷ *adj* requiring or using great effort in order to achieve results quickly

CRASHED > CRASH

CRASHER > CRASH

CRASHERS > CRASH

CRASHES > CRASH

CRASHING *adj* extreme

CRASHLAND n land an aircraft in an emergency causing damage

CRASHPAD n place to sleep or live temporarily

CRASHPADS >CRASHPAD

CRASIS n fusion or contraction of two adjacent vowels into one

CRASS adj stupid and insensitive

CRASSER >CRASS

CRASSEST >CRASS

CRASSLY >CRASS

CRASSNESS >CRASS

CRATCH n rack for holding fodder for cattle, etc

CRATCHES >CRATCH

CRATE n large wooden container for packing goods ▷ vb put in a crate

CRATED >CRATE

CRATEFUL >CRATE

CRATEFULS >CRATE

CRATER n bowl-shaped opening at the top of a volcano vb make or form craters

CRATERED >CRATER

CRATERING >CRATER

CRATERLET n small crater

CRATEROUS >CRATER

CRATERS >CRATER

CRATES >CRATE

CRATING >CRATE

CRATON n stable part of the earth's continental crust or lithosphere that has not been deformed significantly for many millions, even hundreds of millions, of years

CRATONIC >CRATON

CRATONS >CRATON

CRATUR n the. whisky or whiskey

CRATURS >CRATUR

CRAUNCH same as >CRUNCH

CRAUNCHED >CRAUNCH

CRAUNCHES >CRAUNCH

CRAUNCHY >CRAUNCH

CRAVAT n man's scarf worn like a tie ▷ vb wear a cravat

CRAVATS >CRAVAT

CRAVATTED >CRAVAT

CRAVE vb desire intensely

CRAVED >CRAVE

CRAVEN adj cowardly ▷ n coward ▷ vb to make cowardly

CRAVENED >CRAVEN

CRAVENING >CRAVEN

CRAVENLY >CRAVEN

CRAVENS >CRAVEN

CRAVER >CRAVE

CRAVERS >CRAVE

CRAVES >CRAVE

CRAVING n intense desire or longing

CRAVINGS >CRAVING

CRAW n pouchlike part of a bird's oesophagus

CRAWDAD n crayfish

CRAWDADDY n crayfish

CRAWDADS >CRAWDAD

CRAWFISH same as >CRAYFISH

CRAWL vb move on one's hands and knees ▷ n crawling motion or pace

CRAWLED >CRAWL

CRAWLER n servile flatterer

CRAWLERS >CRAWLER

CRAWLIER >CRAWLY

CRAWLIEST >CRAWLY

CRAWLING n defect in freshly applied paint or varnish characterized by bare patches and ridging

CRAWLINGS >CRAWLING

CRAWLS >CRAWL

CRAWLWAY n in a mine, low passageway that can only be negotiated by crawling

CRAWLWAYS >CRAWLWAY

CRAWLY adj feeling or causing a sensation like creatures crawling on one's skin

CRAWS >CRAW

CRAY n crayfish

CRAYER same as >CRARE

CRAYERS >CRAYER

CRAYFISH n edible shellfish like a lobster

CRAYON n a stick or pencil of coloured wax or clay ▷ vb draw or colour with a crayon

CRAYONED >CRAYON

CRAYONER >CRAYON

CRAYONERS >CRAYON

CRAYONING >CRAYON

CRAYONIST >CRAYON

CRAYONS >CRAYON

CRAYS >CRAY

CRAYTHUR variant of >CRATUR

CRAYTHURS >CRAYTHUR

CRAZE n short-lived fashion or enthusiasm ▷ vb make mad

CRAZED adj wild and uncontrolled

CRAZES >CRAZE

CRAZIER >CRAZY

CRAZIES >CRAZY

CRAZIEST >CRAZY

CRAZILY >CRAZY

CRAZINESS >CRAZY

CRAZING >CRAZE

CRAZY adj ridiculous ▷ n crazy person ▷ n crazy person

CRAZYWEED n locoweed

CREACH same as >CREAGH

CREACHS >CREACH

CREAGH n foray

CREAGHS >CREAGH

CREAK n (make) a harsh squeaking sound ▷ vb make or move with a harsh squeaking sound

CREAKED >CREAK

CREAKIER >CREAK

CREAKIEST >CREAK

CREAKILY >CREAK

CREAKING >CREAK

CREAKS >CREAK

CREAKY >CREAK

CREAM n fatty part of milk ▷ adj yellowish-white ▷ vb beat to a creamy consistency

CREAMCUPS n Californian papaveraceous plant, Platystemon californicus, with small cream-coloured or yellow flowers on long flower stalks

CREAMED >CREAM

CREAMER n powdered milk substitute for use in coffee

CREAMERS >CREAMER

CREAMERY n place where dairy products are made or sold

CREAMIER >CREAMY

CREAMIEST >CREAMY

CREAMILY >CREAMY

CREAMING >CREAM

CREAMLAID adj (of laid paper) cream-coloured and of a ribbed appearance

CREAMLIKE >CREAM

CREAMPUFF n puff pastry filled with cream

CREAMS >CREAM

CREAMWARE n type of earthenware with a deep cream body developed about 1720 and widely produced

CREAMWOVE adj (of wove paper) cream-coloured and even-surfaced

CREAMY adj resembling cream in colour, taste, or consistency

CREANCE n long light cord used in falconry

CREANCES >CREANCE

CREANT adj formative

CREASE n line made by folding or pressing ▷ vb crush or line

CREASED >CREASE

CREASER >CREASE

CREASERS >CREASE

CREASES >CREASE

CREASIER >CREASE

CREASIEST >CREASE

CREASING >CREASE

CREASOTE same as >CREOSOTE

CREASOTED >CREASOTE

CREASOTES >CREASOTE

CREASY >CREASE

CREATABLE >CREATE

CREATE vb make, cause to exist

CREATED >CREATE

CREATES >CREATE

CREATIC adj relating to flesh or meat

CREATIN same as >CREATINE

CREATINE n important metabolite involved in many biochemical reactions and present in

many types of living cells

CREATINES >CREATINE

CREATING >CREATE

CREATINS >CREATIN

CREATION n creating or being created

CREATIONS >CREATION

CREATIVE adj imaginative or inventive ▷ n person who is creative professionally

CREATIVES >CREATIVE

CREATOR n person who creates

CREATORS >CREATOR

CREATRESS >CREATOR

CREATRIX >CREATOR

CREATURAL >CREATURE

CREATURE n animal, person, or other being

CREATURES >CREATURE

CRECHE n place where small children are looked after while their parents are working, shopping, etc

CRECHES >CRECHE

CRED n short for credibility

CREDAL >CREED

CREDENCE n belief in the truth or accuracy of a statement

CREDENCES >CREDENCE

CREDENDA >CREDENDUM

CREDENDUM n article of faith

CREDENT adj believing or believable

CREDENZA n type of small sideboard

CREDENZAS >CREDENZA

CREDIBLE adj believable

CREDIBLY >CREDIBLE

CREDIT n system of allowing customers to receive goods and pay later ▷ vb enter as a credit in an account

CREDITED >CREDIT

CREDITING >CREDIT

CREDITOR n person to whom money is owed

CREDITORS >CREDITOR

CREDITS pl n list of people responsible for the production of a film, programme, or record

CREDO n creed

CREDOS >CREDO

CREDS >CRED

CREDULITY n willingness to believe something on little evidence

CREDULOUS adj too willing to believe

CREE vb to soften grain by boiling or soaking

CREED n statement or system of (Christian) beliefs or principles

CREEDAL >CREED

CREEDS >CREED

CREEING >CREE

CREEK n narrow inlet or bay

CREEKIER >CREEKY

173

**CREEKIEST** >CREEKY

**CREEKS** >CREEK

**CREEKY** *adj* abounding in creeks

**CREEL** *n* wicker basket used by anglers ▷ *vb* to fish using creels

**CREELED** >CREEL

**CREELING** >CREEL

**CREELS** >CREEL

**CREEP** *vb* move quietly and cautiously ▷ *n* creeping movement

**CREEPAGE** *n* imperceptible movement

**CREEPAGES** >CREEPAGE

**CREEPED** >CREEP

**CREEPER** *n* creeping plant ▷ *vb* train a plant to creep

**CREEPERED** >CREEPER

**CREEPERS** >CREEPER

**CREEPIE** *n* low stool

**CREEPIER** >CREEPY

**CREEPIES** >CREEPIE

**CREEPIEST** >CREEPY

**CREEPILY** >CREEPY

**CREEPING** >CREEP

**CREEPS** >CREEP

**CREEPY** *adj* causing a feeling of fear or disgust

**CREES** >CREE

**CREESE** *a rare spelling of* >KRIS *vb* >to stab with a creese (or kris)

**CREESED** >CREESE

**CREESES** >CREESE

**CREESH** *vb* to lubricate

**CREESHED** >CREESH

**CREESHES** >CREESH

**CREESHIER** >CREESHY

**CREESHING** >CREESH

**CREESHY** *adj* greasy

**CREESING** >CREESE

**CREM** *n* crematorium

**CREMAINS** *n* cremated remains of a body

**CREMANT** *adj* (of wine) moderately sparkling

**CREMASTER** *n* muscle which raises and lowers the scrotum

**CREMATE** *vb* burn (a corpse) to ash

**CREMATED** >CREMATE

**CREMATES** >CREMATE

**CREMATING** >CREMATE

**CREMATION** >CREMATE

**CREMATOR** *n* furnace for cremating corpses

**CREMATORS** >CREMATOR

**CREMATORY** *adj* of or relating to cremation or crematoriums

**CREME** *n* cream ▷ *adj* (of a liqueur) rich and sweet

**CREMES** >CREME

**CREMINI** *n* variety of mushroom

**CREMINIS** >CREMINI

**CREMOCARP** *n* any fruit, such as anise or fennel, consisting of two united carpels

**CREMONA** *same*

*as* >CROMORNA

**CREMONAS** >CREMONA

**CREMOR** *n* cream

**CREMORNE** *n* penis

**CREMORNES** >CREMORNE

**CREMORS** >CREMOR

**CREMOSIN** *adj* crimson

**CREMS** >CREM

**CREMSIN** *same*

*as* >CREMOSIN

**CRENA** *n* cleft or notch

**CRENAS** >CRENA

**CRENATE** *adj* having a scalloped margin, as certain leaves

**CRENATED** *same*

*as* >CRENATE

**CRENATELY** >CRENATE

**CRENATION** *n* any of the rounded teeth or the notches between them on a crenate structure

**CRENATURE** *same*

*as* >CRENATION

**CRENEL** *n* any of a set of openings formed in the top of a wall or parapet and having slanting sides, as in a battlement ▷ *vb* to crenelate

**CRENELATE** *vb* supply with battlements

**CRENELED** >CRENEL

**CRENELING** >CRENEL

**CRENELLE** *same as* >CRENEL

**CRENELLED** >CRENEL

**CRENELLES** >CRENELLE

**CRENELS** >CRENEL

**CRENSHAW** *n* variety of melon

**CRENSHAWS** >CRENSHAW

**CRENULATE** *adj* having a margin very finely notched with rounded projections, as certain leaves

**CREODONT** *n* any of a group of extinct Tertiary mammals some of which are thought to have been the ancestors of modern carnivores: order *Carnivora*

**CREODONTS** >CREODONT

**CREOLE** *n* language developed from a mixture of languages ▷ *adj* of or relating to a creole

**CREOLES** >CREOLE

**CREOLIAN** *n* Creole

**CREOLIANS** >CREOLIAN

**CREOLISE** *vb* (of a pidgin language) to become the native language of a speech community

**CREOLISED** *same*

*as* >CREOLIZED

**CREOLISES** >CREOLISE

**CREOLIST** *n* student of creole languages

**CREOLISTS** >CREOLIST

**CREOLIZE** *same*

*as* >CREOLISE

**CREOLIZED** *adj* (of a language) incorporating a considerable range of features from one or more unrelated languages, as the result of contact between language communities

**CREOLIZES** >CREOLIZE

**CREOPHAGY** *n* act of eating meat

**CREOSOL** *n* colourless or pale yellow insoluble oily liquid with a smoky odour and a burning taste

**CREOSOLS** >CREOSOL

**CREOSOTE** *n* dark oily liquid made from coal tar and used for preserving wood ▷ *vb* treat with creosote

**CREOSOTED** >CREOSOTE

**CREOSOTES** >CREOSOTE

**CREOSOTIC** >CREOSOTE

**CREPANCE** *n* injury to a horse's hind leg caused by being struck by the shoe of the other hind foot

**CREPANCES** >CREPANCE

**CREPE** *n* fabric or rubber with a crinkled texture ▷ *vb* cover or drape with crepe ▷ *vb* to crimp or frizz

**CREPED** >CREPE

**CREPERIE** *n* eating establishment that specializes in pancakes

**CREPERIES** >CREPERIE

**CREPES** >CREPE

**CREPEY** *same as* >CREPY

**CREPIER** >CREPY

**CREPIEST** >CREPY

**CREPINESS** >CREPY

**CREPING** >CREPE

**CREPITANT** >CREPITATE

**CREPITATE** *vb* make a rattling or crackling sound

**CREPITUS** *n* crackling chest sound heard in pneumonia and other lung diseases

**CREPOLINE** *n* light silk material used in dressmaking

**CREPON** *n* thin material made of fine wool and/or silk

**CREPONS** >CREPON

**CREPT** >CREEP

**CREPUSCLE** *n* twilight

**CREPY** *adj* (esp of the skin) having a dry wrinkled appearance like crepe

**CRESCENDI** >CRESCENDO

**CRESCENDO** *n* gradual increase in loudness, esp in music ▷ *adv* gradually getting louder ▷ *vb* increase in loudness or force

**CRESCENT** *n* (curved shape of) the moon as seen in its first or last quarter ▷ *adj* crescent-shaped

**CRESCENTS** >CRESCENT

**CRESCIVE** *adj* increasing

**CRESOL** *n* aromatic compound derived from phenol, existing in three isomeric forms: found in coal tar and creosote and used in making synthetic resins and as an antiseptic and disinfectant

**CRESOLS** >CRESOL

**CRESS** *n* plant with strong-tasting leaves, used in salads

**CRESSES** >CRESS

**CRESSET** *n* metal basket mounted on a pole in which oil or pitch was burned for illumination

**CRESSETS** >CRESSET

**CRESSY** >CRESS

**CREST** *n* top of a mountain, hill, or wave ▷ *vb* come to or be at the top of

**CRESTA** as in *cresta run* high-speed tobogganing down a steep narrow passage of compacted snow and ice

**CRESTAL** >CREST

**CRESTED** >CREST

**CRESTING** *same as* >CREST

**CRESTINGS** >CREST

**CRESTLESS** >CREST

**CRESTON** *n* hogback

**CRESTONS** >CRESTON

**CRESTS** >CREST

**CRESYL** *n* tolyl

**CRESYLIC** *adj* of, concerned with, or containing creosote or cresol

**CRESYLS** >CRESYL

**CRETIC** *n* metrical foot consisting of three syllables, the first long, the second short, and the third long

**CRETICS** >CRETIC

**CRETIN** *n* stupid person

**CRETINISE** *vb* make (someone) a cretin

**CRETINISM** *n* condition arising from a deficiency of thyroid hormone, present from birth, characterized by dwarfism and mental retardation

**CRETINIZE** *same*

*as* >CRETINISE

**CRETINOID** >CRETIN

**CRETINOUS** >CRETIN

**CRETINS** >CRETIN

**CRETISM** *n* lying

**CRETISMS** >CRETISM

**CRETONNE** *n* heavy printed cotton fabric used in furnishings

**CRETONNES** >CRETONNE

**CREUTZER** *n* former copper and silver coin of Germany or Austria

**CREUTZERS** >CREUTZER

**CREVALLE** *n* any fish of the family Carangidae

**CREVALLES** >CREVALLE

**CREVASSE** *n* deep open crack in a glacier ▷ *vb*

make a break or fissure in
(a dyke, wall, etc)
**CREVASSED** > CREVASSE
**CREVASSES** > CREVASSE
**CREVETTE** n shrimp
**CREVETTES** > CREVETTE
**CREVICE** n narrow crack or
gap in rock
**CREVICED** > CREVICE
**CREVICES** > CREVICE
**CREW** n people who work
on a ship or aircraft ▷ vb
serve as a crew member
(on)
**CREWCUT** n very short
haircut
**CREWCUTS** > CREWCUT
**CREWE** n type of pot
**CREWED** > CREW
**CREWEL** n fine worsted yarn
used in embroidery ▷ vb
to embroider in crewel
**CREWELIST** > CREWEL
**CREWELLED** > CREWEL
**CREWELS** > CREWEL
**CREWES** > CREWE
**CREWING** > CREW
**CREWLESS** adj lacking a
crew
**CREWMAN** n member of a
ship's crew
**CREWMATE** n colleague on
the crew of a boat or ship
**CREWMATES** > CREWMATE
**CREWMEN** > CREWMAN
**CREWNECK** n plain round
neckline in sweaters
**CREWNECKS** > CREWNECK
**CREWS** > CREW
**CRIANT** adj garish
**CRIB** n piece of writing
stolen from elsewhere
▷ vb copy (someone's
work) dishonestly
**CRIBBAGE** n card game for
two to four players
**CRIBBAGES** > CRIBBAGE
**CRIBBED** > CRIB
**CRIBBER** > CRIB
**CRIBBERS** > CRIB
**CRIBBING** > CRIB
**CRIBBINGS** > CRIB
**CRIBBLE** vb to sift
**CRIBBLED** > CRIBBLE
**CRIBBLES** > CRIBBLE
**CRIBBLING** > CRIBBLE
**CRIBELLA** > CRIBELLUM
**CRIBELLAR** > CRIBELLUM
**CRIBELLUM** n sievelike
spinning organ in certain
spiders that occurs
between the spinnerets
**CRIBLE** adj dotted
**CRIBRATE** adj sievelike
**CRIBROSE** adj pierced with
holes
**CRIBROUS** > CRIBROSE
**CRIBS** > CRIB
**CRIBWORK** > CRIB
**CRIBWORKS** > CRIBWORK
**CRICETID** n any member of
the family Cricetidae, such
as the hamster and vole
**CRICETIDS** > CRICETID

**CRICK** n muscle spasm or
cramp in the back or neck
▷ vb cause a crick in
**CRICKED** > CRICK
**CRICKET** n outdoor game
played with bats, a ball,
and wickets by two teams
of eleven ▷ vb play cricket
**CRICKETED** > CRICKET
**CRICKETER** > CRICKET
**CRICKETS** > CRICKET
**CRICKEY** same as > CRIKEY
**CRICKING** > CRICK
**CRICKS** > CRICK
**CRICKY** same as > CRIKEY
**CRICOID** adj of or relating
to the ring-shaped
lowermost cartilage of the
larynx ▷ n this cartilage
**CRICOIDS** > CRICOID
**CRIED** > CRY
**CRIER** n (formerly)
official who made public
announcements
**CRIERS** > CRIER
**CRIES** > CRY
**CRIKEY** interj expression of
surprise
**CRIM** short for > CRIMINAL
**CRIME** n unlawful act ▷ vb
charge with a crime
**CRIMED** > CRIME
**CRIMEFUL** adj criminal
**CRIMELESS** adj innocent
**CRIMEN** n crime
**CRIMES** > CRIME
**CRIMEWAVE** n period of
increased criminal activity
**CRIMINA** > CRIMEN
**CRIMINAL** n person guilty
of a crime ▷ adj of crime
**CRIMINALS** > CRIMINAL
**CRIMINATE** vb charge with
a crime
**CRIMINE** interj expression
of surprise
**CRIMING** > CRIME
**CRIMINI** same as > CRIMINE
**CRIMINIS** n accomplice in
crime
**CRIMINOUS** adj criminal
**CRIMINY** interj cry of
surprise
**CRIMMER** a variant spelling
of > KRIMMER
**CRIMMERS** > CRIMMER
**CRIMP** vb fold or press into
ridges ▷ n act or result of
crimping
**CRIMPED** > CRIMP
**CRIMPER** > CRIMP
**CRIMPERS** > CRIMP
**CRIMPIER** > CRIMP
**CRIMPIEST** > CRIMP
**CRIMPING** > CRIMP
**CRIMPLE** vb crumple,
wrinkle, or curl
**CRIMPLED** > CRIMPLE
**CRIMPLES** > CRIMPLE
**CRIMPLING** > CRIMPLE
**CRIMPS** > CRIMP
**CRIMPY** > CRIMP
**CRIMS** > CRIM
**CRIMSON** adj deep purplish-

red ▷ n deep or vivid
red colour ▷ vb make or
become crimson
**CRIMSONED** > CRIMSON
**CRIMSONS** > CRIMSON
**CRINAL** adj relating to the
hair
**CRINATE** adj having hair
**CRINATED** same
as > CRINATE
**CRINE** vb to shrivel
**CRINED** > CRINE
**CRINES** > CRINE
**CRINGE** vb flinch in fear ▷ n
act of cringing
**CRINGED** > CRINGE
**CRINGER** > CRINGE
**CRINGERS** > CRINGE
**CRINGES** > CRINGE
**CRINGING** > CRINGE
**CRINGINGS** > CRINGE
**CRINGLE** n eye at the
edge of a sail, usually
formed from a thimble or
grommet
**CRINGLES** > CRINGLE
**CRINING** > CRINE
**CRINITE** adj covered with
soft hairs or tufts ▷ n
sedimentary rock
**CRINITES** > CRINITE
**CRINKLE** n wrinkle, crease,
or fold ▷ vb become
slightly creased or folded
**CRINKLED** > CRINKLE
**CRINKLES** > CRINKLE
**CRINKLIER** > CRINKLY
**CRINKLIES** > CRINKLY
**CRINKLING** > CRINKLE
**CRINKLY** adj wrinkled ▷ n
old person
**CRINOID** n any primitive
echinoderm of the class
Crinoidea, having delicate
feathery arms radiating
from a central disc. The
group includes the free-
swimming feather stars,
the sessile sea lilies, and
many stemmed fossil
forms ▷ adj of, relating
to, or belonging to the
Crinoidea
**CRINOIDAL** > CRINOID
**CRINOIDS** > CRINOID
**CRINOLINE** n hooped
petticoat
**CRINOSE** adj hairy
**CRINUM** n any plant of
the mostly tropical
amaryllidaceous genus
Crinum, having straplike
leaves and clusters of lily-
like flowers
**CRINUMS** > CRINUM
**CRIOLLO** n native or
inhabitant of Latin
America of European
descent, esp of Spanish
descent ▷ adj of, relating
to, or characteristic of a
criollo or criollos
**CRIOLLOS** > CRIOLLO
**CRIOS** n multicoloured

woven woollen belt
traditionally worn by men
in the Aran Islands
**CRIOSES** > CRIOS
**CRIPE** variant of > CRIPES
**CRIPES** interj expression of
surprise
**CRIPPLE** n offensive word
for a person who is lame or
disabled ▷ vb make lame
or disabled
**CRIPPLED** > CRIPPLE
**CRIPPLER** > CRIPPLE
**CRIPPLERS** > CRIPPLE
**CRIPPLES** > CRIPPLE
**CRIPPLING** adj damaging
or injurious
**CRIS** variant of > KRIS
**CRISE** n crisis
**CRISES** > CRISIS
**CRISIC** adj relating to a
crisis
**CRISIS** n crucial stage,
turning point
**CRISP** adj fresh and firm
▷ n very thin slice of
potato fried till crunchy
▷ vb make or become crisp
**CRISPATE** adj having
a curled or waved
appearance
**CRISPATED** same
as > CRISPATE
**CRISPED** same as > CRISPATE
**CRISPEN** vb to make crisp
**CRISPENED** > CRISPEN
**CRISPENS** > CRISPEN
**CRISPER** n compartment
in a refrigerator for storing
salads, vegetables, etc, in
order to keep them fresh
**CRISPERS** > CRISPER
**CRISPEST** > CRISP
**CRISPHEAD** n variety of
lettuce
**CRISPIER** > CRISPY
**CRISPIEST** > CRISPY
**CRISPILY** > CRISPY
**CRISPIN** n cobbler
**CRISPING** > CRISP
**CRISPINS** > CRISPIN
**CRISPLY** > CRISP
**CRISPNESS** > CRISP
**CRISPS** > CRISP
**CRISPY** adj hard and
crunchy
**CRISSA** > CRISSUM
**CRISSAL** > CRISSUM
**CRISSUM** n area or feathers
surrounding the cloaca of
a bird
**CRISTA** n structure
resembling a ridge
or crest, such as that
formed by folding of the
inner membrane of a
mitochondrion
**CRISTAE** > CRISTA
**CRISTATE** adj having a
crest
**CRISTATED** same
as > CRISTATE
**CRIT** abbreviation
of > CRITICISM

CRITERIA >CRITERION
CRITERIAL >CRITERION
CRITERION n standard of judgment
CRITERIUM n type of bicycle race, involving many laps of a short course
CRITH n unit of weight for gases
CRITHS >CRITH
CRITIC n professional judge of any of the arts
CRITICAL adj very important or dangerous
CRITICISE same as >CRITICIZE
CRITICISM n fault-finding
CRITICIZE vb find fault with
CRITICS >CRITIC
CRITIQUE n critical essay ▷ vb to review critically
CRITIQUED >CRITIQUE
CRITIQUES >CRITIQUE
CRITS >CRIT
CRITTER a dialect word for >CREATURE
CRITTERS >CRITTER
CRITTUR same as >CRITTER
CRITTURS >CRITTUR
CRIVENS interj expression of surprise
CRIVVENS same as >CRIVENS
CROAK vb (of a frog or crow) give a low hoarse cry ▷ n low hoarse sound
CROAKED >CROAK
CROAKER n animal, bird, etc, that croaks
CROAKERS >CROAKER
CROAKIER >CROAK
CROAKIEST >CROAK
CROAKILY >CROAK
CROAKING >CROAK
CROAKINGS >CROAK
CROAKS >CROAK
CROAKY >CROAK
CROC short for >CROCODILE
CROCEATE adj saffron-coloured
CROCEIN n any one of a group of red or orange acid azo dyes
CROCEINE same as >CROCEIN
CROCEINES >CROCEIN
CROCEINS >CROCEIN
CROCEOUS adj saffron-coloured
CROCHE n knob at the top of a deer's horn
CROCHES >CROCHE
CROCHET vb make by looping and intertwining yarn with a hooked needle ▷ n work made in this way
CROCHETED >CROCHET
CROCHETER >CROCHET
CROCHETS >CROCHET
CROCI >CROCUS
CROCINE adj relating to the crocus
CROCK n earthenware pot

or jar ▷ vb become or cause to become weak or disabled
CROCKED adj injured
CROCKERY n dishes
CROCKET n carved ornament in the form of a curled leaf or cusp, used in Gothic architecture
CROCKETED >CROCKET
CROCKETS >CROCKET
CROCKING >CROCK
CROCKPOT n tradename for a brand of slow cooker
CROCKPOTS >CROCKPOT
CROCKS >CROCK
CROCODILE n large amphibious tropical reptile
CROCOITE n rare orange secondary mineral
CROCOITES >CROCOITE
CROCOSMIA n any plant of the cormous S. African genus Crocosmia, including the plant known to gardeners as montbretia: family Iridaceae
CROCS >CROC
CROCUS n flowering plant
CROCUSES >CROCUS
CROFT n small farm worked by one family in Scotland
CROFTER n owner or tenant of a small farm, esp in Scotland or northern England
CROFTERS >CROFTER
CROFTING n system or occupation of working land in crofts
CROFTINGS >CROFTING
CROFTS >CROFT
CROG vb ride on a bicycle as a passenger
CROGGED >CROG
CROGGIES >CROGGY
CROGGING >CROG
CROGGY n ride on a bicycle as a passenger
CROGS >CROG
CROISSANT n rich flaky crescent-shaped roll
CROJIK n triangular sail
CROJIKS >CROJIK
CROKINOLE n board game popular in Canada in which players flick wooden discs
CROMACK same as >CRUMMOCK
CROMACKS >CROMACK
CROMB same as >CROME
CROMBEC n any African Old World warbler of the genus Sylvietta, having colourful plumage
CROMBECS >CROMBEC
CROMBED >CROMB
CROMBING >CROMB
CROMBS >CROMB
CROME n hook ▷ vb use a crome
CROMED >CROME

CROMES >CROME
CROMING >CROME
CROMLECH n circle of prehistoric standing stones
CROMLECHS >CROMLECH
CROMORNA n one of the reed stops in an organ
CROMORNAS >CROMORNA
CROMORNE variant of >CROMORNA
CROMORNES >CROMORNE
CRONE n witchlike old woman
CRONES >CRONE
CRONET n hair which grows over the top of a horse's hoof
CRONETS >CRONET
CRONIES >CRONY
CRONISH >CRONE
CRONK adj unfit
CRONKER >CRONK
CRONKEST >CRONK
CRONY n close friend
CRONYISM n practice of appointing friends to high-level, esp political, posts regardless of their suitability
CRONYISMS >CRONYISM
CROODLE vb to nestle close
CROODLED >CROODLE
CROODLES >CROODLE
CROODLING >CROODLE
CROOK n dishonest person ▷ vb bend or curve
CROOKBACK a rare word for >HUNCHBACK
CROOKED adj bent or twisted
CROOKEDER >CROOKED
CROOKEDLY >CROOKED
CROOKER >CROOK
CROOKERY n illegal or dishonest activity
CROOKEST >CROOK
CROOKING >CROOK
CROOKNECK n any type of summer squash
CROOKS >CROOK
CROOL vb spoil
CROOLED >CROOL
CROOLING >CROOL
CROOLS >CROOL
CROON vb sing, hum, or speak in a soft low tone ▷ n soft low singing or humming
CROONED >CROON
CROONER >CROON
CROONERS >CROON
CROONING >CROON
CROONINGS >CROON
CROONS >CROON
CROOVE n animal enclosure
CROOVES >CROOVE
CROP n cultivated plant ▷ vb cut very short
CROPBOUND n poultry disease causing a pendulous crop
CROPFUL n quantity that can be held in the craw

CROPFULL adj satiated
CROPFULS >CROPFUL
CROPLAND n land on which crops are grown
CROPLANDS >CROPLAND
CROPLESS adj without crops
CROPPED >CROP
CROPPER n person who cultivates or harvests a crop
CROPPERS >CROPPER
CROPPIE same as >CROPPY
CROPPIES >CROPPY
CROPPING >CROP
CROPPINGS >CROP
CROPPY n rebel in the Irish rising of 1798
CROPS >CROP
CROPSICK adj sick from excessive food or drink
CROQUANTE n crisp nut-filled chocolate or cake
CROQUET n game played on a lawn in which balls are hit through hoops ▷ vb drive away (another player's ball) by hitting one's own ball when the two are in contact
CROQUETED >CROQUET
CROQUETS >CROQUET
CROQUETTE n fried cake of potato, meat, or fish
CROQUIS n rough sketch
CRORE n (in Indian English) ten million
CRORES >CRORE
CROSIER n staff surmounted by a crook or cross, carried by bishops as a symbol of pastoral office ▷ vb bear or carry such a cross
CROSIERED >CROSIER
CROSIERS >CROSIER
CROSS vb move or go across (something) ▷ n structure, symbol, or mark of two intersecting lines ▷ adj angry, annoyed
CROSSABLE adj capable of being crossed
CROSSARM n in mining, horizontal bar on which a drill is mounted
CROSSARMS >CROSSARM
CROSSBAND vb to set the grain of layers of wood at right angles to one another
CROSSBAR n horizontal bar across goalposts or on a bicycle ▷ vb provide with crossbars
CROSSBARS >CROSSBAR
CROSSBEAM n beam that spans from one support to another
CROSSBILL n finch that has a bill with crossed tips
CROSSBIT >CROSSBITE
CROSSBITE vb to trick
CROSSBOW n weapon

consisting of a bow fixed across a wooden stock

**CROSSBOWS** > CROSSBOW

**CROSSBRED** adj bred from two different types of animal or plant ▷ n crossbred plant or animal, esp an animal resulting from a cross between two pure breeds

**CROSSBUCK** n US roadsign used at railroad crossings

**CROSSCUT** vb cut across ▷ adj cut across ▷ n transverse cut or course

**CROSSCUTS** > CROSSCUT

**CROSSE** n light staff with a triangular frame to which a network is attached, used in playing lacrosse

**CROSSED** > CROSS

**CROSSER** > CROSS

**CROSSERS** > CROSS

**CROSSES** > CROSS

**CROSSEST** > CROSS

**CROSSETTE** n in architecture, return in a corner of the architrave of a window or door

**CROSSFALL** n camber of a road

**CROSSFIRE** n gunfire crossing another line of fire

**CROSSFISH** n starfish

**CROSSHAIR** n one of two fine wires that cross in the focal plane of a gunsight or other optical instrument, used to define the line of sight

**CROSSHEAD** n subsection or paragraph heading printed within the body of the text

**CROSSING** n place where a street may be crossed safely

**CROSSINGS** > CROSSING

**CROSSISH** > CROSS

**CROSSJACK** n square sail on a ship's mizzenmast

**CROSSLET** n cross having a smaller cross near the end of each arm

**CROSSLETS** > CROSSLET

**CROSSLY** > CROSS

**CROSSNESS** > CROSS

**CROSSOVER** n place at which a crossing is made ▷ adj (of music, fashion, art, etc) combining two distinct styles

**CROSSROAD** n road that crosses another road

**CROSSRUFF** n alternate trumping of each other's leads by two partners, or by declarer and dummy ▷ vb trump alternately in two hands of a partnership

**CROSSTALK** n rapid or witty talk

**CROSSTIE** n railway

sleeper

**CROSSTIED** adj tied with ropes going across

**CROSSTIES** > CROSSTIE

**CROSSTOWN** adj going across town

**CROSSTREE** n either of a pair of wooden or metal braces on the head of a mast to support the topmast, etc

**CROSSWALK** n place marked where pedestrians may cross a road

**CROSSWAY** same as > CROSSROAD

**CROSSWAYS** same as > CROSSWISE

**CROSSWIND** n wind that blows at right angles to the direction of travel

**CROSSWISE** adv across ▷ adj across

**CROSSWORD** n puzzle in which the solver deduces words suggested by clues and writes them into a grid

**CROSSWORT** n herbaceous perennial Eurasian rubiaceous plant, Galium cruciata, with pale yellow flowers and whorls of hairy leaves

**CROST** > CROSS

**CROSTINI** > CROSTINO

**CROSTINIS** > CROSTINO

**CROSTINO** n piece of toasted bread served with a savoury topping

**CROTAL** n any of various lichens used in dyeing wool, esp for the manufacture of tweeds

**CROTALA** > CROTALUM

**CROTALINE** adj relating to rattlesnakes

**CROTALISM** n posoining due to ingestion of plants of the genus Crotalaria

**CROTALS** > CROTAL

**CROTALUM** n ancient castanet-like percussion instrument

**CROTCH** n part of the body between the tops of the legs ▷ vb have crotch (usu of a piece of clothing) removed

**CROTCHED** > CROTCH

**CROTCHES** > CROTCH

**CROTCHET** n musical note half the length of a minim

**CROTCHETS** > CROTCHET

**CROTCHETY** adj bad-tempered

**CROTON** n any shrub or tree of the chiefly tropical euphorbiaceous genus Croton, esp C. tiglium, the seeds of which yield croton oil

**CROTONBUG** n species of cockroach

**CROTONIC** as in crotonic acid type of colourless acid

**CROTONS** > CROTON

**CROTTLE** same as > CROTAL

**CROTTLES** > CROTTLE

**CROUCH** vb bend low with the legs and body close ▷ n this position

**CROUCHED** > CROUCH

**CROUCHES** > CROUCH

**CROUCHING** > CROUCH

**CROUP** n throat disease of children, with a cough ▷ vb have croup

**CROUPADE** n leap by a horse, pulling the hind legs towards the belly

**CROUPADES** > CROUPADE

**CROUPE** same as > CROUP

**CROUPED** > CROUP

**CROUPER** obsolete variant of > CRUPPER

**CROUPERS** > CROUPER

**CROUPES** > CROUPE

**CROUPIER** n person who collects bets and pays out winnings at a gambling table in a casino

**CROUPIERS** > CROUPIER

**CROUPIEST** > CROUP

**CROUPILY** > CROUP

**CROUPING** > CROUP

**CROUPON** n type of highly-polished flexible leather

**CROUPONS** > CROUPON

**CROUPOUS** > CROUP

**CROUPS** > CROUP

**CROUPY** > CROUP

**CROUSE** adj lively, confident, or saucy

**CROUSELY** > CROUSE

**CROUSTADE** n pastry case in which food is served

**CROUT** n sauerkraut

**CROUTE** n small round of toasted bread on which a savoury mixture is served

**CROUTES** > CROUTE

**CROUTON** n small piece of fried or toasted bread served in soup

**CROUTONS** > CROUTON

**CROUTS** > CROUT

**CROW** n large black bird with a harsh call ▷ vb (of a cock) make a shrill squawking sound

**CROWBAR** n iron bar used as a lever ▷ vb use a crowbar to lever (something)

**CROWBARS** > CROWBAR

**CROWBERRY** n low-growing N temperate evergreen shrub, Empetrum nigrum, with small purplish flowers and black berry-like fruit: family Empetraceae

**CROWBOOT** n type of Inuit boot made of fur and leather

**CROWBOOTS** > CROWBOOT

**CROWD** n large group of people or things ▷ vb

gather together in large numbers

**CROWDED** > CROWD

**CROWDEDLY** > CROWD

**CROWDER** > CROWD

**CROWDERS** > CROWD

**CROWDIE** n porridge of meal and water

**CROWDIES** > CROWDIE

**CROWDING** > CROWD

**CROWDS** > CROWD

**CROWDY** same as > CROWDIE

**CROWEA** n Australian shrub of the genus Crowea, having pink flowers

**CROWEAS** > CROWEA

**CROWED** > CROW

**CROWER** > CROW

**CROWERS** > CROW

**CROWFEET** > CROWFOOT

**CROWFOOT** n type of plant

**CROWFOOTS** > CROWFOOT

**CROWING** > CROW

**CROWINGLY** > CROW

**CROWN** n monarch's headdress of gold and jewels ▷ vb put a crown on the head of (someone) to proclaim him or her monarch

**CROWNED** > CROWN

**CROWNER** n promotional label consisting of a shaped printed piece of card or paper attached to a product on display

**CROWNERS** > CROWNER

**CROWNET** n coronet

**CROWNETS** > CROWNET

**CROWNING** n stage of labour when the infant's head is passing through the vaginal opening

**CROWNINGS** > CROWNING

**CROWNLAND** n large administrative division of the former empire of Austria-Hungary

**CROWNLESS** > CROWN

**CROWNLET** n small crown

**CROWNLETS** > CROWNLET

**CROWNS** > CROWN

**CROWNWORK** n manufacture of artificial crowns for teeth

**CROWS** > CROW

**CROWSFEET** > CROWSFOOT

**CROWSFOOT** n wrinkle at side of eye

**CROWSTEP** n set of steps to the top of a gable on a building

**CROWSTEPS** > CROWSTEP

**CROZE** n recess cut at the end of a barrel or cask to receive the head

**CROZER** n machine which cuts grooves in cask staves

**CROZERS** > CROZER

**CROZES** > CROZE

**CROZIER** same as > CROSIER

**CROZIERS** > CROZIER

**CROZZLED** adj blackened or burnt at the edges

CRU n (in France) a vineyard, group of vineyards, or wine-producing region

CRUBEEN n pig's trotter

CRUBEENS > CRUBEEN

CRUCES > CRUX

CRUCIAL adj very important

CRUCIALLY > CRUCIAL

CRUCIAN n European cyprinid fish, Carassius carassius, with a dark-green back, a golden-yellow undersurface, and reddish dorsal and tail fins: an aquarium fish

CRUCIANS > CRUCIAN

CRUCIATE adj shaped or arranged like a cross

CRUCIBLE n pot in which metals are melted

CRUCIBLES > CRUCIBLE

CRUCIFER n any plant of the family Brassicaceae (formerly Cruciferae), having a corolla of four petals arranged like a cross and a fruit called a siliqua. The family includes the brassicas, mustard, cress, and wallflower

CRUCIFERS > CRUCIFER

CRUCIFIED > CRUCIFY

CRUCIFIER > CRUCIFY

CRUCIFIES > CRUCIFY

CRUCIFIX n model of Christ on the Cross

CRUCIFORM adj cross-shaped ▷ n geometric curve, shaped like a cross, that has four similar branches asymptotic to two mutually perpendicular pairs of lines. Equation: $x^2y^2 - a^2x^2 - a^2y^2 = 0$, where $x = y = \pm a$ are the four lines.

CRUCIFY vb put to death by fastening to a cross

CRUCK n one of a pair of curved wooden timbers supporting the end of the roof in certain types of building

CRUCKS > CRUCK

CRUD n sticky or encrusted substance ▷ interj expression of disgust, disappointment, etc ▷ vb cover with a sticky or encrusted substance

CRUDDED > CRUD

CRUDDIER > CRUDDY

CRUDDIEST > CRUDDY

CRUDDING > CRUD

CRUDDLE vb to curdle

CRUDDLED > CRUDDLE

CRUDDLES > CRUDDLE

CRUDDLING > CRUDDLE

CRUDDY adj dirty or unpleasant

CRUDE adj rough and simple ▷ n crude oil

CRUDELY > CRUDE

CRUDENESS > CRUDE

CRUDER > CRUDE

CRUDES > CRUDE

CRUDEST > CRUDE

CRUDITES pl n selection of raw vegetables often served with a variety of dips before a meal

CRUDITIES > CRUDE

CRUDITY > CRUDE

CRUDS > CRUD

CRUDY adj raw

CRUE obsolete variant of > CREW

CRUEL adj delighting in others' pain

CRUELER > CRUEL

CRUELEST > CRUEL

CRUELLER > CRUEL

CRUELLEST > CRUEL

CRUELLS same as > CRUELS

CRUELLY > CRUEL

CRUELNESS > CRUEL

CRUELS n disease of cattle and sheep, caused by infection with an Actinobacillus lignieresii and characterized by soft tissue lesions, esp of the tongue

CRUELTIES > CRUELTY

CRUELTY n deliberate infliction of pain or suffering

CRUES > CREW

CRUET n small container for salt, pepper, etc, at table

CRUETS > CRUET

CRUISE n sail for pleasure ▷ vb sail from place to place for pleasure

CRUISED > CRUISE

CRUISER n fast warship

CRUISERS > CRUISER

CRUISES > CRUISE

CRUISEWAY n canal used for recreational purposes

CRUISIE same as > CRUIZIE

CRUISIES > CRUISIE

CRUISING > CRUISE

CRUISINGS > CRUISE

CRUIVE n animal enclosure

CRUIVES > CRUIVE

CRUIZIE n oil lamp

CRUIZIES > CRUIZIE

CRULLER n light sweet ring-shaped cake, fried in deep fat

CRULLERS > CRULLER

CRUMB n small fragment of bread or other dry food ▷ vb prepare or cover (food) with breadcrumbs ▷ adj (esp of pie crusts) made with a mixture of biscuit crumbs, sugar, etc

CRUMBED > CRUMB

CRUMBER > CRUMB

CRUMBERS > CRUMB

CRUMBIER > CRUMBY

CRUMBIEST > CRUMBY

CRUMBING > CRUMB

CRUMBLE vb break into fragments ▷ n pudding of stewed fruit with a crumbly topping

CRUMBLED > CRUMBLE

CRUMBLES > CRUMBLE

CRUMBLIER > CRUMBLY

CRUMBLIES n elderly people

CRUMBLING > CRUMBLE

CRUMBLY adj easily crumbled or crumbling

CRUMBS interj expression of dismay or surprise

CRUMBUM n rogue

CRUMBUMS > CRUMBUM

CRUMBY adj full of crumbs

CRUMEN n deer's larmier or tear-pit

CRUMENAL n purse

CRUMENALS > CRUMENAL

CRUMENS > CRUMEN

CRUMHORN n medieval woodwind instrument of bass pitch, consisting of an almost cylindrical tube curving upwards and blown through a double reed covered by a pierced cap

CRUMHORNS > CRUMHORN

CRUMMACK same as > CRUMMOCK

CRUMMACKS > CRUMMACK

CRUMMIE n cow with a crumpled horn

CRUMMIER > CRUMMY

CRUMMIES > CRUMMY

CRUMMIEST > CRUMMY

CRUMMOCK n stick with a crooked head

CRUMMOCKS > CRUMMOCK

CRUMMY adj of poor quality ▷ n lorry that carries loggers to work from their camp

CRUMP vb thud or explode with a loud dull sound ▷ n crunching, thudding, or exploding noise ▷ adj crooked

CRUMPED > CRUMP

CRUMPER > CRUMP

CRUMPEST > CRUMP

CRUMPET n round soft yeast cake, eaten buttered

CRUMPETS > CRUMPET

CRUMPIER > CRUMPY

CRUMPIEST > CRUMPY

CRUMPING > CRUMP

CRUMPLE vb crush, crease ▷ n untidy crease or wrinkle

CRUMPLED > CRUMPLE

CRUMPLES > CRUMPLE

CRUMPLIER > CRUMPLE

CRUMPLING > CRUMPLE

CRUMPLY > CRUMPLE

CRUMPS > CRUMP

CRUMPY adj crisp

CRUNCH vb bite or chew with a noisy crushing sound ▷ n crunching sound

CRUNCHED > CRUNCH

CRUNCHER > CRUNCH

CRUNCHERS > CRUNCH

CRUNCHES > CRUNCH

CRUNCHIE n derogatory word for an Afrikaner

CRUNCHIER > CRUNCH

CRUNCHIES > CRUNCHIE

CRUNCHILY > CRUNCH

CRUNCHING > CRUNCH

CRUNCHY > CRUNCH

CRUNKLE Scots variant of > CRINKLE

CRUNKLED > CRUNKLE

CRUNKLES > CRUNKLE

CRUNKLING > CRUNKLE

CRUNODAL > CRUNODE

CRUNODE n point at which two branches of a curve intersect, each branch having a distinct tangent

CRUNODES > CRUNODE

CRUOR n blood clot

CRUORES > CRUOR

CRUORS > CRUOR

CRUPPER n strap that passes from the back of a saddle under a horse's tail

CRUPPERS > CRUPPER

CRURA > CRUS

CRURAL adj of or relating to the leg or thigh

CRUS n leg, esp from the knee to the foot

CRUSADE n medieval Christian war to recover the Holy Land from the Muslims ▷ vb take part in a crusade

CRUSADED > CRUSADE

CRUSADER > CRUSADE

CRUSADERS > CRUSADE

CRUSADES > CRUSADE

CRUSADING > CRUSADE

CRUSADO n former gold or silver coin of Portugal bearing on its reverse the figure of a cross

CRUSADOES > CRUSADO

CRUSADOS > CRUSADO

CRUSE n small earthenware jug or pot

CRUSES > CRUSE

CRUSET n goldsmith's crucible

CRUSETS > CRUSET

CRUSH vb compress so as to injure, break, or crumple ▷ n dense crowd

CRUSHABLE > CRUSH

CRUSHED > CRUSH

CRUSHER > CRUSH

CRUSHERS > CRUSH

CRUSHES > CRUSH

CRUSHING > CRUSH

CRUSIAN variant of > CRUCIAN

CRUSIANS > CRUSIAN

CRUSIE same as > CRUIZIE

CRUSIES > CRUSIE

CRUSILY adj (in heraldry) strewn with crosses

CRUST n hard outer part of something, esp bread ▷ vb cover with or form a crust

**CRUSTA** n hard outer layer

**CRUSTACEA** n members of the Crustacea class of arthropods including the lobster

**CRUSTAE** > CRUSTA

**CRUSTAL** adj of or relating to the earth's crust

**CRUSTATE** adj covered with a crust

**CRUSTATED** same as > CRUSTATE

**CRUSTED** > CRUST

**CRUSTIER** > CRUSTY

**CRUSTIES** > CRUSTY

**CRUSTIEST** > CRUSTY

**CRUSTILY** > CRUSTY

**CRUSTING** > CRUST

**CRUSTLESS** adj lacking a crust

**CRUSTOSE** adj having a crustlike appearance

**CRUSTS** > CRUST

**CRUSTY** adj having a crust ▷ n dirty type of punk or hippy whose lifestyle involves travelling and squatting

**CRUSY** same as > CRUIZIE

**CRUTCH** n long sticklike support with a rest for the armpit, used by a lame person ▷ vb support or sustain (a person or thing) as with a crutch

**CRUTCHED** > CRUTCH

**CRUTCHES** > CRUTCH

**CRUTCHING** > CRUTCH

**CRUVE** same as > CRUIVE

**CRUVES** > CRUVE

**CRUX** n crucial or decisive point

**CRUXES** > CRUX

**CRUZADO** same as > CRUSADO

**CRUZADOES** > CRUZADO

**CRUZADOS** > CRUZADO

**CRUZEIRO** n former monetary unit of Brazil, replaced by the cruzeiro real

**CRUZEIROS** > CRUZEIRO

**CRUZIE** same as > CRUIZIE

**CRUZIES** > CRUIZIE

**CRWTH** n ancient stringed instrument of Celtic origin similar to the cithara but bowed in later types

**CRWTHS** > CRWTH

**CRY** vb shed tears ▷ n fit of weeping

**CRYBABIES** > CRYBABY

**CRYBABY** n person, esp a child, who cries too readily

**CRYING** > CRY

**CRYINGLY** > CRY

**CRYINGS** > CRY

**CRYOBANK** n place for storing genetic material at low temperature

**CRYOBANKS** > CRYOBANK

**CRYOCABLE** n highly conducting electrical cable cooled with a refrigerant such as liquid nitrogen

**CRYOGEN** n substance used to produce low temperatures

**CRYOGENIC** adj of the branch of physics concerned with the production of very low temperatures

**CRYOGENS** > CRYOGEN

**CRYOGENY** n cryogenic science

**CRYOLITE** n white or colourless mineral

**CRYOLITES** > CRYOLITE

**CRYOMETER** n thermometer for measuring low temperatures

**CRYOMETRY** > CRYOMETER

**CRYONIC** > CRYONICS

**CRYONICS** n practice of freezing a human corpse in the hope of restoring it to life in the future

**CRYOPHYTE** n organism, esp an alga or moss, that grows on snow or ice

**CRYOPROBE** n supercooled instrument used in surgery

**CRYOSCOPE** n any instrument used to determine the freezing point of a substance

**CRYOSCOPY** n determination of freezing points, esp for the determination of molecular weights by measuring the lowering of the freezing point of a solvent when a known quantity of solute is added

**CRYOSTAT** n apparatus for maintaining a constant low temperature or a vessel in which a substance is stored at a low temperature

**CRYOSTATS** > CRYOSTAT

**CRYOTRON** n miniature switch working at the temperature of liquid helium and depending for its action on the production and destruction of superconducting properties in the conductor

**CRYOTRONS** > CRYOTRON

**CRYPT** n vault under a church, esp one used as a burial place

**CRYPTADIA** n things to be kept hidden

**CRYPTAL** > CRYPT

**CRYPTIC** adj obscure in meaning, secret

**CRYPTICAL** same as > CRYPTIC

**CRYPTO** n person who is a secret member of an organization or sect

**CRYPTOGAM** n plant that reproduces by spores not seeds

**CRYPTON** n krypton

**CRYPTONS** > CRYPTON

**CRYPTONYM** n code name

**CRYPTOS** > CRYPTO

**CRYPTS** > CRYPT

**CRYSTAL** n (single grain of) a symmetrically shaped solid formed naturally by some substances ▷ adj bright and clear

**CRYSTALS** > CRYSTAL

**CSARDAS** n type of Hungarian folk dance

**CSARDASES** > CSARDAS

**CTENE** n locomotor organ found in ctenophores (or comb jellies)

**CTENES** > CTENE

**CTENIDIA** > CTENIDIUM

**CTENIDIUM** n one of the comblike respiratory gills of molluscs

**CTENIFORM** adj comblike

**CTENOID** adj toothed like a comb, as the scales of perches

**CUADRILLA** n matador's assistants in a bullfight

**CUATRO** n four-stringed guitar

**CUATROS** > CUATRO

**CUB** n young wild animal such as a bear or fox ▷ adj young or inexperienced ▷ vb give birth to cubs

**CUBAGE** same as > CUBATURE

**CUBAGES** > CUBATURE

**CUBANE** n rare octahedral hydrocarbon

**CUBANELLE** n variety of pepper

**CUBANES** > CUBANE

**CUBATURE** n determination of the cubic contents of something

**CUBATURES** > CUBATURE

**CUBBED** > CUB

**CUBBIES** > CUBBY

**CUBBING** > CUB

**CUBBINGS** > CUB

**CUBBISH** > CUB

**CUBBISHLY** > CUB

**CUBBY** same as > CUBBYHOLE

**CUBBYHOLE** n small enclosed space or room

**CUBE** n object with six equal square sides ▷ vb cut into cubes

**CUBHOOD** n state of being a cub

**CUBHOODS** > CUBHOOD

**CUBIC** adj having three

dimensions ▷ n cubic equation, such as $x^3 + x + 2 = 0$

**CUBICA** n fine shalloon-like fabric

**CUBICAL** adj of or related to volume

**CUBICALLY** > CUBICAL

**CUBICAS** > CUBICA

**CUBICITY** n property of being cubelike

**CUBICLE** n enclosed part of a large room, screened for privacy

**CUBICLES** > CUBICLE

**CUBICLY** > CUBIC

**CUBICS** > CUBIC

**CUBICULA** > CUBICULUM

**CUBICULUM** n underground burial chamber in Imperial Rome, such as those found in the catacombs

**CUBIFORM** adj having the shape of a cube

**CUBING** > CUBE

**CUBISM** n style of art in which objects are represented by geometrical shapes

**CUBISMS** > CUBISM

**CUBIST** > CUBISM

**CUBISTIC** > CUBISM

**CUBISTS** > CUBISM

**CUBIT** n old measure of length based on the length of the forearm

**CUBITAL** adj of or relating to the forearm

**CUBITI** adj of elbow

**CUBITS** > CUBIT

**CUBITUS** n elbow

**CUBITUSES** > CUBITUS

**CUBLESS** adj having no cubs

**CUBOID** adj shaped like a cube ▷ n geometric solid whose six faces are rectangles

**CUBOIDAL** same as > CUBOID

**CUBOIDS** > CUBOID

**CUBS** > CUB

**CUCKING** as in cucking stool stool to which suspected witches, etc, were tied and pelted or ducked into water as punishment

**CUCKOLD** n man whose wife has been unfaithful ▷ vb be unfaithful to (one's husband)

**CUCKOLDED** > CUCKOLD

**CUCKOLDLY** adj possessing the qualities of a cuckold

**CUCKOLDOM** n state of being a cuckold

**CUCKOLDRY** > CUCKOLD

**CUCKOLDS** > CUCKOLD

**CUCKOO** n migratory bird with a characteristic two-note call, which lays its eggs in the nests of other birds ▷ adj insane or foolish ▷ interj imitation or representation of the call of a cuckoo ▷ *vb* repeat over and over

**CUCKOOED** >CUCKOO

**CUCKOOING** >CUCKOO

**CUCKOOS** >CUCKOO

**CUCULLATE** *adj* shaped like a hood or having a hoodlike part

**CUCUMBER** *n* long green-skinned fleshy fruit used in salads

**CUCUMBERS** >CUCUMBER

**CUCURBIT** *n* any creeping flowering plant of the mainly tropical and subtropical family *Cucurbitaceae*, which includes the pumpkin, cucumber, squashes, and gourds

**CUCURBITS** >CUCURBIT

**CUD** *n* partially digested food which a ruminant brings back into its mouth to chew again

**CUDBEAR** *another name for* >ORCHIL

**CUDBEARS** >CUDBEAR

**CUDDEN** *n* young coalfish

**CUDDENS** >CUDDEN

**CUDDIE** *same as* >CUDDY

**CUDDIES** >CUDDY

**CUDDIN** *same as* >CUDDEN

**CUDDINS** >CUDDIN

**CUDDLE** *n* hug ▷ *vb* hold (another person or thing) close or (of two people, etc) to hold each other close, as for affection, comfort, or warmth

**CUDDLED** >CUDDLE

**CUDDLER** >CUDDLE

**CUDDLERS** >CUDDLE

**CUDDLES** >CUDDLE

**CUDDLIER** >CUDDLE

**CUDDLIEST** >CUDDLE

**CUDDLING** >CUDDLE

**CUDDLY** >CUDDLE

**CUDDY** *n* small cabin in a boat

**CUDGEL** *n* short thick stick used as a weapon ▷ *vb* use a cudgel

**CUDGELED** >CUDGEL

**CUDGELER** >CUDGEL

**CUDGELERS** >CUDGEL

**CUDGELING** >CUDGEL

**CUDGELLED** >CUDGEL

**CUDGELLER** >CUDGEL

**CUDGELS** >CUDGEL

**CUDGERIE** *n* large tropical rutaceous tree, *Flindersia schottina*, having light-coloured wood

**CUDGERIES** >CUDGERIE

**CUDS** >CUD

**CUDWEED** *n* any of various temperate woolly plants of the genus *Gnaphalium*, having clusters of whitish or yellow button-like flowers: family *Asteraceae* (composites)

**CUDWEEDS** >CUDWEED

**CUE** *n* signal to an actor or musician to begin speaking or playing ▷ *vb* give a cue to

**CUED** >CUE

**CUEING** >CUE

**CUEIST** *n* snooker or billiards player

**CUEISTS** >CUEIST

**CUES** >CUE

**CUESTA** *n* long low ridge with a steep scarp slope and a gentle back slope, formed by the differential erosion of strata of differing hardness

**CUESTAS** >CUESTA

**CUFF** *n* end of a sleeve ▷ *vb* hit with an open hand

**CUFFED** >CUFF

**CUFFIN** *n* man

**CUFFING** >CUFF

**CUFFINS** >CUFFIN

**CUFFLE** *vb* scuffle

**CUFFLED** >CUFFLE

**CUFFLES** >CUFFLE

**CUFFLESS** *adj* having no cuff(s)

**CUFFLING** >CUFFLE

**CUFFLINK** *n* detachable fastener for shirt cuff

**CUFFLINKS** >CUFFLINK

**CUFFO** *adv* free of charge

**CUFFS** >CUFF

**CUFFUFFLE** *same as* >KERFUFFLE

**CUIF** *same as* >COOF

**CUIFS** >CUIF

**CUING** >CUE

**CUIRASS** *n* piece of armour, of leather or metal covering the chest and back ▷ *vb* equip with a cuirass

**CUIRASSED** >CUIRASS

**CUIRASSES** >CUIRASS

**CUISH** *same as* >CUISSE

**CUISHES** >CUISH

**CUISINART** *n* tradename for a type of food processor

**CUISINE** *n* style of cooking

**CUISINES** >CUISINE

**CUISINIER** *n* cook

**CUISSE** *n* piece of armour for the thigh

**CUISSER** *same as* >COOSER

**CUISSERS** >CUISSER

**CUISSES** >CUISSE

**CUIT** *n* ankle

**CUITER** *vb* to pamper

**CUITERED** >CUITER

**CUITERING** >CUITER

**CUITERS** >CUITER

**CUITIKIN** *n* gaiter

**CUITIKINS** >CUITIKIN

**CUITS** >CUIT

**CUITTLE** *vb* to wheedle

**CUITTLED** >CUITTLE

**CUITTLES** >CUITTLE

**CUITTLING** >CUITTLE

**CUKE** *n* cucumber

**CUKES** >CUKE

**CULCH** *n* mass of broken stones, shells, and gravel

that forms the basis of an oyster bed

**CULCHES** >CULCH

**CULCHIE** *n* rough or unsophisticated country-dweller from outside Dublin

**CULCHIES** >CULCHIE

**CULET** *n* flat face at the bottom of a gem

**CULETS** >CULET

**CULEX** *n* any mosquito of the genus *Culex*, such as *C. pipiens*, the common mosquito

**CULEXES** >CULEX

**CULICES** >CULEX

**CULICID** *n* any dipterous insect of the family *Culicidae*, which comprises the mosquitoes ▷ *adj* of, relating to, or belonging to the *Culicidae*

**CULICIDS** >CULICID

**CULICINE** *n* any member of the genus *Culex* containing mosquitoes

**CULICINES** >CULICINE

**CULINARY** *adj* of kitchens or cookery

**CULL** *vb* choose, gather ▷ *n* culling

**CULLAY** *n* soapbark tree

**CULLAYS** >CULLAY

**CULLED** >CULL

**CULLENDER** *same as* >COLANDER

**CULLER** *n* person employed to cull animals

**CULLERS** >CULLER

**CULLET** *n* waste glass for melting down to be reused

**CULLETS** >CULLET

**CULLIED** >CULLY

**CULLIES** >CULLY

**CULLING** >CULL

**CULLINGS** >CULL

**CULLION** *n* rascal

**CULLIONLY** >CULLION

**CULLIONS** >CULLION

**CULLIS** *same as* >COULISSE

**CULLISES** >CULLIS

**CULLS** >CULL

**CULLY** *n* pal ▷ *vb* to trick

**CULLYING** >CULLY

**CULLYISM** *n* state of being a dupe

**CULLYISMS** >CULLYISM

**CULM** *n* coal-mine waste ▷ *vb* to form a culm or grass stem

**CULMED** >CULM

**CULMEN** *n* summit

**CULMENS** >CULMEN

**CULMINANT** *adj* highest or culminating

**CULMINATE** *vb* reach the highest point or climax

**CULMING** >CULM

**CULMS** >CULM

**CULOTTE** >CULOTTES

**CULOTTES** *pl n* women's knee-length trousers cut to look like a skirt

**CULPA** *n* act of neglect

**CULPABLE** *adj* deserving blame

**CULPABLY** >CULPABLE

**CULPAE** >CULPA

**CULPATORY** *adj* expressing blame

**CULPRIT** *n* person guilty of an offence or misdeed

**CULPRITS** >CULPRIT

**CULT** *n* specific system of worship ▷ *adj* very popular among a limited group of people

**CULTCH** *same as* >CULTCH

**CULTCHES** >CULTCH

**CULTER** *same as* >COULTER

**CULTERS** >CULTER

**CULTI** >CULTUS

**CULTIC** *adj* of or relating to a religious cult

**CULTIER** >CULTY

**CULTIEST** >CULTY

**CULTIGEN** *n* species of plant that is known only as a cultivated form and did not originate from a wild type

**CULTIGENS** >CULTIGEN

**CULTISH** *adj* intended to appeal to a small group of fashionable people

**CULTISHLY** >CULTISH

**CULTISM** >CULT

**CULTISMS** >CULT

**CULTIST** >CULT

**CULTISTS** >CULT

**CULTIVAR** *n* variety of a plant that was produced from a natural species and is maintained by cultivation

**CULTIVARS** >CULTIVAR

**CULTIVATE** *vb* prepare (land) to grow crops

**CULTLIKE** *adj* resembling a cult

**CULTRATE** *adj* shaped like a knife blade

**CULTRATED** *same as* >CULTRATE

**CULTS** >CULT

**CULTURAL** *adj* of or relating to artistic or social pursuits or events considered to be valuable or enlightened

**CULTURATI** *n* people interested in cultural activities

**CULTURE** *n* ideas, customs, and art of a particular society ▷ *vb* grow (bacteria) for study

**CULTURED** *adj* showing good taste or manners

**CULTURES** >CULTURE

**CULTURING** >CULTURE

**CULTURIST** >CULTURE

**CULTUS** *another word for* >CULT

**CULTUSES** >CULTUS

**CULTY** *same as* >CULTISH

**CULVER** *an archaic or poetic*

*name for* > PIGEON
CULVERIN *n* long-range medium to heavy cannon used during the 15th, 16th, and 17th centuries
CULVERINS > CULVERIN
CULVERS > CULVER
CULVERT *n* drain under a road or railway
CULVERTS > CULVERT
CUM *prep* with
CUMACEAN *n* any small malacostracan marine crustacean of the *Cumacea* family, mostly dwelling on the sea bed but sometimes found among the plankton ▷ *adj* of, relating to, or belonging to the *Cumacea*
CUMACEANS > CUMACEAN
CUMARIC > CUMARIN
CUMARIN *same as* > COUMARIN
CUMARINS > CUMARIN
CUMARONE *variant spelling of* > COUMARONE
CUMARONES > CUMARONE
CUMBENT *adj* lying down
CUMBER *vb* obstruct or hinder ▷ *n* hindrance or burden
CUMBERED > CUMBER
CUMBERER > CUMBER
CUMBERERS > CUMBER
CUMBERING > CUMBER
CUMBERS > CUMBER
CUMBIA *n* Colombian style of music
CUMBIAS > CUMBIA
CUMBRANCE *n* burden, obstacle, or hindrance
CUMBROUS *adj* awkward because of size, weight, or height
CUMBUNGI *n* any of various tall Australian marsh plants of the genus *Typha*
CUMBUNGIS > CUMBUNGI
CUMEC *n* unit of volumetric rate of flow
CUMECS > CUMEC
CUMIN *n* sweet-smelling seeds of a Mediterranean plant, used in cooking
CUMINS > CUMIN
CUMMER *n* gossip
CUMMERS > CUMMER
CUMMIN *same as* > CUMIN
CUMMINS > CUMMIN
CUMQUAT *same as* > KUMQUAT
CUMQUATS > CUMQUAT
CUMSHAW *n* (used, esp formerly, by beggars in Chinese ports) a present or tip
CUMSHAWS > CUMSHAW
CUMULATE *vb* accumulate ▷ *adj* heaped up
CUMULATED > CUMULATE
CUMULATES > CUMULATE
CUMULET *n* variety of domestic fancy pigeon, pure white or white with

light red markings
CUMULETS > CUMULET
CUMULI > CUMULUS
CUMULOSE *adj* full of heaps
CUMULOUS *adj* resembling or consisting of cumulus clouds
CUMULUS *n* thick white or dark grey cloud
CUNABULA *n* cradle
CUNCTATOR *n* person in habit of being late
CUNDIES > CUNDY
CUNDUM *n* early form of condom
CUNDUMS > CUNDUM
CUNDY *n* sewer
CUNEAL *same as* > CUNEIFORM
CUNEATE *adj* wedge-shaped: cuneate leaves are attached at the narrow end
CUNEATED *same as* > CUNEATE
CUNEATELY > CUNEATE
CUNEATIC *adj* cuneiform
CUNEI > CUNEUS
CUNEIFORM *adj* (written in) an ancient system of writing using wedge-shaped characters ▷ *n* ancient system of writing using wedge-shaped characters
CUNETTE *n* small trench dug in the main ditch of a fortification
CUNETTES > CUNETTE
CUNEUS *n* small wedge-shaped area of the cerebral cortex
CUNIFORM *same as* > CUNIFORM
CUNIFORMS > CUNIFORM
CUNJEVOI *n* plant of tropical Asia and Australia with small flowers, cultivated for its edible rhizome
CUNJEVOIS > CUNJEVOI
CUNNER *n* fish of the wrasse family
CUNNERS > CUNNER
CUNNING *adj* clever at deceiving ▷ *n* cleverness at deceiving
CUNNINGER > CUNNING
CUNNINGLY > CUNNING
CUNNINGS > CUNNING
CUNT *n* taboo word for female genitals
CUNTS > CUNT
CUP *n* small bowl-shaped drinking container with a handle ▷ *vb* form (one's hands) into the shape of a cup
CUPBEARER *n* attendant who fills and serves wine cups, as in a royal household
CUPBOARD *n* piece of furniture or alcove with a

door, for storage ▷ *vb* to store in a cupboard
CUPBOARDS > CUPBOARD
CUPCAKE *n* small cake baked in a cup-shaped foil or paper case
CUPCAKES > CUPCAKE
CUPEL *n* refractory pot in which gold or silver is refined ▷ *vb* refine (gold or silver) by means of cupellation
CUPELED > CUPEL
CUPELER > CUPEL
CUPELERS > CUPEL
CUPELING > CUPEL
CUPELLED > CUPEL
CUPELLER > CUPEL
CUPELLERS > CUPEL
CUPELLING > CUPEL
CUPELS > CUPEL
CUPFERRON *n* compound used in chemical analysis
CUPFUL *n* amount a cup will hold
CUPFULS > CUPFUL
CUPGALL *n* gall found on oak leaves
CUPGALLS > CUPGALL
CUPHEAD *n* type of bolt or rivet with a cup-shaped head
CUPHEADS > CUPHEAD
CUPID *n* figure representing the Roman god of love
CUPIDITY *n* greed for money or possessions
CUPIDS > CUPID
CUPLIKE > CUP
CUPMAN *n* drinking companion
CUPMEN > CUPMAN
CUPOLA *n* domed roof or ceiling ▷ *vb* to provide with a cupola
CUPOLAED > CUPOLA
CUPOLAING > CUPOLA
CUPOLAR > CUPOLA
CUPOLAS > CUPOLA
CUPOLATED > CUPOLA
CUPPA *n* cup of tea
CUPPAS > CUPPA
CUPPED > CUP
CUPPER *same as* > CUPPA
CUPPERS > CUPPER
CUPPIER > CUPPY
CUPPIEST > CUPPY
CUPPING > CUP
CUPPINGS > CUP
CUPPY *adj* cup-shaped
CUPREOUS *adj* of copper
CUPRESSUS *n* any tree of the genus *Cupressus*
CUPRIC *adj* of or containing copper in the divalent state
CUPRITE *n* red secondary mineral
CUPRITES > CUPRITE
CUPROUS *adj* of or containing copper in the monovalent state
CUPRUM *an obsolete name*

*for* > COPPER
CUPRUMS > CUPRUM
CUPS > CUP
CUPSFUL > CUPFUL
CUPULA *n* dome-shaped structure, esp the sensory structure within the semicircular canals of the ear
CUPULAE > CUPULA
CUPULAR *same as* > CUPULATE
CUPULATE *adj* shaped like a small cup
CUPULE *n* cup-shaped part or structure, such as the cup around the base of an acorn
CUPULES > CUPULE
CUR *n* mongrel dog
CURABLE *adj* capable of being cured
CURABLY > CURABLE
CURACAO *n* orange-flavoured liqueur
CURACAOS > CURACAO
CURACIES > CURACY
CURACOA *same as* > CURACAO
CURACOAS > CURACAO
CURACY *n* work or position of a curate
CURAGH *same as* > CURRACH
CURAGHS > CURAGH
CURANDERA *n* female faith healer
CURANDERO *n* male faith healer
CURARA *same as* > CURARE
CURARAS > CURARA
CURARE *n* poisonous resin of a S American tree, used as a muscle relaxant in medicine
CURARES > CURARE
CURARI *same as* > CURARE
CURARINE *n* alkaloid extracted from curare, used as a muscle relaxant in surgery
CURARINES > CURARINE
CURARIS > CURARI
CURARISE *same as* > CURARIZE
CURARISED > CURARISE
CURARISES > CURARISE
CURARIZE *vb* paralyse or treat with curare
CURARIZED > CURARIZE
CURARIZES > CURARIZE
CURASSOW *n* gallinaceous ground-nesting bird with long legs and tails and, typically, a distinctive crest of curled feathers
CURASSOWS > CURASSOW
CURAT *n* cuirass
CURATE *n* clergyman who assists a parish priest ▷ *vb* be in charge of (an art exhibition or museum) ▷ *vb* to act as a curator
CURATED > CURATE
CURATES > CURATE
CURATING > CURATE

**CURATIVE** n something able to cure ▷ adj able to cure

**CURATIVES** >CURATIVE

**CURATOR** n person in charge of a museum or art gallery

**CURATORS** >CURATOR

**CURATORY** >CURATOR

**CURATRIX** n female curator

**CURATS** >CURAT

**CURB** n something that restrains ▷ vb control, restrain

**CURBABLE** adj capable of being restrained

**CURBED** >CURB

**CURBER** >CURB

**CURBERS** >CURB

**CURBING** the US spelling of >KERBING

**CURBINGS** >CURBING

**CURBLESS** adj having no restraint

**CURBS** >CURB

**CURBSIDE** n pavement

**CURBSIDES** >CURBSIDE

**CURBSTONE** the US spelling of >KERBSTONE

**CURCH** n woman's plain cap or kerchief

**CURCHEF** same as >CURCH

**CURCHEFS** >CURCHEF

**CURCHES** >CURCH

**CURCULIO** n type of American weevil

**CURCULIOS** >CURCULIO

**CURCUMA** n type of tropical Asian tuberous plant

**CURCUMAS** >CURCUMA

**CURCUMIN** n yellow dye derived from turmeric

**CURCUMINE** same as >CURCUMIN

**CURCUMINS** >CURCUMIN

**CURD** n coagulated milk, used to make cheese ▷ vb turn into or become curd

**CURDED** >CURD

**CURDIER** >CURD

**CURDIEST** >CURD

**CURDINESS** >CURD

**CURDING** >CURD

**CURDLE** vb turn into curd, coagulate

**CURDLED** >CURDLE

**CURDLER** >CURDLE

**CURDLERS** >CURDLE

**CURDLES** >CURDLE

**CURDLING** >CURDLE

**CURDS** >CURD

**CURDY** >CURD

**CURE** vb get rid of (an illness or problem) ▷ n (treatment causing) curing of an illness or person

**CURED** >CURE

**CURELESS** >CURE

**CURER** >CURE

**CURERS** >CURE

**CURES** >CURE

**CURET** same as >CURETTE

**CURETS** >CURET

**CURETTAGE** n process of using a curette

**CURETTE** n surgical instrument for scraping tissue from body cavities ▷ vb scrape with a curette

**CURETTED** >CURETTE

**CURETTES** >CURETTE

**CURETTING** >CURETTE

**CURF** n type of limestone

**CURFEW** n law ordering people to stay inside their homes after a specific time at night

**CURFEWS** >CURFEW

**CURFS** >CURF

**CURFUFFLE** vb make a kerfuffle

**CURIA** n papal court and government of the Roman Catholic Church

**CURIAE** >CURIA

**CURIAL** >CURIA

**CURIALISM** n ultramontanism

**CURIALIST** >CURIALISM

**CURIAS** >CURIA

**CURIE** n standard unit of radioactivity

**CURIES** >CURIE

**CURIET** n cuirass

**CURIETS** >CURIET

**CURING** >CURE

**CURIO** n rare or unusual object valued as a collector's item

**CURIOS** >CURIO

**CURIOSA** n curiosities

**CURIOSITY** n eagerness to know or find out

**CURIOUS** adj eager to learn or know

**CURIOUSER** >CURIOUS

**CURIOUSLY** >CURIOUS

**CURITE** n oxide of uranium and lead

**CURITES** >CURITE

**CURIUM** n radioactive element artificially produced from plutonium

**CURIUMS** >CURIUM

**CURL** n curved piece of hair ▷ vb make (hair) into curls or (of hair) grow in curls

**CURLED** >CURL

**CURLER** n pin or small tube for curling hair

**CURLERS** >CURLER

**CURLEW** n long-billed wading bird

**CURLEWS** >CURLEW

**CURLI** pl n curled hairlike processes on the surface of the bacterium Escherichia coli by means of which the bacterium adheres to and infects wounds

**CURLICUE** n ornamental curl or twist ▷ vb to curl or twist elaborately, as in curlicues

**CURLICUED** >CURLICUE

**CURLICUES** >CURLICUE

**CURLIER** >CURLY

**CURLIEST** >CURLY

**CURLILY** >CURLY

**CURLINESS** >CURLY

**CURLING** n game like bowls, played with heavy stones on ice

**CURLINGS** >CURLING

**CURLPAPER** n strip of paper used to roll up and set a section of hair, usually wetted, into a curl

**CURLS** >CURL

**CURLY** adj tending to curl

**CURLYCUE** same as >CURLICUE

**CURLYCUES** >CURLYCUE

**CURN** n grain (of corn etc)

**CURNEY** same as >CURNY

**CURNIER** >CURNY

**CURNIEST** >CURNY

**CURNS** >CURN

**CURNY** adj granular

**CURPEL** same as >CRUPPER

**CURPELS** >CURPEL

**CURR** vb to purr

**CURRACH** a Scot or Irish name for >CORACLE

**CURRACHS** >CURRACH

**CURRAGH** same as >CURRACH

**CURRAGHS** >CURRAGH

**CURRAJONG** same as >KURRAJONG

**CURRAN** n black bun

**CURRANS** >CURRAN

**CURRANT** n small dried grape

**CURRANTS** >CURRANT

**CURRANTY** >CURRANT

**CURRAWONG** n Australian songbird

**CURRED** >CURR

**CURREJONG** as >KURRAJONG

**CURRENCY** n money in use in a particular country

**CURRENT** adj of the immediate present ▷ n flow of water or air in one direction

**CURRENTLY** >CURRENT

**CURRENTS** >CURRENT

**CURRICLE** n two-wheeled open carriage drawn by two horses side by side

**CURRICLES** >CURRICLE

**CURRICULA** n plural form of singular curriculum: course of study in one subject at school or college

**CURRIE** same as >CURRY

**CURRIED** >CURRY

**CURRIER** n person who curries leather

**CURRIERS** >CURRIER

**CURRIERY** n trade, work, or place of occupation of a currier

**CURRIES** >CURRY

**CURRIJONG** same as >KURRAJONG

**CURRING** >CURR

**CURRISH** adj of or like a cur

**CURRISHLY** >CURRISH

**CURRS** >CURR

**CURRY** n Indian dish of meat or vegetables in a hot spicy sauce ▷ vb prepare (food) with curry powder

**CURRYCOMB** n ridged comb used for grooming horses

**CURRYING** >CURRY

**CURRYINGS** >CURRY

**CURS** >CUR

**CURSAL** >CURSUS

**CURSE** vb swear (at) ▷ n swearword

**CURSED** >CURSE

**CURSEDER** >CURSE

**CURSEDEST** >CURSE

**CURSEDLY** >CURSE

**CURSENARY** same as >CURSORARY

**CURSER** >CURSE

**CURSERS** >CURSE

**CURSES** >CURSE

**CURSI** >CURSUS

**CURSING** >CURSE

**CURSINGS** >CURSE

**CURSITOR** n clerk in the Court of Chancery

**CURSITORS** >CURSITOR

**CURSITORY** >CURSITOR

**CURSIVE** n (handwriting) done with joined letters ▷ adj of handwriting or print in which letters are joined in a flowing style

**CURSIVELY** >CURSIVE

**CURSIVES** >CURSIVE

**CURSOR** n movable point of light that shows a specific position on a visual display unit

**CURSORARY** adj cursory

**CURSORES** >CURSOR

**CURSORIAL** adj adapted for running

**CURSORILY** >CURSORY

**CURSORS** >CURSOR

**CURSORY** adj quick and superficial

**CURST** >CURSE

**CURSTNESS** n peevishness

**CURSUS** n Neolithic parallel earthworks

**CURT** adj brief and rather rude

**CURTAIL** vb cut short

**CURTAILED** >CURTAIL

**CURTAILER** >CURTAIL

**CURTAILS** >CURTAIL

**CURTAIN** n piece of cloth hung at a window or opening as a screen ▷ vb provide with curtains

**CURTAINED** >CURTAIN

**CURTAINS** pl n death or ruin

**CURTAL** adj cut short ▷ n animal whose tail has been docked

**CURTALAX** same as >CURTALAXE

**CURTALAXE** n cutlass

**CURTALS** >CURTAL

**CURTANA** n unpointed sword carried before an English sovereign at a

coronation as an emblem of mercy
**CURTANAS** >CURTANA
**CURTATE** *adj* shortened
**CURTATION** >CURTATE
**CURTAXE** *same as* >CURTALAXE
**CURTAXES** >CURTAXE
**CURTER** >CURT
**CURTESIES** >CURTESY
**CURTEST** >CURT
**CURTESY** *n* widower's life interest in his wife's estate
**CURTILAGE** *n* enclosed area of land adjacent to a dwelling house
**CURTLY** >CURT
**CURTNESS** >CURT
**CURTSEY** *same as* >CURTSY
**CURTSEYED** >CURTSEY
**CURTSEYS** >CURTSEY
**CURTSIED** >CURTSY
**CURTSIES** >CURTSY
**CURTSY** *n* woman's gesture of respect made by bending the knees and bowing the head ▷ *vb* make a curtsy
**CURTSYING** >CURTSY
**CURULE** *adj* (in ancient Rome) of the highest rank, esp one entitled to use a curule chair
**CURVATE** *adj* curved
**CURVATED** *same as* >CURVATE
**CURVATION** >CURVATE
**CURVATIVE** *adj* having curved edges
**CURVATURE** *n* curved shape
**CURVE** *n* continuously bending line with no straight parts ▷ *vb* form or move in a curve
**CURVEBALL** *n* in baseball, a ball pitched in a curving path ▷ *vb* pitch a curveball
**CURVED** >CURVE
**CURVEDLY** >CURVE
**CURVES** >CURVE
**CURVESOME** *adj* curvaceous
**CURVET** *n* horse's low leap with all four feet off the ground ▷ *vb* make such a leap
**CURVETED** >CURVET
**CURVETING** >CURVET
**CURVETS** >CURVET
**CURVETTED** >CURVET
**CURVEY** *same as* >CURVY
**CURVIER** >CURVE
**CURVIEST** >CURVE
**CURVIFORM** *adj* having a curved form
**CURVING** >CURVE
**CURVITAL** *adj* relating to curvature
**CURVITIES** >CURVITY
**CURVITY** *n* curvedness
**CURVY** >CURVE
**CUSCUS** *n* large Australian nocturnal possum
**CUSCUSES** >CUSCUS

**CUSEC** *n* unit of flow equal to 1 cubic foot per second
**CUSECS** >CUSEC
**CUSH** *n* cushion
**CUSHAT** *n* wood pigeon
**CUSHATS** >CUSHAT
**CUSHAW** *same as* >CASHAW
**CUSHAWS** >CUSHAW
**CUSHES** >CUSH
**CUSHIE** *same as* >CUSHAT
**CUSHIER** >CUSHY
**CUSHIES** >CUSHIE
**CUSHIEST** >CUSHY
**CUSHILY** >CUSHY
**CUSHINESS** >CUSHY
**CUSHION** *n* bag filled with soft material, to make a seat more comfortable ▷ *vb* lessen the effects of
**CUSHIONED** >CUSHION
**CUSHIONET** *n* small cushion
**CUSHIONS** >CUSHION
**CUSHIONY** >CUSHION
**CUSHTY** *interj* exclamation of pleasure, agreement, approval, etc
**CUSHY** *adj* easy
**CUSK** *n* gadoid food fish, *Brosmius brosme*, of northern coastal waters, having a single long dorsal fin
**CUSKS** >CUSK
**CUSP** *n* pointed end, esp on a tooth
**CUSPAL** >CUSP
**CUSPATE** *adj* having a cusp or cusps
**CUSPATED** *same as* >CUSPATE
**CUSPED** *same as* >CUSPATE
**CUSPID** *n* tooth having one point
**CUSPIDAL** *same as* >CUSPIDATE
**CUSPIDATE** *adj* having a cusp or cusps
**CUSPIDES** >CUSPIS
**CUSPIDOR** *another word (esp US) for* >SPITTOON
**CUSPIDORE** *same as* >CUSPIDOR
**CUSPIDORS** >CUSPIDOR
**CUSPIDS** >CUSPID
**CUSPIS** *n* in anatomy, tapering structure
**CUSPS** >CUSP
**CUSS** *n* curse, oath ▷ *vb* swear (at)
**CUSSED** *adj* obstinate
**CUSSEDLY** >CUSSED
**CUSSER** *same as* >COOSER
**CUSSERS** >CUSSER
**CUSSES** >CUSS
**CUSSING** >CUSS
**CUSSO** *n* tree of the rose family
**CUSSOS** >CUSSO
**CUSSWORD** *n* swearword
**CUSSWORDS** >CUSSWORD
**CUSTARD** *n* sweet yellow sauce made from milk and eggs

**CUSTARDS** >CUSTARD
**CUSTARDY** >CUSTARD
**CUSTOCK** *same as* >CASTOCK
**CUSTOCKS** >CUSTOCK
**CUSTODE** *n* custodian
**CUSTODES** >CUSTODE
**CUSTODIAL** >CUSTODY
**CUSTODIAN** *n* person in charge of a public building
**CUSTODIER** *n* custodian
**CUSTODIES** >CUSTODY
**CUSTODY** *n* protective care
**CUSTOM** *n* long-established activity or action ▷ *adj* made to the specifications of an individual customer
**CUSTOMARY** *adj* usual ▷ *n* statement in writing of customary laws and practices
**CUSTOMED** *adj* accustomed
**CUSTOMER** *n* person who buys goods or services
**CUSTOMERS** >CUSTOMER
**CUSTOMISE** *same as* >CUSTOMIZE
**CUSTOMIZE** *vb* make (something) according to a customer's individual requirements
**CUSTOMS** *n* duty charged on imports or exports
**CUSTOS** *n* superior in the Franciscan religious order
**CUSTREL** *n* knave
**CUSTRELS** >CUSTREL
**CUSTUMAL** *another word for* >CUSTOMARY
**CUSTUMALS** >CUSTUMAL
**CUSTUMARY** *n* customary
**CUT** *vb* open up, penetrate, wound, or divide with a sharp instrument ▷ *n* act of cutting
**CUTANEOUS** *adj* of the skin
**CUTAWAY** *adj* (of a drawing or model) having part of the outside omitted to reveal the inside ▷ *n* man's coat cut diagonally from the front waist to the back of the knees
**CUTAWAYS** >CUTAWAY
**CUTBACK** *n* decrease or reduction ▷ *vb* shorten by cutting
**CUTBACKS** >CUTBACK
**CUTBANK** *n* steep banking at a bend in a river
**CUTBANKS** >CUTBANK
**CUTCH** *same as* >CATECHU
**CUTCHA** *adj* crude
**CUTCHERRY** *n* (formerly, in India) government offices and law courts collectively
**CUTCHERY** *same as* >CUTCHERRY
**CUTCHES** >CUTCH
**CUTDOWN** *n* decrease
**CUTDOWNS** >CUTDOWN
**CUTE** *adj* appealing or attractive
**CUTELY** >CUTE
**CUTENESS** >CUTE

**CUTER** >CUTE
**CUTES** >CUTIS
**CUTESIE** *same as* >CUTESY
**CUTESIER** >CUTESY
**CUTESIEST** >CUTESY
**CUTEST** >CUTE
**CUTESY** *adj* affectedly cute or coy
**CUTEY** *same as* >CUTIE
**CUTEYS** >CUTEY
**CUTGLASS** *adj* (of an accent) upper-class
**CUTGRASS** *n* any grass of the genus Leersia
**CUTICLE** *n* skin at the base of a fingernail or toenail
**CUTICLES** >CUTICLE
**CUTICULA** *n* cuticle
**CUTICULAE** >CUTICULA
**CUTICULAR** >CUTICLE
**CUTIE** *n* person regarded as appealing or attractive, esp a girl or woman
**CUTIES** >CUTIE
**CUTIKIN** *same as* >CUTIKIN
**CUTIKINS** >CUTIKIN
**CUTIN** *n* waxy waterproof substance, consisting of derivatives of fatty acids, that is the main constituent of the plant cuticle
**CUTINISE** *same as* >CUTINIZE
**CUTINISED** >CUTINISE
**CUTINISES** >CUTINISE
**CUTINIZE** *vb* become or cause to become covered or impregnated with cutin
**CUTINIZED** >CUTINIZE
**CUTINIZES** >CUTINIZE
**CUTINS** >CUTIN
**CUTIS** *a technical name for the* >SKIN
**CUTISES** >CUTIS
**CUTLAS** *same as* >CUTLASS
**CUTLASES** >CUTLAS
**CUTLASS** *n* curved one-edged sword formerly used by sailors
**CUTLASSES** >CUTLASS
**CUTLER** *n* maker of cutlery
**CUTLERIES** >CUTLERY
**CUTLERS** >CUTLER
**CUTLERY** *n* knives, forks, and spoons
**CUTLET** *n* small piece of meat like a chop
**CUTLETS** >CUTLET
**CUTLINE** *n* caption
**CUTLINES** >CUTLINE
**CUTOFF** *n* limit or termination
**CUTOFFS** >CUTOFF
**CUTOUT** *n* something that has been cut out from something else
**CUTOUTS** >CUTOUT
**CUTOVER** *n* transitional period in IT system changeover, during which old and new systems are working concurrently
**CUTOVERS** >CUTOVER

CUTPURSE n pickpocket
CUTPURSES > CUTPURSE
CUTS > CUT
CUTTABLE adj capable of being cut
CUTTAGE n propagation by using parts taken from growing plants
CUTTAGES > CUTTAGE
CUTTER n person or tool that cuts
CUTTERS > CUTTER
CUTTHROAT n person who cuts throats
CUTTIER > CUTTY
CUTTIES > CUTTY
CUTTIEST > CUTTY
CUTTING > CUT
CUTTINGLY > CUT
CUTTINGS > CUT
CUTTLE vb to whisper
CUTTLED > CUTTLE
CUTTLES > CUTTLE
CUTTLING > CUTTLE
CUTTO n large knife
CUTTOE same as > CUTTO
CUTTOES > CUTTO
CUTTY adj short or cut short ▷ n something cut short, such as a spoon or short-stemmed tobacco pipe
CUTUP n joker or prankster
CUTUPS > CUTUP
CUTWATER n forward part of the stem of a vessel, which cuts through the water
CUTWATERS > CUTWATER
CUTWORK n openwork embroidery in which the pattern is cut away from the background
CUTWORKS > CUTWORK
CUTWORM n caterpillar of various noctuid moths, esp those of the genus Argrotis, which is a pest of young crop plants in North America
CUTWORMS > CUTWORM
CUVEE n individual batch or blend of wine
CUVEES > CUVEE
CUVETTE n shallow dish or vessel for holding liquid
CUVETTES > CUVETTE
CUZ n cousin
CUZZES > CUZ
CWM same as > CIRQUE
CWMS > CWM
CWTCH vb be snuggled up
CWTCHED > CWTCH
CWTCHES > CWTCH
CWTCHING > CWTCH
CYAN n highly saturated green-blue that is the complementary colour of red and forms, with magenta and yellow, a set of primary colours ▷ adj of this colour
CYANAMID same as > CYANAMIDE

CYANAMIDE n white or colourless crystalline soluble weak dibasic acid, which can be hydrolysed to urea
CYANAMIDS > CYANAMID
CYANATE n any salt or ester of cyanic acid
CYANATES > CYANATE
CYANIC as in cyanic acid colourless poisonous volatile liquid acid
CYANID same as > CYANIDE
CYANIDE n extremely poisonous chemical compound ▷ vb treat with cyanide
CYANIDED > CYANIDE
CYANIDES > CYANIDE
CYANIDING > CYANIDE
CYANIDS > CYANID
CYANIN same as > CYANINE
CYANINE n blue dye used to extend the sensitivity of photographic emulsions to colours other than blue and ultraviolet
CYANINES > CYANINE
CYANINS > CYANIN
CYANISE vb to turn into cyanide
CYANISED > CYANISE
CYANISES > CYANISE
CYANISING > CYANISE
CYANITE a variant spelling of > KYANITE
CYANITES > CYANITE
CYANITIC > CYANITE
CYANIZE same as > CYANISE
CYANIZED > CYANIZE
CYANIZES > CYANIZE
CYANIZING > CYANIZE
CYANO adj containing cyanogen
CYANOGEN n poisonous colourless flammable gas
CYANOGENS > CYANOGEN
CYANOSED adj affected by cyanosis
CYANOSES > CYANOSIS
CYANOSIS n blueness of the skin, caused by a deficiency of oxygen in the blood
CYANOTIC > CYANOSIS
CYANOTYPE another name for > BLUEPRINT
CYANS > CYAN
CYANURATE n chemical derived from cyanide
CYANURET n cyanide
CYANURETS > CYANURET
CYATHI > CYATHUS
CYATHIA > CYATHIUM
CYATHIUM n inflorescence of the type found on the poinsettia
CYATHUS n ancient measure of wine
CYBER adj involving computers
CYBERCAFE n café equipped with computer terminals which

customers can use to access the internet
CYBERCAST same as > WEBCAST
CYBERNATE vb control (a manufacturing process) with a servomechanism or (of a process) to be controlled by a servomechanism
CYBERNAUT n person using internet
CYBERPET n electronic toy that simulates the activities of a pet, requiring the owner to feed, discipline, and entertain it
CYBERPETS > CYBERPET
CYBERPORN n pornography on Internet
CYBERPUNK n genre of science fiction that features rebellious computer hackers and is set in a dystopian society integrated by computer networks
CYBERSEX n exchanging of sexual messages or information via the internet
CYBERWAR n information warfare
CYBERWARS > CYBERWAR
CYBORG n (in science fiction) a living being whose powers are enhanced by computer implants
CYBORGS > CYBORG
CYBRARIAN n person in charge of computer archives
CYBRID n cytoplasmic hybrid (hybrid resulting from the fusion of a cytoplast and a whole cell)
CYBRIDS > CYBRID
CYCAD n any tropical or subtropical gymnosperm plant of the phylum Cycadophyta, having an unbranched stem with fernlike leaves crowded at the top
CYCADEOID n (now extinct) plant with a woody stem and tough leaves
CYCADS > CYCAD
CYCAS n palm tree of the genus Cycas
CYCASES > CYCAS
CYCASIN n glucoside, toxic to mammals, occurring in cycads
CYCASINS > CYCASIN
CYCLAMATE n salt or ester of cyclamic acid. Certain of the salts have a very sweet taste and were formerly used as food additives and sugar substitutes
CYCLAMEN n plant with

red, pink, or white flowers ▷ adj of a dark reddish-purple colour
CYCLAMENS > CYCLAMEN
CYCLASE n enzyme which acts as a catalyst in the formation of a cyclic compound
CYCLASES > CYCLASE
CYCLE vb ride a bicycle ▷ n bicycle
CYCLECAR n any light car with an engine capacity of 1100cc or less
CYCLECARS > CYCLECAR
CYCLED > CYCLE
CYCLER same as > CYCLIST
CYCLERIES > CYCLERY
CYCLERS > CYCLIST
CYCLERY n business dealing in bicycles and bicycle accessories
CYCLES > CYCLE
CYCLEWAY n path or way designed, and reserved for, cyclists
CYCLEWAYS > CYCLEWAY
CYCLIC adj recurring or revolving in cycles
CYCLICAL same as > CYCLIC n short-term trend, of which reversal is expected
CYCLICALS > CYCLIC
CYCLICISM > CYCLIC
CYCLICITY > CYCLIC
CYCLICLY > CYCLIC
CYCLIN n type of protein
CYCLING > CYCLE
CYCLINGS > CYCLE
CYCLINS > CYCLIN
CYCLISE same as > CYCLIZE
CYCLISED > CYCLISE
CYCLISES > CYCLISE
CYCLISING > CYCLISE
CYCLIST n person who rides a bicycle
CYCLISTS > CYCLIST
CYCLITOL n alicyclic compound
CYCLITOLS > CYCLITOL
CYCLIZE vb be cyclical
CYCLIZED > CYCLIZE
CYCLIZES > CYCLIZE
CYCLIZINE n drug used to relieve the symptoms of motion sickness
CYCLIZING > CYCLIZE
CYCLO n type of rickshaw
CYCLOGIRO n aircraft lifted and propelled by pivoted blades rotating parallel to roughly horizontal transverse axes
CYCLOID adj resembling a circle ▷ n curve described by a point on the circumference of a circle as the circle rolls along a straight line
CYCLOIDAL > CYCLOID
CYCLOIDS > CYCLOID
CYCLOLITH n stone circle
CYCLONAL > CYCLONE
CYCLONE n violent wind

moving round a central area

CYCLONES > CYCLONE

CYCLONIC > CYCLONE

CYCLONITE n white crystalline insoluble explosive prepared by the action of nitric acid on hexamethylenetetramine

CYCLOPEAN adj of or relating to the Cyclops

CYCLOPES > CYCLOPS

CYCLOPIAN > CYCLOPS

CYCLOPIC > CYCLOPS

CYCLOPS n any copepod of the genus Cyclops, characterized by having one eye

CYCLORAMA n large picture, such as a battle scene, on the interior wall of a cylindrical room, designed to appear in natural perspective to a spectator in the centre

CYCLOS > CYCLO

CYCLOSES > CYCLOSIS

CYCLOSIS n circulation of cytoplasm or cell organelles, such as food vacuoles in some protozoans

CYCLOTRON n apparatus that accelerates charged particles by means of a strong vertical magnetic field

CYCLUS n cycle

CYCLUSES > CYCLUS

CYDER same as > CIDER

CYDERS > CYDER

CYESES > CYESIS

CYESIS the technical name for > PREGNANCY

CYGNET n young swan

CYGNETS > CYGNET

CYLICES > CYLIX

CYLINDER n solid or hollow body with straight sides and circular ends

CYLINDERS > CYLINDER

CYLINDRIC adj shaped like, or characteristic of a cylinder

CYLIX a variant of > KYLIX

CYMA n moulding with a double curve, part concave and part convex

CYMAE > CYMA

CYMAGRAPH same as > CYMOGRAPH

CYMAR n woman's short fur-trimmed jacket, popular in the 17th and 18th centuries

CYMARS > CYMAR

CYMAS > CYMA

CYMATIA > CYMATIUM

CYMATICS n theory and practice of a therapy whereby sound waves are directed at the body, with the aim of promoting health

CYMATIUM n top moulding

of a classical cornice or entablature

CYMBAL n percussion instrument consisting of a brass plate which is struck against another or hit with a stick

CYMBALEER > CYMBAL

CYMBALER > CYMBAL

CYMBALERS > CYMBAL

CYMBALIST > CYMBAL

CYMBALO another name for > DULCIMER

CYMBALOES > CYMBALO

CYMBALOM same as > CIMBALOM

CYMBALOMS > CYMBALOM

CYMBALOS > CYMBALO

CYMBALS > CYMBAL

CYMBIDIA > CYMBIDIUM

CYMBIDIUM n any orchid of the genus Cymbidium

CYMBIFORM adj shaped like a boat

CYMBLING same as > CYMLING

CYMBLINGS > CYMLING

CYME n flower cluster which has a single flower on the end of each stem and of which the central flower blooms first

CYMENE n colourless insoluble liquid with an aromatic odour that exists in three isomeric forms

CYMENES > CYMENE

CYMES > CYME

CYMLIN same as > CYMLING

CYMLING n pattypan squash

CYMLINGS > CYMLING

CYMLINS > CYMLIN

CYMOGENE n mixture of volatile flammable hydrocarbons, mainly butane, obtained in the distillation of petroleum

CYMOGENES > CYMOGENE

CYMOGRAPH n instrument for tracing the outline of an architectural moulding

CYMOID adj resembling a cyme or cyma

CYMOL same as > CYMENE

CYMOLS > CYMOL

CYMOPHANE n yellow or green opalescent variety of chrysoberyl

CYMOSE adj having the characteristics of a cyme

CYMOSELY > CYMOSE

CYMOUS adj relating to a cyme

CYNANCHE n any disease characterised by inflammation and swelling of the throat

CYNANCHES > CYNANCHE

CYNEGETIC adj relating to hunting

CYNIC n person who believes that people always act selfishly ▷ adj

of or relating to Sirius, the Dog Star

CYNICAL adj believing that people always act selfishly

CYNICALLY > CYNICAL

CYNICISM n attitude or beliefs of a cynic

CYNICISMS > CYNICISM

CYNICS > CYNIC

CYNODONT n carnivorous mammal-like reptile of the late Permian and Triassic periods, whose specialized teeth were well developed

CYNODONTS > CYNODONT

CYNOMOLGI n plural form of singular cynomolgus: type of monkey

CYNOSURAL > CYNOSURE

CYNOSURE n centre of attention

CYNOSURES > CYNOSURE

CYPHER same as > CIPHER

CYPHERED > CYPHER

CYPHERING > CYPHER

CYPHERS > CYPHER

CYPRES n legal doctrine stating that a testator's intentions should be carried out as closely as possible

CYPRESES > CYPRES

CYPRESS n evergreen tree with dark green leaves

CYPRESSES > CYPRESS

CYPRIAN n prostitute or dancer

CYPRIANS > CYPRIAN

CYPRID n cypris

CYPRIDES > CYPRIS

CYPRIDS > CYPRID

CYPRINE adj relating to carp

CYPRINID n any teleost fish of the mainly freshwater family Cyprinidae, typically having toothless jaws and cycloid scales and including such food and game fishes as the carp, tench, roach, rudd, and dace ▷ adj of, relating to, or belonging to the Cyprinidae

CYPRINIDS > CYPRINID

CYPRINOID adj of, relating to, or belonging to the Cyprinoidea, a large suborder of teleost fishes including the cyprinids, characins, electric eels, and loaches ▷ n any fish belonging to the Cyprinoidea

CYPRIS n member of the genus Cypris (small bivalve freshwater crustaceans)

CYPRUS same as > CYPRESS

CYPRUSES > CYPRUS

CYPSELA n dry one-seeded fruit of the daisy and related plants, which resembles an achene but is surrounded by a calyx

sheath

CYPSELAE > CYPSELA

CYST n (abnormal) sac in the body containing fluid or soft matter

CYSTEIN same as > CYSTEINE

CYSTEINE n sulphur-containing amino acid

CYSTEINES > CYSTEINE

CYSTEINIC > CYSTEINE

CYSTEINS > CYSTEIN

CYSTIC adj of, relating to, or resembling a cyst

CYSTID n cystidean

CYSTIDEAN n any echinoderm of the class Cystoidea, an extinct order of sea lilies

CYSTIDS > CYSTID

CYSTIFORM adj having the form of a cyst

CYSTINE n sulphur-containing amino acid

CYSTINES > CYSTINE

CYSTITIS n inflammation of the bladder

CYSTOCARP n reproductive body in red algae, developed after fertilization and consisting of filaments bearing carpospores

CYSTOCELE n hernia of the urinary bladder, esp one protruding into the vagina

CYSTOID adj resembling a cyst or bladder ▷ n tissue mass, such as a tumour, that resembles a cyst but lacks an outer membrane

CYSTOIDS > CYSTOID

CYSTOLITH n knoblike deposit of calcium carbonate in the epidermal cells of such plants as the stinging nettle

CYSTOTOMY n surgical incision into the gall bladder or urinary bladder

CYSTS > CYST

CYTASE n cellulose-dissolving enzyme

CYTASES > CYTASE

CYTASTER another word for > ASTER

CYTASTERS > CYTASTER

CYTE n biological cell

CYTES > CYTE

CYTIDINE n nucleoside formed by the condensation of cytosine and ribose

CYTIDINES > CYTIDINE

CYTIDYLIC as in cytidylic acid nucleotide that is found in DNA

CYTISI > CYTISUS

CYTISINE n poisonous alkaloid found in laburnum seeds

CYTISINES > CYTISINE

CYTISUS n any plant of the

broom genus, Cytisus
**CYTODE** *n* mass of protoplasm without a nucleus
**CYTODES** > CYTODE
**CYTOGENY** *n* origin and development of plant cells
**CYTOID** *adj* resembling a cell
**CYTOKINE** *n* any of various proteins, secreted by cells, that carry signals to neighbouring cells. Cytokines include interferon
**CYTOKINES** > CYTOKINE
**CYTOKININ** *n* any of a group of plant hormones that promote cell division and retard ageing in plants
**CYTOLOGIC** > CYTOLOGY
**CYTOLOGY** *n* study of plant and animal cells
**CYTOLYSES** > CYTOLYSIS
**CYTOLYSIN** *n* substance that can partially or completely destroy animal cells
**CYTOLYSIS** *n* dissolution of cells, esp by the destruction of their membranes
**CYTOLYTIC** > CYTOLYSIS
**CYTOMETER** *n* glass slide used to count and measure blood cells
**CYTOMETRY** *n* counting of blood cells using a cytometer
**CYTON** *n* main part of a neuron
**CYTONS** > CYTON
**CYTOPENIA** *n* blood disorder where there is a deficiency in the blood cells
**CYTOPLASM** *n* protoplasm of a cell excluding the nucleus
**CYTOPLAST** *n* intact cytoplasm of a single cell
**CYTOSINE** *n* white crystalline pyrimidine occurring in nucleic acids
**CYTOSINES** > CYTOSINE
**CYTOSOL** *n* solution of proteins and metabolites inside a biological cell, in which the organelles are suspended
**CYTOSOLIC** > CYTOSOL
**CYTOSOLS** > CYTOSOL
**CYTOSOME** *n* body of a cell excluding its nucleus
**CYTOSOMES** > CYTOSOME
**CYTOTAXES** > CYTOTAXIS
**CYTOTAXIS** *n* movement of cells due to external stimulation
**CYTOTOXIC** *adj* poisonous to living cells: denoting certain drugs used in the treatment of leukaemia and other cancers

**CYTOTOXIN** *n* any substance that is poisonous to living cells
**CZAPKA** *n* leather and felt peaked military helmet of Polish origin
**CZAPKAS** > CZAPKA
**CZAR** *same as* > TSAR
**CZARDAS** *n* Hungarian national dance of alternating slow and fast sections
**CZARDASES** > CZARDAS
**CZARDOM** > CZAR
**CZARDOMS** > CZAR
**CZAREVICH** *n* son of a czar
**CZAREVNA** *a variant spelling (esp US) of* > TSAREVNA
**CZAREVNAS** > CZAREVNA
**CZARINA** *variant spellings (esp US) of* > TSARINA
**CZARINAS** > CZARINA
**CZARISM** *a variant spelling (esp US) of* > TSARISM
**CZARISMS** > CZARISM
**CZARIST** > CZARISM
**CZARISTS** > CZARISM
**CZARITSA** *n* Russian empress
**CZARITSAS** > CZARITSA
**CZARITZA** *same as* > CZARINA
**CZARITZAS** > CZARINA
**CZARS** > CZAR

# Dd

**DA** *n* Burmese knife
**DAB** *vb* pat lightly ▷ *n* small amount of something soft or moist
**DABBA** *n* in Indian cookery, round metal box used to transport hot food
**DABBAS** > DABBA
**DABBED** > DAB
**DABBER** *n* pad used by printers for applying ink by hand
**DABBERS** > DABBER
**DABBING** > DAB
**DABBITIES** > DABBITY
**DABBITY** *n* temporary tattoo
**DABBLE** *vb* be involved in something superficially
**DABBLED** > DABBLE
**DABBLER** > DABBLE
**DABBLERS** > DABBLE
**DABBLES** > DABBLE
**DABBLING** > DABBLE
**DABBLINGS** > DABBLE
**DABCHICK** *n* any of several small grebes of the genera *Podiceps* and *Podilymbus*, such as *Podiceps ruficollis* of the Old World
**DABCHICKS** > DABCHICK
**DABS** > DAB
**DABSTER** *n* incompetent or amateurish worker
**DABSTERS** > DABSTER
**DACE** *n* small European freshwater fish
**DACES** > DACE
**DACHA** *n* country cottage in Russia
**DACHAS** > DACHA
**DACHSHUND** *n* dog with a long body and short legs

**DACITE** *n* volcanic rock
**DACITES** > DACITE
**DACK** *vb* remove the trousers from (someone) by force
**DACKED** > DACK
**DACKER** *vb* walk slowly
**DACKERED** > DACKER
**DACKERING** > DACKER
**DACKERS** > DACKER
**DACKING** > DACK
**DACKS** > DACK
**DACOIT** *n* (in India and Myanmar) a member of a gang of armed robbers
**DACOITAGE** *n* robbery by armed gang
**DACOITIES** > DACOITY
**DACOITS** > DACOIT
**DACOITY** *n* (in India and Myanmar) robbery by an armed gang
**DACQUOISE** *n* cake with meringue layers
**DACRON** *n* US tradename for a synthetic polyester fibre or fabric characterized by lightness and crease resistance
**DACRONS** > DACRON
**DACTYL** *n* metrical foot of three syllables, one long followed by two short
**DACTYLAR** *adj* poetry term
**DACTYLI** > DACTYLUS
**DACTYLIC** *same as* > DACTYL
**DACTYLICS** > DACTYLIC
**DACTYLIST** *n* poet
**DACTYLS** > DACTYL
**DACTYLUS** *n* tip of a squid's tentacular club
**DAD** *n* father ▷ *vb* act or treat as a father

**DADA** *n* nihilistic artistic movement of the early 20th century
**DADAH** *n* illegal drugs
**DADAHS** > DADAH
**DADAISM** *same as* > DADA
**DADAISMS** > DADAISM
**DADAIST** > DADA
**DADAISTIC** > DADA
**DADAISTS** > DADA
**DADAS** > DADA
**DADDED** > DAD
**DADDIES** > DADDY
**DADDING** > DAD
**DADDLE** *vb* walk unsteadily
**DADDLED** > DADDLE
**DADDLES** > DADDLE
**DADDLING** > DADDLE
**DADDOCK** *n* core of a dead tree
**DADDOCKS** > DADDOCK
**DADDY** *n* father
**DADGUM** *mild form of* > DAMNED
**DADO** *n* lower part of an interior wall, below a rail, decorated differently from the upper part ▷ *vb* provide with a dado
**DADOED** > DADO
**DADOES** > DADO
**DADOING** > DADO
**DADOS** > DADO
**DADS** > DAD
**DAE** *a Scot word for* > DO
**DAEDAL** *adj* skilful or intricate
**DAEDALEAN** *same as* > DAEDALIAN
**DAEDALIAN** *adj* of, relating to, or resembling the work of Daedalus, the Athenian architect and inventor of

Greek mythology
**DAEDALIC** *same as* > DAEDALIAN
**DAEING** > DAE
**DAEMON** *same as* > DEMON
**DAEMONES** > DAEMON
**DAEMONIC** > DAEMON
**DAEMONS** > DAEMON
**DAES** > DAE
**DAFF** *vb* frolic
**DAFFED** > DAFF
**DAFFIER** > DAFFY
**DAFFIES** > DAFFY
**DAFFIEST** > DAFFY
**DAFFILY** > DAFFY
**DAFFINESS** > DAFFY
**DAFFING** > DAFF
**DAFFINGS** > DAFF
**DAFFODIL** *n* yellow trumpet-shaped flower that blooms in spring ▷ *adj* brilliant yellow
**DAFFODILS** > DAFFODIL
**DAFFS** > DAFF
**DAFFY** *another word for* > DAFT
**DAFT** *adj* foolish or crazy
**DAFTAR** *Indian word for* > OFFICE
**DAFTARS** > DAFTAR
**DAFTER** > DAFT
**DAFTEST** > DAFT
**DAFTIE** *n* foolish person
**DAFTIES** > DAFTIE
**DAFTLY** > DAFT
**DAFTNESS** > DAFT
**DAG** *n* character ▷ *vb* cut daglocks from sheep
**DAGABA** *n* shrine for Buddhist relics
**DAGABAS** > DAGABA
**DAGGA** *n* cannabis
**DAGGAS** > DAGGA

DAGGED > DAG
DAGGER > DAG
DAGGERED > DAG
DAGGERING > DAG
DAGGERS > DAG
DAGGIER > DAGGY
DAGGIEST > DAGGY
DAGGING > DAG
DAGGINGS > DAG
DAGGLE vb trail through water
DAGGLED > DAGGLE
DAGGLES > DAGGLE
DAGGLING > DAGGLE
DAGGY adj amusing
DAGLOCK n dung-caked lock of wool around the hindquarters of a sheep
DAGLOCKS > DAGLOCK
DAGO n offensive term for a member of a Latin race, esp a Spaniard or Portuguese
DAGOBA n dome-shaped shrine containing relics of the Buddha or a Buddhist saint
DAGOBAS > DAGOBA
DAGOES > DAGO
DAGOS > DAGO
DAGS > DAG
DAGWOOD n European shrub
DAGWOODS > DAGWOOD
DAH n long sound used in combination with the short sound dit, in the spoken representation of Morse and other telegraphic codes
DAHABEAH n houseboat used on the Nile
DAHABEAHS > DAHABEAH
DAHABEEAH n Egyptian houseboat
DAHABIAH same as > DAHABEAH
DAHABIAHS > DAHABIAH
DAHABIEH n Egyptian houseboat
DAHABIEHS > DAHABIEH
DAHABIYA n Egyptian houseboat
DAHABIYAH n Egyptian houseboat
DAHABIYAS > DAHABIYA
DAHABIYEH n Egyptian houseboat
DAHL same as > DHAL
DAHLIA n brightly coloured garden flower
DAHLIAS > DAHLIA
DAHLS > DAHL
DAHOON n evergreen shrub
DAHOONS > DAHOON
DAHS > DAH
DAIDLE vb waddle about
DAIDLED > DAIDLE
DAIDLES > DAIDLE
DAIDLING > DAIDLE
DAIDZEIN n type of protein
DAIDZEINS > DAIDZEIN
DAIKER vb walk slowly
DAIKERED > DAIKER
DAIKERING > DAIKER

DAIKERS > DAIKER
DAIKON another name for > MOOLI
DAIKONS > DAIKON
DAILIES > DAILY
DAILINESS > DAILY
DAILY adj occurring every day or every weekday ▷ adv every day ▷ n daily newspaper
DAILYNESS > DAILY
DAIMEN adj occasional
DAIMIO same as > DAIMYO
DAIMIOS > DAIMIO
DAIMOKU n Nichiren Buddhist chant
DAIMOKUS > DAIMOKU
DAIMON same as > DEMON
DAIMONES pl n disembodied souls
DAIMONIC > DAIMON
DAIMONS > DAIMON
DAIMYO n (in Japan) one of the territorial magnates who dominated much of the country from about the 11th to the 19th century
DAIMYOS > DAIMYO
DAINE vb condescend
DAINED > DAINE
DAINES > DAINE
DAINING > DAINE
DAINT adj dainty
DAINTIER > DAINTY
DAINTIES > DAINTY
DAINTIEST > DAINTY
DAINTILY > DAINTY
DAINTY adj delicate or elegant ▷ n small cake or sweet
DAIQUIRI n iced drink containing rum, lime juice, and sugar
DAIQUIRIS > DAIQUIRI
DAIRIES > DAIRY
DAIRY n place for the processing or sale of milk and its products ▷ adj of milk or its products
DAIRYING n business of producing, processing, and selling dairy products
DAIRYINGS > DAIRYING
DAIRYMAID n (formerly) woman employed to milk cows
DAIRYMAN n man employed to look after cows
DAIRYMEN > DAIRYMAN
DAIS n raised platform in a hall, used by a speaker
DAISES > DAIS
DAISHIKI n upper garment
DAISHIKIS > DAISHIKI
DAISIED > DAISY
DAISIES > DAISY
DAISY n small wild flower with a yellow centre and white petals
DAK n system of mail delivery or passenger transport by relays of bearers or horses

stationed at intervals along a route
DAKER vb walk slowly
DAKERED > DAKER
DAKERHEN n European bird
DAKERHENS > DAKERHEN
DAKERING > DAKER
DAKERS > DAKER
DAKOIT same as > DACOIT
DAKOITI > DAKOIT
DAKOITIES > DAKOIT
DAKOITIS > DAKOIT
DAKOITS > DAKOIT
DAKOITY n armed robbery
DAKS an informal name for > TROUSERS
DAL same as > DECALITRE
DALAPON n herbicide
DALAPONS > DALAPON
DALASI n standard monetary unit of The Gambia, divided into 100 bututs
DALASIS > DALASI
DALE n (esp in N England) valley
DALED same as > DALETH
DALEDH n letter of Hebrew alphabet
DALEDHS > DALEDH
DALEDS > DALED
DALES > DALE
DALESMAN n person living in a dale, esp in the dales of N England
DALESMEN > DALESMAN
DALETH n fourth letter of the Hebrew alphabet, transliterated as d or, when final, dh
DALETHS > DALETH
DALGYTE another name for > BILBY
DALGYTES > DALGYTE
DALI n type of tree
DALIS > DALI
DALLE > DALLES
DALLES pl n stretch of a river between high rock walls, with rapids and dangerous currents
DALLIANCE n flirtation
DALLIED > DALLY
DALLIER > DALLY
DALLIERS > DALLY
DALLIES > DALLY
DALLOP n semisolid lump
DALLOPS > DALLOP
DALLY vb waste time
DALLYING > DALLY
DALMAHOY n bushy wig
DALMAHOYS > DALMAHOY
DALMATIAN n breed of dog characterized by its striking spotted markings
DALMATIC n wide-sleeved tunic-like vestment open at the sides, worn by deacons and bishops
DALMATICS > DALMATIC
DALS > DAL
DALT n foster child
DALTON n atomic mass unit
DALTONIAN > DALTON

DALTONIC > DALTONISM
DALTONISM n colour blindness, esp the confusion of red and green
DALTONS > DALTON
DALTS > DALT
DAM n barrier built across a river to create a lake ▷ vb build a dam across (a river)
DAMAGE vb harm, spoil ▷ n harm to a person or thing
DAMAGED > DAMAGE
DAMAGER > DAMAGE
DAMAGERS > DAMAGE
DAMAGES pl n money awarded as compensation for injury or loss
DAMAGING > DAMAGE
DAMAN n esp the Syrian rock hyrax
DAMANS > DAMAN
DAMAR same as > DAMMAR
DAMARS > DAMMAR
DAMASCENE vb ornament (metal, esp steel) by etching or by inlaying, usually with gold or silver ▷ n design or article produced by this process ▷ adj of or relating to this process
DAMASK n fabric with a pattern woven into it, used for tablecloths etc ▷ vb ornament (metal) by etching or inlaying, usually with gold or silver
DAMASKED > DAMASK
DAMASKEEN vb decorate metal
DAMASKIN vb decorate metal
DAMASKING > DAMASK
DAMASKINS > DAMASKIN
DAMASKS > DAMASK
DAMASQUIN vb decorate metal
DAMASSIN n patterned damask
DAMASSINS > DAMASSIN
DAMBOARD n draughtboard
DAMBOARDS > DAMBOARD
DAMBROD n draughtboard
DAMBRODS > DAMBROD
DAME n woman
DAMES > DAME
DAMEWORT n sweet-scented perennial plant with mauve or white flowers
DAMEWORTS > DAMEWORT
DAMFOOL adj foolish
DAMIANA n herbal medicine
DAMIANAS > DAMIANA
DAMMAR n any of various resins obtained from SE Asian trees used for varnishes, lacquers, bases for oil paints, etc
DAMMARS > DAMMAR
DAMME interj exclamation of surprise
DAMMED > DAM
DAMMER same as > DAMMAR
DAMMERS > DAMMER

**DAMMING** > DAM
**DAMMIT** *interj* exclamation of surprise
**DAMN** *interj* exclamation of annoyance ▷ *adj* extreme(ly) ▷ *vb* condemn as bad or worthless
**DAMNABLE** *adj* annoying
**DAMNABLY** *adv* in a detestable manner
**DAMNATION** *interj* exclamation of anger ▷ *n* eternal punishment
**DAMNATORY** *adj* threatening or occasioning condemnation
**DAMNDEST** *n* utmost
**DAMNDESTS** > DAMNDEST
**DAMNED** *adj* condemned to hell ▷ *adv* extreme or extremely
**DAMNDER** > DAMNED
**DAMNEDEST** *n* utmost
**DAMNER** *n* person who damns
**DAMNERS** > DAMNER
**DAMNIFIED** > DAMNIFY
**DAMNIFIES** > DAMNIFY
**DAMNIFY** *vb* cause loss or damage to (a person)
**DAMNING** > DAMN
**DAMNINGLY** > DAMN
**DAMNS** > DAMN
**DAMOISEL** *same as* > DAMSEL
**DAMOISELS** > DAMOISEL
**DAMOSEL** *same as* > DAMSEL
**DAMOSELS** > DAMOSEL
**DAMOZEL** *same as* > DAMOISELLE
**DAMOZELS** > DAMOZEL
**DAMP** *adj* slightly wet ▷ *n* slight wetness, moisture ▷ *vb* make damp
**DAMPED** > DAMP
**DAMPEN** *vb* reduce the intensity of
**DAMPENED** > DAMPEN
**DAMPENER** > DAMPEN
**DAMPENERS** > DAMPEN
**DAMPENING** > DAMPEN
**DAMPENS** > DAMPEN
**DAMPER** *n* movable plate to regulate the draught in a fire
**DAMPERS** > DAMPER
**DAMPEST** > DAMP
**DAMPIER** > DAMPY
**DAMPIEST** > DAMPY
**DAMPING** *n* moistening or wetting
**DAMPINGS** > DAMPING
**DAMPISH** > DAMP
**DAMPLY** > DAMP
**DAMPNESS** > DAMP
**DAMPS** > DAMP
**DAMPY** *adj* damp
**DAMS** > DAM
**DAMSEL** *n* young woman
**DAMSELFLY** *n* any insect of the suborder *Zygoptera*, similar to but smaller than dragonflies and usually resting with the wings closed over the back: order

*Odonata*
**DAMSELS** > DAMSEL
**DAMSON** *n* small blue-black plumlike fruit
**DAMSONS** > DAMSON
**DAN** *n* in judo, any of the 10 black-belt grades of proficiency
**DANAZOL** *n* type of drug
**DANAZOLS** > DANAZOL
**DANCE** *vb* move the feet and body rhythmically in time to music ▷ *n* series of steps and movements in time to music
**DANCEABLE** > DANCE
**DANCED** > DANCE
**DANCEHALL** *n* style of dance-oriented reggae
**DANCER** > DANCE
**DANCERS** > DANCE
**DANCES** > DANCE
**DANCETTE** *another name for* > CHEVRON
**DANCETTEE** *adj* having a zigzag pattern
**DANCETTES** > DANCETTE
**DANCETTY** *adj* having a zigzag pattern
**DANCEY** *adj* of, relating to, or resembling dance music
**DANCIER** > DANCEY
**DANCIEST** > DANCEY
**DANCING** > DANCE
**DANCINGS** > DANCE
**DANDELION** *n* yellow-flowered wild plant
**DANDER** *n* stroll ▷ *vb* stroll
**DANDERED** > DANDER
**DANDERING** > DANDER
**DANDERS** > DANDER
**DANDIACAL** *adj* like a dandy
**DANDIER** > DANDY
**DANDIES** > DANDY
**DANDIEST** > DANDY
**DANDIFIED** > DANDIFY
**DANDIFIES** > DANDIFY
**DANDIFY** *vb* dress like or cause to resemble a dandy
**DANDILY** > DANDY
**DANDIPRAT** *n* small English coin minted in the 16th century
**DANDLE** *vb* move (a child) up and down on one's knee
**DANDLED** > DANDLE
**DANDLER** > DANDLE
**DANDLERS** > DANDLE
**DANDLES** > DANDLE
**DANDLING** > DANDLE
**DANDRIFF** *same as* > DANDRUFF
**DANDRIFFS** > DANDRIFF
**DANDRUFF** *n* loose scales of dry dead skin shed from the scalp
**DANDRUFFS** > DANDRUFF
**DANDRUFFY** > DANDRUFF
**DANDY** *n* man who is overconcerned with the elegance of his appearance ▷ *adj* very good
**DANDYFUNK** *n* ship's biscuit
**DANDYISH** > DANDY

**DANDYISM** > DANDY
**DANDYISMS** > DANDY
**DANDYPRAT** *n* English coin
**DANEGELD** *n* tax levied in Anglo-Saxon England to provide protection money for, or to finance forces to oppose, Viking invaders
**DANEGELDS** > DANEGELD
**DANEGELT** *same as* > DANEGELD
**DANEGELTS** > DANEGELT
**DANELAGH** *same as* > DANELAW
**DANELAGHS** > DANELAGH
**DANELAW** *n* Danish law and customs of northern, central, and eastern parts of Anglo-Saxon England
**DANELAWS** > DANELAW
**DANEWEED** *n* dwarf elder
**DANEWEEDS** > DANEWEED
**DANEWORT** *n* dwarf elder
**DANEWORTS** > DANEWORT
**DANG** *a euphemistic word for* > DAMN
**DANGED** > DANG
**DANGER** *n* possibility of being injured or killed ▷ *vb* in archaic usage, endanger
**DANGERED** > DANGER
**DANGERING** > DANGER
**DANGEROUS** *adj* likely or able to cause injury or harm
**DANGERS** > DANGER
**DANGING** > DANG
**DANGLE** *vb* hang loosely ▷ *n* act of dangling or something that dangles
**DANGLED** > DANGLE
**DANGLER** > DANGLE
**DANGLERS** > DANGLE
**DANGLES** > DANGLE
**DANGLIER** > DANGLE
**DANGLIEST** > DANGLE
**DANGLING** > DANGLE
**DANGLINGS** > DANGLE
**DANGLY** > DANGLE
**DANGS** > DANG
**DANIO** *n* any brightly coloured tropical freshwater cyprinid fish of the genus *Danio* and related genera: popular aquarium fishes
**DANIOS** > DANIO
**DANISH** *n* sweet pastry
**DANISHES** > DANISH
**DANK** *adj* unpleasantly damp and chilly ▷ *n* unpleasant damp and chilliness
**DANKER** > DANK
**DANKEST** > DANK
**DANKISH** > DANK
**DANKLY** > DANK
**DANKNESS** > DANK
**DANKS** > DANK
**DANNEBROG** *n* Danish flag
**DANNIES** > DANNY
**DANNY** *n* hand (used esp when addressing children)
**DANS** > DAN

**DANSEUR** *n* male ballet dancer
**DANSEURS** > DANSEUR
**DANSEUSE** *n* female ballet dancer
**DANSEUSES** > DANSEUSE
**DANT** *vb* intimidate
**DANTED** > DANT
**DANTHONIA** *n* any of various grasses of the genus *Danthonia*, of N temperate regions and South America
**DANTING** > DANT
**DANTON** *same as* > DAUNTON
**DANTONED** > DANTON
**DANTONING** > DANTON
**DANTONS** > DANTON
**DANTS** > DANT
**DAP** *vb* fish with a natural or artificial fly on a floss silk line so that the wind makes the fly bob on and off the surface of the water
**DAPHNE** *n* any shrub of the Eurasian thymelaeaceous genus *Daphne*, such as the mezereon and spurge laurel: ornamentals with shiny evergreen leaves and clusters of small bell-shaped flowers
**DAPHNES** > DAPHNE
**DAPHNIA** *n* any water flea of the genus *Daphnia*, having a rounded body enclosed in a transparent shell and bearing branched swimming antennae
**DAPHNIAS** > DAPHNIA
**DAPHNID** *n* water flea
**DAPHNIDS** > DAPHNID
**DAPPED** > DAP
**DAPPER** *adj* (of a man) neat in appearance ▷ *n* fisherman or -woman who uses a bobbing bait
**DAPPERER** > DAPPER
**DAPPEREST** > DAPPER
**DAPPERLY** > DAPPER
**DAPPERS** > DAPPER
**DAPPING** > DAP
**DAPPLE** *vb* mark or become marked with spots or patches of a different colour ▷ *n* mottled or spotted markings ▷ *adj* marked with dapples or spots
**DAPPLED** > DAPPLE
**DAPPLES** > DAPPLE
**DAPPLING** > DAPPLE
**DAPS** > DAP
**DAPSONE** *n* antimicrobial drug used to treat leprosy and certain types of dermatitis
**DAPSONES** > DAPSONE
**DAQUIRI** *n* rum cocktail
**DAQUIRIS** > DAQUIRI
**DARAF** *n* unit of elastance equal to a reciprocal farad
**DARAFS** > DARAF
**DARB** *n* something

excellent

**DARBAR** *n* hall in Sikh temple

**DARBARS** > DARBAR

**DARBIES** > HANDCUFFS

**DARBS** > DARB

**DARCIES** > DARCY

**DARCY** *n* unit expressing the permeability coefficient of rock

**DARCYS** > DARCY

**DARE** *vb* be courageous enough to try (to do something) ▷ *n* challenge to do something risky

**DARED** > DARE

**DAREDEVIL** *n* recklessly bold person ▷ *adj* recklessly bold or daring

**DAREFUL** *adj* daring

**DARER** > DARE

**DARERS** > DARE

**DARES** > DARE

**DARESAY** *vb* venture to say

**DARG** *n* day's work

**DARGA** *n* Muslim shrine

**DARGAH** *n* tomb of a Muslim saint

**DARGAHS** > DARGAH

**DARGAS** > DARGA

**DARGLE** *n* wooded hollow

**DARGLES** > DARGLE

**DARGS** > DARG

**DARI** *n* variety of sorghum

**DARIC** *n* gold coin of ancient Persia

**DARICS** > DARIC

**DARING** *adj* willing to take risks ▷ *n* courage to do dangerous things

**DARINGLY** > DARING

**DARINGS** > DARING

**DARIOLE** *n* small cup-shaped mould used for making individual sweet or savoury dishes

**DARIOLES** > DARIOLE

**DARIS** > DARI

**DARK** *adj* having little or no light ▷ *n* absence of light ▷ *vb* in archaic usage, darken

**DARKED** > DARK

**DARKEN** *vb* make or become dark or darker

**DARKENED** > DARKEN

**DARKENER** > DARKEN

**DARKENERS** > DARKEN

**DARKENING** > DARKEN

**DARKENS** > DARKEN

**DARKER** > DARK

**DARKEST** > DARK

**DARKEY** *same as* > DARKY

**DARKEYS** > DARKEY

**DARKIE** *same as* > DARKY

**DARKIES** > DARKY

**DARKING** > DARK

**DARKISH** > DARK

**DARKLE** *vb* grow dark

**DARKLED** > DARKLE

**DARKLES** > DARKLE

**DARKLIER** > DARK

**DARKLIEST** > DARK

**DARKLING** *adj* in the dark

or night

**DARKLINGS** *adv* in darkness

**DARKLY** > DARK

**DARKMANS** *n* slang term for night-time

**DARKNESS** > DARK

**DARKROOM** *n* darkened room for processing photographic film

**DARKROOMS** > DARKROOM

**DARKS** > DARK

**DARKSOME** *adj* dark or darkish

**DARKY** *n* offensive word for a Black person

**DARLING** *n* much-loved person ▷ *adj* much-loved

**DARLINGLY** > DARLING

**DARLINGS** > DARLING

**DARN** *vb* mend (a garment) with a series of interwoven stitches ▷ *n* patch of darned work

**DARNATION** *mild form of* > DAMNATION

**DARNDEST** *n* utmost

**DARNDESTS** > DARNDEST

**DARNED** *adj* damned

**DARNEDER** > DARNED

**DARNEDEST** *a euphemistic word for* > DAMNEDEST

**DARNEL** *n* weed that grows in grain fields

**DARNELS** > DARNEL

**DARNER** > DARN

**DARNERS** > DARN

**DARNING** > DARN

**DARNINGS** > DARN

**DARNS** > DARN

**DAROGHA** *n* in India, manager

**DAROGHAS** > DAROGHA

**DARRAIGN** *same as* > DERAIGN

**DARRAIGNE** *vb* clear from guilt

**DARRAIGNS** > DARRAIGN

**DARRAIN** *vb* clear of guilt

**DARRAINE** *vb* clear of guilt

**DARRAINED** > DARRAINE

**DARRAINES** > DARRAINE

**DARRAINS** > DARRAIN

**DARRAYN** *vb* clear of guilt

**DARRAYNED** > DARRAYN

**DARRAYNS** > DARRAYN

**DARRE** *vb* dare

**DARRED** > DARRE

**DARRES** > DARRE

**DARRING** > DARRE

**DARSHAN** *n* Hindu blessing

**DARSHANS** > DARSHAN

**DART** *n* small narrow pointed missile that is thrown or shot, esp in the game of darts ▷ *vb* move or direct quickly and suddenly

**DARTBOARD** *n* circular board used as the target in the game of darts

**DARTED** > DART

**DARTER** *n* any aquatic bird of the genus *Anhinga* and family *Anhingidae*, of

tropical and subtropical inland waters, having a long slender neck and bill: order *Pelecaniformes* (pelicans, cormorants, etc)

**DARTERS** > DARTER

**DARTING** > DART

**DARTINGLY** > DART

**DARTLE** *vb* move swiftly

**DARTLED** > DARTLE

**DARTLES** > DARTLE

**DARTLING** > DARTLE

**DARTRE** *n* skin disease

**DARTRES** > DARTRE

**DARTROUS** *adj* having a skin disease

**DARTS** *n* game in which darts are thrown at a dartboard

**DARZI** *n* tailor in India

**DARZIS** > DARZI

**DAS** > DA

**DASH** *vb* move quickly ▷ *n* sudden quick movement

**DASHBOARD** *n* instrument panel in a vehicle

**DASHED** > DASH

**DASHEEN** *another name for* > TARO

**DASHEENS** > DASHEEN

**DASHEKI** *n* upper garment

**DASHEKIS** > DASHEKI

**DASHER** *n* one of the boards surrounding an ice-hockey rink

**DASHERS** > DASHER

**DASHES** > DASH

**DASHI** *n* clear stock made from dried fish and kelp

**DASHIER** > DASHY

**DASHIEST** > DASHY

**DASHIKI** *n* large loose-fitting buttonless upper garment worn esp by Blacks in the US, Africa, and the Caribbean

**DASHIKIS** > DASHIKI

**DASHING** *adj* stylish and attractive

**DASHINGLY** > DASHING

**DASHIS** > DASHI

**DASHPOT** *n* device for damping vibrations

**DASHPOTS** > DASHPOT

**DASHY** *adj* showy

**DASSIE** *n* type of hoofed rodent-like animal

**DASSIES** > DASSIE

**DASTARD** *n* contemptible sneaking coward

**DASTARDLY** *adj* wicked and cowardly

**DASTARDS** > DASTARD

**DASTARDY** *n* cowardice

**DASYMETER** *n* device for measuring density of gases

**DASYPOD** *n* armadillo

**DASYPODS** > DASYPOD

**DASYURE** *n* small marsupial of Australia, New Guinea, and adjacent islands

**DASYURES** > DASYURE

**DATA** *n* information

consisting of observations, measurements, or facts

**DATABANK** *n* store of a large amount of information, esp in a form that can be handled by a computer

**DATABANKS** > DATABANK

**DATABASE** *n* store of information in a form that can be easily handled by a computer ▷ *vb* put data into a database

**DATABASED** > DATABASE

**DATABASES** > DATABASE

**DATABLE** > DATE

**DATABUS** *n* computing term

**DATABUSES** > DATABUS

**DATACARD** *n* smart card

**DATACARDS** > DATACARD

**DATACOMMS** *n* computing term

**DATAFLOW** as in *dataflow architecture* means of arranging computer data processing in which operations are governed by the data present and the processing it requires rather than by a prewritten program that awaits data to be processed

**DATAGLOVE** *n* computing term

**DATAL** *adj* slow-witted ▷ *n* day labour

**DATALLER** *n* worker paid by the day

**DATALLERS** > DATALLER

**DATALS** > DATAL

**DATARIA** *n* Roman Catholic office

**DATARIAS** > DATARIA

**DATARIES** > DATARY

**DATARY** *n* head of the dataria, the papal office that assesses candidates for benefices reserved to the Holy See

**DATCHA** *same as* > DACHA

**DATCHAS** > DATCHA

**DATE** *n* specified day of the month ▷ *vb* mark with the date

**DATEABLE** > DATE

**DATEBOOK** *n* list of forthcoming events

**DATEBOOKS** > DATEBOOK

**DATED** *adj* old-fashioned

**DATEDLY** > DATED

**DATEDNESS** > DATED

**DATELESS** > DATE

**DATELINE** *n* information about the place and time a story was written, placed at the top of the article

**DATELINED** > DATELINE

**DATELINES** > DATELINE

**DATER** *n* person who dates

**DATERS** > DATER

**DATES** > DATE

**DATING** *n* any of several

techniques, such as radioactive dating, dendrochronology, or varve dating, for establishing the age of rocks, palaeontological or archaeological specimens, etc

**DATINGS** > DATING

**DATIVAL** > DATIVE

**DATIVE** adj denoting a case of nouns, pronouns, and adjectives used to express the indirect object ▷ n this grammatical case

**DATIVELY** > DATIVE

**DATIVES** > DATIVE

**DATO** n chief of any of certain Muslim tribes in the Philippine Islands

**DATOLITE** n colourless mineral

**DATOLITES** > DATOLITE

**DATOS** > DATO

**DATTO** n Datsun car

**DATTOS** > DATTO

**DATUM** n single piece of information in the form of a fact or statistic

**DATUMS** > DATUM

**DATURA** n any of various chiefly Indian solanaceous plants of the genus Datura, such as the moonflower and thorn apple, having large trumpet-shaped flowers, prickly pods, and narcotic properties

**DATURAS** > DATURA

**DATURIC** > DATURA

**DATURINE** n poisonous alkaloid

**DATURINES** > DATURINE

**DAUB** vb smear or spread quickly or clumsily ▷ n crude or badly done painting

**DAUBE** n braised meat stew

**DAUBED** > DAUB

**DAUBER** > DAUB

**DAUBERIES** > DAUBERY

**DAUBERS** > DAUB

**DAUBERY** n act or an instance of daubing

**DAUBES** > DAUBE

**DAUBIER** > DAUB

**DAUBIEST** > DAUB

**DAUBING** > DAUB

**DAUBINGLY** > DAUB

**DAUBINGS** > DAUB

**DAUBRIES** > DAUBRY

**DAUBRY** n unskilful painting

**DAUBS** > DAUB

**DAUBY** > DAUB

**DAUD** n lump or chunk of something ▷ vb (in dialect) whack

**DAUDED** > DAUD

**DAUDING** > DAUD

**DAUDS** > DAUD

**DAUGHTER** n female child ▷ adj denoting a cell, chromosome, etc

produced by the division of one of its own kind

**DAUGHTERS** > DAUGHTER

**DAULT** n foster child

**DAULTS** > DAULT

**DAUNDER** vb stroll

**DAUNDERED** > DAUNDER

**DAUNDERS** > DAUNDER

**DAUNER** vb stroll

**DAUNERED** > DAUNER

**DAUNERING** > DAUNER

**DAUNERS** > DAUNER

**DAUNT** vb intimidate

**DAUNTED** > DAUNT

**DAUNTER** > DAUNT

**DAUNTERS** > DAUNT

**DAUNTING** adj intimidating or worrying

**DAUNTLESS** adj fearless

**DAUNTON** vb dishearten

**DAUNTONED** > DAUNTON

**DAUNTONS** > DAUNTON

**DAUNTS** > DAUNT

**DAUPHIN** n (formerly) eldest son of the king of France

**DAUPHINE** n wife of a dauphin

**DAUPHINES** > DAUPHINE

**DAUPHINS** > DAUPHIN

**DAUR** a Scot word for > DARE

**DAURED** > DAUR

**DAURING** > DAUR

**DAURS** > DAUR

**DAUT** vb fondle

**DAUTED** > DAUT

**DAUTIE** n darling

**DAUTIES** > DAUTIE

**DAUTING** > DAUT

**DAUTS** > DAUT

**DAVEN** vb pray

**DAVENED** > DAVEN

**DAVENING** > DAVEN

**DAVENPORT** n small writing table with drawers

**DAVENS** > DAVEN

**DAVIDIA** n Chinese shrub

**DAVIDIAS** > DAVIDIA

**DAVIES** > DAVY

**DAVIT** n crane, usu. one of a pair, at a ship's side, for lowering and hoisting a lifeboat

**DAVITS** > DAVIT

**DAVY** n miner's safety lamp

**DAW** n an archaic, dialect, or poetic name for a jackdaw ▷ vb old word for dawn

**DAWAH** n practice of educating non-Muslims about the message of Islam

**DAWAHS** > DAWAH

**DAWBAKE** n foolish or slow-witted person

**DAWBAKES** > DAWBAKE

**DAWBRIES** > DAWBRY

**DAWBRY** n unskilful painting

**DAWCOCK** n male jackdaw

**DAWCOCKS** > DAWCOCK

**DAWD** vb thump

**DAWDED** > DAWD

**DAWDING** > DAWD

**DAWDLE** vb walk slowly, lag behind

**DAWDLED** > DAWDLE

**DAWDLER** > DAWDLE

**DAWDLERS** > DAWDLE

**DAWDLES** > DAWDLE

**DAWDLING** > DAWDLE

**DAWDS** > DAWD

**DAWED** > DAW

**DAWEN** > DAW

**DAWING** > DAW

**DAWISH** > DAW

**DAWK** same as > DAK

**DAWKS** > DAWK

**DAWN** n daybreak ▷ vb begin to grow light

**DAWNED** > DAWN

**DAWNER** vb stroll

**DAWNERED** > DAWNER

**DAWNERING** > DAWNER

**DAWNERS** > DAWNER

**DAWNEY** adj (of a person) dull or slow

**DAWNING** > DAWN

**DAWNINGS** > DAWN

**DAWNLIKE** > DAWN

**DAWNS** > DAWN

**DAWS** > DAW

**DAWSONITE** n mineral

**DAWT** vb fondle

**DAWTED** > DAWT

**DAWTIE** n darling

**DAWTIES** > DAWTIE

**DAWTING** > DAWT

**DAWTS** > DAWT

**DAY** n period of 24 hours

**DAYAN** n senior rabbi, esp one who sits in a religious court

**DAYANIM** > DAYAN

**DAYANS** > DAYAN

**DAYBED** n narrow bed with a head piece and sometimes a foot piece and back, for day use

**DAYBEDS** > DAYBED

**DAYBOOK** n book in which the transactions of each day are recorded as they occur

**DAYBOOKS** > DAYBOOK

**DAYBOY** n boy who attends a boarding school daily, but returns home each evening

**DAYBOYS** > DAYBOY

**DAYBREAK** n time in the morning when light first appears

**DAYBREAKS** > DAYBREAK

**DAYCARE** n occupation, treatment, or supervision during the working day for people who might be at risk if left on their own, or whose usual carers need daytime relief

**DAYCARES** > DAYCARE

**DAYCENTRE** n building used for daycare or other welfare services

**DAYCH** vb thatch

**DAYCHED** > DAYCH

**DAYCHES** > DAYCH

**DAYCHING** > DAYCH

**DAYDREAM** n pleasant fantasy indulged in while awake ▷ vb indulge in idle fantasy

**DAYDREAMS** > DAYDREAM

**DAYDREAMT** > DAYDREAM

**DAYDREAMY** > DAYDREAM

**DAYFLIES** > DAYFLY

**DAYFLOWER** n any of various tropical and subtropical plants of the genus Commelina, having jointed creeping stems, narrow pointed leaves, and blue or purplish flowers which wilt quickly: family Commelinaceae

**DAYFLY** another name for > MAYFLY

**DAYGLO** n fluorescent colours

**DAYGLOW** n fluorescent colours

**DAYGLOWS** > DAYGLOW

**DAYLIGHT** n light from the sun

**DAYLIGHTS** pl n consciousness or wits

**DAYLILIES** > DAYLILY

**DAYLILY** n any of various plants having lily-like flowers that typically last only one day before being succeeded by others

**DAYLIT** > DAYLIGHT

**DAYLONG** adv lasting the entire day

**DAYMARE** n bad dream during the day

**DAYMARES** > DAYMARE

**DAYMARK** n navigation aid

**DAYMARKS** > DAYMARK

**DAYNT** adj dainty

**DAYROOM** n communal living room in a residential institution

**DAYROOMS** > DAYROOM

**DAYS** adv during the day, esp regularly

**DAYSACK** n rucksack

**DAYSACKS** > DAYSACK

**DAYSHELL** n thistle

**DAYSHELLS** > DAYSHELL

**DAYSIDE** n side of a planet nearest the sun

**DAYSIDES** > DAYSIDE

**DAYSMAN** n umpire

**DAYSMEN** > DAYSMAN

**DAYSPRING** a poetic word for > DAWN

**DAYSTAR** a poetic word for > SUN

**DAYSTARS** > DAYSTAR

**DAYTALE** n day labour

**DAYTALER** n worker paid by the day

**DAYTALERS** > DAYTALER

**DAYTALES** > DAYTALE

**DAYTIME** n time from sunrise to sunset

**DAYTIMES** > DAYTIME

**DAYWORK** n daytime work

**DAYWORKER** > DAYWORK

**DAYWORKS** > DAYWORK
**DAZE** vb stun, by a blow or shock ▷ n state of confusion or shock
**DAZED** > DAZE
**DAZEDLY** > DAZE
**DAZEDNESS** > DAZE
**DAZER** > DAZE
**DAZERS** > DAZE
**DAZES** > DAZE
**DAZING** > DAZE
**DAZZLE** vb impress greatly ▷ n bright light that dazzles
**DAZZLED** > DAZZLE
**DAZZLER** > DAZZLE
**DAZZLERS** > DAZZLE
**DAZZLES** > DAZZLE
**DAZZLING** > DAZZLE
**DAZZLINGS** > DAZZLING
**DE** prep of or from
**DEACIDIFY** vb removal acid from
**DEACON** n ordained minister ranking immediately below a priest ▷ vb make a deacon of
**DEACONED** > DEACON
**DEACONESS** n (in the early church and in some modern Churches) a female member of the laity with duties similar to those of a deacon
**DEACONING** > DEACON
**DEACONRY** n office or status of a deacon
**DEACONS** > DEACON
**DEAD** adj no longer alive ▷ n period during which coldness or darkness is most intense ▷ adv extremely ▷ vb in archaic usage, die or kill
**DEADBEAT** n lazy useless person
**DEADBEATS** > DEADBEAT
**DEADBOLT** n bolt operated without a spring
**DEADBOLTS** > DEADBOLT
**DEADBOY** same as > DEADMAN
**DEADBOYS** > DEADBOY
**DEADED** > DEAD
**DEADEN** vb make less intense
**DEADENED** > DEADEN
**DEADENER** > DEADEN
**DEADENERS** > DEADEN
**DEADENING** > DEADEN
**DEADENS** > DEADEN
**DEADER** > DEAD
**DEADERS** > DEAD
**DEADEST** > DEAD
**DEADEYE** n either of a pair of disclike wooden blocks, supported by straps in grooves around them, between which a line is rove so as to draw them together to tighten a shroud
**DEADEYES** > DEADEYE

**DEADFALL** n type of trap, used esp for catching large animals, in which a heavy weight falls to crush the prey
**DEADFALLS** > DEADFALL
**DEADHEAD** n person who does not pay on a bus, at a game, etc ▷ vb cut off withered flowers from (a plant)
**DEADHEADS** > DEADHEAD
**DEADHOUSE** n mortuary
**DEADING** > DEAD
**DEADLIER** > DEADLY
**DEADLIEST** > DEADLY
**DEADLIFT** vb weightlifting term
**DEADLIFTS** > DEADLIFT
**DEADLIGHT** n bull's-eye let into the deck or hull of a vessel to admit light to a cabin
**DEADLINE** n time limit ▷ vb put a time limit on an action, decision, etc
**DEADLINED** > DEADLINE
**DEADLINES** > DEADLINE
**DEADLOCK** n point in a dispute at which no agreement can be reached ▷ vb bring or come to a deadlock
**DEADLOCKS** > DEADLOCK
**DEADLY** adj likely to cause death ▷ adv extremely
**DEADMAN** n heavy plate, wall, or block buried in the ground that acts as an anchor for a retaining wall, sheet pile, etc, by a tie connecting the two
**DEADMEN** > DEADMAN
**DEADNESS** > DEAD
**DEADPAN** adj showing no emotion or expression ▷ adj deliberately emotionless ▷ n deadpan expression or manner
**DEADPANS** > DEADPAN
**DEADS** > DEAD
**DEADSTOCK** n farm equipment
**DEADWOOD** n dead trees or branches
**DEADWOODS** > DEADWOOD
**DEAERATE** vb remove air from
**DEAERATED** > DEAERATE
**DEAERATES** > DEAERATE
**DEAERATOR** > DEAERATE
**DEAF** adj unable to hear
**DEAFBLIND** adj unable to hear or see
**DEAFEN** vb make deaf, esp temporarily
**DEAFENED** > DEAFEN
**DEAFENING** n excessively loud
**DEAFENS** > DEAFEN
**DEAFER** > DEAF
**DEAFEST** > DEAF
**DEAFISH** > DEAF
**DEAFLY** > DEAF

**DEAFNESS** > DEAF
**DEAIR** vb reove air from
**DEAIRED** > DEAIR
**DEAIRING** > DEAIR
**DEAIRS** > DEAIR
**DEAL** n agreement or transaction ▷ vb inflict (a blow) on ▷ adj of fir or pine
**DEALATE** adj (of ants and other insects) having lost their wings, esp by biting or rubbing them off after mating ▷ n insect that has shed its wings
**DEALATED** same as > DEALATE
**DEALATES** > DEALATE
**DEALATION** > DEALATE
**DEALBATE** adj bleached
**DEALER** n person whose business involves buying and selling
**DEALERS** > DEALER
**DEALFISH** n long thin fish
**DEALING** > DEAL
**DEALINGS** pl n transactions or business relations
**DEALS** > DEAL
**DEALT** > DEAL
**DEAMINASE** n enzyme that breaks down amino compounds
**DEAMINATE** vb remove one or more amino groups from (a molecule)
**DEAMINISE** same as > DEAMINATE
**DEAMINIZE** same as > DEAMINATE
**DEAN** n chief administrative official of a college or university faculty ▷ vb punish (a student) by sending them to the dean
**DEANED** > DEAN
**DEANER** n shilling
**DEANERIES** > DEANERY
**DEANERS** > DEANER
**DEANERY** n office or residence of a dean
**DEANING** > DEAN
**DEANS** > DEAN
**DEANSHIP** > DEAN
**DEANSHIPS** > DEAN
**DEAR** n someone regarded with affection ▷ adj much-loved
**DEARE** vb harm
**DEARED** > DEARE
**DEARER** > DEAR
**DEARES** > DEARE
**DEAREST** > DEAR
**DEARIE** same as > DEARY
**DEARIES** > DEARY
**DEARING** > DEARE
**DEARLING** n darling
**DEARLINGS** > DEARLING
**DEARLY** adv very much
**DEARN** vb hide
**DEARNESS** > DEAR
**DEARNFUL** adj secret
**DEARNLY** > DEARN

**DEARNS** > DEARN
**DEARS** > DEAR
**DEARTH** n inadequate amount, scarcity
**DEARTHS** > DEARTH
**DEARY** n term of affection: now often sarcastic or facetious
**DEASH** vb remove ash from
**DEASHED** > DEASH
**DEASHES** > DEASH
**DEASHING** > DEASH
**DEASIL** adv in the direction of the apparent course of the sun ▷ n motion in this direction
**DEASILS** > DEASIL
**DEASIUL** n motion towards the sun
**DEASIULS** > DEASIUL
**DEASOIL** n motion towards the sun
**DEASOILS** > DEASOIL
**DEATH** n permanent end of life in a person or animal
**DEATHBED** n bed where a person is about to die or has just died
**DEATHBEDS** > DEATHBED
**DEATHBLOW** n thing or event that destroys hope
**DEATHCUP** n poisonous fungus
**DEATHCUPS** > DEATHCUP
**DEATHFUL** adj murderous
**DEATHIER** > DEATH
**DEATHIEST** > DEATH
**DEATHLESS** adj everlasting, because of fine qualities
**DEATHLIER** > DEATHLY
**DEATHLIKE** > DEATH
**DEATHLY** adv like death ▷ adj resembling death
**DEATHS** > DEATH
**DEATHSMAN** n executioner
**DEATHSMEN** > DEATHSMAN
**DEATHTRAP** n building, vehicle, etc, that is considered very unsafe
**DEATHWARD** adv heading towards death
**DEATHY** > DEATH
**DEAVE** vb deafen
**DEAVED** > DEAVE
**DEAVES** > DEAVE
**DEAVING** > DEAVE
**DEAW** n dew
**DEAWIE** > DEAW
**DEAWS** > DEAW
**DEAWY** > DEAW
**DEB** n debutante
**DEBACLE** n disastrous failure
**DEBACLES** > DEBACLE
**DEBAG** vb remove the trousers from (someone) by force
**DEBAGGED** > DEBAG
**DEBAGGING** > DEBAG
**DEBAGS** > DEBAG
**DEBAR** vb prevent, bar
**DEBARK** vb remove the bark from (a tree)
**DEBARKED** > DEBARK

**DEBARKER** > DEBARK
**DEBARKERS** > DEBARK
**DEBARKING** > DEBARK
**DEBARKS** > DEBARK
**DEBARMENT** > DEBAR
**DEBARRASS** vb relieve
**DEBARRED** > DEBAR
**DEBARRING** > DEBAR
**DEBARS** > DEBAR
**DEBASE** vb lower in value, quality, or character
**DEBASED** > DEBASE
**DEBASER** > DEBASE
**DEBASERS** > DEBASE
**DEBASES** > DEBASE
**DEBASING** > DEBASE
**DEBATABLE** adj not absolutely certain
**DEBATABLY** > DEBATABLE
**DEBATE** n discussion ▷ vb discuss formally
**DEBATED** > DEBATE
**DEBATEFUL** adj quarrelsome
**DEBATER** > DEBATE
**DEBATERS** > DEBATE
**DEBATES** > DEBATE
**DEBATING** > DEBATE
**DEBAUCH** vb make (someone) bad or corrupt, esp sexually ▷ n instance or period of extreme dissipation
**DEBAUCHED** > DEBAUCH
**DEBAUCHEE** n man who leads a life of reckless drinking, promiscuity, and self-indulgence
**DEBAUCHER** > DEBAUCH
**DEBAUCHES** > DEBAUCH
**DEBBIER** > DEBBY
**DEBBIES** > DEBBY
**DEBBIEST** > DEBBY
**DEBBY** n debutante ▷ adj of, or resembling a debutante
**DEBE** n tin
**DEBEAK** vb remove part of the beak of poultry to reduce the risk of such habits as feather-picking or cannibalism
**DEBEAKED** > DEBEAK
**DEBEAKING** > DEBEAK
**DEBEAKS** > DEBEAK
**DEBEARD** vb remove beard from mussel
**DEBEARDED** > DEBEARD
**DEBEARDS** > DEBEARD
**DEBEL** vb beat in war
**DEBELLED** > DEBEL
**DEBELLING** > DEBEL
**DEBELS** > DEBEL
**DEBENTURE** n long-term bond bearing fixed interest, issued by a company or a government agency
**DEBES** > DEBE
**DEBILE** adj lacking strength
**DEBILITY** n weakness, infirmity
**DEBIT** n acknowledgment

of a sum owing by entry on the left side of an account ▷ vb charge (an account) with a debt
**DEBITED** > DEBIT
**DEBITING** > DEBIT
**DEBITOR** n person in debt
**DEBITORS** > DEBITOR
**DEBITS** > DEBIT
**DEBONAIR** adj (of a man) charming and refined
**DEBONAIRE** adj sauve and refined
**DEBONE** vb remove bones from
**DEBONED** > DEBONE
**DEBONER** > DEBONE
**DEBONERS** > DEBONE
**DEBONES** > DEBONE
**DEBONING** > DEBONE
**DEBOSH** vb debauch
**DEBOSHED** > DEBOSH
**DEBOSHES** > DEBOSH
**DEBOSHING** > DEBOSH
**DEBOSS** vb carve a design into
**DEBOSSED** > DEBOSS
**DEBOSSES** > DEBOSS
**DEBOSSING** > DEBOSS
**DEBOUCH** vb move out from a narrow place to a wider one ▷ n outlet or passage, as for the exit of troops
**DEBOUCHE** same as > DEBOUCH
**DEBOUCHED** > DEBOUCH
**DEBOUCHES** > DEBOUCH
**DEBRIDE** vb remove dead tissue from
**DEBRIDED** > DEBRIDE
**DEBRIDES** > DEBRIDE
**DEBRIDING** > DEBRIDE
**DEBRIEF** vb receive a report from (a soldier, diplomat, etc) after an event
**DEBRIEFED** > DEBRIEF
**DEBRIEFER** > DEBRIEF
**DEBRIEFS** > DEBRIEF
**DEBRIS** n fragments of something destroyed
**DEBRUISE** vb (in heraldry) overlay or partly cover
**DEBRUISED** > DEBRUISE
**DEBRUISES** > DEBRUISE
**DEBS** > DEB
**DEBT** n something owed, esp money
**DEBTED** adj in debt
**DEBTEE** n person owed a debt
**DEBTEES** > DEBTEE
**DEBTLESS** > DEBT
**DEBTOR** n person who owes money
**DEBTORS** > DEBTOR
**DEBTS** > DEBT
**DEBUD** same as > DISBUD
**DEBUDDED** > DEBUD
**DEBUDDING** > DEBUD
**DEBUDS** > DEBUD
**DEBUG** vb find and remove defects in (a computer program) ▷ n something,

esp a computer program, that locates and removes defects in a device, system, etc
**DEBUGGED** > DEBUG
**DEBUGGER** > DEBUG
**DEBUGGERS** > DEBUG
**DEBUGGING** > DEBUG
**DEBUGS** > DEBUG
**DEBUNK** vb expose the falseness of
**DEBUNKED** > DEBUNK
**DEBUNKER** > DEBUNK
**DEBUNKERS** > DEBUNK
**DEBUNKING** > DEBUNK
**DEBUNKS** > DEBUNK
**DEBURR** vb remove burrs from (a workpiece)
**DEBURRED** > DEBURR
**DEBURRING** > DEBURR
**DEBURRS** > DEBURR
**DEBUS** vb unload (goods) or (esp of troops) to alight from a motor vehicle
**DEBUSED** > DEBUS
**DEBUSES** > DEBUS
**DEBUSING** > DEBUS
**DEBUSSED** > DEBUS
**DEBUSSES** > DEBUS
**DEBUSSING** > DEBUS
**DEBUT** n first public appearance of a performer ▷ vb make a debut
**DEBUTANT** n person who is making a first appearance in a particular capacity, such as a sportsperson playing in a first game for a team
**DEBUTANTE** n young upper-class woman being formally presented to society
**DEBUTANTS** > DEBUTANT
**DEBUTED** > DEBUT
**DEBUTING** > DEBUT
**DEBUTS** > DEBUT
**DEBYE** n unit of electric dipole moment
**DEBYES** > DEBYE
**DECACHORD** n instrument with ten strings
**DECAD** n ten years
**DECADAL** > DECADE
**DECADE** n period of ten years
**DECADENCE** n deterioration in morality or culture
**DECADENCY** same as > DECADENCE
**DECADENT** adj characterized by decay or decline, as in being self-indulgent or morally corrupt ▷ n decadent person
**DECADENTS** > DECADENT
**DECADES** > DECADE
**DECADS** > DECAD
**DECAF** n decaffeinated coffee ▷ adj decaffeinated
**DECAFF** n decaffeinated coffee
**DECAFFS** > DECAFF

**DECAFS** > DECAF
**DECAGON** n geometric figure with ten faces
**DECAGONAL** > DECAGON
**DECAGONS** > DECAGON
**DECAGRAM** n ten grams
**DECAGRAMS** > DECAGRAM
**DECAHEDRA** n plural form of singular decahedron: solid figure with ten plane faces
**DECAL** vb transfer (a design) by decalcomania
**DECALCIFY** vb remove calcium or lime from (bones, teeth, etc)
**DECALED** > DECAL
**DECALING** > DECAL
**DECALITER** same as > DECALITRE
**DECALITRE** n measure of volume equivalent to 10 litres
**DECALLED** > DECAL
**DECALLING** > DECAL
**DECALOG** same as > DECALOGUE
**DECALOGS** > DECALOG
**DECALOGUE** n Ten Commandments
**DECALS** > DECAL
**DECAMETER** same as > DECAMETRE
**DECAMETRE** n unit of length equal to ten metres
**DECAMP** vb depart secretly or suddenly
**DECAMPED** > DECAMP
**DECAMPING** > DECAMP
**DECAMPS** > DECAMP
**DECANAL** adj of or relating to a dean or deanery
**DECANALLY** > DECANAL
**DECANE** n liquid alkane hydrocarbon
**DECANES** > DECANE
**DECANI** adv be sung by the decanal side of a choir
**DECANOIC** as in decanoic acid white crystalline insoluble carboxylic acid with an unpleasant odour, used in perfumes and for making fruit flavours
**DECANT** vb pour (a liquid) from one container to another
**DECANTATE** vb decant
**DECANTED** > DECANT
**DECANTER** n stoppered bottle for wine or spirits
**DECANTERS** > DECANTER
**DECANTING** > DECANT
**DECANTS** > DECANT
**DECAPOD** n creature, such as a crab, with five pairs of walking limbs ▷ adj of, relating to, or belonging to these creatures
**DECAPODAL** > DECAPOD
**DECAPODAN** > DECAPOD
**DECAPODS** > DECAPOD
**DECARB** vb decoke
**DECARBED** > DECARB
**DECARBING** > DECARB

DECARBS > DECARB

DECARE *n* ten ares or 1000 square metres

DECARES > DECARE

DECASTERE *n* ten steres

DECASTICH *n* poem with ten lines

DECASTYLE *n* portico consisting of ten columns

DECATHLON *n* athletic contest with ten events

DECAUDATE *vb* remove the tail from

DECAY *vb* become weaker or more corrupt ▷ *n* process of decaying

DECAYABLE > DECAY

DECAYED > DECAY

DECAYER > DECAY

DECAYERS > DECAY

DECAYING > DECAY

DECAYLESS *adj* immortal

DECAYS > DECAY

DECCIE *n* decoration

DECCIES > DECCIE

DECEASE *n* death

DECEASED *adj* dead ▷ *n* dead person

DECEASES > DECEASE

DECEASING > DECEASE

DECEDENT *n* deceased person

DECEDENTS > DECEDENT

DECEIT *n* behaviour intended to deceive

DECEITFUL *adj* full of deceit

DECEITS > DECEIT

DECEIVE *vb* mislead by lying

DECEIVED > DECEIVE

DECEIVER > DECEIVE

DECEIVERS > DECEIVE

DECEIVES > DECEIVE

DECEIVING > DECEIVE

DECELERON *n* type of aileron

DECEMVIR *n* (in ancient Rome) a member of a board of ten magistrates, esp either of the two commissions established in 451 and 450 BC to revise the laws

DECEMVIRI > DECEMVIR

DECEMVIRS > DECEMVIR

DECENARY *adj* of or relating to a tithing

DECENCIES *pl n* generally accepted standards of good behaviour

DECENCY *n* conformity to the prevailing standards of what is right

DECENNARY *same as* > DECENARY

DECENNIA > DECENNIUM

DECENNIAL *adj* lasting for ten years ▷ *n* tenth anniversary or its celebration

DECENNIUM *a less common word for* > DECADE

DECENT *adj* (of a person)

polite and morally acceptable

DECENTER *vb* put out of centre

DECENTERS > DECENTER

DECENTEST > DECENT

DECENTLY > DECENT

DECENTRE *vb* put out of centre

DECENTRED > DECENTRE

DECENTRES > DECENTRE

DECEPTION *n* deceiving

DECEPTIVE *adj* likely or designed to deceive

DECEPTORY *adj* deceiving

DECERN *vb* decree or adjudge

DECERNED > DECERN

DECERNING > DECERN

DECERNS > DECERN

DECERTIFY *vb* withdraw or remove a certificate or certification from (a person, organization, or country)

DECESSION *n* departure

DECHEANCE *n* forfeiting

DECIARE *n* one tenth of an are or 10 square metres

DECIARES > DECIARE

DECIBEL *n* unit for measuring the intensity of sound

DECIBELS > DECIBEL

DECIDABLE *adj* able to be decided

DECIDE *vb* (cause to) reach a decision

DECIDED *adj* unmistakable

DECIDEDLY > DECIDED

DECIDER *n* point, goal, game, etc, that determines who wins a match or championship

DECIDERS > DECIDER

DECIDES > DECIDE

DECIDING > DECIDE

DECIDUA *n* specialized mucous membrane that lines the uterus of some mammals during pregnancy: is shed, with the placenta, at parturition

DECIDUAE > DECIDUA

DECIDUAL > DECIDUA

DECIDUAS > DECIDUA

DECIDUATE > DECIDUA

DECIDUOUS *adj* (of a tree) shedding its leaves annually

DECIGRAM *n* tenth of a gram

DECIGRAMS > DECIGRAM

DECILE *n* one of nine actual or notional values of a variable dividing its distribution into ten groups with equal frequencies: the ninth decile is the value below which 90% of the population lie

DECILES > DECILE

DECILITER *same as* > DECILITRE

DECILITRE *n* measure of volume equivalent to one tenth of a litre

DECILLION *n* (in Britain, France, and Germany) the number represented as one followed by 60 zeros ($10^{60}$)

DECIMAL *n* fraction written in the form of a dot followed by one or more numbers ▷ *adj* relating to or using powers of ten

DECIMALLY > DECIMAL

DECIMALS > DECIMAL

DECIMATE *vb* destroy or kill a large proportion of

DECIMATED > DECIMATE

DECIMATES > DECIMATE

DECIMATOR > DECIMATE

DECIME *n* a former French coin

DECIMES > DECIME

DECIMETER *same as* > DECIMETRE

DECIMETRE *n* unit of length equal to one tenth of a metre

DECIPHER *vb* work out the meaning of (something illegible or in code)

DECIPHERS > DECIPHER

DECISION *n* judgment, conclusion, or resolution

DECISIONS > DECISION

DECISIVE *adj* having a definite influence

DECISORY *adj* deciding

DECISTERE *n* tenth of a stere

DECK *n* area of a ship that forms a floor ▷ *dress or decorate*

DECKCHAIR *n* folding wooden and canvas chair designed for use outside

DECKED *adj* having a wooden deck or platform

DECKEL *same as* > DECKLE

DECKELS > DECKEL

DECKER > DECK

DECKERS > DECK

DECKHAND *n* seaman assigned various duties, such as mooring and cargo handling, on the deck of a ship

DECKHANDS > DECKHAND

DECKHOUSE *n* houselike cabin on the deck of a ship

DECKING *n* wooden platform in a garden

DECKINGS > DECKING

DECKLE *n* frame used to contain pulp on the mould in the making of handmade paper

DECKLED > DECKLE

DECKLES > DECKLE

DECKO *n* look ▷ *vb* have a look

DECKOED > DECKO

DECKOING > DECKO

DECKOS > DECKO

DECKS > DECK

DECLAIM *vb* speak loudly and dramatically

DECLAIMED > DECLAIM

DECLAIMER > DECLAIM

DECLAIMS > DECLAIM

DECLARANT *n* person who makes a declaration

DECLARE *vb* state firmly and forcefully

DECLARED > DECLARE

DECLARER *n* person who declares

DECLARERS > DECLARER

DECLARES > DECLARE

DECLARING > DECLARE

DECLASS *vb* lower in social status or position

DECLASSE *adj* having lost social standing or status

DECLASSED > DECLASS

DECLASSEE *adj* (of a woman) having lost social standing or status

DECLASSES > DECLASS

DECLAW *vb* remove claws from

DECLAWED > DECLAW

DECLAWING > DECLAW

DECLAWS > DECLAW

DECLINAL *adj* bending down

DECLINANT *adj* heraldry term

DECLINATE *adj* (esp of plant parts) descending from the horizontal in a curve

DECLINE *vb* become smaller, weaker, or less important ▷ *n* gradual weakening or loss

DECLINED > DECLINE

DECLINER > DECLINE

DECLINERS > DECLINE

DECLINES > DECLINE

DECLINING > DECLINE

DECLINIST *n* person believing something is in decline

DECLIVITY *n* downward slope

DECLIVOUS *adj* steep

DECLUTCH *vb* disengage the clutch of a motor vehicle

DECLUTTER *vb* simplify or get rid of mess, disorder, complications, etc

DECO as in *art deco* style of art, jewellery, design, etc

DECOCT *vb* extract the essence from (a substance) by boiling

DECOCTED > DECOCT

DECOCTING > DECOCT

DECOCTION *n* extraction by boiling

DECOCTIVE > DECOCT

DECOCTS > DECOCT

DECOCTURE *n* substance obtained by decoction

DECODE *vb* convert from code into ordinary language

DECODED > DECODE

DECODER > DECODE

DECODERS > DECODE

DECODES > DECODE

DECODING > DECODE

DECOHERER *n* electrical device

DECOKE *same as* > DECARBONIZE

DECOKED > DECOKE

DECOKES > DECOKE

DECOKING > DECOKE

DECOLLATE *vb* separate (continuous stationery, etc) into individual forms

DECOLLETE *adj* (of a woman's garment) low-cut ▷ *n* low-cut neckline

DECOLOR *vb* bleach

DECOLORED > DECOLOR

DECOLORS > DECOLOR

DECOLOUR *vb* deprive of colour, as by bleaching

DECOLOURS > DECOLOUR

DECOMMIT *vb* withdraw from a commitment or agreed course of action

DECOMMITS > DECOMMIT

DECOMPLEX *adj* repeatedly compound

DECOMPOSE *vb* be broken down through chemical or bacterial action

DECONGEST *vb* relieve congestion in

DECONTROL *vb* free of restraints or controls, esp government controls

DECOR *n* style in which a room or house is decorated

DECORATE *vb* make more attractive by adding something ornamental

DECORATED > DECORATE

DECORATES > DECORATE

DECORATOR *n* person whose profession is the painting and wallpapering of buildings

DECOROUS *adj* polite, calm, and sensible in behaviour

DECORS > DECOR

DECORUM *n* polite and socially correct behaviour

DECORUMS > DECORUM

DECOS > DECO

DECOUPAGE *n* art or process of decorating a surface with shapes or illustrations cut from paper, card, etc

DECOUPLE *vb* separate (joined or coupled subsystems) thereby enabling them to exist and operate separately

DECOUPLED > DECOUPLE

DECOUPLER > DECOUPLE

DECOUPLES > DECOUPLE

DECOY *n* person or thing used to lure someone into danger ▷ *vb* lure away by means of a trick

DECOYED > DECOY

DECOYER > DECOY

DECOYERS > DECOY

DECOYING > DECOY

DECOYS > DECOY

DECREASE *vb* make or become less ▷ *n* lessening, reduction

DECREASED > DECREASE

DECREASES > DECREASE

DECREE *n* law made by someone in authority ▷ *vb* order by decree

DECREED > DECREE

DECREEING > DECREE

DECREER > DECREE

DECREERS > DECREE

DECREES > DECREE

DECREET *n* final judgment or sentence of a court

DECREETS > DECREET

DECREMENT *n* act of decreasing

DECREPIT *adj* weakened or worn out by age or long use

DECRETAL *n* papal decree ▷ *adj* of or relating to a decretal or a decree

DECRETALS > DECRETAL

DECRETIST *n* law student

DECRETIVE *adj* of a decree

DECRETORY *adj* of a decree

DECREW *vb* decrease

DECREWED > DECREW

DECREWING > DECREW

DECREWS > DECREW

DECRIAL > DECRY

DECRIALS > DECRY

DECRIED > DECRY

DECRIER > DECRY

DECRIERS > DECRY

DECRIES > DECRY

DECROWN *vb* depose

DECROWNED > DECROWN

DECROWNS > DECROWN

DECRY *vb* express disapproval of

DECRYING > DECRY

DECRYPT *vb* decode (a message) with or without previous knowledge of its key

DECRYPTED > DECRYPT

DECRYPTS > DECRYPT

DECTET *n* ten musicians

DECTETS > DECTET

DECUBITAL > DECUBITUS

DECUBITII > DECUBITUS

DECUBITUS *n* posture adopted when lying down

DECUMAN *n* large wave

DECUMANS > DECUMAN

DECUMBENT *adj* lying down or lying flat

DECUPLE *vb* increase by ten times ▷ *n* amount ten times as large as a given reference ▷ *adj* increasing tenfold

DECUPLED > DECUPLE

DECUPLES > DECUPLE

DECUPLING > DECUPLE

DECURIA *n* group of ten

DECURIAS > DECURIA

DECURIES > DECURY

DECURION *n* local councillor

DECURIONS > DECURION

DECURRENT *adj* extending down the stem, esp (of a leaf) having the base of the blade extending down the stem as two wings

DECURSION *n* state of being decurrent

DECURSIVE *adj* extending downwards

DECURVE *vb* curve downwards

DECURVED *adj* bent or curved downwards

DECURVES > DECURVE

DECURVING > DECURVE

DECURY *n* (in ancient Rome) a body of ten men

DECUSSATE *vb* cross or cause to cross in the form of the letter X ▷ *adj* in the form of the letter X

DEDAL *same as* > DAEDAL

DEDALIAN *adj* of Daedalus

DEDANS *n* open gallery at the server's end of the court

DEDICANT *n* person who dedicates

DEDICANTS > DEDICANT

DEDICATE *vb* commit (oneself or one's time) wholly to a special purpose or cause

DEDICATED *adj* devoted to a particular purpose or cause

DEDICATEE > DEDICATE

DEDICATES > DEDICATE

DEDICATOR > DEDICATE

DEDIMUS *n* legal term

DEDIMUSES > DEDIMUS

DEDUCE *vb* reach (a conclusion) by reasoning from evidence

DEDUCED > DEDUCE

DEDUCES > DEDUCE

DEDUCIBLE > DEDUCE

DEDUCIBLY > DEDUCE

DEDUCING > DEDUCE

DEDUCT *vb* subtract

DEDUCTED > DEDUCT

DEDUCTING > DEDUCT

DEDUCTION *n* deducting

DEDUCTIVE *adj* of or relating to deduction

DEDUCTS > DEDUCT

DEE *a Scot word for* > DIE

DEED *n* something that is done ▷ *vb* convey or transfer (property) by deed ▷ *adj* Scots form of dead

DEEDED > DEED

DEEDER > DEED

DEEDEST > DEED

DEEDFUL *adj* full of exploits

DEEDIER > DEEDY

DEEDIEST > DEEDY

DEEDILY > DEEDY

DEEDING > DEED

DEEDLESS *adj* without exploits

DEEDS > DEED

DEEDY *adj* hard-working

DEEING > DEE

DEEJAY *n* disc jockey ▷ *vb* work or act as a disc jockey

DEEJAYED > DEEJAY

DEEJAYING > DEEJAY

DEEJAYS > DEEJAY

DEEK *vb* look at

DEELY as in *deely boppers* hairband with two bobbing antennae-like attachments

DEEM *vb* consider, judge

DEEMED > DEEM

DEEMING > DEEM

DEEMS > DEEM

DEEMSTER *n* title of one of the two justices in the Isle of Man

DEEMSTERS > DEEMSTER

DEEN *n* din

DEENS > DEEN

DEEP *adj* extending or situated far down, inwards, backwards, or sideways ▷ *n* any deep place on land or under water

DEEPEN *vb* make or become deeper or more intense

DEEPENED > DEEPEN

DEEPENER > DEEPEN

DEEPENERS > DEEPEN

DEEPENING > DEEPEN

DEEPENS > DEEPEN

DEEPER > DEEP

DEEPEST > DEEP

DEEPFELT *adj* sincere

DEEPFROZE *vb* froze in a freezer

DEEPIE *n* 3D film

DEEPIES > DEEPIE

DEEPLY > DEEP

DEEPMOST *adj* deepest

DEEPNESS > DEEP

DEEPS > DEEP

DEEPWATER *adj* seagoing

DEER *n* large wild animal, the male of which has antlers

DEERBERRY *n* huckleberry

DEERE *adj* serious

DEERFLIES > DEERFLY

DEERFLY *n* insect related to the horsefly

DEERGRASS *n* perennial cyperaceous plant, *Trichophorum caespitosum*, that grows in dense tufts in peat bogs of temperate regions

DEERHORN *n* deer's antler

DEERHORNS > DEERHORN

DEERHOUND *n* very large rough-coated breed of dog of the greyhound type

DEERLET *n* ruminant mammal

**DEERLETS** > DEERLET
**DEERLIKE** *adj* like a deer
**DEERS** > DEER
**DEERSKIN** *n* hide of a deer
**DEERSKINS** > DEERSKIN
**DEERWEED** *n* forage plant
**DEERWEEDS** > DEERWEED
**DEERYARD** *n* gathering place for deer
**DEERYARDS** > DEERYARD
**DEES** > DEE
**DEET** *n* insect-repellent
**DEETS** > DEET
**DEEV** *n* mythical monster
**DEEVE** *vb* deafen
**DEEVED** > DEEVE
**DEEVES** > DEEVE
**DEEVING** > DEEVE
**DEEVS** > DEEV
**DEEWAN** *n* chief of a village in India
**DEEWANS** > DEEWAN
**DEF** *adj* very good
**DEFACE** *vb* deliberately spoil the appearance of
**DEFACED** > DEFACE
**DEFACER** > DEFACE
**DEFACERS** > DEFACE
**DEFACES** > DEFACE
**DEFACING** > DEFACE
**DEFAECATE** *same as* > DEFECATE
**DEFALCATE** *vb* make wrong use of funds entrusted to one
**DEFAME** *vb* attack the good reputation of
**DEFAMED** > DEFAME
**DEFAMER** > DEFAME
**DEFAMERS** > DEFAME
**DEFAMES** > DEFAME
**DEFAMING** > DEFAME
**DEFAMINGS** > DEFAME
**DEFANG** *vb* remove the fangs of
**DEFANGED** > DEFANG
**DEFANGING** > DEFANG
**DEFANGS** > DEFANG
**DEFAST** *adj* defaced
**DEFASTE** *adj* defaced
**DEFAT** *vb* remove fat from
**DEFATS** > DEFAT
**DEFATTED** > DEFAT
**DEFATTING** > DEFAT
**DEFAULT** *n* failure to do something ▷ *vb* fail to fulfil an obligation
**DEFAULTED** > DEFAULT
**DEFAULTER** *n* person who defaults
**DEFAULTS** > DEFAULT
**DEFEAT** *vb* win a victory over ▷ *n* defeating
**DEFEATED** > DEFEAT
**DEFEATER** > DEFEAT
**DEFEATERS** > DEFEAT
**DEFEATING** > DEFEAT
**DEFEATISM** *n* ready acceptance or expectation of defeat
**DEFEATIST** > DEFEATISM
**DEFEATS** > DEFEAT
**DEFEATURE** *vb* deform
**DEFECATE** *vb* discharge

waste from the body through the anus
**DEFECATED** > DEFECATE
**DEFECATES** > DEFECATE
**DEFECATOR** > DEFECATE
**DEFECT** *n* imperfection, blemish ▷ *vb* desert one's cause or country to join the opposing forces
**DEFECTED** > DEFECT
**DEFECTING** > DEFECT
**DEFECTION** *n* act or an instance of defecting
**DEFECTIVE** *adj* imperfect, faulty
**DEFECTOR** > DEFECT
**DEFECTORS** > DEFECT
**DEFECTS** > DEFECT
**DEFENCE** *n* resistance against attack
**DEFENCED** > DEFENCE
**DEFENCES** > DEFENCE
**DEFENCING** > DEFENCE
**DEFEND** *vb* protect from harm or danger
**DEFENDANT** *n* person accused of a crime ▷ *adj* making a defence
**DEFENDED** > DEFEND
**DEFENDER** > DEFEND
**DEFENDERS** > DEFEND
**DEFENDING** > DEFEND
**DEFENDS** > DEFEND
**DEFENSE** *same as* > DEFENCE
**DEFENSED** > DEFENSE
**DEFENSES** > DEFENSE
**DEFENSING** > DEFENSE
**DEFENSIVE** *adj* intended for defence
**DEFER** *vb* delay (something) until a future time
**DEFERABLE** > DEFER
**DEFERENCE** *n* polite and respectful behaviour
**DEFERENT** *adj* (esp of a bodily nerve, vessel, or duct) conveying an impulse, fluid, etc, outwards, down, or away ▷ *n* (in the Ptolemaic system) a circle centred on the earth around which the centre of the epicycle was thought to move
**DEFERENTS** > DEFERENT
**DEFERMENT** *n* act of deferring or putting off until another time
**DEFERRAL** *same as* > DEFERMENT
**DEFERRALS** > DEFERRAL
**DEFERRED** *adj* withheld over a certain period
**DEFERRER** > DEFER
**DEFERRERS** > DEFER
**DEFERRING** > DEFER
**DEFERS** > DEFER
**DEFFER** > DEF
**DEFFEST** > DEF
**DEFFLY** *archaic word meaning the same as* > DEFTLY
**DEFFO** *interj* definitely: an

expression of agreement or consent
**DEFI** *n* challenge
**DEFIANCE** *n* open resistance or disobedience
**DEFIANCES** > DEFIANCE
**DEFIANT** *adj* marked by resistance or bold opposition, as to authority
**DEFIANTLY** > DEFIANT
**DEFICIENT** *adj* lacking some essential thing or quality
**DEFICIT** *n* amount by which a sum of money is too small
**DEFICITS** > DEFICIT
**DEFIED** > DEFY
**DEFIER** > DEFY
**DEFIERS** > DEFY
**DEFIES** > DEFY
**DEFILADE** *n* protection provided by obstacles against enemy crossfire from the rear, or observation ▷ *vb* provide protection for by defilade
**DEFILADED** > DEFILADE
**DEFILADES** > DEFILADE
**DEFILE** *vb* treat (something sacred or important) without respect ▷ *n* narrow valley or pass
**DEFILED** > DEFILE
**DEFILER** > DEFILE
**DEFILERS** > DEFILE
**DEFILES** > DEFILE
**DEFILING** > DEFILE
**DEFINABLE** > DEFINE
**DEFINABLY** > DEFINE
**DEFINE** *vb* state precisely the meaning of
**DEFINED** > DEFINE
**DEFINER** > DEFINE
**DEFINERS** > DEFINE
**DEFINES** > DEFINE
**DEFINIENS** *n* word or words used to define or give an account of the meaning of another word, as in a dictionary entry
**DEFINING** > DEFINE
**DEFINITE** *adj* firm, clear, and precise
**DEFIS** > DEFI
**DEFLATE** *vb* (cause to) collapse through the release of air
**DEFLATED** > DEFLATE
**DEFLATER** > DEFLATE
**DEFLATERS** > DEFLATE
**DEFLATES** > DEFLATE
**DEFLATING** > DEFLATE
**DEFLATION** *n* reduction in economic activity resulting in lower output and investment
**DEFLATOR** > DEFLATE
**DEFLATORS** > DEFLATE
**DEFLEA** *vb* remove fleas from
**DEFLEAED** > DEFLEA
**DEFLEAING** > DEFLEA

**DEFLEAS** > DEFLEA
**DEFLECT** *vb* (cause to) turn aside from a course
**DEFLECTED** > DEFLECT
**DEFLECTOR** > DEFLECT
**DEFLECTS** > DEFLECT
**DEFLEX** *vb* turn downwards
**DEFLEXED** > DEFLEX
**DEFLEXES** > DEFLEX
**DEFLEXING** > DEFLEX
**DEFLEXION** *same as* > DEFLECTION
**DEFLEXURE** *n* act of deflecting
**DEFLORATE** *vb* deflower
**DEFLOWER** *vb* deprive (a woman) of her virginity
**DEFLOWERS** > DEFLOWER
**DEFLUENT** *adj* running downwards
**DEFLUXION** *n* discharge
**DEFOAM** *vb* remove foam from
**DEFOAMED** > DEFOAM
**DEFOAMER** > DEFOAM
**DEFOAMERS** > DEFOAM
**DEFOAMING** > DEFOAM
**DEFOAMS** > DEFOAM
**DEFOCUS** *vb* put out of focus
**DEFOCUSED** > DEFOCUS
**DEFOCUSES** > DEFOCUS
**DEFOG** *vb* clear of vapour
**DEFOGGED** > DEFOG
**DEFOGGER** > DEFOG
**DEFOGGERS** > DEFOG
**DEFOGGING** > DEFOG
**DEFOGS** > DEFOG
**DEFOLIANT** *n* chemical sprayed or dusted onto trees to cause their leaves to fall, esp to remove cover from an enemy in warfare
**DEFOLIATE** *vb* deprive (a plant) of its leaves ▷ *adj* (of a plant) having shed its leaves
**DEFORCE** *vb* withhold (property, esp land) wrongfully or by force from the rightful owner
**DEFORCED** > DEFORCE
**DEFORCER** > DEFORCE
**DEFORCERS** > DEFORCE
**DEFORCES** > DEFORCE
**DEFORCING** > DEFORCE
**DEFOREST** *vb* clear of trees
**DEFORESTS** > DEFOREST
**DEFORM** *vb* put out of shape or spoil the appearance of
**DEFORMED** *adj* disfigured or misshapen
**DEFORMER** > DEFORM
**DEFORMERS** > DEFORM
**DEFORMING** > DEFORM
**DEFORMITY** *n* distortion of a body part
**DEFORMS** > DEFORM
**DEFOUL** *vb* defile
**DEFOULED** > DEFOUL
**DEFOULING** > DEFOUL
**DEFOULS** > DEFOUL
**DEFRAG** *vb* defragment

**DEFRAGGED** > DEFRAG
**DEFRAGGER** > DEFRAG
**DEFRAGS** > DEFRAG
**DEFRAUD** vb cheat out of money, property, etc
**DEFRAUDED** > DEFRAUD
**DEFRAUDER** > DEFRAUD
**DEFRAUDS** > DEFRAUD
**DEFRAY** vb provide money for (costs or expenses)
**DEFRAYAL** > DEFRAY
**DEFRAYALS** > DEFRAY
**DEFRAYED** > DEFRAY
**DEFRAYER** > DEFRAY
**DEFRAYERS** > DEFRAY
**DEFRAYING** > DEFRAY
**DEFRAYS** > DEFRAY
**DEFREEZE** vb defrost
**DEFREEZES** > DEFREEZE
**DEFROCK** vb deprive (a priest) of priestly status
**DEFROCKED** > DEFROCK
**DEFROCKS** > DEFROCK
**DEFROST** vb make or become free of ice
**DEFROSTED** > DEFROST
**DEFROSTER** n device by which the de-icing process of a refrigerator is accelerated, usually by circulating the refrigerant without the expansion process
**DEFROSTS** > DEFROST
**DEFROZE** > DEFREEZE
**DEFROZEN** > DEFREEZE
**DEFT** adj quick and skilful in movement
**DEFTER** > DEFT
**DEFTEST** > DEFT
**DEFTLY** > DEFT
**DEFTNESS** > DEFT
**DEFUEL** vb remove fuel from
**DEFUELED** > DEFUEL
**DEFUELING** > DEFUEL
**DEFUELLED** > DEFUEL
**DEFUELS** > DEFUEL
**DEFUNCT** adj no longer existing or operative ▷ n deceased person
**DEFUNCTS** > DEFUNCT
**DEFUND** vb stop funds to
**DEFUNDED** > DEFUND
**DEFUNDING** > DEFUND
**DEFUNDS** > DEFUND
**DEFUSE** vb remove the fuse of (an explosive device)
**DEFUSED** > DEFUSE
**DEFUSER** > DEFUSE
**DEFUSERS** > DEFUEL
**DEFUSES** > DEFUSE
**DEFUSING** > DEFUSE
**DEFUZE** same as > DEFUSE
**DEFUZED** > DEFUZE
**DEFUZES** > DEFUZE
**DEFUZING** > DEFUZE
**DEFY** vb resist openly and boldly
**DEFYING** > DEFY
**DEG** vb water (a plant, etc)
**DEGAGE** adj unconstrained in manner
**DEGAME** n tree of South and Central America
**DEGAMES** > DEGAME
**DEGAMI** same as > DEGAME
**DEGAMIS** > DEGAMI
**DEGARNISH** vb remove ornament from
**DEGAS** vb remove gas from (a container, vacuum tube, liquid, adsorbent, etc)
**DEGASES** > DEGAS
**DEGASSED** > DEGAS
**DEGASSER** > DEGAS
**DEGASSERS** > DEGAS
**DEGASSES** > DEGAS
**DEGASSING** > DEGAS
**DEGAUSS** same as > DEMAGNETIZE
**DEGAUSSED** > DEGAUSS
**DEGAUSSER** > DEGAUSS
**DEGAUSSES** > DEGAUSS
**DEGEARING** n process in which a company replaces some or all of its fixed-interest loan stock with ordinary shares
**DEGENDER** vb remove reference to gender from
**DEGENDERS** > DEGENDER
**DEGERM** vb remove germs from
**DEGERMED** > DEGERM
**DEGERMING** > DEGERM
**DEGERMS** > DEGERM
**DEGGED** > DEG
**DEGGING** > DEG
**DEGLAZE** vb dilute meat sediments in (a pan) in order to make a sauce or gravy
**DEGLAZED** > DEGLAZE
**DEGLAZES** > DEGLAZE
**DEGLAZING** > DEGLAZE
**DEGOUT** n disgust
**DEGOUTS** > DEGOUT
**DEGRADE** vb reduce to dishonour or disgrace
**DEGRADED** > DEGRADE
**DEGRADER** > DEGRADE
**DEGRADERS** > DEGRADE
**DEGRADES** > DEGRADE
**DEGRADING** adj causing humiliation
**DEGRAS** n emulsion used for dressing hides
**DEGREASE** vb remove grease from
**DEGREASED** > DEGREASE
**DEGREASER** > DEGREASE
**DEGREASES** > DEGREASE
**DEGREE** n stage in a scale of relative amount or intensity
**DEGREED** adj having a degree
**DEGREES** > DEGREE
**DEGS** > DEG
**DEGUM** vb remove gum from
**DEGUMMED** > DEGUM
**DEGUMMING** > DEGUM
**DEGUMS** > DEGUM
**DEGUST** vb taste, esp with care or relish
**DEGUSTATE** same as > DEGUST

**DEGUSTED** > DEGUST
**DEGUSTING** > DEGUST
**DEGUSTS** > DEGUST
**DEHISCE** vb (of the seed capsules of some plants) to burst open spontaneously
**DEHISCED** > DEHISCE
**DEHISCENT** adj (of fruits, anthers, etc) opening spontaneously to release seeds or pollen
**DEHISCES** > DEHISCE
**DEHISCING** > DEHISCE
**DEHORN** vb remove or prevent the growth of the horns of (cattle, sheep, or goats)
**DEHORNED** > DEHORN
**DEHORNER** > DEHORN
**DEHORNERS** > DEHORN
**DEHORNING** > DEHORN
**DEHORNS** > DEHORN
**DEHORT** vb dissuade
**DEHORTED** > DEHORT
**DEHORTER** > DEHORT
**DEHORTERS** > DEHORT
**DEHORTING** > DEHORT
**DEHORTS** > DEHORT
**DEHYDRATE** vb remove water from (food) to preserve it
**DEI** > DEUS
**DEICE** vb to free or be freed of ice
**DEICED** > DEICE
**DEICER** > DEICE
**DEICERS** > DEICE
**DEICES** > DEICE
**DEICIDAL** > DEICIDE
**DEICIDE** n act of killing a god
**DEICIDES** > DEICIDE
**DEICING** > DEICE
**DEICTIC** adj proving by direct argument
**DEICTICS** > DEICTIC
**DEID** a Scot word for > DEAD
**DEIDER** > DEID
**DEIDEST** > DEID
**DEIDS** > DEID
**DEIF** a Scot word for > DEAF
**DEIFER** > DEIF
**DEIFEST** > DEIF
**DEIFIC** adj making divine or exalting to the position of a god
**DEIFICAL** adj divine
**DEIFIED** > DEIFY
**DEIFIER** > DEIFY
**DEIFIERS** > DEIFY
**DEIFIES** > DEIFY
**DEIFORM** adj having the form or appearance of a god
**DEIFY** vb treat or worship as a god
**DEIFYING** > DEIFY
**DEIGN** vb agree (to do something), but as if doing someone a favour
**DEIGNED** > DEIGN
**DEIGNING** > DEIGN
**DEIGNS** > DEIGN
**DEIL** a Scot word for > DEVIL

**DEILS** > DEIL
**DEINDEX** vb cause to become no longer index-linked
**DEINDEXED** > DEINDEX
**DEINDEXES** > DEINDEX
**DEINOSAUR** n dinosaur
**DEIONISE** same as > DEIONIZE
**DEIONISED** > DEIONISE
**DEIONISER** > DEIONISE
**DEIONISES** > DEIONISE
**DEIONIZE** vb to remove ions from (water, etc), esp by ion exchange
**DEIONIZED** > DEIONIZE
**DEIONIZER** > DEIONIZE
**DEIONIZES** > DEIONIZE
**DEIPAROUS** adj giving birth to a god
**DEISEAL** n clockwise motion
**DEISEALS** > DEISEAL
**DEISHEAL** n clockwise motion
**DEISHEALS** > DEISHEAL
**DEISM** n belief in God but not in divine revelation
**DEISMS** > DEISM
**DEIST** > DEISM
**DEISTIC** > DEISM
**DEISTICAL** > DEISM
**DEISTS** > DEISM
**DEITIES** > DEITY
**DEITY** n god or goddess
**DEIXES** > DEIXIS
**DEIXIS** n use or reference of a deictic word
**DEIXISES** > DEIXIS
**DEJECT** vb have a depressing effect on ▷ adj downcast
**DEJECTA** pl n waste products excreted through the anus
**DEJECTED** adj unhappy
**DEJECTING** > DEJECT
**DEJECTION** n lowness of spirits
**DEJECTORY** adj causing dejection
**DEJECTS** > DEJECT
**DEJEUNE** n lunch
**DEJEUNER** n lunch
**DEJEUNERS** > DEJEUNER
**DEJEUNES** > DEJEUNE
**DEKAGRAM** n ten grams
**DEKAGRAMS** > DEKAGRAM
**DEKALITER** n ten litres
**DEKALITRE** n ten litres
**DEKALOGY** n series of ten related works
**DEKAMETER** n ten meters
**DEKAMETRE** n ten metres
**DEKARE** n unit of measurement equal to ten ares
**DEKARES** > DEKARE
**DEKE** vb (in ice hockey or box lacrosse) to draw (a defending player) out of position by faking a shot or movement ▷ n such a shot or movement

DEKED > DEKE
DEKEING > DEKE
DEKES > DEKE
DEKING > DEKE
DEKKO n look ▷ vb have a look
DEKKOED > DEKKO
DEKKOING > DEKKO
DEKKOS > DEKKO
DEL n differential operator
DELAINE n sheer wool or wool and cotton fabric
DELAINES > DELAINE
DELAPSE vb be inherited
DELAPSED > DELAPSE
DELAPSES > DELAPSE
DELAPSING > DELAPSE
DELAPSION n falling down
DELATE vb (formerly) to bring a charge against
DELATED > DELATE
DELATES > DELATE
DELATING > DELATE
DELATION > DELATE
DELATIONS > DELATE
DELATOR > DELATE
DELATORS > DELATE
DELAY vb put off to a later time ▷ n act of delaying
DELAYABLE > DELAY
DELAYED > DELAY
DELAYER > DELAY
DELAYERS > DELAY
DELAYING > DELAY
DELAYS > DELAY
DELE n sign indicating that typeset matter is to be deleted ▷ vb mark (matter to be deleted) with a dele
DELEAD vb remove lead from
DELEADED > DELEAD
DELEADING > DELEAD
DELEADS > DELEAD
DELEAVE vb separate copies
DELEAVED > DELEAVE
DELEAVES > DELEAVE
DELEAVING > DELEAVE
DELEBLE adj able to be deleted
DELECTATE vb delight
DELED > DELE
DELEGABLE > DELEGATE
DELEGACY n elected standing committee at some British universities
DELEGATE n person chosen to represent others, esp at a meeting ▷ vb entrust (duties or powers) to someone
DELEGATED > DELEGATE
DELEGATEE > DELEGATE
DELEGATES > DELEGATE
DELEGATOR > DELEGATE
DELEING > DELE
DELENDA pl n items for deleting
DELES > DELE
DELETABLE > DELETE
DELETE vb remove (something written or printed)

DELETED > DELETE
DELETES > DELETE
DELETING > DELETE
DELETION n act of deleting or fact of being deleted
DELETIONS > DELETION
DELETIVE > DELETE
DELETORY > DELETE
DELF n kind of earthenware
DELFS > DELF
DELFT n tin-glazed earthenware, typically having blue designs on white
DELFTS > DELFT
DELFTWARE same as > DELFT
DELI n delicatessen
DELIBATE vb taste
DELIBATED > DELIBATE
DELIBATES > DELIBATE
DELIBLE adj able to be deleted
DELICACY n being delicate
DELICATE adj fine or subtle in quality or workmanship ▷ n delicacy
DELICATES > DELICATE
DELICE n delicacy
DELICES > DELICE
DELICIOUS adj very appealing to taste or smell
DELICT n wrongful act for which the person injured has the right to a civil remedy
DELICTS > DELICT
DELIGHT n (source of) great pleasure ▷ vb please greatly
DELIGHTED adj greatly pleased ▷ sentence substitute I should be delighted to!
DELIGHTER > DELIGHT
DELIGHTS > DELIGHT
DELIME vb remove lime from
DELIMED > DELIME
DELIMES > DELIME
DELIMING > DELIME
DELIMIT vb mark or lay down the limits of
DELIMITED > DELIMIT
DELIMITER > DELIMIT
DELIMITS > DELIMIT
DELINEATE vb show by drawing
DELIQUIUM n loss of consciousness
DELIRIA > DELIRIUM
DELIRIANT > DELIRIUM
DELIRIOUS adj suffering from delirium
DELIRIUM n state of excitement and mental confusion, often with hallucinations
DELIRIUMS > DELIRIUM
DELIS > DELI
DELISH adj delicious
DELIST vb remove from a list
DELISTED > DELIST

DELISTING > DELIST
DELISTS > DELIST
DELIVER vb carry (goods etc) to a destination
DELIVERED > DELIVER
DELIVERER > DELIVER
DELIVERLY adv quickly
DELIVERS > DELIVER
DELIVERY n delivering
DELL n small wooded hollow
DELLIES > DELLY
DELLS > DELL
DELLY n delicatessen
DELO an informal word for > DELEGATE
DELOPE vb shoot into the air
DELOPED > DELOPE
DELOPES > DELOPE
DELOPING > DELOPE
DELOS > DELO
DELOUSE vb rid (a person or animal) of lice
DELOUSED > DELOUSE
DELOUSER > DELOUSE
DELOUSERS > DELOUSE
DELOUSES > DELOUSE
DELOUSING > DELOUSE
DELPH n kind of earthenware
DELPHIC adj obscure or ambiguous
DELPHIN n fatty substance from dolphin oil
DELPHINIA n plural form of singular delphinium: garden plant with blue, white or pink flowers
DELPHS > DELPH
DELS > DEL
DELT n deltoid muscle
DELTA n fourth letter in the Greek alphabet
DELTAIC > DELTA
DELTAS > DELTA
DELTIC > DELTA
DELTOID n thick muscle forming the rounded contour of the outer edge of the shoulder and acting to raise the arm ▷ adj shaped like a Greek capital delta
DELTOIDEI n deltoid
DELTOIDS > DELTOID
DELTS > DELT
DELUBRUM n shrine
DELUBRUMS > DELUBRUM
DELUDABLE > DELUDE
DELUDE vb deceive
DELUDED > DELUDE
DELUDER > DELUDE
DELUDERS > DELUDE
DELUDES > DELUDE
DELUDING > DELUDE
DELUGE n great flood ▷ vb flood
DELUGED > DELUGE
DELUGES > DELUGE
DELUGING > DELUGE
DELUNDUNG n spotted mammal
DELUSION n mistaken idea

or belief
DELUSIONS > DELUSION
DELUSIVE > DELUSION
DELUSORY > DELUSION
DELUSTER vb remove the lustre from
DELUSTERS > DELUSTER
DELUXE adj rich, elegant, superior, or sumptuous
DELVE vb research deeply (for information)
DELVED > DELVE
DELVER > DELVE
DELVERS > DELVE
DELVES > DELVE
DELVING > DELVE
DEMAGOG same as > DEMAGOGUE
DEMAGOGED > DEMAGOG
DEMAGOGIC adj of, characteristic of, relating to, or resembling a demagogue
DEMAGOGS > DEMAGOG
DEMAGOGUE n political agitator who appeals to the prejudice and passions of the mob
DEMAGOGY n demagoguery
DEMAIN n demesne
DEMAINE n demesne
DEMAINES > DEMAINE
DEMAINS > DEMAIN
DEMAN vb reduce the workforce of (a plant, industry, etc)
DEMAND vb request forcefully ▷ n forceful request
DEMANDANT n (formerly) the plaintiff in an action relating to real property
DEMANDED > DEMAND
DEMANDER > DEMAND
DEMANDERS > DEMAND
DEMANDING adj requiring a lot of time or effort
DEMANDS > DEMAND
DEMANNED > DEMAN
DEMANNING > DEMAN
DEMANS > DEMAN
DEMANTOID n bright green variety of andradite garnet
DEMARCATE vb mark, fix, or draw the boundaries, limits, etc, of
DEMARCHE n move, step, or manoeuvre, esp in diplomatic affairs
DEMARCHES > DEMARCHE
DEMARK vb demarcate
DEMARKED > DEMARK
DEMARKET vb discourage consumers from buying (a particular product), either because it is faulty or because it could jeopardize the seller's reputation
DEMARKETS > DEMARKET
DEMARKING > DEMARK
DEMARKS > DEMARK
DEMAST vb remove the mast from

DEMASTED > DEMAST
DEMASTING > DEMAST
DEMASTS > DEMAST
DEMAYNE n demesne
DEMAYNES > DEMAYNE
DEME n (in preclassical Greece) the territory inhabited by a tribe
DEMEAN vb lower (oneself) in dignity, status, or character
DEMEANE n demesne
DEMEANED > DEMEAN
DEMEANES n demesne
DEMEANING > DEMEAN
DEMEANOR same
  as > DEMEANOUR
DEMEANORS > DEMEANOR
DEMEANOUR n way a person behaves
DEMEANS > DEMEAN
DEMENT vb deteriorate mentally, esp because of old age
DEMENTATE vb deteriorate mentally
DEMENTED adj mad
DEMENTI n denial
DEMENTIA n state of serious mental deterioration
DEMENTIAL > DEMENTIA
DEMENTIAS > DEMENTIA
DEMENTING > DEMENT
DEMENTIS > DEMENTI
DEMENTS > DEMENT
DEMERARA n brown crystallized cane sugar from the Caribbean and nearby countries
DEMERARAN adj from Demerara
DEMERARAS > DEMERARA
DEMERGE vb separate a company from another with which it was previously merged
DEMERGED > DEMERGE
DEMERGER n separation of two or more companies which have previously been merged
DEMERGERS > DEMERGER
DEMERGES > DEMERGE
DEMERGING > DEMERGE
DEMERIT n fault, disadvantage ▷ vb deserve
DEMERITED > DEMERIT
DEMERITS > DEMERIT
DEMERSAL adj living or occurring on the bottom of a sea or a lake
DEMERSE vb immerse
DEMERSED > DEMERSE
DEMERSES > DEMERSE
DEMERSING > DEMERSE
DEMERSION > DEMERSE
DEMES > DEME
DEMESNE n land surrounding a house
DEMESNES > DEMESNE
DEMETON n insecticide
DEMETONS > DEMETON

DEMIC adj of population
DEMIES > DEMY
DEMIGOD n being who is part mortal, part god
DEMIGODS > DEMIGOD
DEMIJOHN n large bottle with a short neck, often encased in wicker
DEMIJOHNS > DEMIJOHN
DEMILUNE n outwork in front of a fort, shaped like a crescent moon
DEMILUNES > DEMILUNE
DEMIMONDE n (esp in the 19th century) class of women considered to be outside respectable society because of promiscuity
DEMIPIQUE n low pique on a saddle
DEMIREP n woman of bad repute, esp a prostitute
DEMIREPS > DEMIREP
DEMISABLE > DEMISE
DEMISE n eventual failure (of something successful) ▷ vb transfer for a limited period
DEMISED > DEMISE
DEMISES > DEMISE
DEMISING > DEMISE
DEMISS adj humble
DEMISSION n relinquishment of or abdication from an office, responsibility, etc
DEMISSIVE adj humble
DEMISSLY > DEMISS
DEMIST vb remove condensation from (a windscreen)
DEMISTED > DEMIST
DEMISTER n device incorporating a heater and/or blower used in a motor vehicle to free the windscreen of condensation
DEMISTERS > DEMISTER
DEMISTING > DEMIST
DEMISTS > DEMIST
DEMIT vb resign (an office, position, etc)
DEMITS > DEMIT
DEMITTED > DEMIT
DEMITTING > DEMIT
DEMIURGE n (in the philosophy of Plato) the creator of the universe
DEMIURGES > DEMIURGE
DEMIURGIC > DEMIURGE
DEMIURGUS n demiurge
DEMIVEG n person who eats poultry and fish, but no red meat ▷ adj denoting a person who eats poultry and fish, but no red meat
DEMIVEGES > DEMIVEG
DEMIVOLT n half turn on

the hind legs
DEMIVOLTE same
  as > DEMIVOLT
DEMIVOLTS > DEMIVOLT
DEMIWORLD n demimonde
DEMO n demonstration, organized expression of public opinion ▷ vb demonstrate
DEMOB vb demobilize ▷ n (as modifier)
DEMOBBED > DEMOB
DEMOBBING > DEMOB
DEMOBS > DEMOB
DEMOCRACY n government by the people or their elected representatives
DEMOCRAT n advocate of democracy
DEMOCRATS > DEMOCRAT
DEMOCRATY n democracy
DEMODE adj out of fashion
DEMODED adj out of fashion
DEMOED > DEMO
DEMOING > DEMO
DEMOLISH vb knock down or destroy (a building)
DEMOLOGY n demography
DEMON n evil spirit
DEMONESS n female demon
DEMONIAC adj appearing to be possessed by a devil ▷ n person possessed by an evil spirit or demon
DEMONIACS > DEMONIAC
DEMONIAN adj of a demon
DEMONIC adj evil
DEMONICAL adj demonic
DEMONISE same
  as > DEMONIZE
DEMONISED > DEMONISE
DEMONISES > DEMONISE
DEMONISM same
  as > DEMONOLOGY
DEMONISMS > DEMONISM
DEMONIST > DEMONISM
DEMONISTS > DEMONISM
DEMONIZE vb make into a demon
DEMONIZED > DEMONIZE
DEMONIZES > DEMONIZE
DEMONRIES > DEMON
DEMONRY > DEMON
DEMONS > DEMON
DEMOS n people of a nation regarded as a political unit
DEMOSES > DEMOS
DEMOTE vb reduce in status or rank
DEMOTED > DEMOTE
DEMOTES > DEMOTE
DEMOTIC adj of the common people ▷ n demotic script of ancient Egypt
DEMOTICS > DEMOTIC
DEMOTING > DEMOTE
DEMOTION > DEMOTE
DEMOTIONS > DEMOTE
DEMOTIST > DEMOTIC
DEMOTISTS > DEMOTIC
DEMOUNT vb remove (a motor, gun, etc) from its mounting or setting

DEMOUNTED > DEMOUNT
DEMOUNTS > DEMOUNT
DEMPSTER same
  as > DEEMSTER
DEMPSTERS > DEMPSTER
DEMPT > DEEM
DEMULCENT adj soothing ▷ n drug or agent that soothes the irritation of inflamed or injured skin surfaces
DEMULSIFY vb undergo or cause to undergo a process in which an emulsion is permanently broken down into its constituents
DEMUR vb raise objections or show reluctance ▷ n act of demurring
DEMURE adj quiet, reserved, and rather shy ▷ vb archaic for look demure ▷ n archaic for demure look
DEMURED > DEMURE
DEMURELY > DEMURE
DEMURER > DEMURE
DEMURES > DEMURE
DEMUREST > DEMURE
DEMURING > DEMURE
DEMURRAGE n delaying of a ship, railway wagon, etc, caused by the charterer's failure to load, unload, etc, before the time of scheduled departure
DEMURRAL n act of demurring
DEMURRALS > DEMURRAL
DEMURRED > DEMUR
DEMURRER n pleading that admits an opponent's point but denies that it is a relevant or valid argument
DEMURRERS > DEMURRER
DEMURRING > DEMUR
DEMURS > DEMUR
DEMY n size of printing paper, 17½ by 22½ inches (444.5 × 571.5 mm)
DEMYSHIP > DEMY
DEMYSHIPS > DEMY
DEMYSTIFY vb remove the mystery from
DEN n home of a wild animal ▷ vb live in or as if in a den
DENAR n standard monetary unit of Macedonia, divided into 100 deni
DENARI > DENAR
DENARIES > DENARIUS
DENARII > DENARIUS
DENARIUS n ancient Roman silver coin, often called a penny in translation
DENARS > DENAR
DENARY adj calculated by tens
DENATURE vb change the nature of
DENATURED > DENATURE

**DENATURES** > DENATURE
**DENAY** vb deny
**DENAYED** > DENAY
**DENAYING** > DENAY
**DENAYS** > DENAY
**DENAZIFY** vb free or declare (people, institutions, etc) freed from Nazi influence or ideology
**DENDRIMER** n chemical compound with treelike molecular structure
**DENDRITE** n any of the short branched threadlike extensions of a nerve cell, which conduct impulses towards the cell body
**DENDRITES** > DENDRITE
**DENDRITIC** > DENDRITE
**DENDROID** adj freely branching
**DENDRON** same as > DENDRITE
**DENDRONS** > DENDRON
**DENE** n narrow wooded valley
**DENERVATE** vb deprive (a tissue or organ) of its nerve supply
**DENES** > DENE
**DENET** vb remove from the Net Book Agreement
**DENETS** > DENET
**DENETTED** > DENET
**DENETTING** > DENET
**DENGUE** n viral disease transmitted by mosquitoes, characterized by headache, fever, pains in the joints, and a rash
**DENGUES** > DENGUE
**DENI** n monetary unit of the Former Yugoslav Republic of Macedonia, worth one hundredth of a denar
**DENIABLE** adj able to be denied
**DENIABLY** > DENIABLE
**DENIAL** n statement that something is not true
**DENIALS** > DENIAL
**DENIED** > DENY
**DENIER** n unit of weight used to measure the fineness of nylon or silk
**DENIERS** > DENIER
**DENIES** > DENY
**DENIGRATE** vb criticize unfairly
**DENIM** n hard-wearing cotton fabric, usu. blue
**DENIMED** adj wearing denim
**DENIMS** pl n jeans or overalls made of denim
**DENIS** > DENI
**DENITRATE** vb undergo or cause to undergo a process in which a compound loses a nitro or nitrate group, nitrogen dioxide, or nitric acid
**DENITRIFY** vb undergo

or cause to undergo loss or removal of nitrogen compounds or nitrogen
**DENIZEN** n inhabitant ▷ vb make a denizen
**DENIZENED** > DENIZEN
**DENIZENS** > DENIZEN
**DENNED** > DEN
**DENNET** n carriage for one horse
**DENNETS** > DENNET
**DENNING** > DEN
**DENOMINAL** adj formed from a noun
**DENOTABLE** > DENOTE
**DENOTATE** vb denote
**DENOTATED** > DENOTATE
**DENOTATES** > DENOTATE
**DENOTE** vb be a sign of
**DENOTED** > DENOTE
**DENOTES** > DENOTE
**DENOTING** > DENOTE
**DENOTIVE** > DENOTE
**DENOUNCE** vb speak vehemently against
**DENOUNCED** > DENOUNCE
**DENOUNCER** > DENOUNCE
**DENOUNCES** > DENOUNCE
**DENS** > DEN
**DENSE** adj closely packed
**DENSELY** > DENSE
**DENSENESS** > DENSE
**DENSER** > DENSE
**DENSEST** > DENSE
**DENSIFIED** > DENSIFY
**DENSIFIER** > DENSIFY
**DENSIFIES** > DENSIFY
**DENSIFY** vb make or become dense
**DENSITIES** > DENSITY
**DENSITY** n degree to which something is filled or occupied
**DENT** n hollow in the surface of something, made by hitting it ▷ vb make a dent in
**DENTAL** adj of teeth or dentistry ▷ n dental consonant
**DENTALIA** > DENTALIUM
**DENTALITY** n use of teeth in pronouncing words
**DENTALIUM** n any scaphopod mollusc of the genus Dentalium
**DENTALLY** > DENTAL
**DENTALS** > DENTAL
**DENTARIA** n botanical term
**DENTARIAS** > DENTARIA
**DENTARIES** > DENTARY
**DENTARY** n lower jawbone with teeth
**DENTATE** adj having teeth or teethlike notches
**DENTATED** adj having teeth
**DENTATELY** > DENTATE
**DENTATION** n state or condition of being dentate
**DENTED** > DENT
**DENTEL** n architectural term
**DENTELLE** n bookbinding term

**DENTELLES** > DENTELLE
**DENTELS** > DENTEL
**DENTEX** n large active predatory sparid fish, Dentex dentex, of Mediterranean and E Atlantic waters, having long sharp teeth and powerful jaws
**DENTEXES** > DENTEX
**DENTICLE** n small tooth or toothlike part, such as any of the placoid scales of sharks
**DENTICLES** > DENTICLE
**DENTIFORM** adj shaped like a tooth
**DENTIL** n one of a set of small square or rectangular blocks evenly spaced to form an ornamental row, usually under a classical cornice on a building, piece of furniture, etc
**DENTILED** > DENTIL
**DENTILS** > DENTIL
**DENTIN** same as > DENTINE
**DENTINAL** > DENTINE
**DENTINE** n hard dense tissue forming the bulk of a tooth
**DENTINES** > DENTINE
**DENTING** > DENT
**DENTINS** > DENTIN
**DENTIST** n person qualified to practise dentistry
**DENTISTRY** n branch of medicine concerned with the teeth and gums
**DENTISTS** > DENTIST
**DENTITION** n typical arrangement of teeth in a species
**DENTOID** adj resembling a tooth
**DENTS** > DENT
**DENTULOUS** adj having teeth
**DENTURAL** > DENTURE
**DENTURE** n false tooth
**DENTURES** > DENTURE
**DENTURIST** n person who makes dentures
**DENUDATE** adj denuded ▷ vb denude
**DENUDATED** > DENUDATE
**DENUDATES** > DENUDATE
**DENUDE** vb remove the covering or protection from
**DENUDED** > DENUDE
**DENUDER** > DENUDE
**DENUDERS** > DENUDE
**DENUDES** > DENUDE
**DENUDING** > DENUDE
**DENY** vb declare to be untrue
**DENYING** > DENY
**DENYINGLY** > DENY
**DEODAND** n (formerly) a thing that had caused a person's death and was forfeited to the crown

for a charitable purpose: abolished 1862
**DEODANDS** > DEODAND
**DEODAR** n Himalayan cedar with drooping branches
**DEODARA** same as > DEODAR
**DEODARAS** > DEODARA
**DEODARS** > DEODAR
**DEODATE** n offering to God
**DEODATES** > DEODATE
**DEODORANT** n substance applied to the body to mask the smell of perspiration
**DEODORISE** same as > DEODORIZE
**DEODORIZE** vb remove or disguise the smell of
**DEONTIC** adj of or relating to such ethical concepts as obligation and permissibility
**DEONTICS** > DEONTIC
**DEORBIT** vb go out of orbit
**DEORBITED** > DEORBIT
**DEORBITS** > DEORBIT
**DEOXIDATE** vb remove oxygen atoms from
**DEOXIDISE** same as > DEOXIDIZE
**DEOXIDIZE** vb remove oxygen atoms from (a compound, molecule, etc)
**DEOXY** adj having less oxygen than a specified related compound
**DEPAINT** vb depict
**DEPAINTED** > DEPAINT
**DEPAINTS** > DEPAINT
**DEPANNEUR** n (in Quebec) a convenience store
**DEPART** vb leave
**DEPARTED** adj dead
**DEPARTEE** > DEPART
**DEPARTEES** > DEPART
**DEPARTER** > DEPART
**DEPARTERS** > DEPART
**DEPARTING** > DEPART
**DEPARTS** > DEPART
**DEPARTURE** n act of departing
**DEPASTURE** vb graze or denude by grazing (a pasture, esp a meadow specially grown for the purpose)
**DEPECHE** n message
**DEPECHES** > DEPECHE
**DEPEINCT** vb paint
**DEPEINCTS** > DEPEINCT
**DEPEND** vb put trust (in)
**DEPENDANT** same as > DEPENDENT
**DEPENDED** > DEPEND
**DEPENDENT** adj depending on someone or something ▷ n element in a phrase or clause that is not the governor
**DEPENDING** > DEPEND
**DEPENDS** > DEPEND
**DEPEOPLE** vb reduce population
**DEPEOPLED** > DEPEOPLE

DEPEOPLES > DEPEOPLE
DEPERM vb demagnetize
DEPERMED > DEPERM
DEPERMING > DEPERM
DEPERMS > DEPERM
DEPICT vb produce a
picture of
DEPICTED > DEPICT
DEPICTERS > DEPICT
DEPICTERS > DEPICT
DEPICTING > DEPICT
DEPICTION > DEPICT
DEPICTIVE > DEPICT
DEPICTOR > DEPICT
DEPICTORS > DEPICT
DEPICTS > DEPICT
DEPICTURE a less common
word for > DEPICT
DEPILATE vb remove the
hair from
DEPILATED > DEPILATE
DEPILATES > DEPILATE
DEPILATOR > DEPILATE
DEPLANE vb disembark
from an aeroplane
DEPLANED > DEPLANE
DEPLANES > DEPLANE
DEPLANING > DEPLANE
DEPLETE vb use up
DEPLETED > DEPLETE
DEPLETER > DEPLETE
DEPLETERS > DEPLETE
DEPLETES > DEPLETE
DEPLETING > DEPLETE
DEPLETION > DEPLETE
DEPLETIVE > DEPLETE
DEPLETORY > DEPLETE
DEPLORE vb condemn
strongly
DEPLORED > DEPLORE
DEPLORER > DEPLORE
DEPLORERS > DEPLORE
DEPLORES > DEPLORE
DEPLORING > DEPLORE
DEPLOY vb organize
(troops or resources)
into a position ready for
immediate action
DEPLOYED > DEPLOY
DEPLOYER > DEPLOY
DEPLOYERS > DEPLOY
DEPLOYING > DEPLOY
DEPLOYS > DEPLOY
DEPLUME vb deprive of
feathers
DEPLUMED > DEPLUME
DEPLUMES > DEPLUME
DEPLUMING > DEPLUME
DEPOLISH vb remove the
polish from
DEPONE vb declare
(something) under oath
DEPONED > DEPONE
DEPONENT n person who
makes a statement on
oath ▷ adj (of a verb,
esp in Latin) having the
inflectional endings of
a passive verb but the
meaning of an active verb
DEPONENTS > DEPONENT
DEPONES > DEPONE
DEPONING > DEPONE
DEPORT vb remove forcibly

from a country
DEPORTED > DEPORT
DEPORTEE n person
deported or awaiting
deportation
DEPORTEES > DEPORTEE
DEPORTER > DEPORT
DEPORTERS > DEPORT
DEPORTING > DEPORT
DEPORTS > DEPORT
DEPOSABLE > DEPOSE
DEPOSAL another word
for > DEPOSITION
DEPOSALS > DEPOSAL
DEPOSE vb remove from an
office or position of power
DEPOSED > DEPOSE
DEPOSER > DEPOSE
DEPOSERS > DEPOSE
DEPOSES > DEPOSE
DEPOSING > DEPOSE
DEPOSIT vb put down ▷ n
sum of money paid into a
bank account
DEPOSITED > DEPOSIT
DEPOSITOR n person who
places or has money on
deposit in a bank or similar
organization
DEPOSITS > DEPOSIT
DEPOT n building where
goods or vehicles are kept
when not in use ▷ adj
(of a drug or drug dose)
designed for gradual
release from the site of an
injection so as to act over a
long period
DEPOTS > DEPOT
DEPRAVE vb make morally
bad
DEPRAVED adj morally bad
DEPRAVER > DEPRAVE
DEPRAVERS > DEPRAVE
DEPRAVES > DEPRAVE
DEPRAVING > DEPRAVE
DEPRAVITY n moral
corruption
DEPRECATE vb express
disapproval of
DEPREDATE vb plunder or
destroy
DEPREHEND vb apprehend
DEPRENYL n drug
combating effects of
ageing
DEPRENYLS > DEPRENYL
DEPRESS vb make sad
DEPRESSED adj low in
spirits
DEPRESSES > DEPRESS
DEPRESSOR n person or
thing that depresses
DEPRIVAL > DEPRIVE
DEPRIVALS > DEPRIVE
DEPRIVE vb prevent from
(having or enjoying)
DEPRIVED adj lacking
adequate living
conditions, education, etc
DEPRIVER > DEPRIVE
DEPRIVERS > DEPRIVE
DEPRIVES > DEPRIVE
DEPRIVING > DEPRIVE

DEPROGRAM same
as > DEPROGRAMME
DEPSIDE n any
ester formed by the
condensation of the
carboxyl group of one
phenolic carboxylic acid
with the hydroxyl group
of another, found in plant
cells
DEPSIDES > DEPSIDE
DEPTH n distance
downwards, backwards,
or inwards
DEPTHLESS adj
immeasurably deep
DEPTHS > DEPTH
DEPURANT same
as > DEPURATIVE
DEPURANTS > DEPURANT
DEPURATE vb cleanse or
purify or to be cleansed or
purified
DEPURATED > DEPURATE
DEPURATES > DEPURATE
DEPURATOR > DEPURATE
DEPUTABLE > DEPUTE
DEPUTE vb appoint
(someone) to act on one's
behalf ▷ n deputy
DEPUTED > DEPUTE
DEPUTES > DEPUTE
DEPUTIES > DEPUTY
DEPUTING > DEPUTE
DEPUTISE same
as > DEPUTIZE
DEPUTISED > DEPUTISE
DEPUTISES > DEPUTISE
DEPUTIZE vb act as deputy
DEPUTIZED > DEPUTIZE
DEPUTIZES > DEPUTIZE
DEPUTY n person
appointed to act on behalf
of another
DERACINE adj uprooted
DERAIGN vb contest (a
claim, suit, etc)
DERAIGNED > DERAIGN
DERAIGNS > DERAIGN
DERAIL vb cause (a train) to
go off the rails ▷ n device
designed to make rolling
stock or locomotives
leave the rails to avoid a
collision or accident
DERAILED > DERAIL
DERAILER same as > DERAIL
DERAILERS > DERAILER
DERAILING > DERAIL
DERAILS > DERAIL
DERANGE vb disturb the
order or arrangement of
DERANGED > DERANGE
DERANGER > DERANGE
DERANGERS > DERANGE
DERANGES > DERANGE
DERANGING > DERANGE
DERAT vb remove rats from
DERATE vb assess the value
of (some types of property,
such as agricultural land)
at a lower rate than others
for local taxation
DERATED > DERATE

DERATES > DERATE
DERATING > DERATE
DERATINGS > DERATE
DERATION vb end rationing
of (food, petrol, etc)
DERATIONS > DERATION
DERATS > DERAT
DERATTED > DERAT
DERATTING > DERAT
DERAY vb go mad
DERAYED > DERAY
DERAYING > DERAY
DERAYS > DERAY
DERBIES > DERBY
DERBY n bowler hat
DERE vb injure
DERED > DERE
DERELICT adj unused
and falling into ruins ▷ n
social outcast, vagrant
DERELICTS > DERELICT
DEREPRESS vb induce
operation of gene
DERES > DERE
DERHAM same as > DIRHAM
DERHAMS > DERHAM
DERIDE vb treat with
contempt or ridicule
DERIDED > DERIDE
DERIDER > DERIDE
DERIDERS > DERIDE
DERIDES > DERIDE
DERIDING > DERIDE
DERIG vb remove
equipment, e.g. from
stage set
DERIGGED > DERIG
DERIGGING > DERIG
DERIGS > DERIG
DERING > DERE
DERINGER same
as > DERRINGER
DERINGERS > DERINGER
DERISIBLE adj subject to
or deserving of derision
DERISION n act of deriding
DERISIONS > DERISION
DERISIVE adj mocking,
scornful
DERISORY adj too small
or inadequate to be
considered seriously
DERIVABLE > DERIVE
DERIVABLY > DERIVE
DERIVATE n derivative
DERIVATES > DERIVATE
DERIVE vb take or develop
(from)
DERIVED > DERIVE
DERIVER > DERIVE
DERIVERS > DERIVE
DERIVES > DERIVE
DERIVING > DERIVE
DERM same as > DERMA
DERMA n beef or fowl
intestine used as a casing
for certain dishes, esp
kishke
DERMAL adj of or relating to
the skin
DERMAS > DERMA
DERMATIC adj of skin
DERMATOID adj resembling
skin

**DERMATOME** n surgical instrument for cutting thin slices of skin, esp for grafting

**DERMESTID** n any beetle of the family Dermestidae, whose members are destructive at both larval and adult stages to a wide range of stored organic materials such as wool, fur, feathers, and meat. They include the bacon (or larder), cabinet, carpet, leather, and museum beetles

**DERMIC** > DERMIS

**DERMIS** another name for > CORIUM

**DERMISES** > DERMIS

**DERMOID** adj of or resembling skin ▷ n congenital cystic tumour whose walls are lined with epithelium

**DERMOIDS** > DERMOID

**DERMS** > DERM

**DERN** n concealment

**DERNFUL** adj sorrowful

**DERNIER** adj last

**DERNLY** adv sorrowfully

**DERNS** > DERN

**DERO** n tramp or derelict

**DEROGATE** vb detract from ▷ adj debased or degraded

**DEROGATED** > DEROGATE

**DEROGATES** > DEROGATE

**DEROS** > DERO

**DERRICK** n simple crane ▷ vb raise or lower the jib of (a crane)

**DERRICKED** > DERRICK

**DERRICKS** > DERRICK

**DERRIERE** > BUTTOCK

**DERRIERES** > DERRIERE

**DERRIES** > DERRY

**DERRINGER** n small large-bored pistol

**DERRIS** n any East Indian leguminous woody climbing plant of the genus Derris, esp D. elliptica, whose roots yield the compound rotenone

**DERRISES** > DERRIS

**DERRO** n vagrant

**DERROS** > DERRO

**DERRY** n derelict house, esp one used by tramps, drug addicts, etc

**DERTH** same as > DEARTH

**DERTHS** > DERTH

**DERV** n diesel oil, when used for road transport

**DERVISH** n member of a Muslim religious order noted for a frenzied whirling dance

**DERVISHES** > DERVISH

**DERVS** > DERV

**DESALT** same as > DESALINATE

**DESALTED** > DESALT

**DESALTER** > DESALT

**DESALTERS** > DESALT

**DESALTING** > DESALT

**DESALTS** > DESALT

**DESAND** vb remove sand from

**DESANDED** > DESAND

**DESANDING** > DESAND

**DESANDS** > DESAND

**DESCALE** vb remove a hard coating from inside (a kettle or pipe)

**DESCALED** > DESCALE

**DESCALES** > DESCALE

**DESCALING** > DESCALE

**DESCANT** n tune played or sung above a basic melody ▷ adj denoting the highest member in a family of musical instruments ▷ vb compose or perform a descant (for a piece of music)

**DESCANTED** > DESCANT

**DESCANTER** > DESCANT

**DESCANTS** > DESCANT

**DESCEND** vb move down (a slope etc)

**DESCENDED** > DESCEND

**DESCENDER** > DESCEND

**DESCENDS** > DESCEND

**DESCENT** n descending

**DESCENTS** > DESCENT

**DESCHOOL** vb separate education from the institution of school and operate through the pupil's life experience as opposed to a set curriculum

**DESCHOOLS** > DESCHOOL

**DESCRIBE** vb give an account of (something or someone) in words

**DESCRIBED** > DESCRIBE

**DESCRIBER** > DESCRIBE

**DESCRIBES** > DESCRIBE

**DESCRIED** > DESCRY

**DESCRIER** > DESCRY

**DESCRIERS** > DESCRY

**DESCRIES** > DESCRY

**DESCRIVE** vb describe

**DESCRIVED** > DESCRIVE

**DESCRIVES** > DESCRIVE

**DESCRY** vb catch sight of

**DESCRYING** > DESCRY

**DESECRATE** vb damage or insult (something sacred)

**DESELECT** vb refuse to select (an MP) for re-election

**DESELECTS** > DESELECT

**DESERT** n region with little or no vegetation because of low rainfall ▷ vb abandon (a person or place) without intending to return

**DESERTED** > DESERT

**DESERTER** > DESERT

**DESERTERS** > DESERT

**DESERTIC** adj (of soil) developing in hot climates

**DESERTIFY** vb turn into desert

**DESERTING** > DESERT

**DESERTION** n act of deserting or abandoning or the state of being deserted or abandoned

**DESERTS** > DESERT

**DESERVE** vb be entitled to or worthy of

**DESERVED** > DESERVE

**DESERVER** > DESERVE

**DESERVERS** > DESERVE

**DESERVES** > DESERVE

**DESERVING** adj worthy of help, praise, or reward ▷ n merit or demerit

**DESEX** same as > DESEXUALIZE

**DESEXED** > DESEX

**DESEXES** > DESEX

**DESEXING** > DESEX

**DESHI** same as > DESI

**DESI** adj in Indian English, indigenous or local

**DESICCANT** adj desiccating or drying ▷ n substance, such as calcium oxide, that absorbs water and is used to remove moisture

**DESICCATE** vb remove most of the water from

**DESIGN** vb work out the structure or form of (something), by making a sketch or plans ▷ n preliminary drawing

**DESIGNATE** vb give a name to ▷ adj appointed but not yet in office

**DESIGNED** > DESIGN

**DESIGNEE** n person designated to do something

**DESIGNEES** > DESIGNEE

**DESIGNER** n person who draws up original sketches or plans from which things are made ▷ adj designed by a well-known designer

**DESIGNERS** > DESIGNER

**DESIGNFUL** adj scheming

**DESIGNING** adj cunning and scheming

**DESIGNS** > DESIGN

**DESILVER** vb remove silver from

**DESILVERS** > DESILVER

**DESINE** same as > DESIGN

**DESINED** > DESINE

**DESINENCE** n ending or termination, esp an inflectional ending of a word

**DESINENT** > DESINENCE

**DESINES** > DESINE

**DESINING** > DESINE

**DESIPIENT** adj foolish

**DESIRABLE** adj worth having ▷ n person or thing that is the object of desire

**DESIRABLY** > DESIRABLE

**DESIRE** vb want very much ▷ n wish, longing

**DESIRED** > DESIRE

**DESIRER** > DESIRE

**DESIRERS** > DESIRE

**DESIRES** > DESIRE

**DESIRING** > DESIRE

**DESIROUS** adj having a desire for

**DESIST** vb stop (doing something)

**DESISTED** > DESIST

**DESISTING** > DESIST

**DESISTS** > DESIST

**DESK** n piece of furniture with a writing surface and drawers

**DESKBOUND** adj engaged in or involving sedentary work, as at an office desk

**DESKFAST** n breakfast eaten at one's desk at work

**DESKFASTS** > DESKFAST

**DESKILL** vb mechanize or computerize (a job) thereby reducing the skill required to do it

**DESKILLED** > DESKILL

**DESKILLS** > DESKILL

**DESKMAN** n police officer in charge in police station

**DESKMEN** > DESKMAN

**DESKNOTE** n small computer

**DESKNOTES** > DESKNOTE

**DESKS** > DESK

**DESKTOP** adj (of a computer) small enough to use at a desk ▷ n denoting a computer system, esp for word processing, that is small enough to use at a desk

**DESKTOPS** > DESKTOP

**DESMAN** n either of two molelike amphibious mammals

**DESMANS** > DESMAN

**DESMID** n any freshwater green alga of the mainly unicellular family Desmidioideae, typically constricted into two symmetrical halves

**DESMIDIAN** > DESMID

**DESMIDS** > DESMID

**DESMINE** n type of mineral

**DESMINES** > DESMINE

**DESMODIUM** n type of plant

**DESMOID** adj resembling a tendon or ligament ▷ n very firm tumour of connective tissue

**DESMOIDS** > DESMOID

**DESMOSOME** n structure in the cell membranes of adjacent cells that binds them together

**DESNOOD** vb remove the snood of a turkey poult to reduce the risk of cannibalism

**DESNOODED** > DESNOOD

**DESNOODS** > DESNOOD

**DESOEUVRE** adj with nothing to do

**DESOLATE** adj uninhabited

and bleak ▷ vb deprive of inhabitants

**DESOLATED** > DESOLATE

**DESOLATER** > DESOLATE

**DESOLATES** > DESOLATE

**DESOLATOR** > DESOLATE

**DESORB** vb change from an adsorbed state on a surface to a gaseous or liquid state

**DESORBED** > DESORB

**DESORBING** > DESORB

**DESORBS** > DESORB

**DESOXY** same as > DEOXY

**DESPAIR** n total loss of hope ▷ vb lose hope

**DESPAIRED** > DESPAIR

**DESPAIRER** n one who despairs

**DESPAIRS** > DESPAIR

**DESPATCH** same as > DISPATCH

**DESPERADO** n reckless person ready to commit any violent illegal act

**DESPERATE** adj in despair and reckless

**DESPIGHT** obsolete form of > DESPITE

**DESPIGHTS** > DESPIGHT

**DESPISAL** > DESPISE

**DESPISALS** > DESPISE

**DESPISE** vb regard with contempt

**DESPISED** > DESPISE

**DESPISER** > DESPISE

**DESPISERS** > DESPISE

**DESPISES** > DESPISE

**DESPISING** > DESPISE

**DESPITE** prep in spite of ▷ n contempt ▷ vb show contempt for

**DESPITED** > DESPITE

**DESPITES** > DESPITE

**DESPITING** > DESPITE

**DESPOIL** vb plunder

**DESPOILED** > DESPOIL

**DESPOILER** > DESPOIL

**DESPOILS** > DESPOIL

**DESPOND** vb lose heart or hope

**DESPONDED** > DESPOND

**DESPONDS** > DESPOND

**DESPOT** n person in power who acts unfairly or cruelly

**DESPOTAT** n despot's domain

**DESPOTATE** same as > DESPOTAT

**DESPOTATS** > DESPOTAT

**DESPOTIC** > DESPOT

**DESPOTISM** n unfair or cruel government or behaviour

**DESPOTS** > DESPOT

**DESPUMATE** vb clarify or purify (a liquid) by skimming a scum from its surface

**DESSE** n desk

**DESSERT** n sweet course served at the end of a meal

**DESSERTS** > DESSERT

**DESSES** > DESSE

**DESTAIN** vb remove stain from

**DESTAINED** > DESTAIN

**DESTAINS** > DESTAIN

**DESTEMPER** same as > DISTEMPER

**DESTINATE** same as > DESTINE

**DESTINE** vb set apart or appoint (for a certain purpose or person, or to do something)

**DESTINED** adj certain to be or to do something

**DESTINES** > DESTINE

**DESTINIES** > DESTINY

**DESTINING** > DESTINE

**DESTINY** n future marked out for a person or thing

**DESTITUTE** adj having no money or possessions

**DESTOCK** vb (of a retailer) to reduce the amount of stock held or cease to stock certain products

**DESTOCKED** > DESTOCK

**DESTOCKS** > DESTOCK

**DESTRIER** an archaic word for > WARHORSE

**DESTRIERS** > DESTRIER

**DESTROY** vb ruin, demolish

**DESTROYED** > DESTROY

**DESTROYER** n small heavily armed warship

**DESTROYS** > DESTROY

**DESTRUCT** vb destroy (one's own missile or rocket) for safety ▷ n act of destructing ▷ adj designed to be capable of destroying itself or the object, system, or installation containing it

**DESTRUCTO** n person who causes havoc or destruction

**DESTRUCTS** > DESTRUCT

**DESUETUDE** n condition of not being in use

**DESUGAR** vb remove sugar from

**DESUGARED** > DESUGAR

**DESUGARS** > DESUGAR

**DESULFUR** same as > DESULPHUR

**DESULFURS** > DESULFUR

**DESULPHUR** vb remove sulphur from

**DESULTORY** adj jumping from one thing to another, disconnected

**DESYATIN** n Russian unit of area

**DESYATINS** > DESYATIN

**DESYNE** same as > DESIGN

**DESYNED** > DESYNE

**DESYNES** > DESYNE

**DESYNING** > DESYNE

**DETACH** vb disengage and separate

**DETACHED** adj (of a house) not joined to another house

**DETACHER** > DETACH

**DETACHERS** > DETACH

**DETACHES** > DETACH

**DETACHING** > DETACH

**DETAIL** n individual piece of information ▷ vb list fully

**DETAILED** adj having many details

**DETAILER** > DETAIL

**DETAILERS** > DETAIL

**DETAILING** > DETAIL

**DETAILS** > DETAIL

**DETAIN** vb delay (someone)

**DETAINED** > DETAIN

**DETAINEE** > DETAIN

**DETAINEES** > DETAIN

**DETAINER** n wrongful withholding of the property of another person

**DETAINERS** > DETAINER

**DETAINING** > DETAIN

**DETAINS** > DETAIN

**DETASSEL** vb remove top part of corn plant

**DETASSELS** > DETASSEL

**DETECT** vb notice

**DETECTED** > DETECT

**DETECTER** > DETECT

**DETECTERS** > DETECT

**DETECTING** > DETECT

**DETECTION** n act of noticing, discovering, or sensing something

**DETECTIVE** n police officer or private agent who investigates crime ▷ adj used in or serving for detection

**DETECTOR** n instrument used to find something

**DETECTORS** > DETECTOR

**DETECTS** > DETECT

**DETENT** n locking piece of a mechanism, often spring-loaded to check the movement of a wheel in one direction only

**DETENTE** n easing of tension between nations

**DETENTES** > DETENTE

**DETENTION** n imprisonment

**DETENTIST** n supporter of detente

**DETENTS** > DETENT

**DETENU** n prisoner

**DETENUE** n female prisoner

**DETENUES** > DETENUE

**DETENUS** > DETENU

**DETER** vb discourage (someone) from doing something by instilling fear or doubt

**DETERGE** vb wash or wipe away

**DETERGED** > DETERGE

**DETERGENT** n chemical substance for washing clothes or dishes ▷ adj having cleansing power

**DETERGER** n detergent

**DETERGERS** > DETERGER

**DETERGES** > DETERGE

**DETERGING** > DETERGE

**DETERMENT** > DETER

**DETERMINE** vb settle (an argument or a question) conclusively

**DETERRED** > DETER

**DETERRENT** n something that deters ▷ adj tending to deter

**DETERRER** > DETER

**DETERRERS** > DETERRER

**DETERRING** > DETER

**DETERS** > DETER

**DETERSION** n act of cleansing

**DETERSIVE** same as > DETERGENT

**DETEST** vb dislike intensely

**DETESTED** > DETEST

**DETESTER** > DETEST

**DETESTERS** > DETEST

**DETESTING** > DETEST

**DETESTS** > DETEST

**DETHATCH** vb remove dead grass from lawn

**DETHRONE** vb remove from a throne or position of power

**DETHRONED** > DETHRONE

**DETHRONER** > DETHRONE

**DETHRONES** > DETHRONE

**DETICK** vb remove ticks from

**DETICKED** > DETICK

**DETICKER** > DETICK

**DETICKERS** > DETICK

**DETICKING** > DETICK

**DETICKS** > DETICK

**DETINUE** n action brought by a plaintiff to recover goods wrongfully detained

**DETINUES** > DETINUE

**DETONABLE** adj that can be detonated

**DETONATE** vb explode

**DETONATED** > DETONATE

**DETONATES** > DETONATE

**DETONATOR** n small amount of explosive, or a device, used to set off an explosion

**DETORSION** > DETORT

**DETORT** vb pervert

**DETORTED** > DETORT

**DETORTING** > DETORT

**DETORTION** > DETORT

**DETORTS** > DETORT

**DETOUR** n route that is not the most direct one ▷ vb deviate or cause to deviate from a direct route or course of action

**DETOURED** > DETOUR

**DETOURING** > DETOUR

**DETOURS** > DETOUR

**DETOX** n treatment to rid the body of poisonous substances ▷ vb undergo treatment to rid the body of poisonous substances, esp alcohol and drugs

**DETOXED** > DETOX

**DETOXES** > DETOX

**DETOXIFY** vb remove poison from

**DETOXING** > DETOX
**DETRACT** *vb* make (something) seem less good
**DETRACTED** > DETRACT
**DETRACTOR** > DETRACT
**DETRACTS** > DETRACT
**DETRAIN** *vb* leave or cause to leave a railway train, as passengers, etc
**DETRAINED** > DETRAIN
**DETRAINS** > DETRAIN
**DETRAQUE** *n* insane person
**DETRAQUEE** *n* female insane person
**DETRAQUES** > DETRAQUE
**DETRIMENT** *n* disadvantage or damage
**DETRITAL** > DETRITUS
**DETRITION** *n* act of rubbing or wearing away by friction
**DETRITUS** *n* loose mass of stones and silt worn away from rocks
**DETRUDE** *vb* force down or thrust away or out
**DETRUDED** > DETRUDE
**DETRUDES** > DETRUDE
**DETRUDING** > DETRUDE
**DETRUSION** > DETRUDE
**DETUNE** *vb* change pitch of (stringed instrument)
**DETUNED** > DETUNE
**DETUNES** > DETUNE
**DETUNING** > DETUNE
**DEUCE** *vb* score deuce in tennis ▷ *n* score of forty all
**DEUCED** *adj* damned
**DEUCEDLY** > DEUCED
**DEUCES** > DEUCE
**DEUCING** > DEUCE
**DEUDDARN** *n* two-tiered Welsh dresser
**DEUDDARNS** > DEUDDARN
**DEUS** *n* god
**DEUTERATE** *vb* treat or combine with deuterium
**DEUTERIC** *adj* (of mineral) formed by metasomatic changes
**DEUTERIDE** *n* compound of deuterium with some other element. It is analogous to a hydride
**DEUTERIUM** *n* isotope of hydrogen twice as heavy as the normal atom
**DEUTERON** *n* nucleus of a deuterium atom, consisting of one proton and one neutron
**DEUTERONS** > DEUTERON
**DEUTON** *old form of* > DEUTERON
**DEUTONS** > DEUTON
**DEUTZIA** *n* shrub with clusters of pink or white flowers
**DEUTZIAS** > DEUTZIA
**DEV** *same as* > DEVA
**DEVA** *n* (in Hinduism and Buddhism) divine being

or god
**DEVALL** *vb* stop
**DEVALLED** > DEVALL
**DEVALLING** > DEVALL
**DEVALLS** > DEVALL
**DEVALUATE** *same as* > DEVALUE
**DEVALUE** *vb* reduce the exchange value of (a currency)
**DEVALUED** > DEVALUE
**DEVALUES** > DEVALUE
**DEVALUING** > DEVALUE
**DEVAS** > DEVA
**DEVASTATE** *vb* destroy
**DEVEIN** *vb* remove vein from
**DEVEINED** > DEVEIN
**DEVEINING** > DEVEIN
**DEVEINS** > DEVEIN
**DEVEL** *same as* > DEVVEL
**DEVELED** > DEVEL
**DEVELING** > DEVEL
**DEVELLED** > DEVEL
**DEVELLING** > DEVEL
**DEVELOP** *vb* grow or bring to a later, more elaborate, or more advanced stage
**DEVELOPE** *old form of* > DEVELOP
**DEVELOPED** > DEVELOP
**DEVELOPER** *n* person who develops property
**DEVELOPES** > DEVELOPE
**DEVELOPPE** *n* ballet position
**DEVELOPS** > DEVELOP
**DEVELS** > DEVEL
**DEVERBAL** *n* word deriving from verb
**DEVERBALS** > DEVERBAL
**DEVEST** *variant spelling of* > DIVEST
**DEVESTED** > DEVEST
**DEVESTING** > DEVEST
**DEVESTS** > DEVEST
**DEVIANCE** *n* act or state of being deviant
**DEVIANCES** > DEVIANCE
**DEVIANCY** *same as* > DEVIANCE
**DEVIANT** *adj* (person) deviating from what is considered acceptable behaviour ▷ *n* person whose behaviour deviates from what is considered to be acceptable
**DEVIANTS** > DEVIANT
**DEVIATE** *vb* differ from others in belief or thought
**DEVIATED** > DEVIATE
**DEVIATES** > DEVIATE
**DEVIATING** > DEVIATE
**DEVIATION** *n* act or result of deviating
**DEVIATIVE** *adj* tending to deviate
**DEVIATOR** > DEVIATE
**DEVIATORS** > DEVIATE
**DEVIATORY** > DEVIATE
**DEVICE** *n* machine or tool used for a specific task
**DEVICEFUL** *adj* full of

devices
**DEVICES** > DEVICE
**DEVIL** *n* evil spirit ▷ *vb* prepare (food) with a highly flavoured spiced mixture
**DEVILDOM** *n* domain of evil spirits
**DEVILDOMS** > DEVILDOM
**DEVILED** > DEVIL
**DEVILESS** *n* female devil
**DEVILET** *n* young devil
**DEVILETS** > DEVILET
**DEVILFISH** *n* manta fish
**DEVILING** > DEVIL
**DEVILINGS** > DEVIL
**DEVILISH** *adj* cruel or unpleasant ▷ *adv* extremely
**DEVILISM** *n* doctrine of devil
**DEVILISMS** > DEVILISM
**DEVILKIN** *n* small devil
**DEVILKINS** > DEVILKIN
**DEVILLED** > DEVIL
**DEVILLING** > DEVIL
**DEVILMENT** *n* mischievous conduct
**DEVILRIES** > DEVILRY
**DEVILRY** *n* mischievousness
**DEVILS** > DEVIL
**DEVILSHIP** *n* character of devil
**DEVILTRY** *same as* > DEVILRY
**DEVILWOOD** *n* small US tree
**DEVIOUS** *adj* insincere and dishonest
**DEVIOUSLY** > DEVIOUS
**DEVISABLE** *adj* (of property, esp realty) capable of being transferred by will
**DEVISAL** *n* act of inventing, contriving, or devising
**DEVISALS** > DEVISAL
**DEVISE** *vb* work out (something) in one's mind ▷ *n* disposition of property by will
**DEVISED** > DEVISE
**DEVISEE** *n* person to whom property, esp realty, is devised by will
**DEVISEES** > DEVISEE
**DEVISER** > DEVISE
**DEVISERS** > DEVISE
**DEVISES** > DEVISE
**DEVISING** > DEVISE
**DEVISOR** *n* person who devises property, esp realty, by will
**DEVISORS** > DEVISOR
**DEVITRIFY** *vb* change from a vitreous state to a crystalline state
**DEVLING** *n* young devil
**DEVLINGS** > DEVLING
**DEVOICE** *vb* make (a voiced speech sound) voiceless
**DEVOICED** > DEVOICE
**DEVOICES** > DEVOICE
**DEVOICING** > DEVOICE

**DEVOID** *adj* completely lacking (in)
**DEVOIR** *n* duty
**DEVOIRS** > DEVOIR
**DEVOLVE** *vb* pass (power or duties) or (of power or duties) be passed to a successor or substitute
**DEVOLVED** > DEVOLVE
**DEVOLVES** > DEVOLVE
**DEVOLVING** > DEVOLVE
**DEVON** *n* bland processed meat in sausage form, eaten cold in slices
**DEVONIAN** *adj* of, denoting, or formed in the fourth period of the Palaeozoic era, between the Silurian and Carboniferous periods
**DEVONPORT** *same as* > DAVENPORT
**DEVONS** > DEVON
**DEVORE** *n* velvet fabric with a raised pattern created by disintegrating some of the pile with chemicals
**DEVORES** > DEVORE
**DEVOT** *n* devotee
**DEVOTE** *vb* apply or dedicate to a particular purpose
**DEVOTED** *adj* showing loyalty or devotion
**DEVOTEDLY** > DEVOTED
**DEVOTEE** *n* person who is very enthusiastic about something
**DEVOTEES** > DEVOTEE
**DEVOTES** > DEVOTE
**DEVOTING** > DEVOTE
**DEVOTION** *n* strong affection for or loyalty to someone or something
**DEVOTIONS** > DEVOTION
**DEVOTS** > DEVOT
**DEVOUR** *vb* eat greedily
**DEVOURED** > DEVOUR
**DEVOURER** > DEVOUR
**DEVOURERS** > DEVOUR
**DEVOURING** > DEVOUR
**DEVOURS** > DEVOUR
**DEVOUT** *adj* deeply religious
**DEVOUTER** > DEVOUT
**DEVOUTEST** > DEVOUT
**DEVOUTLY** > DEVOUT
**DEVS** > DEV
**DEVVEL** *vb* strike with blow
**DEVVELLED** > DEVVEL
**DEVVELS** > DEVVEL
**DEW** *n* drops of water that form on the ground at night from vapour in the air ▷ *vb* moisten with or as with dew
**DEWAN** *n* (formerly in India) the chief minister or finance minister of a state ruled by an Indian prince
**DEWANI** *n* post of dewan
**DEWANIS** > DEWANI
**DEWANNIES** > DEWANNY
**DEWANNY** *same as* > DEWANI
**DEWANS** > DEWAN
**DEWAR** *as in* *dewar flask*

type of vacuum flask
DEWARS > DEWAR
DEWATER vb remove water from
DEWATERED > DEWATER
DEWATERER > DEWATER
DEWATERS > DEWATER
DEWAX vb remove wax from
DEWAXED > DEWAX
DEWAXES > DEWAX
DEWAXING > DEWAX
DEWBERRY n type of bramble with blue-black fruits
DEWCLAW n nonfunctional claw on a dog's leg
DEWCLAWED > DEWCLAW
DEWCLAWS > DEWCLAW
DEWDROP n drop of dew
DEWDROPS > DEWDROP
DEWED > DEW
DEWFALL n formation of dew
DEWFALLS > DEWFALL
DEWFULL obsolete form of > DUE
DEWIER > DEWY
DEWIEST > DEWY
DEWILY > DEWY
DEWINESS > DEWY
DEWING > DEW
DEWITT vb kill, esp hang unlawfully
DEWITTED > DEWITT
DEWITTING > DEWITT
DEWITTS > DEWITT
DEWLAP n loose fold of skin hanging under the throat in dogs, cattle, etc
DEWLAPPED > DEWLAP
DEWLAPS > DEWLAP
DEWLAPT > DEWLAP
DEWLESS > DEW
DEWOOL vb remove wool from
DEWOOLED > DEWOOL
DEWOOLING > DEWOOL
DEWOOLS > DEWOOL
DEWORM vb rid of worms
DEWORMED > DEWORM
DEWORMER > DEWORM
DEWORMERS > DEWORM
DEWORMING > DEWORM
DEWORMS > DEWORM
DEWPOINT n temperature at which water vapour in the air becomes saturated and water droplets begin to form
DEWPOINTS > DEWPOINT
DEWS > DEW
DEWY adj moist with or as with dew
DEX n dextroamphetamine
DEXES > DEX
DEXIE n pill containing dextroamphetamine
DEXIES > DEXIE
DEXTER adj of or on the right side of a shield, etc, from the bearer's point of view ▷ n small breed of red or black beef cattle, originally from Ireland

DEXTERITY n skill in using one's hands
DEXTEROUS adj possessing or done with dexterity
DEXTERS > DEXTER
DEXTRAL adj of, relating to, or located on the right side, esp of the body
DEXTRALLY > DEXTRAL
DEXTRAN n polysaccharide produced by the action of bacteria on sucrose: used as a substitute for plasma in blood transfusions
DEXTRANS > DEXTRAN
DEXTRIN n sticky substance obtained from starch, used as a thickening agent in food
DEXTRINE same as > DEXTRIN
DEXTRINES > DEXTRINE
DEXTRINS > DEXTRIN
DEXTRO adj dextrorotatory or rotating to the right
DEXTRORSE adj (of some climbing plants) growing upwards in a helix from left to right or anticlockwise
DEXTROSE n glucose occurring in fruit, honey, and the blood of animals
DEXTROSES > DEXTROSE
DEXTROUS same as > DEXTEROUS
DEXY same as > DEXIE
DEY n title given to commanders or (from 1710) governors of the Janissaries of Algiers (1671–1830)
DEYS > DEY
DEZINC vb remove zinc from
DEZINCED > DEZINC
DEZINCING > DEZINC
DEZINCKED > DEZINC
DEZINCS > DEZINC
DHAK n tropical Asian leguminous tree, Butea frondosa, that has bright red flowers and yields a red resin, used as an astringent
DHAKS > DHAK
DHAL n curry made from lentils or beans
DHALS > DHAL
DHAMMA variant of > DHARMA
DHAMMAS > DHAMMA
DHANSAK n any of a variety of Indian dishes consisting of meat or vegetables braised with water or stock and lentils
DHANSAKS > DHANSAK
DHARMA n moral law or behaviour
DHARMAS > DHARMA
DHARMIC > DHARMA
DHARMSALA n Indian hostel
DHARNA n (in India) a method of obtaining justice, as the payment of

a debt, by sitting, fasting, at the door of the person from whom reparation is sought
DHARNAS > DHARNA
DHOBI n (in India, Malaya, East Africa, etc, esp formerly) a washerman
DHOBIS > DHOBI
DHOL n type of Indian drum
DHOLE n fierce canine mammal, Cuon alpinus, of the forests of central and SE Asia, having a reddish-brown coat and rounded ears: hunts in packs
DHOLES > DHOLE
DHOLL same as > DHAL
DHOLLS > DHOLL
DHOLS > DHOL
DHOOLIES > DHOOLY
DHOOLY same as > DOOLIE
DHOORA same as > DURRA
DHOORAS > DHOORA
DHOOTI same as > DHOTI
DHOOTIE same as > DHOTI
DHOOTIES > DHOOTIE
DHOOTIS > DHOOTI
DHOTI n long loincloth worn by men in India
DHOTIS > DHOTI
DHOURRA same as > DURRA
DHOURRAS > DHOURRA
DHOW n Arab sailing ship
DHOWS > DHOW
DHURNA same as > DHARNA
DHURNAS > DHURNA
DHURRA same as > DURRA
DHURRAS > DHURRA
DHURRIE same as > DURRIE
DHURRIES > DHURRIE
DHUTI same as > DHOTI
DHUTIS > DHUTI
DI > DEUS
DIABASE n altered dolerite
DIABASES > DIABASE
DIABASIC > DIABASE
DIABETES n disorder in which an abnormal amount of urine containing an excess of sugar is excreted
DIABETIC n person who has diabetes ▷ adj of or having diabetes
DIABETICS > DIABETIC
DIABLE n type of sauce
DIABLERIE n magic or witchcraft connected with devils
DIABLERY same as > DIABLERIE
DIABLES > DIABLE
DIABOLIC adj of the Devil
DIABOLISE same as > DIABOLIZE
DIABOLISM n witchcraft, devil worship
DIABOLIST > DIABOLISM
DIABOLIZE vb make (someone or something) diabolical
DIABOLO n game in which one throws and catches

a spinning top on a cord fastened to two sticks held in the hands
DIABOLOGY n study of devils
DIABOLOS > DIABOLO
DIACETYL n aromatic compound
DIACETYLS > DIACETYL
DIACHRONY n change over time
DIACHYLON n acid or salt that contains two acidic hydrogen atoms
DIACHYLUM n plaster containing glycerin with lead salts
DIACID n lead plaster
DIACIDIC adj (of a base, such as calcium hydroxide $Ca(OH)_2$) capable of neutralizing two protons with one of its molecules
DIACIDS > DIACID
DIACODION n herbal remedy aiding sleep
DIACODIUM n syrup of poppies
DIACONAL adj of or associated with a deacon or the diaconate
DIACONATE n position or period of office of a deacon
DIACRITIC n sign above or below a character to indicate phonetic value or stress
DIACT n two-rayed
DIACTINAL adj having two pointed ends
DIACTINE adj two-rayed
DIACTINIC adj able to transmit photochemically active radiation
DIADEM n crown ▷ vb adorn or crown with or as with a diadem
DIADEMED > DIADEM
DIADEMING > DIADEM
DIADEMS > DIADEM
DIADOCHI pl n the six Macedonian generals who, after the death of Alexander the Great, fought for control of his empire
DIADOCHY n replacement of one element in a crystal by another
DIADROM n complete course of pendulum
DIADROMS > DIADROM
DIAERESES > DIAERESIS
DIAERESIS n mark (¨) placed over a vowel to show that it is pronounced separately from the preceding one, for example in Noël
DIAERETIC > DIAERESIS
DIAGLYPH n figure cut into stone
DIAGLYPHS > DIAGLYPH
DIAGNOSE vb determine by

diagnosis

**DIAGNOSED** > DIAGNOSE

**DIAGNOSES** > DIAGNOSIS

**DIAGNOSIS** *n* discovery and identification of diseases from the examination of symptoms

**DIAGONAL** *adj* from corner to corner ▷ *n* diagonal line

**DIAGONALS** > DIAGONAL

**DIAGRAM** *n* sketch showing the form or workings of something ▷ *vb* show in or as if in a diagram

**DIAGRAMED** > DIAGRAM

**DIAGRAMS** > DIAGRAM

**DIAGRAPH** *n* device for enlarging or reducing maps, plans, etc

**DIAGRAPHS** > DIAGRAPH

**DIAGRID** *n* diagonal structure network

**DIAGRIDS** > DIAGRID

**DIAL** *n* face of a clock or watch ▷ *vb* operate the dial or buttons on a telephone in order to contact (a number)

**DIALECT** *n* form of a language spoken in a particular area

**DIALECTAL** > DIALECT

**DIALECTIC** *n* logical debate by question and answer to resolve differences between two views ▷ *adj* of or relating to logical disputation

**DIALECTS** > DIALECT

**DIALED** > DIAL

**DIALER** > DIAL

**DIALERS** > DIAL

**DIALING** > DIAL

**DIALINGS** > DIAL

**DIALIST** *n* dial-maker

**DIALISTS** > DIALIST

**DIALLAGE** *n* green or brownish-black variety of the mineral augite in the form of layers of platelike crystals

**DIALLAGES** > DIALLAGE

**DIALLAGIC** > DIALLAGE

**DIALLED** > DIAL

**DIALLEL** *n* interbreeding among a group of parents

**DIALLER** > DIAL

**DIALLERS** > DIAL

**DIALLING** > DIAL

**DIALLINGS** > DIAL

**DIALLIST** *same as* > DIALIST

**DIALLISTS** > DIALLIST

**DIALOG** *same as* > DIALOGUE

**DIALOGED** > DIALOG

**DIALOGER** > DIALOG

**DIALOGERS** > DIALOG

**DIALOGIC** > DIALOGUE

**DIALOGING** > DIALOG

**DIALOGISE** *same as* > DIALOGIZE

**DIALOGISM** *n* deduction with one premise and a disjunctive conclusion

**DIALOGIST** *n* person who writes or takes part in a dialogue

**DIALOGITE** *n* carbonate mineral

**DIALOGIZE** *vb* carry on a dialogue

**DIALOGS** > DIALOG

**DIALOGUE** *n* conversation between two people, esp in a book, film, or play ▷ *vb* put into the form of a dialogue

**DIALOGUED** > DIALOGUE

**DIALOGUER** > DIALOGUE

**DIALOGUES** > DIALOGUE

**DIALS** > DIAL

**DIALYSATE** *n* liquid used in dialysis

**DIALYSE** *vb* separate by dialysis

**DIALYSED** > DIALYSE

**DIALYSER** *n* machine that performs dialysis, esp one that removes impurities from the blood of patients with malfunctioning kidneys

**DIALYSERS** > DIALYSER

**DIALYSES** > DIALYSIS

**DIALYSING** > DIALYSE

**DIALYSIS** *n* filtering of blood through a membrane to remove waste products

**DIALYTIC** > DIALYSIS

**DIALYZATE** *same as* > DIALYSATE

**DIALYZE** *same as* > DIALYSE

**DIALYZED** > DIALYZE

**DIALYZER** *same as* > DIALYSER

**DIALYZERS** > DIALYZER

**DIALYZES** > DIALYZE

**DIALYZING** > DIALYZE

**DIAMAGNET** *n* substance exhibiting diamagnetism

**DIAMANTE** *adj* decorated with artificial jewels or sequins ▷ *n* fabric so covered

**DIAMANTES** > DIAMANTE

**DIAMETER** *n* (length of) a straight line through the centre of a circle or sphere

**DIAMETERS** > DIAMETER

**DIAMETRAL** *same as* > DIAMETRIC

**DIAMETRIC** *adj* of a diameter

**DIAMIDE** *n* compound containing two amido groups

**DIAMIDES** > DIAMIDE

**DIAMIN** *same as* > DIAMIN

**DIAMINE** *n* any chemical compound containing two amino groups in its molecules

**DIAMINES** > DIAMINE

**DIAMINS** > DIAMIN

**DIAMOND** *n* exceptionally hard, usu. colourless, precious stone ▷ *adj* (of an anniversary) the sixtieth ▷ *vb* stud or decorate with diamonds

**DIAMONDED** > DIAMOND

**DIAMONDS** > DIAMOND

**DIAMYL** *adj* with two amyl groups

**DIANDRIES** > DIANDRY

**DIANDROUS** *adj* (of some flowers or flowering plants) having two stamens

**DIANDRY** *n* practice of having two husbands

**DIANODAL** *adj* going through a node

**DIANOETIC** *adj* of or relating to thought, esp to discursive reasoning rather than intuition

**DIANOIA** *n* perception and experience regarded as lower modes of knowledge

**DIANOIAS** > DIANOIA

**DIANTHUS** *n* any Eurasian caryophyllaceous plant of the widely cultivated genus *Dianthus*, such as the carnation, pink, and sweet william

**DIAPASE** *same as* > DIAPASON

**DIAPASES** > DIAPASE

**DIAPASON** *n* either of two stops found throughout the range of a pipe organ

**DIAPASONS** > DIAPASON

**DIAPAUSE** *vb* undergo diapause ▷ *n* period of suspended development and growth accompanied by decreased metabolism in insects and some other animals. It is correlated with seasonal changes

**DIAPAUSED** > DIAPAUSE

**DIAPAUSES** > DIAPAUSE

**DIAPENTE** *n* (in classical Greece) the interval of a perfect fifth

**DIAPENTES** > DIAPENTE

**DIAPER** *n* nappy ▷ *vb* decorate with a geometric pattern

**DIAPERED** > DIAPER

**DIAPERING** > DIAPER

**DIAPERS** > DIAPER

**DIAPHONE** *n* set of all realizations of a given phoneme in a language

**DIAPHONES** > DIAPHONE

**DIAPHONIC** > DIAPHONY

**DIAPHONY** *n* style of two-part polyphonic singing

**DIAPHRAGM** *n* muscular partition that separates the abdominal cavity and chest cavity

**DIAPHYSES** > DIAPHYSIS

**DIAPHYSIS** *n* shaft of a long bone

**DIAPIR** *n* anticlinal fold in which the brittle overlying rock has been pierced by

material, such as salt, from beneath

**DIAPIRIC** > DIAPIR

**DIAPIRISM** > DIAPIR

**DIAPIRS** > DIAPIR

**DIAPSID** *n* reptile with two holes in rear of skull

**DIAPSIDS** > DIAPSID

**DIAPYESES** > DIAPYESIS

**DIAPYESIS** *n* discharge of pus

**DIAPYETIC** > DIAPYESIS

**DIARCH** *adj* (of a vascular bundle) having two strands of xylem

**DIARCHAL** > DIARCHY

**DIARCHIC** > DIARCHY

**DIARCHIES** > DIARCHY

**DIARCHY** *n* government by two states, individuals, etc

**DIARIAL** > DIARY

**DIARIAN** > DIARY

**DIARIES** > DIARY

**DIARISE** *same as* > DIARIZE

**DIARISED** > DIARISE

**DIARISES** > DIARISE

**DIARISING** > DIARISE

**DIARIST** *n* person who writes a diary

**DIARISTIC** > DIARIST

**DIARISTS** > DIARIST

**DIARIZE** *vb* record in diary

**DIARIZED** > DIARIZE

**DIARIZES** > DIARIZE

**DIARIZING** > DIARIZE

**DIARRHEA** *same as* > DIARRHOEA

**DIARRHEAL** > DIARRHEA

**DIARRHEAS** > DIARRHEA

**DIARRHEIC** > DIARRHEA

**DIARRHOEA** *n* frequent discharge of abnormally liquid faeces

**DIARY** *n* (book for) a record of daily events, appointments, or observations

**DIASCOPE** *n* optical projector used to display transparencies

**DIASCOPES** > DIASCOPE

**DIASPORA** *n* dispersion or spreading, as of people originally belonging to one nation or having a common culture

**DIASPORAS** > DIASPORA

**DIASPORE** *n* white, yellowish, or grey mineral

**DIASPORES** > DIASPORE

**DIASPORIC** > DIASPORE

**DIASTASE** *n* enzyme that converts starch into sugar

**DIASTASES** > DIASTASIS

**DIASTASIC** > DIASTASE

**DIASTASIS** *n* separation of an epiphysis from the long bone to which it is normally attached without fracture of the bone

**DIASTATIC** > DIASTASIS

**DIASTEM** *same as* > DIASTEMA

DIASTEMA n abnormal space, fissure, or cleft in a bodily organ or part

DIASTEMAS > DIASTEMA

DIASTEMS > DIASTEM

DIASTER n stage in cell division at which the chromosomes are in two groups at the poles of the spindle before forming daughter nuclei

DIASTERS > DIASTER

DIASTOLE n dilation of the chambers of the heart

DIASTOLES > DIASTOLE

DIASTOLIC > DIASTOLE

DIASTRAL > DIASTER

DIASTYLE adj having columns about three diameters apart ▷ n diastyle building

DIASTYLES > DIASTYLE

DIATHERMY n local heating of the body tissues with an electric current for medical or surgical purposes

DIATHESES > DIATHESIS

DIATHESIS n hereditary or acquired susceptibility of the body to one or more diseases

DIATHETIC > DIATHESIS

DIATOM n microscopic unicellular alga

DIATOMIC adj containing two atoms

DIATOMIST n specialist in diatoms

DIATOMITE n soft very fine-grained whitish rock consisting of the siliceous remains of diatoms deposited in the ocean or in ponds or lakes. It is used as an absorbent, filtering medium, insulator, filler, etc

DIATOMS > DIATOM

DIATONIC adj of a regular major or minor scale

DIATRETUM n Roman glass bowl

DIATRIBE n bitter critical attack

DIATRIBES > DIATRIBE

DIATRON n circuit that uses diodes

DIATRONS > DIATRON

DIATROPIC adj relating to a type of response in plants to an external stimulus

DIAXON n bipolar cell

DIAXONS > DIAXON

DIAZEPAM n chemical compound used as a minor tranquillizer and muscle relaxant and to treat acute epilepsy

DIAZEPAMS > DIAZEPAM

DIAZEUXES > DIAZEUXIS

DIAZEUXIS n separation of two tetrachords by interval of a tone

DIAZIN same as > DIAZINE

DIAZINE n organic compound

DIAZINES > DIAZINE

DIAZINON n type of insecticide

DIAZINONS > DIAZINON

DIAZINS > DIAZIN

DIAZO adj of, or relating to the reproduction of documents using the bleaching action of ultraviolet radiation on diazonium salts ▷ n document produced by this method

DIAZOES > DIAZO

DIAZOLE n type of organic compound

DIAZOLES > DIAZOLE

DIAZONIUM n type of chemical group

DIAZOS > DIAZO

DIAZOTISE same as > DIAZOTIZE

DIAZOTIZE vb cause (an aryl amine) to react with nitrous acid to produce a diazonium salt

DIB vb fish by allowing the bait to bob and dip on the surface

DIBASIC adj (of an acid, such as sulphuric acid, $H_2SO_4$) containing two acidic hydrogen atoms

DIBBED > DIB

DIBBER same as > DIBBLE

DIBBERED > DIBBER

DIBBERING > DIBBER

DIBBERS > DIBBER

DIBBING > DIB

DIBBLE n small hand tool used to make holes in the ground for seeds or plants ▷ vb make a hole in (the ground) with a dibble

DIBBLED > DIBBLE

DIBBLER > DIBBLE

DIBBLERS > DIBBLE

DIBBLES > DIBBLE

DIBBLING > DIBBLE

DIBBS n money

DIBBUK variant spelling of > DYBBUK

DIBBUKIM > DIBBUK

DIBBUKKIM > DIBBUK

DIBBUKS > DIBBUK

DIBROMIDE n chemical compound that contains two bromine atoms per molecule

DIBS > DIB

DIBUTYL adj with two butyl groups

DICACIOUS adj teasing

DICACITY n playful teasing

DICACODYL n oily slightly water-soluble poisonous liquid with garlic-like odour

DICAMBA n type of weedkiller

DICAMBAS > DICAMBA

DICAST n (in ancient

Athens) a juror in the popular courts chosen by lot from a list of citizens

DICASTERY another word for > CONGREGATION

DICASTIC > DICAST

DICASTS > DICAST

DICE n small cube each of whose sides has a different number of spots (1 to 6), used in games of chance ▷ vb cut (food) into small cubes

DICED > DICE

DICENTRA n any Asian or North American plant of the genus Dicentra, such as bleeding heart and Dutchman's-breeches, having finely divided leaves and ornamental clusters of drooping flowers: family Fumariaceae

DICENTRAS > DICENTRA

DICENTRIC n abnormal chromosome with two centromeres

DICER > DICE

DICERS > DICE

DICES > DICE

DICEY adj dangerous or risky

DICH interj archaic expression meaning "may it do"

DICHASIA > DICHASIUM

DICHASIAL > DICHASIUM

DICHASIUM n cymose inflorescence in which each branch bearing a flower gives rise to two other flowering branches, as in the stitchwort

DICHOGAMY n maturation of male and female parts of a flower at different times, preventing automatic self-pollination

DICHONDRA n creeping perennial herb

DICHOPTIC adj having the eyes distinctly separate

DICHORD n two-stringed musical instrument

DICHORDS > DICHORD

DICHOTIC adj relating to or involving the stimulation of each ear simultaneously by different sounds

DICHOTOMY n division into two opposed groups or parts

DICHROIC adj having or consisting of only two colours

DICHROISM n property of a uniaxial crystal, such as tourmaline, of showing a perceptible difference in colour when viewed along two different axes in transmitted white light

DICHROITE n grey or violet-blue dichroic material

DICHROMAT n person able to distinguish only two colours

DICHROMIC adj of or involving only two colours

DICHT vb wipe

DICHTED > DICHT

DICHTING > DICHT

DICHTS > DICHT

DICIER > DICEY

DICIEST > DICEY

DICING > DICE

DICINGS > DICE

DICK n penis ▷ vb penetrate with a penis

DICKED > DICK

DICKENS n euphemism for devil

DICKENSES > DICKENS

DICKER vb trade (goods) by bargaining ▷ n petty bargain or barter

DICKERED > DICKER

DICKERING > DICKER

DICKERS > DICKER

DICKEY same as > DICKY

DICKEYS > DICKY

DICKHEAD n stupid or despicable man or boy

DICKHEADS > DICKHEAD

DICKIE same as > DICKY

DICKIER > DICKY

DICKIES > DICKY

DICKIEST > DICKY

DICKING > DICK

DICKS > DICK

DICKTIER > DICKTY

DICKTIEST > DICKTY

DICKTY same as > DICTY

DICKY n false shirt front ▷ adj shaky or weak

DICKYBIRD See > DICKY

DICLINIES > DICLINOUS

DICLINISM > DICLINOUS

DICLINOUS adj (of flowering plants) bearing unisexual flowers

DICLINY > DICLINOUS

DICOT n type of flowering plant

DICOTS > DICOT

DICOTYL n a type of flowering plant; dicotyledon

DICOTYLS > DICOTYL

DICROTAL same as > DICROTIC

DICROTIC adj having or relating to a double pulse for each heartbeat

DICROTISM > DICROTIC

DICROTOUS same as > DICROTIC

DICT vb dictate

DICTA > DICTUM

DICTATE vb say aloud for someone else to write down ▷ n authoritative command

DICTATED > DICTATE

DICTATES > DICTATE

DICTATING > DICTATE

DICTATION n act of dictating words to be

taken down in writing

**DICTATOR** *n* ruler who has complete power

**DICTATORS** > DICTATOR

**DICTATORY** *adj* tending to dictate

**DICTATRIX** > DICTATOR

**DICTATURE** *n* dictatorship

**DICTED** > DICT

**DICTIER** > DICTY

**DICTIEST** > DICTY

**DICTING** > DICT

**DICTION** *n* manner of pronouncing words and sounds

**DICTIONAL** > DICTION

**DICTIONS** > DICTION

**DICTS** > DICT

**DICTUM** *n* formal statement

**DICTUMS** > DICTUM

**DICTY** *adj* conceited; snobbish

**DICTYOGEN** *n* plant with net-veined leaves

**DICUMAROL** *n* anticoagulant drug

**DICYCLIC** *adj* having the perianth arranged in two whorls

**DICYCLIES** > DICYCLIC

**DICYCLY** > DICYCLIC

**DID** > DO

**DIDACT** *n* instructive person

**DIDACTIC** *adj* intended to instruct

**DIDACTICS** *n* art or science of teaching

**DIDACTS** > DIDACT

**DIDACTYL** *adj* having only two toes on each foot ▷ *n* animal with only two toes on each foot

**DIDACTYLS** > DIDACTYL

**DIDAKAI** *same as* > DIDICOY

**DIDAKAIS** > DIDAKAI

**DIDAKEI** *same as* > DIDICOY

**DIDAKEIS** > DIDAKEI

**DIDAPPER** *n* small grebe

**DIDAPPERS** > DIDAPPER

**DIDDER** *vb* shake with fear

**DIDDERED** > DIDDER

**DIDDERING** > DIDDER

**DIDDERS** > DIDDER

**DIDDICOY** *same as* > DIDICOY

**DIDDICOYS** > DIDDICOY

**DIDDIER** > DIDDY

**DIDDIES** > DIDDY

**DIDDIEST** > DIDDY

**DIDDLE** *vb* swindle

**DIDDLED** > DIDDLE

**DIDDLER** > DIDDLE

**DIDDLERS** > DIDDLE

**DIDDLES** > DIDDLE

**DIDDLEY** *n* worthless amount

**DIDDLEYS** > DIDDLEY

**DIDDLIES** > DIDDLY

**DIDDLING** > DIDDLE

**DIDDLY** *n* worthless amount

**DIDDY** *n* female breast or nipple ▷ *adj* of or relating to a diddy

**DIDELPHIC** *adj* with two genital tubes or ovaries

**DIDELPHID** *n* marsupial

**DIDICOI** *same as* > DIDICOY

**DIDICOIS** > DIDICOI

**DIDICOY** *n* (in Britain) one of a group of caravan-dwelling roadside people who live like Gypsies but are not true Romanies

**DIDICOYS** > DIDICOY

**DIDIE** *same as* > DIDY

**DIDIES** > DIDY

**DIDJERIDU** *n* Australian Aboriginal wind instrument

**DIDO** *n* antic

**DIDOES** > DIDO

**DIDOS** > DIDO

**DIDRACHM** *n* two-drachma piece

**DIDRACHMA** *same as* > DIDRACHM

**DIDRACHMS** > DIDRACHM

**DIDST** *form of the past tense of* > DO

**DIDY** *n* woman's breast

**DIDYMIUM** *n* mixture of the metallic rare earths neodymium and praseodymium, once thought to be an element

**DIDYMIUMS** > DIDYMIUM

**DIDYMOUS** *adj* in pairs or in two parts

**DIDYNAMY** *n* (of stamens) being in two unequal pairs

**DIE** *vb* (of a person, animal, or plant) cease all biological activity permanently ▷ *n* shaped block used to cut or form metal

**DIEB** *n* N African jackal

**DIEBACK** *n* disease of trees and shrubs characterized by death of the young shoots, which spreads to the larger branches: caused by injury to the roots or attack by bacteria or fungi ▷ *vb* (of plants) to suffer from dieback

**DIEBACKS** > DIEBACK

**DIEBS** > DIEB

**DIECIOUS** *same as* > DIOECIOUS

**DIED** > DIE

**DIEDRAL** *same as* > DIHEDRAL

**DIEDRALS** > DIEDRAL

**DIEDRE** *n* large shallow groove or corner in a rock face

**DIEDRES** > DIEDRE

**DIEGESES** > DIEGESIS

**DIEGESIS** *n* utterance of fact

**DIEHARD** *n* person who resists change or who holds on to an outdated attitude

**DIEHARDS** > DIEHARD

**DIEING** > DIE

**DIEL** *n* 24-hour period

**DIELDRIN** *n* highly toxic insecticide

**DIELDRINS** > DIELDRIN

**DIELYTRA** *n* genus of herbaceous plants

**DIELYTRAS** > DIELYTRA

**DIEMAKER** *n* one who makes dies

**DIEMAKERS** > DIEMAKER

**DIENE** *n* hydrocarbon that contains two carbon-to-carbon double bonds in its molecules

**DIENES** > DIENE

**DIEOFF** *n* process of dying in large numbers

**DIEOFFS** > DIEOFF

**DIERESES** > DIERESIS

**DIERESIS** *same as* > DIAERESIS

**DIERETIC** > DIERESIS

**DIES** > DIE

**DIESEL** *vb* drive diesel-fueled vehicle ▷ *n* diesel engine

**DIESELED** > DIESEL

**DIESELING** > DIESEL

**DIESELISE** *same as* > DIESELIZE

**DIESELIZE** *vb* be equipped with diesel engine

**DIESELS** > DIESEL

**DIESES** > DIESIS

**DIESINKER** *n* person who engraves dies

**DIESIS** *n* (in ancient Greek theory) any interval smaller than a whole tone, esp a semitone in the Pythagorean scale

**DIESTER** *n* synthetic lubricant

**DIESTERS** > DIESTER

**DIESTOCK** *n* device holding the dies used to cut an external screw thread

**DIESTOCKS** > DIESTOCK

**DIESTROUS** *same as* > DIOESTRUS

**DIESTRUM** *another word for* > DIESTROUS

**DIESTRUMS** > DIESTRUM

**DIESTRUS** *same as* > DIOESTRUS

**DIET** *n* food that a person or animal regularly eats ▷ *vb* follow a special diet so as to lose weight ▷ *adj* (of food) suitable for a weight-reduction diet

**DIETARIAN** *n* dieter

**DIETARIES** > DIETARY

**DIETARILY** > DIETARY

**DIETARY** *adj* of or relating to a diet ▷ *n* regulated diet

**DIETED** > DIET

**DIETER** > DIET

**DIETERS** > DIET

**DIETETIC** *adj* prepared for special dietary requirements

**DIETETICS** *n* study of diet

and nutrition

**DIETHER** *n* chemical compound

**DIETHERS** > DIETHER

**DIETHYL** as in *diethyl ether same as* > ETHER

**DIETHYLS** > DIETHYL

**DIETICIAN** *n* person who specializes in dietetics

**DIETINE** *n* low-ranking diet

**DIETINES** > DIETINE

**DIETING** > DIET

**DIETINGS** > DIET

**DIETIST** *another word for* > DIETITIAN

**DIETISTS** > DIETIST

**DIETITIAN** *same as* > DIETICIAN

**DIETS** > DIET

**DIF** *same as* > DIFF

**DIFF** *shortening of* > DIFFERENCE

**DIFFER** *vb* be unlike

**DIFFERED** > DIFFER

**DIFFERENT** *adj* unlike

**DIFFERING** > DIFFER

**DIFFERS** > DIFFER

**DIFFICILE** *adj* difficult

**DIFFICULT** *adj* requiring effort or skill to do or understand

**DIFFIDENT** *adj* lacking self-confidence

**DIFFLUENT** *adj* flowing; not fixed

**DIFFORM** *adj* irregular in form

**DIFFRACT** *vb* cause to undergo diffraction

**DIFFRACTS** > DIFFRACT

**DIFFS** > DIFF

**DIFFUSE** *vb* spread over a wide area ▷ *adj* widely spread

**DIFFUSED** > DIFFUSE

**DIFFUSELY** > DIFFUSE

**DIFFUSER** *n* person or thing that diffuses

**DIFFUSERS** > DIFFUSER

**DIFFUSES** > DIFFUSE

**DIFFUSING** > DIFFUSE

**DIFFUSION** *n* act of diffusing or the fact of being diffused

**DIFFUSIVE** *adj* characterized by diffusion

**DIFFUSOR** *same as* > DIFFUSER

**DIFFUSORS** > DIFFUSOR

**DIFS** > DIF

**DIG** *vb* cut into, break up, and turn over or remove (earth), esp with a spade ▷ *n* digging

**DIGAMIES** > DIGAMY

**DIGAMIST** > DIGAMY

**DIGAMISTS** > DIGAMY

**DIGAMMA** *n* letter of the Greek alphabet that became obsolete before the classical period of the language.

**DIGAMMAS** > DIGAMMA

**DIGAMOUS** > DIGAMY
**DIGAMY** n second marriage contracted after the termination of the first by death or divorce
**DIGASTRIC** adj (of certain muscles) having two fleshy portions joined by a tendon ▷ n muscle of the mandible that assists in lowering the lower jaw
**DIGENESES** > DIGENESIS
**DIGENESIS** n ability to alternate sexual and asexual means of reproduction
**DIGENETIC** adj of or relating to digenesis
**DIGERATI** pl n people who earn large amounts of money through internet-related business
**DIGEST** vb subject to a process of digestion ▷ n shortened version of a book, report, or article
**DIGESTANT** same as > DIGESTIVE
**DIGESTED** > DIGEST
**DIGESTER** n apparatus or vessel, such as an autoclave, in which digestion is carried out
**DIGESTERS** > DIGESTER
**DIGESTIF** n something, esp a drink, taken as an aid to digestion, either before or after a meal
**DIGESTIFS** > DIGESTIF
**DIGESTING** > DIGEST
**DIGESTION** n (body's system for) breaking down food into easily absorbed substances
**DIGESTIVE** adj relating to digestion
**DIGESTOR** same as > DIGESTER
**DIGESTORS** > DIGESTOR
**DIGESTS** > DIGEST
**DIGGABLE** adj that can be dug
**DIGGED** a past tense of > DIG
**DIGGER** n machine used for digging
**DIGGERS** > DIGGER
**DIGGING** > DIG
**DIGGINGS** pl n material that has been dug out
**DIGHT** vb adorn or equip, as for battle
**DIGHTED** > DIGHT
**DIGHTING** > DIGHT
**DIGHTS** > DIGHT
**DIGICAM** n digital camera
**DIGICAMS** > DIGICAM
**DIGIT** n finger or toe
**DIGITAL** adj displaying information as numbers rather than with hands and a dial ▷ n one of the keys on the manuals of an organ or on a piano, harpsichord, etc

**DIGITALIN** n poisonous amorphous crystalline mixture of glycosides extracted from digitalis leaves and formerly used in treating heart disease.
**DIGITALIS** n drug made from foxglove leaves, used as a heart stimulant
**DIGITALLY** > DIGITAL
**DIGITALS** > DIGITAL
**DIGITATE** adj (of leaves) having leaflets in the form of a spread hand
**DIGITATED** same as > DIGITATE
**DIGITISE** same as > DIGITIZE
**DIGITISED** > DIGITIZE
**DIGITISER** > DIGITIZE
**DIGITISES** > DIGITIZE
**DIGITIZE** vb transcribe (data) into a digital form for processing by a computer
**DIGITIZED** adj recorded or stored in digital form
**DIGITIZER** > DIGITIZE
**DIGITIZES** > DIGITIZE
**DIGITONIN** n type of glycoside
**DIGITOXIN** same as > DIGOXIN
**DIGITRON** n type of tube, for displaying information, having a common anode and several cathodes shaped in the form of characters, which can be lit by a glow discharge
**DIGITRONS** > DIGITRON
**DIGITS** > DIGIT
**DIGITULE** n any small finger-like process
**DIGITULES** > DIGITULE
**DIGLOSSIA** n existence in a language of a high, or socially prestigious, and a low, or everyday, form, as German and Swiss German in Switzerland
**DIGLOSSIC** > DIGLOSSIA
**DIGLOT** n bilingual book
**DIGLOTS** > DIGLOT
**DIGLOTTIC** > DIGLOT
**DIGLYPH** n ornament in Doric frieze with two grooves
**DIGLYPHS** > DIGLYPH
**DIGNIFIED** adj calm, impressive, and worthy of respect
**DIGNIFIES** > DIGNIFY
**DIGNIFY** vb add distinction to
**DIGNITARY** n person of high official position
**DIGNITIES** > DIGNITY
**DIGNITY** n serious, calm, and controlled behaviour or manner
**DIGONAL** adj of or relating to a symmetry operation

in which the original figure is reconstructed after a 180° turn about an axis
**DIGOXIN** n glycoside extracted from the leaves of the woolly foxglove
**DIGOXINS** > DIGOXIN
**DIGRAPH** n two letters used to represent a single sound, such as gh in tough
**DIGRAPHIC** > DIGRAPH
**DIGRAPHS** > DIGRAPH
**DIGRESS** vb depart from the main subject in speech or writing
**DIGRESSED** > DIGRESS
**DIGRESSER** > DIGRESS
**DIGRESSES** > DIGRESS
**DIGS** > DIG
**DIGYNIAN** adj relating to plant class Digynia
**DIGYNOUS** another word for > DIGYNIAN
**DIHEDRA** > DIHEDRON
**DIHEDRAL** adj having or formed by two intersecting planes ▷ n figure formed by two intersecting planes
**DIHEDRALS** > DIHEDRAL
**DIHEDRON** same as > DIHEDRAL
**DIHEDRONS** > DIHEDRON
**DIHYBRID** n offspring of two individuals that differ with respect to two pairs of genes
**DIHYBRIDS** > DIHYBRID
**DIHYDRIC** adj (of an alcohol) containing two hydroxyl groups per molecule
**DIKA** n wild mango
**DIKAS** > DIKA
**DIKAST** same as > DICAST
**DIKASTS** > DIKAST
**DIKDIK** n small African antelope
**DIKDIKS** > DIKDIK
**DIKE** same as > DYKE
**DIKED** > DIKE
**DIKER** n builder of dikes
**DIKERS** > DIKER
**DIKES** > DIKE
**DIKEY** adj (of a lesbian) masculine
**DIKIER** > DIKEY
**DIKIEST** > DIKEY
**DIKING** > DIKE
**DIKKOP** n any of several brownish shore birds of the family Burhinidae, esp Burhinus oedicnemus, having a large head and eyes: order Charadriiformes
**DIKKOPS** > DIKKOP
**DIKTAT** n dictatorial decree
**DIKTATS** > DIKTAT
**DILATABLE** > DILATE
**DILATABLY** > DILATE
**DILATANCY** n phenomenon caused by the nature

of the stacking or fitting together of particles or granules in a heterogeneous system, such as the solidification of certain sols under pressure, and the thixotropy of certain gels
**DILATANT** adj tending to dilate ▷ n something, such as a catheter, that causes dilation
**DILATANTS** > DILATANT
**DILATATE** same as > DILATE
**DILATATOR** same as > DILATOR
**DILATE** vb make or become wider or larger
**DILATED** > DILATE
**DILATER** same as > DILATOR
**DILATERS** > DILATER
**DILATES** > DILATE
**DILATING** > DILATE
**DILATION** > DILATE
**DILATIONS** > DILATE
**DILATIVE** > DILATE
**DILATOR** n something that dilates an object, esp a surgical instrument for dilating a bodily cavity
**DILATORS** > DILATOR
**DILATORY** adj tending or intended to waste time
**DILDO** n object used as a substitute for an erect penis
**DILDOE** same as > DILDO
**DILDOES** > DILDOE
**DILDOS** > DILDO
**DILEMMA** n situation offering a choice between two equally undesirable alternatives
**DILEMMAS** > DILEMMA
**DILEMMIC** > DILEMMA
**DILIGENCE** n steady and careful application
**DILIGENT** adj careful and persevering in carrying out duties
**DILL** vb flavour with dill ▷ n sweet-smelling herb
**DILLED** > DILL
**DILLI** n dilly bag; small bag, esp one made of plaited grass and used for carrying food
**DILLIER** > DILLY
**DILLIES** > DILLY
**DILLIEST** > DILLY
**DILLING** > DILL
**DILLINGS** > DILL
**DILLIS** > DILLI
**DILLS** > DILL
**DILLY** adj foolish ▷ n person or thing that is remarkable
**DILTIAZEM** n drug used to treat angina
**DILUENT** adj causing dilution or serving to dilute ▷ n substance used for or causing dilution
**DILUENTS** > DILUENT

**DILUTABLE** > DILUTE
**DILUTE** vb make (a liquid) less concentrated, esp by adding water ▷ adj (of a liquid) thin and watery
**DILUTED** > DILUTE
**DILUTEE** > DILUTE
**DILUTEES** > DILUTE
**DILUTER** > DILUTE
**DILUTERS** > DILUTE
**DILUTES** > DILUTE
**DILUTING** > DILUTE
**DILUTION** n act of diluting or state of being diluted
**DILUTIONS** > DILUTION
**DILUTIVE** adj having effect of decreasing earnings per share
**DILUTOR** n having diluting effect
**DILUTORS** > DILUTOR
**DILUVIA** > DILUVIUM
**DILUVIAL** adj of a flood, esp the great Flood described in the Old Testament
**DILUVIAN** same as > DILUVIAL
**DILUVION** same as > DILUVIUM
**DILUVIONS** > DILUVION
**DILUVIUM** n glacial drift
**DILUVIUMS** > DILUVIUM
**DIM** adj badly lit ▷ vb make or become dim
**DIMBLE** n wooded hollow; dingle
**DIMBLES** > DIMBLE
**DIME** n coin of the US and Canada, worth ten cents
**DIMENSION** n measurement of the size of something in a particular direction ▷ vb shape or cut to specified dimensions
**DIMER** n molecule made up of two identical molecules bonded together
**DIMERIC** adj of a dimer
**DIMERISE** same as > DIMERIZE
**DIMERISED** > DIMERISE
**DIMERISES** > DIMERISE
**DIMERISM** > DIMEROUS
**DIMERISMS** > DIMEROUS
**DIMERIZE** vb react or cause to react to form a dimer
**DIMERIZED** > DIMERIZE
**DIMERIZES** > DIMERIZE
**DIMEROUS** adj consisting of or divided into two segments, as the tarsi of some insects
**DIMERS** > DIMER
**DIMES** > DIME
**DIMETER** n line of verse consisting of two metrical feet or a verse written in this metre
**DIMETERS** > DIMETER
**DIMETHYL** n ethane
**DIMETHYLS** > DIMETHYL
**DIMETRIC** adj of, relating

to, or shaped like a quadrilateral
**DIMIDIATE** adj divided in halves ▷ vb halve (two bearings) so that they can be represented on the same shield
**DIMINISH** vb make or become smaller, fewer, or less
**DIMISSORY** adj granting permission to be ordained
**DIMITIES** > DIMITY
**DIMITY** n light strong cotton fabric with woven stripes or squares
**DIMLY** > DIM
**DIMMABLE** adj that can be dimmed
**DIMMED** > DIM
**DIMMER** > DIM
**DIMMERS** > DIM
**DIMMEST** > DIM
**DIMMING** > DIM
**DIMMISH** > DIM
**DIMNESS** > DIM
**DIMNESSES** > DIM
**DIMORPH** n either of two forms of a substance that exhibits dimorphism
**DIMORPHIC** > DIMORPHISM
**DIMORPHS** > DIMORPH
**DIMOUT** n reduction of lighting
**DIMOUTS** > DIMOUT
**DIMP** n in Northern English dialect, a cigarette butt
**DIMPLE** n small natural dent, esp in the cheeks or chin ▷ vb produce dimples by smiling
**DIMPLED** > DIMPLE
**DIMPLES** > DIMPLE
**DIMPLIER** > DIMPLE
**DIMPLIEST** > DIMPLE
**DIMPLING** > DIMPLE
**DIMPLY** > DIMPLE
**DIMPS** > DIMP
**DIMPSIES** > DIMPSY
**DIMPSY** n twilight
**DIMS** > DIM
**DIMWIT** n stupid person
**DIMWITS** > DIMWIT
**DIMWITTED** > DIMWIT
**DIMYARIAN** adj with two adductor muscles
**DIN** n loud unpleasant confused noise ▷ vb instil (something) into someone by constant repetition
**DINAR** n monetary unit of various Balkan, Middle Eastern, and North African countries
**DINARCHY** same as > DIARCHY
**DINARS** > DINAR
**DINDLE** another word for > DINNLE
**DINDLED** > DINDLE
**DINDLES** > DINDLE
**DINDLING** > DINDLE
**DINE** vb eat dinner
**DINED** > DINE

**DINER** n person eating a meal
**DINERIC** adj of or concerned with the interface between immiscible liquids
**DINERO** n money
**DINEROS** > DINERO
**DINERS** > DINER
**DINES** > DINE
**DINETTE** n alcove or small area for use as a dining room
**DINETTES** > DINETTE
**DINFUL** adj noisy
**DING** n small dent in a vehicle ▷ vb ring or cause to ring, esp with tedious repetition
**DINGBAT** n any unnamed object, esp one used as a missile
**DINGBATS** > DINGBAT
**DINGDONG** n sound of a bell or bells ▷ vb make such a sound
**DINGDONGS** > DINGDONG
**DINGE** n dent ▷ vb make a dent in (something)
**DINGED** > DINGE
**DINGER** n (in baseball) home run
**DINGERS** > DINGER
**DINGES** n jocular word for something whose name is unknown or forgotten
**DINGESES** > DINGES
**DINGEY** same as > DINGHY
**DINGEYS** > DINGEY
**DINGHIES** > DINGHY
**DINGHY** n small boat, powered by sails, oars, or a motor
**DINGIER** > DINGY
**DINGIES** > DINGY
**DINGIEST** > DINGY
**DINGILY** > DINGY
**DINGINESS** > DINGY
**DINGING** > DINGE
**DINGLE** n small wooded hollow or valley
**DINGLES** > DINGLE
**DINGO** n Australian wild dog ▷ vb act in a cowardly manner
**DINGOED** > DINGO
**DINGOES** > DINGO
**DINGOING** > DINGO
**DINGS** > DING
**DINGUS** same as > DINGES
**DINGUSES** > DINGUS
**DINGY** adj lacking light
**DINIC** n remedy for vertigo
**DINICS** > DINIC
**DINING** > DINE
**DINITRO** adj containing two nitro groups
**DINK** adj neat or neatly dressed ▷ vb carry (a second person) on a horse, bicycle, etc ▷ n ball struck delicately
**DINKED** > DINK
**DINKER** > DINK

**DINKEST** > DINK
**DINKEY** n small locomotive
**DINKEYS** > DINKEY
**DINKIE** n affluent married childless person ▷ adj designed for or appealing to dinkies
**DINKIER** > DINKY
**DINKIES** > DINKIE
**DINKIEST** > DINKY
**DINKING** > DINK
**DINKLY** adj neat
**DINKS** > DINK
**DINKUM** n truth or genuineness
**DINKUMS** > DINKUM
**DINKY** adj small and neat
**DINMONT** n neutered sheep
**DINMONTS** > DINMONT
**DINNA** vb a Scots word for do not
**DINNED** > DIN
**DINNER** vb dine ▷ n main meal of the day, eaten either in the evening or at midday
**DINNERED** > DINNER
**DINNERING** > DINNER
**DINNERS** > DINNER
**DINNING** > DIN
**DINNLE** vb shake
**DINNLED** > DINNLE
**DINNLES** > DINNLE
**DINNLING** > DINNLE
**DINO** n dinosaur
**DINOCERAS** another name for a > UINTATHERE
**DINOMANIA** n strong interest in dinosaurs
**DINOS** > DINO
**DINOSAUR** n type of extinct prehistoric reptile, many of which were of gigantic size
**DINOSAURS** > DINOSAUR
**DINOTHERE** n any extinct late Tertiary elephant-like mammal of the genus Dinotherium (or Deinotherium), having a down-turned jaw with tusks curving downwards and backwards
**DINS** > DIN
**DINT** variant of > DENT
**DINTED** > DINT
**DINTING** > DINT
**DINTLESS** > DINT
**DINTS** > DINT
**DIOBOL** n ancient Greek coin
**DIOBOLON** same as > DIOBOL
**DIOBOLONS** > DIOBOLON
**DIOBOLS** > DIOBOL
**DIOCESAN** adj of or relating to a diocese ▷ n bishop of a diocese
**DIOCESANS** > DIOCESAN
**DIOCESE** n district over which a bishop has control
**DIOCESES** > DIOCESE
**DIODE** n semiconductor device for converting alternating current to

direct current
**DIODES** > DIODE
**DIOECIES** > DIOECY
**DIOECIOUS** *adj* (of plants) having the male and female reproductive organs on separate plants
**DIOECISM** > DIOECIOUS
**DIOECISMS** > DIOECIOUS
**DIOECY** *n* state of being dioecious
**DIOESTRUS** *n* period in mammal's oestral cycle
**DIOICOUS** same *as* > DIOECIOUS
**DIOL** *n* any of a class of alcohols that have two hydroxyl groups in each molecule
**DIOLEFIN** *n* type of polymer
**DIOLEFINS** > DIOLEFIN
**DIOLS** > DIOL
**DIONYSIAC** same *as* > DIONYSIAN
**DIONYSIAN** *adj* wild or orgiastic
**DIOPSIDE** *n* colourless or pale-green pyroxene mineral
**DIOPSIDES** > DIOPSIDE
**DIOPSIDIC** > DIOPSIDE
**DIOPTASE** *n* green glassy mineral
**DIOPTASES** > DIOPTASE
**DIOPTER** same *as* > DIOPTRE
**DIOPTERS** > DIOPTER
**DIOPTRAL** > DIOPTRE
**DIOPTRATE** *adj* (of compound eye) divided by transverse line
**DIOPTRE** *n* unit for measuring the refractive power of a lens
**DIOPTRES** > DIOPTRE
**DIOPTRIC** *adj* of or concerned with dioptrics
**DIOPTRICS** *n* branch of geometrical optics concerned with the formation of images by lenses
**DIORAMA** *n* miniature three-dimensional scene, in which models of figures are seen against a three-dimensional background
**DIORAMAS** > DIORAMA
**DIORAMIC** > DIORAMA
**DIORISM** *n* definition; clarity
**DIORISMS** > DIORISM
**DIORISTIC** > DIORISM
**DIORITE** *n* dark coarse-grained igneous plutonic rock consisting of plagioclase feldspar and ferromagnesian minerals such as hornblende
**DIORITES** > DIORITE
**DIORITIC** > DIORITE
**DIOSGENIN** *n* yam-based substance used in hormone therapy

**DIOTA** *n* type of ancient vase
**DIOTAS** > DIOTA
**DIOXAN** *n* colourless insoluble toxic liquid made by heating ethanediol with sulphuric acid
**DIOXANE** same *as* > DIOXAN
**DIOXANES** > DIOXANE
**DIOXANS** > DIOXAN
**DIOXID** same *as* > DIOXIDE
**DIOXIDE** *n* oxide containing two oxygen atoms per molecule
**DIOXIDES** > DIOXIDE
**DIOXIDS** > DIOXID
**DIOXIN** *n* any of a number of mostly poisonous chemical by-products of the manufacture of certain herbicides and bactericides, esp the extremely toxic 2,3,7,8-tetrachlorodibenzo-para-dioxin
**DIOXINS** > DIOXIN
**DIP** *vb* plunge quickly or briefly into a liquid ▷ *n* dipping
**DIPCHICK** same *as* > DABCHICK
**DIPCHICKS** > DIPCHICK
**DIPEPTIDE** *n* compound consisting of two linked amino acids
**DIPHASE** *adj* of, having, or concerned with two phases
**DIPHASIC** same *as* > DIPHASE
**DIPHENYL** another name *for* > BIPHENYL
**DIPHENYLS** > DIPHENYL
**DIPHONE** *n* combination of two speech sounds
**DIPHONES** > DIPHONE
**DIPHTHONG** *n* union of two vowel sounds in a single compound sound
**DIPHYSITE** *n* belief in Christ having both divine and human natures
**DIPLEGIA** *n* paralysis of corresponding parts on both sides of the body
**DIPLEGIAS** > DIPLEGIA
**DIPLEGIC** > DIPLEGIA
**DIPLEX** *adj* (in telecommunications) permitting the transmission of simultaneous signals in both directions
**DIPLEXER** *n* device that enables the simultaneous transmission of more than one signal
**DIPLEXERS** > DIPLEXER
**DIPLOE** *n* spongy bone separating the two layers of compact bone of the skull
**DIPLOES** > DIPLOE
**DIPLOGEN** *n* heavy

hydrogen
**DIPLOGENS** > DIPLOGEN
**DIPLOIC** *adj* relating to diploe
**DIPLOID** *adj* denoting a cell or organism with pairs of homologous chromosomes ▷ *n* diploid cell or organism
**DIPLOIDIC** > DIPLOID
**DIPLOIDS** > DIPLOID
**DIPLOIDY** > DIPLOID
**DIPLOMA** *vb* bestow diploma on ▷ *n* qualification awarded by a college on successful completion of a course
**DIPLOMACY** *n* conduct of the relations between nations by peaceful means
**DIPLOMAED** > DIPLOMA
**DIPLOMAS** > DIPLOMA
**DIPLOMAT** *n* official engaged in diplomacy
**DIPLOMATA** > DIPLOMA
**DIPLOMATE** *n* any person who has been granted a diploma, esp a physician certified as a specialist
**DIPLOMATS** > DIPLOMAT
**DIPLON** another name *for* > DEUTERON
**DIPLONEMA** *a less common name for* > DIPLOTENE
**DIPLONS** > DIPLON
**DIPLONT** *n* animal or plant that has the diploid number of chromosomes in its somatic cells
**DIPLONTIC** > DIPLONT
**DIPLONTS** > DIPLONT
**DIPLOPIA** *n* visual defect in which a single object is seen in duplicate
**DIPLOPIAS** > DIPLOPIA
**DIPLOPIC** > DIPLOPIA
**DIPLOPOD** *n* any arthropod of the class *Diplopoda*, which includes the millipedes
**DIPLOPODS** > DIPLOPOD
**DIPLOSES** > DIPLOSIS
**DIPLOSIS** *n* doubling of the haploid number of chromosomes that occurs during fusion of gametes to form a diploid zygote
**DIPLOTENE** *n* fourth stage of the prophase of meiosis, during which the paired homologous chromosomes separate except at the places where genetic exchange has occurred
**DIPLOZOA** *n* type of parasitic worm
**DIPLOZOIC** *adj* (of certain animals) bilaterally symmetrical
**DIPLOZOON** *n* type of parasitic worm
**DIPNET** *vb* fish using fishing net on pole

**DIPNETS** > DIPNET
**DIPNETTED** > DIPNET
**DIPNOAN** *adj* of, relating to, or belonging to the *Dipnoi*, a subclass of bony fishes comprising the lungfishes ▷ *n* any lungfish
**DIPNOANS** > DIPNOAN
**DIPNOOUS** *adj* having lungs and gills
**DIPODIC** > DIPODY
**DIPODIES** > DIPODY
**DIPODY** *n* metrical unit consisting of two feet
**DIPOLAR** > DIPOLE
**DIPOLE** *n* two equal but opposite electric charges or magnetic poles separated by a small distance
**DIPOLES** > DIPOLE
**DIPPABLE** > DIP
**DIPPED** > DIP
**DIPPER** *n* ladle used for dipping
**DIPPERFUL** *n* amount held by scoop
**DIPPERS** > DIPPER
**DIPPIER** > DIPPY
**DIPPIEST** > DIPPY
**DIPPINESS** > DIPPY
**DIPPING** > DIP
**DIPPINGS** > DIP
**DIPPY** *adj* odd, eccentric, or crazy
**DIPROTIC** *adj* having two hydrogen atoms
**DIPS** > DIP
**DIPSADES** > DIPSAS
**DIPSAS** *n* type of snake
**DIPSHIT** *n* stupid person
**DIPSHITS** > DIPSHIT
**DIPSO** same *as* > DIPSOMANIAC
**DIPSOS** > DIPSO
**DIPSTICK** *n* notched rod dipped into a container to measure the level of a liquid
**DIPSTICKS** > DIPSTICK
**DIPT** > DIP
**DIPTERA** *n* order of insects with two wings
**DIPTERAL** *adj* having a double row of columns
**DIPTERAN** *n* dipterous insect ▷ *adj* having two wings or winglike parts
**DIPTERANS** > DIPTERAN
**DIPTERAS** > DIPTERA
**DIPTERIST** *n* fly expert
**DIPTEROI** > DIPTEROS
**DIPTERON** same *as* > DIPTERAN
**DIPTERONS** > DIPTERON
**DIPTEROS** *n* Greek building with double columns
**DIPTEROUS** *adj* having two wings or winglike parts
**DIPTYCA** same *as* > DIPTYCH
**DIPTYCAS** > DIPTYCA
**DIPTYCH** *n* painting on two hinged panels
**DIPTYCHS** > DIPTYCH

**DIQUARK** *n* low-energy configuration of two quarks attracted to one another by virtue of having antisymmetric colours and spins
**DIQUARKS** > DIQUARK
**DIQUAT** *n* type of herbicide
**DIQUATS** > DIQUAT
**DIRAM** *n* money unit of Tajikistan
**DIRAMS** > DIRAM
**DIRDAM** *same as* > DIRDUM
**DIRDAMS** > DIRDAM
**DIRDUM** *n* tumult
**DIRDUMS** > DIRDUM
**DIRE** *adj* disastrous, urgent, or terrible
**DIRECT** *adj* (of a route) shortest, straight ▷ *adv* in a direct manner ▷ *vb* lead and organize
**DIRECTED** *adj* (of a number, line, or angle) having either a positive or negative sign to distinguish measurement in one direction or orientation from that in the opposite direction or orientation
**DIRECTER** > DIRECT
**DIRECTEST** > DIRECT
**DIRECTING** > DIRECT
**DIRECTION** *n* course or line along which a person or thing moves, points, or lies
**DIRECTIVE** *n* instruction, order ▷ *adj* tending to direct
**DIRECTLY** *adv* in a direct manner
**DIRECTOR** *n* person or thing that directs or controls
**DIRECTORS** > DIRECTOR
**DIRECTORY** *n* book listing names, addresses, and telephone numbers ▷ *adj* directing
**DIRECTRIX** *n* fixed reference line, situated on the convex side of a conic section, that is used when defining or calculating its eccentricity
**DIRECTS** > DIRECT
**DIREFUL** *same as* > DIRE
**DIREFULLY** > DIREFUL
**DIRELY** > DIRE
**DIREMPT** *vb* separate with force
**DIREMPTED** > DIREMPT
**DIREMPTS** > DIREMPT
**DIRENESS** > DIRE
**DIRER** > DIRE
**DIREST** > DIRE
**DIRGE** *n* slow sad song of mourning
**DIRGEFUL** > DIRGE
**DIRGELIKE** > DIRGE
**DIRGES** > DIRGE
**DIRHAM** *n* standard monetary unit of Morocco,

divided into 100 centimes
**DIRHAMS** > DIRHAM
**DIRHEM** *same as* > DIRHAM
**DIRHEMS** > DIRHEM
**DIRIGE** *n* dirge
**DIRIGENT** *adj* directing
**DIRIGES** > DIRIGE
**DIRIGIBLE** *adj* able to be steered ▷ *n* airship
**DIRIGISM** *same as* > DIRIGISME
**DIRIGISME** *n* control by the state of economic and social matters
**DIRIGISMS** > DIRIGISM
**DIRIGISTE** > DIRIGISME
**DIRIMENT** *adj* (of an impediment to marriage in canon law) totally invalidating
**DIRK** *n* dagger, formerly worn by Scottish Highlanders ▷ *vb* stab with a dirk
**DIRKE** *variant of* > DIRK
**DIRKED** > DIRK
**DIRKES** > DIRKE
**DIRKING** > DIRK
**DIRKS** > DIRK
**DIRL** *vb* tingle; vibrate
**DIRLED** > DIRL
**DIRLING** > DIRL
**DIRLS** > DIRL
**DIRNDL** *n* full gathered skirt originating from Tyrolean peasant wear
**DIRNDLS** > DIRNDL
**DIRT** *vb* soil ▷ *n* unclean substance, filth
**DIRTBAG** *n* filthy person
**DIRTBAGS** > DIRTBAG
**DIRTED** > DIRT
**DIRTIED** > DIRTY
**DIRTIER** > DIRTY
**DIRTIES** > DIRTY
**DIRTIEST** > DIRTY
**DIRTILY** > DIRTY
**DIRTINESS** > DIRTY
**DIRTING** > DIRT
**DIRTS** > DIRT
**DIRTY** *adj* covered or marked with dirt ▷ *vb* make dirty
**DIRTYING** > DIRTY
**DIS** *same as* > DISS
**DISA** *n* type of orchid
**DISABLE** *vb* make ineffective, unfit, or incapable
**DISABLED** *adj* lacking a physical power, such as the ability to walk
**DISABLER** > DISABLE
**DISABLERS** > DISABLE
**DISABLES** > DISABLE
**DISABLING** > DISABLE
**DISABUSAL** > DISABUSE
**DISABUSE** *vb* rid (someone) of a mistaken idea
**DISABUSED** > DISABUSE
**DISABUSES** > DISABUSE
**DISACCORD** *n* lack of agreement or harmony ▷ *vb* be out of agreement

**DISADORN** *vb* deprive of ornamentation
**DISADORNS** > DISADORN
**DISAFFECT** *vb* cause to lose loyalty or affection
**DISAFFIRM** *vb* deny or contradict (a statement)
**DISAGREE** *vb* argue or have different opinions
**DISAGREED** > DISAGREE
**DISAGREES** > DISAGREE
**DISALLIED** > DISALLY
**DISALLIES** > DISALLY
**DISALLOW** *vb* reject as untrue or invalid
**DISALLOWS** > DISALLOW
**DISALLY** *vb* separate
**DISANCHOR** *vb* raise anchor of
**DISANNEX** *vb* disunite
**DISANNUL** *vb* cancel
**DISANNULS** > DISANNUL
**DISANOINT** *vb* invalidate anointment of
**DISAPPEAR** *vb* cease to be visible
**DISAPPLY** *vb* make (law) invalid
**DISARM** *vb* deprive of weapons
**DISARMED** > DISARM
**DISARMER** > DISARM
**DISARMERS** > DISARM
**DISARMING** *adj* removing hostility or suspicion
**DISARMS** > DISARM
**DISARRAY** *n* confusion and lack of discipline ▷ *vb* throw into confusion
**DISARRAYS** > DISARRAY
**DISAS** > DISA
**DISASTER** *n* occurrence that causes great distress or destruction
**DISASTERS** > DISASTER
**DISATTIRE** *vb* remove clothes from
**DISATTUNE** *vb* render out of tune
**DISAVOUCH** *archaic form of* > DISAVOW
**DISAVOW** *vb* deny connection with or responsibility for
**DISAVOWAL** > DISAVOW
**DISAVOWED** > DISAVOW
**DISAVOWER** > DISAVOW
**DISAVOWS** > DISAVOW
**DISBAND** *vb* (cause to) cease to function as a group
**DISBANDED** > DISBAND
**DISBANDS** > DISBAND
**DISBAR** *vb* deprive (a barrister) of the right to practise
**DISBARK** *same as* > DISEMBARK
**DISBARKED** > DISBARK
**DISBARKS** > DISBARK
**DISBARRED** > DISBAR
**DISBARS** > DISBAR
**DISBELIEF** *n* refusal or reluctance to believe

**DISBENCH** *vb* remove from bench
**DISBODIED** *adj* disembodied
**DISBOSOM** *vb* disclose
**DISBOSOMS** > DISBOSOM
**DISBOUND** *adj* unbound
**DISBOWEL** *vb* disembowel
**DISBOWELS** > DISBOWEL
**DISBRANCH** *vb* remove or cut a branch or branches from (a tree)
**DISBUD** *vb* remove superfluous buds, flowers, or shoots from (a plant, esp a fruit tree)
**DISBUDDED** > DISBUD
**DISBUDS** > DISBUD
**DISBURDEN** *vb* remove a load from (a person or animal)
**DISBURSAL** > DISBURSE
**DISBURSE** *vb* pay out
**DISBURSED** > DISBURSE
**DISBURSER** > DISBURSE
**DISBURSES** > DISBURSE
**DISC** *n* flat circular object ▷ *vb* work (land) with a disc harrow
**DISCAGE** *vb* release from cage
**DISCAGED** > DISCAGE
**DISCAGES** > DISCAGE
**DISCAGING** > DISCAGE
**DISCAL** *adj* relating to or resembling a disc
**DISCALCED** *adj* barefooted: used to denote friars and nuns who wear sandals
**DISCANDIE** *same as* > DISCANDY
**DISCANDY** *vb* melt; dissolve
**DISCANT** *same as* > DESCANT
**DISCANTED** > DISCANT
**DISCANTER** > DISCANT
**DISCANTS** > DISCANT
**DISCARD** *vb* get rid of (something or someone) as useless or undesirable ▷ *n* person or thing that has been cast aside
**DISCARDED** > DISCARD
**DISCARDER** > DISCARD
**DISCARDS** > DISCARD
**DISCASE** *vb* remove case from
**DISCASED** > DISCASE
**DISCASES** > DISCASE
**DISCASING** > DISCASE
**DISCED** > DISC
**DISCEPT** *vb* discuss
**DISCEPTED** > DISCEPT
**DISCEPTS** > DISCEPT
**DISCERN** *vb* see or be aware of (something) clearly
**DISCERNED** > DISCERN
**DISCERNER** > DISCERN
**DISCERNS** > DISCERN
**DISCERP** *vb* divide
**DISCERPED** > DISCERP
**DISCERPS** > DISCERP
**DISCHARGE** *vb* release, allow to go ▷ *n* substance that comes out from a

place
DISCHURCH *vb* deprive of church membership
DISCI > DISCUS
DISCIDE *vb* split
DISCIDED > DISCIDE
DISCIDES > DISCIDE
DISCIDING > DISCIDE
DISCIFORM *adj* disc-shaped
DISCINCT *adj* loosely dressed, without belt
DISCING > DISC
DISCIPLE *vb* teach ▷ *n* follower of the doctrines of a teacher, esp Jesus Christ
DISCIPLED > DISCIPLE
DISCIPLES > DISCIPLE
DISCLAIM *vb* deny (responsibility for or knowledge of something)
DISCLAIMS > DISCLAIM
DISCLIKE > DISC
DISCLIMAX *n* climax community resulting from the activities of man or domestic animals in climatic and other conditions that would otherwise support a different type of community
DISCLOSE *vb* make known
DISCLOSED > DISCLOSE
DISCLOSER > DISCLOSE
DISCLOSES > DISCLOSE
DISCLOST > DISCLOSE
DISCO *vb* go to a disco ▷ *n* nightclub where people dance to amplified pop records
DISCOBOLI *pl n* discus throwers
DISCOED > DISCO
DISCOER > DISCO
DISCOERS > DISCO
DISCOID *adj* like a disc ▷ *n* disclike object
DISCOIDAL *adj* like a disc
DISCOIDS > DISCOID
DISCOING > DISCO
DISCOLOGY *n* study of gramophone records
DISCOLOR *same as* > DISCOLOUR
DISCOLORS > DISCOLOR
DISCOLOUR *vb* change in colour, fade
DISCOMFIT *vb* make uneasy or confused
DISCOMMON *vb* deprive (land) of the character and status of common, as by enclosure
DISCORD *n* lack of agreement or harmony between people ▷ *vb* disagree
DISCORDED > DISCORD
DISCORDS > DISCORD
DISCOS > DISCO
DISCOUNT *vb* take no account of (something) because it is considered to

be unreliable, prejudiced, or irrelevant ▷ *n* deduction from the full price of something
DISCOUNTS > DISCOUNT
DISCOURE *vb* discover
DISCOURED > DISCOURE
DISCOURES > DISCOURE
DISCOURSE *n* conversation ▷ *vb* speak or write (about) at length
DISCOVER *vb* be the first to find or to find out about
DISCOVERS > DISCOVER
DISCOVERT *adj* (of a woman) not under the protection of a husband
DISCOVERY *n* discovering
DISCREDIT *vb* damage the reputation of ▷ *n* damage to someone's reputation
DISCREET *adj* careful to avoid embarrassment, esp by keeping confidences secret
DISCRETE *adj* separate, distinct
DISCRETER > DISCRETE
DISCROWN *vb* deprive of a crown
DISCROWNS > DISCROWN
DISCS > DISC
DISCUMBER *vb* disencumber
DISCURE *old form of* > DISCOVER
DISCURED > DISCURE
DISCURES > DISCURE
DISCURING > DISCURE
DISCURSUS *n* discursive reasoning
DISCUS *n* heavy disc-shaped object thrown in sports competitions
DISCUSES > DISCUS
DISCUSS *vb* consider (something) by talking it over
DISCUSSED > DISCUSS
DISCUSSER > DISCUSS
DISCUSSES > DISCUSS
DISDAIN *n* feeling of superiority and dislike ▷ *vb* refuse with disdain
DISDAINED > DISDAIN
DISDAINS > DISDAIN
DISEASE *vb* make uneasy ▷ *n* illness, sickness
DISEASED *adj* having or affected with disease
DISEASES > DISEASE
DISEASING > DISEASE
DISEDGE *vb* render blunt
DISEDGED > DISEDGE
DISEDGES > DISEDGE
DISEDGING > DISEDGE
DISEMBARK *vb* get off a ship, aircraft, or bus
DISEMBODY *vb* free from the body or from physical form
DISEMPLOY *vb* dismiss from employment
DISENABLE *vb* cause to

become incapable
DISENDOW *vb* take away an endowment from
DISENDOWS > DISENDOW
DISENGAGE *vb* release from a connection
DISENROL *vb* remove from register
DISENROLS > DISENROL
DISENTAIL *vb* free (an estate) from entail ▷ *n* act of disentailing
DISENTOMB *vb* disinter
DISESTEEM *vb* think little of ▷ *n* lack of esteem
DISEUR *same as* > DISEUSE
DISEURS > DISEUR
DISEUSE *n* (esp formerly) an actress who presents dramatic recitals, usually sung accompanied by music
DISEUSES > DISEUSE
DISFAME *n* discredit
DISFAMES > DISFAME
DISFAVOR *same as* > DISFAVOUR
DISFAVORS > DISFAVOR
DISFAVOUR *n* disapproval or dislike ▷ *vb* regard or treat with disapproval or dislike
DISFIGURE *vb* spoil the appearance of
DISFLESH *vb* reduce flesh of
DISFLUENT *adj* lacking fluency in speech
DISFOREST *same as* > DEFOREST
DISFORM *vb* change form of
DISFORMED > DISFORM
DISFORMS > DISFORM
DISFROCK *another word for* > UNFROCK
DISFROCKS > DISFROCK
DISGAVEL *vb* deprive of quality of gavelkind
DISGAVELS > DISGAVEL
DISGEST *vb* digest
DISGESTED > DISGEST
DISGESTS > DISGEST
DISGODDED *adj* deprived of religion
DISGORGE *vb* empty out, discharge
DISGORGED > DISGORGE
DISGORGER *n* thin notched metal implement for removing hooks from a fish
DISGORGES > DISGORGE
DISGOWN *vb* remove gown from
DISGOWNED > DISGOWN
DISGOWNS > DISGOWN
DISGRACE *n* condition of shame, loss of reputation, or dishonour ▷ *vb* bring shame upon (oneself or others)
DISGRACED > DISGRACE
DISGRACER > DISGRACE
DISGRACES > DISGRACE

DISGRADE *vb* degrade
DISGRADED > DISGRADE
DISGRADES > DISGRADE
DISGUISE *vb* change the appearance or manner in order to conceal the identity of (someone or something) ▷ *n* mask, costume, or manner that disguises
DISGUISED > DISGUISE
DISGUISER > DISGUISE
DISGUISES > DISGUISE
DISGUST *n* great loathing or distaste ▷ *vb* sicken, fill with loathing
DISGUSTED > DISGUST
DISGUSTS > DISGUST
DISH *n* shallow container used for holding or serving food ▷ *vb* put into a dish
DISHABIT *vb* dislodge
DISHABITS > DISHABIT
DISHABLE *obsolete form of* > DISABLE
DISHABLED > DISHABLE
DISHABLES > DISHABLE
DISHALLOW *vb* make unholy
DISHCLOTH *n* cloth for washing dishes
DISHCLOUT *same as* > DISHCLOTH
DISHDASHA *n* long-sleeved collarless white garment worn by some Muslim men
DISHED *adj* shaped like a dish
DISHELM *vb* remove helmet from
DISHELMED > DISHELM
DISHELMS > DISHELM
DISHERIT *vb* disinherit
DISHERITS > DISHERIT
DISHES > DISH
DISHEVEL *vb* disarrange (the hair or clothes) of (someone)
DISHEVELS > DISHEVEL
DISHFUL *n* the amount that a dish is able to hold
DISHFULS > DISHFUL
DISHIER > DISHY
DISHIEST > DISHY
DISHING > DISH
DISHINGS > DISH
DISHLIKE > DISH
DISHOME *vb* deprive of home
DISHOMED > DISHOME
DISHOMES > DISHOME
DISHOMING > DISHOME
DISHONEST *adj* not honest or fair
DISHONOR *same as* > DISHONOUR
DISHONORS > DISHONOR
DISHONOUR *vb* treat with disrespect ▷ *n* lack of respect
DISHORN *vb* remove horns from
DISHORNED > DISHORN

213

DISHORNS > DISHORN
DISHORSE vb dismount
DISHORSED > DISHORSE
DISHORSES > DISHORSE
DISHOUSE vb deprive of home
DISHOUSED > DISHOUSE
DISHOUSES > DISHOUSE
DISHPAN n large pan for washing dishes, pots, etc
DISHPANS > DISHPAN
DISHRAG n dishcloth
DISHRAGS > DISHRAG
DISHTOWEL n towel for drying dishes and kitchen utensils
DISHUMOUR vb upset; offend
DISHWARE n tableware
DISHWARES > DISHWARE
DISHWATER n water in which dishes and kitchen utensils are or have been washed
DISHY adj good-looking
DISILLUDE vb remove illusions from
DISIMMURE vb release
DISINFECT vb rid of harmful germs, chemically
DISINFEST vb rid of vermin
DISINFORM vb give wrong information
DISINHUME vb dig up
DISINTER vb dig up
DISINTERS > DISINTER
DISINURE vb render unaccustomed
DISINURED > DISINURE
DISINURES > DISINURE
DISINVEST vb remove investment (from)
DISINVITE vb retract invitation to
DISJASKIT adj fatigued
DISJECT vb break apart
DISJECTED > DISJECT
DISJECTS > DISJECT
DISJOIN vb disconnect or become disconnected
DISJOINED > DISJOIN
DISJOINS > DISJOIN
DISJOINT vb take apart or come apart at the joints ▷ adj (of two sets) having no members in common
DISJOINTS > DISJOINT
DISJUNCT adj not united or joined ▷ n one of the propositions or formulas in a disjunction
DISJUNCTS > DISJUNCT
DISJUNE n breakfast
DISJUNES > DISJUNE
DISK same as > DISC
DISKED > DISK
DISKETTE n floppy disk
DISKETTES > DISKETTE
DISKING > DISK
DISKLESS > DISK
DISKLIKE > DISK
DISKS > DISK
DISLEAF vb remove leaf or leaves from

DISLEAFED > DISLEAF
DISLEAFS > DISLEAF
DISLEAL archaic form of > DISLOYAL
DISLEAVE variant of > DISLEAF
DISLEAVED > DISLEAVE
DISLEAVES > DISLEAVE
DISLIKE vb consider unpleasant or disagreeable ▷ n feeling of not liking something or someone
DISLIKED > DISLIKE
DISLIKEN vb render dissimilar to
DISLIKENS > DISLIKEN
DISLIKER > DISLIKE
DISLIKERS > DISLIKE
DISLIKES > DISLIKE
DISLIKING > DISLIKE
DISLIMB vb remove limbs from
DISLIMBED > DISLIMB
DISLIMBS > DISLIMB
DISLIMN vb efface
DISLIMNED > DISLIMN
DISLIMNS > DISLIMN
DISLINK vb disunite
DISLINKED > DISLINK
DISLINKS > DISLINK
DISLOAD vb unload
DISLOADED > DISLOAD
DISLOADS > DISLOAD
DISLOCATE vb displace (a bone or joint) from its normal position
DISLODGE vb remove (something) from a previously fixed position
DISLODGED > DISLODGE
DISLODGES > DISLODGE
DISLOIGN vb put at a distance
DISLOIGNS > DISLOIGN
DISLOYAL adj not loyal, deserting one's allegiance
DISLUSTRE vb remove lustre from
DISMAL adj gloomy and depressing
DISMALER > DISMAL
DISMALEST > DISMAL
DISMALITY > DISMAL
DISMALLER > DISMAL
DISMALLY > DISMAL
DISMALS pl n gloomy state of mind
DISMAN vb remove men from
DISMANNED > DISMAN
DISMANS > DISMAN
DISMANTLE vb take apart piece by piece
DISMASK vb remove mask from
DISMASKED > DISMASK
DISMASKS > DISMASK
DISMAST vb break off the mast or masts of (a sailing vessel)
DISMASTED > DISMAST
DISMASTS > DISMAST
DISMAY vb fill with alarm

or depression ▷ n alarm mixed with sadness
DISMAYD > DISMAY
DISMAYED > DISMAY
DISMAYFUL > DISMAY
DISMAYING > DISMAY
DISMAYL vb remove a coat of mail from
DISMAYLED > DISMAYL
DISMAYLS > DISMAYL
DISMAYS > DISMAY
DISME old form of > DIME
DISMEMBER vb remove the limbs of
DISMES > DISME
DISMISS vb remove (an employee) from a job ▷ sentence substitute order to end an activity or give permission to disperse
DISMISSAL n official notice of discharge from employment or service
DISMISSED > DISMISS
DISMISSES > DISMISS
DISMODED adj no longer fashionable
DISMOUNT vb get off a horse or bicycle ▷ n act of dismounting
DISMOUNTS > DISMOUNT
DISNEST vb remove from nest
DISNESTED > DISNEST
DISNESTS > DISNEST
DISOBEY vb neglect or refuse to obey
DISOBEYED > DISOBEY
DISOBEYER > DISOBEY
DISOBEYS > DISOBEY
DISOBLIGE vb disregard the desires of
DISOMIC adj having an extra chromosome in the haploid state that is homologous to an existing chromosome in this set
DISOMIES > DISOMIC
DISOMY > DISOMIC
DISORBED adj thrown out of orbit
DISORDER n state of untidiness and disorganization ▷ vb upset the order of
DISORDERS > DISORDER
DISORIENT same as > DISORIENTATE
DISOWN vb deny any connection with (someone)
DISOWNED > DISOWN
DISOWNER > DISOWN
DISOWNERS > DISOWN
DISOWNING > DISOWN
DISOWNS > DISOWN
DISPACE vb move or travel about
DISPACED > DISPACE
DISPACES > DISPACE
DISPACING > DISPACE
DISPARAGE vb speak contemptuously of
DISPARATE adj completely

different ▷ n unlike things or people
DISPARITY n inequality or difference
DISPARK vb release
DISPARKED > DISPARK
DISPARKS > DISPARK
DISPART vb separate
DISPARTED > DISPART
DISPARTS > DISPART
DISPATCH vb send off to a destination or to perform a task ▷ n official communication or report, sent in haste
DISPATHY obsolete spelling of > DYSPATHY
DISPAUPER vb state that someone is no longer a pauper
DISPEACE n absence of peace
DISPEACES > DISPEACE
DISPEL vb destroy or remove
DISPELLED > DISPEL
DISPELLER > DISPEL
DISPELS > DISPEL
DISPENCE same as > DISPENSE
DISPENCED > DISPENCE
DISPENCES > DISPENCE
DISPEND vb spend
DISPENDED > DISPEND
DISPENDS > DISPEND
DISPENSE vb distribute in portions
DISPENSED > DISPENSE
DISPENSER n device, such as a vending machine, that automatically dispenses a single item or a measured quantity
DISPENSES > DISPENSE
DISPEOPLE vb remove inhabitants from
DISPERSAL n act of dispersing or the condition of being dispersed
DISPERSE vb scatter over a wide area ▷ adj of or consisting of the particles in a colloid or suspension
DISPERSED > DISPERSE
DISPERSER > DISPERSE
DISPERSES > DISPERSE
DISPIRIT vb make downhearted
DISPIRITS > DISPIRIT
DISPLACE vb move from the usual location
DISPLACED > DISPLACE
DISPLACER > DISPLACE
DISPLACES > DISPLACE
DISPLANT vb displace
DISPLANTS > DISPLANT
DISPLAY vb make visible or noticeable ▷ n displaying
DISPLAYED > DISPLAY
DISPLAYER > DISPLAY
DISPLAYS > DISPLAY
DISPLE vb punish
DISPLEASE vb annoy or

upset
DISPLED > DISPLE
DISPLES > DISPLE
DISPLING > DISPLE
DISPLODE *obsolete word for* > EXPLODE
DISPLODED > DISPLODE
DISPLODES > DISPLODE
DISPLUME *vb* remove feathers from
DISPLUMED > DISPLUME
DISPLUMES > DISPLUME
DISPONDEE *n* (poetry) double foot of two long syllables
DISPONE *vb* transfer ownership
DISPONED > DISPONE
DISPONEE *vb* person whom something is disponed to
DISPONEES > DISPONEE
DISPONER > DISPONE
DISPONERS > DISPONE
DISPONES > DISPONE
DISPONGE *same as* > DISPUNGE
DISPONGED > DISPONGE
DISPONGES > DISPONGE
DISPONING > DISPONE
DISPORT *vb* indulge (oneself) in pleasure ▷ *n* amusement
DISPORTED > DISPORT
DISPORTS > DISPORT
DISPOSAL *n* getting rid of something
DISPOSALS > DISPOSAL
DISPOSE *vb* place in a certain order
DISPOSED *adj* willing or eager
DISPOSER > DISPOSE
DISPOSERS > DISPOSE
DISPOSES > DISPOSE
DISPOSING > DISPOSE
DISPOST *vb* remove from post
DISPOSTED > DISPOST
DISPOSTS > DISPOST
DISPOSURE *a rare word for* > DISPOSAL
DISPRAD *old form of* > DISPREAD
DISPRAISE *vb* express disapproval or condemnation of ▷ *n* disapproval, etc, expressed
DISPREAD *vb* spread out
DISPREADS > DISPREAD
DISPRED *old spelling of* > DISPREAD
DISPREDS > DISPRED
DISPRISON *vb* release from captivity
DISPRIZE *vb* scorn
DISPRIZED > DISPRIZE
DISPRIZES > DISPRIZE
DISPROFIT *n* loss
DISPROOF *n* facts that disprove something
DISPROOFS > DISPROOF
DISPROOVE *vb* disapprove of
DISPROVAL > DISPROVE

DISPROVE *vb* show (an assertion or claim) to be incorrect
DISPROVED > DISPROVE
DISPROVEN > DISPROVE
DISPROVER > DISPROVE
DISPROVES > DISPROVE
DISPUNGE *vb* expunge
DISPUNGED > DISPUNGE
DISPUNGES > DISPUNGE
DISPURSE *another word for* > DISBURSE
DISPURSED > DISPURSE
DISPURSES > DISPURSE
DISPURVEY *vb* strip of equipment, provisions, etc
DISPUTANT *n* person who argues ▷ *adj* engaged in argument
DISPUTE *n* disagreement, argument ▷ *vb* argue about (something)
DISPUTED > DISPUTE
DISPUTER > DISPUTE
DISPUTERS > DISPUTE
DISPUTES > DISPUTE
DISPUTING > DISPUTE
DISQUIET *n* feeling of anxiety ▷ *vb* make (someone) anxious ▷ *adj* uneasy or anxious
DISQUIETS > DISQUIET
DISRANK *vb* demote
DISRANKED > DISRANK
DISRANKS > DISRANK
DISRATE *vb* punish (an officer) by lowering in rank
DISRATED > DISRATE
DISRATES > DISRATE
DISRATING > DISRATE
DISREGARD *vb* give little or no attention to ▷ *n* lack of attention or respect
DISRELISH *vb* have a feeling of aversion for ▷ *n* such a feeling
DISREPAIR *n* condition of being worn out or in poor working order
DISREPUTE *n* loss or lack of good reputation
DISROBE *vb* undress
DISROBED > DISROBE
DISROBER > DISROBE
DISROBERS > DISROBE
DISROBES > DISROBE
DISROBING > DISROBE
DISROOT *vb* uproot
DISROOTED > DISROOT
DISROOTS > DISROOT
DISRUPT *vb* interrupt the progress of
DISRUPTED > DISRUPT
DISRUPTER > DISRUPT
DISRUPTOR > DISRUPT
DISRUPTS > DISRUPT
DISS *vb* treat (a person) with contempt
DISSAVE *vb* spend savings
DISSAVED > DISSAVE
DISSAVES > DISSAVE
DISSAVING > DISSAVE
DISSEAT *vb* unseat
DISSEATED > DISSEAT

DISSEATS > DISSEAT
DISSECT *vb* cut open (a corpse) to examine it
DISSECTED *adj* in the form of narrow lobes or segments
DISSECTOR > DISSECT
DISSECTS > DISSECT
DISSED > DISS
DISSEISE *vb* deprive of seisin
DISSEISED > DISSEISE
DISSEISEE *n* person who is disseised
DISSEISES > DISSEISE
DISSEISIN *n* act of disseising or state of being disseised
DISSEISOR > DISSEISE
DISSEIZE *same as* > DISSEISE
DISSEIZED > DISSEIZE
DISSEIZEE *n* person who is disseized
DISSEIZES > DISSEIZE
DISSEIZIN *same as* > DISSEISIN
DISSEIZOR > DISSEIZE
DISSEMBLE *vb* conceal one's real motives or emotions by pretence
DISSEMBLY *n* dismantling
DISSENSUS *n* disagreement within group
DISSENT *vb* disagree ▷ *n* disagreement
DISSENTED > DISSENT
DISSENTER > DISSENT
DISSENTS > DISSENT
DISSERT *n* give or make a dissertation; dissertate
DISSERTED > DISSERT
DISSERTS > DISSERT
DISSERVE *vb* do a disservice to
DISSERVED > DISSERVE
DISSERVES > DISSERVE
DISSES > DISS
DISSEVER *vb* break off or become broken off
DISSEVERS > DISSEVER
DISSHIVER *vb* break in pieces
DISSIDENT *n* person who disagrees with and criticizes the government ▷ *adj* disagreeing with the government
DISSIGHT *n* eyesore
DISSIGHTS > DISSIGHT
DISSIMILE *n* comparison using contrast
DISSING > DISS
DISSIPATE *vb* waste or squander
DISSOCIAL *same as* > DISSOCIABLE
DISSOLUTE *adj* leading an immoral life
DISSOLVE *vb* (cause to) become liquid ▷ *n* scene filmed or televised by dissolving

DISSOLVED > DISSOLVE
DISSOLVER > DISSOLVE
DISSOLVES > DISSOLVE
DISSONANT *adj* discordant
DISSUADE *vb* deter (someone) by persuasion from doing something
DISSUADED > DISSUADE
DISSUADER > DISSUADE
DISSUADES > DISSUADE
DISSUNDER *vb* separate
DISTAFF *n* rod on which wool etc is wound for spinning
DISTAFFS > DISTAFF
DISTAIN *vb* stain; tarnish
DISTAINED > DISTAIN
DISTAINS > DISTAIN
DISTAL *adj* (of a muscle, bone, limb, etc) situated farthest from the centre, median line, or point of attachment or origin
DISTALLY > DISTAL
DISTANCE *n* space between two points
DISTANCED > DISTANCE
DISTANCES > DISTANCE
DISTANT *adj* far apart
DISTANTLY > DISTANT
DISTASTE *n* dislike, disgust
DISTASTED > DISTASTE
DISTASTES > DISTASTE
DISTAVES > DISTAFF
DISTEMPER *n* highly contagious viral disease of dogs ▷ *vb* paint with distemper
DISTEND *vb* (of part of the body) swell
DISTENDED > DISTEND
DISTENDER > DISTEND
DISTENDS > DISTEND
DISTENT *adj* bloated; swollen
DISTHENE *n* bluish-green mineral
DISTHENES > DISTHENE
DISTHRONE *vb* remove from throne
DISTICH *n* unit of two verse lines
DISTICHAL > DISTICH
DISTICHS > DISTICH
DISTIL *vb* subject to or obtain by distillation
DISTILL *same as* > DISTIL
DISTILLED > DISTIL
DISTILLER *n* person or company that makes strong alcoholic drink, esp whisky
DISTILLS > DISTILL
DISTILS > DISTIL
DISTINCT *adj* not the same
DISTINGUE *adj* distinguished or noble
DISTOME *n* parasitic flatworm
DISTOMES > DISTOME
DISTORT *vb* misrepresent (the truth or facts)
DISTORTED > DISTORT

**DISTORTER** > DISTORT
**DISTORTS** > DISTORT
**DISTRACT** vb draw the attention of (a person) away from something
**DISTRACTS** > DISTRACT
**DISTRAIL** n trail made by aircraft flying through cloud
**DISTRAILS** > DISTRAIL
**DISTRAIN** vb seize (personal property) to enforce payment of a debt
**DISTRAINS** > DISTRAIN
**DISTRAINT** n act or process of distraining
**DISTRAIT** adj absent-minded or preoccupied
**DISTRAITE** feminine form of > DISTRAIT
**DISTRESS** n extreme unhappiness ▷ vb upset badly
**DISTRICT** n area of land regarded as an administrative or geographical unit ▷ vb divide into districts
**DISTRICTS** > DISTRICT
**DISTRIX** n splitting of the ends of hairs
**DISTRIXES** > DISTRIX
**DISTRUST** vb regard as untrustworthy ▷ n feeling of suspicion or doubt
**DISTRUSTS** > DISTRUST
**DISTUNE** vb cause to be out of tune
**DISTUNED** > DISTUNE
**DISTUNES** > DISTUNE
**DISTUNING** > DISTUNE
**DISTURB** vb intrude on
**DISTURBED** adj emotionally upset or maladjusted
**DISTURBER** > DISTURB
**DISTURBS** > DISTURB
**DISTYLE** n temple with two columns
**DISTYLES** > DISTYLE
**DISULFATE** n chemical compound containing two sulfate ions
**DISULFID** same as > DISULFIDE
**DISULFIDE** n compound of a base with two atoms of sulfur
**DISULFIDS** > DISULFID
**DISUNION** > DISUNITE
**DISUNIONS** > DISUNITE
**DISUNITE** vb cause disagreement among
**DISUNITED** > DISUNITE
**DISUNITER** > DISUNITE
**DISUNITES** > DISUNITE
**DISUNITY** n dissension or disagreement
**DISUSAGE** n disuse
**DISUSAGES** > DISUSAGE
**DISUSE** vb stop using ▷ n state of being no longer used
**DISUSED** adj no longer used

**DISUSES** > DISUSE
**DISUSING** > DISUSE
**DISVALUE** vb belittle
**DISVALUED** > DISVALUE
**DISVALUES** > DISVALUE
**DISVOUCH** vb dissociate oneself from
**DISYOKE** vb unyoke
**DISYOKED** > DISYOKE
**DISYOKES** > DISYOKE
**DISYOKING** > DISYOKE
**DIT** vb stop something happening ▷ n short sound used, in combination with the long sound dah, in the spoken representation of Morse and other telegraphic codes
**DITA** n apocynaceous shrub, Alstonia scholaris, of tropical Africa and Asia, having large shiny whorled leaves and medicinal bark
**DITAL** n key for raising pitch of lute string
**DITALS** > DITAL
**DITAS** > DITA
**DITCH** n narrow channel dug in the earth for drainage or irrigation ▷ vb abandon
**DITCHED** > DITCH
**DITCHER** > DITCH
**DITCHERS** > DITCH
**DITCHES** > DITCH
**DITCHING** > DITCH
**DITCHLESS** > DITCH
**DITE** vb set down in writing
**DITED** > DITE
**DITES** > DITE
**DITHECAL** adj having two thecae
**DITHECOUS** another word for > DITHECAL
**DITHEISM** n belief in two equal gods
**DITHEISMS** > DITHEISM
**DITHEIST** > DITHEISM
**DITHEISTS** > DITHEISM
**DITHELETE** n one believing that Christ had two wills
**DITHELISM** n belief that Christ had two wills
**DITHER** vb be uncertain or indecisive ▷ n state of indecision or agitation
**DITHERED** > DITHER
**DITHERER** > DITHER
**DITHERERS** > DITHER
**DITHERIER** > DITHER
**DITHERING** > DITHER
**DITHERS** > DITHER
**DITHERY** > DITHER
**DITHIOL** n chemical compound
**DITHYRAMB** n (in ancient Greece) a passionate choral hymn in honour of Dionysus
**DITING** > DITE
**DITOKOUS** adj producing two eggs

**DITONE** n interval of two tones
**DITONES** > DITONE
**DITROCHEE** n double metrical foot
**DITS** > DIT
**DITSIER** > DITSY
**DITSIEST** > DITSY
**DITSINESS** > DITSY
**DITSY** same as > DITZY
**DITT** same as > DIT
**DITTANDER** n plant, Lepidium latifolium, of coastal regions of Europe, N Africa, and SW Asia, with clusters of small white flowers: family Brassicaceae (crucifers)
**DITTANIES** > DITTANY
**DITTANY** n aromatic Cretan plant, Origanum dictamnus, with pink drooping flowers: formerly credited with great medicinal properties: family Lamiaceae (labiates)
**DITTAY** n accusation; charge
**DITTAYS** > DITTAY
**DITTED** > DIT
**DITTIED** > DITTY
**DITTIES** > DITTY
**DITTING** > DIT
**DITTIT** > DIT
**DITTO** n same ▷ adv in the same way ▷ sentence substitute used to avoid repeating or to confirm agreement or to confirm agreement with an immediately preceding sentence ▷ vb copy
**DITTOED** > DITTO
**DITTOING** > DITTO
**DITTOLOGY** n interpretation in two ways
**DITTOS** > DITTO
**DITTS** > DITT
**DITTY** vb set to music ▷ n short simple poem or song
**DITTYING** > DITTY
**DITZ** n silly scatterbrained person
**DITZES** > DITZ
**DITZIER** > DITZY
**DITZIEST** > DITZY
**DITZINESS** > DITZY
**DITZY** adj silly and scatterbrained
**DIURESES** > DIURESIS
**DIURESIS** n excretion of an unusually large quantity of urine
**DIURETIC** n drug that increases the flow of urine ▷ adj acting to increase the flow of urine
**DIURETICS** > DIURETIC
**DIURNAL** adj happening during the day or daily ▷ n service book containing all the canonical hours except matins
**DIURNALLY** > DIURNAL
**DIURNALS** > DIURNAL

**DIURON** n type of herbicide
**DIURONS** > DIURON
**DIUTURNAL** adj long-lasting
**DIV** n stupid or foolish person
**DIVA** n distinguished female singer
**DIVAGATE** vb digress or wander
**DIVAGATED** > DIVAGATE
**DIVAGATES** > DIVAGATE
**DIVALENCE** > DIVALENT
**DIVALENCY** > DIVALENT
**DIVALENT** n element that can unite with two atoms ▷ adj having two valencies or a valency of two
**DIVALENTS** > DIVALENT
**DIVAN** n low backless bed
**DIVANS** > DIVAN
**DIVAS** > DIVA
**DIVE** vb plunge headfirst into water ▷ n diving
**DIVEBOMB** vb bomb while making steep dives
**DIVEBOMBS** > DIVEBOMB
**DIVED** > DIVE
**DIVELLENT** adj separating
**DIVER** n person who works or explores underwater
**DIVERGE** vb separate and go in different directions
**DIVERGED** > DIVERGE
**DIVERGENT** adj diverging or causing divergence
**DIVERGES** > DIVERGE
**DIVERGING** > DIVERGE
**DIVERS** adj various ▷ determiner various
**DIVERSE** vb turn away ▷ adj having variety, assorted
**DIVERSED** > DIVERSE
**DIVERSELY** > DIVERSE
**DIVERSES** > DIVERSE
**DIVERSIFY** vb create different forms of
**DIVERSING** > DIVERSE
**DIVERSION** n official detour used by traffic when a main route is closed
**DIVERSITY** n quality of being different or varied
**DIVERSLY** > DIVERS
**DIVERT** vb change the direction of
**DIVERTED** > DIVERT
**DIVERTER** > DIVERT
**DIVERTERS** > DIVERT
**DIVERTING** > DIVERT
**DIVERTIVE** > DIVERT
**DIVERTS** > DIVERT
**DIVES** > DIVE
**DIVEST** vb strip (of clothes)
**DIVESTED** > DIVEST
**DIVESTING** > DIVEST
**DIVESTS** > DIVEST
**DIVESTURE** > DIVEST
**DIVI** alternative spelling of > DIVVY
**DIVIDABLE** > DIVIDE
**DIVIDANT** adj distinct

DIVIDE vb separate into parts ▷ n division, split

DIVIDED adj split

DIVIDEDLY > DIVIDED

DIVIDEND n sum of money representing part of the profit made, paid by a company to its shareholders

DIVIDENDS > DIVIDEND

DIVIDER n screen used to divide a room into separate areas

DIVIDERS pl n compasses with two pointed arms, used for measuring or dividing lines

DIVIDES > DIVIDE

DIVIDING > DIVIDE

DIVIDINGS > DIVIDE

DIVIDIVI n tropical tree

DIVIDIVIS > DIVIDIVI

DIVIDUAL adj divisible

DIVIDUOUS adj divided

DIVINABLE > DIVINE

DIVINATOR n diviner

DIVINE adj of God or a god ▷ vb discover (something) by intuition or guessing ▷ n priest who is learned in theology

DIVINED > DIVINE

DIVINELY > DIVINE

DIVINER > DIVINE

DIVINERS > DIVINE

DIVINES > DIVINE

DIVINEST > DIVINE

DIVING > DIVE

DIVINGS > DIVE

DIVINIFY vb give divine status to

DIVINING > DIVINE

DIVINISE same as > DIVINIZE

DIVINISED > DIVINISE

DIVINISES > DIVINISE

DIVINITY n study of religion

DIVINIZE vb make divine

DIVINIZED > DIVINIZE

DIVINIZES > DIVINIZE

DIVIS > DIVI

DIVISIBLE adj capable of being divided

DIVISIBLY > DIVISIBLE

DIVISIM adv separately

DIVISION n dividing, sharing out

DIVISIONS > DIVISION

DIVISIVE adj tending to cause disagreement

DIVISOR n number to be divided into another number

DIVISORS > DIVISOR

DIVORCE n legal ending of a marriage ▷ vb legally end one's marriage (to)

DIVORCED > DIVORCE

DIVORCEE n person who is divorced

DIVORCEES > DIVORCEE

DIVORCER > DIVORCE

DIVORCERS > DIVORCE

DIVORCES > DIVORCE

DIVORCING > DIVORCE

DIVORCIVE > DIVORCE

DIVOT n small piece of turf

DIVOTS > DIVOT

DIVS > DIV

DIVULGATE vb make publicly known

DIVULGE vb make known, disclose

DIVULGED > DIVULGE

DIVULGER > DIVULGE

DIVULGERS > DIVULGE

DIVULGES > DIVULGE

DIVULGING > DIVULGE

DIVULSE vb tear apart

DIVULSED > DIVULSE

DIVULSES > DIVULSE

DIVULSING > DIVULSE

DIVULSION n tearing or pulling apart

DIVULSIVE > DIVULSION

DIVVIED > DIVVY

DIVVIES > DIVVY

DIVVY vb divide and share ▷ n stupid person

DIVVYING > DIVVY

DIWAN same as > DEWAN

DIWANS > DIWAN

DIXI interj I have spoken

DIXIE n large metal pot for cooking, brewing tea, etc

DIXIES > DIXIE

DIXIT n statement

DIXITS > DIXIT

DIXY same as > DIXIE

DIZAIN n ten-line poem

DIZAINS > DIZAIN

DIZEN archaic word for > BEDIZEN

DIZENED > DIZEN

DIZENING > DIZEN

DIZENMENT > DIZEN

DIZENS > DIZEN

DIZYGOTIC adj developed from two separately fertilized eggs

DIZYGOUS another word for > DIZYGOTIC

DIZZARD n dunce

DIZZARDS > DIZZARD

DIZZIED > DIZZY

DIZZIER > DIZZY

DIZZIES > DIZZY

DIZZIEST > DIZZY

DIZZILY > DIZZY

DIZZINESS > DIZZY

DIZZY adj having or causing a whirling sensation ▷ vb make dizzy

DIZZYING > DIZZY

DJEBEL a variant spelling of > JEBEL

DJEBELS > DJEBEL

DJELLABA n kind of loose cloak with a hood, worn by men esp in North Africa and the Middle East

DJELLABAH same as > DJELLABA

DJELLABAS > DJELLABA

DJEMBE n W African drum played by beating with the hand

DJEMBES > DJEMBE

DJIBBAH same as > JUBBAH

DJIBBAHS > DJIBBAH

DJIN same as same as > JINN

DJINN > DJINNI

DJINNI same as > JINNI

DJINNS > DJINN

DJINNY same as same as > JINNI

DJINS > DJIN

DO vb perform or complete (a deed or action) ▷ n party, celebration

DOAB n alluvial land between two converging rivers, esp the area between the Ganges and Jumna in N India

DOABLE adj capable of being done

DOABS > DOAB

DOAT same as > DOTE

DOATED > DOAT

DOATER > DOAT

DOATERS > DOAT

DOATING > DOAT

DOATINGS > DOAT

DOATS > DOAT

DOB as in dob in inform against or report

DOBBED > DOB

DOBBER n informant or traitor

DOBBERS > DOBBER

DOBBIE same as > DOBBY

DOBBIES > DOBBY

DOBBIN n name for a horse, esp a workhorse, often used in children's tales, etc

DOBBING > DOB

DOBBINS > DOBBIN

DOBBY n attachment to a loom, used in weaving small figures

DOBCHICK same as > DABCHICK

DOBCHICKS > DOBCHICK

DOBHASH n interpreter

DOBHASHES > DOBHASH

DOBIE n cannabis

DOBIES > DOBIE

DOBLA n medieval Spanish gold coin, probably worth 20 maravedis

DOBLAS > DOBLA

DOBLON a variant spelling of > DOUBLOON

DOBLONES > DOBLON

DOBLONS > DOBLON

DOBRA n standard monetary unit of São Tomé e Principe, divided into 100 cêntimos

DOBRAS > DOBRA

DOBRO n tradename for a type of acoustic guitar having a metal resonator built into the body

DOBROS > DOBRO

DOBS > DOB

DOBSON n larva of dobsonfly

DOBSONFLY n large N American insect

DOBSONS > DOBSON

DOBY same as > DOBIE

DOC same as > DOCTOR

DOCENT n voluntary worker who acts as a guide in a museum, art gallery, etc

DOCENTS > DOCENT

DOCETIC adj believer in docetism: a heresy that the humanity of Christ was apparent rather than real

DOCHMIAC > DOCHMIUS

DOCHMII > DOCHMIUS

DOCHMIUS n five-syllable foot

DOCHT > DOW

DOCIBLE adj easily tamed

DOCILE adj (of a person or animal) easily controlled

DOCILELY > DOCILE

DOCILER > DOCILE

DOCILEST > DOCILE

DOCILITY > DOCILE

DOCIMASY n close examination

DOCK n enclosed area of water where ships are loaded, unloaded, or repaired ▷ vb bring or be brought into dock

DOCKAGE n charge levied upon a vessel for using a dock

DOCKAGES > DOCKAGE

DOCKED > DOCK

DOCKEN n something of no value or importance

DOCKENS > DOCKEN

DOCKER n person employed to load and unload ships

DOCKERS > DOCKER

DOCKET n label on a package or other delivery, stating contents, delivery instructions, etc ▷ vb fix a docket to (a package or other delivery)

DOCKETED > DOCKET

DOCKETING > DOCKET

DOCKETS > DOCKET

DOCKHAND n dock labourer

DOCKHANDS > DOCKHAND

DOCKING > DOCK

DOCKINGS > DOCK

DOCKISE same as > DOCKIZE

DOCKISED > DOCKISE

DOCKISES > DOCKISE

DOCKISING > DOCKISE

DOCKIZE vb convert into docks

DOCKIZED > DOCKIZE

DOCKIZES > DOCKIZE

DOCKIZING > DOCKIZE

DOCKLAND n area around the docks

DOCKLANDS > DOCKLAND

DOCKS > DOCK

DOCKSIDE n area next to dock

DOCKSIDES > DOCKSIDE

DOCKYARD n place where ships are built or repaired

DOCKYARDS > DOCKYARD

DOCO short

for > DOCUMENTARY
**DOCOS** > DOCO
**DOCQUET** *same as* > DOCKET
**DOCQUETED** > DOCQUET
**DOCQUETS** > DOCQUET
**DOCS** > DOC
**DOCTOR** *n* person licensed to practise medicine ▷ *vb* alter in order to deceive
**DOCTORAL** > DOCTOR
**DOCTORAND** *n* student working towards doctorate
**DOCTORATE** *n* highest academic degree in any field of knowledge
**DOCTORED** > DOCTOR
**DOCTORESS** *n* female doctor
**DOCTORIAL** > DOCTOR
**DOCTORING** > DOCTOR
**DOCTORLY** > DOCTOR
**DOCTORS** > DOCTOR
**DOCTRESS** *same as* > DOCTORESS
**DOCTRINAL** > DOCTRINE
**DOCTRINE** *n* body of teachings of a religious, political, or philosophical group
**DOCTRINES** > DOCTRINE
**DOCUDRAMA** *n* film or television programme based on true events, presented in a dramatized form
**DOCUMENT** *n* piece of paper providing an official record of something ▷ *vb* record or report (something) in detail
**DOCUMENTS** > DOCUMENT
**DOD** *vb* clip
**DODDARD** *adj* archaic word for missing branches; rotten
**DODDED** > DOD
**DODDER** *vb* move unsteadily ▷ *n* any rootless parasitic plant of the convolvulaceous genus *Cuscuta*, lacking chlorophyll and having slender twining stems with suckers for drawing nourishment from the host plant, scalelike leaves, and whitish flowers
**DODDERED** > DODDER
**DODDERER** > DODDER
**DODDERERS** > DODDER
**DODDERIER** > DODDER
**DODDERING** *adj* shaky, feeble, or infirm, esp from old age
**DODDERS** > DODDER
**DODDERY** > DODDER
**DODDIER** > DODDY
**DODDIES** > DODDY
**DODDIEST** > DODDY
**DODDING** > DOD
**DODDIPOLL** *same as* > DODDYPOLL
**DODDLE** *n* something easily accomplished
**DODDLES** > DODDLE
**DODDY** *n* bad mood ▷ *adj* sulky
**DODDYPOLL** *n* dunce
**DODECAGON** *n* geometric figure with twelve sides
**DODGE** *vb* avoid (a blow, being seen, etc) by moving suddenly ▷ *n* cunning or deceitful trick
**DODGEBALL** *n* game in which the players form a circle and try to hit opponents in the circle with a large ball
**DODGED** > DODGE
**DODGEM** *n* bumper car
**DODGEMS** > DODGEM
**DODGER** *n* person who evades a responsibility or duty
**DODGERIES** > DODGERY
**DODGERS** > DODGER
**DODGERY** *n* deception
**DODGES** > DODGE
**DODGIER** > DODGY
**DODGIEST** > DODGY
**DODGINESS** > DODGY
**DODGING** > DODGE
**DODGINGS** > DODGE
**DODGY** *adj* dangerous, risky
**DODKIN** *n* coin of little value
**DODKINS** > DODKIN
**DODMAN** *n* snail
**DODMANS** > DODMAN
**DODO** *n* large flightless extinct bird
**DODOES** > DODO
**DODOISM** > DODO
**DODOISMS** > DODO
**DODOS** > DODO
**DODS** > DOD
**DOE** *n* female deer, hare, or rabbit
**DOEK** *n* square of cloth worn on the head by women
**DOEKS** > DOEK
**DOEN** > DO
**DOER** *n* active or energetic person
**DOERS** > DOER
**DOES** > DO
**DOESKIN** *n* skin of a deer, lamb, or sheep
**DOESKINS** > DOESKIN
**DOEST** > DO
**DOETH** > DO
**DOF** *informal South African word for* > STUPID
**DOFF** *vb* take off or lift (one's hat) in polite greeting
**DOFFED** > DOFF
**DOFFER** > DOFF
**DOFFERS** > DOFF
**DOFFING** > DOFF
**DOFFS** > DOFF
**DOG** *n* domesticated four-legged mammal of many different breeds ▷ *vb* follow (someone) closely

**DOGARESSA** *n* wife of doge
**DOGATE** *n* office of doge
**DOGATES** > DOGATE
**DOGBANE** *n* any of several North American apocynaceous plants of the genus *Apocynum*, esp *A. androsaemifolium*, having bell-shaped white or pink flowers: thought to be poisonous to dogs
**DOGBANES** > DOGBANE
**DOGBERRY** *n* any of certain plants that have berry-like fruits, such as the European dogwood or the bearberry
**DOGBOLT** *n* bolt on cannon
**DOGBOLTS** > DOGBOLT
**DOGCART** *n* light horse-drawn two-wheeled cart
**DOGCARTS** > DOGCART
**DOGDAYS** *pl n* hot period of the summer reckoned in ancient times from the heliacal rising of Sirius (the Dog Star)
**DOGDOM** *n* world of dogs
**DOGDOMS** > DOGDOM
**DOGE** *n* (formerly) chief magistrate of Venice or Genoa
**DOGEAR** *vb* fold down the corner of (a page) ▷ *n* folded-down corner of a page
**DOGEARED** > DOGEAR
**DOGEARING** > DOGEAR
**DOGEARS** > DOGEAR
**DOGEATE** *n* office of doge
**DOGEATES** > DOGEATE
**DOGEDOM** *n* domain of doge
**DOGEDOMS** > DOGEDOM
**DOGES** > DOGE
**DOGESHIP** > DOGE
**DOGESHIPS** > DOGE
**DOGEY** *same as* > DOGIE
**DOGEYS** > DOGEY
**DOGFACE** *n* WW2 US soldier
**DOGFACES** > DOGFACE
**DOGFIGHT** *vb* fight in confused way ▷ *n* close-quarters combat between fighter aircraft
**DOGFIGHTS** > DOGFIGHT
**DOGFISH** *n* small shark
**DOGFISHES** > DOGFISH
**DOGFOUGHT** > DOGFIGHT
**DOGFOX** *n* male fox
**DOGFOXES** > DOGFOX
**DOGGED** > DOG
**DOGGEDER** > DOG
**DOGGEDEST** > DOG
**DOGGEDLY** > DOG
**DOGGER** *n* Dutch fishing vessel with two masts
**DOGGEREL** *n* poorly written poetry, usu. comic
**DOGGERELS** > DOGGEREL
**DOGGERIES** > DOGGERY
**DOGGERMAN** *n* sailor on dogger
**DOGGERMEN** > DOGGERMAN
**DOGGERS** > DOGGER

**DOGGERY** *n* surly behaviour
**DOGGESS** *n* female dog
**DOGGESSES** > DOGGESS
**DOGGIE** *same as* > DOGGY
**DOGGIER** > DOGGY
**DOGGIES** > DOGGY
**DOGGIEST** > DOGGY
**DOGGINESS** > DOGGY
**DOGGING** > DOG
**DOGGINGS** > DOG
**DOGGISH** *adj* of or like a dog
**DOGGISHLY** > DOGGISH
**DOGGO** *adv* in hiding and keeping quiet
**DOGGONE** *interj* exclamation of annoyance, disappointment, etc ▷ *vb* damn ▷ *adj* damnedest
**DOGGONED** > DOGGONE
**DOGGONER** > DOGGONE
**DOGGONES** > DOGGONE
**DOGGONEST** > DOGGONE
**DOGGONING** > DOGGONE
**DOGGREL** *same as* > DOGGEREL
**DOGGRELS** > DOGGREL
**DOGGY** *n* child's word for a dog ▷ *adj* of or like a dog
**DOGHANGED** *same as* > HANGDOG
**DOGHOLE** *n* squalid dwelling place
**DOGHOLES** > DOGHOLE
**DOGHOUSE** *n* kennel
**DOGHOUSES** > DOGHOUSE
**DOGIE** *n* motherless calf
**DOGIES** > DOGY
**DOGLEG** *n* sharp bend ▷ *vb* go off at an angle ▷ *adj* of or with the shape of a dogleg
**DOGLEGGED** > DOGLEG
**DOGLEGS** > DOGLEG
**DOGLIKE** > DOG
**DOGMA** *n* doctrine or system of doctrines proclaimed by authority as true
**DOGMAN** *n* person who directs the operation of a crane whilst riding on an object being lifted by it
**DOGMAS** > DOGMA
**DOGMATA** > DOGMA
**DOGMATIC** *adj* habitually stating one's opinions forcefully or arrogantly
**DOGMATICS** *n* study of religious dogmas and doctrines
**DOGMATISE** *same as* > DOGMATIZE
**DOGMATISM** > DOGMATIZE
**DOGMATIST** *n* dogmatic person
**DOGMATIZE** *vb* say or state (something) in a dogmatic manner
**DOGMATORY** > DOGMA
**DOGMEN** > DOGMAN
**DOGNAP** *vb* carry off and hold (a dog), usually for ransom
**DOGNAPED** > DOGNAP
**DOGNAPER** > DOGNAP

**DOGNAPERS** > DOGNAP
**DOGNAPING** > DOGNAP
**DOGNAPPED** > DOGNAP
**DOGNAPPER** > DOGNAP
**DOGNAPS** > DOGNAP
**DOGROBBER** *n* army cook
**DOGS** > DOG
**DOGSBODY** *n* person who carries out boring tasks for others ▷ *vb* act as a dogsbody
**DOGSHIP** *n* condition of being a dog
**DOGSHIPS** > DOGSHIP
**DOGSHORES** *n* pieces of wood to prop up boat
**DOGSKIN** *n* leather from dog's skin
**DOGSKINS** > DOGSKIN
**DOGSLED** *n* sleigh drawn by dogs
**DOGSLEDS** > DOGSLED
**DOGSLEEP** *n* feigned sleep
**DOGSLEEPS** > DOGSLEEP
**DOGTEETH** > DOGTOOTH
**DOGTOOTH** *n* carved ornament in the form of four leaflike projections radiating from a raised centre, used in England in the 13th century
**DOGTOWN** *n* community of prairie dogs
**DOGTOWNS** > DOGTOWN
**DOGTROT** *n* gently paced trot
**DOGTROTS** > DOGTROT
**DOGVANE** *n* light windvane consisting of a feather or a piece of cloth or yarn mounted on the side of a vessel
**DOGVANES** > DOGVANE
**DOGWATCH** *n* either of two watches aboard ship, from four to six pm or from six to eight pm
**DOGWOOD** *n* any of various cornaceous trees or shrubs of the genus *Cornus*, esp *C. sanguinea*, a European shrub with clusters of small white flowers and black berries: the shoots are red in winter
**DOGWOODS** > DOGWOOD
**DOGY** *same as* > DOGIE
**DOH** *n* in tonic sol-fa, first degree of any major scale ▷ *interj* exclamation of annoyance when something goes wrong
**DOHS** > DOH
**DOHYO** *n* sumo wrestling ring
**DOHYOS** > DOHYO
**DOILED** *same as* > DOILT
**DOILIES** > DOILY
**DOILT** *adj* foolish
**DOILTER** > DOILT
**DOILTEST** > DOILT
**DOILY** *n* decorative lacy paper mat, laid on a plate
**DOING** > DO

**DOINGS** *pl n* deeds or actions
**DOIT** *n* former small copper coin of the Netherlands
**DOITED** *adj* foolish or childish, as from senility
**DOITIT** *same as* > DOITED
**DOITKIN** *same as* > DOIT
**DOITKINS** > DOITKIN
**DOITS** > DOIT
**DOJO** *n* room or hall for the practice of martial arts
**DOJOS** > DOJO
**DOL** *n* unit of pain intensity, as measured by dolorimetry
**DOLABRATE** *adj* shaped like a hatchet or axe head
**DOLCE** *n* dessert ▷ *adv* (to be performed) gently and sweetly
**DOLCES** > DOLCE
**DOLCETTO** *n* variety of grape for making wine
**DOLCETTOS** > DOLCETTO
**DOLCI** > DOLCE
**DOLDRUMS** *pl n* depressed state of mind
**DOLE** *n* money received from the state while unemployed ▷ *vb* distribute in small quantities
**DOLED** > DOLE
**DOLEFUL** *adj* dreary, unhappy
**DOLEFULLY** > DOLEFUL
**DOLENT** *adj* sad
**DOLENTE** *adv* (to be performed) in a sorrowful manner
**DOLERITE** *n* dark basic intrusive igneous rock consisting of plagioclase feldspar and a pyroxene, such as augite
**DOLERITES** > DOLERITE
**DOLERITIC** > DOLERITE
**DOLES** > DOLE
**DOLESOME** *same as* > DOLEFUL
**DOLIA** > DOLIUM
**DOLICHOS** *n* tropical vines
**DOLICHURI** *n* poetic term
**DOLINA** *same as* > DOLINE
**DOLINAS** > DOLINA
**DOLINE** *n* shallow usually funnel-shaped depression of the ground surface formed by solution in limestone regions
**DOLINES** > DOLINE
**DOLING** > DOLE
**DOLIUM** *n* genus of molluscs
**DOLL** *n* small model of a human being, used as a toy ▷ *vb* as in *doll up* dress up
**DOLLAR** *n* standard monetary unit of many countries
**DOLLARED** *adj* flagged with a dollar sign
**DOLLARISE** *same*

*as* > DOLLARIZE
**DOLLARIZE** *vb* replace a country's currency with US dollar
**DOLLARS** > DOLLAR
**DOLLDOM** > DOLL
**DOLLDOMS** > DOLL
**DOLLED** > DOLL
**DOLLHOOD** > DOLL
**DOLLHOODS** > DOLL
**DOLLHOUSE** *n* toy house in which dolls and miniature furniture can be put
**DOLLIED** > DOLLY
**DOLLIER** *n* person who operates a dolly
**DOLLIERS** > DOLLIER
**DOLLIES** > DOLLY
**DOLLINESS** > DOLLY
**DOLLING** > DOLL
**DOLLISH** > DOLL
**DOLLISHLY** > DOLL
**DOLLOP** *n* lump (of food) ▷ *vb* serve out (food)
**DOLLOPED** > DOLLOP
**DOLLOPING** > DOLLOP
**DOLLOPS** > DOLLOP
**DOLLS** > DOLL
**DOLLY** *adj* attractive and unintelligent ▷ *n* wheeled support on which a camera may be mounted; shaped block of lead used to hammer dents out of sheet metal ▷ *vb* wheel (a camera) backwards or forwards on a dolly
**DOLLYBIRD** *n* pretty and fashionable young woman
**DOLLYING** > DOLLY
**DOLMA** *n* vine leaf stuffed with a filling of meat and rice
**DOLMADES** > DOLMA
**DOLMAN** *n* long Turkish outer robe
**DOLMANS** > DOLMAN
**DOLMAS** > DOLMA
**DOLMEN** *n* prehistoric monument consisting of a horizontal stone supported by vertical stones
**DOLMENIC** > DOLMEN
**DOLMENS** > DOLMEN
**DOLOMITE** *n* mineral consisting of calcium magnesium carbonate
**DOLOMITES** > DOLOMITE
**DOLOMITIC** > DOLOMITE
**DOLOR** *same as* > DOLOUR
**DOLORIFIC** *adj* causing pain or sadness
**DOLOROSO** *adv* (to be performed) in a sorrowful manner
**DOLOROUS** *adj* sad, mournful
**DOLORS** > DOLOR
**DOLOS** *n* knucklebone of a sheep, buck, etc, used esp by diviners
**DOLOSSE** > DOLOS
**DOLOSTONE** *n* rock

composed of the mineral dolomite
**DOLOUR** *n* grief or sorrow
**DOLOURS** > DOLOUR
**DOLPHIN** *n* sea mammal of the whale family, with a beaklike snout
**DOLPHINET** *n* female dolphin
**DOLPHINS** > DOLPHIN
**DOLS** > DOL
**DOLT** *n* stupid person
**DOLTISH** > DOLT
**DOLTISHLY** > DOLT
**DOLTS** > DOLT
**DOM** *n* title given to Benedictine, Carthusian, and Cistercian monks and to certain of the canons regular
**DOMAIN** *n* field of knowledge or activity
**DOMAINAL** > DOMAIN
**DOMAINE** *n* French estate where wine is made
**DOMAINES** > DOMAINE
**DOMAINS** > DOMAIN
**DOMAL** *adj* of a house
**DOMANIAL** > DOMAIN
**DOMATIA** > DOMATIUM
**DOMATIUM** *n* plant cavity inhabited by commensal insects or mites or, occasionally, microorganisms
**DOME** *n* rounded roof built on a circular base ▷ *vb* cover with or as if with a dome
**DOMED** > DOME
**DOMELIKE** > DOME
**DOMES** > DOME
**DOMESDAY** *same as* > DOOMSDAY
**DOMESDAYS** > DOMESDAY
**DOMESTIC** *adj* of one's own country or a specific country ▷ *n* person whose job is to do housework in someone else's house
**DOMESTICS** > DOMESTIC
**DOMETT** *n* wool and cotton cloth
**DOMETTS** > DOMETT
**DOMIC** *adj* dome-shaped
**DOMICAL** > DOME
**DOMICALLY** > DOME
**DOMICIL** *same as* > DOMICILE
**DOMICILE** *n* place where one lives ▷ *vb* establish or be established in a dwelling place
**DOMICILED** > DOMICILE
**DOMICILES** > DOMICILE
**DOMICILS** > DOMICIL
**DOMIER** > DOMY
**DOMIEST** > DOMY
**DOMINANCE** *n* control
**DOMINANCY** > DOMINANCE
**DOMINANT** *adj* having authority or influence ▷ *n* dominant allele or character

DOMINANTS > DOMINANT
DOMINATE vb control or govern
DOMINATED > DOMINATE
DOMINATES > DOMINATE
DOMINATOR > DOMINATE
DOMINE n clergyman
DOMINEE n minister of the Dutch Reformed Church
DOMINEER vb act with arrogance or tyranny
DOMINEERS > DOMINEER
DOMINEES > DOMINEE
DOMINES > DOMINE
DOMING > DOME
DOMINICAL adj of, relating to, or emanating from Jesus Christ as Lord
DOMINICK n breed of chicken
DOMINICKS > DOMINICK
DOMINIE n minister or clergyman: also used as a term of address
DOMINIES > DOMINIE
DOMINION same as > DOMINIUM
DOMINIONS > DOMINION
DOMINIQUE n type of chicken
DOMINIUM n ownership or right to possession of property, esp realty
DOMINIUMS > DOMINIUM
DOMINO n small rectangular block marked with dots, used in dominoes
DOMINOES n game in which dominoes with matching halves are laid together
DOMINOS > DOMINO
DOMS > DOM
DOMY adj having a dome or domes
DON vb put on (clothing) ▷ n member of the teaching staff at a university or college
DONA n Spanish lady
DONAH n woman
DONAHS > DONAH
DONARIES > DONARY
DONARY n thing given for holy use
DONAS > DONA
DONATARY n recipient
DONATE vb give, esp to a charity or organization
DONATED > DONATE
DONATES > DONATE
DONATING > DONATE
DONATION n donating
DONATIONS > DONATION
DONATISM n doctrine and beliefs relating to a schismatic heretical Christian sect originating in N Africa in 311 AD
DONATISMS > DONATISM
DONATIVE n gift or donation ▷ adj of or like a donation
DONATIVES > DONATIVE
DONATOR > DONATE

DONATORS > DONATE
DONATORY n recipient
DONDER vb beat (someone) up ▷ n wretch
DONDERED > DONDER
DONDERING > DONDER
DONDERS > DONDER
DONE > DO
DONEE n person who receives a gift
DONEES > DONEE
DONENESS n extent to which something is cooked
DONER as in doner kebab grilled meat and salad served in pitta bread with chilli sauce
DONG n deep reverberating sound of a large bell ▷ vb (of a bell) to make a deep reverberating sound
DONGA n steep-sided gully created by soil erosion
DONGAS > DONGA
DONGED > DONG
DONGING > DONG
DONGLE n electronic device that accompanies a software item to prevent the unauthorized copying of programs
DONGLES > DONGLE
DONGOLA n leather tanned using a particular method
DONGOLAS > DONGOLA
DONGS > DONG
DONING n act of giving blood
DONINGS > DONING
DONJON n heavily fortified central tower of a castle
DONJONS > DONJON
DONKEY n long-eared member of the horse family
DONKEYS > DONKEY
DONKO n tearoom or cafeteria in a factory, wharf area, etc
DONKOS > DONKO
DONNA n Italian lady
DONNARD same as > DONNERT
DONNART same as > DONNERT
DONNAS > DONNA
DONNAT n lazy person
DONNATS > DONNAT
DONNE same as > DONNEE
DONNED > DON
DONNEE n subject or theme
DONNEES > DONNEE
DONNERD adj stupid
DONNERED same as > DONNERT
DONNERT adj stunned
DONNES > DONNE
DONNICKER n toilet
DONNIES > DONNY
DONNIKER same as > DONNICKER
DONNIKERS > DONNIKER
DONNING > DON

DONNISH adj serious and academic
DONNISHLY > DONNISH
DONNISM n loftiness
DONNISMS > DONNISM
DONNOT n lazy person
DONNOTS > DONNOT
DONNY same as > DANNY
DONOR n person who gives blood or organs for use in the treatment of another person
DONORS > DONOR
DONORSHIP > DONOR
DONS > DON
DONSHIP n state or condition of being a don
DONSHIPS > DONSHIP
DONSIE adj rather unwell
DONSIER > DONSIE
DONSIEST > DONSIE
DONSY same as > DONSIE
DONUT same as > DOUGHNUT
DONUTS > DONUT
DONUTTED > DONUT
DONUTTING > DONUT
DONZEL n man of high birth
DONZELS > DONZEL
DOO a Scot word for > DOVE
DOOB n cannabis cigarette
DOOBIE same as > DOOB
DOOBIES > DOOBIE
DOOBS > DOOB
DOOCED as in get dooced be dismissed on account of indiscretions written in a blog or on a website
DOOCOT n dovecote
DOOCOTS > DOOCOT
DOODAD same as > DOODAH
DOODADS > DOODAD
DOODAH n unnamed thing, esp an object the name of which is unknown or uncertain
DOODAHS > DOODAH
DOODIES > DOODY
DOODLE vb scribble or draw aimlessly ▷ n shape or picture drawn aimlessly
DOODLEBUG n diviner's rod
DOODLED > DOODLE
DOODLER > DOODLE
DOODLERS > DOODLE
DOODLES > DOODLE
DOODLING > DOODLE
DOODOO n excrement
DOODOOS > DOODOO
DOODY same as > DOODOO
DOOFER n thingamajig
DOOFERS > DOOFER
DOOFUS n slow-witted or stupid person
DOOFUSES > DOOFUS
DOOHICKEY another name for > DOODAH
DOOK n wooden plug driven into a wall to hold a nail, screw, etc ▷ vb dip or plunge
DOOKED > DOOK
DOOKET n dovecote
DOOKETS > DOOKET
DOOKING > DOOK

DOOKS > DOOK
DOOL n boundary marker
DOOLALLY adj out of one's mind
DOOLAN n Roman Catholic
DOOLANS > DOOLAN
DOOLE same as > DOOL
DOOLEE same as > DOOLIE
DOOLEES > DOOLEE
DOOLES > DOOLE
DOOLIE n enclosed couch on poles for carrying passengers
DOOLIES > DOOLIE
DOOLS > DOOL
DOOLY same as > DOOLIE
DOOM n death or a terrible fate ▷ vb destine or condemn to death or a terrible fate
DOOMED > DOOM
DOOMFUL > DOOM
DOOMFULLY > DOOM
DOOMIER > DOOMY
DOOMIEST > DOOMY
DOOMILY > DOOMY
DOOMING > DOOM
DOOMS > DOOM
DOOMSAYER n pessimist
DOOMSDAY n day on which the Last Judgment will occur
DOOMSDAYS > DOOMSDAY
DOOMSMAN n pessimist
DOOMSMEN > DOOMSMAN
DOOMSTER n person habitually given to predictions of impending disaster or doom
DOOMSTERS > DOOMSTER
DOOMWATCH n surveillance of the environment to warn of and prevent harm to it from human factors such as pollution or overpopulation
DOOMY adj despondent or pessimistic
DOON same as > DOWN
DOONA n large quilt used as a bed cover in place of the top sheet and blankets
DOONAS > DOONA
DOOR n hinged or sliding panel for closing the entrance to a building, room, etc
DOORBELL n device for visitors to announce presence at a door
DOORBELLS > DOORBELL
DOORCASE same as > DOORFRAME
DOORCASES > DOORCASE
DOORFRAME n frame that supports a door
DOORJAMB n vertical post forming one side of a door frame
DOORJAMBS > DOORJAMB
DOORKNOB n knob for opening and closing a door
DOORKNOBS > DOORKNOB
DOORKNOCK n fund-raising

campaign for charity conducted by seeking donations from door to door

**DOORLESS** > DOOR

**DOORMAN** *n* man employed to be on duty at the entrance to a large public building

**DOORMAT** *n* mat for wiping dirt from shoes before going indoors

**DOORMATS** > DOORMAT

**DOORMEN** > DOORMAN

**DOORN** *n* thorn

**DOORNAIL** as in *dead as a doornail* dead beyond any doubt

**DOORNAILS** > DOORNAIL

**DOORNS** > DOORN

**DOORPLATE** *n* name-plate on door

**DOORPOST** *same as* > DOORJAMB

**DOORPOSTS** > DOORPOST

**DOORS** > DOOR

**DOORSILL** *n* horizontal member of wood, stone, etc, forming the bottom of a doorframe

**DOORSILLS** > DOORSILL

**DOORSMAN** *n* doorkeeper

**DOORSMEN** > DOORSMAN

**DOORSTEP** *n* step in front of a door

**DOORSTEPS** > DOORSTEP

**DOORSTONE** *n* stone of threshold

**DOORSTOP** *n* heavy object or one fixed to the floor, which prevents a door from closing or from striking a wall

**DOORSTOPS** > DOORSTOP

**DOORWAY** *n* opening into a building or room

**DOORWAYS** > DOORWAY

**DOORWOMAN** *n* female doorman

**DOORWOMEN** > DOORWOMAN

**DOORYARD** *n* yard in front of the front or back door of a house

**DOORYARDS** > DOORYARD

**DOOS** > DOO

**DOOSRA** *n* in cricket, a delivery, bowled by an off-spinner, that turns the opposite way from an off-break

**DOOSRAS** > DOOSRA

**DOOWOP** *n* style of singing in harmony

**DOOWOPS** > DOOWOP

**DOOZER** *same as* > DOOZY

**DOOZERS** > DOOZER

**DOOZIE** *same as* > DOOZY

**DOOZIES** > DOOZIE

**DOOZY** *n* something excellent

**DOP** *vb* curtsy ⊳ *n* tot or small drink, usually alcoholic ⊳ *vb* fail to reach the required standard in

(an examination, course, etc)

**DOPA** *n* precursor to dopamine

**DOPAMINE** *n* chemical found in the brain that acts as a neurotransmitter

**DOPAMINES** > DOPAMINE

**DOPANT** *n* element or compound used to dope a semiconductor

**DOPANTS** > DOPANT

**DOPAS** > DOPA

**DOPATTA** *n* headscarf

**DOPATTAS** > DOPATTA

**DOPE** *n* illegal drug, usu. cannabis ⊳ *vb* give a drug to, esp in order to improve performance in a race ⊳ *adj* excellent

**DOPED** > DOPE

**DOPEHEAD** *n* habitual drug user

**DOPEHEADS** > DOPEHEAD

**DOPER** *n* person who administers dope

**DOPERS** > DOPER

**DOPES** > DOPE

**DOPESHEET** *n* document giving information on horse races

**DOPESTER** *n* person who makes predictions, esp in sport or politics

**DOPESTERS** > DOPESTER

**DOPEY** *adj* half-asleep, drowsy

**DOPEYNESS** > DOPEY

**DOPIAZA** *n* Indian meat or fish dish cooked in onion sauce

**DOPIAZAS** > DOPIAZA

**DOPIER** > DOPY

**DOPIEST** > DOPY

**DOPILY** > DOPEY

**DOPINESS** > DOPEY

**DOPING** > DOPE

**DOPINGS** > DOPE

**DOPPED** > DOP

**DOPPER** *n* member of an Afrikaner church that practises a stict Calvinism

**DOPPERS** > DOPPER

**DOPPIE** *n* cartridge case

**DOPPIES** > DOPPIE

**DOPPING** > DOP

**DOPPINGS** > DOP

**DOPPIO** *n* double measure, esp of espresso coffee

**DOPPIOS** > DOPPIO

**DOPS** > DOP

**DOPY** *same as* > DOPEY

**DOR** *n* any European dung beetle of the genus *Geotrupes* and related genera, esp *G. stercorarius*, having a droning flight

**DORAD** *n* South American river fish

**DORADO** *n* large marine percoid fish

**DORADOS** > DORADO

**DORADS** > DORAD

**DORB** *same as* > DORBA

**DORBA** *n* stupid, inept, or clumsy person

**DORBAS** > DORBA

**DORBEETLE** *same as* > DOR

**DORBS** > DORB

**DORBUG** *n* type of beetle

**DORBUGS** > DORBUG

**DORE** *n* walleye fish

**DOREE** *n* type of fish

**DOREES** > DOREE

**DORHAWK** *n* nightjar

**DORHAWKS** > DORHAWK

**DORIC** *adj* rustic

**DORIDOID** *n* shell-less mollusc

**DORIDOIDS** > DORIDOID

**DORIES** > DORY

**DORIS** *n* woman

**DORISE** *same as* > DORIZE

**DORISED** > DORISE

**DORISES** > DORISE

**DORISING** > DORISE

**DORIZE** *vb* become Doric

**DORIZED** > DORIZE

**DORIZES** > DORIZE

**DORIZING** > DORIZE

**DORK** *n* stupid person

**DORKIER** > DORK

**DORKIEST** > DORK

**DORKINESS** > DORK

**DORKS** > DORK

**DORKY** > DORK

**DORLACH** *n* quiver of arrows

**DORLACHS** > DORLACH

**DORM** *same as* > DORMITORY

**DORMANCY** > DORMANT

**DORMANT** *n* supporting beam ⊳ *adj* temporarily quiet, inactive, or not being used

**DORMANTS** > DORMANT

**DORMER** *n* window that sticks out from a sloping roof

**DORMERED** *adj* having dormer windows

**DORMERS** > DORMER

**DORMICE** > DORMOUSE

**DORMIE** *adj* (of a player or side) as many holes ahead of an opponent as there are still to play

**DORMIENT** *adj* dormant

**DORMIN** *n* hormone found in plants

**DORMINS** > DORMIN

**DORMITION** *n* Mary's assumption to heaven

**DORMITIVE** *adj* sleep-inducing

**DORMITORY** *n* large room, esp at a school, containing several beds ⊳ *adj* (of a town or suburb) having many inhabitants who travel to work in a nearby city

**DORMOUSE** *n* small mouselike rodent with a furry tail

**DORMS** > DORM

**DORMY** *same as* > DORMIE

**DORNECK** *same as* > DORNICK

**DORNECKS** > DORNECK

**DORNICK** *n* heavy damask cloth, formerly used for vestments, curtains, etc

**DORNICKS** > DORNICK

**DORNOCK** *n* type of coarse fabric

**DORNOCKS** > DORNOCK

**DORONICUM** *n* any plant of the Eurasian and N African genus *Doronicum*, such as leopard's-bane, having yellow daisy-like flower heads: family *Asteraceae* (composites)

**DORP** *n* small town

**DORPER** *n* breed of sheep

**DORPERS** > DORPER

**DORPS** > DORP

**DORR** *same as* > DOR

**DORRED** > DOR

**DORRING** > DOR

**DORRS** > DOR

**DORS** > DOR

**DORSA** > DORSUM

**DORSAD** *adj* towards the back or dorsal aspect

**DORSAL** *adj* of or on the back ⊳ *n* dorsal fin

**DORSALLY** > DORSAL

**DORSALS** > DORSAL

**DORSE** *n* type of small fish

**DORSEL** *another word for* > DOSSAL

**DORSELS** > DORSEL

**DORSER** *n* hanging tapestry

**DORSERS** > DORSER

**DORSES** > DORSE

**DORSIFLEX** *adj* bending towards the back

**DORSUM** *n* the back

**DORT** *vb* sulk

**DORTED** > DORT

**DORTER** *n* dormitory

**DORTERS** > DORTER

**DORTIER** > DORTY

**DORTIEST** > DORTY

**DORTINESS** > DORTY

**DORTING** > DORT

**DORTOUR** *same as* > DORTER

**DORTOURS** > DORTOUR

**DORTS** > DORT

**DORTY** *adj* haughty, or sullen

**DORY** *n* spiny-finned edible sea fish

**DOS** > DO

**DOSAGE** *same as* > DOSE

**DOSAGES** > DOSAGE

**DOSE** *n* specific quantity of a medicine taken at one time ⊳ *vb* give a dose to

**DOSED** > DOSE

**DOSEH** *n* former Egyptian religious ceremony

**DOSEHS** > DOSEH

**DOSEMETER** *same as* > DOSIMETER

**DOSER** > DOSE

**DOSERS** > DOSE

**DOSES** > DOSE

**DOSH** *n* money

**DOSHES** > DOSH

**DOSIMETER** *n* instrument for measuring the dose of

221

X-rays or other radiation absorbed by matter or the intensity of a source of radiation

**DOSIMETRY** > DOSIMETER

**DOSING** > DOSE

**DOSIOLOGY** n study of doses

**DOSOLOGY** same as > DOSIOLOGY

**DOSS** vb sleep, esp in a dosshouse ▷ n bed, esp in a dosshouse

**DOSSAL** n ornamental hanging, placed at the back of an altar or at the sides of a chancel

**DOSSALS** > DOSSAL

**DOSSED** > DOSS

**DOSSEL** same as > DOSSAL

**DOSSELS** > DOSSEL

**DOSSER** n bag or basket for carrying objects on the back

**DOSSERET** n stone above column supporting an arch

**DOSSERETS** > DOSSERET

**DOSSERS** > DOSSER

**DOSSES** > DOSS

**DOSSHOUSE** n cheap lodging house for homeless people

**DOSSIER** n collection of documents about a subject or person

**DOSSIERS** > DOSSIER

**DOSSIL** n lint for dressing wound

**DOSSILS** > DOSSIL

**DOSSING** > DOSS

**DOST** a singular form of the present tense (indicative mood) of > DO

**DOT** n small round mark ▷ vb mark with a dot

**DOTAGE** n weakness as a result of old age

**DOTAGES** > DOTAGE

**DOTAL** > DOT

**DOTANT** another word for > DOTARD

**DOTANTS** > DOTANT

**DOTARD** n person who is feeble-minded through old age

**DOTARDLY** > DOTARD

**DOTARDS** > DOTARD

**DOTATION** n act of giving a dowry

**DOTATIONS** > DOTATION

**DOTCOM** n company that does most of its business on the Internet

**DOTCOMMER** n person who carries out business on the internet

**DOTCOMS** > DOTCOM

**DOTE** vb love to an excessive or foolish degree

**DOTED** > DOTE

**DOTER** > DOTE

**DOTERS** > DOTE

**DOTES** > DOTE

**DOTH** a singular form of the present tense of > DO

**DOTIER** > DOTY

**DOTIEST** > DOTY

**DOTING** > DOTE

**DOTINGLY** > DOTE

**DOTINGS** > DOTE

**DOTISH** adj foolish

**DOTS** > DOT

**DOTTED** > DOT

**DOTTEL** same as > DOTTLE

**DOTTELS** > DOTTEL

**DOTTER** > DOT

**DOTTEREL** n rare kind of plover

**DOTTERELS** > DOTTEREL

**DOTTERS** > DOT

**DOTTIER** > DOTTY

**DOTTIEST** > DOTTY

**DOTTILY** > DOTTY

**DOTTINESS** > DOTTY

**DOTTING** > DOT

**DOTTLE** n tobacco left in a pipe after smoking ▷ adj relating to dottle

**DOTTLED** adj foolish

**DOTTLER** > DOTTLE

**DOTTLES** > DOTTLE

**DOTTLEST** > DOTTLE

**DOTTREL** same as > DOTTEREL

**DOTTRELS** > DOTTREL

**DOTTY** adj rather eccentric

**DOTY** adj (of wood) rotten

**DOUANE** n customs house

**DOUANES** > DOUANE

**DOUANIER** n customs officer

**DOUANIERS** > DOUANIER

**DOUAR** same as > DUAR

**DOUARS** > DOUAR

**DOUBLE** adj as much again in number, amount, size, etc ▷ adv twice over ▷ n twice the number, amount, size, etc ▷ vb make or become twice as much or as many

**DOUBLED** > DOUBLE

**DOUBLER** > DOUBLE

**DOUBLERS** > DOUBLE

**DOUBLES** n game between two pairs of players

**DOUBLET** n man's close-fitting jacket, with or without sleeves

**DOUBLETON** n original holding of two cards only in a suit

**DOUBLETS** > DOUBLET

**DOUBLING** > DOUBLE

**DOUBLINGS** > DOUBLE

**DOUBLOON** n former Spanish gold coin

**DOUBLOONS** > DOUBLOON

**DOUBLURE** n decorative lining of vellum or leather, etc, on the inside of a book cover

**DOUBLURES** > DOUBLURE

**DOUBLY** adv in a greater degree, quantity, or measure

**DOUBT** n uncertainty

about the truth, facts, or existence of something ▷ vb question the truth of

**DOUBTABLE** > DOUBT

**DOUBTABLY** > DOUBT

**DOUBTED** > DOUBT

**DOUBTER** > DOUBT

**DOUBTERS** > DOUBT

**DOUBTFUL** adj unlikely ▷ n person who is undecided or uncertain about an issue

**DOUBTFULS** > DOUBTFUL

**DOUBTING** > DOUBT

**DOUBTINGS** > DOUBT

**DOUBTLESS** adv probably or certainly ▷ adj certain

**DOUBTS** > DOUBT

**DOUC** n Old World monkey, Pygathrix nemaeus, of SE Asia, with a bright yellow face surrounded by tufts of reddish-brown fur, a white tail, and white hindquarters: one of the langurs

**DOUCE** adj quiet

**DOUCELY** > DOUCE

**DOUCENESS** > DOUCE

**DOUCEPERE** same as > DOUZEPER

**DOUCER** > DOUCE

**DOUCEST** > DOUCE

**DOUCET** n former flute-like instrument

**DOUCETS** > DOUCET

**DOUCEUR** n gratuity, tip, or bribe

**DOUCEURS** > DOUCEUR

**DOUCHE** n (instrument for applying) a stream of water directed onto or into the body for cleansing or medical purposes ▷ vb cleanse or treat by means of a douche

**DOUCHEBAG** n despicable person

**DOUCHED** > DOUCHE

**DOUCHES** > DOUCHE

**DOUCHING** > DOUCHE

**DOUCINE** n type of moulding for cornice

**DOUCINES** > DOUCINE

**DOUCS** > DOUC

**DOUGH** n thick mixture of flour and water or milk, used for making bread etc

**DOUGHBOY** n infantryman, esp in World War I

**DOUGHBOYS** > DOUGHBOY

**DOUGHFACE** n Northern Democrat who sided with the South in the American Civil War

**DOUGHIER** > DOUGHY

**DOUGHIEST** > DOUGHY

**DOUGHLIKE** > DOUGH

**DOUGHNUT** n small cake of sweetened dough fried in deep fat ▷ vb (of Members of Parliament) to surround (a speaker) during the televising of Parliament to

give the impression that the chamber is crowded or the speaker is well supported

**DOUGHNUTS** > DOUGHNUT

**DOUGHS** > DOUGH

**DOUGHT** > DOW

**DOUGHTIER** > DOUGHTY

**DOUGHTILY** > DOUGHTY

**DOUGHTY** adj brave and determined

**DOUGHY** adj resembling dough in consistency, colour, etc

**DOUK** same as > DOOK

**DOUKED** > DOUK

**DOUKING** > DOUK

**DOUKS** > DOUK

**DOULA** n woman who is trained to provide support to women and their families during pregnancy, childbirth, and the period of time following the birth

**DOULAS** > DOULA

**DOULEIA** same as > DULIA

**DOULEIAS** > DOULEIA

**DOUM** as in doum palm variety of palm tree

**DOUMA** same as > DUMA

**DOUMAS** > DOUMA

**DOUMS** > DOUM

**DOUN** same as > DOWN

**DOUP** n bottom

**DOUPIONI** n type of fabric

**DOUPIONIS** > DOUPIONI

**DOUPPIONI** n type of silk yarn

**DOUPS** > DOUP

**DOUR** adj sullen and unfriendly

**DOURA** same as > DURRA

**DOURAH** same as > DURRA

**DOURAHS** > DOURAH

**DOURAS** > DOURA

**DOURER** > DOUR

**DOUREST** > DOUR

**DOURINE** n infectious venereal disease of horses characterized by swollen glands, inflamed genitals, and paralysis of the hindquarters, caused by the protozoan Trypanosoma equiperdum contracted during copulation

**DOURINES** > DOURINE

**DOURLY** > DOUR

**DOURNESS** > DOUR

**DOUSE** vb drench with water or other liquid ▷ n immersion

**DOUSED** > DOUSE

**DOUSER** > DOUSE

**DOUSERS** > DOUSE

**DOUSES** > DOUSE

**DOUSING** > DOUSE

**DOUT** vb extinguish

**DOUTED** > DOUT

**DOUTER** > DOUT

**DOUTERS** > DOUT

**DOUTING** > DOUT

**DOUTS** > DOUT

**DOUX** adj sweet

**DOUZEPER** n distinguished person

**DOUZEPERS** > DOUZEPER

**DOVE** vb be semi-conscious ▷ n bird with a heavy body, small head, and short legs

**DOVECOT** same as > DOVECOTE

**DOVECOTE** n structure for housing pigeons

**DOVECOTES** > DOVECOTE

**DOVECOTS** > DOVECOT

**DOVED** > DOVE

**DOVEISH** adj dovelike

**DOVEKEY** same as > DOVEKIE

**DOVEKEYS** > DOVEKEY

**DOVEKIE** n small short-billed auk

**DOVEKIES** > DOVEKIE

**DOVELET** n small dove

**DOVELETS** > DOVELET

**DOVELIKE** > DOVE

**DOVEN** vb pray

**DOVENED** > DOVEN

**DOVENING** > DOVEN

**DOVENS** > DOVEN

**DOVER** vb doze ▷ n doze

**DOVERED** > DOVER

**DOVERING** > DOVER

**DOVERS** > DOVER

**DOVES** > DOVE

**DOVETAIL** n joint containing wedge-shaped tenons ▷ vb fit together neatly

**DOVETAILS** > DOVETAIL

**DOVIE** Scots word for > STUPID

**DOVIER** > DOVIE

**DOVIEST** > DOVIE

**DOVING** > DOVE

**DOVISH** > DOVE

**DOW** vb archaic word meaning be of worth

**DOWABLE** adj capable of being endowed

**DOWAGER** n widow possessing property or a title obtained from her husband

**DOWAGERS** > DOWAGER

**DOWAR** same as > DUAR

**DOWARS** > DOWAR

**DOWD** n woman who wears unfashionable clothes

**DOWDIER** > DOWDY

**DOWDIES** > DOWDY

**DOWDIEST** > DOWDY

**DOWDILY** > DOWDY

**DOWDINESS** > DOWDY

**DOWDS** > DOWD

**DOWDY** adj dull and old-fashioned ▷ n dowdy woman

**DOWDYISH** > DOWDY

**DOWDYISM** > DOWD

**DOWDYISMS** > DOWD

**DOWED** > DOW

**DOWEL** n wooden or metal peg that fits into two corresponding holes to join two adjacent parts ▷ vb join pieces of wood using dowels

**DOWELED** > DOWEL

**DOWELING** n joining of two pieces of wood using dowels

**DOWELLED** > DOWEL

**DOWELLING** same as > DOWELING

**DOWELS** > DOWEL

**DOWER** n life interest in a part of her husband's estate allotted to a widow by law ▷ vb endow

**DOWERED** > DOWER

**DOWERIES** > DOWERY

**DOWERING** > DOWER

**DOWERLESS** > DOWER

**DOWERS** > DOWER

**DOWERY** same as > DOWRY

**DOWF** adj dull; listless

**DOWFNESS** > DOWF

**DOWIE** adj dull and dreary

**DOWIER** > DOWIE

**DOWIEST** > DOWIE

**DOWING** > DOW

**DOWITCHER** n either of two snipelike shore birds, *Limnodromus griseus* or *L. scolopaceus*, of arctic and subarctic North America: family Scolopacidae (sandpipers, etc), order Charadriiformes

**DOWL** n fluff

**DOWLAS** n coarse fabric

**DOWLASES** > DOWLAS

**DOWLE** same as > DOWL

**DOWLES** > DOWLE

**DOWLIER** > DOWLY

**DOWLIEST** > DOWLY

**DOWLNE** obsolete form of > DOWN

**DOWLNES** > DOWLNE

**DOWLNEY** > DOWLNE

**DOWLS** > DOWL

**DOWLY** adj dull

**DOWN** adv indicating movement to or position in a lower place ▷ adj depressed, unhappy ▷ vb drink quickly ▷ n soft fine feathers

**DOWNA** obsolete Scots form of > CANNOT

**DOWNBEAT** adj gloomy ▷ n first beat of a bar

**DOWNBEATS** > DOWNBEAT

**DOWNBOW** n (in music) a downward stroke of the bow across the strings

**DOWNBOWS** > DOWNBOW

**DOWNBURST** n very high-speed downward movement of turbulent air in a limited area for a short time. Near the ground it spreads out from its centre with high horizontal velocities

**DOWNCAST** adj sad, dejected ▷ n ventilation shaft

**DOWNCASTS** > DOWNCAST

**DOWNCOME** same as > DOWNCOMER

**DOWNCOMER** n pipe that connects a cistern to a WC, wash basin, etc

**DOWNCOMES** > DOWNCOME

**DOWNCOURT** adj in far end a of court

**DOWNDRAFT** n downward air current

**DOWNED** > DOWN

**DOWNER** n barbiturate, tranquillizer, or narcotic

**DOWNERS** > DOWNER

**DOWNFALL** same as > DEADFALL

**DOWNFALLS** > DOWNFALL

**DOWNFIELD** adj at far end of field

**DOWNFLOW** n something that flows down

**DOWNFLOWS** > DOWNFLOW

**DOWNFORCE** n force produced by air resistance plus gravity that increases the stability of an aircraft or motor vehicle by pressing it downwards

**DOWNGRADE** vb reduce in importance or value

**DOWNHAUL** n line for hauling down a sail or for increasing the tension at its luff

**DOWNHAULS** > DOWNHAUL

**DOWNHILL** adj going or sloping down ▷ adv towards the bottom of a hill ▷ n downward slope

**DOWNHILLS** > DOWNHILL

**DOWNHOLE** adj (in the oil industry) denoting any piece of equipment that is used in the well itself

**DOWNIER** > DOWNY

**DOWNIEST** > DOWNY

**DOWNINESS** > DOWNY

**DOWNING** > DOWN

**DOWNLAND** same as > DOWNS

**DOWNLANDS** > DOWNLAND

**DOWNLESS** > DOWN

**DOWNLIGHT** n lamp shining downwards

**DOWNLIKE** > DOWN

**DOWNLINK** n satellite transmission channel

**DOWNLINKS** > DOWNLINK

**DOWNLOAD** vb transfer (data) from the memory of one computer to that of another, especially over the Internet ▷ n file transferred in such a way

**DOWNLOADS** > DOWNLOAD

**DOWNMOST** adj lowest

**DOWNPIPE** n pipe for carrying rainwater from a roof gutter to the ground or to a drain

**DOWNPIPES** > DOWNPIPE

**DOWNPLAY** vb play down

**DOWNPLAYS** > DOWNPLAY

**DOWNPOUR** n heavy fall of rain

**DOWNPOURS** > DOWNPOUR

**DOWNRANGE** adv in the direction of the intended flight path of a rocket or missile

**DOWNRIGHT** adv extreme(ly) ▷ adj absolute

**DOWNRIVER** adv in direction of current

**DOWNRUSH** n instance of rushing down

**DOWNS** pl n low grassy hills, esp in S England

**DOWNSCALE** vb reduce in scale

**DOWNSHIFT** vb reduce work hours

**DOWNSIDE** n disadvantageous aspect of a situation

**DOWNSIDES** > DOWNSIDE

**DOWNSIZE** vb reduce the number of people employed by (a company)

**DOWNSIZED** > DOWNSIZE

**DOWNSIZES** > DOWNSIZE

**DOWNSLIDE** n downward trend

**DOWNSLOPE** adv towards the bottom of a slope

**DOWNSPIN** n sudden downturn

**DOWNSPINS** > DOWNSPIN

**DOWNSPOUT** same as > DOWNPIPE

**DOWNSTAGE** adj or at the front part of the stage ▷ adv at or towards the front of the stage ▷ n front half of the stage

**DOWNSTAIR** adj situated on lower floor

**DOWNSTATE** adj in, or relating to the part of the state away from large cities, esp the southern part ▷ adv towards the southern part of a state ▷ n southern part of a state

**DOWNSWING** n statistical downward trend in business activity, the death rate, etc

**DOWNTHROW** n state of throwing down or being thrown down

**DOWNTICK** n small decrease

**DOWNTICKS** > DOWNTICK

**DOWNTIME** n time during which a computer or other machine is not working

**DOWNTIMES** > DOWNTIME

**DOWNTOWN** n central or lower part of a city, esp the main commercial area ▷ adv towards, to, or into this area ▷ adj of, relating to, or situated in the downtown area

**DOWNTOWNS** > DOWNTOWN

**DOWNTREND** n downward trend

**DOWNTROD** same as > DOWNTRODDEN

**DOWNTURN** n drop in the success of an economy or a

business
**DOWNTURNS** > DOWNTURN
**DOWNWARD** same
as > DOWNWARDS
**DOWNWARDS** adv from a
higher to a lower level,
condition, or position
**DOWNWASH** n downward
deflection of an airflow,
esp one caused by an
aircraft wing
**DOWNWIND** adj in the same
direction towards which
the wind is blowing
**DOWNY** adj covered with soft
fine hair or feathers
**DOWNZONE** vb reduce
density of housing in area
**DOWNZONED** > DOWNZONE
**DOWNZONES** > DOWNZONE
**DOWP** same as > DOUP
**DOWPS** > DOWP
**DOWRIES** > DOWRY
**DOWRY** n property brought
by a woman to her
husband at marriage
**DOWS** > DOW
**DOWSABEL** obsolete word
for > SWEETHEART
**DOWSABELS** > DOWSABEL
**DOWSE** same as > DOUSE
**DOWSED** > DOWSE
**DOWSER** > DOWSE
**DOWSERS** > DOWSE
**DOWSES** > DOWSE
**DOWSET** same as > DOUCET
**DOWSETS** > DOWSET
**DOWSING** > DOWSE
**DOWT** n cigarette butt
**DOWTS** > DOWT
**DOXASTIC** adj of or relating
to belief
**DOXIE** same as > DOXY
**DOXIES** > DOXY
**DOXOLOGY** n short hymn of
praise to God
**DOXY** n opinion or doctrine,
esp concerning religious
matters
**DOY** n beloved person: used
esp as an endearment
**DOYEN** n senior member
of a group, profession, or
society
**DOYENNE** > DOYEN
**DOYENNES** > DOYEN
**DOYENS** > DOYEN
**DOYLEY** same as > DOILY
**DOYLEYS** > DOYLEY
**DOYLIES** > DOYLY
**DOYLY** same as > DOILY
**DOYS** > DOY
**DOZE** vb sleep lightly or
briefly ▷ n short sleep
**DOZED** adj (of timber or
rubber) rotten or decayed
**DOZEN** vb stun
**DOZENED** > DOZEN
**DOZENING** > DOZEN
**DOZENS** > DOZEN
**DOZENTH** > DOZEN
**DOZENTHS** > DOZEN
**DOZER** > DOZE
**DOZERS** > DOZE

**DOZES** > DOZE
**DOZIER** > DOZY
**DOZIEST** > DOZY
**DOZILY** > DOZY
**DOZINESS** > DOZY
**DOZING** > DOZE
**DOZINGS** > DOZE
**DOZY** adj feeling sleepy
**DRAB** adj dull and dreary
▷ n light olive-brown
colour ▷ vb consort with
prostitutes
**DRABBED** > DRAB
**DRABBER** n one who
frequents low women
**DRABBERS** > DRABBER
**DRABBEST** > DRAB
**DRABBET** n yellowish-
brown fabric of coarse
linen
**DRABBETS** > DRABBET
**DRABBIER** > DRABBY
**DRABBIEST** > DRABBY
**DRABBING** > DRAB
**DRABBISH** adj promiscuous
**DRABBLE** vb make or
become wet or dirty
**DRABBLED** > DRABBLE
**DRABBLER** n part fixed to
bottom of sail
**DRABBLERS** > DRABBLER
**DRABBLES** > DRABBLE
**DRABBLING** > DRABBLE
**DRABBY** adj promiscuous
**DRABETTE** n type of rough
linen fabric
**DRABETTES** > DRABETTE
**DRABLER** same as > DRABBLE
**DRABLERS** > DRABLER
**DRABLY** > DRAB
**DRABNESS** > DRAB
**DRABS** > DRAB
**DRAC** same as > DRACK
**DRACAENA** n any tropical
plant of the genus
Dracaena: some species
are cultivated as house
plants for their decorative
foliage: family Agavaceae
**DRACAENAS** > DRACAENA
**DRACENA** same
as > DRACAENA
**DRACENAS** > DRACENA
**DRACHM** same as > DRAM
**DRACHMA** n former
monetary unit of Greece
**DRACHMAE** > DRACHMA
**DRACHMAI** > DRACHMA
**DRACHMAS** > DRACHMA
**DRACHMS** > DRACHM
**DRACK** adj (esp of a woman)
unattractive
**DRACO** as in draco lizard
flying lizard
**DRACONE** n large flexible
cylindrical container
towed by a ship, used for
transporting liquids
**DRACONES** > DRACONE
**DRACONIAN** adj severe,
harsh
**DRACONIC** same
as > DRACONIAN
**DRACONISM** > DRACONIAN

**DRACONTIC** same
as > DRACONIC
**DRAD** > DREAD
**DRAFF** n residue of husks
after fermentation of the
grain used in brewing,
used as a food for cattle
**DRAFFIER** > DRAFF
**DRAFFIEST** > DRAFF
**DRAFFISH** adj worthless
**DRAFFS** > DRAFF
**DRAFFY** > DRAFF
**DRAFT** same as > DRAUGHT
**DRAFTABLE** > DRAFT
**DRAFTED** > DRAFT
**DRAFTEE** n conscript
**DRAFTEES** > DRAFTEE
**DRAFTER** > DRAFT
**DRAFTERS** > DRAFT
**DRAFTIER** > DRAFTY
**DRAFTIEST** > DRAFTY
**DRAFTILY** > DRAFTY
**DRAFTING** > DRAFT
**DRAFTINGS** > DRAFT
**DRAFTS** > DRAFT
**DRAFTSMAN** same
as > DRAUGHTSMAN
**DRAFTSMEN** > DRAFTSMAN
**DRAFTY** same as > DRAUGHTY
**DRAG** vb pull with force,
esp along the ground ▷ n
person or thing that slows
up progress
**DRAGEE** n sweet made of a
nut, fruit, etc, coated with
a hard sugar icing
**DRAGEES** > DRAGEE
**DRAGGED** > DRAG
**DRAGGER** > DRAG
**DRAGGERS** > DRAG
**DRAGGIER** > DRAGGY
**DRAGGIEST** > DRAGGY
**DRAGGING** > DRAG
**DRAGGLE** vb make or
become wet or dirty by
trailing on the ground
**DRAGGLED** > DRAGGLE
**DRAGGLES** > DRAGGLE
**DRAGGLING** > DRAGGLE
**DRAGGY** adj slow or boring
**DRAGHOUND** n hound used
to follow an artificial trail
of scent in a drag hunt
**DRAGLINE** same
as > DRAGROPE
**DRAGLINES** > DRAGLINE
**DRAGNET** n net used to
scour the bottom of a
pond or river to search for
something
**DRAGNETS** > DRAGNET
**DRAGOMAN** n (in some
Middle Eastern countries)
professional interpreter
or guide
**DRAGOMANS** > DRAGOMAN
**DRAGOMEN** > DRAGOMAN
**DRAGON** n mythical fire-
breathing monster like a
huge lizard
**DRAGONESS** > DRAGON
**DRAGONET** n any small
spiny-finned fish of the
family Callionymidae,

having a flat head and a
slender tapering brightly
coloured body and living at
the bottom of shallow seas
**DRAGONETS** > DRAGONET
**DRAGONFLY** n brightly
coloured insect with a
long slender body and two
pairs of wings
**DRAGONISE** same
as > DRAGONIZE
**DRAGONISH** > DRAGON
**DRAGONISM** n vigilance
**DRAGONIZE** vb turn into
dragon
**DRAGONNE** adj dragonlike
**DRAGONS** > DRAGON
**DRAGOON** n heavily armed
cavalryman ▷ vb coerce,
force
**DRAGOONED** > DRAGOON
**DRAGOONS** > DRAGOON
**DRAGROPE** n rope used to
drag military equipment,
esp artillery
**DRAGROPES** > DRAGROPE
**DRAGS** > DRAG
**DRAGSMAN** n carriage driver
**DRAGSMEN** > DRAGSMAN
**DRAGSTER** n car specially
built or modified for drag
racing
**DRAGSTERS** > DRAGSTER
**DRAGSTRIP** n track for drag
racing
**DRAIL** n weighted hook
used in trolling ▷ vb fish
with a drail
**DRAILED** > DRAIL
**DRAILING** > DRAIL
**DRAILS** > DRAIL
**DRAIN** n pipe or channel
that carries off water or
sewage ▷ vb draw off or
remove liquid from
**DRAINABLE** > DRAIN
**DRAINAGE** n system of
drains
**DRAINAGES** > DRAINAGE
**DRAINED** > DRAIN
**DRAINER** n person or thing
that drains
**DRAINERS** > DRAINER
**DRAINING** > DRAIN
**DRAINPIPE** > DOWNPIPE
**DRAINS** > DRAIN
**DRAISENE** same
as > DRAISINE
**DRAISENES** > DRAISENE
**DRAISINE** n light rail
vehicle
**DRAISINES** > DRAISINE
**DRAKE** n male duck
**DRAKES** > DRAKE
**DRAM** n small amount of a
strong alcoholic drink, esp
whisky ▷ vb drink a dram
**DRAMA** n serious play for
theatre, television, or
radio
**DRAMADIES** > DRAMEDY
**DRAMADY** same
as > DRAMEDY
**DRAMAS** > DRAMA

**DRAMATIC** *adj* of or like drama
**DRAMATICS** *n* art of acting or producing plays
**DRAMATISE** *same as* > DRAMATIZE
**DRAMATIST** *n* person who writes plays
**DRAMATIZE** *vb* rewrite (a book) in the form of a play
**DRAMATURG** *n* literary adviser at a theatre
**DRAMEDIES** > DRAMEDY
**DRAMEDY** *n* television or film drama in which there are important elements of comedy
**DRAMMACH** *n* oatmeal mixed with cold water
**DRAMMACHS** > DRAMMACH
**DRAMMED** > DRAM
**DRAMMING** > DRAM
**DRAMMOCK** *same as* > DRAMMACH
**DRAMMOCKS** > DRAMMOCK
**DRAMS** > DRAM
**DRAMSHOP** *n* bar
**DRAMSHOPS** > DRAMSHOP
**DRANGWAY** *n* narrow lane
**DRANGWAYS** > DRANGWAY
**DRANK** > DRINK
**DRANT** *vb* drone
**DRANTED** > DRANT
**DRANTING** > DRANT
**DRANTS** > DRANT
**DRAP** *a Scot word for* > DROP
**DRAPABLE** > DRAPE
**DRAPE** *vb* cover with material, usu. in folds ▷ *n* piece of cloth hung at a window or opening as a screen
**DRAPEABLE** > DRAPE
**DRAPED** > DRAPE
**DRAPER** *n* person who sells fabrics and sewing materials
**DRAPERIED** > DRAPERY
**DRAPERIES** > DRAPERY
**DRAPERS** > DRAPER
**DRAPERY** *n* fabric or clothing arranged and draped
**DRAPES** *pl n* material hung at an opening or window to shut out light or to provide privacy
**DRAPET** *n* cloth
**DRAPETS** > DRAPET
**DRAPEY** *adj* hanging in loose folds
**DRAPIER** *n* draper
**DRAPIERS** > DRAPIER
**DRAPING** > DRAPE
**DRAPPED** > DRAP
**DRAPPIE** *n* little drop, esp a small amount of spirits
**DRAPPIES** > DRAPPIE
**DRAPPING** > DRAP
**DRAPPY** *n* drop (of liquid)
**DRAPS** > DRAP
**DRASTIC** *n* strong purgative ▷ *adj* strong and severe

**DRASTICS** > DRASTIC
**DRAT** *interj* exclamation of annoyance ▷ *vb* curse
**DRATCHELL** *n* low woman
**DRATS** > DRAT
**DRATTED** *adj* wretched
**DRATTING** > DRAT
**DRAUGHT** *vb* make preliminary plan ▷ *n* current of cold air, esp in an enclosed space ▷ *adj* (of an animal) used for pulling heavy loads
**DRAUGHTED** > DRAUGHT
**DRAUGHTER** > DRAUGHT
**DRAUGHTS** *n* game for two players using a draughtboard and 12 draughtsmen each
**DRAUGHTY** *adj* exposed to draughts of air
**DRAUNT** *same as* > DRANT
**DRAUNTED** > DRAUNT
**DRAUNTING** > DRAUNT
**DRAUNTS** > DRAUNT
**DRAVE** *archaic past of* > DRIVE
**DRAW** *vb* sketch (a figure, picture, etc) with a pencil or pen ▷ *n* raffle or lottery
**DRAWABLE** > DRAW
**DRAWBACK** *n* disadvantage ▷ *vb* move backwards
**DRAWBACKS** > DRAWBACK
**DRAWBAR** *n* strong metal bar on a tractor, locomotive, etc, bearing a hook or link and pin to attach a trailer, wagon, etc
**DRAWBARS** > DRAWBAR
**DRAWBORE** *n* hole bored through tenon
**DRAWBORES** > DRAWBORE
**DRAWDOWN** *n* decrease
**DRAWDOWNS** > DRAWDOWN
**DRAWEE** *n* person or organization on which a cheque or other order for payment is drawn
**DRAWEES** > DRAWEE
**DRAWER** *n* sliding box-shaped part of a piece of furniture, used for storage
**DRAWERFUL** *n* amount contained in drawer
**DRAWERS** *pl n* undergarment worn on the lower part of the body
**DRAWING** > DRAW
**DRAWINGS** > DRAW
**DRAWKNIFE** *n* woodcutting tool with two handles at right angles to the blade, used to shave wood
**DRAWL** *vb* speak slowly, with long vowel sounds ▷ *n* drawling manner of speech
**DRAWLED** > DRAWL
**DRAWLER** > DRAWL
**DRAWLERS** > DRAWL
**DRAWLIER** > DRAWL
**DRAWLIEST** > DRAWL
**DRAWLING** > DRAWL

**DRAWLS** > DRAWL
**DRAWLY** > DRAWL
**DRAWN** > DRAW
**DRAWNWORK** *n* type of ornamental needlework
**DRAWPLATE** *n* plate used to reduce the diameter of wire by drawing it through conical holes
**DRAWS** > DRAW
**DRAWSHAVE** *same as* > DRAWKNIFE
**DRAWTUBE** *n* tube, such as one of the component tubes of a telescope, fitting coaxially within another tube through which it can slide
**DRAWTUBES** > DRAWTUBE
**DRAY** *vb* pull using cart ▷ *n* low cart used for carrying heavy loads
**DRAYAGE** *n* act of transporting something a short distance by lorry or other vehicle
**DRAYAGES** > DRAYAGE
**DRAYED** > DRAY
**DRAYHORSE** *n* large powerful horse used for drawing a dray
**DRAYING** > DRAY
**DRAYMAN** *n* driver of a dray
**DRAYMEN** > DRAYMAN
**DRAYS** > DRAY
**DRAZEL** *n* low woman
**DRAZELS** > DRAZEL
**DREAD** *vb* anticipate with apprehension or fear ▷ *n* great fear ▷ *adj* awesome
**DREADED** > DREAD
**DREADER** > DREAD
**DREADERS** > DREAD
**DREADFUL** *n* cheap, often lurid or sensational book or magazine ▷ *adj* very disagreeable or shocking
**DREADFULS** > DREADFUL
**DREADING** > DREAD
**DREADLESS** > DREAD
**DREADLOCK** *n* Rastafarian hair braid
**DREADLY** > DREAD
**DREADS** > DREAD
**DREAM** *n* imagined series of events experienced in the mind while asleep ▷ *vb* see imaginary pictures in the mind while asleep ▷ *adj* ideal
**DREAMBOAT** *n* exceptionally attractive person or thing, esp a person of the opposite sex
**DREAMED** > DREAM
**DREAMER** *n* person who dreams habitually
**DREAMERS** > DREAMER
**DREAMERY** *n* dream world
**DREAMFUL** > DREAM
**DREAMHOLE** *n* light-admitting hole in a tower
**DREAMIER** > DREAMY
**DREAMIEST** > DREAMY

**DREAMILY** > DREAMY
**DREAMING** > DREAM
**DREAMINGS** > DREAM
**DREAMLAND** *n* ideal land existing in dreams or in the imagination
**DREAMLESS** > DREAM
**DREAMLIKE** > DREAM
**DREAMS** > DREAM
**DREAMT** > DREAM
**DREAMTIME** *n* time when the world was new and fresh
**DREAMY** *adj* vague or impractical
**DREAR** *same as* > DREARY
**DREARE** *obsolete form of* > DREAR
**DREARER** > DREAR
**DREARES** > DREARE
**DREAREST** > DREAR
**DREARIER** > DREARY
**DREARIES** > DREARY
**DREARIEST** > DREARY
**DREARILY** > DREARY
**DREARING** *n* sorrow
**DREARINGS** > DREARING
**DREARS** > DREAR
**DREARY** *adj* dull, boring ▷ *n* a dreary thing or person
**DRECK** *n* rubbish
**DRECKIER** > DRECK
**DRECKIEST** > DRECK
**DRECKS** > DRECK
**DRECKSILL** *n* doorstep
**DRECKY** > DRECK
**DREDGE** *vb* clear or search (a river bed or harbour) by removing silt or mud ▷ *n* machine used to scoop or suck up silt or mud from a river bed or harbour
**DREDGED** > DREDGE
**DREDGER** *same as* > DREDGE
**DREDGERS** > DREDGER
**DREDGES** > DREDGE
**DREDGING** > DREDGE
**DREDGINGS** > DREDGE
**DREE** *vb* endure
**DREED** > DREE
**DREEING** > DREE
**DREES** > DREE
**DREG** *n* small quantity
**DREGGIER** > DREGGY
**DREGGIEST** > DREGGY
**DREGGISH** *adj* foul
**DREGGY** *adj* like or full of dregs
**DREGS** *pl n* solid particles that settle at the bottom of some liquids
**DREICH** *adj* dreary
**DREICHER** > DREICH
**DREICHEST** > DREICH
**DREIDEL** *n* spinning top
**DREIDELS** > DREIDEL
**DREIDL** *same as* > DREIDEL
**DREIDLS** > DREIDL
**DREIGH** *same as* > DREICH
**DREK** *same as* > DRECK
**DREKS** > DREK
**DRENCH** *vb* make completely wet ▷ *n* act or an instance of drenching

DRENCHED > DRENCH
DRENCHER > DRENCH
DRENCHERS > DRENCH
DRENCHES > DRENCH
DRENCHING > DRENCH
DRENT > DRENCH
DREPANID *n* any moth of the superfamily Drepanoidae (family Drepanidae): it comprises the hook-tip moths
DREPANIDS > DREPANID
DREPANIUM *n* type of flower cluster
DRERE *obsolete form of* > DREAR
DRERES > DRERE
DRERIHEAD *n* obsolete word for dreary
DRESS *n* one-piece garment for a woman or girl, consisting of a skirt and bodice and sometimes sleeves ▷ *vb* put clothes on ▷ *adj* suitable for a formal occasion
DRESSAGE *n* training of a horse to perform manoeuvres in response to the rider's body signals
DRESSAGES > DRESSAGE
DRESSED > DRESS
DRESSER *n* piece of furniture with shelves and with cupboards, for storing or displaying dishes
DRESSERS > DRESSER
DRESSES > DRESS
DRESSIER > DRESSY
DRESSIEST > DRESSY
DRESSILY > DRESSY
DRESSING *n* sauce for salad
DRESSINGS *pl n* dressed stonework, mouldings, and carved ornaments used to form quoins, keystones, sills, and similar features
DRESSMADE > DRESSMAKE
DRESSMAKE *vb* make clothes
DRESSY *adj* (of clothes) elegant
DREST > DRESS
DREVILL *n* offensive person
DREVILLS > DREVILL
DREW > DRAW
DREY *n* squirrel's nest
DREYS > DREY
DRIB *vb* flow in drops
DRIBBED > DRIB
DRIBBER > DRIB
DRIBBERS > DRIB
DRIBBING > DRIB
DRIBBLE *vb* (allow to) flow in drops ▷ *n* small quantity of liquid falling in drops
DRIBBLED > DRIBBLE
DRIBBLER > DRIBBLE
DRIBBLERS > DRIBBLE
DRIBBLES > DRIBBLE

DRIBBLET *same as* > DRIBLET
DRIBBLETS > DRIBBLET
DRIBBLIER > DRIBBLE
DRIBBLING > DRIBBLE
DRIBBLY > DRIBBLE
DRIBLET *n* small amount
DRIBLETS > DRIBLET
DRIBS > DRIB
DRICE *n* pellets of frozen carbon dioxide
DRICES > DRICE
DRICKSIE *same as* > DRUXY
DRICKSIER > DRICKSIE
DRIED > DRY
DRIEGH *adj* tedious
DRIER > DRY
DRIERS > DRY
DRIES > DRY
DRIEST > DRY
DRIFT *vb* be carried along by currents of air or water ▷ *n* something piled up by the wind or current, such as a snowdrift
DRIFTAGE *n* act of drifting
DRIFTAGES > DRIFTAGE
DRIFTED > DRIFT
DRIFTER *n* person who moves aimlessly from place to place or job to job
DRIFTERS > DRIFTER
DRIFTIER > DRIFT
DRIFTIEST > DRIFT
DRIFTING > DRIFT
DRIFTLESS > DRIFT
DRIFTPIN *same as* > DRIFT
DRIFTPINS > DRIFTPIN
DRIFTS > DRIFT
DRIFTWOOD *n* wood floating on or washed ashore by the sea
DRIFTY > DRIFT
DRILL *n* tool or machine for boring holes ▷ *vb* bore a hole in (something) with or as if with a drill
DRILLABLE > DRILL
DRILLED > DRILL
DRILLER > DRILL
DRILLERS > DRILL
DRILLING > DRILL
DRILLINGS > DRILL
DRILLS > DRILL
DRILLSHIP *n* floating drilling platform
DRILY *adv* in a dry manner
DRINK *vb* swallow (a liquid) ▷ *n* (portion of) a liquid suitable for drinking
DRINKABLE > DRINK
DRINKABLY > DRINK
DRINKER *n* person who drinks, esp a person who drinks alcohol habitually
DRINKERS > DRINKER
DRINKING > DRINK
DRINKINGS > DRINK
DRINKS > DRINK
DRIP *vb* (let) fall in drops ▷ *n* falling of drops of liquid
DRIPLESS > DRIP
DRIPPED > DRIP

DRIPPER > DRIP
DRIPPERS > DRIP
DRIPPIER > DRIPPY
DRIPPIEST > DRIPPY
DRIPPILY > DRIPPY
DRIPPING > DRIP
DRIPPINGS > DRIP
DRIPPY *adj* mawkish, insipid, or inane
DRIPS > DRIP
DRIPSTONE *n* form of calcium carbonate existing in stalactites or stalagmites
DRIPT > DRIP
DRISHEEN *n* pudding made of sheep's intestines filled with meal and sheep's blood
DRISHEENS > DRISHEEN
DRIVABLE > DRIVE
DRIVE *vb* guide the movement of (a vehicle) ▷ *n* journey by car, van, etc
DRIVEABLE > DRIVE
DRIVEL *n* foolish talk ▷ *vb* speak foolishly
DRIVELED > DRIVEL
DRIVELER > DRIVEL
DRIVELERS > DRIVEL
DRIVELINE *n* transmission line from engine to wheels of vehicle
DRIVELING > DRIVEL
DRIVELLED > DRIVEL
DRIVELLER > DRIVEL
DRIVELS > DRIVEL
DRIVEN > DRIVE
DRIVER *n* person who drives a vehicle
DRIVERS > DRIVER
DRIVES > DRIVE
DRIVEWAY *n* path for vehicles connecting a building to a public road
DRIVEWAYS > DRIVEWAY
DRIVING > DRIVE
DRIVINGLY > DRIVE
DRIVINGS > DRIVE
DRIZZLE *n* very light rain ▷ *vb* rain lightly
DRIZZLED > DRIZZLE
DRIZZLES > DRIZZLE
DRIZZLIER > DRIZZLE
DRIZZLING > DRIZZLE
DRIZZLY > DRIZZLE
DROGER *n* W Indian boat
DROGERS > DROGER
DROGHER *same as* > DROGER
DROGHERS > DROGHER
DROGUE *n* any funnel-like device, esp one of canvas, used as a sea anchor
DROGUES > DROGUE
DROGUET *n* woollen fabric
DROGUETS > DROGUET
DROICH *n* dwarf
DROICHIER > DROICHY
DROICHS > DROICH
DROICHY *adj* dwarfish
DROID *same as* > ANDROID
DROIDS > DROID
DROIL *vb* carry out boring menial work

DROILED > DROIL
DROILING > DROIL
DROILS > DROIL
DROIT *n* legal or moral right or claim
DROITS > DROIT
DROLE *adj* amusing ▷ *n* scoundrel
DROLER > DROLE
DROLES > DROLE
DROLEST > DROLE
DROLL *vb* speak wittily ▷ *adj* quaintly amusing
DROLLED > DROLL
DROLLER > DROLL
DROLLERY *n* humour
DROLLEST > DROLL
DROLLING > DROLL
DROLLINGS > DROLL
DROLLISH *adj* somewhat droll
DROLLNESS > DROLL
DROLLS > DROLL
DROLLY > DROLL
DROME *n* informal word for > AERODROME
DROMEDARE *obsolete form of* > DROMEDARY
DROMEDARY *n* camel with a single hump
DROMES > DROME
DROMIC *adj* relating to running track
DROMICAL *same as* > DROMIC
DROMOI > DROMOS
DROMON *same as* > DROMOND
DROMOND *n* large swift sailing vessel of the 12th to 15th centuries
DROMONDS > DROMOND
DROMONS > DROMON
DROMOS *n* Greek passageway
DRONE *n* male bee ▷ *vb* make a monotonous low dull sound
DRONED > DRONE
DRONER > DRONE
DRONERS > DRONE
DRONES > DRONE
DRONGO *n* tropical songbird with a glossy black plumage, a forked tail, and a stout bill
DRONGOES > DRONGO
DRONGOS > DRONGO
DRONIER > DRONY
DRONIEST > DRONY
DRONING > DRONE
DRONINGLY > DRONE
DRONISH > DRONE
DRONISHLY > DRONE
DRONKLAP *n* South African word for a drunkard
DRONKLAPS > DRONKLAP
DRONY *adj* monotonous
DROOB *n* pathetic person
DROOBS > DROOB
DROOG *n* ruffian
DROOGISH > DROOG
DROOGS > DROOG
DROOK *same as* > DROUK
DROOKED > DROOK
DROOKING > DROOK

DROOKINGS > DROOK
DROOKIT *same as* > DROUKIT
DROOKS > DROOK
DROOL *vb* show excessive enthusiasm (for)
DROOLED > DROOL
DROOLIER > DROOLY
DROOLIEST > DROOLY
DROOLING > DROOL
DROOLS > DROOL
DROOLY *adj* tending to drool
DROOME *obsolete form of* > DRUM
DROOMES > DRUM
DROOP *vb* hang downwards loosely ▷ *n* act or state of drooping
DROOPED > DROOP
DROOPIER > DROOPY
DROOPIEST > DROOPY
DROOPILY > DROOPY
DROOPING > DROOP
DROOPS > DROOP
DROOPY *adj* hanging or sagging downwards
DROP *vb* (allow to) fall vertically ▷ *n* small quantity of liquid forming a round shape
DROPCLOTH *n* cloth spread on floor to catch drips while painting
DROPFLIES > DROPFLY
DROPFLY *n* (angling) artificial fly
DROPFORGE *vb* forge metal between two dies
DROPHEAD *as in* *drophead coupe* two-door car with a folding roof and sloping back
DROPHEADS > DROPHEAD
DROPKICK *n* (in certain ball games) a kick in which the ball is first dropped then kicked as it bounces from the ground
DROPKICKS > DROPKICK
DROPLET *n* very small drop of liquid
DROPLETS > DROPLET
DROPLIGHT *n* electric light that may be raised or lowered by means of a pulley or other mechanism
DROPOUT *n* person who rejects conventional society ▷ *vb* abandon or withdraw (from an institution or group)
DROPOUTS > DROPOUT
DROPPABLE > DROP
DROPPED > DROP
DROPPER *n* small tube with a rubber part at one end for drawing up and dispensing drops of liquid
DROPPERS > DROPPER
DROPPING > DROP
DROPPINGS *pl n* faeces of certain animals, such as rabbits or birds
DROPPLE *n* trickle

DROPPLES > DROPPLE
DROPS > DROP
DROPSHOT *n* (in tennis) shot in which a softly returned ball just clears the net before falling abruptly
DROPSHOTS > DROPSHOT
DROPSICAL > DROPSY
DROPSIED > DROPSY
DROPSIES > DROPSY
DROPSONDE *n* radiosonde dropped by parachute
DROPSTONE *n* calcium carbonate in stalactites
DROPSY *n* illness in which watery fluid collects in the body
DROPT > DROP
DROPWISE *adv* in form of a drop
DROPWORT *See also* > MEADOWSWEET
DROPWORTS > DROPWORT
DROSERA *n* insectivorous plant
DROSERAS > DROSERA
DROSHKIES > DROSHKY
DROSHKY *n* open four-wheeled horse-drawn passenger carriage, formerly used in Russia
DROSKIES > DROSKY
DROSKY *same as* > DROSHKY
DROSS *n* scum formed on the surfaces of molten metals
DROSSES > DROSS
DROSSIER > DROSS
DROSSIEST > DROSS
DROSSY > DROSS
DROSTDIES > DROSTDY
DROSTDY *n* office of landdrost
DROSTDYS > DROSTDY
DROUGHT *n* prolonged shortage of rainfall
DROUGHTS > DROUGHT
DROUGHTY > DROUGHT
DROUK *vb* drench
DROUKED > DROUK
DROUKING > DROUK
DROUKINGS > DROUK
DROUKIT *adj* drenched
DROUKS > DROUK
DROUTH *same as* > DROUGHT
DROUTHIER > DROUTHY
DROUTHS > DROUTH
DROUTHY *adj* thirsty or dry
DROVE > DRIVE
DROVED > DRIVE
DROVER *n* person who drives sheep or cattle
DROVERS > DROVER
DROVES > DRIVE
DROVING > DRIVE
DROVINGS > DRIVE
DROW *n* sea fog
DROWN *vb* die or kill by immersion in liquid
DROWND *dialect form of* > DROWN
DROWNDED > DROWND
DROWNDING > DROWND

DROWNDS > DROWND
DROWNED > DROWN
DROWNER > DROWN
DROWNERS > DROWN
DROWNING > DROWN
DROWNINGS > DROWN
DROWNS > DROWN
DROWS > DROW
DROWSE *vb* be sleepy, dull, or sluggish ▷ *n* state of being drowsy
DROWSED > DROWSE
DROWSES > DROWSE
DROWSIER > DROWSY
DROWSIEST > DROWSY
DROWSIHED *adj* old form of drowsy
DROWSILY > DROWSY
DROWSING > DROWSE
DROWSY *adj* feeling sleepy
DRUB *vb* beat as with a stick ▷ *n* blow, as from a stick
DRUBBED > DRUB
DRUBBER > DRUB
DRUBBERS > DRUB
DRUBBING > DRUB
DRUBBINGS > DRUB
DRUBS > DRUB
DRUCKEN *adj* drunken
DRUDGE *n* person who works hard at uninteresting tasks ▷ *vb* work at such tasks
DRUDGED > DRUDGE
DRUDGER > DRUDGE
DRUDGERS > DRUDGE
DRUDGERY *n* uninteresting work that must be done
DRUDGES > DRUDGE
DRUDGING > DRUDGE
DRUDGISM > DRUDGE
DRUDGISMS > DRUDGE
DRUG *n* substance used in the treatment or prevention of disease ▷ *vb* give a drug to (a person or animal) to cause sleepiness or unconsciousness
DRUGGED > DRUG
DRUGGER *n* druggist
DRUGGERS > DRUGGER
DRUGGET *n* coarse fabric used as a protective floor-covering, etc
DRUGGETS > DRUGGET
DRUGGIE *n* drug addict
DRUGGIER > DRUG
DRUGGIES > DRUGGIE
DRUGGIEST > DRUG
DRUGGING > DRUG
DRUGGIST *n* pharmacist
DRUGGISTS > DRUGGIST
DRUGGY > DRUG
DRUGLORD *n* criminal who controls the distribution and sale of large quantities of illegal drugs
DRUGLORDS > DRUGLORD
DRUGMAKER *n* manufacturer of drugs
DRUGS > DRUG
DRUGSTORE *n* pharmacy where a wide range of

goods are available
DRUID *n* member of an ancient order of priests in Gaul, Britain, and Ireland in the pre-Christian era
DRUIDESS > DRUID
DRUIDIC > DRUID
DRUIDICAL > DRUID
DRUIDISM > DRUID
DRUIDISMS > DRUID
DRUIDRIES > DRUID
DRUIDRY > DRUID
DRUIDS > DRUID
DRUM *n* percussion instrument sounded by striking a membrane stretched across the opening of a hollow cylinder ▷ *vb* play (music) on a drum
DRUMBEAT *n* sound made by beating a drum
DRUMBEATS > DRUMBEAT
DRUMBLE *vb* be inactive
DRUMBLED > DRUMBLE
DRUMBLES > DRUMBLE
DRUMBLING > DRUMBLE
DRUMFIRE *n* heavy, rapid, and continuous gunfire, the sound of which resembles rapid drumbeats
DRUMFIRES > DRUMFIRE
DRUMFISH *n* one of several types of fish that make a drumming sound
DRUMHEAD *n* part of a drum that is struck
DRUMHEADS > DRUMHEAD
DRUMLIER > DRUMLY
DRUMLIEST > DRUMLY
DRUMLIKE > DRUM
DRUMLIN *n* streamlined mound of glacial drift, rounded or elongated in the direction of the original flow of ice
DRUMLINS > DRUMLIN
DRUMLY *adj* dismal; dreary
DRUMMED > DRUM
DRUMMER *n* person who plays a drum or drums
DRUMMERS > DRUMMER
DRUMMIES > DRUMMY
DRUMMING > DRUM
DRUMMOCK *same as* > DRAMMOCK
DRUMMOCKS > DRUMMOCK
DRUMMY *n* (in South Africa) drum majorette
DRUMROLL *n* continued repeated sound of drum
DRUMROLLS > DRUMROLL
DRUMS > DRUM
DRUMSTICK *n* stick used for playing a drum
DRUNK > DRINK
DRUNKARD *n* person who frequently gets drunk
DRUNKARDS > DRUNKARD
DRUNKEN *adj* drunk or frequently drunk
DRUNKENLY > DRUNKEN
DRUNKER > DRINK

**DRUNKEST** > DRINK
**DRUNKS** > DRINK
**DRUPE** n fleshy fruit with a stone, such as the peach or cherry
**DRUPEL** same as > DRUPELET
**DRUPELET** n small drupe, usually one of a number forming a compound fruit
**DRUPELETS** > DRUPELET
**DRUPELS** > DRUPEL
**DRUPES** > DRUPE
**DRUSE** n aggregate of small crystals within a cavity in, esp those lining a cavity in a rock or mineral
**DRUSES** > DRUSE
**DRUSIER** > DRUSY
**DRUSIEST** > DRUSY
**DRUSY** adj made of tiny crystals
**DRUTHERS** n preference
**DRUXIER** > DRUXY
**DRUXIEST** > DRUXY
**DRUXY** adj (of wood) having decayed white spots
**DRY** adj lacking moisture ▷ vb make or become dry
**DRYABLE** > DRY
**DRYAD** n wood nymph
**DRYADES** > DRYAD
**DRYADIC** > DRYAD
**DRYADS** > DRYAD
**DRYASDUST** adj boringly bookish
**DRYBEAT** vb beat severely
**DRYBEATEN** > DRYBEAT
**DRYBEATS** > DRYBEAT
**DRYER** > DRY
**DRYERS** > DRY
**DRYEST** > DRY
**DRYING** > DRY
**DRYINGS** > DRY
**DRYISH** adj fairly dry
**DRYLAND** adj of an arid area
**DRYLOT** n livestock enclosure
**DRYLOTS** > DRYLOT
**DRYLY** same as > DRILY
**DRYMOUTH** n condition of insufficient saliva
**DRYMOUTHS** > DRYMOUTH
**DRYNESS** > DRY
**DRYNESSES** > DRY
**DRYPOINT** n copper engraving technique using a hard steel needle
**DRYPOINTS** > DRYPOINT
**DRYS** > DRY
**DRYSALTER** n dealer in certain chemical products, such as dyestuffs and gums, and in dried, tinned, or salted foods and edible oils
**DRYSTONE** adj (of a wall) made without mortar
**DRYWALL** n wall built without mortar ▷ vb build a wall without mortar
**DRYWALLED** > DRYWALL
**DRYWALLS** > DRYWALL
**DRYWELL** n type of sewage disposal system

**DRYWELLS** > DRYWELL
**DSO** same as > ZHO
**DSOBO** same as > ZOBO
**DSOBOS** > DSOBO
**DSOMO** same as > ZHOMO
**DSOMOS** > DSOMO
**DSOS** > DSO
**DUAD** a rare word for > PAIR
**DUADS** > DUAD
**DUAL** adj having two parts, functions, or aspects ▷ n dual number ▷ vb make (a road) into a dual carriageway
**DUALIN** n explosive substance
**DUALINS** > DUALIN
**DUALISE** same as > DUALIZE
**DUALISED** > DUALISE
**DUALISES** > DUALISE
**DUALISING** > DUALISE
**DUALISM** n state of having or being believed to have two distinct parts or aspects
**DUALISMS** > DUALISM
**DUALIST** > DUALISM
**DUALISTIC** > DUALISM
**DUALISTS** > DUALISM
**DUALITIES** > DUALITY
**DUALITY** n state or quality of being two or in two parts
**DUALIZE** vb cause to have two parts
**DUALIZED** > DUALIZE
**DUALIZES** > DUALIZE
**DUALIZING** > DUALIZE
**DUALLED** > DUAL
**DUALLING** > DUAL
**DUALLY** > DUAL
**DUALS** > DUAL
**DUAN** n poem
**DUANS** > DUAN
**DUAR** n Arab camp
**DUARCHIES** > DUARCHY
**DUARCHY** same as > DIARCHY
**DUARS** > DUAR
**DUATHLON** n athletic contest in which each athlete competes in running and cycling events
**DUATHLONS** > DUATHLON
**DUB** vb give (a person or place) a name or nickname ▷ n style of reggae record production involving exaggeration of instrumental parts, echo, etc
**DUBBED** > DUB
**DUBBER** > DUB
**DUBBERS** > DUB
**DUBBIN** n thick grease applied to leather to soften and waterproof it
**DUBBING** > DUB
**DUBBINGS** > DUB
**DUBBINS** > DUBBIN
**DUBBO** adj stupid ▷ n stupid person
**DUBBOS** > DUBBO
**DUBIETIES** > DUBIETY
**DUBIETY** n state of being

doubtful
**DUBIOSITY** same as > DUBIETY
**DUBIOUS** adj feeling or causing doubt
**DUBIOUSLY** > DUBIOUS
**DUBITABLE** adj open to doubt
**DUBITABLY** > DUBITABLE
**DUBITANCY** > DUBITATE
**DUBITATE** vb doubt
**DUBITATED** > DUBITATE
**DUBITATES** > DUBITATE
**DUBNIUM** n element produced in minute quantities by bombarding plutonium with high-energy neon ions
**DUBNIUMS** > DUBNIUM
**DUBONNET** n dark purplish-red colour
**DUBONNETS** > DUBONNET
**DUBS** > DUB
**DUCAL** adj of a duke
**DUCALLY** > DUCAL
**DUCAT** n former European gold or silver coin
**DUCATOON** n former silver coin
**DUCATOONS** > DUCATOON
**DUCATS** > DUCAT
**DUCDAME** interj Shakespearean nonsense word
**DUCE** n leader
**DUCES** > DUCE
**DUCHESS** n woman who holds the rank of duke ▷ vb overwhelm with flattering attention
**DUCHESSE** n type of satin
**DUCHESSED** > DUCHESS
**DUCHESSES** > DUCHESS
**DUCHIES** > DUCHY
**DUCHY** n territory of a duke or duchess
**DUCI** > DUCE
**DUCK** n water bird with short legs, webbed feet, and a broad blunt bill ▷ vb move (the head or body) quickly downwards, to avoid being seen or to dodge a blow
**DUCKBILL** n duckbilled platypus
**DUCKBILLS** > DUCKBILL
**DUCKBOARD** n board or boards laid so as to form a floor or path over wet or muddy ground
**DUCKED** > DUCK
**DUCKER** > DUCK
**DUCKERS** > DUCK
**DUCKFOOT** as in duckfoot quote chevron-shaped quotation mark
**DUCKIE** same as > DUCKY
**DUCKIER** > DUCKY
**DUCKIES** > DUCKY
**DUCKIEST** > DUCKY
**DUCKING** > DUCK
**DUCKINGS** > DUCK
**DUCKLING** n baby duck

**DUCKLINGS** > DUCKLING
**DUCKMOLE** another word for > DUCKBILL
**DUCKMOLES** > DUCKMOLE
**DUCKPIN** n short bowling pin
**DUCKPINS** > DUCKPIN
**DUCKS** > DUCK
**DUCKSHOVE** vb evade responsibility
**DUCKTAIL** n Teddy boy's hairstyle
**DUCKTAILS** > DUCKTAIL
**DUCKWALK** vb walk in a squatting posture
**DUCKWALKS** > DUCKWALK
**DUCKWEED** n any of various small stemless aquatic plants of the family Lemnaceae, esp any of the genus Lemna, that have rounded leaves and occur floating on still water in temperate regions
**DUCKWEEDS** > DUCKWEED
**DUCKY** n darling or dear: used as a term of endearment among women, but now often used in imitation of the supposed usage of homosexual men ▷ adj delightful
**DUCT** vb convey via a duct ▷ n tube, pipe, or channel through which liquid or gas is conveyed
**DUCTAL** > DUCT
**DUCTED** > DUCT
**DUCTILE** adj (of a metal) able to be shaped into sheets or wires
**DUCTILELY** > DUCTILE
**DUCTILITY** > DUCTILE
**DUCTING** > DUCT
**DUCTINGS** > DUCT
**DUCTLESS** > DUCT
**DUCTS** > DUCT
**DUCTULE** n small duct
**DUCTULES** > DUCTULE
**DUCTWORK** n system of ducts
**DUCTWORKS** > DUCTWORK
**DUD** n ineffectual person or thing ▷ adj bad or useless
**DUDDER** n door-to-door salesman
**DUDDERIES** > DUDDERY
**DUDDERS** > DUDDER
**DUDDERY** n place where old clothes are sold
**DUDDIE** adj ragged
**DUDDIER** > DUDDIE
**DUDDIEST** > DUDDIE
**DUDDY** same as > DUDDIE
**DUDE** vb dress fashionably ▷ n man
**DUDED** > DUDE
**DUDEEN** n clay pipe with a short stem
**DUDEENS** > DUDEEN
**DUDES** > DUDE
**DUDGEON** n anger or resentment

**DUDGEONS** > DUDGEON
**DUDHEEN** *n* type of pipe
**DUDHEENS** > DUDHEEN
**DUDING** > DUDE
**DUDISH** > DUDE
**DUDISHLY** > DUDE
**DUDISM** *n* being a dude
**DUDISMS** > DUDISM
**DUDS** > DUD
**DUE** *vb* supply with ▷ *adj* expected or scheduled to be present or arrive ▷ *n* something that is owed or required ▷ *adv* directly or exactly
**DUECENTO** *n* thirteenth century (in Italian art)
**DUECENTOS** > DUECENTO
**DUED** > DUE
**DUEFUL** *adj* proper
**DUEL** *n* formal fight with deadly weapons between two people, to settle a quarrel ▷ *vb* fight in a duel
**DUELED** > DUEL
**DUELER** > DUEL
**DUELERS** > DUEL
**DUELING** > DUEL
**DUELIST** > DUEL
**DUELISTS** > DUEL
**DUELLED** > DUEL
**DUELLER** > DUEL
**DUELLERS** > DUEL
**DUELLI** > DUELLO
**DUELLING** > DUEL
**DUELLINGS** > DUEL
**DUELLIST** > DUEL
**DUELLISTS** > DUEL
**DUELLO** *n* art of duelling
**DUELLOS** > DUELLO
**DUELS** > DUEL
**DUELSOME** *adj* given to duelling
**DUENDE** *n* Spanish goblin
**DUENDES** > DUENDE
**DUENESS** > DUE
**DUENESSES** > DUE
**DUENNA** *n* (esp in Spain) elderly woman acting as chaperone to a young woman
**DUENNAS** > DUENNA
**DUES** *pl n* membership fees paid to a club or organization
**DUET** *n* piece of music for two performers ▷ *vb* perform a duet
**DUETED** > DUET
**DUETING** > DUET
**DUETS** > DUET
**DUETT** *same as* > DUET
**DUETTED** > DUET
**DUETTI** > DUETTO
**DUETTING** > DUET
**DUETTINO** *n* simple duet
**DUETTINOS** > DUETTINO
**DUETTIST** > DUET
**DUETTISTS** > DUET
**DUETTO** *same as* > DUET
**DUETTOS** > DUETTO
**DUETTS** > DUETT
**DUFF** *adj* broken or useless ▷ *vb* change the

appearance of or give a false appearance to (old or stolen goods) ▷ *n* rump or buttocks
**DUFFED** > DUFF
**DUFFEL** *n* heavy woollen cloth with a thick nap
**DUFFELS** > DUFFEL
**DUFFER** *n* dull or incompetent person
**DUFFERDOM** *n* condition of being a duffer
**DUFFERISM** *same as* > DUFFERDOM
**DUFFERS** > DUFFER
**DUFFEST** > DUFF
**DUFFING** > DUFF
**DUFFINGS** > DUFF
**DUFFLE** *same as* > DUFFEL
**DUFFLES** > DUFFLE
**DUFFS** > DUFF
**DUFUS** *same as* > DOOFUS
**DUFUSES** > DUFUS
**DUG** > DIG
**DUGITE** *n* medium-sized Australian venomous snake
**DUGITES** > DUGITE
**DUGONG** *n* whalelike mammal of tropical waters
**DUGONGS** > DUGONG
**DUGOUT** *n* (at a sports ground) covered bench where managers and substitutes sit
**DUGOUTS** > DUGOUT
**DUGS** > DIG
**DUH** *interj* ironic response to a question or statement, implying that the speaker is stupid or that the reply is obvious
**DUHKHA** *same as* > DUKKHA
**DUHKHAS** > DUHKHA
**DUI** > DUO
**DUIKER** *n* small African antelope
**DUIKERBOK** *same as* > DUIKER
**DUIKERS** > DUIKER
**DUING** > DUE
**DUIT** *n* former Dutch coin
**DUITS** > DUIT
**DUKA** *n* shop
**DUKAS** > DUKA
**DUKE** *vb* fight with fists ▷ *n* nobleman of the highest rank
**DUKED** > DUKE
**DUKEDOM** *n* title, rank, or position of a duke
**DUKEDOMS** > DUKEDOM
**DUKELING** *n* low-ranking duke
**DUKELINGS** > DUKELING
**DUKERIES** > DUKERY
**DUKERY** *n* duke's domain
**DUKES** *pl n* fists
**DUKESHIP** > DUKE
**DUKESHIPS** > DUKE
**DUKING** > DUKE
**DUKKA** *n* mix of ground roast nuts and spices,

originating in Egypt, and used for sprinkling on meat or as a dip
**DUKKAH** *same as* > DUKKA
**DUKKAHS** > DUKKAH
**DUKKAS** > DUKKA
**DUKKHA** *n* (in Theravada Buddhism) the belief that all things are suffering, due to the desire to seek permanence or recognise the self when neither exist: one of the three basic characteristics of existence
**DUKKHAS** > DUKKHA
**DULCAMARA** *n* orange-fruited vine
**DULCET** *adj* (of a sound) soothing or pleasant ▷ *n* soft organ stop
**DULCETLY** > DULCET
**DULCETS** > DULCET
**DULCIAN** *n* precursor to the bassoon
**DULCIANA** *n* sweet-toned organ stop, controlling metal pipes of narrow scale
**DULCIANAS** > DULCIANA
**DULCIANS** > DULCIAN
**DULCIFIED** > DULCIFY
**DULCIFIES** > DULCIFY
**DULCIFY** *vb* make pleasant or agreeable
**DULCIMER** *n* tuned percussion instrument consisting of a set of strings stretched over a sounding board and struck with hammers
**DULCIMERS** > DULCIMER
**DULCIMORE** *former name for* > DULCIMER
**DULCINEA** *n* a man's sweetheart
**DULCINEAS** > DULCINEA
**DULCITE** *n* sweet substance
**DULCITES** > DULCITE
**DULCITOL** *another word for* > DULCITE
**DULCITOLS** > DULCITOL
**DULCITUDE** *n* sweetness
**DULCOSE** *another word for* > DULCITE
**DULCOSES** > DULCOSE
**DULE** *n* suffering; misery
**DULES** > DULE
**DULIA** *n* veneration accorded to saints in the Roman Catholic and Eastern Churches, as contrasted with hyperdulia and latria
**DULIAS** > DULIA
**DULL** *adj* not interesting ▷ *vb* make or become dull
**DULLARD** *n* dull or stupid person
**DULLARDS** > DULLARD
**DULLED** > DULL
**DULLER** > DULL
**DULLEST** > DULL

**DULLIER** > DULL
**DULLIEST** > DULL
**DULLING** > DULL
**DULLISH** > DULL
**DULLISHLY** > DULL
**DULLNESS** > DULL
**DULLS** > DULL
**DULLY** > DULL
**DULNESS** > DULL
**DULNESSES** > DULL
**DULOCRACY** *n* rule by slaves
**DULOSES** > DULOSIS
**DULOSIS** *n* practice of some ants, in which one species forces members of a different species to do the work of the colony
**DULOTIC** > DULOSIS
**DULSE** *n* seaweed with large red edible fronds
**DULSES** > DULSE
**DULY** *adv* in a proper manner
**DUMA** *n* elective legislative assembly established by Tsar Nicholas II in 1905: overthrown by the Bolsheviks in 1917
**DUMAIST** *n* member of duma
**DUMAISTS** > DUMAIST
**DUMAS** > DUMA
**DUMB** *vb* silence ▷ *adj* lacking the power to speak
**DUMBBELL** *n* short bar with a heavy ball or disc at each end, used for physical exercise
**DUMBBELLS** > DUMBBELL
**DUMBCANE** *n* West Indian aroid plant
**DUMBCANES** > DUMBCANE
**DUMBED** > DUMB
**DUMBER** > DUMB
**DUMBEST** > DUMB
**DUMBFOUND** *vb* strike dumb with astonishment
**DUMBHEAD** *n* dunce
**DUMBHEADS** > DUMBHEAD
**DUMBING** > DUMB
**DUMBLY** > DUMB
**DUMBNESS** > DUMB
**DUMBO** *n* slow-witted unintelligent person
**DUMBOS** > DUMBO
**DUMBS** > DUMB
**DUMBSHIT** *n* taboo slang word for a stupid person
**DUMBSHITS** > DUMBSHIT
**DUMDUM** *n* soft-nosed bullet that expands on impact and causes serious wounds
**DUMDUMS** > DUMDUM
**DUMELA** *sentence substitute* hello
**DUMFOUND** *same as* > DUMBFOUND
**DUMFOUNDS** > DUMFOUND
**DUMKA** *n* Slavonic lyrical song
**DUMKY** > DUMKA
**DUMMERER** *n* person who pretends to be dumb

**DUMMERERS** > DUMMERER
**DUMMIED** > DUMMY
**DUMMIER** > DUMMY
**DUMMIES** > DUMMY
**DUMMIEST** > DUMMY
**DUMMINESS** > DUMMY
**DUMMKOPF** *n* stupid person
**DUMMKOPFS** > DUMMKOPF
**DUMMY** *adj* sham ▷ *n* figure representing the human form, used for displaying clothes etc ▷ *adj* imitation, substitute ▷ *vb* prepare a dummy of (a proposed book, page, etc)
**DUMMYING** > DUMMY
**DUMOSE** *adj* bushlike
**DUMOSITY** > DUMOSE
**DUMOUS** *same as* > DUMOSE
**DUMP** *vb* drop or let fall in a careless manner ▷ *n* place where waste materials are left
**DUMPBIN** *n* free-standing unit in a bookshop in which a particular publisher's books are displayed
**DUMPBINS** > DUMPBIN
**DUMPCART** *n* cart for dumping without handling
**DUMPCARTS** > DUMPCART
**DUMPED** > DUMP
**DUMPER** > DUMP
**DUMPERS** > DUMP
**DUMPIER** > DUMPY
**DUMPIES** > DUMPY
**DUMPIEST** > DUMPY
**DUMPILY** > DUMPY
**DUMPINESS** > DUMPY
**DUMPING** > DUMP
**DUMPINGS** > DUMP
**DUMPISH** *same as* > DUMPY
**DUMPISHLY** > DUMPISH
**DUMPLE** *vb* form into dumpling shape
**DUMPLED** > DUMPLE
**DUMPLES** > DUMPLE
**DUMPLING** *n* small ball of dough cooked and served with stew
**DUMPLINGS** > DUMPLING
**DUMPS** *pl n* state of melancholy or depression
**DUMPSITE** *n* location of dump
**DUMPSITES** > DUMPSITE
**DUMPSTER** *n* refuse skip
**DUMPSTERS** > DUMPSTER
**DUMPTRUCK** *n* lorry with a tipping container
**DUMPY** *n* dumpy person ▷ *adj* short and plump
**DUN** *adj* brownish-grey ▷ *vb* demand payment from (a debtor) ▷ *n* demand for payment
**DUNAM** *n* unit of area measurement
**DUNAMS** > DUNAM
**DUNCE** *n* person who is stupid or slow to learn
**DUNCEDOM** > DUNCE

**DUNCEDOMS** > DUNCE
**DUNCELIKE** > DUNCE
**DUNCERIES** > DUNCERY
**DUNCERY** *n* duncelike behaviour
**DUNCES** > DUNCE
**DUNCH** *vb* push against gently
**DUNCHED** > DUNCH
**DUNCHES** > DUNCH
**DUNCHING** > DUNCH
**DUNCICAL** *adj* duncelike
**DUNCISH** *adj* duncelike
**DUNCISHLY** > DUNCE
**DUNDER** *n* cane juice lees
**DUNDERS** > DUNDER
**DUNE** *n* mound or ridge of drifted sand
**DUNELAND** *n* land characterized by dunes
**DUNELANDS** > DUNELAND
**DUNELIKE** > DUNE
**DUNES** > DUNE
**DUNG** *n* faeces from animals such as cattle ▷ *vb* cover (ground) with manure
**DUNGAREE** *n* coarse cotton fabric used chiefly for work clothes, etc
**DUNGAREED** *adj* wearing dungarees
**DUNGAREES** > DUNGAREE
**DUNGED** > DUNG
**DUNGEON** *vb* hold captive in dungeon ▷ *n* underground prison cell
**DUNGEONED** > DUNGEON
**DUNGEONER** *n* jailer
**DUNGEONS** > DUNGEON
**DUNGER** *n* old decrepit car
**DUNGERS** > DUNGER
**DUNGHILL** *n* heap of dung
**DUNGHILLS** > DUNGHILL
**DUNGIER** > DUNG
**DUNGIEST** > DUNG
**DUNGING** > DUNG
**DUNGMERE** *n* cesspool
**DUNGMERES** > DUNGMERE
**DUNGS** > DUNG
**DUNGY** > DUNG
**DUNITE** *n* ultrabasic igneous rock consisting mainly of olivine
**DUNITES** > DUNITE
**DUNITIC** > DUNITE
**DUNK** *vb* dip (a biscuit or bread) in a drink or soup before eating it
**DUNKED** > DUNK
**DUNKER** > DUNK
**DUNKERS** > DUNK
**DUNKING** > DUNK
**DUNKS** > DUNK
**DUNLIN** *n* small sandpiper with a brown back found in northern regions
**DUNLINS** > DUNLIN
**DUNNAGE** *n* loose material used for packing cargo
**DUNNAGES** > DUNNAGE
**DUNNAKIN** *n* lavatory
**DUNNAKINS** > DUNNAKIN
**DUNNART** *n* mouselike insectivorous marsupial

of the genus *Sminthopsis* of Australia and New Guinea
**DUNNARTS** > DUNNART
**DUNNED** > DUN
**DUNNER** > DUN
**DUNNESS** > DUN
**DUNNESSES** > DUN
**DUNNEST** > DUN
**DUNNIER** > DUNNY
**DUNNIES** > DUNNY
**DUNNIEST** > DUNNY
**DUNNING** > DUN
**DUNNINGS** > DUN
**DUNNISH** > DUN
**DUNNITE** *n* explosive containing ammonium picrate
**DUNNITES** > DUNNITE
**DUNNO** *vb* slang for don't know
**DUNNOCK** *n* hedge sparrow
**DUNNOCKS** > DUNNOCK
**DUNNY** *n* in Australia, toilet ▷ *adj* relating to dunny
**DUNS** > DUN
**DUNSH** *same as* > DUNCH
**DUNSHED** > DUNSH
**DUNSHES** > DUNSH
**DUNSHING** > DUNSH
**DUNT** *n* blow ▷ *vb* strike or hit
**DUNTED** > DUNT
**DUNTING** > DUNT
**DUNTS** > DUNT
**DUO** *same as* > DUET
**DUOBINARY** *adj* denoting a communications system for coding digital data in which three data bands are used, 0, +1, −1
**DUODECIMO** *n* book size resulting from folding a sheet of paper into twelve leaves
**DUODENA** > DUODENUM
**DUODENAL** > DUODENUM
**DUODENARY** *adj* of or relating to the number 12
**DUODENUM** *n* first part of the small intestine, just below the stomach
**DUODENUMS** > DUODENUM
**DUOLOG** *same as* > DUOLOGUE
**DUOLOGS** > DUOLOG
**DUOLOGUE** *n* (in drama) conversation between only two speakers
**DUOLOGUES** > DUOLOGUE
**DUOMI** > DUOMO
**DUOMO** *n* cathedral in Italy
**DUOMOS** > DUOMO
**DUOPOLIES** > DUOPOLY
**DUOPOLY** *n* situation in which control of a commodity or service in a particular market is vested in just two producers or suppliers
**DUOPSONY** *n* two rival buyers controlling sellers
**DUOS** > DUO
**DUOTONE** *n* process for producing halftone

illustrations using two shades of a single colour or black and a colour
**DUOTONES** > DUOTONE
**DUP** *vb* open
**DUPABLE** > DUPE
**DUPATTA** *n* scarf worn in India
**DUPATTAS** > DUPATTA
**DUPE** *vb* deceive or cheat ▷ *n* person who is easily deceived
**DUPED** > DUPE
**DUPER** > DUPE
**DUPERIES** > DUPE
**DUPERY** > DUPE
**DUPES** > DUPE
**DUPING** > DUPE
**DUPION** *n* silk fabric made from the threads of double cocoons
**DUPIONS** > DUPION
**DUPLE** *adj* having two beats in a bar
**DUPLET** *n* pair of electrons shared between two atoms in a covalent bond
**DUPLETS** > DUPLET
**DUPLEX** *vb* duplicate ▷ *n* apartment on two floors ▷ *adj* having two parts
**DUPLEXED** > DUPLEX
**DUPLEXER** *n* telecommunications system
**DUPLEXERS** > DUPLEXER
**DUPLEXES** > DUPLEX
**DUPLEXING** > DUPLEX
**DUPLEXITY** > DUPLEX
**DUPLICAND** *n* feu duty doubled
**DUPLICATE** *adj* copied exactly from an original ▷ *n* exact copy ▷ *vb* make an exact copy of
**DUPLICITY** *n* deceitful behaviour
**DUPLIED** > DUPLY
**DUPLIES** > DUPLY
**DUPLY** *vb* give a second reply
**DUPLYING** > DUPLY
**DUPONDII** > DUPONDIUS
**DUPONDIUS** *n* brass coin of ancient Rome worth half a sesterce
**DUPPED** > DUP
**DUPPIES** > DUPPY
**DUPPING** > DUP
**DUPPY** *n* spirit or ghost
**DUPS** > DUP
**DURA** *same as* > DURRA
**DURABLE** *adj* long-lasting
**DURABLES** *pl n* goods that require infrequent replacement
**DURABLY** > DURABLE
**DURAL** *n* alloy of aluminium and copper
**DURALS** > DURAL
**DURALUMIN** *n* light and strong aluminium alloy containing copper,

silicon, magnesium, and manganese

**DURAMEN** *another name for* > HEARTWOOD

**DURAMENS** > DURAMEN

**DURANCE** *n* imprisonment

**DURANCES** > DURANCE

**DURANT** *n* tough, leathery cloth

**DURANTS** > DURANT

**DURAS** > DURA

**DURATION** *n* length of time that something lasts

**DURATIONS** > DURATION

**DURATIVE** *adj* denoting an aspect of verbs that includes the imperfective and the progressive ▷ *n* durative aspect of a verb

**DURATIVES** > DURATIVE

**DURBAR** *n* (formerly) the court of a native ruler or a governor in India

**DURBARS** > DURBAR

**DURDUM** *same as* > DIRDUM

**DURDUMS** > DURDUM

**DURE** *vb* endure

**DURED** > DURE

**DUREFUL** *adj* lasting

**DURES** > DURE

**DURESS** *n* compulsion by use of force or threats

**DURESSE** *same as* > DURESS

**DURESSES** > DURESS

**DURGAH** *same as* > DARGAH

**DURGAHS** > DURGAH

**DURGAN** *n* dwarf

**DURGANS** > DURGAN

**DURGIER** > DURGY

**DURGIEST** > DURGY

**DURGY** *adj* dwarflike

**DURIAN** *n* SE Asian bombacaceous tree, *Durio zibethinus*, having very large oval fruits with a hard spiny rind containing seeds surrounded by edible evil-smelling aril

**DURIANS** > DURIAN

**DURICRUST** *another name for* > CALICHE

**DURING** *prep* throughout or within the limit of (a period of time)

**DURION** *same as* > DURIAN

**DURIONS** > DURION

**DURMAST** *n* large Eurasian oak tree, *Quercus petraea*, with lobed leaves and sessile acorns

**DURMASTS** > DURMAST

**DURN** *vb* variant of > DARN

**DURNDEST** *same as* > DARNEDEST

**DURNED** > DURN

**DURNEDER** > DURN

**DURNEDEST** > DURN

**DURNING** > DURN

**DURNS** > DURN

**DURO** *n* silver peso of Spain or Spanish America

**DUROC** *n* breed of pig

**DUROCS** > DUROC

**DUROMETER** *n* instrument

for measuring hardness

**DUROS** > DURO

**DUROY** *n* coarse woollen fabric

**DUROYS** > DUROY

**DURR** *same as* > DURRA

**DURRA** *n* Old World variety of sorghum, *Sorghum vulgare durra*, with erect hairy flower spikes and round seeds: cultivated for grain and fodder

**DURRAS** > DURRA

**DURRIE** *n* cotton carpet made in India, often in rectangular pieces fringed at the ends: sometimes used as a sofa cover, wall hanging, etc

**DURRIES** > DURRY

**DURRS** > DURR

**DURRY** *n* cigarette

**DURST** *a past tense of* > DARE

**DURUKULI** *n* S American monkey

**DURUKULIS** > DURUKULI

**DURUM** *n* variety of wheat, *Triticum durum*, with a high gluten content, cultivated mainly in the Mediterranean region, and used chiefly to make pastas

**DURUMS** > DURUM

**DURZI** *n* Indian tailor

**DURZIS** > DURZI

**DUSH** *vb* strike hard

**DUSHED** > DUSH

**DUSHES** > DUSH

**DUSHING** > DUSH

**DUSK** *n* time just before nightfall, when it is almost dark ▷ *adj* shady ▷ *vb* make or become dark

**DUSKED** > DUSK

**DUSKEN** *vb* grow dark

**DUSKENED** > DUSKEN

**DUSKENING** > DUSKEN

**DUSKENS** > DUSKEN

**DUSKER** > DUSK

**DUSKEST** > DUSK

**DUSKIER** > DUSKY

**DUSKIEST** > DUSKY

**DUSKILY** > DUSKY

**DUSKINESS** > DUSKY

**DUSKING** > DUSK

**DUSKISH** > DUSK

**DUSKISHLY** > DUSK

**DUSKLY** > DUSK

**DUSKNESS** > DUSK

**DUSKS** > DUSK

**DUSKY** *adj* dark in colour

**DUST** *n* small dry particles of earth, sand, or dirt ▷ *vb* remove dust from (furniture) by wiping

**DUSTBIN** *n* large container for household rubbish

**DUSTBINS** > DUSTBIN

**DUSTCART** *n* truck for collecting household rubbish

**DUSTCARTS** > DUSTCART

**DUSTCOVER** *same*

*as* > DUSTSHEET

**DUSTED** > DUST

**DUSTER** *n* cloth used for dusting

**DUSTERS** > DUSTER

**DUSTHEAP** *n* accumulation of refuse

**DUSTHEAPS** > DUSTHEAP

**DUSTIER** > DUSTY

**DUSTIEST** > DUSTY

**DUSTILY** > DUSTY

**DUSTINESS** > DUSTY

**DUSTING** > DUST

**DUSTINGS** > DUST

**DUSTLESS** > DUST

**DUSTLIKE** > DUST

**DUSTMAN** *n* man whose job is to collect household rubbish

**DUSTMEN** > DUSTMAN

**DUSTOFF** *n* casualty evacuation helicopter

**DUSTOFFS** > DUSTOFF

**DUSTPAN** *n* short-handled shovel into which dust is swept from floors

**DUSTPANS** > DUSTPAN

**DUSTPROOF** *adj* repelling dust

**DUSTRAG** *n* cloth for dusting

**DUSTRAGS** > DUSTRAG

**DUSTS** > DUST

**DUSTSHEET** *n* large cloth cover to protect furniture from dust

**DUSTSTORM** *n* storm with whirling column of dust

**DUSTUP** *n* quarrel, fight, or argument

**DUSTUPS** > DUSTUP

**DUSTY** *adj* covered with dust

**DUTCH** *n* wife

**DUTCHES** > DUTCH

**DUTCHMAN** *n* piece of wood, metal, etc, used to repair or patch faulty workmanship

**DUTCHMEN** > DUTCHMAN

**DUTEOUS** *adj* dutiful or obedient

**DUTEOUSLY** > DUTEOUS

**DUTIABLE** *adj* (of goods) requiring payment of duty

**DUTIED** *adj* liable for duty

**DUTIES** > DUTY

**DUTIFUL** *adj* doing what is expected

**DUTIFULLY** > DUTIFUL

**DUTY** *n* work or a task performed as part of one's job

**DUUMVIR** *n* one of two coequal magistrates or officers

**DUUMVIRAL** > DUUMVIR

**DUUMVIRI** > DUUMVIR

**DUUMVIRS** > DUUMVIR

**DUVET** *same as* > DOONA

**DUVETINE** *same*

*as* > DUVETYN

**DUVETINES** > DUVETINE

**DUVETS** > DUVET

**DUVETYN** *n* soft napped velvety fabric of cotton, silk, wool, or rayon

**DUVETYNE** *same as* > DUVETYN

**DUVETYNES** > DUVETYNE

**DUVETYNS** > DUVETYN

**DUX** *n* (in Scottish and certain other schools) the top pupil in a class or school

**DUXELLES** *n* paste of mushrooms and onions

**DUXES** > DUX

**DUYKER** *same as* > DUIKER

**DUYKERS** > DUYKER

**DVANDVA** *n* class of compound words consisting of two elements having a coordinate relationship as if connected by *and*

**DVANDVAS** > DVANDVA

**DVORNIK** *n* Russian doorkeeper

**DVORNIKS** > DVORNIK

**DWAAL** *n* state of absent-mindedness

**DWAALS** > DWAAL

**DWALE** *n* deadly nightshade

**DWALES** > DWALE

**DWALM** *vb* faint

**DWALMED** > DWALM

**DWALMING** > DWALM

**DWALMS** > DWALM

**DWAM** *n* stupor or daydream ▷ *vb* faint or fall ill

**DWAMMED** > DWAM

**DWAMMING** > DWAM

**DWAMS** > DWAM

**DWANG** *n* short piece of wood inserted in a timber-framed wall

**DWANGS** > DWANG

**DWARF** *adj* undersized ▷ *n* person who is smaller than average ▷ *adj* (of an animal or plant) much smaller than the usual size for the species ▷ *vb* cause (someone or something) to seem small by being much larger

**DWARFED** > DWARF

**DWARFER** > DWARF

**DWARFEST** > DWARF

**DWARFING** > DWARF

**DWARFISH** > DWARF

**DWARFISM** *n* condition of being a dwarf

**DWARFISMS** > DWARFISM

**DWARFLIKE** > DWARF

**DWARFNESS** > DWARF

**DWARFS** > DWARF

**DWARVES** > DWARF

**DWAUM** *same as* > DWAM

**DWAUMED** > DWAUM

**DWAUMING** > DWAUM

**DWAUMS** > DWAUM

**DWEEB** *n* stupid or uninteresting person

**DWEEBIER** > DWEEBY

**DWEEBIEST** > DWEEBY

**DWEEBISH** > DWEEB

DWEEBS > DWEEB
DWEEBY adj like or typical of a dweeb
DWELL vb live, reside ▷ n regular pause in the operation of a machine
DWELLED > DWELL
DWELLER > DWELL
DWELLERS > DWELL
DWELLING > DWELL
DWELLINGS > DWELL
DWELLS > DWELL
DWELT > DWELL
DWILE n floor cloth
DWILES > DWILE
DWINDLE vb grow less in size, strength, or number
DWINDLED > DWINDLE
DWINDLES > DWINDLE
DWINDLING > DWINDLE
DWINE vb languish
DWINED > DWINE
DWINES > DWINE
DWINING > DWINE
DYABLE > DYE
DYAD n operator that is the unspecified product of two vectors. It can operate on a vector to produce either a scalar or vector product
DYADIC adj of or relating to a dyad ▷ n sum of a particular number of dyads
DYADICS > DYADIC
DYADS > DYAD
DYARCHAL > DIARCHY
DYARCHIC > DYARCHY
DYARCHIES > DYARCHY
DYARCHY same as > DIARCHY
DYBBUK n (in the folklore of the cabala) the soul of a dead sinner that has transmigrated into the body of a living person
DYBBUKIM > DYBBUK
DYBBUKKIM > DYBBUK
DYBBUKS > DYBBUK
DYE n colouring substance ▷ vb colour (hair or fabric) by applying a dye
DYEABLE > DYE
DYED > DYE
DYEING > DYE
DYEINGS > DYE
DYELINE same as > DIAZO
DYELINES > DYELINE
DYER > DYE
DYERS > DYE
DYES > DYE
DYESTER n dyer
DYESTERS > DYESTER
DYESTUFF n substance that can be used as a dye or from which a dye can be obtained
DYESTUFFS > DYESTUFF
DYEWEED n plant that produces dye
DYEWEEDS > DYEWEED
DYEWOOD n any wood, such as brazil, from which dyes and pigments can be obtained

DYEWOODS > DYEWOOD
DYING > DIE
DYINGLY > DIE
DYINGNESS > DIE
DYINGS > DIE
DYKE n wall built to prevent flooding ▷ vb embankment or wall built to confine a river to a particular course
DYKED > DYKE
DYKES > DYKE
DYKEY same as > DIKEY
DYKIER > DYKEY
DYKIEST > DYKEY
DYKING > DYKE
DYNAMETER n instrument for determining the magnifying power of telescopes
DYNAMIC adj full of energy, ambition, and new ideas ▷ n energetic or driving force
DYNAMICAL same as > DYNAMIC
DYNAMICS n branch of mechanics concerned with the forces that change or produce the motions of bodies
DYNAMISE same as > DYNAMIZE
DYNAMISED > DYNAMISE
DYNAMISES > DYNAMISE
DYNAMISM n great energy and enthusiasm
DYNAMISMS > DYNAMISM
DYNAMIST > DYNAMISM
DYNAMISTS > DYNAMISM
DYNAMITE n explosive made of nitroglycerine ▷ vb blow (something) up with dynamite
DYNAMITED > DYNAMITE
DYNAMITER > DYNAMITE
DYNAMITES > DYNAMITE
DYNAMITIC > DYNAMITE
DYNAMIZE vb cause to be dynamic
DYNAMIZED > DYNAMIZE
DYNAMIZES > DYNAMIZE
DYNAMO n device for converting mechanical energy into electrical energy
DYNAMOS > DYNAMO
DYNAMOTOR n electrical machine having a single magnetic field and two independent armature windings of which one acts as a motor and the other a generator: used to convert direct current from a battery into alternating current
DYNAST n hereditary ruler
DYNASTIC > DYNASTY
DYNASTIES > DYNASTY
DYNASTS > DYNAST
DYNASTY n sequence of hereditary rulers
DYNATRON as in dynatron

oscillator type of oscillator
DYNATRONS > DYNATRON
DYNE n cgs unit of force
DYNEIN n class of proteins
DYNEINS > DYNEIN
DYNEL n trade name for synthetic fibre
DYNELS > DYNEL
DYNES > DYNE
DYNODE n electrode onto which a beam of electrons can fall, causing the emission of a greater number of electrons by secondary emission. They are used in photomultipliers to amplify the signal
DYNODES > DYNODE
DYNORPHIN n drug used to treat cocaine addiction
DYSBINDIN n gene associated with schizophrenia
DYSCHROA n discolouration of skin
DYSCHROAS > DYSCHROA
DYSCHROIA same as > DYSCHROA
DYSCRASIA n any abnormal physiological condition, esp of the blood
DYSCRASIC > DYSCRASIA
DYSCRATIC > DYSCRASIA
DYSENTERY n infection of the intestine causing severe diarrhoea
DYSGENIC adj of, relating to, or contributing to a degeneration or deterioration in the fitness and quality of a race or strain
DYSGENICS n study of factors capable of reducing the quality of a race or strain, esp the human race
DYSLALIA n defective speech characteristic of those affected by aphasia
DYSLALIAS > DYSLALIA
DYSLECTIC > DYSLEXIA
DYSLEXIA n disorder causing impaired ability to read
DYSLEXIAS > DYSLEXIA
DYSLEXIC > DYSLEXIA
DYSLEXICS > DYSLEXIA
DYSLOGIES > DYSLOGY
DYSLOGY n uncomplimentary remarks
DYSMELIA n condition of missing or stunted limbs
DYSMELIAS > DYSMELIA
DYSMELIC > DYSMELIA
DYSODIL n yellow or green mineral
DYSODILE same as > DYSODIL
DYSODILES > DYSODILE
DYSODILS > DYSODIL
DYSODYLE same as > DYSODIL

DYSODYLES > DYSODYLE
DYSPATHY n dislike
DYSPEPSIA n indigestion
DYSPEPSY same as > DYSPEPSIA
DYSPEPTIC adj relating to or suffering from dyspepsia ▷ n person suffering from dyspepsia
DYSPHAGIA n difficulty in swallowing, caused by obstruction or spasm of the oesophagus
DYSPHAGIC > DYSPHAGIA
DYSPHAGY same as > DYSPHAGIA
DYSPHASIA n disorder of language caused by a brain lesion
DYSPHASIC > DYSPHASIA
DYSPHONIA n any impairment in the ability to speak normally, as from spasm or strain of the vocal cords
DYSPHONIC > DYSPHONIA
DYSPHORIA n feeling of being ill at ease
DYSPHORIC > DYSPHORIA
DYSPLASIA n abnormal development of an organ or part of the body, including congenital absence
DYSPNEA same as > DYSPNOEA
DYSPNEAL > DYSPNEA
DYSPNEAS > DYSPNEA
DYSPNEIC > DYSPNEA
DYSPNOEA n difficulty in breathing or in catching the breath
DYSPNOEAL > DYSPNOEA
DYSPNOEAS > DYSPNOEA
DYSPNOEIC > DYSPNOEA
DYSPNOIC > DYSPNOEA
DYSPRAXIA n impairment in the control of the motor system
DYSTAXIA n lack of muscular coordination resulting in shaky limb movements and unsteady gait
DYSTAXIAS > DYSTAXIA
DYSTECTIC adj difficult to fuse together
DYSTHESIA n unpleasant skin sensation
DYSTHETIC > DYSTHESIA
DYSTHYMIA n characteristics of the neurotic and introverted, including anxiety, depression, and compulsive behaviour
DYSTHYMIC > DYSTHYMIA
DYSTOCIA n abnormal, slow, or difficult childbirth, usually because of disordered or ineffective contractions of the uterus
DYSTOCIAL > DYSTOCIA
DYSTOCIAS > DYSTOCIA

**DYSTONIA** *n* neurological disorder, caused by disease of the basal ganglia, in which the muscles of the trunk, shoulders, and neck go into spasm, so that the head and limbs are held in unnatural positions

**DYSTONIAS** > DYSTONIA

**DYSTONIC** > DYSTONIA

**DYSTOPIA** *n* imaginary place where everything is as bad as it can be

**DYSTOPIAN** > DYSTOPIA

**DYSTOPIAS** > DYSTOPIA

**DYSTROPHY** *n* any of various bodily disorders, characterized by wasting of tissues

**DYSURIA** *n* difficult or painful urination

**DYSURIAS** > DYSURIA

**DYSURIC** > DYSURIA

**DYSURIES** > DYSURY

**DYSURY** *same as* > DYSURIA

**DYTISCID** *n* any carnivorous aquatic beetle of the family *Dytiscidae*, having large flattened back legs used for swimming ▷ *adj* of, relating to, or belonging to the *Dytiscidae*

**DYTISCIDS** > DYTISCID

**DYVOUR** *n* debtor

**DYVOURIES** > DYVOURY

**DYVOURS** > DYVOUR

**DYVOURY** *n* bankruptcy

**DZEREN** *n* Chinese yellow antelope

**DZERENS** > DZEREN

**DZHO** *same as* > ZHO

**DZHOS** > DZHO

**DZIGGETAI** *a variant of* > CHIGETAI

**DZO** *a variant spelling of* > ZO

**DZOS** > ZO

# Ee

**EA** *n* river

**EACH** *pron* every (one) taken separately ▷ *determiner* every (one) of two or more considered individually ▷ *adv* for, to, or from each one

**EACHWHERE** *adv* everywhere

**EADISH** *n* aftermath

**EADISHES** > EADISH

**EAGER** *adj* showing or feeling great desire, keen ▷ *n* eagre

**EAGERER** > EAGER

**EAGEREST** > EAGER

**EAGERLY** > EAGER

**EAGERNESS** > EAGER

**EAGERS** > EAGER

**EAGLE** *n* bird of prey ▷ *vb* in golf, score two strokes under par for a hole

**EAGLED** > EAGLE

**EAGLES** > EAGLE

**EAGLET** *n* young eagle

**EAGLETS** > EAGLET

**EAGLEWOOD** *n* Asian thymelaeaceous tree with fragrant wood that yields a resin used as a perfume

**EAGLING** > EAGLE

**EAGRE** *n* tidal bore, esp of the Humber or Severn estuaries

**EAGRES** > EAGRE

**EALDORMAN** *n* official of Anglo-Saxon England, appointed by the king, who was responsible for law, order, and justice in his shire and for leading his local fyrd in battle

**EALDORMEN** > EALDORMAN

**EALE** *n* beast in Roman legend

**EALES** > EALE

**EAN** *vb* give birth

**EANED** > EAN

**EANING** > EAN

**EANLING** *n* newborn lamb

**EANLINGS** > EANLING

**EANS** > EAN

**EAR** *n* organ of hearing, esp the external part of it ▷ *vb* (of cereal plants) to develop such parts

**EARACHE** *n* pain in the ear

**EARACHES** > EARACHE

**EARBALL** *n* (in acupressure) a small ball kept in position in the ear and pressed when needed to relieve stress

**EARBALLS** > EARBALL

**EARBASH** *vb* talk incessantly

**EARBASHED** > EARBASH

**EARBASHER** > EARBASH

**EARBASHES** > EARBASH

**EARBOB** *n* earring

**EARBOBS** > EARBOB

**EARBUD** *n* small earphone

**EARBUDS** > EARBUD

**EARCON** *n* sound representing object or event

**EARCONS** > EARCON

**EARD** *vb* bury

**EARDED** > EARD

**EARDING** > EARD

**EARDROP** *n* pendant earring

**EARDROPS** *pl n* liquid medication for inserting into the external ear

**EARDRUM** *n* thin piece of skin inside the ear which enables one to hear sounds

**EARDRUMS** > EARDRUM

**EARDS** > EARD

**EARED** *adj* having an ear or ears

**EARFLAP** *n* either of two pieces of fabric or fur attached to a cap, which can be let down to keep the ears warm

**EARFLAPS** > EARFLAP

**EARFUL** *n* scolding or telling-off

**EARFULS** > EARFUL

**EARING** *n* line fastened to a corner of a sail for reefing

**EARINGS** > EARING

**EARL** *n* British nobleman ranking next below a marquess

**EARLAP** *same as* > EARFLAP

**EARLAPS** > EARLAP

**EARLDOM** *n* rank, title, or dignity of an earl or countess

**EARLDOMS** > EARLDOM

**EARLESS** > EAR

**EARLIER** > EARLY

**EARLIES** > EARLY

**EARLIEST** > EARLY

**EARLIKE** > EAR

**EARLINESS** > EARLY

**EARLOBE** *n* fleshy lower part of the outer ear

**EARLOBES** > EARLOBE

**EARLOCK** *n* curl of hair close to ear

**EARLOCKS** > EARLOCK

**EARLS** > EARL

**EARLSHIP** *n* title or position of earl

**EARLSHIPS** > EARLSHIP

**EARLY** *adv* before the expected or usual time ▷ *adj* occurring or arriving before the correct or expected time ▷ *n* something which is early

**EARLYWOOD** *n* light wood made by tree in spring

**EARMARK** *vb* set (something) aside for a specific purpose ▷ *n* distinguishing mark

**EARMARKED** > EARMARK

**EARMARKS** > EARMARK

**EARMUFF** *n* one of a pair of pads of fur or cloth, joined by a headband, for keeping the ears warm

**EARMUFFS** > EARMUFF

**EARN** *vb* obtain by work or merit

**EARNED** > EARN

**EARNER** > EARN

**EARNERS** > EARN

**EARNEST** *adj* serious and sincere ▷ *n* part payment given in advance, esp to confirm a contract

**EARNESTLY** > EARNEST

**EARNESTS** > EARNEST

**EARNING** > EARN

**EARNINGS** *pl n* money earned

**EARNS** > EARN

**EARPHONE** *n* receiver for a radio etc, held to or put in the ear

**EARPHONES** > EARPHONE

**EARPICK** *n* instrument for removing ear wax

**EARPICKS** > EARPICK

**EARPIECE** *n* earphone in a telephone receiver

**EARPIECES** > EARPIECE
**EARPLUG** n piece of soft material placed in the ear to keep out water or noise
**EARPLUGS** > EARPLUG
**EARRING** n ornament for the lobe of the ear
**EARRINGED** adj wearing earrings
**EARRINGS** > EARRING
**EARS** > EAR
**EARSHOT** n hearing range
**EARSHOTS** > EARSHOT
**EARST** adv first; previously
**EARSTONE** n calcium carbonate crystal in the ear
**EARSTONES** > EARSTONE
**EARTH** n planet that we live on ▷ vb connect (a circuit) to earth
**EARTHBORN** adj of earthly origin
**EARTHED** > EARTH
**EARTHEN** adj made of baked clay or earth
**EARTHFALL** n landslide
**EARTHFAST** adj method of building
**EARTHFLAX** n type of asbestos
**EARTHIER** > EARTHY
**EARTHIEST** > EARTHY
**EARTHILY** > EARTHY
**EARTHING** > EARTH
**EARTHLIER** > EARTHLY
**EARTHLIES** > EARTHLY
**EARTHLIKE** > EARTH
**EARTHLING** n (esp in poetry or science fiction) an inhabitant of the earth
**EARTHLY** adj conceivable or possible ▷ n a chance
**EARTHMAN** n (esp in science fiction) an inhabitant or native of the earth
**EARTHMEN** > EARTHMAN
**EARTHNUT** n perennial umbelliferous plant of Europe and Asia, with edible dark brown tubers
**EARTHNUTS** > EARTHNUT
**EARTHPEA** n peanut; groundnut
**EARTHPEAS** > EARTHPEA
**EARTHRISE** n rising of the earth above the lunar horizon, as seen from a spacecraft emerging from the lunar farside
**EARTHS** > EARTH
**EARTHSET** n setting of the earth below the lunar horizon, as seen from a spacecraft emerging from the lunar farside
**EARTHSETS** > EARTHSET
**EARTHSTAR** n any of various basidiomycetous saprotrophic woodland fungi of the genus Geastrum, whose brown onion-shaped reproductive body splits

into a star shape to release the spores
**EARTHWARD** adv towards the earth
**EARTHWAX** n ozocerite
**EARTHWOLF** n aardvark
**EARTHWORK** n fortification made of earth
**EARTHWORM** n worm which burrows in the soil
**EARTHY** adj coarse or crude
**EARWAX** nontechnical name for > CERUMEN
**EARWAXES** > EARWAX
**EARWIG** n small insect with a pincer-like tail ▷ vb eavesdrop
**EARWIGGED** > EARWIG
**EARWIGGY** > EARWIG
**EARWIGS** > EARWIG
**EARWORM** n irritatingly catchy tune
**EARWORMS** > EARWORM
**EAS** > EA
**EASE** n freedom from difficulty, discomfort, or worry ▷ vb give bodily or mental ease to
**EASED** > EASE
**EASEFUL** adj characterized by or bringing ease
**EASEFULLY** > EASEFUL
**EASEL** n frame to support an artist's canvas or a blackboard
**EASELED** adj mounted on easel
**EASELESS** > EASE
**EASELS** > EASEL
**EASEMENT** n right enjoyed by a landowner of making limited use of his neighbour's land, as by crossing it to reach his own property
**EASEMENTS** > EASEMENT
**EASER** > EASE
**EASERS** > EASE
**EASES** > EASE
**EASIED** > EASY
**EASIER** > EASY
**EASIES** > EASY
**EASIEST** > EASY
**EASILY** adv without difficulty
**EASINESS** n quality or condition of being easy to accomplish, do, obtain, etc
**EASING** > EASE
**EASLE** n hot ash
**EASLES** > EASLE
**EASSEL** adv easterly
**EASSIL** adv easterly
**EAST** n (direction towards) the part of the horizon where the sun rises ▷ adj in the east ▷ adv in, to, or towards the east ▷ vb move or turn east
**EASTBOUND** adj going towards the east
**EASTED** > EAST
**EASTER** n most important festival of the Christian

Church, commemorating the Resurrection of Christ
**EASTERLY** adj of or in the east ▷ adv towards the east ▷ n wind from the east
**EASTERN** adj situated in or towards the east
**EASTERNER** n person from the east of a country or area
**EASTERS** > EASTER
**EASTING** n net distance eastwards made by a vessel moving towards the east
**EASTINGS** > EASTING
**EASTLAND** n land to east
**EASTLANDS** > EASTLAND
**EASTLIN** adj easterly
**EASTLING** adj easterly
**EASTLINGS** adv eastward
**EASTLINS** adv eastward
**EASTMOST** adj furthest east
**EASTS** > EAST
**EASTWARD** same as > EASTWARDS
**EASTWARDS** adv towards the east
**EASY** adj not needing much work or effort ▷ vb stop rowing
**EASYGOING** adj relaxed in manner
**EASYING** > EASY
**EAT** vb take (food) into the mouth and swallow it
**EATABLE** adj fit or suitable for eating
**EATABLES** pl n food
**EATAGE** n grazing rights
**EATAGES** > EATAGE
**EATCHE** n adze
**EATCHES** > EATCHE
**EATEN** > EAT
**EATER** > EAT
**EATERIE** same as > EATERY
**EATERIES** > EATERY
**EATERS** > EAT
**EATERY** n restaurant or eating house
**EATH** adj easy
**EATHE** same as > EATH
**EATHLY** > EATH
**EATING** > EAT
**EATINGS** > EAT
**EATS** > EAT
**EAU** same as > EA
**EAUS** > EAU
**EAUX** > EAU
**EAVE** vb form eaves
**EAVED** > EAVE
**EAVES** pl n overhanging edges of a roof
**EAVESDRIP** n water dropping from eaves
**EAVESDROP** vb listen secretly to a private conversation
**EAVING** > EAVE
**EBAUCHE** n rough sketch
**EBAUCHES** > EBAUCHE
**EBAYER** n any person who buys or sells using the

internet auction site, eBay
**EBAYERS** > EBAYER
**EBAYING** n buying or selling using the internet auction site eBay
**EBAYINGS** > EBAYING
**EBB** vb (of tide water) flow back ▷ n flowing back of the tide
**EBBED** > EBB
**EBBET** n type of newt
**EBBETS** > EBBET
**EBBING** > EBB
**EBBLESS** > EBB
**EBBS** > EBB
**EBBTIDE** n ebbing tide
**EBBTIDES** > EBBTIDE
**EBENEZER** n chapel
**EBENEZERS** > EBENEZER
**EBENISTE** n cabinetmaker
**EBENISTES** > EBENISTE
**EBIONISE** same as > EBIONIZE
**EBIONISED** > EBIONISE
**EBIONISES** > EBIONISE
**EBIONISM** n doctrine that the poor shall be saved
**EBIONISMS** > EBIONISM
**EBIONITIC** > EBIONISM
**EBIONIZE** vb preach ebionism
**EBIONIZED** > EBIONIZE
**EBIONIZES** > EBIONIZE
**EBON** poetic word for > EBONY
**EBONICS** n dialect used by African-Americans
**EBONIES** > EBONY
**EBONISE** same as > EBONIZE
**EBONISED** > EBONISE
**EBONISES** > EBONISE
**EBONISING** > EBONISE
**EBONIST** n carver of ebony
**EBONISTS** > EBONIST
**EBONITE** another name for > VULCANITE
**EBONITES** > EBONITE
**EBONIZE** vb stain or otherwise finish in imitation of ebony
**EBONIZED** > EBONIZE
**EBONIZES** > EBONIZE
**EBONIZING** > EBONIZE
**EBONS** > EBON
**EBONY** n hard black wood ▷ adj deep black
**EBOOK** n book in electronic form
**EBOOKS** > EBOOK
**EBRIATE** adj drunk
**EBRIATED** > EBRIATE
**EBRIETIES** > EBRIETY
**EBRIETY** n drunkenness
**EBRILLADE** n jerk on rein, when horse refuses to turn
**EBRIOSE** adj drunk
**EBRIOSITY** > EBRIOSE
**EBULLIENT** adj full of enthusiasm or excitement
**EBURNEAN** adj made of ivory
**EBURNEOUS** adj like ivory
**ECAD** n organism whose form has been affected by its environment

**ECADS** > ECAD
**ECARINATE** *adj* having no carina or keel
**ECARTE** *n* card game for two, played with 32 cards and king high
**ECARTES** > ECARTE
**ECAUDATE** *adj* tailless
**ECBOLE** *n* digression
**ECBOLES** > ECBOLE
**ECBOLIC** *adj* hastening labour or abortion ⊳ *n* drug or agent that hastens labour or abortion
**ECBOLICS** > ECBOLIC
**ECCE** *interj* behold
**ECCENTRIC** *adj* odd or unconventional ⊳ *n* eccentric person
**ECCLESIA** *n* (in formal Church usage) a congregation
**ECCLESIAE** > ECCLESIA
**ECCLESIAL** *adj* ecclesiastical
**ECCO** *interj* look there
**ECCRINE** *adj* of or denoting glands that secrete externally, esp the numerous sweat glands on the human body
**ECCRISES** > ECCRISIS
**ECCRISIS** *n* excrement
**ECCRITIC** *n* purgative
**ECCRITICS** > ECCRITIC
**ECDEMIC** *adj* not indigenous or endemic
**ECDYSES** > ECDYSIS
**ECDYSIAL** > ECDYSIS
**ECDYSIAST** *facetious word for* > STRIPPER
**ECDYSIS** *n* periodic shedding of the cuticle in insects and other arthropods or the outer epidermal layer in reptiles
**ECDYSON** > ECDYSONE
**ECDYSONE** *n* hormone secreted by the prothoracic gland of insects that controls ecdysis and stimulates metamorphosis
**ECDYSONES** > ECDYSONE
**ECDYSONS** > ECDYSON
**ECESIC** > ECESIS
**ECESIS** *n* establishment of a plant in a new environment
**ECESISES** > ECESIS
**ECH** *same as* > ECHE
**ECHAPPE** *n* leap in ballet
**ECHAPPES** > ECHAPPE
**ECHARD** *n* water that is present in the soil but cannot be absorbed or otherwise utilized by plants
**ECHARDS** > ECHARD
**ECHE** *vb* eke out
**ECHED** > ECHE
**ECHELLE** *n* ladder; scale
**ECHELLES** > ECHELLE
**ECHELON** *n* level of power

or responsibility ⊳ *vb* assemble in echelon
**ECHELONED** > ECHELON
**ECHELONS** > ECHELON
**ECHES** > ECHE
**ECHEVERIA** *n* any of various tropical American crassulaceous plants of the genus *Echeveria*, cultivated for their colourful foliage
**ECHIDNA** *n* Australian spiny egg-laying mammal
**ECHIDNAE** > ECHIDNA
**ECHIDNAS** > ECHIDNA
**ECHIDNINE** *n* snake poison
**ECHINACEA** *n* either of the two N American plants of the genus *Echinacea*, having flower heads with purple rays and black centres: family *Compositae* (composites)
**ECHINATE** *adj* covered with spines, bristles, or bristle-like outgrowths
**ECHINATED** *same as* > ECHINATE
**ECHING** > ECHE
**ECHINI** > ECHINUS
**ECHINOID** *n* any of the echinoderms constituting the class *Echinoidea*, typically having a rigid ovoid body. The class includes the sea urchins and sand dollars ⊳ *adj* of or belonging to this class
**ECHINOIDS** > ECHINOID
**ECHINUS** *n* ovolo moulding between the shaft and the abacus of a Doric column
**ECHINUSES** > ECHINUS
**ECHIUM** *n* any plant of the Eurasian and African genus *Echium*
**ECHIUMS** > ECHIUM
**ECHIUROID** *n* marine worm
**ECHO** *n* repetition of sounds by reflection of sound waves off a surface ⊳ *vb* repeat or be repeated as an echo
**ECHOED** > ECHO
**ECHOER** > ECHO
**ECHOERS** > ECHO
**ECHOEY** > ECHO
**ECHOGRAM** *n* record made by echography
**ECHOGRAMS** > ECHOGRAM
**ECHOIC** *adj* characteristic of or resembling an echo
**ECHOING** > ECHO
**ECHOISE** *same as* > ECHOIZE
**ECHOISED** > ECHOISE
**ECHOISES** > ECHOISE
**ECHOISING** > ECHOISE
**ECHOISM** *n* onomatopoeia as a source of word formation
**ECHOISMS** > ECHOISM
**ECHOIST** > ECHOISM
**ECHOISTS** > ECHOISM

**ECHOIZE** *vb* repeat like echo
**ECHOIZED** > ECHOIZE
**ECHOIZES** > ECHOIZE
**ECHOIZING** > ECHOIZE
**ECHOLALIA** *n* tendency to repeat mechanically words just spoken by another person: can occur in cases of brain damage, mental retardation, and schizophrenia
**ECHOLALIC** > ECHOLALIA
**ECHOLESS** > ECHO
**ECHOS** > ECHO
**ECHOVIRUS** *n* any of a group of viruses that can cause symptoms of mild meningitis, the common cold, or infections of the intestinal and respiratory tracts
**ECHT** *adj* real
**ECLAIR** *n* finger-shaped pastry filled with cream and covered with chocolate
**ECLAIRS** > ECLAIR
**ECLAMPSIA** *n* serious condition that can develop towards the end of a pregnancy, causing high blood pressure, swelling, and convulsions
**ECLAMPSY** *same as* > ECLAMPSIA
**ECLAMPTIC** > ECLAMPSIA
**ECLAT** *n* brilliant success
**ECLATS** > ECLAT
**ECLECTIC** *adj* selecting from various styles, ideas, or sources ⊳ *n* person who takes an eclectic approach
**ECLECTICS** > ECLECTIC
**ECLIPSE** *n* temporary obscuring of one star or planet by another ⊳ *vb* surpass or outclass
**ECLIPSED** > ECLIPSE
**ECLIPSER** > ECLIPSE
**ECLIPSERS** > ECLIPSE
**ECLIPSES** > ECLIPSIS
**ECLIPSING** > ECLIPSE
**ECLIPSIS** *same as* > ELLIPSIS
**ECLIPTIC** *n* apparent path of the sun ⊳ *adj* of or relating to an eclipse
**ECLIPTICS** > ECLIPTIC
**ECLOGITE** *n* rare coarse-grained basic rock consisting principally of garnet and pyroxene. Quartz, feldspar, etc, may also be present. It is thought to originate by metamorphism or igneous crystallization at extremely high pressure
**ECLOGITES** > ECLOGITE
**ECLOGUE** *n* pastoral or idyllic poem, usually in the form of a conversation or soliloquy

**ECLOGUES** > ECLOGUE
**ECLOSE** *vb* emerge
**ECLOSED** > ECLOSE
**ECLOSES** > ECLOSE
**ECLOSING** > ECLOSE
**ECLOSION** *n* emergence of an insect larva from the egg or an adult from the pupal case
**ECLOSIONS** > ECLOSION
**ECO** *n* ecology activist
**ECOCIDAL** > ECOCIDE
**ECOCIDE** *n* total destruction of an area of the natural environment, esp by human agency
**ECOCIDES** > ECOCIDE
**ECOD** *same as* > EGAD
**ECOFREAK** *n* environmentalist
**ECOFREAKS** > ECOFREAK
**ECOLOGIC** > ECOLOGY
**ECOLOGIES** > ECOLOGY
**ECOLOGIST** > ECOLOGY
**ECOLOGY** *n* study of the relationships between living things and their environment
**ECOMMERCE** *n* business transactions conducted on the internet
**ECONOBOX** *n* fuel efficient utility vehicle
**ECONOMIC** *adj* of economics
**ECONOMICS** *n* social science concerned with the production and consumption of goods and services
**ECONOMIES** > ECONOMY
**ECONOMISE** *same as* > ECONOMIZE
**ECONOMISM** *n* political theory that regards economics as the main factor in society, ignoring or reducing to simplistic economic terms other factors such as culture, nationality, etc
**ECONOMIST** *n* specialist in economics
**ECONOMIZE** *vb* reduce expense or waste
**ECONOMY** *n* system of interrelationship of money, industry, and employment in a country ⊳ *adj* denoting a class of air travel that is cheaper than first-class
**ECONUT** *n* environmentalist
**ECONUTS** > ECONUT
**ECOPHOBIA** *n* fear of home
**ECORCHE** *n* anatomical figure without the skin, so that the muscular structure is visible
**ECORCHES** > ECORCHE
**ECOREGION** *n* area defined by its environmental conditions, esp climate, landforms, and soil characteristics

ECOS > ECO

ECOSPHERE n planetary ecosystem, consisting of all living organisms and their environment

ECOSSAISE n lively dance in two-four time

ECOSTATE adj with no ribs or nerves

ECOSYSTEM n system involving interactions between a community and its environment

ECOTAGE n sabotage for ecological motives

ECOTAGES > ECOTAGE

ECOTONAL > ECOTONE

ECOTONE n zone between two major ecological communities

ECOTONES > ECOTONE

ECOTOUR n holiday taking care not to damage environment

ECOTOURS > ECOTOUR

ECOTOXIC adj harmful to animals, plants or the environment

ECOTYPE n group of organisms within a species that is adapted to particular environmental conditions and therefore exhibits behavioural, structural, or physiological differences from other members of the species

ECOTYPES > ECOTYPE

ECOTYPIC > ECOTYPE

ECRASEUR n surgical device consisting of a heavy wire loop placed around a part to be removed and tightened until it cuts through

ECRASEURS > ECRASEUR

ECRITOIRE n writing desk with compartments and drawers

ECRU adj pale creamy-brown ▷ n greyish-yellow to a light greyish colour

ECRUS > ECRU

ECSTASES > ECSTASIS

ECSTASIED > ECSTASY

ECSTASIES > ECSTASY

ECSTASIS same as > ECSTASY

ECSTASISE same as > ECSTASIZE

ECSTASIZE vb make or become ecstatic

ECSTASY n state of intense delight

ECSTATIC adj in a trancelike state of great rapture or delight ▷ n person who has periods of intense trancelike joy

ECSTATICS pl n fits of delight or rapture

ECTASES > ECTASIS

ECTASIA n distension or dilation of a duct, vessel, or

hollow viscus

ECTASIAS > ECTASIA

ECTASIS same as > ECTASIA

ECTATIC > ECTASIA

ECTHYMA n local inflammation of the skin characterized by flat ulcerating pustules

ECTHYMAS > ECTHYMA

ECTHYMATA > ECTHYMA

ECTOBLAST same as > EPIBLAST

ECTOCRINE n substance that is released by an organism into the external environment and influences the development, behaviour, etc, of members of the same or different species

ECTODERM n outer germ layer of an animal embryo, which gives rise to epidermis and nervous tissue

ECTODERMS > ECTODERM

ECTOGENIC adj capable of developing outside the host

ECTOGENY n (of bacteria, etc) development outside the host

ECTOMERE n any of the blastomeres that later develop into ectoderm

ECTOMERES > ECTOMERE

ECTOMERIC > ECTOMERE

ECTOMORPH n person with a thin body build: said to be correlated with cerebrotonia

ECTOPHYTE n parasitic plant that lives on the surface of its host

ECTOPIA n congenital displacement or abnormal positioning of an organ or part

ECTOPIAS > ECTOPIA

ECTOPIC > ECTOPIA

ECTOPIES > ECTOPY

ECTOPLASM n substance that supposedly is emitted from the body of a medium during a trance

ECTOPROCT another word for > BRYOZOAN

ECTOPY same as > ECTOPIA

ECTOSARC n ectoplasm of an amoeba or any other protozoan

ECTOSARCS > ECTOSARC

ECTOTHERM n animal whose body temperature is determined by ambient temperature

ECTOZOA > ECTOZOON

ECTOZOAN same as > ECTOZOON

ECTOZOANS > ECTOZOON

ECTOZOIC > ECTOZOON

ECTOZOON n parasitic organism that lives on the outside of its host

ECTROPIC > ECTROPION

ECTROPION n condition in which the eyelid turns over exposing some of the inner lid

ECTROPIUM same as > ECTROPION

ECTYPAL > ECTYPE

ECTYPE n copy as distinguished from a prototype

ECTYPES > ECTYPE

ECU n any of various former French gold or silver coins

ECUELLE n covered soup bowl with handles

ECUELLES > ECUELLE

ECUMENIC adj tending to promote unity among Churches

ECUMENICS > ECUMENIC

ECUMENISM n aim of unity among Christian churches throughout the world

ECUMENIST > ECUMENISM

ECURIE n team of motor-racing cars

ECURIES > ECURIE

ECUS > ECU

ECZEMA n skin disease causing intense itching

ECZEMAS > ECZEMA

ED n editor

EDACIOUS adj devoted to eating

EDACITIES > EDACIOUS

EDACITY > EDACIOUS

EDAPHIC adj of or relating to the physical and chemical conditions of the soil, esp in relation to the plant and animal life it supports

EDDIED > EDDY

EDDIES > EDDY

EDDISH n pasture grass

EDDISHES > EDDISH

EDDO same as > TARO

EDDOES > EDDO

EDDY n circular movement of air, water, etc ▷ vb move with a circular motion

EDDYING > EDDY

EDELWEISS n alpine plant with white flowers

EDEMA same as > OEDEMA

EDEMAS > EDEMA

EDEMATA > EDEMA

EDEMATOSE > EDEMA

EDEMATOUS > EDEMA

EDENIC adj delightful, like the Garden of Eden

EDENTAL adj having few or no teeth

EDENTATE n mammal with few or no teeth, such as an armadillo or a sloth ▷ adj denoting such a mammal

EDENTATES > EDENTATE

EDGE n border or line where something ends or begins ▷ vb provide an edge or border for

EDGEBONE n aitchbone

EDGEBONES > EDGEBONE

EDGED > EDGE

EDGELESS > EDGE

EDGER > EDGE

EDGERS > EDGE

EDGES > EDGE

EDGEWAYS adv with the edge forwards or uppermost

EDGEWISE same as > EDGEWAYS

EDGIER > EDGY

EDGIEST > EDGY

EDGILY > EDGY

EDGINESS > EDGY

EDGING n anything placed along an edge to finish it ▷ adj relating to or used for making an edge

EDGINGS > EDGING

EDGY adj nervous or irritable

EDH n character of the runic alphabet used to represent the voiced dental fricative as in then, mother, bathe

EDHS > EDH

EDIBILITY > EDIBLE

EDIBLE adj fit to be eaten

EDIBLES pl n articles fit to eat

EDICT n order issued by an authority

EDICTAL > EDICT

EDICTALLY > EDICT

EDICTS > EDICT

EDIFICE n large building

EDIFICES > EDIFICE

EDIFICIAL > EDIFICE

EDIFIED > EDIFY

EDIFIER > EDIFY

EDIFIERS > EDIFY

EDIFIES > EDIFY

EDIFY vb improve morally by instruction

EDIFYING > EDIFY

EDILE variant spelling of > AEDILE

EDILES > EDILE

EDIT vb prepare (a book, film, etc) for publication or broadcast ▷ n act of editing

EDITABLE > EDIT

EDITED > EDIT

EDITING > EDIT

EDITINGS > EDIT

EDITION n number of copies of a new publication printed at one time ▷ vb produce multiple copies of (an original work of art)

EDITIONS > EDITION

EDITOR n person who edits

EDITORIAL n newspaper article stating the opinion of the editor ▷ adj of editing or editors

EDITORS > EDITOR

EDITRESS n female editor

EDITRICES > EDITRIX

EDITRIX n female editor

**EDITRIXES** > EDITRIX

**EDITS** > EDIT

**EDS** > ED

**EDUCABLE** *adj* capable of being trained or educated ▷ *n* mentally retarded person who is capable of being educated

**EDUCABLES** > EDUCABLE

**EDUCATE** *vb* teach

**EDUCATED** *adj* having an education, esp a good one

**EDUCATES** > EDUCATE

**EDUCATING** > EDUCATE

**EDUCATION** *n* process of acquiring knowledge and understanding

**EDUCATIVE** *adj* educating

**EDUCATOR** *n* person who educates

**EDUCATORS** > EDUCATOR

**EDUCATORY** *adj* educative or educational

**EDUCE** *vb* evolve or develop, esp from a latent or potential state

**EDUCED** > EDUCE

**EDUCEMENT** > EDUCE

**EDUCES** > EDUCE

**EDUCIBLE** > EDUCE

**EDUCING** > EDUCE

**EDUCT** *n* substance separated from another substance without chemical change

**EDUCTION** *n* something educed

**EDUCTIONS** > EDUCTION

**EDUCTIVE** > EDUCE

**EDUCTOR** > EDUCE

**EDUCTORS** > EDUCE

**EDUCTS** > EDUCT

**EDUSKUNTA** *n* Finnish parliament

**EE** *Scots word for* > EYE

**EECH** *same as* > ECHE

**EECHED** > EECH

**EECHES** > EECH

**EECHING** > EECH

**EEJIT** *Scots and Irish word for* > IDIOT

**EEJITS** > EEJIT

**EEK** *interj* indicating shock or fright

**EEL** *n* snakelike fish

**EELFARE** *n* young eel

**EELFARES** > EELFARE

**EELGRASS** *n* any of several perennial submerged marine plants of the genus *Zostera*, esp *Z. marina*, having grasslike leaves: family *Zosteraceae*

**EELIER** > EEL

**EELIEST** > EEL

**EELLIKE** *adj* resembling an eel

**EELPOUT** *n* marine eel-like blennioid fish

**EELPOUTS** > EELPOUT

**EELS** > EEL

**EELWORM** *n* any of various nematode worms, esp the wheatworm and the

vinegar eel

**EELWORMS** > EELWORM

**EELWRACK** *n* grasslike plant growing in seawater

**EELWRACKS** > EELWRACK

**EELY** > EEL

**EEN** > EE

**EERIE** *adj* uncannily frightening or disturbing

**EERIER** > EERIE

**EERIEST** > EERIE

**EERILY** > EERIE

**EERINESS** > EERIE

**EERY** *same as* > EERIE

**EEVEN** *n* evening

**EEVENS** > EEVEN

**EEVN** *n* evening

**EEVNING** *n* evening

**EEVNINGS** > EEVNING

**EEVNS** > EEVN

**EF** *n* sixth letter of Roman alphabet

**EFF** *vb* say the word 'fuck'

**EFFABLE** *adj* capable of being expressed in words

**EFFACE** *vb* remove by rubbing

**EFFACED** > EFFACE

**EFFACER** > EFFACE

**EFFACERS** > EFFACE

**EFFACES** > EFFACE

**EFFACING** > EFFACE

**EFFECT** *n* change or result caused by someone or something ▷ *vb* cause to happen, accomplish

**EFFECTED** > EFFECT

**EFFECTER** > EFFECT

**EFFECTERS** > EFFECT

**EFFECTING** > EFFECT

**EFFECTIVE** *adj* producing a desired result ▷ *n* serviceman who is equipped and prepared for action

**EFFECTOR** *n* nerve ending that terminates in a muscle or gland and provides neural stimulation causing contraction or secretion

**EFFECTORS** > EFFECTOR

**EFFECTS** *pl n* personal belongings

**EFFECTUAL** *adj* producing the intended result

**EFFED** > EFF

**EFFEIR** *vb* suit

**EFFEIRED** > EFFEIR

**EFFEIRING** > EFFEIR

**EFFEIRS** > EFFEIR

**EFFENDI** *n* (in the Ottoman Empire) a title of respect used to address men of learning or social standing

**EFFENDIS** > EFFENDI

**EFFERE** *same as* > EFFEIR

**EFFERED** > EFFERE

**EFFERENCE** > EFFERENT

**EFFERENT** *adj* carrying or conducting outwards from a part or an organ of the body, esp from the brain or spinal cord ▷ *n* nerve that

carries impulses outwards from the brain or spinal cord

**EFFERENTS** > EFFERENT

**EFFERES** > EFFERE

**EFFERING** > EFFERE

**EFFETE** *adj* powerless, feeble

**EFFETELY** > EFFETE

**EFFICACY** *n* quality of being successful in producing an intended result

**EFFICIENT** *adj* functioning effectively with little waste of effort

**EFFIERCE** *vb* archaic word meaning make fierce

**EFFIERCED** > EFFIERCE

**EFFIERCES** > EFFIERCE

**EFFIGIAL** > EFFIGY

**EFFIGIES** > EFFIGY

**EFFIGY** *n* image or likeness of a person

**EFFING** > EFF

**EFFINGS** > EFF

**EFFLUENCE** *n* act or process of flowing out

**EFFLUENT** *n* liquid discharged as waste ▷ *adj* flowing out or forth

**EFFLUENTS** > EFFLUENT

**EFFLUVIA** > EFFLUVIUM

**EFFLUVIAL** ≥ EFFLUVIUM

**EFFLUVIUM** *n* unpleasant smell, as of decaying matter or gaseous waste

**EFFLUX** *same as* > EFFLUENCE

**EFFLUXES** > EFFLUX

**EFFLUXION** *same as* > EFFLUX

**EFFORCE** *vb* force

**EFFORCED** > EFFORCE

**EFFORCES** > EFFORCE

**EFFORCING** > EFFORCE

**EFFORT** *n* physical or mental exertion

**EFFORTFUL** > EFFORT

**EFFORTS** > EFFORT

**EFFRAIDE** *same as* > AFRAID

**EFFRAY** *same as* > AFFRAY

**EFFRAYS** > EFFRAY

**EFFS** > EFF

**EFFULGE** *vb* radiate

**EFFULGED** > EFFULGE

**EFFULGENT** *adj* radiant

**EFFULGES** > EFFULGE

**EFFULGING** > EFFULGE

**EFFUSE** *vb* pour or flow out ▷ *adj* (esp of an inflorescence) spreading out loosely

**EFFUSED** > EFFUSE

**EFFUSES** > EFFUSE

**EFFUSING** > EFFUSE

**EFFUSION** *n* unrestrained outburst

**EFFUSIONS** > EFFUSION

**EFFUSIVE** *adj* openly emotional, demonstrative

**EFS** > EF

**EFT** *n* dialect or archaic name for a newt ▷ *adv*

again

**EFTEST** *adj* nearest at hand

**EFTS** > EFT

**EFTSOON** > EFTSOONS

**EFTSOONS** *adv* soon afterwards

**EGAD** *n* mild oath or expression of surprise

**EGADS** > EGAD

**EGAL** *adj* equal

**EGALITE** *n* equality

**EGALITES** > EGALITY

**EGALITIES** > EGALITY

**EGALITY** *n* equality

**EGALLY** > EGAL

**EGAREMENT** *n* confusion

**EGENCE** *n* need

**EGENCES** > EGENCE

**EGENCIES** > EGENCY

**EGENCY** *same as* > EGENCE

**EGER** *same as* > EAGRE

**EGERS** > EGER

**EGEST** *vb* excrete (waste material)

**EGESTA** *pl n* anything egested, as waste material from the body

**EGESTED** > EGEST

**EGESTING** > EGEST

**EGESTION** > EGEST

**EGESTIONS** > EGEST

**EGESTIVE** > EGEST

**EGESTS** > EGEST

**EGG** *n* oval or round object laid by the females of birds and other creatures, containing a developing embryo ▷ *vb* urge or incite, esp to daring or foolish acts

**EGGAR** *same as* > EGGER

**EGGARS** > EGGAR

**EGGBEATER** *n* kitchen utensil for beating eggs, whipping cream, etc

**EGGCUP** *n* cup for holding a boiled egg

**EGGCUPS** > EGGCUP

**EGGED** > EGG

**EGGER** *n* any of various widely distributed moths having brown bodies and wings

**EGGERIES** > EGGERY

**EGGERS** > EGGER

**EGGERY** *n* place where eggs are laid

**EGGFRUIT** *n* fruit of eggplant

**EGGFRUITS** > EGGFRUIT

**EGGHEAD** *n* intellectual person

**EGGHEADED** > EGGHEAD

**EGGHEADS** > EGGHEAD

**EGGIER** > EGGY

**EGGIEST** > EGGY

**EGGING** > EGG

**EGGLER** *n* egg dealer: sometimes itinerant

**EGGLERS** > EGGLER

**EGGLESS** > EGG

**EGGMASS** *n* intelligentsia

**EGGMASSES** > EGGMASS

**EGGNOG** *n* drink made of

raw eggs, milk, sugar,
spice, and brandy or rum
**EGGNOGS** > EGGNOG
**EGGPLANT** n dark purple
tropical fruit, cooked and
eaten as a vegetable
**EGGPLANTS** > EGGPLANT
**EGGS** > EGG
**EGGSHELL** n hard covering
round the egg of a bird or
animal ▷ adj (of paint)
having a very slight sheen
**EGGSHELLS** > EGGSHELL
**EGGWASH** n beaten egg for
brushing on pastry
**EGGWASHES** > EGGWASH
**EGGWHISK** same
as > EGGBEATER
**EGGWHISKS** > EGGWHISK
**EGGY** adj soaked in or
tasting of egg
**EGIS** rare spelling of > AEGIS
**EGISES** > EGIS
**EGLANTINE** n Eurasian rose
**EGLATERE** archaic name
for > EGLANTINE
**EGLATERES** > EGLATERE
**EGLOMISE** n gilding
**EGMA** mispronunciation
of > ENIGMA
**EGMAS** > EGMA
**EGO** n conscious mind of an
individual
**EGOISM** n excessive
concern for one's own
interests
**EGOISMS** > EGOISM
**EGOIST** n person who is
preoccupied with his own
interests
**EGOISTIC** > EGOIST
**EGOISTS** > EGOIST
**EGOITIES** > EGOITY
**EGOITY** n essence of the
ego
**EGOLESS** adj without an
ego
**EGOMANIA** n obsessive
concern with fulfilling
one's own needs and
desires, regardless of the
effect on other people
**EGOMANIAC** > EGOMANIA
**EGOMANIAS** > EGOMANIA
**EGOS** > EGO
**EGOTHEISM** n making god
of oneself
**EGOTISE** same as > EGOTIZE
**EGOTISED** > EGOTISE
**EGOTISES** > EGOTISE
**EGOTISING** > EGOTISE
**EGOTISM** n concern only for
one's own interests and
feelings
**EGOTISMS** > EGOTISM
**EGOTIST** n conceited
boastful person
**EGOTISTIC** > EGOTIST
**EGOTISTS** > EGOTIST
**EGOTIZE** vb talk or write in
self-important way
**EGOTIZED** > EGOTIZE
**EGOTIZES** > EGOTIZE
**EGOTIZING** > EGOTIZE

**EGREGIOUS** adj
outstandingly bad
**EGRESS** same as > EMERSION
**EGRESSED** > EGRESS
**EGRESSES** > EGRESS
**EGRESSING** > EGRESS
**EGRESSION** same
as > EGRESS
**EGRET** n lesser white heron
**EGRETS** > EGRET
**EGYPTIAN** n type of
typeface
**EGYPTIANS** > EGYPTIAN
**EH** interj exclamation of
surprise or inquiry, or to
seek confirmation of a
statement or question
▷ vb say 'eh'
**EHED** > EH
**EHING** > EH
**EHS** > EH
**EIDE** adj enhanced
integrated drive
electronics
**EIDENT** adj diligent
**EIDER** n Arctic duck
**EIDERDOWN** n quilt
(orig. stuffed with eider
feathers)
**EIDERS** > EIDER
**EIDETIC** adj (of visual,
or sometimes auditory,
images) exceptionally
vivid and allowing detailed
recall of something
previously perceived ▷ n
person with eidetic ability
**EIDETICS** > EIDETIC
**EIDOGRAPH** n device for
copying drawings
**EIDOLA** > EIDOLON
**EIDOLIC** > EIDOLON
**EIDOLON** n unsubstantial
image
**EIDOLONS** > EIDOLON
**EIDOS** n intellectual
character of a culture or a
social group
**EIGENMODE** n
characteristic vibration
pattern
**EIGENTONE** n
characteristic acoustic
resonance frequency of a
system
**EIGHT** n one more than
seven ▷ adj amounting
to eight
**EIGHTBALL** n black ball in
pool
**EIGHTEEN** n eight and
ten ▷ adj amounting to
eighteen ▷ determiner
amounting to eighteen
**EIGHTEENS** > EIGHTEEN
**EIGHTFOIL** n eight leaved
flower shape in heraldry
**EIGHTFOLD** adj having
eight times as many or
as much ▷ adv by eight
times as many or as much
**EIGHTFOOT** adj measuring
eight feet
**EIGHTH** n (of) number

eight in a series ▷ adj
coming after the seventh
and before the ninth in
numbering or counting
order, position, time, etc
▷ adv after the seventh
person, position, event,
etc
**EIGHTHLY** same as > EIGHTH
**EIGHTHS** > EIGHTH
**EIGHTIES** > EIGHTY
**EIGHTIETH** n one of 80
approximately equal parts
of something
**EIGHTS** > EIGHT
**EIGHTSMAN** n member of
an eight-man team
**EIGHTSMEN** > EIGHTSMAN
**EIGHTSOME** n group of
eight people
**EIGHTVO** another word
for > OCTAVO
**EIGHTVOS** > EIGHTVO
**EIGHTY** n eight times ten
▷ adj amounting to eighty
▷ determiner amounting
to eighty
**EIGNE** adj firstborn
**EIK** variant form of > EKE
**EIKED** > EIK
**EIKING** > EIK
**EIKON** variant spelling
of > ICON
**EIKONES** > EIKON
**EIKONS** > EIKON
**EIKS** > EIK
**EILD** n old age
**EILDING** n fuel
**EILDINGS** > EILDING
**EILDS** > EILD
**EINA** interj exclamation of
pain
**EINE** pl n eyes
**EINKORN** n variety of wheat
of Greece and SW Asia
**EINKORNS** > EINKORN
**EINSTEIN** n scientific
genius
**EINSTEINS** > EINSTEIN
**EIRACK** n young hen
**EIRACKS** > EIRACK
**EIRENIC** variant spelling
of > IRENIC
**EIRENICAL** same
as > IRENIC
**EIRENICON** n proposition
that attempts to
harmonize conflicting
viewpoints
**EISEGESES** > EISEGESIS
**EISEGESIS** n
interpretation of a text,
esp a biblical text, using
one's own ideas
**EISEL** n vinegar
**EISELL** same as > EISEL
**EISELLS** > EISELL
**EISELS** > EISEL
**EISH** interj South African
exclamation expressive
of surprise, agreement,
disapproval, etc
**EISWEIN** n wine made
from grapes frozen on the

vine
**EISWEINS** > EISWEIN
**EITHER** pron one or the
other (of two) ▷ adv
likewise ▷ determiner one
or the other (of two)
**EJACULATE** vb eject
(semen)
**EJECT** vb force out, expel
**EJECTA** pl n matter thrown
out of a crater by an
erupting volcano or during
a meteorite impact
**EJECTABLE** > EJECT
**EJECTED** > EJECT
**EJECTING** > EJECT
**EJECTION** > EJECT
**EJECTIONS** > EJECT
**EJECTIVE** adj relating to
or causing ejection ▷ n
ejective consonant
**EJECTIVES** > EJECTIVE
**EJECTMENT** n (formerly)
an action brought by a
wrongfully dispossessed
owner seeking to recover
possession of his land
**EJECTOR** n person or thing
that ejects
**EJECTORS** > EJECTOR
**EJECTS** > EJECT
**EKE** vb increase, enlarge, or
lengthen
**EKED** > EKE
**EKES** > EKE
**EKING** > EKE
**EKISTIC** > EKISTICS
**EKISTICAL** > EKISTICS
**EKISTICS** n science
or study of human
settlements
**EKKA** n type of one-horse
carriage
**EKKAS** > EKKA
**EKLOGITE** same
as > ECLOGITE
**EKLOGITES** > EKLOGITE
**EKPHRASES** > EKPHRASIS
**EKPHRASIS** n description
of a visual work of art
**EKPWELE** n former
monetary unit of
Equatorial Guinea
**EKPWELES** > EKPWELE
**EKTEXINE** n in pollen and
spores, the outer of the
two layers that make up
the exine
**EKTEXINES** > EKTEXINE
**EKUELE** same as > EKPWELE
**EL** n American elevated
railway
**ELABORATE** adj with a lot
of fine detail ▷ vb expand
upon
**ELAEOLITE** n nephelite
**ELAIN** same as > TRIOLEIN
**ELAINS** > ELAIN
**ELAIOSOME** n oil-rich body
on seeds or fruits that
attracts ants, which act as
dispersal agents
**ELAN** n style and vigour
**ELANCE** vb throw a lance

**ELANCED** > ELANCE
**ELANCES** > ELANCE
**ELANCING** > ELANCE
**ELAND** n large antelope of southern Africa
**ELANDS** > ELAND
**ELANET** n bird of prey
**ELANETS** > ELANET
**ELANS** > ELAN
**ELAPHINE** adj of or like a red deer
**ELAPID** n any venomous snake of the mostly tropical family Elapidae
**ELAPIDS** > ELAPID
**ELAPINE** adj of or like an elapid
**ELAPSE** vb (of time) pass by
**ELAPSED** > ELAPSE
**ELAPSES** > ELAPSE
**ELAPSING** > ELAPSE
**ELASTANCE** n reciprocal of capacitance
**ELASTANE** n synthetic fibre that is able to return to its original shape after being stretched
**ELASTANES** > ELASTANE
**ELASTASE** n enzyme that digests elastin
**ELASTASES** > ELASTASE
**ELASTIC** adj resuming normal shape after distortion ▷ n tape or fabric containing interwoven strands of flexible rubber
**ELASTICS** > ELASTIC
**ELASTIN** n fibrous scleroprotein constituting the major part of elastic tissue, such as the walls of arteries
**ELASTINS** > ELASTIN
**ELASTOMER** n any material, such as natural or synthetic rubber, that is able to resume its original shape when a deforming force is removed
**ELATE** vb fill with high spirits, exhilaration, pride or optimism
**ELATED** ▷ adj extremely happy and excited
**ELATEDLY** > ELATED
**ELATER** n elaterid beetle
**ELATERID** n any of the beetles constituting the widely distributed family Elateridae (click beetles)
**ELATERIDS** > ELATERID
**ELATERIN** n white crystalline substance found in elaterium, used as a purgative
**ELATERINS** > ELATERIN
**ELATERITE** n dark brown naturally occurring bitumen resembling rubber
**ELATERIUM** n greenish sediment prepared from the juice of the squirting

cucumber, used as a purgative
**ELATERS** > ELATER
**ELATES** > ELATE
**ELATING** > ELATE
**ELATION** n feeling of great happiness and excitement
**ELATIONS** > ELATION
**ELATIVE** adj (in the grammar of Finnish and other languages) denoting a case of nouns expressing a relation of motion or direction, usually translated by the English prepositions out of or away from ▷ n elative case
**ELATIVES** > ELATIVE
**ELBOW** n joint between the upper arm and the forearm ▷ vb shove or strike with the elbow
**ELBOWED** > ELBOW
**ELBOWING** > ELBOW
**ELBOWROOM** n sufficient scope to move or function
**ELBOWS** > ELBOW
**ELCHEE** n ambassador
**ELCHEES** > ELCHEE
**ELCHI** same as > ELCHEE
**ELCHIS** > ELCHI
**ELD** n old age
**ELDER** adj older ▷ n older person
**ELDERCARE** n care of elderly
**ELDERLIES** > ELDERLY
**ELDERLY** adj (fairly) old
**ELDERS** > ELDER
**ELDERSHIP** > ELDER
**ELDEST** adj oldest
**ELDIN** n fuel
**ELDING** same as > ELDIN
**ELDINGS** > ELDING
**ELDINS** > ELDIN
**ELDORADO** n place of great riches or fabulous opportunity
**ELDORADOS** > ELDORADO
**ELDRESS** n woman elder
**ELDRESSES** > ELDRESS
**ELDRICH** same as > ELDRITCH
**ELDRITCH** adj weird, uncanny
**ELDS** > ELD
**ELECT** vb choose by voting ▷ adj appointed but not yet in office
**ELECTABLE** > ELECT
**ELECTED** > ELECT
**ELECTEE** n someone who is elected
**ELECTEES** > ELECTEE
**ELECTING** > ELECT
**ELECTION** n choosing of representatives by voting
**ELECTIONS** > ELECTION
**ELECTIVE** adj chosen by election ▷ n optional course or hospital placement undertaken by a medical student
**ELECTIVES** > ELECTIVE
**ELECTOR** n someone who

has the right to vote in an election
**ELECTORAL** adj of or relating to elections
**ELECTORS** > ELECTOR
**ELECTRESS** n female elector
**ELECTRET** n permanently polarized dielectric material
**ELECTRETS** > ELECTRET
**ELECTRIC** adj produced by, transmitting, or powered by electricity ▷ n electric train, car, etc
**ELECTRICS** > ELECTRIC
**ELECTRIFY** vb adapt for operation by electric power
**ELECTRISE** same as > ELECTRIZE
**ELECTRIZE** vb electrify
**ELECTRO** vb (in printing) make a metallic copy of a page
**ELECTRODE** n conductor through which an electric current enters or leaves a battery, vacuum tube, etc
**ELECTROED** > ELECTRO
**ELECTRON** n elementary particle in all atoms that has a negative electrical charge
**ELECTRONS** > ELECTRON
**ELECTROS** > ELECTRO
**ELECTRUM** n alloy of gold (55–88 per cent) and silver used for jewellery and ornaments
**ELECTRUMS** > ELECTRUM
**ELECTS** > ELECT
**ELECTUARY** n paste taken orally, containing a drug mixed with syrup or honey
**ELEDOISIN** n substance extracted from the salivary glands of a small octopus for medical applications
**ELEGANCE** n dignified grace in appearance, movement, or behaviour
**ELEGANCES** > ELEGANCE
**ELEGANCY** same as > ELEGANCE
**ELEGANT** adj pleasing or graceful in dress, style, or design
**ELEGANTLY** > ELEGANT
**ELEGIAC** adj mournful or plaintive ▷ n elegiac couplet or stanza
**ELEGIACAL** > ELEGIAC
**ELEGIACS** > ELEGIAC
**ELEGIAST** n writer of elegies
**ELEGIASTS** > ELEGIAST
**ELEGIES** > ELEGY
**ELEGISE** same as > ELEGIZE
**ELEGISED** > ELEGISE
**ELEGISES** > ELEGISE
**ELEGISING** > ELEGISE
**ELEGIST** > ELEGIZE
**ELEGISTS** > ELEGIZE

**ELEGIT** n writ delivering debtor's property to plaintiff
**ELEGITS** > ELEGIT
**ELEGIZE** vb compose an elegy or elegies (in memory of)
**ELEGIZED** > ELEGIZE
**ELEGIZES** > ELEGIZE
**ELEGIZING** > ELEGIZE
**ELEGY** n mournful poem, esp a lament for the dead
**ELEMENT** n component part
**ELEMENTAL** adj of primitive natural forces or passions ▷ n spirit or force that is said to appear in physical form
**ELEMENTS** > ELEMENT
**ELEMI** n any of various fragrant resins obtained from tropical trees, esp trees of the family Burseraceae: used in making varnishes, ointments, inks, etc
**ELEMIS** > ELEMI
**ELENCH** n refutation in logic
**ELENCHI** > ELENCHUS
**ELENCHIC** > ELENCHUS
**ELENCHS** > ELENCH
**ELENCHTIC** same as > ELENCTIC
**ELENCHUS** n refutation of an argument by proving the contrary of its conclusion, esp syllogistically
**ELENCTIC** adj refuting an argument by proving the falsehood of its conclusion
**ELEOPTENE** n liquid part of a volatile oil
**ELEPHANT** n huge four-footed thick-skinned animal with ivory tusks and a long trunk
**ELEPHANTS** adj in Australia, a slang word for drunk
**ELEUTHERI** pl n secret society
**ELEVATE** vb raise in rank or status
**ELEVATED** adj higher than normal ▷ n railway that runs on an elevated structure
**ELEVATEDS** > ELEVATED
**ELEVATES** > ELEVATE
**ELEVATING** > ELEVATE
**ELEVATION** n raising
**ELEVATOR** n lift for carrying people
**ELEVATORS** > ELEVATOR
**ELEVATORY** > ELEVATE
**ELEVEN** n one more than ten ▷ adj amounting to eleven ▷ determiner amounting to eleven
**ELEVENS** > ELEVEN
**ELEVENSES** n mid-morning snack

**ELEVENTH** n (of) number eleven in a series ▷ adj coming after the tenth in numbering or counting order, position, time, etc

**ELEVENTHS** > ELEVENTH

**ELEVON** n aircraft control surface that combines the functions of an elevator and aileron, usually fitted to tailless or delta-wing aircraft

**ELEVONS** > ELEVON

**ELF** n (in folklore) small mischievous fairy ▷ vb entangle (esp hair)

**ELFED** > ELF

**ELFHOOD** > ELF

**ELFHOODS** > ELF

**ELFIN** adj small and delicate ▷ n young elf

**ELFING** > ELF

**ELFINS** > ELFIN

**ELFISH** adj of, relating to, or like an elf or elves ▷ n supposed language of elves

**ELFISHLY** > ELFISH

**ELFLAND** another name for > FAIRYLAND

**ELFLANDS** > ELFLAND

**ELFLIKE** > ELF

**ELFLOCK** n lock of hair, fancifully regarded as having been tangled by the elves

**ELFLOCKS** > ELFLOCK

**ELFS** > ELF

**ELHI** adj informal word for or relating to elementary high school

**ELIAD** n glance

**ELIADS** > ELIAD

**ELICHE** n pasta in the form of spirals

**ELICHES** > ELICHE

**ELICIT** vb bring about (a response or reaction)

**ELICITED** > ELICIT

**ELICITING** > ELICIT

**ELICITOR** > ELICIT

**ELICITORS** > ELICIT

**ELICITS** > ELICIT

**ELIDE** vb omit (a vowel or syllable) from a spoken word

**ELIDED** > ELIDE

**ELIDES** > ELIDE

**ELIDIBLE** > ELIDE

**ELIDING** > ELIDE

**ELIGIBLE** adj meeting the requirements or qualifications needed ▷ n eligible person or thing

**ELIGIBLES** > ELIGIBLE

**ELIGIBLY** > ELIGIBLE

**ELIMINANT** > ELIMINATE

**ELIMINATE** vb get rid of

**ELINT** n electronic intelligence

**ELINTS** > ELINT

**ELISION** n omission of a syllable or vowel from a spoken word

**ELISIONS** > ELISION

**ELITE** n most powerful, rich, or gifted members of a group ▷ adj of, relating to, or suitable for an elite

**ELITES** > ELITE

**ELITISM** n belief that society should be governed by a small group of superior people

**ELITISMS** > ELITISM

**ELITIST** > ELITISM

**ELITISTS** > ELITISM

**ELIXIR** n imaginary liquid that can prolong life or turn base metals into gold

**ELIXIRS** > ELIXIR

**ELK** n large deer of N Europe and Asia

**ELKHOUND** n powerful breed of dog of the spitz type with a thick grey coat and tightly curled tail

**ELKHOUNDS** > ELKHOUND

**ELKS** > ELK

**ELL** n obsolete unit of length equal to approximately 45 inches

**ELLAGIC** adj of an acid derived from gallnuts

**ELLIPSE** n oval shape

**ELLIPSES** > ELLIPSIS

**ELLIPSIS** n omission of letters or words in a sentence

**ELLIPSOID** n surface whose plane sections are ellipses or circles

**ELLIPTIC** adj relating to or having the shape of an ellipse

**ELLOPS** same as > ELOPS

**ELLOPSES** > ELLOPS

**ELLS** > ELL

**ELLWAND** n stick for measuring lengths

**ELLWANDS** > ELLWAND

**ELM** n tree with serrated leaves

**ELMEN** adj of or relating to elm trees

**ELMIER** > ELMY

**ELMIEST** > ELMY

**ELMS** > ELM

**ELMWOOD** n wood from an elm tree

**ELMWOODS** > ELMWOOD

**ELMY** adj of or relating to elm trees

**ELOCUTE** vb speak as if practising elocution

**ELOCUTED** > ELOCUTE

**ELOCUTES** > ELOCUTE

**ELOCUTING** > ELOCUTE

**ELOCUTION** n art of speaking clearly in public

**ELOCUTORY** > ELOCUTION

**ELODEA** n type of American plant

**ELODEAS** > ELODEA

**ELOGE** same as > EULOGY

**ELOGES** > ELOGE

**ELOGIES** > ELOGY

**ELOGIST** > ELOGY

**ELOGISTS** > ELOGY

**ELOGIUM** same as > EULOGY

**ELOGIUMS** > ELOGIUM

**ELOGY** same as > EULOGY

**ELOIGN** vb remove (oneself, one's property, etc) to a distant place

**ELOIGNED** > ELOIGN

**ELOIGNER** > ELOIGN

**ELOIGNERS** > ELOIGN

**ELOIGNING** > ELOIGN

**ELOIGNS** > ELOIGN

**ELOIN** same as > ELOIGN

**ELOINED** > ELOIN

**ELOINER** > ELOIN

**ELOINERS** > ELOIN

**ELOINING** > ELOIN

**ELOINMENT** > ELOIN

**ELOINS** > ELOIN

**ELONGATE** vb make or become longer ▷ adj long and narrow

**ELONGATED** > ELONGATE

**ELONGATES** > ELONGATE

**ELOPE** vb (of two people) run away secretly to get married

**ELOPED** > ELOPE

**ELOPEMENT** > ELOPE

**ELOPER** > ELOPE

**ELOPERS** > ELOPE

**ELOPES** > ELOPE

**ELOPING** > ELOPE

**ELOPS** n type of fish

**ELOPSES** > ELOPS

**ELOQUENCE** n fluent powerful use of language

**ELOQUENT** adj (of speech or writing) fluent and persuasive

**ELPEE** n LP, long-playing record

**ELPEES** > ELPEE

**ELS** > EL

**ELSE** adv in addition or more

**ELSEWHERE** adv in or to another place

**ELSEWISE** adv otherwise

**ELSHIN** n cobbler's awl

**ELSHINS** > ELSHIN

**ELSIN** variant of > ELSHIN

**ELSINS** > ELSIN

**ELT** n young female pig

**ELTCHI** variant of > ELCHEE

**ELTCHIS** > ELTCHI

**ELTS** > ELT

**ELUANT** same as > ELUENT

**ELUANTS** > ELUANT

**ELUATE** n solution of adsorbed material in the eluent obtained during the process of elution

**ELUATES** > ELUATE

**ELUCIDATE** vb make (something difficult) clear

**ELUDE** vb escape from by cleverness or quickness

**ELUDED** > ELUDE

**ELUDER** > ELUDE

**ELUDERS** > ELUDE

**ELUDES** > ELUDE

**ELUDIBLE** adj able to be eluded

**ELUDING** > ELUDE

**ELUENT** n solvent used for eluting

**ELUENTS** > ELUENT

**ELUSION** > ELUDE

**ELUSIONS** > ELUDE

**ELUSIVE** adj difficult to catch or remember

**ELUSIVELY** > ELUSIVE

**ELUSORY** adj avoiding the issue

**ELUTE** vb wash out (a substance) by the action of a solvent, as in chromatography

**ELUTED** > ELUTE

**ELUTES** > ELUTE

**ELUTING** > ELUTE

**ELUTION** > ELUTE

**ELUTIONS** > ELUTE

**ELUTOR** > ELUTE

**ELUTORS** > ELUTE

**ELUTRIATE** vb purify or separate (a substance or mixture) by washing and straining or decanting

**ELUVIA** > ELUVIUM

**ELUVIAL** > ELUVIUM

**ELUVIATE** vb remove material suspended in water in a layer of soil by the action of rainfall

**ELUVIATED** > ELUVIATE

**ELUVIATES** > ELUVIATE

**ELUVIUM** n mass of sand, silt, etc: a product of the erosion of rocks that has remained in its place of origin

**ELUVIUMS** > ELUVIUM

**ELVAN** n type of rock

**ELVANITE** variant of > ELVAN

**ELVANITES** > ELVANITE

**ELVANS** > ELVAN

**ELVER** n young eel

**ELVERS** > ELVER

**ELVES** > ELF

**ELVISH** same as > ELFISH

**ELVISHLY** > ELVISH

**ELYSIAN** adj delightful, blissful

**ELYTRA** > ELYTRUM

**ELYTRAL** > ELYTRON

**ELYTROID** > ELYTRON

**ELYTRON** n either of the horny front wings of beetles and some other insects, which cover and protect the hind wings

**ELYTROUS** > ELYTRON

**ELYTRUM** same as > ELYTRON

**EM** n square of a body of any size of type, used as a unit of measurement

**EMACIATE** vb become or cause to become abnormally thin

**EMACIATED** adj abnormally thin

**EMACIATES** > EMACIATE

**EMACS** n powerful computer program used for creating and editing

text
EMACSEN > EMACS
EMAIL n electronic mail
  ▷ vb send a message by
  electronic mail
EMAILED > EMAIL
EMAILING > EMAIL
EMAILS > EMAIL
EMANANT > EMANATE
EMANATE vb issue, proceed
  from a source
EMANATED > EMANATE
EMANATES > EMANATE
EMANATING > EMANATE
EMANATION n act or
  instance of emanating
EMANATIST > EMANATE
EMANATIVE > EMANATE
EMANATOR > EMANATE
EMANATORS > EMANATE
EMANATORY > EMANATE
EMBACE variant of > EMBASE
EMBACED > EMBACE
EMBACES > EMBACE
EMBACING > EMBACE
EMBAIL vb enclose in a
  circle
EMBAILED > EMBAIL
EMBAILING > EMBAIL
EMBAILS > EMBAIL
EMBALE vb bind
EMBALED > EMBALE
EMBALES > EMBALE
EMBALING > EMBALE
EMBALL vb enclose in a
  circle
EMBALLED > EMBALL
EMBALLING > EMBALL
EMBALLS > EMBALL
EMBALM vb preserve (a
  corpse) from decay by the
  use of chemicals etc
EMBALMED > EMBALM
EMBALMER > EMBALM
EMBALMERS > EMBALM
EMBALMING > EMBALM
EMBALMS > EMBALM
EMBANK vb protect, enclose,
  or confine (a waterway,
  road, etc) with an
  embankment
EMBANKED > EMBANK
EMBANKER > EMBANK
EMBANKERS > EMBANK
EMBANKING > EMBANK
EMBANKS > EMBANK
EMBAR vb close in with bars
EMBARGO n order by a
  government prohibiting
  trade with a country ▷ vb
  put an embargo on
EMBARGOED > EMBARGO
EMBARGOES > EMBARGO
EMBARK vb board a ship or
  aircraft
EMBARKED > EMBARK
EMBARKING > EMBARK
EMBARKS > EMBARK
EMBARRASS vb cause to feel
  self-conscious or ashamed
EMBARRED > EMBAR
EMBARRING > EMBAR
EMBARS > EMBAR
EMBASE vb degrade or

debase
EMBASED > EMBASE
EMBASES > EMBASE
EMBASING > EMBASE
EMBASSADE n embassy
EMBASSAGE n work of an
  embassy
EMBASSIES > EMBASSY
EMBASSY n offices or
  official residence of an
  ambassador
EMBASTE > EMBASE
EMBATHE vb bathe with
  water
EMBATHED > EMBATHE
EMBATHES > EMBATHE
EMBATHING > EMBATHE
EMBATTLE vb deploy
  (troops) for battle
EMBATTLED adj having a lot
  of difficulties
EMBATTLES > EMBATTLE
EMBAY vb form into a bay
EMBAYED > EMBAY
EMBAYING > EMBAY
EMBAYLD > EMBAIL
EMBAYMENT n shape
  resembling a bay
EMBAYS > EMBAY
EMBED vb fix firmly in
  something solid ▷ n
  journalist accompanying
  an active military unit
EMBEDDED > EMBED
EMBEDDING n practice
  of assigning or being
  assigned a journalist to
  accompany an active
  military unit
EMBEDMENT > EMBED
EMBEDS > EMBED
EMBELLISH vb decorate
EMBER n glowing piece of
  wood or coal in a dying fire
EMBERS > EMBER
EMBEZZLE vb steal money
  that has been entrusted
  to one
EMBEZZLED > EMBEZZLE
EMBEZZLER > EMBEZZLE
EMBEZZLES > EMBEZZLE
EMBITTER vb make (a
  person) resentful or bitter
EMBITTERS > EMBITTER
EMBLAZE vb cause to light
  up
EMBLAZED > EMBLAZE
EMBLAZER > EMBLAZE
EMBLAZERS > EMBLAZE
EMBLAZES > EMBLAZE
EMBLAZING > EMBLAZE
EMBLAZON vb decorate
  with bright colours
EMBLAZONS > EMBLAZON
EMBLEM n object or design
  that symbolizes a quality,
  type, or group ▷ vb
  represent or signify
EMBLEMA n mosaic
  decoration
EMBLEMATA > EMBLEMA
EMBLEMED > EMBLEM
EMBLEMING > EMBLEM
EMBLEMISE same

as > EMBLEMIZE
EMBLEMIZE vb function as
  an emblem of
EMBLEMS > EMBLEM
EMBLIC n type of Indian
  tree
EMBLICS > EMBLIC
EMBLOOM vb adorn with
  blooms
EMBLOOMED > EMBLOOM
EMBLOOMS > EMBLOOM
EMBLOSSOM vb adorn with
  blossom
EMBODIED > EMBODY
EMBODIER > EMBODY
EMBODIERS > EMBODY
EMBODIES > EMBODY
EMBODY vb be an example
  or expression of
EMBODYING > EMBODY
EMBOG vb sink down into
  a bog
EMBOGGED > EMBOG
EMBOGGING > EMBOG
EMBOGS > EMBOG
EMBOGUE vb go out through
  a narrow channel or
  passage
EMBOGUED > EMBOGUE
EMBOGUES > EMBOGUE
EMBOGUING > EMBOGUE
EMBOIL vb enrage or be
  enraged
EMBOILED > EMBOIL
EMBOILING > EMBOIL
EMBOILS > EMBOIL
EMBOLDEN vb encourage
  (someone)
EMBOLDENS > EMBOLDEN
EMBOLI > EMBOLUS
EMBOLIC adj of or
  relating to an embolus or
  embolism
EMBOLIES > EMBOLY
EMBOLISE same
as > EMBOLIZE
EMBOLISED > EMBOLISE
EMBOLISES > EMBOLISE
EMBOLISM n blocking of a
  blood vessel by a blood clot
  or air bubble
EMBOLISMS > EMBOLISM
EMBOLIZE vb cause
  embolism in (a blood
  vessel)
EMBOLIZED > EMBOLIZE
EMBOLIZES > EMBOLIZE
EMBOLUS n material, such
  as a blood clot, that blocks
  a blood vessel
EMBOLUSES > EMBOLUS
EMBOLY n infolding of the
  outer layer of cells of an
  organism or part of an
  organism so as to form a
  pocket in the surface
EMBORDER vb edge or
  border
EMBORDERS > EMBORDER
EMBOSCATA n sudden
  attack or raid
EMBOSK vb hide or cover
EMBOSKED > EMBOSK
EMBOSKING > EMBOSK

EMBOSKS > EMBOSK
EMBOSOM vb enclose or
  envelop, esp protectively
EMBOSOMED > EMBOSOM
EMBOSOMS > EMBOSOM
EMBOSS vb mould or carve
  a decoration on (a surface)
  so that it stands out from
  the surface
EMBOSSED adj (of a design
  or pattern) standing out
  from a surface
EMBOSSER > EMBOSS
EMBOSSERS > EMBOSS
EMBOSSES > EMBOSS
EMBOSSING > EMBOSS
EMBOST > EMBOSS
EMBOUND vb surround or
  encircle
EMBOUNDED > EMBOUND
EMBOUNDS > EMBOUND
EMBOW vb design or create
  (a structure) in the form of
  an arch or vault
EMBOWED > EMBOW
EMBOWEL vb bury or embed
  deeply
EMBOWELED > EMBOWEL
EMBOWELS > EMBOWEL
EMBOWER vb enclose in or as
  in a bower
EMBOWERED > EMBOWER
EMBOWERS > EMBOWER
EMBOWING > EMBOW
EMBOWMENT > EMBOW
EMBOWS > EMBOW
EMBOX vb put in a box
EMBOXED > EMBOX
EMBOXES > EMBOX
EMBOXING > EMBOX
EMBRACE vb clasp in the
  arms, hug ▷ n act of
  embracing
EMBRACED > EMBRACE
EMBRACEOR n person guilty
  of embracery
EMBRACER > EMBRACE
EMBRACERS > EMBRACE
EMBRACERY n offence of
  attempting by corrupt
  means to influence a jury
  or juror, as by bribery or
  threats
EMBRACES > EMBRACE
EMBRACING > EMBRACE
EMBRACIVE > EMBRACE
EMBRAID vb braid or
  interweave
EMBRAIDED > EMBRAID
EMBRAIDS > EMBRAID
EMBRANGLE vb confuse or
  entangle
EMBRASOR n one who
  embraces
EMBRASORS > EMBRASOR
EMBRASURE n door or
  window having splayed
  sides so that the opening
  is larger on the inside
EMBRAVE vb adorn or
  decorate
EMBRAVED > EMBRAVE
EMBRAVES > EMBRAVE
EMBRAVING > EMBRAVE

EMBRAZURE *variant of* > EMBRASURE
EMBREAD *vb* braid
EMBREADED > EMBREAD
EMBREADS > EMBREAD
EMBREATHE *vb* breathe in air
EMBRITTLE *vb* become brittle
EMBROCATE *vb* apply a liniment or lotion to (a part of the body)
EMBROGLIO *same as* > IMBROGLIO
EMBROIDER *vb* decorate with needlework
EMBROIL *vb* involve (a person) in problems
EMBROILED > EMBROIL
EMBROILER > EMBROIL
EMBROILS > EMBROIL
EMBROWN *vb* make or become brown
EMBROWNED > EMBROWN
EMBROWNS > EMBROWN
EMBRUE *variant spelling of* > IMBRUE
EMBRUED > EMBRUE
EMBRUES > EMBRUE
EMBRUING > EMBRUE
EMBRUTE *variant of* > IMBRUTE
EMBRUTED > EMBRUTE
EMBRUTES > EMBRUTE
EMBRUTING > EMBRUTE
EMBRYO *n* unborn creature in the early stages of development
EMBRYOID > EMBRYO
EMBRYOIDS > EMBRYO
EMBRYON *variant of* > EMBRYO
EMBRYONAL *same as* > EMBRYONIC
EMBRYONIC *adj* at an early stage
EMBRYONS > EMBRYON
EMBRYOS > EMBRYO
EMBRYOTIC *variant of* > EMBRYONIC
EMBUS *vb* cause (troops) to board or (of troops) to board a transport vehicle
EMBUSED > EMBUS
EMBUSES > EMBUS
EMBUSIED > EMBUSY
EMBUSIES > EMBUSY
EMBUSING > EMBUS
EMBUSQUE *n* man who avoids military conscription by obtaining a government job
EMBUSQUES > EMBUSQUE
EMBUSSED > EMBUS
EMBUSSES > EMBUS
EMBUSSING > EMBUS
EMBUSY *vb* keep occupied
EMBUSYING > EMBUSY
EMCEE *n* master of ceremonies ▷ *vb* act as master of ceremonies (for or at)
EMCEED > EMCEE
EMCEEING > EMCEE

EMCEES > EMCEE
EMDASH *n* long dash in punctuation
EMDASHES > EMDASH
EME *n* uncle
EMEER *variant of* > EMIR
EMEERATE *variant of* > EMIRATE
EMEERATES > EMEERATE
EMEERS > EMEER
EMEND *vb* remove errors from
EMENDABLE > EMEND
EMENDALS *pl n* funds put aside for repairs
EMENDATE *vb* make corrections
EMENDATED > EMENDATE
EMENDATES > EMENDATE
EMENDATOR *n* one who emends a text
EMENDED > EMEND
EMENDER > EMEND
EMENDERS > EMEND
EMENDING > EMEND
EMENDS > EMEND
EMERALD *n* bright green precious stone ▷ *adj* bright green
EMERALDS > EMERALD
EMERAUDE *archaic variant of* > EMERALD
EMERAUDES > EMERAUDE
EMERGE *vb* come into view
EMERGED > EMERGE
EMERGENCE *n* act or process of emerging
EMERGENCY *n* sudden unforeseen occurrence needing immediate action
EMERGENT *adj* coming into being or notice ▷ *n* aquatic plant with stem and leaves above the water
EMERGENTS > EMERGENT
EMERGES > EMERGE
EMERGING > EMERGE
EMERIED > EMERY
EMERIES > EMERY
EMERITA *adj* retired, but retaining an honorary title ▷ *n* woman who is retired, but retains an honorary title
EMERITAE > EMERITA
EMERITAS > EMERITA
EMERITI > EMERITUS
EMERITUS *adj* retired, but retaining an honorary title ▷ *n* man who is retired, but retains an honorary title
EMEROD *n* haemorrhoid
EMERODS > EMEROD
EMEROID *variant of* > EMEROD
EMEROIDS > EMEROID
EMERSED *adj* (of the leaves or stems of aquatic plants) protruding above the surface of the water
EMERSION *n* act or an instance of emerging
EMERSIONS > EMERSION

EMERY *n* hard mineral used for smoothing and polishing ▷ *vb* apply emery to
EMERYING > EMERY
EMES > EME
EMESES > EMESIS
EMESIS *technical name for* > VOMITING
EMETIC *n* substance that causes vomiting ▷ *adj* causing vomiting
EMETICAL *same as* > EMETIC
EMETICS > EMETIC
EMETIN *same as* > EMETINE
EMETINE *n* white bitter poisonous alkaloid
EMETINES > EMETINE
EMETINS > EMETIN
EMEU *variant of* > EMU
EMEUS > EMEU
EMEUTE *n* uprising or rebellion
EMEUTES > EMEUTE
EMIC *adj* of or relating to a significant linguistic unit
EMICANT > EMICATE
EMICATE *vb* twinkle
EMICATED > EMICATE
EMICATES > EMICATE
EMICATING > EMICATE
EMICATION > EMICATE
EMICTION *n* passing of urine
EMICTIONS > EMICTION
EMICTORY > EMICTION
EMIGRANT *n* person who leaves one place or country, esp a native country, to settle in another
EMIGRANTS > EMIGRANT
EMIGRATE *vb* go and settle in another country
EMIGRATED > EMIGRATE
EMIGRATES > EMIGRATE
EMIGRE *n* someone who has left his native country for political reasons
EMIGRES > EMIGRE
EMINENCE *n* position of superiority or fame
EMINENCES > EMINENCE
EMINENCY *same as* > EMINENCE
EMINENT *adj* distinguished, well-known
EMINENTLY > EMINENT
EMIR *n* Muslim ruler
EMIRATE *n* emir's country
EMIRATES > EMIRATE
EMIRS > EMIR
EMISSARY *n* agent sent on a mission by a government ▷ *adj* (of veins) draining blood from sinuses in the dura mater to veins outside the skull
EMISSILE *adj* able to be emitted
EMISSION *n* act of giving out heat, light, a smell, etc
EMISSIONS > EMISSION
EMISSIVE > EMISSION

EMIT *vb* give out
EMITS > EMIT
EMITTANCE > EMIT
EMITTED > EMIT
EMITTER *n* person or thing that emits
EMITTERS > EMITTER
EMITTING > EMIT
EMLETS *as in* *blood-drop emlets* Chilean plant with red-spotted yellow flowers
EMMA *n* former communications code for the letter A
EMMARBLE *vb* decorate with marble
EMMARBLED > EMMARBLE
EMMARBLES > EMMARBLE
EMMAS > EMMA
EMMER *n* variety of wheat grown in mountainous parts of Europe
EMMERS > EMMER
EMMESH *variant of* > ENMESH
EMMESHED > EMMESH
EMMESHES > EMMESH
EMMESHING > EMMESH
EMMET *n* tourist or holiday-maker
EMMETROPE *n* person whose vision is normal
EMMETS > EMMET
EMMEW *vb* restrict
EMMEWED > EMMEW
EMMEWING > EMMEW
EMMEWS > EMMEW
EMMOVE *vb* cause emotion in
EMMOVED > EMMOVE
EMMOVES > EMMOVE
EMMOVING > EMMOVE
EMMY *n* (in the US) one of the gold-plated statuettes awarded annually for outstanding television performances and productions
EMMYS > EMMY
EMO *n* type of music combining hard rock with emotional lyrics
EMODIN *n* type of chemical compound
EMODINS > EMODIN
EMOLLIATE *vb* make soft or smooth
EMOLLIENT *adj* softening, soothing ▷ *n* substance which softens or soothes the skin
EMOLUMENT *n* fees or wages from employment
EMONG *variant of* > AMONG
EMONGES *variant of* > AMONG
EMONGEST *variant of* > AMONGST
EMONGST *variant of* > AMONGST
EMOS > EMO
EMOTE *vb* display exaggerated emotion, as if acting
EMOTED > EMOTE
EMOTER > EMOTE

**EMOTERS** > EMOTE

**EMOTES** > EMOTE

**EMOTICON** n any of several combinations of symbols used in electronic mail and text messaging to indicate the state of mind of the writer, such as :-) to express happiness

**EMOTICONS** > EMOTICON

**EMOTING** > EMOTE

**EMOTION** n strong feeling

**EMOTIONAL** adj readily affected by or appealing to the emotions

**EMOTIONS** > EMOTION

**EMOTIVE** adj tending to arouse emotion

**EMOTIVELY** > EMOTIVE

**EMOTIVISM** n theory that moral utterances do not have a truth value but express the feelings of the speaker, so that *murder is wrong* is equivalent to *down with murder*

**EMOTIVITY** > EMOTIVE

**EMOVE** vb cause to feel emotion

**EMOVED** > EMOVE

**EMOVES** > EMOVE

**EMOVING** > EMOVE

**EMPACKET** vb wrap up

**EMPACKETS** > EMPACKET

**EMPAESTIC** adj embossed

**EMPAIRE** variant of > IMPAIR

**EMPAIRED** > EMPAIRE

**EMPAIRES** > EMPAIRE

**EMPAIRING** > EMPAIRE

**EMPALE** less common spelling of > IMPALE

**EMPALED** > EMPALE

**EMPALER** > EMPALE

**EMPALERS** > EMPALE

**EMPALES** > EMPALE

**EMPALING** > EMPALE

**EMPANADA** n Spanish meat-filled pastry

**EMPANADAS** > EMPANADA

**EMPANEL** vb enter on a list (names of persons to be summoned for jury service)

**EMPANELED** > EMPANEL

**EMPANELS** > EMPANEL

**EMPANOPLY** vb put armour on

**EMPARE** variant of > IMPAIR

**EMPARED** > EMPARE

**EMPARES** > EMPARE

**EMPARING** > EMPARE

**EMPARL** variant of > IMPARL

**EMPARLED** > EMPARL

**EMPARLING** > EMPARL

**EMPARLS** > EMPARL

**EMPART** variant of > IMPART

**EMPARTED** > EMPART

**EMPARTING** > EMPART

**EMPARTS** > EMPART

**EMPATHIC** adj of or relating to empathy

**EMPATHIES** > EMPATHY

**EMPATHISE** same as > EMPATHIZE

**EMPATHIST** > EMPATHY

**EMPATHIZE** vb sense and understand someone else's feelings as if they were one's own

**EMPATHY** n ability to understand someone else's feelings as if they were one's own

**EMPATRON** vb treat in the manner of a patron

**EMPATRONS** > EMPATRON

**EMPAYRE** variant of > IMPAIR

**EMPAYRED** > EMPAYRE

**EMPAYRES** > EMPAYRE

**EMPAYRING** > EMPAYRE

**EMPEACH** variant of > IMPEACH

**EMPEACHED** > EMPEACH

**EMPEACHES** > EMPEACH

**EMPENNAGE** n rear part of an aircraft, comprising the fin, rudder, and tailplane

**EMPEOPLE** vb bring people into

**EMPEOPLED** > EMPEOPLE

**EMPEOPLES** > EMPEOPLE

**EMPERCE** variant of > EMPIERCE

**EMPERCED** > EMPERCE

**EMPERCES** > EMPERCE

**EMPERCING** > EMPERCE

**EMPERIES** > EMPERY

**EMPERISE** variant of > EMPERIZE

**EMPERISED** > EMPERISE

**EMPERISES** > EMPERISE

**EMPERISH** vb damage or harm

**EMPERIZE** vb act like an emperor

**EMPERIZED** > EMPERIZE

**EMPERIZES** > EMPERIZE

**EMPEROR** n ruler of an empire

**EMPERORS** > EMPEROR

**EMPERY** n dominion or power

**EMPHASES** > EMPHASIS

**EMPHASIS** n special importance or significance

**EMPHASISE** same as > EMPHASIZE

**EMPHASIZE** vb give emphasis or prominence to

**EMPHATIC** adj showing emphasis ▷ n emphatic consonant, as used in Arabic

**EMPHATICS** > EMPHATIC

**EMPHLYSES** > EMPHLYSIS

**EMPHLYSIS** n outbreak of blisters on the body

**EMPHYSEMA** n condition in which the air sacs of the lungs are grossly enlarged, causing breathlessness

**EMPIERCE** vb pierce or cut

**EMPIERCED** > EMPIERCE

**EMPIERCES** > EMPIERCE

**EMPIGHT** adj attached or positioned

**EMPIRE** n group of territories under the rule of one state or person

**EMPIRES** > EMPIRE

**EMPIRIC** n person who relies on empirical methods

**EMPIRICAL** adj relying on experiment or experience, not on theory ▷ n posterior probability of an event derived on the basis of its observed frequency in a sample

**EMPIRICS** > EMPIRIC

**EMPLACE** vb put in place or position

**EMPLACED** > EMPLACE

**EMPLACES** > EMPLACE

**EMPLACING** > EMPLACE

**EMPLANE** vb board or put on board an aeroplane

**EMPLANED** > EMPLANE

**EMPLANES** > EMPLANE

**EMPLANING** > EMPLANE

**EMPLASTER** vb cover with plaster

**EMPLASTIC** adj sticky

**EMPLEACH** variant of > IMPLEACH

**EMPLECTON** n type of masonry filled with rubbish

**EMPLECTUM** variant of > EMPLECTON

**EMPLONGE** variant of > IMPLUNGE

**EMPLONGED** > EMPLONGE

**EMPLONGES** > EMPLONGE

**EMPLOY** vb engage or make use of the services of (a person) in return for money ▷ n state of being employed

**EMPLOYE** same as > EMPLOYEE

**EMPLOYED** > EMPLOY

**EMPLOYEE** n person who is hired to work for someone in return for payment

**EMPLOYEES** > EMPLOYEE

**EMPLOYER** n person or organization that employs someone

**EMPLOYERS** > EMPLOYER

**EMPLOYES** > EMPLOYE

**EMPLOYING** > EMPLOY

**EMPLOYS** > EMPLOY

**EMPLUME** vb put a plume on

**EMPLUMED** > EMPLUME

**EMPLUMES** > EMPLUME

**EMPLUMING** > EMPLUME

**EMPOISON** vb embitter or corrupt

**EMPOISONS** > EMPOISON

**EMPOLDER** variant spelling of > IMPOLDER

**EMPOLDERS** > EMPOLDER

**EMPORIA** > EMPORIUM

**EMPORIUM** n large general shop

**EMPORIUMS** > EMPORIUM

**EMPOWER** vb enable, authorize

**EMPOWERED** > EMPOWER

**EMPOWERS** > EMPOWER

**EMPRESS** n woman who rules an empire

**EMPRESSE** adj keen; zealous

**EMPRESSES** > EMPRESS

**EMPRISE** n chivalrous or daring enterprise

**EMPRISES** > EMPRISE

**EMPRIZE** variant of > EMPRISE

**EMPRIZES** > EMPRIZE

**EMPT** vb empty

**EMPTED** > EMPT

**EMPTIABLE** > EMPTY

**EMPTIED** > EMPTY

**EMPTIER** > EMPTY

**EMPTIERS** > EMPTY

**EMPTIES** > EMPTY

**EMPTIEST** > EMPTY

**EMPTILY** > EMPTY

**EMPTINESS** > EMPTY

**EMPTING** > EMPT

**EMPTINGS** variant of > EMPTINS

**EMPTINS** pl n liquid leavening agent made from potatoes

**EMPTION** n process of buying something

**EMPTIONAL** > EMPTION

**EMPTIONS** > EMPTION

**EMPTS** > EMPT

**EMPTY** adj containing nothing ▷ vb make or become empty ▷ n empty container, esp a bottle

**EMPTYING** > EMPTY

**EMPTYINGS** > EMPTY

**EMPTYSES** > EMPTYSIS

**EMPTYSIS** n act of spitting up blood

**EMPURPLE** vb make or become purple

**EMPURPLED** > EMPURPLE

**EMPURPLES** > EMPURPLE

**EMPUSA** n goblin in Greek mythology

**EMPUSAS** > EMPUSA

**EMPUSE** variant of > EMPUSA

**EMPUSES** > EMPUSE

**EMPYEMA** n collection of pus in a body cavity, esp in the chest

**EMPYEMAS** > EMPYEMA

**EMPYEMATA** > EMPYEMA

**EMPYEMIC** > EMPYEMA

**EMPYESES** > EMPYESIS

**EMPYESIS** n pus-filled boil on the skin

**EMPYREAL** variant of > EMPYREAN

**EMPYREAN** n heavens or sky ▷ adj of or relating to the sky or the heavens

**EMPYREANS** > EMPYREAN

**EMPYREUMA** n smell and taste associated with burning vegetable and animal matter

**EMS** > EM

**EMU** n large Australian flightless bird with long

legs
**EMULATE** *vb* attempt to equal or surpass by imitating
**EMULATED** > EMULATE
**EMULATES** > EMULATE
**EMULATING** > EMULATE
**EMULATION** *n* act of emulating or imitating
**EMULATIVE** > EMULATE
**EMULATOR** > EMULATE
**EMULATORS** > EMULATE
**EMULE** *variant of* > EMULATE
**EMULED** > EMULE
**EMULES** > EMULE
**EMULGE** *vb* remove liquid from
**EMULGED** > EMULGE
**EMULGENCE** > EMULGE
**EMULGENT** > EMULGE
**EMULGES** > EMULGE
**EMULGING** > EMULGE
**EMULING** > EMULE
**EMULOUS** *adj* desiring or aiming to equal or surpass another
**EMULOUSLY** > EMULOUS
**EMULSIBLE** > EMULSIFY
**EMULSIFY** *vb* (of two liquids) join together
**EMULSIN** *n* enzyme that is found in almonds
**EMULSINS** > EMULSIN
**EMULSION** *n* light-sensitive coating on photographic film ▷ *vb* paint with emulsion paint
**EMULSIONS** > EMULSION
**EMULSIVE** > EMULSION
**EMULSOID** *n* sol with a liquid disperse phase
**EMULSOIDS** > EMULSOID
**EMULSOR** *n* device that emulsifies
**EMULSORS** > EMULSOR
**EMUNCTION** > EMUNCTORY
**EMUNCTORY** *adj* of or relating to a bodily organ or duct having an excretory function ▷ *n* excretory organ or duct, such as a skin pore
**EMUNGE** *vb* clean or clear out
**EMUNGED** > EMUNGE
**EMUNGES** > EMUNGE
**EMUNGING** > EMUNGE
**EMURE** *variant of* > IMMURE
**EMURED** > EMURE
**EMURES** > EMURE
**EMURING** > EMURE
**EMUS** > EMU
**EMYD** *n* freshwater tortoise or terrapin
**EMYDE** *same as* > EMYD
**EMYDES** > EMYDE
**EMYDS** > EMYD
**EMYS** *n* freshwater tortoise or terrapin
**EN** *n* unit of measurement, half the width of an em
**ENABLE** *vb* provide (a person) with the means, opportunity, or authority

(to do something)
**ENABLED** > ENABLE
**ENABLER** > ENABLE
**ENABLERS** > ENABLE
**ENABLES** > ENABLE
**ENABLING** > ENABLE
**ENACT** *vb* establish by law
**ENACTABLE** > ENACT
**ENACTED** > ENACT
**ENACTING** > ENACT
**ENACTION** > ENACT
**ENACTIONS** > ENACT
**ENACTIVE** > ENACT
**ENACTMENT** > ENACT
**ENACTOR** > ENACT
**ENACTORS** > ENACT
**ENACTORY** > ENACT
**ENACTS** > ENACT
**ENACTURE** > ENACT
**ENACTURES** > ENACT
**ENALAPRIL** *n* ACE inhibitor used to treat high blood pressure and congestive heart failure
**ENALLAGE** *n* act of using one grammatical form in the place of another
**ENALLAGES** > ENALLAGE
**ENAMEL** *n* glasslike coating applied to metal etc to preserve the surface ▷ *vb* cover with enamel
**ENAMELED** > ENAMEL
**ENAMELER** > ENAMEL
**ENAMELERS** > ENAMEL
**ENAMELING** > ENAMEL
**ENAMELIST** > ENAMEL
**ENAMELLED** > ENAMEL
**ENAMELLER** > ENAMEL
**ENAMELS** > ENAMEL
**ENAMINE** *n* type of unsaturated compound
**ENAMINES** > ENAMINE
**ENAMOR** *same as* > ENAMOUR
**ENAMORADO** *n* beloved one, lover
**ENAMORED** *same as* > ENAMOURED
**ENAMORING** > ENAMOR
**ENAMORS** > ENAMOR
**ENAMOUR** *vb* inspire with love
**ENAMOURED** *adj* inspired with love
**ENAMOURS** > ENAMOUR
**ENARCH** *variant of* > INARCH
**ENARCHED** > ENARCH
**ENARCHES** > ENARCH
**ENARCHING** > ENARCH
**ENARM** *vb* provide with arms
**ENARMED** > ENARM
**ENARMING** > ENARM
**ENARMS** > ENARM
**ENATE** *adj* growing out or outwards ▷ *n* relative on the mother's side
**ENATES** > ENATE
**ENATIC** *adj* related on one's mother's side
**ENATION** > ENATE
**ENATIONS** > ENATE
**ENAUNTER** *conj* in case that
**ENCAENIA** *n* festival

of dedication or commemoration
**ENCAENIAS** > ENCAENIA
**ENCAGE** *vb* confine in or as in a cage
**ENCAGED** > ENCAGE
**ENCAGES** > ENCAGE
**ENCAGING** > ENCAGE
**ENCALM** *vb* becalm, settle
**ENCALMED** > ENCALM
**ENCALMING** > ENCALM
**ENCALMS** > ENCALM
**ENCAMP** *vb* set up in a camp
**ENCAMPED** > ENCAMP
**ENCAMPING** > ENCAMP
**ENCAMPS** > ENCAMP
**ENCANTHIS** *n* tumour of the eye
**ENCAPSULE** *vb* enclose or be enclosed in or as if in a capsule
**ENCARPUS** *n* decoration of fruit or flowers on a frieze
**ENCASE** *vb* enclose or cover completely
**ENCASED** > ENCASE
**ENCASES** > ENCASE
**ENCASH** *vb* exchange (a cheque) for cash
**ENCASHED** > ENCASH
**ENCASHES** > ENCASH
**ENCASHING** > ENCASH
**ENCASING** > ENCASE
**ENCASTRE** *adj* (of a beam) fixed at the ends
**ENCAUSTIC** *adj* decorated by any process involving burning in colours, esp by inlaying coloured clays and baking or by fusing wax colours to the surface ▷ *n* process of burning in colours
**ENCAVE** *variant of* > INCAVE
**ENCAVED** > ENCAVE
**ENCAVES** > ENCAVE
**ENCAVING** > ENCAVE
**ENCEINTE** *n* boundary wall enclosing a defended area
**ENCEINTES** > ENCEINTE
**ENCEPHALA** *n* brains
**ENCHAFE** *vb* heat up
**ENCHAFED** > ENCHAFE
**ENCHAFES** > ENCHAFE
**ENCHAFING** > ENCHAFE
**ENCHAIN** *vb* bind with chains
**ENCHAINED** > ENCHAIN
**ENCHAINS** > ENCHAIN
**ENCHANT** *vb* delight and fascinate
**ENCHANTED** > ENCHANT
**ENCHANTER** > ENCHANT
**ENCHANTS** > ENCHANT
**ENCHARGE** *vb* give into the custody of
**ENCHARGED** > ENCHARGE
**ENCHARGES** > ENCHARGE
**ENCHARM** *vb* enchant
**ENCHARMED** > ENCHARM
**ENCHARMS** > ENCHARM
**ENCHASE** *less common word for* > CHASE
**ENCHASED** > ENCHASE

**ENCHASER** > ENCHASE
**ENCHASERS** > ENCHASE
**ENCHASES** > ENCHASE
**ENCHASING** > ENCHASE
**ENCHEASON** *n* reason
**ENCHEER** *vb* cheer up
**ENCHEERED** > ENCHEER
**ENCHEERS** > ENCHEER
**ENCHILADA** *n* Mexican dish of a tortilla filled with meat, served with chilli sauce
**ENCHORIAL** *adj* of or used in a particular country: used esp of the popular (demotic) writing of the ancient Egyptians
**ENCHORIC** *same as* > ENCHORIAL
**ENCIERRO** *n* Spanish bull run
**ENCIERROS** > ENCIERRO
**ENCINA** *n* type of oak
**ENCINAL** > ENCINA
**ENCINAS** > ENCINA
**ENCIPHER** *vb* convert (a message, document, etc) from plain text into code or cipher
**ENCIPHERS** > ENCIPHER
**ENCIRCLE** *vb* form a circle around
**ENCIRCLED** > ENCIRCLE
**ENCIRCLES** > ENCIRCLE
**ENCLASP** *vb* clasp
**ENCLASPED** > ENCLASP
**ENCLASPS** > ENCLASP
**ENCLAVE** *n* part of a country entirely surrounded by foreign territory ▷ *vb* hold in an enclave
**ENCLAVED** > ENCLAVE
**ENCLAVES** > ENCLAVE
**ENCLAVING** > ENCLAVE
**ENCLISES** > ENCLISIS
**ENCLISIS** *n* state of being enclitic
**ENCLITIC** *adj* denoting or relating to a monosyllabic word or form that is treated as a suffix of the preceding word, as Latin *-que* in *populusque* ▷ *n* enclitic word or linguistic form
**ENCLITICS** > ENCLITIC
**ENCLOSE** *vb* surround completely
**ENCLOSED** > ENCLOSE
**ENCLOSER** > ENCLOSE
**ENCLOSERS** > ENCLOSE
**ENCLOSES** > ENCLOSE
**ENCLOSING** > ENCLOSE
**ENCLOSURE** *n* area of land enclosed by a fence, wall, or hedge
**ENCLOTHE** *vb* clothe
**ENCLOTHED** > ENCLOTHE
**ENCLOTHES** > ENCLOTHE
**ENCLOUD** *vb* hide with clouds
**ENCLOUDED** > ENCLOUD
**ENCLOUDS** > ENCLOUD

**ENCODABLE** >ENCODE
**ENCODE** *vb* convert (a message) into code
**ENCODED** >ENCODE
**ENCODER** >ENCODE
**ENCODERS** >ENCODE
**ENCODES** >ENCODE
**ENCODING** >ENCODE
**ENCOLOUR** *vb* give a colour to
**ENCOLOURS** >ENCOLOUR
**ENCOLPION** *n* religious symbol worn on the breast
**ENCOLPIUM** *variant of* >ENCOLPION
**ENCOLURE** *n* mane of a horse
**ENCOLURES** >ENCOLURE
**ENCOMIA** >ENCOMIUM
**ENCOMIAST** *n* person who speaks or writes an encomium
**ENCOMION** *variant of* >ENCOMIUM
**ENCOMIUM** *n* formal expression of praise
**ENCOMIUMS** >ENCOMIUM
**ENCOMPASS** *vb* surround
**ENCORE** *interj* again, once more ▷ *n* extra performance due to enthusiastic demand ▷ *vb* demand an extra or repeated performance of (a work, piece of music, etc) by (a performer)
**ENCORED** >ENCORE
**ENCORES** >ENCORE
**ENCORING** >ENCORE
**ENCOUNTER** *vb* meet unexpectedly ▷ *n* unexpected meeting
**ENCOURAGE** *vb* inspire with confidence
**ENCRADLE** *vb* put in a cradle
**ENCRADLED** >ENCRADLE
**ENCRADLES** >ENCRADLE
**ENCRATIES** >ENCRATY
**ENCRATY** *n* control of one's desires, actions, etc
**ENCREASE** *variant form of* >INCREASE
**ENCREASED** >ENCREASE
**ENCREASES** >ENCREASE
**ENCRIMSON** *vb* make crimson
**ENCRINAL** >ENCRINITE
**ENCRINIC** >ENCRINITE
**ENCRINITE** *n* sedimentary rock formed almost exclusively from the skeletal plates of crinoids
**ENCROACH** *vb* intrude gradually on a person's rights or land
**ENCRUST** *vb* cover with a layer of something
**ENCRUSTED** >ENCRUST
**ENCRUSTS** >ENCRUST
**ENCRYPT** *vb* put (a message) into code
**ENCRYPTED** >ENCRYPT
**ENCRYPTS** >ENCRYPT
**ENCUMBER** *vb* hinder or impede

**ENCUMBERS** >ENCUMBER
**ENCURTAIN** *vb* cover or surround with curtains
**ENCYCLIC** *n* letter sent by the Pope to all bishops
**ENCYCLICS** >ENCYCLIC
**ENCYST** *vb* enclose or become enclosed by a cyst, thick membrane, or shell
**ENCYSTED** >ENCYST
**ENCYSTING** >ENCYST
**ENCYSTS** >ENCYST
**END** *n* furthest point or part ▷ *vb* bring or come to a finish
**ENDAMAGE** *vb* cause injury to
**ENDAMAGED** >ENDAMAGE
**ENDAMAGES** >ENDAMAGE
**ENDAMEBA** *same as* >ENDAMOEBA
**ENDAMEBAE** >ENDAMEBA
**ENDAMEBAS** >ENDAMEBA
**ENDAMEBIC** >ENDAMEBA
**ENDAMOEBA** *same as* >ENTAMOEBA
**ENDANGER** *vb* put in danger
**ENDANGERS** >ENDANGER
**ENDARCH** *adj* (of a xylem strand) having the first-formed xylem internal to that formed later
**ENDARCHY** *n* state of being endarch
**ENDART** *variant of* >INDART
**ENDARTED** >ENDART
**ENDARTING** >ENDART
**ENDARTS** >ENDART
**ENDASH** *n* short dash in punctuation
**ENDASHES** >ENDASH
**ENDBRAIN** *n* part of the brain
**ENDBRAINS** >ENDBRAIN
**ENDEAR** *vb* cause to be liked
**ENDEARED** >ENDEAR
**ENDEARING** *adj* giving rise to love or esteem
**ENDEARS** >ENDEAR
**ENDEAVOR** *same as* >ENDEAVOUR
**ENDEAVORS** >ENDEAVOR
**ENDEAVOUR** *vb* try ▷ *n* effort
**ENDECAGON** *n* figure with eleven sides
**ENDED** >END
**ENDEICTIC** >ENDEIXIS
**ENDEIXES** >ENDEIXIS
**ENDEIXIS** *n* sign or mark
**ENDEMIAL** *same as* >ENDEMIC
**ENDEMIC** *adj* present within a localized area or peculiar to a particular group of people ▷ *n* endemic disease or plant
**ENDEMICAL** *adj* endemic
**ENDEMICS** >ENDEMIC
**ENDEMISM** >ENDEMIC
**ENDEMISMS** >ENDEMIC
**ENDENIZEN** *vb* make a denizen

**ENDER** >END
**ENDERMIC** *adj* (of a medicine) acting by absorption through the skin
**ENDERON** *variant of* >ANDIRON
**ENDERONS** >ENDERON
**ENDERS** >END
**ENDEW** *variant of* >ENDUE
**ENDEWED** >ENDEW
**ENDEWING** >ENDEW
**ENDEWS** >ENDEW
**ENDEXINE** *n* inner layer of an exine
**ENDEXINES** >ENDEXINE
**ENDGAME** *n* closing stage of a game of chess, in which only a few pieces are left on the board
**ENDGAMES** >ENDGAME
**ENDING** *n* last part or conclusion of something
**ENDINGS** >ENDING
**ENDIRON** *variant of* >ANDIRON
**ENDIRONS** >ENDIRON
**ENDITE** *variant of* >INDICT
**ENDITED** >ENDITE
**ENDITES** >ENDITE
**ENDITING** >ENDITE
**ENDIVE** *n* curly-leaved plant used in salads
**ENDIVES** >ENDIVE
**ENDLANG** *variant of* >ENDLONG
**ENDLEAF** *n* endpaper in a book
**ENDLEAFS** >ENDLEAF
**ENDLEAVES** >ENDLEAF
**ENDLESS** *adj* having no end
**ENDLESSLY** >ENDLESS
**ENDLONG** *adv* lengthways or on end
**ENDMOST** *adj* nearest the end
**ENDNOTE** *n* note at the end of a section of writing
**ENDNOTES** >ENDNOTE
**ENDOBLAST** *less common name for* >ENDODERM
**ENDOCARP** *n* inner, usually woody, layer of the pericarp of a fruit, such as the stone of a peach or cherry
**ENDOCARPS** >ENDOCARP
**ENDOCAST** *n* cast made of the inside of a cranial cavity to show the size and shape of a brain
**ENDOCASTS** >ENDOCAST
**ENDOCRINE** *adj* relating to the glands which secrete hormones directly into the bloodstream ▷ *n* endocrine gland
**ENDOCYTIC** *adj* involving absorption of cells
**ENDODERM** *n* inner germ layer of an animal embryo, which gives rise to the lining of the digestive and respiratory tracts

**ENDODERMS** >ENDODERM
**ENDODYNE** *same as* >AUTODYNE
**ENDOERGIC** *adj* (of a nuclear reaction) occurring with absorption of energy, as opposed to *exoergic*
**ENDOGAMIC** >ENDOGAMY
**ENDOGAMY** *n* marriage within one's own tribe or similar unit
**ENDOGEN** *n* plant that increases in size by internal growth
**ENDOGENIC** >ENDOGEN
**ENDOGENS** >ENDOGEN
**ENDOGENY** *n* development by internal growth
**ENDOLYMPH** *n* fluid that fills the membranous labyrinth of the internal ear
**ENDOMIXES** >ENDOMIXIS
**ENDOMIXIS** *n* reorganization of certain nuclei with some protozoa
**ENDOMORPH** *n* person with a fat and heavy body build: said to be correlated with viscerotonia
**ENDOPHAGY** *n* cannibalism within the same group or tribe
**ENDOPHYTE** *n* fungus, or occasionally an alga or other organism, that lives within a plant
**ENDOPLASM** *n* inner cytoplasm in some cells, esp protozoa, which is more granular and fluid than the outer cytoplasm
**ENDOPOD** *n* inner branch of a two-branched crustacean
**ENDOPODS** >ENDOPOD
**ENDOPROCT** *n* small animal living in water
**ENDORPHIN** *n* chemical occurring in the brain, which has a similar effect to morphine
**ENDORSE** *vb* give approval to
**ENDORSED** >ENDORSE
**ENDORSEE** *n* person in whose favour a negotiable instrument is endorsed
**ENDORSEES** >ENDORSEE
**ENDORSER** >ENDORSE
**ENDORSERS** >ENDORSE
**ENDORSES** >ENDORSE
**ENDORSING** >ENDORSE
**ENDORSIVE** >ENDORSE
**ENDORSOR** >ENDORSE
**ENDORSORS** >ENDORSE
**ENDOSARC** *same as* >ENDOPLASM
**ENDOSARCS** >ENDOSARC
**ENDOSCOPE** *n* long slender medical instrument used for examining the interior of hollow organs including

the lung, stomach, bladder and bowel
**ENDOSCOPY** > ENDOSCOPE
**ENDOSMOS** *same as* > ENDOSMOSE
**ENDOSMOSE** *n* osmosis in which water enters a cell or organism from the surrounding solution
**ENDOSOME** *n* sac within a biological cell
**ENDOSOMES** > ENDOSOME
**ENDOSPERM** *n* tissue within the seed of a flowering plant that surrounds and nourishes the developing embryo.
**ENDOSPORE** *n* small asexual spore produced by some bacteria and algae
**ENDOSS** *vb* endorse
**ENDOSSED** > ENDOSS
**ENDOSSES** > ENDOSS
**ENDOSSING** > ENDOSS
**ENDOSTEA** > ENDOSTEUM
**ENDOSTEAL** > ENDOSTEUM
**ENDOSTEUM** *n* highly vascular membrane lining the marrow cavity of long bones, such as the femur and humerus
**ENDOSTYLE** *n* groove or fold in the pharynx of various chordates
**ENDOTHERM** *n* animal with warm blood
**ENDOTOXIC** > ENDOTOXIN
**ENDOTOXIN** *n* toxin contained within the protoplasm of an organism, esp a bacterium, and liberated only at death
**ENDOW** *vb* provide permanent income for
**ENDOWED** > ENDOW
**ENDOWER** > ENDOW
**ENDOWERS** > ENDOW
**ENDOWING** > ENDOW
**ENDOWMENT** *n* money given to an institution, such as a hospital
**ENDOWS** > ENDOW
**ENDOZOA** > ENDOZOON
**ENDOZOIC** *adj* (of a plant) living within an animal
**ENDOZOON** *variant of* > ENTOZOON
**ENDPAPER** *n* either of two leaves at the front and back of a book pasted to the inside of the cover
**ENDPAPERS** > ENDPAPER
**ENDPLATE** *n* any usually flat platelike structure at the end of something
**ENDPLATES** > ENDPLATE
**ENDPLAY** *n* way of playing the last few tricks in a hand so that an opponent is forced to make a particular lead ▷ *vb* force (an opponent) to make a particular lead near the

end of a hand
**ENDPLAYED** > ENDPLAY
**ENDPLAYS** > ENDPLAY
**ENDPOINT** *n* point at which anything is complete
**ENDPOINTS** > ENDPOINT
**ENDRIN** *n* type of insecticide
**ENDRINS** > ENDRIN
**ENDS** > END
**ENDSHIP** *n* small village
**ENDSHIPS** > ENDSHIP
**ENDUE** *vb* invest or provide, as with some quality or trait
**ENDUED** > ENDUE
**ENDUES** > ENDUE
**ENDUING** > ENDUE
**ENDUNGEON** *vb* put in a dungeon
**ENDURABLE** > ENDURE
**ENDURABLY** > ENDURE
**ENDURANCE** *n* act or power of enduring
**ENDURE** *vb* bear (hardship) patiently
**ENDURED** > ENDURE
**ENDURER** > ENDURE
**ENDURERS** > ENDURE
**ENDURES** > ENDURE
**ENDURING** *adj* long-lasting
**ENDURO** *n* long-distance race for vehicles, intended to test endurance
**ENDUROS** > ENDURO
**ENDWAYS** *adv* having the end forwards or upwards ▷ *adj* vertical or upright
**ENDWISE** *same as* > ENDWAYS
**ENDYSES** > ENDYSIS
**ENDYSIS** *n* formation of new layers of integument after ecdysis
**ENE** *variant of* > EVEN
**ENEMA** *n* medicine injected into the rectum to empty the bowels
**ENEMAS** > ENEMA
**ENEMATA** > ENEMA
**ENEMIES** > ENEMY
**ENEMY** *n* hostile person or nation, opponent ▷ *adj* of or belonging to an enemy
**ENERGETIC** *adj* having or showing energy and enthusiasm
**ENERGIC** > ENERGY
**ENERGID** *n* nucleus and the cytoplasm associated with it in a syncytium
**ENERGIDS** > ENERGID
**ENERGIES** > ENERGY
**ENERGISE** *same as* > ENERGIZE
**ENERGISED** > ENERGISE
**ENERGISER** > ENERGISE
**ENERGISES** > ENERGISE
**ENERGIZE** *vb* give vigour to
**ENERGIZED** > ENERGIZE
**ENERGIZER** > ENERGIZE
**ENERGIZES** > ENERGIZE
**ENERGUMEN** *n* person thought to be possessed

by an evil spirit
**ENERGY** *n* capacity for intense activity
**ENERVATE** *vb* deprive of strength or vitality ▷ *adj* deprived of strength or vitality
**ENERVATED** > ENERVATE
**ENERVATES** > ENERVATE
**ENERVATOR** > ENERVATE
**ENERVE** *vb* enervate
**ENERVED** > ENERVE
**ENERVES** > ENERVE
**ENERVING** > ENERVE
**ENES** > ENE
**ENEW** *vb* force a bird into water
**ENEWED** > ENEW
**ENEWING** > ENEW
**ENEWS** > ENEW
**ENFACE** *vb* write, print, or stamp (something) on the face of (a document)
**ENFACED** > ENFACE
**ENFACES** > ENFACE
**ENFACING** > ENFACE
**ENFANT** *n* French child
**ENFANTS** > ENFANT
**ENFEEBLE** *vb* weaken
**ENFEEBLED** > ENFEEBLE
**ENFEEBLER** > ENFEEBLE
**ENFEEBLES** > ENFEEBLE
**ENFELON** *vb* infuriate
**ENFELONED** > ENFELON
**ENFELONS** > ENFELON
**ENFEOFF** *vb* invest (a person) with possession of a freehold estate in land
**ENFEOFFED** > ENFEOFF
**ENFEOFFS** > ENFEOFF
**ENFESTED** *adj* made bitter
**ENFETTER** *vb* fetter
**ENFETTERS** > ENFETTER
**ENFEVER** *vb* make feverish
**ENFEVERED** > ENFEVER
**ENFEVERS** > ENFEVER
**ENFIERCE** *vb* make ferocious
**ENFIERCED** > ENFIERCE
**ENFIERCES** > ENFIERCE
**ENFILADE** *n* burst of gunfire sweeping from end to end along a line of troops ▷ *vb* attack with an enfilade
**ENFILADED** > ENFILADE
**ENFILADES** > ENFILADE
**ENFILED** *adj* passed through
**ENFIRE** *vb* set alight
**ENFIRED** > ENFIRE
**ENFIRES** > ENFIRE
**ENFIRING** > ENFIRE
**ENFIX** *variant of* > INFIX
**ENFIXED** > ENFIX
**ENFIXES** > ENFIX
**ENFIXING** > ENFIX
**ENFLAME** *variant of* > INFLAME
**ENFLAMED** > ENFLAME
**ENFLAMES** > ENFLAME
**ENFLAMING** > ENFLAME
**ENFLESH** *vb* make flesh
**ENFLESHED** > ENFLESH

**ENFLESHES** > ENFLESH
**ENFLOWER** *vb* put flowers on
**ENFLOWERS** > ENFLOWER
**ENFOLD** *vb* cover by wrapping something around
**ENFOLDED** > ENFOLD
**ENFOLDER** > ENFOLD
**ENFOLDERS** > ENFOLD
**ENFOLDING** > ENFOLD
**ENFOLDS** > ENFOLD
**ENFORCE** *vb* impose obedience (to a law etc)
**ENFORCED** > ENFORCE
**ENFORCER** > ENFORCE
**ENFORCERS** > ENFORCE
**ENFORCES** > ENFORCE
**ENFORCING** > ENFORCE
**ENFOREST** *vb* make into a forest
**ENFORESTS** > ENFOREST
**ENFORM** *variant of* > INFORM
**ENFORMED** > ENFORM
**ENFORMING** > ENFORM
**ENFORMS** > ENFORM
**ENFRAME** *vb* put inside a frame
**ENFRAMED** > ENFRAME
**ENFRAMES** > ENFRAME
**ENFRAMING** > ENFRAME
**ENFREE** *vb* release, make free
**ENFREED** > ENFREE
**ENFREEDOM** *variant of* > ENFREE
**ENFREEING** > ENFREE
**ENFREES** > ENFREE
**ENFREEZE** *vb* freeze
**ENFREEZES** > ENFREEZE
**ENFROSEN** > ENFREEZE
**ENFROZE** > ENFREEZE
**ENFROZEN** > ENFREEZE
**ENG** *another name for* > AGMA
**ENGAGE** *vb* take part, participate ▷ *adj* (of a writer or artist, esp a man) morally or politically committed to some ideology
**ENGAGED** *adj* pledged to be married
**ENGAGEDLY** > ENGAGED
**ENGAGEE** *adj* (of a female writer or artist) morally or politically committed to some ideology
**ENGAGER** > ENGAGE
**ENGAGERS** > ENGAGE
**ENGAGES** > ENGAGE
**ENGAGING** *adj* charming
**ENGAOL** *vb* put into gaol
**ENGAOLED** > ENGAOL
**ENGAOLING** > ENGAOL
**ENGAOLS** > ENGAOL
**ENGARLAND** *vb* cover with garlands
**ENGENDER** *vb* produce, cause to occur
**ENGENDERS** > ENGENDER
**ENGENDURE** > ENGENDER
**ENGILD** *vb* cover with or as if with gold
**ENGILDED** > ENGILD

ENGILDING > ENGILD
ENGILDS > ENGILD
ENGILT > ENGILD
ENGINE n any machine which converts energy into mechanical work ▷ vb put an engine in
ENGINED > ENGINE
ENGINEER n person trained in any branch of engineering ▷ vb plan in a clever manner
ENGINEERS > ENGINEER
ENGINER > ENGINE
ENGINERS > ENGINE
ENGINERY n collection or assembly of engines
ENGINES > ENGINE
ENGINING > ENGINE
ENGINOUS adj ingenious or clever
ENGIRD vb surround
ENGIRDED > ENGIRD
ENGIRDING > ENGIRD
ENGIRDLE variant of > ENGIRD
ENGIRDLED > ENGIRDLE
ENGIRDLES > ENGIRDLE
ENGIRDS > ENGIRD
ENGIRT > ENGIRD
ENGISCOPE variant of > ENGYSCOPE
ENGLACIAL adj embedded in, carried by, or running through a glacier
ENGLISH vb put a spinning movement on a billiard ball
ENGLISHED > ENGLISH
ENGLISHES > ENGLISH
ENGLOBE vb surround as if in a globe
ENGLOBED > ENGLOBE
ENGLOBES > ENGLOBE
ENGLOBING > ENGLOBE
ENGLOOM vb make dull or dismal
ENGLOOMED > ENGLOOM
ENGLOOMS > ENGLOOM
ENGLUT vb devour ravenously
ENGLUTS > ENGLUT
ENGLUTTED > ENGLUT
ENGOBE n liquid put on pottery before glazing
ENGOBES > ENGOBE
ENGORE vb pierce or wound
ENGORED > ENGORE
ENGORES > ENGORE
ENGORGE vb clog with blood
ENGORGED > ENGORGE
ENGORGES > ENGORGE
ENGORGING > ENGORGE
ENGORING > ENGORE
ENGOULED adj (in heraldry) with ends coming from the mouths of animals
ENGOUMENT n obsessive liking
ENGRACE vb give grace to
ENGRACED > ENGRACE
ENGRACES > ENGRACE
ENGRACING > ENGRACE

ENGRAFF variant of > ENGRAFT
ENGRAFFED > ENGRAFF
ENGRAFFS > ENGRAFF
ENGRAFT vb graft (a shoot, bud, etc) onto a stock
ENGRAFTED > ENGRAFT
ENGRAFTS > ENGRAFT
ENGRAIL vb decorate or mark (the edge of) (a coin) with small carved notches
ENGRAILED > ENGRAIL
ENGRAILS > ENGRAIL
ENGRAIN variant spelling of > INGRAIN
ENGRAINED > ENGRAIN
ENGRAINER > ENGRAIN
ENGRAINS > ENGRAIN
ENGRAM n physical basis of an individual memory in the brain
ENGRAMMA variant of > ENGRAM
ENGRAMMAS > ENGRAMMA
ENGRAMME variant of > ENGRAM
ENGRAMMES > ENGRAMME
ENGRAMMIC > ENGRAM
ENGRAMS > ENGRAM
ENGRASP vb grasp or seize
ENGRASPED > ENGRASP
ENGRASPS > ENGRASP
ENGRAVE vb carve (a design) onto a hard surface
ENGRAVED > ENGRAVE
ENGRAVEN > ENGRAVE
ENGRAVER > ENGRAVE
ENGRAVERS > ENGRAVE
ENGRAVERY > ENGRAVE
ENGRAVES > ENGRAVE
ENGRAVING n print made from an engraved plate
ENGRENAGE n act of putting into gear
ENGRIEVE vb grieve
ENGRIEVED > ENGRIEVE
ENGRIEVES > ENGRIEVE
ENGROOVE vb put a groove in
ENGROOVED > ENGROOVE
ENGROOVES > ENGROOVE
ENGROSS vb occupy the attention of (a person) completely
ENGROSSED > ENGROSS
ENGROSSER > ENGROSS
ENGROSSES > ENGROSS
ENGS > ENG
ENGUARD vb protect or defend
ENGUARDED > ENGUARD
ENGUARDS > ENGUARD
ENGULF vb cover or surround completely
ENGULFED > ENGULF
ENGULFING > ENGULF
ENGULFS > ENGULF
ENGULPH variant of > ENGULF
ENGULPHED > ENGULPH
ENGULPHS > ENGULPH
ENGYSCOPE n microscope
ENHALO vb surround with

or as if with a halo
ENHALOED > ENHALO
ENHALOES > ENHALO
ENHALOING > ENHALO
ENHALOS > ENHALO
ENHANCE vb increase in quality, value, or attractiveness
ENHANCED > ENHANCE
ENHANCER > ENHANCE
ENHANCERS > ENHANCE
ENHANCES > ENHANCE
ENHANCING > ENHANCE
ENHANCIVE > ENHANCE
ENHEARSE variant of > INHEARSE
ENHEARSED > ENHEARSE
ENHEARSES > ENHEARSE
ENHEARTEN vb give heart to, encourage
ENHUNGER vb cause to be hungry
ENHUNGERS > ENHUNGER
ENHYDRITE n type of mineral
ENHYDROS n piece of chalcedony that contains water
ENHYDROUS > ENHYDROS
ENIAC n early type of computer built in the 1940s
ENIACS > ENIAC
ENIGMA n puzzling thing or person
ENIGMAS > ENIGMA
ENIGMATA > ENIGMA
ENIGMATIC > ENIGMA
ENISLE vb put on or make into an island
ENISLED > ENISLE
ENISLES > ENISLE
ENISLING > ENISLE
ENJAMB vb (of a line of verse) run over into the next line
ENJAMBED > ENJAMB
ENJAMBING > ENJAMB
ENJAMBS > ENJAMB
ENJOIN vb order (someone) to do something
ENJOINDER n order
ENJOINED > ENJOIN
ENJOINER > ENJOIN
ENJOINERS > ENJOIN
ENJOINING > ENJOIN
ENJOINS > ENJOIN
ENJOY vb take joy in
ENJOYABLE > ENJOY
ENJOYABLY > ENJOY
ENJOYED > ENJOY
ENJOYER > ENJOY
ENJOYERS > ENJOY
ENJOYING > ENJOY
ENJOYMENT n act or condition of receiving pleasure from something
ENJOYS > ENJOY
ENKERNEL vb put inside a kernel
ENKERNELS > ENKERNEL
ENKINDLE vb set on fire
ENKINDLED > ENKINDLE
ENKINDLER > ENKINDLE

ENKINDLES > ENKINDLE
ENLACE vb bind or encircle with or as with laces
ENLACED > ENLACE
ENLACES > ENLACE
ENLACING > ENLACE
ENLARD vb put lard on
ENLARDED > ENLARD
ENLARDING > ENLARD
ENLARDS > ENLARD
ENLARGE vb make or grow larger
ENLARGED > ENLARGE
ENLARGEN variant of > ENLARGE
ENLARGENS > ENLARGEN
ENLARGER n optical instrument for making enlarged photographic prints in which a negative is brightly illuminated and its enlarged image is focused onto a sheet of sensitized paper
ENLARGERS > ENLARGER
ENLARGES > ENLARGE
ENLARGING > ENLARGE
ENLEVE adj having been abducted
ENLIGHT vb light up
ENLIGHTED > ENLIGHT
ENLIGHTEN vb give information to
ENLIGHTS > ENLIGHT
ENLINK vb link together
ENLINKED > ENLINK
ENLINKING > ENLINK
ENLINKS > ENLINK
ENLIST vb enter the armed forces
ENLISTED > ENLIST
ENLISTEE > ENLIST
ENLISTEES > ENLIST
ENLISTER > ENLIST
ENLISTERS > ENLIST
ENLISTING > ENLIST
ENLISTS > ENLIST
ENLIT > ENLIGHT
ENLIVEN vb make lively or cheerful
ENLIVENED > ENLIVEN
ENLIVENER > ENLIVEN
ENLIVENS > ENLIVEN
ENLOCK vb lock or secure
ENLOCKED > ENLOCK
ENLOCKING > ENLOCK
ENLOCKS > ENLOCK
ENLUMINE vb illuminate
ENLUMINED > ENLUMINE
ENLUMINES > ENLUMINE
ENMESH vb catch or involve in or as if in a net or snare
ENMESHED > ENMESH
ENMESHES > ENMESH
ENMESHING > ENMESH
ENMEW variant of > EMMEW
ENMEWED > ENMEW
ENMEWING > ENMEW
ENMEWS > ENMEW
ENMITIES > ENMITY
ENMITY n ill will, hatred
ENMOSSED adj having a covering of moss
ENMOVE variant

*of* > EMMOVE
**ENMOVED** > ENMOVE
**ENMOVES** > ENMOVE
**ENMOVING** > ENMOVE
**ENNAGE** *n* total number of ens in a piece of matter to be set in type
**ENNAGES** > ENNAGE
**ENNEAD** *n* group or series of nine
**ENNEADIC** > ENNEAD
**ENNEADS** > ENNEAD
**ENNEAGON** *another name for* > NONAGON
**ENNEAGONS** > ENNEAGON
**ENNOBLE** *vb* make noble, elevate
**ENNOBLED** > ENNOBLE
**ENNOBLER** > ENNOBLE
**ENNOBLERS** > ENNOBLE
**ENNOBLES** > ENNOBLE
**ENNOBLING** > ENNOBLE
**ENNOG** *n* back alley
**ENNOGS** > ENNOG
**ENNUI** *n* boredom, dissatisfaction ▷ *vb* bore
**ENNUIED** > ENNUI
**ENNUIS** > ENNUI
**ENNUYE** *adj* bored
**ENNUYED** > ENNUI
**ENNUYEE** *same as* > ENNUYE
**ENNUYING** > ENNUI
**ENODAL** *adj* having no nodes
**ENOKI** *variant of* > ENOKITAKE
**ENOKIDAKE** *variant of* > ENOKITAKE
**ENOKIS** > ENOKI
**ENOKITAKE** *n* Japanese mushroom
**ENOL** *n* any organic compound containing the group -CH:CO-, often existing in chemical equilibrium with the corresponding keto form
**ENOLASE** *n* type of enzyme
**ENOLASES** > ENOLASE
**ENOLIC** > ENOL
**ENOLOGIES** > ENOLOGY
**ENOLOGIST** *n* wine expert
**ENOLOGY** *usual US spelling of* > OENOLOGY
**ENOLS** > ENOL
**ENOMOTIES** > ENOMOTY
**ENOMOTY** *n* division of the Spartan army in ancient Greece
**ENOPHILE** *n* lover of wine
**ENOPHILES** > ENOPHILE
**ENORM** *variant of* > ENORMOUS
**ENORMITY** *n* great wickedness
**ENORMOUS** *adj* very big, vast
**ENOSES** > ENOSIS
**ENOSIS** *n* union of Greece and Cyprus
**ENOSISES** > ENOSIS
**ENOUGH** *adj* as much or as many as necessary ▷ *n* sufficient quantity ▷ *adv* sufficiently

**ENOUGHS** > ENOUGH
**ENOUNCE** *vb* enunciate
**ENOUNCED** > ENOUNCE
**ENOUNCES** > ENOUNCE
**ENOUNCING** > ENOUNCE
**ENOW** *archaic word for* > ENOUGH
**ENOWS** > ENOW
**ENPLANE** *vb* board an aircraft
**ENPLANED** > ENPLANE
**ENPLANES** > ENPLANE
**ENPLANING** > ENPLANE
**ENPRINT** *n* standard photographic print produced from a negative
**ENPRINTS** > ENPRINT
**ENQUIRE** *same as* > INQUIRE
**ENQUIRED** > ENQUIRE
**ENQUIRER** > ENQUIRE
**ENQUIRERS** > ENQUIRE
**ENQUIRES** > ENQUIRE
**ENQUIRIES** > ENQUIRE
**ENQUIRING** > ENQUIRE
**ENQUIRY** > ENQUIRE
**ENRACE** *vb* bring in a race of people
**ENRACED** > ENRACE
**ENRACES** > ENRACE
**ENRACING** > ENRACE
**ENRAGE** *vb* make extremely angry
**ENRAGED** > ENRAGE
**ENRAGEDLY** > ENRAGE
**ENRAGES** > ENRAGE
**ENRAGING** > ENRAGE
**ENRANCKLE** *vb* upset, make irate
**ENRANGE** *vb* arrange, organize
**ENRANGED** > ENRANGE
**ENRANGES** > ENRANGE
**ENRANGING** > ENRANGE
**ENRANK** *vb* put in a row
**ENRANKED** > ENRANK
**ENRANKING** > ENRANK
**ENRANKS** > ENRANK
**ENRAPT** > ENRAPTURE
**ENRAPTURE** *vb* fill with delight
**ENRAUNGE** *variant of* > ENRANGE
**ENRAUNGED** > ENRAUNGE
**ENRAUNGES** > ENRAUNGE
**ENRAVISH** *vb* enchant
**ENRHEUM** *vb* pass a cold on to
**ENRHEUMED** > ENRHEUM
**ENRHEUMS** > ENRHEUM
**ENRICH** *vb* improve in quality
**ENRICHED** > ENRICH
**ENRICHER** > ENRICH
**ENRICHERS** > ENRICH
**ENRICHES** > ENRICH
**ENRICHING** > ENRICH
**ENRIDGED** *adj* ridged
**ENRING** *vb* put a ring round
**ENRINGED** > ENRING
**ENRINGING** > ENRING
**ENRINGS** > ENRING
**ENRIVEN** *adj* ripped
**ENROBE** *vb* dress in or as if in a robe

**ENROBED** > ENROBE
**ENROBER** > ENROBE
**ENROBERS** > ENROBE
**ENROBES** > ENROBE
**ENROBING** > ENROBE
**ENROL** *vb* (cause to) become a member
**ENROLL** *same as* > ENROL
**ENROLLED** > ENROL
**ENROLLEE** > ENROL
**ENROLLEES** > ENROL
**ENROLLER** > ENROL
**ENROLLERS** > ENROL
**ENROLLING** > ENROLL
**ENROLLS** > ENROLL
**ENROLMENT** *n* act of enrolling or state of being enrolled
**ENROLS** > ENROL
**ENROOT** *vb* establish (plants) by fixing their roots in the earth
**ENROOTED** > ENROOT
**ENROOTING** > ENROOT
**ENROOTS** > ENROOT
**ENROUGH** *vb* roughen
**ENROUGHED** > ENROUGH
**ENROUGHS** > ENROUGH
**ENROUND** *vb* encircle
**ENROUNDED** > ENROUND
**ENROUNDS** > ENROUND
**ENS** *n* being or existence in the most general abstract sense
**ENSAMPLE** *n* example ▷ *vb* make an example
**ENSAMPLED** > ENSAMPLE
**ENSAMPLES** > ENSAMPLE
**ENSATE** *adj* shaped like a sword
**ENSCONCE** *vb* settle firmly or comfortably
**ENSCONCED** > ENSCONCE
**ENSCONCES** > ENSCONCE
**ENSCROLL** *variant of* > INSCROLL
**ENSCROLLS** > ENSCROLL
**ENSEAL** *vb* seal up
**ENSEALED** > ENSEAL
**ENSEALING** > ENSEAL
**ENSEALS** > ENSEAL
**ENSEAM** *vb* put a seam on
**ENSEAMED** > ENSEAM
**ENSEAMING** > ENSEAM
**ENSEAMS** > ENSEAM
**ENSEAR** *vb* dry
**ENSEARED** > ENSEAR
**ENSEARING** > ENSEAR
**ENSEARS** > ENSEAR
**ENSEMBLE** *n* all the parts of something taken together ▷ *adv* all together or at once ▷ *adj* (of a film or play) involving several separate but often interrelated story lines
**ENSEMBLES** > ENSEMBLE
**ENSERF** *vb* enslave
**ENSERFED** > ENSERF
**ENSERFING** > ENSERF
**ENSERFS** > ENSERF
**ENSEW** *variant of* > ENSUE
**ENSEWED** > ENSEW
**ENSEWING** > ENSEW

**ENSEWS** > ENSEW
**ENSHEATH** *variant of* > INSHEATHE
**ENSHEATHE** *variant of* > INSHEATHE
**ENSHEATHS** > ENSHEATH
**ENSHELL** *variant of* > INSHELL
**ENSHELLED** > ENSHELL
**ENSHELLS** > ENSHELL
**ENSHELTER** *vb* shelter
**ENSHIELD** *vb* protect
**ENSHIELDS** > ENSHIELD
**ENSHRINE** *vb* cherish or treasure
**ENSHRINED** > ENSHRINE
**ENSHRINEE** > ENSHRINE
**ENSHRINES** > ENSHRINE
**ENSHROUD** *vb* cover or hide as with a shroud
**ENSHROUDS** > ENSHROUD
**ENSIFORM** *adj* shaped like a sword blade
**ENSIGN** *n* naval flag ▷ *vb* mark with a sign
**ENSIGNCY** > ENSIGN
**ENSIGNED** > ENSIGN
**ENSIGNING** > ENSIGN
**ENSIGNS** > ENSIGN
**ENSILAGE** *n* process of ensiling green fodder ▷ *vb* make into silage
**ENSILAGED** > ENSILAGE
**ENSILAGES** > ENSILAGE
**ENSILE** *vb* store and preserve (green fodder) in an enclosed pit or silo
**ENSILED** > ENSILE
**ENSILES** > ENSILE
**ENSILING** > ENSILE
**ENSKIED** > ENSKY
**ENSKIES** > ENSKY
**ENSKY** *vb* put in the sky
**ENSKYED** > ENSKY
**ENSKYING** > ENSKY
**ENSLAVE** *vb* make a slave of (someone)
**ENSLAVED** > ENSLAVE
**ENSLAVER** > ENSLAVE
**ENSLAVERS** > ENSLAVE
**ENSLAVES** > ENSLAVE
**ENSLAVING** > ENSLAVE
**ENSNARE** *vb* catch in or as if in a snare
**ENSNARED** > ENSNARE
**ENSNARER** > ENSNARE
**ENSNARERS** > ENSNARE
**ENSNARES** > ENSNARE
**ENSNARING** > ENSNARE
**ENSNARL** *vb* become tangled in
**ENSNARLED** > ENSNARL
**ENSNARLS** > ENSNARL
**ENSORCEL** *vb* enchant
**ENSORCELL** *variant of* > ENSORCEL
**ENSORCELS** > ENSORCEL
**ENSOUL** *vb* endow with a soul
**ENSOULED** > ENSOUL
**ENSOULING** > ENSOUL
**ENSOULS** > ENSOUL
**ENSPHERE** *vb* enclose in or as if in a sphere

ENSPHERED > ENSPHERE
ENSPHERES > ENSPHERE
ENSTAMP vb imprint with
a stamp
ENSTAMPED > ENSTAMP
ENSTAMPS > ENSTAMP
ENSTATITE n grey, green,
yellow, or brown pyroxene
mineral consisting of
magnesium silicate in
orthorhombic crystalline
form
ENSTEEP vb soak in water
ENSTEEPED > ENSTEEP
ENSTEEPS > ENSTEEP
ENSTYLE vb give a name to
ENSTYLED > ENSTYLE
ENSTYLES > ENSTYLE
ENSTYLING > ENSTYLE
ENSUE vb come next, result
ENSUED > ENSUE
ENSUES > ENSUE
ENSUING adj following
subsequently or in order
ENSURE vb make certain
or sure
ENSURED > ENSURE
ENSURER > ENSURE
ENSURERS > ENSURE
ENSURES > ENSURE
ENSURING > ENSURE
ENSWATHE vb bind or wrap
ENSWATHED > ENSWATHE
ENSWATHES > ENSWATHE
ENSWEEP vb sweep across
ENSWEEPS > ENSWEEP
ENSWEPT > ENSWEEP
ENTAIL vb bring about
or impose inevitably ▷ n
restriction imposed by
entailing an estate
ENTAILED > ENTAIL
ENTAILER > ENTAIL
ENTAILERS > ENTAIL
ENTAILING > ENTAIL
ENTAILS > ENTAIL
ENTAME vb make tame
ENTAMEBA same
as > ENTAMOEBA
ENTAMEBAE > ENTAMEBA
ENTAMEBAS > ENTAMEBA
ENTAMED > ENTAME
ENTAMES > ENTAME
ENTAMING > ENTAME
ENTAMOEBA n parasitic
amoeba that lives in the
intestines of man and
causes amoebic dysentery
ENTANGLE vb catch or
involve in or as if in a
tangle
ENTANGLED > ENTANGLE
ENTANGLER > ENTANGLE
ENTANGLES > ENTANGLE
ENTASES > ENTASIS
ENTASIA same as > ENTASIS
ENTASIAS > ENTASIA
ENTASIS n slightly convex
curve given to the shaft of
a column, pier, or similar
structure, to correct the
illusion of concavity
produced by a straight
shaft

ENTASTIC adj (of a disease)
characterized by spasms
ENTAYLE variant of > ENTAIL
ENTAYLED > ENTAYLE
ENTAYLES > ENTAYLE
ENTAYLING > ENTAYLE
ENTELECHY n (in the
philosophy of Aristotle)
actuality as opposed to
potentiality
ENTELLUS n langur of S
Asia
ENTENDER vb make more
tender
ENTENDERS > ENTENDER
ENTENTE n friendly
understanding between
nations
ENTENTES > ENTENTE
ENTER vb come or go in
ENTERA > ENTERON
ENTERABLE > ENTER
ENTERAL same as > ENTERIC
ENTERALLY > ENTERIC
ENTERATE adj with an
intestine separate from
the outer wall of the body
ENTERED > ENTER
ENTERER > ENTER
ENTERERS > ENTER
ENTERIC adj intestinal ▷ n
infectious disease of the
intestines
ENTERICS > ENTERIC
ENTERING > ENTER
ENTERINGS > ENTER
ENTERITIS n
inflammation of the
intestine, causing
diarrhoea
ENTERON n alimentary
canal, esp of an embryo or
a coelenterate
ENTERONS > ENTERON
ENTERS > ENTER
ENTERTAIN vb amuse
ENTERTAKE vb entertain
ENTERTOOK > ENTERTAKE
ENTETE adj obsessed
ENTETEE variant
of > ENTETE
ENTHALPY n
thermodynamic property
of a system equal to the
sum of its internal energy
and the product of its
pressure and volume
ENTHETIC adj (esp of
infectious diseases)
introduced into the body
from without
ENTHRAL vb hold the
attention of
ENTHRALL same
as > ENTHRAL
ENTHRALLS > ENTHRALL
ENTHRALS > ENTHRAL
ENTHRONE vb place
(someone) on a throne
ENTHRONED > ENTHRONE
ENTHRONES > ENTHRONE
ENTHUSE vb (cause to)
show enthusiasm
ENTHUSED > ENTHUSE

ENTHUSES > ENTHUSE
ENTHUSING > ENTHUSE
ENTHYMEME n incomplete
syllogism, in which one
or more premises are
unexpressed as their truth
is considered to be self-
evident
ENTIA > ENS
ENTICE vb attract by
exciting hope or desire,
tempt
ENTICED > ENTICE
ENTICER > ENTICE
ENTICERS > ENTICE
ENTICES > ENTICE
ENTICING > ENTICE
ENTICINGS > ENTICE
ENTIRE adj including every
detail, part, or aspect of
something ▷ n state of
being entire
ENTIRELY adv without
reservation or exception
ENTIRES > ENTIRE
ENTIRETY n state of being
entire or whole
ENTITIES > ENTITY
ENTITLE vb give a right to
ENTITLED > ENTITLE
ENTITLES > ENTITLE
ENTITLING > ENTITLE
ENTITY n separate distinct
thing
ENTOBLAST less common
name for > ENDODERM
ENTODERM same
as > ENDODERM
ENTODERMS > ENTODERM
ENTOIL archaic word
for > ENSNARE
ENTOILED > ENTOIL
ENTOILING > ENTOIL
ENTOILS > ENTOIL
ENTOMB vb place (a corpse)
in a tomb
ENTOMBED > ENTOMB
ENTOMBING > ENTOMB
ENTOMBS > ENTOMB
ENTOMIC adj denoting or
relating to insects
ENTOPHYTE variant
of > ENDOPHYTE
ENTOPIC adj situated in its
normal place or position
ENTOPROCT n type of
marine animal
ENTOPTIC adj (of visual
sensation) resulting from
structures within the eye
itself
ENTOPTICS n study of
entoptic visions
ENTOTIC adj of or relating
to the inner ear
ENTOURAGE n group of
people who assist an
important person
ENTOZOA > ENTOZOON
ENTOZOAL > ENTOZOON
ENTOZOAN same
as > ENTOZOON
ENTOZOANS > ENTOZOAN
ENTOZOIC adj of or relating

to an entozoon
ENTOZOON n internal
parasite
ENTRAIL vb twist or
entangle
ENTRAILED > ENTRAIL
ENTRAILS pl n intestines
ENTRAIN vb board or put
aboard a train
ENTRAINED > ENTRAIN
ENTRAINER > ENTRAIN
ENTRAINS > ENTRAIN
ENTRALL variant
of > ENTRAILS
ENTRALLES variant
of > ENTRAILS
ENTRAMMEL vb hamper or
obstruct by entangling
ENTRANCE n way into a
place ▷ vb delight ▷ adj
necessary in order to enter
something
ENTRANCED > ENTRANCE
ENTRANCES > ENTRANCE
ENTRANT n person who
enters a university,
contest, etc
ENTRANTS > ENTRANT
ENTRAP vb trick into
difficulty etc
ENTRAPPED > ENTRAP
ENTRAPPER > ENTRAP
ENTRAPS > ENTRAP
ENTREAT vb ask earnestly
ENTREATED > ENTREAT
ENTREATS > ENTREAT
ENTREATY n earnest
request
ENTRECHAT n leap in ballet
during which the dancer
repeatedly crosses his feet
or beats them together
ENTRECOTE n beefsteak cut
from between the ribs
ENTREE n dish served
before a main course
ENTREES > ENTREE
ENTREMES variant
of > ENTREMETS
ENTREMETS n dessert
ENTRENCH vb establish
firmly
ENTREPOT n warehouse for
commercial goods
ENTREPOTS > ENTREPOT
ENTRESOL another name
for > MEZZANINE
ENTRESOLS > ENTRESOL
ENTREZ interj enter
ENTRIES > ENTRY
ENTRISM variant
of > ENTRYVISM
ENTRISMS > ENTRISM
ENTRIST > ENTRYVISM
ENTRISTS > ENTRYVISM
ENTROLD adj surrounded
ENTROPIC > ENTROPY
ENTROPIES > ENTROPY
ENTROPION n turning
inwards of the edge of the
eyelid
ENTROPIUM variant
of > ENTROPION
ENTROPY n lack of

organization

**ENTRUST** vb put into the care or protection of

**ENTRUSTED** > ENTRUST

**ENTRUSTS** > ENTRUST

**ENTRY** n entrance ▷ adj necessary in order to enter something

**ENTRYISM** n policy or practice of members of a particular political group joining an existing political party with the intention of changing its principles and policies, instead of forming a new party

**ENTRYISMS** > ENTRYISM

**ENTRYIST** > ENTRYISM

**ENTRYISTS** > ENTRYISM

**ENTRYWAY** n entrance passage

**ENTRYWAYS** > ENTRYWAY

**ENTWINE** vb twist together or around

**ENTWINED** > ENTWINE

**ENTWINES** > ENTWINE

**ENTWINING** > ENTWINE

**ENTWIST** vb twist together or around

**ENTWISTED** > ENTWIST

**ENTWISTS** > ENTWIST

**ENUCLEATE** vb remove the nucleus from (a cell) ▷ adj (of cells) deprived of their nuclei

**ENUF** common intentional literary misspelling of > ENOUGH

**ENUMERATE** vb name one by one

**ENUNCIATE** vb pronounce clearly

**ENURE** variant spelling of > INURE

**ENURED** > ENURE

**ENUREMENT** > ENURE

**ENURES** > ENURE

**ENURESES** > ENURESIS

**ENURESIS** n involuntary discharge of urine, esp during sleep

**ENURETIC** > ENURESIS

**ENURETICS** > ENURESIS

**ENURING** > ENURE

**ENVASSAL** vb make a vassal of

**ENVASSALS** > ENVASSAL

**ENVAULT** vb enclose in a vault; entomb

**ENVAULTED** > ENVAULT

**ENVAULTS** > ENVAULT

**ENVEIGLE** same as > INVEIGLE

**ENVEIGLED** > ENVEIGLE

**ENVEIGLES** > ENVEIGLE

**ENVELOP** vb wrap up, enclose

**ENVELOPE** n folded gummed paper cover for a letter

**ENVELOPED** > ENVELOP

**ENVELOPER** > ENVELOP

**ENVELOPES** > ENVELOPE

**ENVELOPS** > ENVELOP

**ENVENOM** vb fill or impregnate with venom

**ENVENOMED** > ENVENOM

**ENVENOMS** > ENVENOM

**ENVERMEIL** vb dye vermilion

**ENVIABLE** adj arousing envy, fortunate

**ENVIABLY** > ENVIABLE

**ENVIED** > ENVY

**ENVIER** > ENVY

**ENVIERS** > ENVY

**ENVIES** > ENVY

**ENVIOUS** adj full of envy

**ENVIOUSLY** > ENVIOUS

**ENVIRO** n environmentalist

**ENVIRON** vb encircle or surround

**ENVIRONED** > ENVIRON

**ENVIRONS** pl n surrounding area, esp of a town

**ENVIROS** > ENVIRO

**ENVISAGE** vb conceive of as a possibility

**ENVISAGED** > ENVISAGE

**ENVISAGES** > ENVISAGE

**ENVISION** vb conceive of as a possibility, esp in the future

**ENVISIONS** > ENVISION

**ENVOI** same as > ENVOY

**ENVOIS** > ENVOI

**ENVOY** n messenger

**ENVOYS** > ENVOY

**ENVOYSHIP** > ENVOY

**ENVY** n feeling of discontent aroused by another's good fortune ▷ vb grudge (another's good fortune, success, or qualities)

**ENVYING** > ENVY

**ENVYINGLY** > ENVY

**ENVYINGS** > ENVY

**ENWALL** vb wall in

**ENWALLED** > ENWALL

**ENWALLING** > ENWALL

**ENWALLOW** vb sink or plunge

**ENWALLOWS** > ENWALLOW

**ENWALLS** > ENWALL

**ENWHEEL** archaic word for > ENCIRCLE

**ENWHEELED** > ENWHEEL

**ENWHEELS** > ENWHEEL

**ENWIND** vb wind or coil around

**ENWINDING** > ENWIND

**ENWINDS** > ENWIND

**ENWOMB** vb enclose in or as if in a womb

**ENWOMBED** > ENWOMB

**ENWOMBING** > ENWOMB

**ENWOMBS** > ENWOMB

**ENWOUND** > ENWIND

**ENWRAP** vb wrap or cover up

**ENWRAPPED** > ENWRAP

**ENWRAPS** > ENWRAP

**ENWREATH** vb surround or encircle with or as with a wreath or wreaths

**ENWREATHE** same as > ENWREATH

**ENWREATHS** > ENWREATH

**ENZIAN** n gentian violet

**ENZIANS** > ENZIAN

**ENZONE** vb enclose in a zone

**ENZONED** > ENZONE

**ENZONES** > ENZONE

**ENZONING** > ENZONE

**ENZOOTIC** adj (of diseases) affecting animals within a limited region ▷ n enzootic disease

**ENZOOTICS** > ENZOOTIC

**ENZYM** same as > ENZYME

**ENZYMATIC** > ENZYME

**ENZYME** n any of a group of complex proteins that act as catalysts in specific biochemical reactions

**ENZYMES** > ENZYME

**ENZYMIC** > ENZYME

**ENZYMS** > ENZYM

**EOAN** adj of or relating to the dawn

**EOBIONT** n hypothetical chemical precursor of a living cell

**EOBIONTS** > EOBIONT

**EOCENE** adj of, denoting, or formed in the second epoch of the Tertiary period

**EOHIPPUS** n earliest horse: an extinct Eocene dog-sized animal of the genus with four-toed forelegs, three-toed hindlegs, and teeth specialized for browsing

**EOLIAN** adj of or relating to the wind

**EOLIENNE** n type of fine cloth

**EOLIENNES** > EOLIENNE

**EOLIPILE** variant of > AEOLIPILE

**EOLIPILES** > EOLIPILE

**EOLITH** n stone, usually crudely broken, used as a primitive tool in Eolithic times

**EOLITHIC** > EOLITH

**EOLITHS** > EOLITH

**EOLOPILE** variant of > AEOLIPILE

**EOLOPILES** > EOLOPILE

**EON** n longest division of geological time, comprising two or more eras

**EONIAN** adj of or relating to an eon

**EONISM** n adoption of female dress and behaviour by a male

**EONISMS** > EONISM

**EONS** > EON

**EORL** n Anglo-Saxon nobleman

**EORLS** > EORL

**EOSIN** n red crystalline water-insoluble derivative of fluorescein

**EOSINE** same as > EOSIN

**EOSINES** > EOSINE

**EOSINIC** > EOSIN

**EOSINS** > EOSIN

**EOTHEN** adv from the East

**EPACRID** n type of heath-like plant

**EPACRIDS** > EPACRID

**EPACRIS** n genus of the epacrids

**EPACRISES** > EPACRIS

**EPACT** n difference in time, about 11 days, between the solar year and the lunar year

**EPACTS** > EPACT

**EPAENETIC** adj eulogistic

**EPAGOGE** n inductive reasoning

**EPAGOGES** > EPAGOGE

**EPAGOGIC** > EPAGOGE

**EPANODOS** n return to main theme after a digression

**EPARCH** n bishop or metropolitan in charge of an eparchy

**EPARCHATE** same as > EPARCHY

**EPARCHIAL** > EPARCHY

**EPARCHIES** > EPARCHY

**EPARCHS** > EPARCH

**EPARCHY** n diocese of the Eastern Christian Church

**EPATANT** adj startling or shocking, esp through being unconventional

**EPAULE** n shoulder of a fortification

**EPAULES** > EPAULE

**EPAULET** same as > EPAULETTE

**EPAULETS** > EPAULET

**EPAULETTE** n shoulder ornament on a uniform

**EPAXIAL** adj above the axis

**EPAZOTE** n type of herb

**EPAZOTES** > EPAZOTE

**EPEDAPHIC** adj of or relating to atmospheric conditions

**EPEE** n straight-bladed sword used in fencing

**EPEEIST** n one who uses or specializes in using an epee

**EPEEISTS** > EPEEIST

**EPEES** > EPEE

**EPEIRA** same as > EPEIRID

**EPEIRAS** > EPEIRA

**EPEIRIC** adj in, of, or relating to a continent

**EPEIRID** n type of spider

**EPEIRIDS** > EPEIRID

**EPENDYMA** n membrane lining the ventricles of the brain and the central canal of the spinal cord

**EPENDYMAL** > EPENDYMA

**EPENDYMAS** > EPENDYMA

**EPEOLATRY** n worship of words

**EPERDU** adj distracted

**EPERDUE** adj distracted

**EPERGNE** n ornamental centrepiece for a table: a stand with holders for

sweetmeats, fruit, flowers, etc
**EPERGNES** > EPERGNE
**EPHA** same as > EPHAH
**EPHAH** n Hebrew unit of dry measure equal to approximately one bushel or about 33 litres
**EPHAHS** > EPHAH
**EPHAS** > EPHA
**EPHEBE** n (in ancient Greece) youth about to enter full citizenship, esp one undergoing military training
**EPHEBES** > EPHEBE
**EPHEBI** > EPHEBE
**EPHEBIC** > EPHEBE
**EPHEBOI** > EPHEBOS
**EPHEBOS** same as > EPHEBE
**EPHEBUS** same as > EPHEBE
**EPHEDRA** n gymnosperm shrub of warm regions of America and Eurasia
**EPHEDRAS** > EPHEDRA
**EPHEDRIN** same as > EPHEDRINE
**EPHEDRINE** n alkaloid used for treatment of asthma and hay fever
**EPHEDRINS** > EPHEDRIN
**EPHELIDES** > EPHELIS
**EPHELIS** n freckle
**EPHEMERA** n something transitory or short-lived
**EPHEMERAE** > EPHEMERA
**EPHEMERAL** adj short-lived ▷ n short-lived organism, such as the mayfly
**EPHEMERAS** > EPHEMERA
**EPHEMERID** n mayfly
**EPHEMERIS** n table giving the future positions of a planet, comet, or satellite
**EPHEMERON** > EPHEMERA
**EPHIALTES** n incubus
**EPHOD** n embroidered vestment believed to resemble an apron with shoulder straps, worn by priests in ancient Israel
**EPHODS** > EPHOD
**EPHOR** n (in ancient Greece) one of a board of senior magistrates in any of several Dorian states, esp the five Spartan ephors, who were elected by the vote of all full citizens and who wielded effective power
**EPHORAL** > EPHOR
**EPHORALTY** > EPHOR
**EPHORATE** > EPHOR
**EPHORATES** > EPHOR
**EPHORI** > EPHOR
**EPHORS** > EPHOR
**EPIBIOSES** > EPIBIOSIS
**EPIBIOSIS** n any relationship between two organisms in which one grows on the other but is not parasitic on it
**EPIBIOTIC** > EPIBIOSIS

**EPIBLAST** n outermost layer of an embryo, which becomes the ectoderm at gastrulation
**EPIBLASTS** > EPIBLAST
**EPIBLEM** n outermost cell layer of a root
**EPIBLEMS** > EPIBLEM
**EPIBOLIC** > EPIBOLY
**EPIBOLIES** > EPIBOLY
**EPIBOLY** n process that occurs during gastrulation in vertebrates, in which cells on one side of the blastula grow over and surround the remaining cells and yolk and eventually form the ectoderm
**EPIC** n long poem, book, or film about heroic events or actions ▷ adj very impressive or ambitious
**EPICAL** > EPIC
**EPICALLY** > EPIC
**EPICALYX** n series of small sepal-like bracts forming an outer calyx beneath the true calyx in some flowers
**EPICANTHI** n folds of skin extending vertically over the inner angles of the eyes
**EPICARDIA** n layers of pericardia in direct contact with the heart
**EPICARP** n outermost layer of the pericarp of fruits: forms the skin of a peach or grape
**EPICARPS** > EPICARP
**EPICEDE** same as > EPICEDIUM
**EPICEDES** > EPICEDE
**EPICEDIA** > EPICEDIUM
**EPICEDIAL** > EPICEDIUM
**EPICEDIAN** > EPICEDIUM
**EPICEDIUM** n funeral ode
**EPICENE** adj having the characteristics of both sexes; hermaphroditic ▷ n epicene person or creature
**EPICENES** > EPICENE
**EPICENISM** > EPICENE
**EPICENTER** same as > EPICENTRE
**EPICENTRA** n epicentres
**EPICENTRE** n point on the earth's surface immediately above the origin of an earthquake
**EPICIER** n grocer
**EPICIERS** > EPICIER
**EPICISM** n style or trope characteristic of epics
**EPICISMS** > EPIC
**EPICIST** n writer of epics
**EPICISTS** > EPIC
**EPICLESES** > EPICLESIS
**EPICLESIS** n invocation of the Holy Spirit to consecrate the bread and wine of the Eucharist
**EPICLIKE** adj resembling or reminiscent of an epic

**EPICOTYL** n part of an embryo plant stem above the cotyledons but beneath the terminal bud
**EPICOTYLS** > EPICOTYL
**EPICRANIA** n tissue covering the cranium
**EPICRISES** > EPICRISIS
**EPICRISIS** n secondary crisis occurring in the course of a disease
**EPICRITIC** adj (of certain nerve fibres of the skin) serving to perceive and distinguish fine variations of temperature or touch
**EPICS** > EPIC
**EPICURE** n person who enjoys good food and drink
**EPICUREAN** adj devoted to sensual pleasures, esp food and drink ▷ n epicure
**EPICURES** > EPICURE
**EPICURISE** same as > EPICURIZE
**EPICURISM** > EPICURE
**EPICURIZE** vb act as an epicure
**EPICYCLE** n (in the Ptolemaic system) a small circle, around which a planet was thought to revolve
**EPICYCLES** > EPICYCLE
**EPICYCLIC** > EPICYCLE
**EPIDEMIC** n widespread occurrence of a disease ▷ adj (esp of a disease) affecting many people in an area
**EPIDEMICS** > EPIDEMIC
**EPIDERM** same as > EPIDERMIS
**EPIDERMAL** > EPIDERMIS
**EPIDERMIC** > EPIDERMIS
**EPIDERMIS** n outer layer of the skin
**EPIDERMS** > EPIDERM
**EPIDICTIC** adj designed to display something, esp the skill of the speaker in rhetoric
**EPIDOSITE** n rock formed of quartz and epidote
**EPIDOTE** n green mineral consisting of hydrated calcium iron aluminium silicate in monoclinic crystalline form: common in metamorphic rocks
**EPIDOTES** > EPIDOTE
**EPIDOTIC** > EPIDOTE
**EPIDURAL** n spinal anaesthetic injected to relieve pain during childbirth ▷ adj on or over the outermost membrane covering the brain and spinal cord
**EPIDURALS** > EPIDURAL
**EPIFAUNA** n animals that live on the surface of the seabed
**EPIFAUNAE** > EPIFAUNA

**EPIFAUNAL** > EPIFAUNA
**EPIFAUNAS** > EPIFAUNA
**EPIFOCAL** adj situated or occurring at an epicentre
**EPIGAEAL** same as > EPIGEAL
**EPIGAEAN** same as > EPIGEAL
**EPIGAEOUS** same as > EPIGEAL
**EPIGAMIC** adj attractive to the opposite sex
**EPIGEAL** adj of or relating to seed germination in which the cotyledons appear above the ground because of the growth of the hypocotyl
**EPIGEAN** same as > EPIGEAL
**EPIGEIC** same as > EPIGEAL
**EPIGENE** adj formed or taking place at or near the surface of the earth
**EPIGENIC** adj pertaining to the theory of the gradual development of the embryo
**EPIGENIST** n one who studies or espouses the theory of the gradual development of the embryo
**EPIGENOUS** adj growing on the surface, esp the upper surface, of an organism or part
**EPIGEOUS** same as > EPIGEAL
**EPIGON** same as > EPIGONE
**EPIGONE** n inferior follower or imitator
**EPIGONES** > EPIGONE
**EPIGONI** > EPIGONE
**EPIGONIC** > EPIGONE
**EPIGONISM** > EPIGONE
**EPIGONOUS** > EPIGONE
**EPIGONS** > EPIGON
**EPIGONUS** same as > EPIGONE
**EPIGRAM** n short witty remark or poem
**EPIGRAMS** > EPIGRAM
**EPIGRAPH** n quotation at the start of a book
**EPIGRAPHS** > EPIGRAPH
**EPIGRAPHY** n study of ancient inscriptions
**EPIGYNIES** > EPIGYNOUS
**EPIGYNOUS** adj (of flowers) having the receptacle enclosing and fused with the gynoecium so that the other floral parts arise above it
**EPIGYNY** > EPIGYNOUS
**EPILATE** vb remove hair from
**EPILATED** > EPILATE
**EPILATES** > EPILATE
**EPILATING** > EPILATE
**EPILATION** > EPILATE
**EPILATOR** n electrical appliance consisting of a metal spiral head that rotates at high speed,

plucking unwanted hair
**EPILATORS** > EPILATOR
**EPILEPSY** n disorder of the nervous system causing loss of consciousness and sometimes convulsions
**EPILEPTIC** adj of or having epilepsy ▷ n person who has epilepsy
**EPILIMNIA** n upper layers of water in lakes
**EPILITHIC** adj (of plants) growing on the surface of rock
**EPILOBIUM** n willow-herb
**EPILOG** same as > EPILOGUE
**EPILOGIC** > EPILOGUE
**EPILOGISE** same as > EPILOGIZE
**EPILOGIST** > EPILOGUE
**EPILOGIZE** vb write or deliver epilogues
**EPILOGS** > EPILOG
**EPILOGUE** n short speech or poem at the end of a literary work, esp a play
**EPILOGUED** adj followed by an epilogue
**EPILOGUES** > EPILOGUE
**EPIMER** n isomer
**EPIMERASE** n enzyme that interconverts epimers
**EPIMERE** n dorsal part of the mesoderm of a vertebrate embryo, consisting of a series of segments
**EPIMERES** > EPIMERE
**EPIMERIC** > EPIMERISM
**EPIMERISM** n optical isomerism in which isomers can form about asymmetric atoms within the molecule
**EPIMERS** > EPIMER
**EPIMYSIA** > EPIMYSIUM
**EPIMYSIUM** n sheath of connective tissue that encloses a skeletal muscle
**EPINAOI** > EPINAOS
**EPINAOS** n rear vestibule
**EPINASTIC** > EPINASTY
**EPINASTY** n increased growth of the upper surface of a plant part, such as a leaf, resulting in a downward bending of the part
**EPINEURAL** adj outside a nerve trunk
**EPINEURIA** n sheaths of connective tissue around bundles of nerve fibres
**EPINICIAN** > EPINICION
**EPINICION** n victory song
**EPINIKIAN** > EPINICION
**EPINIKION** same as > EPINICION
**EPINOSIC** adj unhealthy
**EPIPHANIC** > EPIPHANY
**EPIPHANY** n moment of great or sudden revelation
**EPIPHRAGM** n disc of calcium phosphate and

mucilage secreted by snails over the aperture of their shells before hibernation
**EPIPHYSES** > EPIPHYSIS
**EPIPHYSIS** n end of a long bone, initially separated from the shaft (diaphysis) by a section of cartilage that eventually ossifies so that the two portions fuse together
**EPIPHYTAL** > EPIPHYTE
**EPIPHYTE** n plant that grows on another plant but is not parasitic on it
**EPIPHYTES** > EPIPHYTE
**EPIPHYTIC** > EPIPHYTE
**EPIPLOIC** > EPIPLOON
**EPIPLOON** n greater omentum
**EPIPLOONS** > EPIPLOON
**EPIPOLIC** > EPIPOLISM
**EPIPOLISM** n fluorescence
**EPIROGENY** n formation and submergence of continents by broad, relatively slow, displacements of the earth's crust
**EPIRRHEMA** n address in Greek comedy
**EPISCIA** n creeping plant
**EPISCIAS** > EPISCIA
**EPISCOPAL** adj of or governed by bishops
**EPISCOPE** n optical device that projects an enlarged image of an opaque object, such as a printed page or photographic print, onto a screen by means of reflected light
**EPISCOPES** > EPISCOPE
**EPISCOPY** n area overseen
**EPISEMON** n emblem
**EPISEMONS** > EPISEMON
**EPISODAL** same as > EPISODIC
**EPISODE** n incident in a series of incidents
**EPISODES** > EPISODE
**EPISODIAL** same as > EPISODIC
**EPISODIC** adj occurring at irregular intervals
**EPISOMAL** > EPISOME
**EPISOME** n unit of genetic material (DNA) in bacteria, such as a plasmid, that can either replicate independently or can be integrated into the host chromosome
**EPISOMES** > EPISOME
**EPISPERM** n protective outer layer of certain seeds
**EPISPERMS** > EPISPERM
**EPISPORE** n outer layer of certain spores
**EPISPORES** > EPISPORE
**EPISTASES** > EPISTASIS
**EPISTASIS** n scum on the surface of a liquid, esp on

an old specimen of urine
**EPISTASY** same as > EPISTASIS
**EPISTATIC** > EPISTASIS
**EPISTAXES** > EPISTAXIS
**EPISTAXIS** technical name for > NOSEBLEED
**EPISTEMIC** adj of or relating to knowledge or epistemology
**EPISTERNA** n parts of the sternums of mammals
**EPISTLE** n letter, esp of an apostle ▷ vb preface
**EPISTLED** > EPISTLE
**EPISTLER** n writer of an epistle or epistles
**EPISTLERS** > EPISTLER
**EPISTLES** > EPISTLE
**EPISTLING** > EPISTLE
**EPISTOLER** same as > EPISTLER
**EPISTOLET** n short letter
**EPISTOLIC** > EPISTLE
**EPISTOME** n area between the mouth and antennae of crustaceans
**EPISTOMES** > EPISTOME
**EPISTYLE** n lowest part of an entablature that bears on the columns
**EPISTYLES** > EPISTYLE
**EPITAPH** n commemorative inscription on a tomb ▷ vb compose an epitaph
**EPITAPHED** > EPITAPH
**EPITAPHER** > EPITAPH
**EPITAPHIC** > EPITAPH
**EPITAPHS** > EPITAPH
**EPITASES** > EPITASIS
**EPITASIS** n (in classical drama) part of a play in which the main action develops
**EPITAXES** > EPITAXIS
**EPITAXIAL** > EPITAXY
**EPITAXIC** > EPITAXY
**EPITAXIES** > EPITAXY
**EPITAXIS** same as > EPITAXY
**EPITAXY** n growth of a thin layer on the surface of a crystal so that the layer has the same structure as the underlying crystal
**EPITHECA** n outer and older layer of the cell wall of a diatom
**EPITHECAE** > EPITHECA
**EPITHELIA** n animal tissues consisting of one or more layers of closely packed cells covering the external and internal surfaces of the body
**EPITHEM** n external topical application
**EPITHEMA** > EPITHEM
**EPITHEMS** > EPITHEM
**EPITHESES** > EPITHESIS
**EPITHESIS** n addition of a letter to the end of a word, so that its sense does not change

**EPITHET** n descriptive word or name ▷ vb name
**EPITHETED** > EPITHET
**EPITHETIC** > EPITHET
**EPITHETON** same as > EPITHET
**EPITHETS** > EPITHET
**EPITOME** n typical example
**EPITOMES** > EPITOME
**EPITOMIC** > EPITOME
**EPITOMISE** same as > EPITOMIZE
**EPITOMIST** > EPITOMIZE
**EPITOMIZE** vb be the epitome of
**EPITONIC** adj undergoing too great a strain
**EPITOPE** n site on an antigen at which a specific antibody becomes attached
**EPITOPES** > EPITOPE
**EPITRITE** n metrical foot with three long syllables and one short one
**EPITRITES** > EPITRITE
**EPIZEUXES** > EPIZEUXIS
**EPIZEUXIS** n deliberate repetition of a word
**EPIZOA** > EPIZOON
**EPIZOAN** same as > EPIZOON
**EPIZOANS** > EPIZOAN
**EPIZOIC** adj (of an animal or plant) growing or living on the exterior of a living animal
**EPIZOISM** > EPIZOIC
**EPIZOISMS** > EPIZOIC
**EPIZOITE** n organism that lives on an animal but is not parasitic on it
**EPIZOITES** > EPIZOITE
**EPIZOON** n animal, such as a parasite, that lives on the body of another animal
**EPIZOOTIC** adj (of a disease) suddenly and temporarily affecting a large number of animals over a large area ▷ n epizootic disease
**EPIZOOTY** n animal disease
**EPOCH** n period of notable events
**EPOCHA** same as > EPOCH
**EPOCHAL** > EPOCH
**EPOCHALLY** > EPOCH
**EPOCHAS** > EPOCHA
**EPOCHS** > EPOCH
**EPODE** n part of a lyric ode that follows the strophe and the antistrophe
**EPODES** > EPODE
**EPODIC** > EPODE
**EPONYM** n name, esp a place name, derived from the name of a real or mythical person, as for example Constantinople from Constantine I
**EPONYMIC** > EPONYM
**EPONYMIES** > EPONYMY
**EPONYMOUS** adj after whom a book, play, etc is named

EPONYMS > EPONYM

EPONYMY n derivation of names of places, etc, from those of persons

EPOPEE n epic poem

EPOPEES > EPOPEE

EPOPOEIA same as > EPOPEE

EPOPOEIAS > EPOPOEIA

EPOPT n one initiated into mysteries

EPOPTS > EPOPT

EPOS n body of poetry in which the tradition of a people is conveyed, esp a group of poems concerned with a common epic theme

EPOSES > EPOS

EPOXIDE n compound containing an oxygen atom joined to two different groups that are themselves joined to other groups

EPOXIDES > EPOXIDE

EPOXIDISE same as > EPOXIDIZE

EPOXIDIZE vb form an epoxide

EPOXIED > EPOXY

EPOXIES > EPOXY

EPOXY adj of or containing an oxygen atom joined to two different groups that are themselves joined to other groups ▷ n epoxy resin ▷ vb glue with epoxy resin

EPOXYED > EPOXY

EPOXYING > EPOXY

EPRIS adj enamoured

EPRISE feminine form of > EPRIS

EPROM n type of computer memory

EPROMS > EPROM

EPSILON n fifth letter of the Greek alphabet, a short vowel, transliterated as e

EPSILONIC adj of or relating to an arbitrary small quantity

EPSILONS > EPSILON

EPSOMITE n sulphate of magnesium

EPSOMITES > EPSOMITE

EPUISE adj exhausted

EPUISEE feminine form of > EPUISE

EPULARY adj of or relating to feasting

EPULATION n feasting

EPULIDES > EPULIS

EPULIS n swelling of the gum, usually as a result of fibrous hyperplasia

EPULISES > EPULIS

EPULOTIC n scarring

EPULOTICS > EPULOTIC

EPURATE vb purify

EPURATED > EPURATE

EPURATES > EPURATE

EPURATING > EPURATE

EPURATION > EPURATE

EPYLLIA > EPYLLION

EPYLLION n miniature epic

EPYLLIONS > EPYLLION

EQUABLE adj even-tempered

EQUABLY > EQUABLE

EQUAL adj identical in size, quantity, degree, etc ▷ n person or thing equal to another ▷ vb be equal to

EQUALED > EQUAL

EQUALI pl n pieces for a group of instruments of the same kind

EQUALING > EQUAL

EQUALISE same as > EQUALIZE

EQUALISED > EQUALISE

EQUALISER same as > EQUALIZER

EQUALISES > EQUALISE

EQUALITY n state of being equal

EQUALIZE vb make or become equal

EQUALIZED > EQUALIZE

EQUALIZER n person or thing that equalizes, esp a device to counterbalance opposing forces

EQUALIZES > EQUALIZE

EQUALLED > EQUAL

EQUALLING > EQUAL

EQUALLY > EQUAL

EQUALNESS n equality

EQUALS > EQUAL

EQUANT n circle in which a planet was formerly believed to move

EQUANTS > EQUANT

EQUATABLE > EQUATE

EQUATE vb make or regard as equivalent

EQUATED > EQUATE

EQUATES > EQUATE

EQUATING > EQUATE

EQUATION n mathematical statement that two expressions are equal

EQUATIONS > EQUATION

EQUATOR n imaginary circle round the earth, equidistant from the poles

EQUATORS > EQUATOR

EQUERRIES > EQUERRY

EQUERRY n officer who acts as an attendant to a member of a royal family

EQUID n any animal of the horse family

EQUIDS > EQUID

EQUIMOLAL adj having an equal number of moles

EQUIMOLAR same as > EQUIMOLAL

EQUINAL same as > EQUINE

EQUINE adj of or like a horse ▷ n any animal of the horse family

EQUINELY > EQUINE

EQUINES > EQUINE

EQUINIA n glanders

EQUINIAS > EQUINIA

EQUINITY n horse-like

nature

EQUINOX n time of year when day and night are of equal length

EQUINOXES > EQUINOX

EQUIP vb provide with supplies, components, etc

EQUIPAGE n horse-drawn carriage, esp one elegantly equipped and attended by liveried footmen ▷ vb equip

EQUIPAGED > EQUIPAGE

EQUIPAGES > EQUIPAGE

EQUIPE n (esp in motor racing) team

EQUIPES > EQUIPE

EQUIPMENT n set of tools or devices used for a particular purpose

EQUIPOISE n perfect balance ▷ vb offset or balance in weight or force

EQUIPPED > EQUIP

EQUIPPER > EQUIP

EQUIPPERS > EQUIP

EQUIPPING > EQUIP

EQUIPS > EQUIP

EQUISETA > EQUISETUM

EQUISETIC > EQUISETUM

EQUISETUM n tracheophyte plant of the genus Equisetum

EQUITABLE adj fair and reasonable

EQUITABLY > EQUITABLE

EQUITANT adj (of a leaf) having the base folded around the stem so that it overlaps the leaf above and opposite

EQUITES pl n cavalry

EQUITIES > EQUITY

EQUITY n fairness

EQUIVALVE adj equipped with identical valves

EQUIVOCAL adj ambiguous

EQUIVOKE same as > EQUIVOQUE

EQUIVOKES > EQUIVOKE

EQUIVOQUE n play on words

ER interj sound made when hesitating in speech

ERA n period of time considered as distinctive

ERADIATE less common word for > RADIATE

ERADIATED > ERADIATE

ERADIATES > ERADIATE

ERADICANT > ERADICATE

ERADICATE vb destroy completely

ERAS > ERA

ERASABLE > ERASE

ERASE vb destroy all traces of

ERASED > ERASE

ERASEMENT > ERASE

ERASER n object for erasing something written

ERASERS > ERASER

ERASES > ERASE

ERASING > ERASE

ERASION n act of erasing

ERASIONS > ERASION

ERASURE n erasing

ERASURES > ERASURE

ERATHEM n stratum of rocks representing a specific geological era

ERATHEMS > ERATHEM

ERBIA n oxide of erbium

ERBIAS > ERBIA

ERBIUM n metallic element of the lanthanide series

ERBIUMS > ERBIUM

ERE prep before ▷ vb plough

ERECT vb build ▷ adj upright

ERECTABLE > ERECT

ERECTED > ERECT

ERECTER same as > ERECTOR

ERECTERS > ERECTER

ERECTILE adj capable of becoming erect from sexual excitement

ERECTING > ERECT

ERECTION n act of erecting or the state of being erected

ERECTIONS > ERECTION

ERECTIVE adj producing erections

ERECTLY > ERECT

ERECTNESS > ERECT

ERECTOR n any muscle that raises a part or makes it erect

ERECTORS > ERECTOR

ERECTS > ERECT

ERED > ERE

ERELONG adv before long

EREMIC adj of or relating to deserts

EREMITAL > EREMITE

EREMITE n Christian hermit

EREMITES > EREMITE

EREMITIC > EREMITE

EREMITISH > EREMITE

EREMITISM > EREMITE

EREMURI > EREMURUS

EREMURUS n type of herb

ERENOW adv long before the present

EREPSIN n mixture of proteolytic enzymes secreted by the small intestine

EREPSINS > EREPSIN

ERES > ERE

ERETHIC > ERETHISM

ERETHISM n abnormally high degree of irritability or sensitivity in any part of the body

ERETHISMS > ERETHISM

ERETHITIC > ERETHISM

EREV n day before

EREVS > EREV

EREWHILE adv short time ago

EREWHILES same as > EREWHILE

ERF n plot of land, usually urban, marked off for

building purposes
**ERG** *same as* > ERGOMETER
**ERGASTIC** *adj* consisting of the non-living by-products of protoplasmic activity
**ERGATANER** *n* wingless male ant
**ERGATE** *n* worker ant
**ERGATES** > ERGATE
**ERGATIVE** *adj* denoting a type of verb that takes the same noun as either direct object or as subject, with equivalent meaning. Thus, "fuse" is an ergative verb: "He fused the lights" and "The lights fused" have equivalent meaning ▷ *n* ergative verb
**ERGATIVES** > ERGATIVE
**ERGATOID** > ERGATE
**ERGO** *same as* > ERGOMETER
**ERGODIC** *adj* of or relating to the probability that any state will recur
**ERGOGENIC** *adj* giving energy
**ERGOGRAM** *n* tracing produced by an ergograph
**ERGOGRAMS** > ERGOGRAM
**ERGOGRAPH** *n* instrument that measures and records the amount of work a muscle does during contraction, its rate of fatigue, etc
**ERGOMANIA** *n* excessive desire to work
**ERGOMETER** *n* dynamometer
**ERGOMETRY** *n* measurement of work done
**ERGON** *n* work
**ERGONOMIC** *adj* designed to minimize effort
**ERGONS** > ERGON
**ERGOS** > ERGO
**ERGOT** *n* fungal disease of cereal
**ERGOTIC** > ERGOT
**ERGOTISE** *same as* > ERGOTIZE
**ERGOTISED** > ERGOTISE
**ERGOTISES** > ERGOTISE
**ERGOTISM** *n* ergot poisoning, producing either burning pains and eventually gangrene in the limbs or itching skin and convulsions
**ERGOTISMS** > ERGOTISM
**ERGOTIZE** *vb* inflict ergotism upon
**ERGOTIZED** > ERGOTIZE
**ERGOTIZES** > ERGOTIZE
**ERGOTS** > ERGOT
**ERGS** > ERG
**ERIACH** *same as* > ERIC
**ERIACHS** > ERIACH
**ERIC** *n* (in old Irish law) fine paid by a murderer to the family of his victim
**ERICA** *n* genus of plants

including heathers
**ERICAS** > ERICA
**ERICK** *same as* > ERIC
**ERICKS** > ERICK
**ERICOID** *adj* (of leaves) small and tough, resembling those of heather
**ERICS** > ERIC
**ERIGERON** *n* any plant of the genus *Erigeron*
**ERIGERONS** > ERIGERON
**ERING** > ERE
**ERINGO** *same as* > ERYNGO
**ERINGOES** > ERINGO
**ERINGOS** > ERINGO
**ERINITE** *n* arsenate of copper
**ERINITES** > ERINITE
**ERINUS** *n* any plant of the scrophulariaceous genus *Erinus*
**ERINUSES** > ERINUS
**ERIOMETER** *n* device for measuring the diameters of minute particles or fibres
**ERIONITE** *n* common form of zeolite
**ERIONITES** > ERIONITE
**ERIOPHYID** *n* type of mite
**ERISTIC** *adj* of, relating, or given to controversy or logical disputation, esp for its own sake ▷ *n* person who engages in logical disputes
**ERISTICAL** *same as* > ERISTIC
**ERISTICS** > ERISTIC
**ERK** *n* aircraftman or naval rating
**ERKS** > ERK
**ERLANG** *n* unit of traffic intensity in a telephone system equal to the intensity for a specific period when the average number of simultaneous calls is unity
**ERLANGS** > ERLANG
**ERLKING** *n* malevolent spirit who carries off children
**ERLKINGS** > ERLKING
**ERMELIN** *n* ermine
**ERMELINS** > ERMELIN
**ERMINE** *n* stoat in northern regions, where it has a white winter coat with a black-tipped tail
**ERMINED** *adj* clad in the fur of the ermine
**ERMINES** > ERMINE
**ERN** *archaic variant of* > EARN
**ERNE** *n* fish-eating (European) sea eagle
**ERNED** > ERN
**ERNES** > ERNE
**ERNING** > ERN
**ERNS** > ERN
**ERODABLE** > ERODE
**ERODE** *vb* wear away
**ERODED** > ERODE

**ERODENT** > ERODE
**ERODENTS** > ERODE
**ERODES** > ERODE
**ERODIBLE** > ERODE
**ERODING** > ERODE
**ERODIUM** *n* type of geranium
**ERODIUMS** > ERODIUM
**EROGENIC** *same as* > EROGENOUS
**EROGENOUS** *adj* sensitive to sexual stimulation
**EROS** *n* lust
**EROSE** *adj* jagged or uneven, as though gnawed or bitten
**EROSELY** > EROSE
**EROSES** > EROS
**EROSIBLE** *adj* able to be eroded
**EROSION** *n* wearing away of rocks or soil by the action of water, ice, or wind
**EROSIONAL** > EROSION
**EROSIONS** > EROSION
**EROSIVE** > EROSION
**EROSIVITY** > EROSION
**EROSTRATE** *adj* without a beak
**EROTEMA** *n* rhetorical question
**EROTEMAS** > EROTEMA
**EROTEME** *same as* > EROTEMA
**EROTEMES** > EROTEME
**EROTESES** > EROTESIS
**EROTESIS** *same as* > EROTEMA
**EROTETIC** *adj* pertaining to a rhetorical question
**EROTIC** *adj* relating to sexual pleasure or desire ▷ *n* person who has strong sexual desires or is especially responsive to sexual stimulation
**EROTICA** *n* sexual literature or art
**EROTICAL** *adj* erotic
**EROTICISE** *same as* > EROTICIZE
**EROTICISM** *n* erotic quality or nature
**EROTICIST** > EROTICISM
**EROTICIZE** *vb* regard or present in a sexual way
**EROTICS** > EROTIC
**EROTISE** *same as* > EROTIZE
**EROTISED** > EROTISE
**EROTISES** > EROTISE
**EROTISING** > EROTISE
**EROTISM** *same as* > EROTICISM
**EROTISMS** > EROTISM
**EROTIZE** *vb* make erotic
**EROTIZED** > EROTIZE
**EROTIZES** > EROTIZE
**EROTIZING** > EROTIZE
**EROTOLOGY** *n* study of erotic stimuli and sexual behaviour
**ERR** *vb* make a mistake
**ERRABLE** *adj* capable of

making a mistake
**ERRANCIES** > ERRANCY
**ERRANCY** *n* state or an instance of erring or a tendency to err
**ERRAND** *n* short trip to do something for someone
**ERRANDS** > ERRAND
**ERRANT** *adj* behaving in a manner considered to be unacceptable ▷ *n* knight-errant
**ERRANTLY** > ERRANT
**ERRANTRY** *n* way of life of a knight errant
**ERRANTS** > ERRANT
**ERRATA** > ERRATUM
**ERRATAS** *informal variant of* > ERRATA
**ERRATIC** *adj* irregular or unpredictable ▷ *n* rock that has been transported by glacial action
**ERRATICAL** *adj* erratic
**ERRATICS** > ERRATIC
**ERRATUM** *n* error in writing or printing
**ERRED** > ERR
**ERRHINE** *adj* causing nasal secretion ▷ *n* errhine drug or agent
**ERRHINES** > ERRHINE
**ERRING** > ERR
**ERRINGLY** > ERR
**ERRINGS** > ERR
**ERRONEOUS** *adj* incorrect, mistaken
**ERROR** *n* mistake, inaccuracy, or misjudgment
**ERRORIST** *n* one who makes errors
**ERRORISTS** > ERRORIST
**ERRORLESS** > ERROR
**ERRORS** > ERROR
**ERRS** > ERR
**ERS** *same as* > ERVIL
**ERSATZ** *adj* made in imitation ▷ *n* ersatz substance or article
**ERSATZES** > ERSATZ
**ERSES** > ERS
**ERST** *adv* long ago
**ERSTWHILE** *adj* former ▷ *adv* formerly
**ERUCIC** *as in erucic acid* crystalline fatty acid derived from rapeseed, mustard seed and wallflower seed
**ERUCIFORM** *adj* resembling a caterpillar
**ERUCT** *vb* belch
**ERUCTATE** *same as* > ERUCT
**ERUCTATED** > ERUCTATE
**ERUCTATES** > ERUCTATE
**ERUCTED** > ERUCT
**ERUCTING** > ERUCT
**ERUCTS** > ERUCT
**ERUDITE** *adj* having great academic knowledge ▷ *n* erudite person
**ERUDITELY** > ERUDITE
**ERUDITES** > ERUDITE

255

ERUDITION > ERUDITE
ERUGO n verdigris
ERUGOS > ERUGO
ERUMPENT adj bursting out or (esp of plant parts) developing as though bursting through an overlying structure
ERUPT vb eject (steam, water, or volcanic material) violently
ERUPTED > ERUPT
ERUPTIBLE > ERUPT
ERUPTING > ERUPT
ERUPTION > ERUPT
ERUPTIONS > ERUPT
ERUPTIVE adj erupting or tending to erupt ▷ n type of volcanic rock
ERUPTIVES > ERUPTIVE
ERUPTS > ERUPT
ERUV n area, circumscribed by a symbolic line, within which certain activities forbidden for > Orthodox Jews on the Sabbath are permitted
ERUVIM > ERUV
ERUVIN > ERUV
ERUVS > ERUV
ERVALENTA n health food made from lentil and barley flour
ERVEN > ERF
ERVIL n type of vetch
ERVILS > ERVIL
ERYNGIUM n any plant of the temperate and subtropical perennial umbelliferous genus Eryngium
ERYNGIUMS > ERYNGIUM
ERYNGO n any umbelliferous plant of the genus Eryngium
ERYNGOES > ERYNGO
ERYNGOS > ERYNGO
ERYTHEMA n patchy inflammation of the skin
ERYTHEMAL > ERYTHEMA
ERYTHEMAS > ERYTHEMA
ERYTHEMIC > ERYTHEMA
ERYTHRINA n tropical tree with red flowers
ERYTHRISM n abnormal red coloration, as in plumage or hair
ERYTHRITE n sweet crystalline compound extacted from certain algae and lichens
ERYTHROID adj red or reddish
ERYTHRON n red blood cells and their related tissues
ERYTHRONS > ERYTHRON
ES n letter S
ESCALADE n assault by the use of ladders, esp on a fortification ▷ vb gain access to (a place) by the use of ladders
ESCALADED > ESCALADE
ESCALADER > ESCALADE

ESCALADES > ESCALADE
ESCALADO n escalade
ESCALATE vb increase in extent or intensity
ESCALATED > ESCALATE
ESCALATES > ESCALATE
ESCALATOR n moving staircase
ESCALIER n staircase
ESCALIERS > ESCALIER
ESCALLOP another word for > SCALLOP
ESCALLOPS > ESCALLOP
ESCALOP another word for > SCALLOP
ESCALOPE n thin slice of meat, esp veal
ESCALOPED > ESCALOP
ESCALOPES > ESCALOPE
ESCALOPS > ESCALOP
ESCAPABLE > ESCAPE
ESCAPADE n mischievous adventure
ESCAPADES > ESCAPADE
ESCAPADO n escaped criminal
ESCAPE vb get free (of) ▷ n act of escaping
ESCAPED > ESCAPE
ESCAPEE n person who has escaped
ESCAPEES > ESCAPEE
ESCAPER > ESCAPE
ESCAPERS > ESCAPE
ESCAPES > ESCAPE
ESCAPING > ESCAPE
ESCAPISM n taking refuge in fantasy to avoid unpleasant reality
ESCAPISMS > ESCAPISM
ESCAPIST > ESCAPISM
ESCAPISTS > ESCAPISM
ESCAR same as > ESKER
ESCARGOT n variety of edible snail, usually eaten with a sauce made of melted butter and garlic
ESCARGOTS > ESCARGOT
ESCAROLE n variety of endive with broad leaves, used in salads
ESCAROLES > ESCAROLE
ESCARP n inner side of the ditch separating besiegers and besieged ▷ vb make into a slope
ESCARPED > ESCARP
ESCARPING > ESCARP
ESCARPS > ESCARP
ESCARS > ESCAR
ESCHALOT another name for a > SHALLOT
ESCHALOTS > ESCHALOT
ESCHAR n dry scab or slough, esp one following a burn or cauterization of the skin
ESCHARS > ESCHAR
ESCHEAT n private possessions that become state property in the absence of an heir ▷ vb attain such property
ESCHEATED > ESCHEAT

ESCHEATOR > ESCHEAT
ESCHEATS > ESCHEAT
ESCHEW vb abstain from, avoid
ESCHEWAL > ESCHEW
ESCHEWALS > ESCHEW
ESCHEWED > ESCHEW
ESCHEWER > ESCHEW
ESCHEWERS > ESCHEW
ESCHEWING > ESCHEW
ESCHEWS > ESCHEW
ESCLANDRE n scandal or notoriety
ESCOLAR n slender spiny-finned fish
ESCOLARS > ESCOLAR
ESCOPETTE n carbine
ESCORT n people or vehicles accompanying another person for protection or as an honour ▷ vb act as an escort to
ESCORTAGE > ESCORT
ESCORTED > ESCORT
ESCORTING > ESCORT
ESCORTS > ESCORT
ESCOT vb maintain
ESCOTED > ESCOT
ESCOTING > ESCOT
ESCOTS > ESCOT
ESCOTTED > ESCOT
ESCOTTING > ESCOT
ESCRIBANO n clerk
ESCRIBE vb draw (a circle) so that it is tangential to one side of a triangle and to the other two sides produced
ESCRIBED > ESCRIBE
ESCRIBES > ESCRIBE
ESCRIBING > ESCRIBE
ESCROC n conman
ESCROCS > ESCROC
ESCROL same as > ESCROLL
ESCROLL n scroll
ESCROLLS > ESCROLL
ESCROLS > ESCROL
ESCROW n money, goods, or a written document, such as a contract bond, delivered to a third party and held by him pending fulfilment of some condition ▷ vb place (money, a document, etc) in escrow
ESCROWED > ESCROW
ESCROWING > ESCROW
ESCROWS > ESCROW
ESCUAGE (in medieval Europe) another word for > SCUTAGE
ESCUAGES > ESCUAGE
ESCUDO n former monetary unit of Portugal
ESCUDOS > ESCUDO
ESCULENT adj edible ▷ n any edible substance
ESCULENTS > ESCULENT
ESEMPLASY n unification
ESERINE n crystalline alkaloid
ESERINES > ESERINE
ESES > ES
ESILE n vinegar

ESILES > ESILE
ESKAR same as > ESKER
ESKARS > ESKAR
ESKER n long winding ridge of gravel, sand, etc, originally deposited by a meltwater stream running under a glacier
ESKERS > ESKER
ESKIES > ESKY
ESKY n portable insulated container for keeping food and drink cool
ESLOIN same as > ELOIGN
ESLOINED > ESLOIN
ESLOINING > ESLOIN
ESLOINS > ESLOIN
ESLOYNE same as > ELOIGN
ESLOYNED > ESLOYNE
ESLOYNES > ESLOYNE
ESLOYNING > ESLOYNE
ESNE n household slave
ESNECIES > ESNECY
ESNECY n right of the eldest daughter to make the first choice when dividing inheritance
ESNES > ESNE
ESOPHAGI > ESOPHAGUS
ESOPHAGUS n part of the alimentary canal between the pharynx and the stomach
ESOTERIC adj understood by only a small number of people with special knowledge
ESOTERICA pl n esoteric things
ESOTERIES > ESOTERIC
ESOTERISM > ESOTERIC
ESOTERY > ESOTERIC
ESOTROPIA n condition in which eye turns inwards
ESOTROPIC > ESOTROPIA
ESPADA n sword
ESPADAS > ESPADA
ESPAGNOLE n tomato and sherry sauce
ESPALIER n shrub or fruit tree trained to grow flat ▷ vb train (a plant) on an espalier
ESPALIERS > ESPALIER
ESPANOL n Spanish person
ESPANOLES > ESPANOL
ESPARTO n grass of S Europe and N Africa used for making rope etc
ESPARTOS > ESPARTO
ESPECIAL adj special
ESPERANCE n hope or expectation
ESPIAL n act or fact of being seen or discovered
ESPIALS > ESPIAL
ESPIED > ESPY
ESPIEGLE adj playful
ESPIER > ESPY
ESPIERS > ESPY
ESPIES > ESPY
ESPIONAGE n spying
ESPLANADE n wide open road used as a public

promenade

**ESPOUSAL** *n* adoption or support

**ESPOUSALS** > ESPOUSAL

**ESPOUSE** *vb* adopt or give support to (a cause etc)

**ESPOUSED** > ESPOUSE

**ESPOUSER** > ESPOUSE

**ESPOUSERS** > ESPOUSE

**ESPOUSES** > ESPOUSE

**ESPOUSING** > ESPOUSE

**ESPRESSO** *n* strong coffee made by forcing steam or boiling water through ground coffee beans

**ESPRESSOS** > ESPRESSO

**ESPRIT** *n* spirit, liveliness, or wit

**ESPRITS** > ESPRIT

**ESPUMOSO** *n* sparkling wine

**ESPUMOSOS** > ESPUMOSO

**ESPY** *vb* catch sight of

**ESPYING** > ESPY

**ESQUIRE** *n* courtesy title placed after a man's name ▷ *vb* escort

**ESQUIRED** > ESQUIRE

**ESQUIRES** > ESQUIRE

**ESQUIRESS** *feminine form of* > ESQUIRE

**ESQUIRING** > ESQUIRE

**ESQUISSE** *n* sketch

**ESQUISSES** > ESQUISSE

**ESS** *n* letter S

**ESSAY** *n* short literary composition ▷ *vb* attempt

**ESSAYED** > ESSAY

**ESSAYER** > ESSAY

**ESSAYERS** > ESSAY

**ESSAYETTE** *n* short essay

**ESSAYING** > ESSAY

**ESSAYISH** > ESSAY

**ESSAYIST** *n* person who writes essays

**ESSAYISTS** > ESSAYIST

**ESSAYS** > ESSAY

**ESSE** *n* existence

**ESSENCE** *n* most important feature of a thing which determines its identity

**ESSENCES** > ESSENCE

**ESSENTIAL** *adj* vitally important ▷ *n* something fundamental or indispensable

**ESSES** > ESS

**ESSIVE** *n* grammatical case

**ESSIVES** > ESSIVE

**ESSOIN** *n* excuse

**ESSOINER** > ESSOIN

**ESSOINERS** > ESSOIN

**ESSOINS** > ESSOIN

**ESSONITE** *variant spelling of* > HESSONITE

**ESSONITES** > ESSONITE

**ESSOYNE** *same as* > ESSOIN

**ESSOYNES** > ESSOYNE

**EST** *n* treatment intended to help people towards psychological growth, in which they spend many hours in large groups,

deprived of food and water and hectored by stewards

**ESTABLISH** *vb* set up on a permanent basis

**ESTACADE** *n* defensive arrangement of stakes

**ESTACADES** > ESTACADE

**ESTAFETTE** *n* mounted courier

**ESTAMINET** *n* small café, bar, or bistro, esp a shabby one

**ESTANCIA** *n* (in Spanish America) a large estate or cattle ranch

**ESTANCIAS** > ESTANCIA

**ESTATE** *n* landed property ▷ *vb* provide with an estate

**ESTATED** > ESTATE

**ESTATES** > ESTATE

**ESTATING** > ESTATE

**ESTEEM** *n* high regard ▷ *vb* think highly of

**ESTEEMED** > ESTEEM

**ESTEEMING** > ESTEEM

**ESTEEMS** > ESTEEM

**ESTER** *n* compound produced by the reaction between an acid and an alcohol

**ESTERASE** *n* any of a group of enzymes that hydrolyse esters into alcohols and acids

**ESTERASES** > ESTERASE

**ESTERIFY** *vb* change or cause to change into an ester

**ESTERS** > ESTER

**ESTHESES** > ESTHESIS

**ESTHESIA** *US spelling of* > AESTHESIA

**ESTHESIAS** > ESTHESIA

**ESTHESIS** *n* esthesia

**ESTHETE** *US spelling of* > AESTHETE

**ESTHETES** > ESTHETE

**ESTHETIC** > ESTHETE

**ESTHETICS** > ESTHETE

**ESTIMABLE** *adj* worthy of respect

**ESTIMABLY** > ESTIMABLE

**ESTIMATE** *vb* calculate roughly ▷ *n* approximate calculation

**ESTIMATED** > ESTIMATE

**ESTIMATES** > ESTIMATE

**ESTIMATOR** *n* person or thing that estimates

**ESTIVAL** *usual US spelling of* > AESTIVAL

**ESTIVATE** *usual US spelling of* > AESTIVATE

**ESTIVATED** > ESTIVATE

**ESTIVATES** > ESTIVATE

**ESTIVATOR** > ESTIVATE

**ESTOC** *n* short stabbing sword

**ESTOCS** > ESTOC

**ESTOILE** *n* heraldic star with wavy points

**ESTOILES** > ESTOILE

**ESTOP** *vb* preclude by

estoppel

**ESTOPPAGE** > ESTOP

**ESTOPPED** > ESTOP

**ESTOPPEL** *n* rule of evidence whereby a person is precluded from denying the truth of a statement of facts he has previously asserted

**ESTOPPELS** > ESTOPPEL

**ESTOPPING** > ESTOP

**ESTOPS** > ESTOP

**ESTOVER** *same as* > ESTOVERS

**ESTOVERS** *pl n* right allowed by law to tenants of land to cut timber, esp for fuel and repairs

**ESTRADE** *n* dais or raised platform

**ESTRADES** > ESTRADE

**ESTRADIOL** *n* most potent estrogenic hormone secreted by the mammalian ovary

**ESTRAGON** *another name for* > TARRAGON

**ESTRAGONS** > ESTRAGON

**ESTRAL** *US spelling of* > OESTRAL

**ESTRANGE** *vb* separate and live apart from (one's spouse)

**ESTRANGED** *adj* no longer living with one's spouse

**ESTRANGER** > ESTRANGE

**ESTRANGES** > ESTRANGE

**ESTRAPADE** *n* attempt by a horse to throw its rider

**ESTRAY** *n* stray domestic animal of unknown ownership ▷ *vb* stray

**ESTRAYED** > ESTRAY

**ESTRAYING** > ESTRAY

**ESTRAYS** > ESTRAY

**ESTREAT** *n* true copy of or extract from a court record ▷ *vb* enforce (a recognizance that has been forfeited) by sending an extract of the court record to the proper authority

**ESTREATED** > ESTREAT

**ESTREATS** > ESTREAT

**ESTREPE** *vb* lay waste

**ESTREPED** > ESTREPE

**ESTREPES** > ESTREPE

**ESTREPING** > ESTREPE

**ESTRICH** *n* ostrich

**ESTRICHES** > ESTRICH

**ESTRIDGE** *n* ostrich

**ESTRIDGES** > ESTRIDGE

**ESTRILDID** *n* weaver finch

**ESTRIN** *US spelling of* > OESTRIN

**ESTRINS** > ESTRIN

**ESTRIOL** *usual US spelling of* > OESTRIOL

**ESTRIOLS** > ESTRIOL

**ESTRO** *n* poetic inspiration

**ESTROGEN** *usual US spelling of* > OESTROGEN

**ESTROGENS** > ESTROGEN

**ESTRONE** *usual US spelling of* > OESTRONE

**ESTRONES** > ESTRONE

**ESTROS** > ESTRO

**ESTROUS** > ESTRUS

**ESTRUAL** > ESTRUS

**ESTRUM** *usual US spelling of* > OESTRUM

**ESTRUMS** > ESTRUM

**ESTRUS** *usual US spelling of* > OESTRUS

**ESTRUSES** > ESTRUS

**ESTS** > EST

**ESTUARIAL** > ESTUARY

**ESTUARIAN** > ESTUARY

**ESTUARIES** > ESTUARY

**ESTUARINE** *adj* formed or deposited in an estuary

**ESTUARY** *n* mouth of a river

**ESURIENCE** > ESURIENT

**ESURIENCY** > ESURIENT

**ESURIENT** *adj* greedy

**ET** *dialect past tense of* > EAT

**ETA** *n* seventh letter in the Greek alphabet, a long vowel sound

**ETACISM** *n* pronunciation of eta as a long vowel sound

**ETACISMS** > ETACISM

**ETAERIO** *n* aggregate fruit, as one consisting of drupes (raspberry) or achenes (traveller's joy)

**ETAERIOS** > ETAERIO

**ETAGE** *n* floor in a multi-storey building

**ETAGERE** *n* stand with open shelves for displaying ornaments, etc

**ETAGERES** > ETAGERE

**ETAGES** > ETAGE

**ETALAGE** *n* display

**ETALAGES** > ETALAGE

**ETALON** *n* device used in spectroscopy to measure wavelengths by interference effects produced by multiple reflections between parallel half-silvered glass or quartz plates

**ETALONS** > ETALON

**ETAMIN** *same as* > ETAMINE

**ETAMINE** *n* cotton or worsted fabric of loose weave, used for clothing, curtains, etc

**ETAMINES** > ETAMINE

**ETAMINS** > ETAMIN

**ETAPE** *n* public storehouse

**ETAPES** > ETAPE

**ETAS** > ETA

**ETAT** *n* state

**ETATISM** *same as* > ETATISME

**ETATISME** *n* authoritarian control by the state

**ETATISMES** > ETATISME

**ETATISMS** > ETATISM

**ETATIST** > ETATISME

**ETATISTE** > ETATISME

**ETATISTES** > ETATISME

**ETATS** > ETAT

257

ETCETERA n number of other items

ETCETERAS pl n miscellaneous extra things or people

ETCH vb wear away or cut the surface of (metal, glass, etc) with acid

ETCHANT n any acid or corrosive used for etching

ETCHANTS > ETCHANT

ETCHED > ETCH

ETCHER > ETCH

ETCHERS > ETCH

ETCHES > ETCH

ETCHING n picture printed from an etched metal plate

ETCHINGS > ETCHING

ETEN n giant

ETENS > ETEN

ETERNAL adj without beginning or end ▷ n eternal thing

ETERNALLY > ETERNAL

ETERNALS > ETERNAL

ETERNE archaic or poetic word for > ETERNAL

ETERNISE same as > ETERNIZE

ETERNISED > ETERNISE

ETERNISES > ETERNISE

ETERNITY n infinite time

ETERNIZE vb make eternal

ETERNIZED > ETERNIZE

ETERNIZES > ETERNIZE

ETESIAN adj (of NW winds) recurring annually in the summer in the E Mediterranean ▷ n etesian wind

ETESIANS > ETESIAN

ETH same as > EDH

ETHAL n cetyl alcohol

ETHALS > ETHAL

ETHANAL n colourless volatile pungent liquid

ETHANALS > ETHANAL

ETHANE n odourless flammable gas obtained from natural gas and petroleum

ETHANES > ETHANE

ETHANOATE same as > ACETATE

ETHANOIC as in ethanoic acid acetic acid

ETHANOL same as > ALCOHOL

ETHANOLS > ETHANOL

ETHANOYL n substance consisting of or containing the monovalent group $CH_3CO-$

ETHANOYLS > ETHANOYL

ETHE adj easy

ETHENE same as > ETHYLENE

ETHENES > ETHENE

ETHEPHON n synthetic plant-growth regulator

ETHEPHONS > ETHEPHON

ETHER n colourless sweet-smelling liquid used as an anaesthetic

ETHERCAP n spider

ETHERCAPS > ETHERCAP

ETHEREAL adj extremely delicate

ETHEREOUS same as > ETHEREAL

ETHERIAL same as > ETHEREAL

ETHERIC > ETHER

ETHERICAL > ETHER

ETHERIFY vb change (a compound, such as an alcohol) into an ether

ETHERION n gas formerly believed to exist in air

ETHERIONS > ETHERION

ETHERISE same as > ETHERIZE

ETHERISED > ETHERISE

ETHERISER > ETHERISE

ETHERISES > ETHERISE

ETHERISH > ETHER

ETHERISM n addiction to ether

ETHERISMS > ETHERISM

ETHERIST > ETHERISM

ETHERISTS > ETHERISM

ETHERIZE vb subject (a person) to the anaesthetic influence of ether fumes

ETHERIZED > ETHERIZE

ETHERIZER > ETHERIZE

ETHERIZES > ETHERIZE

ETHERS > ETHER

ETHIC n moral principle

ETHICAL adj of or based on a system of moral beliefs about right and wrong ▷ n drug available only by prescription

ETHICALLY > ETHICAL

ETHICALS > ETHICAL

ETHICIAN > ETHICS

ETHICIANS > ETHICS

ETHICISE same as > ETHICIZE

ETHICISED > ETHICISE

ETHICISES > ETHICISE

ETHICISM > ETHICS

ETHICISMS > ETHICS

ETHICIST > ETHICS

ETHICISTS > ETHICS

ETHICIZE vb make or consider as ethical

ETHICIZED > ETHICIZE

ETHICIZES > ETHICIZE

ETHICS n code of behaviour

ETHINYL same as > ETHYNYL

ETHINYLS > ETHINYL

ETHION n type of pesticide

ETHIONINE n type of amino acid

ETHIONS > ETHION

ETHIOPS n dark-coloured chemical compound

ETHIOPSES > ETHIOPS

ETHMOID adj denoting or relating to a bone of the skull that forms part of the eye socket and the nasal cavity ▷ n ethmoid bone

ETHMOIDAL same as > ETHMOID

ETHMOIDS > ETHMOID

ETHNARCH n ruler of a people or province, as in parts of the Roman and Byzantine Empires

ETHNARCHS > ETHNARCH

ETHNARCHY > ETHNARCH

ETHNIC adj relating to a people or group that shares a culture, religion, or language ▷ n member of an ethnic group, esp a minority group

ETHNICAL same as > ETHNIC

ETHNICISM n paganism

ETHNICITY > ETHNIC

ETHNICS > ETHNIC

ETHNOCIDE n extermination of a race

ETHNOGENY n branch of ethnology that deals with the origin of races or peoples

ETHNOLOGY n study of human races

ETHNONYM n name of ethnic group

ETHNONYMS > ETHNONYM

ETHNOS n ethnic group

ETHNOSES > ETHNOS

ETHOGRAM n description of animal's behaviour

ETHOGRAMS > ETHOGRAM

ETHOLOGIC > ETHOLOGY

ETHOLOGY n study of the behaviour of animals in their normal environment

ETHONONE another name for > KETENE

ETHONONES > ETHONONE

ETHOS n distinctive spirit and attitudes of a people, culture, etc

ETHOSES > ETHOS

ETHOXIDE n any of a class of saltlike compounds

ETHOXIDES > ETHOXIDE

ETHOXIES > ETHOXY

ETHOXY > ETHOXYL

ETHOXYL n univalent radical

ETHOXYLS > ETHOXYL

ETHS > ETH

ETHYL adj type of chemical hydrocarbon group

ETHYLATE same as > ETHOXIDE

ETHYLATED > ETHYLATE

ETHYLATES > ETHYLATE

ETHYLENE n poisonous gas used as an anaesthetic and as fuel

ETHYLENES > ETHYLENE

ETHYLENIC > ETHYLENE

ETHYLIC > ETHYL

ETHYLS > ETHYL

ETHYNE another name for > ACETYLENE

ETHYNES > ETHYNE

ETHYNYL n univalent radical

ETHYNYLS > ETHYNYL

ETIC adj (in linguistics) of or relating to items analyzed without

consideration of their structural function

ETIOLATE vb become pale and weak

ETIOLATED > ETIOLATE

ETIOLATES > ETIOLATE

ETIOLIN n yellow pigment

ETIOLINS > ETIOLIN

ETIOLOGIC > ETIOLOGY

ETIOLOGY n study of the causes of diseases

ETIQUETTE n conventional code of conduct

ETNA n container used to heat liquids

ETNAS > ETNA

ETOILE n star

ETOILES > ETOILE

ETOUFFEE n spicy Cajun stew

ETOUFFEES > ETOUFFEE

ETOURDI adj foolish

ETOURDIE feminine form of > ETOURDI

ETRANGER n foreigner

ETRANGERE feminine form of > ETRANGER

ETRANGERS > ETRANGER

ETRENNE n New Year's gift

ETRENNES > ETRENNE

ETRIER n short portable ladder or set of webbing loops that can be attached to a karabiner or fifi hook

ETRIERS > ETRIER

ETTERCAP n spider

ETTERCAPS > ETTERCAP

ETTIN n giant

ETTINS > ETTIN

ETTLE vb intend

ETTLED > ETTLE

ETTLES > ETTLE

ETTLING > ETTLE

ETUDE n short musical composition for a solo instrument, esp intended as a technical exercise

ETUDES > ETUDE

ETUI n small usually ornamented case for holding needles, cosmetics, or other small articles

ETUIS > ETUI

ETWEE same as > ETUI

ETWEES > ETUI

ETYMA > ETYMON

ETYMIC > ETYMON

ETYMOLOGY n study of the sources and development of words

ETYMON n form of a word or morpheme, usually the earliest recorded form or a reconstructed form, from which another word or morpheme is derived: the etymon of English "ewe" is Indo-European "owi"

ETYMONS > ETYMON

ETYPIC n unable to conform to type

ETYPICAL same as > ETYPIC

EUCAIN same as > EUCAINE

**EUCAINE** n crystalline optically active substance formerly used as a local anaesthetic
**EUCAINES** > EUCAINE
**EUCAINS** > EUCAIN
**EUCALYPT** n myrtaceous tree
**EUCALYPTI** n eucalypts
**EUCALYPTS** > EUCALYPT
**EUCARYON** same as > EUKARYOTE
**EUCARYONS** > EUCARYON
**EUCARYOT** same as > EUKARYOTE
**EUCARYOTE** same as > EUKARYOTE
**EUCARYOTS** > EUCARYOT
**EUCHARIS** n any amaryllidaceous plant of the South American genus Eucharis, cultivated for their large white fragrant flowers
**EUCHLORIC** > EUCHLORIN
**EUCHLORIN** n explosive gaseous mixture of chlorine and chlorine dioxide
**EUCHOLOGY** n prayer formulary
**EUCHRE** n US and Canadian card game similar to écarté for two to four players, using a poker pack with joker ▷ vb prevent (a player) from making his contracted tricks
**EUCHRED** > EUCHRE
**EUCHRES** > EUCHRE
**EUCHRING** > EUCHRE
**EUCLASE** n brittle green gem
**EUCLASES** > EUCLASE
**EUCLIDEAN** adj of or relating to Euclid (Greek mathematician of Alexandria, 3rd century BC), esp his system of geometry
**EUCLIDIAN** same as > EUCLIDEAN
**EUCRITE** n type of stony meteorite
**EUCRITES** > EUCRITE
**EUCRITIC** > EUCRITE
**EUCRYPHIA** n any tree or shrub of the mostly evergreen genus Eucryphia, native to Australia and S America, having leaves of a dark lustrous green and white flowers: family Eucryphiaceae
**EUCYCLIC** adj (of plants) having the same number of leaves in each whorl
**EUDAEMON** same as > EUDEMON
**EUDAEMONS** > EUDAEMON
**EUDAEMONY** same as > EUDEMONIA
**EUDAIMON** same as > EUDAEMON

**EUDAIMONS** > EUDAIMON
**EUDEMON** n benevolent spirit or demon
**EUDEMONIA** n happiness, esp (in the philosophy of Aristotle) that resulting from a rational active life
**EUDEMONIC** > EUDEMONIA
**EUDEMONS** > EUDEMON
**EUDIALYTE** n brownish-red mineral
**EUGARIE** another name for > PIPI
**EUGARIES** > EUGARIE
**EUGE** interj well done!
**EUGENIA** n plant of the clove family
**EUGENIAS** > EUGENIA
**EUGENIC** > EUGENICS
**EUGENICAL** > EUGENICS
**EUGENICS** n study of methods of improving the human race
**EUGENISM** > EUGENICS
**EUGENISMS** > EUGENICS
**EUGENIST** > EUGENICS
**EUGENISTS** > EUGENICS
**EUGENOL** n colourless or pale yellow oily liquid substance with a spicy taste and an odour of cloves, used in perfumery
**EUGENOLS** > EUGENOL
**EUGH** archaic form of > YEW
**EUGHEN** archaic form of > YEW
**EUGHS** > EUGH
**EUGLENA** n any freshwater unicellular organism of the genus Euglena, moving by means of flagella and typically having holophytic nutrition. It has been variously regarded as an alga or a protozoan but is now usually classified as a protoctist (phylum Euglenophyta)
**EUGLENAS** > EUGLENA
**EUGLENID** same as > EUGLENA
**EUGLENIDS** > EUGLENID
**EUGLENOID** > EUGLENA
**EUK** vb itch
**EUKARYON** same as > EUKARYOTE
**EUKARYONS** > EUKARYON
**EUKARYOT** same as > EUKARYOTE
**EUKARYOTE** n any member of the Eukarya, a domain of organisms having cells each with a distinct nucleus within which the genetic material is contained
**EUKARYOTS** > EUKARYOT
**EUKED** > EUK
**EUKING** > EUK
**EUKS** > EUK
**EULACHAN** same as > EULACHON
**EULACHANS** > EULACHAN
**EULACHON** n salmonoid

food fish
**EULACHONS** > EULACHON
**EULOGIA** n blessed bread distributed to members of the congregation after the liturgy, esp to those who have not communed
**EULOGIAE** > EULOGIA
**EULOGIAS** > EULOGIA
**EULOGIES** > EULOGY
**EULOGISE** same as > EULOGIZE
**EULOGISED** > EULOGISE
**EULOGISER** > EULOGISE
**EULOGISES** > EULOGISE
**EULOGIST** > EULOGIZE
**EULOGISTS** > EULOGIZE
**EULOGIUM** same as > EULOGY
**EULOGIUMS** > EULOGIUM
**EULOGIZE** vb praise (a person or thing) highly in speech or writing
**EULOGIZED** > EULOGIZE
**EULOGIZER** > EULOGIZE
**EULOGIZES** > EULOGIZE
**EULOGY** n speech or writing in praise of a person
**EUMELANIN** n dark melanin
**EUMERISM** n collection of similar parts
**EUMERISMS** > EUMERISM
**EUMONG** same as > EUMUNG
**EUMONGS** > EUMONG
**EUMUNG** n any of various Australian acacias
**EUMUNGS** > EUMUNG
**EUNUCH** n castrated man, esp (formerly) a guard in a harem
**EUNUCHISE** same as > EUNUCHIZE
**EUNUCHISM** > EUNUCH
**EUNUCHIZE** vb castrate
**EUNUCHOID** n one suffering from deficient sexual development
**EUNUCHS** > EUNUCH
**EUOI** n cry of Bacchic frenzy
**EUONYMIN** n extract derived from the bark of the euonymus
**EUONYMINS** > EUONYMIN
**EUONYMUS** n any tree or shrub of the N temperate genus Euonymus
**EUOUAE** n cry of Bacchic frenzy
**EUOUAES** > EUOUAE
**EUPAD** n antiseptic powder
**EUPADS** > EUPAD
**EUPATRID** n (in ancient Greece) hereditary noble or landowner
**EUPATRIDS** > EUPATRID
**EUPEPSIA** n good digestion
**EUPEPSIAS** > EUPEPSIA
**EUPEPSIES** > EUPEPSY
**EUPEPSY** same as > EUPEPSIA
**EUPEPTIC** > EUPEPSIA
**EUPHAUSID** n small pelagic shrimplike crustacean
**EUPHEMISE** same as > EUPHEMIZE

**EUPHEMISM** n inoffensive word or phrase substituted for one considered offensive or upsetting
**EUPHEMIST** > EUPHEMISM
**EUPHEMIZE** vb speak in euphemisms or refer to by means of a euphemism
**EUPHENIC** n of or pertaining to biological improvement
**EUPHENICS** n science of biological improvement
**EUPHOBIA** n fear of good news
**EUPHOBIAS** > EUPHOBIA
**EUPHON** n glass harmonica
**EUPHONIA** same as > EUPHONY
**EUPHONIAS** > EUPHONIA
**EUPHONIC** adj denoting or relating to euphony
**EUPHONIES** > EUPHONY
**EUPHONISE** same as > EUPHONIZE
**EUPHONISM** n use of pleasant-sounding words
**EUPHONIUM** n brass musical instrument, tenor tuba
**EUPHONIZE** vb make pleasant to hear
**EUPHONS** > EUPHON
**EUPHONY** n pleasing sound
**EUPHORBIA** n any plant of the genus Euphorbia
**EUPHORIA** n sense of elation
**EUPHORIAS** > EUPHORIA
**EUPHORIC** > EUPHORIA
**EUPHORIES** > EUPHORY
**EUPHORY** same as > EUPHORIA
**EUPHOTIC** adj denoting or relating to the uppermost part of a sea or lake down to about 100 metres depth, which receives enough light to enable photosynthesis to take place
**EUPHRASY** same as > EYEBRIGHT
**EUPHROE** n wooden block with holes through which the lines of a crowfoot are rove
**EUPHROES** > EUPHROE
**EUPHUISE** same as > EUPHUIZE
**EUPHUISED** > EUPHUISE
**EUPHUISES** > EUPHUISE
**EUPHUISM** n artificial prose style of the Elizabethan period, marked by extreme use of antithesis, alliteration, and extended similes and allusions
**EUPHUISMS** > EUPHUISM
**EUPHUIST** > EUPHUISM
**EUPHUISTS** > EUPHUISM
**EUPHUIZE** vb write in euphuism
**EUPHUIZED** > EUPHUIZE

**EUPHUIZES** > EUPHUIZE
**EUPLASTIC** adj healing quickly and well
**EUPLOID** adj having chromosomes present in an exact multiple of the haploid number ▷ n euploid cell or individual
**EUPLOIDS** > EUPLOID
**EUPLOIDY** > EUPLOID
**EUPNEA** same as > EUPNOEA
**EUPNEAS** > EUPNEA
**EUPNEIC** > EUPNOEA
**EUPNOEA** n normal relaxed breathing
**EUPNOEAS** > EUPNOEA
**EUPNOEIC** > EUPNOEA
**EUREKA** n exclamation of triumph at finding something
**EUREKAS** > EUREKA
**EURHYTHMY** n rhythmic movement
**EURIPI** > EURIPUS
**EURIPUS** n strait or channel with a strong current or tide
**EURIPUSES** > EURIPUS
**EURO** n unit of the single currency of the European Union
**EUROBOND** n bond issued in a eurocurrency
**EUROBONDS** > EUROBOND
**EUROCRAT** n member, esp a senior member, of the administration of the European Union
**EUROCRATS** > EUROCRAT
**EUROCREEP** n gradual introduction of the euro into use in Britain
**EUROKIES** > EUROKY
**EUROKOUS** > EUROKY
**EUROKY** n ability of an organism to live under different conditions
**EURONOTE** n form of euro-commercial paper consisting of short-term negotiable bearer notes
**EURONOTES** > EURONOTE
**EUROPHILE** n person who admires Europe, Europeans, or the European Union
**EUROPIUM** n silvery-white element of the lanthanide series
**EUROPIUMS** > EUROPIUM
**EUROS** > EURO
**EURYBATH** n organism that can live at different depths underwater
**EURYBATHS** > EURYBATH
**EURYOKIES** > EURYOKY
**EURYOKOUS** > EURYOKY
**EURYOKY** same as > EUROKY
**EURYTHERM** n organism that can tolerate widely differing temperatures
**EURYTHMIC** adj having a pleasing and harmonious rhythm, order, or structure

**EURYTHMY** > EURYTHMICS
**EURYTOPIC** adj (of a species) able to tolerate a wide range of environments
**EUSOCIAL** adj using division of labour
**EUSOL** n solution of eupad in water
**EUSOLS** > EUSOL
**EUSTACIES** > EUSTATIC
**EUSTACY** > EUSTATIC
**EUSTASIES** > EUSTATIC
**EUSTASY** > EUSTATIC
**EUSTATIC** adj denoting or relating to worldwide changes in sea level, caused by the melting of ice sheets, movements of the ocean floor, sedimentation, etc
**EUSTELE** n central cylinder of a seed plant
**EUSTELES** > EUSTELE
**EUSTYLE** n building with columns optimally spaced
**EUSTYLES** > EUSTYLE
**EUTAXIA** n condition of being easily melted
**EUTAXIAS** > EUTAXIA
**EUTAXIES** > EUTAXY
**EUTAXITE** n banded volcanic rock
**EUTAXITES** > EUTAXITE
**EUTAXITIC** > EUTAXITE
**EUTAXY** n good order
**EUTECTIC** adj (of a mixture of substances, esp an alloy) having the lowest freezing point of all possible mixtures of the substances ▷ n eutectic mixture
**EUTECTICS** > EUTECTIC
**EUTECTOID** n mixture of substances similar to a eutectic, but forming two or three constituents from a solid instead of from a melt ▷ adj concerned with or suitable for eutectoid mixtures
**EUTEXIA** same as > EUTAXIA
**EUTEXIAS** > EUTEXIA
**EUTHANASY** n the act of killing someone painlessly
**EUTHANISE** same as > EUTHANIZE
**EUTHANIZE** vb put (someone, esp one suffering from a terminal illness) to death painlessly
**EUTHENICS** n study of the control of the environment, esp with a view to improving the health and living standards of the human race
**EUTHENIST** > EUTHENICS
**EUTHERIAN** adj of, relating to, or belonging to the Eutheria, a subclass of mammals all of which have a placenta and

reach an advanced state of development before birth ▷ n any eutherian mammal
**EUTHYMIA** n pleasant state of mind
**EUTHYMIAS** > EUTHYMIA
**EUTHYROID** n condition of having thyroid glands that function normally
**EUTRAPELY** n conversational skill
**EUTROPHIC** adj (of lakes and similar habitats) rich in organic and mineral nutrients and supporting an abundant plant life, which in the process of decaying depletes the oxygen supply for animal life
**EUTROPHY** > EUTROPHIC
**EUTROPIC** > EUTROPY
**EUTROPIES** > EUTROPY
**EUTROPOUS** > EUTROPY
**EUTROPY** n regular variation of the crystalline structure of a series of compounds according to atomic number
**EUXENITE** n rare brownish-black mineral containing erbium, cerium, uranium, columbium, and yttrium
**EUXENITES** > EUXENITE
**EVACUANT** adj serving to promote excretion, esp of the bowels ▷ n evacuant agent
**EVACUANTS** > EVACUANT
**EVACUATE** vb send (someone) away from a place of danger
**EVACUATED** > EVACUATE
**EVACUATES** > EVACUATE
**EVACUATOR** > EVACUATE
**EVACUEE** n person evacuated from a place of danger, esp in wartime
**EVACUEES** > EVACUEE
**EVADABLE** > EVADE
**EVADE** vb get away from or avoid
**EVADED** > EVADE
**EVADER** > EVADE
**EVADERS** > EVADE
**EVADES** > EVADE
**EVADIBLE** > EVADE
**EVADING** > EVADE
**EVADINGLY** > EVADE
**EVAGATION** n digression
**EVAGINATE** vb turn (an organ or part) inside out
**EVALUABLE** > EVALUATE
**EVALUATE** vb find or judge the value of
**EVALUATED** > EVALUATE
**EVALUATES** > EVALUATE
**EVALUATOR** > EVALUATE
**EVANESCE** vb fade gradually from sight
**EVANESCED** > EVANESCE
**EVANESCES** > EVANESCE
**EVANGEL** n gospel of

Christianity
**EVANGELIC** adj of, based upon, or following from the gospels
**EVANGELS** > EVANGEL
**EVANGELY** n gospel
**EVANISH** poetic word for > VANISH
**EVANISHED** > EVANISH
**EVANISHES** > EVANISH
**EVANITION** > EVANISH
**EVAPORATE** vb change from a liquid or solid to a vapour
**EVAPORITE** n any sedimentary rock, such as rock salt, gypsum, or anhydrite, formed by evaporation of former seas or salt-water lakes
**EVASIBLE** > EVASION
**EVASION** n act of evading something, esp a duty or responsibility, by cunning or illegal means
**EVASIONAL** > EVASION
**EVASIONS** > EVASION
**EVASIVE** adj not straightforward
**EVASIVELY** > EVASIVE
**EVE** n evening or day before some special event
**EVECTION** n irregularity in the moon's motion caused by perturbations of the sun and planets
**EVECTIONS** > EVECTION
**EVEJAR** n nightjar
**EVEJARS** > EVEJAR
**EVEN** adj flat or smooth ▷ adv equally ▷ vb make even ▷ n eve
**EVENED** > EVEN
**EVENEMENT** n event
**EVENER** > EVEN
**EVENERS** > EVEN
**EVENEST** > EVEN
**EVENFALL** n early evening
**EVENFALLS** > EVENFALL
**EVENING** n end of the day or early part of the night ▷ adj of or in the evening
**EVENINGS** adv in the evening, esp regularly
**EVENLY** > EVEN
**EVENNESS** > EVEN
**EVENS** adv (of a bet) winning the same as the amount staked if successful
**EVENSONG** n evening prayer
**EVENSONGS** > EVENSONG
**EVENT** n anything that takes place ▷ vb take part or ride (a horse) in eventing
**EVENTED** > EVENT
**EVENTER** > EVENTING
**EVENTERS** > EVENTING
**EVENTFUL** adj full of exciting incidents
**EVENTIDE** n evening
**EVENTIDES** > EVENTIDE
**EVENTING** n riding competitions, usu.

involving cross-country, jumping, and dressage
**EVENTINGS** > EVENTING
**EVENTISE** *same as* > EVENTIZE
**EVENTISED** > EVENTISE
**EVENTISES** > EVENTISE
**EVENTIZE** *vb* arrange an occasion so that it is seen as being a special event
**EVENTIZED** > EVENTIZE
**EVENTIZES** > EVENTIZE
**EVENTLESS** > EVENT
**EVENTRATE** *vb* open the belly of
**EVENTS** > EVENT
**EVENTUAL** *adj* ultimate
**EVENTUATE** *vb* result ultimately (in)
**EVER** *adv* at any time
**EVERGLADE** *n* large area of submerged marshland
**EVERGREEN** *adj* (tree or shrub) having leaves throughout the year ▷ *n* evergreen tree or shrub
**EVERMORE** *adv* for all time to come
**EVERNET** *n* hypothetical form of internet that is continuously accessible using a wide variety of devices
**EVERNETS** > EVERNET
**EVERSIBLE** > EVERT
**EVERSION** > EVERT
**EVERSIONS** > EVERT
**EVERT** *vb* turn (an eyelid, the intestines, or some other bodily part) outwards or inside out
**EVERTED** > EVERT
**EVERTING** > EVERT
**EVERTOR** *n* any muscle that turns a part outwards
**EVERTORS** > EVERTOR
**EVERTS** > EVERT
**EVERWHERE** *adv* to or in all parts or places
**EVERWHICH** *dialect version of* > WHICHEVER
**EVERY** *adj* each without exception
**EVERYBODY** *pron* every person
**EVERYDAY** *adj* usual or ordinary ▷ *n* ordinary day
**EVERYDAYS** > EVERYDAY
**EVERYMAN** *n* ordinary person; common man
**EVERYMEN** > EVERYMAN
**EVERYONE** *pron* every person
**EVERYWAY** *adv* in every way
**EVERYWHEN** *adv* to or in all parts or places
**EVES** > EVE
**EVET** *n* eft
**EVETS** > EVET
**EVHOE** *interj* cry of Bacchic frenzy
**EVICT** *vb* legally expel (someone) from his or her home

**EVICTED** > EVICT
**EVICTEE** > EVICT
**EVICTEES** > EVICT
**EVICTING** > EVICT
**EVICTION** > EVICT
**EVICTIONS** > EVICT
**EVICTOR** > EVICT
**EVICTORS** > EVICT
**EVICTS** > EVICT
**EVIDENCE** *n* ground for belief ▷ *vb* demonstrate, prove
**EVIDENCED** > EVIDENCE
**EVIDENCES** > EVIDENCE
**EVIDENT** *adj* easily seen or understood ▷ *n* item of evidence
**EVIDENTLY** *adv* without question
**EVIDENTS** > EVIDENT
**EVIL** *n* wickedness ▷ *adj* harmful ▷ *adv* in an evil manner
**EVILDOER** *n* wicked person
**EVILDOERS** > EVILDOER
**EVILDOING** > EVILDOER
**EVILER** > EVIL
**EVILEST** > EVIL
**EVILLER** > EVIL
**EVILLEST** > EVIL
**EVILLY** > EVIL
**EVILNESS** > EVIL
**EVILS** > EVIL
**EVINCE** *vb* make evident
**EVINCED** > EVINCE
**EVINCES** > EVINCE
**EVINCIBLE** > EVINCE
**EVINCIBLY** > EVINCE
**EVINCING** > EVINCE
**EVINCIVE** > EVINCE
**EVIRATE** *vb* castrate
**EVIRATED** > EVIRATE
**EVIRATES** > EVIRATE
**EVIRATING** > EVIRATE
**EVITABLE** *adj* able to be avoided
**EVITATE** *archaic word for* > AVOID
**EVITATED** > EVITATE
**EVITATES** > EVITATE
**EVITATING** > EVITATE
**EVITATION** > EVITATE
**EVITE** *archaic word for* > AVOID
**EVITED** > EVITE
**EVITERNAL** *adj* eternal
**EVITES** > EVITE
**EVITING** > EVITE
**EVO** *informal word for* > EVENING
**EVOCABLE** > EVOKE
**EVOCATE** *vb* evoke
**EVOCATED** > EVOCATE
**EVOCATES** > EVOCATE
**EVOCATING** > EVOCATE
**EVOCATION** *n* act of evoking
**EVOCATIVE** *adj* tending or serving to evoke
**EVOCATOR** *n* person or thing that evokes
**EVOCATORS** > EVOCATOR
**EVOCATORY** *adj* evocative
**EVOE** *interj* cry of Bacchic

frenzy
**EVOHE** *interj* cry of Bacchic frenzy
**EVOKE** *vb* call or summon up (a memory, feeling, etc)
**EVOKED** > EVOKE
**EVOKER** > EVOKE
**EVOKERS** > EVOKE
**EVOKES** > EVOKE
**EVOKING** > EVOKE
**EVOLUE** *n* (in the African former colonies of Belgium and France) African person educated according to European principles
**EVOLUES** > EVOLUE
**EVOLUTE** *n* geometric curve that describes the locus of the centres of curvature of another curve ▷ *adj* having the margins rolled outwards ▷ *vb* evolve
**EVOLUTED** > EVOLUTE
**EVOLUTES** > EVOLUTE
**EVOLUTING** > EVOLUTE
**EVOLUTION** *n* gradual change in the characteristics of living things over successive generations, esp to a more complex form
**EVOLUTIVE** *adj* relating to, tending to, or promoting evolution
**EVOLVABLE** > EVOLVE
**EVOLVE** *vb* develop gradually
**EVOLVED** > EVOLVE
**EVOLVENT** *adj* evolving
**EVOLVER** > EVOLVE
**EVOLVERS** > EVOLVE
**EVOLVES** > EVOLVE
**EVOLVING** > EVOLVE
**EVONYMUS** *same as* > EUONYMUS
**EVOS** > EVO
**EVOVAE** *n* cry of Bacchic frenzy
**EVOVAES** > EVOVAE
**EVULGATE** *vb* make public
**EVULGATED** > EVULGATE
**EVULGATES** > EVULGATE
**EVULSE** *vb* extract by force
**EVULSED** > EVULSE
**EVULSES** > EVULSE
**EVULSING** > EVULSE
**EVULSION** *n* act of extracting by force
**EVULSIONS** > EVULSION
**EVZONE** *n* soldier in an elite Greek infantry regiment
**EVZONES** > EVZONE
**EWE** *n* female sheep
**EWER** *n* large jug with a wide mouth
**EWERS** > EWER
**EWES** > EWE
**EWEST** *Scots word for* > NEAR
**EWFTES** *Spenserian plural of* > EFT
**EWGHEN** *archaic form of* > YEW
**EWHOW** *interj* expression of pity or regret

**EWK** *vb* itch
**EWKED** > EWK
**EWKING** > EWK
**EWKS** > EWK
**EWT** *archaic form of* > NEWT
**EWTS** > EWT
**EX** *prep* not including ▷ *vb* cross out or delete
**EXABYTE** *n* very large unit of computer memory
**EXABYTES** > EXABYTE
**EXACT** *adj* correct and complete in every detail ▷ *vb* demand (payment or obedience)
**EXACTA** *n* horse-racing bet in which the first and second horses must be named in the correct order
**EXACTABLE** > EXACT
**EXACTAS** > EXACTA
**EXACTED** > EXACT
**EXACTER** > EXACT
**EXACTERS** > EXACT
**EXACTEST** > EXACT
**EXACTING** *adj* making rigorous or excessive demands
**EXACTION** *n* act of obtaining or demanding money as a right
**EXACTIONS** > EXACTION
**EXACTLY** *adv* precisely, in every respect ▷ *interj* just so! precisely!
**EXACTMENT** *n* condition of being exact
**EXACTNESS** > EXACT
**EXACTOR** > EXACT
**EXACTORS** > EXACT
**EXACTRESS** > EXACT
**EXACTS** > EXACT
**EXACUM** *n* any plant of the annual or perennial tropical genus *Exacum*; some are grown as greenhouse biennials for their bluish-purple platter-shaped flowers: family *Gentianaceae*
**EXACUMS** > EXACUM
**EXAHERTZ** *n* very large unit of frequency
**EXALT** *vb* praise highly
**EXALTED** *adj* high or elevated in rank, position, dignity, etc
**EXALTEDLY** > EXALTED
**EXALTER** > EXALT
**EXALTERS** > EXALT
**EXALTING** > EXALT
**EXALTS** > EXALT
**EXAM** *n* examination
**EXAMEN** *n* examination of conscience, usually made daily by Jesuits and others
**EXAMENS** > EXAMEN
**EXAMINANT** *n* examiner
**EXAMINATE** *n* examinee
**EXAMINE** *vb* look at closely
**EXAMINED** > EXAMINE
**EXAMINEE** *n* person who sits an exam
**EXAMINEES** > EXAMINEE

EXAMINER > EXAMINE
EXAMINERS > EXAMINE
EXAMINES > EXAMINE
EXAMINING > EXAMINE
EXAMPLAR *archaic form of* > EXEMPLAR
EXAMPLARS > EXAMPLAR
EXAMPLE *n* specimen typical of its group
EXAMPLED > EXAMPLE
EXAMPLES > EXAMPLE
EXAMPLING > EXAMPLE
EXAMS > EXAM
EXANIMATE *adj* lacking life
EXANTHEM *same as* > EXANTHEMA
EXANTHEMA *n* skin eruption or rash occurring as a symptom in a disease such as measles or scarlet fever
EXANTHEMS > EXANTHEM
EXAPTED *adj* biologically adapted
EXAPTIVE *adj* involving biological adaptation
EXARATE *adj* (of the pupa of such insects as ants and bees) having legs, wings, antennae, etc, free and movable
EXARATION *n* writing
EXARCH *n* head of certain autonomous Orthodox Christian Churches, such as that of Bulgaria and Cyprus ▷ *adj* (of a xylem strand) having the first-formed xylem external to that formed later
EXARCHAL > EXARCH
EXARCHATE *n* office, rank, or jurisdiction of an exarch
EXARCHIES > EXARCHY
EXARCHIST *n* supporter of an exarch
EXARCHS > EXARCH
EXARCHY *same as* > EXARCHATE
EXCAMB *vb* exchange
EXCAMBED > EXCAMB
EXCAMBING > EXCAMB
EXCAMBION *n* exchange, esp of land
EXCAMBIUM *same as* > EXCAMBION
EXCAMBS > EXCAMB
EXCARNATE *vb* remove flesh from
EXCAUDATE *adj* having no tail or tail-like process
EXCAVATE *vb* unearth buried objects from (a piece of land) methodically to learn about the past
EXCAVATED > EXCAVATE
EXCAVATES > EXCAVATE
EXCAVATOR *n* large machine used for digging
EXCEED *vb* be greater than
EXCEEDED > EXCEED
EXCEEDER > EXCEED
EXCEEDERS > EXCEED
EXCEEDING *adj* very great
EXCEEDS > EXCEED

EXCEL *vb* be superior to
EXCELLED > EXCEL
EXCELLENT *adj* exceptionally good
EXCELLING > EXCEL
EXCELS > EXCEL
EXCELSIOR *n* excellent: used as a motto and as a trademark for various products, esp in the US for fine wood shavings used for packing breakable objects
EXCENTRIC *same as* > ECCENTRIC
EXCEPT *prep* other than, not including ▷ *vb* leave out; omit; exclude
EXCEPTANT *n* person taking exception
EXCEPTED > EXCEPT
EXCEPTING *prep* except
EXCEPTION *n* excepting
EXCEPTIVE *adj* relating to or forming an exception
EXCEPTOR > EXCEPT
EXCEPTORS > EXCEPT
EXCEPTS > EXCEPT
EXCERPT *n* passage taken from a book, speech, etc ▷ *vb* take a passage from a book, speech, etc
EXCERPTA > EXCERPTUM
EXCERPTED > EXCERPT
EXCERPTER > EXCERPT
EXCERPTOR > EXCERPT
EXCERPTS > EXCERPT
EXCERPTUM *n* excerpt
EXCESS *n* state or act of exceeding the permitted limits ▷ *vb* make (a position) redundant
EXCESSED > EXCESS
EXCESSES > EXCESS
EXCESSING > EXCESS
EXCESSIVE *adj* exceeding the normal or permitted extents or limits
EXCHANGE *vb* give or receive (something) in return for something else ▷ *n* act of exchanging
EXCHANGED > EXCHANGE
EXCHANGER *n* person or thing that exchanges
EXCHANGES > EXCHANGE
EXCHEAT *same as* > ESCHEAT
EXCHEATS > EXCHEAT
EXCHEQUER *n* (in Britain and certain other countries) accounting department of the Treasury, responsible for receiving and issuing funds
EXCIDE *vb* cut out
EXCIDED > EXCIDE
EXCIDES > EXCIDE
EXCIDING > EXCIDE
EXCIMER *n* excited dimer formed by the association of excited and unexcited molecules, which would remain dissociated in the

ground state
EXCIMERS > EXCIMER
EXCIPIENT *n* substance, such as sugar or gum, used to prepare a drug or drugs in a form suitable for administration
EXCIPLE *n* part of a lichen
EXCIPLES > EXCIPLE
EXCISABLE > EXCISE
EXCISE *n* tax on goods produced for the home market ▷ *vb* cut out or away
EXCISED > EXCISE
EXCISEMAN *n* (formerly) a government agent who collected excise and prevented smuggling
EXCISEMEN > EXCISEMAN
EXCISES > EXCISE
EXCISING > EXCISE
EXCISION > EXCISE
EXCISIONS > EXCISE
EXCITABLE *adj* easily excited
EXCITABLY > EXCITABLE
EXCITANCY *n* ability to excite
EXCITANT *adj* able to excite or stimulate ▷ *n* something, such as a drug or other agent, able to excite
EXCITANTS > EXCITANT
EXCITE *vb* arouse to strong emotion
EXCITED *adj* emotionally aroused, esp to pleasure or agitation
EXCITEDLY > EXCITED
EXCITER *n* person or thing that excites
EXCITERS > EXCITER
EXCITES > EXCITER
EXCITING *adj* causing excitement
EXCITON *n* mobile neutral entity in a crystalline solid consisting of an excited electron bound to the hole produced by its excitation
EXCITONIC > EXCITON
EXCITONS > EXCITON
EXCITOR *n* nerve that, when stimulated, causes increased activity in the organ or part it supplies
EXCITORS > EXCITOR
EXCLAIM *vb* speak suddenly, cry out
EXCLAIMED > EXCLAIM
EXCLAIMER > EXCLAIM
EXCLAIMS > EXCLAIM
EXCLAVE *n* part of a country entirely surrounded by foreign territory: viewed from the position of the home country
EXCLAVES > EXCLAVE
EXCLOSURE *n* area of land, esp in a forest, fenced round to keep out

unwanted animals
EXCLUDE *vb* keep out, leave out
EXCLUDED > EXCLUDE
EXCLUDEE > EXCLUDE
EXCLUDEES > EXCLUDE
EXCLUDER > EXCLUDE
EXCLUDERS > EXCLUDE
EXCLUDES > EXCLUDE
EXCLUDING *prep* excepting
EXCLUSION *n* act or an instance of excluding or the state of being excluded
EXCLUSIVE *adj* excluding everything else ▷ *n* story reported in only one newspaper
EXCLUSORY > EXCLUDE
EXCORIATE *vb* censure severely
EXCREMENT *n* waste matter discharged from the body
EXCRETA *n* excrement
EXCRETAL > EXCRETA
EXCRETE *vb* discharge (waste matter) from the body
EXCRETED > EXCRETE
EXCRETER > EXCRETE
EXCRETERS > EXCRETE
EXCRETES > EXCRETE
EXCRETING > EXCRETE
EXCRETION > EXCRETE
EXCRETIVE > EXCRETE
EXCRETORY > EXCRETE
EXCUBANT *adj* keeping guard
EXCUDIT *sentence substitute* (named person) made this
EXCULPATE *vb* free from blame or guilt
EXCURRENT *adj* having an outward flow, as certain pores in sponges, ducts, etc
EXCURSE *vb* wander
EXCURSED > EXCURSE
EXCURSES > EXCURSE
EXCURSING > EXCURSE
EXCURSION *n* short journey, esp for pleasure
EXCURSIVE *adj* tending to digress
EXCURSUS *n* incidental digression from the main topic under discussion or from the main story in a narrative
EXCUSABLE > EXCUSE
EXCUSABLY > EXCUSE
EXCUSAL > EXCUSE
EXCUSALS > EXCUSE
EXCUSE *n* explanation offered to justify (a fault etc) ▷ *vb* put forward a reason or justification for (a fault etc)
EXCUSED > EXCUSE
EXCUSER > EXCUSE
EXCUSERS > EXCUSE
EXCUSES > EXCUSE
EXCUSING > EXCUSE
EXCUSIVE *adj* excusing
EXEAT *n* leave of absence

from school or some other institution

**EXEATS** > EXEAT

**EXEC** *n* executive

**EXECRABLE** *adj* of very poor quality

**EXECRABLY** > EXECRABLE

**EXECRATE** *vb* feel and express loathing and hatred of (someone or something)

**EXECRATED** > EXECRATE

**EXECRATES** > EXECRATE

**EXECRATOR** > EXECRATE

**EXECS** > EXEC

**EXECUTANT** *n* performer, esp of musical works

**EXECUTARY** *n* person whose job comprises tasks appropriate to a middle-management executive as well as those traditionally carried out by a secretary

**EXECUTE** *vb* put (a condemned person) to death

**EXECUTED** > EXECUTE

**EXECUTER** > EXECUTE

**EXECUTERS** > EXECUTE

**EXECUTES** > EXECUTE

**EXECUTING** > EXECUTE

**EXECUTION** *n* act of executing

**EXECUTIVE** *n* person or group in an administrative position ▷ *adj* having the function of carrying out plans, orders, laws, etc

**EXECUTOR** *n* person appointed to perform the instructions of a will

**EXECUTORS** > EXECUTOR

**EXECUTORY** *adj* (of a law, agreement, etc) coming into operation at a future date

**EXECUTRIX** *n* female executor

**EXECUTRY** *n* condition of being an executor

**EXED** > EX

**EXEDRA** *n* building, room, portico, or apse containing a continuous bench, used in ancient Greece and Rome for holding discussions

**EXEDRAE** > EXEDRA

**EXEEM** *same as* > EXEME

**EXEEMED** > EXEEM

**EXEEMING** > EXEEM

**EXEEMS** > EXEEM

**EXEGESES** > EXEGESIS

**EXEGESIS** *n* explanation of a text, esp of the Bible

**EXEGETE** *n* person who practises exegesis

**EXEGETES** > EXEGETE

**EXEGETIC** *adj* of or relating to exegesis

**EXEGETICS** *n* scientific study of exegesis and exegetical methods

**EXEGETIST** *same*

*as* > EXEGETE

**EXEME** *vb* set free

**EXEMED** > EXEME

**EXEMES** > EXEME

**EXEMING** > EXEME

**EXEMPLA** > EXEMPLUM

**EXEMPLAR** *n* person or thing to be copied, model

**EXEMPLARS** > EXEMPLAR

**EXEMPLARY** *adj* being a good example

**EXEMPLE** *same as* > EXAMPLE

**EXEMPLES** > EXEMPLE

**EXEMPLIFY** *vb* show an example of

**EXEMPLUM** *n* anecdote that supports a moral point or sustains an argument, used esp in medieval sermons

**EXEMPT** *adj* not subject to an obligation etc ▷ *vb* release from an obligation etc ▷ *n* person who is exempt from an obligation, tax, etc

**EXEMPTED** > EXEMPT

**EXEMPTING** > EXEMPT

**EXEMPTION** > EXEMPT

**EXEMPTIVE** > EXEMPT

**EXEMPTS** > EXEMPT

**EXEQUATUR** *n* official authorization issued by a host country to a consular agent, permitting him to perform his official duties

**EXEQUIAL** > EXEQUY

**EXEQUIES** > EXEQUY

**EXEQUY** *n* funeral rite

**EXERCISE** *n* activity to train the body or mind ▷ *vb* make use of

**EXERCISED** > EXERCISE

**EXERCISER** *n* device with springs or elasticated cords for muscular exercise

**EXERCISES** > EXERCISE

**EXERCYCLE** *n* exercise bicycle

**EXERGONIC** *adj* (of a biochemical reaction) producing energy and therefore occurring spontaneously

**EXERGUAL** > EXERGUE

**EXERGUE** *n* space on the reverse of a coin or medal below the central design, often containing the date, place of minting, etc

**EXERGUES** > EXERGUE

**EXERT** *vb* use (influence, authority, etc) forcefully or effectively

**EXERTED** > EXERT

**EXERTING** > EXERT

**EXERTION** > EXERT

**EXERTIONS** > EXERT

**EXERTIVE** > EXERT

**EXERTS** > EXERT

**EXES** > EX

**EXEUNT** *vb* (they) go out

**EXFOLIANT** *n* cosmetic

removing dead skin

**EXFOLIATE** *vb* peel in scales or layers

**EXHALABLE** > EXHALE

**EXHALANT** *adj* emitting a vapour or liquid ▷ *n* organ or vessel that emits a vapour or liquid

**EXHALANTS** > EXHALANT

**EXHALE** *vb* breathe out

**EXHALED** > EXHALE

**EXHALENT** *same as* > EXHALANT

**EXHALENTS** > EXHALANT

**EXHALES** > EXHALE

**EXHALING** > EXHALE

**EXHAUST** *vb* tire out ▷ *n* gases ejected from an engine as waste products

**EXHAUSTED** > EXHAUST

**EXHAUSTER** > EXHAUST

**EXHAUSTS** > EXHAUST

**EXHEDRA** *same as* > EXEDRA

**EXHEDRAE** > EXHEDRA

**EXHIBIT** *vb* display to the public ▷ *n* object exhibited to the public

**EXHIBITED** > EXHIBIT

**EXHIBITER** > EXHIBIT

**EXHIBITOR** *n* person or thing that exhibits

**EXHIBITS** > EXHIBIT

**EXHORT** *vb* urge earnestly

**EXHORTED** > EXHORT

**EXHORTER** > EXHORT

**EXHORTERS** > EXHORT

**EXHORTING** > EXHORT

**EXHORTS** > EXHORT

**EXHUMATE** *same as* > EXHUME

**EXHUMATED** > EXHUMATE

**EXHUMATES** > EXHUMATE

**EXHUME** *vb* dig up (something buried, esp a corpse)

**EXHUMED** > EXHUME

**EXHUMER** > EXHUME

**EXHUMERS** > EXHUME

**EXHUMES** > EXHUME

**EXHUMING** > EXHUME

**EXIES** *n* hysterics

**EXIGEANT** *adj* exacting

**EXIGEANTE** *same as* > EXIGEANT

**EXIGENCE** *same as* > EXIGENCY

**EXIGENCES** > EXIGENCE

**EXIGENCY** *n* urgent demand or need

**EXIGENT** *adj* urgent ▷ *n* emergency

**EXIGENTLY** > EXIGENT

**EXIGENTS** > EXIGENT

**EXIGIBLE** *adj* liable to be exacted or required

**EXIGUITY** > EXIGUOUS

**EXIGUOUS** *adj* scanty or meagre

**EXILABLE** > EXILE

**EXILE** *n* prolonged, usu. enforced, absence from one's country ▷ *vb* expel from one's country

**EXILED** > EXILE

**EXILEMENT** *same as* > EXILE

**EXILER** > EXILE

**EXILERS** > EXILE

**EXILES** > EXILE

**EXILIAN** > EXILE

**EXILIC** > EXILE

**EXILING** > EXILE

**EXILITIES** > EXILITY

**EXILITY** *n* poverty or meagreness

**EXIMIOUS** *adj* select and distinguished

**EXINE** *n* outermost coat of a pollen grain or a spore

**EXINES** > EXINE

**EXING** > EX

**EXIST** *vb* have being or reality

**EXISTED** > EXIST

**EXISTENCE** *n* fact or state of being real, live, or actual

**EXISTENT** *adj* in existence ▷ *n* person or a thing that exists

**EXISTENTS** > EXISTENT

**EXISTING** > EXIST

**EXISTS** > EXIST

**EXIT** *n* way out ▷ *vb* go out

**EXITANCE** *n* measure of the ability of a surface to emit radiation

**EXITANCES** > EXITANCE

**EXITED** > EXIT

**EXITING** > EXIT

**EXITLESS** > EXIT

**EXITS** > EXIT

**EXO** *informal word for* > EXCELLENT

**EXOCARP** *same as* > EPICARP

**EXOCARPS** > EXOCARP

**EXOCRINE** *adj* relating to a gland, such as the sweat gland, that secretes externally through a duct ▷ *n* exocrine gland

**EXOCRINES** > EXOCRINE

**EXOCYCLIC** *adj* (of a sea urchin) having the anus situated outside the apical disc

**EXOCYTIC** *adj* outside biological cell

**EXOCYTOSE** *vb* secrete substance from within cell

**EXODE** *n* exodus

**EXODERM** *same as* > ECTODERM

**EXODERMAL** > EXODERM

**EXODERMIS** *same as* > ECTODERM

**EXODERMS** > EXODERM

**EXODES** > EXODE

**EXODIC** > EXODE

**EXODIST** > EXODUS

**EXODISTS** > EXODUS

**EXODOI** > EXODOS

**EXODONTIA** *n* branch of dental surgery concerned with the extraction of teeth

**EXODOS** *n* processional song performed at the end of a play

**EXODUS** n departure of a large number of people

**EXODUSES** > EXODUS

**EXOENZYME** n extracellular enzyme

**EXOERGIC** adj (of a nuclear reaction) occurring with evolution of energy

**EXOGAMIC** > EXOGAMY

**EXOGAMIES** > EXOGAMY

**EXOGAMOUS** > EXOGAMY

**EXOGAMY** n custom or an act of marrying a person belonging to another tribe, clan, or similar social unit

**EXOGEN** n plant with a stem that develops through the growth of new layers on its outside

**EXOGENISM** > EXOGENOUS

**EXOGENOUS** adj having an external origin

**EXOGENS** > EXOGEN

**EXOMION** same as > EXOMIS

**EXOMIONS** > EXOMION

**EXOMIS** n sleeveless jacket

**EXOMISES** > EXOMIS

**EXON** n one of the four officers who command the Yeomen of the Guard

**EXONERATE** vb free from blame or a criminal charge

**EXONIC** > EXON

**EXONS** > EXON

**EXONUMIA** n objects of interest to numismatists that are not coins, such as medals and tokens

**EXONUMIST** n collector of medals and tokens

**EXONYM** n name given to a place by foreigners

**EXONYMS** > EXONYM

**EXOPHAGY** n (among cannibals) custom of eating only members of other tribes

**EXOPHORIC** adj denoting or relating to a pronoun such as "I" or "you", the meaning of which is determined by reference outside the discourse rather than by a preceding or following expression

**EXOPLANET** n planet that orbits a star in a solar system other than that of Earth

**EXOPLASM** another name for > ECTOPLASM

**EXOPLASMS** > EXOPLASM

**EXOPOD** same as > EXOPODITE

**EXOPODITE** n outer projection on the hind legs of some crustaceans

**EXOPODS** > EXOPOD

**EXORABLE** adj able to be persuaded or moved by pleading

**EXORATION** n plea

**EXORCISE** same

as > EXORCIZE

**EXORCISED** > EXORCISE

**EXORCISER** > EXORCISE

**EXORCISES** > EXORCISE

**EXORCISM** > EXORCIZE

**EXORCISMS** > EXORCIZE

**EXORCIST** > EXORCIZE

**EXORCISTS** > EXORCIZE

**EXORCIZE** vb expel (evil spirits) by prayers and religious rites

**EXORCIZED** > EXORCIZE

**EXORCIZER** > EXORCIZE

**EXORCIZES** > EXORCIZE

**EXORDIA** > EXORDIUM

**EXORDIAL** > EXORDIUM

**EXORDIUM** n introductory part or beginning, esp of an oration or discourse

**EXORDIUMS** > EXORDIUM

**EXOSMIC** > EXOSMOSIS

**EXOSMOSE** same

as > EXOSMOSIS

**EXOSMOSES** > EXOSMOSIS

**EXOSMOSIS** n osmosis in which water flows from a cell or organism into the surrounding solution

**EXOSMOTIC** > EXOSMOSIS

**EXOSPHERE** n outermost layer of the earth's atmosphere

**EXOSPORAL** > EXOSPORE

**EXOSPORE** n outer layer of the spores of some algae and fungi

**EXOSPORES** > EXOSPORE

**EXOSPORIA** n exospores

**EXOSTOSES** > EXOSTOSIS

**EXOSTOSIS** n abnormal bony outgrowth from the surface of a bone

**EXOTERIC** adj intelligible to or intended for more than a select or initiated minority

**EXOTIC** adj having a strange allure or beauty ▷ n non-native plant

**EXOTICA** pl n (collection of) exotic objects

**EXOTICISM** > EXOTIC

**EXOTICIST** > EXOTIC

**EXOTICS** > EXOTIC

**EXOTISM** > EXOTIC

**EXOTISMS** > EXOTIC

**EXOTOXIC** > EXOTOXIN

**EXOTOXIN** n toxin produced by a microorganism and secreted into the surrounding medium

**EXOTOXINS** > EXOTOXIN

**EXOTROPIA** n condition in which eye turns outwards

**EXOTROPIC** > EXOTROPIA

**EXPAND** vb make or become larger

**EXPANDED** adj (of printer's type) wider than usual for a particular height

**EXPANDER** n device for exercising and developing the muscles of the body

**EXPANDERS** > EXPANDER

**EXPANDING** > EXPAND

**EXPANDOR** same

as > EXPANDER

**EXPANDORS** > EXPANDOR

**EXPANDS** > EXPAND

**EXPANSE** n uninterrupted wide area

**EXPANSES** > EXPANSE

**EXPANSILE** adj able to expand or cause expansion

**EXPANSION** n act of expanding

**EXPANSIVE** adj wide or extensive

**EXPAT** n short for

**EXPATIATE** vb speak or write at great length (on)

**EXPATS** > EXPAT

**EXPECT** vb regard as probable

**EXPECTANT** adj expecting or hopeful ▷ n person who expects something

**EXPECTED** > EXPECT

**EXPECTER** n person who expects

**EXPECTERS** > EXPECTER

**EXPECTING** adj pregnant

**EXPECTS** > EXPECT

**EXPEDIENT** n something that achieves a particular purpose ▷ adj suitable to the circumstances, appropriate

**EXPEDITE** vb hasten the progress of ▷ adj unimpeded or prompt

**EXPEDITED** > EXPEDITE

**EXPEDITER** n person who expedites something, esp a person employed in an industry to ensure that work on each job progresses efficiently

**EXPEDITES** > EXPEDITE

**EXPEDITOR** same

as > EXPEDITER

**EXPEL** vb drive out with force

**EXPELLANT** adj forcing out or having the capacity to force out ▷ n medicine used to expel undesirable substances or organisms from the body, esp worms from the digestive tract

**EXPELLED** > EXPEL

**EXPELLEE** > EXPEL

**EXPELLEES** > EXPEL

**EXPELLENT** same

as > EXPELLANT

**EXPELLER** > EXPEL

**EXPELLERS** pl n residue remaining after an oilseed has been crushed to expel the oil, used for animal fodder

**EXPELLING** > EXPEL

**EXPELS** > EXPEL

**EXPEND** vb spend, use up

**EXPENDED** > EXPEND

**EXPENDER** > EXPEND

**EXPENDERS** > EXPEND

**EXPENDING** > EXPEND

**EXPENDS** > EXPEND

**EXPENSE** n cost

**EXPENSED** > EXPENSE

**EXPENSES** > EXPENSE

**EXPENSING** > EXPENSE

**EXPENSIVE** adj high-priced

**EXPERT** n person with extensive skill or knowledge in a particular field ▷ adj skilful or knowledgeable ▷ vb experience

**EXPERTED** > EXPERT

**EXPERTING** > EXPERT

**EXPERTISE** same

as > EXPERTIZE

**EXPERTISM** > EXPERTIZE

**EXPERTIZE** vb act as an expert or give an expert opinion (on)

**EXPERTLY** > EXPERT

**EXPERTS** > EXPERT

**EXPIABLE** adj capable of being expiated or atoned for

**EXPIATE** vb make amends for

**EXPIATED** > EXPIATE

**EXPIATES** > EXPIATE

**EXPIATING** > EXPIATE

**EXPIATION** n act, process, or a means of expiating

**EXPIATOR** > EXPIATE

**EXPIATORS** > EXPIATE

**EXPIATORY** adj capable of making expiation

**EXPIRABLE** > EXPIRE

**EXPIRANT** n one who expires

**EXPIRANTS** > EXPIRANT

**EXPIRE** vb finish or run out

**EXPIRED** > EXPIRE

**EXPIRER** > EXPIRE

**EXPIRERS** > EXPIRE

**EXPIRES** > EXPIRE

**EXPIRIES** > EXPIRY

**EXPIRING** > EXPIRE

**EXPIRY** n end, esp of a contract period

**EXPISCATE** vb find; fish out

**EXPLAIN** vb make clear and intelligible

**EXPLAINED** > EXPLAIN

**EXPLAINER** > EXPLAIN

**EXPLAINS** > EXPLAIN

**EXPLANT** vb transfer (living tissue) from its natural site to a new site or to a culture medium ▷ n piece of tissue treated in this way

**EXPLANTED** > EXPLANT

**EXPLANTS** > EXPLANT

**EXPLETIVE** n swearword ▷ adj expressing no particular meaning, esp when filling out a line of verse

**EXPLETORY** adj expletive

**EXPLICATE** vb explain

**EXPLICIT** adj precisely and clearly expressed ▷ n word used to indicate the end of a book

EXPLICITS > EXPLICIT
EXPLODE vb burst with great violence, blow up
EXPLODED > EXPLODE
EXPLODER > EXPLODE
EXPLODERS > EXPLODE
EXPLODES > EXPLODE
EXPLODING > EXPLODE
EXPLOIT vb take advantage of for one's own purposes ▷ n notable feat or deed
EXPLOITED > EXPLOIT
EXPLOITER > EXPLOIT
EXPLOITS > EXPLOIT
EXPLORE vb investigate
EXPLORED > EXPLORE
EXPLORER > EXPLORE
EXPLORERS > EXPLORE
EXPLORES > EXPLORE
EXPLORING > EXPLORE
EXPLOSION n exploding
EXPLOSIVE adj tending to explode ▷ n substance that causes explosions
EXPO n exposition, large public exhibition
EXPONENT n person who advocates an idea, cause, etc ▷ adj offering a declaration, explanation, or interpretation
EXPONENTS > EXPONENT
EXPONIBLE adj able to be explained
EXPORT n selling or shipping of goods to a foreign country ▷ vb sell or ship (goods) to a foreign country
EXPORTED > EXPORT
EXPORTER > EXPORT
EXPORTERS > EXPORT
EXPORTING > EXPORT
EXPORTS > EXPORT
EXPOS > EXPO
EXPOSABLE > EXPOSE
EXPOSAL > EXPOSE
EXPOSALS > EXPOSE
EXPOSE vb uncover or reveal ▷ n bringing of a crime, scandal, etc to public notice
EXPOSED adj not concealed
EXPOSER > EXPOSE
EXPOSERS > EXPOSE
EXPOSES > EXPOSE
EXPOSING > EXPOSE
EXPOSIT vb state
EXPOSITED > EXPOSIT
EXPOSITOR n person who expounds
EXPOSITS > EXPOSIT
EXPOSTURE n exposure
EXPOSURE n exposing
EXPOSURES > EXPOSURE
EXPOUND vb explain in detail
EXPOUNDED > EXPOUND
EXPOUNDER > EXPOUND
EXPOUNDS > EXPOUND
EXPRESS vb put into words ▷ adj explicitly stated ▷ n fast train or bus stopping

at only a few stations ▷ adv by express delivery
EXPRESSED > EXPRESS
EXPRESSER > EXPRESS
EXPRESSES > EXPRESS
EXPRESSLY adv definitely
EXPRESSO variant of > ESPRESSO
EXPRESSOS > EXPRESSO
EXPUGN vb storm
EXPUGNED > EXPUGN
EXPUGNING > EXPUGN
EXPUGNS > EXPUGN
EXPULSE vb expel
EXPULSED > EXPULSE
EXPULSES > EXPULSE
EXPULSING > EXPULSE
EXPULSION n act of expelling or the fact of being expelled
EXPULSIVE adj tending or serving to expel
EXPUNCT vb expunge
EXPUNCTED > EXPUNCT
EXPUNCTS > EXPUNCT
EXPUNGE vb delete, erase, blot out
EXPUNGED > EXPUNGE
EXPUNGER > EXPUNGE
EXPUNGERS > EXPUNGE
EXPUNGES > EXPUNGE
EXPUNGING > EXPUNGE
EXPURGATE vb remove objectionable parts from (a book etc)
EXPURGE vb purge
EXPURGED > EXPURGE
EXPURGES > EXPURGE
EXPURGING > EXPURGE
EXQUISITE adj of extreme beauty or delicacy ▷ n dandy
EXSCIND vb cut off or out
EXSCINDED > EXSCIND
EXSCINDS > EXSCIND
EXSECANT n trigonometric function
EXSECANTS > EXSECANT
EXSECT vb cut out
EXSECTED > EXSECT
EXSECTING > EXSECT
EXSECTION > EXSECT
EXSECTS > EXSECT
EXSERT vb thrust out ▷ adj protruded, stretched out, or (esp of stamens) projecting beyond the corolla of a flower
EXSERTED > EXSERT
EXSERTILE > EXSERT
EXSERTING > EXSERT
EXSERTION > EXSERT
EXSERTS > EXSERT
EXSICCANT > EXSICCATE
EXSICCATE vb dry up
EXSTROPHY n congenital eversion of a hollow organ, esp the urinary bladder
EXSUCCOUS adj without sap or juice
EXTANT adj still existing
EXTASIES > EXTASY
EXTASY same as > ECSTASY
EXTATIC same as > ECSTATIC

EXTEMPORE adj without planning or preparation ▷ adv without planning or preparation
EXTEND vb draw out or be drawn out, stretch
EXTENDANT adj (in heraldry) with wings spread
EXTENDED same as > EXPANDED
EXTENDER n person or thing that extends
EXTENDERS > EXTENDER
EXTENDING > EXTEND
EXTENDS > EXTEND
EXTENSE adj extensive
EXTENSILE adj capable of being extended
EXTENSION n room or rooms added to an existing building ▷ adj denoting something that can be extended or that extends another object
EXTENSITY n that part of sensory perception relating to the spatial aspect of objects
EXTENSIVE adj having a large extent, widespread
EXTENSOR n muscle that extends a part of the body
EXTENSORS > EXTENSOR
EXTENT n range over which something extends, area
EXTENTS > EXTENT
EXTENUATE vb make (an offence or fault) less blameworthy
EXTERIOR n part or surface on the outside ▷ adj of, on, or coming from the outside
EXTERIORS > EXTERIOR
EXTERMINE vb exterminate
EXTERN n person, such as a physician at a hospital, who has an official connection with an institution but does not reside in it
EXTERNAL adj of, situated on, or coming from the outside ▷ n external circumstance or aspect, esp one that is superficial or inessential
EXTERNALS > EXTERNAL
EXTERNAT n day school
EXTERNATS > EXTERNAT
EXTERNE same as > EXTERN
EXTERNES > EXTERNE
EXTERNS > EXTERN
EXTINCT adj having died out ▷ vb extinguish
EXTINCTED > EXTINCT
EXTINCTS > EXTINCT
EXTINE same as > EXINE
EXTINES > EXTINE
EXTIRP vb extirpate
EXTIRPATE vb destroy utterly
EXTIRPED > EXTIRP

EXTIRPING > EXTIRP
EXTIRPS > EXTIRP
EXTOL vb praise highly
EXTOLD archaic past participle of > EXTOL
EXTOLL same as > EXTOL
EXTOLLED > EXTOLL
EXTOLLER > EXTOL
EXTOLLERS > EXTOL
EXTOLLING > EXTOLL
EXTOLLS > EXTOLL
EXTOLMENT > EXTOL
EXTOLS > EXTOL
EXTORSIVE adj intended or tending to extort
EXTORT vb get (something) by force or threats
EXTORTED > EXTORT
EXTORTER > EXTORT
EXTORTERS > EXTORT
EXTORTING > EXTORT
EXTORTION n act of securing money, favours, etc by intimidation or violence
EXTORTIVE > EXTORT
EXTORTS > EXTORT
EXTRA adj more than is usual, expected or needed ▷ n additional person or thing ▷ adv unusually or exceptionally
EXTRABOLD n very bold typeface
EXTRACT vb pull out by force ▷ n something extracted, such as a passage from a book etc
EXTRACTED > EXTRACT
EXTRACTOR n person or thing that extracts
EXTRACTS > EXTRACT
EXTRADITE vb send (an accused person) back to his or her own country for trial
EXTRADOS n outer curve or surface of an arch or vault
EXTRAIT n extracts
EXTRAITS > EXTRAIT
EXTRALITY n diplomatic immunity
EXTRANET n intranet that is modified to allow outsiders access to it, esp one belonging to a business that allows access to customers
EXTRANETS > EXTRANET
EXTRAPOSE vb move (a word or words) to the end of a clause or sentence
EXTRAS > EXTRA
EXTRAUGHT old past participle of > EXTRACT
EXTRAVERT same as > EXTROVERT
EXTREAT n extraction
EXTREATS > EXTREAT
EXTREMA > EXTREMUM
EXTREMAL n clause in a recursive definition that specifies that no items other than those

generated by the stated rules fall within the definition, as in 1 *is an integer, if n is an integer so is n+1, and nothing else is*

**EXTREMALS** > EXTREMAL

**EXTREME** *adj* of a high or the highest degree or intensity ▷ *n* either of the two limits of a scale or range

**EXTREMELY** > EXTREME

**EXTREMER** > EXTREME

**EXTREMES** > EXTREME

**EXTREMEST** > EXTREME

**EXTREMISM** > EXTREMIST

**EXTREMIST** *n* person who favours immoderate methods ▷ *adj* holding extreme opinions

**EXTREMITY** *n* farthest point

**EXTREMUM** *n* extreme point

**EXTRICATE** *vb* free from complication or difficulty

**EXTRINSIC** *adj* not contained or included within

**EXTRORSAL** *same as* > EXTRORSE

**EXTRORSE** *adj* turned or opening outwards or away from the axis

**EXTROVERT** *adj* lively and outgoing ▷ *n* extrovert person

**EXTRUDE** *vb* squeeze or force out

**EXTRUDED** > EXTRUDE

**EXTRUDER** > EXTRUDE

**EXTRUDERS** > EXTRUDE

**EXTRUDES** > EXTRUDE

**EXTRUDING** > EXTRUDE

**EXTRUSION** *n* act or process of extruding

**EXTRUSIVE** *adj* tending to extrude

**EXTRUSORY** > EXTRUDE

**EXTUBATE** *vb* remove tube from hollow organ

**EXTUBATED** > EXTUBATE

**EXTUBATES** > EXTUBATE

**EXUBERANT** *adj* high-spirited

**EXUBERATE** *vb* be exuberant

**EXUDATE** *same as* > EXUDATION

**EXUDATES** > EXUDATE

**EXUDATION** *n* act of exuding or oozing out

**EXUDATIVE** > EXUDATION

**EXUDE** *vb* (of a liquid or smell) seep or flow out slowly and steadily

**EXUDED** > EXUDE

**EXUDES** > EXUDE

**EXUDING** > EXUDE

**EXUL** *n* exile

**EXULS** > EXUL

**EXULT** *vb* be joyful or jubilant

**EXULTANCE** > EXULTANT

**EXULTANCY** > EXULTANT

**EXULTANT** *adj* elated or jubilant, esp because of triumph or success

**EXULTED** > EXULT

**EXULTING** > EXULT

**EXULTS** > EXULT

**EXURB** *n* residential area beyond suburbs

**EXURBAN** > EXURBIA

**EXURBIA** *n* region outside the suburbs of a city, consisting of residential areas that are occupied predominantly by rich commuters

**EXURBIAS** > EXURBIA

**EXURBS** > EXURB

**EXUVIA** *n* cast-off exoskeleton of animal

**EXUVIAE** > EXUVIA

**EXUVIAL** > EXUVIA

**EXUVIATE** *vb* shed (a skin or similar outer covering)

**EXUVIATED** > EXUVIATE

**EXUVIATES** > EXUVIATE

**EXUVIUM** *n* cast-off exoskeleton of animal

**EYALET** *n* province of Ottoman Empire

**EYALETS** > EYALET

**EYAS** *n* nestling hawk or falcon, esp one reared for training in falconry

**EYASES** > EYAS

**EYASS** *same as* > EYAS

**EYASSES** > EYASS

**EYE** *n* organ of sight ▷ *vb* look at carefully or warily

**EYEABLE** *adj* pleasant to look at

**EYEBALL** *n* ball-shaped part of the eye ▷ *vb* eye

**EYEBALLED** > EYEBALL

**EYEBALLS** > EYEBALL

**EYEBANK** *n* place in which corneas are stored for use in corneal grafts

**EYEBANKS** > EYEBANK

**EYEBAR** *n* bar with flattened ends with holes for connecting pins

**EYEBARS** > EYEBAR

**EYEBATH** *same as* > EYECUP

**EYEBATHS** > EYEBATH

**EYEBEAM** *n* glance

**EYEBEAMS** > EYEBEAM

**EYEBLACK** *another name for* > MASCARA

**EYEBLACKS** > EYEBLACK

**EYEBLINK** *n* very small amount of time

**EYEBLINKS** > EYEBLINK

**EYEBOLT** *n* threaded bolt, the head of which is formed into a ring or eye for lifting, pulling, or securing

**EYEBOLTS** > EYEBOLT

**EYEBRIGHT** *n* any scrophulariaceous annual plant of the genus *Euphrasia*, esp *E. nemorosa*, having small white-and-purple two-lipped flowers:

formerly used in the treatment of eye disorders

**EYEBROW** *n* line of hair on the bony ridge above the eye ▷ *vb* equip with artificial eyebrows

**EYEBROWED** > EYEBROW

**EYEBROWS** > EYEBROW

**EYECUP** *same as* > EYEBATH

**EYECUPS** > EYECUP

**EYED** > EYE

**EYEDNESS** > EYE

**EYEDROPS** *n* medicine applied to the eyes in drops

**EYEFOLD** *n* fold of skin above eye

**EYEFOLDS** > EYEFOLD

**EYEFUL** *n* view

**EYEFULS** > EYEFUL

**EYEGLASS** *n* lens for aiding defective vision

**EYEHOLE** *n* hole through which something, such as a rope, hook, or bar, is passed

**EYEHOLES** > EYEHOLE

**EYEHOOK** *n* hook attached to a ring at the extremity of a rope or chain

**EYEHOOKS** > EYEHOOK

**EYEING** > EYE

**EYELASH** *n* short hair that grows out from the eyelid

**EYELASHES** > EYELASH

**EYELESS** > EYE

**EYELET** *n* small hole for a lace or cord to be passed through ▷ *vb* supply with an eyelet or eyelets

**EYELETED** > EYELET

**EYELETEER** *n* small bodkin or other pointed tool for making eyelet holes

**EYELETING** > EYELET

**EYELETS** > EYELET

**EYELETTED** > EYELET

**EYELEVEL** *adj* level with a person's eyes

**EYELIAD** *same as* > OEILLADE

**EYELIADS** > EYELIAD

**EYELID** *n* fold of skin that covers the eye when it is closed

**EYELIDS** > EYELID

**EYELIFT** *n* cosmetic surgery for eyes

**EYELIFTS** > EYELIFT

**EYELIKE** > EYE

**EYELINER** *n* cosmetic used to outline the eyes

**EYELINERS** > EYELINER

**EYEN** *pl n* eyes

**EYEOPENER** *n* something surprising

**EYEPIECE** *n* lens in a microscope, telescope, etc, into which the person using it looks

**EYEPIECES** > EYEPIECE

**EYEPOINT** *n* position of a lens at which the sharpest image is obtained

**EYEPOINTS** > EYEPOINT

**EYEPOPPER** *n* something that excites the eye

**EYER** *n* someone who eyes

**EYERS** > EYER

**EYES** > EYE

**EYESHADE** *n* opaque or tinted translucent visor, worn on the head like a cap to protect the eyes from glare

**EYESHADES** > EYESHADE

**EYESHADOW** *n* coloured cosmetic put around the eyes so as to enhance their colour or shape

**EYESHINE** *n* reflection of light from animal eye at night

**EYESHINES** > EYESHINE

**EYESHOT** *n* range of vision

**EYESHOTS** > EYESHOT

**EYESIGHT** *n* ability to see

**EYESIGHTS** > EYESIGHT

**EYESOME** *adj* attractive

**EYESORE** *n* ugly object

**EYESORES** > EYESORE

**EYESPOT** *n* small area of light-sensitive pigment in some protozoans, algae, and other simple organisms

**EYESPOTS** > EYESPOT

**EYESTALK** *n* movable stalk bearing a compound eye at its tip: occurs in crustaceans and some molluscs

**EYESTALKS** > EYESTALK

**EYESTONE** *n* device for removing foreign body from eye

**EYESTONES** > EYESTONE

**EYESTRAIN** *n* fatigue or irritation of the eyes, caused by tiredness or a failure to wear glasses

**EYESTRING** *n* tendon holding eye in place

**EYETEETH** > EYETOOTH

**EYETOOTH** *n* either of the two canine teeth in the upper jaw

**EYEWASH** *n* nonsense

**EYEWASHES** > EYEWASH

**EYEWATER** *n* lotion for the eyes

**EYEWATERS** > EYEWATER

**EYEWEAR** *n* spectacles; glasses

**EYEWINK** *n* wink of the eye; instant

**EYEWINKS** > EYEWINK

**EYING** > EYE

**EYLIAD** *same as* > OEILLADE

**EYLIADS** > EYLIAD

**EYNE** *poetic plural of* > EYE

**EYOT** *n* island

**EYOTS** > EYOT

**EYRA** *n* reddish-brown variety of the jaguarondi

**EYRAS** > EYRA

**EYRE** *n* any of the circuit courts held in each shire

from 1176 until the late 13th
century
**EYRES** > EYRE
**EYRIE** *n* nest of an eagle
**EYRIES** > EYRIE
**EYRIR** *n* Icelandic
monetary unit worth one
hundredth of a krona
**EYRY** *same as* > EYRIE

# Ff

FA *same as* > FAH
FAA *Scot word for* > FALL
FAAN > FAA
FAAS > FAA
FAB *adj* excellent ▷ *n* excellent thing
FABACEOUS *less common term for* > LEGUMINOUS
FABBER > FAB
FABBEST > FAB
FABLE *n* story with a moral ▷ *vb* relate or tell (fables)
FABLED *adj* made famous in legend
FABLER > FABLE
FABLERS > FABLE
FABLES > FABLE
FABLIAU *n* comic usually ribald verse tale, of a kind popular in France in the 12th and 13th centuries
FABLIAUX > FABLIAU
FABLING > FABLE
FABLINGS > FABLE
FABRIC *n* knitted or woven cloth
FABRICANT *n* manufacturer
FABRICATE *vb* make up (a story or lie)
FABRICKED *adj* built
FABRICS > FABRIC
FABS > FAB
FABULAR *adj* relating to fables
FABULATE *vb* make up fables
FABULATED > FABULATE
FABULATES > FABULATE
FABULATOR > FABULATE
FABULISE *vb* make up fables
FABULISED > FABULISE

FABULISES > FABULISE
FABULIST *n* person who invents or recounts fables
FABULISTS > FABULIST
FABULIZE *vb* make up fables
FABULIZED > FABULIZE
FABULIZES > FABULIZE
FABULOUS *adj* excellent
FABURDEN *n* early form of counterpoint
FABURDENS > FABURDEN
FACADE *n* front of a building
FACADES > FACADE
FACE *n* front of the head ▷ *vb* look or turn towards
FACEABLE > FACE
FACEBAR *n* wrestling hold in which a wrestler stretches the skin on his opponent's face backwards
FACEBARS > FACEBAR
FACECLOTH *n* small piece of cloth used to wash the face and hands
FACED > FACE
FACEDOWN *vb* confront and force (someone or something) to back down
FACEDOWNS > FACEDOWN
FACELESS *adj* impersonal, anonymous
FACELIFT *n* cosmetic surgery for the face
FACELIFTS > FACELIFT
FACEMAIL *n* computer program which uses an electronically generated face to deliver messages on screen
FACEMAILS > FACEMAIL

FACEMAN *n* miner who works at the coalface
FACEMASK *n* protective mask for the face
FACEMASKS > FACEMASK
FACEMEN > FACEMAN
FACEPLATE *n* perforated circular metal plate that can be attached to the headstock of a lathe in order to hold flat or irregularly shaped workpieces
FACEPRINT *n* digitally recorded representation of a person's face that can be used for security purposes because it is as individual as a fingerprint
FACER *n* difficulty or problem
FACERS > FACER
FACES > FACE
FACET *n* aspect ▷ *vb* cut facets in (a gemstone)
FACETE *adj* witty and humorous
FACETED > FACET
FACETELY > FACETE
FACETIAE *pl n* humorous or witty sayings
FACETING > FACET
FACETIOUS *adj* funny or trying to be funny, esp at inappropriate times
FACETS > FACET
FACETTED > FACET
FACETTING > FACET
FACEUP *adj* with the face or surface exposed
FACIA *same as* > FASCIA
FACIAE > FACIA
FACIAL *adj* of or relating

to the face ▷ *n* beauty treatment for the face
FACIALLY > FACIAL
FACIALS > FACIAL
FACIAS > FACIA
FACIEND *n* multiplicand
FACIENDS > FACIEND
FACIES *n* general form and appearance of an individual or a group of plants or animals
FACILE *adj* (of a remark, argument, etc) superficial and showing lack of real thought
FACILELY > FACILE
FACILITY *n* skill
FACING *n* lining or covering for decoration or reinforcement
FACINGS > FACING
FACONNE *adj* denoting a fabric with the design woven in ▷ *n* such a fabric
FACONNES > FACONNE
FACSIMILE *n* exact copy ▷ *vb* make an exact copy of
FACT *n* event or thing known to have happened or existed
FACTFUL > FACT
FACTICE *n* soft rubbery material made by reacting sulphur or sulphur chloride with vegetable oil
FACTICES > FACTICE
FACTICITY *n* philosophical process
FACTION *n* (dissenting) minority group within a larger body
FACTIONAL > FACTION
FACTIONS > FACTION

**FACTIOUS** adj of or producing factions
**FACTIS** variant of > FACTICE
**FACTISES** > FACTIS
**FACTITIVE** adj denoting a verb taking a direct object as well as a noun in apposition, as for example elect in They elected John president, where John is the direct object and president is the complement
**FACTIVE** adj (of a linguistic context) giving rise to the presupposition that a sentence occurring in that context is true, as John regrets that Mary did not attend
**FACTOID** n piece of unreliable information believed to be true because of the way it is presented or repeated in print
**FACTOIDAL** > FACTOID
**FACTOIDS** > FACTOID
**FACTOR** n element contributing to a result ▷ vb engage in the business of a factor
**FACTORAGE** n commission payable to a factor
**FACTORED** > FACTOR
**FACTORIAL** n product of all the integers from one to a given number ▷ adj of factorials or factors
**FACTORIES** > FACTORY
**FACTORING** n business of a factor
**FACTORISE** same as > FACTORIZE
**FACTORIZE** vb calculate the factors of (a number)
**FACTORS** > FACTOR
**FACTORY** n building where goods are manufactured
**FACTOTUM** n person employed to do all sorts of work
**FACTOTUMS** > FACTOTUM
**FACTS** > FACT
**FACTSHEET** n printed sheet containing information relating to items covered in a television or radio programme
**FACTUAL** adj concerning facts rather than opinions or theories
**FACTUALLY** > FACTUAL
**FACTUM** n something done, deed
**FACTUMS** > FACTUM
**FACTURE** n construction
**FACTURES** > FACTURE
**FACULA** n any of the bright areas on the sun's surface, usually appearing just before a sunspot and subject to the same 11-year cycle
**FACULAE** > FACULA
**FACULAR** > FACULA

**FACULTIES** > FACULTY
**FACULTY** n physical or mental ability
**FACUNDITY** n eloquence, fluency of speech
**FAD** n short-lived fashion
**FADABLE** > FADE
**FADAISE** n silly remark
**FADAISES** > FADAISE
**FADDIER** > FADDY
**FADDIEST** > FADDY
**FADDINESS** n excessive fussiness
**FADDISH** > FAD
**FADDISHLY** > FAD
**FADDISM** > FAD
**FADDISMS** > FAD
**FADDIST** > FAD
**FADDISTS** > FAD
**FADDLE** vb mess around, toy with
**FADDLED** > FADDLE
**FADDLES** > FADDLE
**FADDLING** > FADDLE
**FADDY** adj unreasonably fussy, particularly about food
**FADE** vb (cause to) lose brightness, colour, or strength ▷ n act or an instance of fading
**FADEAWAY** n fading to the point of disappearance
**FADEAWAYS** > FADEAWAY
**FADED** > FADE
**FADEDLY** > FADE
**FADEDNESS** > FADE
**FADEIN** n gradual appearance of image on film
**FADEINS** > FADEIN
**FADELESS** adj not subject to fading
**FADEOUT** n gradual disappearance of image on film
**FADEOUTS** > FADEOUT
**FADER** > FADE
**FADERS** > FADE
**FADES** > FADE
**FADEUR** n blandness, insipidness
**FADEURS** > FADEUR
**FADGE** vb agree ▷ n package of wool in a wool-bale that weighs less than 100 kilograms
**FADGED** > FADGE
**FADGES** > FADGE
**FADGING** > FADGE
**FADIER** > FADY
**FADIEST** > FADY
**FADING** n variation in the strength of received radio signals due to variations in the conditions of the transmission medium
**FADINGS** > FADING
**FADLIKE** > FAD
**FADO** n type of melancholy Portuguese folk song
**FADOMETER** n instrument used to determine the resistance to fading of a

pigment or dye
**FADOS** > FADO
**FADY** adj faded
**FAE** Scot word for > FROM
**FAECAL** adj of, relating to, or consisting of faeces
**FAECES** pl n waste matter discharged from the anus
**FAENA** n matador's final series of passes with sword and cape before the kill
**FAENAS** > FAENA
**FAERIE** n land of fairies
**FAERIES** > FAERY
**FAERY** same as > FAERIE
**FAFF** vb dither or fuss
**FAFFED** > FAFF
**FAFFING** > FAFF
**FAFFS** > FAFF
**FAG** same as > FAGGOT
**FAGACEOUS** adj of, relating to, or belonging to the Fagaceae, a family of trees, including beech, oak, and chestnut, whose fruit is partly or wholly enclosed in a husk (cupule)
**FAGGED** > FAG
**FAGGERIES** > FAGGERY
**FAGGERY** n offensive term for homosexuality
**FAGGIER** > FAG
**FAGGIEST** > FAG
**FAGGING** > FAG
**FAGGINGS** > FAG
**FAGGOT** n ball of chopped liver, herbs, and bread ▷ vb collect into a bundle or bundles
**FAGGOTED** > FAGGOT
**FAGGOTING** n decorative needlework done by tying vertical threads together in bundles
**FAGGOTRY** n offensive term for homosexuality
**FAGGOTS** > FAGGOT
**FAGGOTY** > FAGGOT
**FAGGY** > FAG
**FAGIN** n criminal
**FAGINS** > FAGIN
**FAGOT** same as > FAGGOT
**FAGOTED** > FAGOT
**FAGOTER** > FAGOT
**FAGOTERS** > FAGOT
**FAGOTING** same as > FAGGOTING
**FAGOTINGS** > FAGOTING
**FAGOTS** > FAGOT
**FAGOTTI** > FAGOTTO
**FAGOTTIST** n bassoon player
**FAGOTTO** n bassoon
**FAGS** > FAG
**FAH** n (in tonic sol-fa) fourth degree of any major scale
**FAHLBAND** n thin bed of schistose rock impregnated with metallic sulphides
**FAHLBANDS** > FAHLBAND

**FAHLERZ** n copper ore
**FAHLERZES** > FAHLERZ
**FAHLORE** n copper ore
**FAHLORES** > FAHLORE
**FAHS** > FAH
**FAIBLE** variant of > FOIBLE
**FAIBLES** > FAIBLE
**FAIENCE** n tin-glazed earthenware
**FAIENCES** > FAIENCE
**FAIK** vb grasp
**FAIKED** > FAIK
**FAIKES** > FAIK
**FAIKING** > FAIK
**FAIKS** > FAIK
**FAIL** vb be unsuccessful ▷ n instance of not passing an exam or test
**FAILED** > FAIL
**FAILING** n weak point ▷ prep in the absence of
**FAILINGLY** > FAILING
**FAILINGS** > FAILING
**FAILLE** n soft light ribbed fabric of silk, rayon, or taffeta
**FAILLES** > FAILLE
**FAILS** > FAIL
**FAILURE** n act or instance of failing
**FAILURES** > FAILURE
**FAIN** adv gladly ▷ adj willing or eager
**FAINE** variant of > FAIN
**FAINEANCE** > FAINEANT
**FAINEANCY** > FAINEANT
**FAINEANT** n lazy person ▷ adj indolent
**FAINEANTS** > FAINEANT
**FAINED** > FAIN
**FAINER** > FAIN
**FAINES** > FAIN
**FAINEST** > FAIN
**FAINING** > FAIN
**FAINITES** interj cry for truce or respite from the rules of a game
**FAINLY** > FAIN
**FAINNE** n small ring-shaped metal badge worn by advocates of the Irish language
**FAINNES** > FAINNE
**FAINNESS** > FAIN
**FAINS** same as > FAINITES
**FAINT** adj lacking clarity, brightness, or volume ▷ vb lose consciousness temporarily ▷ n temporary loss of consciousness
**FAINTED** > FAINT
**FAINTER** > FAINT
**FAINTERS** > FAINT
**FAINTEST** > FAINT
**FAINTIER** > FAINTY
**FAINTIEST** > FAINTY
**FAINTING** > FAINT
**FAINTINGS** > FAINT
**FAINTISH** > FAINT
**FAINTLY** > FAINT
**FAINTNESS** > FAINT
**FAINTS** > FAINT
**FAINTY** > FAINT

**FAIR** _adj_ unbiased and reasonable ▷ _adv_ fairly ▷ _n_ travelling entertainment with sideshows, rides, and amusements ▷ _vb_ join together so as to form a smooth or regular shape or surface
**FAIRED** > FAIR
**FAIRER** > FAIR
**FAIREST** > FAIR
**FAIRFACED** _adj_ (of brickwork) having a neat smooth unplastered surface
**FAIRGOER** _n_ person attending fair
**FAIRGOERS** > FAIRGOER
**FAIRIES** > FAIRY
**FAIRILY** > FAIRY
**FAIRING** _n_ curved metal structure fitted round part of a car, aircraft, etc to reduce drag
**FAIRINGS** > FAIRING
**FAIRISH** _adj_ moderately good, well, etc
**FAIRISHLY** > FAIRISH
**FAIRLEAD** _n_ block or ring through which a line is rove to keep it clear of obstructions, prevent chafing, or maintain it at an angle
**FAIRLEADS** > FAIRLEAD
**FAIRLY** _adv_ moderately
**FAIRNESS** > FAIR
**FAIRS** > FAIR
**FAIRWAY** _n_ smooth area between the tee and the green
**FAIRWAYS** > FAIRWAY
**FAIRY** _n_ imaginary small creature with magic powers
**FAIRYDOM** > FAIRY
**FAIRYDOMS** > FAIRY
**FAIRYHOOD** > FAIRY
**FAIRYISM** > FAIRY
**FAIRYISMS** > FAIRY
**FAIRYLAND** _n_ imaginary place where fairies live
**FAIRYLIKE** > FAIRY
**FAIRYTALE** _n_ story about fairies or other mythical or magical beings, esp one of traditional origin told to children
**FAITH** _n_ strong belief, esp without proof
**FAITHCURE** _n_ healing through prayer
**FAITHED** _adj_ having faith or a faith
**FAITHER** _Scot word for_ > FATHER
**FAITHERS** > FAITHER
**FAITHFUL** _adj_ loyal
**FAITHFULS** > FAITHFUL
**FAITHING** _n_ practising a faith
**FAITHLESS** _adj_ disloyal or dishonest

**FAITHS** > FAITH
**FAITOR** _n_ traitor, impostor
**FAITORS** > FAITOR
**FAITOUR** _n_ impostor
**FAITOURS** > FAITOUR
**FAIX** _n_ faith
**FAJITA** > FAJITAS
**FAJITAS** _pl n_ Mexican dish of soft tortillas wrapped around fried strips of meat or vegetables
**FAKE** _vb_ cause something not genuine to appear real or more valuable by fraud ▷ _n_ person, thing, or act that is not genuine ▷ _adj_ not genuine
**FAKED** > FAKE
**FAKEER** _same as_ > FAKIR
**FAKEERS** > FAKEER
**FAKEMENT** _n_ something false, counterfeit
**FAKEMENTS** > FAKEMENT
**FAKER** > FAKE
**FAKERIES** > FAKE
**FAKERS** > FAKE
**FAKERY** > FAKE
**FAKES** > FAKE
**FAKEY** _n_ skateboarding term
**FAKING** > FAKE
**FAKIR** _n_ Muslim who spurns worldly possessions
**FAKIRISM** > FAKIR
**FAKIRISMS** > FAKIR
**FAKIRS** > FAKIR
**FALAFEL** _n_ ball or cake of ground spiced chickpeas, deep-fried and often served with pitta bread
**FALAFELS** > FALAFEL
**FALAJ** _n_ water channel
**FALANGISM** > FALANGIST
**FALANGIST** _n_ member of the Fascist movement founded in Spain in 1933
**FALBALA** _n_ gathered flounce, frill, or ruffle
**FALBALAS** > FALBALA
**FALCADE** _n_ movement of a horse
**FALCADES** > FALCADE
**FALCATE** _adj_ shaped like a sickle
**FALCATED** > FALCATE
**FALCATION** > FALCATE
**FALCES** > FALX
**FALCHION** _n_ short and slightly curved medieval sword broader towards the point
**FALCHIONS** > FALCHION
**FALCIFORM** _same as_ > FALCATE
**FALCON** _n_ small bird of prey
**FALCONER** _n_ person who breeds or trains hawks or who follows the sport of falconry
**FALCONERS** > FALCONER
**FALCONET** _n_ any of various small falcons, esp any of the Asiatic genus

_Microhierax_
**FALCONETS** > FALCONET
**FALCONINE** _adj_ of, relating to, or resembling a falcon
**FALCONOID** _n_ chemical thought to resist cancer
**FALCONRY** _n_ art of training falcons
**FALCONS** > FALCON
**FALCULA** _n_ sharp curved claw, esp of a bird
**FALCULAE** > FALCULA
**FALCULAS** > FALCULA
**FALCULATE** > FALCULA
**FALDAGE** _n_ feudal right
**FALDAGES** > FALDAGE
**FALDERAL** _n_ showy but worthless trifle
**FALDERALS** > FALDERAL
**FALDEROL** _same as_ > FALDERAL
**FALDEROLS** > FALDEROL
**FALDETTA** _n_ Maltese woman's garment with a stiffened hood
**FALDETTAS** > FALDETTA
**FALDSTOOL** _n_ backless seat, sometimes capable of being folded, used by bishops and certain other prelates
**FALL** _vb_ drop from a higher to a lower place through the force of gravity ▷ _n_ falling
**FALLACIES** > FALLACY
**FALLACY** _n_ false belief
**FALLAL** _n_ showy ornament, trinket, or article of dress
**FALLALERY** > FALLAL
**FALLALS** > FALLAL
**FALLAWAY** _n_ friendship that has been withdrawn
**FALLAWAYS** > FALLAWAY
**FALLBACK** _n_ something that recedes or retreats
**FALLBACKS** > FALLBACK
**FALLBOARD** _n_ cover for piano keyboard
**FALLEN** > FALL
**FALLER** _n_ any device that falls or operates machinery by falling, as in a spinning machine
**FALLERS** > FALLER
**FALLFISH** _n_ large North American freshwater cyprinid fish, _Semotilus corporalis_, resembling the chub
**FALLIBLE** _adj_ (of a person) liable to make mistakes
**FALLIBLY** > FALLIBLE
**FALLING** > FALL
**FALLINGS** > FALL
**FALLOFF** _n_ decline or drop
**FALLOFFS** > FALLOFF
**FALLOUT** _n_ radioactive particles spread as a result of a nuclear explosion ▷ _vb_ disagree and quarrel ▷ _sentence substitute_ order to leave a parade or

disciplinary formation
**FALLOUTS** > FALLOUT
**FALLOW** _adj_ (of land) ploughed but left unseeded to regain fertility ▷ _n_ land treated in this way ▷ _vb_ leave (land) unseeded after ploughing and harrowing it
**FALLOWED** > FALLOW
**FALLOWER** > FALLOW
**FALLOWEST** > FALLOW
**FALLOWING** > FALLOW
**FALLOWS** > FALLOW
**FALLS** > FALL
**FALSE** _adj_ not true or correct ▷ _adv_ in a false or dishonest manner ▷ _vb_ falsify
**FALSED** > FALSE
**FALSEFACE** _n_ mask
**FALSEHOOD** _n_ quality of being untrue
**FALSELY** > FALSE
**FALSENESS** > FALSE
**FALSER** > FALSE
**FALSERS** _n_ colloquial term for false teeth
**FALSES** > FALSE
**FALSEST** > FALSE
**FALSETTO** _n_ voice pitched higher than one's natural range
**FALSETTOS** > FALSETTO
**FALSEWORK** _n_ framework supporting something under construction
**FALSIE** _n_ pad used to enlarge breast shape
**FALSIES** > FALSIE
**FALSIFIED** > FALSIFY
**FALSIFIER** > FALSIFY
**FALSIFIES** > FALSIFY
**FALSIFY** _vb_ alter fraudulently
**FALSING** > FALSE
**FALSISH** > FALSE
**FALSISM** > FALSE
**FALSISMS** > FALSE
**FALSITIES** > FALSITY
**FALSITY** _n_ state of being false
**FALTBOAT** _n_ collapsible boat made of waterproof material stretched over a light framework
**FALTBOATS** > FALTBOAT
**FALTER** _vb_ be hesitant, weak, or unsure ▷ _n_ uncertainty or hesitancy in speech or action
**FALTERED** > FALTER
**FALTERER** > FALTER
**FALTERERS** > FALTER
**FALTERING** > FALTER
**FALTERS** > FALTER
**FALX** _n_ sickle-shaped anatomical structure
**FAME** _n_ state of being widely known or recognized ▷ _vb_ make known or famous
**FAMED** > FAME

FAMELESS > FAME
FAMES > FAME
FAMILIAL *adj* of or relating to the family
FAMILIAR *adj* well-known ▷ *n* demon supposed to attend a witch
FAMILIARS *n* attendant demons
FAMILIES > FAMILY
FAMILISM *n* practice of a mystical Christian religious sect of the 16th and 17th centuries based upon love
FAMILISMS > FAMILISM
FAMILLE *n* type of Chinese porcelain
FAMILLES > FAMILLE
FAMILY *n* group of parents and their children ▷ *adj* suitable for parents and children together
FAMINE *n* severe shortage of food
FAMINES > FAMINE
FAMING > FAME
FAMISH *vb* be or make very hungry or weak
FAMISHED *adj* very hungry
FAMISHES > FAMISH
FAMISHING > FAMISH
FAMOUS *adj* very well-known ▷ *vb* make famous
FAMOUSED > FAMOUS
FAMOUSES > FAMOUS
FAMOUSING > FAMOUS
FAMOUSLY *adv* excellently
FAMULI > FAMULUS
FAMULUS *n* (formerly) the attendant of a sorcerer or scholar
FAMULUSES > FAMULUS
FAN *n* hand-held or mechanical object used to create a current of air for ventilation or cooling ▷ *vb* blow or cool with a fan
FANAL *n* lighthouse
FANALS > FANAL
FANATIC *n* person who is excessively enthusiastic about something ▷ *adj* excessively enthusiastic
FANATICAL *adj* surpassing what is normal or accepted in enthusiasm for or belief in something
FANATICS > FANATIC
FANBASE *n* body of admirers of a particular pop singer, sports team, etc
FANBASES > FANBASE
FANCIABLE *adj* sexually attractive
FANCIED *adj* imaginary
FANCIER *n* person who is interested in and often breeds plants or animals
FANCIERS > FANCIER
FANCIES > FANCY
FANCIEST > FANCY
FANCIFIED > FANCIFY

FANCIFIES > FANCIFY
FANCIFUL *adj* not based on fact
FANCIFY *vb* make more beautiful
FANCILESS > FANCY
FANCILY > FANCY
FANCINESS > FANCY
FANCY *adj* elaborate, not plain ▷ *n* sudden irrational liking or desire ▷ *vb* be sexually attracted to
FANCYING > FANCY
FANCYWORK *n* ornamental needlework
FAND *vb* try
FANDANGLE *n* elaborate ornament
FANDANGO *n* lively Spanish dance
FANDANGOS > FANDANGO
FANDED > FAND
FANDING > FAND
FANDOM *n* collectively, the fans of a sport, pastime or person
FANDOMS > FANDOM
FANDS > FAND
FANE *n* temple or shrine
FANEGA *n* Spanish unit of measurement
FANEGADA *n* Spanish unit of land area
FANEGADAS > FANEGADA
FANEGAS > FANEGA
FANES > FANE
FANFARADE *n* fanfare
FANFARE *n* short loud tune played on brass instruments ▷ *vb* perform a fanfare
FANFARED > FANFARE
FANFARES > FANFARE
FANFARING > FANFARE
FANFARON *n* braggart
FANFARONA *n* gold chain
FANFARONS > FANFARON
FANFIC *n* fiction written around previously established characters invented by other authors
FANFICS > FANFIC
FANFOLD *vb* fold (paper) like a fan
FANFOLDED > FANFOLD
FANFOLDS > FANFOLD
FANG *n* snake's tooth which injects poison ▷ *vb* seize
FANGA *same as* > FANEGA
FANGAS > FANGA
FANGED > FANG
FANGING > FANG
FANGLE *vb* fashion
FANGLED > FANGLE
FANGLES > FANGLE
FANGLESS > FANG
FANGLIKE > FANG
FANGLING > FANGLE
FANGO *n* mud from thermal springs in Italy, used in the treatment of rheumatic disease
FANGOS > FANGO

FANGS > FANG
FANION *n* small flag used by surveyors to mark stations
FANIONS > FANION
FANJET *same as* > TURBOFAN
FANJETS > FANJET
FANK *n* sheep pen
FANKLE *vb* entangle ▷ *n* tangle
FANKLED > FANKLE
FANKLES > FANKLE
FANKLING > FANKLE
FANKS > FANK
FANLIGHT *n* semicircular window over a door or window
FANLIGHTS > FANLIGHT
FANLIKE > FAN
FANNED > FAN
FANNEL *n* ecclesiastical vestment
FANNELL *variant of* > FANNEL
FANNELLS > FANNELL
FANNELS > FANNEL
FANNER > FAN
FANNIES > FANNY
FANNING > FAN
FANNINGS > FAN
FANNY *n* taboo word for female genitals
FANO *same as* > FANON
FANON *n* collar-shaped vestment worn by the pope when celebrating mass
FANONS > FANON
FANOS > FANO
FANS > FAN
FANTAD *n* nervous, agitated state
FANTADS > FANTAD
FANTAIL *n* small New Zealand bird with a tail like a fan
FANTAILED *adj* having a tail like a fan
FANTAILS > FANTAIL
FANTASIA *n* musical composition of an improvised nature
FANTASIAS > FANTASIA
FANTASIE *same as* > FANTASY
FANTASIED > FANTASY
FANTASIES > FANTASY
FANTASISE *same as* > FANTASIZE
FANTASIST *n* person who indulges in fantasies
FANTASIZE *vb* indulge in daydreams
FANTASM *archaic spelling of* > PHANTASM
FANTASMAL > FANTASM
FANTASMIC > FANTASM
FANTASMS > FANTASM
FANTASQUE *n* fantasy
FANTAST *n* dreamer or visionary
FANTASTIC *adj* very good ▷ *n* person who dresses or

behaves eccentrically
FANTASTRY *n* condition of being fantastic
FANTASTS > FANTAST
FANTASY *n* far-fetched notion ▷ *adj* of a competition in which a participant selects players for an imaginary, ideal team and points are awarded according to the actual performances of the chosen players ▷ *vb* fantasize
FANTEEG *n* nervous, agitated state
FANTEEGS > FANTEEG
FANTIGUE *variant of* > FANTEEG
FANTIGUES > FANTIGUE
FANTOD *n* crotchety or faddish behaviour
FANTODS > FANTOD
FANTOM *archaic spelling of* > PHANTOM
FANTOMS > FANTOM
FANTOOSH *adj* pretentious
FANUM *n* temple
FANUMS > FANUM
FANWISE *adj* like a fan
FANWORT *n* aquatic plant
FANWORTS > FANWORT
FANZINE *n* magazine produced by fans of a specific interest, soccer club, etc, for fellow fans
FANZINES > FANZINE
FAP *adj* drunk
FAQIR *same as* > FAKIR
FAQIRS > FAQIR
FAQUIR *variant of* > FAQIR
FAQUIRS > FAQUIR
FAR *adv* at, to, or from a great distance ▷ *adj* remote in space or time ▷ *vb* go far
FARAD *n* unit of electrical capacitance
FARADAIC *same as* > FARADIC
FARADAY *n* quantity of electricity, used in electrochemical calculations
FARADAYS > FARADAY
FARADIC *adj* of or concerned with an intermittent asymmetric alternating current such as that induced in the secondary winding of an induction coil
FARADISE *same as* > FARADIZE
FARADISED > FARADISE
FARADISER > FARADISE
FARADISES > FARADISE
FARADISM *n* therapeutic use of faradic currents
FARADISMS > FARADISM
FARADIZE *vb* treat (an organ or part) with faradic currents
FARADIZED > FARADIZE

FARADIZER > FARADIZE

FARADIZES > FARADIZE

FARADS > FARAD

FARAND n manner, fashion

FARANDINE n silk and wool cloth

FARANDOLE n lively dance in six-eight or four-four time from Provence

FARAWAY adj very distant

FARAWAYS same as > FARAWAY

FARCE n boisterous comedy ▷ vb enliven (a speech, etc) with jokes

FARCED > FARCE

FARCEMEAT > FORCEMEAT

FARCER same as > FARCEUR

FARCERS > FARCER

FARCES > FARCE

FARCEUR n writer of or performer in farces

FARCEURS > FARCEUR

FARCEUSE n female farceur

FARCEUSES > FARCEUSE

FARCI adj (of food) stuffed

FARCICAL adj ludicrous

FARCIE same as > FARCI

FARCIED adj afflicted with farcy

FARCIES > FARCY

FARCIFIED > FARCIFY

FARCIFIES > FARCIFY

FARCIFY vb turn into a farce

FARCIN n equine disease

FARCING > FARCE

FARCINGS > FARCE

FARCINS > FARCIN

FARCY n form of glanders in which lymph vessels near the skin become thickened, with skin lesions and abscess-forming nodules, caused by a bacterium, Burkholderia mallei

FARD n paint for the face, esp white paint ▷ vb paint (the face) with fard

FARDAGE n material laid beneath or between cargo

FARDAGES > FARDAGE

FARDED > FARD

FARDEL n bundle or burden

FARDELS > FARDEL

FARDEN n farthing

FARDENS > FARDEN

FARDING > FARD

FARDINGS > FARD

FARDS > FARD

FARE n charge for a passenger's journey ▷ vb get on (as specified)

FAREBOX n box where money for bus fares is placed

FAREBOXES > FAREBOX

FARED > FARE

FARER > FARE

FARERS > FARE

FARES > FARE

FAREWELL interj goodbye ▷ n act of saying goodbye

and leaving ▷ vb say goodbye ▷ adj parting or closing ▷ sentence substitute goodbye

FAREWELLS > FAREWELL

FARFAL same as > FELAFEL

FARFALLE n pasta in bow shapes

FARFALS > FARFAL

FARFEL same as > FELAFEL

FARFELS same as > FARFEL

FARFET adj far-fetched

FARINA n flour or meal made from any kind of cereal grain

FARINAS > FARINA

FARING > FARE

FARINHA n cassava meal

FARINHAS > FARINHA

FARINOSE adj similar to or yielding farina

FARL n thin cake of oatmeal, often triangular in shape

FARLE same as > FARL

FARLES > FARLE

FARLS > FARL

FARM n area of land for growing crops or rearing livestock ▷ vb cultivate (land)

FARMABLE > FARM

FARMED adj (of fish or game) reared on a farm rather than caught in the wild

FARMER n person who owns or runs a farm

FARMERESS n female farmer

FARMERIES > FARMERY

FARMERS > FARMER

FARMERY n farm buildings

FARMHAND n person who is hired to work on a farm

FARMHANDS > FARMHAND

FARMHOUSE n house attached to a farm

FARMING n business or skill of agriculture

FARMINGS > FARMING

FARMLAND n land that is used for or suitable for farming

FARMLANDS > FARMLAND

FARMOST > FAR

FARMS > FARM

FARMSTEAD n farm and its buildings

FARMWIFE n woman who works on a farm

FARMWIVES > FARMWIFE

FARMWORK n tasks carried out on a farm

FARMWORKS > FARMWORK

FARMYARD n small area of land enclosed by or around the farm buildings

FARMYARDS > FARMYARD

FARNARKEL vb spend time or act in a careless or inconsequential manner

FARNESOL n colourless aromatic sesquiterpene

alcohol found in many essential oils and used in the form of its derivatives in perfumery

FARNESOLS > FARNESOL

FARNESS > FAR

FARNESSES > FAR

FARO n gambling game in which players bet against the dealer on what cards he will turn up

FAROLITO n votive candle

FAROLITOS > FAROLITO

FAROS > FARO

FAROUCHE adj sullen or shy

FARRAGO n jumbled mixture of things

FARRAGOES > FARRAGO

FARRAGOS > FARRAGO

FARRAND variant of > FARAND

FARRANT variant of > FARAND

FARRED > FAR

FARREN n allotted ground

FARRENS > FARREN

FARRIER n person who shoes horses

FARRIERS > FARRIER

FARRIERY n art, work, or establishment of a farrier

FARRING > FAR

FARROW n litter of piglets ▷ vb (of a sow) give birth ▷ adj (of a cow) not calving in a given year

FARROWED > FARROW

FARROWING > FARROW

FARROWS > FARROW

FARRUCA n flamenco dance performed by men

FARRUCAS > FARRUCA

FARS > FAR

FARSE vb insert into

FARSED > FARSE

FARSEEING adj having shrewd judgment

FARSES > FARSE

FARSIDE n part of the Moon facing away from the Earth

FARSIDES > FARSIDE

FARSING > FARSE

FART n emission of gas from the anus ▷ vb emit gas from the anus

FARTED > FART

FARTHEL same as > FARL

FARTHELS > FARTHEL

FARTHER > FAR

FARTHEST > FAR

FARTHING n former British coin equivalent to a quarter of a penny

FARTHINGS > FARTHING

FARTING > FART

FARTLEK n in sport, another name for interval training

FARTLEKS > FARTLEK

FARTS > FART

FAS > FA

FASCES pl n (in ancient Rome) a bundle of rods

containing an axe with its blade pointing out

FASCI > FASCIO

FASCIA n outer surface of a dashboard

FASCIAE > FASCIA

FASCIAL > FASCIA

FASCIAS > FASCIA

FASCIATE adj (of stems and branches) abnormally flattened due to coalescence

FASCIATED same as > FASCIATE

FASCICLE same as > FASCICULE

FASCICLED adj in instalments

FASCICLES > FASCICLE

FASCICULE n one part of a printed work that is published in instalments

FASCICULI > FASCICULE

FASCIITIS n inflammation of the fascia of a muscle

FASCINATE vb attract and interest strongly

FASCINE n bundle of long sticks used for filling in ditches and in the construction of embankments, roads, fortifications, etc

FASCINES > FASCINE

FASCIO n political group

FASCIOLA n band

FASCIOLAS > FASCIOLA

FASCIOLE n band

FASCIOLES > FASCIOLE

FASCIS > FASCI

FASCISM n right-wing totalitarian political system characterized by state control and extreme nationalism

FASCISMI > FASCISMO

FASCISMO Italian word for > FASCISM

FASCISMS > FASCISM

FASCIST n adherent or practitioner of fascism ▷ adj characteristic of or relating to fascism

FASCISTA Italian word for > FASCIST

FASCISTI > FASCISTA

FASCISTIC > FASCIST

FASCISTS > FASCIST

FASCIITIS same as > FASCIITIS

FASH n worry ▷ vb trouble

FASHED > FASH

FASHERIES > FASHERY

FASHERY n difficulty, trouble

FASHES > FASH

FASHING > FASH

FASHION n style in clothes, hairstyle, etc, popular at a particular time ▷ vb form or make into a particular shape

FASHIONED > FASHION

FASHIONER > FASHION
FASHIONS > FASHION
FASHIONY adj of or relating to fashion
FASHIOUS adj troublesome
FAST adj (capable of) acting or moving quickly ▷ adv quickly ▷ vb go without food, esp for religious reasons ▷ n period of fasting
FASTBACK n car having a back that forms one continuous slope from roof to rear
FASTBACKS > FASTBACK
FASTBALL n ball pitched at the pitcher's top speed
FASTBALLS > FASTBALL
FASTED > FAST
FASTEN vb make or become firmly fixed or joined
FASTENED > FASTEN
FASTENER > FASTEN
FASTENERS > FASTEN
FASTENING n something that fastens something, such as a clasp or lock
FASTENS > FASTEN
FASTER > FAST
FASTERS > FAST
FASTEST > FAST
FASTI n in ancient Rome, days when business could legally be carried out
FASTIE n deceitful act
FASTIES > FASTIE
FASTIGIUM n highest point
FASTING > FAST
FASTINGS > FAST
FASTISH > FAST
FASTLY > FAST
FASTNESS n fortress, safe place
FASTS > FAST
FASTUOUS adj arrogant
FAT adj having excess flesh on the body ▷ n extra flesh on the body
FATAL adj causing death or ruin
FATALISM n belief that all events are predetermined and people are powerless to change their destinies
FATALISMS > FATALISM
FATALIST > FATALISM
FATALISTS > FATALISM
FATALITY n death caused by an accident or disaster
FATALLY adv resulting in death or disaster
FATALNESS > FATAL
FATBACK n fat, usually salted, from the upper part of a side of pork
FATBACKS > FATBACK
FATBIRD n nocturnal bird
FATBIRDS > FATBIRD
FATE n power supposed to predetermine events ▷ vb predetermine
FATED adj destined
FATEFUL adj having

important, usu disastrous, consequences
FATEFULLY > FATEFUL
FATES > FATE
FATHEAD n stupid person
FATHEADED adj stupid
FATHEADS > FATHEAD
FATHER n male parent ▷ vb be the father of (offspring)
FATHERED > FATHER
FATHERING > FATHER
FATHERLY adj kind or protective, like a father
FATHERS > FATHER
FATHOM n unit of length, used in navigation, equal to six feet (1.83 metres) ▷ vb understand
FATHOMED > FATHOM
FATHOMER > FATHOM
FATHOMERS > FATHOM
FATHOMING > FATHOM
FATHOMS > FATHOM
FATIDIC adj prophetic
FATIDICAL same as > FATIDIC
FATIGABLE > FATIGUE
FATIGATE vb fatigue
FATIGATED > FATIGATE
FATIGATES > FATIGATE
FATIGUE n extreme physical or mental tiredness ▷ vb tire out
FATIGUED > FATIGUE
FATIGUES > FATIGUE
FATIGUING > FATIGUE
FATING > FATE
FATISCENT > FATISCENCE
FATLESS > FAT
FATLIKE > FAT
FATLING n young farm animal fattened for killing
FATLINGS > FATLING
FATLY > FAT
FATNESS > FAT
FATNESSES > FAT
FATS > FAT
FATSIA n any shrub of the araliaceous genus Fatsia, esp F. japonica, with large deeply palmate leaves and umbels of white flowers
FATSIAS > FATSIA
FATSO n fat person: used as an insulting or disparaging term of address
FATSOES > FATSO
FATSOS > FATSO
FATSTOCK n livestock fattened and ready for market
FATSTOCKS > FATSTOCK
FATTED > FAT
FATTEN vb (cause to) become fat
FATTENED > FATTEN
FATTENER > FATTEN
FATTENERS > FATTEN
FATTENING > FATTEN
FATTENS > FATTEN
FATTER > FAT
FATTEST > FAT
FATTIER > FATTY

FATTIES > FATTY
FATTIEST > FATTY
FATTILY > FATTY
FATTINESS > FATTY
FATTING > FAT
FATTISH > FAT
FATTISM n discrimination on the basis of weight, esp prejudice against those considered to be overweight
FATTISMS > FATTISM
FATTIST > FATTISM
FATTISTS > FATTISM
FATTRELS n ends of ribbon
FATTY adj containing fat ▷ n fat person
FATUITIES > FATUITY
FATUITOUS > FATUITY
FATUITY n foolish thoughtlessness
FATUOUS adj foolish
FATUOUSLY > FATUOUS
FATWA n religious decree issued by a Muslim leader ▷ vb issue a fatwa
FATWAED > FATWA
FATWAH same as > FATWA
FATWAHED > FATWAH
FATWAHING > FATWAH
FATWAHS > FATWAH
FATWAING > FATWA
FATWAS > FATWA
FATWOOD n wood used for kindling
FATWOODS > FATWOOD
FAUBOURG n suburb or quarter, esp of a French city
FAUBOURGS > FAUBOURG
FAUCAL adj of or relating to the fauces
FAUCALS > FAUCAL
FAUCES n area between the cavity of the mouth and the pharynx, including the surrounding tissues
FAUCET n tap
FAUCETS > FAUCET
FAUCHION n short sword
FAUCHIONS > FAUCHION
FAUCHON variant of > FAUCHION
FAUCHONS > FAUCHON
FAUCIAL same as > FAUCAL
FAUGH interj exclamation of disgust, scorn, etc
FAULCHION variant of > FAUCHION
FAULD n piece of armour
FAULDS > FAULD
FAULT n responsibility for something wrong ▷ vb criticize or blame
FAULTED > FAULT
FAULTFUL > FAULT
FAULTIER > FAULTY
FAULTIEST > FAULTY
FAULTILY > FAULTY
FAULTING > FAULT
FAULTLESS adj without fault
FAULTS > FAULT
FAULTY adj badly designed

or not working properly
FAUN n (in Roman legend) creature with a human face and torso and a goat's horns and legs
FAUNA n animals of a given place or time
FAUNAE > FAUNA
FAUNAL > FAUNA
FAUNALLY > FAUNA
FAUNAS > FAUNA
FAUNIST > FAUNA
FAUNISTIC > FAUNA
FAUNISTS > FAUNA
FAUNLIKE > FAUN
FAUNS > FAUN
FAUNULA n fauna of a small single environment
FAUNULAE > FAUNULA
FAUNULE same as > FAUNULA
FAUNULES > FAUNULE
FAUR Scot word for > FAR
FAURD adj favoured
FAURER > FAUR
FAUREST > FAUR
FAUSTIAN adj of or relating to Faust, esp reminiscent of his bargain with the devil
FAUT Scot word for > FAULT
FAUTED > FAUT
FAUTEUIL n armchair, the sides of which are not upholstered
FAUTEUILS > FAUTEUIL
FAUTING > FAUT
FAUTOR n patron
FAUTORS > FAUTOR
FAUTS > FAUT
FAUVE adj of the style of the Fauve art movement
FAUVES > FAUVE
FAUVETTE n singing bird, warbler
FAUVETTES > FAUVETTE
FAUVISM > FAUVE
FAUVISMS > FAUVISM
FAUVIST n artist following the Fauve style of painting
FAUVISTS > FAUVIST
FAUX adj false
FAVA n type of bean
FAVAS > FAVA
FAVE short for > FAVOURITE
FAVEL n dun-coloured horse
FAVELA n (in Brazil) a shanty or shantytown
FAVELAS > FAVELA
FAVELL variant of > FAVEL
FAVELLA n group of spores
FAVELLAS > FAVELLA
FAVEOLATE adj pitted with cell-like cavities
FAVER > FAVE
FAVES > FAVE
FAVEST > FAVE
FAVISM n type of anaemia
FAVISMS > FAVISM
FAVONIAN adj of or relating to the west wind
FAVOR same as > FAVOUR
FAVORABLE same as > FAVOURABLE

FAVORABLY > FAVOURABLE
FAVORED > FAVOR
FAVORER > FAVOUR
FAVORERS > FAVOUR
FAVORING > FAVOR
FAVORITE same
  as > FAVOURITE
FAVORITES > FAVORITE
FAVORLESS > FAVOR
FAVORS same as > FAVOURS
FAVOSE same
  as > FAVEOLATE
FAVOUR n approving
  attitude ▷ vb prefer
FAVOURED > FAVOUR
FAVOURER > FAVOUR
FAVOURERS > FAVOUR
FAVOURING > FAVOUR
FAVOURITE adj most liked
  ▷ n preferred person or
  thing
FAVOURS pl n sexual
  intimacy, as when
  consented to by a woman
FAVOUS adj resembling
  honeycomb
FAVRILE n type of
  iridescent glass
FAVRILES > FAVRILE
FAVUS n infectious
  fungal skin disease of
  man and some domestic
  animals, characterized
  by formation of a
  honeycomb-like mass of
  roundish dry cup-shaped
  crusts
FAVUSES > FAVUS
FAW n gypsy
FAWN n young deer ▷ adj
  light yellowish-brown
  ▷ vb seek attention from
  (someone) by insincere
  flattery
FAWNED > FAWN
FAWNER > FAWN
FAWNERS > FAWN
FAWNIER > FAWNY
FAWNIEST > FAWNY
FAWNING > FAWN
FAWNINGLY > FAWN
FAWNINGS > FAWN
FAWNLIKE > FAWN
FAWNS > FAWN
FAWNY adj of a fawn colour
FAWS > FAW
FAX n electronic system
  for sending facsimiles of
  documents by telephone
  ▷ vb send (a document) by
  this system
FAXED > FAX
FAXES > FAX
FAXING > FAX
FAY n fairy or sprite ▷ adj
  of or resembling a fay ▷ vb
  fit or be fitted closely or
  tightly
FAYALITE n rare brown or
  black mineral
FAYALITES > FAYALITE
FAYED > FAY
FAYENCE variant
  of > FAIENCE

FAYENCES > FAYENCE
FAYER > FAY
FAYEST > FAY
FAYING > FAY
FAYNE vb pretend
FAYNED > FAYNE
FAYNES > FAYNE
FAYNING > FAYNE
FAYRE pseudo-archaic
  spelling of > FAIR
FAYRES > FAYRE
FAYS > FAY
FAZE vb disconcert or
  fluster
FAZED adj worried or
  disconcerted
FAZENDA n large estate or
  ranch
FAZENDAS > FAZENDA
FAZES > FAZE
FAZING > FAZE
FE same as > FEE
FEAGUE vb whip or beat
FEAGUED > FEAGUE
FEAGUES > FEAGUE
FEAGUING > FEAGUE
FEAL vb conceal
FEALED > FEAL
FEALING > FEAL
FEALS > FEAL
FEALTIES > FEALTY
FEALTY n (in feudal
  society) subordinate's
  loyalty to his ruler or lord
FEAR n distress or alarm
  caused by impending
  danger or pain ▷ vb be
  afraid of (something or
  someone)
FEARE n companion,
  spouse
FEARED > FEAR
FEARER > FEAR
FEARERS > FEAR
FEARES > FEARE
FEARFUL adj feeling fear
FEARFULLY adv in a fearful
  manner
FEARING > FEAR
FEARLESS > FEAR
FEARS > FEAR
FEARSOME adj terrifying
FEASANCE n performance
  of an act
FEASANCES > FEASANCE
FEASE vb perform an act
FEASED > FEASE
FEASES > FEASE
FEASIBLE adj able to be
  done, possible
FEASIBLY > FEASIBLE
FEASING > FEASE
FEAST n lavish meal ▷ vb
  eat a feast
FEASTED > FEAST
FEASTER > FEAST
FEASTERS > FEAST
FEASTFUL adj festive
FEASTING > FEAST
FEASTINGS > FEAST
FEASTLESS > FEAST
FEASTS > FEAST
FEAT n remarkable, skilful,
  or daring action

FEATED > FEAT
FEATEOUS adj neat
FEATER > FEAT
FEATEST > FEAT
FEATHER n one of the
  barbed shafts forming the
  plumage of birds ▷ vb fit
  or cover with feathers
FEATHERED > FEATHER
FEATHERS > FEATHER
FEATHERY > FEATHER
FEATING > FEAT
FEATLIER > FEAT
FEATLIEST > FEAT
FEATLY > FEAT
FEATOUS variant
  of > FEATEOUS
FEATS > FEAT
FEATUOUS variant
  of > FEATEOUS
FEATURE n part of the face,
  such as the eyes ▷ vb have
  as a feature or be a feature
  in
FEATURED adj having
  features as specified
FEATURELY adj handsome
FEATURES > FEATURE
FEATURING > FEATURE
FEAZE same as > FEEZE
FEAZED > FEAZE
FEAZES > FEAZE
FEAZING > FEAZE
FEBLESSE n feebleness
FEBLESSES > FEBLESSE
FEBRICITY n condition of
  having a fever
FEBRICULA n slight
  transient fever
FEBRICULE variant
  of > FEBRICULA
FEBRIFIC adj causing or
  having a fever
FEBRIFUGE n any drug or
  agent for reducing fever
  ▷ adj serving to reduce
  fever
FEBRILE adj very active
  and nervous
FEBRILITY > FEBRILE
FECAL same as > FAECAL
FECES same as > FAECES
FECHT Scot word for > FIGHT
FECHTER > FECHT
FECHTERS > FECHT
FECHTING > FECHT
FECHTS > FECHT
FECIAL adj heraldic
FECIALS > FECIAL
FECIT (he or she) made it:
  used formerly on works
  of art next to the artist's
  name
FECK n worth
FECKIN same as > FECKING
FECKING adj slang word for
  absolute
FECKLESS adj ineffectual
  or irresponsible
FECKLY > FECK
FECKS > FECK
FECULA n starch obtained
  by washing the crushed
  parts of plants, such as the

  potato
FECULAE > FECULA
FECULAS > FECULA
FECULENCE > FECULENT
FECULENCY > FECULENT
FECULENT adj filthy,
  scummy, muddy, or foul
FECUND adj fertile
FECUNDATE vb make
  fruitful
FECUNDITY n fertility
FED n FBI agent
FEDARIE n accomplice
FEDARIES > FEDARIE
FEDAYEE n (in Arab states)
  a commando, esp one
  fighting against Israel
FEDAYEEN > FEDAYEE
FEDELINI n type of pasta
FEDELINIS > FEDELINI
FEDERACY n alliance
FEDERAL adj of a system
  in which power is divided
  between one central
  government and several
  regional governments ▷ n
  supporter of federal union
  or federation
FEDERALLY > FEDERAL
FEDERALS > FEDERAL
FEDERARIE variant
  of > FEDARIE
FEDERARY variant
  of > FEDARIE
FEDERATE vb unite in a
  federation ▷ adj federal
FEDERATED > FEDERATE
FEDERATES > FEDERATE
FEDERATOR > FEDERATE
FEDEX vb send by FedEx
FEDEXED > FEDEX
FEDEXES > FEDEX
FEDEXING > FEDEX
FEDORA n man's soft hat
  with a brim
FEDORAS > FEDORA
FEDS > FEE
FEE n charge paid to be
  allowed to do something
  ▷ vb pay a fee to
FEEB n contemptible
  person
FEEBLE adj lacking physical
  or mental power ▷ vb
  make feeble
FEEBLED > FEEBLE
FEEBLER > FEEBLE
FEEBLES > FEEBLE
FEEBLEST > FEEBLE
FEEBLING > FEEBLE
FEEBLISH > FEEBLE
FEEBLY > FEEBLE
FEEBS > FEEB
FEED vb give food to ▷ n
  act of feeding
FEEDABLE > FEE
FEEDBACK n information
  received in response to
  something done ▷ adv
  return (part of the output
  of a system) to its input
FEEDBACKS > FEEDBACK
FEEDBAG n any bag in
  which feed for livestock is

sacked
**FEEDBAGS** > FEEDBAG
**FEEDBOX** trough, manger
**FEEDBOXES** > FEEDBOX
**FEEDER** n baby's bib
**FEEDERS** > FEEDER
**FEEDGRAIN** n cereal grown
to feed livestock
**FEEDHOLE** n small hole
through which cable etc is
inserted
**FEEDHOLES** > FEEDHOLE
**FEEDING** > FEED
**FEEDINGS** > FEED
**FEEDLOT** n area or building
where livestock are
fattened rapidly for market
**FEEDLOTS** > FEEDLOT
**FEEDS** > FEED
**FEEDSTOCK** n main raw
material used in the
manufacture of a product
**FEEDSTUFF** n any material
used as a food, esp for
animals
**FEEDWATER** n water,
previously purified to
prevent scale deposit
or corrosion, that is
fed to boilers for steam
generation
**FEEDYARD** n place where
cattle are kept and fed
**FEEDYARDS** > FEEDYARD
**FEEING** > FEE
**FEEL** vb have a physical or
emotional sensation of
▷ n act of feeling
**FEELBAD** n something
inducing depression
**FEELBADS** > FEELBAD
**FEELER** n organ of touch in
some animals
**FEELERS** > FEELER
**FEELESS** > FEE
**FEELGOOD** adj causing or
characterized by a feeling
of self-satisfaction
**FEELGOODS** > FEELGOOD
**FEELING** > FEEL
**FEELINGLY** > FEEL
**FEELINGS** > FEEL
**FEELS** > FEEL
**FEEN** n in Irish dialect, an
informal word for 'man'
**FEENS** > FEEN
**FEER** vb make a furrow
**FEERED** > FEER
**FEERIE** n fairyland
**FEERIES** > FEERIE
**FEERIN** n furrow
**FEERING** > FEER
**FEERINGS** > FEER
**FEERINS** > FEERIN
**FEERS** > FEER
**FEES** > FEE
**FEESE** vb perturb
**FEESED** > FEESE
**FEESES** > FEESE
**FEESING** > FEESE
**FEET** > FOOT
**FEETFIRST** adv with the
feet coming first
**FEETLESS** > FOOT

**FEEZE** vb beat ▷ n rush
**FEEZED** > FEEZE
**FEEZES** > FEEZE
**FEEZING** > FEEZE
**FEG** same as > FIG
**FEGARIES** > FEGARY
**FEGARY** variant of > VAGARY
**FEGS** > FEG
**FEH** n Hebrew coin
**FEHM** n medieval German
court
**FEHME** > FEHM
**FEHMIC** > FEHM
**FEHS** > FEH
**FEIGN** vb pretend
**FEIGNED** > FEIGN
**FEIGNEDLY** > FEIGN
**FEIGNER** > FEIGN
**FEIGNERS** > FEIGN
**FEIGNING** > FEIGN
**FEIGNINGS** > FEIGN
**FEIGNS** > FEIGN
**FEIJOA** n evergreen
myrtaceous shrub of S
America
**FEIJOAS** > FEIJOA
**FEINT** n sham attack or
blow meant to distract an
opponent ▷ vb make a
feint ▷ adj printing term
meaning ruled with faint
lines
**FEINTED** > FEINT
**FEINTER** > FEINT
**FEINTEST** > FEINT
**FEINTING** > FEINT
**FEINTS** pl n leavings of
the second distillation of
Scotch malt whisky
**FEIRIE** adj nimble
**FEIS** n Irish music and
dance festival
**FEISEANNA** > FEIS
**FEIST** n small aggressive
dog
**FEISTIER** > FEISTY
**FEISTIEST** > FEISTY
**FEISTILY** > FEISTY
**FEISTS** > FEIST
**FEISTY** adj showing
courage or spirit
**FELAFEL** same as > FALAFEL
**FELAFELS** > FELAFEL
**FELDGRAU** n ordinary
German soldier (from
uniform colour)
**FELDGRAUS** > FELDGRAU
**FELDSCHAR** same
as > FELDSHER
**FELDSCHER** same
as > FELDSHER
**FELDSHER** n (in Russia) a
medical doctor's assistant
**FELDSHERS** > FELDSHER
**FELDSPAR** n hard
mineral that is the main
constituent of igneous
rocks
**FELDSPARS** > FELDSPAR
**FELDSPATH** variant
of > FELDSPAR
**FELICIA** n type of African
herb
**FELICIAS** > FELICIA

**FELICIFIC** adj making or
tending to make happy
**FELICITER** > FELICITY
**FELICITY** n happiness
**FELID** n any animal
belonging to the family
Felidae; a cat
**FELIDS** > FELID
**FELINE** adj of cats ▷ n
member of the cat family
**FELINELY** > FELINE
**FELINES** > FELINE
**FELINITY** > FELINE
**FELL** vb cut or knock down
▷ adj cruel or deadly
**FELLA** nonstandard variant
of > FELLOW
**FELLABLE** > FALL
**FELLAH** n peasant in Arab
countries
**FELLAHEEN** > FELLAH
**FELLAHIN** > FELLAH
**FELLAHS** > FELLAH
**FELLAS** > FELLA
**FELLATE** vb perform
fellatio on (a person)
**FELLATED** > FELLATE
**FELLATES** > FELLATE
**FELLATING** > FELLATE
**FELLATIO** n sexual
activity in which the
penis is stimulated by the
partner's mouth
**FELLATION** same
as > FELLATIO
**FELLATIOS** > FELLATIO
**FELLATOR** > FELLATIO
**FELLATORS** > FELLATIO
**FELLATRIX** > FELLATIO
**FELLED** > FELL
**FELLER** n person or thing
that fells
**FELLERS** > FELLER
**FELLEST** > FELL
**FELLIES** > FELLY
**FELLING** > FELL
**FELLNESS** > FELL
**FELLOE** n (segment of) the
rim of a wheel
**FELLOES** > FELLOE
**FELLOW** n man or boy ▷ adj
in the same group or
condition
**FELLOWED** > FELLOW
**FELLOWING** > FELLOW
**FELLOWLY** adj friendly,
companionable
**FELLOWMAN** n companion
**FELLOWMEN** > FELLOWMAN
**FELLOWS** > FELLOW
**FELLS** > FELL
**FELLY** same as > FELLOE
**FELON** n (formerly) person
guilty of a felony ▷ adj evil
**FELONIES** > FELONY
**FELONIOUS** adj of,
involving, or constituting
a felony
**FELONOUS** adj wicked
**FELONRIES** > FELONRY
**FELONRY** n felons
collectively
**FELONS** > FELON
**FELONY** n serious crime

**FELSIC** adj relating to
igneous rock
**FELSITE** n any fine-
grained igneous rock
consisting essentially of
quartz and feldspar
**FELSITES** > FELSITE
**FELSITIC** > FELSITE
**FELSPAR** same
as > FELDSPAR
**FELSPARS** > FELSPAR
**FELSTONE** same as > FELSITE
**FELSTONES** > FELSTONE
**FELT** n matted fabric ▷ vb
become matted
**FELTED** > FELT
**FELTER** vb mat together
**FELTERED** > FELTER
**FELTERING** > FELTER
**FELTERS** > FELTER
**FELTIER** > FELT
**FELTIEST** > FELT
**FELTING** n felted material
**FELTINGS** > FELTING
**FELTLIKE** > FEEL
**FELTS** > FELT
**FELTY** > FELT
**FELUCCA** n narrow
lateen-rigged vessel of the
Mediterranean
**FELUCCAS** > FELUCCA
**FELWORT** n biennial
gentianaceous plant,
Gentianella amarella, of
Europe and SW China,
having purple flowers and
rosettes of leaves
**FELWORTS** > FELWORT
**FEM** n passive homosexual
**FEMAL** adj effeminate ▷ n
effeminate person
**FEMALE** adj of the sex which
bears offspring ▷ n female
person or animal
**FEMALES** > FEMALE
**FEMALITY** > FEMALE
**FEMALS** > FEMAL
**FEME** n woman or wife
**FEMERALL** n ventilator or
smoke outlet on a roof
**FEMERALLS** > FEMERALL
**FEMES** > FEME
**FEMETARY** variant
of > FUMITORY
**FEMINACY** n feminine
character
**FEMINAL** adj feminine,
female
**FEMINAZI** n militant
feminist
**FEMINAZIS** > FEMINAZI
**FEMINEITY** n quality of
being feminine
**FEMINIE** n women
collectively
**FEMININE** adj having
qualities traditionally
regarded as suitable for,
or typical of, women ▷ n
short for feminine noun
**FEMININES** > FEMININE
**FEMINISE** same
as > FEMINIZE
**FEMINISED** > FEMINISE

275

FEMINISES > FEMINISE
FEMINISM n advocacy of equal rights for women
FEMINISMS > FEMINISM
FEMINIST n person who advocates equal rights for women ▷ adj of, relating to, or advocating feminism
FEMINISTS > FEMINIST
FEMINITY > FEMINAL
FEMINIZE vb make or become feminine
FEMINIZED > FEMINIZE
FEMINIZES > FEMINIZE
FEMITER variant of > FUMITORY
FEMITERS > FEMITER
FEMME n woman or wife
FEMMES > FEMME
FEMMIER > FEMMY
FEMMIEST > FEMMY
FEMMY adj markedly or exaggeratedly feminine in appearance, manner, etc
FEMORA > FEMUR
FEMORAL adj of the thigh
FEMS > FEM
FEMUR n thighbone
FEMURS > FEMUR
FEN n low-lying flat marshy land
FENAGLE variant of > FINAGLE
FENAGLED > FENAGLE
FENAGLES > FENAGLE
FENAGLING > FENAGLE
FENCE n barrier of posts linked by wire or wood, enclosing an area ▷ vb enclose with or as if with a fence
FENCED > FENCE
FENCELESS > FENCE
FENCELIKE > FENCE
FENCER n person who fights with a sword, esp one who practises the art of fencing
FENCEROW n uncultivated land flanking a fence
FENCEROWS > FENCEROW
FENCERS > FENCER
FENCES > FENCE
FENCIBLE n (formerly) a person who undertook military service in immediate defence of his homeland only
FENCIBLES > FENCIBLE
FENCING n sport of fighting with swords
FENCINGS > FENCING
FEND vb give support (to someone, esp oneself) ▷ n shift or effort
FENDED > FEND
FENDER n low metal frame in front of a fireplace
FENDERED adj having a fender
FENDERS > FENDER
FENDIER > FENDY
FENDIEST > FENDY

FENDING > FEND
FENDS > FEND
FENDY adj thrifty
FENESTRA n small opening in or between bones, esp one of the openings between the middle and inner ears
FENESTRAE > FENESTRA
FENESTRAL > FENESTRA
FENESTRAS > FENESTRA
FENI n Goan alcoholic drink
FENIS > FENI
FENITAR variant of > FUMITORY
FENITARS > FENITAR
FENKS n whale blubber
FENLAND > FEN
FENLANDS > FEN
FENMAN > FEN
FENMEN > FEN
FENNEC n very small nocturnal fox, Fennecus zerda, inhabiting deserts of N Africa and Arabia, having pale fur and enormous ears
FENNECS > FENNEC
FENNEL n fragrant plant whose seeds, leaves, and root are used in cookery
FENNELS > FENNEL
FENNIER > FENNY
FENNIES > FENNY
FENNIEST > FENNY
FENNISH > FEN
FENNY adj boggy or marshy ▷ n feni
FENS > FEN
FENT n piece of waste fabric
FENTANYL n narcotic drug used in medicine to relieve pain
FENTANYLS > FENTANYL
FENTHION n type of pesticide
FENTHIONS > FENTHION
FENTS > FENT
FENUGREEK n Mediterranean plant grown for its heavily scented seeds
FENURON n type of herbicide
FENURONS > FENURON
FEOD same as > FEUD
FEODAL > FEOD
FEODARIES > FEOD
FEODARY > FEOD
FEODS > FEOD
FEOFF same as > FIEF
FEOFFED > FEOFF
FEOFFEE n (in feudal society) a vassal granted a fief by his lord
FEOFFEES > FEOFFEE
FEOFFER > FEOFF
FEOFFERS > FEOFF
FEOFFING > FEOFF
FEOFFMENT n (in medieval Europe) a lord's act of granting a fief to his man

FEOFFOR > FEOFF
FEOFFORS > FEOFF
FEOFFS > FEOFF
FER same as > FAR
FERACIOUS adj fruitful
FERACITY > FERACIOUS
FERAL adj wild ▷ n person who displays such tendencies and appearance
FERALISED same as > FERALIZED
FERALIZED adj once domesticated, but now wild
FERALS > FERAL
FERBAM n black slightly water-soluble fluffy powder used as a fungicide
FERBAMS > FERBAM
FERE n companion ▷ adj fierce
FERER > FERE
FERES > FERE
FEREST > FERE
FERETORY n shrine, usually portable, for a saint's relics
FERIA n weekday, other than Saturday, on which no feast occurs
FERIAE > FERIA
FERIAL adj of or relating to a feria
FERIAS > FERIA
FERINE same as > FERAL
FERITIES > FERAL
FERITY > FERAL
FERLIE same as > FERLY
FERLIED > FERLY
FERLIER > FERLY
FERLIES > FERLY
FERLIEST > FERLY
FERLY adj wonderful ▷ n wonder ▷ vb wonder
FERLYING > FERLY
FERM variant of > FARM
FERMATA another word for > PAUSE
FERMATAS > FERMATA
FERMATE > FERMATA
FERMENT n any agent that causes fermentation ▷ vb (cause to) undergo fermentation
FERMENTED > FERMENT
FERMENTER > FERMENT
FERMENTOR > FERMENT
FERMENTS > FERMENT
FERMI n unit of length used in nuclear physics equal to $10^{-15}$ metre
FERMION n any of a group of elementary particles, such as a nucleon, that has half-integral spin and obeys Fermi-Dirac statistics
FERMIONIC > FERMION
FERMIONS > FERMION
FERMIS > FERMI
FERMIUM n element artificially produced by neutron bombardment of plutonium

FERMIUMS > FERMIUM
FERMS > FERM
FERN n flowerless plant with fine fronds
FERNBIRD n small brown and white New Zealand swamp bird, Bowdleria punctata, with a fernlike tail
FERNBIRDS > FERNBIRD
FERNERIES > FERNERY
FERNERY n place where ferns are grown
FERNIER > FERN
FERNIEST > FERN
FERNING n production of a fern-like pattern
FERNINGS > FERNING
FERNINST same as > FORNENST
FERNLESS > FERN
FERNLIKE > FERN
FERNS > FERN
FERNSHAW n fern thicket
FERNSHAWS > FERNSHAW
FERNTICLE variant of > FERNTICKLE
FERNY > FERN
FEROCIOUS adj savagely fierce or cruel
FEROCITY > FEROCIOUS
FERRATE n type of salt
FERRATES > FERRATE
FERREL variant of > FERRULE
FERRELED > FERREL
FERRELING > FERREL
FERRELLED > FERREL
FERRELS > FERREL
FERREOUS adj containing or resembling iron
FERRET n tamed polecat used to catch rabbits or rats ▷ vb hunt with ferrets
FERRETED > FERRET
FERRETER > FERRET
FERRETERS > FERRET
FERRETING > FERRET
FERRETS > FERRET
FERRETY > FERRET
FERRIAGE n transportation by ferry
FERRIAGES > FERRIAGE
FERRIC adj of or containing iron
FERRIED > FERRY
FERRIES > FERRY
FERRITE n any of a group of ferromagnetic highly resistive ceramic compounds
FERRITES > FERRITE
FERRITIC > FERRITE
FERRITIN n protein that contains iron and plays a part in the storage of iron in the body. It occurs in the liver and spleen
FERRITINS > FERRITIN
FERROCENE n reddish-orange insoluble crystalline compound
FERROTYPE n photographic print produced directly in a

camera by exposing a sheet of iron or tin coated with a sensitized enamel

**FERROUS** *adj* of or containing iron in the divalent state

**FERRUGO** *n* disease affecting plants

**FERRUGOS** > FERRUGO

**FERRULE** *n* metal cap to strengthen the end of a stick ▷ *vb* equip (a stick, etc) with a ferrule

**FERRULED** > FERRULE

**FERRULES** > FERRULE

**FERRULING** > FERRULE

**FERRUM** *Latin word for* > IRON

**FERRUMS** > FERRUM

**FERRY** *n* boat for transporting people and vehicles ▷ *vb* carry by ferry

**FERRYBOAT** *same as* > FERRY

**FERRYING** > FERRY

**FERRYMAN** *n* someone who provides a ferry service

**FERRYMEN** > FERRYMAN

**FERTIGATE** *vb* fertilize and irrigate at the same time

**FERTILE** *adj* capable of producing young, crops, or vegetation

**FERTILELY** > FERTILE

**FERTILER** > FERTILE

**FERTILEST** > FERTILE

**FERTILISE** *same as* > FERTILIZE

**FERTILITY** *n* ability to produce offspring, esp abundantly

**FERTILIZE** *vb* provide (an animal or plant) with sperm or pollen to bring about fertilization

**FERULA** *n* any large umbelliferous plant of the Mediterranean genus *Ferula*, having thick stems and dissected leaves: cultivated as the source of several strongly-scented gum resins, such as galbanum

**FERULAE** > FERULA

**FERULAS** > FERULA

**FERULE** *same as* > FERRULE

**FERULED** > FERULE

**FERULES** > FERULE

**FERULING** > FERULE

**FERVENCY** *another word for* > FERVOUR

**FERVENT** *adj* intensely passionate and sincere

**FERVENTER** > FERVENT

**FERVENTLY** > FERVENT

**FERVID** *same as* > FERVENT

**FERVIDER** > FERVID

**FERVIDEST** > FERVID

**FERVIDITY** > FERVID

**FERVIDLY** > FERVID

**FERVOR** *same as* > FERVOUR

**FERVOROUS** > FERVOUR

**FERVORS** > FERVOR

**FERVOUR** *n* intensity of

feeling

**FERVOURS** > FERVOUR

**FES** > FE

**FESCUE** *n* pasture and lawn grass with stiff narrow leaves

**FESCUES** > FESCUE

**FESS** *same as* > FESSE

**FESSE** *n* ordinary consisting of a horizontal band across a shield, conventionally occupying a third of its length and being wider than a bar

**FESSED** > FESS

**FESSES** > FESSE

**FESSING** > FESS

**FESSWISE** *adv* in heraldry, with a horizontal band across the shield

**FEST** *n* event at which the emphasis is on a particular activity

**FESTA** *n* festival

**FESTAL** *adj* festive ▷ *n* festivity

**FESTALLY** > FESTAL

**FESTALS** > FESTAL

**FESTAS** > FESTA

**FESTER** *vb* grow worse and increasingly hostile ▷ *n* small ulcer or sore containing pus

**FESTERED** > FESTER

**FESTERING** > FESTER

**FESTERS** > FESTER

**FESTIER** > FESTY

**FESTIEST** > FESTY

**FESTILOGY** *n* treatise about church festivals

**FESTINATE** *vb* hurry

**FESTIVAL** *n* organized series of special events or performances

**FESTIVALS** > FESTIVAL

**FESTIVE** *adj* of or like a celebration

**FESTIVELY** > FESTIVE

**FESTIVITY** *n* happy celebration

**FESTIVOUS** > FESTIVE

**FESTOLOGY** *variant of* > FESTILOGY

**FESTOON** *vb* hang decorations in loops ▷ *n* decorative chain of flowers or ribbons suspended in loops

**FESTOONED** > FESTOON

**FESTOONS** > FESTOON

**FESTS** > FEST

**FESTY** *adj* dirty

**FET** *vb* fetch

**FETA** *n* white salty Greek cheese

**FETAL** *adj* of, relating to, or resembling a fetus

**FETAS** > FETA

**FETATION** *n* state of pregnancy

**FETATIONS** > FETATION

**FETCH** *vb* go after and bring back ▷ *n* ghost or apparition of a living

person

**FETCHED** > FETCH

**FETCHER** *n* person or animal that fetches

**FETCHERS** > FETCHER

**FETCHES** > FETCH

**FETCHING** *adj* attractive

**FETE** *n* gala, bazaar, etc, usu held outdoors ▷ *vb* honour or entertain regally

**FETED** > FETE

**FETERITA** *n* type of sorghum

**FETERITAS** > FETERITA

**FETES** > FETE

**FETIAL** *n* (in ancient Rome) any of the 20 priestly heralds involved in declarations of war and in peace negotiations ▷ *adj* of or relating to the fetiales

**FETIALES** > FETIAL

**FETIALIS** *n* priest in ancient Rome

**FETIALS** > FETIAL

**FETICH** *same as* > FETISH

**FETICHE** *variant of* > FETICH

**FETICHES** > FETICH

**FETICHISE** *variant of* > FETICHIZE

**FETICHISM** *same as* > FETISHISM

**FETICHIST** > FETISHISM

**FETICHIZE** *vb* be excessively or irrationally devoted to an object, activity, etc

**FETICIDAL** > FETICIDE

**FETICIDE** *n* destruction of a fetus in the uterus

**FETICIDES** > FETICIDE

**FETID** *adj* stinking

**FETIDER** > FETID

**FETIDEST** > FETID

**FETIDITY** > FETID

**FETIDLY** > FETID

**FETIDNESS** > FETID

**FETING** > FETE

**FETISH** *n* form of behaviour in which sexual pleasure is derived from looking at or handling an inanimate object

**FETISHES** > FETISH

**FETISHISE** *same as* > FETISHIZE

**FETISHISM** *n* condition in which the handling of an inanimate object or a specific part of the body other than the sexual organs is a source of sexual satisfaction

**FETISHIST** > FETISHISM

**FETISHIZE** *vb* be excessively or irrationally devoted to (an object, activity, etc)

**FETLOCK** *n* projection behind and above a horse's hoof

**FETLOCKED** *adj* having fetlocks

**FETLOCKS** > FETLOCK

**FETOLOGY** *n* branch of medicine concerned with the fetus in the uterus

**FETOR** *n* offensive stale or putrid odour

**FETORS** > FETOR

**FETOSCOPE** *n* fibreoptic instrument that can be passed through the abdomen of a pregnant woman to enable examination of the fetus and withdrawal of blood for sampling in prenatal diagnosis

**FETOSCOPY** > FETOSCOPE

**FETS** > FET

**FETT** *variant of* > FET

**FETTA** *variant of* > FETA

**FETTAS** > FETTA

**FETTED** > FET

**FETTER** *n* chain or shackle for the foot ▷ *vb* restrict

**FETTERED** > FETTER

**FETTERER** > FETTER

**FETTERERS** > FETTER

**FETTERING** > FETTER

**FETTERS** > FETTER

**FETTING** > FET

**FETTLE** *same as* > FETTLING

**FETTLED** > FETTLE

**FETTLER** *n* person employed to maintain railway tracks

**FETTLERS** > FETTLER

**FETTLES** > FETTLE

**FETTLING** *n* refractory material used to line the hearth of puddling furnaces

**FETTLINGS** > FETTLING

**FETTS** > FETT

**FETTUCINE** *n* type of pasta in the form of narrow ribbons

**FETTUCINI** *same as* > FETTUCINE

**FETUS** *n* embryo of a mammal in the later stages of development

**FETUSES** > FETUS

**FETWA** *variant of* > FATWA

**FETWAS** > FETWA

**FEU** *n* (in Scotland) right of use of land in return for a fixed annual payment

**FEUAR** *n* tenant of a feu

**FEUARS** > FEUAR

**FEUD** *n* long bitter hostility between two people or groups ▷ *vb* carry on a feud

**FEUDAL** *adj* of or like feudalism

**FEUDALISE** *same as* > FEUDALIZE

**FEUDALISM** *n* medieval system in which people held land from a lord, and in return worked and fought for him

**FEUDALIST** > FEUDALISM

**FEUDALITY** *n* state or

quality of being feudal
**FEUDALIZE** vb make feudal
**FEUDALLY** > FEUDAL
**FEUDARIES** > FEUDARY
**FEUDARY** n holder of land through feudal right
**FEUDATORY** n person holding a fief ▷ adj relating to or characteristic of the relationship between lord and vassal
**FEUDED** > FEUD
**FEUDING** > FEUD
**FEUDINGS** > FEUD
**FEUDIST** n person who takes part in a feud or quarrel
**FEUDISTS** > FEUDIST
**FEUDS** > FEUD
**FEUED** > FEU
**FEUILLETE** n puff pastry
**FEUING** > FEU
**FEUS** > FEU
**FEUTRE** vb place in a resting position
**FEUTRED** > FEUTRE
**FEUTRES** > FEUTRE
**FEUTRING** > FEUTRE
**FEVER** n (illness causing) high body temperature ▷ vb affect with or as if with fever
**FEVERED** > FEVER
**FEVERFEW** n bushy European strong-scented perennial plant, *Tanacetum parthenium*, with white flower heads, formerly used medicinally: family *Asteraceae* (composites)
**FEVERFEWS** > FEVERFEW
**FEVERING** > FEVER
**FEVERISH** adj suffering from fever
**FEVERLESS** > FEVER
**FEVEROUS** same as > FEVERISH
**FEVERROOT** n American wild plant
**FEVERS** > FEVER
**FEVERWEED** n plant thought to be medicinal
**FEVERWORT** n any of several plants considered to have medicinal properties, such as horse gentian and boneset
**FEW** adj not many
**FEWER** > FEW
**FEWEST** > FEW
**FEWMET** variant of > FUMET
**FEWMETS** > FEWMET
**FEWNESS** > FEW
**FEWNESSES** > FEW
**FEWTER** variant of > FEUTRE
**FEWTERED** > FEUTRE
**FEWTERING** > FEUTRE
**FEWTERS** > FEUTRE
**FEWTRILS** n trifles, trivia
**FEY** adj whimsically strange ▷ vb clean out
**FEYED** > FEY
**FEYER** > FEY

**FEYEST** > FEY
**FEYING** > FEY
**FEYLY** > FEY
**FEYNESS** > FEY
**FEYNESSES** > FEY
**FEYS** > FEY
**FEZ** n brimless tasselled cap, orig. from Turkey
**FEZES** > FEZ
**FEZZED** adj wearing a fez
**FEZZES** > FEZ
**FEZZY** > FEZ
**FIACRE** n small four-wheeled horse-drawn carriage, usually with a folding roof
**FIACRES** > FIACRE
**FIANCE** n man engaged to be married
**FIANCEE** n woman who is engaged to be married
**FIANCEES** > FIANCEE
**FIANCES** > FIANCE
**FIAR** n property owner
**FIARS** n legally fixed price of corn
**FIASCHI** > FIASCO
**FIASCO** n ridiculous or humiliating failure
**FIASCOES** > FIASCO
**FIASCOS** > FIASCO
**FIAT** n arbitrary order ▷ vb issue a fiat
**FIATED** > FIAT
**FIATING** > FIAT
**FIATS** > FIAT
**FIAUNT** n fiat
**FIAUNTS** > FIAUNT
**FIB** n trivial lie ▷ vb tell a lie
**FIBBED** > FIB
**FIBBER** > FIB
**FIBBERIES** > FIB
**FIBBERS** > FIB
**FIBBERY** > FIB
**FIBBING** > FIB
**FIBER** same as > FIBRE
**FIBERED** > FIBRE
**FIBERFILL** same as > FIBREFILL
**FIBERISE** same as > FIBERIZE
**FIBERISED** > FIBERISE
**FIBERISES** > FIBERISE
**FIBERIZE** vb break into fibres
**FIBERIZED** > FIBERIZE
**FIBERIZES** > FIBERIZE
**FIBERLESS** > FIBRE
**FIBERLIKE** > FIBER
**FIBERS** > FIBER
**FIBRANNE** n synthetic fabric
**FIBRANNES** > FIBRANNE
**FIBRE** n thread that can be spun into yarn
**FIBRED** > FIBRE
**FIBREFILL** n synthetic fibre used as a filling for pillows, quilted materials, etc
**FIBRELESS** > FIBRE
**FIBRES** > FIBRE
**FIBRIFORM** adj having the

form of a fibre or fibres
**FIBRIL** n small fibre
**FIBRILAR** > FIBRIL
**FIBRILLA** same as > FIBRIL
**FIBRILLAE** > FIBRILLA
**FIBRILLAR** > FIBRIL
**FIBRILLIN** n kind of protein
**FIBRILS** > FIBRIL
**FIBRIN** n white insoluble elastic protein formed when blood clots
**FIBRINOID** > FIBRIN
**FIBRINOUS** adj of, containing, or resembling fibrin
**FIBRINS** > FIBRIN
**FIBRO** n mixture of cement and asbestos fibre, used in sheets for building
**FIBROCYTE** n type of fibroblast
**FIBROID** adj (of structures or tissues) containing or resembling fibres ▷ n benign tumour composed of fibrous connective tissue
**FIBROIDS** > FIBROID
**FIBROIN** n tough elastic protein that is the principal component of spiders' webs and raw silk
**FIBROINS** > FIBROIN
**FIBROLINE** n type of yarn
**FIBROLITE** n trademark name for a type of building board containing asbestos and cement
**FIBROMA** n benign tumour derived from fibrous connective tissue
**FIBROMAS** > FIBROMA
**FIBROMATA** > FIBROMA
**FIBROS** > FIBRO
**FIBROSE** vb become fibrous
**FIBROSED** > FIBROSE
**FIBROSES** > FIBROSE
**FIBROSING** > FIBROSE
**FIBROSIS** n formation of an abnormal amount of fibrous tissue
**FIBROTIC** > FIBROSIS
**FIBROUS** adj consisting of, containing, or resembling fibres
**FIBROUSLY** > FIBROUS
**FIBS** > FIB
**FIBSTER** n fibber
**FIBSTERS** > FIBSTER
**FIBULA** n slender outer bone of the lower leg
**FIBULAE** > FIBULA
**FIBULAR** > FIBULA
**FIBULAS** > FIBULA
**FICE** n small aggressive dog
**FICES** > FICE
**FICHE** n sheet of film for storing publications in miniaturized form
**FICHES** > FICHE
**FICHU** n woman's shawl

or scarf of some light material, worn esp in the 18th century
**FICHUS** > FICHU
**FICIN** n enzyme
**FICINS** > FICIN
**FICKLE** adj changeable, inconstant ▷ vb puzzle
**FICKLED** > FICKLE
**FICKLER** > FICKLE
**FICKLES** > FICKLE
**FICKLEST** > FICKLE
**FICKLING** > FICKLE
**FICKLY** > FICKLE
**FICO** n worthless trifle
**FICOES** > FICO
**FICOS** > FICO
**FICTILE** adj moulded or capable of being moulded from clay
**FICTION** n literary works of the imagination, such as novels
**FICTIONAL** > FICTION
**FICTIONS** > FICTION
**FICTIVE** adj of, relating to, or able to create fiction
**FICTIVELY** > FICTIVE
**FICTOR** n sculptor
**FICTORS** > FICTOR
**FICUS** n any plant of the genus *Ficus*, which includes the edible fig and several greenhouse and house plants
**FICUSES** > FICUS
**FID** n spike for separating strands of rope in splicing
**FIDDIOUS** vb treat someone as Coriolanus, in the eponymous play, dealt with Aufidius
**FIDDLE** n violin ▷ vb play the violin
**FIDDLED** > FIDDLE
**FIDDLER** n person who plays the fiddle
**FIDDLERS** > FIDDLER
**FIDDLES** > FIDDLE
**FIDDLEY** n vertical space above a vessel's engine room extending into its stack
**FIDDLEYS** > FIDDLEY
**FIDDLIER** > FIDDLY
**FIDDLIEST** > FIDDLY
**FIDDLING** adj trivial
**FIDDLY** adj awkward to do or use
**FIDEISM** n theological doctrine that religious truth is a matter of faith and cannot be established by reason
**FIDEISMS** > FIDEISM
**FIDEIST** > FIDEISM
**FIDEISTIC** > FIDEISM
**FIDEISTS** > FIDEISM
**FIDELISMO** n belief in, adherence to, or advocacy of the principles of Fidel Castro, the Cuban Communist statesman (born 1927)

FIDELISTA n advocate of fidelism; a fidelist
FIDELITY n faithfulness
FIDGE obsolete word for > FIDGET
FIDGED > FIDGE
FIDGES > FIDGE
FIDGET vb move about restlessly ▷ n person who fidgets
FIDGETED > FIDGET
FIDGETER > FIDGET
FIDGETERS > FIDGET
FIDGETIER > FIDGET
FIDGETING > FIDGET
FIDGETS > FIDGET
FIDGETY > FIDGET
FIDGING > FIDGE
FIDIBUS n spill for lighting a candle or pipe
FIDIBUSES > FIDIBUS
FIDO n generic term for a dog
FIDOS > FIDO
FIDS > FID
FIDUCIAL adj used as a standard of reference or measurement
FIDUCIARY n person bound to act for someone else's benefit, as a trustee ▷ adj of a trust or trustee
FIE interj exclamation of disapproval
FIEF n land granted by a lord in return for war service
FIEFDOM n (in Feudal Europe) the property owned by a lord
FIEFDOMS > FIEFDOM
FIEFS > FIEF
FIELD n piece of land, usu enclosed with a fence or hedge, and used for pasture or growing crops ▷ vb stop, catch, or return (the ball) as a fielder
FIELDED > FIELD
FIELDER n (in certain sports) player whose task is to field the ball
FIELDERS > FIELDER
FIELDFARE n type of large Old World thrush
FIELDING > FIELD
FIELDINGS > FIELD
FIELDMICE pl n nocturnal mice
FIELDS > FIELD
FIELDSMAN n fielder
FIELDSMEN > FIELDSMAN
FIELDVOLE n small rodent
FIELDWARD adv towards a field or fields
FIELDWORK n investigation made in the field as opposed to the classroom or the laboratory
FIEND n evil spirit
FIENDISH adj of or like a fiend
FIENDLIKE > FIEND
FIENDS > FIEND

FIENT n fiend
FIENTS > FIENT
FIER same as > FERE
FIERCE adj wild or aggressive
FIERCELY > FIERCE
FIERCER > FIERCE
FIERCEST > FIERCE
FIERE > FERE
FIERES > FERE
FIERIER > FIERY
FIERIEST > FIERY
FIERILY > FIERY
FIERINESS > FIERY
FIERS > FIER
FIERY adj consisting of or like fire
FIEST > FIE
FIESTA n religious festival, carnival
FIESTAS > FIESTA
FIFE n small high-pitched flute ▷ vb play (music) on a fife
FIFED > FIFE
FIFER > FIFE
FIFERS > FIFE
FIFES > FIFE
FIFI n type of mountaineering hook
FIFING > FIFE
FIFTEEN n five and ten ▷ adj amounting to fifteen ▷ determiner amounting to fifteen
FIFTEENER n fifteen-syllable line of poetry
FIFTEENS > FIFTEEN
FIFTEENTH adj coming after the fourteenth in order, position, time, etc. Often written: 15th ▷ n one of 15 equal or nearly equal parts of something
FIFTH n (of) number five in a series ▷ adj of or being number five in a series ▷ adv after the fourth person, position, event, etc
FIFTHLY same as > FIFTH
FIFTHS > FIFTH
FIFTIES > FIFTY
FIFTIETH adj being the ordinal number of fifty in order, position, time, etc. Often written: 50th ▷ n one of 50 equal or approximately equal parts of something
FIFTIETHS > FIFTIETH
FIFTY n five times ten ▷ adj amounting to fifty ▷ determiner amounting to fifty
FIFTYISH > FIFTY
FIG n soft pear-shaped fruit ▷ vb dress (up) or rig (out)
FIGEATER n large beetle
FIGEATERS > FIGEATER
FIGGED > FIG
FIGGERIES > FIGGERY
FIGGERY n adornment,

ornament
FIGGING > FIG
FIGHT vb struggle (against) in battle or physical combat ▷ n aggressive conflict between two (groups of) people
FIGHTABLE > FIGHT
FIGHTBACK n act or campaign of resistance
FIGHTER n boxer
FIGHTERS > FIGHTER
FIGHTING > FIGHT
FIGHTINGS > FIGHT
FIGHTS > FIGHT
FIGJAM n very conceited person
FIGJAMS > FIGJAM
FIGMENT n fantastic notion, invention, or fabrication
FIGMENTS > FIGMENT
FIGO variant of > FICO
FIGOS > FIGO
FIGS > FIG
FIGULINE adj of or resembling clay ▷ n article made of clay
FIGULINES > FIGULINE
FIGURABLE > FIGURE
FIGURAL adj composed of or relating to human or animal figures
FIGURALLY > FIGURAL
FIGURANT n ballet dancer who does group work but no solo roles
FIGURANTE n female figurant
FIGURANTS > FIGURANT
FIGURATE adj exhibiting or produced by figuration
FIGURE n numerical symbol ▷ vb calculate (sums or amounts)
FIGURED adj decorated with a design
FIGUREDLY > FIGURED
FIGURER > FIGURE
FIGURERS > FIGURE
FIGURES > FIGURE
FIGURINE n statuette
FIGURINES > FIGURINE
FIGURING > FIGURE
FIGURIST n user of numbers
FIGURISTS > FIGURIST
FIGWORT n any scrophulariaceous plant of the N temperate genus Scrophularia, having square stems and small brown or greenish flowers
FIGWORTS > FIGWORT
FIKE vb fidget
FIKED > FIKE
FIKERIES > FIKERY
FIKERY n fuss
FIKES > FIKE
FIKIER > FIKY
FIKIEST > FIKY
FIKING > FIKE
FIKISH adj fussy
FIKY adj fussy

FIL same as > FILS
FILA > FILUM
FILABEG variant of > FILIBEG
FILABEGS > FILABEG
FILACEOUS adj made of threads
FILACER n formerly, English legal officer
FILACERS > FILACER
FILAGREE same as > FILIGREE
FILAGREED > FILAGREE
FILAGREES > FILAGREE
FILAMENT n fine wire in a light bulb that gives out light
FILAMENTS > FILAMENT
FILANDER n species of kangaroo
FILANDERS > FILANDER
FILAR adj of thread
FILAREE n type of storksbill, a weed
FILAREES > FILAREE
FILARIA n any parasitic nematode worm of the family Filariidae, living in the blood and tissues of vertebrates and transmitted by insects: the cause of filariasis
FILARIAE > FILARIA
FILARIAL > FILARIA
FILARIAN > FILARIA
FILARIAS > FILARIA
FILARIID adj of or relating to a family of threadlike roundworms
FILARIIDS > FILARIID
FILASSE n vegetable fibre such as jute
FILASSES > FILASSE
FILATORY n machine for making threads
FILATURE n act or process of spinning silk, etc, into threads
FILATURES > FILATURE
FILAZER variant of > FILACER
FILAZERS > FILAZER
FILBERD variant of > FILBERT
FILBERDS > FILBERD
FILBERT n hazelnut
FILBERTS > FILBERT
FILCH vb steal (small amounts)
FILCHED > FILCH
FILCHER > FILCH
FILCHERS > FILCH
FILCHES > FILCH
FILCHING > FILCH
FILCHINGS > FILCH
FILE n box or folder used to keep documents in order ▷ vb place (a document) in a file
FILEABLE > FILE
FILECARD n type of brush with sharp steel bristles, used for cleaning the teeth of a file
FILECARDS > FILECARD

**FILED** > FILE
**FILEFISH** n any tropical triggerfish, such as *Alutera scripta*, having a narrow compressed body and a very long dorsal spine
**FILEMOT** n type of brown colour
**FILEMOTS** > FILEMOT
**FILENAME** n arrangement of characters that enables a computer system to permit the user to have access to a particular file
**FILENAMES** > FILENAME
**FILER** > FILE
**FILERS** > FILE
**FILES** > FILE
**FILET** variant of > FILLET
**FILETED** > FILET
**FILETING** > FILET
**FILETS** > FILET
**FILFOT** variant of > FYLFOT
**FILFOTS** > FILFOT
**FILIAL** adj of or befitting a son or daughter
**FILIALLY** > FILIAL
**FILIATE** vb fix judicially the paternity of (a child, esp one born out of wedlock)
**FILIATED** > FILIATE
**FILIATES** > FILIATE
**FILIATING** > FILIATE
**FILIATION** n line of descent
**FILIBEG** n kilt worn by Scottish Highlanders
**FILIBEGS** > FILIBEG
**FILICIDAL** > FILICIDE
**FILICIDE** n act of killing one's own son or daughter
**FILICIDES** > FILICIDE
**FILIFORM** adj having the form of a thread
**FILIGRAIN** n filigree
**FILIGRANE** variant of > FILIGRAIN
**FILIGREE** n delicate ornamental work of gold or silver wire ▷ adj made of filigree ▷ vb decorate with or as if with filigree
**FILIGREED** > FILIGREE
**FILIGREES** > FILIGREE
**FILING** > FILE
**FILINGS** pl n shavings removed by a file
**FILIOQUE** n theological term found in the Nicene Creed
**FILIOQUES** > FILIOQUE
**FILISTER** same as > FILLISTER
**FILISTERS** > FILISTER
**FILL** vb make or become full
**FILLABLE** > FILL
**FILLAGREE** same as > FILIGREE
**FILLE** n girl
**FILLED** > FILL
**FILLER** n substance that fills a gap or increases bulk

**FILLERS** > FILLER
**FILLES** > FILLE
**FILLESTER** same as > FILLISTER
**FILLET** n boneless piece of meat or fish ▷ vb remove the bones from
**FILLETED** > FILLET
**FILLETING** > FILLET
**FILLETS** > FILLET
**FILLIBEG** same as > FILIBEG
**FILLIBEGS** > FILLIBEG
**FILLIES** > FILLY
**FILLING** n substance that fills a gap or cavity, esp in a tooth ▷ adj (of food) substantial and satisfying
**FILLINGS** > FILLING
**FILLIP** n something that adds stimulation or enjoyment ▷ vb stimulate or excite
**FILLIPED** > FILLIP
**FILLIPEEN** n philopoena
**FILLIPING** > FILLIP
**FILLIPS** > FILLIP
**FILLISTER** n adjustable plane for cutting rabbets, grooves, etc
**FILLO** variant of > FILO
**FILLOS** > FILLO
**FILLS** > FILL
**FILLY** n young female horse
**FILM** n sequence of images projected on a screen, creating the illusion of movement ▷ vb photograph with a movie or video camera ▷ adj connected with films or the cinema
**FILMABLE** > FILM
**FILMCARD** n cinema loyalty card
**FILMCARDS** > FILMCARD
**FILMDOM** n cinema industry
**FILMDOMS** > FILMDOM
**FILMED** > FILM
**FILMER** n film-maker
**FILMERS** > FILMER
**FILMGOER** n person who goes regularly to the cinema
**FILMGOERS** > FILMGOER
**FILMGOING** > FILMGOER
**FILMI** adj in Indian English, of or relating to the Indian film industry or Indian films
**FILMIC** adj of or suggestive of films or the cinema
**FILMIER** > FILMY
**FILMIEST** > FILMY
**FILMILY** > FILMY
**FILMINESS** > FILMY
**FILMING** > FILM
**FILMIS** > FILMI
**FILMISH** > FILM
**FILMLAND** n cinema industry
**FILMLANDS** > FILMLAND
**FILMLESS** > FILM

**FILMLIKE** > FILM
**FILMMAKER** n person who makes films
**FILMS** > FILM
**FILMSET** vb set (type matter) by filmsetting
**FILMSETS** > FILMSET
**FILMSTRIP** n strip of film composed of different images projected separately as slides
**FILMY** adj very thin, delicate
**FILO** n type of flaky Greek pastry in very thin sheets
**FILOPLUME** n any of the hairlike feathers that lack vanes and occur between the contour feathers
**FILOPODIA** n plural form of singular filopodium: ectoplasmic pseudopodium
**FILOS** > FILO
**FILOSE** adj resembling or possessing a thread or threadlike process
**FILOSELLE** n soft silk thread, used esp for embroidery
**FILOVIRUS** n any member of a family of viruses that includes the agents responsible for Ebola virus disease and Marburg disease
**FILS** n fractional monetary unit of Bahrain, Iraq, Jordan, and Kuwait, worth one thousandth of a dinar
**FILTER** n material or device permitting fluid to pass but retaining solid particles ▷ vb remove impurities from (a substance) with a filter
**FILTERED** > FILTER
**FILTERER** > FILTER
**FILTERERS** > FILTER
**FILTERING** > FILTER
**FILTERS** > FILTER
**FILTH** n disgusting dirt
**FILTHIER** > FILTHY
**FILTHIEST** > FILTHY
**FILTHILY** > FILTHY
**FILTHS** > FILTH
**FILTHY** adj characterized by or full of filth ▷ adv extremely
**FILTRABLE** adj capable of being filtered
**FILTRATE** n filtered gas or liquid ▷ vb remove impurities with a filter
**FILTRATED** > FILTRATE
**FILTRATES** > FILTRATE
**FILUM** n any threadlike structure or part
**FIMBLE** n male plant of the hemp, which matures before the female plant
**FIMBLES** > FIMBLE
**FIMBRIA** n fringe or fringelike margin or

border, esp at the opening of the Fallopian tubes
**FIMBRIAE** > FIMBRIA
**FIMBRIAL** > FIMBRIA
**FIMBRIATE** adj having a fringed margin, as some petals, antennae, etc
**FIN** n any of the firm appendages that are the organs of locomotion and balance in fishes and some other aquatic mammals ▷ vb provide with fins
**FINABLE** adj liable to a fine
**FINAGLE** vb get or achieve by craftiness or trickery
**FINAGLED** > FINAGLE
**FINAGLER** > FINAGLE
**FINAGLERS** > FINAGLE
**FINAGLES** > FINAGLE
**FINAGLING** > FINAGLE
**FINAL** adj at the end ▷ n deciding contest between winners of previous rounds in a competition
**FINALE** n concluding part of a dramatic performance or musical work
**FINALES** > FINALE
**FINALIS** n musical finishing note
**FINALISE** same as > FINALIZE
**FINALISED** > FINALISE
**FINALISER** > FINALISE
**FINALISES** > FINALISE
**FINALISM** n doctrine that final causes determine the course of all events
**FINALISMS** > FINALISM
**FINALIST** n competitor in a final
**FINALISTS** > FINALIST
**FINALITY** n condition or quality of being final or settled
**FINALIZE** vb put into final form
**FINALIZED** > FINALIZE
**FINALIZER** > FINALIZE
**FINALIZES** > FINALIZE
**FINALLY** adv after a long delay
**FINALS** pl n deciding part of a competition
**FINANCE** vb provide or obtain funds for ▷ n system of money, credit, and investment
**FINANCED** > FINANCE
**FINANCES** > FINANCE
**FINANCIAL** adj of or relating to finance, finances, or people who manage money
**FINANCIER** n person involved in large-scale financial business
**FINANCING** > FINANCE
**FINBACK** another name for > RORQUAL
**FINBACKS** > FINBACK
**FINCA** n Spanish villa
**FINCAS** > FINCA

FINCH n small songbird with a short strong beak
FINCHED adj with streaks or spots on the back
FINCHES > FINCH
FIND vb discover by chance ▷ n person or thing found, esp when valuable
FINDABLE > FIND
FINDER n small telescope fitted to a larger one
FINDERS > FINDER
FINDING > FIND
FINDINGS > FIND
FINDRAM variant of > FINNAN
FINDRAMS > FINDRAM
FINDS > FIND
FINE adj very good ▷ n payment imposed as a penalty ▷ vb impose a fine on
FINEABLE same as > FINABLE
FINED > FINE
FINEER variant of > VENEER
FINEERED > FINEER
FINEERING > FINEER
FINEERS > FINEER
FINEISH > FINE
FINELESS > FINE
FINELY adv into small pieces
FINENESS n state or quality of being fine
FINER > FINE
FINERIES > FINERY
FINERS > FINE
FINERY n showy clothing
FINES > FINE
FINESPUN adj spun or drawn out to a fine thread
FINESSE n delicate skill ▷ vb bring about with finesse
FINESSED > FINESSE
FINESSER > FINESSE
FINESSERS > FINESSE
FINESSES > FINESSE
FINESSING > FINESSE
FINEST > FINE
FINFISH n fish with fins, as opposed to shellfish
FINFISHES > FINFISH
FINFOOT n any aquatic bird of the tropical and subtropical family Heliornithidae, having broadly lobed toes, a long slender head and neck, and pale brown plumage: order Gruiformes (cranes, rails etc)
FINFOOTS > FINFOOT
FINGAN variant of > FINJAN
FINGANS > FINGAN
FINGER n one of the four long jointed parts of the hand ▷ vb touch or handle with the fingers
FINGERED adj marked or dirtied by handling
FINGERER > FINGER
FINGERERS > FINGER

FINGERING n technique of using the fingers in playing a musical instrument
FINGERS > FINGER
FINGERTIP n end joint or tip of a finger
FINI n end; finish
FINIAL n ornament at the apex of a gable or spire
FINIALED adj having a finial or finials
FINIALS > FINIAL
FINICAL another word for > FINICKY
FINICALLY > FINICAL
FINICKETY adj fussy or tricky
FINICKIER > FINICKY
FINICKIN variant of > FINICKY
FINICKING same as > FINICKY
FINICKY adj excessively particular, fussy
FINIKIN variant of > FINICKY
FINIKING variant of > FINICKY
FINING n process of removing undissolved gas bubbles from molten glass
FININGS > FINING
FINIS > FINI
FINISES > FINIS
FINISH vb bring to an end, stop ▷ n end, last part
FINISHED adj perfected
FINISHER n craftsman who carries out the final tasks in a manufacturing process
FINISHERS > FINISHER
FINISHES > FINISH
FINISHING n act or skill of goal scoring
FINITE adj having limits in space, time, or size
FINITELY > FINITE
FINITES > FINITE
FINITISM n view that only those entities may be admitted to mathematics that can be constructed in a finite number of steps, and only those propositions entertained whose truth can be proved in a finite number of steps
FINITISMS > FINITISM
FINITO adj finished
FINITUDE > FINITE
FINITUDES > FINITE
FINJAN n small, handleless coffee cup
FINJANS > FINJAN
FINK n strikebreaker ▷ vb inform (on someone), as to the police
FINKED > FINK
FINKING > FINK
FINKS > FINK
FINLESS > FIN
FINLIKE > FIN

FINMARK n monetary unit of Finland
FINMARKS > FINMARK
FINNAC variant of > FINNOCK
FINNACK variant of > FINNOCK
FINNACKS > FINNACK
FINNACS > FINNAC
FINNAN n smoked haddock
FINNANS > FINNAN
FINNED > FIN
FINNER another name for > RORQUAL
FINNERS > FINNER
FINNESKO n reindeer-skin boot
FINNICKY variant of > FINICKY
FINNIER > FINNY
FINNIEST > FINNY
FINNING > FIN
FINNMARK n Finnish monetary unit
FINNMARKS > FINNMARK
FINNOCHIO variant of > FINOCCHIO
FINNOCK n young sea trout on its first return to fresh water
FINNOCKS > FINNOCK
FINNSKO variant of > FINNESKO
FINNY adj relating to or containing many fishes
FINO n very dry sherry
FINOCCHIO n variety of fennel, Foeniculum vulgare dulce, with thickened stalks that resemble celery and are eaten as a vegetable, esp in S Europe
FINOCHIO same as > FINOCCHIO
FINOCHIOS > FINOCHIO
FINOS > FINO
FINS > FIN
FINSKO variant of > FINNESKO
FIORATURA same as > FIORITURA
FIORD same as > FJORD
FIORDS > FIORD
FIORIN n temperate perennial grass, Agrostis stolonifera
FIORINS > FIORIN
FIORITURA n embellishment, esp ornamentation added by the performer
FIORITURE > FIORITURA
FIPPENCE n fivepence
FIPPENCES > FIPPENCE
FIPPLE n wooden plug forming a flue in the end of a pipe, as the mouthpiece of a recorder
FIPPLES > FIPPLE
FIQUE n hemp
FIQUES > FIQUE
FIR n pyramid-shaped tree with needle-like leaves and erect cones

FIRE n state of combustion producing heat, flames, and smoke ▷ vb operate (a weapon) so that a bullet or missile is released
FIREABLE > FIRE
FIREARM n rifle, pistol, or shotgun
FIREARMED adj carrying firearm
FIREARMS > FIREARM
FIREBACK n ornamental iron slab against the back wall of a hearth
FIREBACKS > FIREBACK
FIREBALL n ball of fire at the centre of an explosion
FIREBALLS > FIREBALL
FIREBASE n artillery base from which heavy fire is directed at the enemy
FIREBASES > FIREBASE
FIREBIRD n any of various songbirds having a bright red plumage, esp the Baltimore oriole
FIREBIRDS > FIREBIRD
FIREBOARD n mantelpiece
FIREBOAT n motor vessel with fire-fighting apparatus
FIREBOATS > FIREBOAT
FIREBOMB n bomb that is designed to cause fires
FIREBOMBS > FIREBOMB
FIREBOX n furnace chamber of a boiler in a steam locomotive
FIREBOXES > FIREBOX
FIREBRAND n person who causes unrest
FIREBRAT n small primitive wingless insect, Thermobia domestica, that occurs in warm buildings, feeding on starchy food scraps, fabric, etc: order Thysanura (bristletails)
FIREBRATS > FIREBRAT
FIREBREAK n strip of cleared land to stop the advance of a fire
FIREBRICK n heat-resistant brick used for lining furnaces, fireplaces, etc
FIREBUG n person who deliberately sets fire to property
FIREBUGS > FIREBUG
FIREBUSH as in Chilean firebush South American shrub with scarlet flowers
FIRECLAY n heat-resistant clay used in the making of firebricks, furnace linings, etc
FIRECLAYS > FIRECLAY
FIRECREST n small European warbler, Regulus ignicapillus, having a crown striped with yellow, black, and white
FIRED > FIRE

**FIREDAMP** n explosive gas, composed mainly of methane, formed in mines
**FIREDAMPS** > FIREDAMP
**FIREDOG** n either of a pair of decorative metal stands used to support logs in an open fire
**FIREDOGS** > FIREDOG
**FIREDRAKE** n fire-breathing dragon
**FIREFANG** vb become overheated through decomposition
**FIREFANGS** > FIREFANG
**FIREFIGHT** n brief small-scale engagement between opposing military ground forces using short-range light weapons
**FIREFLIES** > FIREFLY
**FIREFLOAT** n boat used for firefighting
**FIREFLOOD** n method of extracting oil from a well by burning some of the oil to increase the rate of flow
**FIREFLY** n beetle that glows in the dark
**FIREGUARD** same as > FIREBREAK
**FIREHALL** n US and Canadian word for fire station
**FIREHALLS** > FIREHALL
**FIREHOUSE** n firestation
**FIRELESS** > FIRE
**FIRELIGHT** n light from a fire
**FIRELIT** adj lit by firelight
**FIRELOCK** n obsolete type of gunlock with a priming mechanism ignited by sparks
**FIRELOCKS** > FIRELOCK
**FIREMAN** n man whose job is to put out fires and rescue people endangered by them
**FIREMANIC** > FIREMAN
**FIREMARK** n plaque indicating that a building is insured
**FIREMARKS** > FIREMARK
**FIREMEN** > FIREMAN
**FIREPAN** n metal container for a fire in a room
**FIREPANS** > FIREPAN
**FIREPINK** n wildflower belonging to the pink family
**FIREPINKS** > FIREPINK
**FIREPLACE** n recess in a room for a fire
**FIREPLUG** n US and New Zealand name for a fire hydrant
**FIREPLUGS** > FIREPLUG
**FIREPOT** n Chinese fondue-like cooking pot
**FIREPOTS** > FIREPOT
**FIREPOWER** n amount of fire that may be delivered

by a unit or weapon
**FIREPROOF** adj capable of resisting damage by fire ▷ vb make resistant to fire
**FIRER** > FIRE
**FIREROOM** n stokehold
**FIREROOMS** > FIREROOM
**FIRERS** > FIRE
**FIRES** > FIRE
**FIRESHIP** n vessel loaded with flammable materials, ignited, and directed among enemy warships to set them alight
**FIRESHIPS** > FIRESHIP
**FIRESIDE** n hearth
**FIRESIDES** > FIRESIDE
**FIRESTONE** n sandstone that withstands intense heat, esp one used for lining kilns, furnaces, etc
**FIRESTORM** n uncontrollable blaze sustained by violent winds that are drawn into the column of rising hot air over the burning area: often the result of heavy bombing
**FIRETHORN** n any rosaceous evergreen spiny shrub of the genus Pyracantha, of SE Europe and Asia, having bright red or orange fruits: cultivated for ornament
**FIRETRAP** n building that would burn easily or one without fire escapes
**FIRETRAPS** > FIRETRAP
**FIRETRUCK** n fire engine
**FIREWALL** n appliance that prevents unauthorized access to a computer network from the internet
**FIREWALLS** > FIREWALL
**FIREWATER** n any alcoholic spirit
**FIREWEED** n any of various plants that appear as first vegetation in burnt-over areas, esp rosebay willowherb
**FIREWEEDS** > FIREWEED
**FIREWOMAN** n female firefighter
**FIREWOMEN** > FIREWOMAN
**FIREWOOD** n wood for burning
**FIREWOODS** > FIREWOOD
**FIREWORK** n device containing chemicals that is ignited to produce spectacular explosions and coloured sparks
**FIREWORKS** pl n show in which fireworks are let off
**FIREWORM** n cranberry worm
**FIREWORMS** > FIREWORM
**FIRIE** n in Australian English, informal word for a firefighter
**FIRIES** > FIRIE

**FIRING** n discharge of a firearm
**FIRINGS** > FIRING
**FIRK** vb beat
**FIRKED** > FIRK
**FIRKIN** n small wooden barrel or similar container
**FIRKING** > FIRK
**FIRKINS** > FIRKIN
**FIRKS** > FIRK
**FIRLOT** n unit of measurement for grain
**FIRLOTS** > FIRLOT
**FIRM** adj not soft or yielding ▷ adv in an unyielding manner ▷ vb make or become firm ▷ n business company
**FIRMAMENT** n sky or the heavens
**FIRMAN** n edict of an Oriental sovereign
**FIRMANS** > FIRMAN
**FIRMED** > FIRM
**FIRMER** > FIRM
**FIRMERS** > FIRM
**FIRMEST** > FIRM
**FIRMING** > FIRM
**FIRMLESS** adj unstable
**FIRMLY** > FIRM
**FIRMNESS** > FIRM
**FIRMS** > FIRM
**FIRMWARE** n fixed form of software programmed into a read-only memory
**FIRMWARES** > FIRMWARE
**FIRN** another name for > NEVE
**FIRNS** > FIRN
**FIRRIER** > FIRRY
**FIRRIEST** > FIRRY
**FIRRING** n wooden battens used in building construction
**FIRRINGS** > FIRRING
**FIRRY** adj of, relating to, or made from fir trees
**FIRS** > FIR
**FIRST** adj earliest in time or order ▷ n person or thing coming before all others ▷ adv before anything else
**FIRSTBORN** adj eldest of the children in a family ▷ n eldest child in a family
**FIRSTHAND** adj from the original source
**FIRSTLING** n first, esp the first offspring
**FIRSTLY** adv coming before other points, questions, etc
**FIRSTNESS** > FIRST
**FIRSTS** pl n saleable goods of the highest quality
**FIRTH** n narrow inlet of the sea, esp in Scotland
**FIRTHS** > FIRTH
**FISC** n state or royal treasury
**FISCAL** adj of government finances, esp taxes ▷ n (in some countries) a public

prosecutor
**FISCALIST** > FISCAL
**FISCALLY** > FISCAL
**FISCALS** > FISCAL
**FISCS** > FISC
**FISGIG** variant of > FISHGIG
**FISGIGS** > FISGIG
**FISH** n cold-blooded vertebrate with gills, that lives in water ▷ vb try to catch fish
**FISHABLE** > FISH
**FISHBALL** n fried ball of flaked fish and mashed potato
**FISHBALLS** > FISHBALL
**FISHBOLT** n bolt used for fastening a fishplate to a rail
**FISHBOLTS** > FISHBOLT
**FISHBONE** n bone of a fish
**FISHBONES** > FISHBONE
**FISHBOWL** n goldfish bowl
**FISHBOWLS** > FISHBOWL
**FISHCAKE** n mixture of flaked fish and mashed potatoes formed into a flat circular shape
**FISHCAKES** > FISHCAKE
**FISHED** > FISH
**FISHER** n fisherman
**FISHERIES** > FISHERY
**FISHERMAN** n person who catches fish for a living or for pleasure
**FISHERMEN** > FISHERMAN
**FISHERS** > FISHER
**FISHERY** n area of the sea used for fishing
**FISHES** > FISH
**FISHEYE** n in photography, a lens of small focal length, having a highly curved protruding front element, that covers an angle of view of almost 180°
**FISHEYES** > FISHEYE
**FISHFUL** adj teeming with fish
**FISHGIG** n pole with barbed prongs for impaling fish
**FISHGIGS** > FISHGIG
**FISHHOOK** n sharp hook used in angling, esp one with a barb
**FISHHOOKS** > FISHHOOK
**FISHIER** > FISHY
**FISHIEST** > FISHY
**FISHIFIED** > FISHIFY
**FISHIFIES** > FISHIFY
**FISHIFY** vb change into fish
**FISHILY** > FISHY
**FISHINESS** > FISHY
**FISHING** n job or pastime of catching fish
**FISHINGS** > FISHING
**FISHKILL** n mass killing of fish by pollution
**FISHKILLS** > FISHKILL
**FISHLESS** > FISH
**FISHLIKE** > FISH
**FISHLINE** n line used on a

**fishing-rod**
**FISHLINES** > FISHLINE
**FISHMEAL** n ground dried fish used as feed for farm animals or as a fertilizer
**FISHMEALS** > FISHMEAL
**FISHNET** n open mesh fabric resembling netting
**FISHNETS** > FISHNET
**FISHPLATE** n metal plate holding rails together
**FISHPOLE** n boom arm for a microphone
**FISHPOLES** > FISHPOLE
**FISHPOND** > FISH
**FISHPONDS** > FISH
**FISHSKIN** n skin of a fish
**FISHSKINS** > FISHSKIN
**FISHTAIL** n nozzle having a long narrow slot at the top, placed over a Bunsen burner to produce a thin fanlike flame ▷ vb slow an aeroplane by moving the tail from side to side
**FISHTAILS** > FISHTAIL
**FISHWAY** n fish ladder
**FISHWAYS** > FISHWAY
**FISHWIFE** n coarse scolding woman
**FISHWIVES** > FISHWIFE
**FISHWORM** n worm used as fishing bait
**FISHWORMS** > FISHWORM
**FISHY** adj of or like fish
**FISHYBACK** n goods supply chain involving container transfer from lorry to ship
**FISK** vb frisk
**FISKED** > FISK
**FISKING** > FISK
**FISKS** > FISK
**FISNOMIE** n physiognomy
**FISNOMIES** > FISNOMIE
**FISSATE** > FISSILE
**FISSILE** adj capable of undergoing nuclear fission
**FISSILITY** > FISSILE
**FISSION** n splitting
**FISSIONAL** > FISSION
**FISSIONED** adj split or broken into parts
**FISSIONS** > FISSION
**FISSIPED** adj having toes that are separated from one another, as dogs, cats, bears, and similar carnivores ▷ n fissiped animal
**FISSIPEDE** > FISSIPED
**FISSIPEDS** > FISSIPED
**FISSIVE** > FISSILE
**FISSLE** vb rustle
**FISSLED** > FISSLE
**FISSLES** > FISSLE
**FISSLING** > FISSLE
**FISSURAL** > FISSURE
**FISSURE** n long narrow cleft or crack ▷ vb crack or split apart
**FISSURED** > FISSURE
**FISSURES** > FISSURE
**FISSURING** > FISSURE
**FIST** n clenched hand ▷ vb

hit with the fist
**FISTED** > FIST
**FISTFIGHT** n fight using bare fists
**FISTFUL** n quantity that can be held in a fist or hand
**FISTFULS** > FISTFUL
**FISTIANA** n world of boxing
**FISTIC** adj of or relating to fisticuffs or boxing
**FISTICAL** > FISTIC
**FISTICUFF** > FISTICUFFS
**FISTIER** > FIST
**FISTIEST** > FIST
**FISTING** > FIST
**FISTMELE** n measure of the width of a hand and the extended thumb, used to calculate the approximate height of the string of a braced bow
**FISTMELES** > FISTMELE
**FISTNOTE** n note in printed text preceded by the fist symbol
**FISTNOTES** > FISTNOTE
**FISTS** > FIST
**FISTULA** n long narrow ulcer
**FISTULAE** > FISTULA
**FISTULAR** same as > FISTULOUS
**FISTULAS** > FISTULA
**FISTULATE** same as > FISTULOUS
**FISTULOSE** variant of > FISTULOUS
**FISTULOUS** adj containing, relating to, or resembling a fistula
**FISTY** > FIST
**FIT** vb be appropriate or suitable for ▷ adj appropriate ▷ n way in which something fits
**FITCH** n fur of the polecat or ferret
**FITCHE** adj pointed
**FITCHEE** variant of > FITCHE
**FITCHES** > FITCH
**FITCHET** same as > FITCH
**FITCHETS** > FITCHET
**FITCHEW** archaic name for > POLECAT
**FITCHEWS** > FITCHEW
**FITCHY** variant of > FITCHE
**FITFUL** adj occurring in irregular spells
**FITFULLY** > FITFUL
**FITLIER** > FITLY
**FITLIEST** > FITLY
**FITLY** adv in a proper manner or place or at a proper time
**FITMENT** n accessory attached to a machine
**FITMENTS** > FITMENT
**FITNA** n state of trouble or chaos
**FITNAS** > FITNA
**FITNESS** n state of being fit
**FITNESSES** > FITNESS
**FITS** > FIT

**FITT** n song
**FITTABLE** > FIT
**FITTE** variant of > FITT
**FITTED** > FIT
**FITTER** > FIT
**FITTERS** > FIT
**FITTES** > FITTE
**FITTEST** > FIT
**FITTING** > FIT
**FITTINGLY** > FIT
**FITTINGS** > FIT
**FITTS** > FITT
**FIVE** n one more than four ▷ adj amounting to five ▷ determiner amounting to five
**FIVEFOLD** adj having five times as many or as much ▷ adv by five times as many or as much
**FIVEPENCE** n five-penny coin
**FIVEPENNY** adj (of a nail) one and three-quarters of an inch in length
**FIVEPIN** > FIVEPINS
**FIVEPINS** n bowling game played esp in Canada
**FIVER** n five-pound note
**FIVERS** > FIVER
**FIVES** n ball game resembling squash but played with bats or the hands
**FIX** vb make or become firm, stable, or secure ▷ n difficult situation
**FIXABLE** > FIX
**FIXATE** vb become or cause to become fixed
**FIXATED** > FIXATE
**FIXATES** > FIXATE
**FIXATIF** variant of > FIXATIVE
**FIXATIFS** > FIXATIF
**FIXATING** > FIXATE
**FIXATION** n obsessive interest in something
**FIXATIONS** > FIXATION
**FIXATIVE** n liquid used to preserve or hold things in place ▷ adj serving or tending to fix
**FIXATIVES** > FIXATIVE
**FIXATURE** n something that holds an object in place
**FIXATURES** > FIXATURE
**FIXED** adj attached or placed so as to be immovable
**FIXEDLY** > FIXED
**FIXEDNESS** > FIXED
**FIXER** n solution used to make a photographic image permanent
**FIXERS** > FIXER
**FIXES** > FIX
**FIXING** n means of attaching one thing to another, as a pipe to a wall, slate to a roof, etc
**FIXINGS** pl n apparatus or equipment

**FIXIT** n solution to a complex problem
**FIXITIES** > FIXITY
**FIXITY** n state or quality of a person's gaze, attitude, or concentration not changing or weakening
**FIXIVE** > FIX
**FIXT** adj fixed
**FIXTURE** n permanently fitted piece of household equipment
**FIXTURES** > FIXTURE
**FIXURE** n firmness
**FIXURES** > FIXURE
**FIZ** variant of > FIZZ
**FIZGIG** same as > FISHGIG
**FIZGIGS** > FIZGIG
**FIZZ** vb make a hissing or bubbling noise ▷ n hissing or bubbling noise
**FIZZED** > FIZZ
**FIZZEN** variant of > FOISON
**FIZZENS** > FIZZEN
**FIZZER** n anything that fizzes
**FIZZERS** > FIZZER
**FIZZES** > FIZZ
**FIZZGIG** variant of > FISHGIG
**FIZZGIGS** > FIZZGIG
**FIZZIER** > FIZZ
**FIZZIEST** > FIZZ
**FIZZINESS** > FIZZ
**FIZZING** > FIZZ
**FIZZINGS** > FIZZ
**FIZZLE** vb make a weak hissing or bubbling sound ▷ n hissing or bubbling sound
**FIZZLED** > FIZZLE
**FIZZLES** > FIZZLE
**FIZZLING** > FIZZLE
**FIZZY** > FIZZ
**FJELD** n high rocky plateau with little vegetation in Scandinavian countries
**FJELDS** > FJELD
**FJORD** n long narrow inlet of the sea between cliffs, esp in Norway
**FJORDIC** > FJORD
**FJORDS** > FJORD
**FLAB** n unsightly body fat
**FLABBIER** > FLABBY
**FLABBIEST** > FLABBY
**FLABBILY** > FLABBY
**FLABBY** adj having flabby flesh
**FLABELLA** > FLABELLUM
**FLABELLUM** n fan-shaped organ or part, such as the tip of the proboscis of a honeybee
**FLABS** > FLAB
**FLACCID** adj soft and limp
**FLACCIDER** > FLACCID
**FLACCIDLY** > FLACCID
**FLACK** vb flutter
**FLACKED** > FLACK
**FLACKER** vb flutter like a bird
**FLACKERED** > FLACKER
**FLACKERS** > FLACKER

**FLACKERY** > FLACK
**FLACKET** n flagon
**FLACKETS** > FLACKET
**FLACKING** > FLACK
**FLACKS** > FLACK
**FLACON** n small stoppered bottle or flask, such as one used for perfume
**FLACONS** > FLACON
**FLAFF** vb flap
**FLAFFED** > FLAFF
**FLAFFER** vb flutter
**FLAFFERED** > FLAFFER
**FLAFFERS** > FLAFFER
**FLAFFING** > FLAFF
**FLAFFS** > FLAFF
**FLAG** n piece of cloth attached to a pole as an emblem or signal ▷ vb mark with a flag or sticker
**FLAGELLA** > FLAGELLUM
**FLAGELLAR** > FLAGELLUM
**FLAGELLIN** n structural protein of bacterial flagella
**FLAGELLUM** n whiplike outgrowth from a cell that acts as an organ of movement
**FLAGEOLET** n small instrument like a recorder
**FLAGGED** > FLAG
**FLAGGER** > FLAG
**FLAGGERS** > FLAG
**FLAGGIER** > FLAGGY
**FLAGGIEST** > FLAGGY
**FLAGGING** > FLAG
**FLAGGINGS** > FLAG
**FLAGGY** adj drooping
**FLAGITATE** vb importune
**FLAGLESS** > FLAG
**FLAGMAN** n person who has charge of, carries, or signals with a flag, esp a railway employee
**FLAGMEN** > FLAGMAN
**FLAGON** n wide bottle for wine or cider
**FLAGONS** > FLAGON
**FLAGPOLE** n pole for a flag
**FLAGPOLES** > FLAGPOLE
**FLAGRANCE** > FLAGRANT
**FLAGRANCY** > FLAGRANT
**FLAGRANT** adj openly outrageous
**FLAGS** > FLAG
**FLAGSHIP** n admiral's ship
**FLAGSHIPS** > FLAGSHIP
**FLAGSTAFF** same as > FLAGPOLE
**FLAGSTICK** n in golf, pole used to indicate position of hole
**FLAGSTONE** n flat slab of hard stone for paving
**FLAIL** vb wave about wildly ▷ n tool formerly used for threshing grain by hand
**FLAILED** > FLAIL
**FLAILING** > FLAIL
**FLAILS** > FLAIL
**FLAIR** n natural ability
**FLAIRS** > FLAIR
**FLAK** n anti-aircraft fire

**FLAKE** n small thin piece, esp chipped off something ▷ vb peel off in flakes
**FLAKED** > FLAKE
**FLAKER** > FLAKE
**FLAKERS** > FLAKE
**FLAKES** > FLAKE
**FLAKEY** same as > FLAKY
**FLAKIER** > FLAKY
**FLAKIES** n dandruff
**FLAKIEST** > FLAKY
**FLAKILY** > FLAKY
**FLAKINESS** > FLAKY
**FLAKING** > FLAKE
**FLAKS** > FLAK
**FLAKY** adj like or made of flakes
**FLAM** n falsehood, deception, or sham ▷ vb cheat or deceive
**FLAMBE** vb cook or serve (food) in flaming brandy ▷ adj (of food, such as steak or pancakes) served in flaming brandy
**FLAMBEAU** n burning torch, as used in night processions
**FLAMBEAUS** > FLAMBEAU
**FLAMBEAUX** > FLAMBEAU
**FLAMBEE** same as > FLAMBE
**FLAMBEED** > FLAMBEE
**FLAMBEES** > FLAMBEE
**FLAMBEING** > FLAMBE
**FLAMBES** > FLAMBE
**FLAME** n luminous burning gas coming from burning material ▷ vb burn brightly
**FLAMED** > FLAME
**FLAMELESS** > FLAME
**FLAMELET** > FLAME
**FLAMELETS** > FLAME
**FLAMELIKE** > FLAME
**FLAMEN** n (in ancient Rome) any of 15 priests who each served a particular deity
**FLAMENCO** n rhythmical Spanish dance accompanied by a guitar and vocalist
**FLAMENCOS** > FLAMENCO
**FLAMENS** > FLAMEN
**FLAMEOUT** n failure of an aircraft jet engine in flight due to extinction of the flame ▷ vb (of a jet engine) to fail in flight or to cause (a jet engine) to fail in flight
**FLAMEOUTS** > FLAMEOUT
**FLAMER** > FLAME
**FLAMERS** > FLAME
**FLAMES** > FLAME
**FLAMFEW** n fantastic trifle
**FLAMFEWS** > FLAMFEW
**FLAMIER** > FLAME
**FLAMIEST** > FLAME
**FLAMINES** > FLAMEN
**FLAMING** adj burning with flames ▷ adv extremely
**FLAMINGLY** > FLAMING
**FLAMINGO** n large pink

wading bird with a long neck and legs
**FLAMINGOS** > FLAMINGO
**FLAMM** variant of > FLAM
**FLAMMABLE** adj easily set on fire
**FLAMMED** > FLAM
**FLAMMING** > FLAM
**FLAMMS** > FLAMM
**FLAMMULE** n small flame
**FLAMMULES** > FLAMMULE
**FLAMS** > FLAM
**FLAMY** > FLAME
**FLAN** n open sweet or savoury tart
**FLANCARD** n armour covering a horse's flank
**FLANCARDS** > FLANCARD
**FLANCH** variant of > FLAUNCH
**FLANCHED** > FLANCH
**FLANCHES** > FLANCH
**FLANCHING** > FLANCH
**FLANERIE** n aimless strolling or lounging
**FLANERIES** > FLANERIE
**FLANES** n arrows
**FLANEUR** n idler or loafer
**FLANEURS** > FLANEUR
**FLANGE** n projecting rim or collar ▷ vb attach or provide (a component) with a flange
**FLANGED** > FLANGE
**FLANGER** > FLANGE
**FLANGERS** > FLANGE
**FLANGES** > FLANGE
**FLANGING** > FLANGE
**FLANK** n part of the side between the hips and ribs ▷ vb be at or move along the side of
**FLANKED** > FLANK
**FLANKEN** n cut of beef
**FLANKER** n one of a detachment of soldiers detailed to guard the flanks, esp of a formation
**FLANKERED** > FLANKER
**FLANKERS** > FLANKER
**FLANKING** > FLANK
**FLANKS** > FLANK
**FLANNEL** n small piece of cloth for washing the face ▷ vb talk evasively
**FLANNELED** > FLANNEL
**FLANNELET** n cotton imitation of flannel
**FLANNELLY** > FLANNEL
**FLANNELS** > FLANNEL
**FLANNEN** adj made of flannel
**FLANNENS** > FLANNEN
**FLANS** > FLAN
**FLAP** vb move back and forwards or up and down ▷ n action or sound of flapping
**FLAPERON** n control flap on aircraft wing
**FLAPERONS** > FLAPERON
**FLAPJACK** n chewy biscuit made with oats
**FLAPJACKS** > FLAPJACK

**FLAPLESS** > FLAP
**FLAPPABLE** > FLAP
**FLAPPED** > FLAP
**FLAPPER** n (in the 1920s) a lively young woman who dressed and behaved unconventionally
**FLAPPERS** > FLAPPER
**FLAPPIER** > FLAPPY
**FLAPPIEST** > FLAPPY
**FLAPPING** > FLAP
**FLAPPINGS** > FLAP
**FLAPPY** adj loose
**FLAPS** > FLAP
**FLAPTRACK** n component in an aircraft wing
**FLARE** vb blaze with a sudden unsteady flame ▷ n sudden unsteady flame
**FLAREBACK** n flame in the breech of a gun when fired
**FLARED** > FLARE
**FLARES** pl n trousers with legs that widen below the knee
**FLAREUP** n outbreak of something
**FLAREUPS** > FLAREUP
**FLARIER** > FLARE
**FLARIEST** > FLARE
**FLARING** > FLARE
**FLARINGLY** > FLARE
**FLARY** > FLARE
**FLASER** n type of sedimentary structure in rock
**FLASERS** > FLASER
**FLASH** n sudden burst of light or flame ▷ adj vulgarly showy ▷ vb (cause to) burst into flame
**FLASHBACK** n scene in a book, play, or film, that shows earlier events ▷ vb return in a novel, film, etc, to a past event
**FLASHBULB** n small light bulb that produces a bright flash of light
**FLASHCARD** n card shown briefly as a memory test
**FLASHCUBE** n in photography, a cube with a bulb that is attached to a camera
**FLASHED** > FLASH
**FLASHER** n man who exposes himself indecently
**FLASHERS** > FLASHER
**FLASHES** > FLASH
**FLASHEST** > FLASH
**FLASHGUN** n type of electronic flash, attachable to or sometimes incorporated in a camera, that emits a very brief flash of light when the shutter is open
**FLASHGUNS** > FLASHGUN
**FLASHIER** > FLASHY
**FLASHIEST** > FLASHY
**FLASHILY** > FLASHY
**FLASHING** n watertight

material used to cover joins in a roof

**FLASHINGS** > FLASHING

**FLASHLAMP** n electric lamp producing a flash of intense light

**FLASHOVER** n electric discharge over or around the surface of an insulator

**FLASHTUBE** n tube used in a flashlamp

**FLASHY** adj showy in a vulgar way

**FLASK** n flat bottle for carrying alcoholic drink in the pocket

**FLASKET** n long shallow basket

**FLASKETS** > FLASKET

**FLASKS** > FLASK

**FLAT** adj level and horizontal ▷ adv in or into a flat position ▷ n flat surface ▷ vb live in a flat

**FLATBACK** n flat-backed ornament, designed for viewing from front

**FLATBACKS** > FLATBACK

**FLATBED** n printing machine on which the type forme is carried on a flat bed under a revolving paper-bearing cylinder

**FLATBEDS** > FLATBED

**FLATBOAT** n flat-bottomed boat for transporting goods on a canal

**FLATBOATS** > FLATBOAT

**FLATBREAD** n type of thin unleavened bread

**FLATCAP** n Elizabethan man's hat with a narrow down-turned brim

**FLATCAPS** > FLATCAP

**FLATCAR** n flatbed

**FLATCARS** > FLATCAR

**FLATETTE** n very small flat

**FLATETTES** > FLATETTE

**FLATFEET** > FLATFOOT

**FLATFISH** n sea fish, such as the sole, which has a flat body

**FLATFOOT** n condition in which the entire sole of the foot is able to touch the ground because of flattening of the instep arch

**FLATFOOTS** > FLATFOOT

**FLATHEAD** n common Australian flatfish

**FLATHEADS** > FLATHEAD

**FLATIRON** n (formerly) an iron for pressing clothes that was heated by being placed on a stove

**FLATIRONS** > FLATIRON

**FLATLAND** n land notable for its levelness

**FLATLANDS** > FLATLAND

**FLATLET** n small flat

**FLATLETS** > FLATLET

**FLATLINE** vb die or be so near death that the

display of one's vital signs on medical monitoring equipment shows a flat line rather than peaks and troughs

**FLATLINED** > FLATLINE

**FLATLINER** > FLATLINE

**FLATLINES** > FLATLINE

**FLATLING** adv in a flat or prostrate position ▷ adj with the flat side, as of a sword

**FLATLINGS** same as > FLATLING

**FLATLONG** adv prostrate

**FLATLY** > FLAT

**FLATMATE** n person with whom one shares a flat

**FLATMATES** > FLATMATE

**FLATNESS** > FLAT

**FLATPACK** n (of a piece of furniture, equipment, or other construction) supplied in pieces packed into a flat box for assembly by the buyer

**FLATPACKS** > FLATPACK

**FLATS** > FLAT

**FLATSHARE** n state of living in a flat where each occupant shares the facilities and expenses ▷ vb live in a flat with other people who are not relatives

**FLATTED** > FLAT

**FLATTEN** vb make or become flat or flatter

**FLATTENED** > FLATTEN

**FLATTENER** > FLATTEN

**FLATTENS** > FLATTEN

**FLATTER** vb praise insincerely

**FLATTERED** > FLATTER

**FLATTERER** > FLATTER

**FLATTERS** > FLATTER

**FLATTERY** n excessive or insincere praise

**FLATTEST** > FLAT

**FLATTIE** n flat tyre

**FLATTIES** > FLATTIE

**FLATTING** > FLAT

**FLATTINGS** > FLAT

**FLATTISH** adj somewhat flat

**FLATTOP** n informal name for an aircraft carrier

**FLATTOPS** > FLATTOP

**FLATTY** n flat shoe

**FLATULENT** adj suffering from or caused by too much gas in the intestines

**FLATUOUS** > FLATUS

**FLATUS** n gas generated in the alimentary canal

**FLATUSES** > FLATUS

**FLATWARE** n cutlery

**FLATWARES** > FLATWARE

**FLATWASH** n laundry that can be ironed mechanically

**FLATWAYS** adv with the flat or broad side down or in contact with another

surface

**FLATWISE** same as > FLATWAYS

**FLATWORK** n laundry that can be ironed mechanically

**FLATWORKS** > FLATWORK

**FLATWORM** n worm, such as a tapeworm, with a flattened body

**FLATWORMS** > FLATWORM

**FLAUGHT** vb flutter

**FLAUGHTED** > FLAUGHT

**FLAUGHTER** vb cut peat

**FLAUGHTS** > FLAUGHT

**FLAUNCH** n cement or mortar slope around a chimney top, manhole, etc, to throw off water ▷ vb cause to slope in this manner

**FLAUNCHED** > FLAUNCH

**FLAUNCHES** > FLAUNCH

**FLAUNE** variant of > FLAM

**FLAUNES** > FLAUNE

**FLAUNT** vb display (oneself or one's possessions) arrogantly ▷ n act of flaunting

**FLAUNTED** > FLAUNT

**FLAUNTER** > FLAUNT

**FLAUNTERS** > FLAUNT

**FLAUNTIER** > FLAUNTY

**FLAUNTILY** > FLAUNTY

**FLAUNTING** > FLAUNT

**FLAUNTS** > FLAUNT

**FLAUNTY** adj characterized by or inclined to ostentatious display or flaunting

**FLAUTA** n tortilla rolled around a filling

**FLAUTAS** > FLAUTA

**FLAUTIST** n flute player

**FLAUTISTS** > FLAUTIST

**FLAVANOL** n type of flavonoid

**FLAVANOLS** > FLAVANOL

**FLAVANONE** n flavone-derived compound

**FLAVIN** n heterocyclic ketone

**FLAVINE** same as > FLAVIN

**FLAVINES** > FLAVINE

**FLAVINS** > FLAVIN

**FLAVONE** n crystalline compound occurring in plants

**FLAVONES** > FLAVONE

**FLAVONOID** n any of a group of organic compounds that occur as pigments in fruit and flowers

**FLAVONOL** n flavonoid that occurs in red wine and is said to offer protection against heart disease

**FLAVONOLS** > FLAVONOL

**FLAVOR** same as > FLAVOUR

**FLAVORED** > FLAVOR

**FLAVORER** > FLAVOR

**FLAVORERS** > FLAVOR

**FLAVORFUL** same

as > FLAVOURFUL

**FLAVORING** same as > FLAVORING

**FLAVORIST** n blender of ingredients, to create or enhance flavours

**FLAVOROUS** adj having flavour

**FLAVORS** > FLAVOR

**FLAVORY** adj flavoursome

**FLAVOUR** n distinctive taste ▷ vb give flavour to

**FLAVOURED** > FLAVOUR

**FLAVOURER** > FLAVOUR

**FLAVOURS** > FLAVOUR

**FLAVOURY** adj flavoursome

**FLAW** n imperfection or blemish ▷ vb make or become blemished, defective, or imperfect

**FLAWED** > FLAW

**FLAWIER** > FLAW

**FLAWIEST** > FLAW

**FLAWING** > FLAW

**FLAWLESS** > FLAW

**FLAWN** variant of > FLAM

**FLAWNS** > FLAWN

**FLAWS** > FLAW

**FLAWY** > FLAW

**FLAX** n plant grown for its stem fibres and seeds

**FLAXEN** adj (of hair) pale yellow

**FLAXES** > FLAX

**FLAXIER** > FLAXY

**FLAXIEST** > FLAXY

**FLAXSEED** n seed of the flax plant, which yields linseed oil

**FLAXSEEDS** > FLAXSEED

**FLAXY** same as > FLAXEN

**FLAY** same as > FLEY

**FLAYED** > FLAY

**FLAYER** > FLAY

**FLAYERS** > FLAY

**FLAYING** > FLAY

**FLAYS** > FLAY

**FLAYSOME** adj frightening

**FLEA** n small wingless jumping bloodsucking insect

**FLEABAG** n dirty or unkempt person, esp a woman

**FLEABAGS** > FLEABAG

**FLEABANE** as in Canadian fleabane

**FLEABANES** > FLEABANE

**FLEABITE** n bite of a flea

**FLEABITES** > FLEABITE

**FLEAM** n lancet used for letting blood

**FLEAMS** > FLEAM

**FLEAPIT** n shabby cinema or theatre

**FLEAPITS** > FLEAPIT

**FLEAS** > FLEA

**FLEASOME** > FLEA

**FLEAWORT** n any of various plants of the genus Senecio, esp S. integrifolius, a European species with yellow daisy-like flowers and rosettes of downy leaves: family *Asteraceae* (composites)

FLEAWORTS > FLEAWORT

FLECHE *n* slender spire, esp over the intersection of the nave and transept ridges of a church roof

FLECHES > FLECHE

FLECHETTE *n* steel dart or missile dropped from an aircraft, as in World War I

FLECK *n* small mark, streak, or speck ▷ *vb* speckle

FLECKED > FLECK

FLECKER *same as* > FLECK

FLECKERED > FLECKER

FLECKERS > FLECKER

FLECKING > FLECK

FLECKLESS > FLECK

FLECKS > FLECK

FLECKY > FLECK

FLECTION *n* act of bending or the state of being bent

FLECTIONS > FLECTION

FLED > FLEE

FLEDGE *vb* feed and care for (a young bird) until it is able to fly

FLEDGED > FLEDGE

FLEDGES > FLEDGE

FLEDGIER > FLEDGY

FLEDGIEST > FLEDGY

FLEDGING > FLEDGE

FLEDGLING *n* young bird ▷ *adj* new or inexperienced

FLEDGY *adj* feathery or feathered

FLEE *vb* run away (from)

FLEECE *n* sheep's coat of wool ▷ *vb* defraud or overcharge

FLEECED > FLEECE

FLEECER > FLEECE

FLEECERS > FLEECE

FLEECES > FLEECE

FLEECH *vb* flatter

FLEECHED > FLEECH

FLEECHES > FLEECH

FLEECHING > FLEECH

FLEECIE *n* person who collects fleeces after shearing and prepares them for baling

FLEECIER > FLEECY

FLEECIES > FLEECIE

FLEECIEST > FLEECY

FLEECILY > FLEECY

FLEECING > FLEECE

FLEECY *adj* made of or like fleece ▷ *n* person who collects fleeces after shearing and prepares them for baling

FLEEIN > FLEE

FLEEING > FLEE

FLEER *vb* grin or laugh at ▷ *n* derisory glance or grin

FLEERED > FLEER

FLEERER > FLEER

FLEERERS > FLEER

FLEERING > FLEER

FLEERINGS > FLEER

FLEERS > FLEER

FLEES > FLEE

FLEET *n* number of warships organized as a unit ▷ *adj* swift in movement ▷ *vb* move rapidly

FLEETED > FLEET

FLEETER > FLEET

FLEETEST > FLEET

FLEETING *adj* rapid and soon passing

FLEETLY > FLEET

FLEETNESS > FLEET

FLEETS > FLEET

FLEG *vb* scare

FLEGGED > FLEG

FLEGGING > FLEG

FLEGS > FLEG

FLEHMEN *vb* (of mammal) grimace

FLEHMENED > FLEHMEN

FLEHMENS > FLEHMEN

FLEISHIG *same as* > FLEISHIK

FLEISHIK *adj* (of food) containing or derived from meat or meat products and therefore to be prepared and eaten separately from dairy foods

FLEME *vb* drive out

FLEMES > FLEME

FLEMING *n* native or inhabitant of Flanders or a Flemish-speaking Belgian

FLEMISH *vb* stow (a rope) in a Flemish coil

FLEMISHED > FLEMISH

FLEMISHES > FLEMISH

FLEMIT > FLEME

FLENCH *same as* > FLENSE

FLENCHED > FLENCH

FLENCHER > FLENCH

FLENCHERS > FLENCH

FLENCHES > FLENCH

FLENCHING > FLENCH

FLENSE *vb* strip (a whale, seal, etc) of (its blubber or skin)

FLENSED > FLENSE

FLENSER > FLENSE

FLENSERS > FLENSE

FLENSES > FLENSE

FLENSING > FLENSE

FLESH *n* soft part of a human or animal body

FLESHED > FLESH

FLESHER *n* person or machine that fleshes hides or skins

FLESHERS > FLESHER

FLESHES > FLESH

FLESHHOOD *n* incarnation

FLESHIER > FLESHY

FLESHIEST > FLESHY

FLESHILY > FLESHY

FLESHING > FLESH

FLESHINGS *pl n* flesh-coloured tights

FLESHLESS > FLESH

FLESHLIER > FLESHLY

FLESHLING *n* voluptuary

FLESHLY *adj* carnal

FLESHMENT *n* act of fleshing

FLESHPOT *n* pot in which meat is cooked

FLESHPOTS *pl n* places, such as brothels and strip clubs, where sexual desires are catered to

FLESHWORM *n* flesh-eating worm

FLESHY *adj* plump

FLETCH *same as* > FLEDGE

FLETCHED > FLETCH

FLETCHER *n* person who makes arrows

FLETCHERS > FLETCHER

FLETCHES > FLETCH

FLETCHING > FLETCH

FLETTON *n* type of brick

FLETTONS > FLETTON

FLEURET *same as* > FLEURETTE

FLEURETS > FLEURET

FLEURETTE *n* ornament resembling a flower

FLEURON *n* decorative piece of pastry

FLEURONS > FLEURON

FLEURY *same as* > FLORY

FLEW > FLY

FLEWED *adj* having large flews

FLEWS *pl n* fleshy hanging upper lip of a bloodhound or similar dog

FLEX *n* flexible insulated electric cable ▷ *vb* bend

FLEXAGON *n* hexagon made from a single pliable strip of triangles

FLEXAGONS > FLEXAGON

FLEXED > FLEX

FLEXES > FLEX

FLEXIBLE *adj* easily bent

FLEXIBLY > FLEXIBLE

FLEXILE *same as* > FLEXIBLE

FLEXING > FLEX

FLEXION *n* act of bending a joint or limb

FLEXIONAL > FLEXION

FLEXIONS > FLEXION

FLEXITIME *n* system permitting variation in starting and finishing times of work

FLEXO *n, adj, adv* flexography

FLEXOR *n* any muscle whose contraction serves to bend a joint or limb

FLEXORS > FLEXOR

FLEXOS > FLEXO

FLEXTIME *same as* > FLEXITIME

FLEXTIMER > FLEXTIME

FLEXTIMES > FLEXTIME

FLEXUOSE *same as* > FLEXUOUS

FLEXUOUS *adj* full of bends or curves

FLEXURAL > FLEXURE

FLEXURE *n* act of flexing or the state of being flexed

FLEXURES > FLEXURE

FLEY *vb* be afraid or cause to be afraid

FLEYED > FLEY

FLEYING > FLEY

FLEYS > FLEY

FLIBBERT *n* small piece or bit

FLIBBERTS > FLIBBERT

FLIC *n* French police officer

FLICHTER *vb* flutter

FLICHTERS > FLICHTER

FLICK *vb* touch or move with the finger or hand in a quick movement ▷ *n* tap or quick stroke

FLICKABLE > FLICK

FLICKED > FLICK

FLICKER *vb* shine unsteadily or intermittently ▷ *n* unsteady brief flight

FLICKERED > FLICKER

FLICKERS > FLICKER

FLICKERY > FLICKER

FLICKING > FLICK

FLICKS > FLICK

FLICS > FLIC

FLIED > FLY

FLIER > FLY

FLIERS > FLY

FLIES > FLY

FLIEST > FLY

FLIGHT *n* journey by air ▷ *vb* cause (a ball, dart, etc) to float slowly or deceptively towards its target

FLIGHTED > FLIGHT

FLIGHTIER > FLIGHTY

FLIGHTILY > FLIGHTY

FLIGHTING > FLIGHT

FLIGHTS > FLIGHT

FLIGHTY *adj* frivolous and fickle

FLIM *n* five-pound note

FLIMFLAM *n* nonsense ▷ *vb* deceive

FLIMFLAMS > FLIMFLAM

FLIMP *vb* steal

FLIMPED > FLIMP

FLIMPING > FLIMP

FLIMPS > FLIMP

FLIMS > FLIM

FLIMSIER > FLIMSY

FLIMSIES > FLIMSY

FLIMSIEST > FLIMSY

FLIMSILY > FLIMSY

FLIMSY *adj* not strong or substantial ▷ *n* thin paper used for making carbon copies of a letter, etc

FLINCH *same as* > FLENSE

FLINCHED > FLINCH

FLINCHER > FLINCH

FLINCHERS > FLINCH

FLINCHES > FLINCH

FLINCHING > FLINCH

FLINDER *n* fragment

FLINDERS > FLINDER

FLING *vb* throw, send, or move forcefully or hurriedly ▷ *n* spell of self-indulgent enjoyment

FLINGER > FLING

FLINGERS > FLING

**FLINGING** > FLING

**FLINGS** > FLING

**FLINKITE** n anhydrous phosphate

**FLINKITES** > FLINKITE

**FLINT** n hard grey stone ▷ vb fit or provide with a flint

**FLINTED** > FLINT

**FLINTHEAD** n American wading bird

**FLINTIER** > FLINTY

**FLINTIEST** > FLINTY

**FLINTIFY** vb turn to flint

**FLINTILY** > FLINTY

**FLINTING** > FLINT

**FLINTLIKE** > FLINT

**FLINTLOCK** n obsolete gun in which the powder was lit by a spark from a flint

**FLINTS** > FLINT

**FLINTY** adj cruel

**FLIP** vb throw (something small or light) carelessly ▷ n snap or tap ▷ adj flippant

**FLIPBOOK** n book of drawings made to seem animated by flipping pages

**FLIPBOOKS** > FLIPBOOK

**FLIPFLOP** n rubber sandal

**FLIPFLOPS** > FLIPFLOP

**FLIPPANCY** > FLIPPANT

**FLIPPANT** adj treating serious things lightly

**FLIPPED** > FLIP

**FLIPPER** n limb of a sea animal adapted for swimming

**FLIPPERS** > FLIPPER

**FLIPPEST** > FLIP

**FLIPPING** > FLIP

**FLIPPY** adj (of clothes) tending to move to and fro as the wearer walks

**FLIPS** > FLIP

**FLIR** n forward looking infrared radar

**FLIRS** > FLIR

**FLIRT** vb behave as if sexually attracted to someone ▷ n person who flirts

**FLIRTED** > FLIRT

**FLIRTER** > FLIRT

**FLIRTERS** > FLIRT

**FLIRTIER** > FLIRT

**FLIRTIEST** > FLIRT

**FLIRTING** > FLIRT

**FLIRTINGS** > FLIRT

**FLIRTISH** > FLIRT

**FLIRTS** > FLIRT

**FLIRTY** > FLIRT

**FLISK** vb skip

**FLISKED** > FLISK

**FLISKIER** > FLISK

**FLISKIEST** > FLISK

**FLISKING** > FLISK

**FLISKS** > FLISK

**FLISKY** > FLISK

**FLIT** vb move lightly and rapidly ▷ n act of flitting

**FLITCH** n side of pork

salted and cured ▷ vb cut (a tree trunk) into flitches

**FLITCHED** > FLITCH

**FLITCHES** > FLITCH

**FLITCHING** > FLITCH

**FLITE** vb scold or rail at ▷ n dispute or scolding

**FLITED** > FLITE

**FLITES** > FLITE

**FLITING** > FLITE

**FLITS** > FLIT

**FLITT** adj fleet

**FLITTED** > FLIT

**FLITTER** > FLIT

**FLITTERED** > FLIT

**FLITTERN** n bark of young oak tree

**FLITTERNS** > FLITTERN

**FLITTERS** > FLIT

**FLITTING** > FLIT

**FLITTINGS** > FLIT

**FLIVVER** n old, cheap, or battered car

**FLIVVERS** > FLIVVER

**FLIX** n fur ▷ vb have fur

**FLIXED** > FLIX

**FLIXES** > FLIX

**FLIXING** > FLIX

**FLOAT** vb rest on the surface of a liquid ▷ n light object used to help someone or something float

**FLOATABLE** > FLOAT

**FLOATAGE** same as > FLOTAGE

**FLOATAGES** > FLOATAGE

**FLOATANT** n substance used in fly-fishing, to help dry flies to float

**FLOATANTS** > FLOATANT

**FLOATCUT** as in floatcut file file with rows of parallel teeth

**FLOATED** > FLOAT

**FLOATEL** same as > FLOTEL

**FLOATELS** > FLOATEL

**FLOATER** n person or thing that floats

**FLOATERS** > FLOATER

**FLOATIER** > FLOATY

**FLOATIEST** > FLOATY

**FLOATING** adj moving about, changing

**FLOATINGS** > FLOATING

**FLOATS** pl n footlights

**FLOATY** adj filmy and light

**FLOC** same as > FLOCK

**FLOCCED** > FLOC

**FLOCCI** > FLOCCUS

**FLOCCING** > FLOC

**FLOCCOSE** adj consisting of or covered with woolly tufts or hairs

**FLOCCULAR** > FLOCCUS

**FLOCCULE** n small aggregate of flocculent material

**FLOCCULES** > FLOCCULE

**FLOCCULI** > FLOCCULUS

**FLOCCULUS** same as > FLOCCULE

**FLOCCUS** n downy or woolly covering, as on

the young of certain birds ▷ adj (of a cloud) having the appearance of woolly tufts at odd intervals in its structure

**FLOCK** n number of animals of one kind together ▷ vb gather in a crowd ▷ adj (of wallpaper) with a velvety raised pattern

**FLOCKED** > FLOCK

**FLOCKIER** > FLOCK

**FLOCKIEST** > FLOCK

**FLOCKING** > FLOCK

**FLOCKINGS** > FLOCK

**FLOCKLESS** > FLOCK

**FLOCKS** > FLOCK

**FLOCKY** > FLOCK

**FLOCS** > FLOC

**FLOE** n sheet of floating ice

**FLOES** > FLOE

**FLOG** vb beat with a whip or stick

**FLOGGABLE** > FLOG

**FLOGGED** > FLOG

**FLOGGER** > FLOG

**FLOGGERS** > FLOG

**FLOGGING** > FLOG

**FLOGGINGS** > FLOG

**FLOGS** > FLOG

**FLOKATI** n Greek hand-woven shaggy woollen rug

**FLOKATIS** > FLOKATI

**FLONG** n material, usually pulped paper or cardboard, used for making moulds in stereotyping

**FLONGS** > FLONG

**FLOOD** n overflow of water onto a normally dry area ▷ vb cover or become covered with water

**FLOODABLE** > FLOOD

**FLOODED** > FLOOD

**FLOODER** > FLOOD

**FLOODERS** > FLOOD

**FLOODGATE** n gate used to control the flow of water

**FLOODING** n submerging of land under water, esp due to heavy rain, a lake or river overflowing, etc

**FLOODINGS** > FLOODING

**FLOODLESS** > FLOOD

**FLOODLIT** adj illuminated with a floodlight

**FLOODMARK** n high-water mark

**FLOODS** > FLOOD

**FLOODTIDE** n rising tide

**FLOODWALL** n wall built as a defence against floods

**FLOODWAY** n conduit for floodwater

**FLOODWAYS** > FLOODWAY

**FLOOEY** adj awry

**FLOOIE** same as > FLOOEY

**FLOOR** n lower surface of a room ▷ vb knock down

**FLOORAGE** n area of floor

**FLOORAGES** > FLOORAGE

**FLOORED** > FLOOR

**FLOORER** n coup de grâce

**FLOORERS** > FLOORER

**FLOORHEAD** n upper side of a floor timber

**FLOORING** > FLOOR

**FLOORINGS** > FLOOR

**FLOORLESS** > FLOOR

**FLOORS** > FLOOR

**FLOORSHOW** n entertainment on floor of nightclub

**FLOOSIE** same as > FLOOZY

**FLOOSIES** > FLOOSIE

**FLOOSY** variant of > FLOOSIE

**FLOOZIE** same as > FLOOZY

**FLOOZIES** > FLOOZY

**FLOOZY** n disreputable woman

**FLOP** vb bend, fall, or collapse loosely or carelessly ▷ n failure

**FLOPHOUSE** n cheap lodging house, esp one used by tramps

**FLOPOVER** n TV visual effect of page being turned

**FLOPOVERS** > FLOPOVER

**FLOPPED** > FLOP

**FLOPPER** > FLOP

**FLOPPERS** > FLOP

**FLOPPIER** > FLOPPY

**FLOPPIES** > FLOPPY

**FLOPPIEST** > FLOPPY

**FLOPPILY** > FLOPPY

**FLOPPING** > FLOP

**FLOPPY** adj hanging downwards, loose ▷ n floppy disk

**FLOPS** > FLOP

**FLOPTICAL** n type of floppy disk

**FLOR** n yeast formed on the surface of sherry after fermentation

**FLORA** n plants of a given place or time

**FLORAE** > FLORA

**FLORAL** adj consisting of or decorated with flowers ▷ n class of perfume

**FLORALLY** > FLORAL

**FLORALS** > FLORAL

**FLORAS** > FLORA

**FLOREANT** > FLOREAT

**FLOREAT** vb may (a person, institution, etc) flourish

**FLOREATED** same as > FLORIATED

**FLORENCE** n type of fennel

**FLORENCES** > FLORENCE

**FLORET** n small flower forming part of a composite flower head

**FLORETS** > FLORET

**FLORIATED** adj having ornamentation based on flowers and leaves

**FLORICANE** n fruiting stem of plant

**FLORID** adj with a red or flushed complexion

**FLORIDEAN** n member of the red seaweed family

**FLORIDER** > FLORID

**FLORIDEST** > FLORID

**FLORIDITY** > FLORID

**FLORIDLY** > FLORID
**FLORIER** > FLORY
**FLORIEST** > FLORY
**FLORIFORM** adj flower-shaped
**FLORIGEN** n hypothetical plant hormone that induces flowering, thought to be synthesized in the leaves as a photoperiodic response and transmitted to the flower buds
**FLORIGENS** > FLORIGEN
**FLORIN** n former British and Australian coin
**FLORINS** > FLORIN
**FLORIST** n seller of flowers
**FLORISTIC** adj of or relating to flowers or a flora
**FLORISTRY** > FLORIST
**FLORISTS** > FLORIST
**FLORS** > FLOR
**FLORUIT** vb (he or she) flourished: used to indicate the period when a historical figure, whose birth and death dates are unknown, was most active
**FLORULA** n flora of a small single environment
**FLORULAE** > FLORULA
**FLORULE** same as > FLORULA
**FLORULES** > FLORULE
**FLORY** adj containing a fleur-de-lys
**FLOSCULAR** > FLOSCULE
**FLOSCULE** n floret
**FLOSCULES** > FLOSCULE
**FLOSH** hopper-shaped box
**FLOSHES** > FLOSH
**FLOSS** n fine silky fibres ▷ vb clean (between the teeth) with dental floss
**FLOSSED** > FLOSS
**FLOSSER** > FLOSS
**FLOSSERS** > FLOSS
**FLOSSES** > FLOSS
**FLOSSIE** variant of > FLOSSY
**FLOSSIER** > FLOSSY
**FLOSSIES** > FLOSSY
**FLOSSIEST** > FLOSSY
**FLOSSILY** > FLOSSY
**FLOSSING** > FLOSS
**FLOSSINGS** > FLOSS
**FLOSSY** adj consisting of or resembling floss ▷ n floozy
**FLOTA** n formerly, Spanish commercial fleet
**FLOTAGE** n act or state of floating
**FLOTAGES** > FLOTAGE
**FLOTANT** adj in heraldry, flying in the air
**FLOTAS** > FLOTA
**FLOTATION** n launching or financing of a business enterprise
**FLOTE** n aquatic perennial grass
**FLOTEL** n (in the oil industry) an oil rig or boat

used as accommodation for workers in off-shore oil fields
**FLOTELS** > FLOTEL
**FLOTES** > FLOTE
**FLOTILLA** n small fleet or fleet of small ships
**FLOTILLAS** > FLOTILLA
**FLOTSAM** n floating wreckage
**FLOTSAMS** > FLOTSAM
**FLOUNCE** vb go with emphatic movements ▷ n flouncing movement
**FLOUNCED** > FLOUNCE
**FLOUNCES** > FLOUNCE
**FLOUNCIER** > FLOUNCE
**FLOUNCING** n material, such as lace or embroidered fabric, used for making flounces
**FLOUNCY** > FLOUNCE
**FLOUNDER** vb move with difficulty, as in mud ▷ n edible flatfish
**FLOUNDERS** > FLOUNDER
**FLOUR** n powder made by grinding grain, esp wheat ▷ vb sprinkle with flour
**FLOURED** > FLOUR
**FLOURIER** > FLOUR
**FLOURIEST** > FLOUR
**FLOURING** > FLOUR
**FLOURISH** vb be active, successful, or widespread ▷ n dramatic waving motion
**FLOURISHY** > FLOURISH
**FLOURLESS** > FLOUR
**FLOURS** > FLOUR
**FLOURY** > FLOUR
**FLOUSE** vb splash
**FLOUSED** > FLOUSE
**FLOUSES** > FLOUSE
**FLOUSH** variant of > FLOUSE
**FLOUSHED** > FLOUSH
**FLOUSHES** > FLOUSH
**FLOUSHING** > FLOUSH
**FLOUSING** > FLOUSE
**FLOUT** vb deliberately disobey (a rule, law, etc)
**FLOUTED** > FLOUT
**FLOUTER** > FLOUT
**FLOUTERS** > FLOUT
**FLOUTING** > FLOUT
**FLOUTS** > FLOUT
**FLOW** vb (of liquid) move in a stream ▷ n act, rate, or manner of flowing
**FLOWAGE** n act of flowing or overflowing or the state of having overflowed
**FLOWAGES** > FLOWAGE
**FLOWCHART** n diagrammatic representation of the sequence of operations or equipment in an industrial process, computer program, etc
**FLOWED** > FLOW
**FLOWER** n part of a plant that produces seeds ▷ vb produce flowers, bloom

**FLOWERAGE** n mass of flowers
**FLOWERBED** n piece of ground for growing flowers
**FLOWERED** adj decorated with a floral design
**FLOWERER** n plant that flowers at a specified time or in a specified way
**FLOWERERS** > FLOWERER
**FLOWERET** another name for > FLORET
**FLOWERETS** > FLOWERET
**FLOWERFUL** adj having plentiful flowers
**FLOWERIER** > FLOWERY
**FLOWERILY** > FLOWERY
**FLOWERING** adj (of certain species of plants) capable of producing conspicuous flowers
**FLOWERPOT** n pot in which plants are grown
**FLOWERS** > FLOWER
**FLOWERY** adj decorated with a floral design
**FLOWING** > FLOW
**FLOWINGLY** > FLOW
**FLOWMETER** n instrument that measures the rate of flow of a liquid or gas within a pipe or tube
**FLOWN** > FLY
**FLOWS** > FLOW
**FLOWSTONE** n type of speleothem
**FLU** n any of various viral infections, esp a respiratory or intestinal infection
**FLUATE** n fluoride
**FLUATES** > FLUATE
**FLUB** vb bungle
**FLUBBED** > FLUB
**FLUBBER** > FLUB
**FLUBBERS** > FLUB
**FLUBBING** > FLUB
**FLUBDUB** n bunkum
**FLUBDUBS** > FLUBDUB
**FLUBS** > FLUB
**FLUCTUANT** adj inclined to vary or fluctuate
**FLUCTUATE** vb change frequently and erratically
**FLUE** n passage or pipe for smoke or hot air
**FLUED** adj having a flue
**FLUELLEN** n type of plant
**FLUELLENS** > FLUELLEN
**FLUELLIN** same as > FLUELLEN
**FLUELLINS** > FLUELLIN
**FLUENCE** > FLUENCY
**FLUENCES** > FLUENCY
**FLUENCIES** > FLUENCY
**FLUENCY** n quality of being fluent, esp facility in speech or writing
**FLUENT** adj able to speak or write with ease ▷ n variable quantity in fluxions
**FLUENTLY** > FLUENT

**FLUENTS** > FLUENT
**FLUERIC** adj of or relating to fluidics
**FLUERICS** pl n fluidics
**FLUES** > FLUE
**FLUEWORK** n collectively, organ stops
**FLUEWORKS** > FLUEWORK
**FLUEY** adj involved in, caused by, or like influenza
**FLUFF** n soft fibres ▷ vb make or become soft and puffy
**FLUFFED** > FLUFF
**FLUFFER** n person employed on a pornographic film set to ensure that male actors are kept aroused
**FLUFFERS** n fluffer
**FLUFFIER** > FLUFFY
**FLUFFIEST** > FLUFFY
**FLUFFILY** > FLUFFY
**FLUFFING** > FLUFF
**FLUFFS** > FLUFF
**FLUFFY** adj of, resembling, or covered with fluff
**FLUGEL** n grand piano or harpsichord
**FLUGELMAN** variant of > FUGLEMAN
**FLUGELMEN** > FLUGELMAN
**FLUGELS** > FLUGEL
**FLUID** n substance able to flow and change its shape ▷ adj able to flow or change shape easily
**FLUIDAL** > FLUID
**FLUIDALLY** > FLUID
**FLUIDIC** > FLUIDICS
**FLUIDICS** n study and use of systems in which the flow of fluids in tubes simulates the flow of electricity in conductors. Such systems are used in place of electronics in certain applications, such as the control of apparatus
**FLUIDIFY** vb make fluid
**FLUIDISE** same as > FLUIDIZE
**FLUIDISED** > FLUIDISE
**FLUIDISER** > FLUIDISE
**FLUIDISES** > FLUIDISE
**FLUIDITY** n state of being fluid
**FLUIDIZE** vb make fluid, esp to make (solids) fluid by pulverizing them so that they can be transported in a stream of gas as if they were liquids
**FLUIDIZED** > FLUIDIZE
**FLUIDIZER** > FLUIDIZE
**FLUIDIZES** > FLUIDIZE
**FLUIDLIKE** > FLUID
**FLUIDLY** > FLUID
**FLUIDNESS** > FLUID
**FLUIDRAM** n British imperial measure
**FLUIDRAMS** > FLUIDRAM
**FLUIDS** > FLUID
**FLUIER** > FLUEY

FLUIEST > FLUEY

FLUISH > FLU

FLUKE *n* accidental stroke of luck ▷ *vb* gain, make, or hit by a fluke

FLUKED > FLUKE

FLUKES > FLUKE

FLUKEY *same as* > FLUKY

FLUKIER > FLUKY

FLUKIEST > FLUKY

FLUKILY > FLUKY

FLUKINESS > FLUKY

FLUKING > FLUKE

FLUKY *adj* done or gained by an accident, esp a lucky one

FLUME *n* narrow sloping channel for water ▷ *vb* transport (logs) in a flume

FLUMED > FLUME

FLUMES > FLUME

FLUMING > FLUME

FLUMMERY *n* silly or trivial talk

FLUMMOX *vb* puzzle or confuse

FLUMMOXED > FLUMMOX

FLUMMOXES > FLUMMOX

FLUMP *vb* move or fall heavily

FLUMPED > FLUMP

FLUMPING > FLUMP

FLUMPS > FLUMP

FLUNG > FLING

FLUNK *vb* fail ▷ *n* low grade below the pass standard

FLUNKED > FLUNK

FLUNKER > FLUNK

FLUNKERS > FLUNK

FLUNKEY *same as* > FLUNKY

FLUNKEYS > FLUNKEY

FLUNKIE *same as* > FLUNKY

FLUNKIES > FLUNKY

FLUNKING > FLUNK

FLUNKS > FLUNK

FLUNKY *n* servile person

FLUNKYISM > FLUNKY

FLUOR > FLUORSPAR

FLUORENE *n* white insoluble crystalline solid

FLUORENES > FLUORENE

FLUORESCE *vb* exhibit fluorescence

FLUORIC *adj* of, concerned with, or produced from fluorine or fluorspar

FLUORID *same as* > FLUORIDE

FLUORIDE *n* compound containing fluorine

FLUORIDES > FLUORIDE

FLUORIDS > FLUORID

FLUORIN *same as* > FLUORINE

FLUORINE *n* toxic yellow gas: most reactive of all the elements

FLUORINES > FLUORINE

FLUORINS > FLUORIN

FLUORITE *same as* > FLUORSPAR

FLUORITES > FLUORITE

FLUOROSES > FLUOROSIS

FLUOROSIS *n* fluoride poisoning, due to ingestion of too much fluoride in drinking water over a long period or to ingestion of pesticides containing fluoride salts. Chronic fluorosis results in mottling of the teeth of children

FLUOROTIC > FLUOROSIS

FLUORS > FLUOR

FLUORSPAR *n* white or colourless mineral, consisting of calcium fluoride in crystalline form: the chief ore of fluorine

FLURR *vb* scatter

FLURRED > FLURR

FLURRIED > FLURRY

FLURRIES > FLURRY

FLURRING > FLURR

FLURRS > FLURR

FLURRY *n* sudden commotion ▷ *vb* confuse

FLURRYING > FLURRY

FLUS > FLU

FLUSH *vb* blush or cause to blush ▷ *n* blush ▷ *adj* level with the surrounding surface ▷ *adv* so as to be level

FLUSHABLE > FLUSH

FLUSHED > FLUSH

FLUSHER > FLUSH

FLUSHERS > FLUSH

FLUSHES > FLUSH

FLUSHEST > FLUSH

FLUSHIER > FLUSHY

FLUSHIEST > FLUSHY

FLUSHING *n* extra feeding given to ewes before mating to increase the lambing percentage

FLUSHINGS > FLUSHING

FLUSHNESS > FLUSH

FLUSHWORK *n* decorative treatment of the surface of an outside wall with flints split to show their smooth black surface, combined with dressed stone to form patterns such as tracery or initials

FLUSHY *adj* ruddy

FLUSTER *vb* make nervous or upset ▷ *n* nervous or upset state

FLUSTERED > FLUSTER

FLUSTERS > FLUSTER

FLUSTERY > FLUSTER

FLUSTRATE *vb* fluster

FLUTE *n* wind instrument consisting of a tube with sound holes and a mouth hole in the side ▷ *vb* utter in a high-pitched tone

FLUTED *adj* having decorative grooves

FLUTELIKE > FLUTE

FLUTER *n* craftsman who makes flutes or fluting

FLUTERS > FLUTER

FLUTES > FLUTE

FLUTEY > FLUTE

FLUTIER > FLUTE

FLUTIEST > FLUTE

FLUTINA *n* type of accordion

FLUTINAS > FLUTINA

FLUTING *n* design of decorative grooves

FLUTINGS > FLUTING

FLUTIST *same as* > FLAUTIST

FLUTISTS > FLUTIST

FLUTTER *vb* wave rapidly ▷ *n* flapping movement

FLUTTERED > FLUTTER

FLUTTERER > FLUTTER

FLUTTERS > FLUTTER

FLUTTERY *adj* flapping rapidly

FLUTY > FLUTE

FLUVIAL *adj* of rivers

FLUVIATIC > FLUVIAL

FLUX *n* constant change or instability ▷ *vb* make or become fluid

FLUXED > FLUX

FLUXES > FLUX

FLUXGATE *n* type of magnetometer

FLUXGATES > FLUXGATE

FLUXING > FLUX

FLUXION *n* rate of change of a function, especially the instantaneous velocity of a moving body

FLUXIONAL > FLUXION

FLUXIONS > FLUXION

FLUXIVE > FLUX

FLUXMETER *n* any instrument for measuring magnetic flux, usually by measuring the charge that flows through a coil when the flux changes

FLUYT *n* Dutch sailing ship

FLUYTS > FLUYT

FLY *vb* move through the air on wings or in an aircraft ▷ *n* fastening at the front of trousers ▷ *adj* sharp and cunning

FLYABLE > FLY

FLYAWAY *adj* (of hair) very fine and soft ▷ *n* person who is frivolous or flighty

FLYAWAYS > FLYAWAY

FLYBACK *n* fast return of the spot on a cathode-ray tube after completion of each trace

FLYBACKS > FLYBACK

FLYBANE *n* type of campion

FLYBANES > FLYBANE

FLYBELT *n* strip of tsetse-infested land

FLYBELTS > FLYBELT

FLYBLEW > FLYBLOW

FLYBLOW *vb* contaminate, esp with the eggs or larvae of the blowfly ▷ *n* egg or young larva of a blowfly, deposited on meat, paper, etc

FLYBLOWN *adj* covered with blowfly eggs

FLYBLOWS > FLYBLOW

FLYBOAT *n* any small swift boat

FLYBOATS > FLYBOAT

FLYBOOK *n* small case or wallet used by anglers for storing artificial flies

FLYBOOKS > FLYBOOK

FLYBOY *n* air force pilot

FLYBOYS > FLYBOY

FLYBRIDGE *n* highest navigational bridge on a ship

FLYBY *n* flight past a particular position or target, esp the close approach of a spacecraft to a planet or satellite for investigation of conditions

FLYBYS > FLYBY

FLYER > FLY

FLYERS > FLY

FLYEST > FLY

FLYHAND *n* device for transferring printed sheets from the press to a flat pile

FLYHANDS > FLYHAND

FLYING > FLY

FLYINGS > FLY

FLYLEAF *n* blank leaf at the beginning or end of a book

FLYLEAVES > FLYLEAF

FLYLESS > FLY

FLYMAKER *n* person who makes fishing flies

FLYMAKERS > FLYMAKER

FLYMAN *n* stagehand who operates the scenery, curtains, etc, in the flies

FLYMEN > FLYMAN

FLYOFF *n* total volume of water transferred from the earth to the atmosphere

FLYOFFS > FLYOFF

FLYOVER *n* road passing over another by a bridge

FLYOVERS > FLYOVER

FLYPAPER *n* paper with a sticky poisonous coating, used to kill flies

FLYPAPERS > FLYPAPER

FLYPAST *n* ceremonial flight of aircraft over a given area

FLYPASTS > FLYPAST

FLYPE *vb* fold back

FLYPED > FLYPE

FLYPES > FLYPE

FLYPING > FLYPE

FLYPITCH *n* area for unlicensed stalls at markets

FLYRODDER *n* angler using artificial fly

FLYSCH *n* marine sedimentary facies consisting of a sequence of sandstones, conglomerates, marls, shales, and clays that were formed by erosion during a period of mountain

building and subsequently
deformed as the mountain
building continued

**FLYSCHES** > FLYSCH

**FLYSCREEN** *n* wire-mesh
screen over a window to
prevent flies from entering
a room

**FLYSHEET** *n* part of tent

**FLYSHEETS** > FLYSHEET

**FLYSPECK** *n* small speck of
the excrement of a fly ▷ *vb*
mark with flyspecks

**FLYSPECKS** > FLYSPECK

**FLYSTRIKE** *n* infestation
of wounded sheep by
blowflies or maggots

**FLYTE** *same as* > FLITE

**FLYTED** > FLYTE

**FLYTES** > FLYTE

**FLYTIER** *n* person who
makes his own fishing flies

**FLYTIERS** > FLYTIER

**FLYTING** > FLYTE

**FLYTINGS** > FLYTE

**FLYTRAP** *n* any of various
insectivorous plants, esp
Venus's flytrap

**FLYTRAPS** > FLYTRAP

**FLYWAY** *n* usual route used
by birds when migrating

**FLYWAYS** > FLYWAY

**FLYWEIGHT** *n* boxer
weighing up to 112lb
(professional) or 51kg
(amateur)

**FLYWHEEL** *n* heavy wheel
regulating the speed of a
machine

**FLYWHEELS** > FLYWHEEL

**FOAL** *n* young of a horse or
related animal ▷ *vb* give
birth to a foal

**FOALED** > FOAL

**FOALFOOT** *n* coltsfoot

**FOALFOOTS** > FOALFOOT

**FOALING** > FOAL

**FOALS** > FOAL

**FOAM** *n* mass of small
bubbles on a liquid ▷ *vb*
produce foam

**FOAMABLE** > FOAM

**FOAMED** > FOAM

**FOAMER** *n* (possibly
obsessive) enthusiast

**FOAMERS** > FOAMER

**FOAMIER** > FOAMY

**FOAMIEST** > FOAMY

**FOAMILY** > FOAMY

**FOAMINESS** > FOAMY

**FOAMING** > FOAM

**FOAMINGLY** > FOAM

**FOAMINGS** > FOAM

**FOAMLESS** > FOAM

**FOAMLIKE** > FOAM

**FOAMS** > FOAM

**FOAMY** *adj* of, resembling,
consisting of, or covered
with foam

**FOB** *n* short watch chain
▷ *vb* cheat

**FOBBED** > FOB

**FOBBING** > FOB

**FOBS** > FOB

**FOCACCIA** *n* flat Italian
bread made with olive oil
and yeast

**FOCACCIAS** > FOCACCIA

**FOCAL** *adj* of or at a focus

**FOCALISE** > FOCUS

**FOCALISED** > FOCUS

**FOCALISES** > FOCUS

**FOCALIZE** *less common word
for* > FOCUS

**FOCALIZED** > FOCALIZE

**FOCALIZES** > FOCALIZE

**FOCALLY** > FOCAL

**FOCI** > FOCUS

**FOCIMETER** *n*
photographic focusing
device

**FOCOMETER** *n* instrument
for measuring the focal
length of a lens

**FOCUS** *n* point at which
light or sound waves
converge ▷ *vb* bring or
come into focus

**FOCUSABLE** > FOCUS

**FOCUSED** > FOCUS

**FOCUSER** > FOCUS

**FOCUSERS** > FOCUS

**FOCUSES** > FOCUS

**FOCUSING** > FOCUS

**FOCUSINGS** > FOCUS

**FOCUSLESS** > FOCUS

**FOCUSSED** > FOCUS

**FOCUSSES** > FOCUS

**FOCUSSING** > FOCUS

**FODDER** *n* feed for livestock
▷ *vb* supply (livestock)
with fodder

**FODDERED** > FODDER

**FODDERER** > FODDER

**FODDERERS** > FODDER

**FODDERING** > FODDER

**FODDERS** > FODDER

**FODGEL** *adj* buxom

**FOE** *n* enemy, opponent

**FOEDARIE** *variant
of* > FEDARIE

**FOEDARIES** > FOEDARIE

**FOEDERATI** > FOEDERATUS

**FOEHN** *same as* > FOHN

**FOEHNS** > FOEHN

**FOEMAN** *n* enemy in war

**FOEMEN** > FOEMAN

**FOEN** > FOE

**FOES** > FOE

**FOETAL** *same as* > FETAL

**FOETATION** *same
as* > FETATION

**FOETICIDE** *same
as* > FETICIDE

**FOETID** *same as* > FETID

**FOETIDER** > FOETID

**FOETIDEST** > FOETID

**FOETIDLY** > FOETID

**FOETOR** *same as* > FETOR

**FOETORS** > FOETOR

**FOETUS** *same as* > FETUS

**FOETUSES** > FOETUS

**FOG** *n* mass of condensed
water vapour in the lower
air, often greatly reducing
visibility ▷ *vb* cover with
steam

**FOGASH** *n* type of

Hungarian pike perch

**FOGASHES** > FOGASH

**FOGBOUND** *adj* prevented
from operating by fog

**FOGBOW** *n* faint arc of light
sometimes seen in a fog
bank

**FOGBOWS** > FOGBOW

**FOGDOG** *n* whitish spot
sometimes seen in fog
near the horizon

**FOGDOGS** > FOGDOG

**FOGEY** *n* old-fashioned
person

**FOGEYDOM** > FOGEY

**FOGEYDOMS** > FOGEY

**FOGEYISH** > FOGEY

**FOGEYISM** > FOGEY

**FOGEYISMS** > FOGEY

**FOGEYS** > FOGEY

**FOGFRUIT** *n* wildflower of
the verbena family

**FOGFRUITS** > FOGFRUIT

**FOGGAGE** *n* grass grown for
winter grazing

**FOGGAGES** > FOGGAGE

**FOGGED** > FOG

**FOGGER** *n* device that
generates a fog

**FOGGERS** > FOGGER

**FOGGIER** > FOG

**FOGGIEST** > FOG

**FOGGILY** > FOG

**FOGGINESS** > FOG

**FOGGING** > FOG

**FOGGY** > FOG

**FOGHORN** *n* large horn
sounded to warn ships
in fog

**FOGHORNS** > FOGHORN

**FOGIE** *variant of* > FOGEY

**FOGIES** > FOGIE

**FOGLE** *n* silk handkerchief

**FOGLES** > FOGLE

**FOGLESS** > FOG

**FOGMAN** *n* person in charge
of railway fog-signals

**FOGMEN** > FOGMAN

**FOGRAM** *n* fogey

**FOGRAMITE** > FOGRAM

**FOGRAMITY** > FOGRAM

**FOGRAMS** > FOGRAM

**FOGS** > FOG

**FOGY** *same as* > FOGEY

**FOGYDOM** > FOGY

**FOGYDOMS** > FOGY

**FOGYISH** > FOGY

**FOGYISM** > FOGY

**FOGYISMS** > FOGY

**FOH** *interj* expression of
disgust

**FOHN** *n* warm dry wind
blowing down the
northern slopes of the Alps

**FOHNS** > FOHN

**FOHS** > FOH

**FOIBLE** *n* minor weakness
or slight peculiarity

**FOIBLES** > FOIBLE

**FOID** *same
as* > FELDSPATHOID

**FOIDS** > FOID

**FOIL** *vb* ruin (someone's
plan) ▷ *n* metal in a thin

sheet, esp for wrapping
food

**FOILABLE** > FOIL

**FOILBORNE** *adj* moving by
means of hydrofoils

**FOILED** > FOIL

**FOILING** > FOIL

**FOILINGS** > FOIL

**FOILS** > FOIL

**FOILSMAN** *n* person who
uses or specializes in using
a foil

**FOILSMEN** > FOILSMAN

**FOIN** *n* thrust or lunge with
a weapon ▷ *vb* thrust
with a weapon

**FOINED** > FOIN

**FOINING** > FOIN

**FOININGLY** > FOIN

**FOINS** > FOIN

**FOISON** *n* plentiful supply
or yield

**FOISONS** > FOISON

**FOIST** *vb* force or impose
on

**FOISTED** > FOIST

**FOISTER** > FOIST

**FOISTERS** > FOIST

**FOISTING** > FOIST

**FOISTS** > FOIST

**FOLACIN** *n* folic acid

**FOLACINS** > FOLACIN

**FOLATE** *n* folic acid

**FOLATES** > FOLIC

**FOLD** *vb* bend so that one
part covers another ▷ *n*
folded piece or part

**FOLDABLE** > FOLD

**FOLDAWAY** *adj* (of a bed)
able to be folded and put
away when not in use

**FOLDAWAYS** > FOLDAWAY

**FOLDBACK** *n* (in multitrack
recording) a process for
returning a signal to a
performer instantly

**FOLDBACKS** > FOLDBACK

**FOLDBOAT** *another name
for* > FALTBOAT

**FOLDBOATS** > FOLDBOAT

**FOLDED** > FOLD

**FOLDER** *n* piece of folded
cardboard for holding
loose papers

**FOLDEROL** *same
as* > FALDERAL

**FOLDEROLS** > FOLDEROL

**FOLDERS** > FOLDER

**FOLDING** > FOLD

**FOLDINGS** > FOLDING

**FOLDOUT** *another name
for* > GATEFOLD

**FOLDOUTS** > FOLDOUT

**FOLDS** > FOLD

**FOLDUP** *n* something that
folds up

**FOLDUPS** > FOLDUP

**FOLEY** *n* footsteps editor

**FOLEYS** > FOLEY

**FOLIA** > FOLIUM

**FOLIAGE** *n* leaves

**FOLIAGED** *adj* having
foliage

**FOLIAGES** > FOLIAGE

**FOLIAR** adj of or relating to a leaf or leaves

**FOLIATE** adj relating to, possessing, or resembling leaves ▷ vb ornament with foliage or with leaf forms such as foils

**FOLIATED** adj ornamented with or made up of foliage or foils

**FOLIATES** > FOLIATE

**FOLIATING** > FOLIATE

**FOLIATION** n process of producing leaves

**FOLIATURE** > FOLIATION

**FOLIC** as in folic acid, any of a group of vitamins of the B complex, including pteroylglutamic acid and its derivatives: used in the treatment of megaloblastic anaemia

**FOLIE** n madness

**FOLIES** > FOLIE

**FOLIO** n sheet of paper folded in half to make two leaves of a book ▷ adj of or made in the largest book size, common esp in early centuries of European printing ▷ vb number the leaves of (a book) consecutively

**FOLIOED** > FOLIO

**FOLIOING** > FOLIO

**FOLIOLATE** adj possessing or relating to leaflets

**FOLIOLE** n part of a compound leaf

**FOLIOLES** > FOLIOLE

**FOLIOLOSE** > FOLIOLE

**FOLIOS** > FOLIO

**FOLIOSE** another word for > FOLIACEOUS

**FOLIOUS** adj foliose

**FOLIUM** n plane geometrical curve consisting of a loop whose two ends, intersecting at a node, are asymptotic to the same line. Standard equation: $x^3 + y^3 = 3axy$ where $x=y+a$ is the equation of the line

**FOLIUMS** > FOLIUM

**FOLK** n people in general ▷ adj originating from or traditional to the common people of a country

**FOLKIE** n devotee of folk music ▷ adj of or relating to folk music

**FOLKIER** > FOLKIE

**FOLKIES** > FOLKIE

**FOLKIEST** > FOLKIE

**FOLKISH** > FOLK

**FOLKLAND** n former type of land tenure

**FOLKLANDS** > FOLKLAND

**FOLKLIFE** n traditional customs, arts, crafts, and other forms of cultural expression of a people

**FOLKLIKE** > FOLK

**FOLKLIVES** > FOLKLIFE

**FOLKLORE** n traditional beliefs and stories of a people

**FOLKLORES** > FOLKLORE

**FOLKLORIC** > FOLKLORE

**FOLKMOOT** n (in early medieval England) an assembly of the people of a district, town, or shire

**FOLKMOOTS** > FOLKMOOT

**FOLKMOT** same as > FOLKMOOT

**FOLKMOTE** same as > FOLKMOOT

**FOLKMOTES** > FOLKMOTE

**FOLKMOTS** > FOLKMOT

**FOLKS** > FOLK

**FOLKSIER** > FOLKSY

**FOLKSIEST** > FOLKSY

**FOLKSILY** > FOLKSY

**FOLKSONG** n traditional song

**FOLKSONGS** > FOLKSONG

**FOLKSY** adj simple and unpretentious

**FOLKTALE** n tale or legend originating among a people and typically becoming part of an oral tradition

**FOLKTALES** > FOLKTALE

**FOLKWAY** singular form of > FOLKWAYS

**FOLKWAYS** pl n traditional and customary ways of living

**FOLKY** same as > FOLKIE

**FOLLES** > FOLLIS

**FOLLICLE** n small cavity in the body, esp one from which a hair grows

**FOLLICLES** > FOLLICLE

**FOLLIED** > FOLLY

**FOLLIES** > FOLLY

**FOLLIS** n Roman coin

**FOLLOW** vb go or come after

**FOLLOWED** > FOLLOW

**FOLLOWER** n disciple or supporter

**FOLLOWERS** > FOLLOWER

**FOLLOWING** adj about to be mentioned ▷ n group of supporters ▷ prep as a result of

**FOLLOWS** > FOLLOW

**FOLLOWUP** n further action

**FOLLOWUPS** > FOLLOWUP

**FOLLY** n foolishness ▷ vb behave foolishly

**FOLLYING** > FOLLY

**FOMENT** vb encourage or stir up (trouble)

**FOMENTED** > FOMENT

**FOMENTER** > FOMENT

**FOMENTERS** > FOMENT

**FOMENTING** > FOMENT

**FOMENTS** > FOMENT

**FOMES** n any material, such as bedding or clothing, that may harbour pathogens and therefore convey disease

**FOMITE** > FOMES

**FOMITES** > FOMES

**FON** vb compel

**FOND** adj tender, loving ▷ n background of a design, as in lace ▷ vb dote

**FONDA** n Spanish hotel

**FONDANT** n (sweet made from) flavoured paste of sugar and water ▷ adj (of a colour) soft

**FONDANTS** > FONDANT

**FONDAS** > FONDA

**FONDED** > FOND

**FONDER** > FOND

**FONDEST** > FOND

**FONDING** > FOND

**FONDLE** vb caress

**FONDLED** > FONDLE

**FONDLER** > FONDLE

**FONDLERS** > FONDLE

**FONDLES** > FONDLE

**FONDLING** > FONDLE

**FONDLINGS** > FONDLE

**FONDLY** > FOND

**FONDNESS** > FOND

**FONDS** > FOND

**FONDU** n ballet movement, lowering the body by bending the leg(s)

**FONDUE** n Swiss dish of a hot melted cheese sauce into which pieces of bread are dipped ▷ vb cook and serve (food) as a fondue

**FONDUED** > FONDUE

**FONDUEING** > FONDUE

**FONDUES** > FONDUE

**FONDUING** > FONDUE

**FONDUS** > FONDU

**FONE** variant of > FOE

**FONLY** adv foolishly

**FONNED** > FON

**FONNING** > FON

**FONS** > FON

**FONT** n bowl in a church for baptismal water

**FONTAL** > FONT

**FONTANEL** same as > FONTANELLE

**FONTANELS** > FONTANEL

**FONTANGE** n type of tall headdress

**FONTANGES** > FONTANGE

**FONTICULI** > FONTICULUS

**FONTINA** n semihard, pale yellow, mild Italian cheese made from cow's milk

**FONTINAS** > FONTINA

**FONTLET** > FONT

**FONTLETS** > FONT

**FONTS** > FONT

**FOOBAR** same as > FUBAR

**FOOD** n what one eats; solid nourishment

**FOODFUL** adj supplying abundant food

**FOODIE** n gourmet

**FOODIES** > FOODIE

**FOODISM** n enthusiasm for and interest in the preparation and consumption of good food

**FOODISMS** > FOODISM

**FOODLESS** > FOOD

**FOODS** > FOOD

**FOODSTUFF** n substance used as food

**FOODWAYS** pl n customs and traditions relating to food and its preparation

**FOODY** same as > FOODIE

**FOOFARAW** n vulgar ornamentation

**FOOFARAWS** > FOOFARAW

**FOOL** n person lacking sense or judgment ▷ vb deceive (someone)

**FOOLED** > FOOL

**FOOLERIES** > FOOLERY

**FOOLERY** n foolish behaviour

**FOOLFISH** n orange filefish or winter flounder

**FOOLHARDY** adj recklessly adventurous

**FOOLING** > FOOL

**FOOLINGS** > FOOL

**FOOLISH** adj unwise, silly, or absurd

**FOOLISHER** > FOOLISH

**FOOLISHLY** > FOOLISH

**FOOLPROOF** adj unable to fail

**FOOLS** > FOOL

**FOOLSCAP** n size of paper, 34.3 x 43.2 centimetres

**FOOLSCAPS** > FOOLSCAP

**FOOSBALL** n US and Canadian name for table football

**FOOSBALLS** > FOOSBALL

**FOOT** n part of the leg below the ankle ▷ vb kick

**FOOTAGE** n amount of film used

**FOOTAGES** > FOOTAGE

**FOOTBAG** n sport of keeping small round object off the ground by kicking it

**FOOTBAGS** > FOOTBAG

**FOOTBALL** n game played by two teams of eleven players kicking a ball in an attempt to score goals

**FOOTBALLS** > FOOTBALL

**FOOTBAR** n any bar designed as a footrest or to be operated by the foot

**FOOTBARS** > FOOTBAR

**FOOTBATH** n vessel for bathing the feet

**FOOTBATHS** > FOOTBATH

**FOOTBOARD** n treadle or foot-operated lever on a machine

**FOOTBOY** n boy servant

**FOOTBOYS** > FOOTBOY

**FOOTCLOTH** obsolete word for > CAPARISON

**FOOTED** > FOOT

**FOOTER** n person who goes on foot ▷ vb potter

**FOOTERED** > FOOTER

**FOOTERING** > FOOTER

**FOOTERS** > FOOTER

**FOOTFALL** n sound of a footstep

**FOOTFALLS** > FOOTFALL

**FOOTFAULT** n fault that occurs when the server fails to keep both feet behind the baseline until he/she has served

**FOOTGEAR** another name for > FOOTWEAR

**FOOTGEARS** > FOOTGEAR

**FOOTHILL** n lower slope of a mountain or a relatively low hill at the foot of a mountain

**FOOTHILLS** > FOOTHILL

**FOOTHOLD** n secure position from which progress may be made

**FOOTHOLDS** > FOOTHOLD

**FOOTIE** same as > FOOTY

**FOOTIER** > FOOTY

**FOOTIES** > FOOTIE

**FOOTIEST** > FOOTY

**FOOTING** n basis or foundation

**FOOTINGS** > FOOTING

**FOOTLE** vb loiter aimlessly ▷ n foolishness

**FOOTLED** > FOOTLE

**FOOTLER** > FOOTLE

**FOOTLERS** > FOOTLE

**FOOTLES** > FOOTLE

**FOOTLESS** > FOOT

**FOOTLIGHT** n light illuminating the front of a stage

**FOOTLIKE** > FOOT

**FOOTLING** adj trivial ▷ n trifle

**FOOTLINGS** > FOOTLING

**FOOTLOOSE** adj free from ties

**FOOTMAN** n male servant in uniform

**FOOTMARK** n mark or trace of mud, wetness, etc, left by a person's foot on a surface

**FOOTMARKS** > FOOTMARK

**FOOTMEN** > FOOTMAN

**FOOTMUFF** n muff used to keep the feet warm

**FOOTMUFFS** > FOOTMUFF

**FOOTNOTE** n note printed at the foot of a page ▷ vb supply (a page, book, etc) with footnotes

**FOOTNOTED** > FOOTNOTE

**FOOTNOTES** > FOOTNOTE

**FOOTPACE** n normal or walking pace

**FOOTPACES** > FOOTPACE

**FOOTPAD** n highwayman, on foot rather than horseback

**FOOTPADS** > FOOTPAD

**FOOTPAGE** n errand-boy

**FOOTPAGES** > FOOTPAGE

**FOOTPATH** n narrow path for walkers only

**FOOTPATHS** > FOOTPATH

**FOOTPLATE** n platform in the cab of a locomotive for the driver

**FOOTPOST** n post delivered on foot

**FOOTPOSTS** > FOOTPOST

**FOOTPRINT** n mark left by a foot

**FOOTRA** variant of > FOUTRA

**FOOTRACE** n race run on foot

**FOOTRACES** > FOOTRACE

**FOOTRAS** > FOOTRA

**FOOTREST** n something that provides a support for the feet, such as a low stool, rail, etc

**FOOTRESTS** > FOOTREST

**FOOTROPE** n part of a boltrope to which the foot of a sail is stitched

**FOOTROPES** > FOOTROPE

**FOOTROT** n contagious fungal disease of the feet of sheep

**FOOTROTS** > FOOTROT

**FOOTRULE** n rigid measure, one foot in length

**FOOTRULES** > FOOTRULE

**FOOTS** pl n sediment that accumulates at the bottom of a vessel containing any of certain liquids, such as vegetable oil or varnish

**FOOTSIE** n flirtation involving the touching together of feet

**FOOTSIES** > FOOTSIE

**FOOTSLOG** vb march

**FOOTSLOGS** > FOOTSLOG

**FOOTSORE** adj having sore or tired feet, esp from much walking

**FOOTSTALK** n small supporting stalk in animals and plants

**FOOTSTALL** n pedestal, plinth, or base of a column, pier, or statue

**FOOTSTEP** n step in walking

**FOOTSTEPS** > FOOTSTEP

**FOOTSTOCK** another name for > TAILSTOCK

**FOOTSTONE** n memorial stone at the foot of a grave

**FOOTSTOOL** n low stool used to rest the feet on while sitting

**FOOTSY** variant of > FOOTSIE

**FOOTWALL** n rocks on the lower side of an inclined fault plane or mineral vein

**FOOTWALLS** > FOOTWALL

**FOOTWAY** n way or path for pedestrians, such as a raised walk along the edge of a bridge

**FOOTWAYS** > FOOTWAY

**FOOTWEAR** n anything worn to cover the feet

**FOOTWEARS** > FOOTWEAR

**FOOTWEARY** adj tired from walking

**FOOTWELL** n part of a car in which the foot pedals are located

**FOOTWELLS** > FOOTWELL

**FOOTWORK** n skilful use of the feet, as in sport or dancing

**FOOTWORKS** > FOOTWORK

**FOOTWORN** adj footsore

**FOOTY** n football ▷ adj mean

**FOOZLE** vb bungle (a shot) ▷ n bungled shot

**FOOZLED** > FOOZLE

**FOOZLER** > FOOZLE

**FOOZLERS** > FOOZLE

**FOOZLES** > FOOZLE

**FOOZLING** > FOOZLE

**FOOZLINGS** > FOOZLE

**FOP** n man excessively concerned with fashion ▷ vb act like a fop

**FOPLING** n vain affected dandy

**FOPLINGS** > FOPLING

**FOPPED** > FOP

**FOPPERIES** > FOPPERY

**FOPPERY** n clothes, affectations, obsessions, etc, of or befitting a fop

**FOPPING** > FOP

**FOPPISH** > FOP

**FOPPISHLY** > FOP

**FOPS** > FOP

**FOR** prep indicating a person intended to benefit from or receive something, span of time or distance, person or thing represented by someone, etc

**FORA** > FORUM

**FORAGE** vb search about (for) ▷ n food for cattle or horses

**FORAGED** > FORAGE

**FORAGER** > FORAGE

**FORAGERS** > FORAGE

**FORAGES** > FORAGE

**FORAGING** > FORAGE

**FORAM** same as > FORAMINIFER

**FORAMEN** n natural hole, esp one in a bone through which nerves pass

**FORAMENS** > FORAMEN

**FORAMINA** > FORAMEN

**FORAMINAL** > FORAMEN

**FORAMS** > FORAM

**FORANE** as in vicar forane, in the Roman Catholic church, vicar or priest appointed to act in a certain area of the diocese

**FORASMUCH** conj since

**FORAY** n brief raid or attack ▷ vb raid or ravage (a town, district, etc)

**FORAYED** > FORAY

**FORAYER** > FORAY

**FORAYERS** > FORAY

**FORAYING** > FORAY

**FORAYS** > FORAY

**FORB** n any herbaceous plant that is not a grass

**FORBAD** > FORBID

**FORBADE** > FORBID

**FORBARE** > FORBEAR

**FORBEAR** vb cease or refrain (from doing something)

**FORBEARER** > FORBEAR

**FORBEARS** > FORBEAR

**FORBID** vb prohibit, refuse to allow

**FORBIDAL** > FORBID

**FORBIDALS** > FORBIDAL

**FORBIDDAL** n prohibition

**FORBIDDEN** adj not permitted by order or law

**FORBIDDER** > FORBID

**FORBIDS** > FORBID

**FORBODE** vb obsolete word meaning forbid ▷ n obsolete word meaning forbidding

**FORBODED** > FORBODE

**FORBODES** > FORBODE

**FORBODING** > FORBODE

**FORBORE** past tense of > FORBEAR

**FORBORNE** > FORBEAR

**FORBS** > FORB

**FORBY** adv besides

**FORBYE** same as > FORBY

**FORCAT** n convict or galley slave

**FORCATS** > FORCAT

**FORCE** n strength or power ▷ vb compel, make (someone) do something

**FORCEABLE** > FORCE

**FORCED** adj compulsory

**FORCEDLY** > FORCE

**FORCEFUL** adj emphatic and confident

**FORCELESS** > FORCE

**FORCEMEAT** n mixture of chopped ingredients used for stuffing

**FORCEPS** pl n surgical pincers

**FORCEPSES** > FORCEPS

**FORCER** > FORCE

**FORCERS** > FORCE

**FORCES** > FORCE

**FORCIBLE** adj involving physical force or violence

**FORCIBLY** > FORCIBLE

**FORCING** > FORCE

**FORCINGLY** > FORCE

**FORCIPATE** > FORCEPS

**FORCIPES** > FORCEPS

**FORD** n shallow place where a river may be crossed ▷ vb cross (a river) at a ford

**FORDABLE** > FORD

**FORDED** > FORD

**FORDID** > FORDO

**FORDING** > FORD

**FORDLESS** > FORD

**FORDO** vb destroy

**FORDOES** > FORDO

**FORDOING** > FORDO

**FORDONE** > FORDO

**FORDS** > FORD

**FORE** adj in, at, or towards the front ▷ n front part ▷ interj golfer's shouted warning to a person in the path of a ball

**FOREANENT** prep opposite

**FOREARM** n arm from the

wrist to the elbow ▷ *vb*
prepare beforehand
**FOREARMED** > FOREARM
**FOREARMS** > FOREARM
**FOREBAY** *n* reservoir or
canal
**FOREBAYS** > FOREBAY
**FOREBEAR** *n* ancestor
**FOREBEARS** > FOREBEAR
**FOREBITT** *n* post at a ship's
foremast for securing
cables
**FOREBITTS** > FOREBITT
**FOREBODE** *vb* warn of or
indicate (an event, result,
etc) in advance
**FOREBODED** > FOREBODE
**FOREBODER** > FOREBODE
**FOREBODES** > FOREBODE
**FOREBODY** *n* part of a ship
forward of the foremast
**FOREBOOM** *n* boom of a
foremast
**FOREBOOMS** > FOREBOOM
**FOREBRAIN**
*nontechnical name*
*for* > PROSENCEPHALON
**FOREBY** *variant of* > FORBY
**FOREBYE** *variant of* > FORBY
**FORECABIN** *n* forward
cabin on a vessel
**FORECAR** *n* three-wheeled
passenger vehicle
attached to a motorcycle
**FORECARS** > FORECAR
**FORECAST** *vb* predict
(weather, events, etc) ▷ *n*
prediction
**FORECASTS** > FORECAST
**FORECHECK** *vb* in ice-
hockey, to try to gain
control of the puck while
at opponents' end of rink
**FORECLOSE** *vb* take
possession of (property
bought with borrowed
money which has not been
repaid)
**FORECLOTH** *n* cloth
hung over the front of
something, especially an
altar
**FORECOURT** *n* courtyard
or open space in front of a
building
**FOREDATE** *vb* antedate
**FOREDATED** > FOREDATE
**FOREDATES** > FOREDATE
**FOREDECK** *n* deck between
the bridge and the
forecastle
**FOREDECKS** > FOREDECK
**FOREDID** > FOREDO
**FOREDO** *same as* > FORDO
**FOREDOES** > FOREDO
**FOREDOING** > FOREDO
**FOREDONE** > FOREDO
**FOREDOOM** *vb* doom or
condemn beforehand
**FOREDOOMS** > FOREDOOM
**FOREFACE** *n* muzzle of an
animal
**FOREFACES** > FOREFACE
**FOREFEEL** *vb* have a

premonition of
**FOREFEELS** > FOREFEEL
**FOREFEET** > FOREFOOT
**FOREFELT** > FOREFEEL
**FOREFEND** *same*
*as* > FORFEND
**FOREFENDS** > FOREFEND
**FOREFOOT** *n* either of the
front feet of an animal
**FOREFRONT** *n* most active
or prominent position
**FOREGLEAM** *n* early or
premonitory inkling or
indication
**FOREGO** *same as* > FORGO
**FOREGOER** > FOREGO
**FOREGOERS** > FOREGO
**FOREGOES** > FOREGO
**FOREGOING** *adj* going
before, preceding
**FOREGONE** *adj* gone or
completed
**FOREGUT** *n* anterior part
of the digestive tract of
vertebrates, between the
buccal cavity and the bile
duct
**FOREGUTS** > FOREGUT
**FOREHAND** *n* stroke played
with the palm of the hand
facing forward ▷ *adj* (of a
stroke) made so that the
racket is held with the
wrist facing the direction
of play ▷ *adv* with a
forehand stroke ▷ *vb* play
(a shot) forehand
**FOREHANDS** > FOREHAND
**FOREHEAD** *n* part of the face
above the eyebrows
**FOREHEADS** > FOREHEAD
**FOREHENT** *vb* seize in
advance
**FOREHENTS** > FOREHENT
**FOREHOCK** *n* foreleg cut of
bacon or pork
**FOREHOCKS** > FOREHOCK
**FOREHOOF** *n* front hoof
**FOREHOOFS** > FOREHOOF
**FOREIGN** *adj* not of, or in,
one's own country
**FOREIGNER** *n* person from
a foreign country
**FOREIGNLY** > FOREIGN
**FOREJUDGE** *same*
*as* > FORJUDGE
**FOREKING** *n* previous king
**FOREKINGS** > FOREKING
**FOREKNEW** > FOREKNOW
**FOREKNOW** *vb* know in
advance
**FOREKNOWN** > FOREKNOW
**FOREKNOWS** > FOREKNOW
**FOREL** *n* type of parchment
**FORELADY** *n* forewoman
of a jury
**FORELAID** > FORELAY
**FORELAIN** > FORELIE
**FORELAND** *n* headland,
cape, or coastal
promontory
**FORELANDS** > FORELAND
**FORELAY** *archaic word*
*for* > AMBUSH

**FORELAYS** > FORELAY
**FORELEG** *n* either of the
front legs of an animal
**FORELEGS** > FORELEG
**FORELEND** *vb* give up
**FORELENDS** > FORELEND
**FORELENT** > FORELEND
**FORELIE** *vb* lie in front of
**FORELIES** > FORELIE
**FORELIFT** *vb* lift up in front
**FORELIFTS** > FORELIFT
**FORELIMB** *n* either of the
front or anterior limbs of a
four-limbed vertebrate: a
foreleg, flipper, or wing
**FORELIMBS** > FORELIMB
**FORELOCK** *n* lock of hair
over the forehead ▷ *vb*
secure (a bolt) by means of
a forelock
**FORELOCKS** > FORELOCK
**FORELS** > FOREL
**FORELYING** > FORELIE
**FOREMAN** *n* person in
charge of a group of
workers
**FOREMAST** *n* mast nearest
the bow of a ship
**FOREMASTS** > FOREMAST
**FOREMEAN** *vb* intend in
advance
**FOREMEANS** > FOREMEAN
**FOREMEANT** > FOREMEAN
**FOREMEN** > FOREMAN
**FOREMILK** *n* first milk
drawn from a cow's udder
prior to milking
**FOREMILKS** > FOREMILK
**FOREMOST** *adv* first in time,
place, or importance ▷ *adj*
first in time, place, or
importance
**FORENAME** *n* first name
**FORENAMED** *adj* named or
mentioned previously
**FORENAMES** > FORENAME
**FORENIGHT** *n* evening
**FORENOON** *n* morning
**FORENOONS** > FORENOON
**FORENSIC** *adj* used in or
connected with courts
of law
**FORENSICS** *n* art or study
of formal debating
**FOREPART** *n* first or front
part in place, order, or time
**FOREPARTS** > FOREPART
**FOREPAST** *adj* bygone
**FOREPAW** *n* either of
the front feet of a land
mammal that does not
have hooves
**FOREPAWS** > FOREPAW
**FOREPEAK** *n* interior part
of a vessel that is furthest
forward
**FOREPEAKS** > FOREPEAK
**FOREPLAN** *vb* plan in
advance
**FOREPLANS** > FOREPLAN
**FOREPLAY** *n* sexual
stimulation before
intercourse
**FOREPLAYS** > FOREPLAY

**FOREPOINT** *vb*
predetermine or indicate
in advance
**FORERAN** > FORERUN
**FORERANK** *n* first rank
**FORERANKS** > FORERANK
**FOREREACH** *vb* keep
moving under momentum
without engine or sails
**FOREREAD** *vb* foretell
**FOREREADS** > FOREREAD
**FORERUN** *vb* serve as a
herald for
**FORERUNS** > FORERUN
**FORES** > FORE
**FORESAID** *less common word*
*for* > AFORESAID
**FORESAIL** *n* main sail on
the foremast of a ship
**FORESAILS** > FORESAIL
**FORESAW** > FORESEE
**FORESAY** *vb* foretell
**FORESAYS** > FORESAY
**FORESEE** *vb* see or know
beforehand
**FORESEEN** > FORESEE
**FORESEER** > FORESEE
**FORESEERS** > FORESEE
**FORESEES** > FORESEE
**FORESHANK** *n* top of the
front leg of an animal
**FORESHEET** *n* sheet of a
foresail
**FORESHEW** *variant*
*of* > FORESHOW
**FORESHEWN** > FORESHEW
**FORESHEWS** > FORESHEW
**FORESHIP** *n* fore part of a
ship
**FORESHIPS** > FORESHIP
**FORESHOCK** *n* relatively
small earthquake
heralding the arrival of a
much larger one. Some
large earthquakes are
preceded by a series of
foreshocks
**FORESHORE** *n* part of the
shore between high- and
low-tide marks
**FORESHOW** *vb* indicate in
advance
**FORESHOWN** > FORESHOW
**FORESHOWS** > FORESHOW
**FORESIDE** *n* front or upper
side or part
**FORESIDES** > FORESIDE
**FORESIGHT** *n* ability to
anticipate and provide for
future needs
**FORESKIN** *n* fold of skin
covering the tip of the
penis
**FORESKINS** > FORESKIN
**FORESKIRT** *n* front skirt of
a garment (as opposed to
the train)
**FORESLACK** *variant*
*of* > FORSLACK
**FORESLOW** *variant*
*of* > FORSLOW
**FORESLOWS** > FORESLOW
**FORESPAKE** > FORESPEAK
**FORESPEAK** *vb* predict

FORESPEND *variant of* > FORSPEND

FORESPENT > FORESPEND

FORESPOKE > FORESPEAK

FOREST *n* large area with a thick growth of trees ▷ *vb* create a forest (in)

FORESTAGE *n* part of a stage in front of the curtain

FORESTAIR *n* external stair

FORESTAL > FOREST

FORESTALL *vb* prevent or guard against in advance

FORESTAY *n* adjustable stay leading from the truck of the foremast to the deck, stem, or bowsprit, for controlling the motion or bending of the mast

FORESTAYS > FORESTAY

FORESTEAL > FOREST

FORESTED > FOREST

FORESTER *n* person skilled in forestry

FORESTERS > FORESTER

FORESTIAL > FOREST

FORESTINE > FOREST

FORESTING > FOREST

FORESTRY *n* science of planting and caring for trees

FORESTS > FOREST

FORESWEAR *vb* forgo

FORESWORE > FORESWEAR

FORESWORN > FORESWEAR

FORETASTE *n* early limited experience of something to come ▷ *vb* have a foretaste of

FORETEACH *vb* teach beforehand

FORETEETH > FORETOOTH

FORETELL *vb* tell or indicate beforehand

FORETELLS > FORETELL

FORETHINK *vb* have prescience

FORETIME *n* time already gone

FORETIMES > FORETIME

FORETOKEN *n* sign of a future event ▷ *vb* foreshadow

FORETOLD > FORETELL

FORETOOTH *another word for an* > INCISOR

FORETOP *n* platform at the top of the foremast

FORETOPS > FORETOP

FOREVER *adv* without end

FOREVERS > FOREVER

FOREWARD *n* vanguard

FOREWARDS > FOREWARD

FOREWARN *vb* warn beforehand

FOREWARNS > FOREWARN

FOREWEIGH *vb* assess in advance

FOREWENT *past tense of* > FOREGO

FOREWIND *n* favourable wind

FOREWINDS > FOREWIND

FOREWING *n* either wing of the anterior pair of an insect's two pairs of wings

FOREWINGS > FOREWING

FOREWOMAN *n* woman in charge of a group of workers

FOREWOMEN > FOREWOMAN

FOREWORD *n* introduction to a book

FOREWORDS > FOREWORD

FOREWORN *same as* > FORWORN

FOREX *n* foreign exchange

FOREXES > FOREX

FOREYARD *n* yard for supporting the foresail of a square-rigger

FOREYARDS > FOREYARD

FORFAIR *vb* perish

FORFAIRED > FORFAIR

FORFAIRN *adj* worn out

FORFAIRS > FORFAIR

FORFAITER *variant of* > FORFEIT

FORFAULT *variant of* > FORFEIT

FORFAULTS > FORFAULT

FORFEIT *n* thing lost or given up as a penalty for a fault or mistake ▷ *adj* lost as a forfeit

FORFEITED > FORFEIT

FORFEITER > FORFEIT

FORFEITS > FORFEIT

FORFEND *vb* protect or secure

FORFENDED > FORFEND

FORFENDS > FORFEND

FORFEX *n* pair of pincers, esp the paired terminal appendages of an earwig

FORFEXES > FORFEX

FORFICATE *adj* (esp of the tails of certain birds) deeply forked

FORFOCHEN *Scots word for* > EXHAUSTED

FORGAT *past tense of* > FORGET

FORGATHER *vb* gather together

FORGAVE > FORGIVE

FORGE *n* place where metal is worked, smithy ▷ *vb* make a fraudulent imitation of (something)

FORGEABLE > FORGE

FORGED > FORGE

FORGEMAN > FORGE

FORGEMEN > FORGE

FORGER > FORGE

FORGERIES > FORGERY

FORGERS > FORGE

FORGERY *n* illegal copy of something

FORGES > FORGE

FORGET *vb* fail to remember

FORGETFUL *adj* tending to forget

FORGETIVE *adj* imaginative and inventive

FORGETS > FORGET

FORGETTER > FORGET

FORGING *n* process of producing a metal component by hammering

FORGINGS > FORGING

FORGIVE *vb* cease to blame or hold resentment against, pardon

FORGIVEN > FORGIVE

FORGIVER > FORGIVE

FORGIVERS > FORGIVE

FORGIVES > FORGIVE

FORGIVING *adj* willing to forgive

FORGO *vb* do without or give up

FORGOER > FORGO

FORGOERS > FORGO

FORGOES > FORGO

FORGOING > FORGO

FORGONE > FORGO

FORGOT *past tense of* > FORGET

FORGOTTEN *past participle of* > FORGET

FORHAILE *vb* distress

FORHAILED > FORHAILE

FORHAILES > FORHAILE

FORHENT *variant of* > FOREHENT

FORHENTS > FORHENT

FORHOO *vb* forsake

FORHOOED > FORHOO

FORHOOIE *variant of* > FORHOO

FORHOOIED > FORHOOIE

FORHOOIES > FORHOOIE

FORHOOING > FORHOO

FORHOOS > FORHOO

FORHOW *variant of* > FORHOO

FORHOWED > FORHOW

FORHOWING > FORHOW

FORHOWS > FORHOW

FORINSEC *adj* foreign

FORINT *n* standard monetary unit of Hungary, divided into 100 fillér

FORINTS > FORINT

FORJASKIT *adj* exhausted

FORJESKIT *variant of* > FORJASKIT

FORJUDGE *vb* deprive of a right by the judgment of a court

FORJUDGED > FORJUDGE

FORJUDGES > FORJUDGE

FORK *n* tool for eating food, with prongs and a handle ▷ *vb* pick up, dig, etc with a fork

FORKBALL *n* method of pitching in baseball

FORKBALLS > FORKBALL

FORKED *adj* having a fork or forklike parts

FORKEDLY > FORKED

FORKER > FORK

FORKERS > FORK

FORKFUL > FORK

FORKFULS > FORK

FORKHEAD *n* forked head of a rod

FORKHEADS > FORKHEAD

FORKIER > FORKY

FORKIEST > FORKY

FORKINESS > FORKY

FORKING > FORK

FORKLESS > FORK

FORKLIFT *n* vehicle having two power-operated horizontal prongs that can be raised and lowered for loading, transporting, and unloading goods, esp goods that are stacked on wooden pallets

FORKLIFTS > FORKLIFT

FORKLIKE > FORK

FORKS > FORK

FORKSFUL > FORK

FORKTAIL *n* bird belonging to the flycatcher family

FORKTAILS > FORKTAIL

FORKY *adj* forked

FORLANA *n* Venetian dance

FORLANAS > FORLANA

FORLEND *variant of* > FORELEND

FORLENDS > FORLEND

FORLENT > FORLEND

FORLESE *vb* lose

FORLESES > FORLESE

FORLESING > FORLESE

FORLORE > FORLESE

FORLORN *adj* lonely and unhappy ▷ *n* forsaken person

FORLORNER > FORLORN

FORLORNLY > FORLORN

FORLORNS > FORLORN

FORM *n* shape or appearance ▷ *vb* give a (particular) shape to or take a (particular) shape

FORMABLE > FORM

FORMABLY > FORM

FORMAL *adj* of or characterized by established conventions of ceremony and behaviour

FORMALIN *n* solution of formaldehyde in water, used as a disinfectant or a preservative for biological specimens

FORMALINS > FORMALIN

FORMALISE *same as* > FORMALIZE

FORMALISM *n* concern with outward appearances and structure at the expense of content

FORMALIST > FORMALISM

FORMALITY *n* requirement of custom or etiquette

FORMALIZE *vb* make official or formal

FORMALLY > FORMAL

FORMALS > FORMAL

FORMAMIDE *n* amide derived from formic acid

FORMANT *n* any of several frequency ranges within which the partials of a sound, esp a vowel sound, are at their strongest, thus imparting to the sound its own special quality, tone colour, or timbre

**FORMANTS** > FORMANT
**FORMAT** n size and shape of a publication ▷ vb arrange in a format
**FORMATE** n any salt or ester of formic acid containing the ion HCOO⁻ or the group HCOO–
**FORMATED** > FORMAT
**FORMATES** > FORMATE
**FORMATING** > FORMAT
**FORMATION** n forming
**FORMATIVE** adj of or relating to development ▷ n inflectional or derivational affix
**FORMATS** > FORMAT
**FORMATTED** > FORMAT
**FORMATTER** > FORMAT
**FORME** n type matter, blocks, etc, assembled in a chase and ready for printing
**FORMED** > FORM
**FORMEE** n type of heraldic cross
**FORMER** adj of an earlier time, previous ▷ n person or thing that forms or shapes
**FORMERLY** adv in the past
**FORMERS** > FORMER
**FORMES** > FORME
**FORMFUL** adj imaginative
**FORMIATE** variant of > FORMATE
**FORMIATES** > FORMIATE
**FORMIC** adj of, relating to, or derived from ants
**FORMICA** n tradename for any of various laminated plastic sheets, containing melamine, used esp for heat-resistant surfaces that can be easily cleaned
**FORMICANT** adj low-tension (of pulse)
**FORMICARY** n ant hill
**FORMICAS** > FORMICA
**FORMICATE** vb crawl around like ants
**FORMING** > FORM
**FORMINGS** > FORM
**FORMLESS** adj without a definite shape or form
**FORMOL** same as > FORMALIN
**FORMOLS** > FORMOL
**FORMS** > FORM
**FORMULA** n group of numbers, letters, or symbols expressing a scientific or mathematical rule
**FORMULAE** > FORMULA
**FORMULAIC** > FORMULA
**FORMULAR** adj of or relating to formulas
**FORMULARY** n book of prescribed formulas ▷ adj of, relating to, or of the nature of a formulary
**FORMULAS** > FORMULA
**FORMULATE** vb plan or describe precisely and

clearly
**FORMULISE** vb express in a formula
**FORMULISM** n adherence to or belief in formulas
**FORMULIST** > FORMULISM
**FORMULIZE** variant of > FORMULISE
**FORMWORK** n arrangement of wooden boards, bolts, etc, used to shape reinforced concrete while it is setting
**FORMWORKS** > FORMWORK
**FORMYL** n of, consisting of, or containing the monovalent group HCO-
**FORMYLS** > FORMYL
**FORNENST** prep situated against or facing towards
**FORNENT** variant of > FORNENST
**FORNICAL** > FORNIX
**FORNICATE** vb have sexual intercourse without being married ▷ adj arched or hoodlike in form
**FORNICES** > FORNIX
**FORNIX** n any archlike structure, esp the arched band of white fibres at the base of the brain
**FORPET** n quarter of a peck (measure)
**FORPETS** > FORPET
**FORPINE** vb waste away
**FORPINED** > FORPINE
**FORPINES** > FORPINE
**FORPINING** > FORPINE
**FORPIT** variant of > FORPET
**FORPITS** > FORPIT
**FORRAD** adv forward
**FORRADER** > FORRAD
**FORRARDER** adv further forward
**FORRAY** archaic variant of > FORAY
**FORRAYED** > FORRAY
**FORRAYING** > FORRAY
**FORRAYS** > FORRAY
**FORREN** adj foreign
**FORRIT** adv forward(s)
**FORSAID** > FORSAY
**FORSAKE** vb withdraw support or friendship from
**FORSAKEN** adj completely deserted or helpless
**FORSAKER** > FORSAKE
**FORSAKERS** > FORSAKE
**FORSAKES** > FORSAKE
**FORSAKING** > FORSAKE
**FORSAY** vb renounce
**FORSAYING** > FORSAY
**FORSAYS** > FORSAY
**FORSLACK** vb be neglectful
**FORSLACKS** > FORSLACK
**FORSLOE** variant of > FORSLOW
**FORSLOED** > FORSLOE
**FORSLOES** > FORSLOE
**FORSLOW** vb hinder
**FORSLOWED** > FORSLOW
**FORSLOWS** > FORSLOW
**FORSOOK** past tense

of > FORSAKE
**FORSOOTH** adv indeed
**FORSPEAK** vb bewitch
**FORSPEAKS** > FORSPEAK
**FORSPEND** vb exhaust
**FORSPENDS** > FORSPEND
**FORSPENT** > FORSPEND
**FORSPOKE** > FORSPEAK
**FORSPOKEN** > FORSPEAK
**FORSWATT** adj sweat-covered
**FORSWEAR** vb renounce or reject
**FORSWEARS** > FORSWEAR
**FORSWINK** vb exhaust through toil
**FORSWINKS** > FORSWINK
**FORSWONCK** variant of > FORSWUNK
**FORSWORE** > FORSWEAR
**FORSWORN** past participle of > FORSWEAR
**FORSWUNK** adj overworked
**FORSYTHIA** n shrub with yellow flowers in spring
**FORT** n fortified building or place ▷ vb fortify
**FORTALICE** n small fort or outwork of a fortification
**FORTE** n thing at which a person excels ▷ adv loudly
**FORTED** > FORT
**FORTES** > FORTIS
**FORTH** adv forwards, out, or away ▷ prep out of
**FORTHCAME** > FORTHCOME
**FORTHCOME** vb come forth
**FORTHINK** vb regret
**FORTHINKS** > FORTHINK
**FORTHWITH** adv at once
**FORTHY** adv therefore
**FORTIES** > FORTY
**FORTIETH** adj being the ordinal number of forty in numbering or counting order, position, time, etc. Often written: 40th ▷ n one of 40 approximately equal parts of something
**FORTIETHS** > FORTIETH
**FORTIFIED** > FORTIFY
**FORTIFIER** > FORTIFY
**FORTIFIES** > FORTIFY
**FORTIFY** vb make (a place) defensible, as by building walls
**FORTILAGE** n small fort
**FORTING** > FORT
**FORTIS** adj (of a consonant) articulated with considerable muscular tension of the speech organs or with a great deal of breath pressure or plosion ▷ n consonant, such as English p or f, pronounced with considerable muscular force or breath pressure
**FORTITUDE** n courage in adversity or pain
**FORTLET** > FORT
**FORTLETS** > FORT
**FORTNIGHT** n two weeks

**FORTRESS** n large fort or fortified town ▷ vb protect with or as if with a fortress
**FORTS** > FORT
**FORTUITY** n chance or accidental occurrence
**FORTUNATE** adj having good luck
**FORTUNE** n luck, esp when favourable ▷ vb befall
**FORTUNED** > FORTUNE
**FORTUNES** > FORTUNE
**FORTUNING** > FORTUNE
**FORTUNISE** same as > FORTUNIZE
**FORTUNIZE** vb make happy
**FORTY** n four times ten ▷ adj amounting to forty ▷ determiner amounting to forty
**FORTYISH** > FORTY
**FORUM** n meeting or medium for open discussion or debate
**FORUMS** > FORUM
**FORWANDER** vb wander far
**FORWARD** same as > FORWARDS
**FORWARDED** > FORWARD
**FORWARDER** n person or thing that forwards
**FORWARDLY** > FORWARD
**FORWARDS** adv towards or at a place further ahead in space or time
**FORWARN** archaic word for > FORBID
**FORWARNED** > FORWARN
**FORWARNS** > FORWARN
**FORWASTE** vb lay waste
**FORWASTED** > FORWASTE
**FORWASTES** > FORWASTE
**FORWEARY** vb exhaust
**FORWENT** past tense of > FORGO
**FORWHY** adv for what reason
**FORWORN** adj weary
**FORZA** n force
**FORZANDI** > FORZANDO
**FORZANDO** another word for > SFORZANDO
**FORZANDOS** > FORZANDO
**FORZAS** > FORZA
**FORZATI** > FORZATO
**FORZATO** variant of > FORZANDO
**FORZATOS** > FORZATO
**FOSCARNET** n drug used to treat AIDS
**FOSS** same as > FOSSE
**FOSSA** n anatomical depression, trench, or hollow area
**FOSSAE** > FOSSA
**FOSSAS** > FOSSA
**FOSSATE** adj having cavities or depressions
**FOSSE** n ditch or moat, esp one dug as a fortification
**FOSSED** adj having a ditch or moat
**FOSSES** > FOSSE

**FOSSETTE** n small depression or fossa, as in a bone

**FOSSETTES** > FOSSETTE

**FOSSICK** vb search, esp for gold or precious stones

**FOSSICKED** > FOSSICK

**FOSSICKER** > FOSSICK

**FOSSICKS** > FOSSICK

**FOSSIL** n hardened remains of a prehistoric animal or plant preserved in rock ▷ adj of, like, or being a fossil

**FOSSILISE** same as > FOSSILIZE

**FOSSILIZE** vb turn into a fossil

**FOSSILS** > FOSSIL

**FOSSOR** n grave digger

**FOSSORIAL** adj (of the forelimbs and skeleton of burrowing animals) adapted for digging

**FOSSORS** > FOSSOR

**FOSSULA** n small fossa

**FOSSULAE** > FOSSULA

**FOSSULATE** adj hollowed

**FOSTER** vb promote the growth or development of ▷ adj of or involved in fostering a child

**FOSTERAGE** n act of caring for or bringing up a foster child

**FOSTERED** > FOSTER

**FOSTERER** > FOSTER

**FOSTERERS** > FOSTER

**FOSTERING** > FOSTER

**FOSTERS** > FOSTER

**FOSTRESS** n female fosterer

**FOTHER** vb stop a leak in a ship's hull

**FOTHERED** > FOTHER

**FOTHERING** > FOTHER

**FOTHERS** > FOTHER

**FOU** adj full ▷ n bushel

**FOUAT** n succulent pink-flowered plant

**FOUATS** > FOUAT

**FOUD** n sheriff in Orkney and Shetland

**FOUDRIE** n foud's district or office

**FOUDRIES** > FOUDRIE

**FOUDS** > FOUD

**FOUER** > FOU

**FOUEST** > FOU

**FOUET** n archaic word for a whip

**FOUETS** > FOUET

**FOUETTE** n step in ballet in which the dancer stands on one foot and makes a whiplike movement with the other

**FOUETTES** > FOUETTE

**FOUGADE** n booby-trapped pit or type of mine

**FOUGADES** > FOUGADE

**FOUGASSE** n type of bread made with olive oil

**FOUGASSES** > FOUGASSE

**FOUGHT** > FIGHT

**FOUGHTEN** > FIGHT

**FOUGHTIER** > FOUGHTY

**FOUGHTY** adj musty

**FOUL** adj loathsome or offensive ▷ n violation of the rules ▷ vb make dirty or polluted

**FOULARD** n soft light fabric of plain-weave or twill-weave silk or rayon, usually with a printed design

**FOULARDS** > FOULARD

**FOULBROOD** n disease of honeybees

**FOULDER** vb flash like lightning

**FOULDERED** > FOULDER

**FOULDERS** > FOULDER

**FOULE** n type of woollen cloth

**FOULED** > FOUL

**FOULER** > FOUL

**FOULES** > FOULE

**FOULEST** > FOUL

**FOULIE** n bad mood

**FOULIES** > FOULIE

**FOULING** > FOUL

**FOULINGS** > FOUL

**FOULLY** > FOUL

**FOULMART** n polecat

**FOULMARTS** > FOULMART

**FOULNESS** n state or quality of being foul

**FOULS** > FOUL

**FOUMART** former name for the > POLECAT

**FOUMARTS** > FOUMART

**FOUND** vb set up or establish (an institution, etc)

**FOUNDED** > FOUND

**FOUNDER** vb break down or fail ▷ n person who establishes an institution, company, society, etc

**FOUNDERED** > FOUNDER

**FOUNDERS** > FOUNDER

**FOUNDING** > FOUND

**FOUNDINGS** > FOUND

**FOUNDLING** n abandoned baby

**FOUNDRESS** > FOUNDER

**FOUNDRIES** > FOUNDRY

**FOUNDRY** n place where metal is melted and cast

**FOUNDS** > FOUND

**FOUNT** same as > FONT

**FOUNTAIN** n jet of water

**FOUNTAINS** > FOUNTAIN

**FOUNTFUL** adj full of springs

**FOUNTS** > FOUNT

**FOUR** n one more than three ▷ adj amounting to four ▷ determiner amounting to four

**FOURBALL** n in golf, match for two pairs in which each player uses his own ball, the better score of each pair being counted at every hole

**FOURBALLS** > FOURBALL

**FOURCHEE** n type of heraldic cross

**FOUREYED** adj wearing spectacles

**FOURFOLD** adj having four times as many or as much ▷ adv by four times as many or as much

**FOURGON** n long covered wagon, used mainly for carrying baggage, supplies, etc

**FOURGONS** > FOURGON

**FOURPENCE** n former English silver coin then worth four pennies

**FOURPENNY** adj blow, esp with the fist

**FOURPLEX** n building that contains four separate dwellings

**FOURS** > FOUR

**FOURSCORE** adj eighty

**FOURSES** n snack eaten at four o'clock

**FOURSOME** n group of four people

**FOURSOMES** > FOURSOME

**FOURTEEN** n four and ten ▷ adj amounting to fourteen ▷ determiner amounting to fourteen

**FOURTEENS** > FOURTEEN

**FOURTH** n (of) number four in a series ▷ adj of or being number four in a series ▷ adv after the third person, position, event, etc

**FOURTHLY** > FOURTH

**FOURTHS** > FOURTH

**FOUS** > FOU

**FOUSSA** n Madagascan civet-like animal

**FOUSSAS** > FOUSSA

**FOUSTIER** > FOUSTY

**FOUSTIEST** > FOUSTY

**FOUSTY** archaic variant of > FUSTY

**FOUTER** same as > FOOTER

**FOUTERED** > FOUTER

**FOUTERING** > FOUTER

**FOUTERS** > FOUTER

**FOUTH** n abundance

**FOUTHS** > FOUTH

**FOUTRA** n fig; expression of contempt

**FOUTRAS** > FOUTRA

**FOUTRE** vb footer

**FOUTRED** > FOUTRE

**FOUTRES** > FOUTRE

**FOUTRING** > FOUTRE

**FOVEA** n any small pit or depression in the surface of a bodily organ or part

**FOVEAE** > FOVEA

**FOVEAL** > FOVEA

**FOVEAS** > FOVEA

**FOVEATE** > FOVEA

**FOVEATED** > FOVEA

**FOVEIFORM** adj shaped like small pit

**FOVEOLA** n small fovea

**FOVEOLAE** > FOVEOLA

**FOVEOLAR** > FOVEOLA

**FOVEOLAS** > FOVEOLA

**FOVEOLATE** > FOVEOLA

**FOVEOLE** same as > FOVEOLA

**FOVEOLES** > FOVEOLE

**FOVEOLET** same as > FOVEOLA

**FOVEOLETS** > FOVEOLET

**FOWL** n domestic cock or hen ▷ vb hunt or snare wild birds

**FOWLED** > FOWL

**FOWLER** > FOWLING

**FOWLERS** > FOWLING

**FOWLING** n shooting or trapping of birds for sport or as a livelihood

**FOWLINGS** > FOWLING

**FOWLPOX** n viral infection of poultry and other birds

**FOWLPOXES** > FOWLPOX

**FOWLS** > FOWL

**FOWTH** variant of > FOUTH

**FOWTHS** > FOWTH

**FOX** n reddish-brown bushy-tailed animal of the dog family ▷ vb perplex or deceive

**FOXBERRY** n lingonberry

**FOXED** > FOX

**FOXES** > FOX

**FOXFIRE** n luminescent glow emitted by certain fungi on rotting wood

**FOXFIRES** > FOXFIRE

**FOXFISH** n type of shark

**FOXFISHES** > FOXFISH

**FOXGLOVE** n tall plant with purple or white flowers

**FOXGLOVES** > FOXGLOVE

**FOXHOLE** n small pit dug for protection

**FOXHOLES** > FOXHOLE

**FOXHOUND** n dog bred for hunting foxes

**FOXHOUNDS** > FOXHOUND

**FOXHUNT** n hunting of foxes with hounds ▷ vb hunt foxes with hounds

**FOXHUNTED** > FOXHUNT

**FOXHUNTER** > FOXHUNT

**FOXHUNTS** > FOXHUNT

**FOXIE** n fox terrier

**FOXIER** > FOXY

**FOXIES** > FOXIE

**FOXIEST** > FOXY

**FOXILY** > FOXY

**FOXINESS** > FOXY

**FOXING** n piece of leather used to reinforce or trim part of the upper of a shoe

**FOXINGS** > FOXING

**FOXLIKE** > FOX

**FOXSHARK** n thresher shark

**FOXSHARKS** > FOXSHARK

**FOXSHIP** n cunning

**FOXSHIPS** > FOXSHIP

**FOXSKIN** adj made from the skin of a fox ▷ n skin of a fox

**FOXSKINS** > FOXSKIN

**FOXTAIL** n any grass of the genus *Alopecurus*, esp *A. pratensis*, of Europe, Asia, and South America, having soft cylindrical spikes of flowers: cultivated as a pasture grass

**FOXTAILS** > FOXTAIL

**FOXTROT** n ballroom dance with slow and quick steps ▷ vb perform this dance

**FOXTROTS** > FOXTROT

**FOXY** adj of or like a fox, esp in craftiness

**FOY** n loyalty

**FOYBOAT** n small rowing boat

**FOYBOATS** > FOYBOAT

**FOYER** n entrance hall in a theatre, cinema, or hotel

**FOYERS** > FOYER

**FOYLE** variant of > FOIL

**FOYLED** > FOYLE

**FOYLES** > FOYLE

**FOYLING** > FOYLE

**FOYNE** variant of > FOIN

**FOYNED** > FOYNE

**FOYNES** > FOYNE

**FOYNING** > FOYNE

**FOYS** > FOY

**FOZIER** > FOZY

**FOZIEST** > FOZY

**FOZINESS** > FOZY

**FOZY** adj spongy

**FRA** n brother: a title given to an Italian monk or friar

**FRAB** vb nag

**FRABBED** > FRAB

**FRABBING** > FRAB

**FRABBIT** adj peevish

**FRABJOUS** adj splendid

**FRABS** > FRAB

**FRACAS** n noisy quarrel

**FRACASES** > FRACAS

**FRACK** adj bold

**FRACKING** n method of releasing oil or gas from rock

**FRACKINGS** > FRACKING

**FRACT** vb break

**FRACTAL** n figure or surface generated by successive subdivisions of a simpler polygon or polyhedron, according to some iterative process ▷ adj of, relating to, or involving such a process

**FRACTALS** > FRACTAL

**FRACTED** > FRACT

**FRACTI** > FRACTUS

**FRACTING** > FRACT

**FRACTION** n numerical quantity that is not a whole number ▷ vb divide

**FRACTIONS** > FRACTION

**FRACTIOUS** adj easily upset and angered

**FRACTS** > FRACT

**FRACTUR** variant of > FRAKTUR

**FRACTURAL** > FRACTURE

**FRACTURE** n breaking, esp of a bone ▷ vb break

**FRACTURED** > FRACTURE

**FRACTURER** > FRACTURE

**FRACTURES** > FRACTURE

**FRACTURS** > FRACTUR

**FRACTUS** n ragged-shaped cloud formation

**FRAE** Scot word for > FROM

**FRAENA** > FRAENUM

**FRAENUM** n fold of membrane or skin, such as the fold beneath the tongue, that supports an organ

**FRAENUMS** > FRAENUM

**FRAG** vb kill or wound (a fellow soldier or superior officer) deliberately with an explosive device

**FRAGGED** > FRAG

**FRAGGING** > FRAG

**FRAGGINGS** > FRAG

**FRAGILE** adj easily broken or damaged

**FRAGILELY** > FRAGILE

**FRAGILER** > FRAGILE

**FRAGILEST** > FRAGILE

**FRAGILITY** > FRAGILE

**FRAGMENT** n piece broken off ▷ vb break into pieces

**FRAGMENTS** > FRAGMENT

**FRAGOR** n sudden sound

**FRAGORS** > FRAGOR

**FRAGRANCE** n pleasant smell

**FRAGRANCY** same as > FRAGRANCE

**FRAGRANT** adj sweet-smelling

**FRAGS** > FRAG

**FRAICHEUR** n freshness

**FRAIL** adj physically weak ▷ n rush basket for figs or raisins

**FRAILER** > FRAIL

**FRAILEST** > FRAIL

**FRAILISH** > FRAIL

**FRAILLY** > FRAIL

**FRAILNESS** > FRAIL

**FRAILS** > FRAIL

**FRAILTEE** variant of > FRAILTY

**FRAILTEES** > FRAILTEE

**FRAILTIES** > FRAILTY

**FRAILTY** n physical or moral weakness

**FRAIM** n stranger

**FRAIMS** > FRAIM

**FRAISE** n neck ruff worn during the 16th century ▷ vb provide a rampart with a palisade

**FRAISED** > FRAISE

**FRAISES** > FRAISE

**FRAISING** > FRAISE

**FRAKTUR** n style of typeface, formerly used in German typesetting for many printed works

**FRAKTURS** > FRAKTUR

**FRAMABLE** > FRAME

**FRAMBESIA** same as > FRAMBOESIA

**FRAMBOISE** n brandy distilled from raspberries in the Alsace-Lorraine region

**FRAME** n structure giving

shape or support ▷ vb put together, construct

**FRAMEABLE** > FRAME

**FRAMED** > FRAME

**FRAMELESS** > FRAME

**FRAMER** > FRAME

**FRAMERS** > FRAME

**FRAMES** > FRAME

**FRAMEWORK** n supporting structure

**FRAMING** n frame, framework, or system of frames

**FRAMINGS** > FRAMING

**FRAMPAL** same as > FRAMPOLD

**FRAMPLER** n quarrelsome person

**FRAMPLERS** > FRAMPLER

**FRAMPOLD** adj peevish

**FRANC** n monetary unit of Switzerland, various African countries, and formerly of France and Belgium

**FRANCHISE** n right to vote ▷ vb grant (a person, firm, etc) a franchise

**FRANCISE** same as > FRANCIZE

**FRANCISED** > FRANCISE

**FRANCISES** > FRANCISE

**FRANCIUM** n radioactive metallic element

**FRANCIUMS** > FRANCIUM

**FRANCIZE** vb make French

**FRANCIZED** > FRANCIZE

**FRANCIZES** > FRANCIZE

**FRANCO** adj post-free

**FRANCOLIN** n any African or Asian partridge of the genus Francolinus

**FRANCS** > FRANC

**FRANGER** n condom

**FRANGERS** > FRANGER

**FRANGIBLE** adj breakable or fragile

**FRANGLAIS** n informal French containing a high proportion of words of English origin

**FRANION** n lover, paramour

**FRANIONS** > FRANION

**FRANK** adj honest and straightforward in speech or attitude ▷ n official mark on a letter permitting delivery ▷ vb put such a mark on (a letter)

**FRANKABLE** > FRANK

**FRANKED** > FRANK

**FRANKER** > FRANK

**FRANKERS** > FRANK

**FRANKEST** > FRANK

**FRANKFORT** same as > FRANKFURT

**FRANKFURT** n light brown smoked sausage

**FRANKING** > FRANK

**FRANKLIN** n (in 14th- and 15th-century England) a substantial landholder of free but not noble birth

**FRANKLINS** > FRANKLIN

**FRANKLY** adv in truth

**FRANKNESS** > FRANK

**FRANKS** > FRANK

**FRANSERIA** n American shrub

**FRANTIC** adj distracted with rage, grief, joy, etc

**FRANTICLY** > FRANTIC

**FRANZIER** > FRANZY

**FRANZIEST** > FRANZY

**FRANZY** adj irritable

**FRAP** vb lash down or together

**FRAPPANT** adj striking, vivid

**FRAPPE** adj (of drinks) chilled ▷ n drink consisting of a liqueur, etc, poured over crushed ice

**FRAPPED** > FRAP

**FRAPPEE** > FRAPPE

**FRAPPES** > FRAPPE

**FRAPPING** > FRAP

**FRAPS** > FRAP

**FRAS** > FRA

**FRASCATI** n dry or semisweet white wine from the Lazio region of Italy

**FRASCATIS** > FRASCATI

**FRASS** n excrement or other refuse left by insects and insect larvae

**FRASSES** > FRASS

**FRAT** n member of a fraternity

**FRATCH** n quarrel ▷ vb quarrel

**FRATCHES** > FRATCH

**FRATCHETY** same as > FRATCHY

**FRATCHIER** > FRATCHY

**FRATCHING** > FRATCH

**FRATCHY** adj quarrelsome

**FRATE** n friar

**FRATER** n mendicant friar or a lay brother in a monastery or priory

**FRATERIES** > FRATER

**FRATERNAL** adj of a brother, brotherly

**FRATERS** > FRATER

**FRATERY** > FRATER

**FRATI** > FRATE

**FRATRIES** > FRATER

**FRATRY** > FRATER

**FRATS** > FRAT

**FRAU** n married German woman

**FRAUD** n (criminal) deception, swindle

**FRAUDFUL** > FRAUD

**FRAUDS** > FRAUD

**FRAUDSMAN** n practitioner of criminal fraud

**FRAUDSMEN** > FRAUDSMAN

**FRAUDSTER** n person who commits a fraud

**FRAUGHAN** Irish word for > WHORTLEBERRY

**FRAUGHANS** > FRAUGHAN

**FRAUGHT** adj tense or

anxious ▷ *vb* archaic word for load ▷ *n* archaic word for freight
**FRAUGHTED** > FRAUGHT
**FRAUGHTER** > FRAUGHT
**FRAUGHTS** > FRAUGHT
**FRAULEIN** *n* unmarried German woman
**FRAULEINS** > FRAULEIN
**FRAUS** > FRAU
**FRAUTAGE** *variant of* > FRAUGHTAGE
**FRAUTAGES** > FRAUTAGE
**FRAWZEY** *n* celebration
**FRAWZEYS** > FRAWZEY
**FRAY** *n* noisy quarrel or conflict ▷ *vb* make or become ragged at the edge
**FRAYED** > FRAY
**FRAYING** > FRAY
**FRAYINGS** > FRAY
**FRAYS** > FRAY
**FRAZIL** *n* small pieces of ice that form in water moving turbulently enough to prevent the formation of a sheet of ice
**FRAZILS** > FRAZIL
**FRAZZLE** *n* exhausted state ▷ *vb* tire out
**FRAZZLED** > FRAZZLE
**FRAZZLES** > FRAZZLE
**FRAZZLING** > FRAZZLE
**FREAK** *n* abnormal person or thing ▷ *adj* abnormal ▷ *vb* streak with colour
**FREAKED** > FREAK
**FREAKERY** as in *control freakery* obsessive need to be in control of events
**FREAKFUL** *variant of* > FREAKISH
**FREAKIER** > FREAKY
**FREAKIEST** > FREAKY
**FREAKILY** > FREAKY
**FREAKING** > FREAK
**FREAKISH** *adj* of, related to, or characteristic of a freak
**FREAKOUT** *n* heightened emotional state
**FREAKOUTS** > FREAKOUT
**FREAKS** > FREAK
**FREAKY** *adj* weird, peculiar
**FRECKLE** *n* small brown spot on the skin ▷ *vb* mark or become marked with freckles
**FRECKLED** > FRECKLE
**FRECKLES** > FRECKLE
**FRECKLIER** > FRECKLE
**FRECKLING** > FRECKLE
**FRECKLY** > FRECKLE
**FREDAINE** *n* escapade
**FREDAINES** > FREDAINE
**FREE** *adj* able to act at will, not compelled or restrained ▷ *vb* release, liberate
**FREEBASE** *n* cocaine that has been refined by heating it in ether or some other solvent ▷ *vb* refine (cocaine) in this way
**FREEBASED** > FREEBASE

**FREEBASER** > FREEBASE
**FREEBASES** > FREEBASE
**FREEBEE** *variant of* > FREEBIE
**FREEBEES** > FREEBEE
**FREEBIE** *n* something provided without charge ▷ *adj* without charge
**FREEBIES** > FREEBIE
**FREEBOARD** *n* space or distance between the deck of a vessel and the water line
**FREEBOOT** *vb* act as a freebooter
**FREEBOOTS** > FREEBOOT
**FREEBOOTY** > FREEBOOT
**FREEBORN** *adj* not born in slavery
**FREED** > FREE
**FREEDMAN** *n* man freed from slavery
**FREEDMEN** > FREEDMAN
**FREEDOM** *n* being free
**FREEDOMS** > FREEDOM
**FREEFORM** *n* irregular flowing shape, often used in industrial or fabric design ▷ *adj* freely flowing, spontaneous
**FREEGAN** *n* person who avoids buying consumer goods, recycling discarded goods instead
**FREEGANS** > FREEGAN
**FREEHAND** *adj* drawn without guiding instruments
**FREEHOLD** *n* tenure of land for life without restrictions ▷ *adj* of or held by freehold
**FREEHOLDS** > FREEHOLD
**FREEING** > FREE
**FREELANCE** *n* (of) a self-employed person doing specific pieces of work for various employers ▷ *vb* work as a freelance ▷ *adv* of or as a freelance
**FREELOAD** *vb* act as a freeloader
**FREELOADS** > FREELOAD
**FREELY** > FREE
**FREEMAN** *n* person who has been given the freedom of a city
**FREEMASON** *n* member of a guild of itinerant skilled stonemasons, who had a system of secret signs and passwords with which they recognized each other
**FREEMEN** > FREEMAN
**FREENESS** > FREE
**FREEPHONE** *n* system of telephone use in which the cost of calls in response to an advertisement is borne by the advertiser
**FREER** *n* liberator
**FREERS** > FREER
**FREES** > FREE

**FREESHEET** *n* newspaper that is distributed free, paid for by its advertisers
**FREESIA** *n* plant with fragrant tubular flowers
**FREESIAS** > FREESIA
**FREEST** > FREE
**FREESTONE** *n* any fine-grained stone, esp sandstone or limestone, that can be cut and worked in any direction without breaking
**FREESTYLE** *n* competition, such as in swimming, in which each participant may use a style of his or her choice
**FREET** *n* omen or superstition
**FREETIER** > FREETY
**FREETIEST** > FREETY
**FREETS** > FREET
**FREETY** *adj* superstitious
**FREEWARE** *n* computer software that may be distributed and used without payment
**FREEWARES** > FREEWARE
**FREEWAY** *n* motorway
**FREEWAYS** > FREEWAY
**FREEWHEEL** *vb* travel downhill on a bicycle without pedalling ▷ *n* device in the rear hub of a bicycle wheel that permits it to rotate freely while the pedals are stationary
**FREEWILL** *n* apparent human ability to make choices that are not externally determined
**FREEWOMAN** *n* woman who is free or at liberty
**FREEWOMEN** > FREEWOMAN
**FREEWRITE** *vb* write freely without stopping or thinking
**FREEWROTE** > FREEWRITE
**FREEZABLE** > FREEZE
**FREEZE** *vb* change from a liquid to a solid by the reduction of temperature, as water to ice ▷ *n* period of very cold weather
**FREEZER** *n* insulated cabinet for cold-storage of perishable foods
**FREEZERS** > FREEZER
**FREEZES** > FREEZE
**FREEZING** > FREEZE
**FREEZINGS** > FREEZE
**FREIGHT** *n* commercial transport of goods ▷ *vb* send by freight
**FREIGHTED** > FREIGHT
**FREIGHTER** *n* ship or aircraft for transporting goods
**FREIGHTS** > FREIGHT
**FREIT** *variant of* > FREET
**FREITIER** > FREITY
**FREITIEST** > FREITY
**FREITS** > FREIT

**FREITY** *adj* superstitious
**FREMD** *adj* alien or strange
**FREMDS** > FREMD
**FREMIT** *same as* > FREMD
**FREMITS** > FREMIT
**FREMITUS** *n* vibration felt by the hand when placed on a part of the body, esp the chest, when the patient is speaking or coughing
**FRENA** > FRENUM
**FRENCH** *vb* (of food) cut into thin strips
**FRENCHED** > FRENCH
**FRENCHES** > FRENCH
**FRENCHIFY** *vb* make or become French in appearance, behaviour, etc
**FRENCHING** > FRENCH
**FRENETIC** *adj* uncontrolled, excited ▷ *n* madman
**FRENETICS** > FRENETIC
**FRENNE** *variant of* > FREMD
**FRENULA** > FRENULUM
**FRENULAR** > FRENULUM
**FRENULUM** *n* strong bristle or group of bristles on the hind wing of some moths and other insects, by which the forewing and hind wing are united during flight
**FRENULUMS** > FRENULUM
**FRENUM** *same as* > FRAENUM
**FRENUMS** > FRENUM
**FRENZICAL** > FRENZY
**FRENZIED** *adj* filled with or as if with frenzy
**FRENZIES** > FRENZY
**FRENZILY** > FRENZY
**FRENZY** *n* violent mental derangement ▷ *vb* make frantic
**FRENZYING** > FRENZY
**FREON** *n* trademark term meaning any of a group of chemically unreactive chlorofluorocarbons used as aerosol propellants, refrigerants, and solvents
**FREONS** > FREON
**FREQUENCE** *same as* > FREQUENCY
**FREQUENCY** *n* rate of occurrence
**FREQUENT** *adj* happening often ▷ *vb* visit habitually
**FREQUENTS** > FREQUENT
**FRERE** *n* friar
**FRERES** > FRERE
**FRESCADE** *n* shady place or cool walk
**FRESCADES** > FRESCADE
**FRESCO** *n* watercolour painting done on wet plaster on a wall ▷ *vb* paint a fresco
**FRESCOED** > FRESCO
**FRESCOER** > FRESCO
**FRESCOERS** > FRESCO
**FRESCOES** > FRESCO
**FRESCOING** > FRESCO

FRESCOIST > FRESCO

FRESCOS > FRESCO

FRESH adj newly made, acquired, etc ▷ adv recently ▷ vb freshen

FRESHED > FRESH

FRESHEN vb make or become fresh or fresher

FRESHENED > FRESHEN

FRESHENER > FRESHEN

FRESHENS > FRESHEN

FRESHER n first-year student

FRESHERS > FRESHER

FRESHES > FRESH

FRESHEST > FRESH

FRESHET n sudden overflowing of a river

FRESHETS > FRESHET

FRESHIE n in Indian English, new immigrant to the UK from the Asian subcontinent

FRESHIES > FRESHIE

FRESHING > FRESH

FRESHISH > FRESH

FRESHLY > FRESH

FRESHMAN same as > FRESHER

FRESHMEN > FRESHMAN

FRESHNESS > FRESH

FRESNEL n unit of frequency equivalent to $10^{12}$ hertz

FRESNELS > FRESNEL

FRET vb be worried ▷ n worried state

FRETBOARD n fingerboard with frets on a stringed musical instrument

FRETFUL adj irritable

FRETFULLY > FRETFUL

FRETLESS > FRET

FRETS > FRET

FRETSAW n fine saw with a narrow blade, used for fretwork

FRETSAWS > FRETSAW

FRETSOME adj vexing

FRETTED > FRET

FRETTER > FRET

FRETTERS > FRET

FRETTIER > FRETTY

FRETTIEST > FRETTY

FRETTING > FRET

FRETTINGS > FRET

FRETTY adj decorated with frets

FRETWORK n decorative carving in wood

FRETWORKS > FRETWORK

FRIABLE adj easily crumbled

FRIAND n small almond cake

FRIANDE variant of > FRIAND

FRIANDES > FRIANDE

FRIANDS > FRIAND

FRIAR n member of a male Roman Catholic religious order

FRIARBIRD n any of various Australian honeyeaters of the genus

Philemon, having a naked head

FRIARIES > FRIARY

FRIARLY > FRIAR

FRIARS > FRIAR

FRIARY n house of friars

FRIB n short heavy-conditioned piece of wool removed from a fleece during classing

FRIBBLE vb fritter away ▷ n wasteful or frivolous person or action ▷ adj frivolous

FRIBBLED > FRIBBLE

FRIBBLER > FRIBBLE

FRIBBLERS > FRIBBLE

FRIBBLES > FRIBBLE

FRIBBLING > FRIBBLE

FRIBBLISH adj trifling

FRIBS > FRIB

FRICADEL variant of > FRIKKADEL

FRICADELS > FRICADEL

FRICANDO same as > FRICANDEAU

FRICASSEE n stewed meat served in a thick white sauce ▷ vb prepare (meat) as a fricassee

FRICATIVE n consonant produced by friction of the breath through a partially open mouth, such as (f) or (z) ▷ adj relating to or being a fricative

FRICHT vb frighten

FRICHTED > FRICHT

FRICHTING > FRICHT

FRICHTS > FRICHT

FRICKING adj slang word for absolute

FRICTION n resistance met with by a body moving over another

FRICTIONS > FRICTION

FRIDGE n apparatus in which food and drinks are kept cool ▷ vb archaic word for chafe

FRIDGED > FRIDGE

FRIDGES > FRIDGE

FRIDGING > FRIDGE

FRIED > FRY

FRIEDCAKE n type of doughnut

FRIEND n person whom one knows well and likes ▷ vb befriend

FRIENDED > FRIEND

FRIENDING > FRIEND

FRIENDLY adj showing or expressing liking ▷ n match played for its own sake and not as part of a competition

FRIENDS > FRIEND

FRIER same as > FRYER

FRIERS > FRIER

FRIES > FRY

FRIEZE n ornamental band on a wall ▷ vb give a nap to (cloth)

FRIEZED > FRIEZE

FRIEZES > FRIEZE

FRIEZING > FRIEZE

FRIG vb taboo word meaning masturbate ▷ n fridge

FRIGATE n medium-sized fast warship

FRIGATES > FRIGATE

FRIGATOON n Venetian sailing ship

FRIGES > FRIG

FRIGGED > FRIG

FRIGGER > FRIG

FRIGGERS > FRIG

FRIGGING > FRIG

FRIGGINGS > FRIG

FRIGHT n sudden fear or alarm

FRIGHTED > FRIGHT

FRIGHTEN vb scare or terrify

FRIGHTENS > FRIGHTEN

FRIGHTFUL adj horrifying

FRIGHTING > FRIGHT

FRIGHTS > FRIGHT

FRIGID adj (of a woman) sexually unresponsive

FRIGIDER > FRIGID

FRIGIDEST > FRIGID

FRIGIDITY > FRIGID

FRIGIDLY > FRIGID

FRIGOT variant of > FRIGATE

FRIGOTS > FRIGOT

FRIGS > FRIG

FRIJOL n variety of bean, esp of the French bean, extensively cultivated for food in Mexico

FRIJOLE variant of > FRIJOL

FRIJOLES > FRIJOL

FRIKKADEL n South African meatball

FRILL n gathered strip of fabric attached at one edge ▷ vb adorn or fit with a frill or frills

FRILLED > FRILL

FRILLER > FRILL

FRILLERS > FRILL

FRILLIER > FRILLY

FRILLIES pl n flimsy women's underwear

FRILLIEST > FRILLY

FRILLING > FRILL

FRILLINGS > FRILL

FRILLS > FRILL

FRILLY adj with a frill or frills

FRINGE n hair cut short and hanging over the forehead ▷ vb decorate with a fringe ▷ adj (of theatre) unofficial or unconventional

FRINGED > FRINGE

FRINGES > FRINGE

FRINGIER > FRINGY

FRINGIEST > FRINGY

FRINGING > FRINGE

FRINGY adj having a fringe

FRIPON n rogue

FRIPONS > FRIPON

FRIPPER n dealer in old clothes

FRIPPERER same as > FRIPPER

FRIPPERS > FRIPPER

FRIPPERY n useless ornamentation

FRIPPET n frivolous or flamboyant young woman

FRIPPETS > FRIPPET

FRIS n frieze

FRISBEE n tradename of a light plastic disc, thrown with a spinning motion for recreation or in competition

FRISBEES > FRISBEE

FRISE n fabric with a long normally uncut nap used for upholstery and rugs

FRISEE n endive

FRISEES > FRISEE

FRISES > FRIS

FRISETTE n curly or frizzed fringe, often an artificial hairpiece, worn by women on the forehead

FRISETTES > FRISETTE

FRISEUR n hairdresser

FRISEURS > FRISEUR

FRISK vb move or leap playfully ▷ n playful movement

FRISKA n in Hungarian music, the fast movement of a piece

FRISKAS > FRISKA

FRISKED > FRISK

FRISKER > FRISK

FRISKERS > FRISK

FRISKET n light rectangular frame, attached to the tympan of a hand printing press, that carries a parchment sheet to protect the nonprinting areas

FRISKETS > FRISKET

FRISKFUL > FRISK

FRISKIER > FRISKY

FRISKIEST > FRISKY

FRISKILY > FRISKY

FRISKING > FRISK

FRISKINGS > FRISK

FRISKS > FRISK

FRISKY adj lively or high-spirited

FRISSON n shiver of fear or excitement

FRISSONS > FRISSON

FRIST archaic word for > POSTPONE

FRISTED > FRIST

FRISTING > FRIST

FRISTS > FRIST

FRISURE n styling the hair into curls

FRISURES > FRISURE

FRIT n basic materials, partially or wholly fused, for making glass, glazes for pottery, enamel, etc ▷ vb fuse (materials) in making frit

FRITES pl n chipped potatoes

**FRITFLIES** > FRITFLY
**FRITFLY** n small black dipterous fly, Oscinella frit, whose larvae are destructive to barley, wheat, rye, oats, etc
**FRITH** same as > FIRTH
**FRITHBORH** n type of pledge
**FRITHS** > FRITH
**FRITS** > FRIT
**FRITT** same as > FRIT
**FRITTATA** n Italian dish made with eggs and chopped vegetables or meat, resembling a flat thick omelette
**FRITTATAS** > FRITTATA
**FRITTED** > FRIT
**FRITTER** n piece of food fried in batter ▷ vb waste or squander
**FRITTERED** > FRITTER
**FRITTERER** > FRITTER
**FRITTERS** > FRITTER
**FRITTING** > FRIT
**FRITTS** > FRITY
**FRITURE** archaic word for > FRITTER
**FRITURES** > FRITURE
**FRITZ** n derogatory term for a German soldier
**FRITZES** > FRITZ
**FRIVOL** vb behave frivolously
**FRIVOLED** > FRIVOL
**FRIVOLER** > FRIVOL
**FRIVOLERS** > FRIVOL
**FRIVOLING** > FRIVOL
**FRIVOLITY** > FRIVOLOUS
**FRIVOLLED** > FRIVOL
**FRIVOLLER** > FRIVOL
**FRIVOLOUS** adj not serious or sensible
**FRIVOLS** > FRIVOL
**FRIZ** variant of > FRIZZ
**FRIZE** n coarse woollen fabric ▷ vb freeze
**FRIZED** > FRIZE
**FRIZER** n person who gives nap to cloth
**FRIZERS** > FRIZER
**FRIZES** > FRIZE
**FRIZETTE** same as > FRISETTE
**FRIZETTES** > FRIZETTE
**FRIZING** > FRIZE
**FRIZZ** vb form (hair) into stiff wiry curls ▷ n hair that has been frizzed
**FRIZZANTE** adj (of wine) slightly effervescent
**FRIZZED** > FRIZZ
**FRIZZER** > FRIZZ
**FRIZZERS** > FRIZZ
**FRIZZES** > FRIZZ
**FRIZZIER** > FRIZZY
**FRIZZIES** n condition of having frizzy hair
**FRIZZIEST** > FRIZZY
**FRIZZILY** > FRIZZY
**FRIZZING** > FRIZZ
**FRIZZLE** vb cook or heat until crisp and shrivelled

▷ n tight curl
**FRIZZLED** > FRIZZLE
**FRIZZLER** > FRIZZLE
**FRIZZLERS** > FRIZZLE
**FRIZZLES** > FRIZZLE
**FRIZZLIER** > FRIZZLE
**FRIZZLING** > FRIZZLE
**FRIZZLY** > FRIZZLE
**FRIZZY** adj (of the hair) in tight crisp wiry curls
**FRO** adv away ▷ n afro
**FROCK** n dress ▷ vb invest (a person) with the office or status of a cleric
**FROCKED** > FROCK
**FROCKING** n coarse material suitable for making frocks or work clothes
**FROCKINGS** > FROCKING
**FROCKLESS** > FROCK
**FROCKS** > FROCK
**FROE** n cutting tool with handle and blade at right angles, used for stripping young trees, etc
**FROES** > FROE
**FROG** n smooth-skinned tailless amphibian with long back legs used for jumping
**FROGBIT** n floating aquatic Eurasian plant
**FROGBITS** > FROGBIT
**FROGEYE** n plant disease
**FROGEYED** adj affected by frogeye
**FROGEYES** > FROGEYE
**FROGFISH** n any angler (fish) of the family Antennariidae, in which the body is covered with fleshy processes, including a fleshy lure on top of the head
**FROGGED** adj decorated with frogging
**FROGGERY** n place where frogs are kept
**FROGGIER** > FROGGY
**FROGGIEST** > FROGGY
**FROGGING** n decorative fastening of looped braid on a coat
**FROGGINGS** > FROGGING
**FROGGY** adj like a frog
**FROGLET** n young frog
**FROGLETS** > FROGLET
**FROGLIKE** > FROG
**FROGLING** n young frog
**FROGLINGS** > FROGLING
**FROGMAN** n swimmer with a rubber suit and breathing equipment for working underwater
**FROGMARCH** vb force (a resisting person) to move by holding his arms ▷ n method of carrying a resisting person in which each limb is held and the victim is face downwards
**FROGMEN** > FROGMAN
**FROGMOUTH** n any

nocturnal insectivorous bird of the genera Podargus and Batrachostomus, of SE Asia and Australia, similar to the nightjars: family Podargidae, order Caprimulgiformes
**FROGS** > FROG
**FROGSPAWN** n jelly-like substance containing frog's eggs
**FROIDEUR** n coldness
**FROIDEURS** > FROIDEUR
**FROING** as in toing and froing going back and forth
**FROINGS** > FROING
**FROISE** n kind of pancake
**FROISES** > FROISE
**FROLIC** vb run and play in a lively way ▷ n lively and merry behaviour ▷ adj full of merriment or fun
**FROLICKED** > FROLIC
**FROLICKER** > FROLIC
**FROLICKY** same as > FROLICSOME
**FROLICS** > FROLIC
**FROM** prep indicating the point of departure, source, distance, cause, change of state, etc
**FROMAGE** as in fromage frais low-fat soft cheese
**FROMAGES** > FROMAGE
**FROMENTY** same as > FRUMENTY
**FROND** n long leaf or leaflike part of a fern, palm, or seaweed
**FRONDAGE** n fronds collectively
**FRONDAGES** > FRONDAGE
**FRONDED** adj having fronds
**FRONDENT** adj leafy
**FRONDEUR** 17th-century French rebel
**FRONDEURS** > FRONDEUR
**FRONDLESS** > FROND
**FRONDOSE** adj leafy or like a leaf
**FRONDOUS** adj leafy or like a leaf
**FRONDS** > FROND
**FRONS** n anterior cuticular plate on the head of some insects, in front of the clypeus
**FRONT** n fore part ▷ adj of or at the front ▷ vb face (onto)
**FRONTAGE** n facade of a building
**FRONTAGER** n owner of a building or land on the front of a street
**FRONTAGES** > FRONTAGE
**FRONTAL** adj of, at, or in the front ▷ n decorative hanging for the front of an altar
**FRONTALLY** > FRONTAL
**FRONTALS** > FRONTAL
**FRONTED** > FRONT

**FRONTENIS** n racket used in Basque ball game
**FRONTER** > FRONT
**FRONTES** > FRONS
**FRONTIER** n area of a country bordering on another
**FRONTIERS** > FRONTIER
**FRONTING** > FRONT
**FRONTLESS** > FRONT
**FRONTLET** n small decorative loop worn on a woman's forehead, projecting from under her headdress, in the 15th century
**FRONTLETS** > FRONTLET
**FRONTLINE** adj of, relating to, or suitable for the front line of a military formation
**FRONTLIST** n list of books about to be published
**FRONTMAN** n nominal leader of an organization, etc, who lacks real power or authority, esp one who lends respectability to some nefarious activity
**FRONTMEN** > FRONTMAN
**FRONTON** n wall against which pelota or jai alai is played
**FRONTONS** > FRONTON
**FRONTOON** variant of > FRONTON
**FRONTOONS** > FRONTOON
**FRONTPAGE** adj on or suitable for the front page of a newspaper
**FRONTS** > FRONT
**FRONTWARD** same as > FRONTWARDS
**FRONTWAYS** adv with the front forward
**FRONTWISE** variant of > FRONTWAYS
**FRORE** adj very cold or frosty
**FROREN** variant of > FRORE
**FRORN** variant of > FRORE
**FRORNE** variant of > FRORE
**FRORY** adj frozen
**FROS** > FRO
**FROSH** n freshman
**FROSHES** > FROSH
**FROST** n white frozen dew or mist ▷ vb become covered with frost
**FROSTBIT** > FROSTBITE
**FROSTBITE** n destruction of tissue, esp of the fingers or ears, by cold ▷ vb affect with frostbite
**FROSTED** adj (of glass) having a rough surface to make it opaque ▷ n type of ice cream dish
**FROSTEDS** > FROSTED
**FROSTFISH** n American fish appearing in frosty weather
**FROSTIER** > FROSTY
**FROSTIEST** > FROSTY
**FROSTILY** > FROSTY

FROSTING n sugar icing
FROSTINGS > FROSTING
FROSTLESS > FROST
FROSTLIKE > FROST
FROSTLINE n depth to which ground freezes in winter
FROSTNIP n milder form of frostbite
FROSTNIPS > FROSTNIP
FROSTS > FROST
FROSTWORK n patterns made by frost on glass, metal, etc
FROSTY adj characterized or covered by frost
FROTH n mass of small bubbles ▷ vb foam
FROTHED > FROTH
FROTHER > FROTH
FROTHERS > FROTH
FROTHERY n anything insubstantial, like froth
FROTHIER > FROTH
FROTHIEST > FROTH
FROTHILY > FROTH
FROTHING > FROTH
FROTHLESS > FROTH
FROTHS > FROTH
FROTHY > FROTH
FROTTAGE n act or process of taking a rubbing from a rough surface, such as wood, for a work of art
FROTTAGES > FROTTAGE
FROTTEUR n person who rubs against another person's body for a sexual thrill
FROTTEURS > FROTTEUR
FROUFROU n swishing sound, as made by a long silk dress
FROUFROUS > FROUFROU
FROUGHIER > FROUGHY
FROUGHY adj rancid
FROUNCE vb wrinkle
FROUNCED > FROUNCE
FROUNCES > FROUNCE
FROUNCING > FROUNCE
FROUZIER > FROUZY
FROUZIEST > FROUZY
FROUZILY > FROUZY
FROUZY same as > FROWZY
FROW same as > FROE
FROWARD adj obstinate
FROWARDLY > FROWARD
FROWARDS > FROWARD
FROWIE variant of > FROUGHY
FROWIER > FROWIE
FROWIEST > FROWIE
FROWN vb wrinkle one's brows in worry, anger, or thought ▷ n frowning expression
FROWNED > FROWN
FROWNER > FROWN
FROWNERS > FROWN
FROWNING > FROWN
FROWNS > FROWN
FROWS > FROW
FROWSIER > FROWSY
FROWSIEST > FROWSY

FROWST n hot and stale atmosphere ▷ vb abandon oneself to such an atmosphere
FROWSTED > FROWST
FROWSTER > FROWST
FROWSTERS > FROWST
FROWSTIER > FROWSTY
FROWSTING > FROWST
FROWSTS > FROWST
FROWSTY adj stale or musty
FROWSY same as > FROWZY
FROWY variant of > FROUGHY
FROWZIER > FROWZY
FROWZIEST > FROWZY
FROWZILY > FROWZY
FROWZY adj dirty or unkempt
FROZE > FREEZE
FROZEN > FREEZE
FROZENLY > FREEZE
FRUCTAN n type of polymer of fructose, present in certain fruits
FRUCTANS > FRUCTAN
FRUCTED adj fruit-bearing
FRUCTIFY vb (cause to) bear fruit
FRUCTIVE adj fruitful
FRUCTOSE n crystalline sugar occurring in many fruits
FRUCTOSES > FRUCTOSE
FRUCTUARY n archaic word for a person who enjoys the fruits of something
FRUCTUATE vb bear fruit
FRUCTUOUS adj productive or fruitful
FRUG vb perform the frug, a 1960s dance
FRUGAL adj thrifty, sparing
FRUGALIST > FRUGAL
FRUGALITY > FRUGAL
FRUGALLY > FRUGAL
FRUGGED > FRUG
FRUGGING > FRUG
FRUGIVORE > FRUGIVOROUS
FRUGS > FRUG
FRUICT obsolete variant of > FRUIT
FRUICTS > FRUICT
FRUIT n part of a plant containing seeds, esp if edible ▷ vb bear fruit
FRUITAGE n process, state, or season of producing fruit
FRUITAGES > FRUITAGE
FRUITCAKE n cake containing dried fruit
FRUITED > FRUIT
FRUITER n fruit grower
FRUITERER n person who sells fruit
FRUITERS > FRUITER
FRUITERY n fruitage
FRUITFUL adj useful or productive
FRUITIER > FRUITY
FRUITIEST > FRUITY
FRUITILY > FRUITY
FRUITING > FRUIT
FRUITINGS > FRUIT

FRUITION n fulfilment of something worked for or desired
FRUITIONS > FRUITION
FRUITIVE adj enjoying
FRUITLESS adj useless or unproductive
FRUITLET n small fruit
FRUITLETS > FRUITLET
FRUITLIKE > FRUIT
FRUITS > FRUIT
FRUITWOOD n wood of a fruit tree
FRUITY adj of or like fruit
FRUMENTY n kind of porridge made from hulled wheat boiled with milk, sweetened, and spiced
FRUMP n dowdy woman ▷ vb mock or taunt
FRUMPED > FRUMP
FRUMPIER > FRUMPY
FRUMPIEST > FRUMPY
FRUMPILY > FRUMPY
FRUMPING > FRUMP
FRUMPISH same as > FRUMPY
FRUMPLE vb wrinkle or crumple
FRUMPLED > FRUMPLE
FRUMPLES > FRUMPLE
FRUMPLING > FRUMPLE
FRUMPS > FRUMP
FRUMPY adj (of a woman, clothes, etc) dowdy, drab, or unattractive
FRUSEMIDE n diuretic used to relieve oedema, for example caused by heart or kidney disease
FRUSH vb break into pieces
FRUSHED > FRUSH
FRUSHES > FRUSH
FRUSHING > FRUSH
FRUST n fragment
FRUSTA > FRUSTUM
FRUSTRATE vb upset or anger ▷ adj frustrated or thwarted
FRUSTS > FRUST
FRUSTULE n hard siliceous cell wall of a diatom
FRUSTULES > FRUSTULE
FRUSTUM n part of a cone or pyramid contained between the base and a plane parallel to the base that intersects the solid
FRUSTUMS > FRUSTUM
FRUTEX n shrub
FRUTICES > FRUTEX
FRUTICOSE same as > FRUTESCENT
FRUTIFIED > FRUTIFY
FRUTIFIES > FRUTIFY
FRUTIFY vb malapropism for notify; used for comic effect by Shakespeare
FRY vb cook or be cooked in fat or oil ▷ n dish of fried food
FRYABLE > FRY
FRYBREAD n Native American fried bread

FRYBREADS > FRYBREAD
FRYER n person or thing that fries
FRYERS > FRYER
FRYING > FRY
FRYINGS > FRY
FRYPAN n long-handled shallow pan used for frying
FRYPANS > FRYPAN
FUB vb cheat
FUBAR adj irreparably damaged or bungled
FUBBED > FUB
FUBBERIES > FUBBERY
FUBBERY n cheating
FUBBIER > FUBBY
FUBBIEST > FUBBY
FUBBING > FUB
FUBBY adj chubby
FUBS > FUB
FUBSIER > FUBSY
FUBSIEST > FUBSY
FUBSY adj short and stout
FUCHSIA n ornamental shrub with hanging flowers
FUCHSIAS > FUCHSIA
FUCHSIN n greenish crystalline substance
FUCHSINE same as > FUCHSIN
FUCHSINES > FUCHSINE
FUCHSINS > FUCHSIN
FUCHSITE n form of mica
FUCHSITES > FUCHSITE
FUCI > FUCUS
FUCK vb taboo word meaning to have sexual intercourse (with) ▷ n taboo word for an act of sexual intercourse
FUCKED > FUCK
FUCKER n taboo word for a despicable or obnoxious person
FUCKERS > FUCKER
FUCKING > FUCK
FUCKINGS > FUCK
FUCKOFF n taboo word for an annoying or unpleasant person
FUCKOFFS > FUCKOFF
FUCKS > FUCK
FUCKUP vb taboo word meaning to damage or bungle ▷ n taboo word meaning an act or an instance of bungling
FUCKUPS > FUCKUP
FUCKWIT n taboo word for a fool or idiot
FUCKWITS > FUCKWIT
FUCOID adj of, relating to, or resembling seaweeds of the genus Fucus ▷ n any seaweed of the genus Fucus
FUCOIDAL adj of, relating to, or resembling seaweeds of the genus Fucus ▷ n any seaweed of the genus Fucus
FUCOIDS > FUCOID
FUCOSE n aldose
FUCOSES > FUCOSE

FUCOUS same as > FUCOIDAL

FUCUS n any seaweed of the genus Fucus, common in the intertidal regions of many shores and typically having greenish-brown slimy fronds

FUCUSED adj archaic word meaning made up with cosmetics

FUCUSES > FUCUS

FUD n rabbit's tail

FUDDIES > FUDDY

FUDDLE vb cause to be intoxicated or confused ▷ n confused state

FUDDLED > FUDDLE

FUDDLER > FUDDLE

FUDDLERS > FUDDLE

FUDDLES > FUDDLE

FUDDLING > FUDDLE

FUDDLINGS > FUDDLE

FUDDY n old-fashioned person

FUDGE n soft caramel-like sweet ▷ vb make (an issue) less clear deliberately ▷ interj mild exclamation of annoyance

FUDGED > FUDGE

FUDGES > FUDGE

FUDGING > FUDGE

FUDS > FUD

FUEHRER n leader: applied esp to Adolf Hitler

FUEHRERS > FUEHRER

FUEL n substance burned or treated to produce heat or power ▷ vb provide with fuel

FUELED > FUEL

FUELER > FUEL

FUELERS > FUEL

FUELING > FUEL

FUELLED > FUEL

FUELLER > FUEL

FUELLERS > FUEL

FUELLING > FUEL

FUELS > FUEL

FUELWOOD n any wood used as a fuel

FUELWOODS > FUELWOOD

FUERO n Spanish code of laws

FUEROS > FUERO

FUFF vb puff

FUFFED > FUFF

FUFFIER > FUFFY

FUFFIEST > FUFFY

FUFFING > FUFF

FUFFS > FUFF

FUFFY adj puffy

FUG n hot stale atmosphere ▷ vb sit in a fug

FUGACIOUS adj passing quickly away

FUGACITY n property of a gas that expresses its tendency to escape or expand

FUGAL adj of, relating to, or in the style of a fugue

FUGALLY > FUGAL

FUGATO adj in the manner

or style of a fugue ▷ n movement, section, or piece in this style

FUGATOS > FUGATO

FUGGED > FUG

FUGGIER > FUG

FUGGIEST > FUG

FUGGILY > FUG

FUGGING > FUG

FUGGY > FUG

FUGHETTA n short fugue

FUGHETTAS > FUGHETTA

FUGIE n runaway

FUGIES > FUGIE

FUGIO n former US copper coin worth one dollar, the first authorized by Congress (1787)

FUGIOS > FUGIO

FUGITIVE n person who flees, esp from arrest or pursuit ▷ adj fleeing

FUGITIVES > FUGITIVE

FUGLE vb act as a fugleman

FUGLED > FUGLE

FUGLEMAN n (formerly) a soldier used as an example for those learning drill

FUGLEMEN > FUGLEMAN

FUGLES > FUGLE

FUGLIER > FUGLY

FUGLIEST > FUGLY

FUGLING > FUGLE

FUGLY adj offensive word for very ugly

FUGS > FUG

FUGU n puffer fish

FUGUE n musical composition in which a theme is repeated in different parts ▷ vb be in a dreamlike, altered state of consciousness

FUGUED > FUGUE

FUGUELIKE > FUGUE

FUGUES > FUGUE

FUGUING > FUGUE

FUGUIST n composer of fugues

FUGUISTS > FUGUIST

FUGUS > FUGU

FUHRER same as > FUEHRER

FUHRERS > FUHRER

FUJI n type of African music

FUJIS > FUJI

FULCRA > FULCRUM

FULCRATE > FULCRUM

FULCRUM n pivot about which a lever turns

FULCRUMS > FULCRUM

FULFIL vb bring about the achievement of (a desire or promise)

FULFILL same as > FULFIL

FULFILLED > FULFILL

FULFILLER > FULFIL

FULFILS > FULFIL

FULFILS > FULFIL

FULGENCY > FULGENT

FULGENT adj shining brilliantly

FULGENTLY > FULGENT

FULGID same as > FULGENT

FULGOR n brilliance

FULGOROUS > FULGOR

FULGORS > FULGOR

FULGOUR variant of > FULGOR

FULGOURS > FULGOUR

FULGURAL > FULGURATE

FULGURANT > FULGURATE

FULGURATE vb flash like lightning

FULGURITE n tube of glassy mineral matter found in sand and rock, formed by the action of lightning

FULGUROUS adj flashing like or resembling lightning

FULHAM n loaded die

FULHAMS > FULHAM

FULL adj containing as much or as many as possible ▷ adv completely ▷ vb clean, shrink, and press cloth

FULLAGE n price charged for fulling cloth

FULLAGES > FULLAGE

FULLAM variant of > FULHAM

FULLAMS > FULLAM

FULLAN variant of > FULHAM

FULLANS > FULLAN

FULLBACK n defensive player

FULLBACKS > FULLBACK

FULLBLOOD n person of unmixed race

FULLED > FULL

FULLER n person who fulls cloth for his living ▷ vb forge (a groove) or caulk (a riveted joint) with a fuller

FULLERED > FULLER

FULLERENE n any of various carbon molecules with a polyhedral structure similar to that of buckminsterfullerene, such as $C_{70}$, $C_{76}$, and $C_{84}$

FULLERIDE n compound of a fullerene in which atoms are trapped inside the cage of carbon atoms

FULLERIES > FULLERY

FULLERING > FULLER

FULLERITE n crystalline form of a fullerene

FULLERS > FULLER

FULLERY n place where fulling is carried out

FULLEST > FULL

FULLFACE n in printing, a letter that takes up full body size

FULLFACES > FULLFACE

FULLING > FULL

FULLISH > FULL

FULLNESS > FULL

FULLS > FULL

FULLY adv greatest degree or extent

FULMAR n Arctic sea bird

FULMARS > FULMAR

FULMINANT adj sudden and violent

FULMINATE vb criticize or denounce angrily ▷ n any salt or ester of fulminic acid, esp the mercury salt, which is used as a detonator

FULMINE vb fulminate

FULMINED > FULMINE

FULMINES > FULMINE

FULMINIC as in fulminic acid, unstable volatile acid known only in solution and in the form of its salts and esters

FULMINING > FULMINE

FULMINOUS adj harshly critical

FULNESS > FULL

FULNESSES > FULL

FULSOME adj distastefully excessive or insincere

FULSOMELY > FULSOME

FULSOMER > FULSOME

FULSOMEST > FULSOME

FULVID variant of > FULVOUS

FULVOUS adj of a dull brownish-yellow colour

FUM n phoenix, in Chinese mythology

FUMADO n salted, smoked fish

FUMADOES > FUMADO

FUMADOS > FUMADO

FUMAGE n hearth money

FUMAGES > FUMAGE

FUMARASE n enzyme

FUMARASES > FUMARASE

FUMARATE n salt of fumaric acid

FUMARATES > FUMARATE

FUMARIC as in fumaric acid, colourless crystalline acid with a fruity taste, found in some plants and manufactured from benzene

FUMAROLE n vent in or near a volcano from which hot gases, esp steam, are emitted

FUMAROLES > FUMAROLE

FUMAROLIC > FUMAROLE

FUMATORIA > FUMATORIUM

FUMATORY same as > FUMATORIUM

FUMBLE vb handle awkwardly ▷ n act of fumbling

FUMBLED > FUMBLE

FUMBLER > FUMBLE

FUMBLERS > FUMBLE

FUMBLES > FUMBLE

FUMBLING > FUMBLE

FUME vb be very angry ▷ pl n pungent smoke or vapour

FUMED adj (of wood, esp oak) having a dark colour and distinctive grain from exposure to ammonia fumes

FUMELESS > FUME

FUMELIKE > FUME

FUMER > FUME

FUMEROLE variant of > FUMAROLE

FUMEROLES > FUMEROLE

FUMERS > FUME

FUMES > FUME

FUMET n strong-flavoured liquor from cooking fish, meat, or game: used to flavour sauces

FUMETS > FUMET

FUMETTE variant of > FUMET

FUMETTES > FUMETTE

FUMETTI > FUMETTO

FUMETTO n speech balloon in a comic or cartoon

FUMIER > FUME

FUMIEST > FUME

FUMIGANT n substance used for fumigating

FUMIGANTS > FUMIGANT

FUMIGATE vb disinfect with fumes

FUMIGATED > FUMIGATE

FUMIGATES > FUMIGATE

FUMIGATOR > FUMIGATE

FUMING > FUME

FUMINGLY > FUME

FUMITORY n any plant of the chiefly European genus Fumaria, esp F. officinalis, having spurred flowers and formerly used medicinally: family Fumariaceae

FUMOSITY > FUME

FUMOUS > FUME

FUMS > FUM

FUMULI > FUMULUS

FUMULUS n smokelike cloud

FUMY > FUME

FUN n enjoyment or amusement ▷ vb trick

FUNBOARD n type of surfboard

FUNBOARDS > FUNBOARD

FUNCTION n purpose something exists for ▷ vb operate or work

FUNCTIONS > FUNCTION

FUNCTOR n performer of a function

FUNCTORS > FUNCTOR

FUND n stock of money for a special purpose ▷ vb provide money to

FUNDABLE > FUND

FUNDAMENT n buttocks

FUNDED > FUND

FUNDER > FUND

FUNDERS > FUND

FUNDI n expert or boffin

FUNDIC > FUNDUS

FUNDIE n fundamentalist Christian

FUNDIES > FUNDIE

FUNDING > FUND

FUNDINGS > FUND

FUNDIS > FUNDI

FUNDLESS > FUND

FUNDRAISE vb raise money for a cause

FUNDS pl n money that is readily available

FUNDUS n base of an organ

or the part farthest away from its opening

FUNDY n fundamentalist

FUNEBRAL variant of > FUNEBRIAL

FUNEBRE adj funereal or mournful

FUNEBRIAL same as > FUNEREAL

FUNERAL n ceremony of burying or cremating a dead person

FUNERALS > FUNERAL

FUNERARY adj of or for a funeral

FUNEREAL adj gloomy or sombre

FUNEST adj lamentable

FUNFAIR n entertainment with machines to ride on and stalls

FUNFAIRS > FUNFAIR

FUNFEST n enjoyable time

FUNFESTS > FUNFEST

FUNG same as > FUNK

FUNGAL adj of, derived from, or caused by a fungus or fungi ▷ n fungus or fungal infection

FUNGALS > FUNGAL

FUNGI > FUNGUS

FUNGIBLE n moveable perishable goods of a sort that may be estimated by number or weight, such as grain, wine, etc ▷ adj having the nature or quality of fungibles

FUNGIBLES > FUNGIBLE

FUNGIC > FUNGUS

FUNGICIDE n substance that destroys fungi

FUNGIFORM adj shaped like a mushroom or similar fungus

FUNGISTAT n substance that inhibits the growth of fungi

FUNGO n in baseball, act of tossing and hitting the ball ▷ vb toss and hit a ball

FUNGOES > FUNGO

FUNGOID adj resembling a fungus

FUNGOIDAL > FUNGOID

FUNGOIDS > FUNGOID

FUNGOSITY > FUNGOUS

FUNGOUS adj appearing suddenly and spreading quickly like a fungus

FUNGS > FUNG

FUNGUS n plant without leaves, flowers, or roots, such as a mushroom or mould

FUNGUSES > FUNGUS

FUNHOUSE n amusing place at fairground

FUNHOUSES > FUNHOUSE

FUNICLE n stalk that attaches an ovule or seed to the wall of the ovary

FUNICLES > FUNICLE

FUNICULAR n cable railway

on a mountainside or cliff ▷ adj relating to or operated by a rope, cable, etc

FUNICULI > FUNICULUS

FUNICULUS same as > FUNICLE

FUNK n style of dance music with a strong beat ▷ vb avoid (doing something) through fear

FUNKED > FUNK

FUNKER > FUNK

FUNKERS > FUNK

FUNKHOLE n dugout

FUNKHOLES > FUNKHOLE

FUNKIA n hosta

FUNKIAS > FUNKIA

FUNKIER > FUNKY

FUNKIEST > FUNKY

FUNKILY > FUNKY

FUNKINESS > FUNKY

FUNKING > FUNK

FUNKS > FUNK

FUNKSTER n performer or fan of funk music

FUNKSTERS > FUNKSTER

FUNKY adj (of music) having a strong beat

FUNNED > FUN

FUNNEL n cone-shaped tube for pouring liquids into a narrow opening ▷ vb (cause to) move through or as if through a funnel

FUNNELED > FUNNEL

FUNNELING > FUNNEL

FUNNELLED > FUNNEL

FUNNELS > FUNNEL

FUNNER > FUN

FUNNEST > FUN

FUNNIER > FUNNY

FUNNIES pl n comic strips in a newspaper

FUNNIEST > FUNNY

FUNNILY > FUNNY

FUNNINESS > FUNNY

FUNNING > FUN

FUNNY adj comical, humorous ▷ n joke or witticism

FUNNYMAN n comedian

FUNNYMEN > FUNNYMAN

FUNPLEX n large amusement centre

FUNPLEXES > FUNPLEX

FUNS > FUN

FUNSTER n funnyman

FUNSTERS > FUNSTER

FUR n soft hair of a mammal ▷ vb cover or become covered with fur

FURACIOUS adj thievish

FURACITY > FURACIOUS

FURAL n furfural

FURALS > FURAL

FURAN n colourless flammable toxic liquid heterocyclic compound

FURANE variant of > FURAN

FURANES > FURANE

FURANOSE n simple sugar containing a furan ring

FURANOSES > FURANOSE

FURANS > FURAN

FURBEARER n mammal hunted for its pelt or fur

FURBELOW n flounce, ruffle, or other ornamental trim ▷ vb put a furbelow on (a garment)

FURBELOWS > FURBELOW

FURBISH vb smarten up

FURBISHED > FURBISH

FURBISHER > FURBISH

FURBISHES > FURBISH

FURCA n any forklike structure, esp in insects

FURCAE > FURCA

FURCAL > FURCA

FURCATE vb divide into two parts ▷ adj forked, branching

FURCATED > FURCATE

FURCATELY > FURCATE

FURCATES > FURCATE

FURCATING > FURCATE

FURCATION > FURCATE

FURCRAEA n plant belonging to the Agave family

FURCRAEAS > FURCRAEA

FURCULA n any forklike part or organ, esp the fused clavicles (wishbone) of birds

FURCULAE > FURCULA

FURCULAR > FURCULA

FURCULUM same as > FURCULA

FURDER same as > FURTHER

FUREUR n rage or anger

FUREURS > FUREUR

FURFAIR variant of > FURFUR

FURFAIRS > FURFAIR

FURFUR n scurf or scaling of the skin

FURFURAL n colourless liquid used as a solvent

FURFURALS > FURFURAL

FURFURAN same as > FURAN

FURFURANS > FURFURAN

FURFURES > FURFUR

FURFUROL variant of > FURFURAL

FURFUROLE variant of > FURFURAL

FURFUROLS > FURFUROL

FURFUROUS > FURFUR

FURFURS > FURFUR

FURIBUND adj furious

FURIES > FURY

FURIOSITY > FURIOUS

FURIOSO adv in a frantically rushing manner ▷ n passage or piece to be performed in this way

FURIOSOS > FURIOSO

FURIOUS adj very angry

FURIOUSLY > FURIOUS

FURKID n companion animal

FURKIDS > FURKID

FURL vb roll up and fasten (a sail, umbrella, or flag) ▷ n act or an instance of

furling
**FURLABLE** >FURL
**FURLANA** *variant of* >FORLANA
**FURLANAS** >FURLANA
**FURLED** >FURL
**FURLER** >FURL
**FURLERS** >FURL
**FURLESS** >FUR
**FURLING** >FURL
**FURLONG** *n* unit of length equal to 220 yards (201.168 metres)
**FURLONGS** >FURLONG
**FURLOUGH** *n* leave of absence ▷ *vb* grant a furlough to
**FURLOUGHS** >FURLOUGH
**FURLS** >FURL
**FURMENTY** *same as* >FRUMENTY
**FURMETIES** >FURMETY
**FURMETY** *same as* >FRUMENTY
**FURMITIES** >FURMITY
**FURMITY** *same as* >FRUMENTY
**FURNACE** *n* enclosed chamber containing a very hot fire ▷ *vb* burn in a furnace
**FURNACED** >FURNACE
**FURNACES** >FURNACE
**FURNACING** >FURNACE
**FURNIMENT** *n* furniture
**FURNISH** *vb* provide (a house or room) with furniture
**FURNISHED** >FURNISH
**FURNISHER** >FURNISH
**FURNISHES** >FURNISH
**FURNITURE** *n* large movable articles such as chairs and wardrobes
**FUROL** *variant of* >FURFURAL
**FUROLE** *variant of* >FURFURAL
**FUROLES** >FUROL
**FUROLS** >FUROL
**FUROR** *same as* >FURORE
**FURORE** *n* very excited or angry reaction
**FURORES** >FURORE
**FURORS** >FUROR
**FURPHIES** >FURPHY
**FURPHY** *n* rumour or fictitious story
**FURR** *vb* furrow
**FURRED** *same as* >FURRY
**FURRIER** *n* dealer in furs
**FURRIERS** >FURRIER
**FURRIERY** *n* occupation of a furrier
**FURRIES** >FURRY
**FURRIEST** >FURRY
**FURRILY** >FURRY
**FURRINER** *n* dialect rendering of foreigner
**FURRINERS** >FURRINER
**FURRINESS** >FURRY
**FURRING** >FUR
**FURRINGS** >FUR
**FURROW** *n* trench made by a plough ▷ *vb* make or

become wrinkled
**FURROWED** >FURROW
**FURROWER** >FURROW
**FURROWERS** >FURROW
**FURROWING** >FURROW
**FURROWS** >FURROW
**FURROWY** >FURROW
**FURRS** >FURR
**FURRY** *adj* like or covered with fur or something furlike ▷ *n* child's fur-covered toy animal
**FURS** >FUR
**FURTH** *adv* out
**FURTHER** *adv* in addition ▷ *adj* more distant ▷ *vb* promote
**FURTHERED** >FURTHER
**FURTHERER** >FURTHER
**FURTHERS** >FURTHER
**FURTHEST** *adv* to the greatest degree ▷ *adj* most distant
**FURTIVE** *adj* sly and secretive
**FURTIVELY** >FURTIVE
**FURUNCLE** *technical name for* >BOIL
**FURUNCLES** >FURUNCLE
**FURY** *n* wild anger
**FURZE** *n* gorse
**FURZES** >FURZE
**FURZIER** >FURZE
**FURZIEST** >FURZE
**FURZY** >FURZE
**FUSAIN** *n* fine charcoal pencil or stick made from the spindle tree
**FUSAINS** >FUSAIN
**FUSARIA** >FUSARIUM
**FUSARIUM** *n* type of fungus
**FUSAROL** *variant of* >FUSAROLE
**FUSAROLE** *n* type of architectural moulding
**FUSAROLES** >FUSAROLE
**FUSAROLS** >FUSAROL
**FUSC** *adj* dark or dark-brown
**FUSCOUS** *adj* of a brownish-grey colour
**FUSE** *n* cord containing an explosive for detonating a bomb ▷ *vb* (cause to) fail as a result of a blown fuse
**FUSED** >FUSE
**FUSEE** *n* (in early clocks and watches) a spirally grooved spindle, functioning as an equalizing force on the unwinding of the mainspring
**FUSEES** >FUSEE
**FUSEL** *n* mixture of amyl alcohols, propanol, and butanol: a by-product in the distillation of fermented liquors used as a source of amyl alcohols
**FUSELAGE** *n* body of an aircraft
**FUSELAGES** >FUSELAGE
**FUSELESS** >FUSE

**FUSELIKE** >FUSE
**FUSELS** >FUSEL
**FUSES** >FUSE
**FUSHION** *n* spirit
**FUSHIONS** >FUSHION
**FUSIBLE** *adj* capable of being melted
**FUSIBLY** >FUSIBLE
**FUSIFORM** *adj* elongated and tapering at both ends
**FUSIL** *n* light flintlock musket
**FUSILE** *adj* easily melted
**FUSILEER** *same as* >FUSILIER
**FUSILEERS** >FUSILEER
**FUSILIER** *n* soldier of certain regiments
**FUSILIERS** >FUSILIER
**FUSILLADE** *n* continuous discharge of firearms ▷ *vb* attack with a fusillade
**FUSILLI** *n* spiral-shaped pasta
**FUSILLIS** >FUSILLI
**FUSILS** >FUSIL
**FUSING** >FUSE
**FUSION** *n* melting ▷ *adj* of a style of cooking that combines traditional Western techniques and ingredients with those used in Eastern cuisine
**FUSIONAL** >FUSION
**FUSIONISM** *n* favouring of coalitions among political groups
**FUSIONIST** >FUSIONISM
**FUSIONS** >FUSION
**FUSS** *n* needless activity or worry ▷ *vb* make a fuss
**FUSSED** >FUSS
**FUSSER** >FUSS
**FUSSERS** >FUSS
**FUSSES** >FUSS
**FUSSIER** >FUSSY
**FUSSIEST** >FUSSY
**FUSSILY** >FUSSY
**FUSSINESS** >FUSSY
**FUSSING** >FUSS
**FUSSPOT** *n* person who is difficult to please and complains often
**FUSSPOTS** >FUSSPOT
**FUSSY** *adj* inclined to fuss
**FUST** *vb* become mouldy
**FUSTED** >FUST
**FUSTET** *n* wood of the Venetian sumach shrub
**FUSTETS** >FUSTET
**FUSTIAN** *n* (formerly) a hard-wearing fabric of cotton mixed with flax or wool ▷ *adj* cheap
**FUSTIANS** >FUSTIAN
**FUSTIC** *n* large tropical American moraceous tree, *Chlorophora tinctoria*
**FUSTICS** >FUSTIC
**FUSTIER** >FUSTY
**FUSTIEST** >FUSTY
**FUSTIGATE** *vb* beat
**FUSTILUGS** *n* fat person
**FUSTILY** >FUSTY

**FUSTINESS** >FUSTY
**FUSTING** >FUST
**FUSTOC** *variant of* >FUSTIC
**FUSTOCS** >FUSTOC
**FUSTS** >FUST
**FUSTY** *adj* stale-smelling
**FUSULINID** *n* any of various extinct foraminifers
**FUSUMA** *n* Japanese sliding door
**FUTCHEL** *n* timber support in a carriage
**FUTCHELS** >FUTCHEL
**FUTHARC** *same as* >FUTHARK
**FUTHARCS** >FUTHARC
**FUTHARK** *n* phonetic alphabet consisting of runes
**FUTHARKS** >FUTHARK
**FUTHORC** *same as* >FUTHARK
**FUTHORCS** >FUTHORC
**FUTHORK** *same as* >FUTHARK
**FUTHORKS** >FUTHORK
**FUTILE** *adj* unsuccessful or useless
**FUTILELY** >FUTILE
**FUTILER** >FUTILE
**FUTILEST** >FUTILE
**FUTILITY** *n* lack of effectiveness or success
**FUTON** *n* Japanese-style bed
**FUTONS** >FUTON
**FUTSAL** *n* form of association football, played indoors with five players on each side
**FUTSALS** >FUTSAL
**FUTTOCK** *n* one of the ribs in the frame of a wooden vessel
**FUTTOCKS** >FUTTOCK
**FUTURAL** *adj* relating to the future
**FUTURE** *n* time to come ▷ *adj* yet to come or be
**FUTURES** *pl n* commodities bought or sold at an agreed price for delivery at a specified future date
**FUTURISM** *n* early 20th-century artistic movement making use of the characteristics of the machine age
**FUTURISMS** >FUTURISM
**FUTURIST** >FUTURISM
**FUTURISTS** >FUTURISM
**FUTURITY** *n* future
**FUTZ** *vb* fritter time away
**FUTZED** >FUTZ
**FUTZES** >FUTZ
**FUTZING** >FUTZ
**FUZE** *same as* >FUSE
**FUZED** >FUZE
**FUZEE** *same as* >FUSEE
**FUZEES** >FUZEE
**FUZES** >FUZE
**FUZIL** *variant of* >FUSIL
**FUZILS** >FUZIL
**FUZING** >FUZE
**FUZZ** *n* mass of fine or curly hairs or fibres ▷ *vb* make or become fuzzy

**FUZZED** > FUZZ
**FUZZES** > FUZZ
**FUZZIER** > FUZZY
**FUZZIEST** > FUZZY
**FUZZILY** > FUZZY
**FUZZINESS** > FUZZY
**FUZZING** > FUZZ
**FUZZLE** *vb* make drunk
**FUZZLED** > FUZZLE
**FUZZLES** > FUZZLE
**FUZZLING** > FUZZLE
**FUZZTONE** *n* device
  distorting electric guitar
  sound
**FUZZTONES** > FUZZTONE
**FUZZY** *adj* of, like, or
  covered with fuzz
**FY** *variant of* > FIE
**FYCE** *variant of* > FICE
**FYCES** > FYCE
**FYKE** *n* fish trap consisting
  of a net suspended over
  a series of hoops, laid
  horizontally in the water
  ▷ *vb* catch fish in this
  manner
**FYKED** > FYKE
**FYKES** > FYKE
**FYKING** > FYKE
**FYLE** *variant of* > FILE
**FYLES** > FYLE
**FYLFOT** *rare word*
  *for* > SWASTIKA
**FYLFOTS** > FYLFOT
**FYNBOS** *n* area of low-
  growing, evergreen
  vegetation
**FYNBOSES** > FYNBOS
**FYRD** *n* local militia of an
  Anglo-Saxon shire, in
  which all freemen had to
  serve
**FYRDS** > FYRD
**FYTTE** *n* song
**FYTTES** > FYTTE

# Gg

GAB *vb* talk or chatter ▷ *n* hook or open notch in a rod or lever that drops over the spindle of a valve to form a temporary connection for operating the valve
GABARDINE *n* strong twill cloth used esp for raincoats
GABBARD *same as* > GABBART
GABBARDS > GABBARD
GABBART *n* Scottish sailing barge
GABBARTS > GABBART
GABBED > GAB
GABBER > GAB
GABBERS > GAB
GABBIER > GABBY
GABBIEST > GABBY
GABBINESS > GABBY
GABBING > GAB
GABBLE *vb* speak rapidly and indistinctly ▷ *n* rapid indistinct speech
GABBLED > GABBLE
GABBLER > GABBLE
GABBLERS > GABBLE
GABBLES > GABBLE
GABBLING > GABBLE
GABBLINGS > GABBLE
GABBRO *n* dark coarse-grained basic plutonic igneous rock consisting of plagioclase feldspar, pyroxene, and often olivine
GABBROIC > GABBRO
GABBROID *adj* gabbro-like
GABBROS > GABBRO
GABBY *adj* talkative
GABELLE *n* salt tax levied until 1790

GABELLED > GABELLE
GABELLER *n* person who collects the gabelle
GABELLERS > GABELLER
GABELLES > GABELLE
GABERDINE *same as* > GABARDINE
GABFEST *n* prolonged gossiping or conversation
GABFESTS > GABFEST
GABIES > GABY
GABION *n* cylindrical metal container filled with stones, used in the construction of underwater foundations
GABIONADE *n* row of gabions submerged in a waterway, stream, river, etc, to control the flow of water
GABIONAGE *n* structure composed of gabions
GABIONED > GABION
GABIONS > GABION
GABLE *n* triangular upper part of a wall between sloping roofs
GABLED > GABLE
GABLELIKE > GABLE
GABLES > GABLE
GABLET *n* small gable
GABLETS > GABLET
GABLING > GABLE
GABNASH *n* chatter
GABNASHES > GABNASH
GABOON *n* dark mahogany-like wood from a western and central African burseraceous tree, *Aucoumea klaineana*, used in plywood, for furniture, and as a veneer

GABOONS > GABOON
GABS > GAB
GABY *n* simpleton
GAD *vb* go about in search of pleasure ▷ *n* carefree adventure (esp in the phrase **on** or **upon the gad**)
GADABOUT *n* pleasure-seeker
GADABOUTS > GADABOUT
GADARENE *adj* headlong
GADDED > GAD
GADDER > GAD
GADDERS > GAD
GADDI *n* cushion on an Indian prince's throne
GADDING > GAD
GADDIS > GADDI
GADE *same as* > GAD
GADES > GADE
GADFLIES > GADFLY
GADFLY *n* fly that bites cattle
GADGE *n* man
GADGES > GADGE
GADGET *n* small mechanical device or appliance
GADGETEER *n* person who delights in gadgetry
GADGETRY *n* gadgets
GADGETS > GADGET
GADGETY > GADGET
GADGIE *n* fellow
GADGIES > GADGIE
GADI *n* Indian throne
GADID *n* any marine teleost fish of the family *Gadidae*, which includes the cod, haddock, whiting, and pollack ▷ *adj* of, relating to, or belonging to the *Gadidae*
GADIDS > GADID

GADIS > GADI
GADJE *same as* > GADGIE
GADJES > GADJE
GADJO *variant of* > GORGIO
GADLING *n* vagabond
GADLINGS > GADLING
GADOID *adj* of the cod family of marine fishes ▷ *n* gadoid fish
GADOIDS > GADOID
GADOLINIC *adj* relating to gadolinium, a silvery white metallic element
GADROON *n* moulding composed of a series of convex flutes and curves joined to form a decorative pattern, used esp as an edge to silver articles
GADROONED > GADROON
GADROONS > GADROON
GADS > GAD
GADSMAN *n* person who uses a gad when driving animals
GADSMEN > GADSMAN
GADSO *n* archaic expression of surprise
GADSOS > GADSO
GADWALL *n* duck, *Anas strepera*, related to the mallard
GADWALLS > GADWALL
GADZOOKS *interj* mild oath
GAE *Scot word for* > GO
GAED > GAE
GAEING > GAE
GAELICISE *vb* adapt to conform to Gaelic spelling and pronunciation
GAELICISM > GAELICISE
GAELICIZE *same as* > GAELICISE

GAEN > GAE

GAES > GAE

GAFF n stick with an iron hook for landing large fish ▷ vb hook or land (a fish) with a gaff

GAFFE n social blunder

GAFFED > GAFF

GAFFER n foreman or boss

GAFFERS > GAFFER

GAFFES > GAFFE

GAFFING > GAFF

GAFFINGS > GAFF

GAFFS > GAFF

GAFFSAIL n quadrilateral fore-and-aft sail on a sailing vessel

GAFFSAILS > GAFFSAIL

GAG vb choke or retch ▷ n cloth etc put into or tied across the mouth

GAGA adj senile

GAGAKU n type of traditional Japanese music

GAGAKUS > GAGAKU

GAGE vb gauge ▷ n (formerly) a glove or other object thrown down to indicate a challenge to fight

GAGEABLE > GAGE

GAGEABLY > GAGE

GAGED > GAGE

GAGER same as > GAUGER

GAGERS > GAGER

GAGES > GAGE

GAGGED > GAG

GAGGER n person or thing that gags

GAGGERIES > GAGGERY

GAGGERS > GAGGER

GAGGERY n practice of telling jokes

GAGGING > GAG

GAGGLE n disorderly crowd ▷ vb (of geese) to cackle

GAGGLED > GAGGLE

GAGGLES > GAGGLE

GAGGLING > GAGGLE

GAGGLINGS > GAGGLE

GAGING > GAGE

GAGMAN n person who writes gags for a comedian

GAGMEN > GAGMAN

GAGS > GAG

GAGSTER n standup comedian

GAGSTERS > GAGSTER

GAHNITE n dark green mineral of the spinel group consisting of zinc aluminium oxide

GAHNITES > GAHNITE

GAID same as > GAD

GAIDS > GAID

GAIETIES > GAIETY

GAIETY n cheerfulness

GAIJIN n (in Japan) a foreigner

GAILLARD same as > GALLIARD

GAILLARDE same as > GAILLARD

GAILY adv merrily

GAIN vb acquire or obtain ▷ n profit or advantage ▷ adj straight or near

GAINABLE > GAIN

GAINED > GAIN

GAINER n person or thing that gains

GAINERS > GAINER

GAINEST > GAIN

GAINFUL adj useful or profitable

GAINFULLY > GAINFUL

GAINING > GAIN

GAININGS pl n profits or earnings

GAINLESS > GAIN

GAINLIER > GAINLY

GAINLIEST > GAINLY

GAINLY adj graceful or well-formed ▷ adv conveniently or suitably

GAINS pl n profits or winnings

GAINSAID > GAINSAY

GAINSAY vb deny or contradict

GAINSAYER > GAINSAY

GAINSAYS > GAINSAY

GAINST short for > AGAINST

GAIR n strip of green grass on a hillside

GAIRFOWL same as > GAREFOWL

GAIRFOWLS > GAIRFOWL

GAIRS > GAIR

GAIT n manner of walking ▷ vb teach (a horse) a particular gait

GAITED > GAIT

GAITER n cloth or leather covering for the lower leg

GAITERS > GAITER

GAITING > GAIT

GAITS > GAIT

GAITT Scots word for > GATE

GAITTS > GAITT

GAJO same as > GORGIO

GAJOS > GAJO

GAL n girl

GALA n festival

GALABEA same as > DJELLABA

GALABEAH same as > DJELLABA

GALABEAHS > GALABEAH

GALABEAS > GALABEA

GALABIA same as > DJELLABA

GALABIAH same as > DJELLABA

GALABIAHS > GALABIAH

GALABIAS > GALABIA

GALABIEH same as > DJELLABA

GALABIEHS > GALABIEH

GALABIYA same as > DJELLABA

GALABIYAH same as > DJELLABA

GALABIYAS > GALABIYA

GALACTIC adj of the Galaxy or other galaxies

GALACTOSE n white water-soluble monosaccharide found in lactose

GALAGE same as > GALOSH

GALAGES > GALAGE

GALAGO another name for > BUSHBABY

GALAGOS > GALAGO

GALAH n Australian cockatoo, Kakatoe roseicapilla, having grey wings, back, and crest and a pink body

GALAHS > GALAH

GALANGA same as > GALINGALE

GALANGAL same as > GALINGALE

GALANGALS > GALANGAL

GALANGAS > GALANGAL

GALANT n 18th-century style of music characterized by homophony and elaborate ornamentation

GALANTINE n cold dish of meat or poultry, which is boned, cooked, stuffed, then pressed into a neat shape and glazed

GALANTY as in galanty show pantomime shadow play, esp one in miniature using figures cut from paper

GALAPAGO n tortoise

GALAPAGOS > GALAPAGO

GALAS > GALA

GALATEA n strong twill-weave cotton fabric, striped or plain, for clothing

GALATEAS > GALATEA

GALAVANT same as > GALLIVANT

GALAVANTS > GALAVANT

GALAX n coltsfoot

GALAXES > GALAX

GALAXIES > GALAXY

GALAXY n system of stars

GALBANUM n bitter aromatic gum resin extracted from any of several Asian umbelliferous plants of the genus Ferula, esp F. galbaniflua, and used in incense and medicinally as a counterirritant

GALBANUMS > GALBANUM

GALDRAGON old Scots word for a > SORCERESS

GALE n strong wind

GALEA n part or organ shaped like a helmet or hood, such as the petals of certain flowers

GALEAE > GALEA

GALEAS > GALEA

GALEATE > GALEA

GALEATED > GALEA

GALEIFORM > GALEA

GALENA n soft bluish-grey mineral consisting of lead sulphide: the chief source of lead

GALENAS > GALENA

GALENGALE same as

as > GALINGALE

GALENIC > GALENA

GALENICAL n any drug prepared from plant or animal tissue, esp vegetables, rather than being chemically synthesized ▷ adj denoting or belonging to this group of drugs

GALENITE same as > GALENA

GALENITES > GALENITE

GALENOID adj pertaining to galena

GALERE n group of people having a common interest, esp a coterie of undesirable people

GALERES > GALERE

GALES > GALE

GALETTE n type of savoury pancake

GALETTES > GALETTE

GALILEE n porch or chapel at the entrance to some medieval churches and cathedrals in England

GALILEES > GALILEE

GALINGALE n European cyperaceous plant, Cyperus longus, with rough-edged leaves, reddish spikelets of flowers, and aromatic roots

GALIONGEE n sailor

GALIOT n small swift galley formerly sailed on the Mediterranean

GALIOTS > GALIOT

GALIPOT n resin obtained from several species of pine

GALIPOTS > GALIPOT

GALIVANT same as > GALLIVANT

GALIVANTS > GALIVANT

GALL n impudence ▷ vb annoy

GALLABEA same as > DJELLABA

GALLABEAH same as > DJELLABA

GALLABEAS > GALLABEA

GALLABIA same as > DJELLABA

GALLABIAH same as > DJELLABA

GALLABIAS > GALLABIA

GALLABIEH same as > DJELLABA

GALLABIYA same as > DJELLABA

GALLAMINE n muscle relaxant used in anaesthesia

GALLANT adj brave and noble ▷ n young man who tried to impress women with his fashionable clothes or daring acts ▷ vb court or flirt (with)

GALLANTED > GALLANT

GALLANTER > GALLANT

GALLANTLY > GALLANT

**GALLANTRY** n showy, attentive treatment of women
**GALLANTS** > GALLANT
**GALLATE** n salt of gallic acid
**GALLATES** > GALLATE
**GALLEASS** n three-masted lateen-rigged galley used as a warship in the Mediterranean from the 15th to the 18th centuries
**GALLED** > GALL
**GALLEIN** n type of dyestuff
**GALLEINS** > GALLEIN
**GALLEON** n large three-masted sailing ship of the 15th–17th centuries
**GALLEONS** > GALLEON
**GALLERIA** n central court through several storeys of a shopping centre or department store onto which shops or departments open at each level
**GALLERIAS** > GALLERIA
**GALLERIED** adj having a gallery or galleries
**GALLERIES** > GALLERY
**GALLERIST** n person who owns or runs an art gallery
**GALLERY** n room or building for displaying works of art ▷ vb tunnel; form an underground gallery
**GALLET** vb (in roofing) use small pieces of slate mixed with mortar to support an upper slate
**GALLETA** n low-growing, coarse grass
**GALLETAS** > GALLETA
**GALLETED** > GALLET
**GALLETING** > GALLET
**GALLETS** > GALLET
**GALLEY** n kitchen of a ship or aircraft
**GALLEYS** > GALLEY
**GALLFLIES** > GALLFLY
**GALLFLY** n any of several small insects that produce galls in plant tissues, such as the gall wasp and gall midge
**GALLIARD** n spirited dance in triple time for two persons, popular in the 16th and 17th centuries ▷ adj lively
**GALLIARDS** > GALLIARD
**GALLIASS** same as > GALLEASS
**GALLIC** adj of or containing gallium in the trivalent state
**GALLICA** n variety of rose
**GALLICAN** adj of or relating to a movement favouring the restriction of papal control and greater autonomy for the French church

**GALLICAS** > GORGIO
**GALLICISE** same as > GALLICIZE
**GALLICISM** n word or idiom borrowed from French
**GALLICIZE** vb make or become French in attitude, language, etc
**GALLIED** > GALLY
**GALLIES** > GALLY
**GALLINAZO** n black vulture
**GALLING** adj annoying or bitterly humiliating
**GALLINGLY** > GALLING
**GALLINULE** n moorhen
**GALLIOT** same as > GALIOT
**GALLIOTS** > GALLIOT
**GALLIPOT** same as > GALIPOT
**GALLIPOTS** > GALLIPOT
**GALLISE** vb add water and sugar to unfermented grape juice to increase the quantity of wine produced
**GALLISED** > GALLISE
**GALLISES** > GALLISE
**GALLISING** > GALLISE
**GALLISISE** vb gallise
**GALLISIZE** same as > GALLISE
**GALLIUM** n soft grey metallic element used in semiconductors
**GALLIUMS** > GALLIUM
**GALLIVANT** vb go about in search of pleasure
**GALLIVAT** n Oriental armed vessel
**GALLIVATS** > GALLIVAT
**GALLIWASP** n any lizard of the Central American genus Diploglossus, esp D. monotropis of the Caribbean: family Anguidae
**GALLIZE** same as > GALLISE
**GALLIZED** > GALLIZE
**GALLIZES** > GALLIZE
**GALLIZING** > GALLIZE
**GALLNUT** n type of plant gall that resembles a nut
**GALLNUTS** > GALLNUT
**GALLOCK** adj left-handed
**GALLON** n liquid measure of eight pints, equal to 4.55 litres
**GALLONAGE** n capacity measured in gallons
**GALLONS** > GALLON
**GALLOON** n narrow band of cord, embroidery, silver or gold braid, etc, used on clothes and furniture
**GALLOONED** > GALLOON
**GALLOONS** > GALLOON
**GALLOOT** same as > GALLOOT
**GALLOOTS** > GALOOT
**GALLOP** n horse's fastest pace ▷ vb go or ride at a gallop
**GALLOPADE** n gallop ▷ vb perform a gallopade
**GALLOPED** > GALLOP
**GALLOPER** > GALLOP

**GALLOPERS** > GALLOP
**GALLOPING** adj progressing at or as if at a gallop
**GALLOPS** > GALLOP
**GALLOUS** adj of or containing gallium in the divalent state
**GALLOW** vb frighten
**GALLOWED** > GALLOW
**GALLOWING** > GALLOW
**GALLOWS** n wooden structure used for hanging criminals
**GALLOWSES** > GALLOWS
**GALLS** > GALL
**GALLSTONE** n hard mass formed in the gall bladder or its ducts
**GALLUMPH** same as > GALUMPH
**GALLUMPHS** > GALLUMPH
**GALLUS** adj bold ▷ n suspender for trousers
**GALLUSED** adj held up by galluses
**GALLUSES** > GALLUS
**GALLY** vb frighten
**GALLYING** > GALLY
**GALOCHE** same as > GALOSH
**GALOCHED** > GALOCHE
**GALOCHES** > GALOCHE
**GALOCHING** > GALOCHE
**GALOOT** n clumsy or uncouth person
**GALOOTS** > GALOOT
**GALOP** n 19th-century dance in quick duple time ▷ vb dance a galop
**GALOPADE** > GALOP
**GALOPADES** > GALOP
**GALOPED** > GALOP
**GALOPIN** n boy who ran errands for a cook
**GALOPING** > GALOP
**GALOPINS** > GALOPIN
**GALOPPED** > GALOP
**GALOPPING** > GALOP
**GALOPS** > GALOP
**GALORE** adv in abundance ▷ adj in abundance ▷ n abundance
**GALORES** > GALORE
**GALOSH** n waterproof overshoe ▷ vb cover with galoshes
**GALOSHE** same as > GALOSH
**GALOSHED** > GALOSH
**GALOSHES** > GALOSH
**GALOSHING** > GALOSH
**GALOWSES** Shakespearean plural for > GALLOWS
**GALRAVAGE** same as > GILRAVAGE
**GALS** > GAL
**GALTONIA** n any plant of the bulbous genus Galtonia, esp G. candicans, with lanceolate leaves, drooping racemes of waxy white flowers, and a fragrant scent: family Liliaceae
**GALTONIAS** > GALTONIA
**GALUMPH** vb leap or move

about clumsily
**GALUMPHED** > GALUMPH
**GALUMPHER** > GALUMPH
**GALUMPHS** > GALUMPH
**GALUT** same as > GALUTH
**GALUTH** n exile of Jews from Palestine
**GALUTHS** > GALUTH
**GALUTS** > GALUT
**GALVANIC** adj of or producing an electric current generated by chemical means
**GALVANISE** same as > GALVANIZE
**GALVANISM** n electricity, esp when produced by chemical means as in a cell or battery
**GALVANIST** > GALVANISM
**GALVANIZE** vb stimulate into action ▷ n galvanized iron, usually in the form of corrugated sheets as used in roofing
**GALVO** n instrument for measuring electric current
**GALVOS** > GALVO
**GALYAC** same as > GALYAK
**GALYACS** > GALYAC
**GALYAK** n smooth glossy fur obtained from the skins of newborn or premature lambs and kids
**GALYAKS** > GALYAK
**GAM** n school of whales ▷ vb (of whales) form a school
**GAMA** n tall perennial grass
**GAMAHUCHE** derogatory term vb practise cunnilingus or fellatio on ▷ n cunnilingus or fellatio
**GAMARUCHE** same as > GAMAHUCHE
**GAMAS** > GAMA
**GAMASH** n type of gaiter
**GAMASHES** > GAMASH
**GAMAY** n red grape variety, or the wine made from it
**GAMAYS** > GAMAY
**GAMB** n in heraldry, the whole foreleg of a beast
**GAMBA** n second-largest member of the viol family
**GAMBADE** same as > GAMBADO
**GAMBADES** > GAMBADE
**GAMBADO** n leap or gambol; caper ▷ vb perform a gambado
**GAMBADOED** > GAMBADO
**GAMBADOES** > GAMBADO
**GAMBADOS** > GAMBADO
**GAMBAS** > GAMBA
**GAMBE** same as > GAMB
**GAMBES** > GAMBE
**GAMBESON** n quilted and padded or stuffed leather or cloth garment worn under mail in the Middle Ages and later as a doublet by men and women
**GAMBESONS** > GAMBESON
**GAMBET** n tattler

GAMBETS >GAMBET
GAMBETTA n redshank
GAMBETTAS >GAMBETTA
GAMBIA same as >GAMBIER
GAMBIAS >GAMBIA
GAMBIER n astringent resinous substance obtained from a rubiaceous tropical Asian woody climbing plant, Uncaria gambir (or U. gambier)
GAMBIERS >GAMBIER
GAMBIR same as >GAMBIER
GAMBIRS >GAMBIR
GAMBIST n person who plays the (viola da) gamba
GAMBISTS >GAMBIST
GAMBIT n opening line or move intended to secure an advantage ▷ vb sacrifice a chess piece, in opening, to gain a better position
GAMBITED >GAMBIT
GAMBITING >GAMBIT
GAMBITS >GAMBIT
GAMBLE vb play games of chance to win money ▷ n risky undertaking
GAMBLED >GAMBLE
GAMBLER >GAMBLE
GAMBLERS >GAMBLE
GAMBLES >GAMBLE
GAMBLING >GAMBLE
GAMBLINGS >GAMBLE
GAMBO n farm cart
GAMBOGE n gum resin used as a yellow pigment and purgative
GAMBOGES >GAMBOGE
GAMBOGIAN >GAMBOGE
GAMBOGIC >GAMBOGE
GAMBOL vb jump about playfully, frolic ▷ n frolic
GAMBOLED >GAMBOL
GAMBOLING >GAMBOL
GAMBOLLED >GAMBOL
GAMBOLS >GAMBOL
GAMBOS >GAMBO
GAMBREL n hock of a horse or similar animal
GAMBRELS >GAMBREL
GAMBROON n type of linen cloth
GAMBROONS >GAMBROON
GAMBS >GAMB
GAMBUSIA n small fish that feeds on mosquito larvae
GAMBUSIAS >GAMBUSIA
GAME n amusement or pastime ▷ vb gamble ▷ adj brave
GAMECOCK n cock bred and trained for fighting
GAMECOCKS >GAMECOCK
GAMED >GAME
GAMELAN n type of percussion orchestra common in the East Indies
GAMELANS >GAMELAN
GAMELIKE >GAME
GAMELY adv in a brave or sporting manner

GAMENESS n courage or bravery
GAMEPLAY n plot of a computer or video game or the way that it is played
GAMEPLAYS >GAMEPLAY
GAMER n person who plays computer games
GAMERS >GAMER
GAMES >GAME
GAMESIER >GAMESY
GAMESIEST >GAMESY
GAMESMAN n one who practises gamesmanship: the art of winning by cunning practices without actually cheating
GAMESMEN >GAMESMAN
GAMESOME adj full of merriment
GAMEST >GAME
GAMESTER n gambler
GAMESTERS >GAMESTER
GAMESY adj sporty
GAMETAL >GAMETE
GAMETE n reproductive cell
GAMETES >GAMETE
GAMETIC >GAMETE
GAMEY adj having the smell or flavour of game
GAMIC adj (esp of reproduction) requiring the fusion of gametes
GAMIER >GAMEY
GAMIEST >GAMEY
GAMILY >GAMEY
GAMIN n street urchin
GAMINE n slim boyish young woman
GAMINERIE n impish behaviour
GAMINES >GAMINE
GAMINESS >GAMEY
GAMING n gambling
GAMINGS >GAMING
GAMINS >GAMIN
GAMMA n third letter of the Greek alphabet
GAMMADIA >GAMMADION
GAMMADION n decorative figure composed of a number of Greek capital gammas, esp radiating from a centre, as in a swastika
GAMMAS >GAMMA
GAMMAT n derogatory term for a Cape Coloured person
GAMMATIA >GAMMATION
GAMMATION same as >GAMMADION
GAMMATS >GAMMAT
GAMME n musical scale
GAMMED >GAM
GAMMER n dialect word for an old woman: now chiefly humorous or contemptuous
GAMMERS >GAMMER
GAMMES >GAMME
GAMMIER >GAMMY
GAMMIEST >GAMMY
GAMMING >GAM
GAMMOCK vb clown around

GAMMOCKED >GAMMOCK
GAMMOCKS >GAMMOCK
GAMMON n cured or smoked ham ▷ vb score a double victory in backgammon over
GAMMONED >GAMMON
GAMMONER >GAMMON
GAMMONERS >GAMMON
GAMMONING >GAMMON
GAMMONS >GAMMON
GAMMY adj (of the leg) lame
GAMODEME n isolated breeding population
GAMODEMES >GAMODEME
GAMONE n any chemical substance secreted by a gamete that attracts another gamete during sexual reproduction
GAMONES >GAMONE
GAMP n umbrella
GAMPISH adj bulging
GAMPS >GAMP
GAMS >GAM
GAMUT n whole range or scale (of music, emotions, etc)
GAMUTS >GAMUT
GAMY same as >GAMEY
GAMYNESS >GAMY
GAN vb go
GANACHE n rich icing or filling made of chocolate and cream
GANACHES >GANACHE
GANCH vb impale
GANCHED >GANCH
GANCHES >GANCH
GANCHING >GANCH
GANDER n male goose ▷ vb look
GANDERED >GANDER
GANDERING >GANDER
GANDERISM >GANDER
GANDERS >GANDER
GANDY adj as in gandy dancer railway track maintenance worker
GANE >GANGUE
GANEF n unscrupulous opportunist who stoops to sharp practice
GANEFS >GANEF
GANEV same as >GANEF
GANEVS >GANEV
GANG n (criminal) group ▷ vb become or act as a gang
GANGBANG n sexual intercourse between one woman and several men one after the other, esp against her will ▷ vb force (a woman) to take part in a gangbang
GANGBANGS >GANGBANG
GANGBOARD n gangway
GANGED >GANG
GANGER n foreman of a gang of labourers
GANGERS >GANGER
GANGING >GANG
GANGINGS >GANG

GANGLAND n criminal underworld
GANGLANDS >GANGLAND
GANGLIA >GANGLION
GANGLIAL >GANGLION
GANGLIAR >GANGLION
GANGLIATE vb form a ganglion
GANGLIER >GANGLY
GANGLIEST >GANGLY
GANGLING adj lanky and awkward
GANGLION n group of nerve cells
GANGLIONS >GANGLION
GANGLY same as >GANGLING
GANGPLANK n portable bridge for boarding or leaving a ship
GANGPLOW n plough designed to produce parallel furrows
GANGPLOWS >GANGPLOW
GANGREL n wandering beggar
GANGRELS >GANGREL
GANGRENE n decay of body tissue as a result of disease or injury ▷ vb become or cause to become affected with gangrene
GANGRENED >GANGRENE
GANGRENES >GANGRENE
GANGS >GANG
GANGSHAG vb participate in group sex with
GANGSHAGS >GANGSHAG
GANGSMAN n foreman
GANGSMEN >GANGSMAN
GANGSTA n member of a street gang
GANGSTAS >GANGSTA
GANGSTER n member of a criminal gang
GANGSTERS >GANGSTER
GANGUE n valueless material in an ore
GANGUES >GANGUE
GANGWAY same as >GANGPLANK
GANGWAYS >GANGWAY
GANISTER n highly refractory siliceous sedimentary rock occurring beneath coal seams: used for lining furnaces
GANISTERS >GANISTER
GANJA n highly potent form of cannabis, usually used for smoking
GANJAH same as >GANJA
GANJAHS >GANJAH
GANJAS >GANJA
GANNED >GAN
GANNET n large sea bird
GANNETRY n gannets' breeding-place
GANNETS >GANNET
GANNING >GAN
GANNISTER same as >GANISTER
GANOF same as >GANEF
GANOFS >GANOF

**GANOID** *adj* (of the scales of certain fishes) consisting of an inner bony layer covered with an enamel-like substance ▷ *n* ganoid fish
**GANOIDS** > GANOID
**GANOIN** *n* substance of which the outer layer of fish scales is composed
**GANOINE** *same as* > GANOIN
**GANOINES** > GANOINE
**GANOINS** > GANOIN
**GANS** > GAN
**GANSEY** *n* jersey or pullover
**GANSEYS** > GANSEY
**GANT** *vb* yawn
**GANTED** > GANT
**GANTELOPE** *same as* > GAUNTLET
**GANTING** > GANT
**GANTLET** *n* section of a railway where two tracks overlap ▷ *vb* make railway tracks form a gantlet
**GANTLETED** > GANTLET
**GANTLETS** > GANTLET
**GANTLINE** *n* line rove through a sheave for hoisting men or gear
**GANTLINES** > GANTLINE
**GANTLOPE** *same as* > GAUNTLET
**GANTLOPES** > GANTLOPE
**GANTRIES** > GANTRY
**GANTRY** *n* structure supporting something such as a crane or rocket
**GANTS** > GANT
**GANYMEDE** *n* catamite
**GANYMEDES** > GANYMEDE
**GAOL** *same as* > JAIL
**GAOLBIRD** *n* person who is or has been confined to gaol, esp repeatedly
**GAOLBIRDS** > GAOLBIRD
**GAOLBREAK** *n* escape from gaol
**GAOLED** > GAOL
**GAOLER** > GAOL
**GAOLERESS** *n* female gaoler
**GAOLERS** > GAOL
**GAOLING** > GAOL
**GAOLLESS** > GAOL
**GAOLS** > GAOL
**GAP** *n* break or opening
**GAPE** *vb* stare in wonder ▷ *n* act of gaping
**GAPED** > GAPE
**GAPER** *n* person or thing that gapes
**GAPERS** > GAPER
**GAPES** *n* disease of young domestic fowl, characterized by gaping or gasping for breath and caused by gapeworms
**GAPESEED** *n* person who stares, mouth agape, at something
**GAPESEEDS** > GAPESEED
**GAPEWORM** *n* parasitic nematode worm, *Syngamus trachea*, that lives

in the trachea of birds
**GAPEWORMS** > GAPEWORM
**GAPING** *adj* wide open ▷ *n* state of having a gaping mouth
**GAPINGLY** > GAPING
**GAPINGS** > GAPING
**GAPLESS** > GAP
**GAPO** *n* forest near a river, regularly flooded in the rainy season
**GAPOS** > GAPO
**GAPOSIS** *n* gap between closed fastenings on a garment
**GAPOSISES** > GAPOSIS
**GAPPED** > GAP
**GAPPER** *n* in British English, person taking a year out between school and further education
**GAPPERS** > GAPPER
**GAPPIER** > GAP
**GAPPIEST** > GAP
**GAPPING** > GAP
**GAPPY** > GAP
**GAPS** > GAP
**GAPY** > GAPES
**GAR** *same as* > GARPIKE
**GARAGE** *n* building used to house cars ▷ *vb* put or keep a car in a garage
**GARAGED** > GARAGE
**GARAGEMAN** *n* car mechanic
**GARAGEMEN** > GARAGEMAN
**GARAGES** > GARAGE
**GARAGING** *n* accommodation for housing a motor vehicle
**GARAGINGS** > GARAGING
**GARAGIST** *n* person who runs a garage
**GARAGISTE** *n* small-scale wine-maker
**GARAGISTS** > GARAGIST
**GARB** *n* clothes ▷ *vb* clothe
**GARBAGE** *n* rubbish
**GARBAGES** > GARBAGE
**GARBAGEY** > GARBAGE
**GARBAGY** > GARBAGE
**GARBANZO** *another name for* > CHICKPEA
**GARBANZOS** > GARBANZO
**GARBE** *n* in heraldry, a wheat-sheaf
**GARBED** > GARB
**GARBES** > GARBE
**GARBING** > GARB
**GARBLE** *vb* jumble (a story, quotation, etc), esp unintentionally ▷ *n* act of garbling
**GARBLED** *adj* (of a story etc) jumbled and confused
**GARBLER** > GARBLE
**GARBLERS** > GARBLE
**GARBLES** > GARBLE
**GARBLESS** > GARB
**GARBLING** > GARBLE
**GARBLINGS** > GARBLE
**GARBO** *n* dustman
**GARBOARD** *n* bottommost plank of a vessel's hull
**GARBOARDS** > GARBOARD

**GARBOIL** *n* confusion or disturbance
**GARBOILS** > GARBOIL
**GARBOLOGY** *n* study of the contents of domestic dustbins to analyse the consumption patterns of households
**GARBOS** > GARBO
**GARBS** > GARB
**GARBURE** *n* thick soup from Bearn in France
**GARBURES** > GARBURE
**GARCINIA** *n* tropical tree
**GARCINIAS** > GARCINIA
**GARCON** *n* waiter
**GARCONS** > GARCON
**GARDA** *n* member of the police force of the Republic of Ireland
**GARDAI** > GARDA
**GARDANT** *same as* > GUARDANT
**GARDANTS** > GUARDANT
**GARDEN** *n* piece of land for growing flowers, fruit, or vegetables ▷ *vb* cultivate a garden
**GARDENED** > GARDEN
**GARDENER** *n* person who works in or takes care of a garden as an occupation or pastime
**GARDENERS** > GARDENER
**GARDENFUL** *n* quantity that will fill a garden
**GARDENIA** *n* large fragrant white waxy flower
**GARDENIAS** > GARDENIA
**GARDENING** *n* planning and cultivation of a garden
**GARDENS** > GARDEN
**GARDEROBE** *n* wardrobe or the contents of a wardrobe
**GARDYLOO** *n* act of throwing slops from a window
**GARDYLOOS** > GARDYLOO
**GARE** *n* filth
**GAREFOWL** *n* great auk
**GAREFOWLS** > GAREFOWL
**GARFISH** *same as* > GARPIKE
**GARFISHES** > GARFISH
**GARGANEY** *n* small Eurasian duck, closely related to the mallard
**GARGANEYS** > GARGANEY
**GARGANTUA** *n* monster in Japanese film
**GARGARISE** *vb* gargle
**GARGARISM** *n* gargle
**GARGARIZE** *same as* > GARGARISE
**GARGET** *n* inflammation of the mammary gland of domestic animals, esp cattle
**GARGETS** > GARGET
**GARGETY** > GARGET
**GARGLE** *vb* wash the throat with (a liquid) by breathing out slowly through the liquid ▷ *n* liquid used for gargling

**GARGLED** > GARGLE
**GARGLER** > GARGLE
**GARGLERS** > GARGLE
**GARGLES** > GARGLE
**GARGLING** > GARGLE
**GARGOYLE** *n* waterspout carved in the form of a grotesque face, esp on a church ▷ *vb* provide with gargoyles
**GARGOYLED** > GARGOYLE
**GARGOYLES** > GARGOYLE
**GARI** *n* thinly sliced pickled ginger, often served with sushi
**GARIAL** *same as* > GAVIAL
**GARIALS** > GARIAL
**GARIBALDI** *n* woman's loose blouse with long sleeves popular in the 1860s, copied from the red flannel shirt worn by Garibaldi's soldiers
**GARIGUE** *n* open shrubby vegetation of dry Mediterranean regions, consisting of spiny or aromatic dwarf shrubs interspersed with colourful ephemeral species
**GARIGUES** > GARIGUE
**GARIS** > GARI
**GARISH** *adj* crudely bright or colourful ▷ *vb* heal
**GARISHED** > GARISH
**GARISHES** > GARISH
**GARISHING** > GARISH
**GARISHLY** > GARISH
**GARJAN** *same as* > GURJUN
**GARJANS** > GARJAN
**GARLAND** *n* wreath of flowers worn or hung as a decoration ▷ *vb* decorate with garlands
**GARLANDED** > GARLAND
**GARLANDRY** *n* collective term for garlands
**GARLANDS** > GARLAND
**GARLIC** *n* pungent bulb of a plant of the onion family, used in cooking
**GARLICKED** *adj* flavoured with garlic
**GARLICKY** *adj* containing or resembling the taste or odour of garlic
**GARLICS** > GARLIC
**GARMENT** *n* article of clothing ▷ *vb* cover or clothe
**GARMENTED** > GARMENT
**GARMENTS** > GARMENT
**GARNER** *vb* collect or store ▷ *n* place for storage or safekeeping
**GARNERED** > GARNER
**GARNERING** > GARNER
**GARNERS** > GARNER
**GARNET** *n* red semiprecious stone
**GARNETS** > GARNET
**GARNI** *adj* garnished
**GARNISH** *vb* decorate (food)

▷ *n* decoration for food
**GARNISHED** > GARNISH
**GARNISHEE** *n* person upon whom a notice of warning has been served ▷ *vb* attach (a debt or other property) by a notice of warning
**GARNISHER** > GARNISH
**GARNISHES** > GARNISH
**GARNISHRY** *n* decoration
**GARNITURE** *n* decoration or embellishment
**GAROTE** *same as* > GARROTTE
**GAROTED** > GAROTE
**GAROTES** > GAROTE
**GAROTING** > GAROTE
**GAROTTE** *same as* > GARROTTE
**GAROTTED** > GAROTTE
**GAROTTER** > GAROTTE
**GAROTTES** > GAROTTE
**GAROTTING** > GAROTTE
**GAROUPA** *in Chinese and SE Asian cookery, another name for* > GROPER
**GAROUPAS** > GAROUPA
**GARPIKE** *n* any primitive freshwater elongated bony fish of the genus *Lepisosteus*, of North and Central America, having very long toothed jaws and a body covering of thick scales
**GARPIKES** > GARPIKE
**GARRAN** *same as* > GARRON
**GARRANS** > GARRAN
**GARRE** *vb* compel
**GARRED** > GAR
**GARRES** > GARRE
**GARRET** *n* attic in a house
**GARRETED** *adj* living in a garret
**GARRETEER** *n* person who lives in a garret
**GARRETS** > GARRET
**GARRIGUE** *same as* > GARIGUE
**GARRIGUES** > GARRIGUE
**GARRING** > GAR
**GARRISON** *n* troops stationed in a town or fort ▷ *vb* station troops in
**GARRISONS** > GARRISON
**GARRON** *n* small sturdy pony bred and used chiefly in Scotland and Ireland
**GARRONS** > GARRON
**GARROT** *n* goldeneye duck
**GARROTE** *same as* > GARROTTE
**GARROTED** > GARROTE
**GARROTER** > GARROTE
**GARROTERS** > GARROTE
**GARROTES** > GARROTE
**GARROTING** > GARROTE
**GARROTS** > GARROT
**GARROTTE** *n* Spanish method of execution by strangling ▷ *vb* kill by this method
**GARROTTED** > GARROTTE

**GARROTTER** > GARROTTE
**GARROTTES** > GARROTTE
**GARRULITY** > GARRULOUS
**GARRULOUS** *adj* talkative
**GARRYA** *n* any ornamental catkin-bearing evergreen shrub of the North American genus *Garrya*: family *Garryaceae*
**GARRYAS** > GARRYA
**GARRYOWEN** *n* (in rugby union) high kick forwards followed by a charge to the place where the ball lands
**GARS** > GAR
**GART** *vb* compel
**GARTER** *n* band worn round the leg to hold up a sock or stocking ▷ *vb* secure with a garter
**GARTERED** > GARTER
**GARTERING** > GARTER
**GARTERS** > GARTER
**GARTH** *n* courtyard surrounded by a cloister
**GARTHS** > GARTH
**GARUDA** *n* Hindu god
**GARUDAS** > GARUDA
**GARUM** *n* fermented fish sauce
**GARUMS** > GARUM
**GARVEY** *n* small flat-bottomed yacht
**GARVEYS** > GARVEY
**GARVIE** *n* sprat
**GARVIES** > GARVIE
**GARVOCK** *n* sprat
**GARVOCKS** > GARVOCK
**GAS** *n* airlike substance that is not liquid or solid ▷ *vb* poison or render unconscious with gas
**GASAHOL** *n* mixture of petrol and alcohol used as fuel
**GASAHOLS** > GASAHOL
**GASALIER** *same as* > GASOLIER
**GASALIERS** > GASALIER
**GASBAG** *n* person who talks too much ▷ *vb* talk in a voluble way, esp about unimportant matters
**GASBAGGED** > GASBAG
**GASBAGS** > GASBAG
**GASCON** *n* boaster
**GASCONADE** *n* boastful talk, bragging, or bluster ▷ *vb* boast, brag, or bluster
**GASCONISM** > GASCON
**GASCONS** > GASCON
**GASEITIES** > GASEITY
**GASEITY** *n* state of being gaseous
**GASELIER** *same as* > GASOLIER
**GASELIERS** > GASELIER
**GASEOUS** *adj* of or like gas
**GASES** > GAS
**GASFIELD** *n* area in which natural gas is found underground
**GASFIELDS** > GASFIELD
**GASH** *vb* make a long deep

cut in ▷ *n* long deep cut ▷ *adj* surplus to requirements ▷ *adj* witty
**GASHED** > GASH
**GASHER** > GASH
**GASHES** > GASH
**GASHEST** > GASH
**GASHFUL** *adj* full of gashes
**GASHING** > GASH
**GASHLY** *adv* wittily
**GASHOLDER** *n* large tank for storing gas
**GASHOUSE** *n* gasworks
**GASHOUSES** > GASHOUSE
**GASIFIED** > GASIFY
**GASIFIER** > GASIFY
**GASIFIERS** > GASIFY
**GASIFIES** > GASIFY
**GASIFORM** *adj* in a gaseous form
**GASIFY** *vb* change into a gas
**GASIFYING** > GASIFY
**GASKET** *n* piece of rubber etc placed between the faces of a metal joint to act as a seal
**GASKETS** > GASKET
**GASKIN** *n* lower part of a horse's thigh, between the hock and the stifle
**GASKING** *same as* > GASKET
**GASKINGS** > GASKING
**GASKINS** > GASKIN
**GASLESS** > GAS
**GASLIGHT** *n* lamp in which light is produced by burning gas
**GASLIGHTS** > GASLIGHT
**GASLIT** *adj* lit by gas
**GASMAN** *n* man employed to read household gas meters and install or repair gas fittings, etc
**GASMEN** > GASMAN
**GASOGENE** *n* siphon bottle
**GASOGENES** > GASOGENE
**GASOHOL** *n* mixture of 80% or 90% petrol with 20% or 10% ethyl alcohol, for use as a fuel in internal-combustion engines
**GASOHOLS** > GASOHOL
**GASOLENE** *same as* > GASOLINE
**GASOLENES** > GASOLENE
**GASOLIER** *n* branched hanging fitting for gaslights
**GASOLIERS** > GASOLIER
**GASOLINE** *n* petrol
**GASOLINES** > GASOLINE
**GASOLINIC** > GASOLINE
**GASOMETER** *same as* > GASHOLDER
**GASOMETRY** *n* measurement of quantities of gases
**GASP** *vb* draw in breath sharply or with difficulty ▷ *n* convulsive intake of breath
**GASPED** > GASP
**GASPER** *n* person who

gasps
**GASPEREAU** *another name for* > ALEWIFE
**GASPERS** > GASPER
**GASPIER** > GASP
**GASPIEST** > GASP
**GASPINESS** > GASP
**GASPING** > GASP
**GASPINGLY** > GASP
**GASPINGS** > GASP
**GASPS** > GASP
**GASPY** > GASP
**GASSED** > GAS
**GASSER** *n* drilling or well that yields natural gas
**GASSERS** > GASSER
**GASSES** > GAS
**GASSIER** > GASSY
**GASSIEST** > GASSY
**GASSILY** > GASSY
**GASSINESS** > GASSY
**GASSING** > GAS
**GASSINGS** > GAS
**GASSY** *adj* filled with gas
**GAST** *vb* frighten
**GASTED** > GAST
**GASTER** > GAST
**GASTERS** > GAST
**GASTFULL** *adj* dismal
**GASTIGHT** *adj* not allowing gas to enter or escape
**GASTING** > GAST
**GASTNESS** *n* dread
**GASTNESSE** *same as* > GASTNESS
**GASTRAEA** *n* hypothetical primeval form posited by Haeckel
**GASTRAEAS** > GASTRAEA
**GASTRAEUM** *n* underside of the body
**GASTRAL** *adj* relating to the stomach
**GASTREA** *same as* > GASTRAEA
**GASTREAS** > GASTREAS
**GASTRIC** *adj* of the stomach
**GASTRIN** *n* polypeptide hormone secreted by the stomach: stimulates secretion of gastric juice
**GASTRINS** > GASTRIN
**GASTRITIC** > GASTRITIS
**GASTRITIS** *n* inflammation of the stomach lining
**GASTROPOD** *n* mollusc, such as a snail, with a single flattened muscular foot ▷ *adj* of, relating to, or belonging to the *Gastropoda*
**GASTRULA** *n* saclike animal embryo consisting of three layers of cells (see ECTODERM, MESODERM, and ENDODERM) surrounding a central cavity (archenteron) with a small opening (blastopore) to the exterior
**GASTRULAE** > GASTRULA

**GASTRULAR** > GASTRULA
**GASTRULAS** > GASTRULA
**GASTS** > GAST
**GASWORKS** n plant where coal gas is made
**GAT** n pistol or revolver
**GATE** n movable barrier, usu hinged, in a wall or fence ▷ vb provide with a gate or gates
**GATEAU** n rich elaborate cake
**GATEAUS** > GATEAU
**GATEAUX** > GATEAU
**GATECRASH** vb gain entry to (a party, concert, etc) without invitation or payment
**GATED** > GATE
**GATEFOLD** n oversize page in a book or magazine that is folded in
**GATEFOLDS** > GATEFOLD
**GATEHOUSE** n building at or above a gateway
**GATELEG** adj (of a table) with one or two drop leaves that are supported when in use by a hinged leg swung out from the frame
**GATELESS** > GATE
**GATELIKE** > GATE
**GATEMAN** n gatekeeper
**GATEMEN** > GATEMAN
**GATEPOST** n post on which a gate is hung
**GATEPOSTS** > GATEPOST
**GATER** variant of > GATOR
**GATERS** > GATER
**GATES** > GATE
**GATEWAY** n entrance with a gate
**GATEWAYS** > GATEWAY
**GATH** n (in Indian music) second section of a raga
**GATHER** vb assemble ▷ n act of gathering
**GATHERED** > GATHER
**GATHERER** > GATHER
**GATHERERS** > GATHER
**GATHERING** n assembly
**GATHERS** > GATHER
**GATHS** > GATH
**GATING** > GATE
**GATINGS** > GATE
**GATOR** shortened form of > ALLIGATOR
**GATORS** > GATOR
**GATS** > GAT
**GATVOL** adj in South African English, fed up
**GAU** n district set up by the Nazi Party during the Third Reich
**GAUCHE** adj socially awkward
**GAUCHELY** > GAUCHE
**GAUCHER** > GAUCHE
**GAUCHERIE** n quality of being gauche
**GAUCHESCO** adj relating to the folk traditions of the gauchos

**GAUCHEST** > GAUCHE
**GAUCHO** n S American cowboy
**GAUCHOS** > GAUCHO
**GAUCIE** variant of > GAUCY
**GAUCIER** > GAUCY
**GAUCIEST** > GAUCY
**GAUCY** adj plump or jolly
**GAUD** n article of cheap finery ▷ vb decorate gaudily
**GAUDEAMUS** n first word of a traditional graduation song, hence the song itself
**GAUDED** > GAUD
**GAUDERIES** > GAUDERY
**GAUDERY** n cheap finery or display
**GAUDGIE** same as > GADGIE
**GAUDGIES** > GADGIE
**GAUDIER** > GAUDY
**GAUDIES** > GAUDY
**GAUDIEST** > GAUDY
**GAUDILY** > GAUDY
**GAUDINESS** > GAUDY
**GAUDING** > GAUD
**GAUDS** > GAUD
**GAUDY** adj vulgarly bright or colourful ▷ n celebratory festival or feast held at some schools and colleges
**GAUFER** n wafer
**GAUFERS** > GAUFER
**GAUFFER** same as > GOFFER
**GAUFFERED** > GAUFFER
**GAUFFERS** > GAUFFER
**GAUFRE** same as > GAUFER
**GAUFRES** > GAUFRE
**GAUGE** vb estimate or judge ▷ n measuring instrument ▷ adj (of a pressure measurement) measured on a pressure gauge that registers zero at atmospheric pressure
**GAUGEABLE** > GAUGE
**GAUGEABLY** > GAUGE
**GAUGED** > GAUGE
**GAUGER** n person or thing that gauges
**GAUGERS** > GAUGER
**GAUGES** > GAUGE
**GAUGING** > GAUGE
**GAUGINGS** > GAUGE
**GAUJE** same as > GADGIE
**GAUJES** > GAUJE
**GAULEITER** n person in a position of authority who behaves in an overbearing authoritarian manner
**GAULT** n stiff compact clay or thick heavy clayey soil
**GAULTER** n person who digs gault
**GAULTERS** > GAULTER
**GAULTS** > GAULT
**GAUM** vb understand
**GAUMED** > GAUM
**GAUMIER** > GAUMY
**GAUMIEST** > GAUMY
**GAUMING** > GAUM
**GAUMLESS** variant spelling of > GORMLESS
**GAUMS** > GAUM

**GAUMY** adj clogged
**GAUN** > GO
**GAUNCH** same as > GANCH
**GAUNCHED** > GAUNCH
**GAUNCHES** > GAUNCH
**GAUNCHING** > GAUNCH
**GAUNT** adj lean and haggard ▷ vb yawn
**GAUNTED** > GAUNT
**GAUNTER** > GAUNT
**GAUNTEST** > GAUNT
**GAUNTING** > GAUNT
**GAUNTLET** n heavy glove with a long cuff ▷ vb run (or cause to run) the gauntlet
**GAUNTLETS** > GAUNTLET
**GAUNTLY** > GAUNT
**GAUNTNESS** > GAUNT
**GAUNTREE** same as > GANTRY
**GAUNTREES** > GAUNTREE
**GAUNTRIES** > GAUNTRY
**GAUNTRY** same as > GANTRY
**GAUNTS** > GAUNT
**GAUP** same as > GAWP
**GAUPED** > GAUP
**GAUPER** > GAUP
**GAUPERS** > GAUP
**GAUPING** > GAUP
**GAUPS** > GAUP
**GAUPUS** same as > GAWPUS
**GAUPUSES** > GAUPUS
**GAUR** n large wild member of the cattle tribe, Bos gaurus, inhabiting mountainous regions of S Asia
**GAURS** > GAUR
**GAUS** > GAU
**GAUSS** n cgs unit of magnetic flux density
**GAUSSES** > GAUSS
**GAUSSIAN** adj of or relating to the principles established by Karl Friedrich Gauss, the German mathematician
**GAUZE** n transparent loosely-woven fabric, often used for surgical dressings
**GAUZELIKE** > GAUZE
**GAUZES** > GAUZE
**GAUZIER** > GAUZY
**GAUZIEST** > GAUZY
**GAUZILY** > GAUZY
**GAUZINESS** > GAUZY
**GAUZY** adj resembling gauze
**GAVAGE** n forced feeding by means of a tube inserted into the stomach through the mouth
**GAVAGES** > GAVAGE
**GAVE** > GIVE
**GAVEL** n small hammer banged on a table by a judge, auctioneer, or chairman to call for attention ▷ vb use a gavel to restore order
**GAVELED** > GAVEL
**GAVELING** > GAVEL
**GAVELKIND** n former

system of land tenure peculiar to Kent based on the payment of rent to the lord instead of the performance of services by the tenant
**GAVELLED** > GAVEL
**GAVELLING** > GAVEL
**GAVELMAN** n gavelkind tenant
**GAVELMEN** > GAVELMAN
**GAVELOCK** n iron crowbar
**GAVELOCKS** > GAVELOCK
**GAVELS** > GAVEL
**GAVIAL** as in false gavial small crocodile
**GAVIALOID** adj of or like gavials
**GAVIALS** > GAVIAL
**GAVOT** same as > GAVOTTE
**GAVOTS** > GAVOT
**GAVOTTE** n old formal dance ▷ vb dance a gavotte
**GAVOTTED** > GAVOTTE
**GAVOTTES** > GAVOTTE
**GAVOTTING** > GAVOTTE
**GAWCIER** > GAWCY
**GAWCIEST** > GAWCY
**GAWCY** same as > GAUCY
**GAWD** same as > GAUD
**GAWDS** > GAWD
**GAWK** vb stare stupidly ▷ n clumsy awkward person
**GAWKED** > GAWK
**GAWKER** > GAWK
**GAWKERS** > GAWK
**GAWKIER** > GAWKY
**GAWKIES** > GAWKY
**GAWKIEST** > GAWKY
**GAWKIHOOD** n state of being gawky
**GAWKILY** > GAWKY
**GAWKINESS** > GAWKY
**GAWKING** > GAWK
**GAWKISH** same as > GAWKY
**GAWKISHLY** > GAWKY
**GAWKS** > GAWK
**GAWKY** adj clumsy or awkward ▷ n simpleton
**GAWP** vb stare stupidly
**GAWPED** > GAWP
**GAWPER** > GAWP
**GAWPERS** > GAWP
**GAWPING** > GAWP
**GAWPS** > GAWP
**GAWPUS** n silly person
**GAWPUSES** > GAWPUS
**GAWSIE** same as > GAUCY
**GAWSIER** > GAWSIE
**GAWSIEST** > GAWSIE
**GAWSY** same as > GAUCY
**GAY** adj homosexual ▷ n homosexual
**GAYAL** n ox of India and Myanmar, Bibos frontalis, possibly a semidomesticated variety of gaur, black or brown with white stockings
**GAYALS** > GAYAL
**GAYDAR** n supposed ability of a homosexual person to determine whether

or not another person is homosexual
**GAYDARS** >GAYDAR
**GAYER** >GAY
**GAYEST** >GAY
**GAYETIES** >GAYETY
**GAYETY** same as >GAIETY
**GAYLY** >GAY
**GAYNESS** >GAY
**GAYNESSES** >GAY
**GAYS** >GAY
**GAYSOME** adj full of merriment
**GAYWINGS** n flowering wintergreen
**GAZABO** n fellow or companion
**GAZABOES** >GAZABO
**GAZABOS** >GAZABO
**GAZAL** same as >GHAZAL
**GAZALS** >GAZAL
**GAZANIA** n any plant of the S African genus Gazania, grown for their rayed flowers in variegated colours
**GAZANIAS** >GAZANIA
**GAZAR** n type of silk cloth
**GAZARS** >GAZAR
**GAZE** vb look fixedly ▷ n fixed look
**GAZEBO** n summerhouse with a good view
**GAZEBOES** >GAZEBO
**GAZEBOS** >GAZEBO
**GAZED** >GAZE
**GAZEFUL** adj gazing
**GAZEHOUND** n hound such as a greyhound that hunts by sight rather than by scent
**GAZELLE** n small graceful antelope
**GAZELLES** >GAZELLE
**GAZEMENT** n view
**GAZEMENTS** >GAZEMENT
**GAZER** >GAZE
**GAZERS** >GAZE
**GAZES** >GAZE
**GAZETTE** n official publication containing announcements ▷ vb announce or report (facts or an event) in a gazette
**GAZETTED** >GAZETTE
**GAZETTEER** n (part of) a book that lists and describes places ▷ vb list in a gazetteer
**GAZETTES** >GAZETTE
**GAZETTING** >GAZETTE
**GAZIER** >GAZY
**GAZIEST** >GAZY
**GAZILLION** n in informal English, an extremely large but unspecified number, quantity, or amount
**GAZING** >GAZE
**GAZINGS** >GAZE
**GAZOGENE** same as >GASOGENE
**GAZOGENES** >GAZOGENE
**GAZON** n sod used to cover a parapet in a fortification

**GAZONS** >GAZON
**GAZOO** n kazoo
**GAZOOKA** same as >GAZOO
**GAZOOKAS** >GAZOOKA
**GAZOON** same as >GAZON
**GAZOONS** >GAZOON
**GAZOOS** >GAZOO
**GAZPACHO** n Spanish soup made from tomatoes, peppers, etc, and served cold
**GAZPACHOS** >GAZPACHO
**GAZUMP** vb raise the price of a property after verbally agreeing it with (a prospective buyer) ▷ n act or an instance of gazumping
**GAZUMPED** >GAZUMP
**GAZUMPER** >GAZUMP
**GAZUMPERS** >GAZUMP
**GAZUMPING** >GAZUMP
**GAZUMPS** >GAZUMP
**GAZUNDER** vb reduce an offer on a property immediately before exchanging contracts having earlier agreed a higher price with the seller ▷ n act or instance of gazundering
**GAZUNDERS** >GAZUNDER
**GAZY** adj prone to gazing
**GEAL** vb congeal
**GEALED** >GEAL
**GEALING** >GEAL
**GEALOUS** Spenserian spelling of >JEALOUS
**GEALOUSY** Spenserian spelling of >JEALOUSY
**GEALS** >GEAL
**GEAN** n white-flowered rosaceous tree, Prunus avium, of Europe, W Asia, and N Africa, the ancestor of the cultivated sweet cherries
**GEANS** >GEAN
**GEAR** n set of toothed wheels connecting with another or with a rack to change the direction or speed of transmitted motion ▷ vb prepare or organize for something
**GEARBOX** n case enclosing a set of gears in a motor vehicle
**GEARBOXES** >GEARBOX
**GEARCASE** n protective casing for gears
**GEARCASES** >GEARCASE
**GEARE** Spenserian spelling of >JEER
**GEARED** >GEAR
**GEARES** >GEARE
**GEARHEAD** n part in engine gear system
**GEARHEADS** >GEARHEAD
**GEARING** n system of gears designed to transmit motion
**GEARINGS** >GEARING
**GEARLESS** >GEAR

**GEARS** >GEAR
**GEARSHIFT** n lever used to move gearwheels relative to each other, esp in a motor vehicle
**GEARWHEEL** n one of the toothed wheels in the gears of a motor vehicle
**GEASON** adj wonderful
**GEAT** n in casting, the channel through which molten metal runs into a mould
**GEATS** >GEAT
**GEBUR** n tenant farmer
**GEBURS** >GEBUR
**GECK** vb beguile
**GECKED** >GECK
**GECKING** >GECK
**GECKO** n small tropical lizard
**GECKOES** >GECKO
**GECKOS** >GECKO
**GECKS** >GECK
**GED** Scots word for >PIKE
**GEDACT** n flutelike stopped metal diapason organ pipe
**GEDACTS** >GEDACT
**GEDDIT** interj exclamation meaning do you understand it?
**GEDECKT** same as >GEDACT
**GEDECKTS** >GEDECKT
**GEDS** >GED
**GEE** interj mild exclamation of surprise, admiration, etc ▷ vb move (an animal, esp a horse) ahead
**GEEBAG** n in Irish slang, a disagreeable woman
**GEEBAGS** >GEEBAG
**GEEBUNG** n Australian tree or shrub with an edible but tasteless fruit
**GEEBUNGS** >GEEBUNG
**GEECHEE** n Black person from the southern states of the US
**GEECHEES** >GEECHEE
**GEED** >GEE
**GEEGAW** same as >GEWGAW
**GEEGAWS** >GEEGAW
**GEEING** >GEE
**GEEK** n boring, unattractive person
**GEEKDOM** >GEEK
**GEEKDOMS** >GEEK
**GEEKED** adj highly excited
**GEEKIER** >GEEK
**GEEKIEST** >GEEK
**GEEKINESS** >GEEK
**GEEKS** >GEEK
**GEEKSPEAK** n slang word for jargon used by geeks, esp computer enthusiasts
**GEEKY** >GEEK
**GEELBEK** n edible marine fish
**GEELBEKS** >GEELBEK
**GEEP** n cross between a goat and a sheep
**GEEPOUND** another name for >SLUG
**GEEPOUNDS** >SLUG

**GEEPS** >GEEP
**GEES** >GEE
**GEESE** >GOOSE
**GEEST** n area of sandy heathland in N Germany and adjacent areas
**GEESTS** >GEEST
**GEEZ** interj expression of surprise
**GEEZAH** variant spelling of >GEEZER
**GEEZAHS** >GEEZAH
**GEEZER** n man
**GEEZERS** >GEEZER
**GEFILTE** as in gefilte fish dish of fish stuffed with various ingredients
**GEFUFFLE** same as >KERFUFFLE
**GEFUFFLED** >GEFUFFLE
**GEFUFFLES** >GEFUFFLE
**GEFULLTE** as in gefullte fish dish of fish stuffed with various ingredients
**GEGGIE** Scottish, esp Glaswegian, slang word for the >MOUTH
**GEGGIES** >GEGGIE
**GEHLENITE** n green mineral consisting of calcium aluminium silicate in tetragonal crystalline form
**GEISHA** n (in Japan) professional female companion for men
**GEISHAS** >GEISHA
**GEIST** n spirit
**GEISTS** >GEIST
**GEIT** n border on clothing
**GEITS** >GEIT
**GEL** n jelly-like substance, esp one used to secure a hairstyle ▷ vb form a gel
**GELABLE** adj capable of forming a gel
**GELADA** n NE African baboon, Theropithecus gelada, with dark brown hair forming a mane over the shoulders, a bare red chest, and a ridge muzzle: family Cercopithecidae
**GELADAS** >GELADA
**GELANDE** as in gelande jump jump made in downhill skiing
**GELANT** same as >GELLANT
**GELANTS** >GELANT
**GELASTIC** adj relating to laughter
**GELATE** vb form a gel
**GELATED** >GELATE
**GELATES** >GELATE
**GELATI** n layered dessert of frozen custard and ice cream
**GELATIN** same as >GELATINE
**GELATINE** n substance made by boiling animal bones
**GELATINES** >GELATINE
**GELATING** >GELATE

**GELATINS** >GELATIN

**GELATION** n act or process of freezing a liquid

**GELATIONS** >GELATION

**GELATIS** >GELATI

**GELATO** n Italian frozen dessert, similar to ice cream

**GELATOS** >GELATO

**GELCAP** n dose of medicine enclosed in a soluble case of gelatine

**GELCAPS** >GELCAP

**GELD** vb castrate ▷ n tax on land levied in late Anglo-Saxon and Norman England

**GELDED** >GELD

**GELDER** >GELD

**GELDERS** >GELD

**GELDING** >GELD

**GELDINGS** >GELD

**GELDS** >GELD

**GELEE** n jelly

**GELEES** >GELEE

**GELID** adj very cold, icy, or frosty

**GELIDER** >GELID

**GELIDEST** >GELID

**GELIDITY** >GELID

**GELIDLY** >GELID

**GELIDNESS** >GELID

**GELIGNITE** n type of dynamite used for blasting

**GELLANT** n compound that forms a solid structure

**GELLANTS** >GELLANT

**GELLED** >GEL

**GELLIES** >GELLY

**GELLING** >GEL

**GELLY** same as >GELIGNITE

**GELOSIES** >GELOSY

**GELOSY** Spenserian spelling of >JEALOUSY

**GELS** >GEL

**GELSEMIA** >GELSEMIUM

**GELSEMINE** n alkaloid obtained from gelsemium

**GELSEMIUM** n any climbing shrub of the loganiaceous genus Gelsemium, of SE Asia and North America, esp the yellow jasmine, having fragrant yellow flowers

**GELT** >GELD

**GELTS** >GELD

**GEM** n precious stone or jewel ▷ vb set or ornament with gems

**GEMATRIA** n numerology of the Hebrew language and alphabet

**GEMATRIAS** >GEMATRIA

**GEMCLIP** n paperclip

**GEMCLIPS** >GEMCLIP

**GEMEL** n in heraldry, parallel bars

**GEMELS** >GEMEL

**GEMFISH** n Australian food fish with a delicate flavour

**GEMFISHES** >GEMFISH

**GEMINAL** adj occurring in pairs

**GEMINALLY** >GEMINAL

**GEMINATE** adj combined in pairs ▷ vb arrange or be arranged in pairs

**GEMINATED** >GEMINATE

**GEMINATES** >GEMINATE

**GEMINI** n expression of surprise

**GEMINIES** >GEMINY

**GEMINOUS** adj in pairs

**GEMINY** n pair

**GEMLIKE** >GEM

**GEMMA** n small asexual reproductive structure in liverworts, mosses, etc, that becomes detached from the parent and develops into a new individual

**GEMMAE** >GEMMA

**GEMMAN** dialect form of >GENTLEMAN

**GEMMATE** adj (of some plants and animals) having or reproducing by gemmae ▷ vb produce or reproduce by gemmae

**GEMMATED** >GEMMATE

**GEMMATES** >GEMMATE

**GEMMATING** >GEMMATE

**GEMMATION** >GEMMATE

**GEMMATIVE** adj relating to gemmation

**GEMMED** >GEM

**GEMMEN** >GEMMAN

**GEMMEOUS** adj gem-like

**GEMMERIES** >GEMMERY

**GEMMERY** n gems collectively

**GEMMIER** >GEM

**GEMMIEST** >GEM

**GEMMILY** >GEM

**GEMMINESS** >GEM

**GEMMING** >GEM

**GEMMOLOGY** same as >GEMOLOGY

**GEMMULE** n cell or mass of cells produced asexually by sponges and developing into a new individual

**GEMMULES** >GEMMULE

**GEMMY** >GEM

**GEMOLOGY** n branch of mineralogy that is concerned with gems and gemstones

**GEMONY** same as >JIMINY

**GEMOT** n (in Anglo-Saxon England) a legal or administrative assembly of a community, such as a shire or hundred

**GEMOTE** same as >GEMOT

**GEMOTES** >GEMOTE

**GEMOTS** >GEMOT

**GEMS** >GEM

**GEMSBOK** same as >ORYX

**GEMSBOKS** >GEMSBOK

**GEMSBUCK** >ORYX

**GEMSBUCKS** >GEMSBUCK

**GEMSHORN** n type of medieval flute

**GEMSHORNS** >GEMSHORN

**GEMSTONE** n precious or semiprecious stone, esp

one which has been cut and polished

**GEMSTONES** >GEMSTONE

**GEMUTLICH** adj having a feeling or atmosphere of warmth and friendliness

**GEN** n information ▷ vb gain information

**GENA** n cheek

**GENAL** >GENA

**GENAPPE** n smooth worsted yarn used for braid, etc

**GENAPPES** >GENAPPE

**GENAS** >GENA

**GENDARME** n member of the French police force

**GENDARMES** >GENDARME

**GENDER** n state of being male or female ▷ vb have sex

**GENDERED** >GENDER

**GENDERING** >GENDER

**GENDERISE** same as >GENDERIZE

**GENDERIZE** vb make distinctions according to gender in or among

**GENDERS** >GENDER

**GENE** n part of a cell which determines inherited characteristics

**GENEALOGY** n (study of) the history and descent of a family or families

**GENERA** >GENUS

**GENERABLE** adj able to be generated

**GENERAL** adj common or widespread ▷ n very senior army officer ▷ vb act as a general

**GENERALCY** n rank of general

**GENERALE** singular form of >GENERALIA

**GENERALIA** n generalities

**GENERALLY** adv usually

**GENERALS** >GENERAL

**GENERANT** n something that generates

**GENERANTS** >GENERANT

**GENERATE** vb produce or bring into being

**GENERATED** >GENERATE

**GENERATES** >GENERATE

**GENERATOR** n machine for converting mechanical energy into electrical energy

**GENERIC** adj of a class, group, or genus ▷ n drug, food product, etc that does not have a trademark

**GENERICAL** same as >GENERIC

**GENERICS** >GENERIC

**GENEROUS** adj free in giving

**GENES** >GENE

**GENESES** >GENESIS

**GENESIS** n beginning or origin

**GENET** n any agile catlike viverrine mammal of the

genus Genetta, inhabiting wooded regions of Africa and S Europe, having an elongated head, thick spotted or blotched fur, and a very long tail

**GENETIC** adj of genes or genetics

**GENETICAL** same as >GENETIC

**GENETICS** n study of heredity and variation in organisms

**GENETRIX** n female progenitor

**GENETS** >GENET

**GENETTE** same as >GENET

**GENETTES** >GENETTE

**GENEVA** n gin

**GENEVAS** >GENEVA

**GENIAL** adj cheerful and friendly

**GENIALISE** vb make genial

**GENIALITY** >GENIAL

**GENIALIZE** same as >GENIALISE

**GENIALLY** >GENIAL

**GENIC** adj of or relating to a gene or genes

**GENICALLY** >GENIC

**GENICULAR** adj of or relating to the knee

**GENIE** n (in fairy tales) servant who appears by magic and grants wishes

**GENIES** >GENIE

**GENII** >GENIUS

**GENIP** same as >GENIPAP

**GENIPAP** n evergreen Caribbean rubiaceous tree, Genipa americana, with reddish-brown edible orange-like fruits

**GENIPAPS** >GENIPAP

**GENIPS** >GENIP

**GENISTA** n any member of the broom family

**GENISTAS** >GENISTA

**GENISTEIN** n substance found in plants, thought to fight cancer

**GENITAL** adj of the sexual organs or reproduction

**GENITALIA** same as >GENITALS

**GENITALIC** >GENITALIA

**GENITALLY** >GENITAL

**GENITALS** pl n external sexual organs

**GENITIVAL** >GENITIVE

**GENITIVE** n grammatical case indicating possession or association ▷ adj denoting a case of nouns, pronouns, and adjectives in inflected languages used to indicate a relation of ownership or association, usually translated by English of

**GENITIVES** >GENITIVE

**GENITOR** n biological father as distinguished from the pater or legal

father
**GENITORS** > GENITOR
**GENITRIX** same
as > GENETRIX
**GENITURE** n birth
**GENITURES** > GENITURE
**GENIUS** n (person with) exceptional ability in a particular field
**GENIUSES** > GENIUS
**GENIZAH** n repository (usually in a synagogue) for books and other sacred objects which can no longer be used but which may not be destroyed
**GENIZAHS** > GENIZAH
**GENLOCK** n generator locking device
**GENLOCKS** > GENLOCK
**GENNAKER** n type of sail for boats
**GENNAKERS** > GENNAKER
**GENNED** > GEN
**GENNEL** same as > GINNEL
**GENNELS** > GENNEL
**GENNET** n female donkey or ass
**GENNETS** > GENNET
**GENNIES** > GENNY
**GENNING** > GEN
**GENNY** same as > GENOA
**GENOA** n large triangular jib sail, often with a foot that extends as far aft as the clew of the mainsail
**GENOAS** > GENOA
**GENOCIDAL** > GENOCIDE
**GENOCIDE** n murder of a race of people
**GENOCIDES** > GENOCIDE
**GENOGRAM** n expanded family tree
**GENOGRAMS** > GENOGRAM
**GENOISE** n rich sponge cake
**GENOISES** > GENOISE
**GENOM** same as > GENOME
**GENOME** n full complement of genetic material within an organism
**GENOMES** > GENOME
**GENOMIC** > GENOME
**GENOMICS** n branch of molecular genetics concerned with the study of genomes
**GENOMS** > GENOM
**GENOTYPE** n genetic constitution of an organism
**GENOTYPES** > GENOTYPE
**GENOTYPIC** > GENOTYPE
**GENRE** n style of literary, musical, or artistic work
**GENRES** > GENRE
**GENRO** n group of highly respected elder statesmen in late 19th- and early 20th-century Japan
**GENROS** > GENRO
**GENS** n (in ancient Rome) any of a group of aristocratic families,

having a common name and claiming descent from a common ancestor in the male line
**GENSENG** same as > GINSENG
**GENSENGS** > GENSENG
**GENT** n gentleman
**GENTEEL** adj affectedly proper and polite
**GENTEELER** > GENTEEL
**GENTEELLY** > GENTEEL
**GENTES** > GENS
**GENTIAN** n mountain plant with deep blue flowers
**GENTIANS** > GENTIAN
**GENTIER** > GENTY
**GENTIEST** > GENTY
**GENTIL** adj gentle
**GENTILE** n non-Jewish (person) ▷ adj denoting an adjective or proper noun used to designate a place or the inhabitants of a place, as Spanish and Spaniard
**GENTILES** > GENTILE
**GENTILIC** adj tribal
**GENTILISE** vb live like a gentile
**GENTILISH** adj heathenish
**GENTILISM** n heathenism
**GENTILITY** n noble birth or ancestry
**GENTILIZE** same as > GENTILISE
**GENTLE** adj mild or kindly ▷ vb tame or subdue (a horse) ▷ n maggot, esp when used as bait in fishing
**GENTLED** > GENTLE
**GENTLEMAN** n polite well-bred man
**GENTLEMEN** > GENTLEMAN
**GENTLER** > GENTLE
**GENTLES** > GENTLE
**GENTLEST** > GENTLE
**GENTLING** > GENTLE
**GENTLY** > GENTLE
**GENTOO** n grey-backed penguin
**GENTOOS** > GENTOO
**GENTRICE** n high birth
**GENTRICES** > GENTRICE
**GENTRIES** > GENTRY
**GENTRIFY** vb change the character of a neighbourhood by restoring property or introducing amenities that appeal to the middle classes
**GENTRY** n informal, often derogatory term for people just below the nobility in social rank
**GENTS** n men's public toilet
**GENTY** adj neat
**GENU** n any knee-like bend in a structure or part
**GENUA** > GENU
**GENUFLECT** vb bend the knee as a sign of reverence or deference

**GENUINE** adj not fake, authentic
**GENUINELY** > GENUINE
**GENUS** n group into which a family of animals or plants is divided
**GENUSES** > GENUS
**GEO** n (esp in Shetland) a small fjord or gully
**GEOBOTANY** n study of plants in relation to their geological habitat
**GEOCARPIC** > GEOCARPY
**GEOCARPY** n ripening of fruits below ground, as occurs in the peanut
**GEOCORONA** n outer layer of earth's atmosphere
**GEODE** n cavity, usually lined with crystals, within a rock mass or nodule
**GEODES** > GEODE
**GEODESIC** adj of the geometry of curved surfaces ▷ n shortest line between two points on a curve
**GEODESICS** > GEODESIC
**GEODESIES** > GEODESY
**GEODESIST** > GEODESY
**GEODESY** n study of the shape and size of the earth
**GEODETIC** same as > GEODESIC
**GEODETICS** same as > GEODETIC
**GEODIC** > GEODE
**GEODUCK** n king clam
**GEODUCKS** > GEODUCK
**GEOFACT** n rock shaped by natural forces, as opposed to a manmade artefact
**GEOFACTS** > GEOFACT
**GEOGENIES** > GEOGENY
**GEOGENY** same as > GEOGONY
**GEOGNOSES** > GEOGNOSY
**GEOGNOSIS** same as > GEOGNOSY
**GEOGNOST** > GEOGNOSY
**GEOGNOSTS** > GEOGNOSY
**GEOGNOSY** n study of the origin and distribution of minerals and rocks in the earth's crust: superseded generally by the term GEOLOGY
**GEOGONIC** > GEOGONY
**GEOGONIES** > GEOGONY
**GEOGONY** n science of the earth's formation
**GEOGRAPHY** n study of the earth's physical features, climate, population, etc
**GEOID** n hypothetical surface that corresponds to mean sea level and extends at the same level under the continents
**GEOIDAL** > GEOID
**GEOIDS** > GEOID
**GEOLATRY** n worship of the earth
**GEOLOGER** > GEOLOGY

**GEOLOGERS** > GEOLOGY
**GEOLOGIAN** > GEOLOGY
**GEOLOGIC** > GEOLOGY
**GEOLOGIES** > GEOLOGY
**GEOLOGISE** same as > GEOLOGIZE
**GEOLOGIST** > GEOLOGY
**GEOLOGIZE** vb study the geological features of (an area)
**GEOLOGY** n study of the earth's origin, structure, and composition
**GEOMANCER** > GEOMANCY
**GEOMANCY** n prophecy from the pattern made when a handful of earth is cast down or dots are drawn at random and connected with lines
**GEOMANT** n geomancer
**GEOMANTIC** > GEOMANCY
**GEOMANTS** > GEOMANT
**GEOMETER** n person who is practised in or who studies geometry
**GEOMETERS** > GEOMETER
**GEOMETRIC** adj of geometry
**GEOMETRID** n any moth of the family Geometridae, the larvae of which are called measuring worms, inchworms, or loopers ▷ adj of, relating to, or belonging to the Geometridae
**GEOMETRY** n branch of mathematics dealing with points, lines, curves, and surfaces
**GEOMYOID** adj relating to burrowing rodents of the genus Geomys
**GEOPHAGIA** same as > GEOPHAGY
**GEOPHAGY** n practice of eating earth, clay, chalk, etc, found in some primitive tribes
**GEOPHILIC** adj soil-loving
**GEOPHONE** n device for recording seismic movement
**GEOPHONES** > GEOPHONE
**GEOPHYTE** n perennial plant that propagates by means of buds below the soil surface
**GEOPHYTES** > GEOPHYTE
**GEOPHYTIC** > GEOPHYTE
**GEOPONIC** adj of or relating to agriculture, esp as a science
**GEOPONICS** n science of agriculture
**GEOPROBE** n probing device used for sampling soil
**GEOPROBES** > GEOPROBE
**GEORGETTE** n fine silky fabric
**GEORGIC** adj agricultural ▷ n poem about rural or agricultural life

**GEORGICAL** *same as* >GEORGIC

**GEORGICS** >GEORGIC

**GEOS** >GEO

**GEOSPHERE** *another name for* >LITHOSPHERE

**GEOSTATIC** *adj* denoting or relating to the pressure exerted by a mass of rock or a similar substance

**GEOTACTIC** >GEOTAXIS

**GEOTAXES** >GEOTAXIS

**GEOTAXIS** *n* movement of an organism in response to the stimulus of gravity

**GEOTHERM** *n* line or surface within or on the earth connecting points of equal temperature

**GEOTHERMS** >GEOTHERM

**GEOTROPIC** *adj* of geotropism: the response of a plant to the stimulus of gravity

**GERAH** *n* ancient Hebrew unit of weight

**GERAHS** >GERAH

**GERANIAL** *n* cis-isomer of citral

**GERANIALS** >GERANIAL

**GERANIOL** *n* colourless or pale yellow terpine alcohol with an odour of roses, found in many essential oils: used in perfumery

**GERANIOLS** >GERANIOL

**GERANIUM** *n* cultivated plant with red, pink, or white flowers

**GERANIUMS** >GERANIUM

**GERARDIA** *n* any plant of the genus Gerardia

**GERARDIAS** >GERARDIA

**GERBE** *same as* >GARBE

**GERBERA** *n* any plant of the perennial genus Gerbera, esp the Barberton daisy from S. Africa, G. jamesonii, grown, usually as a greenhouse plant, for its large brightly coloured daisy-like flowers: family Asteraceae

**GERBERAS** >GERBERA

**GERBES** >GARBE

**GERBIL** *n* burrowing desert rodent of Asia and Africa

**GERBILLE** *same as* >GERBIL

**GERBILLES** >GERBILLE

**GERBILS** >GERBIL

**GERE** Spenserian spelling of >GEAR

**GERENT** *n* person who rules or manages

**GERENTS** >GERENT

**GERENUK** *n* slender E African antelope, Litocranius walleri, with a long thin neck and backward-curving horns

**GERENUKS** >GERENUK

**GERES** >GEAR

**GERFALCON** *same as* >GYRFALCON

**GERIATRIC** *n* derogatory term for old person ▷ *adj* of geriatrics or old people

**GERLE** Spenserian spelling of >GIRL

**GERLES** >GERLE

**GERM** *n* microbe, esp one causing disease ▷ *vb* sprout

**GERMAIN** *same as* >GERMEN

**GERMAINE** *same as* >GERMEN

**GERMAINES** >GERMAINE

**GERMAINS** >GERMAIN

**GERMAN** *n* dance consisting of complicated figures and changes of partners ▷ *adj* having the same parents as oneself

**GERMANDER** *n* any of several plants of the genus Teucrium

**GERMANE** *adj* relevant

**GERMANELY** >GERMANE

**GERMANIC** *adj* of or containing germanium in the tetravalent state

**GERMANISE** *same as* >GERMANIZE

**GERMANITE** *n* mineral consisting of a complex copper arsenic sulphide containing germanium, gallium, iron, zinc, and lead: an ore of germanium and gallium

**GERMANIUM** *n* brittle grey element that is a semiconductor

**GERMANIZE** *vb* adopt or cause to adopt German customs, speech, institutions, etc

**GERMANOUS** *adj* of or containing germanium in the divalent state

**GERMANS** >GERMAN

**GERMED** >GERM

**GERMEN** *n* mass of undifferentiated cells that gives rise to the germ cells

**GERMENS** >GERMEN

**GERMFREE** >GERM

**GERMICIDE** *n* substance that kills germs

**GERMIER** >GERMY

**GERMIEST** >GERMY

**GERMIN** *same as* >GERMEN

**GERMINA** >GERMEN

**GERMINAL** *adj* of or in the earliest stage of development

**GERMINANT** *adj* in the process of germinating

**GERMINATE** *vb* (cause to) sprout or begin to grow

**GERMINESS** >GERMY

**GERMING** >GERM

**GERMINS** >GERMIN

**GERMLIKE** >GERM

**GERMPLASM** *n* plant genetic material

**GERMPROOF** *adj* protected against the penetration of germs

**GERMS** >GERM

**GERMY** *adj* full of germs

**GERNE** *vb* grin

**GERNED** >GERNE

**GERNES** >GERNE

**GERNING** >GERNE

**GERONIMO** *interj* shout given by US paratroopers as they jump into battle

**GERONTIC** *adj* of or relating to the senescence of an organism

**GEROPIGA** *n* grape syrup used to sweeten inferior port wines

**GEROPIGAS** >GEROPIGA

**GERT** *adv* in dialect, great or very big

**GERTCHA** *interj* get out of here!

**GERUND** *n* noun formed from a verb

**GERUNDIAL** >GERUND

**GERUNDIVE** *n* (in Latin grammar) an adjective formed from a verb, expressing the desirability of the activity denoted by the verb ▷ *adj* of or relating to the gerund or gerundive

**GERUNDS** >GERUND

**GESNERIA** *n* any plant of the mostly tuberous-rooted S. American genus Gesneria, grown as a greenhouse plant for its large leaves and showy tubular flowers in a range of bright colours: family Gesneriaceae

**GESNERIAD** >GESNERIA

**GESNERIAS** >GESNERIA

**GESSAMINE** *another word for* >JASMINE

**GESSE** Spenserian spelling of >GUESS

**GESSED** >GESS

**GESSES** >GESS

**GESSING** >GESS

**GESSO** *n* plaster used for painting or in sculpture ▷ *vb* apply gesso to

**GESSOED** >GESSO

**GESSOES** >GESSO

**GEST** *n* notable deed or exploit

**GESTALT** *n* perceptual pattern or structure possessing qualities as a whole that cannot be described merely as a sum of its parts

**GESTALTEN** >GESTALT

**GESTALTS** >GESTALT

**GESTANT** *adj* laden

**GESTAPO** *n* any secret state police organization

**GESTAPOS** >GESTAPO

**GESTATE** *vb* carry (developing young) in the uterus during pregnancy

**GESTATED** >GESTATE

**GESTATES** >GESTATE

**GESTATING** >GESTATE

**GESTATION** *n* (period of) carrying of young in the womb between conception and birth

**GESTATIVE** >GESTATION

**GESTATORY** >GESTATION

**GESTE** *same as* >GEST

**GESTES** >GESTE

**GESTIC** *adj* consisting of gestures

**GESTICAL** >GESTIC

**GESTS** >GEST

**GESTURAL** >GESTURE

**GESTURE** *n* movement to convey meaning ▷ *vb* gesticulate

**GESTURED** >GESTURE

**GESTURER** >GESTURE

**GESTURERS** >GESTURE

**GESTURES** >GESTURE

**GESTURING** >GESTURE

**GET** *vb* obtain or receive

**GETA** *n* type of Japanese wooden sandal

**GETABLE** >GET

**GETAS** >GETA

**GETATABLE** *adj* accessible

**GETAWAY** *n* used in escape

**GETAWAYS** >GETAWAY

**GETS** >GET

**GETTABLE** >GET

**GETTER** *n* person or thing that gets ▷ *vb* remove (a gas) by the action of a getter

**GETTERED** >GETTER

**GETTERING** >GETTER

**GETTERS** >GETTER

**GETTING** >GET

**GETTINGS** >GET

**GETUP** *n* outfit

**GETUPS** >GETUP

**GEUM** *n* any herbaceous plant of the rosaceous genus Geum, having compound leaves and red, orange, or white flowers

**GEUMS** >GEUM

**GEWGAW** *n* showy but valueless trinket ▷ *adj* showy and valueless

**GEWGAWED** *adj* decorated gaudily

**GEWGAWS** >GEWGAW

**GEY** *adv* extremely ▷ *adj* gallant

**GEYAN** *adv* somewhat

**GEYER** >GEY

**GEYEST** >GEY

**GEYSER** *n* spring that discharges steam and hot water

**GEYSERITE** *n* mineral form of hydrated silica resembling opal, deposited from the waters of geysers and hot springs

**GEYSERS** >GEYSER

**GHARIAL** *same as* >GAVIAL

**GHARIALS** >GHARIAL

**GHARRI** *same as* >GHARRY

**GHARRIES** >GHARRY

**GHARRIS** > GHARRI
**GHARRY** n (in India) horse-drawn vehicle available for hire
**GHAST** vb terrify
**GHASTED** > GHAST
**GHASTFUL** adj dismal
**GHASTING** > GHAST
**GHASTLIER** > GHASTLY
**GHASTLY** adj unpleasant ▷ adv unhealthily
**GHASTNESS** n dread
**GHASTS** > GHAST
**GHAT** n (in India) steps leading down to a river
**GHATS** > GHAT
**GHAUT** n small cleft in a hill through which a rivulet runs down to the sea
**GHAUTS** > GHAUT
**GHAZAL** n Arabic love poem
**GHAZALS** > GHAZAL
**GHAZEL** same as > GHAZAL
**GHAZELS** > GHAZEL
**GHAZI** n Muslim fighter against infidels
**GHAZIES** > GHAZI
**GHAZIS** > GHAZI
**GHEE** n (in Indian cookery) clarified butter
**GHEES** > GHEE
**GHERAO** n form of industrial action in India in which workers imprison their employers on the premises until their demands are met ▷ vb trap an employer in his office, to indicate the workforce's discontent
**GHERAOED** > GHERAO
**GHERAOES** > GHERAO
**GHERAOING** > GHERAO
**GHERAOS** > GHERAO
**GHERKIN** n small pickled cucumber
**GHERKINS** > GHERKIN
**GHESSE** Spenserian spelling of > GUESS
**GHESSED** > GHESS
**GHESSES** > GHESS
**GHESSING** > GHESS
**GHEST** > GHESS
**GHETTO** n slum area inhabited by a deprived minority ▷ vb ghettoize
**GHETTOED** > GHETTO
**GHETTOES** > GHETTO
**GHETTOING** > GHETTO
**GHETTOISE** same as > GHETTOIZE
**GHETTOIZE** vb confine (someone or something) to a particular area or category
**GHETTOS** > GHETTO
**GHI** same as > GHEE
**GHIBLI** n fiercely hot wind of North Africa
**GHIBLIS** > GHIBLI
**GHILGAI** same as > GILGAI
**GHILGAIS** > GHILGAI
**GHILLIE** n type of tongueless shoe with lacing up the instep,

originally worn by the Scots ▷ vb act as a g(h)illie
**GHILLIED** > GHILLIE
**GHILLIES** > GHILLIE
**GHILLYING** > GHILLIE
**GHIS** > GHI
**GHOST** n disembodied spirit of a dead person ▷ vb ghostwrite
**GHOSTED** > GHOST
**GHOSTIER** > GHOSTY
**GHOSTIEST** > GHOSTY
**GHOSTING** > GHOST
**GHOSTINGS** > GHOST
**GHOSTLIER** > GHOSTLY
**GHOSTLIKE** > GHOST
**GHOSTLY** adj frightening in appearance or effect
**GHOSTS** > GHOST
**GHOSTY** adj pertaining to ghosts
**GHOUL** n person with morbid interests
**GHOULIE** n goblin
**GHOULIES** > GHOULIE
**GHOULISH** adj of or relating to ghouls
**GHOULS** > GHOUL
**GHYLL** same as > GILL
**GHYLLS** > GHYLL
**GI** n loose-fitting white suit worn in judo, karate, and other martial arts
**GIAMBEUX** n jambeaux; leg armour
**GIANT** n mythical being of superhuman size ▷ adj huge
**GIANTESS** same as > GIANT
**GIANTHOOD** n condition of being a giant
**GIANTISM** same as > GIANTISM
**GIANTISMS** > GIANTISM
**GIANTLIER** > GIANTLY
**GIANTLIKE** > GIANT
**GIANTLY** adj giantlike
**GIANTRIES** > GIANTRY
**GIANTRY** n collective term for giants
**GIANTS** > GIANT
**GIANTSHIP** n style of address for a giant
**GIAOUR** n derogatory term for a non-Muslim, esp a Christian, used esp by the Turks
**GIAOURS** > GIAOUR
**GIARDIA** n species of parasite
**GIARDIAS** > GIARDIA
**GIB** n metal wedge, pad, or thrust bearing, esp a brass plate let into a steam engine crosshead ▷ vb fasten or supply with a gib
**GIBBED** > GIB
**GIBBER** vb speak or utter rapidly and unintelligibly ▷ n boulder
**GIBBERED** > GIBBER
**GIBBERING** > GIBBER
**GIBBERISH** n rapid unintelligible talk

**GIBBERS** > GIBBER
**GIBBET** n gallows for displaying executed criminals ▷ vb put to death by hanging on a gibbet
**GIBBETED** > GIBBET
**GIBBETING** > GIBBET
**GIBBETS** > GIBBET
**GIBBETTED** > GIBBET
**GIBBING** > GIB
**GIBBON** n agile tree-dwelling ape of S Asia
**GIBBONS** > GIBBON
**GIBBOSE** same as > GIBBOUS
**GIBBOSITY** n state of being gibbous
**GIBBOUS** adj (of the moon) more than half but less than fully illuminated
**GIBBOUSLY** > GIBBOUS
**GIBBSITE** n mineral consisting of hydrated aluminium oxide
**GIBBSITES** > GIBBSITE
**GIBE** vb make jeering or scoffing remarks (at) ▷ n derisive or provoking remark
**GIBED** > GIBE
**GIBEL** n Prussian carp
**GIBELS** > GIBEL
**GIBER** > GIBE
**GIBERS** > GIBE
**GIBES** > GIBE
**GIBING** > GIBE
**GIBINGLY** > GIBE
**GIBLET** > GIBLETS
**GIBLETS** pl n gizzard, liver, heart, and neck of a fowl
**GIBLI** same as > GHIBLI
**GIBLIS** > GIBLI
**GIBS** > GIB
**GIBSON** n martini garnished with onion
**GIBSONS** > GIBSON
**GIBUS** n collapsible top hat operated by a spring
**GIBUSES** > GIBUS
**GID** n disease of sheep characterized by an unsteady gait and staggering, caused by infestation of the brain with tapeworms (Taenia caenuris)
**GIDDAP** interj exclamation used to make a horse go faster
**GIDDAY** interj expression of greeting
**GIDDIED** > GIDDY
**GIDDIER** > GIDDY
**GIDDIES** > GIDDY
**GIDDIEST** > GIDDY
**GIDDILY** > GIDDY
**GIDDINESS** > GIDDY
**GIDDUP** same as > GIDDYUP
**GIDDY** adj having or causing a feeling of dizziness ▷ vb make giddy
**GIDDYAP** same as > GIDDYUP
**GIDDYING** > GIDDY
**GIDDYUP** interj exclamation

used to make a horse go faster
**GIDGEE** n small acacia tree, which at times emits an unpleasant smell
**GIDGEES** > GIDGEE
**GIDJEE** same as > GIDGEE
**GIDJEES** > GIDJEE
**GIDS** > GID
**GIE** Scot word for > GIVE
**GIED** > GIVE
**GIEING** > GIVE
**GIEN** > GIVE
**GIES** > GIVE
**GIF** obsolete word for > IF
**GIFT** n present ▷ vb make a present of
**GIFTABLE** adj suitable as gift ▷ n something suitable as gift
**GIFTABLES** > GIFTABLE
**GIFTED** adj talented
**GIFTEDLY** > GIFTED
**GIFTEE** n person given a gift
**GIFTEES** > GIFTEE
**GIFTING** > GIFT
**GIFTLESS** > GIFT
**GIFTS** > GIFT
**GIFTSHOP** n shop selling articles suitable for gifts
**GIFTSHOPS** > GIFTSHOP
**GIFTWARE** n anything that may be given as a present
**GIFTWARES** > GIFTWARE
**GIFTWRAP** vb wrap (a gift) in decorative wrapping paper
**GIFTWRAPS** > GIFTWRAP
**GIG** n single performance by pop or jazz musicians ▷ vb play a gig or gigs
**GIGA** same as > GIGUE
**GIGABIT** n unit of information in computing
**GIGABITS** > GIGABIT
**GIGABYTE** n one thousand and twenty-four megabytes
**GIGABYTES** > GIGABYTE
**GIGACYCLE** same as > GIGAHERTZ
**GIGAFLOP** n measure of processing speed, consisting of a thousand million floating-point operations a second
**GIGAFLOPS** > GIGAFLOP
**GIGAHERTZ** n unit of frequency equal to $10^9$ hertz.
**GIGANTEAN** adj gigantic
**GIGANTIC** adj enormous
**GIGANTISM** n excessive growth of the entire body, caused by overproduction of growth hormone by the pituitary gland during childhood or adolescence
**GIGAS** > GIGA
**GIGATON** n unit of explosive force
**GIGATONS** > GIGATON
**GIGAWATT** n unit of power

equal to 1 billion watts

**GIGAWATTS** >GIGAWATT

**GIGGED** >GIG

**GIGGING** >GIG

**GIGGIT** *vb* move quickly

**GIGGITED** >GIGGIT

**GIGGITING** >GIGGIT

**GIGGITS** >GIGGIT

**GIGGLE** *vb* laugh nervously or foolishly ▷ *n* such a laugh

**GIGGLED** >GIGGLE

**GIGGLER** >GIGGLE

**GIGGLERS** >GIGGLE

**GIGGLES** >GIGGLE

**GIGGLIER** >GIGGLE

**GIGGLIEST** >GIGGLE

**GIGGLING** >GIGGLE

**GIGGLINGS** >GIGGLE

**GIGGLY** >GIGGLE

**GIGHE** >GIGA

**GIGLET** *n* flighty girl

**GIGLETS** >GIGLET

**GIGLOT** *same as* >GIGLET

**GIGLOTS** >GIGLOT

**GIGMAN** *n* one who places great importance on respectability

**GIGMANITY** >GIGMAN

**GIGMEN** >GIGMAN

**GIGOLO** *n* man paid by an older woman to be her escort or lover

**GIGOLOS** >GIGOLO

**GIGOT** *n* leg of lamb or mutton

**GIGOTS** >GIGOT

**GIGS** >GIG

**GIGUE** *n* piece of music, usually in six-eight time and often fugal, incorporated into the classical suite

**GIGUES** >GIGUE

**GILA** *n* large venomous brightly coloured lizard

**GILAS** >GILA

**GILBERT** *n* unit of magnetomotive force

**GILBERTS** >GILBERT

**GILCUP** *same as* >GILTCUP

**GILCUPS** >GILCUP

**GILD** *vb* put a thin layer of gold on

**GILDED** >GILD

**GILDEN** *adj* gilded

**GILDER** >GILD

**GILDERS** >GILD

**GILDHALL** *same as* >GUILDHALL

**GILDHALLS** >GILDHALL

**GILDING** >GILD

**GILDINGS** >GILD

**GILDS** >GILD

**GILDSMAN** >GILD

**GILDSMEN** >GILD

**GILET** *n* waist- or hip-length garment, usually sleeveless, fastening up the front

**GILETS** >GILET

**GILGAI** *n* natural water hole

**GILGAIS** >GILGAI

**GILGIE** *n* type of freshwater crayfish

**GILGIES** >GILGIE

**GILL** *n* radiating structure beneath the cap of a mushroom ▷ *vb* catch (fish) or (of fish) to be caught in a gill net

**GILLAROO** *n* type of brown trout

**GILLAROOS** >GILLAROO

**GILLED** >GILL

**GILLER** >GILL

**GILLERS** >GILL

**GILLET** *n* mare

**GILLETS** >GILLET

**GILLFLIRT** *n* flirtatious woman

**GILLIE** *n* (in Scotland) attendant for hunting or fishing ▷ *vb* act as a gillie

**GILLIED** >GILLIE

**GILLIES** >GILLY

**GILLING** >GILL

**GILLION** *n* (no longer in technical use) one thousand million

**GILLIONS** >GILLION

**GILLNET** *n* net designed to catch fish by the gills ▷ *vb* fish using a gillnet

**GILLNETS** >GILLNET

**GILLS** *pl n* breathing organs in fish and other water creatures

**GILLY** *vb* act as a gillie

**GILLYING** >GILLY

**GILLYVOR** *n* type of carnation

**GILLYVORS** >GILLYVOR

**GILPEY** *n* mischievous, frolicsome boy or girl

**GILPEYS** >GILPEY

**GILPIES** >GILPIE

**GILPY** *same as* >GILPEY

**GILRAVAGE** *vb* make merry, especially to excess

**GILSONITE** *n* very pure form of asphalt found in Utah and Colorado

**GILT** >GILD

**GILTCUP** *n* buttercup

**GILTCUPS** >GILTCUP

**GILTHEAD** *n* sparid fish, *Sparus aurata*, of Mediterranean and European Atlantic waters, having a gold-coloured band between the eyes

**GILTHEADS** >GILTHEAD

**GILTS** >GILD

**GILTWOOD** *adj* made of wood and gilded

**GIMBAL** *vb* support on gimbals

**GIMBALED** >GIMBAL

**GIMBALING** >GIMBAL

**GIMBALLED** >GIMBAL

**GIMBALS** *pl n* set of pivoted rings which allow nautical instruments to remain horizontal at sea

**GIMCRACK** *adj* showy but cheap ▷ *n* cheap showy

trifle or gadget

**GIMCRACKS** >GIMCRACK

**GIMEL** *n* third letter of the Hebrew alphabet

**GIMELS** >GIMEL

**GIMLET** *n* small tool with a screwlike tip for boring holes in wood ▷ *adj* penetrating or piercing ▷ *vb* make holes in (wood) using a gimlet

**GIMLETED** >GIMLET

**GIMLETING** >GIMLET

**GIMLETS** >GIMLET

**GIMMAL** *n* ring composed of interlocking rings ▷ *vb* provide with gimmals

**GIMMALLED** >GIMMAL

**GIMMALS** >GIMMAL

**GIMME** *interj* give me! ▷ *n* short putt that one is excused by one's opponent from playing because it is considered too easy to miss

**GIMMER** *n* year-old ewe

**GIMMERS** >GIMMER

**GIMMES** >GIMME

**GIMMICK** *n* something designed to attract attention or publicity ▷ *vb* make gimmicky

**GIMMICKED** >GIMMICK

**GIMMICKRY** >GIMMICK

**GIMMICKS** >GIMMICK

**GIMMICKY** >GIMMICK

**GIMMIE** *n* in golf, an easy putt conceded to one's opponent

**GIMMIES** >GIMMIE

**GIMMOR** *n* mechanical device

**GIMMORS** >GIMMOR

**GIMP** *n* tapelike trimming of silk, wool, or cotton, often stiffened with wire ▷ *vb* derogatory term for limp

**GIMPED** >GIMP

**GIMPIER** >GIMPY

**GIMPIEST** >GIMPY

**GIMPING** >GIMP

**GIMPS** >GIMP

**GIMPY** *same as* >GAMMY

**GIN** *n* spirit flavoured with juniper berries ▷ *vb* free (cotton) of seeds with a gin; begin

**GING** *n* child's catapult

**GINGAL** *n* type of musket mounted on a swivel

**GINGALL** *same as* >GINGAL

**GINGALLS** >GINGALL

**GINGALS** >GINGAL

**GINGE** *n* person with ginger hair

**GINGELEY** *same as* >GINGILI

**GINGELEYS** >GINGELEY

**GINGELI** *same as* >GINGILI

**GINGELIES** >GINGELY

**GINGELIS** >GINGELI

**GINGELLI** *same as* >GINGILI

**GINGELLIS** >GINGILI

**GINGELLY** *same as* >GINGILI

**GINGELY** *same as* >GINGILI

**GINGER** *n* root of a tropical plant, used as a spice ▷ *adj* light reddish-brown ▷ *vb* add the spice ginger to (a dish)

**GINGERADE** *n* fizzy drink flavoured with ginger

**GINGERED** >GINGER

**GINGERING** >GINGER

**GINGERLY** *adv* cautiously ▷ *adj* cautious

**GINGEROUS** *adj* reddish

**GINGERS** >GINGER

**GINGERY** *adj* like or tasting of ginger

**GINGES** >GINGE

**GINGHAM** *n* cotton cloth, usu checked or striped

**GINGHAMS** >GINGHAM

**GINGILI** *n* oil obtained from sesame seeds

**GINGILIS** >GINGILI

**GINGILLI** *same as* >GINGILI

**GINGILLIS** >GINGILI

**GINGIVA** *same as* >GUM

**GINGIVAE** >GINGIVA

**GINGIVAL** >GINGIVA

**GINGKO** *same as* >GINKGO

**GINGKOES** >GINGKO

**GINGKOS** >GINGKO

**GINGLE** *same as* >JINGLE

**GINGLES** >GINGLE

**GINGLYMI** >GINGLYMUS

**GINGLYMUS** *n* hinge joint

**GINGS** >GING

**GINHOUSE** *n* building where cotton is ginned

**GINHOUSES** >GINHOUSE

**GINK** *n* man or boy, esp one considered to be odd

**GINKGO** *n* ornamental Chinese tree

**GINKGOES** >GINKGO

**GINKGOS** >GINKGO

**GINKS** >GINK

**GINN** *same as* >JINN

**GINNED** >GIN

**GINNEL** *n* narrow passageway between buildings

**GINNELS** >GINNEL

**GINNER** >GIN

**GINNERIES** >GINHOUSE

**GINNERS** >GIN

**GINNERY** *another word for* >GINHOUSE

**GINNIER** >GINNY

**GINNIEST** >GINNY

**GINNING** >GIN

**GINNINGS** >GIN

**GINNY** *adj* relating to the spirit gin

**GINORMOUS** *adj* very large

**GINS** >GIN

**GINSENG** *n* (root of) a plant believed to have tonic and energy-giving properties

**GINSENGS** >GINSENG

**GINSHOP** *n* tavern

**GINSHOPS** >GINSHOP

**GINZO** *n* disparaging term for person of Italian descent

GINZOES > GINZO
GIO same as > GEO
GIOCOSO adv (of music) to be expressed joyfully or playfully
GIOS > GIO
GIP same as > GYP
GIPON another word for > JUPON
GIPONS > GIPON
GIPPED > GIP
GIPPER > GIP
GIPPERS > GIP
GIPPIES > GIPPY
GIPPING > GIP
GIPPO same as > GIPPY
GIPPOES > GIPPO
GIPPOS > GIPPO
GIPPY n starling
GIPS > GIP
GIPSEN obsolete word for > GYPSY
GIPSENS > GIPSEN
GIPSIED > GIPSY
GIPSIES > GIPSY
GIPSY n member of a nomadic people scattered throughout Europe and North America ▷ vb live like a gypsy
GIPSYDOM > GIPSY
GIPSYDOMS > GIPSY
GIPSYHOOD > GIPSY
GIPSYING > GIPSY
GIPSYISH > GIPSY
GIPSYWORT n hairy Eurasian plant, Lycopus europaeus, having two-lipped white flowers with purple dots on the lower lip: family Lamiaceae (labiates)
GIRAFFE n African ruminant mammal with a spotted yellow skin and long neck and legs
GIRAFFES > GIRAFFE
GIRAFFID adj giraffe-like
GIRAFFINE adj relating to a giraffe
GIRAFFISH > GIRAFFE
GIRAFFOID adj giraffe-like
GIRANDOLA same as > GIRANDOLE
GIRANDOLE n ornamental branched wall candleholder, usually incorporating a mirror
GIRASOL n type of opal that has a red or pink glow in bright light
GIRASOLE same as > GIRASOL
GIRASOLES > GIRASOLE
GIRASOLS > GIRASOL
GIRD vb put a belt round ▷ n blow or stroke
GIRDED > GIRD
GIRDER n large metal beam
GIRDERS > GIRDER
GIRDING > GIRD
GIRDINGLY > GIRD
GIRDINGS > GIRD
GIRDLE n woman's elastic

corset ▷ vb surround or encircle
GIRDLED > GIRDLE
GIRDLER n person or thing that girdles
GIRDLERS > GIRDLER
GIRDLES > GIRDLE
GIRDLING > GIRDLE
GIRDS > GIRD
GIRKIN same as > GHERKIN
GIRKINS > GIRKIN
GIRL n female child
GIRLHOOD n state or time of being a girl
GIRLHOODS > GIRLHOOD
GIRLIE adj (of a magazine, calendar, etc) featuring pictures of naked or scantily clad women ▷ n little girl
GIRLIER > GIRLY
GIRLIES > GIRLIE
GIRLIEST > GIRLY
GIRLISH adj of or like a girl in looks, behaviour, innocence, etc
GIRLISHLY > GIRLISH
GIRLOND obsolete word for > GARLAND
GIRLONDS > GIRLOND
GIRLS > GIRL
GIRLY same as > GIRLIE
GIRN vb snarl
GIRNED > GIRN
GIRNEL n large chest for storing meal
GIRNELS > GIRNEL
GIRNER > GIRN
GIRNERS > GIRN
GIRNIE adj peevish
GIRNIER > GIRNIE
GIRNIEST > GIRNIE
GIRNING > GIRN
GIRNS > GIRN
GIRO n (in some countries) system of transferring money within a post office or bank directly from one account to another
GIROLLE another word for > CHANTERELLE
GIROLLES > GIROLLE
GIRON n charge consisting of the lower half of a diagonally divided quarter, usually in the top left corner of the shield
GIRONIC > GIRON
GIRONNY adj divided into segments from the fesse point
GIRONS > GIRON
GIROS > GIRO
GIROSOL same as > GIRASOL
GIROSOLS > GIROSOL
GIRR same as > GIRD
GIRRS > GIRR
GIRSH n currency unit of Saudi Arabia
GIRSHES > GIRSH
GIRT vb gird; bind
GIRTED > GIRD
GIRTH n measurement round something ▷ vb

fasten a girth on (a horse)
GIRTHED > GIRTH
GIRTHING > GIRTH
GIRTHLINE same as > GIRTLINE
GIRTHS > GIRTH
GIRTING > GIRD
GIRTLINE n gantline
GIRTLINES > GIRTLINE
GIRTS > GIRT
GIS > GI
GISARME n long-shafted battle-axe with a sharp point on the back of the axe head
GISARMES > GISARME
GISM n semen
GISMO same as > GIZMO
GISMOLOGY same as > GIZMOLOGY
GISMOS > GISMO
GISMS > GISM
GIST n substance or main point of a matter
GISTS > GIST
GIT n contemptible person ▷ vb dialect version of get
GITANA n female gypsy
GITANAS > GITANA
GITANO n male gypsy
GITANOS > GITANO
GITE n self-catering holiday cottage for let in France
GITES > GITE
GITS > GIT
GITTARONE n acoustic bass guitar
GITTED > GIT
GITTERN n obsolete medieval stringed instrument resembling the guitar ▷ vb play the gittern
GITTERNED > GITTERN
GITTERNS > GITTERN
GITTIN n Jewish divorce
GITTING > GIT
GIUST same as > JOUST
GIUSTED > GIUST
GIUSTING > GIUST
GIUSTO adv be observed strictly
GIUSTS > GIUST
GIVABLE > GIVE
GIVE vb present (something) to another person ▷ n resilience or elasticity
GIVEABLE > GIVE
GIVEAWAY n something that reveals hidden feelings or intentions ▷ adj very cheap or free
GIVEAWAYS > GIVEAWAY
GIVEBACK n reduction in wages in return for some other benefit, in time of recession
GIVEBACKS > GIVEBACK
GIVED same as > GYVED
GIVEN n assumed fact
GIVENNESS n condition of being given

GIVENS > GIVEN
GIVER > GIVE
GIVERS > GIVE
GIVES > GIVE
GIVING > GIVE
GIVINGS > GIVE
GIZMO n device
GIZMOLOGY n study of gadgets
GIZMOS > GIZMO
GIZZ n wig
GIZZARD n part of a bird's stomach
GIZZARDS > GIZZARD
GIZZEN vb (of wood) to warp
GIZZENED > GIZZEN
GIZZENING > GIZZEN
GIZZENS > GIZZEN
GIZZES > GIZZ
GJETOST n type of Norwegian cheese
GJETOSTS > GJETOST
GJU n type of violin used in Shetland
GJUS > GJU
GLABELLA n smooth elevation of the frontal bone just above the bridge of the nose: a reference point in physical anthropology or craniometry
GLABELLAE > GLABELLA
GLABELLAR > GLABELLA
GLABRATE same as > GLABROUS
GLABROUS adj without hair or a similar growth
GLACE adj preserved in a thick sugary syrup ▷ vb ice or candy (cakes, fruits, etc)
GLACEED > GLACE
GLACEING > GLACE
GLACES > GLACE
GLACIAL adj of ice or glaciers ▷ n ice age
GLACIALLY > GLACIAL
GLACIALS > GLACIAL
GLACIATE vb cover or become covered with glaciers or masses of ice
GLACIATED > GLACIATE
GLACIATES > GLACIATE
GLACIER n slow-moving mass of ice formed by accumulated snow
GLACIERED adj having a glacier or glaciers
GLACIERS > GLACIER
GLACIS n slight incline
GLACISES > GLACIS
GLAD adj pleased and happy ▷ vb become glad ▷ n gladiolus
GLADDED > GLAD
GLADDEN vb make glad
GLADDENED > GLADDEN
GLADDENER > GLADDEN
GLADDENS > GLADDEN
GLADDER > GLAD
GLADDEST > GLAD
GLADDIE same as > GLAD

GLADDIES > GLADDIE
GLADDING > GLAD
GLADDON n stinking iris
GLADDONS > GLADDON
GLADE n open space in a forest
GLADELIKE > GLADE
GLADES > GLADE
GLADFUL adj full of gladness
GLADIATE adj shaped like a sword
GLADIATOR n (in ancient Rome) man trained to fight in arenas to provide entertainment
GLADIER > GLADE
GLADIEST > GLADE
GLADIOLA same as > GLADIOLUS
GLADIOLAR > GLADIOLUS
GLADIOLAS > GLADIOLA
GLADIOLE same as > GLADIOLUS
GLADIOLES > GLADIOLE
GLADIOLI > GLADIOLUS
GLADIOLUS n garden plant with sword-shaped leaves
GLADIUS n short sword used by Roman legionaries
GLADIUSES > GLADIUS
GLADLIER > GLAD
GLADLIEST > GLAD
GLADLY > GLAD
GLADNESS > GLAD
GLADS > GLAD
GLADSOME adj joyous or cheerful
GLADSOMER > GLADSOME
GLADSTONE n light four-wheeled horse-drawn vehicle
GLADWRAP n in New Zealand English, thin film for wrapping food ▷ vb cover with gladwrap
GLADWRAPS > GLADWRAP
GLADY > GLADE
GLAIK n prank
GLAIKET same as > GLAIKIT
GLAIKIT adj foolish
GLAIKS > GLAIK
GLAIR n white of egg, esp when used as a size, glaze, or adhesive, usually in bookbinding ▷ vb apply glair to (something)
GLAIRE same as > GLAIR
GLAIRED > GLAIR
GLAIREOUS > GLAIR
GLAIRES > GLAIRE
GLAIRIER > GLAIR
GLAIRIEST > GLAIR
GLAIRIN n viscous deposit found in some mineral waters
GLAIRING > GLAIR
GLAIRINS > GLAIRIN
GLAIRS > GLAIR
GLAIRY > GLAIR
GLAIVE archaic word for > SWORD
GLAIVED adj armed with a sword

GLAIVES > GLAIVE
GLAM n magical illusion
GLAMOR same as > GLAMOUR
GLAMORED > GLAMOR
GLAMORING > GLAMOR
GLAMORISE same as > GLAMORIZE
GLAMORIZE vb cause to be or seem glamorous
GLAMOROUS adj alluring
GLAMORS > GLAMOR
GLAMOUR n alluring charm or fascination ▷ vb bewitch
GLAMOURED > GLAMOUR
> GLAMOUROUSNESS
GLAMOURS > GLAMOUR
GLAMS > GLAM
GLANCE vb look rapidly or briefly ▷ n brief look
GLANCED > GLANCE
GLANCER n log or pole used to protect standing trees from damage
GLANCERS > GLANCER
GLANCES > GLANCE
GLANCING > GLANCE
GLANCINGS > GLANCE
GLAND n organ that produces and secretes substances in the body
GLANDERED > GLANDERS
GLANDERS n highly infectious bacterial disease of horses, sometimes transmitted to man, caused by Actinobacillus mallei and characterized by inflammation and ulceration of the mucous membranes of the air passages, skin, and lymph glands
GLANDES > GLANS
GLANDLESS > GLAND
GLANDLIKE > GLAND
GLANDS > GLAND
GLANDULAR adj of or affecting a gland or glands
GLANDULE n small gland
GLANDULES > GLANDULE
GLANS n any small rounded body or glandlike mass, such as the head of the penis
GLARE vb stare angrily ▷ n angry stare ▷ adj smooth and glassy
GLAREAL adj (of a plant) growing in cultivated land
GLARED > GLARE
GLARELESS > GLARE
GLAREOUS adj resembling the white of an egg
GLARES > GLARE
GLARIER > GLARE
GLARIEST > GLARE
GLARINESS > GLARE
GLARING adj conspicuous
GLARINGLY > GLARING
GLARY > GLARE
GLASNOST n policy of openness and

accountability, esp, formerly, in the USSR
GLASNOSTS > GLASNOST
GLASS n hard brittle, usu transparent substance consisting of metal silicates or similar compounds ▷ vb cover with, enclose in, or fit with glass
GLASSED > GLASS
GLASSEN adj glassy
GLASSES pl n pair of lenses for correcting faulty vision, in a frame that rests on the nose and hooks behind the ears
GLASSFUL n amount held by a full glass
GLASSFULS > GLASSFUL
GLASSIE same as > GLASSY
GLASSIER > GLASSY
GLASSIES > GLASSY
GLASSIEST > GLASSY
GLASSIFY vb turn into glass
GLASSILY > GLASSY
GLASSINE n glazed translucent paper used for book jackets
GLASSINES > GLASSINE
GLASSING > GLASS
GLASSLESS > GLASS
GLASSLIKE > GLASS
GLASSMAN n man whose work is making or selling glassware
GLASSMEN > GLASSMAN
GLASSWARE n articles made of glass
GLASSWORK n production of glassware
GLASSWORM n larva of gnat
GLASSWORT n any plant of the chenopodiaceous genus Salicornia, of salt marshes, having fleshy stems and scalelike leaves: formerly used as a source of soda for glass-making
GLASSY adj like glass ▷ n glass marble
GLAUCOMA n eye disease
GLAUCOMAS > GLAUCOMA
GLAUCOUS adj covered with a bluish waxy or powdery bloom
GLAUM vb snatch
GLAUMED > GLAUM
GLAUMING > GLAUM
GLAUMS > GLAUM
GLAUR n mud or mire
GLAURIER > GLAUR
GLAURIEST > GLAUR
GLAURS > GLAUR
GLAURY > GLAUR
GLAZE vb fit or cover with glass ▷ n transparent coating
GLAZED > GLAZE
GLAZEN adj glazed
GLAZER > GLAZE
GLAZERS > GLAZE
GLAZES > GLAZE

GLAZIER n person who fits windows with glass
GLAZIERS > GLAZIER
GLAZIERY > GLAZIER
GLAZIEST > GLAZE
GLAZILY > GLAZE
GLAZINESS > GLAZE
GLAZING n surface of a glazed object
GLAZINGS > GLAZING
GLAZY > GLAZE
GLEAM n small beam or glow of light ▷ vb emit a gleam
GLEAMED > GLEAM
GLEAMER n mirror used to cheat in card games
GLEAMERS > GLEAMER
GLEAMIER > GLEAM
GLEAMIEST > GLEAM
GLEAMING > GLEAM
GLEAMINGS > GLEAM
GLEAMS > GLEAM
GLEAMY > GLEAM
GLEAN vb gather (facts etc) bit by bit
GLEANABLE > GLEAN
GLEANED > GLEAN
GLEANER > GLEAN
GLEANERS > GLEAN
GLEANING > GLEAN
GLEANINGS pl n pieces of information that have been gleaned
GLEANS > GLEAN
GLEAVE same as > SWORD
GLEAVES > GLEAVE
GLEBA n mass of spores
GLEBAE > GLEBA
GLEBE n land granted to a member of the clergy as part of his or her benefice
GLEBELESS > GLEBE
GLEBES > GLEBE
GLEBOUS adj gleby
GLEBY adj relating to a glebe
GLED n kite
GLEDE same as > GLED
GLEDES > GLEDE
GLEDGE vb glance sideways
GLEDGED > GLEDGE
GLEDGES > GLEDGE
GLEDGING > GLEDGE
GLEDS > GLED
GLEE n triumph and delight ▷ vb be full of glee
GLEED n burning ember or hot coal
GLEEDS > GLEED
GLEEFUL adj merry or joyful, esp over someone else's mistake or misfortune
GLEEFULLY > GLEEFUL
GLEEING > GLEE
GLEEK vb jeer
GLEEKED > GLEEK
GLEEKING > GLEEK
GLEEKS > GLEEK
GLEEMAN n minstrel
GLEEMEN > GLEEMAN
GLEENIE n guinea fowl
GLEENIES > GLEENIE

GLEES >GLEE
GLEESOME adj full of glee
GLEET n inflammation of the urethra with a slight discharge of thin pus and mucus: a stage of chronic gonorrhoea ▷ vb discharge gleet
GLEETED >GLEET
GLEETIER >GLEET
GLEETIEST >GLEET
GLEETING >GLEET
GLEETS >GLEET
GLEETY >GLEET
GLEG adj quick
GLEGGER >GLEG
GLEGGEST >GLEG
GLEGLY >GLEG
GLEGNESS >GLEG
GLEI same as >GLEY
GLEIS >GLEI
GLEN n deep narrow valley, esp in Scotland
GLENGARRY n brimless Scottish cap with a crease down the crown
GLENLIKE >GLEN
GLENOID adj resembling or having a shallow cavity ▷ n shallow cavity
GLENOIDAL >GLENOID
GLENOIDS >GLENOID
GLENS >GLEN
GLENT same as >GLINT
GLENTED >GLENT
GLENTING >GLENT
GLENTS >GLENT
GLEY n bluish-grey compact sticky soil occurring in certain humid regions ▷ vb squint
GLEYED >GLEY
GLEYING >GLEY
GLEYINGS >GLEY
GLEYS >GLEY
GLIA n delicate web of connective tissue that surrounds and supports nerve cells
GLIADIN n protein of cereals, esp wheat, with a high proline content: forms a sticky mass with water that binds flour into dough
GLIADINE same as >GLIADIN
GLIADINES >GLIADINE
GLIADINS >GLIADIN
GLIAL >GLIA
GLIAS >GLIA
GLIB adj fluent but insincere or superficial ▷ vb castrate
GLIBBED >GLIB
GLIBBER >GLIB
GLIBBERY adj slippery
GLIBBEST >GLIB
GLIBBING >GLIB
GLIBLY >GLIB
GLIBNESS >GLIB
GLIBS >GLIB
GLID adj moving smoothly and easily
GLIDDER >GLID

GLIDDERY adj slippery
GLIDDEST >GLID
GLIDE vb move easily and smoothly ▷ n smooth easy movement
GLIDED >GLIDE
GLIDEPATH n path followed by aircraft coming in to land
GLIDER n flying phalanger
GLIDERS >GLIDER
GLIDES >GLIDE
GLIDING n sport of flying gliders
GLIDINGLY >GLIDE
GLIDINGS >GLIDING
GLIFF vb slap
GLIFFING >GLIFF
GLIFFINGS >GLIFF
GLIFFS >GLIFF
GLIFT n moment
GLIFTS >GLIFT
GLIKE same as >GLEEK
GLIKES >GLIKE
GLIM n light or lamp
GLIME vb glance sideways
GLIMED >GLIME
GLIMES >GLIME
GLIMING >GLIME
GLIMMER vb shine faintly, flicker ▷ n faint gleam
GLIMMERED >GLIMMER
GLIMMERS >GLIMMER
GLIMMERY >GLIMMER
GLIMPSE n brief or incomplete view ▷ vb catch a glimpse of
GLIMPSED >GLIMPSE
GLIMPSER >GLIMPSE
GLIMPSERS >GLIMPSE
GLIMPSES >GLIMPSE
GLIMPSING >GLIMPSE
GLIMS >GLIM
GLINT vb gleam brightly ▷ n bright gleam
GLINTED >GLINT
GLINTIER >GLINT
GLINTIEST >GLINT
GLINTING >GLINT
GLINTS >GLINT
GLINTY >GLINT
GLIOMA n tumour of the brain and spinal cord, composed of neuroglia cells and fibres
GLIOMAS >GLIOMA
GLIOMATA >GLIOMA
GLIOSES >GLIOSIS
GLIOSIS n process leading to scarring in the central nervous system
GLISK n glimpse
GLISKS >GLISK
GLISSADE n gliding step in ballet ▷ vb perform a glissade
GLISSADED >GLISSADE
GLISSADER >GLISSADE
GLISSADES >GLISSADE
GLISSANDI >GLISSANDO
GLISSANDO n slide between two notes in which all intermediate notes are played

GLISTEN vb gleam by reflecting light ▷ n gleam or gloss
GLISTENED >GLISTEN
GLISTENS >GLISTEN
GLISTER archaic word for >GLITTER
GLISTERED >GLISTER
GLISTERS >GLISTER
GLIT n slimy matter
GLITCH n small problem that stops something from working properly
GLITCHES >GLITCH
GLITCHIER >GLITCH
GLITCHY >GLITCH
GLITS >GLIT
GLITTER vb shine with bright flashes ▷ n sparkle or brilliance
GLITTERED >GLITTER
GLITTERS >GLITTER
GLITTERY >GLITTER
GLITZ n ostentatious showiness ▷ vb make something more attractive
GLITZED >GLITZ
GLITZES >GLITZ
GLITZIER >GLITZY
GLITZIEST >GLITZY
GLITZILY >GLITZY
GLITZING >GLITZ
GLITZY adj showily attractive
GLOAM n dusk
GLOAMING n twilight
GLOAMINGS >GLOAMING
GLOAMS >GLOAM
GLOAT vb regard one's own good fortune or the misfortune of others with smug or malicious pleasure ▷ n act of gloating
GLOATED >GLOAT
GLOATER >GLOAT
GLOATERS >GLOAT
GLOATING >GLOAT
GLOATS >GLOAT
GLOB n rounded mass of thick fluid
GLOBAL adj worldwide
GLOBALISE same as >GLOBALIZE
GLOBALISM n policy which is worldwide in scope
GLOBALIST >GLOBALISM
GLOBALIZE vb put (something) into effect worldwide
GLOBALLY >GLOBAL
GLOBATE adj shaped like a globe
GLOBATED same as >GLOBATE
GLOBBIER >GLOBBY
GLOBBIEST >GLOBBY
GLOBBY adj thick and lumpy
GLOBE n sphere with a map of the earth on it ▷ vb form or cause to form into a globe

GLOBED >GLOBE
GLOBEFISH another name for >PUFFER
GLOBELIKE >GLOBE
GLOBES >GLOBE
GLOBESITY n informal word for obesity seen as a worldwide social problem
GLOBETROT vb regularly travel internationally
GLOBI >GLOBUS
GLOBIN n protein component of the pigments myoglobin and haemoglobin
GLOBING >GLOBE
GLOBINS >GLOBIN
GLOBOID adj shaped approximately like a globe ▷ n globoid body, such as any of those occurring in certain plant granules
GLOBOIDS >GLOBOID
GLOBOSE adj spherical or approximately spherical ▷ n globose object
GLOBOSELY >GLOBOSE
GLOBOSES >GLOBOSE
GLOBOSITY >GLOBOSE
GLOBOUS same as >GLOBOSE
GLOBS >GLOB
GLOBULAR adj shaped like a globe or globule ▷ n globular star cluster
GLOBULARS >GLOBULAR
GLOBULE n small round drop
GLOBULES >GLOBULE
GLOBULET n small globule
GLOBULETS >GLOBULET
GLOBULIN n simple protein found in living tissue
GLOBULINS >GLOBULIN
GLOBULITE n spherical form of crystallite
GLOBULOUS same as >GLOBULAR
GLOBUS n any spherelike structure
GLOBY adj round
GLOCHID n barbed spine on a plant
GLOCHIDIA n, plural form of singular glochidium, a barbed hair on some plants
GLOCHIDS >GLOCHID
GLODE >GLIDE
GLOGG n hot alcoholic mixed drink, originally from Sweden, consisting of sweetened brandy, red wine, bitters or other flavourings, and blanched almonds
GLOGGS >GLOGG
GLOIRE n glory
GLOIRES >GLOIRE
GLOM vb attach oneself to or associate oneself with
GLOMERA >GLOMUS
GLOMERATE adj gathered into a compact rounded mass ▷ vb wind into a ball

**GLOMERULE** n cymose inflorescence in the form of a ball-like cluster of flowers
**GLOMERULI** n, plural of singular glomerulus: a knot of blood vessels in the kidney
**GLOMMED** > GLOM
**GLOMMING** > GLOM
**GLOMS** > GLOM
**GLOMUS** n small anastomosis in an artery or vein
**GLONOIN** n nitroglycerin
**GLONOINS** > GLONOIN
**GLOOM** n melancholy or depression ▷ vb look sullen or depressed
**GLOOMED** > GLOOM
**GLOOMFUL** > GLOOM
**GLOOMIER** > GLOOMY
**GLOOMIEST** > GLOOMY
**GLOOMILY** > GLOOMY
**GLOOMING** > GLOOM
**GLOOMINGS** > GLOOM
**GLOOMLESS** > GLOOM
**GLOOMS** > GLOOM
**GLOOMY** adj despairing or sad
**GLOOP** vb cover with a viscous substance
**GLOOPED** > GLOOP
**GLOOPIER** > GLOOP
**GLOOPIEST** > GLOOP
**GLOOPING** > GLOOP
**GLOOPS** > GLOOP
**GLOOPY** > GLOOP
**GLOP** vb cover with a viscous substance
**GLOPPED** > GLOP
**GLOPPIER** > GLOP
**GLOPPIEST** > GLOP
**GLOPPING** > GLOP
**GLOPPY** > GLOP
**GLOPS** > GLOP
**GLORIA** n silk, wool, cotton, or nylon fabric used esp for umbrellas
**GLORIAS** > GLORIA
**GLORIED** > GLORY
**GLORIES** > GLORY
**GLORIFIED** > GLORIFY
**GLORIFIER** > GLORIFY
**GLORIFIES** > GLORIFY
**GLORIFY** vb make (something) seem more worthy than it is
**GLORIOLE** another name for a > HALO
**GLORIOLES** > GLORIOLE
**GLORIOSA** n bulbous African tropical plant
**GLORIOSAS** > GLORIOSA
**GLORIOUS** adj brilliantly beautiful
**GLORY** n praise or honour ▷ vb triumph or exalt
**GLORYING** > GLORY
**GLOSS** n surface shine or lustre ▷ vb make glossy
**GLOSSA** n paired tonguelike lobe in the labium of an insect

**GLOSSAE** > GLOSSA
**GLOSSAL** > GLOSSA
**GLOSSARY** n list of special or technical words with definitions
**GLOSSAS** > GLOSSA
**GLOSSATOR** n writer of glosses and commentaries, esp (in the Middle Ages) an interpreter of Roman and Canon Law
**GLOSSED** > GLOSS
**GLOSSEME** n smallest meaningful unit of a language, such as stress, form, etc
**GLOSSEMES** > GLOSSEME
**GLOSSER** > GLOSS
**GLOSSERS** > GLOSS
**GLOSSES** > GLOSS
**GLOSSIER** > GLOSSY
**GLOSSIES** > GLOSSY
**GLOSSIEST** > GLOSSY
**GLOSSILY** > GLOSSY
**GLOSSINA** n tsetse fly
**GLOSSINAS** > GLOSSINA
**GLOSSING** > GLOSS
**GLOSSIST** same as > GLOSSATOR
**GLOSSISTS** > GLOSSIST
**GLOSSITIC** > GLOSSITIS
**GLOSSITIS** n inflammation of the tongue
**GLOSSLESS** > GLOSS
**GLOSSY** adj smooth and shiny ▷ n expensively produced magazine
**GLOST** n lead glaze used for pottery
**GLOSTS** > GLOST
**GLOTTAL** adj of the glottis
**GLOTTIC** adj of or relating to the tongue or the glottis
**GLOTTIDES** > GLOTTIS
**GLOTTIS** n vocal cords and the space between them
**GLOTTISES** > GLOTTIS
**GLOUT** vb look sullen
**GLOUTED** > GLOUT
**GLOUTING** > GLOUT
**GLOUTS** > GLOUT
**GLOVE** n covering for the hand with individual sheaths for each finger and the thumb
**GLOVED** > GLOVE
**GLOVELESS** > GLOVE
**GLOVER** n person who makes or sells gloves
**GLOVERS** > GLOVER
**GLOVES** > GLOVE
**GLOVING** > GLOVE
**GLOVINGS** > GLOVE
**GLOW** vb emit light and heat without flames ▷ n glowing light
**GLOWED** > GLOW
**GLOWER** n scowl ▷ vb stare angrily
**GLOWERED** > GLOWER
**GLOWERING** > GLOWER
**GLOWERS** > GLOWER

**GLOWFLIES** > GLOWFLY
**GLOWFLY** n firefly
**GLOWING** adj full of praise
**GLOWINGLY** > GLOWING
**GLOWLAMP** n small light consisting of two or more electrodes in an inert gas
**GLOWLAMPS** > GLOWLAMP
**GLOWS** > GLOW
**GLOWSTICK** n plastic tube containing a luminescent material, waved or held aloft esp at gigs, raves, etc
**GLOWWORM** n European beetle, the females and larvae of which bear luminescent organs producing a greenish light
**GLOWWORMS** > GLOWWORM
**GLOXINIA** n tropical plant with large bell-shaped flowers
**GLOXINIAS** > GLOXINIA
**GLOZE** vb explain away ▷ n flattery or deceit
**GLOZED** > GLOZE
**GLOZES** > GLOZE
**GLOZING** > GLOZE
**GLOZINGS** > GLOZE
**GLUCAGON** n polypeptide hormone, produced in the pancreas by the islets of Langerhans, that stimulates the release of glucose into the blood
**GLUCAGONS** > GLUCAGON
**GLUCAN** n any polysaccharide consisting of a polymer of glucose, such as cellulose or starch
**GLUCANS** > GLUCAN
**GLUCINA** n oxide of glucinum
**GLUCINAS** > GLUCINA
**GLUCINIC** > GLUCINIUM
**GLUCINIUM** former name of > BERYLLIUM
**GLUCINUM** same as > GLUCINIUM
**GLUCINUMS** > GLUCINUM
**GLUCONATE** n compound formed when a mineral is bound to gluconic acid
**GLUCOSE** n kind of sugar found in fruit
**GLUCOSES** > GLUCOSE
**GLUCOSIC** > GLUCOSE
**GLUCOSIDE** n any of a large group of glycosides that yield glucose on hydrolysis
**GLUE** n natural or synthetic sticky substance used as an adhesive ▷ vb fasten with glue
**GLUED** > GLUE
**GLUEING** > GLUE
**GLUELIKE** > GLUE
**GLUEPOT** n container for holding glue
**GLUEPOTS** > GLUEPOT
**GLUER** > GLUE
**GLUERS** > GLUE
**GLUES** > GLUE
**GLUEY** > GLUE

**GLUEYNESS** > GLUE
**GLUG** n word representing a gurgling sound, as of liquid being poured from a bottle or swallowed ▷ vb drink noisily, taking big gulps
**GLUGGABLE** adj (of wine) easy and pleasant to drink
**GLUGGED** > GLUG
**GLUGGING** > GLUG
**GLUGS** > GLUG
**GLUHWEIN** n mulled wine
**GLUHWEINS** > GLUHWEIN
**GLUIER** > GLUE
**GLUIEST** > GLUE
**GLUILY** > GLUE
**GLUINESS** > GLUE
**GLUING** > GLUE
**GLUISH** > GLUE
**GLUM** adj sullen or gloomy
**GLUME** n one of a pair of dry membranous bracts at the base of the spikelet of grasses
**GLUMELIKE** > GLUME
**GLUMELLA** n palea
**GLUMELLAS** > GLUMELLA
**GLUMES** > GLUME
**GLUMLY** > GLUM
**GLUMMER** > GLUM
**GLUMMEST** > GLUM
**GLUMNESS** > GLUM
**GLUMPIER** > GLUMPY
**GLUMPIEST** > GLUMPY
**GLUMPILY** > GLUMPY
**GLUMPISH** > GLUMPY
**GLUMPS** n state of sulking
**GLUMPY** adj sullen
**GLUMS** n gloomy feelings
**GLUNCH** vb look sullen
**GLUNCHED** > GLUNCH
**GLUNCHES** > GLUNCH
**GLUNCHING** > GLUNCH
**GLUON** n hypothetical particle believed to be exchanged between quarks in order to bind them together to form particles
**GLUONS** > GLUON
**GLURGE** n stories, often sent by email, that are supposed to be true and uplifting, but which are often fabricated and sentimental
**GLURGES** > GLURGE
**GLUT** n excessive supply ▷ vb oversupply
**GLUTAEAL** > GLUTAEUS
**GLUTAEI** > GLUTAEUS
**GLUTAEUS** same as > GLUTEUS
**GLUTAMATE** n any salt of glutamic acid, esp its sodium salt
**GLUTAMIC** as in glutamic acid nonessential amino acid that plays a part in nitrogen metabolism
**GLUTAMINE** n nonessential amino acid occurring in proteins: plays an

important role in protein metabolism

**GLUTE** *n same as* > GLUTEUS

**GLUTEAL** > GLUTEUS

**GLUTEI** > GLUTEUS

**GLUTELIN** *n* any of a group of water-insoluble plant proteins found in cereals. They are precipitated by alcohol and are not coagulated by heat

**GLUTELINS** > GLUTELIN

**GLUTEN** *n* protein found in cereal grain

**GLUTENIN** *n* type of protein

**GLUTENINS** > GLUTENIN

**GLUTENOUS** > GLUTEN

**GLUTENS** > GLUTEN

**GLUTES** > GLUTE

**GLUTEUS** *n* any of the three muscles of the buttock

**GLUTINOUS** *adj* sticky or gluey

**GLUTS** > GLUT

**GLUTTED** > GLUT

**GLUTTING** > GLUT

**GLUTTON** *n* greedy person

**GLUTTONS** > GLUTTON

**GLUTTONY** *n* practice of eating too much

**GLYCAEMIA** *n* presence of glucose in blood

**GLYCAEMIC** > GLYCAEMIA

**GLYCAN** *n* polysaccharide

**GLYCANS** > GLYCAN

**GLYCEMIA** *US spelling of* > GLYCAEMIA

**GLYCEMIAS** > GLYCEMIA

**GLYCEMIC** > GLYCEMIA

**GLYCERIA** *n* manna grass

**GLYCERIAS** > GLYCERIA

**GLYCERIC** *adj* of, containing, or derived from glycerol

**GLYCERIDE** *n* any fatty-acid ester of glycerol

**GLYCERIN** *same as* > GLYCEROL

**GLYCERINE** *same as* > GLYCEROL

**GLYCERINS** > GLYCERIN

**GLYCEROL** *n* colourless odourless syrupy liquid obtained from animal and vegetable fats, used as a solvent, antifreeze, and sweetener, and in explosives

**GLYCEROLS** > GLYCEROL

**GLYCERYL** *n* (something) derived from glycerol by replacing or removing one or more of its hydroxyl groups

**GLYCERYLS** > GLYCERYL

**GLYCIN** *same as* > GLYCINE

**GLYCINE** *n* nonessential amino acid occurring in most proteins

**GLYCINES** > GLYCINE

**GLYCINS** > GLYCIN

**GLYCOCOLL** *n* glycine

**GLYCOGEN** *n* starchlike carbohydrate stored in

the liver and muscles of humans and animals

**GLYCOGENS** > GLYCOGEN

**GLYCOL** *n* another name (not in technical usage) for or a diol

**GLYCOLIC** > GLYCOL

**GLYCOLLIC** > GLYCOL

**GLYCOLS** > GLYCOL

**GLYCONIC** *n* verse consisting of a spondee, choriamb and pyrrhic

**GLYCONICS** > GLYCONIC

**GLYCOSE** *n* any of various monosaccharides

**GLYCOSES** > GLYCOSE

**GLYCOSIDE** *n* any of a group of substances, such as digitoxin, derived from monosaccharides by replacing the hydroxyl group by another group

**GLYCOSYL** *n* glucose-derived radical

**GLYCOSYLS** > GLYCOSYL

**GLYCYL** *n* radical of glycine

**GLYCYLS** > GLYCYL

**GLYPH** *n* carved channel or groove, esp a vertical one as used on a Doric frieze

**GLYPHIC** > GLYPH

**GLYPHS** > GLYPH

**GLYPTAL** *n* alkyd resin obtained from polyhydric alcohols and polybasic organic acids or their anhydrides

**GLYPTALS** > GLYPTAL

**GLYPTIC** *adj* of or relating to engraving or carving, esp on precious stones

**GLYPTICS** *n* art of engraving precious stones

**GMELINITE** *n* zeolitic mineral

**GNAMMA** *variant of* > NAMMA

**GNAR** *same as* > GNARL

**GNARL** *n* any knotty protuberance or swelling on a tree ▷ *vb* knot or cause to knot

**GNARLED** *adj* rough, twisted, and knobbly

**GNARLIER** > GNARLY

**GNARLIEST** > GNARLY

**GNARLING** > GNARL

**GNARLS** > GNARL

**GNARLY** *adj* good

**GNARR** *same as* > GNARL

**GNARRED** > GNARR

**GNARRING** > GNARR

**GNARRS** > GNARR

**GNASH** *vb* grind (the teeth) together in anger or pain ▷ *n* act of gnashing the teeth

**GNASHED** > GNASH

**GNASHER** *n* tooth

**GNASHERS** *pl n* teeth, esp false ones

**GNASHES** > GNASH

**GNASHING** > GNASH

**GNAT** *n* small biting two-

winged fly

**GNATHAL** *same as* > GNATHIC

**GNATHIC** *adj* of or relating to the jaw

**GNATHION** *n* lowest point of the midline of the lower jaw: a reference point in craniometry

**GNATHIONS** > GNATHION

**GNATHITE** *n* appendage of an arthropod that is specialized for grasping or chewing

**GNATHITES** > GNATHITE

**GNATHONIC** *adj* deceitfully flattering

**GNATLIKE** > GNAT

**GNATLING** *n* small gnat

**GNATLINGS** > GNATLING

**GNATS** > GNAT

**GNATTIER** > GNATTY

**GNATTIEST** > GNATTY

**GNATTY** *adj* infested with gnats

**GNAW** *vb* bite or chew steadily ▷ *n* act or an instance of gnawing

**GNAWABLE** > GNAW

**GNAWED** > GNAW

**GNAWER** > GNAW

**GNAWERS** > GNAW

**GNAWING** > GNAW

**GNAWINGLY** > GNAW

**GNAWINGS** > GNAW

**GNAWN** > GNAW

**GNAWS** > GNAW

**GNEISS** *n* coarse-grained metamorphic rock

**GNEISSES** > GNEISS

**GNEISSIC** > GNEISS

**GNEISSOID** > GNEISS

**GNEISSOSE** > GNEISS

**GNOCCHI** *n* dumplings made of pieces of semolina pasta, or sometimes potato, used to garnish soup or served alone with sauce

**GNOCCHIS** > GNOCCHI

**GNOMAE** > GNOME

**GNOME** *n* imaginary creature like a little old man

**GNOMELIKE** > GNOME

**GNOMES** > GNOME

**GNOMIC** *adj* of pithy sayings

**GNOMICAL** *same as* > GNOMIC

**GNOMISH** > GNOME

**GNOMIST** *n* writer of pithy sayings

**GNOMISTS** > GNOMIST

**GNOMON** *n* stationary arm that projects the shadow on a sundial

**GNOMONIC** > GNOMON

**GNOMONICS** > GNOMON

**GNOMONS** > GNOMON

**GNOSES** > GNOSIS

**GNOSIS** *n* supposedly revealed knowledge of various spiritual truths, esp that said to have been possessed by ancient

Gnostics

**GNOSTIC** *adj* of, relating to, or possessing knowledge, esp esoteric spiritual knowledge ▷ *n* one who knows

**GNOSTICAL** *same as* > GNOSTIC

**GNOSTICS** > GNOSTIC

**GNOW** *n* Australian wild bird

**GNOWS** > GNOW

**GNU** *n* ox-like S African antelope

**GNUS** > GNU

**GO** *vb* move to or from a place ▷ *n* attempt

**GOA** *n* gazelle, *Procapra picticauda*, inhabiting the plains of the Tibetan plateau, having a brownish-grey coat and backward-curving horns

**GOAD** *vb* provoke (someone) to take some kind of action, usu in anger ▷ *n* spur or provocation

**GOADED** > GOAD

**GOADING** > GOAD

**GOADLIKE** > GOAD

**GOADS** > GOAD

**GOADSMAN** *n* person who uses a goad

**GOADSMEN** > GOADSMAN

**GOADSTER** *n* goadsman

**GOADSTERS** > GOADSTER

**GOAF** *n* waste left in old mine workings

**GOAFS** > GOAF

**GOAL** *n* posts through which the ball or puck has to be propelled to score ▷ *vb* in rugby, to convert a try into a goal

**GOALBALL** *n* game played by two teams who compete to score goals by throwing a ball that emits audible sound when in motion. Players, who may be blind or sighted, are blindfolded during play

**GOALBALLS** > GOALBALL

**GOALED** > GOAL

**GOALIE** *n* goalkeeper

**GOALIES** > GOALIE

**GOALING** > GOAL

**GOALLESS** > GOAL

**GOALMOUTH** *n* area in front of the goal

**GOALPOST** *n* one of the two posts marking the limit of a goal

**GOALPOSTS** > GOALPOST

**GOALS** > GOAL

**GOALWARD** *adv* towards a goal

**GOANNA** *n* large Australian lizard

**GOANNAS** > GOANNA

**GOARY** *variant spelling of* > GORY

**GOAS** > GOA

**GOAT** *n* sure-footed ruminant animal with

horns
**GOATEE** n pointed tuft-like beard
**GOATEED** > GOATEE
**GOATEES** > GOATEE
**GOATFISH** n red mullet
**GOATHERD** n person who looks after a herd of goats
**GOATHERDS** > GOATHERD
**GOATIER** > GOAT
**GOATIEST** > GOAT
**GOATISH** adj of, like, or relating to a goat
**GOATISHLY** > GOATISH
**GOATLIKE** > GOAT
**GOATLING** n young goat
**GOATLINGS** > GOATLING
**GOATS** > GOAT
**GOATSKIN** n leather made from the skin of a goat
**GOATSKINS** > GOATSKIN
**GOATWEED** n plant of the genus Capraria
**GOATWEEDS** > GOATWEED
**GOATY** > GOAT
**GOB** n lump of a soft substance ▷ vb spit
**GOBAN** n board on which go is played
**GOBANG** n Japanese board-game
**GOBANGS** > GOBANG
**GOBANS** > GOBAN
**GOBBED** > GOB
**GOBBELINE** same as > GOBLIN
**GOBBET** n lump, esp of food
**GOBBETS** > GOBBET
**GOBBI** > GOBBO
**GOBBIER** > GOBBY
**GOBBIEST** > GOBBY
**GOBBING** > GOB
**GOBBLE** vb eat hastily and greedily ▷ n rapid gurgling cry of the male turkey ▷ interj imitation of this sound
**GOBBLED** > GOBBLE
**GOBBLER** n turkey
**GOBBLERS** > GOBBLER
**GOBBLES** > GOBBLE
**GOBBLING** > GOBBLE
**GOBBO** n hunchback
**GOBBY** adj loudmouthed and offensive
**GOBIES** > GOBY
**GOBIID** n member of the genus Gobius
**GOBIIDS** > GOBIID
**GOBIOID** adj of or relating to the Gobioidea, a suborder of spiny-finned teleost fishes that includes gobies and mudskippers (family Gobiidae) and sleepers (family Eleotridae) ▷ n any gobioid fish
**GOBIOIDS** > GOBIOID
**GOBLET** n drinking cup without handles
**GOBLETS** > GOBLET
**GOBLIN** n (in folklore) small malevolent creature
**GOBLINS** > GOBLIN

**GOBO** n shield placed around a microphone to exclude unwanted sounds
**GOBOES** > GOBO
**GOBONEE** same as > GOBONY
**GOBONY** adj in heraldry, composed of a row of small, alternately-coloured, squares
**GOBOS** > GOBO
**GOBS** > GOB
**GOBSHITE** n stupid person
**GOBSHITES** > GOBSHITE
**GOBURRA** n kookaburra
**GOBURRAS** > GOBURRA
**GOBY** n small spiny-finned fish
**GOD** n spirit or being worshipped as having supernatural power ▷ vb deify
**GODCHILD** n child for whom a person stands as godparent
**GODDAM** vb damn
**GODDAMMED** > GODDAM
**GODDAMN** interj oath expressing anger, surprise, etc ▷ adj extremely ▷ vb damn
**GODDAMNED** > GODDAMN
**GODDAMNS** > GODDAMN
**GODDAMS** > GODDAM
**GODDED** > GOD
**GODDEN** n evening greeting
**GODDENS** > GODDEN
**GODDESS** n female divinity
**GODDESSES** > GODDESS
**GODDING** > GOD
**GODET** n triangular piece of material inserted into a garment, such as into a skirt to create a flare
**GODETIA** n plant with showy flowers
**GODETIAS** > GODETIA
**GODETS** > GODET
**GODFATHER** n male godparent ▷ vb be a godfather to
**GODHEAD** n essential nature and condition of being a god
**GODHEADS** > GODHEAD
**GODHOOD** n state of being divine
**GODHOODS** > GODHOOD
**GODLESS** adj wicked or unprincipled
**GODLESSLY** > GODLESS
**GODLIER** > GODLY
**GODLIEST** > GODLY
**GODLIKE** adj resembling or befitting a god or God
**GODLILY** > GODLY
**GODLINESS** > GODLY
**GODLING** n little god
**GODLINGS** > GODLING
**GODLY** adj devout or pious
**GODMOTHER** n female godparent
**GODOWN** n (in East Asia and India) warehouse
**GODOWNS** > GODOWN

**GODPARENT** n person who promises at a child's baptism to bring the child up as a Christian
**GODROON** same as > GADROON
**GODROONED** > GODROON
**GODROONS** > GODROON
**GODS** > GOD
**GODSEND** n something unexpected but welcome
**GODSENDS** > GODSEND
**GODSHIP** n divinity
**GODSHIPS** > GODSHIP
**GODSLOT** n time in a television or radio schedule traditionally reserved for religious broadcasts
**GODSLOTS** > GODSLOT
**GODSO** same as > GADSO
**GODSON** n male godchild
**GODSONS** > GODSON
**GODSOS** > GODSO
**GODSPEED** n expression of one's good wishes for a person's success and safety
**GODSPEEDS** > GODSPEED
**GODSQUAD** n informal, sometimes derogatory term for any group of evangelical Christians, members of which are regarded as intrusive and exuberantly pious
**GODSQUADS** > GODSQUAD
**GODWARD** adv towards God
**GODWARDS** same as > GODWARD
**GODWIT** n shore bird with long legs and an upturned bill
**GODWITS** > GODWIT
**GOE** same as > GO
**GOEL** n in Jewish law, blood-avenger
**GOELS** > GOEL
**GOER** n person who attends something regularly
**GOERS** > GOER
**GOES** > GO
**GOETHITE** n black, brown, or yellow mineral consisting of hydrated iron oxide in the form of orthorhombic crystals or fibrous masses
**GOETHITES** > GOETHITE
**GOETIC** > GOETY
**GOETIES** > GOETY
**GOETY** n witchcraft
**GOEY** adj go-ahead
**GOFER** n employee or assistant whose duties include menial tasks such as running errands
**GOFERS** > GOFER
**GOFF** obsolete variant of > GOLF
**GOFFED** > GOFF
**GOFFER** vb press pleats into (a frill) ▷ n ornamental frill made by pressing pleats

**GOFFERED** > GOFFER
**GOFFERING** > GOFFER
**GOFFERS** > GOFFER
**GOFFING** > GOFF
**GOFFS** > GOFF
**GOGGA** n any small insect
**GOGGAS** > GOGGA
**GOGGLE** vb (of the eyes) bulge ▷ n fixed or bulging stare
**GOGGLEBOX** n television set
**GOGGLED** > GOGGLE
**GOGGLER** n big-eyed scad
**GOGGLERS** > GOGGLER
**GOGGLES** > GOGGLE
**GOGGLIER** > GOGGLE
**GOGGLIEST** > GOGGLE
**GOGGLING** > GOGGLE
**GOGGLINGS** > GOGGLE
**GOGGLY** > GOGGLE
**GOGLET** n long-necked water-cooling vessel of porous earthenware, used esp in India
**GOGLETS** > GOGLET
**GOGO** n disco
**GOGOS** > GOGO
**GOHONZON** n (in Nichiren Buddhism) paper scroll to which devotional chanting is directed
**GOHONZONS** > GOHONZON
**GOIER** > GOEY
**GOIEST** > GOEY
**GOING** > GO
**GOINGS** > GO
**GOITER** same as > GOITRE
**GOITERED** > GOITRE
**GOITERS** > GOITRE
**GOITRE** n swelling of the thyroid gland in the neck
**GOITRED** > GOITRE
**GOITRES** > GOITRE
**GOITROGEN** n substance that induces the formation of a goitre
**GOITROUS** > GOITRE
**GOLCONDA** n source of wealth or riches, esp a mine
**GOLCONDAS** > GOLCONDA
**GOLD** n yellow precious metal ▷ adj made of gold
**GOLDARN** euphemistic variant of > GODDAMN
**GOLDARNS** > GODDAMN
**GOLDBRICK** vb swindle
**GOLDBUG** n American beetle with a bright metallic lustre
**GOLDBUGS** > GOLDBUG
**GOLDCREST** n small bird with a yellow crown
**GOLDEN** adj made of gold ▷ vb gild
**GOLDENED** > GOLDEN
**GOLDENER** > GOLDEN
**GOLDENEST** > GOLDEN
**GOLDENEYE** n either of two black-and-white diving ducks, Bucephala clangula or B. islandica, of northern regions
**GOLDENING** > GOLDEN

**GOLDENLY** > GOLDEN
**GOLDENROD** n tall plant with spikes of small yellow flowers
**GOLDENS** > GOLDEN
**GOLDER** > GOLD
**GOLDEST** > GOLD
**GOLDEYE** n North American clupeoid fish, *Hiodon alosoides*, with yellowish eyes, silvery sides, and a dark blue back: family *Hiodontidae* (mooneyes)
**GOLDEYES** > GOLDEYE
**GOLDFIELD** n area in which there are gold deposits
**GOLDFINCH** n kind of finch, the male of which has yellow-and-black wings
**GOLDFINNY** same as > GOLDSINNY
**GOLDFISH** n orange fish kept in ponds or aquariums
**GOLDIER** > GOLDY
**GOLDIEST** > GOLDY
**GOLDISH** > GOLD
**GOLDLESS** > GOLD
**GOLDMINER** n miner who works in a gold mine
**GOLDS** > GOLD
**GOLDSINNY** n any of various small European wrasses, esp the brightly coloured *Ctenolabrus rupestris*
**GOLDSIZE** n adhesive used to fix gold leaf to a surface
**GOLDSIZES** > GOLDSIZE
**GOLDSMITH** n dealer in or maker of gold articles
**GOLDSPINK** n goldfinch
**GOLDSTICK** n colonel in the Life Guards who carries out ceremonial duties
**GOLDSTONE** another name for > AVENTURINE
**GOLDTAIL** as in *goldtail moth* European moth with white wings and a soft white furry body with a yellow tail tuft
**GOLDTONE** adj gold-coloured
**GOLDURN** variant of > GODDAMN
**GOLDURNS** > GOLDURN
**GOLDY** adj gold-like
**GOLE** obsolete spelling of > GOAL
**GOLEM** n (in Jewish legend) artificially created human being brought to life by supernatural means
**GOLEMS** > GOLEM
**GOLES** > GOLE
**GOLF** n outdoor game in which a ball is struck with clubs into a series of holes ⊳ vb play golf
**GOLFED** > GOLF
**GOLFER** n person who plays golf
**GOLFERS** > GOLFER

**GOLFIANA** n golfing collectibles
**GOLFIANAS** > GOLFIANA
**GOLFING** > GOLF
**GOLFINGS** > GOLF
**GOLFS** > GOLF
**GOLGOTHA** n place of burial
**GOLGOTHAS** > GOLGOTHA
**GOLIARD** n one of a number of wandering scholars in 12th- and 13th-century Europe famed for their riotous behaviour, intemperance, and composition of satirical and ribald Latin verse
**GOLIARDIC** > GOLIARD
**GOLIARDS** > GOLIARD
**GOLIARDY** > GOLIARD
**GOLIAS** vb behave outrageously
**GOLIASED** > GOLIAS
**GOLIASES** > GOLIAS
**GOLIASING** > GOLIAS
**GOLIATH** n giant
**GOLIATHS** > GOLIATH
**GOLLAN** n yellow flower
**GOLLAND** same as > GOLLAN
**GOLLANDS** > GOLLAN
**GOLLANS** > GOLLAN
**GOLLAR** same as > GOLLER
**GOLLARED** > GOLLAR
**GOLLARING** > GOLLAR
**GOLLARS** > GOLLAR
**GOLLER** vb roar
**GOLLERED** > GOLLER
**GOLLERING** > GOLLER
**GOLLERS** > GOLLER
**GOLLIED** > GOLLY
**GOLLIES** > GOLLY
**GOLLIWOG** n soft black-faced doll
**GOLLIWOGG** same as > GOLLIWOG
**GOLLIWOGS** > GOLLIWOG
**GOLLOP** vb eat or drink (something) quickly or greedily
**GOLLOPED** > GOLLOP
**GOLLOPER** > GOLLOP
**GOLLOPERS** > GOLLOP
**GOLLOPING** > GOLLOP
**GOLLOPS** > GOLLOP
**GOLLY** interj exclamation of mild surprise ⊳ n short for GOLLIWOG: used chiefly by children ⊳ vb spit
**GOLLYING** > GOLLY
**GOLLYWOG** same as > GOLLIWOG
**GOLLYWOGS** > GOLLYWOG
**GOLOMYNKA** n oily fish found only in Lake Baikal
**GOLOSH** same as > GALOSH
**GOLOSHE** same as > GALOSH
**GOLOSHED** > GOLOSH
**GOLOSHES** > GOLOSH
**GOLOSHING** > GOLOSH
**GOLOSHOES** > GOLOSH
**GOLP** same as > GOLPE
**GOLPE** n in heraldry, a purple circle
**GOLPES** > GOLPE
**GOLPS** > GOLP

**GOMBEEN** n usury
**GOMBEENS** > GOMBEEN
**GOMBO** same as > GUMBO
**GOMBOS** > GOMBO
**GOMBRO** same as > GUMBO
**GOMBROON** n Persian and Chinese pottery and porcelain wares
**GOMBROONS** > GOMBROON
**GOMBROS** > GOMBRO
**GOMER** n unwanted hospital patient
**GOMERAL** same as > GOMERIL
**GOMERALS** > GOMERAL
**GOMEREL** same as > GOMERIL
**GOMERELS** > GOMEREL
**GOMERIL** n slow-witted or stupid person
**GOMERILS** > GOMERIL
**GOMERS** > GOMER
**GOMOKU** another word for > GOBANG
**GOMOKUS** > GOMOKU
**GOMPA** n Tibetan monastery
**GOMPAS** > GOMPA
**GOMPHOSES** > GOMPHOSIS
**GOMPHOSIS** n form of immovable articulation in which a peglike part fits into a cavity, as in the setting of a tooth in its socket
**GOMUTI** n East Indian feather palm, *Arenga pinnata*, whose sweet sap is a source of sugar
**GOMUTIS** > GOMUTI
**GOMUTO** same as > GOMUTI
**GOMUTOS** > GOMUTO
**GON** n geometrical grade
**GONAD** n organ producing reproductive cells, such as a testicle or ovary
**GONADAL** > GONAD
**GONADIAL** > GONAD
**GONADIC** > GONAD
**GONADS** > GONAD
**GONDELAY** same as > GONDOLA
**GONDELAYS** > GONDELAY
**GONDOLA** n long narrow boat used in Venice
**GONDOLAS** > GONDOLA
**GONDOLIER** n person who propels a gondola
**GONE** > GO
**GONEF** same as > GANEF
**GONEFS** > GONEF
**GONENESS** n faintness from hunger
**GONER** n person or thing beyond help or recovery
**GONERS** > GONER
**GONFALON** n banner hanging from a crossbar, used esp by certain medieval Italian republics or in ecclesiastical processions
**GONFALONS** > GONFALON
**GONFANON** same as > GONFALON
**GONFANONS** > GONFANON

**GONG** n rimmed metal disc that produces a note when struck ⊳ vb sound a gong
**GONGED** > GONG
**GONGING** > GONG
**GONGLIKE** > GONG
**GONGS** > GONG
**GONGSTER** n person who strikes a gong
**GONGSTERS** > GONGSTER
**GONGYO** n (in Nichiren Buddhism) ceremony, performed twice a day, involving reciting parts of the Lotus Sutra and chanting the Daimoku to the Gohonzon
**GONGYOS** > GONGYO
**GONIA** > GONION
**GONIATITE** n any extinct cephalopod mollusc of the genus *Goniatites* and related genera, similar to ammonites
**GONIDIA** > GONIDIUM
**GONIDIAL** > GONIDIUM
**GONIDIC** > GONIDIUM
**GONIDIUM** n green algal cell in the thallus of a lichen
**GONIF** same as > GANEF
**GONIFF** same as > GANEF
**GONIFFS** > GONIFF
**GONIFS** > GANIF
**GONION** n point or apex of the angle of the lower jaw
**GONIUM** n immature reproductive cell
**GONK** n stuffed toy, often used as a mascot
**GONKS** > GONK
**GONNA** vb going to
**GONOCOCCI** n, plural of singular gonococcus: bacterium that causes gonorrhea
**GONOCYTE** n oocyte or spermatocyte
**GONOCYTES** > GONOCYTE
**GONODUCT** n duct leading from a gonad to the exterior, through which gametes pass
**GONODUCTS** > GONODUCT
**GONOF** same as > GANEF
**GONOFS** > GANOF
**GONOPH** same as > GANEF
**GONOPHORE** n polyp in certain coelenterates that bears gonads
**GONOPHS** > GONOPH
**GONOPOD** n either member of a pair of appendages that are the external reproductive organs of insects and some other arthropods
**GONOPODS** > GONOPOD
**GONOPORE** n external pore in insects, earthworms, etc, through which the gametes are extruded
**GONOPORES** > GONOPORE
**GONORRHEA** n infectious venereal disease

**GONOSOME** n individuals, collectively, in a colonial animal that are involved with reproduction
**GONOSOMES** > GONOSOME
**GONS** > GON
**GONYS** n lower outline of a bird's bill
**GONYSES** > GONYS
**GONZO** adj wild or crazy
**GOO** n sticky substance
**GOOBER** another name for > PEANUT
**GOOBERS** > GOOBER
**GOOBIES** > GOOBY
**GOOBY** n spittle
**GOOD** adj giving pleasure ▷ n benefit
**GOODBY** same as > GOODBYE
**GOODBYE** n expression used on parting ▷ interj expression used on parting ▷ sentence substitute farewell: a conventional expression used at leave-taking or parting with people and at the loss or rejection of things or ideas
**GOODBYES** > GOODBYE
**GOODBYS** > GOODBY
**GOODFACED** adj with a handsome face
**GOODIE** same as > GOODY
**GOODIER** > GOODY
**GOODIES** > GOODY
**GOODIEST** > GOODY
**GOODINESS** > GOODY
**GOODISH** > GOOD
**GOODLIER** > GOODLY
**GOODLIEST** > GOODLY
**GOODLY** adj considerable
**GOODMAN** n husband
**GOODMEN** > GOODMAN
**GOODNESS** n quality of being good ▷ interj exclamation of surprise
**GOODNIGHT** n conventional expression of farewell used in the evening or at night
**GOODS** > GOOD
**GOODSIRE** n grandfather
**GOODSIRES** > GOODSIRE
**GOODTIME** adj wildly seeking pleasure
**GOODWIFE** n mistress of a household
**GOODWILL** n kindly feeling
**GOODWILLS** > GOODWILL
**GOODWIVES** > GOODWIFE
**GOODY** n hero in a book or film ▷ interj child's exclamation of pleasure ▷ adj smug and sanctimonious
**GOODYEAR** n euphemistic term for the Devil
**GOODYEARS** > GOODYEAR
**GOOEY** adj sticky and soft
**GOOEYNESS** > GOOEY
**GOOF** n mistake ▷ vb make a mistake
**GOOFBALL** n barbiturate sleeping pill

**GOOFBALLS** > GOOFBALL
**GOOFED** > GOOF
**GOOFIER** > GOOFY
**GOOFIEST** > GOOFY
**GOOFILY** > GOOFY
**GOOFINESS** > GOOFY
**GOOFING** > GOOF
**GOOFS** > GOOF
**GOOFY** adj silly or ridiculous
**GOOG** n egg
**GOOGLE** vb search for (something) on the internet using a search engine
**GOOGLED** > GOOGLE
**GOOGLES** > GOOGLE
**GOOGLIES** > GOOGLY
**GOOGLING** > GOOGLE
**GOOGLY** n ball that spins unexpectedly from off to leg on the bounce
**GOOGOL** n number represented as one followed by 100 zeros ($10^{100}$)
**GOOGOLS** > GOOGOL
**GOOGS** > GOOG
**GOOIER** > GOOEY
**GOOIEST** > GOOEY
**GOOILY** > GOOEY
**GOOK** n derogatory word for a person from a Far Eastern country
**GOOKS** > GOOK
**GOOKY** adj sticky and messy
**GOOL** n corn marigold
**GOOLD** Scots word for > GOLD
**GOOLDS** > GOOLD
**GOOLEY** same as > GOOLIE
**GOOLEYS** > GOOLEY
**GOOLIE** n testicle
**GOOLIES** > GOOLIE
**GOOLS** > GOOL
**GOOLY** same as > GOOLIE
**GOOMBAH** n patron or mentor
**GOOMBAHS** > GOOMBAH
**GOOMBAY** n Bahamian soft drink
**GOOMBAYS** > GOOMBAY
**GOON** n stupid person
**GOONDA** n (in India) habitual criminal
**GOONDAS** > GOONDA
**GOONEY** n albatross
**GOONEYS** > GOONEY
**GOONIE** Scots word for a > GOWN
**GOONIER** > GOON
**GOONIES** > GOONIE
**GOONIEST** > GOON
**GOONS** > GOON
**GOONY** > GOON
**GOOP** n rude or ill-mannered person
**GOOPIER** > GOOP
**GOOPIEST** > GOOP
**GOOPS** > GOOP
**GOOPY** > GOOP
**GOOR** same as > GUR
**GOORAL** same as > GORAL
**GOORALS** > GOORAL
**GOORIE** See > KURI
**GOORIES** > GOORIE

**GOOROO** same as > GURU
**GOOROOS** > GOOROO
**GOORS** > GOOR
**GOORY** > GOOR
**GOOS** > GOO
**GOOSANDER** n type of duck
**GOOSE** n web-footed bird like a large duck ▷ vb prod (someone) playfully in the bottom
**GOOSED** > GOOSE
**GOOSEFISH** another name for > MONKFISH
**GOOSEFOOT** n any typically weedy chenopodiaceous plant of the genus Chenopodium, having small greenish flowers and leaves shaped like a goose's foot
**GOOSEGOB** > GOOSEBERRY
**GOOSEGOBS** > GOOSEBERRY
**GOOSEGOG** dialect or informal word for > GOOSEGOG
**GOOSEGOGS** > GOOSEGOG
**GOOSEHERD** n person who herds geese
**GOOSENECK** n pivot between the forward end of a boom and a mast, to allow the boom to swing freely
**GOOSERIES** > GOOSERY
**GOOSERY** n place for keeping geese
**GOOSES** > GOOSE
**GOOSEY** same as > GOOSY
**GOOSEYS** > GOOSEY
**GOOSIER** > GOOSY
**GOOSIES** > GOOSY
**GOOSIEST** > GOOSY
**GOOSINESS** > GOOSY
**GOOSING** > GOOSE
**GOOSY** adj of or like a goose
**GOPAK** n spectacular high-leaping Russian peasant dance for men
**GOPAKS** > GOPAK
**GOPHER** n American burrowing rodent ▷ vb burrow
**GOPHERED** > GOPHER
**GOPHERING** > GOPHER
**GOPHERS** > GOPHER
**GOPIK** n money unit of Azerbaijan
**GOPURA** n gateway tower of an Indian temple
**GOPURAM** same as > GOPURA
**GOPURAMS** > GOPURA
**GOPURAS** > GOPURA
**GOR** interj God!
**GORA** n (in informal Indian English) White or fair-skinned male
**GORAL** n small goat antelope, Naemorhedus goral, inhabiting mountainous regions of S Asia. It has a yellowish-grey and black coat and small conical horns
**GORALS** > GORAL
**GORAMIES** > GORAMY

**GORAMY** same as > GOURAMI
**GORAS** > GORA
**GORBELLY** n large belly
**GORBLIMEY** interj exclamation of surprise or annoyance
**GORBLIMY** same as > GORBLIMEY
**GORCOCK** n male of the red grouse
**GORCOCKS** > GORCOCK
**GORCROW** n carrion crow
**GORCROWS** > GORCROW
**GORDITA** n small thick tortilla
**GORDITAS** > GORDITA
**GORE** n blood from a wound ▷ vb pierce with horns
**GORED** > GORE
**GOREHOUND** n enthusiast of gory horror films
**GORES** > GORE
**GORGE** n deep narrow valley ▷ vb eat greedily
**GORGEABLE** > GORGE
**GORGED** > GORGE
**GORGEDLY** > GORGE
**GORGEOUS** adj strikingly beautiful or attractive
**GORGER** > GORGE
**GORGERIN** another name for > NECKING
**GORGERINS** > GORGERIN
**GORGERS** > GORGE
**GORGES** > GORGE
**GORGET** n collar-like piece of armour worn to protect the throat
**GORGETED** > GORGET
**GORGETS** > GORGET
**GORGIA** n improvised sung passage
**GORGIAS** > GORGIA
**GORGING** > GORGE
**GORGIO** n word used by gypsies for a non-gypsy
**GORGIOS** > GORGIO
**GORGON** n terrifying or repulsive woman
**GORGONEIA** n plural of gorgoneion: representation of a Gorgon's head
**GORGONIAN** n any coral of the order Gorgonacea, having a horny or calcareous branching skeleton: includes the sea fans and red corals ▷ adj of, relating to, or belonging to the Gorgonacea
**GORGONISE** vb turn to stone
**GORGONIZE** same as > GORGONISE
**GORGONS** > GORGON
**GORHEN** n female red grouse
**GORHENS** > GORHEN
**GORI** n in informal Indian English, a White or fair-skinned female
**GORIER** > GORY

GORIEST > GORY

GORILLA n largest of the apes, found in Africa

GORILLAS > GORILLA

GORILLIAN > GORILLA

GORILLINE > GORILLA

GORILLOID > GORILLA

GORILY > GORY

GORINESS > GORY

GORING > GORE

GORINGS > GORE

GORIS > GORI

GORM n foolish person ▷ vb understand

GORMAND same as > GOURMAND

GORMANDS > GOURMAND

GORMED > GORM

GORMIER > GORMY

GORMIEST > GORMY

GORMING > GORM

GORMLESS adj stupid

GORMS > GORM

GORMY adj gormless

GORP same as > GAWP

GORPED > GAWP

GORPING > GAWP

GORPS > GAWP

GORSE n prickly yellow-flowered shrub

GORSEDD n meeting of bards and druids held daily before an eisteddfod

GORSEDDS > GORSEDD

GORSES > GORSE

GORSIER > GORSE

GORSIEST > GORSE

GORSOON n young boy

GORSOONS > GORSOON

GORSY > GORSE

GORY adj horrific or bloodthirsty

GOS > GO

GOSH interj exclamation of mild surprise or wonder

GOSHAWK n large hawk

GOSHAWKS > GOSHAWK

GOSHT n Indian meat dish

GOSHTS > GOSHT

GOSLARITE n hydrated zinc sulphate

GOSLET n pygmy goose

GOSLETS > GOSLET

GOSLING n young goose

GOSLINGS > GOSLING

GOSPEL n any of the first four books of the New Testament ▷ adj denoting a kind of religious music originating in the churches of the Black people in the Southern US ▷ vb teach the gospel

GOSPELER same as > GOSPELLER

GOSPELERS > GOSPELER

GOSPELISE vb evangelise

GOSPELIZE same as > GOSPELISE

GOSPELLED > GOSPEL

GOSPELLER n person who reads or chants the Gospel in a religious service

GOSPELLY > GOSPEL

GOSPELS > GOSPEL

GOSPODA > GOSPODIN

GOSPODAR n hospodar

GOSPODARS > GOSPODAR

GOSPODIN n Russian title of address, often indicating respect, equivalent to sir when used alone or to Mr when before a name

GOSPORT n aeroplane communication device

GOSPORTS > GOSPORT

GOSS vb spit

GOSSAMER n very fine fabric

GOSSAMERS > GOSSAMER

GOSSAMERY > GOSSAMER

GOSSAN n oxidised portion of a mineral vein in rock

GOSSANS > GOSSAN

GOSSE variant of > GORSE

GOSSED > GOSS

GOSSES > GOSSE

GOSSIB n gossip

GOSSIBS > GOSSIB

GOSSING > GOSS

GOSSIP n idle talk, esp about other people ▷ vb engage in gossip

GOSSIPED > GOSSIP

GOSSIPER > GOSSIP

GOSSIPERS > GOSSIP

GOSSIPING > GOSSIP

GOSSIPPED > GOSSIP

GOSSIPPER > GOSSIP

GOSSIPRY n idle talk

GOSSIPS > GOSSIP

GOSSIPY > GOSSIP

GOSSOON n boy, esp a servant boy

GOSSOONS > GOSSOON

GOSSYPINE adj cottony

GOSSYPOL n toxic crystalline pigment that is a constituent of cottonseed oil

GOSSYPOLS > GOSSYPOL

GOSTER vb laugh uncontrollably

GOSTERED > GOSTER

GOSTERING > GOSTER

GOSTERS > GOSTER

GOT > GET

GOTCHA as in gotcha lizard Australian name for a crocodile

GOTCHAS > GOTCHA

GOTH n aficionado of Goth music and fashion

GOTHIC adj of or relating to a literary style characterized by gloom, the grotesque, and the supernatural ▷ n family of heavy script typefaces

GOTHICISE same as > GOTHICIZE

GOTHICISM > GOTHIC

GOTHICIZE vb make gothic in style

GOTHICS > GOTHIC

GOTHITE same as > GOETHITE

GOTHITES > GOTHITE

GOTHS > GOTH

GOTTA vb got to

GOTTEN past participle of > GET

GOUACHE n (painting using) watercolours mixed with glue

GOUACHES > GOUACHE

GOUGE vb scoop or force out ▷ n hole or groove

GOUGED > GOUGE

GOUGER n person or tool that gouges

GOUGERE n choux pastry flavoured with cheese

GOUGERES > GOUGERE

GOUGERS > GOUGER

GOUGES > GOUGE

GOUGING > GOUGE

GOUJEERS same as > GOODYEAR

GOUJON n small strip of fish or chicken, coated in breadcrumbs and deep-fried

GOUJONS > GOUJON

GOUK same as > GOWK

GOUKS > GOUK

GOULASH n rich stew seasoned with paprika

GOULASHES > GOULASH

GOURA n large, crested ground pigeon found in New Guinea

GOURAMI n large SE Asian labyrinth fish, Osphronemus goramy, used for food and (when young) as an aquarium fish

GOURAMIES > GOURAMI

GOURAMIS > GOURAMI

GOURAS > GOURA

GOURD n fleshy fruit of a climbing plant

GOURDE n standard monetary unit of Haiti, divided into 100 centimes

GOURDES > GOURDE

GOURDIER > GOURDY

GOURDIEST > GOURDY

GOURDLIKE > GOURD

GOURDS > GOURD

GOURDY adj (of horses) swollen-legged

GOURMAND n person who is very keen on food and drink

GOURMANDS > GOURMAND

GOURMET n connoisseur of food and drink

GOURMETS > GOURMET

GOUSTIER > GOUSTY

GOUSTIEST > GOUSTY

GOUSTROUS adj stormy

GOUSTY adj dismal

GOUT n disease causing inflammation of the joints

GOUTFLIES > GOUTFLY

GOUTFLY n fly whose larvae infect crops

GOUTIER > GOUT

GOUTIEST > GOUT

GOUTILY > GOUT

GOUTINESS > GOUT

GOUTS > GOUT

GOUTTE n in heraldry, charge shaped like a drop of liquid

GOUTTES > GOUTTE

GOUTWEED n widely naturalized Eurasian umbelliferous plant, Aegopodium podagraria, with white flowers and creeping underground stems

GOUTWEEDS > GOUTWEED

GOUTWORT n bishop's weed

GOUTWORTS > GOUTWORT

GOUTY > GOUT

GOV n boss

GOVERN vb rule, direct, or control > GOVERNABLENESS

GOVERNALL n government

GOVERNED > GOVERN

GOVERNESS n woman teacher in a private household ▷ vb act as a governess

GOVERNING > GOVERN

GOVERNOR n official governing a province or state

GOVERNORS > GOVERNOR

GOVERNS > GOVERN

GOVS > GOV

GOWAN n any of various yellow or white flowers growing in fields, esp the common daisy

GOWANED > GOWAN

GOWANS > GOWAN

GOWANY > GOWAN

GOWD Scots word for > GOWD

GOWDER > GOWD

GOWDEST > GOWD

GOWDS > GOWD

GOWDSPINK n goldfinch

GOWF vb strike

GOWFED > GOWF

GOWFER > GOWF

GOWFERS > GOWF

GOWFING > GOWF

GOWFS > GOWF

GOWK n stupid person

GOWKS > GOWK

GOWL n substance often found in the corner of the eyes after sleep ▷ vb howl

GOWLAN same as > GOLLAN

GOWLAND same as > GOLLAN

GOWLANDS > GOWLAND

GOWLANS > GOWLAN

GOWLED > GOWL

GOWLING > GOWL

GOWLS > GOWL

GOWN n woman's long formal dress ▷ vb supply with or dress in a gown

GOWNBOY n foundationer schoolboy who wears a gown

GOWNBOYS > GOWNBOY

GOWNED > GOWN

GOWNING > GOWN

GOWNMAN n professional person, such as a lawyer, who wears a gown

GOWNMEN > GOWNMAN
GOWNS > GOWN
GOWNSMAN same
as > GOWNMAN
GOWNSMEN > GOWNSMAN
GOWPEN n pair of cupped
hands
GOWPENFUL n amount
that can be contained in
cupped hands
GOWPENS > GOWPEN
GOX n gaseous oxygen
GOXES > GOX
GOY n Jewish word for a
non-Jew
GOYIM > GOY
GOYISCH > GOY
GOYISH > GOY
GOYS > GOY
GOZZAN same as > GOSSAN
GOZZANS > GOZZAN
GRAAL n holy grail
GRAALS > GRAAL
GRAB vb grasp suddenly,
snatch ▷ n sudden snatch
GRABBABLE > GRAB
GRABBED > GRAB
GRABBER > GRAB
GRABBERS > GRAB
GRABBIER > GRABBY
GRABBIEST > GRABBY
GRABBING > GRAB
GRABBLE vb scratch or feel
about with the hands
GRABBLED > GRABBLE
GRABBLER > GRABBLE
GRABBLERS > GRABBLE
GRABBLES > GRABBLE
GRABBLING > GRABBLE
GRABBY adj greedy or
selfish
GRABEN n elongated
trough of land produced by
subsidence of the earth's
crust between two faults
GRABENS > GRABEN
GRABS > GRAB
GRACE n beauty and
elegance ▷ vb honour
GRACED > GRACE
GRACEFUL adj having
beauty of movement,
style, or form
GRACELESS adj lacking
elegance
GRACES > GRACE
GRACILE adj gracefully thin
or slender
GRACILES > GRACILIS
GRACILIS n thin muscle on
the inner thigh
GRACILITY > GRACILE
GRACING > GRACE
GRACIOSO n clown in
Spanish comedy
GRACIOSOS > GRACIOSO
GRACIOUS adj kind
and courteous ▷ interj
expression of mild
surprise or wonder ▷ interj
expression of surprise
GRACKLE n any American
songbird of the genera
Quiscalus and Cassidix,

having a dark iridescent
plumage: family Icteridae
(American orioles)
GRACKLES > GRACKLE
GRAD n graduate
GRADABLE adj capable of
being graded ▷ n word of
this kind
GRADABLES > GRADABLE
GRADATE vb change
or cause to change
imperceptibly, as from one
colour, tone, or degree to
another
GRADATED > GRADATE
GRADATES > GRADATE
GRADATIM adv step by step
GRADATING > GRADATE
GRADATION n (stage in) a
series of degrees or steps
GRADATORY adj moving
step by step
GRADDAN vb dress corn
GRADDANED > GRADDAN
GRADDANS > GRADDAN
GRADE n place on a scale of
quality, rank, or size ▷ vb
arrange in grades
GRADED > GRADE
GRADELESS > GRADE
GRADELIER > GRADELY
GRADELY adj fine
GRADER n person or thing
that grades
GRADERS > GRADER
GRADES > GRADE
GRADIENT n (degree
of) slope ▷ adj sloping
uniformly
GRADIENTS > GRADIENT
GRADIN n ledge above or
behind an altar on which
candles, a cross, or other
ornaments stand
GRADINE same as > GRADIN
GRADINES > GRADINE
GRADING > GRADE
GRADINI > GRADINO
GRADINO n step above an
altar
GRADINS > GRADIN
GRADS > GRAD
GRADUAL adj occurring,
developing, or moving in
small stages ▷ n antiphon
or group of several
antiphons, usually from
the Psalms, sung or recited
immediately after the
epistle at Mass
GRADUALLY > GRADUAL
GRADUALS > GRADUAL
GRADUAND n person who is
about to graduate
GRADUANDS > GRADUAND
GRADUATE vb receive a
degree or diploma ▷ n
holder of a degree
GRADUATED > GRADUATE
GRADUATES > GRADUATE
GRADUATOR > GRADUATE
GRADUS n book of études
or other musical exercises
arranged in order of

increasing difficulty
GRADUSES > GRADUS
GRAECISE same
as > GRAECIZE
GRAECISED > GRAECISE
GRAECISES > GRAECISE
GRAECIZE vb make or
become like the ancient
Greeks
GRAECIZED > GRAECIZE
GRAECIZES > GRAECIZE
GRAFF same as > GRAF
GRAFFED > GRAFF
GRAFFING > GRAFF
GRAFFITI pl n words or
drawings scribbled or
sprayed on walls etc
GRAFFITIS > GRAFFITI
GRAFFITO n instance of
graffiti
GRAFFS > GRAFF
GRAFT n surgical transplant
of skin or tissue ▷ vb
transplant (living tissue)
surgically
GRAFTAGE n in
horticulture, the art of
grafting
GRAFTAGES > GRAFTAGE
GRAFTED > GRAFT
GRAFTER > GRAFT
GRAFTERS > GRAFT
GRAFTING > GRAFT
GRAFTINGS > GRAFT
GRAFTS > GRAFT
GRAHAM n made of graham
flour
GRAHAMS > GRAHAM
GRAIL n any desired
ambition or goal
GRAILE same as > GRAIL
GRAILES > GRAILE
GRAILS > GRAIL
GRAIN n seedlike fruit of a
cereal plant ▷ vb paint in
imitation of the grain of
wood or leather
GRAINAGE n duty paid on
grain
GRAINAGES > GRAINAGE
GRAINE n eggs of the
silkworm
GRAINED > GRAIN
GRAINER > GRAIN
GRAINERS > GRAIN
GRAINES > GRAINE
GRAINIER > GRAINY
GRAINIEST > GRAINY
GRAINING n pattern or
texture of the grain of
wood, leather, etc
GRAININGS > GRAINING
GRAINLESS > GRAIN
GRAINS > GRAIN
GRAINY adj resembling, full
of, or composed of grain
GRAIP n long-handled
gardening fork
GRAIPS > GRAIP
GRAITH vb clothe
GRAITHED > GRAITH
GRAITHING > GRAITH
GRAITHLY > GRAITH
GRAITHS > GRAITH

GRAKLE same as > GRACKLE
GRAKLES > GRAKLE
GRALLOCH n entrails of a
deer ▷ vb disembowel (a
deer killed in a hunt)
GRALLOCHS > GRALLOCH
GRAM n metric unit of mass
equal to one thousandth
of a kilogram
GRAMA n any of various
grasses of the genus
Bouteloua, of W North
America and South
America: often used as
pasture grasses
GRAMARIES > GRAMARY
GRAMARY same
as > GRAMARYE
GRAMARYE n magic,
necromancy, or occult
learning
GRAMARYES > GRAMARYE
GRAMAS > GRAMA
GRAMASH n type of gaiter
GRAMASHES > GRAMASH
GRAME n sorrow
GRAMERCY interj many
thanks
GRAMES > GRAME
GRAMMA n pasture grass of
the South American plains
GRAMMAGE n weight of
paper expressed as grams
per square metre
GRAMMAGES > GRAMMAGE
GRAMMAR n branch of
linguistics dealing with
the form, function, and
order of words
GRAMMARS > GRAMMAR
GRAMMAS > GRAMMA
GRAMMATIC adj of or
relating to grammar
GRAMME same as > GRAME
GRAMMES > GRAM
GRAMOCHE same
as > GRAMASH
GRAMOCHES > GRAMOCHE
GRAMP n grandfather
GRAMPA variant
of > GRANDPA
GRAMPAS > GRAMPA
GRAMPS > GRAMP
GRAMPUS n dolphin-like
mammal
GRAMPUSES > GRAMPUS
GRAMS > GRAM
GRAN n grandmother
GRANA > GRANUM
GRANARIES > GRANARY
GRANARY n storehouse for
grain
GRAND adj large or
impressive, imposing
▷ n thousand pounds or
dollars
GRANDAD n grandfather
GRANDADDY same
as > GRANDAD
GRANDADS > GRANDAD
GRANDAM archaic word
for > GRANDMOTHER
GRANDAME same
as > GRANDAM

**GRANDAMES** >GRANDAME
**GRANDAMS** >GRANDAM
**GRANDAUNT** n great-aunt
**GRANDBABY** n very young grandchild
**GRANDDAD** same as >GRANDDAD
**GRANDDADS** >GRANDAD
**GRANDDAM** same as >GRANDAM
**GRANDDAMS** >GRANDDAM
**GRANDE** feminine form of >GRAND
**GRANDEE** n Spanish nobleman of the highest rank
**GRANDEES** >GRANDEE
**GRANDER** >GRAND
**GRANDEST** >GRAND
**GRANDEUR** n magnificence
**GRANDEURS** >GRANDEUR
**GRANDIOSE** adj imposing
**GRANDIOSO** adv (to be played) in a grand manner
**GRANDKID** n grandchild
**GRANDKIDS** >GRANDKID
**GRANDLY** >GRAND
**GRANDMA** n grandmother
**GRANDMAMA** same as >GRANDMA
**GRANDMAS** >GRANDMA
**GRANDNESS** >GRAND
**GRANDPA** n grandfather
**GRANDPAPA** same as >GRANDPA
**GRANDPAS** >GRANDPA
**GRANDS** >GRAND
**GRANDSIR** same as >GRANDSIRE
**GRANDSIRE** n grandfather
**GRANDSIRS** >GRANDSIR
**GRANDSON** n male grandchild
**GRANDSONS** >GRANDSON
**GRANFER** n grandfather
**GRANFERS** >GRANFER
**GRANGE** n country house with farm buildings
**GRANGER** n keeper or member of a grange
**GRANGERS** >GRANGER
**GRANGES** >GRANGE
**GRANITA** n Italian iced drink
**GRANITAS** >GRANITA
**GRANITE** n very hard igneous rock often used in building
**GRANITES** >GRANITE
**GRANITIC** >GRANITE
**GRANITISE** vb form granite
**GRANITITE** n any granite with a high content of biotite
**GRANITIZE** same as >GRANITISE
**GRANITOID** >GRANITE
**GRANIVORE** n animal that feeds on seeds and grain
**GRANNAM** n old woman
**GRANNAMS** >GRANNAM
**GRANNIE** vb defeat (in a game or contest) so that one's opponent does not

score a single point
**GRANNIED** >GRANNIE
**GRANNIES** pl n Granny Smith apples
**GRANNOM** n widespread caddis fly, Brachycentrus subnubilus, the larvae of which attach their cases to vegetation under running water and are esteemed as a bait by anglers
**GRANNOMS** >GRANNOM
**GRANNY** n grandmother ▷ vb defeat (in a game or contest) so that one's opponent does not score a single point
**GRANNYING** >GRANNY
**GRANNYISH** adj typical of or suitable for an elderly woman
**GRANOLA** n muesli-like breakfast cereal
**GRANOLAS** >GRANOLA
**GRANOLITH** n paving material consisting of a mixture of cement and crushed granite or granite chippings
**GRANS** >GRAN
**GRANT** vb consent to fulfil (a request) ▷ n sum of money provided by a government for a specific purpose, such as education
**GRANTABLE** >GRANT
**GRANTED** >GRANT
**GRANTEE** n person to whom a grant is made
**GRANTEES** >GRANTEE
**GRANTER** >GRANT
**GRANTERS** >GRANT
**GRANTING** >GRANT
**GRANTOR** n person who makes a grant
**GRANTORS** >GRANTOR
**GRANTS** >GRANT
**GRANTSMAN** n student who specializes in obtaining grants
**GRANTSMEN** >GRANTSMAN
**GRANULAR** adj of or like grains
**GRANULARY** adj granular
**GRANULATE** vb make into grains
**GRANULE** n small grain
**GRANULES** >GRANULE
**GRANULITE** n granular foliated metamorphic rock in which the minerals form a mosaic of equal-sized granules
**GRANULOMA** n tumour composed of granulation tissue produced in response to chronic infection, inflammation, a foreign body, or to unknown causes
**GRANULOSE** less common word for > GRANULAR
**GRANULOUS** adj consisting

of grains or granules
**GRANUM** n membrane layers in a chloroplast
**GRAPE** n small juicy green or purple berry, eaten raw or used to produce wine, raisins, currants, or sultanas ▷ vb grope
**GRAPED** >GRAPE
**GRAPELESS** >GRAPE
**GRAPELIKE** >GRAPE
**GRAPERIES** >GRAPERY
**GRAPERY** n building where grapes are grown
**GRAPES** n abnormal growth, resembling a bunch of grapes, on the fetlock of a horse
**GRAPESEED** n seed of the grape
**GRAPESHOT** n bullets which scatter when fired
**GRAPETREE** n sea grape, a shrubby plant resembling a grapevine
**GRAPEVINE** n grape-bearing vine
**GRAPEY** >GRAPE
**GRAPH** n drawing showing the relation of different numbers or quantities plotted against a set of axes ▷ vb draw or represent in a graph
**GRAPHED** >GRAPH
**GRAPHEME** n one of a set of orthographic symbols (letters or combinations of letters) in a given language that serve to distinguish one word from another and usually correspond to or represent phonemes, e.g. the f in fun, the ph in phantom, and the gh in laugh
**GRAPHEMES** >GRAPHEME
**GRAPHEMIC** >GRAPHEME
**GRAPHIC** adj vividly descriptive
**GRAPHICAL** same as >GRAPHIC
**GRAPHICLY** >GRAPHIC
**GRAPHICS** pl n diagrams, graphs, etc, esp as used on a television programme or computer screen
**GRAPHING** >GRAPH
**GRAPHITE** n soft black form of carbon, used in pencil leads
**GRAPHITES** >GRAPHITE
**GRAPHITIC** >GRAPHITE
**GRAPHIUM** n stylus (for writing)
**GRAPHIUMS** >GRAPHIUM
**GRAPHS** >GRAPH
**GRAPIER** >GRAPE
**GRAPIEST** >GRAPE
**GRAPINESS** >GRAPE
**GRAPING** >GRAPE
**GRAPLE** same as >GRAPPLE
**GRAPLES** >GRAPLE
**GRAPLIN** same as >GRAPNEL

**GRAPLINE** same as >GRAPNEL
**GRAPLINES** >GRAPLINE
**GRAPLINS** >GRAPLIN
**GRAPNEL** n device with several hooks, used to grasp or secure things
**GRAPNELS** >GRAPNEL
**GRAPPA** n spirit distilled from the fermented remains of grapes after pressing
**GRAPPAS** >GRAPPA
**GRAPPLE** vb try to cope with (something difficult) ▷ n grapnel
**GRAPPLED** >GRAPPLE
**GRAPPLER** >GRAPPLE
**GRAPPLERS** >GRAPPLE
**GRAPPLES** >GRAPPLE
**GRAPPLING** n act of gripping or seizing, as in wrestling
**GRAPY** >GRAPE
**GRASP** vb grip something firmly ▷ n grip or clasp
**GRASPABLE** >GRASP
**GRASPED** >GRASP
**GRASPER** >GRASP
**GRASPERS** >GRASP
**GRASPING** adj greedy or avaricious
**GRASPLESS** adj relaxed
**GRASPS** >GRASP
**GRASS** n common type of plant with jointed stems and long narrow leaves, including cereals and bamboo ▷ vb cover with grass
**GRASSED** >GRASS
**GRASSER** n police informant
**GRASSERS** >GRASSER
**GRASSES** >GRASS
**GRASSHOOK** another name for > SICKLE
**GRASSIER** >GRASSY
**GRASSIEST** >GRASSY
**GRASSILY** >GRASSY
**GRASSING** >GRASS
**GRASSINGS** >GRASS
**GRASSLAND** n land covered with grass
**GRASSLESS** >GRASS
**GRASSLIKE** >GRASS
**GRASSPLOT** n plot of ground overgrown with grass
**GRASSQUIT** n any tropical American finch of the genus Tiaris and related genera, such as T. olivacea (yellow-faced grassquit)
**GRASSROOT** adj relating to the ordinary people, especially as part of the electorate
**GRASSUM** n in Scots law, lump sum paid when taking up a lease
**GRASSUMS** >GRASSUM
**GRASSY** adj covered with, containing, or resembling

grass
GRASTE *archaic past participle of* >GRACE
GRAT >GREET
GRATE *vb* rub into small bits on a rough surface ⊳ *n* framework of metal bars for holding fuel in a fireplace
GRATED >GRATE
GRATEFUL *adj* feeling or showing gratitude
GRATELESS >GRATE
GRATER *n* tool with a sharp surface for grating food
GRATERS >GRATER
GRATES >GRATE
GRATICULE *n* grid of intersecting lines, esp of latitude and longitude on which a map is drawn
GRATIFIED >GRATIFY
GRATIFIER >GRATIFY
GRATIFIES >GRATIFY
GRATIFY *vb* satisfy or please ⊳ *adj* giving one satisfaction or pleasure
GRATIN *n* crust of browned breadcrumbs
GRATINATE *vb* cook until the juice is absorbed and the surface crisps
GRATINE *adj* cooked au gratin
GRATINEE *vb* cook au gratin
GRATINEED >GRATINEE
GRATINEES >GRATINEE
GRATING *adj* harsh or rasping ⊳ *n* framework of metal bars covering an opening
GRATINGLY >GRATING
GRATINGS >GRATING
GRATINS >GRATIN
GRATIS *adj* free, for nothing
GRATITUDE *n* feeling of being thankful for a favour or gift
GRATTOIR *n* scraper made of flint
GRATTOIRS >GRATTOIR
GRATUITY *n* money given for services rendered, tip
GRATULANT >GRATULATE
GRATULATE *vb* greet joyously
GRAUNCH *vb* crush or destroy
GRAUNCHED >GRAUNCH
GRAUNCHER >GRAUNCH
GRAUNCHES >GRAUNCH
GRAUPEL *n* soft hail or snow pellets
GRAUPELS >GRAUPEL
GRAV *n* unit of acceleration equal to the standard acceleration of free fall
GRAVADLAX *same as* >GRAVLAX
GRAVAMEN *n* that part of an accusation weighing most heavily against an accused

GRAVAMENS >GRAVAMEN
GRAVAMINA >GRAVAMEN
GRAVE *n* hole for burying a corpse ⊳ *adj* causing concern ⊳ *vb* cut, carve, sculpt, or engrave ⊳ *adv* to be performed in a solemn manner
GRAVED >GRAVE
GRAVEL *n* mixture of small stones and coarse sand ⊳ *vb* cover with gravel
GRAVELED >GRAVEL
GRAVELESS >GRAVE
GRAVELIKE >GRAVE
GRAVELING >GRAVEL
GRAVELISH >GRAVEL
GRAVELLED >GRAVEL
GRAVELLY *adj* covered with gravel
GRAVELS >GRAVEL
GRAVELY >GRAVE
GRAVEN >GRAVE
GRAVENESS >GRAVE
GRAVER *n* any of various engraving, chasing, or sculpting tools, such as a burin
GRAVERS >GRAVER
GRAVES >GRAVE
GRAVESIDE *n* area surrounding a grave
GRAVESITE *n* site of grave
GRAVEST >GRAVE
GRAVEWARD *adj* moving towards grave
GRAVEYARD *n* cemetery
GRAVID *adj* pregnant
GRAVIDA *n* pregnant woman
GRAVIDAE >GRAVIDA
GRAVIDAS >GRAVIDA
GRAVIDITY >GRAVID
GRAVIDLY >GRAVID
GRAVIES >GRAVY
GRAVING >GRAVE
GRAVINGS >GRAVE
>GRAVIPERCEPTION
GRAVIS *adj* as in *myasthenia gravis* chronic muscle-weakening disease
GRAVITAS *n* seriousness or solemnity
GRAVITATE *vb* be influenced or drawn towards
GRAVITIES >GRAVITY
GRAVITINO *n* hypothetical subatomic particle
GRAVITON *n* postulated quantum of gravitational energy
GRAVITONS >GRAVITON
GRAVITY *n* force of attraction of one object for another, esp of objects to the earth
GRAVLAKS *same as* >GRAVLAX
GRAVLAX *n* dry-cured salmon, marinated in salt, sugar, and spices, as served in Scandinavia
GRAVLAXES >GRAVLAX

GRAVS >GRAV
GRAVURE *n* method of intaglio printing using a plate with many small etched recesses
GRAVURES >GRAVURE
GRAVY *n* juices from meat in cooking
GRAY *same as* >GREY
GRAYBACK *same as* >GREYBACK
GRAYBACKS >GRAYBACK
GRAYBEARD *same as* >GREYBEARD
GRAYED >GRAY
GRAYER >GRAY
GRAYEST >GRAY
GRAYFISH *n* dogfish
GRAYFLIES >GRAYFLY
GRAYFLY *n* trumpet fly
GRAYHOUND *US spelling of* >GREYHOUND
GRAYING >GRAY
GRAYISH >GRAY
GRAYLAG *same as* >GREYLAG
GRAYLAGS >GRAYLAG
GRAYLE *n* holy grail
GRAYLES >GRAYLE
GRAYLING *n* fish of the salmon family
GRAYLINGS >GRAYLING
GRAYLY >GRAY
GRAYMAIL *n* tactic to avoid prosecution in espionage case by threatening to expose state secrets during trial
GRAYMAILS >GRAYMAIL
GRAYNESS >GREY
GRAYOUT *n* in aeronautics, impairment of vision due to lack of oxygen
GRAYOUTS >GRAYOUT
GRAYS >GRAY
GRAYSCALE *adj* in shades of grey
GRAYWACKE *same as* >GREYWACKE
GRAYWATER *n* water that has been used
GRAZABLE >GRAZE
GRAZE *vb* feed on grass ⊳ *n* slight scratch or scrape
GRAZEABLE >GRAZE
GRAZED >GRAZE
GRAZER >GRAZE
GRAZERS >GRAZE
GRAZES >GRAZE
GRAZIER *n* person who feeds cattle for market
GRAZIERS >GRAZIER
GRAZING *n* land on which grass for livestock is grown
GRAZINGLY >GRAZE
GRAZINGS >GRAZING
GRAZIOSO *adv* (of music) to be played gracefully
GREASE *n* soft melted animal fat ⊳ *vb* apply grease to
GREASED >GREASE
GREASER *n* mechanic, esp of motor vehicles
GREASERS >GREASER

GREASES >GREASE
GREASIER >GREASY
GREASIES >GREASY
GREASIEST >GREASY
GREASILY >GREASY
GREASING >GREASE
GREASY *adj* covered with or containing grease ⊳ *n* shearer
GREAT *adj* large in size or number ⊳ *n* distinguished person
GREATCOAT *n* heavy overcoat
GREATEN *vb* make or become great
GREATENED >GREATEN
GREATENS >GREATEN
GREATER >GREAT
GREATEST *n* most outstanding individual in a given field
GREATESTS >GREATEST
GREATLY >GREAT
GREATNESS >GREAT
GREATS >GREAT
GREAVE *n* piece of armour for the shin ⊳ *vb* grieve
GREAVED >GREAVE
GREAVES *pl n* residue left after the rendering of tallow
GREAVING >GREAVE
GREBE *n* diving water bird
GREBES >GREBE
GRECE *n* flight of steps
GRECES >GRECE
GRECIAN *same as* >GRECE
GRECIANS >GRECIAN
GRECISE *same as* >GRAECIZE
GRECISED >GRECISE
GRECISES >GRECISE
GRECISING >GRECISE
GRECIZE *same as* >GRAECIZE
GRECIZED >GRECIZE
GRECIZES >GRECIZE
GRECIZING >GRECIZE
GRECQUE *n* ornament of Greek origin
GRECQUES >GRECQUE
GREE *n* superiority or victory ⊳ *vb* come or cause to come to agreement or harmony
GREEBO *n* unkempt or dirty-looking young man
GREEBOES >GREEBO
GREECE *same as* >GRECE
GREECES >GREECE
GREED *n* excessive desire for food, wealth, etc
GREEDIER >GREEDY
GREEDIEST >GREEDY
GREEDILY >GREEDY
GREEDLESS >GREED
GREEDS >GREED
GREEDSOME *same as* >GREEDY
GREEDY *adj* having an excessive desire for something, such as food or money

GREEGREE *same as* >GRIGRI

GREEGREES >GREEGREE

GREEING >GREE

GREEK *vb* represent text as grey lines on a computer screen

GREEKED >GREEK

GREEKING >GREEK

GREEKINGS >GREEK

GREEN *adj* of a colour between blue and yellow ▷ *n* colour between blue and yellow ▷ *vb* make or become green

GREENBACK *n* inconvertible legal-tender US currency note originally issued during the Civil War in 1862

GREENBELT *n* zone of farmland, parks, and open country surrounding a town or city

GREENBONE *another name for* >BUTTERFISH

GREENBUG *n* common name for Schizaphis graminum

GREENBUGS >GREENBUG

GREENED >GREEN

GREENER *n* recent immigrant

GREENERS >GREENER

GREENERY *n* vegetation

GREENEST >GREEN

GREENFLY *n* green aphid, a common garden pest

GREENGAGE *n* sweet green plum

GREENHAND *n* greenhorn

GREENHEAD *n* male mallard

GREENHORN *n* novice

GREENIE *n* conservationist

GREENIER >GREEN

GREENIES >GREENIE

GREENIEST >GREEN

GREENING *n* process of making or becoming more aware of environmental considerations

GREENINGS >GREENING

GREENISH >GREEN

GREENLET *n* vireo, esp one of the genus Hylophilus

GREENLETS >GREENLET

GREENLING *n* any scorpaenoid food fish of the family Hexagrammidae of the North Pacific Ocean

GREENLIT *adj* given permission to proceed

GREENLY >GREEN

GREENMAIL *n* practice of a company buying sufficient shares in another company to threaten takeover and making a quick profit as a result of the threatened company buying back its shares at a higher price ▷ *vb* carry out the practice of greenmail

GREENNESS >GREEN

GREENROOM *n* backstage room in a theatre where

performers rest or receive visitors

GREENS >GREEN

GREENSAND *n* olive-green sandstone consisting mainly of quartz and glauconite

GREENSICK *adj* suffering from greensickness: same as chlorosis

GREENSOME *n* match for two pairs in which each of the four players tees off and after selecting the better drive the partners of each pair play that ball alternately

GREENTH *n* greenness

GREENTHS >GREENTH

GREENWASH *n* superficial or insincere display of concern for the environment that is shown by an organization ▷ *vb* adopt a 'greenwash' policy

GREENWAY *n* linear open space, with pedestrian and cycle paths

GREENWAYS >GREENWAY

GREENWEED *n* woodwaxen

GREENWING *n* teal

GREENWOOD *n* forest or wood when the leaves are green

GREENY >GREEN

GREES >GREE

GREESE *same as* >GRECE

GREESES >GREESE

GREESING >GREESE

GREESINGS >GREESE

GREET *vb* meet with expressions of welcome ▷ *n* weeping

GREETE *same as* >GREET

GREETED >GREET

GREETER *n* person who greets people at the entrance of a shop, restaurant, casino, etc

GREETERS >GREETER

GREETES >GREETE

GREETING *n* act or words of welcoming on meeting

GREETINGS >GREETING

GREETS >GREET

GREFFIER *n* registrar

GREFFIERS >GREFFIER

GREGALE *n* northeasterly wind occurring in the Mediterranean

GREGALES >GREGALE

GREGARIAN *adj* gregarious

GREGARINE *n* any parasitic protozoan of the order Gregarinida, typically occurring in the digestive tract and body cavity of other invertebrates: phylum Apicomplexa (sporozoans) ▷ *adj* of, relating to, or belonging to the Gregarinida

GREGATIM *adv* in flocks or

crowds

GREGE *vb* make heavy

GREGO *n* short, thick jacket

GREGOS >GREGO

GREIGE *adj* (of a fabric or material) not yet dyed ▷ *n* unbleached or undyed cloth or yarn

GREIGES >GREIGE

GREIN *vb* desire fervently

GREINED >GREIN

GREINING >GREIN

GREINS >GREIN

GREISEN *n* light-coloured metamorphic rock consisting mainly of quartz, white mica, and topaz formed by the pneumatolysis of granite

GREISENS >GREISEN

GREISLY *same as* >GRISLY

GREMIAL *n* cloth spread upon the lap of a bishop when seated during Mass

GREMIALS >GREMIAL

GREMLIN *n* imaginary being blamed for mechanical malfunctions

GREMLINS >GREMLIN

GREMMIE *n* young surfer

GREMMIES >GREMMIE

GREMMY *same as* >GREMMIE

GREMOLATA *n* garnish of finely chopped parsley, garlic and lemon

GREN *same as* >GRIN

GRENADE *n* small bomb thrown by hand or fired from a rifle

GRENADES >GRENADE

GRENADIER *n* soldier of a regiment formerly trained to throw grenades

GRENADINE *n* syrup made from pomegranates

GRENNED >GREN

GRENNING >GREN

GRENS >GREN

GRENZ *as in* grenz rays X-rays of long wavelength produced in a device when electrons are accelerated through 25 kilovolts or less

GRESE *same as* >GRECE

GRESES >GRESE

GRESSING *same as* >GRECE

GRESSINGS >GRESSING

GREVE *same as* >GREAVE

GREVES >GREVE

GREVILLEA *n* any of various Australian evergreen trees and shrubs

GREW *vb* shudder

GREWED >GROW

GREWHOUND *n* greyhound

GREWING >GROW

GREWS >GROW

GREWSOME *archaic or US spelling of* >GRUESOME

GREWSOMER >GREWSOME

GREX *n* group of plants that has arisen from the same hybrid parent group

GREXES >GREX

GREY *adj* of a colour between black and white ▷ *n* grey colour ▷ *vb* become or make grey

GREYBACK *n* any of various animals having a grey back, such as the grey whale and the hooded crow

GREYBACKS >GREYBACK

GREYBEARD *n* old man, esp a sage

GREYED >GREY

GREYER >GREY

GREYEST >GREY

GREYHEN *n* female of the black grouse

GREYHENS >GREYHEN

GREYHOUND *n* swift slender dog used in racing

GREYING >GREY

GREYINGS >GREY

GREYISH >GREY

GREYLAG *n* large grey goose

GREYLAGS >GREYLAG

GREYLIST *vb* hold (someone) in suspicion, without actually excluding him or her from a particular activity

GREYLISTS >GREYLIST

GREYLY >GREY

GREYNESS >GREY

GREYS >GREY

GREYSTONE *n* type of grey rock

GREYWACKE *n* any dark sandstone or grit having a matrix of clay minerals

GRIBBLE *n* any small marine isopod crustacean of the genus Limnoria, which bores into and damages wharves and other submerged wooden structures

GRIBBLES >GRIBBLE

GRICE *vb* (of a railway enthusiast) to collect objects or visit places connected with trains and railways ▷ *n* object collected or place visited by a railway enthusiast

GRICER >GRICE

GRICERS >GRICE

GRICES >GRICE

GRICING >GRICE

GRICINGS >GRICE

GRID *n* network of horizontal and vertical lines, bars, etc

GRIDDED >GRID

GRIDDER *n* American football player

GRIDDERS >GRIDDER

GRIDDLE *n* flat iron plate for cooking ▷ *vb* cook (food) on a griddle

GRIDDLED >GRIDDLE

GRIDDLES >GRIDDLE

GRIDDLING >GRIDDLE

GRIDE *vb* grate or scrape harshly ▷ *n* harsh or

piercing sound
**GRIDED** >GRIDE
**GRIDELIN** n greyish violet colour
**GRIDELINS** >GRIDELIN
**GRIDES** >GRIDE
**GRIDING** >GRIDE
**GRIDIRON** n frame of metal bars for grilling food ▷ vb cover with parallel lines
**GRIDIRONS** >GRIDIRON
**GRIDLOCK** n situation where traffic is not moving ▷ vb (of traffic) to obstruct (an area)
**GRIDLOCKS** >GRIDLOCK
**GRIDS** >GRID
**GRIECE** same as >GRECE
**GRIECED** >GRIECE
**GRIECES** >GRIECE
**GRIEF** n deep sadness
**GRIEFER** n online game player who intentionally spoils the game for other players
**GRIEFERS** >GRIEFER
**GRIEFFUL** adj stricken with grief
**GRIEFLESS** >GRIEF
**GRIEFS** >GRIEF
**GRIESIE** same as >GRISY
**GRIESLY** same as >GRISLY
**GRIESY** same as >GRISY
**GRIEVANCE** n real or imaginary cause for complaint
**GRIEVANT** n any person with a grievance
**GRIEVANTS** >GRIEVANT
**GRIEVE** vb (cause to) feel grief ▷ n farm manager or overseer
**GRIEVED** >GRIEVE
**GRIEVER** >GRIEVE
**GRIEVERS** >GRIEVE
**GRIEVES** >GRIEVE
**GRIEVING** >GRIEVE
**GRIEVINGS** >GRIEVE
**GRIEVOUS** adj very severe or painful
**GRIFF** n information
**GRIFFE** n carved ornament at the base of a column, often in the form of a claw
**GRIFFES** >GRIFFE
**GRIFFIN** n mythical monster with an eagle's head and wings and a lion's body
**GRIFFINS** >GRIFFIN
**GRIFFON** same as >GRIFFIN
**GRIFFONS** >GRIFFON
**GRIFFS** >GRIFF
**GRIFT** vb swindle
**GRIFTED** >GRIFT
**GRIFTER** >GRIFT
**GRIFTERS** >GRIFT
**GRIFTING** >GRIFT
**GRIFTS** >GRIFT
**GRIG** n lively person ▷ vb fish for grigs
**GRIGGED** >GRIG
**GRIGGING** >GRIG
**GRIGRI** n African talisman,

amulet, or charm
**GRIGRIS** >GRIGRI
**GRIGS** >GRIG
**GRIKE** n solution fissure, a vertical crack about 0.5 m wide formed by the dissolving of limestone by water, that divides an exposed limestone surface into sections or clints
**GRIKES** >GRIKE
**GRILL** n device on a cooker that radiates heat downwards ▷ vb cook under a grill
**GRILLADE** n grilled food
**GRILLADES** >GRILLADE
**GRILLAGE** n arrangement of beams and crossbeams used as a foundation on soft ground
**GRILLAGES** >GRILLAGE
**GRILLE** n grating over an opening
**GRILLED** adj cooked on a grill or gridiron
**GRILLER** >GRILL
**GRILLERS** >GRILL
**GRILLERY** n place where food is grilled
**GRILLES** >GRILLE
**GRILLING** >GRILL
**GRILLINGS** >GRILL
**GRILLION** n extremely large but unspecified number, quantity, or amount ▷ determiner amounting to a grillion
**GRILLIONS** >GRILLION
**GRILLROOM** n restaurant serving grilled foods
**GRILLS** >GRILL
**GRILLWORK** same as >GRILL
**GRILSE** n salmon on its first return from the sea to fresh water
**GRILSES** >GRILSE
**GRIM** adj stern
**GRIMACE** n ugly or distorted facial expression of pain, disgust, etc ▷ vb make a grimace
**GRIMACED** >GRIMACE
**GRIMACER** >GRIMACE
**GRIMACERS** >GRIMACE
**GRIMACES** >GRIMACE
**GRIMACING** >GRIMACE
**GRIMALKIN** n old cat, esp an old female cat
**GRIME** n ingrained dirt ▷ vb make very dirty
**GRIMED** >GRIME
**GRIMES** >GRIME
**GRIMIER** >GRIME
**GRIMIEST** >GRIME
**GRIMILY** >GRIME
**GRIMINESS** >GRIME
**GRIMING** >GRIME
**GRIMLY** >GRIM
**GRIMMER** >GRIM
**GRIMMEST** >GRIM
**GRIMNESS** >GRIM
**GRIMOIRE** n textbook of sorcery and magic

**GRIMOIRES** >GRIMOIRE
**GRIMY** >GRIME
**GRIN** vb smile broadly, showing the teeth ▷ n broad smile
**GRINCH** n person whose lack of enthusiasm or bad temper has a depressing effect on others
**GRINCHES** >GRINCH
**GRIND** vb crush or rub to a powder ▷ n hard work
**GRINDED** obsolete past participle of >GRIND
**GRINDELIA** n any coarse plant of the American genus Grindelia, having yellow daisy-like flower heads: family Asteraceae (composites)
**GRINDER** n device for grinding substances
**GRINDERS** >GRINDER
**GRINDERY** n place in which tools and cutlery are sharpened
**GRINDING** >GRIND
**GRINDINGS** >GRIND
**GRINDS** >GRIND
**GRINGA** n female gringo
**GRINGAS** >GRINGA
**GRINGO** n person from an English-speaking country: used as a derogatory term by Latin Americans
**GRINGOS** >GRINGO
**GRINNED** >GRIN
**GRINNER** >GRIN
**GRINNERS** >GRIN
**GRINNING** >GRIN
**GRINS** >GRIN
**GRIOT** n (in Western Africa) member of a caste responsible for maintaining an oral record of tribal history in the form of music, poetry, and storytelling
**GRIOTS** >GRIOT
**GRIP** n firm hold or grasp ▷ vb grasp or hold tightly
**GRIPE** vb complain persistently ▷ n complaint
**GRIPED** >GRIPE
**GRIPER** >GRIPE
**GRIPERS** >GRIPE
**GRIPES** >GRIPE
**GRIPEY** adj causing gripes
**GRIPIER** >GRIPEY
**GRIPIEST** >GRIPEY
**GRIPING** >GRIPE
**GRIPINGLY** >GRIPE
**GRIPLE** same as >GRIPPLE
**GRIPMAN** n cable-car operator
**GRIPMEN** >GRIPMAN
**GRIPPE** former name for >INFLUENZA
**GRIPPED** >GRIP
**GRIPPER** >GRIP
**GRIPPERS** >GRIP
**GRIPPES** >GRIPPE
**GRIPPIER** >GRIPPY

**GRIPPIEST** >GRIPPY
**GRIPPING** >GRIP
**GRIPPLE** adj greedy ▷ n hook
**GRIPPLES** >GRIPPLE
**GRIPPY** adj having grip
**GRIPS** >GRIP
**GRIPSACK** n travel bag
**GRIPSACKS** >GRIPSACK
**GRIPT** archaic variant of >GRIPPED
**GRIPTAPE** n rough tape for sticking to a surface to provide a greater grip
**GRIPTAPES** >GRIPTAPE
**GRIPY** same as >GRIPEY
**GRIS** same as >GRECE
**GRISAILLE** n technique of monochrome painting in shades of grey, as in an oil painting or a wall decoration, imitating the effect of relief
**GRISE** vb shudder
**GRISED** >GRISE
**GRISELY** same as >GRISLY
**GRISEOUS** adj streaked or mixed with grey
**GRISES** >GRISE
**GRISETTE** n (esp formerly) a French working-class girl, esp a pretty or flirtatious one
**GRISETTES** >GRISETTE
**GRISGRIS** same as >GRIGRI
**GRISING** >GRISE
**GRISKIN** n lean part of a loin of pork
**GRISKINS** >GRISKIN
**GRISLED** another word for >GRIZZLED
**GRISLIER** >GRISLY
**GRISLIES** >GRISLY
**GRISLIEST** >GRISLY
**GRISLY** adj horrifying or ghastly ▷ n large American bear
**GRISON** n either of two musteline mammals, Grison (or Galictis) cuja or G. vittata, of Central and South America, having a greyish back and black face and underparts
**GRISONS** >GRISON
**GRISSINI** pl n thin crisp breadsticks
**GRIST** n grain for grinding
**GRISTER** n device for grinding grain
**GRISTERS** >GRISTER
**GRISTLE** n tough stringy animal tissue found in meat
**GRISTLES** >GRISTLE
**GRISTLIER** >GRISTLE
**GRISTLY** >GRISTLE
**GRISTMILL** n mill, esp one equipped with large grinding stones for grinding grain
**GRISTS** >GRIST
**GRISY** adj grim
**GRIT** n rough particles

of sand ▷ *vb* spread grit on (an icy road etc) ▷ *adj* great

GRITH *n* security, peace, or protection, guaranteed either in a certain place, such as a church, or for a period of time

GRITHS >GRITH

GRITLESS >GRIT

GRITS >GRIT

GRITSTONE *same as* >GRIT

GRITTED >GRIT

GRITTER *n* vehicle that spreads grit on the roads in icy weather

GRITTERS >GRITTER

GRITTEST >GRIT

GRITTIER >GRITTY

GRITTIEST >GRITTY

GRITTILY >GRITTY

GRITTING >GRIT

GRITTY *adj* courageous and tough

GRIVATION *n* (in navigation) grid variation

GRIVET *n* E African variety of a common guenon monkey, *Cercopithecus aethiops*, having long white tufts of hair on either side of the face

GRIVETS >GRIVET

GRIZE *same as* >GRECE

GRIZES >GRIZE

GRIZZLE *vb* whine or complain ▷ *n* grey colour

GRIZZLED *adj* grey-haired

GRIZZLER >GRIZZLE

GRIZZLERS >GRIZZLE

GRIZZLES >GRIZZLE

GRIZZLIER >GRIZZLY

GRIZZLIES >GRIZZLY

GRIZZLING >GRIZZLE

GRIZZLY *n* large American bear ▷ *adj* somewhat grey

GROAN *n* deep sound of grief or pain ▷ *vb* utter a groan

GROANED >GROAN

GROANER *n* person or thing that groans

GROANERS >GROANER

GROANFUL *adj* sad

GROANING >GROAN

GROANINGS >GROAN

GROANS >GROAN

GROAT *n* fourpenny piece

GROATS *pl n* hulled and crushed grain of various cereals

GROCER *n* shopkeeper selling foodstuffs

GROCERIES *pl n* food and other household supplies

GROCERS >GROCER

GROCERY *n* business or premises of a grocer

GROCKLE *n* tourist, esp one from the Midlands or the North of England

GROCKLES >GROCKLE

GRODIER >GRODY

GRODIEST >GRODY

GRODY *adj* unpleasant

GROG *n* spirit, usu rum, and water ▷ *vb* drink grog

GROGGED >GROG

GROGGERY *n* grogshop

GROGGIER >GROGGY

GROGGIEST >GROGGY

GROGGILY >GROGGY

GROGGING >GROG

GROGGY *adj* faint, shaky, or dizzy

GROGRAM *n* coarse fabric of silk, wool, or silk mixed with wool or mohair, often stiffened with gum, formerly used for clothing

GROGRAMS >GROGRAM

GROGS >GROG

GROGSHOP *n* drinking place, esp one of disreputable character

GROGSHOPS >GROGSHOP

GROIN *n* place where the legs join the abdomen ▷ *vb* provide or construct with groins

GROINED >GROIN

GROINING >GROIN

GROININGS >GROIN

GROINS >GROIN

GROK *vb* understand completely and intuitively

GROKKED >GROK

GROKKING >GROK

GROKS >GROK

GROMA *n* Roman surveying instrument

GROMAS >GROMA

GROMET *same as* >GROMMET

GROMETS >GROMET

GROMMET *n* ring or eyelet

GROMMETED *adj* having grommets

GROMMETS >GROMMET

GROMWELL *n* any of various hairy plants of the boraginaceous genus *Lithospermum*, esp *L. officinale*, having small greenish-white, yellow, or blue flowers, and smooth nutlike fruits

GROMWELLS >GROMWELL

GRONE *obsolete word for* >GROAN

GRONED >GRONE

GRONEFULL *same as* >GROANFUL

GRONES >GRONE

GRONING >GRONE

GROOF *n* face, or front of the body

GROOFS >GROOF

GROOLIER >GROOLY

GROOLIEST >GROOLY

GROOLY *adj* gruesome

GROOM *n* person who looks after horses ▷ *vb* make or keep one's clothes and appearance neat and tidy

GROOMED >GROOM

GROOMER >GROOM

GROOMERS >GROOM

GROOMING >GROOM

GROOMINGS >GROOM

GROOMS >GROOM

GROOMSMAN *n* man who attends the bridegroom at a wedding, usually the best man

GROOMSMEN >GROOMSMAN

GROOVE *n* long narrow channel in a surface

GROOVED >GROOVE

GROOVER *n* device that makes grooves

GROOVERS >GROOVER

GROOVES >GROOVE

GROOVIER >GROOVY

GROOVIEST >GROOVY

GROOVING >GROOVE

GROOVY *adj* attractive or exciting

GROPE *vb* feel about or search uncertainly ▷ *n* instance of groping

GROPED >GROPE

GROPER *n* any large marine serranid fish of the genus *Epinephelus* and related genera, of warm and tropical seas

GROPERS >GROPER

GROPES >GROPE

GROPING >GROPE

GROPINGLY >GROPE

GROSBEAK *n* finch with a large powerful bill

GROSBEAKS >GROSBEAK

GROSCHEN *n* former Austrian monetary unit worth one hundredth of a schilling

GROSCHENS >GROSCHEN

GROSER *n* gooseberry

GROSERS >GROSER

GROSERT *another word for* >GROSER

GROSERTS >GROSERT

GROSET *another word for* >GROSER

GROSETS >GROSET

GROSGRAIN *n* heavy ribbed silk or rayon fabric

GROSS *adj* flagrant ▷ *n* twelve dozen ▷ *vb* make as total revenue before deductions ▷ *interj* exclamation indicating disgust

GROSSART *another word for* >GROSER

GROSSARTS >GROSSART

GROSSED >GROSS

GROSSER >GROSS

GROSSERS >GROSS

GROSSES >GROSS

GROSSEST >GROSS

GROSSING >GROSS

GROSSLY >GROSS

GROSSNESS >GROSS

GROSSULAR *n* type of garnet

GROSZ *n* Polish monetary unit worth one hundredth of a zloty

GROSZE >GROSZ

GROSZY >GROSZ

GROT *n* rubbish

GROTESQUE *adj* strangely distorted ▷ *n* grotesque person or thing

GROTS >GROT

GROTTIER >GROTTY

GROTTIEST >GROTTY

GROTTO *n* small picturesque cave

GROTTOED *adj* having grotto

GROTTOES >GROTTO

GROTTOS >GROTTO

GROTTY *adj* nasty or in bad condition

GROUCH *vb* grumble or complain ▷ *n* person who is always complaining

GROUCHED >GROUCH

GROUCHES >GROUCH

GROUCHIER >GROUCHY

GROUCHILY >GROUCHY

GROUCHING >GROUCH

GROUCHY *adj* bad-tempered

GROUF *same as* >GROOF

GROUFS >GROUF

GROUGH *n* natural channel or fissure in a peat moor

GROUGHS >GROUGH

GROUND *n* surface of the earth ▷ *adj* on or of the ground ▷ *vb* base or establish

GROUNDAGE *n* fee levied on a vessel entering a port or anchored off a shore

GROUNDED *adj* sensible and down-to-earth

GROUNDEN *obsolete variant of* >GROUND

GROUNDER *n* (in baseball) ball that travels along the ground

GROUNDERS >GROUNDER

GROUNDHOG *another name for* >WOODCHUCK

GROUNDING *n* basic knowledge of a subject

GROUNDMAN *n* groundsman

GROUNDMEN >GROUNDMAN

GROUNDNUT *n* peanut

GROUNDOUT *n* (in baseball) being put out after hitting a grounder that is fielded and thrown to first base

GROUNDS >GROUND

GROUNDSEL *n* yellow-flowered weed

GROUP *n* number of people or things regarded as a unit ▷ *vb* place or form into a group

GROUPABLE >GROUP

GROUPAGE *n* gathering people or objects into a group or groups

GROUPAGES >GROUPAGE

GROUPED >GROUP

GROUPER *n* large edible sea fish

GROUPERS >GROUPER

GROUPIE *n* ardent fan of a celebrity or of a sport or activity

GROUPIES >GROUPIE

**GROUPING** n set of people or organizations who act or work together to achieve a shared aim
**GROUPINGS** > GROUPING
**GROUPIST** n follower of a group
**GROUPISTS** > GROUPIST
**GROUPLET** n small group
**GROUPLETS** > GROUPLET
**GROUPOID** n magma
**GROUPOIDS** > GROUPOID
**GROUPS** > GROUP
**GROUPWARE** n software that enables computers within a group or organization to work together, allowing users to exchange electronic-mail messages, access shared files and databases, use video conferencing, etc
**GROUPY** same as > GROUPIE
**GROUSE** n stocky game bird ▷ vb grumble or complain ▷ adj fine or excellent ▷ adj excellent
**GROUSED** > GROUSE
**GROUSER** > GROUSE
**GROUSERS** > GROUSE
**GROUSES** > GROUSE
**GROUSEST** > GROUSE
**GROUSING** > GROUSE
**GROUT** n thin mortar ▷ vb fill up with grout
**GROUTED** > GROUT
**GROUTER** > GROUT
**GROUTERS** > GROUT
**GROUTIER** > GROUTY
**GROUTIEST** > GROUTY
**GROUTING** > GROUT
**GROUTINGS** > GROUT
**GROUTS** pl n sediment or grounds, as from making coffee
**GROUTY** adj sullen or surly
**GROVE** n small group of trees
**GROVED** > GROVE
**GROVEL** vb behave humbly in order to win a superior's favour
**GROVELED** > GROVEL
**GROVELER** > GROVEL
**GROVELERS** > GROVEL
**GROVELESS** > GROVE
**GROVELING** > GROVEL
**GROVELLED** > GROVEL
**GROVELLER** > GROVEL
**GROVELS** > GROVEL
**GROVES** > GROVE
**GROVET** n wrestling hold in which a wrestler in a kneeling position grips the head of his kneeling opponent with one arm and forces his shoulders down with the other
**GROVETS** > GROVET
**GROW** vb develop physically
**GROWABLE** adj able to be cultivated
**GROWER** n person who grows plants

**GROWERS** > GROWER
**GROWING** > GROW
**GROWINGLY** > GROW
**GROWINGS** > GROW
**GROWL** vb make a low rumbling sound ▷ n growling sound
**GROWLED** > GROWL
**GROWLER** n person, animal, or thing that growls
**GROWLERS** > GROWLER
**GROWLERY** n place to retreat to, alone, when ill-humoured
**GROWLIER** > GROWL
**GROWLIEST** > GROWL
**GROWLING** > GROWL
**GROWLINGS** > GROWL
**GROWLS** > GROWL
**GROWLY** > GROWL
**GROWN** > GROW
**GROWNUP** n adult
**GROWNUPS** > GROWNUP
**GROWS** > GROW
**GROWTH** n growing ▷ adj of or relating to growth
**GROWTHIER** > GROWTHY
**GROWTHIST** n advocate of the importance of economic growth
**GROWTHS** > GROWTH
**GROWTHY** adj rapid-growing
**GROYNE** n wall built out from the shore to control erosion
**GROYNES** > GROYNE
**GROZING** as in grazing iron iron for smoothing joints between lead pipes
**GRUB** n legless insect larva ▷ vb search carefully for something by digging or by moving things about
**GRUBBED** > GRUB
**GRUBBER** n person who grubs
**GRUBBERS** > GRUBBER
**GRUBBIER** > GRUBBY
**GRUBBIEST** > GRUBBY
**GRUBBILY** > GRUBBY
**GRUBBING** > GRUB
**GRUBBLE** same as > GRABBLE
**GRUBBLED** > GRUBBLE
**GRUBBLES** > GRUBBLE
**GRUBBLING** > GRUBBLE
**GRUBBY** adj dirty
**GRUBS** > GRUB
**GRUBSTAKE** n supplies provided for a prospector on the condition that the donor has a stake in any finds ▷ vb furnish with such supplies
**GRUBWORM** another word for > GRUB
**GRUBWORMS** > GRUBWORM
**GRUDGE** vb be unwilling to give or allow ▷ n resentment ▷ adj planned or carried out in order to settle a grudge
**GRUDGED** > GRUDGE
**GRUDGEFUL** adj envious
**GRUDGER** > GRUDGE

**GRUDGERS** > GRUDGE
**GRUDGES** > GRUDGE
**GRUDGING** > GRUDGE
**GRUDGINGS** > GRUDGE
**GRUE** n shiver or shudder ▷ vb shiver or shudder
**GRUED** > GRUE
**GRUEING** > GRUE
**GRUEL** n thin porridge ▷ vb subject to exhausting experiences
**GRUELED** > GRUEL
**GRUELER** > GRUEL
**GRUELERS** > GRUEL
**GRUELING** same as > GRUELLING
**GRUELINGS** > GRUELING
**GRUELLED** > GRUEL
**GRUELLER** > GRUEL
**GRUELLERS** > GRUEL
**GRUELLING** adj exhausting or severe ▷ n severe experience, esp punishment
**GRUELS** > GRUEL
**GRUES** > GRUE
**GRUESOME** adj causing horror and disgust
**GRUESOMER** > GRUESOME
**GRUFE** same as > GROOF
**GRUFES** > GRUFE
**GRUFF** adj rough or surly in manner or voice ▷ vb talk gruffly
**GRUFFED** > GRUFF
**GRUFFER** > GRUFF
**GRUFFEST** > GRUFF
**GRUFFIER** > GRUFFY
**GRUFFIEST** > GRUFFY
**GRUFFILY** > GRUFFY
**GRUFFING** > GRUFF
**GRUFFISH** > GRUFF
**GRUFFLY** > GRUFF
**GRUFFNESS** > GRUFF
**GRUFFS** > GRUFF
**GRUFFY** adj gruff
**GRUFTED** adj dirty
**GRUGRU** n any of several tropical American palms, esp Acrocomia sclerocarpa, which has a spiny trunk and leaves and edible nuts
**GRUGRUS** > GRUGRU
**GRUIFORM** adj relating to an order of birds, including cranes and bustards
**GRUING** > GRUE
**GRUM** adj surly
**GRUMBLE** vb complain ▷ n complaint
**GRUMBLED** > GRUMBLE
**GRUMBLER** > GRUMBLE
**GRUMBLERS** > GRUMBLE
**GRUMBLES** > GRUMBLE
**GRUMBLIER** > GRUMBLE
**GRUMBLING** > GRUMBLE
**GRUMBLY** > GRUMBLE
**GRUME** n clot
**GRUMES** > GRUME
**GRUMLY** > GRUM
**GRUMMER** > GRUM
**GRUMMEST** > GRUM
**GRUMMET** same as > GROMMET

**GRUMMETED** adj having grummets
**GRUMMETS** > GRUMMET
**GRUMNESS** > GRUM
**GRUMOSE** same as > GRUMOUS
**GRUMOUS** adj (esp of plant parts) consisting of granular tissue
**GRUMP** n surly or bad-tempered person ▷ vb complain or grumble
**GRUMPED** > GRUMP
**GRUMPH** vb grunt
**GRUMPHED** > GRUMPH
**GRUMPHIE** n pig
**GRUMPHIES** > GRUMPHIE
**GRUMPHING** > GRUMPH
**GRUMPHS** > GRUMPH
**GRUMPHY** same as > GRUMPHIE
**GRUMPIER** > GRUMPY
**GRUMPIEST** > GRUMPY
**GRUMPILY** > GRUMPY
**GRUMPING** > GRUMP
**GRUMPISH** same as > GRUMPY
**GRUMPS** > GRUMP
**GRUMPY** adj bad-tempered
**GRUNDIES** pl n men's underpants
**GRUNGE** n style of rock music with a fuzzy guitar sound
**GRUNGER** n fan of grunge music
**GRUNGERS** > GRUNGER
**GRUNGES** > GRUNGE
**GRUNGIER** > GRUNGY
**GRUNGIEST** > GRUNGY
**GRUNGY** adj squalid or seedy
**GRUNION** n Californian marine teleost fish, Leuresthes tenuis, that spawns on beaches: family Atherinidae (silversides)
**GRUNIONS** > GRUNION
**GRUNT** vb make a low short gruff sound, like a pig ▷ n pig's sound
**GRUNTED** > GRUNT
**GRUNTER** n person or animal that grunts, esp a pig
**GRUNTERS** > GRUNTER
**GRUNTING** > GRUNT
**GRUNTINGS** > GRUNT
**GRUNTLE** vb grunt or groan
**GRUNTLED** > GRUNTLE
**GRUNTLES** > GRUNTLE
**GRUNTLING** > GRUNTLE
**GRUNTS** > GRUNT
**GRUPPETTI** > GRUPPETTO
**GRUPPETTO** n turn
**GRUSHIE** adj healthy and strong
**GRUTCH** vb grudge
**GRUTCHED** > GRUTCH
**GRUTCHES** > GRUTCH
**GRUTCHING** > GRUTCH
**GRUTTEN** > GREET
**GRUYERE** n hard flat whole-milk cheese with holes
**GRUYERES** > GRUYERE

**GRYCE** same as >GRICE
**GRYCES** >GRYCE
**GRYDE** same as >GRYDE
**GRYDED** >GRYDE
**GRYDES** >GRYDE
**GRYDING** >GRYDE
**GRYESY** adj grey
**GRYFON** same as >GRIFFIN
**GRYFONS** >GRYFON
**GRYKE** same as >GRIKE
**GRYKES** >GRYKE
**GRYPE** same as >GRIPE
**GRYPES** >GRIPE
**GRYPHON** same as >GRIFFIN
**GRYPHONS** >GRYPHON
**GRYPT** archaic form of >GRIPPED
**GRYSBOK** n either of two small antelopes, *Raphicerus melanotis* or *R. sharpei*, of central and southern Africa, having small straight horns
**GRYSBOKS** >GRYSBOK
**GRYSELY** same as >GRISLY
**GRYSIE** same as >GRISY
**GU** same as >GJU
**GUACAMOLE** n spread of mashed avocado, tomato pulp, mayonnaise, and seasoning
**GUACHARO** another name for >OILBIRD
**GUACHAROS** >GUACHARO
**GUACO** n any of several tropical American plants whose leaves are used as an antidote to snakebite
**GUACOS** >GUACO
**GUAIAC** same as >GUAIACUM
**GUAIACOL** n yellowish oily creosote-like liquid extracted from guaiacum resin and hardwood tar, used medicinally as an expectorant
**GUAIACOLS** >GUAIACOL
**GUAIACS** >GUAIACUM
**GUAIACUM** n any tropical American evergreen tree of the zygophyllaceous genus *Guaiacum*, such as the lignum vitae
**GUAIACUMS** >GUAIACUM
**GUAIOCUM** same as >GUAIACUM
**GUAIOCUMS** >GUAIOCUM
**GUAN** n any gallinaceous bird of the genera *Penelope*, *Pipile*, etc, of Central and South America
**GUANA** another word for >IGUANA
**GUANABANA** n tropical tree or its fruit
**GUANACO** n S American animal related to the llama
**GUANACOS** >GUANACO
**GUANAS** >GUANA
**GUANASE** n enzyme that converts guanine to xanthine by removal of an amino group
**GUANASES** >GUANASE

**GUANAY** n type of cormorant
**GUANAYS** >GUANAY
**GUANAZOLO** n form of guanine
**GUANGO** n rain tree
**GUANGOS** >GUANGO
**GUANIDIN** same as >GUANIDINE
**GUANIDINE** n strongly alkaline crystalline substance, soluble in water and found in plant and animal tissues
**GUANIDINS** >GUANIDIN
**GUANIN** same as >GUANINE
**GUANINE** n white almost insoluble compound: one of the purine bases in nucleic acids
**GUANINES** >GUANINE
**GUANINS** >GUANINE
**GUANO** n dried sea-bird manure, used as fertilizer
**GUANOS** >GUANO
**GUANOSINE** n nucleoside consisting of guanine and ribose
**GUANS** >GUAN
**GUANXI** n Chinese social concept based on the exchange of favours
**GUANXIS** >GUANXI
**GUANYLIC** as in *guanylic acid* nucleotide consisting of guanine, ribose or deoxyribose, and a phosphate group
**GUAR** n leguminous Indian plant, *Cyamopsis tetragonolobus*, grown as a fodder crop and for the gum obtained from its seeds
**GUARANA** n type of shrub native to Venezuela
**GUARANAS** >GUARANA
**GUARANI** n standard monetary unit of Paraguay, divided into 100 céntimos
**GUARANIES** >GUARANI
**GUARANIS** >GUARANI
**GUARANTEE** n formal assurance, esp in writing, that a product will meet certain standards ▷ vb give a guarantee
**GUARANTOR** n person who gives or is bound by a guarantee
**GUARANTY** n pledge of responsibility for fulfilling another person's obligations in case of default
**GUARD** vb watch over to protect or to prevent escape ▷ n person or group that guards
**GUARDABLE** >GUARD
**GUARDAGE** n state of being in the care of a guardian
**GUARDAGES** >GUARDAGE

**GUARDANT** adj (of a beast) shown full face ▷ n guardian
**GUARDANTS** >GUARDANT
**GUARDDOG** n dog trained to protect premises
**GUARDDOGS** >GUARDDOG
**GUARDED** adj cautious or noncommittal
**GUARDEDLY** >GUARDED
**GUARDEE** n guardsman, esp considered as representing smartness and dash
**GUARDEES** >GUARDEE
**GUARDER** >GUARD
**GUARDERS** >GUARD
**GUARDIAN** n keeper or protector ▷ adj protecting or safeguarding
**GUARDIANS** >GUARDIAN
**GUARDING** >GUARD
**GUARDLESS** >GUARD
**GUARDLIKE** >GUARD
**GUARDRAIL** n railing at the side of a staircase, road, etc, as a safety barrier
**GUARDROOM** n room used by guards
**GUARDS** >GUARD
**GUARDSHIP** n warship responsible for the safety of other ships in its company
**GUARDSMAN** n member of the Guards
**GUARDSMEN** >GUARDSMAN
**GUARISH** vb heal
**GUARISHED** >GUARISH
**GUARISHES** >GUARISH
**GUARS** >GUAR
**GUAVA** n yellow-skinned tropical American fruit
**GUAVAS** >GUAVA
**GUAYABERA** n type of embroidered men's shirt
**GUAYULE** n bushy shrub, *Parthenium argentatum*, of the southwestern US: family *Asteraceae* (composites)
**GUAYULES** >GUAYULE
**GUB** n white man
**GUBBAH** same as >GUB
**GUBBAHS** >GUBBAH
**GUBBINS** n object of little or no value
**GUBBINSES** >GUBBINS
**GUBERNIYA** n territorial division of imperial Russia
**GUBS** >GUB
**GUCK** n slimy matter
**GUCKIER** >GUCKY
**GUCKIEST** >GUCKY
**GUCKS** >GUCK
**GUCKY** adj slimy and mucky
**GUDDLE** vb catch (fish) by groping with the hands under the banks or stones of a stream ▷ n muddle
**GUDDLED** >GUDDLE
**GUDDLES** >GUDDLE
**GUDDLING** >GUDDLE
**GUDE** Scots word for >GOOD

**GUDEMAN** n male householder
**GUDEMEN** >GUDEMAN
**GUDES** n goods
**GUDESIRE** n grandfather
**GUDESIRES** >GUDESIRE
**GUDEWIFE** n female householder
**GUDEWIVES** >GUDEWIFE
**GUDGEON** n small freshwater fish ▷ vb trick or cheat
**GUDGEONED** >GUDGEON
**GUDGEONS** >GUDGEON
**GUE** same as >GJU
**GUENON** n any slender agile Old World monkey of the genus *Cercopithecus*, inhabiting wooded regions of Africa and having long hind limbs and tail and long hair surrounding the face
**GUENONS** >GUENON
**GUERDON** n reward or payment ▷ vb give a guerdon to
**GUERDONED** >GUERDON
**GUERDONER** >GUERDON
**GUERDONS** >GUERDON
**GUEREZA** n handsome colobus monkey of the mountain forests of Ethiopia
**GUEREZAS** >GUEREZA
**GUERIDON** n small ornately-carved table
**GUERIDONS** >GUERIDON
**GUERILLA** same as >GUERRILLA
**GUERILLAS** >GUERILLA
**GUERITE** n turret used by a sentry
**GUERITES** >GUERITE
**GUERNSEY** n seaman's knitted woolen sweater
**GUERNSEYS** >GUERNSEY
**GUERRILLA** n member of an unofficial armed force fighting regular forces
**GUES** >GUE
**GUESS** vb estimate or draw a conclusion without proper knowledge ▷ n estimate or conclusion reached by guessing
**GUESSABLE** >GUESS
**GUESSED** >GUESS
**GUESSER** >GUESS
**GUESSERS** >GUESS
**GUESSES** >GUESS
**GUESSING** >GUESS
**GUESSINGS** >GUESS
**GUESSWORK** n process or results of guessing
**GUEST** n person entertained at another's house or at another's expense ▷ vb appear as a visiting player or performer
**GUESTED** >GUEST
**GUESTEN** vb stay as a guest in someone's house

**GUESTENED** > GUESTEN
**GUESTENS** > GUESTEN
**GUESTING** > GUEST
**GUESTS** > GUEST
**GUESTWISE** *adv* as, or in the manner of, a guest
**GUFF** *n* nonsense
**GUFFAW** *n* crude noisy laugh ▷ *vb* laugh in this way
**GUFFAWED** > GUFFAW
**GUFFAWING** > GUFFAW
**GUFFAWS** > GUFFAW
**GUFFIE** *Scots word for* > PIG
**GUFFIES** > GUFFIE
**GUFFS** > GUFF
**GUGA** *n* gannet chick
**GUGAS** > GUGA
**GUGGLE** *vb* drink making a gurgling sound
**GUGGLED** > GUGGLE
**GUGGLES** > GUGGLE
**GUGGLING** > GUGGLE
**GUGLET** *same as* > GOGLET
**GUGLETS** > GUGLET
**GUICHET** *n* grating, hatch, or small opening in a wall, esp a ticket-office window
**GUICHETS** > GUICHET
**GUID** *Scot word for* > GOOD
**GUIDABLE** > GUIDE
**GUIDAGE** *n* guidance
**GUIDAGES** > GUIDAGE
**GUIDANCE** *n* leadership, instruction, or advice
**GUIDANCES** > GUIDANCE
**GUIDE** *n* person who conducts tour expeditions ▷ *vb* act as a guide for
**GUIDEBOOK** *n* handbook with information for visitors to a place
**GUIDED** > GUIDE
**GUIDELESS** > GUIDE
**GUIDELINE** *n* set principle for doing something
**GUIDEPOST** *n* sign on a post by a road indicating directions
**GUIDER** > GUIDE
**GUIDERS** > GUIDE
**GUIDES** > GUIDE
**GUIDESHIP** *n* supervision
**GUIDEWAY** *n* track controlling the motion of something
**GUIDEWAYS** > GUIDEWAY
**GUIDEWORD** *n* word at top of dictionary page indicating first entry on page
**GUIDING** > GUIDE
**GUIDINGS** > GUIDE
**GUIDON** *n* small pennant, used as a marker or standard, esp by cavalry regiments
**GUIDONS** > GUIDON
**GUIDS** *n* possessions
**GUILD** *n* organization or club
**GUILDER** *n* former monetary unit of the Netherlands
**GUILDERS** > GUILDER

**GUILDHALL** *n* hall where members of a guild meet
**GUILDRIES** > GUILDRY
**GUILDRY** *n* in Scotland, corporation of merchants in a burgh
**GUILDS** > GUILD
**GUILDSHIP** *n* condition of being a member of a guild
**GUILDSMAN** *n* man who is a member of a guild
**GUILDSMEN** > GUILDSMAN
**GUILE** *n* cunning or deceit ▷ *vb* deceive
**GUILED** > GUILE
**GUILEFUL** > GUILE
**GUILELESS** *adj* free from guile
**GUILER** *n* deceiver
**GUILERS** > GUILER
**GUILES** > GUILE
**GUILING** > GUILE
**GUILLEMET** *n* (in printing) a duckfoot quote
**GUILLEMOT** *n* black-and-white diving sea bird of N hemisphere
**GUILLOCHE** *n* ornamental band or border with a repeating pattern of two or more interwoven wavy lines, as in architecture ▷ *vb* decorate with guilloches·
**GUILT** *n* fact or state of having done wrong
**GUILTIER** > GUILTY
**GUILTIEST** > GUILTY
**GUILTILY** > GUILTY
**GUILTLESS** *adj* innocent
**GUILTS** > GUILT
**GUILTY** *adj* responsible for an offence or misdeed
**GUIMBARD** *n* Jew's harp
**GUIMBARDS** > GUIMBARD
**GUIMP** *same as* > GUIMPE
**GUIMPE** *n* short blouse with sleeves worn under a pinafore dress ▷ *vb* make with gimp
**GUIMPED** > GUIMPE
**GUIMPES** > GUIMPE
**GUIMPING** > GUIMPE
**GUIMPS** > GUIMP
**GUINEA** *n* former British monetary unit worth 21 shillings (1.05 pounds)
**GUINEAS** > GUINEA
**GUIPURE** *n* heavy lace that has its pattern connected by threads, rather than supported on a net mesh
**GUIPURES** > GUIPURE
**GUIRO** *n* percussion instrument made from a hollow gourd
**GUIROS** > GUIRO
**GUISARD** *n* guiser
**GUISARDS** > GUISARD
**GUISE** *n* false appearance ▷ *vb* disguise or be disguised in fancy dress
**GUISED** > GUISE
**GUISER** *n* mummer, esp at

Christmas or Halloween revels
**GUISERS** > GUISER
**GUISES** > GUISE
**GUISING** > GUISE
**GUISINGS** > GUISE
**GUITAR** *n* stringed instrument with a flat back and a long neck, played by plucking or strumming
**GUITARIST** > GUITAR
**GUITARS** > GUITAR
**GUITGUIT** *n* bird belonging to the family Coerebidae
**GUITGUITS** > GUITGUIT
**GUIZER** *same as* > GUISER
**GUIZERS** > GUIZER
**GUL** *n* design used in oriental carpets
**GULA** *n* gluttony
**GULAG** *n* forced-labour camp
**GULAGS** > GULAG
**GULAR** *adj* of, relating to, or situated in the throat or oesophagus
**GULAS** > GULA
**GULCH** *n* deep narrow valley ▷ *vb* swallow fast
**GULCHED** > GULCH
**GULCHES** > GULCH
**GULCHING** > GULCH
**GULDEN** *same as* > GUILDER
**GULDENS** > GULDEN
**GULE** *Scots word for* > MARIGOLD
**GULES** *n* red in heraldry
**GULF** *n* large deep bay ▷ *vb* swallow up
**GULFED** > GULF
**GULFIER** > GULF
**GULFIEST** > GULF
**GULFING** > GULF
**GULFLIKE** > GULF
**GULFS** > GULF
**GULFWEED** *n* any brown seaweed of the genus *Sargassum*
**GULFWEEDS** > GULFWEED
**GULFY** > GULF
**GULL** *n* long-winged sea bird ▷ *vb* cheat or deceive
**GULLABLE** *same as* > GULLIBLE
**GULLABLY** > GULLABLE
**GULLED** > GULL
**GULLER** *n* deceiver
**GULLERIES** > GULLERY
**GULLERS** > GULLER
**GULLERY** *n* breeding-place for gulls
**GULLET** *n* muscular tube through which food passes from the mouth to the stomach
**GULLETS** > GULLET
**GULLEY** *same as* > GULLY
**GULLEYED** > GULLEY
**GULLEYING** > GULLEY
**GULLEYS** > GULLEY
**GULLIBLE** *adj* easily tricked
**GULLIBLY** > GULLIBLE
**GULLIED** > GULLY

**GULLIES** > GULLY
**GULLING** > GULL
**GULLISH** *adj* stupid
**GULLS** > GULL
**GULLWING** *adj* (of vehicle door) opening upwards
**GULLY** *n* channel cut by running water ▷ *vb* make (channels) in (the ground, sand, etc)
**GULLYING** > GULLY
**GULOSITY** *n* greed or gluttony
**GULP** *vb* swallow hastily ▷ *n* gulping
**GULPED** > GULP
**GULPER** > GULP
**GULPERS** > GULP
**GULPH** *archaic word for* > GULF
**GULPHS** > GULPH
**GULPIER** > GULP
**GULPIEST** > GULP
**GULPING** > GULP
**GULPINGLY** > GULP
**GULPS** > GULP
**GULPY** > GULP
**GULS** > GUL
**GULY** *adj* relating to gules
**GUM** *n* firm flesh in which the teeth are set ▷ *vb* stick with gum
**GUMBALL** *n* round piece of chewing gum
**GUMBALLS** > GUMBALL
**GUMBO** *n* mucilaginous pods of okra
**GUMBOIL** *n* abscess on the gum
**GUMBOILS** > GUMBOIL
**GUMBOOT** *n* rubber boot
**GUMBOOTS** *pl n* Wellington boots
**GUMBOS** > GUMBO
**GUMBOTIL** *n* sticky clay formed by the weathering of glacial drift
**GUMBOTILS** > GUMBOTIL
**GUMDROP** *n* hard jelly-like sweet
**GUMDROPS** > GUMDROP
**GUMLANDS** *pl n* infertile land from which the original kauri bush has been removed or burnt producing only kauri gum
**GUMLESS** > GUM
**GUMLIKE** > GUM
**GUMLINE** *n* line where gums meet teeth
**GUMLINES** > GUMLINE
**GUMMA** *n* rubbery tumour characteristic of advanced syphilis, occurring esp on the skin, liver, brain or heart
**GUMMAS** > GUMMA
**GUMMATA** > GUMMA
**GUMMATOUS** > GUMMA
**GUMMED** > GUM
**GUMMER** *n* punch-cutting tool
**GUMMERS** > GUMMER
**GUMMIER** > GUMMY

GUMMIES > GUMMY
GUMMIEST > GUMMY
GUMMILY > GUMMY
GUMMINESS > GUMMY
GUMMING > GUM
GUMMINGS > GUM
GUMMITE n orange or
  yellowish amorphous
  secondary mineral
  consisting of hydrated
  uranium oxides
GUMMITES > GUMMITE
GUMMOSE same
  as > GUMMOUS
GUMMOSES > GUMMOSE
GUMMOSIS n abnormal
  production of excessive
  gum in certain trees, esp
  fruit trees, as a result of
  wounding, infection,
  adverse weather
  conditions, severe
  pruning, etc
GUMMOSITY > GUMMOUS
GUMMOUS adj resembling or
  consisting of gum
GUMMY adj toothless ▷ n
  small crustacean-eating
  shark, Mustelus antarcticus,
  with bony ridges
  resembling gums in its
  mouth
GUMNUT n hardened seed
  container of the gumtree
GUMNUTS > GUMNUT
GUMP vb guddle
GUMPED > GUMP
GUMPHION n funeral banner
GUMPHIONS > GUMPHION
GUMPING > GUMP
GUMPS > GUMP
GUMPTION n
  resourcefulness
GUMPTIONS > GUMPTION
GUMPTIOUS > GUMPTION
GUMS > GUM
GUMSHIELD n plate or strip
  of soft waxy substance
  used by boxers to protect
  the teeth and gums
GUMSHOE n waterproof
  overshoe ▷ vb act
  stealthily
GUMSHOED > GUMSHOE
GUMSHOES > GUMSHOE
GUMSUCKER n native-born
  Australian
GUMTREE n any of various
  trees that yield gum, such
  as the eucalyptus, sweet
  gum, and sour gum
GUMTREES > GUMTREE
GUMWEED n any of several
  American yellow-flowered
  plants that have sticky
  flower heads
GUMWEEDS > GUMWEED
GUMWOOD same
  as > GUMTREE
GUMWOODS > GUMWOOD
GUN n weapon with a metal
  tube from which missiles
  are fired by explosion ▷ vb
  cause (an engine) to run at

high speed
GUNBOAT n small warship
GUNBOATS > GUNBOAT
GUNCOTTON n form of
  cellulose nitrate used as an
  explosive
GUNDIES > GUNDY
GUNDOG n dog trained to
  work with a hunter or
  gamekeeper
GUNDOGS > GUNDOG
GUNDY n toffee
GUNFIGHT n fight between
  persons using firearms
  ▷ vb fight with guns
GUNFIGHTS > GUNFIGHT
GUNFIRE n repeated firing
  of guns
GUNFIRES > GUNFIRE
GUNFLINT n piece of flint in
  a flintlock's hammer used
  to strike the spark that
  ignites the charge
GUNFLINTS > GUNFLINT
GUNFOUGHT > GUNFIGHT
GUNG adj as in gung ho
  extremely or excessively
  enthusiastic about
  something
GUNGE n sticky unpleasant
  substance ▷ vb block or
  encrust with gunge
GUNGED > GUNGE
GUNGES > GUNGE
GUNGIER > GUNGE
GUNGIEST > GUNGE
GUNGING > GUNGE
GUNGY > GUNGE
GUNHOUSE n on a warship,
  an armoured rotatable
  enclosure for guns
GUNHOUSES > GUNHOUSE
GUNITE n cement-sand
  mortar that is sprayed
  onto formwork, walls, or
  rock by a compressed air
  ejector giving a very dense
  strong concrete layer:
  used to repair reinforced
  concrete, to line tunnel
  walls or mine airways, etc
GUNITES > GUNITE
GUNK n slimy or filthy
  substance
GUNKHOLE vb make a series
  of short boat excursions
GUNKHOLED > GUNKHOLE
GUNKHOLES > GUNKHOLE
GUNKIER > GUNK
GUNKIEST > GUNK
GUNKS > GUNK
GUNKY > GUNK
GUNLAYER n person who
  aims a ship's gun
GUNLAYERS > GUNLAYER
GUNLESS > GUN
GUNLOCK n mechanism in
  some firearms that causes
  the charge to be exploded
GUNLOCKS > GUNLOCK
GUNMAKER n person who
  makes guns
GUNMAKERS > GUNMAKER
GUNMAN n armed criminal

GUNMEN > GUNMAN
GUNMETAL n alloy of copper,
  tin, and zinc ▷ adj dark
  grey
GUNMETALS > GUNMETAL
GUNNAGE n number of guns
  carried by a warship
GUNNAGES > GUNNAGE
GUNNED > GUN
GUNNEL same as > GUNWALE
GUNNELS > GUNNEL
GUNNEN > GUN
GUNNER n artillery soldier
GUNNERA n any herbaceous
  perennial plant of the
  genus Gunnera, found
  throughout the S
  hemisphere and cultivated
  for its large leaves
GUNNERAS > GUNNERA
GUNNERIES > GUNNERY
GUNNERS > GUNNER
GUNNERY n use or science of
  large guns
GUNNIES > GUNNY
GUNNING > GUN
GUNNINGS > GUN
GUNNY n strong coarse
  fabric used for sacks
GUNNYBAG same
  as > GUNNYSACK
GUNNYBAGS > GUNNYBAG
GUNNYSACK n sack made
  from gunny
GUNPAPER n cellulose
  nitrate explosive made by
  treating paper with nitric
  acid
GUNPAPERS > GUNPAPER
GUNPLAY n use of firearms,
  as by criminals
GUNPLAYS > GUNPLAY
GUNPOINT n muzzle of a
  gun
GUNPOINTS > GUNPOINT
GUNPORT n porthole, or
  other, opening for a gun
GUNPORTS > GUNPORT
GUNPOWDER n explosive
  mixture of potassium
  nitrate, sulphur, and
  charcoal
GUNROOM n (esp in the Royal
  Navy) the mess allocated
  to subordinate or junior
  officers
GUNROOMS > GUNROOM
GUNRUNNER n person
  who smuggles guns and
  ammunition
GUNS > GUN
GUNSEL n catamite
GUNSELS > GUNSEL
GUNSHIP n ship or
  helicopter armed with
  heavy guns
GUNSHIPS > GUNSHIP
GUNSHOT n shot or range
  of a gun
GUNSHOTS > GUNSHOT
GUNSMITH n person who
  manufactures or repairs
  firearms, esp portable
  guns

GUNSMITHS > GUNSMITH
GUNSTICK n ramrod
GUNSTICKS > GUNSTICK
GUNSTOCK n wooden
  handle to which the barrel
  of a rifle is attached
GUNSTOCKS > GUNSTOCK
GUNSTONE n cannonball
GUNSTONES > GUNSTONE
GUNTER n type of gaffing in
  which the gaff is hoisted
  parallel to the mast
GUNTERS > GUNTER
GUNWALE n top of a ship's
  side
GUNWALES > GUNWALE
GUNYAH n hut or shelter in
  the bush
GUNYAHS > GUNYAH
GUP n gossip
GUPPIES > GUPPY
GUPPY n small colourful
  aquarium fish
GUPS > GUP
GUR n unrefined cane sugar
GURAMI same as > GOURAMI
GURAMIS > GURAMI
GURDWARA n Sikh place of
  worship
GURDWARAS > GURDWARA
GURGE vb swallow up
GURGED > GURGE
GURGES > GURGE
GURGING > GURGE
GURGLE n bubbling noise
  ▷ vb (of water) to make
  low bubbling noises when
  flowing
GURGLED > GURGLE
GURGLES > GURGLE
GURGLET same as > GOGLET
GURGLETS > GURGLET
GURGLING > GURGLE
GURGOYLE same
  as > GARGOYLE
GURGOYLES > GURGOYLE
GURJUN n any of
  several S or SE Asian
  dipterocarpaceous trees
  of the genus Dipterocarpus
  that yield a resin
GURJUNS > GURJUN
GURL vb snarl
GURLED > GURL
GURLET n type of pickaxe
GURLETS > GURLET
GURLIER > GURLY
GURLIEST > GURLY
GURLING > GURL
GURLS > GURL
GURLY adj stormy
GURN variant spelling
  of > GIRN
GURNARD n spiny armour-
  headed sea fish
GURNARDS > GURNARD
GURNED > GURN
GURNET same as > GURNARD
GURNETS > GURNARD
GURNEY n wheeled
  stretcher for transporting
  hospital patients
GURNEYS > GURNEY
GURNING > GURN

GURNS >GURN

GURRAH n type of coarse muslin

GURRAHS >GURRAH

GURRIER n low-class tough ill-mannered person

GURRIERS >GURRIER

GURRIES >GURRY

GURRY n dog-fight

GURS >GUR

GURSH n unit of currency in Saudi Arabia

GURSHES >GURSH

GURU n Hindu or Sikh religious teacher or leader

GURUDOM n state of being a guru

GURUDOMS >GURUDOM

GURUISM >GURU

GURUISMS >GURU

GURUS >GURU

GURUSHIP >GURU

GURUSHIPS >GURU

GUS >GU

GUSH vb flow out suddenly and profusely ▷ n sudden copious flow

GUSHED >GUSH

GUSHER n spurting oil well

GUSHERS >GUSHER

GUSHES >GUSH

GUSHIER >GUSHY

GUSHIEST >GUSHY

GUSHILY >GUSHY

GUSHINESS >GUSHY

GUSHING >GUSH

GUSHINGLY >GUSH

GUSHY adj displaying excessive admiration or sentimentality

GUSLA n Balkan single-stringed musical instrument

GUSLAR n player of the gusla

GUSLARS >GUSLAR

GUSLAS >GUSLA

GUSLE same as >GUSLA

GUSLES >GUSLE

GUSLI n Russian harp-like musical instrument

GUSLIS >GUSLI

GUSSET n piece of material sewn into a garment to strengthen it ▷ vb put a gusset in (a garment)

GUSSETED >GUSSET

GUSSETING >GUSSET

GUSSETS >GUSSET

GUSSIE n young pig

GUSSIED >GUSSY

GUSSIES >GUSSY

GUSSY vb dress elaborately

GUSSYING >GUSSY

GUST n sudden blast of wind ▷ vb blow in gusts

GUSTABLE n anything that can be tasted

GUSTABLES >GUSTABLE

GUSTATION n act of tasting or the faculty of taste

GUSTATIVE >GUSTATION

GUSTATORY >GUSTATION

GUSTED >GUST

GUSTFUL adj tasty

GUSTIE adj tasty

GUSTIER >GUSTY

GUSTIEST >GUSTY

GUSTILY >GUSTY

GUSTINESS >GUSTY

GUSTING >GUST

GUSTLESS adj tasteless

GUSTO n enjoyment or zest

GUSTOES >GUSTO

GUSTOS >GUSTO

GUSTS >GUST

GUSTY adj blowing or occurring in gusts or characterized by blustery weather

GUT n intestine ▷ vb remove the guts from ▷ adj basic or instinctive

GUTBUCKET n highly emotional style of jazz playing

GUTCHER n grandfather

GUTCHERS >GUTCHER

GUTFUL n bellyful

GUTFULS >GUTFUL

GUTLESS adj cowardly

GUTLIKE >GUT

GUTROT n diarrhoea

GUTROTS >GUTROT

GUTS >GUT vb devour greedily

GUTSED >GUTS

GUTSER as in come a gutser fall heavily to the ground

GUTSERS >GUTSER

GUTSES >GUTS

GUTSFUL n bellyful

GUTSFULS >GUTSFUL

GUTSIER >GUTSY

GUTSIEST >GUTSY

GUTSILY >GUTSY

GUTSINESS >GUTSY

GUTSING >GUTS

GUTSY adj courageous

GUTTA n one of a set of small drop-like ornaments, esp as used on the architrave of a Doric entablature ▷ n rubber substance obtained from the coagulated latex of the guttapercha tree

GUTTAE >GUTTA

GUTTAS >GUTTA

GUTTATE adj (esp of plants) covered with small drops or drop-like markings, esp oil glands ▷ vb exude droplets of liquid

GUTTATED same as >GUTTATE

GUTTATES >GUTTATE

GUTTATING >GUTTATE

GUTTATION >GUTTATE

GUTTED >GUT

GUTTER n shallow channel for carrying away water from a roof or roadside ▷ vb (of a candle) burn unsteadily, with wax running down the sides

GUTTERED >GUTTER

GUTTERING n material for gutters

GUTTERS >GUTTER

GUTTERY >GUTTER

GUTTIER >GUTTY

GUTTIES >GUTTY

GUTTIEST >GUTTY

GUTTING >GUT

GUTTLE vb eat greedily

GUTTLED >GUTTLE

GUTTLER >GUTTLE

GUTTLERS >GUTTLE

GUTTLES >GUTTLE

GUTTLING >GUTTLE

GUTTURAL adj (of a sound) produced at the back of the throat ▷ n guttural consonant

>GUTTURALISATION

>GUTTURALIZATION

GUTTURALS >GUTTURAL

GUTTY n urchin or delinquent ▷ adj courageous

GUTZER n bad fall

GUTZERS >GUTZER

GUV informal name for >GOVERNOR

GUVS >GUV

GUY n man or boy ▷ vb make fun of

GUYED >GUY

GUYING >GUY

GUYLE same as >GUILE

GUYLED >GUYLE

GUYLER >GUYLE

GUYLERS >GUYLE

GUYLES >GUYLE

GUYLINE n guy rope

GUYLINES >GUYLINE

GUYLING >GUYLE

GUYOT n flat-topped submarine mountain, common in the Pacific Ocean, usually an extinct volcano whose summit did not reach above the sea surface

GUYOTS >GUYOT

GUYS >GUY

GUYSE same as >GUISE

GUYSES >GUYSE

GUZZLE vb eat or drink greedily

GUZZLED >GUZZLE

GUZZLER n person or thing that guzzles

GUZZLERS >GUZZLER

GUZZLES >GUZZLE

GUZZLING >GUZZLE

GWEDUC same as >GEODUCK

GWEDUCK same as >GEODUCK

GWEDUCKS >GWEDUCK

GWEDUCS >GWEDUCK

GWINE dialect form of >GOING

GWINIAD n powan

GWINIADS >GWINIAD

GWYNIAD n freshwater white fish, Coregonus pennantii, occurring in Lake Bala in Wales: related to the powan

GWYNIADS >GWYNIAD

GYAL same as >GAYAL

GYALS >GYAL

GYBE vb (of a fore-and-aft sail) swing suddenly from one side to the other ▷ n instance of gybing

GYBED >GYBE

GYBES >GYBE

GYBING >GYBE

GYELD n guild

GYELDS >GYELD

GYLDEN adj golden

GYM n gymnasium

GYMBAL same as >GIMBAL

GYMBALS >GYMBAL

GYMKHANA n horse-riding competition

GYMKHANAS >GYMKHANA

GYMMAL same as >GIMMAL

GYMMALS >GYMMAL

GYMNASIA >GYMNASIUM

GYMNASIAL >GYMNASIUM

GYMNASIC >GYMNASIUM

GYMNASIEN >GYMNASIUM

GYMNASIUM n large room with equipment for physical training

GYMNAST n expert in gymnastics

GYMNASTIC adj of, relating to, like, or involving gymnastics

GYMNASTS >GYMNAST

GYMNIC adj gymnastic

GYMNOSOPH n adherent of gymnosophy: belief that food and clothing are detrimental to purity of thought

GYMP same as >GIMP

GYMPED >GYMP

GYMPIE n tall tree with stinging hairs on its leaves

GYMPIES >GYMPIE

GYMPING >GYMP

GYMPS >GYMP

GYMS >GYM

GYMSLIP n tunic or pinafore formerly worn by schoolgirls

GYMSLIPS >GYMSLIP

GYNAE adj gynaecological ▷ n gynaecology

GYNAECEA >GYNAECIUM

GYNAECEUM same as >GYNAECIA

GYNAECIA >GYNAECIUM

GYNAECIUM. same as >GYNOECIUM

GYNAECOID adj resembling, relating to, or like a woman

GYNAES >GYNAE

GYNANDRY n hermaphroditism

GYNARCHIC >GYNARCHY

GYNARCHY n government by women

GYNECIA >GYNECIUM

GYNECIC adj relating to the female sex

GYNECIUM same as >GYNOECIUM

GYNECOID same as >GYNAECOID

GYNIATRY *n* gynaecology: medicine concerned with diseases in women
GYNIE *n* gynaecology
GYNIES > GYNIE
GYNNEY *n* guinea hen
GYNNEYS > GYNNEY
GYNNIES > GYNNY
GYNNY *same as* > GYNNEY
GYNOCRACY *n* government by women
GYNOECIA > GYNOECIUM
GYNOECIUM *n* carpels of a flowering plant collectively
GYNOPHOBE *n* person who hates or fears women
GYNOPHORE *n* stalk in some plants that bears the gynoecium above the level of the other flower parts
GYNY *n* gynaecology
GYOZA *n* Japanese fried dumpling
GYOZAS > GYOZA
GYP *vb* swindle, cheat, or defraud ▷ *n* act of cheating
GYPLURE *n* synthetic version of the gypsy moth sex pheromone
GYPLURES > GYPLURE
GYPPED > GYP
GYPPER > GYP
GYPPERS > GYP
GYPPIE *same as* > GIPPY
GYPPIES > GYPPY
GYPPING > GYP
GYPPO *n* derogatory term for a gypsy
GYPPOS > GYPPO
GYPPY *same as* > GIPPY
GYPS > GYP
GYPSEIAN *adj* relating to gypsies
GYPSEOUS > GYPSUM
GYPSIED > GYPSY
GYPSIES > GYPSY
GYPSTER *n* swindler
GYPSTERS > GYPSTER
GYPSUM *n* chalklike mineral used to make plaster of Paris
GYPSUMS > GYPSUM
GYPSY *n* member of a nomadic people scattered throughout Europe and North America ▷ *vb* live like a gypsy
GYPSYDOM > GYPSY
GYPSYDOMS > GYPSYDOM
GYPSYHOOD > GYPSY
GYPSYING > GYPSY
GYPSYISH > GYPSY
GYPSYISM *n* state of being a gypsy
GYPSYISMS > GYPSYISM
GYPSYWORT *n* type of Eurasian herb with white flowers
GYRAL *adj* having a circular, spiral, or rotating motion
GYRALLY > GYRAL
GYRANT *adj* gyrating

GYRASE *n* topoisomerase enzyme
GYRASES > GYRASE
GYRATE *vb* rotate or spiral about a point or axis ▷ *adj* curved or coiled into a circle
GYRATED > GYRATE
GYRATES > GYRATE
GYRATING > GYRATE
GYRATION *n* act or process of gyrating
GYRATIONS > GYRATION
GYRATOR *n* electronic circuit that inverts the impedance
GYRATORS > GYRATOR
GYRATORY > GYRATE
GYRE *n* circular or spiral movement or path ▷ *vb* whirl
GYRED > GYRE
GYRENE *n* nickname for a member of the US Marine Corps
GYRENES > GYRENE
GYRES > GYRE
GYRFALCON *n* very large rare falcon of northern regions
GYRI > GYRUS
GYRING > GYRE
GYRO *n* gyrocompass: nonmagnetic compass that uses a motor-driven gyroscope to indicate true north
GYROCAR *n* two-wheeled car
GYROCARS > GYROCAR
GYRODYNE *n* aircraft that uses a powered rotor to take off and manoeuvre, but uses autorotation when cruising
GYRODYNES > GYRODYNE
GYROIDAL *adj* spiral
GYROLITE *n* silicate
GYROLITES > GYROLITE
GYROMANCY *n* divination by spinning in a circle, then falling on any of various letters that have been written on the ground
GYRON *same as* > GIRON
GYRONIC > GYRON
GYRONNY *same as* > GIRONNY
GYRONS > GYRON
GYROPILOT *n* type of automatic pilot
GYROPLANE *another name for* > AUTOGIRO
GYROS > GYRO
GYROSCOPE *n* disc rotating on an axis that can turn in any direction, so the disc maintains the same position regardless of the movement of the surrounding structure
GYROSE *adj* marked with sinuous lines
GYROSTAT *same as* > GYROSCOPE

GYROSTATS > GYROSTAT
GYROUS *adj* gyrose
GYROVAGUE *n* peripatetic monk
GYRUS *another name for* > CONVOLUTION
GYRUSES > GYRUS
GYTE *n* goat
GYTES > GYTE
GYTRASH *n* spirit that haunts lonely roads
GYTRASHES > GYTRASH
GYTTJA *n* sediment on lake bottom
GYTTJAS > GYTTJA
GYVE *vb* shackle or fetter ▷ *n* fetters
GYVED > GYVE
GYVES > GYVE
GYVING > GYVE

# Hh

HA *interj* exclamation expressing triumph, surprise, or scorn
HAAF *n* deep-sea fishing ground off the Shetland and Orkney Islands
HAAFS > HAAF
HAANEPOOT *same as* > HANEPOOT
HAAR *n* cold sea mist or fog off the North Sea
HAARS > HAAR
HABANERA *n* slow Cuban dance in duple time
HABANERAS > HABANERA
HABANERO *n* variety of chilli pepper
HABANEROS > HABANERO
HABDABS *n* highly nervous state
HABDALAH *n* prayer at end of Jewish sabbath
HABDALAHS > HABDALAH
HABERDINE *n* dried cod
HABERGEON *n* light sleeveless coat of mail worn in the 14th century under the plated hauberk
HABILABLE *adj* able to wear clothes
HABILE *adj* skilful
HABIT *n* established way of behaving ▷ *vb* clothe
HABITABLE *adj* fit to be lived in
HABITABLY > HABITABLE
HABITAN *same as* > HABITANT
HABITANS > HABITAN
HABITANT *n* early French settler in Canada or Louisiana or a descendant of one, esp a farmer

HABITANTS > HABITANT
HABITAT *n* natural home of an animal or plant
HABITATS > HABITAT
HABITED *adj* dressed in a habit
HABITING > HABIT
HABITS > HABIT
HABITUAL *adj* done regularly and repeatedly ▷ *vb* accustom
HABITUALS > HABITUAL
HABITUATE *vb* accustom
HABITUDE *n* habit or tendency
HABITUDES > HABITUDE
HABITUE *n* frequent visitor to a place
HABITUES > HABITUE
HABITUS *n* general physical state, esp with regard to susceptibility to disease
HABLE *old form of* > ABLE
HABOOB *n* sandstorm
HABOOBS > HABOOB
HABU *n* large venomous snake
HABUS > HABU
HACEK *n* pronunciation symbol in Slavonic language
HACEKS > HACEK
HACENDADO *n* owner of hacienda
HACHIS *n* hash
HACHURE *n* shading of short lines drawn on a map to indicate the degree of steepness of a hill ▷ *vb* mark or show by hachures
HACHURED > HACHURE
HACHURES > HACHURE
HACHURING > HACHURE

HACIENDA *n* ranch or large estate in Latin America
HACIENDAS > HACIENDA
HACK *vb* cut or chop violently ▷ *n* (inferior) writer or journalist ▷ *adj* unoriginal or of a low standard
HACKABLE > HACK
HACKAMORE *n* rope or rawhide halter used for unbroken foals
HACKBERRY *n* American tree or shrub with edible cherry-like fruits
HACKBOLT *n* shearwater
HACKBOLTS > HACKBOLT
HACKBUT *another word for* > ARQUEBUS
HACKBUTS > HACKBUT
HACKED > HACK
HACKEE *n* chipmunk
HACKEES > HACKEE
HACKER *n* computer enthusiast, esp one who breaks into the computer system of a company or government
HACKERIES > HACKERY
HACKERS > HACKER
HACKERY *n* journalism
HACKETTE *n* informal, derogatory term for female journalist
HACKETTES > HACKETTE
HACKIE *n* US word meaning cab driver
HACKIES > HACKIE
HACKING > HACK
HACKINGS > HACK
HACKLE *same as* > HECKLE
HACKLED > HACKLE
HACKLER > HACKLE

HACKLERS > HACKLE
HACKLES *pl n* hairs on the back of the neck and the back of a dog, cat, etc, which rise when the animal is angry or afraid
HACKLET *n* kittiwake
HACKLETS > HACKLET
HACKLIER > HACKLY
HACKLIEST > HACKLY
HACKLING > HACKLE
HACKLY *adj* rough or jagged
HACKMAN *n* taxi driver
HACKMEN > HACKMAN
HACKNEY *n* taxi ▷ *vb* make commonplace and banal by too frequent use
HACKNEYED *adj* (of a word or phrase) unoriginal and overused
HACKNEYS > HACKNEY
HACKS > HACK
HACKSAW *n* small saw for cutting metal ▷ *vb* cut with a hacksaw
HACKSAWED > HACKSAW
HACKSAWN > HACKSAW
HACKSAWS > HACKSAW
HACKWORK *n* dull repetitive work
HACKWORKS > HACKWORK
HACQUETON *n* padded jacket worn under chain mail
HAD *vb* Scots form of hold
HADAL *adj* of, relating to, or constituting very deep zones of the oceans
HADARIM > HEDER
HADAWAY *sentence substitute* exclamation urging the hearer to refrain from delay in the execution of

a task
**HADDEN** > HAVE
**HADDEST** *same as* > HADST
**HADDIE** *n* finnan haddock
**HADDIES** > HADDIE
**HADDING** > HAVE
**HADDOCK** *n* edible sea fish of N Atlantic
**HADDOCKS** > HADDOCK
**HADE** *n* angle made to the vertical by the plane of a fault or vein ▷ *vb* incline from the vertical
**HADED** > HADE
**HADEDAH** *n* large grey-green S African ibis
**HADEDAHS** > HADEDAH
**HADES** > HADE
**HADING** > HADE
**HADITH** *n* body of tradition and legend about Mohammed and his followers, used as a basis of Islamic law
**HADITHS** > HADITH
**HADJ** *same as* > HAJJ
**HADJEE** *same as* > HADJI
**HADJEES** > HADJEE
**HADJES** > HADJ
**HADJI** *same as* > HAJJI
**HADJIS** > HADJI
**HADROME** *n* part of xylem
**HADROMES** > HADROME
**HADRON** *n* any elementary particle capable of taking part in a strong nuclear interaction and therefore excluding leptons and photons
**HADRONIC** > HADRON
**HADRONS** > HADRON
**HADROSAUR** *n* any one of a large group of duck-billed partly aquatic bipedal dinosaurs
**HADS** > HAVE
**HADST** *singular form of the past tense (indicative mood) of* > HAVE
**HAE** *Scot variant of* > HAVE
**HAECCEITY** *n* property that uniquely identifies an object
**HAED** > HAE
**HAEING** > HAE
**HAEM** *n* complex red organic pigment containing ferrous iron, present in haemoglobin
  > HAEMAGGLUTINATE
  > HAEMAGGLUTINATE
  > HAEMAGGLUTINATE
**HAEMAL** *adj* of the blood
**HAEMATAL** *same as* > HAEMAL
**HAEMATEIN** *n* dark purple water-insoluble crystalline substance obtained from logwood and used as an indicator and biological stain
**HAEMATIC** *n* agent that stimulates the production of red blood cells

**HAEMATICS** > HAEMATIC
**HAEMATIN** *n* dark bluish or brownish pigment containing iron in the ferric state, obtained by the oxidation of haem
**HAEMATINS** > HAEMATIN
**HAEMATITE** *same as* > HEMATITE
**HAEMATOID** *adj* resembling blood
**HAEMATOMA** *n* tumour of clotted or partially clotted blood
**HAEMIC** *same as* > HAEMATIC
**HAEMIN** *n* haematin chloride
**HAEMINS** > HAEMIN
**HAEMOCOEL** *n* body cavity of many invertebrates, including arthropods and molluscs, developed from part of the blood system
**HAEMOCYTE** *n* any blood cell, esp a red blood cell
  > HAEMOFLAGELLATE
**HAEMOID** *same as* > HAEMATOID
**HAEMONIES** > HAEMONY
**HAEMONY** *n* plant mentioned in Milton's poetry
**HAEMOSTAT** *n* surgical instrument that stops bleeding by compression of a blood vessel
**HAEMS** > HAEM
**HAEN** > HAE
**HAEREDES** > HAERES
**HAEREMAI** *interj* Māori expression of welcome
**HAERES** *same as* > HERES
**HAES** > HAE
**HAET** *n* whit
**HAETS** > HAET
**HAFF** *n* lagoon
**HAFFET** *n* side of head
**HAFFETS** > HAFFET
**HAFFIT** *same as* > HAFFET
**HAFFITS** > HAFFIT
**HAFFLIN** *same as* > HALFLING
**HAFFLINS** > HAFFLIN
**HAFFS** > HAFF
**HAFIZ** *n* title for a person who knows the Koran by heart
**HAFIZES** > HAFIZ
**HAFNIUM** *n* metallic element found in zirconium ores
**HAFNIUMS** > HAFNIUM
**HAFT** *n* handle of an axe, knife, or dagger ▷ *vb* provide with a haft
**HAFTARA** *same as* > HAFTARAH
**HAFTARAH** *n* (in Judaism) short reading from the Prophets which follows the reading from the Torah on Sabbaths and festivals
**HAFTARAHS** > HAFTARAH
**HAFTARAS** > HAFTARA

**HAFTAROT** > HAFTARAH
**HAFTAROTH** > HAFTARAH
**HAFTED** > HAFT
**HAFTER** > HAFT
**HAFTERS** > HAFT
**HAFTING** > HAFT
**HAFTORAH** *same as* > HAFTARAH
**HAFTORAHS** > HAFTORAH
**HAFTOROS** > HAFTORAH
**HAFTOROT** > HAFTORAH
**HAFTOROTH** > HAFTORAH
**HAFTS** > HAFT
**HAG** *n* ugly old woman ▷ *vb* hack
**HAGADIC** > HAGGAD
**HAGADIST** *same as* > HAGGADIST
**HAGADISTS** > HAGADIST
**HAGBERRY** *same as* > HACKBERRY
**HAGBOLT** *same as* > HACKBOLT
**HAGBOLTS** > HAGBOLT
**HAGBORN** *adj* born of witch
**HAGBUSH** *same as* > ARQUEBUS
**HAGBUSHES** > HAGBUSH
**HAGBUT** > HAGBUT
**HAGBUTEER** > HAGBUT
**HAGBUTS** > HAGBUT
**HAGBUTTER** > HAGBUT
**HAGDEN** *same as* > HACKBOLT
**HAGDENS** > HAGDEN
**HAGDON** *same as* > HACKBOLT
**HAGDONS** > HAGDON
**HAGDOWN** *same as* > HACKBOLT
**HAGDOWNS** > HAGDOWN
**HAGFISH** *n* any of various primitive eel-like marine vertebrates
**HAGFISHES** > HAGFISH
**HAGG** *n* boggy place
**HAGGADA** *same as* > HAGGADAH
**HAGGADAH** *n* book containing the order of service of the traditional Jewish Passover meal
**HAGGADAHS** > HAGGADAH
**HAGGADAS** > HAGGADA
**HAGGADIC** > HAGGADAH
**HAGGADIST** *n* writer of Aggadoth
**HAGGADOT** > HAGGADAH
**HAGGADOTH** > HAGGADAH
**HAGGARD** *adj* looking tired and ill ▷ *n* hawk that has reached maturity before being caught
**HAGGARDLY** > HAGGARD
**HAGGARDS** > HAGGARD
**HAGGED** > HAG
**HAGGING** > HAG
**HAGGIS** *n* Scottish dish made from sheep's offal, oatmeal, suet, and seasonings, boiled in a bag made from the sheep's stomach
**HAGGISES** > HAGGIS
**HAGGISH** > HAG
**HAGGISHLY** > HAG

**HAGGLE** *vb* bargain or wrangle over a price
**HAGGLED** > HAGGLE
**HAGGLER** > HAGGLE
**HAGGLERS** > HAGGLE
**HAGGLES** > HAGGLE
**HAGGLING** > HAGGLE
**HAGGS** > HAGG
**HAGIARCHY** *n* government by saints, holy men, or men in holy orders
**HAGIOLOGY** *n* literature about the lives and legends of saints
**HAGLET** *same as* > HACKLET
**HAGLETS** > HAGLET
**HAGLIKE** > HAG
**HAGRIDDEN** > HAGRIDE
**HAGRIDE** *vb* torment or obsess
**HAGRIDER** > HAGRIDE
**HAGRIDERS** > HAGRIDE
**HAGRIDES** > HAGRIDE
**HAGRIDING** > HAGRIDE
**HAGRODE** > HAGRIDE
**HAGS** > HAG
**HAH** *same as* > HA
**HAHA** *n* wall or other boundary marker that is set in a ditch so as not to interrupt the landscape
**HAHAS** > HAHA
**HAHNIUM** *n* transuranic element artificially produced from californium
**HAHNIUMS** > HAHNIUM
**HAHS** > HAH
**HAICK** *same as* > HAIK
**HAICKS** > HAICK
**HAIDUK** *n* rural brigand
**HAIDUKS** > HAIDUK
**HAIK** *n* Arab's outer garment of cotton, wool, or silk, for the head and body
**HAIKA** > HAIK
**HAIKAI** *same as* > HAIKU
**HAIKS** > HAIK
**HAIKU** *n* Japanese verse form in 17 syllables
**HAIKUS** > HAIKU
**HAIL** *n* (shower of) small pellets of ice ▷ *vb* fall as or like hail ▷ *sentence substitute* exclamation of greeting
**HAILED** > HAIL
**HAILER** > HAIL
**HAILERS** > HAIL
**HAILIER** > HAIL
**HAILIEST** > HAIL
**HAILING** > HAIL
**HAILS** > HAIL
**HAILSHOT** *n* small scattering shot
**HAILSHOTS** > HAILSHOT
**HAILSTONE** *n* pellet of hail
**HAILSTORM** *n* storm during which hail falls
**HAILY** > HAIL
**HAIMISH** *same as* > HEIMISH
**HAIN** *vb* Scots word meaning save
**HAINCH** *Scots form*

*of* > HAUNCH
**HAINCHED** > HAINCH
**HAINCHES** > HAINCH
**HAINCHING** > HAINCH
**HAINED** > HAIN
**HAINING** > HAIN
**HAININGS** > HAIN
**HAINS** > HAIN
**HAINT** *same as* > HAUNT
**HAINTS** > HAINT
**HAIQUE** *same as* > HAIK
**HAIQUES** > HAIK
**HAIR** *n* threadlike growth on the skin ▷ *vb* provide with hair
**HAIRBALL** *n* compact mass of hair that forms in the stomach of cats, calves, etc, as a result of licking and swallowing the fur, and causes vomiting, coughing, bloat, weight loss, and depression
**HAIRBALLS** > HAIRBALL
**HAIRBAND** *n* band worn around head to control hair
**HAIRBANDS** > HAIRBAND
**HAIRBELL** *same as* > HAREBELL
**HAIRBELLS** > HAIRBELL
**HAIRBRUSH** *n* brush for grooming the hair
**HAIRCAP** *n* type of moss
**HAIRCAPS** > HAIRCAP
**HAIRCLOTH** *n* cloth woven from horsehair, used in upholstery
**HAIRCUT** *n* act or an instance of cutting the hair
**HAIRCUTS** > HAIRCUT
**HAIRDO** *n* hairstyle
**HAIRDOS** > HAIRDO
**HAIRDRIER** *same as* > HAIRDRYER
**HAIRDRYER** *n* hand-held electric device that blows out hot air and is used to dry and, sometimes, assist in styling the hair, as in blow-drying
**HAIRED** *adj* with hair
**HAIRGRIP** *n* small bent clasp used to fasten the hair
**HAIRGRIPS** > HAIRGRIP
**HAIRIER** > HAIRY
**HAIRIEST** > HAIRY
**HAIRIF** *another name for* > CLEAVERS
**HAIRIFS** > HAIRIF
**HAIRINESS** > HAIRY
**HAIRING** > HAIR
**HAIRLESS** *adj* having little or no hair
**HAIRLIKE** > HAIR
**HAIRLINE** *n* edge of hair at the top of the forehead ▷ *adj* very fine or narrow
**HAIRLINES** > HAIRLINE
**HAIRLOCK** *n* lock of hair
**HAIRLOCKS** > HAIRLOCK
**HAIRNET** *n* any of several

kinds of light netting worn over the hair to keep it in place
**HAIRNETS** > HAIRNET
**HAIRPIECE** *n* section of false hair added to a person's real hair
**HAIRPIN** *n* U-shaped wire used to hold the hair in place
**HAIRPINS** > HAIRPIN
**HAIRS** > HAIR
**HAIRSPRAY** *n* fixative solution sprayed onto the hair to keep a hairstyle in shape
**HAIRST** *Scots form of* > HARVEST
**HAIRSTED** > HAIRST
**HAIRSTING** > HAIRST
**HAIRSTS** > HAIRST
**HAIRSTYLE** *n* cut and arrangement of a person's hair
**HAIRTAIL** *n* any of various marine spiny-finned fish having a long whiplike scaleless body and long sharp teeth
**HAIRTAILS** > HAIRTAIL
**HAIRWORK** *n* thing made from hair
**HAIRWORKS** > HAIRWORK
**HAIRWORM** *n* any of various hairlike nematode worms
**HAIRWORMS** > HAIRWORM
**HAIRY** *adj* covered with hair
**HAIRYBACK** *n* offensive word for an Afrikaner
**HAITH** *interj* Scots oath
**HAJ** *same as* > HADJ
**HAJES** > HAJ
**HAJI** *same as* > HAJJI
**HAJIS** > HAJI
**HAJJ** *n* pilgrimage a Muslim makes to Mecca
**HAJJAH** *n* Muslim woman who has made a pilgrimage to Mecca
**HAJJAHS** > HAJJAH
**HAJJES** > HAJJ
**HAJJI** *n* Muslim who has made a pilgrimage to Mecca
**HAJJIS** > HAJJI
**HAKA** *n* ceremonial Māori dance with chanting
**HAKAM** *n* text written by a rabbi
**HAKAMS** > HAKAM
**HAKARI** *n* Māori ritual feast
**HAKAS** > HAKA
**HAKE** *n* edible sea fish of N hemisphere
**HAKEA** *n* Australian tree or shrub with hard woody fruit
**HAKEAS** > HAKEA
**HAKEEM** *same as* > HAKIM
**HAKEEMS** > HAKEEM
**HAKES** > HAKE
**HAKIM** *n* Muslim judge, ruler, or administrator

**HAKIMS** > HAKIM
**HAKU** *in New Zealand English, same as* > KINGFISH
**HAKUS** > HAKU
**HALACHA** *n* Jewish religious law
**HALACHAS** > HALACHA
**HALACHIC** > HALACHA
**HALACHIST** > HALACHA
**HALACHOT** > HALACHA
**HALACHOTH** > HALACHA
**HALAKAH** *same as* > HALACHA
**HALAKAHS** > HALAKAH
**HALAKHA** *same as* > HALACHA
**HALAKHAH** *same as* > HALACHA
**HALAKHAHS** > HALAKHAH
**HALAKHAS** > HALAKHA
**HALAKHIC** > HALAKHAH
**HALAKHIST** > HALAKHAH
**HALAKHOT** > HALAKHA
**HALAKHOTH** > HALAKHA
**HALAKIC** > HALAKHA
**HALAKIST** > HALAKHA
**HALAKISTS** > HALAKHA
**HALAKOTH** > HALAKHA
**HALAL** *n* meat from animals slaughtered according to Muslim law ▷ *adj* of or relating to such meat ▷ *vb* kill (animals) in this way
**HALALA** *n* money unit in Saudi Arabia
**HALALAH** *same as* > HALALA
**HALALAHS** > HALALAH
**HALALAS** > HALALA
**HALALLED** > HALAL
**HALALLING** > HALAL
**HALALS** > HALAL
**HALATION** *n* fogging usually seen as a bright ring surrounding a source of light: caused by reflection from the back of the film
**HALATIONS** > HALATION
**HALAVAH** *same as* > HALVAH
**HALAVAHS** > HALAVAH
**HALAZONE** *n* type of disinfectant
**HALAZONES** > HALAZONE
**HALBERD** *n* spear with an axe blade
**HALBERDS** > HALBERD
**HALBERT** *same as* > HALBERD
**HALBERTS** > HALBERT
**HALCYON** *adj* peaceful and happy ▷ *n* (in Greek mythology) fabulous bird associated with the winter solstice
**HALCYONIC** *adj* peaceful and happy
**HALCYONS** > HALCYON
**HALE** *adj* healthy, robust ▷ *vb* pull or drag
**HALED** > HALE
**HALENESS** > HALE
**HALER** *same as* > HELLER
**HALERS** > HALER
**HALERU** > HALER
**HALES** > HALE
**HALEST** > HALE
**HALF** *n* either of two equal

parts ▷ *adj* denoting one of two equal parts ▷ *adv* to the extent of half
**HALFA** *n* African grass
**HALFAS** > HALFA
**HALFBACK** *n* player positioned immediately behind the forwards
**HALFBACKS** > HALFBACK
**HALFBEAK** *n* type of fish with an elongated body, a short upper jaw, and a long protruding lower jaw
**HALFBEAKS** > HALFBEAK
**HALFEN** > HALF
**HALFLIFE** *n* time taken for half of the atoms in a radioactive material to undergo decay
**HALFLIN** *same as* > HALFLING
**HALFLING** *n* person only half-grown
**HALFLINGS** > HALFLING
**HALFLINS** > HALFLIN
**HALFLIVES** > HALFLIFE
**HALFNESS** > HALF
**HALFPACE** *n* landing on staircase
**HALFPACES** > HALFPACE
**HALFPENCE** > HALFPENNY
**HALFPENNY** *n* former British coin worth half an old penny
**HALFPIPE** *n* U-shaped object used in skateboarding stunts
**HALFPIPES** > HALFPIPE
**HALFS** > HALF
**HALFTIME** *n* rest period between the two halves of a game
**HALFTIMES** > HALFTIME
**HALFTONE** *n* illustration showing lights and shadows by means of very small dots ▷ *adj* relating to, used in, or made by halftone
**HALFTONES** > HALFTONE
**HALFTRACK** *n* vehicle with caterpillar tracks and wheels
**HALFWAY** *adj* at or to half the distance
**HALFWIT** *n* foolish or stupid person
**HALFWITS** > HALFWIT
**HALIBUT** *n* large edible flatfish of N Atlantic
**HALIBUTS** > HALIBUT
**HALICORE** *n* dugong
**HALICORES** > HALICORE
**HALID** *same as* > HALIDE
**HALIDE** *n* binary compound containing a halogen atom or ion in combination with a more electropositive element
**HALIDES** > HALIDE
**HALIDOM** *n* holy place or thing
**HALIDOME** *same as* > HALIDOM

**HALIDOMES** > HALIDOME
**HALIDOMS** > HALIDOM
**HALIDS** > HALID
**HALIEUTIC** *adj* of fishing
**HALIMOT** *n* court held by lord
**HALIMOTE** *same as* > HALIMOT
**HALIMOTES** > HALIMOTE
**HALIMOTS** > HALIMOT
**HALING** > HALE
**HALIOTIS** *n* type of shellfish
**HALITE** *n* colourless or white mineral sometimes tinted by impurities, found in beds as an evaporite
**HALITES** > HALITE
**HALITOSES** > HALITOSIS
**HALITOSIS** *n* unpleasant-smelling breath
**HALITOTIC** > HALITUS
**HALITOUS** > HALITUS
**HALITUS** *n* vapour
**HALITUSES** > HALITUS
**HALL** *n* entrance passage
**HALLAH** *variant spelling of* > CHALLAH
**HALLAHS** > HALLAH
**HALLAL** *same as* > HALAL
**HALLALI** *n* bugle call
**HALLALIS** > HALLALI
**HALLALLED** > HALLAL
**HALLALOO** *same as* > HALLOO
**HALLALOOS** > HALLALOO
**HALLALS** > HALLAL
**HALLAN** *n* partition in cottage
**HALLANS** > HALLAN
**HALLEL** *n* (in Judaism) section of the liturgy consisting of Psalms 113–18, read during the morning service on festivals, Chanukah, and Rosh Chodesh
**HALLELS** > HALLEL
**HALLIAN** *same as* > HALLION
**HALLIANS** > HALLIAN
**HALLIARD** *same as* > HALYARD
**HALLIARDS** > HALLIARD
**HALLING** *n* Norwegian country dance
**HALLINGS** > HALLING
**HALLION** *n* lout
**HALLIONS** > HALLION
**HALLMARK** *n* typical feature ▷ *vb* stamp with a hallmark
**HALLMARKS** > HALLMARK
**HALLO** *same as* > HALLOO
**HALLOA** *same as* > HALLOO
**HALLOAED** > HALLOA
**HALLOAING** > HALLOA
**HALLOAS** > HALLOA
**HALLOED** > HALLO
**HALLOES** > HALLO
**HALLOING** > HALLO
**HALLOO** *interj* shout used to call hounds at a hunt ▷ *sentence substitute* shout to attract attention, esp

to call hounds at a hunt ▷ *n* shout of "halloo" ▷ *vb* shout (something) to (someone)
**HALLOOED** > HALLOO
**HALLOOING** > HALLOO
**HALLOOS** > HALLOO
**HALLOS** > HALLO
**HALLOT** > HALLAH
**HALLOTH** *same as* > CHALLAH
**HALLOUMI** *n* salty white sheep's cheese from Greece or Turkey, usually eaten grilled
**HALLOUMIS** > HALLOUMI
**HALLOW** *vb* consecrate or set apart as being holy
**HALLOWED** *adj* regarded as holy
**HALLOWER** > HALLOW
**HALLOWERS** > HALLOW
**HALLOWING** > HALLOW
**HALLOWS** > HALLOW
**HALLS** > HALL
**HALLSTAND** *n* piece of furniture on which are hung coats, hats, etc
**HALLUCAL** > HALLUX
**HALLUCES** > HALLUX
**HALLUX** *n* first digit on the hind foot of a mammal, bird, reptile, or amphibian
**HALLWAY** *n* entrance area
**HALLWAYS** > HALLWAY
**HALLYON** *same as* > HALLION
**HALLYONS** > HALLYON
**HALM** *same as* > HAULM
**HALMA** *n* board game in which players attempt to transfer their pieces from their own to their opponents' bases
**HALMAS** > HALMA
**HALMS** > HALM
**HALO** *n* ring of light round the head of a sacred figure ▷ *vb* surround with a halo
**HALOBIONT** *n* plant or animal that lives in a salty environment such as the sea
**HALOCLINE** *n* gradient in salinity of sea
**HALOED** > HALO
**HALOES** > HALO
**HALOGEN** *n* any of a group of nonmetallic elements including chlorine and iodine
**HALOGENS** > HALOGEN
**HALOGETON** *n* herbaceous plant
**HALOID** *adj* resembling or derived from a halogen ▷ *n* compound containing halogen atoms in its molecules
**HALOIDS** > HALOID
**HALOING** > HALO
**HALOLIKE** > HALO
**HALON** *n* any of a class of chemical compounds derived from hydrocarbons by replacing one or more

hydrogen atoms by bromine atoms and other hydrogen atoms by other halogen atoms (chlorine, fluorine, or iodine). Halons are stable compounds that are used in fire extinguishers, although they may contribute to depletion of the ozone layer
**HALONS** > HALON
**HALOPHILE** *n* organism that thrives in an extremely salty environment, such as the Dead Sea
**HALOPHILY** *n* ability to live in salty environment
**HALOPHOBE** *n* plant unable to live in salty soil
**HALOPHYTE** *n* plant that grows in very salty soil, as in a salt marsh
**HALOS** > HALO
**HALOSERE** *n* plant community that originates and develops in conditions of high salinity
**HALOSERES** > HALOSERE
**HALOTHANE** *n* colourless volatile slightly soluble liquid with an odour resembling that of chloroform
**HALOUMI** *same as* > HALLOUMI
**HALOUMIS** > HALOUMI
**HALSE** *vb* embrace
**HALSED** > HALSE
**HALSER** > HALSE
**HALSERS** > HALSE
**HALSES** > HALSE
**HALSING** > HALSE
**HALT** *vb* come or bring to a stop ▷ *n* temporary stop ▷ *adj* lame
**HALTED** > HALT
**HALTER** *n* strap round a horse's head with a rope to lead it with ▷ *vb* put a halter on (a horse)
**HALTERE** *n* one of a pair of short projections in dipterous insects that are modified hind wings, used for maintaining equilibrium during flight
**HALTERED** > HALTER
**HALTERES** > HALTERE
**HALTERING** > HALTER
**HALTERS** > HALTER
**HALTING** > HALT
**HALTINGLY** > HALT
**HALTINGS** > HALT
**HALTLESS** > HALT
**HALTS** > HALT
**HALUTZ** *variant spelling of* > CHALUTZ
**HALUTZIM** > HALUTZ
**HALVA** *same as* > HALVAH
**HALVAH** *n* Eastern Mediterranean, Middle Eastern, or Indian

sweetmeat made of honey and containing sesame seeds, nuts, rose water, saffron, etc
**HALVAHS** > HALVAH
**HALVAS** > HALVA
**HALVE** *vb* divide in half
**HALVED** > HALVE
**HALVER** > HALVE
**HALVERS** > HALVE
**HALVES** > HALVE
**HALVING** > HALVE
**HALYARD** *n* rope for raising a ship's sail or flag
**HALYARDS** > HALYARD
**HAM** *n* smoked or salted meat from a pig's thigh ▷ *vb* overact
**HAMADA** *n* rocky plateau in desert
**HAMADAS** > HAMADA
**HAMADRYAD** *n* one of a class of nymphs, each of which inhabits a tree and dies with it
**HAMADRYAS** *n* type of baboon
**HAMAL** *n* (in Middle Eastern countries) a porter, bearer, or servant
**HAMALS** > HAMAL
**HAMAMELIS** *n* any of several trees or shrubs native to E Asia and North America and cultivated as ornamentals
**HAMARTIA** *n* flaw in character which leads to the downfall of the protagonist in a tragedy
**HAMARTIAS** > HAMARTIA
**HAMATE** *adj* hook-shaped ▷ *n* small bone in the wrist
**HAMATES** > HAMATE
**HAMAUL** *same as* > HAMAL
**HAMAULS** > HAMAUL
**HAMBA** *interj* usually offensive term for go away
**HAMBLE** *vb* mutilate
**HAMBLED** > HAMBLE
**HAMBLES** > HAMBLE
**HAMBLING** > HAMBLE
**HAMBONE** *vb* strike body to provide percussion
**HAMBONED** > HAMBONE
**HAMBONES** > HAMBONE
**HAMBONING** *same as* > HAMBONE
**HAMBURG** *same as* > HAMBURGER
**HAMBURGER** *n* minced beef shaped into a flat disc, cooked and usually served in a bread roll
**HAMBURGS** > HAMBURG
**HAME** *n* either of the two curved bars holding the traces of the harness, attached to the collar of a draught animal
**HAMED** > HAME
**HAMES** > HAME
**HAMEWITH** *adv* Scots word meaning homewards
**HAMFATTER** *n* inferior actor

or musician

**HAMING** > HAME

**HAMLET** n small village

**HAMLETS** > HAMLET

**HAMMADA** same as > HAMADA

**HAMMADAS** > HAMMADA

**HAMMAL** same as > HAMAL

**HAMMALS** > HAMMAL

**HAMMAM** n bathing establishment, such as a Turkish bath

**HAMMAMS** > HAMMAM

**HAMMED** > HAM

**HAMMER** n tool with a heavy metal head and a wooden handle, used to drive in nails etc ▷ vb hit (as if) with a hammer

**HAMMERED** > HAMMER

**HAMMERER** > HAMMER

**HAMMERERS** > HAMMER

**HAMMERING** > HAMMER

**HAMMERKOP** n shark with hammer-shaped head

**HAMMERMAN** n person working with hammer

**HAMMERMEN** > HAMMERMAN

**HAMMERS** > HAMMER

**HAMMERTOE** n condition in which the toe is permanently bent at the joint

**HAMMIER** > HAMMY

**HAMMIEST** > HAMMY

**HAMMILY** > HAMMY

**HAMMINESS** > HAMMY

**HAMMING** > HAM

**HAMMOCK** same as > HUMMOCK

**HAMMOCKS** > HAMMOCK

**HAMMY** adj (of an actor) overacting or tending to overact

**HAMOSE** adj shaped like hook

**HAMOUS** same as > HAMOSE

**HAMPER** vb make it difficult for (someone or something) to move or progress ▷ n large basket with a lid

**HAMPERED** > HAMPER

**HAMPERER** > HAMPER

**HAMPERERS** > HAMPER

**HAMPERING** > HAMPER

**HAMPERS** > HAMPER

**HAMPSTER** same as > HAMSTER

**HAMPSTERS** > HAMPSTER

**HAMS** > HAM

**HAMSTER** n small rodent with a short tail and cheek pouches

**HAMSTERS** > HAMSTER

**HAMSTRING** n tendon at the back of the knee ▷ vb make it difficult for (someone) to take any action

**HAMSTRUNG** > HAMSTRING

**HAMULAR** > HAMULUS

**HAMULATE** > HAMULUS

**HAMULI** > HAMULUS

**HAMULOSE** > HAMULUS

**HAMULOUS** > HAMULUS

**HAMULUS** n hook or hooklike process at the end of some bones or between the fore and hind wings of a bee or similar insect

**HAMZA** n sign used in Arabic to represent the glottal stop

**HAMZAH** same as > HAMZA

**HAMZAHS** > HAMZAH

**HAMZAS** > HAMZA

**HAN** archaic inflected form of > HAVE

**HANAP** n medieval drinking cup

**HANAPER** n small wickerwork basket, often used to hold official papers

**HANAPERS** > HANAPER

**HANAPS** > HANAP

**HANCE** same as > HAUNCH

**HANCES** > HANCE

**HANCH** vb try to bite

**HANCHED** > HANCH

**HANCHES** > HANCH

**HANCHING** > HANCH

**HAND** n part of the body at the end of the arm, consisting of a palm, four fingers, and a thumb ▷ vb pass, give

**HANDAX** n small axe held in one hand

**HANDAXES** > HANDAX

**HANDBAG** n woman's small bag for carrying personal articles in

**HANDBAGS** pl n incident in which people, esp sportsmen, fight or threaten to fight, but without real intent to inflict harm

**HANDBALL** n game in which two teams of seven players try to throw a ball into their opponent's goal ▷ vb pass (the ball) with a blow of the fist

**HANDBALLS** > HANDBALL

**HANDBELL** n bell rung by hand, esp one of a tuned set used in musical performance

**HANDBELLS** > HANDBELL

**HANDBILL** n small printed notice

**HANDBILLS** > HANDBILL

**HANDBLOWN** adj (of glass) made by hand

**HANDBOOK** n small reference or instruction book

**HANDBOOKS** > HANDBOOK

**HANDBRAKE** n brake in a motor vehicle operated by a hand lever

**HANDCAR** n small railway vehicle propelled by hand-pumped mechanism

**HANDCARS** > HANDCAR

**HANDCART** n simple cart

pushed or pulled by hand, used for transporting goods

**HANDCARTS** > HANDCART

**HANDCLAP** n act of clapping hands

**HANDCLAPS** > HANDCLAP

**HANDCLASP** another word for > HANDSHAKE

**HANDCRAFT** same as > HANDICRAFT

**HANDCUFF** n one of a linked pair of metal rings designed to be locked round a prisoner's wrists by the police ▷ vb put handcuffs on

**HANDCUFFS** > HANDCUFF

**HANDED** > HAND

**HANDER** > HAND

**HANDERS** > HAND

**HANDFAST** n agreement, esp of marriage, confirmed by a handshake ▷ vb betroth or marry (two persons or another person) by joining the hands

**HANDFASTS** > HANDFAST

**HANDFED** > HANDFEED

**HANDFEED** vb feed (a person or an animal) by hand

**HANDFEEDS** > HANDFEED

**HANDFUL** n amount that can be held in the hand

**HANDFULS** > HANDFUL

**HANDGRIP** n covering, usually of towelling or rubber, that makes the handle of a racket or club easier to hold

**HANDGRIPS** > HANDGRIP

**HANDGUN** n firearm that can be held, carried, and fired with one hand, such as a pistol

**HANDGUNS** > HANDGUN

**HANDHELD** adj held in position by the hand ▷ n computer that can be held in the hand

**HANDHELDS** > HANDHELD

**HANDHOLD** n object, crevice, etc, that can be used as a grip or support, as in climbing

**HANDHOLDS** > HANDHOLD

**HANDICAP** n physical or mental disability ▷ vb make it difficult for (someone) to do something

**HANDICAPS** > HANDICAP

**HANDIER** > HANDY

**HANDIEST** > HANDY

**HANDILY** adv in a handy way or manner

**HANDINESS** > HANDY

**HANDING** > HAND

**HANDISM** n discrimination against people on the grounds of whether they are left-handed or right-handed

**HANDISMS** > HANDISM

**HANDIWORK** n result of someone's work or activity

**HANDJAR** n Persian dagger

**HANDJARS** > HANDJAR

**HANDLE** n part of an object that is held so that it can be used ▷ vb hold, feel, or move with the hands

**HANDLEBAR** as in handlebar moustache: bushy extended moustache with curled ends that resembles the handlebars of a bicycle

**HANDLED** > HANDLE

**HANDLER** n person who controls an animal

**HANDLERS** > HANDLER

**HANDLES** > HANDLE

**HANDLESS** > HAND

**HANDLIKE** > HAND

**HANDLING** n act or an instance of picking up, turning over, or touching something

**HANDLINGS** > HANDLING

**HANDLIST** n rough list

**HANDLISTS** > HANDLIST

**HANDLOOM** n weaving device operated by hand

**HANDLOOMS** > HANDLOOM

**HANDMADE** adj made by hand, not by machine

**HANDMAID** n person or thing that serves as a useful but subordinate purpose

**HANDMAIDS** > HANDMAID

**HANDOFF** n (in rugby) act of warding off an opposing player with the open hand

**HANDOFFS** > HANDOFF

**HANDOUT** n clothing, food, or money given to a needy person

**HANDOUTS** > HANDOUT

**HANDOVER** n transfer or surrender

**HANDOVERS** > HANDOVER

**HANDPHONE** n in SE Asian English, mobile phone

**HANDPICK** vb choose or select with great care, as for a special job or purpose

**HANDPICKS** > HANDPICK

**HANDPLAY** n fighting with fists

**HANDPLAYS** > HANDPLAY

**HANDPRESS** n printing press operated by hand

**HANDPRINT** n print of hand

**HANDRAIL** n rail alongside a stairway, to provide support

**HANDRAILS** > HANDRAIL

**HANDROLL** n large dried-seaweed cone filled with cold rice and other ingredients

**HANDROLLS** > HANDROLL

**HANDS** > HAND

**HANDSAW** n any saw for use in one hand only

**HANDSAWS** > HANDSAW

**HANDSEL** n gift for good

luck at the beginning of a new year, new venture, etc ▷ vb give a handsel to (a person)
**HANDSELED** > HANDSEL
**HANDSELS** > HANDSEL
**HANDSET** n telephone mouthpiece and earpiece in a single unit
**HANDSETS** > HANDSET
**HANDSEWN** adj sewn by hand
**HANDSFUL** > HANDFUL
**HANDSHAKE** n act of grasping and shaking a person's hand, such as in greeting or when agreeing on a deal
**HANDSOME** adj (esp of a man) good-looking ▷ n term of endearment for a beloved person
**HANDSOMER** > HANDSOME
**HANDSPIKE** n bar or length of pipe used as a lever
**HANDSTAFF** n staff held in hand
**HANDSTAMP** vb stamp by hand
**HANDSTAND** n act of supporting the body on the hands in an upside-down position
**HANDSTURN** n slightest amount of work
**HANDTOWEL** n towel for drying hands
**HANDWHEEL** n wheel operated by hand
**HANDWORK** n work done by hand rather than by machine
**HANDWORKS** > HANDWORK
**HANDWOVEN** adj woven by hand
**HANDWRIT** > HANDWRITE
**HANDWRITE** vb write by hand
**HANDWROTE** > HANDWRITE
**HANDY** adj convenient, useful
**HANDYMAN** n man who is good at making or repairing things
**HANDYMEN** > HANDYMAN
**HANDYWORK** same as > HANDIWORK
**HANEPOOT** n variety of muscat grape
**HANEPOOTS** > HANEPOOT
**HANG** vb attach or be attached at the top with the lower part free
**HANGABLE** adj suitable for hanging
**HANGAR** n large shed for storing aircraft ▷ vb put in a hangar
**HANGARED** > HANGAR
**HANGARING** > HANGAR
**HANGARS** > HANGAR
**HANGBIRD** n any bird, esp the Baltimore oriole, that builds a hanging nest

**HANGBIRDS** > HANGBIRD
**HANGDOG** adj guilty, ashamed ▷ n furtive or sneaky person
**HANGDOGS** > HANGDOG
**HANGED** > HANG
**HANGER** n curved piece of wood, wire, or plastic, with a hook, for hanging up clothes
**HANGERS** > HANGER
**HANGFIRE** n failure to fire
**HANGFIRES** > HANGFIRE
**HANGI** n Māori oven consisting of a hole in the ground filled with hot stones
**HANGING** > HANG
**HANGINGS** > HANG
**HANGIS** > HANGI
**HANGMAN** n man who executes people by hanging
**HANGMEN** > HANGMAN
**HANGNAIL** n piece of skin partly torn away from the base or side of a fingernail
**HANGNAILS** > HANGNAIL
**HANGNEST** same as > HANGBIRD
**HANGNESTS** > HANGNEST
**HANGOUT** n place where one lives or that one frequently visits
**HANGOUTS** > HANGOUT
**HANGOVER** n headache and nausea as a result of drinking too much alcohol
**HANGOVERS** > HANGOVER
**HANGS** > HANG
**HANGTAG** n attached label
**HANGTAGS** > HANGTAG
**HANGUL** n Korean language
**HANGUP** n emotional or psychological preoccupation or problem
**HANGUPS** > HANGUP
**HANIWA** n Japanese funeral offering
**HANJAR** same as > HANDJAR
**HANJARS** > HANJAR
**HANK** n coil, esp of yarn ▷ vb attach (a sail) to a stay by hanks
**HANKED** > HANK
**HANKER** vb desire intensely
**HANKERED** > HANKER
**HANKERER** > HANKER
**HANKERERS** > HANKER
**HANKERING** > HANKER
**HANKERS** > HANKER
**HANKIE** same as > HANKY
**HANKIES** > HANKY
**HANKING** > HANK
**HANKS** > HANK
**HANKY** n handkerchief
**HANSA** same as > HANSE
**HANSAS** > HANSA
**HANSE** n medieval guild of merchants
**HANSEATIC** > HANSA
**HANSEL** same as > HANDSEL
**HANSELED** > HANSEL
**HANSELING** > HANSEL

**HANSELLED** > HANSEL
**HANSELS** > HANSEL
**HANSES** > HANSE
**HANSOM** n formerly, a two-wheeled one-horse carriage with a fixed hood
**HANSOMS** > HANSOM
**HANT** same as > HAUNT
**HANTED** > HANT
**HANTING** > HANT
**HANTLE** n good deal
**HANTLES** > HANTLE
**HANTS** > HANT
**HANUKIAH** n candelabrum having nine branches that is lit during the festival of Hanukkah
**HANUKIAHS** > HANUKIAH
**HANUMAN** n type of monkey
**HANUMANS** > HANUMAN
**HAO** n monetary unit of Vietnam, worth one tenth of a đông
**HAOLE** n Hawaiian word for white person
**HAOLES** > HAOLE
**HAOMA** n type of ritual drink
**HAOMAS** > HAOMA
**HAP** n luck ▷ vb cover up
**HAPAX** n word that only appears in once in a work of literature, or in a body of work by a particular author
**HAPAXES** > HAPAX
**HAPHAZARD** adj not organized or planned ▷ n chance
**HAPHTARA** same as > HAFTARAH
**HAPHTARAH** same as > HAFTARAH
**HAPHTARAS** > HAPHTARA
**HAPHTAROT** > HAPHTARA
**HAPKIDO** n Korean martial art
**HAPKIDOS** > HAPKIDO
**HAPLESS** adj unlucky
**HAPLESSLY** > HAPLESS
**HAPLITE** variant of > APLITE
**HAPLITES** > HAPLITE
**HAPLITIC** > HAPLITE
**HAPLOID** adj denoting a cell or organism with unpaired chromosomes ▷ n haploid cell or organism
**HAPLOIDIC** adj denoting a cell or organism with unpaired chromosomes
**HAPLOIDS** > HAPLOID
**HAPLOIDY** > HAPLOID
**HAPLOLOGY** n omission of a repeated occurrence of a sound or syllable in fluent speech
**HAPLONT** n organism, esp a plant, that has the haploid number of chromosomes in its somatic cells
**HAPLONTIC** > HAPLONT
**HAPLONTS** > HAPLONT
**HAPLOPIA** n normal single vision
**HAPLOPIAS** > HAPLOPIA

**HAPLOSES** > HAPLOSIS
**HAPLOSIS** n production of a haploid number of chromosomes during meiosis
**HAPLOTYPE** n collection of genetic markers usually inherited together
**HAPLY** archaic word for > PERHAPS
**HAPPED** > HAP
**HAPPEN** vb take place, occur
**HAPPENED** > HAPPEN
**HAPPENING** n event, occurrence ▷ adj fashionable and up-to-the-minute
**HAPPENS** > HAPPEN
**HAPPIED** > HAPPY
**HAPPIER** > HAPPY
**HAPPIES** > HAPPY
**HAPPIEST** > HAPPY
**HAPPILY** > HAPPY
**HAPPINESS** > HAPPY
**HAPPING** > HAP
**HAPPY** adj feeling or causing joy ▷ vb make happy
**HAPPYING** > HAPPY
**HAPS** > HAP
**HAPTEN** n incomplete antigen that can stimulate antibody production only when it is chemically combined with a particular protein
**HAPTENE** same as > HAPTEN
**HAPTENES** > HAPTENE
**HAPTENIC** > HAPTENE
**HAPTENS** > HAPTEN
**HAPTERON** n cell or group of cells that occurs in certain plants, esp seaweeds, and attaches the plant to its substratum
**HAPTERONS** > HAPTERON
**HAPTIC** adj relating to or based on the sense of touch
**HAPTICAL** same as > HAPTIC
**HAPTICS** n science of sense of touch
**HAPU** n subtribe
**HAPUKA** another name for > GROPER
**HAPUKAS** > HAPUKA
**HAPUKU** same as > HAPUKA
**HAPUKUS** > HAPUKU
**HAPUS** > HAPU
**HAQUETON** same as > HACQUETON
**HAQUETONS** > HAQUETON
**HARAKEKE** in New Zealand English, another name for > FLAX
**HARAKEKES** > HARAKEKE
**HARAM** n anything that is forbidden by Islamic law
**HARAMBEE** n work chant used on the E African coast ▷ interj cry of harambee
**HARAMBEES** > HARAMBEE
**HARAMDA** same as > HARAMZADA

HARAMDAS > HARAMDA
HARAMDI same
as > HARAMZADI
HARAMDIS > HARAMDI
HARAMS > HARAM
HARAMZADA n in Indian
English, slang word for an
illegitimate male
HARAMZADI n in Indian
English, slang word for an
illegitimate female
HARANGUE vb address
angrily or forcefully ▷ n
angry or forceful speech
HARANGUED > HARANGUE
HARANGUER > HARANGUE
HARANGUES > HARANGUE
HARASS vb annoy or trouble
constantly
HARASSED > HARASS
HARASSER > HARASS
HARASSERS > HARASS
HARASSES > HARASS
HARASSING > HARASS
HARBINGER n someone
or something that
announces the approach
of something ▷ vb
announce the approach or
arrival of
HARBOR same as > HARBOUR
HARBORAGE same
as > HARBOURAGE
HARBORED > HARBOR
HARBORER > HARBOR
HARBORERS > HARBOR
HARBORFUL n amount a
harbour can hold
HARBORING > HARBOR
HARBOROUS adj hospitable
HARBORS > HARBOR
HARBOUR n sheltered port
▷ vb maintain secretly in
the mind
HARBOURED > HARBOUR
HARBOURER > HARBOUR
HARBOURS > HARBOUR
HARD adj firm, solid, or rigid
▷ adv with great energy
or effort
HARDASS n tough person
HARDASSES > HARDASS
HARDBACK n book with
a stiff cover ▷ adj of or
denoting a hardback
HARDBACKS > HARDBACK
HARDBAG n rigid container
on motorcycle
HARDBAGS > HARDBAG
HARDBAKE n almond toffee
HARDBAKES > HARDBAKE
HARDBALL as in play
hardball act in a ruthless or
uncompromising way
HARDBALLS > HARDBALL
HARDBEAM same
as > HORNBEAM
HARDBEAMS > HARDBEAM
HARDBOARD n thin stiff
board made of compressed
sawdust and wood chips
HARDBOOT n type of skiing
boot
HARDBOOTS > HARDBOOT

HARDBOUND same
as > HARDBACK
HARDCASE n tough person
HARDCORE n style of rock
music with short fast
songs and little melody
HARDCORES > HARDCORE
HARDCOURT adj (of tennis)
played on hard surface
HARDCOVER same
as > HARDBACK
HARDEDGE n style of
painting in which vividly
coloured subjects are
clearly delineated ▷ adj of,
relating to, or denoting
this style of painting
HARDEDGES > HARDEDGE
HARDEN vb make or become
hard ▷ n rough fabric
made from hards
HARDENED adj toughened
by experience
HARDENER n person or
thing that hardens
HARDENERS > HARDENER
HARDENING n act or process
of becoming or making
hard
HARDENS > HARDEN
HARDER > HARD
HARDEST > HARD
HARDFACE n
uncompromising person
HARDFACES > HARDFACE
HARDGOODS same
as > HARDWARE
HARDGRASS n coarse grass
HARDHACK n woody North
American rosaceous plant
with downy leaves and
clusters of small pink or
white flowers
HARDHACKS > HARDHACK
HARDHAT n hat made
of a hard material for
protection, worn esp by
construction workers,
equestrians, etc ▷ adj (in
US English) characteristic
of the presumed
conservative attitudes
and prejudices typified by
construction workers
HARDHATS > HARDHAT
HARDHEAD same
as > HARDHEADS
HARDHEADS n thistle-like
plant
HARDIER > HARDY
HARDIES > HARDY
HARDIEST > HARDY
HARDIHEAD same
as > HARDIHOOD
HARDIHOOD n courage or
daring
HARDILY adv in a hardy
manner
HARDIMENT same
as > HARDIHOOD
HARDINESS n condition
or quality of being hardy,
robust, or bold
HARDISH > HARD

HARDLINE adj
uncompromising
HARDLINER > HARDLINE
HARDLY adv scarcely or not
at all
HARDMAN n tough, ruthless,
or violent man
HARDMEN > HARDMAN
HARDNESS n quality or
condition of being hard
HARDNOSE n tough person
HARDNOSED adj tough,
shrewd, and practical
HARDNOSES > HARDNOSE
HARDOKE n burdock
HARDOKES > HARDOKE
HARDPACK n rigid backpack
HARDPACKS > HARDPACK
HARDPAN n hard
impervious layer of clay
below the soil, resistant to
drainage and root growth
HARDPANS > HARDPAN
HARDPARTS n skeleton
HARDROCK adj (of mining)
concerned with extracting
minerals other than coal,
usually from solid rock ▷ n
tough uncompromising
man
HARDROCKS > HARDROCK
HARDS pl n coarse fibres
and other refuse from flax
and hemp
HARDSET adj in difficulties
HARDSHELL adj having a
shell or carapace that is
thick, heavy, or hard
HARDSHIP n suffering
HARDSHIPS > HARDSHIP
HARDSTAND n hard surface
on which vehicles may be
parked
HARDTACK n kind of hard
saltless biscuit, formerly
eaten by sailors
HARDTACKS > HARDTACK
HARDTOP n car equipped
with a metal or plastic
roof that is sometimes
detachable
HARDTOPS > HARDTOP
HARDWARE n metal tools or
implements
HARDWARES > HARDWARE
HARDWIRE vb instal
permanently in computer
HARDWIRED adj (of a
circuit or instruction)
permanently wired into
a computer, replacing
separate software
HARDWIRES > HARDWIRE
HARDWOOD n wood of a
broad-leaved tree such as
oak or ash
HARDWOODS > HARDWOOD
HARDY adj able to stand
difficult conditions ▷ n
any blacksmith's tool
made with a square shank
so that it can be lodged in a
square hole in an anvil
HARE n animal like a large

rabbit, with longer ears
and legs ▷ vb run (away)
quickly
HAREBELL n bluebell-
shaped flower
HAREBELLS > HAREBELL
HARED > HARE
HAREEM same as > HAREM
HAREEMS > HAREEM
HARELD n long-tailed duck
HARELDS > HARELD
HARELIKE > HARE
HARELIP n slight split in
the upper lip
HARELIPS > HARELIP
HAREM n (apartments of) a
Muslim man's wives and
concubines
HAREMS > HAREM
HARES > HARE
HARESTAIL n species of
cotton grass
HAREWOOD n sycamore
wood that has been
stained for use in furniture
making
HAREWOODS > HAREWOOD
HARIANA n Indian breed of
cattle
HARIANAS > HARIANA
HARICOT n variety of
French bean with light-
coloured edible seeds,
which can be dried and
stored
HARICOTS > HARICOT
HARIGALDS pl n intestines
HARIGALS same
as > HARIGALDS
HARIJAN n member of
an Indian caste once
considered untouchable
HARIJANS > HARIJAN
HARIM same as > HAREM
HARIMS > HARIM
HARING > HARE
HARIOLATE vb practise
divination
HARIRA n Moroccan soup
made from a variety of
vegetables with lentils,
chickpeas, and coriander
HARIRAS > HARIRA
HARISH adj like hare
HARISSA n hot paste
made from chilli peppers,
tomatoes, spices, and
olive oil
HARISSAS > HARISSA
HARK vb listen
HARKED > HARK
HARKEN same as > HEARKEN
HARKENED > HARKEN
HARKENER > HARKEN
HARKENERS > HARKEN
HARKENING > HARKEN
HARKENS > HARKEN
HARKING > HARK
HARKS > HARK
HARL same as > HERL
HARLED > HARL
HARLEQUIN n stock comic
character with a diamond-
patterned costume and

mask ▷ *adj* in many colours

**HARLING** > HARL

**HARLINGS** > HARL

**HARLOT** *n* prostitute ▷ *adj* of or like a harlot

**HARLOTRY** > HARLOT

**HARLOTS** > HARLOT

**HARLS** > HARL

**HARM** *vb* injure physically, mentally, or morally ▷ *n* physical, mental, or moral injury

**HARMALA** *n* African plant

**HARMALAS** > HARMALA

**HARMALIN** *n* chemical derived from harmala

**HARMALINE** *same as* > HARMALIN

**HARMALINS** > HARMALIN

**HARMAN** *n* constable

**HARMANS** > HARMAN

**HARMATTAN** *n* dry dusty wind from the Sahara blowing towards the W African coast, esp from November to March

**HARMDOING** *n* doing of harm

**HARMED** > HARM

**HARMEL** *same as* > HARMALA

**HARMELS** > HARMEL

**HARMER** > HARM

**HARMERS** > HARM

**HARMFUL** *adj* causing or tending to cause harm, esp to a person's health

**HARMFULLY** > HARMFUL

**HARMIN** *same as* > HARMALIN

**HARMINE** *same as* > HARMALIN

**HARMINES** > HARMINE

**HARMING** > HARM

**HARMINS** > HARMIN

**HARMLESS** *adj* safe to use, touch, or be near

**HARMONIC** *adj* of harmony ▷ *n* overtone of a musical note produced when that note is played, but not usually heard as a separate note

**HARMONICA** *n* small wind instrument played by sucking and blowing

**HARMONICS** *n* science of musical sounds

**HARMONIES** > HARMONY

**HARMONISE** *same as* > HARMONIZE

**HARMONIST** *n* person skilled in the art and techniques of harmony

**HARMONIUM** *n* keyboard instrument like a small organ

**HARMONIZE** *vb* sing or play in harmony

**HARMONY** *n* peaceful agreement and cooperation

**HARMOST** *n* Spartan governor

**HARMOSTS** > HARMOST

**HARMOSTY** *n* office of a harmost

**HARMOTOME** *n* mineral of the zeolite group

**HARMS** > HARM

**HARN** *n* coarse linen

**HARNESS** *n* arrangement of straps for attaching a horse to a cart or plough ▷ *vb* put a harness on

**HARNESSED** > HARNESS

**HARNESSER** > HARNESS

**HARNESSES** > HARNESS

**HARNS** > HARN

**HARO** *interj* cry meaning alas

**HAROS** > HARO

**HAROSET** *n* Jewish dish eaten at Passover

**HAROSETH** *same as* > HAROSET

**HAROSETHS** > HAROSETH

**HAROSETS** > HAROSET

**HARP** *n* large triangular stringed instrument played with the fingers ▷ *vb* play the harp

**HARPED** > HARP

**HARPER** > HARP

**HARPERS** > HARP

**HARPIES** > HARPY

**HARPIN** *n* type of protein

**HARPING** > HARP

**HARPINGS** *pl n* wooden members used for strengthening the bow of a vessel

**HARPINS** *same as* > HARPINGS

**HARPIST** > HARP

**HARPISTS** > HARP

**HARPOON** *n* barbed spear attached to a rope used for hunting whales ▷ *vb* spear with a harpoon

**HARPOONED** > HARPOON

**HARPOONER** > HARPOON

**HARPOONS** > HARPOON

**HARPS** > HARP

**HARPY** *n* nasty or bad-tempered woman

**HARPYLIKE** > HARPY

**HARQUEBUS** *variant of* > ARQUEBUS

**HARRIDAN** *n* nagging or vicious woman

**HARRIDANS** > HARRIDAN

**HARRIED** > HARRY

**HARRIER** *n* cross-country runner

**HARRIERS** > HARRIER

**HARRIES** > HARRY

**HARROW** *n* implement used to break up lumps of soil ▷ *vb* draw a harrow over

**HARROWED** > HARROW

**HARROWER** > HARROW

**HARROWERS** > HARROW

**HARROWING** > HARROW

**HARROWS** > HARROW

**HARRUMPH** *vb* clear or make the noise of clearing the throat

**HARRUMPHS** > HARRUMPH

**HARRY** *vb* keep asking (someone) to do something, pester

**HARRYING** > HARRY

**HARSH** *adj* severe and difficult to cope with

**HARSHEN** *vb* make harsh

**HARSHENED** > HARSHEN

**HARSHENS** > HARSHEN

**HARSHER** > HARSH

**HARSHEST** > HARSH

**HARSHLY** > HARSH

**HARSHNESS** > HARSH

**HARSLET** *same as* > HASLET

**HARSLETS** > HARSLET

**HART** *n* adult male deer

**HARTAL** *n* (in India) the act of closing shops or suspending work, esp in political protest

**HARTALS** > HARTAL

**HARTBEES** *same as* > HARTBEEST

**HARTBEEST** *n* African antelope

**HARTELY** *archaic spelling of* > HEARTILY

**HARTEN** *same as* > HEARTEN

**HARTENED** > HARTEN

**HARTENING** > HARTEN

**HARTENS** > HARTEN

**HARTLESSE** *same as* > HEARTLESS

**HARTS** > HART

**HARTSHORN** *n* sal volatile

**HARUMPH** *same as* > HARRUMPH

**HARUMPHED** > HARUMPH

**HARUMPHS** > HARUMPH

**HARUSPEX** *n* (in ancient Rome) a priest who practised divination, esp by examining the entrails of animals

**HARUSPICY** > HARUSPEX

**HARVEST** *n* (season for) the gathering of crops ▷ *vb* gather (a ripened crop)

**HARVESTED** > HARVEST

**HARVESTER** *n* harvesting machine, esp a combine harvester

**HARVESTS** > HARVEST

**HAS** > HAVE

**HASBIAN** *n* former lesbian who has become heterosexual or bisexual

**HASBIANS** > HASBIAN

**HASH** *n* dish of diced cooked meat and vegetables reheated ▷ *vb* chop into small pieces

**HASHED** > HASH

**HASHEESH** *same as* > HASHISH

**HASHES** > HASH

**HASHHEAD** *n* regular marijuana user

**HASHHEADS** > HASHHEAD

**HASHIER** > HASH

**HASHIEST** > HASH

**HASHING** > HASH

**HASHISH** *n* drug made

from the cannabis plant, smoked for its intoxicating effects

**HASHISHES** > HASHISH

**HASHMARK** *n* character (#)

**HASHMARKS** > HASHMARK

**HASHY** > HASH

**HASK** *n* archaic name for a basket for transporting fish

**HASKS** > HASK

**HASLET** *n* loaf of cooked minced pig's offal, eaten cold

**HASLETS** > HASLET

**HASP** *n* clasp that fits over a staple and is secured by a bolt or padlock, used as a fastening ▷ *vb* secure (a door, window, etc) with a hasp

**HASPED** > HASP

**HASPING** > HASP

**HASPS** > HASP

**HASSAR** *n* South American catfish

**HASSARS** > HASSAR

**HASSEL** *variant of* > HASSLE

**HASSELS** > HASSEL

**HASSIUM** *n* element synthetically produced in small quantities by high-energy ion bombardment

**HASSIUMS** > HASSIUM

**HASSLE** *n* trouble, bother ▷ *vb* bother or annoy

**HASSLED** > HASSLE

**HASSLES** > HASSLE

**HASSLING** > HASSLE

**HASSOCK** *n* cushion for kneeling on in church

**HASSOCKS** > HASSOCK

**HASSOCKY** > HASSOCK

**HAST** *singular form of the present tense (indicative mood) of* > HAVE

**HASTA** *Spanish for* > UNTIL

**HASTATE** *adj* (of a leaf) having a pointed tip and two outward-pointing lobes at the base

**HASTATED** *same as* > HASTATE

**HASTATELY** > HASTATE

**HASTE** *n* (excessive) quickness ▷ *vb* hasten

**HASTED** > HASTE

**HASTEFUL** > HASTE

**HASTEN** *vb* (cause to) hurry

**HASTENED** > HASTEN

**HASTENER** > HASTEN

**HASTENERS** > HASTEN

**HASTENING** > HASTEN

**HASTENS** > HASTEN

**HASTES** > HASTE

**HASTIER** > HASTY

**HASTIEST** > HASTY

**HASTILY** > HASTY

**HASTINESS** > HASTY

**HASTING** > HASTE

**HASTINGS** > HASTE

**HASTY** *adj* (too) quick

**HAT** *n* covering for the head, often with a brim

▷ *vb* supply (a person) with a hat or put a hat on (someone)

**HATABLE** > HATE

**HATBAND** *n* band or ribbon around the base of the crown of a hat

**HATBANDS** > HATBAND

**HATBOX** *n* box or case for a hat or hats

**HATBOXES** > HATBOX

**HATBRUSH** *n* brush for hats

**HATCH** *vb* (cause to) emerge from an egg ▷ *n* hinged door covering an opening in a floor or wall

**HATCHABLE** > HATCH

**HATCHBACK** *n* car with a lifting door at the back

**HATCHECK** *n* cloakroom

**HATCHECKS** > HATCHECK

**HATCHED** > HATCH

**HATCHEL** *same as* > HECKLE

**HATCHELED** > HATCHEL

**HATCHELS** > HATCHEL

**HATCHER** > HATCH

**HATCHERS** > HATCH

**HATCHERY** *n* place where eggs are hatched under artificial conditions

**HATCHES** > HATCH

**HATCHET** *n* small axe

**HATCHETS** > HATCHET

**HATCHETY** *adj* like a hatchet

**HATCHING** > HATCH

**HATCHINGS** > HATCH

**HATCHLING** *n* young animal that has newly hatched from an egg

**HATCHMENT** *n* diamond-shaped tablet displaying the coat of arms of a dead person

**HATCHWAY** *n* opening in the deck of a ship

**HATCHWAYS** > HATCHWAY

**HATE** *vb* dislike intensely ▷ *n* intense dislike

**HATEABLE** > HATE

**HATED** > HATE

**HATEFUL** *adj* causing or deserving hate

**HATEFULLY** > HATEFUL

**HATELESS** > HATE

**HATER** > HATE

**HATERENT** *same as* > HATRED

**HATERENTS** > HATERENT

**HATERS** > HATE

**HATES** > HATE

**HATFUL** *n* amount a hat will hold

**HATFULS** > HATFUL

**HATGUARD** *n* string to keep a hat from blowing off

**HATGUARDS** > HATGUARD

**HATH** *form of the present tense (indicative mood) of* > HAVE

**HATHA** *as in* hatha yoga form of yoga

**HATING** > HATE

**HATLESS** > HAT

**HATLIKE** > HAT

**HATMAKER** *n* maker of hats

**HATMAKERS** > HATMAKER

**HATPEG** *n* peg to hang hat on

**HATPEGS** > HATPEG

**HATPIN** *n* sturdy pin used to secure a woman's hat to her hair, often having a decorative head

**HATPINS** > HATPIN

**HATRACK** *n* rack for hanging hats on

**HATRACKS** > HATRACK

**HATRED** *n* intense dislike

**HATREDS** > HATRED

**HATS** > HAT

**HATSFUL** > HATFUL

**HATSTAND** *n* frame or pole equipped with hooks or arms for hanging up hats, coats, etc

**HATSTANDS** > HATSTAND

**HATTED** > HAT

**HATTER** *n* person who makes and sells hats ▷ *vb* annoy

**HATTERED** > HATTER

**HATTERIA** *n* species of reptile

**HATTERIAS** > HATTERIA

**HATTERING** > HATTER

**HATTERS** > HATTER

**HATTING** > HAT

**HATTINGS** > HAT

**HATTOCK** *n* small hat

**HATTOCKS** > HATTOCK

**HAUBERK** *n* long sleeveless coat of mail

**HAUBERKS** > HAUBERK

**HAUBOIS** *same as* > HAUTBOY

**HAUD** *Scot word for* > HOLD

**HAUDEN** > HAUD

**HAUDING** > HAUD

**HAUDS** > HAUD

**HAUF** *Scot word for* > HALF

**HAUFS** > HAUF

**HAUGH** *n* low-lying often alluvial riverside meadow

**HAUGHS** > HAUGH

**HAUGHT** *same as* > HAUGHTY

**HAUGHTIER** > HAUGHTY

**HAUGHTILY** > HAUGHTY

**HAUGHTY** *adj* proud, arrogant

**HAUL** *vb* pull or drag with effort ▷ *n* hauling

**HAULAGE** *n* (charge for) transporting goods

**HAULAGES** > HAULAGE

**HAULD** *Scots word for* > HOLD

**HAULDS** > HAULD

**HAULED** > HAUL

**HAULER** *same as* > HAULIER

**HAULERS** > HAULER

**HAULIER** *n* firm or person that transports goods by road

**HAULIERS** > HAULIER

**HAULING** > HAUL

**HAULM** *n* stalks of beans, peas, or potatoes collectively

**HAULMIER** > HAULMY

**HAULMIEST** > HAULMY

**HAULMS** > HAULM

**HAULMY** *adj* having haulms

**HAULS** > HAUL

**HAULST** *same as* > HALSE

**HAULT** *same as* > HAUGHTY

**HAULYARD** *same as* > HALYARD

**HAULYARDS** > HAULYARD

**HAUNCH** *n* human hip or fleshy hindquarter of an animal ▷ *vb* in archaic usage, cause (an animal) to come down on its haunches

**HAUNCHED** > HAUNCH

**HAUNCHES** > HAUNCH

**HAUNCHING** > HAUNCH

**HAUNT** *vb* visit in the form of a ghost ▷ *n* place visited frequently

**HAUNTED** *adj* frequented by ghosts

**HAUNTER** > HAUNT

**HAUNTERS** > HAUNT

**HAUNTING** *adj* memorably beautiful or sad

**HAUNTINGS** > HAUNT

**HAUNTS** > HAUNT

**HAURIANT** *adj* rising

**HAURIENT** *same as* > HAURIANT

**HAUSE** *same as* > HALSE

**HAUSED** > HAUSE

**HAUSEN** *n* variety of sturgeon

**HAUSENS** > HAUSEN

**HAUSES** > HAUSE

**HAUSFRAU** *n* German housewife

**HAUSFRAUS** > HAUSFRAU

**HAUSING** > HAUSE

**HAUSTELLA** *n* pl of haustellum: tip of the proboscis of an insect

**HAUSTORIA** *n* pl of haustorium: organ of a parasitic plant that absorbs food and water from host tissues

**HAUT** *same as* > HAUGHTY

**HAUTBOIS** *same as* > HAUTBOY

**HAUTBOY** *n* oboe

**HAUTBOYS** > HAUTBOY

**HAUTE** *adj* French word meaning high

**HAUTEUR** *n* haughtiness

**HAUTEURS** > HAUTEUR

**HAUYNE** *n* blue mineral containing calcium

**HAUYNES** > HAUYNE

**HAVARTI** *n* Danish cheese

**HAVARTIS** > HAVARTI

**HAVDALAH** *n* ceremony marking the end of the sabbath or of a festival, including the blessings over wine, candles, and spices

**HAVDALAHS** > HAVDALAH

**HAVDOLOH** *same as* > HAVDALAH

**HAVDOLOHS** > HAVDOLOH

**HAVE** *vb* possess, hold

**HAVELOCK** *n* light-coloured cover for a service cap with a flap extending over the back of the neck to protect the head and neck from the sun

**HAVELOCKS** > HAVELOCK

**HAVEN** *n* place of safety ▷ *vb* secure or shelter in or as if in a haven

**HAVENED** > HAVEN

**HAVENING** > HAVEN

**HAVENLESS** > HAVEN

**HAVENS** > HAVEN

**HAVEOUR** *same as* > HAVIOR

**HAVEOURS** > HAVEOUR

**HAVER** *vb* talk nonsense ▷ *n* nonsense

**HAVERED** > HAVER

**HAVEREL** *n* fool

**HAVERELS** > HAVEREL

**HAVERING** > HAVER

**HAVERINGS** > HAVER

**HAVERS** > HAVER

**HAVERSACK** *n* canvas bag carried on the back or shoulder

**HAVERSINE** *n* half the value of the versed sine

**HAVES** > HAVE

**HAVILDAR** *n* noncommissioned officer in the Indian army, equivalent in rank to sergeant

**HAVILDARS** > HAVILDAR

**HAVING** > HAVE

**HAVINGS** > HAVE

**HAVIOR** *same as* > HAVIOUR

**HAVIORS** > HAVIOR

**HAVIOUR** *n* possession

**HAVIOURS** > HAVIOUR

**HAVOC** *n* disorder and confusion ▷ *vb* lay waste

**HAVOCKED** > HAVOC

**HAVOCKER** > HAVOC

**HAVOCKERS** > HAVOC

**HAVOCKING** > HAVOC

**HAVOCS** > HAVOC

**HAW** *n* hawthorn berry ▷ *vb* make an inarticulate utterance

**HAWALA** *n* Middle Eastern system of money transfer

**HAWALAS** > HAWALA

**HAWBUCK** *n* bumpkin

**HAWBUCKS** > HAWBUCK

**HAWED** > HAW

**HAWFINCH** *n* European finch with a stout bill and brown plumage with black-and-white wings

**HAWING** > HAW

**HAWK** *n* bird of prey with a short hooked bill and very good eyesight ▷ *vb* offer (goods) for sale in the street or door-to-door

**HAWKBELL** *n* bell fitted to a hawk's leg

**HAWKBELLS** > HAWKBELL

**HAWKBILL** *same as* > HAWKSBILL

**HAWKBILLS** > HAWKBILL

HAWKBIT n any of three perennial plants with yellow dandelion-like flowers

HAWKBITS > HAWKBIT

HAWKED > HAWK

HAWKER n person who travels from place to place selling goods

HAWKERS > HAWKER

HAWKEY same as > HOCKEY

HAWKEYED adj having extremely keen sight

HAWKEYS > HAWKEY

HAWKIE n cow with white stripe on face

HAWKIES > HAWKIE

HAWKING another name for > FALCONRY

HAWKINGS > HAWKING

HAWKISH adj favouring the use or display of force rather than diplomacy to achieve foreign policy goals

HAWKISHLY > HAWKISH

HAWKIT adj having a white streak

HAWKLIKE > HAWK

HAWKMOTH n powerful narrow-winged moth with the ability to hover over flowers when feeding from the nectar

HAWKMOTHS > HAWKMOTH

HAWKNOSE n hooked nose

HAWKNOSES > HAWKNOSE

HAWKS > HAWK

HAWKSBILL n type of turtle

HAWKSHAW n private detective

HAWKSHAWS > HAWKSHAW

HAWKWEED n hairy plant with clusters of dandelion-like flowers

HAWKWEEDS > HAWKWEED

HAWM vb be idle and relaxed

HAWMED > HAWM

HAWMING > HAWM

HAWMS > HAWM

HAWS > HAW

HAWSE vb of boats, pitch violently when at anchor

HAWSED > HAWSE

HAWSEHOLE n one of the holes in the upper part of the bows of a vessel through which the anchor ropes pass

HAWSEPIPE n strong metal pipe through which an anchor rope passes

HAWSER n large rope used on a ship

HAWSERS > HAWSER

HAWSES > HAWSE

HAWSING > HAWSE

HAWTHORN n thorny shrub or tree

HAWTHORNS > HAWTHORN

HAWTHORNY > HAWTHORN

HAY n grass cut and dried as fodder ▷ vb cut, dry, and store (grass, clover, etc) as

fodder

HAYBAND n rope made by twisting hay together

HAYBANDS > HAYBAND

HAYBOX n airtight box full of hay or other insulating material used to keep partially cooked food warm and allow cooking by retained heat

HAYBOXES > HAYBOX

HAYCOCK n small cone-shaped pile of hay left in the field until dry enough to carry to the rick or barn

HAYCOCKS > HAYCOCK

HAYED > HAY

HAYER n person who makes hay

HAYERS > HAYER

HAYEY > HAY

HAYFIELD n field of hay

HAYFIELDS > HAYFIELD

HAYFORK n long-handled fork with two long curved prongs, used for moving or turning hay

HAYFORKS > HAYFORK

HAYING > HAY

HAYINGS > HAY

HAYLAGE n type of hay for animal fodder

HAYLAGES > HAYLAGE

HAYLE n welfare

HAYLES > HAYLE

HAYLOFT n loft for storing hay

HAYLOFTS > HAYLOFT

HAYMAKER n person who helps to cut, turn, toss, spread, or carry hay

HAYMAKERS > HAYMAKER

HAYMAKING > HAYMAKER

HAYMOW n part of a barn where hay is stored

HAYMOWS > HAYMOW

HAYRACK n rack for holding hay for feeding to animals

HAYRACKS > HAYRACK

HAYRICK same as > HAYSTACK

HAYRICKS > HAYRICK

HAYRIDE n pleasure trip in hay wagon

HAYRIDES > HAYRIDE

HAYS > HAY

HAYSEED n seeds or fragments of grass or straw

HAYSEEDS > HAYSEED

HAYSEL n season for making hay

HAYSELS > HAYSEL

HAYSTACK n large pile of stored hay

HAYSTACKS > HAYSTACK

HAYWARD n parish officer in charge of enclosures and fences

HAYWARDS > HAYWARD

HAYWIRE adj (of things) not functioning properly ▷ n wire for binding hay

HAYWIRES > HAYWIRE

HAZAN same as > CANTOR

HAZANIM > HAZAN

HAZANS > HAZAN

HAZARD n something that could be dangerous ▷ vb put in danger

HAZARDED > HAZARD

HAZARDER > HAZARD

HAZARDERS > HAZARD

HAZARDING > HAZARD

HAZARDIZE same as > HAZARD

HAZARDOUS adj involving great risk

HAZARDRY n taking of risks

HAZARDS > HAZARD

HAZE n mist, often caused by heat ▷ vb make or become hazy

HAZED > HAZE

HAZEL n small tree producing edible nuts ▷ adj (of eyes) greenish-brown

HAZELHEN n type of grouse

HAZELHENS > HAZELHEN

HAZELLY > HAZEL

HAZELNUT n nut of a hazel shrub, which has a smooth shiny hard shell

HAZELNUTS > HAZELNUT

HAZELS > HAZEL

HAZER > HAZE

HAZERS > HAZE

HAZES > HAZE

HAZIER > HAZY

HAZIEST > HAZY

HAZILY > HAZY

HAZINESS > HAZY

HAZING > HAZE

HAZINGS > HAZE

HAZMAT n hazardous material

HAZMATS > HAZMAT

HAZY adj not clear, misty

HAZZAN same as > CANTOR

HAZZANIM > HAZZAN

HAZZANS > HAZZAN

HE pron male person or animal ▷ n male person or animal ▷ interj expression of amusement or derision

HEAD n upper or front part of the body, containing the sense organs and the brain ▷ adj chief, principal ▷ vb be at the top or front of

HEADACHE n continuous pain in the head

HEADACHES > HEADACHE

HEADACHEY same as > HEADACHY

HEADACHY adj suffering from, caused by, or likely to cause a headache

HEADAGE n payment to farmer based on number of animals kept

HEADAGES > HEADAGE

HEADBAND n ribbon or band worn around the head

HEADBANDS > HEADBAND

HEADBANG vb nod one's head violently to the beat

of loud rock music

HEADBANGS > HEADBANG

HEADBOARD n vertical board at the top end of a bed

HEADCASE n insane person

HEADCASES > HEADCASE

HEADCHAIR n chair with support for the head

HEADCLOTH n kerchief worn on the head

HEADCOUNT n count of number of people present

HEADDRESS n decorative head covering

HEADED adj having a head or heads

HEADEND n facility from which cable television is transmitted

HEADENDS > HEADEND

HEADER n striking a ball with the head

HEADERS > HEADER

HEADFAST n mooring rope at the bows of a ship

HEADFASTS > HEADFAST

HEADFIRST adv with the head foremost

HEADFISH same as > SUNFISH

HEADFRAME n structure supporting winding machinery at mine

HEADFUCK n taboo slang for experience that is wildly exciting or impressive

HEADFUCKS > HEADFUCK

HEADFUL n amount head will hold

HEADFULS > HEADFUL

HEADGATE n a gate that is used to control the flow of water at the upper end of a lock or conduit

HEADGATES > HEADGATE

HEADGEAR n hats collectively

HEADGEARS > HEADGEAR

HEADGUARD n padded helmet worn to protect the head in contact sports

HEADHUNT vb recruit employee from another company

HEADHUNTS > HEADHUNT

HEADIER > HEADY

HEADIEST > HEADY

HEADILY > HEADY

HEADINESS > HEADY

HEADING same as > HEAD

HEADINGS > HEADING

HEADLAMP same as > HEADLIGHT

HEADLAMPS > HEADLAMP

HEADLAND n area of land jutting out into the sea

HEADLANDS > HEADLAND

HEADLEASE n main lease often subdivided

HEADLESS adj without a head

HEADLIGHT n powerful light on the front of a

vehicle
**HEADLIKE** > HEAD
**HEADLINE** n title at the top of a newspaper article, esp on the front page
**HEADLINED** > HEADLINE
**HEADLINER** n performer given prominent billing
**HEADLINES** > HEADLINE
**HEADLOCK** n wrestling hold in which a wrestler locks his opponent's head between the crook of his elbow and the side of his body
**HEADLOCKS** > HEADLOCK
**HEADLONG** adj with the head first ▷ adv with the head foremost
**HEADMAN** n chief or leader
**HEADMARK** n characteristic
**HEADMARKS** > HEADMARK
**HEADMEN** > HEADMAN
**HEADMOST** less common word for > FOREMOST
**HEADNOTE** n note at book chapter head
**HEADNOTES** > HEADNOTE
**HEADPEACE** archaic form of > HEADPIECE
**HEADPHONE** n small loudspeaker held against the ear
**HEADPIECE** n decorative band at the top of a page, chapter, etc
**HEADPIN** another word for > KINGPIN
**HEADPINS** > HEADPIN
**HEADRACE** n channel that carries water to a water wheel, turbine, etc
**HEADRACES** > HEADRACE
**HEADRAIL** n end of the table from which play is started, nearest the baulkline
**HEADRAILS** > HEADRAIL
**HEADREACH** n distance made to windward while tacking ▷ vb gain distance over (another boat) when tacking
**HEADREST** n support for the head, as on a dentist's chair or car seat
**HEADRESTS** > HEADREST
**HEADRIG** n edge of ploughed field
**HEADRIGS** > HEADRIG
**HEADRING** n African head decoration
**HEADRINGS** > HEADRING
**HEADROOM** n space below a roof or bridge which allows an object to pass or stay underneath it without touching it
**HEADROOMS** > HEADROOM
**HEADROPE** n rope round an animal's head
**HEADROPES** > HEADROPE
**HEADS** adv with the side of a coin which has a portrait

of a head on it uppermost
**HEADSAIL** n any sail set forward of the foremast
**HEADSAILS** > HEADSAIL
**HEADSCARF** n scarf for the head, often worn tied under the chin
**HEADSET** n pair of headphones, esp with a microphone attached
**HEADSETS** > HEADSET
**HEADSHAKE** n gesture of shaking head
**HEADSHIP** n position or state of being a leader, esp the head teacher of a school
**HEADSHIPS** > HEADSHIP
**HEADSHOT** n photo of person's head
**HEADSHOTS** > HEADSHOT
**HEADSMAN** n (formerly) an executioner who beheaded condemned persons
**HEADSMEN** > HEADSMAN
**HEADSPACE** n space between bolt and cartridge in a rifle
**HEADSTALL** n part of a bridle that fits round a horse's head
**HEADSTAND** n act or an instance of balancing on the head, usually with the hands as support
**HEADSTAY** n rope from mast to bow on ship
**HEADSTAYS** > HEADSTAY
**HEADSTICK** n piece of wood formerly used in typesetting
**HEADSTOCK** n part of a machine that supports and transmits the drive to the chuck
**HEADSTONE** n memorial stone on a grave
**HEADWARD** same as > HEADWARDS
**HEADWARDS** adv backwards beyond the original source
**HEADWATER** n highest part of river
**HEADWAY** same as > HEADROOM
**HEADWAYS** > HEADWAY
**HEADWIND** n wind blowing against the course of an aircraft or ship
**HEADWINDS** > HEADWIND
**HEADWORD** n key word placed at the beginning of a line, paragraph, etc, as in a dictionary entry
**HEADWORDS** > HEADWORD
**HEADWORK** n mental work
**HEADWORKS** > HEADWORK
**HEADY** adj intoxicating or exciting
**HEAL** vb make or become well
**HEALABLE** > HEAL
**HEALD** same as > HEDDLE

**HEALDED** > HEALD
**HEALDING** > HEALD
**HEALDS** > HEALD
**HEALED** > HEAL
**HEALEE** n person who is being healed
**HEALEES** > HEALEE
**HEALER** > HEAL
**HEALERS** > HEAL
**HEALING** > HEAL
**HEALINGLY** > HEAL
**HEALINGS** > HEAL
**HEALS** > HEAL
**HEALSOME** Scots word for > WHOLESOME
**HEALTH** n normal (good) condition of someone's body ▷ interj exclamation wishing someone good health as part of a toast
**HEALTHFUL** same as > HEALTHY
**HEALTHIER** > HEALTHY
**HEALTHILY** > HEALTHY
**HEALTHISM** n lifestyle that prioritizes health and fitness over anything else
**HEALTHS** > HEALTH
**HEALTHY** adj having good health
**HEAME** old form of > HOME
**HEAP** n pile of things one on top of another ▷ vb gather into a pile
**HEAPED** > HEAP
**HEAPER** > HEAP
**HEAPERS** > HEAP
**HEAPIER** > HEAPY
**HEAPIEST** > HEAPY
**HEAPING** adj (of a spoonful) heaped
**HEAPS** > HEAP
**HEAPSTEAD** n buildings at mine
**HEAPY** adj having many heaps
**HEAR** vb perceive (a sound) by ear
**HEARABLE** > HEAR
**HEARD** same as > HERD
**HEARDS** > HERD
**HEARE** old form of > HAIR
**HEARER** > HEAR
**HEARERS** > HEAR
**HEARES** > HEARE
**HEARIE** old form of > HAIRY
**HEARING** > HEAR
**HEARINGS** > HEAR
**HEARKEN** vb listen
**HEARKENED** > HEARKEN
**HEARKENER** > HEARKEN
**HEARKENS** > HEARKEN
**HEARS** > HEAR
**HEARSAY** n gossip, rumour
**HEARSAYS** > HEARSAY
**HEARSE** n funeral car used to carry a coffin ▷ vb put in hearse
**HEARSED** > HEARSE
**HEARSES** > HEARSE
**HEARSIER** > HEARSY
**HEARSIEST** > HEARSY
**HEARSING** > HEARSE
**HEARSY** adj like a hearse

**HEART** n organ that pumps blood round the body ▷ vb (of vegetables) form a heart
**HEARTACHE** n intense anguish
**HEARTBEAT** n one complete pulsation of the heart
**HEARTBURN** n burning sensation in the chest caused by indigestion
**HEARTED** > HEART
**HEARTEN** vb encourage, make cheerful
**HEARTENED** > HEARTEN
**HEARTENER** > HEARTEN
**HEARTENS** > HEARTEN
**HEARTFELT** adj felt sincerely or strongly
**HEARTFREE** adj not in love
**HEARTH** n floor of a fireplace
**HEARTHRUG** n rug laid before fireplace
**HEARTHS** > HEARTH
**HEARTIER** > HEARTY
**HEARTIES** > HEARTY
**HEARTIEST** > HEARTY
**HEARTIKIN** n little heart
**HEARTILY** adv thoroughly or vigorously
**HEARTING** > HEART
**HEARTLAND** n central region of a country or continent
**HEARTLESS** adj cruel, unkind
**HEARTLET** n little heart
**HEARTLETS** > HEART
**HEARTLING** n little heart
**HEARTLY** adv vigorously
**HEARTPEA** same as > HEARTSEED
**HEARTPEAS** > HEARTPEA
**HEARTS** n card game in which players must avoid winning tricks containing hearts or the queen of spades
**HEARTSEED** n type of vine
**HEARTSICK** adj deeply dejected or despondent
**HEARTSOME** adj cheering or encouraging
**HEARTSORE** adj greatly distressed
**HEARTWOOD** n central core of dark hard wood in tree trunks
**HEARTWORM** n parasitic nematode worm that lives in the heart and bloodstream of vertebrates
**HEARTY** adj substantial, nourishing ▷ n comrade, esp a sailor
**HEAST** same as > HEST
**HEASTE** same as > HEST
**HEASTES** > HEASTE
**HEASTS** > HEAST
**HEAT** vb make or become hot ▷ n state of being hot
**HEATABLE** > HEAT

**HEATED** adj angry and excited
**HEATEDLY** > HEATED
**HEATER** n device for supplying heat
**HEATERS** > HEATER
**HEATH** n area of open uncultivated land
**HEATHBIRD** n black grouse
**HEATHCOCK** same as > BLACKCOCK
**HEATHEN** n (of) a person who does not believe in an established religion ▷ adj of or relating to heathen peoples
**HEATHENRY** > HEATHEN
**HEATHENS** > HEATHEN
**HEATHER** n low-growing plant with small purple, pinkish, or white flowers, growing on heaths and mountains ▷ adj of a heather colour
**HEATHERED** > HEATHER
**HEATHERS** > HEATHER
**HEATHERY** > HEATHER
**HEATHFOWL** Compare > MOORFOWL
**HEATHIER** > HEATH
**HEATHIEST** > HEATH
**HEATHLAND** n area of heath
**HEATHLESS** > HEATH
**HEATHLIKE** > HEATH
**HEATHS** > HEATH
**HEATHY** > HEATH
**HEATING** n device or system for supplying heat, esp central heating, to a building
**HEATINGS** > HEATING
**HEATLESS** > HEAT
**HEATPROOF** > HEAT
**HEATS** > HEAT
**HEATSPOT** n spot on skin produced by heat
**HEATSPOTS** > HEATSPOT
**HEAUME** n (in the 12th and 13th centuries) a large helmet reaching and supported by the shoulders
**HEAUMES** > HEAUME
**HEAVE** vb lift with effort ▷ n heaving
**HEAVED** > HEAVE
**HEAVEN** n place believed to be the home of God, where good people go when they die
**HEAVENLY** adj of or like heaven
**HEAVENS** > HEAVEN
**HEAVER** > HEAVE
**HEAVERS** > HEAVE
**HEAVES** > HEAVE
**HEAVIER** > HEAVY
**HEAVIES** > HEAVY
**HEAVIEST** > HEAVY
**HEAVILY** > HEAVY
**HEAVINESS** > HEAVY
**HEAVING** > HEAVE
**HEAVINGS** > HEAVE
**HEAVY** adj of great weight

**HEAVYSET** adj stockily built
**HEBDOMAD** n number seven or a group of seven
**HEBDOMADS** > HEBDOMAD
**HEBE** n any of various flowering shrubs
**HEBEN** old form of > EBONY
**HEBENON** n source of poison
**HEBENONS** > HEBENON
**HEBENS** > HEBEN
**HEBES** > HEBE
**HEBETANT** adj causing dullness
**HEBETATE** adj (of plant parts) having a blunt or soft point ▷ vb make or become blunted
**HEBETATED** > HEBETATE
**HEBETATES** > HEBETATE
**HEBETIC** adj of or relating to puberty
**HEBETUDE** n mental dullness or lethargy
**HEBETUDES** > HEBETUDE
**HEBONA** same as > HEBENON
**HEBONAS** > HEBONA
**HEBRAISE** same as > HEBRAIZE
**HEBRAISED** > HEBRAISE
**HEBRAISES** > HEBRAISE
**HEBRAIZE** vb become or cause to become Hebrew or Hebraic
**HEBRAIZED** > HEBRAIZE
**HEBRAIZES** > HEBRAIZE
**HECATOMB** n (in ancient Greece or Rome) any great public sacrifice and feast, originally one in which 100 oxen were sacrificed
**HECATOMBS** > HECATOMB
**HECH** interj expression of surprise
**HECHT** same as > HIGHT
**HECHTING** > HECHT
**HECHTS** > HECHT
**HECK** interj mild exclamation of surprise, irritation, etc ▷ n frame for obstructing the passage of fish in a river
**HECKLE** vb interrupt (a public speaker) with comments, questions, or taunts ▷ n instrument for combing flax or hemp
**HECKLED** > HECKLE
**HECKLER** > HECKLE
**HECKLERS** > HECKLE
**HECKLES** > HECKLE
**HECKLING** > HECKLE
**HECKLINGS** > HECKLE
**HECKS** > HECK
**HECOGENIN** n plant chemical used in drugs
**HECTARE** n one hundred ares or 10 000 square metres (2.471 acres)
**HECTARES** > HECTARE
**HECTIC** adj rushed or busy ▷ n hectic fever or flush
**HECTICAL** same as > HECTIC
**HECTICLY** > HECTIC
**HECTICS** > HECTIC

**HECTOGRAM** n one hundred grams. 1 hectogram is equivalent to 3.527 ounces.
**HECTOR** vb bully ▷ n blustering bully
**HECTORED** > HECTOR
**HECTORER** > HECTOR
**HECTORERS** > HECTOR
**HECTORING** > HECTOR
**HECTORISM** > HECTOR
**HECTORLY** > HECTOR
**HECTORS** > HECTOR
**HEDDLE** n one of a set of frames of vertical wires on a loom, each wire having an eye through which a warp thread can be passed ▷ vb pass thread through heddle
**HEDDLED** > HEDDLE
**HEDDLES** > HEDDLE
**HEDDLING** > HEDDLE
**HEDER** variant spelling of > CHEDER
**HEDERA** See > IVY
**HEDERAL** > HEDERA
**HEDERAS** > HEDERA
**HEDERATED** adj honoured with crown of ivy
**HEDERS** > HEDER
**HEDGE** n row of bushes forming a barrier or boundary ▷ vb be evasive or noncommittal
**HEDGEBILL** n tool for pruning a hedge
**HEDGED** > HEDGE
**HEDGEHOG** n small mammal with a protective covering of spines
**HEDGEHOGS** > HEDGEHOG
**HEDGEHOP** vb (of an aircraft) to fly close to the ground, as in crop spraying
**HEDGEHOPS** > HEDGEHOP
**HEDGEPIG** same as > HEDGEHOG
**HEDGEPIGS** > HEDGEPIG
**HEDGER** > HEDGE
**HEDGEROW** n bushes forming a hedge
**HEDGEROWS** > HEDGEROW
**HEDGERS** > HEDGE
**HEDGES** > HEDGE
**HEDGIER** > HEDGE
**HEDGIEST** > HEDGE
**HEDGING** > HEDGE
**HEDGINGLY** > HEDGE
**HEDGINGS** > HEDGE
**HEDGY** > HEDGE
**HEDONIC** > HEDONISM
**HEDONICS** n branch of psychology concerned with the study of pleasant and unpleasant sensations
**HEDONISM** n doctrine that pleasure is the most important thing in life
**HEDONISMS** > HEDONISM
**HEDONIST** > HEDONISM
**HEDONISTS** > HEDONISM
**HEDYPHANE** n variety of lead ore
**HEED** n careful attention

▷ vb pay careful attention to
**HEEDED** > HEED
**HEEDER** > HEED
**HEEDERS** > HEED
**HEEDFUL** > HEED
**HEEDFULLY** > HEED
**HEEDINESS** > HEED
**HEEDING** > HEED
**HEEDLESS** adj taking no notice
**HEEDS** > HEED
**HEEDY** > HEED
**HEEHAW** interj representation of the braying sound of a donkey ▷ vb make braying sound
**HEEHAWED** > HEEHAW
**HEEHAWING** > HEEHAW
**HEEHAWS** > HEEHAW
**HEEL** n back part of the foot ▷ vb repair the heel of (a shoe)
**HEELBALL** n mixture of beeswax and lampblack used by shoemakers
**HEELBALLS** > HEELBALL
**HEELED** > HEEL
**HEELER** n dog that herds cattle by biting at their heels
**HEELERS** > HEELER
**HEELING** > HEEL
**HEELINGS** > HEEL
**HEELLESS** > HEEL
**HEELPIECE** n piece of a shoe, stocking, etc, designed to fit the heel
**HEELPLATE** n reinforcing piece of metal
**HEELPOST** n post for carrying the hinges of a door or gate
**HEELPOSTS** > HEELPOST
**HEELS** > HEEL
**HEELTAP** n layer of leather, etc, in the heel of a shoe
**HEELTAPS** > HEELTAP
**HEEZE** Scots word for > HOIST
**HEEZED** > HEEZE
**HEEZES** > HEEZE
**HEEZIE** n act of lifting
**HEEZIES** > HEEZIE
**HEEZING** > HEEZE
**HEFT** vb assess the weight of (something) by lifting ▷ n weight
**HEFTE** same as > HEAVE
**HEFTED** > HEFT
**HEFTER** > HEFT
**HEFTERS** > HEFT
**HEFTIER** > HEFTY
**HEFTIEST** > HEFTY
**HEFTILY** > HEFTY
**HEFTINESS** > HEFTY
**HEFTING** > HEFT
**HEFTS** > HEFT
**HEFTY** adj large, heavy, or strong
**HEGARI** n African sorghum
**HEGARIS** > HEGARI
**HEGEMON** n person in authority
**HEGEMONIC** > HEGEMONY

**HEGEMONS** > HEGEMON
**HEGEMONY** n political domination
**HEGIRA** n emigration escape or flight
**HEGIRAS** > HEGIRA
**HEGUMEN** n head of a monastery of the Eastern Church
**HEGUMENE** n head of Greek nunnery
**HEGUMENES** > HEGUMENE
**HEGUMENOI** > HEGUMENOS
**HEGUMENOS** same as > HEGUMEN
**HEGUMENS** > HEGUMEN
**HEGUMENY** n office of hegumen
**HEH** interj exclamation of surprise or inquiry
**HEHS** > HEH
**HEID** Scot word for > HEAD
**HEIDS** > HEID
**HEIFER** n young cow
**HEIFERS** > HEIFER
**HEIGH** same as > HEY
**HEIGHT** n distance from base to top
**HEIGHTEN** vb make or become higher or more intense
**HEIGHTENS** > HEIGHTEN
**HEIGHTH** obsolete form of > HEIGHT
**HEIGHTHS** > HEIGHTH
**HEIGHTISM** n discrimination based on people's heights
**HEIGHTS** > HEIGHT
**HEIL** vb give a German greeting
**HEILED** > HEIL
**HEILING** > HEIL
**HEILS** > HEIL
**HEIMISH** adj comfortable
**HEINIE** n buttocks
**HEINIES** > HEINIE
**HEINOUS** adj evil and shocking
**HEINOUSLY** > HEINOUS
**HEIR** n person entitled to inherit property or rank ▷ vb inherit
**HEIRDOM** n succession by right of blood
**HEIRDOMS** > HEIRDOM
**HEIRED** > HEIR
**HEIRESS** n woman who inherits or expects to inherit great wealth
**HEIRESSES** > HEIRESS
**HEIRING** > HEIR
**HEIRLESS** > HEIR
**HEIRLOOM** n object that has belonged to a family for generations
**HEIRLOOMS** > HEIRLOOM
**HEIRS** > HEIR
**HEIRSHIP** n state or condition of being an heir
**HEIRSHIPS** > HEIRSHIP
**HEISHI** n Native American shell jewellery
**HEIST** n robbery ▷ vb steal

or burgle
**HEISTED** > HEIST
**HEISTER** > HEIST
**HEISTERS** > HEIST
**HEISTING** > HEIST
**HEISTS** > HEIST
**HEITIKI** n Māori neck ornament of greenstone
**HEITIKIS** > HEITIKI
**HEJAB** same as > HIJAB
**HEJABS** > HEJAB
**HEJIRA** same as > HEGIRA
**HEJIRAS** > HEJIRA
**HEJRA** same as > HEGIRA
**HEJRAS** > HEJRA
**HEKETARA** n small shrub that has flowers with white petals and yellow centres
**HEKETARAS** > HEKETARA
**HEKTARE** same as > HECTARE
**HEKTARES** > HEKTARE
**HEKTOGRAM** same as > HECTOGRAM
**HELCOID** adj having ulcers
**HELD** > HOLD
**HELE** as in hele in dialect expression meaning insert (cuttings, shoots, etc) into soil before planting to keep them moist
**HELED** > HELE
**HELENIUM** n plant with daisy-like yellow or variegated flowers
**HELENIUMS** > HELENIUM
**HELES** > HELE
**HELIAC** same as > HELIACAL
**HELIACAL** as in heliacal rising rising of a celestial object at approximately the same time as the rising of the sun
**HELIAST** n ancient Greek juror
**HELIASTS** > HELIAST
**HELIBORNE** adj carried in helicopter
**HELIBUS** n helicopter carrying passengers
**HELIBUSES** > HELIBUS
**HELICAL** adj spiral
**HELICALLY** > HELICAL
**HELICES** > HELIX
**HELICITY** n projection of the spin of an elementary particle on the direction of propagation
**HELICLINE** n spiral-shaped ramp
**HELICOID** adj shaped like a spiral ▷ n any surface resembling that of a screw thread
**HELICOIDS** > HELICOID
**HELICON** n bass tuba made to coil over the shoulder of a band musician
**HELICONIA** n tropical flowering plant
**HELICONS** > HELICON
**HELICOPT** vb transport using a helicopter
**HELICOPTS** > HELICOPT

**HELICTITE** n twisted stalactite
**HELIDECK** n landing deck for helicopters on ships, oil platforms, etc
**HELIDECKS** > HELIDECK
**HELIDROME** n small airport for helicopters
**HELILIFT** vb transport by helicopter
**HELILIFTS** > HELILIFT
**HELIMAN** n helicopter pilot
**HELIMEN** > HELIMAN
**HELING** > HELE
**HELIO** n instrument for sending messages in Morse code by reflecting the sun's rays
**HELIODOR** n clear yellow form of beryl used as a gemstone
**HELIODORS** > HELIODOR
**HELIOGRAM** n message sent by reflecting the sun's rays in a mirror
**HELIOLOGY** n study of sun
**HELIOS** > HELIO
**HELIOSES** > HELIOSIS
**HELIOSIS** n bad effect of overexposure to the sun
**HELIOSTAT** n astronomical instrument used to reflect the light of the sun in a constant direction
**HELIOTYPE** n printing process in which an impression is taken in ink from a gelatine surface that has been exposed under a negative and prepared for printing
**HELIOTYPY** same as > HELIOTYPE
**HELIOZOAN** n type of protozoan, typically having a siliceous shell and stiff radiating cytoplasmic projections
**HELIOZOIC** > HELIOZOAN
**HELIPAD** n place for helicopters to land and take off
**HELIPADS** > HELIPAD
**HELIPILOT** n helicopter pilot
**HELIPORT** n airport for helicopters
**HELIPORTS** > HELIPORT
**HELISTOP** n landing place for helicopter
**HELISTOPS** > HELISTOP
**HELIUM** n very light colourless odourless gas
**HELIUMS** > HELIUM
**HELIX** n spiral
**HELIXES** > HELIX
**HELL** n place believed to be where wicked people go when they die ▷ vb act wildly
**HELLBENT** adj intent
**HELLBOX** n (in printing) container for broken type
**HELLBOXES** > HELLBOX

**HELLBROTH** n evil concoction
**HELLCAT** n spiteful fierce-tempered woman
**HELLCATS** > HELLCAT
**HELLDIVER** n small greyish-brown North American grebe
**HELLEBORE** n plant with white flowers that bloom in winter
**HELLED** > HELL
**HELLENISE** same as > HELLENIZE
**HELLENIZE** vb make or become like the ancient Greeks
**HELLER** n monetary unit of the Czech Republic and Slovakia
**HELLERI** n Central American fish
**HELLERIES** > HELLERY
**HELLERIS** > HELLERI
**HELLERS** > HELLER
**HELLERY** n wild or mischievous behaviour
**HELLFIRE** n torment of hell, imagined as eternal fire
**HELLFIRES** > HELLFIRE
**HELLHOLE** n unpleasant or evil place
**HELLHOLES** > HELLHOLE
**HELLHOUND** n hound of hell
**HELLICAT** n evil creature
**HELLICATS** > HELLICAT
**HELLIER** n slater
**HELLIERS** > HELLIER
**HELLING** > HELL
**HELLION** n rough or rowdy person, esp a child
**HELLIONS** > HELLION
**HELLISH** adj very unpleasant ▷ adv (intensifier)
**HELLISHLY** > HELLISH
**HELLKITE** n bird of prey from hell
**HELLKITES** > HELLKITE
**HELLO** interj expression of greeting or surprise ▷ n act of saying 'hello' ▷ sentence substitute expression of greeting used on meeting a person or at the start of a telephone call ▷ vb say hello
**HELLOED** > HELLO
**HELLOES** > HELLO
**HELLOING** > HELLO
**HELLOS** > HELLO
**HELLOVA** same as > HELLUVA
**HELLS** > HELL
**HELLUVA** adj (intensifier)
**HELLWARD** adj towards hell
**HELLWARDS** adv towards hell
**HELM** n tiller or wheel for steering a ship ▷ vb direct or steer
**HELMED** > HELM
**HELMER** n film director

**HELMERS** >HELMER
**HELMET** n hard hat worn for protection
**HELMETED** >HELMET
**HELMETING** n wearing or provision of a helmet
**HELMETS** >HELMET
**HELMING** >HELM
**HELMINTH** n any parasitic worm, esp a nematode or fluke
**HELMINTHS** >HELMINTH
**HELMLESS** >HELM
**HELMS** >HELM
**HELMSMAN** n person at the helm who steers the ship
**HELMSMEN** >HELMSMAN
**HELO** n helicopter
**HELOPHYTE** n any perennial marsh plant that bears its overwintering buds in the mud below the surface
**HELOS** >HELO
**HELOT** n serf or slave
**HELOTAGE** same as >HELOTISM
**HELOTAGES** >HELOTAGE
**HELOTISM** n condition or quality of being a helot
**HELOTISMS** >HELOTISM
**HELOTRIES** >HELOTRY
**HELOTRY** n serfdom or slavery
**HELOTS** >HELOT
**HELP** vb make something easier, better, or quicker for (someone) ▷ n assistance or support
**HELPABLE** >HELP
**HELPDESK** n place where advice is given by telephone
**HELPDESKS** >HELPDESK
**HELPED** >HELP
**HELPER** >HELP
**HELPERS** >HELP
**HELPFUL** adj giving help
**HELPFULLY** >HELPFUL
**HELPING** n single portion of food
**HELPINGS** >HELPING
**HELPLESS** adj weak or incapable
**HELPLINE** n telephone line set aside for callers to contact an organization for help with a problem
**HELPLINES** >HELPLINE
**HELPMATE** n companion and helper, esp a husband or wife
**HELPMATES** >HELPMATE
**HELPMEET** less common word for >HELPMATE
**HELPMEETS** >HELPMEET
**HELPS** >HELP
**HELVE** n handle of a hand tool such as an axe or pick ▷ vb fit a helve to (a tool)
**HELVED** >HELVE
**HELVES** >HELVE
**HELVETIUM** same as >ASTATINE
**HELVING** >HELVE

**HEM** n bottom edge of a garment, folded under and stitched down ▷ vb provide with a hem >HEMAGGLUTINATE
**HEMAGOG** same as >HEMAGOGUE
**HEMAGOGS** >HEMAGOGUE
**HEMAGOGUE** n haemagogue: drug that promotes the flow of blood
**HEMAL** same as >HAEMAL
**HEMATAL** same as >HEMAL
**HEMATEIN** same as >HAEMATEIN
**HEMATEINS** >HEMATEIN
**HEMATIC** same as >HAEMATIC
**HEMATICS** >HEMATIC
**HEMATIN** same as >HAEMATIN
**HEMATINE** n red dye
**HEMATINES** >HEMATINE
**HEMATINIC** same as >HAEMATIC
**HEMATINS** >HEMATIN
**HEMATITE** n red, grey, or black mineral
**HEMATITES** >HEMATITE
**HEMATITIC** >HEMATITE
**HEMATOID** same as >HAEMATOID
**HEMATOMA** same as >HAEMATOMA
**HEMATOMAS** >HEMATOMA
**HEMATOSES** >HEMATOSIS
**HEMATOSIS** n haematosis: oxygenation of venous blood in the lungs
**HEMATOZOA** n plural of hematozoon: protozoan that is parasitic in the blood
**HEMATURIA** same as >HAEMATURIA
**HEMATURIC** >HEMATURIA
**HEME** same as >HAEM
**HEMELYTRA** n plural of hemelytron: forewing of plant bugs
**HEMES** >HEME
**HEMIALGIA** n pain limited to one side of the body
**HEMIC** >HAEMATIC
**HEMICYCLE** n semicircular structure, room, arena, wall, etc
**HEMIHEDRY** n state of crystal having certain kind of symmetry
**HEMIN** same as >HAEMIN
**HEMINA** n old liquid measure
**HEMINAS** >HEMINA
**HEMINS** >HEMIN
**HEMIOLA** n rhythmic device involving the superimposition of, for example, two notes in the time of three
**HEMIOLAS** >HEMIOLA
**HEMIOLIA** same as >HEMIOLA
**HEMIOLIAS** >HEMIOLIA

**HEMIOLIC** >HEMIOLA
**HEMIONE** same as >HEMIONUS
**HEMIONES** >HEMIONE
**HEMIONUS** n Asian wild ass
**HEMIOPIA** n defective vision seeing only halves of things
**HEMIOPIAS** >HEMIOPIA
**HEMIOPIC** >HEMIOPIA
**HEMIOPSIA** same as >HEMIOPIA
**HEMIPOD** same as >HEMIPODE
**HEMIPODE** n button quail
**HEMIPODES** >HEMIPODE
**HEMIPODS** >HEMIPOD
**HEMIPTER** n insect with beaklike mouthparts
**HEMIPTERS** >HEMIPTER
**HEMISPACE** n area in brain
**HEMISTICH** n half line of verse
**HEMITROPE** another name for >TWIN
**HEMITROPY** n state of being a twin
**HEMLINE** n level to which the hem of a skirt hangs
**HEMLINES** >HEMLINE
**HEMLOCK** n poison made from a plant with spotted stems and small white flowers
**HEMLOCKS** >HEMLOCK
**HEMMED** >HEM
**HEMMER** n attachment on a sewing machine for hemming
**HEMMERS** >HEMMER
**HEMMING** >HEM
**HEMOCOEL** same as >HAEMOCOEL
**HEMOCOELS** >HEMOCOEL
**HEMOCYTE** same as >HAEMOCYTE
**HEMOCYTES** >HEMOCYTE
**HEMOID** same as >HAEMATOID
**HEMOLYMPH** n blood-like fluid in invertebrates
**HEMOLYSE** vb break down so that haemoglobulin is released
**HEMOLYSED** >HEMOLYSE
**HEMOLYSES** >HEMOLYSIS
**HEMOLYSIN** n haemolysis: substance that breaks down red blood cells
**HEMOLYSIS** n haemolysis: disintegration of red blood cells
**HEMOLYTIC** >HEMOLYSIS
**HEMOLYZE** vb undergo or make undergo hemolysis
**HEMOLYZED** >HEMOLYZE
**HEMOLYZES** >HEMOLYZE
**HEMOPHILE** n haemophile: person with haemophilia
**HEMOSTAT** same as >HAEMOSTAT
**HEMOSTATS** >HEMOSTAT
**HEMOTOXIC** >HEMOTOXIN
**HEMOTOXIN** n substance

that destroys red blood cells
**HEMP** n Asian plant with tough fibres
**HEMPEN** >HEMP
**HEMPIE** variant of >HEMPY
**HEMPIER** >HEMPY
**HEMPIES** >HEMPY
**HEMPIEST** >HEMPY
**HEMPLIKE** >HEMP
**HEMPS** >HEMP
**HEMPSEED** n seed of hemp
**HEMPSEEDS** >HEMPSEED
**HEMPWEED** n climbing weed
**HEMPWEEDS** >HEMPWEED
**HEMPY** adj of or like hemp ▷ n rogue
**HEMS** >HEM
**HEMSTITCH** n decorative edging stitch, usually for a hem, in which the cross threads are stitched in groups ▷ vb decorate (a hem, etc) with hemstitches
**HEN** n female domestic fowl ▷ vb lose one's courage
**HENBANE** n poisonous plant with sticky hairy leaves
**HENBANES** >HENBANE
**HENBIT** n European plant with small dark red flowers
**HENBITS** >HENBIT
**HENCE** adv from this time ▷ interj begone! away!
**HENCHMAN** n person employed by someone powerful to carry out orders
**HENCHMEN** >HENCHMAN
**HENCOOP** n cage for poultry
**HENCOOPS** >HENCOOP
**HEND** vb seize
**HENDED** >HEND
**HENDIADYS** n rhetorical device by which two nouns joined by a conjunction are used instead of a noun and modifier
**HENDING** >HEND
**HENDS** >HEND
**HENEQUEN** n agave plant native to Yucatán
**HENEQUENS** >HENEQUEN
**HENEQUIN** same as >HENEQUEN
**HENEQUINS** >HENEQUIN
**HENGE** n circular monument, often containing a circle of stones, dating from the Neolithic and Bronze Ages
**HENGES** >HENGE
**HENHOUSE** n coop for hens
**HENHOUSES** >HENHOUSE
**HENIQUEN** same as >HENEQUEN
**HENIQUENS** >HENIQUEN
**HENIQUIN** same as >HENIQUIN
**HENIQUINS** >HENIQUIN
**HENLEY** n type of sweater
**HENLEYS** >HENLEY

**HENLIKE** >HEN
**HENNA** n reddish dye made from a shrub or tree ▷ vb dye (the hair) with henna
**HENNAED** >HENNA
**HENNAING** >HENNA
**HENNAS** >HENNA
**HENNED** >HEN
**HENNER** n challenge
**HENNERIES** >HENNERY
**HENNERS** >HENNER
**HENNERY** n place or farm for keeping poultry
**HENNIER** >HENNY
**HENNIES** >HENNY
**HENNIEST** >HENNY
**HENNIN** n former women's hat
**HENNING** >HEN
**HENNINS** >HENNIN
**HENNISH** >HEN
**HENNISHLY** >HEN
**HENNY** adj like hen ▷ n cock that looks like hen
**HENOTIC** adj acting to reconcile
**HENPECK** vb (of a woman) to harass or torment (a man, esp her husband) by persistent nagging
**HENPECKED** adj (of a man) dominated by his wife
**HENPECKS** >HENPECK
**HENRIES** >HENRY
**HENRY** n unit of electrical inductance
**HENRYS** >HENRY
**HENS** >HEN
**HENT** vb seize ▷ n anything that has been grasped, esp by the mind
**HENTED** >HENT
**HENTING** >HENT
**HENTS** >HENT
**HEP** same as >HIP
**HEPAR** n compound containing sulphur
**HEPARIN** n polysaccharide, containing sulphate groups, present in most body tissues: an anticoagulant used in the treatment of thrombosis
**HEPARINS** >HEPARIN
**HEPARS** >HEPAR
**HEPATIC** adj of the liver ▷ n any of various drugs for use in treating diseases of the liver
**HEPATICA** n woodland plant with white, mauve, or pink flowers
**HEPATICAE** >HEPATICA
**HEPATICAL** same as >HEPATIC
**HEPATICAS** >HEPATICA
**HEPATICS** >HEPATIC
**HEPATISE** same as >HEPATIZE
**HEPATISED** >HEPATISE
**HEPATISES** >HEPATISE
**HEPATITE** n mineral containing sulphur
**HEPATITES** >HEPATITE

**HEPATITIS** n inflammation of the liver
**HEPATIZE** vb turn into liver
**HEPATIZED** >HEPATIZE
**HEPATIZES** >HEPATIZE
**HEPATOMA** n cancer of liver
**HEPATOMAS** >HEPATOMA
**HEPCAT** n person who is hep, esp a player or admirer of jazz and swing in the 1940s
**HEPCATS** >HEPCAT
**HEPPER** >HEP
**HEPPEST** >HEP
**HEPS** >HEP
**HEPSTER** same as >HIPSTER
**HEPSTERS** >HEPSTER
**HEPT** archaic spelling of >HEAPED
**HEPTAD** n group or series of seven
**HEPTADS** >HEPTAD
**HEPTAGLOT** n book in seven languages
**HEPTAGON** n geometric figure with seven sides
**HEPTAGONS** >HEPTAGON
**HEPTANE** n alkane found in petroleum and used as an anaesthetic
**HEPTANES** >HEPTANE
**HEPTAPODY** n verse with seven beats in rhythm
**HEPTARCH** >HEPTARCHY
**HEPTARCHS** >HEPTARCHY
**HEPTARCHY** n government by seven rulers
**HEPTOSE** n any monosaccharide that has seven carbon atoms per molecule
**HEPTOSES** >HEPTOSE
**HER** pron refers to a female person or animal or anything personified as feminine when the object of a sentence or clause ▷ adj belonging to her ▷ determiner of, belonging to, or associated with her
**HERALD** n person who announces important news ▷ vb signal the approach of
**HERALDED** >HERALD
**HERALDIC** adj of or relating to heraldry
**HERALDING** >HERALD
**HERALDIST** >HERALDRY
**HERALDRY** n study of coats of arms and family trees
**HERALDS** >HERALD
**HERB** n plant used for flavouring in cookery, and in medicine
**HERBAGE** n herbaceous plants collectively, esp those on which animals graze
**HERBAGED** adj with grass growing on it
**HERBAGES** >HERBAGE
**HERBAL** adj of or relating to herbs, usually culinary or

medicinal herbs ▷ n book describing and listing the properties of plants
**HERBALISM** n use of herbal medicine
**HERBALIST** n person who grows or specializes in the use of medicinal herbs
**HERBALS** >HERBAL
**HERBAR** same as >HERBARY
**HERBARIA** >HERBARIUM
**HERBARIAL** >HERBARIUM
**HERBARIAN** same as >HERBALIST
**HERBARIES** >HERBARY
**HERBARIUM** n collection of dried plants that are mounted and classified systematically
**HERBARS** >HERBAR
**HERBARY** n herb garden
**HERBED** adj flavoured with herbs
**HERBELET** same as >HERBLET
**HERBELETS** >HERBELET
**HERBICIDE** n chemical used to destroy plants, esp weeds
**HERBIER** >HERBY
**HERBIEST** >HERBY
**HERBIST** same as >HERBALIST
**HERBISTS** >HERBIST
**HERBIVORA** n animals that eat grass
**HERBIVORE** n animal that eats only plants
**HERBIVORY** >HERBIVORE
**HERBLESS** >HERB
**HERBLET** n little herb
**HERBLETS** >HERBLET
**HERBLIKE** >HERB
**HERBOLOGY** n use or study of herbal medicine
**HERBORISE** same as >HERBORIZE
**HERBORIST** same as >HERBALIST
**HERBORIZE** vb collect herbs
**HERBOSE** same as >HERBOUS
**HERBOUS** adj with abundance of herbs
**HERBS** >HERB
**HERBY** adj abounding in herbs
**HERCOGAMY** n prevention of flower pollination
**HERCULEAN** adj requiring great strength or effort
**HERCULES** as in hercules beetle very large tropical American beetle
**HERCYNITE** n mineral containing iron
**HERD** n group of animals feeding and living together ▷ vb collect into a herd
**HERDBOY** n boy who looks after herd
**HERDBOYS** >HERDBOY
**HERDED** >HERD

**HERDEN** n type of coarse cloth
**HERDENS** >HERDEN
**HERDER** same as >HERDSMAN
**HERDERS** >HERDER
**HERDESS** n female herder
**HERDESSES** >HERDESS
**HERDIC** n small horse-drawn carriage with a rear entrance and side seats
**HERDICS** >HERDIC
**HERDING** >HERD
**HERDLIKE** >HERD
**HERDMAN** same as >HERDSMAN
**HERDMEN** >HERDMAN
**HERDS** >HERD
**HERDSMAN** n man who looks after a herd of animals
**HERDSMEN** >HERDSMAN
**HERDWICK** n hardy breed of sheep
**HERDWICKS** >HERDWICK
**HERE** adv in, at, or to this place or point
**HEREABOUT** same as >HEREABOUTS
**HEREAFTER** adv after this point or time ▷ n life after death
**HEREAT** adv because of this
**HEREAWAY** same as >HEREABOUT
**HEREAWAYS** dialect form of >HERE
**HEREBY** adv by means of or as a result of this
**HEREDES** >HERES
**HEREDITY** n passing on of characteristics from one generation to another
**HEREFROM** adv from here
**HEREIN** adv in this place, matter, or document
**HEREINTO** adv into this place, circumstance, etc
**HERENESS** n state of being here
**HEREOF** adv of or concerning this
**HEREON** archaic word for >HEREUPON
**HERES** n heir
**HERESIES** >HERESY
**HERESY** n opinion contrary to accepted opinion or belief
**HERETIC** n person who holds unorthodox opinions
**HERETICAL** >HERETIC
**HERETICS** >HERETIC
**HERETO** adv this place, matter, or document
**HERETRIX** n in Scots law, female inheritor
**HEREUNDER** adv (in documents, etc) below this
**HEREUNTO** archaic word for >HERETO
**HEREUPON** adv following

HEREWITH *adv* with this
HERIED > HERY
HERIES > HERY
HERIOT *n* (in medieval England) a death duty paid by villeins and free tenants to their lord, often consisting of the dead man's best beast or chattel
HERIOTS > HERIOT
HERISSE *adj* with bristles
HERISSON *n* spiked beam used as fortification
HERISSONS > HERISSON
HERITABLE *adj* capable of being inherited
HERITABLY > HERITABLE
HERITAGE *n* something inherited
HERITAGES > HERITAGE
HERITOR *n* person who inherits
HERITORS > HERITOR
HERITRESS > HERITOR
HERITRIX > HERITOR
HERKOGAMY *same as* > HERCOGAMY
HERL *n* barb or barbs of a feather, used to dress fishing flies
HERLING *n* Scots word for a type of fish
HERLINGS > HERL
HERLS > HERL
HERM *n* (in ancient Greece) a stone head of Hermes surmounting a square stone pillar
HERMA *same as* > HERM
HERMAE > HERMA
HERMAEAN *adj* type of statue
HERMAI > HERMA
HERMANDAD *n* organization of middle classes in Spain
HERMETIC *adj* sealed so as to be airtight
HERMETICS *n* alchemy
HERMETISM *n* belief in pagan mystical knowledge
HERMETIST > HERMETISM
HERMIT *n* person living in solitude, esp for religious reasons
HERMITAGE *n* home of a hermit
HERMITESS *n* female hermit
HERMITIC > HERMIT
HERMITISM *n* act of living as hermit
HERMITRY *n* life as hermit
HERMITS > HERMIT
HERMS > HERM
HERN *archaic or dialect word for* > HERON
HERNIA *n* protrusion of an organ or part through the lining of the surrounding body cavity
HERNIAE > HERNIA
HERNIAL > HERNIA
HERNIAS > HERNIA

HERNIATE *n* form hernia
HERNIATED > HERNIA
HERNIATES > HERNIATE
HERNS > HERN
HERNSHAW *same as* > HERONSHAW
HERNSHAWS > HERNSHAW
HERO *n* principal character in a film, book, etc
HEROE *variant of* > HERO
HEROES > HERO
HEROIC *adj* courageous
HEROICAL *same as* > HEROIC
HEROICISE *same as* > HEROICIZE
HEROICIZE *same as* > HEROIZE
HEROICLY > HEROIC
HEROICS *pl n* extravagant behaviour
HEROIN *n* highly addictive drug derived from morphine
HEROINE *n* principal female character in a novel, play, etc
HEROINES > HEROINE
HEROINISM *n* addiction to heroin
HEROINS > HEROIN
HEROISE *same as* > HEROIZE
HEROISED > HEROISE
HEROISES > HEROISE
HEROISING > HEROISE
HEROISM *n* great courage and bravery
HEROISMS > HEROISM
HEROIZE *vb* make into hero
HEROIZED > HEROIZE
HEROIZES > HEROIZE
HEROIZING > HEROIZE
HERON *n* long-legged wading bird
HERONRIES > HERONRY
HERONRY *n* colony of breeding herons
HERONS > HERON
HERONSEW *same as* > HERONSHAW
HERONSEWS > HERONSEW
HERONSHAW *n* young heron
HEROON *n* temple or monument dedicated to hero
HEROONS > HEROON
HEROS > HERO
HEROSHIP > HERO
HEROSHIPS > HERO
HERPES *n* any of several inflammatory skin diseases, including shingles and cold sores
HERPESES > HERPES
HERPETIC *adj* of or relating to any of the herpes diseases ▷ *n* person suffering from any of the herpes diseases
HERPETICS > HERPETIC
HERPETOID *adj* like reptile
HERPTILE *adj* denoting, relating to, or characterizing both reptiles and amphibians

HERRIED > HERRY
HERRIES > HERRY
HERRIMENT *n* act of plundering
HERRING *n* important food fish of northern seas
HERRINGER *n* person or boat catching herring
HERRINGS > HERRING
HERRY *vb* harry
HERRYING > HERRY
HERRYMENT *same as* > HERRIMENT
HERS *pron* something belonging to her
HERSALL *n* rehearsal
HERSALLS > HERSALL
HERSE *n* harrow
HERSED *adj* arranged like a harrow
HERSELF *pron* feminine singular reflexive form
HERSES > HERSE
HERSHIP *n* act of plundering
HERSHIPS > HERSHIP
HERSTORY *n* history from a female point of view or as it relates to women
HERTZ *n* unit of frequency
HERTZES > HERTZ
HERY *vb* praise
HERYE *same as* > HERY
HERYED > HERYE
HERYES > HERYE
HERYING > HERY
HES > HE
HESITANCE > HESITANT
HESITANCY > HESITANT
HESITANT *adj* undecided or wavering
HESITATE *vb* be slow or uncertain in doing something
HESITATED > HESITATE
HESITATER > HESITATE
HESITATES > HESITATE
HESITATOR > HESITATE
HESP *same as* > HASP
HESPED > HESP
HESPERID *n* species of butterfly
HESPERIDS > HESPERID
HESPING > HESP
HESPS > HESP
HESSIAN *n* coarse jute fabric
HESSIANS > HESSIAN
HESSITE *n* black or grey metallic mineral consisting of silver telluride in cubic crystalline form
HESSITES > HESSITE
HESSONITE *n* orange-brown variety of grossularite garnet
HEST *archaic word for* > BEHEST
HESTERNAL *adj* belonging to yesterday
HESTS > HEST
HET *n* short for heterosexual ▷ *past tense*

*and past participle of heat* ▷ *adj* Scot word for hot
HETAERA *n* (esp in ancient Greece) a female prostitute, esp an educated courtesan
HETAERAE > HETAERA
HETAERAS > HETAERA
HETAERIC > HETAERA
HETAERISM *n* state of being a concubine
HETAERIST > HETAERISM
HETAIRA *same as* > HETAERA
HETAIRAI > HETAIRA
HETAIRAS > HETAIRA
HETAIRIA *n* society
HETAIRIAS > HETAIRIA
HETAIRIC > HETAERA
HETAIRISM *same as* > HETAERISM
HETAIRIST > HETAERISM
HETE *same as* > HIGHT
HETERO *short for* > HETEROSEXUAL
HETERODOX *adj* differing from accepted doctrines or beliefs
HETERONYM *n* one of two or more words pronounced differently but spelt alike
HETEROPOD *n* marine invertebrate with a foot for swimming
HETEROS > HETERO
HETEROSES > HETEROSIS
HETEROSIS *n* increased size, strength, etc, of a hybrid as compared to either of its parents
HETEROTIC > HETEROSIS
HETES > HETE
HETH *n* eighth letter of the Hebrew alphabet
HETHER *same as* > HITHER
HETHS > HETH
HETING > HETE
HETMAN *another word for* > ATAMAN
HETMANATE > HETMAN
HETMANS > HETMAN
HETS > HET
HEUCH *Scots word for* > CRAG
HEUCHERA *n* N American plant with heart-shaped leaves and mostly red flowers
HEUCHERAS > HEUCHERA
HEUCHS > HEUCH
HEUGH *same as* > HEUCH
HEUGHS > HEUGH
HEUREKA *same as* > EUREKA
HEUREKAS > HEUREKA
HEURETIC *same as* > HEURISTIC
HEURETICS *n* use of logic
HEURISM *n* use of logic
HEURISMS > HEURISM
HEURISTIC *adj* involving learning by investigation ▷ *n* science of heuristic procedure
HEVEA *n* rubber-producing South American tree
HEVEAS > HEVEA

**HEW** *vb* cut with an axe
**HEWABLE** > HEW
**HEWED** > HEW
**HEWER** > HEW
**HEWERS** > HEW
**HEWGH** *interj* sound made to imitate the flight of an arrow
**HEWING** > HEW
**HEWINGS** > HEW
**HEWN** > HEW
**HEWS** > HEW
**HEX** *adj* of or relating to hexadecimal notation ▷ *n* evil spell ▷ *vb* bewitch
**HEXACHORD** *n* (in medieval musical theory) any of three diatonic scales based upon C, F, and G, each consisting of six notes, from which solmization was developed
**HEXACT** *n* part of a sponge with six rays
**HEXACTS** > HEXACT
**HEXAD** *n* group or series of six
**HEXADE** *same as* > HEXAD
**HEXADES** > HEXADE
**HEXADIC** > HEXAD
**HEXADS** > HEXAD
**HEXAFOIL** *n* pattern with six lobes
**HEXAFOILS** > HEXAFOIL
**HEXAGLOT** *n* book in six languages
**HEXAGON** *n* geometrical figure with six sides
**HEXAGONAL** *adj* having six sides and six angles
**HEXAGONS** > HEXAGON
**HEXAGRAM** *n* star formed by extending the sides of a regular hexagon to meet at six points
**HEXAGRAMS** > HEXAGRAM
**HEXAHEDRA** *n* plural of hexahedron: solid figure with six plane faces
**HEXAMERAL** *adj* arranged in six groups
**HEXAMETER** *n* verse line consisting of six metrical feet
**HEXAMINE** *n* type of fuel produced in small solid blocks or tablets for use in miniature camping stoves
**HEXAMINES** > HEXAMINE
**HEXANE** *n* liquid alkane existing in five isomeric forms that are found in petroleum and used as solvents
**HEXANES** > HEXANE
**HEXANOIC** as in *hexanoic acid* insoluble oily carboxylic acid found in coconut and palm oils and in milk
**HEXAPLA** *n* edition of the Old Testament compiled by Origen, containing six versions of the text

**HEXAPLAR** > HEXAPLA
**HEXAPLAS** > HEXAPLA
**HEXAPLOID** *adj* with six times the normal number of chromosomes
**HEXAPOD** *n* six-footed arthropod
**HEXAPODIC** > HEXAPODY
**HEXAPODS** > HEXAPOD
**HEXAPODY** *n* verse measure consisting of six metrical feet
**HEXARCH** *adj* (of plant) with six veins
**HEXARCHY** *n* alliance of six states
**HEXASTICH** *n* poem, stanza, or strophe that consists of six lines
**HEXASTYLE** *n* portico or façade with six columns ▷ *adj* having six columns
**HEXED** > HEX
**HEXENE** *same as* > HEXYLENE
**HEXENES** > HEXENE
**HEXER** > HEX
**HEXEREI** *n* witchcraft
**HEXEREIS** > HEXEREI
**HEXERS** > HEX
**HEXES** > HEX
**HEXING** > HEX
**HEXINGS** > HEX
**HEXONE** *n* colourless insoluble liquid ketone used as a solvent for organic compounds
**HEXONES** > HEXONE
**HEXOSAN** *n* any of a group of polysaccharides that yield hexose on hydrolysis
**HEXOSANS** > HEXOSAN
**HEXOSE** *n* monosaccharide, such as glucose, that contains six carbon atoms per molecule
**HEXOSES** > HEXOSE
**HEXYL** *adj* of, consisting of, or containing the group of atoms $C_6H_{13}$, esp the isomeric form of this group, $CH_3(CH_2)_4CH_2$-
**HEXYLENE** *n* chemical compound similar to ethylene
**HEXYLENES** > HEXYLENE
**HEXYLIC** > HEXYL
**HEXYLS** > HEXYL
**HEY** *interj* expression of surprise or for catching attention ▷ *vb* perform a country dance
**HEYDAY** *n* time of greatest success, prime
**HEYDAYS** > HEYDAY
**HEYDEY** *variant of* > HEYDAY
**HEYDEYS** > HEYDEY
**HEYDUCK** *same as* > HAIDUK
**HEYDUCKS** > HEYDUCK
**HEYED** > HEY
**HEYING** > HEY
**HEYS** > HEY
**HI** *interj* hello
**HIANT** *adj* gaping
**HIATAL** > HIATUS

**HIATUS** *n* pause or interruption in continuity
**HIATUSES** > HIATUS
**HIBACHI** *n* portable brazier for heating and cooking food
**HIBACHIS** > HIBACHI
**HIBAKUSHA** *n* survivor of either of the atomic-bomb attacks on Hiroshima and Nagasaki in 1945
**HIBERNAL** *adj* of or occurring in winter
**HIBERNATE** *vb* (of an animal) pass the winter as if in a deep sleep
**HIBERNISE** > HIBERNIZE
**HIBERNIZE** *vb* make Irish
**HIBISCUS** *n* tropical plant with large brightly coloured flowers
**HIC** *interj* representation of the sound of a hiccup
**HICATEE** *same as* > HICCATEE
**HICATEES** > HICATEE
**HICCATEE** *n* tortoise of West Indies
**HICCATEES** > HICCATEE
**HICCOUGH** *same as* > HICCUP
**HICCOUGHS** > HICCOUGH
**HICCUP** *n* spasm of the breathing organs with a sharp coughlike sound ▷ *vb* make a hiccup
**HICCUPED** > HICCUP
**HICCUPING** > HICCUP
**HICCUPPED** > HICCUP
**HICCUPS** > HICCUP
**HICCUPY** > HICCUP
**HICK** *n* unsophisticated country person
**HICKEY** *n* object or gadget: used as a name when the correct name is forgotten, etc
**HICKEYS** > HICKEY
**HICKIE** *same as* > HICKEY
**HICKIES** > HICKIE
**HICKISH** > HICK
**HICKORIES** > HICKORY
**HICKORY** *n* N American nut-bearing tree
**HICKS** > HICK
**HICKWALL** *n* green woodpecker
**HICKWALLS** > HICKWALL
**HICKYMAL** *n* titmouse
**HICKYMALS** > HICKYMAL
**HID** > HIDE
**HIDABLE** > HIDE
**HIDAGE** *n* former tax on land
**HIDAGES** > HIDAGE
**HIDALGA** *n* Spanish noblewoman
**HIDALGAS** > HIDALGA
**HIDALGO** *n* member of the lower nobility in Spain
**HIDALGOS** > HIDALGO
**HIDDEN** > HIDE
**HIDDENITE** *n* green transparent variety of the mineral spodumene, used

as a gemstone
**HIDDENLY** > HIDE
**HIDDER** *n* young ram
**HIDDERS** > HIDDER
**HIDE** *vb* put (oneself or an object) somewhere difficult to see or find ▷ *n* place of concealment, esp for a bird-watcher
**HIDEAWAY** *n* private place
**HIDEAWAYS** > HIDEAWAY
**HIDEBOUND** *adj* unwilling to accept new ideas
**HIDED** > HIDE
**HIDELESS** > HIDE
**HIDEOSITY** > HIDEOUS
**HIDEOUS** *adj* ugly, revolting
**HIDEOUSLY** > HIDEOUS
**HIDEOUT** *n* hiding place, esp a remote place used by outlaws, etc; hideaway
**HIDEOUTS** > HIDEOUT
**HIDER** > HIDE
**HIDERS** > HIDE
**HIDES** > HIDE
**HIDING** > HIDE
**HIDINGS** > HIDE
**HIDLING** *n* hiding place
**HIDLINGS** *adv* in secret
**HIDLINS** *same as* > HIDLINGS
**HIDROSES** > HIDROSIS
**HIDROSIS** *n* any skin disease affecting the sweat glands
**HIDROTIC** > HIDROSIS
**HIDROTICS** > HIDROSIS
**HIE** *vb* hurry
**HIED** > HIE
**HIEING** > HIE
**HIELAMAN** *n* Australian Aboriginal shield
**HIELAMANS** > HIELAMAN
**HIELAND** *adj* characteristic of Highlanders, esp alluding to their supposed gullibility or foolishness in towns or cities
**HIEMAL** *less common word for* > HIBERNAL
**HIEMS** *n* winter
**HIERACIUM** *n* plant of hawkweed family
**HIERARCH** *n* person in a position of high-priestly authority
**HIERARCHS** > HIERARCH
**HIERARCHY** *n* system of people or things arranged in a graded order
**HIERATIC** *adj* of or relating to priests ▷ *n* hieratic script of ancient Egypt
**HIERATICA** *n* type of papyrus
**HIEROCRAT** *n* person who believes in government by religious leaders
**HIERODULE** *n* (in ancient Greece) a temple slave, esp a sacral prostitute
**HIEROGRAM** *n* sacred symbol
**HIEROLOGY** *n* sacred

literature
**HIERURGY** *n* performance of religious drama or music
**HIES** > HIE
**HIFALUTIN** *adj* pompous or pretentious
**HIGGLE** *less common word for* > HAGGLE
**HIGGLED** > HIGGLE
**HIGGLER** > HIGGLE
**HIGGLERS** > HIGGLE
**HIGGLES** > HIGGLE
**HIGGLING** > HIGGLE
**HIGGLINGS** > HIGGLE
**HIGH** *adj* being a relatively great distance from top to bottom; tall ▷ *adv* at or to a height ▷ *n* a high place or level ▷ *vb* hie
**HIGHBALL** *n* tall drink of whiskey with soda water or ginger ale and ice ▷ *vb* move at great speed
**HIGHBALLS** > HIGHBALL
**HIGHBORN** *adj* of noble or aristocratic birth
**HIGHBOY** *n* tall chest of drawers in two sections, the lower section being a lowboy
**HIGHBOYS** > HIGHBOY
**HIGHBRED** *adj* of noble breeding
**HIGHBROW** *often disparaging n* intellectual and serious person ▷ *adj* concerned with serious, intellectual subjects
**HIGHBROWS** > HIGHBROW
**HIGHBUSH** *adj* (of bush) growing tall
**HIGHCHAIR** *n* long-legged chair with a tray attached, used by a very young child at mealtimes
**HIGHED** > HIGH
**HIGHER** *n* advanced level of the Scottish Certificate of Education ▷ *vb* raise up
**HIGHERED** > HIGHER
**HIGHERING** > HIGHER
**HIGHERS** > HIGHER
**HIGHEST** > HIGH
**HIGHFLIER** *same as* > HIGHFLYER
**HIGHFLYER** *n* person who is extreme in aims, ambition, etc
**HIGHING** > HIGH
**HIGHISH** > HIGH
**HIGHJACK** *same as* > HIJACK
**HIGHJACKS** > HIGHJACK
**HIGHLAND** *n* relatively high ground
**HIGHLANDS** > HIGHLAND
**HIGHLIFE** *n* style of music combining West African elements with US jazz forms, found esp in the cities of West Africa
**HIGHLIFES** > HIGHLIFE
**HIGHLIGHT** *n* outstanding part or feature ▷ *vb* give

emphasis to
**HIGHLY** *adv* extremely
**HIGHMAN** *n* dice weighted to make it fall in particular way
**HIGHMEN** > HIGHMAN
**HIGHMOST** *adj* highest
**HIGHNESS** *n* condition of being high or lofty
**HIGHRISE** *n* tall building
**HIGHRISES** > HIGHRISE
**HIGHROAD** *n* main road
**HIGHROADS** > HIGHROAD
**HIGHS** > HIGH
**HIGHSPOT** *n* highlight
**HIGHSPOTS** > HIGHSPOT
**HIGHT** *vb* archaic word for name or call
**HIGHTAIL** *vb* go or move in a great hurry
**HIGHTAILS** > HIGHTAIL
**HIGHTED** > HIGHT
**HIGHTH** *old form of* > HEIGHT
**HIGHTHS** > HIGHTH
**HIGHTING** *n* oath
**HIGHTOP** *n* top of ship's mast
**HIGHTOPS** > HIGHTOP
**HIGHTS** > HIGHT
**HIGHVELD** *n* high-altitude grassland region of E South Africa
**HIGHVELDS** > HIGHVELD
**HIGHWAY** *n* main road
**HIGHWAYS** > HIGHWAY
**HIJAB** *n* covering for the head and face, worn by Muslim women
**HIJABS** > HIJAB
**HIJACK** *vb* seize control of (an aircraft or other vehicle) while travelling ▷ *n* instance of hijacking
**HIJACKED** > HIJACK
**HIJACKER** > HIJACK
**HIJACKERS** > HIJACK
**HIJACKING** > HIJACK
**HIJACKS** > HIJACK
**HIJINKS** *n* lively enjoyment
**HIJRA** *same as* > HIJRAH
**HIJRAH** *same as* > HEGIRA
**HIJRAHS** > HIJRAH
**HIJRAS** > HIJRA
**HIKE** *n* long walk in the country, esp for pleasure ▷ *vb* go for a long walk
**HIKED** > HIKE
**HIKER** > HIKE
**HIKERS** > HIKE
**HIKES** > HIKE
**HIKING** > HIKE
**HIKOI** *n* walk or march, esp a Māori protest march ▷ *vb* take part in such a march
**HIKOIED** > HIKOI
**HIKOIING** > HIKOI
**HIKOIS** > HIKOI
**HILA** > HILUM
**HILAR** > HILUS
**HILARIOUS** *adj* very funny
**HILARITY** *n* mirth and merriment

**HILCH** *vb* hobble
**HILCHED** > HILCH
**HILCHES** > HILCH
**HILCHING** > HILCH
**HILD** *same as* > HOLD
**HILDING** *n* coward
**HILDINGS** > HILDING
**HILI** > HILUS
**HILL** *n* raised part of the earth's surface, less high than a mountain ▷ *vb* form into a hill or mound
**HILLBILLY** *n* usually disparaging term for an unsophisticated country person
**HILLCREST** *n* crest of hill
**HILLED** > HILL
**HILLER** > HILL
**HILLERS** > HILL
**HILLFOLK** *n* people living in the hills
**HILLFORT** *n* hilltop fortified with ramparts and ditches, dating from the second millennium BC
**HILLFORTS** > HILLFORT
**HILLIER** > HILL
**HILLIEST** > HILL
**HILLINESS** > HILL
**HILLING** > HILL
**HILLMEN** *same as* > HILLFOLK
**HILLO** *same as* > HELLO
**HILLOA** *same as* > HALLOA
**HILLOAED** > HILLOA
**HILLOAING** > HILLOA
**HILLOAS** > HILLOA
**HILLOCK** *n* small hill
**HILLOCKED** > HILLOCK
**HILLOCKS** > HILLOCK
**HILLOCKY** > HILLOCK
**HILLOED** > HILLO
**HILLOES** > HILLO
**HILLOING** > HILLO
**HILLOS** > HILLO
**HILLS** > HILL
**HILLSIDE** *n* side of a hill
**HILLSIDES** > HILLSIDE
**HILLSLOPE** *same as* > HILLSIDE
**HILLTOP** *n* top of hill
**HILLTOPS** > HILLTOP
**HILLY** > HILL
**HILT** *n* handle of a sword or knife ▷ *vb* supply with a hilt
**HILTED** > HILT
**HILTING** > HILT
**HILTLESS** > HILT
**HILTS** > HILT
**HILUM** *n* scar on a seed marking its point of attachment to the seed vessel
**HILUS** *rare word for* > HILUM
**HIM** *pron* refers to a male person or animal when the object of a sentence or clause ▷ *n* male person
**HIMATIA** > HIMATION
**HIMATION** *n* (in ancient Greece) a cloak draped around the body

**HIMATIONS** > HIMATION
**HIMBO** *n* slang, usually derogarory term for an attractive but empty-headed man
**HIMBOS** > HIMBO
**HIMS** > HIM
**HIMSELF** *pron* masculine singular reflexive form
**HIN** *n* Hebrew unit of capacity equal to about 12 pints or 3.5 litres
**HINAHINA** *same as* > MAHOE
**HINAU** *n* New Zealand tree
**HIND** *adj* situated at the back ▷ *n* female deer
**HINDBERRY** *n* raspberry
**HINDBRAIN** *nontechnical name for* > RHOMBENCEPHALON: part of the brain comprising the cerbellum, pons and medulla oblongata
**HINDER** *vb* get in the way of ▷ *adj* situated at the back
**HINDERED** > HINDER
**HINDERER** > HINDER
**HINDERERS** > HINDER
**HINDERING** > HINDER
**HINDERS** > HINDER
**HINDFEET** > HINDFOOT
**HINDFOOT** *n* back foot
**HINDGUT** *n* part of the vertebrate digestive tract comprising the colon and rectum
**HINDGUTS** > HINDGUT
**HINDHEAD** *n* back of head
**HINDHEADS** > HINDHEAD
**HINDLEG** *n* back leg
**HINDLEGS** > HINDLEG
**HINDMOST** > HIND
**HINDRANCE** *n* obstruction or snag
**HINDS** > HIND
**HINDSHANK** *n* meat from animal's hind leg
**HINDSIGHT** *n* ability to understand, after something has happened, what should have been done
**HINDWARD** *adj* at back
**HINDWING** *n* back wing
**HINDWINGS** > HINDWING
**HING** *n* asafoetida
**HINGE** *n* device for holding together two parts so that one can swing freely ▷ *vb* depend (on)
**HINGED** > HINGE
**HINGELESS** > HINGE
**HINGELIKE** > HINGE
**HINGER** *n* tool for making hinges
**HINGERS** > HINGER
**HINGES** > HINGE
**HINGING** > HINGE
**HINGS** > HING
**HINKIER** > HINKY
**HINKIEST** > HINKY
**HINKY** *adj* strange
**HINNIED** > HINNY

HINNIES > HINNY

HINNY n offspring of a male horse and a female donkey ▷ vb whinny

HINNYING > HINNY

HINS > HIN

HINT n indirect suggestion ▷ vb suggest indirectly

HINTED > HINT

HINTER > HINT

HINTERS > HINT

HINTING > HINT

HINTINGLY > HINT

HINTINGS > HINT

HINTS > HINT

HIOI n New Zealand plant of the mint family

HIOIS > HIOI

HIP n either side of the body between the pelvis and the thigh ▷ adj aware of or following the latest trends ▷ interj exclamation used to introduce cheers

HIPBONE n either of the two bones that form the sides of the pelvis

HIPBONES > HIPBONE

HIPHUGGER adj (of trousers) having a low waist

HIPLESS > HIP

HIPLIKE > HIP

HIPLINE n widest part of a person's hips

HIPLINES > HIPLINE

HIPLY > HIP

HIPNESS > HIP

HIPNESSES > HIP

HIPPARCH n (in ancient Greece) a cavalry commander

HIPPARCHS > HIPPARCH

HIPPED adj having a hip or hips

HIPPEN n baby's nappy

HIPPENS > HIPPEN

HIPPER > HIP

HIPPEST > HIP

HIPPIATRY n treatment of disease in horses

HIPPIC adj of horses

HIPPIE same as > HIPPY

HIPPIEDOM > HIPPIE

HIPPIEISH > HIPPIE

HIPPIER > HIPPY

HIPPIES > HIPPY

HIPPIEST > HIPPY

HIPPIN same as > HIPPEN

HIPPINESS > HIPPY

HIPPING same as > HIPPEN

HIPPINGS > HIPPING

HIPPINS > HIPPIN

HIPPISH adj in low spirits

HIPPO n hippopotamus

HIPPOCRAS n old English drink of wine flavoured with spices

HIPPODAME n sea horse

HIPPOLOGY n study of horses

HIPPOS > HIPPO

HIPPURIC as in hippuric acid crystalline solid excreted in the urine of mammals

HIPPURITE n type of fossil

HIPPUS n spasm of eye

HIPPUSES > HIPPUS

HIPPY n (esp in the 1960s) person whose behaviour and dress imply a rejection of conventional values ▷ adj having large hips

HIPPYDOM > HIPPY

HIPPYDOMS > HIPPY

HIPS > HIP

HIPSHOT adj having a dislocated hip

HIPSTER n enthusiast of modern jazz

HIPSTERS pl n trousers cut so that the top encircles the hips

HIPT > HIP

HIRABLE > HIRE

HIRAGANA n one of the Japanese systems of syllabic writing based on Chinese cursive ideograms. The more widely used of the two current systems, it is employed in newspapers and general literature

HIRAGANAS > HIRAGANA

HIRAGE n fee for hiring

HIRAGES > HIRAGE

HIRCINE adj of or like a goat, esp in smell

HIRCOSITY n quality of being like a goat

HIRE vb pay to have temporary use of ▷ n hiring

HIREABLE > HIRE

HIREAGE same as > HIRAGE

HIREAGES > HIREAGE

HIRED > HIRE

HIREE n hired person

HIREES > HIREE

HIRELING n derogatory term for a person who works only for wages

HIRELINGS > HIRELING

HIRER > HIRE

HIRERS > HIRE

HIRES > HIRE

HIRING > HIRE

HIRINGS > HIRE

HIRLING n Scots word for a type of fish

HIRLINGS > HIRLING

HIRPLE vb limp ▷ n limping gait

HIRPLED > HIRPLE

HIRPLES > HIRPLE

HIRPLING > HIRPLE

HIRRIENT n trilled sound

HIRRIENTS > HIRRIENT

HIRSEL vb sort into groups

HIRSELED > HIRSEL

HIRSELING > HIRSEL

HIRSELLED > HIRSEL

HIRSELS > HIRSEL

HIRSLE vb wriggle or fidget

HIRSLED > HIRSLE

HIRSLES > HIRSLE

HIRSLING > HIRSLE

HIRSTIE adj dry

HIRSUTE adj hairy

HIRSUTISM > HIRSUTE

HIRUDIN n anticoagulant extracted from the mouth glands of leeches

HIRUDINS > HIRUDIN

HIRUNDINE adj of or resembling a swallow

HIS adj belonging to him

HISH same as > HISS

HISHED > HISH

HISHES > HISH

HISHING > HISH

HISN dialect form of > HIS

HISPANISM n Spanish turn of phrase

HISPID adj covered with stiff hairs or bristles

HISPIDITY > HISPID

HISS n sound like that of a long s (as an expression of contempt) ▷ vb utter a hiss ▷ interj exclamation of derision or disapproval

HISSED > HISS

HISSELF dialect form of > HIMSELF

HISSER > HISS

HISSERS > HISS

HISSES > HISS

HISSIER > HISSY

HISSIES > HISSY

HISSIEST > HISSY

HISSING > HISS

HISSINGLY > HISS

HISSINGS > HISS

HISSY n temper tantrum ▷ adj sound similar to a hiss

HIST interj exclamation used to attract attention or as a warning to be silent ▷ vb make hist sound

HISTAMIN variant of > HISTAMINE

HISTAMINE n substance released by the body tissues in allergic reactions

HISTAMINS > HISTAMIN

HISTED > HIST

HISTIDIN variant of > HISTIDINE

HISTIDINE n nonessential amino acid that occurs in most proteins: a precursor of histamine

HISTIDINS > HISTIDIN

HISTIE same as > HIRSTIE

HISTING > HIST

HISTIOID same as > HISTOID

HISTOGEN n (formerly) any of three layers in an apical meristem that were thought to give rise to the different parts of the plant: the apical meristem is now regarded as comprising two layers

HISTOGENS > HISTOGEN

HISTOGENY > HISTOGEN

HISTOGRAM n statistical graph in which the frequency of values is represented by vertical bars of varying heights and widths

HISTOID adj (esp of a tumour)

HISTOLOGY n study of the tissues of an animal or plant

HISTONE n any of a group of basic proteins present in cell nuclei and implicated in the spatial organization of DNA

HISTONES > HISTONE

HISTORIAN n writer of history

HISTORIC adj famous or significant in history

HISTORIED adj recorded in history

HISTORIES > HISTORY

HISTORIFY vb make part of history

HISTORISM n idea that history influences present

HISTORY n (record or account of) past events and developments

HISTRIO n actor

HISTRION same as > HISTRIO

HISTRIONS > HISTRION

HISTRIOS > HISTRIO

HISTS > HIST

HIT vb strike, touch forcefully ▷ n hitting

HITCH n minor problem ▷ vb obtain (a lift) by hitchhiking

HITCHED > HITCH

HITCHER > HITCH

HITCHERS > HITCH

HITCHES > HITCH

HITCHHIKE vb travel by obtaining free lifts

HITCHIER > HITCH

HITCHIEST > HITCH

HITCHILY > HITCH

HITCHING > HITCH

HITCHY > HITCH

HITHE n small harbour

HITHER adv or towards this place ▷ vb come

HITHERED > HITHER

HITHERING > HITHER

HITHERS > HITHER

HITHERTO adv until this time

HITHES > HITHE

HITLESS > HIT

HITMAN n professional killer

HITMEN > HITMAN

HITS > HIT

HITTABLE > HIT

HITTER n boxer who has a hard punch rather than skill or finesse

HITTERS > HITTER

HITTING > HIT

HIVE n structure in which

social bees live and rear their young ▷ *vb* cause (bees) to collect or (of bees) to collect inside a hive

**HIVED** > HIVE

**HIVELESS** > HIVE

**HIVELIKE** > HIVE

**HIVER** *n* person who keeps beehives

**HIVERS** > HIVER

**HIVES** *n* allergic reaction in which itchy red or whitish patches appear on the skin

**HIVEWARD** *adj* towards hive

**HIVEWARDS** *adv* towards hive

**HIVING** > HIVE

**HIYA** *sentence substitute* informal term of greeting

**HIZEN** *n* type of Japanese porcelain

**HIZENS** > HIZEN

**HIZZ** *same as* > HISS

**HIZZED** > HIZZ

**HIZZES** > HIZZ

**HIZZING** > HIZZ

**HIZZONER** *n* nickname for mayor

**HIZZONERS** > HIZZONER

**HM** *interj* sound made to express hesitation or doubt

**HMM** *same as* > HM

**HO** *n* derogatory term for a woman ▷ *interj* imitation or representation of the sound of a deep laugh ▷ *vb* halt

**HOA** *same as* > HO

**HOACTZIN** *same as* > HOATZIN

**HOACTZINS** > HOACTZIN

**HOAED** > HOA

**HOAGIE** *n* sandwich made with long bread roll

**HOAGIES** > HOAGIE

**HOAGY** *same as* > HOAGIE

**HOAING** > HOA

**HOAR** *adj* covered with hoarfrost ▷ *vb* make hoary

**HOARD** *n* store hidden away for future use ▷ *vb* save or store

**HOARDED** > HOARD

**HOARDER** > HOARD

**HOARDERS** > HOARD

**HOARDING** *n* large board for displaying advertisements

**HOARDINGS** > HOARDING

**HOARDS** > HOARD

**HOARED** > HOAR

**HOARFROST** *n* white ground frost

**HOARHEAD** *n* person with white hair

**HOARHEADS** > HOARHEAD

**HOARHOUND** *same as* > HOREHOUND

**HOARIER** > HOARY

**HOARIEST** > HOARY

**HOARILY** > HOARY

**HOARINESS** > HOARY

**HOARING** > HOAR

**HOARS** > HOAR

**HOARSE** *adj* (of a voice) rough and unclear

**HOARSELY** > HOARSE

**HOARSEN** *vb* make or become hoarse

**HOARSENED** > HOARSEN

**HOARSENS** > HOARSEN

**HOARSER** > HOARSE

**HOARSEST** > HOARSE

**HOARY** *adj* grey or white(-haired)

**HOAS** > HOA

**HOAST** *n* cough ▷ *vb* cough

**HOASTED** > HOAST

**HOASTING** > HOAST

**HOASTMAN** *n* shipper of coal

**HOASTMEN** > HOASTMAN

**HOASTS** > HOAST

**HOATCHING** *adj* infested

**HOATZIN** *n* South American bird with a brownish plumage and very small crested head

**HOATZINES** > HOATZIN

**HOATZINS** > HOATZIN

**HOAX** *n* deception or trick ▷ *vb* deceive or play a trick upon

**HOAXED** > HOAX

**HOAXER** > HOAX

**HOAXERS** > HOAX

**HOAXES** > HOAX

**HOAXING** > HOAX

**HOB** *n* flat top part of a cooker, or a separate flat surface, containing gas or electric rings for cooking on ▷ *vb* cut or form with a hob

**HOBBED** > HOB

**HOBBER** *n* machine used in making gears

**HOBBERS** > HOBBER

**HOBBIES** > HOBBY

**HOBBING** > HOB

**HOBBISH** *adj* like a clown

**HOBBIT** *n* one of an imaginary race of half-size people living in holes

**HOBBITRY** > HOBBIT

**HOBBITS** > HOBBIT

**HOBBLE** *vb* walk lamely ▷ *n* strap, rope, etc, used to hobble a horse

**HOBBLED** > HOBBLE

**HOBBLER** > HOBBLE

**HOBBLERS** > HOBBLE

**HOBBLES** > HOBBLE

**HOBBLING** > HOBBLE

**HOBBLINGS** > HOBBLE

**HOBBY** *n* activity pursued in one's spare time

**HOBBYISM** > HOBBY

**HOBBYISMS** > HOBBY

**HOBBYIST** > HOBBY

**HOBBYISTS** > HOBBY

**HOBBYLESS** > HOBBY

**HOBDAY** *vb* alleviate (a breathing problem in certain horses) by the surgical operation of removing soft tissue ventricles to pull back the vocal fold

**HOBDAYED** > HOBDAY

**HOBDAYING** > HOBDAY

**HOBDAYS** > HOBDAY

**HOBGOBLIN** *n* mischievous goblin

**HOBJOB** *vb* do odd jobs

**HOBJOBBED** > HOBJOB

**HOBJOBBER** > HOBJOB

**HOBJOBS** > HOBJOB

**HOBLIKE** > HOB

**HOBNAIL** *n* short nail with a large head for protecting the soles of heavy footwear ▷ *vb* provide with hobnails

**HOBNAILED** > HOBNAIL

**HOBNAILS** > HOBNAIL

**HOBNOB** *vb* be on friendly terms (with)

**HOBNOBBED** > HOBNOB

**HOBNOBBER** > HOBNOB

**HOBNOBBY** > HOBNOB

**HOBNOBS** > HOBNOB

**HOBO** *n* tramp or vagrant ▷ *vb* live as hobo

**HOBODOM** > HOBO

**HOBODOMS** > HOBO

**HOBOED** > HOBO

**HOBOES** > HOBO

**HOBOING** > HOBO

**HOBOISM** > HOBO

**HOBOISMS** > HOBO

**HOBOS** > HOBO

**HOBS** > HOB

**HOC** *adj* Latin for this

**HOCK** *n* joint in the back leg of an animal such as a horse that corresponds to the human ankle ▷ *vb* pawn

**HOCKED** > HOCK

**HOCKER** > HOCK

**HOCKERS** > HOCK

**HOCKEY** *n* team game played on a field with a ball and curved sticks

**HOCKEYS** > HOCKEY

**HOCKING** > HOCK

**HOCKLE** *vb* spit

**HOCKLED** > HOCKLE

**HOCKLES** > HOCKLE

**HOCKLING** > HOCKLE

**HOCKS** > HOCK

**HOCKSHOP** *n* pawnshop

**HOCKSHOPS** > HOCKSHOP

**HOCUS** *vb* take in

**HOCUSED** > HOCUS

**HOCUSES** > HOCUS

**HOCUSING** > HOCUS

**HOCUSSED** > HOCUS

**HOCUSSES** > HOCUS

**HOCUSSING** > HOCUS

**HOD** *n* open wooden box attached to a pole, for carrying bricks or mortar ▷ *vb* bob up and down

**HODAD** *n* person who pretends to be a surfer

**HODADDIES** > HODADDY

**HODADDY** *same as* > HODAD

**HODADS** > HODAD

**HODDED** > HOD

**HODDEN** *n* coarse homespun cloth produced in Scotland: hodden grey is made by mixing black and white wools

**HODDENS** > HODDEN

**HODDIN** *same as* > HODDEN

**HODDING** > HOD

**HODDINS** > HODDIN

**HODDLE** *vb* waddle

**HODDLED** > HODDLE

**HODDLES** > HODDLE

**HODDLING** > HODDLE

**HODIERNAL** *adj* of the present day

**HODJA** *n* respectful Turkish form of address

**HODJAS** > HODJA

**HODMAN** *n* hod carrier

**HODMANDOD** *n* snail

**HODMEN** > HODMAN

**HODOGRAPH** *n* curve of which the radius vector represents the velocity of a moving particle

**HODOMETER** *another name for* > ODOMETER

**HODOMETRY** > HODOMETER

**HODOSCOPE** *n* any device for tracing the path of a charged particle, esp a particle found in cosmic rays

**HODS** > HOD

**HOE** *n* long-handled tool used for loosening soil or weeding ▷ *vb* scrape or weed with a hoe

**HOECAKE** *n* maize cake

**HOECAKES** > HOECAKE

**HOED** > HOE

**HOEDOWN** *n* boisterous square dance

**HOEDOWNS** > HOEDOWN

**HOEING** > HOE

**HOELIKE** > HOE

**HOER** > HOE

**HOERS** > HOE

**HOES** > HOE

**HOG** *n* castrated male pig ▷ *vb* take more than one's share of

**HOGAN** *n* wooden dwelling covered with earth, typical of the Navaho Indians of N America

**HOGANS** > HOGAN

**HOGBACK** *n* narrow ridge that consists of steeply inclined rock strata

**HOGBACKS** > HOGBACK

**HOGEN** *n* strong alcoholic drink

**HOGENS** > HOGEN

**HOGFISH** *n* type of fish

**HOGFISHES** > HOGFISH

**HOGG** *same as* > HOG

**HOGGED** > HOG

**HOGGER** > HOG

**HOGGEREL** *n* year-old sheep

**HOGGERELS** > HOGGEREL

**HOGGERIES** > HOGGERY

**HOGGERS** > HOG

**HOGGERY** *n* hogs collectively

**HOGGET** n sheep up to the age of one year that has yet to be sheared
**HOGGETS** > HOGGET
**HOGGIN** n finely sifted gravel containing enough clay binder for it to be used in its natural form for making paths or roads
**HOGGING** same as > HOGGIN
**HOGGINGS** > HOGGING
**HOGGINS** > HOGGIN
**HOGGISH** adj selfish, gluttonous, or dirty
**HOGGISHLY** > HOGGISH
**HOGGS** > HOGG
**HOGH** n ridge of land
**HOGHOOD** n condition of being hog
**HOGHOODS** > HOGHOOD
**HOGHS** > HOGH
**HOGLIKE** > HOG
**HOGMANAY** n New Year's Eve
**HOGMANAYS** > HOGMANAY
**HOGMANE** n short stiff mane
**HOGMANES** > HOGMANE
**HOGMENAY** variant of > HOGMANAY
**HOGMENAYS** > HOGMENAY
**HOGNOSE** as in hognose snake puff adder
**HOGNOSED** as in hognosed skunk any of several American skunks having a broad snoutlike nose
**HOGNOSES** > HOGNOSE
**HOGNUT** another name for > PIGNUT
**HOGNUTS** > HOGNUT
**HOGS** > HOG
**HOGSHEAD** n large cask
**HOGSHEADS** > HOGSHEAD
**HOGTIE** vb tie together the legs or the arms and legs of
**HOGTIED** > HOGTIE
**HOGTIEING** > HOGTIE
**HOGTIES** > HOGTIE
**HOGTYING** > HOGTIE
**HOGWARD** n person looking after hogs
**HOGWARDS** > HOGWARD
**HOGWASH** n nonsense
**HOGWASHES** > HOGWASH
**HOGWEED** n any of several coarse weedy umbelliferous plants, esp cow parsnip
**HOGWEEDS** > HOGWEED
**HOH** same as > HO
**HOHA** n nuisance
**HOHED** > HOH
**HOHING** > HOH
**HOHS** > HOH
**HOI** same as > HOY
**HOICK** vb raise abruptly and sharply
**HOICKED** > HOICK
**HOICKING** > HOICK
**HOICKS** interj cry used to encourage hounds to hunt ▷ vb shout hoicks
**HOICKSED** > HOICKS
**HOICKSES** > HOICKS
**HOICKSING** > HOICKS

**HOIDEN** same as > HOYDEN
**HOIDENED** > HOIDEN
**HOIDENING** > HOIDEN
**HOIDENISH** > HOIDEN
**HOIDENS** > HOIDEN
**HOIK** same as > HOICK
**HOIKED** > HOIK
**HOIKING** > HOIK
**HOIKS** > HOIK
**HOING** > HO
**HOISE** same as > HOIST
**HOISED** > HOISE
**HOISES** > HOISE
**HOISIN** n Chinese sweet spicy reddish-brown sauce made from soya beans, sugar, vinegar, and garlic
**HOISING** > HOISE
**HOISINS** > HOISIN
**HOIST** vb raise or lift up ▷ n device for lifting things
**HOISTED** > HOIST
**HOISTER** > HOIST
**HOISTERS** > HOIST
**HOISTING** > HOIST
**HOISTINGS** > HOIST
**HOISTMAN** n person operating a hoist
**HOISTMEN** > HOISTMAN
**HOISTS** > HOIST
**HOISTWAY** n shaft for a hoist
**HOISTWAYS** > HOISTWAY
**HOKA** n red cod
**HOKE** vb overplay (a part, etc)
**HOKED** > HOKE
**HOKES** > HOKE
**HOKEY** adj corny
**HOKEYNESS** > HOKEY
**HOKI** n fish of New Zealand waters
**HOKIER** > HOKEY
**HOKIEST** > HOKEY
**HOKILY** > HOKEY
**HOKINESS** > HOKEY
**HOKING** > HOKE
**HOKIS** > HOKI
**HOKKU** same as > HAIKU
**HOKONUI** n illicit whisky
**HOKONUIS** > HOKONUI
**HOKUM** n rubbish, nonsense
**HOKUMS** > HOKUM
**HOKYPOKY** n trickery
**HOLANDRIC** adj relating to Y-chromosomal genes
**HOLARCHY** n system composed of interacting holons
**HOLARD** n amount of water contained in soil
**HOLARDS** > HOLARD
**HOLD** vb keep or support in or with the hands or arms ▷ n act or way of holding
**HOLDABLE** > HOLD
**HOLDALL** n large strong travelling bag
**HOLDALLS** > HOLDALL
**HOLDBACK** n strap of the harness joining the breeching to the shaft, so that the horse can hold back the vehicle

**HOLDBACKS** > HOLDBACK
**HOLDDOWN** n control function in a computer
**HOLDDOWNS** > HOLDDOWN
**HOLDEN** past participle of > HOLD
**HOLDER** n person or thing that holds
**HOLDERBAT** n part of pipe used as fastening
**HOLDERS** > HOLDER
**HOLDFAST** n act of gripping strongly
**HOLDFASTS** > HOLDFAST
**HOLDING** > HOLD
**HOLDINGS** > HOLD
**HOLDOUT** n (in US English) person, country, organization, etc, that continues to resist or refuses to change
**HOLDOUTS** > HOLDOUT
**HOLDOVER** n (in US and Canadian English) elected official who continues in office after his term has expired
**HOLDOVERS** > HOLDOVER
**HOLDS** > HOLD
**HOLDUP** n robbery, esp an armed one
**HOLDUPS** > HOLDUP
**HOLE** n area hollowed out in a solid ▷ vb make holes in
**HOLED** > HOLE
**HOLELESS** > HOLE
**HOLES** > HOLE
**HOLESOM** same as > HOLESOME
**HOLESOME** same as > WHOLESOME
**HOLEY** adj full of holes
**HOLEYER** > HOLEY
**HOLEYEST** > HOLEY
**HOLIBUT** same as > HALIBUT
**HOLIBUTS** > HOLIBUT
**HOLIDAY** n time spent away from home for rest or recreation ▷ vb spend a holiday
**HOLIDAYED** > HOLIDAY
**HOLIDAYER** > HOLIDAY
**HOLIDAYS** > HOLIDAY
**HOLIER** > HOLY
**HOLIES** > HOLY
**HOLIEST** > HOLY
**HOLILY** adv in a holy, devout, or sacred manner
**HOLINESS** n state of being holy
**HOLING** > HOLE
**HOLINGS** > HOLE
**HOLISM** n view that a whole is greater than the sum of its parts
**HOLISMS** > HOLISM
**HOLIST** > HOLISM
**HOLISTIC** adj considering the complete person, physically and mentally, in the treatment of an illness
**HOLISTS** > HOLISM
**HOLK** vb dig

**HOLKED** > HOLK
**HOLKING** > HOLK
**HOLKS** > HOLK
**HOLLA** same as > HOLLO
**HOLLAED** > HOLLA
**HOLLAING** > HOLLA
**HOLLAND** n coarse linen cloth, used esp for furnishing
**HOLLANDS** > HOLLAND
**HOLLAS** > HOLLA
**HOLLER** n shout, yell ▷ vb shout or yell
**HOLLERED** > HOLLER
**HOLLERING** > HOLLER
**HOLLERS** > HOLLER
**HOLLIDAM** same as > HALIDOM
**HOLLIDAMS** > HOLLIDAM
**HOLLIES** > HOLLY
**HOLLO** interj cry for attention, or of encouragement ▷ vb shout
**HOLLOA** same as > HOLLO
**HOLLOAED** > HOLLOA
**HOLLOAING** > HOLLOA
**HOLLOAS** > HOLLOA
**HOLLOED** > HOLLO
**HOLLOES** > HOLLO
**HOLLOING** > HOLLO
**HOLLOO** same as > HALLOO
**HOLLOOED** > HOLLOO
**HOLLOOING** > HOLLOO
**HOLLOOS** > HOLLOO
**HOLLOS** > HOLLO
**HOLLOW** adj having a hole or space inside ▷ n cavity or space ▷ vb form a hollow in
**HOLLOWARE** n hollow utensils such as cups
**HOLLOWED** > HOLLOW
**HOLLOWER** > HOLLOW
**HOLLOWEST** > HOLLOW
**HOLLOWING** > HOLLOW
**HOLLOWLY** > HOLLOW
**HOLLOWS** > HOLLOW
**HOLLY** n evergreen tree with prickly leaves and red berries
**HOLLYHOCK** n tall garden plant with spikes of colourful flowers
**HOLM** n island in a river, lake, or estuary
**HOLMIA** n oxide of holmium
**HOLMIAS** > HOLMIA
**HOLMIC** adj of or containing holmium
**HOLMIUM** n silver-white metallic element, the compounds of which are highly magnetic
**HOLMIUMS** > HOLMIUM
**HOLMS** > HOLM
**HOLOCAUST** n destruction or loss of life on a massive scale
**HOLOCENE** adj of, denoting, or formed in the second and most recent epoch of the Quaternary period, which began 10 000

years ago at the end of the Pleistocene

**HOLOCRINE** *adj* (of the secretion of glands) characterized by disintegration of the entire glandular cell in releasing its product, as in sebaceous glands

**HOLOGAMY** *n* condition of having gametes like ordinary cells

**HOLOGRAM** *n* three-dimensional photographic image

**HOLOGRAMS** > HOLOGRAM

**HOLOGRAPH** *n* document handwritten by the author

**HOLOGYNIC** *adj* passed down through females

**HOLOGYNY** *n* inheritance of genetic traits through females only

**HOLOHEDRA** *n* geometrical forms with particular symmetry

**HOLON** *n* autonomous self-reliant unit, esp in manufacturing

**HOLONIC** > HOLON

**HOLONS** > HOLON

**HOLOPHOTE** *n* device for directing light from lighthouse

**HOLOPHYTE** *n* plant capable of synthesizing food from inorganic molecules

**HOLOPTIC** *adj* with eyes meeting at the front

**HOLOTYPE** *n* original specimen from which a description of a new species is made

**HOLOTYPES** > HOLOTYPE

**HOLOTYPIC** > HOLOTYPE

**HOLOZOIC** *adj* (of animals) obtaining nourishment by feeding on plants or other animals

**HOLP** *past tense of* > HELP

**HOLPEN** *past participle of* > HELP

**HOLS** *pl n* holidays

**HOLSTEIN** *n* breed of cattle

**HOLSTEINS** > HOLSTEIN

**HOLSTER** *n* leather case for a pistol, hung from a belt ▷ *vb* return (a pistol) to its holster

**HOLSTERED** > HOLSTER

**HOLSTERS** > HOLSTER

**HOLT** *n* otter's lair

**HOLTS** > HOLT

**HOLY** *adj* of God or a god

**HOLYDAM** *same as* > HALIDOM

**HOLYDAME** *same as* > HALIDOM

**HOLYDAMES** > HOLYDAME

**HOLYDAMS** > HOLYDAM

**HOLYDAY** *n* day on which a religious festival is observed

**HOLYDAYS** > HOLYDAY

**HOLYSTONE** *n* soft sandstone used for scrubbing the decks of a vessel ▷ *vb* scrub (a vessel's decks) with a holystone

**HOLYTIDE** *n* time for special religious observance

**HOLYTIDES** > HOLYTIDE

**HOM** *n* sacred plant of the Parsees and ancient Persians

**HOMA** *same as* > HOM

**HOMAGE** *n* show of respect or honour towards someone or something ▷ *vb* render homage to

**HOMAGED** > HOMAGE

**HOMAGER** > HOMAGE

**HOMAGERS** > HOMAGE

**HOMAGES** > HOMAGE

**HOMAGING** > HOMAGE

**HOMALOID** *n* geometrical plane

**HOMALOIDS** > HOMALOID

**HOMAS** > HOMA

**HOMBRE** *slang word for* > MAN

**HOMBRES** > HOMBRE

**HOMBURG** *n* man's soft felt hat with a dented crown and a stiff upturned brim

**HOMBURGS** > HOMBURG

**HOME** *n* place where one lives ▷ *adj* of one's home, birthplace, or native country ▷ *adv* to or at home ▷ *vb* direct towards (a point or target)

**HOMEBIRTH** *n* act of giving birth to a child in one's own home

**HOMEBODY** *n* person whose life and interests are centred on the home

**HOMEBOUND** *adj* heading for home

**HOMEBOY** *n* close friend

**HOMEBOYS** > HOMEBOY

**HOMEBRED** *adj* raised or bred at home ▷ *n* animal bred at home

**HOMEBREDS** > HOMEBRED

**HOMEBREW** *n* home-made beer

**HOMEBREWS** > HOMEBREW

**HOMEBUILT** *adj* built at home

**HOMEBUYER** *n* person buying a home

**HOMECOMER** *n* person coming home

**HOMECRAFT** *n* skills used in the home

**HOMED** > HOME

**HOMEFELT** *adj* felt personally

**HOMEGIRL** > HOMEBOY

**HOMEGIRLS** > HOMEBOY

**HOMEGROWN** *adj* (esp of fruit and vegetables) produced in one's own country, district, estate, or garden

**HOMELAND** *n* country from

which a person's ancestors came

**HOMELANDS** > HOMELAND

**HOMELESS** *adj* having nowhere to live ▷ *pl n* people who have nowhere to live

**HOMELIER** > HOMELY

**HOMELIEST** > HOMELY

**HOMELIKE** > HOME

**HOMELILY** > HOMELY

**HOMELY** *adj* simple, ordinary, and comfortable

**HOMELYN** *n* species of ray

**HOMELYNS** > HOMELYN

**HOMEMADE** *adj* (esp of cakes, jam, and other foods) made at home or on the premises, esp of high-quality ingredients

**HOMEMAKER** *n* person, esp a housewife, who manages a home

**HOMEOBOX** *adj* of genes that regulate cell development

**HOMEOMERY** *n* condition of being made up of similar parts

**HOMEOPATH** *n* person who treats disease by the use of small amounts of a drug that produces symptoms like those of the disease being treated

**HOMEOSES** > HOMEOSIS

**HOMEOSIS** *n* process of one part coming to resemble another

**HOMEOTIC** > HOMEOSIS

**HOMEOWNER** *n* person who owns the home in which he or she lives

**HOMEPAGE** *n* main page of website

**HOMEPAGES** > HOMEPAGE

**HOMEPLACE** *n* person's home

**HOMEPORT** *n* port where vessel is registered

**HOMEPORTS** > HOMEPORT

**HOMER** *n* homing pigeon ▷ *vb* score a home run in baseball

**HOMERED** > HOMER

**HOMERIC** *adj* grand or heroic

**HOMERING** > HOMER

**HOMEROOM** *n* common room at school

**HOMEROOMS** > HOMEROOM

**HOMERS** > HOMER

**HOMES** > HOME

**HOMESICK** *adj* sad because missing one's home and family

**HOMESITE** *n* site for building house

**HOMESITES** > HOMESITE

**HOMESPUN** *adj* (of philosophies or opinions) plain and unsophisticated ▷ *n* cloth made at home or made of yarn spun at home

**HOMESPUNS** > HOMESPUN

**HOMESTALL** *same as* > HOMESTEAD

**HOMESTAND** *n* series of games played at a team's home ground

**HOMESTAY** *n* period spent living as a guest in someone's home

**HOMESTAYS** > HOMESTAY

**HOMESTEAD** *n* farmhouse plus the adjoining land

**HOMETOWN** *n* town where one lives or was born

**HOMETOWNS** > HOMETOWN

**HOMEWARD** *adj* going home ▷ *adv* towards home

**HOMEWARDS** *adv* towards home

**HOMEWARE** *n* crockery, furniture, and furnishings with which a house, room, etc, is furnished

**HOMEWARES** > HOMEWARE

**HOMEWORK** *n* school work done at home

**HOMEWORKS** > HOMEWORK

**HOMEY** *same as* > HOMY

**HOMEYNESS** > HOMEY

**HOMEYS** > HOMEY

**HOMICIDAL** *adj* of, involving, or characterized by homicide

**HOMICIDE** *n* killing of a human being

**HOMICIDES** > HOMICIDE

**HOMIE** *short for* > HOMEBOY

**HOMIER** > HOMY

**HOMIES** > HOMIE

**HOMIEST** > HOMY

**HOMILETIC** *adj* of or relating to a homily or sermon

**HOMILIES** > HOMILY

**HOMILIST** > HOMILY

**HOMILISTS** > HOMILY

**HOMILY** *n* speech telling people how they should behave

**HOMINES** > HOMO

**HOMINESS** > HOMY

**HOMING** *adj* denoting the ability to return home after travelling great distances ▷ *n* relating to the ability to return home after travelling great distances

**HOMINGS** > HOMING

**HOMINIAN** *same as* > HOMINID

**HOMINIANS** > HOMINIAN

**HOMINID** *n* man or any extinct forerunner of man ▷ *adj* of or belonging to this family

**HOMINIDS** > HOMINID

**HOMINIES** > HOMINY

**HOMININE** *adj* characteristic of humans

**HOMINISE** *same as* > HOMINIZE

**HOMINISED** > HOMINISE

**HOMINISES** > HOMINISE

**HOMINIZE** *vb* make

suitable for humans
**HOMINIZED** > HOMINIZE
**HOMINIZES** > HOMINIZE
**HOMINOID** *n* manlike
animal ▷ *adj* of or like
man
**HOMINOIDS** > HOMINOID
**HOMINY** *n* coarsely ground
maize prepared as a food
by boiling in milk or water
**HOMME** *French word for* > MAN
**HOMMES** > HOMME
**HOMMOCK** *same*
*as* > HUMMOCK
**HOMMOCKS** > HOMMOCK
**HOMMOS** *same as* > HUMMUS
**HOMMOSES** > HOMMOS
**HOMO** *n* homogenized milk
**HOMOCERCY** *n* condition
in fish of having a
symmetrical tail
**HOMODONT** *adj* (of most
nonmammalian
vertebrates) having teeth
that are all of the same
type
**HOMODYNE** *adj* of
strengthened radio waves
**HOMOEOBOX** *same*
*as* > HOMEOBOX
**HOMOEOSES** > HOMOEOSIS
**HOMOEOSIS** *n* condition of
controlling a system from
within
**HOMOEOTIC** > HOMOEOSIS
**HOMOGAMIC** > HOMOGAMY
**HOMOGAMY** *n* condition
in which all the flowers
of an inflorescence are
either of the same sex or
hermaphrodite
**HOMOGENY** *n* similarity in
structure of individuals or
parts because of common
ancestry
**HOMOGONY** *n* condition in
a plant of having stamens
and styles of the same
length in all the flowers
**HOMOGRAFT** *n* tissue
graft obtained from an
organism of the same
species as the recipient
**HOMOGRAPH** *n* word spelt
the same as another, but
with a different meaning
**HOMOLOG** *same*
*as* > HOMOLOGUE
**HOMOLOGIC** *adj* having a
related or similar position,
structure, etc
**HOMOLOGS** > HOMOLOG
**HOMOLOGUE** *n* homologous
part or organ
**HOMOLOGY** *n* condition of
being homologous
**HOMOLYSES** > HOMOLYSIS
**HOMOLYSIS** *n* dissociation
of a molecule into two
neutral fragments
**HOMOLYTIC** > HOMOLYSIS
**HOMOMORPH** *n* thing same
in form as something else
**HOMONYM** *n* word spelt or

pronounced the same
as another, but with a
different meaning
**HOMONYMIC** > HOMONYM
**HOMONYMS** > HOMONYM
**HOMONYMY** > HOMONYMITY
**HOMOPHILE** *n* rare word for
homosexual: person who
is sexually attracted to
members of the same sex
**HOMOPHOBE** *n* person who
has an intense hatred of
homosexuality
**HOMOPHONE** *n* word
pronounced the same
as another, but with a
different meaning or
spelling
**HOMOPHONY** *n* linguistic
phenomenon whereby
words of different origins
become identical in
pronunciation
**HOMOPHYLY** *n* resemblance
due to common ancestry
**HOMOPLASY** *n* state of being
derived from an individual
of the same species as the
recipient
**HOMOPOLAR** *adj* of uniform
charge
**HOMOS** > HOMO
**HOMOSEX** *n* sexual activity
between homosexuals
**HOMOSEXES** > HOMOSEX
**HOMOSPORY** *n* state of
producing spores of one
kind only
**HOMOSTYLY** *n* (in flowers)
existence of styles of only
one length
**HOMOTAXES** > HOMOTAXIS
**HOMOTAXIC** > HOMOTAXIS
**HOMOTAXIS** *n* similarity
of composition and
arrangement in rock strata
of different ages or in
different regions
**HOMOTONIC** *adj* of same
tone
**HOMOTONY** > HOMOTONIC
**HOMOTYPAL** *adj* of normal
type
**HOMOTYPE** *n* something
with same structure as
something else
**HOMOTYPES** > HOMOTYPE
**HOMOTYPIC** *same*
*as* > HOMOTYPAL
**HOMOTYPY** > HOMOTYPE
**HOMOUSIAN** *adj* believing
God the Son and God the
Father to be of the same
essence
**HOMS** > HOM
**HOMUNCLE** *n* homunculus
**HOMUNCLES** > HOMUNCLE
**HOMUNCULE** *n* homunculus
**HOMUNCULI** *n* plural of
homunculus: miniature
man
**HOMY** *adj* like a home
**HON** *short for* > HONEY
**HONAN** *n* silk fabric of rough

weave
**HONANS** > HONAN
**HONCHO** *n* person in charge
▷ *vb* supervise or be in
charge of
**HONCHOED** > HONCHO
**HONCHOING** > HONCHO
**HONCHOS** > HONCHO
**HOND** *old form of* > HAND
**HONDA** *n* loop through
which rope is threaded to
make a lasso
**HONDAS** > HONDA
**HONDLE** *vb* negotiate on
price
**HONDLED** > HONDLE
**HONDLES** > HONDLE
**HONDLING** > HONDLE
**HONDS** > HOND
**HONE** *vb* sharpen ▷ *n*
fine whetstone used for
sharpening edged tools
and knives
**HONED** > HONE
**HONER** > HONE
**HONERS** > HONE
**HONES** > HONE
**HONEST** *adj* truthful and
moral
**HONESTER** > HONEST
**HONESTEST** > HONEST
**HONESTIES** > HONESTY
**HONESTLY** *adv* in an
honest manner ▷ *interj*
expression of disgust,
surprise, etc
**HONESTY** *n* quality of being
honest
**HONEWORT** *n* European
plant that has clusters of
small white flowers
**HONEWORTS** > HONEWORT
**HONEY** *n* sweet edible
sticky substance made by
bees from nectar; term of
endearment ▷ *vb* sweeten
with or as if with honey
**HONEYBEE** *n* bee widely
domesticated as a source
of honey and beeswax
**HONEYBEES** > HONEYBEE
**HONEYBUN** *n* term of
endearment
**HONEYBUNS** > HONEYBUN
**HONEYCOMB** *n* waxy
structure of six-sided cells
in which honey is stored
by bees in a beehive ▷ *vb*
pierce or fill with holes,
cavities, etc
**HONEYDEW** *n* sugary
substance excreted by
aphids and similar insects
**HONEYDEWS** > HONEYDEW
**HONEYED** > HONEY
**HONEYEDLY** > HONEY
**HONEYFUL** *adj* full of honey
**HONEYING** > HONEY
**HONEYLESS** > HONEY
**HONEYMOON** *n* holiday taken
by a newly married couple
▷ *vb* take a honeymoon
**HONEYPOT** *n* container for
honey

**HONEYPOTS** > HONEYPOT
**HONEYS** > HONEY
**HONEYTRAP** *n* scheme in
which a victim is lured into
a compromising sexual
situation that provides the
opportunity for blackmail
**HONG** *n* (in China) a factory,
warehouse, etc ▷ *vb*
archaic form of hang
**HONGI** *n* Māori greeting in
which people touch noses
▷ *vb* touch noses
**HONGIED** > HONGI
**HONGIES** > HONGI
**HONGIING** > HONGI
**HONGING** > HONG
**HONGIS** > HONGI
**HONGS** > HONG
**HONIED** > HONEY
**HONIEDLY** > HONEY
**HONING** > HONE
**HONK** *n* sound made by a car
horn ▷ *vb* (cause to) make
this sound
**HONKED** > HONK
**HONKER** *n* person or thing
that honks
**HONKERS** > HONKER
**HONKEY** *same as* > HONKY
**HONKEYS** > HONKEY
**HONKIE** *same as* > HONKY
**HONKIES** > HONKY
**HONKING** > HONK
**HONKS** > HONK
**HONKY** *n* derogatory slang
for White man or White
men collectively
**HONOR** *same as* > HONOUR
**HONORABLE** *adj* possessing
high principles
**HONORABLY** > HONOURABLE
**HONORAND** *n* person being
honoured
**HONORANDS** > HONORAND
**HONORARIA** *n* fee pain for a
nominally free service
**HONORARY** *adj* held or given
only as an honour
**HONORED** > HONOR
**HONOREE** *same*
*as* > HONORAND
**HONOREES** > HONOREE
**HONORER** > HONOUR
**HONORERS** > HONOUR
**HONORIFIC** *adj* showing
respect
**HONORING** > HONOR
**HONORLESS** > HONOUR
**HONORS** *same as* > HONOURS
**HONOUR** *n* sense of honesty
and fairness ▷ *vb* give
praise and attention to
**HONOURED** > HONOUR
**HONOURER** > HONOUR
**HONOURERS** > HONOUR
**HONOURING** > HONOUR
**HONOURS** > HONOUR
**HONS** > HON
**HOO** *pron* she
**HOOCH** *n* alcoholic drink,
esp illicitly distilled spirits
**HOOCHES** > HOOCH
**HOOCHIE** *n* immoral

woman
**HOOCHIES** > HOOCHIE
**HOOD** *n* head covering, often attached to a coat or jacket ▷ *vb* cover with or as if with a hood
**HOODED** *adj* (of a garment) having a hood
**HOODIA** *n* any of several southern African succulent plants whose sap has appetite-suppressing properties
**HOODIAS** > HOODIA
**HOODIE** *n* hooded sweatshirt
**HOODIER** > HOOD
**HOODIES** > HOODIE
**HOODIEST** > HOOD
**HOODING** > HOOD
**HOODLESS** > HOOD
**HOODLIKE** > HOOD
**HOODLUM** *n* violent criminal, gangster
**HOODLUMS** > HOODLUM
**HOODMAN** *n* blindfolded person in blindman's buff
**HOODMEN** > HOODMAN
**HOODMOLD** *n* moulding over door or window
**HOODMOLDS** > HOODMOLD
**HOODOO** *n* (cause of) bad luck ▷ *vb* bring bad luck to
**HOODOOED** > HOODOO
**HOODOOING** > HOODOO
**HOODOOISM** > HOODOO
**HOODOOS** > HOODOO
**HOODS** > HOOD
**HOODWINK** *vb* trick, deceive
**HOODWINKS** > HOODWINK
**HOODY** > HOOD
**HOOEY** *n* nonsense ▷ *interj* nonsense
**HOOEYS** > HOOEY
**HOOF** *n* horny covering of the foot of a horse, deer, etc ▷ *vb* kick or trample with the hooves
**HOOFBEAT** *n* sound made by hoof on the ground
**HOOFBEATS** > HOOFBEAT
**HOOFBOUND** *adj* (of a horse) having dry contracted hooves, with resultant pain and lameness
**HOOFED** *adj* having a hoof or hoofs
**HOOFER** *n* professional dancer
**HOOFERS** > HOOFER
**HOOFING** > HOOF
**HOOFLESS** > HOOF
**HOOFLIKE** > HOOF
**HOOFPRINT** *n* mark made by hoof on ground
**HOOFROT** *n* disease of hoof
**HOOFROTS** > HOOFROT
**HOOFS** > HOOF
**HOOK** *n* curved piece of metal, plastic, etc, used to hang, hold, or pull something ▷ *vb* fasten or catch (as if) with a hook
**HOOKA** *same as* > HOOKAH

**HOOKAH** *n* oriental pipe in which smoke is drawn through water and a long tube
**HOOKAHS** > HOOKAH
**HOOKAS** > HOOKA
**HOOKCHECK** *n* in ice hockey, act of hooking an opposing player
**HOOKED** *adj* bent like a hook
**HOOKER** *n* prostitute
**HOOKERS** > HOOKER
**HOOKEY** *same as* > HOOKY
**HOOKEYS** > HOOKEY
**HOOKIER** > HOOKY
**HOOKIES** > HOOKY
**HOOKIEST** > HOOKY
**HOOKING** > HOOK
**HOOKLESS** > HOOK
**HOOKLET** *n* little hook
**HOOKLETS** > HOOKLET
**HOOKLIKE** > HOOK
**HOOKNOSE** *n* nose with a pronounced outward and downward curve
**HOOKNOSED** > HOOKNOSE
**HOOKNOSES** > HOOKNOSE
**HOOKS** > HOOK
**HOOKUP** *n* contact of an aircraft in flight with the refuelling hose of a tanker aircraft
**HOOKUPS** > HOOKUP
**HOOKWORM** *n* blood-sucking worm with hooked mouthparts
**HOOKWORMS** > HOOKWORM
**HOOKY** *n* truancy, usually from school (esp in the phrase play hooky) ▷ *adj* hooklike
**HOOLACHAN** *n* Highland reel
**HOOLEY** *n* lively party
**HOOLEYS** > HOOLEY
**HOOLICAN** *same as* > HOOLACHAN
**HOOLICANS** > HOOLICAN
**HOOLIE** *same as* > HOOLEY
**HOOLIER** > HOOLY
**HOOLIES** > HOOLIE
**HOOLIEST** > HOOLY
**HOOLIGAN** *n* rowdy young person
**HOOLIGANS** > HOOLIGAN
**HOOLOCK** *n* Indian gibbon
**HOOLOCKS** > HOOLOCK
**HOOLY** *adj* careful or gentle
**HOON** *n* loutish youth who drives irresponsibly ▷ *vb* drive irresponsibly
**HOONS** > HOON
**HOOP** *n* rigid circular band, used esp as a child's toy or for animals to jump through in the circus ▷ *vb* surround with or as if with a hoop
**HOOPED** > HOOP
**HOOPER** *rare word for* > COOPER
**HOOPERS** > HOOPER
**HOOPING** > HOOP
**HOOPLA** *n* fairground game in which hoops are thrown

over objects in an attempt to win them
**HOOPLAS** > HOOPLA
**HOOPLESS** > HOOP
**HOOPLIKE** > HOOP
**HOOPOE** *n* bird with a pinkish-brown plumage and a fanlike crest
**HOOPOES** > HOOPOE
**HOOPOO** *same as* > HOOPOE
**HOOPOOS** > HOOPOO
**HOOPS** > HOOP
**HOOPSKIRT** *n* skirt stiffened by hoops
**HOOPSTER** *n* basketball player
**HOOPSTERS** > HOOPSTER
**HOORAH** *same as* > HURRAH
**HOORAHED** > HOORAH
**HOORAHING** > HOORAH
**HOORAHS** > HOORAH
**HOORAY** *same as* > HURRAH
**HOORAYED** > HOORAY
**HOORAYING** > HOORAY
**HOORAYS** > HOORAY
**HOORD** *same as* > HOARD
**HOORDS** > HOORD
**HOOROO** *same as* > HURRAH
**HOOSEGOW** *slang word for* > JAIL
**HOOSEGOWS** > HOOSEGOW
**HOOSGOW** > JAIL
**HOOSGOWS** > JAIL
**HOOSH** *vb* shoo away
**HOOSHED** > HOOSH
**HOOSHES** > HOOSH
**HOOSHING** > HOOSH
**HOOT** *n* sound of a car horn ▷ *vb* sound (a car horn) ▷ *interj* exclamation of impatience or dissatisfaction: a supposed Scotticism
**HOOTCH** *same as* > HOOCH
**HOOTCHES** > HOOTCH
**HOOTED** > HOOT
**HOOTER** *n* device that hoots
**HOOTERS** > HOOTER
**HOOTIER** > HOOT
**HOOTIEST** > HOOT
**HOOTING** > HOOT
**HOOTNANNY** *n* informal performance by folk singers
**HOOTS** *same as* > HOOT
**HOOTY** > HOOT
**HOOVE** *same as* > HEAVE
**HOOVED** > HOOVE
**HOOVEN** > HOOVE
**HOOVER** *vb* vacuum-clean (a carpet, furniture, etc)
**HOOVERED** > HOOVER
**HOOVERING** > HOOVER
**HOOVERS** > HOOVER
**HOOVES** > HOOF
**HOOVING** > HOOVE
**HOP** *vb* jump on one foot ▷ *n* instance of hopping
**HOPBIND** *n* stalk of the hop
**HOPBINDS** > HOPBIND
**HOPBINE** *same as* > HOPBIND
**HOPBINES** > HOPBINE
**HOPDOG** *n* species of

caterpillar
**HOPDOGS** > HOPDOG
**HOPE** *vb* want (something) to happen or be true ▷ *n* expectation of something desired
**HOPED** > HOPE
**HOPEFUL** *adj* having, expressing, or inspiring hope ▷ *n* person considered to be on the brink of success
**HOPEFULLY** *adv* in a hopeful manner
**HOPEFULS** > HOPEFUL
**HOPELESS** *adj* having or offering no hope
**HOPER** > HOPE
**HOPERS** > HOPE
**HOPES** > HOPE
**HOPHEAD** *n* heroin or opium addict
**HOPHEADS** > HOPHEAD
**HOPING** > HOPE
**HOPINGLY** > HOPE
**HOPLITE** *n* (in ancient Greece) a heavily armed infantryman
**HOPLITES** > HOPLITE
**HOPLITIC** > HOPLITE
**HOPLOLOGY** *n* study of weapons or armour
**HOPPED** > HOP
**HOPPER** *n* container for storing substances such as grain or sand
**HOPPERCAR** *same as* > HOPPER
**HOPPERS** > HOPPER
**HOPPIER** > HOPPY
**HOPPIEST** > HOPPY
**HOPPING** > HOP
**HOPPINGS** > HOP
**HOPPLE** *same as* > HOBBLE
**HOPPLED** > HOPPLE
**HOPPLER** > HOPPLE
**HOPPLERS** > HOPPLE
**HOPPLES** > HOPPLE
**HOPPLING** > HOPPLE
**HOPPY** *adj* tasting of hops
**HOPS** > HOP
**HOPSACK** *n* roughly woven fabric of wool, cotton, etc, used for clothing
**HOPSACKS** > HOPSACK
**HOPSCOTCH** *n* children's game of hopping in a pattern drawn on the ground
**HOPTOAD** *n* toad
**HOPTOADS** > HOPTOAD
**HORA** *n* traditional Israeli or Romanian circle dance
**HORAH** *same as* > HORA
**HORAHS** > HORAH
**HORAL** *less common word for* > HOURLY
**HORARY** *adj* relating to the hours
**HORAS** > HORA
**HORDE** *n* large crowd ▷ *vb* form, move in, or live in a horde
**HORDED** > HORDE

HORDEIN n simple protein, rich in proline, that occurs in barley

HORDEINS > HORDEIN

HORDEOLA > HORDEOLUM

HORDEOLUM n (in medicine) stye

HORDES > HORDE

HORDING > HORDE

HORDOCK same as > HARDOKE

HORDOCKS > HORDOCK

HORE same as > HOAR

HOREHOUND n plant that produces a bitter juice formerly used as a cough medicine

HORI derogatory term n Māori ⊳ adj of or relating to the Māori

HORIATIKI n traditional Greek salad consisting of tomatoes, cucumber, onion, olives, and feta cheese

HORIS > HORI

HORIZON n apparent line that divides the earth and the sky

HORIZONAL > HORIZON

HORIZONS > HORIZON

HORKEY same as > HOCKEY

HORKEYS > HORKEY

HORLICKS as in make a horlicks make a mistake or a mess

HORME n (in the psychology of C. G. Jung) fundamental vital energy

HORMES > HORME

HORMIC > HORME

HORMONAL > HORMONE

HORMONE n substance secreted by certain glands which stimulates certain organs of the body

HORMONES > HORMONE

HORMONIC > HORMONE

HORN n one of a pair of bony growths sticking out of the heads of cattle, sheep, etc ⊳ vb provide with a horn or horns

HORNBAG n in Australian slang, a promiscuous woman

HORNBAGS > HORNBAG

HORNBEAK n garfish

HORNBEAKS > HORNBEAK

HORNBEAM n tree with smooth grey bark

HORNBEAMS > HORNBEAM

HORNBILL n bird with a bony growth on its large beak

HORNBILLS > HORNBILL

HORNBOOK n page bearing a religious text or the alphabet, held in a frame with a thin window of flattened cattle horn over it

HORNBOOKS > HORNBOOK

HORNBUG n stag beetle

HORNBUGS > HORNBUG

HORNED adj having a horn, horns, or hornlike parts

HORNER n dealer in horn

HORNERS > HORNER

HORNET n large wasp with a severe sting

HORNETS > HORNET

HORNFELS n hard compact fine-grained metamorphic rock formed by the action of heat from a magmatic intrusion on neighbouring sedimentary rocks

HORNFUL n amount a horn will hold

HORNFULS > HORNFUL

HORNGELD n feudal rent based on number of cattle

HORNGELDS > HORNGELD

HORNIER > HORNY

HORNIEST > HORNY

HORNILY > HORNY

HORNINESS > HORNY

HORNING > HORN

HORNINGS > HORN

HORNISH adj like horn

HORNIST n horn player

HORNISTS > HORNIST

HORNITO n small vent in volcano

HORNITOS > HORNITO

HORNLESS > HORN

HORNLET n small horn

HORNLETS > HORNLET

HORNLIKE > HORN

HORNPIPE n (music for) a solo dance, traditionally performed by sailors

HORNPIPES > HORNPIPE

HORNPOUT n catfish

HORNPOUTS > HORNPOUT

HORNS > HORN

HORNSTONE same as > HORNFELS

HORNTAIL n wasplike insect

HORNTAILS > HORNTAIL

HORNWORK n bastion in fortifications

HORNWORKS > HORNWORK

HORNWORM n caterpillar of hawk moth

HORNWORMS > HORNWORM

HORNWORT n aquatic plant

HORNWORTS > HORNWORT

HORNWRACK n yellowish bryozoan or sea mat sometimes found on beaches after a storm

HORNY adj of or like horn

HORNYHEAD n species of fish

HORNYWINK n lapwing

HOROEKA n New Zealand tree

HOROKAKA n low-growing New Zealand plant with fleshy leaves and pink or white flowers

HOROLOGE rare word for > TIMEPIECE

HOROLOGER same as > HOROLOGIST

HOROLOGES > HOROLOGE

HOROLOGIA n plural of horologium: clocktower

HOROLOGIC > HOROLOGY

HOROLOGY n art of making clocks and watches or of measuring time

HOROMETRY n measurement of time

HOROPITO n New Zealand plant

HOROPITOS > HOROPITO

HOROPTER n locus of all points in space that stimulate points on each eye that yield the same visual direction as each other

HOROPTERS > HOROPTER

HOROSCOPE n prediction of a person's future based on the positions of the planets, sun, and moon at his or her birth

HOROSCOPY n casting and interpretation of horoscopes

HORRENT adj bristling

HORRIBLE adj disagreeable, unpleasant ⊳ n horrible thing

HORRIBLES > HORRIBLE

HORRIBLY adv in a horrible manner

HORRID adj disagreeable, unpleasant

HORRIDER > HORRID

HORRIDEST > HORRID

HORRIDLY > HORRID

HORRIFIC adj causing horror

HORRIFIED adj terrified

HORRIFIES > HORRIFY

HORRIFY vb cause to feel horror or shock

HORROR n (thing or person causing) terror or hatred ⊳ adj having a frightening subject, usually concerned with the supernatural

HORRORS pl n fit of depression or anxiety ⊳ interj expression of dismay, sometimes facetious

HORS as in hors d'oeuvre appetizer

HORSE n large animal with hooves, a mane, and a tail, used for riding and pulling carts etc ⊳ vb provide with a horse

HORSEBACK n horse's back

HORSEBEAN n broad bean

HORSEBOX n trailer used for transporting horses

HORSECAR n streetcar drawn by horses

HORSECARS > HORSECAR

HORSED > HORSE

HORSEFLY n large bloodsucking fly

HORSEHAIR n hair from the tail or mane of a horse

HORSEHIDE n hide of a horse

HORSELESS > HORSE

HORSELIKE > HORSE

HORSEMAN n person skilled in riding

HORSEMEAT n flesh of the horse used as food

HORSEMEN > HORSEMAN

HORSEMINT n European mint plant

HORSEPLAY n rough or rowdy play

HORSEPOND n pond where horses drink

HORSEPOX n viral infection of horses

HORSERACE n race for horses

HORSES > HORSE

HORSESHIT n rubbish

HORSESHOD > HORSESHOE

HORSESHOE n protective U-shaped piece of iron nailed to a horse's hoof, regarded as a symbol of good luck ⊳ vb fit with a horseshoe

HORSETAIL n plant with small dark toothlike leaves

HORSEWAY n road for horses

HORSEWAYS > HORSEWAY

HORSEWEED n US name for Canadian fleabane

HORSEWHIP n whip with a long thong, used for managing horses ⊳ vb beat (a person or animal) with such a whip

HORSEY adj very keen on horses

HORSIER > HORSY

HORSIEST > HORSY

HORSILY > HORSEY

HORSINESS > HORSEY

HORSING > HORSE

HORSINGS > HORSE

HORSON same as > WHORESON

HORSONS > HORSON

HORST n ridge of land that has been forced upwards between two parallel faults

HORSTE variant of > HORST

HORSTES > HORST

HORSTS > HORST

HORSY same as > HORSEY

HORTATION > HORTATORY

HORTATIVE same as > HORTATORY

HORTATORY adj encouraging

HOS > HO

HOSANNA interj exclamation of praise to God ⊳ n act of crying "hosanna" ⊳ vb cry hosanna

HOSANNAED > HOSANNA

HOSANNAH same as > HOSANNA

HOSANNAHS > HOSANNAH

HOSANNAS > HOSANNA

HOSE n flexible pipe for conveying liquid ⊳ vb

water with a hose
**HOSED** > HOSE
**HOSEL** n socket in head of golf club
**HOSELIKE** > HOSE
**HOSELS** > HOSEL
**HOSEMAN** n fireman in charge of hose
**HOSEMEN** > HOSEMAN
**HOSEN** > HOSE
**HOSEPIPE** n hose
**HOSEPIPES** > HOSEPIPE
**HOSER** n person who swindles or deceives others
**HOSERS** > HOSER
**HOSES** > HOSE
**HOSEY** vb claim possession
**HOSEYED** > HOSEY
**HOSEYING** > HOSEY
**HOSEYS** > HOSEY
**HOSIER** n person who sells stockings, etc
**HOSIERIES** > HOSIERY
**HOSIERS** > HOSIER
**HOSIERY** n stockings, socks, and tights collectively
**HOSING** > HOSE
**HOSPICE** n nursing home for the terminally ill
**HOSPICES** > HOSPICE
**HOSPITAGE** n behaviour of guest
**HOSPITAL** n place where people who are ill are looked after and treated
**HOSPITALE** n lodging
**HOSPITALS** > HOSPITAL
**HOSPITIA** > HOSPITIUM
**HOSPITIUM** same as > HOSPICE
**HOSPODAR** n (formerly) the governor or prince of Moldavia or Wallachia under Ottoman rule
**HOSPODARS** > HOSPODAR
**HOSS** n horse
**HOSSES** > HOSS
**HOST** n person who entertains guests, esp in his own home ▷ vb be the host of
**HOSTA** n ornamental plant
**HOSTAGE** n person who is illegally held prisoner until certain demands are met by other people
**HOSTAGES** > HOSTAGE
**HOSTAS** > HOSTA
**HOSTED** > HOST
**HOSTEL** n building providing accommodation at a low cost for a specific group of people such as students, travellers, homeless people, etc ▷ vb stay in hostels
**HOSTELED** > HOSTEL
**HOSTELER** same as > HOSTELLER
**HOSTELERS** > HOSTELER
**HOSTELING** > HOSTEL
**HOSTELLED** > HOSTEL

**HOSTELLER** n person who stays at youth hostels
**HOSTELRY** n inn, pub
**HOSTELS** > HOSTEL
**HOSTESS** n woman who receives and entertains guests, esp in her own house ▷ vb act as hostess
**HOSTESSED** > HOSTESS
**HOSTESSES** > HOSTESS
**HOSTIE** n informal Australian word for an air hostess
**HOSTIES** > HOSTIE
**HOSTILE** adj unfriendly ▷ n hostile person
**HOSTILELY** > HOSTILE
**HOSTILES** > HOSTILE
**HOSTILITY** n unfriendly and aggressive feelings or behaviour
**HOSTING** > HOST
**HOSTINGS** > HOST
**HOSTLER** another name (esp Brit) for > OSTLER
**HOSTLERS** > HOSTLER
**HOSTLESSE** adj inhospitable
**HOSTLY** > HOST
**HOSTRIES** > HOSTRY
**HOSTRY** n lodging
**HOSTS** > HOST
**HOT** adj having a high temperature
**HOTBED** n any place encouraging a particular activity
**HOTBEDS** > HOTBED
**HOTBLOOD** n type of horse
**HOTBLOODS** > HOTBLOOD
**HOTBOX** n closed room where marijuana is smoked
**HOTBOXES** > HOTBOX
**HOTCAKE** n pancake
**HOTCAKES** > HOTCAKE
**HOTCH** vb jog
**HOTCHED** > HOTCH
**HOTCHES** > HOTCH
**HOTCHING** > HOTCH
**HOTCHPOT** n collecting of property so that it may be redistributed in equal shares, esp on the intestacy of a parent who has given property to his children in his lifetime
**HOTCHPOTS** > HOTCHPOT
**HOTDOG** vb perform a series of manoeuvres in skiing, surfing, etc, esp in a showy manner
**HOTDOGGED** > HOTDOG
**HOTDOGGER** > HOTDOG
**HOTDOGS** > HOTDOG
**HOTE** > HIGHT
**HOTEL** n commercial establishment providing lodging and meals
**HOTELDOM** n hotel business
**HOTELDOMS** > HOTELDOM
**HOTELIER** n owner or manager of a hotel
**HOTELIERS** > HOTELIER

**HOTELMAN** n hotel owner
**HOTELMEN** > HOTELMAN
**HOTELS** > HOTEL
**HOTEN** > HIGHT
**HOTFOOT** adv quickly and eagerly ▷ vb move quickly
**HOTFOOTED** > HOTFOOT
**HOTFOOTS** > HOTFOOT
**HOTHEAD** n excitable or fiery person
**HOTHEADED** adj impetuous, rash, or hot-tempered
**HOTHEADS** > HOTHEAD
**HOTHOUSE** n greenhouse
**HOTHOUSED** adj taught intensively
**HOTHOUSES** > HOTHOUSE
**HOTLINE** n direct telephone link for emergency use
**HOTLINES** > HOTLINE
**HOTLINK** n area on website connecting to another site
**HOTLINKS** > HOTLINK
**HOTLY** > HOT
**HOTNESS** > HOT
**HOTNESSES** > HOT
**HOTPLATE** n heated metal surface on an electric cooker
**HOTPLATES** > HOTPLATE
**HOTPOT** n casserole of meat and vegetables, topped with potatoes
**HOTPOTS** > HOTPOT
**HOTPRESS** vb subject (paper, cloth, etc) to heat and pressure to give it a smooth surface or extract oil
**HOTROD** n car with an engine that has been radically modified to produce increased power
**HOTRODS** > HOTROD
**HOTS** as in the hots feeling of lust
**HOTSHOT** n important person or expert, esp when showy
**HOTSHOTS** > HOTSHOT
**HOTSPOT** n place where wireless broadband services are provided through a wireless local area network
**HOTSPOTS** > HOTSPOT
**HOTSPUR** n impetuous or fiery person
**HOTSPURS** > HOTSPUR
**HOTTED** > HOT
**HOTTENTOT** as in hottentot fig perennial plant with fleshy leaves, showy yellow or purple flowers, and edible fruits
**HOTTER** vb simmer
**HOTTERED** > HOTTER
**HOTTERING** > HOTTER
**HOTTERS** > HOTTER
**HOTTEST** > HOT
**HOTTIE** n sexually attractive person
**HOTTIES** > HOTTIE

**HOTTING** n practice of stealing fast cars and putting on a show of skilful but dangerous driving
**HOTTINGS** > HOTTING
**HOTTISH** adj fairly hot
**HOTTY** same as > HOTTIE
**HOUDAH** same as > HOWDAH
**HOUDAHS** > HOUDAH
**HOUDAN** n breed of light domestic fowl originally from France, with a distinctive full crest
**HOUDANS** > HOUDAN
**HOUF** same as > HOWF
**HOUFED** > HOUF
**HOUFF** same as > HOWF
**HOUFFED** > HOUFF
**HOUFFING** > HOUFF
**HOUFFS** > HOUFF
**HOUFING** > HOUF
**HOUFS** > HOUF
**HOUGH** n in Scotland, a cut of meat corresponding to shin ▷ vb hamstring (cattle, horses, etc)
**HOUGHED** > HOUGH
**HOUGHING** > HOUGH
**HOUGHS** > HOUGH
**HOUHERE** n small evergreen New Zealand tree
**HOUMMOS** same as > HUMMUS
**HOUMMOSES** > HOUMMOS
**HOUMOUS** > HUMMUS
**HOUMOUSES** > HOUMOUS
**HOUMUS** same as > HUMMUS
**HOUMUSES** > HOUMUS
**HOUND** n hunting dog ▷ vb pursue relentlessly
**HOUNDED** > HOUND
**HOUNDER** > HOUND
**HOUNDERS** > HOUND
**HOUNDFISH** n name given to various small sharks or dogfish
**HOUNDING** > HOUND
**HOUNDS** > HOUND
**HOUNGAN** n voodoo priest
**HOUNGANS** > HOUNGAN
**HOUR** n twenty-fourth part of a day, sixty minutes
**HOURGLASS** n device with two glass compartments, containing a quantity of sand that takes an hour to trickle from the top section to the bottom one
**HOURI** n any of the nymphs of paradise
**HOURIS** > HOURI
**HOURLIES** > HOURLY
**HOURLONG** adj lasting an hour
**HOURLY** adv (happening) every hour ▷ adj of, occurring, or done once every hour ▷ n something that is done by the hour; someone who is paid by the hour
**HOURPLATE** n dial of clock
**HOURS** pl n indefinite time
**HOUSE** n building used

as a home ▷ *vb* give accommodation to ▷ *adj* (of wine) sold in a restaurant at a lower price than wines on the wine list

**HOUSEBOAT** *n* stationary boat used as a home

**HOUSEBOY** *n* male domestic servant

**HOUSEBOYS** > HOUSEBOY

**HOUSECARL** *n* (in medieval Europe) a household warrior of Danish kings and noblemen

**HOUSECOAT** *n* woman's long loose coat-shaped garment for wearing at home

**HOUSED** > HOUSE

**HOUSEFLY** *n* common fly often found in houses

**HOUSEFUL** *n* full amount or number that can be accommodated in a particular house

**HOUSEFULS** > HOUSEFUL

**HOUSEHOLD** *n* all the people living in a house ▷ *adj* relating to the running of a household

**HOUSEKEEP** *vb* run household

**HOUSEKEPT** > HOUSEKEEP

**HOUSEL** *vb* give the Eucharist to (someone)

**HOUSELED** > HOUSEL

**HOUSELEEK** *n* plant that has a rosette of succulent leaves and pinkish flowers and grows on walls

**HOUSELESS** > HOUSE

**HOUSELINE** *n* tarred marline

**HOUSELING** > HOUSEL

**HOUSELLED** > HOUSEL

**HOUSELS** > HOUSEL

**HOUSEMAID** *n* female servant employed to do housework

**HOUSEMAN** *n* junior hospital doctor

**HOUSEMATE** *n* person who is not part of the same family, but with whom one shares a house

**HOUSEMEN** > HOUSEMAN

**HOUSER** > HOUSE

**HOUSEROOM** *n* room for storage or lodging

**HOUSERS** > HOUSE

**HOUSES** > HOUSE

**HOUSESAT** > HOUSESIT

**HOUSESIT** *vb* live in and look after a house during the absence of its owner or owners

**HOUSESITS** > HOUSESIT

**HOUSETOP** *n* rooftop

**HOUSETOPS** > HOUSETOP

**HOUSEWIFE** *n* woman who runs her own household and does not have a job

**HOUSEWORK** *n* work of running a home, such as cleaning, cooking, and shopping

**HOUSEY** *adj* of or like house music

**HOUSIER** > HOUSEY

**HOUSIEST** > HOUSEY

**HOUSING** *n* (providing of) houses

**HOUSINGS** > HOUSING

**HOUSLING** *adj* of sacrament

**HOUSTONIA** *n* small North American plant with blue, white or purple flowers

**HOUT** *same as* > HOOT

**HOUTED** > HOUT

**HOUTING** *n* type of fish that lives in salt water but spawns in freshwater lakes and is valued for its edible flesh

**HOUTINGS** > HOUTING

**HOUTS** > HOUT

**HOVE** > HEAVE

**HOVEA** *n* Australian plant with purple flowers

**HOVEAS** > HOVEA

**HOVED** > HEAVE

**HOVEL** *n* small dirty house or hut ▷ *vb* shelter or be sheltered in a hovel

**HOVELED** > HOVEL

**HOVELING** > HOVEL

**HOVELLED** > HOVEL

**HOVELLER** *n* man working on boat

**HOVELLERS** > HOVELLER

**HOVELLING** > HOVEL

**HOVELS** > HOVEL

**HOVEN** > HEAVE

**HOVER** *vb* (of a bird etc) remain suspended in one place in the air ▷ *n* act of hovering

**HOVERED** > HOVER

**HOVERER** > HOVER

**HOVERERS** > HOVER

**HOVERFLY** *n* hovering wasp-like fly

**HOVERING** > HOVER

**HOVERPORT** *n* port for hovercraft

**HOVERS** > HOVER

**HOVES** > HEAVE

**HOVING** > HEAVE

**HOW** *adv* in what way, by what means ▷ *n* the way a thing is done ▷ *sentence substitute* greeting supposed to be or have been used by American Indians and often used humorously

**HOWBE** *same as* > HOWBEIT

**HOWBEIT** *adv* in archaic usage, however

**HOWDAH** *n* canopied seat on an elephant's back

**HOWDAHS** > HOWDAH

**HOWDIE** *n* midwife

**HOWDIED** > HOWDY

**HOWDIES** > HOWDY

**HOWDY** *vb* greet someone

**HOWDYING** > HOWDY

**HOWE** *n* depression in the earth's surface, such as a basin or valley

**HOWES** > HOWE

**HOWEVER** *adv* nevertheless

**HOWF** *n* haunt, esp a public house ▷ *vb* visit place frequently

**HOWFED** > HOWF

**HOWFF** *vb* visit place frequently

**HOWFFED** > HOWFF

**HOWFFING** > HOWFF

**HOWFFS** > HOWFF

**HOWFING** > HOWF

**HOWFS** > HOWF

**HOWITZER** *n* large gun firing shells at a steep angle

**HOWITZERS** > HOWITZER

**HOWK** *vb* dig (out or up)

**HOWKED** > HOWK

**HOWKER** > HOWK

**HOWKERS** > HOWK

**HOWKING** > HOWK

**HOWKS** > HOWK

**HOWL** *n* loud wailing cry ▷ *vb* utter a howl

**HOWLBACK** *same as* > HOWLROUND

**HOWLBACKS** > HOWLBACK

**HOWLED** > HOWL

**HOWLER** *n* stupid mistake

**HOWLERS** > HOWLER

**HOWLET** *another word for* > OWL

**HOWLETS** > HOWLET

**HOWLING** *adj* great

**HOWLINGLY** > HOWL

**HOWLINGS** > HOWL

**HOWLROUND** *n* condition, resulting in a howling noise, when sound from a loudspeaker is fed back into the microphone of a public-address or recording system

**HOWLS** > HOWL

**HOWRE** *same as* > HOUR

**HOWRES** > HOWRE

**HOWS** > HOW

**HOWSO** *same as* > HOWSOEVER

**HOWSOEVER** *less common word for* > HOWEVER

**HOWTOWDIE** *n* Scottish dish of boiled chicken with poached eggs and spinach

**HOWZAT** > HOW

**HOWZIT** *informal word for* > HELLO

**HOX** *vb* hamstring

**HOXED** > HOX

**HOXES** > HOX

**HOXING** > HOX

**HOY** *interj* cry used to attract someone's attention ▷ *n* freight barge ▷ *vb* drive animal with cry

**HOYA** *n* any of various E Asian or Australian plants

**HOYAS** > HOYA

**HOYDEN** *n* wild or boisterous girl ▷ *vb* behave like a hoyden

**HOYDENED** > HOYDEN

**HOYDENING** > HOYDEN

**HOYDENISH** > HOYDEN

**HOYDENISM** > HOYDEN

**HOYDENS** > HOYDEN

**HOYED** > HOY

**HOYING** > HOY

**HOYLE** *n* archer's mark used as a target

**HOYLES** > HOYLE

**HOYS** > HOY

**HRYVNA** *n* standard monetary unit of Ukraine, divided into 100 kopiykas

**HRYVNAS** > HRYVNA

**HRYVNIA** *n* money unit of Ukraine

**HRYVNIAS** > HRYVNIA

**HRYVNYA** *same as* > HRYVNA

**HRYVNYAS** > HRYVNYA

**HUANACO** *same as* > GUANACO

**HUANACOS** > HUANACO

**HUAQUERO** *n* Central American tomb robber

**HUAQUEROS** > HUAQUERO

**HUARACHE** *n* Mexican sandal

**HUARACHES** > HUARACHE

**HUARACHO** *same as* > HUARACHE

**HUARACHOS** > HUARACHO

**HUB** *n* centre of a wheel, through which the axle passes

**HUBBIES** > HUBBY

**HUBBLY** *adj* having an irregular surface

**HUBBUB** *n* confused noise of many voices

**HUBBUBOO** *same as* > HUBBUB

**HUBBUBOOS** > HUBBUBOO

**HUBBUBS** > HUBBUB

**HUBBY** *n* husband

**HUBCAP** *n* metal disc that fits on to and protects the hub of a wheel, esp on a car

**HUBCAPS** > HUBCAP

**HUBRIS** *n* pride, arrogance

**HUBRISES** > HUBRIS

**HUBRISTIC** > HUBRIS

**HUBS** > HUB

**HUCK** *same as* > HUCKABACK

**HUCKABACK** *n* coarse absorbent linen or cotton fabric used for towels and informal shirts, etc

**HUCKERY** *adj* ugly

**HUCKLE** *n* hip or haunch

**HUCKLES** > HUCKLE

**HUCKS** > HUCK

**HUCKSTER** *n* person using aggressive methods of selling ▷ *vb* peddle

**HUCKSTERS** > HUCKSTER

**HUCKSTERY** > HUCKSTER

**HUDDEN** > HAUD

**HUDDLE** *vb* hunch (oneself) through cold or fear ▷ *n* small group

**HUDDLED** > HUDDLE

**HUDDLER** > HUDDLE

**HUDDLERS** > HUDDLE

HUDDLES > HUDDLE
HUDDLING > HUDDLE
HUDDUP interj get up
HUDNA n truce or ceasefire for a fixed duration
HUDNAS > HUDNA
HUDUD n set of laws and punishments specified by Allah in the Koran
HUDUDS > HUDUD
HUE n colour, shade
HUED adj having a hue or colour as specified
HUELESS > HUE
HUER n pilchard fisherman
HUERS > HUER
HUES > HUE
HUFF n passing mood of anger or resentment ▷ vb blow or puff heavily
HUFFED > HUFF
HUFFER > HUFFING
HUFFERS > HUFFING
HUFFIER > HUFF
HUFFIEST > HUFF
HUFFILY > HUFF
HUFFINESS > HUFF
HUFFING n practice of inhaling toxic fumes from glue and other household products for their intoxicating effects
HUFFINGS > HUFFING
HUFFISH > HUFF
HUFFISHLY > HUFF
HUFFKIN n type of muffin
HUFFKINS > HUFFKIN
HUFFS > HUFF
HUFFY > HUFF
HUG vb clasp tightly in the arms, usu with affection ▷ n tight or fond embrace
HUGE adj very big
HUGELY adv very much
HUGENESS > HUGE
HUGEOUS same as > HUGE
HUGEOUSLY > HUGEOUS
HUGER > HUGE
HUGEST > HUGE
HUGGABLE > HUG
HUGGED > HUG
HUGGER > HUG
HUGGERS > HUG
HUGGIER > HUGGY
HUGGIEST > HUGGY
HUGGING > HUG
HUGGY adj sensitive and caring
HUGS > HUG
HUGY same as > HUGE
HUH interj exclamation of derision, bewilderment, or inquiry
HUHU n type of hairy New Zealand beetle
HUHUS > HUHU
HUI n meeting of Māori people
HUIA n extinct bird of New Zealand, prized by early Māoris for its distinctive tail feathers
HUIAS > HUIA
HUIC interj in hunting, a call

to hounds
HUIPIL n Mayan woman's blouse
HUIPILES > HUIPIL
HUIPILS > HUIPIL
HUIS > HUI
HUISACHE n American tree
HUISACHES > HUISACHE
HUISSIER n doorkeeper
HUISSIERS > HUISSIER
HUITAIN n verse of eighteen lines
HUITAINS > HUITAIN
HULA n swaying Hawaiian dance
HULAS > HULA
HULE same as > ULE
HULES > HULE
HULK n body of an abandoned ship ▷ vb move clumsily
HULKED > HULK
HULKIER > HULKY
HULKIEST > HULKY
HULKING adj bulky, unwieldy
HULKS > HULK
HULKY same as > HULKING
HULL n main body of a boat ▷ vb remove the hulls from
HULLED > HULL
HULLER > HULL
HULLERS > HULL
HULLIER > HULLY
HULLIEST > HULLY
HULLING > HULL
HULLO same as > HELLO
HULLOA same as > HALLOA
HULLOAED > HULLOA
HULLOAING > HULLOA
HULLOAS > HULLOA
HULLOED > HULLO
HULLOES > HULLO
HULLOING > HULLO
HULLOO same as > HALLOO
HULLOOED > HULLOO
HULLOOING > HULLOO
HULLOOS > HULLOO
HULLOS > HULLO
HULLS > HULL
HULLY adj having husks
HUM vb make a low continuous vibrating sound ▷ n humming sound
HUMA n mythical bird
HUMAN adj of or typical of people ▷ n human being
HUMANE adj kind or merciful
HUMANELY > HUMANE
HUMANER > HUMANE
HUMANEST > HUMANE
HUMANHOOD n state of being human
HUMANISE same as > HUMANIZE
HUMANISED > HUMANISE
HUMANISER > HUMANISE
HUMANISES > HUMANISE
HUMANISM n belief in human effort rather than religion
HUMANISMS > HUMANISM
HUMANIST > HUMANISM

HUMANISTS > HUMANISM > HUMANITARIANIST
HUMANITY n human race
HUMANIZE vb make human or humane
HUMANIZED > HUMANIZE
HUMANIZER > HUMANIZE
HUMANIZES > HUMANIZE
HUMANKIND n human race
HUMANLIKE > HUMAN
HUMANLY adv by human powers or means
HUMANNESS > HUMAN
HUMANOID adj resembling a human being in appearance ▷ n (in science fiction) a robot or creature resembling a human being
HUMANOIDS > HUMANOID
HUMANS > HUMAN
HUMAS > HUMA
HUMATE n decomposed plants used as fertilizer
HUMATES > HUMATE
HUMBLE adj conscious of one's failings ▷ vb cause to feel humble, humiliate
HUMBLEBEE another name for the > BUMBLEBEE
HUMBLED > HUMBLE
HUMBLER > HUMBLE
HUMBLERS > HUMBLE
HUMBLES > HUMBLE
HUMBLESSE n quality of being humble
HUMBLEST > HUMBLE
HUMBLING > HUMBLE
HUMBLINGS > HUMBLE
HUMBLY > HUMBLE
HUMBUCKER n twin-coil guitar pick-up
HUMBUG n hard striped peppermint sweet ▷ vb cheat or deceive (someone)
HUMBUGGED > HUMBUG
HUMBUGGER > HUMBUG
HUMBUGS > HUMBUG
HUMBUZZ n type of beetle
HUMBUZZES > HUMBUZZ
HUMDINGER n excellent person or thing
HUMDRUM adj ordinary, dull ▷ n monotonous routine, task, or person
HUMDRUMS > HUMDRUM
HUMECT vb make moist
HUMECTANT adj producing moisture ▷ n substance added to another substance to keep it moist
HUMECTATE vb produce moisture
HUMECTED > HUMECT
HUMECTING > HUMECT
HUMECTIVE > HUMECT
HUMECTS > HUMECT
HUMEFIED > HUMEFY
HUMEFIES > HUMEFY
HUMEFY same as > HUMIFY
HUMEFYING > HUMEFY
HUMERAL adj of or relating to the humerus ▷ n silk

shawl worn by a priest at High Mass; humeral veil
HUMERALS > HUMERAL
HUMERI > HUMERUS
HUMERUS n bone from the shoulder to the elbow
HUMF same as > HUMPH
HUMFED > HUMF
HUMFING > HUMF
HUMFS > HUMF
HUMHUM n Indian cotton cloth
HUMHUMS > HUMHUM
HUMIC adj of, relating to, derived from, or resembling humus
HUMICOLE n any plant that thrives on humus
HUMICOLES > HUMICOLE
HUMID adj damp and hot
HUMIDER > HUMID
HUMIDEST > HUMID
HUMIDEX n system of measuring discomfort showing the combined effect of humidity and temperature
HUMIDEXES > HUMIDEX
HUMIDICES > HUMIDEX
HUMIDIFY vb make the air in (a room) more humid or damp
HUMIDITY n dampness
HUMIDLY > HUMID
HUMIDNESS > HUMID
HUMIDOR n humid place or container for storing cigars, tobacco, etc
HUMIDORS > HUMIDOR
HUMIFIED > HUMIFY
HUMIFIES > HUMIFY
HUMIFY vb convert or be converted into humus
HUMIFYING > HUMIFY
HUMILIANT adj humiliating
HUMILIATE vb lower the dignity or hurt the pride of
HUMILITY n quality of being humble
HUMINT n human intelligence
HUMINTS > HUMINT
HUMITE n mineral containing magnesium
HUMITES > HUMITE
HUMITURE n measure of both humidity and temperature
HUMITURES > HUMITURE
HUMLIE n hornless cow
HUMLIES > HUMLIE
HUMMABLE > HUM
HUMMAUM same as > HAMMAM
HUMMAUMS > HUMMAUM
HUMMED > HUM
HUMMEL adj (of cattle) hornless ▷ vb remove horns from
HUMMELLED > HUMMEL
HUMMELLER > HUMMEL
HUMMELS > HUMMEL
HUMMER > HUM
HUMMERS > HUM

HUMMING > HUM

HUMMINGS > HUM

HUMMOCK n very small hill ▷ vb form into a hummock or hummocks

HUMMOCKED > HUMMOCK

HUMMOCKS > HUMMOCK

HUMMOCKY > HUMMOCK

HUMMUM same as > HAMMAM

HUMMUMS > HUMMUM

HUMMUS n creamy dip originating in the Middle East, made from puréed chickpeas

HUMMUSES > HUMMUS

HUMOGEN n type of fertilizer

HUMOGENS > HUMOGEN

HUMONGOUS same as > HUMUNGOUS

HUMOR same as > HUMOUR

HUMORAL adj denoting or relating to a type of immunity caused by free antibodies circulating in the blood

HUMORALLY > HUMORAL

HUMORED > HUMOR

HUMORESK n humorous musical composition

HUMORESKS > HUMORESK

HUMORFUL > HUMOR

HUMORING > HUMOR

HUMORIST n writer or entertainer who uses humour in his or her work

HUMORISTS > HUMORIST

HUMORLESS > HUMOR

HUMOROUS adj amusing, esp in a witty or clever way

HUMORS > HUMOR

HUMORSOME same as > HUMOURSOME

HUMOUR n ability to say or perceive things that are amusing ▷ vb be kind and indulgent to

HUMOURED > HUMOUR

HUMOURFUL > HUMOUR

HUMOURING > HUMOUR

HUMOURS > HUMOUR

HUMOUS same as > HUMUS

HUMP n raised piece of ground ▷ vb carry or heave

HUMPBACK same as > HUNCHBACK

HUMPBACKS > HUMPBACK

HUMPED > HUMP

HUMPEN n old German drinking glass

HUMPENS > HUMPEN

HUMPER > HUMP

HUMPERS > HUMP

HUMPH interj exclamation of annoyance or scepticism ▷ vb exclaim humph

HUMPHED > HUMPH

HUMPHING > HUMPH

HUMPHS > HUMPH

HUMPIER > HUMPY

HUMPIES > HUMPY

HUMPIEST > HUMPY

HUMPINESS > HUMPY

HUMPING > HUMP

HUMPLESS > HUMP

HUMPLIKE > HUMP

HUMPS > HUMP

HUMPTIES > HUMPTY

HUMPTY n low padded seat

HUMPY adj full of humps ▷ n primitive hut

HUMS > HUM

HUMSTRUM n medieval musical instrument

HUMSTRUMS > HUMSTRUM

HUMUNGOUS adj very large

HUMUS n decomposing vegetable and animal mould in the soil

HUMUSES > HUMUS

HUMUSY > HUMUS

HUMVEE n military vehicle

HUMVEES > HUMVEE

HUN n member of any of several Asiatic nomadic peoples speaking Mongoloid or Turkic languages

HUNCH n feeling or suspicion not based on facts ▷ vb draw (one's shoulders) up or together

HUNCHBACK n person with an abnormal curvature of the spine

HUNCHED > HUNCH

HUNCHES > HUNCH

HUNCHING > HUNCH

HUNDRED n ten times ten ▷ adj amounting to a hundred

HUNDREDER n inhabitant of a hundred

HUNDREDOR same as > HUNDREDER

HUNDREDS > HUNDRED

HUNDREDTH adj being the ordinal number of 100 in numbering or counting order, position, time, etc ▷ n one of 100 approximately equal parts of something

HUNG > HANG

HUNGAN same as > HOUNGAN

HUNGANS > HUNGAN

HUNGER n discomfort or weakness from lack of food ▷ vb want very much

HUNGERED > HUNGER

HUNGERFUL adj hungry

HUNGERING > HUNGER

HUNGERLY adj hungry

HUNGERS > HUNGER

HUNGOVER adj suffering from hangover

HUNGRIER > HUNGRY

HUNGRIEST > HUNGRY

HUNGRILY > HUNGRY

HUNGRY adj desiring food

HUNH same as > HUH

HUNK n large piece

HUNKER vb squat

HUNKERED > HUNKER

HUNKERING > HUNKER

HUNKERS pl n haunches

HUNKEY n person of Hungarian descent

HUNKEYS > HUNKEY

HUNKIE same as > HUNKEY

HUNKIER > HUNKY

HUNKIES > HUNKY

HUNKIEST > HUNKY

HUNKS n crotchety old person

HUNKSES > HUNKS

HUNKY adj excellent

HUNS > HUN

HUNT vb seek out and kill (wild animals) for food or sport ▷ n hunting

HUNTABLE > HUNT

HUNTAWAY n sheepdog trained to drive sheep by barking

HUNTAWAYS > HUNTAWAY

HUNTED adj harassed and worn

HUNTEDLY > HUNT

HUNTER n person or animal that hunts wild animals for food or sport

HUNTERS > HUNTER

HUNTING n pursuit and killing or capture of game and wild animals, regarded as a sport

HUNTINGS > HUNTING

HUNTRESS same as > HUNTER

HUNTS > HUNT

HUNTSMAN n man who hunts wild animals, esp foxes

HUNTSMEN > HUNTSMAN

HUP n cry hup to get a horse to move

HUPIRO in New Zealand English, same as > STINKWOOD

HUPPAH variant spelling of > CHUPPAH

HUPPAHS > HUPPAH

HUPPED > HUP,

HUPPING > HUP

HUPS > HUP

HURCHEON same as > URCHIN

HURCHEONS > HURCHEON

HURDEN same as > HARDEN

HURDENS > HURDEN

HURDIES pl n buttocks or haunches

HURDLE n light barrier for jumping over in some races ▷ vb jump over (something)

HURDLED > HURDLE

HURDLER > HURDLE

HURDLERS > HURDLE

HURDLES > HURDLE

HURDLING > HURDLE

HURDLINGS > HURDLE

HURDS same as > HARDS

HURL vb throw or utter forcefully ▷ n act or an instance of hurling

HURLBAT same as > WHIRLBAT

HURLBATS > HURLBAT

HURLED > HURL

HURLER > HURL

HURLERS > HURL

HURLEY n another word for HURLING (the game)

HURLEYS > HURLEY

HURLIES > HURLY

HURLING n Irish game like hockey

HURLINGS > HURLING

HURLS > HURL

HURLY n wheeled barrow

HURRA same as > HURRAH

HURRAED > HURRA

HURRAH interj exclamation of joy or applause ▷ n cheer of joy or victory ▷ vb shout "hurrah"

HURRAHED > HURRAH

HURRAHING > HURRAH

HURRAHS > HURRAH

HURRAING > HURRA

HURRAS > HURRA

HURRAY same as > HURRAH

HURRAYED > HURRAY

HURRAYING > HURRAY

HURRAYS > HURRAY

HURRICANE n very strong, often destructive, wind or storm

HURRICANO same as > HURRICANE

HURRIED adj done quickly or too quickly

HURRIEDLY > HURRIED

HURRIER > HURRY

HURRIERS > HURRY

HURRIES > HURRY

HURRY vb (cause to) move or act very quickly ▷ n doing something quickly or the need to do something quickly

HURRYING > HURRY

HURRYINGS > HURRY

HURST n wood

HURSTS > HURST

HURT vb cause physical or mental pain to ▷ n physical or mental pain ▷ adj injured or pained

HURTER > HURT

HURTERS > HURT

HURTFUL adj unkind

HURTFULLY > HURTFUL

HURTING > HURT

HURTLE vb move quickly or violently

HURTLED > HURTLE

HURTLES > HURTLE

HURTLESS adj uninjured

HURTLING > HURTLE

HURTS > HURT

HUSBAND n woman's partner in marriage ▷ vb use economically

HUSBANDED > HUSBAND

HUSBANDER > HUSBAND

HUSBANDLY > HUSBAND

HUSBANDRY n farming

HUSBANDS > HUSBAND

HUSH vb make or be silent ▷ n stillness or silence ▷ interj plea or demand for silence

HUSHABIED > HUSHABY

HUSHABIES > HUSHABY

HUSHABY *interj* used in quietening a baby or child to sleep ▷ *n* lullaby ▷ *vb* quieten to sleep
HUSHED > HUSH
HUSHEDLY > HUSH
HUSHER *same as* > USHER
HUSHERED > HUSHER
HUSHERING > HUSHER
HUSHERS > HUSHER
HUSHES > HUSH
HUSHFUL *adj* quiet
HUSHIER > HUSHY
HUSHIEST > HUSHY
HUSHING > HUSH
HUSHPUPPY *n* snack of deep-fried dough
HUSHY *adj* secret
HUSK *n* outer covering of certain seeds and fruits ▷ *vb* remove the husk from
HUSKED > HUSK
HUSKER > HUSK
HUSKERS > HUSK
HUSKIER > HUSKY
HUSKIES > HUSKY
HUSKIEST > HUSKY
HUSKILY > HUSKY
HUSKINESS > HUSKY
HUSKING > HUSK
HUSKINGS > HUSK
HUSKLIKE > HUSK
HUSKS > HUSK
HUSKY *adj* slightly hoarse ▷ *n* Arctic sledge dog with thick hair and a curled tail
HUSO *n* sturgeon
HUSOS > HUSO
HUSS *n* flesh of the European dogfish, when used as food
HUSSAR *n* lightly armed cavalry soldier
HUSSARS > HUSSAR
HUSSES > HUSS
HUSSIES > HUSSY
HUSSIF *n* sewing kit
HUSSIFS > HUSSIF
HUSSY *n* immodest or promiscuous woman
HUSTINGS *pl n* political campaigns and speeches before an election
HUSTLE *vb* push about, jostle ▷ *n* lively activity or bustle
HUSTLED > HUSTLE
HUSTLER > HUSTLE
HUSTLERS > HUSTLE
HUSTLES > HUSTLE
HUSTLING > HUSTLE
HUSTLINGS > HUSTLE
HUSWIFE *same as* > HOUSEWIFE
HUSWIFES > HUSWIFE
HUSWIVES > HUSWIFE
HUT *n* small house, shelter, or shed
HUTCH *n* cage for pet rabbits etc ▷ *vb* store or keep in or as if in a hutch
HUTCHED > HUTCH
HUTCHES > HUTCH
HUTCHIE *n* groundsheet

draped over an upright stick, used as a temporary shelter
HUTCHIES > HUTCHIE
HUTCHING > HUTCH
HUTIA *n* rodent of West Indies
HUTIAS > HUTIA
HUTLIKE > HUT
HUTMENT *n* number or group of huts
HUTMENTS > HUTMENT
HUTS > HUT
HUTTED > HUT
HUTTING > HUT
HUTTINGS > HUT
HUTZPA *same as* > HUTZPAH
HUTZPAH *variant spelling of* > CHUTZPAH
HUTZPAHS > HUTZPAH
HUTZPAS > HUTZPA
HUZOOR *n* person of rank in India
HUZOORS > HUZOOR
HUZZA *same as* > HUZZAH
HUZZAED > HUZZA
HUZZAH *archaic word for* > HURRAH
HUZZAHED > HUZZAH
HUZZAHING > HUZZAH
HUZZAHS > HUZZAH
HUZZAING > HUZZA
HUZZAS > HUZZA
HUZZIES > HUZZY
HUZZY *same as* > HUSSY
HWAN *another name for* > WON
HWYL *n* emotional fervour, as in the recitation of poetry
HWYLS > HWYL
HYACINE *same as* > HYACINTH
HYACINES > HYACINE
HYACINTH *n* sweet-smelling spring flower that grows from a bulb
HYACINTHS > HYACINTH
HYAENA *same as* > HYENA
HYAENAS > HYAENA
HYAENIC > HYAENA
HYALIN *n* glassy translucent substance, such as occurs in certain degenerative skin conditions or in hyaline cartilage
HYALINE *adj* clear and translucent, with no fibres or granules ▷ *n* glassy transparent surface
HYALINES > HYALINE
HYALINISE *same as* > HYALINIZE
HYALINIZE *vb* give a glassy consistency to
HYALINS > HYALIN
HYALITE *n* clear and colourless variety of opal in globular form
HYALITES > HYALITE
HYALOGEN *n* insoluble substance in body structures

HYALOGENS > HYALOGEN
HYALOID *adj* clear and transparent ▷ *n* delicate transparent membrane enclosing the vitreous humour of the eye
HYALOIDS > HYALOID
HYALONEMA *n* species of sponge
HYBRID *n* offspring of two plants or animals of different species ▷ *adj* mixed origin
HYBRIDISE *same as* > HYBRIDIZE
HYBRIDISM > HYBRID
HYBRIDIST > HYBRID
HYBRIDITY > HYBRID
HYBRIDIZE *vb* produce or cause (species) to produce hybrids
HYBRIDOMA *n* hybrid cell formed by the fusion of two different types of cell, esp one capable of producing antibodies, but of limited lifespan, fused with an immortal tumour cell
HYBRIDOUS > HYBRID
HYBRIDS > HYBRID
HYBRIS *same as* > HUBRIS
HYBRISES > HYBRIS
HYBRISTIC > HYBRIS
HYDANTOIN *n* colourless odourless crystalline compound present in beet molasses and used in the manufacture of pharmaceuticals and synthetic resins
HYDATHODE *n* pore in plants, esp on the leaves, specialized for excreting water
HYDATID *n* cyst containing tapeworm larvae
HYDATIDS > HYDATID
HYDATOID *adj* watery
HYDRA *n* mythical many-headed water serpent
HYDRACID *n* acid, such as hydrochloric acid, that does not contain oxygen
HYDRACIDS > HYDRACID
HYDRAE > HYDRA
HYDRAEMIA *n* wateriness of blood
HYDRAGOG *n* drug that removes water
HYDRAGOGS > HYDRAGOG
HYDRANGEA *n* ornamental shrub with clusters of pink, blue, or white flowers
HYDRANT *n* outlet from a water main with a nozzle for a hose
HYDRANTH *n* polyp in a colony of hydrozoan coelenterates that is specialized for feeding rather than reproduction
HYDRANTHS > HYDRANTH

HYDRANTS > HYDRANT
HYDRAS > HYDRA
HYDRASE *n* enzyme that removes water
HYDRASES > HYDRASE
HYDRASTIS *n* any of various Japanese and E North American plants, such as goldenseal, having showy foliage and ornamental red fruits
HYDRATE *n* chemical compound of water with another substance ▷ *vb* treat or impregnate with water
HYDRATED *adj* (of a compound) chemically bonded to water molecules
HYDRATES > HYDRATE
HYDRATING > HYDRATE
HYDRATION > HYDRATE
HYDRATOR > HYDRATE
HYDRATORS > HYDRATE
HYDRAULIC *adj* operated by pressure forced through a pipe by a liquid such as water or oil
HYDRAZIDE *n* any of a class of chemical compounds that result when hydrogen in hydrazine or any of its derivatives is replaced by an acid radical
HYDRAZINE *n* colourless basic liquid made from sodium hypochlorite and ammonia: a strong reducing agent, used chiefly as a rocket fuel
HYDRAZOIC *as in hydrazoic acid* colourless highly explosive liquid
HYDREMIA *same as* > HYDRAEMIA
HYDREMIAS > HYDREMIA
HYDRIA *n* (in ancient Greece and Rome) a large water jar
HYDRIAE > HYDRIA
HYDRIC *adj* of or containing hydrogen
HYDRID *same as* > HYDROID
HYDRIDE *n* compound of hydrogen with another element
HYDRIDES > HYDRIDE
HYDRIDS > HYDRID
HYDRILLA *n* aquatic plant used as an oxygenator in aquaria and pools
HYDRILLAS > HYDRILLA
HYDRIODIC *as in hydriodic acid* colourless or pale yellow aqueous solution of hydrogen iodide: a strong acid
HYDRO *n* hotel offering facilities for hydropathy ▷ *adj* electricity as supplied to a residence, business, etc
HYDROCAST *n* gathering of

water samples for analysis

**HYDROCELE** n abnormal collection of fluid in any saclike space, esp around the testicles

**HYDROFOIL** n fast light boat with its hull raised out of the water on one or more pairs of fins

**HYDROGEL** n gel in which the liquid constituent is water

**HYDROGELS** > HYDROGEL

**HYDROGEN** n light flammable colourless gas that combines with oxygen to form water
> HYDROGENISATION
> HYDROGENIZATION

**HYDROGENS** > HYDROGEN

**HYDROID** adj of or relating to an order of colonial hydrozoan coelenterates that have the polyp phase dominant ▷ n hydroid colony or individual

**HYDROIDS** > HYDROID

**HYDROLASE** n enzyme, such as an esterase, that controls hydrolysis

**HYDROLOGY** n study of the distribution, conservation, and use of the water of the earth and its atmosphere

**HYDROLYSE** vb subject to or undergo hydrolysis

**HYDROLYTE** n substance subjected to hydrolysis

**HYDROLYZE** same as > HYDROLYSE

**HYDROMA** same as > HYGROMA

**HYDROMAS** > HYDROMA

**HYDROMATA** > HYDROMA

**HYDROMEL** n another word for MEAD (the drink)

**HYDROMELS** > HYDROMEL

**HYDRONAUT** n person trained to operate deep submergence vessels

**HYDRONIC** adj using hot water in heating system

**HYDRONIUM** as in hydronium ion positive ion, formed by the attachment of a proton to a water molecule: occurs in solutions of acids and behaves like a hydrogen ion

**HYDROPATH** > HYDROPATHY

**HYDROPIC** > HYDROPSY

**HYDROPS** n anaemia in a fetus

**HYDROPSES** > HYDROPS

**HYDROPSY** same as > DROPSY

**HYDROPTIC** > HYDROPSY

**HYDROPULT** n type of water pump

**HYDROS** > HYDRO

**HYDROSERE** n sere that begins in an aquatic environment

**HYDROSKI** n hydrofoil

used on some seaplanes to provide extra lift when taking off

**HYDROSKIS** > HYDROSKI

**HYDROSOL** n sol that has water as its liquid phase

**HYDROSOLS** > HYDROSOL

**HYDROSOMA** same as > HYDROSOME

**HYDROSOME** n body of a colonial hydrozoan

**HYDROSTAT** n device that detects the presence of water as a prevention against drying out, overflow, etc, esp one used as a warning in a steam boiler

**HYDROUS** adj containing water

**HYDROVANE** n vane on a seaplane conferring stability on water (a sponson) or facilitating take-off (a hydrofoil)

**HYDROXIDE** n compound containing a hydroxyl group or ion

**HYDROXY** adj (of a chemical compound) containing one or more hydroxyl groups

**HYDROXYL** adj of or containing the monovalent group –OH or the ion OH⁻ ▷ n of, consisting of, or containing the monovalent group -OH or the ion OH⁻

**HYDROXYLS** > HYDROXYL

**HYDROZOA** > HYDROZOON

**HYDROZOAN** n any colonial or solitary coelenterate of the class *Hydrozoa*, which includes the hydra, Portuguese man-of-war, and the sertularians ▷ adj of, relating to, or belonging to the *Hydrozoa*

**HYDROZOON** same as > HYDROZOAN

**HYDYNE** n type of rocket fuel

**HYDYNES** > HYDYNE

**HYE** same as > HIE

**HYED** > HYE

**HYEING** > HYE

**HYEN** same as > HYENA

**HYENA** n scavenging doglike mammal of Africa and S Asia

**HYENAS** > HYENA

**HYENIC** > HYENA

**HYENINE** adj of hyenas

**HYENOID** adj of or like hyenas

**HYENS** > HYEN

**HYES** > HYE

**HYETAL** adj of or relating to rain, rainfall, or rainy regions

**HYETOLOGY** n study of rainfall

**HYGEIST** same as > HYGIENIST

**HYGEISTS** > HYGEIST

**HYGIEIST** same as > HYGIENIST

**HYGIEISTS** > HYGIEIST

**HYGIENE** n principles and practice of health and cleanliness

**HYGIENES** > HYGIENE

**HYGIENIC** adj promoting health or cleanliness

**HYGIENICS** same as > HYGIENE

**HYGIENIST** n person skilled in the practice of hygiene

**HYGRISTOR** n electronic component the resistance of which varies with humidity

**HYGRODEIK** n type of thermometer

**HYGROLOGY** n study of humidity of air

**HYGROMA** n swelling in the soft tissue that occurs over a joint, usually caused by repeated injury

**HYGROMAS** > HYGROMA

**HYGROMATA** > HYGROMA

**HYGROPHIL** adj moisture-loving

**HYGROSTAT** same as > HUMIDISTAT

**HYING** > HIE

**HYKE** same as > HAIK

**HYKES** > HYKE

**HYLA** n type of tropical American tree frog

**HYLAS** > HYLA

**HYLDING** same as > HILDING

**HYLDINGS** > HYLDING

**HYLE** n wood

**HYLEG** n dominant planet when someone is born

**HYLEGS** > HYLEG

**HYLES** > HYLE

**HYLIC** adj solid

**HYLICISM** n materialism

**HYLICISMS** > HYLICISM

**HYLICIST** > HYLICISM

**HYLICISTS** > HYLICISM

**HYLISM** same as > HYLICISM

**HYLISMS** > HYLISM

**HYLIST** > HYLISM

**HYLISTS** > HYLISM

**HYLOBATE** n gibbon

**HYLOBATES** > HYLOBATE

**HYLOIST** n materialist

**HYLOISTS** > HYLOIST

**HYLOPHYTE** n plant that grows in woods

**HYLOZOIC** > HYLOZOISM

**HYLOZOISM** n philosophical doctrine that life is one of the properties of matter

**HYLOZOIST** > HYLOZOISM

**HYMEN** n membrane partly covering the opening of a girl's vagina, which breaks before puberty or at the first occurrence of sexual intercourse

**HYMENAEAL** same as > HYMENEAL

**HYMENAEAN** > HYMEN

**HYMENAL** > HYMEN

**HYMENEAL** adj of or relating to marriage ▷ n wedding song or poem

**HYMENEALS** > HYMENEAL

**HYMENEAN** > HYMEN

**HYMENIA** > HYMENIUM

**HYMENIAL** > HYMENIUM

**HYMENIUM** n (in basidiomycetous and ascomycetous fungi) a layer of cells some of which produce the spores

**HYMENIUMS** > HYMENIUM

**HYMENS** > HYMEN

**HYMN** n Christian song of praise sung to God or a saint ▷ vb express (praises, thanks, etc) by singing hymns

**HYMNAL** n book of hymns ▷ adj of, relating to, or characteristic of hymns

**HYMNALS** > HYMNAL

**HYMNARIES** > HYMNARY

**HYMNARY** same as > HYMNAL

**HYMNBOOK** n book containing the words and music of hymns

**HYMNBOOKS** > HYMNBOOK

**HYMNED** > HYMN

**HYMNIC** > HYMN

**HYMNING** > HYMN

**HYMNIST** n person who composes hymns

**HYMNISTS** > HYMNIST

**HYMNLESS** > HYMN

**HYMNLIKE** > HYMN

**HYMNODIES** > HYMNODY

**HYMNODIST** same as > HYMNIST

**HYMNODY** n composition or singing of hymns

**HYMNOLOGY** same as > HYMNODY

**HYMNS** > HYMN

**HYNDE** same as > HIND

**HYNDES** > HYNDE

**HYOID** adj of or relating to the hyoid bone ▷ n horseshoe-shaped bone that lies at the base of the tongue and above the thyroid cartilage

**HYOIDAL** adj of or relating to the hyoid bone

**HYOIDEAN** same as > HYOIDAL

**HYOIDS** > HYOID

**HYOSCINE** another name for > SCOPOLAMINE

**HYOSCINES** > HYOSCINE

**HYP** same as > HYPOTENUSE

**HYPALGIA** n reduced ability to feel pain

**HYPALGIAS** > HYPALGIA

**HYPALLAGE** n figure of speech in which the natural relations of two words in a statement are interchanged, as in *the fire*

*spread the wind*

**HYPANTHIA** *n* plural of hypanthium: cup-shaped receptacle of perigynous or epigynous flowers

**HYPATE** *n* string of lyre

**HYPATES** > HYPATE

**HYPE** *n* intensive or exaggerated publicity or sales promotion ▷ *vb* promote (a product) using intensive or exaggerated publicity

**HYPED** > HYPE

**HYPER** > HYPE

**HYPERACID** *adj* having excess acidity

**HYPERARID** *adj* extremely dry

**HYPERBOLA** *n* curve produced when a cone is cut by a plane at a steeper angle to its base than its side

**HYPERBOLE** *n* deliberate exaggeration for effect

**HYPERCUBE** *n* figure in a space of four or more dimensions having all its sides equal and all its angles right angles

**HYPEREMIA** *n* excessive blood in an organ or part

**HYPEREMIC** > HYPEREMIA

**HYPERFINE** as in *hyperfine structure* splitting of a spectral line of an atom or molecule into two or more closely spaced components as a result of interaction of the electrons with the magnetic moments of the nuclei

**HYPERGAMY** *n* custom that forbids a woman to marry a man of lower social status

**HYPERGOL** *n* type of fuel

**HYPERGOLS** > HYPERGOL

**HYPERICUM** *n* herbaceous plant or shrub

**HYPERLINK** *n* link from a hypertext file that gives users instant access to related material in another file ▷ *vb* link (files) in this way

**HYPERMART** *n* very large supermarket

**HYPERNOVA** *n* exploding star that produces even more energy and light than a supernova

**HYPERNYM** *n* superordinate

**HYPERNYMS** > HYPERNYM

**HYPERNYMY** > HYPERNYM

**HYPERON** *n* any baryon that is not a nucleon

**HYPERONS** > HYPERON

**HYPEROPE** *n* person with hyperopia

**HYPEROPES** > HYPEROPE

**HYPEROPIA** *n* inability to see near objects clearly because the images received by the eye are focused behind the retina

**HYPEROPIC** > HYPEROPIA

**HYPERPNEA** *n* increase in breathing rate

**HYPERPURE** *adj* extremely pure

**HYPERREAL** *adj* involving or characterized by particularly realistic graphic representation ▷ *n* that which constitutes hyperreality

**HYPERS** > HYPE

**HYPERTEXT** *n* computer software and hardware that allows users to store and view text and move between related items easily

**HYPES** > HYPE

**HYPESTER** *n* person or organization that gives an idea or product intense publicity in order to promote it

**HYPESTERS** > HYPESTER

**HYPETHRAL** *adj* having no roof

**HYPHA** *n* any of the filaments that constitute the body (mycelium) of a fungus

**HYPHAE** > HYPHA

**HYPHAL** > HYPHA

**HYPHEMIA** *n* bleeding inside eye

**HYPHEMIAS** > HYPHEMIA

**HYPHEN** *n* punctuation mark (-) indicating that two words or syllables are connected ▷ *vb* hyphenate

**HYPHENATE** *vb* separate (words) with a hyphen

**HYPHENED** > HYPHEN

**HYPHENIC** > HYPHEN

**HYPHENING** > HYPHEN

**HYPHENISE** *same as* > HYPHENIZE

**HYPHENISM** > HYPHEN

**HYPHENIZE** *same as* > HYPHENATE

**HYPHENS** > HYPHEN

**HYPING** > HYPE

**HYPINOSES** > HYPINOSIS

**HYPINOSIS** *n* protein deficiency in blood

**HYPNIC** *n* sleeping drug

**HYPNICS** > HYPNIC

**HYPNOGENY** *n* hypnosis

**HYPNOID** *adj* of or relating to a state resembling sleep or hypnosis

**HYPNOIDAL** *same as* > HYPNOID

**HYPNOLOGY** *n* study of sleep and hypnosis

**HYPNONE** *n* sleeping drug

**HYPNONES** > HYPNONE

**HYPNOSES** > HYPNOSIS

**HYPNOSIS** *n* artificially induced state of relaxation in which the mind is more than usually receptive to suggestion

**HYPNOTEE** *n* person being hypnotized

**HYPNOTEES** > HYPNOTEE

**HYPNOTIC** *adj* of or (as if) producing hypnosis ▷ *n* drug that induces sleep

**HYPNOTICS** > HYPNOTIC

**HYPNOTISE** *same as* > HYPNOTIZE

**HYPNOTISM** *n* inducing hypnosis in someone

**HYPNOTIST** *n* person skilled in the theory and practice of hypnosis

**HYPNOTIZE** *vb* induce hypnosis in (a person)

**HYPNOTOID** *adj* like hypnosis

**HYPNUM** *n* species of moss

**HYPNUMS** > HYPNUM

**HYPO** *vb* inject with a hypodermic syringe

**HYPOACID** *adj* abnormally acidic

**HYPOBARIC** *adj* below normal pressure

**HYPOBLAST** *n* inner layer of an embryo at an early stage of development that becomes the endoderm at gastrulation

**HYPOBOLE** *n* act of anticipating objection

**HYPOBOLES** > HYPOBOLE

**HYPOCAUST** *n* ancient Roman heating system in which hot air circulated under the floor and between double walls

**HYPOCIST** *n* type of juice

**HYPOCISTS** > HYPOCIST

**HYPOCOTYL** *n* part of an embryo plant between the cotyledons and the radicle

**HYPOCRISY** *n* (instance of) pretence of having standards or beliefs that are contrary to one's real character or actual behaviour

**HYPOCRITE** *n* person who pretends to be what he or she is not

**HYPODERM** *n* layer of thick-walled tissue in some plants

**HYPODERMA** *n* layer of skin tissue

**HYPODERMS** > HYPODERM

**HYPOED** > HYPO

**HYPOGAEA** > HYPOGAEUM

**HYPOGAEAL** > HYPOGAEUM

**HYPOGAEAN** > HYPOGAEUM

**HYPOGAEUM** *same as* > HYPOGEUM

**HYPOGEA** > HYPOGEUM

**HYPOGEAL** *adj* occurring or living below the surface of the ground

**HYPOGEAN** > HYPOGEUM

**HYPOGENE** *adj* formed, taking place, or originating beneath the surface of the earth

**HYPOGENIC** > HYPOGENE

**HYPOGEOUS** *same as* > HYPOGEAL

**HYPOGEUM** *n* underground vault, esp one used for burials

**HYPOGYNY** *adj* having the gynoecium above the other floral parts

**HYPOID** as in *hypoid gear* gear having a tooth form generated by a hypocycloidal curve; used extensively in motor vehicle transmissions to withstand a high surface loading

**HYPOING** > HYPO

**HYPOMANIA** *n* abnormal condition of extreme excitement, milder than mania but characterized by great optimism and overactivity and often by reckless spending of money

**HYPOMANIC** > HYPOMANIA

**HYPOMORPH** *n* mutant gene

**HYPONASTY** *n* increased growth of the lower surface of a plant part, resulting in an upward bending of the part

**HYPONEA** *same as* > HYPOPNEA

**HYPONEAS** > HYPONEA

**HYPONOIA** *n* underlying meaning

**HYPONOIAS** > HYPONOIA

**HYPONYM** *n* word whose meaning is included in that of another word

**HYPONYMS** > HYPONYM

**HYPONYMY** > HYPONYM

**HYPOPHYGE** *another name for* > APOPHYGE

**HYPOPLOID** *adj* having or designating a chromosome number that is less than a multiple of the haploid number

**HYPOPNEA** *same as* > HYPOPNOEA

**HYPOPNEAS** > HYPOPNEA

**HYPOPNEIC** > HYPOPNEA

**HYPOPNOEA** *n* abnormally shallow breathing, usually accompanied by a decrease in the breathing rate

**HYPOPYON** *n* pus in eye

**HYPOPYONS** > HYPOPYON

**HYPOS** > HYPO

**HYPOSTOME** *n* invertebrate body part

**HYPOSTYLE** *adj* having a roof supported by columns ▷ *n* building constructed in this way

**HYPOTAXES** > HYPOTAXIS

**HYPOTAXIS** *n*
subordination of one
clause to another by a
conjunction
**HYPOTHEC** *n* charge on
property in favour of a
creditor
**HYPOTHECA** *n* inner and
younger layer of the cell
wall of a diatom
**HYPOTHECS** > HYPOTHEC
**HYPOTONIA** *n* state of being
hypnotized
**HYPOTONIC** *adj* (of muscles)
lacking normal tone or
tension
**HYPOXEMIA** *n* lack of
oxygen in blood
**HYPOXEMIC** > HYPOXEMIA
**HYPOXIA** *n* deficiency in
the amount of oxygen
delivered to the body
tissues
**HYPOXIAS** > HYPOXIA
**HYPOXIC** > HYPOXIA
**HYPPED** > HYP
**HYPPING** > HYP
**HYPS** > HYP
**HYPURAL** *adj* below the tail
**HYRACES** > HYRAX
**HYRACOID** *adj* of, relating
to, or belonging to
the mammalian order
*Hyracoidea*, which contains
the hyraxes ▷ *n* hyrax
**HYRACOIDS** > HYRACOID
**HYRAX** *n* type of hoofed
rodent-like animal of
Africa and Asia
**HYRAXES** > HYRAX
**HYSON** *n* Chinese green tea
**HYSONS** > HYSON
**HYSSOP** *n* sweet-smelling
herb used in folk medicine
**HYSSOPS** > HYSSOP
**HYSTERIA** *n* state of
uncontrolled excitement,
anger, or panic
**HYSTERIAS** > HYSTERIA
**HYSTERIC** *adj* of or
suggesting hysteria
**HYSTERICS** *pl n* attack of
hysteria
**HYSTEROID** *adj* resembling
hysteria
**HYTE** *adj* insane
**HYTHE** *same as* > HITHE
**HYTHES** > HYTHE

# Ii

**IAMB** *n* metrical foot of two syllables, a short one followed by a long one

**IAMBI** >IAMBUS

**IAMBIC** *adj* written in metrical units of one short and one long syllable ▷ *n* iambic foot, line, or stanza

**IAMBICS** >IAMBIC

**IAMBIST** *n* one who writes iambs

**IAMBISTS** >IAMBIST

**IAMBS** >IAMB

**IAMBUS** *same as* >IAMB

**IAMBUSES** >IAMBUS

**IANTHINE** *adj* violet

**IATRIC** *adj* relating to medicine or physicians

**IATRICAL** *same as* >IATRIC

**IATROGENY** *n* disease caused by medical intervention

**IBERIS** *n* plant with white or purple flowers

**IBERISES** >IBERIS

**IBEX** *n* wild goat with large backward-curving horns

**IBEXES** >IBEX

**IBICES** >IBEX

**IBIDEM** *adv* in the same place

**IBIS** *n* large wading bird with long legs

**IBISES** >IBIS

**IBOGAINE** *n* dopamine blocker

**IBOGAINES** >IBOGAINE

**IBUPROFEN** *n* drug that relieves pain and reduces inflammation

**ICE** *n* water in the solid state, formed by freezing liquid water ▷ *vb* form or cause to form ice

**ICEBALL** *n* ball of ice

**ICEBALLS** >ICEBALL

**ICEBERG** *n* large floating mass of ice

**ICEBERGS** >ICEBERG

**ICEBLINK** *n* yellowish-white reflected glare in the sky over an ice field

**ICEBLINKS** >ICEBLINK

**ICEBOAT** *n* boat that breaks up bodies of ice in water

**ICEBOATER** >ICEBOAT

**ICEBOATS** >ICEBOAT

**ICEBOUND** *adj* covered or made immobile by ice

**ICEBOX** *n* refrigerator

**ICEBOXES** >ICEBOX

**ICECAP** *n* mass of ice permanently covering an area

**ICECAPPED** *adj* having an icecap

**ICECAPS** >ICECAP

**ICED** *adj* covered with icing

**ICEFALL** *n* very steep part of a glacier that has deep crevasses and resembles a frozen waterfall

**ICEFALLS** >ICEFALL

**ICEFIELD** *n* very large flat expanse of ice floating in the sea; large ice floe

**ICEFIELDS** >ICEFIELD

**ICEHOUSE** *n* building for storing ice

**ICEHOUSES** >ICEHOUSE

**ICEKHANA** *n* motor race on a frozen lake

**ICEKHANAS** >ICEKHANA

**ICELESS** >ICE

**ICELIKE** >ICE

**ICEMAKER** *n* device for making ice

**ICEMAKERS** >ICEMAKER

**ICEMAN** *n* person who sells or delivers ice

**ICEMEN** >ICEMAN

**ICEPACK** *n* bag or folded cloth containing ice, applied to a part of the body, esp the head, to cool, reduce swelling, etc

**ICEPACKS** >ICEPACK

**ICER** *n* person who ices cakes

**ICERS** >ICER

**ICES** >ICE

**ICESTONE** *n* cryolite

**ICESTONES** >ICESTONE

**ICEWINE** *n* dessert wine made from grapes that have frozen before being harvested

**ICEWINES** >ICEWINE

**ICH** *archaic form of* >EKE

**ICHABOD** *interj* the glory has departed

**ICHED** >ICH

**ICHES** >ICH

**ICHING** >ICH

**ICHNEUMON** *n* greyish-brown mongoose

**ICHNITE** *n* trace fossil

**ICHNITES** >ICHNITE

**ICHNOLITE** *same as* >ICHNITE

**ICHNOLOGY** *n* study of trace fossils

**ICHOR** *n* fluid said to flow in the veins of the gods

**ICHOROUS** >ICHOR

**ICHORS** >ICHOR

**ICHS** >ICH

**ICHTHIC** *same as* >ICHTHYIC

**ICHTHYIC** *adj* of, relating to, or characteristic of fishes

**ICHTHYOID** *adj* resembling a fish ▷ *n* fishlike vertebrate

**ICHTHYS** *n* early Christian emblem

**ICHTHYSES** >ICHTHYS

**ICICLE** *n* tapering spike of ice hanging where water has dripped

**ICICLED** *adj* covered with icicles

**ICICLES** >ICICLE

**ICIER** >ICY

**ICIEST** >ICY

**ICILY** *adv* in an icy or reserved manner

**ICINESS** *n* condition of being icy or very cold

**ICINESSES** >ICINESS

**ICING** *n* mixture of sugar and water etc, used to cover and decorate cakes

**ICINGS** >ICING

**ICK** *interj* expression of disgust

**ICKER** *n* ear of corn

**ICKERS** >ICKER

**ICKIER** >ICKY

**ICKIEST** >ICKY

**ICKILY** >ICKY

**ICKINESS** >ICKY

**ICKLE** *ironically childish word for* >LITTLE

**ICKLER** >ICKLE

**ICKLEST** >ICKLE

**ICKY** *adj* sticky

**ICON** *n* picture of Christ or another religious figure, regarded as holy in the

Orthodox Church
**ICONES** >ICON
**ICONIC** adj relating to, resembling, or having the character of an icon
**ICONICAL** same as >ICONIC
**ICONICITY** >ICONIC
**ICONIFIED** >ICONIFY
**ICONIFIES** >ICONIFY
**ICONIFY** vb render as an icon
**ICONISE** same as >ICONIZE
**ICONISED** >ICONISE
**ICONISES** >ICONISE
**ICONISING** >ICONISE
**ICONIZE** vb render as an icon
**ICONIZED** >ICONIZE
**ICONIZES** >ICONIZE
**ICONIZING** >ICONIZE
**ICONOLOGY** n study or field of art history concerning icons
**ICONOSTAS** same as >ICONOSTASIS
**ICONS** >ICON
**ICTAL** >ICTUS
**ICTERIC** >ICTERUS
**ICTERICAL** >ICTERUS
**ICTERICS** >ICTERUS
**ICTERID** n bird of the oriole family
**ICTERIDS** >ICTERID
**ICTERINE** >ICTERID
**ICTERUS** n yellowing of plant leaves, caused by excessive cold or moisture
**ICTERUSES** >ICTERUS
**ICTIC** >ICTUS
**ICTUS** n metrical or rhythmic stress in verse feet, as contrasted with the stress accent on words
**ICTUSES** >ICTUS
**ICY** adj very cold
**ID** n mind's instinctive unconscious energies
**IDANT** n chromosome
**IDANTS** >IDANT
**IDE** n silver orfe fish
**IDEA** n plan or thought formed in the mind ▷ vb have or form an idea
**IDEAED** >IDEA
**IDEAL** adj most suitable ▷ n conception of something that is perfect
**IDEALESS** >IDEA
**IDEALISE** same as >IDEALIZE
**IDEALISED** >IDEALISE
**IDEALISER** >IDEALISE
**IDEALISES** >IDEALISE
**IDEALISM** n tendency to seek perfection in everything
**IDEALISMS** >IDEALISM
**IDEALIST** >IDEALISM
**IDEALISTS** >IDEALISM
**IDEALITY** >IDEAL
**IDEALIZE** vb regard or portray as perfect or nearly perfect
**IDEALIZED** >IDEALIZE

**IDEALIZER** >IDEALIZE
**IDEALIZES** >IDEALIZE
**IDEALLESS** >IDEAL
**IDEALLY** >IDEAL
**IDEALNESS** >IDEAL
**IDEALOGUE** corruption of >IDEOLOGUE
**IDEALOGY** corruption of >IDEOLOGY
**IDEALS** >IDEAL
**IDEAS** >IDEA
**IDEATA** >IDEATUM
**IDEATE** vb form or have an idea of
**IDEATED** >IDEATE
**IDEATES** >IDEATE
**IDEATING** >IDEATE
**IDEATION** >IDEATE
**IDEATIONS** >IDEATE
**IDEATIVE** >IDEATE
**IDEATUM** n objective reality with which human ideas are supposed to correspond
**IDEE** n idea
**IDEES** >IDEE
**IDEM** adj same: used to refer to an article, chapter, or book already quoted
**IDENT** n short visual image employed between television programmes that works as a logo to locate the viewer to the channel
**IDENTIC** adj (esp of opinions expressed by two or more governments) having the same wording or intention regarding another power
**IDENTICAL** adj exactly the same
**IDENTIFY** vb prove or recognize as being a certain person or thing
**IDENTIKIT** n trademark name for a set of transparencies of various typical facial characteristics that can be superimposed on one another to build up a picture of a person sought by the police
**IDENTITY** n state of being a specified person or thing
**IDENTS** >IDENT
**IDEOGRAM** n character or symbol that directly represents a concept or thing, rather than the sounds that form its name
**IDEOGRAMS** >IDEOGRAM
**IDEOGRAPH** same as >IDEOGRAM
**IDEOLOGIC** >IDEOLOGY
**IDEOLOGUE** same as >IDEOLOGIST
**IDEOLOGY** n body of ideas and beliefs of a group, nation, etc
**IDEOMOTOR** adj designating automatic

muscular movements stimulated by ideas
**IDEOPHONE** n sound that represents a complete idea
**IDES** n (in the Ancient Roman calendar) the 15th of March, May, July, or October, or the 13th of other months
**IDIOBLAST** n plant cell that differs from those around it in the same tissue
**IDIOCIES** >IDIOCY
**IDIOCY** n utter stupidity
**IDIOGRAM** another name for >KARYOGRAM
**IDIOGRAMS** >IDIOGRAM
**IDIOLECT** n variety or form of a language used by an individual
**IDIOLECTS** >IDIOLECT
**IDIOM** n group of words which when used together have a different meaning from the words individually
**IDIOMATIC** >IDIOM
**IDIOMS** >IDIOM
**IDIOPATHY** n any disease of unknown cause
**IDIOPHONE** n percussion instrument, such as a cymbal or xylophone, made of naturally sonorous material
**IDIOPLASM** n germ plasm
**IDIOT** n foolish or stupid person
**IDIOTCIES** >IDIOTCY
**IDIOTCY** same as >IDIOCY
**IDIOTIC** adj of or resembling an idiot
**IDIOTICAL** same as >IDIOTIC
**IDIOTICON** n dictionary of dialect
**IDIOTISH** same as >IDIOTIC
**IDIOTISM** archaic word for >IDIOCY
**IDIOTISMS** >IDIOTISM
**IDIOTS** >IDIOT
**IDIOTYPE** n unique part of antibody
**IDIOTYPES** >IDIOTYPE
**IDIOTYPIC** >IDIOTYPE
**IDLE** adj not doing anything ▷ vb spend (time) doing very little
**IDLED** >IDLE
**IDLEHOOD** >IDLE
**IDLEHOODS** >IDLE
**IDLENESS** >IDLE
**IDLER** n person who idles
**IDLERS** >IDLER
**IDLES** >IDLE
**IDLESSE** >IDLE
**IDLESSES** >IDLE
**IDLEST** >IDLE
**IDLING** >IDLE
**IDLY** >IDLE
**IDOCRASE** n green, brown, or yellow mineral

**IDOCRASES** >IDOCRASE
**IDOL** n object of excessive devotion
**IDOLA** >IDOLUM
**IDOLATER** >IDOLATRY
**IDOLATERS** >IDOLATRY
**IDOLATOR** >IDOLATRY
**IDOLATORS** >IDOLATRY
**IDOLATRY** n worship of idols
**IDOLISE** same as >IDOLIZE
**IDOLISED** >IDOLISE
**IDOLISER** >IDOLISE
**IDOLISERS** >IDOLISE
**IDOLISES** >IDOLISE
**IDOLISING** >IDOLISE
**IDOLISM** >IDOLIZE
**IDOLISMS** >IDOL
**IDOLIST** >IDOLIZE
**IDOLISTS** >IDOLIZE
**IDOLIZE** vb love or admire excessively
**IDOLIZED** >IDOLIZE
**IDOLIZER** >IDOLIZE
**IDOLIZERS** >IDOLIZE
**IDOLIZES** >IDOLIZE
**IDOLIZING** >IDOLIZE
**IDOLS** >IDOL
**IDOLUM** n mental picture
**IDONEITY** >IDONEOUS
**IDONEOUS** adj appropriate
**IDS** >ID
**IDYL** same as >IDYLL
**IDYLIST** same as >IDYLLIST
**IDYLISTS** >IDYLIST
**IDYLL** n scene or time of great peace and happiness
**IDYLLIAN** same as >IDYLLIC
**IDYLLIC** adj of or relating to an idyll
**IDYLLIST** n writer of idylls
**IDYLLISTS** >IDYLLIST
**IDYLLS** >IDYLL
**IDYLS** >IDYL
**IF** n uncertainty or doubt
**IFF** n military system using radar transmissions to which equipment carried by friendly forces automatically responds with a precoded signal
**IFFIER** >IFFY
**IFFIEST** >IFFY
**IFFINESS** >IFFY
**IFFY** adj doubtful, uncertain
**IFS** >IF
**IFTAR** n meal eaten by Muslims to break their fast after sunset every day during Ramadan
**IFTARS** >IFTAR
**IGAD** same as >EGAD
**IGAPO** n flooded forest
**IGAPOS** >IGAPO
**IGARAPE** n canoe route
**IGARAPES** >IGARAPE
**IGG** vb antagonize
**IGGED** >IGG
**IGGING** >IGG
**IGGS** >IGG
**IGLOO** n dome-shaped Inuit house made of snow and ice

IGLOOS >IGLOO
IGLU same as >IGLOO
IGLUS >IGLU
IGNARO n ignoramus
IGNAROES >IGNARO
IGNAROS >IGNARO
IGNATIA n dried seed
IGNATIAS >IGNATIA
IGNEOUS adj (of rock)
formed as molten rock
cools and hardens
IGNESCENT adj giving
off sparks when struck,
as a flint ▷ n ignescent
substance
IGNIFIED >IGNIFY
IGNIFIES >IGNIFY
IGNIFY vb turn into fire
IGNIFYING >IGNIFY
IGNITABLE >IGNITE
IGNITE vb catch fire or set
fire to
IGNITED >IGNITE
IGNITER n person or thing
that ignites
IGNITERS >IGNITER
IGNITES >IGNITE
IGNITIBLE >IGNITE
IGNITING >IGNITE
IGNITION n system that
ignites the fuel-and-air
mixture to start an engine
IGNITIONS >IGNITION
IGNITOR same as >IGNITER
IGNITORS >IGNITER
IGNITRON n mercury-arc
rectifier controlled by a
subsidiary electrode
IGNITRONS >IGNITRON
IGNOBLE adj dishonourable
IGNOBLER >IGNOBLE
IGNOBLEST >IGNOBLE
IGNOBLY >IGNOBLE
IGNOMIES >IGNOMY
IGNOMINY n humiliating
disgrace
IGNOMY Shakespearean
variant of >IGNOMINY
IGNORABLE >IGNORE
IGNORAMI >IGNORAMUS
IGNORAMUS n ignorant
person
IGNORANCE n lack of
knowledge or education
IGNORANT adj lacking
knowledge ▷ n ignorant
person
IGNORANTS >IGNORANT
IGNORE vb refuse to notice,
disregard deliberately ▷ n
disregard
IGNORED >IGNORE
IGNORER >IGNORE
IGNORERS >IGNORE
IGNORES >IGNORE
IGNORING >IGNORE
IGUANA n large tropical
American lizard
IGUANAS >IGUANA
IGUANIAN >IGUANA
IGUANIANS >IGUANA
IGUANID same as >IGUANA
IGUANIDS >IGUANID
IGUANODON n massive

herbivorous long-tailed
bipedal dinosaur
IHRAM n customary white
robes worn by Muslim
pilgrims to Mecca,
symbolizing a sacred or
consecrated state
IHRAMS >IHRAM
IJTIHAD n effort of a
Muslim scholar to derive a
legal ruling from the Koran
IJTIHADS >IJTIHAD
IKAN n (in Malaysia) fish
used esp in names of
cooked dishes
IKANS >IKAN
IKAT n method of creating
patterns in fabric by tie-
dyeing the yarn before
weaving
IKATS >IKAT
IKEBANA n Japanese art of
flower arrangement
IKEBANAS >IKEBANA
IKON same as >ICON
IKONS >IKON
ILEA >ILEUM
ILEAC adj of or relating to
the ileum
ILEAL same as >ILEAC
ILEITIDES >ILEITIS
ILEITIS n inflammation
of the ileum
ILEITISES >ILEITIS
ILEOSTOMY n surgical
formation of a permanent
opening through the
abdominal wall into the
ileum
ILEUM n lowest part of the
small intestine
ILEUS n obstruction of the
intestine, esp the ileum, by
mechanical occlusion or as
the result of distension of
the bowel following loss of
muscular action
ILEUSES >ILEUS
ILEX n any of a genus
of trees or shrubs that
includes holly
ILEXES >ILEX
ILIA >ILIUM
ILIAC adj of or relating to
the ilium
ILIACUS n iliac
ILIACUSES >ILIACUS
ILIAD n epic poem
ILIADS >ILIAD
ILIAL >ILIUM
ILICES >ILEX
ILIUM n uppermost
and widest of the three
sections of the hipbone
ILK n type ▷ determiner
each
ILKA same as >ILK
ILKADAY n every day
ILKADAYS >ILKADAY
ILKS >ILK
ILL adj not in good health
▷ n evil, harm ▷ adv badly
ILLAPSE vb slide in
ILLAPSED >ILLAPSE

ILLAPSES >ILLAPSE
ILLAPSING >ILLAPSE
ILLATION rare word
for >INFERENCE
ILLATIONS >ILLATION
ILLATIVE adj of or relating
to illation ▷ n illative case
ILLATIVES >ILLATIVE
ILLEGAL adj against the
law ▷ n person who has
entered or attempted to
enter a country illegally
ILLEGALLY >ILLEGAL
ILLEGALS >ILLEGAL
ILLEGIBLE adj unable to
be read or deciphered
ILLEGIBLY >ILLEGIBLE
ILLER >ILL
ILLEST >ILL
ILLIAD n wink
ILLIADS >ILLIAD
ILLIBERAL adj narrow-
minded, intolerant
ILLICIT adj illegal
ILLICITLY >ILLICIT
ILLIMITED adj infinite
ILLINIUM n type of
radioactive element
ILLINIUMS >ILLINIUM
ILLIPE n Asian tree
ILLIPES >ILLIPE
ILLIQUID adj (of an asset)
not easily convertible into
cash
ILLISION n act of striking
against
ILLISIONS >ILLISION
ILLITE n clay mineral of
the mica group, found in
shales and mudstones
ILLITES >ILLITE
ILLITIC >ILLITE
ILLNESS n disease or
indisposition
ILLNESSES >ILLNESS
ILLOGIC n reasoning
characterized by lack of
logic
ILLOGICAL adj
unreasonable
ILLOGICS >ILLOGIC
ILLS >ILL
ILLTH n condition of
poverty or misery
ILLTHS >ILLTH
ILLUDE vb trick or deceive
ILLUDED >ILLUDE
ILLUDES >ILLUDE
ILLUDING >ILLUDE
ILLUME vb illuminate
ILLUMED >ILLUME
ILLUMES >ILLUME
ILLUMINE vb throw light
in or into
ILLUMINED >ILLUMINE
ILLUMINER n illuminator
ILLUMINES >ILLUMINE
ILLUMING >ILLUME
ILLUPI same as >ILLIPE
ILLUPIS >ILLUPI
ILLUSION n deceptive
appearance or belief
ILLUSIONS >ILLUSION
ILLUSIVE same

as >ILLUSORY
ILLUSORY adj seeming to
be true, but actually false
ILLUVIA >ILLUVIUM
ILLUVIAL >ILLUVIUM
ILLUVIATE vb deposit
illuvium
ILLUVIUM n material,
which includes colloids
and mineral salts, that is
washed down from one
layer of soil to a lower layer
ILLUVIUMS >ILLUVIUM
ILLY adv badly
ILMENITE n black mineral
found in igneous rocks as
layered deposits and in
veins
ILMENITES >ILMENITE
IMAGE n mental picture of
someone or something
▷ vb picture in the mind
IMAGEABLE >IMAGE
IMAGED >IMAGE
IMAGELESS >IMAGE
IMAGER n device that
produces images
IMAGERIES >IMAGERY
IMAGERS >IMAGER
IMAGERY n images
collectively, esp in the arts
IMAGES >IMAGE
IMAGINAL adj of, relating
to, or resembling an imago
IMAGINARY adj existing
only in the imagination
IMAGINE vb form a mental
image of ▷ sentence
substitute exclamation of
surprise
IMAGINED >IMAGINE
IMAGINER >IMAGINE
IMAGINERS >IMAGINE
IMAGINES >IMAGO
IMAGING >IMAGE
IMAGINGS >IMAGE
IMAGINING >IMAGINE
IMAGINIST n imaginative
person
IMAGISM n poetic
movement in England
and America between 1912
and 1917
IMAGISMS >IMAGISM
IMAGIST >IMAGISM
IMAGISTIC >IMAGISM
IMAGISTS >IMAGISM
IMAGO n sexually mature
adult insect
IMAGOES >IMAGO
IMAGOS >IMAGO
IMAM n leader of prayers in
a mosque
IMAMATE n region or
territory governed by an
imam
IMAMATES >IMAMATE
IMAMS >IMAM
IMARET n (in Turkey) a
hospice for pilgrims or
travellers
IMARETS >IMARET
IMARI n Japanese porcelain
IMARIS >IMARI

**IMAUM** *same as* >IMAM
**IMAUMS** >IMAUM
**IMBALANCE** n lack of balance or proportion
**IMBALM** *same as* >EMBALM
**IMBALMED** >IMBALM
**IMBALMER** >IMBALM
**IMBALMERS** >IMBALM
**IMBALMING** >IMBALM
**IMBALMS** >IMBALM
**IMBAR** vb bar in
**IMBARK** vb cover in bark
**IMBARKED** >IMBARK
**IMBARKING** >IMBARK
**IMBARKS** >IMBARK
**IMBARRED** >IMBAR
**IMBARRING** >IMBAR
**IMBARS** >IMBAR
**IMBASE** vb degrade
**IMBASED** >IMBASE
**IMBASES** >IMBASE
**IMBASING** >IMBASE
**IMBATHE** vb bathe
**IMBATHED** >IMBATHE
**IMBATHES** >IMBATHE
**IMBATHING** >IMBATHE
**IMBECILE** n stupid person ▷ adj stupid or senseless
**IMBECILES** >IMBECILE
**IMBECILIC** >IMBECILE
**IMBED** *same as* >EMBED
**IMBEDDED** >IMBED
**IMBEDDING** >IMBED
**IMBEDS** >IMBED
**IMBIBE** vb drink (alcoholic drinks)
**IMBIBED** >IMBIBE
**IMBIBER** >IMBIBE
**IMBIBERS** >IMBIBE
**IMBIBES** >IMBIBE
**IMBIBING** >IMBIBE
**IMBITTER** *same as* >EMBITTER
**IMBITTERS** >IMBITTER
**IMBIZO** n meeting, esp a gathering of the Zulu people called by the king or a traditional leader
**IMBIZOS** >IMBIZO
**IMBLAZE** vb depict heraldically
**IMBLAZED** >IMBLAZE
**IMBLAZES** >IMBLAZE
**IMBLAZING** >IMBLAZE
**IMBODIED** >IMBODY
**IMBODIES** >IMBODY
**IMBODY** *same as* >EMBODY
**IMBODYING** >IMBODY
**IMBOLDEN** *same as* >EMBOLDEN
**IMBOLDENS** >IMBOLDEN
**IMBORDER** vb enclose in a border
**IMBORDERS** >IMBORDER
**IMBOSK** vb conceal
**IMBOSKED** >IMBOSK
**IMBOSKING** >IMBOSK
**IMBOSKS** >IMBOSK
**IMBOSOM** vb hold in one's heart
**IMBOSOMED** >IMBOSOM
**IMBOSOMS** >IMBOSOM
**IMBOSS** *same as* >EMBOSS
**IMBOSSED** >IMBOSS

**IMBOSSES** >IMBOSS
**IMBOSSING** >IMBOSS
**IMBOWER** vb enclose in a bower
**IMBOWERED** >IMBOWER
**IMBOWERS** >IMBOWER
**IMBRANGLE** vb entangle
**IMBRAST** *Spenserian past participle of* > EMBRACE
**IMBREX** n curved tile
**IMBRICATE** adj having tiles or slates that overlap ▷ vb decorate with a repeating pattern resembling scales or overlapping tiles
**IMBRICES** >IMBREX
**IMBROGLIO** n confusing and complicated situation
**IMBROWN** vb make brown
**IMBROWNED** >IMBROWN
**IMBROWNS** >IMBROWN
**IMBRUE** vb stain, esp with blood
**IMBRUED** >IMBRUE
**IMBRUES** >IMBRUE
**IMBRUING** >IMBRUE
**IMBRUTE** vb reduce to a bestial state
**IMBRUTED** >IMBRUTE
**IMBRUTES** >IMBRUTE
**IMBRUTING** >IMBRUTE
**IMBUE** vb fill or inspire with (ideals or principles)
**IMBUED** >IMBUE
**IMBUEMENT** >IMBUE
**IMBUES** >IMBUE
**IMBUING** >IMBUE
**IMBURSE** vb pay
**IMBURSED** >IMBURSE
**IMBURSES** >IMBURSE
**IMBURSING** >IMBURSE
**IMID** n immunomodulatory drug
**IMIDAZOLE** n white crystalline basic heterocyclic compound
**IMIDE** n any of a class of organic compounds
**IMIDES** >IMIDE
**IMIDIC** >IMIDE
**IMIDO** >IMIDE
**IMIDS** >IMID
**IMINAZOLE** *same as* >IMIDAZOLE
**IMINE** n any of a class of organic compounds
**IMINES** >IMINE
**IMINO** >IMINE
**IMINOUREA** *another name for* >GUANIDINE
**IMITABLE** >IMITATE
**IMITANCY** n tendency to imitate
**IMITANT** *same as* >IMITATION
**IMITANTS** >IMITANT
**IMITATE** vb take as a model
**IMITATED** >IMITATE
**IMITATES** >IMITATE
**IMITATING** >IMITATE
**IMITATION** n copy of an original ▷ adj made to look like a material of superior quality

**IMITATIVE** adj imitating or tending to copy
**IMITATOR** >IMITATE
**IMITATORS** >IMITATE
**IMMANACLE** vb fetter
**IMMANE** adj monstrous
**IMMANELY** >IMMANE
**IMMANENCE** >IMMANENT
**IMMANENCY** >IMMANENT
**IMMANENT** adj present within and throughout something
**IMMANITY** >IMMANE
**IMMANTLE** vb cover with a mantle
**IMMANTLED** >IMMANTLE
**IMMANTLES** >IMMANTLE
**IMMASK** vb disguise
**IMMASKED** >IMMASK
**IMMASKING** >IMMASK
**IMMASKS** >IMMASK
**IMMATURE** n young animal ▷ adj not fully developed
**IMMATURES** >IMMATURE
**IMMEDIACY** >IMMEDIATE
**IMMEDIATE** adj occurring at once
**IMMENSE** adj extremely large
**IMMENSELY** >IMMENSE
**IMMENSER** >IMMENSE
**IMMENSEST** >IMMENSE
**IMMENSITY** n state or quality of being immense
**IMMERGE** *archaic word for* >IMMERSE
**IMMERGED** >IMMERGE
**IMMERGES** >IMMERGE
**IMMERGING** >IMMERGE
**IMMERSE** vb involve deeply, engross
**IMMERSED** adj sunk or submerged
**IMMERSER** >IMMERSE
**IMMERSERS** >IMMERSE
**IMMERSES** >IMMERSE
**IMMERSING** >IMMERSE
**IMMERSION** n form of baptism in which part or the whole of a person's body is submerged in the water
**IMMERSIVE** adj providing information or stimulation for a number of senses, not only sight and sound
**IMMESH** *variant of* > ENMESH
**IMMESHED** >IMMESH
**IMMESHES** >IMMESH
**IMMESHING** >IMMESH
**IMMEW** vb confine
**IMMEWED** >IMMEW
**IMMEWING** >IMMEW
**IMMEWS** >IMMEW
**IMMIES** >IMMY
**IMMIGRANT** n person who comes to a foreign country in order to settle there
**IMMIGRATE** vb come to a place or country of which one is not a native in order to settle there
**IMMINENCE** >IMMINENT

**IMMINENCY** >IMMINENT
**IMMINENT** adj about to happen
**IMMINGLE** vb blend or mix together
**IMMINGLED** >IMMINGLE
**IMMINGLES** >IMMINGLE
**IMMINUTE** adj reduced
**IMMISSION** n insertion
**IMMIT** vb insert
**IMMITS** >IMMIT
**IMMITTED** >IMMIT
**IMMITTING** >IMMIT
**IMMIX** vb mix in
**IMMIXED** >IMMIX
**IMMIXES** >IMMIX
**IMMIXING** >IMMIX
**IMMIXTURE** >IMMIX
**IMMOBILE** adj not moving
**IMMODEST** adj behaving in an indecent or improper manner
**IMMODESTY** >IMMODEST
**IMMOLATE** vb kill as a sacrifice
**IMMOLATED** >IMMOLATE
**IMMOLATES** >IMMOLATE
**IMMOLATOR** >IMMOLATE
**IMMOMENT** adj of no value
**IMMORAL** adj morally wrong, corrupt
**IMMORALLY** >IMMORAL
**IMMORTAL** adj living forever ▷ n person whose fame will last for all time
**IMMORTALS** >IMMORTAL
**IMMOTILE** adj (esp of living organisms or their parts) not capable of moving spontaneously and independently.
**IMMOVABLE** adj unable to be moved
**IMMOVABLY** >IMMOVABLE
**IMMUNE** adj protected against a specific disease ▷ n immune person or animal
**IMMUNES** >IMMUNE
**IMMUNISE** *same as* >IMMUNIZE
**IMMUNISED** >IMMUNISE
**IMMUNISER** >IMMUNISE
**IMMUNISES** >IMMUNISE
**IMMUNITY** n ability to resist disease
**IMMUNIZE** vb make immune to a disease
**IMMUNIZED** >IMMUNIZE
**IMMUNIZER** >IMMUNIZE
**IMMUNIZES** >IMMUNIZE
**IMMUNOGEN** n any substance that evokes an immune response
**IMMURE** vb imprison
**IMMURED** >IMMURE
**IMMURES** >IMMURE
**IMMURING** >IMMURE
**IMMUTABLE** adj unchangeable
**IMMUTABLY** >IMMUTABLE
**IMMY** n image-orthicon camera
**IMP** n (in folklore)

mischievous small creature with magical powers ▷ *vb* insert (new feathers) into the stumps of broken feathers in order to repair the wing of a hawk or falcon

**IMPACABLE** *adj* incapable of being placated or pacified

**IMPACT** *n* strong effect ▷ *vb* have a strong effect on

**IMPACTED** >IMPACT

**IMPACTER** >IMPACT

**IMPACTERS** >IMPACT

**IMPACTFUL** >IMPACT

**IMPACTING** >IMPACT

**IMPACTION** >IMPACT

**IMPACTITE** *n* glassy rock formed in a meteor collision

**IMPACTIVE** *adj* of or relating to a physical impact

**IMPACTOR** >IMPACT

**IMPACTORS** >IMPACT

**IMPACTS** >IMPACT

**IMPAINT** *vb* paint

**IMPAINTED** >IMPAINT

**IMPAINTS** >IMPAINT

**IMPAIR** *vb* weaken or damage

**IMPAIRED** >IMPAIR

**IMPAIRER** >IMPAIR

**IMPAIRERS** >IMPAIR

**IMPAIRING** >IMPAIR

**IMPAIRS** >IMPAIR

**IMPALA** *n* southern African antelope

**IMPALAS** >IMPALA

**IMPALE** *vb* pierce with a sharp object

**IMPALED** >IMPALE

**IMPALER** >IMPALE

**IMPALERS** >IMPALE

**IMPALES** >IMPALE

**IMPALING** >IMPALE

**IMPANATE** *adj* embodied in bread

**IMPANEL** *variant spelling (esp US) of* >EMPANEL

**IMPANELED** >IMPANEL

**IMPANELS** >IMPANEL

**IMPANNEL** *same as* >IMPANEL

**IMPANNELS** >IMPANEL

**IMPARITY** *less common word for* >DISPARITY

**IMPARK** *vb* make into a park

**IMPARKED** >IMPARK

**IMPARKING** >IMPARK

**IMPARKS** >IMPARK

**IMPARL** *vb* parley

**IMPARLED** >IMPARL

**IMPARLING** >IMPARL

**IMPARLS** >IMPARL

**IMPART** *vb* communicate (information)

**IMPARTED** >IMPART

**IMPARTER** >IMPART

**IMPARTERS** >IMPART

**IMPARTIAL** *adj* not favouring one side or the other

**IMPARTING** >IMPART

**IMPARTS** >IMPART

**IMPASSE** *n* situation in which progress is impossible

**IMPASSES** >IMPASSE

**IMPASSION** *vb* arouse the passions of

**IMPASSIVE** *adj* showing no emotion, calm

**IMPASTE** *vb* apply paint thickly to

**IMPASTED** >IMPASTE

**IMPASTES** >IMPASTE

**IMPASTING** >IMPASTE

**IMPASTO** *n* technique of applying paint thickly, so that brush marks are evident ▷ *vb* apply impasto

**IMPASTOED** >IMPASTO

**IMPASTOS** >IMPASTO

**IMPATIENS** *n* plant such as balsam, touch-me-not, busy Lizzie, and policeman's helmet

**IMPATIENT** *adj* irritable at any delay or difficulty

**IMPAVE** *vb* set in a pavement

**IMPAVED** >IMPAVE

**IMPAVES** >IMPAVE

**IMPAVID** *adj* fearless

**IMPAVIDLY** >IMPAVID

**IMPAVING** >IMPAVE

**IMPAWN** *vb* pawn

**IMPAWNED** >IMPAWN

**IMPAWNING** >IMPAWN

**IMPAWNS** >IMPAWN

**IMPEACH** *vb* charge with a serious crime against the state

**IMPEACHED** >IMPEACH

**IMPEACHER** >IMPEACH

**IMPEACHES** >IMPEACH

**IMPEARL** *vb* adorn with pearls

**IMPEARLED** >IMPEARL

**IMPEARLS** >IMPEARL

**IMPECCANT** *adj* not sinning

**IMPED** >IMP

**IMPEDANCE** *n* measure of the opposition to the flow of an alternating current

**IMPEDE** *vb* hinder in action or progress

**IMPEDED** >IMPEDE

**IMPEDER** >IMPEDE

**IMPEDERS** >IMPEDE

**IMPEDES** >IMPEDE

**IMPEDING** >IMPEDE

**IMPEDOR** *n* component, such as an inductor or resistor, that offers impedance

**IMPEDORS** >IMPEDOR

**IMPEL** *vb* push or force (someone) to do something

**IMPELLED** >IMPEL

**IMPELLENT** >IMPEL

**IMPELLER** *n* vaned rotating disc of a centrifugal pump, compressor, etc

**IMPELLERS** >IMPELLER

**IMPELLING** >IMPEL

**IMPELLOR** *same as* >IMPELLER

**IMPELLORS** >IMPELLOR

**IMPELS** >IMPEL

**IMPEND** *vb* (esp of something threatening) to be about to happen

**IMPENDED** >IMPEND

**IMPENDENT** >IMPEND

**IMPENDING** >IMPEND

**IMPENDS** >IMPEND

**IMPENNATE** *adj* (of birds) lacking true functional wings or feathers

**IMPERATOR** *n* (in imperial Rome) a title of the emperor

**IMPERFECT** *adj* having faults or mistakes ▷ *n* imperfect tense

**IMPERIA** >IMPERIUM

**IMPERIAL** *adj* of or like an empire or emperor ▷ *n* wine bottle holding the equivalent of eight normal bottles

**IMPERIALS** >IMPERIAL

**IMPERIL** *vb* put in danger

**IMPERILED** >IMPERIL

**IMPERILS** >IMPERIL

**IMPERIOUS** *adj* proud and domineering

**IMPERIUM** *n* (in ancient Rome) the supreme power, held esp by consuls and emperors, to command and administer in military, judicial, and civil affairs

**IMPERIUMS** >IMPERIUM

**IMPETICOS** *vb* put in a pocket

**IMPETIGO** *n* contagious skin disease

**IMPETIGOS** >IMPETIGO

**IMPETRATE** *vb* supplicate or entreat for, esp by prayer

**IMPETUOUS** *adj* done or acting without thought, rash

**IMPETUS** *n* incentive, impulse

**IMPETUSES** >IMPETUS

**IMPHEE** *n* African sugar cane

**IMPHEES** >IMPHEE

**IMPI** *n* group of Zulu warriors

**IMPIES** >IMPI

**IMPIETIES** >IMPIETY

**IMPIETY** *n* lack of respect or religious reverence

**IMPING** >IMP

**IMPINGE** *vb* affect or restrict

**IMPINGED** >IMPINGE

**IMPINGENT** >IMPINGE

**IMPINGER** >IMPINGE

**IMPINGERS** >IMPINGE

**IMPINGES** >IMPINGE

**IMPINGING** >IMPINGE

**IMPINGS** >IMP

**IMPIOUS** *adj* showing a

lack of respect or reverence

**IMPIOUSLY** >IMPIOUS

**IMPIS** >IMPI

**IMPISH** *adj* mischievous

**IMPISHLY** >IMPISH

**IMPLANT** *n* something put into someone's body, usu. by surgical operation ▷ *vb* put (something) into someone's body, usu. by surgical operation

**IMPLANTED** >IMPLANT

**IMPLANTER** >IMPLANT

**IMPLANTS** >IMPLANT

**IMPLATE** *vb* sheathe

**IMPLATED** >IMPLATE

**IMPLATES** >IMPLATE

**IMPLATING** >IMPLATE

**IMPLEACH** *vb* intertwine

**IMPLEAD** *vb* sue or prosecute

**IMPLEADED** >IMPLEAD

**IMPLEADER** >IMPLEAD

**IMPLEADS** >IMPLEAD

**IMPLED** >IMPLEAD

**IMPLEDGE** *vb* pledge

**IMPLEDGED** >IMPLEDGE

**IMPLEDGES** >IMPLEDGE

**IMPLEMENT** *vb* carry out (instructions etc) ▷ *n* tool, instrument

**IMPLETE** *vb* fill

**IMPLETED** >IMPLETE

**IMPLETES** >IMPLETE

**IMPLETING** >IMPLETE

**IMPLETION** >IMPLETE

**IMPLEX** *n* part of an arthropod

**IMPLEXES** >IMPLEX

**IMPLEXION** *n* complication

**IMPLICATE** *vb* show to be involved, esp in a crime

**IMPLICIT** *adj* expressed indirectly

**IMPLICITY** >IMPLICIT

**IMPLIED** *adj* hinted at or suggested

**IMPLIEDLY** >IMPLIED

**IMPLIES** >IMPLY

**IMPLODE** *vb* collapse inwards

**IMPLODED** >IMPLODE

**IMPLODENT** *n* sound of an implosion

**IMPLODES** >IMPLODE

**IMPLODING** >IMPLODE

**IMPLORE** *vb* beg earnestly

**IMPLORED** >IMPLORE

**IMPLORER** >IMPLORE

**IMPLORERS** >IMPLORE

**IMPLORES** >IMPLORE

**IMPLORING** >IMPLORE

**IMPLOSION** *n* act or process of imploding

**IMPLOSIVE** *n* consonant pronounced in a particular way

**IMPLUNGE** *vb* submerge

**IMPLUNGED** >IMPLUNGE

**IMPLUNGES** >IMPLUNGE

**IMPLUVIA** >IMPLUVIUM

**IMPLUVIUM** *n* rain-filled water tank

**IMPLY** *vb* indicate by

hinting, suggest
**IMPLYING** > IMPLY
**IMPOCKET** *vb* put in a pocket
**IMPOCKETS** > IMPOCKET
**IMPOLDER** *vb* make into a polder
**IMPOLDERS** > IMPOLDER
**IMPOLICY** *n* act or an instance of being unjudicious or impolitic
**IMPOLITE** *adj* showing bad manners
**IMPOLITER** > IMPOLITE
**IMPOLITIC** *adj* unwise or inadvisable
**IMPONE** *vb* impose
**IMPONED** > IMPONE
**IMPONENT** *n* person who imposes a duty, etc
**IMPONENTS** > IMPONENT
**IMPONES** > IMPONE
**IMPONING** > IMPONE
**IMPOROUS** *adj* not porous
**IMPORT** *vb* bring in (goods) from another country ▷ *n* something imported
**IMPORTANT** *adj* of great significance or value
**IMPORTED** > IMPORT
**IMPORTER** > IMPORT
**IMPORTERS** > IMPORT
**IMPORTING** > IMPORT
**IMPORTS** > IMPORT
**IMPORTUNE** *vb* harass with persistent requests
**IMPOSABLE** > IMPOSE
**IMPOSE** *vb* force the acceptance of
**IMPOSED** > IMPOSE
**IMPOSER** > IMPOSE
**IMPOSERS** > IMPOSE
**IMPOSES** > IMPOSE
**IMPOSING** *adj* grand, impressive
**IMPOST** *n* tax, esp a customs duty ▷ *vb* classify (imported goods) according to the duty payable on them
**IMPOSTED** > IMPOST
**IMPOSTER** > IMPOST
**IMPOSTERS** > IMPOST
**IMPOSTING** > IMPOST
**IMPOSTOR** *n* person who cheats or swindles by pretending to be someone else
**IMPOSTORS** > IMPOSTOR
**IMPOSTS** > IMPOST
**IMPOSTUME** *archaic word for* > ABSCESS
**IMPOSTURE** *n* deception, esp by pretending to be someone else
**IMPOT** *n* slang term for the act of imposing
**IMPOTENCE** > IMPOTENT
**IMPOTENCY** > IMPOTENT
**IMPOTENT** *n* one who is impotent ▷ *adj* powerless
**IMPOTENTS** > IMPOTENT
**IMPOTS** > IMPOT
**IMPOUND** *vb* take legal

possession of, confiscate
**IMPOUNDED** > IMPOUND
**IMPOUNDER** > IMPOUND
**IMPOUNDS** > IMPOUND
**IMPOWER** *less common spelling of* > EMPOWER
**IMPOWERED** > IMPOWER
**IMPOWERS** > IMPOWER
**IMPRECATE** *vb* swear, curse, or blaspheme
**IMPRECISE** *adj* inexact or inaccurate
**IMPREGN** *vb* impregnate
**IMPREGNED** > IMPREGN
**IMPREGNS** > IMPREGN
**IMPRESA** *n* heraldic device
**IMPRESARI** *n* impresarios
**IMPRESAS** > IMPRESA
**IMPRESE** *same as* > IMPRESA
**IMPRESES** > IMPRESE
**IMPRESS** *vb* affect strongly, usu. favourably ▷ *n* impressing
**IMPRESSE** *n* heraldic device
**IMPRESSED** > IMPRESS
**IMPRESSER** > IMPRESS
**IMPRESSES** > IMPRESS
**IMPREST** *n* fund of cash from which a department or other unit pays incidental expenses, topped up periodically from central funds
**IMPRESTS** > IMPREST
**IMPRIMIS** *adv* in the first place
**IMPRINT** *n* mark made by printing or stamping ▷ *vb* produce (a mark) by printing or stamping
**IMPRINTED** > IMPRINT
**IMPRINTER** > IMPRINT
**IMPRINTS** > IMPRINT
**IMPRISON** *vb* put in prison
**IMPRISONS** > IMPRISON
**IMPROBITY** *n* dishonesty or wickedness
**IMPROMPTU** *adj* without planning or preparation ▷ *adv* in a spontaneous or improvised way ▷ *n* short piece of instrumental music resembling improvisation
**IMPROPER** *adj* indecent
**IMPROV** *n* improvisational comedy
**IMPROVE** *vb* make or become better
**IMPROVED** > IMPROVE
**IMPROVER** > IMPROVE
**IMPROVERS** > IMPROVE
**IMPROVES** > IMPROVE
**IMPROVING** > IMPROVE
**IMPROVISE** *vb* make use of whatever materials are available
**IMPROVS** > IMPROV
**IMPRUDENT** *adj* not sensible or wise
**IMPS** > IMP
**IMPSONITE** *n* asphaltite compound

**IMPUDENCE** *n* quality of being impudent
**IMPUDENCY** *same as* > IMPUDENCE
**IMPUDENT** *adj* cheeky, disrespectful
**IMPUGN** *vb* challenge the truth or validity of
**IMPUGNED** > IMPUGN
**IMPUGNER** > IMPUGN
**IMPUGNERS** > IMPUGN
**IMPUGNING** > IMPUGN
**IMPUGNS** > IMPUGN
**IMPULSE** *vb* give an impulse to ▷ *n* sudden urge to do something
**IMPULSED** > IMPULSE
**IMPULSES** > IMPULSE
**IMPULSING** > IMPULSE
**IMPULSION** *n* act of impelling or the state of being impelled
**IMPULSIVE** *adj* acting or done without careful consideration
**IMPUNDULU** *n* mythical bird associated with witchcraft, frequently manifested as the secretary bird
**IMPUNITY** *n* exemption or immunity from punishment or recrimination
**IMPURE** *adj* having dirty or unwanted substances mixed in
**IMPURELY** > IMPURE
**IMPURER** > IMPURE
**IMPUREST** > IMPURE
**IMPURITY** *n* impure element or thing
**IMPURPLE** *vb* colour purple
**IMPURPLED** > IMPURPLE
**IMPURPLES** > IMPURPLE
**IMPUTABLE** *adj* capable of being imputed
**IMPUTABLY** > IMPUTABLE
**IMPUTE** *vb* attribute responsibility to
**IMPUTED** > IMPUTE
**IMPUTER** > IMPUTE
**IMPUTERS** > IMPUTE
**IMPUTES** > IMPUTE
**IMPUTING** > IMPUTE
**IMSHI** *interj* go away!
**IMSHY** *same as* > IMSHI
**IN** *prep* indicating position inside, state or situation, etc ▷ *adv* indicating position inside, entry into, etc ▷ *adj* fashionable ▷ *n* way of approaching or befriending a person
**INABILITY** *n* lack of means or skill to do something
**INACTION** *n* act of doing nothing
**INACTIONS** > INACTION
**INACTIVE** *adj* idle
**INAIDABLE** *adj* beyond help
**INAMORATA** *n* woman with whom one is in love

**INAMORATO** *n* man with whom one is in love
**INANE** *adj* senseless, silly ▷ *n* something that is inane
**INANELY** > INANE
**INANENESS** > INANE
**INANER** > INANE
**INANES** > INANE
**INANEST** > INANE
**INANGA** *n* common type of New Zealand grass tree
**INANGAS** > INANGA
**INANIMATE** *adj* not living
**INANITIES** > INANITY
**INANITION** *n* exhaustion or weakness, as from lack of food
**INANITY** *n* lack of intelligence or imagination
**INAPT** *adj* not apt or fitting
**INAPTLY** > INAPT
**INAPTNESS** > INAPT
**INARABLE** *adj* not arable
**INARCH** *vb* graft (a plant) by uniting stock and scion while both are still growing independently
**INARCHED** > INARCH
**INARCHES** > INARCH
**INARCHING** > INARCH
**INARM** *vb* embrace
**INARMED** > INARM
**INARMING** > INARM
**INARMS** > INARM
**INASMUCH** as in *inasmuch as*, in view of the fact that
**INAUDIBLE** *adj* not loud enough to be heard
**INAUDIBLY** > INAUDIBLE
**INAUGURAL** *adj* of or for an inauguration ▷ *n* speech made at an inauguration
**INAURATE** *adj* gilded
**INBEING** *n* existence in something else
**INBEINGS** > INBEING
**INBENT** *adj* bent inwards
**INBOARD** *adj* (of a boat's engine) inside the hull ▷ *adv* within the sides of or towards the centre of a vessel or aircraft
**INBOARDS** *same as* > INBOARD
**INBORN** *adj* existing from birth, natural
**INBOUND** *vb* pass into the playing area from outside it ▷ *adj* coming in
**INBOUNDED** > INBOUND
**INBOUNDS** > INBOUND
**INBREAK** *n* breaking in
**INBREAKS** > INBREAK
**INBREATHE** *vb* infuse or imbue
**INBRED** *n* inbred person or animal ▷ *adj* produced as a result of inbreeding
**INBREDS** > INBRED
**INBREED** *vb* breed from closely related individuals
**INBREEDER** > INBREED

INBREEDS >INBREED
INBRING vb bring in
INBRINGS >INBRING
INBROUGHT >INBRING
INBUILT adj present from the start
INBURNING adj burning within
INBURST n irruption
INBURSTS >INBURST
INBY adv into the house or an inner room ▷ adj located near or nearest to the house
INBYE adv near the house
INCAGE vb confine in or as in a cage
INCAGED >INCAGE
INCAGES >INCAGE
INCAGING >INCAGE
INCANT vb chant (a spell)
INCANTED >INCANT
INCANTING >INCANT
INCANTS >INCANT
INCAPABLE adj unable (to do something)
INCAPABLY >INCAPABLE
INCARNATE adj in human form ▷ vb give a bodily or concrete form to
INCASE variant spelling of >ENCASE
INCASED >INCASE
INCASES >INCASE
INCASING >INCASE
INCAUTION n act of not being cautious
INCAVE vb hide
INCAVED >INCAVE
INCAVES >INCAVE
INCAVI >INCAVO
INCAVING >INCAVE
INCAVO n incised part of a carving
INCEDE vb advance
INCEDED >INCEDE
INCEDES >INCEDE
INCEDING >INCEDE
INCENSE vb make very angry ▷ n substance that gives off a sweet perfume when burned
INCENSED >INCENSE
INCENSER n incense burner
INCENSERS >INCENSER
INCENSES >INCENSE
INCENSING >INCENSE
INCENSOR n incense burner
INCENSORS >INCENSOR
INCENSORY less common name for >CENSER
INCENT vb provide incentive
INCENTED >INCENT
INCENTER same as >INCENTRE
INCENTERS >INCENTER
INCENTING >INCENT
INCENTIVE n something that encourages effort or action ▷ adj encouraging greater effort
INCENTRE n centre of an inscribed circle

INCENTRES >INCENTRE
INCENTS >INCENT
INCEPT vb (of organisms) to ingest (food) ▷ n rudimentary organ
INCEPTED >INCEPT
INCEPTING >INCEPT
INCEPTION n beginning
INCEPTIVE adj beginning ▷ n type of verb
INCEPTOR >INCEPT
INCEPTORS >INCEPT
INCEPTS >INCEPT
INCERTAIN archaic form of >UNCERTAIN
INCESSANT adj never stopping
INCEST n sexual intercourse between two people too closely related to marry
INCESTS >INCEST
INCH n unit of length equal to one twelfth of a foot or 2.54 centimetres ▷ vb move slowly and gradually
INCHASE same as >ENCHASE
INCHASED >INCHASE
INCHASES >INCHASE
INCHASING >INCHASE
INCHED >INCH
INCHER n something measuring given amount of inches
INCHERS >INCHER
INCHES >INCH
INCHING >INCH
INCHMEAL adv gradually
INCHOATE adj just begun and not yet properly developed ▷ vb begin
INCHOATED >INCHOATE
INCHOATES >INCHOATE
INCHPIN n cervine sweetbread
INCHPINS >INCHPIN
INCHWORM n larva of a type of moth
INCHWORMS >INCHWORM
INCIDENCE n extent or frequency of occurrence
INCIDENT n something that happens ▷ adj related (to) or dependent (on)
INCIDENTS >INCIDENT
INCIPIENT adj just starting to appear or happen
INCIPIT n Latin introductory phrase
INCIPITS >INCIPIT
INCISAL adj relating to the cutting edge of incisors and cuspids
INCISE vb cut into with a sharp tool
INCISED >INCISE
INCISES >INCISE
INCISING >INCISE
INCISION n cut, esp one made during a surgical operation
INCISIONS >INCISION

INCISIVE adj direct and forceful
INCISOR n front tooth, used for biting into food
INCISORS >INCISOR
INCISORY >INCISOR
INCISURAL >INCISURE
INCISURE n incision or notch in an organ or part
INCISURES >INCISURE
INCITABLE >INCITE
INCITANT n something that incites
INCITANTS >INCITANT
INCITE vb stir up, provoke
INCITED >INCITE
INCITER >INCITE
INCITERS >INCITE
INCITES >INCITE
INCITING >INCITE
INCIVIL archaic form of >UNCIVIL
INCIVISM n neglect of a citizen's duties
INCIVISMS >INCIVISM
INCLASP vb clasp
INCLASPED >INCLASP
INCLASPS >INCLASP
INCLE same as >INKLE
INCLEMENT adj (of weather) stormy or severe
INCLES >INCLE
INCLINE vb lean, slope ▷ n slope
INCLINED adj having a disposition
INCLINER >INCLINE
INCLINERS >INCLINE
INCLINES >INCLINE
INCLINING >INCLINE
INCLIP vb embrace
INCLIPPED >INCLIP
INCLIPS >INCLIP
INCLOSE less common spelling of >ENCLOSE
INCLOSED >INCLOSE
INCLOSER >INCLOSE
INCLOSERS >INCLOSE
INCLOSES >INCLOSE
INCLOSING >INCLOSE
INCLOSURE >INCLOSE
INCLUDE vb have as part of the whole
INCLUDED adj (of the stamens or pistils of a flower) not protruding beyond the corolla
INCLUDES >INCLUDE
INCLUDING >INCLUDE
INCLUSION n including or being included
INCLUSIVE adj including everything (specified)
INCOG n incognito
INCOGNITA n female who is in disguise or unknown
INCOGNITO adv having adopted a false identity ▷ n false identity ▷ adj under an assumed name or appearance
INCOGS >INCOG
INCOME n amount of money earned from work,

investments, etc
INCOMER n person who comes to live in a place in which he or she was not born
INCOMERS >INCOMER
INCOMES >INCOME
INCOMING adj coming in ▷ n act of coming in
INCOMINGS >INCOMING
INCOMMODE vb cause inconvenience to
INCOMPACT adj not compact
INCONDITE adj poorly constructed or composed
INCONIE adj fine or delicate
INCONNU n whitefish of Arctic waters
INCONNUE n unknown woman
INCONNUES >INCONNUE
INCONNUS >INCONNU
INCONY adj fine or delicate
INCORPSE vb incorporate
INCORPSED >INCORPSE
INCORPSES >INCORPSE
INCORRECT adj wrong
INCORRUPT adj free from corruption
INCREASE vb make or become greater in size, number, etc ▷ n rise in number, size, etc
INCREASED >INCREASE
INCREASER >INCREASE
INCREASES >INCREASE
INCREATE adj (esp of gods) never having been created
INCREMATE vb cremate
INCREMENT n increase in money or value, esp a regular salary increase
INCRETION n direct secretion into the bloodstream, esp of a hormone from an endocrine gland
INCRETORY >INCRETION
INCROSS n plant or animal produced by continued inbreeding ▷ vb inbreed or produce by inbreeding
INCROSSED >INCROSS
INCROSSES >INCROSS
INCRUST same as >ENCRUST
INCRUSTED >INCRUST
INCRUSTS >INCRUST
INCUBATE vb (of a bird) hatch (eggs) by sitting on them
INCUBATED >INCUBATE
INCUBATES >INCUBATE
INCUBATOR n heated enclosed apparatus for rearing premature babies
INCUBI >INCUBUS
INCUBOUS adj (of a liverwort) having the leaves arranged so that the upper margin of each leaf lies above the lower margin of the next leaf

along

**INCUBUS** n (in folklore) demon believed to have sex with sleeping women

**INCUBUSES** > INCUBUS

**INCUDAL** > INCUS

**INCUDATE** > INCUS

**INCUDES** > INCUS

**INCULCATE** vb fix in someone's mind by constant repetition

**INCULPATE** vb cause (someone) to be blamed for a crime

**INCULT** adj (of land) uncultivated

**INCUMBENT** n person who holds a particular office or position ▷ adj morally binding as a duty

**INCUMBER** less common spelling of > ENCUMBER

**INCUMBERS** > INCUMBER

**INCUNABLE** n early printed book

**INCUR** vb cause (something unpleasant) to happen

**INCURABLE** adj not able to be cured ▷ n person with an incurable disease

**INCURABLY** > INCURABLE

**INCURIOUS** adj showing no curiosity or interest

**INCURRED** > INCUR

**INCURRENT** adj (of anatomical ducts, tubes, channels, etc) having an inward flow

**INCURRING** > INCUR

**INCURS** > INCUR

**INCURSION** n sudden brief invasion

**INCURSIVE** > INCURSION

**INCURVATE** vb curve or cause to curve inwards ▷ adj curved inwards

**INCURVE** vb curve or cause to curve inwards

**INCURVED** > INCURVE

**INCURVES** > INCURVE

**INCURVING** > INCURVE

**INCURVITY** > INCURVE

**INCUS** n central of the three small bones in the middle ear of mammals

**INCUSE** n design stamped or hammered onto a coin ▷ vb impress (a design) in a coin or to impress (a coin) with a design by hammering or stamping ▷ adj stamped or hammered onto a coin

**INCUSED** > INCUSE

**INCUSES** > INCUSE

**INCUSING** > INCUSE

**INCUT** adj cut or etched in

**INDABA** n (among native peoples of southern Africa) a meeting to discuss a serious topic

**INDABAS** > INDABA

**INDAGATE** vb investigate

**INDAGATED** > INDAGATE

**INDAGATES** > INDAGATE

**INDAGATOR** > INDAGATE

**INDAMIN** same as > INDAMINE

**INDAMINE** n organic base used in the production of the dye safranine

**INDAMINES** > INDAMINE

**INDAMINS** > INDAMIN

**INDART** vb dart in

**INDARTED** > INDART

**INDARTING** > INDART

**INDARTS** > INDART

**INDEBTED** adj owing gratitude for help or favours

**INDECENCY** n state or quality of being indecent

**INDECENT** adj morally or sexually offensive

**INDECORUM** n indecorous behaviour or speech

**INDEED** adv really, certainly ▷ interj expression of indignation or surprise

**INDELIBLE** adj impossible to erase or remove

**INDELIBLY** > INDELIBLE

**INDEMNIFY** vb secure against loss, damage, or liability

**INDEMNITY** n insurance against loss or damage

**INDENE** n colourless liquid hydrocarbon extracted from petroleum and coal tar and used in making synthetic resins

**INDENES** > INDENE

**INDENT** vb make a dent in

**INDENTED** > INDENT

**INDENTER** > INDENT

**INDENTERS** > INDENT

**INDENTING** > INDENT

**INDENTION** n space between a margin and the start of the line of text

**INDENTOR** > INDENT

**INDENTORS** > INDENT

**INDENTS** > INDENT

**INDENTURE** n contract, esp one binding an apprentice to his or her employer ▷ vb bind (an apprentice) by indenture

**INDEVOUT** adj not devout

**INDEW** same as > INDUE

**INDEWED** > INDEW

**INDEWING** > INDEW

**INDEWS** > INDEW

**INDEX** n alphabetical list of names or subjects dealt with in a book ▷ vb provide (a book) with an index

**INDEXABLE** > INDEX

**INDEXAL** > INDEX

**INDEXED** > INDEX

**INDEXER** > INDEX

**INDEXERS** > INDEX

**INDEXES** > INDEX

**INDEXICAL** adj arranged as or relating to an index or indexes ▷ n term whose reference depends on the context of utterance, such as I, you, here, now, or tomorrow

**INDEXING** > INDEX

**INDEXINGS** > INDEX

**INDEXLESS** > INDEX

**INDICAN** n compound secreted in the urine, usually in the form of its potassium salt

**INDICANS** > INDICAN

**INDICANT** n something that indicates

**INDICANTS** > INDICANT

**INDICATE** vb be a sign or symptom of

**INDICATED** > INDICATE

**INDICATES** > INDICATE

**INDICATOR** n something acting as a sign or indication

**INDICES** plural of > INDEX

**INDICIA** > INDICIUM

**INDICIAL** > INDICIUM

**INDICIAS** > INDICIUM

**INDICIUM** n notice

**INDICIUMS** > INDICIUM

**INDICT** vb formally charge with a crime

**INDICTED** > INDICT

**INDICTEE** > INDICT

**INDICTEES** > INDICT

**INDICTER** > INDICT

**INDICTERS** > INDICT

**INDICTING** > INDICT

**INDICTION** n recurring fiscal period of 15 years, often used as a unit for dating events

**INDICTOR** > INDICT

**INDICTORS** > INDICT

**INDICTS** > INDICT

**INDIE** adj (of rock music) released by an independent record company ▷ n independent record company

**INDIES** > INDIE

**INDIGEN** same as > INDIGENE

**INDIGENCE** > INDIGENT

**INDIGENCY** > INDIGENT

**INDIGENE** n indigenous person, animal, or thing

**INDIGENES** > INDIGENE

**INDIGENS** > INDIGEN

**INDIGENT** adj extremely poor ▷ n impoverished person

**INDIGENTS** > INDIGENT

**INDIGEST** n undigested mass

**INDIGESTS** > INDIGEST

**INDIGN** adj undeserving

**INDIGNANT** adj feeling or showing indignation

**INDIGNIFY** vb treat in a humiliating manner

**INDIGNITY** n embarrassing or humiliating treatment

**INDIGNLY** > INDIGN

**INDIGO** adj deep violet-blue ▷ n dye of this colour

**INDIGOES** > INDIGO

**INDIGOID** adj of, concerned with, or resembling indigo or its blue colour ▷ n any of a number of synthetic dyes or pigments related in chemical structure to indigo

**INDIGOIDS** > INDIGOID

**INDIGOS** > INDIGO

**INDIGOTIC** > INDIGO

**INDIGOTIN** same as > INDIGO

**INDINAVIR** n drug used to treat AIDS

**INDIRECT** adj done or caused by someone or something else

**INDIRUBIN** n isomer of indigotin

**INDISPOSE** vb make unwilling or opposed

**INDITE** vb write

**INDITED** > INDITE

**INDITER** > INDITE

**INDITERS** > INDITE

**INDITES** > INDITE

**INDITING** > INDITE

**INDIUM** n soft silvery-white metallic element

**INDIUMS** > INDIUM

**INDIVIDUA** pl n indivisible entities

**INDOCIBLE** same as > INDOCILE

**INDOCILE** adj difficult to discipline or instruct

**INDOL** same as > INDOLE

**INDOLE** n white or yellowish crystalline heterocyclic compound extracted from coal tar and used in perfumery, medicine, and as a flavouring agent

**INDOLENCE** > INDOLENT

**INDOLENCY** > INDOLENT

**INDOLENT** adj lazy

**INDOLES** > INDOLE

**INDOLS** > INDOL

**INDOOR** adj inside a building

**INDOORS** adj inside or into a building

**INDORSE** variant spelling of > ENDORSE

**INDORSED** > INDORSE

**INDORSEE** > INDORSE

**INDORSEES** > INDORSE

**INDORSER** > INDORSE

**INDORSERS** > INDORSE

**INDORSES** > INDORSE

**INDORSING** > INDORSE

**INDORSOR** > INDORSE

**INDORSORS** > INDORSE

**INDOW** archaic variant of > INDOW

**INDOWED** > INDOW

**INDOWING** > INDOW

**INDOWS** > INDOW

**INDOXYL** n yellow water-soluble crystalline

compound occurring in woad as its glucoside and in urine as its ester

**INDOXYLS** >INDOXYL

**INDRAFT** same as >INDRAUGHT

**INDRAFTS** >INDRAFT

**INDRAUGHT** n act of drawing or pulling in

**INDRAWN** adj drawn or pulled in

**INDRENCH** vb submerge

**INDRI** same as >INDRIS

**INDRIS** n large Madagascan arboreal lemuroid primate

**INDRISES** >INDRIS

**INDUBIOUS** adj certain

**INDUCE** vb persuade or influence

**INDUCED** >INDUCE

**INDUCER** >INDUCE

**INDUCERS** >INDUCE

**INDUCES** >INDUCE

**INDUCIAE** n time limit for a defendant to appear in court

**INDUCIBLE** >INDUCE

**INDUCING** >INDUCE

**INDUCT** vb formally install (someone, esp a clergyman) in office

**INDUCTED** >INDUCT

**INDUCTEE** n military conscript

**INDUCTEES** >INDUCTEE

**INDUCTILE** adj not ductile, pliant, or yielding

**INDUCTING** >INDUCT

**INDUCTION** >INDUCT

**INDUCTIVE** adj of or using induction

**INDUCTOR** n device designed to create inductance in an electrical circuit

**INDUCTORS** >INDUCTOR

**INDUCTS** >INDUCT

**INDUE** variant spelling of >ENDUE

**INDUED** >INDUE

**INDUES** >INDUE

**INDUING** >INDUE

**INDULGE** vb allow oneself pleasure

**INDULGED** >INDULGE

**INDULGENT** adj kind or lenient, often to excess

**INDULGER** >INDULGE

**INDULGERS** >INDULGE

**INDULGES** >INDULGE

**INDULGING** >INDULGE

**INDULIN** same as >INDULINE

**INDULINE** n any of a class of blue dyes obtained from aniline and aminoazobenzene

**INDULINES** >INDULINE

**INDULINS** >INDULIN

**INDULT** n faculty granted by the Holy See allowing a specific deviation from the Church's common law

**INDULTS** >INDULT

**INDUMENTA** pl n outer coverings of feather, fur, etc

**INDUNA** n (in South Africa) a Black African overseer in a factory, mine, etc

**INDUNAS** >INDUNA

**INDURATE** vb make or become hard or callous ▷ adj hardened, callous, or unfeeling

**INDURATED** >INDURATE

**INDURATES** >INDURATE

**INDUSIA** >INDUSIUM

**INDUSIAL** >INDUSIUM

**INDUSIATE** adj covered in indusia

**INDUSIUM** n membranous outgrowth on the undersurface of fern leaves that covers and protects the developing sporangia

**INDUSTRY** n manufacture of goods

**INDUVIAE** pl n withered leaves

**INDUVIAL** >INDUVIAE

**INDUVIATE** >INDUVIAE

**INDWELL** vb (of a spirit, principle, etc) to inhabit

**INDWELLER** >INDWELL

**INDWELLS** >INDWELL

**INDWELT** >INDWELL

**INEARTH** poetic word for >BURY

**INEARTHED** >INEARTH

**INEARTHS** >INEARTH

**INEBRIANT** adj causing intoxication, esp drunkenness ▷ n something that inebriates

**INEBRIATE** adj (person who is) habitually drunk ▷ n person who is habitually drunk ▷ vb make drunk

**INEBRIETY** >INEBRIATE

**INEBRIOUS** adj drunk

**INEDIBLE** adj not fit to be eaten

**INEDIBLY** >INEDIBLE

**INEDITA** pl n unpublished writings

**INEDITED** adj not edited

**INEFFABLE** adj too great for words

**INEFFABLY** >INEFFABLE

**INELASTIC** adj not elastic

**INELEGANT** adj lacking elegance or refinement

**INEPT** adj clumsy, lacking skill

**INEPTER** >INEPT

**INEPTEST** >INEPT

**INEPTLY** >INEPT

**INEPTNESS** >INEPT

**INEQUABLE** adj unfair

**INEQUITY** n injustice or unfairness

**INERM** adj without thorns

**INERMOUS** same as >INERM

**INERRABLE** adj not liable to error ▷ n person or thing

that is incapable of error

**INERRABLY** >INERRABLE

**INERRANCY** >INERRABLE

**INERRANT** same as >INERRABLE

**INERT** n inert thing ▷ adj without the power of motion or resistance

**INERTER** >INERT

**INERTEST** >INERT

**INERTIA** n feeling of unwillingness to do anything

**INERTIAE** >INERTIA

**INERTIAL** >INERTIA

**INERTIAS** >INERTIA

**INERTLY** >INERT

**INERTNESS** >INERT

**INERTS** >INERT

**INERUDITE** adj not erudite

**INESSIVE** n grammatical case in Finnish

**INESSIVES** >INESSIVE

**INEXACT** adj not exact or accurate

**INEXACTLY** >INEXACT

**INEXPERT** n unskilled person ▷ adj lacking skill

**INEXPERTS** >INEXPERT

**INFALL** vb move towards a black hole, etc, under the influence of gravity

**INFALLING** >INFALL

**INFALLS** >INFALL

**INFAME** vb defame

**INFAMED** >INFAME

**INFAMES** >INFAME

**INFAMIES** >INFAMY

**INFAMING** >INFAME

**INFAMISE** same as >INFAMIZE

**INFAMISED** >INFAMISE

**INFAMISES** >INFAMISE

**INFAMIZE** vb make infamous

**INFAMIZED** >INFAMIZE

**INFAMIZES** >INFAMIZE

**INFAMOUS** adj well-known for something bad

**INFAMY** n state of being infamous

**INFANCIES** >INFANCY

**INFANCY** n early childhood

**INFANT** n very young child ▷ adj of, relating to, or designed for young children

**INFANTA** n (formerly) daughter of a king of Spain or Portugal

**INFANTAS** >INFANTA

**INFANTE** n (formerly) any son of a king of Spain or Portugal, except the heir to the throne

**INFANTES** >INFANTE

**INFANTILE** adj childish

**INFANTINE** adj infantile

**INFANTRY** n soldiers who fight on foot

**INFANTS** >INFANT

**INFARCT** n localized area of dead tissue (necrosis) resulting from obstruction

of the blood supply to that part, esp by an embolus ▷ vb obstruct the blood supply to part of a body

**INFARCTED** >INFARCT

**INFARCTS** >INFARCT

**INFARE** vb enter

**INFARES** >INFARE

**INFATUATE** vb inspire or fill with an intense and unreasoning passion ▷ n person who is infatuated

**INFAUNA** n animals that live in ocean and river beds

**INFAUNAE** >INFAUNA

**INFAUNAL** >INFAUNA

**INFAUNAS** >INFAUNA

**INFAUST** adj unlucky

**INFECT** vb affect with a disease ▷ adj contaminated or polluted with or as if with a disease

**INFECTANT** n something that infects

**INFECTED** >INFECT

**INFECTER** >INFECT

**INFECTERS** >INFECT

**INFECTING** >INFECT

**INFECTION** n infectious disease

**INFECTIVE** adj capable of causing infection

**INFECTOR** >INFECT

**INFECTORS** >INFECT

**INFECTS** >INFECT

**INFECUND** less common word for >INFERTILE

**INFEFT** vb give possession of heritable property

**INFEFTED** >INFEFT

**INFEFTING** >INFEFT

**INFEFTS** >INFEFT

**INFELT** adj heartfelt

**INFEOFF** same as >ENFEOFF

**INFEOFFED** >INFEOFF

**INFEOFFS** >INFEOFF

**INFER** vb work out from evidence

**INFERABLE** >INFER

**INFERABLY** >INFER

**INFERE** adv together

**INFERENCE** n act or process of reaching a conclusion by reasoning from evidence

**INFERIAE** pl n offerings made to the spirits of the dead

**INFERIBLE** >INFER

**INFERIOR** adj lower in quality, position, or status ▷ n person of lower position or status

**INFERIORS** >INFERIOR

**INFERNAL** adj of hell

**INFERNO** n intense raging fire

**INFERNOS** >INFERNO

**INFERRED** >INFER

**INFERRER** >INFER

**INFERRERS** >INFER

**INFERRING** >INFER

**INFERS** >INFER

INFERTILE *adj* unable to produce offspring
INFEST *vb* inhabit or overrun in unpleasantly large numbers
INFESTANT *n* parasite
INFESTED >INFEST
INFESTER >INFEST
INFESTERS >INFEST
INFESTING >INFEST
INFESTS >INFEST
INFICETE *adj* not witty
INFIDEL *n* person with no religion ▷ *adj* of unbelievers or unbelief
INFIDELIC >INFIDEL
INFIDELS >INFIDEL
INFIELD *n* area of the field near the pitch
INFIELDER *n* player positioned in the infield
INFIELDS >INFIELD
INFIGHT *vb* box at close quarters
INFIGHTER >INFIGHT
INFIGHTS >INFIGHT
INFILL *vb* fill in ▷ *n* act of filling or closing gaps, etc, in something, such as a row of buildings
INFILLED >INFILL
INFILLING >INFILL
INFILLS >INFILL
INFIMA >INFIMUM
INFIMUM *n* greatest lower bound
INFIMUMS >INFIMUM
INFINITE *adj* without any limit or end ▷ *n* something without any limit or end
INFINITES >INFINITE
INFINITY *n* endless space, time, or number
INFIRM *vb* make infirm ▷ *adj* physically or mentally weak
INFIRMARY *n* hospital
INFIRMED >INFIRM
INFIRMER >INFIRM
INFIRMEST >INFIRM
INFIRMING >INFIRM
INFIRMITY *n* state of being infirm
INFIRMLY >INFIRM
INFIRMS >INFIRM
INFIX *vb* fix firmly in ▷ *n* affix inserted into the middle of a word
INFIXED >INFIX
INFIXES >INFIX
INFIXING >INFIX
INFIXION >INFIX
INFIXIONS >INFIX
INFLAME *vb* make angry or excited
INFLAMED >INFLAME
INFLAMER >INFLAME
INFLAMERS >INFLAME
INFLAMES >INFLAME
INFLAMING >INFLAME
INFLATE *vb* expand by filling with air or gas
INFLATED >INFLATE

INFLATER >INFLATE
INFLATERS >INFLATE
INFLATES >INFLATE
INFLATING >INFLATE
INFLATION *n* inflating
INFLATIVE *adj* causing inflation
INFLATOR >INFLATE
INFLATORS >INFLATE
INFLATUS *n* act of breathing in
INFLECT *vb* change (the voice) in tone or pitch
INFLECTED >INFLECT
INFLECTOR >INFLECT
INFLECTS >INFLECT
INFLEXED *adj* curved or bent inwards and downwards towards the axis
INFLEXION *n* modulation of the voice
INFLEXURE *same as* >INFLEXION
INFLICT *vb* impose (something unpleasant) on
INFLICTED >INFLICT
INFLICTER >INFLICT
INFLICTOR >INFLICT
INFLICTS >INFLICT
INFLIGHT *adj* provided during flight in an aircraft
INFLOW *n* something, such as liquid or gas, that flows in ▷ *vb* flow in
INFLOWING >INFLOW
INFLOWS >INFLOW
INFLUENCE *n* effect of one person or thing on another ▷ *vb* have an effect on
INFLUENT *adj* flowing in ▷ *n* something flowing in, esp a tributary
INFLUENTS >INFLUENT
INFLUENZA *n* contagious viral disease causing headaches, muscle pains, and fever
INFLUX *n* arrival or entry of many people or things
INFLUXES >INFLUX
INFLUXION *same as* >INFLUX
INFO *n* information
INFOBAHN *same as* >INTERNET
INFOBAHNS >INFOBAHN
INFOLD *variant spelling of* >ENFOLD
INFOLDED >INFOLD
INFOLDER >INFOLD
INFOLDERS >INFOLD
INFOLDING >INFOLD
INFOLDS >INFOLD
INFOMANIA *n* obsessive devotion to gathering information
INFORCE *same as* >ENFORCE
INFORCED >INFORCE
INFORCES >INFORCE
INFORCING >INFORCE
INFORM *vb* tell ▷ *adj*

without shape
INFORMAL *adj* relaxed and friendly
INFORMANT *n* person who gives information
INFORMED >INFORM
INFORMER *n* person who informs to the police
INFORMERS >INFORMER
INFORMING >INFORM
INFORMS >INFORM
INFORTUNE *n* misfortune
INFOS >INFO
INFOUGHT >INFIGHT
INFRA *adv* (esp in textual annotation) below
INFRACT *vb* violate or break (a law, an agreement, etc)
INFRACTED >INFRACT
INFRACTOR >INFRACT
INFRACTS >INFRACT
INFRARED *adj* of or using rays below the red end of the visible spectrum ▷ *n* infrared part of the spectrum
INFRAREDS >INFRARED
INFRINGE *vb* break (a law or agreement)
INFRINGED >INFRINGE
INFRINGER >INFRINGE
INFRINGES >INFRINGE
INFRUGAL *adj* wasteful
INFULA *singular of* >INFULAE
INFULAE *pl n* two ribbons hanging from the back of a bishop's mitre
INFURIATE *vb* make very angry ▷ *adj* furious
INFUSCATE *adj* (esp of the wings of an insect) tinged with brown
INFUSE *vb* fill (with an emotion or quality)
INFUSED >INFUSE
INFUSER *n* any device used to make an infusion, esp a tea maker
INFUSERS >INFUSER
INFUSES >INFUSE
INFUSIBLE *adj* unable to be fused or melted
INFUSING >INFUSE
INFUSION *n* infusing
INFUSIONS >INFUSION
INFUSIVE >INFUSION
INFUSORIA *pl n* tiny water-dwelling animals
INFUSORY *adj* containing infusoria
INGAN *Scots word for* >ONION
INGANS >INGAN
INGATE *n* entrance
INGATES >INGATE
INGATHER *vb* gather together or in (a harvest)
INGATHERS >INGATHER
INGENER *Shakespearean form of* >ENGINEER
INGENERS >INGENER
INGENIOUS *adj* showing

cleverness and originality
INGENIUM *n* genius
INGENIUMS >INGENIUM
INGENU *n* artless or inexperienced boy or young man
INGENUE *n* artless or inexperienced girl or young woman
INGENUES >INGENUE
INGENUITY *n* cleverness at inventing things
INGENUOUS *adj* unsophisticated and trusting
INGENUS >INGENU
INGEST *vb* take (food or liquid) into the body
INGESTA *pl n* nourishment taken into the body through the mouth
INGESTED >INGEST
INGESTING >INGEST
INGESTION >INGEST
INGESTIVE >INGEST
INGESTS >INGEST
INGINE *n* genius
INGINES >INGINE
INGLE *n* fire in a room or a fireplace
INGLENEUK *same as* >INGLENOOK
INGLENOOK *n* corner by a fireplace
INGLES >INGLE
INGLOBE *vb* shape as a sphere
INGLOBED >INGLOBE
INGLOBES >INGLOBE
INGLOBING >INGLOBE
INGLUVIAL >INGLUVIES
INGLUVIES *n* bird's craw
INGO *vb* reveal
INGOES >INGO
INGOING >INGO
INGOINGS >INGO
INGOT *n* oblong block of cast metal ▷ *vb* shape (metal) into ingots
INGOTED >INGOT
INGOTING >INGOT
INGOTS >INGOT
INGRAFT *variant spelling of* >ENGRAFT
INGRAFTED >INGRAFT
INGRAFTS >INGRAFT
INGRAIN *vb* impress deeply on the mind or nature ▷ *adj* (of carpets) made of dyed yarn or of fibre that is dyed before being spun into yarn ▷ *n* carpet made from ingrained yarn
INGRAINED >INGRAIN
INGRAINS >INGRAIN
INGRAM *adj* ignorant
INGRATE *n* ungrateful person ▷ *adj* ungrateful
INGRATELY >INGRATE
INGRATES >INGRATE
INGRESS *n* entrance
INGRESSES >INGRESS
INGROOVE *vb* cut a groove into

INGROOVED >INGROOVE
INGROOVES >INGROOVE
INGROSS archaic form
of >ENGROSS
INGROSSED >INGROSS
INGROSSES >INGROSS
INGROUND adj sunk into
ground
INGROUP n highly cohesive
and relatively closed social
group
INGROUPS >INGROUP
INGROWING adj (of
a toenail) growing
abnormally into the flesh
INGROWN adj (esp of a
toenail) grown abnormally
into the flesh
INGROWTH n act of growing
inwards
INGROWTHS >INGROWTH
INGRUM adj ignorant
INGUINAL adj of or relating
to the groin
INGULF variant spelling
of >ENGULF
INGULFED >INGULF
INGULFING >INGULF
INGULFS >INGULF
INGULPH archaic form
of >ENGULF
INGULPHED >INGULPH
INGULPHS >INGULPH
INHABIT vb live in
INHABITED >INHABIT
INHABITER n inhabitant
INHABITOR n inhabitant
INHABITS >INHABIT
INHALANT n medical
preparation inhaled to
help breathing problems
▷ adj inhaled for its
soothing or therapeutic
effect
INHALANTS >INHALANT
INHALATOR n device for
converting drugs into a
fine spray for inhaling
INHALE vb breathe in (air,
smoke, etc)
INHALED >INHALE
INHALER n container for an
inhalant
INHALERS >INHALER
INHALES >INHALE
INHALING >INHALE
INHARMONY n discord
INHAUL n line for hauling
in a sail
INHAULER >INHAUL
INHAULERS >INHAULER
INHAULS >INHAUL
INHAUST vb drink in
INHAUSTED >INHAUST
INHAUSTS >INHAUST
INHEARSE vb bury
INHEARSED >INHEARSE
INHEARSES >INHEARSE
INHERCE same
as >INHEARSE
INHERCED >INHERCE
INHERCES >INHERCE
INHERCING >INHERCE
INHERE vb be an

inseparable part (of)
INHERED >INHERE
INHERENCE n state or
condition of being
inherent
INHERENCY same
as >INHERENCE
INHERENT adj existing as
an inseparable part
INHERES >INHERE
INHERING >INHERE
INHERIT vb receive (money
etc) from someone who
has died
INHERITED >INHERIT
INHERITOR >INHERIT
INHERITS >INHERIT
INHESION less common word
for >INHERENCE
INHESIONS >INHESION
INHIBIN n peptide
hormone
INHIBINS >INHIBIN
INHIBIT vb restrain (an
impulse or desire)
INHIBITED >INHIBIT
INHIBITER same
as >INHIBITOR
INHIBITOR n person or
thing that inhibits
INHIBITS >INHIBIT
INHOLDER n inhabitant
INHOLDERS >INHOLDER
INHOLDING n privately
owned land inside a
federal reserve
INHOOP vb confine
INHOOPED >INHOOP
INHOOPING >INHOOP
INHOOPS >INHOOP
INHUMAN adj cruel or brutal
INHUMANE same
as >INHUMAN
INHUMANLY >INHUMAN
INHUMATE vb bury
INHUMATED >INHUMATE
INHUMATES >INHUMATE
INHUME vb inter
INHUMED >INHUME
INHUMER >INHUME
INHUMERS >INHUME
INHUMES >INHUME
INHUMING >INHUME
INIA >INION
INIMICAL adj unfavourable
or hostile
INION n most prominent
point at the back of the
head, used as a point
of measurement in
craniometry
INIONS >INION
INIQUITY n injustice or
wickedness
INISLE vb put on or make
into an island
INISLED >INISLE
INISLES >INISLE
INISLING >INISLE
INITIAL adj first, at the
beginning ▷ n first letter,
esp of a person's name ▷ vb
sign with one's initials
INITIALED >INITIAL

INITIALER >INITIAL
INITIALLY >INITIAL
INITIALS >INITIAL
INITIATE vb begin or
set going ▷ n recently
initiated person ▷ adj
initiated
INITIATED >INITIATE
INITIATES >INITIATE
INITIATOR n person or
thing that initiates
INJECT vb put (a fluid) into
the body with a syringe
INJECTANT n injected
substance
INJECTED >INJECT
INJECTING >INJECT
INJECTION n fluid injected
into the body, esp for
medicinal purposes
INJECTIVE >INJECTION
INJECTOR >INJECT
INJECTORS >INJECT
INJECTS >INJECT
INJELLIED >INJELLY
INJELLIES >INJELLY
INJELLY vb place in jelly
INJERA n white Ethiopian
flatbread, similar to a
crepe
INJERAS >INJERA
INJOINT vb join
INJOINTED >INJOINT
INJOINTS >INJOINT
INJUNCT vb issue a legal
injunction against (a
person)
INJUNCTED >INJUNCT
INJUNCTS >INJUNCT
INJURABLE >INJURE
INJURE vb hurt physically
or mentally
INJURED >INJURE
INJURER >INJURE
INJURERS >INJURE
INJURES >INJURE
INJURIES >INJURY
INJURING >INJURE
INJURIOUS adj causing
harm
INJURY n physical hurt
INJUSTICE n unfairness
INK n coloured liquid used
for writing or printing ▷ vb
mark in ink (something
already marked in pencil)
INKBERRY n North
American holly tree
INKBLOT n abstract
patch of ink, one often
commonly used in the
Rorschach test
INKBLOTS >INKBLOT
INKED >INK
INKER >INK
INKERS >INK
INKHOLDER same
as >INKHORN
INKHORN n (formerly) a
small portable container
for ink, usually made from
horn
INKHORNS >INKHORN
INKIER >INKY

INKIEST >INKY
INKINESS >INKY
INKING >INK
INKJET n method of
printing streams of
electrically charged ink
INKLE n kind of linen tape
used for trimmings
INKLED adj trimmed with
inkle
INKLES >INKLE
INKLESS >INK
INKLIKE >INK
INKLING n slight idea or
suspicion
INKLINGS >INKLING
INKPOT n ink-bottle
INKPOTS >INKPOT
INKS >INK
INKSPOT n ink stain
INKSPOTS >INKSPOT
INKSTAND n stand or tray
for holding writing tools
and containers for ink
INKSTANDS >INKSTAND
INKSTONE n stone used in
making ink
INKSTONES >INKSTONE
INKWELL n small container
for ink, often fitted into
the surface of a desk
INKWELLS >INKWELL
INKWOOD n type of tree
INKWOODS >INKWOOD
INKY adj dark or black
INLACE variant spelling
of >ENLACE
INLACED >INLACE
INLACES >INLACE
INLACING >INLACE
INLAID >INLAY
INLAND adv in or towards
the interior of a country,
away from the sea ▷ adj
of or in the interior of a
country or region, away
from a sea or border ▷ n
interior of a country or
region
INLANDER >INLAND
INLANDERS >INLAND
INLANDS >INLAND
INLAY n inlaid substance or
pattern ▷ vb decorate (an
article, esp of furniture) by
inserting pieces of wood,
ivory, or metal so that the
surfaces are smooth and
flat
INLAYER >INLAY
INLAYERS >INLAY
INLAYING >INLAY
INLAYINGS >INLAY
INLAYS >INLAY
INLET n narrow strip of
water extending from
the sea into the land ▷ vb
insert or inlay
INLETS >INLET
INLETTING >INLET
INLIER n outcrop of rocks
that is entirely surrounded
by younger rocks
INLIERS >INLIER

INLOCK *vb* lock up
INLOCKED >INLOCK
INLOCKING >INLOCK
INLOCKS >INLOCK
INLY *adv* inwardly
INLYING *adj* situated within or inside
INMATE *n* person living in an institution such as a prison
INMATES >INMATE
INMESH *variant spelling of* >ENMESH
INMESHED >INMESH
INMESHES >INMESH
INMESHING >INMESH
INMIGRANT *adj* coming in from another area of the same country ▷ *n* inmigrant person or animal
INMOST *adj* innermost
INN *n* pub or small hotel, esp in the country ▷ *vb* stay at an inn
INNAGE *n* measurement from bottom of container to surface of liquid
INNAGES >INNAGE
INNARDS *pl n* internal organs
INNATE *adj* being part of someone's nature, inborn
INNATELY >INNATE
INNATIVE *adj* native
INNED >INN
INNER *adj* happening or located inside ▷ *n* red innermost ring on a target
INNERLY >INNER
INNERMOST *adj* furthest inside
INNERNESS >INNER
INNERS >INNER
INNERSOLE *same as* >INSOLE
INNERVATE *vb* supply nerves to (a bodily organ or part)
INNERVE *vb* supply with nervous energy
INNERVED >INNERVE
INNERVES >INNERVE
INNERVING >INNERVE
INNERWEAR *n* underwear
INNING *n* division of the game consisting of a turn at batting and a turn in the field for each side
INNINGS >INNING
INNKEEPER *n* owner or manager of an inn
INNLESS *adj* without inns
INNOCENCE *n* quality or state of being innocent
INNOCENCY *same as* >INNOCENCE
INNOCENT *adj* not guilty of a crime ▷ *n* innocent person, esp a child
INNOCENTS >INNOCENT
INNOCUITY >INNOCUOUS
INNOCUOUS *adj* not harmful
INNOVATE *vb* introduce

new ideas or methods
INNOVATED >INNOVATE
INNOVATES >INNOVATE
INNOVATOR >INNOVATE
INNOXIOUS *adj* not noxious
INNS >INN
INNUENDO *n* (remark making) an indirect reference to something rude or unpleasant
INNUENDOS >INNUENDO
INNYARD *n* courtyard of an inn
INNYARDS >INNYARD
INOCULA >INOCULUM
INOCULANT *same as* >INOCULUM
INOCULATE *vb* protect against disease by injecting with a vaccine
INOCULUM *n* substance used in giving an inoculation
INOCULUMS >INOCULUM
INODOROUS *adj* odourless
INOPINATE *adj* unexpected
INORB *vb* enclose in or as if in an orb
INORBED >INORB
INORBING >INORB
INORBS >INORB
INORGANIC *adj* not having the characteristics of living organisms
INORNATE *adj* simple
INOSINE *n* type of molecule making up cell
INOSINES >INOSINE
INOSITE *same as* >INOSITOL
INOSITES >INOSITE
INOSITOL *n* cyclic alcohol
INOSITOLS >INOSITOL
INOTROPIC *adj* affecting or controlling the contraction of muscles, esp those of the heart
INPATIENT *n* patient who stays in a hospital for treatment
INPAYMENT *n* money paid into a bank account
INPHASE *adj* in the same phase
INPOUR *vb* pour in
INPOURED >INPOUR
INPOURING >INPOUR
INPOURS >INPOUR
INPUT *n* resources put into a project etc ▷ *vb* enter (data) in a computer
INPUTS >INPUT
INPUTTED >INPUT
INPUTTER >INPUT
INPUTTERS >INPUT
INPUTTING >INPUT
INQILAB *n* (in India, Pakistan, etc) revolution
INQILABS >INQILAB
INQUERE *Spenserian form of* >INQUIRE
INQUERED >INQUERE
INQUERES >INQUERE
INQUERING >INQUERE

INQUEST *n* official inquiry into a sudden death
INQUESTS >INQUEST
INQUIET *vb* disturb
INQUIETED >INQUIET
INQUIETLY >INQUIET
INQUIETS >INQUIET
INQUILINE *n* animal that lives in close association with another animal without harming it ▷ *adj* of or living as an inquiline
INQUINATE *vb* corrupt
INQUIRE *vb* seek information or ask (about)
INQUIRED >INQUIRE
INQUIRER >INQUIRE
INQUIRERS >INQUIRE
INQUIRES >INQUIRE
INQUIRIES >INQUIRY
INQUIRING >INQUIRE
INQUIRY *n* question
INQUORATE *adj* without enough people present to make a quorum
INRO *n* Japanese seal-box
INROAD *n* invasion or hostile attack
INROADS >INROAD
INRUN *n* slope down which ski jumpers ski
INRUNS >INRUN
INRUSH *n* sudden and overwhelming inward flow ▷ *vb* flow or rush suddenly and overwhelmingly
INRUSHES >INRUSH
INRUSHING >INRUSH
INS >IN
INSANE *adj* mentally ill
INSANELY >INSANE
INSANER >INSANE
INSANEST >INSANE
INSANIE *n* insanity
INSANIES >INSANIE
INSANITY *n* state of being insane
INSATIATE *adj* not able to be satisfied
INSATIETY *n* insatiability
INSCAPE *n* essential inner nature of a person, an object, etc
INSCAPES >INSCAPE
INSCIENCE *n* ignorance
INSCIENT *adj* ignorant
INSCONCE *vb* fortify
INSCONCED >INSCONCE
INSCONCES >INSCONCE
INSCRIBE *vb* write or carve words on
INSCRIBED >INSCRIBE
INSCRIBER >INSCRIBE
INSCRIBES >INSCRIBE
INSCROLL *vb* write on a scroll
INSCROLLS >INSCROLL
INSCULP *vb* engrave
INSCULPED >INSCULP
INSCULPS >INSCULP
INSCULPT *adj* engraved
INSEAM *vb* contain
INSEAMED >INSEAM

INSEAMING >INSEAM
INSEAMS >INSEAM
INSECT *n* small animal with six legs and usu. wings, such as an ant or fly
INSECTAN >INSECT
INSECTARY *n* place where insects are kept
INSECTEAN >INSECT
INSECTILE >INSECT
INSECTION *n* incision
INSECTS >INSECT
INSECURE *adj* anxious, not confident
INSEEM *vb* cover with grease
INSEEMED >INSEEM
INSEEMING >INSEEM
INSEEMS >INSEEM
INSELBERG *n* isolated rocky hill rising abruptly from a flat plain
INSENSATE *adj* without sensation, unconscious
INSERT *vb* put inside or include ▷ *n* something inserted
INSERTED *adj* (of a muscle) attached to the bone that it moves
INSERTER >INSERT
INSERTERS >INSERT
INSERTING >INSERT
INSERTION *n* act of inserting
INSERTS >INSERT
INSET *n* small picture inserted within a larger one ▷ *vb* place in or within ▷ *adj* decorated with something inserted
INSETS >INSET
INSETTED >INSET
INSETTER >INSET
INSETTERS >INSET
INSETTING >INSET
INSHALLAH *sentence substitute* if Allah wills it
INSHEATH *vb* sheathe
INSHEATHE *vb* sheathe
INSHEATHS >INSHEATH
INSHELL *vb* retreat, as into a shell
INSHELLED >INSHELL
INSHELLS >INSHELL
INSHELTER *vb* put in a shelter
INSHIP *vb* travel or send by ship
INSHIPPED >INSHIP
INSHIPS >INSHIP
INSHORE *adj* close to the shore ▷ *adv* towards the shore
INSHRINE *variant spelling of* >ENSHRINE
INSHRINED >INSHRINE
INSHRINES >INSHRINE
INSIDE *prep* in or to the interior of ▷ *adj* on or of the inside ▷ *adv* on, in, or to the inside, indoors ▷ *n* inner side, surface, or part
INSIDER *n* member of a

group who has privileged
knowledge about it
**INSIDERS** >INSIDER
**INSIDES** >INSIDE
**INSIDIOUS** adj subtle or
unseen but dangerous
**INSIGHT** n deep
understanding
**INSIGHTS** >INSIGHT
**INSIGNE** same as >INSIGNIA
**INSIGNIA** n badge or
emblem of honour or
office
**INSIGNIAS** >INSIGNIA
**INSINCERE** adj showing
false feelings, not genuine
**INSINEW** vb connect
or strengthen, as with
sinews
**INSINEWED** >INSINEW
**INSINEWS** >INSINEW
**INSINUATE** vb suggest
indirectly
**INSIPID** adj lacking
interest, spirit, or flavour
**INSIPIDLY** >INSIPID
**INSIPIENT** adj lacking
wisdom
**INSIST** vb demand or state
firmly
**INSISTED** >INSIST
**INSISTENT** adj making
persistent demands
**INSISTER** >INSIST
**INSISTERS** >INSIST
**INSISTING** >INSIST
**INSISTS** >INSIST
**INSNARE** less common
spelling of >ENSNARE
**INSNARED** >INSNARE
**INSNARER** >INSNARE
**INSNARERS** >INSNARE
**INSNARES** >INSNARE
**INSNARING** >INSNARE
**INSOFAR** adv to the extent
**INSOLATE** vb expose to
sunlight, as for bleaching
**INSOLATED** >INSOLATE
**INSOLATES** >INSOLATE
**INSOLE** n inner sole of a
shoe or boot
**INSOLENCE** >INSOLENT
**INSOLENT** n insolent
person ▷ adj rude and
disrespectful
**INSOLENTS** >INSOLENT
**INSOLES** >INSOLE
**INSOLUBLE** adj incapable
of being solved
**INSOLUBLY** >INSOLUBLE
**INSOLVENT** adj unable to
pay one's debts ▷ n person
who is insolvent
**INSOMNIA** n inability to
sleep
**INSOMNIAC** adj exhibiting
or causing insomnia ▷ n
person experiencing
insomnia
**INSOMNIAS** >INSOMNIA
**INSOMUCH** adv such an
extent
**INSOOTH** adv indeed
**INSOUL** variant of >ENSOUL

**INSOULED** >INSOUL
**INSOULING** >INSOUL
**INSOULS** >INSOUL
**INSPAN** vb harness
(animals) to (a vehicle)
**INSPANNED** >INSPAN
**INSPANS** >INSPAN
**INSPECT** vb check closely
or officially
**INSPECTED** >INSPECT
**INSPECTOR** n person who
inspects
**INSPECTS** >INSPECT
**INSPHERE** variant spelling
of >ENSPHERE
**INSPHERED** >INSPHERE
**INSPHERES** >INSPHERE
**INSPIRE** vb fill with
enthusiasm, stimulate
**INSPIRED** adj brilliantly
creative
**INSPIRER** >INSPIRE
**INSPIRERS** >INSPIRE
**INSPIRES** >INSPIRE
**INSPIRING** >INSPIRE
**INSPIRIT** vb fill with
vigour
**INSPIRITS** >INSPIRIT
**INSTABLE** less common word
for >UNSTABLE
**INSTAL** same as >INSTALL
**INSTALL** vb put in and
prepare (equipment) for
use
**INSTALLED** >INSTALL
**INSTALLER** >INSTALL
**INSTALLS** >INSTALL
**INSTALS** >INSTAL
**INSTANCE** n particular
example ▷ vb mention as
an example
**INSTANCED** >INSTANCE
**INSTANCES** >INSTANCE
**INSTANCY** n quality of
being urgent or imminent
**INSTANT** n very brief time
▷ adj happening at once
**INSTANTER** adv without
delay
**INSTANTLY** adv
immediately
**INSTANTS** >INSTANT
**INSTAR** vb decorate with
stars ▷ n stage in the
development of an insect
between any two moults
**INSTARRED** >INSTAR
**INSTARS** >INSTAR
**INSTATE** vb place in a
position or office
**INSTATED** >INSTATE
**INSTATES** >INSTATE
**INSTATING** >INSTATE
**INSTEAD** adv as a
replacement or substitute
**INSTEP** n part of the foot
forming the arch between
the ankle and toes
**INSTEPS** >INSTEP
**INSTIGATE** vb cause to
happen
**INSTIL** vb introduce (an
idea etc) gradually into
someone's mind

**INSTILL** same as >INSTIL
**INSTILLED** >INSTILL
**INSTILLER** >INSTIL
**INSTILLS** >INSTILL
**INSTILS** >INSTIL
**INSTINCT** n inborn
tendency to behave
in a certain way ▷ adj
animated or impelled (by)
**INSTINCTS** >INSTINCT
**INSTITUTE** n organization
set up for a specific
purpose, esp research or
teaching ▷ vb start or
establish
**INSTRESS** vb create or
sustain
**INSTROKE** n inward stroke
**INSTROKES** >INSTROKE
**INSTRUCT** vb order to do
something
**INSTRUCTS** >INSTRUCT
**INSUCKEN** adj of a sucken
**INSULA** n pyramid-shaped
area of the brain within
each cerebral hemisphere
beneath parts of the
frontal and temporal lobes
**INSULAE** >INSULA
**INSULANT** same
as >INSULATION
**INSULANTS** >INSULANT
**INSULAR** adj not open
to new ideas, narrow-
minded ▷ n islander
**INSULARLY** >INSULAR
**INSULARS** >INSULAR
**INSULAS** >INSULA
**INSULATE** vb prevent or
reduce the transfer of
electricity, heat, or sound
by surrounding or lining
with a nonconducting
material
**INSULATED** >INSULATE
**INSULATES** >INSULATE
**INSULATOR** n any material
or device that insulates
**INSULIN** n hormone
produced in the pancreas
that controls the amount
of sugar in the blood
**INSULINS** >INSULIN
**INSULSE** adj stupid
**INSULSITY** n stupidity
**INSULT** vb behave rudely
to, offend ▷ n insulting
remark or action
**INSULTANT** adj insulting
**INSULTED** >INSULT
**INSULTER** >INSULT
**INSULTERS** >INSULT
**INSULTING** >INSULT
**INSULTS** >INSULT
**INSURABLE** >INSURE
**INSURANCE** n agreement
by which one makes
regular payments to a
company who pay an
agreed sum if damage,
loss, or death occurs
**INSURANT** n holder of an
insurance policy
**INSURANTS** >INSURANT

**INSURE** vb protect by
insurance
**INSURED** adj covered by
insurance ▷ n person,
persons, or organization
covered by an insurance
policy
**INSUREDS** >INSURED
**INSURER** n person or
company that sells
insurance
**INSURERS** >INSURER
**INSURES** >INSURE
**INSURGENT** adj in revolt
against an established
authority ▷ n person who
takes part in a rebellion
**INSURING** >INSURE
**INSWATHE** vb bind or wrap
**INSWATHED** >INSWATHE
**INSWATHES** >INSWATHE
**INSWEPT** adj narrowed
towards the front
**INSWING** n movement of a
bowled ball from off to leg
through the air
**INSWINGER** n ball bowled
so as to move from off to
leg through the air
**INSWINGS** >INSWING
**INTACT** adj not changed or
damaged in any way
**INTACTLY** >INTACT
**INTAGLI** >INTAGLIO
**INTAGLIO** n (gem carved
with) an engraved design
**INTAGLIOS** >INTAGLIO
**INTAKE** n amount or
number taken in
**INTAKES** >INTAKE
**INTARSIA** n decorative or
pictorial mosaic of inlaid
wood or sometimes ivory
of a style developed in the
Italian Renaissance and
used esp on wooden wall
panels
**INTARSIAS** >INTARSIA
**INTEGER** n positive or
negative whole number
or zero
**INTEGERS** >INTEGER
**INTEGRAL** adj being an
essential part of a whole
▷ n sum of a large number
of very small quantities
**INTEGRALS** >INTEGRAL
**INTEGRAND** n
mathematical function to
be integrated
**INTEGRANT** adj part of a
whole ▷ n integrant thing
or part
**INTEGRATE** vb combine
into a whole ▷ adj made
up of parts
**INTEGRITY** n quality
of having high moral
principles
**INTEL** n US military
intelligence
**INTELLECT** n power of
thinking and reasoning
**INTELS** >INTEL

**INTENABLE** *adj* untenable
**INTEND** *vb* propose or plan (to do something)
**INTENDANT** *n* provincial or colonial official of France, Spain, or Portugal
**INTENDED** *adj* planned or future ▷ *n* person whom one is to marry
**INTENDEDS** > INTENDED
**INTENDER** > INTEND
**INTENDERS** > INTEND
**INTENDING** > INTEND
**INTENDS** > INTEND
**INTENIBLE** *adj* incapable of holding
**INTENSATE** *vb* intensify
**INTENSE** *adj* of great strength or degree
**INTENSELY** > INTENSE
**INTENSER** > INTENSE
**INTENSEST** > INTENSE
**INTENSIFY** *vb* make or become more intense
**INTENSION** *n* set of characteristics or properties by which the referent or referents of a given word are determined
**INTENSITY** *n* state or quality of being intense
**INTENSIVE** *adj* using or needing concentrated effort or resources ▷ *n* intensifier or intensive pronoun or grammatical construction
**INTENT** *n* intention ▷ *adj* paying close attention
**INTENTION** *n* something intended
**INTENTIVE** *adj* intent
**INTENTLY** > INTENT
**INTENTS** > INTENT
**INTER** *vb* bury (a corpse)
**INTERACT** *vb* act on or in close relation with each other
**INTERACTS** > INTERACT
**INTERAGE** *adj* between different ages
**INTERARCH** *vb* have intersecting arches
**INTERBANK** *adj* conducted between or involving two or more banks
**INTERBED** *vb* lie between strata of different minerals
**INTERBEDS** > INTERBED
**INTERBRED** *adj* having been bred within a single family or strain so as to produce particular characteristics
**INTERCEDE** *vb* try to end a dispute between two people or groups
**INTERCELL** *adj* occurring between cells
**INTERCEPT** *vb* seize or stop in transit ▷ *n* point at which two figures intersect
**INTERCITY** *adj* (in Britain)

denoting a fast train or passenger rail service, esp between main towns
**INTERCLAN** *adj* occurring between clans
**INTERCLUB** *adj* of, relating to, or conducted between two or more clubs
**INTERCOM** *n* internal communication system with loudspeakers
**INTERCOMS** > INTERCOM
**INTERCROP** *n* crop grown between the rows of another crop ▷ *vb* grow (one crop) between the rows of (another)
**INTERCUT** another word for > CROSSCUT
**INTERCUTS** > INTERCUT
**INTERDASH** *vb* dash between
**INTERDEAL** *vb* intrigue or plot
**INTERDICT** *n* official prohibition or restraint ▷ *vb* prohibit or forbid
**INTERDINE** *vb* eat together
**INTERESS** *vb* interest
**INTERESSE** *vb* interest
**INTEREST** *n* desire to know or hear more about something ▷ *vb* arouse the interest of
**INTERESTS** > INTEREST
**INTERFACE** *n* area where two things interact or link ▷ *vb* connect or be connected with by interface
**INTERFERE** *vb* try to influence other people's affairs where one is not involved or wanted
**INTERFILE** *vb* place (one or more items) among other items in a file or arrangement
**INTERFIRM** *adj* occurring between companies
**INTERFLOW** *vb* flow together
**INTERFOLD** *vb* fold together
**INTERFUSE** *vb* mix or become mixed
**INTERGANG** *adj* occurring between gangs
**INTERGREW** > INTERGROW
**INTERGROW** *vb* grow among
**INTERIM** *adj* temporary, provisional, or intervening ▷ *n* intervening time ▷ *adv* meantime
**INTERIMS** > INTERIM
**INTERIOR** *n* inside ▷ *adj* inside, inner
**INTERIORS** > INTERIOR
**INTERJECT** *vb* make (a remark) suddenly or as an interruption
**INTERJOIN** *vb* join together

**INTERKNIT** *vb* knit together
**INTERKNOT** *vb* knot together
**INTERLACE** *vb* join together as if by weaving
**INTERLAID** > INTERLAY
**INTERLAP** less common word for > OVERLAP
**INTERLAPS** > INTERLAP
**INTERLARD** *vb* insert in or occur throughout
**INTERLAY** *vb* insert (layers) between ▷ *n* material, such as paper, placed between a printing plate and its base
**INTERLAYS** > INTERLAY
**INTERLEAF** *n* extra leaf which is inserted
**INTERLEND** *vb* lend between libraries
**INTERLENT** > INTERLEND
**INTERLINE** *vb* write or print (matter) between the lines of (a text or book)
**INTERLINK** *vb* connect together
**INTERLOAN** *n* loan between one library and another
**INTERLOCK** *vb* join firmly together ▷ *n* device used to prevent a mechanism from operating independently or unsafely ▷ *adj* (of fabric) closely knitted
**INTERLOOP** *vb* loop together
**INTERLOPE** *vb* intrude
**INTERLUDE** *n* short rest or break in an activity or event
**INTERMALE** *adj* occurring between males
**INTERMAT** *n* patch of seabed devoid of vegetation
**INTERMATS** > INTERMAT
**INTERMENT** *n* burial
**INTERMESH** *vb* net together
**INTERMIT** *vb* suspend (activity) or (of activity) to be suspended temporarily or at intervals
**INTERMITS** > INTERMIT
**INTERMIX** *vb* mix together
**INTERMONT** *adj* located between mountains
**INTERMURE** *vb* wall in
**INTERN** *vb* imprison, esp during a war ▷ *n* trainee doctor in a hospital
**INTERNAL** *adj* of or on the inside ▷ *n* medical examination of the vagina, uterus, or rectum
**INTERNALS** > INTERNAL
**INTERNE** same as > INTERN
**INTERNED** > INTERN
**INTERNEE** *n* person who is interned
**INTERNEES** > INTERNEE
**INTERNES** > INTERNE

**INTERNET** *n* worldwide computer network
**INTERNETS** > INTERNET
**INTERNING** > INTERN
**INTERNIST** *n* physician who specializes in internal medicine
**INTERNODE** *n* part of a plant stem between two nodes
**INTERNS** > INTERN
**INTERPAGE** *vb* print (matter) on intervening pages
**INTERPLAY** *n* action and reaction of two things upon each other
**INTERPLED** *adj* having instituted a particular type of proceedings
**INTERPONE** *vb* interpose
**INTERPOSE** *vb* insert between or among things
**INTERPRET** *vb* explain the meaning of
**INTERRACE** *adj* between races
**INTERRAIL** *vb* travel on an international rail pass
**INTERRED** > INTER
**INTERREX** *n* person who governs during an interregnum
**INTERRING** > INTER
**INTERROW** *adj* occurring between rows
**INTERRUPT** *vb* break into (a conversation etc) ▷ *n* signal to initiate the stopping of the running of one computer program in order to run another
**INTERS** > INTER
**INTERSECT** *vb* (of roads) meet and cross
**INTERSERT** *vb* insert between
**INTERSEX** *n* condition of having characteristics intermediate between those of a male and a female
**INTERTERM** *adj* occurring between terms
**INTERTEXT** *adj* text seen as modifying another text in literary theory
**INTERTIE** *n* short roofing timber
**INTERTIES** > INTERTIE
**INTERTILL** *vb* cultivate between rows of crops
**INTERUNIT** *adj* occurring between units
**INTERVAL** *n* time between two particular moments or events
**INTERVALE** *dialect form of* > INTERVAL
**INTERVALS** > INTERVAL
**INTERVEIN** *vb* intersect
**INTERVENE** *vb* involve oneself in a situation, esp to prevent conflict

**INTERVIEW** n formal discussion, esp between a job-seeker and an employer ▷ vb conduct an interview with
**INTERWAR** adj of or happening in the period between World War I and World War II
**INTERWIND** vb wind together
**INTERWORK** same as > INTERWEAVE
**INTERWOVE** adj having been woven together
**INTERZONE** n area between two occupied zones
**INTESTACY** > INTESTATE
**INTESTATE** adj not having made a will ▷ n person who dies without having made a will
**INTESTINE** n lower part of the alimentary canal between the stomach and the anus
**INTHRAL** archaic form of > ENTHRAL
**INTHRALL** archaic form of > ENTHRAL
**INTHRALLS** > INTHRALL
**INTHRALS** > INTHRALL
**INTHRONE** archaic form of > ENTHRONE
**INTHRONED** > INTHRONE
**INTHRONES** > INTHRONE
**INTI** n former monetary unit of Peru
**INTIFADA** n Palestinian uprising against Israel in the West Bank and Gaza Strip
**INTIFADAH** same as > INTIFADA
**INTIFADAS** > INTIFADA
**INTIFADEH** same as > INTIFADA
**INTIL** Scot form of > INTO
**INTIMA** n innermost layer of an organ or part, esp of a blood vessel
**INTIMACY** n close or warm friendship
**INTIMAE** > INTIMA
**INTIMAL** > INTIMA
**INTIMAS** > INTIMA
**INTIMATE** adj having a close personal relationship ▷ n close friend ▷ vb hint at or suggest
**INTIMATED** > INTIMATE
**INTIMATER** > INTIMATE
**INTIMATES** > INTIMATE
**INTIME** adj intimate
**INTIMISM** n school of impressionist painting
**INTIMISMS** > INTIMISM
**INTIMIST** > INTIMISM
**INTIMISTE** > INTIMISM
**INTIMISTS** > INTIMISM
**INTIMITY** n intimacy
**INTINE** n inner wall of a pollen grain or a spore
**INTINES** > INTINE

**INTIRE** archaic form of > ENTIRE
**INTIS** > INTI
**INTITLE** archaic form of > ENTITLE
**INTITLED** > INTITLE
**INTITLES** > INTITLE
**INTITLING** > INTITLE
**INTITULE** vb (in Britain) to entitle (an act of parliament)
**INTITULED** > INTITULE
**INTITULES** > INTITULE
**INTO** prep indicating motion towards the centre, result of a change, division, etc
**INTOED** adj having inward-turning toes
**INTOMB** same as > ENTOMB
**INTOMBED** > INTOMB
**INTOMBING** > INTOMB
**INTOMBS** > INTOMB
**INTONACO** n wet plaster surface on which frescoes are painted
**INTONACOS** > INTONACO
**INTONATE** vb pronounce or articulate (continuous connected speech) with a characteristic rise and fall of the voice
**INTONATED** > INTONATE
**INTONATES** > INTONATE
**INTONATOR** > INTONATE
**INTONE** vb speak or recite in an unvarying tone of voice
**INTONED** > INTONE
**INTONER** > INTONE
**INTONERS** > INTONE
**INTONES** > INTONE
**INTONING** > INTONE
**INTONINGS** > INTONE
**INTORSION** n spiral twisting in plant stems or other parts
**INTORT** vb twist inward
**INTORTED** > INTORT
**INTORTING** > INTORT
**INTORTION** > INTORT
**INTORTS** > INTORT
**INTOWN** adj infield
**INTRA** prep within
**INTRACITY** same as > INTERCITY
**INTRADA** n prelude
**INTRADAS** > INTRADA
**INTRADAY** adj occurring within one day
**INTRADOS** n inner curve or surface of an arch or vault
**INTRANET** n internal network that makes use of Internet technology
**INTRANETS** > INTRANET
**INTRANT** n one who enters
**INTRANTS** > INTRANT
**INTREAT** archaic spelling of > ENTREAT
**INTREATED** > INTREAT
**INTREATS** > INTREAT
**INTRENCH** less common spelling of > ENTRENCH

**INTREPID** adj fearless, bold
**INTRICACY** > INTRICATE
**INTRICATE** adj involved or complicated
**INTRIGANT** n person who intrigues
**INTRIGUE** vb make interested or curious ▷ n secret plotting
**INTRIGUED** > INTRIGUE
**INTRIGUER** > INTRIGUE
**INTRIGUES** > INTRIGUE
**INTRINCE** adj intricate
**INTRINSIC** adj essential to the basic nature of something
**INTRO** n introduction
**INTRODUCE** vb present (someone) by name (to another person)
**INTROFIED** > INTROFY
**INTROFIES** > INTROFY
**INTROFY** vb increase the wetting properties
**INTROIT** n short prayer said or sung as the celebrant is entering the sanctuary to celebrate Mass
**INTROITAL** > INTROIT
**INTROITS** > INTROIT
**INTROITUS** n entrance to a body cavity
**INTROJECT** vb (esp of a child) to incorporate ideas of others, or (in fantasy) of objects
**INTROLD** variant of > ENTROLD
**INTROMIT** vb enter or insert or allow to enter or be inserted
**INTROMITS** > INTROMIT
**INTRON** n stretch of DNA that interrupts a gene and does not contribute to the specification of a protein
**INTRONS** > INTRON
**INTRORSE** adj turned inwards or towards the axis
**INTROS** > INTRO
**INTROVERT** n person concerned more with his or her thoughts and feelings than with the outside world ▷ adj shy and quiet ▷ vb turn (a hollow organ or part) inside out
**INTRUDE** vb come in or join in without being invited
**INTRUDED** > INTRUDE
**INTRUDER** n person who enters a place without permission
**INTRUDERS** > INTRUDER
**INTRUDES** > INTRUDE
**INTRUDING** > INTRUDE
**INTRUSION** n act of intruding
**INTRUSIVE** adj characterized by intrusion or tending to intrude

**INTRUST** same as > ENTRUST
**INTRUSTED** > INTRUST
**INTRUSTS** > INTRUST
**INTUBATE** vb insert a tube or cannula into (a hollow organ)
**INTUBATED** > INTUBATE
**INTUBATES** > INTUBATE
**INTUIT** vb know or discover by intuition
**INTUITED** > INTUIT
**INTUITING** > INTUIT
**INTUITION** n instinctive knowledge or insight without conscious reasoning
**INTUITIVE** adj of, possessing, or resulting from intuition
**INTUITS** > INTUIT
**INTUMESCE** vb swell or become swollen
**INTURN** n inward turn
**INTURNED** adj turned inward
**INTURNS** > INTURN
**INTUSE** n contusion
**INTUSES** > INTUSE
**INTWINE** less common spelling of > ENTWINE
**INTWINED** > INTWINE
**INTWINES** > INTWINE
**INTWINING** > INTWINE
**INTWIST** vb twist together
**INTWISTED** > INTWIST
**INTWISTS** > INTWIST
**INUKSHUIT** > INUKSHUK
**INUKSHUK** n stone used by Inuit people to mark a location
**INUKSHUKS** > INUKSHUK
**INULA** n plant of the elecampane genus
**INULAS** > INULA
**INULASE** n enzyme that hydrolyses inulin to fructose
**INULASES** > INULASE
**INULIN** n fructose polysaccharide present in the tubers and rhizomes of some plants
**INULINS** > INULIN
**INUMBRATE** vb shade
**INUNCTION** n application of an ointment to the skin, esp by rubbing
**INUNDANT** > INUNDATE
**INUNDATE** vb flood
**INUNDATED** > INUNDATE
**INUNDATES** > INUNDATE
**INUNDATOR** > INUNDATE
**INURBANE** adj not urbane
**INURE** vb cause to accept or become hardened to
**INURED** > INURE
**INUREMENT** > INURE
**INURES** > INURE
**INURING** > INURE
**INURN** vb place (esp cremated ashes) in an urn
**INURNED** > INURN
**INURNING** > INURN
**INURNMENT** > INURN

INURNS > INURN

INUSITATE adj out of use

INUST adj burnt in

INUSTION > INUST

INUSTIONS > INUST

INUTILE adj useless

INUTILELY > INUTILE

INUTILITY > INUTILE

INVADABLE > INVADE

INVADE vb enter (a country) by military force

INVADED > INVADE

INVADER > INVADE

INVADERS > INVADE

INVADES > INVADE

INVADING > INVADE

INVALID n disabled or chronically ill person ▷ vb dismiss from active service because of illness or injury ▷ adj having no legal force

INVALIDED > INVALID

INVALIDLY > INVALID

INVALIDS > INVALID

INVAR n alloy made from iron and nickel

INVARIANT n entity, quantity, etc, that is unaltered by a particular transformation of coordinates

INVARS > INVAR

INVASION n invading

INVASIONS > INVASION

INVASIVE adj of or relating to an invasion, intrusion, etc

INVEAGLE archaic form of > INVEIGLE

INVEAGLED > INVEAGLE

INVEAGLES > INVEAGLE

INVECKED same as > INVECTED

INVECTED adj bordered with small convex curves

INVECTIVE n abusive speech or writing ▷ adj characterized by or using abusive language, bitter sarcasm, etc

INVEIGH vb criticize strongly

INVEIGHED > INVEIGH

INVEIGHER > INVEIGH

INVEIGHS > INVEIGH

INVEIGLE vb coax by cunning or trickery

INVEIGLED > INVEIGLE

INVEIGLER > INVEIGLE

INVEIGLES > INVEIGLE

INVENIT (he or she) designed it: used formerly on objects such as pocket watches next to the designer's name

INVENT vb think up or create (something new)

INVENTED > INVENT

INVENTER same as > INVENTOR

INVENTERS > INVENTER

INVENTING > INVENT

INVENTION n something invented

INVENTIVE adj creative and resourceful

INVENTOR n person who invents, esp as a profession

INVENTORS > INVENTOR

INVENTORY n detailed list of goods or furnishings ▷ vb make a list of

INVENTS > INVENT

INVERITY n untruth

INVERNESS n type of cape

INVERSE vb make something opposite or contrary in effect ▷ adj reversed in effect, sequence, direction, etc ▷ n exact opposite

INVERSED > INVERSE

INVERSELY > INVERSE

INVERSES > INVERSE

INVERSING > INVERSE

INVERSION n act of inverting or state of being inverted

INVERSIVE > INVERSION

INVERT vb turn upside down or inside out ▷ n homosexual

INVERTASE n enzyme, occurring in the intestinal juice of animals and in yeasts

INVERTED > INVERT

INVERTER n any device for converting a direct current into an alternating current

INVERTERS > INVERTER

INVERTIN same as > INVERTASE

INVERTING > INVERT

INVERTINS > INVERTIN

INVERTOR same as > INVERTER

INVERTORS > INVERTOR

INVERTS > INVERT

INVEST vb spend (money, time, etc) on something with the expectation of profit

INVESTED > INVEST

INVESTING > INVEST

INVESTOR > INVEST

INVESTORS > INVEST

INVESTS > INVEST

INVEXED adj concave

INVIABLE adj not viable, esp financially

INVIABLY > INVIABLE

INVIDIOUS adj likely to cause resentment

INVIOLACY > INVIOLATE

INVIOLATE adj unharmed, unaffected

INVIOUS adj without paths or roads

INVIRILE adj unmanly

INVISCID adj not viscid

INVISIBLE adj not able to be seen ▷ n invisible item of trade

INVISIBLY > INVISIBLE

INVITAL adj not vital

INVITE vb request the company of ▷ n invitation

INVITED > INVITE

INVITEE n one who is invited

INVITEES > INVITEE

INVITER > INVITE

INVITERS > INVITE

INVITES > INVITE

INVITING adj tempting, attractive ▷ n old word for invitation

INVITINGS > INVITING

INVOCABLE > INVOKE

INVOCATE archaic word for > INVOKE

INVOCATED > INVOCATE

INVOCATES > INVOCATE

INVOCATOR > INVOCATE

INVOICE n (present with) a bill for goods or services supplied ▷ vb present (a customer) with an invoice

INVOICED > INVOICE

INVOICES > INVOICE

INVOICING > INVOICE

INVOKE vb put (a law or penalty) into operation

INVOKED > INVOKE

INVOKER > INVOKE

INVOKERS > INVOKE

INVOKES > INVOKE

INVOKING > INVOKE

INVOLUCEL n ring of bracts at the base of the florets of a compound umbel

INVOLUCRA > involucres

INVOLUCRE n ring of bracts at the base of an inflorescence in such plants as the composites

INVOLUTE adj complex, intricate, or involved ▷ n curve described by the free end of a thread as it is wound around another curve on the same plane ▷ vb become involute

INVOLUTED > INVOLUTE

INVOLUTES > INVOLUTE

INVOLVE vb include as a necessary part

INVOLVED > INVOLVE

INVOLVER > INVOLVE

INVOLVERS > INVOLVE

INVOLVES > INVOLVE

INVOLVING > INVOLVE

INWALL vb surround with a wall

INWALLED > INWALL

INWALLING > INWALL

INWALLS > INWALL

INWARD adj directed towards the middle ▷ adv towards the inside or middle ▷ n inward part

INWARDLY adv within the private thoughts or feelings

INWARDS adv towards the inside or middle of something

INWEAVE vb weave together into or as if into a design, fabric, etc

INWEAVED > INWEAVE

INWEAVES > INWEAVE

INWEAVING > INWEAVE

INWICK vb perform a curling stroke in which the stone bounces off another stone

INWICKED > INWICK

INWICKING > INWICK

INWICKS > INWICK

INWIND vb wind or coil around

INWINDING > INWIND

INWINDS > INWIND

INWIT n conscience

INWITH adv within

INWITS > INWIT

INWORK vb work in

INWORKED > INWORK

INWORKING > INWORK

INWORKS > INWORK

INWORN adj worn in

INWOUND > INWIND

INWOVE > INWEAVE

INWOVEN > INWEAVE

INWRAP less common spelling of > ENWRAP

INWRAPPED > INWRAP

INWRAPS > INWRAP

INWREATHE same as > ENWREATHE

INWROUGHT adj worked or woven into material, esp decoratively

INYALA n antelope

INYALAS > INYALA

IO n type of moth

IODATE same as > IODIZE

IODATED > IODATE

IODATES > IODATE

IODATING > IODATE

IODATION > IODATE

IODATIONS > IODATE

IODIC adj of or containing iodine

IODID same as > IODIDE

IODIDE n compound containing an iodine atom, such as methyl iodide

IODIDES > IODIDE

IODIDS > IODID

IODIN same as > IODINE

IODINATE vb cause to combine with iodine

IODINATED > IODINATE

IODINATES > IODINATE

IODINE n bluish-black element used in medicine and photography

IODINES > IODINE

IODINS > IODIN

IODISE same as > IODIZE

IODISED > IODISE

IODISER > IODISE

IODISERS > IODISE

IODISES > IODISE

IODISING > IODISE

IODISM n poisoning induced by ingestion of iodine or its compounds

IODISMS > IODISM

IODIZE vb treat with iodine

IODIZED > IODIZE

**IODIZER** > IODIZE
**IODIZERS** > IODIZE
**IODIZES** > IODIZE
**IODIZING** > IODIZE
**IODOFORM** n yellow crystalline insoluble volatile solid
**IODOFORMS** > IODOFORM
**IODOMETRY** n procedure used in volumetric analysis for determining the quantity of substance present that contains iodine
**IODOPHILE** adj taking an intense iodine stain
**IODOPHOR** n substance in which iodine is combined with an agent that renders it soluble
**IODOPHORS** > IODOPHOR
**IODOPSIN** n violet light-sensitive pigment in the cones of the retina of the eye that is responsible for colour vision
**IODOPSINS** > IODOPSIN
**IODOUS** adj of or containing iodine, esp in the trivalent state
**IODURET** n iodide
**IODURETS** > IODURET
**IODYRITE** n silver iodide
**IODYRITES** > IODYRITE
**IOLITE** n grey or violet-blue dichroic mineral
**IOLITES** > IOLITE
**ION** n electrically charged atom
**IONIC** adj of or in the form of ions
**IONICITY** n ionic character
**IONICS** pl n study of ions
**IONISABLE** > IONISE
**IONISE** same as > IONIZE
**IONISED** > IONISE
**IONISER** same as > IONIZER
**IONISERS** > IONISER
**IONISES** > IONISE
**IONISING** > IONISE
**IONIUM** n naturally occurring radioisotope of thorium
**IONIUMS** > IONIUM
**IONIZABLE** > IONIZE
**IONIZE** vb change into ions
**IONIZED** > IONIZE
**IONIZER** n person or thing that ionizes, esp an electrical device used within a room to refresh its atmosphere by restoring negative ions
**IONIZERS** > IONIZER
**IONIZES** > IONIZE
**IONIZING** > IONIZE
**IONOGEN** n compound that exists as ions when dissolved
**IONOGENIC** adj forming ions
**IONOGENS** > IONOGEN
**IONOMER** n thermoplastic

with ionic bonding between polymer chains
**IONOMERS** > IONOMER
**IONONE** n yellowish liquid mixture of two isomers with an odour of violets
**IONONES** > IONONE
**IONOPAUSE** n transitional zone in the atmosphere between the ionosphere and the exosphere
**IONOPHORE** n chemical compound capable of forming a complex with an ion and transporting it through a biological membrane
**IONOSONDE** n instrument measuring ionization
**IONOTROPY** n reversible interconversion of a pair of organic isomers as a result of the migration of an ionic part of the molecule
**IONS** > ION
**IOS** > IO
**IOTA** n ninth letter in the Greek alphabet
**IOTACISM** n pronunciation tendency in Modern Greek
**IOTACISMS** > IOTACISM
**IOTAS** > IOTA
**IPECAC** n type of S American shrub
**IPECACS** > IPECAC
**IPOMOEA** n tropical or subtropical convolvulaceous plant
**IPOMOEAS** > IPOMOEA
**IPPON** n winning point awarded in a judo or karate competition
**IPPONS** > IPPON
**IPRINDOLE** n antidepressant
**IRACUND** adj easily angered
**IRADE** n written edict of a Muslim ruler
**IRADES** > IRADE
**IRASCIBLE** adj easily angered
**IRASCIBLY** > IRASCIBLE
**IRATE** adj very angry
**IRATELY** > IRATE
**IRATENESS** > IRATE
**IRATER** > IRATE
**IRATEST** > IRATE
**IRE** vb anger ▷ n anger
**IRED** > IRE
**IREFUL** > IRE
**IREFULLY** > IRE
**IRELESS** > IRE
**IRENIC** adj tending to conciliate or promote peace
**IRENICAL** same as > IRENIC
**IRENICISM** > IRENICS
**IRENICON** variant spelling of > EIRENICON
**IRENICONS** > IRENICON
**IRENICS** n that branch of theology that is concerned with unity between Christian sects and

denominations
**IRENOLOGY** n study of peace
**IRES** > IRE
**IRID** n type of iris
**IRIDAL** > IRID
**IRIDEAL** > IRID
**IRIDES** > IRIS
**IRIDIAL** > IRID
**IRIDIAN** > IRID
**IRIDIC** adj of or containing iridium, esp in the tetravalent state
**IRIDISE** vb make iridescent
**IRIDISED** > IRIDISE
**IRIDISES** > IRIDISE
**IRIDISING** > IRIDISE
**IRIDIUM** n very hard corrosion-resistant metal
**IRIDIUMS** > IRIDIUM
**IRIDIZE** vb make iridescent
**IRIDIZED** > IRIDIZE
**IRIDIZES** > IRIDIZE
**IRIDIZING** > IRIDIZE
**IRIDOCYTE** n cell in the skin of fish that gives them iridescence
**IRIDOLOGY** n technique used in complementary medicine to diagnose illness by studying a patient's eyes
**IRIDOTOMY** n surgical incision into the iris, esp to create an artificial pupil
**IRIDS** > IRID
**IRING** > IRE
**IRIS** n coloured circular membrane of the eye containing the pupil ▷ vb display iridescence
**IRISATE** vb make iridescent
**IRISATED** > IRISATE
**IRISATES** > IRISATE
**IRISATING** > IRISATE
**IRISATION** > IRISATE
**IRISCOPE** n instrument that displays the prismatic colours
**IRISCOPES** > IRISCOPE
**IRISED** > IRIS
**IRISES** > IRIS
**IRISING** > IRIS
**IRITIC** > IRITIS
**IRITIS** n inflammation of the iris of the eye
**IRITISES** > IRITIS
**IRK** vb irritate, annoy
**IRKED** > IRK
**IRKING** > IRK
**IRKS** > IRK
**IRKSOME** adj irritating, annoying
**IRKSOMELY** > IRKSOME
**IROKO** n tropical African hardwood tree
**IROKOS** > IROKO
**IRON** n strong silvery-white metallic element, widely used for structural and engineering purposes

▷ adj made of iron ▷ vb smooth (clothes or fabric) with an iron
**IRONBARK** n Australian eucalyptus with hard rough bark
**IRONBARKS** > IRONBARK
**IRONBOUND** adj bound with iron
**IRONCLAD** adj covered or protected with iron ▷ n large wooden 19th-century warship with armoured plating
**IRONCLADS** > IRONCLAD
**IRONE** n fragrant liquid
**IRONED** > IRON
**IRONER** > IRON
**IRONERS** > IRON
**IRONES** > IRONE
**IRONIC** adj using irony
**IRONICAL** same as > IRONIC
**IRONIER** > IRONY
**IRONIES** > IRONY
**IRONIEST** > IRONY
**IRONING** n clothes to be ironed
**IRONINGS** > IRONING
**IRONISE** same as > IRONIZE
**IRONISED** > IRONISE
**IRONISES** > IRONISE
**IRONISING** > IRONISE
**IRONIST** > IRONIZE
**IRONISTS** > IRONIZE
**IRONIZE** vb use or indulge in irony
**IRONIZED** > IRONIZE
**IRONIZES** > IRONIZE
**IRONIZING** > IRONIZE
**IRONLESS** > IRON
**IRONLIKE** > IRON
**IRONMAN** n very strong man
**IRONMEN** > IRONMAN
**IRONNESS** > IRON
**IRONS** > IRON
**IRONSIDE** n person with great stamina or resistance
**IRONSIDES** > IRONSIDE
**IRONSMITH** adj blacksmith
**IRONSTONE** n rock consisting mainly of iron ore
**IRONWARE** n domestic articles made of iron
**IRONWARES** > IRONWARE
**IRONWEED** n plant with purplish leaves
**IRONWEEDS** > IRONWEED
**IRONWOMAN** n very strong woman
**IRONWOMEN** > IRONWOMAN
**IRONWOOD** n any of various trees, such as hornbeam, with exceptionally hard wood
**IRONWOODS** > IRONWOOD
**IRONWORK** n work done in iron, esp decorative work
**IRONWORKS** n building in which iron is smelted, cast, or wrought
**IRONY** n mildly sarcastic use of words to imply the

opposite of what is said
▷ *adj* of, resembling, or
containing iron
**IRRADIANT** *adj* radiating
light
**IRRADIATE** *vb* subject to or
treat with radiation
**IRREAL** *adj* unreal
**IRREALITY** *n* unreality
**IRREDENTA** *variant*
*of* > IRRIDENTA
**IRREGULAR** *adj* not regular
or even ▷ *n* soldier not in a
regular army
**IRRELATED** *adj* irrelevant
**IRRIDENTA** *n* region that
is ethnically or historically
tied to one country, but
which is ruled by another
**IRRIGABLE** > IRRIGATE
**IRRIGABLY** > IRRIGATE
**IRRIGATE** *vb* supply (land)
with water by artificial
channels or pipes
**IRRIGATED** > IRRIGATE
**IRRIGATES** > IRRIGATE
**IRRIGATOR** > IRRIGATE
**IRRIGUOUS** *adj* well-
watered
**IRRISION** *n* mockery
**IRRISIONS** > IRRISION
**IRRISORY** *adj* mocking
**IRRITABLE** *adj* easily
annoyed
**IRRITABLY** > IRRITABLE
**IRRITANCY** > IRRITANT
**IRRITANT** *adj* causing
irritation ▷ *n* something
that annoys or irritates
**IRRITANTS** > IRRITANT
**IRRITATE** *vb* annoy, anger
**IRRITATED** > IRRITATE
**IRRITATES** > IRRITATE
**IRRITATOR** > IRRITATE
**IRRUPT** *vb* enter forcibly or
suddenly
**IRRUPTED** > IRRUPT
**IRRUPTING** > IRRUPT
**IRRUPTION** > IRRUPT
**IRRUPTIVE** *adj* irrupting or
tending to irrupt
**IRRUPTS** > IRRUPT
**IS** *third person singular*
*present tense of* > BE
**ISABEL** *n* brown yellow
colour
**ISABELLA** *same as* > ISABEL
**ISABELLAS** > ISABELLA
**ISABELS** > ISABEL
**ISAGOGE** *n* academic
introduction to a
specialized subject field or
area of research
**ISAGOGES** > ISAGOGE
**ISAGOGIC** > ISAGOGICS
**ISAGOGICS** *n* introductory
studies, esp in the history
of the Bible
**ISALLOBAR** *n* line on a map
connecting places with
equal pressure changes
**ISARITHM** *n* line on a map
connecting places with
the same population

density
**ISARITHMS** > ISARITHM
**ISATIN** *n* yellowish-red
crystalline compound
soluble in hot water, used
for the preparation of vat
dyes
**ISATINE** *same as* > ISATIN
**ISATINES** > ISATINE
**ISATINIC** > ISATIN
**ISATINS** > ISATIN
**ISBA** *n* log hut
**ISBAS** > ISBA
**ISCHAEMIA** *n* inadequate
supply of blood to an
organ or part, as from an
obstructed blood flow
**ISCHAEMIC** > ISCHAEMIA
**ISCHEMIA** *same*
*as* > ISCHAEMIA
**ISCHEMIAS** > ISCHEMIA
**ISCHEMIC** > ISCHAEMIA
**ISCHIA** > ISCHIUM
**ISCHIADIC** > ISCHIUM
**ISCHIAL** > ISCHIUM
**ISCHIATIC** > ISCHIUM
**ISCHIUM** *n* one of the three
sections of the hipbone,
situated below the ilium
**ISCHURIA** *n* retention of
urine
**ISCHURIAS** > ISCHURIA
**ISEIKONIA** *n* seeing of
same image in both eyes
**ISEIKONIC** > ISEIKONIA
**ISENERGIC** *adj* of equal
energy
**ISH** *n* issue
**ISHES** > ISH
**ISINGLASS** *n* kind of
gelatine obtained from
some freshwater fish
**ISIT** *sentence substitute*
expression used to
seek confirmation of
something or show one is
listening
**ISLAND** *n* piece of land
surrounded by water ▷ *vb*
cause to become an island
**ISLANDED** > ISLAND
**ISLANDER** *n* person who
lives on an island
**ISLANDERS** > ISLANDER
**ISLANDING** > ISLAND
**ISLANDS** > ISLAND
**ISLE** *vb* make an isle of ▷ *n*
island
**ISLED** > ISLE
**ISLELESS** *adj* without
islands
**ISLEMAN** *n* islander
**ISLEMEN** > ISLEMAN
**ISLES** > ISLE
**ISLESMAN** *same*
*as* > ISLEMAN
**ISLESMEN** > ISLESMAN
**ISLET** *n* small island
**ISLETED** *adj* having islets
**ISLETS** > ISLET
**ISLING** > ISLE
**ISLOMANIA** *n* obsessional
enthusiasm or partiality
for islands

**ISM** *n* doctrine, system, or
practice
**ISMATIC** *adj* following
fashionable doctrines
**ISMATICAL** *same*
*as* > ISMATIC
**ISMS** > ISM
**ISNA** *vb* is not
**ISNAE** *same as* > ISNA
**ISO** *n* short segment of film
that can be replayed easily
**ISOAMYL** as in *isoamyl*
*acetate*, colourless
volatile compound
used as a solvent for
cellulose lacquers and as a
flavouring
**ISOAMYLS** > ISOAMYL
**ISOBAR** *n* line on a map
connecting places of equal
atmospheric pressure
**ISOBARE** *same as* > ISOBAR
**ISOBARES** > ISOBARE
**ISOBARIC** *adj* having equal
atmospheric pressure
**ISOBARISM** > ISOBAR
**ISOBARS** > ISOBAR
**ISOBASE** *n* line connecting
points of equal land
upheaval
**ISOBASES** > ISOBASE
**ISOBATH** *n* line on a map
connecting points of equal
underwater depth
**ISOBATHIC** > ISOBATH
**ISOBATHS** > ISOBATH
**ISOBRONT** *n* line
connecting points of
simultaneous storm
development
**ISOBRONTS** > ISOBRONT
**ISOBUTANE** *n* form of
butane
**ISOBUTENE** *n* isomer of
butene
**ISOBUTYL** as in *methyl*
*isobutyl ketone* colourless
insoluble liquid ketone
used as a solvent for
organic compounds
**ISOBUTYLS** > ISOBUTYL
**ISOCHASM** *n* line
connecting points of equal
aurorae frequency
**ISOCHASMS** > ISOCHASM
**ISOCHEIM** *n* line on a map
connecting places with
the same mean winter
temperature
**ISOCHEIMS** > ISOCHEIM
**ISOCHIMAL** > ISOCHIME
**ISOCHIME** *same*
*as* > ISOCHEIM
**ISOCHIMES** > ISOCHIME
**ISOCHOR** *n* line on a graph
showing the variation
of the temperature of a
fluid with its pressure,
when the volume is kept
constant
**ISOCHORE** *same*
*as* > ISOCHOR
**ISOCHORES** > ISOCHORE
**ISOCHORIC** > ISOCHOR

**ISOCHORS** > ISOCHOR
**ISOCHRON** *n* line on an
isotope ratio diagram
denoting a suite of rock
or mineral samples all
formed at the same time
**ISOCHRONE** *n* line on a map
or diagram connecting
places from which it takes
the same time to travel to
a certain point
**ISOCHRONS** > ISOCHRON
**ISOCLINAL** *adj* sloping in
the same direction and
at the same angle ▷ *n*
imaginary line connecting
points on the earth's
surface having equal
angles of dip
**ISOCLINE** *same*
*as* > ISOCLINAL
**ISOCLINES** > ISOCLINE
**ISOCLINIC** *same*
*as* > ISOCLINAL
**ISOCRACY** *n* form of
government in which all
people have equal powers
**ISOCRATIC** > ISOCRACY
**ISOCRYMAL** *same*
*as* > ISOCRYME
**ISOCRYME** *n* line
connecting points of equal
winter temperature
**ISOCRYMES** > ISOCRYME
**ISOCYANIC** as in *isocyanic*
*acid*, hypothetical acid
known only in the form of
its compounds
**ISOCYCLIC** *adj* containing
a closed ring of atoms of
the same kind, esp carbon
atoms
**ISODICA** > ISODICON
**ISODICON** *n* short anthem
**ISODOMA** > ISODOMON
**ISODOMON** *n* masonry
formed of uniform blocks,
with courses are of equal
height
**ISODOMONS** > ISODOMON
**ISODOMOUS** > ISODOMON
**ISODOMUM** *same*
*as* > ISODOMON
**ISODONT** *n* animal in which
the teeth are of similar size
**ISODONTAL** *same*
*as* > ISONDONT
**ISODONTS** > ISODONT
**ISODOSE** *n* dose of
radiation applied to
a part of the body in
radiotherapy that is equal
to the dose applied to a
different part
**ISODOSES** > ISODOSE
**ISOENZYME** *same*
*as* > ISOZYME
**ISOETES** *n* quillwort
**ISOFORM** *n* protein similar
in function but not form to
another
**ISOFORMS** > ISOFORM
**ISOGAMETE** *n* gamete that
is similar in size and form

to the one with which it unites in fertilization

**ISOGAMIC** > ISOGAMY

**ISOGAMIES** > ISOGAMY

**ISOGAMOUS** > ISOGAMY

**ISOGAMY** n (in some algae and fungi) sexual fusion of gametes of similar size and form

**ISOGENEIC** same
as > ISOGENIC

**ISOGENIC** same
as > ISOGENOUS

**ISOGENIES** > ISOGENOUS

**ISOGENOUS** adj of similar origin, as parts derived from the same embryonic tissue

**ISOGENY** > ISOGENOUS

**ISOGLOSS** n line drawn on a map around the area in which a linguistic feature is to be found, such as a particular pronunciation of a given word

**ISOGON** n equiangular polygon

**ISOGONAL** same
as > ISOGONIC

**ISOGONALS** > ISOGONAL

**ISOGONE** same
as > ISOGONIC

**ISOGONES** > ISOGONE

**ISOGONIC** adj having, making, or involving equal angles ▷ n imaginary line connecting points on the earth's surface having equal magnetic declination

**ISOGONICS** > ISOGONIC

**ISOGONIES** > ISOGONIC

**ISOGONS** > ISOGON

**ISOGONY** > ISOGONIC

**ISOGRAFT** vb grafting tissue from a donor genetically identical to the recipient

**ISOGRAFTS** > ISOGRAFT

**ISOGRAM** same
as > ISOPLETH

**ISOGRAMS** > ISOGRAM

**ISOGRAPH** n line connecting points of the same linguistic usage

**ISOGRAPHS** > ISOGRAPH

**ISOGRIV** n line connecting points of equal angular difference between magnetic north and grid north

**ISOGRIVS** > ISOGRIV

**ISOHEL** n line on a map connecting places with an equal period of sunshine

**ISOHELS** > ISOHEL

**ISOHYDRIC** adj having the same acidity or hydrogen-ion concentration

**ISOHYET** n line on a map connecting places having equal rainfall

**ISOHYETAL** > ISOHYET

**ISOHYETS** > ISOHYET

**ISOKONT** same
as > ISOKONTAN

**ISOKONTAN** n alga whose zoophores have equal cilia

**ISOKONTS** > ISOKONT

**ISOLABLE** > ISOLATE

**ISOLATE** vb place apart or alone ▷ n isolated person or group

**ISOLATED** > ISOLATE

**ISOLATES** > ISOLATE

**ISOLATING** > ISOLATE

**ISOLATION** > ISOLATE

**ISOLATIVE** adj concerned with isolation

**ISOLATOR** > ISOLATE

**ISOLATORS** > ISOLATE

**ISOLEAD** n line on a ballistic graph

**ISOLEADS** > ISOLEAD

**ISOLEX** n isogloss marking off the area in which a particular item of vocabulary is found

**ISOLEXES** > ISOLEX

**ISOLINE** same
as > ISOPLETH

**ISOLINES** > ISOLINE

**ISOLOG** > ISOLOGOUS

**ISOLOGOUS** adj (of two or more organic compounds) having a similar structure but containing different atoms of the same valency

**ISOLOGS** > ISOLOGOUS

**ISOLOGUE** > ISOLOGOUS

**ISOLOGUES** > ISOLOGOUS

**ISOMER** n substance whose molecules contain the same atoms as another but in a different arrangement

**ISOMERASE** n any enzyme that catalyses the conversion of one isomeric form of a compound to another

**ISOMERE** same as > ISOMER

**ISOMERES** > ISOMERE

**ISOMERIC** > ISOMER

**ISOMERISE** same
as > ISOMERIZE

**ISOMERISM** n existence of two or more compounds having the same molecular formula but a different arrangement of atoms within the molecule

**ISOMERIZE** vb change or cause to change from one isomer to another

**ISOMEROUS** adj having an equal number of parts or markings

**ISOMERS** > ISOMER

**ISOMETRIC** adj relating to muscular contraction without shortening of the muscle ▷ n drawing made in this way

**ISOMETRY** n rigid motion of a plane or space such that the distance between any two points before

and after this motion is unaltered

**ISOMORPH** n substance or organism that exhibits isomorphism

**ISOMORPHS** > ISOMORPH

**ISONIAZID** n soluble colourless crystalline compound used to treat tuberculosis

**ISONOME** n line on a chart connecting points of equal abundance values of a plant species sampled in different sections of an area

**ISONOMES** > ISONOME

**ISONOMIC** > ISONOMY

**ISONOMIES** > ISONOMY

**ISONOMOUS** > ISONOMY

**ISONOMY** n equality before the law of the citizens of a state

**ISOOCTANE** n colourless liquid alkane hydrocarbon produced from petroleum and used in standardizing petrol

**ISOPACH** n line on a map connecting points below which a particular rock stratum has the same thickness

**ISOPACHS** > ISOPACH

**ISOPHONE** n isogloss marking off an area in which a particular feature of pronunciation is found

**ISOPHONES** > ISOPHONE

**ISOPHOTAL** > ISOPHOTE

**ISOPHOTE** n line on a diagram or image of a galaxy, nebula, or other celestial object joining points of equal surface brightness

**ISOPHOTES** > ISOPHOTE

**ISOPLETH** n line on a map connecting places registering the same amount or ratio of some geographical or meteorological phenomenon or phenomena

**ISOPLETHS** > ISOPLETH

**ISOPOD** n type of crustacean including woodlice and pill bugs ▷ adj of this type of crustacean

**ISOPODAN** > ISOPOD

**ISOPODANS** > ISOPOD

**ISOPODOUS** > ISOPOD

**ISOPODS** > ISOPOD

**ISOPOLITY** n equality of political rights

**ISOPRENE** n colourless volatile liquid with a penetrating odour

**ISOPRENES** > ISOPRENE

**ISOPROPYL** n group of atoms

**ISOPYCNAL** n line on a map

connecting points of equal atmospheric density

**ISOPYCNIC** same
as > ISOPYCNAL

**ISOS** > ISO

**ISOSCELES** adj (of a triangle) having two sides of equal length

**ISOSMOTIC** same
as > ISOTONIC

**ISOSPIN** n internal quantum number used in the classification of elementary particles

**ISOSPINS** > ISOSPIN

**ISOSPORY** n condition of having spores of only one kind

**ISOSTACY** n state of balance in earth's crust

**ISOSTASY** n state of balance, or equilibrium, which sections of the earth's lithosphere are thought ultimately to achieve when the vertical forces upon them remain unchanged

**ISOSTATIC** > ISOSTASY

**ISOSTERIC** adj (of two different molecules) having the same number of atoms and the same number and configuration of valency electrons

**ISOTACH** n line on a map connecting points of equal wind speed

**ISOTACHS** > ISOTACH

**ISOTACTIC** adj (of a stereospecific polymer) having identical steric configurations of the groups on each asymmetric carbon atom on the chain

**ISOTHERAL** > ISOTHERE

**ISOTHERE** n line on a map linking places with the same mean summer temperature

**ISOTHERES** > ISOTHERE

**ISOTHERM** n line on a map connecting points of equal temperature

**ISOTHERMS** > ISOTHERM

**ISOTONE** n one of two or more atoms of different atomic number that contain the same number of neutrons

**ISOTONES** > ISOTONE

**ISOTONIC** adj (of two or more muscles) having equal tension

**ISOTOPE** n one of two or more atoms with the same number of protons in the nucleus but a different number of neutrons

**ISOTOPES** > ISOTOPE

**ISOTOPIC** > ISOTOPE

**ISOTOPIES** > ISOTOPE

**ISOTOPY** > ISOTOPE

**ISOTRON** *n* device for separating small quantities of isotopes by ionizing them and separating the ions by a mass spectrometer
**ISOTRONS** > ISOTRON
**ISOTROPIC** *adj* having uniform physical properties, such as elasticity or conduction in all directions
**ISOTROPY** > ISOTROPIC
**ISOTYPE** *n* presentation of statistical information in a row of diagrams
**ISOTYPES** > ISOTYPE
**ISOTYPIC** > ISOTYPE
**ISOZYME** *n* any of a set of structural variants of an enzyme occurring in different tissues in a single species
**ISOZYMES** > ISOZYME
**ISOZYMIC** > ISOZYME
**ISPAGHULA** *n* dietary fibre derived the seed husks and used as a thickener or stabilizer in the food industry
**ISSEI** *n* first-generation Japanese immigrant
**ISSEIS** > ISSEI
**ISSUABLE** *adj* capable of issuing or being issued
**ISSUABLY** > ISSUABLE
**ISSUANCE** *n* act of issuing
**ISSUANCES** > ISSUANCE
**ISSUANT** *adj* emerging or issuing
**ISSUE** *n* topic of interest or discussion ▷ *vb* make (a statement etc) publicly
**ISSUED** > ISSUE
**ISSUELESS** > ISSUE
**ISSUER** > ISSUE
**ISSUERS** > ISSUE
**ISSUES** > ISSUE
**ISSUING** > ISSUE
**ISTANA** *n* (in Malaysia) a royal palace
**ISTANAS** > ISTANA
**ISTHMI** > ISTHMUS
**ISTHMIAN** *n* inhabitant of an isthmus ▷ *adj* relating to or situated in an isthmus
**ISTHMIANS** > ISTHMIAN
**ISTHMIC** > ISTHMUS
**ISTHMOID** > ISTHMUS
**ISTHMUS** *n* narrow strip of land connecting two areas of land
**ISTHMUSES** > ISTHMUS
**ISTLE** *n* fibre obtained from various tropical American agave and yucca trees used in making carpets, cord, etc
**ISTLES** > ISTLE
**IT** *pron* refers to a nonhuman, animal, plant, or inanimate object ▷ *n* player whose turn it is

to catch the others in children's games
**ITA** *n* type of palm
**ITACISM** *n* pronunciation of the Greek letter eta as in Modern Greek
**ITACISMS** > ITACISM
**ITACONIC** as in *itaconic acid*, white colourless crystalline carboxylic acid
**ITALIC** *adj* (of printing type) sloping to the right ▷ *n* style of printing type modelled on this, chiefly used to indicate emphasis, a foreign word, etc
**ITALICISE** *same as* > ITALICIZE
**ITALICIZE** *vb* put in italics
**ITALICS** > ITALIC
**ITAS** > ITA
**ITCH** *n* skin irritation causing a desire to scratch ▷ *vb* have an itch
**ITCHED** > ITCH
**ITCHES** > ITCH
**ITCHIER** > ITCH
**ITCHIEST** > ITCH
**ITCHILY** > ITCH
**ITCHINESS** > ITCH
**ITCHING** > ITCH
**ITCHINGS** > ITCH
**ITCHWEED** *n* white hellebore
**ITCHWEEDS** > ITCHWEED
**ITCHY** > ITCH
**ITEM** *n* single thing in a list or collection ▷ *adv* likewise ▷ *vb* itemize
**ITEMED** > ITEM
**ITEMING** > ITEM
**ITEMISE** *same as* > ITEMIZE
**ITEMISED** > ITEMISE
**ITEMISER** > ITEMISE
**ITEMISERS** > ITEMISE
**ITEMISES** > ITEMISE
**ITEMISING** > ITEMISE
**ITEMIZE** *vb* make a list of
**ITEMIZED** > ITEMIZE
**ITEMIZER** > ITEMIZE
**ITEMIZERS** > ITEMIZE
**ITEMIZES** > ITEMIZE
**ITEMIZING** > ITEMIZE
**ITEMS** > ITEM
**ITERANCE** > ITERATE
**ITERANCES** > ITERATE
**ITERANT** > ITERATE
**ITERATE** *vb* repeat
**ITERATED** > ITERATE
**ITERATES** > ITERATE
**ITERATING** > ITERATE
**ITERATION** > ITERATE
**ITERATIVE** *adj* repetitious or frequent
**ITERUM** *adv* again
**ITHER** *Scot word for* > OTHER
**ITINERACY** *same as* > ITINERANCY
**ITINERANT** *adj* travelling from place to place ▷ *n* itinerant worker or other person
**ITINERARY** *n* detailed plan of a journey ▷ *adj* of or

relating to travel or routes of travel
**ITINERATE** *vb* travel from place to place
**ITS** *pron* belonging to it ▷ *adj* of or belonging to it
**ITSELF** *pron* reflexive form of it
**IURE** *adv* by law
**IVIED** *adj* covered with ivy
**IVIES** > IVY
**IVORIED** > IVORY
**IVORIES** *pl n* keys of a piano
**IVORIST** *n* worker in ivory
**IVORISTS** > IVORIST
**IVORY** *n* hard white bony substance forming the tusks of elephants ▷ *adj* yellowish-white
**IVORYBILL** *n* large American woodpecker
**IVORYLIKE** > IVORY
**IVORYWOOD** *n* yellowish-white wood of an Australian tree, used for engraving, inlaying, and turnery
**IVRESSE** *n* drunkenness
**IVRESSES** > IVRESSE
**IVY** *n* evergreen climbing plant
**IVYLIKE** > IVY
**IWI** *n* Māori tribe
**IWIS** *archaic word for* > CERTAINLY
**IXIA** *n* southern African plant of the iris family with showy ornamental funnel-shaped flowers
**IXIAS** > IXIA
**IXODIASES** > IXODIASIS
**IXODIASIS** *n* disease transmitted by ticks
**IXODID** *n* hard-bodied tick
**IXODIDS** > IXODID
**IXORA** *n* flowering shrub
**IXORAS** > IXORA
**IXTLE** *same as* > ISTLE
**IXTLES** > IXTLE
**IZAR** *n* long garment worn by Muslim women
**IZARD** *n* type of goat-antelope
**IZARDS** > IZARD
**IZARS** > IZAR
**IZVESTIA** *n* news
**IZVESTIAS** > IZVESTIA
**IZVESTIYA** *same as* > IZVESTIA
**IZZARD** *n* letter Z
**IZZARDS** > IZZARD
**IZZAT** *n* honour or prestige
**IZZATS** > IZZAT

# Jj

**JA** *interj* yes ▷ *sentence substitute* yes
**JAAP** *n* S African offensive word for a simpleton or country bumpkin
**JAAPS** > JAAP
**JAB** *vb* poke sharply ▷ *n* quick punch or poke
**JABBED** > JAB
**JABBER** *vb* talk rapidly or incoherently ▷ *n* rapid or incoherent talk
**JABBERED** > JABBER
**JABBERER** > JABBER
**JABBERERS** > JABBER
**JABBERING** > JABBER
**JABBERS** > JABBER
**JABBING** > JAB
**JABBINGLY** > JAB
**JABBLE** *vb* ripple
**JABBLED** > JABBLE
**JABBLES** > JABBLE
**JABBLING** > JABBLE
**JABERS** *interj* Irish exclamation
**JABIRU** *n* large white-and-black Australian stork
**JABIRUS** > JABIRU
**JABORANDI** *n* any of several tropical American rutaceous shrubs
**JABOT** *n* frill or ruffle on the front of a blouse or shirt
**JABOTS** > JABOT
**JABS** > JAB
**JACAL** *n* Mexican daub hut
**JACALES** > JACAL
**JACALS** > JACAL
**JACAMAR** *n* tropical American bird with an iridescent plumage
**JACAMARS** > JACAMAR
**JACANA** *n* long-legged

long-toed bird of tropical and subtropical marshy regions
**JACANAS** > JACANA
**JACARANDA** *n* tropical tree with sweet-smelling wood
**JACARE** *another name for* > CAYMAN
**JACARES** > JACARE
**JACCHUS** *n* small monkey
**JACCHUSES** > JACCHUS
**JACENT** *adj* lying
**JACINTH** *another name for* > HYACINTH
**JACINTHE** *n* hyacinth
**JACINTHES** > JACINTHE
**JACINTHS** > JACINTH
**JACK** *n* device for raising a motor vehicle or other heavy object ▷ *vb* lift or push (an object) with a jack
**JACKAL** *n* doglike wild animal of Africa and Asia ▷ *vb* behave like a jackal
**JACKALLED** > JACKAL
**JACKALS** > JACKAL
**JACKAROO** *same as* > JACKEROO
**JACKAROOS** > JACKAROO
**JACKASS** *n* fool
**JACKASSES** > JACKASS
**JACKBOOT** *n* high military boot ▷ *vb* oppress
**JACKBOOTS** > JACKBOOT
**JACKDAW** *n* black-and-grey Eurasian bird of the crow family
**JACKDAWS** > JACKDAW
**JACKED** > JACK
**JACKEEN** *n* slick self-assertive lower-class Dubliner

**JACKEENS** > JACKEEN
**JACKER** *n* labourer
**JACKEROO** *n* young male management trainee on a sheep or cattle station ▷ *vb* work as a jackeroo
**JACKEROOS** > JACKEROO
**JACKERS** > JACKER
**JACKET** *n* short coat ▷ *vb* put a jacket on (someone or something)
**JACKETED** > JACKET
**JACKETING** > JACKET
**JACKETS** > JACKET
**JACKFISH** *n* small pike fish
**JACKFRUIT** *n* tropical Asian tree
**JACKIES** > JACKY
**JACKING** > JACK
**JACKINGS** > JACK
**JACKKNIFE** *vb* (of an articulated truck) go out of control so that the trailer swings round at a sharp angle to the cab ▷ *n* large clasp knife
**JACKLEG** *n* unskilled worker
**JACKLEGS** > JACKLEG
**JACKLIGHT** > JACK
**JACKMAN** *n* retainer
**JACKMEN** > JACKMAN
**JACKPLANE** *n* large woodworking plane
**JACKPOT** *n* largest prize that may be won in a game
**JACKPOTS** > JACKPOT
**JACKROLL** *vb* gang-rape
**JACKROLLS** > JACKROLL
**JACKS** *n* game in which metal, bone, or plastic pieces are thrown and then picked up between

throws of a small ball
**JACKSCREW** *n* lifting device
**JACKSHAFT** *n* short length of shafting that transmits power from an engine or motor to a machine
**JACKSIE** *n* buttocks or anus
**JACKSIES** > JACKSIE
**JACKSMELT** *n* food fish of the North Pacific
**JACKSMITH** *n* smith who makes jacks
**JACKSNIPE** *n* small Eurasian short-billed snipe
**JACKSTAY** *n* metal rod, wire rope, or wooden batten to which an edge of a sail is fastened along a yard
**JACKSTAYS** > JACKSTAY
**JACKSTONE** > JACK
**JACKSTRAW** *n* straw mannequin
**JACKSY** *same as* > JACKSIE
**JACKY** *n* offensive word for a native Australian
**JACOBIN** *n* variety of fancy pigeon with a hood of feathers swept up over and around the head
**JACOBINS** > JACOBIN
**JACOBUS** *n* English gold coin minted in the reign of James I
**JACOBUSES** > JACOBUS
**JACONET** *n* light cotton fabric used for clothing, bandages, etc
**JACONETS** > JACONET
**JACQUARD** *n* fabric in which the design is incorporated into the weave instead of

393

being printed or dyed on

**JACQUARDS** > JACQUARD

**JACQUERIE** n peasant rising or revolt

**JACTATION** n act of boasting

**JACULATE** vb hurl

**JACULATED** > JACULATE

**JACULATES** > JACULATE

**JACULATOR** > JACULATE

**JACUZZI** n bath or pool equipped with a system of underwater jets

**JACUZZIS** > JACUZZI

**JADE** n ornamental semiprecious stone, usu dark green ▷ adj bluish-green ▷ vb exhaust or make exhausted from work or use

**JADED** adj tired and unenthusiastic

**JADEDLY** > JADED

**JADEDNESS** > JADED

**JADEITE** n usually green or white mineral, found in igneous and metamorphic rocks

**JADEITES** > JADEITE

**JADELIKE** > JADE

**JADERIES** > JADERY

**JADERY** n shrewishness

**JADES** > JADE

**JADING** > JADE

**JADISH** > JADE

**JADISHLY** > JADE

**JADITIC** > JADE

**JAEGER** n marksman in certain units of the German or Austrian armies

**JAEGERS** > JAEGER

**JAFA** n offensive name for a person from Auckland

**JAFAS** > JAFA

**JAG** n period of uncontrolled indulgence in an activity ▷ vb cut unevenly

**JAGA** n guard ▷ vb guard or watch

**JAGAED** > JAGA

**JAGAING** > JAGA

**JAGAS** > JAGA

**JAGER** same as > JAEGER

**JAGERS** > JAGER

**JAGG** same as > JAG

**JAGGARIES** > JAGGARY

**JAGGARY** same as > JAGGERY

**JAGGED** > JAG

**JAGGEDER** > JAG

**JAGGEDEST** > JAG

**JAGGEDLY** > JAG

**JAGGER** n pedlar

**JAGGERIES** > JAGGERY

**JAGGERS** > JAGGER

**JAGGERY** n coarse brown sugar made in the East Indies from the sap of the date palm

**JAGGHERY** same as > JAGGERY

**JAGGIER** > JAGGY

**JAGGIES** > JAGGY

**JAGGIEST** > JAGGY

**JAGGING** > JAG

**JAGGS** > JAG

**JAGGY** adj prickly ▷ n jagged computer image

**JAGHIR** n Indian regional governance

**JAGHIRDAR** n Indian regional governor

**JAGHIRE** n Indian regional governance

**JAGHIRES** > JAGHIRE

**JAGHIRS** > JAGHIR

**JAGIR** n Indian regional governance

**JAGIRS** > JAGIR

**JAGRA** n Hindu festival

**JAGRAS** > JAGRA

**JAGS** > JAG

**JAGUAR** n large S American spotted cat

**JAGUARS** > JAGUAR

**JAI** n victory (to)

**JAIL** n prison ▷ vb send to prison

**JAILABLE** > JAIL

**JAILBAIT** n young woman, or young women collectively, considered sexually attractive but below the age of consent

**JAILBIRD** n person who has often been in prison

**JAILBIRDS** > JAILBIRD

**JAILBREAK** n escape from jail

**JAILED** > JAIL

**JAILER** n person in charge of a jail

**JAILERESS** > JAILER

**JAILERS** > JAILER

**JAILHOUSE** n jail

**JAILING** > JAIL

**JAILLESS** > JAIL

**JAILOR** same as > JAILER

**JAILORESS** > JAILOR

**JAILORS** > JAILOR

**JAILS** > JAIL

**JAIS** > JAI

**JAK** > JACK

**JAKE** adj slang word meaning all right

**JAKES** n human excrement

**JAKESES** > JAKES

**JAKEY** n derogatory Scots word for a homeless alcoholic

**JAKEYS** > JAKEY

**JAKFRUIT** same as > JACKFRUIT

**JAKFRUITS** > JAKFRUIT

**JAKS** > JACK

**JAL** as in Ganga jal sacred water from the Ganges

**JALAP** n Mexican convolvulaceous plant

**JALAPENO** n very hot type of green chilli pepper, used esp in Mexican cookery

**JALAPENOS** > JALAPENO

**JALAPIC** > JALAP

**JALAPIN** n purgative resin

**JALAPINS** > JALAPIN

**JALAPS** > JALAP

**JALOP** same as > JALAP

**JALOPIES** > JALOPY

**JALOPPIES** > JALOPPY

**JALOPPY** same as > JALOPY

**JALOPS** > JALOP

**JALOPY** n old car

**JALOUSE** vb suspect

**JALOUSED** > JALOUSE

**JALOUSES** > JALOUSE

**JALOUSIE** n window blind or shutter constructed from angled slats of wood, plastic, etc

**JALOUSIED** > JALOUSIE

**JALOUSIES** > JALOUSIE

**JALOUSING** > JALOUSE

**JAM** vb pack tightly into a place ▷ n fruit preserve or hold-up of traffic

**JAMADAR** n Indian army officer

**JAMADARS** > JAMADAR

**JAMB** n side post of a door or window frame ▷ vb climb up a crack in rock

**JAMBALAYA** n Creole dish made of shrimps, ham, rice, onions, etc

**JAMBART** same as > GREAVE

**JAMBARTS** > JAMBART

**JAMBE** same as > JAMB

**JAMBEAU** another word for > GREAVE

**JAMBEAUX** > JAMBEAU

**JAMBED** > JAMB

**JAMBEE** n light cane

**JAMBEES** > JAMBEE

**JAMBER** same as > GREAVE

**JAMBERS** > JAMBER

**JAMBES** > JAMBE

**JAMBEUX** > JAMBEAU

**JAMBIER** n greave

**JAMBIERS** > JAMBIER

**JAMBING** > JAMB

**JAMBIYA** n curved dagger

**JAMBIYAH** same as > JAMBIYA

**JAMBIYAHS** > JAMBIYAH

**JAMBIYAS** > JAMBIYA

**JAMBO** sentence substitute E African salutation

**JAMBOK** same as > SJAMBOK

**JAMBOKKED** > JAMBOK

**JAMBOKS** > JAMBOK

**JAMBOLAN** n Asian tree

**JAMBOLANA** same as > JAMBOLAN

**JAMBOLANS** > JAMBOLAN

**JAMBONE** n type of play in the card game euchre

**JAMBONES** > JAMBONE

**JAMBOOL** same as > JAMBOLAN

**JAMBOOLS** > JAMBOOL

**JAMBOREE** n large gathering or celebration

**JAMBOREES** > JAMBOREE

**JAMBOS** > JAMBO

**JAMBS** > JAMB

**JAMBU** same as > JAMBOLAN

**JAMBUL** same as > JAMBOLAN

**JAMBULS** > JAMBUL

**JAMBUS** > JAMBU

**JAMDANI** n patterned

muslin

**JAMDANIS** > JAMDANI

**JAMES** n jemmy

**JAMESES** > JAMES

**JAMJAR** n container for preserves

**JAMJARS** > JAMJAR

**JAMLIKE** > JAM

**JAMMABLE** > JAM

**JAMMED** > JAM

**JAMMER** > JAM

**JAMMERS** > JAM

**JAMMIER** > JAMMY

**JAMMIES** informal word for > PYJAMAS

**JAMMIEST** > JAMMY

**JAMMING** > JAM

**JAMMY** adj lucky

**JAMPACKED** adj very crowded

**JAMPAN** n type of sedan chair used in India

**JAMPANEE** n jampan bearer

**JAMPANEES** > JAMPANEE

**JAMPANI** same as > JAMPANEE

**JAMPANIS** > JAMPANI

**JAMPANS** > JAMPAN

**JAMPOT** n container for preserves

**JAMPOTS** > JAMPOT

**JAMS** > JAM

**JANDAL** n sandal with a strap between the toes

**JANDALS** > JANDAL

**JANE** n girl or woman

**JANES** > JANE

**JANGLE** vb (cause to) make a harsh ringing noise ▷ n harsh ringing noise

**JANGLED** > JANGLE

**JANGLER** > JANGLE

**JANGLERS** > JANGLE

**JANGLES** > JANGLE

**JANGLIER** > JANGLY

**JANGLIEST** > JANGLY

**JANGLING** > JANGLE

**JANGLINGS** > JANGLE

**JANGLY** adj making a jangling sound

**JANIFORM** adj with two faces

**JANISARY** same as > JANISSARY

**JANISSARY** n infantryman in the Turkish army, originally a member of the sovereign's personal guard, from the 14th to the early 19th century

**JANITOR** n caretaker of a school or other building

**JANITORS** > JANITOR

**JANITRESS** > JANITOR

**JANITRIX** > JANITOR

**JANIZAR** same as > JANISSARY

**JANIZARS** > JANIZAR

**JANIZARY** same as > JANISSARY

**JANKER** n device for transporting logs

**JANKERS** > JANKER

**JANN** n lesser jinn

JANNIES > JANNY
JANNOCK *same as* > JONNOCK
JANNOCKS > JANNOCK
JANNS > JANN
JANNY *n* janitor
JANSKY *n* unit of flux density used predominantly in radio and infrared astronomy
JANSKYS > JANSKY
JANTEE *archaic version of* > JAUNTY
JANTIER > JANTY
JANTIES > JANTY
JANTIEST > JANTY
JANTY *n* petty officer ▷ *adj* (in archaic usage) jaunty
JAP *vb* splash
JAPAN *n* very hard varnish, usu black ▷ *vb* cover with this varnish ▷ *adj* relating to or varnished with japan
JAPANISE *same as* > JAPANIZE
JAPANISED > JAPANISE
JAPANISES > JAPANISE
JAPANIZE *vb* make Japanese
JAPANIZED > JAPANIZE
JAPANIZES > JAPANIZE
JAPANNED > JAPAN
JAPANNER > JAPAN
JAPANNERS > JAPAN
JAPANNING > JAPAN
JAPANS > JAPAN
JAPE *n* joke or prank ▷ *vb* joke or jest (about)
JAPED > JAPE
JAPER > JAPE
JAPERIES > JAPE
JAPERS > JAPE
JAPERY > JAPE
JAPES > JAPE
JAPING > JAPE
JAPINGLY > JAPE
JAPINGS > JAPE
JAPONICA *n* shrub with red flowers
JAPONICAS > JAPONICA
JAPPED > JAP
JAPPING > JAP
JAPS > JAP
JAR *n* wide-mouthed container, usu round and made of glass ▷ *vb* have a disturbing or unpleasant effect
JARARACA *n* South American snake
JARARACAS > JARARACA
JARARAKA *same as* > JARARACA
JARARAKAS > JARARAKA
JARFUL *same as* > JAR
JARFULS > JARFUL
JARGON *n* specialized technical language of a particular subject ▷ *vb* use or speak in jargon
JARGONED > JARGON
JARGONEER *n* user of jargon
JARGONEL *n* pear
JARGONELS > JARGONEL
JARGONING > JARGON

JARGONISE *same as* > JARGONIZE
JARGONISH > JARGON
JARGONIST > JARGON
JARGONIZE *vb* render into jargon
JARGONS > JARGON
JARGONY > JARGON
JARGOON *same as* > JARGON
JARGOONS > JARGOON
JARHEAD *n* US Marine
JARHEADS > JARHEAD
JARINA *n* South American palm tree
JARINAS > JARINA
JARK *n* seal or pass
JARKMAN *n* forger of passes or licences
JARKMEN > JARKMAN
JARKS > JARK
JARL *n* Scandinavian chieftain or noble
JARLDOM *n* JARL
JARLDOMS > JARL
JARLS > JARL
JARLSBERG *n* Norwegian cheese
JAROOL *n* Indian tree
JAROOLS > JAROOL
JAROSITE *n* yellow to brown mineral
JAROSITES > JAROSITE
JAROVISE *same as* > JAROVIZE
JAROVISED > JAROVISE
JAROVISES > JAROVISE
JAROVIZE *vb* vernalize
JAROVIZED > JAROVIZE
JAROVIZES > JAROVIZE
JARP *vb* strike or smash, esp to break the shell of (an egg) at Easter
JARPED > JARP
JARPING > JARP
JARPS > JARP
JARRAH *n* Australian eucalypt yielding valuable timber
JARRAHS > JARRAH
JARRED > JAR
JARRING > JAR
JARRINGLY > JAR
JARRINGS > JAR
JARS > JAR
JARSFUL > JARFUL
JARTA *n* heart
JARTAS > JARTA
JARUL *variant of* > JAROOL
JARULS > JARUL
JARVEY *n* hackney coachman
JARVEYS > JARVEY
JARVIE *same as* > JARVEY
JARVIES > JARVIE
JASEY *n* wig
JASEYS > JASEY
JASIES > JASEY
JASMIN *same as* > JASMINE
JASMINE *n* shrub with sweet-smelling yellow or white flowers
JASMINES > JASMINE
JASMINS > JASMIN
JASP *another word*

*for* > JASPER
JASPE *adj* resembling jasper ▷ *n* subtly striped woven fabric
JASPER *n* red, yellow, dark green, or brown variety of quartz
JASPERISE *same as* > JASPERIZE
JASPERIZE *vb* turn into jasper
JASPEROUS > JASPER
JASPERS > JASPER
JASPERY > JASPER
JASPES > JASPE
JASPIDEAN > JASPER
JASPILITE *n* rock like jasper
JASPIS *archaic word for* > JASPER
JASPISES > JASPIS
JASPS > JASP
JASS *obsolete variant of* > JAZZ
JASSES > JASS
JASSID *n* leafhopper
JASSIDS > JASSID
JASY *n* wig
JATAKA *n* text describing the birth of Buddha
JATAKAS > JATAKA
JATO *n* jet-assisted takeoff
JATOS > JATO
JAUK *vb* dawdle
JAUKED > JAUK
JAUKING > JAUK
JAUKS > JAUK
JAUNCE *vb* prance
JAUNCED > JAUNCE
JAUNCES > JAUNCE
JAUNCING > JAUNCE
JAUNDICE *n* disease marked by yellowness of the skin ▷ *vb* distort (the judgment, etc) adversely
JAUNDICED > JAUNDICE
JAUNDICES > JAUNDICE
JAUNSE *same as* > JAUNCE
JAUNSED > JAUNSE
JAUNSES > JAUNSE
JAUNSING > JAUNSE
JAUNT *n* short journey for pleasure ▷ *vb* make such a journey
JAUNTED > JAUNT
JAUNTEE *old spelling of* > JAUNTY
JAUNTIE *old spelling of* > JAUNTY
JAUNTIER > JAUNTY
JAUNTIES > JAUNTY
JAUNTIEST > JAUNTY
JAUNTILY > JAUNTY
JAUNTING > JAUNT
JAUNTS > JAUNT
JAUNTY *adj* sprightly and cheerful ▷ *n* master-at-arms on a naval ship
JAUP *same as* > JARP
JAUPED > JAUP
JAUPING > JAUP
JAUPS > JAUP
JAVA *n* coffee or a variety of it

JAVAS > JAVA
JAVEL *as in javel water* aqueous solution containing sodium hypochlorite and some sodium chloride, used as a bleach and disinfectant
JAVELIN *n* light spear thrown in sports competitions ▷ *vb* spear with a javelin
JAVELINA *n* collared peccary
JAVELINAS > JAVELINA
JAVELINED > JAVELIN
JAVELINS > JAVELIN
JAVELS > JAVEL
JAW *n* one of the bones in which the teeth are set ▷ *vb* talk lengthily
JAWAN *n* (in India) a soldier
JAWANS > JAWAN
JAWARI *n* variety of sorghum
JAWARIS > JAWARI
JAWBATION *n* scolding
JAWBONE *n* lower jaw of a person or animal ▷ *vb* try to persuade or bring pressure to bear (on) by virtue of one's high office or position, esp in urging compliance with official policy
JAWBONED > JAWBONE
JAWBONER > JAWBONE
JAWBONERS > JAWBONE
JAWBONES > JAWBONE
JAWBONING > JAWBONE
JAWBOX *n* metal sink
JAWBOXES > JAWBOX
JAWED > JAW
JAWFALL *n* depression
JAWFALLS > JAWFALL
JAWHOLE *n* cesspit
JAWHOLES > JAWHOLE
JAWING > JAW
JAWINGS > JAW
JAWLESS > JAW
JAWLIKE > JAW
JAWLINE *n* outline of the jaw
JAWLINES > JAWLINE
JAWS > JAW
JAXIE *same as* > JACKSIE
JAXIES > JAXIE
JAXY *same as* > JACKSIE
JAY *n* bird with a pinkish body and blue-and-black wings
JAYBIRD *n* jay
JAYBIRDS > JAYBIRD
JAYGEE *n* lieutenant junior grade in the US army
JAYGEES > JAYGEE
JAYHAWKER *n* Unionist guerrilla in US Civil War
JAYS > JAY
JAYVEE *n* junior varsity sports team
JAYVEES > JAYVEE
JAYWALK *vb* cross or walk in a street recklessly or illegally

**JAYWALKED** > JAYWALK
**JAYWALKER** > JAYWALK
**JAYWALKS** > JAYWALK
**JAZERANT** n coat of metal plates sewn onto cloth
**JAZERANTS** > JAZERANT
**JAZIES** > JAZY
**JAZY** n wig
**JAZZ** n kind of music with an exciting rhythm, usu involving improvisation ▷ vb play or dance to jazz music
**JAZZBO** n jazz musician or fan
**JAZZBOS** > JAZZBO
**JAZZED** > JAZZ
**JAZZER** > JAZZ
**JAZZERS** > JAZZ
**JAZZES** > JAZZ
**JAZZIER** > JAZZY
**JAZZIEST** > JAZZY
**JAZZILY** > JAZZY
**JAZZINESS** > JAZZY
**JAZZING** > JAZZ
**JAZZLIKE** > JAZZ
**JAZZMAN** > JAZZ
**JAZZMEN** > JAZZ
**JAZZY** adj flashy or showy
**JEALOUS** adj fearful of losing a partner or possession to a rival
**JEALOUSE** vb be jealous of
**JEALOUSED** > JEALOUSE
**JEALOUSES** > JEALOUSE
**JEALOUSLY** > JEALOUS
**JEALOUSY** n state of or an instance of feeling jealous
**JEAN** n tough twill-weave cotton fabric used for hard-wearing trousers, overalls, etc
**JEANED** adj wearing jeans
**JEANETTE** n light jean cloth
**JEANETTES** > JEANETTE
**JEANS** pl n casual denim trousers
**JEAT** n jet
**JEATS** > JEAT
**JEBEL** n hill or mountain in an Arab country
**JEBELS** > JEBEL
**JEDI** n person claiming to live according to a philosophy based on that of the fictional Jedi, from the Star Wars films
**JEDIS** > JEDI
**JEE** variant of > GEE
**JEED** > JEE
**JEEING** > JEE
**JEEL** vb make into jelly
**JEELED** > JEEL
**JEELIE** same as > JEELY
**JEELIED** > JEELY
**JEELIEING** > JEELIE
**JEELIES** > JEELY
**JEELING** > JEEL
**JEELS** > JEEL
**JEELY** n jelly ▷ vb make into jelly
**JEELYING** > JEELY
**JEEP** n small military four-

wheel drive road vehicle ▷ vb travel in a jeep
**JEEPED** > JEEP
**JEEPERS** interj mild exclamation of surprise
**JEEPING** > JEEP
**JEEPNEY** n Filipino bus converted from a jeep
**JEEPNEYS** > JEEPNEY
**JEEPS** > JEEP
**JEER** vb scoff or deride ▷ n cry of derision
**JEERED** > JEER
**JEERER** > JEER
**JEERERS** > JEER
**JEERING** > JEER
**JEERINGLY** > JEER
**JEERINGS** > JEER
**JEERS** > JEER
**JEES** > JEE
**JEEZ** interj expression of surprise or irritation
**JEFE** n (in Spanish-speaking countries) a military or political leader
**JEFES** > JEFE
**JEFF** vb downsize or close down (an organization)
**JEFFED** > JEFF
**JEFFING** > JEFF
**JEFFS** > JEFF
**JEHAD** same as > JIHAD
**JEHADI** same as > JIHADI
**JEHADIS** > JEHADI
**JEHADISM** same as > JIHADISM
**JEHADISMS** > JEHADISM
**JEHADIST** > JEHADISM
**JEHADISTS** > JEHADISM
**JEHADS** > JEHAD
**JEHU** n fast driver
**JEHUS** > JEHU
**JEJUNA** > JEJUNUM
**JEJUNAL** > JEJUNUM
**JEJUNE** adj simple or naive
**JEJUNELY** > JEJUNE
**JEJUNITY** > JEJUNE
**JEJUNUM** n part of the small intestine between the duodenum and the ileum
**JELAB** same as > JELLABA
**JELABS** > JELAB
**JELL** vb form into a jelly-like substance
**JELLABA** n loose robe with a hood, worn by some Arab men
**JELLABAH** same as > JELLABA
**JELLABAHS** > JELLABAH
**JELLABAS** > JELLABA
**JELLED** > JELL
**JELLIED** > JELLY
**JELLIES** > JELLY
**JELLIFIED** > JELLIFY
**JELLIFIES** > JELLIFY
**JELLIFY** vb make into or become jelly
**JELLING** > JELL
**JELLO** n (in US English) fruit-flavoured clear dessert set with gelatine
**JELLOS** > JELLO
**JELLS** > JELL
**JELLY** n fruit-flavoured

clear dessert set with gelatine ▷ vb jellify
**JELLYBEAN** n bean-shaped sweet with a brightly coloured coating around a gelatinous filling
**JELLYFISH** n small jelly-like sea animal
**JELLYING** > JELLY
**JELLYLIKE** > JELLY
**JELLYROLL** n type of cake
**JELUTONG** n Malaysian tree
**JELUTONGS** > JELUTONG
**JEMADAR** n native junior officer belonging to a locally raised regiment serving as mercenaries in India, esp with the British Army (until 1947)
**JEMADARS** > JEMADAR
**JEMBE** n hoe
**JEMBES** > JEMBE
**JEMIDAR** same as > JEMADAR
**JEMIDARS** > JEMIDAR
**JEMIMA** n boot with elastic sides
**JEMIMAS** > JEMIMA
**JEMMIED** > JEMMY
**JEMMIER** > JEMMY
**JEMMIES** > JEMMY
**JEMMIEST** > JEMMY
**JEMMINESS** > JEMMY
**JEMMY** n short steel crowbar used by burglars ▷ vb prise (something) open with a jemmy ▷ adj neat
**JEMMYING** > JEMMY
**JENNET** n female donkey or ass
**JENNETING** n early-season apple
**JENNETS** > JENNET
**JENNIES** > JENNY
**JENNY** same as > JENNET
**JEOFAIL** n oversight in legal pleading
**JEOFAILS** > JEOFAIL
**JEON** n Korean pancake
**JEOPARD** vb put in jeopardy
**JEOPARDED** > JEOPARD
**JEOPARDER** > JEOPARD
**JEOPARDS** > JEOPARD
**JEOPARDY** n danger ▷ vb put in jeopardy
**JEQUERITY** same as > JEQUIRITY
**JEQUIRITY** n seed of the Indian liquorice
**JERBIL** variant spelling of > GERBIL
**JERBILS** > JERBIL
**JERBOA** n small mouselike rodent with long hind legs
**JERBOAS** > JERBOA
**JEREED** same as > JERID
**JEREEDS** > JEREED
**JEREMIAD** n long mournful complaint
**JEREMIADS** > JEREMIAD
**JEREPIGO** n sweet fortified wine similar to port
**JEREPIGOS** > JEREPIGO
**JERFALCON** variant

of > GYRFALCON
**JERID** n wooden javelin used in Muslim countries in military displays on horseback
**JERIDS** > JERID
**JERK** vb move or throw abruptly ▷ n sharp or abruptly stopped movement
**JERKED** > JERK
**JERKER** > JERK
**JERKERS** > JERK
**JERKIER** > JERKY
**JERKIES** > JERKY
**JERKIEST** > JERKY
**JERKILY** > JERKY
**JERKIN** n sleeveless jacket
**JERKINESS** > JERKY
**JERKING** > JERK
**JERKINGLY** > JERK
**JERKINGS** > JERK
**JERKINS** > JERKIN
**JERKS** > JERK
**JERKWATER** adj inferior and insignificant
**JERKY** adj characterized by jerks ▷ n type of cured meat
**JEROBOAM** n wine bottle holding the equivalent of four normal bottles (approximately 104 ounces)
**JEROBOAMS** > JEROBOAM
**JERQUE** vb search for contraband
**JERQUED** > JERQUE
**JERQUER** > JERQUE
**JERQUERS** > JERQUE
**JERQUES** > JERQUE
**JERQUING** > JERQUE
**JERQUINGS** > JERQUE
**JERREED** variant spelling of > JERID
**JERREEDS** > JERREED
**JERRICAN** n five-gallon fuel can
**JERRICANS** > JERRICAN
**JERRID** n blunt javelin
**JERRIDS** > JERRID
**JERRIES** > JERRY
**JERRY** short for > JEROBOAM
**JERRYCAN** n flat-sided can used for storing or transporting liquids, esp motor fuel
**JERRYCANS** > JERRYCAN
**JERSEY** n knitted jumper ▷ vb pull an ice-hockey player's jersey over his or her head
**JERSEYED** > JERSEY
**JERSEYING** > JERSEY
**JERSEYS** > JERSEY
**JESS** n short leather strap, one end of which is permanently attached to the leg of a hawk or falcon while the other can be attached to a leash ▷ vb put jesses on (a hawk or falcon)
**JESSAMIES** > JESSAMY

JESSAMINE *same as* >JASMINE

JESSAMY *n* fop

JESSANT *adj* emerging

JESSE *same as* >JESS

JESSED >JESS

JESSERANT *n* coat of metal plates sewn onto cloth

JESSES >JESS

JESSIE *n* effeminate, weak, or cowardly boy or man

JESSIES >JESSIE

JESSING >JESS

JEST *vb* joke ▷ *n* something done or said for amusement

JESTBOOK *n* book of amusing stories

JESTBOOKS >JESTBOOK

JESTED >JEST

JESTEE *n* person about whom a joke is made

JESTEES >JESTEE

JESTER *n* professional clown at court

JESTERS >JESTER

JESTFUL >JEST

JESTING >JEST

JESTINGLY >JEST

JESTINGS >JEST

JESTS >JEST

JESUIT *n* offensive term for a person given to subtle and equivocating arguments

JESUITIC >JESUIT

JESUITISM >JESUIT

JESUITRY >JESUIT

JESUITS >JESUIT

JESUS *n* French paper size

JET *n* aircraft driven by jet propulsion ▷ *vb* fly by jet aircraft

JETBEAD *n* ornamental shrub

JETBEADS >JETBEAD

JETE *n* step in which the dancer springs from one leg and lands on the other

JETES >JETE

JETFOIL *n* type of hydrofoil that is propelled by water jets

JETFOILS >JETFOIL

JETLAG *n* tiredness caused by crossing timezones in jet flight

JETLAGS >JETLAG

JETLIKE >JET

JETLINER *n* commercial airliner powered by jet engines

JETLINERS >JETLINER

JETON *n* gambling chip

JETONS >JETON

JETPLANE *n* aircraft powered by one or more jet engines

JETPLANES >JETPLANE

JETPORT *n* airport for jet planes

JETPORTS >JETPORT

JETS >JET

JETSAM *n* goods thrown overboard to lighten a ship

JETSAMS >JETSAM

JETSOM *same as* >JETSAM

JETSOMS >JETSOM

JETSON *archaic form of* >JETSAM

JETSONS >JETSON

JETSTREAM *n* narrow belt of high-altitude winds moving east at high speeds

JETTATURA *n* evil eye

JETTED >JET

JETTIED >JETTY

JETTIER >JETTY

JETTIES >JETTY

JETTIEST >JETTY

JETTINESS >JETTY

JETTING >JET

JETTISON *vb* abandon

JETTISONS >JETTISON

JETTON *n* counter or token, esp a chip used in such gambling games as roulette

JETTONS >JETTON

JETTY *n* small pier ▷ *adj* of or resembling jet, esp in colour or polish ▷ *vb* equip with a cantilevered floor

JETTYING >JETTY

JETWAY *n* tradename of a mobile elevated gangway connecting an aircraft to a departure gate, allowing passengers to board and disembark

JETWAYS >JETWAY

JEU *n* game

JEUNE *adj* young

JEUX >JEU

JEW *vb* obsolete offensive word for haggle ▷ *n* obsolete offensive word for a haggler

JEWED >JEW

JEWEL *n* precious or semiprecious stone ▷ *vb* fit or decorate with a jewel or jewels

JEWELED >JEWEL

JEWELER *same as* >JEWELLER

JEWELERS >JEWELER

JEWELFISH *n* beautifully coloured fish popular in aquaria

JEWELING >JEWEL

JEWELLED >JEWEL

JEWELLER *n* dealer in jewels

JEWELLERS >JEWELLER

JEWELLERY *n* objects decorated with precious stones

JEWELLIKE >JEWEL

JEWELLING >JEWEL

JEWELRIES >JEWELRY

JEWELRY *same as* >JEWELLERY

JEWELS >JEWEL

JEWELWEED *n* small bushy plant

JEWFISH *n* freshwater catfish

JEWFISHES >JEWFISH

JEWIE *n* jewfish

JEWIES >JEWIE

JEWING >JEW

JEWS >JEW

JEZAIL *n* Afghan musket

JEZAILS >JEZAIL

JEZEBEL *n* shameless or scheming woman

JEZEBELS >JEZEBEL

JHALA *n* Indian musical style

JHALAS >JHALA

JHATKA *n* slaughter of animals for food according to Sikh law

JHATKAS >JHATKA

JIAO *n* Chinese currency unit

JIAOS >JIAO

JIB *same as* >JIBE

JIBB *same as* >JIBE

JIBBAH *same as* >JUBBAH

JIBBAHS >JIBBAH

JIBBED >JIBB

JIBBER *variant of* >GIBBER

JIBBERED >JIBBER

JIBBERING >JIBBER

JIBBERS >JIBBER

JIBBING >JIBB

JIBBINGS >JIBB

JIBBONS *pl n* spring onions

JIBBOOM *n* spar forming an extension of the bowsprit

JIBBOOMS >JIBBOOM

JIBBS >JIBB

JIBE *vb* taunt or jeer ▷ *n* insulting or taunting remark

JIBED >JIBE

JIBER >JIBE

JIBERS >JIBE

JIBES >JIBE

JIBING >JIBE

JIBINGLY >JIBE

JIBS >JIB

JICAMA *n* pale brown turnip with crisp sweet flesh, originating in Mexico

JICAMAS >JICAMA

JICKAJOG *vb* engage in sexual intercourse

JICKAJOGS >JICKAJOG

JIFF *same as* >JIFFY

JIFFIES >JIFFY

JIFFS >JIFF

JIFFY *n* very short period of time

JIG *n* type of lively dance ▷ *vb* dance a jig

JIGABOO *n* offensive term for a Black person

JIGABOOS >JIGABOO

JIGAJIG *vb* engage in sexual intercourse

JIGAJIGS >JIGAJIG

JIGAJOG *variant of* >JIGAJIG

JIGAJOGS >JIGAJOG

JIGAMAREE *n* thing

JIGGED >JIG

JIGGER *n* small whisky glass ▷ *vb* interfere or alter

JIGGERED >JIGGER

JIGGERING >JIGGER

JIGGERS >JIGGER

JIGGIER >JIGGY

JIGGIEST >JIGGY

JIGGING >JIG

JIGGINGS >JIG

JIGGISH >JIG

JIGGLE *vb* move up and down with short jerky movements ▷ *n* short jerky motion

JIGGLED >JIGGLE

JIGGLES >JIGGLE

JIGGLIER >JIGGLE

JIGGLIEST >JIGGLE

JIGGLING >JIGGLE

JIGGLY >JIGGLE

JIGGUMBOB *n* thing

JIGGY *adj* resembling a jig

JIGJIG *variant of* >JIGAJIG

JIGJIGGED >JIGJIG

JIGJIGS >JIGJIG

JIGLIKE >JIG

JIGOT *same as* >GIGOT

JIGOTS >JIGOT

JIGS >JIG

JIGSAW *n* picture cut into interlocking pieces, which the user tries to fit together again ▷ *vb* cut with a jigsaw

JIGSAWED >JIGSAW

JIGSAWING >JIGSAW

JIGSAWN >JIGSAW

JIGSAWS >JIGSAW

JIHAD *n* Islamic holy war against unbelievers

JIHADI *n* person who takes part in a jihad

JIHADIS >JIHADI

JIHADISM *n* Islamic fundamentalist movement that favours the pursuit of jihads in defence of the Islamic faith

JIHADISMS >JIHADISM

JIHADIST >JIHADISM

JIHADISTS >JIHADISM

JIHADS >JIHAD

JILBAB *n* long robe worn by Muslim women

JILBABS >JILBAB

JILGIE *n* freshwater crayfish

JILGIES >JILGIE

JILL *variant spelling of* >GILL

JILLAROO *n* female jackeroo

JILLAROOS >JILLAROO

JILLET *n* wanton woman

JILLETS >JILLET

JILLFLIRT *same as* >JILLET

JILLION *n* extremely large number or amount

JILLIONS >JILLION

JILLIONTH >JILLION

JILLS >JILL

JILT *vb* leave or reject (one's lover) ▷ *n* woman

who jilts a lover
JILTED >JILT
JILTER >JILT
JILTERS >JILT
JILTING >JILT
JILTS >JILT
JIMCRACK same as >GIMCRACK
JIMCRACKS >JIMCRACK
JIMINY interj expression of surprise
JIMJAM >JIMJAMS
JIMJAMS pl n state of nervous tension, excitement, or anxiety
JIMMIE same as >JIMMY
JIMMIED >JIMMY
JIMMIES >JIMMY
JIMMINY interj expression of surprise
JIMMY same as >JEMMY
JIMMYING >JIMMY
JIMP adj handsome
JIMPER >JIMP
JIMPEST >JIMP
JIMPIER >JIMPY
JIMPIEST >JIMPY
JIMPLY adv neatly
JIMPNESS >JIMP
JIMPY adj neat and tidy
JIMSON as in jimson weed type of poisonous plant with white flowers and shiny fruits
JIN n Chinese unit of weight
JINGAL n swivel-mounted gun
JINGALL same as >JINGAL
JINGALLS >JINGAL
JINGALS >JINGAL
JINGBANG n entirety of something
JINGBANGS >JINGBANG
JINGKO same as >GINGKO
JINGKOES >JINGKO
JINGLE n catchy verse or song used in a radio or television advert ▷ vb (cause to) make a gentle ringing sound
JINGLED >JINGLE
JINGLER >JINGLE
JINGLERS >JINGLE
JINGLES >JINGLE
JINGLET n sleigh-bell clapper
JINGLETS >JINGLET
JINGLIER >JINGLE
JINGLIEST >JINGLE
JINGLING >JINGLE
JINGLY >JINGLE
JINGO n loud and bellicose patriot; chauvinism
JINGOES >JINGO
JINGOISH >JINGO
JINGOISM n aggressive nationalism
JINGOISMS >JINGOISM
JINGOIST >JINGOISM
JINGOISTS >JINGOISM
JINJILI n type of sesame
JINJILIS >JINJILI
JINK vb move quickly or

jerkily in order to dodge someone ▷ n jinking movement
JINKED >JINK
JINKER n vehicle for transporting timber, consisting of a tractor and two sets of wheels for supporting the logs
JINKERS >JINKER
JINKING >JINK
JINKS >JINK
JINN >JINNI
JINNE interj South African exclamation expressing surprise, admiration, shock, etc
JINNEE same as >JINNI
JINNI n spirit in Muslim mythology
JINNIS >JINNI
JINNS >JINNI
JINRIKSHA same as >RICKSHAW
JINS >JIN
JINX n person or thing bringing bad luck ▷ vb be or put a jinx on
JINXED >JINX
JINXES >JINX
JINXING >JINX
JIPIJAPA n palmlike Central and South American plant whose fanlike leaves are bleached for making panama hats
JIPIJAPAS >JIPIJAPA
JIPYAPA same as >JIPIJAPA
JIPYAPAS >JIPYAPA
JIRBLE vb pour carelessly
JIRBLED >JIRBLE
JIRBLES >JIRBLE
JIRBLING >JIRBLE
JIRD n gerbil
JIRDS >JIRD
JIRGA n Afghan council
JIRGAS >JIRGA
JIRKINET n bodice
JIRKINETS >JIRKINET
JIRRE same as >JINNE
JISM slang word for >SEMEN
JISMS >JISM
JISSOM slang word for >SEMEN
JISSOMS >JISSOM
JITNEY n small bus that carries passengers for a low price, originally five cents
JITNEYS >JITNEY
JITTER vb be anxious or nervous
JITTERBUG n fast jerky American dance that was popular in the 1940s ▷ vb dance the jitterbug
JITTERED >JITTER
JITTERIER >JITTERY
JITTERING >JITTER
JITTERS >JITTER
JITTERY adj nervous
JIUJITSU variant spelling of >JUJITSU
JIUJITSUS >JIUJITSU

JIUJUTSU same as >JUJITSU
JIUJUTSUS >JIUJUTSU
JIVE n lively dance of the 1940s and '50s ▷ vb dance the jive
JIVEASS adj misleading or phoney
JIVED >JIVE
JIVER >JIVE
JIVERS >JIVE
JIVES >JIVE
JIVEY >JIVE
JIVIER >JIVE
JIVIEST >JIVE
JIVING >JIVE
JIVY >JIVE
JIZ n wig
JIZZ n term for the total combination of characteristics that serve to identify a particular species of bird or plant
JIZZES >JIZZ
JNANA n type of yoga
JNANAS >JNANA
JO n Scots word for sweetheart
JOANNA n piano
JOANNAS >JOANNA
JOANNES same as >JOHANNES
JOANNESES >JOANNES
JOB n occupation or paid employment ▷ vb work at casual jobs
JOBATION n scolding
JOBATIONS >JOBATION
JOBBED >JOB
JOBBER n person who jobs
JOBBERIES >JOBBERY
JOBBERS >JOBBER
JOBBERY n practice of making private profit out of a public office
JOBBIE n piece of excrement
JOBBIES >JOBBIE
JOBBING adj doing individual jobs for payment ▷ n act of seeking work
JOBBINGS >JOBBING
JOBCENTRE n office where unemployed people can find out about job vacancies
JOBE vb scold
JOBED >JOBE
JOBERNOWL n stupid person
JOBES >JOBE
JOBHOLDER n person who has a job
JOBING >JOBE
JOBLESS pl n unemployed people ▷ adj unemployed
JOBNAME n title of position
JOBNAMES >JOBNAME
JOBS >JOB
JOBSEEKER n person looking for employment
JOBSHARE n arrangement in which two or more people divide the duties

and payment for one position between them, working at different times
JOBSHARES >JOBSHARE
JOBSWORTH n person in a position of minor authority who invokes the letter of the law in order to avoid any action requiring initiative, cooperation, etc
JOCK n athlete
JOCKETTE n female athlete
JOCKETTES >JOCKETTE
JOCKEY n person who rides horses in races, esp as a profession or for hire ▷ vb ride (a horse) in a race
JOCKEYED >JOCKEY
JOCKEYING >JOCKEY
JOCKEYISH n skills and practices of jockeys
JOCKEYS >JOCKEY
JOCKNEY n Scots dialect influenced by cockney speech patterns
JOCKNEYS >JOCKNEY
JOCKO n chimpanzee
JOCKOS >JOCKO
JOCKS >JOCK
JOCKSTRAP n belt with a pouch to support the genitals, worn by male athletes
JOCKTELEG n clasp knife
JOCO adj relaxed
JOCOSE adj playful or humorous
JOCOSELY >JOCOSE
JOCOSITY >JOCOSE
JOCULAR adj fond of joking
JOCULARLY >JOCULAR
JOCULATOR n joker
JOCUND adj merry or cheerful
JOCUNDITY >JOCUND
JOCUNDLY >JOCUND
JODEL same as >YODEL
JODELLED >JODEL
JODELLING >JODEL
JODELS >JODEL
JODHPUR as in jodphur boots ankle-length leather riding boots
JODHPURS pl n riding breeches, loose-fitting around the hips and tight-fitting from the thighs to the ankles
JOE same as >JO
JOES >JOE
JOEY n young kangaroo
JOEYS >JOEY
JOG vb run at a gentle pace, esp for exercise ▷ n slow run
JOGGED >JOG
JOGGER n person who runs at a jog trot over some distance for exercise, usually regularly
JOGGERS >JOGGER
JOGGING >JOG
JOGGINGS >JOG

JOGGLE *vb* shake or move jerkily ▷ *n* act of joggling

JOGGLED >JOGGLE

JOGGLER >JOGGLE

JOGGLERS >JOGGLE

JOGGLES >JOGGLE

JOGGLING >JOGGLE

JOGPANTS *pl n* trousers worn for jogging

JOGS >JOG

JOGTROT *n* easy bouncy gait, esp of a horse, midway between a walk and a trot

JOGTROTS >JOGTROT

JOHANNES *n* Portuguese gold coin minted in the early 18th century

JOHN *n* toilet

JOHNBOAT *n* small flat-bottomed boat

JOHNBOATS >JOHNBOAT

JOHNNIE *same as* >JOHNNY

JOHNNY *n* chap

JOHNS >JOHN

JOHNSON *slang word for* >PENIS

JOHNSONS >JOHNSON

JOIN *vb* become a member (of) ▷ *n* place where two things are joined

JOINABLE >JOIN

JOINDER *n* act of joining, esp in legal contexts

JOINDERS >JOINDER

JOINED >JOIN

JOINER *n* maker of finished woodwork

JOINERIES >JOINERY

JOINERS >JOINER

JOINERY *n* joiner's work

JOINING >JOIN

JOININGS >JOIN

JOINS >JOIN

JOINT *adj* shared by two or more ▷ *n* place where bones meet but can move ▷ *vb* divide meat into joints

JOINTED *adj* having a joint or joints

JOINTEDLY >JOINTED

JOINTER *n* tool for pointing mortar joints, as in brickwork

JOINTERS >JOINTER

JOINTING >JOINT

JOINTLESS >JOINT

JOINTLY >JOINT

JOINTNESS >JOINT

JOINTRESS *n* woman entitled to a jointure

JOINTS >JOINT

JOINTURE *n* provision made by a husband for his wife by settling property upon her at marriage for her use after his death

JOINTURED >JOINTURE

JOINTURES >JOINTURE

JOINTWEED *n* American wild plant

JOINTWORM *n* larva of chalcid flies which form galls on the stems of cereal plants

JOIST *n* horizontal beam that helps support a floor or ceiling ▷ *vb* construct (a floor, roof, etc) with joists

JOISTED >JOIST

JOISTING >JOIST

JOISTS >JOIST

JOJOBA *n* shrub of SW North America whose seeds yield oil used in cosmetics

JOJOBAS >JOJOBA

JOKE *n* thing said or done to cause laughter ▷ *vb* make jokes

JOKED >JOKE

JOKER *n* person who jokes

JOKERS >JOKER

JOKES >JOKE

JOKESMITH *n* comedian

JOKESOME >JOKE

JOKESTER *n* person who makes jokes

JOKESTERS >JOKESTER

JOKEY *adj* intended as a joke

JOKIER >JOKEY

JOKIEST >JOKEY

JOKILY >JOKE

JOKINESS >JOKE

JOKING >JOKE

JOKINGLY >JOKE

JOKOL *Shetland word for* >YES

JOKY *same as* >JOKEY

JOL *n* party ▷ *vb* have a good time

JOLE *vb* knock

JOLED >JOLE

JOLES >JOLE

JOLING >JOLE

JOLL *variant of* >JOLE

JOLLED >JOL

JOLLEY *same as* >JOLLY

JOLLEYER >JOLLEY

JOLLEYERS >JOLLEY

JOLLEYING >JOLLEY

JOLLEYS >JOLLEY

JOLLIED >JOLLY

JOLLIER *n* joker

JOLLIERS >JOLLIER

JOLLIES >JOLLY

JOLLIEST >JOLLY

JOLLIFIED >JOLLIFY

JOLLIFIES >JOLLIFY

JOLLIFY *vb* be or cause to be jolly

JOLLILY >JOLLY

JOLLIMENT >JOLLY

JOLLINESS >JOLLY

JOLLING >JOL

JOLLITIES >JOLLITY

JOLLITY *n* condition of being jolly

JOLLOP *n* cream or unguent

JOLLOPS >JOLLOP

JOLLS >JOLL

JOLLY *adj* full of good humour ▷ *adv* extremely

▷ *vb* try to make or keep (someone) cheerful ▷ *n* festivity or celebration

JOLLYBOAT *n* small boat used as a utility tender for a vessel

JOLLYER >JOLLY

JOLLYERS >JOLLY

JOLLYHEAD *same as* >JOLLITY

JOLLYING >JOLLY

JOLLYINGS >JOLLY

JOLS >JOL

JOLT *n* unpleasant surprise or shock ▷ *vb* surprise or shock

JOLTED >JOLT

JOLTER >JOLT

JOLTERS >JOLT

JOLTHEAD *n* fool

JOLTHEADS >JOLTHEAD

JOLTIER >JOLT

JOLTIEST >JOLT

JOLTILY >JOLT

JOLTING >JOLT

JOLTINGLY >JOLT

JOLTS >JOLT

JOLTY >JOLT

JOMO *same as* >ZO

JOMON *n* particular era in Japanese history

JOMOS >JOMO

JONCANOE *n* Jamaican ceremony

JONCANOES >JONCANOE

JONES *vb* desire

JONESED >JONES

JONESES >JONES

JONESING >JONES

JONG *n* friend, often used in direct address

JONGLEUR *n* (in medieval France) an itinerant minstrel

JONGLEURS >JONGLEUR

JONNOCK *adj* genuine ▷ *adv* honestly

JONNYCAKE *n* type of flat bread

JONQUIL *n* fragrant narcissus

JONQUILS >JONQUIL

JONTIES >JONTY

JONTY *n* petty officer

JOOK *vb* poke or puncture (the skin) ▷ *n* jab or the resulting wound

JOOKED >JOOK

JOOKERIES >JOOKERY

JOOKERY *n* mischief

JOOKING >JOOK

JOOKS >JOOK

JOR *n* movement in Indian music

JORAM *same as* >JORUM

JORAMS >JORAM

JORDAN *n* chamber pot

JORDANS >JORDAN

JORDELOO *same as* >GARDYLOO

JORDELOOS >JORDELOO

JORS >JOR

JORUM *n* large drinking bowl or vessel or its

contents

JORUMS >JORUM

JOSEPH *n* woman's floor-length riding coat with a small cape, worn esp in the 18th century

JOSEPHS >JOSEPH

JOSH *vb* tease ▷ *n* teasing or bantering joke

JOSHED >JOSH

JOSHER >JOSH

JOSHERS >JOSH

JOSHES >JOSH

JOSHING >JOSH

JOSHINGLY >JOSH

JOSKIN *n* bumpkin

JOSKINS >JOSKIN

JOSS *n* Chinese deity worshipped in the form of an idol

JOSSER *n* simpleton

JOSSERS >JOSSER

JOSSES >JOSS

JOSTLE *vb* knock or push against ▷ *n* act of jostling

JOSTLED >JOSTLE

JOSTLER >JOSTLE

JOSTLERS >JOSTLE

JOSTLES >JOSTLE

JOSTLING >JOSTLE

JOSTLINGS >JOSTLE

JOT *vb* write briefly ▷ *n* very small amount

JOTA *n* Spanish dance with castanets in fast triple time, usually to a guitar and voice accompaniment

JOTAS >JOTA

JOTS >JOT

JOTTED >JOT

JOTTER *n* notebook

JOTTERS >JOTTER

JOTTING >JOT

JOTTINGS >JOT

JOTTY >JOT

JOTUN *n* giant

JOTUNN *same as* >JOTUN

JOTUNNS >JOTUNN

JOTUNS >JOTUN

JOUAL *n* nonstandard variety of Canadian French

JOUALS >JOUAL

JOUGS *pl n* iron ring, fastened by a chain to a wall, post, or tree, in which an offender was held by the neck

JOUISANCE *n* joy

JOUK *vb* duck or dodge ▷ *n* sudden evasive movement

JOUKED >JOUK

JOUKERIES >JOUKERY

JOUKERY *same as* >JOOKERY

JOUKING >JOUK

JOUKS >JOUK

JOULE *n* unit of work or energy ▷ *vb* knock

JOULED >JOULE

JOULES >JOULE

JOULING >JOULE

JOUNCE *vb* shake or jolt or cause to shake or jolt ▷ *n* jolting movement

JOUNCED >JOUNCE

JOUNCES >JOUNCE
JOUNCIER >JOUNCE
JOUNCIEST >JOUNCE
JOUNCING >JOUNCE
JOUNCY >JOUNCE
JOUR n day
JOURNAL n daily
newspaper or magazine
▷ vb record in a journal
JOURNALED >JOURNAL
JOURNALS >JOURNAL
JOURNEY n act or process of
travelling from one place
to another ▷ vb travel
JOURNEYED >JOURNEY
JOURNEYER >JOURNEY
JOURNEYS >JOURNEY
JOURNO n journalist
JOURNOS >JOURNO
JOURS >JOUR
JOUST n combat with
lances between two
mounted knights ▷ vb
fight on horseback using
lances
JOUSTED >JOUST
JOUSTER >JOUST
JOUSTERS >JOUST
JOUSTING >JOUST
JOUSTS >JOUST
JOVIAL adj happy and
cheerful
JOVIALITY >JOVIAL
JOVIALLY >JOVIAL
JOVIALTY same as >JOVIAL
JOW vb ring (a bell)
JOWAR n variety of sorghum
JOWARI same as >JOWAR
JOWARIS >JOWAR
JOWARS >JOWAR
JOWED >JOW
JOWING >JOW
JOWL n lower jaw ▷ vb
knock
JOWLED >JOWL
JOWLER n dog with
prominent jowls
JOWLERS >JOWLER
JOWLIER >JOWL
JOWLIEST >JOWL
JOWLINESS >JOWL
JOWLING >JOWL
JOWLS >JOWL
JOWLY >JOWL
JOWS >JOW
JOY n feeling of great
delight or pleasure ▷ vb
feel joy
JOYANCE n joyous feeling
or festivity
JOYANCES >JOYANCE
JOYED >JOY
JOYFUL adj feeling or
bringing great joy
JOYFULLER >JOYFUL
JOYFULLY >JOYFUL
JOYING >JOY
JOYLESS adj feeling or
bringing no joy
JOYLESSLY >JOYLESS
JOYOUS adj extremely
happy and enthusiastic
JOYOUSLY >JOYOUS
JOYPOP vb take addictive

drugs occasionally
without becoming
addicted
JOYPOPPED >JOYPOP
JOYPOPPER >JOYPOP
JOYPOPS >JOYPOP
JOYRIDDEN >JOYRIDE
JOYRIDE n drive in a car
one has stolen ▷ vb take
such a ride
JOYRIDER >JOYRIDE
JOYRIDERS >JOYRIDE
JOYRIDES >JOYRIDE
JOYRIDING >JOYRIDE
JOYRODE >JOYRIDE
JOYS >JOY
JOYSTICK n control device
for an aircraft or computer
JOYSTICKS >JOYSTICK
JUBA n lively African-
American dance developed
in the southern US
JUBAS >JUBA
JUBATE adj possessing a
mane
JUBBAH n long loose
outer garment with wide
sleeves, worn by Muslim
men and women, esp in
India
JUBBAHS >JUBBAH
JUBE n gallery or loft over
the rood screen in a church
or cathedral
JUBES >JUBE
JUBHAH same as >JUBBAH
JUBHAHS >JUBHAH
JUBILANCE >JUBILANT
JUBILANCY >JUBILANT
JUBILANT adj feeling or
expressing great joy
JUBILATE vb have or
express great joy
JUBILATED >JUBILATE
JUBILATES >JUBILATE
JUBILE same as >JUBILEE
JUBILEE n special
anniversary, esp 25th or
50th
JUBILEES >JUBILEE
JUBILES >JUBILE
JUCO n junior college in
America
JUCOS >JUCO
JUD n large block of coal
JUDAS n peephole or a very
small window in a door
JUDASES >JUDAS
JUDDER vb vibrate violently
▷ n violent vibration
JUDDERED >JUDDER
JUDDERING >JUDDER
JUDDERS >JUDDER
JUDGE n public official who
tries cases and passes
sentence in a court of law
▷ vb act as a judge
JUDGEABLE >JUDGE
JUDGED >JUDGE
JUDGELESS >JUDGE
JUDGELIKE >JUDGE
JUDGEMENT same
as >JUDGMENT
JUDGER >JUDGE

JUDGERS >JUDGE
JUDGES >JUDGE
JUDGESHIP n position,
office, or function of a
judge
JUDGING >JUDGE
JUDGINGLY >JUDGE
JUDGMATIC adj judicious
JUDGMENT n opinion
reached after careful
thought
JUDGMENTS >JUDGMENT
JUDICABLE adj capable
of being judged, esp in a
court of law
JUDICATOR n person who
acts as a judge
JUDICIAL adj of or by a
court or judge
JUDICIARY n system of
courts and judges ▷ adj of
or relating to courts of law,
judgment, or judges
JUDICIOUS adj well-judged
and sensible
JUDIES >JUDY
JUDO n sport in which two
opponents try to throw
each other to the ground
JUDOGI n white two-piece
cotton costume worn
during judo contests
JUDOGIS >JUDOGI
JUDOIST >JUDO
JUDOISTS >JUDO
JUDOKA n competitor or
expert in judo
JUDOKAS >JUDOKA
JUDOS >JUDO
JUDS >JUD
JUDY n woman
JUG n container for liquids,
with a handle and small
spout ▷ vb stew or boil
(meat, esp hare) in an
earthenware container
JUGA >JUGUM
JUGAL adj of or relating to
the zygomatic bone ▷ n
cheekbone
JUGALS >JUGAL
JUGATE adj (esp of
compound leaves) having
parts arranged in pairs
JUGFUL same as >JUG
JUGFULS >JUGFUL
JUGGED >JUG
JUGGING >JUG
JUGGINGS >JUG
JUGGINS n silly person
JUGGINSES >JUGGINS
JUGGLE vb throw and
catch (several objects) so
that most are in the air at
the same time ▷ n act of
juggling
JUGGLED >JUGGLE
JUGGLER n person who
juggles, esp a professional
entertainer
JUGGLERS >JUGGLER
JUGGLERY >JUGGLE
JUGGLES >JUGGLE
JUGGLING >JUGGLE

JUGGLINGS >JUGGLE
JUGHEAD n clumsy person
JUGHEADS >JUGHEAD
JUGLET n small jug
JUGLETS >JUGLET
JUGS >JUG
JUGSFUL >JUGFUL
JUGULA >JUGULUM
JUGULAR n one of three
large veins of the neck that
return blood from the head
to the heart
JUGULARS >JUGULAR
JUGULATE vb check (a
disease) by extreme
measures or remedies
JUGULATED >JUGULATE
JUGULATES >JUGULATE
JUGULUM n lower throat
JUGUM n small process at
the base of each forewing
in certain insects by which
the forewings are united
to the hindwings during
flight
JUGUMS >JUGUM
JUICE n liquid part of
vegetables, fruit, or meat
▷ vb extract juice from
fruits and vegetables
JUICED >JUICE
JUICEHEAD n alcoholic
JUICELESS >JUICE
JUICER n kitchen
appliance, usually
operated by electricity, for
extracting juice from fruits
and vegetables
JUICERS >JUICER
JUICES >JUICE
JUICIER >JUICY
JUICIEST >JUICY
JUICILY >JUICY
JUICINESS >JUICY
JUICING >JUICE
JUICY adj full of juice
JUJITSU n Japanese art of
wrestling and self-defence
JUJITSUS >JUJITSU
JUJU n W African magic
charm or fetish
JUJUBE n chewy sweet
made of flavoured gelatine
JUJUBES >JUJUBE
JUJUISM >JUJU
JUJUISMS >JUJU
JUJUIST >JUJU
JUJUISTS >JUJU
JUJUS >JUJU
JUJUTSU same as >JUJITSU
JUJUTSUS >JUJUTSU
JUKE vb dance or play
dance music
JUKEBOX n coin-operated
machine on which records,
CDs, or videos can be
played
JUKEBOXES >JUKEBOX
JUKED >JUKE
JUKES >JUKE
JUKING >JUKE
JUKSKEI n game in which
a peg is thrown over a fixed
distance at a stake fixed

into the ground
**JUKSKEIS** > JUKE
**JUKU** *n* Japanese martial art
**JUKUS** > JUKU
**JULEP** *n* sweet alcoholic drink
**JULEPS** > JULEP
**JULIENNE** *adj* (of vegetables or meat) cut into thin shreds ▷ *n* clear soup containing thinly shredded vegetables ▷ *vb* cut into thin pieces
**JULIENNED** > JULIENNE
**JULIENNES** > JULIENNE
**JUMAR** *n* clamp with a handle that can move freely up a rope on which it is clipped but locks when downward pressure is applied ▷ *vb* climb (up a fixed rope) using jumars
**JUMARED** > JUMAR
**JUMARING** > JUMAR
**JUMARRED** > JUMAR
**JUMARRING** > JUMAR
**JUMARS** > JUMAR
**JUMART** *n* mythical offspring of a bull and a mare
**JUMARTS** > JUMART
**JUMBAL** *same as* > JUMBLE
**JUMBALS** > JUMBAL
**JUMBIE** *n* Caribbean ghost
**JUMBIES** > JUMBIE
**JUMBLE** *n* confused heap or state ▷ *vb* mix in a disordered way
**JUMBLED** > JUMBLE
**JUMBLER** > JUMBLE
**JUMBLERS** > JUMBLE
**JUMBLES** > JUMBLE
**JUMBLIER** > JUMBLE
**JUMBLIEST** > JUMBLE
**JUMBLING** > JUMBLE
**JUMBLY** > JUMBLE
**JUMBO** *adj* very large ▷ *n* large jet airliner
**JUMBOISE** *same as* > JUMBOIZE
**JUMBOISED** > JUMBOISE
**JUMBOISES** > JUMBOISE
**JUMBOIZE** *vb* extend (a ship, esp a tanker) by cutting out the middle part and inserting a new larger part between the original bow and stern
**JUMBOIZED** > JUMBOIZE
**JUMBOIZES** > JUMBOIZE
**JUMBOS** > JUMBO
**JUMBUCK** *n* sheep
**JUMBUCKS** > JUMBUCK
**JUMBY** *n* Caribbean ghost
**JUMELLE** *n* paired objects
**JUMELLES** > JUMELLE
**JUMP** *vb* leap or spring into the air using the leg muscles ▷ *n* act of jumping
**JUMPABLE** > JUMP
**JUMPED** > JUMP
**JUMPER** *n* sweater or

pullover
**JUMPERS** > JUMPER
**JUMPIER** > JUMPY
**JUMPIEST** > JUMPY
**JUMPILY** > JUMPY
**JUMPINESS** > JUMPY
**JUMPING** > JUMP
**JUMPINGLY** > JUMP
**JUMPINGS** > JUMP
**JUMPOFF** *n* extra round in a showjumping contest when two or more horses are equal first, the fastest round deciding the winner
**JUMPOFFS** > JUMPOFF
**JUMPS** > JUMP
**JUMPSUIT** *n* one-piece garment of combined trousers and jacket or shirt
**JUMPSUITS** > JUMPSUIT
**JUMPY** *adj* nervous
**JUN** *variant of* > CHON
**JUNCATE** *same as* > JUNKET
**JUNCATES** > JUNCATE
**JUNCO** *n* North American bunting
**JUNCOES** > JUNCO
**JUNCOS** > JUNCO
**JUNCTION** *n* place where routes, railway lines, or roads meet
**JUNCTIONS** > JUNCTION
**JUNCTURAL** > JUNCTURE
**JUNCTURE** *n* point in time, esp a critical one
**JUNCTURES** > JUNCTURE
**JUNCUS** *n* type of rush
**JUNCUSES** > JUNCUS
**JUNEATING** *n* early-season apple
**JUNGLE** *n* tropical forest of dense tangled vegetation
**JUNGLED** *adj* covered with jungle
**JUNGLEGYM** *n* climbing frame for children
**JUNGLES** > JUNGLE
**JUNGLI** *n* uncultured person
**JUNGLIER** > JUNGLE
**JUNGLIEST** > JUNGLE
**JUNGLIS** > JUNGLI
**JUNGLIST** *n* jungle-music enthusiast
**JUNGLISTS** > JUNGLIST
**JUNGLY** > JUNGLE
**JUNIOR** *adj* of lower standing ▷ *n* junior person
**JUNIORATE** *n* preparatory course for candidates for religious orders
**JUNIORITY** *n* condition of being junior
**JUNIORS** > JUNIOR
**JUNIPER** *n* evergreen shrub with purple berries
**JUNIPERS** > JUNIPER
**JUNK** *n* discarded or useless objects ▷ *vb* discard as junk
**JUNKANOO** *n* Bahamian ceremony
**JUNKANOOS** > JUNKANOO

**JUNKED** > JUNK
**JUNKER** *n* (formerly) young German nobleman
**JUNKERS** > JUNKER
**JUNKET** *n* excursion by public officials paid for from public funds ▷ *vb* (of a public official, committee, etc) to go on a junket
**JUNKETED** > JUNKET
**JUNKETEER** > JUNKET
**JUNKETER** > JUNKET
**JUNKETERS** > JUNKET
**JUNKETING** > JUNKET
**JUNKETS** > JUNKET
**JUNKETTED** > JUNKET
**JUNKETTER** > JUNKET
**JUNKIE** *n* drug addict
**JUNKIER** > JUNKY
**JUNKIES** > JUNKY
**JUNKIEST** > JUNKY
**JUNKINESS** > JUNKY
**JUNKING** > JUNK
**JUNKMAN** *n* man who buys and sells discarded clothing, furniture, etc
**JUNKMEN** > JUNKMAN
**JUNKS** > JUNK
**JUNKY** *n* drug addict ▷ *adj* of low quality
**JUNKYARD** *n* place where junk is stored or collected for sale
**JUNKYARDS** > JUNKYARD
**JUNTA** *n* group of military officers holding power in a country, esp after a coup
**JUNTAS** > JUNTA
**JUNTO** *same as* > JUNTA
**JUNTOS** > JUNTO
**JUPATI** *n* type of palm tree
**JUPATIS** > JUPATI
**JUPE** *n* sleeveless jacket
**JUPES** > JUPE
**JUPON** *n* short close-fitting sleeveless padded garment, used in the late 14th and early 15th centuries with armour
**JUPONS** > JUPON
**JURA** > JUS
**JURAL** *adj* of or relating to law or to the administration of justice
**JURALLY** > JURAL
**JURANT** *n* person taking oath
**JURANTS** > JURANT
**JURASSIC** *adj* of, denoting, or formed in the second period of the Mesozoic era, between the Triassic and Cretaceous periods, lasting for 55 million years during which dinosaurs and ammonites flourished
**JURAT** *n* statement at the foot of an affidavit, naming the parties, stating when, where, and before whom it was sworn, etc
**JURATORY** *adj* of, relating

to, or expressed in an oath
**JURATS** > JURAT
**JURE** *adv* by legal right
**JUREL** *n* edible fish found in warm American Atlantic waters
**JURELS** > JUREL
**JURIDIC** *same as* > JURIDICAL
**JURIDICAL** *adj* of law or the administration of justice
**JURIED** > JURY
**JURIES** > JURY
**JURIST** *n* expert in law
**JURISTIC** *adj* of or relating to jurists
**JURISTS** > JURIST
**JUROR** *n* member of a jury
**JURORS** > JUROR
**JURY** *n* group of people sworn to deliver a verdict in a court of law ▷ *adj* makeshift ▷ *vb* evaluate by jury
**JURYING** > JURY
**JURYLESS** > JURY
**JURYMAN** *n* member of a jury, esp a man
**JURYMAST** *n* replacement mast
**JURYMASTS** > JURYMAST
**JURYMEN** > JURYMAN
**JURYWOMAN** *n* female member of a jury
**JURYWOMEN** > JURYWOMAN
**JUS** *n* right, power, or authority
**JUSSIVE** *n* mood of verbs used for giving orders; imperative
**JUSSIVES** > JUSSIVE
**JUST** *adv* very recently ▷ *adj* fair or impartial in action or judgment ▷ *vb* joust
**JUSTED** > JUST
**JUSTER** > JUST
**JUSTERS** > JUST
**JUSTEST** > JUST
**JUSTICE** *n* quality of being just
**JUSTICER** *n* magistrate
**JUSTICERS** > JUSTICER
**JUSTICES** > JUSTICE
**JUSTICIAR** *n* chief political and legal officer from the time of William I to that of Henry III, who deputized for the king in his absence and presided over the kings' courts
**JUSTIFIED** > JUSTIFY
**JUSTIFIER** > JUSTIFY
**JUSTIFIES** > JUSTIFY
**JUSTIFY** *vb* prove right or reasonable
**JUSTING** > JOUST
**JUSTLE** *less common word for* > JOSTLE
**JUSTLED** > JUSTLE
**JUSTLES** > JUSTLE
**JUSTLING** > JUSTLE
**JUSTLY** > JUST

**JUSTNESS** > JUST
**JUSTS** *same as* > JOUST
**JUT** *vb* project or stick out
▷ *n* something that juts
out
**JUTE** *n* plant fibre, used for
rope, canvas, etc
**JUTELIKE** > JUTE
**JUTES** > JUTE
**JUTS** > JUT
**JUTTED** > JUT
**JUTTIED** > JUTTY
**JUTTIES** > JUTTY
**JUTTING** > JUT
**JUTTINGLY** > JUT
**JUTTY** *vb* project beyond
**JUTTYING** > JUTTY
**JUVE** *same as* > JUVENILE
**JUVENAL** *variant spelling (esp
US) of* > JUVENILE
**JUVENALS** > JUVENAL
**JUVENILE** *adj* young ▷ *n*
young person or child
**JUVENILES** > JUVENILE
**JUVENILIA** *pl n* works
produced in an author's
youth
**JUVES** > JUVE
**JUXTAPOSE** *vb* put side by
side
**JYMOLD** *n* ring made of two
interlocking rings
**JYMOLDS** > JYMOLD
**JYNX** *n* woodpecker
**JYNXES** > JYNX

# Kk

KA *n* (in ancient Egypt) attendant spirit supposedly dwelling as a vital force in a man or statue ▷ *vb* (in archaic usage) help
KAAL *adj* naked
KAAMA *n* large African antelope with lyre-shaped horns
KAAMAS > KAAMA
KAAS *n* Dutch cabinet or wardrobe
KAB *variant spelling of* > CAB
KABAB *same as* > KEBAB
KABABBED > KABAB
KABABBING > KABAB
KABABS > KABAB
KABADDI *n* game in which players try to touch opposing players but avoid being captured by them
KABADDIS > KABADDI
KABAKA *n* any of the former rulers of the Baganda people of S Uganda
KABAKAS > KABAKA
KABALA *same as* > KABBALAH
KABALAS > KABALA
KABALISM > KABALA
KABALISMS > KABALA
KABALIST > KABALA
KABALISTS > KABALA
KABAR *archaic form of* > CABER
KABARS > KABAR
KABAYA *n* tunic
KABAYAS > KABAYA
KABBALA *same as* > KABBALAH
KABBALAH *n* ancient Jewish mystical tradition
KABBALAHS > KABBALAH

KABBALAS > KABBALA
KABBALISM > KABBALAH
KABBALIST > KABBALAH
KABELE *same as* > KEBELE
KABELES > KABELE
KABELJOU *n* large fish that is an important food fish of South African waters
KABELJOUS > KABELJOU
KABELJOUW *same as* > KABELJOU
KABIKI *n* fruit tree found in India
KABIKIS > KABIKI
KABOB *same as* > KEBAB
KABOBBED > KABOB
KABOBBING > KABOB
KABOBS > KABOB
KABS > KAB
KABUKI *n* form of Japanese drama based on popular legends and characterized by elaborate costumes, stylized acting, and the use of male actors for all roles
KABUKIS > KABUKI
KACCHA *same as* > KACHA
KACCHAS > KACCHA
KACHA *n* short trousers traditionally worn by Sikhs as a symbol of their religious and cultural loyalty
KACHAHRI *n* Indian courthouse
KACHAHRIS > KACHAHRI
KACHAS > KACHA
KACHCHA *same as* > KACHA
KACHCHAS > KACHCHA
KACHERA *same as* > KACHA
KACHERAS > KACHERA
KACHERI *same*

*as* > KACHAHRI
KACHERIS > KACHERI
KACHINA *n* any of the supernatural beings believed by the Hopi Indians to be the ancestors of living humans
KACHINAS > KACHINA
KADAITCHA *n* (in certain Central Australian Aboriginal tribes) man with the mission of avenging the death of a tribesman
KADDISH *n* ancient Jewish liturgical prayer
KADDISHES > KADDISH
KADDISHIM > KADDISH
KADE *same as* > KED
KADES > KADE
KADI *variant spelling of* > CADI
KADIS > KADI
KAE *n* dialect word for jackdaw or jay ▷ *vb* (in archaic usage) help
KAED > KAE
KAEING > KAE
KAES > KAE
KAF *n* letter of the Hebrew alphabet
KAFFIR *n* Southern African variety of sorghum, cultivated in dry regions for its grain and as fodder
KAFFIRS > KAFFIR
KAFFIYAH *same as* > KAFFIYEH
KAFFIYAHS > KAFFIYAH
KAFFIYEH *same as* > KEFFIYEH
KAFFIYEHS > KAFFIYEH
KAFILA *n* caravan

KAFILAS > KAFILA
KAFIR *same as* > KAFFIR
KAFIRS > KAFIR
KAFS > KAF
KAFTAN *n* long loose Eastern garment
KAFTANS > KAFTAN
KAGO *n* Japanese sedan chair
KAGOOL *variant spelling of* > CAGOULE
KAGOOLS > KAGOOL
KAGOS > KAGO
KAGOUL *variant spelling of* > CAGOULE
KAGOULE *same as* > KAGOUL
KAGOULES > KAGOULE
KAGOULS > KAGOUL
KAGU *n* crested nocturnal bird of New Caledonia with a red bill and greyish plumage
KAGUS > KAGU
KAHAL *n* Jewish community
KAHALS > KAHAL
KAHAWAI *n* food and game fish of New Zealand
KAHAWAIS > KAHAWAI
KAHIKATEA *n* tall New Zealand coniferous tree
KAHIKATOA *n* tall New Zealand coniferous tree
KAHUNA *n* Hawaiian priest, shaman, or expert
KAHUNAS > KAHUNA
KAI *n* food
KAIAK *same as* > KAYAK
KAIAKED > KAIAK
KAIAKING > KAIAK
KAIAKS > KAIAK
KAID *n* North African chieftan or leader
KAIDS > KAID

403

**KAIE** archaic form of > KEY
**KAIES** > KAIE
**KAIF** same as > KIF
**KAIFS** > KAIF
**KAIK** same as > KAINGA
**KAIKA** same as > KAINGA
**KAIKAI** n food
**KAIKAIS** > KAIKAI
**KAIKAS** > KAIKA
**KAIKAWAKA** n small pyramid-shaped New Zealand conifer
**KAIKOMAKO** n small New Zealand tree with white flowers and black fruit
**KAIKS** > KAIK
**KAIL** same as > KALE
**KAILS** > KAIL
**KAILYAIRD** same as > KALEYARD
**KAILYARD** same as > KALEYARD
**KAILYARDS** > KAILYARD
**KAIM** same as > KAME
**KAIMAKAM** n Turkish governor
**KAIMAKAMS** > KAIMAKAM
**KAIMS** > KAIM
**KAIN** variant spelling of > CAIN
**KAING** > KA
**KAINGA** n (in New Zealand) a Māori village or small settlement
**KAINGAS** > KAINGA
**KAINIT** same as > KAINITE
**KAINITE** n white mineral consisting of potassium chloride and magnesium sulphate: a fertilizer and source of potassium salts
**KAINITES** > KAINITE
**KAINITS** > KAINIT
**KAINS** > KAIN
**KAIROMONE** n substance secreted by animal
**KAIS** > KAI
**KAISER** n German or Austro-Hungarian emperor
**KAISERDOM** > KAISER
**KAISERIN** n empress
**KAISERINS** > KAISERIN
**KAISERISM** > KAISER
**KAISERS** > KAISER
**KAIZEN** n philosophy of continuous improvement of working practices that underlies total quality management and just-in-time business techniques
**KAIZENS** > KAIZEN
**KAJAWAH** n type of seat or panier used on a camel
**KAJAWAHS** > KAJAWAH
**KAJEPUT** n variety of Australian melaleuca
**KAJEPUTS** > KAJEPUT
**KAK** n South African slang word for faeces
**KAKA** n parrot of New Zealand
**KAKAPO** n ground-living nocturnal New Zealand parrot that resembles an owl
**KAKAPOS** > KAKAPO
**KAKARIKI** n green-feathered New Zealand parrot
**KAKAS** > KAKA
**KAKEMONO** n Japanese paper or silk wall hanging, usually long and narrow, with a picture or inscription on it and a roller at the bottom
**KAKEMONOS** > KAKEMONO
**KAKI** n Asian persimmon tree
**KAKIEMON** n type of 17th century Japanese porcelain
**KAKIEMONS** > KAKIEMON
**KAKIS** > KAKI
**KAKODYL** variant spelling of > CACODYL
**KAKODYLS** > KAKODYL
**KAKS** > KAK
**KALAM** n discussion and debate, especially relating to Islamic theology
**KALAMATA** as in kalamata olive aubergine-coloured Greek olive
**KALAMATAS** > KALAMATA
**KALAMDAN** n Persian box in which to keep pens
**KALAMDANS** > KALAMDAN
**KALAMKARI** n Indian cloth printing and printed Indian cloth
**KALAMS** > KALAM
**KALANCHOE** n tropical succulent plant having small brightly coloured flowers and dark shiny leaves
**KALE** n cabbage with crinkled leaves
**KALENDAR** variant form of > CALENDAR
**KALENDARS** > KALENDAR
**KALENDS** same as > CALENDS
**KALES** > KALE
**KALEWIFE** n Scots word for a female vegetable or cabbage seller
**KALEWIVES** > KALEWIFE
**KALEYARD** n vegetable garden
**KALEYARDS** > KALEYARD
**KALI** another name for > SALTWORT
**KALIAN** another name for > HOOKAH
**KALIANS** > KALIAN
**KALIF** variant spelling of > CALIPH
**KALIFATE** same as > CALIPHATE
**KALIFATES** > KALIFATE
**KALIFS** > KALIF
**KALIMBA** n musical instrument
**KALIMBAS** > KALIMBA
**KALINITE** n alum
**KALINITES** > KALINITE

**KALIPH** variant spelling of > CALIPH
**KALIPHATE** same as > CALIPHATE
**KALIPHS** > KALIPH
**KALIS** > KALI
**KALIUM** n Latin for potassium
**KALIUMS** > KALIUM
**KALLIDIN** n type of peptide
**KALLIDINS** > KALLIDIN
**KALLITYPE** n old printing process
**KALMIA** n N American evergreen ericaceous shrub with showy clusters of white or pink flowers
**KALMIAS** > KALMIA
**KALONG** n fruit bat
**KALONGS** > KALONG
**KALOTYPE** variant spelling of > CALOTYPE
**KALOTYPES** > KALOTYPE
**KALPA** n (in Hindu cosmology) period in which the universe experiences a cycle of creation and destruction
**KALPAC** same as > CALPAC
**KALPACS** > KALPAC
**KALPAK** variant spelling of > CALPAC
**KALPAKS** > KALPAK
**KALPAS** > KALPA
**KALPIS** n Greek water jar
**KALPISES** > KALPIS
**KALSOMINE** variant of > CALCIMINE
**KALUMPIT** n type of Filipino fruit tree or its fruit
**KALUMPITS** > KALUMPIT
**KALYPTRA** n Greek veil
**KALYPTRAS** > KALYPTRA
**KAM** Shakespearean word for > CROOKED
**KAMA** n large African antelope with lyre-shaped horns
**KAMAAINA** n Hawaiian local
**KAMAAINAS** > KAMAAINA
**KAMACITE** n alloy of iron and nickel, occurring in meteorites
**KAMACITES** > KAMACITE
**KAMAHI** n tall New Zealand hardwood tree with pinkish flowers
**KAMALA** n East Indian tree
**KAMALAS** > KAMALA
**KAMAS** > KAMA
**KAME** n irregular mound or ridge of gravel, sand, etc, deposited by water derived from melting glaciers
**KAMEES** > KAMEEZ
**KAMEESES** > KAMEES
**KAMEEZ** n long tunic worn in the Indian subcontinent, often with shalwar
**KAMEEZES** > KAMEEZ
**KAMELA** same as > KAMALA
**KAMELAS** > KAMELA

**KAMERAD** interj shout of surrender ▷ vb surrender
**KAMERADED** > KAMERAD
**KAMERADS** > KAMERAD
**KAMES** > KAME
**KAMI** n divine being or spiritual force in Shinto
**KAMICHI** n South American bird
**KAMICHIS** > KAMICHI
**KAMIK** n traditional Inuit boot made of caribou hide or sealskin
**KAMIKAZE** n (in World War II) Japanese pilot who performed a suicide mission ▷ adj (of an action) undertaken in the knowledge that it will kill or injure the person performing it
**KAMIKAZES** > KAMIKAZE
**KAMIKS** > KAMIK
**KAMILA** same as > KAMALA
**KAMILAS** > KAMILA
**KAMIS** same as > KAMEEZ
**KAMISES** > KAMIS
**KAMME** same as > KAM
**KAMOKAMO** n kind of marrow found in New Zealand
**KAMPONG** n (in Malaysia) village
**KAMPONGS** > KAMPONG
**KAMSEEN** same as > KHAMSIN
**KAMSEENS** > KAMSEEN
**KAMSIN** same as > KAMSEEN
**KAMSINS** > KAMSIN
**KANA** n Japanese syllabary, which consists of two written varieties
**KANAE** n grey mullet
**KANAKA** n Australian word for any native of the South Pacific islands, esp (formerly) one abducted to work in Australia
**KANAKAS** > KANAKA
**KANAMYCIN** n type of antibiotic
**KANAS** > KANA
**KANBAN** n just-in-time manufacturing process in which the movements of materials through a process are recorded on specially designed cards
**KANBANS** > KANBAN
**KANDIES** > KANDY
**KANDY** same as > CANDIE
**KANE** n Hawaiian man or boy
**KANEH** n 6-cubit Hebrew measure
**KANEHS** > KANEH
**KANES** > KANE
**KANG** n Chinese heatable platform used for sleeping and sitting on
**KANGA** n piece of gaily decorated thin cotton cloth used as a garment by women in E Africa
**KANGAROO** n Australian

marsupial which moves by jumping with its powerful hind legs ▷ *vb* (of a car) move forward or to cause (a car) to move forward with short sudden jerks, as a result of improper use of the clutch
**KANGAROOS** > KANGAROO
**KANGAS** > KANGA
**KANGHA** *n* comb traditionally worn by Sikhs as a symbol of their religious and cultural loyalty
**KANGHAS** > KANGHA
**KANGS** > KANG
**KANJI** *n* Japanese writing system using characters mainly derived from Chinese ideograms
**KANJIS** > KANJI
**KANS** *n* Indian wild sugar cane
**KANSES** > KANS
**KANT** *archaic spelling of* > CANT
**KANTAR** *n* unit of weight used in E Mediterranean countries, equivalent to 100 pounds or 45 kilograms but varying from place to place
**KANTARS** > KANTAR
**KANTED** > KANT
**KANTELA** *same as* > KANTELE
**KANTELAS** > KANTELA
**KANTELE** *n* Finnish stringed instrument
**KANTELES** > KANTELE
**KANTEN** *same as* > AGAR
**KANTENS** > KANTEN
**KANTHA** *n* Bengali embroidered quilt
**KANTHAS** > KANTHA
**KANTIKOY** *vb* dance ceremonially
**KANTIKOYS** > KANTIKOY
**KANTING** > KANT
**KANTS** > KANT
**KANUKA** *n* New Zealand myrtaceous tree
**KANZU** *n* long garment, usually white, with long sleeves, worn by E African men
**KANZUS** > KANZU
**KAOLIANG** *n* any of various E Asian varieties of sorghum
**KAOLIANGS** > KAOLIANG
**KAOLIN** *n* fine white clay used to make porcelain and in some medicines
**KAOLINE** *same as* > KAOLIN
**KAOLINES** > KAOLINE
**KAOLINIC** > KAOLIN
**KAOLINISE** *same as* > KAOLINIZE
**KAOLINITE** *n* white or grey clay mineral consisting of hydrated aluminium silicate in triclinic crystalline form, the main

constituent of kaolin
**KAOLINIZE** *vb* change into kaolin
**KAOLINS** > KAOLIN
**KAON** *n* meson that has a positive or negative charge and a rest mass of about 966 electron masses, or no charge and a rest mass of 974 electron masses
**KAONIC** > KAON
**KAONS** > KAON
**KAPA** *n* Hawaiian cloth made from beaten mulberry bark
**KAPAS** > KAPA
**KAPH** *n* 11th letter of the Hebrew alphabet
**KAPHS** > KAPH
**KAPOK** *n* fluffy fibre from a tropical tree, used to stuff cushions etc
**KAPOKS** > KAPOK
**KAPPA** *n* tenth letter in the Greek alphabet
**KAPPAS** > KAPPA
**KAPUKA** *same as* > BROADLEAF
**KAPUT** *adj* ruined or broken
**KAPUTT** *same as* > KAPUT
**KARA** *n* steel bangle traditionally worn by Sikhs as a symbol of their religious and cultural loyalty
**KARABINER** *n* metal clip with a spring for attaching to a piton, belay, etc
**KARAISM** *n* beliefs and doctrines of a Jewish sect rejecting Rabbinism
**KARAISMS** > KARAISM
**KARAIT** *same as* > KRAIT
**KARAITS** > KRAIT
**KARAKA** *n* New Zealand tree
**KARAKAS** > KARAKA
**KARAKIA** *n* prayer
**KARAKIAS** > KARAKIA
**KARAKUL** *n* sheep of central Asia, the lambs of which have soft curled dark hair
**KARAKULS** > KARAKUL
**KARAMU** *n* small New Zealand tree with glossy leaves and orange fruit
**KARAMUS** > KARAMU
**KARANGA** *n* call or chant of welcome, sung by a female elder ▷ *vb* perform a karanga
**KARANGAED** > KARANGA
**KARANGAS** > KARANGA
**KARAOKE** *n* form of entertainment in which people sing over a prerecorded backing tape
**KARAOKES** > KARAOKE
**KARAS** > KARA
**KARAT** *n* measure of the proportion of gold in an alloy, expressed as the number of parts of gold in 24 parts of the alloy

**KARATE** *n* Japanese system of unarmed combat using blows with the feet, hands, elbows, and legs
**KARATEIST** *same as* > KARATEKA
**KARATEKA** *n* competitor or expert in karate
**KARATEKAS** > KARATEKA
**KARATES** > KARATE
**KARATS** > KARAT
**KAREAREA** *n* New Zealand falcon
**KARENGO** *n* edible type of Pacific seaweed
**KARENGOS** > KARENGO
**KARITE** *n* shea tree
**KARITES** > KARITE
**KARK** *variant spelling of* > CARK
**KARKED** > KARK
**KARKING** > KARK
**KARKS** > KARK
**KARMA** *n* person's actions affecting his or her fate in the next reincarnation
**KARMAS** > KARMA
**KARMIC** > KARMA
**KARN** *old word for* > CAIRN
**KARNS** > KARN
**KARO** *n* small New Zealand tree or shrub with sweet-smelling brown flowers
**KAROO** *n* high arid plateau
**KAROOS** > KAROO
**KARORO** *n* large seagull with black feathers on its back
**KAROROS** > KARORO
**KAROSHI** *n* (in Japan) death caused by overwork
**KAROSHIS** > KAROSHI
**KAROSS** *n* blanket made of animal skins sewn together
**KAROSSES** > KAROSS
**KARRI** *n* Australian eucalypt
**KARRIS** > KARRI
**KARROO** *same as* > KAROO
**KARROOS** > KARROO
**KARSEY** *variant spelling of* > KHAZI
**KARSEYS** > KARSEY
**KARSIES** > KARSY
**KARST** *n* denoting the characteristic scenery of a limestone region, including underground streams, gorges, etc
**KARSTIC** > KARST
**KARSTIFY** *vb* become karstic
**KARSTS** > KARST
**KARSY** *variant spelling of* > KHAZI
**KART** *n* light low-framed vehicle with small wheels and engine used for recreational racing
**KARTER** > KART
**KARTERS** > KART
**KARTING** > KART
**KARTINGS** > KART

**KARTS** > KART
**KARYOGAMY** *n* fusion of two gametic nuclei during fertilization
**KARYOGRAM** *n* diagram or photograph of the chromosomes of a cell, arranged in homologous pairs and in a numbered sequence
**KARYOLOGY** *n* study of cell nuclei, esp with reference to the number and shape of the chromosomes
**KARYON** *n* nucleus of a cell
**KARYONS** > KARYON
**KARYOSOME** *n* any of the dense aggregates of chromatin in the nucleus of a cell
**KARYOTIN** *less common word for* > CHROMATIN
**KARYOTINS** > KARYOTIN
**KARYOTYPE** *n* appearance of the chromosomes in a somatic cell of an individual or species, with reference to their number, size, shape, etc ▷ *vb* determine the karyotype of (a cell)
**KARZIES** > KARZY
**KARZY** *variant spelling of* > KHAZI
**KAS** > KA
**KASBAH** *n* citadel of any of various North African cities
**KASBAHS** > KASBAH
**KASHA** *n* dish originating in Eastern Europe, consisting of boiled or baked buckwheat
**KASHAS** > KASHA
**KASHER** *vb* make fit for use
**KASHERED** > KASHER
**KASHERING** > KASHER
**KASHERS** > KASHER
**KASHMIR** *variant spelling of* > CASHMERE
**KASHMIRS** > KASHMIR
**KASHRUS** *same as* > KASHRUTH
**KASHRUSES** > KASHRUS
**KASHRUT** *same as* > KASHRUTH
**KASHRUTH** *n* condition of being fit for ritual use in general
**KASHRUTHS** > KASHRUTH
**KASHRUTS** > KASHRUT
**KASME** *interj* (in Indian English) I swear
**KAT** *same as* > KHAT
**KATA** *n* exercise consisting of a sequence of the specific movements of a martial art, used in training and designed to show skill in technique
**KATABASES** > KATABASIS
**KATABASIS** *n* retreat of the Greek mercenaries of Cyrus the Younger, after

his death at Cunaxa, from the Euphrates to the Black Sea in 401–400 BC under the leadership of Xenophon

**KATABATIC** *adj* (of winds) blowing downhill through having become denser with cooling, esp at night when heat is lost from the earth's surface

**KATABOLIC** *same as* > CATABOLIC

**KATAKANA** *n* one of the two systems of syllabic writing employed for the representation of Japanese, based on Chinese ideograms. It is used mainly for foreign or foreign-derived words

**KATAKANAS** > KATAKANA

**KATANA** *n* Japanese samurai sword

**KATANAS** > KATANA

**KATAS** > KATA

**KATCHINA** *variant spelling of* > KACHINA

**KATCHINAS** > KATCHINA

**KATCINA** *variant spelling of* > KACHINA

**KATCINAS** > KATCINA

**KATHAK** *n* form of N Indian classical dancing that tells a story

**KATHAKALI** *n* form of dance drama of S India using mime and based on Hindu literature

**KATHAKS** > KATHAK

**KATHARSES** > KATHARSIS

**KATHARSIS** *variant spelling of* > CATHARSIS

**KATHODAL** > KATHODE

**KATHODE** *variant spelling of* > CATHODE

**KATHODES** > KATHODE

**KATHODIC** > KATHODE

**KATI** *variant spelling of* > CATTY

**KATION** *variant spelling of* > CATION

**KATIONS** > KATION

**KATIPO** *n* small poisonous New Zealand spider

**KATIPOS** > KATIPO

**KATIS** > KATI

**KATORGA** *n* labour camp in Imperial Russia or the Soviet Union

**KATORGAS** > KATORGA

**KATS** > KAT

**KATSURA** *n* Asian tree

**KATSURAS** > KATSURA

**KATTI** *variant spelling of* > CATTY

**KATTIS** > KATTI

**KATYDID** *n* large green grasshopper of N America

**KATYDIDS** > KATYDID

**KAUGH** *same as* > KIAUGH

**KAUGHS** > KAUGH

**KAUMATUA** *n* senior member of a tribe

**KAUMATUAS** > KAUMATUA

**KAUPAPA** *n* strategy, policy, or cause

**KAUPAPAS** > KAUPAPA

**KAURI** *n* large NZ conifer that yields valuable timber and resin

**KAURIES** > KAURY

**KAURIS** > KAURI

**KAURU** *n* edible stem of the cabbage tree

**KAURY** *variant spelling of* > KAURI

**KAVA** *n* Polynesian shrub

**KAVAKAVA** *same as* > KAVA

**KAVAKAVAS** > KAVAKAVA

**KAVAS** > KAVA

**KAVASS** *n* armed Turkish constable

**KAVASSES** > KAVASS

**KAW** *variant spelling of* > CAW

**KAWA** *n* protocol or etiquette, particularly in a Māori tribal meeting place

**KAWAKAWA** *n* aromatic shrub or small tree of New Zealand

**KAWAKAWAS** > KAWAKAWA

**KAWAS** > KAWA

**KAWAU** *n* New Zealand name for black shag

**KAWED** > KAW

**KAWING** > KAW

**KAWS** > KAW

**KAY** *n* name of the letter K

**KAYAK** *n* Inuit canoe made of sealskins stretched over a frame ▷ *vb* travel by kayak

**KAYAKED** > KAYAK

**KAYAKER** > KAYAK

**KAYAKERS** > KAYAK

**KAYAKING** > KAYAK

**KAYAKINGS** > KAYAK

**KAYAKS** > KAYAK

**KAYLE** *n* one of a set of ninepins

**KAYLES** *pl n* ninepins

**KAYLIED** *adj* (in British slang) intoxicated or drunk

**KAYO** *another term for* > KNOCKOUT

**KAYOED** > KAYO

**KAYOES** > KAYO

**KAYOING** > KAYO

**KAYOINGS** > KAYO

**KAYOS** > KAYO

**KAYS** > KAY

**KAZACHKI** *same as* > KAZACHOK

**KAZACHOK** *n* Russian folk dance in which the performer executes high kicks from a squatting position

**KAZATSKI** *same as* > KAZACHOK

**KAZATSKY** *same as* > KAZACHOK

**KAZATZKA** *same as* > KAZACHOK

**KAZATZKAS** > KAZACHOK

**KAZI** *variant spelling of* > KHAZI

**KAZILLION** *same as* > GAZILLION

**KAZIS** > KAZI

**KAZOO** *n* cigar-shaped metal musical instrument that produces a buzzing sound when the player hums into it

**KAZOOS** > KAZOO

**KBAR** *n* kilobar

**KBARS** > KBAR

**KEA** *n* large brownish-green parrot of NZ

**KEAS** > KEA

**KEASAR** *archaic variant of* > KAISER

**KEASARS** > KEASAR

**KEAVIE** *n* archaic or dialect word for a type of crab

**KEAVIES** > KEAVIE

**KEB** *vb* Scots word meaning miscarry or reject a lamb

**KEBAB** *n* dish of small pieces of meat grilled on skewers ▷ *vb* skewer

**KEBABBED** > KEBAB

**KEBABBING** > KEBAB

**KEBABS** > KEBAB

**KEBAR** *n* Scots word for beam or rafter

**KEBARS** > KEBAR

**KEBBED** > KEB

**KEBBIE** *n* Scots word for shepherd's crook

**KEBBIES** > KEBBIE

**KEBBING** > KEB

**KEBBOCK** *n* Scots word for a cheese

**KEBBOCKS** > CHEESE

**KEBBOCK** *same as* > KEBBOCK

**KEBBUCKS** > KEBBUCK

**KEBELE** *n* Ethiopian local council

**KEBELES** > KEBELE

**KEBLAH** *same as* > KIBLAH

**KEBLAHS** > KEBLAH

**KEBOB** *same as* > KEBAB

**KEBOBBED** > KEBOB

**KEBOBBING** > KEBOB

**KEBOBS** > KEBOB

**KEBS** > KEB

**KECK** *vb* retch or feel nausea

**KECKED** > KECK

**KECKING** > KECK

**KECKLE** *Scots variant of* > CACKLE

**KECKLED** > KECKLE

**KECKLES** > KECKLE

**KECKLING** > KECKLE

**KECKLINGS** > KECKLE

**KECKS** *pl n* trousers

**KECKSES** > KECKS

**KECKSIES** > KECKSY

**KECKSY** *n* dialect word meaning hollow plant stalk

**KED** *as in* *sheep ked* sheep tick

**KEDDAH** *same as* > KHEDA

**KEDDAHS** > KEDDAH

**KEDGE** *vb* move (a ship) along by hauling in on the cable of a light anchor

▷ *n* light anchor used for kedging

**KEDGED** > KEDGE

**KEDGER** *n* small anchor

**KEDGEREE** *n* dish of fish with rice and eggs

**KEDGEREES** > KEDGEREE

**KEDGERS** > KEDGER

**KEDGES** > KEDGE

**KEDGIER** > KEDGY

**KEDGIEST** > KEDGY

**KEDGING** > KEDGE

**KEDGY** *adj* dialect word for happy or lively

**KEDS** > KED

**KEECH** *n* old word for lump of fat

**KEECHES** > KEECH

**KEEF** *same as* > KIF

**KEEFS** > KEEF

**KEEK** *Scot word for* > PEEP

**KEEKED** > KEEK

**KEEKER** > KEEK

**KEEKERS** > KEEK

**KEEKING** > KEEK

**KEEKS** > KEEK

**KEEL** *n* main lengthways timber or steel support along the base of a ship ▷ *vb* mark with this stain

**KEELAGE** *n* fee charged by certain ports to allow a ship to dock

**KEELAGES** > KEELAGE

**KEELBOAT** *n* river boat with a shallow draught and a keel, used for freight and moved by towing, punting, or rowing

**KEELBOATS** > KEELBOAT

**KEELED** > KEEL

**KEELER** *n* bargeman

**KEELERS** > KEELER

**KEELHALE** *same as* > KEELHAUL

**KEELHALED** > KEELHALE

**KEELHALES** > KEELHALE

**KEELHAUL** *vb* reprimand (someone) harshly

**KEELHAULS** > KEELHAUL

**KEELIE** *n* kestrel

**KEELIES** > KEELIE

**KEELING** > KEEL

**KEELINGS** > KEEL

**KEELIVINE** *Scots word for* > PENCIL

**KEELLESS** > KEEL

**KEELMAN** *n* bargeman

**KEELMEN** > KEELMAN

**KEELS** > KEEL

**KEELSON** *n* lengthways beam fastened to the keel of a ship for strength

**KEELSONS** > KEELSON

**KEELYVINE** *same as* > KEELIVINE

**KEEN** *adj* eager or enthusiastic ▷ *vb* wail over the dead ▷ *n* lament for the dead

**KEENED** > KEEN

**KEENER** > KEEN

**KEENERS** > KEEN

**KEENEST** > KEEN

KEENING > KEEN
KEENINGS > KEEN
KEENLY > KEEN
KEENNESS > KEEN
KEENO same as > KENO
KEENOS > KEENO
KEENS > KEEN
KEEP vb have or retain possession of ▷ n cost of food and everyday expenses
KEEPABLE > KEEP
KEEPER n person who looks after animals in a zoo
KEEPERS > KEEPER
KEEPING > KEEP
KEEPINGS > KEEP
KEEPNET n cylindrical net strung on wire hoops and sealed at one end, suspended in water by anglers to keep alive the fish they have caught
KEEPNETS > KEEPNET
KEEPS > KEEP
KEEPSAKE n gift treasured for the sake of the giver
KEEPSAKES > KEEPSAKE
KEEPSAKY > KEEPSAKE
KEESHOND n breed of dog of the spitz type with a shaggy greyish coat and tightly curled tail, originating in Holland
KEESHONDS > KEESHOND
KEESTER same as > KEISTER
KEESTERS > KEESTER
KEET short for > PARAKEET
KEETS > KEET
KEEVE n tub or vat
KEEVES > KEEVE
KEF same as > KIF
KEFFEL dialect word for > HORSE
KEFFELS > KEFFEL
KEFFIYAH same as > KAFFIYEH
KEFFIYAHS > KEFFIYAH
KEFFIYEH n cotton headdress worn by Arabs
KEFFIYEHS > KEFFIYEH
KEFIR n effervescent drink of the Caucasus made from fermented milk
KEFIRS > KEFIR
KEFS > KEF
KEFTEDES n Greek dish of meatballs cooked with herbs and onions
KEFUFFLE same as > KERFUFFLE
KEFUFFLED > KEFUFFLE
KEFUFFLES > KEFUFFLE
KEG n small metal beer barrel ▷ vb put in kegs
KEGELER same as > KEGLER
KEGELERS > KEGELER
KEGGED > KEG
KEGGER > KEG
KEGGERS > KEG
KEGGING > KEG
KEGLER n participant in a game of tenpin bowling
KEGLERS > KEGLER

KEGLING n bowling
KEGLINGS > KEGLING
KEGS > KEG
KEHUA n ghost or spirit
KEHUAS > KEHUA
KEIGHT > KETCH
KEIR same as > KIER
KEIRETSU n group of Japanese businesses
KEIRETSUS > KEIRETSU
KEIRS > KEIR
KEISTER n rump
KEISTERS > KEISTER
KEITLOA n southern African black two-horned rhinoceros
KEITLOAS > KEITLOA
KEKENO n New Zealand fur seal
KEKERENGU n Māori bug
KEKS same as > KECKS
KEKSYE same as > KEX
KEKSYES > KEKSYE
KELEP n large ant found in Central and South America
KELEPS > KELEP
KELIM same as > KILIM
KELIMS > KELIM
KELL dialect word for > HAIRNET
KELLAUT same as > KHILAT
KELLAUTS > KELLAUT
KELLIES > KELLY
KELLS > KELL
KELLY n part of a drill system
KELOID n hard smooth pinkish raised growth of scar tissue at the site of an injury, tending to occur more frequently in dark-skinned races
KELOIDAL > KELOID
KELOIDS > KELOID
KELP n large brown seaweed ▷ vb burn seaweed to make a type of ash used as a source for iodine and potash
KELPED > KELP
KELPER n Falkland Islander
KELPERS > KELPER
KELPIE n Australian sheepdog with a smooth coat and upright ears
KELPIES > KELPY
KELPING > KELP
KELPS > KELP
KELPY same as > KELPIE
KELSON same as > KEELSON
KELSONS > KELSON
KELT n salmon that has recently spawned
KELTER same as > KILTER
KELTERS > KELTER
KELTIE variant spelling of > KELTY
KELTIES > KELTY
KELTS > KELT
KELTY n old Scots word for an extra drink imposed on someone not thought to be drinking enough
KELVIN n SI unit of

temperature
KELVINS > KELVIN
KEMB old word for > COMB
KEMBED > KEMB
KEMBING > KEMB
KEMBLA n small change
KEMBLAS > KEMBLA
KEMBO same as > KIMBO
KEMBOED > KEMBO
KEMBOING > KEMBO
KEMBOS > KEMBO
KEMBS > KEMB
KEMP n coarse hair or strand of hair, esp one in a fleece that resists dyeing ▷ vb dialect word meaning to compete or try to come first
KEMPED > KEMP
KEMPER > KEMP
KEMPERS > KEMP
KEMPIER > KEMPY
KEMPIEST > KEMPY
KEMPING > KEMP
KEMPINGS > KEMP
KEMPLE n variable Scottish measure for hay or straw
KEMPLES > KEMPLE
KEMPS > KEMP
KEMPT adj (of hair) tidy
KEMPY > KEMP
KEN vb know ▷ n range of knowledge or perception
KENAF another name for > AMBARY
KENAFS > KENAF
KENCH n bin for salting and preserving fish
KENCHES > KENCH
KENDO n Japanese sport of fencing using wooden staves
KENDOS > KENDO
KENNED > KEN
KENNEL n hutlike shelter for a dog ▷ vb put or go into a kennel
KENNELED > KENNEL
KENNELING > KENNEL
KENNELLED > KENNEL
KENNELS > KENNEL
KENNER > KEN
KENNERS > KEN
KENNET n old word for a small hunting dog
KENNETS > KENNET
KENNETT vb spoil or destroy ruthlessly
KENNETTED > KENNETT
KENNETTS > KENNETT
KENNING > KEN
KENNINGS > KEN
KENO n game of chance similar to bingo
KENOS > KENO
KENOSES > KENOSIS
KENOSIS n Christ's voluntary renunciation of certain divine attributes, in order to identify himself with mankind
KENOSISES > KENOSIS
KENOTIC > KENOSIS
KENOTRON n signal-

amplifying device
KENOTRONS > KENOTRON
KENS > KEN
KENSPECK adj Scots for easily seen or recognized
KENT dialect word for > PUNT
KENTE n brightly coloured handwoven cloth of Ghana, usually with some gold thread
KENTED > KENT
KENTES > KENTE
KENTIA n plant name formerly used to include palms now allotted to several different genera
KENTIAS > KENTIA
KENTING > KENT
KENTLEDGE n scrap metal used as ballast in a vessel
KENTS > KENT
KEP vb catch
KEPHALIC variant spelling of > CEPHALIC
KEPHALICS > KEPHALIC
KEPHALIN same as > CEPHALIN
KEPHALINS > KEPHALIN
KEPHIR same as > KEFIR
KEPHIRS > KEPHIR
KEPI n French military cap with a flat top and a horizontal peak
KEPIS > KEPI
KEPPED > KEP
KEPPEN > KEP
KEPPING > KEP
KEPPIT > KEP
KEPS > KEP
KEPT > KEEP
KERAMIC rare variant of > CERAMIC
KERAMICS rare variant of > CERAMICS
KERATIN n fibrous protein found in the hair and nails
KERATINS > KERATIN
KERATITIS n inflammation of the cornea
KERATOID adj resembling horn
KERATOMA n horny growth on the skin
KERATOMAS > KERATOMA
KERATOSE adj (esp of certain sponges) having a horny skeleton
KERATOSES > KERATOSIS
KERATOSIC > KERATOSE
KERATOSIS n any skin condition marked by a horny growth, such as a wart
KERATOTIC > KERATOSIS
KERB n edging to a footpath ▷ vb provide with or enclose with a kerb
KERBAYA n blouse worn by Malay women
KERBAYAS > KERBAYA
KERBED > KERB
KERBING n material used for a kerb

KERBINGS > KERBING

KERBS > KERB

KERBSIDE n edge of a pavement where it drops to the level of the road

KERBSIDES > KERBSIDE

KERBSTONE n one of a series of stones that form a kerb

KERCHIEF n piece of cloth worn over the head or round the neck

KERCHIEFS > KERCHIEF

KERCHOO interj atishoo

KEREL n chap or fellow

KERELS > KEREL

KERERU n New Zealand pigeon

KERF n cut made by a saw, an axe, etc ▷ vb cut

KERFED > KERF

KERFING > KERF

KERFLOOEY adv into state of destruction or malfunction

KERFS > KERF

KERFUFFLE n commotion or disorder ▷ vb put into disorder or disarray

KERKIER > KERKY

KERKIEST > KERKY

KERKY adj stupid

KERMA n quotient of the sum of the initial kinetic energies of all the charged particles liberated by indirectly ionizing radiation in a volume element of a material divided by the mass of the volume element

KERMAS > KERMA

KERMES n dried bodies of female scale insects, used as a red dyestuff

KERMESITE n red antimony

KERMESS same as > KERMIS

KERMESSE same as > KERMIS

KERMESSES > KERMESSE

KERMIS n (formerly, esp in Holland and Northern Germany) annual country festival or carnival

KERMISES > KERMIS

KERN n part of the character on a piece of printer's type that projects beyond the body ▷ vb furnish (a typeface) with a kern

KERNE same as > KERN

KERNED > KERNE

KERNEL n seed of a nut, cereal, or fruit stone ▷ vb form kernels

KERNELED > KERNEL

KERNELING > KERNEL

KERNELLED > KERNEL

KERNELLY adj with or like kernels

KERNELS > KERNEL

KERNES > KERNE

KERNING n adjustment of space between the letters

of words to improve the appearance of text matter

KERNINGS > KERNING

KERNISH adj of, belonging to, or resembling an armed foot soldier or peasant

KERNITE n light soft colourless or white mineral consisting of a hydrated sodium borate in monoclinic crystalline form: an important source of borax and other boron compounds

KERNITES > KERNITE

KERNS > KERN

KERO short for > KEROSENE

KEROGEN n solid organic material found in some rocks, such as oil shales, that produces hydrocarbons similar to petroleum when heated

KEROGENS > KEROGEN

KEROS > KERO

KEROSENE n liquid mixture distilled from petroleum and used as a fuel or solvent

KEROSENES > KEROSENE

KEROSINE same as > KEROSENE

KEROSINES > KEROSINE

KERPLUNK vb land noisily

KERPLUNKS > KERPLUNK

KERRIA n type of shrub with yellow flowers

KERRIAS > KERRIA

KERRIES > KERRY

KERRY n breed of dairy cattle

KERSEY n smooth woollen cloth used for overcoats, etc

KERSEYS > KERSEY

KERVE dialect word for > CARVE

KERVED > KERVE

KERVES > KERVE

KERVING > KERVE

KERYGMA n essential news of Jesus, as preached by the early Christians to elicit faith rather than to educate or instruct

KERYGMAS > KERYGMA

KERYGMATA > KERYGMA

KESAR old variant of > KAISER

KESARS > KESAR

KESH n beard and uncut hair, covered by the turban, traditionally worn by Sikhs as a symbol of their religious and cultural loyalty

KESHES > KESH

KEST old form of > CAST

KESTING > KEST

KESTREL n type of small falcon

KESTRELS > KESTREL

KESTS > KEST

KET n dialect word for carrion

KETA n type of salmon

KETAMINE n drug, chemically related to PCP, that is used in medicine as a general anaesthetic, being administered by injection

KETAMINES > KETAMINE

KETAS > KETA

KETCH n two-masted sailing vessel ▷ vb (in archaic usage) catch

KETCHES > KETCH

KETCHING > KETCH

KETCHUP n thick cold sauce, usu made of tomatoes

KETCHUPS > KETCHUP

KETE n basket woven from flax

KETENE n colourless irritating toxic gas used as an acetylating agent in organic synthesis

KETENES > KETENE

KETMIA as in bladder ketmia plant with pale yellow flowers and a bladder-like calyx

KETMIAS > KETMIA

KETO as in keto form form of tautomeric compounds when they are ketones rather than enol

KETOGENIC adj forming or able to stimulate the production of ketone bodies

KETOL n nitrogenous substance

KETOLS > KETOL

KETONE n type of organic solvent

KETONEMIA n excess of ketone bodies in the blood

KETONES > KETONE

KETONIC > KETONE

KETONURIA n presence of ketone bodies in the urine

KETOSE n any monosaccharide that contains a ketone group

KETOSES > KETOSIS

KETOSIS n high concentration of ketone bodies in the blood

KETOTIC > KETOSIS

KETOXIME n oxime formed by reaction between hydroxylamine and a ketone

KETOXIMES > KETOXIME

KETS > KET

KETTLE n container with a spout and handle used for boiling water

KETTLEFUL > KETTLE

KETTLES > KETTLE

KETUBAH n contract that states the obligations within Jewish marriage

KETUBAHS > KETUBAH

KETUBOT > KETUBAH

KETUBOTH > KETUBAH

KEVEL n strong bitt or bollard for securing heavy hawsers

KEVELS > KEVEL

KEVIL old variant of > KEVEL

KEVILS > KEVIL

KEWL nonstandard variant spelling of > COOL

KEWLER > KEWL

KEWLEST > KEWL

KEWPIE as in kewpie doll (in US and Canadian English) brightly coloured doll, commonly given as a prize at carnival

KEWPIES > KEWPIE

KEX n any of several large hollow-stemmed umbelliferous plants, such as cow parsnip and chervil

KEXES > KEX

KEY n device for operating a lock by moving a bolt ▷ adj of great importance ▷ vb enter (text) using a keyboard

KEYBOARD n set of keys on a piano, computer, etc ▷ vb enter (text) using a keyboard

KEYBOARDS > KEYBOARD

KEYBUGLE n bugle with keys

KEYBUGLES > KEYBUGLE

KEYBUTTON n on a keyboard, an object which, when pressed, causes the letter, number, or symbol shown on it to be printed in a document

KEYCARD n card with an electronic strip or code on it that allows it to open a corresponding keycard-operated door

KEYCARDS > KEYCARD

KEYED > KEY

KEYHOLE n opening for inserting a key into a lock

KEYHOLES > KEYHOLE

KEYING > KEY

KEYINGS > KEY

KEYLESS > KEY

KEYLINE n outline image of something on artwork or plans to show where it is to be placed

KEYLINES > KEYLINE

KEYLOGGER n device or software application used for covertly recording and monitoring keystrokes made on a remote computer

KEYNOTE adj central or dominating ▷ n dominant idea of a speech etc ▷ vb deliver a keynote address to (a political convention, etc)

KEYNOTED > KEYNOTE

KEYNOTER n person delivering a keynote address

**KEYNOTERS** > KEYNOTER
**KEYNOTES** > KEYNOTE
**KEYNOTING** > KEYNOTE
**KEYPAD** *n* small panel with a set of buttons for operating a Teletext system, electronic calculator, etc
**KEYPADS** > KEYPAD
**KEYPAL** *n* person with whom one regularly exchanges emails for fun
**KEYPALS** > KEYPAL
**KEYPUNCH** *n* device having a keyboard that is operated manually to transfer data onto punched cards, paper tape, etc ▷ *vb* transfer (data) onto punched cards, paper tape, etc, by using a key punch
**KEYRING** *n* split ring designed for holding keys
**KEYS** *interj* children's cry for truce or respite from the rules of a game
**KEYSET** *n* set of computer keys used for a particular purpose
**KEYSETS** > KEYSET
**KEYSTER** *same as* > KEISTER
**KEYSTERS** > KEYSTER
**KEYSTONE** *n* most important part of a process, organization, etc ▷ *vb* project or provide with a distorted image
**KEYSTONED** > KEYSTONE
**KEYSTONES** > KEYSTONE
**KEYSTROKE** *n* single operation of the mechanism of a typewriter or keyboard-operated typesetting machine by the action of a key ▷ *vb* enter or cause to be recorded by pressing a key
**KEYWAY** *n* longitudinal slot cut into a component to accept a key that engages with a similar slot on a mating component to prevent relative motion of the two components
**KEYWAYS** > KEYWAY
**KEYWORD** *n* word or phrase that a computer will search for in order to locate the information or file that the computer user has requested
**KEYWORDS** > KEYWORD
**KGOTLA** *n* (in South African English) meeting place for village assemblies, court cases, and meetings of village leaders
**KGOTLAS** > KGOTLA
**KHADDAR** *n* cotton cloth of plain weave, produced in India
**KHADDARS** > KHADDAR

**KHADI** *same as* > KHADDAR
**KHADIS** > KHADI
**KHAF** *n* letter of the Hebrew alphabet
**KHAFS** > KHAF
**KHAKI** *adj* dull yellowish-brown ▷ *n* hard-wearing fabric of this colour used for military uniforms
**KHAKILIKE** > KHAKI
**KHAKIS** > KHAKI
**KHALAT** *same as* > KHILAT
**KHALATS** > KHALAT
**KHALIF** *variant spelling of* > CALIPH
**KHALIFA** *same as* > CALIPH
**KHALIFAH** *same as* > CALIPH
**KHALIFAHS** > KHALIFAH
**KHALIFAS** > KHALIFA
**KHALIFAT** *same as* > CALIPHATE
**KHALIFATE** *same as* > CALIPHATE
**KHALIFATS** > KHALIFAT
**KHALIFS** > KHALIF
**KHAMSEEN** *same as* > KHAMSIN
**KHAMSEENS** > KHAMSEEN
**KHAMSIN** *n* hot southerly wind blowing from about March to May, esp in Egypt
**KHAMSINS** > KHAMSIN
**KHAN** *n* title of respect in Afghanistan and central Asia
**KHANATE** *n* territory ruled by a khan
**KHANATES** > KHANATE
**KHANDA** *n* double-edged sword that appears as the emblem on the Sikh flag and is used in the Amrit ceremony to stir the amrit
**KHANDAS** > KHANDA
**KHANGA** *same as* > KANGA
**KHANGAS** > KHANGA
**KHANJAR** *n* type of dagger
**KHANJARS** > KHANJAR
**KHANS** > KHAN
**KHANSAMA** *same as* > KHANSAMAH
**KHANSAMAH** *n* Indian cook or other male servant
**KHANSAMAS** > KHANSAMA
**KHANUM** *feminine form of* > KHAN
**KHANUMS** > KHANUM
**KHAPH** *n* letter of the Hebrew alphabet
**KHAPHS** > KHAPH
**KHARIF** *n* (in Pakistan, India, etc) crop that is harvested at the beginning of winter
**KHARIFS** > KHARIF
**KHAT** *n* white-flowered evergreen shrub of Africa and Arabia whose leaves have narcotic properties
**KHATS** > KHAT
**KHAYA** *n* type of African tree
**KHAYAL** *n* kind of Indian classical vocal music
**KHAYALS** > KHAYAL

**KHAYAS** > KHAYA
**KHAZEN** *same as* > CHAZAN
**KHAZENIM** > KHAZEN
**KHAZENS** > KHAZEN
**KHAZI** *n* lavatory
**KHAZIS** > KHAZI
**KHEDA** *n* (in India, Myanmar, etc) enclosure into which wild elephants are driven to be captured
**KHEDAH** *same as* > KHEDA
**KHEDAHS** > KHEDAH
**KHEDAS** > KHEDA
**KHEDIVA** *n* khedive's wife
**KHEDIVAL** > KHEDIVE
**KHEDIVAS** > KHEDIVA
**KHEDIVATE** > KHEDIVE
**KHEDIVE** *n* viceroy of Egypt under Ottoman suzerainty
**KHEDIVES** > KHEDIVE
**KHEDIVIAL** > KHEDIVE
**KHET** *n* Thai district
**KHETH** *same as* > HETH
**KHETHS** > KHETH
**KHETS** > KHET
**KHI** *n* letter of the Greek alphabet
**KHILAFAT** *same as* > CALIPHATE
**KHILAFATS** > KHILAFAT
**KHILAT** *n* (in the Middle East) robe or other gift given to someone by a superior as a mark of honour
**KHILATS** > KHILAT
**KHILIM** *same as* > KILIM
**KHILIMS** > KHILIM
**KHIRKAH** *n* dervish's woollen or cotton outer garment
**KHIRKAHS** > KHIRKAH
**KHIS** > KHI
**KHODJA** *same as* > KHOJA
**KHODJAS** > KHODJA
**KHOJA** *n* teacher in a Muslim school
**KHOJAS** > KHOJA
**KHOR** *n* watercourse
**KHORS** > KHOR
**KHOTBAH** *same as* > KHUTBAH
**KHOTBAHS** > KHOTBAH
**KHOTBEH** *same as* > KHUTBAH
**KHOTBEHS** > KHOTBEH
**KHOUM** *n* Mauritanian monetary unit
**KHOUMS** > KHOUM
**KHUD** *n* Indian ravine
**KHUDS** > KHUD
**KHURTA** *same as* > KURTA
**KHURTAS** > KHURTA
**KHUSKHUS** *n* aromatic perennial Indian grass whose roots are woven into mats, fans, and baskets
**KHUTBAH** *n* sermon in a Mosque, especially on a Friday
**KHUTBAHS** > KHUTBAH
**KI** *n* Japanese martial art
**KIAAT** *n* tropical African

leguminous tree
**KIAATS** > KIAAT
**KIANG** *n* variety of wild ass that occurs in Tibet and surrounding regions
**KIANGS** > KIANG
**KIAUGH** *n* (in Scots) anxiety
**KIAUGHS** > KIAUGH
**KIBBE** *n* Middle Eastern dish made with minced meat and bulgur
**KIBBEH** *same as* > KIBBE
**KIBBEHS** > KIBBEH
**KIBBES** > KIBBE
**KIBBI** *same as* > KIBBE
**KIBBIS** > KIBBI
**KIBBITZ** *same as* > KIBITZ
**KIBBITZED** > KIBBITZ
**KIBBITZER** > KIBBITZ
**KIBBITZES** > KIBBITZ
**KIBBLE** *n* bucket used in wells or in mining for hoisting ▷ *vb* grind into small pieces
**KIBBLED** > KIBBLE
**KIBBLES** > KIBBLE
**KIBBLING** > KIBBLE
**KIBBUTZ** *n* communal farm or factory in Israel
**KIBBUTZIM** > KIBBUTZ
**KIBE** *n* chilblain, esp an ulcerated one on the heel
**KIBEI** *n* someone of Japanese ancestry born in the US and educated in Japan
**KIBEIS** > KIBEI
**KIBES** > KIBE
**KIBITKA** *n* (in Russia) covered sledge or wagon
**KIBITKAS** > KIBITKA
**KIBITZ** *vb* interfere or offer unwanted advice, esp as a spectator at a card game
**KIBITZED** > KIBITZ
**KIBITZER** > KIBITZ
**KIBITZERS** > KIBITZ
**KIBITZES** > KIBITZ
**KIBITZING** > KIBITZ
**KIBLA** *same as* > KIBLAH
**KIBLAH** *n* direction of Mecca, to which Muslims turn in prayer, indicated in mosques by a niche (mihrab) in the wall
**KIBLAHS** > KIBLAH
**KIBLAS** > KIBLA
**KIBOSH** *vb* put a stop to
**KIBOSHED** > KIBOSH
**KIBOSHES** > KIBOSH
**KIBOSHING** > KIBOSH
**KICK** *vb* drive, push, or strike with the foot ▷ *n* thrust or blow with the foot
**KICKABLE** > KICK
**KICKABOUT** *n* informal game of soccer
**KICKBACK** *n* money paid illegally for favours done ▷ *vb* have a strong reaction
**KICKBACKS** > KICKBACK
**KICKBALL** *n* children's ball

game or the large ball used
in it
**KICKBALLS** > KICKBALL
**KICKBOARD** n type of float
held on to by a swimmer
when practising leg
strokes
**KICKBOX** vb box with hands
and feet
**KICKBOXED** > KICKBOX
**KICKBOXER** n someone
who practises kickboxing,
a martial art that
resembles boxing but in
which kicks are permitted
**KICKBOXES** > KICKBOX
**KICKDOWN** n method
of changing gear in a
car with automatic
transmission, by fully
depressing the accelerator
**KICKDOWNS** > KICKDOWN
**KICKED** > KICK
**KICKER** n person or thing
that kicks
**KICKERS** > KICKER
**KICKIER** > KICKY
**KICKIEST** > KICKY
**KICKING** > KICK
**KICKOFF** n kick from the
centre of the field that
starts a game of football
**KICKOFFS** > KICKOFF
**KICKS** > KICK
**KICKSHAW** n valueless
trinket
**KICKSHAWS** same
as > KICKSHAW
**KICKSTAND** n short metal
bar on a motorcycle, which
when kicked into a vertical
position holds the cycle
upright when stationary
**KICKSTART** vb start by
kicking pedal
**KICKUP** n fuss
**KICKUPS** > KICKUP
**KICKY** adj excitingly
unusual and different
**KID** n child ▷ vb tease or
deceive (someone) ▷ adj
younger
**KIDDED** > KID
**KIDDER** > KID
**KIDDERS** > KID
**KIDDIE** same as > KIDDY
**KIDDIED** > KIDDY
**KIDDIER** n old word for a
market trader
**KIDDIERS** > KIDDIER
**KIDDIES** > KIDDY
**KIDDING** > KID
**KIDDINGLY** > KID
**KIDDISH** > KID
**KIDDLE** n device, esp a
barrier constructed of nets
and stakes, for catching
fish in a river or in the sea
**KIDDLES** > KIDDLE
**KIDDO** n very informal term
of address for a young
person
**KIDDOES** > KIDDO
**KIDDOS** > KIDDO

**KIDDUSH** n (in Judaism)
special blessing said
before a meal on sabbaths
and festivals
**KIDDUSHES** > KIDDUSH
**KIDDY** n affectionate word
for a child ▷ vb tease or
deceive
**KIDDYING** > KIDDY
**KIDDYWINK** n humorous
word for a child
**KIDEL** same as > KIDDLE
**KIDELS** > KIDEL
**KIDGE** dialect word
for > LIVELY
**KIDGIE** adj dialect word for
friendly and welcoming
**KIDGIER** > KIDGIE
**KIDGIEST** > KIDGIE
**KIDGLOVE** adj overdelicate
or overrefined
**KIDLET** n humorous word
for small child
**KIDLETS** > KIDLET
**KIDLIKE** > KID
**KIDLING** n young kid
**KIDLINGS** > KIDLING
**KIDNAP** vb seize and hold (a
person) to ransom
**KIDNAPED** > KIDNAP
**KIDNAPEE** > KIDNAP
**KIDNAPEES** > KIDNAP
**KIDNAPER** > KIDNAP
**KIDNAPERS** > KIDNAP
**KIDNAPING** > KIDNAP
**KIDNAPPED** > KIDNAP
**KIDNAPPEE** > KIDNAP
**KIDNAPPER** > KIDNAP
**KIDNAPS** > KIDNAP
**KIDNEY** n either of the pair
of organs that filter waste
products from the blood to
produce urine
**KIDNEYS** > KIDNEY
**KIDOLOGY** n practice of
bluffing or deception
in order to gain a
psychological advantage
over someone
**KIDS** > KID
**KIDSKIN** n soft smooth
leather made from the
hide of a young goat
**KIDSKINS** > KIDSKIN
**KIDSTAKES** pl n pretence
**KIDULT** n adult who is
interested in forms of
entertainment such
as computer games,
television programmes,
etc that are intended for
children ▷ adj aimed at
or suitable for kidults, or
both children and adults
**KIDULTS** > KIDULT
**KIDVID** n informal word
for children's video or
television
**KIDVIDS** > KIDVID
**KIEF** same as > KIF
**KIEFS** > KIEF
**KIEKIE** n climbing bush
plant of New Zealand
**KIEKIES** > KIEKIE

**KIELBASA** n Polish sausage
**KIELBASAS** > KIELBASA
**KIELBASI** same
as > KIELBASA
**KIELBASY** same
as > KIELBASA
**KIER** n vat in which cloth is
bleached
**KIERIE** n South African
cudgel
**KIERIES** > KIERIE
**KIERS** > KIER
**KIESELGUR** n type of
mineral
**KIESERITE** n white
mineral consisting of
hydrated magnesium
sulphate
**KIESTER** same as > KEISTER
**KIESTERS** > KIESTER
**KIEVE** same as > KEEVE
**KIEVES** > KIEVE
**KIF** n any drug or agent
that when smoked is
capable of producing a
euphoric condition
**KIFF** adj South African
slang for excellent
**KIFS** > KIF
**KIGHT** n archaic spelling of
kite, the bird of prey
**KIGHTS** > KIGHT
**KIKE** n offensive word for a
Jewish person
**KIKES** > KIKE
**KIKOI** n piece of cotton
cloth with coloured bands,
worn wrapped around the
body
**KIKOIS** > KIKOI
**KIKUMON** n
chrysanthemum emblem
of the imperial family of
Japan
**KIKUMONS** > KIKUMON
**KIKUYU** n type of grass
**KIKUYUS** > KIKUYU
**KILD** old spelling of > KILLED
**KILDERKIN** n obsolete unit
of liquid capacity equal to
16 or 18 Imperial gallons or
of dry capacity equal to 16
or 18 wine gallons
**KILERG** n 1000 ergs
**KILERGS** > KILERG
**KILEY** same as > KYLIE
**KILEYS** > KILEY
**KILIM** n pileless woven rug
of intricate design made in
the Middle East
**KILIMS** > KILIM
**KILL** vb cause the death of
▷ n act of killing
**KILLABLE** > KILL
**KILLADAR** n fort
commander or governor
**KILLADARS** > KILLADAR
**KILLAS** n Cornish clay slate
**KILLASES** > KILLAS
**KILLCOW** n important
person
**KILLCOWS** > KILLCOW
**KILLCROP** n ever-hungry
baby, thought to be a fairy

changeling
**KILLCROPS** > KILLCROP
**KILLDEE** same
as > KILLDEER
**KILLDEER** n large
brown-and-white North
American plover with a
noisy cry
**KILLDEERS** > KILLDEER
**KILLDEES** > KILLDEE
**KILLED** > KILL
**KILLER** n person or animal
that kills, esp habitually
**KILLERS** > KILLER
**KILLICK** n small anchor,
esp one made of a heavy
stone
**KILLICKS** > KILLICK
**KILLIE** same as > KILLIFISH
**KILLIES** > KILLIE
**KILLIFISH** n any of
various chiefly American
minnow-like fishes
**KILLING** adj very tiring ▷ n
sudden financial success
**KILLINGLY** > KILLING
**KILLINGS** > KILLING
**KILLJOY** n person who
spoils others' pleasure
**KILLJOYS** > KILLJOY
**KILLOCK** same as > KILLICK
**KILLOCKS** > KILLOCK
**KILLOGIE** n sheltered
place in front of a kiln
**KILLOGIES** > KILLOGIE
**KILLS** > KILL
**KILLUT** same as > KHILAT
**KILLUTS** > KILLUT
**KILN** n oven for baking,
drying, or processing
pottery, bricks, etc ▷ vb
fire or process in a kiln
**KILNED** > KILN
**KILNING** > KILN
**KILNS** > KILN
**KILO** n code word for the
letter k
**KILOBAR** n 1000 bars
**KILOBARS** > KILOBAR
**KILOBASE** n unit of
measurement for DNA and
RNA equal to 1000 base
pairs
**KILOBASES** > KILOBASE
**KILOBAUD** n 1000 baud
**KILOBAUDS** > KILOBAUD
**KILOBIT** n 1024 bits
**KILOBITS** > KILOBIT
**KILOBYTE** n 1024 units of
information
**KILOBYTES** > KILOBYTE
**KILOCURIE** n unit of
thousand curies
**KILOCYCLE** n short for
kilocycle per second: a
former unit of frequency
equal to 1 kilohertz
**KILOGAUSS** n 1000 gauss
**KILOGRAM** n one thousand
grams
**KILOGRAMS** > KILOGRAM
**KILOGRAY** n 1000 gray
**KILOGRAYS** > KILOGRAY
**KILOHERTZ** n one

thousand hertz

**KILOJOULE** *n* 1000 joules

**KILOLITER** *US spelling of* > KILOLITRE

**KILOLITRE** *n* 1000 litres

**KILOMETER** *same as* > KILOMETRE

**KILOMETRE** *n* one thousand metres

**KILOMOLE** *n* 1000 moles

**KILOMOLES** > KILOMOLE

**KILORAD** *n* 1000 rads

**KILORADS** > KILORAD

**KILOS** > KILO

**KILOTON** *n* one thousand tons

**KILOTONS** > KILOTON

**KILOVOLT** *n* one thousand volts

**KILOVOLTS** > KILOVOLT

**KILOWATT** *n* one thousand watts

**KILOWATTS** > KILOWATT

**KILP** *dialect form of* > KELP

**KILPS** > KILP

**KILT** *n* knee-length pleated tartan skirt-like garment worn orig. by Scottish Highlanders ▷ *vb* put pleats in (cloth)

**KILTED** > KILT

**KILTER** *n* working order or alignment

**KILTERS** > KILTER

**KILTIE** *n* someone wearing a kilt

**KILTIES** > KILTIE

**KILTING** > KILT

**KILTINGS** > KILT

**KILTLIKE** > KILT

**KILTS** > KILT

**KILTY** *same as* > KILTIE

**KIMBO** *vb* place akimbo

**KIMBOED** > KIMBO

**KIMBOING** > KIMBO

**KIMBOS** > KIMBO

**KIMCHEE** *same as* > KIMCHI

**KIMCHEES** > KIMCHEE

**KIMCHI** *n* Korean dish made from fermented cabbage or other vegetables, garlic, and chillies

**KIMCHIS** > KIMCHI

**KIMMER** *same as* > CUMMER

**KIMMERS** > KIMMER

**KIMONO** *n* loose wide-sleeved Japanese robe, fastened with a sash

**KIMONOED** > KIMONO

**KIMONOS** > KIMONO

**KIN** *n* person's relatives collectively ▷ *adj* related by blood

**KINA** *n* standard monetary unit of Papua New Guinea, divided into 100 toea

**KINAKINA** *same as* > QUININE

**KINAKINAS** > KINAKINA

**KINARA** *n* African candle holder

**KINARAS** > KINARA

**KINAS** > KINA

**KINASE** *n* any enzyme that can convert an inactive zymogen to the corresponding enzyme

**KINASES** > KINASE

**KINCHIN** *old slang word for* > CHILD

**KINCHINS** > KINCHIN

**KINCOB** *n* fine silk fabric embroidered with threads of gold or silver, of a kind made in India

**KINCOBS** > KINCOB

**KIND** *adj* considerate, friendly, and helpful ▷ *n* class or group with common characteristics ▷ *vb* old word for beget or father

**KINDA** *adv* very informal shortening of kind of

**KINDED** > KIND

**KINDER** *adj* more kind ▷ *n* kindergarten or nursery school

**KINDERS** > KIND

**KINDEST** > KIND

**KINDIE** *same as* > KINDY

**KINDIES** > KINDY

**KINDING** > KIND

**KINDLE** *vb* set (a fire) alight

**KINDLED** > KINDLE

**KINDLER** > KINDLE

**KINDLERS** > KINDLE

**KINDLES** > KINDLE

**KINDLESS** *adj* heartless

**KINDLIER** > KINDLY

**KINDLIEST** > KINDLY

**KINDLILY** > KINDLY

**KINDLING** *n* dry wood or straw for starting fires

**KINDLINGS** > KINDLING

**KINDLY** *adj* having a warm-hearted nature ▷ *adv* in a considerate way

**KINDNESS** *n* quality of being kind

**KINDRED** *adj* having similar qualities ▷ *n* blood relationship

**KINDREDS** > KINDRED

**KINDS** > KIND

**KINDY** *n* kindergarten

**KINE** *pl n* cows or cattle ▷ *n* Japanese pestle

**KINEMA** *same as* > CINEMA

**KINEMAS** > KINEMA

**KINEMATIC** *adj* of or relating to the study of the motion of bodies without reference to mass or force

**KINES** *n* > KINE

**KINESCOPE** *n* US name for a television tube ▷ *vb* record on film

**KINESES** > KINESIS

**KINESIC** *adj* of or relating to kinesics

**KINESICS** *n* study of the role of body movements, such as winking, shrugging, etc, in communication

**KINESIS** *n* nondirectional

movement of an organism or cell in response to a stimulus, the rate of movement being dependent on the strength of the stimulus

**KINETIC** *adj* relating to or caused by motion

**KINETICAL** *same as* > KINETIC

**KINETICS** *n* branch of mechanics concerned with the study of bodies in motion

**KINETIN** *n* plant hormone

**KINETINS** > KINETIN

**KINFOLK** *another word for* > KINSFOLK

**KINFOLKS** > KINFOLK

**KING** *n* male ruler of a monarchy ▷ *vb* make king

**KINGBIRD** *n* any of several large American flycatchers

**KINGBIRDS** > KINGBIRD

**KINGBOLT** *n* pivot bolt that connects the body of a horse-drawn carriage to the front axle and provides the steering joint

**KINGBOLTS** > KINGBOLT

**KINGCRAFT** *n* art of ruling as a king, esp by diplomacy and cunning

**KINGCUP** *n* yellow-flowered plant

**KINGCUPS** > KINGCUP

**KINGDOM** *n* state ruled by a king or queen

**KINGDOMED** *adj* old word for with a kingdom

**KINGDOMS** > KINGDOM

**KINGED** > KING

**KINGFISH** *n* food and game fish occurring in warm American Atlantic coastal waters

**KINGHOOD** > KING

**KINGHOODS** > KING

**KINGING** > KING

**KINGKLIP** *n* edible eel-like marine fish of S Africa

**KINGKLIPS** > KINGKLIP

**KINGLE** *n* Scots word for a type of hard rock

**KINGLES** > KINGLE

**KINGLESS** > KING

**KINGLET** *n* king of a small or insignificant territory

**KINGLETS** > KINGLET

**KINGLIER** > KINGLY

**KINGLIEST** > KINGLY

**KINGLIKE** > KING

**KINGLING** *n* minor king

**KINGLINGS** > KINGLING

**KINGLY** *adj* appropriate to a king ▷ *adv* in a manner appropriate to a king

**KINGMAKER** *n* person who has control over appointments to positions of authority

**KINGPIN** *n* most important person in an organization

**KINGPINS** > KINGPIN

**KINGPOST** *n* vertical post connecting the apex of a triangular roof truss to the tie beam

**KINGPOSTS** > KINGPOST

**KINGS** > KING

**KINGSHIP** *n* position or authority of a king

**KINGSHIPS** > KINGSHIP

**KINGSIDE** *n* (in chess) side of the board on which a particular king is at the start of a game as opposed to the side the queen is on

**KINGSIDES** > KINGSIDE

**KINGSNAKE** *n* North American snake

**KINGWOOD** *n* hard fine-grained violet-tinted wood of a Brazilian leguminous tree

**KINGWOODS** > KINGWOOD

**KININ** *n* any of a group of polypeptides in the blood that cause dilation of the blood vessels and make smooth muscles contract

**KININS** > KININ

**KINK** *n* twist or bend in rope, wire, hair, etc ▷ *vb* form or cause to form a kink

**KINKAJOU** *n* arboreal fruit-eating mammal of Central and South America, with a long prehensile tail

**KINKAJOUS** > KINKAJOU

**KINKED** > KINK

**KINKIER** > KINKY

**KINKIEST** > KINKY

**KINKILY** > KINKY

**KINKINESS** > KINKY

**KINKING** > KINK

**KINKLE** *n* little kink

**KINKLES** > KINKLE

**KINKS** > KINK

**KINKY** *adj* given to unusual sexual practices

**KINLESS** *adj* without any relatives

**KINO** *same as* > KENO

**KINONE** *n* benzoquinone, a yellow crystalline water-soluble ketone used in the production of dyestuffs

**KINONES** > KINONE

**KINOS** > KINO

**KINRED** *old form of* > KINDRED

**KINREDS** > KINRED

**KINS** > KIN

**KINSFOLK** *pl n* one's family or relatives

**KINSFOLKS** > KINSFOLK

**KINSHIP** *n* blood relationship

**KINSHIPS** > KINSHIP

**KINSMAN** *n* relative

**KINSMEN** > KINSMAN

**KINSWOMAN** > KINSMAN

**KINSWOMEN** > KINSMAN

**KIORE** *n* small brown rat native to New Zealand

**KIOSK** *n* small booth

selling drinks, cigarettes, newspapers, etc

**KIOSKS** > KIOSK

**KIP** vb sleep ▷ n sleep or slumber

**KIPE** n dialect word for a basket for catching fish

**KIPES** > KIPE

**KIPP** uncommon variant of > KIP

**KIPPA** n skullcap worn by orthodox male Jews at all times and by others for prayer, esp a crocheted one worn by those with a specifically religious Zionist affiliation

**KIPPAGE** n Scots word for a state of anger or excitement

**KIPPAGES** > KIPPAGE

**KIPPAS** > KIPPA

**KIPPED** > KIP

**KIPPEN** > KEP

**KIPPER** n cleaned, salted, and smoked herring ▷ vb cure (a herring) by salting and smoking it

**KIPPERED** adj (of fish, esp herring) having been cleaned, salted, and smoked

**KIPPERER** > KIPPER

**KIPPERERS** > KIPPER

**KIPPERING** > KIPPER

**KIPPERS** > KIPPER

**KIPPING** > KIP

**KIPPS** > KIPP

**KIPS** > KIP

**KIPSKIN** same as > KIP

**KIPSKINS** > KIPSKIN

**KIR** n drink made from dry white wine and cassis

**KIRBEH** n leather bottle

**KIRBEHS** > KIRBEH

**KIRBIGRIP** n hairgrip

**KIRBY** as in kirby grip hairgrip consisting of a piece of wire bent back on itself and partly bent into ridges

**KIRIGAMI** n art, originally Japanese, of folding and cutting paper into decorative shapes

**KIRIGAMIS** > KIRIGAMI

**KIRIMON** n Japanese imperial crest

**KIRIMONS** > KIRIMON

**KIRK** Scot word for > CHURCH

**KIRKED** > KIRK

**KIRKING** > KIRK

**KIRKINGS** > KIRK

**KIRKMAN** n member or strong upholder of the Kirk

**KIRKMEN** > KIRKMAN

**KIRKS** > KIRK

**KIRKTON** n village or town with a parish church

**KIRKTONS** > KIRKTON

**KIRKWARD** adv towards the church

**KIRKYAIRD** same as > KIRKYARD

**KIRKYARD** n churchyard

**KIRKYARDS** > KIRKYARD

**KIRMESS** same as > KERMIS

**KIRMESSES** > KIRMESS

**KIRN** dialect word for > CHURN

**KIRNED** > KIRN

**KIRNING** > KIRN

**KIRNS** > KIRN

**KIRPAN** n short sword traditionally carried by Sikhs as a symbol of their religious and cultural loyalty

**KIRPANS** > KIRPAN

**KIRRI** n Hottentot stick

**KIRRIS** > KIRRI

**KIRS** > KIR

**KIRSCH** n cherry brandy

**KIRSCHES** > KIRSCH

**KIRTAN** n devotional singing, usually accompanied by musical instruments

**KIRTANS** > KIRTAN

**KIRTLE** n woman's skirt or dress ▷ vb dress with a kirtle

**KIRTLED** > KIRTLE

**KIRTLES** > KIRTLE

**KIS** > KI

**KISAN** n peasant or farmer

**KISANS** > KISAN

**KISH** n graphite formed on the surface of molten iron that contains a large amount of carbon

**KISHES** > KISH

**KISHKA** same as > KISHKE

**KISHKAS** > KISHKA

**KISHKE** n beef or fowl intestine or skin stuffed with flour, onion, etc, and boiled and roasted

**KISHKES** > KISHKE

**KISMAT** same as > KISMET

**KISMATS** > KISMAT

**KISMET** n fate or destiny

**KISMETIC** > KISMET

**KISMETS** > KISMET

**KISS** vb touch with the lips in affection or greeting ▷ n touch with the lips

**KISSABLE** > KISS

**KISSABLY** > KISS

**KISSAGRAM** n greetings service in which a messenger kisses the person celebrating

**KISSED** > KISS

**KISSEL** n Russian dessert of sweetened fruit purée thickened with arrowroot

**KISSELS** > KISSEL

**KISSER** n mouth or face

**KISSERS** > KISSER

**KISSES** > KISS

**KISSING** > KISS

**KISSOGRAM** same as > KISSAGRAM

**KISSY** adj showing exaggerated affection, esp by frequent touching or kissing

**KIST** n large wooden chest ▷ vb place in a coffin

**KISTED** > KIST

**KISTFUL** > KIST

**KISTFULS** > KIST

**KISTING** > KIST

**KISTS** > KIST

**KISTVAEN** n stone tomb

**KISTVAENS** > KISTVAEN

**KIT** n outfit or equipment for a specific purpose ▷ vb fit or provide

**KITBAG** n bag for a soldier's or traveller's belongings

**KITBAGS** > KITBAG

**KITCHEN** n room used for cooking ▷ vb (in archaic usage) provide with food

**KITCHENED** > KITCHEN

**KITCHENER** n someone employed in kitchen work

**KITCHENET** n small kitchen or part of another room equipped for use as a kitchen

**KITCHENS** > KITCHEN

**KITE** n light frame covered with a thin material flown on a string in the wind ▷ vb soar and glide

**KITED** > KITE

**KITELIKE** > KITE

**KITENGE** n thick cotton cloth

**KITENGES** > KITENGE

**KITER** > KITE

**KITERS** > KITE

**KITES** > KITE

**KITH** n one's friends and acquaintances

**KITHARA** variant of > CITHARA

**KITHARAS** > KITHARA

**KITHE** same as > KYTHE

**KITHED** > KITHE

**KITHES** > KITHE

**KITHING** > KITHE

**KITHS** > KITH

**KITING** > KITE

**KITINGS** > KITE

**KITLING** dialect word for > KITTEN

**KITLINGS** > KITLING

**KITS** > KIT

**KITSCH** n art or literature with popular sentimental appeal ▷ n object or art that is tawdry, vulgarized, oversentimental or pretentious

**KITSCHES** > KITSCH

**KITSCHIER** > KITSCH

**KITSCHIFY** vb make kitsch

**KITSCHILY** > KITSCH

**KITSCHY** > KITSCH

**KITSET** n New Zealand word for a piece of furniture supplied in pieces for the purchaser to assemble

**KITSETS** > KITSET

**KITTED** > KIT

**KITTEL** n white garment worn for certain Jewish rituals or burial

**KITTELS** > KITTEL

**KITTEN** n young cat ▷ vb (of cats) give birth

**KITTENED** > KITTEN

**KITTENING** > KITTEN

**KITTENISH** adj lively and flirtatious

**KITTENS** > KITTEN

**KITTENY** > KITTEN

**KITTIES** > KITTY

**KITTING** > KIT

**KITTIWAKE** n type of seagull

**KITTLE** adj capricious and unpredictable ▷ vb be troublesome or puzzling to (someone)

**KITTLED** > KITTLE

**KITTLER** > KITTLE

**KITTLES** > KITTLE

**KITTLEST** > KITTLE

**KITTLIER** > KITTLY

**KITTLIEST** > KITTLY

**KITTLING** > KITTLE

**KITTLY** Scots word for > TICKLISH

**KITTUL** n type of palm from which jaggery sugar comes

**KITTULS** > KITTUL

**KITTY** n communal fund

**KIVA** n large underground or partly underground room in a Pueblo Indian village, used chiefly for religious ceremonies

**KIVAS** > KIVA

**KIWI** n New Zealand flightless bird with a long beak and no tail

**KIWIFRUIT** n edible oval fruit of the kiwi plant

**KIWIS** > KIWI

**KLANG** n (in music) kind of tone

**KLANGS** > KLANG

**KLAP** vb slap or spank

**KLAPPED** > KLAP

**KLAPPING** > KLAP

**KLAPS** > KLAP

**KLATCH** n gathering, especially over coffee

**KLATCHES** > KLATCH

**KLATSCH** same as > KLATCH

**KLATSCHES** > KLATSCH

**KLAVERN** n local Ku Klux Klan group

**KLAVERNS** > KLAVERN

**KLAVIER** same as > CLAVIER

**KLAVIERS** > KLAVIER

**KLAXON** n loud horn used on emergency vehicles as a warning signal ▷ vb hoot with a klaxon

**KLAXONED** > KLAXON

**KLAXONING** > KLAXON

**KLAXONS** > KLAXON

**KLEAGLE** n person with a particular rank in the Ku Klux Klan

**KLEAGLES** > KLEAGLE

**KLEENEX** n tradename for a kind of soft paper tissue,

used esp as a handkerchief

**KLEENEXES** > KLEENEX

**KLENDUSIC** *adj* disease-resistant

**KLEPHT** *n* any of the Greeks who fled to the mountains after the 15th-century Turkish conquest of Greece and whose descendants survived as brigands into the 19th century

**KLEPHTIC** > KLEPHT

**KLEPHTISM** > KLEPHT

**KLEPHTS** > KLEPHT

**KLEPTO** *n* compulsive thief

**KLEPTOS** > KLEPTO

**KLEZMER** *n* Jewish folk musician, usually a member of a small band

**KLEZMERS** > KLEZMER

**KLEZMORIM** > KLEZMER

**KLICK** *n* kilometre

**KLICKS** > KLICK

**KLIEG** as in *klieg light* intense carbon-arc light used for illumination in producing films

**KLIK** *US military slang word for* > KILOMETRE

**KLIKS** > KLIK

**KLINKER** *n* type of brick used in paving

**KLINKERS** > KLINKER

**KLINOSTAT** *n* rotating and tilting plant holder for studying and experimenting with plant growth

**KLIPDAS** *n* rock hyrax

**KLIPDASES** > KLIPDAS

**KLISTER** *n* type of ski dressing for improving grip on snow

**KLISTERS** > KLISTER

**KLONDIKE** *n* rich source of something ▷ *vb* transfer (bulk loads of fish) to factory ships at sea for processing

**KLONDIKED** > KLONDIKE

**KLONDIKER** *same as* > KLONDYKER

**KLONDIKES** > KLONDIKE

**KLONDYKE** *n* rich source of something ▷ *vb* transfer (bulk loads of fish) to factory ships at sea for processing

**KLONDYKED** > KLONDYKE

**KLONDYKER** *n* East European factory ship

**KLONDYKES** > KLONDYKE

**KLONG** *n* type of canal in Thailand

**KLONGS** > KLONG

**KLOOCH** *same as* > KLOOCHMAN

**KLOOCHES** > KLOOCH

**KLOOCHMAN** *n* North American Indian woman

**KLOOCHMEN** > KLOOCHMAN

**KLOOF** *n* mountain pass or gorge

**KLOOFS** > KLOOF

**KLOOTCH** *same as* > KLOOCHMAN

**KLOOTCHES** > KLOOTCH

**KLUDGE** *n* untidy solution involving a variety of cobbled-together elements ▷ *vb* cobble something together

**KLUDGED** > KLUDGE

**KLUDGES** > KLUDGE

**KLUDGEY** > KLUDGE

**KLUDGIER** > KLUDGE

**KLUDGIEST** > KLUDGE

**KLUDGING** > KLUDGE

**KLUDGY** > KLUDGE

**KLUGE** *same as* > KLUDGE

**KLUGED** > KLUGE

**KLUGES** > KLUGE

**KLUGING** > KLUGE

**KLUTZ** *n* clumsy or stupid person

**KLUTZES** > KLUTZ

**KLUTZIER** > KLUTZ

**KLUTZIEST** > KLUTZ

**KLUTZY** > KLUTZ

**KLYSTRON** *n* electron tube for the amplification or generation of microwaves by means of velocity modulation

**KLYSTRONS** > KLYSTRON

**KNACK** *n* skilful way of doing something ▷ *vb* dialect word for crack or snap

**KNACKED** *adj* broken or worn out

**KNACKER** *n* buyer of old horses for killing ▷ *vb* exhaust

**KNACKERED** *adj* extremely tired

**KNACKERS** > KNACKER

**KNACKERY** *n* slaughterhouse for horses

**KNACKIER** > KNACKY

**KNACKIEST** > KNACKY

**KNACKING** > KNACK

**KNACKISH** *adj* old word meaning cunning or artful

**KNACKS** > KNACK

**KNACKY** *adj* old or dialect word for cunning or artful

**KNAG** *n* knot in wood

**KNAGGIER** > KNAGGY

**KNAGGIEST** > KNAGGY

**KNAGGY** *adj* knotty

**KNAGS** > KNAG

**KNAIDEL** *same as* > KNEIDEL

**KNAIDLACH** > KNAIDEL

**KNAP** *n* crest of a hill ▷ *vb* hit, hammer, or chip

**KNAPPED** > KNAP

**KNAPPER** > KNAP

**KNAPPERS** > KNAP

**KNAPPING** > KNAP

**KNAPPLE** *old word for* > NIBBLE

**KNAPPLED** > KNAPPLE

**KNAPPLES** > KNAPPLE

**KNAPPLING** > KNAPPLE

**KNAPS** > KNAP

**KNAPSACK** *n* soldier's or traveller's bag worn

strapped on the back

**KNAPSACKS** > KNAPSACK

**KNAPWEED** *n* plant with purplish thistle-like flowers

**KNAPWEEDS** > KNAPWEED

**KNAR** *old spelling of* > GNAR

**KNARL** *old spelling of* > GNARL

**KNARLS** > KNARL

**KNARLY** *same as* > GNARLY

**KNARRED** > KNAR

**KNARRING** > KNAR

**KNARRY** > KNAR

**KNARS** > KNAR

**KNAUR** *variant form of* > KNUR

**KNAURS** > KNAUR

**KNAVE** *n* jack at cards

**KNAVERIES** > KNAVERY

**KNAVERY** *n* dishonest behaviour

**KNAVES** > KNAVE

**KNAVESHIP** *n* old Scottish legal term for the small proportion of milled grain due to the person doing the milling

**KNAVISH** > KNAVE

**KNAVISHLY** > KNAVE

**KNAWE** *same as* > KNAWEL

**KNAWEL** *n* any of several Old World caryophyllaceous plants of the genus *Scleranthus*, having heads of minute petal-less flowers

**KNAWELS** > KNAWEL

**KNAWES** > KNAWE

**KNEAD** *vb* work (dough) into a smooth mixture with the hands

**KNEADABLE** > KNEAD

**KNEADED** > KNEAD

**KNEADER** > KNEAD

**KNEADERS** > KNEAD

**KNEADING** > KNEAD

**KNEADS** > KNEAD

**KNEE** *n* joint between thigh and lower leg ▷ *vb* strike or push with the knee

**KNEECAP** *nontechnical name for* > PATELLA

**KNEECAPS** > KNEECAP

**KNEED** > KNEE

**KNEEHOLE** *n* space for the knees, esp under a desk

**KNEEHOLES** > KNEEHOLE

**KNEEING** > KNEE

**KNEEJERK** *adj* (of a reply or reaction) automatic and predictable

**KNEEL** *vb* fall or rest on one's knees ▷ *n* act or position of kneeling

**KNEELED** > KNEEL

**KNEELER** > KNEEL

**KNEELERS** > KNEEL

**KNEELING** > KNEEL

**KNEELS** > KNEEL

**KNEEPAD** *n* any of several types of protective covering for the knees

**KNEEPADS** > KNEEPAD

**KNEEPAN** *another word*

*for* > PATELLA

**KNEEPANS** > KNEEPAN

**KNEEPIECE** *n* knee-shaped piece of timber in ship

**KNEES** > KNEE

**KNEESIES** *n* flirtatious touching of knees under table

**KNEESOCK** *n* type of sock that comes up to the knee

**KNEESOCKS** > KNEESOCK

**KNEIDEL** *n* (in Jewish cookery) small dumpling, usually served in chicken soup

**KNEIDLACH** > KNEIDEL

**KNELL** *n* sound of a bell, esp at a funeral or death ▷ *vb* ring a knell

**KNELLED** > KNELL

**KNELLING** > KNELL

**KNELLS** > KNELL

**KNELT** > KNEEL

**KNESSET** *n* parliament or assembly

**KNESSETS** > KNESSET

**KNEVELL** *vb* old Scots word meaning beat

**KNEVELLED** > KNEVELL

**KNEVELLS** > KNEVELL

**KNEW** > KNOW

**KNICKER** *n* woman's or girl's undergarment covering the lower trunk and having legs or legholes

**KNICKERED** > KNICKER

**KNICKERS** *pl n* woman's or girl's undergarment covering the lower trunk and having legs or legholes

**KNICKS** *pl n* knickers

**KNIFE** *n* cutting tool or weapon consisting of a sharp-edged blade with a handle ▷ *vb* cut or stab with a knife

**KNIFED** > KNIFE

**KNIFELESS** > KNIFE

**KNIFELIKE** > KNIFE

**KNIFEMAN** *n* man who is armed with a knife

**KNIFEMEN** > KNIFEMAN

**KNIFER** > KNIFE

**KNIFEREST** *n* support on which a carving knife or carving fork is placed at the table

**KNIFERS** > KNIFE

**KNIFES** > KNIFE

**KNIFING** > KNIFE

**KNIFINGS** > KNIFE

**KNIGHT** *n* man who has been given a knighthood ▷ *vb* award a knighthood to

**KNIGHTAGE** *n* group of knights or knights collectively

**KNIGHTED** > KNIGHT

**KNIGHTING** > KNIGHT

**KNIGHTLY** *adj* of, resembling, or appropriate for a knight

**KNIGHTS** > KNIGHT

**KNIPHOFIA** n any of several perennial southern African flowering plants

**KNISH** n piece of dough stuffed with potato, meat, or some other filling and baked or fried

**KNISHES** > KNISH

**KNIT** vb make (a garment) by interlocking a series of loops in wool or other yarn ▷ n fabric made by knitting

**KNITCH** dialect word for > BUNDLE

**KNITCHES** > KNITCH

**KNITS** > KNIT

**KNITTABLE** > KNIT

**KNITTED** > KNIT

**KNITTER** > KNIT

**KNITTERS** > KNIT

**KNITTING** > KNIT

**KNITTINGS** > KNIT

**KNITTLE** n old word for string or cord

**KNITTLES** > KNITTLE

**KNITWEAR** n knitted clothes, such as sweaters

**KNITWEARS** > KNITWEAR

**KNIVE** rare variant of > KNIFE

**KNIVED** > KNIVE

**KNIVES** > KNIFE

**KNIVING** > KNIVE

**KNOB** n rounded projection, such as a switch on a radio ▷ vb supply with knobs

**KNOBBED** > KNOB

**KNOBBER** n two-year-old male deer

**KNOBBERS** > KNOBBER

**KNOBBIER** > KNOB

**KNOBBIEST** > KNOB

**KNOBBING** > KNOB

**KNOBBLE** n small knob ▷ vb dialect word meaning strike

**KNOBBLED** same as > KNOBBLY

**KNOBBLES** > KNOBBLE

**KNOBBLIER** > KNOBBLY

**KNOBBLING** > KNOBBLE

**KNOBBLY** adj covered with small bumps

**KNOBBY** > KNOB

**KNOBHEAD** n stupid person

**KNOBHEADS** > KNOBHEAD

**KNOBLIKE** > KNOB

**KNOBS** > KNOB

**KNOBSTICK** n stick with a round knob at the end, used as a club or missile by South African tribesmen

**KNOCK** vb give a blow or push to ▷ n blow or rap

**KNOCKDOWN** adj (of a price) very low

**KNOCKED** > KNOCK

**KNOCKER** n metal fitting for knocking on a door

**KNOCKERS** > KNOCKER

**KNOCKING** > KNOCK

**KNOCKINGS** > KNOCK

**KNOCKLESS** > KNOCK

**KNOCKOFF** n informal word for a cheap, often illegal, copy of something

**KNOCKOFFS** > KNOCKOFF

**KNOCKOUT** n blow that renders an opponent unconscious ▷ vb render (someone) unconscious

**KNOCKOUTS** > KNOCKOUT

**KNOCKS** > KNOCK

**KNOLL** n small rounded hill ▷ vb (in archaic or dialect usage) knell

**KNOLLED** > KNOLL

**KNOLLER** > KNOLL

**KNOLLERS** > KNOLL

**KNOLLING** > KNOLL

**KNOLLS** > KNOLL

**KNOLLY** > KNOLL

**KNOP** n knob, esp an ornamental one

**KNOPPED** > KNOP

**KNOPS** > KNOP

**KNOSP** n budlike architectural feature

**KNOSPS** > KNOSP

**KNOT** n fastening made by looping and pulling tight strands of string, cord, or rope ▷ vb tie with or into a knot

**KNOTGRASS** n polygonaceous weedy plant whose small green flowers produce numerous seeds

**KNOTHOLE** n hole in a piece of wood where a knot has been

**KNOTHOLES** > KNOTHOLE

**KNOTLESS** > KNOT

**KNOTLIKE** > KNOT

**KNOTS** > KNOT

**KNOTTED** > KNOT

**KNOTTER** > KNOT

**KNOTTERS** > KNOT

**KNOTTIER** > KNOTTY

**KNOTTIEST** > KNOTTY

**KNOTTILY** > KNOTTY

**KNOTTING** > KNOT

**KNOTTINGS** > KNOT

**KNOTTY** adj full of knots

**KNOTWEED** n any of several polygonaceous plants of the genus Polygonum, having small flowers and jointed stems

**KNOTWEEDS** > KNOTWEED

**KNOTWORK** n ornamentation consisting of a mass of intertwined and knotted cords

**KNOTWORKS** > KNOTWORK

**KNOUT** n stout whip used formerly in Russia as an instrument of punishment ▷ vb whip

**KNOUTED** > KNOUT

**KNOUTING** > KNOUT

**KNOUTS** > KNOUT

**KNOW** vb be or feel certain of the truth of (information etc)

**KNOWABLE** > KNOW

**KNOWE** same as > KNOLL

**KNOWER** > KNOW

**KNOWERS** > KNOW

**KNOWES** > KNOW

**KNOWHOW** n ingenuity, knack, or skill

**KNOWHOWS** > KNOWHOW

**KNOWING** > KNOW

**KNOWINGER** > KNOW

**KNOWINGLY** > KNOW

**KNOWINGS** > KNOW

**KNOWLEDGE** n facts, feelings or experiences known by a person or group of people ▷ vb (in archaic usage) acknowledge

**KNOWN** > KNOW

**KNOWNS** > KNOW

**KNOWS** > KNOW

**KNUB** dialect word for > KNOB

**KNUBBIER** > KNUB

**KNUBBIEST** > KNUB

**KNUBBLE** vb dialect word for beat or pound using one's fists

**KNUBBLED** > KNUBBLE

**KNUBBLES** > KNUBBLE

**KNUBBLIER** > KNUBBLY

**KNUBBLING** > KNUBBLE

**KNUBBLY** adj having small lumps or protuberances

**KNUBBY** adj knub

**KNUBS** > KNUB

**KNUCKLE** n bone at the finger joint

**KNUCKLED** > KNUCKLE

**KNUCKLER** n type of throw in baseball

**KNUCKLERS** > KNUCKLER

**KNUCKLES** > KNUCKLE

**KNUCKLIER** > KNUCKLE

**KNUCKLING** > KNUCKLE

**KNUCKLY** > KNUCKLE

**KNUR** n knot or protuberance in a tree trunk or in wood

**KNURL** n small ridge, often one of a series ▷ vb impress with a series of fine ridges or serrations

**KNURLED** > KNURL

**KNURLIER** > KNURLY

**KNURLIEST** > KNURLY

**KNURLING** > KNURL

**KNURLINGS** > KNURL

**KNURLS** > KNURL

**KNURLY** rare word for > GNARLED

**KNURR** same as > KNUR

**KNURRS** > KNURR

**KNURS** > KNUR

**KNUT** n dandy

**KNUTS** > KNUT

**KO** n (in New Zealand) traditional digging tool

**KOA** n Hawaiian leguminous tree

**KOALA** n tree-dwelling Australian marsupial with dense grey fur

**KOALAS** > KOALA

**KOAN** n (in Zen Buddhism) problem or riddle that admits no logical solution

**KOANS** > KOAN

**KOAP** n (in Papua New Guinean slang) sexual intercourse

**KOAPS** > KOAP

**KOAS** > KOA

**KOB** n any of several waterbuck-like species of African antelope

**KOBAN** n old oval-shaped Japanese gold coin

**KOBANG** same as > KOBAN

**KOBANGS** > KOBANG

**KOBANS** > KOBAN

**KOBO** n Nigerian monetary unit, worth one hundredth of a naira

**KOBOLD** n mischievous household sprite

**KOBOLDS** > KOBOLD

**KOBOS** > KOBO

**KOBS** > KOB

**KOCHIA** n any of several plants whose foliage turns dark red in late summer

**KOCHIAS** > KOCHIA

**KOEKOEA** n long-tailed cuckoo of New Zealand

**KOEL** n any of several parasitic cuckoos of S and SE Asia and Australia

**KOELS** > KOEL

**KOFF** n Dutch masted merchant vessel

**KOFFS** > KOFF

**KOFTA** n Indian dish of seasoned minced meat shaped into small balls and cooked

**KOFTAS** > KOFTA

**KOFTGAR** n (in India) person skilled in the art of inlaying steel with gold

**KOFTGARI** n ornamental Indian metalwork

**KOFTGARIS** > KOFTGARI

**KOFTGARS** > KOFTGAR

**KOFTWORK** same as > KOFTGARI

**KOFTWORKS** > KOFTWORK

**KOHA** n gift or donation, esp of cash

**KOHAS** > KOHA

**KOHEKOHE** n New Zealand tree with large glossy leaves and reddish wood

**KOHL** n cosmetic powder used to darken the edges of the eyelids

**KOHLRABI** n type of cabbage with an edible stem

**KOHLRABIS** > KOHLRABI

**KOHLS** > KOHL

**KOI** n any of various ornamental forms of the common carp

**KOINE** n common language among speakers of different languages

**KOINES** > KOINE

**KOIS** > KOI

**KOJI** n Japanese steamed rice

**KOJIS** > KOJI

**KOKAKO** n dark grey long-tailed wattled crow of New Zealand
**KOKAKOS** > KOKAKO
**KOKANEE** n freshwater salmon of lakes and rivers in W North America
**KOKANEES** > KOKANEE
**KOKER** n Guyanese sluice
**KOKERS** > KOKER
**KOKIRI** n rough-skinned New Zealand triggerfish, *Parika scaber*
**KOKOBEH** adj (of certain fruit) having a rough skin
**KOKOPU** n any of several small freshwater fish of New Zealand
**KOKOWAI** n type of clay used in decoration because of its red colour
**KOKOWAIS** > KOKOWAI
**KOKRA** n type of wood
**KOKRAS** > KOKRA
**KOKUM** n tropical tree
**KOKUMS** > KOKUM
**KOLA** as in *kola nut* caffeine-containing seed used in medicine and soft drinks
**KOLACKY** n sweet bun with a fruit, jam, or nut filling
**KOLAS** > KOLA
**KOLBASI** same as > KOLBASSI
**KOLBASIS** > KOLBASI
**KOLBASSI** n type of sausage
**KOLBASSIS** > KOLBASSI
**KOLHOZ** same as > KOLKHOZ
**KOLHOZES** > KOLHOZ
**KOLHOZY** same as > KOLKHOZ
**KOLINSKI** same as > KOLINSKY
**KOLINSKY** n Asian mink
**KOLKHOS** same as > KOLKHOZ
**KOLKHOSES** > KOLKHOS
**KOLKHOSY** > KOLKHOS
**KOLKHOZ** n (formerly) collective farm in the Soviet Union
**KOLKHOZES** > KOLKHOZ
**KOLKHOZY** > KOLKHOZ
**KOLKOZ** same as > KOLKHOZ
**KOLKOZES** > KOLKOZ
**KOLKOZY** > KOLKOZ
**KOLO** n Serbian folk dance in which a circle of people dance slowly around one or more dancers in the centre
**KOLOS** > KOLO
**KOMATIK** n sledge with wooden runners and crossbars bound with animal hides
**KOMATIKS** > KOMATIK
**KOMBU** n dark brown seaweed, the leaves of which are dried and used esp in Japanese cookery
**KOMBUS** > KOMBU

**KOMISSAR** same as > COMMISSAR
**KOMISSARS** > KOMISSAR
**KOMITAJI** n rebel or revolutionary
**KOMITAJIS** > KOMITAJI
**KOMONDOR** n large powerful dog of an ancient Hungarian breed, originally used for sheep herding
**KOMONDORS** > KOMONDOR
**KON** old word for > KNOW
**KONAKI** same as > KONEKE
**KONBU** same as > KOMBU
**KONBUS** > KONBU
**KOND** > KON
**KONDO** n (in Uganda) thief or armed robber
**KONDOS** > KONDO
**KONEKE** n farm vehicle with runners in front and wheels at the rear
**KONFYT** n South African fruit preserve
**KONFYTS** > KONFYT
**KONGONI** n E African hartebeest, *Alcelaphus buselaphus*
**KONIMETER** n device for measuring airborne dust concentration in which samples are obtained by sucking the air through a hole and allowing it to pass over a glass plate coated with grease on which the particles collect
**KONINI** n edible dark purple berry of the kotukutuku or tree fuchsia
**KONIOLOGY** n study of atmospheric dust and its effects
**KONISCOPE** n device for detecting and measuring dust in the air
**KONK** same as > CONK
**KONKED** > KONK
**KONKING** > KONK
**KONKS** > KONK
**KONNING** > KON
**KONS** > KON
**KOODOO** same as > KUDU
**KOODOOS** > KOODOO
**KOOK** n eccentric person ▷ vb dialect word for vanish
**KOOKED** > KOOK
**KOOKIE** same as > KOOKY
**KOOKIER** > KOOKY
**KOOKIEST** > KOOKY
**KOOKINESS** > KOOKY
**KOOKING** > KOOK
**KOOKS** > KOOK
**KOOKY** adj crazy, eccentric, or foolish
**KOOLAH** old form of > KOALA
**KOOLAHS** > KOOLAH
**KOORI** n Australian Aborigine
**KOORIES** > KOORI
**KOORIS** > KOORI
**KOP** n prominent isolated

hill or mountain in southern Africa
**KOPASETIC** same as > COPACETIC
**KOPECK** n former Russian monetary unit, one hundredth of a rouble
**KOPECKS** > KOPECK
**KOPEK** same as > KOPECK
**KOPEKS** > KOPEK
**KOPH** n 19th letter in the Hebrew alphabet
**KOPHS** > KOPH
**KOPIYKA** n monetary unit of Ukraine, worth one hundredth of a hryvna
**KOPIYKAS** > KOPIYKA
**KOPJE** n small hill
**KOPJES** > KOPJE
**KOPPA** n consonantal letter in the Greek alphabet pronounced like kappa (K) with the point of articulation further back in the throat
**KOPPAS** > KOPPA
**KOPPIE** same as > KOPJE
**KOPPIES** > KOPPIE
**KOPS** > KOP
**KOR** n ancient Hebrew unit of capacity
**KORA** n West African instrument with twenty-one strings, combining features of the harp and the lute
**KORAI** > KORE
**KORARI** n native New Zealand flax plant, *Phormium tenax*
**KORAS** > KORA
**KORAT** as in *korat cat* rare blue-grey breed of cat with brilliant green eyes
**KORATS** > KORAT
**KORE** n ancient Greek statue of a young woman wearing clothes
**KORERO** n talk or discussion ▷ vb speak or converse
**KOREROED** > KORERO
**KOREROING** > KORERO
**KOREROS** > KORERO
**KORES** > KORE
**KORFBALL** n game similar to basketball, in which each team consists of six men and six women
**KORFBALLS** > KORFBALL
**KORIMAKO** another name for > BELLBIRD
**KORKIR** n variety of lichen used in dyeing
**KORKIRS** > KORKIR
**KORMA** n type of mild Indian dish consisting of meat or vegetables cooked in water, yoghurt, or cream
**KORMAS** > KORMA
**KORO** n elderly Māori man
**KOROMIKO** n flowering New Zealand shrub, *Hebe salicifolia*
**KORORA** n small New

Zealand penguin
**KORORAS** > KORORA
**KOROWAI** n decorative woven cloak worn by a Māori chief
**KORS** > KOR
**KORU** n stylized curved pattern used esp in carving
**KORUN** > KORUNA
**KORUNA** n standard monetary unit of the Czech Republic and Slovakia, divided into 100 hellers
**KORUNAS** > KORUNA
**KORUNY** > KORUNA
**KORUS** > KORU
**KOS** n Indian unit of distance having different values in different localities
**KOSES** > KOS
**KOSHER** adj conforming to Jewish religious law, esp (of food) to Jewish dietary law ▷ n kosher food ▷ vb prepare in accordance with Jewish dietary rules
**KOSHERED** > KOSHER
**KOSHERING** > KOSHER
**KOSHERS** > KOSHER
**KOSMOS** variant form of > COSMOS
**KOSMOSES** > KOSMOS
**KOSS** same as > KOS
**KOSSES** > KOSS
**KOTARE** n small greenish-blue kingfisher found in New Zealand, Australia, and some Pacific islands to the north
**KOTCH** vb South African slang for vomit
**KOTCHED** > KOTCH
**KOTCHES** > KOTCH
**KOTCHING** > KOTCH
**KOTO** n Japanese stringed instrument, consisting of a rectangular wooden body over which are stretched silk strings, which are plucked with plectrums or a nail-like device
**KOTOS** > KOTO
**KOTOW** same as > KOWTOW
**KOTOWED** > KOTOW
**KOTOWER** > KOTOW
**KOTOWERS** > KOTOW
**KOTOWING** > KOTOW
**KOTOWS** > KOTOW
**KOTTABOS** > COTTABUS
**KOTUKU** n white heron with brilliant white plumage, black legs and yellow eyes and bill
**KOTWAL** n senior police officer or magistrate in an Indian town
**KOTWALS** > KOTWAL
**KOULAN** same as > KULAN
**KOULANS** > KOULAN
**KOUMIS** same as > KUMISS
**KOUMISES** > KOUMIS

**KOUMISS** *same as* > KUMISS
**KOUMISSES** > KOUMISS
**KOUMYS** *same as* > KUMISS
**KOUMYSES** > KOUMYS
**KOUMYSS** *same as* > KUMISS
**KOUMYSSES** > KOUMYSS
**KOUPREY** *n* large wild SE Asian ox
**KOUPREYS** > KOUPREY
**KOURA** *n* New Zealand freshwater crayfish
**KOURBASH** *same as* > KURBASH
**KOUROI** > KOUROS
**KOUROS** *n* ancient Greek statue of a young man
**KOUSKOUS** *same as* > COUSCOUS
**KOUSSO** *n* Abyssinian tree whose flowers have useful antiparasitic properties
**KOUSSOS** > KOUSSO
**KOW** *old variant of* > COW
**KOWHAI** *n* New Zealand tree with clusters of yellow flowers
**KOWHAIS** > KOWHAI
**KOWS** > KOW
**KOWTOW** *vb* be servile (towards) ▷ *n* act of kowtowing
**KOWTOWED** > KOWTOW
**KOWTOWER** > KOWTOW
**KOWTOWERS** > KOWTOW
**KOWTOWING** > KOWTOW
**KOWTOWS** > KOWTOW
**KRAAL** *n* S African village surrounded by a strong fence ▷ *adj* denoting or relating to the tribal aspects of the Black African way of life ▷ *vb* enclose (livestock) in a kraal
**KRAALED** > KRAAL
**KRAALING** > KRAAL
**KRAALS** > KRAAL
**KRAB** *same as* > KARABINER
**KRABS** > KRAB
**KRAFT** *n* strong wrapping paper, made from pulp processed with a sulphate solution
**KRAFTS** > KRAFT
**KRAIT** *n* any nonaggressive brightly coloured venomous elapid snake of the genus *Bungarus*, of S and SE Asia
**KRAITS** > KRAIT
**KRAKEN** *n* legendary sea monster
**KRAKENS** > KRAKEN
**KRAKOWIAK** *n* Polish dance
**KRAMERIA** *another name for* > RHATANY
**KRAMERIAS** > KRAMERIA
**KRANG** *n* dead whale from which the blubber has been removed
**KRANGS** > KRANG
**KRANS** *n* sheer rock face
**KRANSES** > KRANS
**KRANTZ** *same as* > KRANS

**KRANTZES** > KRANTZ
**KRANZ** *same as* > KRANS
**KRANZES** > KRANS
**KRATER** *same as* > CRATER
**KRATERS** > KRATER
**KRAUT** *n* sauerkraut
**KRAUTS** > KRAUT
**KREASOTE** *same as* > CREOSOTE
**KREASOTED** > KREASOTE
**KREASOTES** > KREASOTE
**KREATINE** *same as* > CREATINE
**KREATINES** > KREATINE
**KREEP** *n* lunar substance that is high in potassium, rare earth elements, and phosphorus
**KREEPS** > KREEP
**KREESE** *same as* > KRIS
**KREESED** > KREESE
**KREESES** > KREESE
**KREESING** > KREESE
**KREMLIN** *n* citadel of any Russian city
**KREMLINS** > KREMLIN
**KRENG** *same as* > KRANG
**KRENGS** > KRENG
**KREOSOTE** *same as* > CREOSOTE
**KREOSOTED** > KREOSOTE
**KREOSOTES** > KREOSOTE
**KREPLACH** *pl n* small filled dough casings usually served in soup
**KREPLECH** *same as* > KREPLACH
**KREUTZER** *n* any of various former copper and silver coins of Germany or Austria
**KREUTZERS** > KREUTZER
**KREUZER** *same as* > KREUTZER
**KREUZERS** > KREUZER
**KREWE** *n* club taking part in New Orleans carnival parade
**KREWES** > KREWE
**KRILL** *n* small shrimplike sea creature
**KRILLS** > KRILL
**KRIMMER** *n* tightly curled light grey fur obtained from the skins of lambs from the Crimean region
**KRIMMERS** > KRIMMER
**KRIS** *n* Malayan and Indonesian stabbing or slashing knife with a scalloped edge ▷ *vb* stab or slash with a kris
**KRISED** > KRIS
**KRISES** > KRIS
**KRISING** > KRIS
**KROMESKY** *n* croquette consisting of a piece of bacon wrapped round minced meat or fish
**KRONA** *n* standard monetary unit of Sweden
**KRONE** *n* standard monetary unit of Norway and Denmark

**KRONEN** > KRONE
**KRONER** > KRONE
**KRONOR** > KRONA
**KRONUR** > KRONA
**KROON** *n* standard monetary unit of Estonia, divided into 100 senti
**KROONI** > KROON
**KROONS** > KROON
**KRUBI** *n* aroid plant with an unpleasant smell
**KRUBIS** > KRUBI
**KRUBUT** *same as* > KRUBI
**KRUBUTS** > KRUBUT
**KRULLER** *variant spelling of* > CRULLER
**KRULLERS** > KRULLER
**KRUMHORN** *variant spelling of* > CRUMHORN
**KRUMHORNS** > KRUMHORN
**KRUMKAKE** *n* Scandinavian biscuit
**KRUMKAKES** > KRUMKAKE
**KRUMMHOLZ** *n* zone of stunted wind-blown trees growing at high altitudes just above the timberline on tropical mountains
**KRUMMHORN** *variant spelling of* > CRUMHORN
**KRYOLITE** *variant spelling of* > CRYOLITE
**KRYOLITES** > KRYOLITE
**KRYOLITH** *same as* > CRYOLITE
**KRYOLITHS** > KRYOLITH
**KRYOMETER** *same as* > CRYOMETER
**KRYPSES** > KRYPSIS
**KRYPSIS** *n* idea that Christ made secret use of his divine attributes
**KRYPTON** *n* colourless gas present in the atmosphere and used in fluorescent lights
**KRYPTONS** > KRYPTON
**KRYTRON** *n* type of fast electronic gas-discharge switch, used as a trigger in nuclear weapons
**KRYTRONS** > KRYTRON
**KSAR** *old form of* > TSAR
**KSARS** > KSAR
**KUCHCHA** *same as* > KACHA
**KUCHEN** *n* breadlike cake containing apple, nuts, and sugar, originating from Germany
**KUCHENS** > KUCHEN
**KUDLIK** *n* Inuit soapstone seal-oil lamp
**KUDLIKS** > KUDLIK
**KUDO** *variant of* > KUDOS
**KUDOS** *n* fame or credit
**KUDOSES** > KUDOS
**KUDU** *n* African antelope with spiral horns
**KUDUS** > KUDU
**KUDZU** *n* hairy leguminous climbing plant of China and Japan, with trifoliate leaves and purple fragrant flowers

**KUDZUS** > KUDZU
**KUE** *n* name of the letter Q
**KUEH** *n* (in Malaysia) any cake of Malay, Chinese, or Indian origin
**KUES** > KUE
**KUFI** *n* cap for Muslim man
**KUFIS** > KUFI
**KUFIYAH** *same as* > KEFFIYEH
**KUFIYAHS** > KUFIYAH
**KUGEL** *n* baked pudding in traditional Jewish cooking
**KUGELS** > KUGEL
**KUIA** *n* Māori female elder or elderly woman
**KUIAS** > KUIA
**KUKRI** *n* heavy, curved knife used by Gurkhas
**KUKRIS** > KUKRI
**KUKU** *n* mussel
**KUKUS** > KUKU
**KULA** *n* ceremonial gift exchange practised among a group of islanders in the W Pacific, used to establish relations between islands
**KULAK** *n* (formerly) property-owning Russian peasant
**KULAKI** > KULAK
**KULAKS** > KULAK
**KULAN** *n* Asiatic wild ass of the Russian steppes, probably a variety of kiang or onager
**KULANS** > KULAN
**KULAS** > KULA
**KULFI** *n* Indian dessert made by freezing milk which has been concentrated by boiling away some of the water in it, and flavoured with nuts and cardamom seeds
**KULFIS** > KULFI
**KULTUR** *n* German civilization
**KULTURS** > KULTUR
**KUMARA** *n* tropical root vegetable with yellow flesh
**KUMARAHOU** *n* New Zealand shrub
**KUMARAS** > KUMARA
**KUMARI** *n* (in Indian English) maiden
**KUMARIS** > KUMARI
**KUMBALOI** *pl n* worry beads
**KUMERA** *same as* > KUMARA
**KUMERAS** > KUMERA
**KUMIKUMI** *same as* > KAMOKAMO
**KUMISS** *n* drink made from fermented mare's or other milk, drunk by certain Asian tribes, esp in Russia or used for dietetic and medicinal purposes
**KUMISSES** > KUMISS
**KUMITE** *n* freestyle sparring or fighting
**KUMITES** > KUMITE

**KUMMEL** n German liqueur flavoured with aniseed and cumin
**KUMMELS** > KUMMEL
**KUMQUAT** n citrus fruit resembling a tiny orange
**KUMQUATS** > KUMQUAT
**KUMYS** same as > KUMISS
**KUMYSES** > KUMYS
**KUNA** n standard monetary unit of Croatia, divided into 100 lipa
**KUNDALINI** n (in yoga) life force that resides at the base of the spine
**KUNE** > KUNA
**KUNJOOS** adj (in Indian English) mean or stingy
**KUNKAR** n type of limestone
**KUNKARS** > KUNKAR
**KUNKUR** same as > KUNKAR
**KUNKURS** > KUNKUR
**KUNZITE** n pink-coloured transparent variety of the mineral spodumene: a gemstone
**KUNZITES** > KUNZITE
**KURBASH** vb whip with a hide whip
**KURBASHED** > KURBASH
**KURBASHES** > KURBASH
**KURFUFFLE** same as > KERFUFFLE
**KURGAN** n Russian burial mound
**KURGANS** > KURGAN
**KURI** n mongrel dog
**KURIS** > KURI
**KURRAJONG** n Australian tree or shrub with tough fibrous bark
**KURRE** old variant of > CUR
**KURRES** > KURRE
**KURSAAL** n public room at a health resort
**KURSAALS** > KURSAAL
**KURTA** n long loose garment like a shirt without a collar worn in India
**KURTAS** > KURTA
**KURTOSES** > KURTOSIS
**KURTOSIS** n measure of the concentration of a distribution around its mean
**KURU** n degenerative disease of the nervous system, restricted to certain tribes in New Guinea, marked by loss of muscular control and thought to be caused by a slow virus
**KURUS** > KURU
**KURVEY** vb (in old South African English) transport goods by ox cart
**KURVEYED** > KURVEY
**KURVEYING** > KURVEY
**KURVEYOR** > KURVEY
**KURVEYORS** > KURVEY
**KURVEYS** > KURVEY
**KUSSO** variant spelling

of > KOUSSO
**KUSSOS** > KUSSO
**KUTA** n (in Indian English) male dog
**KUTAS** > KUTA
**KUTCH** same as > CATECHU
**KUTCHA** adj makeshift or not solid
**KUTCHES** > KUTCH
**KUTI** n (in Indian English) female dog or bitch
**KUTIS** > KUTI
**KUTU** n body louse
**KUTUS** > KUTU
**KUVASZ** n breed of dog from Hungary
**KUVASZOK** > KUVASZ
**KUZU** same as > KUDZU
**KUZUS** > KUZU
**KVAS** same as > KVASS
**KVASES** > KVAS
**KVASS** n alcoholic drink of low strength made in Russia and E Europe from cereals and stale bread
**KVASSES** > KVASS
**KVELL** vb US word meaning be happy
**KVELLED** > KVELL
**KVELLING** > KVELL
**KVELLS** > KVELL
**KVETCH** vb complain or grumble
**KVETCHED** > KVETCH
**KVETCHER** > KVETCH
**KVETCHERS** > KVETCH
**KVETCHES** > KVETCH
**KVETCHIER** > KVETCHY
**KVETCHILY** > KVETCHY
**KVETCHING** > KVETCH
**KVETCHY** adj tending to grumble or complain
**KWACHA** n standard monetary unit of Zambia, divided into 100 ngwee
**KWACHAS** > KWACHA
**KWAITO** n type of South African pop music with lyrics spoken over an instrumental backing usually consisting of slowed-down house music layered with African percussion and melodies
**KWAITOS** > KWAITO
**KWANZA** n standard monetary unit of Angola, divided into 100 lwei
**KWANZAS** > KWANZA
**KWELA** n type of pop music popular among the Black communities of South Africa
**KWELAS** > KWELA
**KY** pl n Scots word for cows
**KYACK** n type of panier
**KYACKS** > KYACK
**KYAK** same as > KAYAK
**KYAKS** > KYAK
**KYANG** same as > KIANG
**KYANGS** > KYANG
**KYANISE** same as > KYANIZE
**KYANISED** > KYANISE
**KYANISES** > KYANISE

**KYANISING** > KYANISE
**KYANITE** n grey, green, or blue mineral consisting of aluminium silicate in triclinic crystalline form
**KYANITES** > KYANITE
**KYANITIC** > KYANITE
**KYANIZE** vb treat (timber) with corrosive sublimate to make it resistant to decay
**KYANIZED** > KYANIZE
**KYANIZES** > KYANIZE
**KYANIZING** > KYANIZE
**KYAR** same as > COIR
**KYARS** > KYAR
**KYAT** n standard monetary unit of Myanmar, divided into 100 pyas
**KYATS** > KYAT
**KYBO** n temporary lavatory constructed for use when camping
**KYBOS** > KYBO
**KYBOSH** same as > KIBOSH
**KYBOSHED** > KYBOSH
**KYBOSHES** > KYBOSH
**KYBOSHING** > KYBOSH
**KYDST** > KYTHE
**KYE** n Korean fundraising meeting
**KYES** > KYE
**KYLE** n narrow strait or channel
**KYLES** > KYLE
**KYLICES** > KYLIX
**KYLIE** n boomerang that is flat on one side and convex on the other
**KYLIES** > KYLIE
**KYLIKES** > KYLIX
**KYLIN** n (in Chinese art) mythical animal of composite form
**KYLINS** > KYLIN
**KYLIX** n shallow two-handled drinking vessel used in ancient Greece
**KYLLOSES** > KYLLOSIS
**KYLLOSIS** n club foot
**KYLOE** n breed of small long-horned long-haired beef cattle from NW Scotland
**KYLOES** > KYLOE
**KYMOGRAM** n image or other visual record created by a kymograph
**KYMOGRAMS** > KYMOGRAM
**KYMOGRAPH** n rotatable drum for holding paper on which a tracking stylus continuously records variations in blood pressure, respiratory movements, etc
**KYND** old variant of > KIND
**KYNDE** old variant of > KIND
**KYNDED** > KYND
**KYNDES** > KYNDE
**KYNDING** > KYND
**KYNDS** > KYND
**KYNE** pl n archaic word for cows

**KYOGEN** n type of Japanese drama
**KYOGENS** > KYOGEN
**KYPE** n hook on the lower jaw of a mature male salmon
**KYPES** > KYPE
**KYPHOSES** > KYPHOSIS
**KYPHOSIS** n backward curvature of the thoracic spine
**KYPHOTIC** > KYPHOSIS
**KYRIE** n type of prayer
**KYRIELLE** n verse form of French origin characterized by repeated lines or words
**KYRIELLES** > KYRIELLE
**KYRIES** > KYRIE
**KYTE** n belly
**KYTES** > KYTE
**KYTHE** vb appear
**KYTHED** > KYTHE
**KYTHES** > KYTHE
**KYTHING** > KYTHE
**KYU** n (in judo) one of the five student grades for inexperienced competitors
**KYUS** > KYU

# L1

**LA** *n* exclamation of surprise or emphasis
**LAAGER** *n* (in Africa) a camp defended by a circular formation of wagons ▷ *vb* form (wagons) into a laager
**LAAGERED** > LAAGER
**LAAGERING** > LAAGER
**LAAGERS** > LAAGER
**LAARI** *same as* > LARI
**LAARIS** > LAARI
**LAB** *n* laboratory
**LABARA** > LABARUM
**LABARUM** *n* standard or banner carried in Christian religious processions
**LABARUMS** > LABARUM
**LABDA** *same as* > LAMBDA
**LABDACISM** *n* excessive use or idiosyncratic pronunciation of (l)
**LABDANUM** *n* dark resinous juice obtained from various rockroses
**LABDANUMS** > LABDANUM
**LABDAS** > LABDA
**LABEL** *n* piece of card or other material fixed to an object to show its ownership, destination, etc ▷ *vb* give a label to
**LABELABLE** > LABEL
**LABELED** > LABEL
**LABELER** > LABEL
**LABELERS** > LABEL
**LABELING** > LABEL
**LABELLA** > LABELLUM
**LABELLATE** > LABELLUM
**LABELLED** > LABEL
**LABELLER** > LABEL
**LABELLERS** > LABEL
**LABELLING** > LABEL

**LABELLIST** *n* person who wears only clothes with fashionable brand names
**LABELLOID** > LABELLUM
**LABELLUM** *n* lip-like part of certain plants
**LABELS** > LABEL
**LABIA** > LABIUM
**LABIAL** *adj* of the lips ▷ *n* speech sound that involves the lips
**LABIALISE** *same as* > LABIALIZE
**LABIALISM** > LABIALIZE
**LABIALITY** > LABIAL
**LABIALIZE** *vb* pronounce with articulation involving rounded lips
**LABIALLY** > LABIAL
**LABIALS** > LABIAL
**LABIATE** *n* any of a family of plants with square stems, aromatic leaves, and a two-lipped flower, such as mint or thyme ▷ *adj* of this family
**LABIATED** *adj* having a lip
**LABIATES** > LABIATE
**LABILE** *adj* (of a compound) prone to chemical change
**LABILITY** > LABILE
**LABIS** *n* cochlear
**LABISES** > LABIS
**LABIUM** *n* lip or liplike structure
**LABLAB** *n* twining leguminous plant
**LABLABS** > LABLAB
**LABOR** *same as* > LABOUR
**LABORED** *same as* > LABOURED
**LABOREDLY** > LABOURED

**LABORER** *same as* > LABOURER
**LABORERS** > LABORER
**LABORING** > LABOR
**LABORIOUS** *adj* involving great prolonged effort
**LABORISM** *same as* > LABOURISM
**LABORISMS** > LABORISM
**LABORIST** *same as* > LABOURIST
**LABORISTS** > LABORIST
**LABORITE** *n* adherent of the Labour party
**LABORITES** > LABORITE
**LABORS** > LABOR
**LABOUR** *n* physical work or exertion ▷ *vb* work hard
**LABOURED** *adj* uttered or done with difficulty
**LABOURER** *n* person who labours, esp someone doing manual work for wages
**LABOURERS** > LABOURER
**LABOURING** > LABOUR
**LABOURISM** *n* dominance of the working classes
**LABOURIST** *n* person who supports workers' rights
**LABOURS** > LABOUR
**LABRA** > LABRUM
**LABRADOR** *n* large retriever dog with a usu gold or black coat
**LABRADORS** > LABRADOR
**LABRET** *n* piece of bone, shell, etc
**LABRETS** > LABRET
**LABRID** *same as* > LABROID
**LABRIDS** > LABRID
**LABROID** *n* type of fish ▷ *adj* of or relating to such

fish
**LABROIDS** > LABROID
**LABROSE** *adj* thick-lipped
**LABRUM** *n* lip or liplike part
**LABRUMS** > LABRUM
**LABRUSCA** *n* grape variety
**LABRYS** *n* type of axe
**LABRYSES** > LABRYS
**LABS** > LAB
**LABURNUM** *n* ornamental tree with yellow hanging flowers
**LABURNUMS** > LABURNUM
**LABYRINTH** *n* complicated network of passages
**LAC** *same as* > LAKH
**LACCOLITE** *same as* > LACCOLITH
**LACCOLITH** *n* dome-shaped body of igneous rock between two layers of older sedimentary rock
**LACE** *n* delicate loosely woven decorative fabric ▷ *vb* fasten with shoelaces, cords, etc
**LACEBARK** *n* small evergreen tree
**LACEBARKS** > LACEBARK
**LACED** > LACE
**LACELESS** > LACE
**LACELIKE** > LACE
**LACER** > LACE
**LACERABLE** > LACERATE
**LACERANT** *adj* painfully distressing
**LACERATE** *vb* tear (flesh) ▷ *adj* having edges that are jagged or torn
**LACERATED** > LACERATE
**LACERATES** > LACERATE
**LACERS** > LACE
**LACERTIAN** *n* type of

reptile

**LACERTID** n type of lizard

**LACERTIDS** > LACERTID

**LACERTINE** adj relating to lacertid

**LACES** > LACE

**LACET** n braidwork

**LACETS** > LACET

**LACEWING** n any of various neuropterous insects

**LACEWINGS** > LACEWING

**LACEWOOD** n wood of sycamore tree

**LACEWOODS** > LACEWOOD

**LACEWORK** n work made from lace

**LACEWORKS** > LACEWORK

**LACEY** same as > LACY

**LACHES** n negligence or unreasonable delay in pursuing a legal remedy

**LACHESES** > LACHES

**LACHRYMAL** same as > LACRIMAL

**LACIER** > LACY

**LACIEST** > LACY

**LACILY** > LACY

**LACINESS** > LACY

**LACING** > LACE

**LACINGS** > LACE

**LACINIA** n narrow fringe on petal

**LACINIAE** > LACINIA

**LACINIATE** adj jagged

**LACK** n shortage or absence of something needed or wanted ▷ vb need or be short of (something)

**LACKADAY** another word for > ALAS

**LACKED** > LACK

**LACKER** variant spelling of > LACQUER

**LACKERED** > LACKER

**LACKERING** > LACKER

**LACKERS** > LACKER

**LACKEY** n servile follower ▷ vb act as a lackey (to)

**LACKEYED** > LACKEY

**LACKEYING** > LACKEY

**LACKEYS** > LACKEY

**LACKING** > LACK

**LACKLAND** n fool

**LACKLANDS** > LACKLAND

**LACKS** > LACK

**LACMUS** n old form of litmus

**LACMUSES** > LACMUS

**LACONIC** adj using only a few words, terse

**LACONICAL** same as > LACONIC

**LACONISM** n economy of expression

**LACONISMS** > LACONISM

**LACQUER** n hard varnish for wood or metal ▷ vb apply lacquer to

**LACQUERED** > LACQUER

**LACQUERER** > LACQUER

**LACQUERS** > LACQUER

**LACQUEY** same as > LACKEY

**LACQUEYED** > LACQUEY

**LACQUEYS** > LACQUEY

**LACRIMAL** adj of tears or

the glands which produce them ▷ n bone near tear gland

**LACRIMALS** > LACRIMAL

**LACRIMOSO** adj tearful

**LACROSSE** n sport in which teams catch and throw a ball using long sticks with a pouched net at the end, in an attempt to score goals

**LACROSSES** > LACROSSE

**LACRYMAL** same as > LACRIMAL

**LACRYMALS** > LACRYMAL

**LACS** > LAC

**LACTAM** n any of a group of inner amides

**LACTAMS** > LACTAM

**LACTARIAN** n vegetarian who eats dairy products

**LACTARY** adj relating to milk

**LACTASE** n any of a group of enzymes that hydrolyse lactose to glucose and galactose

**LACTASES** > LACTASE

**LACTATE** vb (of mammals) to secrete milk ▷ n ester or salt of lactic acid

**LACTATED** > LACTATE

**LACTATES** > LACTATE

**LACTATING** > LACTATE

**LACTATION** n secretion of milk by female mammals to feed young

**LACTEAL** adj of or like milk ▷ n any of the lymphatic vessels that convey chyle from the small intestine to the blood

**LACTEALLY** > LACTEAL

**LACTEALS** > LACTEAL

**LACTEAN** another word for > LACTEOUS

**LACTEOUS** adj milky

**LACTIC** adj of or derived from milk

**LACTIFIC** adj yielding milk

**LACTONE** n any of a class of organic compounds

**LACTONES** > LACTONE

**LACTONIC** > LACTONE

**LACTOSE** n white crystalline sugar found in milk

**LACTOSES** > LACTOSE

**LACUNA** n gap or missing part, esp in a document or series

**LACUNAE** > LACUNA

**LACUNAL** > LACUNA

**LACUNAR** n ceiling, soffit, or vault having coffers ▷ adj of, relating to, or containing a lacuna or lacunas

**LACUNARIA** > LACUNAR

**LACUNARS** > LACUNAR

**LACUNARY** > LACUNA

**LACUNAS** > LACUNA

**LACUNATE** > LACUNA

**LACUNE** n hiatus

**LACUNES** > LACUNE

**LACUNOSE** > LACUNA

**LACY** adj fine, like lace

**LAD** n boy or young man

**LADANUM** same as > LABDANUM

**LADANUMS** > LADANUM

**LADDER** n frame of two poles connected by horizontal steps used for climbing ▷ vb have or cause to have such a line of undone stitches

**LADDERED** > LADDER

**LADDERING** > LADDER

**LADDERS** > LADDER

**LADDERY** > LADDER

**LADDIE** n familiar term for a male, esp a young man

**LADDIES** > LADDIE

**LADDISH** adj informal word for behaving in a macho or immature manner

**LADE** vb put cargo on board (a ship) or (of a ship) to take on cargo ▷ n watercourse, esp a millstream

**LADED** > LADE

**LADEN** adj loaded ▷ vb load with cargo

**LADENED** > LADEN

**LADENING** > LADEN

**LADENS** > LADEN

**LADER** > LADE

**LADERS** > LADE

**LADES** > LADE

**LADETTE** n young woman whose social behaviour is similar to that of male adolescents or young men

**LADETTES** > LADETTE

**LADHOOD** > LAD

**LADHOODS** > LAD

**LADIES** n women's public toilet

**LADIFIED** > LADIFY

**LADIFIES** > LADIFY

**LADIFY** same as > LADYFY

**LADIFYING** > LADIFY

**LADING** > LADE

**LADINGS** > LADE

**LADINO** n Italian variety of white clover

**LADINOS** > LADINO

**LADLE** n spoon with a long handle and a large bowl, used for serving soup etc ▷ vb serve out

**LADLED** > LADLE

**LADLEFUL** > LADLE

**LADLEFULS** > LADLE

**LADLER** n person who serves with a ladle

**LADLERS** > LADLER

**LADLES** > LADLE

**LADLING** > LADLE

**LADRON** same as > LADRONE

**LADRONE** n thief

**LADRONES** > LADRONE

**LADRONS** > LADRON

**LADS** > LAD

**LADY** n woman regarded

as having characteristics of good breeding or high rank ▷ adj female

**LADYBIRD** n small red beetle with black spots

**LADYBIRDS** > LADYBIRD

**LADYBOY** n transvestite or transsexual, esp one from the Far East

**LADYBOYS** > LADYBOY

**LADYBUG** same as > LADYBIRD

**LADYBUGS** > LADYBUG

**LADYCOW** another word for > LADYBIRD

**LADYCOWS** > LADYCOW

**LADYFIED** > LADYFY

**LADYFIES** > LADYFY

**LADYFISH** n type of game fish

**LADYFLIES** > LADYFLY

**LADYFLY** another word for > LADYBIRD

**LADYFY** vb make a lady of (someone)

**LADYFYING** > LADYFY

**LADYHOOD** > LADY

**LADYHOODS** > LADY

**LADYISH** > LADY

**LADYISM** > LADY

**LADYISMS** > LADY

**LADYKIN** n endearing form of lady

**LADYKINS** > LADYKIN

**LADYLIKE** adj polite and dignified

**LADYLOVE** n beloved woman

**LADYLOVES** > LADYLOVE

**LADYPALM** n small palm, grown indoors

**LADYPALMS** > LADYPALM

**LADYSHIP** n title of a peeress

**LADYSHIPS** > LADYSHIP

**LAER** another word for > LAAGER

**LAERED** > LAER

**LAERING** > LAER

**LAERS** > LAER

**LAESIE** old form of > LAZY

**LAETARE** n fourth Sunday of Lent

**LAETARES** > LAETARE

**LAETRILE** n drug used to treat cancer

**LAETRILES** > LAETRILE

**LAEVIGATE** same as > LEVIGATE

**LAEVO** adj on the left

**LAEVULIN** n polysaccharide occurring in the tubers of certain helianthus plants

**LAEVULINS** > LAEVULIN

**LAEVULOSE** n fructose

**LAG** vb go too slowly, fall behind ▷ n delay between events

**LAGAN** n goods or wreckage on the sea bed, sometimes attached to a buoy to permit recovery

**LAGANS** > LAGAN

LAGENA *n* bottle with a narrow neck
LAGENAS > LAGENA
LAGEND *same as* > LAGAN
LAGENDS > LAGEND
LAGER *n* light-bodied beer ▷ *vb* ferment into lager
LAGERED > LAGER
LAGERING > LAGER
LAGERS > LAGER
LAGGARD *n* person who lags behind ▷ *adj* sluggish, slow, or dawdling
LAGGARDLY > LAGGARD
LAGGARDS > LAGGARD
LAGGED > LAG
LAGGEN *n* spar of a barrel
LAGGENS > LAGGEN
LAGGER *n* person who lags pipes
LAGGERS > LAGGER
LAGGIN *same as* > LAGGEN
LAGGING > LAG
LAGGINGLY > LAG
LAGGINGS > LAG
LAGGINS > LAGGIN
LAGNAPPE *same as* > LAGNIAPPE
LAGNAPPES > LAGNAPPE
LAGNIAPPE *n* small gift, esp one given to a customer who makes a purchase
LAGOMORPH *n* any placental mammal of the order *Lagomorpha*
LAGOON *n* body of water cut off from the open sea by coral reefs or sand bars
LAGOONAL > LAGOON
LAGOONS > LAGOON
LAGRIMOSO *adj* mournful
LAGS > LAG
LAGUNA *n* lagoon
LAGUNAS > LAGUNA
LAGUNE *same as* > LAGOON
LAGUNES > LAGUNE
LAH *n* (in tonic sol-fa) sixth degree of any major scale
LAHAR *n* landslide of volcanic debris and water
LAHARS > LAHAR
LAHS > LAH
LAIC *adj* laical ▷ *n* layman
LAICAL *adj* secular
LAICALLY > LAIC
LAICH *n* low-lying piece of land
LAICHS > LAICH
LAICISE *same as* > LAICIZE
LAICISED > LAICISE
LAICISES > LAICISE
LAICISING > LAICISE
LAICISM > LAIC
LAICISMS > LAIC
LAICITIES > LAICITY
LAICITY *n* state of being laical
LAICIZE *vb* withdraw clerical or ecclesiastical character or status from (an institution, building, etc)
LAICIZED > LAICIZE

LAICIZES > LAICIZE
LAICIZING > LAICIZE
LAICS > LAIC
LAID *Scots form of* > LOAD
LAIDED > LAID
LAIDING > LAID
LAIDLY *adj* very ugly
LAIDS > LAID
LAIGH *adj* low-lying ▷ *n* area of low-lying ground
LAIGHER > LAIGH
LAIGHEST > LAIGH
LAIGHS > LAIGH
LAIK *vb* play (a game, etc)
LAIKA *n* type of small dog
LAIKAS > LAIKA
LAIKED > LAIK
LAIKER > LAIK
LAIKERS > LAIK
LAIKING > LAIK
LAIKS > LAIK
LAIN > LIE
LAIPSE *vb* beat soundly
LAIPSED > LAIPSE
LAIPSES > LAIPSE
LAIPSING > LAIPSE
LAIR *n* resting place of an animal ▷ *vb* (esp of a wild animal) to retreat to or rest in a lair
LAIRAGE *n* accommodation for farm animals, esp at docks or markets
LAIRAGES > LAIRAGE
LAIRD *n* Scottish landowner
LAIRDLY *adj* pertaining to laird or lairds
LAIRDS > LAIRD
LAIRDSHIP *n* state of being laird
LAIRED > LAIR
LAIRIER > LAIRY
LAIRIEST > LAIRY
LAIRING > LAIR
LAIRISE *same as* > LAIRIZE
LAIRISED > LAIRISE
LAIRISES > LAIRISE
LAIRISING > LAIRISE
LAIRIZE *vb* show off
LAIRIZED > LAIRIZE
LAIRIZES > LAIRIZE
LAIRIZING > LAIRIZE
LAIRS > LAIR
LAIRY *adj* gaudy or flashy
LAISSE *n* type of rhyme scheme
LAISSES > LAISSE
LAITANCE *n* white film forming on drying concrete
LAITANCES > LAITANCE
LAITH *Scots form of* > LOATH
LAITHLY *same as* > LAIDLY
LAITIES > LAITY
LAITY *n* people who are not members of the clergy
LAKE *n* expanse of water entirely surrounded by land ▷ *vb* take time away from work
LAKEBED *n* bed of lake
LAKEBEDS > LAKEBED

LAKED > LAKE
LAKEFRONT *n* area at edge of lake
LAKELAND *n* countryside with a lot of lakes
LAKELANDS > LAKELAND
LAKELET *n* small lake
LAKELETS > LAKELET
LAKELIKE > LAKE
LAKEPORT *n* port on lake
LAKEPORTS > LAKEPORT
LAKER *n* cargo vessel used on lakes
LAKERS > LAKER
LAKES > LAKE
LAKESHORE *n* area at edge of lake
LAKESIDE *n* area at edge of lake
LAKESIDES > LAKESIDE
LAKH *n* (in India) 100 000, esp referring to this sum of rupees
LAKHS > LAKH
LAKIER > LAKY
LAKIEST > LAKY
LAKIN *short form of* > LADYKIN
LAKING > LAKE
LAKINGS > LAKE
LAKINS > LAKIN
LAKISH *adj* similar to poetry of Lake poets
LAKSA *n* (in Malaysia) a dish of Chinese origin consisting of rice noodles served in curry or hot soup
LAKSAS > LAKSA
LAKY *adj* of the reddish colour of the pigment lake
LALANG *n* coarse weedy Malaysian grass
LALANGS > LALANG
LALDIE *n* great gusto
LALDIES > LALDIE
LALDY *same as* > LALDIE
LALIQUE *n* type of ornamental glass
LALIQUES > LALIQUE
LALL *vb* make imperfect 'l' or 'r' sounds
LALLAN *n* literary version of the English spoken in Lowland Scotland
LALLAND *same as* > LALLAN
LALLANDS > LALLAND
LALLANS > LALLAN
LALLATION *n* defect of speech consisting of the pronunciation of 'r' as 'l'
LALLED > LALL
LALLING > LALL
LALLINGS > LALL
LALLS > LALL
LALLYGAG *vb* loiter aimlessly
LALLYGAGS > LALLYGAG
LAM *vb* attack vigorously
LAMA *n* Buddhist priest in Tibet or Mongolia
LAMAISTIC *adj* relating to the Mahayana form of Buddhism
LAMANTIN *another word*

*for* > MANATEE
LAMANTINS > LAMANTIN
LAMAS > LAMA
LAMASERAI *same as* > LAMASERY
LAMASERY *n* monastery of lamas
LAMB *n* young sheep ▷ *vb* (of sheep) give birth to a lamb or lambs
LAMBADA *n* erotic Brazilian dance
LAMBADAS > LAMBADA
LAMBAST *vb* beat or thrash
LAMBASTE *same as* > LAMBAST
LAMBASTED > LAMBAST
LAMBASTES > LAMBASTE
LAMBASTS > LAMBAST
LAMBDA *n* 11th letter of the Greek alphabet
LAMBDAS > LAMBDA
LAMBDOID *adj* having the shape of the Greek letter lambda
LAMBED > LAMB
LAMBENCY > LAMBENT
LAMBENT *adj* (of a flame) flickering softly
LAMBENTLY > LAMBENT
LAMBER *n* person that attends to lambing ewes
LAMBERS > LAMBER
LAMBERT *n* cgs unit of illumination, equal to 1 lumen per square centimetre
LAMBERTS > LAMBERT
LAMBIE *same as* > LAMBKIN
LAMBIER > LAMBY
LAMBIES > LAMBIE
LAMBIEST > LAMBY
LAMBING *n* birth of lambs at the end of winter
LAMBINGS > LAMBING
LAMBITIVE *n* medicine taken by licking
LAMBKILL *n* N American dwarf shrub
LAMBKILLS > LAMBKILL
LAMBKIN *n* small or young lamb
LAMBKINS > LAMBKIN
LAMBLIKE > LAMB
LAMBLING *n* small lamb
LAMBLINGS > LAMBLING
LAMBOYS *n* skirt-like piece of armour made from metal strips
LAMBRUSCO *n* Italian sparkling wine
LAMBS > LAMB
LAMBSKIN *n* skin of a lamb, usually with the wool still on, used to make coats, slippers, etc
LAMBSKINS > LAMBSKIN
LAMBY *adj* lamb-like
LAME *adj* having an injured or disabled leg or foot ▷ *vb* make lame ▷ *n* fabric interwoven with gold or silver threads
LAMEBRAIN *n* stupid or

slow-witted person
**LAMED** *n* 12th letter in the Hebrew alphabet
**LAMEDH** *same as* > LAMED
**LAMEDHS** > LAMEDH
**LAMEDS** > LAMED
**LAMELLA** *n* thin layer, plate, or membrane, esp any of the calcified layers of which bone is formed
**LAMELLAE** > LAMELLA
**LAMELLAR** > LAMELLA
**LAMELLAS** > LAMELLA
**LAMELLATE** > LAMELLA
**LAMELLOID** *another word for* > LAMELLA
**LAMELLOSE** > LAMELLA
**LAMELY** > LAME
**LAMENESS** > LAME
**LAMENT** *vb* feel or express sorrow (for) ▷ *n* passionate expression of grief
**LAMENTED** *adj* grieved for
**LAMENTER** > LAMENT
**LAMENTERS** > LAMENT
**LAMENTING** > LAMENT
**LAMENTS** > LAMENT
**LAMER** > LAME
**LAMES** > LAME
**LAMEST** > LAME
**LAMETER** *Scots form of* > LAMIGER
**LAMETERS** > LAMETER
**LAMIA** *n* one of a class of female monsters depicted with a snake's body and a woman's head and breasts
**LAMIAE** > LAMIA
**LAMIAS** > LAMIA
**LAMIGER** *n* disabled person
**LAMIGERS** > LAMIGER
**LAMINA** *n* thin plate, esp of bone or mineral
**LAMINABLE** > LAMINATE
**LAMINAE** > LAMINA
**LAMINAL** *n* consonant articulated with blade of tongue
**LAMINALS** > LAMINAL
**LAMINAR** > LAMINA
**LAMINARIA** *n* any brown seaweed of the genus *Laminaria*
**LAMINARIN** *n* carbohydrate, consisting of repeated glucose units, that is the main storage product of brown algae
**LAMINARY** > LAMINA
**LAMINAS** > LAMINA
**LAMINATE** *vb* make (a sheet of material) by sticking together thin sheets ▷ *n* laminated sheet ▷ *adj* composed of lamina
**LAMINATED** *adj* composed of many layers stuck together
**LAMINATES** > LAMINATE
**LAMINATOR** > LAMINATE
**LAMING** > LAME
**LAMINGTON** *n* sponge cake coated with a sweet

coating
**LAMININ** *n* type of protein
**LAMININS** > LAMININ
**LAMINITIS** *n* (in animals with hooves) inflammation of the tissue to which the hoof is attached
**LAMINOSE** > LAMINA
**LAMINOUS** > LAMINA
**LAMISH** *adj* rather lame
**LAMISTER** *n* fugitive
**LAMISTERS** > LAMISTER
**LAMITER** *same as* > LAMETER
**LAMITERS** > LAMITER
**LAMMED** > LAM
**LAMMER** *Scots word for* > AMBER
**LAMMERS** > LAMMER
**LAMMIE** *same as* > LAMMY
**LAMMIES** > LAMMY
**LAMMIGER** *same as* > LAMIGER
**LAMMIGERS** > LAMIGER
**LAMMING** > LAM
**LAMMINGS** > LAM
**LAMMY** *n* thick woollen jumper
**LAMP** *n* device which produces light from electricity, oil, or gas ▷ *vb* go quickly with long steps
**LAMPAD** *n* candlestick
**LAMPADARY** *n* person who lights the lamps in an Orthodox Greek Church
**LAMPADIST** *n* prize-winner in race run by young men with torches
**LAMPADS** > LAMPAD
**LAMPAS** *n* swelling of the mucous membrane of the hard palate of horses
**LAMPASES** > LAMPAS
**LAMPASSE** *same as* > LAMPAS
**LAMPASSES** > LAMPASSE
**LAMPBLACK** *n* fine black soot used as a pigment in paint and ink
**LAMPED** > LAMP
**LAMPER** *n* lamprey
**LAMPERN** *n* migratory European lamprey
**LAMPERNS** > LAMPERN
**LAMPERS** > LAMPER
**LAMPERSES** > LAMPERS
**LAMPHOLE** *n* hole in ground for lowering lamp into sewer
**LAMPHOLES** > LAMPHOLE
**LAMPING** > LAMP
**LAMPINGS** > LAMP
**LAMPION** *n* oil-burning lamp
**LAMPIONS** > LAMPION
**LAMPLIGHT** *n* light produced by lamp
**LAMPOON** *n* humorous satire ridiculing someone ▷ *vb* satirize or ridicule
**LAMPOONED** > LAMPOON
**LAMPOONER** > LAMPOON
**LAMPOONS** > LAMPOON
**LAMPPOST** *n* post

supporting a lamp in the street
**LAMPPOSTS** > LAMPPOST
**LAMPREY** *n* eel-like fish with a round sucking mouth
**LAMPREYS** > LAMPREY
**LAMPS** > LAMP
**LAMPSHADE** *n* shade used to reduce light shed by light bulb
**LAMPSHELL** *n* brachiopod
**LAMPUKA** *same as* > LAMPUKI
**LAMPUKAS** > LAMPUKA
**LAMPUKI** *n* type of fish
**LAMPUKIS** > LAMPUKI
**LAMPYRID** *n* firefly
**LAMPYRIDS** > LAMPYRID
**LAMS** > LAM
**LAMSTER** *n* fugitive
**LAMSTERS** > LAMSTER
**LANA** *n* wood from genipap tree
**LANAI** *Hawaiian word for* > VERANDA
**LANAIS** > LANAI
**LANAS** > LANA
**LANATE** *adj* having or consisting of a woolly covering of hairs
**LANATED** *same as* > LANATE
**LANCE** *n* long spear used by a mounted soldier ▷ *vb* pierce (a boil or abscess) with a lancet
**LANCED** > LANCE
**LANCEGAY** *n* kind of ancient spear
**LANCEGAYS** > LANCEGAY
**LANCEJACK** *n* lance corporal
**LANCELET** *n* any of several marine animals of the genus *Branchiostoma*
**LANCELETS** > LANCELET
**LANCEOLAR** *adj* narrow and tapering to a point at each end
**LANCER** *n* formerly, cavalry soldier armed with a lance
**LANCERS** *n* quadrille for eight or sixteen couples
**LANCES** > LANCE
**LANCET** *n* pointed two-edged surgical knife
**LANCETED** *adj* having one or more lancet arches or windows
**LANCETS** > LANCET
**LANCEWOOD** *n* New Zealand tree with slender leaves
**LANCH** *obsolete form of* > LAUNCH
**LANCHED** > LANCH
**LANCHES** > LANCH
**LANCHING** > LANCH
**LANCIERS** *pl n* type of dance
**LANCIFORM** *adj* in the form of a lance
**LANCINATE** *adj* (esp of pain) sharp or cutting
**LANCING** > LANCE
**LAND** *n* solid part of the

earth's surface ▷ *vb* come or bring to earth after a flight, jump, or fall
**LANDAMMAN** *n* chairman of the governing council in some Swiss cantons
**LANDAU** *n* four-wheeled carriage with two folding hoods
**LANDAULET** *n* small landau
**LANDAUS** > LANDAU
**LANDBOARD** *n* narrow board, with wheels larger than those on a skateboard, usually ridden while standing
**LANDDAMNE** *vb* Shakespearian word for make (a person's life) unbearable
**LANDDROS** *n* sheriff
**LANDDROST** *n* South African magistrate
**LANDE** *n* type of moorland in SW France
**LANDED** *adj* possessing or consisting of lands
**LANDER** *n* spacecraft designed to land on a planet or other body
**LANDERS** > LANDER
**LANDES** > LANDE
**LANDFALL** *n* ship's first landing after a voyage
**LANDFALLS** > LANDFALL
**LANDFILL** *n* disposing of rubbish by covering it with earth
**LANDFILLS** > LANDFILL
**LANDFORCE** *n* body of people trained for land warfare
**LANDFORM** *n* any natural feature of the earth's surface, such as valleys and mountains
**LANDFORMS** > LANDFORM
**LANDGRAB** *n* sudden attempt to establish ownership of or copyright on something in advance of competitors
**LANDGRABS** > LANDGRAB
**LANDGRAVE** *n* (from the 13th century to 1806) a count who ruled over a specified territory
**LANDING** *n* floor area at the top of a flight of stairs
**LANDINGS** > LANDING
**LANDLADY** *n* woman who owns and leases property
**LANDLER** *n* Austrian country dance in which couples spin and clap
**LANDLERS** > LANDLER
**LANDLESS** > LAND
**LANDLINE** *n* telecommunications cable laid over land
**LANDLINES** > LANDLINE
**LANDLOPER** *n* vagabond or vagrant
**LANDLORD** *n* person who

rents out land, houses, etc
**LANDLORDS** > LANDLORD
**LANDMAN** n person who lives and works on land
**LANDMARK** n prominent object in or feature of a landscape
**LANDMARKS** > LANDMARK
**LANDMASS** n large continuous area of land
**LANDMEN** > LANDMAN
**LANDOWNER** n person who owns land
**LANDRACE** n white very long-bodied lop-eared breed of pork pig
**LANDRACES** > LANDRACE
**LANDRAIL** n type of bird
**LANDRAILS** > LANDRAIL
**LANDS** pl n holdings in land
**LANDSCAPE** n extensive piece of inland scenery seen from one place ▷ vb improve natural features of (a piece of land) ▷ adj (of a publication or an illustration in a publication) of greater width than height
**LANDSHARK** n person who makes inordinate profits by buying and selling land
**LANDSIDE** n part of an airport farthest from the aircraft
**LANDSIDES** > LANDSIDE
**LANDSKIP** another word for > LANDSCAPE
**LANDSKIPS** > LANDSKIP
**LANDSLEIT** > LANDSMAN
**LANDSLID** > LANDSLIDE
**LANDSLIDE** vb cause land or rock to fall from hillside
**LANDSLIP** same as > LANDSLIDE
**LANDSLIPS** > LANDSLIP
**LANDSMAN** n person who works or lives on land, as distinguished from a seaman
**LANDSMEN** > LANDSMAN
**LANDWARD** same as > LANDWARDS
**LANDWARDS** adv towards land
**LANDWIND** n wind that comes from the land
**LANDWINDS** > LANDWIND
**LANE** n narrow road
**LANELY** Scots form of > LONELY
**LANES** > LANE
**LANEWAY** n lane
**LANEWAYS** > LANEWAY
**LANG** Scot word for > LONG
**LANGAHA** n type of Madagascan snake
**LANGAHAS** > LANGAHA
**LANGAR** n dining hall in a gurdwara
**LANGARS** > LANGAR
**LANGER** informal Irish word for > PENIS
**LANGERED** adj drunk

**LANGERS** > LANGER
**LANGEST** > LANG
**LANGLAUF** n cross-country skiing
**LANGLAUFS** > LANGLAUF
**LANGLEY** n unit of solar radiation
**LANGLEYS** > LANGLEY
**LANGOUSTE** n spiny lobster
**LANGRAGE** n shot consisting of scrap iron packed into a case, formerly used in naval warfare
**LANGRAGES** > LANGRAGE
**LANGREL** same as > LANGRAGE
**LANGRELS** > LANGREL
**LANGRIDGE** same as > LANGRAGE
**LANGSHAN** n breed of chicken
**LANGSHANS** > LANGSHAN
**LANGSPEL** n type of Scandinavian stringed instrument
**LANGSPELS** > LANGSPEL
**LANGSPIEL** same as > LANGSPEL
**LANGSYNE** adv long ago ▷ n times long past, esp those fondly remembered
**LANGSYNES** > LANGSYNE
**LANGUAGE** n system of sounds, symbols, etc for communicating thought ▷ vb express in language
**LANGUAGED** > LANGUAGE
**LANGUAGES** > LANGUAGE
**LANGUE** n language considered as an abstract system or a social institution
**LANGUED** adj having a tongue
**LANGUES** > LANGUE
**LANGUET** n anything resembling a tongue in shape or function
**LANGUETS** > LANGUET
**LANGUETTE** same as > LANGUET
**LANGUID** adj lacking energy or enthusiasm
**LANGUIDLY** > LANGUID
**LANGUISH** vb suffer neglect or hardship
**LANGUOR** n state of dreamy relaxation
**LANGUORS** > LANGUOR
**LANGUR** n any of various agile arboreal Old World monkeys of the genus Presbytis
**LANGURS** > LANGUR
**LANIARD** same as > LANYARD
**LANIARDS** > LANIARD
**LANIARIES** > LANIARY
**LANIARY** adj (esp of canine teeth) adapted for tearing ▷ n tooth adapted for tearing
**LANITAL** n fibre used in production of synthetic

wool
**LANITALS** > LANITAL
**LANK** adj (of hair) straight and limp ▷ vb become or cause to become lank
**LANKED** > LANK
**LANKER** > LANK
**LANKEST** > LANK
**LANKIER** > LANKY
**LANKIEST** > LANKY
**LANKILY** > LANKY
**LANKINESS** > LANKY
**LANKING** > LANK
**LANKLY** > LANK
**LANKNESS** > LANK
**LANKS** > LANK
**LANKY** adj ungracefully tall and thin
**LANNER** n large falcon of Mediterranean regions, N Africa, and S Asia
**LANNERET** n male or tercel of the lanner falcon
**LANNERETS** > LANNERET
**LANNERS** > LANNER
**LANOLATED** > LANOLIN
**LANOLIN** n grease from sheep's wool used in ointments etc
**LANOLINE** same as > LANOLIN
**LANOLINES** > LANOLINE
**LANOLINS** > LANOLIN
**LANOSE** same as > LANATE
**LANOSITY** > LANOSE
**LANT** n stale urine
**LANTANA** n shrub with orange or yellow flowers, considered a weed in Australia
**LANTANAS** > LANTANA
**LANTERLOO** n old card game
**LANTERN** n light in a transparent protective case ▷ vb supply with lantern
**LANTERNED** > LANTERN
**LANTERNS** > LANTERN
**LANTHANON** n one of a group of chemical elements
**LANTHANUM** n silvery-white metallic element
**LANTHORN** archaic word for > LANTERN
**LANTHORNS** > LANTHORN
**LANTS** > LANT
**LANTSKIP** another word for > LANDSCAPE
**LANTSKIPS** > LANTSKIP > LANUGO
**LANUGO** n layer of fine hairs, esp the covering of the human fetus before birth
**LANUGOS** > LANUGO
**LANX** n dish; plate
**LANYARD** n cord worn round the neck to hold a knife or whistle
**LANYARDS** > LANYARD
**LAODICEAN** adj indifferent, esp in religious matters ▷ n person having a

lukewarm attitude towards religious matters
**LAOGAI** n forced labour camp in China
**LAOGAIS** > LAOGAI
**LAP** n part between the waist and knees of a person when sitting ▷ vb overtake an opponent so as to be one or more circuits ahead
**LAPBOARD** n flat board that can be used on the lap as a makeshift table or desk
**LAPBOARDS** > LAPBOARD
**LAPDOG** n small pet dog
**LAPDOGS** > LAPDOG
**LAPEL** n part of the front of a coat or jacket folded back towards the shoulders
**LAPELED** > LAPEL
**LAPELLED** > LAPEL
**LAPELS** > LAPEL
**LAPFUL** same as > LAP
**LAPFULS** > LAPFUL
**LAPHELD** adj (esp of a personal computer) small enough to be used on one's lap
**LAPIDARY** adj of or relating to stones ▷ n person who cuts, polishes, sets, or deals in gemstones
**LAPIDATE** vb pelt with stones
**LAPIDATED** > LAPIDATE
**LAPIDATES** > LAPIDATE
**LAPIDEOUS** adj having appearance or texture of stone
**LAPIDES** > LAPIS
**LAPIDIFIC** adj transforming into stone
**LAPIDIFY** vb change into stone
**LAPIDIST** n cutter and engraver of precious stones
**LAPIDISTS** > LAPIDIST
**LAPILLI** > LAPILLUS
**LAPILLUS** n small piece of lava thrown from a volcano
**LAPIN** n castrated rabbit
**LAPINS** > LAPIN
**LAPIS** as in lapis lazuli brilliant blue mineral used as a gemstone
**LAPISES** > LAPIS
**LAPJE** same as > LAPPIE
**LAPJES** > LAPJE
**LAPPED** > LAP
**LAPPEL** same as > LAPEL
**LAPPELS** > LAPPEL
**LAPPER** n one that laps ▷ vb curdle
**LAPPERED** > LAPPER
**LAPPERING** > LAPPER
**LAPPERS** > LAPPER
**LAPPET** n small hanging flap or piece of lace
**LAPPETED** > LAPPET
**LAPPETS** > LAPPET
**LAPPIE** n rag

**LAPPIES** > LAPPIE
**LAPPING** > LAP
**LAPPINGS** > LAP
**LAPS** > LAP
**LAPSABLE** > LAPSE
**LAPSANG** n smoky-tasting Chinese tea
**LAPSANGS** > LAPSANG
**LAPSE** n temporary drop in a standard, esp through forgetfulness or carelessness ▷ vb drop in standard
**LAPSED** > LAPSE
**LAPSER** > LAPSE
**LAPSERS** > LAPSE
**LAPSES** > LAPSE
**LAPSIBLE** > LAPSE
**LAPSING** > LAPSE
**LAPSTONE** n device used by a cobbler on which leather is beaten
**LAPSTONES** > LAPSTONE
**LAPSTRAKE** n clinker-built boat
**LAPSTREAK** same as > LAPSTRAKE
**LAPSUS** n lapse or error
**LAPTOP** adj small enough to fit on a user's lap ▷ n computer small enough to fit on a user's lap
**LAPTOPS** > LAPTOP
**LAPTRAY** n tray with a cushioned underside, designed to rest in a person's lap while supporting reading material, etc
**LAPTRAYS** > LAPTRAY
**LAPWING** n plover with a tuft of feathers on the head
**LAPWINGS** > LAPWING
**LAPWORK** n work with lapping edges
**LAPWORKS** > LAPWORK
**LAQUEARIA** n ceiling made of panels
**LAR** n boy or young man
**LARBOARD** n port (side of a ship)
**LARBOARDS** > LARBOARD
**LARCENER** > LARCENY
**LARCENERS** > LARCENY
**LARCENIES** > LARCENY
**LARCENIST** > LARCENY
**LARCENOUS** > LARCENY
**LARCENY** n theft
**LARCH** n deciduous coniferous tree
**LARCHEN** adj of larch
**LARCHES** > LARCH
**LARD** n soft white fat obtained from a pig ▷ vb insert strips of bacon in (meat) before cooking
**LARDALITE** n type of mineral
**LARDED** > LARD
**LARDER** n storeroom for food
**LARDERER** n person in charge of larder
**LARDERERS** > LARDERER

**LARDERS** > LARDER
**LARDIER** > LARDY
**LARDIEST** > LARDY
**LARDING** > LARD
**LARDLIKE** > LARD
**LARDON** n strip or cube of fat or bacon used in larding meat
**LARDONS** > LARDON
**LARDOON** same as > LARDON
**LARDOONS** > LARDOON
**LARDS** > LARD
**LARDY** adj fat
**LARE** another word for > LORE
**LAREE** n Asian fish-hook formerly used as currency
**LAREES** > LAREE
**LARES** > LARE
**LARGANDO** adv (music) growing slower and more marked
**LARGE** adj great in size, number, or extent ▷ n formerly, musical note of particular length
**LARGELY** adv principally
**LARGEN** another word for > ENLARGE
**LARGENED** > LARGEN
**LARGENESS** > LARGE
**LARGENING** > LARGEN
**LARGENS** > LARGEN
**LARGER** > LARGE
**LARGES** > LARGE
**LARGESS** same as > LARGESSE
**LARGESSE** n generous giving, esp of money
**LARGESSES** > LARGESSE
**LARGEST** > LARGE
**LARGHETTO** adv be performed moderately slowly ▷ n piece or passage to be performed in this way
**LARGISH** adj fairly large
**LARGITION** n act of being generous
**LARGO** adv in a slow and dignified manner ▷ n piece or passage to be performed in a slow and stately manner
**LARGOS** > LARGO
**LARI** n standard monetary unit of Georgia, divided into 100 tetri
**LARIAT** n lasso ▷ vb tether with lariat
**LARIATED** > LARIAT
**LARIATING** > LARIAT
**LARIATS** > LARIAT
**LARINE** adj of, relating to, or resembling a gull
**LARIS** > LARI
**LARK** n small brown songbird, skylark ▷ vb have a good time by frolicking
**LARKED** > LARK
**LARKER** > LARK
**LARKERS** > LARK
**LARKIER** > LARKY
**LARKIEST** > LARKY

**LARKINESS** > LARKY
**LARKING** > LARK
**LARKISH** > LARK
**LARKS** > LARK
**LARKSOME** adj mischievous
**LARKSPUR** n plant with spikes of blue, pink, or white flowers with spurs
**LARKSPURS** > LARKSPUR
**LARKY** adj frolicsome or mischievous
**LARMIER** n pouch under lower eyelid of deer
**LARMIERS** > LARMIER
**LARN** vb learn
**LARNAKES** > LARNAX
**LARNAX** n coffin made of terracotta
**LARNED** > LARN
**LARNEY** n white person ▷ adj (of clothes) smart
**LARNEYS** > LARNEY
**LARNIER** > LARNEY
**LARNIEST** > LARNEY
**LARNING** > LARN
**LARNS** > LARN
**LAROID** adj relating to Larus genus of gull family
**LARRIGAN** n knee-high oiled leather moccasin boot worn by trappers, etc
**LARRIGANS** > LARRIGAN
**LARRIKIN** n mischievous or unruly person
**LARRIKINS** > LARRIKIN
**LARRUP** vb beat or flog
**LARRUPED** > LARRUP
**LARRUPER** > LARRUP
**LARRUPERS** > LARRUP
**LARRUPING** > LARRUP
**LARRUPPED** > LARRUP
**LARRUPS** > LARRUP
**LARS** > LAR
**LARUM** archaic word for > ALARM
**LARUMS** > LARUM
**LARVA** n insect in an immature stage, often resembling a worm
**LARVAE** > LARVA
**LARVAL** > LARVA
**LARVAS** > LARVA
**LARVATE** adj masked; concealed
**LARVATED** same as > LARVATE
**LARVICIDE** n chemical used for killing larvae
**LARVIFORM** adj in the form of a larva
**LARVIKITE** n type of mineral
**LARYNGAL** adj laryngeal ▷ n sound articulated in the larynx
**LARYNGALS** > LARYNGAL
**LARYNGEAL** adj of or relating to the larynx
**LARYNGES** > LARYNX
**LARYNX** n part of the throat containing the vocal cords
**LARYNXES** > LARYNX
**LAS** > LA
**LASAGNA** same as > LASAGNE

**LASAGNAS** > LASAGNA
**LASAGNE** n pasta in wide flat sheets
**LASAGNES** > LASAGNE
**LASCAR** n East Indian seaman
**LASCARS** > LASCAR
**LASE** vb (of a substance, such as carbon dioxide or ruby) to be capable of acting as a laser
**LASED** > LASE
**LASER** n device that produces a very narrow intense beam of light, used for cutting very hard materials and in surgery etc
**LASERDISC** n disk similar in size to a long-playing record, on which data is stored in pits in a similar way to data storage on a compact disk
**LASERDISK** same as > LASERDISC
**LASERS** > LASER
**LASERWORT** n type of plant
**LASES** > LASE
**LASH** n eyelash ▷ vb hit with a whip
**LASHED** > LASH
**LASHER** > LASH
**LASHERS** > LASH
**LASHES** > LASH
**LASHING** > LASH
**LASHINGLY** > LASH
**LASHINGS** pl n great amount of
**LASHINS** variant of > LASHINGS
**LASHKAR** n troop of Indian men with weapons
**LASHKARS** > LASHKAR
**LASING** > LASE
**LASINGS** > LASE
**LASKET** n loop at the foot of a sail onto which an extra sail may be fastened
**LASKETS** > LASKET
**LASQUE** n flat-cut diamond
**LASQUES** > LASQUE
**LASS** n girl
**LASSES** > LASS
**LASSI** n cold drink made with yoghurt or buttermilk and flavoured with sugar, salt, or a mild spice
**LASSIE** n little lass
**LASSIES** > LASSIE
**LASSIS** > LASSI
**LASSITUDE** n physical or mental weariness
**LASSLORN** adj abandoned by a young girl
**LASSO** n rope with a noose for catching cattle and horses ▷ vb catch with a lasso
**LASSOCK** another word for > LASS
**LASSOCKS** > LASSOCK
**LASSOED** > LASSO

**LASSOER** > LASSO
**LASSOERS** > LASSO
**LASSOES** > LASSO
**LASSOING** > LASSO
**LASSOS** > LASSO
**LASSU** n slow part of csárdás folk dance
**LASSUS** > LASSU
**LAST** adv coming at the end or after all others ▷ adj only remaining ▷ n last person or thing ▷ vb continue
**LASTAGE** n space for storing goods in ship
**LASTAGES** > LASTAGE
**LASTBORN** n last child to be born
**LASTBORNS** > LASTBORN
**LASTED** > LAST
**LASTER** > LAST
**LASTERS** > LAST
**LASTING** adj existing or remaining effective for a long time ▷ n strong durable closely woven fabric used for shoe uppers, etc
**LASTINGLY** > LASTING
**LASTINGS** > LASTING
**LASTLY** adv at the end or at the last point
**LASTS** > LAST
**LAT** n former coin of Latvia
**LATAH** n psychological condition in which a traumatized individual becomes anxious and suggestible
**LATAHS** > LATAH
**LATAKIA** n type of Turkish tobacco
**LATAKIAS** > LATAKIA
**LATCH** n fastening for a door with a bar and lever ▷ vb fasten with a latch
**LATCHED** > LATCH
**LATCHES** > LATCH
**LATCHET** n shoe fastening, such as a thong or lace
**LATCHETS** > LATCHET
**LATCHING** > LATCH
**LATCHKEY** n key for an outside door or gate, esp one that lifts a latch
**LATCHKEYS** > LATCHKEY
**LATE** adj after the normal or expected time ▷ adv after the normal or expected time
**LATECOMER** n person or thing that comes late
**LATED** archaic word for > BELATED
**LATEEN** adj denoting a rig with a triangular sail bent to a yard hoisted to the head of a low mast
**LATEENER** n lateen-rigged ship
**LATEENERS** > LATEEN
**LATEENS** > LATEEN
**LATEN** vb become or cause

to become late
**LATENCE** > LATENT
**LATENCES** > LATENCE
**LATENCIES** > LATENT
**LATENCY** > LATENT
**LATENED** > LATEN
**LATENESS** > LATE
**LATENING** > LATEN
**LATENS** > LATEN
**LATENT** adj hidden and not yet developed ▷ n fingerprint that is not visible to the eye
**LATENTLY** > LATENT
**LATENTS** > LATENT
**LATER** adv afterwards
**LATERA** > LATUS
**LATERAD** adv towards the side
**LATERAL** adj of or relating to the side or sides ▷ n lateral object, part, passage, or movement ▷ vb pass laterally
**LATERALED** > LATERAL
**LATERALLY** > LATERAL
**LATERALS** > LATERAL
**LATERBORN** adj born later
**LATERISE** same as > LATERIZE
**LATERISED** > LATERISE
**LATERISES** > LATERISE
**LATERITE** n any of a group of deposits consisting of residual insoluble ferric and aluminium oxides
**LATERITES** > LATERITE
**LATERITIC** > LATERITE
**LATERIZE** vb develop into a laterite
**LATERIZED** > LATERIZE
**LATERIZES** > LATERIZE
**LATESCENT** n becoming latent
**LATEST** n the most recent news, fashion, etc
**LATESTS** > LATEST
**LATEWAKE** n vigil held over corpse
**LATEWAKES** > LATEWAKE
**LATEWOOD** n wood formed later in tree's growing season
**LATEWOODS** > LATEWOOD
**LATEX** n milky fluid found in some plants, esp the rubber tree, used in making rubber
**LATEXES** > LATEX
**LATH** n thin strip of wood used to support plaster, tiles, etc ▷ vb attach laths to (a ceiling, roof, floor, etc)
**LATHE** n machine for turning wood or metal while it is being shaped ▷ vb shape, bore, or cut a screw thread in or on (a workpiece) on a lathe
**LATHED** > LATHE
**LATHEE** same as > LATHI
**LATHEES** > LATHEE
**LATHEN** adj covered with

laths
**LATHER** n froth of soap and water ▷ vb make frothy
**LATHERED** > LATHER
**LATHERER** > LATHER
**LATHERERS** > LATHER
**LATHERIER** > LATHER
**LATHERING** > LATHER
**LATHERS** > LATHER
**LATHERY** > LATHER
**LATHES** > LATHE
**LATHI** n long heavy wooden stick used as a weapon in India, esp by the police
**LATHIER** > LATHY
**LATHIEST** > LATHY
**LATHING** > LATHE
**LATHINGS** > LATHE
**LATHIS** > LATHI
**LATHLIKE** > LATH
**LATHS** > LATH
**LATHWORK** n work made of laths
**LATHWORKS** > LATHWORK
**LATHY** adj resembling a lath, esp in being tall and thin
**LATHYRISM** n neurological disease often resulting in weakness and paralysis of the legs
**LATHYRUS** n genus of climbing plant
**LATI** > LATUS
**LATICES** > LATEX
**LATICIFER** n cell or group of cells in a plant that contains latex
**LATICLAVE** n broad stripe on Roman senator's tunic
**LATIFONDI** pl n large agricultural estates in ancient Rome
**LATIGO** n strap on horse's saddle
**LATIGOES** > LATIGO
**LATIGOS** > LATIGO
**LATILLA** n stick making up part of ceiling
**LATILLAS** > LATILLA
**LATIMERIA** n any coelacanth fish of the genus Latimeria
**LATINA** n female inhabitant of the US who is of Latin American origin
**LATINAS** > LATINA
**LATINISE** same as > LATINIZE
**LATINISED** > LATINISE
**LATINISES** > LATINISE
**LATINITY** n facility in the use of Latin
**LATINIZE** vb translate into Latin
**LATINIZED** > LATINIZE
**LATINIZES** > LATINIZE
**LATINO** n male inhabitant of the US who is of Latin American origin
**LATINOS** > LATINO
**LATISH** adv rather late ▷ adj rather late

**LATITANCY** > LATITANT
**LATITANT** adj concealed
**LATITAT** n writ presuming that person accused was hiding
**LATITATS** > LATITAT
**LATITUDE** n angular distance measured in degrees N or S of the equator
**LATITUDES** > LATITUDE
**LATKE** n crispy Jewish pancake
**LATKES** > LATKE
**LATOSOL** n type of deep, well-drained soil
**LATOSOLIC** > LATOSOL
**LATOSOLS** > LATOSOL
**LATRANT** adj barking
**LATRATION** n instance of barking
**LATRIA** n adoration that may be offered to God alone
**LATRIAS** > LATRIA
**LATRINE** n toilet in a barracks or camp
**LATRINES** > LATRINE
**LATROCINY** n banditry
**LATRON** n bandit
**LATRONS** > LATRON
**LATS** > LAT
**LATTE** n coffee made with hot milk
**LATTEN** n metal or alloy, esp brass, made in thin sheets
**LATTENS** > LATTEN
**LATTER** adj second of two
**LATTERLY** adv recently
**LATTES** > LATTE
**LATTICE** n framework of intersecting strips of wood, metal, etc ▷ vb make, adorn, or supply with a lattice
**LATTICED** > LATTICE
**LATTICES** > LATTICE
**LATTICING** > LATTICE
**LATTICINI** > LATTICINO
**LATTICINO** n type of Italian glass
**LATTIN** n brass alloy beaten into a thin sheet
**LATTINS** > LATTIN
**LATU** n type of seaweed
**LATUS** as in latus rectum (in geometry) chord that passes through the focus of a conic and is perpendicular to the major axis
**LAUAN** n type of wood used in furniture-making
**LAUANS** > LAUAN
**LAUCH** Scots form of > LAUGH
**LAUCHING** > LAUCH
**LAUCHS** > LAUCH
**LAUD** vb praise or glorify ▷ n praise or glorification
**LAUDABLE** adj praiseworthy
**LAUDABLY** > LAUDABLE
**LAUDANUM** n opium-based

sedative
**LAUDANUMS** > LAUDANUM
**LAUDATION** *formal word for* > PRAISE
**LAUDATIVE** *same as* > LAUDATORY
**LAUDATOR** *n* one who praises highly
**LAUDATORS** > LAUDATOR
**LAUDATORY** *adj* praising or glorifying
**LAUDED** > LAUD
**LAUDER** > LAUD
**LAUDERS** > LAUD
**LAUDING** > LAUD
**LAUDS** *n* traditional morning prayer of the Western Church, constituting with matins the first of the seven canonical hours
**LAUF** *n* run in bobsleighing
**LAUFS** > LAUF
**LAUGH** *vb* make inarticulate sounds with the voice expressing amusement, merriment, or scorn ▷ *n* act or instance of laughing
**LAUGHABLE** *adj* ridiculously inadequate
**LAUGHABLY** > LAUGHABLE
**LAUGHED** > LAUGH
**LAUGHER** > LAUGH
**LAUGHFUL** > LAUGH
**LAUGHIER** > LAUGHY
**LAUGHIEST** > LAUGHY
**LAUGHING** > LAUGH
**LAUGHINGS** > LAUGH
**LAUGHLINE** *n* funny line in dialogue
**LAUGHS** > LAUGH
**LAUGHSOME** *adj* causing laughter
**LAUGHTER** *n* sound or action of laughing
**LAUGHTERS** > LAUGHTER
**LAUGHY** *adj* tending to laugh a lot
**LAUNCE** *old form of* > LANCE
**LAUNCED** > LAUNCE
**LAUNCES** > LAUNCE
**LAUNCH** *vb* put (a ship or boat) into the water, esp for the first time ▷ *n* launching
**LAUNCHED** > LAUNCH
**LAUNCHER** *n* any installation, vehicle, or other device for launching rockets, missiles, or other projectiles
**LAUNCHERS** > LAUNCHER
**LAUNCHES** > LAUNCH
**LAUNCHING** > LAUNCH
**LAUNCHPAD** *n* platform from which a spacecraft is launched
**LAUNCING** > LAUNCE
**LAUND** *n* open grassy space
**LAUNDER** *vb* wash and iron (clothes and linen) ▷ *n* water trough, esp one used for washing ore in

mining
**LAUNDERED** > LAUNDER
**LAUNDERER** > LAUNDER
**LAUNDERS** > LAUNDER
**LAUNDRESS** *n* woman who launders clothes, sheets, etc, for a living
**LAUNDRIES** > LAUNDRY
**LAUNDRY** *n* clothes etc for washing or which have recently been washed
**LAUNDS** > LAUND
**LAURA** *n* group of monastic cells
**LAURAE** > LAURA
**LAURAS** > LAURA
**LAUREATE** *adj* crowned with laurel leaves as a sign of honour ▷ *n* person honoured with an award for art or science ▷ *vb* crown with laurel
**LAUREATED** > LAUREATE
**LAUREATES** > LAUREATE
**LAUREL** *n* glossy-leaved shrub, bay tree ▷ *vb* crown with laurel
**LAURELED** > LAUREL
**LAURELING** > LAUREL
**LAURELLED** > LAUREL
**LAURELS** > LAUREL
**LAURIC** *as in lauric acid* dodecanoic acid
**LAURYL** *as in lauryl alcohol* crystalline solid used to make detergents
**LAURYLS** > LAURYL
**LAUWINE** *n* avalanche
**LAUWINES** > LAUWINE
**LAV** *short for* > LAVATORY
**LAVA** *n* molten rock thrown out by volcanoes, which hardens as it cools
**LAVABO** *n* ritual washing of the celebrant's hands after the offertory at Mass
**LAVABOES** > LAVABO
**LAVABOS** > LAVABO
**LAVAFORM** *n* in form of lava
**LAVAGE** *n* washing out of a hollow organ by flushing with water
**LAVAGES** > LAVAGE
**LAVALAVA** *n* draped skirtlike garment worn by Polynesians
**LAVALAVAS** > LAVALAVA
**LAVALIER** *n* decorative pendant worn on chain
**LAVALIERE** *same as* > LAVALIER
**LAVALIERS** > LAVALIER
**LAVALIKE** > LAVA
**LAVAS** > LAVA
**LAVASH** *n* Armenian flat bread
**LAVASHES** > LAVASH
**LAVATERA** *n* any plant of the genus *Lavatera*, closely resembling mallow
**LAVATERAS** > LAVATERA
**LAVATION** *n* act or process of washing
**LAVATIONS** > LAVATION

**LAVATORY** *n* toilet
**LAVE** *archaic word for* > WASH
**LAVED** > LAVE
**LAVEER** *vb* (in sailing) tack
**LAVEERED** > LAVEER
**LAVEERING** > LAVEER
**LAVEERS** > LAVEER
**LAVEMENT** *n* washing with injections of water
**LAVEMENTS** > LAVEMENT
**LAVENDER** *n* shrub with fragrant flowers ▷ *adj* bluish-purple
**LAVENDERS** > LAVENDER
**LAVER** *n* large basin of water used by priests for ritual ablutions
**LAVEROCK** *Scot and northern English dialect word for* > SKYLARK
**LAVEROCKS** > LAVEROCK
**LAVERS** > LAVER
**LAVES** > LAVE
**LAVING** > LAVE
**LAVISH** *adj* great in quantity or richness ▷ *vb* give or spend generously
**LAVISHED** > LAVISH
**LAVISHER** > LAVISH
**LAVISHERS** > LAVISH
**LAVISHES** > LAVISH
**LAVISHEST** > LAVISH
**LAVISHING** > LAVISH
**LAVISHLY** > LAVISH
**LAVOLT** *same as* > LAVOLTA
**LAVOLTA** *n* Italian dance of the 16th and 17th centuries ▷ *vb* dance the lavolta
**LAVOLTAED** > LAVOLTA
**LAVOLTAS** > LAVOLTA
**LAVOLTED** > LAVOLT
**LAVOLTING** > LAVOLT
**LAVOLTS** > LAVOLT
**LAVRA** *same as* > LAURA
**LAVRAS** > LAVRA
**LAVROCK** *same as* > LAVEROCK
**LAVROCKS** > LAVROCK
**LAVS** > LAV
**LAW** *n* rule binding on a community ▷ *vb* prosecute ▷ *adj* (in archaic usage) low
**LAWBOOK** *n* book on subject of law
**LAWBOOKS** > LAWBOOK
**LAWED** > LAW
**LAWER** > LAW
**LAWEST** > LAW
**LAWFUL** *adj* allowed by law
**LAWFULLY** > LAWFUL
**LAWGIVER** *n* giver of a code of laws
**LAWGIVERS** > LAWGIVER
**LAWGIVING** > LAWGIVER
**LAWIN** *n* bill or reckoning
**LAWINE** *n* avalanche
**LAWINES** > LAWINE
**LAWING** *same as* > LAWIN
**LAWINGS** > LAWING
**LAWINS** > LAWIN
**LAWK** *interj* used to show surprise

**LAWKS** *same as* > LAWK
**LAWLAND** *same as* > LOWLAND
**LAWLANDS** > LAWLAND
**LAWLESS** *adj* breaking the law, esp in a violent way
**LAWLESSLY** > LAWLESS
**LAWLIKE** > LAW
**LAWMAKER** *same as* > LAWGIVER
**LAWMAKERS** > LAWMAKER
**LAWMAKING** *n* process of legislating
**LAWMAN** *n* officer of the law, such as a policeman or sheriff
**LAWMEN** > LAWMAN
**LAWMONGER** *n* inferior lawyer
**LAWN** *n* area of tended and mown grass
**LAWNIER** > LAWN
**LAWNIEST** > LAWN
**LAWNMOWER** *n* machine for cutting grass on lawns
**LAWNS** > LAWN
**LAWNY** > LAWN
**LAWS** > LAW
**LAWSUIT** *n* court case brought by one person or group against another
**LAWSUITS** > LAWSUIT
**LAWYER** *n* professionally qualified legal expert ▷ *vb* act as lawyer
**LAWYERED** > LAWYER
**LAWYERING** > LAWYER
**LAWYERLY** > LAWYER
**LAWYERS** > LAWYER
**LAX** *adj* not strict ▷ *n* laxative
**LAXATION** *n* act of making lax or the state of being lax
**LAXATIONS** > LAXATION
**LAXATIVE** *adj* (medicine) inducing the emptying of the bowels ▷ *n* medicine that induces the emptying of the bowels
**LAXATIVES** > LAXATIVE
**LAXATOR** *n* muscle that loosens body part
**LAXATORS** > LAXATOR
**LAXER** > LAX
**LAXES** > LAX
**LAXEST** > LAX
**LAXISM** > LAXIST
**LAXISMS** > LAXIST
**LAXIST** *n* lenient or tolerant person
**LAXISTS** > LAXIST
**LAXITIES** > LAX
**LAXITY** > LAX
**LAXLY** > LAX
**LAXNESS** > LAX
**LAXNESSES** > LAX
**LAY** > LIE
**LAYABOUT** *n* lazy person ▷ *vb* hit out with violent and repeated blows in all directions
**LAYABOUTS** > LAYABOUT
**LAYAWAY** *n* merchandise reserved for future delivery

LAYAWAYS > LAYAWAY
LAYBACK n technique for climbing cracks by pulling on one side of the crack with the hands and pressing on the other with the feet ▷ vb in climbing, use layback technique
LAYBACKED > LAYBACK
LAYBACKS > LAYBACK
LAYDEEZ pl n jocular spelling of ladies, as pronounced in a mid-Atlantic accent
LAYED > LAY
LAYER n single thickness of some substance, as a cover or coating on a surface ▷ vb form a layer
LAYERAGE n covering stem or branch with soil to encourage new roots
LAYERAGES > LAYERAGE
LAYERED > LAYER
LAYERING n method of propagation that induces a shoot or branch to take root while it is still attached to the parent plant
LAYERINGS > LAYERING
LAYERS > LAYER
LAYETTE n clothes for a newborn baby
LAYETTES > LAYETTE
LAYIN n basketball score made by dropping ball into basket
LAYING > LAY
LAYINGS > LAY
LAYINS > LAYIN
LAYLOCK old form of > LILAC
LAYLOCKS > LAYLOCK
LAYMAN n person who is not a member of the clergy
LAYMEN > LAYMAN
LAYOFF n act of suspending employees
LAYOFFS > LAYOFF
LAYOUT n arrangement, esp of matter for printing or of a building
LAYOUTS > LAYOUT
LAYOVER n break in a journey
LAYOVERS > LAYOVER
LAYPEOPLE > LAYPERSON
LAYPERSON n person who is not a member of the clergy
LAYS > LIE
LAYSHAFT n auxiliary shaft in a gearbox
LAYSHAFTS > LAYSHAFT
LAYSTALL n place where waste is deposited
LAYSTALLS > LAYSTALL
LAYTIME n time allowed for loading cargo
LAYTIMES > LAYTIME
LAYUP n period of incapacity through illness
LAYUPS > LAYUP
LAYWOMAN n woman who is

not a member of the clergy
LAYWOMEN > LAYWOMAN
LAZAR archaic word for > LEPER
LAZARET same as > LAZARETTO
LAZARETS > LAZARET
LAZARETTE same as > LAZARETTO
LAZARETTO n small locker at the stern of a boat or a storeroom between decks of a ship
LAZARS > LAZAR
LAZE vb be idle or lazy ▷ n time spent lazing
LAZED > LAZE
LAZES > LAZE
LAZIED > LAZY
LAZIER > LAZY
LAZIES > LAZY
LAZIEST > LAZY
LAZILY > LAZY
LAZINESS > LAZY
LAZING > LAZE
LAZO another word for > LASSO
LAZOED > LAZO
LAZOES > LAZO
LAZOING > LAZO
LAZOS > LAZO
LAZULI n lapis lazuli
LAZULIS > LAZULI
LAZULITE n blue mineral, consisting of hydrated magnesium iron phosphate, occurring in metamorphic rocks
LAZULITES > LAZULITE
LAZURITE n rare blue mineral consisting of a sodium–calcium–aluminium silicate
LAZURITES > LAZURITE
LAZY vb laze ▷ adj not inclined to work or exert oneself
LAZYBONES n lazy person
LAZYING > LAZY
LAZYISH > LAZY
LAZZARONE n Italian street beggar
LAZZARONI > LAZZARONE
LAZZI > LAZZO
LAZZO n comic routine in the commedia dell'arte
LEA n meadow
LEACH vb remove or be removed from a substance by a liquid passing through it ▷ n act or process of leaching
LEACHABLE > LEACH
LEACHATE n water that carries salts dissolved out of materials through which it has percolated
LEACHATES > LEACHATE
LEACHED > LEACH
LEACHER > LEACH
LEACHERS > LEACH
LEACHES > LEACH
LEACHIER > LEACHY
LEACHIEST > LEACHY

LEACHING > LEACH
LEACHINGS > LEACH
LEACHOUR old form of > LECHER
LEACHOURS > LEACHOUR
LEACHY adj porous
LEAD vb guide or conduct ▷ n first or most prominent place ▷ adj acting as a leader or lead
LEADED adj (of windows) made from many small panes of glass held together by lead strips
LEADEN adj heavy or sluggish ▷ vb become or cause to become leaden
LEADENED > LEADEN
LEADENING > LEADEN
LEADENLY > LEADEN
LEADENS > LEADEN
LEADER n person who leads
LEADERENE n strong female leader
LEADERS > LEADER
LEADIER > LEADY
LEADIEST > LEADY
LEADING > LEAD
LEADINGLY > LEAD
LEADINGS > LEAD
LEADLESS adj without lead
LEADMAN n man who leads
LEADMEN > LEADMAN
LEADOFF n initial move or action
LEADOFFS > LEADOFF
LEADPLANT n N American shrub
LEADS > LEAD
LEADSCREW n threaded rod in a lathe
LEADSMAN n sailor who takes soundings with a lead line
LEADSMEN > LEADSMAN
LEADWORK n maintenance work involving lead pipes, etc
LEADWORKS > LEADWORK
LEADWORT n any shrub of the plumbaginaceous genus Plumbago
LEADWORTS > LEADWORT
LEADY adj like lead
LEAF n flat usu green blade attached to the stem of a plant ▷ vb turn (pages) cursorily
LEAFAGE n leaves of plants
LEAFAGES > LEAFAGE
LEAFBUD n bud producing leaves rather than flowers
LEAFBUDS > LEAFBUD
LEAFED > LEAF
LEAFERIES > LEAFERY
LEAFERY n foliage
LEAFIER > LEAFY
LEAFIEST > LEAFY
LEAFINESS > LEAFY
LEAFING > LEAF
LEAFLESS > LEAF
LEAFLET n sheet of printed matter for distribution ▷ vb distribute leaflets (to)

LEAFLETED > LEAFLET
LEAFLETER > LEAFLET
LEAFLETS > LEAFLET
LEAFLIKE > LEAF
LEAFS > LEAF
LEAFSTALK n stalk attaching a leaf to a stem or branch
LEAFWORM n cotton plant pest
LEAFWORMS > LEAFWORM
LEAFY adj covered with leaves
LEAGUE n association promoting the interests of its members
LEAGUED > LEAGUE
LEAGUER vb harass; beset ▷ n encampment, esp of besiegers
LEAGUERED > LEAGUER
LEAGUERS > LEAGUER
LEAGUES > LEAGUE
LEAGUING > LEAGUE
LEAK n hole or defect that allows the escape or entrance of liquid, gas, radiation, etc ▷ vb let liquid etc in or out
LEAKAGE n act or instance of leaking
LEAKAGES > LEAKAGE
LEAKED > LEAK
LEAKER > LEAK
LEAKERS > LEAK
LEAKIER > LEAKY
LEAKIEST > LEAKY
LEAKILY > LEAKY
LEAKINESS > LEAKY
LEAKING > LEAK
LEAKLESS > LEAK
LEAKPROOF adj not likely to leak
LEAKS > LEAK
LEAKY adj leaking or tending to leak
LEAL adj loyal
LEALER > LEAL
LEALEST > LEAL
LEALLY > LEAL
LEALTIES > LEAL
LEALTY > LEAL
LEAM vb shine
LEAMED > LEAM
LEAMING > LEAM
LEAMS > LEAM
LEAN vb rest (against) ▷ adj thin but healthy-looking ▷ n lean part of meat
LEANED > LEAN
LEANER > LEAN
LEANERS > LEAN
LEANEST > LEAN
LEANING > LEAN
LEANINGS > LEAN
LEANLY > LEAN
LEANNESS > LEAN
LEANS > LEAN
LEANT > LEAN
LEANY old form of > LEAN
LEAP vb make a sudden powerful jump ▷ n sudden powerful jump
LEAPED > LEAP

**LEAPER** > LEAP

**LEAPEROUS** old form of > LEPROUS

**LEAPERS** > LEAP

**LEAPFROG** n game in which a player vaults over another bending down ▷ vb play leapfrog

**LEAPFROGS** > LEAPFROG

**LEAPING** > LEAP

**LEAPOROUS** old form of > LEPROUS

**LEAPROUS** old form of > LEPROUS

**LEAPS** > LEAP

**LEAPT** > LEAP

**LEAR** vb instruct

**LEARE** same as > LEAR

**LEARED** > LEAR

**LEARES** > LEARE

**LEARIER** > LEARY

**LEARIEST** > LEARY

**LEARINESS** > LEARY

**LEARING** > LEAR

**LEARN** vb gain skill or knowledge by study, practice, or teaching

**LEARNABLE** > LEARN

**LEARNED** > LEARN

**LEARNEDLY** > LEARN

**LEARNER** n someone who is learning something

**LEARNERS** > LEARNER

**LEARNING** > LEARN

**LEARNINGS** > LEARN

**LEARNS** > LEARN

**LEARNT** > LEARN

**LEARS** > LEAR

**LEARY** same as > LEERY

**LEAS** > LEA

**LEASABLE** > LEASE

**LEASE** n contract by which land or property is rented for a stated time by the owner to a tenant ▷ vb let or rent by lease

**LEASEBACK** n property transaction in which the buyer leases the property to the seller

**LEASED** > LEASE

**LEASEHOLD** adj (land or property) held on lease ▷ n land or property held under a lease

**LEASER** > LEASE

**LEASERS** > LEASE

**LEASES** > LEASE

**LEASH** n lead for a dog ▷ vb control by a leash

**LEASHED** > LEASH

**LEASHES** > LEASH

**LEASHING** > LEASH

**LEASING** > LEASE

**LEASINGS** > LEASE

**LEASOW** vb pasture

**LEASOWE** same as > LEASOW

**LEASOWED** > LEASOW

**LEASOWES** > LEASOWE

**LEASOWING** > LEASOW

**LEASOWS** > LEASOW

**LEAST** n smallest amount ▷ adj smallest ▷ n smallest one ▷ adv in the smallest degree

**LEASTS** > LEAST

**LEASTWAYS** adv at least

**LEASTWISE** same as > LEASTWAYS

**LEASURE** old form of > LEISURE

**LEASURES** > LEASURE

**LEAT** n trench or ditch that conveys water to a mill wheel

**LEATHER** n material made from specially treated animal skins ▷ adj made of leather ▷ vb beat or thrash

**LEATHERED** > LEATHER

**LEATHERN** adj made of or resembling leather

**LEATHERS** > LEATHER

**LEATHERY** adj like leather, tough

**LEATS** > LEAT

**LEAVE** vb go away from ▷ n permission to be absent from work or duty

**LEAVED** adj with leaves

**LEAVEN** n substance that causes dough to rise ▷ vb raise with leaven

**LEAVENED** > LEAVEN

**LEAVENING** > LEAVEN

**LEAVENOUS** adj containing leaven

**LEAVENS** > LEAVEN

**LEAVER** > LEAVE

**LEAVERS** > LEAVE

**LEAVES** > LEAF

**LEAVIER** > LEAVY

**LEAVIEST** > LEAVY

**LEAVING** > LEAVE

**LEAVINGS** pl n something remaining, such as refuse

**LEAVY** same as > LEAFY

**LEAZE** same as > LEASE

**LEAZES** > LEAZE

**LEBBEK** n type of timber tree

**LEBBEKS** > LEBBEK

**LEBEN** n semiliquid food made from curdled milk in N Africa and the Levant

**LEBENS** > LEBEN

**LEBKUCHEN** n biscuit, originating from Germany, usually containing honey, spices, etc

**LECANORA** n type of lichen

**LECANORAS** > LECANORA

**LECCIES** > LECCY

**LECCY** n electricity

**LECH** vb behave lecherously (towards) ▷ n lecherous act or indulgence

**LECHAIM** interj drinking toast ▷ n small drink with which to toast something or someone

**LECHAIMS** > LECHAIM

**LECHAYIM** same as > LECHAIM

**LECHAYIMS** > LECHAYIM

**LECHED** > LECH

**LECHER** n man who has or

shows excessive sexual desire ▷ vb behave lecherously

**LECHERED** > LECHER

**LECHERIES** > LECHERY

**LECHERING** > LECHER

**LECHEROUS** adj (of a man) having or showing excessive sexual desire

**LECHERS** > LECHER

**LECHERY** n unrestrained and promiscuous sexuality

**LECHES** > LECH

**LECHING** > LECH

**LECHWE** n African antelope

**LECHWES** > LECHWE

**LECITHIN** n yellow-brown compound found in plant and animal tissues

**LECITHINS** > LECITHIN

**LECTERN** n sloping reading desk, esp in a church

**LECTERNS** > LECTERN

**LECTIN** n type of protein possessing high affinity for a specific sugar

**LECTINS** > LECTIN

**LECTION** n variant reading of a passage in a particular copy or edition of a text

**LECTIONS** > LECTION

**LECTOR** n lecturer or reader in certain universities

**LECTORATE** > LECTOR

**LECTORS** > LECTOR

**LECTOTYPE** n specimen designated by author after the publication of a species name

**LECTRESS** n female reader

**LECTURE** n informative talk to an audience on a subject ▷ vb give a talk

**LECTURED** > LECTURE

**LECTURER** n person who lectures, esp in a university or college

**LECTURERS** > LECTURER

**LECTURES** > LECTURE

**LECTURING** > LECTURE

**LECTURN** old form of > LECTERN

**LECTURNS** > LECTURN

**LECYTHI** > LECYTHUS

**LECYTHIS** n genus of very tall trees

**LECYTHUS** n (in ancient Greece) a vase with a narrow neck

**LED** > LEAD

**LEDDEN** n language; speech

**LEDDENS** > LEDDEN

**LEDGE** n narrow shelf sticking out from a wall

**LEDGED** > LEDGE

**LEDGER** n book of debit and credit accounts of a firm ▷ vb fish using a wire trace that allows the bait to float freely while the weight sinks

**LEDGERED** > LEDGER

**LEDGERING** > LEDGER

**LEDGERS** > LEDGER

**LEDGES** > LEDGE

**LEDGIER** > LEDGE

**LEDGIEST** > LEDGE

**LEDGY** > LEDGE

**LEDUM** n evergreen shrub

**LEDUMS** > LEDUM

**LEE** n sheltered side ▷ vb (Scots) lie

**LEEAR** Scots form of > LIAR

**LEEARS** > LEEAR

**LEEBOARD** n one of two paddle-like boards that can be lowered along the lee side of a vessel to reduce sideways drift

**LEEBOARDS** > LEEBOARD

**LEECH** n species of bloodsucking worm ▷ vb use leeches to suck the blood of

**LEECHDOM** n remedy

**LEECHDOMS** > LEECHDOM

**LEECHED** > LEECH

**LEECHEE** same as > LITCHI

**LEECHEES** > LEECHEE

**LEECHES** > LEECH

**LEECHING** > LEECH

**LEECHLIKE** > LEECH

**LEED** > LEE

**LEEING** > LEE

**LEEK** n vegetable of the onion family with a long bulb and thick stem

**LEEKS** > LEEK

**LEEP** vb boil; scald

**LEEPED** > LEEP

**LEEPING** > LEEP

**LEEPS** > LEEP

**LEER** vb look or grin at in a sneering or suggestive manner ▷ n sneering or suggestive look or grin

**LEERED** > LEER

**LEERIER** > LEERY

**LEERIEST** > LEERY

**LEERILY** > LEERY

**LEERINESS** > LEERY

**LEERING** > LEER

**LEERINGLY** > LEER

**LEERINGS** > LEER

**LEERS** > LEER

**LEERY** adj suspicious or wary (of)

**LEES** pl n sediment of wine

**LEESE** old form of > LOOSE

**LEESES** > LEESE

**LEESING** > LEESE

**LEET** n list of candidates for an office

**LEETLE** form of > LITTLE

**LEETS** > LEET

**LEEWARD** n lee side ▷ adv towards this side ▷ adj of, in, or moving in the direction towards which the wind blows

**LEEWARDLY** > LEEWARD

**LEEWARDS** adv towards the lee side

**LEEWAY** n room for free movement within limits

**LEEWAYS** > LEEWAY

**LEFT** adj on the opposite side from right ▷ n left

side

LEFTE *old past tense of* > LIFT

LEFTER > LEFT

LEFTEST > LEFT

LEFTIE *same as* > LEFTY

LEFTIES > LEFTY

LEFTISH > LEFT

LEFTISM > LEFTIST

LEFTISMS > LEFTIST

LEFTIST *adj* (person) of the political left ▷ *n* person who supports the political left

LEFTISTS > LEFTIST

LEFTMOST > LEFT

LEFTMOSTS > LEFT

LEFTOVER *n* unused portion of food or material ▷ *adj* left as an unused portion

LEFTOVERS > LEFTOVER

LEFTS > LEFT

LEFTWARD *same as* > LEFTWARDS

LEFTWARDS *adv* towards or on the left

LEFTWING *adj* of or relating to the leftist faction of a party, etc

LEFTY *n* left-winger

LEG *n* one of the limbs on which a person or animal walks, runs, or stands

LEGACIES > LEGACY

LEGACY *n* thing left in a will

LEGAL *adj* established or permitted by law ▷ *n* legal expert

LEGALESE *n* conventional language in which legal documents are written

LEGALESES > LEGALESE

LEGALISE *same as* > LEGALIZE

LEGALISED > LEGALISE

LEGALISER > LEGALISE

LEGALISES > LEGALISE

LEGALISM *n* strict adherence to the letter of the law

LEGALISMS > LEGALISM

LEGALIST > LEGALISM

LEGALISTS > LEGALISM

LEGALITY *n* state or quality of being legal or lawful

LEGALIZE *vb* make legal

LEGALIZED > LEGALIZE

LEGALIZER > LEGALIZE

LEGALIZES > LEGALIZE

LEGALLY > LEGAL

LEGALS > LEGAL

LEGATARY *n* legatee

LEGATE *n* messenger or representative, esp from the Pope ▷ *vb* leave as legacy

LEGATED > LEGATE

LEGATEE *n* recipient of a legacy

LEGATEES > LEGATEE

LEGATES > LEGATE

LEGATINE > LEGATE

LEGATING > LEGATE

LEGATION *n* diplomatic minister and his staff

LEGATIONS > LEGATION

LEGATO *adv* (piece to be played) smoothly ▷ *n* style of playing with no gaps between notes

LEGATOR *n* person who gives a legacy or makes a bequest

LEGATORS > LEGATOR

LEGATOS > LEGATO

LEGEND *n* traditional story or myth

LEGENDARY *adj* famous

LEGENDISE *same as* > LEGENDIZE

LEGENDIST *n* writer of legends

LEGENDIZE *vb* make into legend

LEGENDRY > LEGEND

LEGENDS > LEGEND

LEGER *variant of* > LEDGER

LEGERING > LEGER

LEGERINGS > LEGER

LEGERITY *n* agility

LEGERS > LEGER

LEGES > LEX

LEGGE *vb* lighten or lessen

LEGGED > LEG

LEGGER *n* man who moves barge through tunnel using legs

LEGGERS > LEGGER

LEGGES > LEGGE

LEGGIER > LEGGY

LEGGIERO *adj* light; delicate

LEGGIEST > LEGGY

LEGGIN *same as* > LEGGING

LEGGINESS > LEGGY

LEGGING *n* extra outer covering for the lower leg

LEGGINGED > LEGGING

LEGGINGS > LEGGING

LEGGINS > LEGGIN

LEGGISM *n* blacklegging

LEGGISMS > LEGGISM

LEGGY *adj* having long legs

LEGHORN *n* type of Italian wheat straw that is woven into hats

LEGHORNS > LEGHORN

LEGIBLE *adj* easily read

LEGIBLY > LEGIBLE

LEGION *n* large military force ▷ *adj* very large or numerous

LEGIONARY *adj* of or relating to a legion ▷ *n* soldier belonging to a legion

LEGIONED *adj* arranged in legions

LEGIONS > LEGION

LEGISLATE *vb* make laws

LEGIST *n* person versed in the law

LEGISTS > LEGIST

LEGIT *n* legitimate or professionally respectable drama ▷ *adj* legitimate

LEGITIM *n* amount

of inheritance due to children from father

LEGITIMS > LEGITIM

LEGITS > LEGIT

LEGLAN *same as* > LEGLIN

LEGLANS > LEGLAN

LEGLEN *same as* > LEGLIN

LEGLENS > LEGLEN

LEGLESS *adj* without legs

LEGLET *n* jewellery worn around the leg

LEGLETS > LEGLET

LEGLIKE > LEG

LEGLIN *n* milk-pail

LEGLINS > LEGLIN

LEGMAN *n* newsman who reports on news stories from the scene of action or original source

LEGMEN > LEGMAN

LEGONG *n* Indonesian dance

LEGONGS > LEGONG

LEGROOM *n* space to move one's legs comfortably, as in a car

LEGROOMS > LEGROOM

LEGS > LEG

LEGUAAN *n* large S African lizard

LEGUAANS > LEGUAAN

LEGUME *n* pod of a plant of the pea or bean family

LEGUMES > LEGUME

LEGUMIN *n* protein obtained mainly from the seeds of leguminous plants

LEGUMINS > LEGUMIN

LEGWARMER *n* one of a pair of garments resembling stockings without feet

LEGWEAR *n* clothing worn on the legs

LEGWEARS > LEGWEAR

LEGWORK *n* work that involves travelling on foot or as if on foot

LEGWORKS > LEGWORK

LEHAIM *same as* > LECHAIM

LEHAIMS > LEHAIM

LEHAYIM *same as* > LEHAIM

LEHAYIMS > LEHAYIM

LEHR *n* long tunnel-shaped oven used for annealing glass

LEHRJAHRE *n* apprenticeship

LEHRS > LEHR

LEHUA *n* flower of Hawaii

LEHUAS > LEHUA

LEI > LEU

LEIDGER *same as* > LEDGER

LEIDGERS > LEIDGER

LEIGER *same as* > LEDGER

LEIGERS > LEIGER

LEIOMYOMA *same as* > FIBROID

LEIPOA *n* Australian bird

LEIPOAS > LEIPOA

LEIR *same as* > LEAR

LEIRED > LEIR

LEIRING > LEIR

LEIRS > LEIR

LEIS > LEU

LEISH *adj* agile

LEISHER > LEISH

LEISHEST > LEISH

LEISLER *n* small bat

LEISLERS > LEISLER

LEISTER *n* spear with three or more prongs for spearing fish, esp salmon ▷ *vb* spear (a fish) with a leister

LEISTERED > LEISTER

LEISTERS > LEISTER

LEISURE *n* time for relaxation or hobbies ▷ *vb* have leisure

LEISURED > LEISURE

LEISURELY *adj* deliberate, unhurried ▷ *adv* slowly

LEISURES > LEISURE

LEISURING > LEISURE

LEITMOTIF *n* recurring theme associated with a person, situation, or thought

LEITMOTIV *same as* > LEITMOTIF

LEK *n* area where birds gather for sexual display and courtship ▷ *vb* (of birds) gather at lek

LEKE old form of > LEAK

LEKGOTLA *n* meeting place for village assemblies, court cases, and meetings of village leaders

LEKGOTLAS > LEKGOTLA

LEKKED > LEK

LEKKER *adj* attractive or nice

LEKKING > LEK

LEKKINGS > LEK

LEKS > LEK

LEKU > LEK

LEKVAR *n* prune or apricot pie filling

LEKVARS > LEKVAR

LEKYTHI > LEKYTHOS

LEKYTHOI > LEKYTHOS

LEKYTHOS *n* Greek flask

LEKYTHUS *same as* > LEKYTHOS

LEMAN *n* beloved

LEMANS > LEMAN

LEME *same as* > LEAM

LEMED > LEME

LEMEL *n* metal filings

LEMELS > LEMEL

LEMES > LEME

LEMING > LEME

LEMMA *n* subsidiary proposition, proved for use in the proof of another proposition

LEMMAS > LEMMA

LEMMATA > LEMMA

LEMMATISE *same as* > LEMMATIZE

LEMMATIZE *vb* group together the inflected forms of (a word) for analysis as a single item

LEMMING *n* rodent of arctic regions, reputed to run

into the sea and drown during mass migrations

**LEMMINGS** > LEMMING

**LEMNISCAL** *adj* relating to a type of closed plane curve

**LEMNISCI** > LEMNISCUS

**LEMNISCUS** *technical name for* > FILLET

**LEMON** *n* yellow oval fruit that grows on trees ▷ *adj* pale-yellow ▷ *vb* flavour with lemon

**LEMONADE** *n* lemon-flavoured soft drink, often fizzy

**LEMONADES** > LEMONADE

**LEMONED** > LEMON

**LEMONFISH** *n* type of game fish

**LEMONIER** > LEMONY

**LEMONIEST** > LEMONY

**LEMONING** > LEMON

**LEMONISH** > LEMON

**LEMONLIKE** > LEMON

**LEMONS** > LEMON

**LEMONWOOD** *n* small tree of New Zealand

**LEMONY** *adj* having or resembling the taste or colour of a lemon

**LEMPIRA** *n* standard monetary unit of Honduras, divided into 100 centavos

**LEMPIRAS** > LEMPIRA

**LEMUR** *n* nocturnal animal like a small monkey, found in Madagascar

**LEMURES** *pl n* spirits of the dead

**LEMURIAN** *same as* > LEMUROID

**LEMURIANS** > LEMURIAN

**LEMURINE** *same as* > LEMUROID

**LEMURINES** > LEMURINE

**LEMURLIKE** > LEMUR

**LEMUROID** *adj* of, relating to, or belonging to the superfamily which includes the lemurs and indrises ▷ *n* animal that resembles or is closely related to a lemur

**LEMUROIDS** > LEMUROID

**LEMURS** > LEMUR

**LEND** *vb* give the temporary use of

**LENDABLE** > LEND

**LENDER** > LEND

**LENDERS** > LEND

**LENDING** > LEND

**LENDINGS** > LEND

**LENDS** > LEND

**LENES** > LENIS

**LENG** *vb* linger ▷ *adj* long

**LENGED** > LENG

**LENGER** > LENG

**LENGEST** > LENG

**LENGING** > LENG

**LENGS** > LENG

**LENGTH** *n* extent or measurement from end

to end

**LENGTHEN** *vb* make or become longer

**LENGTHENS** > LENGTHEN

**LENGTHFUL** > LENGTH

**LENGTHIER** > LENGTHY

**LENGTHILY** > LENGTHY

**LENGTHMAN** *n* person whose job it is to maintain a particular length of road or railway line

**LENGTHMEN** > LENGTHMAN

**LENGTHS** > LENGTH

**LENGTHY** *adj* very long or tiresome

**LENIENCE** > LENIENT

**LENIENCES** > LENIENT

**LENIENCY** > LENIENT

**LENIENT** *adj* tolerant, not strict or severe ▷ *n* lenient person

**LENIENTLY** > LENIENT

**LENIENTS** > LENIENT

**LENIFIED** > LENIFY

**LENIFIES** > LENIFY

**LENIFY** *vb* make lenient

**LENIFYING** > LENIFY

**LENIS** *adj* (of a consonant) pronounced with little muscular tension ▷ *n* consonant pronounced like this

**LENITE** *vb* undergo lenition

**LENITED** > LENITE

**LENITES** > LENITE

**LENITIES** > LENITY

**LENITING** > LENITE

**LENITION** *n* weakening of consonant sound

**LENITIONS** > LENITION

**LENITIVE** *adj* soothing or alleviating of pain or distress ▷ *n* lenitive drug

**LENITIVES** > LENITIVE

**LENITY** *n* mercy or clemency

**LENO** *n* (in textiles) a weave in which the warp yarns are twisted together in pairs between the weft or filling yarns

**LENOS** > LENO

**LENS** *n* piece of glass or similar material with one or both sides curved, used to bring together or spread light rays in cameras, spectacles, telescopes, etc

**LENSE** *same as* > LENS

**LENSED** *adj* incorporating a lens

**LENSES** > LENS

**LENSING** *n* materials which colour and diffuse light

**LENSLESS** > LENS

**LENSMAN** *n* camera operator

**LENSMEN** > LENSMAN

**LENT** > LEND

**LENTANDO** *adv* slowing down

**LENTEN** *adj* of or relating

to Lent

**LENTI** > LENTO

**LENTIC** *adj* of, relating to, or inhabiting still water

**LENTICEL** *n* any of numerous pores in the stem of a woody plant

**LENTICELS** > LENTICEL

**LENTICLE** *n* lens-shaped layer of mineral or rock embedded in a matrix of different constitution

**LENTICLES** > LENTICLE

**LENTICULE** *n* small lentil

**LENTIFORM** *adj* shaped like a biconvex lens

**LENTIGO** *technical name for a* > FRECKLE

**LENTIL** *n* edible seed of a leguminous Asian plant

**LENTILS** > LENTIL

**LENTISK** *n* mastic tree

**LENTISKS** > LENTISK

**LENTO** *adv* slowly ▷ *n* movement or passage performed slowly

**LENTOID** *adj* lentiform ▷ *n* lentiform object

**LENTOIDS** > LENTOID

**LENTOR** *n* lethargy

**LENTORS** > LENTOR

**LENTOS** > LENTO

**LENTOUS** *adj* lethargic

**LENVOY** *another word for* > ENVOY

**LENVOYS** > LENVOY

**LEONE** *n* standard monetary unit of Sierra Leone, divided into 100 cents

**LEONES** > LEONE

**LEONINE** *adj* like a lion

**LEOPARD** *n* large spotted carnivorous animal of the cat family

**LEOPARDS** > LEOPARD

**LEOTARD** *n* tight-fitting garment covering the upper body, worn for dancing or exercise

**LEOTARDED** *adj* wearing a leotard

**LEOTARDS** > LEOTARD

**LEP** *dialect word for* > LEAP

**LEPER** *n* person suffering from leprosy

**LEPERS** > LEPER

**LEPID** *adj* amusing

**LEPIDOTE** *adj* covered with scales, scaly leaves, or spots ▷ *n* lepidote person, creature, or thing

**LEPIDOTES** > LEPIDOTE

**LEPORID** *adj* of, relating to, or belonging to the family of mammals that includes rabbits and hares ▷ *n* any animal belonging to this family

**LEPORIDAE** > LEPORID

**LEPORIDS** > LEPORID

**LEPORINE** *adj* of, relating to, or resembling a hare

**LEPPED** > LEP

**LEPPING** > LEP

**LEPRA** *n* leprosy

**LEPRAS** > LEPRA

**LEPROSE** *adj* having or denoting a whitish scurfy surface

**LEPROSERY** *n* hospital for leprosy sufferers

**LEPROSIES** > LEPROSY

**LEPROSITY** *n* state of being leprous

**LEPROSY** *n* disease attacking the nerves and skin, resulting in loss of feeling in the affected parts

**LEPROTIC** *adj* relating to leprosy

**LEPROUS** *adj* having leprosy

**LEPROUSLY** > LEPROUS

**LEPS** > LEP

**LEPT** > LEAP

**LEPTA** > LEPTON

**LEPTIN** *n* protein, produced by fat cells in the body, that acts on the brain to regulate the amount of additional fat laid down in the body

**LEPTINS** > LEPTIN

**LEPTOME** *n* tissue of plant conducting food

**LEPTOMES** > LEPTOME

**LEPTON** *n* any of a group of elementary particles with weak interactions

**LEPTONIC** > LEPTON

**LEPTONS** > LEPTON

**LEPTOPHOS** *n* type of pesticide

**LEPTOSOME** *n* person with a small bodily frame and a slender physique

**LEPTOTENE** *n* (in reproduction) early stage in cell division

**LEQUEAR** *same as* > LACUNAR

**LEQUEARS** > LEQUEAR

**LERE** *same as* > LEAR

**LERED** > LERE

**LERES** > LERE

**LERING** > LERE

**LERNAEAN** *adj* relating to Lerna

**LERNEAN** *same as* > LERNAEAN

**LERP** *n* crystallized honeydew

**LERPS** > LERP

**LES** *short form of* > LESBIAN

**LESBIAN** *n* homosexual woman ▷ *adj* of homosexual women

**LESBIANS** > LESBIAN

**LESBIC** *adj* relating to lesbians

**LESBO** *n* lesbian

**LESBOS** > LESBO

**LESES** > LES

**LESION** *n* structural change in an organ of the body caused by illness or injury ▷ *vb* cause lesions

**LESIONED** > LESION

LESIONING > LESION
LESIONS > LESION
LESPEDEZA n bush clover
LESS n smaller amount
▷ adj smaller in extent,
degree, or duration ▷ pron
smaller part or quantity
▷ adv smaller extent
or degree ▷ prep after
deducting, minus
LESSEE n person to whom
a lease is granted
LESSEES > LESSEE
LESSEN vb make or become
smaller or not as much
LESSENED > LESSEN
LESSENING > LESSEN
LESSENS > LESSEN
LESSER adj not as great in
quantity, size, or worth
LESSES > LESS
LESSON n class or single
period of instruction in a
subject ▷ vb censure or
punish
LESSONED > LESSON
LESSONING > LESSON
LESSONS > LESSON
LESSOR n person who
grants a lease of property
LESSORS > LESSOR
LEST conj so as to prevent
any possibility that ▷ vb
listen
LESTED > LEST
LESTING > LEST
LESTS > LEST
LET n act of letting
property ▷ vb obstruct
LETCH same as > LECH
LETCHED > LETCH
LETCHES > LETCH
LETCHING > LETCH
LETCHINGS > LETCH
LETDOWN n
disappointment
LETDOWNS > LETDOWN
LETHAL adj deadly ▷ n
weapon, etc capable of
causing death
LETHALITY > LETHAL
LETHALLY > LETHAL
LETHALS > LETHAL
LETHARGIC > LETHARGY
LETHARGY n sluggishness
or dullness
LETHE n forgetfulness
LETHEAN > LETHE
LETHEE n life-blood
LETHEES > LETHEE
LETHES > LETHE
LETHIED adj forgetful
LETS > LET
LETTABLE > LET
LETTED > LET
LETTER n written message,
usu sent by post ▷ vb
inscribe letters on
LETTERBOX n slot through
which letters are delivered
into a building
LETTERED adj learned
LETTERER > LETTER
LETTERERS > LETTER

LETTERING n act, art, or
technique of inscribing
letters on to something
LETTERMAN n successful
college sportsman
LETTERMEN > LETTERMAN
LETTERN another word
for > LECTERN
LETTERNS > LETTERN
LETTERS pl n literary
knowledge or ability
LETTERSET n method of
rotary printing in which
ink is transferred from
raised surfaces to paper
via a rubber-covered
cylinder
LETTING > LET
LETTINGS > LET
LETTRE n letter
LETTRES > LETTRE
LETTUCE n plant with large
green leaves used in salads
LETTUCES > LETTUCE
LETUP n lessening or
abatement
LETUPS > LETUP
LEU n standard monetary
unit of Romania and
Moldova, divided into 100
bani
LEUCAEMIA same
as > LEUKAEMIA
LEUCAEMIC > LEUCAEMIA
LEUCEMIA same
as > LEUKAEMIA
LEUCEMIAS > LEUCEMIA
LEUCEMIC > LEUCEMIA
LEUCH > LAUCH
LEUCHEN > LAUCH
LEUCIN same as > LEUCINE
LEUCINE n essential
amino acid found in many
proteins
LEUCINES > LEUCINE
LEUCINS > LEUCIN
LEUCITE n grey or white
mineral consisting of
potassium aluminium
silicate
LEUCITES > LEUCITE
LEUCITIC > LEUCITE
LEUCO as in leuco base
colourless compound
formed by reducing a dye
LEUCOCYTE n white blood
cell
LEUCOMA n white opaque
scar of the cornea
LEUCOMAS > LEUCOMA
LEUCOSIN n albumin in
cereal grains
LEUCOSINS > LEUCOSIN
LEUCOTOME n needle used
in leucotomy
LEUCOTOMY n surgical
operation of cutting some
of the nerve fibres in the
frontal lobes of the brain
LEUD Scots word
for > BREADTH
LEUDES > LEUD
LEUDS > LEUD
LEUGH > LAUCH

LEUGHEN > LAUCH
LEUKAEMIA n disease
caused by uncontrolled
overproduction of white
blood cells
LEUKEMIA same
as > LEUKAEMIA
LEUKEMIAS > LEUKEMIA
LEUKEMIC > LEUKEMIA
LEUKEMICS > LEUKEMIA
LEUKEMOID adj resembling
leukaemia
LEUKOCYTE same
as > LEUCOCYTE
LEUKOMA same
as > LEUCOMA
LEUKOMAS > LEUKOMA
LEUKON n white blood cell
count
LEUKONS > LEUKON
LEUKOSES > LEUKOSIS
LEUKOSIS n abnormal
growth of white blood
cells
LEUKOTIC > LEUKOSIS
LEUKOTOMY n lobotomy
LEV n standard monetary
unit of Bulgaria, divided
into 100 stotinki
LEVA > LEV
LEVANT n type of leather
made from the skins of
goats, sheep, or seals ▷ vb
bolt or abscond, esp to
avoid paying debts
LEVANTED > LEVANT
LEVANTER n easterly wind
in the W Mediterranean
area, esp in the late
summer
LEVANTERS > LEVANTER
LEVANTINE n cloth of
twilled silk
LEVANTING > LEVANT
LEVANTS > LEVANT
LEVATOR n any of various
muscles that raise a part of
the body
LEVATORES > LEVATOR
LEVATORS > LEVATOR
LEVE adj darling ▷ adv
gladly
LEVEE n natural or artificial
river embankment ▷ vb
go to the reception of
LEVEED > LEVEE
LEVEEING > LEVEE
LEVEES > LEVEE
LEVEL adj horizontal ▷ vb
make even or horizontal
▷ n horizontal line or
surface
LEVELED > LEVEL
LEVELER same
as > LEVELLER
LEVELERS > LEVELER
LEVELING > LEVEL
LEVELLED > LEVEL
LEVELLER n person or
thing that levels
LEVELLERS > LEVELLER
LEVELLEST > LEVEL
LEVELLING > LEVEL
LEVELLY > LEVEL

LEVELNESS > LEVEL
LEVELS > LEVEL
LEVER n handle used to
operate machinery ▷ vb
prise or move with a lever
LEVERAGE n action or
power of a lever ▷ vb
borrow capital required
LEVERAGED > LEVERAGE
LEVERAGES > LEVERAGE
LEVERED > LEVER
LEVERET n young hare
LEVERETS > LEVERET
LEVERING > LEVER
LEVERS > LEVER
LEVIABLE adj (of taxes,
tariffs, etc) liable to be
levied
LEVIATHAN n sea monster
LEVIED > LEVY
LEVIER > LEVY
LEVIERS > LEVY
LEVIES > LEVY
LEVIGABLE > LEVIGATE
LEVIGATE vb grind into a
fine powder or a smooth
paste ▷ adj having a
smooth polished surface
LEVIGATED > LEVIGATE
LEVIGATES > LEVIGATE
LEVIGATOR > LEVIGATE
LEVIN archaic word
for > LIGHTNING
LEVINS > LEVIN
LEVIRATE n practice,
required by Old Testament
law, of marrying the
widow of one's brother
LEVIRATES > LEVIRATE
LEVIRATIC > LEVIRATE
LEVIS n jeans
LEVITATE vb rise or cause
to rise into the air
LEVITATED > LEVITATE
LEVITATES > LEVITATE
LEVITATOR > LEVITATE
LEVITE n Christian
clergyman
LEVITES > LEVITE
LEVITIC > LEVITE
LEVITICAL > LEVITE
LEVITIES > LEVITY
LEVITY n inclination to
make a joke of serious
matters
LEVO adj anticlockwise
LEVODOPA n substance
occurring naturally in the
bopy and used to treat
Parkinson's disease
LEVODOPAS > LEVODOPA
LEVOGYRE n
counterclockwise spiral
LEVULIN n substance
obtained from certain
bulbs
LEVULINS > LEVULIN
LEVULOSE n fructose
LEVULOSES > LEVULOSE
LEVY vb impose and collect
(a tax) ▷ n imposition or
collection of taxes
LEVYING > LEVY
LEW adj tepid

LEWD adj lustful or indecent
LEWDER > LEWD
LEWDEST > LEWD
LEWDLY > LEWD
LEWDNESS > LEWD
LEWDSBIES > LEWDSBY
LEWDSBY another word for > LEWDSTER
LEWDSTER n lewd person
LEWDSTERS > LEWDSTER
LEWIS n lifting device for heavy stone or concrete blocks
LEWISES > LEWIS
LEWISIA n type of herb
LEWISIAS > LEWISIA
LEWISITE n colourless oily poisonous liquid
LEWISITES > LEWISITE
LEWISSON same as > LEWIS
LEWISSONS > LEWISSON
LEX n system or body of laws
LEXEME n minimal meaningful unit of language, the meaning of which cannot be understood from that of its component morphemes
LEXEMES > LEXEME
LEXEMIC > LEXEME
LEXES > LEX
LEXICA > LEXICON
LEXICAL adj relating to the vocabulary of a language
LEXICALLY > LEXICAL
LEXICON n dictionary
LEXICONS > LEXICON
LEXIGRAM n figure or symbol that represents a word
LEXIGRAMS > LEXIGRAM
LEXIS n totality of vocabulary items in a language, including all forms having lexical meaning or grammatical function
LEXISES > LEXIS
LEY n land temporarily under grass
LEYLANDI same as > LEYLANDII
LEYLANDII n type of fast-growing cypress tree
LEYLANDIS > LEYLANDI
LEYS > LEY
LEZ short form of > LESBIAN
LEZES > LEZ
LEZZ short form of > LESBIAN
LEZZA same as > LEZZIE
LEZZAS > LEZZA
LEZZES > LEZZ
LEZZIE n lesbian
LEZZIES > LEZZIE
LEZZY short form of > LESBIAN
LI n Chinese measurement of distance
LIABILITY n hindrance or disadvantage
LIABLE adj legally obliged or responsible
LIAISE vb establish and

maintain communication (with)
LIAISED > LIAISE
LIAISES > LIAISE
LIAISING > LIAISE
LIAISON n communication and contact between groups
LIAISONS > LIAISON
LIANA n climbing plant in tropical forests
LIANAS > LIANA
LIANE same as > LIANA
LIANES > LIANE
LIANG n Chinese unit of weight
LIANGS > LIANG
LIANOID > LIANA
LIAR n person who tells lies
LIARD adj grey ⊳ n former small coin of various European countries
LIARDS > LIARD
LIARS > LIAR
LIART Scots form of > LIARD
LIAS n lowest series of rocks of the Jurassic system
LIASES > LIAS
LIATRIS n type of North American plant with small white flowers
LIATRISES > LIATRIS
LIB n informal, sometimes derogatory word for liberation ⊳ vb geld
LIBANT adj touching lightly
LIBATE vb offer as gift to the gods
LIBATED > LIBATE
LIBATES > LIBATE
LIBATING > LIBATE
LIBATION n drink poured as an offering to the gods
LIBATIONS > LIBATION
LIBATORY > LIBATE
LIBBARD another word for > LEOPARD
LIBBARDS > LIBBARD
LIBBED > LIB
LIBBER n liberationist
LIBBERS > LIBBER
LIBBING > LIB
LIBECCHIO same as > LIBECCIO
LIBECCIO n strong westerly or southwesterly wind blowing onto the W coast of Corsica
LIBECCIOS > LIBECCIO
LIBEL n published statement falsely damaging a person's reputation ⊳ vb falsely damage the reputation of (someone)
LIBELANT same as > LIBELLANT
LIBELANTS > LIBELANT
LIBELED > LIBEL
LIBELEE same as > LIBELLEE
LIBELEES > LIBELEE
LIBELER > LIBEL

LIBELERS > LIBEL
LIBELING > LIBEL
LIBELINGS > LIBEL
LIBELIST > LIBEL
LIBELISTS > LIBEL
LIBELLANT n party who brings an action in the ecclesiastical courts by presenting a libel
LIBELLED > LIBEL
LIBELLEE n person against whom a libel has been filed in an ecclesiastical court
LIBELLEES > LIBELLEE
LIBELLER > LIBEL
LIBELLERS > LIBEL
LIBELLING > LIBEL
LIBELLOUS > LIBEL
LIBELOUS > LIBEL
LIBELS > LIBEL
LIBER n tome or book
LIBERAL adj having social and political views that favour progress and reform ⊳ n person who has liberal ideas or opinions
LIBERALLY > LIBERAL
LIBERALS > LIBERAL
LIBERATE vb set free
LIBERATED adj not bound by traditional sexual and social roles
LIBERATES > LIBERATE
LIBERATOR > LIBERATE
LIBERO another name for > SWEEPER
LIBEROS > LIBERO
LIBERS > LIBER
LIBERTIES > LIBERTY
LIBERTINE n morally dissolute person ⊳ adj promiscuous and unscrupulous
LIBERTY n freedom
LIBIDINAL > LIBIDO
LIBIDO n psychic energy
LIBIDOS > LIBIDO
LIBKEN n lodging
LIBKENS > LIBKEN
LIBLAB n 19th century British liberal
LIBLABS > LIBLAB
LIBRA n ancient Roman unit of weight corresponding to 1 pound, but equal to about 12 ounces
LIBRAE > LIBRA
LIBRAIRE n bookseller
LIBRAIRES > LIBRAIRE
LIBRAIRIE n bookshop
LIBRARIAN n keeper of or worker in a library
LIBRARIES > LIBRARY
LIBRARY n room or building where books are kept
LIBRAS > LIBRA
LIBRATE vb oscillate or waver
LIBRATED > LIBRATE
LIBRATES > LIBRATE
LIBRATING > LIBRATE
LIBRATION n act or an

instance of oscillating
LIBRATORY > LIBRATE
LIBRETTI > LIBRETTO
LIBRETTO n words of an opera
LIBRETTOS > LIBRETTO
LIBRI > LIBER
LIBRIFORM adj (of a fibre of woody tissue) elongated and having a pitted thickened cell wall
LIBS > LIB
LICE > LOUSE
LICENCE n document giving official permission to do something ⊳ vb (in the US) give permission to
LICENCED > LICENCE
LICENCEE same as > LICENSEE
LICENCEES > LICENCEE
LICENCER > LICENCE
LICENCERS > LICENCE
LICENCES > LICENCE
LICENCING > LICENCE
LICENSE vb grant or give a licence for
LICENSED > LICENSE
LICENSEE n holder of a licence, esp to sell alcohol
LICENSEES > LICENSEE
LICENSER > LICENSE
LICENSERS > LICENSE
LICENSES > LICENSE
LICENSING > LICENSE
LICENSOR > LICENSE
LICENSORS > LICENSE
LICENSURE n act of conferring licence
LICENTE adj permitted; allowed
LICH n dead body
LICHANOS n note played using forefinger
LICHEE same as > LITCHI
LICHEES > LICHEE
LICHEN n small flowerless plant forming a crust on rocks, trees, etc ⊳ vb cover with lichen
LICHENED > LICHEN
LICHENIN n complex polysaccharide occurring in certain species of moss
LICHENING > LICHEN
LICHENINS > LICHENIN
LICHENISM n type of fungus
LICHENIST n person who studies lichens
LICHENOID > LICHEN
LICHENOSE > LICHEN
LICHENOUS > LICHEN
LICHENS > LICHEN
LICHES > LICH
LICHGATE n roofed gate to a churchyard
LICHGATES > LICHGATE
LICHI same as > LITCHI
LICHIS > LICHI
LICHT Scot word for > LIGHT
LICHTED > LICHT
LICHTER > LICHT
LICHTEST > LICHT

431

LICHTING > LICHT

LICHTLIED > LICHTLY

LICHTLIES > LICHTLY

LICHTLY *vb* treat discourteously

LICHTS > LICHT

LICHWAKE *n* night vigil over a dead body

LICHWAKES > LICHWAKE

LICHWAY *n* path used to carry coffin into church

LICHWAYS > LICHWAY

LICIT *adj* lawful, permitted

LICITLY > LICIT

LICITNESS > LICIT

LICK *vb* pass the tongue over ▷ *n* licking

LICKED > LICK

LICKER > LICK

LICKERISH *adj* lecherous or lustful

LICKERS > LICK

LICKING *n* beating

LICKINGS > LICKING

LICKPENNY *n* something that uses up large amounts of money

LICKS > LICK

LICKSPIT *n* flattering or servile person

LICKSPITS > LICKSPIT

LICORICE *same as* > LIQUORICE

LICORICES > LICORICE

LICTOR *n* one of a group of ancient Roman officials

LICTORIAN > LICTOR

LICTORS > LICTOR

LID *n* movable cover

LIDAR *n* radar-type instrument

LIDARS > LIDAR

LIDDED > LID

LIDDING *n* lids

LIDGER *variant form of* > LEDGER

LIDGERS > LEDGER

LIDLESS *adj* having no lid or top

LIDO *n* open-air centre for swimming and water sports

LIDOCAINE *n* powerful local anaesthetic administered by injection

LIDOS > LIDO

LIDS > LID

LIE *vb* make a deliberately false statement ▷ *n* deliberate falsehood

LIED *n* setting for solo voice and piano of a poem

LIEDER > LIED

LIEF *adv* gladly ▷ *adj* ready ▷ *n* beloved person

LIEFER > LIEF

LIEFEST > LIEF

LIEFLY > LIEF

LIEFS > LIEF

LIEGE *adj* bound to give or receive feudal service ▷ *n* lord

LIEGEDOM > LIEGE

LIEGEDOMS > LIEGE

LIEGELESS > LIEGE

LIEGEMAN *n* (formerly) the subject of a sovereign or feudal lord

LIEGEMEN > LIEGEMAN

LIEGER *same as* > LEDGER

LIEGERS > LIEGER

LIEGES > LIEGE

LIEN *n* right to hold another's property until a debt is paid

LIENABLE *adj* that can be subject of a lien

LIENAL *adj* of or relating to the spleen

LIENS > LIEN

LIENTERIC > LIENTERY

LIENTERY *n* passage of undigested food in the faeces

LIER *n* person who lies down

LIERNE *n* short secondary rib that connects the intersections of the primary ribs, esp as used in Gothic vaulting

LIERNES > LIERNE

LIERS > LIER

LIES > LIE

LIEU *n* stead

LIEUS > LIEU

LIEVE *same as* > LEVE

LIEVER > LIEVE

LIEVEST > LIEVE

LIFE *n* state of living beings, characterized by growth, reproduction, and response to stimuli

LIFEBELT *n* ring filled with air, used to keep a person afloat when in danger of drowning

LIFEBELTS > LIFEBELT

LIFEBLOOD *n* blood vital to life

LIFEBOAT *n* boat used for rescuing people at sea

LIFEBOATS > LIFEBOAT

LIFEBUOY *n* any of various kinds of buoyant device for keeping people afloat

LIFEBUOYS > LIFEBUOY

LIFECARE *n* care of person's health and welfare

LIFECARES > LIFECARE

LIFEFUL *adj* full of life

LIFEGUARD *n* person who saves people from drowning ▷ *vb* work as lifeguard

LIFEHOLD *adj* (of land) held while one is alive

LIFELESS *adj* dead

LIFELIKE *adj* closely resembling or representing life

LIFELINE *n* means of contact or support

LIFELINES > LIFELINE

LIFELONG *adj* lasting all of a person's life

LIFER *n* prisoner sentenced to imprisonment for life

LIFERS > LIFER

LIFES as in *still lifes* paintings or drawings of inanimate objects

LIFESAVER *n* saver of a person's life

LIFESOME *adj* full of life

LIFESPAN *n* period of time during which a person or animal may be expected to live

LIFESPANS > LIFESPAN

LIFESTYLE *n* particular attitudes, habits, etc ▷ *adj* suggestive of a fashionable or desirable lifestyle

LIFETIME *n* length of time a person is alive

LIFETIMES > LIFETIME

LIFEWAY *n* way of life

LIFEWAYS > LIFEWAY

LIFEWORK *n* work to which a person has devoted their life

LIFEWORKS > LIFEWORK

LIFEWORLD *n* way individual experiences world

LIFT *vb* move upwards in position, status, volume, etc ▷ *n* cage raised and lowered in a vertical shaft to transport people or goods

LIFTABLE > LIFT

LIFTBACK *n* hatchback

LIFTBACKS > LIFTBACK

LIFTBOY *n* person who operates a lift, esp in large public or commercial buildings and hotels

LIFTBOYS > LIFTBOY

LIFTED > LIFT

LIFTER > LIFT

LIFTERS > LIFT

LIFTGATE *n* rear opening of hatchback

LIFTGATES > LIFTGATE

LIFTING > LIFT

LIFTMAN *same as* > LIFTBOY

LIFTMEN > LIFTMAN

LIFTOFF *n* moment a rocket leaves the ground ▷ *vb* (of a rocket) to leave its launch pad

LIFTOFFS > LIFTOFF

LIFTS > LIFT

LIFULL *obsolete form of* > LIFEFUL

LIG *n* (esp in the media) a function with free entertainment and refreshments ▷ *vb* attend such a function

LIGAMENT *n* band of tissue joining bones

LIGAMENTS > LIGAMENT

LIGAN *same as* > LAGAN

LIGAND *n* atom, molecule, radical, or ion forming a complex with a central atom

LIGANDS > LIGAND

LIGANS > LIGAN

LIGASE *n* any of a class of enzymes

LIGASES > LIGASE

LIGATE *vb* tie up or constrict (something) with a ligature

LIGATED > LIGATE

LIGATES > LIGATE

LIGATING > LIGATE

LIGATION > LIGATE

LIGATIONS > LIGATE

LIGATIVE > LIGATE

LIGATURE *n* link, bond, or tie ▷ *vb* bind with a ligature

LIGATURED > LIGATURE

LIGATURES > LIGATURE

LIGER *n* hybrid offspring of a female tiger and a male lion

LIGERS > LIGER

LIGGE *obsolete form of* > LIE

LIGGED > LIG

LIGGEN > LIG

LIGGER > LIG

LIGGERS > LIG

LIGGES > LIGGE

LIGGING > LIG

LIGGINGS > LIG

LIGHT *n* electromagnetic radiation by which things are visible ▷ *adj* bright ▷ *vb* ignite ▷ *adv* with little equipment or luggage

LIGHTBULB *n* glass bulb containing gas that emits light when a current is passed through it

LIGHTED > LIGHT

LIGHTEN *vb* make less dark

LIGHTENED > LIGHTEN

LIGHTENER > LIGHTEN

LIGHTENS > LIGHTEN

LIGHTER *n* device for lighting cigarettes etc ▷ *vb* convey in a type of flat-bottomed barge

LIGHTERED > LIGHTER

LIGHTERS > LIGHTER

LIGHTEST > LIGHT

LIGHTFACE *n* weight of type in printing

LIGHTFAST *adj* (of a dye) unaffected by light

LIGHTFUL *adj* full of light

LIGHTING > LIGHT

LIGHTINGS > LIGHT

LIGHTISH > LIGHT

LIGHTLESS > LIGHT

LIGHTLIED > LIGHTLY

LIGHTLIES > LIGHTLY

LIGHTLY *adv* in a light way ▷ *vb* belittle

LIGHTNESS *n* quality of being light

LIGHTNING *n* visible discharge of electricity in the atmosphere ▷ *adj* fast and sudden

LIGHTS > LIGHT
LIGHTSHIP n moored ship used as a lighthouse
LIGHTSOME adj lighthearted
LIGHTWAVE n wave of light
LIGHTWOOD n Australian acacia
LIGNAGE another word for > LINEAGE
LIGNAGES > LIGNAGE
LIGNALOES another name for > EAGLEWOOD
LIGNAN n beneficial substance found in plants
LIGNANS > LIGNAN
LIGNE n unit of measurement
LIGNEOUS adj of or like wood
LIGNES > LIGNE
LIGNICOLE adj growing or living in wood
LIGNIFIED > LIGNIFY
LIGNIFIES > LIGNIFY
LIGNIFORM adj having the appearance of wood
LIGNIFY vb make or become woody as a result of the deposition of lignin in the cell walls
LIGNIN n complex polymer occurring in certain plant cell walls making the plant rigid
LIGNINS > LIGNIN
LIGNITE n woody textured rock used as fuel
LIGNITES > LIGNITE
LIGNITIC > LIGNITE
LIGNOSE n explosive compound
LIGNOSES > LIGNOSE
LIGNUM n wood
LIGNUMS > LIGNUM
LIGROIN n volatile fraction of petroleum that is used as a solvent
LIGROINE same as > LIGROIN
LIGROINES > LIGROINE
LIGROINS > LIGROIN
LIGS > LIG
LIGULA same as > LIGULE
LIGULAE > LIGULA
LIGULAR > LIGULA
LIGULAS > LIGULA
LIGULATE adj having the shape of a strap
LIGULATED same as > LIGULATE
LIGULE n membranous outgrowth at the junction between the leaf blade and sheath in many grasses and sedges
LIGULES > LIGULE
LIGULOID > LIGULE
LIGURE n any of the 12 precious stones used in the breastplates of high priests
LIGURES > LIGURE
LIKABLE adj easy to like

LIKE adj similar ▷ vb find enjoyable ▷ n favourable feeling, desire, or preference
LIKEABLE same as > LIKABLE
LIKED > LIKE
LIKELIER > LIKELY
LIKELIEST > LIKELY
LIKELY adj tending or inclined ▷ adv probably
LIKEN vb compare
LIKENED > LIKEN
LIKENESS n resemblance
LIKENING > LIKEN
LIKENS > LIKEN
LIKER > LIKE
LIKERS > LIKE
LIKES > LIKE
LIKEST > LIKE
LIKEWAKE same as > LYKEWAKE
LIKEWAKES > LIKEWAKE
LIKEWALK same as > LYKEWAKE
LIKEWALKS > LIKEWALK
LIKEWISE adv similarly
LIKIN n historically, Chinese tax
LIKING n fondness
LIKINGS > LIKING
LIKINS > LIKIN
LIKUTA n (formerly) a coin used in Zaïre
LILAC n shrub with pale mauve or white flowers ▷ adj light-purple
LILACS > LILAC
LILANGENI n standard monetary unit of Swaziland, divided into 100 cents
LILIED adj decorated with lilies
LILIES > LILY
LILL obsolete form of > LOLL
LILLED > LILL
LILLING > LILL
LILLIPUT adj tiny ▷ n tiny person or being
LILLIPUTS > LILLIPUTIAN
LILLS > LILL
LILO n trademark for a type of inflatable plastic mattress
LILOS > LILO
LILT n pleasing musical quality in speaking ▷ vb speak with a lilt
LILTED > LILT
LILTING > LILT
LILTINGLY > LILT
LILTS > LILT
LILY n plant which grows from a bulb and has large, often white, flowers
LILYLIKE adj resembling a lily
LIMA n type of edible bean
LIMACEL n small shell inside some kinds of slug
LIMACELS > LIMACEL
LIMACEOUS adj relating to the slug

LIMACES > LIMAX
LIMACINE adj of, or relating to slugs, esp those of the genus Limax
LIMACON n heart-shaped curve
LIMACONS > LIMACON
LIMAIL same as > LEMEL
LIMAILS > LIMAIL
LIMAN n lagoon
LIMANS > LIMAN
LIMAS > LIMA
LIMATION n polishing
LIMATIONS > LIMATION
LIMAX n slug
LIMB n arm, leg, or wing ▷ vb dismember
LIMBA n type of African tree
LIMBAS > LIMBA
LIMBATE adj having an edge or border of a different colour from the rest
LIMBEC obsolete form of > ALEMBIC
LIMBECK obsolete form of > ALEMBIC
LIMBECKS > LIMBECK
LIMBECS > LIMBEC
LIMBED > LIMB
LIMBER vb loosen stiff muscles by exercising ▷ adj pliant or supple ▷ n part of a gun carriage, consisting of an axle, pole, and two wheels
LIMBERED > LIMBER
LIMBERER > LIMBER
LIMBEREST > LIMBER
LIMBERING > LIMBER
LIMBERLY > LIMBER
LIMBERS > LIMBER
LIMBI > LIMBUS
LIMBIC > LIMBUS
LIMBIER > LIMBY
LIMBIEST > LIMBY
LIMBING > LIMB
LIMBLESS > LIMB
LIMBMEAL adv piece by piece
LIMBO n supposed region intermediate between Heaven and Hell for the unbaptized
LIMBOS > LIMBO
LIMBOUS adj with overlapping edges
LIMBS > LIMB
LIMBUS n border
LIMBUSES > LIMBUS
LIMBY adj with long legs, stem, branches, etc
LIME n calcium compound used as a fertilizer or in making cement ▷ vb spread a calcium compound upon (land) ▷ adj having the flavour of lime fruit
LIMEADE n drink made from sweetened lime juice and plain or carbonated water
LIMEADES > LIMEADE

LIMED > LIME
LIMEKILN n kiln in which calcium carbonate is burned to produce quicklime
LIMEKILNS > LIMEKILN
LIMELESS > LIME
LIMELIGHT n glare of publicity ▷ vb illuminate with limelight
LIMELIT > LIMELIGHT
LIMEN another term for > THRESHOLD
LIMENS > LIMEN
LIMEPIT n pit containing lime in which hides are placed to remove the hair
LIMEPITS > LIMEPIT
LIMERICK n humorous verse of five lines
LIMERICKS > LIMERICK
LIMES n fortified boundary of the Roman Empire
LIMESCALE n flaky deposit left in containers such as kettles by the action of heat on water containing calcium salts
LIMESTONE n sedimentary rock used in building
LIMEWASH n mixture of lime and water used to whitewash walls, ceilings, etc
LIMEWATER n clear colourless solution of calcium hydroxide in water
LIMEY n British person ▷ adj British
LIMEYS > LIMEY
LIMIER > LIMY
LIMIEST > LIMY
LIMINA > LIMEN
LIMINAL adj relating to the point (or threshold) beyond which a sensation becomes too faint to be experienced
LIMINESS > LIMY
LIMING > LIME
LIMINGS > LIME
LIMIT n ultimate extent, degree, or amount of something ▷ vb restrict or confine
LIMITABLE > LIMIT
LIMITARY adj of, involving, or serving as a limit
LIMITED adj having a limit ▷ n limited train, bus, etc
LIMITEDLY > LIMITED
LIMITEDS > LIMITED
LIMITER n electronic circuit that produces an output signal whose positive or negative amplitude, or both, is limited to some predetermined value above which the peaks become flattened
LIMITERS > LIMITER
LIMITES > LIMES

LIMITING > LIMIT
LIMITINGS > LIMIT
LIMITLESS > LIMIT
LIMITS > LIMIT
LIMMA n semitone
LIMMAS > LIMMA
LIMMER n scoundrel
LIMMERS > LIMMER
LIMN vb represent in
drawing or painting
LIMNAEID n type of snail
LIMNAEIDS > LIMNAEID
LIMNED > LIMN
LIMNER > LIMN
LIMNERS > LIMN
LIMNETIC adj of, relating
to, or inhabiting the open
water of lakes down to the
depth of light penetration
LIMNIC adj relating to lakes
LIMNING > LIMN
LIMNOLOGY n study of
bodies of fresh water with
reference to their plant
and animal life, physical
properties, geographical
features, etc
LIMNS > LIMN
LIMO short for > LIMOUSINE
LIMONENE n liquid optically
active terpene with a
lemon-like odour
LIMONENES > LIMONENE
LIMONITE n common
brown, black, or yellow
amorphous secondary
mineral
LIMONITES > LIMONITE
LIMONITIC > LIMONITE
LIMOS > LIMO
LIMOSES > LIMOSIS
LIMOSIS n excessive
hunger
LIMOUS adj muddy
LIMOUSINE n large
luxurious car
LIMP vb walk with an
uneven step ▷ n limping
walk ▷ adj without
firmness or stiffness
LIMPA n type of rye bread
LIMPAS > LIMPA
LIMPED > LIMP
LIMPER > LIMP
LIMPERS > LIMP
LIMPEST > LIMP
LIMPET n shellfish which
sticks tightly to rocks ▷ adj
denoting certain weapons
that are magnetically
attached to their targets
and resist removal
LIMPETS > LIMPET
LIMPID adj clear or
transparent
LIMPIDITY > LIMPID
LIMPIDLY > LIMPID
LIMPING > LIMP
LIMPINGLY > LIMP
LIMPINGS > LIMP
LIMPKIN n rail-like wading
bird
LIMPKINS > LIMPKIN
LIMPLY > LIMP

LIMPNESS > LIMP
LIMPS > LIMP
LIMPSEY same as > LIMPSY
LIMPSIER > LIMPSY
LIMPSIEST > LIMPSY
LIMPSY adj limp
LIMULI > LIMULUS
LIMULOID n type of crab
LIMULOIDS > LIMULOID
LIMULUS n any horseshoe
crab of the genus Limulus
LIMULUSES > LIMULUS
LIMY adj of, like, or smeared
with birdlime
LIN vb cease
LINABLE > LINE
LINAC n linear accelerator
LINACS > LINAC
LINAGE n number of lines
in written or printed
matter
LINAGES > LINAGE
LINALOL same
as > LINALOOL
LINALOLS > LINALOL
LINALOOL n optically
active colourless fragrant
liquid
LINALOOLS > LINALOOL
LINCH n ledge
LINCHES > LINCH
LINCHET another word
for > LINCH
LINCHETS > LINCHET
LINCHPIN n pin to hold a
wheel on its axle
LINCHPINS > LINCHPIN
LINCRUSTA n type of
wallpaper having a hard
embossed surface
LINCTURE n medicine
taken by licking
LINCTURES > LINCTURE
LINCTUS n syrupy cough
medicine
LINCTUSES > LINCTUS
LIND variant of > LINDEN
LINDANE n white
poisonous crystalline
powder
LINDANES > LINDANE
LINDEN n large tree with
heart-shaped leaves and
fragrant yellowish flowers
LINDENS > LINDEN
LINDIES > LINDY
LINDS > LIND
LINDWORM n wingless
serpent-like dragon
LINDWORMS > LINDWORM
LINDY n lively dance
LINE n long narrow mark
▷ vb mark with lines
LINEABLE > LINE
LINEAGE n descent from an
ancestor
LINEAGES > LINEAGE
LINEAL adj in direct line of
descent
LINEALITY > LINEAL
LINEALLY > LINEAL
LINEAMENT n facial feature
LINEAR adj of or in lines
LINEARISE same

as > LINEARIZE
LINEARITY > LINEAR
LINEARIZE vb make linear
LINEARLY > LINEAR
LINEATE adj marked with
lines
LINEATED same
as > LINEATE
LINEATION n act of
marking with lines
LINEBRED adj having an
ancestor that is common
to sire and dam
LINECUT n method of relief
printing
LINECUTS > LINECUT
LINED > LINE
LINELIKE > LINE
LINEMAN same
as > LINESMAN
LINEMEN > LINEMAN
LINEN n cloth or thread
made from flax
LINENS > LINEN
LINENY > LINEN
LINEOLATE adj marked
with very fine parallel lines
LINER n large passenger
ship or aircraft
LINERLESS > LINER
LINERS > LINER
LINES > LINE
LINESMAN n (in some
sports) an official who
helps the referee or umpire
LINESMEN > LINESMAN
LINEUP n row or
arrangement of people or
things
LINEUPS > LINEUP
LINEY > LINE
LING n slender food fish
LINGA same as > LINGAM
LINGAM n (in Sanskrit
grammar) the masculine
gender
LINGAMS > LINGAM
LINGAS > LINGA
LINGBERRY same
as > COWBERRY
LINGCOD n any
scorpaenoid food fish of
the family Ophiodontidae
LINGCODS > LINGCOD
LINGEL n strong
shoemaker's thread
LINGELS > LINGEL
LINGER vb delay or prolong
departure
LINGERED > LINGER
LINGERER > LINGER
LINGERERS > LINGER
LINGERIE n women's
underwear or nightwear
LINGERIES > LINGERIE
LINGERING > LINGER
LINGERS > LINGER
LINGIER > LINGY
LINGIEST > LINGY
LINGLE same as > LINGEL
LINGLES > LINGLE
LINGO n foreign or
unfamiliar language or
jargon

LINGOES > LINGO
LINGOT n ingot
LINGOTS > LINGOT
LINGS > LING
LINGSTER n person able to
communicate with aliens
LINGSTERS > LINGSTER
LINGUA n any tongue-like
structure
LINGUAE > LINGUA
LINGUAL adj of the tongue
▷ n lingual consonant,
such as Scots (r)
LINGUALLY > LINGUAL
LINGUALS > LINGUAL
LINGUAS > LINGUA
LINGUICA n Portuguese
sausage
LINGUICAS > LINGUICA
LINGUINE n kind of pasta
in the shape of thin flat
strands
LINGUINES > LINGUINE
LINGUINI same
as > LINGUINE
LINGUINIS > LINGUINI
LINGUISA same
as > LINGUICA
LINGUISAS > LINGUISA
LINGUIST n person skilled
in foreign languages
LINGUISTS > LINGUIST
LINGULA n small tongue
LINGULAE > LINGULA
LINGULAR > LINGULA
LINGULAS > LINGULA
LINGULATE adj shaped like
a tongue
LINGY adj heather-covered
LINHAY n farm building
with an open front
LINHAYS > LINHAY
LINIER > LINE
LINIEST > LINE
LINIMENT n medicated
liquid rubbed on the skin
to relieve pain or stiffness
LINIMENTS > LINIMENT
LININ n network of viscous
material in the nucleus
of a cell that connects the
chromatin granules
LINING n layer of cloth
attached to the inside of a
garment etc
LININGS > LINING
LININS > LININ
LINISH vb polish metal
LINISHED > LINISH
LINISHER > LINISH
LINISHERS > LINISH
LINISHES > LINISH
LINISHING > LINISH
LINK n any of the rings
forming a chain ▷ vb
connect with or as if with
links
LINKABLE > LINK
LINKAGE n act of linking or
the state of being linked
LINKAGES > LINKAGE
LINKBOY n (formerly) a boy
who carried a torch for
pedestrians in dark streets

LINKBOYS > LINKBOY
LINKED > LINK
LINKER n person or thing that links
LINKERS > LINKER
LINKING > LINK
LINKMAN same as > LINKBOY
LINKMEN > LINKMAN
LINKS > LINK
LINKSLAND n land near sea used for golf
LINKSMAN same as > LINKBOY
LINKSMEN > LINKSMAN
LINKSTER n interpreter
LINKSTERS > LINKSTER
LINKUP n establishing of a connection or union between objects, groups, organizations, etc
LINKUPS > LINKUP
LINKWORK n something made up of links
LINKWORKS > LINKWORK
LINKY adj (of countryside) consisting of links
LINN n waterfall or a pool at the foot of it
LINNED > LIN
LINNET n songbird of the finch family
LINNETS > LINNET
LINNEY same as > LINHAY
LINNEYS > LINNEY
LINNIES > LINNY
LINNING > LIN
LINNS > LINN
LINNY same as > LINHAY
LINO same as > LINOLEUM
LINOCUT n design cut in relief in linoleum mounted on a block of wood
LINOCUTS > LINOCUT
LINOLEATE n ester or salt of linoleic acid
LINOLEIC as in linoleic acid colourless oily essential fatty acid found in linseed
LINOLENIC as in linolenic acid colourless unsaturated essential fatty acid
LINOLEUM n type of floor covering
LINOLEUMS > LINOLEUM
LINOS > LINO
LINOTYPE n line of metal type produced by machine ▷ vb set as line of type
LINOTYPED > LINOTYPE
LINOTYPER > LINOTYPE
LINOTYPES > LINOTYPE
LINS > LIN
LINSANG n any of several forest-dwelling viverrine mammals
LINSANGS > LINSANG
LINSEED n seed of the flax plant
LINSEEDS > LINSEED
LINSEY n type of cloth
LINSEYS > LINSEY
LINSTOCK n long staff holding a lighted match,

formerly used to fire a cannon
LINSTOCKS > LINSTOCK
LINT n soft material for dressing a wound
LINTED adj having lint
LINTEL n horizontal beam at the top of a door or window
LINTELLED adj having a lintel
LINTELS > LINTEL
LINTER n machine for stripping the short fibres of ginned cotton seeds
LINTERS > LINTER
LINTIE Scot word for > LINNET
LINTIER > LINT
LINTIES > LINTIE
LINTIEST > LINT
LINTING n process of making lint
LINTLESS > LINT
LINTOL same as > LINTEL
LINTOLS > LINTEL
LINTS > LINT
LINTSEED same as > LINSEED
LINTSEEDS > LINTSEED
LINTSTOCK same as > LINSTOCK
LINTWHITE n linnet
LINTY > LINT
LINUM n any plant of the annual or perennial genus Linum
LINUMS > LINUM
LINURON n type of herbicide
LINURONS > LINURON
LINUX n nonproprietary computer operating system suitable for use on personal computers
LINUXES > LINUX
LINY > LINE
LION n large animal of the cat family, the male of which has a shaggy mane
LIONCEL n (heraldry) small lion
LIONCELLE same as > LIONCEL
LIONCELS > LIONCEL
LIONEL same as > LIONCEL
LIONELS > LIONEL
LIONESS n female lion
LIONESSES > LIONESS
LIONET n young lion
LIONETS > LIONET
LIONFISH n any of various scorpion fishes of the Pacific > LIONHEARTEDNESS
LIONISE same as > LIONIZE
LIONISED > LIONISE
LIONISER > LIONISE
LIONISERS > LIONISE
LIONISES > LIONISE
LIONISING > LIONISE
LIONISM n lion-like appearance of leprosy
LIONISMS > LIONISM

LIONIZE vb treat as a celebrity
LIONIZED > LIONIZE
LIONIZER > LIONIZE
LIONIZERS > LIONIZE
LIONIZES > LIONIZE
LIONIZING > LIONIZE
LIONLIKE > LION
LIONLY > LION
LIONS > LION
LIP n either of the fleshy edges of the mouth ▷ vb touch with the lips
LIPA n monetary unit of Croatia worth one hundredth of a kuna
LIPAEMIA n abnormally large amount of fat in the blood
LIPARITE n type of igneous rock
LIPARITES > LIPARITE
LIPASE n any of a group of enzymes that digest fat
LIPASES > LIPASE
LIPE n lurch
LIPECTOMY n surgical operation to remove fat
LIPEMIA same as > LIPAEMIA
LIPEMIAS > LIPEMIA
LIPID n any of a group of organic compounds including fats, oils, waxes, and sterols
LIPIDE same as > LIPID
LIPIDES > LIPIDE
LIPIDIC > LIPID
LIPIDS > LIPID
LIPIN n family of nuclear proteins
LIPINS > LIPIN
LIPLESS > LIP
LIPLIKE > LIP
LIPO n liposuction
LIPOCYTE n fat-storing cell
LIPOCYTES > LIPOCYTE
LIPOGRAM n piece of writing in which all words containing a particular letter have been deliberately omitted
LIPOGRAMS > LIPOGRAM
LIPOIC as in lipoic acid sulphur-containing fatty acid
LIPOID n fatlike substance, such as wax
LIPOIDAL > LIPOID
LIPOIDS > LIPOID
LIPOLITIC same as > LIPOLYTIC
LIPOLYSES > LIPOLYSIS
LIPOLYSIS n hydrolysis of fats resulting in the production of carboxylic acids and glycerol
LIPOLYTIC adj fat-burning
LIPOMA n benign tumour composed of fatty tissue
LIPOMAS > LIPOMA
LIPOMATA > LIPOMA
LIPOPLAST n small particle in plant cytoplasm, esp that of seeds, in which fat

is stored
LIPOS > LIPO
LIPOSOMAL > LIPOSOME
LIPOSOME n particle formed by lipids
LIPOSOMES > LIPOSOME
LIPOSUCK vb subject to liposuction
LIPOSUCKS > LIPOSUCK
LIPOTROPY n breaking down of fat in body
LIPPED > LIP
LIPPEN vb trust
LIPPENED > LIPPEN
LIPPENING > LIPPEN
LIPPENS > LIPPEN
LIPPER Scots word for > RIPPLE
LIPPERED > LIPPER
LIPPERING > LIPPER
LIPPERS > LIPPER
LIPPIE variant of > LIPPY
LIPPIER > LIPPY
LIPPIES > LIPPIE
LIPPIEST > LIPPY
LIPPINESS > LIPPY
LIPPING > LIP
LIPPINGS > LIP
LIPPITUDE n state of having bleary eyes
LIPPY adj insolent or cheeky ▷ n lipstick
LIPREAD vb follow what someone says by watching their lips
LIPREADER > LIPREAD
LIPREADS > LIPREAD
LIPS > LIP
LIPSTICK n cosmetic in stick form, for colouring the lips ▷ vb put lipstick on
LIPSTICKS > LIPSTICK
LIPURIA n presence of fat in the urine
LIPURIAS > LIPURIA
LIQUABLE adj that can be melted
LIQUATE vb separate one component of (an alloy, impure metal, or ore) by heating so that the more fusible part melts
LIQUATED > LIQUATE
LIQUATES > LIQUATE
LIQUATING > LIQUATE
LIQUATION > LIQUATE
LIQUEFIED > LIQUEFY
LIQUEFIER > LIQUEFY
LIQUEFIES > LIQUEFY
LIQUEFY vb make or become liquid
LIQUESCE vb become liquid
LIQUESCED > LIQUESCE
LIQUESCES > LIQUESCE
LIQUEUR n flavoured and sweetened alcoholic spirit ▷ vb flavour with liqueur
LIQUEURED > LIQUEUR
LIQUEURS > LIQUEUR
LIQUID n substance in a physical state which can change shape but not size

▷ *adj* of or being a liquid
**LIQUIDATE** *vb* pay (a debt)
**LIQUIDISE** *same as* > LIQUIDIZE
**LIQUIDITY** *n* state of being able to meet financial obligations
**LIQUIDIZE** *vb* make or become liquid
**LIQUIDLY** > LIQUID
**LIQUIDS** > LIQUID
**LIQUIDUS** *n* line on graph above which a substance is in liquid form
**LIQUIFIED** > LIQUIFY
**LIQUIFIES** > LIQUIFY
**LIQUIFY** *same as* > LIQUEFY
**LIQUOR** *n* alcoholic drink, esp spirits ▷ *vb* steep (malt) in warm water to form wort in brewing
**LIQUORED** > LIQUOR
**LIQUORICE** *n* black substance used in medicine and as a sweet
**LIQUORING** > LIQUOR
**LIQUORISH** *same as* > LICKERISH
**LIQUORS** > LIQUOR
**LIRA** *n* monetary unit of Turkey, Malta, and formerly of Italy
**LIRAS** > LIRA
**LIRE** > LIRA
**LIRI** > LIRA
**LIRIOPE** *n* grasslike plant
**LIRIOPES** > LIRIOPE
**LIRIPIPE** *n* tip of a graduate's hood
**LIRIPIPES** > LIRIPIPE
**LIRIPOOP** *same as* > LIRIPIPE
**LIRIPOOPS** > LIRIPOOP
**LIRK** *vb* wrinkle
**LIRKED** > LIRK
**LIRKING** > LIRK
**LIRKS** > LIRK
**LIROT** > LIRA
**LIROTH** > LIRA
**LIS** *n* fleur-de-lis
**LISENTE** > SENTE
**LISK** *Yorkshire dialect for* > GROIN
**LISKS** > LISK
**LISLE** *n* strong fine cotton thread or fabric
**LISLES** > LISLE
**LISP** *n* speech defect in which s and z are pronounced th ▷ *vb* speak or utter with a lisp
**LISPED** > LISP
**LISPER** > LISP
**LISPERS** > LISP
**LISPING** > LISP
**LISPINGLY** > LISP
**LISPINGS** > LISP
**LISPOUND** *n* unit of weight
**LISPOUNDS** > LISPOUND
**LISPS** > LISP
**LISPUND** *same as* > LISPOUND
**LISPUNDS** > LISPUND
**LISSES** > LIS
**LISSOM** *adj* supple, agile

**LISSOME** *same as* > LISSOM
**LISSOMELY** > LISSOM
**LISSOMLY** > LISSOM
**LIST** *n* item-by-item record of names or things, usu written one below another ▷ *vb* make a list of
**LISTABLE** > LIST
**LISTED** > LIST
**LISTEE** *n* person on list
**LISTEES** > LISTEE
**LISTEL** *another name for* > FILLET
**LISTELS** > LISTEL
**LISTEN** *vb* concentrate on hearing something
**LISTENED** > LISTEN
**LISTENER** > LISTEN
**LISTENERS** > LISTEN
**LISTENING** > LISTEN
**LISTENS** > LISTEN
**LISTER** *n* plough with a double mouldboard designed to throw soil to either side of a central furrow
**LISTERIA** *n* any rodlike Gram-positive bacterium of the genus *Listeria*
**LISTERIAL** > LISTERIA
**LISTERIAS** > LISTERIA
**LISTERS** > LISTER
**LISTETH** > LIST
**LISTFUL** *adj* paying attention
**LISTING** *n* list or an entry in a list
**LISTINGS** > LISTING
**LISTLESS** *adj* lacking interest or energy
**LISTS** *pl n* field of combat in a tournament
**LISTSERV** *n* service on the internet that provides an electronic mailing to subscribers with similar interests
**LISTSERVS** > LISTSERV
**LIT** *n* archaic word for dye or colouring
**LITAI** > LITAS
**LITANIES** > LITANY
**LITANY** *n* prayer with responses from the congregation
**LITAS** *n* standard monetary unit of Lithuania, divided into 100 centai
**LITCHI** *n* Chinese sapindaceous tree cultivated for its round edible fruits
**LITCHIS** > LITCHI
**LITE** *same as* > LIGHT
**LITED** > LIGHT
**LITENESS** > LITE
**LITER** *same as* > LITRE
**LITERACY** *n* ability to read and write
**LITERAL** *adj* according to the explicit meaning of a word or text, not figurative ▷ *n* misprint or

misspelling in a text
**LITERALLY** *adv* in a literal manner
**LITERALS** > LITERAL
**LITERARY** *adj* of or knowledgeable about literature
**LITERATE** *adj* able to read and write ▷ *n* literate person
**LITERATES** > LITERATE
**LITERATI** *pl n* literary people
**LITERATIM** *adv* letter for letter
**LITERATO** > LITERATI
**LITERATOR** *n* professional writer
**LITERATUS** > LITERATI
**LITEROSE** *adj* affectedly literary
**LITERS** > LITER
**LITES** > LITE
**LITH** *n* limb or joint
**LITHARGE** *n* lead monoxide
**LITHARGES** > LITHARGE
**LITHATE** *n* salt of uric acid
**LITHATES** > LITHATE
**LITHE** *adj* flexible or supple, pliant ▷ *vb* listen
**LITHED** > LITHE
**LITHELY** > LITHE
**LITHEMIA** *n* gout
**LITHEMIAS** > LITHEMIA
**LITHEMIC** > LITHEMIA
**LITHENESS** > LITHE
**LITHER** > LITHE
**LITHERLY** *adj* crafty; cunning
**LITHES** > LITHE
**LITHESOME** *less common word for* > LISSOM
**LITHEST** > LITHE
**LITHIA** *n* lithium present in mineral waters as lithium salts
**LITHIAS** > LITHIA
**LITHIASES** > LITHIASIS
**LITHIASIS** *n* formation of a calculus
**LITHIC** *adj* of, relating to, or composed of stone
**LITHIFIED** > LITHIFY
**LITHIFIES** > LITHIFY
**LITHIFY** *vb* turn into rock
**LITHING** > LITHE
**LITHISTID** *n* type of sponge
**LITHITE** *n* part of cell with sensory element
**LITHITES** > LITHITE
**LITHIUM** *n* chemical element, the lightest known metal
**LITHIUMS** > LITHIUM
**LITHO** *n* lithography ▷ *vb* print using lithography
**LITHOCYST** *n* sac containing otoliths
**LITHOED** > LITHO
**LITHOID** *adj* resembling stone or rock
**LITHOIDAL** *same as* > LITHOID

**LITHOING** > LITHO
**LITHOLOGY** *n* physical characteristics of a rock
**LITHOPONE** *n* white pigment consisting of a mixture of zinc sulphide, zinc oxide, and barium sulphate
**LITHOPS** *n* fleshy-leaved plant
**LITHOS** > LITHO
**LITHOSOL** *n* type of azonal soil consisting chiefly of unweathered or partly weathered rock fragments
**LITHOSOLS** > LITHOSOL
**LITHOTOME** *n* instrument used in lithotomy operation
**LITHOTOMY** *n* surgical removal of a calculus, esp one in the urinary bladder
**LITHS** > LITH
**LITIGABLE** *adj* that may be the subject of litigation
**LITIGANT** *n* person involved in a lawsuit ▷ *adj* engaged in litigation
**LITIGANTS** > LITIGANT
**LITIGATE** *vb* bring or contest a law suit
**LITIGATED** > LITIGATE
**LITIGATES** > LITIGATE
**LITIGATOR** > LITIGATE
**LITIGIOUS** *adj* frequently going to law
**LITING** > LITE
**LITMUS** *n* blue dye turned red by acids and restored to blue by alkalis
**LITMUSES** > LITMUS
**LITORAL** *same as* > LITTORAL
**LITOTES** *n* ironical understatement used for effect
**LITOTIC** > LITOTES
**LITRE** *n* unit of liquid measure equal to 1000 cubic centimetres or 1.76 pints
**LITRES** > LITRE
**LITS** > LIT
**LITTEN** *adj* lighted
**LITTER** *n* untidy rubbish dropped in public places ▷ *vb* strew with litter
**LITTERBAG** *n* bag for putting rubbish in
**LITTERBUG** *n* person who tends to drop rubbish in public places
**LITTERED** > LITTER
**LITTERER** *n* one who litters
**LITTERERS** > LITTERER
**LITTERING** > LITTER
**LITTERS** > LITTER
**LITTERY** *adj* covered in litter
**LITTLE** *adj* small or smaller than average ▷ *adv* not a lot ▷ *n* small amount, extent, or duration
**LITTLER** > LITTLE

LITTLES > LITTLE
LITTLEST > LITTLE
LITTLIE n young child
LITTLIES > LITTLIE
LITTLIN same as > LITTLING
LITTLING n child
LITTLINGS > LITTLING
LITTLINS > LITTLIN
LITTLISH adj rather small
LITTORAL adj of or by the seashore ▷ n coastal district
LITTORALS > LITTORAL
LITU > LITAS
LITURGIC > LITURGY
LITURGICS n study of liturgies
LITURGIES > LITURGY
LITURGISM > LITURGIST
LITURGIST n student or composer of liturgical forms
LITURGY n prescribed form of public worship
LITUUS n type of curved trumpet
LITUUSES > LITUUS
LIVABLE adj tolerable or pleasant to live (with)
LIVE vb be alive ▷ adj living, alive ▷ adv in the form of a live performance
LIVEABLE same as > LIVABLE
LIVED > LIVE
LIVEDO n reddish discoloured patch on the skin
LIVEDOS > LIVEDO
LIVELIER > LIVELY
LIVELIEST > LIVELY
LIVELILY > LIVELY
LIVELOD n livelihood
LIVELODS > LIVELOD
LIVELONG adj long or seemingly long
LIVELONGS > LIVELONG
LIVELOOD n livelihood
LIVELOODS > LIVELOOD
LIVELY adj full of life or vigour
LIVEN vb make or become lively
LIVENED > LIVEN
LIVENER > LIVEN
LIVENERS > LIVEN
LIVENESS n state of being alive
LIVENING > LIVEN
LIVENS > LIVEN
LIVER n person who lives in a specified way
LIVERED adj having liver
LIVERIED adj wearing livery
LIVERIES > LIVERY
LIVERING n process of liquid becoming lumpy
LIVERISH adj having a disorder of the liver
LIVERLEAF n woodland plant
LIVERLESS > LIVER
LIVERS > LIVER
LIVERWORT n plant

resembling seaweed or leafy moss
LIVERY n distinctive dress, esp of a servant or servants ▷ adj of or resembling liver
LIVERYMAN n member of a livery company
LIVERYMEN > LIVERYMAN
LIVES > LIFE
LIVEST > LIVE
LIVESTOCK n farm animals
LIVETRAP n box constructed to trap an animal without injuring it
LIVETRAPS > LIVETRAP
LIVEWARE n programmers, systems analysts, operating staff, and other personnel working in a computer system
LIVEWARES > LIVEWARE
LIVEYER n (in Newfoundland) a full-time resident
LIVEYERE same as > LIVEYER
LIVEYERES > LIVEYERE
LIVEYERS > LIVEYER
LIVID adj angry or furious
LIVIDER > LIVID
LIVIDEST > LIVID
LIVIDITY n state of being livid
LIVIDLY > LIVID
LIVIDNESS > LIVID
LIVIER same as > LIVEYER
LIVIERS > LIVIER
LIVING adj possessing life, not dead or inanimate ▷ n condition of being alive
LIVINGLY > LIVING
LIVINGS > LIVING
LIVOR another word for > LIVIDITY
LIVORS > LIVOR
LIVRAISON n one of the numbers of a book published in parts
LIVRE n former French unit of money of account, equal to 1 pound of silver
LIVRES > LIVRE
LIVYER same as > LIVEYER
LIVYERS > LIVYER
LIXIVIA > LIXIVIUM
LIXIVIAL > LIXIVIATE
LIXIVIATE less common word for > LEACH
LIXIVIOUS > LIXIVIUM
LIXIVIUM n alkaline solution obtained by leaching wood ash with water
LIXIVIUMS > LIXIVIUM
LIZARD n four-footed reptile with a long body and tail
LIZARDS > LIZARD
LIZZIE as in busy lizzie plant with pink, white, or red flowers
LIZZIES > LIZZIE
LLAMA n woolly animal of the camel family used as a beast of burden in S

America
LLAMAS > LLAMA
LLANERO n native of llanos
LLANEROS > LLANERO
LLANO n extensive grassy treeless plain, esp in South America
LLANOS > LLANO
LO interj look!
LOACH n carplike freshwater fish
LOACHES > LOACH
LOAD n burden or weight ▷ vb put a load on or into
LOADED adj (of a question) containing a hidden trap or implication
LOADEN vb load
LOADENED > LOADEN
LOADENING > LOADEN
LOADENS > LOADEN
LOADER n person who loads a gun or other firearm
LOADERS > LOADER
LOADING n load or burden
LOADINGS > LOADING
LOADS pl n lots or a lot
LOADSPACE n area in a motor vehicle where a load can be carried
LOADSTAR same as > LODESTAR
LOADSTARS > LOADSTAR
LOADSTONE same as > LODESTONE
LOAF n shaped mass of baked bread ▷ vb idle, loiter
LOAFED > LOAF
LOAFER n person who avoids work
LOAFERISH > LOAFER
LOAFERS > LOAFER
LOAFING > LOAF
LOAFINGS > LOAF
LOAFS > LOAF
LOAM n fertile soil ▷ vb cover, treat, or fill with loam
LOAMED > LOAM
LOAMIER > LOAM
LOAMIEST > LOAM
LOAMINESS > LOAM
LOAMING > LOAM
LOAMLESS > LOAM
LOAMS > LOAM
LOAMY > LOAM
LOAN n money lent at interest ▷ vb lend
LOANABLE > LOAN
LOANBACK n facility by which an individual can borrow from his or her pension fund ▷ vb make use of this facility
LOANBACKS > LOANBACK
LOANED > LOAN
LOANER > LOAN
LOANERS > LOAN
LOANING > LOAN
LOANINGS > LOANING
LOANS > LOAN
LOANSHIFT n adaptation of word from one language

by another
LOANWORD n word adopted from one language into another
LOANWORDS > LOANWORD
LOAST > LOOSE
LOATH adj unwilling or reluctant (to)
LOATHE vb hate, be disgusted by
LOATHED > LOATHE
LOATHER > LOATHE
LOATHERS > LOATHE
LOATHES > LOATHE
LOATHEST > LOATH
LOATHFUL adj causing loathing
LOATHING n strong disgust
LOATHINGS > LOATHING
LOATHLY adv with reluctance
LOATHNESS > LOATH
LOATHSOME adj causing loathing
LOATHY obsolete form of > LOATHSOME
LOAVE vb make into the form of a loaf
LOAVED > LOAVE
LOAVES > LOAF
LOAVING > LOAVE
LOB n ball struck or thrown in a high arc ▷ vb strike or throw (a ball) in a high arc
LOBAR adj of or affecting a lobe
LOBATE adj with or like lobes
LOBATED same as > LOBATE
LOBATELY > LOBATE
LOBATION n division into lobes
LOBATIONS > LOBATION
LOBBED > LOB
LOBBER n one who lobs
LOBBERS > LOBBER
LOBBIED > LOBBY
LOBBIES > LOBBY
LOBBING > LOB
LOBBY n corridor into which rooms open ▷ vb try to influence (legislators) in the formulation of policy
LOBBYER > LOBBY
LOBBYERS > LOBBY
LOBBYGOW n errand boy
LOBBYGOWS > LOBBYGOW
LOBBYING > LOBBY
LOBBYINGS > LOBBY
LOBBYISM > LOBBYIST
LOBBYISMS > LOBBYIST
LOBBYIST n person who lobbies on behalf of a particular interest
LOBBYISTS > LOBBYIST
LOBE n rounded projection
LOBECTOMY n surgical removal of a lobe from any organ or gland in the body
LOBED > LOBE
LOBEFIN n type of fish
LOBEFINS > LOBEFIN
LOBELET n small lobe

437

LOBELETS > LOBELET
LOBELIA n garden plant with blue, red, or white flowers
LOBELIAS > LOBELIA
LOBELINE n crystalline alkaloid extracted from the seeds of the Indian tobacco plant
LOBELINES > LOBELINE
LOBES > LOBE
LOBI > LOBUS
LOBING n formation of lobes
LOBINGS > LOBING
LOBIPED adj with lobed toes
LOBLOLLY n southern US pine tree
LOBO n timber wolf
LOBOLA n (in African custom) price paid by a bridegroom's family to his bride's family
LOBOLAS > LOBOLA
LOBOLO same as > LOBOLA
LOBOLOS > LOBOLO
LOBOS > LOBO
LOBOSE another word for > LOBATE
LOBOTOMY n surgical incision into a lobe of the brain to treat mental disorders
LOBS > LOB
LOBSCOUSE n sailor's stew of meat, vegetables, and hardtack
LOBSTER n shellfish with a long tail and claws, which turns red when boiled ▷ vb fish for lobsters
LOBSTERED > LOBSTER
LOBSTERER n person who catches lobsters
LOBSTERS > LOBSTER
LOBSTICK n tree used as landmark
LOBSTICKS > LOBSTICK
LOBULAR > LOBULE
LOBULARLY > LOBULE
LOBULATE > LOBULE
LOBULATED > LOBULE
LOBULE n small lobe or a subdivision of a lobe
LOBULES > LOBULE
LOBULI > LOBULUS
LOBULOSE > LOBULE
LOBULUS n small lobe
LOBUS n lobe
LOBWORM same as > LUGWORM
LOBWORMS > LOBWORM
LOCA > LOCUS
LOCAL adj of or existing in a particular place ▷ n person belonging to a particular district
LOCALE n scene of an event
LOCALES > LOCALE
LOCALISE same as > LOCALIZE
LOCALISED > LOCALISE
LOCALISER > LOCALISE

LOCALISES > LOCALISE
LOCALISM n pronunciation, phrase, etc, peculiar to a particular locality
LOCALISMS > LOCALISM
LOCALIST > LOCALISM
LOCALISTS > LOCALISM
LOCALITE n resident of an area
LOCALITES > LOCALITE
LOCALITY n neighbourhood or area
LOCALIZE vb restrict to a particular place
LOCALIZED > LOCALIZE
LOCALIZER > LOCALIZE
LOCALIZES > LOCALIZE
LOCALLY adv within a particular area or place
LOCALNESS > LOCAL
LOCALS > LOCAL
LOCATABLE > LOCATE
LOCATE vb discover the whereabouts of
LOCATED > LOCATE
LOCATER > LOCATE
LOCATERS > LOCATE
LOCATES > LOCATE
LOCATING > LOCATE
LOCATION n site or position
LOCATIONS > LOCATION
LOCATIVE adj (of a word or phrase) indicating place or direction ▷ n locative case
LOCATIVES > LOCATIVE
LOCATOR n part of index that indicates where to look for information
LOCATORS > LOCATOR
LOCELLATE adj split into secondary cells
LOCH n lake
LOCHAN n small inland loch
LOCHANS > LOCHAN
LOCHIA n vaginal discharge of cellular debris, mucus, and blood following childbirth
LOCHIAL > LOCHIA
LOCHS > LOCH
LOCI > LOCUS
LOCK n appliance for fastening a door, case, etc ▷ vb fasten or become fastened securely
LOCKABLE > LOCK
LOCKAGE n system of locks in a canal
LOCKAGES > LOCKAGE
LOCKAWAY n investment intended to be held for a relatively long time
LOCKAWAYS > LOCKAWAY
LOCKBOX n system of collecting funds from companies by banks
LOCKBOXES > LOCKBOX
LOCKDOWN n device used to secure equipment, etc
LOCKDOWNS > LOCKDOWN
LOCKED > LOCK

LOCKER n small cupboard with a lock
LOCKERS > LOCKER
LOCKET n small hinged pendant for a portrait etc
LOCKETS > LOCKET
LOCKFAST adj securely fastened with a lock
LOCKFUL n sufficient to fill a canal lock
LOCKFULS > LOCKFUL
LOCKHOUSE n house of lock-keeper
LOCKING > LOCK
LOCKINGS > LOCK
LOCKJAW n tetanus
LOCKJAWS > LOCKJAW
LOCKMAKER n maker of locks
LOCKMAN n lock-keeper
LOCKMEN > LOCKMAN
LOCKNUT n supplementary nut screwed down upon a primary nut to prevent it from shaking loose
LOCKNUTS > LOCKNUT
LOCKOUT n closing of a workplace by an employer to force workers to accept terms
LOCKOUTS > LOCKOUT
LOCKPICK another word for > PICKLOCK
LOCKPICKS > LOCKPICK
LOCKRAM n type of linen cloth
LOCKRAMS > LOCKRAM
LOCKS > LOCK
LOCKSET n hardware used to lock door
LOCKSETS > LOCKSET
LOCKSMAN same as > LOCKMAN
LOCKSMEN > LOCKSMAN
LOCKSMITH n person who makes and mends locks
LOCKSTEP n method of marching in step as closely as possible
LOCKSTEPS > LOCKSTEP
LOCKUP n prison
LOCKUPS > LOCKUP
LOCO n locomotive ▷ adj insane ▷ vb poison with locoweed
LOCOED > LOCO
LOCOES > LOCO
LOCOFOCO n match
LOCOFOCOS > LOCOFOCO
LOCOING > LOCO
LOCOISM n disease of cattle, sheep, and horses caused by eating locoweed
LOCOISMS > LOCOISM
LOCOMAN n railwayman, esp an engine-driver
LOCOMEN > LOCOMAN
LOCOMOTE vb move from one place to another
LOCOMOTED > LOCOMOTE
LOCOMOTES > LOCOMOTE
LOCOMOTOR adj of or relating to locomotion
LOCOPLANT another word

for > LOCOWEED
LOCOS > LOCO
LOCOWEED n any of several perennial leguminous plants
LOCOWEEDS > LOCOWEED
LOCULAR adj divided into compartments by septa
LOCULATE same as > LOCULAR
LOCULATED same as > LOCULATE
LOCULE n any of the chambers of an ovary or anther
LOCULED adj having locules
LOCULES > LOCULE
LOCULI > LOCULUS
LOCULUS same as > LOCULE
LOCUM n temporary stand-in for a doctor or clergyman
LOCUMS > LOCUM
LOCUPLETE adj well-stored
LOCUS n area or place where something happens
LOCUST n destructive insect that flies in swarms and eats crops ▷ vb ravage, as locusts
LOCUSTA n flower cluster unit in grasses
LOCUSTAE > LOCUSTA
LOCUSTAL > LOCUSTA
LOCUSTED > LOCUST
LOCUSTING > LOCUST
LOCUSTS > LOCUST
LOCUTION n manner or style of speech
LOCUTIONS > LOCUTION
LOCUTORY adj room intended for conversation
LOD n type of logarithm
LODE n vein of ore
LODEN n thick heavy waterproof woollen cloth with a short pile, used to make garments, esp coats
LODENS > LODEN
LODES > LODE
LODESMAN n pilot
LODESMEN > LODESMAN
LODESTAR n star used in navigation or astronomy as a point of reference
LODESTARS > LODESTAR
LODESTONE n magnetic iron ore
LODGE n gatekeeper's house ▷ vb live in another's house at a fixed charge
LODGEABLE > LODGE
LODGED > LODGE
LODGEMENT same as > LODGMENT
LODGEPOLE n type of pine tree
LODGER n person who pays rent in return for accommodation in someone else's home
LODGERS > LODGER
LODGES > LODGE

**LODGING** *n* temporary residence
**LODGINGS** *pl n* rented room or rooms in which to live, esp in another person's house
**LODGMENT** *n* act of lodging or the state of being lodged
**LODGMENTS** > LODGMENT
**LODICULA** *n* delicate scale in grass
**LODICULAE** > LODICULA
**LODICULE** *n* any of two or three minute scales at the base of the ovary in grass flowers that represent the corolla
**LODICULES** > LODICULE
**LODS** > LOD
**LOERIE** *same as* > LOURIE
**LOERIES** > LOERIE
**LOESS** *n* fine-grained soil, found mainly in river valleys, originally deposited by the wind
**LOESSAL** > LOESS
**LOESSES** > LOESS
**LOESSIAL** > LOESS
**LOFT** *n* space between the top storey and roof of a building ▷ *vb* strike, throw, or kick (a ball) high into the air
**LOFTED** > LOFT
**LOFTER** *n* type of golf club
**LOFTERS** > LOFTER
**LOFTIER** > LOFTY
**LOFTIEST** > LOFTY
**LOFTILY** > LOFTY
**LOFTINESS** > LOFTY
**LOFTING** > LOFT
**LOFTLESS** > LOFT
**LOFTLIKE** > LOFT
**LOFTS** > LOFT
**LOFTSMAN** *n* person who reproduces in actual size a draughtsman's design for a ship or an aircraft
**LOFTSMEN** > LOFTSMAN
**LOFTY** *adj* of great height
**LOG** *n* portion of a felled tree stripped of branches ▷ *vb* saw logs from a tree
**LOGAN** *another name for* > BOGAN
**LOGANIA** *n* type of Australian plant
**LOGANIAS** > LOGANIA
**LOGANS** > LOGAN
**LOGAOEDIC** *adj* of or relating to verse in which mixed metres are combined within a single line to give the effect of prose ▷ *n* line or verse of this kind
**LOGARITHM** *n* one of a series of arithmetical functions used to make certain calculations easier
**LOGBOARD** *n* board used for logging a ship's records
**LOGBOARDS** > LOGBOARD

**LOGBOOK** *n* book recording the details about a car or a ship's journeys
**LOGBOOKS** > LOGBOOK
**LOGE** *n* small enclosure or box in a theatre or opera house
**LOGES** > LOGE
**LOGGAT** *n* small piece of wood
**LOGGATS** > LOGGAT
**LOGGED** > LOG
**LOGGER** *n* tractor or crane for handling logs
**LOGGERS** > LOGGER
**LOGGETS** *n* old-fashioned game played with sticks
**LOGGIA** *n* covered gallery at the side of a building
**LOGGIAS** > LOGGIA
**LOGGIE** > LOGGIA
**LOGGIER** > LOGGY
**LOGGIEST** > LOGGY
**LOGGING** > LOG
**LOGGINGS** > LOG
**LOGGISH** > LOG
**LOGGY** *adj* slow, sluggish, or listless
**LOGIA** > LOGION
**LOGIC** *n* philosophy of reasoning
**LOGICAL** *adj* of logic
**LOGICALLY** > LOGICAL
**LOGICIAN** *n* person who specializes in or is skilled at logic
**LOGICIANS** > LOGICIAN
**LOGICISE** *same as* > LOGICIZE
**LOGICISED** > LOGICISE
**LOGICISES** > LOGICISE
**LOGICISM** *n* philosophical theory that all of mathematics can be deduced from logic
**LOGICISMS** > LOGICISM
**LOGICIST** > LOGICISM
**LOGICISTS** > LOGICISM
**LOGICIZE** *vb* present reasons for or against
**LOGICIZED** > LOGICIZE
**LOGICIZES** > LOGICIZE
**LOGICLESS** > LOGIC
**LOGICS** > LOGIC
**LOGIE** *n* fire-place of a kiln
**LOGIER** > LOGY
**LOGIES** > LOGIE
**LOGIEST** > LOGY
**LOGILY** > LOGY
**LOGIN** *n* process by which a computer user logs on
**LOGINESS** > LOGY
**LOGINS** > LOGIN
**LOGION** *n* saying of Christ regarded as authentic
**LOGIONS** > LOGION
**LOGISTIC** *n* uninterpreted calculus or system of symbolic logic ▷ *adj* (of a curve) having a particular form of equation
**LOGISTICS** *n* detailed planning and organization of a large, esp military,

operation
**LOGJAM** *n* blockage caused by the crowding together of a number of logs floating in a river ▷ *vb* cause a logjam
**LOGJAMMED** > LOGJAM
**LOGJAMS** > LOGJAM
**LOGJUICE** *n* poor quality port wine
**LOGJUICES** > LOGJUICE
**LOGLINE** *n* synopsis of screenplay
**LOGLINES** > LOGLINE
**LOGLOG** *n* logarithm of a logarithm (in equations, etc)
**LOGLOGS** > LOGLOG
**LOGNORMAL** *adj* (maths) having a natural logarithm with normal distribution
**LOGO** *same as* > LOGOTYPE
**LOGOFF** *n* process by which a computer user logs out
**LOGOFFS** > LOGOFF
**LOGOGRAM** *n* single symbol representing an entire morpheme, word, or phrase
**LOGOGRAMS** > LOGOGRAM
**LOGOGRAPH** *same as* > LOGOGRAM
**LOGOGRIPH** *n* word puzzle, esp one based on recombination of the letters of a word
**LOGOI** > LOGOS
**LOGOMACH** *n* one who argues over words
**LOGOMACHS** > LOGOMACH
**LOGOMACHY** *n* argument about words or the meaning of words
**LOGON** *variant of* > LOGIN
**LOGONS** > LOGON
**LOGOPEDIC** *adj* of or relating to speech therapy
**LOGOPHILE** *n* one who loves words
**LOGORRHEA** *n* excessive or uncontrollable talkativeness
**LOGOS** *n* reason or the rational principle expressed in words and things, argument, or justification
**LOGOTHETE** *n* officer of Byzantine empire
**LOGOTYPE** *n* piece of type with several uncombined characters cast on it
**LOGOTYPES** > LOGOTYPE
**LOGOTYPY** > LOGOTYPE
**LOGOUT** *variant of* > LOGOFF
**LOGOUTS** > LOGOUT
**LOGROLL** *vb* use logrolling in order to procure the passage of (legislation)
**LOGROLLED** > LOGROLL
**LOGROLLER** > LOGROLL
**LOGROLLS** > LOGROLL
**LOGS** > LOG
**LOGWAY** *another name*

*for* > GANGWAY
**LOGWAYS** > LOGWAY
**LOGWOOD** *n* leguminous tree of the Caribbean and Central America
**LOGWOODS** > LOGWOOD
**LOGY** *adj* dull or listless
**LOHAN** *another word for* > ARHAT
**LOHANS** > LOHAN
**LOID** *vb* open (a lock) using a celluloid strip
**LOIDED** > LOID
**LOIDING** > LOID
**LOIDS** > LOID
**LOIN** *n* part of the body between the ribs and the hips
**LOINCLOTH** *n* piece of cloth covering the loins only
**LOINS** *pl n* hips and the inner surface of the legs where they join the body
**LOIPE** *n* cross-country skiing track
**LOIPEN** > LOIPE
**LOIR** *n* large dormouse
**LOIRS** > LOIR
**LOITER** *vb* stand or wait aimlessly or idly
**LOITERED** > LOITER
**LOITERER** > LOITER
**LOITERERS** > LOITER
**LOITERING** > LOITER
**LOITERS** > LOITER
**LOKE** *n* track
**LOKES** > LOKE
**LOKSHEN** *pl n* noodles
**LOLIGO** *n* type of squid
**LOLIGOS** > LOLIGO
**LOLIUM** *n* type of grass
**LOLIUMS** > LOLIUM
**LOLL** *vb* lounge lazily ▷ *n* act or instance of lolling
**LOLLED** > LOLL
**LOLLER** > LOLL
**LOLLERS** > LOLL
**LOLLIES** > LOLLY
**LOLLING** > LOLL
**LOLLINGLY** > LOLL
**LOLLIPOP** *n* boiled sweet on a small wooden stick
**LOLLIPOPS** > LOLLIPOP
**LOLLOP** *vb* move clumsily
**LOLLOPED** > LOLLOP
**LOLLOPING** > LOLLOP
**LOLLOPS** > LOLLOP
**LOLLOPY** > LOLLOP
**LOLLS** > LOLL
**LOLLY** *n* lollipop or ice lolly
**LOLLYGAG** *same as* > LALLYGAG
**LOLLYGAGS** > LOLLYGAG
**LOLLYPOP** *same as* > LOLLIPOP
**LOLLYPOPS** > LOLLYPOP
**LOLOG** *same as* > LOGLOG
**LOLOGS** > LOLOG
**LOMA** *n* lobe
**LOMAS** > LOMA
**LOMATA** > LOMA
**LOME** *vb* cover with lome
**LOMED** > LOME
**LOMEIN** *n* Chinese dish

**LOMEINS** > LOMEIN
**LOMENT** n pod of certain leguminous plants
**LOMENTA** > LOMENTUM
**LOMENTS** > LOMENT
**LOMENTUM** same as > LOMENT
**LOMENTUMS** > LOMENTUM
**LOMES** > LOME
**LOMING** > LOME
**LOMPISH** another word for > LUMPISH
**LONE** adj solitary
**LONELIER** > LONELY
**LONELIEST** > LONELY
**LONELILY** > LONELY
**LONELY** adj sad because alone
**LONENESS** > LONE
**LONER** n person who prefers to be alone
**LONERS** > LONER
**LONESOME** adj lonely ▷ n own
**LONESOMES** > LONESOME
**LONG** adj having length, esp great length, in space or time ▷ adv for a certain time ▷ vb have a strong desire (for)
**LONGA** n long note
**LONGAEVAL** adj long-lived
**LONGAN** n sapindaceous tree of tropical and subtropical Asia
**LONGANS** > LONGAN
**LONGAS** > LONGA
**LONGBOARD** n type of surfboard
**LONGBOAT** n largest boat carried on a ship
**LONGBOATS** > LONGBOAT
**LONGBOW** n large powerful bow
**LONGBOWS** > LONGBOW
**LONGCASE** as in longcase clock grandfather clock
**LONGCLOTH** n fine plain-weave cotton cloth made in long strips
**LONGE** n rope used in training a horse ▷ vb train using a longe
**LONGED** > LONG
**LONGEING** > LONGE
**LONGER** n line of barrels on a ship
**LONGERON** n main longitudinal structural member of an aircraft
**LONGERONS** > LONGERON
**LONGERS** > LONGER
**LONGES** > LONGE
**LONGEST** > LONG
**LONGEVAL** another word for > LONGAEVAL
**LONGEVITY** n long life
**LONGEVOUS** > LONGEVITY
**LONGHAIR** n cat with long hair
**LONGHAIRS** > LONGHAIR
**LONGHAND** n ordinary writing, not shorthand or typing

**LONGHANDS** > LONGHAND
**LONGHEAD** n person with long head
**LONGHEADS** > LONGHEAD
**LONGHORN** n British breed of beef cattle with long curved horns
**LONGHORNS** > LONGHORN
**LONGHOUSE** n long communal dwelling of Native American peoples
**LONGICORN** n any beetle of the family Cerambycidae ▷ adj having or designating long antennae
**LONGIES** n long johns
**LONGING** n yearning ▷ adj having or showing desire
**LONGINGLY** > LONGING
**LONGINGS** > LONGING
**LONGISH** adj rather long
**LONGITUDE** n distance east or west from a standard meridian
**LONGJUMP** n jumping contest decided by length
**LONGJUMPS** > LONGJUMP
**LONGLEAF** n North American pine tree
**LONGLINE** n (tennis) straight stroke played down court
**LONGLINES** > LONGLINE
**LONGLY** > LONG
**LONGNECK** n US, Canadian and Australian word for a 330-ml beer bottle with a long narrow neck
**LONGNECKS** > LONGNECK
**LONGNESS** > LONG
**LONGS** pl n full-length trousers
**LONGSHIP** n narrow open boat with oars and a square sail, used by the Vikings
**LONGSHIPS** > LONGSHIP
**LONGSHORE** adj situated on, relating to, or along the shore
**LONGSOME** adj slow; boring
**LONGSPUR** n any of various Arctic and North American buntings
**LONGSPURS** > LONGSPUR
**LONGTIME** adj of long standing
**LONGUEUR** n period of boredom or dullness
**LONGUEURS** > LONGUEUR
**LONGWALL** n long face in coal mine
**LONGWALLS** > LONGWALL
**LONGWAYS** adv lengthways
**LONGWISE** same as > LONGWAYS
**LONICERA** n honeysuckle
**LONICERAS** > LONICERA
**LOO** n informal word meaning lavatory ▷ vb Scots word meaning love
**LOOBIER** > LOOBY
**LOOBIES** > LOOBY

**LOOBIEST** > LOOBY
**LOOBILY** > LOOBY
**LOOBY** adj foolish ▷ n foolish or stupid person
**LOOED** > LOO
**LOOEY** n lieutenant
**LOOEYS** > LOOEY
**LOOF** n part of ship's side
**LOOFA** same as > LOOFAH
**LOOFAH** n sponge made from the dried pod of a gourd
**LOOFAHS** > LOOFAH
**LOOFAS** > LOOFA
**LOOFFUL** n handful
**LOOFFULS** > LOOFFUL
**LOOFS** > LOOF
**LOOIE** same as > LOOEY
**LOOIES** > LOOIE
**LOOING** > LOO
**LOOK** vb direct the eyes or attention (towards) ▷ n instance of looking
**LOOKALIKE** n person who is the double of another
**LOOKDOWN** n way paper appears when looked at under reflected light
**LOOKDOWNS** > LOOKDOWN
**LOOKED** > LOOK
**LOOKER** n person who looks
**LOOKERS** > LOOKER
**LOOKING** > LOOK
**LOOKISM** n discrimination against a person on the grounds of physical appearance
**LOOKISMS** > LOOKISM
**LOOKIST** > LOOKISM
**LOOKISTS** > LOOKISM
**LOOKOUT** n act of watching for danger or for an opportunity ▷ vb be careful
**LOOKOUTS** > LOOKOUT
**LOOKOVER** n inspection, esp a brief one
**LOOKOVERS** > LOOKOVER
**LOOKS** > LOOK
**LOOKSISM** same as > LOOKISM
**LOOKSISMS** > LOOKSISM
**LOOKUP** n act of looking up information, esp on the internet
**LOOKUPS** > LOOKUP
**LOOM** n machine for weaving cloth ▷ vb appear dimly
**LOOMED** > LOOM
**LOOMING** > LOOM
**LOOMS** > LOOM
**LOON** n diving bird
**LOONEY** same as > LOONY
**LOONEYS** > LOONY
**LOONIE** n Canadian dollar coin with a loon bird on one of its faces
**LOONIER** > LOONY
**LOONIES** > LOONY
**LOONIEST** > LOONY
**LOONILY** > LOONY
**LOONINESS** > LOONY
**LOONING** n cry of the loon

**LOONINGS** > LOONING
**LOONS** > LOON
**LOONY** adj foolish or insane ▷ n foolish or insane person
**LOOP** n rounded shape made by a curved line or rope crossing itself ▷ vb form or fasten with a loop
**LOOPED** > LOOP
**LOOPER** n person or thing that loops or makes loops
**LOOPERS** > LOOPER
**LOOPHOLE** n means of evading a rule without breaking it ▷ vb provide with loopholes
**LOOPHOLED** > LOOPHOLE
**LOOPHOLES** > LOOPHOLE
**LOOPIER** > LOOPY
**LOOPIEST** > LOOPY
**LOOPILY** > LOOPY
**LOOPINESS** > LOOPY
**LOOPING** > LOOP
**LOOPINGS** > LOOP
**LOOPS** > LOOP
**LOOPY** adj slightly mad or crazy
**LOOR** > LIEF
**LOORD** obsolete word for > LOUT
**LOORDS** > LOORD
**LOOS** > LOO
**LOOSE** adj not tight, fastened, fixed, or tense ▷ adv in a loose manner ▷ vb free
**LOOSEBOX** n enclosed stall with a door in which an animal can be kept
**LOOSED** > LOOSE
**LOOSELY** > LOOSE
**LOOSEN** vb make loose
**LOOSENED** > LOOSEN
**LOOSENER** > LOOSEN
**LOOSENERS** > LOOSEN
**LOOSENESS** > LOOSE
**LOOSENING** > LOOSEN
**LOOSENS** > LOOSEN
**LOOSER** > LOOSE
**LOOSES** > LOOSE
**LOOSEST** > LOOSE
**LOOSIE** n informal word for loose forward
**LOOSIES** pl n cigarettes sold individually
**LOOSING** n celebration of one's 21st birthday
**LOOSINGS** > LOOSING
**LOOT** vb pillage ▷ n goods stolen during pillaging
**LOOTED** > LOOT
**LOOTEN** Scots past form of > LET
**LOOTER** > LOOT
**LOOTERS** > LOOT
**LOOTING** > LOOT
**LOOTINGS** > LOOT
**LOOTS** > LOOT
**LOOVES** > LOOF
**LOP** vb cut away (twigs and branches) ▷ n part or parts lopped off, as from a tree

LOPE *vb* run with long easy strides ▷ *n* loping stride
LOPED > LOPE
LOPER > LOPE
LOPERS > LOPE
LOPES > LOPE
LOPGRASS *n* smooth-bladed grass
LOPHODONT *adj* (of teeth) having elongated ridges
LOPING > LOPE
LOPOLITH *n* saucer- or lens-shaped body of intrusive igneous rock
LOPOLITHS > LOPOLITH
LOPPED > LOP
LOPPER *n* tool for lopping ▷ *vb* curdle
LOPPERED > LOPPER
LOPPERING > LOPPER
LOPPERS > LOPPER
LOPPIER > LOPPY
LOPPIES > LOPPY
LOPPIEST > LOPPY
LOPPING > LOP
LOPPINGS > LOP
LOPPY *adj* floppy ▷ *n* man employed to do maintenance tasks on a ranch
LOPS > LOP
LOPSIDED *adj* greater in height, weight, or size on one side
LOPSTICK *variant of* > LOBSTICK
LOPSTICKS > LOPSTICK
LOQUACITY *n* tendency to talk a great deal
LOQUAT *n* ornamental evergreen rosaceous tree
LOQUATS > LOQUAT
LOQUITUR *n* stage direction meaning *he or she speaks*
LOR *interj* exclamation of surprise or dismay
LORAL *adj* of part of side of bird's head
LORAN *n* radio navigation system operating over long distances
LORANS > LORAN
LORATE *adj* like a strap
LORAZEPAM *n* type of tranquillizer
LORCHA *n* junk-rigged vessel
LORCHAS > LORCHA
LORD *n* person with power over others, such as a monarch or master ▷ *vb* act in a superior manner
LORDED > LORD
LORDING *n* gentleman
LORDINGS > LORDING
LORDKIN *n* little lord
LORDKINS > LORDKIN
LORDLESS > LORD
LORDLIER > LORDLY
LORDLIEST > LORDLY
LORDLIKE > LORD
LORDLING *n* young lord
LORDLINGS > LORDLING

LORDLY *adj* imperious, proud ▷ *adv* in the manner of a lord
LORDOMA *same as* > LORDOSIS
LORDOMAS > LORDOMA
LORDOSES > LORDOSIS
LORDOSIS *n* forward curvature of the lumbar spine
LORDOTIC > LORDOSIS
LORDS > LORD
LORDSHIP *n* position or authority of a lord
LORDSHIPS > LORDSHIP
LORDY *interj* exclamation of surprise or dismay
LORE *n* body of traditions on a subject
LOREAL *adj* concerning or relating to lore
LOREL *another word for* > LOSEL
LORELS > LOREL
LORES > LORE
LORETTE *n* concubine
LORETTES > LORETTE
LORGNETTE *n* pair of spectacles mounted on a long handle
LORGNON *n* monocle or pair of spectacles
LORGNONS > LORGNON
LORIC > LORICA
LORICA *n* hard outer covering of rotifers, ciliate protozoans, and similar organisms
LORICAE > LORICA
LORICATE > LORICA
LORICATED > LORICA
LORICATES > LORICA
LORICS > LORICA
LORIES > LORY
LORIKEET *n* small brightly coloured Australian parrot
LORIKEETS > LORIKEET
LORIMER *n* (formerly) a person who made bits, spurs, and other small metal objects
LORIMERS > LORIMER
LORINER *same as* > LORIMER
LORINERS > LORINER
LORING *n* teaching
LORINGS > LORING
LORIOT *n* golden oriole (bird)
LORIOTS > LORIOT
LORIS *n* any of several omnivorous nocturnal slow-moving prosimian primates
LORISES > LORIS
LORN *adj* forsaken or wretched
LORNNESS > LORN
LORRELL *obsolete word for* > LOSEL
LORRELLS > LORRELL
LORRIES > LORRY
LORRY *n* large vehicle for transporting loads by road
LORY *n* any of various small

brightly coloured parrots of Australia and Indonesia
LOS *n* approval
LOSABLE > LOOSE
LOSE *vb* part with or come to be without
LOSED > LOSE
LOSEL *n* worthless person ▷ *adj* (of a person) worthless, useless, or wasteful
LOSELS > LOSEL
LOSEN > LOOSE
LOSER *n* person or thing that loses
LOSERS > LOSER
LOSES > LOSE
LOSH *interj* lord
LOSING > LOSE
LOSINGLY > LOSE
LOSINGS *pl n* losses, esp money lost in gambling
LOSLYF *n* South African slang for a promiscuous female
LOSLYFS > LOSLYF
LOSS *n* losing
LOSSES > LOSS
LOSSIER > LOSSY
LOSSIEST > LOSSY
LOSSLESS > LOSS
LOSSMAKER *n* organization, industry, or enterprise that consistently fails to make a profit
LOSSY *adj* (of a dielectric material, transmission line, etc) designed to have a high attenuation
LOST *adj* missing
LOSTNESS > LOST
LOT *pron* great number ▷ *n* collection of people or things ▷ *vb* draw lots for
LOTA *n* globular water container, usually of brass, used in India, Myanmar, etc
LOTAH *same as* > LOTA
LOTAHS > LOTAH
LOTAS > LOTA
LOTE *another word for* > LOTUS
LOTES > LOTE
LOTH *same as* > LOATH
LOTHARIO *n* rake, libertine, or seducer
LOTHARIOS > LOTHARIO
LOTHEFULL *obsolete form of* > LOATHFULL
LOTHER > LOTH
LOTHEST > LOTH
LOTHFULL *obsolete form of* > LOATHFULL
LOTHNESS > LOTH
LOTHSOME *same as* > LOATHSOME
LOTI *n* standard monetary unit of Lesotho, divided into 100 lisente
LOTIC *adj* of, relating to, or designating natural communities living in rapidly flowing water

LOTION *n* medical or cosmetic liquid for use on the skin
LOTIONS > LOTION
LOTO *same as* > LOTTO
LOTOS *same as* > LOTUS
LOTOSES > LOTOS
LOTS > LOT
LOTTE *n* type of fish
LOTTED > LOT
LOTTER *n* someone who works an allotment
LOTTERIES > LOTTERY
LOTTERS > LOTTER
LOTTERY *n* method of raising money by selling tickets that win prizes by chance
LOTTES > LOTTE
LOTTING > LOT
LOTTO *n* game of chance like bingo
LOTTOS > LOTTO
LOTUS *n* legendary plant whose fruit induces forgetfulness
LOTUSES > LOTUS
LOTUSLAND *n* idyllic place of contentment
LOU *Scot word for* > LOVE
LOUCHE *adj* shifty or disreputable
LOUCHELY > LOUCHE
LOUD *adj* relatively great in volume
LOUDEN *vb* make or become louder
LOUDENED > LOUDEN
LOUDENING > LOUDEN
LOUDENS > LOUDEN
LOUDER > LOUD
LOUDEST > LOUD
LOUDISH *adj* fairly loud
LOUDLIER > LOUD
LOUDLIEST > LOUD
LOUDLY > LOUD
LOUDMOUTH *n* person who talks too much, esp in a boastful or indiscreet way
LOUDNESS > LOUD
LOUED > LOU
LOUGH *n* loch
LOUGHS > LOUGH
LOUIE *same as* > LOOEY
LOUIES > LOUIE
LOUING > LOU
LOUIS *n* former French gold coin
LOUMA *n* weekly market in rural areas of developing countries
LOUMAS > LOUMA
LOUN *same as* > LOWN
LOUND > LOUN
LOUNDED > LOUND
LOUNDER *vb* beat severely
LOUNDERED > LOUNDER
LOUNDERS > LOUNDER
LOUNDING > LOUND
LOUNDS > LOUND
LOUNED > LOUN
LOUNGE *n* living room in a private house ▷ *vb* sit, lie, or stand in a relaxed

manner
**LOUNGED** >LOUNGE
**LOUNGER** n comfortable sometimes adjustable couch or extending chair designed for someone to relax on
**LOUNGERS** >LOUNGER
**LOUNGES** >LOUNGE
**LOUNGING** >LOUNGE
**LOUNGINGS** >LOUNGE
**LOUNGY** adj casual; relaxed
**LOUNING** >LOUN
**LOUNS** >LOUN
**LOUP** Scot word for >LEAP
**LOUPE** n magnifying glass used by jewellers, horologists, etc
**LOUPED** >LOUP
**LOUPEN** >LOUP
**LOUPES** >LOUPE
**LOUPING** >LOUP
**LOUPIT** >LOUP
**LOUPS** >LOUP
**LOUR** vb (esp of the sky, weather, etc) to be overcast, dark, and menacing ▷n menacing scowl or appearance
**LOURE** n slow, former French dance
**LOURED** >LOUR
**LOURES** >LOURE
**LOURIE** n type of African bird with either crimson or grey plumage
**LOURIER** >LOURY
**LOURIES** >LOURIE
**LOURIEST** >LOURY
**LOURING** >LOUR
**LOURINGLY** >LOUR
**LOURINGS** >LOUR
**LOURS** >LOUR
**LOURY** adj sombre
**LOUS** >LOU
**LOUSE** n wingless parasitic insect ▷vb ruin or spoil
**LOUSED** >LOUSE
**LOUSER** n mean nasty person
**LOUSERS** >LOUSER
**LOUSES** >LOUSE
**LOUSEWORT** n any of various N temperate scrophulariaceous plants
**LOUSIER** >LOUSY
**LOUSIEST** >LOUSY
**LOUSILY** >LOUSY
**LOUSINESS** >LOUSY
**LOUSING** >LOUSE
**LOUSY** adj mean or unpleasant
**LOUT** n crude, oafish, or aggressive person ▷vb bow or stoop
**LOUTED** >LOUT
**LOUTING** >LOUT
**LOUTISH** adj characteristic of a lout
**LOUTISHLY** >LOUTISH
**LOUTS** >LOUT
**LOUVAR** n large silvery whalelike scombroid fish
**LOUVARS** >LOUVAR

**LOUVER** same as >LOUVRE
**LOUVERED** same as >LOUVRED
**LOUVERS** >LOUVER
**LOUVRE** n one of a set of parallel slats slanted to admit air but not rain
**LOUVRED** adj (of a window, door, etc) having louvres
**LOUVRES** >LOUVRE
**LOVABLE** adj attracting or deserving affection
**LOVABLY** >LOVABLE
**LOVAGE** n European plant used for flavouring food
**LOVAGES** >LOVAGE
**LOVAT** n yellowish-green or bluish-green mixture, esp in tweeds or woollens
**LOVATS** >LOVAT
**LOVE** vb have a great affection for ▷n great affection
**LOVEABLE** same as >LOVABLE
**LOVEABLY** >LOEVABLE
**LOVEBIRD** n small parrot
**LOVEBIRDS** >LOVEBIRD
**LOVEBITE** n temporary red mark left on a person's skin by someone biting or sucking it
**LOVEBITES** >LOVEBITE
**LOVEBUG** n small US flying insect
**LOVEBUGS** >LOVEBUG
**LOVED** >LOVE
**LOVEFEST** n event when people talk about loving one another
**LOVEFESTS** >LOVEFEST
**LOVELESS** adj without love
**LOVELIER** >LOVELY
**LOVELIES** >LOVELY
**LOVELIEST** >LOVELY
**LOVELIGHT** n brightness of eyes of one in love
**LOVELILY** >LOVELY
**LOVELOCK** n long lock of hair worn on the forehead
**LOVELOCKS** >LOVELOCK
**LOVELORN** adj miserable because of unhappiness in love
**LOVELY** adj very attractive ▷n attractive woman
**LOVEMAKER** n one involved in lovemaking
**LOVER** n person having a sexual relationship outside marriage
**LOVERED** adj having a lover
**LOVERLESS** >LOVER
**LOVERLY** adj loverlike
**LOVERS** >LOVER
**LOVES** >LOVE
**LOVESEAT** n armchair for two people
**LOVESEATS** >LOVESEAT
**LOVESICK** adj pining or languishing because of love
**LOVESOME** adj full of love
**LOVEVINE** n leafless

parasitic vine
**LOVEVINES** >LOVEVINE
**LOVEY** another word for >LOVE
**LOVEYS** >LOVEY
**LOVIES** >LOVEY
**LOVING** adj affectionate, tender
**LOVINGLY** >LOVING
**LOVINGS** >LOVING
**LOW** adj not tall, high, or elevated ▷adv in or to a low position, level, or degree ▷n low position, level, or degree ▷vb moo
**LOWAN** n type of Australian bird
**LOWANS** >LOWAN
**LOWBALL** vb deliberately under-charge
**LOWBALLED** >LOWBALL
**LOWBALLS** >LOWBALL
**LOWBORN** adj of ignoble or common parentage
**LOWBOY** n table fitted with drawers
**LOWBOYS** >LOWBOY
**LOWBRED** same as >LOWBORN
**LOWBROW** disparaging term adj with nonintellectual tastes and interests ▷n person with uncultivated or nonintellectual tastes
**LOWBROWED** >LOWBROW
**LOWBROWS** >LOWBROW
**LOWDOWN** n inside information
**LOWDOWNS** >LOWDOWN
**LOWE** variant of >LOW
**LOWED** >LOW
**LOWER** adj below one or more other things ▷vb cause or allow to move down
**LOWERABLE** >LOWER
**LOWERCASE** n small letters ▷adj non-capitalized
**LOWERED** >LOWER
**LOWERIER** >LOWERY
**LOWERIEST** >LOWERY
**LOWERING** >LOWER
**LOWERINGS** >LOWER
**LOWERMOST** adj lowest
**LOWERS** >LOWER
**LOWERY** adj sombre
**LOWES** >LOWE
**LOWEST** >LOW
**LOWING** >LOW
**LOWINGS** >LOW
**LOWISH** >LOW
**LOWLAND** n low-lying country ▷adj of a lowland or lowlands
**LOWLANDER** >LOWLAND
**LOWLANDS** >LOWLAND
**LOWLIER** >LOWLY
**LOWLIEST** >LOWLY
**LOWLIFE** n member or members of the underworld
**LOWLIFER** >LOWLIFE
**LOWLIFERS** >LOWLIFE
**LOWLIFES** >LOWLIFE

**LOWLIGHT** n unenjoyable or unpleasant part of an event
**LOWLIGHTS** >LOWLIGHT
**LOWLIHEAD** n state of being humble
**LOWLILY** >LOWLY
**LOWLINESS** >LOWLY
**LOWLIVES** >LOWLIFE
**LOWLY** adj modest, humble ▷adv in a low or lowly manner
**LOWN** vb calm
**LOWND** same as >LOWN
**LOWNDED** >LOWND
**LOWNDING** >LOWND
**LOWNDS** >LOWND
**LOWNE** same as >LOON
**LOWNED** >LOWN
**LOWNES** >LOWNE
**LOWNESS** >LOW
**LOWNESSES** >LOW
**LOWNING** >LOWN
**LOWNS** >LOWN
**LOWP** same as >LOUP
**LOWPED** >LOWP
**LOWPING** >LOWP
**LOWPS** >LOWP
**LOWRIDER** n car with body close to ground
**LOWRIDERS** >LOWRIDER
**LOWRIE** another name for same as >LORY
**LOWRIES** >LOWRY
**LOWRY** another name for >LORY
**LOWS** >LOW
**LOWSE** vb release or loose ▷adj loose
**LOWSED** >LOWSE
**LOWSENING** same as >LOOSING
**LOWSER** >LOWSE
**LOWSES** >LOWSE
**LOWSEST** >LOWSE
**LOWSING** >LOWSE
**LOWSIT** >LOWSE
**LOWT** same as >LOUT
**LOWTED** >LOWT
**LOWTING** >LOWT
**LOWTS** >LOWT
**LOWVELD** n low ground in S Africa
**LOWVELDS** >LOWVELD
**LOX** vb load fuel tanks of spacecraft with liquid oxygen ▷n kind of smoked salmon
**LOXED** >LOX
**LOXES** >LOX
**LOXING** >LOX
**LOXODROME** n line on globe crossing all meridians at same angle
**LOXODROMY** n technique of navigating using rhumb lines
**LOXYGEN** n liquid oxygen
**LOXYGENS** >LOXYGEN
**LOY** n narrow spade with a single footrest
**LOYAL** adj faithful to one's friends, country, or government

LOYALER > LOYAL

LOYALEST > LOYAL

LOYALISM > LOYALIST

LOYALISMS > LOYALIST

LOYALIST n patriotic supporter of the sovereign or government

LOYALISTS > LOYALIST

LOYALLER > LOYAL

LOYALLEST > LOYAL

LOYALLY > LOYAL

LOYALNESS > LOYAL

LOYALTIES > LOYALTY

LOYALTY n quality of being loyal

LOYS > LOY

LOZELL obsolete form of > LOSEL

LOZELLS > LOZELL

LOZEN n window pane

LOZENGE n medicated tablet held in the mouth until it dissolves

LOZENGED adj decorated with lozenges

LOZENGES > LOZENGE

LOZENGY adj divided by diagonal lines to form a lattice

LOZENS > LOZEN

LUACH n calendar that shows the dates of festivals and, usually, the times of start and finish of the Sabbath

LUAU n feast of Hawaiian food

LUAUS > LUAU

LUBBARD same as > LUBBER

LUBBARDS > LUBBARD

LUBBER n big, awkward, or stupid person

LUBBERLY > LUBBER

LUBBERS > LUBBER

LUBE n lubricating oil ▷ vb lubricate with oil

LUBED > LUBE

LUBES > LUBE

LUBFISH n type of fish

LUBFISHES > LUBFISH

LUBING > LUBE

LUBRA n Aboriginal woman

LUBRAS > LUBRA

LUBRIC adj slippery

LUBRICAL same as > LUBRIC

LUBRICANT n lubricating substance, such as oil ▷ adj serving to lubricate

LUBRICATE vb oil or grease to lessen friction

LUBRICITY n lewdness or salaciousness

LUBRICOUS adj lewd or lascivious

LUCARNE n type of dormer window

LUCARNES > LUCARNE

LUCE another name for > PIKE

LUCENCE > LUCENT

LUCENCES > LUCENT

LUCENCIES > LUCENT

LUCENCY > LUCENT

LUCENT adj brilliant, shining, or translucent

LUCENTLY > LUCENT

LUCERN same as > LUCERNE

LUCERNE n alfalfa

LUCERNES > LUCERNE

LUCERNS > LUCERN

LUCES > LUCE

LUCHOT pl n engraved tablets of stone

LUCHOTH same as > LUCHOT

LUCID adj clear and easily understood

LUCIDER > LUCID

LUCIDEST > LUCID

LUCIDITY > LUCID

LUCIDLY > LUCID

LUCIDNESS > LUCID

LUCIFER n friction match

LUCIFERIN n substance occurring in bioluminescent organisms, such as glow-worms and fireflies

LUCIFERS > LUCIFER

LUCIGEN n lamp burning oil mixed with hot air

LUCIGENS > LUCIGEN

LUCITE n brand name of a type of transparent acrylic-based plastic

LUCITES > LUCITE

LUCK n fortune, good or bad ▷ vb have good fortune

LUCKED > LUCK

LUCKEN adj shut

LUCKIE same as > LUCKY

LUCKIER > LUCKY

LUCKIES > LUCKIE

LUCKIEST > LUCKY

LUCKILY > LUCKY

LUCKINESS > LUCKY

LUCKING > LUCK

LUCKLESS adj having bad luck

LUCKPENNY n coin kept for luck

LUCKS > LUCK

LUCKY adj having or bringing good luck ▷ n old woman

LUCRATIVE adj very profitable

LUCRE n money or wealth

LUCRES > LUCRE

LUCTATION n effort; struggle

LUCUBRATE vb write or study, esp at night

LUCULENT adj easily understood

LUCUMA n type of S American tree

LUCUMAS > LUCUMA

LUCUMO n Etruscan king

LUCUMONES > LUCUMO

LUCUMOS > LUCUMO

LUD n lord ▷ interj exclamation of dismay or surprise

LUDE n slang word for drug for relieving anxiety

LUDERICK n Australian fish, usu black or dark brown in colour

LUDERICKS > LUDERICK

LUDES > LUDE

LUDIC adj playful

LUDICALLY > LUDIC

LUDICROUS adj absurd or ridiculous

LUDO n game played with dice and counters on a board

LUDOS > LUDO

LUDS > LUD

LUDSHIP > LUD

LUDSHIPS > LUD

LUES n any venereal disease

LUETIC > LUES

LUETICS > LUES

LUFF vb sail (a ship) towards the wind ▷ n leading edge of a fore-and-aft sail

LUFFA same as > LOOFAH

LUFFAS > LUFFA

LUFFED > LUFF

LUFFING > LUFF

LUFFS > LUFF

LUG vb carry or drag with great effort ▷ n projection serving as a handle

LUGE n racing toboggan on which riders lie on their backs, descending feet first ▷ vb ride on a luge

LUGED > LUGE

LUGEING > LUGE

LUGEINGS > LUGE

LUGER n tradename for a type of German automatic pistol

LUGERS > LUGER

LUGES > LUGE

LUGGABLE n unwieldy portable computer

LUGGABLES > LUGGABLE

LUGGAGE n suitcases, bags, etc

LUGGAGES > LUGGAGE

LUGGED > LUG

LUGGER n small working boat with an oblong sail

LUGGERS > LUGGER

LUGGIE n wooden bowl with handles

LUGGIES > LUGGIE

LUGGING > LUG

LUGHOLE informal word for > EAR

LUGHOLES > LUGHOLE

LUGING > LUGE

LUGINGS > LUGE

LUGS > LUG

LUGSAIL n four-sided sail bent and hoisted on a yard

LUGSAILS > LUGSAIL

LUGWORM n large worm used as bait

LUGWORMS > LUGWORM

LUIT Scots past form of > LET

LUITEN > LET

LUKE variant of > LUKEWARM

LUKEWARM adj moderately warm, tepid

LULIBUB obsolete form of > LOLLIPOP

LULIBUBS > LULIBUB

LULL vb soothe (someone) by soft sounds or motions ▷ n brief time of quiet in a storm etc

LULLABIED > LULLABY

LULLABIES > LULLABY

LULLABY n quiet song to send a child to sleep ▷ vb quiet or soothe with or as if with a lullaby

LULLED > LULL

LULLER > LULL

LULLERS > LULL

LULLING > LULL

LULLS > LULL

LULU n person or thing considered to be outstanding in size, appearance, etc

LULUS > LULU

LUM n chimney

LUMA n black and white element of TV signal

LUMAS > LUMA

LUMBAGO n pain in the lower back

LUMBAGOS > LUMBAGO

LUMBANG n type of tree

LUMBANGS > LUMBANG

LUMBAR adj of the part of the body between the lowest ribs and the hipbones ▷ n old-fashioned kind of ship

LUMBARS > LUMBAR

LUMBER n unwanted disused household articles ▷ vb burden with something unpleasant

LUMBERED > LUMBER

LUMBERER > LUMBER

LUMBERERS > LUMBER

LUMBERING n business or trade of cutting, transporting, preparing, or selling timber ▷ adj awkward in movement

LUMBERLY adj heavy; clumsy

LUMBERMAN n person whose work involves felling trees

LUMBERMEN > LUMBERMAN

LUMBERS > LUMBER

LUMBRICAL adj relating to any of the the four wormlike muscles in the hand or foot

LUMBRICI > LUMBRICUS

LUMBRICUS n type of worm

LUMEN n derived SI unit of luminous flux

LUMENAL > LUMEN

LUMENS > LUMEN

LUMINA > LUMEN

LUMINAIRE n light fixture

LUMINAL > LUMEN

LUMINANCE n state or quality of radiating or reflecting light

LUMINANT n something used to give light

LUMINANTS > LUMINANT

LUMINARIA n type of candle
LUMINARY n famous person ▷ adj of, involving, or characterized by light or enlightenment
LUMINE vb illuminate
LUMINED > LUMINE
LUMINES > LUMINE
LUMINESCE vb exhibit luminescence
LUMINING > LUMINE
LUMINISM n US artistic movement
LUMINISMS > LUMINISM
LUMINIST > LUMINISM
LUMINISTS > LUMINISM
LUMINOUS adj reflecting or giving off light
LUMME interj exclamation of surprise or dismay
LUMMIER > LUMMY
LUMMIEST > LUMMY
LUMMOX n clumsy or stupid person
LUMMOXES > LUMMOX
LUMMY interj exclamation of surprise ▷ adj excellent
LUMP n shapeless piece or mass ▷ vb consider as a single group
LUMPED > LUMP
LUMPEN adj stupid or unthinking ▷ n member of underclass
LUMPENLY > LUMPEN
LUMPENS > LUMPEN
LUMPER n stevedore
LUMPERS > LUMPER
LUMPFISH n North Atlantic scorpaenoid fish
LUMPIER > LUMPY
LUMPIEST > LUMPY
LUMPILY > LUMPY
LUMPINESS > LUMPY
LUMPING > LUMP
LUMPINGLY > LUMP
LUMPISH adj stupid or clumsy
LUMPISHLY > LUMPISH
LUMPKIN n lout
LUMPKINS > LUMPKIN
LUMPS > LUMP
LUMPY adj full of or having lumps
LUMS > LUM
LUNA n type of large American moth
LUNACIES > LUNACY
LUNACY n foolishness
LUNANAUT same as > LUNARNAUT
LUNANAUTS > LUNANAUT
LUNAR adj relating to the moon ▷ n lunar distance
LUNARIAN n inhabitant of the moon
LUNARIANS > LUNARIAN
LUNARIES > LUNARY
LUNARIST n one believing the moon influences weather
LUNARISTS > LUNARIST
LUNARNAUT n astronaut

who travels to moon
LUNARS > LUNAR
LUNARY n moonwort herb
LUNAS > LUNA
LUNATE adj shaped like a crescent ▷ n crescent-shaped bone forming part of the wrist
LUNATED variant of > LUNATE
LUNATELY > LUNATE
LUNATES > LUNATE
LUNATIC adj foolish and irresponsible ▷ n foolish or annoying person
LUNATICAL variant of > LUNATIC
LUNATICS > LUNATIC
LUNATION See > MONTH
LUNATIONS > LUNATION
LUNCH n meal taken in the middle of the day ▷ vb eat lunch
LUNCHBOX n container for carrying a packed lunch
LUNCHED > LUNCH
LUNCHEON n formal lunch
LUNCHEONS > LUNCHEON
LUNCHER > LUNCH
LUNCHERS > LUNCH
LUNCHES > LUNCH
LUNCHING > LUNCH
LUNCHMEAT n mixture of meat and cereal
LUNCHROOM n room where lunch is served or people may eat lunches they bring
LUNCHTIME n time at which lunch is usually eaten
LUNE same as > LUNETTE
LUNES > LUNE
LUNET n small moon or satellite
LUNETS > LUNET
LUNETTE n anything that is shaped like a crescent
LUNETTES > LUNETTE
LUNG n organ that allows an animal or bird to breathe air
LUNGAN same as > LONGAN
LUNGANS > LUNGAN
LUNGE n sudden forward motion ▷ vb move with or make a lunge
LUNGED > LUNGE
LUNGEE same as > LUNGI
LUNGEES > LUNGEE
LUNGEING > LUNGE
LUNGER > LUNGE
LUNGERS > LUNGE
LUNGES > LUNGE
LUNGFISH n freshwater bony fish with an air-breathing lung
LUNGFUL > LUNG
LUNGFULS > LUNG
LUNGI n long piece of cotton cloth worn as a loincloth, sash, or turban by Indian men or as a skirt
LUNGIE n guillemot
LUNGIES > LUNGIE

LUNGING > LUNGE
LUNGIS > LUNGI
LUNGS > LUNG
LUNGWORM n any parasitic nematode worm of the family Metastrongylidae
LUNGWORMS > LUNGWORM
LUNGWORT n any of several Eurasian plants of the boraginaceous genus Pulmonaria
LUNGWORTS > LUNGWORT
LUNGYI same as > LUNGI
LUNGYIS > LUNGYI
LUNIER > LUNY
LUNIES > LUNY
LUNIEST > LUNY
LUNINESS > LUNY
LUNISOLAR adj resulting from or based on the combined gravitational attraction of the sun and moon
LUNITIDAL adj of or relating to tidal phenomena as produced by the moon
LUNK n awkward, heavy, or stupid person
LUNKER n very large fish, esp bass
LUNKERS > LUNKER
LUNKHEAD n stupid person
LUNKHEADS > LUNKHEAD
LUNKS > LUNK
LUNT vb produce smoke
LUNTED > LUNT
LUNTING > LUNT
LUNTS > LUNT
LUNULA n white crescent-shaped area at the base of the human fingernail
LUNULAE > LUNULA
LUNULAR same as > LUNULATE
LUNULATE adj having markings shaped like crescents
LUNULATED same as > LUNULATE
LUNULE same as > LUNULA
LUNULES > LUNULE
LUNY same as > LOONY
LUNYIE same as > LUNGIE
LUNYIES > LUNYIE
LUPANAR n brothel
LUPANARS > LUPANAR
LUPIN n garden plant with tall spikes of flowers
LUPINE adj like a wolf ▷ n lupin
LUPINES > LUPINE
LUPINS > LUPIN
LUPOUS adj relating to lupus
LUPPEN > SCOTS PAST FORM OF > LEAP
LUPULIN n resinous powder extracted from the female flowers of the hop plant
LUPULINE adj relating to lupulin
LUPULINIC same

as > LUPULINE
LUPULINS > LUPULIN
LUPUS n ulcerous skin disease
LUPUSES > LUPUS
LUR n large bronze musical horn found in Danish peat bogs
LURCH vb tilt or lean suddenly to one side ▷ n lurching movement
LURCHED > LURCH
LURCHER n crossbred dog trained to hunt silently
LURCHERS > LURCHER
LURCHES > LURCH
LURCHING > LURCH
LURDAN n stupid or dull person ▷ adj dull or stupid
LURDANE same as > LURDAN
LURDANES > LURDANE
LURDANS > LURDAN
LURDEN same as > LURDAN
LURDENS > LURDEN
LURE vb tempt or attract by the promise of reward ▷ n person or thing that lures
LURED > LURE
LURER > LURE
LURERS > LURE
LURES > LURE
LUREX n thin glittery thread
LUREXES > LUREX
LURGI same as > LURGY
LURGIES > LURGY
LURGIS > LURGI
LURGY n any undetermined illness
LURID adj vivid in shocking detail, sensational
LURIDER > LURID
LURIDEST > LURID
LURIDLY > LURID
LURIDNESS > LURID
LURING > LURE
LURINGLY > LURE
LURK vb lie hidden or move stealthily, esp for sinister purposes
LURKED > LURK
LURKER > LURK
LURKERS > LURK
LURKING adj lingering but almost unacknowledged
LURKINGLY > LURKING
LURKINGS > LURKING
LURKS > LURK
LURRIES > LURRY
LURRY n confused jumble
LURS > LUR
LURVE n love
LURVES > LURVE
LUSCIOUS adj extremely pleasurable to taste or smell
LUSER n user of a computer system, as considered by a systems administator or other member of a technical support team
LUSERS > LUSER
LUSH adj (of grass etc) growing thickly and

healthily ▷ n alcoholic ▷ vb drink (alcohol) to excess
LUSHED > LUSH
LUSHER adj more lush ▷ n drunkard
LUSHERS > LUSHER
LUSHES > LUSH
LUSHEST > LUSH
LUSHIER > LUSHY
LUSHING > LUSH
LUSHLY > LUSH
LUSHNESS > LUSH
LUSHY adj slightly intoxicated
LUSK vb lounge around
LUSKED > LUSK
LUSKING > LUSK
LUSKISH adj lazy
LUSKS > LUSK
LUST n strong sexual desire ▷ vb have passionate desire (for)
LUSTED > LUST
LUSTER same as > LUSTRE
LUSTERED > LUSTER
LUSTERING > LUSTER
LUSTERS > LUSTER
LUSTFUL adj driven by lust
LUSTFULLY > LUSTFUL
LUSTICK obsolete word for > LUSTY
LUSTIER > LUSTY
LUSTIEST > LUSTY
LUSTIHEAD n vigour
LUSTIHOOD n vigour
LUSTILY > LUSTY
LUSTINESS > LUSTY
LUSTING > LUST
LUSTIQUE obsolete word for > LUSTY
LUSTLESS > LUST
LUSTRA > LUSTRUM
LUSTRAL adj of or relating to a ceremony of purification
LUSTRATE vb purify by means of religious rituals or ceremonies
LUSTRATED > LUSTRATE
LUSTRATES > LUSTRATE
LUSTRE n gloss, sheen ▷ vb make, be, or become lustrous
LUSTRED > LUSTRE
LUSTRES > LUSTRE
LUSTRINE same as > LUSTRING
LUSTRINES > LUSTRINE
LUSTRING n glossy silk cloth, formerly used for clothing, upholstery, etc
LUSTRINGS > LUSTRING
LUSTROUS > LUSTRE
LUSTRUM n period of five years
LUSTRUMS > LUSTRUM
LUSTS > LUST
LUSTY adj vigorous, healthy
LUSUS n freak, mutant, or monster
LUSUSES > LUSUS

LUTANIST same as > LUTENIST
LUTANISTS > LUTANIST
LUTE n ancient guitar-like musical instrument with a body shaped like a half pear ▷ vb seal (a joint or surface) with a mixture of cement and clay
LUTEA adj yellow
LUTEAL adj relating to or characterized by the development of the corpus luteum
LUTECIUM same as > LUTETIUM
LUTECIUMS > LUTECIUM
LUTED > LUTE
LUTEFISK n Scandinavian fish dish
LUTEFISKS > LUTEFISK
LUTEIN n xanthophyll pigment that has a light-absorbing function in photosynthesis
LUTEINISE same as > LUTEINIZE
LUTEINIZE vb develop into part of corpus luteum
LUTEINS > LUTEIN
LUTENIST n person who plays the lute
LUTENISTS > LUTENIST
LUTEOLIN n yellow crystalline compound found in many plants
LUTEOLINS > LUTEOLIN
LUTEOLOUS > LUTEOLIN
LUTEOUS adj of a light to moderate greenish-yellow colour
LUTER n lute player
LUTERS > LUTER
LUTES > LUTE
LUTESCENT adj yellowish in colour
LUTETIUM n silvery-white metallic element
LUTETIUMS > LUTETIUM
LUTEUM adj yellow
LUTFISK same as > LUTEFISK
LUTFISKS > LUTFISK
LUTHERN another name for > DORMER
LUTHERNS > LUTHERN
LUTHIER n lute-maker
LUTHIERS > LUTHIER
LUTING n mixture of cement and clay
LUTINGS > LUTING
LUTIST same as > LUTENIST
LUTISTS > LUTIST
LUTITE another name for > PELITE
LUTITES > LUTITE
LUTTEN > LOOT
LUTZ n jump in which the skater takes off from the back outside edge of one skate, makes one, two, or three turns in the air, and lands on the back outside edge of the other skate
LUTZES > LUTZ

LUV n love
LUVS > LOVE
LUVVIE n person who is involved in acting or the theatre
LUVVIES > LUVVY
LUVVY same as > LUVVIE
LUX n unit of illumination
LUXATE vb put (a shoulder, knee, etc) out of joint
LUXATED > LUXATE
LUXATES > LUXATE
LUXATING > LUXATE
LUXATION > LUXATE
LUXATIONS > LUXATE
LUXE as in de luxe rich, elegant, or sumptuous
LUXES > LUXE
LUXMETER n device for measuring light
LUXMETERS > LUXMETER
LUXURIANT adj rich and abundant
LUXURIATE vb take self-indulgent pleasure (in)
LUXURIES > LUXURY
LUXURIOUS adj full of luxury, sumptuous
LUXURIST n lover of luxury
LUXURISTS > LUXURIST
LUXURY n enjoyment of rich, very comfortable living ▷ adj of or providing luxury
LUZ n supposedly indestructible bone of the human body
LUZERN n alfalfa
LUZERNS > LUZERN
LUZZES > LUZ
LWEI n Angolan monetary unit
LWEIS > LWEI
LYAM n leash
LYAMS > LYAM
LYARD same as > LIARD
LYART same as > LIARD
LYASE n any enzyme that catalyses the separation of two parts of a molecule
LYASES > LYASE
LYCEA > LYCEUM
LYCEE n secondary school
LYCEES > LYCEE
LYCEUM n public building for events such as concerts and lectures
LYCEUMS > LYCEUM
LYCH same as > LICH
LYCHEE same as > LITCHI
LYCHEES > LYCHEE
LYCHES > LYCH
LYCHGATE same as > LICHGATE
LYCHGATES > LYCHGATE
LYCHNIS n any caryophyllaceous plant of the genus Lychnis
LYCHNISES > LYCHNIS
LYCOPENE n red pigment
LYCOPENES > LYCOPENE
LYCOPOD n type of moss
LYCOPODS > LYCOPOD
LYCRA n tradename for a

type of synthetic elastic fabric and fibre used for tight-fitting garments, such as swimming costumes
LYCRAS > LYCRA
LYDDITE n explosive consisting chiefly of fused picric acid
LYDDITES > LYDDITE
LYE n caustic solution obtained by leaching wood ash
LYES > LYE
LYFULL obsolete form of > LIFEFULL
LYING > LIE
LYINGLY > LIE
LYINGS > LIE
LYKEWAKE n watch held over a dead person, often with festivities
LYKEWAKES > LYKEWAKE
LYKEWALK variant of > LYKEWAKE
LYKEWALKS > LYKEWALK
LYM obsolete form of > LYAM
LYME as in lyme grass type of perennial dune grass
LYMES > LYME
LYMITER same as > LIMITER
LYMITERS > LIMITER
LYMPH n colourless bodily fluid consisting mainly of white blood cells
LYMPHAD n ancient rowing boat
LYMPHADS > LYMPHAD
LYMPHATIC adj of, relating to, or containing lymph ▷ n lymphatic vessel
LYMPHOID adj of or resembling lymph, or relating to the lymphatic system
LYMPHOMA n any form of cancer of the lymph nodes
LYMPHOMAS > LYMPHOMA
LYMPHS n lymph
LYMS > LYM
LYNAGE obsolete form of > LINEAGE
LYNAGES > LYNAGE
LYNCEAN adj of or resembling a lynx
LYNCH vb put to death without a trial
LYNCHED > LYNCH
LYNCHER > LYNCH
LYNCHERS > LYNCH
LYNCHES > LYNCH
LYNCHET n terrace or ridge formed in prehistoric or medieval times by ploughing a hillside
LYNCHETS > LYNCHET
LYNCHING > LYNCH
LYNCHINGS > LYNCH
LYNCHPIN same as > LINCHPIN
LYNCHPINS > LYNCHPIN
LYNE n flax
LYNES > LYNE
LYNX n animal of the cat

family with tufted ears
and a short tail
**LYNXES** > LYNX
**LYNXLIKE** > LYNX
**LYOLYSES** > LYOLYSIS
**LYOLYSIS** *n* formation of
an acid and a base from the
interaction of a salt with a
solvent
**LYOMEROUS** *adj* relating to
Lyomeri fish
**LYONNAISE** *adj* (of food)
cooked or garnished with
onions, usually fried
**LYOPHIL** *same*
*as* > LYOPHILIC
**LYOPHILE** *same*
*as* > LYOPHILIC
**LYOPHILED** *adj* lyophiliized
**LYOPHILIC** *adj* (of a
colloid) having a dispersed
phase with a high affinity
for the continuous phase
**LYOPHOBE** *same*
*as* > LYOPHOBIC
**LYOPHOBIC** *adj* (of a
colloid) having a dispersed
phase with little or no
affinity for the continuous
phase
**LYRA** as in *lyra viol* lutelike
musical instrument of the
16th and 17th centuries
**LYRATE** *adj* shaped like a
lyre
**LYRATED** *same as* > LYRATE
**LYRATELY** > LYRATE
**LYRE** *n* ancient musical
instrument like a U-
shaped harp
**LYREBIRD** *n* Australian
bird, the male of which
spreads its tail into the
shape of a lyre
**LYREBIRDS** > LYREBIRD
**LYRES** > LYRE
**LYRIC** *adj* (of poetry)
expressing personal
emotion in songlike
style ▷ *n* short poem in a
songlike style
**LYRICAL** *same as* > LYRIC
**LYRICALLY** > LYRIC
**LYRICISE** *same*
*as* > LYRICIZE
**LYRICISED** > LYRICISE
**LYRICISES** > LYRICISE
**LYRICISM** *n* quality or style
of lyric poetry
**LYRICISMS** > LYRICISM
**LYRICIST** *n* person who
writes the words of songs
or musicals
**LYRICISTS** > LYRICIST
**LYRICIZE** *vb* write lyrics
**LYRICIZED** > LYRICIZE
**LYRICIZES** > LYRICIZE
**LYRICON** *n* wind
synthesizer
**LYRICONS** > LYRICON
**LYRICS** > LYRIC
**LYRIFORM** *adj* lyre-shaped
**LYRISM** *n* art or technique
of playing the lyre

**LYRISMS** > LYRISM
**LYRIST** *same as* > LYRICIST
**LYRISTS** > LYRIST
**LYSATE** *n* material formed
by lysis
**LYSATES** > LYSATE
**LYSE** *vb* undergo or cause
to undergo lysis
**LYSED** > LYSE
**LYSERGIC** as in *lysergic
acid* crystalline compound
used in medical research
**LYSERGIDE** *n* LSD
**LYSES** > LYSIS
**LYSIGENIC** *adj* caused by
breaking down of cells
**LYSIMETER** *n* instrument
for determining solubility,
esp the amount of water-
soluble matter in soil
**LYSIN** *n* any of a group
of antibodies that cause
dissolution of cells against
which they are directed
**LYSINE** *n* essential
amino acid that occurs in
proteins
**LYSINES** > LYSINE
**LYSING** > LYSE
**LYSINS** > LYSIN
**LYSIS** *n* destruction or
dissolution of cells by the
action of a particular lysin
**LYSOGEN** *n* lysis-inducing
agent
**LYSOGENIC** > LYSOGEN
**LYSOGENS** > LYSOGEN
**LYSOGENY** > LYSOGEN
**LYSOL** *n* tradename
for a solution used
as an antiseptic and
disinfectant
**LYSOLS** > LYSOL
**LYSOSOMAL** > LYSOSOME
**LYSOSOME** *n* any of
numerous small particles
that are present in the
cytoplasm of most cells
**LYSOSOMES** > LYSOSOME
**LYSOZYME** *n* enzyme
occurring in tears, certain
body tissues, and egg
white
**LYSOZYMES** > LYSOZYME
**LYSSA** *less common word
for* > RABIES
**LYSSAS** > LYSSA
**LYTE** *vb* dismount
**LYTED** > LYTE
**LYTES** > LYTE
**LYTHE** *n* type of fish
**LYTHES** > LYTHE
**LYTIC** *adj* relating to,
causing, or resulting from
lysis
**LYTICALLY** > LYTIC
**LYTING** > LYTE
**LYTTA** *n* rodlike mass of
cartilage beneath the
tongue in the dog and
other carnivores
**LYTTAE** > LYTTA
**LYTTAS** > LYTTA

# Mm

**MA** n mother
**MAA** vb (of goats) bleat
**MAAED** > MAA
**MAAING** > MAA
**MAAR** n coneless volcanic crater that has been formed by a single explosion
**MAARE** > MAAR
**MAARS** > MAAR
**MAAS** n thick soured milk
**MAATJES** n pickled herring
**MABE** n type of pearl
**MABELA** n ground kaffir corn used for making porridge
**MABELAS** > MABELAS
**MABES** > MABE
**MAC** n macintosh
**MACABER** same as > MACABRE
**MACABRE** adj strange and horrible, gruesome
**MACABRELY** > MACABRE
**MACACO** n any of various lemurs, esp *Lemur macaco*, the males of which are usually black and the females brown
**MACACOS** > MACACO
**MACADAM** n road surface of pressed layers of small broken stones
**MACADAMIA** n Australian tree with edible nuts
**MACADAMS** > MACADAM
**MACAHUBA** n South American palm tree
**MACAHUBAS** > MACAHUBA
**MACALLUM** n ice cream with raspberry sauce
**MACALLUMS** > MACALLUM
**MACAQUE** n monkey of Asia and Africa with cheek

pouches and either a short tail or no tail
**MACAQUES** > MACAQUE
**MACARISE** vb congratulate
**MACARISED** > MACARISE
**MACARISES** > MACARISE
**MACARISM** n blessing
**MACARISMS** > MACARISM
**MACARIZE** same
   as > MACARISE
**MACARIZED** > MACARIZE
**MACARIZES** > MACARIZE
**MACARONI** n pasta in short tube shapes
**MACARONIC** adj (of verse) characterized by a mixture of vernacular words jumbled together with Latin words or Latinized words or with words from one or more other foreign languages ▷ n macaronic verse
**MACARONIS** > MACARONI
**MACAROON** n small biscuit or cake made with ground almonds
**MACAROONS** > MACAROON
**MACASSAR** n oily preparation formerly put on the hair to make it smooth and shiny
**MACASSARS** > MACASSAR
**MACAW** n large tropical American parrot
**MACAWS** > MACAW
**MACCABAW** same
   as > MACCABOY
**MACCABAWS** > MACCABAW
**MACCABOY** n dark rose-scented snuff
**MACCABOYS** > MACCABOY
**MACCARONI** same

as > MACARONI
**MACCHIA** n thicket in Italy
**MACCHIATO** n espresso coffee served with a dash of hot or cold milk
**MACCHIE** > MACCHIA
**MACCOBOY** same
   as > MACCABOY
**MACCOBOYS** > MACCOBOY
**MACE** n club, usually having a spiked metal head, used esp in the Middle Ages ▷ vb use a mace
**MACED** > MACE
**MACEDOINE** n hot or cold mixture of diced vegetables
**MACER** n macebearer, esp (in Scotland) an official who acts as usher in a court of law
**MACERAL** n any of the organic units that constitute coal: equivalent to any of the mineral constituents of a rock
**MACERALS** > MACERAL
**MACERATE** vb soften by soaking
**MACERATED** > MACERATE
**MACERATER** > MACERATE
**MACERATES** > MACERATE
**MACERATOR** > MACERATE
**MACERS** > MACER
**MACES** > MACE
**MACH** n ratio of the speed of a body in a particular medium to the speed of sound in that medium
**MACHAIR** n (in the western Highlands of Scotland) a strip of sandy, grassy, often lime-rich land just above

the high-water mark at a sandy shore: used as grazing or arable land
**MACHAIRS** > MACHAIR
**MACHAN** n (in India) a raised platform used in tiger hunting
**MACHANS** > MACHAN
**MACHE** n papier-mâché
**MACHER** n important or influential person: often used ironically
**MACHERS** > MACHER
**MACHES** > MACHE
**MACHETE** n broad heavy knife used for cutting or as a weapon
**MACHETES** > MACHETE
**MACHI** as in *machi chips* in Indian English, fish and chips
**MACHINATE** vb contrive, plan, or devise (schemes, plots, etc)
**MACHINE** n apparatus, usu. powered by electricity, designed to perform a particular task ▷ vb make or produce by machine
**MACHINED** > MACHINE
**MACHINERY** n machines or machine parts collectively
**MACHINES** > MACHINE
**MACHINING** > MACHINE
**MACHINIST** n person who operates a machine
**MACHISMO** n exaggerated or strong masculinity
**MACHISMOS** > MACHISMO
**MACHMETER** n instrument for measuring the Mach number of an aircraft in flight

**MACHO** *adj* strongly or exaggeratedly masculine ▷ *n* strong or exaggerated masculinity
**MACHOISM** > MACHO
**MACHOISMS** > MACHO
**MACHOS** > MACHO
**MACHREE** *n* Irish form of address meaning my dear
**MACHREES** > MACHREE
**MACHS** > MACH
**MACHZOR** *n* Jewish prayer book containing prescribed holiday rituals
**MACHZORIM** > MACHZOR
**MACHZORS** > MACHZOR
**MACING** > MACE
**MACINTOSH** *n* waterproof raincoat
**MACK** *same as* > MAC
**MACKEREL** *n* edible sea fish
**MACKERELS** > MACKEREL
**MACKINAW** *n* thick short double-breasted plaid coat
**MACKINAWS** > MACKINAW
**MACKLE** *n* double or blurred impression caused by shifting paper or type ▷ *vb* mend hurriedly or in a makeshift way
**MACKLED** > MACKLE
**MACKLES** > MACKLE
**MACKLING** > MACKLE
**MACKS** > MACK
**MACLE** *n* crystal consisting of two parts
**MACLED** > MACLE
**MACLES** > MACLE
**MACON** *n* red or white wine from the Mâcon area, heavier than the other burgundies
**MACONS** > MACON
**MACOYA** *n* South American tree
**MACOYAS** > MACOYA
**MACRAME** *n* ornamental work of knotted cord
**MACRAMES** > MACRAME
**MACRAMI** *same as* > MACRAME
**MACRAMIS** > MACRAMI
**MACRO** *n* close-up lens
**MACROBIAN** *adj* long-lived
**MACROCODE** *n* computer instruction that triggers many other instructions
**MACROCOPY** *n* enlargement of printed material for easier reading
**MACROCOSM** *n* universe
**MACROCYST** *n* unusually large cyst
**MACROCYTE** *n* abnormally large red blood cell
**MACRODOME** *n* dome shape in crystal structure
**MACRODONT** *adj* having large teeth
**MACROGLIA** *n* one of the two types of non-nervous tissue (glia) found in the central nervous system: includes astrocytes

**MACROLOGY** *n* verbose but meaningless talk
**MACROMERE** *n* any of the large yolk-filled cells formed by unequal cleavage of a fertilized ovum
**MACROMOLE** *n* large chemistry mole
**MACRON** *n* mark placed over a letter to represent a long vowel
**MACRONS** > MACRON
**MACROPOD** *n* member of kangaroo family
**MACROPODS** > MACROPOD
**MACROPSIA** *n* condition of seeing everything in the field of view as larger than it really is, which can occur in diseases of the retina or in some brain disorders
**MACROS** > MACRO
**MACROTOUS** *adj* having large ears
**MACRURAL** > MACRURAN
**MACRURAN** *n* any decapod crustacean of the group (formerly suborder) *Macrura*, which includes the lobsters, prawns, and crayfish ▷ *adj* of, relating to, or belonging to the *Macrura*
**MACRURANS** > MACRURAN
**MACRUROID** > MACRURAN
**MACRUROUS** > MACRURAN
**MACS** > MAC
**MACTATION** *n* sacrificial killing
**MACULA** *n* small spot or area of distinct colour, such as a freckle
**MACULAE** > MACULA
**MACULAR** > MACULA
**MACULAS** > MACULA
**MACULATE** *vb* spot, stain, or pollute ▷ *adj* spotted or polluted
**MACULATED** > MACULATE
**MACULATES** > MACULATE
**MACULE** *same as* > MACKLE
**MACULED** > MACULE
**MACULES** > MACULE
**MACULING** > MACULE
**MACULOSE** *adj* having spots
**MACUMBA** *n* religious cult in Brazil that combines Christian and voodoo elements
**MACUMBAS** > MACUMBA
**MAD** *adj* mentally deranged, insane ▷ *vb* make mad
**MADAFU** *n* coconut milk
**MADAFUS** > MADAFU
**MADAM** *n* polite term of address for a woman ▷ *vb* call someone madam
**MADAME** *n* French title equivalent to *Mrs*
**MADAMED** > MADAM
**MADAMES** > MADAME
**MADAMING** > MADAM
**MADAMS** > MADAM

**MADAROSES** > MADAROSIS
**MADAROSIS** *n* abnormal loss of eyebrows or eyelashes
**MADBRAIN** *adj* insane
**MADCAP** *adj* foolish or reckless ▷ *n* impulsive or reckless person
**MADCAPS** > MADCAP
**MADDED** > MAD
**MADDEN** *vb* infuriate or irritate
**MADDENED** > MADDEN
**MADDENING** *adj* serving to send mad
**MADDENS** > MADDEN
**MADDER** *n* type of rose
**MADDERS** > MADAM
**MADDEST** > MAD
**MADDING** > MAD
**MADDINGLY** > MAD
**MADDISH** > MAD
**MADDOCK** *same as* > MATTOCK
**MADDOCKS** > MADDOCK
**MADE** > MAKE
**MADEFIED** > MADEFY
**MADEFIES** > MADEFY
**MADEFY** *vb* make moist
**MADEFYING** > MADEFY
**MADEIRA** *n* kind of rich sponge cake
**MADEIRAS** > MADEIRA
**MADELEINE** *n* small fancy sponge cake
**MADERISE** *vb* become reddish
**MADERISED** > MADERISE
**MADERISES** > MADERISE
**MADERIZE** *same as* > MADERISE
**MADERIZED** > MADERIZE
**MADERIZES** > MADERIZE
**MADGE** *n* type of hammer
**MADGES** > MADGE
**MADHOUSE** *n* place filled with uproar or confusion
**MADHOUSES** > MADHOUSE
**MADID** *adj* wet
**MADISON** *n* type of cycle relay race
**MADISONS** > MADISON
**MADLING** *n* insane person
**MADLINGS** > MADLING
**MADLY** *adv* with great speed and energy
**MADMAN** *n* person who is insane
**MADMEN** > MADMAN
**MADNESS** *n* insanity
**MADNESSES** > MADNESS
**MADONNA** *n* picture or statue of the Virgin Mary
**MADONNAS** > MADONNA
**MADOQUA** *n* Ethiopian antelope
**MADOQUAS** > MADOQUA
**MADRAS** *n* medium-hot curry
**MADRASA** *same as* > MADRASAH
**MADRASAH** *n* educational institution, particularly for Islamic religious instruction

**MADRASAHS** > MADRASAH
**MADRASAS** > MADRASA
**MADRASES** > MADRAS
**MADRASSA** *same as* > MADRASAH
**MADRASSAH** *same as* > MADRASAH
**MADRASSAS** > MADRASSA
**MADRE** *Spanish word for* > MOTHER
**MADREPORE** *n* any coral of the genus *Madrepora*, many of which occur in tropical seas and form large coral reefs: order *Zoantharia*
**MADRES** > MADRE
**MADRIGAL** *n* 16th–17th-century part song for unaccompanied voices
**MADRIGALS** > MADRIGAL
**MADRILENE** *n* cold consommé flavoured with tomato juice
**MADRONA** *n* ericaceous North American evergreen tree or shrub, *Arbutus menziesii*, with white flowers and red berry-like fruits
**MADRONAS** > MADRONA
**MADRONE** *same as* > MADRONA
**MADRONES** > MADRONE
**MADRONO** *same as* > MADRONA
**MADRONOS** > MADRONO
**MADS** > MAD
**MADTOM** *n* species of catfish
**MADTOMS** > MADTOM
**MADURO** *adj* (of cigars) dark and strong ▷ *n* cigar of this type
**MADUROS** > MADURO
**MADWOMAN** *n* woman who is insane, esp one who behaves violently
**MADWOMEN** > MADWOMAN
**MADWORT** *n* low-growing Eurasian boraginaceous plant, *Asperugo procumbens*, with small blue flowers
**MADWORTS** > MADWORT
**MADZOON** *same as* > MATZOON
**MADZOONS** > MADZOON
**MAE** *as in mae west* inflatable life jacket, esp as issued to the US armed forces for emergency use
**MAELID** *n* mythical spirit of apple
**MAELIDS** > MAELID
**MAELSTROM** *n* great whirlpool
**MAENAD** *n* female disciple of Dionysus, the Greek god of wine
**MAENADES** > MAENAD
**MAENADIC** > MAENAD
**MAENADISM** > MAENAD
**MAENADS** > MAENAD
**MAES** > MAE
**MAESTOSO** *adv* be performed majestically

▷ n piece or passage directed to be played in this way

**MAESTOSOS** > MAESTOSO

**MAESTRI** > MAESTRO

**MAESTRO** n outstanding musician or conductor

**MAESTROS** > MAESTRO

**MAFFIA** same as > MAFIA

**MAFFIAS** > MAFFIA

**MAFFICK** vb celebrate extravagantly and publicly

**MAFFICKED** > MAFFICK

**MAFFICKER** > MAFFICK

**MAFFICKS** > MAFFICK

**MAFFLED** adj baffled

**MAFFLIN** n half-witted person

**MAFFLING** same as > MAFFLIN

**MAFFLINGS** > MAFFLING

**MAFFLINS** > MAFFLIN

**MAFIA** n international secret organization founded in Sicily, probably in opposition to tyranny. It developed into a criminal organization and in the late 19th century was carried to the US by Italian immigrants

**MAFIAS** > MAFIA

**MAFIC** n collective term for minerals present in igneous rock

**MAFICS** > MAFIC

**MAFIOSI** > MAFIOSO

**MAFIOSO** n member of the Mafia

**MAFIOSOS** > MAFIOSO

**MAFTED** adj suffering under oppressive heat

**MAFTIR** n final section of the weekly Torah reading

**MAFTIRS** > MAFTIR

**MAG** vb talk ▷ n talk

**MAGAININ** n any of a series of related substances with antibacterial properties, derived from the skins of frogs

**MAGAININS** > MAGAININ

**MAGALOG** same as > MAGALOGUE

**MAGALOGS** > MAGALOG

**MAGALOGUE** n combination of a magazine and a catalogue

**MAGAZINE** n periodical publication with articles by different writers

**MAGAZINES** > MAGAZINE

**MAGDALEN** n reformed prostitute

**MAGDALENE** same as > MAGDALEN

**MAGDALENS** > MAGDALEN

**MAGE** archaic word for > MAGICIAN

**MAGENTA** adj deep purplish-red ▷ n deep purplish red that is the complementary colour of green and, with yellow and cyan, forms a set of primary colours

**MAGENTAS** > MAGENTA

**MAGES** > MAGE

**MAGESHIP** > MAGE

**MAGESHIPS** > MAGE

**MAGG** same as > MAG

**MAGGED** > MAG

**MAGGIE** n magpie

**MAGGIES** > MAGGIE

**MAGGING** > MAG

**MAGGOT** n larva of an insect

**MAGGOTIER** > MAGGOTY

**MAGGOTS** > MAGGOT

**MAGGOTY** adj relating to, resembling, or ridden with maggots

**MAGGS** > MAGG

**MAGI** > MAGUS

**MAGIAN** > MAGUS

**MAGIANISM** > MAGUS

**MAGIANS** > MAGUS

**MAGIC** n supposed art of invoking supernatural powers to influence events ▷ vb to transform or produce by or as if by magic ▷ adj of, using, or like magic

**MAGICAL** > MAGIC

**MAGICALLY** > MAGIC

**MAGICIAN** n conjuror

**MAGICIANS** > MAGICIAN

**MAGICKED** > MAGIC

**MAGICKING** > MAGIC

**MAGICS** > MAGIC

**MAGILP** same as > MEGILP

**MAGILPS** > MAGILP

**MAGISM** > MAGUS

**MAGISMS** > MAGUS

**MAGISTER** n person entitled to teach in medieval university

**MAGISTERS** > MAGISTER

**MAGISTERY** n agency or substance, such as the philosopher's stone, believed to transmute other substances

**MAGISTRAL** adj of, relating to, or characteristic of a master ▷ n fortification in a determining position

**MAGLEV** n type of high-speed train that runs on magnets supported by a magnetic field generated around the track

**MAGLEVS** > MAGLEV

**MAGMA** n molten rock inside the earth's crust

**MAGMAS** > MAGMA

**MAGMATA** > MAGMA

**MAGMATIC** > MAGMA

**MAGMATISM** > MAGMA

**MAGNALIUM** n alloy of magnesium and aluminium

**MAGNATE** n influential or wealthy person, esp in industry

**MAGNATES** > MAGNATE

**MAGNES** n magnetic iron ore

**MAGNESES** > MAGNES

**MAGNESIA** n white tasteless substance used as an antacid and a laxative

**MAGNESIAL** > MAGNESIA

**MAGNESIAN** > MAGNESIA

**MAGNESIAS** > MAGNESIA

**MAGNESIC** > MAGNESIA

**MAGNESITE** n white, colourless, or lightly tinted mineral

**MAGNESIUM** n silvery-white metallic element

**MAGNET** n piece of iron or steel capable of attracting iron and pointing north when suspended

**MAGNETAR** n type of neutron star that has a very intense magnetic field, over 1000 times greater than that of a pulsar

**MAGNETARS** > MAGNETAR

**MAGNETIC** adj having the properties of a magnet

**MAGNETICS** n branch of physics concerned with magnetism

**MAGNETISE** same as > MAGNETIZE

**MAGNETISM** n magnetic property

**MAGNETIST** > MAGNETISM

**MAGNETITE** n black magnetizable mineral that is an important source of iron

**MAGNETIZE** vb make into a magnet

**MAGNETO** n apparatus for ignition in an internal-combustion engine

**MAGNETON** n unit of magnetic moment

**MAGNETONS** > MAGNETON

**MAGNETOS** > MAGNETO

**MAGNETRON** n electronic valve used with a magnetic field to generate microwave oscillations, used, esp in radar

**MAGNETS** > MAGNET

**MAGNIFIC** adj magnificent, grandiose, or pompous

**MAGNIFICO** n magnate

**MAGNIFIED** > MAGNIFY

**MAGNIFIER** > MAGNIFY

**MAGNIFIES** > MAGNIFY

**MAGNIFY** vb increase in apparent size, as with a lens

**MAGNITUDE** n relative importance or size

**MAGNOLIA** n shrub or tree with showy white or pink flowers

**MAGNOLIAS** > MAGNOLIA

**MAGNON** n short for Cro-Magnon

**MAGNONS** > MAGNON

**MAGNOX** n alloy composed mainly of magnesium, used in fuel elements of some nuclear reactors

**MAGNOXES** > MAGNOX

**MAGNUM** n large wine bottle holding about 1.5 litres

**MAGNUMS** > MAGNUM

**MAGNUS** as in magnus hitch knot similar to a clove hitch but having one more turn

**MAGOT** n Chinese or Japanese figurine in a crouching position, usually grotesque

**MAGOTS** > MAGOT

**MAGPIE** n black-and-white bird

**MAGPIES** > MAGPIE

**MAGS** > MAG

**MAGSMAN** n raconteur

**MAGSMEN** > MAGSMAN

**MAGUEY** n any of various tropical American agave plants of the genera Agave or Furcraea, esp one that yields a fibre or is used in making an alcoholic beverage

**MAGUEYS** > MAGUEY

**MAGUS** n Zoroastrian priest of the ancient Medes and Persians

**MAGYAR** adj of or relating to a style of sleeve cut in one piece with the bodice

**MAHARAJA** same as > MAHARAJAH

**MAHARAJAH** n former title of some Indian princes

**MAHARAJAS** > MAHARAJA

**MAHARANEE** same as > MAHARANI

**MAHARANI** n wife of a maharaja

**MAHARANIS** > MAHARANI

**MAHARISHI** n Hindu religious teacher or mystic

**MAHATMA** n person revered for holiness and wisdom

**MAHATMAS** > MAHATMA

**MAHEWU** n (in South Africa) fermented liquid mealie-meal porridge, used as a stimulant, esp by Black Africans

**MAHEWUS** > MAHEWU

**MAHIMAHI** n Pacific fish

**MAHIMAHIS** > MAHIMAHI

**MAHJONG** n game of Chinese origin, usually played by four people, in which tiles bearing various designs are drawn and discarded until one player has an entire hand of winning combinations

**MAHJONGG** same as > MAHJONG

**MAHJONGGS** > MAHJONGG

**MAHJONGS** > MAHJONG

**MAHLSTICK** same as > MAULSTICK

**MAHMAL** n litter used in Muslim ceremony

**MAHMALS** > MAHMAL
**MAHOE** n New Zealand tree
**MAHOES** > MAHOE
**MAHOGANY** n hard reddish-brown wood of several tropical trees ▷ adj reddish-brown
**MAHONIA** n any evergreen berberidaceous shrub of the Asian and American genus *Mahonia*, esp *M. aquifolium*: cultivated for their ornamental spiny divided leaves and clusters of small yellow flowers
**MAHONIAS** > MAHONIA
**MAHOUT** n (in India and the East Indies) elephant driver or keeper
**MAHOUTS** > MAHOUT
**MAHSEER** n any of various large freshwater Indian cyprinid fishes, such as *Barbus tor*
**MAHSEERS** > MAHSEER
**MAHSIR** same as > MAHSEER
**MAHSIRS** > MAHSIR
**MAHUA** n Indian tree
**MAHUANG** n herbal medicine from shrub
**MAHUANGS** > MAHUANG
**MAHUAS** > MAHUA
**MAHWA** same as > MAHUA
**MAHWAS** > MAHWA
**MAHZOR** same as > MACHZOR
**MAHZORIM** > MAHZOR
**MAHZORS** > MAHZOR
**MAIASAUR** same as > MAIASAURA
**MAIASAURA** n species of dinosaur
**MAIASAURS** > MAIASAUR
**MAID** n female servant ▷ vb work as maid
**MAIDAN** n (in Pakistan, India, etc) an open space used for meetings, sports, etc
**MAIDANS** > MAIDAN
**MAIDED** > MAID
**MAIDEN** n young unmarried woman ▷ adj unmarried
**MAIDENISH** > MAIDEN
**MAIDENLY** adj modest
**MAIDENS** > MAIDEN
**MAIDHOOD** > MAID
**MAIDHOODS** > MAID
**MAIDING** > MAID
**MAIDISH** > MAID
**MAIDISM** n pellagra
**MAIDISMS** > MAIDISM
**MAIDLESS** > MAID
**MAIDS** > MAID
**MAIEUTIC** adj of or relating to the Socratic method of eliciting knowledge by a series of questions and answers
**MAIEUTICS** n Socratic method
**MAIGRE** adj not containing flesh, and so permissible as food on days of religious abstinence ▷ n species

of fish
**MAIGRES** > MAIGRE
**MAIHEM** same as > MAYHEM
**MAIHEMS** > MAIHEM
**MAIK** n old halfpenny
**MAIKO** n apprentice geisha
**MAIKOS** > MAIKO
**MAIKS** > MAIK
**MAIL** n letters and packages transported and delivered by the post office ▷ vb send by mail
**MAILABLE** > MAIL
**MAILBAG** n large bag for transporting or delivering mail
**MAILBAGS** > MAILBAG
**MAILBOX** n box into which letters and parcels are delivered
**MAILBOXES** > MAILBOX
**MAILCAR** same as > MAILCOACH
**MAILCARS** > MAILCAR
**MAILCOACH** n railway coach specially constructed for the transportation of mail
**MAILE** n halfpenny
**MAILED** > MAIL
**MAILER** n person who addresses or mails letters, etc
**MAILERS** > MAILER
**MAILES** > MAILE
**MAILGRAM** n telegram
**MAILGRAMS** > MAILGRAM
**MAILING** > MAIL
**MAILINGS** > MAILING
**MAILL** n Scots word meaning rent
**MAILLESS** > MAIL
**MAILLOT** n tights worn for ballet, gymnastics, etc
**MAILLOTS** > MAILLOT
**MAILLS** > MAILL
**MAILMAN** n postman
**MAILMEN** > MAILMAN
**MAILMERGE** n computer program for sending mass mailings
**MAILPOUCH** same as > MAILBAG
**MAILROOM** n room where mail to and from building is dealt with
**MAILROOMS** > MAILROOM
**MAILS** > MAIL
**MAILSACK** same as > MAILBAG
**MAILSACKS** > MAILSACK
**MAILSHOT** n posting of advertising material to many selected people at once
**MAILSHOTS** > MAILSHOT
**MAILVAN** n vehicle used to transport post
**MAILVANS** > MAILVAN
**MAIM** vb cripple or mutilate ▷ n injury or defect
**MAIMED** > MAIM
**MAIMER** > MAIM
**MAIMERS** > MAIM

**MAIMING** > MAIM
**MAIMINGS** > MAIM
**MAIMS** > MAIM
**MAIN** adj chief or principal ▷ n principal pipe or line carrying water, gas, or electricity ▷ vb lower sails
**MAINBOOM** spar for mainsail
**MAINBOOMS** > MAINBOOM
**MAINBRACE** n brace attached to the mainyard
**MAINDOOR** n door from street into house
**MAINDOORS** > MAINDOOR
**MAINED** > MAIN
**MAINER** > MAIN
**MAINEST** > MAIN
**MAINFRAME** adj denoting a high-speed general-purpose computer ▷ n high-speed general-purpose computer, with a large store capacity
**MAINING** > MAIN
**MAINLAND** n stretch of land which forms the main part of a country
**MAINLANDS** > MAINLAND
**MAINLINE** n the trunk route between two points, usually fed by branch lines ▷ vb to inject a drug into a vein ▷ adj having an important position, esp having responsibility for the main areas of activity
**MAINLINED** > MAINLINE
**MAINLINER** > MAINLINE
**MAINLINES** > MAINLINE
**MAINLY** adv for the most part, chiefly
**MAINMAST** n chief mast of a ship
**MAINMASTS** > MAINMAST
**MAINOR** n act of doing something
**MAINORS** > MAINOR
**MAINOUR** same as > MAINOR
**MAINOURS** > MAINOUR
**MAINPRISE** n former legal surety
**MAINS** > MAIN
**MAINSAIL** n largest sail on a mainmast
**MAINSAILS** > MAINSAIL
**MAINSHEET** n line used to control the angle of the mainsail to the wind
**MAINSTAY** n chief support
**MAINSTAYS** > MAINSTAY
**MAINTAIN** vb continue or keep in existence
**MAINTAINS** > MAINTAIN
**MAINTOP** n top or platform at the head of the mainmast
**MAINTOPS** > MAINTOP
**MAINYARD** n yard for a square mainsail
**MAINYARDS** > MAINYARD
**MAIOLICA** same as > MAJOLICA
**MAIOLICAS** > MAIOLICA
**MAIR** Scots form of > MORE

**MAIRE** n New Zealand tree
**MAIREHAU** n small aromatic shrub of New Zealand
**MAIREHAUS** > MAIREHAU
**MAIRES** > MAIRE
**MAIRS** > MAIR
**MAISE** n measure of herring
**MAISES** > MAISE
**MAIST** Scot word for > MOST
**MAISTER** Scots word for > MASTER
**MAISTERED** > MAISTER
**MAISTERS** > MAISTER
**MAISTRIES** > MAISTER
**MAISTRING** > MAISTER
**MAISTRY** > MAISTER
**MAISTS** > MAIST
**MAIZE** n type of corn with spikes of yellow grains
**MAIZES** > MAIZE
**MAJAGUA** same as > MAHOE
**MAJAGUAS** > MAJAGUA
**MAJESTIC** adj beautiful, dignified, and impressive
**MAJESTIES** > MAJESTY
**MAJESTY** n stateliness or grandeur
**MAJLIS** n (in various N African and Middle Eastern countries) an assembly; council
**MAJLISES** > MAJLIS
**MAJOLICA** n type of ornamented Italian pottery
**MAJOLICAS** > MAJOLICA
**MAJOR** adj greater in number, quality, or extent ▷ n middle-ranking army officer ▷ vb do one's principal study in (a particular subject)
**MAJORAT** n estate, the right to which is that of the first born child of a family
**MAJORATS** > MAJORAT
**MAJORDOMO** n chief steward or butler of a great household
**MAJORED** > MAJOR
**MAJORETTE** n one of a group of girls who practise formation marching and baton twirling
**MAJORING** > MAJOR
**MAJORITY** n greater number
**MAJORLY** adv very
**MAJORS** > MAJOR
**MAJORSHIP** > MAJOR
**MAJUSCULE** n large letter, either capital or uncial, used in printing or writing ▷ adj relating to, printed, or written in such letters
**MAK** Scot word for > MAKE
**MAKABLE** > MAKE
**MAKAR** same as > MAKER
**MAKARS** > MAKAR
**MAKE** vb create, construct, or establish ▷ n brand, type, or style
**MAKEABLE** > MAKE
**MAKEBATE** n troublemaker

MAKEBATES > MAKEBATE

MAKEFAST *n* strong support to which a vessel is secured

MAKEFASTS > MAKEFAST

MAKELESS > MAKE

MAKEOVER *vb* to transfer the title or possession of (property, etc) ▷ *n* a series of alterations, including beauty treatments and new clothes, intended to make a noticeable improvement in a person's appearance

MAKEOVERS > MAKEOVER

MAKER *n* person or company that makes something

MAKEREADY *n* process of preparing the forme and the cylinder or platen packing to achieve the correct impression all over the forme

MAKERS > MAKER

MAKES > MAKE

MAKESHIFT *adj* serving as a temporary substitute ▷ *n* something serving in this capacity

MAKEUP *n* cosmetics, such as powder, lipstick, etc, applied to the face to improve its appearance ▷ *vb* devise, construct, or compose, sometimes with the intent to deceive

MAKEUPS > MAKEUP

MAKI *n* in Japanese cuisine, rice and other ingredients wrapped in a short seaweed roll

MAKIMONO *n* Japanese scroll

MAKIMONOS > MAKIMONO

MAKING > MAKE

MAKINGS *pl n* potentials, qualities, or materials

MAKIS > MAKI

MAKO *n* powerful shark of the Atlantic and Pacific Oceans

MAKOS > MAKO

MAKS > MAK

MAKUTA *plural of* > LIKUTA

MAKUTU *n* Polynesian witchcraft ▷ *vb* cast a spell on

MAKUTUED > MAKUTU

MAKUTUING > MAKUTU

MAKUTUS > MAKUTU

MAL *n* illness

MALA *n* string of beads or knots, used in praying and meditating

MALACCA *n* stem of the rattan palm

MALACCAS > MALACCA

MALACHITE *n* green mineral

MALACIA *n* pathological softening of an organ or tissue, such as bone

MALACIAS > MALACIA

MALADIES > MALADY

MALADROIT *adj* clumsy or awkward

MALADY *n* disease or illness

MALAGUENA *n* Spanish dance similar to the fandango

MALAISE *n* something wrong which affects a section of society or area of activity

MALAISES > MALAISE

MALAM *same as* > MALLAM

MALAMS > MALAM

MALAMUTE *n* Alaskan sled dog of the spitz type, having a dense usually greyish coat

MALAMUTES > MALAMUTE

MALANDER *same as* > MALANDERS

MALANDERS *pl n* disease of horses characterized by an eczematous inflammation behind the knee

MALANGA *same as* > COCOYAM

MALANGAS > MALANGA

MALAPERT *adj* saucy or impudent ▷ *n* saucy or impudent person

MALAPERTS > MALAPERT

MALAPROP *n* a word unintentionally confused with one of similar sound, esp when creating a ridiculous effect, as in *I am not under the affluence of alcohol*

MALAPROPS > MALAPROP

MALAR *n* cheekbone ▷ *adj* of or relating to the cheek or cheekbone

MALARIA *n* infectious disease caused by the bite of some mosquitoes

MALARIAL > MALARIA

MALARIAN > MALARIA

MALARIAS > MALARIA

MALARIOUS > MALARIA

MALARKEY *n* nonsense or rubbish

MALARKEYS > MALARKEY

MALARKIES > MALARKY

MALARKY *same as* > MALARKEY

MALAROMA *n* bad smell

MALAROMAS > MALAROMA

MALARS > MALAR

MALAS > MALA

MALATE *n* any salt or ester of malic acid

MALATES > MALATE

MALATHION *n* yellow organophosphorus insecticide used as a dust or mist for the control of house flies and garden pests

MALAX *vb* soften

MALAXAGE > MALAX

MALAXAGES > MALAX

MALAXATE *same as* > MALAX

MALAXATED > MALAXATE

MALAXATES > MALAXATE

MALAXATOR *n* machine for kneading or grinding

MALAXED > MALAX

MALAXES > MALAX

MALAXING > MALAX

MALE *adj* of the sex which can fertilize female reproductive cells ▷ *n* male person or animal

MALEATE *n* any salt or ester of maleic acid

MALEATES > MALEATE

MALEDICT *vb* utter a curse against ▷ *adj* cursed or detestable

MALEDICTS > MALEDICT

MALEFFECT *n* bad effect

MALEFIC *adj* causing evil

MALEFICE *n* wicked deed

MALEFICES > MALEFICE

MALEIC *as in maleic acid* colourless soluble crystalline substance used to synthesize other compounds

MALEMIUT *same as* > MALAMUTE

MALEMIUTS > MALEMIUT

MALEMUTE *same as* > MALAMUTE

MALEMUTES > MALEMUTE

MALENESS > MALE

MALENGINE *n* wicked plan

MALES > MALE

MALFED *adj* having malfunctioned

MALFORMED *adj* deformed

MALGRADO *prep* in spite of

MALGRE *same as* > MAUGRE

MALGRED > MALGRE

MALGRES > MALGRE

MALGRING > MALGRE

MALI *n* member of an Indian caste

MALIBU *as in malibu board* lightweight surfboard

MALIC *as in malic acid* colourless crystalline compound occurring in apples and other fruit

MALICE *n* desire to cause harm to others ▷ *vb* wish harm to

MALICED > MALICE

MALICES > MALICE

MALICHO *n* mischief

MALICHOS > MALICHO

MALICING > MALICE

MALICIOUS *adj* characterized by malice

MALIGN *vb* slander or defame ▷ *adj* evil in influence or effect

MALIGNANT *adj* seeking to harm others

MALIGNED > MALIGN

MALIGNER > MALIGN

MALIGNERS > MALIGN

MALIGNING > MALIGN

MALIGNITY *n* evil disposition

MALIGNLY > MALIGN

MALIGNS > MALIGN

MALIHINI *n* (in Hawaii) a foreigner or stranger

MALIHINIS > MALIHINI

MALIK *n* person of authority in India

MALIKS > MALIK

MALINE *n* stiff net

MALINES > MALINE

MALINGER *vb* feign illness to avoid work

MALINGERS > MALINGER

MALINGERY > MALINGER

MALIS > MALI

MALISM *n* belief that evil dominates world

MALISMS > MALISM

MALISON *archaic or poetic word for* > CURSE

MALISONS > MALISON

MALIST > MALISM

MALKIN *archaic or dialect name for a* > CAT

MALKINS > MALKIN

MALL *n* street or shopping area closed to vehicles ▷ *vb* maul

MALLAM *n* (in Islamic W Africa) a man learned in Koranic studies

MALLAMS > MALLAM

MALLANDER *same as* > MALANDERS

MALLARD *n* wild duck

MALLARDS > MALLARD

MALLEABLE *adj* capable of being hammered or pressed into shape

MALLEABLY > MALLEABLE

MALLEATE *vb* hammer

MALLEATED > MALLEATE

MALLEATES > MALLEATE

MALLECHO *same as* > MALICHO

MALLECHOS > MALLECHO

MALLED > MALL

MALLEE *n* low-growing eucalypt in dry regions

MALLEES > MALLEE

MALLEI > MALLEUS

MALLEMUCK *n* any of various sea birds, such as the albatross, fulmar, or shearwater

MALLENDER *same as* > MALANDERS

MALLEOLAR > MALLEOLUS

MALLEOLI > MALLEOLUS

MALLEOLUS *n* either of two rounded bony projections of the tibia and fibula on the sides of each ankle joint

MALLET *n* (wooden) hammer

MALLETS > MALLET

MALLEUS *n* outermost and largest of the three small bones in the middle ear of mammals

MALLEUSES > MALLEUS

MALLING > MALL

MALLINGS > MALL

MALLOW *n* plant with pink or purple flowers

MALLOWS > MALLOW
MALLS > MALL
MALM n soft greyish limestone that crumbles easily
MALMAG n Asian monkey
MALMAGS > MALMAG
MALMIER > MALMY
MALMIEST > MALMY
MALMS > MALM
MALMSEY n sweet Madeira wine
MALMSEYS > MALMSEY
MALMSTONE same as > MALM
MALMY adj looking like malm
MALODOR same as > MALODOUR
MALODORS > MALODOR
MALODOUR n unpleasant smell
MALODOURS > MALODOUR
MALONATE n salt of malonic acid
MALONATES > MALONATE
MALONIC as in malonic acid colourless crystalline compound occurring in sugar beet
MALOTI plural of > LOTI
MALPIGHIA n tropical shrub
MALPOSED adj in abnormal position
MALS > MAL
MALSTICK same as > MAULSTICK
MALSTICKS > MALSTICK
MALT n grain, such as barley, prepared for use in making beer or whisky ▷ vb make into or make with malt
MALTALENT n evil intention
MALTASE n enzyme that hydrolyses maltose and similar glucosides to glucose
MALTASES > MALTASE
MALTED > MALT
MALTEDS > MALT
MALTHA n any of various naturally occurring mixtures of hydrocarbons, such as ozocerite
MALTHAS > MALTHA
MALTIER > MALTY
MALTIEST > MALTY
MALTINESS > MALTY
MALTING n building in which malt is made or stored
MALTINGS > MALTING
MALTMAN same as > MALTSTER
MALTMEN > MALTMAN
MALTOL n food additive
MALTOLS > MALTOL
MALTOSE n sugar formed by the action of enzymes on starch
MALTOSES > MALTOSE
MALTREAT vb treat badly
MALTREATS > MALTREAT

MALTS > MALT
MALTSTER n person who makes or deals in malt
MALTSTERS > MALTSTER
MALTWORM n heavy drinker
MALTWORMS > MALTWORM
MALTY adj of, like, or containing malt
MALVA n mallow plant
MALVAS > MALVA
MALVASIA n type of grape used to make malmsey
MALVASIAN > MALVASIA
MALVASIAS > MALVASIA
MALVESIE same as > MALMSEY
MALVESIES > MALVESIE
MALVOISIE n amber dessert wine made in France, similar to malmsey
MALWA n Ugandan drink brewed from millet
MALWARE n computer program designed to cause damage or disruption to a system
MALWARES > MALWARE
MALWAS > MALWA
MAM same as > MOTHER
MAMA n mother
MAMAGUY vb deceive or tease, either in jest or by deceitful flattery ▷ n instance of such deception or flattery
MAMAGUYED > MAMAGUY
MAMAGUYS > MAMAGUY
MAMAKAU same as > MAMAKU
MAMAKO same as > MAMAKU
MAMAKU n tall edible New Zealand tree fern
MAMALIGA same as > POLENTA
MAMALIGAS > MAMALIGA
MAMAS > MAMA
MAMBA n deadly S African snake
MAMBAS > MAMBA
MAMBO n Latin American dance resembling the rumba ▷ vb perform this dance
MAMBOED > MAMBO
MAMBOES > MAMBO
MAMBOING > MAMBO
MAMBOS > MAMBO
MAMEE same as > MAMEY
MAMEES > MAMEE
MAMELON n small rounded hillock
MAMELONS > MAMELON
MAMELUCO n Brazilian of mixed European and South American descent
MAMELUCOS > MAMELUCO
MAMELUKE n member of a military class, originally of Turkish slaves, ruling in Egypt from about 1250 to 1517 and remaining powerful until crushed in 1811
MAMELUKES > MAMELUKE
MAMEY n tropical tree

MAMEYES > MAMEY
MAMEYS > MAMEY
MAMIE n tropical tree
MAMIES > MAMIE
MAMILLA n nipple or teat
MAMILLAE > MAMILLA
MAMILLAR adj of breast
MAMILLARY > MAMILLA
MAMILLATE adj having nipples or nipple-like protuberances
MAMLUK same as > MAMELUKE
MAMLUKS > MAMLUK
MAMMA n buxom and voluptuous woman
MAMMAE > MAMMA
MAMMAL n animal of the type that suckles its young
MAMMALIAN > MAMMAL
MAMMALITY > MAMMAL
MAMMALOGY n branch of zoology concerned with the study of mammals
MAMMALS > MAMMAL
MAMMARY adj of the breasts or milk-producing glands
MAMMAS > MAMMA
MAMMATE adj having breasts
MAMMATI > MAMMATUS
MAMMATUS n breast-shaped cloud
MAMMEE same as > MAMEY
MAMMEES > MAMMEE
MAMMER vb hesitate
MAMMERED > MAMMER
MAMMERING > MAMMER
MAMMERS > MAMMER
MAMMET same as > MAUMET
MAMMETRY n worship of idols
MAMMETS > MAMMET
MAMMEY same as > MAMEY
MAMMEYS > MAMMEY
MAMMIE same as > MAMMY
MAMMIES > MAMMY
MAMMIFER same as > MAMMAL
MAMMIFERS > MAMMIFER
MAMMIFORM adj in form of breast
MAMMILLA same as > MAMILLA
MAMMILLAE > MAMMILLA
MAMMITIS same as > MASTITIS
MAMMOCK n fragment ▷ vb tear or shred
MAMMOCKED > MAMMOCK
MAMMOCKS > MAMMOCK
MAMMOGRAM n xray to examine the breasts in early detection of cancer
MAMMON n wealth regarded as a source of evil
MAMMONISH > MAMMON
MAMMONISM > MAMMON
MAMMONIST > MAMMON
MAMMONITE > MAMMON
MAMMONS > MAMMON
MAMMOTH n extinct elephant-like mammal ▷ adj colossal
MAMMOTHS > MAMMOTH

MAMMY n Black woman employed as a nurse or servant to a White family
MAMPARA n foolish person, idiot
MAMPARAS > MAMPARA
MAMPOER n home-distilled brandy made from peaches, prickly pears, etc
MAMPOERS > MAMPOER
MAMS > MAM
MAMSELLE n mademoiselle
MAMSELLES > MAMSELLE
MAMZER n child of an incestuous or adulterous union
MAMZERIM > MAMZER
MAMZERS > MAMZER
MAN n adult male ▷ vb supply with sufficient people for operation or defence
MANA n authority, influence
MANACLE vb handcuff or fetter ▷ n metal ring or chain put round the wrists or ankles, used to restrict the movements of a prisoner or convict
MANACLED > MANACLE
MANACLES > MANACLE
MANACLING > MANACLE
MANAGE vb succeed in doing
MANAGED > MANAGE
MANAGER n person in charge of a business, institution, actor, sports team, etc
MANAGERS > MANAGER
MANAGES > MANAGE
MANAGING adj having administrative control or authority
MANAIA n common figure in Māori carving consisting of a human body and a bird-like head
MANAKIN same as > MANIKIN
MANAKINS > MANAKIN
MANANA n tomorrow ▷ adv tomorrow
MANANAS > MANANA
MANAS > MANA
MANAT n standard monetary unit of Azerbaijan, divided into 100 gopik
MANATEE n large tropical plant-eating aquatic mammal
MANATEES > MANATEE
MANATI same as > MANATEE
MANATIS > MANATI
MANATOID > MANATEE
MANATS > MANAT
MANATU n large flowering deciduous New Zealand tree
MANAWA in New Zealand, same as > MANGROVE
MANAWAS > MANAWA
MANCALA n African and Asian board game

**MANCALAS** > MANCALA
**MANCANDO** *adv* musical direction meaning fading away
**MANCHE** *n* long sleeve
**MANCHES** > MANCHE
**MANCHET** *n* type of bread
**MANCHETS** > MANCHET
**MANCIPATE** *vb* make legal transfer in ancient Rome
**MANCIPLE** *n* steward who buys provisions, esp in a college, Inn of Court, or monastery
**MANCIPLES** > MANCIPLE
**MANCUS** *n* former English coin
**MANCUSES** > MANCUS
**MAND** > MAN
**MANDALA** *n* circular design symbolizing the universe
**MANDALAS** > MANDALA
**MANDALIC** > MANDALA
**MANDAMUS** *n* formerly a writ from, now an order of, a superior court commanding an inferior tribunal, public official, corporation, etc, to carry out a public duty
**MANDARIN** *n* high-ranking government official
**MANDARINE** *same as* > MANDARIN
**MANDARINS** > MANDARIN
**MANDATARY** *same as* > MANDATORY
**MANDATE** *n* official or authoritative command ▷ *vb* give authority to
**MANDATED** > MANDATE
**MANDATES** > MANDATE
**MANDATING** > MANDATE
**MANDATOR** > MANDATE
**MANDATORS** > MANDATE
**MANDATORY** *adj* compulsory ▷ *n* person or state holding a mandate
**MANDI** *n* (in India) a big market
**MANDIBLE** *n* lower jawbone or jawlike part
**MANDIBLES** > MANDIBLE
**MANDILION** *same as* > MANDYLION
**MANDIOC** *same as* > MANIOC
**MANDIOCA** *same as* > MANIOC
**MANDIOCAS** > MANDIOCA
**MANDIOCCA** *same as* > MANIOC
**MANDIOCS** > MANDIOC
**MANDIR** *n* Hindu or Jain temple
**MANDIRA** *same as* > MANDIR
**MANDIRAS** > MANDIRA
**MANDIRS** > MANDIR
**MANDIS** > MANDI
**MANDOLA** *n* early type of mandolin
**MANDOLAS** > MANDOLA
**MANDOLIN** *n* musical instrument with four pairs of strings
**MANDOLINE** *same*

*as* > MANDOLIN
**MANDOLINS** > MANDOLIN
**MANDOM** *n* mankind
**MANDOMS** > MANDOM
**MANDORA** *n* ancestor of mandolin
**MANDORAS** > MANDORA
**MANDORLA** *n* (in painting, sculpture, etc) an almond-shaped area of light, usually surrounding the resurrected Christ or the Virgin at the Assumption
**MANDORLAS** > MANDORLA
**MANDRAKE** *n* plant with a forked root, formerly used as a narcotic
**MANDRAKES** > MANDRAKE
**MANDREL** *n* shaft on which work is held in a lathe
**MANDRELS** > MANDREL
**MANDRIL** *same*

*as* > MANDREL
**MANDRILL** *n* large blue-faced baboon
**MANDRILLS** > MANDRILL
**MANDRILS** > MANDRIL
**MANDUCATE** *vb* eat or chew
**MANDYLION** *n* loose garment formerly worn over armour
**MANE** *n* long hair on the neck of a horse, lion, etc
**MANED** > MANE
**MANEGE** *n* art of training horses and riders ▷ *vb* train horse
**MANEGED** > MANEGE
**MANEGES** > MANEGE
**MANEGING** > MANEGE
**MANEH** *same as* > MINA
**MANEHS** > MANEH
**MANELESS** > MANE
**MANENT** > MANET
**MANES** *pl n* spirits of the dead, often revered as minor deities
**MANET** *vb* theatre direction, remain on stage
**MANEUVER** *same*

*as* > MANOEUVRE
**MANEUVERS** > MANEUVER
**MANFUL** *adj* determined and brave
**MANFULLY** > MANFUL
**MANG** *vb* speak
**MANGA** *n* type of Japanese comic book with an adult theme
**MANGABEY** *n* any of several large agile arboreal Old World monkeys of the genus *Cercocebus*, of central Africa, having long limbs and tail and white upper eyelids
**MANGABEYS** > MANGABEY
**MANGABIES** > MANGABY
**MANGABY** *same*

*as* > MANGABEY
**MANGAL** *n* Turkish brazier
**MANGALS** > MANGAL
**MANGANATE** *n* salt of manganic acid

**MANGANESE** *n* brittle greyish-white metallic element
**MANGANIC** *adj* of or containing manganese in the trivalent state
**MANGANIN** *n* copper-based alloy
**MANGANINS** > MANGANIN
**MANGANITE** *n* blackish mineral
**MANGANOUS** *adj* of or containing manganese in the divalent state
**MANGAS** > MANGA
**MANGE** *n* skin disease of domestic animals
**MANGEAO** *n* small New Zealand tree with glossy leaves
**MANGED** *adj* having mange
**MANGEL** *n* Eurasian variety of the beet plant, *Beta vulgaris*, cultivated as a cattle food, having a large yellowish root
**MANGELS** > MANGEL
**MANGER** *n* eating trough in a stable or barn
**MANGERS** > MANGER
**MANGES** > MANGE
**MANGETOUT** *n* variety of pea with an edible pod
**MANGEY** *same as* > MANGY
**MANGIER** > MANGY
**MANGIEST** > MANGY
**MANGILY** > MANGY
**MANGINESS** > MANGY
**MANGING** > MANG
**MANGLE** *vb* destroy by crushing and twisting ▷ *n* machine with rollers for squeezing water from washed clothes
**MANGLED** > MANGLE
**MANGLER** > MANGLE
**MANGLERS** > MANGLE
**MANGLES** > MANGLE
**MANGLING** > MANGLE
**MANGO** *n* tropical fruit with sweet juicy yellow flesh
**MANGOES** > MANGO
**MANGOLD** *n* type of root vegetable
**MANGOLDS** > MANGOLD
**MANGONEL** *n* war engine for hurling stones
**MANGONELS** > MANGONEL
**MANGOS** > MANGO
**MANGOSTAN** *n* East Indian tree with thick leathery leaves and edible fruit
**MANGOUSTE** *same*

*as* > MONGOOSE
**MANGROVE** *n* tropical tree with exposed roots, which grows beside water
**MANGROVES** > MANGROVE
**MANGS** > MANG
**MANGULATE** *vb* bend or twist out of shape
**MANGY** *adj* having mange
**MANHANDLE** *vb* treat roughly

**MANHATTAN** *n* mixed drink consisting of four parts whisky, one part vermouth, and a dash of bitters
**MANHOLE** *n* hole with a cover, through which a person can enter a drain or sewer
**MANHOLES** > MANHOLE
**MANHOOD** *n* state or quality of being a man or being manly
**MANHOODS** > MANHOOD
**MANHUNT** *n* organized search, usu. by police, for a wanted man or a fugitive
**MANHUNTER** > MANHUNT
**MANHUNTS** > MANHUNT
**MANI** *n* place to pray
**MANIA** *n* extreme enthusiasm
**MANIAC** *n* mad person
**MANIACAL** *adj* affected with or characteristic of mania
**MANIACS** > MANIAC
**MANIAS** > MANIA
**MANIC** *adj* extremely excited or energetic ▷ *n* person afflicted with mania
**MANICALLY** > MANIC
**MANICOTTI** *pl n* large tubular noodles, usually stuffed with ricotta cheese and baked in a tomato sauce
**MANICS** > MANIC
**MANICURE** *n* cosmetic care of the fingernails and hands ▷ *vb* care for (the fingernails and hands) in this way
**MANICURED** > MANICURE
**MANICURES** > MANICURE
**MANIES** > MANY
**MANIFEST** *adj* easily noticed, obvious ▷ *vb* show plainly ▷ *n* list of cargo or passengers for customs
**MANIFESTO** *n* declaration of policy as issued by a political party ▷ *vb* issued manifesto
**MANIFESTS** > MANIFEST
**MANIFOLD** *adj* numerous and varied ▷ *n* pipe with several outlets, esp in an internal-combustion engine ▷ *vb* duplicate (a page, book, etc)
**MANIFOLDS** > MANIFOLD
**MANIFORM** *adj* like hand
**MANIHOC** *variation of* > MANIOC
**MANIHOCS** > MANIHOC
**MANIHOT** *n* tropical American plant
**MANIHOTS** > MANIHOT
**MANIKIN** *n* little man or dwarf
**MANIKINS** > MANIKIN
**MANILA** *n* strong brown

paper used for envelopes

**MANILAS** > MANILA

**MANILLA** n early currency in W Africa in the form of a small bracelet

**MANILLAS** > MANILLA

**MANILLE** n (in ombre and quadrille) the second best trump

**MANILLES** > MANILLE

**MANIOC** same as > CASSAVA

**MANIOCA** same as > MANIOC

**MANIOCAS** > MANIOCA

**MANIOCS** > MANIOC

**MANIPLE** n (in ancient Rome) a unit of 120 to 200 foot soldiers

**MANIPLES** > MANIPLE

**MANIPLIES** same as > MANYPLIES

**MANIPULAR** adj of or relating to an ancient Roman maniple

**MANIS** n pangolin

**MANITO** same as > MANITOU

**MANITOS** > MANITO

**MANITOU** n (among the Algonquian Indians) a deified spirit or force

**MANITOUS** > MANITOU

**MANITU** same as > MANITOU

**MANITUS** > MANITU

**MANJACK** n single individual

**MANJACKS** > MANJACK

**MANKIER** > MANKY

**MANKIEST** > MANKY

**MANKIND** n human beings collectively

**MANKINDS** > MANKIND

**MANKY** adj worthless, rotten, or in bad taste

**MANLESS** > MAN

**MANLIER** > MANLY

**MANLIEST** > MANLY

**MANLIKE** adj resembling or befitting a man

**MANLIKELY** > MANLIKE

**MANLILY** > MANLY

**MANLINESS** > MANLY

**MANLY** adj (possessing qualities) appropriate to a man

**MANMADE** adj made or produced by man

**MANNA** n miraculous food which sustained the Israelites in the wilderness

**MANNAN** n drug derived from mannose

**MANNANS** > MANNAN

**MANNAS** > MANNA

**MANNED** > MAN

**MANNEQUIN** n woman who models clothes at a fashion show

**MANNER** n way a thing happens or is done

**MANNERED** adj affected

**MANNERISM** n person's distinctive habit or trait

**MANNERIST** > MANNERISM

**MANNERLY** adj having good manners, polite ▷ adv

with good manners

**MANNERS** pl n person's social conduct viewed in the light of whether it is regarded as polite or acceptable or not

**MANNIKIN** same as > MANIKIN

**MANNIKINS** > MANNIKIN

**MANNING** > MAN

**MANNISH** adj (of a woman) like a man

**MANNISHLY** > MANNISH

**MANNITE** same as > MANNITOL

**MANNITES** > MANNITE

**MANNITIC** > MANNITOL

**MANNITOL** n white crystalline water-soluble sweet-tasting alcohol

**MANNITOLS** > MANNITOL

**MANNOSE** n hexose sugar

**MANNOSES** > MANNOSE

**MANO** n stone for grinding grain

**MANOAO** n New Zealand shrub

**MANOAOS** > MANOAO

**MANOEUVRE** n skilful movement ▷ vb manipulate or contrive skilfully or cunningly

**MANOMETER** n instrument for comparing pressures

**MANOMETRY** > MANOMETER

**MANOR** n large country house and its lands

**MANORIAL** > MANOR

**MANORS** > MANOR

**MANOS** > MANO

**MANOSCOPY** n measurement of the densities of gases

**MANPACK** n load carried by one person

**MANPACKS** > MANPACK

**MANPOWER** n available number of workers

**MANPOWERS** > MANPOWER

**MANQUE** adj would-be

**MANRED** n homage

**MANREDS** > MANRED

**MANRENT** same as > MANRED

**MANRENTS** > MANRENT

**MANRIDER** n train carrying miners in coal mine

**MANRIDERS** > MANRIDER

**MANRIDING** adj carrying people rather than goods

**MANROPE** n rope railing

**MANROPES** > MANROPE

**MANS** > MAN

**MANSARD** n roof with two slopes on both sides and both ends, the lower slopes being steeper than the upper

**MANSARDED** adj having mansard roof

**MANSARDS** > MANSARD

**MANSE** n house provided for a minister in some religious denominations

**MANSES** > MANSE

**MANSHIFT** n work done by one person in one shift

**MANSHIFTS** > MANSHIFT

**MANSION** n large house

**MANSIONS** > MANSION

**MANSLAYER** n person who kills man

**MANSONRY** n mansions collectively

**MANSUETE** adj gentle

**MANSWORN** adj perjured

**MANTA** n any large ray (fish) of the family Mobulidae, having very wide winglike pectoral fins and feeding on plankton

**MANTAS** > MANTA

**MANTEAU** n cloak or mantle

**MANTEAUS** > MANTEAU

**MANTEAUX** > MANTEAU

**MANTEEL** n cloak

**MANTEELS** > MANTEEL

**MANTEL** n structure round a fireplace ▷ vb construct a mantel

**MANTELET** n woman's short mantle, often lace-trimmed, worn in the mid-19th century

**MANTELETS** > MANTELET

**MANTELS** > MANTEL

**MANTES** > MANTIS

**MANTIC** adj of or relating to divination and prophecy

**MANTICORA** same as > MANTICORE

**MANTICORE** n mythical monster with body of lion and human head

**MANTID** same as > MANTIS

**MANTIDS** > MANTID

**MANTIES** > MANTY

**MANTILLA** n (in Spain) a lace scarf covering a woman's head and shoulders

**MANTILLAS** > MANTILLA

**MANTIS** n carnivorous insect like a grasshopper

**MANTISES** > MANTIS

**MANTISSA** n part of a common logarithm consisting of the decimal point and the figures following it

**MANTISSAS** > MANTISSA

**MANTLE** same as > MANTEL

**MANTLED** > MANTLE

**MANTLES** > MANTLE

**MANTLET** same as > MANTELET

**MANTLETS** > MANTLET

**MANTLING** n drapery or scrollwork around a shield

**MANTLINGS** > MANTLING

**MANTO** same as > MANTEAU

**MANTOES** > MANTO

**MANTOS** > MANTO

**MANTRA** n any sacred word or syllable used as an object of concentration

**MANTRAM** same as > MANTRA

**MANTRAMS** > MANTRAM

**MANTRAP** n snare for

catching people, esp trespassers

**MANTRAPS** > MANTRAP

**MANTRAS** > MANTRA

**MANTRIC** > MANTRA

**MANTUA** n loose gown of the 17th and 18th centuries, worn open in front to show the underskirt

**MANTUAS** > MANTUA

**MANTY** Scots variant of > MANTUA

**MANUAL** adj of or done with the hands ▷ n handbook

**MANUALLY** > MANUAL

**MANUALS** > MANUAL

**MANUARY** same as > MANUAL

**MANUBRIA** > MANUBRIUM

**MANUBRIAL** > MANUBRIUM

**MANUBRIUM** n any handle-shaped part, esp the upper part of the sternum

**MANUHIRI** n visitor to a Māori marae

**MANUHIRIS** > MANUHIRI

**MANUKA** n New Zealand tree with strong elastic wood and aromatic leaves

**MANUKAS** > MANUKA

**MANUL** n Asian wildcat

**MANULS** > MANUL

**MANUMEA** n pigeon of Samoa

**MANUMEAS** > MANUMEA

**MANUMIT** vb free from slavery

**MANUMITS** > MANUMIT

**MANURANCE** n cultivation of land

**MANURE** n animal excrement used as a fertilizer ▷ vb fertilize (land) with this

**MANURED** > MANURE

**MANURER** > MANURE

**MANURERS** > MANURE

**MANURES** > MANURE

**MANURIAL** > MANURE

**MANURING** > MANURE

**MANURINGS** > MANURE

**MANUS** n wrist and hand

**MANWARD** adv towards humankind

**MANWARDS** same as > MANWARD

**MANWISE** adv in human way

**MANY** adj numerous ▷ n large number

**MANYATA** same as > MANYATTA

**MANYATAS** > MANYATA

**MANYATTA** n settlement of Masai people

**MANYATTAS** > MANYATTA

**MANYFOLD** adj many in number

**MANYPLIES** n third component of the stomach of ruminants

**MANZANITA** n Californian plant

**MANZELLO** n instrument like saxophone

**MANZELLOS** > MANZELLO

**MAOMAO** n fish of New Zealand seas

**MAORMOR** same

*as* > MORMAOR

**MAORMORS** > MAORMOR

**MAP** n representation of the earth's surface or some part of it, showing geographical features ▷ vb make a map of

**MAPAU** n small New Zealand tree with reddish bark, aromatic leaves, and dark berries

**MAPLE** n tree with broad leaves, a variety of which yields sugar

**MAPLELIKE** > MAPLE

**MAPLES** > MAPLE

**MAPLESS** > MAP

**MAPLIKE** > MAP

**MAPMAKER** n person who draws maps

**MAPMAKERS** > MAPMAKER

**MAPMAKING** > MAPMAKER

**MAPPABLE** > MAP

**MAPPED** > MAP

**MAPPEMOND** n map of world

**MAPPER** > MAP

**MAPPERIES** > MAPPERY

**MAPPERS** > MAP

**MAPPERY** n making of maps

**MAPPING** > MAP

**MAPPINGS** > MAP

**MAPPIST** > MAP

**MAPPISTS** > MAP

**MAPS** > MAP

**MAPSTICK** same

*as* > MOPSTICK

**MAPSTICKS** > MAPSTICK

**MAPWISE** adv like map

**MAQUETTE** n sculptor's small preliminary model or sketch

**MAQUETTES** > MAQUETTE

**MAQUI** n Chilean shrub

**MAQUILA** n US-owned factory in Mexico

**MAQUILAS** > MAQUILA

**MAQUIS** n French underground movement that fought against the German occupying forces in World War II

**MAQUISARD** n member of French maquis

**MAR** vb spoil or impair ▷ n disfiguring mark

**MARA** n harelike South American rodent, *Dolichotis patagonum*, inhabiting the pampas of Argentina: family *Caviidae* (cavies)

**MARABI** n kind of music popular in S African townships in the 1930s

**MARABIS** > MARABI

**MARABOU** n large black-and-white African stork

**MARABOUS** > MARABOU

**MARABOUT** n Muslim holy man or hermit of North Africa

**MARABOUTS** > MARABOUT

**MARABUNTA** n any of several social wasps

**MARACA** n shaken percussion instrument made from a gourd containing dried seeds etc

**MARACAS** > MARACA

**MARAE** n enclosed space in front of a Māori meeting house

**MARAES** > MARAE

**MARAGING** as in *maraging steel* strong low-carbon steel containing nickel and small amounts of titanium, aluminium, and niobium, produced by transforming to a martensitic structure and heating at 500°C

**MARAGINGS** > MARAGING

**MARAH** n bitterness

**MARAHS** > MARAH

**MARANATHA** n member of Christian sect

**MARANTA** n any plant of the tropical American rhizomatous genus *Maranta*, some species of which are grown as pot plants for their showy leaves in variegated shades of green: family *Marantaceae*

**MARANTAS** > MARANTA

**MARARI** n eel-like blennoid food fish

**MARARIS** > MARARI

**MARAS** > MARA

**MARASCA** n European cherry tree, *Prunus cerasus marasca*, with red acid-tasting fruit from which maraschino is made

**MARASCAS** > MARASCA

**MARASMIC** > MARASMUS

**MARASMOID** > MARASMUS

**MARASMUS** n general emaciation and wasting, esp of infants, thought to be associated with severe malnutrition or impaired utilization of nutrients

**MARATHON** n long-distance race of 26 miles 385 yards (42.195 kilometres) ▷ adj of or relating to a race on foot of 26 miles 385 yards (42.195 kilometres)

**MARATHONS** > MARATHON

**MARAUD** vb wander or raid in search of plunder

**MARAUDED** > MARAUD

**MARAUDER** > MARAUD

**MARAUDERS** > MARAUD

**MARAUDING** adj wandering or raiding in search of plunder

**MARAUDS** > MARAUD

**MARAVEDI** n any of various Spanish coins of copper or gold

**MARAVEDIS** > MARAVEDI

**MARBELISE** same

*as* > MARBLEIZE

**MARBELIZE** same

*as* > MARBLEIZE

**MARBLE** n kind of limestone with a mottled appearance, which can be highly polished ▷ vb mottle with variegated streaks in imitation of marble

**MARBLED** > MARBLE

**MARBLEISE** same

*as* > MARBLEIZE

**MARBLEIZE** vb give a marble-like appearance to

**MARBLER** > MARBLE

**MARBLERS** > MARBLE

**MARBLES** n game in which marble balls are rolled at one another

**MARBLIER** > MARBLE

**MARBLIEST** > MARBLE

**MARBLING** n mottled effect or pattern resembling marble

**MARBLINGS** > MARBLING

**MARBLY** > MARBLE

**MARC** n remains of grapes or other fruit that have been pressed for wine-making

**MARCASITE** n crystals of iron pyrites, used in jewellery

**MARCATO** adj (of notes) heavily accented ▷ adv with each note heavily accented

**MARCATOS** > MARCATO

**MARCEL** n hairstyle characterized by repeated regular waves, popular in the 1920s ▷ vb make such waves in (the hair) with special hot irons

**MARCELLA** n type of fabric

**MARCELLAS** > MARCELLA

**MARCELLED** > MARCEL

**MARCELLER** > MARCEL

**MARCELS** > MARCEL

**MARCH** vb walk with a military step ▷ n action of marching

**MARCHED** > MARCH

**MARCHEN** n German story

**MARCHER** n person who marches

**MARCHERS** > MARCHER

**MARCHES** > MARCH

**MARCHESA** n (in Italy) the wife or widow of a marchese

**MARCHESAS** > MARCHESA

**MARCHESE** n (in Italy) a nobleman ranking below a prince and above a count

**MARCHESES** > MARCHESE

**MARCHESI** > MARCHESE

**MARCHING** > MARCH

**MARCHLAND** n border land

**MARCHLIKE** adj like march in rhythm

**MARCHMAN** n person living on border

**MARCHMEN** > MARCHMAN

**MARCHPANE** same

*as* > MARZIPAN

**MARCONI** vb communicate by wireless

**MARCONIED** > MARCONI

**MARCONIS** > MARCONI

**MARCS** > MARC

**MARD** > MAR

**MARDIED** > MARDY

**MARDIER** > MARDY

**MARDIES** > MARDY

**MARDIEST** > MARDY

**MARDY** adj (of a child) spoilt ▷ vb behave in mardy way

**MARDYING** > MARDY

**MARE** n female horse or zebra

**MAREMMA** n marshy unhealthy region near the shore, esp in Italy

**MAREMMAS** > MAREMMA

**MAREMME** > MAREMMA

**MARENGO** adj browned in oil and cooked with tomatoes, mushrooms, garlic, wine, etc

**MARES** > MARE

**MARESCHAL** same

*as* > MARSHAL

**MARG** short for > MARGARINE

**MARGARIC** adj of or resembling pearl

**MARGARIN** n ester of margaric acid

**MARGARINE** n butter substitute made from animal or vegetable fats

**MARGARINS** > MARGARIN

**MARGARITA** n mixed drink consisting of tequila and lemon juice

**MARGARITE** n pink pearly micaceous mineral

**MARGAY** n feline mammal, *Felis wiedi*, of Central and South America, having a dark-striped coat

**MARGAYS** > MARGAY

**MARGE** n margarine

**MARGENT** same as > MARGIN

**MARGENTED** > MARGENT

**MARGENTS** > MARGENT

**MARGES** > MARGE

**MARGIN** n edge or border ▷ vb provide with a margin

**MARGINAL** adj insignificant, unimportant ▷ n marginal constituency

**MARGINALS** > MARGINAL

**MARGINATE** vb provide with a margin or margins ▷ adj having a margin of a distinct colour or form

**MARGINED** > MARGIN

**MARGINING** > MARGIN

**MARGINS** > MARGIN

**MARGOSA** n Indian tree

**MARGOSAS** > MARGOSA

**MARGRAVE** n (formerly) a German nobleman ranking above a count

MARGRAVES > MARGRAVE
MARGS > MARG
MARIA > MARE
MARIACHI n small ensemble of street musicians in Mexico
MARIACHIS > MARIACHI
MARIALITE n silicate mineral
MARID n spirit in Muslim mythology
MARIDS > MARID
MARIES > MARY
MARIGOLD n plant with yellow or orange flowers
MARIGOLDS > MARIGOLD
MARIGRAM n graphic record of the tide levels at a particular coastal station
MARIGRAMS > MARIGRAM
MARIGRAPH n gauge for recording the levels of the tides
MARIHUANA same as > MARIJUANA
MARIJUANA n dried flowers and leaves of the cannabis plant, used as a drug, esp in cigarettes
MARIMBA n Latin American percussion instrument resembling a xylophone
MARIMBAS > MARIMBA
MARIMBIST > MARIMBA
MARINA n harbour for yachts and other pleasure boats
MARINADE n seasoned liquid in which fish or meat is soaked before cooking
MARINADED > MARINADE
MARINADES > MARINADE
MARINARA n Italian pasta sauce
MARINARAS > MARINARA
MARINAS > MARINA
MARINATE vb soak in marinade
MARINATED > MARINATE
MARINATES > MARINATE
MARINE adj of the sea or shipping ▷ n (esp in Britain and the US) soldier trained for land and sea combat
MARINER n sailor
MARINERA n folk dance of Peru
MARINERAS > MARINERA
MARINERS > MARINER
MARINES > MARINE
MARINIERE adj served in white wine and onion sauce
MARIPOSA n any of several liliaceous plants of the genus Calochortus, of the southwestern US and Mexico, having brightly coloured tulip-like flowers
MARIPOSAS > MARIPOSA
MARISCHAL Scots variant of > MARSHAL

MARISH n marsh
MARISHES > MARISH
MARITAGE n right of a lord to choose the spouses of his wards
MARITAGES > MARITAGE
MARITAL adj relating to marriage
MARITALLY > MARITAL
MARITIME adj relating to shipping
MARJORAM n aromatic herb used for seasoning food and in salads
MARJORAMS > MARJORAM
MARK n line, dot, scar, etc visible on a surface ▷ vb make a mark on
MARKA n unit of currency introduced as an interim currency in Bosnia-Herzegovina
MARKAS > MARKA
MARKDOWN n price reduction ▷ vb reduce in price
MARKDOWNS > MARKDOWN
MARKED adj noticeable
MARKEDLY > MARKED
MARKER n object used to show the position of something
MARKERS > MARKER
MARKET n assembly or place for buying and selling ▷ vb offer or produce for sale
MARKETED > MARKET
MARKETEER n supporter of the European Union and of Britain's membership of it
MARKETER > MARKET
MARKETERS > MARKET
MARKETING n part of a business that controls the way that goods or services are sold
MARKETS > MARKET
MARKHOOR same as > MARKHOR
MARKHOORS > MARKHOOR
MARKHOR n large wild Himalayan goat, Capra falconeri, with a reddish-brown coat and large spiralled horns
MARKHORS > MARKHOR
MARKING n arrangement of colours on an animal or plant
MARKINGS > MARKING
MARKKA n former standard monetary unit of Finland, divided into 100 penniä
MARKKAA > MARKKA
MARKKAS > MARKKA
MARKMAN n person owning land
MARKMEN > MARKMAN
MARKS > MARK
MARKSMAN n person skilled at shooting
MARKSMEN > MARKSMAN
MARKUP n percentage or amount added to the cost

of a commodity to provide the seller with a profit and to cover overheads, costs, etc ▷ vb increase the price of
MARKUPS > MARKUP
MARL n soil formed of clay and lime, used as fertilizer ▷ vb fertilize (land) with marl
MARLE same as > MARVEL
MARLED > MARL
MARLES > MARLE
MARLIER > MARLY
MARLIEST > MARLY
MARLIN same as > MARLINE
MARLINE n light rope, usually tarred, made of two strands laid left-handed
MARLINES > MARLINE
MARLING same as > MARLINE
MARLINGS > MARLING
MARLINS > MARLIN
MARLITE n type of marl that contains clay and calcium carbonate and is resistant to the decomposing action of air
MARLITES > MARLITE
MARLITIC > MARLITE
MARLS > MARL
MARLSTONE same as > MARLITE
MARLY adj marl-like
MARM same as > MADAM
MARMALADE n jam made from citrus fruits ▷ adj (of cats) streaked orange and yellow and brown
MARMALISE vb beat soundly or defeat utterly
MARMALIZE same as > MARMALISE
MARMARISE same as > MARMARIZE
MARMARIZE vb turn to marble
MARMELISE same as > MARMELIZE
MARMELIZE vb beat soundly
MARMITE n large cooking pot
MARMITES > MARMITE
MARMOREAL adj of or like marble
MARMOREAN same as > MARMOREAL
MARMOSE n South American opossum
MARMOSES > MARMOSE
MARMOSET n small bushy-tailed monkey
MARMOSETS > MARMOSET
MARMOT n burrowing rodent
MARMOTS > MARMOT
MARMS > MARM
MAROCAIN n fabric of ribbed crepe
MAROCAINS > MAROCAIN
MARON n freshwater crustacean

MARONS > MARON
MAROON adj reddish-purple ▷ vb abandon ashore, esp on an island ▷ n exploding firework or flare used as a warning signal
MAROONED > MAROON
MAROONER > MAROON
MAROONERS > MAROON
MAROONING > MAROON
MAROONS > MAROON
MAROQUIN n morocco leather
MAROQUINS > MAROQUIN
MAROR n Jewish ceremonial dish of bitter herbs
MARORS > MAROR
MARPLOT n person interfering with plot
MARPLOTS > MARPLOT
MARQUE n brand of product, esp of a car
MARQUEE n large tent used for a party or exhibition
MARQUEES > MARQUEE
MARQUES > MARQUE
MARQUESS n nobleman of the rank below a duke
MARQUETRY n ornamental inlaid work of wood
MARQUIS n (in some European countries) nobleman of the rank above a count
MARQUISE same as > MARQUEE
MARQUISES > MARQUISE
MARRAM as in marram grass any of several grasses of the genus that grow on sandy shores and can withstand drying
MARRAMS > MARRAM
MARRANO n Spanish or Portuguese Jew of the late Middle Ages who was converted to Christianity, esp one forcibly converted but secretly adhering to Judaism
MARRANOS > MARRANO
MARRED > MAR
MARRELS same as > MERILS
MARRER > MAR
MARRERS > MAR
MARRI n species of eucalyptus, Eucalyptus calophylla, of Western Australia, widely cultivated for its coloured flowers
MARRIAGE n state of being married
MARRIAGES > MARRIAGE
MARRIED > MARRY
MARRIEDS pl n married people
MARRIER > MARRY
MARRIERS > MARRY
MARRIES > MARRY
MARRING > MAR
MARRIS > MARRI
MARRON n large edible sweet chestnut

**MARRONS** > MARRON
**MARROW** n fatty substance inside bones ▷ vb be mate to
**MARROWED** > MARROW
**MARROWFAT** n variety of large pea
**MARROWING** > MARROW
**MARROWISH** > MARROW
**MARROWS** > MARROW
**MARROWSKY** n spoonerism
**MARROWY** > MARROW
**MARRUM** same as > MARRAM
**MARRUMS** > MARRUM
**MARRY** vb take as a husband or wife ▷ interj exclamation of surprise or anger
**MARRYING** > MARRY
**MARRYINGS** > MARRY
**MARS** > MAR
**MARSALA** n dark sweet dessert wine made in Sicily
**MARSALAS** > MARSALA
**MARSE** same as > MASTER
**MARSEILLE** n strong cotton fabric with a raised pattern, used for bedspreads, etc
**MARSES** > MARSE
**MARSH** n low-lying wet land
**MARSHAL** n officer of the highest rank ▷ vb arrange in order
**MARSHALCY** > MARSHAL
**MARSHALED** > MARSHAL
**MARSHALER** > MARSHAL
**MARSHALL** n shortened form of Marshall Plan, programme of US economic aid for the reconstruction of post-World War II Europe (1948–52)
**MARSHALLS** > MARSHALL
**MARSHALS** > MARSHAL
**MARSHBUCK** n antelope of the central African swamplands, *Strepsiceros spekei*, with spreading hoofs adapted to boggy ground
**MARSHES** > MARSH
**MARSHIER** > MARSHY
**MARSHIEST** > MARSHY
**MARSHLAND** n land consisting of marshes
**MARSHLIKE** > MARSH
**MARSHWORT** n prostrate creeping aquatic perennial umbelliferous plant of the genus *Apium*, esp *A. inundatum*, having small white flowers: related to wild celery
**MARSHY** adj of, involving, or like a marsh
**MARSPORT** n spoilsport
**MARSPORTS** > MARSPORT
**MARSQUAKE** n Martian equivalent of earthquake
**MARSUPIA** > MARSUPIUM
**MARSUPIAL** n animal that

carries its young in a pouch, such as a kangaroo ▷ adj of or like a marsupial
**MARSUPIAN** > MARSUPIAL
**MARSUPIUM** n external pouch in most female marsupials within which the newly born offspring are suckled and complete their development
**MART** n market ▷ vb sell or trade
**MARTAGON** n Eurasian lily plant, *Lilium martagon*, cultivated for its mottled purplish-red flowers with reflexed petals
**MARTAGONS** > MARTAGON
**MARTED** > MART
**MARTEL** n hammer-shaped weapon ▷ vb use such a weapon
**MARTELLED** > MARTEL
**MARTELLO** n small circular tower for coastal defence, formerly much used in Europe
**MARTELLOS** > MARTELLO
**MARTELS** > MARTEL
**MARTEN** n weasel-like animal
**MARTENS** > MARTEN
**MARTEXT** n preacher who makes many mistakes
**MARTEXTS** > MARTEXT
**MARTIAL** adj of war, warlike
**MARTIALLY** > MARTIAL
**MARTIAN** n inhabitant of Mars
**MARTIANS** > MARTIAN
**MARTIN** n bird with a slightly forked tail
**MARTINET** n person who maintains strict discipline
**MARTINETS** > MARTINET
**MARTING** > MART
**MARTINGAL** n strap of a horse's harness
**MARTINI** n cocktail of vermouth and gin
**MARTINIS** > MARTINI
**MARTINS** > MARTIN
**MARTLET** n footless bird often found in coats of arms, standing for either a martin or a swallow
**MARTLETS** > MARTLET
**MARTS** > MART
**MARTYR** n person who dies or suffers for his or her beliefs ▷ vb make a martyr of
**MARTYRDOM** n sufferings or death of a martyr
**MARTYRED** > MARTYR
**MARTYRIA** > MARTYRIUM
**MARTYRIES** > MARTYRY
**MARTYRING** > MARTYR
**MARTYRISE** > MARTYR
**MARTYRIUM** same as > MARTYRY
**MARTYRIZE** > MARTYR
**MARTYRLY** > MARTYR
**MARTYRS** > MARTYR

**MARTYRY** n shrine or chapel erected in honour of a martyr
**MARVEL** vb be filled with wonder ▷ n wonderful thing
**MARVELED** > MARVEL
**MARVELING** > MARVEL
**MARVELLED** > MARVEL
**MARVELOUS** adj causing great wonder
**MARVELS** > MARVEL
**MARVER** vb roll molten glass on slab
**MARVERED** > MARVER
**MARVERING** > MARVER
**MARVERS** > MARVER
**MARVY** shortened form of > MARVELOUS
**MARXISANT** adj sympathetic to Marxism
**MARY** shortened form of > MARYJANE
**MARYBUD** n bud of marigold
**MARYBUDS** > MARYBUD
**MARYJANE** n slang for marijuana
**MARYJANES** > MARYJANE
**MARZIPAN** n paste of ground almonds, sugar, and egg whites ▷ modifier of or relating to the stratum of middle managers in a financial institution or other business
**MARZIPANS** > MARZIPAN
**MAS** > MA
**MASA** n Mexican maize dough
**MASALA** n mixture of spices ground into a paste ▷ adj spicy
**MASALAS** > MASALA
**MASAS** > MASA
**MASCARA** n cosmetic for darkening the eyelashes
**MASCARAED** adj wearing mascara
**MASCARAS** > MASCARA
**MASCARON** n in architecture, a face carved in stone or metal
**MASCARONS** n grotesque face used as decoration
**MASCLE** n charge consisting of a lozenge with a lozenge-shaped hole in the middle
**MASCLED** > MASCLE
**MASCLES** > MASCLE
**MASCON** n any of several lunar regions of high gravity
**MASCONS** > MASCON
**MASCOT** n person, animal, or thing supposed to bring good luck
**MASCOTS** > MASCOT
**MASCULINE** adj relating to males
**MASCULIST** n advocate of rights of men
**MASCULY** > MASCLE

**MASE** vb function as maser
**MASED** > MASE
**MASER** n device for amplifying microwaves
**MASERS** > MASER
**MASES** > MASE
**MASH** n soft pulpy mass ▷ vb crush into a soft mass
**MASHALLAH** interj what Allah wishes
**MASHED** > MASH
**MASHER** > MASH
**MASHERS** > MASH
**MASHES** > MASH
**MASHGIACH** n person who ensures adherence to kosher rules
**MASHGIAH** same as > MASHGIACH
**MASHGIHIM** > MASHGIACH
**MASHIACH** n messiah
**MASHIACHS** > MASHIACH
**MASHIE** n (formerly) a club, corresponding to the modern No. 5 or No. 6 iron, used for approach shots
**MASHIER** > MASHY
**MASHIES** > MASHIE
**MASHIEST** > MASHY
**MASHING** > MASH
**MASHINGS** > MASH
**MASHLAM** same as > MASLIN
**MASHLAMS** > MASHLAM
**MASHLIM** same as > MASLIN
**MASHLIMS** > MASHLIM
**MASHLIN** same as > MASLIN
**MASHLINS** > MASHLIN
**MASHLOCH** same as > MASLIN
**MASHLOCHS** > MASHLOCH
**MASHLUM** same as > MASLIN
**MASHLUMS** > MASHLUM
**MASHMAN** n brewery worker
**MASHMEN** > MASHMAN
**MASHUA** n South American plant
**MASHUAS** > MASHUA
**MASHUP** n piece of recorded or live music in which a producer or DJ blends together two or more tracks, often of contrasting genres
**MASHUPS** > MASHUP
**MASHY** adj like mash
**MASING** > MASE
**MASJID** same as > MOSQUE
**MASJIDS** > MASJID
**MASK** n covering for the face, as a disguise or protection ▷ vb cover with a mask
**MASKABLE** > MASK
**MASKED** adj disguised or covered by or as if by a mask
**MASKEG** n North American bog
**MASKEGS** > MASKEG
**MASKER** n person who wears a mask or takes part in a masque
**MASKERS** > MASKER
**MASKING** n act or practice of masking

**MASKINGS** > MASKING
**MASKLIKE** > MASK
**MASKS** > MASK
**MASLIN** n mixture of wheat, rye or other grain
**MASLINS** > MASLIN
**MASOCHISM** n condition in which (sexual) pleasure is obtained from feeling pain or from being humiliated
**MASOCHIST** > MASOCHISM
**MASON** n person who works with stone ▷ vb construct or strengthen with masonry
**MASONED** > MASON
**MASONIC** adj of, characteristic of, or relating to Freemasons or Freemasonry
**MASONING** > MASON
**MASONITE** n tradename for a kind of dark brown hardboard used for partitions, lining, etc
**MASONITES** > MASONITE
**MASONRIED** adj built of masonry
**MASONRIES** > MASONRY
**MASONRY** n stonework
**MASONS** > MASON
**MASOOLAH** n Indian boat used in surf
**MASOOLAHS** > MASOOLAH
**MASQUE** n 16th–17th-century form of dramatic entertainment
**MASQUER** same as > MASKER
**MASQUERS** > MASQUER
**MASQUES** > MASQUE
**MASS** n coherent body of matter ▷ adj large-scale ▷ vb form into a mass
**MASSA** old fashioned variant of > MASTER
**MASSACRE** n indiscriminate killing of large numbers of people ▷ vb kill in large numbers
**MASSACRED** > MASSACRE
**MASSACRER** > MASSACRE
**MASSACRES** > MASSACRE
**MASSAGE** n rubbing and kneading of parts of the body to reduce pain or stiffness ▷ vb give a massage to
**MASSAGED** > MASSAGE
**MASSAGER** > MASSAGE
**MASSAGERS** > MASSAGE
**MASSAGES** > MASSAGE
**MASSAGING** > MASSAGE
**MASSAGIST** > MASSAGE
**MASSAS** > MASSA
**MASSCULT** n culture of masses
**MASSCULTS** > MASSCULT
**MASSE** n stroke made by hitting the cue ball off centre with the cue held nearly vertically, esp so as to make the ball move in a curve around another ball before hitting the object ball

**MASSED** > MASS
**MASSEDLY** > MASS
**MASSES** pl n body of common people
**MASSETER** n muscle of the cheek used in moving the jaw, esp in chewing
**MASSETERS** > MASSETER
**MASSEUR** n person who gives massages
**MASSEURS** > MASSEUR
**MASSEUSE** n woman who gives massages, esp as a profession
**MASSEUSES** > MASSEUSE
**MASSICOT** n yellow earthy secondary mineral
**MASSICOTS** > MASSICOT
**MASSIER** > MASSY
**MASSIEST** > MASSY
**MASSIF** n connected group of mountains
**MASSIFS** > MASSIF
**MASSINESS** > MASSY
**MASSING** > MASS
**MASSIVE** adj large and heavy ▷ n group of friends or associates
**MASSIVELY** > MASSIVE
**MASSLESS** > MASS
**MASSOOLA** same as > MASOOLAH
**MASSOOLAS** > MASSOOLA
**MASSY** literary word for > MASSIVE
**MASSYMORE** n underground prison
**MAST** n tall pole for supporting something, esp a ship's sails
**MASTABA** n mud-brick superstructure above tombs in ancient Egypt
**MASTABAH** same as > MASTABA
**MASTABAHS** > MASTABAH
**MASTABAS** > MASTABA
**MASTED** > MAST
**MASTER** n person in control, such as an employer or an owner of slaves or animals ▷ adj overall or controlling ▷ vb acquire knowledge of or skill in ▷ modifier overall or controlling
**MASTERATE** n status of master
**MASTERDOM** > MASTER
**MASTERED** > MASTER
**MASTERFUL** adj domineering
**MASTERIES** > MASTERY
**MASTERING** > MASTER
**MASTERLY** adj showing great skill
**MASTERS** > MASTER
**MASTERY** n expertise
**MASTFUL** > MAST
**MASTHEAD** n head of a mast ▷ vb send (a sailor) to the masthead as a punishment
**MASTHEADS** > MASTHEAD

**MASTHOUSE** n place for storing masts
**MASTIC** n gum obtained from certain trees
**MASTICATE** vb chew
**MASTICH** same as > MASTIC
**MASTICHE** same as > MASTIC
**MASTICHES** > MASTICHE
**MASTICHS** > MASTICH
**MASTICOT** same as > MASSICOT
**MASTICOTS** > MASTICOT
**MASTICS** > MASTIC
**MASTIER** > MAST
**MASTIEST** > MAST
**MASTIFF** n large dog
**MASTIFFS** > MASTIFF
**MASTING** > MAST
**MASTITIC** > MASTITIS
**MASTITIS** n inflammation of a breast or udder
**MASTIX** n type of gum
**MASTIXES** > MASTIX
**MASTLESS** > MAST
**MASTLIKE** > MAST
**MASTODON** n extinct elephant-like mammal
**MASTODONS** > MASTODON
**MASTODONT** > MASTODON
**MASTOID** n projection of the bone behind the ear ▷ adj shaped like a nipple or breast
**MASTOIDAL** > MASTOID
**MASTOIDS** > MASTOID
**MASTOPEXY** n cosmetic surgery of breasts
**MASTS** > MAST
**MASTY** > MAST
**MASU** n Japanese salmon
**MASULA** same as > MASOOLAH
**MASULAS** > MASULA
**MASURIUM** n silver-grey metallic element
**MASURIUMS** > MASURIUM
**MASUS** > MASU
**MAT** n piece of fabric used as a floor covering or to protect a surface ▷ vb tangle or become tangled into a dense mass ▷ adj having a dull, lustreless, or roughened surface
**MATACHIN** n dancer with sword
**MATACHINA** n feamale matachin
**MATACHINI** > MATACHIN
**MATADOR** n man who kills the bull in bullfights
**MATADORA** n female matador
**MATADORAS** > MATADORA
**MATADORE** n form of dominoes game
**MATADORES** > MATADORE
**MATADORS** > MATADOR
**MATAGOURI** n thorny bush of New Zealand, Discaria toumatou, that forms thickets in open country
**MATAI** n New Zealand tree, the wood of which is used

for timber for building
**MATAIS** > MATAI
**MATAMATA** (in Malaysia) a former name for > POLICE
**MATAMATAS** > MATAMATA
**MATAMBALA** > TAMBALA
**MATATA** same as > FERNBIRD
**MATCH** n contest in a game or sport ▷ vb be exactly like, equal to, or in harmony with
**MATCHABLE** > MATCH
**MATCHBOOK** n number of carboard matches attached in folder
**MATCHBOX** n small box for holding matches
**MATCHED** > MATCH
**MATCHER** > MATCH
**MATCHERS** > MATCH
**MATCHES** > MATCH
**MATCHET** same as > MACHETE
**MATCHETS** > MATCHET
**MATCHING** > MATCH
**MATCHLESS** adj unequalled
**MATCHLOCK** n obsolete type of gunlock igniting the powder by means of a slow match
**MATCHMADE** > MATCHMAKE
**MATCHMAKE** vb bring suitable people together for marriage
**MATCHMARK** n mark made on mating components of an engine, machine, etc, to ensure that the components are assembled in the correct relative positions ▷ vb stamp (an object) with matchmarks
**MATCHUP** n sports match
**MATCHUPS** > MATCHUP
**MATCHWOOD** n small splinters
**MATE** n friend ▷ vb pair (animals) or (of animals) be paired for reproduction
**MATED** > MATE
**MATELASSE** adj (in textiles) having a raised design, as quilting
**MATELESS** > MATE
**MATELOT** n sailor
**MATELOTE** n fish served with a sauce of wine, onions, seasonings, and fish stock
**MATELOTES** > MATELOTE
**MATELOTS** > MATELOT
**MATELOTTE** same as > MATELOTE
**MATER** n mother: often used facetiously
**MATERIAL** n substance of which a thing is made ▷ adj of matter or substance
**MATERIALS** pl n equipment necessary for a particular activity
**MATERIEL** n materials

and equipment of an organization, esp of a military force
**MATERIELS** > MATERIEL
**MATERNAL** *adj* of a mother
**MATERNITY** *n* motherhood ▷ *adj* of or for pregnant women
**MATERS** > MATER
**MATES** > MATE
**MATESHIP** *n* comradeship of friends, usually male, viewed as an institution
**MATESHIPS** > MATESHIP
**MATEY** *adj* friendly or intimate ▷ *n* friend or fellow: usually used in direct address
**MATEYNESS** > MATEY
**MATEYS** > MATEY
**MATFELON** *n* knapweed
**MATFELONS** > MATFELON
**MATGRASS** *n* widespread perennial European grass with dense tufts of bristly leaves, characteristic of peaty moors
**MATH** *same as* > MATHS
**MATHESES** > MATHESIS
**MATHESIS** *n* learning or wisdom
**MATHS** *same as* > MATH
**MATICO** *n* Peruvian shrub
**MATICOS** > MATICO
**MATIER** > MATY
**MATIES** > MATY
**MATIEST** > MATY
**MATILDA** *n* bushman's swag
**MATILDAS** > MATILDA
**MATILY** > MATY
**MATIN** *adj* of or relating to matins
**MATINAL** *same as* > MATIN
**MATINEE** *n* afternoon performance in a theatre or cinema
**MATINEES** > MATINEE
**MATINESS** > MATY
**MATING** > MATE
**MATINGS** > MATE
**MATINS** *pl n* early morning service in various Christian Churches
**MATIPO** *n* New Zealand shrub
**MATIPOS** > MATIPO
**MATJES** *same as* > MAATJES
**MATLESS** > MAT
**MATLO** *same as* > MATELOT
**MATLOS** > MATLO
**MATLOW** *same as* > MATELOT
**MATLOWS** > MATLOW
**MATOKE** *n* (in Uganda) the flesh of bananas, boiled and mashed as a food
**MATOKES** > MATOKE
**MATOOKE** *same as* > MATOKE
**MATOOKES** > MATOOKE
**MATRASS** *n* long-necked glass flask, used for distilling, dissolving substances, etc
**MATRASSES** > MATRASS

**MATRES** > MATER
**MATRIARCH** *n* female head of a tribe or family
**MATRIC** *n* matriculation
**MATRICE** *same as* > MATRIX
**MATRICES** > MATRIX
**MATRICIDE** *n* crime of killing one's mother
**MATRICS** > MATRIC
**MATRICULA** *n* register
**MATRILINY** *n* attention to descent of kinship through the female line
**MATRIMONY** *n* marriage
**MATRIX** *n* substance or situation in which something originates, takes form, or is enclosed
**MATRIXES** > MATRIX
**MATRON** *n* staid or dignified married woman
**MATRONAGE** *n* state of being a matron
**MATRONAL** > MATRON
**MATRONISE** *same as* > MATRONIZE
**MATRONIZE** *vb* make matronly
**MATRONLY** *adj* (of a woman) middle-aged and plump
**MATRONS** > MATRON
**MATROSS** *n* gunner's assitant
**MATROSSES** > MATROSS
**MATS** > MAT
**MATSAH** *same as* > MATZO
**MATSAHS** > MATSAH
**MATSURI** *n* Japanese religious ceremony
**MATSURIS** > MATSURI
**MATSUTAKE** *n* Japanese mushroom
**MATT** *adj* dull, not shiny
**MATTAMORE** *n* subterranean storehouse or dwelling
**MATTE** *same as* > MATT
**MATTED** > MAT
**MATTEDLY** > MAT
**MATTER** *n* substance of which something is made ▷ *vb* be of importance
**MATTERED** > MATTER
**MATTERFUL** > MATTER
**MATTERING** > MATTER
**MATTERS** > MATTER
**MATTERY** *adj* discharging pus
**MATTES** > MATTE
**MATTIE** *n* young herring
**MATTIES** > MATTIE
**MATTIFIED** > MATTIFY
**MATTIFIES** > MATTIFY
**MATTIFY** *vb* make (the skin of the face) less oily or shiny using cosmetics
**MATTIN** *same as* > MATIN
**MATTING** > MAT
**MATTINGS** > MAT
**MATTINS** *same as* > MATINS
**MATTOCK** *n* large pick with one of its blade ends flattened for loosening soil
**MATTOCKS** > MATTOCK
**MATTOID** *n* person

displaying eccentric behaviour and mental characteristics that approach the psychotic
**MATTOIDS** > MATTOID
**MATTRASS** *same as* > MATRASS
**MATTRESS** *n* large stuffed flat case, often with springs, used on or as a bed
**MATTS** > MATT
**MATURABLE** > MATURE
**MATURATE** *vb* mature or bring to maturity
**MATURATED** > MATURATE
**MATURATES** > MATURATE
**MATURE** *adj* fully developed or grown-up ▷ *vb* make or become mature
**MATURED** > MATURE
**MATURELY** > MATURE
**MATURER** > MATURE
**MATURERS** > MATURE
**MATURES** > MATURE
**MATUREST** > MATURE
**MATURING** > MATURE
**MATURITY** *n* state of being mature
**MATUTINAL** *adj* of, occurring in, or during the morning
**MATUTINE** *same as* > MATUTINAL
**MATWEED** *n* grass found on moors
**MATWEEDS** > MATWEED
**MATY** *same as* > MATEY
**MATZA** *same as* > MATZO
**MATZAH** *same as* > MATZO
**MATZAHS** > MATZAH
**MATZAS** > MATZA
**MATZO** *n* large very thin biscuit of unleavened bread, traditionally eaten by Jews during Passover
**MATZOH** *same as* > MATZO
**MATZOHS** > MATZOH
**MATZOON** *n* fermented milk product similar to yogurt
**MATZOONS** > MATZOON
**MATZOS** > MATZO
**MATZOT** > MATZO
**MATZOTH** > MATZOH
**MAUBIES** > MAUBY
**MAUBY** *n* (in the E Caribbean) a bittersweet drink made from the bark of a rhamnaceous tree
**MAUD** *n* shawl or rug of grey wool plaid formerly worn in Scotland
**MAUDLIN** *adj* foolishly or tearfully sentimental
**MAUDLINLY** > MAUDLIN
**MAUDS** > MAUD
**MAUGER** *same as* > MAUGRE
**MAUGRE** *prep* in spite of ▷ *vb* behave spitefully towards
**MAUGRED** > MAUGRE
**MAUGRES** > MAUGRE
**MAUGRING** > MAUGRE
**MAUL** *vb* handle roughly ▷ *n* loose scrum
**MAULED** > MAUL

**MAULER** > MAUL
**MAULERS** *pl n* hands
**MAULGRE** *same as* > MAUGRE
**MAULGRED** > MAULGRE
**MAULGRES** > MAULGRE
**MAULGRING** > MAULGRE
**MAULING** > MAUL
**MAULS** > MAUL
**MAULSTICK** *n* long stick used by artists to steady the hand holding the brush
**MAULVI** *n* expert in Islamic law
**MAULVIS** > MAULVI
**MAUMET** *n* false god
**MAUMETRY** > MAUMET
**MAUMETS** > MAUMET
**MAUN** *dialect word for* > MUST
**MAUND** *n* unit of weight used in Asia, esp India, having different values in different localities. A common value in India is 82 pounds or 37 kilograms ▷ *vb* beg
**MAUNDED** > MAUND
**MAUNDER** *vb* talk or act aimlessly or idly
**MAUNDERED** > MAUNDER
**MAUNDERER** > MAUNDER
**MAUNDERS** > MAUNDER
**MAUNDIES** > MAUNDY
**MAUNDING** > MAUND
**MAUNDS** > MAUND
**MAUNDY** *n* ceremonial washing of the feet of poor persons in commemoration of Jesus' washing of his disciples' feet (John 13:4–34) re-enacted in some churches on Maundy Thursday
**MAUNGIER** > MAUNGY
**MAUNGIEST** > MAUNGY
**MAUNGY** *adj* (esp of a child) sulky, bad-tempered, or peevish
**MAUNNA** *vb* Scots term meaning must not
**MAURI** *n* soul
**MAURIS** > MAURI
**MAUSOLEA** > MAUSOLEUM
**MAUSOLEAN** > MAUSOLEUM
**MAUSOLEUM** *n* stately tomb
**MAUT** *same as* > MAHOUT
**MAUTHER** *n* girl
**MAUTHERS** > MAUTHER
**MAUTS** > MAUT
**MAUVAIS** *adj* bad
**MAUVAISE** *feminine form of* > MAUVAIS
**MAUVE** *adj* pale purple ▷ *n* any of various pale to moderate pinkish-purple or bluish-purple colours
**MAUVEIN** *same as* > MAUVEINE
**MAUVEINE** *same as* > MAUVE
**MAUVEINES** > MAUVEINE
**MAUVEINS** > MAUVEIN
**MAUVER** > MAUVE
**MAUVES** > MAUVE
**MAUVEST** > MAUVE

459

MAUVIN *same as* > MAUVEINE

MAUVINE *same as* > MAUVEINE

MAUVINES > MAUVEINE

MAUVINS > MAUVIN

MAVEN *n* expert or connoisseur

MAVENS > MAVEN

MAVERICK *adj* independent and unorthodox (person) ▷ *n* person of independent or unorthodox views ▷ *vb* take illegally

MAVERICKS > MAVERICK

MAVIE *n* type of thrush

MAVIES > MAVIE

MAVIN *same as* > MAVEN

MAVINS > MAVIN

MAVIS *n* song thrush

MAVISES > MAVIS

MAVOURNIN *n* Irish form of address meaning my darling

MAW *n* animal's mouth, throat, or stomach ▷ *vb* eat or bite

MAWBOUND *adj* (of cattle) constipated

MAWED > MAW

MAWGER *adj* (of persons or animals) thin or lean

MAWING > MAW

MAWK *n* maggot

MAWKIER > MAWK

MAWKIEST > MAWK

MAWKIN *n* slovenly woman

MAWKINS > MAWKIN

MAWKISH *adj* foolishly sentimental

MAWKISHLY > MAWKISH

MAWKS > MAWK

MAWKY > MAWK

MAWMET *same as* > MAUMET

MAWMETRY > MAWMET

MAWMETS > MAWMET

MAWN *n* dialect word for a quantity

MAWPUS *same as* > MOPUS

MAWPUSES > MAWPUS

MAWR *same as* > MAUTHER

MAWRS > MAWR

MAWS > MAW

MAWSEED *n* poppy seed

MAWSEEDS > MAWSEED

MAWTHER *same as* > MAUTHER

MAWTHERS > MAWTHER

MAX *vb* reach the full extent

MAXED > MAX

MAXES > MAX

MAXI *adj* (of a garment) very long ▷ *n* type of large racing yacht

MAXICOAT *n* long coat

MAXICOATS > MAXICOAT

MAXILLA *n* upper jawbone of a vertebrate

MAXILLAE > MAXILLA

MAXILLAR > MAXILLA

MAXILLARY > MAXILLA

MAXILLAS > MAXILLA

MAXILLULA *n* jaw in crustacean

MAXIM *n* general truth or principle

MAXIMA > MAXIMUM

MAXIMAL *adj* maximum ▷ *n* maximum

MAXIMALLY > MAXIMAL

MAXIMALS > MAXIMAL

MAXIMIN *n* highest of a set of minimum values

MAXIMINS > MAXIMIN

MAXIMISE *same as* > MAXIMIZE

MAXIMISED > MAXIMISE

MAXIMISER > MAXIMIZE

MAXIMISES > MAXIMISE

MAXIMIST > MAXIM

MAXIMISTS > MAXIM

MAXIMITE *n* type of explosive

MAXIMITES > MAXIMITE

MAXIMIZE *vb* increase to a maximum

MAXIMIZED > MAXIMIZE

MAXIMIZER > MAXIMIZE

MAXIMIZES > MAXIMIZE

MAXIMS > MAXIM

MAXIMUM *n* greatest possible (amount or number) ▷ *adj* of, being, or showing a maximum or maximums

MAXIMUMLY > MAXIMUM

MAXIMUMS > MAXIMUM

MAXIMUS *n* method rung on twelve bells

MAXIMUSES > MAXIMUS

MAXING > MAX

MAXIS > MAXI

MAXIXE *n* Brazilian dance in duple time, a precursor of the tango

MAXIXES > MAXIXE

MAXWELL *n* cgs unit of magnetic flux

MAXWELLS > MAXWELL

MAY *vb* used as an auxiliary to express possibility, permission, opportunity, etc ▷ *vb* gather may

MAYA *n* illusion, esp the material world of the senses regarded as illusory

MAYAN > MAYA

MAYAPPLE *n* American plant

MAYAPPLES > MAYAPPLE

MAYAS > MAYA

MAYBE *adv* perhaps, possibly ▷ *sentence substitute* possibly

MAYBES > MAYBE

MAYBIRD *n* American songbird

MAYBIRDS > MAYBIRD

MAYBUSH *n* flowering shrub

MAYBUSHES > MAYBUSH

MAYDAY *n* international radiotelephone distress signal

MAYDAYS > MAYDAY

MAYED > MAY

MAYEST *same as* > MAYST

MAYFLIES > MAYFLY

MAYFLOWER *n* any of various plants that bloom in May

MAYFLY *n* short-lived aquatic insect

MAYHAP *archaic word for* > PERHAPS

MAYHAPPEN *same as* > MAYHAP

MAYHEM *n* violent destruction or confusion

MAYHEMS > MAYHEM

MAYING > MAY

MAYINGS > MAYING

MAYO *n* mayonnaise

MAYOR *n* head of a municipality

MAYORAL > MAYOR

MAYORALTY *n* (term of) office of a mayor

MAYORESS *n* mayor's wife

MAYORS > MAYOR

MAYORSHIP > MAYOR

MAYOS > MAYO

MAYPOLE *n* pole set up for dancing round on the first day of May to celebrate spring

MAYPOLES > MAYPOLE

MAYPOP *n* American wild flower

MAYPOPS > MAYPOP

MAYS > MAY

MAYST *singular form of the present tense of* > MAY

MAYSTER *same as* > MASTER

MAYSTERS > MAYSTER

MAYVIN *same as* > MAVEN

MAYVINS > MAYVIN

MAYWEED *n* widespread Eurasian weedy plant, having evil-smelling leaves and daisy-like flower heads

MAYWEEDS > MAYWEED

MAZAEDIA > MAZAEDIUM

MAZAEDIUM *n* part of lichen

MAZARD *same as* > MAZER

MAZARDS > MAZARD

MAZARINE *n* blue colour

MAZARINES > MAZARINE

MAZE *n* complex network of paths or lines designed to puzzle

MAZED > MAZE

MAZEDLY *adv* in bewildered way

MAZEDNESS *n* bewilderment

MAZEFUL > MAZE

MAZELIKE > MAZE

MAZELTOV *interj* congratulations

MAZEMENT > MAZE

MAZEMENTS > MAZE

MAZER *n* large hardwood drinking bowl

MAZERS > MAZER

MAZES > MAZE

MAZEY *adj* dizzy

MAZHBI *n* low-caste Sikh

MAZHBIS > MAZHBI

MAZIER > MAZY

MAZIEST > MAZY

MAZILY > MAZY

MAZINESS > MAZY

MAZING > MAZE

MAZOURKA *same as* > MAZURKA

MAZOURKAS > MAZOURKA

MAZOUT *same as* > MAZUT

MAZOUTS > MAZOUT

MAZUMA *n* money

MAZUMAS > MAZUMA

MAZURKA *n* lively Polish dance

MAZURKAS > MAZURKA

MAZUT *n* residue left after distillation of petrol

MAZUTS > MAZUT

MAZY *adj* of or like a maze

MAZZARD *same as* > MAZARD

MAZZARDS > MAZARD

MBAQANGA *n* style of Black popular music of urban South Africa

MBAQANGAS > MBAQANGA

MBIRA *n* African musical instrument consisting of tuned metal strips attached to a resonating box, which are plucked with the thumbs

MBIRAS > MBIRA

ME *n* (in tonic sol-fa) third degree of any major scale ▷ *pron* refers to the speaker or writer

MEACOCK *n* timid person

MEACOCKS > MEACOCK

MEAD *n* alcoholic drink made from honey

MEADOW *n* piece of grassland

MEADOWS > MEADOW

MEADOWY > MEADOW

MEADS > MEAD

MEAGER *same as* > MEAGRE

MEAGERLY > MEAGRE

MEAGRE *adj* scanty or insufficient ▷ *n* Mediterranean fish

MEAGRELY > MEAGRE

MEAGRER > MEAGRE

MEAGRES > MEAGRE

MEAGREST > MEAGRE

MEAL *n* occasion when food is served and eaten ▷ *vb* cover with meal

MEALED > MEAL

MEALER *n* person eating but not lodging at boarding house

MEALERS > MEALER

MEALIE *n* maize

MEALIER > MEALY

MEALIES *South African word for* > MAIZE

MEALIEST > MEALY

MEALINESS > MEALY

MEALING > MEAL

MEALLESS > MEAL

MEALS > MEAL

MEALTIME *n* time for meal

MEALTIMES > MEALTIME

MEALWORM *n* larva of various beetles of the genus *Tenebrio*, esp *T. molitor*, feeding on meal, flour, and similar stored

foods: family *Tenebrionidae*
**MEALWORMS** > MEALWORM
**MEALY** *adj* resembling meal
**MEALYBUG** *n* plant-eating homopterous insect
**MEALYBUGS** > MEALYBUG
**MEAN** *vb* intend to convey or express ▷ *adj* miserly, ungenerous, or petty ▷ *n* middle point between two extremes
**MEANDER** *vb* follow a winding course ▷ *n* winding course
**MEANDERED** > MEANDER
**MEANDERER** > MEANDER
**MEANDERS** > MEANDER
**MEANDRIAN** > MEANDER
**MEANDROUS** > MEANDER
**MEANE** *vb* moan
**MEANED** > MEANE
**MEANER** > MEAN
**MEANERS** > MEAN
**MEANES** > MEANE
**MEANEST** > MEAN
**MEANIE** *n* unkind or miserly person
**MEANIES** > MEANY
**MEANING** *n* what something means
**MEANINGLY** > MEAN
**MEANINGS** > MEANING
**MEANLY** > MEAN
**MEANNESS** > MEAN
**MEANS** > MEAN
**MEANT** > MEAN
**MEANTIME** *n* intervening period ▷ *adv* meanwhile
**MEANTIMES** > MEANTIME
**MEANWHILE** *adv* during the intervening period
**MEANY** *same as* > MEANIE
**MEARE** *same as* > MERE
**MEARES** > MEARE
**MEARING** *adj* forming boundary
**MEASE** *vb* assuage
**MEASED** > MEASE
**MEASES** > MEASE
**MEASING** > MEASE
**MEASLE** *vb* infect with measles
**MEASLED** *adj* (of cattle, sheep, or pigs) infested with tapeworm larvae
**MEASLES** *n* infectious disease producing red spots
**MEASLIER** > MEASLY
**MEASLIEST** > MEASLY
**MEASLING** > MEASLE
**MEASLY** *adj* meagre
**MEASURE** *n* size or quantity ▷ *vb* determine the size or quantity of
**MEASURED** *adj* slow and steady
**MEASURER** > MEASURE
**MEASURERS** > MEASURE
**MEASURES** *pl n* rock strata that contain a particular type of deposit
**MEASURING** *adj* used to measure quantities, esp in

cooking
**MEAT** *n* animal flesh as food
**MEATAL** > MEATUS
**MEATAXE** *n* meat cleaver
**MEATAXES** > MEATAXE
**MEATBALL** *n* minced beef, shaped into a ball before cooking
**MEATBALLS** > MEATBALL
**MEATED** *adj* fattened
**MEATH** *same as* > MEAD
**MEATHE** *same as* > MEAD
**MEATHEAD** *n* stupid person
**MEATHEADS** > MEATHEAD
**MEATHES** > MEATHE
**MEATHS** > MEATH
**MEATIER** > MEATY
**MEATIEST** > MEATY
**MEATILY** > MEATY
**MEATINESS** > MEATY
**MEATLESS** > MEAT
**MEATLOAF** *n* chopped meat served in loaf-shaped mass
**MEATMAN** *n* meat seller
**MEATMEN** > MEATMAN
**MEATS** > MEAT
**MEATSPACE** *n* real physical world, as contrasted with the world of cyberspace
**MEATUS** *n* natural opening or channel, such as the canal leading from the outer ear to the eardrum
**MEATUSES** > MEATUS
**MEATY** *adj* (tasting) of or like meat
**MEAWES** *same as* > MEWS
**MEAZEL** *same as* > MESEL
**MEAZELS** > MEAZEL
**MEBOS** *n* South African dried apricots
**MEBOSES** > MEBOS
**MECCA** *n* place that attracts many visitors
**MECCAS** > MECCA
**MECHANIC** *n* person skilled in repairing or operating machinery
**MECHANICS** *n* scientific study of motion and force
**MECHANISE** *same as* > MECHANIZE
**MECHANISM** *n* way a machine works
**MECHANIST** *same as* > MECHANIC
**MECHANIZE** *vb* equip with machinery
**MECHITZA** *n* screen in synagogue separating men and women
**MECHITZAS** > MECHITZA
**MECHITZOT** > MECHITZA
**MECK** *same as* > MAIK
**MECKS** > MECK
**MECLIZINE** *n* drug used to treat motion sickness
**MECONATE** *n* salt of meconic acid
**MECONATES** > MECONATE
**MECONIC** *adj* derived from poppies
**MECONIN** *n* substance found in opium

**MECONINS** > MECONIN
**MECONIUM** *n* dark green mucoid material that forms the first faeces of a newborn infant
**MECONIUMS** > MECONIUM
**MED** *n* doctor
**MEDACCA** *n* Japanese freshwater fish
**MEDACCAS** > MEDACCA
**MEDAILLON** *n* small round thin piece of food
**MEDAKA** *same as* > MEDACCA
**MEDAKAS** > MEDAKA
**MEDAL** *n* piece of metal with an inscription etc, given as a reward or memento ▷ *vb* honour with a medal
**MEDALED** > MEDAL
**MEDALET** *n* small medal
**MEDALETS** > MEDALET
**MEDALING** > MEDAL
**MEDALIST** *same as* > MEDALLIST
**MEDALISTS** > MEDALIST
**MEDALLED** > MEDAL
**MEDALLIC** > MEDAL
**MEDALLING** > MEDAL
**MEDALLION** *n* disc-shaped ornament worn on a chain round the neck
**MEDALLIST** *n* winner of a medal
**MEDALS** > MEDAL
**MEDCINAL** *same as* > MEDICINAL
**MEDDLE** *vb* interfere annoyingly
**MEDDLED** > MEDDLE
**MEDDLER** > MEDDLE
**MEDDLERS** > MEDDLE
**MEDDLES** > MEDDLE
**MEDDLING** > MEDDLE
**MEDDLINGS** > MEDDLE
**MEDEVAC** *n* evacuation of casualties from forward areas to the nearest hospital or base ▷ *vb* transport (a wounded or sick person) to hospital by medevac
**MEDEVACED** > MEDEVAC
**MEDEVACS** > MEDEVAC
**MEDFLIES** > MEDFLY
**MEDFLY** *n* Mediterranean fruit fly
**MEDIA** > MEDIUM
**MEDIACIES** > MEDIACY
**MEDIACY** *n* quality or state of being mediate
**MEDIAD** *adj* situated near the median line or plane of an organism
**MEDIAE** > MEDIUM
**MEDIAEVAL** *adj* of, relating to, or in the style of the Middle Ages ▷ *n* person living in medieval times
**MEDIAL** *adj* of or in the middle ▷ *n* speech sound between being fortis and lenis
**MEDIALLY** > MEDIAL

**MEDIALS** > MEDIAL
**MEDIAN** *n* middle (point or line) ▷ *adj* of, relating to, situated in, or directed towards the middle
**MEDIANLY** > MEDIAN
**MEDIANS** > MEDIAN
**MEDIANT** *n* third degree of a major or minor scale
**MEDIANTS** > MEDIANT
**MEDIAS** > MEDIUM
**MEDIATE** *vb* intervene in a dispute to bring about agreement ▷ *adj* occurring as a result of or dependent upon mediation
**MEDIATED** > MEDIATE
**MEDIATELY** > MEDIATE
**MEDIATES** > MEDIATE
**MEDIATING** > MEDIATE
**MEDIATION** *n* act of mediating
**MEDIATISE** *same as* > MEDIATIZE
**MEDIATIVE** > MEDIATE
**MEDIATIZE** *vb* annex (a state) to another state, allowing the former ruler to retain his title and some authority
**MEDIATOR** > MEDIATE
**MEDIATORS** > MEDIATE
**MEDIATORY** > MEDIATE
**MEDIATRIX** *n* female mediator
**MEDIC** *n* doctor or medical student
**MEDICABLE** *adj* potentially able to be treated or cured medically
**MEDICABLY** > MEDICABLE
**MEDICAID** *n* health assistance programme financed by federal, state, and local taxes to help pay hospital and medical costs for persons of low income
**MEDICAIDS** > MEDICAID
**MEDICAL** *adj* of the science of medicine ▷ *n* medical examination
**MEDICALLY** > MEDICAL
**MEDICALS** > MEDICAL
**MEDICANT** *n* medicinal substance
**MEDICANTS** > MEDICANT
**MEDICARE** *n* (in the US) a federally sponsored health insurance programme for persons of 65 or older
**MEDICARES** > MEDICARE
**MEDICATE** *vb* treat with a medicinal substance
**MEDICATED** *adj* (of a patient) having been treated with a medicine or drug
**MEDICATES** > MEDICATE
**MEDICIDE** *n* suicide assisted by doctor
**MEDICIDES** > MEDICIDE
**MEDICINAL** *adj* having therapeutic properties ▷ *n*

medicinal substance
**MEDICINE** n substance used to treat disease ▷ vb treat with medicine
**MEDICINED** > MEDICINE
**MEDICINER** n physician
**MEDICINES** > MEDICINE
**MEDICK** n any small leguminous plant of the genus *Medicago*, such as black medick or sickle medick, having yellow or purple flowers and trifoliate leaves
**MEDICKS** > MEDICK
**MEDICO** n doctor or medical student
**MEDICOS** > MEDICO
**MEDICS** > MEDIC
**MEDIEVAL** adj of the Middle Ages ▷ n person living in medieval times
**MEDIEVALS** > MEDIEVAL
**MEDIGAP** n private health insurance
**MEDIGAPS** > MEDIGAP
**MEDII** > MEDIUS
**MEDINA** n ancient quarter of any of various North African cities
**MEDINAS** > MEDINA
**MEDIOCRE** adj average in quality
**MEDITATE** vb reflect deeply, esp on spiritual matters
**MEDITATED** > MEDITATE
**MEDITATES** > MEDITATE
**MEDITATOR** > MEDITATE
**MEDIUM** adj midway between extremes, average ▷ n middle state, degree, or condition
**MEDIUMS** pl n medium-dated gilt-edged securities
**MEDIUSES** > MEDIUS
**MEDIUS** n middle finger
**MEDIVAC** variant spelling of > MEDEVAC
**MEDIVACED** > MEDIVAC
**MEDIVACS** > MEDIVAC
**MEDLAR** n apple-like fruit of a small tree, eaten when it begins to decay
**MEDLARS** > MEDLAR
**MEDLE** same as > MEDDLE
**MEDLED** > MEDLE
**MEDLES** > MEDLE
**MEDLEY** n miscellaneous mixture ▷ adj of, being, or relating to a mixture or variety
**MEDLEYS** > MEDLEY
**MEDLING** > MEDLE
**MEDRESE** same as > MADRASAH
**MEDRESES** > MEDRESE
**MEDRESSEH** same as > MADRASAH
**MEDS** > MED
**MEDULLA** n marrow, pith, or inner tissue
**MEDULLAE** > MEDULLA
**MEDULLAR** > MEDULLA
**MEDULLARY** > MEDULLA

**MEDULLAS** > MEDULLA
**MEDULLATE** adj having medulla
**MEDUSA** n jellyfish
**MEDUSAE** > MEDUSA
**MEDUSAL** > MEDUSA
**MEDUSAN** > MEDUSA
**MEDUSANS** > MEDUSA
**MEDUSAS** > MEDUSA
**MEDUSOID** same as > MEDUSA
**MEDUSOIDS** > MEDUSOID
**MEE** n Malaysian noodle dish
**MEED** n recompense
**MEEDS** > MEED
**MEEK** adj submissive or humble
**MEEKEN** vb make meek
**MEEKENED** > MEEKEN
**MEEKENING** > MEEKEN
**MEEKENS** > MEEKEN
**MEEKER** > MEEK
**MEEKEST** > MEEK
**MEEKLY** > MEEK
**MEEKNESS** > MEEK
**MEEMIE** n hysterical person
**MEEMIES** > MEEMIE
**MEER** same as > MERE
**MEERCAT** same as > MEERKAT
**MEERCATS** > MEERCAT
**MEERED** > MEER
**MEERING** > MEER
**MEERKAT** n S African mongoose
**MEERKATS** > MEERKAT
**MEERS** > MEER
**MEES** > MEE
**MEET** vb come together (with) ▷ n meeting, esp a sports meeting ▷ adj fit or suitable
**MEETER** > MEET
**MEETERS** > MEET
**MEETEST** > MEET
**MEETING** > MEET
**MEETINGS** > MEET
**MEETLY** > MEET
**MEETNESS** n properness
**MEETS** > MEET
**MEFF** dialect word for > TRAMP
**MEFFS** > MEFF
**MEG** short for > MEGABYTE
**MEGA** adj extremely good, great, or successful
**MEGABAR** n unit of million bars
**MEGABARS** > MEGABAR
**MEGABIT** n one million bits
**MEGABITS** > MEGABIT
**MEGABUCK** n million dollars
**MEGABUCKS** > MEGABUCK
**MEGABYTE** n 2S2So or 1048 576 bytes
**MEGABYTES** > MEGABYTE
**MEGACITY** n city with over 10 million inhabitants
**MEGACURIE** n unit of million curies
**MEGACYCLE** same as > MEGAHERTZ
**MEGADEAL** n very good deal
**MEGADEALS** > MEGADEAL

**MEGADEATH** n death of a million people, esp in a nuclear war or attack
**MEGADOSE** n very large dose, as of a medicine, vitamin, etc
**MEGADOSES** > MEGADOSE
**MEGADYNE** n unit of million dynes
**MEGADYNES** > MEGADYNE
**MEGAFARAD** n unit of million farads
**MEGAFAUNA** n component of the fauna of a region or period that comprises the larger terrestrial animals
**MEGAFLOP** n measure of processing speed, consisting of a million floating-point operations a second
**MEGAFLOPS** > MEGAFLOP
**MEGAFLORA** n plants large enough to be seen by naked eye
**MEGAFOG** n amplified fog signal
**MEGAFOGS** > MEGAFOG
**MEGAGAUSS** n unit of million gauss
**MEGAHERTZ** n one million hertz
**MEGAHIT** n great success
**MEGAHITS** > MEGAHIT
**MEGAJOULE** n unit of million joules
**MEGALITH** n great stone, esp as part of a prehistoric monument
**MEGALITHS** > MEGALITH
**MEGALITRE** n one million litres
**MEGALOPIC** adj having large eyes
**MEGALOPS** n crab in larval stage
**MEGAPHONE** n cone-shaped instrument used to amplify the voice ▷ vb speak through megaphone
**MEGAPHYLL** n relatively large type of leaf produced by ferns and seed plants
**MEGAPIXEL** n one million pixels
**MEGAPLEX** n cinema complex containing a large number of separate screens, and usually a restaurant or bar
**MEGAPOD** same as > MEGAPODE
**MEGAPODE** n bird of Australia, New Guinea, and adjacent islands
**MEGAPODES** > MEGAPODE
**MEGAPODS** > MEGAPOD
**MEGARA** > MEGARON
**MEGARAD** n unit of million rads
**MEGARADS** > MEGARAD
**MEGARON** n tripartite rectangular room

containing a central hearth surrounded by four pillars, found in Bronze Age Greece and Asia Minor
**MEGARONS** > MEGARON
**MEGASCOPE** n type of image projector
**MEGASPORE** n larger of the two types of spore produced by some spore-bearing plants, which develops into the female gametophyte
**MEGASS** another name for > BAGASSE
**MEGASSE** same as > MEGASS
**MEGASSES** > MEGASS
**MEGASTAR** n very well-known personality in the entertainment business
**MEGASTARS** > MEGASTAR
**MEGASTORE** n very large store
**MEGATHERE** n any of various gigantic extinct American sloths of the genus *Megatherium* and related genera, common in late Cenozoic times
**MEGATON** n explosive power equal to that of one million tons of TNT
**MEGATONIC** > MEGATON
**MEGATONS** > MEGATON
**MEGAVOLT** n one million volts
**MEGAVOLTS** > MEGAVOLT
**MEGAWATT** n one million watts
**MEGAWATTS** > MEGAWATT
**MEGILLA** same as > MEGILLAH
**MEGILLAH** n scroll of the Book of Esther, read on the festival of Purim
**MEGILLAHS** > MEGILLAH
**MEGILLAS** > MEGILLA
**MEGILLOTH** > MEGILLAH
**MEGILP** n oil-painting medium of linseed oil mixed with mastic varnish or turpentine
**MEGILPH** same as > MEGILP
**MEGILPHS** > MEGILPH
**MEGILPS** > MEGILP
**MEGOHM** n one million ohms.
**MEGOHMS** > MEGOHM
**MEGRIM** n caprice
**MEGRIMS** n fit of depression
**MEGS** > MEG
**MEHNDI** n (esp in India) the practice of painting designs on the hands, feet, etc using henna
**MEHNDIS** > MEHNDI
**MEIBOMIAN** as in *meibomian gland* any of the small sebaceous glands in the eyelid, beneath the conjunctiva
**MEIKLE** adj Scots word meaning large
**MEIN** Scots word for > MOAN

**MEINED** > MEIN
**MEINEY** same as > MEINY
**MEINEYS** > MEINEY
**MEINIE** same as > MEINY
**MEINIES** > MEINY
**MEINING** > MEIN
**MEINS** > MEIN
**MEINT** same as > MING
**MEINY** n retinue or household
**MEIOCYTE** n cell that divides by meiosis to produce four haploid spores
**MEIOCYTES** > MEIOCYTE
**MEIOFAUNA** n component of the fauna of a sea or lake bed comprising small (but not microscopic) animals, such as tiny worms and crustaceans
**MEIONITE** n mineral containing silica
**MEIONITES** > MEIONITE
**MEIOSES** > MEIOSIS
**MEIOSIS** n type of cell division in which reproductive cells are produced, each containing half the chromosome number of the parent nucleus
**MEIOSPORE** n haploid spore
**MEIOTIC** > MEIOSIS
**MEISHI** n business card in Japan
**MEISHIS** > MEISHI
**MEISTER** n person who excels at a particular activity
**MEISTERS** > MEISTER
**MEITH** n landmark
**MEITHS** > MEITH
**MEJLIS** same as > MAJLIS
**MEJLISES** > MEJLIS
**MEKKA** same as > MECCA
**MEKKAS** > MEKKA
**MEKOMETER** n device for measuring distance
**MEL** n pure form of honey formerly used in pharmaceutical products
**MELA** n Asian cultural or religious fair or festival
**MELALEUCA** n Australian shrub or tree with a white trunk and black branches
**MELAMDIM** > MELAMED
**MELAMED** n Hebrew teacher
**MELAMINE** n colourless crystalline compound used in making synthetic resins
**MELAMINES** > MELAMINE
**MELAMPODE** n poisonous plant
**MELANGE** n mixture
**MELANGES** > MELANGE
**MELANIAN** n freshwater mollusc
**MELANIC** adj relating to melanism or melanosis ▷ n darker form of creature
**MELANICS** > MELANIC

**MELANIN** n dark pigment found in the hair, skin, and eyes of humans and animals
**MELANINS** > MELANIN
**MELANISE** same as > MELANIZE
**MELANISED** > MELANISE
**MELANISES** > MELANISE
**MELANISM** same as > MELANOSIS
**MELANISMS** > MELANISM
**MELANIST** > MELANISM
**MELANISTS** > MELANISM
**MELANITE** n black variety of andradite garnet
**MELANITES** > MELANITE
**MELANITIC** > MELANITE
**MELANIZE** vb turn into melanin
**MELANIZED** > MELANIZE
**MELANIZES** > MELANIZE
**MELANO** n person with abnormally dark skin
**MELANOID** adj resembling melanin ▷ n dark substance formed in skin
**MELANOIDS** > MELANOID
**MELANOMA** n tumour composed of dark-coloured cells, occurring in some skin cancers
**MELANOMAS** > MELANOMA
**MELANOS** > MELANO
**MELANOSES** > MELANOSIS
**MELANOSIS** n skin condition characterized by excessive deposits of melanin
**MELANOTIC** > MELANOSIS
**MELANOUS** adj having a dark complexion and black hair
**MELANURIA** n presence of melanin in urine
**MELANURIC** > MELANURIA
**MELAPHYRE** n type of weathered amygdaloidal basalt or andesite
**MELAS** > MELA
**MELASTOME** n tropical flowering plant
**MELATONIN** n hormone-like secretion of the pineal gland, causing skin colour changes in some animals and thought to be involved in reproductive function
**MELD** vb merge or blend ▷ n act of melding
**MELDED** > MELD
**MELDER** > MELD
**MELDERS** > MELD
**MELDING** > MELD
**MELDS** > MELD
**MELEE** n noisy confused fight or crowd
**MELEES** > MELEE
**MELENA** n excrement or vomit stained by blood
**MELENAS** > MELENA
**MELIC** adj (of poetry, esp ancient Greek lyric poems) intended to be sung ▷ n tpye of grass

**MELICK** n either of two pale green perennial grasses
**MELICKS** > MELICK
**MELICS** > MELIC
**MELIK** same as > MALIK
**MELIKS** > MELIK
**MELILITE** n mineral containing calcium
**MELILITES** > MELILITE
**MELILOT** n any leguminous plant of the Old World genus Melilotus, having narrow clusters of small white or yellow fragrant flowers
**MELILOTS** > MELILOT
**MELINITE** n high explosive made from picric acid
**MELINITES** > MELINITE
**MELIORATE** vb improve
**MELIORISM** n notion that the world can be improved by human effort
**MELIORIST** > MELIORISM
**MELIORITY** n improved state
**MELISMA** n expressive vocal phrase or passage consisting of several notes sung to one syllable
**MELISMAS** > MELISMA
**MELISMATA** > MELISMA
**MELL** vb mix
**MELLAY** same as > MELEE
**MELLAYS** > MELLAY
**MELLED** > MELL
**MELLIFIC** adj forming or producing honey
**MELLING** > MELL
**MELLITE** n soft yellow mineral
**MELLITES** > MELLITE
**MELLITIC** > MELLITE
**MELLOTRON** n musical synthesizer
**MELLOW** adj soft, not harsh ▷ vb make or become mellow
**MELLOWED** > MELLOW
**MELLOWER** > MELLOW
**MELLOWEST** > MELLOW
**MELLOWING** > MELLOW
**MELLOWLY** > MELLOW
**MELLOWS** > MELLOW
**MELLOWY** same as > MELLOW
**MELLS** > MELL
**MELOCOTON** n variety of peach
**MELODEON** n small accordion
**MELODEONS** > MELODEON
**MELODIA** same as > MELODICA
**MELODIAS** > MELODIA
**MELODIC** adj of melody
**MELODICA** n type of flute
**MELODICAS** > MELODICA
**MELODICS** n study of melody
**MELODIES** > MELODY
**MELODION** same as > MELODEON
**MELODIONS** > MELODION
**MELODIOUS** adj pleasing to

the ear
**MELODISE** same as > MELODIZE
**MELODISED** > MELODISE
**MELODISER** > MELODISE
**MELODISES** > MELODISE
**MELODIST** n composer of melodies
**MELODISTS** > MELODIST
**MELODIZE** vb provide with a melody
**MELODIZED** > MELODIZE
**MELODIZER** > MELODIZE
**MELODIZES** > MELODIZE
**MELODRAMA** n play full of extravagant action and emotion
**MELODRAME** same as > MELODRAMA
**MELODY** n series of musical notes which make a tune
**MELOID** n any long-legged beetle of the family Meloidae, which includes the blister beetles and oil beetles ▷ adj of, relating to, or belonging to the Meloidae
**MELOIDS** > MELOID
**MELOMANIA** n great enthusiasm for music
**MELOMANIC** > MELOMANIA
**MELON** n large round juicy fruit with a hard rind
**MELONGENE** n aubergine
**MELONS** > MELON
**MELPHALAN** n drug used to treat leukaemia
**MELS** > MEL
**MELT** vb (cause to) become liquid by heat ▷ n act or process of melting
**MELTABLE** > MELT
**MELTAGE** n process or result of melting or the amount melted
**MELTAGES** > MELTAGE
**MELTDOWN** n (in a nuclear reactor) melting of the fuel rods, with the possible release of radiation
**MELTDOWNS** > MELTDOWN
**MELTED** > MELT
**MELTEMI** n northerly wind in the northeast Mediterranean
**MELTEMIS** > MELTEMI
**MELTER** > MELT
**MELTERS** > MELT
**MELTIER** > MELTY
**MELTIEST** > MELTY
**MELTING** > MELT
**MELTINGLY** > MELT
**MELTINGS** > MELT
**MELTITH** n meal
**MELTITHS** > MELTITH
**MELTON** n heavy smooth woollen fabric with a short nap, used esp for overcoats
**MELTONS** > MELTON
**MELTS** > MELT
**MELTWATER** n melted snow or ice
**MELTY** adj tending to melt

**MELUNGEON** n any of a dark-skinned group of people of the Appalachians in E Tennessee, of mixed Indian, White, and Black ancestry

**MEM** n 13th letter in the Hebrew alphabet, transliterated as m

**MEMBER** n individual making up a body or society ▷ adj (of a country or group) belonging to an organization or alliance

**MEMBERED** adj having members

**MEMBERS** > MEMBER

**MEMBRAL** adj of limbs

**MEMBRANAL** > MEMBRANE

**MEMBRANE** n thin flexible tissue in a plant or animal body

**MEMBRANED** adj having membrane

**MEMBRANES** > MEMBRANE

**MEME** n idea or element of social behaviour passed on through generations in a culture, esp by imitation

**MEMENTO** n thing serving to remind, souvenir

**MEMENTOES** > MEMENTO

**MEMENTOS** > MEMENTO

**MEMES** > MEME

**MEMETICS** n study of gentic transmission of culture

**MEMO** n memorandum

**MEMOIR** n biography or historical account based on personal knowledge

**MEMOIRISM** n writing of memoirs

**MEMOIRIST** > MEMOIRISM

**MEMOIRS** pl n collection of reminiscences about a period or series of events, written from personal experience

**MEMORABLE** adj worth remembering, noteworthy

**MEMORABLY** > MEMORABLE

**MEMORANDA** n plural of memorandum: written statement of communications

**MEMORIAL** n something serving to commemorate a person or thing ▷ adj serving as a memorial

**MEMORIALS** > MEMORIAL

**MEMORIES** > MEMORY

**MEMORISE** same as > MEMORIZE

**MEMORISED** > MEMORISE

**MEMORISER** > MEMORISE

**MEMORISES** > MEMORISE

**MEMORITER** adv from memory

**MEMORIZE** vb commit to memory

**MEMORIZED** > MEMORIZE

**MEMORIZER** > MEMORIZE

**MEMORIZES** > MEMORIZE

**MEMORY** n ability to remember

**MEMOS** > MEMO

**MEMS** > MEM

**MEMSAHIB** n (formerly, in India) term of respect used for a European married woman

**MEMSAHIBS** > MEMSAHIB

**MEN** > MAN

**MENACE** n threat ▷ vb threaten, endanger

**MENACED** > MENACE

**MENACER** > MENACE

**MENACERS** > MENACE

**MENACES** > MENACE

**MENACING** > MENACE

**MENAD** same as > MAENAD

**MENADIONE** n yellow crystalline compound

**MENADS** > MENAD

**MENAGE** old form of > MANAGE

**MENAGED** > MENAGE

**MENAGERIE** n collection of wild animals for exhibition

**MENAGES** > MENAGE

**MENAGING** > MENAGE

**MENARCHE** n first occurrence of menstruation in a woman's life

**MENARCHES** > MENARCHE

**MENAZON** n type of insecticide

**MENAZONS** > MENAZON

**MEND** vb repair or patch ▷ n mended area

**MENDABLE** > MEND

**MENDACITY** n (tendency to) untruthfulness

**MENDED** > MEND

**MENDER** > MEND

**MENDERS** > MEND

**MENDICANT** adj begging ▷ n beggar

**MENDICITY** > MENDICANT

**MENDIGO** n Spanish beggar or vagrant

**MENDIGOS** > MENDIGO

**MENDING** n something to be mended, esp clothes

**MENDINGS** > MENDING

**MENDS** > MEND

**MENE** Scots form of > MOAN

**MENED** > MENE

**MENEER** n South African title of address equivalent to sir when used alone or Mr when placed before a name

**MENEERS** > MENEER

**MENES** > MENE

**MENFOLK** pl n men collectively, esp the men of a particular family

**MENFOLKS** same as > MENFOLK

**MENG** vb mix

**MENGE** same as > MENG

**MENGED** > MENG

**MENGES** > MENGE

**MENGING** > MENG

**MENGS** > MENG

**MENHADEN** n marine North American fish, Brevoortia tyrannus: source of fishmeal, fertilizer, and oil: family Clupeidae (herrings, etc)

**MENHADENS** > MENHADEN

**MENHIR** n single upright prehistoric stone

**MENHIRS** > MENHIR

**MENIAL** adj involving boring work of low status ▷ n person with a menial job

**MENIALLY** > MENIAL

**MENIALS** > MENIAL

**MENILITE** n liver opal

**MENILITES** > MENILITE

**MENING** > MENE

**MENINGEAL** > MENINX

**MENINGES** > MENINX

**MENINX** n one of three membranes that envelop the brain and spinal cord

**MENISCAL** > MENISCUS

**MENISCATE** > MENISCUS

**MENISCI** > MENISCUS

**MENISCOID** > MENISCUS

**MENISCUS** n curved surface of a liquid

**MENO** adv (esp preceding a dynamic or tempo marking) to be played less quickly, less softly, etc

**MENOLOGY** n ecclesiastical calendar of the months

**MENOMINEE** n whitefish, found in N America and Siberia

**MENOMINI** same as > MENOMINEE

**MENOMINIS** > MENOMINI

**MENOPAUSE** n time when a woman's menstrual cycle ceases

**MENOPOLIS** n informal word for an area with a high proportion of single men

**MENOPOME** n American salamander

**MENOPOMES** > MENOPOME

**MENORAH** n seven-branched candelabrum used as an emblem of Judaism

**MENORAHS** > MENORAH

**MENORRHEA** n normal bleeding in menstruation

**MENSA** n faint constellation in the S hemisphere lying between Hydrus and Volans and containing part of the Large Magellanic Cloud

**MENSAE** n star of the mensa constellation

**MENSAL** adj monthly

**MENSAS** > MENSA

**MENSCH** n decent person

**MENSCHEN** > MENSCH

**MENSCHES** > MENSCH

**MENSCHY** > MENSCH

**MENGING** > MENG

**MENGS** > MENG

**MENHADEN** n marine North

**MENSE** vb grace

**MENSED** > MENSE

**MENSEFUL** adj gracious

**MENSELESS** adj graceless

**MENSES** n menstruation

**MENSH** vb mention

**MENSHED** > MENSH

**MENSHEN** n Chinese door god

**MENSHES** > MENSH

**MENSHING** > MENSH

**MENSING** > MENSE

**MENSTRUA** > MENSTRUUM

**MENSTRUAL** adj of or relating to menstruation

**MENSTRUUM** n solvent, esp one used in the preparation of a drug

**MENSUAL** same as > MENSAL

**MENSURAL** adj of or involving measure

**MENSWEAR** n clothing for men

**MENSWEARS** > MENSWEAR

**MENT** same as > MING

**MENTA** > MENTUM

**MENTAL** adj of, in, or done by the mind

**MENTALESE** n picturing of concepts in mind without words

**MENTALISM** n doctrine that mind is the fundamental reality and that objects of knowledge exist only as aspects of the subject's consciousness

**MENTALIST** > MENTALISM

**MENTALITY** n way of thinking

**MENTALLY** > MENTAL

**MENTATION** n process or result of mental activity

**MENTEE** n person trained by mentor

**MENTEES** > MENTEE

**MENTHENE** n liquid obtained from menthol

**MENTHENES** > MENTHENE

**MENTHOL** n organic compound found in peppermint, used medicinally

**MENTHOLS** > MENTHOL

**MENTICIDE** n destruction of person's mental independence

**MENTION** vb refer to briefly ▷ n brief reference to a person or thing

**MENTIONED** > MENTION

**MENTIONER** > MENTION

**MENTIONS** > MENTION

**MENTO** n Jamaican song

**MENTOR** n adviser or guide ▷ vb act as a mentor to (someone) ▷ vb act as mentor for

**MENTORED** > MENTOR

**MENTORIAL** > MENTOR

**MENTORING** n (in business) the practice of assigning a junior member of staff to the care of a more

experienced person who
assists him in his career
**MENTORS** > MENTOR
**MENTOS** > MENTO
**MENTUM** *n* chin
**MENU** *n* list of dishes to be
served, or from which to
order
**MENUDO** *n* Mexican soup
**MENUDOS** > MENUDO
**MENUISIER** *n* joiner
**MENUS** > MENU
**MENYIE** *same as* > MEINIE
**MENYIES** > MENYIE
**MEOU** *same as* > MEOW
**MEOUED** > MEOU
**MEOUING** > MEOU
**MEOUS** > MEOU
**MEOW** *vb* (of a cat) to make
a characteristic crying
sound ▷ *interj* imitation
of this sound
**MEOWED** > MEOW
**MEOWING** > MEOW
**MEOWS** > MEOW
**MEPACRINE** *n* drug formerly
widely used to treat
malaria
**MEPHITIC** *adj* poisonous
**MEPHITIS** *n* foul-smelling
discharge
**MEPHITISM** *n* poisoning
**MERANTI** *n* wood from any
of several Malaysian trees
of the dipterocarpaceous
genus *Shorea*
**MERANTIS** > MERANTI
**MERBROMIN** *n* green
iridescent crystalline
compound
**MERC** *n* mercenary
**MERCAPTAN** *another name*
*(not in technical usage)*
*for* > THIOL
**MERCAPTO** *adj* of a
particular chemical group
**MERCAT** *Scots word*
*for* > MARKET
**MERCATS** > MERCAT
**MERCENARY** *adj* influenced
by greed ▷ *n* hired soldier
**MERCER** *n* dealer in textile
fabrics and fine cloth
**MERCERIES** > MERCER
**MERCERISE** *same*
*as* > MERCERIZE
**MERCERIZE** *vb* treat
(cotton yarn) with an
alkali to increase its
strength and reception to
dye and impart a lustrous
silky appearance
**MERCERS** > MERCER
**MERCERY** > MERCER
**MERCES** > MERC
**MERCH** *n* merchandise
**MERCHANT** *n* person
engaged in trade,
wholesale trader ▷ *adj*
of ships involved in
commercial trade or their
crews ▷ *vb* conduct trade
in
**MERCHANTS** > MERCHANT

**MERCHES** > MERCH
**MERCHET** *n* (in feudal
England) a fine paid by a
tenant, esp a villein, to
his lord for allowing the
marriage of his daughter
**MERCHETS** > MERCHET
**MERCHILD** *n* mythical
creature with upper body
of child and lower body
of fish
**MERCIABLE** *adj* merciful
**MERCIES** > MERCY
**MERCIFIDE** > MERCIFY
**MERCIFIED** > MERCIFY
**MERCIFIES** > MERCIFY
**MERCIFUL** *adj*
compassionate
**MERCIFY** *vb* show mercy to
**MERCILESS** *adj* without
mercy
**MERCS** > MERC
**MERCURATE** *vb* treat or mix
with mercury
**MERCURIAL** *adj* lively,
changeable ▷ *n* any salt
of mercury for use as a
medicine
**MERCURIC** *adj* of or
containing mercury in the
divalent state
**MERCURIES** > MERCURY
**MERCURISE** *same*
*as* > MERCURATE
**MERCURIZE** *same*
*as* > MERCURISE
**MERCUROUS** *adj* of or
containing mercury in the
monovalent state
**MERCURY** *n* silvery liquid
metal
**MERCY** *n* compassionate
treatment of an offender
or enemy who is in one's
power
**MERDE** *French word*
*for* > EXCREMENT
**MERDES** > MERDE
**MERE** *adj* nothing more
than ▷ *n* lake ▷ *vb* old
form of survey
**MERED** *adj* forming a
boundary
**MEREL** *same as* > MERIL
**MERELL** *same as* > MERIL
**MERELLS** *same as* > MERILS
**MERELS** > MERILS
**MERELY** *adv* only
**MERENGUE** *n* type of lively
dance music originating in
the Dominican Republic,
which combines African
and Spanish elements
**MERENGUES** > MERENGUE
**MEREOLOGY** *n* formal study
of the logical properties
of the relation of part and
whole
**MERER** > MERE
**MERES** > MERE
**MERESMAN** *n* man who
decides on boundaries
**MERESMEN** > MERESMAN
**MEREST** > MERE

**MERESTONE** *n* stone
marking boundary
**MERFOLK** *n* mermaids and
mermen
**MERFOLKS** > MERFOLK
**MERGANSER** *n* large crested
diving duck
**MERGE** *vb* combine or blend
**MERGED** > MERGE
**MERGEE** *n* business taken
over by merger
**MERGEES** > MERGEE
**MERGENCE** > MERGE
**MERGENCES** > MERGE
**MERGER** *n* combination of
business firms into one
**MERGERS** > MERGER
**MERGES** > MERGE
**MERGING** > MERGE
**MERGINGS** > MERGE
**MERI** *n* Māori war club
**MERICARP** *n* part of plant
fruit
**MERICARPS** > MERICARP
**MERIDIAN** *n* imaginary
circle of the earth passing
through both poles ▷ *adj*
along or relating to a
meridian
**MERIDIANS** > MERIDIAN
**MERIL** *n* counter used in
merils
**MERILS** *n* old board game
**MERIMAKE** *n* merrymaking
**MERIMAKES** > MERIMAKE
**MERING** > MERE
**MERINGS** > MERING
**MERINGUE** *n* baked mixture
of egg whites and sugar
**MERINGUES** > MERINGUE
**MERINO** *n* breed of sheep
with fine soft wool
**MERINOS** > MERINO
**MERIS** > MERI
**MERISES** > MERISIS
**MERISIS** *n* growth by
division of cells
**MERISM** *n* duplication of
biological parts
**MERISMS** > MERISM
**MERISTEM** *n* plant tissue
responsible for growth,
whose cells divide and
differentiate to form the
tissues and organs of the
plant
**MERISTEMS** > MERISTEM
**MERISTIC** *adj* of or relating
to the number of organs or
parts in an animal or plant
body
**MERIT** *n* excellence or
worth ▷ *vb* deserve
**MERITED** > MERIT
**MERITING** > MERIT
**MERITLESS** > MERIT
**MERITS** > MERIT
**MERK** *n* old Scots coin
**MERKIN** *n* artificial
hairpiece for the
pudendum
**MERKINS** > MERKIN
**MERKS** > MERK
**MERL** *same as* > MERLE

**MERLE** *adj* (of a dog, esp
a collie) having a bluish-
grey coat with speckles or
streaks of black
**MERLES** > MERLE
**MERLIN** *n* small falcon
**MERLING** *n* whiting
**MERLINGS** > MERLING
**MERLINS** > MERLIN
**MERLON** *n* solid upright
section in a crenellated
battlement
**MERLONS** > MERLON
**MERLOT** *n* black grape
grown in France and
now throughout the
wine-producing world,
used, often in a blend, for
making wine
**MERLOTS** > MERLOT
**MERLS** > MERL
**MERMAID** *n* imaginary sea
creature with the upper
part of a woman and the
lower part of a fish
**MERMAIDEN** *same*
*as* > MERMAID
**MERMAIDS** > MERMAID
**MERMAN** *n* male counterpart
of the mermaid
**MERMEN** > MERMAN
**MEROCRINE** *adj* (of the
secretion of glands)
characterized by
formation of the product
without undergoing
disintegration
**MEROGONY** *n* development
of embryo from part of
ovum
**MEROISTIC** *adj* producing
yolk and ova
**MEROME** *same*
*as* > MEROSOME
**MEROMES** > MEROME
**MERONYM** *n* part of
something used to refer
to the whole, such as
*faces* meaning *people*, as
in *they've seen a lot of faces*
*come and go*
**MERONYMS** > MERONYM
**MERONYMY** > MERONYM
**MEROPIA** *n* partial
blindness
**MEROPIAS** > MEROPIA
**MEROPIC** > MEROPIA
**MEROPIDAN** *n* bird of bee-
eater family
**MEROSOME** *n* segment in
body of worm
**MEROSOMES** > MEROSOME
**MEROZOITE** *n* any of the
cells formed by fission
of a schizont during the
life cycle of sporozoan
protozoans, such as the
malaria parasite
**MERPEOPLE** *same*
*as* > MERFOLK
**MERRIER** > MERRY
**MERRIES** > MERRY
**MERRIEST** > MERRY
**MERRILY** > MERRY

**MERRIMENT** n gaiety, fun, or mirth
**MERRINESS** > MERRY
**MERRY** adj cheerful or jolly ▷ n gean
**MERRYMAN** n jester
**MERRYMEN** > MERRYMAN
**MERSALYL** n salt of sodium
**MERSALYLS** > MERSALYL
**MERSE** n low level ground by a river or shore, often alluvial and fertile
**MERSES** > MERSE
**MERSION** n dipping in water
**MERSIONS** > MERSION
**MERYCISM** n rumination
**MERYCISMS** > MERYCISM
**MES** > ME
**MESA** n flat-topped hill found in arid regions
**MESAIL** n visor
**MESAILS** > MESAIL
**MESAL** same as > MESIAL
**MESALLY** > MESAL
**MESARAIC** adj of mesentery
**MESARCH** adj (of a xylem strand) having the first-formed xylem surrounded by that formed later, as in fern stems
**MESAS** > MESA
**MESCAL** n spineless globe-shaped cactus of Mexico and the SW of the USA
**MESCALIN** same as > MESCALINE
**MESCALINE** n hallucinogenic drug obtained from the tops of mescals
**MESCALINS** > MESCALIN
**MESCALISM** n addiction to mescal
**MESCALS** > MESCAL
**MESCLUM** same as > MESCLUN
**MESCLUMS** > MESCLUM
**MESCLUN** n type of green salad
**MESCLUNS** > MESCLUN
**MESDAMES** > MADAM
**MESE** n middle string on lyre
**MESEEMED** > MESEEMS
**MESEEMETH** same as > MESEEMS
**MESEEMS** vb it seems to me
**MESEL** n leper
**MESELED** adj afflicted by leprosy
**MESELS** > MESEL
**MESENTERA** > MESENTERON
**MESENTERY** n double layer of peritoneum that is attached to the back wall of the abdominal cavity and supports most of the small intestine
**MESES** > MESE
**MESETA** n plateau in Spain
**MESETAS** > MESETA
**MESH** n network or net ▷ vb (of gear teeth) engage

▷ adj made from mesh
**MESHED** > MESH
**MESHES** > MESH
**MESHIER** > MESH
**MESHIEST** > MESH
**MESHING** > MESH
**MESHINGS** > MESH
**MESHUGA** adj crazy
**MESHUGAAS** n madness
**MESHUGAH** same as > MESHUGA
**MESHUGAS** adj crazy
**MESHUGGA** same as > MESHUGA
**MESHUGGAH** same as > MESHUGA
**MESHUGGE** same as > MESHUGA
**MESHWORK** n network
**MESHWORKS** > MESHWORK
**MESHY** > MESH
**MESIAD** adj relating to or situated at the middle or centre
**MESIAL** another word for > MEDIAL
**MESIALLY** > MESIAL
**MESIAN** same as > MESIAL
**MESIC** > MESON
**MESICALLY** > MESON
**MESMERIC** adj holding (someone) as if spellbound
**MESMERISE** same as > MESMERIZE
**MESMERISM** n hypnotic state induced by the operator's imposition of his will on that of the patient
**MESMERIST** > MESMERISM
**MESMERIZE** vb hold spellbound
**MESNALTY** n lands of a mesne lord
**MESNE** adj in Law, intermediate or intervening: used esp of any assignment of property before the last
**MESNES** > MESNE
**MESOBLAST** another name for > MESODERM
**MESOCARP** n middle layer of the pericarp of a fruit, such as the flesh of a peach
**MESOCARPS** > MESOCARP
**MESOCRANY** n medium skull breadth
**MESODERM** n middle germ layer of an animal embryo, giving rise to muscle, blood, bone, connective tissue, etc
**MESODERMS** > MESODERM
**MESOGLEA** n gelatinous material between the outer and inner cellular layers of jellyfish and other coelenterates
**MESOGLEAL** > MESOGLEA
**MESOGLEAS** > MESOGLEA
**MESOGLOEA** same as > MESOGLEA
**MESOLITE** n type of mineral

**MESOLITES** > MESOLITE
**MESOMERE** n cell in fertilized ovum
**MESOMERES** > MESOMERE
**MESOMORPH** n person with a muscular body build: said to be correlated with somatotonia
**MESON** n elementary atomic particle
**MESONIC** > MESON
**MESONS** > MESON
**MESOPAUSE** n zone of minimum temperature between the mesosphere and the thermosphere
**MESOPHILE** n ideal growth temperature of 20-45 degrees
**MESOPHYL** same as > MESOPHYLL
**MESOPHYLL** n soft chlorophyll-containing tissue of a leaf between the upper and lower layers of epidermis: involved in photosynthesis
**MESOPHYLS** > MESOPHYL
**MESOPHYTE** n any plant that grows in surroundings receiving an average supply of water
**MESOSCALE** adj of weather phenomena of medium duration
**MESOSOME** n part of bacterial cell
**MESOSOMES** > MESOSOME
**MESOTRON** same as > MESON
**MESOTRONS** > MESOTRON
**MESOZOAN** n type of parasite
**MESOZOANS** > MESOZOAN
**MESOZOIC** adj of, denoting, or relating to an era of geological time
**MESPRISE** same as > MISPRISE
**MESPRISES** > MESPRISE
**MESPRIZE** same as > MISPRISE
**MESPRIZES** > MESPRIZE
**MESQUIN** adj mean
**MESQUINE** same as > MESQUIN
**MESQUIT** same as > MESQUITE
**MESQUITE** n small tree whose sugary pods are used as animal fodder
**MESQUITES** > MESQUITE
**MESQUITS** > MESQUIT
**MESS** n untidy or dirty confusion ▷ vb muddle or dirty
**MESSAGE** n communication sent ▷ vb send as a message
**MESSAGED** > MESSAGE
**MESSAGES** > MESSAGE
**MESSAGING** n sending and receving of messages
**MESSALINE** n light lustrous twilled-silk fabric

**MESSAN** Scots word for > DOG
**MESSANS** > MESSAN
**MESSED** > MESS
**MESSENGER** n bearer of a message ▷ vb send by messenger
**MESSES** > MESS
**MESSIAH** n exceptional or hoped for liberator of a country or people
**MESSIAHS** > MESSIAH
**MESSIANIC** adj of or relating to the Messiah, his awaited deliverance of the Jews, or the new age of peace expected to follow this
**MESSIAS** same as > MESSIAH
**MESSIASES** > MESSIAS
**MESSIER** > MESSY
**MESSIEST** > MESSY
**MESSIEURS** > MONSIEUR
**MESSILY** > MESSY
**MESSINESS** > MESSY
**MESSING** > MESS
**MESSMAN** n sailor working in ship's mess
**MESSMATE** n person with whom one shares meals in a mess, esp in the army
**MESSMATES** > MESSMATE
**MESSMEN** > MESSMAN
**MESSUAGE** n dwelling house together with its outbuildings, curtilage, and the adjacent land appropriated to its use
**MESSUAGES** > MESSUAGE
**MESSY** adj dirty, confused, or untidy
**MESTEE** same as > MUSTEE
**MESTEES** > MESTEE
**MESTER** n master: used as a term of address for a man who is the head of a house
**MESTERS** > MESTER
**MESTESO** n Spanish music genre
**MESTESOES** > MESTESO
**MESTESOS** > MESTESO
**MESTINO** n person of mixed race
**MESTINOES** > MESTINO
**MESTINOS** > MESTINO
**MESTIZA** > MESTIZO
**MESTIZAS** > MESTIZO
**MESTIZO** n person of mixed parentage, esp the offspring of a Spanish American and an American Indian
**MESTIZOES** > MESTIZO
**MESTIZOS** > MESTIZO
**MESTO** adj sad
**MESTOM** same as > MESTOME
**MESTOME** n conducting tissue associated with parenchyma
**MESTOMES** > MESTOME
**MESTOMS** > MESTOM
**MESTRANOL** n synthetic oestrogen
**MET** n measuring stick
**META** n indicating change,

alteration, or alternation
**METABASES** > METABASIS
**METABASIS** n change
**METABATIC** > METABASIS
**METABOLIC** adj of or related to the sum total of the chemical processes that occurs in living organisms, resulting in growth, production of energy, elimination of waste material, etc
**METABOLY** n ability of some cells, esp protozoans, to alter their shape
**METACARPI** n skeleton of the hand between the wrist and the fingers
**METAGE** n official measuring of weight or contents
**METAGENIC** adj of or relating to the production within the life cycle of an organism of alternating asexual and sexual reproductive forms
**METAGES** > METAGE
**METAIRIE** n area of land on which farmer pays rent in kind
**METAIRIES** > METAIRIE
**METAL** n chemical element, such as iron or copper, that is malleable and capable of conducting heat and electricity ▷ adj made of metal ▷ vb fit or cover with metal
**METALED** > METAL
**METALHEAD** n fan of heavy metal music
**METALING** > METAL
**METALISE** same
as > METALLIZE
**METALISED** > METALISE
**METALISES** > METALISE
**METALIST** same
as > METALLIST
**METALISTS** > METALIST
**METALIZE** same
as > METALLIZE
**METALIZED** > METALIZE
**METALIZES** > METALIZE
**METALLED** > METAL
**METALLIC** adj of or consisting of metal ▷ n something metallic
**METALLICS** > METALLIC
**METALLIKE** > METAL
**METALLINE** adj of, resembling, or relating to metals
**METALLING** > METAL
**METALLISE** same
as > METALLIZE
**METALLIST** n person who works with metals
**METALLIZE** vb make metallic or to coat or treat with metal
**METALLOID** n nonmetallic element, such as arsenic or silicon, that has some

of the properties of a metal ▷ adj of or being a metalloid
**METALLY** adj like metal
**METALMARK** n variety of butterfly
**METALS** > METAL
**METALWARE** n items made of metal
**METALWORK** n craft of making objects from metal
**METAMALE** n sterile male organism, esp a fruit fly (Drosophila) that has one X chromosome and three sets of autosomes
**METAMALES** > METAMALE
**METAMER** n any of two or more isomeric compounds exhibiting metamerism
**METAMERAL** > METAMERE
**METAMERE** n one of the similar body segments into which earthworms, crayfish, and similar animals are divided longitudinally
**METAMERES** > METAMERE
**METAMERIC** adj divided into or consisting of metameres
**METAMERS** > METAMER
**METAMICT** adj of or denoting the amorphous state of a substance that has lost its crystalline structure as a result of the radioactivity of uranium or thorium within it
**METANOIA** n repentance
**METANOIAS** > METANOIA
**METAPELET** n foster mother
**METAPHASE** n second stage of mitosis during which the condensed chromosomes attach to the centre of the spindle
**METAPHOR** n figure of speech in which a term is applied to something it does not literally denote in order to imply a resemblance
**METAPHORS** > METAPHOR
**METAPLASM** n nonliving constituents, such as starch and pigment granules, of the cytoplasm of a cell
**METAPLOT** > METAPELET
**METARCHON** n nontoxic substance, such as a chemical to mask pheromones, that reduces the persistence of a pest
**METASOMA** n posterior part of an arachnid's abdomen (opisthosoma) that never carries appendages
**METASOMAS** > METASOMA
**METATAG** n element of HTML describing the

contents of a web page and used by search engines to index pages by subject
**METATAGS** > METATAG
**METATARSI** pl n skeleton of human foot between toes and tarsus
**METATE** n stone for grinding grain on
**METATES** > METATE
**METAXYLEM** n xylem tissue that consists of rigid thick-walled cells and occurs in parts of the plant that have finished growing
**METAYAGE** n farming in which rent is paid in kind
**METAYAGES** > METAYAGE
**METAYER** n farmer who pays rent in kind
**METAYERS** > METAYER
**METAZOA** > METAZOAN
**METAZOAL** > METAZOAN
**METAZOAN** n any animal having a body composed of many cells: includes all animals except sponges and protozoans ▷ adj of the metazoans
**METAZOANS** > METAZOAN
**METAZOIC** adj of, relating to, or belonging to the Metazoa
**METAZOON** same
as > METAZOAN
**METCAST** n weather forecast
**METCASTS** > METCAST
**METE** vb deal out as punishment ▷ n (to) measure
**METED** > METE
**METEOR** n small fast-moving heavenly body, visible as a streak of incandescence if it enters the earth's atmosphere
**METEORIC** adj of a meteor
**METEORISM** another name for > TYMPANITES
**METEORIST** n person who studies meteors
**METEORITE** n meteor that has fallen to earth
**METEOROID** n any of the small celestial bodies that are thought to orbit the sun. When they enter the earth's atmosphere, they become visible as meteors
**METEOROUS** > METEOR
**METEORS** > METEOR
**METEPA** n type of pesticide
**METEPAS** > METEPA
**METER** same as > METRE
**METERAGE** n act of measuring
**METERAGES** > METERAGE
**METERED** > METER
**METERING** > METER
**METERS** > METER
**METES** > METE
**METESTICK** n measuring

rod
**METESTRUS** n period in the oestrous cycle following oestrus, characterized by lack of sexual activity
**METEWAND** same
as > METESTICK
**METEWANDS** > METEWAND
**METEYARD** same
as > METESTICK
**METEYARDS** > METEYARD
**METFORMIN** n drug used to treat diabetes
**METH** n variety of amphetamine
**METHADON** same
as > METHADONE
**METHADONE** n drug similar to morphine, sometimes prescribed as a heroin substitute
**METHADONS** > METHADON
**METHANAL** n colourless poisonous irritating gas with a pungent characteristic odour, made by the oxidation of methanol and used as formalin and in the manufacture of synthetic resins
**METHANALS** > METHANAL
**METHANE** n colourless inflammable gas
**METHANES** > METHANE
**METHANOIC** as in methanoic acid systematic name for formic acid
**METHANOL** n colourless poisonous liquid used as a solvent and fuel
**METHANOLS** > METHANOL
**METHEGLIN** n (esp formerly) spiced or medicated mead
**METHINK** same
as > METHINKS
**METHINKS** vb it seems to me
**METHO** n methylated spirits
**METHOD** n way or manner
**METHODIC** > METHOD
**METHODISE** same
as > METHODIZE
**METHODISM** n system and practices of the Methodist Church, developed by the English preacher John Wesley (1703–91) and his followers
**METHODIST** > METHODISM
**METHODIZE** vb organize according to a method
**METHODS** > METHOD
**METHOS** > METHO
**METHOUGHT** > METHINKS
**METHOXIDE** n saltlike compound in which the hydrogen atom in the hydroxyl group of methanol has been replaced by a metal atom, usually an alkali metal atom as in sodium

methoxide, NaOCH₃
**METHOXY** *n* steroid drug
**METHOXYL** *n* chemical compound of methyl and hydroxyl
**METHS** *n* methylated spirits
**METHYL** *n* compound containing a saturated hydrocarbon group of atoms
**METHYLAL** *n* colourless volatile flammable liquid
**METHYLALS** > METHYLAL
**METHYLASE** *n* enzyme
**METHYLATE** *vb* mix with methanol
**METHYLENE** *adj* of, consisting of, or containing the divalent group of atoms =CH₂
**METHYLIC** > METHYL
**METHYLS** > METHYL
**METHYSES** > METHYSIS
**METHYSIS** *n* drunkenness
**METHYSTIC** *adj* intoxicating
**METIC** *n* (in ancient Greece) an alien having some rights of citizenship in the city in which he lives
**METICAIS** > METICAL
**METICAL** *n* money unit in Mozambique
**METICALS** > METICAL
**METICS** > METIC
**METIER** *n* profession or trade
**METIERS** > METIER
**METIF** *n* person of mixed race
**METIFS** > METIF
**METING** > METE
**METIS** *n* person of mixed parentage
**METISSE** > METIS
**METISSES** > METIS
**METOL** *n* colourless soluble organic substance used, in the form of its sulphate, as a photographic developer
**METOLS** > METOL
**METONYM** *n* word used in a metonymy. For example *the bottle* is a metonym for *alcoholic drink*
**METONYMIC** > METONYMY
**METONYMS** > METONYM
**METONYMY** *n* figure of speech in which one thing is replaced by another associated with it, such as 'the Crown' for 'the queen'
**METOPAE** > METOPE
**METOPE** *n* square space between two triglyphs in a Doric frieze
**METOPES** > METOPE
**METOPIC** *adj* of or relating to the forehead
**METOPISM** *n* congenital disfigurement of forehead
**METOPISMS** > METOPISM

**METOPON** *n* painkilling drug
**METOPONS** > METOPON
**METOPRYL** *n* type of anaesthetic
**METOPRYLS** > METOPRYL
**METRALGIA** *n* pain in the uterus
**METRAZOL** *n* drug used to improve blood circulation
**METRAZOLS** > METRAZOL
**METRE** *n* basic unit of length equal to about 1.094 yards (100 centimetres) ▷ *vb* express in poetry
**METRED** > METRE
**METRES** > METRE
**METRIC** *adj* of the decimal system of weights and measures based on the metre
**METRICAL** *adj* of measurement
**METRICATE** *vb* convert a measuring system or instrument to metric units
**METRICIAN** *n* writer of metrical verse
**METRICISE** *vb* study metre of poetry
**METRICISM** > METRICISE
**METRICIST** *same as* > METRICIAN
**METRICIZE** *same as* > METRICISE
**METRICS** *n* art of using poetic metre
**METRIFIED** > METRIFY
**METRIFIER** > METRIFY
**METRIFIES** > METRIFY
**METRIFY** *vb* render into poetic metre
**METRING** > METRE
**METRIST** *n* person skilled in the use of poetic metre
**METRISTS** > METRIST
**METRITIS** *n* inflammation of the uterus
**METRO** *n* underground railway system, esp in Paris
**METROLOGY** *n* science of weights and measures
**METRONOME** *n* instrument which marks musical time by means of a ticking pendulum
**METROPLEX** *n* large urban area
**METROS** > METRO
**METS** > MET
**METTLE** *n* courage or spirit
**METTLED** *adj* spirited, courageous, or valiant
**METTLES** > METTLE
**METUMP** *n* band for carrying a load or burden
**METUMPS** > METUMP
**MEU** *another name for* > SPIGNEL
**MEUNIERE** *adj* (of fish) dredged with flour, fried in butter, and served with butter, lemon juice, and parsley

**MEUS** > MEU
**MEUSE** *n* gap (in fence, wall etc) through which an animal passed ▷ *vb* go through this gap
**MEUSED** > MEUSE
**MEUSES** > MEUSE
**MEUSING** > MEUSE
**MEVE** *same as* > MOVE
**MEVED** > MEVE
**MEVES** > MEVE
**MEVING** > MEVE
**MEVROU** *n* South African title of address equivalent to *Mrs* when placed before a surname or *madam* when used alone
**MEVROUS** > MEVROU
**MEW** *n* cry of a cat ▷ *vb* utter this cry
**MEWED** > MEW
**MEWING** > MEW
**MEWL** *vb* (esp of a baby) to cry weakly ▷ *n* weak or whimpering cry
**MEWLED** > MEWL
**MEWLER** > MEWL
**MEWLERS** > MEWL
**MEWLING** > MEWL
**MEWLS** > MEWL
**MEWS** *same as* > MEUSE
**MEWSED** > MEWS
**MEWSES** > MEWS
**MEWSING** > MEWS
**MEYNT** > MING
**MEZAIL** *same as* > MESAIL
**MEZAILS** > MEZAIL
**MEZCAL** *variant spelling of* > MESCAL
**MEZCALINE** *variant spelling of* > MESCALINE
**MEZCALS** > MEZCAL
**MEZE** *n* type of hors d'oeuvre eaten esp with an apéritif or other drink in Greece and the Near East
**MEZEREON** *same as* > MEZEREUM
**MEZEREONS** > MEZEREON
**MEZEREUM** *n* dried bark of certain shrubs of the genus *Daphne*, esp mezereon, formerly used as a vesicant and to treat arthritis
**MEZEREUMS** > MEZEREUM
**MEZES** > MEZE
**MEZQUIT** *same as* > MESQUITE
**MEZQUITE** *same as* > MESQUITE
**MEZQUITES** > MEZQUITE
**MEZQUITS** > MEZQUIT
**MEZUZA** *same as* > MEZUZAH
**MEZUZAH** *n* piece of parchment inscribed with biblical passages and fixed to the doorpost of the rooms of a Jewish house
**MEZUZAHS** > MEZUZAH
**MEZUZAS** > MEZUZA
**MEZUZOT** > MEZUZAH
**MEZUZOTH** > MEZUZAH

**MEZZ** *same as* > MEZZANINE
**MEZZALUNA** *n* half-moon shaped kitchen chopper
**MEZZANINE** *n* intermediate storey, esp between the ground and first floor ▷ *adj* of or relating to an intermediate stage in a financial process
**MEZZE** *same as* > MEZE
**MEZZES** > MEZZE
**MEZZO** *adv* moderately
**MEZZOS** > MEZZO
**MEZZOTINT** *n* method of engraving by scraping the roughened surface of a metal plate ▷ *vb* engrave (a copper plate) in this fashion
**MGANGA** *n* witch doctor
**MGANGAS** > MGANGA
**MHO** *former name for* > SIEMENS
**MHORR** *n* African gazelle
**MHORRS** > MHORR
**MHOS** > MHO
**MI** *n* (in tonic sol-fa) the third degree of any major scale
**MIAOU** *same as* > MEOW
**MIAOUED** > MIAOU
**MIAOUING** > MIAOU
**MIAOUS** > MIAOU
**MIAOW** *same as* > MEOW
**MIAOWED** > MIAOW
**MIAOWING** > MIAOW
**MIAOWS** > MIAOW
**MIASM** *same as* > MIASMA
**MIASMA** *n* unwholesome or foreboding atmosphere
**MIASMAL** > MIASMA
**MIASMAS** > MIASMA
**MIASMATA** > MIASMA
**MIASMATIC** > MIASMA
**MIASMIC** > MIASMA
**MIASMOUS** > MIASMA
**MIASMS** > MIASM
**MIAUL** *same as* > MEOW
**MIAULED** > MIAUL
**MIAULING** > MIAUL
**MIAULS** > MIAUL
**MIB** *n* marble used in games
**MIBS** > MIB
**MIC** *n* microphone
**MICA** *n* glasslike mineral used as an electrical insulator
**MICACEOUS** > MICA
**MICAS** > MICA
**MICATE** *vb* add mica to
**MICATED** > MICATE
**MICATES** > MICATE
**MICATING** > MICATE
**MICAWBER** *n* person who idles and trusts to fortune
**MICAWBERS** > MICAWBER
**MICE** > MOUSE
**MICELL** *same as* > MICELLE
**MICELLA** *same as* > MICELLE
**MICELLAE** > MICELLA
**MICELLAR** > MICELLE
**MICELLAS** > MICELLA
**MICELLE** *n* charged

aggregate of molecules of colloidal size in a solution
**MICELLES** > MICELLE
**MICELLS** > MICELL
**MICH** *same as* > MITCH
**MICHE** *same as* > MICH
**MICHED** > MICH
**MICHER** > MICH
**MICHERS** > MICH
**MICHES** > MICH
**MICHIGAN** US name for > NEWMARKET
**MICHIGANS** > MICHIGAN
**MICHING** > MICH
**MICHINGS** > MICH
**MICHT** n Scots word for might
**MICHTS** > MICHT
**MICK** n derogatory term for an Irish person
**MICKEY** n young bull, esp one that is wild and unbranded ▷ vb drug person's drink
**MICKEYED** > MICKEY
**MICKEYING** > MICKEY
**MICKEYS** > MICKEY
**MICKIES** > MICKY
**MICKLE** adj large or abundant ▷ adv much ▷ n great amount
**MICKLER** > MICKLE
**MICKLES** > MICKLE
**MICKLEST** > MICKLE
**MICKS** > MICK
**MICKY** *same as* > MICKEY
**MICO** n marmoset
**MICOS** > MICO
**MICRA** > MICRON
**MICRIFIED** > MICRIFY
**MICRIFIES** > MICRIFY
**MICRIFY** vb make very small
**MICRO** n small computer
**MICROBAR** n millionth of bar of pressure
**MICROBARS** > MICROBAR
**MICROBE** n minute organism, esp one causing disease
**MICROBEAM** n X-ray machine with narrow focussed beam
**MICROBES** > MICROBE
**MICROBIAL** > MICROBE
**MICROBIAN** > MICROBE
**MICROBIC** > MICROBE
**MICROBREW** n beer made in small brewery
**MICROBUS** n small bus
**MICROCAP** adj (of investments) involving very small amount of capital
**MICROCAR** n small car
**MICROCARD** n card containing microprint
**MICROCARS** > MICROCAR
**MICROCHIP** n small wafer of silicon containing electronic circuits ▷ vb implant (an animal) with a microchip tag linked to a national computer

network for purposes of identification
**MICROCODE** n set of computer instructions
**MICROCOPY** n greatly reduced photographic copy of a printed page, drawing, etc, on microfilm or microfiche
**MICROCOSM** n miniature representation of something
**MICROCYTE** n unusually small red blood cell
**MICRODONT** adj having unusually small teeth
**MICRODOT** n photographic copy of a document reduced to pinhead size
**MICRODOTS** > MICRODOT
**MICROFILM** n miniaturized recording of books or documents on a roll of film ▷ vb photograph a page or document on microfilm
**MICROFORM** n method of storing symbolic information by using photographic reduction techniques, such as microfilm, microfiche, etc
**MICROGLIA** n one of the two types of non-nervous tissue (glia) found in the central nervous system, having macrophage activity
**MICROGRAM** n photograph or drawing of an object as viewed through a microscope
**MICROHM** n millionth of ohm
**MICROHMS** > MICROHM
**MICROINCH** n millionth of inch
**MICROJET** n light jet-propelled aircraft
**MICROJETS** > MICROJET
**MICROLITE** n small private aircraft carrying no more than two people, with an empty weight of not more than 150 kg and a wing area not less than 10 square metres: used in pleasure flying and racing
**MICROLITH** n small Mesolithic flint tool which was made from a blade and formed part of hafted tools
**MICROLOAN** n very small loan
**MICROLOGY** n study of microscopic things
**MICROLUX** n millionth of a lux
**MICROMERE** n any of the small cells formed by unequal cleavage of a fertilized ovum
**MICROMESH** n very fine mesh

**MICROMHO** n millionth of mho
**MICROMHOS** > MICROMHO
**MICROMINI** n very short skirt
**MICROMOLE** n millionth of mole
**MICRON** n unit of length equal to $10^{-6}$ metre
**MICRONISE** *same as* > MICRONIZE
**MICRONIZE** vb break down to very small particles
**MICRONS** > MICRON
**MICROPORE** n very small pore
**MICROPSIA** n defect of vision in which objects appear to be smaller than they appear to a person with normal vision
**MICROPUMP** n small pump inserted in skin to automatically deliver medicine
**MICROPYLE** n small opening in the integuments of a plant ovule through which the male gametes pass
**MICROS** > MICRO
**MICROSITE** n website that is intended for a specific limited purpose and is often temporary
**MICROSOME** n any of the small particles consisting of ribosomes and fragments of attached endoplasmic reticulum that can be isolated from cells by centrifugal action
**MICROTOME** n instrument used for cutting thin sections, esp of biological material, for microscopical examination
**MICROTOMY** n cutting of sections with a microtome
**MICROTONE** n any musical interval smaller than a semitone
**MICROVOLT** n millionth of volt
**MICROWATT** n millionth of watt
**MICROWAVE** n electromagnetic wave with a wavelength of a few centimetres, used in radar and cooking ▷ vb cook in a microwave oven
**MICROWIRE** n very fine wire
**MICRURGY** n manipulation and examination of single cells under a microscope
**MICS** > MIC
**MICTION** n urination
**MICTIONS** > MICTION
**MICTURATE** vb urinate
**MID** adj intermediate, middle ▷ n middle ▷ prep amid
**MIDAIR** n some point

above ground level, in the air
**MIDAIRS** > MIDAIR
**MIDBRAIN** n part of the brain that develops from the middle portion of the embryonic neural tube
**MIDBRAINS** > MIDBRAIN
**MIDCAP** adj (of investments) involving very small amount
**MIDCOURSE** adj in middle of course
**MIDCULT** n middlebrow culture
**MIDCULTS** > MIDCULT
**MIDDAY** n noon
**MIDDAYS** > MIDDAY
**MIDDEN** n dunghill or rubbish heap
**MIDDENS** > MIDDEN
**MIDDEST** adj in middle
**MIDDIE** n glass or bottle containing 285ml of beer
**MIDDIES** > MIDDY
**MIDDLE** adj equidistant from two extremes ▷ n middle point or part ▷ vb place in the middle
**MIDDLED** > MIDDLE
**MIDDLEMAN** n trader who buys from the producer and sells to the consumer
**MIDDLEMEN** > MIDDLEMAN
**MIDDLER** n pupil in middle years at school
**MIDDLERS** > MIDDLER
**MIDDLES** > MIDDLE
**MIDDLING** adj mediocre ▷ adv moderately
**MIDDLINGS** pl n poorer or coarser part of flour or other products
**MIDDORSAL** adj in middle or back
**MIDDY** n middle-sized glass of beer
**MIDFIELD** n area between the two opposing defences
**MIDFIELDS** > MIDFIELD
**MIDGE** n small mosquito-like insect
**MIDGES** > MIDGE
**MIDGET** n very small person or thing ▷ adj much smaller than normal
**MIDGETS** > MIDGET
**MIDGIE** n informal word for a small winged biting insect such as the midge or sandfly
**MIDGIES** > MIDGIE
**MIDGUT** n middle part of the digestive tract of vertebrates, including the small intestine
**MIDGUTS** > MIDGUT
**MIDGY** > MIDGE
**MIDI** adj (of a skirt, coat, etc) reaching to below the knee or midcalf
**MIDINETTE** n Parisian seamstress or salesgirl in a clothes shop

**MIDIRON** n club, usually a No. 5, 6, or 7 iron, used for medium-length approach shots
**MIDIRONS** > MIDIRON
**MIDIS** > MIDI
**MIDISKIRT** n skirt of medium length
**MIDLAND** n middle part of a country
**MIDLANDS** > MIDLAND
**MIDLEG** n middle of leg
**MIDLEGS** > MIDLEG
**MIDLIFE** as in *midlife crisis* crisis that may be experienced in middle age involving frustration, panic, and feelings of pointlessness, sometimes resulting in radical and often ill-advised changes of lifestyle
**MIDLIFER** n middle-aged person
**MIDLIFERS** > MIDLIFER
**MIDLINE** n line at middle of something
**MIDLINES** > MIDLINE
**MIDLIST** n books in publisher's range that sell reasonably well
**MIDLISTS** > MIDLIST
**MIDLIVES** > MIDLIFE
**MIDMONTH** n middle of month
**MIDMONTHS** > MIDMONTH
**MIDMOST** adv in the middle or midst
**MIDMOSTS** > MIDMOST
**MIDNIGHT** n twelve o'clock at night
**MIDNIGHTS** > MIDNIGHT
**MIDNOON** n noon
**MIDNOONS** > MIDNOON
**MIDPOINT** n point on a line equally distant from either end
**MIDPOINTS** > MIDPOINT
**MIDRANGE** n part of loudspeaker
**MIDRANGES** > MIDRANGE
**MIDRASH** n homily on a scriptural passage derived by traditional Jewish exegetical methods and consisting usually of embellishment of the scriptural narrative
**MIDRASHIC** > MIDRASH
**MIDRASHIM** > MIDRASH
**MIDRASHOT** > MIDRASH
**MIDRIB** n main vein of a leaf, running down the centre of the blade
**MIDRIBS** > MIDRIB
**MIDRIFF** n middle part of the body
**MIDRIFFS** > MIDRIFF
**MIDS** > MID
**MIDSHIP** adj in, of, or relating to the middle of a vessel ▷ n middle of a vessel
**MIDSHIPS** See > AMIDSHIPS

**MIDSIZE** adj medium-sized
**MIDSIZED** same as > MIDSIZE
**MIDSOLE** n layer between the inner and the outer sole of a shoe, contoured for absorbing shock
**MIDSOLES** > MIDSOLE
**MIDSPACE** n area in middle of space
**MIDSPACES** > MIDSPACE
**MIDST** See > AMID
**MIDSTORY** n level of forest trees between smallest and tallest
**MIDSTREAM** n middle of a stream or river ▷ adj in or towards the middle of a stream or river
**MIDSTS** > MIDST
**MIDSUMMER** n middle of summer
**MIDTERM** n middle of a term in a school, university, etc
**MIDTERMS** > MIDTERM
**MIDTOWN** n centre of a town
**MIDTOWNS** > MIDTOWN
**MIDWATCH** n naval watch period beginning at midnight
**MIDWAY** adv halfway ▷ adj in or at the middle of the distance ▷ n place in a fair, carnival, etc, where sideshows are located
**MIDWAYS** > MIDWAY
**MIDWEEK** n middle of the week
**MIDWEEKLY** > MIDWEEK
**MIDWEEKS** > MIDWEEK
**MIDWIFE** n trained person who assists at childbirth ▷ vb act as midwife
**MIDWIFED** > MIDWIFE
**MIDWIFERY** n art or practice of a midwife
**MIDWIFES** > MIDWIFE
**MIDWIFING** > MIDWIFE
**MIDWINTER** n middle or depth of winter
**MIDWIVE** vb act as midwife
**MIDWIVED** > MIDWIVE
**MIDWIVES** > MIDWIFE
**MIDWIVING** > MIDWIVE
**MIDYEAR** n middle of the year
**MIDYEARS** > MIDYEAR
**MIELIE** same as > MEALIE
**MIELIES** > MIELIE
**MIEN** n person's bearing, demeanour, or appearance
**MIENS** > MIEN
**MIEVE** same as > MOVE
**MIEVED** > MIEVE
**MIEVES** > MIEVE
**MIEVING** > MIEVE
**MIFF** vb take offence or offend ▷ n petulant mood
**MIFFED** > MIFF
**MIFFIER** > MIFFY
**MIFFIEST** > MIFFY
**MIFFILY** > MIFFY
**MIFFINESS** > MIFFY
**MIFFING** > MIFF

**MIFFS** > MIFF
**MIFFY** adj easily upset
**MIFTY** same as > MIFFY
**MIG** n marble used in games
**MIGG** same as > MIG
**MIGGLE** n US word for playing marble
**MIGGLES** > MIGGLE
**MIGGS** > MIGG
**MIGHT** > MAY
**MIGHTEST** > MAY
**MIGHTFUL** same as > MIGHTY
**MIGHTIER** > MIGHTY
**MIGHTIEST** > MIGHTY
**MIGHTILY** adv great extent, amount, or degree
**MIGHTS** > MAY
**MIGHTST** > MAY
**MIGHTY** adj powerful ▷ adv very
**MIGMATITE** n composite rock body containing two types of rock (esp igneous and metamorphic rock) that have interacted with each other but are nevertheless still distinguishable
**MIGNON** adj small and pretty ▷ n tender boneless cut of meat
**MIGNONNE** > MIGNON
**MIGNONS** > MIGNON
**MIGRAINE** n severe headache, often with nausea and visual disturbances
**MIGRAINES** > MIGRAINE
**MIGRANT** n person or animal that moves from one place to another ▷ adj moving from one place to another
**MIGRANTS** > MIGRANT
**MIGRATE** vb move from one place to settle in another
**MIGRATED** > MIGRATE
**MIGRATES** > MIGRATE
**MIGRATING** > MIGRATE
**MIGRATION** n act or an instance of migrating
**MIGRATOR** > MIGRATE
**MIGRATORS** > MIGRATE
**MIGRATORY** adj (of an animal) migrating every year
**MIGS** > MIG
**MIHA** n young fern frond which has not yet opened
**MIHI** n Māori ceremonial greeting ▷ vb greet
**MIHIED** > MIHI
**MIHIING** > MIHI
**MIHIS** > MIHI
**MIHRAB** n niche in a mosque showing the direction of Mecca
**MIHRABS** > MIHRAB
**MIJNHEER** same as > MYNHEER
**MIJNHEERS** > MIJNHEER
**MIKADO** n Japanese emperor

**MIKADOS** > MIKADO
**MIKE** n microphone
**MIKED** > MIKE
**MIKES** > MIKE
**MIKING** > MIKE
**MIKRA** > MIKRON
**MIKRON** same as > MICRON
**MIKRONS** > MIKRON
**MIKVAH** n pool used esp by women for ritual purification after their monthly period
**MIKVAHS** > MIKVAH
**MIKVEH** same as > MIKVAH
**MIKVEHS** > MIKVEH
**MIKVOS** > MIKVEH
**MIKVOT** > MIKVEH
**MIKVOTH** > MIKVAH
**MIL** n unit of length equal to one thousandth of an inch
**MILADI** same as > MILADY
**MILADIES** > MILADY
**MILADIS** > MILADI
**MILADY** n (formerly) a continental title for an English gentlewoman
**MILAGE** same as > MILEAGE
**MILAGES** > MILAGE
**MILCH** adj (of a cow) giving milk
**MILCHIG** same as > MILCHIK
**MILCHIK** adj containing or used in the preparation of milk products and so not to be used with meat products
**MILD** adj not strongly flavoured ▷ n dark beer flavoured with fewer hops than bitter ▷ vb become gentle
**MILDED** > MILD
**MILDEN** vb make or become mild or milder
**MILDENED** > MILDEN
**MILDENING** > MILDEN
**MILDENS** > MILDEN
**MILDER** > MILD
**MILDEST** > MILD
**MILDEW** same as > MOULD
**MILDEWED** > MILDEW
**MILDEWING** > MILDEW
**MILDEWS** > MILDEW
**MILDEWY** > MILDEW
**MILDING** > MILD
**MILDLY** > MILD
**MILDNESS** > MILD
**MILDS** > MILD
**MILE** n unit of length equal to 1760 yards or 1.609 kilometres
**MILEAGE** n distance travelled in miles
**MILEAGES** > MILEAGE
**MILEPOST** n signpost that shows the distance in miles to or from a place
**MILEPOSTS** > MILEPOST
**MILER** n athlete, horse, etc, that specializes in races of one mile
**MILERS** > MILER
**MILES** > MILE

MILESIAN n Irishman

MILESIMO n Spanish word meaning thousandth

MILESIMOS > MILESIMO

MILESTONE same as > MILEPOST

MILFOIL same as > YARROW

MILFOILS > MILFOIL

MILIA > MILIUM

MILIARIA n acute itching eruption of the skin, caused by blockage of the sweat glands

MILIARIAL > MILIARIA

MILIARIAS > MILIARIA

MILIARY adj resembling or relating to millet seeds

MILIEU n environment or surroundings

MILIEUS > MILIEU

MILIEUX > MILIEU

MILITANCE > MILITANT

MILITANCY > MILITANT

MILITANT adj aggressive or vigorous in support of a cause ▷ n militant person

MILITANTS > MILITANT

MILITAR same as > MILITARY

MILITARIA pl n items of military interest, such as weapons, uniforms, medals, etc, esp from the past

MILITARY adj of or for soldiers, armies, or war ▷ n armed services

MILITATE vb have a strong influence or effect

MILITATED > MILITATE

MILITATES > MILITATE

MILITIA n military force of trained citizens for use in emergency only

MILITIAS > MILITIA

MILIUM n pimple

MILK n white fluid produced by female mammals to feed their young ▷ vb draw milk from

MILKED > MILK

MILKEN adj of or like milk

MILKER n cow, goat, etc, that yields milk, esp of a specified quality or amount

MILKERS > MILKER

MILKFISH n large silvery tropical clupeoid food and game fish, Chanos chanos: family Chanidae

MILKIER > MILKY

MILKIEST > MILKY

MILKILY > MILKY

MILKINESS > MILKY

MILKING > MILK

MILKINGS > MILKING

MILKLESS > MILK

MILKLIKE > MILK

MILKMAID n (esp in former times) woman who milks cows

MILKMAIDS > MILKMAID

MILKMAN n man who delivers milk to people's houses

MILKMEN > MILKMAN

MILKO informal name for > MILKMAN

MILKOS > MILKO

MILKS > MILK

MILKSHAKE n drink of flavoured milk

MILKSHED n area where milk is produced

MILKSHEDS > MILKSHED

MILKSOP n feeble man

MILKSOPPY > MILKSOP

MILKSOPS > MILKSOP

MILKTOAST n meek, submissive, or timid person

MILKWEED same as > MONARCH

MILKWEEDS > MILKWEED

MILKWOOD n tree producing latex

MILKWOODS > MILKWOOD

MILKWORT n any of several plants of the genus Polygala, having small blue, pink, or white flowers with two petal-like sepals: family Polygalaceae. They were formerly believed to increase milk production in cows

MILKWORTS > MILKWORT

MILKY adj of or like milk

MILL n factory ▷ vb grind, press, or process in or as if in a mill

MILLABLE > MILL

MILLAGE adj American tax rate calculated in thousandths per dollar

MILLAGES > MILLAGE

MILLBOARD n strong pasteboard, used esp in book covers

MILLCAKE n food for livestock

MILLCAKES > MILLCAKE

MILLDAM n dam built in a stream to raise the water level sufficiently for it to turn a millwheel

MILLDAMS > MILLDAM

MILLE French word for > THOUSAND

MILLED adj crushed or ground in a mill

MILLENARY adj of or relating to a thousand or to a thousand years ▷ n adherent of millenarianism

MILLENNIA n plural of millennium: period or cycle of one thousand years

MILLEPED same as > MILLEPEDE

MILLEPEDE same as > MILLIPEDE

MILLEPEDS > MILLEPED

MILLEPORE n any tropical colonial coral-like medusoid hydrozoan of the order Milleporina, esp of the genus Millepora, having a calcareous skeleton

MILLER n person who works in a mill

MILLERITE n yellow mineral consisting of nickel sulphide

MILLERS > MILLER

MILLES > MILLE

MILLET n type of cereal grass

MILLETS > MILLET

MILLHOUSE n house attached to mill

MILLIARD n one thousand millions

MILLIARDS > MILLIARD

MILLIARE n ancient Roman unit of distance

MILLIARES > MILLIARE

MILLIARY adj relating to or marking a distance equal to an ancient Roman mile of a thousand paces

MILLIBAR n unit of atmospheric pressure

MILLIBARS > MILLIBAR

MILLIE n derogatory name for a young working-class woman

MILLIEME n Tunisian monetary unit worth one thousandth of a dinar

MILLIEMES > MILLIEME

MILLIER n metric weight of million grams

MILLIERS > MILLIER

MILLIES > MILLIE

MILLIGAL n unit of gravity

MILLIGALS > MILLIGAL

MILLIGRAM n thousandth part of a gram

MILLILUX n thousandth of lux

MILLIME same as > MILLIEME

MILLIMES > MILLIME

MILLIMHO n thousandth of mho

MILLIMHOS > MILLIMHO

MILLIMOLE n thousandth of mole

MILLINE n measurement of advertising space

MILLINER n maker or seller of women's hats

MILLINERS > MILLINER

MILLINERY n hats, trimmings, etc, sold by a milliner

MILLINES > MILLINE

MILLING n act or process of grinding, cutting, pressing, or crushing in a mill

MILLINGS > MILLING

MILLIOHM n thousandth of ohm

MILLIOHMS > MILLIOHM

MILLION n one thousand thousands

MILLIONS > MILLION

MILLIONTH n one of 1 000 000 approximately equal parts of something ▷ adj being the ordinal number of 1 000 000 in numbering or counting order, etc

MILLIPED same as > MILLIPEDE

MILLIPEDE n small animal with a jointed body and many pairs of legs

MILLIPEDS > MILLIPED

MILLIREM n unit of radiation

MILLIREMS > MILLIREM

MILLIVOLT n thousandth of volt

MILLIWATT n thousandth of watt

MILLOCRAT n member of a government of millowners

MILLPOND n pool which provides water to turn a millwheel

MILLPONDS > MILLPOND

MILLRACE n current of water that turns a millwheel

MILLRACES > MILLRACE

MILLRIND n iron support fitted across an upper millstone

MILLRINDS > MILLRIND

MILLRUN same as > MILLRACE

MILLRUNS > MILLRUN

MILLS > MILL

MILLSCALE n scale on metal being heated

MILLSTONE n flat circular stone for grinding corn

MILLTAIL n channel carrying water away from mill

MILLTAILS > MILLTAIL

MILLWHEEL n waterwheel that drives a mill

MILLWORK n work done in a mill

MILLWORKS > MILLWORK

MILNEB n type of pesticide

MILNEBS > MILNEB

MILO n any of various early-growing cultivated varieties of sorghum with heads of yellow or pinkish seeds resembling millet

MILOMETER n device that records the number of miles that a bicycle or motor vehicle has travelled

MILOR same as > MILORD

MILORD n (formerly) a continental title used for an English gentleman

MILORDS > MILORD

MILORS > MILOR

MILOS > MILO

MILPA n form of subsistence agriculture in Mexico

MILPAS > MILPA

MILREIS n former monetary unit of Portugal

and Brazil, divided into
1000 reis
**MILS** > MIL
**MILSEY** n milk strainer
**MILSEYS** > MILSEY
**MILT** n sperm of fish ▷ vb
fertilize (the roe of a
female fish) with milt, esp
artificially
**MILTED** > MILT
**MILTER** n male fish that is
mature and ready to breed
**MILTERS** > MILTER
**MILTIER** > MILTY
**MILTIEST** > MILTY
**MILTING** > MILT
**MILTONIA** n tropical
American orchid
**MILTONIAS** > MILTONIA
**MILTS** > MILT
**MILTY** adj full of milt
**MILTZ** same as > MILT
**MILTZES** > MILTZ
**MILVINE** adj of kites and
related birds
**MIM** adj prim, modest, or
demure
**MIMBAR** n pulpit in mosque
**MIMBARS** > MIMBAR
**MIME** n acting without the
use of words ▷ vb act in
mime
**MIMED** > MIME
**MIMEO** vb mimeograph
**MIMEOED** > MIMEO
**MIMEOING** > MIMEO
**MIMEOS** > MIMEO
**MIMER** > MIME
**MIMERS** > MIME
**MIMES** > MIME
**MIMESES** > MIMESIS
**MIMESIS** n imitative
representation of nature
or human behaviour
**MIMESISES** > MIMESIS
**MIMESTER** > MIME
**MIMESTERS** > MIME
**MIMETIC** adj imitating or
representing something
**MIMETICAL** > MIMETIC
**MIMETITE** n rare secondary
mineral
**MIMETITES** > MIMETITE
**MIMIC** vb imitate (a
person or manner), esp
for satirical effect ▷ n
person or animal that is
good at mimicking ▷ adj
of, relating to, or using
mimicry
**MIMICAL** > MIMIC
**MIMICKED** > MIMIC
**MIMICKER** > MIMIC
**MIMICKERS** > MIMIC
**MIMICKING** > MIMIC
**MIMICRIES** > MIMICRY
**MIMICRY** n act or art of
copying or imitating
closely
**MIMICS** > MIMIC
**MIMING** > MIME
**MIMMER** > MIM
**MIMMEST** > MIM
**MIMMICK** same as > MINNICK

**MIMMICKED** > MIMMICK
**MIMMICKS** > MIMMICK
**MIMOSA** n shrub with
fluffy yellow flowers and
sensitive leaves
**MIMOSAS** > MIMOSA
**MIMSEY** same as > MIMSY
**MIMSIER** > MIMSY
**MIMSIEST** > MIMSY
**MIMSY** adj prim,
underwhelming, and
ineffectual
**MIMULUS** n plants
cultivated for their yellow
or red flowers
**MIMULUSES** > MIMULUS
**MINA** n ancient unit of
weight and money, used
in Asia Minor, equal to one
sixtieth of a talent
**MINABLE** > MINE
**MINACIOUS** adj
threatening
**MINACITY** > MINACIOUS
**MINAE** > MINA
**MINAR** n tower
**MINARET** n tall slender
tower of a mosque
**MINARETED** > MINARET
**MINARETS** > MINARET
**MINARS** > MINAR
**MINAS** > MINA
**MINATORY** adj threatening
or menacing
**MINBAR** same as > MIMBAR
**MINBARS** > MINBAR
**MINCE** vb cut or grind into
very small pieces ▷ n
minced meat
**MINCED** > MINCE
**MINCEMEAT** n sweet
mixture of dried fruit and
spices
**MINCER** n machine for
mincing meat
**MINCERS** > MINCER
**MINCES** > MINCE
**MINCEUR** adj (of food)
low-fat
**MINCIER** > MINCY
**MINCIEST** > MINCY
**MINCING** adj affected in
manner
**MINCINGLY** > MINCING
**MINCINGS** > MINCING
**MINCY** adj effeminate
**MIND** n thinking faculties
▷ vb take offence at
**MINDED** adj having an
inclination as specified
**MINDER** n aide or
bodyguard
**MINDERS** > MINDER
**MINDFUCK** n taboo term
for deliberate infliction of
psychological damage
**MINDFUCKS** > MINDFUCK
**MINDFUL** adj heedful
**MINDFULLY** > MINDFUL
**MINDING** > MIND
**MINDINGS** > MIND
**MINDLESS** adj stupid
**MINDS** > MIND
**MINDSET** n ideas and

attitudes with which
a person approaches a
situation, esp when these
are seen as being difficult
to alter
**MINDSETS** > MINDSET
**MINDSHARE** n level of
awareness in the minds
of consumers that a
particular product
commands
**MINE** pron belonging to me
▷ n deep hole for digging
out coal, ores, etc ▷ vb dig
for minerals
**MINEABLE** > MINE
**MINED** > MINE
**MINEFIELD** n area of land
or water containing mines
**MINELAYER** n warship or
aircraft for carrying and
laying mines
**MINEOLA** same
as > MINNEOLA
**MINEOLAS** > MINEOLA
**MINER** n person who works
in a mine
**MINERAL** n naturally
occurring inorganic
substance, such as metal
▷ adj of, containing, or like
minerals
**MINERALS** > MINERAL
**MINERS** > MINER
**MINES** > MINE
**MINESHAFT** n vertical
entrance into mine
**MINESTONE** n ore
**MINETTE** n type of rock
**MINETTES** > MINETTE
**MINEVER** same as > MINIVER
**MINEVERS** > MINEVER
**MING** vb mix
**MINGE** n taboo word fore
female genitals
**MINGED** > MING
**MINGER** n unattractive
person
**MINGERS** > MINGER
**MINGES** > MINGE
**MINGIER** > MINGY
**MINGIEST** > MINGY
**MINGIN** same as > MINGING
**MINGINESS** > MINGY
**MINGING** adj unattractive
or unpleasant
**MINGLE** vb mix or blend
**MINGLED** > MINGLE
**MINGLER** > MINGLE
**MINGLERS** > MINGLE
**MINGLES** > MINGLE
**MINGLING** > MINGLE
**MINGLINGS** > MINGLE
**MINGS** > MING
**MINGY** adj miserly
**MINI** same as > MINIDRESS
**MINIATE** vb paint with
minium
**MINIATED** > MINIATE
**MINIATES** > MINIATE
**MINIATING** > MINIATE
**MINIATION** > MINIATE
**MINIATURE** n small
portrait, model, or copy

▷ adj small-scale ▷ vb
reproduce in miniature
**MINIBAR** n selection of
drinks and confectionery
provided in a hotel room
**MINIBARS** > MINIBAR
**MINIBIKE** n light
motorcycle
**MINIBIKER** > MINIBIKE
**MINIBIKES** > MINIBIKE
**MINIBREAK** n short holiday
**MINIBUS** n small bus
**MINIBUSES** > MINIBUS
**MINICAB** n ordinary car
used as a taxi
**MINICABS** > MINICAB
**MINICAM** n portable
television camera
**MINICAMP** n period spent
together in isolation by
sports team
**MINICAMPS** > MINICAMP
**MINICAMS** > MINICAM
**MINICAR** n small car
**MINICARS** > MINICAR
**MINICOM** n device used by
deaf and hard-of-hearing
people, allowing typed
telephone messages to be
sent and received
**MINICOMS** > MINICOM
**MINIDISC** n small
recordable compact disc
**MINIDISCS** > MINIDISC
**MINIDISH** n small
parabolic aerial for
reception or transmission
to a communications
satellite
**MINIDISK** same
as > MINIDISC
**MINIDISKS** > MINIDISK
**MINIDRESS** n very short
dress, at least four inches
above the knee
**MINIER** > MINY
**MINIEST** > MINY
**MINIFIED** > MINIFY
**MINIFIES** > MINIFY
**MINIFY** vb minimize
or lessen the size
or importance of
(something)
**MINIFYING** > MINIFY
**MINIKIN** n small, dainty,
or affected person or thing
▷ adj dainty, prim, or
affected
**MINIKINS** > MINIKIN
**MINILAB** n equipment for
processing photographic
film
**MINILABS** > MINILAB
**MINIM** n note half the
length of a semibreve ▷ adj
very small
**MINIMA** > MINIMUM
**MINIMAL** adj minimum ▷ n
small surfboard
**MINIMALLY** > MINIMAL
**MINIMALS** > MINIMAL
**MINIMAX** n lowest of a set
of maximum values ▷ vb
make maximum as low as

possible
**MINIMAXED** > MINIMAX
**MINIMAXES** > MINIMAX
**MINIMENT** same
as > MUNIMENT
**MINIMENTS** > MINIMENT
**MINIMILL** n small mill
**MINIMILLS** > MINIMILL
**MINIMISE** same
as > MINIMIZE
**MINIMISED** > MINIMISE
**MINIMISER** > MINIMIZE
**MINIMISES** > MINIMISE
**MINIMISM** n desire to
reduce to minimum
**MINIMISMS** > MINIMISM
**MINIMIST** > MINIMISM
**MINIMISTS** > MINIMISM
**MINIMIZE** vb reduce to a
minimum
**MINIMIZED** > MINIMIZE
**MINIMIZER** > MINIMIZE
**MINIMIZES** > MINIMIZE
**MINIMOTO** n reduced-size
replica motorcycle used for
racing
**MINIMOTOS** > MINIMOTO
**MINIMS** > MINIM
**MINIMUM** n least possible
(amount or number) ▷ adj
of, being, or showing a
minimum or minimums
**MINIMUMS** > MINIMUM
**MINIMUS** adj youngest:
sometimes used after the
surname of a schoolboy
having elder brothers at
the same school
**MINIMUSES** > MINIMUS
**MINING** n act, process, or
industry of extracting coal
or ores from the earth
**MININGS** > MINING
**MINION** n servile assistant
▷ adj dainty, pretty, or
elegant
**MINIONS** > MINION
**MINIPARK** n small park
**MINIPARKS** > MINIPARK
**MINIPILL** n low-dose oral
contraceptive containing
a progestogen only
**MINIPILLS** > MINIPILL
**MINIRUGBY** n version of
rugby with fewer players
**MINIS** > MINI
**MINISCULE** same
as > MINUSCULE
**MINISH** vb diminish
**MINISHED** > MINISH
**MINISHES** > MINISH
**MINISHING** > MINISH
**MINISKI** n short ski
**MINISKIRT** n very short
skirt
**MINISKIS** > MINISKI
**MINISTATE** n small
independent state
**MINISTER** n head of a
government department
▷ vb attend to the needs of
**MINISTERS** > MINISTER
**MINISTRY** n profession or
duties of a clergyman

**MINITOWER** n computer in
small vertical cabinet
**MINITRACK** n satellite
tracking system
**MINIUM** n bright red
poisonous insoluble oxide
of lead usually obtained
as a powder by heating
litharge in air
**MINIUMS** > MINIUM
**MINIVAN** n small van, esp
one with seats in the back
for carrying passengers
**MINIVANS** > MINIVAN
**MINIVER** n white fur, used
in ceremonial costumes
**MINIVERS** > MINIVER
**MINIVET** n any brightly
coloured tropical Asian
cuckoo shrike of the genus
Pericrocotus
**MINIVETS** > MINIVET
**MINK** n stoatlike animal
**MINKE** as in minke whale
type of small whalebone
whale or rorqual
**MINKES** > MINKE
**MINKS** > MINK
**MINNEOLA** n juicy citrus
fruit that is a cross
between a tangerine and a
grapefruit
**MINNEOLAS** > MINNEOLA
**MINNICK** vb behave in fussy
way
**MINNICKED** > MINNICK
**MINNICKS** > MINNICK
**MINNIE** n mother
**MINNIES** > MINNIE
**MINNOCK** same as > MINNICK
**MINNOCKED** > MINNOCK
**MINNOCKS** > MINNOCK
**MINNOW** n small freshwater
fish
**MINNOWS** > MINNOW
**MINNY** same as > MINNIE
**MINO** same as > MYNAH
**MINOR** adj lesser ▷ n
person regarded legally as
a child ▷ vb take a minor
**MINORCA** n breed of light
domestic fowl with glossy
white, black, or blue
plumage
**MINORCAS** > MINORCA
**MINORED** > MINOR
**MINORING** > MINOR
**MINORITY** n lesser number
**MINORS** > MINOR
**MINORSHIP** > MINOR
**MINOS** > MINO
**MINOXIDIL** n drug used to
counter baldness
**MINSHUKU** n guesthouse
in Japan
**MINSHUKUS** > MINSHUKU
**MINSTER** n cathedral or
large church
**MINSTERS** > MINSTER
**MINSTREL** n medieval
singer or musician
**MINSTRELS** > MINSTREL
**MINT** n plant with aromatic
leaves used for seasoning

and flavouring ▷ vb make
(coins)
**MINTAGE** n process of
minting
**MINTAGES** > MINTAGE
**MINTED** > MINT
**MINTER** > MINT
**MINTERS** > MINT
**MINTIER** > MINT
**MINTIEST** > MINT
**MINTING** > MINT
**MINTS** > MINT
**MINTY** > MINT
**MINUEND** n number from
which another number is
to be subtracted
**MINUENDS** > MINUEND
**MINUET** n stately dance
**MINUETS** > MINUET
**MINUS** adj indicating
subtraction ▷ n sign (-)
denoting subtraction or
a number less than zero
▷ prep reduced by the
subtraction of
**MINUSCULE** adj very small
▷ n lower-case letter
**MINUSES** > MINUS
**MINUTE** n 60th part of an
hour or degree ▷ vb record
in the minutes ▷ adj very
small
**MINUTED** > MINUTE
**MINUTELY** adv in great
detail ▷ adj occurring
every minute
**MINUTEMAN** n (in the War of
American Independence)
colonial militiaman who
promised to be ready
to fight at one minute's
notice
**MINUTEMEN** > MINUTEMAN
**MINUTER** > MINUTE
**MINUTES** pl n official record
of the proceedings of a
meeting or conference
**MINUTEST** > MINUTE
**MINUTIA** singular noun
of > MINUTIAE
**MINUTIAE** pl n trifling or
precise details
**MINUTIAL** > MINUTIAE
**MINUTING** > MINUTE
**MINUTIOSE** > MINUTIAE
**MINX** n bold or flirtatious
girl
**MINXES** > MINX
**MINXISH** > MINX
**MINY** adj of or like mines
**MINYAN** n number of
persons required by Jewish
law to be present for a
religious service, namely,
at least ten males over
thirteen years of age
**MINYANIM** > MINYAN
**MINYANS** > MINYAN
**MIOCENE** adj of, denoting,
or formed in the fourth
epoch of the Tertiary
period, between the
Oligocene and Pliocene
epochs, which lasted for 19

million years
**MIOMBO** n (in E Africa) a dry
wooded area with sparse
deciduous growth
**MIOMBOS** > MIOMBO
**MIOSES** > MIOSIS
**MIOSIS** n excessive
contraction of the pupil of
the eye, as in response to
drugs
**MIOTIC** > MIOSIS
**MIOTICS** > MIOSIS
**MIPS** n million instructions
per second: a unit used
to express the speed of
a computer's central
processing unit
**MIQUELET** n type of lock on
old firearm
**MIQUELETS** > MIQUELET
**MIR** n peasant commune in
prerevolutionary Russia
**MIRABELLE** n small sweet
yellow-orange fruit that is
a variety of greengage
**MIRABILIA** n wonders
**MIRABILIS** n tropical
American plant
**MIRABLE** adj wonderful
**MIRACIDIA** n plural form
of singular miracidium:
flat ciliated larva of flukes
that hatches from the egg
and gives rise asexually to
other larval forms
**MIRACLE** n wonderful
supernatural event
**MIRACLES** > MIRACLE
**MIRADOR** n window,
balcony, or turret
**MIRADORS** > MIRADOR
**MIRAGE** n optical illusion,
esp one caused by hot air
**MIRAGES** > MIRAGE
**MIRANDIZE** vb (in USA)
inform arrested person of
rights
**MIRBANE** n substance used
in perfumes
**MIRBANES** > MIRBANE
**MIRCHI** Indian English word
for > HOT
**MIRE** n swampy ground
▷ vb sink or be stuck in a
mire
**MIRED** > MIRE
**MIREPOIX** n mixture of
sautéed root vegetables
used as a base for braising
meat or for various sauces
**MIRES** > MIRE
**MIREX** n type of insecticide
**MIREXES** > MIREX
**MIRI** > MIR
**MIRIER** > MIRE
**MIRIEST** > MIRE
**MIRIFIC** adj achieving
wonderful things
**MIRIFICAL** same
as > MIRIFIC
**MIRIN** n Japanese rice wine
**MIRINESS** > MIRE
**MIRING** > MIRE
**MIRINS** > MIRIN

**MIRITI** *n* South American palm
**MIRITIS** > MIRITI
**MIRK** *same as* > MURK
**MIRKER** > MIRK
**MIRKEST** > MIRK
**MIRKIER** > MIRK
**MIRKIEST** > MURKY
**MIRKILY** > MIRK
**MIRKINESS** > MIRK
**MIRKS** > MIRK
**MIRKY** > MIRK
**MIRLIER** > MIRLY
**MIRLIEST** > MIRLY
**MIRLIGOES** *n* dizzy feeling
**MIRLITON** *another name (chiefly US) for* > CHAYOTE
**MIRLITONS** > MIRLITON
**MIRLY** *same as* > MARLY
**MIRO** *n* tall New Zealand tree
**MIROMIRO** *n* small New Zealand bird
**MIRROR** *n* coated glass surface for reflecting images ▷ *vb* reflect in or as if in a mirror
**MIRRORED** > MIRROR
**MIRRORING** > MIRROR
**MIRRORS** > MIRROR
**MIRS** > MIR
**MIRTH** *n* laughter, merriment, or gaiety
**MIRTHFUL** > MIRTH
**MIRTHLESS** > MIRTH
**MIRTHS** > MIRTH
**MIRV** *n* missile that has several warheads, each one being directed to different enemy targets ▷ *vb* arm with mirvs
**MIRVED** > MIRV
**MIRVING** > MIRV
**MIRVS** > MIRV
**MIRY** > MIRE
**MIRZA** *n* title of respect placed before the surname of an official, scholar, or other distinguished man
**MIRZAS** > MIRZA
**MIS** > MI
**MISACT** *vb* act wrongly
**MISACTED** > MISACT
**MISACTING** > MISACT
**MISACTS** > MISACT
**MISADAPT** *vb* adapt badly
**MISADAPTS** > MISADAPT
**MISADD** *vb* add badly
**MISADDED** > MISADD
**MISADDING** > MISADD
**MISADDS** > MISADD
**MISADJUST** *vb* adjust wrongly
**MISADVICE** *n* bad advice
**MISADVISE** *vb* give bad advice to
**MISAGENT** *n* bad agent
**MISAGENTS** > MISAGENT
**MISAIM** *vb* aim badly
**MISAIMED** > MISAIM
**MISAIMING** > MISAIM
**MISAIMS** > MISAIM
**MISALIGN** *vb* align badly
**MISALIGNS** > MISALIGN

**MISALLEGE** *vb* allege wrongly
**MISALLIED** > MISALLY
**MISALLIES** > MISALLY
**MISALLOT** *vb* allot wrongly
**MISALLOTS** > MISALLOT
**MISALLY** *vb* form unsuitable alliance
**MISALTER** *vb* alter wrongly
**MISALTERS** > MISALTER
**MISANDRY** *n* hatred of men
**MISAPPLY** *vb* use something for a purpose for which it is not intended or is not suited
**MISARRAY** *n* disarray
**MISARRAYS** > MISARRAY
**MISASSAY** *vb* assay wrongly
**MISASSAYS** > MISASSAY
**MISASSIGN** *vb* assign wrongly
**MISATE** > MISEAT
**MISATONE** *vb* atone wrongly
**MISATONED** > MISATONE
**MISATONES** > MISATONE
**MISAUNTER** *n* misadventure
**MISAVER** *vb* claim wrongly
**MISAVERS** > MISAVER
**MISAVISED** *adj* badly advised
**MISAWARD** *vb* award wrongly
**MISAWARDS** > MISAWARD
**MISBECAME** > MISBECOME
**MISBECOME** *vb* be unbecoming to or unsuitable for
**MISBEGAN** > MISBEGIN
**MISBEGIN** *vb* begin badly
**MISBEGINS** > MISBEGIN
**MISBEGOT** *adj* illegitimate
**MISBEGUN** > MISBEGIN
**MISBEHAVE** *vb* behave badly
**MISBELIEF** *n* false or unorthodox belief
**MISBESEEM** *vb* be unsuitable for
**MISBESTOW** *vb* bestow wrongly
**MISBIAS** *vb* prejudice wrongly
**MISBIASED** > MISBIAS
**MISBIASES** > MISBIAS
**MISBILL** *vb* present inaccurate bill
**MISBILLED** > MISBILL
**MISBILLS** > MISBILL
**MISBIND** *vb* bind wrongly
**MISBINDS** > MISBIND
**MISBIRTH** *n* abortion
**MISBIRTHS** > MISBIRTH
**MISBORN** *adj* abortive
**MISBOUND** > MISBIND
**MISBRAND** *vb* put misleading label on
**MISBRANDS** > MISBRAND
**MISBUILD** *vb* build badly
**MISBUILDS** > MISBUILD
**MISBUILT** > MISBUILD
**MISBUTTON** *vb* button

wrongly
**MISCALL** *vb* call by the wrong name
**MISCALLED** > MISCALL
**MISCALLER** > MISCALL
**MISCALLS** > MISCALL
**MISCARRY** *vb* have a miscarriage
**MISCAST** *vb* cast (a role or actor) in (a play or film) inappropriately
**MISCASTS** > MISCAST
**MISCEGEN** *n* person of mixed race
**MISCEGENE** *same as* > MISCEGEN
**MISCEGENS** > MISCEGEN
**MISCEGINE** *same as* > MISCEGEN
**MISCH** as in *misch metal* alloy of cerium and other rare earth metals, used esp as a flint in cigarette lighters
**MISCHANCE** *n* unlucky event
**MISCHANCY** *adj* unlucky
**MISCHARGE** *vb* charge wrongly
**MISCHIEF** *n* annoying but not malicious behaviour
**MISCHIEFS** > MISCHIEF
**MISCHOICE** *n* bad choice
**MISCHOOSE** *vb* make bad choice
**MISCHOSE** > MISCHOOSE
**MISCHOSEN** > MISCHOOSE
**MISCIBLE** *adj* able to be mixed
**MISCITE** *vb* cite wrongly
**MISCITED** > MISCITE
**MISCITES** > MISCITE
**MISCITING** > MISCITE
**MISCLAIM** *vb* claim wrongly
**MISCLAIMS** > MISCLAIM
**MISCLASS** *adj* class badly
**MISCODE** *vb* code wrongly
**MISCODED** > MISCODE
**MISCODES** > MISCODE
**MISCODING** > MISCODE
**MISCOIN** *vb* coin wrongly
**MISCOINED** > MISCOIN
**MISCOINS** > MISCOIN
**MISCOLOR** *same as* > MISCOLOUR
**MISCOLORS** > MISCOLOR
**MISCOLOUR** *vb* give wrong colour to
**MISCOOK** *vb* cook badly
**MISCOOKED** > MISCOOK
**MISCOOKS** > MISCOOK
**MISCOPIED** > MISCOPY
**MISCOPIES** > MISCOPY
**MISCOPY** *vb* copy badly
**MISCOUNT** *vb* count or calculate incorrectly ▷ *n* false count or calculation
**MISCOUNTS** > MISCOUNT
**MISCREANT** *n* wrongdoer ▷ *adj* evil or villainous
**MISCREATE** *vb* create (something) badly or incorrectly ▷ *adj* badly

or unnaturally formed or made
**MISCREDIT** *vb* disbelieve
**MISCREED** *n* false creed
**MISCREEDS** > MISCREED
**MISCUE** *n* faulty stroke in which the cue tip slips off the cue ball or misses it altogether ▷ *vb* make a miscue
**MISCUED** > MISCUE
**MISCUEING** > MISCUE
**MISCUES** > MISCUE
**MISCUING** > MISCUE
**MISCUT** *n* cut wrongly
**MISCUTS** > MISCUT
**MISDATE** *vb* date (a letter, event, etc) wrongly
**MISDATED** > MISDATE
**MISDATES** > MISDATE
**MISDATING** > MISDATE
**MISDEAL** *vb* deal out cards incorrectly ▷ *n* faulty deal
**MISDEALER** > MISDEAL
**MISDEALS** > MISDEAL
**MISDEALT** > MISDEAL
**MISDEED** *n* wrongful act
**MISDEEDS** > MISDEED
**MISDEEM** *vb* form bad opinion of
**MISDEEMED** > MISDEEM
**MISDEEMS** > MISDEEM
**MISDEFINE** *vb* define badly
**MISDEMEAN** *rare word for* > MISBEHAVE
**MISDEMPT** > MISDEEM
**MISDESERT** *n* quality of being undeserving
**MISDIAL** *vb* dial telephone number incorrectly
**MISDIALED** > MISDIAL
**MISDIALS** > MISDIAL
**MISDID** > MISDO
**MISDIET** *n* wrong diet
**MISDIETS** > MISDIET
**MISDIGHT** *adj* done badly
**MISDIRECT** *vb* give (someone) wrong directions or instructions
**MISDIVIDE** *vb* divide wrongly
**MISDO** *vb* do badly or wrongly
**MISDOER** > MISDO
**MISDOERS** > MISDO
**MISDOES** > MISDO
**MISDOING** > MISDO
**MISDOINGS** > MISDO
**MISDONE** *adj* done badly
**MISDONNE** *same as* > MISDONE
**MISDOUBT** *archaic word for* > DOUBT
**MISDOUBTS** > MISDOUBT
**MISDRAW** *vb* draw poorly
**MISDRAWN** > MISDRAW
**MISDRAWS** > MISDRAW
**MISDREAD** *n* fear of approaching evil
**MISDREADS** > MISDREAD
**MISDREW** > MISDRAW
**MISDRIVE** *vb* drive badly
**MISDRIVEN** > MISDRIVE
**MISDRIVES** > MISDRIVE

MISDROVE > MISDRIVE
MISE n issue in the obsolete writ of right
MISEASE n unease
MISEASES > MISEASE
MISEAT vb eat unhealthy food
MISEATEN > MISEAT
MISEATING > MISEAT
MISEATS > MISEAT
MISEDIT vb edit badly
MISEDITED > MISEDIT
MISEDITS > MISEDIT
MISEMPLOY vb employ badly
MISENROL vb enrol wrongly
MISENROLL same
   as > MISENROL
MISENROLS > MISENROL
MISENTER vb enter wrongly
MISENTERS > MISENTER
MISENTRY n wrong or mistaken entry
MISER n person who hoards money and hates spending it
MISERABLE adj very unhappy, wretched ▷ n wretched person
MISERABLY > MISERABLE
MISERE n call in solo whist and other card games declaring a hand that will win no tricks
MISERERE n type of psalm
MISERERES > MISERERE
MISERES > MISERE
MISERIES > MISERY
MISERLIER > MISERLY
MISERLY adj of or resembling a miser
MISERS > MISER
MISERY n great unhappiness
MISES > MISE
MISESTEEM n lack of respect
MISEVENT n mishap
MISEVENTS > MISEVENT
MISFAITH n distrust
MISFAITHS > MISFAITH
MISFALL vb happen as piece of bad luck
MISFALLEN > MISFALL
MISFALLS > MISFALL
MISFALNE > MISFALL
MISFARE vb get on badly
MISFARED > MISFARE
MISFARES > MISFARE
MISFARING > MISFARE
MISFEASOR n someone who carries out the improper performance of an act that is lawful in itself
MISFED > MISFEED
MISFEED vb feed wrongly
MISFEEDS > MISFEED
MISFEIGN vb feign with evil motive
MISFEIGNS > MISFEIGN
MISFELL > MISFALL
MISFIELD vb fail to field properly

MISFIELDS > MISFIELD
MISFILE vb file (papers, records, etc) wrongly
MISFILED > MISFILE
MISFILES > MISFILE
MISFILING > MISFILE
MISFIRE vb (of a firearm or engine) fail to fire correctly ▷ n act or an instance of misfiring
MISFIRED > MISFIRE
MISFIRES > MISFIRE
MISFIRING > MISFIRE
MISFIT n person not suited to his or her social environment ▷ vb fail to fit or be fitted
MISFITS > MISFIT
MISFITTED > MISFIT
MISFOCUS n wrong or poor focus
MISFORM vb form badly
MISFORMED > MISFORM
MISFORMS > MISFORM
MISFRAME vb frame wrongly
MISFRAMED > MISFRAME
MISFRAMES > MISFRAME
MISGAUGE vb gauge badly
MISGAUGED > MISGAUGE
MISGAUGES > MISGAUGE
MISGAVE > MISGIVE
MISGIVE vb make or be apprehensive or suspicious
MISGIVEN > MISGIVE
MISGIVES > MISGIVE
MISGIVING n feeling of fear or doubt
MISGO vb go wrong way
MISGOES > MISGO
MISGOING > MISGO
MISGONE > MISGO
MISGOTTEN adj obtained dishonestly
MISGOVERN vb govern badly
MISGRADE vb grade wrongly
MISGRADED > MISGRADE
MISGRADES > MISGRADE
MISGRAFF adj badly done
MISGRAFT vb graft wrongly
MISGRAFTS > MISGRAFT
MISGREW > MISGROW
MISGROW vb grow in unsuitable way
MISGROWN > MISGROW
MISGROWS > MISGROW
MISGROWTH > MISGROW
MISGUESS vb guess wrongly
MISGUGGLE vb handle incompetently
MISGUIDE vb guide or direct wrongly or badly
MISGUIDED adj mistaken or unwise
MISGUIDER > MISGUIDE
MISGUIDES > MISGUIDE
MISHANDLE vb handle badly or inefficiently
MISHANTER n misfortune
MISHAP n minor accident

▷ vb happen as bad luck
MISHAPPED > MISHAP
MISHAPPEN vb happen as bad luck
MISHAPS > MISHAP
MISHAPT same
   as > MISSHAPEN
MISHEAR vb hear (what someone says) wrongly
MISHEARD > MISHEAR
MISHEARS > MISHEAR
MISHEGAAS same
   as > MESHUGAAS
MISHEGOSS same
   as > MESHUGAAS
MISHIT n faulty shot, kick, or stroke ▷ vb hit or kick a ball with a faulty stroke
MISHITS > MISHIT
MISHMASH n confused collection or mixture
MISHMEE n root of Asian plant
MISHMEES > MISHMEE
MISHMI n evergreen perennial plant
MISHMIS > MISHMI
MISHMOSH same
   as > MISHMASH
MISINFER vb infer wrongly
MISINFERS > MISINFER
MISINFORM vb give incorrect information to
MISINTEND vb intend to harm
MISINTER vb bury wrongly
MISINTERS > MISINTER
MISJOIN vb join badly
MISJOINED > MISJOIN
MISJOINS > MISJOIN
MISJUDGE vb judge wrongly or unfairly
MISJUDGED > MISJUDGE
MISJUDGER > MISJUDGE
MISJUDGES > MISJUDGE
MISKAL n unit of weight in Iran
MISKALS > MISKAL
MISKEEP vb keep wrongly
MISKEEPS > MISKEEP
MISKEN vb be unaware of
MISKENNED > MISKEN
MISKENS > MISKEN
MISKENT > MISKEN
MISKEPT > MISKEEP
MISKEY vb key wrongly
MISKEYED > MISKEY
MISKEYING > MISKEY
MISKEYS > MISKEY
MISKICK vb fail to kick properly
MISKICKED > MISKICK
MISKICKS > MISKICK
MISKNEW vb > MISKNOW
MISKNOW have wrong idea about
MISKNOWN > MISKNOW
MISKNOWS > MISKNOW
MISLABEL vb label badly
MISLABELS > MISLABEL
MISLABOR vb labour wrongly
MISLABORS > MISLABOR
MISLAID > MISLAY

MISLAIN > MISLAY
MISLAY vb lose (something) temporarily
MISLAYER > MISLAY
MISLAYERS > MISLAY
MISLAYING > MISLAY
MISLAYS > MISLAY
MISLEAD vb give false or confusing information to
MISLEADER > MISLEAD
MISLEADS > MISLEAD
MISLEARED adj badly brought up
MISLEARN vb learn wrongly
MISLEARNS > MISLEARN
MISLEARNT > MISLEARN
MISLED > MISLEAD
MISLEEKE same
   as > MISLIKE
MISLEEKED > MISLEEKE
MISLEEKES > MISLEEKE
MISLETOE same
   as > MISTLETOE
MISLETOES > MISLETOE
MISLIE vb lie wrongly
MISLIES > MISLIE
MISLIGHT vb use light to lead astray
MISLIGHTS > MISLIGHT
MISLIKE vb dislike ▷ n dislike or aversion
MISLIKED > MISLIKE
MISLIKER > MISLIKE
MISLIKERS > MISLIKE
MISLIKES > MISLIKE
MISLIKING > MISLIKE
MISLIPPEN vb distrust
MISLIT > MISLIGHT
MISLIVE vb live wickedly
MISLIVED > MISLIVE
MISLIVES > MISLIVE
MISLIVING > MISLIVE
MISLOCATE vb put in wrong place
MISLODGE vb lodge wrongly
MISLODGED > MISLODGE
MISLODGES > MISLODGE
MISLUCK vb have bad luck
MISLUCKED > MISLUCK
MISLUCKS > MISLUCK
MISLYING > MISLIE
MISMADE > MISMAKE
MISMAKE vb make badly
MISMAKES > MISMAKE
MISMAKING > MISMAKE
MISMANAGE vb organize or run (something) badly
MISMARK vb mark wrongly
MISMARKED > MISMARK
MISMARKS > MISMARK
MISMARRY vb make unsuitable marriage
MISMATCH vb form an unsuitable partner, opponent, or set ▷ n unsuitable match
MISMATE vb mate wrongly
MISMATED > MISMATE
MISMATES > MISMATE
MISMATING > MISMATE
MISMEET vb fail to meet
MISMEETS > MISMEET
MISMET > MISMEET

MISMETRE *vb* fail to follow metre of poem

MISMETRED > MISMETRE

MISMETRES > MISMETRE

MISMOVE *vb* move badly

MISMOVED > MISMOVE

MISMOVES > MISMOVE

MISMOVING > MISMOVE

MISNAME *vb* name badly

MISNAMED > MISNAME

MISNAMES > MISNAME

MISNAMING > MISNAME

MISNOMER *n* incorrect or unsuitable name ▷ *vb* apply misnomer to

MISNOMERS > MISNOMER

MISNUMBER *vb* number wrongly

MISO *n* thick brown salty paste made from soya beans, used to flavour savoury dishes, esp soups

MISOCLERE *adj* hostile to clergy

MISOGAMIC > MISOGAMY

MISOGAMY *n* hatred of marriage

MISOGYNIC > MISOGYNY

MISOGYNY *n* hatred of women

MISOLOGY *n* hatred of reasoning or reasoned argument

MISONEISM *n* hatred of anything new

MISONEIST > MISONEISM

MISORDER *vb* order badly

MISORDERS > MISORDER

MISORIENT *vb* orient incorrectly

MISOS > MISO

MISPAGE *vb* page wrongly

MISPAGED > MISPAGE

MISPAGES > MISPAGE

MISPAGING > MISPAGE

MISPAINT *vb* paint badly or wrongly

MISPAINTS > MISPAINT

MISPARSE *vb* parse wrongly

MISPARSED > MISPARSE

MISPARSES > MISPARSE

MISPART *vb* part wrongly

MISPARTED > MISPART

MISPARTS > MISPART

MISPATCH *vb* patch wrongly

MISPEN *vb* write wrongly

MISPENNED > MISPEN

MISPENS > MISPEN

MISPHRASE *vb* phrase badly

MISPICKEL *n* white or grey metallic mineral consisting of a sulphide of iron and arsenic that forms monoclinic crystals with an orthorhombic shape: an ore of arsenic

MISPLACE *vb* mislay

MISPLACED *adj* (of an emotion or action) directed towards a person or thing that does not deserve it

MISPLACES > MISPLACE

MISPLAN *vb* plan badly or wrongly

MISPLANS > MISPLAN

MISPLANT *vb* plant badly or wrongly

MISPLANTS > MISPLANT

MISPLAY *vb* play badly or wrongly in games or sports ▷ *n* wrong or unskilful play

MISPLAYED > MISPLAY

MISPLAYS > MISPLAY

MISPLEAD *vb* plead incorrectly

MISPLEADS > MISPLEAD

MISPLEASE *vb* displease

MISPLED > MISPLEAD

MISPOINT *vb* punctuate badly

MISPOINTS > MISPOINT

MISPOISE *n* lack of poise ▷ *vb* lack poise

MISPOISED > MISPOISE

MISPOISES > MISPOISE

MISPRAISE *vb* fail to praise properly

MISPRICE *vb* give wrong price to

MISPRICED > MISPRICE

MISPRICES > MISPRICE

MISPRINT *n* printing error ▷ *vb* print a letter incorrectly

MISPRINTS > MISPRINT

MISPRISE *same as* > MISPRIZE

MISPRISED > MISPRISE

MISPRISER > MISPRISE

MISPRISES > MISPRISE

MISPRIZE *vb* fail to appreciate the value of

MISPRIZED > MISPRIZE

MISPRIZER > MISPRIZE

MISPRIZES > MISPRIZE

MISPROUD *adj* undeservedly proud

MISQUOTE *vb* quote inaccurately

MISQUOTED > MISQUOTE

MISQUOTER > MISQUOTE

MISQUOTES > MISQUOTE

MISRAISE *vb* raise wrongly or excessively

MISRAISED > MISRAISE

MISRAISES > MISRAISE

MISRATE *vb* rate wrongly

MISRATED > MISRATE

MISRATES > MISRATE

MISRATING > MISRATE

MISREAD *vb* misinterpret (a situation etc)

MISREADS > MISREAD

MISRECKON *vb* reckon wrongly

MISRECORD *vb* record wrongly

MISREFER *vb* refer wrongly

MISREFERS > MISREFER

MISREGARD *n* lack of attention

MISRELATE *vb* relate badly

MISRELIED > MISRELY

MISRELIES > MISRELY

MISRELY *vb* rely wrongly

MISRENDER *vb* render wrongly

MISREPORT *vb* report falsely or inaccurately ▷ *n* inaccurate or false report

MISRHYMED *adj* badly rhymed

MISROUTE *vb* send wrong way

MISROUTED > MISROUTE

MISROUTES > MISROUTE

MISRULE *vb* govern inefficiently or unjustly ▷ *n* inefficient or unjust government

MISRULED > MISRULE

MISRULES > MISRULE

MISRULING > MISRULE

MISS *vb* fail to notice, hear, hit, reach, find, or catch ▷ *n* fact or instance of missing

MISSA *n* Roman Catholic mass

MISSABLE > MISS

MISSAE > MISSA

MISSAID > MISSAY

MISSAL *n* book containing the prayers and rites of the Mass

MISSALS > MISSAL

MISSAW > MISSEE

MISSAY *vb* say wrongly

MISSAYING > MISSAY

MISSAYS > MISSAY

MISSEAT *vb* seat wrongly

MISSEATED > MISSEAT

MISSEATS > MISSEAT

MISSED > MISS

MISSEE *vb* see wrongly

MISSEEING > MISSEE

MISSEEM *vb* be unsuitable for

MISSEEMED > MISSEEM

MISSEEMS > MISSEEM

MISSEEN > MISSEE

MISSEES > MISSEE

MISSEL *as in missel thrush* large European thrush with a brown back and spotted breast, noted for feeding on mistletoe berries

MISSELS > MISSEL

MISSEND *vb* send wrongly

MISSENDS > MISSEND

MISSENSE *n* type of genetic mutation

MISSENSES > MISSENSE

MISSENT > MISSEND

MISSES > MISS

MISSET *vb* set wrongly

MISSETS > MISSET

MISSHAPE *vb* shape badly ▷ *n* something that is badly shaped

MISSHAPED > MISSHAPE

MISSHAPEN *adj* badly shaped, deformed

MISSHAPER > MISSHAPE

MISSHAPES > MISSHAPE

MISSHOD *adj* badly shod

MISSHOOD *n* state of being unmarried woman

MISSHOODS > MISSHOOD

MISSIER > MISSY

MISSIES > MISSY

MISSIEST > MISSY

MISSILE *n* rocket with an exploding warhead, used as a weapon

MISSILEER *n* serviceman or servicewoman who is responsible for firing missiles

MISSILERY *n* missiles collectively

MISSILES > MISSILE

MISSILRY *same as* > MISSILERY

MISSING *adj* lost or absent

MISSINGLY > MISSING

MISSION *n* specific task or duty ▷ *vb* direct a mission to or establish a mission in (a given region)

MISSIONAL *adj* emphasizing preaching of gospel

MISSIONED > MISSION

MISSIONER *n* person heading a parochial mission in a Christian country

MISSIONS > MISSION

MISSIS *same as* > MISSUS

MISSISES > MISSIS

MISSISH *adj* like schoolgirl

MISSIVE *n* letter ▷ *adj* sent or intended to be sent

MISSIVES > MISSIVE

MISSORT *vb* sort wrongly

MISSORTED > MISSORT

MISSORTS > MISSORT

MISSOUND *vb* sound wrongly

MISSOUNDS > MISSOUND

MISSOUT *n* someone who has been overlooked

MISSOUTS > MISSOUT

MISSPACE *vb* space out wrongly

MISSPACED > MISSPACE

MISSPACES > MISSPACE

MISSPEAK *vb* speak wrongly

MISSPEAKS > MISSPEAK

MISSPELL *vb* spell (a word) wrongly

MISSPELLS > MISSPELL

MISSPELT > MISSPELL

MISSPEND *vb* waste or spend unwisely

MISSPENDS > MISSPEND

MISSPENT > MISSPEND

MISSPOKE > MISSPEAK

MISSPOKEN > MISSPEAK

MISSTAMP *vb* stamp badly

MISSTAMPS > MISSTAMP

MISSTART *vb* start wrongly

MISSTARTS > MISSTART

MISSTATE *vb* state incorrectly

MISSTATED > MISSTATE

MISSTATES > MISSTATE

MISSTEER *vb* steer badly

MISSTEERS > MISSTEER

**MISSTEP** *n* false step ▷ *vb* take false step

**MISSTEPS** > MISSTEP

**MISSTOP** *vb* stop wrongly

**MISSTOPS** > MISSTOP

**MISSTRIKE** *vb* fail to strike properly

**MISSTRUCK** > MISSTRIKE

**MISSTYLE** *vb* call by wrong name

**MISSTYLED** > MISSTYLE

**MISSTYLES** > MISSTYLE

**MISSUIT** *vb* be unsuitable for

**MISSUITED** > MISSUIT

**MISSUITS** > MISSUIT

**MISSUS** *n* one's wife or the wife of the person addressed or referred to

**MISSUSES** > MISSUS

**MISSY** *n* affectionate or disparaging form of address to a girl ▷ *adj* missish

**MIST** *n* thin fog ▷ *vb* cover or be covered with mist

**MISTAKE** *n* error or blunder ▷ *vb* misunderstand

**MISTAKEN** *adj* wrong in judgment or opinion

**MISTAKER** > MISTAKE

**MISTAKERS** > MISTAKE

**MISTAKES** > MISTAKE

**MISTAKING** > MISTAKE

**MISTAL** *n* cow shed

**MISTALS** > MISTAL

**MISTAUGHT** > MISTEACH

**MISTBOW** *same as* > FOGBOW

**MISTBOWS** > MISTBOW

**MISTEACH** *vb* teach badly

**MISTED** > MIST

**MISTELL** *vb* tell wrongly

**MISTELLS** > MISTELL

**MISTEMPER** *vb* make disordered

**MISTEND** *vb* tend wrongly

**MISTENDED** > MISTEND

**MISTENDS** > MISTEND

**MISTER** *n* informal form of address for a man ▷ *vb* call (someone) mister

**MISTERED** > MISTER

**MISTERIES** > MISTERY

**MISTERING** > MISTER

**MISTERM** *vb* term badly

**MISTERMED** > MISTERM

**MISTERMS** > MISTERM

**MISTERS** > MISTER

**MISTERY** *same as* > MYSTERY

**MISTEUK** *Scots variant of* > MISTOOK

**MISTFUL** > MIST

**MISTHINK** *vb* have poor opinion of

**MISTHINKS** > MISTHINK

**MISTHREW** > MISTHROW

**MISTHROW** *vb* fail to throw properly

**MISTHROWN** > MISTHROW

**MISTHROWS** > MISTHROW

**MISTICO** *n* small Mediterranean sailing ship

**MISTICOS** > MISTICO

**MISTIER** > MISTY

**MISTIEST** > MISTY

**MISTIGRIS** *n* joker or a blank card used as a wild card in a variety of draw poker

**MISTILY** > MISTY

**MISTIME** *vb* do (something) at the wrong time

**MISTIMED** > MISTIME

**MISTIMES** > MISTIME

**MISTIMING** > MISTIME

**MISTINESS** > MISTY

**MISTING** *n* application of a fake suntan by spray

**MISTINGS** > MISTING

**MISTITLE** *vb* name badly

**MISTITLED** > MISTITLE

**MISTITLES** > MISTITLE

**MISTLE** *same as* > MIZZLE

**MISTLED** > MISTLE

**MISTLES** > MISTLE

**MISTLETOE** *n* evergreen plant with white berries growing as a parasite on trees

**MISTLING** > MISTLE

**MISTOLD** > MISTELL

**MISTOOK** *past tense of* > MISTAKE

**MISTOUCH** *vb* fail to touch properly

**MISTRACE** *vb* trace wrongly

**MISTRACED** > MISTRACE

**MISTRACES** > MISTRACE

**MISTRAIN** *vb* train wrongly

**MISTRAINS** > MISTRAIN

**MISTRAL** *n* strong dry northerly wind of S France

**MISTRALS** > MISTRAL

**MISTREAT** *vb* treat (a person or animal) badly

**MISTREATS** > MISTREAT

**MISTRESS** *n* woman who has a continuing sexual relationship with a married man ▷ *vb* make into mistress

**MISTRIAL** *n* trial made void because of some error

**MISTRIALS** > MISTRIAL

**MISTRUST** *vb* have doubts or suspicions about ▷ *n* lack of trust

**MISTRUSTS** > MISTRUST

**MISTRUTH** *n* something untrue

**MISTRUTHS** > MISTRUTH

**MISTRYST** *vb* fail to keep appointment with

**MISTRYSTS** > MISTRYST

**MISTS** > MIST

**MISTUNE** *vb* fail to tune properly

**MISTUNED** > MISTUNE

**MISTUNES** > MISTUNE

**MISTUNING** > MISTUNE

**MISTUTOR** *vb* instruct badly

**MISTUTORS** > MISTUTOR

**MISTY** *adj* full of mist

**MISTYPE** *vb* type badly

**MISTYPED** > MISTYPE

**MISTYPES** > MISTYPE

**MISTYPING** > MISTYPE

**MISUNION** *n* wrong or bad union

**MISUNIONS** > MISUNION

**MISUSAGE** > MISUSE

**MISUSAGES** > MISUSE

**MISUSE** *n* incorrect, improper, or careless use ▷ *vb* use wrongly

**MISUSED** > MISUSE

**MISUSER** *n* abuse of some right, privilege, office, etc, such as one that may lead to its forfeiture

**MISUSERS** > MISUSER

**MISUSES** > MISUSE

**MISUSING** > MISUSE

**MISUST** > MISUSE

**MISVALUE** *vb* value badly

**MISVALUED** > MISVALUE

**MISVALUES** > MISVALUE

**MISWEEN** *vb* assess wrongly

**MISWEENED** > MISWEEN

**MISWEENS** > MISWEEN

**MISWEND** *vb* become lost

**MISWENDS** > MISWEND

**MISWENT** > MISWEND

**MISWORD** *vb* word badly

**MISWORDED** > MISWORD

**MISWORDS** > MISWORD

**MISWRIT** > MISWRITE

**MISWRITE** *vb* write badly

**MISWRITES** > MISWRITE

**MISWROTE** > MISWRITE

**MISYOKE** *vb* join wrongly

**MISYOKED** > MISYOKE

**MISYOKES** > MISYOKE

**MISYOKING** > MISYOKE

**MITCH** *vb* play truant from school

**MITCHED** > MITCH

**MITCHES** > MITCH

**MITCHING** > MITCH

**MITE** *n* very small spider-like animal

**MITER** *same as* > MITRE

**MITERED** > MITER

**MITERER** > MITER

**MITERERS** > MITER

**MITERING** > MITER

**MITERS** > MITER

**MITERWORT** *same as* > MITREWORT

**MITES** > MITE

**MITHER** *vb* fuss over or moan about something

**MITHERED** > MITHER

**MITHERING** > MITHER

**MITHERS** > MITHER

**MITICIDAL** > MITICIDE

**MITICIDE** *n* any drug or agent that destroys mites

**MITICIDES** > MITICIDE

**MITIER** > MITY

**MITIEST** > MITY

**MITIGABLE** > MITIGATE

**MITIGANT** *adj* acting to mitigate

**MITIGATE** *vb* make less severe

**MITIGATED** > MITIGATE

**MITIGATES** > MITIGATE

**MITIGATOR** > MITIGATE

**MITIS** *n* malleable iron, fluid enough for casting, made by adding a small amount of aluminium to wrought iron

**MITISES** > MITIS

**MITOGEN** *n* any agent that induces mitosis

**MITOGENIC** > MITOGEN

**MITOGENS** > MITOGEN

**MITOMYCIN** *n*

**MITOSES** > MITOSIS

**MITOSIS** *n* type of cell division in which the nucleus divides into two nuclei which each contain the same number of chromosomes as the original nucleus

**MITOTIC** > MITOSIS

**MITRAILLE** *n* hail of bullets

**MITRAL** *adj* of or like a mitre

**MITRE** *n* bishop's pointed headdress ▷ *vb* join with a mitre joint

**MITRED** > MITRE

**MITRES** > MITRE

**MITREWORT** *n* any of several Asian and North American saxifragaceous plants of the genus *Mitella*, having clusters of small white flowers and capsules resembling a bishop's mitre

**MITRIFORM** *adj* shaped like mitre

**MITRING** > MITRE

**MITSVAH** *same as* > MITZVAH

**MITSVAHS** > MITSVAH

**MITSVOTH** > MITSVAH

**MITT** *same as* > MITTEN

**MITTEN** *n* glove with one section for the thumb and one for the four fingers together

**MITTENED** *adj* wearing mittens

**MITTENS** > MITTEN

**MITTIMUS** *n* warrant of commitment to prison or a command to a jailer directing him to hold someone in prison

**MITTS** > MITT

**MITUMBA** *n* used clothes imported for sale in African countries

**MITUMBAS** > MITUMBA

**MITY** *adj* having mites

**MITZVAH** *n* commandment or precept, esp one found in the Bible

**MITZVAHS** > MITZVAH

**MITZVOTH** > MITZVAH

**MIURUS** *n* type of rhythm in poetry

**MIURUSES** > MIURUS

**MIX** *vb* combine or blend into one mass ▷ *n* mixture

**MIXABLE** > MIX

**MIXDOWN** *n* (in sound recording) the transfer of a multitrack master mix to two-track stereo tape

**MIXDOWNS** > MIXDOWN
**MIXED** *adj* formed or blended together by mixing
**MIXEDLY** > MIXED
**MIXEDNESS** > MIXED
**MIXEN** *n* dunghill
**MIXENS** > MIXEN
**MIXER** *n* kitchen appliance used for mixing foods
**MIXERS** > MIXER
**MIXES** > MIX
**MIXIBLE** > MIX
**MIXIER** > MIX
**MIXIEST** > MIX
**MIXING** > MIX
**MIXMASTER** *n* disc jockey
**MIXOLOGY** *n* art of mixing cocktails
**MIXT** > MIX
**MIXTE** *adj* of or denoting a type of bicycle frame, usually for women, in which angled twin lateral tubes run back to the rear axle
**MIXTION** *n* amber-based mixture used in making gold leaf
**MIXTIONS** > MIXTION
**MIXTURE** *n* something mixed
**MIXTURES** > MIXTURE
**MIXUP** *vb* confuse or confound ▷ *n* something that is mixed up
**MIXUPS** > MIXUP
**MIXY** *adj* mixed
**MIZ** *shortened form of* > MISERY
**MIZEN** *same as* > MIZZEN
**MIZENMAST** *n* (on a yawl, ketch, or dandy) the after mast
**MIZENS** > MIZEN
**MIZMAZE** *n* maze
**MIZMAZES** > MIZMAZE
**MIZUNA** *n* Japanese variety of lettuce having crisp green leaves
**MIZUNAS** > MIZUNA
**MIZZ** *same as* > MIZ
**MIZZEN** *n* sail set on a mizzenmast ▷ *adj* of or relating to any kind of gear used with a mizzenmast
**MIZZENS** > MIZZEN
**MIZZES** > MIZ
**MIZZLE** *vb* decamp
**MIZZLED** > MIZZLE
**MIZZLES** > MIZZLE
**MIZZLIER** > MIZZLE
**MIZZLIEST** > MIZZLE
**MIZZLING** > MIZZLE
**MIZZLINGS** > MIZZLE
**MIZZLY** > MIZZLE
**MIZZONITE** *n* mineral containing sodium
**MIZZY** as in *mizzy maze* dialect expression meaning state of confusion
**MM** *interj* expression of enjoyment of taste or

smell
**MNA** *same as* > MINA
**MNAS** > MNA
**MNEME** *n* ability to retain memory
**MNEMES** > MNEME
**MNEMIC** > MNEME
**MNEMON** *n* unit of memory
**MNEMONIC** *adj* intended to help the memory ▷ *n* something, for instance a verse, intended to help the memory
**MNEMONICS** *n* art or practice of improving or of aiding the memory
**MNEMONIST** > MNEMONICS
**MNEMONS** > MNEMON
**MO** *n* moment
**MOA** *n* large extinct flightless New Zealand bird
**MOAI** *n* any of the gigantic carved stone figures found on Easter Island (Rapa Nui)
**MOAN** *n* low cry of pain ▷ *vb* make or utter with a moan
**MOANED** > MOAN
**MOANER** > MOAN
**MOANERS** > MOAN
**MOANFUL** > MOAN
**MOANFULLY** > MOAN
**MOANING** > MOAN
**MOANINGLY** > MOAN
**MOANS** > MOAN
**MOAS** > MOA
**MOAT** *n* deep wide ditch, esp round a castle ▷ *vb* surround with or as if with a moat
**MOATED** > MOAT
**MOATING** > MOAT
**MOATLIKE** > MOAT
**MOATS** > MOAT
**MOB** *n* disorderly crowd ▷ *vb* surround in a mob to acclaim or attack
**MOBBED** > MOB
**MOBBER** > MOB
**MOBBERS** > MOB
**MOBBIE** *same as* > MOBBY
**MOBBIES** > MOBBY
**MOBBING** > MOB
**MOBBINGS** > MOB
**MOBBISH** > MOB
**MOBBISHLY** > MOB
**MOBBISM** *n* behaviour as mob
**MOBBISMS** > MOBBISM
**MOBBLE** *same as* > MOBLE
**MOBBLED** > MOBBLE
**MOBBLES** > MOBBLE
**MOBBLING** > MOBBLE
**MOBBY** *n* West Indian drink
**MOBCAP** *n* woman's 18th-century cotton cap with a pouched crown
**MOBCAPS** > MOBCAP
**MOBE** *n* mobile phone
**MOBES** > MOBE
**MOBIE** *n* mobile phone
**MOBIES** > MOBY
**MOBILE** *adj* able to move ▷ *n* hanging structure

designed to move in air currents
**MOBILES** > MOBILE
**MOBILISE** *same as* > MOBILIZE
**MOBILISED** > MOBILISE
**MOBILISER** > MOBILISE
**MOBILISES** > MOBILISE
**MOBILITY** *n* ability to move physically
**MOBILIZE** *vb* (of the armed services) prepare for active service
**MOBILIZED** > MOBILIZE
**MOBILIZER** > MOBILIZE
**MOBILIZES** > MOBILIZE
**MOBLE** *vb* muffle
**MOBLED** > MOBLE
**MOBLES** > MOBLE
**MOBLING** > MOBLE
**MOBLOG** *n* chronicle, which may be shared with others, of someone's thoughts and experiences recorded in the form of mobile phone calls, text messages, and photographs
**MOBLOGGER** > MOBLOG
**MOBLOGS** > MOBLOG
**MOBOCRACY** *n* rule or domination by a mob
**MOBOCRAT** > MOBOCRACY
**MOBOCRATS** > MOBOCRACY
**MOBS** > MOB
**MOBSMAN** *n* person in mob
**MOBSMEN** > MOBSMAN
**MOBSTER** *n* member of a criminal organization
**MOBSTERS** > MOBSTER
**MOBY** *n* mobile phone
**MOC** *shortening of* > MOCCASIN
**MOCCASIN** *same as* > MOCCASIN
**MOCCASIN** *n* soft leather shoe
**MOCCASINS** > MOCCASIN
**MOCCIES** *pl n* informal Australian word for moccasins
**MOCH** *n* spell of humid weather
**MOCHA** *n* kind of strong dark coffee
**MOCHAS** > MOCHA
**MOCHELL** *same as* > MUCH
**MOCHELLS** > MOCHELL
**MOCHIE** *adj* damp or humid
**MOCHIER** > MOCHIE
**MOCHIEST** > MOCHIE
**MOCHILA** *n* South American shoulder bag
**MOCHILAS** > MOCHILA
**MOCHINESS** > MOCHIE
**MOCHS** > MOCH
**MOCHY** *same as* > MOCHIE
**MOCK** *vb* make fun of ▷ *adj* sham or imitation ▷ *n* act of mocking
**MOCKABLE** > MOCK
**MOCKADO** *n* imitation velvet
**MOCKADOES** > MOCKADO
**MOCKAGE** *same*

*as* > MOCKERY
**MOCKAGES** > MOCKAGE
**MOCKED** > MOCK
**MOCKER** > MOCK
**MOCKERIES** > MOCKERY
**MOCKERNUT** *n* species of smooth-barked hickory, *Carya tomentosa*, with fragrant foliage that turns bright yellow in autumn
**MOCKERS** > MOCK
**MOCKERY** *n* derision
**MOCKING** > MOCK
**MOCKINGLY** > MOCK
**MOCKINGS** > MOCK
**MOCKNEY** *n* person who affects a cockney accent ▷ *adj* denoting an affected cockney accent or a person who has one
**MOCKNEYS** > MOCKNEY
**MOCKS** > MOCK
**MOCKTAIL** *n* cocktail without alcohol
**MOCKTAILS** > MOCKTAIL
**MOCKUP** *n* working full-scale model of a machine, apparatus, etc, for testing, research, etc
**MOCKUPS** > MOCKUP
**MOCOCK** *n* Native American birchbark container
**MOCOCKS** > MOCOCK
**MOCS** > MOC
**MOCUCK** *same as* > MOCOCK
**MOCUCKS** > MOCUCK
**MOCUDDUM** *same as* > MUQADDAM
**MOCUDDUMS** > MOCUDDUM
**MOD** *n* member of a group of young people, orig. in the mid-1960s, who were very clothes-conscious and rode motor scooters
**MODAL** *adj* of or relating to mode or manner ▷ *n* modal word
**MODALISM** *n* type of Christian doctrine
**MODALISMS** > MODALISM
**MODALIST** > MODALISM
**MODALISTS** > MODALISM
**MODALITY** *n* condition of being modal
**MODALLY** > MODAL
**MODALS** > MODAL
**MODE** *n* method or manner
**MODEL** *n* (miniature) representation ▷ *adj* excellent or perfect ▷ *vb* make a model of
**MODELED** > MODEL
**MODELER** > MODEL
**MODELERS** > MODEL
**MODELING** *same as* > MODELLING
**MODELINGS** > MODELING
**MODELIST** *n* person who constructs models
**MODELISTS** > MODELIST
**MODELLED** > MODEL
**MODELLER** > MODEL
**MODELLERS** > MODEL
**MODELLI** > MODELLO

**MODELLING** n act or an instance of making a model
**MODELLO** n artist's preliminary sketch or model
**MODELLOS** > MODELLO
**MODELS** > MODEL
**MODEM** n device for connecting two computers by a telephone line ▷ vb send or receive by modem
**MODEMED** > MODEM
**MODEMING** > MODEM
**MODEMS** > MODEM
**MODENA** n popular variety of domestic fancy pigeon originating in Modena
**MODENAS** > MODENA
**MODER** n intermediate layer in humus
**MODERATE** adj not extreme ▷ n person of moderate views ▷ vb make or become less violent or extreme
**MODERATED** > MODERATE
**MODERATES** > MODERATE
**MODERATO** adv at a moderate speed ▷ n moderato piece
**MODERATOR** n (Presbyterian Church) minister appointed to preside over a Church court, general assembly, etc
**MODERATOS** > MODERATO
**MODERN** adj of present or recent times ▷ n contemporary person
**MODERNE** adj of or relating to the style of architecture and design, prevalent in Europe and the US in the late 1920s and 1930s, typified by the use of straight lines, tubular chromed steel frames, contrasting inlaid woods, etc
**MODERNER** > MODERN
**MODERNES** n being modern
**MODERNEST** > MODERN
**MODERNISE** same as > MODERNIZE
**MODERNISM** n (support of) modern tendencies, thoughts, or styles
**MODERNIST** > MODERNISM
**MODERNITY** n quality or state of being modern
**MODERNIZE** vb bring up to date
**MODERNLY** > MODERN
**MODERNS** > MODERN
**MODERS** > MODER
**MODES** > MODE
**MODEST** adj not vain or boastful
**MODESTER** > MODEST
**MODESTEST** > MODEST
**MODESTIES** > MODESTY
**MODESTLY** > MODEST

**MODESTY** n quality or condition of being modest
**MODGE** vb do shoddily
**MODGED** > MODGE
**MODGES** > MODGE
**MODGING** > MODGE
**MODI** > MODUS
**MODICA** > MODICUM
**MODICUM** n small quantity
**MODICUMS** > MODICUM
**MODIFIED** > MODIFY
**MODIFIER** n word that qualifies the sense of another
**MODIFIERS** > MODIFIER
**MODIFIES** > MODIFY
**MODIFY** vb change slightly
**MODIFYING** > MODIFY
**MODII** > MODIUS
**MODILLION** n one of a set of ornamental brackets under a cornice, esp as used in the Corinthian order
**MODIOLAR** > MODIOLUS
**MODIOLI** > MODIOLUS
**MODIOLUS** n central bony pillar of the cochlea
**MODISH** adj in fashion
**MODISHLY** > MODISH
**MODIST** n follower of fashion
**MODISTE** n fashionable dressmaker or milliner
**MODISTES** > MODISTE
**MODISTS** > MODIST
**MODIUS** n ancient Roman quantity measure
**MODIWORT** Scots variant of > MOULDWARP
**MODIWORTS** > MODIWORT
**MODS** > MOD
**MODULAR** adj of, consisting of, or resembling a module or modulus ▷ n thing comprised of modules
**MODULARLY** > MODULAR
**MODULARS** > MODULAR
**MODULATE** vb vary in tone
**MODULATED** > MODULATE
**MODULATES** > MODULATE
**MODULATOR** > MODULATE
**MODULE** n self-contained unit, section, or component with a specific function
**MODULES** > MODULE
**MODULI** > MODULUS
**MODULO** adv with reference to modulus
**MODULUS** n coefficient expressing a specified property, for instance elasticity, of a specified substance
**MODUS** n way of doing something
**MOE** same as > MORE
**MOELLON** n rubble
**MOELLONS** > MOELLON
**MOER** n in South Africa, slang word for the womb ▷ vb in South Africa, attack (someone or

something) violently
**MOERED** > MOER
**MOERING** > MOER
**MOERS** > MOER
**MOES** > MOE
**MOFETTE** n opening in a region of nearly extinct volcanic activity, through which carbon dioxide, nitrogen, and other gases pass
**MOFETTES** > MOFETTE
**MOFFETTE** same as > MOFETTE
**MOFFETTES** > MOFETTE
**MOFFIE** n homosexual ▷ adj homosexual
**MOFFIES** > MOFFIE
**MOFO** n offensive term, a shortened form of motherfucker
**MOFOS** > MOFO
**MOFUSSIL** n provincial area in India
**MOFUSSILS** > MOFUSSIL
**MOG** vb go away
**MOGGAN** n stocking without foot
**MOGGANS** > MOGGAN
**MOGGED** > MOG
**MOGGIE** same as > MOGGY
**MOGGIES** > MOGGY
**MOGGING** > MOG
**MOGGY** n cat
**MOGHUL** same as > MOGUL
**MOGHULS** > MOGHUL
**MOGS** > MOG
**MOGUL** n important or powerful person
**MOGULED** adj having moguls
**MOGULS** > MOGUL
**MOHAIR** n fine hair of the Angora goat
**MOHAIRS** > MOHAIR
**MOHALIM** same as > MOHELIM
**MOHAWK** n half turn from either edge of either skate to the corresponding edge of the other skate
**MOHAWKS** > MOHAWK
**MOHEL** n man qualified to conduct circumcisions
**MOHELIM** > MOHEL
**MOHELS** > MOHEL
**MOHICAN** n punk hairstyle
**MOHICANS** > MOHICAN
**MOHR** same as > MHORR
**MOHRS** > MOHR
**MOHUA** n small New Zealand bird with a yellow head and breast
**MOHUR** n former Indian gold coin worth 15 rupees
**MOHURS** > MOHUR
**MOI** > ME
**MOIDER** same as > MOITHER
**MOIDERED** > MOIDER
**MOIDERING** > MOIDER
**MOIDERS** > MOIDER
**MOIDORE** n former Portuguese gold coin
**MOIDORES** > MOIDORE

**MOIETIES** > MOIETY
**MOIETY** n half
**MOIL** vb moisten or soil or become moist, soiled, etc ▷ n toil
**MOILED** > MOIL
**MOILER** > MOIL
**MOILERS** > MOIL
**MOILING** > MOIL
**MOILINGLY** > MOIL
**MOILS** > MOIL
**MOINEAU** n small fortification
**MOINEAUS** > MOINEAU
**MOIRA** n fate
**MOIRAI** > MOIRA
**MOIRE** adj having a watered or wavelike pattern ▷ n any fabric that has such a pattern
**MOIRES** > MOIRE
**MOISER** n informer
**MOISERS** > MOISER
**MOIST** adj slightly wet ▷ vb moisten
**MOISTED** > MOIST
**MOISTEN** vb make or become moist
**MOISTENED** > MOISTEN
**MOISTENER** > MOISTEN
**MOISTENS** > MOISTEN
**MOISTER** > MOIST
**MOISTEST** > MOIST
**MOISTFUL** adj full of moisture
**MOISTIFY** vb moisten
**MOISTING** > MOIST
**MOISTLY** > MOIST
**MOISTNESS** > MOIST
**MOISTS** > MOIST
**MOISTURE** n liquid diffused as vapour or condensed in drops
**MOISTURES** > MOISTURE
**MOIT** same as > MOTE
**MOITHER** vb bother or bewilder
**MOITHERED** > MOITHER
**MOITHERS** > MOITHER
**MOITS** > MOIT
**MOJARRA** n tropical American sea fish
**MOJARRAS** > MOJARRA
**MOJO** n charm or magic spell
**MOJOES** > MOJO
**MOJOS** > MOJO
**MOKADDAM** same as > MUQADDAM
**MOKADDAMS** > MOKADDAM
**MOKE** n donkey
**MOKES** > MOKE
**MOKI** n either of two edible sea fish of New Zealand, the blue cod (Percis colias) or the bastard trumpeter (Latridopsis ciliaris)
**MOKIHI** n Māori raft
**MOKIS** > MOKI
**MOKO** n Māori tattoo or tattoo pattern
**MOKOMOKO** n type of skink found in New Zealand
**MOKOPUNA** n grandchild or

young person
MOKOPUNAS > MOKOPUNA
MOKORO n (in Botswana)
the traditional dugout
canoe of the people of the
Okavango Delta
MOKOROS > MOKORO
MOKOS > MOKO
MOKSHA n freedom from
the endless cycle of
transmigration into a
state of bliss
MOKSHAS > MOKSHA
MOL same as > MOLE
MOLA another name
for > SUNFISH
MOLAL adj of or consisting
of a solution containing
one mole of solute per
thousand grams of solvent
MOLALITY n (not in
technical usage) a
measure of concentration
equal to the number
of moles of solute in a
thousand grams of solvent
MOLAR n large back tooth
used for grinding ▷ adj of
any of these teeth
MOLARITY n concentration
MOLARS > MOLAR
MOLAS > MOLA
MOLASSE n soft sediment
produced by the erosion of
mountain ranges after the
final phase of mountain
building
MOLASSES n dark syrup,
a by-product of sugar
refining
MOLD same as > MOULD
MOLDABLE > MOLD
MOLDAVITE n green
tektite found in the Czech
Republic, thought to be
the product of an ancient
meteorite impact in
Germany
MOLDBOARD n curved blade
of a plough
MOLDED > MOLD
MOLDER same as > MOULDER
MOLDERED > MOLDER
MOLDERING > MOLDER
MOLDERS > MOLDER
MOLDIER > MOLDY
MOLDIEST > MOLDY
MOLDINESS > MOLDY
MOLDING same
as > MOULDING
MOLDINGS > MOLDING
MOLDS > MOLD
MOLDWARP same
as > MOULDWARP
MOLDWARPS > MOLDWARP
MOLDY same as > MOULDY
MOLE n small dark raised
–spot on the skin
MOLECAST n molehill
MOLECASTS > MOLECAST
MOLECULAR adj of or
relating to molecules
MOLECULE n simplest freely
existing chemical unit,

composed of two or more
atoms
MOLECULES > MOLECULE
MOLEHILL n small mound
of earth thrown up by a
burrowing mole
MOLEHILLS > MOLEHILL
MOLEHUNT n hunt for moles
MOLEHUNTS > MOLEHUNT
MOLERAT n any burrowing
molelike African rodent of
the famil
MOLERATS > MOLERAT
MOLES > MOLE
MOLESKIN n dark grey
dense velvety pelt of a
mole, used as a fur
MOLESKINS pl n clothing of
moleskin
MOLEST vb interfere with
sexually
MOLESTED > MOLEST
MOLESTER > MOLEST
MOLESTERS > MOLEST
MOLESTFUL adj molesting
MOLESTING > MOLEST
MOLESTS > MOLEST
MOLIES > MOLY
MOLIMEN n effort needed to
perform bodily function
MOLIMENS > MOLIMEN
MOLINE adj (of a cross)
having arms of equal
length, forked and curved
back at the ends ▷ n
moline cross
MOLINES > MOLINE
MOLINET n stick for
whipping chocolate
MOLINETS > MOLINET
MOLL n gangster's female
accomplice
MOLLA same as > MOLLAH
MOLLAH same as > MULLAH
MOLLAHS > MOLLAH
MOLLAS > MOLLA
MOLLIE same as > MOLLY
MOLLIES > MOLLY
MOLLIFIED > MOLLIFY
MOLLIFIER > MOLLIFY
MOLLIFIES > MOLLIFY
MOLLIFY vb pacify or
soothe
MOLLITIES n softness
MOLLS > MOLL
MOLLUSC n soft-bodied,
usu. hard-shelled, animal,
such as a snail or oyster
MOLLUSCA n molluscs
collectively
MOLLUSCAN > MOLLUSC
MOLLUSCS > MOLLUSC
MOLLUSCUM n viral skin
infection
MOLLUSK same as > MOLLUSC
MOLLUSKAN > MOLLUSK
MOLLUSKS > MOLLUSK
MOLLY n any brightly
coloured tropical or
subtropical American
freshwater cyprinodont
fish of the genus Molliensia
MOLLYHAWK n juvenile of
the southern black-backed

gull (Larus dominicanus)
MOLLYMAWK informal name
for > MALLEMUCK
MOLOCH n spiny Australian
desert-living lizard, Moloch
horridus, that feeds on ants:
family Agamidae (agamas)
MOLOCHISE vb sacrifice to
deity
MOLOCHIZE same
as > MOLOCHISE
MOLOCHS > MOLOCH
MOLOSSI > MOLOSSUS
MOLOSSUS n division of
metre in poetry
MOLS > MOL
MOLT same as > MOULT
MOLTED > MOLT
MOLTEN > MELT
MOLTENLY > MELT
MOLTER > MOLT
MOLTERS > MOLT
MOLTING > MOLT
MOLTO adv very
MOLTS > MOLT
MOLY n magic herb given
by Hermes to Odysseus to
nullify the spells of Circe
MOLYBDATE n salt or ester
of a molybdic acid
MOLYBDIC adj of or
containing molybdenum
in the trivalent or
hexavalent state
MOLYBDOUS adj of or
containing molybdenum,
esp in a low valence state
MOM same as > MOTHER
MOME n fool
MOMENT n short space of
time
MOMENTA > MOMENTUM
MOMENTANY same
as > MOMENTARY
MOMENTARY adj lasting only
a moment
MOMENTLY same
as > MOMENT
MOMENTO same
as > MEMENTO
MOMENTOES > MOMENTO
MOMENTOS > MOMENTO
MOMENTOUS adj of great
significance
MOMENTS > MOMENT
MOMENTUM n impetus to go
forward, develop, or get
stronger
MOMENTUMS > MOMENTUM
MOMES > MOME
MOMI same as > MOM
MOMISM n excessive
domination of a child by
his or her mother
MOMISMS > MOMISM
MOMMA same as > MAMMA
MOMMAS > MOMMA
MOMMET same as > MAMMET
MOMMETS > MOMMET
MOMMIES > MOMMY
MOMMY same as > MOM
MOMS > MOM
MOMSER same as > MOMZER
MOMSERS > MOMSER

MOMUS n person who
ridicules
MOMUSES > MOMUS
MOMZER same as > MAMZER
MOMZERIM > MOMZER
MOMZERS > MOMZER
MON dialect variant of > MAN
MONA n W African guenon
monkey, Cercopithecus
mona, with dark fur on the
back and white or yellow
underparts
MONACHAL less common word
for > MONASTIC
MONACHISM > MONACHAL
MONACHIST > MONACHAL
MONACID same
as > MONOACID
MONACIDIC same
as > MONACID
MONACIDS > MONACID
MONACT adj (of sponge)
with single-spiked
structures in skeleton
MONACTINE > MONACT
MONAD n any fundamental
singular metaphysical
entity
MONADAL > MONAD
MONADES > MONAS
MONADIC adj being or
relating to a monad
MONADICAL > MONAD
MONADISM n (esp in the
writings of Gottfried
Leibnitz, the German
rationalist philosopher
and mathematician (1646–
1716)) the philosophical
doctrine that monads
are the ultimate units of
reality
MONADISMS > MONADISM
MONADNOCK n residual hill
that consists of hard rock
in an otherwise eroded
area
MONADS > MONAD
MONAL n any of several S
Asian pheasants of the
genus Lophophorus, the
males of which have
a brilliantly coloured
plumage
MONALS > MONAL
MONANDRY n preference
of only one male sexual
partner over a period of
time
MONARCH n sovereign ruler
of a state
MONARCHAL > MONARCH
MONARCHIC > MONARCH
MONARCHS > MONARCH
MONARCHY n government
by or a state ruled by a
sovereign
MONARDA n any mintlike
North American plant of
the genus Monarda: family
Lamiaceae (labiates)
MONARDAS > MONARDA
MONAS same as > MONAD
MONASES > MONAS

**MONASTERY** *n* residence of a community of monks
**MONASTIC** *adj* of monks, nuns, or monasteries ▷ *n* person who is committed to this way of life, esp a monk
**MONASTICS** > MONASTIC
**MONATOMIC** *adj* consisting of single atoms
**MONAUL** *same as* > MONAL
**MONAULS** > MONAUL
**MONAURAL** *adj* relating to, having, or hearing with only one ear
**MONAXIAL** *another word for* > UNIAXIAL
**MONAXON** *n* type of sponge
**MONAXONIC** > MONAXON
**MONAXONS** > MONAXON
**MONAZITE** *n* yellow to reddish-brown mineral consisting of a phosphate of thorium, cerium, and lanthanum in monoclinic crystalline form
**MONAZITES** > MONAZITE
**MONDAIN** *n* man who moves in fashionable society ▷ *adj* characteristic of fashionable society
**MONDAINE** *n* woman who moves in fashionable society ▷ *adj* characteristic of fashionable society
**MONDAINES** > MONDAINE
**MONDAINS** > MONDAIN
**MONDE** *n* French word meaning world or society
**MONDES** > MONDE
**MONDIAL** *adj* of or involving the whole world
**MONDO** *n* Buddhist questioning technique
**MONDOS** > MONDO
**MONECIAN** *same as* > MONECIOUS
**MONECIOUS** *adj* (of some flowering plants) having the male and female reproductive organs in separate flowers on the same plant
**MONELLIN** *n* sweet protein
**MONELLINS** > MONELLIN
**MONEME** *less common word for* > MORPHEME
**MONEMES** > MONEME
**MONER** *n* hypothetical simple organism
**MONERA** > MONER
**MONERAN** *n* type of bacterium
**MONERANS** > MONERAN
**MONERGISM** *n* Christian doctrine on spiritual regeneration
**MONERON** *same as* > MONER
**MONETARY** *adj* of money or currency
**MONETH** *same as* > MONTH
**MONETHS** > MONETH
**MONETISE** *same*

*as* > MONETIZE
**MONETISED** > MONETISE
**MONETISES** > MONETISE
**MONETIZE** *vb* establish as the legal tender of a country
**MONETIZED** > MONETIZE
**MONETIZES** > MONETIZE
**MONEY** *n* medium of exchange, coins or banknotes
**MONEYBAG** *n* bag for money
**MONEYBAGS** *n* very rich person
**MONEYED** *adj* rich
**MONEYER** *n* person who coins money
**MONEYERS** > MONEYER
**MONEYLESS** > MONEY
**MONEYMAN** *n* person supplying money
**MONEYMEN** > MONEY
**MONEYS** > MONEY
**MONEYWORT** *n* European and North American creeping primulaceous plant, *Lysimachia nummularia*, with round leaves and yellow flowers
**MONG** *n* stupid or foolish person
**MONGCORN** *same as* > MASLIN
**MONGCORNS** > MONGCORN
**MONGED** *adj* under the influence of drugs
**MONGEESE** > MONGOOSE
**MONGER** *n* trader or dealer ▷ *vb* deal in
**MONGERED** > MONGER
**MONGERIES** > MONGER
**MONGERING** > MONGER
**MONGERS** > MONGER
**MONGERY** > MONGER
**MONGO** *same as* > MUNGO
**MONGOE** *same as* > MONGO
**MONGOES** > MONGOE
**MONGOL** *adj* offensive word for a person affected by Down's syndrome
**MONGOLIAN** *adj* offensive term meaning affected by Down's syndrome
**MONGOLISM** > MONGOL
**MONGOLOID** *adj* offensive term meaning characterized by Down's syndrome ▷ *n* offensive word for a person affected by Down's syndrome
**MONGOLS** > MONGOL
**MONGOOSE** *n* stoatlike mammal of Asia and Africa that kills snakes
**MONGOOSES** > MONGOOSE
**MONGOS** > MONGO
**MONGREL** *n* animal, esp a dog, of mixed breed ▷ *adj* of mixed breed or origin
**MONGRELLY** > MONGREL
**MONGRELS** > MONGREL
**MONGS** > MONG
**MONGST** *short for* > AMONGST
**MONIAL** *n* mullion
**MONIALS** > MONIAL

**MONICKER** *same as* > MONIKER
**MONICKERS** > MONICKER
**MONIE** *Scots word for* > MANY
**MONIED** *same as* > MONEYED
**MONIES** > MONEY
**MONIKER** *n* person's name or nickname
**MONIKERS** > MONIKER
**MONILIA** *n* type of fungus
**MONILIAL** *adj* denoting a thrush infection, caused by the fungus *Candida* (formerly *Monilia*) *albicans*
**MONILIAS** > MONILIA
**MONIMENT** *same as* > MONUMENT
**MONIMENTS** > MONIMENT
**MONIPLIES** *same as* > MANYPLIES
**MONISH** *same as* > ADMONISH
**MONISHED** > MONISH
**MONISHES** > MONISH
**MONISHING** > MONISH
**MONISM** *n* doctrine that reality consists of only one basic substance or element, such as mind or matter
**MONISMS** > MONISM
**MONIST** > MONISM
**MONISTIC** > MONISM
**MONISTS** > MONISM
**MONITION** *n* warning or caution
**MONITIONS** > MONITION
**MONITIVE** *adj* reproving
**MONITOR** *n* person or device that checks, controls, warns, or keeps a record of something ▷ *vb* watch and check on
**MONITORED** > MONITOR
**MONITORS** > MONITOR
**MONITORY** *adj* acting as or giving a warning ▷ *n* letter containing a monition
**MONITRESS** > MONITOR
**MONK** *n* member of an all-male religious community bound by vows
**MONKERIES** > MONKERY
**MONKERY** *n* derogatory word for monastic life or practices
**MONKEY** *n* long-tailed primate ▷ *vb* meddle or fool
**MONKEYED** > MONKEY
**MONKEYING** > MONKEY
**MONKEYISH** > MONKEY
**MONKEYISM** *n* practice of behaving like monkey
**MONKEYPOD** *n* Central American tree
**MONKEYPOT** *n* any of various tropical trees of the genus *Lecythis*: family *Lecythidaceae*
**MONKEYS** > MONKEY
**MONKFISH** *n* any of various fish of the genus *Lophius*

**MONKHOOD** *n* condition of being a monk
**MONKHOODS** > MONKHOOD
**MONKISH** *adj* of, relating to, or resembling a monk or monks
**MONKISHLY** > MONKISH
**MONKS** > MONK
**MONKSHOOD** *n* poisonous plant with hooded flowers
**MONO** *n* monophonic sound
**MONOACID** *adj* a base which is capable of reacting with only one molecule of a monobasic acid
**MONOACIDS** > MONOACID
**MONOAMINE** *n* substance, such as adrenaline, noradrenaline, or serotonin, that contains a single amine group
**MONOAO** *n* New Zealand plant with rigid leaves
**MONOBASIC** *adj* (of an acid, such as hydrogen chloride) having only one replaceable hydrogen atom per molecule
**MONOBROW** *n* appearance of a single eyebrow as a result of the eyebrows joining above a person's nose
**MONOBROWS** > MONOBROW
**MONOCARP** *n* plant that is monocarpic
**MONOCARPS** > MONOCARP
**MONOCEROS** *n* faint constellation on the celestial equator crossed by the Milky Way and lying close to Orion and Canis Major
**MONOCHORD** *n* instrument employed in acoustic analysis or investigation, consisting usually of one string stretched over a resonator of wood
**MONOCLE** *n* eyeglass for one eye only
**MONOCLED** > MONOCLE
**MONOCLES** > MONOCLE
**MONOCLINE** *n* fold in stratified rocks in which the strata are inclined in the same direction from the horizontal
**MONOCOQUE** *n* vehicle body moulded from a single piece of material with no separate load-bearing parts ▷ *adj* of or relating to the design characteristic of a monocoque
**MONOCOT** *n* any flowering plant of the class *Monocotyledonae*, having a single embryonic seed leaf, leaves with parallel veins, and flowers with parts in threes: includes grasses, lilies, palms, and orchids
**MONOCOTS** > MONOCOT

**MONOCOTYL** same as > MONOCOT

**MONOCRACY** n government by one person

**MONOCRAT** > MONOCRACY

**MONOCRATS** > MONOCRACY

**MONOCULAR** adj having or for one eye only ▷ n device for use with one eye, such as a field glass

**MONOCYCLE** another name for > UNICYCLE

**MONOCYTE** n large phagocytic leucocyte with a spherical nucleus and clear cytoplasm

**MONOCYTES** > MONOCYTE

**MONOCYTIC** > MONOCYTE

**MONODIC** > MONODY

**MONODICAL** > MONODY

**MONODIES** > MONODY

**MONODIST** > MONODY

**MONODISTS** > MONODY

**MONODONT** adj (of certain animals, esp the male narwhal) having a single tooth throughout life

**MONODRAMA** n play or other dramatic piece for a single performer

**MONODY** n (in Greek tragedy) an ode sung by a single actor

**MONOECIES** > MONOECY

**MONOECISM** n being both male and female

**MONOECY** same as > MONOECISM

**MONOESTER** n type of ester

**MONOFIL** n synthetic thread or yarn composed of a single strand rather than twisted fibres

**MONOFILS** > MONOFIL

**MONOFUEL** n single type of fuel

**MONOFUELS** > MONOFUEL

**MONOGAMIC** > MONOGAMY

**MONOGAMY** n custom of being married to one person at a time

**MONOGENIC** adj of or relating to an inherited character difference that is controlled by a single gene

**MONOGENY** n the hypothetical descent of all organisms from a single cell or organism

**MONOGERM** adj containing single seed

**MONOGLOT** n person speaking only one language

**MONOGLOTS** > MONOGLOT

**MONOGONY** n asexual reproduction

**MONOGRAM** n design of combined letters, esp a person's initials ▷ vb decorate (clothing, stationery, etc) with a monogram

**MONOGRAMS** > MONOGRAM

**MONOGRAPH** n book or paper on a single subject ▷ vb write a monograph on

**MONOGYNY** n custom of having only one female sexual partner over a period of time

**MONOHULL** n sailing vessel with a single hull

**MONOHULLS** > MONOHULL

**MONOICOUS** adj (of some flowering plants) having the male and female reproductive organs in separate flowers on the same plant

**MONOKINE** n type of protein

**MONOKINES** > MONOKINE

**MONOKINI** n bottom half of bikini

**MONOKINIS** > MONOKINI

**MONOLATER** > MONOLATRY

**MONOLATRY** n exclusive worship of one god without excluding the existence of others

**MONOLAYER** n single layer of atoms or molecules adsorbed on a surface

**MONOLITH** n large upright block of stone

**MONOLITHS** > MONOLITH

**MONOLOG** same as > MONOLOGUE

**MONOLOGIC** > MONOLOGUE

**MONOLOGS** > MONOLOG

**MONOLOGUE** n long speech by one person

**MONOLOGY** > MONOLOGUE

**MONOMACHY** n combat between two individuals

**MONOMANIA** n obsession with one thing

**MONOMARK** n series of letters or figures to identify goods, personal articles, etc

**MONOMARKS** > MONOMARK

**MONOMER** n compound whose molecules can join together to form a polymer

**MONOMERIC** > MONOMER

**MONOMERS** > MONOMER

**MONOMETER** n line of verse consisting of one metrical foot

**MONOMIAL** n expression consisting of a single term, such as 5ax ▷ adj consisting of a single algebraic term

**MONOMIALS** > MONOMIAL

**MONOMODE** adj denoting or relating to a type of optical fibre with a core less than 10 micrometres in diameter

**MONONYM** n person who is famous enough to be known only by one name, usually the first name

**MONONYMS** > MONONYM

**MONOPHAGY** n feeding on only one type of food

**MONOPHASE** adj having single alternating electric current

**MONOPHONY** > MONO

**MONOPHYLY** n group of ancestor and all descendants

**MONOPITCH** adj (of roof) having only one slope

**MONOPLANE** n aeroplane with one pair of wings

**MONOPLOID** less common word for > HAPLOID

**MONOPOD** same as > MONOPODE

**MONOPODE** n member of a legendary one-legged race of Africa

**MONOPODES** > MONOPODE

**MONOPODIA** n plural of monopodium: the main axis of growth in the pine tree and similar plants: the main stem, which elongates from the tip and gives rise to lateral branches

**MONOPODS** > MONOPOD

**MONOPODY** n single-foot measure in poetry

**MONOPOLE** n magnetic pole considered in isolation

**MONOPOLES** > MONOPOLE

**MONOPOLY** n exclusive possession of or right to do something

**MONOPSONY** n situation in which the entire market demand for a product or service consists of only one buyer

**MONOPTERA** n plural of monopteron: circular classical building, esp a temple, that has a single ring of columns surrounding it

**MONOPTOTE** n word with only one form

**MONOPULSE** n radar transmitting single pulse only

**MONORAIL** n single-rail railway

**MONORAILS** > MONORAIL

**MONORCHID** adj having only one testicle ▷ n animal or person with only one testicle

**MONORHINE** adj having single nostril

**MONORHYME** n poem in which all lines rhyme

**MONOS** > MONO

**MONOSEMY** n fact of having only a single meaning

**MONOSES** > MONOSIS

**MONOSIES** > MONOSY

**MONOSIS** n abnormal separation

**MONOSKI** n wide ski on which the skier stands with both feet

**MONOSKIER** > MONOSKI

**MONOSKIS** > MONOSKI

**MONOSOME** n unpaired chromosome, esp an X-chromosome in an otherwise diploid cell

**MONOSOMES** > MONOSOME

**MONOSOMIC** > MONOSOME

**MONOSOMY** n condition with missing pair of chromosomes

**MONOSTELE** n type of plant tissue

**MONOSTELY** > MONOSTELE

**MONOSTICH** n poem of a single line

**MONOSTOME** adj having only one mouth, pore, or similar opening

**MONOSTYLE** adj having single shaft

**MONOSY** same as > MONOSIS

**MONOTINT** n black-and-white photograph or transparency

**MONOTINTS** > MONOTINT

**MONOTONE** n unvaried pitch in speech or sound ▷ adj unvarying ▷ vb speak in monotone

**MONOTONED** > MONOTONE

**MONOTONES** > MONOTONE

**MONOTONIC** same as > MONOTONE

**MONOTONY** n wearisome routine, dullness

**MONOTREME** n any mammal of the primitive order Monotremata, of Australia and New Guinea: egg-laying toothless animals with a single opening (cloaca) for the passage of eggs or sperm, faeces, and urine. The group contains only the echidnas and the platypus

**MONOTROCH** n wheelbarrow

**MONOTYPE** n single print made from a metal or glass plate on which a picture has been painted

**MONOTYPES** > MONOTYPE

**MONOTYPIC** adj (of a genus or species) consisting of only one type of animal or plant

**MONOVULAR** adj of single ovum

**MONOXIDE** n oxide that contains one oxygen atom per molecule

**MONOXIDES** > MONOXIDE

**MONOXYLON** n canoe made from one log

**MONS** > MON

**MONSIEUR** n French title of address equivalent to sir or Mr

**MONSIGNOR** n ecclesiastical title attached to certain offices or distinctions usually bestowed by the Pope

**MONSOON** n seasonal wind

of SE Asia

**MONSOONAL** > MONSOON

**MONSOONS** > MONSOON

**MONSTER** n imaginary, usu. frightening, beast ▷ adj huge ▷ vb criticize (a person or group) severely

**MONSTERA** n any plant of the tropical climbing genus Monstera, some species of which are grown as greenhouse or pot plants for their unusual leathery perforated leaves: family Araceae. M. deliciosa is the Swiss cheese plant

**MONSTERAS** > MONSTERA

**MONSTERED** > MONSTER

**MONSTERS** > MONSTER

**MONSTROUS** adj unnatural or ugly

**MONTADALE** n breed of sheep

**MONTAGE** n (making of) a picture composed from pieces of others ▷ vb make as montage

**MONTAGED** > MONTAGE

**MONTAGES** > MONTAGE

**MONTAGING** > MONTAGE

**MONTAN** as in montan wax hard wax obtained from lignite and peat used in polishes and candles

**MONTANE** n area of mountain dominated by vegetation ▷ adj of or inhabiting mountainous regions

**MONTANES** > MONTANE

**MONTANT** n vertical part in woodwork

**MONTANTO** n rising blow

**MONTANTOS** > MONTANTO

**MONTANTS** > MONTANT

**MONTARIA** n Brazilian canoe

**MONTARIAS** > MONTARIA

**MONTE** n gambling card game of Spanish origin

**MONTEITH** n large ornamental bowl, usually of silver, for cooling wineglasses, which are suspended from the notched rim

**MONTEITHS** > MONTEITH

**MONTEM** n former money-raising practice at Eton school

**MONTEMS** > MONTEM

**MONTERO** n round cap with a flap at the back worn by hunters, esp in Spain in the 17th and 18th centuries

**MONTEROS** > MONTERO

**MONTES** > MONTE

**MONTH** n one of the twelve divisions of the calendar year

**MONTHLIES** > MONTHLY

**MONTHLING** n month-old child

**MONTHLONG** adj lasting all

month

**MONTHLY** adj happening or payable once a month ▷ adv once a month ▷ n monthly magazine

**MONTHS** > MONTH

**MONTICLE** same as > MONTICULE

**MONTICLES** > MONTICLE

**MONTICULE** n small hill or mound, such as a secondary volcanic cone

**MONTIES** > MONTY

**MONTRE** n pipes of organ

**MONTRES** > MONTRE

**MONTURE** n mount or frame

**MONTURES** > MONTURE

**MONTY** n complete form of something

**MONUMENT** n something, esp a building or statue, that commemorates something

**MONUMENTS** > MONUMENT

**MONURON** n type of weedkiller

**MONURONS** > MONURON

**MONY** Scot word for > MANY

**MONYPLIES** same as > MANYPLIES

**MONZONITE** n coarse-grained plutonic igneous rock consisting of equal amounts of plagioclase and orthoclase feldspar, with ferromagnesian minerals

**MOO** n long deep cry of a cow ▷ vb make this noise ▷ interj instance or imitation of this sound

**MOOCH** vb loiter about aimlessly

**MOOCHED** > MOOCH

**MOOCHER** > MOOCH

**MOOCHERS** > MOOCH

**MOOCHES** > MOOCH

**MOOCHING** > MOOCH

**MOOD** n temporary (gloomy) state of mind

**MOODIED** > MOODY

**MOODIER** > MOODY

**MOODIES** > MOODY

**MOODIEST** > MOODY

**MOODILY** > MOODY

**MOODINESS** > MOODY

**MOODS** > MOOD

**MOODY** adj sullen or gloomy ▷ vb flatter

**MOODYING** > MOODY

**MOOED** > MOO

**MOOI** adj pleasing or nice

**MOOING** > MOO

**MOOK** n person regarded with contempt, esp a stupid person

**MOOKS** > MOOK

**MOOKTAR** same as > MUKHTAR

**MOOKTARS** > MOOKTAR

**MOOL** same as > MOULD

**MOOLA** same as > MOOLAH

**MOOLAH** slang word for > MONEY

**MOOLAHS** > MOOLAH

**MOOLAS** > MOOLA

**MOOLED** > MOOL

**MOOLEY** same as > MOOLY

**MOOLEYS** > MOOLEY

**MOOLI** n type of large white radish

**MOOLIES** > MOOLY

**MOOLING** > MOOL

**MOOLIS** > MOOLI

**MOOLOO** n person from the Waikato

**MOOLOOS** > MOOLOO

**MOOLS** > MOOL

**MOOLVI** same as > MOOLVIE

**MOOLVIE** n (esp in India) a Muslim doctor of the law, teacher, or learned man also used as a title of respect

**MOOLVIES** > MOOLVIE

**MOOLVIS** > MOOLVI

**MOOLY** same as > MULEY

**MOON** n natural satellite of the earth ▷ vb be idle in a listless or dreamy way

**MOONBEAM** n ray of moonlight

**MOONBEAMS** > MOONBEAM

**MOONBLIND** adj (in horses), having a disorder which causes inflammation of the eyes and sometimes blindness

**MOONBOW** n rainbow made by moonlight

**MOONBOWS** > MOONBOW

**MOONCALF** n born fool

**MOONCHILD** n someone who is born under the Cancer star sign

**MOONDUST** n dust on surface of moon

**MOONDUSTS** > MOONDUST

**MOONED** adj decorated with a moon

**MOONER** > MOON

**MOONERS** > MOON

**MOONEYE** n any of several North American large-eyed freshwater clupeoid fishes of the family Hiodontidae, esp Hiodon tergisus

**MOONEYES** > MOONEYE

**MOONFACE** n big round face ▷ vb have a moon face

**MOONFACED** > MOONFACE

**MOONFACES** > MOONFACE

**MOONFISH** n any of several deep-bodied silvery carangid fishes, occurring in warm and tropical American coastal waters

**MOONIER** > MOONY

**MOONIES** > MOONY

**MOONIEST** > MOONY

**MOONILY** > MOONY

**MOONINESS** > MOONY

**MOONING** > MOON

**MOONISH** > MOON

**MOONISHLY** > MOON

**MOONLESS** > MOON

**MOONLET** n small moon

**MOONLETS** > MOONLET

**MOONLIGHT** n light from the moon ▷ adj illuminated by the moon ▷ vb work at a secondary job, esp illegally

**MOONLIKE** > MOON

**MOONLIT** adj illuminated by the moon

**MOONPHASE** n phase of moon

**MOONPORT** n place from which flights leave for moon

**MOONPORTS** > MOONPORT

**MOONQUAKE** n light tremor of the moon, detected on the moon's surface

**MOONRAKER** n small square sail set above a skysail

**MOONRISE** n moment when the moon appears above the horizon

**MOONRISES** > MOONRISE

**MOONROCK** n rock from moon

**MOONROCKS** > MOONROCK

**MOONROOF** same as > SUNROOF

**MOONROOFS** > MOONROOF

**MOONS** > MOON

**MOONSAIL** n small sail high on mast

**MOONSAILS** > MOONSAIL

**MOONSCAPE** n surface of the moon or a picture or model of it

**MOONSEED** n any menispermaceous climbing plant of the genus Menispermum and related genera, having red or black fruits with crescent-shaped or ring-shaped seeds

**MOONSEEDS** > MOONSEED

**MOONSET** n moment when the moon disappears below the horizon

**MOONSETS** > MOONSET

**MOONSHEE** same as > MUNSHI

**MOONSHEES** > MOONSHEE

**MOONSHINE** same as > MOONLIGHT

**MOONSHINY** > MOONSHINE

**MOONSHOT** n launching of a spacecraft to the moon

**MOONSHOTS** > MOONSHOT

**MOONSTONE** n translucent semiprecious stone

**MOONWALK** n instance of walking on moon

**MOONWALKS** > MOONWALK

**MOONWARD** adj towards moon

**MOONWARDS** adv towards moon

**MOONWORT** n any of various ferns of the genus Botrychium, esp B. lunaria, which has crescent-shaped leaflets

**MOONWORTS** > MOONWORT

**MOONY** adj dreamy or listless ▷ n crazy or foolish person

**MOOP** same as > MOUP

**MOOPED** > MOOP

**MOOPING** > MOOP

**MOOPS** > MOOP

**MOOR** n tract of open uncultivated ground covered with grass and heather ▷ vb secure (a ship) with ropes etc

**MOORAGE** n place for mooring a vessel

**MOORAGES** > MOORAGE

**MOORBURN** n practice of burning off old growth on a heather moor to encourage new growth for grazing

**MOORBURNS** > MOORBURN

**MOORCOCK** n male of the red grouse

**MOORCOCKS** > MOORCOCK

**MOORED** > MOOR

**MOORFOWL** n red grouse

**MOORFOWLS** > MOORFOWL

**MOORHEN** n small black water bird

**MOORHENS** > MOORHEN

**MOORIER** > MOOR

**MOORIEST** > MOOR

**MOORILL** n disease of cattle on moors

**MOORILLS** > MOORILL

**MOORING** n place for mooring a ship

**MOORINGS** pl n ropes and anchors used in mooring a vessel

**MOORISH** adj of or relating to the Moor people of North Africa

**MOORLAND** n area of moor

**MOORLANDS** > MOORLAND

**MOORLOG** n rotted wood below surface of moor

**MOORLOGS** > MOOR

**MOORMAN** n person living on moor

**MOORMEN** > MOORMAN

**MOORS** > MOOR

**MOORVA** same as > MURVA

**MOORVAS** > MOORVA

**MOORWORT** n low-growing pink-flowered shrub that grows in peaty bogs

**MOORWORTS** > MOORWORT

**MOORY** > MOOR

**MOOS** > MOO

**MOOSE** n large N American deer

**MOOSEBIRD** n North American jay

**MOOSEWOOD** n North American tree

**MOOSEYARD** n place where moose spend winter

**MOOT** adj debatable ▷ vb bring up for discussion ▷ n (in Anglo-Saxon England) a local administrative assembly

**MOOTABLE** > MOOT

**MOOTED** > MOOT

**MOOTER** > MOOT

**MOOTERS** > MOOT

**MOOTEST** > MOOT

**MOOTING** > MOOT

**MOOTINGS** > MOOT

**MOOTMAN** n person taking part in moot

**MOOTMEN** > MOOTMAN

**MOOTNESS** > MOOT

**MOOTS** > MOOT

**MOOVE** same as > MOVE

**MOOVED** > MOOVE

**MOOVES** > MOOVE

**MOOVING** > MOOVE

**MOP** n long stick with twists of cotton or a sponge on the end, used for cleaning ▷ vb clean or soak up with or as if with a mop

**MOPANE** same as > MOPANI

**MOPANES** > MOPANE

**MOPANI** n leguminous tree, Colophospermum (or Copaifera) mopane, native to southern Africa, that is highly resistant to drought and produces very hard wood

**MOPANIS** > MOPANI

**MOPBOARD** n wooden border fixed round the base of an interior wall

**MOPBOARDS** > MOPBOARD

**MOPE** vb be gloomy and apathetic ▷ n gloomy person

**MOPED** n light motorized cycle

**MOPEDS** > MOPED

**MOPEHAWK** same as > MOPEHAWK

**MOPEHAWKS** > MOPEHAWK

**MOPER** > MOPE

**MOPERIES** > MOPERY

**MOPERS** > MOPE

**MOPERY** n gloominess

**MOPES** pl n the. low spirits

**MOPEY** > MOPE

**MOPHEAD** n person with shaggy hair

**MOPHEADS** > MOPHEAD

**MOPIER** > MOPE

**MOPIEST** > MOPE

**MOPINESS** > MOPE

**MOPING** > MOPE

**MOPINGLY** > MOPE

**MOPISH** > MOPE

**MOPISHLY** > MOPE

**MOPOKE** n species of owl

**MOPOKES** > MOPOKE

**MOPPED** > MOP

**MOPPER** > MOP

**MOPPERS** > MOP

**MOPPET** same as > POPPET

**MOPPETS** > MOPPET

**MOPPIER** > MOPPY

**MOPPIEST** > MOPPY

**MOPPING** > MOP

**MOPPY** adj drunk

**MOPS** > MOP

**MOPSIES** > MOPSY

**MOPSTICK** n mop handle

**MOPSTICKS** > MOPSTICK

**MOPSY** n untidy or dowdy person

**MOPUS** n person who mopes

**MOPUSES** > MOPUS

**MOPY** > MOPE

**MOQUETTE** n thick velvety fabric used for carpets and upholstery

**MOQUETTES** > MOQUETTE

**MOR** n layer of acidic humus formed in cool moist areas where decomposition is slow

**MORA** n quantity of a short syllable in verse

**MORACEOUS** adj of, relating to, or belonging to the Moraceae, mostly tropical and subtropical family of trees and shrubs, including fig, mulberry, breadfruit, and hop, many of which have latex in the stems and heads enclosed in a fleshy receptacle

**MORAE** > MORA

**MORAINAL** > MORAINE

**MORAINE** n accumulated mass of debris deposited by a glacier

**MORAINES** > MORAINE

**MORAINIC** > MORAINE

**MORAL** adj concerned with right and wrong conduct ▷ n lesson to be obtained from a story or event ▷ vb moralize

**MORALE** n degree of confidence or hope of a person or group

**MORALES** > MORALE

**MORALISE** same as > MORALIZE

**MORALISED** > MORALISE

**MORALISER** > MORALIZE

**MORALISES** > MORALISE

**MORALISM** n habit or practice of moralizing

**MORALISMS** > MORALISM

**MORALIST** n person with a strong sense of right and wrong

**MORALISTS** > MORALIST

**MORALITY** n good moral conduct

**MORALIZE** vb make moral pronouncements

**MORALIZED** > MORALIZE

**MORALIZER** > MORALIZE

**MORALIZES** > MORALIZE

**MORALL** same as > MURAL

**MORALLED** > MORALL

**MORALLER** > MORAL

**MORALLERS** > MORAL

**MORALLING** > MORALL

**MORALLS** > MORALL

**MORALLY** > MORAL

**MORALS** > MORAL

**MORAS** > MORA

**MORASS** n marsh

**MORASSES** > MORASS

**MORASSY** > MORASS

**MORAT** n drink containing mulberry juice

**MORATORIA** n plural form of singular moratorium: legally authorized postponement of the fulfilment of an obligation

**MORATORY** > MORATORIA

**MORATS** > MORAT

**MORAY** n large voracious eel

**MORAYS** > MORAY

**MORBID** adj unduly interested in death or unpleasant events

**MORBIDER** > MORBID

**MORBIDEST** > MORBID

**MORBIDITY** n state of being morbid

**MORBIDLY** > MORBID

**MORBIFIC** adj causing disease

**MORBILLI** same as > MEASLES

**MORBUS** n disease

**MORBUSES** > MORBUS

**MORCEAU** n fragment or morsel

**MORCEAUX** > MORCEAU

**MORCHA** n (in India) a hostile demonstration against the government

**MORCHAS** > MORCHA

**MORDACITY** n quality of sarcasm

**MORDANCY** > MORDANT

**MORDANT** adj sarcastic or scathing ▷ n substance used to fix dyes ▷ vb treat (a fabric, yarn, etc) with a mordant

**MORDANTED** > MORDANT

**MORDANTLY** > MORDANT

**MORDANTS** > MORDANT

**MORDENT** n melodic ornament consisting of the rapid alternation of a note with a note one degree lower than it

**MORDENTS** > MORDENT

**MORE** adj greater in amount or degree ▷ adv greater extent ▷ pron greater or additional amount or number

**MOREEN** n heavy, usually watered, fabric of wool or wool and cotton, used esp in furnishing

**MOREENS** > MOREEN

**MOREISH** adj (of food) causing a desire for more

**MOREL** n edible mushroom with a pitted cap

**MORELLE** n nightshade

**MORELLES** > MORELLE

**MORELLO** n variety of small very dark sour cherry

**MORELLOS** > MORELLO

**MORELS** > MOREL

**MORENDO** adv (in music) dying away

**MORENESS** > MORE

**MOREOVER** adv in addition to what has already been said

**MOREPORK** same

*as* > MOPOKE

MOREPORKS > MOREPORK

MORES *pl n* customs and conventions embodying the fundamental values of a community

MORESQUE *adj* (esp of decoration and architecture) of Moorish style ▷ *n* Moorish design or decoration

MORESQUES > MORESQUE

MORGAN *n* American breed of small compact saddle horse

MORGANITE *n* pink variety of beryl, used as a gemstone

MORGANS > MORGAN

MORGAY *n* small dogfish

MORGAYS > MORGAY

MORGEN *n* South African unit of area, equal to about two acres or o.8 hectare

MORGENS > MORGEN

MORGUE *same as* > MORTUARY

MORGUES > MORGUE

MORIA *n* folly

MORIAS > MORIA

MORIBUND *adj* without force or vitality

MORICHE *same as* > MIRITI

MORICHES > MORICHE

MORION *n* 16th-century helmet with a brim and wide comb

MORIONS > MORION

MORISCO *n* a morris dance

MORISCOES > MORISCO

MORISCOS > MORISCO

MORISH *same as* > MOREISH

MORKIN *n* animal dying in accident

MORKINS > MORKIN

MORLING *n* sheep killed by disease

MORLINGS > MORLING

MORMAOR *n* former high-ranking Scottish nobleman

MORMAORS > MORMAOR

MORN *n* morning

MORNAY *adj* served with a cheese sauce

MORNAYS > MORNAY

MORNE *same as* > MOURN

MORNED > MORNE

MORNES > MORNE

MORNING *n* part of the day before noon

MORNINGS > MORNING

MORNS > MORN

MOROCCO *n* goatskin leather

MOROCCOS > MOROCCO

MORON *n* foolish or stupid person

MORONIC > MORON

MORONISM > MORON

MORONISMS > MORON

MORONITY > MORON

MORONS > MORON

MOROSE *adj* sullen or moody

MOROSELY > MOROSE

MOROSER > MOROSE

MOROSEST > MOROSE

MOROSITY > MOROSE

MORPH *n* phonological representation of a morpheme ▷ *vb* undergo or cause to undergo morphing

MORPHEAN *adj* of or relating to Morpheus, the god of sleep and dreams

MORPHED > MORPH

MORPHEME *n* speech element having a meaning or grammatical function that cannot be subdivided into further such elements

MORPHEMES > MORPHEME

MORPHEMIC > MORPHEME

MORPHETIC *same as* > MORPHEAN

MORPHEW *n* blemish on skin

MORPHEWS > MORPHEW

MORPHIA *same as* > MORPHINE

MORPHIAS > MORPHIA

MORPHIC as in *morphic resonance* idea that, through a telepathic effect or sympathetic vibration, an event or act can lead to similar events or acts in the future or an idea conceived in one mind can then arise in another

MORPHIN *variant form of* > MORPHINE

MORPHINE *n* drug extracted from opium, used as an anaesthetic and sedative

MORPHINES > MORPHINE

MORPHING *n* computer technique used for graphics and in films, in which one image is gradually transformed into another image without individual changes being noticeable in the process

MORPHINGS > MORPHING

MORPHINIC > MORPHINE

MORPHINS > MORPHINE

MORPHO *n* type of butterfly

MORPHOGEN *n* chemical in body that influences growth

MORPHOS > MORPHO

MORPHOSES > MORPHOSIS

MORPHOSIS *n* development in an organism or its parts characterized by structural change

MORPHOTIC > MORPHOSIS

MORPHS > MORPH

MORRA *same as* > MORA

MORRAS > MORRA

MORRELL *n* tall eucalyptus, *Eucalyptus longicornis*, of SW Australia, having pointed buds

MORRELLS > MORRELL

MORRHUA *n* cod

MORRHUAS > MORRHUA

MORRICE *same as* > MORRIS

MORRICES > MORRICE

MORRION *same as* > MORION

MORRIONS > MORRION

MORRIS *vb* perform morris dance

MORRISED > MORRIS

MORRISES > MORRIS

MORRISING > MORRIS

MORRO *n* rounded hill or promontory

MORROS > MORRO

MORROW *n* next day

MORROWS > MORROW

MORS > MOR

MORSAL > MORSURE

MORSE *n* clasp or fastening on a cope

MORSEL *n* small piece, esp of food ▷ *vb* divide into morsels

MORSELED > MORSEL

MORSELING > MORSEL

MORSELLED > MORSEL

MORSELS > MORSEL

MORSES > MORSE

MORSURE *n* bite

MORSURES > MORSURE

MORT *n* call blown on a hunting horn to signify the death of the animal hunted

MORTAL *adj* subject to death ▷ *n* human being

MORTALISE *same as* > MORTALIZE

MORTALITY *n* state of being mortal

MORTALIZE *vb* make mortal

MORTALLY > MORTAL

MORTALS > MORTAL

MORTAR *n* small cannon with a short range ▷ *vb* fire on with mortars

MORTARED > MORTAR

MORTARING > MORTAR

MORTARMAN *n* person firing mortar

MORTARMEN > MORTAR

MORTARS > MORTAR

MORTARY *adj* of or like mortar

MORTBELL *n* bell rung for funeral

MORTBELLS > MORTBELL

MORTCLOTH *n* cloth spread over coffin

MORTGAGE *n* conditional pledging of property, esp a house, as security for the repayment of a loan ▷ *vb* pledge (property) as security thus ▷ *adj* of or relating to a mortgage

MORTGAGED > MORTGAGE

MORTGAGEE *n* creditor in a mortgage

MORTGAGER *same as* > MORTGAGOR

MORTGAGES > MORTGAGE

MORTGAGOR *n* debtor in a mortgage

MORTICE *same as* > MORTISE

MORTICED > MORTICE

MORTICER > MORTICE

MORTICERS > MORTICE

MORTICES > MORTICE

MORTICIAN *n* undertaker

MORTICING > MORTICE

MORTIFIC *adj* causing death

MORTIFIED > MORTIFY

MORTIFIER > MORTIFY

MORTIFIES > MORTIFY

MORTIFY *vb* humiliate

MORTISE *n* slot or recess, usually rectangular, cut into a piece of wood, stone, etc, to receive a matching projection (tenon) of another piece, or a mortise lock ▷ *vb* cut a slot or recess in (a piece of wood, stone, etc)

MORTISED > MORTISE

MORTISER > MORTISE

MORTISERS > MORTISE

MORTISES > MORTISE

MORTISING > MORTISE

MORTLING *n* corpse

MORTLINGS > MORTLING

MORTMAIN *n* state or condition of lands, buildings, etc, held inalienably, as by an ecclesiastical or other corporation

MORTMAINS > MORTMAIN

MORTS > MORT

MORTSAFE *n* heavy iron cage or grille placed over the grave of a newly deceased person during the 19th century in order to deter body snatchers

MORTSAFES > MORTSAFE

MORTUARY *n* building where corpses are kept before burial or cremation ▷ *adj* of or relating to death or burial

MORULA *n* solid ball of cells resulting from cleavage of a fertilized ovum

MORULAE > MORULA

MORULAR > MORULA

MORULAS > MORULA

MORWONG *n* food fish of Australasian coastal waters belonging to the *Cheilodactylidae* family

MORWONGS > MORWONG

MORYAH *interj* exclamation of annoyance, disbelief, etc

MOS > MO

MOSAIC *n* design or decoration using small pieces of coloured stone or glass

MOSAICISM *n* occurrence of different types of tissue side by side

MOSAICIST > MOSAIC

MOSAICKED *adj* arranged in mosaic form

MOSAICS > MOSAIC

MOSASAUR n any of various extinct Cretaceous giant marine lizards of the genus *Mosasaurus* and related genera, typically having paddle-like limbs

MOSASAURI > MOSASAUR

MOSASAURS > MOSASAUR

MOSCHATE n odour like musk

MOSCHATEL n small N temperate plant, *Adoxa moschatellina*, with greenish-white musk-scented flowers on top of the stem, arranged as four pointing sideways at right angles to each other and one facing upwards: family *Adoxaceae*

MOSE vb have glanders

MOSED > MOSE

MOSELLE n German white wine from the Moselle valley

MOSELLES > MOSELLE

MOSES > MOSE

MOSEY vb walk in a leisurely manner

MOSEYED > MOSEY

MOSEYING > MOSEY

MOSEYS > MOSEY

MOSH n type of dance, performed to loud rock music, in which people throw themselves about in a frantic and violent manner ▷ vb dance in this manner

MOSHAV n cooperative settlement in Israel, consisting of a number of small farms

MOSHAVIM > MOSHAV

MOSHED > MOSH

MOSHER > MOSH

MOSHERS > MOSH

MOSHES > MOSH

MOSHING > MOSH

MOSHINGS > MOSH

MOSHPIT n area at a rock-music concert, usually in front of the stage, where members of the audience dance in a frantic and violent manner

MOSHPITS > MOSHPIT

MOSING > MOSE

MOSK same as > MOSQUE

MOSKONFYT n South African grape syrup

MOSKS > MOSK

MOSLINGS n shavings from animal skin being prepared

MOSQUE n Muslim temple

MOSQUES > MOSQUE

MOSQUITO n blood-sucking flying insect

MOSQUITOS > MOSQUITO

MOSS n small flowerless plant growing in masses on moist surfaces ▷ vb

gather moss

MOSSBACK n old turtle, shellfish, etc, that has a growth of algae on its back

MOSSBACKS > MOSSBACK

MOSSED > MOSS

MOSSER > MOSS

MOSSERS > MOSS

MOSSES > MOSS

MOSSGROWN adj covered in moss

MOSSIE n common sparrow

MOSSIER > MOSS

MOSSIES > MOSSIE

MOSSIEST > MOSS

MOSSINESS > MOSS

MOSSING > MOSS

MOSSLAND n land covered in peat

MOSSLANDS > MOSSLAND

MOSSLIKE > MOSS

MOSSO adv to be performed with rapidity

MOSSPLANT n individual plant in moss

MOSSY > MOSS

MOST n greatest number or degree ▷ adj greatest in number or degree ▷ adv in the greatest degree

MOSTE > MOTE

MOSTEST > MOST

MOSTESTS > MOST

MOSTLY adv for the most part, generally

MOSTS > MOST

MOSTWHAT adv mostly

MOT n girl or young woman, esp one's girlfriend

MOTE n tiny speck ▷ vb may or might

MOTED adj containing motes

MOTEL n roadside hotel for motorists

MOTELIER n person running motel

MOTELIERS > MOTELIER

MOTELS > MOTEL

MOTEN > MOTE

MOTES > MOTE

MOTET n short sacred choral song

MOTETS > MOTET

MOTETT same as > MOTET

MOTETTIST > MOTET

MOTETTS > MOTET

MOTEY adj containing motes

MOTH n nocturnal insect like a butterfly

MOTHBALL n small ball of camphor or naphthalene used to repel moths from stored clothes ▷ vb store (something operational) for future use

MOTHBALLS > MOTHBALL

MOTHED adj damaged by moths

MOTHER n female parent ▷ adj native or inborn ▷ vb look after as a mother

MOTHERED > MOTHER

MOTHERESE n simplified and repetitive type of speech, with exaggerated intonation and rhythm, often used by adults when speaking to babies

MOTHERING > MOTHER

MOTHERLY adj of or resembling a mother, esp in warmth, or protectiveness

MOTHERS > MOTHER

MOTHERY > MOTHER

MOTHIER > MOTHY

MOTHIEST > MOTHY

MOTHLIKE > MOTH

MOTHPROOF adj (esp of clothes) chemically treated so as to repel clothes moths ▷ vb make mothproof

MOTHS > MOTH

MOTHY adj ragged

MOTI n derogatory Indian English word for a fat woman or girl

MOTIER > MOTEY

MOTIEST > MOTEY

MOTIF n (recurring) theme or design

MOTIFIC adj causing motion

MOTIFS > MOTIF

MOTILE adj capable of independent movement ▷ n person whose mental imagery strongly reflects movement, esp his own

MOTILES > MOTILE

MOTILITY > MOTILE

MOTION n process, action, or way of moving ▷ vb direct (someone) by gesture

MOTIONAL > MOTION

MOTIONED > MOTION

MOTIONER > MOTION

MOTIONERS > MOTION

MOTIONING > MOTION

MOTIONIST n person proposing many motions

MOTIONS > MOTION

MOTIS > MOTI

MOTIVATE vb give incentive to

MOTIVATED > MOTIVATE

MOTIVATES > MOTIVATE

MOTIVATOR > MOTIVATE

MOTIVE n reason for a course of action ▷ adj causing motion ▷ vb motivate

MOTIVED > MOTIVE

MOTIVES > MOTIVE

MOTIVIC adj of musical motif

MOTIVING > MOTIVE

MOTIVITY n power of moving or of initiating motion

MOTLEY adj miscellaneous ▷ n costume of a jester

MOTLEYER > MOTLEY

MOTLEYEST > MOTLEY

MOTLEYS > MOTLEY

MOTLIER > MOTLEY

MOTLIEST > MOTLEY

MOTMOT n any tropical American bird of the family *Momotidae*, having a long tail and blue and brownish-green plumage: order *Coraciiformes* (kingfishers, etc)

MOTMOTS > MOTMOT

MOTOCROSS n motorcycle race over a rough course

MOTOR n engine, esp of a vehicle ▷ vb travel by car ▷ adj of or relating to cars and other vehicles powered by petrol or diesel engines

MOTORABLE adj (of a road) suitable for use by motor vehicles

MOTORAIL n transport of cars by train

MOTORAILS > MOTORAIL

MOTORBIKE n motorcycle

MOTORBOAT n any boat powered by a motor

MOTORBUS n bus driven by an internal-combustion engine

MOTORCADE n procession of cars carrying important people

MOTORCAR n self-propelled electric railway car

MOTORCARS > MOTORCAR

MOTORDOM n world of motor cars

MOTORDOMS > MOTORDOM

MOTORED > MOTOR

MOTORHOME n large motor vehicle with living quarters behind the driver's compartment

MOTORIAL > MOTOR

MOTORIC > MOTOR

MOTORING > MOTOR

MOTORINGS > MOTOR

MOTORISE same as > MOTORIZE

MOTORISED > MOTORISE

MOTORISES > MOTORISE

MOTORIST n driver of a car

MOTORISTS > MOTORIST

MOTORIUM n area of nervous system involved in movement

MOTORIUMS > MOTORIUM

MOTORIZE vb equip with a motor

MOTORIZED > MOTORIZE

MOTORIZES > MOTORIZE

MOTORLESS > MOTOR

MOTORMAN n driver of an electric train

MOTORMEN > MOTORMAN

MOTORS > MOTOR

MOTORSHIP n ship with motor

MOTORWAY n main road for fast-moving traffic

MOTORWAYS > MOTORWAY

**MOTORY** > MOTOR
**MOTOSCAFI** > MOTOSCAFO
**MOTOSCAFO** n motorboat
**MOTS** > MOT
**MOTSER** n large sum of money, esp a gambling win
**MOTSERS** > MOTSER
**MOTT** n clump of trees
**MOTTE** n mound on which a castle was built
**MOTTES** > MOTTE
**MOTTIER** > MOTTY
**MOTTIES** > MOTTY
**MOTTIEST** > MOTTY
**MOTTLE** vb colour with streaks or blotches of different shades ▷ n mottled appearance, as of the surface of marble
**MOTTLED** > MOTTLE
**MOTTLER** n paintbrush for mottled effects
**MOTTLERS** > MOTTLER
**MOTTLES** > MOTTLE
**MOTTLING** > MOTTLE
**MOTTLINGS** > MOTTLE
**MOTTO** n saying expressing an ideal or rule of conduct
**MOTTOED** adj having motto
**MOTTOES** > MOTTO
**MOTTOS** > MOTTO
**MOTTS** > MOTT
**MOTTY** n target at which coins are aimed in pitch-and-toss ▷ adj containing motes
**MOTU** n derogatory Indian English word for a fat man or boy
**MOTUCA** n Brazilian fly
**MOTUCAS** > MOTUCA
**MOTUS** > MOTU
**MOTZA** same as > MOTSER
**MOTZAS** > MOTZA
**MOU** Scots word for > MOUTH
**MOUCH** same as > MOOCH
**MOUCHARD** n police informer
**MOUCHARDS** > MOUCHARD
**MOUCHED** > MOUCH
**MOUCHER** > MOUCH
**MOUCHERS** > MOUCH
**MOUCHES** > MOUCH
**MOUCHING** > MOUCH
**MOUCHOIR** n handkerchief
**MOUCHOIRS** > MOUCHOIR
**MOUDIWART** same as > MOULDWARP
**MOUDIWORT** same as > MOULDWARP
**MOUE** n disdainful or pouting look
**MOUES** > MOUE
**MOUFFLON** same as > MOUFLON
**MOUFFLONS** > MOUFFLON
**MOUFLON** n wild short-fleeced mountain sheep, Ovis musimon, of Corsica and Sardinia
**MOUFLONS** > MOUFLON
**MOUGHT** > MOTE
**MOUILLE** adj palatalized, as

in the sounds represented by Spanish ll or ñ
**MOUJIK** same as > MUZHIK
**MOUJIKS** > MOUJIK
**MOULAGE** n mould making
**MOULAGES** > MOULAGE
**MOULD** n hollow container in which metal etc is cast ▷ vb shape
**MOULDABLE** > MOULD
**MOULDED** > MOULD
**MOULDER** vb decay into dust ▷ n person who moulds or makes moulds
**MOULDERED** > MOULDER
**MOULDERS** > MOULDER
**MOULDIER** > MOULDY
**MOULDIEST** > MOULDY
**MOULDING** n moulded ornamental edging
**MOULDINGS** > MOULDING
**MOULDS** > MOULD
**MOULDWARP** archaic or dialect name for a > MOLE
**MOULDY** adj stale or musty
**MOULIN** n vertical shaft in a glacier, maintained by a constant descending stream of water and debris
**MOULINET** n device for bending crossbow
**MOULINETS** > MOULINET
**MOULINS** > MOULIN
**MOULS** Scots word for > MOULD
**MOULT** vb shed feathers, hair, or skin to make way for new growth ▷ n process of moulting
**MOULTED** > MOULT
**MOULTEN** adj having moulted
**MOULTER** > MOULT
**MOULTERS** > MOULT
**MOULTING** > MOULT
**MOULTINGS** > MOULT
**MOULTS** > MOULT
**MOUND** n heap, esp of earth or stones ▷ vb gather into a mound
**MOUNDBIRD** n Australian bird laying eggs in mounds
**MOUNDED** > MOUND
**MOUNDING** > MOUND
**MOUNDS** > MOUND
**MOUNSEER** same as > MONSIEUR
**MOUNSEERS** > MOUNSEER
**MOUNT** vb climb or ascend ▷ n backing or support on which something is fixed
**MOUNTABLE** > MOUNT
**MOUNTAIN** n hill of great size ▷ adj of, found on, or for use on a mountain or mountains
**MOUNTAINS** > MOUNTAIN
**MOUNTAINY** > MOUNTAIN
**MOUNTANT** n adhesive for mounting pictures
**MOUNTANTS** > MOUNTANT
**MOUNTED** adj riding horses
**MOUNTER** > MOUNT
**MOUNTERS** > MOUNT

**MOUNTING** same as > MOUNT
**MOUNTINGS** > MOUNTING
**MOUNTS** > MOUNT
**MOUP** n nibble
**MOUPED** > MOUP
**MOUPING** > MOUP
**MOUPS** > MOUP
**MOURN** vb feel or express sorrow for (a dead person or lost thing)
**MOURNED** > MOURN
**MOURNER** n person attending a funeral
**MOURNERS** > MOURNER
**MOURNFUL** adj sad or dismal
**MOURNING** n grieving ▷ adj of or relating to mourning
**MOURNINGS** > MOURNING
**MOURNIVAL** n card game
**MOURNS** > MOURN
**MOUS** > MOU
**MOUSAKA** same as > MOUSSAKA
**MOUSAKAS** > MOUSAKA
**MOUSE** n small long-tailed rodent ▷ vb stalk and catch mice
**MOUSEBIRD** another name for > COLY
**MOUSED** > MOUSE
**MOUSEKIN** n little mouse
**MOUSEKINS** > MOUSEKIN
**MOUSELIKE** > MOUSE
**MOUSEMAT** n piece of material on which a computer mouse is moved
**MOUSEMATS** > MOUSEMAT
**MOUSEOVER** n on a web page, any item that changes or pops up when the pointer of a mouse moves over it
**MOUSEPAD** n pad for computer mouse
**MOUSEPADS** > MOUSEPAD
**MOUSER** n cat used to catch mice
**MOUSERIES** > MOUSERY
**MOUSERS** > MOUSER
**MOUSERY** n place infested with mice
**MOUSES** > MOUSE
**MOUSETAIL** n any of various N temperate ranunculaceous plants of the genus Myosurus, esp M. minimus, with tail-like flower spikes
**MOUSETRAP** n spring-loaded trap for killing mice
**MOUSEY** same as > MOUSY
**MOUSIE** n little mouse
**MOUSIER** > MOUSY
**MOUSIES** > MOUSIE
**MOUSIEST** > MOUSY
**MOUSILY** > MOUSY
**MOUSINESS** > MOUSY
**MOUSING** n lashing, shackle, etc, for closing off a hook to prevent a load from slipping off
**MOUSINGS** > MOUSING
**MOUSLE** vb handle roughly
**MOUSLED** > MOUSLE

**MOUSLES** > MOUSLE
**MOUSLING** > MOUSLE
**MOUSME** n Japanese girl
**MOUSMEE** same as > MOUSME
**MOUSMEES** > MOUSMEE
**MOUSMES** > MOUSME
**MOUSSAKA** n dish made with meat, aubergines, and tomatoes, topped with cheese sauce
**MOUSSAKAS** > MOUSSAKA
**MOUSSE** n dish of flavoured cream whipped and set ▷ vb apply mousse to
**MOUSSED** > MOUSSE
**MOUSSES** > MOUSSE
**MOUSSING** > MOUSSE
**MOUST** same as > MUST
**MOUSTACHE** n hair on the upper lip
**MOUSTED** > MOUST
**MOUSTING** > MOUST
**MOUSTS** > MOUST
**MOUSY** adj like a mouse, esp in hair colour
**MOUTAN** n variety of peony
**MOUTANS** > MOUTAN
**MOUTER** same as > MULTURE
**MOUTERED** > MOUTER
**MOUTERER** > MOUTER
**MOUTERERS** > MOUTER
**MOUTERING** > MOUTER
**MOUTERS** > MOUTER
**MOUTH** n opening in the head for eating and issuing sounds ▷ vb form (words) with the lips without speaking
**MOUTHABLE** adj able to be recited
**MOUTHED** > MOUTH
**MOUTHER** > MOUTH
**MOUTHERS** > MOUTH
**MOUTHFEEL** n texture of a substance as it is perceived in the mouth
**MOUTHFUL** n amount of food or drink put into the mouth at any one time when eating or drinking
**MOUTHFULS** > MOUTHFUL
**MOUTHIER** > MOUTHY
**MOUTHIEST** > MOUTHY
**MOUTHILY** > MOUTHY
**MOUTHING** > MOUTH
**MOUTHLESS** > MOUTH
**MOUTHLIKE** > MOUTH
**MOUTHPART** n any of the paired appendages in arthropods that surround the mouth and are specialized for feeding
**MOUTHS** > MOUTH
**MOUTHWASH** n medicated liquid for gargling and cleansing the mouth
**MOUTHY** adj bombastic
**MOUTON** n sheepskin processed to resemble the fur of another animal, esp beaver or seal
**MOUTONNEE** n rounded by action of glacier
**MOUTONS** > MOUTON

MOVABLE adj able to be moved or rearranged ▷ n movable article, esp a piece of furniture
MOVABLES > MOVABLE
MOVABLY > MOVABLE
MOVE vb change in place or position ▷ n moving
MOVEABLE same as > MOVABLE
MOVEABLES > MOVEABLE
MOVEABLY > MOVEABLE
MOVED > MOVE
MOVELESS adj immobile
MOVEMENT n action or process of moving
MOVEMENTS > MOVEMENT
MOVER n person or animal that moves in a particular way
MOVERS > MOVER
MOVES > MOVE
MOVIE n cinema film
MOVIEDOM n world of cinema
MOVIEDOMS > MOVIEDOM
MOVIEGOER n person who goes to cinema
MOVIELAND same as > MOVIEDOM
MOVIEOKE n entertainment in which people act out well-known scenes from movies that are silently playing in the background
MOVIEOKES > MOVIEOKE
MOVIEOLA same as > MOVIOLA
MOVIEOLAS > MOVIEOLA
MOVIES > MOVIE
MOVING adj arousing or touching the emotions
MOVINGLY > MOVING
MOVIOLA n viewing machine used in cutting and editing film
MOVIOLAS > MOVIOLA
MOW vb cut (grass or crops) ▷ n part of a barn where hay, straw, etc, is stored
MOWA same as > MAHUA
MOWAS > MOWA
MOWBURN vb heat up in mow
MOWBURNED > MOWBURN
MOWBURNS > MOWBURN
MOWBURNT adj (of hay, straw, etc) damaged by overheating in a mow
MOWDIE Scot words for > MOLE
MOWDIES > MOWDIE
MOWED > MOW
MOWER > MOW
MOWERS > MOW
MOWING > MOW
MOWINGS > MOW
MOWN > MOW
MOWRA same as > MAHUA
MOWRAS > MOWRA
MOWS > MOW
MOXA n downy material obtained from various plants and used in

Oriental medicine by being burned on the skin as a cauterizing agent or counterirritant for the skin
MOXAS > MOXA
MOXIE n courage, nerve, or vigour
MOXIES > MOXIE
MOY n coin
MOYA n mud emitted from a volcano
MOYAS > MOYA
MOYGASHEL n type of linen
MOYITIES > MOIETY
MOYITY same as > MOIETY
MOYL same as > MOYLE
MOYLE vb toil
MOYLED > MOYLE
MOYLES > MOYLE
MOYLING > MOYLE
MOYLS > MOYL
MOYS > MOY
MOZ n hex ▷ vb jinx someone or something
MOZE vb give nap to
MOZED > MOZE
MOZES > MOZ
MOZETTA same as > MOZZETTA
MOZETTAS > MOZETTA
MOZETTE > MOZETTA
MOZING > MOZE
MOZO n porter in southwest USA
MOZOS > MOZO
MOZZ same as > MOZ
MOZZES > MOZZ
MOZZETTA n short hooded cape worn by the pope, cardinals, etc
MOZZETTAS > MOZZETTA
MOZZETTE > MOZZETTA
MOZZIE same as > MOSSIE
MOZZIES > MOZZIE
MOZZLE n luck
MOZZLES > MOZZLE
MPRET n former Albanian ruler
MPRETS > MPRET
MRIDAMGAM same as > MRIDANG
MRIDANG n drum used in Indian music
MRIDANGA same as > MRIDANG
MRIDANGAM same as > MRIDANG
MRIDANGAS > MRIDANGA
MRIDANGS > MRIDANG
MU n 12th letter in the Greek alphabet, a consonant, transliterated as m
MUCATE n salt of mucic acid
MUCATES > MUCATE
MUCH adj large amount or degree of ▷ n large amount or degree ▷ adv great degree
MUCHACHO n young man
MUCHACHOS > MUCHACHO
MUCHEL same as > MUCH
MUCHELL same as > MUCH
MUCHELLS > MUCHELL
MUCHELS > MUCHEL

MUCHES > MUCH
MUCHLY > MUCH
MUCHNESS n magnitude
MUCHO adv Spanish for very
MUCIC as in mucic acid colourless crystalline solid carboxylic acid found in milk sugar and used in the manufacture of pyrrole
MUCID adj mouldy, musty, or slimy
MUCIDITY > MUCID
MUCIDNESS > MUCID
MUCIGEN n substance present in mucous cells that is converted into mucin
MUCIGENS > MUCIGEN
MUCILAGE n gum or glue
MUCILAGES > MUCILAGE
MUCIN n any of a group of nitrogenous mucoproteins occurring in saliva, skin, tendon, etc, that produce a very viscous solution in water
MUCINOGEN n substance forming mucin
MUCINOID adj of or like mucin
MUCINOUS > MUCIN
MUCINS > MUCIN
MUCK n dirt, filth
MUCKAMUCK n food ▷ vb consume food
MUCKED > MUCK
MUCKENDER n handkerchief
MUCKER n person who shifts broken rock or waste ▷ vb hoard
MUCKERED > MUCKER
MUCKERING > MUCKER
MUCKERISH > MUCKER
MUCKERS > MUCKER
MUCKHEAP n dunghill
MUCKHEAPS > MUCKHEAP
MUCKIER > MUCKY
MUCKIEST > MUCKY
MUCKILY > MUCKY
MUCKINESS > MUCKY
MUCKING > MUCK
MUCKLE same as > MICKLE
MUCKLES > MUCKLE
MUCKLUCK same as > MUKLUK
MUCKLUCKS > MUCKLUCK
MUCKRAKE n agricultural rake for spreading manure ▷ vb seek out and expose scandal, esp concerning public figures
MUCKRAKED > MUCKRAKE
MUCKRAKER > MUCKRAKE
MUCKRAKES > MUCKRAKE
MUCKS > MUCK
MUCKSWEAT n profuse sweat
MUCKWORM n any larva or worm that lives in mud
MUCKWORMS > MUCKWORM
MUCKY adj dirty or muddy
MUCLUC same as > MUKLUK
MUCLUCS > MUCLUC
MUCOID adj of the nature of

or resembling mucin ▷ n substance like mucin
MUCOIDAL same as > MUCOID
MUCOIDS > MUCOID
MUCOLYTIC adj breaking down mucus
MUCOR n any fungus belonging to the genus Mucor, which comprises many common moulds
MUCORS > MUCOR
MUCOSA n mucous membrane: mucus-secreting membrane that lines body cavities or passages that are open to the external environment
MUCOSAE > MUCOSA
MUCOSAL > MUCOSA
MUCOSAS > MUCOSA
MUCOSE same as > MUCOUS
MUCOSITY > MUCOUS
MUCOUS adj of, resembling, or secreting mucus
MUCRO n short pointed projection from certain parts or organs, as from the tip of a leaf
MUCRONATE adj terminating in a sharp point
MUCRONES > MUCRO
MUCROS > MUCRO
MUCULENT adj like mucus
MUCUS n slimy secretion of the mucous membranes
MUCUSES > MUCUS
MUD n wet soft earth ▷ vb cover in mud
MUDBATH n medicinal bath in heated mud
MUDBATHS > MUDBATH
MUDBUG n crayfish
MUDBUGS > MUDBUG
MUDCAP vb use explosive charge in blasting
MUDCAPPED > MUDCAP
MUDCAPS > MUDCAP
MUDCAT n any of several large North American catfish living in muddy rivers, esp in the Mississippi valley
MUDCATS > MUDCAT
MUDDED > MUD
MUDDER n horse that runs well in mud
MUDDERS > MUDDER
MUDDIED > MUDDY
MUDDIER > MUDDY
MUDDIES > MUDDY
MUDDIEST > MUDDY
MUDDILY > MUDDY
MUDDINESS > MUDDY
MUDDING > MUD
MUDDLE vb confuse ▷ n state of confusion
MUDDLED > MUDDLE
MUDDLER n person who muddles or muddles through
MUDDLERS > MUDDLER
MUDDLES > MUDDLE

MUDDLING > MUDDLE

MUDDLY > MUDDLE

MUDDY *adj* covered or filled with mud ▷ *vb* make muddy

MUDDYING > MUDDY

MUDEJAR *n* Spanish Moor, esp one permitted to stay in Spain after the Christian reconquest ▷ *adj* of or relating to a style of architecture originated by Mudéjares

MUDEJARES > MUDEJAR

MUDEYE *n* larva of the dragonfly, commonly used as a fishing bait

MUDEYES > MUDEYE

MUDFISH *n* any of various fishes, such as the bowfin and cichlids, that live at or frequent the muddy bottoms of rivers, lakes, etc

MUDFISHES > MUDFISH

MUDFLAP *n* flap above wheel to deflect mud

MUDFLAPS > MUDFLAP

MUDFLAT *n* tract of low muddy land, esp near an estuary, that is covered at high tide and exposed at low tide

MUDFLATS > MUDFLAT

MUDFLOW *n* flow of soil or fine-grained sediment mixed with water down a steep unstable slope

MUDFLOWS > MUDFLOW

MUDGE *vb* speak vaguely

MUDGED > MUDGE

MUDGER > MUDGE

MUDGERS > MUDGE

MUDGES > MUDGE

MUDGING > MUDGE

MUDGUARD *n* cover over a wheel to prevent mud or water being thrown up by it

MUDGUARDS > MUDGUARD

MUDHEN *n* water bird living in muddy place

MUDHENS > MUDHEN

MUDHOLE *n* hole with mud at bottom

MUDHOLES > MUDHOLE

MUDHOOK *n* anchor

MUDHOOKS > MUDHOOK

MUDIR *n* local governor

MUDIRIA *n* province of mudir

MUDIRIAS > MUDIRIA

MUDIRIEH *same as* > MUDIRIA

MUDIRIEHS > MUDIRIEH

MUDIRS > MUDIR

MUDLARK *n* street urchin ▷ *vb* play in mud

MUDLARKED > MUDLARK

MUDLARKS > MUDLARK

MUDLOGGER *n* person checking mud for traces of oil

MUDPACK *n* cosmetic paste

applied to the face to improve the complexion

MUDPACKS > MUDPACK

MUDPUPPY *n* aquatic North American salamander of the genus with red feathery external gills and other persistent larval features

MUDRA *n* any of various ritual hand movements in Hindu religious dancing

MUDRAS > MUDRA

MUDROCK *n* type of sedimentary rock

MUDROCKS > MUDROCK

MUDROOM *n* room where muddy shoes may be left

MUDROOMS > MUDROOM

MUDS > MUD

MUDSCOW *n* boat for travelling over mudflats

MUDSCOWS > MUDSCOW

MUDSILL *n* support for building at or below ground

MUDSILLS > MUDSILL

MUDSLIDE *n* landslide of mud

MUDSLIDES > MUDSLIDE

MUDSTONE *n* dark grey clay rock similar to shale but with the lamination less well developed

MUDSTONES > MUDSTONE

MUDWORT *n* plant growing in mud

MUDWORTS > MUDWORT

MUEDDIN *same as* > MUEZZIN

MUEDDINS > MUEDDIN

MUENSTER *n* whitish-yellow semihard whole milk cheese, often flavoured with caraway or aniseed

MUENSTERS > MUENSTER

MUESLI *n* mixture of grain, nuts, and dried fruit, eaten with milk

MUESLIS > MUESLI

MUEZZIN *n* official who summons Muslims to prayer

MUEZZINS > MUEZZIN

MUFF *n* tube-shaped covering to keep the hands warm ▷ *vb* bungle (an action)

MUFFED > MUFF

MUFFIN *n* light round flat yeast cake

MUFFINEER *n* muffin dish

MUFFING > MUFF

MUFFINS > MUFFIN

MUFFISH > MUFF

MUFFLE *vb* wrap up for warmth or to deaden sound ▷ *n* something that muffles

MUFFLED > MUFFLE

MUFFLER *n* scarf

MUFFLERED *adj* with muffler

MUFFLERS > MUFFLER

MUFFLES > MUFFLE

MUFFLING > MUFFLE

MUFFS > MUFF

MUFLON *same as* > MOUFFLON

MUFLONS > MUFLON

MUFTI *n* civilian clothes worn by a person who usually wears a uniform

MUFTIS > MUFTI

MUG *n* large drinking cup ▷ *vb* attack in order to rob

MUGEARITE *n* crystalline rock

MUGFUL *same as* > MUG

MUGFULS > MUGFUL

MUGG *same as* > MUG

MUGGA *n* Australian eucalyptus tree with dark bark and pink flowers, *Eucalyptus sideroxylon*

MUGGAR *same as* > MUGGER

MUGGARS > MUGGAR

MUGGAS > MUGGA

MUGGED > MUG

MUGGEE *n* mugged person

MUGGEES > MUGGEE

MUGGER *n* person who commits robbery with violence, esp in the street

MUGGERS > MUGGER

MUGGIER > MUGGY

MUGGIEST > MUGGY

MUGGILY > MUGGY

MUGGINESS > MUGGY

MUGGING > MUG

MUGGINGS > MUG

MUGGINS *n* stupid or gullible person

MUGGINSES > MUGGINS

MUGGISH *same as* > MUGGY

MUGGS > MUG

MUGGUR *same as* > MUGGER

MUGGURS > MUGGUR

MUGGY *adj* (of weather) damp and stifling

MUGHAL *same as* > MOGUL

MUGHALS > MUGHAL

MUGS > MUG

MUGSHOT *n* police photograph of person's face

MUGSHOTS > MUGSHOT

MUGWORT *n* temperate perennial herbaceous plant, *Artemisia vulgaris*, with aromatic leaves and clusters of small greenish-white flowers: family *Asteraceae* (composites)

MUGWORTS > MUGWORT

MUGWUMP *n* neutral or independent person, esp in politics

MUGWUMPS > MUGWUMP

MUHLIES > MUHLY

MUHLY *n* American grass

MUID *n* former French measure of capacity

MUIDS > MUID

MUIL *same as* > MULE

MUILS > MUIL

MUIR *Scots word for* > MOOR

MUIRBURN *same*

*as* > MOORBURN

MUIRBURNS > MUIRBURN

MUIRS > MUIR

MUIST *same as* > MUST

MUISTED > MUIST

MUISTING > MUIST

MUISTS > MUIST

MUJAHEDIN *n* Muslim guerrilla

MUJAHIDIN *same as* > MUJAHEDIN

MUJIK *same as* > MUZHIK

MUJIKS > MUJIK

MUKHTAR *n* lawyer in India

MUKHTARS > MUKHTAR

MUKLUK *n* soft boot, usually of sealskin, worn in the American Arctic

MUKLUKS > MUKLUK

MUKTUK *n* thin outer skin of the beluga, used as food

MUKTUKS > MUKTUK

MULATTA *n* female mulatto

MULATTAS > MULATTA

MULATTO *n* child of one Black and one White parent ▷ *adj* of a light brown colour

MULATTOES > MULATTO

MULATTOS > MULATTO

MULBERRY *n* tree whose leaves are used to feed silkworms ▷ *adj* dark purple

MULCH *n* mixture of wet straw, leaves, etc, used to protect the roots of plants ▷ *vb* cover (land) with mulch

MULCHED > MULCH

MULCHES > MULCH

MULCHING > MULCH

MULCT *vb* cheat or defraud ▷ *n* fine or penalty

MULCTED > MULCT

MULCTING > MULCT

MULCTS > MULCT

MULE *n* offspring of a horse and a donkey ▷ *vb* strike coin with different die on each side

MULED > MULE

MULES *vb* surgically remove folds of skin from a sheep

MULESED > MULES

MULESES > MULES

MULESING > MULES

MULETA *n* small cape attached to a stick used by the matador during the final stages of a bullfight

MULETAS > MULETA

MULETEER *n* mule driver

MULETEERS > MULETEER

MULEY *adj* (of cattle) having no horns ▷ *n* any hornless cow

MULEYS > MULEY

MULGA *n* Australian acacia shrub growing in desert regions

MULGAS > MULGA

MULING > MULE

MULISH *adj* obstinate

489

**MULISHLY** > MULISH
**MULL** vb think (over) or ponder ▷ n promontory or headland
**MULLA** same as > MULLAH
**MULLAH** n Muslim scholar, teacher, or religious leader
**MULLAHISM** n rule by mullahs
**MULLAHS** > MULLAH
**MULLARKY** same as > MALARKEY
**MULLAS** > MULLA
**MULLED** > MULL
**MULLEIN** n type of European plant
**MULLEINS** > MULLEIN
**MULLEN** same as > MULLEIN
**MULLENS** > MULLEN
**MULLER** n flat heavy implement of stone or iron used to grind material against a slab of stone
**MULLERED** adj drunk
**MULLERS** > MULLER
**MULLET** n edible sea fish
**MULLETS** > MULLET
**MULLEY** same as > MULEY
**MULLEYS** > MULLEY
**MULLIGAN** n stew made from odds and ends of food
**MULLIGANS** > MULLIGAN
**MULLING** > MULL
**MULLION** n vertical dividing bar in a window ▷ vb furnish (a window, screen, etc) with mullions
**MULLIONED** > MULLION
**MULLIONS** > MULLION
**MULLITE** n colourless mineral
**MULLITES** > MULLITE
**MULLOCK** n waste material from a mine
**MULLOCKS** > MULLOCK
**MULLOCKY** > MULLOCK
**MULLOWAY** n large Australian sea fish, valued for sport and food
**MULLOWAYS** > MULLOWAY
**MULLS** > MULL
**MULMUL** n muslin
**MULMULL** same as > MULMUL
**MULMULLS** > MULMULL
**MULMULS** > MULMUL
**MULSE** n drink containing honey
**MULSES** > MULSE
**MULSH** same as > MULCH
**MULSHED** > MULSH
**MULSHES** > MULSH
**MULSHING** > MULSH
**MULTEITY** n manifoldness
**MULTIAGE** adj involving different age groups
**MULTIATOM** adj involving many atoms
**MULTIBAND** adj involving more than one waveband
**MULTIBANK** adj involving more than one bank
**MULTICAR** adj involving several cars
**MULTICAST** n broadcast

from one source simultaneously to several receivers on a network
**MULTICELL** adj involving many cells
**MULTICIDE** n mass murder
**MULTICITY** adj involving more than one city
**MULTICOPY** adj involving many copies
**MULTIDAY** adj involving more than one day
**MULTIDISC** adj involving more than one disc
**MULTIDRUG** adj involving more than one drug
**MULTIFID** adj having or divided into many lobes or similar segments
**MULTIFIL** n fibre made up of many filaments
**MULTIFILS** > MULTIFIL
**MULTIFOIL** n ornamental design having a large number of foils
**MULTIFOLD** adj many times doubled
**MULTIFORM** adj having many shapes or forms
**MULTIGERM** adj (of plants) having the ability to multiply germinate
**MULTIGRID** adj involving several grids
**MULTIGYM** n exercise apparatus incorporating a variety of weights, used for toning the muscles
**MULTIGYMS** > MULTIGYM
**MULTIHUED** adj having many colours
**MULTIHULL** n sailing vessel with two or more hulls
**MULTIJET** adj involving more than one jet
**MULTILANE** adj having several lanes
**MULTILINE** adj involving several lines
**MULTILOBE** adj having more than one lobe
**MULTIMODE** adj involving several modes
**MULTIPACK** n form of packaging of foodstuffs, etc, that contains several units and is offered at a price below that of the equivalent number of units
**MULTIPAGE** adj involving many pages
**MULTIPARA** n woman who has given birth to more than one viable fetus or living child
**MULTIPART** adj involving many parts
**MULTIPATH** adj relating to television or radio signals that travel by more than one route from a transmitter and arrive at slightly different times,

causing ghost images or audio distortion
**MULTIPED** adj having many feet ▷ n insect or animal having many feet
**MULTIPEDE** same as > MULTIPED
**MULTIPEDS** > MULTIPED
**MULTIPION** adj involving many pions
**MULTIPLE** adj having many parts ▷ n quantity which contains another an exact number of times
**MULTIPLES** > MULTIPLE
**MULTIPLET** n set of closely spaced lines in a spectrum, resulting from small differences between the energy levels of atoms or molecules
**MULTIPLEX** n purpose-built complex containing several cinemas and usu. restaurants and bars ▷ adj having many elements, complex ▷ vb send (messages or signals) or (of messages or signals) be sent by multiplex
**MULTIPLY** vb increase in number or degree
**MULTIPOLE** adj involving more than one pole
**MULTIPORT** adj involving more than one port
**MULTIROLE** adj having a number of roles, functions, etc
**MULTIROOM** adj having many rooms
**MULTISITE** adj involving more than one site
**MULTISIZE** adj involving more than size
**MULTISTEP** adj involving several steps
**MULTITASK** vb work at several different tasks simultaneously
**MULTITON** adj weighing several tons
**MULTITONE** adj involving more than one tone
**MULTITUDE** n great number
**MULTIUNIT** adj involving more than one unit
**MULTIUSE** adj suitable for more than one use
**MULTIUSER** > MULTIUSE
**MULTIWALL** adj involving several layers
**MULTIYEAR** adj involving more than one year
**MULTUM** n substance used in brewing
**MULTUMS** > MULTUM
**MULTURE** n fee formerly paid to a miller for grinding grain ▷ vb take multure
**MULTURED** > MULTURE
**MULTURER** > MULTURE

**MULTURERS** > MULTURE
**MULTURES** > MULTURE
**MULTURING** > MULTURE
**MUM** n mother ▷ vb act in a mummer's play
**MUMBLE** vb speak indistinctly, mutter ▷ n indistinct utterance
**MUMBLED** > MUMBLE
**MUMBLER** > MUMBLE
**MUMBLERS** > MUMBLE
**MUMBLES** > MUMBLE
**MUMBLING** > MUMBLE
**MUMBLINGS** > MUMBLE
**MUMBLY** > MUMBLE
**MUMCHANCE** adj silent
**MUMM** same as > MUM
**MUMMED** > MUM
**MUMMER** n actor in a traditional English folk play or mime
**MUMMERIES** > MUMMERY
**MUMMERS** > MUMMER
**MUMMERY** n performance by mummers
**MUMMIA** n mummified flesh used as medicine
**MUMMIAS** > MUMMIA
**MUMMICHOG** n small American fish
**MUMMIED** > MUMMY
**MUMMIES** > MUMMY
**MUMMIFIED** > MUMMIFY
**MUMMIFIES** > MUMMIFY
**MUMMIFORM** adj like mummy
**MUMMIFY** vb preserve the body of (a human or animal) as a mummy
**MUMMING** > MUM
**MUMMINGS** > MUM
**MUMMOCK** same as > MAMMOCK
**MUMMOCKS** > MUMMOCK
**MUMMS** > MUMM
**MUMMY** n body embalmed and wrapped for burial in ancient Egypt ▷ vb mummify
**MUMMYING** > MUMMY
**MUMP** vb be silent
**MUMPED** > MUMP
**MUMPER** > MUMP
**MUMPERS** > MUMP
**MUMPING** > MUMP
**MUMPISH** > MUMPS
**MUMPISHLY** > MUMPS
**MUMPS** n infectious disease with swelling in the glands of the neck
**MUMPSIMUS** n opinion held obstinately
**MUMS** > MUM
**MUMSIER** > MUMSY
**MUMSIEST** > MUMSY
**MUMSY** adj out of fashion
**MUMU** n oven in Papua New Guinea
**MUMUS** > MUMU
**MUN** same as > MAUN
**MUNCH** vb chew noisily and steadily
**MUNCHABLE** > MUNCH
**MUNCHED** > MUNCH

MUNCHER > MUNCH
MUNCHERS > MUNCH
MUNCHES > MUNCH
MUNCHIES pl n the. craving for food, induced by alcohol or drugs
MUNCHING > MUNCH
MUNCHKIN n undersized person or a child, esp an appealing one
MUNCHKINS > MUNCHKIN
MUNDANE adj everyday
MUNDANELY > MUNDANE
MUNDANER > MUNDANE
MUNDANEST > MUNDANE
MUNDANITY > MUNDANE
MUNDIC n iron pyrites
MUNDICS > MUNDIC
MUNDIFIED > MUNDIFY
MUNDIFIES > MUNDIFY
MUNDIFY vb cleanse
MUNDUNGO n tripe in Spain
MUNDUNGOS > MUNDUNGO
MUNDUNGUS n smelly tobacco
MUNG vb process (computer data)
MUNGA n army canteen
MUNGAS > MUNGA
MUNGCORN n maslin
MUNGCORNS > MUNGCORN
MUNGED > MUNG
MUNGING > MUNG
MUNGO n cheap felted fabric made from waste wool
MUNGOES > MUNGO
MUNGOOSE same as > MONGOOSE
MUNGOOSES > MUNGOOSE
MUNGOS > MUNGO
MUNGS > MUNG
MUNI n municipal radio broadcast
MUNICIPAL adj relating to a city or town
MUNIFIED > MUNIFY
MUNIFIES > MUNIFY
MUNIFY vb fortify
MUNIFYING > MUNIFY
MUNIMENT n means of defence
MUNIMENTS pl n title deeds or similar documents
MUNIS > MUNI
MUNITE vb strengthen
MUNITED > MUNITE
MUNITES > MUNITE
MUNITING > MUNITE
MUNITION vb supply with munitions
MUNITIONS pl n military stores
MUNNION archaic word for > MULLION
MUNNIONS > MUNNION
MUNS > MUN
MUNSHI n secretary in India
MUNSHIS > MUNSHI
MUNSTER variant of > MUENSTER
MUNSTERS > MUNSTER
MUNT n derogatory word for a Black African
MUNTER n unattractive person
MUNTERS > MUNTER
MUNTIN n supporting or strengthening bar for a glass window, door, etc
MUNTING same as > MUNTIN
MUNTINGS > MUNTING
MUNTINS > MUNTIN
MUNTJAC n any small Asian deer of the genus Muntiacus, typically having a chestnut-brown coat, small antlers, and a barklike cry
MUNTJACS > MUNTJAC
MUNTJAK same as > MUNTJAC
MUNTJAKS > MUNTJAK
MUNTRIE n Australian shrub with green-red edible berries
MUNTRIES > MUNTRIE
MUNTS > MUNT
MUNTU same as > MUNT
MUNTUS > MUNTU
MUON n positive or negative elementary particle with a mass 207 times that of an electron
MUONIC > MUON
MUONIUM n form of hydrogen
MUONIUMS > MUONIUM
MUONS > MUON
MUPPET n stupid person
MUPPETS > MUPPET
MUQADDAM n person of authority in India
MUQADDAMS > MUQADDAM
MURA n group of people living together in Japanese countryside
MURAENA n moray eel
MURAENAS > MURAENA
MURAENID n eel of moray family
MURAENIDS > MURAENID
MURAGE n tax levied for the construction or maintenance of town walls
MURAGES > MURAGE
MURAL n painting on a wall ▷ adj of or relating to a wall
MURALED same as > MURALLED
MURALIST > MURAL
MURALISTS > MURAL
MURALLED adj decorated with mural
MURALS > MURAL
MURAS > MURA
MURDABAD vb down with
MURDER n unlawful intentional killing of a human being ▷ vb kill in this way
MURDERED > MURDER
MURDEREE n murder victim
MURDEREES > MURDEREE
MURDERER > MURDER
MURDERERS > MURDER
MURDERESS > MURDER
MURDERING > MURDER

MURDEROUS adj intending, capable of, or guilty of murder
MURDERS > MURDER
MURE archaic or literary word for > IMMURE
MURED > MURE
MUREIN n polymer found in cells
MUREINS > MUREIN
MURENA same as > MURAENA
MURENAS > MURENA
MURES > MURE
MUREX n any of various spiny-shelled marine gastropods of the genus Murex and related genera: formerly used as a source of the dye Tyrian purple
MUREXES > MUREX
MURGEON vb grimace at
MURGEONED > MURGEON
MURGEONS > MURGEON
MURIATE obsolete name for a > CHLORIDE
MURIATED > MURIATE
MURIATES > MURIATE
MURIATIC as in muriatic acid former name for a strong acid used in many industrial processes
MURICATE adj having a surface roughened by numerous short points
MURICATED same as > MURICATE
MURICES > MUREX
MURID n animal of mouse family
MURIDS > MURID
MURIFORM adj like mouse
MURINE adj of, relating to, or belonging to the Muridae, an Old World family of rodents, typically having long hairless tails: includes rats and mice ▷ n any animal belonging to the Muridae
MURINES > MURINE
MURING > MURE
MURK n thick darkness ▷ adj dark or gloomy
MURKER > MURK
MURKEST > MURK
MURKIER > MURKY
MURKIEST > MURKY
MURKILY > MURKY
MURKINESS > MURKY
MURKISH > MURK
MURKLY > MURK
MURKS > MURK
MURKSOME > MURK
MURKY adj dark or gloomy
MURL vb crumble
MURLAIN n type of basket
MURLAINS > MURLAIN
MURLAN same as > MURLAIN
MURLANS > MURLAN
MURLED > MURL
MURLIER > MURL
MURLIEST > MURL
MURLIN same as > MURLAIN
MURLING > MURL

MURLINS > MURLIN
MURLS > MURL
MURLY > MURL
MURMUR vb speak or say in a quiet indistinct way ▷ n continuous low indistinct sound
MURMURED > MURMUR
MURMURER > MURMUR
MURMURERS > MURMUR
MURMURING > MURMUR
MURMUROUS > MURMUR
MURMURS > MURMUR
MURPHIES > MURPHY
MURPHY dialect or informal word for > POTATO
MURR n former name for a cold
MURRA same as > MURRHINE
MURRAGH n type of large caddis fly
MURRAGHS > MURRAGH
MURRAIN n cattle plague
MURRAINED > MURRAIN
MURRAINS > MURRAIN
MURRAM n type of gravel
MURRAMS > MURRAM
MURRAS > MURRA
MURRAY n large Australian freshwater fish
MURRAYS > MURRAY
MURRE n any guillemot of the genus Uria
MURREE n native Australian
MURREES > MURREE
MURRELET n any of several small diving birds of the genus Brachyramphus and related genera, similar and related to the auks: family Alcidae, order Charadriiformes
MURRELETS > MURRELET
MURREN same as > MURRAIN
MURRENS > MURREN
MURRES > MURRE
MURREY adj mulberry colour
MURREYS > MURREY
MURRHA same as > MURRA
MURRHAS > MURRHA
MURRHINE adj of or relating to an unknown substance used in ancient Rome to make vases, cups, etc ▷ n substance so used
MURRI same as > MURREE
MURRIES > MURRY
MURRIN same as > MURRAIN
MURRINE same as > MURRHINE
MURRINS > MURRIN
MURRION same as > MURRAIN
MURRIONS > MURRION
MURRIS > MURRI
MURRS > MURR
MURRY same as > MORAY
MURTHER same as > MURDER
MURTHERED > MURTHER
MURTHERER > MURTHER
MURTHERS > MURTHER
MURTI n image of a deity, which itself is considered divine once consecrated

**MURTIS** >MURTI
**MURVA** n type of hemp
**MURVAS** >MURVA
**MUS** >MU
**MUSACEOUS** adj of, relating to, a family of tropical flowering plants with large leaves and clusters of elongated berry fruits: includes the banana, edible plantain, and Manila hemp
**MUSANG** n catlike aninal of Malaysia
**MUSANGS** >MUSANG
**MUSAR** n rabbinic literature concerned with ethics, right conduct, etc
**MUSARS** >MUSAR
**MUSCA** n small constellation in the S hemisphere lying between the Southern Cross and Chamaeleon
**MUSCADEL** same as >MUSCATEL
**MUSCADELS** >MUSCADEL
**MUSCADET** n white grape, grown esp in the Loire valley, used for making wine
**MUSCADETS** >MUSCADET
**MUSCADIN** n Parisian dandy
**MUSCADINE** n woody climbing vitaceous plant, Vitis rotundifolia, of the southeastern US
**MUSCADINS** >MUSCADIN
**MUSCAE** >MUSCA
**MUSCARINE** n poisonous alkaloid occurring in certain mushrooms
**MUSCAT** same as >MUSCATEL
**MUSCATEL** n rich sweet wine made from muscat grapes
**MUSCATELS** >MUSCATEL
**MUSCATS** >MUSCAT
**MUSCAVADO** same as >MUSCOVADO
**MUSCID** n any fly of the dipterous family Muscidae, including the housefly and tsetse fly ▷ adj of, relating to, or belonging to the Muscidae
**MUSCIDS** >MUSCID
**MUSCLE** n tissue in the body which produces movement by contracting ▷ vb force one's way (in)
**MUSCLED** >MUSCLE
**MUSCLEMAN** n man with highly developed muscles
**MUSCLEMEN** >MUSCLEMAN
**MUSCLES** >MUSCLE
**MUSCLIER** >MUSCLE
**MUSCLIEST** >MUSCLE
**MUSCLING** >MUSCLE
**MUSCLINGS** >MUSCLE
**MUSCLY** >MUSCLE
**MUSCOID** adj of family of plants
**MUSCOLOGY** n branch of botany

**MUSCONE** same as >MUSKONE
**MUSCONES** >MUSCONE
**MUSCOSE** adj like moss
**MUSCOVADO** n raw sugar obtained from the juice of sugar cane by evaporating the molasses
**MUSCOVITE** n pale brown, or green, or colourless mineral of the mica group
**MUSCULAR** adj with well-developed muscles
**MUSCULOUS** adj muscular
**MUSE** vb ponder quietly ▷ n state of abstraction
**MUSED** >MUSE
**MUSEFUL** >MUSE
**MUSEFULLY** >MUSE
**MUSEOLOGY** n science of museum organization
**MUSER** >MUSE
**MUSERS** >MUSE
**MUSES** >MUSE
**MUSET** same as >MUSIT
**MUSETS** >MUSET
**MUSETTE** n type of bagpipe with a bellows popular in France during the 17th and 18th centuries
**MUSETTES** >MUSETTE
**MUSEUM** n building where natural, artistic, historical, or scientific objects are exhibited and preserved
**MUSEUMS** >MUSEUM
**MUSH** n soft pulpy mass ▷ interj order to dogs in a sled team to start up or go faster ▷ vb travel by or drive a dogsled
**MUSHA** interj Irish exclamation of surprise
**MUSHED** >MUSH
**MUSHER** >MUSH
**MUSHERS** >MUSH
**MUSHES** >MUSH
**MUSHIER** >MUSHY
**MUSHIEST** >MUSHY
**MUSHILY** >MUSHY
**MUSHINESS** >MUSHY
**MUSHING** >MUSH
**MUSHMOUTH** n person speaking indistinctly
**MUSHROOM** n edible fungus with a stem and cap ▷ vb grow rapidly
**MUSHROOMS** >MUSHROOM
**MUSHY** adj soft and pulpy
**MUSIC** n art form using a melodious and harmonious combination of notes ▷ vb play music
**MUSICAL** adj of or like music ▷ n play or film with songs and dancing
**MUSICALE** n party or social evening with a musical programme
**MUSICALES** >MUSICALE
**MUSICALLY** >MUSICAL
**MUSICALS** >MUSICAL

**MUSICIAN** n person who plays or composes music, esp as a profession
**MUSICIANS** >MUSICIAN
**MUSICK** same as >MUSIC
**MUSICKED** >MUSIC
**MUSICKER** >MUSIC
**MUSICKERS** >MUSIC
**MUSICKING** >MUSIC
**MUSICKS** >MUSICK
**MUSICLESS** >MUSIC
**MUSICS** >MUSIC
**MUSIMON** same as >MOUFFLON
**MUSIMONS** >MUSIMON
**MUSING** >MUSE
**MUSINGLY** >MUSE
**MUSINGS** >MUSE
**MUSIT** n gap in fence
**MUSITS** >MUSIT
**MUSIVE** adj mosaic
**MUSJID** same as >MASJID
**MUSJIDS** >MUSJID
**MUSK** n scent obtained from a gland of the musk deer or produced synthetically ▷ vb perfume with musk
**MUSKED** >MUSK
**MUSKEG** n area of undrained boggy land
**MUSKEGS** >MUSKEG
**MUSKET** n long-barrelled gun
**MUSKETEER** n (formerly) a soldier armed with a musket
**MUSKETOON** n small musket
**MUSKETRY** n (use of) muskets
**MUSKETS** >MUSKET
**MUSKIE** n large North American freshwater game fish
**MUSKIER** >MUSKIE
**MUSKIES** >MUSKIE
**MUSKIEST** >MUSKIE
**MUSKILY** >MUSKY
**MUSKINESS** >MUSKY
**MUSKING** >MUSK
**MUSKIT** same as >MESQUITE
**MUSKITS** >MUSKIT
**MUSKLE** same as >MUSSEL
**MUSKLES** >MUSKLE
**MUSKMELON** n any of several varieties of melon, such as the cantaloupe and honeydew
**MUSKONE** n substance in musk
**MUSKONES** >MUSKONE
**MUSKOX** n large Canadian mammal
**MUSKOXEN** >MUSKOX
**MUSKRAT** n N American beaver-like rodent
**MUSKRATS** >MUSKRAT
**MUSKROOT** same as >MOSCHATEL
**MUSKROOTS** >MUSKROOT
**MUSKS** >MUSK
**MUSKY** same as >MUSKIE
**MUSLIN** n fine cotton fabric
**MUSLINED** adj wearing muslin

**MUSLINET** n coarse muslin
**MUSLINETS** >MUSLINET
**MUSLINS** >MUSLIN
**MUSMON** same as >MUSIMON
**MUSMONS** >MUSMON
**MUSO** n musician, esp a pop musician, regarded as being overconcerned with technique rather than musical content or expression
**MUSOS** >MUSO
**MUSPIKE** n Canadian freshwater fish
**MUSPIKES** >MUSPIKE
**MUSQUASH** same as >MUSKRAT
**MUSROL** n part of bridle
**MUSROLS** >MUSROL
**MUSS** vb make untidy ▷ n state of disorder
**MUSSE** same as >MUSS
**MUSSED** >MUSS
**MUSSEL** n edible shellfish with a dark hinged shell
**MUSSELLED** adj poisoned through eating bad mussels
**MUSSELS** >MUSSEL
**MUSSES** >MUSS
**MUSSIER** >MUSSY
**MUSSIEST** >MUSSY
**MUSSILY** >MUSSY
**MUSSINESS** >MUSSY
**MUSSING** >MUSS
**MUSSITATE** vb mutter
**MUSSY** adj untidy or disordered
**MUST** vb used as an auxiliary to express obligation, certainty, or resolution ▷ n essential or necessary thing ▷ vb powder
**MUSTACHE** same as >MOUSTACHE
**MUSTACHED** >MUSTACHE
**MUSTACHES** >MUSTACHE
**MUSTACHIO** n moustache, esp a bushy or elaborate one
**MUSTANG** n wild horse of SW USA
**MUSTANGS** >MUSTANG
**MUSTARD** n paste made from the powdered seeds of a plant, used as a condiment ▷ adj brownish-yellow
**MUSTARDS** >MUSTARD
**MUSTARDY** >MUSTARD
**MUSTED** >MUST
**MUSTEE** n offspring of a White and a quadroon
**MUSTEES** >MUSTEE
**MUSTELID** n member of weasel family
**MUSTELIDS** >MUSTELID
**MUSTELINE** adj of, relating to, or belonging to the Mustelidae, family of typically predatory mammals including weasels, ferrets, minks,

polecats, badgers, skunks, and otters: order *Carnivora* (carnivores) ▷ *n* any musteline animal
**MUSTER** *vb* summon up (strength, energy, or support) ▷ *n* assembly of military personnel
**MUSTERED** > MUSTER
**MUSTERER** > MUSTER
**MUSTERERS** > MUSTER
**MUSTERING** > MUSTER
**MUSTERS** > MUSTER
**MUSTH** *n* state of frenzied sexual excitement in the males of certain large mammals, esp elephants, associated with discharge from a gland between the ear and eye
**MUSTHS** > MUSTH
**MUSTIER** > MUSTY
**MUSTIEST** > MUSTY
**MUSTILY** > MUSTY
**MUSTINESS** > MUSTY
**MUSTING** > MUST
**MUSTS** > MUST
**MUSTY** *adj* smelling mouldy and stale
**MUT** another word for > EM
**MUTABLE** *adj* liable to change
**MUTABLY** > MUTABLE
**MUTAGEN** *n* any substance that can induce genetic mutation
**MUTAGENIC** > MUTAGEN
**MUTAGENS** > MUTAGEN
**MUTANDA** > MUTANDUM
**MUTANDUM** *n* something to be changed
**MUTANT** *n* mutated animal, plant, etc ▷ *adj* of or resulting from mutation
**MUTANTS** > MUTANT
**MUTASE** *n* type of enzyme
**MUTASES** > MUTASE
**MUTATE** *vb* (cause to) undergo mutation
**MUTATED** > MUTATE
**MUTATES** > MUTATE
**MUTATING** > MUTATE
**MUTATION** same as > MUTANT
**MUTATIONS** > MUTATION
**MUTATIVE** > MUTATE
**MUTATORY** *adj* subject to change
**MUTCH** *n* close-fitting linen cap formerly worn by women and children in Scotland ▷ *vb* cadge
**MUTCHED** > MUTCH
**MUTCHES** > MUTCH
**MUTCHING** > MUTCH
**MUTCHKIN** *n* Scottish unit of liquid measure equal to slightly less than one pint
**MUTCHKINS** > MUTCHKIN
**MUTE** *adj* silent ▷ *n* person who is unable to speak ▷ *vb* reduce the volume or soften the tone of a musical instrument by

means of a mute or soft pedal
**MUTED** *adj* (of sound or colour) softened
**MUTEDLY** > MUTED
**MUTELY** > MUTE
**MUTENESS** > MUTE
**MUTER** > MUTE
**MUTES** > MUTE
**MUTEST** > MUTE
**MUTHA** *n* taboo slang word derived from motherfucker
**MUTHAS** > MUTHA
**MUTI** *n* medicine, esp herbal medicine
**MUTICATE** same as > MUTICOUS
**MUTICOUS** *adj* lacking an awn, spine, or point
**MUTILATE** *vb* deprive of a limb or other part
**MUTILATED** > MUTILATE
**MUTILATES** > MUTILATE
**MUTILATOR** > MUTILATE
**MUTINE** *vb* mutiny
**MUTINED** > MUTINE
**MUTINEER** *n* person who mutinies
**MUTINEERS** > MUTINEER
**MUTINES** > MUTINE
**MUTING** > MUTE
**MUTINIED** > MUTINY
**MUTINIES** > MUTINY
**MUTINING** > MUTINE
**MUTINOUS** *adj* openly rebellious
**MUTINY** *n* rebellion against authority, esp by soldiers or sailors ▷ *vb* commit mutiny
**MUTINYING** > MUTINY
**MUTIS** > MUTI
**MUTISM** *n* state of being mute
**MUTISMS** > MUTISM
**MUTON** *n* part of gene
**MUTONS** > MUTON
**MUTOSCOPE** *n* early form of cine camera
**MUTS** > MUT
**MUTT** *n* mongrel dog
**MUTTER** *vb* utter or speak indistinctly ▷ *n* muttered sound or grumble
**MUTTERED** > MUTTER
**MUTTERER** > MUTTER
**MUTTERERS** > MUTTER
**MUTTERING** > MUTTER
**MUTTERS** > MUTTER
**MUTTON** *n* flesh of sheep, used as food
**MUTTONS** > MUTTON
**MUTTONY** > MUTTON
**MUTTS** > MUTT
**MUTUAL** *adj* felt or expressed by each of two people about the other ▷ *n* mutual company
**MUTUALISE** same as > MUTUALIZE
**MUTUALISM** another name for > SYMBIOSIS
**MUTUALIST** > MUTUALISM

**MUTUALITY** > MUTUAL
**MUTUALIZE** *vb* make or become mutual
**MUTUALLY** > MUTUAL
**MUTUALS** > MUTUAL
**MUTUCA** same as > MOTUCA
**MUTUCAS** > MUTUCA
**MUTUEL** *n* system of betting in which those who have bet on the winners of a race share in the total amount wagered less a percentage for the management
**MUTUELS** > MUTUEL
**MUTULAR** > MUTULE
**MUTULE** *n* one of a set of flat blocks below the corona of a Doric cornice
**MUTULES** > MUTULE
**MUTUUM** *n* contract for loan of goods
**MUTUUMS** > MUTUUM
**MUUMUU** *n* loose brightly-coloured dress worn by women in Hawaii
**MUUMUUS** > MUUMUU
**MUX** *vb* spoil
**MUXED** > MUX
**MUXES** > MUX
**MUXING** > MUX
**MUZAKY** *adj* having a bland sound
**MUZHIK** *n* Russian peasant, esp under the tsars
**MUZHIKS** > MUZHIK
**MUZJIK** same as > MUZHIK
**MUZJIKS** > MUZJIK
**MUZZ** *vb* make (something) muzzy
**MUZZED** > MUZZ
**MUZZES** > MUZZ
**MUZZIER** > MUZZY
**MUZZIEST** > MUZZY
**MUZZILY** > MUZZY
**MUZZINESS** > MUZZY
**MUZZING** > MUZZ
**MUZZLE** *n* animal's mouth and nose ▷ *vb* prevent from being heard or noticed
**MUZZLED** > MUZZLE
**MUZZLER** > MUZZLE
**MUZZLERS** > MUZZLE
**MUZZLES** > MUZZLE
**MUZZLING** > MUZZLE
**MUZZY** *adj* confused or muddled
**MVULE** *n* tropical African tree
**MVULES** > MVULE
**MWALIMU** *n* teacher
**MWALIMUS** > MWALIMU
**MY** *adj* belonging to me ▷ *interj* exclamation of surprise or awe ▷ *determiner* of, belonging to, or associated with the speaker or writer (me)
**MYAL** > MYALISM
**MYALGIA** *n* pain in a muscle or a group of muscles
**MYALGIAS** > MYALGIA
**MYALGIC** > MYALGIA

**MYALISM** *n* kind of witchcraft, similar to obi, practised esp in the Caribbean
**MYALISMS** > MYALISM
**MYALIST** > MYALISM
**MYALISTS** > MYALISM
**MYALL** *n* Australian acacia with hard scented wood
**MYALLS** > MYALL
**MYASES** > MYASIS
**MYASIS** same as > MYIASIS
**MYC** *n* oncogene that aids the growth of tumorous cells
**MYCELE** *n* microscopic spike-like structure in mucus
**MYCELES** > MYCELE
**MYCELIA** > MYCELIUM
**MYCELIAL** > MYCELIUM
**MYCELIAN** > MYCELIUM
**MYCELIUM** *n* mass forming the body of a fungus
**MYCELLA** *n* blue-veined Danish cream cheese, less strongly flavoured than Danish blue
**MYCELLAS** > MYCELLA
**MYCELOID** > MYCELIUM
**MYCETES** *n* fungus
**MYCETOMA** *n* chronic fungal infection, esp of the foot, characterized by swelling, usually resulting from a wound
**MYCETOMAS** > MYCETOMA
**MYCOBIONT** *n* fungal constituent of a lichen
**MYCOFLORA** *n* all fungus growing in particular place
**MYCOLOGIC** > MYCOLOGY
**MYCOLOGY** *n* study of fungi
**MYCOPHAGY** *n* eating of mushrooms
**MYCOPHILE** *n* person who likes eating mushrooms
**MYCORHIZA** *n* association of a fungus and a plant in which the fungus lives within or on the outside of the plant's roots forming a symbiotic or parasitic relationship
**MYCOSES** > MYCOSIS
**MYCOSIS** *n* any infection or disease caused by fungus
**MYCOTIC** > MYCOSIS
**MYCOTOXIN** *n* any of various toxic substances produced by fungi some of which may affect food and others of which are alleged to have been used in warfare
**MYCOVIRUS** *n* virus attacking fungi
**MYCS** > MYC
**MYDRIASES** > MYDRIASIS
**MYDRIASIS** *n* abnormal dilation of the pupil of the eye, produced by drugs, coma, etc

**MYDRIATIC** adj relating to or causing mydriasis ▷ n mydriatic drug

**MYELIN** n white tissue forming an insulating sheath around certain nerve fibres

**MYELINE** same as > MYELIN

**MYELINES** > MYELINE

**MYELINIC** > MYELIN

**MYELINS** > MYELIN

**MYELITIS** n inflammation of the spinal cord or of the bone marrow

**MYELOCYTE** n immature granulocyte, normally occurring in the bone marrow but detected in the blood in certain diseases

**MYELOGRAM** n X-ray of the spinal cord, after injection with a radio-opaque medium

**MYELOID** adj of or relating to the spinal cord or the bone marrow

**MYELOMA** n tumour of the bone marrow

**MYELOMAS** > MYELOMA

**MYELOMATA** > MYELOMA

**MYELON** n spinal cord

**MYELONS** > MYELON

**MYGALE** n large American spider

**MYGALES** > MYGALE

**MYIASES** > MYIASIS

**MYIASIS** n infestation of the body by the larvae of flies

**MYIOPHILY** same as > MYOPHILY

**MYLAR** n tradename for a kind of strong polyester film

**MYLARS** > MYLAR

**MYLODON** n prehistoric giant sloth

**MYLODONS** > MYLODON

**MYLODONT** same as > MYLODON

**MYLODONTS** > MYLODONT

**MYLOHYOID** n muscle in neck

**MYLONITE** n fine-grained metamorphic rock, often showing banding and micaceous fracture, formed by the crushing, grinding, or rolling of the original structure

**MYLONITES** > MYLONITE

**MYLONITIC** > MYLONITE

**MYNA** same as > MYNAH

**MYNAH** n tropical Asian starling which can mimic human speech

**MYNAHS** > MYNAH

**MYNAS** > MYNA

**MYNHEER** n Dutch title of addres

**MYNHEERS** > MYNHEER

**MYOBLAST** n cell from which muscle develops

**MYOBLASTS** > MYOBLAST

**MYOCARDIA** pl n muscular tissues of the heart

**MYOCLONIC** > MYOCLONUS

**MYOCLONUS** n sudden involuntary muscle contraction

**MYOFIBRIL** n type of cell in muscle

**MYOGEN** n albumin found in muscle

**MYOGENIC** adj originating in or forming muscle tissue

**MYOGENS** > MYOGEN

**MYOGLOBIN** n protein that is the main oxygen-carrier of muscle

**MYOGRAM** n tracings of muscular contractions

**MYOGRAMS** > MYOGRAM

**MYOGRAPH** n instrument for recording tracings of muscular contractions

**MYOGRAPHS** > MYOGRAPH

**MYOGRAPHY** > MYOGRAPH

**MYOID** adj like muscle

**MYOLOGIC** > MYOLOGY

**MYOLOGIES** > MYOLOGY

**MYOLOGIST** > MYOLOGY

**MYOLOGY** n branch of medical science concerned with the structure and diseases of muscles

**MYOMA** n benign tumour composed of muscle tissue

**MYOMANCY** n divination through observing mice

**MYOMANTIC** > MYOMANCY

**MYOMAS** > MYOMA

**MYOMATA** > MYOMA

**MYOMATOUS** > MYOMA

**MYONEURAL** adj involving muscle and nerve

**MYOPATHIC** > MYOPATHY

**MYOPATHY** n any disease affecting muscles or muscle tissue

**MYOPE** n any person afflicted with myopia

**MYOPES** > MYOPE

**MYOPHILY** n pollination of plants by flies

**MYOPIA** n short-sightedness

**MYOPIAS** > MYOPIA

**MYOPIC** n shortsighted person

**MYOPICS** > MYOPIC

**MYOPIES** > MYOPY

**MYOPS** same as > MYOPE

**MYOPSES** > MYOPS

**MYOPY** same as > MYOPIA

**MYOSCOPE** n electrical instrument for stimulating muscles

**MYOSCOPES** > MYOSCOPE

**MYOSES** > MYOSIS

**MYOSIN** n chief protein of muscle that interacts with actin to form actomyosin during muscle contraction

**MYOSINS** > MYOSIN

**MYOSIS** same as > MIOSIS

**MYOSITIS** n inflammation of muscle

**MYOSOTE** same as > MYOSOTIS

**MYOSOTES** > MYOSOTE

**MYOSOTIS** n any plant of the boraginaceous genus Myosotis

**MYOTIC** > MIOSIS

**MYOTICS** > MIOSIS

**MYOTOME** n any segment of embryonic mesoderm that develops into skeletal muscle in the adult

**MYOTOMES** > MYOTOME

**MYOTONIA** n lack of muscle tone, frequently including muscle spasm or rigidity

**MYOTONIAS** > MYOTONIA

**MYOTONIC** > MYOTONIA

**MYOTUBE** n cylindrical cell in muscle

**MYOTUBES** > MYOTUBE

**MYRBANE** same as > MIRBANE

**MYRBANES** > MYRBANE

**MYRIAD** adj innumerable ▷ n large indefinite number

**MYRIADS** > MYRIAD

**MYRIADTH** > MYRIAD

**MYRIADTHS** > MYRIAD

**MYRIAPOD** n invertebrate with a long segmented body and many legs, such as a centipede ▷ adj of, relating to, or belonging to the Myriapoda

**MYRIAPODS** > MYRIAPOD

**MYRICA** n dried root bark of the wax myrtle, used as a tonic and to treat diarrhoea

**MYRICAS** > MYRICA

**MYRINGA** n eardrum

**MYRINGAS** > MYRINGA

**MYRIOPOD** same as > MYRIAPOD

**MYRIOPODS** > MYRIOPOD

**MYRIORAMA** n picture made up of different parts

**MYRISTIC** adj of nutmeg plant family

**MYRMECOID** adj like ant

**MYRMIDON** n follower or henchman

**MYRMIDONS** > MYRMIDON

**MYROBALAN** n dried plumlike fruit of various tropical trees of the genus Terminalia, used in dyeing, tanning, ink, and medicine

**MYRRH** n aromatic gum used in perfume, incense, and medicine

**MYRRHIC** > MYRRH

**MYRRHINE** > MURRA

**MYRRHOL** n oil of myrrh

**MYRRHOLS** > MYRRHOL

**MYRRHS** > MYRRH

**MYRTLE** n flowering evergreen shrub

**MYRTLES** > MYRTLE

**MYSELF** pron reflexive form of I or me

**MYSID** n small shrimplike crustacean

**MYSIDS** > MYSID

**MYSOST** n Norwegian cheese

**MYSOSTS** > MYSOST

**MYSTAGOG** n person instructing others in religious mysteries

**MYSTAGOGS** > MYSTAGOG

**MYSTAGOGY** n instruction of those who are preparing for initiation into the mysteries

**MYSTERIES** > MYSTERY

**MYSTERY** n strange or inexplicable event or phenomenon

**MYSTIC** n person who seeks spiritual knowledge ▷ adj mystical

**MYSTICAL** adj having a spiritual or religious significance beyond human understanding

**MYSTICETE** n species of whale

**MYSTICISM** n belief in or experience of a reality beyond normal human understanding or experience

**MYSTICLY** > MYSTIC

**MYSTICS** > MYSTIC

**MYSTIFIED** > MYSTIFY

**MYSTIFIER** > MYSTIFY

**MYSTIFIES** > MYSTIFY

**MYSTIFY** vb bewilder or puzzle

**MYSTIQUE** n aura of mystery or power

**MYSTIQUES** > MYSTIQUE

**MYTH** n tale with supernatural characters, usu. of how the world and mankind began

**MYTHI** > MYTHUS

**MYTHIC** same as > MYTHICAL

**MYTHICAL** adj of or relating to myth

**MYTHICISE** same as > MYTHICIZE

**MYTHICISM** n theory that explains miracles as myths

**MYTHICIST** > MYTHICIZE

**MYTHICIZE** vb make into or treat as a myth

**MYTHIER** > MYTHY

**MYTHIEST** > MYTHY

**MYTHISE** same as > MYTHIZE

**MYTHISED** > MYTHISE

**MYTHISES** > MYTHISE

**MYTHISING** > MYTHISE

**MYTHISM** same as > MYTHICISM

**MYTHISMS** > MYTHISM

**MYTHIST** > MYTHISM

**MYTHISTS** > MYTHISM

**MYTHIZE** same as > MYTHICIZE

**MYTHIZED** > MYTHIZE

**MYTHIZES** > MYTHIZE

**MYTHIZING** > MYTHIZE

**MYTHMAKER** n person who

creates myth

**MYTHOI** > MYTHOS

**MYTHOLOGY** *n* myths
collectively

**MYTHOMANE** *n* obsession
with lying, exaggerating,
or relating incredible
imaginary adventures as if
they had really happened

**MYTHOPEIC** *adj* of myths

**MYTHOPOET** *n* poet writing
on mythical theme

**MYTHOS** *n* complex of
beliefs, values, attitudes,
etc, characteristic of a
specific group or society

**MYTHS** > MYTH

**MYTHUS** *same as* > MYTHOS

**MYTHY** *adj* of or like myth

**MYTILOID** *adj* like mussel

**MYXAMEBA** *same
as* > MYXAMOEBA

**MYXAMEBAE** > MYXAMEBA

**MYXAMEBAS** > MYXAMEBA

**MYXAMOEBA** *n* cell produced
by spore

**MYXEDEMA** *same
as* > MYXOEDEMA

**MYXEDEMAS** > MYXEDEMA

**MYXEDEMIC** > MYXOEDEMA

**MYXO** *n* infectious and
usually fatal viral disease
of rabbits characterized
by swelling of the mucous
membranes and formation
of skin tumours

**MYXOCYTE** *n* cell in mucous
tissue

**MYXOCYTES** > MYXOCYTE

**MYXOEDEMA** *n* disease
caused by an underactive
thyroid gland,
characterized by puffy
eyes, face, and hands, and
mental sluggishness

**MYXOID** *adj* containing
mucus

**MYXOMA** *n* tumour
composed of mucous
connective tissue, usually
situated in subcutaneous
tissue

**MYXOMAS** > MYXOMA

**MYXOMATA** > MYXOMA

**MYXOS** > MYXO

**MYXOVIRAL** > MYXOVIRUS

**MYXOVIRUS** *n* any of a
group of viruses that cause
influenza, mumps, and
certain other diseases

**MZEE** *n* old person ▷ *adj*
advanced in years

**MZEES** > MZEE

**MZUNGU** *n* White person

**MZUNGUS** > MZUNGU

# Nn

NA *same as* > NAE
NAAM *same as* > NAM
NAAMS > NAAM
NAAN *n* slightly leavened flat Indian bread
NAANS > NAAN
NAARTJE *same as* > NAARTJIE
NAARTJES > NAARTJIE
NAARTJIE *n* tangerine
NAARTJIES > NAARTJIE
NAB *vb* arrest (someone)
NABBED > NAB
NABBER *n* thief
NABBERS > NABBER
NABBING > NAB
NABE *n* Japanese hotpot
NABES > NABE
NABIS *n* Parisian art movement
NABK *n* edible berry
NABKS > NABK
NABLA *another name for* > DEL
NABLAS > NABLA
NABOB *same as* > NAWAB
NABOBERY > NABOB
NABOBESS *n* rich, powerful, or important woman
NABOBISH > NABOB
NABOBISM > NABOB
NABOBISMS > NABOB
NABOBS > NABOB
NABS > NAB
NACARAT *n* red-orange colour
NACARATS > NACARAT
NACELLE *n* streamlined enclosure on an aircraft, esp one housing an engine
NACELLES > NACELLE
NACH *n* Indian dance
NACHAS *n* pleasure
NACHE *n* rump

NACHES *same as* > NACHAS
NACHO *n* snack of a piece of tortilla topped with cheese, peppers, etc
NACHOS > NACHO
NACHTMAAL *same as* > NAGMAAL
NACKET *n* light lunch, snack
NACKETS > NACKET
NACRE *n* mother of pearl
NACRED > NACRE
NACREOUS *adj* relating to or consisting of mother-of-pearl
NACRES > NACRE
NACRITE *n* mineral
NACRITES > NACRITE
NACROUS > NACRE
NADA *n* nothing
NADAS > NADA
NADIR *n* point in the sky opposite the zenith
NADIRAL > NADIR
NADIRS > NADIR
NADORS *n* thirst brought on by excessive consumption of alcohol
NADS *pl n* testicles
NAE *Scot word for* > NO
NAEBODIES > NAEBODY
NAEBODY *Scots variant of* > NOBODY
NAETHING *Scots variant of* > NOTHING
NAETHINGS > NAETHING
NAEVE *n* birthmark
NAEVES > NAEVUS
NAEVI > NAEVUS
NAEVOID > NAEVUS
NAEVUS *n* birthmark or mole
NAFF *adj* lacking quality or taste ▷ *vb* go away

NAFFED > NAFF
NAFFER > NAFF
NAFFEST > NAFF
NAFFING > NAFF
NAFFLY > NAFF
NAFFNESS > NAFF
NAFFS > NAFF
NAG *vb* scold or find fault constantly ▷ *n* person who nags
NAGA *n* cobra
NAGANA *n* disease of all domesticated animals of central and southern Africa
NAGANAS > NAGANA
NAGAPIE *n* bushbaby
NAGAPIES > NAGAPIE
NAGARI *n* set of scripts used as the writing systems for several languages of India
NAGARIS > NAGARI
NAGAS > NAGA
NAGGED > NAG
NAGGER > NAG
NAGGERS > NAG
NAGGIER > NAG
NAGGIEST > NAG
NAGGING > NAG
NAGGINGLY > NAG
NAGGY > NAG
NAGMAAL *n* Communion
NAGMAALS > NAGMAAL
NAGOR *another name for* > REEDBUCK
NAGORS > NAGOR
NAGS > NAG
NAH *same as* > NO
NAHAL *n* agricultural settlement run by an Israeli military youth organization

NAHALS > NAHAL
NAIAD *n* nymph living in a lake or river
NAIADES > NAIAD
NAIADS > NAIAD
NAIANT *adj* swimming
NAIF *less common word for* > NAIVE
NAIFER > NAIF
NAIFEST > NAIF
NAIFLY > NAIVE
NAIFNESS > NAIVE
NAIFS > NAIF
NAIK *n* chief
NAIKS > NAIK
NAIL *n* pointed piece of metal with a head, hit with a hammer to join two objects together ▷ *vb* attach (something) with nails
NAILBITER *n* person who bites his or her nails
NAILBRUSH *n* small stiff-bristled brush for cleaning the fingernails
NAILED > NAIL
NAILER > NAIL
NAILERIES > NAILERY
NAILERS > NAIL
NAILERY *n* nail factory
NAILFILE *n* small metal file used to shape and smooth the nails
NAILFILES > NAILFILE
NAILFOLD *n* skin at base of fingernail
NAILFOLDS > NAILFOLD
NAILHEAD *n* decorative device, as on tooled leather, resembling the round head of a nail
NAILHEADS > NAILHEAD

**NAILING** > NAIL
**NAILINGS** > NAIL
**NAILLESS** > NAIL
**NAILS** > NAIL
**NAILSET** n punch for driving the head of a nail below the surrounding surface
**NAILSETS** > NAILSET
**NAIN** adj own
**NAINSELL** n own self
**NAINSELLS** > NAINSELL
**NAINSOOK** n light soft plain-weave cotton fabric, used esp for babies' wear
**NAINSOOKS** > NAINSOOK
**NAIRA** n standard monetary unit of Nigeria, divided into 100 kobo
**NAIRAS** > NAIRA
**NAIRU** n Non-Accelerating Inflation Rate of Unemployment
**NAIRUS** > NAIRU
**NAISSANCE** French for > BIRTH
**NAISSANT** adj (of a beast) having only the forepart shown above a horizontal division of a shield
**NAIVE** adj innocent and gullible ▷ n person who is naive, esp in artistic style
**NAIVELY** > NAIVE
**NAIVENESS** > NAIVE
**NAIVER** > NAIVE
**NAIVES** > NAIVE
**NAIVEST** > NAIVE
**NAIVETE** variant of > NAIVETY
**NAIVETES** > NAIVETE
**NAIVETIES** > NAIVETY
**NAIVETY** n state or quality of being naive
**NAIVIST** > NAIVE
**NAKED** adj without clothes
**NAKEDER** > NAKED
**NAKEDEST** > NAKED
**NAKEDLY** > NAKED
**NAKEDNESS** > NAKED
**NAKER** n one of a pair of small kettledrums used in medieval music
**NAKERS** > NAKER
**NAKFA** n standard currency unit of Eritrea
**NAKFAS** > NAKFA
**NALA** n ravine
**NALAS** > NALA
**NALED** n type of insecticide
**NALEDS** > NALED
**NALLA** n ravine
**NALLAH** same as > NALLA
**NALLAHS** > NALLAH
**NALLAS** > NALLA
**NALOXONE** n chemical substance that counteracts the effects of opiates by binding to opiate receptors on cells
**NALOXONES** > NALOXONE
**NAM** n distraint
**NAMABLE** > NAME
**NAMASKAR** n salutation

used in India
**NAMASKARS** > NAMASKAR
**NAMASTE** n Indian greeting
**NAMASTES** > NAMASTE
**NAMAYCUSH** n North American freshwater fish
**NAME** n word by which a person or thing is known ▷ vb give a name to
**NAMEABLE** > NAME
**NAMECHECK** vb mention (someone) by name ▷ n mention of someone's name, for example on a radio programme
**NAMED** > NAME
**NAMELESS** adj without a name
**NAMELY** adv that is to say
**NAMEPLATE** n small sign on or by a door giving the occupant's name and, sometimes, profession
**NAMER** > NAME
**NAMERS** > NAME
**NAMES** > NAME
**NAMESAKE** n person with the same name as another
**NAMESAKES** > NAMESAKE
**NAMETAG** n identification badge
**NAMETAGS** > NAMETAG
**NAMETAPE** n narrow cloth tape bearing the owner's name and attached to an article
**NAMETAPES** > NAMETAPE
**NAMING** > NAME
**NAMINGS** > NAME
**NAMMA** as in namma hole Australian word for a natural well in rock
**NAMS** > NAM
**NAMU** n black New Zealand sandfly
**NAN** n grandmother
**NANA** same as > NAN
**NANAS** > NANA
**NANCE** n homosexual man
**NANCES** > NANCE
**NANCIES** > NANCY
**NANCIFIED** adj effeminate
**NANCY** n effeminate or homosexual boy or man
**NANDIN** n type of shrub
**NANDINA** n type of shrub
**NANDINAS** > NANDINA
**NANDINE** n African palm civet
**NANDINES** > NANDINE
**NANDINS** > NANDIN
**NANDOO** > NANDU
**NANDOOS** > NANDOO
**NANDU** n type of ostrich
**NANDUS** > NANDU
**NANE** Scot word for > NONE
**NANISM** n dwarfism
**NANISMS** > NANISM
**NANKEEN** n hard-wearing buff-coloured cotton fabric
**NANKEENS** > NANKEEN
**NANKIN** same as > NANKEEN
**NANKINS** > NANKIN

**NANNA** same as > NAN
**NANNAS** > NANNA
**NANNIE** same as > NANNY
**NANNIED** > NANNY
**NANNIES** > NANNY
**NANNY** n woman whose job is looking after young children ▷ vb be too protective towards
**NANNYGAI** n edible sea fish of Australia which is red in colour and has large prominent eyes
**NANNYGAIS** > NANNYGAI
**NANNYING** > NANNY
**NANNYISH** > NANNY
**NANOBE** n microbe that is smaller than the smallest known bacterium
**NANOBES** > NANOBE
**NANODOT** n microscopic cluster of several hundred nickel atoms used to store large amounts of data in a computer chip
**NANODOTS** > NANODOT
**NANOGRAM** n unit of measurement
**NANOGRAMS** > NANOGRAM
**NANOMETER** same as > NANOMETRE
**NANOMETRE** n one thousand-millionth of a metre
**NANOOK** n polar bear
**NANOOKS** > NANOOK
**NANOSCALE** adj on very small scale
**NANOTECH** n technology of very small objects
**NANOTECHS** > NANOTECH
**NANOTESLA** n unit of measurement
**NANOTUBE** n cylindrical molecule of carbon
**NANOTUBES** > NANOTUBE
**NANOWATT** n unit of measurement
**NANOWATTS** > NANOWATT
**NANOWORLD** n world at a microscopic level, as dealt with by nanotechnology
**NANS** > NAN
**NANUA** same as > MOKI
**NAOI** > NAOS
**NAOS** n ancient classical temple
**NAOSES** > NAOS
**NAP** n short sleep ▷ vb have a short sleep
**NAPA** n type of leather
**NAPALM** n highly inflammable jellied petrol, used in bombs ▷ vb attack (people or places) with napalm
**NAPALMED** > NAPALM
**NAPALMING** > NAPALM
**NAPALMS** > NAPALM
**NAPAS** > NAPA
**NAPE** n back of the neck ▷ vb attack with napalm
**NAPED** > NAPE
**NAPERIES** > NAPERY

**NAPERY** n household linen, esp table linen
**NAPES** > NAPE
**NAPHTHA** n liquid mixture distilled from coal tar or petroleum, used as a solvent and in petrol
**NAPHTHAS** > NAPHTHA
**NAPHTHENE** n any of a class of cycloalkanes found in petroleum
**NAPHTHOL** n white crystalline solid used in dyes
**NAPHTHOLS** > NAPHTHOL
**NAPHTHOUS** > NAPHTHA
**NAPHTHYL** n of, consisting of, or containing either of two forms of the monovalent group $C_{10}H_7-$
**NAPHTHYLS** > NAPHTHYL
**NAPHTOL** same as > NAPHTHOL
**NAPHTOLS** > NAPHTHOL
**NAPIFORM** adj shaped like a turnip
**NAPING** > NAPE
**NAPKIN** same as > NAPPY
**NAPKINS** > NAPKIN
**NAPLESS** adj threadbare
**NAPOLEON** n former French gold coin worth 20 francs
**NAPOLEONS** > NAPOLEON
**NAPOO** vb kill
**NAPOOED** > NAPOO
**NAPOOING** > NAPOO
**NAPOOS** > NAPOO
**NAPPA** n soft leather, used in gloves and clothes, made from sheepskin, lambskin, or kid
**NAPPAS** > NAPPA
**NAPPE** n large sheet or mass of rock that has been thrust from its original position by earth movements
**NAPPED** > NAP
**NAPPER** n person or thing that raises the nap on cloth
**NAPPERS** > NAPPER
**NAPPES** > NAPPE
**NAPPIE** same as > NAPPY
**NAPPIER** > NAPPY
**NAPPIES** > NAPPY
**NAPPIEST** > NAPPY
**NAPPINESS** > NAPPY
**NAPPING** > NAP
**NAPPY** n piece of absorbent material fastened round a baby's lower torso to absorb urine and faeces ▷ adj having a nap
**NAPRON** same as > APRON
**NAPRONS** > NAPRON
**NAPROXEN** n pain-killing drug
**NAPROXENS** > NAPROXEN
**NAPS** > NAP
**NARAS** same as > NARRAS
**NARASES** > NARAS
**NARC** n narcotics agent
**NARCEEN** same

*as* > NARCEINE
**NARCEENS** > NARCEEN
**NARCEIN** *same*
*as* > NARCEINE
**NARCEINE** *n* narcotic alkaloid that occurs in opium
**NARCEINES** > NARCEINE
**NARCEINS** > NARCEIN
**NARCISM** *n* exceptional admiration for oneself
**NARCISMS** > NARCISM
**NARCISSI** > NARCISSUS
**NARCISSUS** *n* yellow, orange, or white flower related to the daffodil
**NARCIST** *same*
*as* > NARCISSIST
**NARCISTIC** *adj* excessively admiring of oneself
**NARCISTS** > NARCIST
**NARCO** *n* officer working in the area of anti-drug operations
**NARCOMA** *n* coma caused by intake of narcotic drugs
**NARCOMAS** > NARCOMA
**NARCOMATA** > NARCOMA
**NARCOS** *n* drug smugglers
**NARCOSE** *same*
*as* > NARCOSIS
**NARCOSES** > NARCOSIS
**NARCOSIS** *n* effect of a narcotic
**NARCOTIC** *adj* of a drug, such as morphine or opium, which produces numbness and drowsiness, used medicinally but addictive ▷ *n* such a drug
**NARCOTICS** > NARCOTIC
**NARCOTINE** *n* type of drug
**NARCOTISE** *same*
*as* > NARCOTIZE
**NARCOTISM** *n* stupor or addiction induced by narcotic drugs
**NARCOTIST** *n* person affected by narcotics
**NARCOTIZE** *vb* place under the influence of a narcotic drug
**NARCS** > NARC
**NARD** *n* any of several plants whose aromatic roots were formerly used in medicine ▷ *vb* anoint with nard oil
**NARDED** > NARD
**NARDINE** > NARD
**NARDING** > NARD
**NARDOO** *n* any of certain cloverlike ferns which grow in swampy areas
**NARDOOS** > NARDOO
**NARDS** > NARD
**NARE** *n* nostril
**NARES** *pl n* nostrils
**NARGHILE** *another name for* > HOOKAH
**NARGHILES** > NARGHILE
**NARGHILLY** *same*
*as* > NARGHILE

**NARGHILY** *same*
*as* > NARGHILE
**NARGILE** *same*
*as* > NARGHILE
**NARGILEH** *same*
*as* > NARGHILE
**NARGILEHS** > NARGILEH
**NARGILES** > NARGILE
**NARGILIES** > NARGILE
**NARGILY** *same*
*as* > NARGHILE
**NARIAL** *adj* of or relating to the nares
**NARIC** > NARE
**NARICORN** *n* bird's nostril
**NARICORNS** > NARICORN
**NARINE** *same as* > NARIAL
**NARIS** > NARES
**NARK** *vb* annoy ▷ *n* informer or spy
**NARKED** > NARK
**NARKIER** > NARKY
**NARKIEST** > NARKY
**NARKING** > NARK
**NARKS** > NARK
**NARKY** *adj* irritable or complaining
**NARQUOIS** *adj* malicious
**NARRAS** *n* type of shrub
**NARRASES** > NARRAS
**NARRATE** *vb* tell (a story)
**NARRATED** > NARRATE
**NARRATER** *same*
*as* > NARRATOR
**NARRATERS** > NARRATER
**NARRATES** > NARRATE
**NARRATING** > NARRATE
**NARRATION** *n* narrating
**NARRATIVE** *n* account, story ▷ *adj* telling a story
**NARRATOR** *n* person who tells a story or gives an account of something
**NARRATORS** > NARRATOR
**NARRATORY** > NARRATIVE
**NARRE** *adj* nearer
**NARROW** *adj* small in breadth in comparison to length ▷ *vb* make or become narrow
**NARROWED** > NARROW
**NARROWER** > NARROW
**NARROWEST** > NARROW
**NARROWING** > NARROW
**NARROWISH** > NARROW
**NARROWLY** > NARROW
**NARROWS** *pl n* narrow part of a strait, river, or current
**NARTHEX** *n* portico at the west end of a basilica or church
**NARTHEXES** > NARTHEX
**NARTJIE** *same as* > NAARTJIE
**NARTJIES** > NARTJIE
**NARWAL** *same as* > NARWHAL
**NARWALS** > NARWAL
**NARWHAL** *n* arctic whale with a long spiral tusk
**NARWHALE** *same*
*as* > NARWHAL
**NARWHALES** > NARWHALE
**NARWHALS** > NARWHAL
**NARY** *adv* not
**NAS** *obsolete contraction of*

has not
**NASAL** *adj* of the nose ▷ *n* nasal speech sound, such as English *m*, *n*, or *ng*
**NASALISE** *same*
*as* > NASALIZE
**NASALISED** > NASALISE
**NASALISES** > NASALISE
**NASALISM** *n* nasal pronunciation
**NASALISMS** > NASALISM
**NASALITY** > NASAL
**NASALIZE** *vb* pronounce nasally
**NASALIZED** > NASALIZE
**NASALIZES** > NASALIZE
**NASALLY** > NASAL
**NASALS** > NASAL
**NASARD** *n* organ stop
**NASARDS** > NASARD
**NASCENCE** > NASCENT
**NASCENCES** > NASCENT
**NASCENCY** > NASCENT
**NASCENT** *adj* starting to grow or develop
**NASEBERRY** *another name for* > SAPODILLA
**NASHGAB** *n* chatter
**NASHGABS** > NASHGAB
**NASHI** *n* fruit of the Japanese pear
**NASHIS** > NASHI
**NASIAL** > NASION
**NASION** *n* craniometric point where the top of the nose meets the ridge of the forehead
**NASIONS** > NASION
**NASSELLA** as in *nassella tussock* type of tussock grass
**NASTALIK** *n* type of script
**NASTALIKS** > NASTALIK
**NASTIC** *adj* (of movement of plants) independent of the direction of the external stimulus
**NASTIER** > NASTY
**NASTIES** > NASTY
**NASTIEST** > NASTY
**NASTILY** > NASTY
**NASTINESS** > NASTY
**NASTY** *adj* unpleasant ▷ *n* something unpleasant
**NASUTE** *n* type of termite
**NASUTES** > NASUTE
**NAT** *n* supporter of nationalism
**NATAL** *adj* of or relating to birth
**NATALITY** *n* birth rate in a given place
**NATANT** *adj* (of aquatic plants) floating on the water
**NATANTLY** *adv* in a floating manner
**NATATION** *n* swimming
**NATATIONS** > NATATION
**NATATORIA** *pl n* indoor swimming pools
**NATATORY** *adj* of or relating to swimming
**NATCH** *sentence substitute*

naturally ▷ *n* notch
**NATCHES** > NATCH
**NATES** *pl n* buttocks
**NATHELESS** *prep* notwithstanding
**NATHEMO** *same*
*as* > NATHEMORE
**NATHEMORE** *adv* nevermore
**NATHLESS** *same*
*as* > NATHELESS
**NATIFORM** *adj* resembling buttocks
**NATION** *n* people of one or more cultures or races organized as a single state
**NATIONAL** *adj* of or serving a nation as a whole ▷ *n* citizen of a nation
**NATIONALS** > NATIONAL
**NATIONS** > NATION
**NATIVE** *adj* relating to a place where a person was born ▷ *n* person born in a specified place
**NATIVELY** > NATIVE
**NATIVES** > NATIVE
**NATIVISM** *n* policy of favouring the natives of a country over the immigrants
**NATIVISMS** > NATIVISM
**NATIVIST** > NATIVISM
**NATIVISTS** > NATIVISM
**NATIVITY** *n* birth or origin
**NATRIUM** *obsolete name for* > SODIUM
**NATRIUMS** > NATRIUM
**NATROLITE** *n* colourless, white, or yellow zeolite mineral
**NATRON** *n* whitish or yellow mineral
**NATRONS** > NATRON
**NATS** > NAT
**NATTER** *vb* talk idly or chatter ▷ *n* long idle chat
**NATTERED** > NATTER
**NATTERER** > NATTER
**NATTERERS** > NATTER
**NATTERING** > NATTER
**NATTERS** > NATTER
**NATTERY** *adj* irritable
**NATTIER** > NATTY
**NATTIEST** > NATTY
**NATTILY** > NATTY
**NATTINESS** > NATTY
**NATTY** *adj* smart and spruce
**NATURA** *n* nature
**NATURAE** > NATURA
**NATURAL** *adj* normal or to be expected ▷ *n* person with an inborn talent or skill
**NATURALLY** > NATURAL
**NATURALS** > NATURAL
**NATURE** *n* whole system of the existence, forces, and events of the physical world that are not controlled by human beings
**NATURED** *adj* having a certain disposition
**NATURES** > NATURE

NATURING adj creative
NATURISM n nudism
NATURISMS > NATURISM
NATURIST > NATURISM
NATURISTS > NATURISM
NAUCH same as > NAUTCH
NAUCHES > NAUCH
NAUGAHYDE n type of vinyl-coated fabric
NAUGHT n nothing ▷ adv not at all
NAUGHTIER > NAUGHTY
NAUGHTIES > NAUGHTY
NAUGHTILY > NAUGHTY
NAUGHTS > NAUGHT
NAUGHTY adj disobedient or mischievous ▷ n act of sexual intercourse
NAUMACHIA n mock sea fight performed as an entertainment
NAUMACHY same as > NAUMACHIA
NAUNT n aunt
NAUNTS > NAUNT
NAUPLIAL > NAUPLIUS
NAUPLII > NAUPLIUS
NAUPLIOID > NAUPLIUS
NAUPLIUS n larva of many crustaceans
NAUSEA n feeling of being about to vomit
NAUSEANT n substance inducing nausea
NAUSEANTS > NAUSEANT
NAUSEAS > NAUSEA
NAUSEATE vb make (someone) feel sick
NAUSEATED > NAUSEATE
NAUSEATES > NAUSEATE
NAUSEOUS adj as if about to vomit
NAUTCH n intricate traditional Indian dance performed by professional dancing girls
NAUTCHES > NAUTCH
NAUTIC same as > NAUTICAL
NAUTICAL adj of the sea or ships
NAUTICS > NAUTIC
NAUTILI > NAUTILUS
NAUTILOID n type of mollusc ▷ adj of this type of mollusc
NAUTILUS n shellfish with many tentacles
NAVAID n navigational aid
NAVAIDS > NAVAID
NAVAL adj of or relating to a navy or ships
NAVALISM n domination of naval interests
NAVALISMS > NAVALISM
NAVALLY > NAVAL
NAVAR n system of air navigation
NAVARCH n admiral
NAVARCHS > NAVARCH
NAVARCHY n navarch's term of office
NAVARHO n aircraft navigation system
NAVARHOS > NAVARHO

NAVARIN n stew of mutton or lamb with root vegetables
NAVARINS > NAVARIN
NAVARS > NAVAR
NAVE n long central part of a church
NAVEL n hollow in the middle of the abdomen where the umbilical cord was attached
NAVELS > NAVEL
NAVELWORT another name for > PENNYWORT
NAVES > NAVE
NAVETTE n gem cut
NAVETTES > NAVETTE
NAVEW another name for > TURNIP
NAVEWS > NAVEW
NAVICERT n certificate specifying the contents of a neutral ship's cargo
NAVICERTS > NAVICERT
NAVICULA n incense holder
NAVICULAR adj shaped like a boat ▷ n small boat-shaped bone of the wrist or foot
NAVICULAS > NAVICULA
NAVIES > NAVY
NAVIGABLE adj wide, deep, or safe enough to be sailed through
NAVIGABLY > NAVIGABLE
NAVIGATE vb direct or plot the path or position of a ship, aircraft, or car
NAVIGATED > NAVIGATE
NAVIGATES > NAVIGATE
NAVIGATOR n person who is skilled in or performs navigation, esp on a ship or aircraft
NAVVIED > NAVVY
NAVVIES > NAVVY
NAVVY n labourer employed on a road or a building site ▷ vb work as a navvy
NAVVYING > NAVVY
NAVY n branch of a country's armed services comprising warships with their crews and organization ▷ adj navy-blue
NAW same as > NO
NAWAB n (formerly) a Muslim ruler or powerful landowner in India
NAWABS > NAWAB
NAY interj no ▷ n person who votes against a motion ▷ adv used for emphasis ▷ sentence substitute no
NAYS > NAY
NAYSAID > NAYSAY
NAYSAY vb say no
NAYSAYER n refuser
NAYSAYERS > NAYSAYER
NAYSAYING > NAYSAY
NAYSAYS > NAYSAY
NAYTHLES same

as > NATHELESS
NAYWARD n towards denial
NAYWARDS same as > NAYWARD
NAYWORD n proverb
NAYWORDS > NAYWORD
NAZE n flat marshy headland
NAZES > NAZE
NAZI n person who thinks or acts in a brutal or dictatorial way
NAZIFIED > NAZIFY
NAZIFIES > NAZIFY
NAZIFY vb make nazi in character
NAZIFYING > NAZIFY
NAZIR n Muslim official
NAZIRS > NAZIR
NAZIS > NAZI
NE conj nor
NEAFE same as > NIEVE
NEAFES > NEAFE
NEAFFE same as > NIEVE
NEAFFES > NEAFFE
NEAL same as > ANNEAL
NEALED > NEAL
NEALING > NEAL
NEALS > NEAL
NEANIC adj of or relating to the early stages in the life cycle of an organism
NEAP adj of, relating to, or constituting a neap tide ▷ vb be grounded by a neap tide
NEAPED > NEAP
NEAPING > NEAP
NEAPS > NEAP
NEAR adj indicating a place or time not far away ▷ vb draw close (to) ▷ prep at or to a place or time not far away from ▷ adv at or to a place or time not far away ▷ n left side of a horse or vehicle
NEARBY adj not far away ▷ adv close at hand
NEARED > NEAR
NEARER > NEAR
NEAREST > NEAR
NEARING > NEAR
NEARLIER > NEARLY
NEARLIEST > NEARLY
NEARLY adv almost
NEARNESS > NEAR
NEARS > NEAR
NEARSHORE n area of coastline water
NEARSIDE n side of a vehicle that is nearer the kerb
NEARSIDES > NEARSIDE
NEAT adj tidy and clean ▷ n domestic bovine animal
NEATEN vb make neat
NEATENED > NEATEN
NEATENING > NEATEN
NEATENS > NEATEN
NEATER > NEAT
NEATEST > NEAT
NEATH short for > BENEATH
NEATHERD n cowherd

NEATHERDS > NEATHERD
NEATLY > NEAT
NEATNESS > NEAT
NEATNIK n very neat and tidy person
NEATNIKS > NEATNIK
NEATS > NEAT
NEB n beak of a bird or the nose of an animal ▷ vb look around nosily
NEBBED > NEB
NEBBICH same as > NEBBISH
NEBBICHS > NEBBICH
NEBBING > NEB
NEBBISH n unfortunate simpleton
NEBBISHE same as > NEBBISH
NEBBISHER same as > NEBBISH
NEBBISHES > NEBBISH
NEBBISHY > NEBBISH
NEBBUK n type of shrub
NEBBUKS > NEBBUK
NEBECK same as > NEBBUK
NEBECKS > NEBECK
NEBEK same as > NEBBUK
NEBEKS > NEBEK
NEBEL n Hebrew musical instrument
NEBELS > NEBEL
NEBENKERN n component of insect sperm
NEBISH same as > NEBBISH
NEBISHES > NEBISH
NEBRIS n fawn-skin
NEBRISES > NEBRIS
NEBS > NEB
NEBULA n hazy cloud of particles and gases
NEBULAE > NEBULA
NEBULAR > NEBULA
NEBULAS > NEBULA
NEBULE n cloud
NEBULES > NEBULE
NEBULISE same as > NEBULIZE
NEBULISED > NEBULISE
NEBULISER same as > NEBULIZER
NEBULISES > NEBULISE
NEBULIUM n element
NEBULIUMS > NEBULIUM
NEBULIZE vb turn (a liquid) into a fine spray
NEBULIZED > NEBULIZE
NEBULIZER n device which turns a drug from a liquid into a fine spray which can be inhaled
NEBULIZES > NEBULIZE
NEBULOSE same as > NEBULOUS
NEBULOUS adj vague and unclear
NEBULY adj wavy
NECESSARY adj needed to obtain the desired result
NECESSITY n circumstances that inevitably require a certain result
NECK n part of the body joining the head to the

shoulders ▷ *vb* kiss and cuddle
**NECKATEE** *n* piece of ornamental cloth worn around the neck
**NECKATEES** > NECKATEE
**NECKBAND** *n* band around the neck of a garment
**NECKBANDS** > NECKBAND
**NECKBEEF** *n* cheap cattle flesh
**NECKBEEFS** > NECKBEEF
**NECKCLOTH** *n* large ornamental usually white cravat worn formerly by men
**NECKED** > NECK
**NECKER** > NECK
**NECKERS** > NECK
**NECKGEAR** *n* any neck covering
**NECKGEARS** > NECKGEAR
**NECKING** *n* activity of kissing and embracing passionately
**NECKINGS** > NECKING
**NECKLACE** *n* decorative piece of jewellery worn around the neck ▷ *vb* kill (someone) by placing a burning tyre round his or her neck
**NECKLACED** > NECKLACE
**NECKLACES** > NECKLACE
**NECKLESS** > NECK
**NECKLET** *n* ornament worn round the neck
**NECKLETS** > NECKLET
**NECKLIKE** > NECK
**NECKLINE** *n* shape or position of the upper edge of a dress or top
**NECKLINES** > NECKLINE
**NECKPIECE** *n* piece of fur, cloth, etc, worn around the neck or neckline
**NECKS** > NECK
**NECKTIE** *same as* > TIE
**NECKTIES** > NECKTIE
**NECKVERSE** *n* verse read to prove clergy membership
**NECKWEAR** *n* articles of clothing, such as ties, scarves, etc, worn around the neck
**NECKWEARS** > NECKWEAR
**NECKWEED** *n* type of plant
**NECKWEEDS** > NECKWEED
**NECROLOGY** *n* list of people recently dead
**NECROPHIL** *n* person who is sexually attracted to dead bodies
**NECROPOLI** *pl n* burial sites or cemeteries
**NECROPSY** *n* postmortem examination ▷ *vb* carry out a necropsy
**NECROSE** *vb* cause or undergo necrosis
**NECROSED** > NECROSE
**NECROSES** > NECROSE
**NECROSING** > NECROSE
**NECROSIS** *n* death of cells

in the body
**NECROTIC** > NECROSIS
**NECROTISE** *same as* > NECROTIZE
**NECROTIZE** *vb* undergo necrosis
**NECROTOMY** *n* dissection of a dead body
**NECTAR** *n* sweet liquid collected from flowers by bees
**NECTAREAL** > NECTAR
**NECTAREAN** > NECTAR
**NECTARED** *adj* filled with nectar
**NECTARIAL** > NECTARY
**NECTARIED** *adj* having nectaries
**NECTARIES** > NECTARY
**NECTARINE** *n* smooth-skinned peach
**NECTAROUS** > NECTAR
**NECTARS** > NECTAR
**NECTARY** *n* any of various glandular structures secreting nectar in a plant
**NED** *n* derogatory name for an adolescent hooligan
**NEDDIER** > NEDDY
**NEDDIES** > NEDDY
**NEDDIEST** > NEDDY
**NEDDISH** > NEDDY
**NEDDY** *n* donkey ▷ *adj* of or relating to neds
**NEDETTE** *n* derogatory name for a female adolescent hooligan
**NEDETTES** > NEDETTE
**NEDS** > NED
**NEE** *prep* indicating the maiden name of a married woman ▷ *adj* indicating the maiden name of a married woman
**NEED** *vb* require or be in want of ▷ *n* condition of lacking something
**NEEDED** > NEED
**NEEDER** > NEED
**NEEDERS** > NEED
**NEEDFIRE** *n* beacon
**NEEDFIRES** > NEEDFIRE
**NEEDFUL** *adj* necessary or required
**NEEDFULLY** > NEEDFUL
**NEEDFULS** *n* must-haves
**NEEDIER** > NEEDY
**NEEDIEST** > NEEDY
**NEEDILY** > NEEDY
**NEEDINESS** *n* state of being needy
**NEEDING** > NEED
**NEEDLE** *n* thin pointed piece of metal with an eye through which thread is passed for sewing ▷ *vb* goad or provoke
**NEEDLED** > NEEDLE
**NEEDLEFUL** *n* length of thread cut for use in a needle
**NEEDLER** *n* needle maker
**NEEDLERS** > NEEDLER
**NEEDLES** > NEEDLE

**NEEDLESS** *adj* unnecessary
**NEEDLIER** > NEEDLE
**NEEDLIEST** > NEEDLE
**NEEDLING** > NEEDLE
**NEEDLINGS** > NEEDLE
**NEEDLY** > NEEDLE
**NEEDMENT** > NEED
**NEEDMENTS** > NEED
**NEEDS** *adv* necessarily ▷ *pl n* what is required
**NEEDY** *adj* poor, in need of financial support
**NEELD** *same as* > NEEDLE
**NEELDS** > NEELD
**NEELE** *same as* > NEEDLE
**NEELES** > NEELE
**NEEM** *n* type of large Indian tree
**NEEMB** *same as* > NEEM
**NEEMBS** > NEEMB
**NEEMS** > NEEM
**NEEP** *dialect name for* > TURNIP
**NEEPS** > NEEP
**NEESBERRY** *same as* > NASEBERRY
**NEESE** *same as* > NEEZE
**NEESED** > NEESE
**NEESES** > NEESE
**NEESING** > NEESE
**NEEZE** *vb* sneeze
**NEEZED** > NEEZE
**NEEZES** > NEEZE
**NEEZING** > NEEZE
**NEF** *n* church nave
**NEFANDOUS** *adj* unmentionable
**NEFARIOUS** *adj* wicked
**NEFAST** *adj* wicked
**NEFS** > NEF
**NEG** *n* photographic negative
**NEGATE** *vb* invalidate
**NEGATED** > NEGATE
**NEGATER** > NEGATE
**NEGATERS** > NEGATE
**NEGATES** > NEGATE
**NEGATING** > NEGATE
**NEGATION** *n* opposite or absence of something
**NEGATIONS** > NEGATION
**NEGATIVE** *adj* expressing a denial or refusal ▷ *n* negative word or statement
**NEGATIVED** > NEGATIVE
**NEGATIVES** > NEGATIVE
**NEGATON** *same as* > NEGATRON
**NEGATONS** > NEGATON
**NEGATOR** > NEGATE
**NEGATORS** > NEGATE
**NEGATORY** > NEGATION
**NEGATRON** *obsolete word for* > ELECTRON
**NEGATRONS** > NEGATRON
**NEGLECT** *vb* take no care of ▷ *n* neglecting or being neglected
**NEGLECTED** > NEGLECT
**NEGLECTER** > NEGLECT
**NEGLECTOR** > NEGLECT
**NEGLECTS** > NEGLECT
**NEGLIGE** *variant*

*of* > NEGLIGEE
**NEGLIGEE** *n* woman's lightweight usu. lace-trimmed dressing gown
**NEGLIGEES** > NEGLIGEE
**NEGLIGENT** *adj* habitually neglecting duties, responsibilities, etc
**NEGLIGES** > NEGLIGE
**NEGOCIANT** *n* wine merchant
**NEGOTIANT** *n* person, nation, organization, etc, involved in a negotiation
**NEGOTIATE** *vb* discuss in order to reach (an agreement)
**NEGRESS** *n* old-fashioned offensive name for a Black woman
**NEGRESSES** > NEGRESS
**NEGRITUDE** *n* fact of being a Negro
**NEGRO** *n* old-fashioned offensive name for a Black man
**NEGROES** > NEGRO
**NEGROHEAD** *n* type of rubber
**NEGROID** *n* member of one of the major racial groups of mankind, which is characterized by brown-black skin and tightly-curled hair
**NEGROIDAL** > NEGROID
**NEGROIDS** > NEGROID
**NEGROISM** > NEGRO
**NEGROISMS** > NEGRO
**NEGRONI** *n* type of cocktail
**NEGRONIS** > NEGRONI
**NEGROPHIL** *n* person who admires Black people and their culture
**NEGS** > NEG
**NEGUS** *n* hot drink of port and lemon juice, usually spiced and sweetened
**NEGUSES** > NEGUS
**NEIF** *same as* > NIEVE
**NEIFS** > NEIF
**NEIGH** *n* loud high-pitched sound made by a horse ▷ *vb* make this sound
**NEIGHBOR** *same as* > NEIGHBOUR
**NEIGHBORS** > NEIGHBOR
**NEIGHBOUR** *n* person who lives or is situated near another ▷ *vb* be or live close (to a person or thing)
**NEIGHED** > NEIGH
**NEIGHING** > NEIGH
**NEIGHS** > NEIGH
**NEINEI** *n* type of plant
**NEINEIS** > NEINEI
**NEIST** *Scots variant of* > NEXT
**NEITHER** *pron* not one nor the other ▷ *adj* not one nor the other (of two)
**NEIVE** *same as* > NIEVE
**NEIVES** > NEIVE
**NEK** *n* mountain pass

NEKS > NEK
NEKTON n population of free-swimming animals that inhabits the middle depths of a sea or lake
NEKTONIC > NEKTON
NEKTONS > NEKTON
NELIES same as > NELIS
NELIS n type of pear
NELLIE n effeminate man
NELLIES > NELLIE
NELLY as in not on your nelly not under any circumstances
NELSON n type of wrestling hold
NELSONS > NELSON
NELUMBIUM same as > NELUMBO
NELUMBO n type of aquatic plant
NELUMBOS > NELUMBO
NEMA n filament
NEMAS > NEMA
NEMATIC adj (of a substance) existing in or having a mesomorphic state in which a linear orientation of the molecules causes anisotropic properties
NEMATODE n slender cylindrical unsegmented worm
NEMATODES > NEMATODE
NEMATOID > NEMATODE
NEMERTEAN n type of ribbon-like marine worm ▷ adj of this worm
NEMERTIAN same as > NEMERTEAN
NEMERTINE same as > NEMERTEAN
NEMESES > NEMESIS
NEMESIA n type of southern African plant
NEMESIAS > NEMESIA
NEMESIS n retribution or vengeance
NEMN vb name
NEMNED > NEMN
NEMNING > NEMN
NEMNS > NEMN
NEMOPHILA n any of a genus of low-growing hairy annual plants
NEMORAL adj of a wood
NEMOROUS adj woody
NEMPT adj named
NENE n rare black-and-grey short-winged Hawaiian goose
NENES > NENE
NENNIGAI same as > NANNYGAI
NENNIGAIS > NENNIGAI
NENUPHAR n type of water lily
NENUPHARS > NENUPHAR
NEOBLAST n worm cell
NEOBLASTS > NEOBLAST
NEOCON n supporter of conservative politics
NEOCONS > NEOCON

NEOCORTEX n part of the brain
NEODYMIUM n silvery-white metallic element of lanthanide series
NEOGENE adj of, denoting, or formed during the Miocene and Pliocene epochs
NEOGOTHIC n style of architecture popular in Britain in the 18th and 19th centuries
NEOLITH n Neolithic stone implement
NEOLITHIC adj relating to the Neolithic period
NEOLITHS > NEOLITH
NEOLOGIAN > NEOLOGY
NEOLOGIC > NEOLOGISM
NEOLOGIES > NEOLOGY
NEOLOGISE same as > NEOLOGIZE
NEOLOGISM n newly-coined word or an established word used in a new sense
NEOLOGIST > NEOLOGISM
NEOLOGIZE vb invent or use neologisms
NEOLOGY same as > NEOLOGISM
NEOMORPH n genetic component
NEOMORPHS > NEOMORPH
NEOMYCIN n type of antibiotic obtained from a bacterium
NEOMYCINS > NEOMYCIN
NEON n colourless odourless gaseous element used in illuminated signs and lights ▷ adj of or illuminated by neon
NEONATAL adj relating to the first few weeks of a baby's life
NEONATE n newborn child, esp in the first week of life and up to four weeks old
NEONATES > NEONATE
NEONED adj lit with neon
NEONOMIAN n Christian religious belief
NEONS > NEON
NEOPAGAN n advocate of the revival of paganism
NEOPAGANS > NEOPAGAN
NEOPHILE n person who welcomes new things
NEOPHILES > NEOPHILE
NEOPHILIA n tendency to like anything new
NEOPHOBE > NEOPHOBIA
NEOPHOBES > NEOPHOBIA
NEOPHOBIA n tendency to dislike anything new
NEOPHOBIC > NEOPHOBIA
NEOPHYTE n beginner or novice
NEOPHYTES > NEOPHYTE
NEOPHYTIC > NEOPHYTE
NEOPILINA n type of mollusc
NEOPLASIA n abnormal

growth of tissue
NEOPLASM n any abnormal new growth of tissue
NEOPLASMS > NEOPLASM
NEOPLASTY n surgical formation of new tissue structures or repair of damaged structures
NEOPRENE n synthetic rubber used in waterproof products
NEOPRENES > NEOPRENE
NEOTEINIA n state of prolonged immaturity
NEOTENIC > NEOTENY
NEOTENIES > NEOTENY
NEOTENOUS > NEOTENY
NEOTENY n persistence of larval or fetal features in the adult form of an animal
NEOTERIC adj belonging to a new fashion or trend ▷ n new writer or philosopher
NEOTERICS > NEOTERIC
NEOTERISE same as > NEOTERIZE
NEOTERISM > NEOTERIC
NEOTERIST > NEOTERIC
NEOTERIZE vb introduce new things
NEOTOXIN n harmful agent
NEOTOXINS > NEOTOXIN
NEOTROPIC adj of tropical America
NEOTYPE n specimen selected to replace a type specimen that has been lost or destroyed
NEOTYPES > NEOTYPE
NEP n catmint
NEPENTHE n drug that ancient writers referred to as a means of forgetting - grief or trouble
NEPENTHES > NEPENTHE
NEPER n unit expressing the ratio of two quantities
NEPERS > NEPER
NEPETA same as > CATMINT
NEPETAS > NEPETA
NEPHALISM n teetotalism
NEPHALIST > NEPHALISM
NEPHELINE n whitish mineral
NEPHELITE same as > NEPHELINE
NEPHEW n son of one's sister or brother
NEPHEWS > NEPHEW
NEPHOGRAM n photograph of a cloud
NEPHOLOGY n study of clouds
NEPHRALGY n pain in a kidney
NEPHRIC adj renal
NEPHRIDIA pl n simple excretory organs of many invertebrates
NEPHRISM n chronic kidney disease
NEPHRISMS > NEPHRISM
NEPHRITE n tough fibrous

amphibole mineral
NEPHRITES > NEPHRITE
NEPHRITIC adj of or relating to the kidneys
NEPHRITIS n inflammation of a kidney
NEPHROID adj kidney-shaped
NEPHRON n minute urine-secreting tubule in the kidney
NEPHRONS > NEPHRON
NEPHROSES > NEPHROSIS
NEPHROSIS n any noninflammatory degenerative kidney disease
NEPHROTIC > NEPHROSIS
NEPIONIC adj of or relating to the juvenile period in the life cycle of an organism
NEPIT same as > NIT
NEPITS > NEPIT
NEPOTIC > NEPOTISM
NEPOTISM n favouritism in business shown to relatives and friends
NEPOTISMS > NEPOTISM
NEPOTIST > NEPOTISM
NEPOTISTS > NEPOTISM
NEPS > NEP
NEPTUNIUM n synthetic radioactive metallic element
NERAL n isomer of citral
NERALS > NERAL
NERD n boring person obsessed with a particular subject
NERDIER > NERD
NERDIEST > NERD
NERDINESS > NERD
NERDISH > NERD
NERDS > NERD
NERDY > NERD
NEREID n sea nymph in Greek mythology
NEREIDES > NEREID
NEREIDS > NEREID
NEREIS n any polychaete worm of the genus Nereis
NERINE n type of S African plant related to the amaryllis
NERINES > NERINE
NERITE n type of sea snail
NERITES > NERITE
NERITIC adj of or formed in the region of shallow seas near a coastline
NERK n fool
NERKA n type of salmon
NERKAS > NERKA
NERKS > NERK
NEROL n scented liquid
NEROLI n brown oil used in perfumery
NEROLIS > NEROLI
NEROLS > NEROL
NERTS interj nuts
NERTZ same as > NERTS
NERVAL > NERVE
NERVATE adj (of leaves)

with veins
**NERVATION** *less common word for* > VENATION
**NERVATURE** *same as* > NERVATION
**NERVE** *n* cordlike bundle of fibres that conducts impulses between the brain and other parts of the body ▷ *vb* give courage to oneself
**NERVED** > NERVE
**NERVELESS** *adj* numb, without feeling
**NERVELET** *n* small nerve
**NERVELETS** > NERVELET
**NERVER** > NERVE
**NERVERS** > NERVE
**NERVES** > NERVE
**NERVIER** > NERVY
**NERVIEST** > NERVY
**NERVILY** > NERVY
**NERVINE** *adj* having a soothing or calming effect upon the nerves ▷ *n* nervine drug or agent
**NERVINES** > NERVINE
**NERVINESS** > NERVY
**NERVING** > NERVE
**NERVINGS** > NERVE
**NERVOSITY** *n* nervousness
**NERVOUS** *adj* apprehensive or worried
**NERVOUSLY** > NERVOUS
**NERVULAR** > NERVULE
**NERVULE** *n* small vein
**NERVULES** > NERVULE
**NERVURE** *n* any of the stiff rods that form the supporting framework of an insect's wing
**NERVURES** > NERVURE
**NERVY** *adj* excitable or nervous
**NESCIENCE** *formal or literary word for* > IGNORANCE
**NESCIENT** > NESCIENCE
**NESCIENTS** > NESCIENCE
**NESH** *adj* sensitive to the cold
**NESHER** > NESH
**NESHEST** > NESH
**NESHNESS** > NESH
**NESS** *n* headland, cape
**NESSES** > NESS
**NEST** *n* place or structure in which birds or certain animals lay eggs or give birth to young ▷ *vb* make or inhabit a nest
**NESTABLE** > NEST
**NESTED** > NEST
**NESTER** > NEST
**NESTERS** > NEST
**NESTFUL** > NEST
**NESTFULS** > NEST
**NESTING** > NEST
**NESTINGS** > NEST
**NESTLE** *vb* snuggle
**NESTLED** > NESTLE
**NESTLER** > NESTLE
**NESTLERS** > NESTLE
**NESTLES** > NESTLE
**NESTLIKE** > NEST

**NESTLING** *n* bird too young to leave the nest
**NESTLINGS** > NESTLING
**NESTOR** *n* wise old man
**NESTORS** > NESTOR
**NESTS** > NEST
**NET** *n* fabric of meshes of string, thread, or wire with many openings ▷ *vb* catch (a fish or animal) in a net ▷ *adj* left after all deductions
**NETBALL** *n* team game in which a ball has to be thrown through a net hanging from a ring at the top of a pole
**NETBALLER** > NETBALL
**NETBALLS** > NETBALL
**NETE** *n* lyre string
**NETES** > NETE
**NETFUL** > NET
**NETFULS** > NET
**NETHEAD** *n* person who is enthusiastic about or an expert on the internet
**NETHEADS** > NETHEAD
**NETHELESS** *same as* > NATHELESS
**NETHER** *adj* lower
**NETIZEN** *n* person who regularly uses the internet
**NETIZENS** > NETIZEN
**NETLESS** > NET
**NETLIKE** > NET
**NETMINDER** *n* goalkeeper
**NETOP** *n* friend
**NETOPS** > NETOP
**NETS** > NET
**NETSPEAK** *n* jargon, abbreviations, and emoticons typically used by frequent internet users
**NETSPEAKS** > NETSPEAK
**NETSUKE** *n* (in Japan) a carved toggle worn dangling from the waist
**NETSUKES** > NETSUKE
**NETT** *same as* > NET
**NETTABLE** > NETT
**NETTED** > NET
**NETTER** *n* person that makes nets
**NETTERS** > NETTER
**NETTIE** *n* habitual and enthusiastic user of the internet
**NETTIER** > NET
**NETTIES** > NETTY
**NETTIEST** > NET
**NETTING** > NET
**NETTINGS** > NET
**NETTLE** *n* plant with stinging hairs on the leaves ▷ *vb* bother or irritate
**NETTLED** > NETTLE
**NETTLER** > NETTLE
**NETTLERS** > NETTLE
**NETTLES** > NETTLE
**NETTLIER** > NETTLE
**NETTLIEST** > NETTLE
**NETTLING** > NETTLE
**NETTLY** > NETTLE

**NETTS** > NETT
**NETTY** *n* lavatory, originally an earth closet
**NETWORK** *n* system of intersecting lines, roads, etc ▷ *vb* broadcast (a programme) over a network
**NETWORKED** > NETWORK
**NETWORKER** *n* person who forms business contacts through informal social meetings
**NETWORKS** > NETWORK
**NEUK** *Scot word for* > NOOK
**NEUKS** > NEUK
**NEUM** *same as* > NEUME
**NEUMATIC** > NEUME
**NEUME** *n* one of a series of notational symbols used before the 14th century
**NEUMES** > NEUME
**NEUMIC** > NEUME
**NEUMS** > NEUM
**NEURAL** *adj* of a nerve or the nervous system
**NEURALGIA** *n* severe pain along a nerve
**NEURALGIC** > NEURALGIA
**NEURALLY** > NEURAL
**NEURATION** *n* arrangement of veins
**NEURAXON** *n* biological cell component
**NEURAXONS** > NEURAXON
**NEURILITY** *n* properties of the nerves
**NEURINE** *n* poisonous alkaloid
**NEURINES** > NEURINE
**NEURISM** *n* nerve force
**NEURISMS** > NEURISM
**NEURITE** *n* biological cell component
**NEURITES** > NEURITE
**NEURITIC** > NEURITIS
**NEURITICS** > NEURITIS
**NEURITIS** *n* inflammation of a nerve or nerves
**NEUROCHIP** *n* semiconductor chip designed for use in an electronic neural network
**NEUROCOEL** *n* cavity in brain
**NEUROGLIA** *another name for* > GLIA
**NEUROGRAM** *same as* > ENGRAM
**NEUROID** *adj* nervelike
**NEUROLOGY** *n* scientific study of the nervous system
**NEUROMA** *n* any tumour composed of nerve tissue
**NEUROMAS** > NEUROMA
**NEUROMAST** *n* sensory cell in fish
**NEUROMATA** > NEUROMA
**NEURON** *same as* > NEURONE
**NEURONAL** > NEURONE
**NEURONE** *n* cell specialized to conduct nerve impulses
**NEURONES** > NEURONE

**NEURONIC** > NEURONE
**NEURONS** > NEURON
**NEUROPATH** *n* person suffering from or predisposed to a disorder of the nervous system
**NEUROPIL** *n* dense network of neurons and glia in the central nervous system
**NEUROPILS** > NEUROPIL
**NEUROSAL** > NEUROSIS
**NEUROSES** > NEUROSIS
**NEUROSIS** *n* mental disorder producing hysteria, anxiety, depression, or obsessive behaviour
**NEUROTIC** *adj* emotionally unstable ▷ *n* neurotic person
**NEUROTICS** > NEUROTIC
**NEUROTOMY** *n* surgical cutting of a nerve, esp to relieve intractable pain
**NEURULA** *n* stage of embryonic development
**NEURULAE** > NEURULA
**NEURULAR** > NEURULA
**NEURULAS** > NEURULA
**NEUSTIC** > NEUSTON
**NEUSTON** *n* organisms, similar to plankton, that float on the surface film of open water
**NEUSTONIC** > NEUSTON
**NEUSTONS** > NEUSTON
**NEUTER** *adj* belonging to a particular class of grammatical inflections in some languages ▷ *vb* castrate (an animal) ▷ *n* neuter gender
**NEUTERED** > NEUTER
**NEUTERING** > NEUTER
**NEUTERS** > NEUTER
**NEUTRAL** *adj* taking neither side in a war or dispute ▷ *n* neutral person or nation
**NEUTRALLY** > NEUTRAL
**NEUTRALS** > NEUTRAL
**NEUTRETTO** *n* neutrino associated with the muon
**NEUTRINO** *n* elementary particle with no mass or electrical charge
**NEUTRINOS** > NEUTRINO
**NEUTRON** *n* electrically neutral elementary particle of about the same mass as a proton
**NEUTRONIC** > NEUTRON
**NEUTRONS** > NEUTRON
**NEVE** *n* mass of porous ice, formed from snow, that has not yet become frozen into glacier ice
**NEVEL** *vb* beat with the fists
**NEVELLED** > NEVEL
**NEVELLING** > NEVEL
**NEVELS** > NEVEL
**NEVER** *adv* at no time ▷ *sentence substitute* at no time ▷ *interj* surely not!

NEVERMIND n difference
NEVERMORE adv never again
NEVES > NEVE
NEVI > NEVUS
NEVOID > NAEVUS
NEVUS same as > NAEVUS
NEW adj not existing before ▷ adv recently ▷ vb make new
NEWBIE n person new to a job, club, etc
NEWBIES > NEWBIE
NEWBORN adj recently or just born ▷ n newborn baby
NEWBORNS > NEWBORN
NEWCOME > NEWCOMER
NEWCOMER n recent arrival or participant
NEWCOMERS > NEWCOMER
NEWED > NEW
NEWEL n post at the top or bottom of a flight of stairs that supports the handrail
NEWELL n new thing
NEWELLED > NEWEL
NEWELLS > NEWEL
NEWELS > NEWEL
NEWER > NEW
NEWEST > NEW
NEWFANGLE adj newly come into existence or fashion
NEWFOUND adj newly or recently discovered
NEWIE n fresh idea or thing
NEWIES > NEWIE
NEWING > NEW
NEWISH adj fairly new
NEWISHLY > NEWISH
NEWLY adv recently
NEWLYWED n recently married person
NEWLYWEDS > NEWLYWED
NEWMARKET n double-breasted waisted coat with a full skirt
NEWMOWN adj freshly cut
NEWNESS > NEW
NEWNESSES > NEW
NEWS n important or interesting new happenings ▷ vb report
NEWSAGENT n shopkeeper who sells newspapers and magazines
NEWSBEAT n particular area of news reporting
NEWSBEATS > NEWSBEAT
NEWSBOY n boy who sells or delivers newspapers
NEWSBOYS > NEWSBOY
NEWSBREAK n newsflash
NEWSCAST n radio or television broadcast of the news
NEWSCASTS > NEWSCAST
NEWSDESK n news gathering and reporting department
NEWSDESKS > NEWSDESK
NEWSED > NEWS
NEWSES > NEWS
NEWSFLASH n brief

important news item, which interrupts a radio or television programme
NEWSGIRL n female newsreader or reporter
NEWSGIRLS > NEWSGIRL
NEWSGROUP n forum where subscribers exchange information about a specific subject by e-mail
NEWSHAWK n newspaper reporter
NEWSHAWKS > NEWSHAWK
NEWSHOUND same as > NEWSHAWK
NEWSIE same as > NEWSY
NEWSIER > NEWSY
NEWSIES > NEWSIE
NEWSIEST > NEWSY
NEWSINESS > NEWSY
NEWSING > NEWS
NEWSLESS > NEWS
NEWSMAKER n person whose activities are reported in news
NEWSMAN n male newsreader or reporter
NEWSMEN > NEWSMAN
NEWSPAPER n weekly or daily publication containing news ▷ vb do newspaper related work
NEWSPEAK n language of politicians and officials regarded as deliberately ambiguous and misleading
NEWSPEAKS > NEWSPEAK
NEWSPRINT n inexpensive paper used for newspapers
NEWSREEL n short film giving news
NEWSREELS > NEWSREEL
NEWSROOM n room where news is received and prepared for publication or broadcasting
NEWSROOMS > NEWSROOM
NEWSSTAND n portable stand from which newspapers are sold
NEWSTRADE n newspaper retail
NEWSWIRE n electronic means of delivering up-to-the-minute news
NEWSWIRES > NEWSWIRE
NEWSWOMAN n female newsreader or reporter
NEWSWOMEN > NEWSWOMAN
NEWSY adj full of news ▷ n newsagent
NEWT n small amphibious creature with a long slender body and tail
NEWTON n unit of force
NEWTONS > NEWTON
NEWTS > NEWT
NEWWAVER n member of new wave
NEWWAVERS > NEWWAVER
NEXT adv immediately following ▷ n next person or thing

NEXTDOOR adj in or at the adjacent house or building
NEXTLY > NEXT
NEXTNESS > NEXT
NEXTS > NEXT
NEXUS n connection or link
NEXUSES > NEXUS
NGAIO n small New Zealand tree
NGAIOS > NGAIO
NGANA same as > NAGANA
NGANAS > NGANA
NGARARA n lizard found in New Zealand
NGATI n (occurring as part of the tribe name) a tribe or clan
NGATIS > NGATI
NGOMA n type of drum
NGOMAS > NGOMA
NGULTRUM n standard monetary unit of Bhutan, divided into 100 chetrum
NGULTRUMS > NGULTRUM
NGWEE n Zambian monetary unit worth one hundredth of a kwacha
NHANDU n type of spider
NHANDUS > NHANDU
NIACIN n vitamin of the B complex that occurs in milk, liver, and yeast
NIACINS > NIACIN
NIAISERIE n simplicity
NIALAMIDE n type of drug
NIB n writing point of a pen ▷ vb provide with a nib
NIBBED > NIB
NIBBING > NIB
NIBBLE vb take little bites (of) ▷ n little bite
NIBBLED > NIBBLE
NIBBLER n person, animal, or thing that nibbles
NIBBLERS > NIBBLER
NIBBLES > NIBBLE
NIBBLING > NIBBLE
NIBBLINGS > NIBBLE
NIBLICK n (formerly) a club, a No. 9 iron, giving a great deal of lift
NIBLICKS > NIBLICK
NIBLIKE > NIB
NIBS > NIB
NICAD n rechargeable dry-cell battery
NICADS > NICAD
NICCOLITE n copper-coloured mineral
NICE adj pleasant
NICEISH > NICE
NICELY > NICE
NICENESS > NICE
NICER > NICE
NICEST > NICE
NICETIES > NICETY
NICETY n subtle point
NICHE n hollow area in a wall ▷ adj of or aimed at a specialist group or market ▷ vb place (a statue) in a niche
NICHED > NICHE
NICHER vb snigger

NICHERED > NICHER
NICHERING > NICHER
NICHERS > NICHER
NICHES > NICHE
NICHING > NICHE
NICHT Scot word for > NIGHT
NICHTS > NICHT
NICISH > NICE
NICK vb make a small cut in ▷ n small cut
NICKAR n hard seed
NICKARS > NICKAR
NICKED > NICK
NICKEL n silvery-white metal often used in alloys ▷ vb plate with nickel
NICKELED > NICKEL
NICKELIC adj of or containing metallic nickel
NICKELINE another name for > NICCOLITE
NICKELING > NICKEL
NICKELISE same as > NICKELIZE
NICKELIZE vb treat with nickel
NICKELLED > NICKEL
NICKELOUS adj of or containing nickel, esp in the divalent state
NICKELS > NICKEL
NICKER n pound sterling ▷ vb (of a horse) to neigh softly
NICKERED > NICKER
NICKERING > NICKER
NICKERS > NICKER
NICKING > NICK
NICKLE same as > NICKEL
NICKLED > NICKLE
NICKLES > NICKLE
NICKLING > NICKLE
NICKNACK n cheap ornament or trinket
NICKNACKS > NICKNACK
NICKNAME n familiar name given to a person or place ▷ vb call by a nickname
NICKNAMED > NICKNAME
NICKNAMER > NICKNAME
NICKNAMES > NICKNAME
NICKPOINT n break in the slope of a river caused by renewed erosion
NICKS > NICK
NICKSTICK n tally
NICKUM n mischievous person
NICKUMS > NICKUM
NICOISE adj prepared with tomatoes, black olives, garlic and anchovies
NICOL n device for producing plane-polarized light
NICOLS > NICOL
NICOMPOOP n stupid person
NICOTIAN n tobacco user
NICOTIANA n any plant of the American and Australian genus Nicotiana, such as tobacco
NICOTIANS > NICOTIAN

NICOTIN same
as > NICOTINE
NICOTINE n poisonous
substance found in
tobacco
NICOTINED > NICOTINE
NICOTINES > NICOTINE
NICOTINIC > NICOTINE
NICOTINS same
as > NICOTIN
NICTATE same
as > NICTITATE
NICTATED > NICTATE
NICTATES > NICTATE
NICTATING > NICTATE
NICTATION n act of
blinking
NICTITANT adj blinking
NICTITATE vb blink
NID same as > NIDE
NIDAL > NIDUS
NIDAMENTA pl n egg
capsules
NIDATE vb undergo
nidation
NIDATED > NIDATE
NIDATES > NIDATE
NIDATING > NIDATE
NIDATION n implantation
NIDATIONS > NIDATION
NIDDERING n coward ▷ adj
cowardly
NIDDICK n nape of the neck
NIDDICKS > NIDDICK
NIDE vb nest
NIDED > NIDE
NIDERING same
as > NIDDERING
NIDERINGS > NIDERING
NIDERLING same
as > NIDDERING
NIDES > NIDE
NIDGET n fool
NIDGETS > NIDGET
NIDI > NIDUS
NIDIFIED > NIDIFY
NIDIFIES > NIDIFY
NIDIFY vb (of a bird) to
make or build a nest
NIDIFYING > NIDIFY
NIDING n coward
NIDINGS > NIDING
NIDOR n cooking smell
NIDOROUS > NIDOR
NIDORS > NIDOR
NIDS > NID
NIDUS n nest in which
insects or spiders deposit
their eggs
NIDUSES > NIDUS
NIE archaic spelling of > NIGH
NIECE n daughter of one's
sister or brother
NIECES > NIECE
NIED > NIE
NIEF same as > NIEVE
NIEFS > NIEF
NIELLATED > NIELLO
NIELLI > NIELLO
NIELLIST > NIELLO
NIELLISTS > NIELLO
NIELLO n black compound
of sulphur and silver, lead,
or copper ▷ vb decorate or

treat with niello
NIELLOED > NIELLO
NIELLOING > NIELLO
NIELLOS > NIELLO
NIES > NIE
NIEVE n closed hand
NIEVEFUL > NIEVE
NIEVEFULS > NIEVE
NIEVES > NIEVE
NIFE n earth's core,
thought to be composed of
nickel and iron
NIFES > NIFE
NIFF n stink ▷ vb stink
NIFFED > NIFF
NIFFER vb barter
NIFFERED > NIFFER
NIFFERING > NIFFER
NIFFERS > NIFFER
NIFFIER > NIFF
NIFFIEST > NIFF
NIFFING > NIFF
NIFFNAFF vb trifle
NIFFNAFFS > NIFFNAFF
NIFFS > NIFF
NIFFY > NIFF
NIFTIER > NIFTY
NIFTIES > NIFTY
NIFTIEST > NIFTY
NIFTILY > NIFTY
NIFTINESS > NIFTY
NIFTY adj neat or smart
▷ n nifty thing
NIGELLA n type of plant the
Mediterranean and W Asia
NIGELLAS > NIGELLA
NIGER n obsolete offensive
term for a Black person
NIGERS > NIGER
NIGGARD n stingy person
▷ adj miserly ▷ vb act in a
niggardly way
NIGGARDED > NIGGARD
NIGGARDLY adj stingy
▷ adv stingily
NIGGARDS > NIGGARD
NIGGER n offensive name
for a Black person ▷ vb
burn
NIGGERDOM > NIGGER
NIGGERED > NIGGER
NIGGERING > NIGGER
NIGGERISH > NIGGER
NIGGERISM n offensive
name for an idiom
supposedly characteristic
of Black people
NIGGERS > NIGGER
NIGGERY > NIGGER
NIGGLE vb worry slightly
▷ n small worry or doubt
NIGGLED > NIGGLE
NIGGLER > NIGGLE
NIGGLERS > NIGGLE
NIGGLES > NIGGLE
NIGGLIER > NIGGLE
NIGGLIEST > NIGGLE
NIGGLING adj petty ▷ n act
or instance of niggling
NIGGLINGS > NIGGLING
NIGGLY > NIGGLE
NIGH prep near ▷ adv
nearly ▷ adj near ▷ vb
approach

NIGHED > NIGH
NIGHER > NIGH
NIGHEST > NIGH
NIGHING > NIGH
NIGHLY > NIGH
NIGHNESS > NIGH
NIGHS > NIGH
NIGHT n time of darkness
between sunset and
sunrise ▷ adj of,
occurring, or working at
night
NIGHTBIRD same
as > NIGHTHAWK
NIGHTCAP n drink taken
just before bedtime
NIGHTCAPS > NIGHTCAP
NIGHTCLUB n
establishment for
dancing, music, etc, open
late at night ▷ vb go to
nightclubs
NIGHTED adj darkened
NIGHTFALL n approach of
darkness
NIGHTFIRE n fire burned
at night
NIGHTGEAR n nightclothes
NIGHTGLOW n faint
light from the upper
atmosphere in the night
sky, esp in low latitudes
NIGHTGOWN n loose dress
worn in bed by women
NIGHTHAWK n type of
American nightjar
NIGHTIE same
as > NIGHTGOWN
NIGHTIES > NIGHTY
NIGHTJAR n nocturnal bird
with a harsh cry
NIGHTJARS > NIGHTJAR
NIGHTLESS > NIGHT
NIGHTLIFE n
entertainment and social
activities available at
night in a town or city
NIGHTLIKE > NIGHT
NIGHTLONG adv
throughout the night
NIGHTLY adv (happening)
each night ▷ adj
happening each night
NIGHTMARE n very bad
dream
NIGHTMARY > NIGHTMARE
NIGHTS adv at night or on
most nights
NIGHTSIDE n dark side
NIGHTSPOT n nightclub
NIGHTTIDE same
as > NIGHTTIME
NIGHTTIME n time from
sunset to sunrise
NIGHTWARD > NIGHT
NIGHTWEAR n apparel worn
in bed or before retiring
to bed
NIGHTY same as > NIGHTIE
NIGIRI n small oval block
of cold rice, wasabi and
fish, sometimes held
together by a seaweed
band

NIGIRIS > NIGIRI
NIGRICANT adj black
NIGRIFIED > NIGRIFY
NIGRIFIES > NIGRIFY
NIGRIFY vb blacken
NIGRITUDE n blackness
NIGROSIN same
as > NIGROSINE
NIGROSINE n type of black
pigment and dye used in
inks and shoe polishes
NIGROSINS > NIGROSIN
NIHIL n nil
NIHILISM n rejection of all
established authority and
institutions
NIHILISMS > NIHILISM
NIHILIST > NIHILISM
NIHILISTS > NIHILISM
NIHILITY n state or
condition of being
nothing
NIHILS > NIHIL
NIHONGA n Japanese form
of painting
NIHONGAS > NIHONGA
NIKAU n palm tree native to
New Zealand
NIKAUS > NIKAU
NIL n nothing, zero
NILGAI n large Indian
antelope
NILGAIS > NILGAI
NILGAU same as > NILGHAU
NILGAUS > NILGAU
NILGHAI same as > NILGAI
NILGHAIS > NILGHAI
NILGHAU same as > NILGAI
NILGHAUS > NILGHAU
NILL vb be unwilling
NILLED > NILL
NILLING > NILL
NILLS > NILL
NILPOTENT n
mathematical term
NILS > NIL
NIM n game in which two
players alternately remove
one or more small items
from one of several rows or
piles ▷ vb steal
NIMB n halo
NIMBED > NIMB
NIMBI > NIMBUS
NIMBLE adj agile and quick
NIMBLER > NIMBLE
NIMBLESSE > NIMBLE
NIMBLEST > NIMBLE
NIMBLEWIT n alert, bright,
and clever person
NIMBLY > NIMBLE
NIMBS > NIMB
NIMBUS n dark grey rain
cloud
NIMBUSED > NIMBUS
NIMBUSES > NIMBUS
NIMBYISM n practice of
objecting to something
that will affect one or take
place in one's locality
NIMBYISMS > NIMBYISM
NIMBYNESS same
as > NIMBYISM
NIMIETIES > NIMIETY

NIMIETY *rare word*
for > EXCESS
NIMIOUS > NIMIETY
NIMMED > NIM
NIMMER > NIM
NIMMERS > NIM
NIMMING > NIM
NIMONIC as in *nimonic alloy*
type of nickel-based alloy
used at high temperature
NIMPS *adj* easy
NIMROD *n* hunter
NIMRODS > NIMROD
NIMS > NIM
NINCOM *same*
*as* > NICOMPOOP
NINCOMS > NINCOM
NINCUM *same*
*as* > NICOMPOOP
NINCUMS > NINCUM
NINE *n* one more than
eight
NINEBARK *n* North
American shrub
NINEBARKS > NINEBARK
NINEFOLD *adj* having nine
times as many or as much
▷ *adv* by nine times as
much or as many
NINEHOLES *n* type of game
NINEPENCE *n* coin worth
nine pennies
NINEPENNY *same*
*as* > NINEPENCE
NINEPIN *n* skittle used in
ninepins
NINEPINS *n* game of
skittles
NINES > NINE
NINESCORE *n* product of
nine times twenty
NINETEEN *n* ten and nine
NINETEENS > NINETEEN
NINETIES > NINETY
NINETIETH *adj* being the
ordinal number of *ninety* in
numbering order ▷ *n* one
of 90 approximately equal
parts of something
NINETY *n* ten times nine
▷ *determiner* amounting to
ninety
NINHYDRIN *n* chemical
reagent used for the
detection and analysis of
primary amines
NINJA *n* person skilled in
ninjutsu
NINJAS > NINJA
NINJITSU *same*
*as* > NINJUTSU
NINJITSUS > NINJITSU
NINJUTSU *n* Japanese
martial art
NINJUTSUS > NINJUTSU
NINNIES > NINNY
NINNY *n* stupid person
NINNYISH > NINNY
NINON *n* fine strong silky
fabric
NINONS > NINON
NINTH *n* (of) number nine
in a series ▷ *adj* coming
after the eighth in

counting order, position,
time, etc ▷ *adv* after the
eighth person, position,
event, etc
NINTHLY *same as* > NINTH
NINTHS > NINTH
NIOBATE *n* type of salt
crystal
NIOBATES > NIOBATE
NIOBIC *adj* of or
containing niobium in the
pentavalent state
NIOBITE *another name*
*for* > COLUMBITE
NIOBITES > NIOBITE
NIOBIUM *n* white
superconductive metallic
element
NIOBIUMS > NIOBIUM
NIOBOUS *adj* of or
containing niobium in the
trivalent state
NIP *vb* hurry ▷ *n* pinch or
light bite
NIPA *n* palm tree of S and
SE Asia
NIPAS > NIPA
NIPCHEESE *n* ship's purser
NIPPED > NIP
NIPPER *n* small child ▷ *vb*
secure with rope
NIPPERED > NIPPER
NIPPERING > NIPPER
NIPPERKIN *n* small
quantity of alcohol
NIPPERS *pl n* instrument
or tool for snipping,
pinching, or squeezing
NIPPIER > NIPPY
NIPPIEST > NIPPY
NIPPILY > NIPPY
NIPPINESS > NIPPY
NIPPING > NIP
NIPPINGLY > NIP
NIPPLE *n* projection in
the centre of a breast ▷ *vb*
provide with a nipple
NIPPLED > NIPPLE
NIPPLES > NIPPLE
NIPPLING > NIPPLE
NIPPY *adj* frosty or chilly
NIPS > NIP
NIPTER *n* type of religious
ceremony
NIPTERS > NIPTER
NIQAB *n* type of veil worn
by some Muslim women
NIQABS > NIQAB
NIRAMIAI *n* sumo
wrestling procedure
NIRAMIAIS > NIRAMIAI
NIRL *vb* shrivel
NIRLED > NIRL
NIRLIE *variant of* > NIRLY
NIRLIER > NIRLY
NIRLIEST > NIRLY
NIRLING > NIRL
NIRLIT > NIRL
NIRLS > NIRL
NIRLY *adj* shrivelled
NIRVANA *n* absolute
spiritual enlightenment
and bliss
NIRVANAS > NIRVANA

NIRVANIC > NIRVANA
NIS *n* friendly goblin
NISBERRY *same*
*as* > NASEBERRY
NISEI *n* native-born
citizen of the US or Canada
whose parents were
Japanese immigrants
NISEIS > NISEI
NISGUL *n* smallest and
weakest bird in a brood of
chickens
NISGULS > NISGUL
NISH *n* nothing
NISHES > NISH
NISI *adj* (of a court order)
coming into effect on a
specified date
NISSE *same as* > NIS
NISSES > NISSE
NISUS *n* impulse towards
or striving after a goal
NIT *n* egg or larva of a louse
NITCHIE *n* offensive term
for a Native American
person
NITCHIES > NITCHIE
NITE *variant of* > NIGHT
NITER *same as* > NITRE
NITERIE *n* nightclub
NITERIES > NITERIE
NITERS > NITER
NITERY > NITER
NITES > NITE
NITHER *vb* shiver
NITHERED > NITHER
NITHERING > NITHER
NITHERS > NITHER
NITHING *n* coward
NITHINGS > NITHING
NITID *adj* bright
NITINOL *n* metal alloy
NITINOLS > NITINOL
NITON *less common name*
*for* > RADON
NITONS > NITON
NITPICK *vb* criticize
unnecessarily
NITPICKED > NITPICK
NITPICKER > NITPICK
NITPICKS > NITPICK
NITPICKY > NITPICK
NITRAMINE *another name*
*for* > TETRYL
NITRATE *n* compound
of nitric acid, used as a
fertilizer ▷ *vb* treat with
nitric acid or a nitrate
NITRATED > NITRATE
NITRATES > NITRATE
NITRATINE *n* type of
mineral
NITRATING > NITRATE
NITRATION > NITRATE
NITRATOR > NITRATE
NITRATORS > NITRATE
NITRE *n* potassium nitrate
NITREOUS as in *nitreous*
*silica* quartz glass
NITRES > NITRE
NITRIC *adj* of or containing
nitrogen
NITRID *same as* > NITRIDE
NITRIDE *n* compound

of nitrogen with a more
electropositive element
▷ *vb* make into a nitride
NITRIDED > NITRIDE
NITRIDES > NITRIDE
NITRIDING > NITRIDE
NITRIDS > NITRID
NITRIFIED > NITRIFY
NITRIFIER > NITRIFY
NITRIFIES > NITRIFY
NITRIFY *vb* treat (a
substance) or cause (a
substance) to react with
nitrogen
NITRIL *same as* > NITRILE
NITRILE *n* any one of a
particular class of organic
compounds
NITRILES > NITRILE
NITRILS > NITRIL
NITRITE *n* salt or ester of
nitrous acid
NITRITES > NITRITE
NITRO *n* nitroglycerine
NITROGEN *n* colourless
odourless gas that forms
four fifths of the air
NITROGENS > NITROGEN
NITROLIC *adj* pertaining
to a group of acids
NITROS > NITRO
NITROSO *adj* of a particular
monovalent group
NITROSYL *another word*
*for* > NITROSO
NITROSYLS > NITROSYL
NITROUS *adj* derived from
or containing nitrogen in a
low valency state
NITROXYL *n* type of
chemical
NITROXYLS > NITROXYL
NITRY *adj* nitrous
NITRYL *n* chemical
compound
NITRYLS > NITRYL
NITS > NIT
NITTIER > NITTY
NITTIEST > NITTY
NITTY *adj* infested with
nits
NITWIT *n* stupid person
NITWITS > NITWIT
NITWITTED > NITWIT
NIVAL *adj* of or growing in
or under snow
NIVATION *n* weathering
of rock around a patch of
snow by alternate freezing
and thawing
NIVATIONS > NIVATION
NIVEOUS *adj* resembling
snow, esp in colour
NIX *sentence substitute* be
careful! watch out! ▷ *n*
rejection or refusal ▷ *vb*
veto, deny, reject, or forbid
(plans, suggestions, etc)
NIXE *n* water sprite
NIXED > NIX
NIXER *n* spare-time job
NIXERS > NIXER
NIXES > NIX
NIXIE *n* female water

sprite, usually unfriendly to humans
**NIXIES** > NIXIE
**NIXING** > NIX
**NIXY** same as > NIXIE
**NIZAM** n (formerly) a Turkish regular soldier
**NIZAMATE** n territory of the nizam
**NIZAMATES** > NIZAMATE
**NIZAMS** > NIZAM
**NKOSI** n term of address to a superior
**NKOSIS** > NKOSI
**NO** interj expresses denial, disagreement, or refusal ▷ adj not any, not a ▷ adv not at all ▷ n answer or vote of 'no'
**NOAH** n shark
**NOAHS** > NOAH
**NOB** n person of wealth or social distinction
**NOBBIER** > NOB
**NOBBIEST** > NOB
**NOBBILY** > NOB
**NOBBINESS** > NOB
**NOBBLE** vb attract the attention of (someone) in order to talk to him or her
**NOBBLED** > NOBBLE
**NOBBLER** > NOBBLE
**NOBBLERS** > NOBBLE
**NOBBLES** > NOBBLE
**NOBBLING** > NOBBLE
**NOBBUT** adv nothing but
**NOBBY** > NOB
**NOBELIUM** n artificially-produced radioactive element
**NOBELIUMS** > NOBELIUM
**NOBILESSE** same as > NOBLESSE
**NOBILIARY** adj of or relating to the nobility
**NOBILITY** n quality of being noble
**NOBLE** adj showing or having high moral qualities ▷ n member of the nobility
**NOBLEMAN** n person of noble rank
**NOBLEMEN** > NOBLEMAN
**NOBLENESS** > NOBLE
**NOBLER** > NOBLE
**NOBLES** > NOBLE
**NOBLESSE** n noble birth or condition
**NOBLESSES** > NOBLESSE
**NOBLEST** > NOBLE
**NOBLY** > NOBLE
**NOBODIES** > NOBODY
**NOBODY** pron no person ▷ n person of no importance
**NOBS** > NOB
**NOCAKE** n Indian meal made from dried corn
**NOCAKES** > NOCAKE
**NOCENT** n guilty person
**NOCENTLY** > NOCENT
**NOCENTS** > NOCENT
**NOCHEL** vb refuse to pay someone else's debt

**NOCHELLED** > NOCHEL
**NOCHELS** > NOCHEL
**NOCK** n notch on an arrow or a bow for the bowstring ▷ vb fit (an arrow) on a bowstring
**NOCKED** > NOCK
**NOCKET** same as > NACKET
**NOCKETS** > NOCKET
**NOCKING** > NOCK
**NOCKS** > NOCK
**NOCTILIO** n type of bat
**NOCTILIOS** > NOCTILIO
**NOCTILUCA** n any bioluminescent marine dinoflagellate of the genus Noctiluca
**NOCTUA** n type of moth
**NOCTUARY** n nightly journal
**NOCTUAS** > NOCTUA
**NOCTUID** n type of nocturnal moth ▷ adj of or relating to this type of moth
**NOCTUIDS** > NOCTUID
**NOCTULE** n any of several large Old World insectivorous bats
**NOCTULES** > NOCTULE
**NOCTUOID** > NOCTUA
**NOCTURIA** n excessive urination during the night
**NOCTURIAS** > NOCTURIA
**NOCTURN** n any of the main sections of the office of matins
**NOCTURNAL** adj of the night ▷ n something active at night
**NOCTURNE** n short dreamy piece of music
**NOCTURNES** > NOCTURNE
**NOCTURNS** > NOCTURN
**NOCUOUS** adj harmful
**NOCUOUSLY** > NOCUOUS
**NOD** vb lower and raise (one's head) briefly in agreement or greeting ▷ n act of nodding
**NODAL** adj of or like a node
**NODALISE** same as > NODALIZE
**NODALISED** same as > NODALISE
**NODALISES** same as > NODALISE
**NODALITY** > NODAL
**NODALIZE** vb make something nodal
**NODALIZED** > NODALIZE
**NODALIZES** > NODALIZE
**NODALLY** > NODAL
**NODATED** adj knotted
**NODATION** n knottiness
**NODATIONS** > NODATION
**NODDED** > NOD
**NODDER** > NOD
**NODDERS** > NOD
**NODDIES** > NODDY
**NODDING** > NOD
**NODDINGLY** > NOD
**NODDINGS** > NOD
**NODDLE** n head ▷ vb nod (the head), as through

drowsiness
**NODDLED** > NODDLE
**NODDLES** > NODDLE
**NODDLING** > NODDLE
**NODDY** n tropical tern with a dark plumage ▷ adj very easy to use or understand
**NODE** n point on a plant stem from which leaves grow
**NODES** > NODE
**NODI** > NODUS
**NODICAL** adj of or relating to the nodes of a celestial body, esp of the moon
**NODOSE** adj having nodes or knotlike swellings
**NODOSITY** > NODOSE
**NODOUS** same as > NODOSE
**NODS** > NOD
**NODULAR** > NODULE
**NODULATED** > NODULE
**NODULE** n small knot or lump
**NODULED** > NODULE
**NODULES** > NODULE
**NODULOSE** > NODULE
**NODULOUS** > NODULE
**NODUS** n problematic idea, situation, etc
**NOEL** n Christmas
**NOELS** > NOEL
**NOES** > NO
**NOESES** > NOESIS
**NOESIS** n exercise of reason, esp in the apprehension of universal forms
**NOESISES** > NOESIS
**NOETIC** adj of or relating to the mind, esp to its rational and intellectual faculties
**NOG** same as > NOGG
**NOGAKU** n Japanese style of drama
**NOGG** same as > NOG
**NOGGED** adj built with timber and brick
**NOGGIN** n head
**NOGGING** n short horizontal timber member used between the studs of a framed partition
**NOGGINGS** > NOGGING
**NOGGINS** > NOGGIN
**NOGGS** > NOGG
**NOGS** > NOG
**NOH** n stylized classic drama of Japan
**NOHOW** adv under any conditions
**NOHOWISH** > NOHOW
**NOIL** n short or knotted fibres that are separated from the long fibres by combing
**NOILS** > NOIL
**NOILY** > NOIL
**NOINT** vb anoint
**NOINTED** > NOINT
**NOINTER** n mischievous child
**NOINTERS** > NOINTER

**NOINTING** > NOINT
**NOINTS** > NOINT
**NOIR** adj (of a film) showing characteristics of a film noir, in plot or style ▷ n film noir
**NOIRISH** > NOIR
**NOIRS** > NOIR
**NOISE** n sound, usu. a loud or disturbing one
**NOISED** > NOISE
**NOISEFUL** > NOISE
**NOISELESS** adj making little or no sound
**NOISENIK** n rock musician who performs loud harsh music
**NOISENIKS** > NOISENIK
**NOISES** > NOISE
**NOISETTE** n hazelnut chocolate ▷ adj flavoured or made with hazelnuts
**NOISETTES** > NOISETTE
**NOISIER** > NOISY
**NOISIEST** > NOISY
**NOISILY** > NOISY
**NOISINESS** > NOISY
**NOISING** > NOISE
**NOISOME** adj (of smells) offensive
**NOISOMELY** > NOISOME
**NOISY** adj making a lot of noise
**NOLE** same as > NOLL
**NOLES** > NOLE
**NOLITION** n unwillingness
**NOLITIONS** > NOLITION
**NOLL** n head
**NOLLS** > NOLL
**NOLO** as in nolo contendere plea indicating that the defendant does not wish to contest the case
**NOLOS** > NOLO
**NOM** n name
**NOMA** n gangrenous inflammation of the mouth, esp one affecting malnourished children
**NOMAD** n member of a tribe with no fixed dwelling place, wanderer
**NOMADE** same as > NOMAD
**NOMADES** > NOMADE
**NOMADIC** adj relating to or characteristic of nomads or their way of life
**NOMADIES** > NOMADY
**NOMADISE** same as > NOMADIZE
**NOMADISED** > NOMADISE
**NOMADISES** > NOMADISE
**NOMADISM** > NOMAD
**NOMADISMS** > NOMAD
**NOMADIZE** vb live as nomads
**NOMADIZED** > NOMADIZE
**NOMADIZES** > NOMADIZE
**NOMADS** > NOMAD
**NOMADY** n practice of living like nomads
**NOMARCH** n head of an ancient Egyptian nome
**NOMARCHS** > NOMARCH

**NOMARCHY** n any of the provinces of modern Greece

**NOMAS** > NOMA

**NOMBLES** variant spelling of > NUMBLES

**NOMBRIL** n point on a shield between the fesse point and the lowest point

**NOMBRILS** > NOMBRIL

**NOME** n any of the former provinces of modern Greece

**NOMEN** n ancient Roman's second name, designating his gens or clan

**NOMES** > NOME

**NOMIC** adj normal or habitual

**NOMINA** > NOMEN

**NOMINABLE** > NOMINATE

**NOMINAL** adj in name only ▷ n nominal element

**NOMINALLY** > NOMINAL

**NOMINALS** > NOMINAL

**NOMINATE** vb suggest as a candidate ▷ adj having a particular name

**NOMINATED** > NOMINATE

**NOMINATES** > NOMINATE

**NOMINATOR** > NOMINATE

**NOMINEE** n candidate

**NOMINEES** > NOMINEE

**NOMISM** n adherence to a law or laws as a primary exercise of religion

**NOMISMS** > NOMISM

**NOMISTIC** > NOMISM

**NOMOCRACY** n government based on the rule of law rather than arbitrary will, terror, etc

**NOMOGENY** n law of life originating as a natural process

**NOMOGRAM** n arrangement of two linear or logarithmic scales

**NOMOGRAMS** > NOMOGRAM

**NOMOGRAPH** same as > NOMOGRAM

**NOMOI** > NOMOS

**NOMOLOGIC** > NOMOLOGY

**NOMOLOGY** n science of law and law-making

**NOMOS** n convention

**NOMOTHETE** n legislator

**NOMS** > NOM

**NON** adv not

**NONA** n sleeping sickness

**NONACID** adj not acid ▷ n nonacid substance

**NONACIDIC** adj not acidic

**NONACIDS** > NONACID

**NONACTING** adj not acting

**NONACTION** n not action

**NONACTIVE** adj not active

**NONACTOR** n person who is not an actor

**NONACTORS** > NONACTOR

**NONADDICT** n person who is not an addict

**NONADULT** n person who is not an adult

**NONADULTS** > NONADULT

**NONAGE** n state of being under full legal age for various actions

**NONAGED** > NONAGE

**NONAGES** > NONAGE

**NONAGON** n geometric figure with nine sides

**NONAGONAL** > NONAGON

**NONAGONS** > NONAGON

**NONANE** n type of chemical compound

**NONANES** > NONANE

**NONANIMAL** adj not animal

**NONANOIC** as in nonanoic acid colourless oily fatty acid with a rancid odour

**NONANSWER** n unsatisfactory reply

**NONARABLE** adj not arable

**NONART** n something that does not constitute art

**NONARTIST** n person who is not an artist

**NONARTS** > NONART

**NONARY** adj based on the number nine

**NONAS** > NONES

**NONATOMIC** adj not atomic

**NONAUTHOR** n person who is not the author

**NONBANK** n business or institution that is not a bank but provides similar services

**NONBANKS** > NONBANK

**NONBASIC** adj not basic

**NONBEING** n philosophical problem relating to the question of existence

**NONBEINGS** > NONBEING

**NONBELIEF** n state of not believing

**NONBINARY** adj not binary

**NONBITING** adj not biting

**NONBLACK** n person or thing that is not black

**NONBLACKS** > NONBLACK

**NONBODIES** > NONBODY

**NONBODY** n nonphysical nature of a person

**NONBONDED** adj not bonded

**NONBOOK** n book with little substance

**NONBOOKS** > NONBOOK

**NONBRAND** adj not produced by a well-known company

**NONBUYING** adj not buying

**NONCAKING** adj not liable to cake

**NONCAMPUS** adj not on campus

**NONCAREER** adj not career-related

**NONCASH** adj other than cash

**NONCASUAL** adj not casual

**NONCAUSAL** adj not causal

**NONCE** n present time or occasion

**NONCEREAL** adj not cereal

**NONCES** > NONCE

**NONCHURCH** adj not related to the church

**NONCLASS** n lack of class

**NONCLING** adj not liable to stick

**NONCODING** adj (of DNA) not containing instructions for making protein

**NONCOITAL** adj not involving sexual intercourse

**NONCOKING** adj not liable to coke

**NONCOLA** n soft drink other than cola

**NONCOLAS** > NONCOLA

**NONCOLOR** n achromatic colour such as black or white

**NONCOLORS** > NONCOLOR

**NONCOM** n person not involved in combat

**NONCOMBAT** adj not involved in combat

**NONCOMS** > NONCOM

**NONCONCUR** vb disagree

**NONCORE** adj not central or essential

**NONCOUNTY** adj not controlled or run by a county

**NONCREDIT** adj relating to an educational course not providing a credit towards a degree

**NONCRIME** n incident that is not a crime

**NONCRIMES** > NONCRIME

**NONCRISES** > NONCRISIS

**NONCRISIS** n situation that is not a crisis

**NONCYCLIC** adj not cyclic

**NONDAIRY** adj not containing dairy products

**NONDANCE** n series of movements that do not constitute a dance

**NONDANCER** n person who is not a dancer

**NONDANCES** > NONDANCE

**NONDEGREE** adj not leading to a degree

**NONDEMAND** adj not involving demand

**NONDESERT** adj not belonging to the desert

**NONDOCTOR** n person who is not a doctor

**NONDOLLAR** adj not involving the dollar

**NONDRIP** adj (of paint) specially formulated to minimize dripping during application

**NONDRIVER** n person who does not drive

**NONDRUG** adj not involving the use of drugs

**NONDRYING** adj not drying

**NONE** pron not any

**NONEDIBLE** n not edible

**NONEGO** n everything that is outside one's conscious self, such as one's environment

**NONEGOS** > NONEGO

**NONELECT** n person not chosen

**NONELITE** adj not elite

**NONEMPTY** adj mathematical term

**NONENDING** adj not ending

**NONENERGY** adj without energy

**NONENTITY** n insignificant person or thing

**NONENTRY** n failure to enter

**NONEQUAL** adj not equal ▷ n person who is not the equal of another person

**NONEQUALS** > NONEQUAL

**NONEROTIC** adj not erotic

**NONES** n (in the Roman calendar) the ninth day before the ides of each month

**NONESUCH** n matchless person or thing

**NONET** n piece of music composed for a group of nine instruments

**NONETHNIC** n not ethnic

**NONETS** > NONET

**NONETTE** same as > NONET

**NONETTES** > NONETTE

**NONETTI** same as > NONET

**NONETTO** same as > NONET

**NONETTOS** > NONETTO

**NONEVENT** n disappointing or insignificant occurrence

**NONEVENTS** > NONEVENT

**NONEXEMPT** adj not exempt

**NONEXOTIC** adj not exotic

**NONEXPERT** n person who is not an expert

**NONEXTANT** adj no longer in existence

**NONFACT** n event or thing not provable

**NONFACTOR** n something that is not a factor

**NONFACTS** > NONFACT

**NONFADING** adj colourfast

**NONFAMILY** n household that does not consist of a family

**NONFAN** n person who is not a fan

**NONFANS** > NONFAN

**NONFARM** adj not connected with a farm

**NONFARMER** n person who is not a farmer

**NONFAT** adj fat free

**NONFATAL** adj not resulting in or capable of causing death

**NONFATTY** adj not fatty

**NONFEUDAL** adj not feudal

**NONFILIAL** adj not involving parent-child relationship

**NONFINAL** adj not final

**NONFINITE** adj not finite

**NONFISCAL** adj not involving government funds

**NONFLUID** adj not fluid ▷ n

something that is not a fluid

**NONFLUIDS** > NONFLUID

**NONFLYING** *adj* not capable of flying

**NONFOCAL** *adj* not focal

**NONFOOD** *n* item that is not food

**NONFORMAL** *adj* not formal

**NONFOSSIL** *adj* not consisting of fossils

**NONFROZEN** *adj* not frozen

**NONFUEL** *adj* not relating to fuel

**NONFUNDED** *adj* not receiving funding

**NONG** *n* stupid or incompetent person

**NONGAME** *adj* not pursued for competitive sport purposes

**NONGAY** *n* person who is not gay

**NONGAYS** > NONGAY

**NONGHETTO** *adj* not belonging to the ghetto

**NONGLARE** *adj* not causing glare ▷ *n* any of various nonglare materials

**NONGLARES** > NONGLARE

**NONGLAZED** *adj* not glazed

**NONGLOSSY** *adj* not glossy

**NONGOLFER** *n* person who is not a golfer

**NONGRADED** *adj* not graded

**NONGREASY** *adj* not greasy

**NONGREEN** *adj* not green

**NONGROWTH** *n* failure to grow

**NONGS** > NONG

**NONGUEST** *n* person who is not a guest

**NONGUESTS** > NONGUEST

**NONGUILT** *n* state of being innocent

**NONGUILTS** > NONGUILT

**NONHARDY** *adj* fragile

**NONHEME** *adj* of dietary iron, obtained from vegetable foods

**NONHERO** *n* person who is not a hero

**NONHEROES** > NONHERO

**NONHEROIC** *adj* not heroic

**NONHOME** *adj* not of the home

**NONHUMAN** *n* something not human

**NONHUMANS** > NONHUMAN

**NONHUNTER** *n* person or thing that does not hunt

**NONI** *n* type of tree of SE Asia and the Pacific islands whose fruit provides a possibly health-promoting juice

**NONIDEAL** *adj* not ideal

**NONILLION** *n* (in Britain, France, and Germany) the number represented as one followed by 54 zeros

**NONIMAGE** *n* person who is not a celebrity

**NONIMAGES** > NONIMAGE

**NONIMMUNE** *adj* not immune

**NONIMPACT** *adj* not involving impact

**NONINERT** *adj* not inert

**NONINJURY** *adj* not involving injury

**NONINSECT** *n* animal that is not an insect

**NONIONIC** *adj* not ionic

**NONIRON** *adj* not requiring ironing

**NONIS** > NONI

**NONISSUE** *n* matter of little importance

**NONISSUES** > NONISSUE

**NONJOINER** *n* person who does not join (an organisation, etc)

**NONJURIES** > NONJURY

**NONJURING** *adj* refusing the oath of allegiance

**NONJUROR** *n* person who refuses to take an oath, as of allegiance

**NONJURORS** > NONJUROR

**NONJURY** *n* trial without a jury

**NONKOSHER** *adj* not kosher

**NONLABOR** *adj* not concerned with labour

**NONLAWYER** *n* person who is not a lawyer

**NONLEADED** *adj* not leaded

**NONLEAFY** *adj* not leafy

**NONLEAGUE** *adj* not belonging to a league

**NONLEGAL** *adj* not legal

**NONLEGUME** *n* not a pod of the pea or bean family

**NONLETHAL** *adj* not resulting in or capable of causing death

**NONLEVEL** *adj* not level

**NONLIABLE** *adj* not liable

**NONLIFE** *n* matter which is not living

**NONLINEAL** *same as* > NONLINEAR

**NONLINEAR** *adj* not of, in, along, or relating to a line

**NONLIQUID** *n* substance which is not liquid

**NONLIVES** > NONLIFE

**NONLIVING** *adj* not living

**NONLOCAL** *adj* not of, affecting, or confined to a limited area or part ▷ *n* person who is not local to an area

**NONLOCALS** > NONLOCAL

**NONLOVING** *adj* not loving

**NONLOYAL** *adj* not loyal

**NONLYRIC** *adj* without lyrics

**NONMAJOR** *n* student who is not majoring in a specified subject

**NONMAJORS** > NONMAJOR

**NONMAN** *n* being that is not a man

**NONMANUAL** *adj* not manual

**NONMARKET** *adj* not relating to markets

**NONMATURE** *adj* not mature

**NONMEAT** *n* not containing meat

**NONMEMBER** *n* person who is not a member of a particular club or organization

**NONMEN** > NONMAN

**NONMENTAL** *adj* not mental

**NONMETAL** *n* chemical element that forms acidic oxides and is a poor conductor of heat and electricity

**NONMETALS** > NONMETAL

**NONMETRIC** *adj* not metric

**NONMETRO** *adj* not metropolitan

**NONMOBILE** *adj* not mobile

**NONMODAL** *adj* not modal

**NONMODERN** *adj* not modern

**NONMONEY** *adj* not involving money

**NONMORAL** *adj* not involving morality

**NONMORTAL** *adj* not fatal

**NONMOTILE** *adj* not capable of movement

**NONMOVING** *adj* not moving

**NONMUSIC** *n* (unpleasant) noise

**NONMUSICS** > NONMUSIC

**NONMUTANT** *n* person or thing that is not mutated

**NONMUTUAL** *adj* not mutual

**NONNASAL** *adj* not nasal

**NONNATIVE** *adj* not native ▷ *n* person who is not native to a place

**NONNAVAL** *adj* not belonging to the navy

**NONNEURAL** *adj* not neural

**NONNEWS** *adj* not concerned with news

**NONNIES** > NONNY

**NONNOBLE** *adj* not noble

**NONNORMAL** *adj* not normal

**NONNOVEL** *n* literary work that is not a novel

**NONNOVELS** > NONNOVEL

**NONNY** *n* meaningless word

**NONOBESE** *adj* not obese

**NONOHMIC** *adj* not having electrical resistance

**NONOILY** *adj* not oily

**NONORAL** *adj* not oral

**NONORALLY** > NONORAL

**NONOWNER** *n* person who is not an owner

**NONOWNERS** > NONOWNER

**NONPAGAN** *n* person who is not a pagan

**NONPAGANS** > NONPAGAN

**NONPAID** *adj* without payment

**NONPAPAL** *adj* not of the pope

**NONPAPIST** *adj* not papist

**NONPAR** *adj* nonparticipating

**NONPAREIL** *n* person or thing that is unsurpassed ▷ *adj* having no match or equal

**NONPARENT** *n* person who is not a parent

**NONPARITY** *n* state of not being equal

**NONPAROUS** *adj* never having given birth

**NONPARTY** *adj* not connected with a political party

**NONPAST** *n* grammatical term

**NONPASTS** > NONPAST

**NONPAYING** *adj* (of guests, customers, etc) not expected or requested to pay

**NONPEAK** *n* period of low demand

**NONPERSON** *n* person regarded as nonexistent or unimportant

**NONPLANAR** *adj* not planar

**NONPLAY** *n* social behaviour that is not classed as play

**NONPLAYER** *n* person not playing

**NONPLAYS** > NONPLAY

**NONPLIANT** *adj* not pliant

**NONPLUS** *vb* put at a loss ▷ *n* state of utter perplexity prohibiting action or speech

**NONPLUSED** > NONPLUS

**NONPLUSES** > NONPLUS

**NONPOETIC** *adj* not poetic

**NONPOINT** *adj* without a specific site

**NONPOLAR** *adj* not polar

**NONPOLICE** *adj* not related to the police

**NONPOOR** *adj* not poor

**NONPOROUS** *adj* not permeable to water, air, or other fluids

**NONPOSTAL** *adj* not postal

**NONPRINT** *adj* published in a format other than print on paper

**NONPROFIT** *n* organization that is not intended to make a profit

**NONPROS** *vb* enter a judgment of non prosequitur against a plaintiff

**NONPROVEN** *adj* not tried and tested

**NONPUBLIC** *adj* not public

**NONQUOTA** *adj* not included in a quota

**NONRACIAL** *adj* not related to racial factors or discrimination

**NONRANDOM** *adj* not random

**NONRATED** *adj* not rated

**NONREADER** *n* person who does not or cannot read

**NONRETURN** *adj* denoting a mechanism that permits flow in a pipe in one direction only

**NONRHOTIC** *adj* denoting or speaking a dialect

of English in which preconsonantal rs are not pronounced

**NONRIGID** adj not rigid

**NONRIOTER** n person who does not participate in a riot

**NONRIVAL** n person or thing not competing for success

**NONRIVALS** > NONRIVAL

**NONROYAL** adj not royal

**NONRUBBER** adj not containing rubber

**NONRULING** adj not ruling

**NONRURAL** adj not rural

**NONSACRED** adj not sacred

**NONSALINE** adj not containing salt

**NONSCHOOL** adj not relating to school

**NONSECRET** adj not sacred

**NONSECURE** adj not secure

**NONSELF** n foreign molecule in the body

**NONSELVES** > NONSELF

**NONSENSE** n something that has or makes no sense ▷ interj exclamation of disagreement

**NONSENSES** > NONSENSE

**NONSERIAL** adj not serial

**NONSEXIST** adj not discriminating on the basis of sex, esp not against women

**NONSEXUAL** adj not of, relating to, or characterized by sex or sexuality

**NONSHRINK** adj not likely to shrink

**NONSIGNER** n person who cannot use sign language

**NONSKATER** n person who does not skate

**NONSKED** n non-scheduled aeroplane

**NONSKEDS** > NONSKED

**NONSKID** adj designed to reduce skidding

**NONSKIER** n person who does not ski

**NONSKIERS** > NONSKIER

**NONSLIP** adj designed to prevent slipping

**NONSMOKER** n person who does not smoke

**NONSOCIAL** adj not social

**NONSOLAR** adj not related to the sun

**NONSOLID** n substance that is not a solid

**NONSOLIDS** > NONSOLID

**NONSPEECH** adj not involving speech

**NONSTAPLE** adj not staple

**NONSTATIC** adj not static

**NONSTEADY** adj not steady

**NONSTICK** adj coated with a substance that food will not stick to when cooked

**NONSTICKY** adj not sticky

**NONSTOP** adv without a

stop ▷ adj without a stop ▷ n nonstop flight

**NONSTOPS** > NONSTOP

**NONSTORY** n story of little substance or importance

**NONSTYLE** n style that cannot be identified

**NONSTYLES** > NONSTYLE

**NONSUCH** same as > NONESUCH

**NONSUCHES** > NONSUCH

**NONSUGAR** n substance that is not a sugar

**NONSUGARS** > NONSUGAR

**NONSUIT** n order of a judge dismissing a suit when the plaintiff fails to show a good cause of action or to produce any evidence ▷ vb order the dismissal of the suit of (a person)

**NONSUITED** > NONSUIT

**NONSUITS** > NONSUIT

**NONSYSTEM** adj having no system

**NONTALKER** n person who does not talk

**NONTARGET** adj not being a target

**NONTARIFF** adj without tariff

**NONTAX** n tax that has little real effect

**NONTAXES** > NONTAX

**NONTHEIST** n person who believes the existence or non-existence of God is irrelevant

**NONTIDAL** adj not having a tide

**NONTITLE** adj without title

**NONTONAL** adj not written in a key

**NONTONIC** adj not tonic

**NONTOXIC** adj not poisonous

**NONTRAGIC** adj not tragic

**NONTRIBAL** adj not tribal

**NONTRUMP** adj not of the trump suit

**NONTRUTH** same as > UNTRUTH

**NONTRUTHS** > NONTRUTH

**NONUNION** adj (of a company) not employing trade union members ▷ n failure of broken bones or bone fragments to heal

**NONUNIONS** > NONUNION

**NONUNIQUE** adj not unique

**NONUPLE** adj ninefold ▷ n ninefold number

**NONUPLES** > NONUPLE

**NONUPLET** n child born in a multiple birth of nine siblings

**NONUPLETS** > NONUPLET

**NONURBAN** adj rural

**NONURGENT** adj not urgent

**NONUSABLE** adj not usable

**NONUSE** n failure to use

**NONUSER** > NONUSE

**NONUSERS** > NONUSE

**NONUSES** > NONUSE

**NONUSING** > NONUSE

**NONVACANT** adj not vacant

**NONVALID** adj not valid

**NONVECTOR** n quantity without size and direction

**NONVENOUS** adj not venous

**NONVERBAL** adj not involving the use of language

**NONVESTED** adj not vested

**NONVIABLE** adj not viable

**NONVIEWER** n person who does not watch (television)

**NONVIRAL** adj not caused by a virus

**NONVIRGIN** n person who is not a virgin

**NONVIRILE** adj not virile

**NONVISUAL** adj not visual

**NONVITAL** adj not vital

**NONVOCAL** n music track without singing

**NONVOCALS** > NONVOCAL

**NONVOTER** n person who does not vote

**NONVOTERS** > NONVOTER

**NONVOTING** adj (of shares in a company) not entitling the owner to vote at company meetings

**NONWAGE** adj not part of wages

**NONWAR** n state of nonviolence

**NONWARS** > NONWAR

**NONWHITE** n person who is not white

**NONWHITES** > NONWHITE

**NONWINGED** adj without wings

**NONWOODY** adj not woody

**NONWOOL** adj not wool

**NONWORD** n series of letters not recognised as a word

**NONWORDS** > NONWORD

**NONWORK** adj not involving work

**NONWORKER** n person who does not work

**NONWOVEN** n material made by a method other than weaving

**NONWOVENS** > NONWOVEN

**NONWRITER** n person who is not a writer

**NONYL** n type of chemical

**NONYLS** > NONYL

**NONZERO** adj not equal to zero

**NOO** n type of Japanese musical drama

**NOODGE** vb annoy persistently

**NOODGED** > NOODGE

**NOODGES** > NOODGE

**NOODGING** > NOODGE

**NOODLE** n simpleton ▷ vb improvise aimlessly on a musical instrument

**NOODLED** > NOODLE

**NOODLEDOM** n state of being a simpleton

**NOODLES** > NOODLE

**NOODLING** n aimless musical improvisation

**NOODLINGS** > NOODLING

**NOOGIE** n act of inflicting pain by rubbing someone's head hard

**NOOGIES** > NOOGIE

**NOOIT** interj South African exclamation of pleased or shocked surprise

**NOOK** n corner or recess

**NOOKIE** same as > NOOKY

**NOOKIER** > NOOKY

**NOOKIES** > NOOKIE

**NOOKIEST** > NOOKY

**NOOKLIKE** > NOOK

**NOOKS** > NOOK

**NOOKY** n sexual intercourse ▷ adj resembling a nook

**NOOLOGIES** > NOOLOGY

**NOOLOGY** n study of intuition

**NOOMETRY** n mind measurement

**NOON** n twelve o'clock midday ▷ vb take a rest at noon

**NOONDAY** adj happening at noon ▷ n middle of the day

**NOONDAYS** > NOONDAY

**NOONED** > NOON

**NOONER** n sexual encounter during a lunch hour

**NOONERS** > NOONER

**NOONING** n midday break for rest or food

**NOONINGS** > NOONING

**NOONS** > NOON

**NOONTIDE** same as > NOONTIME

**NOONTIDES** > NOONTIDE

**NOONTIME** n middle of the day

**NOONTIMES** > NOONTIME

**NOOP** n point of the elbow

**NOOPS** > NOOP

**NOOSE** n loop in the end of a rope, tied with a slipknot

**NOOSED** > NOOSE

**NOOSER** n person who uses a noose

**NOOSERS** > NOOSER

**NOOSES** > NOOSE

**NOOSING** > NOOSE

**NOOSPHERE** n sphere of human thought

**NOOTROPIC** adj acting on mind

**NOPAL** n type of cactus

**NOPALES** > NOPAL

**NOPALITO** n small cactus

**NOPALITOS** > NOPALITO

**NOPALS** > NOPAL

**NOPE** interj no

**NOPLACE** same as > NOWHERE

**NOR** prep and not

**NORDIC** adj of competitions in cross-country racing and ski-jumping

**NORI** n edible seaweed often used in Japanese cookery, esp for wrapping sushi or rice balls

**NORIA** n water wheel with buckets attached to its rim for raising water from a stream into irrigation canals

**NORIAS** > NORIA

**NORIMON** n Japanese passenger vehicle

**NORIMONS** > NORIMON

**NORIS** > NORI

**NORITE** n variety of gabbro composed mainly of hypersthene and labradorite feldspar

**NORITES** > NORITE

**NORITIC** > NORITE

**NORK** n female breast

**NORKS** > NORK

**NORLAND** n north part of a country or the earth

**NORLANDS** > NORLAND

**NORM** n standard that is regarded as normal

**NORMA** n norm or standard

**NORMAL** adj usual, regular, or typical ▷ n usual or regular state, degree or form

**NORMALCY** > NORMAL

**NORMALISE** same as > NORMALIZE

**NORMALITY** > NORMAL

**NORMALIZE** vb make or become normal

**NORMALLY** adv as a rule

**NORMALS** > NORMAL

**NORMAN** n post used for winding on a ship

**NORMANDE** n type of cattle

**NORMANS** > NORMAN

**NORMAS** > NORMA

**NORMATIVE** adj of or setting a norm or standard

**NORMED** n mathematical term

**NORMLESS** adj without a norm

**NORMS** > NORM

**NORSEL** vb fit with short lines for fastening hooks

**NORSELLED** > NORSEL

**NORSELLER** > NORSEL

**NORSELS** > NORSEL

**NORTENA** same as > NORTENO

**NORTENAS** > NORTENA

**NORTENO** n type of Mexican music

**NORTENOS** > NORTENO

**NORTH** n direction towards the North Pole, opposite south ▷ adj or in the north ▷ adv in, to, or towards the north ▷ vb move north

**NORTHEAST** adv (in or to) direction between north and east ▷ n point of the compass or direction midway between north and east ▷ adj of or denoting the northeastern part of a specified country, area, etc

**NORTHED** > NORTH

**NORTHER** n wind or storm from the north ▷ vb move north

**NORTHERED** > NORTHER

**NORTHERLY** adj of or in the north ▷ adv towards the north ▷ n wind from the north

**NORTHERN** adj situated in or towards the north ▷ n person from the north

**NORTHERNS** > NORTHERN

**NORTHERS** > NORTHER

**NORTHING** n movement or distance covered in a northerly direction

**NORTHINGS** > NORTHING

**NORTHLAND** n lands that are far to the north

**NORTHMOST** adj situated furthest north

**NORTHS** > NORTH

**NORTHWARD** adv towards the north

**NORTHWEST** adv (in or to) direction between north and west ▷ n point of the compass or direction midway between north and west ▷ adj of or denoting the northwestern part of a specified country, area, etc

**NORWARD** same as > NORTHWARD

**NORWARDS** same as > NORWARD

**NOS** > NO

**NOSE** n organ of smell, used also in breathing ▷ vb move forward slowly and carefully

**NOSEAN** n type of mineral

**NOSEANS** > NOSEAN

**NOSEBAG** n bag containing feed fastened round a horse's head

**NOSEBAGS** > NOSEBAG

**NOSEBAND** n part of a horse's bridle that goes around the nose

**NOSEBANDS** > NOSEBAND

**NOSEBLEED** n bleeding from the nose

**NOSED** > NOSE

**NOSEDIVE** vb (of an aircraft) plunge suddenly with the nose pointing downwards

**NOSEDIVED** > NOSEDIVE

**NOSEDIVES** > NOSEDIVE

**NOSEDOVE** > NOSEDIVE

**NOSEGAY** n small bunch of flowers

**NOSEGAYS** > NOSEGAY

**NOSEGUARD** n position in American football

**NOSELESS** > NOSE

**NOSELIKE** > NOSE

**NOSELITE** same as > NOSEAN

**NOSELITES** > NOSELITE

**NOSEPIECE** same

as > NOSEBAND

**NOSER** n strong headwind

**NOSERS** > NOSER

**NOSES** > NOSE

**NOSEWHEEL** n wheel fitted under the nose of an aircraft

**NOSEY** adj prying or inquisitive ▷ n nosey person

**NOSEYS** > NOSEY

**NOSH** n food ▷ vb eat

**NOSHED** > NOSH

**NOSHER** > NOSH

**NOSHERIE** same as > NOSHERY

**NOSHERIES** > NOSHERIE

**NOSHERS** > NOSH

**NOSHERY** n restaurant or other place where food is served

**NOSHES** > NOSH

**NOSHING** > NOSH

**NOSIER** > NOSY

**NOSIES** > NOSY

**NOSIEST** > NOSY

**NOSILY** > NOSY

**NOSINESS** > NOSY

**NOSING** n edge of a step or stair tread that projects beyond the riser

**NOSINGS** > NOSING

**NOSODE** n homeopathic remedy

**NOSODES** > NOSODE

**NOSOLOGIC** > NOSOLOGY

**NOSOLOGY** n branch of medicine concerned with the classification of diseases

**NOSTALGIA** n sentimental longing for the past

**NOSTALGIC** adj of or characterized by nostalgia ▷ n person who indulges in nostalgia

**NOSTOC** n type of bacterium occurring in moist places

**NOSTOCS** > NOSTOC

**NOSTOI** > NOSTOS

**NOSTOLOGY** n scientific study of ageing

**NOSTOS** n story of a return home

**NOSTRIL** n one of the two openings at the end of the nose

**NOSTRILS** > NOSTRIL

**NOSTRO** as in nostro account bank account conducted by a British bank with a foreign bank

**NOSTRUM** n quack medicine

**NOSTRUMS** > NOSTRUM

**NOSY** adj prying or inquisitive

**NOT** adv expressing negation, refusal, or denial

**NOTA** > NOTUM

**NOTABILIA** n things worthy of notice

**NOTABLE** adj worthy of being noted, remarkable

▷ n person of distinction

**NOTABLES** > NOTABLE

**NOTABLY** adv particularly or especially

**NOTAEUM** n back of a bird's body

**NOTAEUMS** > NOTAEUM

**NOTAL** > NOTUM

**NOTANDA** > NOTANDUM

**NOTANDUM** n notable fact

**NOTAPHILY** n study of paper money

**NOTARIAL** > NOTARY

**NOTARIES** > NOTARY

**NOTARISE** same as > NOTARIZE

**NOTARISED** > NOTARISE

**NOTARISES** > NOTARISE

**NOTARIZE** vb attest to or authenticate (a document, contract, etc), as a notary

**NOTARIZED** > NOTARIZE

**NOTARIZES** > NOTARIZE

**NOTARY** n person authorized to witness the signing of legal documents

**NOTATE** vb write (esp music) in notation

**NOTATED** > NOTATE

**NOTATES** > NOTATE

**NOTATING** > NOTATE

**NOTATION** n representation of numbers or quantities in a system by a series of symbols

**NOTATIONS** > NOTATION

**NOTCH** n V-shaped cut ▷ vb make a notch in

**NOTCHBACK** n type of car

**NOTCHED** > NOTCH

**NOTCHEL** vb refuse to pay another person's debts

**NOTCHELS** > NOTCHEL

**NOTCHER** n person who cuts notches

**NOTCHERS** > NOTCHER

**NOTCHES** > NOTCH

**NOTCHIER** > NOTCHY

**NOTCHIEST** > NOTCHY

**NOTCHING** > NOTCH

**NOTCHINGS** > NOTCH

**NOTCHY** adj (of a motor vehicle gear mechanism) requiring careful gear-changing

**NOTE** n short letter ▷ vb notice, pay attention to

**NOTEBOOK** n book for writing in

**NOTEBOOKS** > NOTEBOOK

**NOTECARD** n greetings card with space to write note

**NOTECARDS** > NOTECARD

**NOTECASE** same as > WALLET

**NOTECASES** > NOTECASE

**NOTED** adj well-known

**NOTEDLY** > NOTED

**NOTEDNESS** > NOTED

**NOTELESS** > NOTE

**NOTELET** n small folded card with a design on the front, used for writing informal letters

**NOTELETS** > NOTELET
**NOTEPAD** n number of sheets of paper fastened together along one edge
**NOTEPADS** > NOTEPAD
**NOTEPAPER** n paper used for writing letters
**NOTER** n person who takes notes
**NOTERS** > NOTER
**NOTES** pl n short descriptive or summarized jottings taken down for future reference
**NOTHER** same as > OTHER
**NOTHING** pron not anything ▷ adv not at all ▷ n person or thing of no importance
**NOTHINGS** > NOTHING
**NOTICE** n observation or attention ▷ vb observe, become aware of
**NOTICED** > NOTICE
**NOTICER** n person who takes notice
**NOTICERS** > NOTICER
**NOTICES** > NOTICE
**NOTICING** > NOTICE
**NOTIFIED** > NOTIFY
**NOTIFIER** > NOTIFY
**NOTIFIERS** > NOTIFY
**NOTIFIES** > NOTIFY
**NOTIFY** vb inform
**NOTIFYING** > NOTIFY
**NOTING** > NOTE
**NOTION** n idea or opinion
**NOTIONAL** adj speculative, imaginary, or unreal
**NOTIONIST** n person whose opinions are merely notions
**NOTIONS** pl n pins, cotton, ribbon, and similar wares used for sewing
**NOTITIA** n register or list, esp of ecclesiastical districts
**NOTITIAE** > NOTITIA
**NOTITIAS** > NOTITIA
**NOTOCHORD** n fibrous longitudinal rod in all embryo and some adult chordate animals
**NOTORIETY** > NOTORIOUS
**NOTORIOUS** adj well known for something bad
**NOTORNIS** n rare flightless rail of New Zealand
**NOTOUR** adj notorious
**NOTT** same as > NOT
**NOTTURNI** > NOTTURNO
**NOTTURNO** n piece of music
**NOTUM** n cuticular plate covering the dorsal surface of a thoracic segment of an insect
**NOUGAT** n chewy sweet containing nuts and fruit
**NOUGATS** > NOUGAT
**NOUGHT** n figure o
**NOUGHTIES** pl n decade from 2000 to 2009
**NOUGHTS** > NOUGHT
**NOUL** same as > NOLL

**NOULD** vb would not
**NOULDE** same as > NOULD
**NOULE** same as > NOLL
**NOULES** > NOULE
**NOULS** > NOUL
**NOUMENA** > NOUMENON
**NOUMENAL** > NOUMENON
**NOUMENON** n (in the philosophy of Kant) a thing as it is in itself, incapable of being known, but only inferred from the nature of experience
**NOUN** n word that refers to a person, place, or thing
**NOUNAL** > NOUN
**NOUNALLY** > NOUN
**NOUNIER** > NOUNY
**NOUNIEST** > NOUNY
**NOUNLESS** > NOUN
**NOUNS** > NOUN
**NOUNY** adj nounlike
**NOUP** n steep headland
**NOUPS** > NOUP
**NOURICE** n nurse
**NOURICES** > NOURICE
**NOURISH** vb feed
**NOURISHED** > NOURISH
**NOURISHER** > NOURISH
**NOURISHES** > NOURISH
**NOURITURE** n nourishment
**NOURSLE** vb nurse
**NOURSLED** > NOURSLE
**NOURSLES** > NOURSLE
**NOURSLING** > NOURSLE
**NOUS** n common sense
**NOUSELL** vb foster
**NOUSELLED** > NOUSELL
**NOUSELLS** > NOUSELL
**NOUSES** > NOUS
**NOUSLE** vb nuzzle
**NOUSLED** > NOUSLE
**NOUSLES** > NOUSLE
**NOUSLING** > NOUSLE
**NOUT** same as > NOUGHT
**NOUVEAU** adj having recently become the thing specified
**NOUVEAUX** same as > NOUVEAU
**NOUVELLE** n long short story
**NOUVELLES** > NOUVELLE
**NOVA** n star that suddenly becomes brighter and then gradually decreases to its original brightness
**NOVAE** > NOVA
**NOVALIA** n newly reclaimed land
**NOVALIKE** adj resembling a nova
**NOVAS** > NOVA
**NOVATED** as in novated lease Australian system of employer-aided car purchase
**NOVATION** n substitution of a new obligation for an old one by mutual agreement between the parties
**NOVATIONS** > NOVATION
**NOVEL** n long fictitious

story in book form ▷ adj fresh, new, or original
**NOVELDOM** n realm of fiction
**NOVELDOMS** > NOVELDOM
**NOVELESE** n style of writing characteristic of poor novels
**NOVELESES** > NOVELESE
**NOVELETTE** n short novel, esp one regarded as trivial or sentimental
**NOVELISE** same as > NOVELIZE
**NOVELISED** > NOVELISE
**NOVELISER** n person who novelizes
**NOVELISES** > NOVELISE
**NOVELISH** adj resembling a novel
**NOVELISM** n innovation
**NOVELISMS** > NOVELISM
**NOVELIST** n writer of novels
**NOVELISTS** > NOVELIST
**NOVELIZE** vb convert (a true story, film, etc) into a novel
**NOVELIZED** > NOVELIZE
**NOVELIZER** n person who novelizes
**NOVELIZES** > NOVELIZE
**NOVELLA** n short novel
**NOVELLAE** > NOVELLA
**NOVELLAS** > NOVELLA
**NOVELLE** > NOVELLA
**NOVELLY** > NOVEL
**NOVELS** > NOVEL
**NOVELTIES** > NOVELTY
**NOVELTY** n newness
**NOVENA** n set of prayers or services on nine consecutive days
**NOVENAE** > NOVENA
**NOVENARY** n set of nine
**NOVENAS** > NOVENA
**NOVENNIAL** adj recurring every ninth year
**NOVERCAL** adj stepmotherly
**NOVERINT** n writ
**NOVERINTS** > NOVERINT
**NOVICE** n beginner
**NOVICES** > NOVICE
**NOVICIATE** same as > NOVITIATE
**NOVITIATE** n period of being a novice
**NOVITIES** > NOVITY
**NOVITY** n novelty
**NOVOCAINE** n tradename of a painkilling substance used as a local anaesthetic
**NOVODAMUS** n type of charter
**NOVUM** n game played with dice
**NOVUMS** > NOVUM
**NOW** adv at or for the present time
**NOWADAYS** adv in these times
**NOWAY** adv in no manner ▷ sentence substitute used

to make an emphatic refusal, denial etc
**NOWAYS** same as > NOWAY
**NOWED** adj knotted
**NOWHENCE** adv from no place
**NOWHERE** adv not anywhere ▷ n nonexistent or insignicant place
**NOWHERES** > NOWHERE
**NOWHITHER** adv no place
**NOWISE** another word for > NOWAY
**NOWL** n crown of the head
**NOWLS** > NOWL
**NOWN** same as > OWN
**NOWNESS** > NOWN
**NOWNESSES** > NOWN
**NOWS** > NOW
**NOWT** n nothing
**NOWTIER** > NOWTY
**NOWTIEST** > NOWTY
**NOWTS** > NOWT
**NOWTY** adj bad-tempered
**NOWY** adj having a small projection at the centre (of a cross)
**NOX** n nitrogen oxide
**NOXAL** adj relating to damage done by something belonging to another
**NOXES** > NOX
**NOXIOUS** adj poisonous or harmful
**NOXIOUSLY** > NOXIOUS
**NOY** vb harrass
**NOYADE** n execution by drowning
**NOYADES** > NOYADE
**NOYANCE** n nuisance
**NOYANCES** > NOYANCE
**NOYAU** n liqueur made from brandy flavoured with nut kernels
**NOYAUS** > NOYAU
**NOYED** > NOY
**NOYES** archaic form of > NOISE
**NOYESES** > NOYES
**NOYING** > NOY
**NOYOUS** > NOY
**NOYS** > NOY
**NOYSOME** > NOY
**NOZZER** n new recruit (in the Navy)
**NOZZERS** > NOZZER
**NOZZLE** n projecting spout through which fluid is discharged
**NOZZLES** > NOZZLE
**NTH** adj of an unspecified number
**NU** n 13th letter in the Greek alphabet
**NUANCE** n subtle difference in colour, meaning, or tone ▷ vb give subtle differences to
**NUANCED** > NUANCE
**NUANCES** > NUANCE
**NUANCING** > NUANCE
**NUB** n point or gist (of a story etc) ▷ vb hang from

the gallows
**NUBBED** > NUB
**NUBBIER** > NUBBY
**NUBBIEST** > NUBBY
**NUBBIN** n something small or undeveloped, esp a fruit or ear of corn
**NUBBINESS** > NUBBY
**NUBBING** > NUB
**NUBBINS** > NUBBIN
**NUBBLE** n small lump
**NUBBLED** > NUBBLE
**NUBBLES** > NUBBLE
**NUBBLIER** > NUBBLE
**NUBBLIEST** > NUBBLE
**NUBBLING** > NUBBLE
**NUBBLY** > NUBBLE
**NUBBY** adj having small lumps or protuberances
**NUBECULA** n small irregular galaxy near the S celestial pole
**NUBECULAE** > NUBECULA
**NUBIA** n fleecy scarf for the head, worn by women
**NUBIAS** > NUBIA
**NUBIFORM** adj cloudlike
**NUBILE** adj sexually attractive
**NUBILITY** > NUBILE
**NUBILOSE** same as > NUBILOUS
**NUBILOUS** adj cloudy
**NUBS** > NUB
**NUBUCK** n type of leather with a velvety finish
**NUBUCKS** > NUBUCK
**NUCELLAR** > NUCELLUS
**NUCELLI** > NUCELLUS
**NUCELLUS** n central part of a plant ovule containing the embryo sac
**NUCHA** n back or nape of the neck
**NUCHAE** > NUCHA
**NUCHAL** n scale on a reptile's neck
**NUCHALS** > NUCHAL
**NUCLEAL** > NUCLEUS
**NUCLEAR** adj of nuclear weapons or energy
**NUCLEASE** n any of a group of enzymes that hydrolyse nucleic acids to simple nucleotides
**NUCLEASES** > NUCLEASE
**NUCLEATE** adj having a nucleus ▷ vb form a nucleus
**NUCLEATED** > NUCLEATE
**NUCLEATES** > NUCLEATE
**NUCLEATOR** > NUCLEATE
**NUCLEI** > NUCLEUS
**NUCLEIC** as in nucleic acid type of complex compound that is a vital constituent of living cells
**NUCLEIDE** same as > NUCLIDE
**NUCLEIDES** > NUCLEIDE
**NUCLEIN** n any of a group of proteins that occur in the nuclei of living cells
**NUCLEINIC** > NUCLEIN

**NUCLEINS** > NUCLEIN
**NUCLEOID** n component of a bacterium
**NUCLEOIDS** > NUCLEOID
**NUCLEOLAR** > NUCLEOLUS
**NUCLEOLE** variant of > NUCLEOLUS
**NUCLEOLES** > NUCLEOLE
**NUCLEOLI** > NUCLEOLUS
**NUCLEOLUS** n small rounded body within a resting nucleus that contains RNA and proteins
**NUCLEON** n proton or neutron
**NUCLEONIC** adj relating to the branch of physics concerned with the applications of nuclear energy
**NUCLEONS** > NUCLEON
**NUCLEUS** n centre, esp of an atom or cell
**NUCLEUSES** > NUCLEUS
**NUCLIDE** n species of atom characterized by its atomic number and its mass number
**NUCLIDES** > NUCLIDE
**NUCLIDIC** > NUCLIDE
**NUCULE** n small seed
**NUCULES** > NUCULE
**NUDATION** n act of stripping
**NUDATIONS** > NUDATION
**NUDDIES** > NUDDY
**NUDDY** as in in the nuddy in the nude
**NUDE** adj naked ▷ n naked figure in painting, sculpture, or photography
**NUDELY** > NUDE
**NUDENESS** > NUDE
**NUDER** > NUDE
**NUDES** > NUDE
**NUDEST** > NUDE
**NUDGE** vb push gently, esp with the elbow ▷ n gentle push or touch
**NUDGED** > NUDGE
**NUDGER** > NUDGE
**NUDGERS** > NUDGE
**NUDGES** > NUDGE
**NUDGING** > NUDGE
**NUDICAUL** adj (of plants) having stems without leaves
**NUDIE** n film, show, or magazine depicting nudity
**NUDIES** > NUDIE
**NUDISM** n practice of not wearing clothes
**NUDISMS** > NUDISM
**NUDIST** > NUDISM
**NUDISTS** > NUDISM
**NUDITIES** > NUDITY
**NUDITY** n state or fact of being nude
**NUDNICK** same as > NUDNIK
**NUDNICKS** > NUDNICK
**NUDNIK** n boring person
**NUDNIKS** > NUDNIK
**NUDZH** same as > NUDGE

**NUDZHED** > NUDZH
**NUDZHES** > NUDZH
**NUDZHING** > NUDZH
**NUFF** slang form of > ENOUGH
**NUFFIN** slang form of > NOTHING
**NUFFINS** > NUFFIN
**NUFFS** > NUFF
**NUGAE** n jests
**NUGATORY** adj of little value
**NUGGAR** n sailing boat used to carry cargo on the Nile
**NUGGARS** > NUGGAR
**NUGGET** n small lump of gold in its natural state ▷ vb polish footwear
**NUGGETED** > NUGGET
**NUGGETING** > NUGGET
**NUGGETS** > NUGGET
**NUGGETTED** > NUGGET
**NUGGETY** adj of or resembling a nugget
**NUISANCE** n something or someone that causes annoyance or bother ▷ adj causing annoyance or bother
**NUISANCER** n person or thing causing a nuisance
**NUISANCES** > NUISANCE
**NUKE** vb attack with nuclear weapons ▷ n nuclear weapon
**NUKED** > NUKE
**NUKES** > NUKE
**NUKING** > NUKE
**NULL** adj without legal force ▷ vb make negative
**NULLA** same as > NULLAH
**NULLAH** n stream or drain
**NULLAHS** > NULLAH
**NULLAS** > NULLA
**NULLED** > NULL
**NULLIFIED** > NULLIFY
**NULLIFIER** > NULLIFY
**NULLIFIES** > NULLIFY
**NULLIFY** vb make ineffective
**NULLING** n knurling
**NULLINGS** > NULLING
**NULLIPARA** n woman who has never borne a child
**NULLIPORE** n any of several red seaweeds
**NULLITIES** > NULLITY
**NULLITY** n state of being null
**NULLNESS** > NULL
**NULLS** > NULL
**NUMB** adj without feeling, as through cold, shock, or fear ▷ vb make numb
**NUMBAT** n small Australian marsupial with a long snout and tongue
**NUMBATS** > NUMBAT
**NUMBED** > NUMB
**NUMBER** n sum or quantity ▷ vb count
**NUMBERED** > NUMBER
**NUMBERER** n person who numbers
**NUMBERERS** > NUMBERER

**NUMBERING** > NUMBER
**NUMBERS** > NUMBER
**NUMBEST** > NUMB
**NUMBFISH** n any of several electric ray fish
**NUMBING** > NUMB
**NUMBINGLY** > NUMB
**NUMBLES** pl n heart, lungs, liver, etc, of a deer or other animal, cooked for food
**NUMBLY** > NUMB
**NUMBNESS** > NUMB
**NUMBS** > NUMB
**NUMBSKULL** n stupid person
**NUMCHUCK** same as > NUNCHAKU
**NUMCHUCKS** > NUMCHUCK
**NUMDAH** n coarse felt made esp in India
**NUMDAHS** > NUMDAH
**NUMEN** n (esp in ancient Roman religion) a deity or spirit presiding over a thing or place
**NUMERABLE** adj able to be numbered or counted
**NUMERABLY** > NUMERABLE
**NUMERACY** n ability to use numbers, esp in arithmetical operations
**NUMERAIRE** n unit in which prices are measured
**NUMERAL** n word or symbol used to express a sum or quantity ▷ adj of, consisting of, or denoting a number
**NUMERALLY** > NUMERAL
**NUMERALS** > NUMERAL
**NUMERARY** adj of or relating to numbers
**NUMERATE** adj able to do basic arithmetic ▷ vb read (a numerical expression)
**NUMERATED** > NUMERATE
**NUMERATES** > NUMERATE
**NUMERATOR** n number above the line in a fraction
**NUMERIC** n number or numeral
**NUMERICAL** adj measured or expressed in numbers
**NUMERICS** > NUMERIC
**NUMEROUS** adj existing or happening in large numbers
**NUMINA** plural of > NUMEN
**NUMINOUS** adj arousing religious or spiritual emotions ▷ n something that arouses religious or spiritual emotions
**NUMMARY** adj of or relating to coins
**NUMMULAR** adj shaped like a coin
**NUMMULARS** > NUMMULAR
**NUMMULINE** > NUMMULAR
**NUMMULITE** n type of large fossil protozoan
**NUMNAH** same as > NUMDAH
**NUMNAHS** > NUMNAH
**NUMPTIES** > NUMPTY

**NUMPTY** n stupid person

**NUMSKULL** same as > NUMBSKULL

**NUMSKULLS** > NUMSKULL

**NUN** n female member of a religious order

**NUNATAK** n isolated mountain peak projecting through the surface of surrounding glacial ice

**NUNATAKER** > NUNATAK

**NUNATAKS** > NUNATAK

**NUNCHAKU** n rice flail used as a weapon

**NUNCHAKUS** > NUNCHAKU

**NUNCHEON** n light snack

**NUNCHEONS** > NUNCHEON

**NUNCIO** n pope's ambassador

**NUNCIOS** > NUNCIO

**NUNCLE** archaic or dialect word for > UNCLE

**NUNCLES** > NUNCLE

**NUNCUPATE** vb declare publicly

**NUNDINAL** > NUNDINE

**NUNDINE** n market day

**NUNDINES** > NUNDINE

**NUNHOOD** n condition, practice, or character of a nun

**NUNHOODS** > NUNHOOD

**NUNLIKE** > NUN

**NUNNATION** n pronunciation of n at the end of words

**NUNNERIES** > NUNNERY

**NUNNERY** n convent

**NUNNISH** > NUN

**NUNNY** as in nunny bag small sealskin haversack used in Canada

**NUNS** > NUN

**NUNSHIP** > NUN

**NUNSHIPS** > NUN

**NUPTIAL** adj relating to marriage

**NUPTIALLY** > NUPTIAL

**NUPTIALS** pl n wedding

**NUR** n wooden ball

**NURAGHE** n Sardinian round tower

**NURAGHI** > NURAGHE

**NURAGHIC** > NURAGHE

**NURD** same as > NERD

**NURDIER** > NERD

**NURDIEST** > NERD

**NURDISH** > NERD

**NURDLE** vb score runs in cricket by deflecting the ball rather than striking it hard

**NURDLED** > NURDLE

**NURDLES** > NURDLE

**NURDLING** > NURDLE

**NURDS** > NURD

**NURDY** > NURD

**NURHAG** n Sardinian round tower

**NURHAGS** > NURHAG

**NURL** variant of > KNURL

**NURLED** > NURL

**NURLING** > NURL

**NURLS** > NURL

**NURR** n wooden ball

**NURRS** > NURR

**NURS** > NUR

**NURSE** n person employed to look after sick people, usu. in a hospital ▷ vb look after (a sick person)

**NURSED** > NURSE

**NURSELIKE** > NURSE

**NURSELING** same as > NURSLING

**NURSEMAID** n woman employed to look after children

**NURSER** n person who treats something carefully

**NURSERIES** > NURSERY

**NURSERS** > NURSER

**NURSERY** n room where children sleep or play

**NURSES** > NURSE

**NURSING** n practice or profession of caring for the sick and injured

**NURSINGS** > NURSING

**NURSLE** vb nuzzle

**NURSLED** > NURSLE

**NURSLES** > NURSLE

**NURSLING** n child or young animal that is being suckled, nursed, or fostered

**NURSLINGS** > NURSLING

**NURTURAL** > NURTURE

**NURTURANT** > NURTURE

**NURTURE** n act or process of promoting the development of a child or young plant ▷ vb promote or encourage the development of

**NURTURED** > NURTURE

**NURTURER** > NURTURE

**NURTURERS** > NURTURE

**NURTURES** > NURTURE

**NURTURING** > NURTURE

**NUS** > NU

**NUT** n fruit consisting of a hard shell and a kernel ▷ vb to gather nuts

**NUTANT** adj having the apex hanging down

**NUTARIAN** n person whose diet is based around nuts

**NUTARIANS** > NUTARIAN

**NUTATE** vb nod

**NUTATED** > NUTATE

**NUTATES** > NUTATE

**NUTATING** > NUTATE

**NUTATION** n periodic variation in the precession of the earth's axis

**NUTATIONS** > NUTATION

**NUTBROWN** adj of a brownish colour, esp a reddish-brown

**NUTBUTTER** n ground nuts blended with butter

**NUTCASE** n insane person

**NUTCASES** > NUTCASE

**NUTGALL** n nut-shaped gall caused by gall wasps on the oak and other trees

**NUTGALLS** > NUTGALL

**NUTGRASS** n type of plant

**NUTHATCH** n small songbird

**NUTHOUSE** n mental hospital or asylum

**NUTHOUSES** > NUTHOUSE

**NUTJOBBER** n nuthatch

**NUTLET** n any of the one-seeded portions of a fruit that fragments when mature

**NUTLETS** > NUTLET

**NUTLIKE** > NUT

**NUTMEAL** n type of grain

**NUTMEALS** > NUTMEAL

**NUTMEAT** n kernel of a nut

**NUTMEATS** > NUTMEAT

**NUTMEG** n spice made from the seed of a tropical tree ▷ vb kick or hit the ball between the legs of (an opposing player)

**NUTMEGGED** > NUTMEG

**NUTMEGGY** > NUTMEG

**NUTMEGS** > NUTMEG

**NUTPECKER** n nuthatch

**NUTPICK** n tool used to dig the meat from nuts

**NUTPICKS** > NUTPICK

**NUTRIA** n fur of the coypu

**NUTRIAS** > NUTRIA

**NUTRIENT** n substance that provides nourishment ▷ adj providing nourishment

**NUTRIENTS** > NUTRIENT

**NUTRIMENT** n food or nourishment required by all living things to grow and stay healthy

**NUTRITION** n process of taking in and absorbing nutrients

**NUTRITIVE** adj of nutrition ▷ n nutritious food

**NUTS** > NUT

**NUTSEDGE** same as > NUTGRASS

**NUTSEDGES** > NUTSEDGE

**NUTSHELL** n shell around the kernel of a nut

**NUTSHELLS** > NUTSHELL

**NUTSIER** > NUTSY

**NUTSIEST** > NUTSY

**NUTSO** adj insane

**NUTSY** adj lunatic

**NUTTED** > NUT

**NUTTER** n insane person

**NUTTERIES** > NUTTERY

**NUTTERS** > NUTTER

**NUTTERY** n place where nut trees grow

**NUTTIER** > NUTTY

**NUTTIEST** > NUTTY

**NUTTILY** > NUTTY

**NUTTINESS** > NUTTY

**NUTTING** n act of gathering nuts

**NUTTINGS** > NUTTING

**NUTTY** adj containing or resembling nuts

**NUTWOOD** n any of various nut-bearing trees, such as walnut

**NUTWOODS** > NUTWOOD

**NUZZER** n present given to a superior in India

**NUZZERS** > NUZZER

**NUZZLE** vb push or rub gently with the nose or snout

**NUZZLED** > NUZZLE

**NUZZLER** n person or thing that nuzzles

**NUZZLERS** > NUZZLER

**NUZZLES** > NUZZLE

**NUZZLING** > NUZZLE

**NY** same as > NIGH

**NYAFF** n small or contemptible person ▷ vb yelp like a small dog

**NYAFFED** > NYAFF

**NYAFFING** > NYAFF

**NYAFFS** > NYAFF

**NYALA** n spiral-horned southern African antelope

**NYALAS** > NYALA

**NYANZA** n (in E Africa) a lake

**NYANZAS** > NYANZA

**NYAS** n young hawk

**NYASES** > NYAS

**NYBBLE** n small byte

**NYBBLES** > NYBBLE

**NYCTALOPS** n person or thing with night-vision

**NYE** n flock of pheasants ▷ vb near

**NYED** > NYE

**NYES** > NYE

**NYING** > NYE

**NYLGHAI** same as > NILGAI

**NYLGHAIS** > NYLGHAI

**NYLGHAU** same as > NILGAI

**NYLGHAUS** > NYLGHAU

**NYLON** n synthetic material used for clothing etc

**NYLONS** pl n stockings made of nylon

**NYMPH** n mythical spirit of nature, represented as a beautiful young woman

**NYMPHA** n either one of the labia minora

**NYMPHAE** > NYMPHA

**NYMPHAEA** n water lily

**NYMPHAEUM** n shrine of the nymphs

**NYMPHAL** > NYMPH

**NYMPHALID** n butterfly of the family that includes the fritillaries and red admirals ▷ adj of this family of butterflies

**NYMPHEAN** > NYMPH

**NYMPHET** n sexually precocious young girl

**NYMPHETIC** > NYMPHET

**NYMPHETS** > NYMPHET

**NYMPHETTE** same as > NYMPHET

**NYMPHIC** > NYMPH

**NYMPHICAL** > NYMPH

**NYMPHISH** > NYMPH

**NYMPHLIKE** > NYMPH

**NYMPHLY** > NYMPH

**NYMPHO** n nymphomaniac

**NYMPHOS** > NYMPHO

**NYMPHS** > NYMPH

**NYS** > NY

**NYSSA** *n* type of tree
**NYSSAS** > NYSSA
**NYSTAGMIC** > NYSTAGMUS
**NYSTAGMUS** *n* involuntary
movement of the eye
comprising a smooth drift
followed by a flick back
**NYSTATIN** *n* type of
antibiotic obtained from a
bacterium
**NYSTATINS** > NYSTATIN

# Oo

OAF *n* stupid or clumsy person
OAFISH > OAF
OAFISHLY > OAF
OAFS > OAF
OAK *n* deciduous forest tree
OAKED *adj* relating to wine that is stored for a time in oak barrels prior to bottling
OAKEN *adj* made of the wood of the oak
OAKENSHAW *n* small forest of oaks
OAKER *same as* > OCHRE
OAKERS > OAKER
OAKIER > OAKY
OAKIES > OAKY
OAKIEST > OAKY
OAKLEAF *n* leaf on oak tree
OAKLEAVES > OAKLEAF
OAKLIKE > OAK
OAKLING *n* young oak
OAKLINGS > OAKLING
OAKMOSS *n* type of lichen
OAKMOSSES > OAKMOSS
OAKS > OAK
OAKUM *n* fibre obtained by unravelling old rope
OAKUMS > OAKUM
OAKY *adj* hard like the wood of an oak ▷ *n* ice cream
OANSHAGH *n* foolish girl or woman
OANSHAGHS > OANSHAGH
OAR *n* pole with a broad blade, used for rowing a boat ▷ *vb* propel with oars
OARAGE *n* use or number of oars
OARAGES > OARAGE
OARED *adj* equipped with oars

OARFISH *n* very long ribbonfish with long slender ventral fins
OARFISHES > OARFISH
OARIER > OARY
OARIEST > OARY
OARING > OAR
OARLESS > OAR
OARLIKE > OAR
OARLOCK *n* swivelling device attached to the gunwale of a boat that holds an oar in place
OARLOCKS > OARLOCK
OARS > OAR
OARSMAN *n* person who rows
OARSMEN > OARSMAN
OARSWOMAN *n* female oarsman
OARSWOMEN > OARSWOMAN
OARWEED *n* type of brown seaweed
OARWEEDS > OARWEED
OARY *adj* of or like an oar
OASES > OASIS
OASIS *n* fertile area in a desert
OAST *n* oven for drying hops
OASTHOUSE *n* building with kilns for drying hops
OASTS > OAST
OAT *n* hard cereal grown as food
OATCAKE *n* thin flat biscuit of oatmeal
OATCAKES > OATCAKE
OATEN *adj* made of oats or oat straw
OATER *n* film about the American Wild West
OATERS > OATER

OATH *n* solemn promise, esp to be truthful in court
OATHABLE *adj* able to take an oath
OATHS > OATH
OATLIKE > OAT
OATMEAL *n* coarse flour made from oats ▷ *adj* pale brownish-cream
OATMEALS > OATMEAL
OATS > OAT
OAVES > OAF
OB *n* expression of opposition
OBA *n* (in W Africa) a Yoruba chief or ruler
OBANG *n* former Japanese coin
OBANGS > OBANG
OBAS > OBA
OBBLIGATI > OBBLIGATO
OBBLIGATO *n* essential part or accompaniment ▷ *adj* not to be omitted in performance
OBCONIC *adj* (of a fruit or similar part) shaped like a cone and attached at the pointed end
OBCONICAL *same as* > OBCONIC
OBCORDATE *adj* heart-shaped and attached at the pointed end
OBDURACY > OBDURATE
OBDURATE *adj* hardhearted or stubborn ▷ *vb* make obdurate
OBDURATED > OBDURATE
OBDURATES > OBDURATE
OBDURE *vb* make obdurate
OBDURED > OBDURE
OBDURES > OBDURE

OBDURING > OBDURE
OBE *n* ancient Laconian village
OBEAH *vb* cast spell on
OBEAHED > OBEAH
OBEAHING > OBEAH
OBEAHISM > OBEAH
OBEAHISMS > OBEAH
OBEAHS > OBEAH
OBECHE *n* African tree
OBECHES > OBECHE
OBEDIENCE *n* condition or quality of being obedient
OBEDIENT *adj* obeying or willing to obey
OBEISANCE *n* attitude of respect
OBEISANT > OBEISANCE
OBEISM *n* belief in obeah
OBEISMS > OBEISM
OBELI > OBELUS
OBELIA *n* type of jellyfish
OBELIAS > OBELIA
OBELION *n* area of skull
OBELISCAL > OBELISK
OBELISE *same as* > OBELIZE
OBELISED > OBELISE
OBELISES > OBELISE
OBELISING > OBELISE
OBELISK *n* four-sided stone column tapering to a pyramid at the top
OBELISKS > OBELISK
OBELISM *n* practice of marking passages in text
OBELISMS > OBELISM
OBELIZE *vb* mark (a word or passage) with an obelus
OBELIZED > OBELIZE
OBELIZES > OBELIZE
OBELIZING > OBELIZE
OBELUS *n* mark used in editions of ancient

documents to indicate spurious words or passages

**OBENTO** _n_ Japanese lunch box

**OBENTOS** > OBENTO

**OBES** > OBE

**OBESE** _adj_ very fat

**OBESELY** > OBESE

**OBESENESS** > OBESE

**OBESER** > OBESE

**OBESEST** > OBESE

**OBESITIES** > OBESITY

**OBESITY** > OBESE

**OBEY** _vb_ carry out instructions or orders

**OBEYABLE** > OBEY

**OBEYED** > OBEY

**OBEYER** > OBEY

**OBEYERS** > OBEY

**OBEYING** > OBEY

**OBEYS** > OBEY

**OBFUSCATE** _vb_ make (something) confusing

**OBI** _n_ broad sash tied in a large flat bow at the back, worn by Japanese women and children ▷ _vb_ bewitch

**OBIA** _same as_ > OBEAH

**OBIAS** > OBIA

**OBIED** > OBI

**OBIING** > OBI

**OBIISM** > OBI

**OBIISMS** > OBI

**OBIIT** _vb_ died

**OBIS** > OBI

**OBIT** _n_ memorial service

**OBITAL** _adj_ of obits

**OBITER** _adv_ by the way

**OBITS** > OBIT

**OBITUAL** _adj_ of obits

**OBITUARY** _n_ announcement of someone's death, esp in a newspaper

**OBJECT** _n_ physical thing ▷ _vb_ express disapproval

**OBJECTED** > OBJECT

**OBJECTIFY** _vb_ represent concretely

**OBJECTING** > OBJECT

**OBJECTION** _n_ expression or feeling of opposition or disapproval

**OBJECTIVE** _n_ aim or purpose ▷ _adj_ not biased

**OBJECTOR** > OBJECT

**OBJECTORS** > OBJECT

**OBJECTS** > OBJECT

**OBJET** _n_ object

**OBJETS** > OBJET

**OBJURE** _vb_ put on oath

**OBJURED** > OBJURE

**OBJURES** > OBJURE

**OBJURGATE** _vb_ scold or reprimand

**OBJURING** > OBJURE

**OBLAST** _n_ administrative division of the constituent republics of Russia

**OBLASTI** > OBLAST

**OBLASTS** > OBLAST

**OBLATE** _adj_ (of a sphere) flattened at the poles ▷ _n_ person dedicated to a monastic or religious life

**OBLATELY** > OBLATE

**OBLATES** > OBLATE

**OBLATION** _n_ religious offering

**OBLATIONS** > OBLATION

**OBLATORY** > OBLATION

**OBLIGABLE** > OBLIGATE

**OBLIGANT** _n_ person promising to pay a sum

**OBLIGANTS** > OBLIGANT

**OBLIGATE** _vb_ compel, constrain, or oblige morally or legally ▷ _adj_ compelled, bound, or restricted

**OBLIGATED** > OBLIGATE

**OBLIGATES** > OBLIGATE

**OBLIGATI** > OBLIGATO

**OBLIGATO** _same as_ > OBBLIGATO

**OBLIGATOR** > OBLIGATE

**OBLIGATOS** > OBLIGATO

**OBLIGE** _vb_ compel (someone) morally or by law to do something

**OBLIGED** > OBLIGE

**OBLIGEE** _n_ person in whose favour an obligation, contract, or bond is created

**OBLIGEES** > OBLIGEE

**OBLIGER** > OBLIGE

**OBLIGERS** > OBLIGE

**OBLIGES** > OBLIGE

**OBLIGING** _adj_ ready to help other people

**OBLIGOR** _n_ person who binds himself by contract to perform some obligation

**OBLIGORS** > OBLIGOR

**OBLIQUE** _adj_ slanting ▷ _n_ symbol (/) ▷ _vb_ take or have an oblique direction

**OBLIQUED** > OBLIQUE

**OBLIQUELY** > OBLIQUE

**OBLIQUER** > OBLIQUE

**OBLIQUES** > OBLIQUE

**OBLIQUEST** > OBLIQUE

**OBLIQUID** _adj_ oblique

**OBLIQUING** > OBLIQUE

**OBLIQUITY** _n_ state or condition of being oblique

**OBLIVION** _n_ state of being forgotten

**OBLIVIONS** > OBLIVION

**OBLIVIOUS** _adj_ unaware

**OBLONG** _adj_ having two long sides, two short sides, and four right angles ▷ _n_ oblong figure

**OBLONGLY** > OBLONG

**OBLONGS** > OBLONG

**OBLOQUIAL** > OBLOQUY

**OBLOQUIES** > OBLOQUY

**OBLOQUY** _n_ verbal abuse

**OBNOXIOUS** _adj_ offensive

**OBO** _n_ ship carrying oil and ore

**OBOE** _n_ double-reeded woodwind instrument

**OBOES** > OBOE

**OBOIST** > OBOE

**OBOISTS** > OBOE

**OBOL** _same as_ > OBOLUS

**OBOLARY** _adj_ very poor

**OBOLE** _n_ former weight unit in pharmacy

**OBOLES** > OBOLE

**OBOLI** > OBOLUS

**OBOLS** > OBOL

**OBOLUS** _n_ modern Greek unit of weight equal to one tenth of a gram

**OBOS** > OBO

**OBOVATE** _adj_ (of a leaf) shaped like the longitudinal section of an egg with the narrower end at the base

**OBOVATELY** > OBOVATE

**OBOVOID** _adj_ (of a fruit) egg-shaped with the narrower end at the base

**OBREPTION** _n_ obtaining of something by giving false information

**OBS** > OB

**OBSCENE** _adj_ portraying sex offensively

**OBSCENELY** > OBSCENE

**OBSCENER** > OBSCENE

**OBSCENEST** > OBSCENE

**OBSCENITY** _n_ state or quality of being obscene

**OBSCURANT** _n_ opposer of reform and enlightenment ▷ _adj_ of or relating to an obscurant

**OBSCURE** _adj_ not well known ▷ _vb_ make (something) obscure

**OBSCURED** > OBSCURE

**OBSCURELY** > OBSCURE

**OBSCURER** > OBSCURE

**OBSCURERS** > OBSCURE

**OBSCURES** > OBSCURE

**OBSCUREST** > OBSCURE

**OBSCURING** > OBSCURE

**OBSCURITY** _n_ state or quality of being obscure

**OBSECRATE** _rare word for_ > BESEECH

**OBSEQUENT** _adj_ (of a river) flowing into a subsequent stream in the opposite direction to the original slope of the land

**OBSEQUIAL** > OBSEQUIES

**OBSEQUIE** _same as_ > OBSEQUY

**OBSEQUIES** _pl n_ funeral rites

**OBSEQUY** _singular of_ > OBSEQUIES

**OBSERVANT** _adj_ quick to notice things

**OBSERVE** _vb_ see or notice

**OBSERVED** > OBSERVE

**OBSERVER** _n_ person who observes, esp one who watches someone or something carefully

**OBSERVERS** > OBSERVER

**OBSERVES** > OBSERVE

**OBSERVING** > OBSERVE

**OBSESS** _vb_ preoccupy (someone) compulsively

**OBSESSED** > OBSESS

**OBSESSES** > OBSESS

**OBSESSING** > OBSESS

**OBSESSION** _n_ something that preoccupies a person to the exclusion of other things

**OBSESSIVE** _adj_ motivated by a persistent overriding idea or impulse ▷ _n_ person subject to obsession

**OBSESSOR** > OBSESS

**OBSESSORS** > OBSESS

**OBSIDIAN** _n_ dark glassy volcanic rock

**OBSIDIANS** > OBSIDIAN

**OBSIGN** _vb_ confirm

**OBSIGNATE** _same as_ > OBSIGN

**OBSIGNED** > OBSIGN

**OBSIGNING** > OBSIGN

**OBSIGNS** > OBSIGN

**OBSOLESCE** _vb_ become obsolete

**OBSOLETE** _adj_ no longer in use ▷ _vb_ make obsolete

**OBSOLETED** > OBSOLETE

**OBSOLETES** > OBSOLETE

**OBSTACLE** _n_ something that makes progress difficult

**OBSTACLES** > OBSTACLE

**OBSTETRIC** _adj_ of or relating to childbirth

**OBSTINACY** _n_ state or quality of being obstinate

**OBSTINATE** _adj_ stubborn

**OBSTRUCT** _vb_ block with an obstacle

**OBSTRUCTS** > OBSTRUCT

**OBSTRUENT** _adj_ causing obstruction, esp of the intestinal tract ▷ _n_ anything that causes obstruction

**OBTAIN** _vb_ acquire intentionally

**OBTAINED** > OBTAIN

**OBTAINER** > OBTAIN

**OBTAINERS** > OBTAIN

**OBTAINING** > OBTAIN

**OBTAINS** > OBTAIN

**OBTECT** _adj_ (of a pupa) encased in a hardened secretion

**OBTECTED** _same as_ > OBTECT

**OBTEMPER** _vb_ comply (with)

**OBTEMPERS** > OBTEMPER

**OBTEND** _vb_ put forward

**OBTENDED** > OBTEND

**OBTENDING** > OBTEND

**OBTENDS** > OBTEND

**OBTENTION** _n_ act of obtaining

**OBTEST** _vb_ beg (someone) earnestly

**OBTESTED** > OBTEST

**OBTESTING** > OBTEST

**OBTESTS** > OBTEST

**OBTRUDE** _vb_ push oneself or one's ideas on others

**OBTRUDED** > OBTRUDE
**OBTRUDER** > OBTRUDE
**OBTRUDERS** > OBTRUDE
**OBTRUDES** > OBTRUDE
**OBTRUDING** > OBTRUDE
**OBTRUSION** > OBTRUDE
**OBTRUSIVE** *adj* unpleasantly noticeable
**OBTUND** *vb* deaden or dull
**OBTUNDED** > OBTUND
**OBTUNDENT** > OBTUND
**OBTUNDING** > OBTUND
**OBTUNDITY** *n* semi-conscious state
**OBTUNDS** > OBTUND
**OBTURATE** *vb* stop up (an opening, esp the breech of a gun)
**OBTURATED** > OBTURATE
**OBTURATES** > OBTURATE
**OBTURATOR** > OBTURATE
**OBTUSE** *adj* mentally slow
**OBTUSELY** > OBTUSE
**OBTUSER** > OBTUSE
**OBTUSEST** > OBTUSE
**OBTUSITY** > OBTUSE
**OBUMBRATE** *vb* overshadow
**OBVENTION** *n* incidental expense
**OBVERSE** *n* opposite way of looking at an idea ▷ *adj* facing or turned towards the observer
**OBVERSELY** > OBVERSE
**OBVERSES** > OBVERSE
**OBVERSION** > OBVERT
**OBVERT** *vb* deduce the obverse of (a proposition)
**OBVERTED** > OBVERT
**OBVERTING** > OBVERT
**OBVERTS** > OBVERT
**OBVIABLE** > OBVIATE
**OBVIATE** *vb* make unnecessary
**OBVIATED** > OBVIATE
**OBVIATES** > OBVIATE
**OBVIATING** > OBVIATE
**OBVIATION** > OBVIATE
**OBVIATOR** > OBVIATE
**OBVIATORS** > OBVIATE
**OBVIOUS** *adj* easy to see or understand, evident
**OBVIOUSLY** *adv* in a way that is easy to see or understand
**OBVOLUTE** *adj* (of leaves or petals in the bud) folded so that the margins overlap each other
**OBVOLUTED** *same as* > OBVOLUTE
**OBVOLVENT** *adj* curving around something
**OCA** *n* any of various South American herbaceous plants
**OCARINA** *n* small oval wind instrument
**OCARINAS** > OCARINA
**OCAS** > OCA
**OCCAM** *n* computer programming language
**OCCAMIES** > OCCAMY
**OCCAMS** > OCCAM

**OCCAMY** *n* type of alloy
**OCCASION** *n* time at which a particular thing happens ▷ *vb* cause
**OCCASIONS** *pl n* needs
**OCCIDENT** *literary or formal word for* > WEST
**OCCIDENTS** > OCCIDENT
**OCCIES** > OCCY
**OCCIPITA** > OCCIPUT
**OCCIPITAL** *adj* of or relating to the back of the head or skull
**OCCIPUT** *n* back of the head
**OCCIPUTS** > OCCIPUT
**OCCLUDE** *vb* obstruct
**OCCLUDED** > OCCLUDE
**OCCLUDENT** > OCCLUDE
**OCCLUDER** > OCCLUDE
**OCCLUDERS** > OCCLUDE
**OCCLUDES** > OCCLUDE
**OCCLUDING** > OCCLUDE
**OCCLUSAL** > OCCLUSION
**OCCLUSION** *n* act or process of occluding or the state of being occluded
**OCCLUSIVE** *adj* of or relating to the act of occlusion ▷ *n* occlusive speech sound
**OCCLUSOR** *n* muscle for closing opening
**OCCLUSORS** > OCCLUSOR
**OCCULT** *adj* relating to the supernatural ▷ *vb* (of a celestial body) to hide (another celestial body) from view
**OCCULTED** > OCCULT
**OCCULTER** *n* something that obscures
**OCCULTERS** > OCCULTER
**OCCULTING** > OCCULT
**OCCULTISM** *n* belief in and the study and practice of magic, astrology, etc
**OCCULTIST** > OCCULTISM
**OCCULTLY** > OCCULT
**OCCULTS** > OCCULT
**OCCUPANCE** *same as* > OCCUPANCY
**OCCUPANCY** *n* (length of) a person's stay in a specified place
**OCCUPANT** *n* person occupying a specified place
**OCCUPANTS** > OCCUPANT
**OCCUPATE** *same as* > OCCUPY
**OCCUPATED** > OCCUPATE
**OCCUPATES** > OCCUPATE
**OCCUPIED** > OCCUPY
**OCCUPIER** *n* person who lives in a particular house, whether as owner or tenant
**OCCUPIERS** > OCCUPIER
**OCCUPIES** > OCCUPY
**OCCUPY** *vb* live or work in (a building)
**OCCUPYING** > OCCUPY
**OCCUR** *vb* happen
**OCCURRED** > OCCUR
**OCCURRENT** *adj* (of a

property) relating to some observable feature of its bearer
**OCCURRING** > OCCUR
**OCCURS** > OCCUR
**OCCY** as in *all over the occy* dialect expression meaning in every direction
**OCEAN** *n* vast area of sea between continents
**OCEANARIA** *pl n* large saltwater aquaria for marine life
**OCEANAUT** *n* undersea explorer
**OCEANAUTS** > OCEANAUT
**OCEANIC** *adj* of or relating to the ocean
**OCEANID** *n* ocean nymph in Greek mythology
**OCEANIDES** > OCEANID
**OCEANIDS** > OCEANID
**OCEANS** > OCEAN
**OCELLAR** > OCELLUS
**OCELLATE** > OCELLUS
**OCELLATED** > OCELLUS
**OCELLI** > OCELLUS
**OCELLUS** *n* simple eye of insects and some other invertebrates
**OCELOID** *adj* of or like an ocelot
**OCELOT** *n* American wild cat with a spotted coat
**OCELOTS** > OCELOT
**OCH** *interj* expression of surprise, annoyance, or disagreement
**OCHE** *n* (in darts) mark on the floor behind which a player must stand
**OCHER** *same as* > OCHRE
**OCHERED** > OCHER
**OCHERING** > OCHER
**OCHEROUS** > OCHER
**OCHERS** > OCHER
**OCHERY** > OCHER
**OCHES** > OCHE
**OCHIDORE** *n* type of crab
**OCHIDORES** > OCHIDORE
**OCHLOCRAT** *n* supporter of rule by the mob
**OCHONE** *interj* expression of sorrow or regret
**OCHRE** *n* brownish-yellow earth ▷ *adj* moderate yellow-orange to orange ▷ *vb* colour with ochre
**OCHREA** *n* cup-shaped structure that sheathes the stems of certain plants
**OCHREAE** > OCHREA
**OCHREATE** *same as* > OCREATE
**OCHRED** > OCHRE
**OCHREOUS** > OCHRE
**OCHRES** > OCHRE
**OCHREY** > OCHRE
**OCHRING** > OCHRE
**OCHROID** > OCHRE
**OCHROUS** > OCHRE
**OCHRY** > OCHRE
**OCICAT** *n* breed of large short-haired cat with a

spotted coat
**OCICATS** > OCICAT
**OCKER** *n* uncultivated or boorish Australian
**OCKERISM** *n* Australian boorishness
**OCKERISMS** > OCKERISM
**OCKERS** > OCKER
**OCKODOLS** *pl n* one's feet when wearing boots
**OCOTILLO** *n* cactus-like tree
**OCOTILLOS** > OCOTILLO
**OCREA** *same as* > OCHREA
**OCREAE** > OCREA
**OCREATE** *adj* possessing an ocrea
**OCTA** *same as* > OKTA
**OCTACHORD** *n* eight-stringed musical instrument
**OCTAD** *n* group or series of eight
**OCTADIC** > OCTAD
**OCTADS** > OCTAD
**OCTAGON** *n* geometric figure with eight sides
**OCTAGONAL** *adj* having eight sides and eight angles
**OCTAGONS** > OCTAGON
**OCTAHEDRA** *pl n* solid eight-sided figures; octahedrons
**OCTAL** *n* number system with a base 8
**OCTALS** > OCTAL
**OCTAMETER** *n* verse line consisting of eight metrical feet
**OCTAN** *n* illness that occurs weekly
**OCTANE** *n* hydrocarbon found in petrol
**OCTANES** > OCTANE
**OCTANGLE** *same as* > OCTAGON
**OCTANGLES** > OCTANGLE
**OCTANOL** *n* alcohol containing eight carbon atoms
**OCTANOLS** > OCTANOL
**OCTANS** > OCTAN
**OCTANT** *n* any of the eight parts into which the three planes containing the Cartesian coordinate axes divide space
**OCTANTAL** > OCTANT
**OCTANTS** > OCTANT
**OCTAPLA** *n* book with eight texts
**OCTAPLAS** > OCTAPLA
**OCTAPLOID** *adj* having eight parts
**OCTAPODIC** > OCTAPODY
**OCTAPODY** *n* line of verse with eight metrical feet
**OCTARCHY** *n* government by eight rulers
**OCTAROON** *same as* > OCTOROON
**OCTAROONS** > OCTAROON
**OCTAS** > OCTA
**OCTASTICH** *n* verse of eight

lines
**OCTASTYLE** *adj* (of building) having eight columns
**OCTAVAL** > OCTAVE
**OCTAVE** *n* (interval between the first and) eighth note of a scale ▷ *adj* consisting of eight parts
**OCTAVES** > OCTAVE
**OCTAVO** *n* book size in which the sheets are folded into eight leaves
**OCTAVOS** > OCTAVO
**OCTENNIAL** *adj* occurring every eight years
**OCTET** *n* group of eight performers
**OCTETS** > OCTET
**OCTETT** *same as* > OCTET
**OCTETTE** *same as* > OCTET
**OCTETTES** > OCTETTE
**OCTETTS** > OCTETT
**OCTILLION** *n* (in Britain and Germany) the number represented as one followed by 48 zeros
**OCTOFID** *adj* divided into eight
**OCTOHEDRA** *same as* > OCTAHEDRA
**OCTONARII** *pl n* lines with eight feet
**OCTONARY** *adj* relating to or based on the number eight ▷ *n* stanza of eight lines
**OCTOPI** > OCTOPUS
**OCTOPLOID** *same as* > OCTAPLOID
**OCTOPOD** *n* type of mollusc ▷ *adj* of these molluscs
**OCTOPODAN** > OCTOPOD
**OCTOPODES** > OCTOPOD
**OCTOPODS** > OCTOPOD
**OCTOPUS** *n* sea creature with a soft body and eight tentacles
**OCTOPUSES** > OCTOPUS
**OCTOPUSH** *n* hockey-like game played underwater
**OCTOROON** *n* person having one quadroon and one White parent
**OCTOROONS** > OCTOROON
**OCTOSTYLE** *same as* > OCTASTYLE
**OCTOTHORP** *n* type of symbol in printing
**OCTROI** *n* duty on various goods brought into certain European towns
**OCTROIS** > OCTROI
**OCTUOR** *n* octet
**OCTUORS** > OCTUOR
**OCTUPLE** *n* quantity or number eight times as great as another ▷ *adj* eight times as much or as many ▷ *vb* multiply by eight
**OCTUPLED** > OCTUPLE
**OCTUPLES** > OCTUPLE
**OCTUPLET** *n* one of eight offspring from one birth

**OCTUPLETS** > OCTUPLET
**OCTUPLEX** *n* something made up of eight parts
**OCTUPLING** > OCTUPLE
**OCTUPLY** *adv* by eight times
**OCTYL** *n* group of atoms
**OCTYLS** > OCTYL
**OCULAR** *adj* relating to the eyes or sight ▷ *n* lens in an optical instrument
**OCULARIST** *n* person who makes artificial eyes
**OCULARLY** > OCULAR
**OCULARS** > OCULAR
**OCULATE** *adj* possessing eyes
**OCULATED** *same as* > OCULATE
**OCULI** > OCULUS
**OCULIST** *n* ophthalmologist
**OCULISTS** > OCULIST
**OCULUS** *n* round window
**OD** *n* hypothetical force formerly thought to be responsible for many natural phenomena
**ODA** *n* room in a harem
**ODAH** *same as* > ODA
**ODAHS** > ODAH
**ODAL** *same as* > UDAL
**ODALIQUE** *same as* > ODALISQUE
**ODALIQUES** > ODALIQUE
**ODALISK** *same as* > ODALISQUE
**ODALISKS** > ODALISK
**ODALISQUE** *n* female slave in a harem
**ODALLER** > ODAL
**ODALLERS** > ODAL
**ODALS** > ODAL
**ODAS** > ODA
**ODD** *adj* unusual
**ODDBALL** *n* eccentric person ▷ *adj* strange or peculiar
**ODDBALLS** > ODDBALL
**ODDER** > ODD
**ODDEST** > ODD
**ODDISH** > ODD
**ODDITIES** > ODDITY
**ODDITY** *n* odd person or thing
**ODDLY** > ODD
**ODDMENT** *n* odd piece or thing
**ODDMENTS** > ODDMENT
**ODDNESS** > ODD
**ODDNESSES** > ODD
**ODDS** *pl n* (ratio showing) the probability of something happening
**ODDSMAKER** *n* person setting odds in betting
**ODDSMAN** *n* umpire
**ODDSMEN** > ODDSMAN
**ODE** *n* lyric poem, usu addressed to a particular subject
**ODEA** > ODEUM
**ODEON** *same as* > ODEUM
**ODEONS** > ODEON
**ODES** > ODE

**ODEUM** *n* (esp in ancient Greece and Rome) a building for musical performances
**ODEUMS** > ODEUM
**ODIC** > OD
**ODIFEROUS** *adj* having odour
**ODIOUS** *adj* offensive
**ODIOUSLY** > ODIOUS
**ODISM** > OD
**ODISMS** > OD
**ODIST** > OD
**ODISTS** > OD
**ODIUM** *n* widespread dislike
**ODIUMS** > ODIUM
**ODOGRAPH** *same as* > ODOMETER
**ODOGRAPHS** > ODOGRAPH
**ODOMETER** *n* device that records the number of miles that a bicycle or motor vehicle has travelled
**ODOMETERS** > ODOMETER
**ODOMETRY** > ODOMETER
**ODONATE** *n* dragonfly or related insect
**ODONATES** > ODONATE
**ODONATIST** *n* dragonfly expert
**ODONTALGY** *n* toothache
**ODONTIC** *adj* of teeth
**ODONTIST** *n* dentist
**ODONTISTS** > ODONTIST
**ODONTOID** *adj* toothlike ▷ *n* bone in the spine
**ODONTOIDS** > ODONTOID
**ODONTOMA** *n* tumour near teeth
**ODONTOMAS** > ODONTOMA
**ODOR** *same as* > ODOUR
**ODORANT** *n* something with a strong smell
**ODORANTS** > ODORANT
**ODORATE** *adj* having a strong smell
**ODORED** *same as* > ODOURED
**ODORFUL** *same as* > ODOURFUL
**ODORISE** *same as* > ODORIZE
**ODORISED** > ODORISE
**ODORISES** > ODORISE
**ODORISING** > ODORISE
**ODORIZE** *vb* give an odour to
**ODORIZED** > ODORIZE
**ODORIZES** > ODORIZE
**ODORIZING** > ODORIZE
**ODORLESS** > ODOR
**ODOROUS** *adj* having or emitting a characteristic smell or odour
**ODOROUSLY** > ODOROUS
**ODORS** > ODOR
**ODOUR** *n* particular smell
**ODOURED** *adj* having odour
**ODOURFUL** *adj* full of odour
**ODOURLESS** > ODOUR
**ODOURS** > ODOUR
**ODS** > OD
**ODSO** *n* cry of suprise
**ODSOS** > ODSO
**ODYL** *same as* > OD
**ODYLE** *same as* > OD

**ODYLES** > ODYLE
**ODYLISM** > ODYL
**ODYLISMS** > ODYL
**ODYLS** > ODYL
**ODYSSEY** *n* long eventful journey
**ODYSSEYS** > ODYSSEY
**ODZOOKS** *interj* cry of surprise
**OE** *n* grandchild
**OECIST** *n* colony founder
**OECISTS** > OECIST
**OECOLOGY** *less common spelling of* > ECOLOGY
**OECUMENIC** *variant of* > ECUMENIC
**OEDEMA** *n* abnormal swelling
**OEDEMAS** > OEDEMA
**OEDEMATA** > OEDEMA
**OEDIPAL** *adj* relating to an Oedipus complex, whereby a male child wants to replace his father
**OEDIPALLY** > OEDIPAL
**OEDIPEAN** *same as* > OEDIPAL
**OEDOMETER** *n* instrument for measuring the consolidation of a soil specimen under pressure
**OEILLADE** *n* amorous or suggestive glance
**OEILLADES** > OEILLADE
**OENANTHIC** *adj* smelling of or like wine
**OENOLOGY** *n* study of wine
**OENOMANCY** *n* divination by studying the colour of wine
**OENOMANIA** *n* craving for wine
**OENOMEL** *n* drink made of wine and honey
**OENOMELS** > OENOMEL
**OENOMETER** *n* device for measuring the strength of wine
**OENOPHIL** *same as* > OENOPHILE
**OENOPHILE** *n* lover or connoisseur of wines
**OENOPHILS** > OENOPHIL
**OENOPHILY** *n* love of wine
**OENOTHERA** *n* type of American plant with yellow flowers that open in the evening
**OERLIKON** *n* type of cannon
**OERLIKONS** > OERLIKON
**OERSTED** *n* cgs unit of magnetic field strength
**OERSTEDS** > OERSTED
**OES** > OE
**OESOPHAGI** *pl n* gullets
**OESTRAL** > OESTRUS
**OESTRIN** *obsolete term for* > OESTROGEN
**OESTRINS** > OESTRIN
**OESTRIOL** *n* weak oestrogenic hormone secreted by the mammalian ovary
**OESTRIOLS** > OESTRIOL

**OESTROGEN** *n* female hormone that controls the reproductive cycle

**OESTRONE** *n* weak oestrogenic hormone secreted by the mammalian ovary

**OESTRONES** > OESTRONE

**OESTROUS** > OESTRUS

**OESTRUM** *same as* > OESTRUS

**OESTRUMS** > OESTRUM

**OESTRUS** *n* regularly occurring period of fertility and sexual receptivity in most female mammals

**OESTRUSES** > OESTRUS

**OEUVRE** *n* work of art, literature, music, etc

**OEUVRES** > OEUVRE

**OF** *prep* belonging to

**OFAY** *n* derogatory term for a White person

**OFAYS** > OFAY

**OFF** *prep* away from ▷ *adv* away ▷ *adj* not operating ▷ *n* side of the field to which the batsman's feet point ▷ *vb* kill

**OFFAL** *n* edible organs of an animal, such as liver or kidneys

**OFFALS** > OFFAL

**OFFBEAT** *adj* unusual or eccentric ▷ *n* any of the normally unaccented beats in a bar

**OFFBEATS** > OFFBEAT

**OFFCAST** *n* cast-off

**OFFCASTS** > OFFCAST

**OFFCUT** *n* piece remaining after the required parts have been cut out

**OFFCUTS** > OFFCUT

**OFFED** > OFF

**OFFENCE** *n* (cause of) hurt feelings or annoyance

**OFFENCES** > OFFENCE

**OFFEND** *vb* hurt the feelings of, insult

**OFFENDED** > OFFEND

**OFFENDER** > OFFEND

**OFFENDERS** > OFFEND

**OFFENDING** > OFFEND

**OFFENDS** > OFFEND

**OFFENSE** *same as* > OFFENCE

**OFFENSES** > OFFENSE

**OFFENSIVE** *adj* disagreeable ▷ *n* position or action of attack

**OFFER** *vb* present (something) for acceptance or rejection ▷ *n* something offered

**OFFERABLE** > OFFER

**OFFERED** > OFFER

**OFFEREE** *n* person to whom an offer is made

**OFFEREES** > OFFEREE

**OFFERER** > OFFER

**OFFERERS** > OFFER

**OFFERING** *n* thing offered

**OFFERINGS** > OFFERING

**OFFEROR** > OFFER

**OFFERORS** > OFFER

**OFFERS** > OFFER

**OFFERTORY** *n* offering of the bread and wine for Communion

**OFFHAND** *adj* casual, curt ▷ *adv* without preparation

**OFFHANDED** *adj* without care oe consideration

**OFFICE** *n* room or building where people work at desks

**OFFICER** *n* person in authority in the armed services ▷ *vb* furnish with officers

**OFFICERED** > OFFICER

**OFFICERS** > OFFICER

**OFFICES** > OFFICE

**OFFICIAL** *adj* of a position of authority ▷ *n* person who holds a position of authority

**OFFICIALS** > OFFICIAL

**OFFICIANT** *n* person who presides and officiates at a religious ceremony

**OFFICIARY** *n* body of officials ▷ *adj* of, relating to, or derived from office

**OFFICIATE** *vb* act in an official role

**OFFICINAL** *adj* (of pharmaceutical products) available without prescription ▷ *n* officinal preparation or plant

**OFFICIOUS** *adj* interfering unnecessarily

**OFFING** *n* area of the sea visible from the shore

**OFFINGS** > OFFING

**OFFISH** *adj* aloof or distant in manner

**OFFISHLY** > OFFISH

**OFFKEY** *adj* out of tune

**OFFLINE** *adj* disconnected from a computer or the internet

**OFFLOAD** *vb* pass responsibility for (something unpleasant) to someone else

**OFFLOADED** > OFFLOAD

**OFFLOADS** > OFFLOAD

**OFFPEAK** *adj* relating to times outside periods of intensive use

**OFFPRINT** *n* separate reprint of an article that originally appeared in a larger publication ▷ *vb* reprint (an article taken from a larger publication) separately

**OFFPRINTS** > OFFPRINT

**OFFPUT** *n* act of putting off

**OFFPUTS** > OFFPUT

**OFFRAMP** *n* road allowing traffic to leave a motorway

**OFFRAMPS** > OFFRAMP

**OFFS** > OFF

**OFFSADDLE** *vb* unsaddle

**OFFSCREEN** *adj* unseen by film viewers

**OFFSCUM** *n* scum

**OFFSCUMS** > OFFSCUM

**OFFSEASON** *n* period of little trade in a business

**OFFSET** *vb* cancel out, compensate for ▷ *n* printing method in which the impression is made onto a surface which transfers it to the paper

**OFFSETS** > OFFSET

**OFFSHOOT** *n* something developed from something else

**OFFSHOOTS** > OFFSHOOT

**OFFSHORE** *adv* away from or at some distance from the shore ▷ *adj* sited or conducted at sea ▷ *n* company operating abroad where the tax system is more advantageous than at home

**OFFSHORES** > OFFSHORE

**OFFSIDE** *adv* (positioned) illegally ahead of the ball ▷ *n* side of a vehicle nearest the centre of the road

**OFFSIDER** *n* partner or assistant

**OFFSIDERS** > OFFSIDER

**OFFSIDES** > OFFSIDE

**OFFSPRING** *n* child

**OFFSTAGE** *adv* out of the view of the audience ▷ *n* something that happens offstage

**OFFSTAGES** > OFFSTAGE

**OFFTAKE** *n* act of taking off

**OFFTAKES** > OFFTAKE

**OFFTRACK** *adj* not at a racetrack

**OFLAG** *n* German prisoner-of-war camp for officers in World War II

**OFLAGS** > OFLAG

**OFT** *adv* often

**OFTEN** *adv* frequently, much of the time

**OFTENER** > OFTEN

**OFTENEST** > OFTEN

**OFTENNESS** > OFTEN

**OFTER** > OFT

**OFTEST** > OFT

**OFTTIMES** *same as* > OFTEN

**OGAM** *same as* > OGHAM

**OGAMIC** > OGAM

**OGAMS** > OGAM

**OGDOAD** *n* group of eight

**OGDOADS** > OGDOAD

**OGEE** *n* moulding having a cross section in the form of a letter S

**OGEES** > OGEE

**OGGIN** *n* sea

**OGGINS** > OGGIN

**OGHAM** *n* ancient alphabetical writing system used by the Celts in Britain and Ireland

**OGHAMIC** > OGHAM

**OGHAMIST** > OGHAM

**OGHAMISTS** > OGHAM

**OGHAMS** > OGHAM

**OGIVAL** > OGIVE

**OGIVE** *n* diagonal rib or groin of a Gothic vault

**OGIVES** > OGIVE

**OGLE** *vb* stare at (someone) lustfully ▷ *n* flirtatious or lewd look

**OGLED** > OGLE

**OGLER** > OGLE

**OGLERS** > OGLE

**OGLES** > OGLE

**OGLING** > OGLE

**OGLINGS** > OGLE

**OGMIC** > OGAM

**OGRE** *n* giant that eats human flesh

**OGREISH** > OGRE

**OGREISHLY** > OGRE

**OGREISM** > OGRE

**OGREISMS** > OGRE

**OGRES** > OGRE

**OGRESS** > OGRE

**OGRESSES** > OGRE

**OGRISH** > OGRE

**OGRISHLY** > OGRE

**OGRISM** > OGRE

**OGRISMS** > OGRE

**OH** *interj* exclamation of surprise, pain, etc ▷ *vb* say oh

**OHED** > OH

**OHIA** *n* Hawaiian plant

**OHIAS** > OHIA

**OHING** > OH

**OHM** *n* unit of electrical resistance

**OHMAGE** *n* electrical resistance in ohms

**OHMAGES** > OHMAGE

**OHMIC** *adj* of or relating to a circuit element

**OHMICALLY** > OHMIC

**OHMMETER** *n* instrument for measuring electrical resistance

**OHMMETERS** > OHMMETER

**OHMS** > OHM

**OHO** *n* exclamation expressing surprise, exultation, or derision

**OHONE** *same as* > OCHONE

**OHOS** > OHO

**OHS** > OH

**OI** *interj* shout to attract attention

**OIDIA** > OIDIUM

**OIDIOID** > OIDIUM

**OIDIUM** *n* type of fungal spore

**OIK** *n* person regarded as inferior because ignorant or lower-class

**OIKIST** *same as* > OECIST

**OIKISTS** > OIKIST

**OIKS** > OIK

**OIL** *n* viscous liquid, insoluble in water and usu flammable ▷ *vb* lubricate (a machine) with oil

**OILBIRD** *n* type of nocturnal gregarious

cave-dwelling bird
**OILBIRDS** > OILBIRD
**OILCAMP** *n* camp for oilworkers
**OILCAMPS** > OILCAMP
**OILCAN** *n* container with a long nozzle for applying oil to machinery
**OILCANS** > OILCAN
**OILCLOTH** *n* waterproof material
**OILCLOTHS** > OILCLOTH
**OILCUP** *n* cup-shaped oil reservoir in a machine providing continuous lubrication for a bearing
**OILCUPS** > OILCUP
**OILED** > OIL
**OILER** *n* person, device, etc, that lubricates or supplies oil
**OILERIES** > OILERY
**OILERS** > OILER
**OILERY** *n* oil business
**OILFIELD** *n* area containing oil reserves
**OILFIELDS** > OILFIELD
**OILFIRED** *adj* using oil as fuel
**OILGAS** *n* gaseous mixture of hydrocarbons used as a fuel
**OILGASES** > OILGAS
**OILHOLE** *n* hole for oil
**OILHOLES** > OILHOLE
**OILIER** > OILY
**OILIEST** > OILY
**OILILY** > OILY
**OILINESS** > OILY
**OILING** > OIL
**OILLET** *same as* > EYELET
**OILLETS** > OILLET
**OILMAN** *n* person who owns or operates oil wells
**OILMEN** > OILMAN
**OILNUT** *n* nut from which oil is extracted
**OILNUTS** > OILNUT
**OILPAPER** *n* oiled paper
**OILPAPERS** > OILPAPER
**OILPROOF** *adj* resistant to oil
**OILS** > OIL
**OILSEED** *n* seed from which oil is extracted
**OILSEEDS** > OILSEED
**OILSKIN** *n* (garment made from) waterproof material
**OILSKINS** > OILSKIN
**OILSTONE** *n* stone with a fine grain lubricated with oil and used for sharpening cutting tools
**OILSTONES** > OILSTONE
**OILTIGHT** *adj* not allowing oil through
**OILWAY** *n* channel for oil
**OILWAYS** > OILWAY
**OILY** *adj* soaked or covered with oil
**OINK** *n* grunt of a pig or an imitation of this ▷ *interj* imitation or representation of the

grunt of a pig ▷ *vb* make noise of pig
**OINKED** > OINK
**OINKING** > OINK
**OINKS** > OINK
**OINOLOGY** *same as* > OENOLOGY
**OINOMEL** *same as* > OENOMEL
**OINOMELS** > OINOMEL
**OINT** *vb* anoint
**OINTED** > OINT
**OINTING** > OINT
**OINTMENT** *n* greasy substance used for healing skin or as a cosmetic
**OINTMENTS** > OINTMENT
**OINTS** > OINT
**OITICICA** *n* South American tree
**OITICICAS** > OITICICA
**OJIME** *n* Japanese bead used to secure cords
**OJIMES** > OJIME
**OKA** *n* unit of weight used in Turkey
**OKAPI** *n* African animal related to the giraffe but with a shorter neck
**OKAPIS** > OKAPI
**OKAS** > OKA
**OKAY** *adj* satisfactory ▷ *vb* approve or endorse ▷ *n* approval or agreement ▷ *interj* expression of approval
**OKAYED** > OKAY
**OKAYING** > OKAY
**OKAYS** > OKAY
**OKE** *same as* > OKA
**OKEH** *variant of* > OKAY
**OKEHS** > OKEH
**OKES** > OKE
**OKEYDOKE** *variant of* > OKAY
**OKEYDOKEY** *variant of* > OKAY
**OKIMONO** *n* Japanese ornamental item
**OKIMONOS** > OKIMONO
**OKRA** *n* tropical plant with edible green pods
**OKRAS** > OKRA
**OKTA** *n* unit used in meteorology to measure cloud cover
**OKTAS** > OKTA
**OLD** *adj* having lived or existed for a long time ▷ *n* earlier or past time
**OLDEN** *adj* old ▷ *vb* grow old
**OLDENED** > OLDEN
**OLDENING** > OLDEN
**OLDENS** > OLDEN
**OLDER** *adj* having lived or existed longer
**OLDEST** > OLD
**OLDIE** *n* old but popular song or film
**OLDIES** > OLDIE
**OLDISH** > OLD
**OLDNESS** > OLD
**OLDNESSES** > OLD
**OLDS** > OLD

**OLDSQUAW** *n* type of long-tailed sea duck
**OLDSQUAWS** > OLDSQUAW
**OLDSTER** *n* older person
**OLDSTERS** > OLDSTER
**OLDSTYLE** *n* printing type style
**OLDSTYLES** > OLDSTYLE
**OLDWIFE** *n* any of various fishes, esp the menhaden or the alewife
**OLDWIVES** > OLDWIFE
**OLDY** *same as* > OLDIE
**OLE** *interj* exclamation of approval or encouragement customary at bullfights ▷ *n* cry of olé
**OLEA** > OLEUM
**OLEACEOUS** *adj* relating to a family of trees and shrubs, including the ash, jasmine, and olive
**OLEANDER** *n* Mediterranean flowering evergreen shrub
**OLEANDERS** > OLEANDER
**OLEARIA** *n* daisy bush
**OLEARIAS** > OLEARIA
**OLEASTER** *n* type of shrub with silver-white twigs and yellow flowers
**OLEASTERS** > OLEASTER
**OLEATE** *n* any salt or ester of oleic acid
**OLEATES** > OLEATE
**OLECRANAL** > OLECRANON
**OLECRANON** *n* bony projection of the ulna behind the elbow joint
**OLEFIANT** *adj* forming oil
**OLEFIN** *same as* > OLEFINE
**OLEFINE** *another name for* > ALKENE
**OLEFINES** > OLEFINE
**OLEFINIC** > OLEFINE
**OLEFINS** > OLEFIN
**OLEIC** as in *oleic acid* colourless oily liquid used in making soap
**OLEIN** *another name for* > TRIOLEIN
**OLEINE** *same as* > OLEIN
**OLEINES** > OLEINE
**OLEINS** > OLEIN
**OLENT** *adj* having smell
**OLEO** as in *oleo oil* oil extracted from beef fat
**OLEOGRAPH** *n* chromolithograph printed in oil colours to imitate the appearance of an oil painting
**OLEORESIN** *n* semisolid mixture of a resin and essential oil
**OLEOS** > OLEO
**OLES** > OLE
**OLESTRA** *n* trademark term for an artificial fat
**OLESTRAS** > OLESTRA
**OLEUM** *n* type of sulphuric acid
**OLEUMS** > OLEUM

**OLFACT** *vb* smell something
**OLFACTED** > OLFACT
**OLFACTING** > OLFACT
**OLFACTION** *n* sense of smell
**OLFACTIVE** *adj* of sense of smell
**OLFACTORY** *adj* relating to the sense of smell ▷ *n* organ or nerve concerned with the sense of smell
**OLFACTS** > OLFACT
**OLIBANUM** *n* frankincense
**OLIBANUMS** > OLIBANUM
**OLICOOK** *n* doughnut
**OLICOOKS** > OLICOOK
**OLID** *adj* foul-smelling
**OLIGAEMIA** *n* reduction in the volume of the blood, as occurs after haemorrhage
**OLIGAEMIC** > OLIGAEMIA
**OLIGARCH** *n* member of an oligarchy
**OLIGARCHS** > OLIGARCH
**OLIGARCHY** *n* government by a small group of people
**OLIGEMIA** *same as* > OLIGAEMIA
**OLIGEMIAS** > OLIGEMIA
**OLIGEMIC** > OLIGAEMIA
**OLIGIST** *n* type of iron ore
**OLIGISTS** > OLIGIST
**OLIGOCENE** *adj* belonging to geological time period
**OLIGOGENE** *n* type of gene
**OLIGOMER** *n* compound of relatively low molecular weight containing up to five monomer units
**OLIGOMERS** > OLIGOMER
**OLIGOPOLY** *n* market situation in which control over the supply of a commodity is held by a small number of producers
**OLIGURIA** *n* excretion of an abnormally small volume of urine
**OLIGURIAS** > OLIGURIA
**OLINGO** *n* South American mammal
**OLINGOS** > OLINGO
**OLIO** *n* dish of many different ingredients
**OLIOS** > OLIO
**OLIPHANT** *archaic variant of* > ELEPHANT
**OLIPHANTS** > OLIPHANT
**OLITORIES** > OLITORY
**OLITORY** *n* kitchen garden
**OLIVARY** *adj* shaped like an olive
**OLIVE** *n* small green or black fruit used as food or pressed for its oil ▷ *adj* greyish-green
**OLIVENITE** *n* green to black rare secondary mineral
**OLIVER** as in *Bath oliver* type of unsweetened biscuit
**OLIVERS** > OLIVER

OLIVES > OLIVE
OLIVET n button shaped like olive
OLIVETS > OLIVET
OLIVINE n olive-green mineral of the olivine group
OLIVINES > OLIVINE
OLIVINIC adj containing olivine
OLLA n cooking pot
OLLAMH n old Irish term for a wise man
OLLAMHS > OLLAMH
OLLAS > OLLA
OLLAV same as > OLLAMH
OLLAVS > OLLAV
OLLER n waste ground
OLLERS > OLLER
OLLIE n (in skateboarding and snowboarding) a jump into the air executed by stamping on the tail of the board
OLLIES > OLLIE
OLM n pale blind eel-like salamander
OLMS > OLM
OLOGIES > OLOGY
OLOGIST n scientist
OLOGISTS > OLOGIST
OLOGOAN vb complain loudly without reason
OLOGOANED > OLOGOAN
OLOGOANS > OLOGOAN
OLOGY n science or other branch of knowledge
OLOLIUQUI n medicinal plant used by the Aztecs
OLOROSO n golden-coloured sweet sherry
OLOROSOS > OLOROSO
OLPAE > OLPE
OLPE n ancient Greek jug
OLPES > OLPE
OLYCOOK same as > OLYKOEK
OLYCOOKS > OLYCOOK
OLYKOEK n American type of doughnut
OLYKOEKS > OLYKOEK
OLYMPIAD n staging of the modern Olympic Games
OLYMPIADS > OLYMPIAD
OLYMPICS pl n modern revival of the ancient Greek games, featuring sporting contests
OM n sacred syllable in Hinduism
OMADHAUN n foolish man or boy
OMADHAUNS > OMADHAUN
OMASA > OMASUM
OMASAL > OMASUM
OMASUM n compartment in the stomach of a ruminant animal
OMBER same as > OMBRE
OMBERS > OMBER
OMBRE n 18th-century card game
OMBRELLA old form of > UMBRELLA

OMBRELLAS > OMBRELLA
OMBRES > OMBRE
OMBROPHIL n plant flourishing in rainy conditions
OMBU n South American tree
OMBUDSMAN n official who investigates complaints against government organizations
OMBUDSMEN > OMBUDSMAN
OMBUS > OMBU
OMEGA n last letter in the Greek alphabet
OMEGAS > OMEGA
OMELET same as > OMELETTE
OMELETS > OMELET
OMELETTE n dish of eggs beaten and fried
OMELETTES > OMELETTE
OMEN n happening or object thought to foretell success or misfortune ▷ vb portend
OMENED > OMEN
OMENING > OMEN
OMENS > OMEN
OMENTA > OMENTUM
OMENTAL > OMENTUM
OMENTUM n double fold of the peritoneum connecting the stomach with other abdominal organs
OMENTUMS > OMENTUM
OMER n ancient Hebrew unit of dry measure equal to one tenth of an ephah
OMERS > OMER
OMERTA n conspiracy of silence
OMERTAS > OMERTA
OMICRON n 15th letter in the Greek alphabet
OMICRONS > OMICRON
OMIGOD interj exclamation of surprise, pleasure, dismay, etc
OMIKRON same as > OMICRON
OMIKRONS > OMIKRON
OMINOUS adj worrying, seeming to foretell misfortune
OMINOUSLY > OMINOUS
OMISSIBLE > OMIT
OMISSION n something that has been left out or passed over
OMISSIONS > OMISSION
OMISSIVE > OMISSION
OMIT vb leave out
OMITS > OMIT
OMITTANCE n omission
OMITTED > OMIT
OMITTER > OMIT
OMITTERS > OMIT
OMITTING > OMIT
OMLAH n staff team in India
OMLAHS > OMLAH
OMMATEA > OMMATEUM
OMMATEUM n insect eye
OMMATIDIA pl n cone-

shaped parts of the eyes of some arthropods
OMNEITIES > OMNEITY
OMNEITY n state of being all
OMNIANA n miscellaneous collection
OMNIARCH n ruler of everything
OMNIARCHS > OMNIARCH
OMNIBUS n several books or TV or radio programmes made into one ▷ adj consisting of or dealing with several different things at once
OMNIBUSES > OMNIBUS
OMNIETIES > OMNIETY
OMNIETY same as > OMNEITY
OMNIFIC adj creating all things
OMNIFIED > OMNIFY
OMNIFIES > OMNIFY
OMNIFORM adj of all forms
OMNIFY vb make something universal
OMNIFYING > OMNIFY
OMNIMODE adj of all functions
OMNIRANGE n very-high-frequency ground radio navigational system
OMNIUM n total value
OMNIUMS > OMNIUM
OMNIVORA n group of omnivorous mammals
OMNIVORE n omnivorous animal
OMNIVORES > OMNIVORE
OMNIVORY n state of being omnivorous
OMOHYOID n muscle in shoulder
OMOHYOIDS > OMOHYOID
OMOPHAGIA n eating of raw food, esp meat
OMOPHAGIC > OMOPHAGIA
OMOPHAGY same as > OMOPHAGIA
OMOPHORIA pl n stole-like bands worn by some bishops
OMOPLATE n shoulder blade
OMOPLATES > OMOPLATE
OMOV n one member one vote: a voting system in which each voter has one vote to cast
OMOVS > OMOV
OMPHACITE n type of mineral
OMPHALI > OMPHALOS
OMPHALIC > OMPHALOS
OMPHALOID adj like navel
OMPHALOS n (in the ancient world) a sacred conical object, esp a stone
OMRAH n Muslim noble
OMRAHS > OMRAH
OMS > OM
ON prep indicating position above, attachment, closeness, etc ▷ adv in

operation ▷ adj operating ▷ n side of the field on which the batsman stands ▷ vb go on
ONAGER n wild ass of Persia
ONAGERS > ONAGER
ONAGRI > ONAGER
ONANISM n withdrawal in sexual intercourse before ejaculation
ONANISMS > ONANISM
ONANIST > ONANISM
ONANISTIC > ONANISM
ONANISTS > ONANISM
ONBEAT n first and third beats in a bar of four-four time
ONBEATS > ONBEAT
ONBOARD adj on a ship or other craft
ONCE adv on one occasion ▷ n one occasion
ONCER n (formerly) a one-pound note
ONCERS > ONCER
ONCES > ONCE
ONCET dialect form of > ONCE
ONCIDIUM n American orchid
ONCIDIUMS > ONCIDIUM
ONCOGEN n substance causing tumours to form
ONCOGENE n gene that can cause cancer when abnormally activated
ONCOGENES > ONCOGENE
ONCOGENIC adj causing the formation of a tumour
ONCOGENS > ONCOGEN
ONCOLOGIC > ONCOLOGY
ONCOLOGY n branch of medicine concerned with the study, classification, and treatment of tumours
ONCOLYSES > ONCOLYSIS
ONCOLYSIS n destruction of tumours
ONCOLYTIC adj destroying tumours
ONCOME n act of coming on
ONCOMES > ONCOME
ONCOMETER n instrument for measuring body organs
ONCOMICE > ONCOMOUSE
ONCOMING adj approaching from the front ▷ n approach or onset
ONCOMINGS > ONCOMING
ONCOMOUSE n mouse bred for cancer treatment research
ONCOST same as > OVERHEADS
ONCOSTMAN n miner paid daily
ONCOSTMEN > ONCOSTMAN
ONCOSTS > ONCOST
ONCOTOMY n surgical cutting of a tumour
ONCOVIRUS n virus causing cancer
ONCUS same as > ONKUS
ONDATRA same as > MUSQUASH

ONDATRAS > ONDATRA
ONDINE same as > UNDINE
ONDINES > ONDINE
ONDING Scots word
for > ONSET
ONDINGS > ONDING
ONDOGRAM n record made
by ondograph
ONDOGRAMS > ONDOGRAM
ONDOGRAPH n instrument
for producing a graphical
recording of an alternating
current
ONE adj single, lone ▷ n
number or figure 1 ▷ pron
any person
ONEFOLD adj simple
ONEIRIC adj of or relating
to dreams
ONELY same as > ONLY
ONENESS n unity
ONENESSES > ONENESS
ONER n single continuous
action
ONERIER > ONERY
ONERIEST > ONERY
ONEROUS adj (of a task)
difficult to carry out
ONEROUSLY > ONEROUS
ONERS > ONER
ONERY same as > ORNERY
ONES > ONE
ONESELF pron reflexive
form of one
ONETIME adj at some time
in the past
ONEYER old form of > ONE
ONEYERS > ONEYER
ONEYRE same as > ONEYER
ONEYRES > ONEYER
ONFALL n attack or onset
ONFALLS > ONFALL
ONFLOW n flowing on
ONFLOWS > ONFLOW
ONGAONGA n New Zealand
nettle with a severe or
fatal sting
ONGAONGAS > ONGAONGA
ONGOING adj in progress,
continuing
ONGOINGS pl n things that
are happening
ONIE variant spelling
of > ONY
ONION n strongly flavoured
edible bulb ▷ vb add
onion to
ONIONED > ONION
ONIONIER > ONION
ONIONIEST > ONION
ONIONING > ONION
ONIONS > ONION
ONIONSKIN n glazed
translucent paper
ONIONY > ONION
ONIRIC same as > ONEIRIC
ONISCOID adj of or like
woodlice
ONIUM as in onium
compound type of chemical
salt
ONIUMS > ONIUM
ONKUS adj bad
ONLAY n artificial veneer

for a tooth
ONLAYS > ONLAY
ONLIEST same as > ONLY
ONLINE adj connected to a
computer or the internet
ONLINER n person who
uses the internet regularly
ONLINERS > ONLINER
ONLOAD vb load files on to a
computer
ONLOADED > ONLOAD
ONLOADING > ONLOAD
ONLOADS > ONLOAD
ONLOOKER n person who
watches without taking
part
ONLOOKERS > ONLOOKER
ONLOOKING > ONLOOKER
ONLY adj alone of its kind
▷ adv exclusively
ONNED > ON
ONNING > ON
ONO n Hawaiian fish
ONOMASTIC adj of or
relating to proper names
ONOS > ONO
ONRUSH n forceful forward
rush or flow
ONRUSHES > ONRUSH
ONRUSHING adj
approaching quickly
ONS > ON
ONSCREEN adj appearing on
screen
ONSET n beginning
ONSETS > ONSET
ONSETTER n attacker
ONSETTERS > ONSET
ONSETTING n attack
ONSHORE adv towards the
land
ONSHORING n practice of
employing white-collar
workers from abroad
ONSIDE adv (of a player in
various sports) in a legal
position ▷ adj taking
one's part or side ▷ n part
of cricket field where a
batsman stands
ONSIDES > ONSIDE
ONSLAUGHT n violent
attack
ONST same as > ONCE
ONSTAGE adj visible by
audience
ONSTEAD Scots word
for > FARMSTEAD
ONSTEADS > ONSTEAD
ONSTREAM adj in operation
ONTIC adj having real
existence
ONTICALLY > ONTIC
ONTO prep a position on
ONTOGENIC > ONTOGENY
ONTOGENY n entire
sequence of events
involved in the
development of an
individual organism
ONTOLOGIC > ONTOLOGY
ONTOLOGY n branch of
philosophy concerned
with existence

ONUS n responsibility or
burden
ONUSES > ONUS
ONWARD same as > ONWARDS
ONWARDLY > ONWARD
ONWARDS adv at or towards
a point or position ahead,
in advance, etc
ONY Scots word for > ANY
ONYCHA n part of mollusc
ONYCHAS > ONYCHA
ONYCHIA n inflammation
of the nails or claws of
animals
ONYCHIAS > ONYCHIA
ONYCHITE n type of stone
ONYCHITES > ONYCHITE
ONYCHITIS n
inflammation of nails
ONYCHIUM n part of insect
foot
ONYCHIUMS > ONYCHIUM
ONYMOUS adj (of a book)
bearing its author's name
ONYX n type of quartz with
coloured layers
ONYXES > ONYX
OO Scots word for > WOOL
OOBIT n hairy caterpillar
OOBITS > OOBIT
OOCYST n type of zygote
OOCYSTS > OOCYST
OOCYTE n immature female
germ cell that gives rise to
an ovum
OOCYTES > OOCYTE
OODLES pl n great
quantities
OODLINS same as > OODLES
OOF n money
OOFIER > OOF
OOFIEST > OOF
OOFS > OOF
OOFTISH n money
OOFTISHES > OOFTISH
OOFY > OOF
OOGAMETE n female gamete
OOGAMETES > OOGAMETE
OOGAMIES > OOGAMY
OOGAMOUS > OOGAMY
OOGAMY n sexual
reproduction involving a
small motile male gamete
and a large much less
motile female gamete
OOGENESES > OOGENESIS
OOGENESIS n formation
and maturation of ova
from undifferentiated cells
in the ovary
OOGENETIC > OOGENESIS
OOGENIES > OOGENY
OOGENY same
as > OOGENESIS
OOGONIA > OOGONIUM
OOGONIAL > OOGONIUM
OOGONIUM n immature
female germ cell forming
oocytes by repeated
divisions
OOGONIUMS > OOGONIUM
OOH interj exclamation of
surprise, pleasure, pain,
etc ▷ vb say ooh

OOHED > OOH
OOHING > OOH
OOHS > OOH
OOIDAL adj shaped like egg
OOLACHAN same
as > EULACHON
OOLACHANS > OOLACHAN
OOLAKAN same
as > EULACHON
OOLAKANS > OOLAKAN
OOLITE n limestone made
up of tiny grains of calcium
carbonate
OOLITES > OOLITE
OOLITH n any of the
tiny spherical grains of
sedimentary rock of which
oolite is composed
OOLITHS > OOLITH
OOLITIC > OOLITE
OOLOGIC > OOLOGY
OOLOGICAL > OOLOGY
OOLOGIES > OOLOGY
OOLOGIST > OOLOGY
OOLOGISTS > OOLOGY
OOLOGY n branch of
ornithology concerned
with the study of birds'
eggs
OOLONG n kind of dark tea
that is partly fermented
before being dried
OOLONGS > OOLONG
OOM n title of respect used
to refer to an elderly man
OOMIAC same as > UMIAK
OOMIACK same as > UMIAK
OOMIACKS > OOMIACK
OOMIACS > OOMIAC
OOMIAK same as > UMIAK
OOMIAKS > OOMIAK
OOMPAH n representation of
the sound made by a deep
brass instrument ▷ vb
make the noise of a brass
instrument
OOMPAHED > OOMPAH
OOMPAHING > OOMPAH
OOMPAHS > OOMPAH
OOMPH n enthusiasm,
vigour, or energy
OOMPHS > OOMPH
OOMS > OOM
OOMYCETE n organism
formerly classified as fungi
OOMYCETES > OOMYCETE
OON Scots word for > OVEN
OONS > OON
OONT n camel
OONTS > OONT
OOP vb Scots word meaning
to bind
OOPED > OOP
OOPHORON n ovary
OOPHORONS > OOPHORON
OOPHYTE n gametophyte
in mosses, liverworts, and
ferns
OOPHYTES > OOPHYTE
OOPHYTIC > OOPHYTE
OOPING > OOP
OOPS interj exclamation of
surprise or apology
OOR Scots form of > OUR

**OORALI** n member of Indian people
**OORALIS** > OORALI
**OORIAL** n Himalayan sheep
**OORIALS** > OORIAL
**OORIE** adj Scots word meaning shabby
**OORIER** > OORIE
**OORIEST** > OORIE
**OOS** > OO
**OOSE** n dust
**OOSES** > OOSE
**OOSIER** > OOSE
**OOSIEST** > OOSE
**OOSPERM** n fertilized ovum
**OOSPERMS** > OOSPERM
**OOSPHERE** n large female gamete produced in the oogonia of algae and fungi
**OOSPHERES** > OOSPHERE
**OOSPORE** n thick-walled sexual spore that develops from a fertilized oosphere
**OOSPORES** > OOSPORE
**OOSPORIC** > OOSPORE
**OOSPOROUS** > OOSPORE
**OOSY** > OOSE
**OOT** Scots word for > OUT
**OOTHECA** n capsule containing eggs that is produced by some insects and molluscs
**OOTHECAE** > OOTHECA
**OOTHECAL** > OOTHECA
**OOTID** n immature female gamete that develops into an ovum
**OOTIDS** > OOTID
**OOTS** > OOT
**OOZE** vb flow slowly ▷ n sluggish flow
**OOZED** > OOZE
**OOZES** > OOZE
**OOZIER** > OOZY
**OOZIEST** > OOZY
**OOZILY** > OOZY
**OOZINESS** > OOZY
**OOZING** > OOZE
**OOZY** adj moist or dripping
**OP** n operation
**OPACIFIED** > OPACIFY
**OPACIFIER** > OPACIFY
**OPACIFIES** > OPACIFY
**OPACIFY** vb become or make opaque
**OPACITIES** > OPACITY
**OPACITY** n state or quality of being opaque
**OPACOUS** same as > OPAQUE
**OPAH** n large soft-finned deep-sea fish
**OPAHS** > OPAH
**OPAL** n iridescent precious stone
**OPALED** adj made like opal
**OPALESCE** vb exhibit a milky iridescence
**OPALESCED** > OPALESCE
**OPALESCES** > OPALESCE
**OPALINE** adj opalescent ▷ n opaque or semiopaque whitish glass
**OPALINES** > OPALINE
**OPALISED** same

as > OPALIZED
**OPALIZED** adj made into opal
**OPALS** > OPAL
**OPAQUE** adj not able to be seen through, not transparent ▷ n opaque pigment used to block out particular areas on a negative ▷ vb make opaque
**OPAQUED** > OPAQUE
**OPAQUELY** > OPAQUE
**OPAQUER** > OPAQUE
**OPAQUES** > OPAQUE
**OPAQUEST** > OPAQUE
**OPAQUING** > OPAQUE
**OPCODE** n computer code containing operating instructions
**OPCODES** > OPCODE
**OPE** archaic or poetic word for > OPEN
**OPED** > OPE
**OPEN** adj not closed ▷ vb (cause to) become open ▷ n competition which all may enter
**OPENABLE** > OPEN
**OPENCAST** as in opencast mining mining by excavating from the surface
**OPENED** > OPEN
**OPENER** n tool for opening cans and bottles
**OPENERS** > OPENER
**OPENEST** > OPEN
**OPENING** n beginning ▷ adj first
**OPENINGS** > OPENING
**OPENLY** > OPEN
**OPENNESS** > OPEN
**OPENS** > OPEN
**OPENSIDE** n in rugby, flanker who plays on the open side of the scrum
**OPENSIDES** > OPENSIDE
**OPENWORK** n ornamental work, as of metal or embroidery, having a pattern of openings or holes
**OPENWORKS** > OPENWORK
**OPEPE** n African tree
**OPEPES** > OPEPE
**OPERA** n drama in which the text is sung to an orchestral accompaniment
**OPERABLE** adj capable of being treated by a surgical operation
**OPERABLY** > OPERABLE
**OPERAGOER** n person who goes to operas
**OPERAND** n quantity, variable, or function upon which an operation is performed
**OPERANDS** > OPERAND
**OPERANT** adj producing effects ▷ n person or thing that operates

**OPERANTLY** > OPERANT
**OPERANTS** > OPERANT
**OPERAS** > OPERA
**OPERATE** vb (cause to) work
**OPERATED** > OPERATE
**OPERATES** > OPERATE
**OPERATIC** adj of or relating to opera
**OPERATICS** n performance of operas
**OPERATING** > OPERATE
**OPERATION** n method or procedure of working
**OPERATISE** same as > OPERATIZE
**OPERATIVE** adj working ▷ n worker with a special skill
**OPERATIZE** vb turn (a play, novel, etc) into an opera
**OPERATOR** n person who operates a machine or instrument
**OPERATORS** > OPERATOR
**OPERCELE** same as > OPERCULE
**OPERCELES** > OPERCELE
**OPERCULA** > OPERCULUM
**OPERCULAR** > OPERCULUM
**OPERCULE** n gill cover
**OPERCULES** > OPERCULE
**OPERCULUM** n covering flap or lidlike structure in animals or plants
**OPERETTA** n light-hearted comic opera
**OPERETTAS** > OPERETTA
**OPERON** n group of adjacent genes in bacteria functioning as a unit
**OPERONS** > OPERON
**OPEROSE** adj laborious
**OPEROSELY** > OPEROSE
**OPEROSITY** > OPEROSE
**OPES** > OPE
**OPGEFOK** adj South African taboo slang for damaged or bungled
**OPHIDIAN** adj snakelike ▷ n any reptile of the suborder Ophidia; a snake
**OPHIDIANS** > OPHIDIAN
**OPHIOLITE** n type of mineral
**OPHIOLOGY** n branch of zoology that is concerned with the study of snakes
**OPHITE** n any of several greenish mottled rocks
**OPHITES** > OPHITE
**OPHITIC** adj having small elongated feldspar crystals enclosed
**OPHIURA** n sea creature like a starfish
**OPHIURAN** same as > OPHIURA
**OPHIURANS** > OPHIURAN
**OPHIURAS** > OPHIURA
**OPHIURID** same as > OPHIURA
**OPHIURIDS** > OPHIURID
**OPHIUROID** adj of or like ophiura

**OPIATE** n narcotic drug containing opium ▷ adj containing or consisting of opium ▷ vb treat with an opiate
**OPIATED** > OPIATE
**OPIATES** > OPIATE
**OPIATING** > OPIATE
**OPIFICER** n craftsman
**OPIFICERS** > OPIFICER
**OPINABLE** adj thinkable
**OPINE** vb express an opinion
**OPINED** > OPINE
**OPINES** > OPINE
**OPING** > OPE
**OPINICUS** n mythical monster
**OPINING** > OPINE
**OPINION** n personal belief or judgment
**OPINIONED** adj having strong opinions
**OPINIONS** > OPINION
**OPIOID** n substance that resembles morphine in its physiological or pharmacological effect
**OPIOIDS** > OPIOID
**OPIUM** n addictive narcotic drug made from poppy seeds
**OPIUMISM** n addiction to opium
**OPIUMISMS** > OPIUMISM
**OPIUMS** > OPIUM
**OPOBALSAM** n soothing ointment
**OPODELDOC** n medical ointment
**OPOPANAX** n medical resin from plant
**OPORICE** n former medicine made from fruit
**OPORICES** > OPORICE
**OPOSSUM** n small marsupial of America or Australasia
**OPOSSUMS** > OPOSSUM
**OPPIDAN** adj of a town ▷ n person living in a town
**OPPIDANS** > OPPIDAN
**OPPILANT** > OPPILATE
**OPPILATE** vb block (the pores, bowels, etc)
**OPPILATED** > OPPILATE
**OPPILATES** > OPPILATE
**OPPO** n counterpart in another organization
**OPPONENCY** > OPPONENT
**OPPONENT** n person one is working against in a contest, battle, or argument ▷ adj opposite, as in position
**OPPONENTS** > OPPONENT
**OPPORTUNE** adj happening at a suitable time
**OPPOS** > OPPO
**OPPOSABLE** adj (of the thumb) capable of touching the tip of all the other fingers
**OPPOSABLY** > OPPOSABLE
**OPPOSE** vb work against

OPPOSED > OPPOSE
OPPOSER > OPPOSE
OPPOSERS > OPPOSE
OPPOSES > OPPOSE
OPPOSING > OPPOSE
OPPOSITE adj situated on the other side ▷ n person or thing that is opposite ▷ prep facing ▷ adv on the other side
OPPOSITES > OPPOSITE
OPPRESS vb control by cruelty or force
OPPRESSED > OPPRESS
OPPRESSES > OPPRESS
OPPRESSOR > OPPRESS
OPPUGN vb call into question
OPPUGNANT adj combative, antagonistic, or contrary
OPPUGNED > OPPUGN
OPPUGNER > OPPUGN
OPPUGNERS > OPPUGN
OPPUGNING > OPPUGN
OPPUGNS > OPPUGN
OPS > OP
OPSIMATH n person who learns late in life
OPSIMATHS > OPSIMATH
OPSIMATHY > OPSIMATH
OPSIN n type of protein
OPSINS > OPSIN
OPSOMANIA n extreme enthusiasm for a particular food
OPSONIC > OPSONIN
OPSONIFY same as > OPSONIZE
OPSONIN n constituent of blood serum
OPSONINS > OPSONIN
OPSONISE same as > OPSONIZE
OPSONISED > OPSONISE
OPSONISES > OPSONISE
OPSONIUM n relish eaten with bread
OPSONIUMS > OPSONIUM
OPSONIZE vb subject (bacteria) to the action of opsonins
OPSONIZED > OPSONIZE
OPSONIZES > OPSONIZE
OPT vb show a preference, choose
OPTANT n person who opts
OPTANTS > OPTANT
OPTATIVE adj indicating or expressing choice, preference, or wish ▷ n optative mood
OPTATIVES > OPTATIVE
OPTED > OPT
OPTER > OPT
OPTERS > OPT
OPTIC adj relating to the eyes or sight
OPTICAL adj of or involving light or optics
OPTICALLY > OPTICAL
OPTICIAN n person qualified to prescribe glasses
OPTICIANS > OPTICIAN

OPTICIST n optics expert
OPTICISTS > OPTICIST
OPTICS n science of sight and light
OPTIMA > OPTIMUM
OPTIMAL adj best or most favourable
OPTIMALLY > OPTIMAL
OPTIMATE n Roman aristocrat
OPTIMATES > OPTIMATE
OPTIME n mathematics student at Cambridge University
OPTIMES > OPTIME
OPTIMISE same as > OPTIMIZE
OPTIMISED > OPTIMISE
OPTIMISER > OPTIMISE
OPTIMISES > OPTIMISE
OPTIMISM n tendency to take the most hopeful view
OPTIMISMS > OPTIMISM
OPTIMIST > OPTIMISM
OPTIMISTS > OPTIMISM
OPTIMIZE vb make the most of
OPTIMIZED > OPTIMIZE
OPTIMIZER > OPTIMIZE
OPTIMIZES > OPTIMIZE
OPTIMUM n best possible conditions ▷ adj most favourable
OPTIMUMS > OPTIMUM
OPTING > OPT
OPTION n choice ▷ vb obtain an option on
OPTIONAL adj possible but not compulsory ▷ n optional thing
OPTIONALS > OPTIONAL
OPTIONED > OPTION
OPTIONEE n holder of a financial option
OPTIONEES > OPTIONEE
OPTIONING > OPTION
OPTIONS > OPTION
OPTOLOGY n science of sight
OPTOMETER n any of various instruments for measuring the refractive power of the eye
OPTOMETRY n science or practice of testing visual acuity and prescribing corrective lenses
OPTOPHONE n device for blind people that converts printed words into sounds
OPTRONICS n science of electronic and light signals
OPTS > OPT
OPULENCE > OPULENT
OPULENCES > OPULENT
OPULENCY > OPULENT
OPULENT adj having or indicating wealth
OPULENTLY > OPULENT
OPULUS n flowering shrub
OPULUSES > OPULUS
OPUNTIA n type of cactus
OPUNTIAS > OPUNTIA

OPUS n artistic creation, esp a musical work
OPUSCLE same as > OPUSCULE
OPUSCLES > OPUSCLE
OPUSCULA > OPUSCULUM
OPUSCULAR > OPUSCULE
OPUSCULE n small or insignificant artistic work
OPUSCULES > OPUSCULE
OPUSCULUM same as > OPUSCULE
OPUSES > OPUS
OQUASSA n American trout
OQUASSAS > OQUASSA
OR prep before ▷ adj of the metal gold ▷ n gold
ORA > OS
ORACH same as > ORACHE
ORACHE n type of plant
ORACHES > ORACHE
ORACIES > ORACY
ORACLE n shrine of an ancient god ▷ vb utter as an oracle
ORACLED > ORACLE
ORACLES > ORACLE
ORACLING > ORACLE
ORACULAR adj of or like an oracle
ORACULOUS adj of an oracle
ORACY n capacity to express oneself in and understand speech
ORAD adv towards the mouth
ORAGIOUS adj stormy
ORAL adj spoken ▷ n spoken examination
ORALISM n oral method of communicating with deaf people
ORALISMS > ORALISM
ORALIST > ORALISM
ORALISTS > ORALISM
ORALITIES > ORALITY
ORALITY n state of being oral
ORALLY > ORAL
ORALS > ORAL
ORANG n orangutan
ORANGE n reddish-yellow citrus fruit ▷ adj reddish-yellow
ORANGEADE n orange-flavoured, usu fizzy drink
ORANGER > ORANGE
ORANGERIE archaic variant of > ORANGERY
ORANGERY n greenhouse for growing orange trees
ORANGES > ORANGE
ORANGEST > ORANGE
ORANGEY > ORANGE
ORANGIER > ORANGE
ORANGIEST > ORANGE
ORANGISH > ORANGE
ORANGS > ORANG
ORANGUTAN n large ape with shaggy reddish-brown hair
ORANGY > ORANGE
ORANT n artistic representation of

worshipper
ORANTS > ORANT
ORARIA > ORARIUM
ORARIAN n person who lives on the coast
ORARIANS > ORARIAN
ORARION n garment worn by Greek clergyman
ORARIONS > ORARION
ORARIUM n handkerchief
ORARIUMS > ORARIUM
ORATE vb make or give an oration
ORATED > ORATE
ORATES > ORATE
ORATING > ORATE
ORATION n formal speech
ORATIONS > ORATION
ORATOR n skilful public speaker
ORATORIAL adj of oratory
ORATORIAN n clergyman of a particular type of church
ORATORIES > ORATORY
ORATORIO n musical composition for choir and orchestra
ORATORIOS > ORATORIO
ORATORS > ORATOR
ORATORY n art of making speeches
ORATRESS n female orator
ORATRICES > ORATRIX
ORATRIX n female orator
ORATRIXES > ORATRIX
ORB n ceremonial decorated sphere with a cross on top, carried by a monarch ▷ vb make or become circular or spherical
ORBED > ORB
ORBICULAR adj circular or spherical
ORBIER > ORBY
ORBIEST > ORBY
ORBING > ORB
ORBIT n curved path of a planet, satellite, or spacecraft around another body ▷ vb move in an orbit around
ORBITA same as > ORBIT
ORBITAL adj of or denoting an orbit ▷ n region surrounding an atomic nucleus
ORBITALLY > ORBITAL
ORBITALS > ORBITAL
ORBITAS > ORBITA
ORBITED > ORBIT
ORBITER n spacecraft or satellite designed to orbit a planet without landing on it
ORBITERS > ORBITER
ORBITIES > ORBITY
ORBITING > ORBIT
ORBITS > ORBIT
ORBITY n bereavement
ORBLESS > ORB
ORBS > ORB
ORBY adj orb-shaped
ORC n any of various

whales, such as the killer and grampus

**ORCA** *n* killer whale

**ORCAS** > ORCA

**ORCEIN** *n* brown crystalline material

**ORCEINS** > ORCEIN

**ORCHARD** *n* area where fruit trees are grown

**ORCHARDS** > ORCHARD

**ORCHAT** *same as* > ORCHARD

**ORCHATS** > ORCHAT

**ORCHEL** *same as* > ORCHIL

**ORCHELLA** *same as* > ORCHIL

**ORCHELLAS** > ORCHELLA

**ORCHELS** > ORCHEL

**ORCHESES** > ORCHESIS

**ORCHESIS** *n* art of dance

**ORCHESTIC** *adj* of dance

**ORCHESTRA** *n* large group of musicians, esp playing a variety of instruments

**ORCHID** *n* plant with flowers that have unusual lip-shaped petals

**ORCHIDIST** *n* orchid grower

**ORCHIDS** > ORCHID

**ORCHIL** *n* any of various lichens

**ORCHILLA** *same as* > ORCHIL

**ORCHILLAS** > ORCHILLA

**ORCHILS** > ORCHIL

**ORCHIS** *n* type of orchid

**ORCHISES** > ORCHIS

**ORCHITIC** > ORCHITIS

**ORCHITIS** *n* inflammation of one or both testicles

**ORCIN** *same as* > ORCINOL

**ORCINE** *same as* > ORCINOL

**ORCINES** > ORCINE

**ORCINOL** *n* colourless crystalline water-soluble solid

**ORCINOLS** > ORCINOL

**ORCINS** > ORCIN

**ORCS** > ORC

**ORD** *n* pointed weapon

**ORDAIN** *vb* make (someone) a member of the clergy

**ORDAINED** > ORDAIN

**ORDAINER** > ORDAIN

**ORDAINERS** > ORDAIN

**ORDAINING** > ORDAIN

**ORDAINS** > ORDAIN

**ORDALIAN** *adj* of an ordeal

**ORDALIUM** *same as* > ORDEAL

**ORDALIUMS** > ORDALIUM

**ORDEAL** *n* painful or difficult experience

**ORDEALS** > ORDEAL

**ORDER** *n* instruction to be carried out ▷ *vb* give an instruction to

**ORDERABLE** > ORDER

**ORDERED** > ORDER

**ORDERER** > ORDER

**ORDERERS** > ORDER

**ORDERING** > ORDER

**ORDERINGS** > ORDER

**ORDERLESS** > ORDER

**ORDERLIES** > ORDERLY

**ORDERLY** *adj* well-organized ▷ *n* hospital attendant ▷ *adv* according to custom or rule

**ORDERS** > ORDER

**ORDINAIRE** *adj* ordinary

**ORDINAL** *adj* denoting a certain position in a sequence of numbers ▷ *n* book containing the forms of services for the ordination of ministers

**ORDINALLY** > ORDINAL

**ORDINALS** > ORDINAL

**ORDINANCE** *n* official rule or order

**ORDINAND** *n* candidate for ordination

**ORDINANDS** > ORDINAND

**ORDINANT** *n* person who ordains

**ORDINANTS** > ORDINANT

**ORDINAR** *Scots word for* > ORDINARY

**ORDINARS** > ORDINAR

**ORDINARY** *adj* usual or normal

**ORDINATE** *n* vertical coordinate of a point in a two-dimensional system of coordinates ▷ *vb* ordain

**ORDINATED** > ORDINATE

**ORDINATES** > ORDINATE

**ORDINEE** *n* person being ordained

**ORDINEES** > ORDINEE

**ORDINES** > ORDO

**ORDNANCE** *n* weapons and military supplies

**ORDNANCES** > ORDNANCE

**ORDO** *n* religious order

**ORDOS** > ORDO

**ORDS** > ORD

**ORDURE** *n* excrement

**ORDURES** > ORDURE

**ORDUROUS** > ORDURE

**ORE** *n* (rock containing) a mineral which yields metal

**OREAD** *n* mountain nymph

**OREADES** > OREAD

**OREADS** > OREAD

**ORECTIC** *adj* of or relating to the desires

**ORECTIVE** > OREXIS

**OREGANO** *n* sweet-smelling herb used in cooking

**OREGANOS** > OREGANO

**OREIDE** *same as* > OROIDE

**OREIDES** > OREIDE

**OREODONT** *n* extinct prehistoric mammal

**OREODONTS** > OREODONT

**OREOLOGY** *same as* > OROLOGY

**OREPEARCH** *same as* > OVERPERCH

**ORES** > ORE

**ORESTUNCK** > OVERSTINK

**OREWEED** *n* seaweed

**OREWEEDS** > OREWEED

**OREXIS** *n* appetite

**OREXISES** > OREXIS

**ORF** *n* infectious disease of sheep and sometimes goats and cattle

**ORFE** *n* small slender European fish

**ORFES** > ORFE

**ORFRAY** *same as* > ORPHREY

**ORFRAYS** > ORFRAY

**ORFS** > ORF

**ORGAN** *n* part of an animal or plant that has a particular function

**ORGANA** > ORGANON

**ORGANDIE** *n* fine cotton fabric

**ORGANDIES** > ORGANDY

**ORGANDY** *same as* > ORGANDIE

**ORGANELLE** *n* structural and functional unit in a cell

**ORGANIC** *adj* of or produced from animals or plants ▷ *n* substance that is derived from animal or vegetable matter

**ORGANICAL** *same as* > ORGANIC

**ORGANICS** > ORGANIC

**ORGANISE** *same as* > ORGANIZE

**ORGANISED** *same as* > ORGANIZED

**ORGANISER** *same as* > ORGANIZER

**ORGANISES** > ORGANISE

**ORGANISM** *n* any living animal or plant

**ORGANISMS** > ORGANISM

**ORGANIST** *n* organ player

**ORGANISTS** > ORGANIST

**ORGANITY** *same as* > ORGANISM

**ORGANIZE** *vb* make arrangements for

**ORGANIZED** > ORGANIZE

**ORGANIZER** *n* person who organizes or is capable of organizing

**ORGANIZES** > ORGANIZE

**ORGANON** *n* system of logical or scientific rules, esp that of Aristotle

**ORGANONS** > ORGANON

**ORGANOSOL** *n* resin-based coating

**ORGANS** > ORGAN

**ORGANUM** *same as* > ORGANON

**ORGANUMS** > ORGANUM

**ORGANZA** *n* thin stiff fabric of silk, cotton, or synthetic fibre

**ORGANZAS** > ORGANZA

**ORGANZINE** *n* strong thread made of twisted strands of raw silk

**ORGASM** *n* most intense point of sexual pleasure ▷ *vb* experience orgasm

**ORGASMED** > ORGASM

**ORGASMIC** > ORGASM

**ORGASMING** > ORGASM

**ORGASMS** > ORGASM

**ORGASTIC** > ORGASM

**ORGEAT** *n* drink made from barley or almonds, and orange flower water

**ORGEATS** > ORGEAT

**ORGIA** *same as* > ORGY

**ORGIAC** > ORGY

**ORGIAS** > ORGIA

**ORGIAST** *n* participant in orgy

**ORGIASTIC** > ORGY

**ORGIASTS** > ORGIAST

**ORGIC** > ORGY

**ORGIES** > ORGY

**ORGILLOUS** *same as* > ORGULOUS

**ORGONE** *n* substance claimed to be needed in people for sexual activity and mental health

**ORGONES** > ORGONE

**ORGUE** *n* number of stakes lashed together

**ORGUES** > ORGUE

**ORGULOUS** *adj* proud

**ORGY** *n* party involving promiscuous sexual activity

**ORIBATID** *n* type of mite

**ORIBATIDS** > ORIBATID

**ORIBI** *n* small African antelope

**ORIBIS** > ORIBI

**ORICALCHE** *same as* > ORICHALC

**ORICHALC** *n* type of alloy

**ORICHALCS** > ORICHALC

**ORIEL** *n* type of bay window

**ORIELLED** *adj* having an oriel

**ORIELS** > ORIEL

**ORIENCIES** > ORIENCY

**ORIENCY** *n* state of being orient

**ORIENT** *vb* position (oneself) according to one's surroundings ▷ *n* eastern sky or the dawn ▷ *adj* eastern

**ORIENTAL** *adj* eastern ▷ *n* native of the orient

**ORIENTALS** > ORIENTAL

**ORIENTATE** *vb* position (oneself) according to one's surroundings

**ORIENTED** > ORIENT

**ORIENTEER** *vb* take part in orienteering ▷ *n* person who takes part in orienteering

**ORIENTER** > ORIENT

**ORIENTERS** > ORIENT

**ORIENTING** > ORIENT

**ORIENTS** > ORIENT

**ORIFEX** *same as* > ORIFICE

**ORIFEXES** > ORIFEX

**ORIFICE** *n* opening or hole

**ORIFICES** > ORIFICE

**ORIFICIAL** > ORIFICE

**ORIFLAMME** *n* scarlet flag

adopted as the national banner of France in the Middle Ages

**ORIGAMI** n Japanese decorative art of paper folding

**ORIGAMIS** > ORIGAMI

**ORIGAN** another name for > MARJORAM

**ORIGANE** same as > ORIGAN

**ORIGANES** > ORIGANE

**ORIGANS** > ORIGAN

**ORIGANUM** n type of aromatic plant

**ORIGANUMS** > ORIGANUM

**ORIGIN** n point from which something develops

**ORIGINAL** adj first or earliest ▷ n first version, from which others are copied

**ORIGINALS** > ORIGINAL

**ORIGINATE** vb come or bring into existence

**ORIGINS** > ORIGIN

**ORIHOU** n small New Zealand tree

**ORILLION** n part of bastion

**ORILLIONS** > ORILLION

**ORINASAL** adj pronounced with simultaneous oral and nasal articulation ▷ n orinasal speech sound

**ORINASALS** > ORINASAL

**ORIOLE** n tropical or American songbird

**ORIOLES** > ORIOLE

**ORISHA** n any of the minor gods or spirits of traditional Yoruba religion

**ORISHAS** > ORISHA

**ORISON** another word for > PRAYER

**ORISONS** > ORISON

**ORIXA** same as > ORISHA

**ORIXAS** > ORIXA

**ORLE** n border around a shield

**ORLEANS** n type of fabric

**ORLEANSES** > ORLEANS

**ORLES** > ORLE

**ORLON** n tradename for a crease-resistant acrylic fibre or fabric used for clothing, furnishings, etc

**ORLONS** > ORLON

**ORLOP** n (in a vessel with four or more decks) the lowest deck

**ORLOPS** > ORLOP

**ORMER** n edible marine mollusc

**ORMERS** > ORMER

**ORMOLU** n gold-coloured alloy used for decoration

**ORMOLUS** > ORMOLU

**ORNAMENT** n decorative object ▷ vb decorate

**ORNAMENTS** > ORNAMENT

**ORNATE** adj highly decorated, elaborate

**ORNATELY** > ORNATE

**ORNATER** > ORNATE

**ORNATEST** > ORNATE

**ORNERIER** > ORNERY

**ORNERIEST** > ORNERY

**ORNERY** adj stubborn or vile-tempered

**ORNIS** less common word for > AVIFAUNA

**ORNISES** > ORNIS

**ORNITHES** n birds in Greek myth

**ORNITHIC** adj of or relating to birds or a bird fauna

**ORNITHINE** n type of amino acid

**ORNITHOID** adj like bird

**OROGEN** n part of earth subject to orogeny

**OROGENIC** > OROGENY

**OROGENIES** > OROGENY

**OROGENS** > OROGEN

**OROGENY** n formation of mountain ranges by intense upward displacement of the earth's crust

**OROGRAPHY** n study or mapping of relief, esp of mountains

**OROIDE** n alloy containing copper, tin, and other metals, used as imitation gold

**OROIDES** > OROIDE

**OROLOGIES** > OROLOGY

**OROLOGIST** > OROROGRAPHY

**OROLOGY** same as > OROGRAPHY

**OROMETER** n aneroid barometer with an altitude scale

**OROMETERS** > OROMETER

**ORONASAL** adj of or relating to the mouth and nose

**OROPESA** n float used in minesweeping

**OROPESAS** > OROPESA

**OROTUND** adj (of the voice) resonant and booming

**ORPHAN** n child whose parents are dead ▷ vb deprive of parents

**ORPHANAGE** n children's home for orphans

**ORPHANED** > ORPHAN

**ORPHANING** > ORPHAN

**ORPHANISM** n state of being an orphan

**ORPHANS** > ORPHAN

**ORPHARION** n large lute in use during the 16th and 17th centuries

**ORPHIC** adj mystical or occult

**ORPHICAL** same as > ORPHIC

**ORPHISM** n style of abstract art

**ORPHISMS** > ORPHISM

**ORPHREY** n richly embroidered band or border

**ORPHREYED** adj emroidered with gold

**ORPHREYS** > ORPHREY

**ORPIMENT** n yellow mineral

**ORPIMENTS** > ORPIMENT

**ORPIN** same as > ORPINE

**ORPINE** n type of plant

**ORPINES** > ORPINE

**ORPINS** > ORPIN

**ORRA** adj odd or unmatched

**ORRAMAN** n man who does odd jobs

**ORRAMEN** > ORRAMAN

**ORRERIES** > ORRERY

**ORRERY** n mechanical model of the solar system

**ORRICE** same as > ORRIS

**ORRICES** > ORRICE

**ORRIS** n kind of iris

**ORRISES** > ORRIS

**ORRISROOT** n rhizome of a type of iris, used as perfume

**ORS** > OR

**ORSEILLE** same as > ORCHIL

**ORSEILLES** > ORSEILLE

**ORSELLIC** > ORSEILLE

**ORT** n fragment

**ORTANIQUE** n hybrid between an orange and a tangerine

**ORTHIAN** adj having high pitch

**ORTHICON** n type of television camera tube

**ORTHICONS** > ORTHICON

**ORTHO** n type of photographic plate

**ORTHOAXES** > ORTHOAXIS

**ORTHOAXIS** n axis in a crystal

**ORTHODOX** adj conforming to established views

**ORTHODOXY** n orthodox belief or practice

**ORTHOEPIC** > ORTHOEPY

**ORTHOEPY** n study of correct or standard pronunciation

**ORTHOPEDY** n treatment of deformity

**ORTHOPOD** n surgeon

**ORTHOPODS** > ORTHOPOD

**ORTHOPTER** n type of aircraft propelled by flapping wings

**ORTHOPTIC** adj relating to normal binocular vision

**ORTHOS** > ORTHO

**ORTHOSES** > ORTHOSIS

**ORTHOSIS** n artificial or mechanical aid to support a weak part of the body

**ORTHOTIC** > ORTHOTICS

**ORTHOTICS** n use of artificial or mechanical aids to assist movement of weak joints or muscles

**ORTHOTIST** n person who is qualified to practise orthotics

**ORTHOTONE** adj (of a word) having an independent accent ▷ n independently accented word

**ORTHROS** n canonical hour in the Greek Church

**ORTHROSES** > ORTHROS

**ORTOLAN** n small European

songbird eaten as a delicacy

**ORTOLANS** > ORTOLAN

**ORTS** pl n scraps or leavings

**ORVAL** n plant of sage family

**ORVALS** > ORVAL

**ORYX** n large African antelope

**ORYXES** > ORYX

**ORZO** n pasta in small grain shapes

**ORZOS** > ORZO

**OS** n mouth or mouthlike part or opening

**OSAR** > OS

**OSCAR** n cash

**OSCARS** > OSCAR

**OSCHEAL** adj of scrotum

**OSCILLATE** vb swing back and forth

**OSCINE** n songbird ▷ adj of songbirds

**OSCINES** > OSCINE

**OSCININE** > OSCINE

**OSCITANCE** same as > OSCITANCY

**OSCITANCY** n state of being drowsy, lazy, or inattentive

**OSCITANT** > OSCITANCY

**OSCITATE** vb yawn

**OSCITATED** > OSCITATE

**OSCITATES** > OSCITATE

**OSCULA** > OSCULUM

**OSCULANT** adj possessing some of the characteristics of two different taxonomic groups

**OSCULAR** adj of or relating to an osculum

**OSCULATE** vb kiss

**OSCULATED** > OSCULATE

**OSCULATES** > OSCULATE

**OSCULE** n small mouth or opening

**OSCULES** > OSCULE

**OSCULUM** n mouthlike aperture

**OSE** same as > ESKER

**OSES** > OSE

**OSETRA** n type of caviar

**OSETRAS** > OSETRA

**OSHAC** n plant smelling of ammonia

**OSHACS** > OSHAC

**OSIER** n willow tree

**OSIERED** adj covered with osiers

**OSIERIES** > OSIERY

**OSIERS** > OSIER

**OSIERY** n work done with osiers

**OSMATE** n salt of osmic acid

**OSMATES** > OSMATE

**OSMATIC** adj relying on sense of smell

**OSMETERIA** pl n glands in some caterpillars that secrete foul-smelling substances to deter predators

**OSMIATE** same as > OSMATE

**OSMIATES** > OSMIATE

**OSMIC** adj of or containing

OSMIUM in a high valence state
**OSMICALLY** > OSMIC
**OSMICS** n science of smell
**OSMIOUS** same as > OSMOUS
**OSMIUM** n heaviest known metallic element
**OSMIUMS** > OSMIUM
**OSMOL** same as > OSMOLE
**OSMOLAL** > OSMOLE
**OSMOLAR** adj containing one osmole per litre
**OSMOLE** n unit of osmotic pressure
**OSMOLES** > OSMOLE
**OSMOLS** > OSMOL
**OSMOMETER** n instrument for measuring osmotic pressure
**OSMOMETRY** > OSMOMETER
**OSMOSE** vb undergo or cause to undergo osmosis
**OSMOSED** > OSMOSE
**OSMOSES** > OSMOSE
**OSMOSING** > OSMOSE
**OSMOSIS** n movement of a liquid through a membrane from a lower to a higher concentration
**OSMOTIC** > OSMOSIS
**OSMOUS** adj of or containing osmium in a low valence state
**OSMUND** same as > OSMUNDA
**OSMUNDA** n type of fern
**OSMUNDAS** > OSMUNDA
**OSMUNDINE** n type of compost
**OSMUNDS** > OSMUND
**OSNABURG** n coarse plain-woven cotton used for sacks, furnishings, etc
**OSNABURGS** > OSNABURG
**OSPREY** n large fish-eating bird of prey
**OSPREYS** > OSPREY
**OSSA** > OS
**OSSARIUM** same as > OSSUARY
**OSSARIUMS** > OSSARIUM
**OSSATURE** n skeleton
**OSSATURES** > OSSATURE
**OSSEIN** n protein that forms the organic matrix of bone
**OSSEINS** > OSSEIN
**OSSELET** n growth on knee of horse
**OSSELETS** > OSSELET
**OSSEOUS** adj consisting of or like bone
**OSSEOUSLY** > OSSEOUS
**OSSETER** n sturgeon
**OSSETERS** > OSSETER
**OSSETRA** same as > OSETRA
**OSSETRAS** > OSSETRA
**OSSIA** conj (in music) or
**OSSICLE** n small bone, esp one of those in the middle ear
**OSSICLES** > OSSICLE
**OSSICULAR** > OSSICLE
**OSSIFIC** adj making something turn to bone

**OSSIFIED** adj converted into bone
**OSSIFIER** > OSSIFY
**OSSIFIERS** > OSSIFY
**OSSIFIES** > OSSIFY
**OSSIFRAGA** n large sea bird
**OSSIFRAGE** n osprey
**OSSIFY** vb (cause to) become bone, harden
**OSSIFYING** > OSSIFY
**OSSUARIES** > OSSUARY
**OSSUARY** n any container for the burial of human bones, such as an urn or vault
**OSTEAL** adj of or relating to bone or to the skeleton
**OSTEITIC** > OSTEITIS
**OSTEITIS** n inflammation of a bone
**OSTENSIVE** adj directly showing or pointing out
**OSTENSORY** n (in the RC Church) receptacle for displaying the consecrated Host
**OSTENT** n appearance
**OSTENTS** > OSTENT
**OSTEOCYTE** n bone cell
**OSTEODERM** n bony area in skin
**OSTEOGEN** n material from which bone forms
**OSTEOGENS** > OSTEOGEN
**OSTEOGENY** n forming of bone
**OSTEOID** adj of or resembling bone ▷ n bony deposit
**OSTEOIDS** > OSTEOID
**OSTEOLOGY** n study of the structure and function of bones
**OSTEOMA** n benign tumour composed of bone or bonelike tissue
**OSTEOMAS** > OSTEOMA
**OSTEOMATA** > OSTEOMA
**OSTEOPATH** n person who practises osteopathy
**OSTEOSES** > OSTEOSIS
**OSTEOSIS** n forming of bony tissue
**OSTEOTOME** n surgical instrument for cutting bone, usually a special chisel
**OSTEOTOMY** n surgical cutting or dividing of bone
**OSTIA** > OSTIUM
**OSTIAL** > OSTIUM
**OSTIARIES** > OSTIARY
**OSTIARY** another word for > PORTER
**OSTIATE** adj having ostium
**OSTINATI** > OSTINATO
**OSTINATO** n persistently repeated phrase or rhythm
**OSTINATOS** > OSTINATO
**OSTIOLAR** > OSTIOLE
**OSTIOLATE** > OSTIOLE
**OSTIOLE** n pore in the reproductive bodies of certain algae and fungi

through which spores pass
**OSTIOLES** > OSTIOLE
**OSTIUM** n any of the pores in sponges through which water enters the body
**OSTLER** n stableman at an inn
**OSTLERESS** n female ostler
**OSTLERS** > OSTLER
**OSTMARK** n currency of the former East Germany
**OSTMARKS** > OSTMARK
**OSTOMATE** n person with an ostomy
**OSTOMATES** > OSTOMATE
**OSTOMIES** > OSTOMY
**OSTOMY** n surgically made opening connecting organ to surface of body
**OSTOSES** > OSTOSIS
**OSTOSIS** n formation of bone
**OSTOSISES** > OSTOSIS
**OSTRACA** > OSTRACON
**OSTRACEAN** adj of oysters
**OSTRACISE** same as > OSTRACIZE
**OSTRACISM** > OSTRACIZE
**OSTRACIZE** vb exclude (a person) from a group
**OSTRACOD** n type of minute crustacean
**OSTRACODE** adj of ostracods
**OSTRACODS** > OSTRACOD
**OSTRACON** n (in ancient Greece) a potsherd used for ostracizing
**OSTRACONS** > OSTRACON
**OSTRAKA** > OSTRAKON
**OSTRAKON** same as > OSTRACON
**OSTREGER** n keeper of hawks
**OSTREGERS** > OSTREGER
**OSTRICH** n large African bird that runs fast but cannot fly
**OSTRICHES** > OSTRICH
**OTAKU** n Japanese computer geeks
**OTALGIA** technical name for > EARACHE
**OTALGIAS** > OTALGIA
**OTALGIC** > OTALGIA
**OTALGIES** > OTALGY
**OTALGY** same as > OTALGIA
**OTARIES** > OTARY
**OTARINE** > OTARY
**OTARY** n seal with ears
**OTHER** adj remaining in a group of which one or some have been specified ▷ n other person or thing
**OTHERNESS** n quality of being different or distinct in appearance, character, etc
**OTHERS** > OTHER
**OTHERWISE** adv differently, in another way ▷ adj of an unexpected nature ▷ pron something different in outcome

**OTIC** adj of or relating to the ear
**OTIOSE** adj not useful
**OTIOSELY** > OTIOSE
**OTIOSITY** > OTIOSE
**OTITIC** > OTITIS
**OTITIDES** > OTITIS
**OTITIS** n inflammation of the ear
**OTITISES** > OTITIS
**OTOCYST** n embryonic structure in vertebrates that develops into the inner ear in the adult
**OTOCYSTIC** > OTOCYST
**OTOCYSTS** > OTOCYST
**OTOLITH** n granule of calcium carbonate in the inner ear of vertebrates
**OTOLITHIC** > OTOLITH
**OTOLITHS** > OTOLITH
**OTOLOGIES** > OTOLOGY
**OTOLOGIST** > OTOLOGY
**OTOLOGY** n branch of medicine concerned with the ear
**OTOPLASTY** n cosmetic surgery on ears
**OTORRHOEA** n discharge from the ears
**OTOSCOPE** another name for > AURISCOPE
**OTOSCOPES** > OTOSCOPE
**OTOSCOPIC** > OTOSCOPY
**OTOSCOPY** n examination of ear using otoscope
**OTOTOXIC** adj toxic to the ear
**OTTAR** variant of > ATTAR
**OTTARS** > OTTAR
**OTTAVA** n interval of an octave
**OTTAVAS** > OTTAVA
**OTTAVINO** n piccolo
**OTTAVINOS** > OTTAVINO
**OTTER** n small brown freshwater mammal that eats fish ▷ vb fish using an otter board
**OTTERED** > OTTER
**OTTERING** > OTTER
**OTTERS** > OTTER
**OTTO** another name for > ATTAR
**OTTOMAN** n storage chest with a padded lid for use as a seat
**OTTOMANS** > OTTOMAN
**OTTOS** > OTTO
**OTTRELITE** n type of mineral
**OU** n man, bloke, or chap
**OUABAIN** n poisonous white crystalline glycoside
**OUABAINS** > OUABAIN
**OUAKARI** n South American monkey
**OUAKARIS** > OUAKARI
**OUBAAS** n man in authority
**OUBAASES** > OUBAAS
**OUBIT** n hairy caterpillar
**OUBITS** > OUBIT
**OUBLIETTE** n dungeon entered only by a trapdoor

**OUCH** *interj* exclamation of sudden pain ▷ *n* brooch or clasp set with gems ▷ *vb* say ouch
**OUCHED** > OUCH
**OUCHES** > OUCH
**OUCHING** > OUCH
**OUCHT** *Scots word for* > ANYTHING
**OUCHTS** > OUCHT
**OUD** *n* Arabic stringed musical instrument resembling a lute or mandolin
**OUDS** > OUD
**OUGHLIED** > OUGHLY
**OUGHLIES** > OUGHLY
**OUGHLY** *variant of* > UGLY
**OUGHLYING** > OUGHLIE
**OUGHT** *vb* have an obligation ▷ *n* zero
**OUGHTED** > OUGHT
**OUGHTING** > OUGHT
**OUGHTNESS** *n* state of being right
**OUGHTS** > OUGHT
**OUGLIE** *variant of* > UGLY
**OUGLIED** > OUGLIE
**OUGLIEING** > OUGLIE
**OUGLIES** > OUGLIE
**OUGUIYA** *n* standard monetary unit of Mauritania
**OUGUIYAS** > OUGUIYA
**OUIJA** *n* tradename for a board through which spirits supposedly answer questions
**OUIJAS** > OUIJA
**OUISTITI** *n* marmoset
**OUISTITIS** > OUISTITI
**OUK** *Scots word for* > WEEK
**OUKS** > OUK
**OULACHON** *same as* > EULACHON
**OULACHONS** > OULACHON
**OULAKAN** *same as* > EULACHON
**OULAKANS** > OULAKAN
**OULD** *Scots or Irish form of* > OLD
**OULDER** > OULD
**OULDEST** > OULD
**OULK** *Scots form of* > WEEK
**OULKS** > OULK
**OULONG** *same as* > OOLONG
**OULONGS** > OULONG
**OUMA** *n* grandmother, often as a title with a surname
**OUMAS** > OUMA
**OUNCE** *n* unit of weight equal to one sixteenth of a pound
**OUNCES** > OUNCE
**OUNDY** *adj* wavy
**OUP** *same as* > OOP
**OUPA** *n* grandfather, often as a title with a surname
**OUPAS** > OUPA
**OUPED** > OUP
**OUPH** *same as* > OAF
**OUPHE** *same as* > OAF
**OUPHES** > OUPHE
**OUPHS** > OUPH

**OUPING** > OUP
**OUPS** > OUP
**OUR** *adj* belonging to us ▷ *determiner* of, belonging to, or associated in some way with us
**OURALI** *n* plant from which curare comes
**OURALIS** > OURALI
**OURANG** *same as* > ORANG
**OURANGS** > OURANG
**OURARI** *same as* > OURALI
**OURARIS** > OURARI
**OUREBI** *same as* > ORIBI
**OUREBIS** > OUREBI
**OURIE** *same as* > OORIE
**OURIER** > OURIE
**OURIEST** > OURIE
**OURN** *dialect form of* > OUR
**OUROBOROS** *n* mythical serpent
**OUROLOGY** *same as* > UROLOGY
**OUROSCOPY** *same as* > UROSCOPY
**OURS** *pron* thing(s) belonging to us
**OURSELF** *pron* formal word for *myself* used by monarchs
**OURSELVES** *pron* reflexive form of *we* or *us*
**OUSEL** *same as* > OUZEL
**OUSELS** > OUSEL
**OUST** *vb* force (someone) out, expel
**OUSTED** > OUST
**OUSTER** *n* act or instance of forcing someone out of a position
**OUSTERS** > OUSTER
**OUSTING** > OUST
**OUSTITI** *n* device for opening locked door
**OUSTITIS** > OUSTITI
**OUSTS** > OUST
**OUT** *adj* denoting movement or distance away from ▷ *vb* name (a public figure) as being homosexual
**OUTACT** *vb* surpass in acting
**OUTACTED** > OUTACT
**OUTACTING** > OUTACT
**OUTACTS** > OUTACT
**OUTADD** *vb* beat or surpass at adding
**OUTADDED** > OUTADD
**OUTADDING** > OUTADD
**OUTADDS** > OUTADD
**OUTAGE** *n* period of power failure
**OUTAGES** > OUTAGE
**OUTARGUE** *vb* defeat in argument
**OUTARGUED** > OUTARGUE
**OUTARGUES** > OUTARGUE
**OUTASIGHT** *adj* excellent or wonderful
**OUTASK** *vb* declare wedding banns
**OUTASKED** > OUTASK
**OUTASKING** > OUTASK

**OUTASKS** > OUTASK
**OUTATE** > OUTEAT
**OUTBACK** *n* remote bush country of Australia
**OUTBACKER** > OUTBACK
**OUTBACKS** > OUTBACK
**OUTBAKE** *vb* bake more or better than
**OUTBAKED** > OUTBAKE
**OUTBAKES** > OUTBAKE
**OUTBAKING** > OUTBAKE
**OUTBAR** *vb* keep out
**OUTBARK** *vb* bark more or louder than
**OUTBARKED** > OUTBARK
**OUTBARKS** > OUTBARK
**OUTBARRED** > OUTBAR
**OUTBARS** > OUTBAR
**OUTBAWL** *vb* bawl more or louder than
**OUTBAWLED** > OUTBAWL
**OUTBAWLS** > OUTBAWL
**OUTBEAM** *vb* beam more or brighter than
**OUTBEAMED** > OUTBEAM
**OUTBEAMS** > OUTBEAM
**OUTBEG** *vb* beg more or better than
**OUTBEGGED** > OUTBEG
**OUTBEGS** > OUTBEG
**OUTBID** *vb* offer a higher price than
**OUTBIDDEN** > OUTBID
**OUTBIDDER** > OUTBID
**OUTBIDS** > OUTBID
**OUTBITCH** *vb* bitch more or better than
**OUTBLAZE** *vb* blaze more or hotter than
**OUTBLAZED** > OUTBLAZE
**OUTBLAZES** > OUTBLAZE
**OUTBLEAT** *vb* bleat more or louder than
**OUTBLEATS** > OUTBLEAT
**OUTBLESS** *vb* bless more than
**OUTBLOOM** *vb* bloom more or better than
**OUTBLOOMS** > OUTBLOOM
**OUTBLUFF** *vb* surpass in bluffing
**OUTBLUFFS** > OUTBLUFF
**OUTBLUSH** *vb* blush more than
**OUTBOARD** *adj* (of a boat's engine) portable, with its own propeller ▷ *adv* away from the centre line of a vessel or aircraft ▷ *n* outboard motor
**OUTBOARDS** > OUTBOARD
**OUTBOAST** *vb* surpass in boasting
**OUTBOASTS** > OUTBOAST
**OUTBOUGHT** > OUTBUY
**OUTBOUND** *adj* going out
**OUTBOUNDS** *n* boundaries
**OUTBOX** *vb* surpass in boxing
**OUTBOXED** > OUTBOX
**OUTBOXES** > OUTBOX
**OUTBOXING** > OUTBOX
**OUTBRAG** *vb* brag more or better than

**OUTBRAGS** > OUTBRAG
**OUTBRAVE** *vb* surpass in bravery
**OUTBRAVED** > OUTBRAVE
**OUTBRAVES** > OUTBRAVE
**OUTBRAWL** *vb* defeat in a brawl
**OUTBRAWLS** > OUTBRAWL
**OUTBRAZEN** *vb* be more brazen than
**OUTBREAK** *n* sudden occurrence (of something unpleasant) ▷ *vb* break out
**OUTBREAKS** > OUTBREAK
**OUTBRED** > OUTBREED
**OUTBREED** *vb* produce offspring through sexual relations outside a particular family or tribe
**OUTBREEDS** > OUTBREED
**OUTBRIBE** *vb* bribe more than
**OUTBRIBED** > OUTBRIBE
**OUTBRIBES** > OUTBRIBE
**OUTBROKE** > OUTBREAK
**OUTBROKEN** > OUTBREAK
**OUTBUILD** *vb* exceed in building
**OUTBUILDS** > OUTBUILD
**OUTBUILT** > OUTBUILD
**OUTBULGE** *vb* bulge outwards
**OUTBULGED** > OUTBULGE
**OUTBULGES** > OUTBULGE
**OUTBULK** *vb* exceed in bulk
**OUTBULKED** > OUTBULK
**OUTBULKS** > OUTBULK
**OUTBULLY** *vb* exceed in bullying
**OUTBURN** *vb* burn longer or brighter than
**OUTBURNED** > OUTBURN
**OUTBURNS** > OUTBURN
**OUTBURNT** > OUTBURN
**OUTBURST** *n* sudden expression of emotion ▷ *vb* burst out
**OUTBURSTS** > OUTBURST
**OUTBUY** *vb* buy more than
**OUTBUYING** > OUTBUY
**OUTBUYS** > OUTBUY
**OUTBY** *adv* outside
**OUTBYE** *same as* > OUTBY
**OUTCALL** *n* visit to customer's home by professional
**OUTCALLS** > OUTCALL
**OUTCAPER** *vb* exceed in capering
**OUTCAPERS** > OUTCAPER
**OUTCAST** *n* person rejected by a particular group ▷ *adj* rejected, abandoned, or discarded
**OUTCASTE** *n* person who has been expelled from a caste ▷ *vb* cause (someone) to lose his caste
**OUTCASTED** > OUTCASTE
**OUTCASTES** > OUTCASTE
**OUTCASTS** > OUTCAST
**OUTCATCH** *vb* catch more than

OUTCAUGHT > OUTCATCH

OUTCAVIL vb exceed in cavilling

OUTCAVILS > OUTCAVIL

OUTCHARGE vb charge more than

OUTCHARM vb exceed in charming

OUTCHARMS > OUTCHARM

OUTCHEAT vb exceed in cheating

OUTCHEATS > OUTCHEAT

OUTCHID > OUTCHIDE

OUTCHIDE vb exceed in chiding

OUTCHIDED > OUTCHIDE

OUTCHIDES > OUTCHIDE

OUTCITIES > OUTCITY

OUTCITY n anywhere outside a city's confines

OUTCLASS vb surpass in quality

OUTCLIMB vb exceed in climbing

OUTCLIMBS > OUTCLIMB

OUTCLOMB > OUTCLIMB

OUTCOACH vb exceed in coaching

OUTCOME n result

OUTCOMES > OUTCOME

OUTCOOK vb cook more or better than

OUTCOOKED > OUTCOOK

OUTCOOKS > OUTCOOK

OUTCOUNT vb exceed in counting

OUTCOUNTS > OUTCOUNT

OUTCRAFTY vb be craftier than

OUTCRAWL vb crawl further or faster than

OUTCRAWLS > OUTCRAWL

OUTCRIED > OUTCRY

OUTCRIES > OUTCRY

OUTCROP n part of a rock formation that sticks out of the earth ▷ vb (of rock strata) to protrude through the surface of the earth

OUTCROPS > OUTCROP

OUTCROSS vb breed (animals or plants of the same breed but different strains) ▷ n animal or plant produced as a result of outcrossing

OUTCROW vb exceed in crowing

OUTCROWD vb have more crowd than

OUTCROWDS > OUTCROWD

OUTCROWED > OUTCROW

OUTCROWS > OUTCROW

OUTCRY n vehement or widespread protest ▷ vb cry louder or make more noise than (someone or something)

OUTCRYING > OUTCRY

OUTCURSE vb exceed in cursing

OUTCURSED > OUTCURSE

OUTCURSES > OUTCURSE

OUTCURVE n baseball thrown to curve away from batter

OUTCURVES > OUTCURVE

OUTDANCE vb surpass in dancing

OUTDANCED > OUTDANCE

OUTDANCES > OUTDANCE

OUTDARE vb be more brave than

OUTDARED > OUTDARE

OUTDARES > OUTDARE

OUTDARING > OUTDARE

OUTDATE vb make or become old-fashioned or obsolete

OUTDATED adj old-fashioned

OUTDATES > OUTDATE

OUTDATING > OUTDATE

OUTDAZZLE vb exceed in dazzling

OUTDEBATE vb exceed in debate

OUTDESIGN vb exceed in designing

OUTDID > OUTDO

OUTDO vb surpass in performance

OUTDODGE vb surpass in dodging

OUTDODGED > OUTDODGE

OUTDODGES > OUTDODGE

OUTDOER > OUTDO

OUTDOERS > OUTDO

OUTDOES > OUTDO

OUTDOING > OUTDO

OUTDONE > OUTDO

OUTDOOR adj taking place, existing, or intended for use in the open air

OUTDOORS adv in(to) the open air ▷ n open air

OUTDOORSY adj taking part in activities relating to the outdoors

OUTDRAG vb beat in drag race

OUTDRAGS > OUTDRAG

OUTDRANK > OUTDRINK

OUTDRAW vb draw (a gun) faster than

OUTDRAWN > OUTDRAW

OUTDRAWS > OUTDRAW

OUTDREAM vb exceed in dreaming

OUTDREAMS > OUTDREAM

OUTDREAMT > OUTDREAM

OUTDRESS vb dress better than

OUTDREW > OUTDRAW

OUTDRINK vb drink more than

OUTDRINKS > OUTDRINK

OUTDRIVE vb exceed in driving

OUTDRIVEN > OUTDRIVE

OUTDRIVES > OUTDRIVE

OUTDROP same as > OUTCROP

OUTDROPS > OUTDROP

OUTDROVE > OUTDRIVE

OUTDRUNK > OUTDRINK

OUTDUEL vb defeat in duel

OUTDUELED > OUTDUEL

OUTDUELS > OUTDUEL

OUTDURE vb last longer than

OUTDURED > OUTDURE

OUTDURES > OUTDURE

OUTDURING > OUTDURE

OUTDWELL vb live outside something

OUTDWELLS > OUTDWELL

OUTDWELT > OUTDWELL

OUTEARN vb earn more than

OUTEARNED > OUTEARN

OUTEARNS > OUTEARN

OUTEAT vb eat more than

OUTEATEN > OUTEAT

OUTEATING > OUTEAT

OUTEATS > OUTEAT

OUTECHO vb echo more than

OUTECHOED > OUTECHO

OUTECHOES > OUTECHO

OUTED > OUT

OUTEDGE n furthest limit

OUTEDGES > OUTEDGE

OUTER adj on the outside ▷ n white outermost ring on a target

OUTERCOAT same as > OVERCOAT

OUTERMOST adj furthest out

OUTERS > OUTER

OUTERWEAR n clothes worn on top of other clothes

OUTFABLE vb exceed in creating fables

OUTFABLED > OUTFABLE

OUTFABLES > OUTFABLE

OUTFACE vb subdue or disconcert (someone) by staring

OUTFACED > OUTFACE

OUTFACES > OUTFACE

OUTFACING > OUTFACE

OUTFALL n mouth of a river or drain

OUTFALLS > OUTFALL

OUTFAST vb fast longer than

OUTFASTED > OUTFAST

OUTFASTS > OUTFAST

OUTFAWN vb exceed in fawning

OUTFAWNED > OUTFAWN

OUTFAWNS > OUTFAWN

OUTFEAST vb exceed in feasting

OUTFEASTS > OUTFEAST

OUTFEEL vb exceed in feeling

OUTFEELS > OUTFEEL

OUTFELT > OUTFEEL

OUTFENCE vb surpass at fencing

OUTFENCED > OUTFENCE

OUTFENCES > OUTFENCE

OUTFIELD n area far from the pitch

OUTFIELDS > OUTFIELD

OUTFIGHT vb surpass in fighting

OUTFIGHTS > OUTFIGHT

OUTFIGURE same

as > OUTTHINK

OUTFIND vb exceed in finding

OUTFINDS > OUTFIND

OUTFIRE vb exceed in firing

OUTFIRED > OUTFIRE

OUTFIRES > OUTFIRE

OUTFIRING > OUTFIRE

OUTFISH vb catch more fish than

OUTFISHED > OUTFISH

OUTFISHES > OUTFISH

OUTFIT n matching set of clothes ▷ vb furnish or be furnished with an outfit, equipment, etc

OUTFITS > OUTFIT

OUTFITTED > OUTFIT

OUTFITTER n supplier of men's clothes

OUTFLANK vb get round the side of (an enemy army)

OUTFLANKS > OUTFLANK

OUTFLASH vb be flashier than

OUTFLEW > OUTFLY

OUTFLIES > OUTFLY

OUTFLING n cutting remark

OUTFLINGS > OUTFLING

OUTFLOAT vb surpass at floating

OUTFLOATS > OUTFLOAT

OUTFLOW n anything that flows out, such as liquid or money ▷ vb flow faster than

OUTFLOWED > OUTFLOW

OUTFLOWN > OUTFLY

OUTFLOWS > OUTFLOW

OUTFLUSH n burst of light

OUTFLY vb fly better or faster than

OUTFLYING > OUTFLY

OUTFOOL vb be more foolish than

OUTFOOLED > OUTFOOL

OUTFOOLS > OUTFOOL

OUTFOOT vb (of a boat) to go faster than (another boat)

OUTFOOTED > OUTFOOT

OUTFOOTS > OUTFOOT

OUTFOUGHT > OUTFIGHT

OUTFOUND > OUTFIND

OUTFOX vb defeat or foil (someone) by being more cunning

OUTFOXED > OUTFOX

OUTFOXES > OUTFOX

OUTFOXING > OUTFOX

OUTFROWN vb dominate by frowning more than

OUTFROWNS > OUTFROWN

OUTFUMBLE vb exceed in fumbling

OUTGAIN vb gain more than

OUTGAINED > OUTGAIN

OUTGAINS > OUTGAIN

OUTGALLOP vb gallop faster than

OUTGAMBLE vb defeat at gambling

OUTGAS vb undergo the

removal of adsorbed or absorbed gas from solids
**OUTGASES** > OUTGAS
**OUTGASSED** > OUTGAS
**OUTGASSES** > OUTGAS
**OUTGATE** n way out
**OUTGATES** > OUTGATE
**OUTGAVE** > OUTGIVE
**OUTGAZE** vb gaze beyond
**OUTGAZED** > OUTGAZE
**OUTGAZES** > OUTGAZE
**OUTGAZING** > OUTGAZE
**OUTGIVE** vb exceed in giving
**OUTGIVEN** > OUTGIVE
**OUTGIVES** > OUTGIVE
**OUTGIVING** > OUTGIVE
**OUTGLARE** vb exceed in glaring
**OUTGLARED** > OUTGLARE
**OUTGLARES** > OUTGLARE
**OUTGLEAM** vb gleam more than
**OUTGLEAMS** > OUTGLEAM
**OUTGLOW** vb glow more than
**OUTGLOWED** > OUTGLOW
**OUTGLOWS** > OUTGLOW
**OUTGNAW** vb exceed in gnawing
**OUTGNAWED** > OUTGNAW
**OUTGNAWN** > OUTGNAW
**OUTGNAWS** > OUTGNAW
**OUTGO** vb exceed or outstrip ▷ n cost
**OUTGOER** > OUTGO
**OUTGOERS** > OUTGO
**OUTGOES** > OUTGO
**OUTGOING** adj leaving ▷ n act of going out
**OUTGOINGS** pl n expenses
**OUTGONE** > OUTGO
**OUTGREW** > OUTGROW
**OUTGRIN** vb exceed in grinning
**OUTGRINS** > OUTGRIN
**OUTGROSS** vb earn more than
**OUTGROUP** n group of people outside one's own group of people
**OUTGROUPS** > OUTGROUP
**OUTGROW** vb become too large or too old for
**OUTGROWN** > OUTGROW
**OUTGROWS** > OUTGROW
**OUTGROWTH** n natural development
**OUTGUARD** n guard furthest away from main party
**OUTGUARDS** > OUTGUARD
**OUTGUESS** vb surpass in guessing
**OUTGUIDE** n folder in filing system ▷ vb beat or surpass at guiding
**OUTGUIDED** > OUTGUIDE
**OUTGUIDES** > OUTGUIDE
**OUTGUN** vb surpass in fire power
**OUTGUNNED** > OUTGUN
**OUTGUNS** > OUTGUN
**OUTGUSH** vb gush out
**OUTGUSHED** > OUTGUSH

**OUTGUSHES** > OUTGUSH
**OUTHANDLE** vb handle better than
**OUTHAUL** n line or cable for tightening the foot of a sail
**OUTHAULER** same as > OUTHAUL
**OUTHAULS** > OUTHAUL
**OUTHEAR** vb exceed in hearing
**OUTHEARD** > OUTHEAR
**OUTHEARS** > OUTHEAR
**OUTHER** same as > OTHER
**OUTHIRE** vb hire out
**OUTHIRED** > OUTHIRE
**OUTHIRES** > OUTHIRE
**OUTHIRING** > OUTHIRE
**OUTHIT** vb hit something further than (someone else)
**OUTHITS** > OUTHIT
**OUTHOMER** vb score more home runs than
**OUTHOMERS** > OUTHOMER
**OUTHOUSE** n building near a main building
**OUTHOUSES** > OUTHOUSE
**OUTHOWL** vb exceed in howling
**OUTHOWLED** > OUTHOWL
**OUTHOWLS** > OUTHOWL
**OUTHUMOR** vb exceed in humouring
**OUTHUMORS** > OUTHUMOR
**OUTHUNT** vb exceed in hunting
**OUTHUNTED** > OUTHUNT
**OUTHUNTS** > OUTHUNT
**OUTHUSTLE** vb be more competitive than
**OUTHYRE** same as > OUTHIRE
**OUTHYRED** > OUTHYRE
**OUTHYRES** > OUTHYRE
**OUTHYRING** > OUTHYRE
**OUTING** n leisure trip
**OUTINGS** > OUTING
**OUTJEST** vb exceed in jesting
**OUTJESTED** > OUTJEST
**OUTJESTS** > OUTJEST
**OUTJET** n projecting part
**OUTJETS** > OUTJET
**OUTJINX** vb exceed in jinxing
**OUTJINXED** > OUTJINX
**OUTJINXES** > OUTJINX
**OUTJOCKEY** vb outwit by deception
**OUTJUGGLE** vb surpass at juggling
**OUTJUMP** vb jump higher or farther than
**OUTJUMPED** > OUTJUMP
**OUTJUMPS** > OUTJUMP
**OUTJUT** vb jut out ▷ n projecting part
**OUTJUTS** > OUTJUT
**OUTJUTTED** > OUTJUT
**OUTKEEP** vb beat or surpass at keeping
**OUTKEEPS** > OUTKEEP
**OUTKEPT** > OUTKEEP
**OUTKICK** vb exceed in

kicking
**OUTKICKED** > OUTKICK
**OUTKICKS** > OUTKICK
**OUTKILL** vb exceed in killing
**OUTKILLED** > OUTKILL
**OUTKILLS** > OUTKILL
**OUTKISS** vb exceed in kissing
**OUTKISSED** > OUTKISS
**OUTKISSES** > OUTKISS
**OUTLAID** > OUTLAY
**OUTLAIN** > OUTLAY
**OUTLAND** adj outlying or distant ▷ n outlying areas of a country or region
**OUTLANDER** n foreigner or stranger
**OUTLANDS** > OUTLAND
**OUTLASH** n sudden attack
**OUTLASHES** > OUTLASH
**OUTLAST** vb last longer than
**OUTLASTED** > OUTLAST
**OUTLASTS** > OUTLAST
**OUTLAUGH** vb laugh longer or louder than
**OUTLAUGHS** > OUTLAUGH
**OUTLAUNCE** same as > OUTLAUNCH
**OUTLAUNCH** vb send out
**OUTLAW** n criminal deprived of legal protection, bandit ▷ vb make illegal
**OUTLAWED** > OUTLAW
**OUTLAWING** > OUTLAW
**OUTLAWRY** n act of outlawing or the state of being outlawed
**OUTLAWS** > OUTLAW
**OUTLAY** n expenditure ▷ vb spend (money)
**OUTLAYING** > OUTLAY
**OUTLAYS** > OUTLAY
**OUTLEAD** vb be better leader than
**OUTLEADS** > OUTLEAD
**OUTLEAP** vb leap higher or farther than
**OUTLEAPED** > OUTLEAP
**OUTLEAPS** > OUTLEAP
**OUTLEAPT** > OUTLEAP
**OUTLEARN** vb exceed in learning
**OUTLEARNS** > OUTLEARN
**OUTLEARNT** > OUTLEARN
**OUTLED** > OUTLEAD
**OUTLER** n farm animal kept out of doors
**OUTLERS** > OUTLER
**OUTLET** n means of expressing emotion
**OUTLETS** > OUTLET
**OUTLIE** vb lie outside a particular place
**OUTLIED** > OUTLIE
**OUTLIER** n outcrop of rocks that is entirely surrounded by older rocks
**OUTLIERS** > OUTLIER
**OUTLIES** > OUTLIE
**OUTLINE** n short general explanation ▷ vb summarize

**OUTLINEAR** > OUTLINE
**OUTLINED** > OUTLINE
**OUTLINER** > OUTLINE
**OUTLINERS** > OUTLINE
**OUTLINES** > OUTLINE
**OUTLINING** > OUTLINE
**OUTLIVE** vb live longer than
**OUTLIVED** > OUTLIVE
**OUTLIVER** > OUTLIVE
**OUTLIVERS** > OUTLIVE
**OUTLIVES** > OUTLIVE
**OUTLIVING** > OUTLIVE
**OUTLOOK** n attitude ▷ vb look out
**OUTLOOKED** > OUTLOOK
**OUTLOOKS** > OUTLOOK
**OUTLOVE** vb exceed in loving
**OUTLOVED** > OUTLOVE
**OUTLOVES** > OUTLOVE
**OUTLOVING** > OUTLOVE
**OUTLUSTRE** vb outshine
**OUTLYING** adj distant from the main area
**OUTMAN** vb surpass in manpower
**OUTMANNED** > OUTMAN
**OUTMANS** > OUTMAN
**OUTMANTLE** vb be better dressed than
**OUTMARCH** vb exceed in marching
**OUTMASTER** vb surpass
**OUTMATCH** vb surpass or outdo (someone)
**OUTMODE** vb make unfashionable
**OUTMODED** adj no longer fashionable or accepted
**OUTMODES** > OUTMODE
**OUTMODING** > OUTMODE
**OUTMOST** another word for > OUTERMOST
**OUTMOVE** vb move faster or better than
**OUTMOVED** > OUTMOVE
**OUTMOVES** > OUTMOVE
**OUTMOVING** > OUTMOVE
**OUTMUSCLE** vb dominate by physical strength
**OUTNAME** vb be more notorious than
**OUTNAMED** > OUTNAME
**OUTNAMES** > OUTNAME
**OUTNAMING** > OUTNAME
**OUTNESS** n state or quality of being external
**OUTNESSES** > OUTNESS
**OUTNIGHT** vb refer to night more often than
**OUTNIGHTS** > OUTNIGHT
**OUTNUMBER** vb exceed in number
**OUTOFFICE** n outbuilding
**OUTPACE** vb go faster than (someone)
**OUTPACED** > OUTPACE
**OUTPACES** > OUTPACE
**OUTPACING** > OUTPACE
**OUTPAINT** vb exceed in painting
**OUTPAINTS** > OUTPAINT
**OUTPART** n remote region

**OUTPARTS** > OUTPART
**OUTPASS** vb exceed in passing
**OUTPASSED** > OUTPASS
**OUTPASSES** > OUTPASS
**OUTPEEP** vb peep out
**OUTPEEPED** > OUTPEEP
**OUTPEEPS** > OUTPEEP
**OUTPEER** vb surpass
**OUTPEERED** > OUTPEER
**OUTPEERS** > OUTPEER
**OUTPEOPLE** vb rid a country of its people
**OUTPITCH** vb exceed in pitching
**OUTPITIED** > OUTPITY
**OUTPITIES** > OUTPITY
**OUTPITY** vb exceed in pitying
**OUTPLACE** vb find job for ex-employee
**OUTPLACED** > OUTPLACE
**OUTPLACER** > OUTPLACE
**OUTPLACES** > OUTPLACE
**OUTPLAN** vb exceed in planning
**OUTPLANS** > OUTPLAN
**OUTPLAY** vb perform better than one's opponent in a sport or game
**OUTPLAYED** > OUTPLAY
**OUTPLAYS** > OUTPLAY
**OUTPLOD** vb exceed in plotting
**OUTPLODS** > OUTPLOD
**OUTPLOT** vb exceed in plotting
**OUTPLOTS** > OUTPLOT
**OUTPOINT** vb score more points than
**OUTPOINTS** > OUTPOINT
**OUTPOLL** vb win more votes than
**OUTPOLLED** > OUTPOLL
**OUTPOLLS** > OUTPOLL
**OUTPORT** n isolated fishing village, esp in Newfoundland
**OUTPORTER** n inhabitant or native of a Newfoundland outport
**OUTPORTS** > OUTPORT
**OUTPOST** n outlying settlement
**OUTPOSTS** > OUTPOST
**OUTPOUR** n act of flowing or pouring out ▷ vb pour or cause to pour out freely or rapidly
**OUTPOURED** > OUTPOUR
**OUTPOURER** > OUTPOUR
**OUTPOURS** > OUTPOUR
**OUTPOWER** vb have more power than
**OUTPOWERS** > OUTPOWER
**OUTPRAY** vb exceed in praying
**OUTPRAYED** > OUTPRAY
**OUTPRAYS** > OUTPRAY
**OUTPREACH** vb outdo in preaching
**OUTPREEN** vb exceed in preening
**OUTPREENS** > OUTPREEN

**OUTPRESS** vb exceed in pressing
**OUTPRICE** vb sell at better price than
**OUTPRICED** > OUTPRICE
**OUTPRICES** > OUTPRICE
**OUTPRIZE** vb prize more highly than
**OUTPRIZED** > OUTPRIZE
**OUTPRIZES** > OUTPRIZE
**OUTPULL** vb exceed in pulling
**OUTPULLED** > OUTPULL
**OUTPULLS** > OUTPULL
**OUTPUNCH** vb punch better than
**OUTPUPIL** n student sent to a different school to the one he or she would normally attend
**OUTPUPILS** > OUTPUPIL
**OUTPURSUE** vb pursue farther than
**OUTPUSH** vb exceed in pushing
**OUTPUSHED** > OUTPUSH
**OUTPUSHES** > OUTPUSH
**OUTPUT** n amount produced ▷ vb produce (data) at the end of a process
**OUTPUTS** > OUTPUT
**OUTPUTTED** > OUTPUT
**OUTQUOTE** vb exceed in quoting
**OUTQUOTED** > OUTQUOTE
**OUTQUOTES** > OUTQUOTE
**OUTRACE** vb surpass in racing
**OUTRACED** > OUTRACE
**OUTRACES** > OUTRACE
**OUTRACING** > OUTRACE
**OUTRAGE** n great moral indignation ▷ vb offend morally
**OUTRAGED** > OUTRAGE
**OUTRAGES** > OUTRAGE
**OUTRAGING** > OUTRAGE
**OUTRAISE** vb raise more money than
**OUTRAISED** > OUTRAISE
**OUTRAISES** > OUTRAISE
**OUTRAN** > OUTRUN
**OUTRANCE** n furthest extreme
**OUTRANCES** > OUTRANCE
**OUTRANG** > OUTRING
**OUTRANGE** vb have a greater range than
**OUTRANGED** > OUTRANGE
**OUTRANGES** > OUTRANGE
**OUTRANK** vb be of higher rank than (someone)
**OUTRANKED** > OUTRANK
**OUTRANKS** > OUTRANK
**OUTRATE** vb offer better rate than
**OUTRATED** > OUTRATE
**OUTRATES** > OUTRATE
**OUTRATING** > OUTRATE
**OUTRAVE** vb outdo in raving
**OUTRAVED** > OUTRAVE
**OUTRAVES** > OUTRAVE
**OUTRAVING** > OUTRAVE

**OUTRE** adj shockingly eccentric
**OUTREACH** vb surpass in reach ▷ n act or process of reaching out
**OUTREAD** vb outdo in reading
**OUTREADS** > OUTREAD
**OUTREASON** vb surpass in reasoning
**OUTRECKON** vb surpass in reckoning
**OUTRED** vb be redder than
**OUTREDDED** > OUTRED
**OUTREDDEN** same as > OUTRED
**OUTREDS** > OUTRED
**OUTREIGN** vb reign for longer than
**OUTREIGNS** > OUTREIGN
**OUTRELIEF** n aid given outdoors
**OUTREMER** n land overseas
**OUTREMERS** > OUTREMER
**OUTRIDDEN** > OUTRIDE
**OUTRIDE** vb outdo by riding faster, farther, or better than ▷ n extra unstressed syllable within a metrical foot
**OUTRIDER** n motorcyclist acting as an escort
**OUTRIDERS** > OUTRIDER
**OUTRIDES** > OUTRIDE
**OUTRIDING** > OUTRIDE
**OUTRIG** vb supply with outfit
**OUTRIGGED** > OUTRIG
**OUTRIGGER** n stabilizing frame projecting from a boat
**OUTRIGHT** adv absolute(ly) ▷ adj complete
**OUTRIGS** > OUTRIG
**OUTRING** vb exceed in ringing
**OUTRINGS** > OUTRING
**OUTRIVAL** vb surpass
**OUTRIVALS** > OUTRIVAL
**OUTRO** n instrumental passage that concludes a piece of music
**OUTROAR** vb roar louder than
**OUTROARED** > OUTROAR
**OUTROARS** > OUTROAR
**OUTROCK** vb outdo in rocking
**OUTROCKED** > OUTROCK
**OUTROCKS** > OUTROCK
**OUTRODE** > OUTRIDE
**OUTROLL** vb exceed in rolling
**OUTROLLED** > OUTROLL
**OUTROLLS** > OUTROLL
**OUTROOP** n auction
**OUTROOPER** > OUTROOP
**OUTROOPS** > OUTROOP
**OUTROOT** vb root out
**OUTROOTED** > OUTROOT
**OUTROOTS** > OUTROOT
**OUTROPE** same as > OUTROOP
**OUTROPER** > OUTROPE

**OUTROPES** > OUTROPE
**OUTROPES** > OUTROPE
**OUTROS** > OUTRO
**OUTROW** vb outdo in rowing
**OUTROWED** > OUTROW
**OUTROWING** > OUTROW
**OUTROWS** > OUTROW
**OUTRUN** vb run faster than
**OUTRUNG** > OUTRING
**OUTRUNNER** n attendant who runs in front of a carriage, etc
**OUTRUNS** > OUTRUN
**OUTRUSH** n flowing or rushing out ▷ vb rush out
**OUTRUSHED** > OUTRUSH
**OUTRUSHES** > OUTRUSH
**OUTS** > OUT
**OUTSAID** > OUTSAY
**OUTSAIL** vb sail better than
**OUTSAILED** > OUTSAIL
**OUTSAILS** > OUTSAIL
**OUTSANG** > OUTSING
**OUTSAT** > OUTSIT
**OUTSAVOR** vb exceed in savouring
**OUTSAVORS** > OUTSAVOR
**OUTSAW** > OUTSEE
**OUTSAY** vb say something out loud
**OUTSAYING** > OUTSAY
**OUTSAYS** > OUTSAY
**OUTSCHEME** vb outdo in scheming
**OUTSCOLD** vb outdo in scolding
**OUTSCOLDS** > OUTSCOLD
**OUTSCOOP** vb outdo in achieving scoops
**OUTSCOOPS** > OUTSCOOP
**OUTSCORE** vb score more than
**OUTSCORED** > OUTSCORE
**OUTSCORES** > OUTSCORE
**OUTSCORN** vb defy with scorn
**OUTSCORNS** > OUTSCORN
**OUTSCREAM** vb scream louder than
**OUTSEE** vb exceed in seeing
**OUTSEEING** > OUTSEE
**OUTSEEN** > OUTSEE
**OUTSEES** > OUTSEE
**OUTSELL** vb be sold in greater quantities than
**OUTSELLS** > OUTSELL
**OUTSERT** another word for > WRAPROUND
**OUTSERTS** > OUTSERT
**OUTSERVE** vb serve better at tennis than
**OUTSERVED** > OUTSERVE
**OUTSERVES** > OUTSERVE
**OUTSET** n beginning
**OUTSETS** > OUTSET
**OUTSHAME** vb greatly shame
**OUTSHAMED** > OUTSHAME
**OUTSHAMES** > OUTSHAME
**OUTSHINE** vb surpass (someone) in excellence
**OUTSHINED** > OUTSHINE
**OUTSHINES** > OUTSHINE
**OUTSHONE** > OUTSHINE

**OUTSHOOT** *vb* surpass or excel in shooting ▷ *n* thing that projects or shoots out
**OUTSHOOTS** > OUTSHOOT
**OUTSHOT** > OUTSHOOT *n* projecting part
**OUTSHOTS** > OUTSHOT
**OUTSHOUT** *vb* shout louder than
**OUTSHOUTS** > OUTSHOUT
**OUTSIDE** *adv* indicating movement to or position on the exterior ▷ *adj* unlikely ▷ *n* external area or surface
**OUTSIDER** *n* person outside a specific group
**OUTSIDERS** > OUTSIDER
**OUTSIDES** > OUTSIDE
**OUTSIGHT** *n* power of seeing
**OUTSIGHTS** > OUTSIGHT
**OUTSIN** *vb* sin more than
**OUTSING** *vb* sing better or louder than
**OUTSINGS** > OUTSING
**OUTSINNED** > OUTSIN
**OUTSINS** > OUTSIN
**OUTSIT** *vb* sit longer than
**OUTSITS** > OUTSIT
**OUTSIZE** *adj* larger than normal ▷ *n* outsize garment
**OUTSIZED** *same as* > OUTSIZE
**OUTSIZES** > OUTSIZE
**OUTSKATE** *vb* skate better than
**OUTSKATED** > OUTSKATE
**OUTSKATES** > OUTSKATE
**OUTSKIRT** *singular of* > OUTSKIRTS
**OUTSKIRTS** *pl n* outer areas, esp of a town
**OUTSLEEP** *vb* sleep longer than
**OUTSLEEPS** > OUTSLEEP
**OUTSLEPT** > OUTSLEEP
**OUTSLICK** *vb* outsmart
**OUTSLICKS** > OUTSLICK
**OUTSMART** *vb* outwit
**OUTSMARTS** > OUTSMART
**OUTSMELL** *vb* surpass in smelling
**OUTSMELLS** > OUTSMELL
**OUTSMELT** > OUTSMELL
**OUTSMILE** *vb* outdo in smiling
**OUTSMILED** > OUTSMILE
**OUTSMILES** > OUTSMILE
**OUTSMOKE** *vb* smoke more than
**OUTSMOKED** > OUTSMOKE
**OUTSMOKES** > OUTSMOKE
**OUTSNORE** *vb* outdo in snoring
**OUTSNORED** > OUTSNORE
**OUTSNORES** > OUTSNORE
**OUTSOAR** *vb* fly higher than
**OUTSOARED** > OUTSOAR
**OUTSOARS** > OUTSOAR
**OUTSOLD** > OUTSELL
**OUTSOLE** *n* outermost sole

of a shoe
**OUTSOLES** > OUTSOLE
**OUTSOURCE** *vb* subcontract (work) to another company
**OUTSPAN** *vb* relax
**OUTSPANS** > OUTSPAN
**OUTSPEAK** *vb* speak better or louder than
**OUTSPEAKS** > OUTSPEAK
**OUTSPED** > OUTSPEED
**OUTSPEED** *vb* go faster than
**OUTSPEEDS** > OUTSPEED
**OUTSPELL** *vb* exceed at spelling
**OUTSPELLS** > OUTSPELL
**OUTSPELT** > OUTSPELL
**OUTSPEND** *vb* spend more than
**OUTSPENDS** > OUTSPEND
**OUTSPENT** > OUTSPEND
**OUTSPOKE** > OUTSPEAK
**OUTSPOKEN** *adj* tending to say what one thinks
**OUTSPORT** *vb* sport in excess of
**OUTSPORTS** > OUTSPORT
**OUTSPRANG** > OUTSPRING
**OUTSPREAD** *adj* spread or stretched out as far as possible ▷ *vb* spread out or cause to spread out ▷ *n* spreading out
**OUTSPRING** *vb* spring out
**OUTSPRINT** *vb* run faster than (someone)
**OUTSPRUNG** > OUTSPRING
**OUTSTAND** *vb* be outstanding or excel
**OUTSTANDS** > OUTSTAND
**OUTSTARE** *vb* stare longer than
**OUTSTARED** > OUTSTARE
**OUTSTARES** > OUTSTARE
**OUTSTART** *vb* jump out ▷ *n* outset
**OUTSTARTS** > OUTSTART
**OUTSTATE** *vb* surpass in stating
**OUTSTATED** > OUTSTATE
**OUTSTATES** > OUTSTATE
**OUTSTAY** *vb* overstay
**OUTSTAYED** > OUTSTAY
**OUTSTAYS** > OUTSTAY
**OUTSTEER** *vb* steer better than
**OUTSTEERS** > OUTSTEER
**OUTSTEP** *vb* step farther than
**OUTSTEPS** > OUTSTEP
**OUTSTOOD** > OUTSTAND
**OUTSTRAIN** *vb* strain too much
**OUTSTRIDE** *vb* surpass in striding
**OUTSTRIKE** *vb* exceed in striking
**OUTSTRIP** *vb* surpass
**OUTSTRIPS** > OUTSTRIP
**OUTSTRIVE** *vb* strive harder than
**OUTSTRODE** > OUTSTRIDE
**OUTSTROKE** *n* outward stroke

**OUTSTROVE** > OUTSTRIVE
**OUTSTRUCK** > OUTSTRIKE
**OUTSTUDY** *vb* outdo in studying
**OUTSTUNT** *vb* outdo in performing stunts
**OUTSTUNTS** > OUTSTUNT
**OUTSULK** *vb* outdo in sulking
**OUTSULKED** > OUTSULK
**OUTSULKS** > OUTSULK
**OUTSUM** *vb* add up to more than
**OUTSUMMED** > OUTSUM
**OUTSUMS** > OUTSUM
**OUTSUNG** > OUTSING
**OUTSWAM** > OUTSWIM
**OUTSWARE** > OUTSWEAR
**OUTSWEAR** *vb* swear more than
**OUTSWEARS** > OUTSWEAR
**OUTSWEEP** *n* outward movement of arms in swimming breaststroke
**OUTSWEEPS** > OUTSWEEP
**OUTSWELL** *vb* exceed in swelling
**OUTSWELLS** > OUTSWELL
**OUTSWEPT** *adj* curving outwards
**OUTSWIM** *vb* outdo in swimming
**OUTSWIMS** > OUTSWIM
**OUTSWING** *n* (in cricket) movement of a ball from leg to off through the air
**OUTSWINGS** > OUTSWING
**OUTSWORE** > OUTSWEAR
**OUTSWORN** > OUTSWEAR
**OUTSWUM** > OUTSWIM
**OUTSWUNG** *adj* made to curve outwards
**OUTTAKE** *n* unreleased take from a recording session, film, or TV programme ▷ *vb* take out
**OUTTAKEN** > OUTTAKE
**OUTTAKES** > OUTTAKE
**OUTTAKING** > OUTTAKE
**OUTTALK** *vb* talk more, longer, or louder than (someone)
**OUTTALKED** > OUTTALK
**OUTTALKS** > OUTTALK
**OUTTASK** *vb* assign task to staff outside organization
**OUTTASKED** > OUTTASK
**OUTTASKS** > OUTTASK
**OUTTELL** *vb* make known
**OUTTELLS** > OUTTELL
**OUTTHANK** *vb* outdo in thanking
**OUTTHANKS** > OUTTHANK
**OUTTHIEVE** *vb* surpass in stealing
**OUTTHINK** *vb* outdo in thinking
**OUTTHINKS** > OUTTHINK
**OUTTHREW** > OUTTHROW
**OUTTHROB** *vb* outdo in throbbing
**OUTTHROBS** > OUTTHROB
**OUTTHROW** *vb* throw better than

**OUTTHROWN** > OUTTHROW
**OUTTHROWS** > OUTTHROW
**OUTTHRUST** *vb* extend outwards
**OUTTOLD** > OUTTELL
**OUTTONGUE** *vb* speak louder than
**OUTTOOK** > OUTTAKE
**OUTTOP** *vb* rise higher than
**OUTTOPPED** > OUTTOP
**OUTTOPS** > OUTTOP
**OUTTOWER** *vb* tower over
**OUTTOWERS** > OUTTOWER
**OUTTRADE** *vb* surpass in trading
**OUTTRADED** > OUTTRADE
**OUTTRADES** > OUTTRADE
**OUTTRAVEL** *vb* outdo in travelling
**OUTTRICK** *vb* outdo in trickery
**OUTTRICKS** > OUTTRICK
**OUTTROT** *vb* exceed at trotting
**OUTTROTS** > OUTTROT
**OUTTRUMP** *vb* count for more than
**OUTTRUMPS** > OUTTRUMP
**OUTTURN** *same as* > OUTPUT
**OUTTURNS** > OUTTURN
**OUTVALUE** *vb* surpass in value
**OUTVALUED** > OUTVALUE
**OUTVALUES** > OUTVALUE
**OUTVAUNT** *vb* outdo in boasting
**OUTVAUNTS** > OUTVAUNT
**OUTVENOM** *vb* surpass in venomousness
**OUTVENOMS** > OUTVENOM
**OUTVIE** *vb* outdo in competition
**OUTVIED** > OUTVIE
**OUTVIES** > OUTVIE
**OUTVOICE** *vb* surpass in noise
**OUTVOICED** > OUTVOICE
**OUTVOICES** > OUTVOICE
**OUTVOTE** *vb* defeat by getting more votes than
**OUTVOTED** > OUTVOTE
**OUTVOTER** > OUTVOTE
**OUTVOTERS** > OUTVOTE
**OUTVOTES** > OUTVOTE
**OUTVOTING** > OUTVOTE
**OUTVYING** > OUTVIE
**OUTWAIT** *vb* wait longer than
**OUTWAITED** > OUTWAIT
**OUTWAITS** > OUTWAIT
**OUTWALK** *vb* walk farther or longer than
**OUTWALKED** > OUTWALK
**OUTWALKS** > OUTWALK
**OUTWAR** *vb* surpass or exceed in warfare
**OUTWARD** *same as* > OUTWARDS
**OUTWARDLY** *adv* in outward appearance
**OUTWARDS** *adv* towards the outside
**OUTWARRED** > OUTWAR
**OUTWARS** > OUTWAR

OUTWASH n mass of gravel carried and deposited by the water derived from melting glaciers
OUTWASHES > OUTWASH
OUTWASTE vb outdo in wasting
OUTWASTED > OUTWASTE
OUTWASTES > OUTWASTE
OUTWATCH vb surpass in watching
OUTWEAR vb use up or destroy by wearing
OUTWEARS > OUTWEAR
OUTWEARY vb exhaust
OUTWEED vb root out
OUTWEEDED > OUTWEED
OUTWEEDS > OUTWEED
OUTWEEP vb outdo in weeping
OUTWEEPS > OUTWEEP
OUTWEIGH vb be more important, significant, or influential than
OUTWEIGHS > OUTWEIGH
OUTWELL vb pour out
OUTWELLED > OUTWELL
OUTWELLS > OUTWELL
OUTWENT > OUTGO
OUTWEPT > OUTWEEP
OUTWHIRL vb surpass at whirling
OUTWHIRLS > OUTWHIRL
OUTWICK vb move one curling stone by striking with another
OUTWICKED > OUTWICK
OUTWICKS > OUTWICK
OUTWILE vb surpass in cunning
OUTWILED > OUTWILE
OUTWILES > OUTWILE
OUTWILING > OUTWILE
OUTWILL vb demonstrate stronger will than
OUTWILLED > OUTWILL
OUTWILLS > OUTWILL
OUTWIN vb get out of
OUTWIND vb unwind
OUTWINDED > OUTWIND
OUTWINDS > OUTWIND
OUTWING vb surpass in flying
OUTWINGED > OUTWING
OUTWINGS > OUTWING
OUTWINS > OUTWIN
OUTWISH vb surpass in wishing
OUTWISHED > OUTWISH
OUTWISHES > OUTWISH
OUTWIT vb get the better of (someone) by cunning
OUTWITH prep outside
OUTWITS > OUTWIT
OUTWITTED > OUTWIT
OUTWON > OUTWIN
OUTWORE > OUTWEAR
OUTWORK n defences which lie outside main defensive works ▷ vb work better, harder, etc, than
OUTWORKED > OUTWORK
OUTWORKER > OUTWORK
OUTWORKS > OUTWORK

OUTWORN adj no longer in use
OUTWORTH vb be more valuable than
OUTWORTHS > OUTWORTH
OUTWOUND > OUTWIND
OUTWREST vb extort
OUTWRESTS > OUTWREST
OUTWRIT > OUTWRITE
OUTWRITE vb outdo in writing
OUTWRITES > OUTWRITE
OUTWROTE > OUTWRITE
OUTYELL vb outdo in yelling
OUTYELLED > OUTYELL
OUTYELLS > OUTYELL
OUTYELP vb outdo in yelping
OUTYELPED > OUTYELP
OUTYELPS > OUTYELP
OUTYIELD vb yield more than
OUTYIELDS > OUTYIELD
OUVERT adj open
OUVERTE feminine form of > OUVERT
OUVRAGE n work
OUVRAGES > OUVRAGE
OUVRIER n worker
OUVRIERE feminine form of > OUVRIER
OUVRIERES > OUVRIERE
OUVRIERS > OUVRIER
OUZEL n type of bird
OUZELS > OUZEL
OUZO n strong aniseed-flavoured spirit from Greece
OUZOS > OUZO
OVA > OVUM
OVAL adj egg-shaped ▷ n anything that is oval in shape
OVALBUMIN n albumin in egg whites
OVALITIES > OVAL
OVALITY > OVAL
OVALLY > OVAL
OVALNESS > OVAL
OVALS > OVAL
OVARIAL > OVARY
OVARIAN > OVARY
OVARIES > OVARY
OVARIOLE n tube in insect ovary
OVARIOLES > OVARIOLE
OVARIOUS adj of eggs
OVARITIS n inflammation of an ovary
OVARY n female egg-producing organ
OVATE adj shaped like an egg ▷ vb give ovation
OVATED > OVATE
OVATELY > OVATE
OVATES > OVATE
OVATING > OVATE
OVATION n enthusiastic round of applause
OVATIONAL > OVATION
OVATIONS > OVATION
OVATOR > OVATE
OVATORS > OVATE

OVEL n mourner, esp during the first seven days after a death
OVELS > OVEL
OVEN n heated compartment or container for cooking or for drying or firing ceramics ▷ vb cook in an oven
OVENABLE adj (of food) suitable for cooking in an oven
OVENBIRD n type of small brownish South American bird
OVENBIRDS > OVENBIRD
OVENED > OVEN
OVENING > OVEN
OVENLIKE > OVEN
OVENPROOF adj able to be used in an oven
OVENS > OVEN
OVENWARE n heat-resistant dishes in which food can be both cooked and served
OVENWARES > OVENWARE
OVENWOOD n pieces of wood for burning in an oven
OVENWOODS > OVENWOOD
OVER adv indicating position on the top of, amount greater than, etc ▷ adj finished ▷ n (in cricket) series of six balls bowled from one end ▷ vb jump over
OVERABLE adj too able
OVERACT vb act in an exaggerated way
OVERACTED > OVERACT
OVERACTS > OVERACT
OVERACUTE adj too acute
OVERAGE adj beyond a specified age ▷ n amount beyond given limit
OVERAGED adj very old
OVERAGES > OVERAGE
OVERALERT adj abnormally alert
OVERALL adv in total ▷ n coat-shaped protective garment ▷ adj from one end to the other
OVERALLED adj wearing overalls
OVERALLS > OVERALL
OVERAPT adj tending excessively
OVERARCH vb form an arch over
OVERARM adv with the arm above the shoulder ▷ adj bowled, thrown, or performed with the arm raised above the shoulder ▷ vb throw (a ball) overarm
OVERARMED > OVERARM
OVERARMS > OVERARM
OVERATE > OVEREAT
OVERAWE vb affect (someone) with an overpowering sense of awe

OVERAWED > OVERAWE
OVERAWES > OVERAWE
OVERAWING > OVERAWE
OVERBAKE vb bake too long
OVERBAKED > OVERBAKE
OVERBAKES > OVERBAKE
OVERBEAR vb dominate or overcome
OVERBEARS > OVERBEAR
OVERBEAT vb beat too much
OVERBEATS > OVERBEAT
OVERBED adj fitting over bed
OVERBET vb bet too much
OVERBETS > OVERBET
OVERBID vb bid for more tricks than one can expect to win ▷ n bid higher than someone else's bid
OVERBIDS > OVERBID
OVERBIG adj too big
OVERBILL vb charge too much money
OVERBILLS > OVERBILL
OVERBITE n extension of the upper front teeth over the lower front teeth when the mouth is closed
OVERBITES > OVERBITE
OVERBLEW > OVERBLOW
OVERBLOW vb blow into (a wind instrument) with greater force than normal
OVERBLOWN adj excessive
OVERBLOWS > OVERBLOW
OVERBOARD adv from a boat into the water
OVERBOIL vb boil too much
OVERBOILS > OVERBOIL
OVERBOLD adj too bold
OVERBOOK vb accept too many bookings
OVERBOOKS > OVERBOOK
OVERBOOT n protective boot worn over an ordinary boot or shoe
OVERBOOTS > OVERBOOT
OVERBORE > OVERBEAR
OVERBORN > OVERBEAR
OVERBORNE > OVERBEAR
OVERBOUND vb jump over
OVERBRAKE vb brake too much
OVERBRED adj produced by too much selective breeding
OVERBREED vb produce by too much selective breeding
OVERBRIEF adj too brief
OVERBRIM vb overflow
OVERBRIMS > OVERBRIM
OVERBROAD adj not specific enough
OVERBROW vb hang over
OVERBROWS > OVERBROW
OVERBUILD vb build over or on top of
OVERBUILT > OVERBUILD
OVERBULK vb loom large over
OVERBULKS > OVERBULK
OVERBURN vb copy

information onto CD
**OVERBURNS** > OVERBURN
**OVERBURNT** > OVERBURN
**OVERBUSY** *adj* too busy
▷ *vb* make too busy
**OVERBUY** *vb* buy too much
or too many
**OVERBUYS** > OVERBUY
**OVERBY** *adv* Scots
expression meaning over
the road or across the way
**OVERCALL** *n* bid higher
than the preceding one
▷ *vb* bid higher than (an
opponent)
**OVERCALLS** > OVERCALL
**OVERCAME** > OVERCOME
**OVERCARRY** *vb* carry too far
or too many
**OVERCAST** *adj* (of the
sky) covered by clouds
▷ *vb* make or become
overclouded or gloomy
▷ *n* covering, as of clouds
or mist
**OVERCASTS** > OVERCAST
**OVERCATCH** *vb* overtake
**OVERCHEAP** *adj* too cheap
**OVERCHECK** *n* thin leather
strap attached to a horse's
bit to keep its head up
**OVERCHILL** *vb* make too
cold
**OVERCIVIL** *adj* too civil
**OVERCLAD** *adj* wearing too
many clothes
**OVERCLAIM** *vb* claim too
much
**OVERCLASS** *n* dominant
group in society
**OVERCLEAN** *adj* too clean
**OVERCLEAR** *adj* too clear
**OVERCLOSE** *adj* too close
**OVERCLOUD** *vb* make or
become covered with
clouds
**OVERCLOY** *vb* weary with
excess
**OVERCLOYS** > OVERCLOY
**OVERCOACH** *vb* coach too
much
**OVERCOAT** *n* heavy coat
**OVERCOATS** > OVERCOAT
**OVERCOLD** *adj* too cold
**OVERCOLOR** *vb* colour too
highly
**OVERCOME** *vb* gain control
over after an effort
**OVERCOMER** > OVERCOME
**OVERCOMES** > OVERCOME
**OVERCOOK** *vb* spoil food by
cooking it for too long
**OVERCOOKS** > OVERCOOK
**OVERCOOL** *vb* cool too
much
**OVERCOOLS** > OVERCOOL
**OVERCOUNT** *vb* outnumber
**OVERCOVER** *vb* cover up
**OVERCOY** *adj* too modest
**OVERCRAM** *vb* fill too full
**OVERCRAMS** > OVERCRAM
**OVERCRAW** *same*
*as* > OVERCROW
**OVERCRAWS** > OVERCRAW

**OVERCROP** *vb* exhaust
(land) by excessive
cultivation
**OVERCROPS** > OVERCROP
**OVERCROW** *vb* crow over
**OVERCROWD** *vb* fill with
more people or things
than is desirable
**OVERCROWS** > OVERCROW
**OVERCURE** *vb* take curing
process too far
**OVERCURED** > OVERCURE
**OVERCURES** > OVERCURE
**OVERCUT** *vb* cut too much
**OVERCUTS** > OVERCUT
**OVERDARE** *vb* dare too
much
**OVERDARED** > OVERDARE
**OVERDARES** > OVERDARE
**OVERDATED** *adj* outdated
**OVERDEAR** *adj* too dear
**OVERDECK** *n* upper deck
**OVERDECKS** > OVERDECK
**OVERDID** > OVERDO
**OVERDIGHT** *adj* covered up
**OVERDO** *vb* do to excess
**OVERDOER** > OVERDO
**OVERDOERS** > OVERDO
**OVERDOES** > OVERDO
**OVERDOG** *n* person or side in
an advantageous position
**OVERDOGS** > OVERDOG
**OVERDOING** > OVERDO
**OVERDONE** > OVERDO
**OVERDOSE** *n* excessive dose
of a drug ▷ *vb* take an
overdose
**OVERDOSED** > OVERDOSE
**OVERDOSES** > OVERDOSE
**OVERDRAFT** *n* overdrawing
**OVERDRANK** > OVERDRINK
**OVERDRAW** *vb* withdraw
more money than is in
(one's bank account)
**OVERDRAWN** > OVERDRAW
**OVERDRAWS** > OVERDRAW
**OVERDRESS** *vb* dress
(oneself or another) too
elaborately or finely ▷ *n*
dress that may be worn
over a jumper, blouse, etc
**OVERDREW** > OVERDRAW
**OVERDRIED** > OVERDRY
**OVERDRIES** > OVERDRY
**OVERDRINK** *vb* drink too
much alcohol
**OVERDRIVE** *n* very high
gear in a motor vehicle
**OVERDROVE** > OVERDRIVE
**OVERDRUNK** > OVERDRINK
**OVERDRY** *vb* dry too much
**OVERDUB** *vb* add (new
sounds) to a tape so
that the old and the new
sounds can be heard ▷ *n*
sound or series of sounds
added by this method
**OVERDUBS** > OVERDUB
**OVERDUE** *adj* still due after
the time allowed
**OVERDUST** *vb* dust too
much
**OVERDUSTS** > OVERDUST
**OVERDYE** *vb* dye (a fabric,

yarn, etc) excessively
**OVERDYED** > OVERDYE
**OVERDYER** > OVERDYE
**OVERDYERS** > OVERDYE
**OVERDYES** > OVERDYE
**OVEREAGER** *adj* excessively
eager or keen
**OVEREASY** *adj* too easy
**OVEREAT** *vb* eat more than
is necessary or healthy
**OVEREATEN** > OVEREAT
**OVEREATER** > OVEREAT
**OVEREATS** > OVEREAT
**OVERED** > OVER
**OVEREDIT** *vb* edit too much
**OVEREDITS** > OVEREDIT
**OVEREGG** *vb* exaggerate
absurdly
**OVEREGGED** > OVEREGG
**OVEREGGS** > OVEREGG
**OVEREMOTE** *vb* emote too
much
**OVEREXERT** *vb* exhaust or
injure (oneself) by doing
too much
**OVEREYE** *vb* survey
**OVEREYED** > OVEREYE
**OVEREYES** > OVEREYE
**OVEREYING** > OVEREYE
**OVERFALL** *n* turbulent
stretch of water caused by
marine currents over an
underwater ridge
**OVERFALLS** > OVERFALL
**OVERFAR** *adv* too far
**OVERFAST** *adj* too fast
**OVERFAT** *adj* too fat
**OVERFAVOR** *vb* favour too
much
**OVERFEAR** *vb* fear too much
**OVERFEARS** > OVERFEAR
**OVERFED** > OVERFEED
**OVERFEED** *vb* give (a
person, plant, or animal)
more food than is
necessary or healthy
**OVERFEEDS** > OVERFEED
**OVERFELL** > OVERFALL
**OVERFILL** *vb* put more into
(something) than there is
room for
**OVERFILLS** > OVERFILL
**OVERFINE** *adj* too fine
**OVERFISH** *vb* fish too much
**OVERFIT** *adj* too fit
**OVERFLEW** > OVERFLY
**OVERFLIES** > OVERFLY
**OVERFLOOD** *vb* flood
excessively
**OVERFLOW** *vb* flow over ▷ *n*
something that overflows
**OVERFLOWN** > OVERFLY
**OVERFLOWS** > OVERFLOW
**OVERFLUSH** *adj* too flush
**OVERFLY** *vb* fly over (a
territory) or past (a point)
**OVERFOCUS** *vb* focus too
much
**OVERFOLD** *n* fold in which
one or both limbs have
been inclined more than
90° from their original
orientation
**OVERFOLDS** > OVERFOLD

**OVERFOND** *adj* excessively
keen (on)
**OVERFOUL** *adj* too foul
**OVERFRANK** *adj* too frank
**OVERFREE** *adj* too forward
**OVERFULL** *adj* excessively
full
**OVERFUND** *vb* supply with
too much money
**OVERFUNDS** > OVERFUND
**OVERFUSSY** *adj* too fussy
**OVERGALL** *vb* make sore
all over
**OVERGALLS** > OVERGALL
**OVERGANG** *vb* dominate
**OVERGANGS** > OVERGANG
**OVERGAVE** > OVERGIVE
**OVERGEAR** *vb* cause (a
company) to have too high
a proportion of loan stock
**OVERGEARS** > OVERGEAR
**OVERGET** *vb* overtake
**OVERGETS** > OVERGET
**OVERGILD** *vb* gild too much
**OVERGILDS** > OVERGILD
**OVERGILT** > OVERGILD
**OVERGIRD** *vb* gird too
tightly
**OVERGIRDS** > OVERGIRD
**OVERGIRT** > OVERGIRD
**OVERGIVE** *vb* give up
**OVERGIVEN** > OVERGIVE
**OVERGIVES** > OVERGIVE
**OVERGLAD** *adj* too glad
**OVERGLAZE** *adj* (of
decoration or colours)
applied to porcelain above
the glaze
**OVERGLOOM** *vb* make
gloomy
**OVERGO** *vb* go beyond
**OVERGOAD** *vb* goad too
much
**OVERGOADS** > OVERGOAD
**OVERGOES** > OVERGO
**OVERGOING** > OVERGO
**OVERGONE** > OVERGO
**OVERGORGE** *vb* overeat
**OVERGOT** > OVERGET
**OVERGRADE** *vb* grade too
highly
**OVERGRAIN** *vb* apply grainy
texture to
**OVERGRASS** *vb* grow grass
on top of
**OVERGRAZE** *vb* graze (land)
too intensively
**OVERGREAT** *adj* too great
**OVERGREEN** *vb* cover with
vegetation
**OVERGREW** > OVERGROW
**OVERGROW** *vb* grow over
or across (an area, path,
lawn, etc)
**OVERGROWN** > OVERGROW
**OVERGROWS** > OVERGROW
**OVERHAILE** *vb* pull over
**OVERHAIR** *n* outer coat of
animal
**OVERHAIRS** > OVERHAIR
**OVERHALE** *same*
*as* > OVERHAILE
**OVERHALED** > OVERHALE
**OVERHALES** > OVERHALE

**OVERHAND** adj thrown or performed with the hand raised above the shoulder ▷ adv with the hand above the shoulder ▷ vb sew with the thread passing over two edges in one direction

**OVERHANDS** > OVERHAND

**OVERHANG** vb project beyond something ▷ n overhanging part

**OVERHANGS** > OVERHANG

**OVERHAPPY** adj too happy

**OVERHARD** adj too hard

**OVERHASTE** n excessive haste

**OVERHASTY** > OVERHASTE

**OVERHATE** vb hate too much

**OVERHATED** > OVERHATE

**OVERHATES** > OVERHATE

**OVERHAUL** vb examine and repair ▷ n examination and repair

**OVERHAULS** > OVERHAUL

**OVERHEAD** adj above one's head ▷ adv over or above head height ▷ n stroke in racket games played from above head height

**OVERHEADS** pl n general cost of maintaining a business

**OVERHEAP** vb supply too much

**OVERHEAPS** > OVERHEAP

**OVERHEAR** vb hear (a speaker or remark) unintentionally

**OVERHEARD** > OVERHEAR

**OVERHEARS** > OVERHEAR

**OVERHEAT** vb make or become excessively hot ▷ n condition of being overheated

**OVERHEATS** > OVERHEAT

**OVERHELD** > OVERHOLD

**OVERHENT** vb overtake

**OVERHENTS** > OVERHENT

**OVERHIGH** adj too high

**OVERHIT** vb hit too strongly

**OVERHITS** > OVERHIT

**OVERHOLD** vb value too highly

**OVERHOLDS** > OVERHOLD

**OVERHOLY** adj too holy

**OVERHONOR** vb honour too highly

**OVERHOPE** vb hope too much

**OVERHOPED** > OVERHOPE

**OVERHOPES** > OVERHOPE

**OVERHOT** adj too hot

**OVERHUNG** > OVERHANG

**OVERHUNT** vb hunt too much

**OVERHUNTS** > OVERHUNT

**OVERHYPE** vb hype too much

**OVERHYPED** > OVERHYPE

**OVERHYPES** > OVERHYPE

**OVERIDLE** adj too idle

**OVERING** > OVER

**OVERINKED** adj printed using too much ink

**OVERISSUE** vb issue (shares, banknotes, etc) in excess of demand or ability to pay ▷ n shares, banknotes, etc, thus issued

**OVERJOY** vb give great delight to

**OVERJOYED** adj extremely pleased

**OVERJOYS** > OVERJOY

**OVERJUMP** vb jump too far

**OVERJUMPS** > OVERJUMP

**OVERJUST** adj too just

**OVERKEEN** adj too keen

**OVERKEEP** vb keep too long

**OVERKEEPS** > OVERKEEP

**OVERKEPT** > OVERKEEP

**OVERKEST** same as > OVERCAST

**OVERKILL** n treatment that is greater than required

**OVERKILLS** > OVERKILL

**OVERKIND** adj too kind

**OVERKING** n supreme king

**OVERKINGS** > OVERKING

**OVERKNEE** adj reaching to above knee

**OVERLABOR** vb spend too much work on

**OVERLADE** vb overburden

**OVERLADED** > OVERLADE

**OVERLADEN** > OVERLADE

**OVERLADES** > OVERLADE

**OVERLAID** > OVERLAY

**OVERLAIN** > OVERLIE

**OVERLAND** adv by land ▷ vb drive (cattle or sheep) overland

**OVERLANDS** > OVERLAND

**OVERLAP** vb share part of the same space or period of time (as) ▷ n area overlapping

**OVERLAPS** > OVERLAP

**OVERLARD** vb cover with lard

**OVERLARDS** > OVERLARD

**OVERLARGE** adj excessively large

**OVERLATE** adj too late

**OVERLAX** adj too lax

**OVERLAY** vb cover with a thin layer ▷ n something that is laid over something else

**OVERLAYS** > OVERLAY

**OVERLEAF** adv on the back of the current page

**OVERLEAP** vb leap too far

**OVERLEAPS** > OVERLEAP

**OVERLEAPT** > OVERLEAP

**OVERLEARN** vb study too intensely

**OVERLEND** vb lend too much

**OVERLENDS** > OVERLEND

**OVERLENT** > OVERLEND

**OVERLET** vb let to too many

**OVERLETS** > OVERLET

**OVERLEWD** adj too lewd

**OVERLIE** vb lie on or cover (something or someone)

**OVERLIER** > OVERLIE

**OVERLIERS** > OVERLIE

**OVERLIES** > OVERLIE

**OVERLIGHT** vb illuminate too brightly

**OVERLIT** > OVERLIGHT

**OVERLIVE** vb live longer than (another person)

**OVERLIVED** > OVERLIVE

**OVERLIVES** > OVERLIVE

**OVERLOAD** vb put too large a load on or in ▷ n excessive load

**OVERLOADS** > OVERLOAD

**OVERLOCK** vb sew fabric with interlocking stitch

**OVERLOCKS** > OVERLOCK

**OVERLONG** adj too or excessively long

**OVERLOOK** vb fail to notice ▷ n high place affording a view

**OVERLOOKS** > OVERLOOK

**OVERLORD** n supreme lord or master

**OVERLORDS** > OVERLORD

**OVERLOUD** adj too loud

**OVERLOVE** vb love too much

**OVERLOVED** > OVERLOVE

**OVERLOVES** > OVERLOVE

**OVERLUSH** adj too lush

**OVERLUSTY** adj too lusty

**OVERLY** adv excessively

**OVERLYING** > OVERLIE

**OVERMAN** vb provide with too many staff ▷ n man who oversees others

**OVERMANS** > OVERMAN

**OVERMANY** adj too many

**OVERMAST** vb provide mast that is too big

**OVERMASTS** > OVERMAST

**OVERMATCH** vb be more than a match for ▷ n person superior in ability

**OVERMEEK** adj too meek

**OVERMELT** vb melt too much

**OVERMELTS** > OVERMELT

**OVERMEN** > OVERMAN

**OVERMERRY** adj very merry

**OVERMILD** adj too mild

**OVERMILK** vb milk too much

**OVERMILKS** > OVERMILK

**OVERMINE** vb mine too much

**OVERMINED** > OVERMINE

**OVERMINES** > OVERMINE

**OVERMIX** vb mix too much

**OVERMIXED** > OVERMIX

**OVERMIXES** > OVERMIX

**OVERMOUNT** vb surmount

**OVERMUCH** adj too much ▷ n excessive amount

**OVERNAME** vb repeat (someone's) name

**OVERNAMED** > OVERNAME

**OVERNAMES** > OVERNAME

**OVERNEAR** adj too near

**OVERNEAT** adj too neat

**OVERNET** vb cover with net

**OVERNETS** > OVERNET

**OVERNEW** adj too new

**OVERNICE** adj too fastidious, precise, etc

**OVERNIGHT** adv (taking place) during one night ▷ adj done in, occurring in, or lasting the night ▷ vb stay the night

**OVERPACK** vb pack too much

**OVERPACKS** > OVERPACK

**OVERPAGE** same as > OVERLEAF

**OVERPAID** > OVERPAY

**OVERPAINT** vb apply too much paint

**OVERPART** vb give an actor too difficult a role

**OVERPARTS** > OVERPART

**OVERPASS** vb pass over, through, or across

**OVERPAST** > OVERPASS

**OVERPAY** vb pay (someone) at too high a rate

**OVERPAYS** > OVERPAY

**OVERPEDAL** vb use piano pedal too much

**OVERPEER** vb look down over

**OVERPEERS** > OVERPEER

**OVERPERCH** vb fly up to perch on

**OVERPERT** adj too insolent

**OVERPITCH** vb bowl (a cricket ball) so that it pitches too close to the stumps

**OVERPLAID** n plaid in double layer

**OVERPLAN** vb plan excessively

**OVERPLANS** > OVERPLAN

**OVERPLANT** vb plant more than is necessary

**OVERPLAST** adj put above

**OVERPLAY** same as > OVERACT

**OVERPLAYS** > OVERPLAY

**OVERPLIED** > OVERPLY

**OVERPLIES** > OVERPLY

**OVERPLOT** vb plot onto existing graph or map

**OVERPLOTS** > OVERPLOT

**OVERPLUS** n surplus or excess quantity

**OVERPLY** vb ply too much

**OVERPOISE** vb weigh more than

**OVERPOST** vb hurry over

**OVERPOSTS** > OVERPOST

**OVERPOWER** vb subdue or overcome (someone)

**OVERPRESS** vb oppress

**OVERPRICE** vb put too high a price on

**OVERPRINT** vb print (additional matter) onto (something already printed) ▷ n additional matter printed onto something already printed

**OVERPRIZE** vb prize too highly
**OVERPROOF** adj containing more alcohol than standard spirit
**OVERPROUD** adj too proud
**OVERPUMP** vb pump too much
**OVERPUMPS** > OVERPUMP
**OVERQUICK** adj too quick
**OVERRACK** vb strain too much
**OVERRACKS** > OVERRACK
**OVERRAKE** vb rake over
**OVERRAKED** > OVERRAKE
**OVERRAKES** > OVERRAKE
**OVERRAN** > OVERRUN
**OVERRANK** adj too rank
**OVERRASH** adj too rash
**OVERRATE** vb have too high an opinion of
**OVERRATED** > OVERRATE
**OVERRATES** > OVERRATE
**OVERREACH** vb defeat or thwart (oneself) by attempting to do or gain too much
**OVERREACT** vb react more strongly than is necessary
**OVERREAD** vb read over
**OVERREADS** > OVERREAD
**OVERRED** vb paint over in red
**OVERREDS** > OVERRED
**OVERREN** same as > OVERRUN
**OVERRENS** > OVERREN
**OVERRICH** adj (of food) excessively flavoursome or fatty
**OVERRIDE** vb overrule ▷ n device or system that can override an automatic control
**OVERRIDER** > OVERRIDE
**OVERRIDES** > OVERRIDE
**OVERRIFE** adj too rife
**OVERRIGID** adj too rigid
**OVERRIPE** adj (of a fruit or vegetable) so ripe that it has started to decay
**OVERRIPEN** vb become overripe
**OVERROAST** vb roast too long
**OVERRODE** > OVERRIDE
**OVERRUDE** adj very rude
**OVERRUFF** vb defeat trump card by playing higher trump
**OVERRUFFS** > OVERRUFF
**OVERRULE** vb reverse the decision of (a person with less power)
**OVERRULED** > OVERRULE
**OVERRULER** > OVERRULE
**OVERRULES** > OVERRULE
**OVERRUN** vb conquer rapidly ▷ n act or an instance of overrunning
**OVERRUNS** > OVERRUN
**OVERS** > OVER
**OVERSAD** adj too sad
**OVERSAIL** vb project

beyond
**OVERSAILS** > OVERSAIL
**OVERSALE** n selling of more than is available
**OVERSALES** > OVERSALE
**OVERSALT** vb put too much salt in
**OVERSALTS** > OVERSALT
**OVERSAUCE** vb put too much sauce on
**OVERSAVE** vb put too much money in savings
**OVERSAVED** > OVERSAVE
**OVERSAVES** > OVERSAVE
**OVERSAW** > OVERSEE
**OVERSCALE** adj at higher scale than standard
**OVERSCORE** vb cancel by drawing a line or lines over or through
**OVERSEA** same as > OVERSEAS
**OVERSEAS** adj to, of, or from a distant country ▷ adv across the sea ▷ n foreign country or foreign countries collectively
**OVERSEE** vb watch over from a position of authority
**OVERSEED** vb plant too much seed in
**OVERSEEDS** > OVERSEED
**OVERSEEN** > OVERSEE
**OVERSEER** n person who oversees others, esp workmen
**OVERSEERS** > OVERSEER
**OVERSEES** > OVERSEE
**OVERSELL** vb exaggerate the merits or abilities of
**OVERSELLS** > OVERSELL
**OVERSET** vb disturb or upset
**OVERSETS** > OVERSET
**OVERSEW** vb sew (two edges) with stitches that pass over them both
**OVERSEWED** > OVERSEW
**OVERSEWN** > OVERSEW
**OVERSEWS** > OVERSEW
**OVERSEXED** adj more interested in sex than is thought decent
**OVERSHADE** vb appear more important than
**OVERSHARP** adj too sharp
**OVERSHINE** vb shine down on
**OVERSHIRT** n shirt worn over lighter clothes
**OVERSHOE** n protective shoe worn over an ordinary shoe
**OVERSHOES** > OVERSHOE
**OVERSHONE** > OVERSHINE
**OVERSHOOT** vb go beyond (a mark or target) ▷ n act or instance of overshooting
**OVERSHOT** adj (of a water wheel) driven by a flow of water that passes over the wheel ▷ n type of fishing rod

**OVERSHOTS** > OVERSHOT
**OVERSICK** adj too sick
**OVERSIDE** adv over the side (of a ship) ▷ n top side
**OVERSIDES** > OVERSIDE
**OVERSIGHT** n mistake caused by not noticing something
**OVERSIZE** adj larger than the usual size ▷ n size larger than the usual or proper size
**OVERSIZED** same as > OVERSIZE
**OVERSIZES** > OVERSIZE
**OVERSKIP** vb skip over
**OVERSKIPS** > OVERSKIP
**OVERSKIRT** n outer skirt, esp one that reveals a decorative underskirt
**OVERSLEEP** vb sleep beyond the intended time
**OVERSLEPT** > OVERSLEEP
**OVERSLIP** vb slip past
**OVERSLIPS** > OVERSLIP
**OVERSLIPT** > OVERSLIP
**OVERSLOW** adj too slow
**OVERSMAN** n overseer
**OVERSMEN** > OVERSMAN
**OVERSMOKE** vb smoke something too much
**OVERSOAK** vb soak too much
**OVERSOAKS** > OVERSOAK
**OVERSOFT** adj too soft
**OVERSOLD** > OVERSELL
**OVERSOON** adv too soon
**OVERSOUL** n universal divine essence
**OVERSOULS** > OVERSOUL
**OVERSOW** vb sow again after first sowing
**OVERSOWED** > OVERSOW
**OVERSOWN** > OVERSOW
**OVERSOWS** > OVERSOW
**OVERSPEND** vb spend more than one can afford ▷ n amount by which someone or something is overspent
**OVERSPENT** > OVERSPEND
**OVERSPICE** vb add too much spice to
**OVERSPILL** n rehousing of people from crowded cities in smaller towns ▷ vb overflow
**OVERSPILT** > OVERSPILL
**OVERSPIN** n forward spinning motion
**OVERSPINS** > OVERSPIN
**OVERSTAFF** vb provide an excessive number of staff for (a factory, hotel, etc)
**OVERSTAIN** vb stain too much
**OVERSTAND** vb remain longer than
**OVERSTANK** > OVERSTINK
**OVERSTARE** vb outstare
**OVERSTATE** vb state too strongly
**OVERSTAY** vb stay beyond the limit or duration of

**OVERSTAYS** > OVERSTAY
**OVERSTEER** vb (of a vehicle) to turn more sharply than is desirable or anticipated
**OVERSTEP** vb go beyond (a certain limit)
**OVERSTEPS** > OVERSTEP
**OVERSTINK** vb exceed in stinking
**OVERSTIR** vb stir too much
**OVERSTIRS** > OVERSTIR
**OVERSTOCK** vb hold or supply (a commodity) in excess of requirements
**OVERSTOOD** > OVERSTAND
**OVERSTORY** n highest level of trees in a rainforest
**OVERSTREW** vb scatter over
**OVERSTUDY** vb study too much
**OVERSTUFF** vb force too much into
**OVERSTUNK** > OVERSTINK
**OVERSUDS** vb produce too much lather
**OVERSUP** vb sup too much
**OVERSUPS** > OVERSUP
**OVERSURE** adj too sure
**OVERSWAM** > OVERSWIM
**OVERSWAY** vb overrule
**OVERSWAYS** > OVERSWAY
**OVERSWEAR** vb swear again
**OVERSWEET** adj too sweet
**OVERSWELL** vb overflow
**OVERSWIM** vb swim across
**OVERSWIMS** > OVERSWIM
**OVERSWING** vb swing too much or too far
**OVERSWORE** > OVERSWEAR
**OVERSWORN** > OVERSWEAR
**OVERSWUM** > OVERSWIM
**OVERSWUNG** > OVERSWING
**OVERT** adj open, not hidden
**OVERTAKE** vb move past (a vehicle or person) travelling in the same direction
**OVERTAKEN** > OVERTAKE
**OVERTAKES** > OVERTAKE
**OVERTALK** vb talk over
**OVERTALKS** > OVERTALK
**OVERTAME** adj too tame
**OVERTART** adj too bitter
**OVERTASK** vb impose too heavy a task upon
**OVERTASKS** > OVERTASK
**OVERTAX** vb put too great a strain on
**OVERTAXED** > OVERTAX
**OVERTAXES** > OVERTAX
**OVERTEACH** vb teach too much
**OVERTEEM** vb be too full of something
**OVERTEEMS** > OVERTEEM
**OVERTHICK** adj too thick
**OVERTHIN** adj too thin
**OVERTHINK** vb give too much thought to
**OVERTHREW** > OVERTHROW
**OVERTHROW** vb defeat and replace ▷ n downfall, destruction
**OVERTIGHT** adj too tight

**OVERTIME** adv in addition to one's normal working hours ▷ n work at a regular job done in addition to regular working hours ▷ vb exceed the required time for (a photographic exposure)
**OVERTIMED** > OVERTIME
**OVERTIMER** > OVERTIME
**OVERTIMES** > OVERTIME
**OVERTIMID** adj too timid
**OVERTIP** vb give too much money as a tip
**OVERTIPS** > OVERTIP
**OVERTIRE** vb make too tired
**OVERTIRED** > OVERTIRE
**OVERTIRES** > OVERTIRE
**OVERTLY** > OVERT
**OVERTNESS** > OVERT
**OVERTOIL** vb work too hard
**OVERTOILS** > OVERTOIL
**OVERTONE** n additional meaning
**OVERTONES** > OVERTONE
**OVERTOOK** > OVERTAKE
**OVERTOP** vb exceed in height
**OVERTOPS** > OVERTOP
**OVERTOWER** vb tower above
**OVERTRADE** vb (of an enterprise) to trade in excess of working capital
**OVERTRAIN** vb train too much
**OVERTREAT** vb give too much medical treatment to
**OVERTRICK** n trick by which a player exceeds his contract
**OVERTRIM** vb trim too much
**OVERTRIMS** > OVERTRIM
**OVERTRIP** vb tread lightly over
**OVERTRIPS** > OVERTRIP
**OVERTRUMP** vb (in cards) play a trump higher than (one previously played to the trick)
**OVERTRUST** vb trust too much
**OVERTURE** n orchestral introduction ▷ vb make or present an overture to
**OVERTURED** > OVERTURE
**OVERTURES** > OVERTURE
**OVERTURN** vb turn upside down ▷ n act of overturning or the state of being overturned
**OVERTURNS** > OVERTURN
**OVERTYPE** vb type over existing text
**OVERTYPED** > OVERTYPE
**OVERTYPES** > OVERTYPE
**OVERURGE** vb urge too strongly
**OVERURGED** > OVERURGE
**OVERURGES** > OVERURGE
**OVERUSE** vb use excessively

▷ n excessive use
**OVERUSED** > OVERUSE
**OVERUSES** > OVERUSE
**OVERUSING** > OVERUSE
**OVERVALUE** vb regard (someone or something) as much more important than is the case
**OVERVEIL** vb cover over
**OVERVEILS** > OVERVEIL
**OVERVIEW** n general survey
**OVERVIEWS** > OVERVIEW
**OVERVIVID** adj too vivid
**OVERVOTE** vb vote more times than is allowed
**OVERVOTED** > OVERVOTE
**OVERVOTES** > OVERVOTE
**OVERWARM** vb make too warm
**OVERWARMS** > OVERWARM
**OVERWARY** adj excessively wary
**OVERWASH** n act of washing over something
**OVERWATCH** vb watch over
**OVERWATER** vb give too much water to
**OVERWEAK** adj too weak
**OVERWEAR** vb wear out
**OVERWEARS** > OVERWEAR
**OVERWEARY** vb make too tired
**OVERWEEN** vb think too highly of
**OVERWEENS** > OVERWEEN
**OVERWEIGH** vb exceed in weight
**OVERWENT** > OVERGO
**OVERWET** vb make too wet
**OVERWETS** > OVERWET
**OVERWHELM** vb overpower, esp emotionally
**OVERWIDE** adj too wide
**OVERWILY** adj too crafty
**OVERWIND** vb wind (a watch) beyond the proper limit
**OVERWINDS** > OVERWIND
**OVERWING** vb fly above
**OVERWINGS** > OVERWING
**OVERWISE** adj too wise
**OVERWORD** n repeated word or phrase
**OVERWORDS** > OVERWORD
**OVERWORE** > OVERWEAR
**OVERWORK** vb work too much ▷ n excessive work
**OVERWORKS** > OVERWORK
**OVERWORN** > OVERWEAR
**OVERWOUND** > OVERWIND
**OVERWREST** vb strain too much
**OVERWRITE** vb write (something) in an excessively ornate or prolix style
**OVERWROTE** > OVERWRITE
**OVERYEAR** vb keep for later year
**OVERYEARS** > OVERYEAR
**OVERZEAL** n excess of zeal
**OVERZEALS** > OVERZEAL
**OVIBOS** n type of ox
**OVIBOSES** > OVIBOS

**OVIBOVINE** > OVIBOS
**OVICIDAL** > OVICIDE
**OVICIDE** n killing of sheep
**OVICIDES** > OVICIDE
**OVIDUCAL** > OVIDUCT
**OVIDUCT** n tube through which eggs are conveyed from the ovary
**OVIDUCTAL** > OVIDUCT
**OVIDUCTS** > OVIDUCT
**OVIFEROUS** adj carrying or producing eggs or ova
**OVIFORM** adj shaped like an egg
**OVIGEROUS** same as > OVIFEROUS
**OVINE** adj of or like a sheep ▷ n member of sheep family
**OVINES** > OVINE
**OVIPARA** n all oviparous animals
**OVIPARITY** > OVIPAROUS
**OVIPAROUS** adj producing eggs that hatch outside the body of the mother
**OVIPOSIT** vb (of insects and fishes) to deposit eggs through an ovipositor
**OVIPOSITS** > OVIPOSIT
**OVIRAPTOR** n egg-eating dinosaur
**OVISAC** n capsule or sac, such as an ootheca, in which egg cells are produced
**OVISACS** > OVISAC
**OVIST** n person believing ovum contains all subsequent generations
**OVISTS** > OVIST
**OVOID** adj egg-shaped ▷ n something that is ovoid
**OVOIDAL** adj ovoid ▷ n something that is ovoid
**OVOIDALS** > OVOIDAL
**OVOIDS** > OVOID
**OVOLI** > OVOLO
**OVOLO** n convex moulding having a cross section in the form of a quarter of a circle or ellipse
**OVOLOS** > OVOLO
**OVONIC** adj using particular electronic storage batteries
**OVONICS** n science of ovonic equipment
**OVOTESTES** > OVOTESTIS
**OVOTESTIS** n reproductive organ of snails
**OVULAR** > OVULE
**OVULARY** > OVULE
**OVULATE** vb produce or release an egg cell from an ovary
**OVULATED** > OVULATE
**OVULATES** > OVULATE
**OVULATING** > OVULATE
**OVULATION** > OVULATE
**OVULATORY** > OVULATE
**OVULE** n plant part that contains the egg cell and becomes the seed after

fertilization
**OVULES** > OVULE
**OVUM** n unfertilized egg cell
**OW** interj exclamation of pain
**OWCHE** same as > OUCH
**OWCHES** > OWCHE
**OWE** vb be obliged to pay (a sum of money) to (a person)
**OWED** > OWE
**OWELTIES** > OWELTY
**OWELTY** n equality, esp in financial transactions
**OWER** Scots word for > OVER
**OWERBY** adv over there
**OWERLOUP** n Scots word meaning encroachment
**OWERLOUPS** > OWERLOUP
**OWES** > OWE
**OWING** > OWE
**OWL** n night bird of prey ▷ vb act like an owl
**OWLED** > OWL
**OWLER** vb smuggler
**OWLERIES** > OWLERY
**OWLERS** > OWLER
**OWLERY** n place where owls live
**OWLET** n young or nestling owl
**OWLETS** > OWLET
**OWLIER** > OWLY
**OWLIEST** > OWLY
**OWLING** > OWL
**OWLISH** adj like an owl
**OWLISHLY** > OWLISH
**OWLLIKE** > OWL
**OWLS** > OWL
**OWLY** same as > OWLISH
**OWN** adj used to emphasize possession ▷ pron thing(s) belonging to a particular person ▷ vb possess
**OWNABLE** adj able to be owned
**OWNED** > OWN
**OWNER** n person who owns
**OWNERLESS** > OWNER
**OWNERS** > OWNER
**OWNERSHIP** n state or fact of being an owner
**OWNING** > OWN
**OWNS** > OWN
**OWRE** same as > OWER
**OWRECOME** n chorus of song
**OWRECOMES** > OWRECOME
**OWRELAY** Scots form of > OVERLAY
**OWRELAYS** > OWRELAY
**OWRES** > OWRE
**OWREWORD** variant of > OVERWORD
**OWREWORDS** > OWREWORD
**OWRIE** same as > OORIE
**OWRIER** > OWRIE
**OWRIEST** > OWRIE
**OWSE** Scots form of > OX
**OWSEN** pl n Scots word for > OXEN
**OWT** dialect word for > ANYTHING
**OWTS** > OWT

**OX** n castrated bull
**OXACILLIN** n antibiotic drug
**OXALATE** n salt or ester of oxalic acid ▷ vb treat with oxalate
**OXALATED** > OXALATE
**OXALATES** > OXALATE
**OXALATING** > OXALATE
**OXALIC** as in oxalic acid poisonous acid found in many plants
**OXALIS** n type of plant
**OXALISES** > OXALIS
**OXAZEPAM** n drug used to relieve anxiety
**OXAZEPAMS** > OXAZEPAM
**OXAZINE** n type of chemical compound
**OXAZINES** > OXAZINE
**OXBLOOD** n dark reddish-brown colour ▷ adj of this colour
**OXBLOODS** > OXBLOOD
**OXBOW** n U-shaped piece of wood fitted around the neck of a harnessed ox and attached to the yoke
**OXBOWS** > OXBOW
**OXCART** n cart pulled by ox
**OXCARTS** > OXCART
**OXEN** > OX
**OXER** n high fence
**OXERS** > OXER
**OXES** > OX
**OXEYE** n daisy-like flower
**OXEYES** > OXEYE
**OXFORD** n type of stout laced shoe with a low heel
**OXFORDS** > OXFORD
**OXGANG** n old measure of farmland
**OXGANGS** > OXGANG
**OXGATE** same as > OXGANG
**OXGATES** > OXGATE
**OXHEAD** n head of an ox
**OXHEADS** > OXHEAD
**OXHEART** n heart-shaped cherry
**OXHEARTS** > OXHEART
**OXHIDE** n leather made from the hide of an ox
**OXHIDES** > OXHIDE
**OXID** same as > OXIDE
**OXIDABLE** adj able to undergo oxidation
**OXIDANT** n substance that acts or is used as an oxidizing agent
**OXIDANTS** > OXIDANT
**OXIDASE** n any of a group of enzymes that bring about biological oxidation
**OXIDASES** > OXIDASE
**OXIDASIC** > OXIDASE
**OXIDATE** another word for > OXIDIZE
**OXIDATED** > OXIDATE
**OXIDATES** > OXIDATE
**OXIDATING** > OXIDATE
**OXIDATION** n oxidizing
**OXIDATIVE** > OXIDATION
**OXIDE** n compound of oxygen and one other

element
**OXIDES** > OXIDE
**OXIDIC** > OXIDE
**OXIDISE** same as > OXIDIZE
**OXIDISED** > OXIDISE
**OXIDISER** same as > OXIDIZER
**OXIDISERS** > OXIDISER
**OXIDISES** > OXIDISE
**OXIDISING** > OXIDISE
**OXIDIZE** vb combine chemically with oxygen, as in burning or rusting
**OXIDIZED** > OXIDIZE
**OXIDIZER** same as > OXIDANT
**OXIDIZERS** > OXIDIZER
**OXIDIZES** > OXIDIZE
**OXIDIZING** > OXIDIZE
**OXIDS** > OXID
**OXIM** same as > OXIME
**OXIME** n type of chemical compound
**OXIMES** > OXIME
**OXIMETER** n instrument for measuring oxygen in blood
**OXIMETERS** > OXIMETER
**OXIMETRY** > OXIMETER
**OXIMS** > OXIM
**OXLAND** same as > OXGANG
**OXLANDS** > OXLAND
**OXLIKE** > OX
**OXLIP** n type of woodland plant with small drooping pale yellow flowers
**OXLIPS** > OXLIP
**OXO** as in oxo acid acid that contains oxygen
**OXONIUM** as in oxonium compound type of salt derived from an organic ether
**OXONIUMS** > OXONIUM
**OXPECKER** n type of African starling
**OXPECKERS** > OXPECKER
**OXSLIP** same as > OXLIP
**OXSLIPS** > OXSLIP
**OXTAIL** n tail of an ox, used in soups and stews
**OXTAILS** > OXTAIL
**OXTER** n armpit ▷ vb grip under arm
**OXTERED** > OXTER
**OXTERING** > OXTER
**OXTERS** > OXTER
**OXTONGUE** n type of plant
**OXTONGUES** > OXTONGUE
**OXY** > OX
**OXYACID** n any acid that contains oxygen
**OXYACIDS** > OXYACID
**OXYCODONE** as in oxycodone hydrochloride opiate drug used as a painkiller
**OXYGEN** n gaseous element essential to life and combustion
**OXYGENASE** n enzyme
**OXYGENATE** vb add oxygen to
**OXYGENIC** > OXYGEN
**OXYGENISE** variant

of > OXYGENIZE
**OXYGENIZE** vb add oxygen to
**OXYGENOUS** > OXYGEN
**OXYGENS** > OXYGEN
**OXYMEL** n mixture of vinegar and honey
**OXYMELS** > OXYMEL
**OXYMORA** > OXYMORON
**OXYMORON** n figure of speech that combines two apparently contradictory ideas
**OXYMORONS** > OXYMORON
**OXYNTIC** adj of or denoting stomach cells that secrete acid
**OXYPHIL** n type of cell found in glands
**OXYPHILE** same as > OXYPHIL
**OXYPHILES** > OXYPHILE
**OXYPHILIC** > OXYPHILE
**OXYPHILS** > OXYPHIL
**OXYSALT** n any salt of an oxyacid
**OXYSALTS** > OXYSALT
**OXYSOME** n group of molecules
**OXYSOMES** > OXYSOME
**OXYTOCIC** adj accelerating childbirth by stimulating uterine contractions ▷ n oxytocic drug or agent
**OXYTOCICS** > OXYTOCIC
**OXYTOCIN** n hormone that stimulates the ejection of milk in mammals
**OXYTOCINS** > OXYTOCIN
**OXYTONE** adj having an accent on the final syllable ▷ n oxytone word
**OXYTONES** > OXYTONE
**OY** n grandchild
**OYE** same as > OY
**OYER** n (in the 13th century) an assize
**OYERS** > OYER
**OYES** same as > OYEZ
**OYESES** > OYES
**OYESSES** > OYES
**OYEZ** interj shouted three times by a public crier calling for attention before a proclamation ▷ n such a cry
**OYEZES** > OYEZ
**OYS** > OY
**OYSTER** n edible shellfish ▷ vb dredge for, gather, or raise oysters
**OYSTERED** > OYSTER
**OYSTERER** n person fishing for oysters
**OYSTERERS** > OYSTERER
**OYSTERING** > OYSTER
**OYSTERMAN** n person who gathers, cultivates, or sells oysters
**OYSTERMEN** > OYSTERMAN
**OYSTERS** > OYSTER
**OYSTRIGE** archaic variant of > OSTRICH
**OYSTRIGES** > OYSTRIGE

**OZAENA** n inflammation of nasal mucous membrane
**OZAENAS** > OZAENA
**OZALID** n method of duplicating writing or illustrations
**OZALIDS** > OZALID
**OZEKI** n sumo wrestling champion
**OZEKIS** > OZEKI
**OZOCERITE** n brown or greyish wax
**OZOKERITE** same as > OZOCERITE
**OZONATE** vb add ozone to
**OZONATED** > OZONATE
**OZONATES** > OZONATE
**OZONATING** > OZONATE
**OZONATION** > OZONATE
**OZONE** n strong-smelling form of oxygen
**OZONES** > OZONE
**OZONIC** > OZONE
**OZONIDE** n type of unstable explosive compound
**OZONIDES** > OZONIDE
**OZONISE** same as > OZONIZE
**OZONISED** > OZONISE
**OZONISER** > OZONISE
**OZONISERS** > OZONISE
**OZONISES** > OZONISE
**OZONISING** > OZONISE
**OZONIZE** vb convert (oxygen) into ozone
**OZONIZER** > OZONIZE
**OZONIZERS** > OZONIZE
**OZONIZES** > OZONIZE
**OZONIZING** > OZONIZE
**OZONOUS** > OZONE
**OZZIE** n hospital
**OZZIES** > OZZIE

# Pp

PA n (formerly) fortified Māori settlement

PAAL n stake driven into the ground

PAALS > PAAL

PABLUM same as > PABULUM

PABLUMS > PABLUM

PABOUCHE n soft shoe

PABOUCHES > PABOUCHE

PABULAR > PABULUM

PABULOUS > PABULUM

PABULUM n food

PABULUMS > PABULUM

PAC n soft shoe

PACA n large burrowing hystricomorph rodent of Central and South America

PACABLE adj easily appeased

PACAS > PACA

PACATION n act of making peace

PACATIONS > PACATION

PACE n single step in walking ▷ vb walk up and down, esp in anxiety ▷ prep with due respect to: used to express polite disagreement

PACED > PACE

PACEMAKER n electronic device surgically implanted in a person with heart disease to regulate the heartbeat

PACER n horse trained to move at a special gait, esp for racing

PACERS > PACER

PACES > PACE

PACEWAY n racecourse for trotting and pacing

PACEWAYS > PACEWAY

PACEY adj fast-moving, quick, lively

PACHA same as > PASHA

PACHADOM n rank of pacha

PACHADOMS > PACHADOM

PACHAK n fragrant roots of Asian plant

PACHAKS > PACHAK

PACHALIC n jurisdiction of pasha

PACHALICS > PACHALIC

PACHAS > PACHA

PACHINKO n Japanese game similar to pinball

PACHINKOS > PACHINKO

PACHISI n Indian game somewhat resembling backgammon, played on a cruciform board using six cowries as dice

PACHISIS > PACHISI

PACHOULI same as > PATCHOULI

PACHOULIS > PACHOULI

PACHUCO n young Mexican living in the US, esp one of low social status who belongs to a street gang

PACHUCOS > PACHUCO

PACHYDERM n thick-skinned animal such as an elephant

PACHYTENE n third stage of the prophase of meiosis during which the chromosomes become shorter and thicker and divide into chromatids

PACIER > PACY

PACIEST > PACY

PACIFIC adj tending to bring peace

PACIFICAL > PACIFIC

PACIFIED > PACIFY

PACIFIER n baby's dummy

PACIFIERS > PACIFIER

PACIFIES > PACIFY

PACIFISM n belief that violence of any kind is unjustifiable and that one should not participate in war

PACIFISMS > PACIFISM

PACIFIST n person who refuses on principle to take part in war ▷ adj advocating, relating to, or characterized by pacifism

PACIFISTS > PACIFIST

PACIFY vb soothe, calm

PACIFYING > PACIFY

PACING > PACE

PACK vb put (clothes etc) together in a suitcase or bag ▷ n bag carried on a person's or animal's back

PACKABLE > PACK

PACKAGE same as > PACKET

PACKAGED > PACKAGE

PACKAGER n independent firm specializing in design and production, as of illustrated books or television programmes which are sold to publishers or television companies as finished products

PACKAGERS > PACKAGER

PACKAGES > PACKAGE

PACKAGING n box or wrapping in which a product is offered for sale

PACKBOARD n frame for carrying goods

PACKED adj completely

filled

PACKER n person or company whose business is to pack goods, esp food

PACKERS > PACKER

PACKET n small container (and contents) ▷ vb wrap up in a packet or as a packet

PACKETED > PACKET

PACKETING > PACKET

PACKETS > PACKET

PACKFONG n Chinese alloy

PACKFONGS > PACKFONG

PACKFRAME n light metal frame with shoulder straps, used for carrying heavy or awkward loads

PACKHORSE n horse used for carrying goods

PACKING n material, such as paper or plastic, used to protect packed goods

PACKINGS > PACKING

PACKLY > PACK

PACKMAN n person carrying pack

PACKMEN > PACKMAN

PACKNESS > PACK

PACKS > PACK

PACKSACK n bag carried strapped on the back or shoulder

PACKSACKS > PACKSACK

PACKSHEET n cover for pack

PACKSTAFF n staff for supporting pack

PACKWAX n neck ligament

PACKWAXES > PACKWAX

PACKWAY n path for pack animals

PACKWAYS > PACKWAY

539

**PACO** *n* S American mammal

**PACOS** > PACO

**PACS** > PAC

**PACT** *n* formal agreement

**PACTA** > PACTUM

**PACTION** *vb* concur with

**PACTIONAL** > PACTION

**PACTIONED** > PACTION

**PACTIONS** > PACTION

**PACTS** > PACT

**PACTUM** *n* pact

**PACY** *same as* > PACEY

**PAD** *n* piece of soft material used for protection, support, absorption of liquid, etc ▷ *vb* protect or fill with soft material

**PADANG** *n* (in Malaysia) playing field

**PADANGS** > PADANG

**PADAUK** *n* tropical African or Asian leguminous tree with reddish wood

**PADAUKS** > PADAUK

**PADDED** > PAD

**PADDER** *n* highwayman who robs on foot

**PADDERS** > PADDER

**PADDIES** > PADDY

**PADDING** > PAD

**PADDINGS** > PAD

**PADDLE** *n* short oar with a broad blade at one or each end ▷ *vb* move (a canoe etc) with a paddle

**PADDLED** > PADDLE

**PADDLER** > PADDLE

**PADDLERS** > PADDLE

**PADDLES** > PADDLE

**PADDLING** > PADDLE

**PADDLINGS** > PADDLE

**PADDOCK** *n* small field or enclosure for horses ▷ *vb* place (a horse) in a paddock

**PADDOCKED** > PADDOCK

**PADDOCKS** > PADDOCK

**PADDY** *n* fit of temper

**PADDYWACK** *vb* spank or smack

**PADELLA** *n* type of candle

**PADELLAS** > PADELLA

**PADEMELON** *n* small Australian wallaby

**PADERERO** *same as* > PATERERO

**PADEREROS** > PADERERO

**PADI** *same as* > PADDY

**PADIS** > PADI

**PADISHAH** *n* Iranian ruler

**PADISHAHS** > PADISHAH

**PADKOS** *n* snacks and provisions for a journey

**PADLE** *another name for* > LUMPFISH

**PADLES** > PADLE

**PADLOCK** *n* detachable lock with a hinged hoop fastened over a ring on the object to be secured ▷ *vb* fasten (something) with a padlock

**PADLOCKED** > PADLOCK

**PADLOCKS** > PADLOCK

**PADMA** *n* type of lotus

**PADMAS** > PADMA

**PADNAG** *n* ambling horse

**PADNAGS** > PADNAG

**PADOUK** *same as* > PADAUK

**PADOUKS** > PADOUK

**PADRE** *n* chaplain to the armed forces

**PADRES** > PADRE

**PADRI** > PADRE

**PADRONE** *n* owner or proprietor of an inn, esp in Italy

**PADRONES** > PADRONE

**PADRONI** > PADRONE

**PADRONISM** *n* system of work controlled by a padrone

**PADS** > PAD

**PADSAW** *n* small narrow saw used for cutting curves

**PADSAWS** > PADSAW

**PADSHAH** *same as* > PADISHAH

**PADSHAHS** > PADSHAH

**PADUASOY** *n* rich strong silk fabric used for hangings, vestments, etc

**PADUASOYS** > PADUASOY

**PADYMELON** *same as* > PADEMELON

**PAEAN** *n* song of triumph or thanksgiving

**PAEANISM** > PAEAN

**PAEANISMS** > PAEAN

**PAEANS** > PAEAN

**PAEDERAST** *same as* > PEDERAST

**PAEDEUTIC** *adj* of or relating to the study of teaching

**PAEDIATRY** *n* branch of medical science concerned with children and their diseases

**PAEDOLOGY** *n* study of the character, growth, and development of children

**PAELLA** *n* Spanish dish of rice, chicken, shellfish, and vegetables

**PAELLAS** > PAELLA

**PAENULA** *n* ancient Roman cloak

**PAENULAE** > PAENULA

**PAENULAS** > PAENULA

**PAEON** *n* metrical foot of four syllables, with one long one and three short ones in any order

**PAEONIC** > PAEON

**PAEONICS** > PAEON

**PAEONIES** > PAEONY

**PAEONS** > PAEON

**PAEONY** *same as* > PEONY

**PAESAN** *n* fellow countryman

**PAESANI** > PAESANO

**PAESANO** *n* Italian-American man

**PAESANOS** > PAESANO

**PAESANS** > PAESAN

**PAGAN** *adj* not belonging to one of the world's main religions ▷ *n* pagan person

**PAGANDOM** > PAGAN

**PAGANDOMS** > PAGAN

**PAGANISE** *same as* > PAGANIZE

**PAGANISED** > PAGANISE

**PAGANISER** > PAGANISE

**PAGANISES** > PAGANISE

**PAGANISH** > PAGAN

**PAGANISM** > PAGAN

**PAGANISMS** > PAGAN

**PAGANIST** > PAGAN

**PAGANISTS** > PAGAN

**PAGANIZE** *vb* become pagan, render pagan, or convert to paganism

**PAGANIZED** > PAGANIZE

**PAGANIZER** > PAGANIZE

**PAGANIZES** > PAGANIZE

**PAGANS** > PAGAN

**PAGE** *n* (one side of) sheet of paper forming a book etc ▷ *vb* summon (someone) by bleeper or loudspeaker, in order to pass on a message

**PAGEANT** *n* parade or display of people in costume, usu illustrating a scene from history

**PAGEANTRY** *n* spectacular display or ceremony

**PAGEANTS** > PAGEANT

**PAGEBOY** *n* hairstyle in which the hair is smooth and the same medium length with the ends curled under

**PAGEBOYS** > PAGEBOY

**PAGED** > PAGE

**PAGEFUL** *n* amount (of text, etc) that a page will hold

**PAGEFULS** > PAGEFUL

**PAGEHOOD** *n* state of being a page

**PAGEHOODS** > PAGEHOOD

**PAGER** *n* small electronic device, capable of receiving short messages

**PAGERS** > PAGER

**PAGES** > PAGE

**PAGEVIEW** *n* electronic page of information displayed at the request of a user

**PAGEVIEWS** > PAGEVIEW

**PAGINAL** *adj* page-for-page

**PAGINATE** *vb* number the pages of (a book, manuscript, etc) in sequence

**PAGINATED** > PAGINATE

**PAGINATES** > PAGINATE

**PAGING** > PAGE

**PAGINGS** > PAGE

**PAGLE** *same as* > PAIGLE

**PAGLES** > PAGLE

**PAGOD** *n* oriental idol

**PAGODA** *n* pyramid-shaped Asian temple or tower

**PAGODAS** > PAGODA

**PAGODS** > PAGOD

**PAGRI** *n* type of turban

**PAGRIS** > PAGRI

**PAGURIAN** *n* any decapod crustacean of the family *Paguridae*, which includes the hermit crabs ▷ *adj* of, relating to, or belonging to the *Paguridae*

**PAGURIANS** > PAGURIAN

**PAGURID** *same as* > PAGURIAN

**PAGURIDS** > PAGURID

**PAH** *same as* > PA

**PAHAUTEA** *same as* > KAIKAWAKA

**PAHLAVI** *n* Iranian coin

**PAHLAVIS** > PAHLAVI

**PAHOEHOE** *n* hardened lava

**PAHOEHOES** > PAHOEHOE

**PAHS** > PAH

**PAID** > PAY

**PAIDEUTIC** *same as* > PAEDEUTIC

**PAIDLE** *Scots variant of* > PADDLE

**PAIDLED** > PAIDLE

**PAIDLES** > PAIDLE

**PAIDLING** > PAIDLE

**PAIGLE** *n* cowslip

**PAIGLES** > PAIGLE

**PAIK** *vb* thump or whack

**PAIKED** > PAIK

**PAIKING** > PAIK

**PAIKS** > PAIK

**PAIL** *n* bucket

**PAILFUL** *same as* > PAIL

**PAILFULS** > PAILFUL

**PAILLARD** *n* thin slice of meat

**PAILLARDS** > PAILLARD

**PAILLASSE** *same as* > PALLIASSE

**PAILLETTE** *n* sequin or spangle sewn onto a costume

**PAILLON** *n* thin leaf of metal

**PAILLONS** > PAILLON

**PAILS** > PAIL

**PAILSFUL** > PAILFUL

**PAIN** *n* physical or mental suffering ▷ *vb* cause (someone) mental or physical suffering

**PAINCH** *Scots variant of* > PAUNCH

**PAINCHES** > PAINCH

**PAINED** *adj* having or suggesting pain or distress

**PAINFUL** *adj* causing pain or distress

**PAINFULLY** > PAINFUL

**PAINIM** *n* heathen or pagan

**PAINIMS** > PAINIM

**PAINING** > PAIN

**PAINLESS** *adj* not causing pain or distress

**PAINS** *pl n* care or trouble

**PAINT** *n* coloured substance, spread on a surface with a brush or roller ▷ *vb* colour or coat with paint

**PAINTABLE** > PAINT

**PAINTBALL** *n* game in which teams of players simulate a military skirmish, shooting each other with paint pellets

**PAINTBOX** *n* box containing a tray of dry watercolour paints

**PAINTED** > PAINT

**PAINTER** *n* rope at the front of a boat, for tying it up

**PAINTERLY** *adj* having qualities peculiar to painting, esp the depiction of shapes by means of solid masses of colour, rather than by lines

**PAINTERS** > PAINTER

**PAINTIER** > PAINT

**PAINTIEST** > PAINT

**PAINTING** *n* picture produced by using paint

**PAINTINGS** > PAINTING

**PAINTRESS** *n* female painter

**PAINTS** > PAINT

**PAINTURE** *n* art of painting

**PAINTURES** > PAINTURE

**PAINTWORK** *n* covering of paint on parts of a vehicle, building, etc

**PAINTY** > PAINT

**PAIOCK** *obsolete word for* > PEACOCK

**PAIOCKE** *obsolete word for* > PEACOCK

**PAIOCKES** > PAIOCKE

**PAIOCKS** > PAIOCK

**PAIR** *n* set of two things matched for use together ▷ *vb* group or be grouped in twos

**PAIRE** *obsolete spelling of* > PAIR

**PAIRED** > PAIR

**PAIRER** > PAIR

**PAIRES** > PAIRE

**PAIREST** > PAIR

**PAIRIAL** *variant of* > PRIAL

**PAIRIALS** > PAIRIAL

**PAIRING** > PAIR

**PAIRINGS** > PAIR

**PAIRS** > PAIR

**PAIRWISE** *adv* in pairs

**PAIS** *n* country

**PAISA** *n* monetary unit of Bangladesh, Bhutan, India, Nepal, and Pakistan worth one hundredth of a rupee

**PAISAN** *n* fellow countryman

**PAISANA** *n* female peasant

**PAISANAS** > PAISANA

**PAISANO** *n* friend

**PAISANOS** > PAISANO

**PAISANS** > PAISAN

**PAISAS** > PAISA

**PAISE** > PAISA

**PAISLEY** *n* pattern of small curving shapes with intricate detailing, usually printed in bright colours

**PAISLEYS** > PAISLEY

**PAITRICK** *Scots word for* > PARTRIDGE

**PAITRICKS** > PAITRICK

**PAJAMA** *same as* > PYJAMA

**PAJAMAED** *adj* wearing pajamas

**PAJAMAS** > PAJAMA

**PAJOCK** *obsolete word for* > PEACOCK

**PAJOCKE** *obsolete word for* > PEACOCK

**PAJOCKES** > PAJOCKE

**PAJOCKS** > PAJOCK

**PAKAHI** *n* acid land that is unsuitable for cultivation

**PAKAHIS** > PAKAHI

**PAKAPOO** *n* Chinese lottery with betting slips marked with Chinese characters

**PAKAPOOS** > PAKAPOO

**PAKEHA** *n* person of European descent, as distinct from a Māori

**PAKEHAS** > PAKEHA

**PAKFONG** *same as* > PACKFONG

**PAKFONGS** > PAKFONG

**PAKIHI** *n* area of swampy infertile land

**PAKIHIS** > PAKIHI

**PAKKA** *variant of* > PUKKA

**PAKOKO** *n* small freshwater fish

**PAKOKOS** > PAKOKO

**PAKORA** *n* Indian dish consisting of pieces of vegetable, chicken, etc, dipped in a spiced batter and deep-fried

**PAKORAS** > PAKORA

**PAKTHONG** *n* white alloy containing copper, zinc, and nickel

**PAKTHONGS** > PAKTHONG

**PAKTONG** *same as* > PAKTHONG

**PAKTONGS** > PAKTONG

**PAL** *n* friend ▷ *vb* associate as friends

**PALABRA** *n* word

**PALABRAS** > PALABRA

**PALACE** *n* residence of a king, bishop, etc

**PALACED** *adj* having palaces

**PALACES** > PALACE

**PALADIN** *n* knight who did battle for a monarch

**PALADINS** > PALADIN

**PALAESTRA** *n* (in ancient Greece or Rome) public place devoted to the training of athletes

**PALAFITTE** *n* prehistoric dwelling

**PALAGI** *n* (in Samoa) European

**PALAGIS** > PALAGI

**PALAIS** *n* dance hall

**PALAMA** *n* webbing on bird's feet

**PALAMAE** > PALAMA

**PALAMATE** > PALAMA

**PALAMINO** *same*

*as* > PALOMINO

**PALAMINOS** > PALAMINO

**PALAMPORE** *same as* > PALEMPORE

**PALANKEEN** *same as* > PALANQUIN

**PALANQUIN** *n* (formerly, in the Orient) covered bed in which someone could be carried on the shoulders of four men

**PALAPA** *n* open-sided tropical building

**PALAPAS** > PALAPA

**PALAS** *n* East Indian tree

**PALASES** > PALAS

**PALATABLE** *adj* pleasant to taste

**PALATABLY** > PALATABLE

**PALATAL** *adj* of or relating to the palate ▷ *n* bony plate that forms the palate

**PALATALLY** > PALATAL

**PALATALS** > PALATAL

**PALATE** *n* roof of the mouth ▷ *vb* perceive by taste

**PALATED** > PALATE

**PALATES** > PALATE

**PALATIAL** *adj* like a palace, magnificent

**PALATINE** *same as* > PALATAL

**PALATINES** > PALATINE

**PALATING** > PALATE

**PALAVER** *n* time-wasting fuss ▷ *vb* (often used humorously) have a conference

**PALAVERED** > PALAVER

**PALAVERER** > PALAVER

**PALAVERS** > PALAVER

**PALAY** *n* type of rubber

**PALAYS** > PALAY

**PALAZZI** > PALAZZO

**PALAZZO** *n* Italian palace

**PALAZZOS** > PALAZZO

**PALE** *adj* light, whitish ▷ *vb* become pale ▷ *n* wooden or metal post used in fences

**PALEA** *n* inner of two bracts surrounding each floret in a grass spikelet

**PALEAE** > PALEA

**PALEAL** > PALEA

**PALEATE** *adj* having scales

**PALEBUCK** *n* small African antelope

**PALEBUCKS** > PALEBUCK

**PALED** > PALE

**PALEFACE** *n* offensive term for a White person, said to have been used by Native Americans of N America

**PALEFACES** > PALEFACE

**PALELY** > PALE

**PALEMPORE** *n* bed covering

**PALENESS** > PALE

**PALEOCENE** *adj* belonging to geological time period

**PALEOGENE** *adj* of early geological time period

**PALEOLITH** *n* Stone Age artefact

**PALEOLOGY** *n* study of prehistory

**PALEOSOL** *n* ancient soil horizon

**PALEOSOLS** > PALEOSOL

**PALEOZOIC** *adj* belonging to geological time period

**PALER** > PALE

**PALES** > PALE

**PALEST** > PALE

**PALESTRA** *same as* > PALAESTRA

**PALESTRAE** > PALESTRA

**PALESTRAL** > PALESTRA

**PALESTRAS** > PALESTRA

**PALET** *n* perpendicular band on escutcheon

**PALETOT** *n* loose outer garment

**PALETOTS** > PALETOT

**PALETS** > PALET

**PALETTE** *n* artist's flat board for mixing colours on

**PALETTES** > PALETTE

**PALEWAYS** *same as* > PALEWISE

**PALEWISE** *adv* by perpendicular lines

**PALFREY** *n* light saddle horse, esp ridden by women ▷ *vb* mount a palfrey

**PALFREYED** > PALFREY

**PALFREYS** > PALFREY

**PALIER** > PALY

**PALIEST** > PALY

**PALIFORM** *adj* shaped like a palus

**PALIKAR** *n* Greek soldier in the war of independence against Turkey

**PALIKARS** > PALIKAR

**PALILALIA** *n* speech disorder in which a word or phrase is rapidly repeated

**PALILLOGY** *n* repetition of word or phrase

**PALIMONY** *n* alimony awarded to a nonmarried partner after the break-up of a long-term relationship

**PALING** *n* wooden or metal post used in fences

**PALINGS** > PALING

**PALINKA** *n* type of apricot brandy, originating in Central and Eastern Europe

**PALINKAS** > PALINKA

**PALINODE** *n* poem in which the poet recants something he has said in a former poem

**PALINODES** > PALINODE

**PALINODY** > PALINODE

**PALINOPIA** *n* visual disorder in which the patient perceives a prolonged afterimage

**PALISADE** *n* fence made of wooden posts driven into the ground ▷ *vb* enclose

with a palisade
PALISADED > PALISADE
PALISADES > PALISADE
PALISADO same
as > PALISADE
PALISH adj rather pale
PALKEE n covered Oriental
litter
PALKEES > PALKEE
PALKI same as > PALKEE
PALKIS > PALKI
PALL n cloth spread over a
coffin ▷ vb become boring
PALLA n ancient Roman
cloak
PALLADIA > PALLADIUM
PALLADIC adj of or
containing palladium in
the trivalent or tetravalent
state
PALLADIUM n silvery-white
element of the platinum
metal group
PALLADOUS adj of or
containing palladium in
the divalent state
PALLAE > PALLA
PALLAH n S African
antelope
PALLAHS > PALLAH
PALLED > PALL
PALLET same as > PALETTE
PALLETED > PALLET
PALLETING > PALLET
PALLETISE same
as > PALLETIZE
PALLETIZE vb stack or
transport on a pallet or
pallets
PALLETS > PALLET
PALLETTE n armpit plate of
a suit of armour
PALLETTES > PALLETTE
PALLIA > PALLIUM
PALLIAL adj relating to
cerebral cortex
PALLIARD n person who
begs
PALLIARDS > PALLIARD
PALLIASSE n straw-filled
mattress
PALLIATE vb lessen the
severity of (something)
without curing it
PALLIATED > PALLIATE
PALLIATES > PALLIATE
PALLIATOR > PALLIATE
PALLID adj pale, esp
because ill or weak
PALLIDER > PALLID
PALLIDEST > PALLID
PALLIDITY > PALLID
PALLIDLY > PALLID
PALLIER > PALLY
PALLIEST > PALLY
PALLING > PALL
PALLIUM n garment worn
by men in ancient Greece
or Rome, made by draping
a large rectangular cloth
about the body
PALLIUMS > PALLIUM
PALLONE n Italian ball
game

PALLONES > PALLONE
PALLOR n paleness of
complexion, usually
because of illness, shock,
or fear
PALLORS > PALLOR
PALLS > PALL
PALLY adj on friendly terms
PALM n inner surface of
the hand ▷ vb conceal in
or about the hand, as in
sleight-of-hand tricks
PALMAR adj of or relating to
the palm of the hand
PALMARIAN adj pre-
eminent
PALMARY adj worthy of
praise
PALMATE adj shaped like an
open hand
PALMATED same
as > PALMATE
PALMATELY > PALMATE
PALMATION n state of being
palmate
PALMED > PALM
PALMER n (in Medieval
Europe) pilgrim bearing
a palm branch as a sign of
his visit to the Holy Land
PALMERS > PALMER
PALMETTE n ornament or
design resembling the
palm leaf
PALMETTES > PALMETTE
PALMETTO n small palm
tree with fan-shaped
leaves
PALMETTOS > PALMETTO
PALMFUL n amount that
can be held in the palm of
a hand
PALMFULS > PALMFUL
PALMHOUSE n greenhouse
for palms, etc
PALMIE n palmtop
computer
PALMIER > PALMY
PALMIES > PALMIE
PALMIEST > PALMY
PALMIET n South African
rush
PALMIETS > PALMIET
PALMING > PALM
PALMIPED n web-footed
bird
PALMIPEDE same
as > PALMIPED
PALMIPEDS > PALMIPED
PALMIST > PALMISTRY
PALMISTER n person
telling fortunes by reading
palms
PALMISTRY n fortune-
telling from lines on the
palm of the hand
PALMISTS > PALMISTRY
PALMITATE n any salt or
ester of palmitic acid
PALMITIC as in palmitic
acid white crystalline solid
that is a saturated fatty
acid
PALMITIN n colourless

glyceride of palmitic acid
PALMITINS > PALMITIN
PALMLIKE > PALM
PALMS > PALM
PALMTOP adj small enough
to be held in the hand ▷ n
computer small enough to
be held in the hand
PALMTOPS > PALMTOP
PALMY adj successful,
prosperous and happy
PALMYRA n tall tropical
Asian palm
PALMYRAS > PALMYRA
PALOLO n polychaete worm
of the S Pacific Ocean
PALOLOS > PALOLO
PALOMINO n gold-coloured
horse with a white mane
and tail
PALOMINOS > PALOMINO
PALOOKA n stupid or
clumsy boxer or other
person
PALOOKAS > PALOOKA
PALOVERDE n thorny
American shrub
PALP n either of a pair of
sensory appendages that
arise from the mouthparts
of crustaceans and insects
▷ vb feel
PALPABLE adj obvious
PALPABLY > PALPABLE
PALPAL > PALP
PALPATE vb examine
(an area of the body) by
touching ▷ adj of, relating
to, or possessing a palp or
palps
PALPATED > PALPATE
PALPATES > PALPATE
PALPATING > PALPATE
PALPATION > PALPATE
PALPATOR n type of beetle
PALPATORS > PALPATOR
PALPATORY > PALPATE
PALPEBRA n eyelid
PALPEBRAE > PALPEBRA
PALPEBRAL adj of or
relating to the eyelid
PALPEBRAS > PALPEBRA
PALPED > PALP
PALPI > PALPUS
PALPING > PALP
PALPITANT > PALPITATE
PALPITATE vb (of the
heart) beat rapidly
PALPS > PALP
PALPUS same as > PALP
PALS > PAL
PALSGRAVE n German
count palatine
PALSHIP n state of being
pals
PALSHIPS > PALSHIP
PALSIED > PALSY
PALSIER > PALSY
PALSIES > PALSY
PALSIEST > PALSY
PALSTAFF variant
of > PALSTAVE
PALSTAFFS > PALSTAFF
PALSTAVE n kind of celt,

usually of bronze, made
to fit into a split wooden
handle rather than having
a socket for the handle
PALSTAVES > PALSTAVE
PALSY n paralysis ▷ vb
paralyse ▷ adj friendly
PALSYING > PALSY
PALSYLIKE > PALSY
PALTER vb act or talk
insincerely
PALTERED > PALTER
PALTERER > PALTER
PALTERERS > PALTER
PALTERING > PALTER
PALTERS > PALTER
PALTRIER > PALTRY
PALTRIEST > PALTRY
PALTRILY > PALTRY
PALTRY adj insignificant
PALUDAL adj of, relating to,
or produced by marshes
PALUDIC adj of malaria
PALUDINAL adj inhabiting
swamps
PALUDINE adj relating to
marsh
PALUDISM rare word
for > MALARIA
PALUDISMS > PALUDISM
PALUDOSE adj growing or
living in marshes
PALUDOUS adj marshy
PALUS n part of the calicle
of certain corals
PALUSTRAL adj marshy
PALY adj vertically striped
PAM n knave of clubs
PAMPA n grassland area
PAMPAS pl n vast grassy
plains in S America
PAMPASES > PAMPAS
PAMPEAN > PAMPAS
PAMPEANS > PAMPAS
PAMPER vb treat (someone)
with great indulgence,
spoil
PAMPERED > PAMPER
PAMPERER > PAMPER
PAMPERERS > PAMPER
PAMPERING > PAMPER
PAMPERO n dry cold wind
in South America blowing
across the pampas from
the south or southwest
PAMPEROS > PAMPERO
PAMPERS > PAMPER
PAMPHLET n thin paper-
covered booklet
PAMPHLETS > PAMPHLET
PAMPHREY n cabbage
PAMPHREYS > PAMPHREY
PAMPOEN n pumpkin
PAMPOENS > PAMPOEN
PAMPOOTIE n rawhide
slipper worn by men in the
Aran Islands
PAMS > PAM
PAN n wide long-handled
metal container used in
cooking ▷ vb sift gravel
from (a river) in a pan to
search for gold
PANACEA n remedy for all

diseases or problems
**PANACEAN** > PANACEA
**PANACEAS** > PANACEA
**PANACHAEA** *variant of* > PANACEA
**PANACHE** *n* confident elegant style
**PANACHES** > PANACHE
**PANADA** *n* mixture of flour, water, etc, or of breadcrumbs soaked in milk, used as a thickening
**PANADAS** > PANADA
**PANAMA** *n* hat made of the plaited leaves of the jipijapa plant
**PANAMAS** > PANAMA
**PANARIES** > PANARY
**PANARY** *n* storehouse for bread
**PANATELA** *same as* > PANATELLA
**PANATELAS** > PANATELA
**PANATELLA** *n* long slender cigar
**PANAX** *n* genus of perennial herbs
**PANAXES** > PANAX
**PANBROIL** *vb* broil in a pan
**PANBROILS** > PANBROIL
**PANCAKE** *n* thin flat circle of fried batter ▷ *vb* cause (an aircraft) to make a pancake landing or (of an aircraft) to make a pancake landing
**PANCAKED** > PANCAKE.
**PANCAKES** > PANCAKE
**PANCAKING** > PANCAKE
**PANCE** *n* pansy
**PANCES** > PANCE
**PANCETTA** *n* lightly spiced cured bacon from Italy
**PANCETTAS** > PANCETTA
**PANCHAX** *n* brightly coloured tropical Asian cyprinodont fish
**PANCHAXES** > PANCHAX
**PANCHAYAT** *n* village council in India
**PANCHEON** *n* shallow bowl
**PANCHEONS** > PANCHEON
**PANCHION** *same as* > PANCHEON
**PANCHIONS** > PANCHION
**PANCOSMIC** *adj* of every cosmos
**PANCRATIA** *n* wrestling and boxing contests
**PANCRATIC** > PANCRATIA
**PANCREAS** *n* large gland behind the stomach that produces insulin and helps digestion
**PAND** *n* valance
**PANDA** *n* large black-and-white bearlike mammal from China
**PANDANI** *n* tropical tree
**PANDANUS** *n* Old World tropical palmlike plant
**PANDAR** *vb* act as a pimp
**PANDARED** > PANDAR
**PANDARING** > PANDAR

**PANDARS** > PANDAR
**PANDAS** > PANDA
**PANDATION** *n* warping
**PANDECT** *n* treatise covering all aspects of a particular subject
**PANDECTS** > PANDECT
**PANDEMIA** *n* epidemic affecting everyone
**PANDEMIAN** *adj* sensual
**PANDEMIAS** > PANDEMIA
**PANDEMIC** *adj* (of a disease) occurring over a wide area ▷ *n* pandemic disease
**PANDEMICS** > PANDEMIC
**PANDER** *vb* indulge (a person his or her desires) ▷ *n* person who procures a sexual partner for someone
**PANDERED** > PANDER
**PANDERER** *n* person who procures a sexual partner for someone
**PANDERERS** > PANDERER
**PANDERESS** *n* female panderer
**PANDERING** > PANDER
**PANDERISM** > PANDER
**PANDERLY** > PANDER
**PANDEROUS** > PANDER
**PANDERS** > PANDER
**PANDIED** > PANDY
**PANDIES** > PANDY
**PANDIT** *same as* > PUNDIT
**PANDITS** > PANDIT
**PANDOOR** *same as* > PANDOUR
**PANDOORS** > PANDOOR
**PANDORA** *n* handsome red sea bream
**PANDORAS** > PANDORA
**PANDORE** *another word for* > BANDORE
**PANDORES** > PANDORE
**PANDOUR** *n* one of an 18th-century force of Croatian soldiers in the Austrian service, notorious for their brutality
**PANDOURS** > PANDOUR
**PANDOWDY** *n* deep-dish pie made from fruit, esp apples, with a cake topping
**PANDS** > PAND
**PANDURA** *n* ancient stringed instrument
**PANDURAS** > PANDURA
**PANDURATE** *adj* (of plant leaves) shaped like the body of a fiddle
**PANDY** *n* (in schools) stroke on the hand with a strap as a punishment ▷ *vb* punish with such strokes
**PANDYING** > PANDY
**PANE** *n* sheet of glass in a window or door ▷ *adj* (of fish, meat, etc) dipped or rolled in breadcrumbs before cooking
**PANED** > PANE
**PANEER** *n* soft white

cheese, used in Indian cookery
**PANEERS** > PANEER
**PANEGOISM** *n* form of scepticism
**PANEGYRIC** *n* formal speech or piece of writing in praise of someone or something
**PANEGYRY** *n* panegyric
**PANEITIES** > PANEITY
**PANEITY** *n* state of being bread
**PANEL** *n* flat distinct section of a larger surface, for example in a door ▷ *vb* cover or decorate with panels ▷ *adj* of a group acting as a panel
**PANELED** > PANEL
**PANELESS** > PANE
**PANELING** *same as* > PANELLING
**PANELINGS** > PANELING
**PANELISED** *same as* > PANELIZED
**PANELIST** *same as* > PANELLIST
**PANELISTS** > PANELIST
**PANELIZED** *adj* made in sections for quick assembly
**PANELLED** > PANEL
**PANELLING** *n* panels collectively, esp on a wall
**PANELLIST** *n* member of a panel
**PANELS** > PANEL
**PANES** > PANE
**PANETELA** *same as* > PANATELA
**PANETELAS** > PANETELA
**PANETELLA** *n* long thin cigar
**PANETTONE** *n* kind of Italian spiced brioche containing sultanas
**PANETTONI** > PANETTONE
**PANFISH** *n* small food fish
**PANFISHES** > PANFISH
**PANFRIED** > PANFRY
**PANFRIES** > PANFRY
**PANFRY** *vb* fry in a pan
**PANFRYING** > PANFRY
**PANFUL** > PAN
**PANFULS** > PAN
**PANG** *n* sudden sharp feeling of pain or sadness ▷ *vb* cause pain
**PANGA** *n* broad heavy knife of E Africa, used as a tool or weapon
**PANGAMIC** > PANGAMY
**PANGAMIES** > PANGAMY
**PANGAMY** *n* unrestricted mating
**PANGAS** > PANGA
**PANGED** > PANG
**PANGEN** *same as* > PANGENE
**PANGENE** *n* hypothetical particle of protoplasm
**PANGENES** > PANGENE
**PANGENS** > PANGEN
**PANGING** > PANG

**PANGLESS** *adj* without pangs
**PANGOLIN** *n* animal of tropical countries with a scaly body and a long snout for eating ants and termites
**PANGOLINS** > PANGOLIN
**PANGRAM** *n* sentence incorporating all the letters of the alphabet
**PANGRAMS** > PANGRAM
**PANGS** > PANG
**PANHANDLE** *n* (in the US) narrow strip of land that projects from one state into another ▷ *vb* accost and beg from (passers-by), esp on the street
**PANHUMAN** *adj* relating to all humanity
**PANIC** *n* sudden overwhelming fear, often affecting a whole group of people ▷ *vb* feel or cause to feel panic ▷ *adj* of or resulting from such terror
**PANICALLY** > PANIC
**PANICK** *old word for* > PANIC
**PANICKED** > PANIC
**PANICKIER** > PANIC
**PANICKING** > PANIC
**PANICKS** > PANICK
**PANICKY** > PANIC
**PANICLE** *n* loose, irregularly branched cluster of flowers
**PANICLED** > PANICLE
**PANICLES** > PANICLE
**PANICS** > PANIC
**PANICUM** *n* type of grass
**PANICUMS** > PANICUM
**PANIER** *same as* > PANNIER
**PANIERS** > PANIER
**PANIM** *n* heathen or pagan
**PANIMS** > PANIM
**PANING** > PANE
**PANINI** > PANINO
**PANINO** *n* Italian sandwich
**PANISC** *n* faun; attendant of Pan
**PANISCS** > PANISC
**PANISK** *same as* > PANISC
**PANISKS** > PANISK
**PANISLAM** *n* all of Islam
**PANISLAMS** > PANISLAM
**PANJANDRA** *n* pompous self-important officials of people of rank
**PANLOGISM** *n* metaphysics of Leibniz
**PANMICTIC** > PANMIXIA
**PANMIXES** > PANMIXIA
**PANMIXIA** *n* (in population genetics) random mating within an interbreeding population
**PANMIXIAS** > PANMIXIA
**PANMIXIS** *same as* > PANMIXIA
**PANNAGE** *n* pasturage for pigs, esp in a forest
**PANNAGES** > PANNAGE
**PANNE** *n* lightweight velvet

fabric
**PANNED** > PAN
**PANNELLED** adj divided into panels
**PANNER** > PAN
**PANNERS** > PAN
**PANNES** > PANNE
**PANNICK** old spelling of the noun > PANIC
**PANNICKS** > PANNICK
**PANNICLE** n thin layer of body tissue
**PANNICLES** > PANNICLE
**PANNIER** n bag fixed on the back of a cycle
**PANNIERED** > PANNIER
**PANNIERS** > PANNIER
**PANNIKEL** n skull
**PANNIKELL** same as > PANNIKEL
**PANNIKELS** > PANNIKEL
**PANNIKIN** n small metal cup or pan
**PANNIKINS** > PANNIKIN
**PANNING** > PAN
**PANNINGS** > PAN
**PANNOSE** adj like felt
**PANNUS** n inflammatory fleshy lesion on the surface of the eye
**PANNUSES** > PANNUS
**PANOCHA** n coarse grade of sugar made in Mexico
**PANOCHAS** > PANOCHA
**PANOCHE** n type of dark sugar
**PANOCHES** > PANOCHE
**PANOISTIC** adj producing ova
**PANOPLIED** > PANOPLY
**PANOPLIES** > PANOPLY
**PANOPLY** n magnificent array
**PANOPTIC** adj taking in all parts, aspects, etc, in a single view
**PANORAMA** n wide unbroken view of a scene
**PANORAMAS** > PANORAMA
**PANORAMIC** > PANORAMA
**PANPIPE** n wind instrument
**PANPIPES** > PANPIPE
**PANS** > PAN
**PANSEXUAL** n person open to any sexual activity
**PANSIED** adj covered with pansies
**PANSIES** > PANSY
**PANSOPHIC** > PANSOPHY
**PANSOPHY** n universal knowledge
**PANSPERMY** n 19th-century evolutionary theory
**PANSY** n small garden flower with velvety purple, yellow, or white petals
**PANT** vb breathe quickly and noisily during or after exertion ▷ n act of panting
**PANTABLE** n soft shoe
**PANTABLES** > PANTABLE
**PANTAGAMY** n marriage to

everyone
**PANTALEON** n percussion instrument
**PANTALET** same as > PANTALETS
**PANTALETS** pl n long drawers, usually trimmed with ruffles, extending below the skirts
**PANTALON** n keyboard instrument
**PANTALONE** n Italian comic character
**PANTALONS** > PANTALON
**PANTALOON** n (in pantomime) absurd old man, the butt of the clown's tricks
**PANTDRESS** n dress with divided skirt
**PANTED** > PANT
**PANTER** n person who pants
**PANTERS** > PANTER
**PANTHEISM** n belief that God is present in everything
**PANTHEIST** > PANTHEISM
**PANTHENOL** n pantothenyl alcohol
**PANTHEON** n (in ancient Greece and Rome) temple built to honour all the gods
**PANTHEONS** > PANTHEON
**PANTHER** n leopard, esp a black one
**PANTHERS** > PANTHER
**PANTIE** same as > PANTY
**PANTIES** pl n women's underpants
**PANTIHOSE** same as > PANTYHOSE
**PANTILE** n roofing tile with an S-shaped cross section ▷ vb tile roof with pantiles
**PANTILED** > PANTILE
**PANTILES** > PANTILE
**PANTILING** > PANTILE
**PANTINE** n pasteboard puppet
**PANTINES** > PANTINE
**PANTING** > PANT
**PANTINGLY** > PANT
**PANTINGS** > PANT
**PANTLER** n pantry servant
**PANTLERS** > PANTLER
**PANTO** same as > PANTOMIME
**PANTOFFLE** same as > PANTOFLE
**PANTOFLE** n kind of slipper
**PANTOFLES** > PANTOFLE
**PANTOMIME** n play based on a fairy tale, performed at Christmas time
**PANTON** n type of horseshoe
**PANTONS** > PANTON
**PANTOS** > PANTO
**PANTOUFLE** same as > PANTOFLE
**PANTOUM** n verse form
**PANTOUMS** > PANTOUM
**PANTRIES** > PANTRY
**PANTROPIC** adj found

throughout tropics
**PANTRY** n small room or cupboard for storing food
**PANTRYMAN** n pantry servant
**PANTRYMEN** > PANTRYMAN
**PANTS** pl n undergarment for the lower part of the body
**PANTSUIT** n woman's suit of a jacket or top and trousers
**PANTSUITS** > PANTSUIT
**PANTUN** n Malayan poetry
**PANTUNS** > PANTUN
**PANTY** n woman's undergarment
**PANTYHOSE** pl n women's tights
**PANZER** n German tank
**PANZERS** > PANZER
**PANZOOTIC** n disease that affects all the animals in a geographical area
**PAOLI** > PAOLO
**PAOLO** n Italian silver coin
**PAP** n soft food for babies or invalids ▷ vb (of the paparazzi) to follow and photograph (a famous person) ▷ vb feed with pap
**PAPA** n father
**PAPABLE** adj suitable for papacy
**PAPACIES** > PAPACY
**PAPACY** n position or term of office of a pope
**PAPADAM** variant of > POPPADOM
**PAPADAMS** > PAPADAM
**PAPADOM** variant of > POPPADOM
**PAPADOMS** > PAPADOM
**PAPADUM** variant of > POPPADOM
**PAPADUMS** > PAPADUM
**PAPAIN** n proteolytic enzyme occurring in the unripe fruit of the papaya tree
**PAPAINS** > PAPAIN
**PAPAL** adj of the pope
**PAPALISE** same as > PAPALIZE
**PAPALISED** > PAPALISE
**PAPALISES** > PAPALISE
**PAPALISM** n papal system
**PAPALISMS** > PAPALISM
**PAPALIST** n supporter of a pope
**PAPALISTS** > PAPALIST
**PAPALIZE** vb make papal
**PAPALIZED** > PAPALIZE
**PAPALIZES** > PAPALIZE
**PAPALLY** > PAPAL
**PAPARAZZI** > PAPARAZZO
**PAPARAZZO** n photographer specializing in candid photographs of famous people
**PAPAS** > PAPA
**PAPAUMA** n New Zealand word for broadleaf

**PAPAW** same as > PAPAYA
**PAPAWS** > PAPAW
**PAPAYA** n large sweet West Indian fruit
**PAPAYAN** > PAPAYA
**PAPAYAS** > PAPAYA
**PAPE** n spiritual father
**PAPER** n material made in sheets from wood pulp or other fibres ▷ vb cover (walls) with wallpaper
**PAPERBACK** n book with covers made of flexible card ▷ adj of a paperback or publication of paperbacks ▷ vb publish in paperback
**PAPERBARK** n Australian tree of swampy regions, with spear-shaped leaves and papery bark
**PAPERBOY** n boy employed to deliver newspapers to people's homes
**PAPERBOYS** > PAPERBOY
**PAPERCLIP** n bent wire clip for holding sheets of paper together
**PAPERED** > PAPER
**PAPERER** > PAPER
**PAPERERS** > PAPER
**PAPERGIRL** n girl employed to deliver newspapers to people's homes
**PAPERIER** > PAPERY
**PAPERIEST** > PAPERY
**PAPERING** > PAPER
**PAPERINGS** > PAPER
**PAPERLESS** adj of, relating to, or denoting a means of communication, record keeping, etc, esp electronic, that does not use paper
**PAPERS** > PAPER
**PAPERWARE** n printed matter
**PAPERWORK** n clerical work, such as writing reports and letters
**PAPERY** adj like paper, esp in thinness, flimsiness, or dryness
**PAPES** > PAPE
**PAPETERIE** n box or case for papers and other writing materials
**PAPHIAN** n prostitute
**PAPHIANS** > PAPHIAN
**PAPILIO** n butterfly
**PAPILIOS** > PAPILIO
**PAPILLA** n small projection of tissue at the base of a hair, tooth, or feather
**PAPILLAE** > PAPILLA
**PAPILLAR** > PAPILLA
**PAPILLARY** > PAPILLA
**PAPILLATE** > PAPILLA
**PAPILLOMA** n benign tumour derived from epithelial tissue and forming a rounded or lobulated mass
**PAPILLON** n breed of toy

spaniel with large ears
**PAPILLONS** > PAPILLON
**PAPILLOSE** > PAPILLA
**PAPILLOTE** n paper frill around cutlets, etc
**PAPILLOUS** > PAPILLA
**PAPILLULE** n tubercle
**PAPISH** n Catholic
**PAPISHER** n derogatory term for a Roman Catholic
**PAPISHERS** > PAPISHER
**PAPISHES** > PAPISH
**PAPISM** n derogatory term for Roman Catholicism
**PAPISMS** > PAPISM
**PAPIST** n derogatory term for a Roman Catholic
**PAPISTIC** > PAPIST
**PAPISTRY** > PAPIST
**PAPISTS** > PAPIST
**PAPOOSE** n Native American child
**PAPOOSES** > PAPOOSE
**PAPPADAM** same as > POPPADOM
**PAPPADAMS** > PAPPADAM
**PAPPADOM** same as > POPPADOM
**PAPPADOMS** > PAPPADOM
**PAPPED** > PAP
**PAPPI** > PAPPUS
**PAPPIER** > PAPPY
**PAPPIES** > PAPPY
**PAPPIEST** > PAPPY
**PAPPING** > PAP
**PAPPOOSE** same as > PAPOOSE
**PAPPOOSES** > PAPPOOSE
**PAPPOSE** > PAPPUS
**PAPPOUS** > PAPPUS
**PAPPUS** n ring of fine feathery hairs surrounding the fruit in composite plants, such as the thistle
**PAPPUSES** > PAPPUS
**PAPPY** adj resembling pap
**PAPRICA** same as > PAPRIKA
**PAPRICAS** > PAPRICA
**PAPRIKA** n mild powdered seasoning made from red peppers
**PAPRIKAS** > PAPRIKA
**PAPS** > PAP
**PAPULA** same as > PAPULE
**PAPULAE** > PAPULA
**PAPULAR** > PAPULE
**PAPULE** n small solid usually round elevation of the skin
**PAPULES** > PAPULE
**PAPULOSE** > PAPULE
**PAPULOUS** > PAPULE
**PAPYRAL** > PAPYRUS
**PAPYRI** > PAPYRUS
**PAPYRIAN** > PAPYRUS
**PAPYRINE** > PAPYRUS
**PAPYRUS** n tall water plant
**PAPYRUSES** > PAPYRUS
**PAR** n usual or average condition ▷ vb play (a golf hole) in par
**PARA** n paratrooper
**PARABASES** > PARABASIS
**PARABASIS** n (in classical

Greek comedy) address from the chorus to the audience
**PARABEMA** n architectural feature
**PARABLAST** n yolk of an egg, such as a hen's egg, that undergoes meroblastic cleavage
**PARABLE** n story that illustrates a religious teaching ▷ vb write parable
**PARABLED** > PARABLE
**PARABLES** > PARABLE
**PARABLING** > PARABLE
**PARABOLA** n regular curve resembling the course of an object thrown forward and up
**PARABOLAS** > PARABOLA
**PARABOLE** n similitude
**PARABOLES** > PARABOLE
**PARABOLIC** adj of, relating to, or shaped like a parabola
**PARABRAKE** n parachute attached to the rear of a vehicle and opened to assist braking
**PARACHOR** n quantity constant over range of temperatures
**PARACHORS** > PARACHOR
**PARACHUTE** n large fabric canopy that slows the descent of a person or object from an aircraft ▷ vb land or drop by parachute
**PARACLETE** n mediator or advocate
**PARACME** n phase where fever lessens
**PARACMES** > PARACME
**PARACRINE** adj of signalling between biological cells
**PARACUSES** > PARACUSIS
**PARACUSIS** n hearing disorder
**PARADE** n procession or march ▷ vb display or flaunt
**PARADED** > PARADE
**PARADER** > PARADE
**PARADERS** > PARADE
**PARADES** > PARADE
**PARADIGM** n example or model
**PARADIGMS** > PARADIGM
**PARADING** > PARADE
**PARADISAL** adj of, relating to, or resembling paradise
**PARADISE** n heaven
**PARADISES** > PARADISE
**PARADISIC** > PARADISE
**PARADOR** n state-run hotel in Spain
**PARADORES** > PARADOR
**PARADORS** > PARADOR
**PARADOS** n bank behind a trench or other fortification, giving

protection from being fired on from the rear
**PARADOSES** > PARADOS
**PARADOX** n person or thing made up of contradictory elements
**PARADOXAL** adj paradoxical
**PARADOXER** n proposer of paradox
**PARADOXES** > PARADOX
**PARADOXY** n state of being paradoxical
**PARADROP** n delivery of personnel or equipment from an aircraft by parachute
**PARADROPS** > PARADROP
**PARAE** n type of fish
**PARAFFIN** n liquid mixture distilled from petroleum and used as a fuel or solvent ▷ vb treat with paraffin or paraffin wax
**PARAFFINE** same as > PARAFFIN
**PARAFFINS** > PARAFFIN
**PARAFFINY** adj like paraffin ▷ vb correspond to
**PARAFFLE** n extravagant display
**PARAFFLES** > PARAFFLE
**PARAFLE** same as > PARAFFLE
**PARAFLES** > PARAFLE
**PARAFOIL** n airfoil used on a paraglider
**PARAFOILS** > PARAFOIL
**PARAFORM** n paraformaldehyde
**PARAFORMS** > PARAFORM
**PARAGE** n type of feudal land tenure
**PARAGES** > PARAGE
**PARAGLIDE** vb glide through the air on a special parachute
**PARAGOGE** n addition of a sound or a syllable to the end of a word, such as st in amongst
**PARAGOGES** > PARAGOGE
**PARAGOGIC** > PARAGOGE
**PARAGOGUE** same as > PARAGOGE
**PARAGON** n model of perfection ▷ vb equal or surpass
**PARAGONED** > PARAGON
**PARAGONS** > PARAGON
**PARAGRAM** n pun
**PARAGRAMS** > PARAGRAM
**PARAGRAPH** n section of a piece of writing starting on a new line ▷ vb put (a piece of writing) into paragraphs
**PARAKEET** n small long-tailed parrot
**PARAKEETS** > PARAKEET
**PARAKELIA** n succulent herb of the genus *Calandrinia*, with purple flowers, that thrives in inland Australia
**PARAKITE** n series of linked

kites
**PARAKITES** > PARAKITE
**PARALALIA** n any of various speech disorders, esp the production of a sound different from that intended
**PARALEGAL** n person trained to assist lawyers but not qualified to practise law ▷ adj of or designating such a person
**PARALEXIA** n disorder of the ability to read in which words and syllables are meaninglessly transposed
**PARALEXIC** > PARALEXIA
**PARALLAX** n apparent change in an object's position due to a change in the observer's position
**PARALLEL** adj separated by an equal distance at every point ▷ n line separated from another by an equal distance at every point ▷ vb correspond to
**PARALLELS** > PARALLEL
**PARALOGIA** n self-deception
**PARALOGY** n anatomical similarity
**PARALYSE** vb affect with paralysis
**PARALYSED** > PARALYSE
**PARALYSER** > PARALYSE
**PARALYSES** > PARALYSIS
**PARALYSIS** n inability to move or feel, because of damage to the nervous system
**PARALYTIC** adj affected with paralysis ▷ n person who is paralysed
**PARALYZE** same as > PARALYSE
**PARALYZED** > PARALYZE
**PARALYZER** > PARALYZE
**PARALYZES** > PARALYZE
**PARAMATTA** n lightweight twill-weave fabric of wool with silk or cotton
**PARAMECIA** n freshwater protozoans
**PARAMEDIC** n person working in support of the medical profession ▷ adj of or designating such a person
**PARAMENT** n ecclesiastical vestment or decorative hanging
**PARAMENTA** > PARAMENT
**PARAMENTS** > PARAMENT
**PARAMESE** n note in ancient Greek music
**PARAMESES** > PARAMESE
**PARAMETER** n limiting factor, boundary
**PARAMO** n high plateau in the Andes between the tree line and the permanent snow line
**PARAMORPH** n mineral

PARAMOS > PARAMO
PARAMOUNT adj of the greatest importance ▷ n supreme ruler
PARAMOUR n lover, esp of a person married to someone else
PARAMOURS > PARAMOUR
PARAMYLUM n starch-like substance
PARANETE n note in ancient Greek music
PARANETES > PARANETE
PARANG n short stout straight-edged knife used by the Dyaks of Borneo
PARANGS > PARANG
PARANOEA same as > PARANOIA
PARANOEAS > PARANOEA
PARANOEIC same as > PARANOIAC
PARANOIA n mental illness causing delusions of grandeur or persecution
PARANOIAC > PARANOIA
PARANOIAS > PARANOIA
PARANOIC > PARANOIA
PARANOICS > PARANOIA
PARANOID adj of, characterized by, or resembling paranoia ▷ n person who shows the behaviour patterns associated with paranoia
PARANOIDS > PARANOID
PARANYM n euphemism
PARANYMPH n bridesmaid or best man
PARANYMS > PARANYM
PARAPARA n small carnivorous New Zealand tree
PARAPENTE n sport of jumping off high mountains wearing skis and a light parachute
PARAPET n low wall or railing along the edge of a balcony or roof ▷ vb provide with a parapet
PARAPETED > PARAPET
PARAPETS > PARAPET
PARAPH n flourish after a signature, originally to prevent forgery ▷ vb embellish signature
PARAPHED > PARAPH
PARAPHING > PARAPH
PARAPHS > PARAPH
PARAPODIA n paired unjointed lateral appendages of polychaete worms
PARAQUAT n yellow extremely poisonous soluble solid used in solution as a weedkiller
PARAQUATS > PARAQUAT
PARAQUET n long-tailed parrot
PARAQUETS > PARAQUET

PARAQUITO n parakeet
PARARHYME n type of rhyme
PARAS > PARA
PARASAIL vb glide through air on parachute towed by boat
PARASAILS > PARASAIL
PARASANG n Persian unit of distance equal to about 5.5 km or 3.4 miles
PARASANGS > PARASANG
PARASCEVE n preparation
PARASHAH n section of the Torah read in the synagogue
PARASHAHS > PARASHAH
PARASHOT > PARASHAH
PARASHOTH > PARASHAH
PARASITE n animal or plant living in or on another
PARASITES > PARASITE
PARASITIC > PARASITE
PARASOL n umbrella-like sunshade
PARASOLED adj having a parasol
PARASOLS > PARASOL
PARATAXES > PARATAXIS
PARATAXIS n juxtaposition of clauses in a sentence without the use of a conjunction
PARATHA n (in Indian cookery) flat unleavened bread, resembling a small nan bread, that is fried on a griddle
PARATHAS > PARATHA
PARATHION n slightly water-soluble toxic oil, odourless and colourless when pure, used as an insecticide
PARATONIC adj (of a plant movement) occurring in response to an external stimulus
PARATROOP n paratrooper
PARAVAIL adj lowest
PARAVANE n torpedo-shaped device towed from the bow of a vessel so that the cables will cut the anchors of any moored mines
PARAVANES > PARAVANE
PARAVANT adv in front
PARAVAUNT same as > PARAVANT
PARAWING n paraglider
PARAWINGS > PARAWING
PARAXIAL adj (of a light ray) parallel to the axis of an optical system
PARAZOA > PARAZOAN
PARAZOAN n sea sponge
PARAZOANS > PARAZOAN
PARAZOON n parasitic animal
PARBAKE vb partially bake
PARBAKED > PARBAKE
PARBAKES > PARBAKE
PARBAKING > PARBAKE

PARBOIL vb boil until partly cooked
PARBOILED > PARBOIL
PARBOILS > PARBOIL
PARBREAK vb vomit
PARBREAKS > PARBREAK
PARBUCKLE n rope sling for lifting or lowering a heavy cylindrical object, such as a cask or tree trunk ▷ vb raise or lower (an object) with such a sling
PARCEL n something wrapped up, package ▷ vb wrap up
PARCELED > PARCEL
PARCELING > PARCEL
PARCELLED > PARCEL
PARCELS > PARCEL
PARCENARY n joint heirship
PARCENER n person who takes an equal share with another or others
PARCENERS > PARCENER
PARCH vb make very hot and dry
PARCHED > PARCH
PARCHEDLY > PARCH
PARCHEESI n modern board game derived from the ancient game of pachisi
PARCHES > PARCH
PARCHESI same as > PARCHEESI
PARCHESIS > PARCHESI
PARCHING > PARCH
PARCHISI same as > PARCHEESI
PARCHISIS > PARCHISI
PARCHMENT n thick smooth writing material made from animal skin
PARCIMONY obsolete variant of > PARSIMONY
PARCLOSE n screen or railing in a church separating off an altar, chapel, etc
PARCLOSES > PARCLOSE
PARD n leopard or panther ▷ vb partner
PARDAH same as > PURDAH
PARDAHS > PARDAH
PARDAL variant spelling of > PARDALE
PARDALE n leopard
PARDALES > PARDALE
PARDALIS n leopard
PARDALOTE n small Australian songbird
PARDALS > PARDAL
PARDED > PARD
PARDEE adv certainly
PARDI same as > PARDEE
PARDIE same as > PARDEE
PARDINE adj spotted
PARDING > PARD
PARDNER n friend or partner: used as a term of address
PARDNERS > PARDNER
PARDON vb forgive, excuse ▷ n forgiveness ▷ interj

sorry ▷ sentence substitute sorry
PARDONED > PARDON
PARDONER n (before the Reformation) person licensed to sell ecclesiastical indulgences
PARDONERS > PARDONER
PARDONING > PARDON
PARDONS > PARDON
PARDS > PARD
PARDY same as > PARDEE
PARE vb cut off the skin or top layer of
PARECIOUS adj having the male and female reproductive organs at different levels on the same stem
PARECISM n state of having male and female organs close together
PARECISMS > PARECISM
PARED > PARE
PAREGORIC n medicine containing opium, benzoic acid, camphor or ammonia, and anise oil
PAREIRA n root of a South American menispermaceous climbing plant
PAREIRAS > PAREIRA
PARELLA n type of lichen
PARELLAS > PARELLA
PARELLE same as > PARELLA
PARELLES > PARELLE
PARENESES > PARENESIS
PARENESIS n exhortation
PARENT n father or mother ▷ vb raise offspring
PARENTAGE n ancestry or family
PARENTAL adj of or relating to a parent or parenthood
PARENTED > PARENT
PARENTING n activity of bringing up children
PARENTS > PARENT
PAREO same as > PAREU
PAREOS > PAREU
PARER > PARE
PARERA n New Zealand duck with grey-edged brown feathers
PARERGA > PARERGON
PARERGON n work that is not one's main employment
PARERS > PARE
PARES > PARE
PARESES > PARESIS
PARESIS n incomplete or slight paralysis of motor functions
PARETIC > PARESIS
PARETICS > PARESIS
PAREU n rectangle of fabric worn by Polynesians as a skirt or loincloth
PAREUS > PAREU
PAREV adj containing neither meat nor milk products and so fit for use

with either meat or milk dishes

**PAREVE** *same as* > PAREV

**PARFAIT** *n* dessert consisting of layers of ice cream, fruit, and sauce, topped with whipped cream, and served in a tall glass

**PARFAITS** > PARFAIT

**PARFLECHE** *n* sheet of rawhide that has been dried after soaking in lye and water to remove the hair

**PARFLESH** *same as* > PARFLECHE

**PARFOCAL** *adj* with focal points in the same plane

**PARGANA** *n* Indian subdistrict

**PARGANAS** > PARGANA

**PARGASITE** *n* dark green mineral

**PARGE** *vb* coat with plaster

**PARGED** > PARGE

**PARGES** > PARGE

**PARGET** *n* plaster, mortar, etc, used to line chimney flues or cover walls ▷ *vb* cover or decorate with parget

**PARGETED** > PARGET

**PARGETER** > PARGET

**PARGETERS** > PARGET

**PARGETING** *same as* > PARGET

**PARGETS** > PARGET

**PARGETTED** > PARGET

**PARGING** > PARGE

**PARGINGS** > PARGE

**PARGO** *n* sea bream

**PARGOS** > PARGO

**PARGYLINE** *n* monoamine oxidase inhibitor

**PARHELIA** > PARHELION

**PARHELIC** > PARHELION

**PARHELION** *n* one of several bright spots on the parhelic circle or solar halo

**PARHYPATE** *n* note in ancient Greek music

**PARIAH** *n* social outcast

**PARIAHS** > PARIAH

**PARIAL** *n* pair royal of playing cards

**PARIALS** > PARIAL

**PARIAN** *n* type of marble or porcelain

**PARIANS** > PARIAN

**PARIES** *n* wall of an organ or bodily cavity

**PARIETAL** *adj* of the walls of a body cavity such as the skull ▷ *n* parietal bone

**PARIETALS** > PARIETAL

**PARIETES** > PARIES

**PARING** *n* piece pared off

**PARINGS** > PARING

**PARIS** *n* type of herb

**PARISCHAN** *variant of* > PAROCHIN

**PARISES** > PARIS

**PARISH** *n* area that has its

own church and a priest or pastor

**PARISHAD** *n* Indian assembly

**PARISHADS** > PARISHAD

**PARISHEN** *n* member of parish

**PARISHENS** > PARISHEN

**PARISHES** > PARISH

**PARISON** *n* unshaped mass of glass before it is moulded into its final form

**PARISONS** > PARISON

**PARITIES** > PARITY

**PARITOR** *n* official who summons witnesses

**PARITORS** > PARITOR

**PARITY** *n* equality or equivalence

**PARK** *n* area of open land for recreational use by the public ▷ *vb* stop and leave (a vehicle) temporarily

**PARKA** *n* large waterproof jacket with a hood

**PARKADE** *n* building used as a car park

**PARKADES** > PARKADE

**PARKAS** > PARKA

**PARKED** > PARK

**PARKEE** *n* Eskimo outer garment

**PARKEES** > PARKEE

**PARKER** > PARK

**PARKERS** > PARK

**PARKETTE** *n* small public car park

**PARKETTES** > PARKETTE

**PARKI** *variant of* > PARKA

**PARKIE** *n* park keeper

**PARKIER** > PARKY

**PARKIES** > PARKIE

**PARKIEST** > PARKY

**PARKIN** *n* moist spicy ginger cake usually containing oatmeal

**PARKING** > PARK

**PARKINGS** > PARK

**PARKINS** > PARKIN

**PARKIS** > PARKI

**PARKISH** *adj* like a park

**PARKLAND** *n* grassland with scattered trees

**PARKLANDS** > PARKLAND

**PARKLIKE** > PARK

**PARKLY** *adj* having many parks or resembling a park

**PARKOUR** *n* sport of running in urban areas performing gymnastics on manmade obstacles

**PARKOURS** > PARKOUR

**PARKS** > PARK

**PARKWARD** *adv* towards a park

**PARKWARDS** *adv* towards a park

**PARKWAY** *n* (in the US and Canada) wide road planted with trees, turf, etc

**PARKWAYS** > PARKWAY

**PARKY** *adj* (of the weather) chilly

**PARLANCE** *n* particular way

of speaking, idiom

**PARLANCES** > PARLANCE

**PARLANDO** *adv* to be performed as though speaking

**PARLANTE** *same as* > PARLANDO

**PARLAY** *vb* stake (winnings from one bet) on a subsequent wager ▷ *n* bet in which winnings from one wager are staked on another, or a series of such bets

**PARLAYED** > PARLAY

**PARLAYING** > PARLAY

**PARLAYS** > PARLAY

**PARLE** *vb* speak

**PARLED** > PARLE

**PARLEMENT** *n* parliament

**PARLES** > PARLE

**PARLEY** *n* meeting between leaders or representatives of opposing forces to discuss terms ▷ *vb* have a parley

**PARLEYED** > PARLEY

**PARLEYER** > PARLEY

**PARLEYERS** > PARLEY

**PARLEYING** > PARLEY

**PARLEYS** > PARLEY

**PARLEYVOO** *vb* speak French ▷ *n* French language

**PARLIES** *pl n* small Scottish biscuits

**PARLING** > PARLE

**PARLOR** *same as* > PARLOUR

**PARLORS** > PARLOR

**PARLOUR** *n* living room for receiving visitors

**PARLOURS** > PARLOUR

**PARLOUS** *adj* dire ▷ *adv* extremely

**PARLOUSLY** > PARLOUS

**PARLY** *n* short form of parliament

**PARMESAN** *n* Italian hard cheese

**PARMESANS** > PARMESAN

**PAROCHIAL** *adj* narrow in outlook

**PAROCHIN** *n* old Scottish parish

**PAROCHINE** *same as* > PAROCHIN

**PAROCHINS** > PAROCHIN

**PARODIC** > PARODY

**PARODICAL** > PARODY

**PARODIED** > PARODY

**PARODIES** > PARODY

**PARODIST** > PARODY

**PARODISTS** > PARODY

**PARODOI** *n* path leading to Greek theatre

**PARODOS** *n* ode sung by Greek chorus

**PARODY** *n* exaggerated and amusing imitation of someone else's style ▷ *vb* make a parody of

**PARODYING** > PARODY

**PAROEMIA** *n* proverb

**PAROEMIAC** *adj* of proverbs

**PAROEMIAL** *adj* of proverbs

**PAROEMIAS** > PAROEMIA

**PAROICOUS** *same as* > PARECIOUS

**PAROL** *n* (formerly) pleadings in an action when presented by word of mouth ▷ *adj* (of a contract, lease, etc) made orally or in writing but not under seal

**PAROLABLE** > PAROLE

**PAROLE** *n* early freeing of a prisoner on condition that he or she behaves well ▷ *vb* put on parole

**PAROLED** > PAROLE

**PAROLEE** > PAROLE

**PAROLEES** > PAROLE

**PAROLES** > PAROLE

**PAROLING** > PAROLE

**PAROLS** > PAROL

**PARONYM** *n* cognate word

**PARONYMIC** > PARONYM

**PARONYMS** > PARONYM

**PARONYMY** > PARONYM

**PAROQUET** *n* small longtailed parrot

**PAROQUETS** > PARROQUET

**PARORE** *n* type of fish found around Australia and New Zealand

**PAROSMIA** *n* any disorder of the sense of smell

**PAROSMIAS** > PAROSMIA

**PAROTIC** *adj* situated near the ear

**PAROTID** *adj* relating to or situated near the parotid gland ▷ *n* parotid gland

**PAROTIDS** > PAROTID

**PAROTIS** *n* parotid gland

**PAROTISES** > PAROTIS

**PAROTITIC** > PAROTITIS

**PAROTITIS** *n* inflammation of the parotid gland

**PAROTOID** *n* any of various warty poison glands on the head and back of certain toads and salamanders ▷ *adj* resembling a parotid gland

**PAROTOIDS** > PAROTOID

**PAROUS** *adj* having given birth

**PAROUSIA** *n* Second Coming

**PAROUSIAS** > PAROUSIA

**PAROXYSM** *n* uncontrollable outburst of rage, delight, etc

**PAROXYSMS** > PAROXYSM

**PARP** *vb* make a honking sound

**PARPANE** *n* parapet on bridge

**PARPANES** > PARPANE

**PARPED** > PARP

**PARPEN** *same as* > PARPEND

**PARPEND** *same as* > PERPEND

**PARPENDS** > PARPEND

**PARPENS** > PARPEN

**PARPENT** *n* parapet on

bridge

**PARPENTS** > PARPENT

**PARPING** > PARP

**PARPOINT** n parapet on bridge

**PARPOINTS** > PARPOINT

**PARPS** > PARP

**PARQUET** n floor covering made of wooden blocks arranged in a geometric pattern ▷ vb cover with parquet

**PARQUETED** > PARQUET

**PARQUETRY** n pieces of wood arranged in a geometric pattern, used to cover floors

**PARQUETS** > PARQUET

**PARR** n salmon up to two years of age

**PARRA** n tourist or non-resident on a beach

**PARRAKEET** same as > PARAKEET

**PARRAL** same as > PARREL

**PARRALS** > PARRAL

**PARRAS** > PARRA

**PARRED** > PAR

**PARREL** n ring that holds the jaws of a boom to the mast but lets it slide up and down

**PARRELS** > PARREL

**PARRHESIA** n boldness of speech

**PARRICIDE** n crime of killing either of one's parents

**PARRIDGE** Scottish variant of > PORRIDGE

**PARRIDGES** > PARRIDGE

**PARRIED** > PARRY

**PARRIER** > PARRY

**PARRIERS** > PARRY

**PARRIES** > PARRY

**PARRING** > PAR

**PARRITCH** Scottish variant of > PORRIDGE

**PARROCK** vb put (an animal) in a small field

**PARROCKED** > PARROCK

**PARROCKS** > PARROCK

**PARROKET** n small long-tailed parrot

**PARROKETS** > PARROKET

**PARROQUET** n small long-tailed parrot

**PARROT** n tropical bird with a short hooked beak and an ability to imitate human speech ▷ vb repeat (someone else's words) without thinking

**PARROTED** > PARROT

**PARROTER** n person who repeats what is said

**PARROTERS** > PARROTER

**PARROTING** > PARROT

**PARROTRY** > PARROT

**PARROTS** > PARROT

**PARROTY** adj like a parrot; chattering

**PARRS** > PARR

**PARRY** vb ward off (an

attack) ▷ n parrying

**PARRYING** > PARRY

**PARS** > PAR

**PARSABLE** > PARSE

**PARSE** vb analyse (a sentence) in terms of grammar

**PARSEC** n unit of astronomical distance

**PARSECS** > PARSEC

**PARSED** > PARSE

**PARSER** n program or part of a program that interprets input to a computer by recognizing key words or analysing sentence structure

**PARSERS** > PARSER

**PARSES** > PARSE

**PARSIMONY** n extreme caution in spending money

**PARSING** > PARSE

**PARSINGS** > PARSE

**PARSLEY** n herb used for seasoning and decorating food ▷ vb garnish with parsley

**PARSLEYED** > PARSLEY

**PARSLEYS** > PARSLEY

**PARSLIED** > PARSLEY

**PARSNEP** same as > PARSNIP

**PARSNEPS** > PARSNEP

**PARSNIP** n long tapering cream-coloured root vegetable

**PARSNIPS** > PARSNIP

**PARSON** n Anglican parish priest

**PARSONAGE** n parson's house

**PARSONIC** > PARSON

**PARSONISH** adj like a parson

**PARSONS** > PARSON

**PART** n one of the pieces that make up a whole ▷ vb divide or separate

**PARTAKE** vb take (food or drink)

**PARTAKEN** > PARTAKE

**PARTAKER** > PARTAKE

**PARTAKERS** > PARTAKE

**PARTAKES** > PARTAKE

**PARTAKING** > PARTAKE

**PARTAN** Scottish word for > CRAB

**PARTANS** > PARTAN

**PARTED** adj divided almost to the base

**PARTER** n thing that parts

**PARTERRE** n formally patterned flower garden

**PARTERRES** > PARTERRE

**PARTERS** > PARTER

**PARTI** n concept of architectural design

**PARTIAL** adj not complete ▷ n any of the component tones of a single musical sound, including both those that belong to the harmonic series of the sound and those that do

not

**PARTIALLY** > PARTIAL

**PARTIALS** > PARTIAL

**PARTIBLE** adj (esp of property or an inheritance) divisible

**PARTICLE** n extremely small piece or amount

**PARTICLES** > PARTICLE

**PARTIED** > PARTY

**PARTIER** n person who parties

**PARTIERS** > PARTIER

**PARTIES** > PARTY

**PARTIM** adv in part

**PARTING** same as > PART

**PARTINGS** > PARTING

**PARTIS** > PARTI

**PARTISAN** n strong supporter of a party or group ▷ adj prejudiced or one-sided

**PARTISANS** > PARTISAN

**PARTITA** n type of suite

**PARTITAS** > PARTITA

**PARTITE** adj composed of or divided into a specified number of parts

**PARTITION** n screen or thin wall that divides a room ▷ vb divide with a partition

**PARTITIVE** adj (of a noun) referring to part of something ▷ n partitive word, such as some or any

**PARTITURA** n music score for several parts

**PARTIZAN** same as > PARTISAN

**PARTIZANS** > PARTIZAN

**PARTLET** n woman's garment covering the neck and shoulders

**PARTLETS** > PARTLET

**PARTLY** adv not completely

**PARTNER** n either member of a couple in a relationship or activity ▷ vb be the partner of

**PARTNERED** > PARTNER

**PARTNERS** > PARTNER

**PARTON** n hypothetical elementary particle postulated as a constituent of neutrons and protons

**PARTONS** > PARTON

**PARTOOK** > PARTAKE

**PARTRIDGE** n game bird of the grouse family

**PARTS** pl n abilities or talents

**PARTURE** n departure

**PARTURES** > PARTURE

**PARTWAY** adv some of the way

**PARTWORK** n series of magazines issued at weekly or monthly intervals, which are designed to be bound together to form a complete course or book

**PARTWORKS** > PARTWORK

**PARTY** n social gathering for pleasure ▷ vb celebrate, have fun ▷ adj (of a shield) divided vertically into two colours, metals, or furs

**PARTYER** n person who parties

**PARTYERS** > PARTYER

**PARTYGOER** n person who goes to party

**PARTYING** > PARTY

**PARTYISM** n devotion to political party

**PARTYISMS** > PARTYISM

**PARULIDES** > PARULIS

**PARULIS** another name for > GUMBOIL

**PARULISES** > PARULIS

**PARURA** same as > PARURE

**PARURAS** > PARURA

**PARURE** n set of jewels or other ornaments

**PARURES** > PARURE

**PARVE** same as > PAREV

**PARVENU** n person newly risen to a position of power or wealth ▷ adj of or characteristic of a parvenu

**PARVENUE** n woman who, having risen socially or economically, is considered to be an upstart or to lack the appropriate refinement for her new position ▷ adj of or characteristic of a parvenue

**PARVENUES** > PARVENUE

**PARVENUS** > PARVENU

**PARVIS** n court or portico in front of a building, esp a church

**PARVISE** same as > PARVIS

**PARVISES** > PARVISE

**PARVO** n disease of cattle and dogs

**PARVOLIN** n substance resulting from the putrefaction of flesh

**PARVOLINE** n liquid derived from coal tar

**PARVOLINS** > PARVOLIN

**PARVOS** > PARVO

**PAS** n dance steps or movement, esp in ballet

**PASCAL** n unit of pressure

**PASCALS** > PASCAL

**PASCHAL** adj of the Passover or Easter ▷ n Passover or Easter

**PASCHALS** > PASCHAL

**PASCUAL** adj relating to pasture

**PASE** n movement of the cape or muleta by a matador to attract the bull's attention and guide its attack

**PASEAR** vb go for a rambling walk

**PASEARED** > PASEAR

PASEARING > PASEAR
PASEARS > PASEAR
PASEO n bullfighters' procession
PASEOS > PASEO
PASES > PASE
PASH n infatuation ▷ vb throw or be thrown and break or be broken to bits
PASHA n high official of the Ottoman Empire
PASHADOM n territory of a pasha
PASHADOMS > PASHADOM
PASHALIC same as > PASHALIK
PASHALICS > PASHALIC
PASHALIK n province or jurisdiction of a pasha
PASHALIKS > PASHALIK
PASHAS > PASHA
PASHED > PASH
PASHES > PASH
PASHIM same as > PASHM
PASHIMS > PASHM
PASHING > PASH
PASHKA n rich Russian dessert made of cottage cheese, cream, almonds, currants, etc
PASHKAS > PASHKA
PASHM n underfur of various Tibetan animals, esp goats, used for cashmere shawls
PASHMINA n type of cashmere scarf or shawl made from the underfur of Tibetan goats
PASHMINAS > PASHMINA
PASHMS > PASHM
PASODOBLE n fast modern ballroom dance
PASPALUM n type of grass with wide leaves
PASPALUMS > PASPALUM
PASPIES > PASPY
PASPY n piece of music in triple time
PASQUIL n abusive lampoon or satire ▷ vb ridicule with pasquil
PASQUILER n person who lampoons
PASQUILS > PASQUIL
PASS vb go by, past, or through ▷ n successful result in a test or examination
PASSABLE adj (just) acceptable
PASSABLY adv fairly
PASSADE n act of moving back and forth in the same place
PASSADES > PASSADE
PASSADO n forward thrust with sword
PASSADOES > PASSADO
PASSADOS > PASSADO
PASSAGE n channel or opening providing a way through ▷ vb move or cause to move at a passage

PASSAGED > PASSAGE
PASSAGER as in passager hawk young hawk or falcon caught while on migration
PASSAGES > PASSAGE
PASSAGING > PASSAGE
PASSALONG adj (of plants) easily propagated and given to others
PASSAMENT vb sew border on garment
PASSANT adj (of a beast) walking, with the right foreleg raised
PASSATA n sauce made from sieved tomatoes, often used in Italian cookery
PASSATAS > PASSATA
PASSBAND n band of frequencies that is transmitted with maximum efficiency through a circuit, filter, etc
PASSBANDS > PASSBAND
PASSBOOK n book issued by a bank or building society for keeping a record of deposits and withdrawals
PASSBOOKS > PASSBOOK
PASSE adj out-of-date
PASSED > PASS
PASSEE adj out of fashion
PASSEL n group or quantity of no fixed number
PASSELS > PASSEL
PASSEMENT vb sew border on garment
PASSENGER n person travelling in a vehicle driven by someone else
PASSEPIED n lively minuet of Breton origin
PASSER n person or thing that passes
PASSERBY n person that is passing or going by, esp on foot
PASSERINE adj belonging to the order of perching birds ▷ n any bird of this order
PASSERS > PASSER
PASSERSBY > PASSERBY
PASSES > PASS
PASSIBLE adj susceptible to emotion or suffering
PASSIBLY > PASSIBLE
PASSIM adv everywhere, throughout
PASSING adj brief or transitory ▷ n death
PASSINGLY > PASSING
PASSINGS > PASSING
PASSION n intense sexual love ▷ vb give passionate character to
PASSIONAL adj of, relating to, or due to passion or the passions ▷ n book recounting the sufferings of Christian martyrs or saints

PASSIONED > PASSION
PASSIONS > PASSION
PASSIVATE vb render (a metal) less susceptible to corrosion by coating the surface with a substance, such as an oxide
PASSIVE adj not playing an active part ▷ n passive form of a verb
PASSIVELY > PASSIVE
PASSIVES > PASSIVE
PASSIVISM n theory, belief, or practice of passive resistance
PASSIVIST > PASSIVISM
PASSIVITY > PASSIVE
PASSKEY n private key
PASSKEYS > PASSKEY
PASSLESS adj having no pass
PASSMAN n student who passes without honours
PASSMEN > PASSMAN
PASSMENT same as > PASSEMENT
PASSMENTS > PASSMENT
PASSOUT n (in ice hockey) pass by an attacking player from behind the opposition goal line
PASSOUTS > PASSOUT
PASSOVER n lamb eaten during Passover
PASSOVERS > PASSOVER
PASSPORT n official document of nationality granting permission to travel abroad
PASSPORTS > PASSPORT
PASSUS n (esp in medieval literature) division or section of a poem, story, etc
PASSUSES > PASSUS
PASSWORD n secret word or phrase that ensures admission
PASSWORDS > PASSWORD
PAST adj of the time before the present ▷ n period of time before the present ▷ adv ago ▷ prep beyond
PASTA n type of food, such as spaghetti, that is made in different shapes from flour and water
PASTALIKE > PASTA
PASTANCE n activity that passes time
PASTANCES > PASTANCE
PASTAS > PASTA
PASTE n moist soft mixture, such as toothpaste ▷ vb fasten with paste
PASTED > PASTE
PASTEDOWN n portion of endpaper pasted to cover of book
PASTEL n coloured chalk crayon for drawing ▷ adj pale and delicate in colour
PASTELIST > PASTEL

PASTELS > PASTEL
PASTER n person or thing that pastes
PASTERN n part of a horse's foot between the fetlock and the hoof
PASTERNS > PASTERN
PASTERS > PASTER
PASTES > PASTE
PASTEUP n assembly of typeset matter, illustrations, etc, pasted on a sheet of paper or board
PASTEUPS > PASTEUP
PASTICCI > PASTICCIO
PASTICCIO n art work borrowing various styles
PASTICHE n work of art that mixes styles or copies the style of another artist
PASTICHES > PASTICHE
PASTIE n decorative cover for nipple
PASTIER > PASTY
PASTIES > PASTY
PASTIEST > PASTY
PASTIL same as > PASTILLE
PASTILLE n small fruit-flavoured and sometimes medicated sweet
PASTILLES > PASTILLE
PASTILS > PASTIL
PASTILY > PASTY
PASTIME n activity that makes time pass pleasantly
PASTIMES > PASTIME
PASTINA n small pieces of pasta
PASTINAS > PASTINA
PASTINESS > PASTY
PASTING n heavy defeat
PASTINGS > PASTING
PASTIS n anise-flavoured alcoholic drink
PASTISES > PASTIS
PASTITSIO n Greek dish consisting of minced meat and macaroni topped with bechamel sauce
PASTITSO n Greek dish of baked pasta
PASTITSOS > PASTITSO
PASTLESS adj having no past
PASTNESS n quality of being past
PASTOR n member of the clergy in charge of a congregation ▷ vb act as a pastor
PASTORAL adj of or depicting country life ▷ n poem or picture portraying country life
PASTORALE n musical composition that suggests country life
PASTORALI > PASTORALE
PASTORALS > PASTORAL
PASTORATE n office or term of office of a pastor
PASTORED > PASTOR

PASTORING > PASTOR
PASTORIUM n residence of pastor
PASTORLY > PASTOR
PASTORS > PASTOR
PASTRAMI n highly seasoned smoked beef
PASTRAMIS > PASTRAMI
PASTRIES > PASTRY
PASTROMI same as > PASTRAMI
PASTROMIS > PASTROMI
PASTRY n baking dough made of flour, fat, and water
PASTS > PAST
PASTURAGE n business of grazing cattle
PASTURAL adj of pasture
PASTURE n grassy land for farm animals to graze on ▷ vb cause (livestock) to graze or (of livestock) to graze (a pasture)
PASTURED > PASTURE
PASTURER n person who tends cattle
PASTURERS > PASTURER
PASTURES > PASTURE
PASTURING > PASTURE
PASTY adj (of a complexion) pale and unhealthy ▷ n round of pastry folded over a savoury filling
PAT vb tap lightly ▷ n gentle tap or stroke ▷ adj quick, ready, or glib
PATACA n monetary unit of Macao
PATACAS > PATACA
PATAGIA > PATAGIUM
PATAGIAL > PATAGIUM
PATAGIUM n web of skin between the neck, limbs, and tail in bats and gliding mammals that functions as a wing
PATAKA n building on stilts, used for storing provisions
PATAMAR n type of boat
PATAMARS > PATAMAR
PATBALL n game like squash but using hands instead of rackets
PATBALLS > PATBALL
PATCH n piece of material sewn on a garment ▷ vb mend with a patch
PATCHABLE > PATCH
PATCHED > PATCH
PATCHER > PATCH
PATCHERS > PATCH
PATCHERY n bungling work
PATCHES > PATCH
PATCHIER > PATCHY
PATCHIEST > PATCHY
PATCHILY > PATCHY
PATCHING > PATCH
PATCHINGS > PATCH
PATCHOCKE Spenserian word for > CLOWN
PATCHOULI n Asiatic tree, the leaves of which yield a heavy fragrant oil

PATCHOULY same as > PATCHOULI
PATCHWORK n needlework made of pieces of different materials sewn together
PATCHY adj of uneven quality or intensity
PATE n head
PATED > PATE
PATELA n flat-bottomed Indian river boat
PATELAS > PATELA
PATELLA n kneecap
PATELLAE > PATELLA
PATELLAR > PATELLA
PATELLAS > PATELLA
PATELLATE adj having the shape of a patella
PATEN n plate, usually made of silver or gold, used for the bread at Communion
PATENCIES > PATENCY
PATENCY n condition of being obvious
PATENS > PATEN
PATENT n document giving the exclusive right to make or sell an invention ▷ adj open to public inspection ▷ vb obtain a patent for
PATENTED > PATENT
PATENTEE n person, group, company, etc, that has been granted a patent
PATENTEES > PATENTEE
PATENTING > PATENT
PATENTLY adv obviously
PATENTOR n person who or official body that grants a patent or patents
PATENTORS > PATENTOR
PATENTS > PATENT
PATER n father
PATERA n shallow ancient Roman bowl
PATERAE > PATERA
PATERCOVE n fraudulent priest
PATERERO n type of cannon
PATEREROS > PATERERO
PATERNAL adj fatherly
PATERNITY n fact or state of being a father
PATERS > PATER
PATES > PATE
PATH n surfaced walk or track ▷ vb make a path
PATHED > PATH
PATHETIC adj causing feelings of pity or sadness ▷ pl n pathetic sentiments ▷ n pathetic person
PATHETICS > PATHETIC
PATHIC n catamite ▷ adj of or relating to a catamite
PATHICS > PATHIC
PATHING > PATH
PATHLESS > PATH
PATHNAME n name of a file or directory together with its position in relation to other directories traced back in a line to the root

PATHNAMES > PATHNAME
PATHOGEN n thing that causes disease
PATHOGENE same as > PATHOGEN
PATHOGENS > PATHOGEN
PATHOGENY n origin, development, and resultant effects of a disease
PATHOLOGY n scientific study of diseases
PATHOS n power of arousing pity or sadness
PATHOSES > PATHOS
PATHS > PATH
PATHWAY n path
PATHWAYS > PATHWAY
PATIBLE adj endurable
PATIENCE n quality of being patient
PATIENCES > PATIENCE
PATIENT adj enduring difficulties or delays calmly ▷ n person receiving medical treatment ▷ vb make calm
PATIENTED > PATIENT
PATIENTER > PATIENT
PATIENTLY > PATIENT
PATIENTS > PATIENT
PATIKI n New Zealand sand flounder or dab
PATIN same as > PATEN
PATINA n fine layer on a surface
PATINAE > PATINA
PATINAED adj having a patina
PATINAS > PATINA
PATINATE vb coat with patina
PATINATED > PATINATE
PATINATES > PATINATE
PATINE vb cover with patina
PATINED > PATINE
PATINES > PATINE
PATINING > PATINE
PATINISE same as > PATINIZE
PATINISED > PATINISE
PATINISES > PATINISE
PATINIZE vb coat with patina
PATINIZED > PATINIZE
PATINIZES > PATINIZE
PATINS > PATIN
PATIO n paved area adjoining a house
PATIOS > PATIO
PATISSIER n pastry chef
PATLY adv fitly
PATNESS n appropriateness
PATNESSES > PATNESS
PATOIS n regional dialect, esp of French
PATONCE adj (of cross) with limbs which broaden from centre
PATOOTIE n person's bottom
PATOOTIES > PATOOTIE

PATRIAL n (in Britain, formerly) person with a right by statute to live in the United Kingdom, and so not subject to immigration control
PATRIALS > PATRIAL
PATRIARCH n male head of a family or tribe
PATRIATE vb bring under the authority of an autonomous country
PATRIATED > PATRIATE
PATRIATES > PATRIATE
PATRICIAN n member of the nobility ▷ adj of noble birth
PATRICIDE n crime of killing one's father
PATRICK n former Irish coin
PATRICKS > PATRICK
PATRICO n fraudulent priest
PATRICOES > PATRICO
PATRILINY n tracing of family descent through males
PATRIMONY n property inherited from ancestors
PATRIOT n person who loves his or her country and supports its interests
PATRIOTIC > PATRIOT
PATRIOTS > PATRIOT
PATRISTIC adj of or relating to the Fathers of the Church, their writings, or the study of these
PATROL n regular circuit by a guard ▷ vb go round on guard, or reconnoitring
PATROLLED > PATROL
PATROLLER > PATROL
PATROLMAN n man, esp a policeman, who patrols a certain area
PATROLMEN > PATROLMAN
PATROLOGY n study of the writings of the Fathers of the Church
PATROLS > PATROL
PATRON n person who gives financial support to charities, artists, etc
PATRONAGE n support given by a patron
PATRONAL > PATRONESS
PATRONESS n woman who sponsors or aids artists, charities, etc
PATRONISE same as > PATRONIZE
PATRONIZE vb treat in a condescending way
PATRONLY > PATRONESS
PATRONNE n woman who owns or manages a hotel, restaurant, or bar
PATRONNES > PATRONNE
PATRONS > PATRON
PATROON n Dutch land-holder in New Netherland and New York with

manorial rights in the colonial era
PATROONS > PATROON
PATS > PAT
PATSIES > PATSY
PATSY n person who is easily cheated, victimized, etc
PATTAMAR n Indian courier
PATTAMARS > PATTAMAR
PATTE n band keeping belt in place
PATTED > PAT
PATTEE adj (of a cross) having triangular arms widening outwards
PATTEN n wooden clog or sandal on a raised wooden platform or metal ring ▷ vb wear pattens
PATTENED > PATTEN
PATTENING > PATTEN
PATTENS > PATTEN
PATTER vb make repeated soft tapping sounds ▷ n quick succession of taps
PATTERED > PATTER
PATTERER > PATTER
PATTERERS > PATTER
PATTERING > PATTER
PATTERN n arrangement of repeated parts or decorative designs ▷ vb model
PATTERNED > PATTERN
PATTERNS > PATTERN
PATTERS > PATTER
PATTES > PATTE
PATTIE same as > PATTY
PATTIES > PATTY
PATTING > PAT
PATTLE dialect for > PADDLE
PATTLES > PATTLE
PATTY n small flattened cake of minced food
PATTYPAN n small round flattish squash
PATTYPANS > PATTYPAN
PATU n short Māori club, now used ceremonially
PATULENT adj spreading widely
PATULIN n toxic antibiotic
PATULINS > PATULIN
PATULOUS adj spreading widely or expanded
PATUS > PATU
PATUTUKI n blue cod
PATUTUKIS > PATUTUKI
PATY adj (of cross) having arms of equal length
PATZER n novice chess player
PATZERS > PATZER
PAUA n edible shellfish of New Zealand, which has a pearly shell used for jewellery
PAUAS > PAUA
PAUCAL n grammatical number occurring in some languages for words in contexts where a few of their referents

are described or referred to ▷ adj relating to or inflected for this number
PAUCALS > PAUCAL
PAUCITIES > PAUCITY
PAUCITY n scarcity
PAUGHTIER > PAUGHTY
PAUGHTY Scots word for > HAUGHTY
PAUL same as > PAWL
PAULDRON n either of two metal plates worn with armour to protect the shoulders
PAULDRONS > PAULDRON
PAULIN n tarpaulin
PAULINS > PAULIN
PAULOWNIA n Japanese tree with large heart-shaped leaves and clusters of purplish or white flowers
PAULS > PAUL
PAUNCE n pansy
PAUNCES > PAUNCE
PAUNCH n protruding belly ▷ vb stab in the stomach
PAUNCHED > PAUNCH
PAUNCHES > PAUNCH
PAUNCHIER > PAUNCHY
PAUNCHING > PAUNCH
PAUNCHY adj having a protruding belly or abdomen
PAUPER n very poor person ▷ vb reduce to beggary
PAUPERED > PAUPER
PAUPERESS n female pauper
PAUPERING > PAUPER
PAUPERISE same as > PAUPERIZE
PAUPERISM > PAUPER
PAUPERIZE vb make a pauper of
PAUPERS > PAUPER
PAUPIETTE n rolled stuffed fish or meat
PAUROPOD n minute myriapod
PAUROPODS > PAUROPOD
PAUSAL > PAUSE
PAUSE vb stop for a time ▷ n stop or rest in speech or action
PAUSED > PAUSE
PAUSEFUL adj taking pauses
PAUSELESS adj without pauses
PAUSER > PAUSE
PAUSERS > PAUSE
PAUSES > PAUSE
PAUSING > PAUSE
PAUSINGLY adv with pauses
PAUSINGS > PAUSE
PAV short for > PAVLOVA
PAVAGE n tax towards paving streets, or the right to levy such a tax
PAVAGES > PAVAGE
PAVAN same as > PAVANE
PAVANE n slow and stately dance of the 16th and 17th

centuries
PAVANES > PAVANE
PAVANS > PAVAN
PAVE vb form (a surface) with stone or brick ▷ n paved surface, esp an uneven one
PAVED > PAVE
PAVEED adj (of jewels) set close together
PAVEMENT n paved path for pedestrians ▷ vb provide with pavement
PAVEMENTS > PAVEMENT
PAVEN same as > PAVANE
PAVENS > PAVEN
PAVER > PAVE
PAVERS > PAVE
PAVES > PAVE
PAVID adj fearful
PAVILION n building on a playing field etc ▷ vb place or set in or as if in a pavilion
PAVILIONS > PAVILION
PAVILLON n bell of wind instrument
PAVILLONS > PAVILLON
PAVIN same as > PAVANE
PAVING n paved surface ▷ adj of or for a paved surface or pavement
PAVINGS > PAVING
PAVINS > PAVIN
PAVIOR same as > PAVIOUR
PAVIORS > PAVIOR
PAVIOUR n person who lays paving
PAVIOURS > PAVIOUR
PAVIS n large square shield, developed in the 15th century, at first portable but later heavy and set up in a permanent position
PAVISE same as > PAVIS
PAVISER n soldier holding pavise
PAVISERS > PAVISER
PAVISES > PAVISE
PAVISSE same as > PAVIS
PAVISSES > PAVISSE
PAVLOVA n meringue cake topped with whipped cream and fruit
PAVLOVAS > PAVLOVA
PAVONAZZO n white Italian marble
PAVONE n peacock
PAVONES > PAVONE
PAVONIAN same as > PAVONINE
PAVONINE adj of or resembling a peacock or the colours, design, or iridescence of a peacock's tail
PAVS > PAV
PAW n animal's foot with claws and pads ▷ vb scrape with the paw or hoof
PAWA old word for > PEACOCK
PAWAS > PAWA

PAWAW vb recite N American incantation
PAWAWED > PAWAW
PAWAWING > PAWAW
PAWAWS > PAWAW
PAWED > PAW
PAWER n person or animal that paws
PAWERS > PAWER
PAWING > PAW
PAWK Scots word for > TRICK
PAWKIER > PAWKY
PAWKIEST > PAWKY
PAWKILY > PAWKY
PAWKINESS > PAWKY
PAWKS > PAWK
PAWKY adj having or characterized by a dry wit
PAWL n pivoted lever shaped to engage with a ratchet to prevent motion in a particular direction
PAWLS > PAWL
PAWN vb deposit (an article) as security for money borrowed ▷ n chessman of the lowest value
PAWNABLE > PAWN
PAWNAGE > PAWN
PAWNAGES > PAWN
PAWNCE old word for > PANSY
PAWNCES > PAWNCE
PAWNED > PAWN
PAWNEE n one who accepts goods in pawn
PAWNEES > PAWNEE
PAWNER n one who pawns his or her possessions
PAWNERS > PAWNER
PAWNING > PAWN
PAWNOR same as > PAWNER
PAWNORS > PAWNOR
PAWNS > PAWN
PAWNSHOP n premises of a pawnbroker
PAWNSHOPS > PAWNSHOP
PAWPAW same as > PAPAW
PAWPAWS > PAWPAW
PAWS > PAW
PAX n kiss of peace ▷ interj call signalling a desire to end hostilities
PAXES > PAX
PAXIUBA n tropical tree
PAXIUBAS > PAXIUBA
PAXWAX n strong ligament in the neck of many mammals, which supports the head
PAXWAXES > PAXWAX
PAY vb give money etc in return for goods or services ▷ n wages or salary
PAYABLE adj due to be paid
PAYABLES n debts to be paid
PAYABLY > PAYABLE
PAYBACK n return on an investment
PAYBACKS > PAYBACK
PAYCHECK n payment for work done
PAYCHECKS > PAYCHECK

551

**PAYDAY** n day on which wages or salaries are paid
**PAYDAYS** > PAYDAY
**PAYED** > PAY
**PAYEE** n person to whom money is paid or due
**PAYEES** > PAYEE
**PAYER** n person who pays
**PAYERS** > PAYER
**PAYFONE** US spelling of > PAYPHONE
**PAYFONES** > PAYFONE
**PAYGRADE** n military rank
**PAYGRADES** > PAYGRADE
**PAYING** > PAY
**PAYINGS** > PAY
**PAYLOAD** n passengers or cargo of an aircraft
**PAYLOADS** > PAYLOAD
**PAYMASTER** n official responsible for the payment of wages and salaries
**PAYMENT** n act of paying
**PAYMENTS** > PAYMENT
**PAYNIM** n heathen or pagan
**PAYNIMRY** n state of being heathen
**PAYNIMS** > PAYNIM
**PAYOFF** n final settlement, esp in retribution
**PAYOFFS** > PAYOFF
**PAYOLA** n bribe to get special treatment, esp to promote a commercial product
**PAYOLAS** > PAYOLA
**PAYOR** same as > PAYER
**PAYORS** > PAYOR
**PAYOUT** n sum of money paid out
**PAYOUTS** > PAYOUT
**PAYPHONE** n coin-operated telephone
**PAYPHONES** > PAYPHONE
**PAYROLL** n list of employees who receive regular pay ▷ vb employ
**PAYROLLED** > PAYROLL
**PAYROLLS** > PAYROLL
**PAYS** > PAY
**PAYSAGE** n landscape
**PAYSAGES** > PAYSAGE
**PAYSAGIST** n painter of landscapes
**PAYSD** Spenserian form of > POISED
**PAYSLIP** n note of payment given to employee
**PAYSLIPS** > PAYSLIP
**PAZAZZ** same as > PIZZAZZ
**PAZAZZES** > PAZAZZ
**PAZZAZZ** same as > PIZZAZZ
**PAZZAZZES** > PAZZAZZ
**PE** n 17th letter in the Hebrew alphabet
**PEA** n climbing plant with seeds growing in pods
**PEABERRY** n coffee berry containing one seed
**PEACE** n calm, quietness
**PEACEABLE** adj inclined towards peace

**PEACEABLY** > PEACEABLE
**PEACED** > PEACE
**PEACEFUL** adj not in a state of war or disagreement
**PEACELESS** adj without peace
**PEACENIK** n activist who opposes war
**PEACENIKS** > PEACENIK
**PEACES** > PEACE
**PEACETIME** n period without war
**PEACH** n soft juicy fruit with a stone and a downy skin ▷ adj pinkish-orange ▷ vb inform against an accomplice
**PEACHBLOW** n type of glaze on porcelain
**PEACHED** > PEACH
**PEACHER** > PEACH
**PEACHERS** > PEACH
**PEACHES** > PEACH
**PEACHIER** > PEACHY
**PEACHIEST** > PEACHY
**PEACHILY** > PEACHY
**PEACHING** > PEACH
**PEACHY** adj of or like a peach, esp in colour or texture
**PEACING** > PEACE
**PEACOAT** n woollen jacket
**PEACOATS** > PEACOAT
**PEACOCK** n large male bird with a brilliantly coloured fanlike tail ▷ vb display (oneself) proudly
**PEACOCKED** > PEACOCK
**PEACOCKS** > PEACOCK
**PEACOCKY** > PEACOCK
**PEACOD** same as > PEASCOD
**PEACODS** > PEACOD
**PEAFOWL** n peacock or peahen
**PEAFOWLS** > PEAFOWL
**PEAG** n (formerly) money used by North American Indians, made of cylindrical shells strung or woven together
**PEAGE** same as > PEAG
**PEAGES** > PEAGE
**PEAGS** > PEAG
**PEAHEN** > PEACOCK
**PEAHENS** > PEACOCK
**PEAK** n pointed top, esp of a mountain ▷ vb form or reach a peak ▷ adj of or at the point of greatest demand
**PEAKED** adj having a peak
**PEAKIER** > PEAK
**PEAKIEST** > PEAK
**PEAKING** > PEAK
**PEAKISH** adj sickly
**PEAKLESS** > PEAK
**PEAKLIKE** > PEAK
**PEAKS** > PEAK
**PEAKY** > PEAK
**PEAL** n long loud echoing sound, esp of bells or thunder ▷ vb sound with a peal or peals
**PEALED** > PEAL

**PEALIKE** > PEA
**PEALING** > PEAL
**PEALS** > PEAL
**PEAN** n paean ▷ vb deliver a pean
**PEANED** > PEAN
**PEANING** > PEAN
**PEANS** > PEAN
**PEANUT** n pea-shaped nut that ripens underground
**PEANUTS** > PEANUT
**PEAPOD** n pod of the pea plant
**PEAPODS** > PEAPOD
**PEAR** n sweet juicy fruit with a narrow top and rounded base
**PEARCE** old spelling of > PIERCE
**PEARCED** > PEARCE
**PEARCES** > PEARCE
**PEARCING** > PEARCE
**PEARE** obsolete spelling of > PEAR
**PEARES** > PEARE
**PEARL** same as > PURL
**PEARLASH** n granular crystalline form of potassium carbonate
**PEARLED** > PEARL
**PEARLER** n person who dives for or trades in pearls ▷ adj excellent
**PEARLERS** > PEARLER
**PEARLIER** > PEARLY
**PEARLIES** > PEARLY
**PEARLIEST** > PEARLY
**PEARLIN** n type of lace used to trim clothes
**PEARLING** > PEARL
**PEARLINGS** > PEARL
**PEARLINS** n type of lace
**PEARLISED** same as > PEARLIZED
**PEARLITE** same as > PERLITE
**PEARLITES** > PEARLITE
**PEARLITIC** > PEARLITE
**PEARLIZED** adj having or given a pearly lustre
**PEARLS** > PEARL
**PEARLWORT** n plant with small white flowers that are spherical in bud
**PEARLY** adj resembling a pearl, esp in lustre ▷ n London costermonger who wears on ceremonial occasions a traditional dress of dark clothes covered with pearl buttons
**PEARMAIN** n any of several varieties of apple having a red skin
**PEARMAINS** > PEARMAIN
**PEARS** > PEAR
**PEARST** archaic variant of > PIERCED
**PEART** adj lively
**PEARTER** > PEART
**PEARTEST** > PEART
**PEARTLY** > PEART
**PEARTNESS** > PEART
**PEARWOOD** n wood from pear tree

**PEARWOODS** > PEARWOOD
**PEAS** > PEA
**PEASANT** n person working on the land, esp in poorer countries or in the past
**PEASANTRY** n peasants collectively
**PEASANTS** > PEASANT
**PEASANTY** adj having qualities ascribed to traditional country life or people
**PEASCOD** same as > COD
**PEASCODS** > PEASCOD
**PEASE** n archaic or dialect word for pea ▷ vb appease
**PEASECOD** n pod of a pea plant
**PEASECODS** > PEASECOD
**PEASED** > PEASE
**PEASEN** obsolete plural of > PEASE
**PEASES** > PEASE
**PEASING** > PEASE
**PEASON** obsolete plural of > PEASE
**PEASOUPER** n thick fog
**PEAT** n decayed vegetable material found in bogs, used as fertilizer or fuel
**PEATARIES** > PEATARY
**PEATARY** n area covered with peat
**PEATERIES** > PEATERY
**PEATERY** same as > PEATARY
**PEATIER** > PEAT
**PEATIEST** > PEAT
**PEATLAND** n area of land consisting of peat bogs, usually containing many species of flora and fauna
**PEATLANDS** > PEATLAND
**PEATMAN** n person who collects peat
**PEATMEN** > PEATMAN
**PEATS** > PEAT
**PEATSHIP** n ship carrying peat
**PEATSHIPS** > PEATSHIP
**PEATY** > PEAT
**PEAVEY** n wooden lever with a metal pointed end and a hinged hook, used for handling logs
**PEAVEYS** > PEAVEY
**PEAVIES** > PEAVY
**PEAVY** same as > PEAVEY
**PEAZE** same as > PEASE
**PEAZED** > PEAZE
**PEAZES** > PEAZE
**PEAZING** > PEAZE
**PEBA** n type of armadillo
**PEBAS** > PEBA
**PEBBLE** n small roundish stone ▷ vb cover with pebbles
**PEBBLED** > PEBBLE
**PEBBLES** > PEBBLE
**PEBBLIER** > PEBBLE
**PEBBLIEST** > PEBBLE
**PEBBLING** n act of spraying the rink with drops of hot water to slow down the stone

PEBBLINGS > PEBBLING
PEBBLY > PEBBLE
PEBRINE n disease of silkworms
PEBRINES > PEBRINE
PEC n pectoral muscle
PECAN n edible nut of a N American tree
PECANS > PECAN
PECCABLE adj liable to sin
PECCANCY > PECCANT
PECCANT adj guilty of an offence
PECCANTLY > PECCANT
PECCARIES > PECCARY
PECCARY n piglike animal of American forests
PECCAVI n confession of guilt
PECCAVIS > PECCAVI
PECH Scottish word for > PANT
PECHAN Scots word for > STOMACH
PECHANS > PECHAN
PECHED > PECH
PECHING > PECH
PECHS > PECH
PECK vb strike or pick up with the beak ▷ n pecking movement
PECKE n quarter of bushel
PECKED > PECK
PECKER n slang word for penis
PECKERS > PECKER
PECKES > PECKE
PECKIER > PECKY
PECKIEST > PECKY
PECKING peck
PECKINGS > PECK
PECKISH adj slightly hungry
PECKISHLY > PECKISH
PECKS > PECK
PECKY adj discoloured
PECORINI > PECORINO
PECORINO n Italian cheese made from ewes' milk
PECORINOS > PECORINO
PECS pl n pectoral muscles
PECTASE n enzyme occurring in certain ripening fruits
PECTASES > PECTASE
PECTATE n salt or ester of pectic acid
PECTATES > PECTATE
PECTEN n comblike structure in the eye of birds and reptiles
PECTENS > PECTEN
PECTIC > PECTIN
PECTIN n substance in fruit that makes jam set
PECTINAL adj resembling a comb
PECTINATE adj shaped like a comb
PECTINEAL adj relating to pubic bone
PECTINES > PECTEN
PECTINOUS > PECTIN
PECTINS > PECTIN

PECTISE same as > PECTIZE
PECTISED > PECTISE
PECTISES > PECTISE
PECTISING > PECTISE
PECTIZE vb change into a jelly
PECTIZED > PECTIZE
PECTIZES > PECTIZE
PECTIZING > PECTIZE
PECTOLITE n silicate of lime and soda
PECTORAL adj of the chest or thorax ▷ n pectoral muscle or fin
PECTORALS > PECTORAL
PECTOSE n insoluble carbohydrate found in the cell walls of unripe fruit that is converted to pectin by enzymic processes
PECTOSES > PECTOSE
PECULATE vb embezzle (public money)
PECULATED > PECULATE
PECULATES > PECULATE
PECULATOR > PECULATE
PECULIA > PECULIUM
PECULIAR adj strange ▷ n special sort, esp an accented letter
PECULIARS > PECULIAR
PECULIUM n property that a father or master allowed his child or slave to hold as his own
PECUNIARY adj relating to, or consisting of, money
PECUNIOUS adj having lots of money
PED n pannier
PEDAGOG same as > PEDAGOGUE
PEDAGOGIC > PEDAGOGUE
PEDAGOGS > PEDAGOG
PEDAGOGUE n schoolteacher, esp a pedantic one
PEDAGOGY n principles, practice, or profession of teaching
PEDAL n foot-operated lever used to control a vehicle or machine, or to modify the tone of a musical instrument ▷ vb propel (a bicycle) by using its pedals ▷ adj of or relating to the foot or the feet
PEDALED > PEDAL
PEDALER > PEDAL
PEDALERS > PEDAL
PEDALFER n type of zonal soil deficient in lime but containing deposits of aluminium and iron
PEDALFERS > PEDALFER
PEDALIER n pedal piano
PEDALIERS > PEDALIER
PEDALING > PEDAL
PEDALLED > PEDAL
PEDALLER n person who pedals
PEDALLERS > PEDALLER

PEDALLING > PEDAL
PEDALO n pleasure craft driven by pedal-operated paddle wheels
PEDALOES > PEDALO
PEDALOS > PEDALO
PEDALS > PEDAL
PEDANT n person who is excessively concerned with details and rules, esp in academic work
PEDANTIC adj of, relating to, or characterized by pedantry
PEDANTISE same as > PEDANTIZE
PEDANTISM > PEDANT
PEDANTIZE vb make pedantic comments
PEDANTRY n practice of being a pedant, esp in the minute observance of petty rules or details
PEDANTS > PEDANT
PEDATE adj (of a plant leaf) divided into several lobes arising at a common point, the lobes often being stalked and the lateral lobes sometimes divided into smaller lobes
PEDATELY > PEDATE
PEDATIFID adj (of a plant leaf) pedately divided, with the divisions less deep than in a pedate leaf
PEDDER old form of > PEDLAR
PEDDERS > PEDDER
PEDDLE vb sell (goods) from door to door
PEDDLED > PEDDLE
PEDDLER same as > PEDLAR
PEDDLERS > PEDDLER
PEDDLERY n business of peddler
PEDDLES > PEDDLE
PEDDLING > PEDDLE
PEDDLINGS > PEDDLE
PEDERAST n man who has homosexual relations with boys
PEDERASTS > PEDERAST
PEDERASTY n homosexual relations between men and boys
PEDERERO n type of cannon
PEDEREROS > PEDERERO
PEDES > PES
PEDESES > PEDESIS
PEDESIS n random motion of small particles
PEDESTAL n base supporting a column, statue, etc
PEDESTALS > PEDESTAL
PEDETIC adj of feet
PEDIATRIC adj of or relating to the medical science of children and their diseases
PEDICAB n pedal-operated tricycle, available for hire, with an attached seat for one or two passengers

PEDICABS > PEDICAB
PEDICEL n stalk bearing a single flower of an inflorescence
PEDICELS > PEDICEL
PEDICLE n any small stalk
PEDICLED > PEDICLE
PEDICLES > PEDICLE
PEDICULAR adj relating to, infested with, or caused by lice
PEDICULI > PEDICULUS
PEDICULUS n wingless parasite
PEDICURE n medical or cosmetic treatment of the feet ▷ vb give a pedicure
PEDICURED > PEDICURE
PEDICURES > PEDICURE
PEDIFORM adj shaped like a foot
PEDIGREE n register of ancestors, esp of a purebred animal
PEDIGREED > PEDIGREE
PEDIGREES > PEDIGREE
PEDIMENT n triangular part over a door etc
PEDIMENTS > PEDIMENT
PEDIPALP n either member of the second pair of head appendages of arachnids
PEDIPALPI > PEDIPALP
PEDIPALPS > PEDIPALP
PEDLAR n person who sells goods from door to door
PEDLARIES > PEDLARY
PEDLARS > PEDLAR
PEDLARY same as > PEDLERY
PEDLER same as > PEDLAR
PEDLERIES > PEDLERY
PEDLERS > PEDLER
PEDLERY n business of pedler
PEDOCAL n type of zonal soil that is rich in lime and characteristic of relatively dry areas
PEDOCALIC > PEDOCAL
PEDOCALS > PEDOCAL
PEDOGENIC adj relating to soil
PEDOLOGIC > PEDOLOGY
PEDOLOGY same as > PAEDOLOGY
PEDOMETER n instrument which measures the distance walked
PEDOPHILE n person who is sexually attracted to children
PEDORTHIC adj (of footwear) designed to alleviate foot problems
PEDRAIL n device replacing wheel on rough surfaces
PEDRAILS > PEDRAIL
PEDRERO n type of cannon
PEDREROES > PEDRERO
PEDREROS > PEDRERO
PEDRO n card game
PEDROS > PEDRO
PEDS > PED
PEDUNCLE same

553

*as* > PEDICEL
**PEDUNCLED** > PEDUNCLE
**PEDUNCLES** > PEDUNCLE
**PEE** *vb* urinate ▷ *n* urine
**PEEBEEN** *n* type of large
evergreen
**PEEBEENS** > PEEBEEN
**PEECE** *obsolete variant
of* > PIECE
**PEECED** > PIECE
**PEECES** > PIECE
**PEECING** > PIECE
**PEED** > PEE
**PEEING** > PEE
**PEEK** *n* peep or glance ▷ *vb*
glance quickly or secretly
**PEEKABOO** *n* game for
young children, in which
one person hides his face
and suddenly reveals it and
cries 'peekaboo' ▷ *adj* (of
a garment) made of fabric
that is almost transparent
or patterned with small
holes
**PEEKABOOS** > PEEKABOO
**PEEKAPOO** *n* dog which is
cross between Pekingese
and poodle
**PEEKAPOOS** > PEEKAPOO
**PEEKED** > PEEK
**PEEKING** > PEEK
**PEEKS** > PEEK
**PEEL** *vb* remove the skin
or rind of (a vegetable or
fruit) ▷ *n* rind or skin
**PEELABLE** > PEEL
**PEELED** > PEEL
**PEELER** *n* special knife or
mechanical device for
peeling vegetables, fruit,
etc
**PEELERS** > PEELER
**PEELING** *n* strip of skin,
rind, bark, etc, that has
been peeled off
**PEELINGS** > PEELING
**PEELS** > PEEL
**PEEN** *n* end of a hammer
head opposite the striking
face, often rounded or
wedge-shaped ▷ *vb* strike
with the peen of a hammer
or with a stream of metal
shot in order to bend or
shape (a sheet of metal)
**PEENED** > PEEN
**PEENGE** *vb* complain
**PEENGED** > PEENGE
**PEENGEING** > PEENGE
**PEENGES** > PEENGE
**PEENGING** > PEENGE
**PEENING** > PEEN
**PEENS** > PEEN
**PEEOY** *n* homemade
firework
**PEEOYS** > PEEOY
**PEEP** *vb* look slyly or quickly
▷ *n* peeping look
**PEEPE** *old spelling of* > PIP
**PEEPED** > PEEP
**PEEPER** *n* person who
peeps
**PEEPERS** > PEEPER

**PEEPES** *archiac spelling
of* > PEEPS
**PEEPHOLE** *n* small
aperture, such as one
in the door of a flat for
observing callers before
opening
**PEEPHOLES** > PEEPHOLE
**PEEPING** > PEEP
**PEEPS** > PEEP
**PEEPSHOW** *n* box
containing a series of
pictures that can be seen
through a small hole
**PEEPSHOWS** > PEEPSHOW
**PEEPUL** *n* Indian
moraceous tree
**PEEPULS** > PEEPUL
**PEER** *n* (in Britain) member
of the nobility ▷ *vb* look
closely and intently
**PEERAGE** *n* whole body of
peers
**PEERAGES** > PEERAGE
**PEERED** > PEER
**PEERESS** *n* (in Britain)
woman holding the rank
of a peer
**PEERESSES** > PEERESS
**PEERIE** *n* spinning top
▷ *adj* small
**PEERIER** > PEERIE
**PEERIES** > PEERIE
**PEERIEST** > PEERIE
**PEERING** > PEER
**PEERLESS** *adj* unequalled,
unsurpassed
**PEERS** > PEER
**PEERY** *n* child's spinning
top
**PEES** > PEE
**PEESWEEP** *n* early spring
storm
**PEESWEEPS** > PEESWEEP
**PEETWEET** *n* spotted
sandpiper
**PEETWEETS** > PEETWEET
**PEEVE** *vb* irritate or annoy
▷ *n* something that
irritates
**PEEVED** > PEEVE
**PEEVER** *n* hopscotch
**PEEVERS** > PEEVER
**PEEVES** > PEEVE
**PEEVING** > PEEVE
**PEEVISH** *adj* fretful or
irritable
**PEEVISHLY** > PEEVISH
**PEEWEE** *same as* > PEWEE
**PEEWEES** > PEEWEE
**PEEWIT** *same as* > LAPWING
**PEEWITS** > PEEWIT
**PEG** *n* pin or clip for joining,
fastening, marking, etc
▷ *vb* fasten with pegs
**PEGASUS** *n* winged horse
**PEGASUSES** > PEGASUS
**PEGBOARD** *n* board with
a pattern of holes into
which small pegs can be
fitted, used for playing
certain games or keeping
a score
**PEGBOARDS** > PEGBOARD

**PEGBOX** *n* part of stringed
instrument that holds
tuning pegs
**PEGBOXES** > PEGBOX
**PEGGED** > PEG
**PEGGIES** > PEGGY
**PEGGING** > PEG
**PEGGINGS** > PEG
**PEGGY** *n* ship's steward
**PEGH** *variant of* > PECH
**PEGHED** > PEGH
**PEGHING** > PEGH
**PEGHS** > PEGH
**PEGLEGGED** *adj* having
wooden leg
**PEGLESS** > PEG
**PEGLIKE** > PEG
**PEGMATITE** *n* exceptionally
coarse-grained intrusive
igneous rock
**PEGS** > PEG
**PEH** *n* letter in the Hebrew
alphabet
**PEHS** > PEH
**PEIGNOIR** *n* woman's light
dressing gown
**PEIGNOIRS** > PEIGNOIR
**PEIN** *same as* > PEEN
**PEINCT** *vb* paint
**PEINCTED** > PEINCT
**PEINCTING** > PEINCT
**PEINCTS** > PEINCT
**PEINED** > PEIN
**PEINING** > PEIN
**PEINS** > PEIN
**PEIRASTIC** *adj*
experimental
**PEISE** *same as* > PEIZE
**PEISED** > PEISE
**PEISES** > PEISE
**PEISHWA** *n* Indian leader
**PEISHWAH** *same
as* > PEISHWA
**PEISHWAHS** > PEISHWAH
**PEISHWAS** > PEISHWA
**PEISING** > PEISE
**PEIZE** *vb* weight or poise
**PEIZED** > PEIZE
**PEIZES** > PEIZE
**PEIZING** > PEIZE
**PEJORATE** *vb* change for
the worse
**PEJORATED** > PEJORATE
**PEJORATES** > PEJORATE
**PEKAN** *n* large North
American marten
**PEKANS** > PEKAN
**PEKE** *n* Pekingese dog
**PEKEPOO** *same
as* > PEEKAPOO
**PEKEPOOS** > PEKEPOO
**PEKES** > PEKE
**PEKIN** *n* silk fabric
**PEKINS** > PEKIN
**PEKOE** *n* high-quality tea
made from the downy tips
of the young buds of the
tea plant
**PEKOES** > PEKOE
**PELA** *n* insect living on wax
**PELAGE** *n* coat of a
mammal, consisting of
hair, wool, fur, etc
**PELAGES** > PELAGE

**PELAGIAL** *adj* of the open
sea
**PELAGIAN** *adj* of or
inhabiting the open sea
▷ *n* pelagic creature
**PELAGIANS** > PELAGIAN
**PELAGIC** *adj* of or relating
to the open sea ▷ *n* any
pelagic creature
**PELAGICS** > PELAGIC
**PELAS** > PELA
**PELE** *Spenserian variant
of* > PEAL
**PELECYPOD** *another word
for* > BIVALVE
**PELERINE** *n* woman's
narrow cape with long
pointed ends in front
**PELERINES** > PELERINE
**PELES** > PELE
**PELF** *n* money or wealth
**PELFS** > PELF
**PELHAM** *n* horse's bit for a
double bridle, less severe
than a curb but more
severe than a snaffle
**PELHAMS** > PELHAM
**PELICAN** *n* large water bird
with a pouch beneath its
bill for storing fish
**PELICANS** > PELICAN
**PELISSE** *n* cloak or loose
coat which is usually fur-
trimmed
**PELISSES** > PELISSE
**PELITE** *n* any argillaceous
rock such as shale
**PELITES** > PELITE
**PELITIC** > PELITE
**PELL** *vb* knock about
**PELLACH** *same as* > PELLACK
**PELLACHS** > PELLACH
**PELLACK** *n* porpoise
**PELLACKS** > PELLACK
**PELLAGRA** *n* disease caused
by lack of vitamin B
**PELLAGRAS** > PELLAGRA
**PELLAGRIN** *n* person who
suffers from pellagra
**PELLED** > PELL
**PELLET** *n* small ball of
something ▷ *vb* strike
with pellets
**PELLETAL** > PELLET
**PELLETED** > PELLET
**PELLETIFY** *vb* shape into
pellets
**PELLETING** > PELLET
**PELLETISE** *vb* shape into
pellets
**PELLETIZE** *vb* shape into
pellets
**PELLETS** > PELLET
**PELLICLE** *n* thin skin or
film
**PELLICLES** > PELLICLE
**PELLING** > PELL
**PELLITORY** *n* urticaceous
plant
**PELLMELL** *n* disorder
**PELLMELLS** > PELLMELL
**PELLOCK** *n* porpoise
**PELLOCKS** > PELLOCK
**PELLS** > PELL

**PELLUCID** *adj* very clear
**PELLUM** *n* dust
**PELLUMS** > PELLUM
**PELMA** *n* sole of the foot
**PELMANISM** *n* memory card game
**PELMAS** > PELMA
**PELMATIC** > PELMA
**PELMET** *n* ornamental drapery or board, concealing a curtain rail
**PELMETS** > PELMET
**PELOID** *n* mud used therapeutically
**PELOIDS** > PELOID
**PELOLOGY** *n* study of therapeutic uses of mud
**PELON** *adj* hairless
**PELORIA** *n* abnormal production of actinomorphic flowers in a plant of a species that usually produces zygomorphic flowers
**PELORIAN** > PELORIA
**PELORIAS** > PELORIA
**PELORIC** > PELORIA
**PELORIES** > PELORY
**PELORISED** *adj* affected by peloria
**PELORISM** *n* floral mutation
**PELORISMS** > PELORISM
**PELORIZED** *same as* > PELORISED
**PELORUS** *n* sighting device used in conjunction with a magnetic compass or a gyrocompass for measuring the relative bearings of observed points
**PELORUSES** > PELORUS
**PELORY** *n* floral mutation
**PELOTA** *n* game played by two players who use a basket strapped to their wrists or a wooden racket to propel a ball against a specially marked wall
**PELOTAS** > PELOTA
**PELOTON** *n* main field of riders in a road race
**PELOTONS** > PELOTON
**PELT** *vb* throw missiles at ▷ *n* skin of a fur-bearing animal
**PELTA** *n* small ancient shield
**PELTAE** > PELTA
**PELTAS** > PELTA
**PELTAST** *n* (in ancient Greece) lightly armed foot soldier
**PELTASTS** > PELTAST
**PELTATE** *adj* (of leaves) having the stalk attached to the centre of the lower surface
**PELTATELY** > PELTATE
**PELTATION** > PELTATE
**PELTED** > PELT
**PELTER** > PELT *vb* rain heavily

**PELTERED** > PELT
**PELTERING** > PELT
**PELTERS** > PELT
**PELTING** > PELT
**PELTINGLY** > PELT
**PELTINGS** > PELT
**PELTLESS** > PELT
**PELTRIES** > PELTRY
**PELTRY** *n* pelts of animals collectively
**PELTS** > PELT
**PELVES** > PELVIS
**PELVIC** *adj* of, near, or relating to the pelvis ▷ *n* pelvic bone
**PELVICS** > PELVIC
**PELVIFORM** *adj* shaped like pelvis
**PELVIS** *n* framework of bones at the base of the spine, to which the hips are attached
**PELVISES** > PELVIS
**PEMBINA** *n* type of cranberry
**PEMBINAS** > PEMBINA
**PEMBROKE** *n* small table
**PEMBROKES** > PEMBROKE
**PEMICAN** *same as* > PEMMICAN
**PEMICANS** > PEMICAN
**PEMMICAN** *n* small pressed cake of shredded dried meat, pounded into paste with fat and berries or dried fruits
**PEMMICANS** > PEMMICAN
**PEMOLINE** *n* mild stimulant
**PEMOLINES** > PEMOLINE
**PEMPHIGUS** *n* any of a group of blistering skin diseases
**PEMPHIX** *n* type of crustacean
**PEMPHIXES** > PEMPHIX
**PEN** *n* instrument for writing in ink ▷ *vb* write or compose
**PENAL** *adj* of or used in punishment
**PENALISE** *same as* > PENALIZE
**PENALISED** > PENALISE
**PENALISES** > PENALISE
**PENALITY** > PENAL
**PENALIZE** *vb* impose a penalty on
**PENALIZED** > PENALIZE
**PENALIZES** > PENALIZE
**PENALLY** > PENAL
**PENALTIES** > PENALTY
**PENALTY** *n* punishment for a crime or offence
**PENANCE** *n* voluntary self-punishment to make amends for wrongdoing ▷ *vb* (of ecclesiastical authorities) impose a penance upon (a sinner)
**PENANCED** > PENANCE
**PENANCES** > PENANCE
**PENANCING** > PENANCE
**PENANG** *variant of* > PINANG
**PENANGS** > PENANG

**PENATES** *pl n* household gods
**PENCE** > PENNY
**PENCEL** *n* small pennon, originally one carried by a knight's squire
**PENCELS** > PENCEL
**PENCES** > PENNY
**PENCHANT** *n* inclination or liking
**PENCHANTS** > PENCHANT
**PENCIL** *n* thin cylindrical instrument containing graphite, for writing or drawing ▷ *vb* draw, write, or mark with a pencil
**PENCILED** > PENCIL
**PENCILER** > PENCIL
**PENCILERS** > PENCIL
**PENCILING** > PENCIL
**PENCILLED** > PENCIL
**PENCILLER** > PENCIL
**PENCILS** > PENCIL
**PENCRAFT** *n* skill in writing
**PENCRAFTS** > PENCRAFT
**PEND** *vb* await judgment or settlement ▷ *n* archway or vaulted passage
**PENDANT** *n* ornament worn on a chain round the neck
**PENDANTLY** > PENDANT
**PENDANTS** > PENDANT
**PENDED** > PEND
**PENDENCY** > PENDENT
**PENDENT** *adj* hanging ▷ *n* pendant
**PENDENTLY** > PENDENT
**PENDENTS** > PENDENT
**PENDICLE** *n* something dependent on another
**PENDICLER** *n* person who rents a croft
**PENDICLES** > PENDICLE
**PENDING** *prep* while waiting for ▷ *adj* not yet decided or settled
**PENDRAGON** *n* supreme war chief or leader of the ancient Britons
**PENDS** > PEND
**PENDU** *adj* in informal Indian English, culturally backward
**PENDULAR** *adj* pendulous
**PENDULATE** *vb* swing as pendulum
**PENDULE** *n* manoeuvre by which a climber on a rope from above swings in a pendulum-like series of movements to reach another line of ascent
**PENDULES** > PENDULE
**PENDULINE** *n* type of titmouse
**PENDULOUS** *adj* hanging, swinging
**PENDULUM** *same as* > PENDULE
**PENDULUMS** > PENDULUM
**PENE** *variant of* > PEEN
**PENED** > PENE
**PENEPLAIN** *n* relatively flat land surface produced by a

long period of erosion
**PENEPLANE** *same as* > PENEPLAIN
**PENES** > PENIS
**PENETRANT** *adj* sharp ▷ *n* substance that lowers the surface tension of a liquid and thus causes it to penetrate or be absorbed more easily
**PENETRATE** *vb* find or force a way into or through
**PENFOLD** *same as* > PINFOLD
**PENFOLDS** > PENFOLD
**PENFUL** *n* contents of pen
**PENFULS** > PENFUL
**PENGO** *n* standard monetary unit of Hungary, replaced by the forint in 1946
**PENGOS** > PENGO
**PENGUIN** *n* flightless black-and-white sea bird of the southern hemisphere
**PENGUINRY** *n* breeding place of penguins
**PENGUINS** > PENGUIN
**PENHOLDER** *n* container for pens
**PENI** *old spelling of* > PENNY
**PENIAL** > PENIS
**PENICIL** *n* small pad for wounds
**PENICILS** > PENICIL
**PENIE** *old spelling of* > PENNY
**PENIES** > PENIE
**PENILE** *adj* of or relating to the penis
**PENILL** > PENILLION
**PENILLION** *pl n* Welsh art or practice of singing poetry in counterpoint to a traditional melody played on the harp
**PENING** > PENE
**PENINSULA** *n* strip of land nearly surrounded by water
**PENIS** *n* organ of copulation and urination in male mammals
**PENISES** > PENIS
**PENISTONE** *n* coarse woollen cloth
**PENITENCE** > PENITENT
**PENITENCY** > PENITENT
**PENITENT** *adj* feeling sorry for having done wrong ▷ *n* someone who is penitent
**PENITENTS** > PENITENT
**PENK** *n* small fish
**PENKNIFE** *n* small knife with blade(s) that fold into the handle
**PENKNIVES** > PENKNIFE
**PENKS** > PENK
**PENLIGHT** *n* small thin flashlight
**PENLIGHTS** > PENLIGHT
**PENLITE** *same as* > PENLIGHT
**PENLITES** > PENLITE
**PENMAN** *n* person skilled in

handwriting
**PENMEN** > PENMAN
**PENNA** n any large feather that has a vane and forms part of the main plumage of a bird
**PENNAE** > PENNA
**PENNAL** n first-year student of Protestant university
**PENNALISM** n menial choring at college
**PENNALS** > PENNAL
**PENNAME** n author's pseudonym
**PENNAMES** > PENNAME
**PENNANT** same as > PENDANT
**PENNANTS** > PENNANT
**PENNATE** adj having feathers, wings, or winglike structures
**PENNATED** same as > PENNATE
**PENNATULA** n sea pen
**PENNE** n pasta in the form of short tubes
**PENNED** > PEN
**PENNEECH** n card game
**PENNEECHS** > PENNEECH
**PENNEECK** same as > PENNEECH
**PENNEECKS** > PENNEECK
**PENNER** n person who writes
**PENNERS** > PENNER
**PENNES** > PENNE
**PENNI** n former Finnish monetary unit worth one hundredth of a markka
**PENNIA** > PENNI
**PENNIED** adj having money
**PENNIES** > PENNY
**PENNIFORM** adj shaped like a feather
**PENNILESS** adj very poor
**PENNILL** n stanza in a Welsh poem
**PENNINE** n mineral found in the Pennine Alps
**PENNINES** > PENNINE
**PENNING** > PEN
**PENNINITE** n bluish-green variety of chlorite occurring in the form of thick crystals
**PENNIS** > PENNI
**PENNON** n triangular or tapering flag
**PENNONCEL** n small narrow flag
**PENNONED** n equipped with a pennon
**PENNONS** > PENNON
**PENNY** n British bronze coin worth one hundredth of a pound
**PENNYBOY** n employee whose duties include menial tasks, such as running errands
**PENNYBOYS** > PENNYBOY
**PENNYFEE** n small payment
**PENNYFEES** > PENNYFEE
**PENNYLAND** n old Scottish division of land

**PENNYWISE** adj careful with small amounts of money
**PENNYWORT** n Eurasian rock plant with whitish-green tubular flowers and rounded leaves
**PENOCHE** n type of fudge
**PENOCHES** > PENOCHE
**PENOLOGY** n study of punishment and prison management
**PENONCEL** n small narrow flag
**PENONCELS** > PENONCEL
**PENPOINT** n tip of pen
**PENPOINTS** > PENPOINT
**PENPUSHER** n person whose work involves a lot of boring paperwork
**PENS** > PEN
**PENSEE** n thought put down on paper
**PENSEES** > PENSEE
**PENSEL** same as > PENCEL
**PENSELS** > PENSEL
**PENSIL** same as > PENCEL
**PENSILE** adj designating or building a hanging nest
**PENSILITY** > PENSILE
**PENSILS** > PENSIL
**PENSION** n regular payment to people above a certain age, retired employees, widows, etc ▷ vb grant a pension to
**PENSIONE** n Italian boarding house
**PENSIONED** > PENSION
**PENSIONER** n person receiving a pension
**PENSIONES** > PENSIONE
**PENSIONS** > PENSION
**PENSIVE** adj deeply thoughtful, often with a tinge of sadness
**PENSIVELY** > PENSIVE
**PENSTEMON** n North American flowering plant with five stamens
**PENSTER** n writer
**PENSTERS** > PENSTER
**PENSTOCK** n conduit that supplies water to a hydroelectric power plant
**PENSTOCKS** > PENSTOCK
**PENSUM** n school exercise
**PENSUMS** > PENSUM
**PENT** n penthouse
**PENTACLE** same as > PENTAGRAM
**PENTACLES** > PENTACLE
**PENTACT** n sponge spicule with five rays
**PENTACTS** > PENTACT
**PENTAD** n group or series of five
**PENTADIC** > PENTAD
**PENTADS** > PENTAD
**PENTAGON** n geometric figure with five sides
**PENTAGONS** > PENTAGON
**PENTAGRAM** n five-pointed star
**PENTALOGY** n combination

of five closely related symptoms
**PENTALPHA** n five-pointed star
**PENTAMERY** n state of consisting of five parts
**PENTANE** n alkane hydrocarbon with three isomers
**PENTANES** > PENTANE
**PENTANGLE** same as > PENTAGRAM
**PENTANOIC** as in pentanoic acid colourless liquid carboxylic acid
**PENTANOL** n colourless oily liquid
**PENTANOLS** > PENTANOL
**PENTAPODY** n series or measure of five feet
**PENTARCH** n member of pentarchy
**PENTARCHS** > PENTARCH
**PENTARCHY** n government by five rulers
**PENTATHLA** n pentathlons
**PENTEL** n ballpoint pen with free-flowing ink
**PENTELS** > PENTEL
**PENTENE** n colourless flammable liquid alkene with several straight-chained isomeric forms
**PENTENES** > PENTENE
**PENTHIA** n child born fifth
**PENTHIAS** > PENTHIA
**PENTHOUSE** n flat built on the roof or top floor of a building
**PENTICE** vb accommodate in a penthouse
**PENTICED** > PENTICE
**PENTICES** > PENTICE
**PENTICING** > PENTICE
**PENTISE** same as > PENTICE
**PENTISED** > PENTISE
**PENTISES** > PENTISE
**PENTISING** > PENTISE
**PENTITI** > PENTITO
**PENTITO** n person involved in organized crime who offers information to the police in return for immunity from prosecution
**PENTODE** n electronic valve having five electrodes: a cathode, anode, and three grids
**PENTODES** > PENTODE
**PENTOMIC** adj denoting or relating to the subdivision of an army division into five battle groups, esp for nuclear warfare
**PENTOSAN** n polysaccharide occuring in plants, humus, etc
**PENTOSANE** same as > PENTOSAN
**PENTOSANS** > PENTOSAN
**PENTOSE** n monosaccharide containing five atoms of

carbon per molecule
**PENTOSES** > PENTOSE
**PENTOSIDE** n compound containing sugar
**PENTOXIDE** n oxide of an element with five atoms of oxygen per molecule
**PENTROOF** n lean-to
**PENTROOFS** > PENTROOF
**PENTS** > PENT
**PENTYL** n one of a particular chemical group
**PENTYLENE** n type of chemical
**PENTYLS** > PENTYL
**PENUCHE** same as > PANOCHA
**PENUCHES** > PENUCHE
**PENUCHI** same as > PANOCHA
**PENUCHIS** > PENUCHI
**PENUCHLE** same as > PINOCHLE
**PENUCHLES** > PENUCHLE
**PENUCKLE** same as > PENUCHLE
**PENUCKLES** > PENUCKLE
**PENULT** n last syllable but one in a word
**PENULTIMA** same as > PENULT
**PENULTS** > PENULT
**PENUMBRA** n (in an eclipse) partially shadowed region which surrounds the full shadow
**PENUMBRAE** > PENUMBRA
**PENUMBRAL** > PENUMBRA
**PENUMBRAS** > PENUMBRA
**PENURIES** > PENURY
**PENURIOUS** adj niggardly with money
**PENURY** n extreme poverty
**PENWOMAN** n female writer
**PENWOMEN** > PENWOMAN
**PEON** n Spanish-American farm labourer or unskilled worker
**PEONAGE** n state of being a peon
**PEONAGES** > PEONAGE
**PEONES** > PEON
**PEONIES** > PEONY
**PEONISM** same as > PEONAGE
**PEONISMS** > PEONISM
**PEONS** > PEON
**PEONY** n garden plant with showy red, pink, or white flowers
**PEOPLE** pl n persons generally ▷ vb provide with inhabitants
**PEOPLED** > PEOPLE
**PEOPLER** n settler
**PEOPLERS** > PEOPLER
**PEOPLES** > PEOPLE
**PEOPLING** > PEOPLE
**PEP** n high spirits, energy, or enthusiasm ▷ vb liven by imbuing with new vigour
**PEPERINO** n type of volcanic rock
**PEPERINOS** > PEPERINO
**PEPEROMIA** n plant from tropical and subtropical

America with slightly fleshy ornamental leaves

**PEPERONI** same as > PEPPERONI

**PEPERONIS** > PEPPERONI

**PEPFUL** adj full of vitality

**PEPINO** n purple-striped yellow fruit

**PEPINOS** > PEPINO

**PEPLA** > PEPLUM

**PEPLOS** n (in ancient Greece) top part of a woman's attire, caught at the shoulders and hanging in folds to the waist

**PEPLOSES** > PEPLOS

**PEPLUM** same as > PEPLOS

**PEPLUMED** > PEPLUM

**PEPLUMS** > PEPLUM

**PEPLUS** same as > PEPLOS

**PEPLUSES** > PEPLUS

**PEPO** n fruit such as the melon, squash, cucumber, or pumpkin

**PEPONIDA** variant of > PEPO

**PEPONIDAS** > PEPO

**PEPONIUM** variant of > PEPO

**PEPONIUMS** > PEPONIUM

**PEPOS** > PEPO

**PEPPED** > PEP

**PEPPER** n sharp hot condiment made from the fruit of an East Indian climbing plant ▷ vb season with pepper

**PEPPERBOX** n container for pepper

**PEPPERED** > PEPPER

**PEPPERER** > PEPPER

**PEPPERERS** > PEPPER

**PEPPERIER** > PEPPERY

**PEPPERING** > PEPPER

**PEPPERONI** n dry sausage of pork and beef spiced with pepper

**PEPPERS** > PEPPER

**PEPPERY** adj tasting of pepper

**PEPPIER** > PEPPY

**PEPPIEST** > PEPPY

**PEPPILY** > PEPPY

**PEPPINESS** > PEPPY

**PEPPING** > PEP

**PEPPY** adj full of vitality

**PEPS** > PEP

**PEPSIN** n enzyme produced in the stomach, which, when activated by acid, breaks down proteins

**PEPSINATE** vb treat (a patient) with pepsin

**PEPSINE** same as > PEPSIN

**PEPSINES** > PEPSINE

**PEPSINS** > PEPSIN

**PEPTALK** n talk meant to inspire ▷ vb give a peptalk to

**PEPTALKED** > PEPTALK

**PEPTALKS** > PEPTALK

**PEPTIC** adj relating to digestion or the digestive juices ▷ n substance that aids digestion

**PEPTICITY** > PEPTIC

**PEPTICS** > PEPTIC

**PEPTID** variant of > PEPTIDE

**PEPTIDASE** n any of a group of proteolytic enzymes that hydrolyse peptides to amino acids

**PEPTIDE** n compound consisting of two or more amino acids linked by chemical bonding between the amino group of one and the carboxyl group of another

**PEPTIDES** > PEPTIDE

**PEPTIDIC** adj of peptides

**PEPTIDS** > PEPTID

**PEPTISE** same as > PEPTIZE

**PEPTISED** > PEPTISE

**PEPTISER** > PEPTISE

**PEPTISERS** > PEPTISE

**PEPTISES** > PEPTISE

**PEPTISING** > PEPTISE

**PEPTIZE** vb disperse (a substance) into a colloidal state, usually to form a sol

**PEPTIZED** > PEPTIZE

**PEPTIZER** > PEPTIZE

**PEPTIZERS** > PEPTIZE

**PEPTIZES** > PEPTIZE

**PEPTIZING** > PEPTIZE

**PEPTONE** n any of a group of compounds that form an intermediary group in the digestion of proteins to amino acids

**PEPTONES** > PEPTONE

**PEPTONIC** > PEPTONE

**PEPTONISE** same as > PEPTONIZE

**PEPTONIZE** vb hydrolyse (a protein) to peptones by enzymic action, esp by pepsin or pancreatic extract

**PEQUISTE** n in Canada, member or supporter of the Parti Québécois

**PEQUISTES** > PEQUISTE

**PER** prep for each

**PERACID** n acid, such as perchloric acid, in which the element forming the acid radical exhibits its highest valency

**PERACIDS** > PERACID

**PERACUTE** adj very acute

**PERAEA** > PERAEON

**PERAEON** same as > PEREION

**PERAEONS** > PERAEON

**PERAEOPOD** same as > PEREIOPOD

**PERAI** another name for > PIRANHA

**PERAIS** > PERAI

**PERBORATE** n salt derived, or apparently derived, from perboric acid

**PERCALE** n close-textured woven cotton fabric, plain or printed, used esp for sheets

**PERCALES** > PERCALE

**PERCALINE** n fine light cotton fabric, used esp for linings

**PERCASE** adv perchance

**PERCE** obsolete word for > PIERCE

**PERCEABLE** adj pierceable

**PERCEANT** adj piercing

**PERCED** > PERCE

**PERCEIVE** vb become aware of (something) through the senses

**PERCEIVED** > PERCEIVE

**PERCEIVER** > PERCEIVE

**PERCEIVES** > PERCEIVE

**PERCEN** > PERCE

**PERCENT** n percentage or proportion

**PERCENTAL** > PERCENT

**PERCENTS** > PERCENT

**PERCEPT** n concept that depends on recognition by the senses, such as sight, of some external object or phenomenon

**PERCEPTS** > PERCEPT

**PERCES** > PERCE

**PERCH** n resting place for a bird ▷ vb alight, rest, or place on or as if on a perch

**PERCHANCE** adv perhaps

**PERCHED** > PERCH

**PERCHER** > PERCH

**PERCHERON** n compact heavy breed of carthorse

**PERCHERS** > PERCH

**PERCHERY** n barn in which hens are allowed to move without restriction

**PERCHES** > PERCH

**PERCHING** > PERCH

**PERCHINGS** > PERCH

**PERCIFORM** adj of perch-like fishes

**PERCINE** adj of perches

**PERCING** > PERCE

**PERCOCT** adj well-cooked

**PERCOID** adj of, relating to, or belonging to the Percoidea, a suborder of spiny-finned teleost fishes ▷ n any fish belonging to the suborder Percoidea

**PERCOIDS** > PERCOID

**PERCOLATE** vb pass or filter through small holes ▷ n product of percolation

**PERCOLIN** n pain-relieving drug

**PERCOLINS** > PERCOLIN

**PERCUSS** vb strike sharply, rapidly, or suddenly

**PERCUSSED** > PERCUSS

**PERCUSSES** > PERCUSS

**PERCUSSOR** > PERCUSS

**PERDENDO** adj (of music) getting gradually quieter and slower

**PERDIE** adv certainly

**PERDITION** n spiritual ruin

**PERDU** adj (of a soldier) placed on hazardous sentry duty ▷ n soldier placed on hazardous sentry duty

**PERDUE** same as > PERDU

**PERDUES** > PERDUE

**PERDURE** vb last for long time

**PERDURED** > PERDURE

**PERDURES** > PERDURE

**PERDURING** > PERDURE

**PERDUS** > PERDU

**PERDY** adv certainly

**PERE** n addition to a French surname to specify the father rather than the son of the same name

**PEREA** > PEREON

**PEREGAL** adj equal

**PEREGRIN** variant spelling of > PEREGRIN

**PEREGRINE** adj coming from abroad

**PEREGRINS** > PEREGRIN

**PEREIA** > PEREION

**PEREION** n thorax of some crustaceans

**PEREIONS** > PEREION

**PEREIOPOD** n appendage of the pereion

**PEREIRA** n bark of a South American apocynaceous tree

**PEREIRAS** > PEREIRA

**PERENNATE** vb (of plants) live from one growing season to another

**PERENNIAL** adj lasting through many years ▷ n plant lasting more than two years

**PERENNITY** n state of being perennial

**PERENTIE** n large dark-coloured Australian monitor lizard

**PERENTIES** > PERENTY

**PERENTY** same as > PERENTIE

**PEREON** same as > PEREION

**PEREONS** > PEREON

**PEREOPOD** same as > PEREIOPOD

**PEREOPODS** > PEREOPOD

**PERES** > PERE

**PERFAY** interj by my faith

**PERFECT** adj having all the essential elements ▷ n perfect tense ▷ vb improve

**PERFECTA** n bet on the order of the first and second in a race

**PERFECTAS** > PERFECTA

**PERFECTED** > PERFECT

**PERFECTER** same as > PERFECTOR

**PERFECTI** n ascetic group of elite Cathars

**PERFECTLY** adv completely, utterly, or absolutely

**PERFECTO** n large cigar that is tapered from both ends

**PERFECTOR** n person who completes or makes something perfect

**PERFECTOS** > PERFECTO

**PERFECTS** > PERFECT

PERFERVID *adj* extremely ardent, enthusiastic, or zealous

PERFERVOR *n* zealous person

PERFET *obsolete variant of* > PERFECT

PERFIDIES > PERFIDY

PERFIDY *n* perfidious act

PERFIN *former name for* > SPIF

PERFING *n* practice of taking early retirement, with financial compensation, from the police force

PERFINS > PERFIN

PERFORANS *adj* perforating or penetrating

PERFORANT *adj* perforating

PERFORATE *vb* make holes in ▷ *adj* pierced by small holes

PERFORCE *adv* of necessity

PERFORM *vb* carry out (an action)

PERFORMED > PERFORM

PERFORMER > PERFORM

PERFORMS > PERFORM

PERFUME *n* liquid cosmetic worn for its pleasant smell ▷ *vb* give a pleasant smell to

PERFUMED > PERFUME

PERFUMER *n* person who makes or sells perfume

PERFUMERS > PERFUMER

PERFUMERY *n* perfumes in general

PERFUMES > PERFUME

PERFUMIER *same as* > PERFUMER

PERFUMING > PERFUME

PERFUMY *adj* like perfume

PERFUSATE *n* fluid flowing through tissue or organ

PERFUSE *vb* permeate (a liquid, colour, etc) through or over (something)

PERFUSED > PERFUSE

PERFUSES > PERFUSE

PERFUSING > PERFUSE

PERFUSION > PERFUSE

PERFUSIVE > PERFUSE

PERGOLA *n* arch or framework of trellis supporting climbing plants

PERGOLAS > PERGOLA

PERGUNNAH *same as* > PARGANA

PERHAPS *adv* possibly, maybe ▷ *sentence substitute* it may happen, be so, etc ▷ *n* something that might have happened

PERHAPSES > PERHAPS

PERI *n* (in Persian folklore) one of a race of beautiful supernatural beings

PERIAGUA *n* dugout canoe

PERIAGUAS > PERIAGUA

PERIAKTOI > PERIAKTOS

PERIAKTOS *n* ancient

device for changing theatre scenery

PERIANTH *n* outer part of a flower

PERIANTHS > PERIANTH

PERIAPSES > PERIAPSIS

PERIAPSIS *n* closest point to a central body reached by a body in orbit

PERIAPT *n* charm or amulet

PERIAPTS > PERIAPT

PERIBLAST *n* tissue surrounding blastoderm in meroblastic eggs

PERIBLEM *n* layer of meristematic tissue in stems and roots that gives rise to the cortex

PERIBLEMS > PERIBLEM

PERIBOLOI > PERIBOLOS

PERIBOLOS *n* enclosed court surrounding ancient temple

PERIBOLUS *same as* > PERIBOLOS

PERICARP *n* part of a fruit enclosing the seed that develops from the wall of the ovary

PERICARPS > PERICARP

PERICLASE *n* mineral consisting of magnesium oxide in the form of isometric crystals or grains

PERICLINE *n* white translucent variety of albite in the form of elongated crystals

PERICON *n* Argentinian dance

PERICONES > PERICON

PERICOPAE > PERICOPE

PERICOPAL > PERICOPE

PERICOPE *n* selection from a book, esp a passage from the Bible read at religious services

PERICOPES > PERICOPE

PERICOPIC > PERICOPE

PERICYCLE *n* layer of plant tissue beneath the endodermis

PERIDERM *n* outer corky protective layer of woody stems and roots

PERIDERMS > PERIDERM

PERIDIA > PERIDIUM

PERIDIAL > PERIDIUM

PERIDINIA *n* genus of flagellate organisms

PERIDIUM *n* distinct outer layer of the spore-bearing organ in many fungi

PERIDIUMS > PERIDIUM

PERIDOT *n* pale green transparent gemstone

PERIDOTE *same as* > PERIDOT

PERIDOTES > PERIDOTE

PERIDOTIC > PERIDOT

PERIDOTS > PERIDOT

PERIDROME *n* space

between the columns and inner room of a classical temple

PERIGEAL > PERIGEE

PERIGEAN > PERIGEE

PERIGEE *n* point in the orbit of the moon or a satellite that is nearest the earth

PERIGEES > PERIGEE

PERIGON *n* angle of 360°

PERIGONE *n* part enclosing the essential organs of a flower

PERIGONES > PERIGONE

PERIGONIA *n* perigones

PERIGONS > PERIGON

PERIGYNY *n* (of a flower) condition of having a concave or flat receptacle with the gynoecium and other floral parts at the same level

PERIHELIA *n* points in the orbits of planets at which they are nearest the sun

PERIKARYA *n* parts of nerve cells that contain the nuclei

PERIL *n* great danger ▷ *vb* expose to danger

PERILED > PERIL

PERILING > PERIL

PERILLA *n* type of mint

PERILLAS > PERILLA

PERILLED > PERIL

PERILLING > PERIL

PERILOUS *adj* very hazardous or dangerous

PERILS > PERIL

PERILUNE *n* point in a lunar orbit when a spacecraft launched from the moon is nearest the moon

PERILUNES > PERILUNE

PERILYMPH *n* fluid filling the space between the membranous and bony labyrinths of the internal ear

PERIMETER *n* outer edge of an area

PERIMETRY > PERIMETER

PERIMORPH *n* mineral that encloses another mineral of a different type

PERIMYSIA *n* sheaths of fibrous connective tissue surrounding the primary bundles of muscle fibres

PERINAEUM *same as* > PERINEUM

PERINATAL *adj* of or in the weeks shortly before or after birth

PERINEA > PERINEUM

PERINEAL > PERINEUM

PERINEUM *n* region of the body between the anus and the genitals

PERINEUMS > PERINEUM

PERIOD *n* particular portion of time ▷ *adj* (of

furniture, dress, a play, etc) dating from or in the style of an earlier time ▷ *vb* divide into periods

PERIODATE *n* any salt or ester of a periodic acid

PERIODED > PERIOD

PERIODIC *adj* recurring at intervals

PERIODID *n* kind of iodide

PERIODIDE *variant of* > PERIODID

PERIODIDS > PERIODID

PERIODING > PERIOD

PERIODS > PERIOD

PERIOST *n* thick fibrous two-layered membrane covering the surface of bones

PERIOSTEA > PERIOSTS

PERIOSTS > PERIOST

PERIOTIC *adj* of or relating to the structures situated around the internal ear ▷ *n* periotic bone

PERIOTICS > PERIOTIC

PERIPATUS *n* wormlike arthropod with a segmented body and short unjointed limbs

PERIPETIA *n* abrupt turn of events or reversal of circumstances

PERIPETY *same as* > PERIPETEIA

PERIPHERY *n* boundary or edge

PERIPLASM *n* region inside wall of biological cell

PERIPLAST *n* nutritive and supporting tissue in animal organ

PERIPLUS *n* circumnavigation

PERIPROCT *n* tough membrane surrounding anus in echinoderms

PERIPTER *n* type of ancient temple

PERIPTERS > PERIPTER

PERIPTERY *n* region surrounding moving body

PERIQUE *n* strong highly-flavoured tobacco cured in its own juices and grown in Louisiana

PERIQUES > PERIQUE

PERIS > PERI

PERISARC *n* outer chitinous layer secreted by colonial hydrozoan coelenterates

PERISARCS > PERISARC

PERISCIAN *adj* person whose shadow moves round every point of compass during day

PERISCOPE *n* instrument used, esp in submarines, to give a view of objects on a different level

PERISH *vb* be destroyed or die

PERISHED *adj* (of a person,

part of the body, etc) extremely cold
**PERISHER** n mischievous person
**PERISHERS** > PERISHER
**PERISHES** > PERISH
**PERISHING** adj very cold
**PERISPERM** n nutritive tissue surrounding the embryo in certain seeds, and developing from the nucellus of the ovule
**PERISTOME** n fringe of pointed teeth surrounding the opening of a moss capsule
**PERISTYLE** n colonnade that surrounds a court or building
**PERITI** > PERITUS
**PERITONEA** n thin translucent serous sacs that line the walls of abdominal cavities and cover the viscera
**PERITRACK** another name for > TAXIWAY
**PERITRICH** n ciliate protozoan in which the cilia are restricted to a spiral around the mouth
**PERITUS** n Catholic theology consultant
**PERIWIG** same as > PERUKE
**PERIWIGS** > PERIWIG
**PERJINK** adj prim or finicky
**PERJURE** vb render (oneself) guilty of perjury
**PERJURED** adj having sworn falsely
**PERJURER** > PERJURE
**PERJURERS** > PERJURE
**PERJURES** > PERJURE
**PERJURIES** > PERJURY
**PERJURING** > PERJURE
**PERJUROUS** > PERJURY
**PERJURY** n act or crime of lying while under oath in a court
**PERK** n incidental benefit gained from a job, such as a company car ▷ adj pert ▷ vb (of coffee) percolate
**PERKED** > PERK
**PERKIER** > PERKY
**PERKIEST** > PERKY
**PERKILY** > PERKY
**PERKIN** same as > PARKIN
**PERKINESS** > PERKY
**PERKING** > PERK
**PERKINS** > PERKIN
**PERKISH** adj perky
**PERKS** > PERK
**PERKY** adj lively or cheerful
**PERLEMOEN** n edible sea creature with a shell lined with mother of pearl
**PERLITE** n variety of obsidian consisting of masses of small pearly globules
**PERLITES** > PERLITE
**PERLITIC** > PERLITE
**PERLOUS** same

as > PERILOUS
**PERM** n long-lasting curly hairstyle produced by treating the hair with chemicals ▷ vb give (hair) a perm
**PERMALLOY** n any of various alloys containing iron and nickel
**PERMANENT** adj lasting forever
**PERMEABLE** adj able to be permeated, esp by liquid
**PERMEABLY** > PERMEABLE
**PERMEANCE** n act of permeating
**PERMEANT** > PERMEANCE
**PERMEASE** n carrier protein
**PERMEASES** > PERMEASE
**PERMEATE** vb pervade or pass through the whole of (something)
**PERMEATED** > PERMEATE
**PERMEATES** > PERMEATE
**PERMEATOR** > PERMEATE
**PERMED** > PERM
**PERMIAN** adj of, denoting, or formed in the last period of the Palaeozoic era
**PERMIE** n person, esp an office worker, employed by a firm on a permanent basis
**PERMIES** > PERMIE
**PERMING** > PERM
**PERMIT** vb give permission, allow ▷ n document giving permission to do something
**PERMITS** > PERMIT
**PERMITTED** > PERMIT
**PERMITTEE** n person given a permit
**PERMITTER** > PERMIT
**PERMS** > PERM
**PERMUTATE** vb alter the sequence or arrangement (of)
**PERMUTE** vb change the sequence of
**PERMUTED** > PERMUTE
**PERMUTES** > PERMUTE
**PERMUTING** > PERMUTE
**PERN** vb make profitable
**PERNANCY** n receiving of rents
**PERNED** > PERN
**PERNING** > PERN
**PERNIO** n chilblain
**PERNIONES** > PERNIO
**PERNOD** n aniseed-flavoured aperitif from France
**PERNODS** > PERNOD
**PERNS** > PERN
**PERONE** n fibula
**PERONEAL** adj of or relating to the fibula or the outer side of the leg
**PERONES** > PERONE
**PERONEUS** n lateral muscle of the leg
**PERORAL** adj administered through mouth

**PERORALLY** > PERORAL
**PERORATE** vb speak at length, esp in a formal manner
**PERORATED** > PERORATE
**PERORATES** > PERORATE
**PERORATOR** > PERORATE
**PEROVSKIA** n Russian sage
**PEROXID** variant of > PEROXIDE
**PEROXIDE** n hydrogen peroxide used as a hair bleach ▷ adj bleached with or resembling peroxide ▷ vb bleach (the hair) with peroxide
**PEROXIDED** > PEROXIDE
**PEROXIDES** > PEROXIDE
**PEROXIDIC** > PEROXIDE
**PEROXIDS** > PEROXID
**PEROXY** adj containing the peroxide group
**PERP** n informal US and Canadian word for someone who has committed a crime
**PERPEND** n large stone that passes through a wall from one side to the other ▷ vb ponder
**PERPENDED** > PERPEND
**PERPENDS** > PERPEND
**PERPENT** same as > PERPEND
**PERPENTS** > PERPENT
**PERPETUAL** adj lasting forever ▷ n (of a crop plant) continually producing edible parts
**PERPLEX** vb puzzle, bewilder
**PERPLEXED** > PERPLEX
**PERPLEXER** > PERPLEX
**PERPLEXES** > PERPLEX
**PERPS** > PERP
**PERRADIAL** adj situated around radii of radiate
**PERRADII** > PERRADIUS
**PERRADIUS** n primary tentacle of a polyp
**PERRIER** n short mortar
**PERRIERS** > PERRIER
**PERRIES** > PERRY
**PERRON** n external flight of steps, esp one at the front entrance of a building
**PERRONS** > PERRON
**PERRUQUE** old spelling of > PERUKE
**PERRUQUES** > PERRUQUE
**PERRY** n alcoholic drink made from fermented pears
**PERSALT** n any salt of a peracid
**PERSALTS** > PERSALT
**PERSANT** adj piercing
**PERSAUNT** adj piercing
**PERSE** old variant of > PIERCE
**PERSECUTE** vb treat cruelly because of race, religion, etc
**PERSEITY** n quality of having substance independently of real

objects
**PERSELINE** same as > PURSLANE
**PERSES** > PERSE
**PERSEVERE** vb keep making an effort despite difficulties
**PERSICO** same as > PERSICOT
**PERSICOS** > PERSICO
**PERSICOT** n cordial made from apricots
**PERSICOTS** > PERSICOT
**PERSIENNE** n printed calico
**PERSIMMON** n sweet red tropical fruit
**PERSING** > PERSE
**PERSIST** vb continue to be or happen, last
**PERSISTED** > PERSIST
**PERSISTER** > PERSIST
**PERSISTS** > PERSIST
**PERSON** n human being
**PERSONA** n someone's personality as presented to others
**PERSONAE** > PERSONA
**PERSONAGE** n important person
**PERSONAL** adj individual or private ▷ n item of movable property
**PERSONALS** > PERSONAL
**PERSONAS** > PERSONA
**PERSONATE** vb assume the identity of (another person) with intent to deceive ▷ adj (of the corollas of certain flowers) having two lips in the form of a face
**PERSONIFY** vb give human characteristics to
**PERSONISE** same as > PERSONIZE
**PERSONIZE** vb personify
**PERSONNED** adj manned
**PERSONNEL** n people employed in an organization
**PERSONS** > PERSON
**PERSPEX** n tradename for any of various clear acrylic resins, used chiefly as a substitute for glass
**PERSPEXES** > PERSPEX
**PERSPIRE** vb sweat
**PERSPIRED** > PERSPIRE
**PERSPIRES** > PERSPIRE
**PERSPIRY** adj perspiring
**PERST** adj perished
**PERSUADE** vb make (someone) do something by argument, charm, etc
**PERSUADED** > PERSUADE
**PERSUADER** > PERSUADE
**PERSUADES** > PERSUADE
**PERSUE** obsolete form of > PURSUE
**PERSUED** > PERSUE
**PERSUES** > PERSUE
**PERSUING** > PERSUE
**PERSWADE** obsolete form of > PERSUADE

**PERSWADED** > PERSWADE
**PERSWADES** > PERSWADE
**PERT** adj saucy and cheeky ▷ n pert person
**PERTAIN** vb belong or be relevant (to)
**PERTAINED** > PERTAIN
**PERTAINS** > PERTAIN
**PERTAKE** obsolete form of > PARTAKE
**PERTAKEN** > PERTAKE
**PERTAKES** > PERTAKE
**PERTAKING** > PERTAKE
**PERTER** > PERT
**PERTEST** > PERT
**PERTHITE** n type of feldspar
**PERTHITES** > PERTHITE
**PERTHITIC** > PERTHITE
**PERTINENT** adj relevant
**PERTLY** > PERT
**PERTNESS** > PERT
**PERTOOK** > PERTAKE
**PERTS** > PERT
**PERTURB** vb disturb greatly
**PERTURBED** > PERTURB
**PERTURBER** > PERTURB
**PERTURBS** > PERTURB
**PERTUSATE** adj pierced at apex
**PERTUSE** adj having holes
**PERTUSED** adj having holes
**PERTUSION** n punched hole
**PERTUSSAL** > PERTUSSIS
**PERTUSSES** > PERTUSSIS
**PERTUSSIS** n whooping cough
**PERUKE** n wig for men worn in the 17th and 18th centuries
**PERUKED** adj wearing wig
**PERUKES** > PERUKE
**PERUSABLE** > PERUSE
**PERUSAL** > PERUSE
**PERUSALS** > PERUSE
**PERUSE** vb read in a careful or leisurely manner
**PERUSED** > PERUSE
**PERUSER** > PERUSE
**PERUSERS** > PERUSE
**PERUSES** > PERUSE
**PERUSING** > PERUSE
**PERV** n pervert ▷ vb give a person an erotic look
**PERVADE** vb spread right through (something)
**PERVADED** > PERVADE
**PERVADER** > PERVADE
**PERVADERS** > PERVADE
**PERVADES** > PERVADE
**PERVADING** > PERVADE
**PERVASION** > PERVADE
**PERVASIVE** adj pervading or tending to pervade
**PERVE** same as > PERV
**PERVED** > PERV
**PERVERSE** adj deliberately doing something different from what is thought normal or proper
**PERVERSER** > PERVERSE
**PERVERT** vb use or alter for a wrong purpose ▷ n person who practises

sexual perversion
**PERVERTED** adj deviating greatly from what is regarded as normal or right
**PERVERTER** > PERVERT
**PERVERTS** > PERVERT
**PERVES** > PERV
**PERVIATE** vb perforate or burrow
**PERVIATED** > PERVIATE
**PERVIATES** > PERVIATE
**PERVICACY** n obstinacy
**PERVING** > PERV
**PERVIOUS** adj able to be penetrated, permeable
**PERVS** > PERV
**PES** n animal part corresponding to the human foot
**PESADE** n position in which the horse stands on the hind legs with the forelegs in the air
**PESADES** > PESADE
**PESANT** obsolete spelling of > PEASANT
**PESANTE** adv to be performed clumsily
**PESANTS** > PESANT
**PESAUNT** obsolete spelling of > PEASANT
**PESAUNTS** > PESAUNT
**PESETA** n former monetary unit of Spain
**PESETAS** > PESETA
**PESEWA** n Ghanaian monetary unit worth one hundredth of a cedi
**PESEWAS** > PESEWA
**PESHWA** same as > PEISHWA
**PESHWAS** > PESHWA
**PESKIER** > PESKY
**PESKIEST** > PESKY
**PESKILY** > PESKY
**PESKINESS** > PESKY
**PESKY** adj troublesome
**PESO** n monetary unit of Argentina, Mexico, etc
**PESOS** > PESO
**PESSARIES** > PESSARY
**PESSARY** n appliance worn in the vagina, either to prevent conception or to support the womb
**PESSIMA** n lowest point
**PESSIMAL** adj (of animal's environment) least favourable for survival
**PESSIMISM** n tendency to expect the worst in all things
**PESSIMIST** > PESSIMISM
**PESSIMUM** same as > PESSIMAL
**PEST** n annoying person
**PESTER** vb annoy or nag continually
**PESTERED** > PESTER
**PESTERER** > PESTER
**PESTERERS** > PESTER
**PESTERING** > PESTER
**PESTEROUS** adj inclined to annoy

**PESTERS** > PESTER
**PESTFUL** adj causing annoyance
**PESTHOLE** n breeding ground for disease
**PESTHOLES** > PESTHOLE
**PESTHOUSE** n hospital for treating persons with infectious diseases
**PESTICIDE** n chemical for killing insect pests
**PESTIER** > PESTY
**PESTIEST** > PESTY
**PESTILENT** adj annoying, troublesome
**PESTLE** n club-shaped implement for grinding things to powder in a mortar ▷ vb pound (a substance or object) with or as if with a pestle
**PESTLED** > PESTLE
**PESTLES** > PESTLE
**PESTLING** > PESTLE
**PESTO** n sauce for pasta, consisting of basil leaves, pine nuts, garlic, oil, and Parmesan cheese, all crushed together
**PESTOLOGY** n study of pests
**PESTOS** > PESTO
**PESTS** > PEST
**PESTY** adj persistently annoying
**PET** n animal kept for pleasure and companionship ▷ adj kept as a pet ▷ vb treat as a pet
**PETABYTE** n in computing, $10^{15}$ or $2^{50}$ bytes
**PETABYTES** > PETABYTE
**PETAHERTZ** n very large unit of electrical frequency
**PETAL** n one of the brightly coloured outer parts of a flower
**PETALED** > PETAL
**PETALINE** > PETAL
**PETALISM** n ostracism in ancient Syracuse
**PETALISMS** > PETALISM
**PETALLED** > PETAL
**PETALLIKE** > PETAL
**PETALODIC** > PETALODY
**PETALODY** n condition in certain plants in which stamens or other parts of the flower assume the form and function of petals
**PETALOID** adj resembling a petal, esp in shape
**PETALOUS** adj bearing or having petals
**PETALS** > PETAL
**PETANQUE** n game, popular in France, in which metal bowls are thrown to land as near as possible to a target ball
**PETANQUES** > PETANQUE
**PETAR** obsolete variant of > PETARD

**PETARA** n clothes basket
**PETARAS** > PETARA
**PETARD** n device containing explosives used to breach a wall, doors, etc
**PETARDS** > PETARD
**PETARIES** > PETARY
**PETARS** > PETAR
**PETARY** n weapon for hurling stones
**PETASOS** same as > PETASUS
**PETASOSES** > PETASOS
**PETASUS** n broad-brimmed hat worn by the ancient Greeks
**PETASUSES** > PETASUS
**PETAURINE** n animal able to glide
**PETAURIST** n flying phalanger
**PETCHARY** n type of kingbird
**PETCOCK** n small valve for checking the water level in a steam boiler or draining condensed steam from the cylinder of a steam engine
**PETCOCKS** > PETCOCK
**PETECHIA** n minute discoloured spot on the surface of the skin or mucous membrane, caused by an underlying ruptured blood vessel
**PETECHIAE** > PETECHIA
**PETECHIAL** > PETECHIA
**PETER** vb fall (off) in volume, intensity, etc, and finally cease ▷ n act of petering
**PETERED** > PETER
**PETERING** > PETER
**PETERMAN** n burglar skilled in safe-breaking
**PETERMEN** > PETERMAN
**PETERS** > PETER
**PETERSHAM** n thick corded ribbon used to stiffen belts, button bands, etc
**PETHER** old variant of > PEDLAR
**PETHERS** > PETHER
**PETHIDINE** n white crystalline water-soluble drug used to relieve pain
**PETILLANT** adj (of wine) slightly effervescent
**PETIOLAR** > PETIOLE
**PETIOLATE** adj (of a plant or leaf) having a leafstalk
**PETIOLE** n stalk which attaches a leaf to a plant
**PETIOLED** > PETIOLE
**PETIOLES** > PETIOLE
**PETIOLULE** n stalk of any of the leaflets making up a compound leaf
**PETIT** adj of little or lesser importance
**PETITE** adj (of a woman) small and dainty ▷ n clothing size for small women

PETITES > PETITE
PETITIO as in *petitio principii* form of fallacious reasoning in which the conclusion has been assumed in the premise
PETITION n formal request, esp one signed by many people and presented to parliament ▷ vb present a petition to
PETITIONS > PETITION
PETITORY adj soliciting
PETNAP vb steal pet
PETNAPER > PETNAP
PETNAPERS > PETNAP
PETNAPING > PETNAP
PETNAPPED > PETNAP
PETNAPPER > PETNAP
PETNAPS > PETNAP
PETRALE n type of sole
PETRALES > PETRALE
PETRARIES > PETRARY
PETRARY n weapon for hurling stones
PETRE same as > SALTPETRE
PETREL n sea bird with a hooked bill and tubular nostrils
PETRELS > PETREL
PETRES > PETRE
PETRIFIC adj petrifying
PETRIFIED > PETRIFY
PETRIFIER > PETRIFY
PETRIFIES > PETRIFY
PETRIFY vb frighten severely
PETROGENY n origin of rocks
PETROGRAM n prehistoric rock painting
PETROL n flammable liquid obtained from petroleum, used as fuel in internal-combustion engines ▷ vb supply with petrol
PETROLAGE n addition of petrol (to a body of water) to get rid of mosquitoes
PETROLEUM n thick dark oil found underground
PETROLEUR n person using petrol to cause explosions
PETROLIC adj of, relating to, containing, or obtained from petroleum
PETROLLED > PETROL
PETROLOGY n study of the composition, origin, structure, and formation of rocks
PETROLS > PETROL
PETRONEL n firearm of large calibre used in the 16th and early 17th centuries, esp by cavalry soldiers
PETRONELS > PETRONEL
PETROSAL adj of, relating to, or situated near the dense part of the temporal bone that surrounds the inner ear ▷ n petrosal bone

PETROSALS > PETROSAL
PETROUS adj denoting the dense part of the temporal bone that surrounds the inner ear
PETS > PET
PETSAI n Chinese cabbage
PETSAIS > PETSAI
PETTABLE > PET
PETTED > PET
PETTEDLY > PET
PETTER > PET
PETTERS > PET
PETTI n petticoat
PETTICOAT n woman's skirt-shaped undergarment
PETTIER > PETTY
PETTIES > PETTI
PETTIEST > PETTY
PETTIFOG vb quibble or fuss over details
PETTIFOGS > PETTIFOG
PETTILY > PETTY
PETTINESS > PETTY
PETTING > PET
PETTINGS > PET
PETTISH adj peevish or fretful
PETTISHLY > PETTISH
PETTITOES pl n pig's trotters, esp when used as food
PETTLE vb pat animal
PETTLED > PETTLE
PETTLES > PETTLE
PETTLING > PETTLE
PETTO n breast of animal
PETTY adj unimportant, trivial
PETULANCE > PETULANT
PETULANCY > PETULANT
PETULANT adj childishly irritable or peevish
PETUNIA n garden plant with funnel-shaped flowers
PETUNIAS > PETUNIA
PETUNTSE n fusible feldspathic mineral used in hard-paste porcelain
PETUNTSES > PETUNTSE
PETUNTZE same as > PETUNTSE
PETUNTZES > PETUNTZE
PEW n fixed benchlike seat in a church
PEWEE n any of several small North American flycatchers of the genus *Contopus*, having a greenish-brown plumage
PEWEES > PEWEE
PEWHOLDER n renter of pew
PEWIT another name for > LAPWING
PEWITS > PEWIT
PEWS > PEW
PEWTER n greyish metal made of tin and lead
PEWTERER > PEWTER
PEWTERERS > PEWTER
PEWTERS > PEWTER
PEYOTE another name

for > MESCAL
PEYOTES > PEYOTE
PEYOTISM n ritual use of peyote
PEYOTISMS > PEYOTISM
PEYOTIST n person who uses peyote
PEYOTISTS > PEYOTIST
PEYOTL same as > PEYOTE
PEYOTLS > PEYOTL
PEYSE vb weight or poise
PEYSED > PEYSE
PEYSES > PEYSE
PEYSING > PEYSE
PEYTRAL same as > PEYTREL
PEYTRALS > PEYTRAL
PEYTREL n breastplate of horse's armour
PEYTRELS > PEYTREL
PEZANT obsolete spelling of > PEASANT
PEZANTS > PEZANT
PEZIZOID adj having cup-like form
PFENNIG n former German monetary unit worth one hundredth of a mark
PFENNIGE > PFENNIG
PFENNIGS > PFENNIG
PFENNING old variant of > PFENNIG
PFENNINGS > PFENNING
PFFT interj sound indicating sudden disappearance of something
PFUI interj phooey
PHACELIA n plant grown for its large, deep blue bell flowers
PHACELIAS > PHACELIA
PHACOID adj lentil- or lens-shaped
PHACOIDAL same as > PHACOID
PHACOLITE n colourless variety of chabazite
PHACOLITH n lens-shaped igneous rock structure
PHAEIC adj (of animals) having dusky coloration
PHAEISM > PHAEIC
PHAEISMS > PHAEIC
PHAENOGAM n seed-bearing plant
PHAETON n light four-wheeled horse-drawn carriage with or without a top
PHAETONS > PHAETON
PHAGE n virus that is parasitic in a bacterium and multiplies within its host, which is destroyed when the new viruses are released
PHAGEDENA n rapidly spreading ulcer that destroys tissues as it increases in size
PHAGES > PHAGE
PHAGOCYTE n cell or protozoan that engulfs particles, such as

microorganisms
PHAGOSOME n part of biological cell
PHALANGAL > PHALANGE
PHALANGE another name for > PHALANX
PHALANGER same as > POSSUM
PHALANGES > PHALANX
PHALANGID n type of arachnid
PHALANX n closely grouped mass of people
PHALANXES > PHALANX
PHALAROPE n aquatic shore bird of northern oceans and lakes
PHALLI > PHALLUS
PHALLIC adj of or resembling a phallus
PHALLIN n poisonous substance from mushroom
PHALLINS > PHALLIN
PHALLISM n worship or veneration of the phallus
PHALLISMS > PHALLISM
PHALLIST > PHALLICISM
PHALLISTS > PHALLICISM
PHALLOID adj resembling penis
PHALLUS n penis, esp as a symbol of reproductive power in primitive rites
PHALLUSES > PHALLUS
PHANG old variant spelling of > FANG
PHANGED > PHANG
PHANGING > PHANG
PHANGS > PHANG
PHANSIGAR n Indian assassin
PHANTASIM same as > PHANTASM
PHANTASM n unreal vision, illusion
PHANTASMA same as > PHANTASM
PHANTASMS > PHANTASM
PHANTAST same as > FANTAST
PHANTASTS > PHANTAST
PHANTASY same as > FANTASY
PHANTOM n ghost ▷ adj deceptive or unreal
PHANTOMS > PHANTOM
PHANTOMY adj of phantoms
PHANTOSME old spelling of > PHANTASM
PHARAOH n ancient Egyptian king
PHARAOHS > PHARAOH
PHARAONIC > PHARAOH
PHARE n beacon tower
PHARES > PHARE
PHARISAIC n righteously hypocritical
PHARISEE n self-righteous or hypocritical person
PHARISEES > PHARISEE
PHARMA n pharmaceutical companies considered together as an industry

PHARMACY n preparation and dispensing of drugs and medicines

PHARMAS > PHARMA

PHARMING n practice of rearing or growing genetically-modified animals or plants in order to develop pharmaceutical products

PHARMINGS > PHARMING

PHAROS n lighthouse

PHAROSES > PHAROS

PHARYNGAL adj of, relating to, or situated in or near the pharynx

PHARYNGES > PHARYNX

PHARYNX n cavity forming the back part of the mouth

PHARYNXES > PHARYNX

PHASE n any distinct or characteristic stage in a development or chain of events ▷ vb arrange or carry out in stages or to coincide with something else

PHASEAL > PHASE

PHASED > PHASE

PHASEDOWN n gradual reduction

PHASELESS > PHASE

PHASEOLIN n anti-fungal substance from kidney bean

PHASEOUT n gradual reduction

PHASEOUTS > PHASEOUT

PHASES > PHASE

PHASIC > PHASE

PHASING n tonal sweep achieved by varying the phase relationship of two similar audio signals by mechanical or electronic means

PHASINGS > PHASING

PHASIS another word for > PHASE

PHASMID n stick insect or leaf insect

PHASMIDS > PHASMID

PHASOR n rotating vector representing a quantity, such as an alternating current or voltage, that varies sinusoidally

PHASORS > PHASOR

PHAT adj terrific

PHATIC adj (of speech, esp of conversational phrases) used to establish social contact and to express sociability rather than specific meaning

PHATTER > PHAT

PHATTEST > PHAT

PHEASANT n game bird with bright plumage

PHEASANTS > PHEASANT

PHEAZAR old variant of > VIZIER

PHEAZARS > PHEAZAR

PHEER same as > FERE

PHEERE same as > FERE

PHEERES > PHEERE

PHEERS > PHEER

PHEESE vb worry

PHEESED > PHEESE

PHEESES > PHEESE

PHEESING > PHEESE

PHEEZE same as > PHEESE

PHEEZED > PHEEZE

PHEEZES > PHEEZE

PHEEZING > PHEEZE

PHELLEM technical name for > CORK

PHELLEMS > PHELLEM

PHELLOGEN n cork cambium

PHELLOID adj like cork

PHELONIA > PHELONION

PHELONION n vestment for an Orthodox priest

PHENACITE n colourless or white glassy mineral

PHENAKISM n deception

PHENAKITE same as > PHENACITE

PHENATE n ester or salt of phenol

PHENATES > PHENATE

PHENAZIN same as > PHENAZINE

PHENAZINE n yellow crystalline tricyclic compound

PHENAZINS > PHENAZIN

PHENE n genetically determined characteristic of organism

PHENES > PHENE

PHENETIC > PHENETICS

PHENETICS n system of classification based on similarities between organisms without regard to their evolutionary relationships

PHENETOL same as > PHENETOLE

PHENETOLE n colourless oily compound

PHENETOLS > PHENETOL

PHENGITE n type of alabaster

PHENGITES > PHENGITE

PHENIC adj of phenol

PHENIX same as > PHOENIX

PHENIXES > PHENIX

PHENOCOPY n noninheritable change in an organism that is caused by environmental influence during development but resembles the effects of a genetic mutation

PHENOGAM same as > PHAENOGAM

PHENOGAMS > PHENOGAM

PHENOL n chemical used in disinfectants and antiseptics

PHENOLATE vb treat or disinfect with phenol

PHENOLIC adj of, containing, or derived from phenol ▷ n derivative of phenol

PHENOLICS > PHENOLIC

PHENOLOGY n study of recurring phenomena, such as animal migration, esp as influenced by climatic conditions

PHENOLS > PHENOL

PHENOM n person or thing of outstanding abilities or qualities

PHENOMENA n phenomenons

PHENOMS > PHENOM

PHENOTYPE n physical form of an organism as determined by the interaction of its genetic make-up and its environment

PHENOXIDE n any of a class of salts of phenol

PHENOXY as in phenoxy resin any of a class of resins dervied from polyhydroxy ethers

PHENYL n chemical substance

PHENYLENE n compound derived from benzene

PHENYLIC > PHENYL

PHENYLS > PHENYL

PHENYTOIN n anticonvulsant drug

PHEON n barbed iron head of dart

PHEONS > PHEON

PHERESES > PHERESIS

PHERESIS n specialized form of blood donation

PHEROMONE n chemical substance, secreted externally by certain animals, such as insects, affecting the behaviour or physiology of other animals of the same species

PHESE same as > PHEESE

PHESED > PHESE

PHESES > PHESE

PHESING > PHESE

PHEW interj exclamation of relief, surprise, etc

PHI n 21st letter in the Greek alphabet

PHIAL n small bottle for medicine etc ▷ vb put in phial

PHIALLED > PHIAL

PHIALLING > PHIAL

PHIALS > PHIAL

PHILABEG same as > FILIBEG

PHILABEGS > PHILABEG

PHILANDER vb (of a man) flirt or have many casual love affairs with women

PHILATELY n stamp collecting

PHILHORSE n last horse in a team

PHILIBEG variant spelling of > FILIBEG

PHILIBEGS > PHILIBEG

PHILIPPIC n bitter or impassioned speech of denunciation, invective

PHILISTIA n domain of cultural philistine

PHILLABEG same as > FILIBEG

PHILLIBEG same as > FILIBEG

PHILOGYNY n fondness for women

PHILOLOGY n science of the structure and development of languages

PHILOMATH n lover of learning

PHILOMEL n nightingale

PHILOMELA same as > PHILOMEL

PHILOMELS > PHILOMEL

PHILOMOT n colour of dead leaf

PHILOMOTS > PHILOMOT

PHILOPENA n gift made as forfeit in game

PHILTER vb drink supposed to arouse love, desire, etc ▷ vb arouse sexual or romantic feelings by means of a philter

PHILTERED > PHILTER

PHILTERS > PHILTER

PHILTRA > PHILTRUM

PHILTRE n magic drink supposed to arouse love in the person who drinks it ▷ vb mix with love potion

PHILTRED > PHILTRE

PHILTRES > PHILTRE

PHILTRING > PHILTRE

PHILTRUM n indentation above the upper lip

PHIMOSES > PHIMOSIS

PHIMOSIS n abnormal tightness of the foreskin, preventing its being retracted over the tip of the penis

PHIMOTIC > PHIMOSIS

PHINNOCK variant spelling of > FINNOCK

PHINNOCKS > PHINNOCK

PHIS > PHI

PHISHING n use of fraudulent e-mails and lookalike websites to extract personal and financial details for criminal purposes

PHISHINGS > PHISHING

PHISNOMY n physiognomy

PHIZ n face or a facial expression

PHIZES > PHIZ

PHIZOG same as > PHIZ

PHIZOGS > PHIZOG

PHIZZES > PHIZ

PHLEBITIC > PHLEBITIS

PHLEBITIS n inflammation of a vein

PHLEGM n thick yellowish substance formed in the nose and throat during a cold

**PHLEGMIER** > PHLEGM

**PHLEGMON** *n* inflammatory mass that may progress to abscess

**PHLEGMONS** > PHLEGMON

**PHLEGMS** > PHLEGM

**PHLEGMY** > PHLEGM

**PHLOEM** *n* plant tissue that acts as a path for the distribution of food substances to all parts of the plant

**PHLOEMS** > PHLOEM

**PHLOMIS** *n* plant of Phlomis genus

**PHLOMISES** > PHLOMIS

**PHLORIZIN** *n* chemical found in root bark of fruit trees

**PHLOX** *n* flowering garden plant

**PHLOXES** > PHLOX

**PHLYCTENA** *n* small blister, vesicle, or pustule

**PHO** *n* Vietnamese noodle soup

**PHOBIA** *n* intense and unreasoning fear or dislike

**PHOBIAS** > PHOBIA

**PHOBIC** *adj* of, relating to, or arising from a phobia ▷ *n* person suffering from a phobia

**PHOBICS** > PHOBIC

**PHOBISM** *n* phobia

**PHOBISMS** > PHOBISM

**PHOBIST** > PHOBISM

**PHOBISTS** > PHOBISM

**PHOCA** *n* genus of seals

**PHOCAE** > PHOCA

**PHOCAS** > PHOCA

**PHOCINE** *adj* of, relating to, or resembling a seal

**PHOCOMELY** *n* congenital deformity resulting from prenatal interference with the development of the fetal limbs, characterized esp by short stubby hands or feet attached close to the body

**PHOEBE** *n* greyish-brown North American flycatcher

**PHOEBES** > PHOEBE

**PHOEBUS** *n* sun

**PHOEBUSES** > PHOEBUS

**PHOENIX** *n* legendary bird said to set fire to itself and rise anew from its ashes

**PHOENIXES** > PHOENIX

**PHOH** *variant of* > FOH

**PHOHS** > PHOH

**PHOLADES** > PHOLAS

**PHOLAS** *n* type of bivalve mollusc

**PHON** *n* unit of loudness

**PHONAL** *adj* relating to voice

**PHONATE** *vb* articulate speech sounds, esp to cause the vocal cords to vibrate in the execution of a voiced speech sound

**PHONATED** > PHONATE

**PHONATES** > PHONATE

**PHONATHON** *n* telephone-based fund-raising campaign

**PHONATING** > PHONATE

**PHONATION** > PHONATE

**PHONATORY** > PHONATE

**PHONE** *vb* telephone ▷ *n* single uncomplicated speech sound

**PHONECAM** *n* digital camera incorporated in a mobile phone

**PHONECAMS** > PHONECAM

**PHONECARD** *n* card used to operate certain public telephones

**PHONED** > PHONE

**PHONEME** *n* one of the set of speech sounds in any given language that serve to distinguish one word from another

**PHONEMES** > PHONEME

**PHONEMIC** *adj* of or relating to the phoneme

**PHONEMICS** *n* classification and analysis of the phonemes of a language

**PHONER** *n* person making a telephone call

**PHONERS** > PHONER

**PHONES** > PHONE

**PHONETIC** *adj* of speech sounds

**PHONETICS** *n* science of speech sounds

**PHONETISE** *same as* > PHONETIZE

**PHONETISM** *n* phonetic writing

**PHONETIST** *n* person who advocates or uses a system of phonetic spelling

**PHONETIZE** *vb* represent by phonetic signs

**PHONEY** *adj* not genuine ▷ *n* phoney person or thing ▷ *vb* fake

**PHONEYED** > PHONEY

**PHONEYING** > PHONEY

**PHONEYS** > PHONEY

**PHONIC** > PHONICS

**PHONICS** *n* method of teaching people to read by training them to associate letters with their phonetic values

**PHONIED** > PHONY

**PHONIER** > PHONY

**PHONIES** > PHONY

**PHONIEST** > PHONY

**PHONILY** > PHONY

**PHONINESS** > PHONY

**PHONING** > PHONE

**PHONMETER** *n* instrument measuring sound levels

**PHONO** *n* phonograph

**PHONOGRAM** *n* any written symbol standing for a sound, syllable, morpheme, or word

**PHONOLITE** *n* fine-grained volcanic igneous rock consisting of alkaline feldspars and nepheline

**PHONOLOGY** *n* study of the speech sounds in a language

**PHONON** *n* quantum of vibrational energy in the acoustic vibrations of a crystal lattice

**PHONONS** > PHONON

**PHONOPORE** *n* device for conveying sound

**PHONOS** > PHONO

**PHONOTYPE** *n* letter or symbol representing a sound

**PHONOTYPY** *n* transcription of speech into phonetic symbols

**PHONS** > PHON

**PHONY** *vb* fake

**PHONYING** > PHONY

**PHOOEY** *interj* exclamation of scorn or contempt

**PHORATE** *n* type of insecticide

**PHORATES** > PHORATE

**PHORESIES** > PHORESY

**PHORESY** *n* association in which one animal clings to another to ensure movement from place to place, as some mites use some insects

**PHORMINX** *n* ancient Greek stringed instrument

**PHORMIUM** *n* New Zealand plant with leathery evergreen leaves and red or yellow flowers in panicles

**PHORMIUMS** > PHORMIUM

**PHORONID** *n* small wormlike marine animal

**PHORONIDS** > PHORONID

**PHOS** > PHO

**PHOSGENE** *n* poisonous gas used in warfare

**PHOSGENES** > PHOSGENE

**PHOSPHATE** *n* compound of phosphorus

**PHOSPHENE** *n* sensation of light caused by pressure on the eyelid of a closed eye or by other mechanical or electrical interference with the visual system

**PHOSPHID** *same as* > PHOSPHIDE

**PHOSPHIDE** *n* any compound of phosphorus with another element, esp a more electropositive element

**PHOSPHIDS** > PHOSPHID

**PHOSPHIN** *same as* > PHOSPHINE

**PHOSPHINE** *n* colourless flammable gas that is slightly soluble in water and has a strong fishy odour

**PHOSPHINS** > PHOSPHIN

**PHOSPHITE** *n* any salt or

ester of phosphorous acid

**PHOSPHOR** *n* substance capable of emitting light when irradiated with particles of electromagnetic radiation

**PHOSPHORE** *same as* > PHOSPHOR

**PHOSPHORI** *n* plural of phosphorus

**PHOSPHORS** > PHOSPHOR

**PHOSSY** as in *phossy jaw* gangrenous condition of the lower jawbone caused by prolonged exposure to phosphorus fumes

**PHOT** *n* unit of illumination equal to one lumen per square centimetre

**PHOTIC** *adj* of or concerned with light

**PHOTICS** *n* science of light

**PHOTINIA** *n* genus of garden plants

**PHOTINIAS** > PHOTINIA

**PHOTISM** *n* sensation of light or colour caused by stimulus of another sense

**PHOTISMS** > PHOTISM

**PHOTO** *n* photograph ▷ *vb* take a photograph of

**PHOTOCELL** *n* cell which produces a current or voltage when exposed to light or other electromagnetic radiation

**PHOTOCOPY** *n* photographic reproduction ▷ *vb* make a photocopy of

**PHOTOED** > PHOTO

**PHOTOFIT** *n* method of combining photographs of facial features, hair, etc, into a composite picture of a face

**PHOTOFITS** > PHOTOFIT

**PHOTOG** *n* photograph

**PHOTOGEN** *same as* > PHOTOGENE

**PHOTOGENE** *n* afterimage

**PHOTOGENS** > PHOTOGEN

**PHOTOGENY** *n* photography

**PHOTOGRAM** *n* picture, usually abstract, produced on a photographic material without the use of a camera, as by placing an object on the material and exposing to light

**PHOTOGS** > PHOTOG

**PHOTOING** > PHOTO

**PHOTOLYSE** *vb* cause to undergo photolysis

**PHOTOLYZE** *same as* > PHOTOLYSE

**PHOTOMAP** *n* map constructed by adding grid lines, place names, etc, to one or more aerial photographs ▷ *vb* map (an area) using aerial photography

**PHOTOMAPS** > PHOTOMAP

**PHOTOMASK** n material on which etching pattern for integrated circuit is drawn

**PHOTON** n quantum of electromagnetic radiation energy, such as light, having both particle and wave behaviour

**PHOTONIC** > PHOTON

**PHOTONICS** n study and design of devices and systems, such as optical fibres, that depend on the transmission, modulation, or amplification of streams of photons

**PHOTONS** > PHOTON

**PHOTOPHIL** n light-seeking organism

**PHOTOPIA** n normal adaptation of the eye to light

**PHOTOPIAS** > PHOTOPIA

**PHOTOPIC** > PHOTOPIA

**PHOTOPLAY** n play filmed as movie

**PHOTOPSIA** n appearance of flashes due to retinal irritation

**PHOTOPSY** same as > PHOTOPSIA

**PHOTOS** > PHOTO

**PHOTOSCAN** n photographic scan

**PHOTOSET** vb set (type matter) by photosetting

**PHOTOSETS** > PHOTOSET

**PHOTOSTAT** n copy made by photocopying machine ▷ vb make a photostat copy (of)

**PHOTOTAXY** n movement of an entire organism in response to light

**PHOTOTUBE** n type of photocell in which radiation falling on a photocathode causes electrons to flow to an anode and thus produce an electric current

**PHOTOTYPE** n printing plate produced by photography ▷ vb reproduce (an illustration) using a phototype

**PHOTOTYPY** n process of producing phototypes

**PHOTS** > PHOT

**PHPHT** interj expressing irritation or reluctance

**PHRASAL** adj of, relating to, or composed of phrases

**PHRASALLY** > PHRASAL

**PHRASE** n group of words forming a unit of meaning, esp within a sentence ▷ vb express in words

**PHRASED** > PHRASE

**PHRASEMAN** n coiner of phrases

**PHRASEMEN** > PHRASEMAN

**PHRASER** > PHRASE

**PHRASERS** > PHRASE

**PHRASES** > PHRASE

**PHRASIER** > PHRASY

**PHRASIEST** > PHRASY

**PHRASING** n exact words used to say or write something

**PHRASINGS** > PHRASING

**PHRASY** adj containing phrases

**PHRATRAL** > PHRATRY

**PHRATRIC** > PHRATRY

**PHRATRIES** > PHRATRY

**PHRATRY** n group of people within a tribe who have a common ancestor

**PHREAK** vb hack into a telecommunications system

**PHREAKED** > PHREAK

**PHREAKER** > PHREAK

**PHREAKERS** > PHREAK

**PHREAKING** > PHREAK

**PHREAKS** > PHREAK

**PHREATIC** adj of or relating to ground water occurring below the water table

**PHRENESES** > PHRENESIS

**PHRENESIS** n mental confusion

**PHRENETIC** obsolete spelling of > FRENETIC

**PHRENIC** adj of or relating to the diaphragm

**PHRENISM** n belief in non-physical life force

**PHRENISMS** > PHRENISM

**PHRENITIC** > PHRENITIS

**PHRENITIS** n state of frenzy

**PHRENSIED** > PHRENSY

**PHRENSIES** > PHRENSY

**PHRENSY** obsolete spelling of > FRENZY

**PHRENTICK** obsolete spelling of > PHRENETIC

**PHRYGANA** another name for > GARIGUE

**PHRYGANAS** > PHRYGANA

**PHT** same as > PHPHT

**PHTHALATE** n salt or ester of phthalic acid

**PHTHALEIN** n any of a class of organic compounds obtained by the reaction of phthalic anhydride with a phenol and used in dyes

**PHTHALIC** as in phthalic anhydride white crystalline substance used mainly in producing dyestuffs

**PHTHALIN** n colourless compound formed by reduction of phthalein

**PHTHALINS** > PHTHALIN

**PHTHISES** > PHTHISIS

**PHTHISIC** adj relating to or affected with phthisis ▷ n person suffering from phthisis

**PHTHISICS** > PHTHISIC

**PHTHISIS** n any disease that causes wasting of the body, esp pulmonary tuberculosis

**PHUT** vb make muffled explosive sound

**PHUTS** > PHUT

**PHUTTED** > PHUT

**PHUTTING** > PHUT

**PHYCOLOGY** n study of algae

**PHYLA** > PHYLUM

**PHYLAE** > PHYLE

**PHYLAR** > PHYLUM

**PHYLARCH** n chief of tribe

**PHYLARCHS** > PHYLARCH

**PHYLARCHY** > PHYLARCH

**PHYLAXIS** n protection against infection

**PHYLE** n tribe or clan of an ancient Greek people such as the Ionians

**PHYLESES** > PHYLESIS

**PHYLESIS** n evolutionary events that modify taxon without causing speciation

**PHYLETIC** adj of or relating to the evolution of a species or group of organisms

**PHYLETICS** n study of the evolution of species

**PHYLIC** > PHYLE

**PHYLLARY** n bract subtending flower head of composite plant

**PHYLLID** n leaf of a liverwort or moss

**PHYLLIDS** > PHYLLID

**PHYLLITE** n compact lustrous metamorphic rock, rich in mica, derived from a shale or other clay-rich rock

**PHYLLITES** > PHYLLITE

**PHYLLITIC** > PHYLLITE

**PHYLLO** variant of > FILO

**PHYLLODE** n flattened leafstalk that resembles and functions as a leaf

**PHYLLODES** > PHYLLODE

**PHYLLODIA** > PHYLLODE

**PHYLLODY** n abnormal development of leaves from parts of flower

**PHYLLOID** adj resembling a leaf ▷ n leaf-like organ

**PHYLLOIDS** > PHYLLOID

**PHYLLOME** n leaf or a leaflike organ

**PHYLLOMES** > PHYLLOME

**PHYLLOMIC** > PHYLLOME

**PHYLLOPOD** n crustacean with leaf-like appendages

**PHYLLOS** > PHYLLO

**PHYLOGENY** n sequence of events involved in the evolution of a species, genus, etc

**PHYLON** n tribe

**PHYLONS** > PHYLON

**PHYLUM** n major taxonomic division of animals and plants that contains one or more classes

**PHYSALIA** n Portuguese man-of-war

**PHYSALIAS** > PHYSALIA

**PHYSALIS** n strawberry tomato

**PHYSED** n physical education

**PHYSEDS** > PHYSED

**PHYSES** > PHYSIS

**PHYSETER** n creature such as the sperm whale

**PHYSETERS** > PHYSETER

**PHYSIATRY** n treatment of injury by physical means

**PHYSIC** n medicine or drug, esp a cathartic or purge ▷ vb treat (a patient) with medicine

**PHYSICAL** adj of the body, as contrasted with the mind or spirit

**PHYSICALS** pl n commodities that can be purchased and used, as opposed to those bought and sold in a futures market

**PHYSICIAN** n doctor of medicine

**PHYSICISM** n belief in the physical as opposed to the spiritual

**PHYSICIST** n person skilled in or studying physics

**PHYSICKED** > PHYSIC

**PHYSICKY** > PHYSIC

**PHYSICS** n science of the properties of matter and energy

**PHYSIO** n physiotherapy

**PHYSIOS** > PHYSIO

**PHYSIQUE** n person's bodily build and muscular development

**PHYSIQUED** adj having particular physique

**PHYSIQUES** > PHYSIQUE

**PHYSIS** n part of bone responsible for lengthening

**PHYTANE** n hydrocarbon found in some fossilised plant remains

**PHYTANES** > PHYTANE

**PHYTIN** n substance from plants used as an energy supplement

**PHYTINS** > PHYTIN

**PHYTOGENY** n branch of botany that is concerned with the detailed description of plants

**PHYTOID** adj resembling plant

**PHYTOL** n alcohol used to synthesize some vitamins

**PHYTOLITH** n microscopic particle in plants

**PHYTOLOGY** rare name for > BOTANY

**PHYTOLS** > PHYTOL

**PHYTON** n unit of plant structure, usually considered as the smallest part of the plant that is capable of growth when detached from the parent plant

**PHYTONIC** > PHYTON

**PHYTONS** > PHYTON

**PHYTOSES** > PHYTOSIS

**PHYTOSIS** n disease caused by vegetable parasite

**PHYTOTOMY** n dissection of plants

**PHYTOTRON** n building in which plants can be grown on a large scale, under controlled conditions

**PI** n. sixteenth letter in the Greek alphabet ▷ vb spill and mix (set type) indiscriminately

**PIA** n innermost of the three membranes that cover the brain and the spinal cord

**PIACEVOLE** adv to be performed in playful manner

**PIACULAR** adj making expiation for a sacrilege

**PIAFFE** n passage done on the spot ▷ vb strut on the spot

**PIAFFED** > PIAFFE

**PIAFFER** > PIAFFE

**PIAFFERS** > PIAFFE

**PIAFFES** > PIAFFE

**PIAFFING** > PIAFFE

**PIAL** adj relating to pia mater

**PIAN** n contagious tropical skin disease

**PIANETTE** n small piano

**PIANETTES** > PIANETTE

**PIANIC** adj of piano

**PIANINO** n small upright piano

**PIANINOS** > PIANINO

**PIANISM** n technique, skill, or artistry in playing the piano

**PIANISMS** > PIANISM

**PIANIST** n person who plays the piano

**PIANISTE** variant of > PIANIST

**PIANISTES** > PIANISTE

**PIANISTIC** > PIANISM

**PIANISTS** > PIANIST

**PIANO** n musical instrument with strings which are struck by hammers worked by a keyboard ▷ adv quietly

**PIANOLIST** n person who plays the Pianola

**PIANOS** > PIANO

**PIANS** > PIAN

**PIARIST** n member of a Roman religious order

**PIARISTS** > PIARIST

**PIAS** > PIA

**PIASABA** same as > PIASSAVA

**PIASABAS** > PIASABA

**PIASAVA** same as > PIASSAVA

**PIASAVAS** > PIASAVA

**PIASSABA** same

as > PIASSAVA

**PIASSABAS** > PIASSABA

**PIASSAVA** n South American palm tree

**PIASSAVAS** > PIASSAVA

**PIASTER** same as > PIASTRE

**PIASTERS** > PIASTER

**PIASTRE** n standard monetary unit of South Vietnam, divided into 100 cents

**PIASTRES** > PIASTRE

**PIAZZA** n square or marketplace, esp in Italy

**PIAZZAS** > PIAZZA

**PIAZZE** > PIAZZA

**PIAZZIAN** > PIAZZA

**PIBAL** n method of measuring wind

**PIBALS** > PIBAL

**PIBROCH** n form of bagpipe music

**PIBROCHS** > PIBROCH

**PIC** n photograph or illustration

**PICA** n abnormal craving to ingest substances such as clay, dirt, and hair

**PICACHO** n pointed solitary mountain

**PICACHOS** > PICACHO

**PICADILLO** n Mexican dish

**PICADOR** n mounted bullfighter with a lance

**PICADORES** > PICADOR

**PICADORS** > PICADOR

**PICAL** adj relating to pica

**PICAMAR** n hydrocarbon extract of beechwood tar

**PICAMARS** > PICAMAR

**PICANINNY** n offensive term for a small Black or Aboriginal child

**PICANTE** adj spicy

**PICARA** n female adventurer

**PICARAS** > PICARA

**PICARIAN** n tree-haunting bird

**PICARIANS** > PICARIAN

**PICARO** n roguish adventurer

**PICAROON** n adventurer or rogue

**PICAROONS** > PICAROON

**PICAROS** > PICARO

**PICAS** > PICA

**PICAYUNE** adj of small value or importance ▷ n any coin of little value, such as a five-cent piece

**PICAYUNES** > PICAYUNE

**PICCADILL** n high stiff collar

**PICCANIN** n offensive word for a Black African child

**PICCANINS** > PICCANIN

**PICCATA** n Italian sauce

**PICCIES** > PICCY

**PICCOLO** n small flute

**PICCOLOS** > PICCOLO

**PICCY** n picture or photograph

**PICE** n former Indian coin

worth one sixty-fourth of a rupee

**PICENE** n type of hydrocarbon

**PICENES** > PICENE

**PICEOUS** adj of, relating to, or resembling pitch

**PICHOLINE** n variety of olive

**PICHURIM** n S American laurel tree

**PICHURIMS** > PICHURIM

**PICIFORM** adj relating to certain tree-haunting birds

**PICINE** adj relating to woodpeckers

**PICK** vb choose ▷ n choice

**PICKABACK** same

as > PIGGYBACK

**PICKABLE** > PICK

**PICKADIL** same

as > PICCADILL

**PICKADILL** same

as > PICCADILL

**PICKADILS** > PICKADIL

**PICKAPACK** same

as > PICKABACK

**PICKAROON** same

as > PICAROON

**PICKAX** same as > PICKAXE

**PICKAXE** n large pick ▷ vb use a pickaxe on (earth, rocks, etc)

**PICKAXED** > PICKAXE

**PICKAXES** > PICKAXE

**PICKAXING** > PICKAXE

**PICKBACK** same

as > PICKABACK

**PICKBACKS** > PICKBACK

**PICKED** > PICK

**PICKEER** vb make raid for booty

**PICKEERED** > PICKEER

**PICKEERER** > PICKEER

**PICKEERS** > PICKEER

**PICKER** n person or thing that picks, esp that gathers fruit, crops, etc

**PICKEREL** n North American freshwater game fish

**PICKERELS** > PICKEREL

**PICKERIES** > PICKERY

**PICKERS** > PICKER

**PICKERY** n petty theft

**PICKET** n person or group standing outside a workplace to deter would-be workers during a strike ▷ vb form a picket outside (a workplace)

**PICKETED** > PICKET

**PICKETER** > PICKET

**PICKETERS** > PICKET

**PICKETING** > PICKET

**PICKETS** > PICKET

**PICKIER** > PICKY

**PICKIEST** > PICKY

**PICKILY** > PICKY

**PICKIN** n small child

**PICKINESS** > PICKY

**PICKING** > PICK

**PICKINGS** pl n money

easily acquired

**PICKINS** > PICKIN

**PICKLE** n food preserved in vinegar or salt water ▷ vb preserve in vinegar or salt water

**PICKLED** adj (of food) preserved

**PICKLER** > PICKLE

**PICKLERS** > PICKLE

**PICKLES** > PICKLE

**PICKLING** > PICKLE

**PICKLOCK** n person who picks locks, esp one who gains unlawful access to premises by this means

**PICKLOCKS** > PICKLOCK

**PICKMAW** n type of gull

**PICKMAWS** > PICKMAW

**PICKOFF** n baseball play

**PICKOFFS** > PICKOFF

**PICKPROOF** adj (of a lock) unable to be picked

**PICKS** > PICK

**PICKTHANK** n flatterer

**PICKUP** n small truck with an open body and low sides

**PICKUPS** > PICKUP

**PICKWICK** n tool for raising the short wick of an oil lamp

**PICKWICKS** > PICKWICK

**PICKY** adj fussy

**PICLORAM** n type of herbicide

**PICLORAMS** > PICLORAM

**PICNIC** n informal meal out of doors ▷ vb have a picnic

**PICNICKED** > PICNIC

**PICNICKER** > PICNIC

**PICNICKY** > PICNIC

**PICNICS** > PICNIC

**PICOCURIE** n unit of radioactivity

**PICOFARAD** n unit of capacitance

**PICOGRAM** n trillionth of gram

**PICOGRAMS** > PICOGRAM

**PICOLIN** variant of > PICOLINE

**PICOLINE** n liquid derivative of pyridine found in bone oil and coal tar

**PICOLINES** > PICOLINE

**PICOLINIC** > PICOLINE

**PICOLINS** > PICOLIN

**PICOMETER** same as > PICOMETRE

**PICOMETRE** n trillionth fraction of metre

**PICOMOLE** n trillionth of a mole

**PICOMOLES** > PICOMOLE

**PICONG** n any teasing or satirical banter, originally a verbal duel in song

**PICONGS** > PICONG

**PICOT** n any of pattern of small loops, as on lace ▷ vb decorate material with

small loops
**PICOTE** adj (of material) picoted
**PICOTED** > PICOT
**PICOTEE** n type of carnation having pale petals edged with a darker colour, usually red
**PICOTEES** > PICOTEE
**PICOTING** > PICOT
**PICOTITE** n dark-brown mineral
**PICOTITES** > PICOTITE
**PICOTS** > PICOT
**PICOWAVE** vb treat food with gamma waves
**PICOWAVED** > PICOWAVE
**PICOWAVES** > PICOWAVE
**PICQUET** vb provide early warning of attack
**PICQUETED** > PICQUET
**PICQUETS** > PICQUET
**PICRA** n powder of aloes and canella
**PICRAS** > PICRA
**PICRATE** n any salt or ester of picric acid, such as sodium picrate
**PICRATED** adj containing picrate
**PICRATES** > PICRATE
**PICRIC** as in picric acid toxic sparingly soluble crystalline yellow acid
**PICRITE** n coarse-grained ultrabasic igneous rock consisting of olivine and augite with small amounts of plagioclase feldspar
**PICRITES** > PICRITE
**PICRITIC** > PICRITE
**PICS** > PIC
**PICTARNIE** Scots word for > TERN
**PICTOGRAM** n picture or symbol standing for a word or group of words, as in written Chinese
**PICTORIAL** adj of or in painting or pictures ▷ n newspaper etc with many pictures
**PICTURAL** n picture
**PICTURALS** > PICTURAL
**PICTURE** n drawing or painting ▷ vb visualize, imagine
**PICTURED** > PICTURE
**PICTURES** > PICTURE
**PICTURING** > PICTURE
**PICTURISE** same as > PICTURIZE
**PICTURIZE** vb adorn with pictures
**PICUL** n unit of weight, used in China, Japan, and SE Asia
**PICULS** > PICUL
**PIDDLE** vb urinate
**PIDDLED** > PIDDLE
**PIDDLER** > PIDDLE
**PIDDLERS** > PIDDLE
**PIDDLES** > PIDDLE

**PIDDLING** adj small or unimportant
**PIDDLY** adj trivial
**PIDDOCK** n marine bivalve that bores into rock, clay, or wood
**PIDDOCKS** > PIDDOCK
**PIDGEON** variant of > PIDGIN
**PIDGEONS** > PIDGEON
**PIDGIN** n language, not a mother tongue, made up of elements of two or more other languages
**PIDGINISE** same as > PIDGINIZE
**PIDGINIZE** vb create pidgin language
**PIDGINS** > PIDGIN
**PIE** n dish of meat, fruit, etc baked in pastry
**PIEBALD** adj (horse) with irregular black-and-white markings ▷ n black-and-white horse
**PIEBALDS** > PIEBALD
**PIECE** n separate bit or part
**PIECED** > PIECE
**PIECELESS** > PIECE
**PIECEMEAL** adv bit by bit ▷ adj fragmentary or unsystematic
**PIECEN** vb join broken threads
**PIECENED** > PIECEN
**PIECENER** > PIECEN
**PIECENERS** > PIECEN
**PIECENING** > PIECEN
**PIECENS** > PIECEN
**PIECER** n person who mends, repairs, or joins something, esp broken threads on a loom
**PIECERS** > PIECER
**PIECES** > PIECE
**PIECEWISE** adv with respect to number of discrete pieces
**PIECEWORK** n work paid for according to the quantity produced
**PIECING** > PIECE
**PIECINGS** > PIECE
**PIECRUST** n pastry used for making pies
**PIECRUSTS** > PIECRUST
**PIED** > PI
**PIEDFORT** n coin thicker than normal
**PIEDFORTS** > PIEDFORT
**PIEDISH** n container for baking pies
**PIEDISHES** > PIEDISH
**PIEDMONT** adj (of glaciers, plains, etc) formed or situated at the foot of a mountain or mountain range ▷ n gentle slope leading from mountains to flat land
**PIEDMONTS** > PIEDMONT
**PIEDNESS** n state of being pied
**PIEFORT** same

as > PIEDFORT
**PIEFORTS** > PIEFORT
**PIEHOLE** n person's mouth
**PIEHOLES** > PIEHOLE
**PIEING** > PIE
**PIEMAN** n seller of pies
**PIEMEN** > PIEMAN
**PIEND** same as > PEEN
**PIENDED** > PIEND
**PIENDING** > PIEND
**PIENDS** > PIEND
**PIEPLANT** n rhubarb
**PIEPLANTS** > PIEPLANT
**PIEPOWDER** n former court for dealing with disputes
**PIER** n platform on stilts sticking out into the sea
**PIERAGE** n accommodation for ships at piers
**PIERAGES** > PIERAGE
**PIERCE** vb make a hole in or through with a sharp instrument
**PIERCED** > PIERCE
**PIERCER** > PIERCE
**PIERCERS** > PIERCE
**PIERCES** > PIERCE
**PIERCING** adj (of a sound) shrill and high-pitched ▷ n art or practice of piercing body parts for the insertion of jewellery
**PIERCINGS** > PIERCING
**PIERID** n type of butterfly
**PIERIDINE** adj > PIERID
**PIERIDS** > PIERID
**PIERIS** n American or Asiatic shrub
**PIERISES** > PIERIS
**PIEROGI** n Polish dumpling
**PIEROGIES** > PIEROGI
**PIERRETTE** n female pierrot
**PIERROT** n clown or masquerader with a whitened face, white costume, and pointed hat
**PIERROTS** > PIERROT
**PIERS** > PIER
**PIERST** archaic spelling of > PIERCED
**PIERT** n small plant with small greenish flowers
**PIERTS** > PIERT
**PIES** > PIE
**PIET** n magpie
**PIETA** n sculpture, painting, or drawing of the dead Christ, supported by the Virgin Mary
**PIETAS** > PIETA
**PIETIES** > PIETY
**PIETISM** n exaggerated piety
**PIETISMS** > PIETISM
**PIETIST** > PIETISM
**PIETISTIC** > PIETISM
**PIETISTS** > PIETISM
**PIETS** > PIET
**PIETY** n deep devotion to God and religion

**PIEZO** adj piezoelectric
**PIFFERARI** > PIFFERARO
**PIFFERARO** n player of piffero
**PIFFERO** n small rustic flute
**PIFFEROS** > PIFFERO
**PIFFLE** n nonsense ▷ vb talk or behave feebly
**PIFFLED** > PIFFLE
**PIFFLER** n talker of nonsense
**PIFFLERS** > PIFFLER
**PIFFLES** > PIFFLE
**PIFFLING** adj worthless
**PIG** n animal kept and killed for pork, ham, and bacon ▷ vb eat greedily
**PIGBOAT** n submarine
**PIGBOATS** > PIGBOAT
**PIGEON** n bird with a heavy body and short legs, sometimes trained to carry messages ▷ vb pigeonhole
**PIGEONED** > PIGEON
**PIGEONING** > PIGEON
**PIGEONITE** n brownish mineral
**PIGEONRY** n loft for keeping pigeons
**PIGEONS** > PIGEON
**PIGFACE** n creeping succulent plant with bright-coloured flowers and red fruits
**PIGFACES** > PIGFACE
**PIGFEED** n food for pigs
**PIGFEEDS** > PIGFEED
**PIGFISH** n grunting fish of the North American Atlantic coast
**PIGFISHES** > PIGFISH
**PIGGED** > PIG
**PIGGERIES** > PIGGERY
**PIGGERY** n place for keeping and breeding pigs
**PIGGIE** same as > PIGGY
**PIGGIER** > PIGGY
**PIGGIES** > PIGGY
**PIGGIEST** > PIGGY
**PIGGIN** n small wooden bucket or tub
**PIGGINESS** > PIGGY
**PIGGING** > PIG
**PIGGINGS** > PIG
**PIGGINS** > PIGGIN
**PIGGISH** adj like a pig, esp in appetite or manners
**PIGGISHLY** > PIGGISH
**PIGGY** n child's word for a pig, esp a piglet ▷ adj like a pig, esp in appetite
**PIGGYBACK** n ride on someone's shoulders ▷ adv carried on someone's shoulders ▷ adj on the back and shoulders of another person ▷ vb give (a person) a piggyback on one's back and shoulders
**PIGHEADED** adj stupidly stubborn
**PIGHT** vb pierce

PIGHTED > PIGHT
PIGHTING > PIGHT
PIGHTLE n small enclosure
PIGHTLES > PIGHTLE
PIGHTS > PIGHT
PIGLET n young pig
PIGLETS > PIGLET
PIGLIKE > PIG
PIGLING n young pig
PIGLINGS > PIGLING
PIGMAEAN same
as > PYGMAEAN
PIGMEAN same
as > PYGMAEAN
PIGMEAT less common name
for > PORK
PIGMEATS > PIGMEAT
PIGMENT n colouring
matter, paint or dye ▷ vb
colour with pigment
PIGMENTAL > PIGMENT
PIGMENTED > PIGMENT
PIGMENTS > PIGMENT
PIGMIES > PIGMY
PIGMOID adj of pygmies
PIGMY same as > PYGMY
PIGNERATE vb pledge or
pawn
PIGNOLI same as > PIGNOLIA
PIGNOLIA n edible seed of
nut pine
PIGNOLIAS > PIGNOLIA
PIGNOLIS > PIGNOLI
PIGNORA > PIGNUS
PIGNORATE same
as > PIGNERATE
PIGNUS n pawn or pledge
PIGNUT n bitter nut of any
of several North American
hickory trees
PIGNUTS > PIGNUT
PIGOUT n binge
PIGOUTS > PIGOUT
PIGPEN same as > PIGSTY
PIGPENS > PIGPEN
PIGS > PIG
PIGSCONCE n foolish
person
PIGSKIN n skin of the
domestic pig ▷ adj made
of pigskin
PIGSKINS > PIGSKIN
PIGSNEY same as > PIGSNY
PIGSNEYS > PIGSNEY
PIGSNIE same as > PIGSNY
PIGSNIES > PIGSNIE
PIGSNY n former pet name
for girl
PIGSNYS > PIGSNY
PIGSTICK vb (esp in India)
hunt and spear wild boar,
esp from horseback
PIGSTICKS > PIGSTICK
PIGSTIES > PIGSTY
PIGSTUCK > PIGSTICK
PIGSTY same as > PIGPEN
PIGSWILL n waste food
or other edible matter fed
to pigs
PIGSWILLS > PIGSWILL
PIGTAIL n plait of hair
hanging from the back or
either side of the head ▷ vb
twist hair into a pigtail

PIGTAILED > PIGTAIL
PIGTAILS > PIGTAIL
PIGWASH n wet feed for
pigs
PIGWASHES > PIGWASH
PIGWEED n coarse
North American
amaranthaceous weed
PIGWEEDS > PIGWEED
PIHOIHOI n variety of New
Zealand pipit
PIING > PI
PIKA n burrowing
lagomorph mammal of
mountainous regions of
North America and Asia
PIKAKE n type of Asian vine
PIKAKES > PIKAKE
PIKAS > PIKA
PIKAU n pack, knapsack, or
rucksack
PIKAUS > PIKAU
PIKE n large predatory
freshwater fish ▷ vb stab
or pierce using a pike ▷ adj
(of the body position of a
diver) bent at the hips but
with the legs straight
PIKED > PIKE
PIKELET n small thick
pancake
PIKELETS > PIKELET
PIKEMAN n (formerly)
soldier armed with a pike
PIKEMEN > PIKEMAN
PIKEPERCH n pikelike
freshwater teleost fish
PIKER n shirker
PIKERS > PIKER
PIKES > PIKE
PIKESTAFF n wooden
handle of a pike
PIKEY n in British English,
derogatory word for gypsy
or vagrant
PIKEYS > PIKEY
PIKI n bread made from
blue cornmeal
PIKING > PIKE
PIKINGS > PIKE
PIKIS > PIKI
PIKUL same as > PICUL
PIKULS > PIKUL
PILA n pillar-like
anatomical structure
PILAE > PILA
PILAF same as > PILAU
PILAFF same as > PILAU
PILAFFS > PILAFF
PILAFS > PILAF
PILAO same as > PILAU
PILAOS > PILAO
PILAR adj relating to hair
PILASTER n square
column, usu set in a wall
PILASTERS > PILASTER
PILAU n Middle Eastern
dish of meat, fish, or
poultry boiled with rice,
spices, etc
PILAUS > PILAU
PILAW same as > PILAU
PILAWS > PILAW
PILCH n outer garment,

originally one made of skin
PILCHARD n small edible
sea fish of the herring
family
PILCHARDS > PILCHARD
PILCHER n scabbard for
sword
PILCHERS > PILCHER
PILCHES > PILCH
PILCORN n type if oat
PILCORNS > PILCORN
PILCROW n paragraph mark
PILCROWS > PILCROW
PILE n number of things
lying on top of each other
▷ vb collect into a pile
PILEA n artillery or
gunpowder plant, which
releases a cloud of pollen
when shaken
PILEAS > PILEA
PILEATE adj (of birds)
having a crest
PILEATED same as > PILEATE
PILED > PILE
PILEI > PILEUS
PILELESS > PILE
PILEOUS adj hairy
PILER n placer of things
on pile
PILERS > PILER
PILES pl n swollen veins in
the rectum, haemorrhoids
PILEUM n top of a bird's
head from the base of the
bill to the occiput
PILEUP n multiple collision
of vehicles
PILEUPS > PILEUP
PILEUS n upper cap-
shaped part of a
mushroom or similar
spore-producing body
PILEWORK n construction
built from heavy stakes or
cylinders
PILEWORKS > PILEWORK
PILEWORT n any of several
plants, such as lesser
celandine, thought to be
effective in treating piles
PILEWORTS > PILEWORT
PILFER vb steal in small
quantities
PILFERAGE n act or
practice of stealing small
quantities or articles
PILFERED > PILFER
PILFERER > PILFER
PILFERERS > PILFER
PILFERIES > PILFERY
PILFERING > PILFER
PILFERS > PILFER
PILFERY n theft
PILGARLIC n bald head or
a man with a bald head
PILGRIM n person who
journeys to a holy place
PILGRIMER n one who
undertakes a pilgrimage
PILGRIMS > PILGRIM
PILI n Philippine tree with
edible seeds resembling
almonds

PILIFORM adj resembling a
long hair
PILING n act of driving
piles
PILINGS > PILING
PILIS > PILI
PILL n small ball of
medicine swallowed
whole ▷ vb peel or skin
(something)
PILLAGE vb steal property
by violence in war ▷ n
violent seizure of goods,
esp in war
PILLAGED > PILLAGE
PILLAGER > PILLAGE
PILLAGERS > PILLAGE
PILLAGES > PILLAGE
PILLAGING > PILLAGE
PILLAR n upright post,
usu supporting a roof ▷ vb
provide or support with
pillars
PILLARED > PILLAR
PILLARING > PILLAR
PILLARIST n recluse who
sat on high pillar
PILLARS > PILLAR
PILLAU same as > PILAU
PILLAUS > PILLAU
PILLBOX n small box for
pills
PILLBOXES > PILLBOX
PILLED > PILL
PILLHEAD n person
addicted to pills
PILLHEADS > PILLHEAD
PILLICOCK n penis
PILLIE n pilchard
PILLIES > PILLIE
PILLING > PILL
PILLINGS > PILL
PILLION n seat for a
passenger behind the rider
of a motorcycle ▷ adv on a
pillion ▷ vb ride pillion
PILLIONED > PILLION
PILLIONS > PILLION
PILLOCK n stupid or
annoying person
PILLOCKS > PILLOCK
PILLORIED > PILLORY
PILLORIES > PILLORY
PILLORISE same
as > PILLORIZE
PILLORIZE vb put in pillory
PILLORY n frame with
holes for the head and
hands in which an
offender was locked and
exposed to public abuse
▷ vb ridicule publicly
PILLOW n stuffed cloth bag
for supporting the head
in bed ▷ vb rest as if on a
pillow
PILLOWED > PILLOW
PILLOWING > PILLOW
PILLOWS > PILLOW
PILLOWY > PILLOW
PILLS > PILL
PILLWORM n worm that
rolls up spirally
PILLWORMS > PILLWORM

**PILLWORT** *n* small Eurasian water fern
**PILLWORTS** > PILLWORT
**PILOMOTOR** *adj* causing movement of hairs
**PILONIDAL** *adj* of crease above buttocks
**PILOSE** *adj* covered with fine soft hairs
**PILOSITY** > PILOSE
**PILOT** *n* person qualified to fly an aircraft or spacecraft ▷ *adj* experimental and preliminary ▷ *vb* act as the pilot of
**PILOTAGE** *n* act of piloting an aircraft or ship
**PILOTAGES** > PILOTAGE
**PILOTED** > PILOT
**PILOTFISH** *n* fish that accompanies sharks
**PILOTI** *n* post that supports a roof
**PILOTING** *n* navigational handling of a ship near land using buoys, soundings, landmarks, etc, or the finding of a ship's position by such means
**PILOTINGS** > PILOTING
**PILOTIS** > PILOTI
**PILOTLESS** > PILOT
**PILOTMAN** *n* railway worker who directs trains through hazardous stretches of track
**PILOTMEN** > PILOTMAN
**PILOTS** > PILOT
**PILOUS** *same as* > PILOSE
**PILOW** *same as* > PILAU
**PILOWS** > PILOW
**PILSENER** *same as* > PILSNER
**PILSENERS** > PILSENER
**PILSNER** *n* type of pale beer with a strong flavour of hops
**PILSNERS** > PILSNER
**PILULA** *n* pill
**PILULAE** > PILULA
**PILULAR** > PILULE
**PILULAS** > PILULA
**PILULE** *n* small pill
**PILULES** > PILULE
**PILUM** *n* ancient Roman javelin
**PILUS** > PILI
**PILY** *adj* like wool or pile
**PIMA** *n* type of cotton
**PIMAS** > PIMA
**PIMENT** *n* wine flavoured with spices
**PIMENTO** *same as* > PIMIENTO
**PIMENTON** *n* smoked chilli powder
**PIMENTONS** > PIMENTON
**PIMENTOS** > PIMENTO
**PIMENTS** > PIMENT
**PIMIENTO** *n* Spanish pepper with a red fruit used as a vegetable
**PIMIENTOS** > PIMIENTO
**PIMP** *n* man who gets

customers for a prostitute in return for a share of his or her earnings ▷ *vb* act as a pimp
**PIMPED** > PIMP
**PIMPERNEL** *n* wild plant with small star-shaped flowers
**PIMPING** > PIMP
**PIMPLE** *n* small pus-filled spot on the skin
**PIMPLED** > PIMPLE
**PIMPLES** > PIMPLE
**PIMPLIER** > PIMPLE
**PIMPLIEST** > PIMPLE
**PIMPLY** > PIMPLE
**PIMPS** > PIMP
**PIN** *n* short thin piece of stiff wire with a point and head, for fastening things ▷ *vb* fasten with a pin
**PINA** *n* cone of silver amalgam
**PINACEOUS** *adj* of, relating to, or belonging to the *Pinaceae*, a family of conifers with needle-like leaves: includes pine, spruce, fir, larch, and cedar
**PINACOID** *n* pair of opposite parallel faces of crystal
**PINACOIDS** > PINACOID
**PINAFORE** *n* apron ▷ *vb* cover clothes with pinafore
**PINAFORED** > PINAFORE
**PINAFORES** > PINAFORE
**PINAKOID** *same as* > PINACOID
**PINAKOIDS** > PINAKOID
**PINANG** *n* areca tree
**PINANGS** > PINANG
**PINAS** > PINA
**PINASTER** *n* Mediterranean pine tree
**PINASTERS** > PINASTER
**PINATA** *n* papier-mâché party decoration filled with sweets, hung up during parties, and struck with a stick until it breaks open
**PINATAS** > PINATA
**PINBALL** *vb* ricochet
**PINBALLED** > PINBALL
**PINBALLS** > PINBALL
**PINBONE** *n* part of sirloin
**PINBONES** > PINBONE
**PINCASE** *n* case for holding pins
**PINCASES** > PINCASE
**PINCER** *vb* grip with pincers
**PINCERED** > PINCER
**PINCERING** > PINCER
**PINCERS** *pl n* tool consisting of two hinged arms, for gripping
**PINCH** *vb* squeeze between finger and thumb ▷ *n* act of pinching
**PINCHBECK** *n* alloy of zinc and copper, used as

imitation gold ▷ *adj* sham or cheap
**PINCHBUG** *n* type of crab
**PINCHBUGS** > PINCHBUG
**PINCHCOCK** *n* clamp used to compress a flexible tube to control the flow of fluid through it
**PINCHECK** *n* small check woven into fabric
**PINCHECKS** > PINCHECK
**PINCHED** > PINCH
**PINCHER** > PINCH
**PINCHERS** > PINCH
**PINCHES** > PINCH
**PINCHFIST** *n* mean person
**PINCHGUT** *n* miserly person
**PINCHGUTS** > PINCHGUT
**PINCHING** > PINCH
**PINCHINGS** > PINCH
**PINDAN** *n* desert region of Western Australia
**PINDANS** > PINDAN
**PINDAREE** *same as* > PINDARI
**PINDAREES** > PINDAREE
**PINDARI** *n* former irregular Indian horseman
**PINDARIS** > PINDARI
**PINDER** *n* person who impounds
**PINDERS** > PINDER
**PINDLING** *adj* peevish or fractious
**PINDOWN** *n* wrestling manoeuvre
**PINDOWNS** > PINDOWN
**PINE** *n* evergreen coniferous tree ▷ *vb* feel great longing (for)
**PINEAL** *adj* resembling a pine cone ▷ *n* pineal gland
**PINEALS** > PINEAL
**PINEAPPLE** *n* large tropical fruit with juicy yellow flesh and a hard skin
**PINECONE** *n* seed-producing structure of a pine tree
**PINECONES** > PINECONE
**PINED** > PINE
**PINEDROPS** *n* parasitic herb of pine trees
**PINELAND** *n* area covered with pine forest
**PINELANDS** > PINELAND
**PINELIKE** > PINE
**PINENE** *n* isomeric terpene found in many essential oils
**PINENES** > PINENE
**PINERIES** > PINERY
**PINERY** *n* place, esp a hothouse, where pineapples are grown
**PINES** > PINE
**PINESAP** *n* red herb of N America
**PINESAPS** > PINESAP
**PINETA** > PINETUM
**PINETUM** *n* area of land where pine trees and other conifers are grown
**PINEWOOD** *n* wood of pine trees

**PINEWOODS** > PINEWOOD
**PINEY** > PINE
**PINFALL** *another name for* > FALL
**PINFALLS** > PINFALL
**PINFISH** *n* small porgy of the SE North American coast of the Atlantic
**PINFISHES** > PINFISH
**PINFOLD** *n* pound for stray cattle ▷ *vb* gather or confine in or as if in a pinfold
**PINFOLDED** > PINFOLD
**PINFOLDS** > PINFOLD
**PING** *n* short high-pitched sound ▷ *vb* make such a noise
**PINGED** > PING
**PINGER** *n* device, esp a timer, that makes a pinging sound
**PINGERS** > PINGER
**PINGING** > PING
**PINGLE** *vb* enclose small area of ground
**PINGLED** > PINGLE
**PINGLER** > PINGLE
**PINGLERS** > PINGLE
**PINGLES** > PINGLE
**PINGLING** > PINGLE
**PINGO** *n* mound of earth or gravel formed through pressure from a layer of water trapped between newly frozen ice and underlying permafrost in Arctic regions
**PINGOES** > PINGO
**PINGOS** > PINGO
**PINGPONG** *n* table tennis
**PINGPONGS** > PINGPONG
**PINGRASS** *n* weed with fernlike leaves
**PINGS** > PING
**PINGUEFY** *vb* become greasy or fat
**PINGUID** *adj* fatty, oily, or greasy
**PINGUIN** *same as* > PENGUIN
**PINGUINS** > PINGUIN
**PINHEAD** *n* head of a pin
**PINHEADED** *adj* stupid or silly
**PINHEADS** > PINHEAD
**PINHOLE** *n* small hole made with or as if with a pin
**PINHOLES** > PINHOLE
**PINHOOKER** *n* trader of young thoroughbred horses
**PINIER** > PINY
**PINIES** > PINY
**PINIEST** > PINY
**PINING** > PINE
**PINION** *n* bird's wing ▷ *vb* immobilize (someone) by tying or holding his or her arms
**PINIONED** > PINION
**PINIONING** > PINION
**PINIONS** > PINION
**PINITE** *n* greyish-green or brown mineral containing

amorphous aluminium and potassium sulphates

**PINITES** > PINITE

**PINITOL** *n* compound found in pinewood

**PINITOLS** > PINITOL

**PINK** *n* pale reddish colour ▷ *adj* of the colour pink ▷ *vb* (of an engine) make a metallic noise because not working properly, knock

**PINKED** > PINK

**PINKEN** *vb* turn pink

**PINKENED** > PINKEN

**PINKENING** > PINKEN

**PINKENS** > PINKEN

**PINKER** > PINK

**PINKERTON** *n* private detective

**PINKEST** > PINK

**PINKEY** *variant of* > PINKY

**PINKEYE** *n* acute contagious inflammation of the conjunctiva of the eye

**PINKEYES** > PINKEYE

**PINKEYS** > PINKEY

**PINKIE** *n* little finger

**PINKIES** > PINKIE

**PINKINESS** *n* quality of being pink

**PINKING** > PINK

**PINKINGS** > PINK

**PINKISH** > PINK

**PINKLY** > PINK

**PINKNESS** > PINK

**PINKO** *n* person regarded as mildly left-wing

**PINKOES** > PINKO

**PINKOS** > PINKO

**PINKROOT** *n* plant with red-and-yellow flowers and pink roots

**PINKROOTS** > PINKROOT

**PINKS** > PINK

**PINKY** *same as* > PINKIE

**PINNA** *n* external part of the ear

**PINNACE** *n* ship's boat

**PINNACES** > PINNACE

**PINNACLE** *n* highest point of fame or success ▷ *vb* set on or as if on a pinnacle

**PINNACLED** > PINNACLE

**PINNACLES** > PINNACLE

**PINNAE** > PINNA

**PINNAL** > PINNA

**PINNAS** > PINNA

**PINNATE** *adj* (of compound leaves) having leaflets growing opposite each other in pairs

**PINNATED** *same as* > PINNATE

**PINNATELY** > PINNATE

**PINNATION** > PINNATE

**PINNED** > PIN

**PINNER** *n* person or thing that pins

**PINNERS** > PINNER

**PINNET** *n* pinnacle

**PINNETS** > PINNET

**PINNIE** *same as* > PINNY

**PINNIES** > PINNIE

**PINNING** > PIN

**PINNINGS** > PIN

**PINNIPED** *n* aquatic placental mammal such as the seal, sea lion, walrus, etc

**PINNIPEDE** *same as* > PINNIPED

**PINNIPEDS** > PINNIPED

**PINNOCK** *n* small bird

**PINNOCKS** > PINNOCK

**PINNOED** *adj* held or bound by the arms

**PINNULA** *same as* > PINNULE

**PINNULAE** > PINNULA

**PINNULAR** > PINNULE

**PINNULAS** > PINNULA

**PINNULATE** > PINNULE

**PINNULE** *n* any of the lobes of a leaflet of a pinnate compound leaf, which is itself pinnately divided

**PINNULES** > PINNULE

**PINNY** *informal or child's name for* > PINAFORE

**PINOCHLE** *n* card game for two to four players similar to bezique

**PINOCHLES** > PINOCHLE

**PINOCLE** *same as* > PINOCHLE

**PINOCLES** > PINOCLE

**PINOCYTIC** *adj* of process of pinocytosis

**PINOLE** *n* (in the southwestern United States) flour made of parched ground corn, mesquite beans, sugar, etc

**PINOLES** > PINOLE

**PINON** *n* low-growing pine

**PINONES** > PINON

**PINONS** > PINON

**PINOT** *n* any of several grape varieties

**PINOTAGE** *n* blended red wine of S Africa

**PINOTAGES** > PINOTAGE

**PINOTS** > PINOT

**PINPOINT** *vb* locate or identify exactly ▷ *adj* exact ▷ *n* insignificant or trifling thing

**PINPOINTS** > PINPOINT

**PINPRICK** *n* small irritation or annoyance ▷ *vb* puncture with or as if with a pin

**PINPRICKS** > PINPRICK

**PINS** > PIN

**PINSCHER** *n* breed of dog

**PINSCHERS** > PINSCHER

**PINSETTER** *n* device that sets pins in bowling alley

**PINSTRIPE** *n* very narrow stripe in fabric

**PINSWELL** *n* small boil

**PINSWELLS** > PINSWELL

**PINT** *n* liquid measure, 1/8 gallon (.568 litre)

**PINTA** *n* pint of milk

**PINTABLE** *n* pinball machine

**PINTABLES** > PINTABLE

**PINTADA** > PINTADO

**PINTADERA** *n* decorative stamp, usually made of clay, found in the Neolithic of the E Mediterranean and in many American cultures

**PINTADO** *n* species of seagoing petrel

**PINTADOES** > PINTADO

**PINTADOS** > PINTADO

**PINTAIL** *n* greyish-brown duck with a pointed tail

**PINTAILED** *adj* having tapered tail

**PINTAILS** > PINTAIL

**PINTANO** *n* tropical reef fish

**PINTANOS** > PINTANO

**PINTAS** > PINTA

**PINTLE** *n* pin or bolt forming the pivot of a hinge

**PINTLES** > PINTLE

**PINTO** *adj* marked with patches of white ▷ *n* pinto horse

**PINTOES** > PINTO

**PINTOS** > PINTO

**PINTS** > PINT

**PINTSIZE** *same as* > PINTSIZED

**PINTSIZED** *adj* very small

**PINUP** *n* picture of a sexually attractive person, esp when partially or totally undressed

**PINUPS** > PINUP

**PINWALE** *n* fabric with narrow ridges

**PINWALES** > PINWALE

**PINWEED** *n* herb with tiny flowers

**PINWEEDS** > PINWEED

**PINWHEEL** *n* cogwheel whose teeth are formed by small pins projecting either axially or radially from the rim of the wheel

**PINWHEELS** > PINWHEEL

**PINWORK** *n* (in needlepoint lace) fine raised stitches

**PINWORKS** > PINWORK

**PINWORM** *n* parasitic nematode worm

**PINWORMS** > PINWORM

**PINWRENCH** *n* wrench with a projection to fit a hole

**PINXIT** *vb* (he or she) painted (it): used formerly on paintings next to the artist's name

**PINY** *variant of* > PEONY

**PINYIN** *n* system of romanized spelling for the Chinese language

**PINYON** *n* low-growing pine

**PINYONS** > PINYON

**PIOLET** *n* type of ice axe

**PIOLETS** > PIOLET

**PION** *n* any of three subatomic particles which are classified as mesons

**PIONED** *adj* abounding in

marsh marigolds

**PIONEER** *n* explorer or early settler of a new country ▷ *vb* be the pioneer or leader of

**PIONEERED** > PIONEER

**PIONEERS** > PIONEER

**PIONER** *obsolete spelling of* > PIONEER

**PIONERS** > PIONER

**PIONEY** *same as* > PEONY

**PIONEYS** > PIONEY

**PIONIC** > PION

**PIONIES** > PIONY

**PIONING** *n* work of pioneers

**PIONINGS** > PIONING

**PIONS** > PION

**PIONY** *same as* > PEONY

**PIOPIO** *n* New Zealand thrush, thought to be extinct

**PIOSITIES** > PIOSITY

**PIOSITY** *n* grandiose display of piety

**PIOTED** *adj* pied

**PIOUS** *adj* deeply religious, devout

**PIOUSLY** > PIOUS

**PIOUSNESS** > PIOUS

**PIOY** *variant of* > PEEOY

**PIOYE** *variant of* > PEEOY

**PIOYES** > PIOYE

**PIOYS** > PIOY

**PIP** *n* small seed in a fruit ▷ *vb* chirp

**PIPA** *n* tongueless South American toad, *Pipa pipa*, that carries its young in pits in the skin of its back

**PIPAGE** *n* pipes collectively

**PIPAGES** > PIPAGE

**PIPAL** *same as* > PEEPUL

**PIPALS** > PIPAL

**PIPAS** > PIPA

**PIPE** *n* tube for conveying liquid or gas ▷ *vb* play on a pipe

**PIPEAGE** *same as* > PIPAGE

**PIPEAGES** > PIPEAGE

**PIPECLAY** *n* fine white pure clay, used in tobacco pipes and pottery and to whiten leather and similar materials ▷ *vb* whiten with pipeclay

**PIPECLAYS** > PIPECLAY

**PIPED** > PIPE

**PIPEFISH** *n* teleost fish with a long tubelike snout and an elongated body covered with bony plates

**PIPEFUL** > PIPE

**PIPEFULS** > PIPE

**PIPELESS** > PIPE

**PIPELIKE** > PIPE

**PIPELINE** *n* long pipe for transporting oil, water, etc

**PIPELINED** > PIPELINE

**PIPELINES** > PIPELINE

**PIPER** *n* player on a pipe or bagpipes

**PIPERIC** > PIPERINE

**PIPERINE** *n* crystalline

insoluble alkaloid that is the active ingredient of pepper
**PIPERINES** > PIPERINE
**PIPERONAL** n white fragrant aldehyde used in flavourings, perfumery, and suntan lotions
**PIPERS** > PIPER
**PIPES** > PIPE
**PIPESTEM** n hollow stem of pipe
**PIPESTEMS** > PIPESTEM
**PIPESTONE** n variety of consolidated red clay used by American Indians to make tobacco pipes
**PIPET** same as > PIPETTE
**PIPETED** > PIPET
**PIPETING** > PIPET
**PIPETS** > PIPET
**PIPETTE** n slender glass tube used to transfer or measure fluids ▷ vb transfer or measure out (a liquid) using a pipette
**PIPETTED** > PIPETTE
**PIPETTES** > PIPETTE
**PIPETTING** > PIPETTE
**PIPEWORK** n stops and flues on pipe organ
**PIPEWORKS** > PIPEWORK
**PIPEWORT** n perennial plant with a twisted flower stalk and a greenish-grey scaly flower head
**PIPEWORTS** > PIPEWORT
**PIPI** n edible mollusc often used as bait
**PIPIER** > PIPE
**PIPIEST** > PIPE
**PIPINESS** n material's suitability for use as pipe
**PIPING** n system of pipes
**PIPINGLY** > PIPING
**PIPINGS** > PIPING
**PIPIS** > PIPI
**PIPISTREL** n species of bat
**PIPIT** n small brownish songbird
**PIPITS** > PIPIT
**PIPKIN** same as > PIGGIN
**PIPKINS** > PIPKIN
**PIPLESS** > PIP
**PIPPED** > PIP
**PIPPIER** > PIPPY
**PIPPIEST** > PIPPY
**PIPPIN** n type of eating apple
**PIPPING** > PIP
**PIPPINS** > PIPPIN
**PIPPY** adj containing many pips
**PIPS** > PIP
**PIPSQUEAK** n insignificant or contemptible person
**PIPUL** n Indian fig tree
**PIPULS** > PIPUL
**PIPY** > PIPE
**PIQUANCE** same as > PIQUANT
**PIQUANCES** > PIQUANT
**PIQUANCY** > PIQUANT

**PIQUANT** adj having a pleasant spicy taste
**PIQUANTLY** > PIQUANT
**PIQUE** n feeling of hurt pride, baffled curiosity, or resentment ▷ vb hurt the pride of
**PIQUED** > PIQUE
**PIQUES** > PIQUE
**PIQUET** n card game for two ▷ vb play game of piquet
**PIQUETED** > PIQUET
**PIQUETING** > PIQUET
**PIQUETS** > PIQUET
**PIQUILLO** n variety of sweet red pepper
**PIQUILLOS** > PIQUILLO
**PIQUING** > PIQUE
**PIR** n Sufi master
**PIRACETAM** n drug used to treat muscle spasm
**PIRACIES** > PIRACY
**PIRACY** n robbery on the seas
**PIRAGUA** same as > PIROGUE
**PIRAGUAS** > PIRAGUA
**PIRAI** n large S American fish
**PIRAIS** > PIRAI
**PIRANA** same as > PIRANHA
**PIRANAS** > PIRANA
**PIRANHA** n small fierce freshwater fish of tropical America
**PIRANHAS** > PIRANHA
**PIRARUCU** n large S American food fish
**PIRARUCUS** > PIRARUCU
**PIRATE** n sea robber ▷ vb sell or reproduce (artistic work etc) illegally
**PIRATED** > PIRATE
**PIRATES** > PIRATE
**PIRATIC** > PIRATE
**PIRATICAL** > PIRATE
**PIRATING** > PIRATE
**PIRAYA** same as > PIRAI
**PIRAYAS** > PIRAYA
**PIRIFORM** adj shaped like pear
**PIRL** vb spin or twist
**PIRLED** > PIRL
**PIRLICUE** same as > PURLICUE
**PIRLICUED** > PIRLICUE
**PIRLICUES** > PIRLICUE
**PIRLING** > PIRL
**PIRLS** > PIRL
**PIRN** n reel or bobbin
**PIRNIE** > STRIPED
**PIRNIT** adj striped
**PIRNS** > PIRN
**PIROG** n large pie filled with meat, vegetables, etc
**PIROGEN** n turnovers made from kneaded dough
**PIROGHI** > PIROG
**PIROGI** > PIROG
**PIROGIES** > PIROG
**PIROGUE** n any of various kinds of dugout canoes
**PIROGUES** > PIROGUE
**PIROJKI** same as > PIROSHKI

**PIROPLASM** n parasite of red blood cells
**PIROQUE** same as > PIROGUE
**PIROQUES** > PIROQUE
**PIROSHKI** same as > PIROZHKI
**PIROUETTE** n spinning turn balanced on the toes of one foot ▷ vb perform a pirouette
**PIROZHKI** > PIROZHOK
**PIROZHOK** n small triangular pastry filled with meat, vegetables, etc
**PIRS** > PIR
**PIS** > PI
**PISCARIES** > PISCARY
**PISCARY** n place where fishing takes place
**PISCATOR** n fisherman
**PISCATORS** > PISCATOR
**PISCATORY** adj of or relating to fish, fishing, or fishermen
**PISCATRIX** n female angler
**PISCIFORM** adj having form of fish
**PISCINA** n stone basin, with a drain, in a church or sacristy where water used at Mass is poured away
**PISCINAE** > PISCINA
**PISCINAL** > PISCINA
**PISCINAS** > PISCINA
**PISCINE** adj of or resembling a fish
**PISCIVORE** n eater of fish
**PISCO** n S American brandy
**PISCOS** > PISCO
**PISE** n rammed earth or clay used to make floors or walls
**PISES** > PISE
**PISH** interj exclamation of impatience or contempt ▷ vb make this exclamation at (someone or something)
**PISHED** > PISH
**PISHER** n Yiddish term for small boy
**PISHERS** > PISHER
**PISHES** > PISH
**PISHING** > PISH
**PISHOGE** same as > PISHOGUE
**PISHOGES** > PISHOGE
**PISHOGUE** n sorcery
**PISHOGUES** > PISHOGUE
**PISIFORM** adj resembling a pea ▷ n small pealike bone on the ulnar side of the carpus
**PISIFORMS** > PISIFORM
**PISKIES** > PISKY
**PISKY** n Cornish fairy
**PISMIRE** archaic or dialect word for > ANT
**PISMIRES** > PISMIRE
**PISO** n peso of the Philippines
**PISOLITE** n sedimentary rock
**PISOLITES** > PISOLITE

**PISOLITH** same as > PISOLITE
**PISOLITHS** > PISOLITH
**PISOLITIC** > PISOLITE
**PISOS** > PISO
**PISS** vb urinate ▷ n act of urinating
**PISSANT** n insignificant person
**PISSANTS** > PISSANT
**PISSED** adj drunk
**PISSER** n someone or something that pisses
**PISSERS** > PISSER
**PISSES** > PISS
**PISSHEAD** n drunkard
**PISSHEADS** > PISSHEAD
**PISSING** > PISS
**PISSOIR** n public urinal, usu enclosed by a wall or screen
**PISSOIRS** > PISSOIR
**PISTACHE** n tree yielding pistachio nut
**PISTACHES** > PISTACHE
**PISTACHIO** n edible nut of a Mediterranean tree ▷ adj of a yellowish-green colour
**PISTAREEN** n Spanish coin, used in the US and the West Indies until the 18th century
**PISTE** n ski slope
**PISTES** > PISTE
**PISTIL** n seed-bearing part of a flower
**PISTILS** > PISTIL
**PISTOL** n short-barrelled handgun ▷ vb shoot with a pistol
**PISTOLE** n any of various gold coins of varying value, formerly used in Europe
**PISTOLED** > PISTOL
**PISTOLEER** n person, esp a soldier, who is armed with or fires a pistol
**PISTOLERO** n shooter of pistols
**PISTOLES** > PISTOLE
**PISTOLET** n small pistol
**PISTOLETS** > PISTOLET
**PISTOLIER** n shooter of pistols
**PISTOLING** > PISTOL
**PISTOLLED** > PISTOL
**PISTOLS** > PISTOL
**PISTON** n cylindrical part in an engine that slides to and fro in a cylinder
**PISTONS** > PISTON
**PISTOU** n French sauce
**PISTOUS** > PISTOU
**PIT** n deep hole in the ground ▷ vb mark with small dents or scars
**PITA** n any of several agave plants yielding a strong fibre
**PITAHAYA** n any giant cactus of Central America and the SW United States
**PITAHAYAS** > PITAHAYA
**PITAPAT** adv with quick

light taps ▷ n such taps
▷ vb make quick light taps
or beats
**PITAPATS** > PITAPAT
**PITARA** variant of > PETARA
**PITARAH** variant of > PETARA
**PITARAHS** > PITARAH
**PITARAS** > PITARA
**PITAS** > PITA
**PITAYA** same as > PITAHAYA
**PITAYAS** > PITAYA
**PITCH** vb throw, hurl
▷ n area marked out for
playing sport
**PITCHBEND** n electronic
device that enables a
player to bend the pitch of
a note being sounded on a
synthesizer, usually with a
pitch wheel, strip, or lever
**PITCHED** > PITCH
**PITCHER** n large jug with a
narrow neck
**PITCHERS** > PITCHER
**PITCHES** > PITCH
**PITCHFORK** n large long-
handled fork for lifting hay
▷ vb thrust abruptly or
violently
**PITCHIER** > PITCHY
**PITCHIEST** > PITCHY
**PITCHILY** > PITCHY
**PITCHING** > PITCH
**PITCHINGS** > PITCH
**PITCHMAN** n itinerant
pedlar of small
merchandise who
operates from a stand at a
fair, etc
**PITCHMEN** > PITCHMAN
**PITCHOUT** n type of
baseball pitch
**PITCHOUTS** > PITCHOUT
**PITCHPINE** n large N
American pine tree
**PITCHPIPE** n small one-
note pipe used for tuning
instruments
**PITCHPOLE** vb turn end
over end
**PITCHY** adj full of or
covered with pitch
**PITEOUS** adj arousing pity
**PITEOUSLY** > PITEOUS
**PITFALL** n hidden
difficulty or danger
**PITFALLS** > PITFALL
**PITH** n soft white lining
of the rind of oranges etc
▷ vb destroy the brain and
spinal cord of (a laboratory
animal) by piercing or
severing
**PITHBALL** n type of
conductor
**PITHBALLS** > PITHBALL
**PITHEAD** n top of a mine
shaft and the buildings
and hoisting gear around
it
**PITHEADS** > PITHEAD
**PITHECOID** adj relating to
apes
**PITHED** > PITH

**PITHFUL** > PITH
**PITHIER** > PITHY
**PITHIEST** > PITHY
**PITHILY** > PITHY
**PITHINESS** > PITHY
**PITHING** > PITH
**PITHLESS** > PITH
**PITHLIKE** > PITH
**PITHOI** > PITHOS
**PITHOS** n large ceramic
container for oil or grain
**PITHS** > PITH
**PITHY** adj short and full of
meaning
**PITIABLE** adj arousing
or deserving pity or
contempt
**PITIABLY** > PITIABLE
**PITIED** > PITY
**PITIER** > PITY
**PITIERS** > PITY
**PITIES** > PITY
**PITIFUL** adj arousing pity
**PITIFULLY** > PITIFUL
**PITILESS** adj feeling no
pity or mercy
**PITMAN** n connecting rod
(in a machine)
**PITMANS** > PITMAN
**PITMEN** > PITMAN
**PITON** n metal spike used
in climbing to secure a
rope
**PITONS** > PITON
**PITPROP** n support beam
in mine shaft
**PITPROPS** > PITPROP
**PITS** > PIT
**PITSAW** n large saw
formerly used for cutting
logs into planks, operated
by two men, one standing
on top of the log and the
other in a pit underneath it
**PITSAWS** > PITSAW
**PITTA** n small brightly
coloured ground-dwelling
tropical bird
**PITTANCE** n very small
amount of money
**PITTANCES** > PITTANCE
**PITTAS** > PITTA
**PITTED** > PIT
**PITTEN** adj having been
put
**PITTER** vb make pattering
sound
**PITTERED** > PITTER
**PITTERING** > PITTER
**PITTERS** > PITTER
**PITTING** > PIT
**PITTINGS** > PIT
**PITTITE** n occupant of a
theatre pit
**PITTITES** > PITTITE
**PITUITA** n thick nasal
secretion
**PITUITARY** n gland at the
base of the brain, that
helps to control growth
▷ adj of or relating to the
pituitary gland
**PITUITAS** > PITUITA
**PITUITE** n mucus

**PITUITES** > PITUITE
**PITUITRIN** n extract from
pituitary gland
**PITURI** n Australian
solanaceous shrub
**PITURIS** > PITURI
**PITY** n sympathy or sorrow
for others' suffering ▷ vb
feel pity for
**PITYING** > PITY
**PITYINGLY** > PITY
**PITYROID** adj resembling
bran
**PIU** adv more (quickly,
softly, etc)
**PIUM** n stinging insect
**PIUMS** > PIUM
**PIUPIU** n skirt made from
the leaves of the New
Zealand flax, worn by
Māoris on ceremonial
occasions
**PIUPIUS** > PIUPIU
**PIVOT** n central shaft on
which something turns
▷ vb provide with or turn
on a pivot
**PIVOTABLE** > PIVOT
**PIVOTAL** adj of crucial
importance
**PIVOTALLY** > PIVOTAL
**PIVOTED** > PIVOT
**PIVOTER** > PIVOT
**PIVOTERS** > PIVOT
**PIVOTING** > PIVOT
**PIVOTINGS** > PIVOT
**PIVOTMAN** n person in
rank around whom others
wheel
**PIVOTMEN** > PIVOTMAN
**PIVOTS** > PIVOT
**PIX** less common spelling
of > PYX
**PIXEL** n any of a number
of very small picture
elements that make up
a picture, as on a visual
display unit
**PIXELS** > PIXEL
**PIXES** > PIX
**PIXIE** n (in folklore) fairy
**PIXIEISH** > PIXIE
**PIXIES** > PIXY
**PIXILATED** adj eccentric or
whimsical
**PIXINESS** > PIXIE
**PIXY** same as > PIXIE
**PIXYISH** > PIXY
**PIZAZZ** same as > PIZZAZZ
**PIZAZZES** > PIZAZZ
**PIZAZZY** > PIZAZZ
**PIZE** vb strike (someone
a blow)
**PIZED** > PIZE
**PIZES** > PIZE
**PIZING** > PIZE
**PIZZA** n flat disc of
dough covered with a
wide variety of savoury
toppings and baked
**PIZZAIOLA** n type of
tomato sauce
**PIZZALIKE** > PIZZA
**PIZZAS** > PIZZA

**PIZZAZ** same as > PZAZZ
**PIZZAZES** > PIZZAZ
**PIZZAZZ** n attractive
combination of energy
and style
**PIZZAZZES** > PIZZAZZ
**PIZZAZZY** > PIZZAZZ
**PIZZELLE** n Italian sweet
wafer
**PIZZELLES** > PIZZELLE
**PIZZERIA** n place where
pizzas are made, sold, or
eaten
**PIZZERIAS** > PIZZERIA
**PIZZICATI** > PIZZICATO
**PIZZICATO** adj played by
plucking the string of a
violin etc with the finger
▷ adv (in music for the
violin family) to be plucked
with the finger ▷ n style
or technique of playing a
normally bowed stringed
instrument in this manner
**PIZZLE** n penis of an
animal, esp a bull
**PIZZLES** > PIZZLE
**PLAAS** n farm
**PLAASES** > PLAAS
**PLACABLE** adj easily
placated or appeased
**PLACABLY** > PLACABLE
**PLACARD** n notice that
is carried or displayed
in public ▷ vb attach
placards to
**PLACARDED** > PLACARD
**PLACARDS** > PLACARD
**PLACATE** vb make
(someone) stop feeling
angry or upset
**PLACATED** > PLACATE
**PLACATER** > PLACATE
**PLACATERS** > PLACATE
**PLACATES** > PLACATE
**PLACATING** > PLACATE
**PLACATION** > PLACATE
**PLACATIVE** same
as > PLACATORY
**PLACATORY** adj placating
or intended to placate
**PLACCAT** variant
of > PLACKET
**PLACCATE** variant
of > PLACKET
**PLACCATES** > PLACCATE
**PLACCATS** > PLACCAT
**PLACE** n particular part of
an area or space ▷ vb put
in a particular place
**PLACEABLE** > PLACE
**PLACEBO** n sugar pill etc
given to an unsuspecting
patient instead of an
active drug
**PLACEBOES** > PLACEBO
**PLACEBOS** > PLACEBO
**PLACED** > PLACE
**PLACEKICK** n (in football)
kick in which the ball is
placed in position before
it is kicked ▷ vb take a
placekick
**PLACELESS** adj not rooted

in a specific place or community

**PLACEMAN** n person who holds a public office, esp for private profit and as a reward for political support

**PLACEMEN** > PLACEMAN

**PLACEMENT** n arrangement

**PLACENTA** n organ formed in the womb during pregnancy, providing nutrients for the fetus

**PLACENTAE** > PLACENTA

**PLACENTAL** adj (esp of animals) having a placenta

**PLACENTAS** > PLACENTA

**PLACER** n surface sediment containing particles of gold or some other valuable mineral

**PLACERS** > PLACER

**PLACES** > PLACE

**PLACET** n vote or expression of assent by saying the word placet

**PLACETS** > PLACET

**PLACID** adj not easily excited or upset, calm

**PLACIDER** > PLACID

**PLACIDEST** > PLACID

**PLACIDITY** > PLACID

**PLACIDLY** > PLACID

**PLACING** n method of issuing securities to the public using an intermediary, such as a stockbroking firm

**PLACINGS** > PLACING

**PLACIT** n decree or dictum

**PLACITA** > PLACITUM

**PLACITORY** > PLACIT

**PLACITS** > PLACIT

**PLACITUM** n court or assembly in Middle Ages

**PLACK** n small former Scottish coin

**PLACKET** n opening at the waist of a dress or skirt for buttons or zips or for access to a pocket

**PLACKETS** > PLACKET

**PLACKLESS** adj lacking money

**PLACKS** > PLACK

**PLACODERM** n extinct bony-plated fishlike vertebrate

**PLACOID** adj platelike or flattened ▷ n fish with placoid scales

**PLACOIDS** > PLACOID

**PLAFOND** n ceiling, esp one having ornamentation

**PLAFONDS** > PLAFOND

**PLAGAL** adj (of a cadence) progressing from the subdominant to the tonic chord, as in the Amen of a hymn

**PLAGE** n bright patch in the sun's chromosphere

**PLAGES** > PLAGE

**PLAGIARY** n person who plagiarizes or a piece of

plagiarism

**PLAGIUM** n crime of kidnapping

**PLAGIUMS** > PLAGIUM

**PLAGUE** n fast-spreading fatal disease ▷ vb trouble or annoy continually

**PLAGUED** > PLAGUE

**PLAGUER** > PLAGUE

**PLAGUERS** > PLAGUE

**PLAGUES** > PLAGUE

**PLAGUEY** same as > PLAGUY

**PLAGUIER** > PLAGUEY

**PLAGUIEST** > PLAGUEY

**PLAGUILY** > PLAGUY

**PLAGUING** > PLAGUE

**PLAGUY** adj disagreeable or vexing ▷ adv disagreeably or annoyingly

**PLAICE** n edible European flatfish

**PLAICES** > PLAICE

**PLAID** n long piece of tartan cloth worn as part of Highland dress ▷ vb weave cloth into plaid

**PLAIDED** > PLAID

**PLAIDING** > PLAID

**PLAIDINGS** > PLAID

**PLAIDMAN** n wearer of plaid

**PLAIDMEN** > PLAIDMAN

**PLAIDS** > PLAID

**PLAIN** adj easy to see or understand ▷ n large stretch of level country ▷ adv clearly or simply ▷ vb complain

**PLAINANT** n plaintiff

**PLAINANTS** > PLAINANT

**PLAINED** > PLAIN

**PLAINER** > PLAIN

**PLAINEST** > PLAIN

**PLAINFUL** adj apt to complain

**PLAINING** > PLAIN

**PLAININGS** > PLAIN

**PLAINISH** > PLAIN

**PLAINLY** > PLAIN

**PLAINNESS** > PLAIN

**PLAINS** pl n extensive tracts of level or almost level treeless countryside

**PLAINSMAN** n person who lives in a plains region, esp in the Great Plains of North America

**PLAINSMEN** > PLAINSMAN

**PLAINSONG** n unaccompanied singing, esp in a medieval church

**PLAINT** n complaint or lamentation

**PLAINTEXT** n (in telecommunications) message set in a directly readable form rather than in coded groups

**PLAINTFUL** adj complaining

**PLAINTIFF** n person who sues in a court of law

**PLAINTIVE** adj sad, mournful

**PLAINTS** > PLAINT

**PLAINWORK** n weaving

**PLAISTER** n plaster

**PLAISTERS** > PLAISTER

**PLAIT** n intertwined length of hair ▷ vb intertwine separate strands in a pattern

**PLAITED** > PLAIT

**PLAITER** > PLAIT

**PLAITERS** > PLAIT

**PLAITING** > PLAIT

**PLAITINGS** > PLAIT

**PLAITS** > PLAIT

**PLAN** n way thought out to do or achieve something ▷ vb arrange beforehand

**PLANAR** adj of or relating to a plane

**PLANARIA** n free-living flatworms

**PLANARIAN** n free-living flatworm

**PLANARITY** > PLANAR

**PLANATE** adj having been flattened

**PLANATION** n erosion of a land surface until it is basically flat

**PLANCH** vb cover with planks

**PLANCHE** same as > PLANCH

**PLANCHED** > PLANCH

**PLANCHES** > PLANCH

**PLANCHET** n piece of metal ready to be stamped as a coin, medal, etc

**PLANCHETS** > PLANCHET

**PLANCHING** > PLANCH

**PLANE** n aeroplane ▷ adj perfectly flat or level ▷ vb glide or skim

**PLANED** > PLANE

**PLANELOAD** n amount or number carried by plane

**PLANENESS** > PLANE

**PLANER** n machine with a cutting tool that makes repeated horizontal strokes across the surface of a workpiece

**PLANERS** > PLANER

**PLANES** > PLANE

**PLANESIDE** n area next to aeroplane

**PLANET** n large body in space that revolves round the sun or another star

**PLANETARY** adj of or relating to a planet ▷ n train of planetary gears

**PLANETIC** > PLANET

**PLANETOID** See > ASTEROID

**PLANETS** > PLANET

**PLANFORM** n outline or silhouette of an object, esp an aircraft, as seen from above

**PLANFORMS** > PLANFORM

**PLANGENCY** > PLANGENT

**PLANGENT** adj (of sounds) mournful and resounding

**PLANING** > PLANE

**PLANISH** vb give a final finish to (metal) by

hammering or rolling to produce a smooth surface

**PLANISHED** > PLANISH

**PLANISHER** > PLANISH

**PLANISHES** > PLANISH

**PLANK** n long flat piece of sawn timber ▷ vb cover or provide (an area) with planks

**PLANKED** > PLANK

**PLANKING** n number of planks

**PLANKINGS** > PLANKING

**PLANKS** > PLANK

**PLANKTER** n organism in plankton

**PLANKTERS** > PLANKTER

**PLANKTON** n minute animals and plants floating in the surface water of a sea or lake

**PLANKTONS** > PLANKTON

**PLANLESS** adj having no plan

**PLANNED** > PLAN

**PLANNER** n person who makes plans, esp for the development of a town, building, etc

**PLANNERS** > PLANNER

**PLANNING** > PLAN

**PLANNINGS** > PLAN

**PLANOSOL** n type of intrazonal soil of humid or subhumid uplands having a strongly leached upper layer overlying a clay hardpan

**PLANOSOLS** > PLANOSOL

**PLANS** > PLAN

**PLANT** n living organism that grows in the ground and has no power to move ▷ vb put in the ground to grow

**PLANTA** n sole of foot

**PLANTABLE** > PLANT

**PLANTAE** > PLANTA

**PLANTAGE** n plants

**PLANTAGES** > PLANTAGE

**PLANTAIN** n low-growing wild plant with broad leaves

**PLANTAINS** > PLANTAIN

**PLANTAR** adj of, relating to, or occurring on the sole of the foot or a corresponding part

**PLANTAS** > PLANTA

**PLANTED** > PLANT

**PLANTER** n owner of a plantation

**PLANTERS** > PLANTER

**PLANTING** > PLANT

**PLANTINGS** > PLANT

**PLANTLESS** > PLANT

**PLANTLET** n small plant

**PLANTLETS** > PLANTLET

**PLANTLIKE** > PLANT

**PLANTLING** n young plant

**PLANTS** > PLANT

**PLANTSMAN** n experienced gardener who specializes in collecting rare or

interesting plants
**PLANTSMEN** > PLANTSMAN
**PLANTULE** n embryo in act
of germination
**PLANTULES** > PLANTULE
**PLANULA** n ciliated
free-swimming larva of
hydrozoan coelenterates
such as the hydra
**PLANULAE** > PLANULA
**PLANULAR** > PLANULA
**PLANULATE** adj flat
**PLANULOID** adj of planula
**PLANURIA** n expulsion
of urine from abnormal
opening
**PLANURIAS** > PLANURIA
**PLANURIES** > PLANURY
**PLANURY** another name
for > PLANURY
**PLANXTIES** > PLANXTY
**PLANXTY** n Celtic melody
for harp
**PLAP** same as > PLOP
**PLAPPED** > PLAP
**PLAPPING** > PLAP
**PLAPS** > PLAP
**PLAQUE** n inscribed
commemorative stone or
metal plate
**PLAQUES** > PLAQUE
**PLAQUETTE** n small plaque
**PLASH** same as > PLEACH
**PLASHED** > PLASH
**PLASHER** n type of farm
tool
**PLASHERS** > PLASHER
**PLASHES** > PLASH
**PLASHET** n small pond
**PLASHETS** > PLASHET
**PLASHIER** > PLASHY
**PLASHIEST** > PLASHY
**PLASHING** > PLASH
**PLASHINGS** > PLASH
**PLASHY** adj wet or marshy
**PLASM** same as > PLASMA
**PLASMA** n clear liquid part
of blood
**PLASMAGEL** another name
for > ECTOPLASM
**PLASMAS** > PLASMA
**PLASMASOL** another name
for > ENDOPLASM
**PLASMATIC** > PLASMA
**PLASMIC** > PLASMA
**PLASMID** n small circle
of bacterial DNA that is
independent of the main
bacterial chromosome
**PLASMIDS** > PLASMID
**PLASMIN** n proteolytic
enzyme that causes
fibrinolysis in blood clots
**PLASMINS** > PLASMIN
**PLASMODIA** n amoeboid
masses of protoplasm,
each containing many
nuclei
**PLASMOID** n section
of a plasma having a
characteristic shape
**PLASMOIDS** > PLASMOID
**PLASMON** n sum total of
plasmagenes in a cell

**PLASMONS** > PLASMON
**PLASMS** > PLASM
**PLAST** archaic past participle
of > PLACE
**PLASTE** archaic past
participle of > PLACE
**PLASTER** n mixture of lime,
sand, etc for coating walls
▷ vb cover with plaster
**PLASTERED** adj drunk
**PLASTERER** > PLASTER
**PLASTERS** > PLASTER
**PLASTERY** > PLASTER
**PLASTIC** n synthetic
material that can be
moulded when soft but
sets in a hard long-lasting
shape ▷ adj made of
plastic
**PLASTICKY** adj made of or
resembling plastic
**PLASTICLY** > PLASTIC
**PLASTICS** > PLASTIC
**PLASTID** n any of various
small particles in the
cytoplasm of the cells of
plants and some animals
**PLASTIDS** > PLASTID
**PLASTIQUE** n easily-
moulded plastic explosive
**PLASTISOL** n suspension
of resin particles
convertible into solid
plastic
**PLASTRAL** > PLASTRON
**PLASTRON** n bony plate
forming the ventral part
of the shell of a tortoise or
turtle
**PLASTRONS** > PLASTRON
**PLASTRUM** variant
of > PLASTRON
**PLASTRUMS** > PLASTRUM
**PLAT** n small area of ground
**PLATAN** n plane tree
**PLATANE** same as > PLATAN
**PLATANES** > PLATANE
**PLATANNA** n S African frog
**PLATANNAS** > PLATANNA
**PLATANS** > PLATAN
**PLATBAND** n border of
flowers in garden
**PLATBANDS** > PLATBAND
**PLATE** n shallow dish for
holding food ▷ vb cover
with a thin coating of gold,
silver, or other metal
**PLATEASM** n talking with
mouth open too wide
**PLATEASMS** > PLATEASM
**PLATEAU** n area of level
high land ▷ vb remain
stable for a long period
**PLATEAUED** > PLATEAU
**PLATEAUS** > PLATEAU
**PLATEAUX** > PLATEAU
**PLATED** adj coated with a
layer of metal
**PLATEFUL** same as > PLATE
**PLATEFULS** > PLATEFUL
**PLATELET** n minute
particle occurring in
blood of vertebrates and
involved in clotting of

blood
**PLATELETS** > PLATELET
**PLATELIKE** > PLATE
**PLATEMAN** n one of crew of
steam train
**PLATEMARK** another name
for > HALLMARK
**PLATEMEN** > PLATEMAN
**PLATEN** n roller of a
typewriter, against which
the paper is held
**PLATENS** > PLATEN
**PLATER** n person or thing
that plates
**PLATERS** > PLATER
**PLATES** > PLATE
**PLATESFUL** > PLATEFUL
**PLATFORM** n raised floor
**PLATFORMS** > PLATFORM
**PLATIER** > PLATY
**PLATIES** > PLATY
**PLATIEST** > PLATY
**PLATINA** n alloy of
platinum and several
other metals, including
palladium, osmium, and
iridium
**PLATINAS** > PLATINA
**PLATING** n coating of
metal
**PLATINGS** > PLATING
**PLATINIC** adj of or
containing platinum, esp
in the tetravalent state
**PLATINISE** same
as > PLATINIZE
**PLATINIZE** vb coat with
platinum
**PLATINOID** adj containing
or resembling platinum
**PLATINOUS** adj of or
containing platinum, esp
in the divalent state
**PLATINUM** n valuable
silvery-white metal
**PLATINUMS** > PLATINUM
**PLATITUDE** n remark that
is true but not interesting
or original
**PLATONIC** adj (of a
relationship) friendly or
affectionate but not sexual
**PLATONISM** n philosophy
of Plato
**PLATOON** n smaller unit
within a company of
soldiers ▷ vb organise
into platoons
**PLATOONED** > PLATOON
**PLATOONS** > PLATOON
**PLATS** > PLAT
**PLATTED** > PLAT
**PLATTER** n large dish
**PLATTERS** > PLATTER
**PLATTING** > PLAT
**PLATTINGS** > PLAT
**PLATY** adj of, relating to,
or designating rocks the
constituents of which
occur in flaky layers ▷ n
small brightly coloured
freshwater cyprinodont
fish
**PLATYFISH** same as > PLATY

**PLATYPI** > PLATYPUS
**PLATYPUS** n Australian
egg-laying amphibious
mammal, with dense
fur, webbed feet, and a
ducklike bill
**PLATYS** > PLATY
**PLATYSMA** n muscle
located on side of neck
**PLATYSMAS** > PLATYSMA
**PLAUDIT** n expression of
enthusiastic approval
**PLAUDITE** interj give a
round of applause!
**PLAUDITS** > PLAUDIT
**PLAUSIBLE** adj apparently
true or reasonable
**PLAUSIBLY** > PLAUSIBLE
**PLAUSIVE** adj expressing
praise or approval
**PLAUSTRAL** adj relating to
wagons
**PLAY** vb occupy oneself in
(a game or recreation) ▷ n
story performed on stage
or broadcast
**PLAYA** n (in the US)
temporary lake, or its dry
often salty bed, in a desert
basin
**PLAYABLE** > PLAY
**PLAYACT** vb pretend or
make believe
**PLAYACTED** > PLAYACT
**PLAYACTOR** > PLAYACT
**PLAYACTS** > PLAYACT
**PLAYAS** > PLAYA
**PLAYBACK** n playing of a
recording on magnetic
tape ▷ vb listen to
or watch (something
recorded)
**PLAYBACKS** > PLAYBACK
**PLAYBILL** n poster or bill
advertising a play
**PLAYBILLS** > PLAYBILL
**PLAYBOOK** n book
containing a range of
possible set plays
**PLAYBOOKS** > PLAYBOOK
**PLAYBOY** n rich man who
lives only for pleasure
**PLAYBOYS** > PLAYBOY
**PLAYBUS** n mobile
playground
**PLAYBUSES** > PLAYBUS
**PLAYDATE** n gathering of
children at house for play
**PLAYDATES** > PLAYDATE
**PLAYDAY** n day given to
play
**PLAYDAYS** > PLAYDAY
**PLAYDOWN** same
as > PLAYOFF
**PLAYDOWNS** > PLAYDOWN
**PLAYED** > PLAY
**PLAYER** n person who plays
a game or sport
**PLAYERS** > PLAYER
**PLAYFIELD** n field for
sports
**PLAYFUL** adj lively
**PLAYFULLY** > PLAYFUL
**PLAYGIRL** n rich woman

573

devoted to pleasure
**PLAYGIRLS** > PLAYGIRL
**PLAYGOER** n person who goes often to the theatre
**PLAYGOERS** > PLAYGOER
**PLAYGOING** > PLAYGOER
**PLAYGROUP** same as > PLAYSCHOOL
**PLAYHOUSE** n theatre
**PLAYING**
**PLAYLAND** US variant of > PLAYGROUND
**PLAYLANDS** > PLAYLAND
**PLAYLESS** > PLAY
**PLAYLET** n short play
**PLAYLETS** > PLAYLET
**PLAYLIKE** > PLAY
**PLAYLIST** n list of records chosen for playing, such as on a radio station ▷ vb put (a song or record) on a playlist
**PLAYLISTS** > PLAYLIST
**PLAYMAKER** n player who creates scoring opportunities for his or her team-mates
**PLAYMATE** n companion in play
**PLAYMATES** > PLAYMATE
**PLAYOFF** n extra contest to decide the winner when two or more competitors are tied
**PLAYOFFS** > PLAYOFF
**PLAYPEN** n small portable enclosure in which a young child can safely be left to play
**PLAYPENS** > PLAYPEN
**PLAYROOM** n recreation room, esp for children
**PLAYROOMS** > PLAYROOM
**PLAYS** > PLAY
**PLAYSOME** adj playful
**PLAYSUIT** n woman's or child's outfit, usually comprising shorts and a top
**PLAYSUITS** > PLAYSUIT
**PLAYTHING** n toy
**PLAYTIME** n time for play or recreation, such as a school break
**PLAYTIMES** > PLAYTIME
**PLAYWEAR** n clothes suitable for playing in
**PLAZA** n open space or square
**PLAZAS** > PLAZA
**PLEA** n serious or urgent request, entreaty
**PLEACH** vb interlace the stems or boughs of (a tree or hedge)
**PLEACHED** > PLEACH
**PLEACHES** > PLEACH
**PLEACHING** > PLEACH
**PLEAD** vb ask urgently or with deep feeling
**PLEADABLE** > PLEAD
**PLEADED** > PLEAD
**PLEADER** > PLEAD
**PLEADERS** > PLEAD

**PLEADING** > PLEAD
**PLEADINGS** > PLEAD
**PLEADS** > PLEAD
**PLEAED** > PLEA
**PLEAING** > PLEA
**PLEAS** > PLEA
**PLEASABLE** > PLEASE
**PLEASANCE** n secluded part of a garden laid out with trees, walks, etc
**PLEASANT** adj pleasing, enjoyable
**PLEASE** vb give pleasure or satisfaction to ▷ adv polite word of request
**PLEASED** > PLEASE
**PLEASEDLY** > PLEASE
**PLEASEMAN** n person who courts favour
**PLEASEMEN** > PLEASEMAN
**PLEASER** > PLEASE
**PLEASERS** > PLEASE
**PLEASES** > PLEASE
**PLEASETH** obsolete inflection of > PLEASE
**PLEASING** adj giving pleasure or satisfaction ▷ n act of giving pleasure
**PLEASINGS** > PLEASING
**PLEASURE** n feeling of happiness and satisfaction ▷ vb give pleasure to or take pleasure (in)
**PLEASURED** > PLEASURE
**PLEASURER** > PLEASURE
**PLEASURES** > PLEASURE
**PLEAT** n fold made by doubling material back on itself ▷ vb arrange (material) in pleats
**PLEATED** > PLEAT
**PLEATER** n attachment on a sewing machine that makes pleats
**PLEATERS** > PLEATER
**PLEATHER** n synthetic leather
**PLEATHERS** > PLEATHER
**PLEATING** > PLEAT
**PLEATLESS** > PLEAT
**PLEATS** > PLEAT
**PLEB** n common vulgar person
**PLEBBIER** > PLEBBY
**PLEBBIEST** > PLEBBY
**PLEBBY** adj common or vulgar
**PLEBE** n member of the lowest class at the US Naval Academy or Military Academy
**PLEBEAN** old variant of > PLEBEIAN
**PLEBEIAN** adj of the lower social classes ▷ n member of the lower social classes
**PLEBEIANS** > PLEBEIAN
**PLEBES** > PLEBE
**PLEBIFIED** > PLEBIFY
**PLEBIFIES** > PLEBIFY
**PLEBIFY** vb make plebeian
**PLEBS** n common people
**PLECTRA** > PLECTRUM
**PLECTRE** variant

of > PLECTRUM
**PLECTRES** > PLECTRE
**PLECTRON** same as > PLECTRUM
**PLECTRONS** > PLECTRON
**PLECTRUM** n small implement for plucking the strings of a guitar etc
**PLECTRUMS** > PLECTRUM
**PLED** > PLEAD
**PLEDGABLE** > PLEDGE
**PLEDGE** n solemn promise ▷ vb promise solemnly
**PLEDGED** > PLEDGE
**PLEDGEE** n person to whom a pledge is given
**PLEDGEES** > PLEDGEE
**PLEDGEOR** same as > PLEDGOR
**PLEDGEORS** > PLEDGEOR
**PLEDGER** same as > PLEDGOR
**PLEDGERS** > PLEDGER
**PLEDGES** > PLEDGE
**PLEDGET** n small flattened pad of wool, cotton, etc, esp for use as a pressure bandage to be applied to wounds or sores
**PLEDGETS** > PLEDGET
**PLEDGING** > PLEDGE
**PLEDGOR** n person who gives or makes a pledge
**PLEDGORS** > PLEDGOR
**PLEIAD** n brilliant or talented group, esp one with seven members
**PLEIADES** > PLEIAD
**PLEIADS** > PLEIAD
**PLEIOCENE** variant spelling of > PLIOCENE
**PLEIOMERY** n state of having more than normal number
**PLEIOTAXY** n increase in whorls in flower
**PLENA** > PLENUM
**PLENARIES** > PLENARY
**PLENARILY** > PLENARY
**PLENARTY** n state of endowed church office when occupied
**PLENARY** adj (of a meeting) attended by all members ▷ n book of the gospels or epistles and homilies read at the Eucharist
**PLENCH** n tool combining wrench and pliers
**PLENCHES** > PLENCH
**PLENILUNE** n full moon
**PLENIPO** n plenipotentiary diplomat
**PLENIPOES** > PLENIPO
**PLENIPOS** > PLENIPO
**PLENISH** vb fill, stock, or resupply
**PLENISHED** > PLENISH
**PLENISHER** > PLENISH
**PLENISHES** > PLENISH
**PLENISM** n philosophical theory
**PLENISMS** > PLENISM
**PLENIST** > PLENISM
**PLENISTS** > PLENISM

**PLENITUDE** n completeness, abundance
**PLENTEOUS** adj plentiful
**PLENTIES** > PLENTY
**PLENTIFUL** adj existing in large amounts or numbers
**PLENTY** n large amount or number ▷ adj very many ▷ adv more than adequately
**PLENUM** n enclosure containing gas at a higher pressure than the surrounding environment
**PLENUMS** > PLENUM
**PLEON** n abdomen of crustacean
**PLEONAL** adj of abdomen or crustacean
**PLEONASM** n use of more words than necessary
**PLEONASMS** > PLEONASM
**PLEONAST** n person using more words than necessary
**PLEONASTE** n type of black mineral
**PLEONASTS** > PLEONAST
**PLEONEXIA** n greed
**PLEONIC** > PLEON
**PLEONS** > PLEON
**PLEOPOD** another name for > SWIMMERET
**PLEOPODS** > PLEOPOD
**PLERION** n filled-centre supernova remnant in which radiation is emitted by the centre as well as the shell
**PLERIONS** > PLERION
**PLEROMA** n abundance
**PLEROMAS** > PLEROMA
**PLEROME** n central column in growing stem or root
**PLEROMES** > PLEROME
**PLESH** n small pool
**PLESHES** > PLESH
**PLESSOR** same as > PLEXOR
**PLESSORS** > PLESSOR
**PLETHORA** n excess
**PLETHORAS** > PLETHORA
**PLETHORIC** > PLETHORA
**PLEUCH** same as > PLEUGH
**PLEUCHED** > PLEUCH
**PLEUCHING** > PLEUCH
**PLEUCHS** > PLEUCH
**PLEUGH** Scottish word for > PLOUGH
**PLEUGHED** > PLEUGH
**PLEUGHING** > PLEUGH
**PLEUGHS** > PLEUGH
**PLEURA** > PLEURON
**PLEURAE** > PLEURON
**PLEURAL** > PLEURON
**PLEURAS** > PLEURON
**PLEURISY** n inflammation of the membrane covering the lungs
**PLEURITIC** > PLEURISY
**PLEURITIS** n pleurisy
**PLEURON** n part of the cuticle of arthropods that covers the lateral surface of a body segment

PLEUSTON n mass of small organisms, esp algae, floating at the surface of shallow pools
PLEUSTONS > PLEUSTON
PLEW n (formerly in Canada) beaver skin used as a standard unit of value in the fur trade
PLEWS > PLEW
PLEX n shortening of multiplex
PLEXAL > PLEXUS
PLEXES > PLEX
PLEXIFORM adj like or having the form of a network or plexus
PLEXOR n small hammer with a rubber head for use in percussion of the chest and testing reflexes
PLEXORS > PLEXOR
PLEXURE n act of weaving together
PLEXURES > PLEXURE
PLEXUS n complex network of nerves or blood vessels
PLEXUSES > PLEXUS
PLIABLE adj easily bent
PLIABLY > PLIABLE
PLIANCIES > PLIANT
PLIANCY > PLIANT
PLIANT adj pliable
PLIANTLY > PLIANT
PLICA n folding over of parts, such as a fold of skin, muscle, peritoneum, etc
PLICAE > PLICA
PLICAL > PLICA
PLICATE adj having or arranged in parallel folds or ridges ▷ vb arrange into parallel folds
PLICATED > PLICATE
PLICATELY > PLICATE
PLICATES > PLICATE
PLICATING > PLICATE
PLICATION n act of folding or the condition of being folded or plicate
PLICATURE same as > PLICATION
PLIE n classic ballet practice posture with back erect and knees bent
PLIED > PLY
PLIER n person who plies a trade
PLIERS pl n tool with hinged arms and jaws for gripping
PLIES > PLY
PLIGHT n difficult or dangerous situation
PLIGHTED > PLIGHT
PLIGHTER > PLIGHT
PLIGHTERS > PLIGHT
PLIGHTFUL > PLIGHT
PLIGHTING > PLIGHT
PLIGHTS > PLIGHT
PLIM vb swell with water
PLIMMED > PLIM
PLIMMING > PLIM
PLIMS > PLIM

PLIMSOL same as > PLIMSOLE
PLIMSOLE same as > PLIMSOLL
PLIMSOLES > PLIMSOLE
PLIMSOLL n light rubber-soled canvas shoe worn for various sports
PLIMSOLLS > PLIMSOLL
PLIMSOLS > PLIMSOL
PLING n (in computer jargon) an exclamation mark
PLINGS > PLING
PLINK n short sharp often metallic sound as of a string on a musical instrument being plucked or a bullet striking metal ▷ vb make such a noise
PLINKED > PLINK
PLINKER > PLINK
PLINKERS > PLINK
PLINKING > PLINK
PLINKS > PLINK
PLINTH n slab forming the base of a statue, column, etc
PLINTHS > PLINTH
PLIOCENE adj of the Pliocene geological time period
PLIOFILM n transparent plastic material
PLIOFILMS > PLIOFILM
PLIOSAUR n type of dinosaur
PLIOSAURS > PLIOSAUR
PLIOTRON n type of vacuum tube
PLIOTRONS > PLIOTRON
PLISKIE n practical joke
PLISKIES > PLISKIE
PLISKY same as > PLISKIE
PLISSE n fabric with a wrinkled finish, achieved by treatment involving caustic soda
PLISSES > PLISSE
PLOAT vb thrash
PLOATED > PLOAT
PLOATING > PLOAT
PLOATS > PLOAT
PLOD vb walk with slow heavy steps ▷ n act of plodding
PLODDED > PLOD
PLODDER n person who plods, esp one who works in a slow and persevering but uninspired manner
PLODDERS > PLODDER
PLODDING > PLOD
PLODDINGS > PLOD
PLODGE vb wade in water, esp the sea ▷ n act of wading
PLODGED > PLODGE
PLODGES > PLODGE
PLODGING > PLODGE
PLODS > PLOD
PLOIDIES > PLOIDY
PLOIDY n number of copies of set of chromosomes

in cell
PLONG obsolete variant of > PLUNGE
PLONGD > PLONG
PLONGE vb clean drains by action of tide
PLONGED > PLONGE
PLONGES > PLONGE
PLONGING > PLONGE
PLONGS > PLONG
PLONK vb put (something) down heavily and carelessly ▷ n cheap inferior wine ▷ interj exclamation imitative of this sound
PLONKED > PLONK
PLONKER n stupid person
PLONKERS > PLONKER
PLONKIER > PLONK
PLONKIEST > PLONK
PLONKING > PLONK
PLONKINGS > PLONK
PLONKO n alcoholic, esp one who drinks wine
PLONKOS > PLONKO
PLONKS > PLONK
PLONKY > PLONK
PLOOK same as > PLOUK
PLOOKIE same as > PLOUKY
PLOOKIER > PLOUK
PLOOKIEST > PLOUK
PLOOKS > PLOOK
PLOOKY same as > PLOUKY
PLOP n sound of an object falling into water without a splash ▷ vb make this sound ▷ interj exclamation imitative of this sound
PLOPPED > PLOP
PLOPPING > PLOP
PLOPS > PLOP
PLOSION n sound of an abrupt break or closure, esp the audible release of a stop
PLOSIONS > PLOSION
PLOSIVE adj pronounced with a sudden release of breath ▷ n plosive consonant
PLOSIVES > PLOSIVE
PLOT n secret plan to do something illegal or wrong ▷ vb plan secretly, conspire
PLOTFUL > PLOT
PLOTLESS > PLOT
PLOTLINE n literary or dramatic plot
PLOTLINES > PLOTLINE
PLOTS > PLOT
PLOTTAGE n land that makes up plot
PLOTTAGES > PLOTTAGE
PLOTTED > PLOT
PLOTTER same as > PLOUTER
PLOTTERED > PLOTTER
PLOTTERS > PLOTTER
PLOTTIE n hot spiced drink
PLOTTIER > PLOTTY
PLOTTIES > PLOTTIE
PLOTTIEST > PLOTTY

PLOTTING > PLOT
PLOTTINGS > PLOT
PLOTTY adj intricately plotted
PLOTZ vb faint or collapse
PLOTZED > PLOTZ
PLOTZES > PLOTZ
PLOTZING > PLOTZ
PLOUGH n agricultural tool for turning over soil ▷ vb turn over (earth) with a plough
PLOUGHBOY n boy who guides the animals drawing a plough
PLOUGHED > PLOUGH
PLOUGHER > PLOUGH
PLOUGHERS > PLOUGH
PLOUGHING > PLOUGH
PLOUGHMAN n man who ploughs
PLOUGHMEN > PLOUGHMAN
PLOUGHS > PLOUGH
PLOUK n pimple
PLOUKIE > PLOUK
PLOUKIER > PLOUK
PLOUKIEST > PLOUK
PLOUKS > PLOUK
PLOUKY > PLOUK
PLOUTER same as > PLOWTER
PLOUTERED > PLOUTER
PLOUTERS > PLOUTER
PLOVER n shore bird with a straight bill and long pointed wings
PLOVERS > PLOVER
PLOVERY > PLOVER
PLOW same as > PLOUGH
PLOWABLE > PLOW
PLOWBACK n reinvestment of profits
PLOWBACKS > PLOWBACK
PLOWBOY same as > PLOUGHBOY
PLOWBOYS > PLOWBOY
PLOWED > PLOW
PLOWER > PLOW
PLOWERS > PLOW
PLOWHEAD n draught iron of plow
PLOWHEADS > PLOWHEAD
PLOWING > PLOW
PLOWLAND n land plowed
PLOWLANDS > PLOWLAND
PLOWMAN same as > PLOUGHMAN
PLOWMEN > PLOWMAN
PLOWS > PLOW
PLOWSHARE n horizontal pointed cutting blade of a mouldboard plow
PLOWSTAFF n one of the handles of a plow
PLOWTER vb work or play in water or mud ▷ n act of plowtering
PLOWTERED > PLOWTER
PLOWTERS > PLOWTER
PLOY n manoeuvre designed to gain an advantage ▷ vb form a column from a line of troops
PLOYED > PLOY

**PLOYING** > PLOY
**PLOYS** > PLOY
**PLU** same as > PLEW
**PLUCK** vb pull or pick off ▷ n courage
**PLUCKED** > PLUCK
**PLUCKER** > PLUCK
**PLUCKERS** > PLUCK
**PLUCKIER** > PLUCKY
**PLUCKIEST** > PLUCKY
**PLUCKILY** > PLUCKY
**PLUCKING** > PLUCK
**PLUCKS** > PLUCK
**PLUCKY** adj brave
**PLUE** same as > PLEW
**PLUES** > PLUE
**PLUFF** vb expel in puffs
**PLUFFED** > PLUFF
**PLUFFIER** > PLUFF
**PLUFFIEST** > PLUFF
**PLUFFING** > PLUFF
**PLUFFS** > PLUFF
**PLUFFY** > PLUFF
**PLUG** n thing fitting into and filling a hole ▷ vb block or seal (a hole or gap) with a plug
**PLUGBOARD** n device with a large number of sockets in which electrical plugs can be inserted to form many different temporary circuits
**PLUGGED** > PLUG
**PLUGGER** > PLUG
**PLUGGERS** > PLUG
**PLUGGING** > PLUG
**PLUGGINGS** > PLUG
**PLUGHOLE** n hole, esp in a bath, basin, or sink, through which water drains and which can be closed with a plug
**PLUGHOLES** > PLUGHOLE
**PLUGLESS** > PLUG
**PLUGOLA** n plugging of products on television
**PLUGOLAS** > PLUGOLA
**PLUGS** > PLUG
**PLUGUGLY** n city tough; ruffian
**PLUM** n oval usu dark red fruit with a stone in the middle ▷ adj dark purplish-red
**PLUMAGE** n bird's feathers
**PLUMAGED** > PLUMAGE
**PLUMAGES** > PLUMAGE
**PLUMATE** adj of, relating to, or possessing one or more feathers or plumes
**PLUMB** vb understand (something obscure) ▷ adv exactly ▷ n weight, usually of lead, suspended at the end of a line and used to determine water depth or verticality
**PLUMBABLE** > PLUMB
**PLUMBAGO** n plant of warm regions with clusters of blue, white, or red flowers
**PLUMBAGOS** > PLUMBAGO
**PLUMBATE** n compound

formed from lead oxide
**PLUMBATES** > PLUMBATE
**PLUMBED** > PLUMB
**PLUMBEOUS** adj made of or relating to lead or resembling lead in colour
**PLUMBER** n person who fits and repairs pipes and fixtures for water and drainage systems
**PLUMBERS** > PLUMBER
**PLUMBERY** same as > PLUMBING
**PLUMBIC** adj of or containing lead in the tetravalent state
**PLUMBING** n pipes and fixtures used in water and drainage systems
**PLUMBINGS** > PLUMBING
**PLUMBISM** n chronic lead poisoning
**PLUMBISMS** > PLUMBISM
**PLUMBITE** n substance containing lead oxide
**PLUMBITES** > PLUMBITE
**PLUMBLESS** adj incapable of being sounded
**PLUMBNESS** > PLUMB
**PLUMBOUS** adj of or containing lead in the divalent state
**PLUMBS** > PLUMB
**PLUMBUM** n obsolete name for lead (the metal)
**PLUMBUMS** > PLUMBUM
**PLUMCOT** n hybrid of apricot and plum
**PLUMCOTS** > PLUMCOT
**PLUMDAMAS** n prune
**PLUME** n feather, esp one worn as an ornament ▷ vb adorn or decorate with feathers or plumes
**PLUMED** > PLUME
**PLUMELESS** > PLUME
**PLUMELET** n small plume
**PLUMELETS** > PLUMELET
**PLUMELIKE** > PLUME
**PLUMERIA** n tropical tree with candelabra-like branches
**PLUMERIAS** > PLUMERIA
**PLUMERIES** > PLUMERY
**PLUMERY** n plumes collectively
**PLUMES** > PLUME
**PLUMIER** > PLUMY
**PLUMIEST** > PLUMY
**PLUMING** > PLUME
**PLUMIPED** n bird with feathered feet
**PLUMIPEDS** > PLUMIPED
**PLUMIST** n person who makes plumes
**PLUMISTS** > PLUMIST
**PLUMLIKE** > PLUM
**PLUMMER** > PLUM
**PLUMMEST** > PLUM
**PLUMMET** vb plunge downward ▷ n weight on a plumb line or fishing line
**PLUMMETED** > PLUMMET
**PLUMMETS** > PLUMMET

**PLUMMIER** > PLUMMY
**PLUMMIEST** > PLUMMY
**PLUMMY** adj of, full of, or like plums
**PLUMOSE** same as > PLUMATE
**PLUMOSELY** > PLUMOSE
**PLUMOSITY** > PLUMOSE
**PLUMOUS** adj having plumes or feathers
**PLUMP** adj moderately or attractively fat ▷ vb sit or fall heavily and suddenly ▷ n heavy abrupt fall or the sound of this ▷ adv suddenly or heavily
**PLUMPED** > PLUMP
**PLUMPEN** vb make or become plump
**PLUMPENED** > PLUMPEN
**PLUMPENS** > PLUMPEN
**PLUMPER** n pad carried in the mouth by actors to round out the cheeks
**PLUMPERS** > PLUMPER
**PLUMPEST** > PLUMP
**PLUMPIER** > PLUMPY
**PLUMPIEST** > PLUMPY
**PLUMPING** > PLUMP
**PLUMPISH** adj on the plump side
**PLUMPLY** > PLUMP
**PLUMPNESS** > PLUMP
**PLUMPS** > PLUMP
**PLUMPY** adj plump
**PLUMS** > PLUM
**PLUMULA** n down feather
**PLUMULAE** > PLUMULA
**PLUMULAR** > PLUMULE
**PLUMULATE** adj covered with soft fine feathers
**PLUMULE** n embryonic shoot of seed-bearing plants
**PLUMULES** > PLUMULE
**PLUMULOSE** adj having hairs branching out like feathers
**PLUMY** adj like a feather
**PLUNDER** vb take by force, esp in time of war ▷ n things plundered, spoils
**PLUNDERED** > PLUNDER
**PLUNDERER** > PLUNDER
**PLUNDERS** > PLUNDER
**PLUNGE** vb put or throw forcibly or suddenly (into) ▷ n plunging dive
**PLUNGED** > PLUNGE
**PLUNGER** n rubber suction cup used to clear blocked pipes
**PLUNGERS** > PLUNGER
**PLUNGES** > PLUNGE
**PLUNGING** > PLUNGE
**PLUNGINGS** > PLUNGE
**PLUNK** vb pluck the strings of (a banjo etc) to produce a twanging sound ▷ n act or sound of plunking ▷ interj exclamation imitative of the sound of something plunking ▷ adv exactly
**PLUNKED** > PLUNK

**PLUNKER** > PLUNK
**PLUNKERS** > PLUNK
**PLUNKIER** > PLUNKY
**PLUNKIEST** > PLUNKY
**PLUNKING** > PLUNK
**PLUNKS** > PLUNK
**PLUNKY** adj sounding like plucked banjo string
**PLURAL** adj of or consisting of more than one ▷ n word indicating more than one
**PLURALISE** same as > PLURALIZE
**PLURALISM** n existence and toleration of a variety of peoples, opinions, etc in a society
**PLURALIST** > PLURALISM
**PLURALITY** n state of being plural
**PLURALIZE** vb make or become plural
**PLURALLY** > PLURAL
**PLURALS** > PLURAL
**PLURIPARA** n woman who has borne more than one child
**PLURISIE** same as > PLEURISY
**PLURISIES** > PLURISIE
**PLURRY** euphemism for > BLOODY
**PLUS** vb make or become greater in value
**PLUSAGE** same as > PLUSSAGE
**PLUSAGES** > PLUSAGE
**PLUSED** > PLUS
**PLUSES** > PLUS
**PLUSH** n fabric with long velvety pile ▷ adj luxurious
**PLUSHER** > PLUSH
**PLUSHES** > PLUSH
**PLUSHEST** > PLUSH
**PLUSHIER** > PLUSHY
**PLUSHIEST** > PLUSHY
**PLUSHILY** > PLUSH
**PLUSHLY** > PLUSH
**PLUSHNESS** > PLUSH
**PLUSHY** same as > PLUSH
**PLUSING** > PLUS
**PLUSSAGE** n amount over and above another amount
**PLUSSAGES** > PLUSSAGE
**PLUSSED** > PLUS
**PLUSSES** > PLUS
**PLUSSING** > PLUS
**PLUTEAL** > PLUTEUS
**PLUTEI** > PLUTEUS
**PLUTEUS** n larva of sea urchin
**PLUTEUSES** > PLUTEUS
**PLUTOCRAT** n person who is powerful because of being very rich
**PLUTOLOGY** n study of wealth
**PLUTON** n any mass of igneous rock that has solidified below the surface of the earth

**PLUTONIAN** *adj* of or relating to the underworld

**PLUTONIC** *adj* (of igneous rocks) formed from molten rock that has cooled and solidified below the earth's surface

**PLUTONISM** *n* theory that the earth's crust was formed by volcanoes

**PLUTONIUM** *n* radioactive metallic element used esp in nuclear reactors and weapons

**PLUTONOMY** *n* economics

**PLUTONS** > PLUTON

**PLUVIAL** *adj* of or caused by the action of rain ▷ *n* of or relating to rainfall or precipitation

**PLUVIALS** > PLUVIAL

**PLUVIAN** *n* crocodile bird

**PLUVIOSE** *same as* > PLUVIOUS

**PLUVIOUS** *adj* of or relating to rain

**PLY** *vb* work at (a job or trade) ▷ *n* thickness of wool, fabric, etc

**PLYER** *n* person who plies trade

**PLYERS** > PLYER

**PLYING** > PLY

**PLYINGLY** > PLY

**PLYWOOD** *n* board made of thin layers of wood glued together

**PLYWOODS** > PLYWOOD

**PNEUMA** *n* person's vital spirit, soul, or creative energy

**PNEUMAS** > PNEUMA

**PNEUMATIC** *adj* worked by or inflated with wind or air

**PNEUMONIA** *n* inflammation of the lungs

**PNEUMONIC** *adj* of, relating to, or affecting the lungs

**PO** *n* chamber pot

**POA** *n* type of grass

**POACEOUS** *adj* of, relating to, or belonging to the plant family *Poaceae* (grasses)

**POACH** *vb* catch (animals) illegally on someone else's land

**POACHABLE** > POACH

**POACHED** > POACH

**POACHER** *n* person who catches animals illegally on someone else's land

**POACHERS** > POACHER

**POACHES** > POACH

**POACHIER** > POACHY

**POACHIEST** > POACHY

**POACHING** > POACH

**POACHINGS** > POACH

**POACHY** *adj* (of land) wet and soft

**POAKA** *n* type of stilt (bird) native to New Zealand

**POAKAS** > POAKA

**POAKE** *n* waste matter from tanning of hides

**POAKES** > POAKE

**POAS** > POA

**POBLANO** *n* variety of chilli pepper

**POBLANOS** > POBLANO

**POBOY** *n* New Orleans sandwich

**POBOYS** > POBOY

**POCHARD** *n* European diving duck

**POCHARDS** > POCHARD

**POCHAY** *n* post chaise: a closed horse-drawn four-wheeled coach

**POCHAYS** > POCHAY

**POCHETTE** *n* envelope-shaped handbag used by women and men

**POCHETTES** > POCHETTE

**POCHOIR** *n* print made from stencils

**POCHOIRS** > POCHOIR

**POCK** *n* pus-filled blister resulting from smallpox ▷ *vb* mark with scars

**POCKARD** *variant of* > POCHARD

**POCKARDS** > POCKARD

**POCKED** > POCK

**POCKET** *n* small bag sewn into clothing for carrying things ▷ *vb* put into one's pocket ▷ *adj* small

**POCKETED** > POCKET

**POCKETER** > POCKET

**POCKETERS** > POCKET

**POCKETFUL** *n* as much as a pocket will hold

**POCKETING** > POCKET

**POCKETS** > POCKET

**POCKIER** > POCK

**POCKIES** *pl n* woollen mittens

**POCKIEST** > POCK

**POCKILY** > POCK

**POCKING** > POCK

**POCKMANKY** *n* portmanteau

**POCKMARK** *n* pitted scar left on the skin after the healing of a smallpox or similar pustule ▷ *vb* scar or pit (a surface) with pockmarks

**POCKMARKS** > POCKMARK

**POCKPIT** *vb* mark with scars

**POCKPITS** > POCKPIT

**POCKS** > POCK

**POCKY** > POCK

**POCO** *adv* little

**POCOSEN** *same as* > POCOSIN

**POCOSENS** > POCOSEN

**POCOSIN** *n* swamp in US upland coastal region

**POCOSINS** > POCOSIN

**POCOSON** *same as* > POCOSIN

**POCOSONS** > POCOSON

**POD** *n* long narrow seed case of peas, beans, etc ▷ *vb* remove the pod from

**PODAGRA** *n* gout of the foot or big toe

**PODAGRAL** > PODAGRA

**PODAGRAS** > PODAGRA

**PODAGRIC** > PODAGRA

**PODAGROUS** > PODAGRA

**PODALIC** *adj* relating to feet

**PODARGUS** *n* bird of SE Asia and Australia

**PODCAST** *n* audio file similar to a radio broadcast, which can be downloaded and listened to on a computer or MP3 player ▷ *vb* make available in this format

**PODCASTED** > PODCAST

**PODCASTER** > PODCAST

**PODCASTS** > PODCAST

**PODDED** > POD

**PODDIE** *n* user of or enthusiast for the iPod, a portable digital music player

**PODDIES** > PODDY

**PODDING** > POD

**PODDLE** *vb* move or travel in a leisurely manner

**PODDLED** > PODDLE

**PODDLES** > PODDLE

**PODDLING** > PODDLE

**PODDY** *n* handfed calf or lamb

**PODESTA** *n* (in modern Italy) subordinate magistrate in some towns

**PODESTAS** > PODESTA

**PODEX** *n* posterior

**PODEXES** > PODEX

**PODGE** *n* short chubby person

**PODGES** > PODGE

**PODGIER** > PODGY

**PODGIEST** > PODGY

**PODGILY** > PODGY

**PODGINESS** > PODGY

**PODGY** *adj* short and fat

**PODIA** > PODIUM

**PODIAL** > PODIUM

**PODIATRIC** > PODIATRY

**PODIATRY** *another word for* > CHIROPODY

**PODITE** *n* crustacean leg

**PODITES** > PODITE

**PODITIC** *n* segment of limb of arthropod

**PODITICS** > PODITIC

**PODIUM** *n* small raised platform for a conductor or speaker

**PODIUMS** > PODIUM

**PODLEY** *n* young coalfish

**PODLEYS** > PODLEY

**PODLIKE** > POD

**PODOCARP** *n* stem supporting fruit

**PODOCARPS** > PODOCARP

**PODOLOGY** *n* study of feet

**PODOMERE** *n* segment of limb of arthropod

**PODOMERES** > PODOMERE

**PODS** > POD

**PODSOL** *same as* > PODZOL

**PODSOLIC** > PODZOL

**PODSOLISE** *same as* > PODZOLIZE

**PODSOLIZE** *same as* > PODZOLIZE

**PODSOLS** > PODSOL

**PODZOL** *n* type of soil characteristic of coniferous forest regions having a greyish-white colour in its upper leached layers

**PODZOLIC** > PODZOL

**PODZOLISE** *same as* > PODZOLIZE

**PODZOLIZE** *vb* make into or form a podzol

**PODZOLS** > PODZOL

**POECHORE** *n* dry region

**POECHORES** > POECHORE

**POEM** *n* imaginative piece of writing in rhythmic lines

**POEMATIC** *adj* of poetry

**POEMS** > POEM

**POENOLOGY** *same as* > PENOLOGY

**POEP** *n* emission of gas from the anus

**POEPOL** *n* South African slang for anus

**POEPOLS** > POEPOL

**POEPS** > POEP

**POESIED** > POESY

**POESIES** > POESY

**POESY** *n* poetry ▷ *vb* write poems

**POESYING** > POESY

**POET** *n* writer of poems

**POETASTER** *n* writer of inferior verse

**POETASTRY** > POETASTER

**POETESS** *n* female poet

**POETESSES** > POETESS

**POETIC** *adj* of or like poetry

**POETICAL** *n* poet

**POETICALS** > POETICAL

**POETICISE** *same as* > POETICIZE

**POETICISM** > POETICISE

**POETICIZE** *vb* put into poetry or make poetic

**POETICIZM** > POETICIZE

**POETICS** *n* principles and forms of poetry or the study of these, esp as a form of literary criticism

**POETICULE** *n* inferior poet

**POETISE** *same as* > POETICIZE

**POETISED** > POETISE

**POETISER** > POETISE

**POETISERS** > POETISE

**POETISES** > POETISE

**POETISING** > POETISE

**POETIZE** *same as* > POETICIZE

**POETIZED** > POETIZE

**POETIZER** > POETIZE

**POETIZERS** > POETIZE

**POETIZES** > POETIZE

**POETIZING** > POETIZE

**POETLESS** > POET

**POETLIKE** > POET

**POETRESSE** *old variant of* > POETESS

**POETRIES** > POETRY

POETRY n poems
POETS > POET
POETSHIP n state of being poet
POETSHIPS > POETSHIP
POFFLE n small piece of land
POFFLES > POFFLE
POGEY n financial or other relief given to the unemployed by the government
POGEYS > POGEY
POGGE n European marine scorpaenoid fish
POGGES > POGGE
POGIES > POGY
POGO vb jump up and down in one spot, as in a punk dance of the 1970s
POGOED > POGO
POGOER > POGO
POGOERS > POGO
POGOING > POGO
POGONIA n orchid with pink or white fragrant flowers
POGONIAS > POGONIA
POGONIP n icy winter fog
POGONIPS > POGONIP
POGOS > POGO
POGROM n organized persecution and massacre ▷ vb carry out a pogrom
POGROMED > POGROM
POGROMING > POGROM
POGROMIST > POGROM
POGROMS > POGROM
POGY same as > POGEY
POH interj exclamation expressing contempt or disgust
POHIRI variant spelling of > POWHIRI
POHIRIS > POHIRI
POI n ball of woven flax swung rhythmically by Māori women during poi dances
POIGNADO old variant of > PONIARD
POIGNANCE > POIGNANT
POIGNANCY > POIGNANT
POIGNANT adj sharply painful to the feelings
POILU n infantryman in the French Army, esp one in the front lines in World War I
POILUS > POILU
POINADO old variant of > PONIARD
POINADOES > POINADO
POINCIANA n tropical leguminous tree with large orange or red flowers
POIND vb take (property of a debtor) in execution or by way of distress
POINDED > POIND
POINDER > POIND
POINDERS > POIND
POINDING > POIND
POINDINGS > POIND

POINDS > POIND
POINT n main idea in a discussion, argument, etc ▷ vb show the direction or position of something or draw attention to it by extending a finger or other pointed object towards it
POINTABLE > POINT
POINTE n tip of the toe
POINTED adj having a sharp end
POINTEDLY > POINTED
POINTEL n engraver's tool
POINTELLE n fabric design in form of chevrons
POINTELS > POINTEL
POINTER n helpful hint
POINTERS > POINTER
POINTES > POINTE
POINTIER > POINTY
POINTIEST > POINTY
POINTILLE n dotted lines and curves impressed on cover of book
POINTING n insertion of mortar between the joints in brickwork
POINTINGS > POINTING
POINTLESS adj meaningless, irrelevant
POINTMAN n soldier who walks at the front of an infantry patrol in combat
POINTMEN > POINTMAN
POINTS > POINT
POINTSMAN n person who operates railway points
POINTSMEN > POINTSMAN
POINTY adj having a sharp point or points
POIS > POI
POISE n calm dignified manner ▷ vb be balanced or suspended
POISED adj absolutely ready
POISER n balancing organ of some insects
POISERS > POISER
POISES > POISE
POISHA n monetary unit of Bangladesh
POISING > POISE
POISON n substance that kills or injures when swallowed or absorbed ▷ vb give poison to
POISONED > POISON
POISONER > POISON
POISONERS > POISON
POISONING > POISON
POISONOUS adj of or like a poison
POISONS > POISON
POISSON n fish
POISSONS > POISSON
POITIN variant spelling of > POTEEN
POITINS > POITIN
POITREL n breastplate of horse's armour
POITRELS > POITREL
POITRINE n woman's

bosom
POITRINES > POITRINE
POKABLE > POKE
POKAL n tall drinking cup
POKALS > POKAL
POKE vb jab or prod with one's finger, a stick, etc ▷ n poking
POKEBERRY same as > POKEWEED
POKED > POKE
POKEFUL n contents of small bag
POKEFULS > POKEFUL
POKELOGAN another name for > BOGAN
POKER n metal rod for stirring a fire
POKERISH adj stiff like poker
POKEROOT same as > POKEWEED
POKEROOTS > POKEROOT
POKERS > POKER
POKERWORK n art of producing pictures or designs on wood by burning it with a heated metal point
POKES > POKE
POKEWEED n tall North American plant that has small white flowers, juicy purple berries, and a poisonous purple root used medicinally
POKEWEEDS > POKEWEED
POKEY same as > POKIE
POKEYS > POKEY
POKIE n poker machine
POKIER > POKY
POKIES > POKY
POKIEST > POKY
POKILY > POKY
POKINESS > POKY
POKING > POKE
POKY adj small and cramped
POL n political campaigner
POLACCA same as > POLACRE
POLACCAS > POLACCA
POLACRE n three-masted sailing vessel used in the Mediterranean
POLACRES > POLACRE
POLAR adj of or near either of the earth's poles ▷ n type of line in geometry
POLARISE same as > POLARIZE
POLARISED > POLARISE
POLARISER same as > POLARIZER
POLARISES > POLARISE
POLARITY n state of having two directly opposite tendencies or opinions
POLARIZE vb form or cause to form into groups with directly opposite views
POLARIZED > POLARIZE
POLARIZER n person or a device that causes polarization

POLARIZES > POLARIZE
POLARON n kind of electron
POLARONS > POLARON
POLARS > POLAR
POLDER n land reclaimed from the sea, esp in the Netherlands ▷ vb reclaim land from the sea
POLDERED > POLDER
POLDERING > POLDER
POLDERS > POLDER
POLE n long rounded piece of wood etc ▷ vb strike or push with a pole
POLEAX same as > POLEAXE
POLEAXE vb hit or stun with a heavy blow ▷ n axe formerly used in battle or used by a butcher
POLEAXED > POLEAXE
POLEAXES > POLEAXE
POLEAXING > POLEAXE
POLECAT n small animal of the weasel family
POLECATS > POLECAT
POLED > POLE
POLEIS > POLIS
POLELESS > POLE
POLEMARCH n (in ancient Greece) civilian official, originally a supreme general
POLEMIC n fierce attack on or defence of a particular opinion, belief, etc ▷ adj of or involving dispute or controversy
POLEMICAL > POLEMIC
POLEMICS n art of dispute
POLEMISE same as > POLEMIZE
POLEMISED > POLEMISE
POLEMISES > POLEMISE
POLEMIST > POLEMIC
POLEMISTS > POLEMIC
POLEMIZE vb engage in controversy
POLEMIZED > POLEMIZE
POLEMIZES > POLEMIZE
POLENTA n thick porridge made in Italy, usually from maize
POLENTAS > POLENTA
POLER n person or thing that poles, esp a punter
POLERS > POLER
POLES > POLE
POLESTAR n guiding principle, rule, standard, etc
POLESTARS > POLESTAR
POLEWARD adv towards a pole
POLEY adj (of cattle) hornless or polled ▷ n animal with horns removed
POLEYN n piece of armour for protecting the knee
POLEYNS > POLEYN
POLEYS > POLEY
POLIANITE n manganese dioxide occurring as hard crystals

POLICE n organized force in a state which keeps law and order ▷ vb control or watch over with police or a similar body

POLICED > POLICE

POLICEMAN n member of a police force

POLICEMEN > POLICEMAN

POLICER n computer device controlling use

POLICERS > POLICER

POLICES > POLICE

POLICIES > POLICY

POLICING > POLICE

POLICINGS > POLICE

POLICY n plan of action adopted by a person, group, or state

POLIES > POLY

POLING > POLE

POLINGS > POLE

POLIO n acute viral disease

POLIOS > POLIO

POLIS n ancient Greek city-state

POLISH vb make smooth and shiny by rubbing ▷ n substance used for polishing

POLISHED adj accomplished

POLISHER > POLISH

POLISHERS > POLISH

POLISHES > POLISH

POLISHING > POLISH

POLITBURO n supreme policy-making authority in most communist countries

POLITE adj showing consideration for others in one's manners, speech, etc

POLITELY > POLITE

POLITER > POLITE

POLITESSE n formal or genteel politeness

POLITEST > POLITE

POLITIC adj wise and likely to prove advantageous

POLITICAL adj of the state, government, or public administration

POLITICK vb engage in politics

POLITICKS > POLITICK

POLITICLY > POLITIC

POLITICO n politician

POLITICOS > POLITICO

POLITICS n winning and using of power to govern society

POLITIES > POLITY

POLITIQUE n 16th-century French moderate

POLITY n politically organized state, church, or society

POLJE n large elliptical depression in karst regions, sometimes containing a marsh or small lake

POLJES > POLJE

POLK vb dance a polka

POLKA n lively 19th-century dance ▷ vb dance a polka

POLKAED > POLKA

POLKAING > POLKA

POLKAS > POLKA

POLKED > POLK

POLKING > POLK

POLKS > POLK

POLL n questioning of a random sample of people to find out general opinion ▷ vb receive (votes)

POLLACK n food fish related to the cod, found in northern seas

POLLACKS > POLLACK

POLLAN n whitefish that occurs in lakes in Northern Ireland

POLLANS > POLLAN

POLLARD n animal that has shed its horns or has had them removed ▷ vb cut off the top of (a tree) to make it grow bushy

POLLARDED > POLLARD

POLLARDS > POLLARD

POLLED adj (of animals, esp cattle) having the horns cut off or being naturally hornless

POLLEE > POLL

POLLEES > POLL

POLLEN n fine dust produced by flowers to fertilize other flowers ▷ vb collect pollen

POLLENATE same as > POLLINATE

POLLENED > POLLEN

POLLENING > POLLEN

POLLENS > POLLEN

POLLENT adj strong

POLLER > POLL

POLLERS > POLL

POLLEX n first digit of the forelimb of amphibians, reptiles, birds, and mammals, such as the thumb of man and other primates

POLLICAL > POLLEX

POLLICES > POLLEX

POLLICIE obsolete spelling of > POLICY

POLLICIES > POLLICIE

POLLICY obsolete spelling of > POLICY

POLLIES > POLLY

POLLINATE vb fertilize with pollen

POLLING n casting or registering of votes at an election

POLLINGS > POLLING

POLLINIA > POLLINIUM

POLLINIC > POLLEN

POLLINISE same as > POLLINIZE

POLLINIUM n mass of cohering pollen grains, produced by plants such as orchids and transported as a whole during pollination

POLLINIZE same as > POLLINATE

POLLIST n one advocating the use of polls

POLLISTS > POLLIST

POLLIWIG same as > POLLIWOG

POLLIWIGS > POLLIWOG

POLLIWOG n sailor who has not crossed the equator

POLLIWOGS > POLLIWOG

POLLMAN n one passing a degree without honours

POLLMEN > POLLMAN

POLLOCK same as > POLLACK

POLLOCKS > POLLOCK

POLLS > POLL

POLLSTER n person who conducts opinion polls

POLLSTERS > POLLSTER

POLLTAKER n person conducting poll

POLLUCITE n colourless rare mineral consisting of a hydrated caesium aluminium silicate

POLLUSION n comic Shakespearian character's version of "allusion"

POLLUTANT n something that pollutes

POLLUTE vb contaminate with something poisonous or harmful

POLLUTED adj made unclean or impure

POLLUTER > POLLUTE

POLLUTERS > POLLUTE

POLLUTES > POLLUTE

POLLUTING > POLLUTE

POLLUTION n act of polluting or the state of being polluted

POLLUTIVE adj causing pollution

POLLY n politician

POLLYANNA n person who is constantly or excessively optimistic

POLLYWIG same as > POLLIWOG

POLLYWIGS > POLLYWIG

POLLYWOG same as > POLLIWOG

POLLYWOGS > POLLYWOG

POLO n game like hockey played by teams of players on horseback

POLOIDAL adj relating to a type of magnetic field

POLOIST n devotee of polo

POLOISTS > POLOIST

POLONAISE n old stately dance

POLONIE same as > POLONY

POLONIES > POLONY

POLONISE same as > POLONIZE

POLONISED > POLONISE

POLONISES > POLONISE

POLONISM > POLONISE

POLONISMS > POLONISE

POLONIUM n radioactive element that occurs in trace amounts in uranium ores

POLONIUMS > POLONIUM

POLONIZE vb make Polish

POLONIZED > POLONIZE

POLONIZES > POLONIZE

POLONY n bologna sausage

POLOS > POLO

POLS > POL

POLT n thump or blow ▷ vb strike

POLTED > POLT

POLTFOOT adj having a club foot

POLTING > POLT

POLTROON n utter coward

POLTROONS > POLTROON

POLTS > POLT

POLVERINE n glassmakers' potash

POLY n polytechnic

POLYACID n alcohol or base with two or more hydroxyl groups

POLYACIDS > POLYACID

POLYACT adj (of a sea creature) having many tentacles or limb-like protrusions

POLYADIC adj (of a relation, operation, etc) having several argument places

POLYAMIDE n synthetic polymeric material

POLYAMINE n compound containing two or more amine groups

POLYANDRY n practice of having more than one husband at the same time

POLYANTHA n type of flower

POLYANTHI n hybrid garden primroses

POLYARCH n member of polyarchy

POLYARCHY n political system in which power is dispersed

POLYAXIAL n joint in which movement occurs in more than one axis

POLYAXON n nerve cell with multiple branches

POLYAXONS > POLYAXON

POLYBASIC adj (of an acid) having two or more replaceable hydrogen atoms per molecule

POLYBRID n hybrid plant with more than two parental groups

POLYBRIDS > POLYBRID

POLYCARPY n condition of being able to produce flowers and fruit several times in successive years or seasons

POLYCHETE n variety of worm

POLYCONIC as in polyconic projection type of projection used in making maps of large areas

POLYCOT n plant that has or appears to have more than two cotyledons

POLYCOTS > POLYCOT

POLYDEMIC adj growing in or inhabiting more than two regions

POLYENE n chemical compound containing a chain of alternating single and double carbon-carbon bonds

POLYENES > POLYENE

POLYENIC > POLYENE

POLYESTER n synthetic material used to make plastics and textile fibres

POLYGALA n herbaceous plant or small shrub

POLYGALAS > POLYGALA

POLYGAM n plant of the Polygamia class

POLYGAMIC > POLYGAMY

POLYGAMS > POLYGAM

POLYGAMY n practice of having more than one husband or wife at the same time

POLYGENE n any of a group of genes that each produce a small quantitative effect on a particular characteristic of the phenotype, such as height

POLYGENES > POLYGENE

POLYGENIC adj of, relating to, or controlled by polygenes

POLYGENY > POLYGENIC

POLYGLOT adj (person) able to speak or write several languages ▷ n person who can speak many languages

POLYGLOTS > POLYGLOT

POLYGLOTT variant of > POLYGLOT

POLYGON n geometrical figure with three or more angles and sides

POLYGONAL > POLYGON

POLYGONS > POLYGON

POLYGONUM n plant with stems with knotlike joints and spikes of small white, green, or pink flowers

POLYGONY > POLYGON

POLYGRAPH n instrument for recording pulse rate and perspiration, used esp as a lie detector

POLYGYNY n practice of having more than one wife at the same time

POLYHEDRA n solid figures, each consisting of four or more plane faces

POLYIMIDE n type of polymer

POLYLEMMA n debate forcing choice between contradictory positions

POLYMASTY n condition in which more than two

breasts are present

POLYMATH n person of great and varied learning

POLYMATHS > POLYMATH

POLYMATHY > POLYMATH

POLYMER n chemical compound with large molecules made of simple molecules of the same kind

POLYMERIC adj of or being a polymer

POLYMERS > POLYMER

POLYMERY > POLYMER

POLYMORPH n species of animal or plant that exhibits polymorphism

POLYMYXIN n polypeptide antibiotic

POLYNIA same as > POLYNYA

POLYNIAS > POLYNIA

POLYNYA n stretch of open water surrounded by ice, esp near the mouths of large rivers, in arctic seas

POLYNYAS > POLYNYA

POLYNYI > POLYNYA

POLYOL n type of alcohol

POLYOLS > POLYOL

POLYOMA n type of tumour caused by virus

POLYOMAS > POLYOMA

POLYOMINO n polygon made from joining identical squares at their edges

POLYONYM n object with many names

POLYONYMS > POLYONYM

POLYONYMY > POLYONYM

POLYP n small simple sea creature with a hollow cylindrical body

POLYPARIA n polyparies

POLYPARY n common base and connecting tissue of a colony of coelenterate polyps, esp coral

POLYPE variant of > POLYP

POLYPED same as > POLYPOD

POLYPEDS > POLYPED

POLYPES > POLYPE

POLYPHAGY n insatiable appetite

POLYPHASE adj (of an electrical system, circuit, or device) having, generating, or using two or more alternating voltages of the same frequency, the phases of which are cyclically displaced by fractions of a period

POLYPHON n musical instrument resembling a lute

POLYPHONE n letter or character with more than one phonetic value

POLYPHONS > POLYPHON

POLYPHONY n polyphonic style of composition or a piece of music using it

POLYPI > POLYPUS

POLYPIDE n polyp forming part of a colonial animal

POLYPIDES > POLYPIDE

POLYPIDOM same as > POLYPARY

POLYPILL n proposed combined medication intended to reduce the likelihood of heart attacks and strokes

POLYPILLS > POLYPILL

POLYPINE adj of or relating to polyps

POLYPITE same as > POLYPIDE

POLYPITES > POLYPITE

POLYPLOID adj (of cells, organisms, etc) having more than twice the basic (haploid) number of chromosomes ▷ n individual or cell of this type

POLYPNEA n rapid breathing

POLYPNEAS > POLYPNEA

POLYPNEIC > POLYPNEA

POLYPOD adj (esp of insect larvae) having many legs or similar appendages ▷ n animal of this type

POLYPODS > POLYPOD

POLYPODY n fern with deeply divided leaves and round naked sori

POLYPOID > POLYP

POLYPORE n type of fungi

POLYPORES > POLYPORE

POLYPOSES > POLYPOSIS

POLYPOSIS n formation of many polyps

POLYPOUS > POLYP

POLYPS > POLYP

POLYPTYCH n altarpiece consisting of more than three panels, set with paintings or carvings, and usually hinged for folding

POLYPUS same as > POLYP

POLYPUSES > POLYPUS

POLYS > POLY

POLYSEME n word with many meanings

POLYSEMES > POLYSEME

POLYSEMIC > POLYSEME

POLYSEMY n existence of several meanings in a single word

POLYSOME n assemblage of ribosomes associated with a messenger RNA molecule

POLYSOMES > POLYSOME

POLYSOMIC adj of, relating to, or designating a basically diploid chromosome complement, in which some but not all the chromosomes are represented more than twice

POLYSOMY > POLYSOME

POLYSTYLE n room with many columns

POLYTENE adj denoting a type of giant-size chromosome consisting of many replicated genes in parallel, found esp in Drosophila larvae

POLYTENY > POLYTENE

POLYTHENE n light plastic used for bags etc

POLYTONAL adj using more than two different tones or keys simultaneously

POLYTYPE n crystal occurring in more than one form

POLYTYPES > POLYTYPE

POLYTYPIC adj existing in, consisting of, or incorporating several different types or forms

POLYURIA n state or condition of discharging abnormally large quantities of urine, often accompanied by a need to urinate frequently

POLYURIAS > POLYURIA

POLYURIC > POLYURIA

POLYVINYL n designating a plastic or resin formed by polymerization of a vinyl derivative

POLYWATER n liquid formerly supposed to be polymeric form of water

POLYZOA n small mosslike aquatic creatures

POLYZOAN another word for > BRYOZOAN

POLYZOANS > POLYZOAN

POLYZOARY n colony of bryozoan animals

POLYZOIC adj (of certain colonial animals) having many zooids or similar polyps

POLYZONAL adj having many zones

POLYZOOID adj resembling a polyzoon

POLYZOON n individual zooid within polyzoan

POM same as > POMMY

POMACE n apple pulp left after pressing for juice

POMACEOUS adj of, relating to, or bearing pomes, such as the apple, pear, and quince trees

POMACES > POMACE

POMADE n perfumed oil put on the hair to make it smooth and shiny ▷ vb put pomade on

POMADED > POMADE

POMADES > POMADE

POMADING > POMADE

POMANDER n mixture of sweet-smelling petals, herbs, etc

POMANDERS > POMANDER

POMATO n hybrid of tomato

and potato

POMATOES > POMATO

POMATUM *same as* > POMADE

POMATUMS > POMATUM

POMBE *n* any alcoholic drink

POMBES > POMBE

POME *n* fleshy fruit of the apple and related plants, consisting of an enlarged receptacle enclosing the ovary and seeds

POMELO *n* edible yellow fruit, like a grapefruit, of a tropical tree

POMELOS > POMELO

POMEROY *n* bullet used to down airships

POMEROYS > POMEROY

POMES > POME

POMFRET *n* small black rounded liquorice sweet

POMFRETS > POMFRET

POMMEE *adj* (of cross) having end of each arm ending in disk

POMMEL *same as* > PUMMEL

POMMELE *adj* having a pommel

POMMELED > POMMEL

POMMELING > POMMEL

POMMELLED > POMMEL

POMMELS > POMMEL

POMMETTY *adj* having a pommel

POMMIE *same as* > POMMY

POMMIES > POMMY

POMMY *n* word used by Australians and New Zealanders for a British person

POMO *n* postmodernism

POMOERIUM *n* space around town within city walls

POMOLOGY *n* branch of horticulture that is concerned with the study and cultivation of fruit

POMOS > POMO

POMP *n* stately display or ceremony

POMPADOUR *n* early 18th-century hairstyle for women, having the front hair arranged over a pad to give it greater height and bulk

POMPANO *n* deep-bodied carangid food fish

POMPANOS > POMPANO

POMPELO *n* large Asian citrus fruit

POMPELOS > POMPELO

POMPEY *vb* mollycoddle

POMPEYED > POMPEY

POMPEYING > POMPEY

POMPEYS > POMPEY

POMPHOLYX *n* type of eczema

POMPIER *adj* slavishly conventional

POMPILID *n* spider-hunting wasp

POMPILIDS > POMPILID

POMPION *n* pumpkin

POMPIONS > POMPION

POMPOM *n* decorative ball of tufted wool, silk, etc

POMPOMS > POMPOM

POMPON *same as* > POMPOM

POMPONS > POMPOM

POMPOON *variant of* > POMPOM

POMPOONS > POMPOON

POMPOSITY *n* vain or ostentatious display of dignity or importance

POMPOUS *adj* foolishly serious and grand, self-important

POMPOUSLY > POMPOUS

POMPS > POMP

POMROY *variant of* > POMEROY

POMROYS > POMROY

POMS > POM

POMWATER *n* kind of apple

POMWATERS > POMWATER

PONCE *n* derogatory word for an effeminate man ▷ *vb* act stupidly or waste time

PONCEAU *n* scarlet red

PONCEAUS > PONCEAU

PONCED > PONCE

PONCES > PONCE

PONCEY *adj* ostentatious, pretentious, or effeminate

PONCHO *n* loose circular cloak with a hole for the head

PONCHOED *adj* wearing poncho

PONCHOS > PONCHO

PONCIER > PONCEY

PONCIEST > PONCEY

PONCING > PONCE

PONCY *same as* > PONCEY

POND *n* small area of still water ▷ *vb* hold back (flowing water)

PONDAGE *n* water held in reservoir

PONDAGES > PONDAGE

PONDED > POND

PONDER *vb* think thoroughly or deeply (about)

PONDERAL *adj* relating to weight

PONDERATE *vb* consider

PONDERED > PONDER

PONDERER > PONDER

PONDERERS > PONDER

PONDERING > PONDER

PONDEROSA *n* N American pine tree

PONDEROUS *adj* serious and dull

PONDERS > PONDER

PONDING > POND

PONDOK *n* (in southern Africa) crudely made house or shack

PONDOKKIE *same as* > PONDOK

PONDOKS > PONDOK

PONDS > POND

PONDWEED *n* plant that

grows in ponds

PONDWEEDS > PONDWEED

PONE *n* bread made of maize

PONENT *n* west wind

PONES > PONE

PONEY *same as* > PONY

PONEYS > PONEY

PONG *n* strong unpleasant smell ▷ *vb* give off a strong unpleasant smell

PONGA *n* tall New Zealand tree fern with large leathery leaves

PONGAS > PONGA

PONGED > PONG

PONGEE *n* thin plain-weave silk fabric from China or India, left in its natural colour

PONGEES > PONGEE

PONGID *n* any primate of the family *Pongidae*, which includes the gibbons and the great apes ▷ *adj* of, relating to, or belonging to the family *Pongidae*

PONGIDS > PONGID

PONGIER > PONG

PONGIEST > PONG

PONGING > PONG

PONGO *n* anthropoid ape, esp an orang-utan or (formerly) a gorilla

PONGOES > PONGO

PONGOS > PONGO

PONGY > PONG

PONIARD *n* small slender dagger ▷ *vb* stab with a poniard

PONIARDED > PONIARD

PONIARDS > PONIARD

PONIED > PONY

PONIES > PONY

PONK *n* evil spirit

PONKS > PONK

PONS *n* bridge of connecting tissue

PONT *n* (in South Africa) river ferry, esp one that is guided by a cable from one bank to the other

PONTAGE *n* tax paid for repairing bridge

PONTAGES > PONTAGE

PONTAL *adj* of or relating to the pons

PONTES > PONS

PONTIANAC *same as* > PONTIANAK

PONTIANAK *n* (in Malay folklore) female vampire

PONTIC *adj* of or relating to the pons

PONTIES > PONTY

PONTIFEX *n* (in ancient Rome) any of the senior members of the Pontifical College

PONTIFF *n* Pope

PONTIFFS > PONTIFF

PONTIFIC > PONTIFF

PONTIFICE *n* structure of

bridge

PONTIFIED > PONTIFY

PONTIFIES > PONTIFY

PONTIFY *vb* speak or behave in a pompous or dogmatic manner

PONTIL *same as* > PUNTY

PONTILE *adj* relating to pons

PONTILS > PONTIL

PONTINE *adj* of or relating to bridges

PONTLEVIS *n* horse rearing repeatedly

PONTON *variant of* > PONTOON

PONTONEER *same as* > PONTONIER

PONTONIER *n* person in charge of or involved in building a pontoon bridge

PONTONS > PONTON

PONTOON *n* floating platform supporting a temporary bridge ▷ *vb* cross a river using pontoons

PONTOONED > PONTOON

PONTOONER > PONTOON

PONTOONS > PONTOON

PONTS > PONT

PONTY *n* rod used for shaping molten glass

PONY *n* small horse ▷ *vb* settle bill or debt

PONYING > PONY

PONYSKIN *n* leather from pony hide

PONYSKINS > PONYSKIN

PONYTAIL *n* long hair tied in one bunch at the back of the head

PONYTAILS > PONYTAIL

PONZU *n* type of Japanese dipping sauce made from orange juice, sake, sugar, soy sauce, and red pepper

PONZUS > PONZU

POO *vb* defecate

POOCH *n* slang word for dog ▷ *vb* bulge or protrude

POOCHED > POOCH

POOCHES > POOCH

POOCHING > POOCH

POOD *n* unit of weight, used in Russia, equal to 36.1 pounds or 16.39 kilograms

POODLE *n* dog with curly hair often clipped fancifully

POODLES > POODLE

POODS > POOD

POOED > POO

POOF *n* derogatory word for a homosexual man

POOFIER > POOF

POOFIEST > POOF

POOFS > POOF

POOFTAH *same as* > POOFTER

POOFTAHS > POOFTAH

POOFTER *n* derogatory word for a man who is considered effeminate or homosexual

POOFTERS > POOFTER
POOFY > POOF
POOGYE n Hindu nose-flute
POOGYES > POOGYE
POOH interj exclamation of disdain, contempt, or disgust ▷ vb make such an exclamation
POOHED > POOH
POOHING > POOH
POOHS > POOH
POOING > POO
POOJA variant of > PUJA
POOJAH variant of > PUJA
POOJAHS > POOJAH
POOJAS > POOJA
POOK vb pluck
POOKA n malevolent Irish spirit
POOKAS > POOKA
POOKING > POOK
POOKIT > POOK
POOKS > POOK
POOL n small body of still water ▷ vb put in a common fund
POOLED > POOL
POOLER n person taking part in pool
POOLERS > POOLER
POOLHALL n room containing pool tables
POOLHALLS > POOLHALL
POOLING > POOL
POOLROOM n hall or establishment where pool, billiards, etc, are played
POOLROOMS > POOLROOM
POOLS pl n organized nationwide principally postal gambling pool betting on the result of football matches
POOLSIDE n area surrounding swimming pool
POOLSIDES > POOLSIDE
POON n SE Asian tree with lightweight hard wood and shiny leathery leaves
POONAC n coconut residue
POONACS > POONAC
POONCE n derogatory word for a homosexual man ▷ vb behave effeminately
POONCED > POONCE
POONCES > POONCE
POONCING > POONCE
POONS > POON
POONTANG n taboo word for the female pudenda
POONTANGS > POONTANG
POOP n raised part at the back of a sailing ship ▷ vb (of a wave or sea) break over the stern of (a vessel)
POOPED > POOP
POOPER as in party pooper person whose behaviour or personality spoils other people's enjoyment
POOPERS > POOPER
POOPING > POOP
POOPS > POOP

POOR adj having little money and few possessions
POORER > POOR
POOREST > POOR
POORHOUSE n (formerly) publicly maintained institution offering accommodation to the poor
POORI n unleavened Indian bread
POORIS > POORI
POORISH > POOR
POORLIER > POORLY
POORLIEST > POORLY
POORLY adv in a poor manner ▷ adj not in good health
POORMOUTH vb complain about being poor
POORNESS > POOR
POORT n (in South Africa) steep narrow mountain pass, usually following a river or stream
POORTITH same as > PUIRTITH
POORTITHS > POORTITH
POORTS > POORT
POORWILL n bird of N America
POORWILLS > POORWILL
POOS > POO
POOT vb break wind
POOTED > POOT
POOTER > POOT
POOTERS > POOT
POOTING > POOT
POOTLE vb travel or go in a relaxed or leisurely manner
POOTLED > POOTLE
POOTLES > POOTLE
POOTLING > POOTLE
POOTS > POOT
POOVE same as > POOF
POOVERIES > POOVERY
POOVERY n derogatory word for homosexuality
POOVES > POOVE
POOVIER > POOVE
POOVIEST > POOVE
POOVY > POOVE
POP vb make or cause to make a small explosive sound ▷ n small explosive sound ▷ adj popular
POPADUM same as > POPPADOM
POPADUMS > POPADUM
POPCORN n grains of maize heated until they puff up and burst
POPCORNS > POPCORN
POPE n bishop of Rome as head of the Roman Catholic Church
POPEDOM n office or dignity of a pope
POPEDOMS > POPEDOM
POPEHOOD > POPE
POPEHOODS > POPE
POPELESS > POPE
POPELIKE > POPE

POPELING n deputy or supporter of pope
POPELINGS > POPELING
POPERA n music drawing on opera or classical music and aiming for popular appeal
POPERAS > POPERA
POPERIES > POPERY
POPERIN n kind of pear
POPERINS > POPERIN
POPERY n derogatory word for Roman Catholicism
POPES > POPE
POPESEYE adj denoting a cut of steak
POPESHIP > POPE
POPESHIPS > POPE
POPETTE n young female fan or performer of pop music
POPETTES > POPETTE
POPEYED adj staring in astonishment
POPGUN n toy gun that fires a pellet or cork by means of compressed air
POPGUNS > POPGUN
POPINJAY n conceited, foppish, or overly talkative person
POPINJAYS > POPINJAY
POPISH adj derogatory word for Roman Catholic
POPISHLY > POPISH
POPJOY vb amuse oneself
POPJOYED > POPJOY
POPJOYING > POPJOY
POPJOYS > POPJOY
POPLAR n tall slender tree
POPLARS > POPLAR
POPLIN n ribbed cotton material
POPLINS > POPLIN
POPLITEAL adj of, relating to, or near the part of the leg behind the knee
POPLITEI > POPLITEUS
POPLITEUS n muscle in leg
POPLITIC same as > POPLITEAL
POPOVER n individual Yorkshire pudding, often served with roast beef
POPOVERS > POPOVER
POPPA same as > PAPA
POPPADOM n thin round crisp Indian bread
POPPADOMS > POPPADOM
POPPADUM same as > POPPADOM
POPPADUMS > POPPADOM
POPPAS > POPPA
POPPED > POP
POPPER n press stud
POPPERING n method of fishing
POPPERS > POPPER
POPPET n term of affection for a small child or sweetheart
POPPETS > POPPET
POPPIED adj covered with poppies

POPPIER > POPPY
POPPIES > POPPY
POPPIEST > POPPY
POPPING > POP
POPPISH adj like pop music
POPPIT n bead used to form necklace
POPPITS > POPPIT
POPPLE vb (of boiling water or a choppy sea) to heave or toss
POPPLED > POPPLE
POPPLES > POPPLE
POPPLIER > POPPLY
POPPLIEST > POPPLY
POPPLING > POPPLE
POPPLY adj covered in small bumps
POPPY n plant with a large red flower ▷ adj reddish-orange
POPPYCOCK n nonsense
POPPYHEAD n hard dry seed-containing capsule of a poppy
POPRIN same as > POPERIN
POPRINS > POPRIN
POPS > POP
POPSICLE n tradename for a kind of ice lolly
POPSICLES > POPSICLE
POPSIE same as > POPSY
POPSIES > POPSY
POPSTER n pop star
POPSTERS > POPSTER
POPSY n attractive young woman
POPULACE n ordinary people
POPULACES > POPULACE
POPULAR adj widely liked and admired ▷ n cheap newspapers with mass circulation
POPULARLY adv by the public as a whole
POPULARS > POPULAR
POPULATE vb live in, inhabit
POPULATED > POPULATE
POPULATES > POPULATE
POPULISM n political strategy based on a calculated appeal to the interests or prejudices of ordinary people
POPULISMS > POPULISM
POPULIST adj (person) appealing to the interests or prejudices of ordinary people ▷ n person, esp a politician, who appeals to the interests or prejudices of ordinary people
POPULISTS > POPULIST
POPULOUS adj densely populated
PORAE n large edible sea fish of New Zealand waters
PORAES > PORAE
PORAL adj relating to pores
PORANGI adj crazy
PORBEAGLE n kind of shark
PORCELAIN n fine china

**PORCH** n covered approach to the entrance of a building
**PORCHES** > PORCH
**PORCINE** adj of or like a pig
**PORCINI** > PORCINO
**PORCINIS** > PORCINO
**PORCINO** n edible woodland fungus
**PORCUPINE** n animal covered with long pointed quills
**PORCUPINY** > PORCUPINE
**PORE** n tiny opening in the skin or in the surface of a plant ▷ vb make a close intent examination or study (of a book, map, etc)
**PORED** > PORE
**PORER** n person who pores
**PORERS** > PORE
**PORES** > PORE
**PORGE** vb cleanse (slaughtered animal) ceremonially
**PORGED** > PORGE
**PORGES** > PORGE
**PORGIE** same as > PORGY
**PORGIES** > PORGY
**PORGING** > PORGE
**PORGY** n any of various sparid fishes, many of which occur in American Atlantic waters
**PORIER** > PORY
**PORIEST** > PORY
**PORIFER** n type of invertebrate
**PORIFERAL** > PORIFERAN
**PORIFERAN** n sponge ▷ adj of, relating to, or belonging to the phylum Porifera
**PORIFERS** > PORIFER
**PORINA** n larva of a moth which causes damage to grassland
**PORINAS** > PORINA
**PORINESS** > PORY
**PORING** > PORE
**PORISM** n type of mathematical proposition, the meaning of which is now obscure
**PORISMS** > PORISM
**PORISTIC** > PORISM
**PORK** vb (of eg a raven) make a croaking sound
**PORKED** > PORK
**PORKER** n pig raised for food
**PORKERS** > PORKER
**PORKIER** > PORKY
**PORKIES** > PORKY
**PORKIEST** > PORKY
**PORKINESS** > PORKY
**PORKING** > PORK
**PORKLING** n pig
**PORKLINGS** > PORKLING
**PORKPIE** n hat with a round flat crown and a brim that can be turned up or down
**PORKPIES** > PORKPIE

**PORKS** > PORK
**PORKWOOD** n wood of small American tree
**PORKWOODS** > PORKWOOD
**PORKY** adj of or like pork ▷ n lie
**PORN** n pornography
**PORNIER** > PORNY
**PORNIEST** > PORNY
**PORNO** same as > PORN
**PORNOMAG** n pornographic magazine
**PORNOMAGS** > PORNOMAG
**PORNOS** > PORNO
**PORNS** > PORN
**PORNY** adj pornographic
**POROGAMIC** > POROGAMY
**POROGAMY** n fertilization of seed plants
**POROMERIC** adj (of a plastic) permeable to water vapour ▷ n substance having this characteristic, esp one based on polyurethane and used in place of leather in making shoe uppers
**POROSCOPE** n instrument for assessing porosity
**POROSCOPY** > POROSCOPE
**POROSE** adj pierced with small pores
**POROSES** > POROSIS
**POROSIS** n porous condition of bones
**POROSITY** n state or condition of being porous
**POROUS** adj allowing liquid to pass through gradually
**POROUSLY** > POROUS
**PORPESS** n type of fish
**PORPESSE** same as > PORPOISE
**PORPESSES** > PORPESS
**PORPHYRIA** n hereditary disease of body metabolism, producing abdominal pain, mental confusion, etc
**PORPHYRIC** > PORPHYRIA
**PORPHYRIN** n any of a group of pigments occurring widely in animal and plant tissues and having a heterocyclic structure formed from four pyrrole rings linked by four methylene groups
**PORPHYRIO** n aquatic bird
**PORPHYRY** n reddish rock with large crystals in it
**PORPOISE** n fishlike sea mammal ▷ vb (of an aeroplane) nose-dive during landing
**PORPOISED** > PORPOISE
**PORPOISES** > PORPOISE
**PORPORATE** adj wearing purple
**PORRECT** adj extended forwards ▷ vb stretch forward
**PORRECTED** > PORRECT
**PORRECTS** > PORRECT

**PORRENGER** same as > PORRINGER
**PORRIDGE** n breakfast food made of oatmeal cooked in water or milk
**PORRIDGES** > PORRIDGE
**PORRIDGY** > PORRIDGE
**PORRIGO** n disease of the scalp
**PORRIGOS** > PORRIGO
**PORRINGER** n small dish, often with a handle, used esp formerly for soup or porridge
**PORT** same as > PORTHOLE
**PORTA** n aperture in an organ, such as the liver, esp one providing an opening for blood vessels
**PORTABLE** adj easily carried ▷ n article designed to be easily carried, such as a television or typewriter
**PORTABLES** > PORTABLE
**PORTABLY** > PORTABLE
**PORTAGE** n (route for) transporting boats and supplies overland between navigable waterways ▷ vb transport (boats and supplies) in this way
**PORTAGED** > PORTAGE
**PORTAGES** > PORTAGE
**PORTAGING** > PORTAGE
**PORTAGUE** n Portuguese gold coin
**PORTAGUES** > PORTAGUE
**PORTAL** n large imposing doorway or gate ▷ adj internet site providing links to other sites ▷ vb go from one internet portal to another
**PORTALED** > PORTAL
**PORTALING** > PORTAL
**PORTALLED** > PORTAL
**PORTALS** > PORTAL
**PORTANCE** n person's bearing
**PORTANCES** > PORTANCE
**PORTAPACK** n combined videotape recorder and camera
**PORTAPAK** same as > PORTAPACK
**PORTAPAKS** > PORTAPAK
**PORTAS** > PORTA
**PORTASES** variant of > PORTESSE
**PORTATE** adj diagonally athwart escutcheon
**PORTATILE** adj portable
**PORTATIVE** adj concerned with the act of carrying
**PORTED** > PORT
**PORTEND** vb be a sign of
**PORTENDED** > PORTEND
**PORTENDS** > PORTEND
**PORTENT** n sign of a future event
**PORTENTS** > PORTENT
**PORTEOUS** variant of > PORTESSE
**PORTER** n man who carries

luggage ▷ vb carry luggage
**PORTERAGE** n work of carrying supplies, goods, etc, done by porters
**PORTERED** > PORTER
**PORTERESS** n female porter
**PORTERING** > PORTER
**PORTERLY** > PORTER
**PORTERS** > PORTER
**PORTESS** variant of > PORTESSE
**PORTESSE** n prayer book
**PORTESSES** > PORTESSE
**PORTFIRE** n (formerly) slow-burning fuse used for firing rockets and fireworks and, in mining, for igniting explosives
**PORTFIRES** > PORTFIRE
**PORTFOLIO** n (flat case for carrying) examples of an artist's work
**PORTHOLE** n small round window in a ship or aircraft
**PORTHOLES** > PORTHOLE
**PORTHORS** same as > PORTESSE
**PORTHOS** same as > PORTESSE
**PORTHOSES** > PORTHOS
**PORTHOUSE** n company producing port
**PORTICO** n porch or covered walkway with columns supporting the roof
**PORTICOED** > PORTICO
**PORTICOES** > PORTICO
**PORTICOS** > PORTICO
**PORTIER** > PORT
**PORTIERE** n curtain hung in a doorway
**PORTIERED** > PORTIERE
**PORTIERES** > PORTIERE
**PORTIEST** > PORT
**PORTIGUE** same as > PORTAGUE
**PORTIGUES** > PORTIGUE
**PORTING** > PORT
**PORTION** n part or share ▷ vb divide (something) into shares
**PORTIONED** > PORTION
**PORTIONER** > PORTION
**PORTIONS** > PORTION
**PORTLAND** n type of rose
**PORTLANDS** > PORTLAND
**PORTLAST** n gunwale of ship
**PORTLASTS** > PORTLAST
**PORTLESS** > PORT
**PORTLIER** > PORTLY
**PORTLIEST** > PORTLY
**PORTLY** adj rather fat
**PORTMAN** n inhabitant of port
**PORTMEN** > PORTMAN
**PORTOISE** same as > PORTLAST
**PORTOISES** > PORTOISE
**PORTOLAN** n book of sailing charts

PORTOLANI > PORTOLANO
PORTOLANO *variant of* > PORTOLAN
PORTOLANS > PORTOLAN
PORTOUS *variant of* > PORTESSE
PORTOUSES > PORTOUS
PORTRAIT *n* picture of a person ▷ *adj* (of a publication or an illustration in a publication) of greater height than width
PORTRAITS > PORTRAIT
PORTRAY *vb* describe or represent by artistic means, as in writing or film
PORTRAYAL > PORTRAY
PORTRAYED > PORTRAY
PORTRAYER > PORTRAY
PORTRAYS > PORTRAY
PORTREEVE *n* Saxon magistrate
PORTRESS *n* female porter, esp a doorkeeper
PORTS > PORT
PORTSIDE *adj* beside port
PORTULACA *n* tropical American plant with yellow, pink, or purple showy flowers
PORTULAN *same as* > PORTOLAN
PORTULANS > PORTULAN
PORTY *adj* like port
PORWIGGLE *n* tadpole
PORY *adj* containing pores
POS > PO
POSABLE > POSE
POSADA *n* inn in a Spanish-speaking country
POSADAS > POSADA
POSAUNE *n* organ chorus reed
POSAUNES > POSAUNE
POSE *vb* place in or take up a particular position to be photographed or drawn ▷ *n* position while posing
POSEABLE *adj* able to be manipulated into poses
POSED > POSE
POSER *n* puzzling question
POSERISH *same as* > POSEY
POSERS > POSER
POSES > POSE
POSEUR *n* person who behaves in an affected way to impress others
POSEURS > POSEUR
POSEUSE *n* female poseur
POSEUSES > POSEUSE
POSEY *adj* (of a place) for, characteristic of, or full of posers
POSH *adj* smart, luxurious ▷ *adv* in a manner associated with the upper class ▷ *vb* make posh
POSHED > POSH
POSHER > POSH
POSHES > POSH
POSHEST > POSH

POSHING > POSH
POSHLY > POSH
POSHNESS > POSH
POSHO *n* corn meal
POSHOS > POSHO
POSHTEEN *same as* > POSTEEN
POSHTEENS > POSHTEEN
POSIER > POSY
POSIES > POSY
POSIEST > POSY
POSIGRADE *n* auxiliary rocket for space craft
POSING > POSE
POSINGLY > POSE
POSINGS > POSE
POSIT *vb* lay down as a basis for argument ▷ *n* fact, idea, etc, that is posited
POSITED > POSIT
POSITIF *n* (on older organs) manual controlling soft stops
POSITIFS > POSITIF
POSITING > POSIT
POSITION *n* place ▷ *vb* place
POSITIONS > POSITION
POSITIVE *same as* > PLUS
POSITIVER > POSITIVE
POSITIVES > POSITIVE
POSITON *n* part of chromosome
POSITONS > POSITON
POSITRON *n* particle with same mass as electron but positive charge
POSITRONS > POSITRON
POSITS > POSIT
POSNET *n* small basin or dish
POSNETS > POSNET
POSOLE *n* hominy
POSOLES > POSOLE
POSOLOGIC > POSOLOGY
POSOLOGY *n* branch of medicine concerned with the determination of appropriate doses of drugs or agents
POSS *vb* wash (clothes) by agitating them with a long rod, pole, etc
POSSE *n* group of men organized to maintain law and order
POSSED > POSS
POSSER *n* short stick used for stirring clothes in a washtub
POSSERS > POSSER
POSSES > POSSE
POSSESS *vb* have as one's property
POSSESSED *adj* owning or having
POSSESSES > POSSESS
POSSESSOR > POSSESS
POSSET *n* drink of hot milk curdled with ale, beer, etc, flavoured with spices, formerly used as a remedy for colds ▷ *vb* treat with

a posset
POSSETED > POSSET
POSSETING > POSSET
POSSETS > POSSET
POSSIBLE *adj* able to exist, happen, or be done ▷ *n* person or thing that might be suitable or chosen
POSSIBLER > POSSIBLE
POSSIBLES > POSSIBLE
POSSIBLY *adv* perhaps, not necessarily
POSSIE *n* place
POSSIES > POSSIE
POSSING > POSS
POSSUM *vb* pretend to be dead, asleep, ignorant, etc, to deceive an opponent
POSSUMED > POSSUM
POSSUMING > POSSUM
POSSUMS > POSSUM
POST *n* official system of delivering letters and parcels ▷ *vb* send by post
POSTAGE *n* charge for sending a letter or parcel by post
POSTAGES > POSTAGE
POSTAL *adj* of a Post Office or the mail-delivery service
POSTALLY > POSTAL
POSTANAL *adj* behind the anus
POSTAXIAL *adj* situated or occurring behind the axis of the body
POSTBAG *n* postman's bag
POSTBAGS > POSTBAG
POSTBASE *adv* (in linguistics) coming immediately after a base word
POSTBOX *n* box into which mail is put for collection by the postal service
POSTBOXES > POSTBOX
POSTBOY *n* man or boy who brings the post round to offices
POSTBOYS > POSTBOY
POSTBURN *adj* after injury from burns
POSTBUS *n* (in Britain, esp in rural districts) vehicle carrying the mail that also carries passengers
POSTBUSES > POSTBUS
POSTCARD *n* card for sending a message by post without an envelope
POSTCARDS > POSTCARD
POSTCAVA *n* inferior vena cava
POSTCAVAE > POSTCAVA
POSTCAVAL > POSTCAVA
POSTCAVAS > POSTCAVA
POSTCODE *n* system of letters and numbers used to aid the sorting of mail ▷ *vb* put a postcode on a letter
POSTCODED > POSTCODE
POSTCODES > POSTCODE

POSTCOUP *adj* after coup
POSTCRASH *adj* after a crash
POSTDATE *vb* write a date on (a cheque) that is later than the actual date
POSTDATED > POSTDATE
POSTDATES > POSTDATE
POSTDIVE *adj* following a dive
POSTDOC *n* postdoctoral degree
POSTDOCS > POSTDOC
POSTDRUG *adj* of time after drug has been taken
POSTED > POST
POSTEEN *n* Afghan leather jacket
POSTEENS > POSTEEN
POSTER *n* large picture or notice stuck on a wall ▷ *vb* cover with posters
POSTERED > POSTER
POSTERING > POSTER
POSTERIOR *n* buttocks ▷ *adj* behind, at the back of
POSTERITY *n* future generations, descendants
POSTERN *n* small back door or gate ▷ *adj* situated at the rear or the side
POSTERNS > POSTERN
POSTERS > POSTER
POSTFACE *n* note added to the end of a text
POSTFACES > POSTFACE
POSTFAULT *adj* after a fault
POSTFIRE *adj* of the period after a fire
POSTFIX *vb* add or append at the end of something
POSTFIXAL > POSTFIX
POSTFIXED > POSTFIX
POSTFIXES > POSTFIX
POSTFORM *vb* mould or shape (plastic) while it hot from reheating
POSTFORMS > POSTFORM
POSTGAME *adj* of period after sports match
POSTGRAD *n* graduate taking further degree
POSTGRADS > POSTGRAD
POSTHASTE *adv* with great speed ▷ *n* great haste
POSTHEAT *n* industrial heating process
POSTHEATS > POSTHEAT
POSTHOLE *n* hole dug in ground to hold fence post
POSTHOLES > POSTHOLE
POSTHORSE *n* horse kept at an inn or posthouse for use by postriders or for hire to travellers
POSTHOUSE *n* house or inn where horses were kept for postriders or for hire to travellers
POSTICAL *adj* (of the position of plant parts) behind another part
POSTICHE *adj* (of architectural ornament)

inappropriately applied
▷ *n* imitation, counterfeit,
or substitute
**POSTICHES** > POSTICHE
**POSTICOUS** *same*
*as* > POSTICAL
**POSTIE** *n* postman
**POSTIES** > POSTIE
**POSTIL** *n* commentary or
marginal note, as in a Bible
▷ *vb* annotate (a biblical
passage)
**POSTILED** > POSTIL
**POSTILING** > POSTIL
**POSTILION** *n* person riding
one of a pair of horses
drawing a carriage
**POSTILLED** > POSTIL
**POSTILLER** > POSTIL
**POSTILS** > POSTIL
**POSTIN** *variant*
*of* > POSTEEN
**POSTING** *n* job to which
someone is assigned by
his or her employer which
involves moving to a
particular town or country
**POSTINGS** > POSTING
**POSTINS** > POSTIN
**POSTIQUE** *variant*
*of* > POSTICHE
**POSTIQUES** > POSTIQUE
**POSTLUDE** *n* final or
concluding piece or
movement
**POSTLUDES** > POSTLUDE
**POSTMAN** *n* person who
collects and delivers post
**POSTMARK** *n* official
mark stamped on letters
showing place and date of
posting ▷ *vb* put such a
mark on (mail)
**POSTMARKS** > POSTMARK
**POSTMEN** > POSTMAN
**POSTNASAL** *adj* situated at
the back of the nose
**POSTNATAL** *adj* occurring
after childbirth
**POSTNATI** *n* those born in
Scotland after its union
with England
**POSTOP** *n* person
recovering from surgery
**POSTOPS** > POSTOP
**POSTORAL** *adj* situated at
the back of the mouth
**POSTPAID** *adj* with the
postage prepaid
**POSTPONE** *vb* put off to a
later time
**POSTPONED** > POSTPONE
**POSTPONER** > POSTPONE
**POSTPONES** > POSTPONE
**POSTPOSE** *vb* place (word
or phrase) after other
constituents in sentence
**POSTPOSED** > POSTPOSE
**POSTPOSES** > POSTPOSE
**POSTPUNK** *adj* (of pop
music) belonging to a style
that followed punk rock
**POSTRACE** *adj* of the period
after a race

**POSTRIDER** *n* (formerly)
person who delivered post
on horseback
**POSTRIOT** *adj* of the period
after a riot
**POSTS** > POST
**POSTSHOW** *adj* of the period
after a show
**POSTSYNC** *vb* add a
sound recording to (and
synchronize with) an
existing video or film
recording
**POSTSYNCS** > POSTSYNC
**POSTTAX** *adj* of the period
after tax is paid
**POSTTEEN** *n* young adult
**POSTTEENS** > POSTTEEN
**POSTTEST** *n* test taken
after a lesson
**POSTTESTS** > POSTTEST
**POSTTRIAL** *adj* of the
period after a trial
**POSTULANT** *n* candidate for
admission to a religious
order
**POSTULATA** *n* things
postulated
**POSTULATE** *vb* assume to
be true as the basis of an
argument or theory ▷ *n*
something postulated
**POSTURAL** > POSTURE
**POSTURE** *n* position or way
in which someone stands,
walks, etc ▷ *vb* behave in
an exaggerated way to get
attention
**POSTURED** > POSTURE
**POSTURER** > POSTURE
**POSTURERS** > POSTURE
**POSTURES** > POSTURE
**POSTURING** > POSTURE
**POSTURISE** *same*
*as* > POSTURIZE
**POSTURIST** > POSTURE
**POSTURIZE** *less common*
*word for* > POSTURE
**POSTVIRAL** as in *postviral*
*syndrome* debilitating
condition occurring as a
sequel to viral illness
**POSTWAR** *adj* occurring or
existing after a war
**POSTWOMAN** *n* woman who
carries and delivers mail as
a profession
**POSTWOMEN** > POSTWOMAN
**POSY** *n* small bunch of
flowers
**POT** *n* round deep container
▷ *vb* plant in a pot
**POTABLE** *adj* drinkable ▷ *n*
something fit to drink
**POTABLES** > POTABLE
**POTAE** *n* hat
**POTAES** > POTAE
**POTAGE** *n* thick soup
**POTAGER** *n* small kitchen
garden
**POTAGERS** > POTAGER
**POTAGES** > POTAGE
**POTAMIC** *adj* of or relating
to rivers

**POTASH** *n* white powdery
substance obtained from
ashes and used as fertilizer
▷ *vb* treat with potash
**POTASHED** > POTASH
**POTASHES** > POTASH
**POTASHING** > POTASH
**POTASS** *abbreviated form*
*of* > POTASSIUM
**POTASSA** *n* potassium
oxide
**POTASSAS** > POTASSA
**POTASSES** > POTASS
**POTASSIC** > POTASSIUM
**POTASSIUM** *n* silvery
metallic element
**POTATION** *n* act of drinking
**POTATIONS** > POTATION
**POTATO** *n* roundish starchy
vegetable that grows
underground
**POTATOBUG** *n* Colorado
beetle
**POTATOES** > POTATO
**POTATORY** *adj* of, relating
to, or given to drinking
**POTBELLY** *n* bulging belly
**POTBOIL** *vb* boil in a pot
**POTBOILED** > POTBOIL
**POTBOILER** *n* inferior work
of art produced quickly to
make money
**POTBOILS** > POTBOIL
**POTBOUND** *adj* (of plant)
unable to grow because
pot is too small
**POTBOY** *n* (esp formerly)
youth or man employed
at a public house to serve
beer, etc
**POTBOYS** > POTBOY
**POTCH** *n* inferior quality
opal used in jewellery for
mounting precious opals
**POTCHE** *vb* stab
**POTCHED** > POTCHE
**POTCHER** > POTCHE
**POTCHERS** > POTCHE
**POTCHES** > POTCH
**POTCHING** > POTCHE
**POTE** *vb* push
**POTED** > POTE
**POTEEN** *n* (in Ireland)
illegally made alcoholic
drink
**POTEENS** > POTEEN
**POTENCE** *same as* > POTENCY
**POTENCES** > POTENCE
**POTENCIES** > POTENCY
**POTENCY** *n* state or quality
of being potent
**POTENT** *adj* having great
power or influence ▷ *n*
potentate or ruler
**POTENTATE** *n* ruler or
monarch
**POTENTIAL** *adj* possible
but not yet actual ▷ *n*
ability or talent not yet
fully used
**POTENTISE** *same*
*as* > POTENTIZE
**POTENTIZE** *vb* make more
potent

**POTENTLY** > POTENT
**POTENTS** > POTENT
**POTES** > POTE
**POTFUL** *n* amount held by
a pot
**POTFULS** > POTFUL
**POTGUN** *n* pot-shaped
mortar
**POTGUNS** > POTGUN
**POTHEAD** *n* habitual user of
cannabis
**POTHEADS** > POTHEAD
**POTHECARY** *n* pharmacist
**POTHEEN** *rare variant*
*of* > POTEEN
**POTHEENS** > POTHEEN
**POTHER** *n* fuss or
commotion ▷ *vb* make or
be troubled or upset
**POTHERB** *n* plant whose
leaves, flowers, or stems
are used in cooking
**POTHERBS** > POTHERB
**POTHERED** > POTHER
**POTHERING** > POTHER
**POTHERS** > POTHER
**POTHERY** *adj* stuffy
**POTHOLDER** *n* piece of
material used to protect
hands while lifting pot
from oven
**POTHOLE** *n* hole in the
surface of a road
**POTHOLED** > POTHOLE
**POTHOLER** > POTHOLING
**POTHOLERS** > POTHOLING
**POTHOLES** > POTHOLE
**POTHOLING** *n* sport of
exploring underground
caves
**POTHOOK** *n* S-shaped hook
for suspending a pot over
a fire
**POTHOOKS** > POTHOOK
**POTHOS** *n* climbing plant
**POTHOUSE** *n* (formerly)
small tavern or pub
**POTHOUSES** > POTHOUSE
**POTHUNTER** *n* person who
hunts for food or for profit
without regard to the rules
of sport
**POTICARY** *obsolete spelling*
*of* > POTHECARY
**POTICHE** *n* tall vase or jar,
as of porcelain, with a
round or polygonal body
that narrows towards the
neck and a detached lid or
cover
**POTICHES** > POTICHE
**POTIN** *n* bronze alloy with
high tin content
**POTING** > POTE
**POTINS** > POTIN
**POTION** *n* dose of medicine
or poison
**POTIONS** > POTION
**POTLACH** *same*
*as* > POTLATCH
**POTLACHE** *same*
*as* > POTLATCH
**POTLACHES** > POTLACHE
**POTLATCH** *n* competitive

ceremonial activity
among certain North
American Indians
POTLIKE > POT
POTLINE n row of
electrolytic cells for
reducing metals
POTLINES > POTLINE
POTLUCK n whatever
food happens to be
available without special
preparation
POTLUCKS > POTLUCK
POTMAN same as > POTBOY
POTMEN > POTMAN
POTOMETER n apparatus
that measures the rate of
water uptake by a plant or
plant part
POTOO n nocturnal tropical
bird
POTOOS > POTOO
POTOROO n Australian
leaping rodent
POTOROOS > POTOROO
POTPIE n meat and
vegetable stew with a pie
crust on top
POTPIES > POTPIE
POTPOURRI n fragrant
mixture of dried flower
petals
POTS > POT
POTSHARD same
as > POTSHERD
POTSHARDS > POTSHARD
POTSHARE same
as > POTSHERD
POTSHARES > POTSHARE
POTSHERD n broken
fragment of pottery
POTSHERDS > POTSHERD
POTSHOP n public house
POTSHOPS > POTSHOP
POTSHOT n chance shot
taken casually, hastily, or
without careful aim
POTSHOTS > POTSHOT
POTSIE same as > POTSY
POTSIES > POTSY
POTSTONE n impure
massive variety of
soapstone, formerly used
for making cooking vessels
POTSTONES > POTSTONE
POTSY n hopscotch
POTT old variant of > POT
POTTAGE n thick soup or
stew
POTTAGES > POTTAGE
POTTED > POT
POTTEEN same as > POTEEN
POTTEENS > POTTEEN
POTTER same as > PUTTER
POTTERED > POTTER
POTTERER > POTTER
POTTERERS > POTTER
POTTERIES > POTTERY
POTTERING > POTTER
POTTERS > POTTER
POTTERY n articles made
from baked clay
POTTIER > POTTY
POTTIES > POTTY

POTTIEST > POTTY
POTTINESS > POTTY
POTTING > POT
POTTINGAR same
as > POTTINGER
POTTINGER n apothecary
POTTLE n liquid measure
equal to half a gallon
POTTLES > POTTLE
POTTO n short-tailed
prosimian primate
POTTOS > POTTO
POTTS > POTT
POTTY adj crazy or silly ▷ n
bowl used by a small child
as a toilet
POTWALLER n man entitled
to the franchise before 1832
by virtue of possession of
his own fireplace
POTZER same as > PATZER
POTZERS > POTZER
POUCH n small bag ▷ vb
place in or as if in a pouch
POUCHED > POUCH
POUCHES > POUCH
POUCHFUL n amount a
pouch will hold
POUCHFULS > POUCHFUL
POUCHIER > POUCH
POUCHIEST > POUCH
POUCHING > POUCH
POUCHY > POUCH
POUDER obsolete spelling
of > POWDER
POUDERS > POUDER
POUDRE old spelling
of > POWDER
POUDRES > POUDRE
POUF n large solid cushion
used as a seat ▷ vb pile up
hair into rolled puffs
POUFED > POUF
POUFFE same as > POUF
POUFFED > POUFFE
POUFFES > POUFFE
POUFFING > POUFFE
POUFFS > POUFFE
POUFFY same as > POOFY
POUFING > POUF
POUFS > POUF
POUFTAH same as > POOFTER
POUFTAHS > POUFTAH
POUFTER same as > POOFTER
POUFTERS > POUFTER
POUK Scots variant of > POKE
POUKE n mischievous spirit
POUKED > POUK
POUKES > POUKE
POUKING > POUK
POUKIT > POUK
POUKS > POUK
POULAINE n tapering toe
of shoe
POULAINES > POULAINE
POULARD n hen that has
been spayed for fattening
POULARDE same
as > POULARD
POULARDES > POULARDE
POULARDS > POULARD
POULDER obsolete spelling
of > POWDER
POULDERED > POULDER

POULDERS > POULDER
POULDRE archaic spelling
of > POWDER
POULDRES > POULDRE
POULDRON same
as > PAULDRON
POULDRONS > POULDRON
POULE n fowl suitable for
slow stewing
POULES > POULE
POULP n octopus
POULPE variant of > POULP
POULPES > POULPE
POULPS > POULP
POULT n young of a
gallinaceous bird, esp of
domestic fowl
POULTER n poultry dealer
POULTERER same
as > POULTER
POULTERS > POULTER
POULTICE n moist
dressing, often heated,
applied to inflamed skin
▷ vb apply poultice to
POULTICED > POULTICE
POULTICES > POULTICE
POULTRIES > POULTRY
POULTRY n domestic fowls
POULTS > POULT
POUNCE vb spring upon
suddenly to attack or
capture ▷ n pouncing
POUNCED > POUNCE
POUNCER > POUNCE
POUNCERS > POUNCE
POUNCES > POUNCE
POUNCET n box with a
perforated top used for
perfume
POUNCETS > POUNCET
POUNCHING old variant
of > PUNCHING
POUNCING > POUNCE
POUND n monetary unit of
Britain and some other
countries ▷ vb hit heavily
and repeatedly
POUNDAGE n charge of so
much per pound of weight
or sterling
POUNDAGES > POUNDAGE
POUNDAL n fps unit of force
POUNDALS > POUNDAL
POUNDCAKE n cake
containing a pound of
each ingredient
POUNDED > POUND
POUNDER > POUND
POUNDERS > POUND
POUNDING > POUND
POUNDS > POUND
POUPE vb make sudden
blowing sound
POUPED > POUPE
POUPES > POUPE
POUPING > POUPE
POUPT > POUPE
POUR vb flow or cause to
flow out in a stream
POURABLE > POUR
POURBOIRE n tip or
gratuity
POURED > POUR

POURER > POUR
POURERS > POUR
POURIE n jug
POURIES > POURIE
POURING > POUR
POURINGLY > POUR
POURINGS > POUR
POURPOINT n man's stuffed
quilted doublet of a kind
worn between the Middle
Ages and the 17th century
POURS > POUR
POURSEW obsolete spelling
of > PURSUE
POURSEWED > POURSEW
POURSEWS > POURSEW
POURSUE obsolete spelling
of > PURSUE
POURSUED > PURSUE
POURSUES > POURSUE
POURSUING > POURSUE
POURSUIT same
as > PURSUIT
POURSUITS > POURSUIT
POURTRAY obsolete spelling
of > PORTRAY
POURTRAYD > POURTRAY
POURTRAYS > POURTRAY
POUSOWDIE n Scottish stew
made from sheep's head
POUSSE same as > PEASE
POUSSES > POUSSE
POUSSETTE n figure in
country dancing in which
couples hold hands and
move up or down the set
to change positions ▷ vb
perform such a figure
POUSSIE old variant
of > PUSSY
POUSSIES > POUSSIE
POUSSIN n young chicken
reared for eating
POUSSINS > POUSSIN
POUT vb thrust out one's
lips, look sulky ▷ n
pouting look
POUTED > POUT
POUTER n pigeon that can
puff out its crop
POUTERS > POUTER
POUTFUL adj tending to
pout
POUTHER Scots variant
of > POWDER
POUTHERED > POUTHER
POUTHERS > POUTHER
POUTIER > POUT
POUTIEST > POUT
POUTINE n dish of chipped
potatoes topped with curd
cheese and a tomato-
based sauce
POUTINES > POUTINE
POUTING > POUT
POUTINGLY > POUT
POUTINGS > POUT
POUTS > POUT
POUTY > POUT
POVERTIES > POVERTY
POVERTY n state of being
without enough food or
money
POW interj exclamation to

indicate that a collision or explosion has taken place ▷ n head or a head of hair

POWAN n freshwater whitefish, *Coregonus clupeoides*, occurring in some Scottish lakes

POWANS > POWAN

POWDER n substance in the form of tiny loose particles ▷ vb apply powder to

POWDERED > POWDER

POWDERER > POWDER

POWDERERS > POWDER

POWDERIER > POWDER

POWDERING > POWDER

POWDERS > POWDER

POWDERY > POWDER

POWELLISE > POWELLIZE

POWELLITE n type of mineral

POWELLIZE vb treat wood with a sugar solution

POWER n ability to do or act ▷ vb give or provide power to

POWERBOAT n fast powerful motorboat

POWERED > POWER

POWERFUL adj having great power or influence ▷ adv extremely

POWERING > POWER

POWERLESS adj without power or authority

POWERPLAY n behaviour intended to maximise person's power

POWERS > POWER

POWFAGGED adj exhausted

POWHIRI n Māori ceremony of welcome, esp to a marae

POWHIRIS > POWHIRI

POWIN n peacock

POWINS > POWIN

POWN variant of > POWIN

POWND obsolete spelling of > POUND

POWNDED > POWND

POWNDING > POWND

POWNDS > POWND

POWNEY old Scots spelling of > PONY

POWNEYS > POWNEY

POWNIE old Scots spelling of > PONY

POWNIES > POWNIE

POWNS > POWN

POWNY old Scots spelling of > PONY

POWRE obsolete spelling of > POWER

POWRED > POWRE

POWRES > POWRE

POWRING > POWRE

POWS > POW

POWSOWDY same as > POUSOWDIE

POWTER same as > POUTER

POWTERS > POWTER

POWWAW n Algonquian priest

POWWAWS > POWWAW

POWWOW n talk or conference ▷ vb hold a powwow

POWWOWED > POWWOW

POWWOWING > POWWOW

POWWOWS > POWWOW

POX n disease in which skin pustules form ▷ vb infect with pox

POXED > POX

POXES > POX

POXIER > POXY

POXIEST > POXY

POXING > POX

POXVIRUS n virus such as smallpox

POXY adj having or having had syphilis

POYNANT old variant of > POIGNANT

POYNT obsolete spelling of > POINT

POYNTED > POYNT

POYNTING > POYNT

POYNTS > POYNT

POYOU n type of armadillo

POYOUS > POYOU

POYSE obsolete variant of > POISE

POYSED > POYSE

POYSES > POYSE

POYSING > POYSE

POYSON obsolete spelling of > POISON

POYSONED > POYSON

POYSONING > POYSON

POYSONS > POYSON

POZ adj positive

POZOLE same as > POSOLE

POZOLES > POZOLE

POZZ adj positive

POZZIES > POZZY

POZZOLAN same as > POZZOLANA

POZZOLANA n type of porous volcanic ash

POZZOLANS > POZZOLAN

POZZY same as > POSSIE

PRAAM same as > PRAM

PRAAMS > PRAAM

PRABBLE variant of > BRABBLE

PRABBLES > PRABBLE

PRACHARAK n (in India) person appointed to propagate a cause through personal contact, meetings, public lectures, etc

PRACTIC adj practical

PRACTICAL adj involving experience or actual use rather than theory ▷ n examination in which something has to be done or made

PRACTICE same as > PRACTISE

PRACTICED > PRACTICE

PRACTICER > PRACTICE

PRACTICES > PRACTICE

PRACTICK obsolete word for > PRACTICE

PRACTICKS > PRACTICK

PRACTICUM n course in which theory is put into practice

PRACTIQUE variant of > PRACTIC

PRACTISE vb do repeatedly so as to gain skill

PRACTISED > PRACTISE

PRACTISER > PRACTISE

PRACTISES > PRACTISE

PRACTIVE obsolete word for > ACTIVE

PRACTOLOL n type of drug

PRAD n horse

PRADS > PRAD

PRAEAMBLE same as > PREAMBLE

PRAECIPE n written request addressed to court

PRAECIPES > PRAECIPE

PRAECOCES n division of birds whose young are able to run when first hatched

PRAEDIAL adj of or relating to land, farming, etc

PRAEFECT same as > PREFECT

PRAEFECTS > PRAEFECT

PRAELECT same as > PRAELECT

PRAELECTS > PRAELECT

PRAELUDIA n musical preludes

PRAENOMEN n ancient Roman's first or given name

PRAESES n Roman governor

PRAESIDIA n presidiums

PRAETOR n (in ancient Rome) senior magistrate ranking just below the consuls

PRAETORS > PRAETOR

PRAGMATIC adj concerned with practical consequences rather than theory

PRAHU same as > PROA

PRAHUS > PRAHU

PRAIRIE n large treeless area of grassland, esp in N America and Canada

PRAIRIES > PRAIRIE

PRAISE vb express approval or admiration of (someone or something) ▷ n something said or written to show approval or admiration

PRAISEACH n type of porridge

PRAISED > PRAISE

PRAISEFUL > PRAISE

PRAISER > PRAISE

PRAISERS > PRAISE

PRAISES > PRAISE

PRAISING > PRAISE

PRAISINGS > PRAISE

PRAJNA n wisdom or understanding considered as the goal of Buddhist contemplation

PRAJNAS > PRAJNA

PRALINE n sweet made of nuts and caramelized sugar

PRALINES > PRALINE

PRAM n four-wheeled carriage for a baby, pushed by hand

PRAMS > PRAM

PRANA n (in Oriental medicine, martial arts, etc) cosmic energy believed to come from the sun and connecting the elements of the universe

PRANAS > PRANA

PRANAYAMA n breath control in yoga

PRANCE vb walk with exaggerated bouncing steps ▷ n act of prancing

PRANCED > PRANCE

PRANCER > PRANCE

PRANCERS > PRANCE

PRANCES > PRANCE

PRANCING > PRANCE

PRANCINGS > PRANCE

PRANCK obsolete variant of > PRANK

PRANCKE obsolete variant of > PRANK

PRANCKED > PRANCK

PRANCKES > PRANCKE

PRANCKING > PRANCK

PRANCKS > PRANCK

PRANDIAL adj of or relating to a meal

PRANG n crash in a car or aircraft ▷ vb crash or damage (an aircraft or car)

PRANGED > PRANG

PRANGING > PRANG

PRANGS > PRANG

PRANK n mischievous trick ▷ vb dress or decorate showily or gaudily

PRANKED > PRANK

PRANKFUL > PRANK

PRANKIER > PRANK

PRANKIEST > PRANK

PRANKING > PRANK

PRANKINGS > PRANK

PRANKISH > PRANK

PRANKLE obsolete variant of > PRANCE

PRANKLED > PRANKLE

PRANKLES > PRANKLE

PRANKLING > PRANKLE

PRANKS > PRANK

PRANKSOME > PRANK

PRANKSTER n practical joker

PRANKY > PRANK

PRAO same as > PROA

PRAOS > PRAO

PRASE n light green translucent variety of chalcedony

PRASES > PRASE

PRAT n stupid person

PRATE vb talk idly and at length ▷ n chatter

PRATED > PRATE

PRATER > PRATE

**PRATERS** > PRATE
**PRATES** > PRATE
**PRATFALL** *n* fall upon one's buttocks
**PRATFALLS** > PRATFALL
**PRATIE** *n* potato
**PRATIES** > PRATIE
**PRATING** > PRATE
**PRATINGLY** > PRATE
**PRATINGS** > PRATE
**PRATIQUE** *n* formal permission given to a vessel to use a foreign port upon satisfying the requirements of local health authorities
**PRATIQUES** > PRATIQUE
**PRATS** > PRAT
**PRATT** *n* buttocks
**PRATTLE** *vb* chatter in a childish or foolish way ▷ *n* childish or foolish talk
**PRATTLED** > PRATTLE
**PRATTLER** > PRATTLE
**PRATTLERS** > PRATTLE
**PRATTLES** > PRATTLE
**PRATTLING** > PRATTLE
**PRATY** *obsolete variant of* > PRETTY
**PRAU** *same as* > PROA
**PRAUNCE** *obsolete variant of* > PRANCE
**PRAUNCED** > PRAUNCE
**PRAUNCES** > PRAUNCE
**PRAUNCING** > PRAUNCE
**PRAUS** > PRAU
**PRAVITIES** > PRAVITY
**PRAVITY** *n* moral degeneracy
**PRAWLE** *n* Shakespearian phonetic spelling of "brawl" meant to indicate that the speaker is Welsh
**PRAWLES** > PRAWLE
**PRAWLIN** *variant of* > PRALINE
**PRAWLINS** > PRAWLIN
**PRAWN** *n* edible shellfish like a large shrimp ▷ *vb* catch prawns
**PRAWNED** > PRAWN
**PRAWNER** > PRAWN
**PRAWNERS** > PRAWN
**PRAWNING** > PRAWN
**PRAWNS** > PRAWN
**PRAXES** > PRAXIS
**PRAXIS** *n* practice as opposed to theory
**PRAXISES** > PRAXIS
**PRAY** *vb* say prayers ▷ *adv* I beg you ▷ *interj* I beg you
**PRAYED** > PRAY
**PRAYER** *n* thanks or appeal addressed to one's God
**PRAYERFUL** *adj* inclined to or characterized by prayer
**PRAYERS** > PRAYER
**PRAYING** > PRAY
**PRAYINGS** > PRAY
**PRAYS** > PRAY
**PRE** *prep* before
**PREABSORB** *vb* absorb beforehand
**PREACCUSE** *vb* accuse

beforehand
**PREACE** *obsolete variant of* > PRESS
**PREACED** > PREACE
**PREACES** > PREACE
**PREACH** *vb* give a talk on a religious theme as part of a church service
**PREACHED** > PREACH
**PREACHER** *n* person who preaches, esp in church
**PREACHERS** > PREACHER
**PREACHES** > PREACH
**PREACHIER** > PREACHY
**PREACHIFY** *vb* preach or moralize in a tedious manner
**PREACHILY** > PREACHY
**PREACHING** > PREACH
**PREACHY** *adj* inclined to or marked by preaching
**PREACING** > PREACE
**PREACT** *vb* act beforehand
**PREACTED** > PREACT
**PREACTING** > PREACT
**PREACTS** > PREACT
**PREADAMIC** *adj* of or relating to the belief that there were people on earth before Adam
**PREADAPT** *vb* adapt beforehand
**PREADAPTS** > PREADAPT
**PREADJUST** *vb* adjust beforehand
**PREADMIT** *vb* prepare patient prior to treatment
**PREADMITS** > PREADMIT
**PREADULT** *n* animal or person who has not reached adulthood
**PREADULTS** > PREADULT
**PREAGED** *adj* treated to appear older
**PREALLOT** *vb* allot beforehand
**PREALLOTS** > PREALLOT
**PREALTER** *vb* alter beforehand
**PREALTERS** > PREALTER
**PREAMBLE** *n* introductory part to something said or written ▷ *vb* write a preamble
**PREAMBLED** > PREAMBLE
**PREAMBLES** > PREAMBLE
**PREAMP** *n* electronic amplifier used to improve the signal-to-noise ratio of an electronic device
**PREAMPS** > PREAMP
**PREANAL** *adj* situated in front of anus
**PREAPPLY** *vb* apply beforehand
**PREARM** *vb* arm beforehand
**PREARMED** > PREARM
**PREARMING** > PREARM
**PREARMS** > PREARM
**PREASE** *vb* crowd or press
**PREASED** > PREASE
**PREASES** > PREASE
**PREASING** > PREASE
**PREASSE** *obsolete spelling*

*of* > PRESS
**PREASSED** > PREASSE
**PREASSES** > PREASSE
**PREASSIGN** *vb* assign beforehand
**PREASSING** > PREASSE
**PREASSURE** *vb* assure beforehand
**PREATOMIC** *adj* before the atomic age
**PREATTUNE** *vb* attune beforehand
**PREAUDIT** *vb* examine contracts before a transaction
**PREAUDITS** > PREAUDIT
**PREAVER** *vb* aver in advance
**PREAVERS** > PREAVER
**PREAXIAL** *adj* situated or occurring in front of the axis of the body
**PREBADE** > PREBID
**PREBAKE** *vb* bake before further cooking
**PREBAKED** > PREBAKE
**PREBAKES** > PREBAKE
**PREBAKING** > PREBAKE
**PREBASAL** > PREBASE
**PREBASE** *n* part of tongue lying anterior to base
**PREBATTLE** *adj* of the period before a battle
**PREBEND** *n* allowance paid by a cathedral or collegiate church to a canon or member of the chapter
**PREBENDAL** > PREBEND
**PREBENDS** > PREBEND
**PREBID** *vb* bid beforehand
**PREBIDDEN** > PREBID
**PREBIDS** > PREBID
**PREBILL** *vb* issue an invoice before the service has been provided
**PREBILLED** > PREBILL
**PREBILLS** > PREBILL
**PREBIND** *n* book that has been previously bound
**PREBINDS** > PREBIND
**PREBIOTIC** *adj* of the period before the existence of life on earth
**PREBIRTH** *n* period of life before birth
**PREBIRTHS** > PREBIRTH
**PREBLESS** *vb* bless a couple before they marry
**PREBOARD** *vb* board an aircraft before other passengers
**PREBOARDS** > PREBOARD
**PREBOIL** *vb* boil beforehand
**PREBOILED** > PREBOIL
**PREBOILS** > PREBOIL
**PREBOOK** *vb* book well in advance
**PREBOOKED** > PREBOOK
**PREBOOKS** > PREBOOK
**PREBOOM** *adj* of the period before an economic boom
**PREBORN** *adj* unborn
**PREBOUGHT** > PREBUY
**PREBOUND** *adj* previously

bound
**PREBUDGET** *adj* before budget
**PREBUILD** *vb* build beforehand
**PREBUILDS** > PREBUILD
**PREBUILT** > PREBUILD
**PREBUTTAL** *n* prepared response to an anticipated criticism
**PREBUY** *vb* buy in advance
**PREBUYING** > PREBUY
**PREBUYS** > PREBUY
**PRECANCEL** *vb* cancel (postage stamps) before placing them on mail ▷ *n* precancelled stamp
**PRECANCER** *n* condition that may develop into cancer
**PRECAST** *adj* (esp of concrete when employed as a structural element in building) cast in a particular form before being used ▷ *vb* cast (concrete) in a particular form before use
**PRECASTS** > PRECAST
**PRECATIVE** *same as* > PRECATORY
**PRECATORY** *adj* of, involving, or expressing entreaty
**PRECAUDAL** *adj* in front of the caudal fin
**PRECAVA** *n* superior vena cava
**PRECAVAE** > PRECAVA
**PRECAVAL** > PRECAVA
**PRECEDE** *vb* go or be before
**PRECEDED** > PRECEDE
**PRECEDENT** *n* previous case or occurrence regarded as an example to be followed ▷ *adj* preceding
**PRECEDES** > PRECEDE
**PRECEDING** *adj* going or coming before
**PRECEESE** *Scots variant of* > PRECISE
**PRECENSOR** *vb* censor (a film, play, book, etc) before its publication
**PRECENT** *vb* issue a command or law
**PRECENTED** > PRECENT
**PRECENTOR** *n* person who leads the singing in a church
**PRECENTS** > PRECENT
**PRECEPIT** *old word for* > PRECIPICE
**PRECEPITS** > PRECEPIT
**PRECEPT** *n* rule of behaviour
**PRECEPTOR** *n* instructor
**PRECEPTS** > PRECEPT
**PRECESS** *vb* undergo or cause to undergo precession
**PRECESSED** > PRECESS
**PRECESSES** > PRECESS
**PRECHARGE** *vb* charge

beforehand

**PRECHECK** *vb* check beforehand

**PRECHECKS** > PRECHECK

**PRECHILL** *vb* chill beforehand

**PRECHILLS** > PRECHILL

**PRECHOOSE** *vb* choose in advance

**PRECHOSE** > PRECHOOSE

**PRECHOSEN** > PRECHOOSE

**PRECIEUSE** *n* pretentious female

**PRECINCT** *n* area in a town closed to traffic

**PRECINCTS** *pl n* surrounding region

**PRECIOUS** *adj* of great value and importance ▷ *adv* very

**PRECIPE** *n* type of legal document

**PRECIPES** > PRECIPE

**PRECIPICE** *n* very steep face of a cliff

**PRECIS** *n* short written summary of a longer piece ▷ *vb* make a precis of

**PRECISE** *adj* exact, accurate in every detail

**PRECISED** > PRECIS

**PRECISELY** *adv* in a precise manner

**PRECISER** > PRECISE

**PRECISES** > PRECIS

**PRECISEST** > PRECISE

**PRECISIAN** *n* punctilious observer of rules or forms, esp in the field of religion

**PRECISING** > PRECIS

**PRECISION** *n* quality of being precise ▷ *adj* accurate

**PRECISIVE** *adj* limiting by cutting off all that is unnecessary

**PRECITED** *adj* cited previously

**PRECLEAN** *vb* clean beforehand

**PRECLEANS** > PRECLEAN

**PRECLEAR** *vb* approve in advance

**PRECLEARS** > PRECLEAR

**PRECLUDE** *vb* make impossible to happen

**PRECLUDED** > PRECLUDE

**PRECLUDES** > PRECLUDE

**PRECOCIAL** *adj* (of the young of some species of birds after hatching) covered with down, having open eyes, and capable of leaving the nest within a few days of hatching ▷ *n* precocial bird

**PRECOCITY** *n* early maturing or development

**PRECODE** *vb* code beforehand

**PRECODED** > PRECODE

**PRECODES** > PRECODE

**PRECODING** > PRECODE

**PRECOITAL** *adj* before sex

**PRECONISE** *same as* > PRECONIZE

**PRECONIZE** *vb* announce or commend publicly

**PRECOOK** *vb* cook (food) beforehand

**PRECOOKED** > PRECOOK

**PRECOOKER** *n* device for preparing food before cooking

**PRECOOKS** > PRECOOK

**PRECOOL** *vb* cool in advance

**PRECOOLED** > PRECOOL

**PRECOOLS** > PRECOOL

**PRECOUP** *adj* of the period before a coup

**PRECRASH** *adj* of the period before a crash

**PRECREASE** *vb* provide with a crease in advance

**PRECRISIS** *adj* occurring before a crisis

**PRECURE** *vb* cure in advance

**PRECURED** > PRECURE

**PRECURES** > PRECURE

**PRECURING** > PRECURE

**PRECURRER** > PRECURE

**PRECURSE** *n* forerunning

**PRECURSES** > PRECURSE

**PRECURSOR** *n* something that precedes and is a signal of something else, forerunner

**PRECUT** *vb* cut in advance

**PRECUTS** > PRECUT

**PREDACITY** *n* predatory nature

**PREDATE** *vb* occur at an earlier date than

**PREDATED** > PREDATE

**PREDATES** > PREDATE

**PREDATING** > PREDATE

**PREDATION** *n* relationship between two species of animal in a community, in which one (the predator) hunts, kills, and eats the other (the prey)

**PREDATISM** *n* state of preying on other animals

**PREDATIVE** > PREDATE

**PREDATOR** *n* predatory animal

**PREDATORS** > PREDATOR

**PREDATORY** *adj* habitually hunting and killing other animals for food

**PREDAWN** *n* period before dawn

**PREDAWNS** > PREDAWN

**PREDEATH** *n* period immediately before death

**PREDEATHS** > PREDEATH

**PREDEBATE** *adj* before a debate

**PREDEDUCT** *vb* deduct beforehand

**PREDEFINE** *vb* define in advance

**PREDELLA** *n* painting or sculpture or a series of small paintings or

sculptures in a long narrow strip forming the lower edge of an altarpiece or the face of an altar step or platform

**PREDELLAS** > PREDELLA

**PREDELLE** > PREDELLA

**PREDESIGN** *vb* design beforehand

**PREDEVOTE** *adj* preordained

**PREDIAL** *same as* > PRAEDIAL

**PREDICANT** *same as* > PREDIKANT

**PREDICATE** *n* part of a sentence in which something is said about the subject ▷ *vb* declare or assert ▷ *adj* of or relating to something that has been predicated

**PREDICT** *vb* tell about in advance, prophesy

**PREDICTED** > PREDICT

**PREDICTER** > PREDICT

**PREDICTOR** *n* person or thing that predicts

**PREDICTS** > PREDICT

**PREDIGEST** *vb* treat (food) artificially to aid subsequent digestion in the body

**PREDIKANT** *n* minister in the Dutch Reformed Church in South Africa

**PREDILECT** *vb* choose beforehand

**PREDINNER** *adj* of the period before dinner

**PREDIVE** *n* diver's preparation

**PREDIVES** > PREDIVE

**PREDOOM** *vb* pronounce (someone or something's) doom beforehand

**PREDOOMED** > PREDOOM

**PREDOOMS** > PREDOOM

**PREDRAFT** *adj* before a draft

**PREDRIED** > PREDRY

**PREDRIES** > PREDRY

**PREDRILL** *vb* drill in advance

**PREDRILLS** > PREDRILL

**PREDRY** *vb* dry beforehand

**PREDRYING** > PREDRY

**PREDUSK** *n* period before dawn

**PREDUSKS** > PREDUSK

**PREDY** *adj* ready; shipshape

**PREDYE** *vb* dye beforehand

**PREDYED** > PREDYE

**PREDYEING** > PREDYE

**PREDYES** > PREDYE

**PREE** *vb* try or taste

**PREED** > PREE

**PREEDIT** *vb* edit beforehand

**PREEDITED** > PREEDIT

**PREEDITS** > PREEDIT

**PREEING** > PREE

**PREELECT** *vb* elect beforehand

**PREELECTS** > PREELECT

**PREEMIE** *n* premature

infant

**PREEMIES** > PREEMIE

**PREEMPT** *vb* acquire in advance of or to the exclusion of others

**PREEMPTED** > PREEMPT

**PREEMPTOR** > PREEMPT

**PREEMPTS** > PREEMPT

**PREEN** *vb* (of a bird) clean or trim (feathers) with the beak ▷ *n* pin, esp a decorative one

**PREENACT** *vb* enact beforehand

**PREENACTS** > PREENACT

**PREENED** > PREEN

**PREENER** > PREEN

**PREENERS** > PREEN

**PREENING** > PREEN

**PREENS** > PREEN

**PREERECT** *vb* erect beforehand

**PREERECTS** > PREERECT

**PREES** > PREE

**PREEVE** *old form of* > PROVE

**PREEVED** > PREEVE

**PREEVES** > PREEVE

**PREEVING** > PREEVE

**PREEXCITE** *vb* stimulate in preparation

**PREEXEMPT** *vb* exempt beforehand

**PREEXILIC** *adj* prior to the Babylonian exile of the Jews

**PREEXIST** *vb* exist beforehand

**PREEXISTS** > PREEXIST

**PREEXPOSE** *vb* expose beforehand

**PREFAB** *n* prefabricated house ▷ *vb* manufacture sections of (building) in factory

**PREFABBED** > PREFAB

**PREFABS** > PREFAB

**PREFACE** *n* introduction to a book ▷ *vb* serve as an introduction to (a book, speech, etc)

**PREFACED** > PREFACE

**PREFACER** > PREFACE

**PREFACERS** > PREFACE

**PREFACES** > PREFACE

**PREFACIAL** *adj* anterior to face

**PREFACING** > PREFACE

**PREFADE** *vb* fade beforehand

**PREFADED** > PREFADE

**PREFADES** > PREFADE

**PREFADING** > PREFADE

**PREFATORY** *adj* concerning a preface

**PREFECT** *n* senior pupil in a school, with limited power over others

**PREFECTS** > PREFECT

**PREFER** *vb* like better

**PREFERRED** > PREFER

**PREFERRER** > PREFER

**PREFERS** > PREFER

**PREFEUDAL** *adj* of the period before the feudal

era
**PREFIGHT** *adj* of the period before a boxing match
**PREFIGURE** *vb* represent or suggest in advance
**PREFILE** *vb* file beforehand
**PREFILED** > PREFILE
**PREFILES** > PREFILE
**PREFILING** > PREFILE
**PREFILL** *vb* fill beforehand
**PREFILLED** > PREFILL
**PREFILLS** > PREFILL
**PREFIRE** *vb* fire beforehand
**PREFIRED** > PREFIRE
**PREFIRES** > PREFIRE
**PREFIRING** > PREFIRE
**PREFIX** *n* letter or group of letters put at the beginning of a word to make a new word, such as un- in *unhappy* ▷ *vb* put as an introduction or prefix (to)
**PREFIXAL** > PREFIX
**PREFIXED** > PREFIX
**PREFIXES** > PREFIX
**PREFIXING** > PREFIX
**PREFIXION** > PREFIX
**PREFLAME** *adj* of the period before combustion
**PREFLIGHT** *adj* of or relating to the period just prior to a plane taking off
**PREFOCUS** *vb* focus in advance
**PREFORM** *vb* form beforehand
**PREFORMAT** *vb* format in advance
**PREFORMED** > PREFORM
**PREFORMS** > PREFORM
**PREFRANK** *vb* frank in advance
**PREFRANKS** > PREFRANK
**PREFREEZE** *vb* freeze beforehand
**PREFROZE** > PREFREEZE
**PREFROZEN** > PREFREEZE
**PREFUND** *vb* pay for in advance
**PREFUNDED** > PREFUND
**PREFUNDS** > PREFUND
**PREGAME** *adj* of the period before a sports match ▷ *n* such a period
**PREGAMES** > PREGAME
**PREGGERS** *informal word for* > PREGNANT
**PREGGIER** > PREGGY
**PREGGIEST** > PREGGY
**PREGGY** *informal word for* > PREGNANT
**PREGNABLE** *adj* capable of being assailed or captured
**PREGNANCE** *obsolete word for* > PREGNANCY
**PREGNANCY** *n* state or condition of being pregnant
**PREGNANT** *adj* carrying a fetus in the womb
**PREGROWTH** *n* period before something begins to grow
**PREGUIDE** *vb* give guidance

in advance
**PREGUIDED** > PREGUIDE
**PREGUIDES** > PREGUIDE
**PREHALLUX** *n* extra first toe
**PREHANDLE** *vb* handle beforehand
**PREHARDEN** *vb* harden beforehand
**PREHEAT** *vb* heat (an oven, grill, pan, etc) beforehand
**PREHEATED** > PREHEAT
**PREHEATER** > PREHEAT
**PREHEATS** > PREHEAT
**PREHEND** *vb* take hold of
**PREHENDED** > PREHEND
**PREHENDS** > PREHEND
**PREHENSOR** *n* part that grasps
**PREHNITE** *n* green mineral
**PREHNITES** > PREHNITE
**PREHUMAN** *n* hominid that predates man
**PREHUMANS** > PREHUMAN
**PREIF** *old form of* > PROOF
**PREIFE** *old form of* > PROOF
**PREIFES** > PREIFE
**PREIFS** > PREIF
**PREIMPOSE** *vb* impose beforehand
**PREINFORM** *vb* inform beforehand
**PREINSERT** *vb* insert beforehand
**PREINVITE** *vb* invite before others
**PREJINK** *variant of* > PERJINK
**PREJUDGE** *vb* judge beforehand without sufficient evidence
**PREJUDGED** > PREJUDGE
**PREJUDGER** > PREJUDGE
**PREJUDGES** > PREJUDGE
**PREJUDICE** *n* unreasonable or unfair dislike or preference ▷ *vb* cause (someone) to have a prejudice
**PRELACIES** > PRELACY
**PRELACY** *n* office or status of a prelate
**PRELATE** *n* bishop or other churchman of high rank
**PRELATES** > PRELATE
**PRELATESS** *n* female prelate
**PRELATIAL** > PRELATE
**PRELATIC** > PRELATE
**PRELATIES** > PRELATY
**PRELATION** *n* setting of one above another
**PRELATISE** *same as* > PRELATIZE
**PRELATISH** > PRELATE
**PRELATISM** *same as* > PRELACY
**PRELATIST** > PRELATISM
**PRELATIZE** *vb* exercise prelatical power
**PRELATURE** *same as* > PRELACY
**PRELATY** *n* prelacy
**PRELAUNCH** *adj* of the period before a launch

**PRELAW** *adj* before taking up study of law
**PRELECT** *vb* lecture or discourse in public
**PRELECTED** > PRELECT
**PRELECTOR** > PRELECT
**PRELECTS** > PRELECT
**PRELEGAL** *adj* of the period before the start of a law course
**PRELIFE** *adj* of the period before life on earth
**PRELIM** *n* event which precedes another
**PRELIMIT** *vb* limit beforehand
**PRELIMITS** > PRELIMIT
**PRELIMS** *pl n* pages of a book, such as the title page and contents, which come before the main text
**PRELOAD** *vb* load beforehand
**PRELOADED** > PRELOAD
**PRELOADS** > PRELOAD
**PRELOCATE** *vb* locate beforehand
**PRELOVED** *adj* previously owned or used
**PRELUDE** *n* introductory movement in music ▷ *vb* act as a prelude to (something)
**PRELUDED** > PRELUDE
**PRELUDER** > PRELUDE
**PRELUDERS** > PRELUDE
**PRELUDES** > PRELUDE
**PRELUDI** > PRELUDIO
**PRELUDIAL** > PRELUDE
**PRELUDING** > PRELUDE
**PRELUDIO** *n* musical prelude
**PRELUNCH** *adj* of the period before lunch
**PRELUSION** > PRELUDE
**PRELUSIVE** > PRELUDE
**PRELUSORY** > PRELUDE
**PREM** *n* informal word for a premature infant
**PREMADE** *adj* made in advance
**PREMAN** *n* Indonesian gangster
**PREMARKET** *adj* of the period before a product is available
**PREMATURE** *adj* happening or done before the normal or expected time
**PREMEAL** *adj* of the period before a meal
**PREMED** *n* premedical student
**PREMEDIC** *same as* > PREMED
**PREMEDICS** > PREMEDIC
**PREMEDS** > PREMED
**PREMEET** *n* meeting prior to another
**PREMEETS** > PREMEET
**PREMEN** > PREMAN
**PREMERGER** *adj* of the period prior to a merger
**PREMIA** > PREMIUM

**PREMIE** *same as* > PREEMIE
**PREMIER** *n* prime minister ▷ *adj* chief, leading
**PREMIERE** *n* first performance of a play, film, etc ▷ *vb* give, or (of a film, play, or opera) be, a premiere
**PREMIERED** > PREMIERE
**PREMIERES** > PREMIERE
**PREMIERS** > PREMIER
**PREMIES** > PREMIE
**PREMISE** *n* statement assumed to be true and used as the basis of reasoning ▷ *vb* state or assume (a proposition) as a premise in an argument, theory, etc
**PREMISED** > PREMISE
**PREMISES** > PREMISE
**PREMISING** > PREMISE
**PREMISS** *same as* > PREMISE
**PREMISSES** > PREMISS
**PREMIUM** *n* additional sum of money, as on a wage or charge
**PREMIUMS** > PREMIUM
**PREMIX** *vb* mix beforehand
**PREMIXED** > PREMIX
**PREMIXES** > PREMIX
**PREMIXING** > PREMIX
**PREMODERN** *adj* of the period before a modern era
**PREMODIFY** *vb* modify in advance
**PREMOLAR** *n* tooth between the canine and first molar in adult humans ▷ *adj* situated before a molar tooth
**PREMOLARS** > PREMOLAR
**PREMOLD** *vb* mold in advance
**PREMOLDED** > PREMOLD
**PREMOLDS** > PREMOLD
**PREMOLT** *n* period before an animal molts
**PREMOLTS** > PREMOLT
**PREMONISH** *vb* admonish beforehand
**PREMORAL** *adj* not governed by sense of right and wrong
**PREMORSE** *adj* appearing as though the end had been bitten off
**PREMOSAIC** *adj* of the period before Moses
**PREMOTION** *n* previous motion
**PREMOVE** *vb* prompt to action
**PREMOVED** > PREMOVE
**PREMOVES** > PREMOVE
**PREMOVING** > PREMOVE
**PREMS** > PREM
**PREMUNE** *adj* having immunity to a disease as a result of latent infection
**PREMY** *variant of* > PREEMIE
**PRENAME** *n* forename
**PRENAMES** > PRENAME
**PRENASAL** *n* bone in the

front of the nose
**PRENASALS** > PRENASAL
**PRENATAL** *adj* before birth, during pregnancy ▷ *n* prenatal examination
**PRENATALS** > PRENATAL
**PRENOMEN** *less common spelling of* > PRAENOMEN
**PRENOMENS** > PRENOMEN
**PRENOMINA** > PRENOMEN
**PRENOON** *adj* of the period before noon
**PRENOTIFY** *vb* notify in advance
**PRENOTION** *n* preconception
**PRENT** *Scots variant of* > PRINT
**PRENTED** > PRENT
**PRENTICE** *vb* bind as an apprentice
**PRENTICED** > PRENTICE
**PRENTICES** > PRENTICE
**PRENTING** > PRENT
**PRENTS** > PRENT
**PRENUBILE** *adj* of the period from birth to puberty
**PRENUMBER** *vb* number in advance
**PRENUP** *n* prenuptial agreement
**PRENUPS** > PRENUP
**PRENZIE** *adj* Shakespearian word, possibly a mistake, supposed by some to mean "princely"
**PREOBTAIN** *vb* obtain in advance
**PREOCCUPY** *vb* fill the thoughts or attention of (someone) to the exclusion of other things
**PREOCULAR** *n* scale in front of eye of reptile or fish
**PREOP** *n* patient being prepared for surgery
**PREOPS** > PREOP
**PREOPTION** *n* right of first choice
**PREORAL** *adj* situated in front of mouth
**PREORDAIN** *vb* ordain, decree, or appoint beforehand
**PREORDER** *vb* order in advance
**PREORDERS** > PREORDER
**PREOWNED** *adj* second-hand
**PREP** *vb* prepare
**PREPACK** *vb* pack in advance of sale
**PREPACKED** *adj* sold already wrapped
**PREPACKS** > PREPACK
**PREPAID** > PREPAY
**PREPARE** *vb* make or get ready
**PREPARED** > PREPARE
**PREPARER** > PREPARE
**PREPARERS** > PREPARE
**PREPARES** > PREPARE
**PREPARING** > PREPARE

**PREPASTE** *vb* paste in advance
**PREPASTED** > PREPASTE
**PREPASTES** > PREPASTE
**PREPAVE** *vb* pave beforehand
**PREPAVED** > PREPAVE
**PREPAVES** > PREPAVE
**PREPAVING** > PREPAVE
**PREPAY** *vb* pay for in advance
**PREPAYING** > PREPAY
**PREPAYS** > PREPAY
**PREPENSE** *adj* (usually in legal contexts) arranged in advance ▷ *vb* consider beforehand
**PREPENSED** > PREPENSE
**PREPENSES** > PREPENSE
**PREPILL** *adj* of the period before the contraceptive pill became available
**PREPLACE** *vb* place in advance
**PREPLACED** > PREPLACE
**PREPLACES** > PREPLACE
**PREPLAN** *vb* plan beforehand
**PREPLANS** > PREPLAN
**PREPLANT** *vb* plant in advance
**PREPLANTS** > PREPLANT
**PREPOLLEX** *n* additional digit on thumb of some animals
**PREPONE** *vb* bring forward to an earlier time
**PREPONED** > PREPONE
**PREPONES** > PREPONE
**PREPONING** > PREPONE
**PREPOSE** *vb* place before
**PREPOSED** > PREPOSE
**PREPOSES** > PREPOSE
**PREPOSING** > PREPOSE
**PREPOSTOR** *n* prefect in certain public shcools
**PREPOTENT** *adj* greater in power, force, or influence
**PREPPED** > PREP
**PREPPIE** *same as* > PREPPY
**PREPPIER** > PREPPY
**PREPPIES** > PREPPY
**PREPPIEST** > PREPPY
**PREPPILY** > PREPPY
**PREPPING** > PREP
**PREPPY** *adj* characteristic of or denoting a fashion style of neat, understated, and often expensive clothes ▷ *n* person exhibiting such style
**PREPREG** *n* material already impregnated with synthetic resin
**PREPREGS** > PREPREG
**PREPRESS** *adj* before printing
**PREPRICE** *vb* price in advance
**PREPRICED** > PREPRICE
**PREPRICES** > PREPRICE
**PREPRINT** *vb* print in advance
**PREPRINTS** > PREPRINT

**PREPS** > PREP
**PREPUBES** > PREPUBIS
**PREPUBIS** *n* animal hip bone
**PREPUCE** *n* foreskin
**PREPUCES** > PREPUCE
**PREPUEBLO** *adj* belonging to the period before the Pueblo Indians
**PREPUNCH** *vb* pierce with holes in advance
**PREPUPA** *n* insect in stage of life before pupa
**PREPUPAE** > PREPUPA
**PREPUPAL** *adj* of the period between the larval and pupal stages
**PREPUPAS** > PREPUPA
**PREPUTIAL** > PREPUCE
**PREQUEL** *n* film or book about an earlier stage of a story or a character's life, released because the later part of it has already been successful
**PREQUELS** > PREQUEL
**PRERACE** *adj* of the period before a race
**PRERADIO** *adj* before the invention of radio
**PRERECORD** *vb* record (music or a programme) in advance so that it can be played or broadcast later
**PRERECTAL** *adj* in front of the rectum
**PREREFORM** *adj* before reform
**PRERENAL** *adj* anterior to kidney
**PRERETURN** *adj* of the period before return
**PREREVIEW** *adj* of the period before review
**PRERINSE** *vb* treat before rinsing
**PRERINSED** > PRERINSE
**PRERINSES** > PRERINSE
**PRERIOT** *adj* of the period before a riot
**PREROCK** *adj* of the era before rock music
**PRERUPT** *adj* abrupt
**PRESA** *n* sign or symbol used in a canon, round, etc, to indicate the entry of each part.
**PRESAGE** *vb* be a sign or warning of ▷ *n* omen
**PRESAGED** > PRESAGE
**PRESAGER** > PRESAGE
**PRESAGERS** > PRESAGE
**PRESAGES** > PRESAGE
**PRESAGING** > PRESAGE
**PRESALE** *n* practice of arranging the sale of a product before it is available
**PRESALES** > PRESALE
**PRESBYOPE** *n* person with presbyopy
**PRESBYOPY** *n* diminishing ability of the eye to focus
**PRESBYTE** *n* person with

presbyopy
**PRESBYTER** *n* (in some episcopal Churches) official with administrative and priestly duties
**PRESBYTES** > PRESBYTE
**PRESBYTIC** > PRESBYTE
**PRESCHOOL** *adj* of or for children below the age of five
**PRESCIENT** *adj* having knowledge of events before they take place
**PRESCIND** *vb* withdraw attention (from something)
**PRESCINDS** > PRESCIND
**PRESCIOUS** *adj* prescient
**PRESCORE** *vb* record (the score of a film) before shooting
**PRESCORED** > PRESCORE
**PRESCORES** > PRESCORE
**PRESCREEN** *vb* screen in advance
**PRESCRIBE** *vb* recommend the use of (a medicine)
**PRESCRIPT** *n* something laid down or prescribed ▷ *adj* prescribed as a rule
**PRESCUTA** > PRESCUTUM
**PRESCUTUM** *n* part of an insect's thorax
**PRESE** > PRESA
**PRESEASON** *n* period before the start of a sport season
**PRESELECT** *vb* select beforehand
**PRESELL** *vb* promote (a product, entertainment, etc) with publicity in advance of its appearance
**PRESELLS** > PRESELL
**PRESENCE** *n* fact of being in a specified place
**PRESENCES** > PRESENCE
**PRESENILE** *adj* occurring before the onset of old age
**PRESENT** *adj* being in a specified place ▷ *n* present time or tense ▷ *vb* introduce formally or publicly
**PRESENTED** > PRESENT
**PRESENTEE** *n* person who is presented, as at court
**PRESENTER** *n* person introducing a TV or radio show
**PRESENTLY** *adv* soon
**PRESENTS** *pl n* used in a deed or document to refer to itself
**PRESERVE** *vb* keep from being damaged, changed, or ended ▷ *n* area of interest restricted to a particular person or group
**PRESERVED** > PRESERVE
**PRESERVER** > PRESERVE
**PRESERVES** > PRESERVE
**PRESES** *variant of* > PRAESES
**PRESET** *vb* set the timer

591

on a piece of equipment
so that it starts to work
at a specific time ▷ adj
(of equipment) with the
controls set in advance ▷ n
control, such as a variable
resistor, that is not as
accessible as the main
controls and is used to set
initial conditions
PRESETS > PRESET
PRESETTLE vb settle
beforehand
PRESHAPE vb shape
beforehand
PRESHAPED > PRESHAPE
PRESHAPES > PRESHAPE
PRESHIP vb ship in
advance
PRESHIPS > PRESHIP
PRESHOW vb show in
advance
PRESHOWED > PRESHOW
PRESHOWN > PRESHOW
PRESHOWS > PRESHOW
PRESHRANK > PRESHRINK
PRESHRINK vb subject to a
shrinking process so that
further shrinkage will not
occur
PRESHRUNK > PRESHRINK
PRESIDE vb be in charge,
esp of a meeting
PRESIDED > PRESIDE
PRESIDENT n head of state
in many countries
PRESIDER > PRESIDE
PRESIDERS > PRESIDE
PRESIDES > PRESIDE
PRESIDIA > PRESIDIUM
PRESIDIAL adj
presidential
PRESIDING > PRESIDE
PRESIDIO n military post
or establishment, esp in
countries under Spanish
control
PRESIDIOS > PRESIDIO
PRESIDIUM n (in
Communist countries)
permanent administrative
committee
PRESIFT vb sift beforehand
PRESIFTED > PRESIFT
PRESIFTS > PRESIFT
PRESIGNAL vb signal in
advance
PRESLEEP adj of the period
before sleep
PRESLICE vb slice in
advance
PRESLICED > PRESLICE
PRESLICES > PRESLICE
PRESOAK vb soak
beforehand
PRESOAKED > PRESOAK
PRESOAKS > PRESOAK
PRESOLD > PRESELL
PRESOLVE vb solve
beforehand
PRESOLVED > PRESOLVE
PRESOLVES > PRESOLVE
PRESONG adj of the period
before a song is sung

PRESORT vb sort in advance
PRESORTED > PRESORT
PRESORTS > PRESORT
PRESPLIT adj of the period
prior to a split
PRESS vb apply force or
weight to ▷ n printing
machine
PRESSED > PRESS
PRESSER > PRESS
PRESSERS > PRESS
PRESSES > PRESS
PRESSFAT n wine vat
PRESSFATS > PRESSFAT
PRESSFUL > PRESS
PRESSGANG n squad of
sailors forcing others into
navy
PRESSIE informal word
for > PRESENT
PRESSIES > PRESSIE
PRESSING adj urgent
▷ n large number of
gramophone records
produced at one time
PRESSINGS > PRESSING
PRESSION n act of pressing
PRESSIONS > PRESSION
PRESSMAN n person who
works for the press
PRESSMARK n location
mark on a book indicating
a specific bookcase
PRESSMEN > PRESSMAN
PRESSOR adj relating to or
producing an increase in
blood pressure
PRESSROOM n room in a
printing establishment
that houses the printing
presses
PRESSRUN n number of
books printed at one time
PRESSRUNS > PRESSRUN
PRESSURE n force produced
by pressing ▷ vb persuade
forcefully
PRESSURED > PRESSURE
PRESSURES > PRESSURE
PRESSWORK n operation of
a printing press
PREST adj prepared for
action or use ▷ n loan of
money ▷ vb give as a loan
PRESTAMP vb stamp in
advance
PRESTAMPS > PRESTAMP
PRESTED > PREST
PRESTER > PREST
PRESTERNA adj anterior to
sternum
PRESTERS > PREST
PRESTIGE n high status
or respect resulting from
success or achievements
PRESTIGES > PRESTIGE
PRESTING > PREST
PRESTO adv very quickly
▷ n passage to be played
very quickly
PRESTORE vb store in
advance
PRESTORED > PRESTORE
PRESTORES > PRESTORE

PRESTOS > PRESTO
PRESTRESS vb apply tensile
stress to (the steel cables,
wires, etc, of a precast
concrete part) before the
load is applied
PRESTRIKE adj of the
period before a strike
PRESTS > PREST
PRESUME vb suppose to be
the case
PRESUMED > PRESUME
PRESUMER > PRESUME
PRESUMERS > PRESUME
PRESUMES > PRESUME
PRESUMING > PRESUME
PRESUMMIT n meeting held
prior to a summit
PRESURVEY vb survey in
advance
PRETAPE vb tape in
advance
PRETAPED > PRETAPE
PRETAPES > PRETAPE
PRETAPING > PRETAPE
PRETASTE vb taste in
advance
PRETASTED > PRETASTE
PRETASTES > PRETASTE
PRETAX adj before tax
PRETEEN n boy or girl
approaching his or her
teens
PRETEENS > PRETEEN
PRETELL vb predict
PRETELLS > PRETELL
PRETENCE n behaviour
intended to deceive,
pretending
PRETENCES > PRETENCE
PRETEND vb claim or
give the appearance of
(something untrue) to
deceive or in play ▷ adj
fanciful
PRETENDED > PRETEND
PRETENDER n person who
makes a false or disputed
claim to a position of
power
PRETENDS > PRETEND
PRETENSE same
as > PRETENCE
PRETENSES > PRETENSE
PRETERIST n person
interested in past
PRETERIT same
as > PRETERITE
PRETERITE n past tense
of verbs, such as jumped,
swam ▷ adj expressing
such a past tense
PRETERITS > PRETERIT
PRETERM n premature baby
PRETERMIT vb overlook
intentionally
PRETERMS > PRETERM
PRETEST vb test
(something) before
presenting it to its
intended public or client
▷ n act or instance of
pretesting
PRETESTED > PRETEST

PRETESTS > PRETEST
PRETEXT n false reason
given to hide the real
one ▷ vb get personal
information under false
pretences
PRETEXTED > PRETEXT
PRETEXTS > PRETEXT
PRETOLD > PRETELL
PRETONIC adj denoting
or relating to the syllable
before the one bearing the
primary stress in a word
PRETOR same as > PRAETOR
PRETORIAL > PRETOR
PRETORIAN n person with
the rank of praetor
PRETORS > PRETOR
PRETRAIN vb train in
advance
PRETRAINS > PRETRAIN
PRETRAVEL adj of the
period before travel
PRETREAT vb treat in
advance
PRETREATS > PRETREAT
PRETRIAL n hearing prior
to a trial
PRETRIALS > PRETRIAL
PRETRIM vb trim in
advance
PRETRIMS > PRETRIM
PRETTIED > PRETTY
PRETTIER > PRETTY
PRETTIES > PRETTY
PRETTIEST > PRETTY
PRETTIFY vb make pretty
PRETTILY > PRETTY
PRETTY adj pleasing to look
at ▷ adv fairly, moderately
▷ vb pretty
PRETTYING > PRETTY
PRETTYISH adj quite pretty
PRETTYISM n affectedly
pretty style
PRETYPE vb type in
advance
PRETYPED > PRETYPE
PRETYPES > PRETYPE
PRETYPING > PRETYPE
PRETZEL n brittle salted
biscuit
PRETZELS > PRETZEL
PREUNION n early form of
trade union
PREUNIONS > PREUNION
PREUNITE vb unite in
advance
PREUNITED > PREUNITE
PREUNITES > PREUNITE
PREVAIL vb gain mastery
PREVAILED > PREVAIL
PREVAILER > PREVAIL
PREVAILS > PREVAIL
PREVALENT adj
widespread, common
PREVALUE vb value
beforehand
PREVALUED > PREVALUE
PREVALUES > PREVALUE
PREVE vb prove
PREVED > PREVE
PREVENE vb come before
PREVENED > PREVENE

PREVENES > PREVENE
PREVENING > PREVENE
PREVENT vb keep from happening or doing
PREVENTED > PREVENT
PREVENTER n person or thing that prevents
PREVENTS > PREVENT
PREVERB n particle preceding root of verb
PREVERBAL > PREVERB
PREVERBS > PREVERB
PREVES > PREVE
PREVIABLE adj not yet viable
PREVIEW n advance showing of a film or exhibition before it is shown to the public ▷ vb view in advance
PREVIEWED > PREVIEW
PREVIEWER > PREVIEW
PREVIEWS > PREVIEW
PREVING > PREVE
PREVIOUS adj coming or happening before
PREVISE vb predict or foresee
PREVISED > PREVISE
PREVISES > PREVISE
PREVISING > PREVISE
PREVISION n act or power of foreseeing
PREVISIT vb visit beforehand
PREVISITS > PREVISIT
PREVISOR > PREVISE
PREVISORS > PREVISE
PREVUE same as > PREVIEW
PREVUED > PREVUE
PREVUES > PREVUE
PREVUING > PREVUE
PREWAR adj relating to the period before a war, esp before World War I or II
PREWARM vb warm beforehand
PREWARMED > PREWARM
PREWARMS > PREWARM
PREWARN vb warn in advance
PREWARNED > PREWARN
PREWARNS > PREWARN
PREWASH vb give a preliminary wash to (clothes), esp in a washing machine ▷ n preliminary wash, esp in a washing machine
PREWASHED > PREWASH
PREWASHES > PREWASH
PREWEIGH vb weigh beforehand
PREWEIGHS > PREWEIGH
PREWIRE vb wire beforehand
PREWIRED > PREWIRE
PREWIRES > PREWIRE
PREWIRING > PREWIRE
PREWORK vb work in advance
PREWORKED > PREWORK
PREWORKS > PREWORK
PREWORN adj (of clothes)

second-hand
PREWRAP vb wrap in advance
PREWRAPS > PREWRAP
PREWYN obsolete spelling of > PRUNE
PREWYNS > PREWYN
PREX same as > PREXY
PREXES > PREX
PREXIES > PREXY
PREXY n US college president
PREY n animal hunted and killed for food by another animal ▷ vb hunt or seize food by killing other animals
PREYED > PREY
PREYER > PREY
PREYERS > PREY
PREYFUL adj rich in prey
PREYING > PREY
PREYS > PREY
PREZ n president
PREZZES > PREZ
PREZZIE same as > PRESSIE
PREZZIES > PREZZIE
PRIAL n pair royal of cards
PRIALS > PRIAL
PRIAPEAN same as > PRIAPIC
PRIAPI > PRIAPUS
PRIAPIC adj phallic
PRIAPISM n prolonged painful erection of the penis, caused by another neurological disorders, obstruction of the penile blood vessels, etc
PRIAPISMS > PRIAPISM
PRIAPUS n representation of the penis
PRIAPUSES > PRIAPUS
PRIBBLE variant of > PRABBLE
PRIBBLES > PRIBBLE
PRICE n amount of money for which a thing is bought or sold ▷ vb fix or ask the price of
PRICEABLE > PRICE
PRICED > PRICE
PRICELESS adj very valuable
PRICER > PRICE
PRICERS > PRICE
PRICES > PRICE
PRICEY adj expensive
PRICIER > PRICY
PRICIEST > PRICY
PRICILY > PRICEY
PRICINESS > PRICEY
PRICING > PRICE
PRICINGS > PRICE
PRICK vb pierce lightly with a sharp point ▷ n sudden sharp pain caused by pricking
PRICKED > PRICK
PRICKER n person or thing that pricks
PRICKERS > PRICKER
PRICKET n male deer in the second year of life having unbranched antlers

PRICKETS > PRICKET
PRICKIER > PRICKY
PRICKIEST > PRICKY
PRICKING > PRICK
PRICKINGS > PRICK
PRICKLE n thorn or spike on a plant ▷ vb have a tingling or pricking sensation
PRICKLED > PRICKLE
PRICKLES > PRICKLE
PRICKLIER > PRICKLY
PRICKLING > PRICKLE
PRICKLY adj having prickles
PRICKS > PRICK
PRICKWOOD n shrub with wood used for skewers
PRICKY adj covered with pricks
PRICY same as > PRICEY
PRIDE n feeling of pleasure and satisfaction when one has done well
PRIDED > PRIDE
PRIDEFUL > PRIDE
PRIDELESS > PRIDE
PRIDES > PRIDE
PRIDIAN adj relating to yesterday
PRIDING > PRIDE
PRIED > PRY
PRIEDIEU n piece of furniture consisting of a low surface for kneeling upon and a narrow front surmounted by a rest for the elbows or for books, for use when praying
PRIEDIEUS > PRIEDIEU
PRIEDIEUX > PRIEDIEU
PRIEF obsolete variant of > PROOF
PRIEFE obsolete variant of > PROOF
PRIEFED > PRIEFE
PRIEFES > PRIEFE
PRIEFING > PRIEFE
PRIEFS > PRIEF
PRIER n person who pries
PRIERS > PRIER
PRIES > PRY
PRIEST n (in the Christian church) person who can administer the sacraments and preach ▷ vb make a priest
PRIESTED > PRIEST
PRIESTESS n female official who offers sacrifice on behalf of the people and peforms various other religious ceremonies
PRIESTING > PRIEST
PRIESTLY adj of, relating to, characteristic of, or befitting a priest
PRIESTS > PRIEST
PRIEVE obsolete variant of > PROOF
PRIEVED > PRIEVE
PRIEVES > PRIEVE
PRIEVING > PRIEVE
PRIG n self-righteous

person who acts as if superior to others
PRIGGED > PRIG
PRIGGER n thief
PRIGGERS > PRIGGER
PRIGGERY > PRIG
PRIGGING > PRIG
PRIGGINGS > PRIG
PRIGGISH > PRIG
PRIGGISM > PRIG
PRIGGISMS > PRIG
PRIGS > PRIG
PRILL vb convert (a material) into a granular free-flowing form ▷ n prilled material
PRILLED > PRILL
PRILLING > PRILL
PRILLS > PRILL
PRIM adj formal, proper, and rather prudish ▷ vb make prim
PRIMA same as > PRIMO
PRIMACIES > PRIMACY
PRIMACY n state of being first in rank, grade, etc
PRIMAEVAL same as > PRIMEVAL
PRIMAGE n tax added to customs duty
PRIMAGES > PRIMAGE
PRIMAL adj of basic causes or origins
PRIMALITY n state of being prime
PRIMALLY > PRIMAL
PRIMARIES > PRIMARY
PRIMARILY adv chiefly or mainly
PRIMARY adj chief, most important ▷ n person or thing that is first in position, time, or importance
PRIMAS > PRIMA
PRIMATAL > PRIMATE
PRIMATE n member of an order of mammals including monkeys and humans ▷ adj of, relating to, or belonging to the order Primates
PRIMATES > PRIMATE
PRIMATIAL > PRIMATE
PRIMATIC > PRIMATE
PRIMAVERA n springtime
PRIME adj main, most important ▷ n time when someone is at his or her best or most vigorous ▷ vb give (someone) information in advance to prepare them for something
PRIMED > PRIME
PRIMELY > PRIME
PRIMENESS > PRIME
PRIMER n special paint applied to bare wood etc before the main paint
PRIMERO n 16th- and 17th-century card game
PRIMEROS > PRIMERO
PRIMERS > PRIMER

**PRIMES** > PRIME
**PRIMETIME** adj occurring during or designed for prime time
**PRIMEUR** n anything (esp fruit) produced early
**PRIMEURS** > PRIMEUR
**PRIMEVAL** adj of the earliest age of the world
**PRIMI** > PRIMO
**PRIMINE** n integument surrounding an ovule or the outer of two such integuments
**PRIMINES** > PRIMINE
**PRIMING** same as > PRIMER
**PRIMINGS** > PRIMING
**PRIMIPARA** n woman who has borne only one child
**PRIMITIA** n first fruit of season
**PRIMITIAE** > PRIMITIA
**PRIMITIAL** > PRIMITIA
**PRIMITIAS** > PRIMITIA
**PRIMITIVE** adj of an early simple stage of development ▷ n primitive person or thing
**PRIMLY** > PRIM
**PRIMMED** > PRIM
**PRIMMER** > PRIM
**PRIMMERS** > PRIM
**PRIMMEST** > PRIM
**PRIMMING** > PRIM
**PRIMNESS** > PRIM
**PRIMO** n upper or right-hand part in a piano duet
**PRIMORDIA** n organs or parts in the earliest stage of development
**PRIMOS** > PRIMO
**PRIMP** vb tidy (one's hair or clothes) fussily
**PRIMPED** > PRIMP
**PRIMPING** > PRIMP
**PRIMPS** > PRIMP
**PRIMROSE** n pale yellow spring flower ▷ adj pale yellow
**PRIMROSED** > PRIMROSE
**PRIMROSES** > PRIMROSE
**PRIMROSY** > PRIMROSE
**PRIMS** > PRIM
**PRIMSIE** Scots variant of > PRIM
**PRIMSIER** > PRIMSIE
**PRIMSIEST** > PRIMSIE
**PRIMULA** n type of primrose with brightly coloured flowers
**PRIMULAS** > PRIMULA
**PRIMULINE** n type of dye
**PRIMUS** n presiding bishop in the Synod
**PRIMUSES** > PRIMUS
**PRIMY** adj prime
**PRINCE** vb act the prince
**PRINCED** > PRINCE
**PRINCEDOM** n dignity, rank, or position of a prince
**PRINCEKIN** n young prince
**PRINCELET** n petty or minor prince
**PRINCELY** adj of or like a

prince ▷ adv in a princely manner
**PRINCES** > PRINCE
**PRINCESS** n female member of a royal family, esp the daughter of the king or queen
**PRINCING** > PRINCE
**PRINCIPAL** adj main, most important ▷ n head of a school or college
**PRINCIPE** n prince
**PRINCIPI** > PRINCIPE
**PRINCIPIA** n principles
**PRINCIPLE** n moral rule guiding behaviour
**PRINCOCK** same as > PRINCOX
**PRINCOCKS** > PRINCOCK
**PRINCOX** n pert youth
**PRINCOXES** > PRINCOX
**PRINK** vb dress (oneself) finely
**PRINKED** > PRINK
**PRINKER** > PRINK
**PRINKERS** > PRINK
**PRINKING** > PRINK
**PRINKS** > PRINK
**PRINT** vb reproduce (a newspaper, book, etc) in large quantities by mechanical or electronic means ▷ n printed words etc
**PRINTABLE** adj capable of being printed or of producing a print
**PRINTED** > PRINT
**PRINTER** n person or company engaged in printing
**PRINTERS** > PRINTER
**PRINTERY** n establishment in which printing is carried out
**PRINTHEAD** n component in a printer that forms a printed character
**PRINTING** n process of producing printed matter
**PRINTINGS** > PRINTING
**PRINTLESS** > PRINT
**PRINTOUT** n printed information produced by a computer output device
**PRINTOUTS** > PRINTOUT
**PRINTS** > PRINT
**PRION** n dovelike petrel with a serrated bill
**PRIONS** > PRION
**PRIOR** adj earlier ▷ n head monk in a priory
**PRIORATE** n office, status, or term of office of a prior
**PRIORATES** > PRIORATE
**PRIORESS** n deputy head nun in a convent
**PRIORIES** > PRIORY
**PRIORITY** n most important thing that must be dealt with first
**PRIORLY** > PRIOR
**PRIORS** > PRIOR
**PRIORSHIP** n office of prior

**PRIORY** n place where certain orders of monks or nuns live
**PRISAGE** n customs duty levied until 1809 upon wine imported into England
**PRISAGES** > PRISAGE
**PRISE** same as > PRY
**PRISED** > PRISE
**PRISER** > PRISE
**PRISERE** n primary sere or succession from bare ground to the community climax
**PRISERES** > PRISERE
**PRISERS** > PRISE
**PRISES** > PRISE
**PRISING** > PRISE
**PRISM** n transparent block usu with triangular ends and rectangular sides, used to disperse light into a spectrum or refract it in optical instruments
**PRISMATIC** adj of or shaped like a prism
**PRISMOID** n prismatoid having an equal number of vertices in each of the two parallel planes and whose sides are trapeziums or parallelograms
**PRISMOIDS** > PRISMOID
**PRISMS** > PRISM
**PRISMY** > PRISM
**PRISON** n building where criminals and accused people are held ▷ vb imprison
**PRISONED** > PRISON
**PRISONER** n person held captive
**PRISONERS** > PRISONER
**PRISONING** > PRISON
**PRISONOUS** > PRISON
**PRISONS** > PRISON
**PRISS** n prissy person ▷ vb act prissily
**PRISSED** > PRISS
**PRISSES** > PRISS
**PRISSIER** > PRISSY
**PRISSIES** > PRISSY
**PRISSIEST** > PRISSY
**PRISSILY** > PRISSY
**PRISSING** > PRISS
**PRISSY** adj prim, correct, and easily shocked ▷ n prissy person
**PRISTANE** n colourless combustible liquid
**PRISTANES** > PRISTANE
**PRISTINE** adj clean, new, and unused
**PRITHEE** interj pray thee
**PRIVACIES** > PRIVACY
**PRIVACY** n condition of being private
**PRIVADO** n close friend
**PRIVADOES** > PRIVADO
**PRIVADOS** > PRIVADO
**PRIVATE** adj for the use of one person or group only ▷ n soldier of the lowest

rank
**PRIVATEER** n privately owned armed vessel authorized by the government to take part in a war ▷ vb competitor, esp in motor racing, who is privately financed rather than sponsored by a manufacturer
**PRIVATELY** > PRIVATE
**PRIVATER** > PRIVATE
**PRIVATES** > PRIVATE
**PRIVATEST** > PRIVATE
**PRIVATION** n loss or lack of the necessities of life
**PRIVATISE** same as > PRIVATIZE
**PRIVATISM** n lack of concern for public life
**PRIVATIST** > PRIVATISM
**PRIVATIVE** adj causing privation
**PRIVATIZE** vb sell (a publicly owned company) to individuals or a private company
**PRIVET** n bushy evergreen shrub used for hedges
**PRIVETS** > PRIVET
**PRIVIER** > PRIVY
**PRIVIES** > PRIVY
**PRIVIEST** > PRIVY
**PRIVILEGE** n advantage or favour that only some people have ▷ vb bestow a privilege or privileges upon
**PRIVILY** adv in a secret way
**PRIVITIES** > PRIVITY
**PRIVITY** n legally recognized relationship existing between two parties, such as that between lessor and lessee and between the parties to a contract
**PRIVY** adj sharing knowledge of something secret ▷ n toilet, esp an outside one
**PRIZABLE** adj of worth
**PRIZE** n reward given for success in a competition etc ▷ adj winning or likely to win a prize ▷ vb value highly
**PRIZED** > PRIZE
**PRIZEMAN** n winner of prize
**PRIZEMEN** > PRIZEMAN
**PRIZER** n contender for prize
**PRIZERS** > PRIZER
**PRIZES** > PRIZE
**PRIZING** > PRIZE
**PRO** prep in favour of ▷ n professional ▷ adv in favour of a motion etc
**PROA** n any of several kinds of canoe-like boats used in the South Pacific, esp one equipped with an

outrigger and sails

**PROACTION** *n* action that initiates change as opposed to reaction to events

**PROACTIVE** *adj* tending to initiate change rather than reacting to events

**PROAS** > PROA

**PROB** *n* problem

**PROBABLE** *adj* likely to happen or be true ▷ *n* person who is likely to be chosen for a team, event, etc

**PROBABLES** > PROBABLE

**PROBABLY** *adv* in all likelihood ▷ *sentence substitute* I believe such a thing or situation may be the case

**PROBALL** *adj* believable

**PROBAND** *n* first patient to be investigated in a family study, to whom all relationships are referred

**PROBANDS** > PROBAND

**PROBANG** *n* long flexible rod, often with a small sponge at one end, for inserting into the oesophagus, as to apply medication

**PROBANGS** > PROBANG

**PROBATE** *n* process of proving the validity of a will ▷ *vb* establish officially the authenticity and validity of (a will)

**PROBATED** > PROBATE

**PROBATES** > PROBATE

**PROBATING** > PROBATE

**PROBATION** *n* system of dealing with law-breakers, esp juvenile ones, by placing them under supervision

**PROBATIVE** *adj* serving to test or designed for testing

**PROBATORY** *same as* > PROBATIVE

**PROBE** *vb* search into or examine closely ▷ *n* surgical instrument used to examine a wound, cavity, etc

**PROBEABLE** > PROBE

**PROBED** > PROBE

**PROBER** > PROBE

**PROBERS** > PROBE

**PROBES** > PROBE

**PROBING** > PROBE

**PROBINGLY** > PROBE

**PROBIOTIC** *n* bacterium that protects the body from harmful bacteria

**PROBIT** *n* statistical measurement

**PROBITIES** > PROBITY

**PROBITS** > PROBIT

**PROBITY** *n* honesty, integrity

**PROBLEM** *n* something difficult to deal with or

solve ▷ *adj* of a literary work that deals with difficult moral questions

**PROBLEMS** > PROBLEM

**PROBOSCIS** *n* long trunk or snout

**PROBS** > PROB

**PROCACITY** *n* insolence

**PROCAINE** *n* colourless or white crystalline water-soluble substance

**PROCAINES** > PROCAINE

**PROCAMBIA** *n* plant part in stem and root

**PROCARP** *n* female reproductive organ in red algae

**PROCARPS** > PROCARP

**PROCARYON** *same as* > PROKARYON

**PROCEDURE** *n* way of doing something, esp the correct or usual one

**PROCEED** *vb* start or continue doing

**PROCEEDED** > PROCEED

**PROCEEDER** > PROCEED

**PROCEEDS** *pl n* money obtained from an event or activity

**PROCERITY** *n* tallness

**PROCESS** *n* series of actions or changes ▷ *vb* handle or prepare by a special method of manufacture

**PROCESSED** > PROCESS

**PROCESSER** *same as* > PROCESSOR

**PROCESSES** > PROCESS

**PROCESSOR** *n* person or thing that carries out a process

**PROCHAIN** *variant of* > PROCHEIN

**PROCHEIN** *adj* next or nearest

**PROCHOICE** *adj* in favour of women's right to abortion

**PROCHURCH** *adj* favourable to church

**PROCIDENT** *adj* relating to prolapsus

**PROCINCT** *n* state of preparedness

**PROCINCTS** > PROCINCT

**PROCLAIM** *vb* declare publicly

**PROCLAIMS** > PROCLAIM

**PROCLISES** > PROCLITIC

**PROCLISIS** > PROCLITIC

**PROCLITIC** *adj* relating to or denoting a monosyllabic word or form having no stress or accent and pronounced as a prefix of the following word, as in English 't for it in 'twas ▷ *n* proclitic word or form

**PROCLIVE** *adj* prone

**PROCONSUL** *n* administrator or governor of a colony, occupied territory, or other dependency

**PROCREANT** > PROCREATE

**PROCREATE** *vb* produce offspring

**PROCTAL** *adj* relating to the rectum

**PROCTITIS** *n* inflammation of the rectum

**PROCTODEA** *pl n* parts of the anus

**PROCTOR** *n* member of the staff of certain universities having duties including the enforcement of discipline ▷ *vb* invigilate (an examination)

**PROCTORED** > PROCTOR

**PROCTORS** > PROCTOR

**PROCURACY** *n* office of a procurator

**PROCURAL** > PROCURE

**PROCURALS** > PROCURE

**PROCURE** *vb* get, provide

**PROCURED** > PROCURE

**PROCURER** *n* person who obtains people to act as prostitutes

**PROCURERS** > PROCURER

**PROCURES** > PROCURE

**PROCURESS** *same as* > PROCURER

**PROCUREUR** *n* law officer in Guernsey

**PROCURING** > PROCURE

**PROD** *vb* poke with something pointed ▷ *n* prodding

**PRODDED** > PROD

**PRODDER** > PROD

**PRODDERS** > PROD

**PRODDING** > PROD

**PRODIGAL** *adj* recklessly extravagant, wasteful ▷ *n* person who spends lavishly or squanders money

**PRODIGALS** > PRODIGAL

**PRODIGIES** > PRODIGY

**PRODIGY** *n* person with some marvellous talent

**PRODITOR** *n* traitor

**PRODITORS** > PRODITOR

**PRODITORY** > PRODITOR

**PRODNOSE** *vb* make uninvited inquiries (about someone else's business, for example)

**PRODNOSED** > PRODNOSE

**PRODNOSES** > PRODNOSE

**PRODROMAL** > PRODROME

**PRODROME** *n* any symptom that signals the impending onset of a disease

**PRODROMES** > PRODROME

**PRODROMI** > PRODROME

**PRODROMIC** > PRODROME

**PRODROMUS** *same as* > PRODROME

**PRODRUG** *n* compound that is itself biologically inactive but is metabolized in the body to produce an active

therapeutic drug

**PRODRUGS** > PRODRUG

**PRODS** > PROD

**PRODUCE** *vb* bring into existence ▷ *n* food grown for sale

**PRODUCED** > PRODUCE

**PRODUCER** *n* person with control over the making of a film, record, etc

**PRODUCERS** > PRODUCER

**PRODUCES** > PRODUCE

**PRODUCING** > PRODUCE

**PRODUCT** *n* something produced

**PRODUCTS** > PRODUCT

**PROEM** *n* introduction or preface

**PROEMBRYO** *n* stage prior to embryo in plants

**PROEMIAL** > PROEM

**PROEMS** > PROEM

**PROENZYME** *n* inactive form of an enzyme

**PROESTRUS** *n* period in the estrous cycle that immediately precedes estrus

**PROETTE** *n* female golfing professional

**PROETTES** > PROETTE

**PROF** *short for* > PROFESSOR

**PROFACE** *interj* much good may it do you

**PROFAMILY** *adj* in favour of family

**PROFANE** *adj* showing disrespect for religion or holy things ▷ *vb* treat (something sacred) irreverently, desecrate

**PROFANED** > PROFANE

**PROFANELY** > PROFANE

**PROFANER** > PROFANE

**PROFANERS** > PROFANE

**PROFANES** > PROFANE

**PROFANING** > PROFANE

**PROFANITY** *n* profane talk or behaviour, blasphemy

**PROFESS** *vb* state or claim (something as true), sometimes falsely

**PROFESSED** *adj* supposed

**PROFESSES** > PROFESS

**PROFESSOR** *n* teacher of the highest rank in a university

**PROFFER** *vb* offer ▷ *n* act of proffering

**PROFFERED** > PROFFER

**PROFFERER** > PROFFER

**PROFFERS** > PROFFER

**PROFILE** *n* outline, esp of the face, as seen from the side ▷ *vb* draw, write, or make a profile of

**PROFILED** > PROFILE

**PROFILER** *n* person or device that creates a profile, esp someone with psychological training who assists police investigations by identifying the likely characteristics of the perpetrator of a particular crime

**PROFILERS** > PROFILER

**PROFILES** > PROFILE

**PROFILING** > PROFILE

**PROFILIST** > PROFILE

**PROFIT** n money gained ▷ vb gain or benefit

**PROFITED** > PROFIT

**PROFITEER** n person who makes excessive profits at the expense of the public ▷ vb make excessive profits

**PROFITER** > PROFIT

**PROFITERS** > PROFIT

**PROFITING** > PROFIT

**PROFITS** > PROFIT

**PROFLUENT** adj flowing smoothly or abundantly

**PROFORMA** n invoice issued before an order is placed or before the goods are delivered giving all the details and the cost of the goods

**PROFORMAS** > PROFORMA

**PROFOUND** adj showing or needing great knowledge ▷ n great depth

**PROFOUNDS** > PROFOUND

**PROFS** > PROF

**PROFUSE** adj plentiful

**PROFUSELY** > PROFUSE

**PROFUSER** > PROFUSE

**PROFUSERS** > PROFUSE

**PROFUSION** > PROFUSE

**PROFUSIVE** same as > PROFUSE

**PROG** vb prowl about for or as if for food or plunder ▷ vb food obtained by begging

**PROGENIES** > PROGENY

**PROGENY** n children

**PROGERIA** n premature old age, a rare condition occurring in children and characterized by small stature, absent or greying hair, wrinkled skin, and other signs of old age

**PROGERIAS** > PROGERIA

**PROGESTIN** n type of steroid hormone

**PROGGED** > PROG

**PROGGER** n fan of progressive rock

**PROGGERS** > PROGGER

**PROGGING** > PROG

**PROGGINS** n proctor

**PROGNOSE** vb predict course of disease

**PROGNOSED** > PROGNOSE

**PROGNOSES** > PROGNOSIS

**PROGNOSIS** n doctor's forecast about the progress of an illness

**PROGRADE** vb (of beach) advance towards sea

**PROGRADED** > PROGRADE

**PROGRADES** > PROGRADE

**PROGRAM** same as > PROGRAMME

**PROGRAMED** > PROGRAM

**PROGRAMER** n US spelling of programmer

**PROGRAMME** same as > PROGRAM

**PROGRAMS** > PROGRAM

**PROGRESS** n improvement, development ▷ vb become more advanced or skilful

**PROGS** > PROG

**PROGUN** adj in favour of public owning firearms

**PROHIBIT** vb forbid or prevent from happening

**PROHIBITS** > PROHIBIT

**PROIGN** same as > PROIN

**PROIGNED** > PROIGN

**PROIGNING** > PROIGN

**PROIGNS** > PROIGN

**PROIN** vb trim or prune

**PROINE** same as > PROIN

**PROINED** > PROIN

**PROINES** > PROINE

**PROINING** > PROIN

**PROINS** > PROIN

**PROJECT** n planned scheme to do or examine something over a period ▷ vb make a forecast based on known data

**PROJECTED** > PROJECT

**PROJECTOR** n apparatus for projecting photographic images, films, or slides on a screen

**PROJECTS** > PROJECT

**PROJET** n draft of a proposed treaty

**PROJETS** > PROJET

**PROKARYON** n nucleus of a prokaryote

**PROKARYOT** n any organism having cells in each of which the genetic material is in a single DNA chain, not enclosed in a nucleus

**PROKE** vb thrust or poke

**PROKED** > PROKE

**PROKER** > PROKE

**PROKERS** > PROKE

**PROKES** > PROKE

**PROKING** > PROKE

**PROLABOR** adj favouring the Labor party

**PROLACTIN** n gonadotrophic hormone secreted by the anterior lobe of the pituitary gland

**PROLAMIN** same as > PROLAMINE

**PROLAMINE** n any of a group of simple plant proteins, including gliadin, hordein, and zein

**PROLAMINS** > PROLAMIN

**PROLAN** n constituent of human pregnancy urine

**PROLANS** > PROLAN

**PROLAPSE** n slipping down of an internal organ of the body from its normal position ▷ vb (of an internal organ) slip from its normal position

**PROLAPSED** > PROLAPSE

**PROLAPSES** > PROLAPSE

**PROLAPSUS** same as > PROLAPSE

**PROLATE** adj having a polar diameter which is longer than the equatorial diameter ▷ vb pronounce or utter

**PROLATED** > PROLATE

**PROLATELY** > PROLATE

**PROLATES** > PROLATE

**PROLATING** > PROLATE

**PROLATION** > PROLATE

**PROLATIVE** > PROLATE

**PROLE** old form of > PROWL

**PROLED** > PROLE

**PROLEG** n any of the short paired unjointed appendages on each abdominal segment of a caterpillar and any of certain other insect larvae

**PROLEGS** > PROLEG

**PROLEPSES** > PROLEPSIS

**PROLEPSIS** n rhetorical device by which objections are anticipated and answered in advance

**PROLEPTIC** > PROLEPSIS

**PROLER** n prowler

**PROLERS** > PROLER

**PROLES** > PROLE

**PROLETARY** n member of the proletariat

**PROLICIDE** n killing of one's child

**PROLIFIC** adj very productive

**PROLINE** n nonessential amino acid that occurs in protein

**PROLINES** > PROLINE

**PROLING** > PROLE

**PROLIX** adj (of speech or a piece of writing) overlong and boring

**PROLIXITY** > PROLIX

**PROLIXLY** > PROLIX

**PROLL** vb prowl or search

**PROLLED** > PROLL

**PROLLER** > PROLL

**PROLLERS** > PROLL

**PROLLING** > PROLL

**PROLLS** > PROLL

**PROLOG** same as > PROLOGUE

**PROLOGED** > PROLOG

**PROLOGING** > PROLOG

**PROLOGISE** same as > PROLOGIZE

**PROLOGIST** n prologue writer

**PROLOGIZE** vb write a prologue

**PROLOGS** > PROLOG

**PROLOGUE** n introduction to a play or book ▷ vb introduce or preface with or as if with a prologue

**PROLOGUED** > PROLOGUE

**PROLOGUES** > PROLOGUE

**PROLONG** vb make

(something) last longer

**PROLONGE** n (formerly) specially fitted rope used as part of the towing equipment of a gun carriage

**PROLONGED** > PROLONG

**PROLONGER** > PROLONG

**PROLONGES** > PROLONGE

**PROLONGS** > PROLONG

**PROLUSION** n preliminary written exercise

**PROLUSORY** > PROLUSION

**PROM** n formal dance held at a high school or college

**PROMACHOS** n defender or champion

**PROMENADE** n paved walkway along the seafront at a holiday resort ▷ vb take a leisurely walk

**PROMETAL** n type of cast iron

**PROMETALS** > PROMETAL

**PROMETRIC** adj in favour of the metric system

**PROMINE** n substance promoting cell growth

**PROMINENT** adj very noticeable

**PROMINES** > PROMINE

**PROMISE** vb say that one will definitely do or not do something ▷ n undertaking to do or not to do something

**PROMISED** > PROMISE

**PROMISEE** n person to whom a promise is made

**PROMISEES** > PROMISEE

**PROMISER** > PROMISE

**PROMISERS** > PROMISE

**PROMISES** > PROMISE

**PROMISING** adj likely to succeed or turn out well

**PROMISOR** n person who makes a promise

**PROMISORS** > PROMISOR

**PROMISSOR** n (in law) person who makes a promise

**PROMMER** n spectator at promenade concert

**PROMMERS** > PROMMER

**PROMO** vb promote (something) using a promo

**PROMODERN** adj in favour of the modern

**PROMOED** > PROMO

**PROMOING** > PROMO

**PROMOS** > PROMO

**PROMOTE** vb help to make (something) happen or increase

**PROMOTED** > PROMOTE

**PROMOTER** n person who organizes or finances an event etc

**PROMOTERS** > PROMOTER

**PROMOTES** > PROMOTE

**PROMOTING** > PROMOTE

**PROMOTION** > PROMOTE

**PROMOTIVE** adj tending to

promote
**PROMOTOR** *variant of* > PROMOTER
**PROMOTORS** > PROMOTOR
**PROMPT** *vb* cause (an action) ▷ *adj* done without delay ▷ *adv* exactly ▷ *n* anything that serves to remind
**PROMPTED** > PROMPT
**PROMPTER** *n* person offstage who prompts actors
**PROMPTERS** > PROMPTER
**PROMPTEST** > PROMPT
**PROMPTING** > PROMPT
**PROMPTLY** > PROMPT
**PROMPTS** > PROMPT
**PROMPTURE** *n* prompting
**PROMS** > PROM
**PROMULGE** *vb* bring to public knowledge
**PROMULGED** > PROMULGE
**PROMULGES** > PROMULGE
**PROMUSCES** > PROMUSCIS
**PROMUSCIS** *n* proboscis of certain insects
**PRONAOI** > PRONAOS
**PRONAOS** *n* inner area of the portico of a classical temple
**PRONATE** *vb* turn (a limb, hand, or foot) so that the palm or sole is directed downwards
**PRONATED** > PRONATE
**PRONATES** > PRONATE
**PRONATING** > PRONATE
**PRONATION** > PRONATE
**PRONATOR** *n* any muscle whose contractions produce or affect pronation
**PRONATORS** > PRONATOR
**PRONE** *n* sermon
**PRONELY** > PRONE
**PRONENESS** > PRONE
**PRONEPHRA** *n* parts of the kidneys of lower vertebrates
**PRONER** > PRONE
**PRONES** > PRONE
**PRONEST** > PRONE
**PRONEUR** *n* flatterer
**PRONEURS** > PRONEUR
**PRONG** *n* one spike of a fork or similar instrument ▷ *vb* prick or spear with or as if with a prong
**PRONGBUCK** *n* horned N American ruminant
**PRONGED** > PRONG
**PRONGHORN** *n* ruminant mammal inhabiting rocky deserts of North America and having small branched horns
**PRONGING** > PRONG
**PRONGS** > PRONG
**PRONK** *vb* jump straight up
**PRONKED** > PRONK
**PRONKING** > PRONK
**PRONKS** > PRONK
**PRONOTA** > PRONOTUM

**PRONOTAL** > PRONOTUM
**PRONOTUM** *n* notum of the prothorax of an insect
**PRONOUN** *n* word, such as *she* or *it*, used to replace a noun
**PRONOUNCE** *vb* form the sounds of (words or letters), esp clearly or in a particular way
**PRONOUNS** > PRONOUN
**PRONTO** *adv* at once
**PRONUCLEI** *n* nuclei of mature ova or spermatozoa before fertilization
**PRONUNCIO** *n* papal ambassador
**PROO** *interj* (to a horse) stop!
**PROOEMION** *n* preface
**PROOEMIUM** *n* preface
**PROOF** *n* evidence that shows that something is true or has happened ▷ *adj* able to withstand ▷ *vb* take a proof from (type matter)
**PROOFED** > PROOF
**PROOFER** *n* reader of proofs
**PROOFERS** > PROOFER
**PROOFING** > PROOF
**PROOFINGS** > PROOF
**PROOFLESS** > PROOF
**PROOFREAD** *vb* read and correct (printer's proofs)
**PROOFROOM** *n* room for proofreading
**PROOFS** > PROOF
**PROOTIC** *n* bone in front of ear
**PROOTICS** > PROOTIC
**PROP** *vb* support (something) so that it stays upright or in place ▷ *n* pole, beam, etc used as a support
**PROPAGATE** *vb* spread (information and ideas)
**PROPAGE** *vb* propagate
**PROPAGED** > PROPAGE
**PROPAGES** > PROPAGE
**PROPAGING** > PROPAGE
**PROPAGULA** > PROPAGULE
**PROPAGULE** *n* plant part, such as a bud, that becomes detached from the rest of the plant and grows into a new plant
**PROPALE** *vb* publish (something)
**PROPALED** > PROPALE
**PROPALES** > PROPALE
**PROPALING** > PROPALE
**PROPANE** *n* flammable gas found in petroleum and used as a fuel
**PROPANES** > PROPANE
**PROPANOIC** as in *propanoic acid* colourless liquid carboxylic acid
**PROPANOL** *n* colourless alcohol
**PROPANOLS** > PROPANOL
**PROPANONE** *n* systematic

name of acetone
**PROPEL** *vb* cause to move forward
**PROPELLED** > PROPEL
**PROPELLER** *n* revolving shaft with blades for driving a ship or aircraft
**PROPELLOR** *same as* > PROPELLER
**PROPELS** > PROPEL
**PROPEND** *vb* be inclined or disposed
**PROPENDED** > PROPEND
**PROPENDS** > PROPEND
**PROPENE** *n* colourless gaseous alkene obtained by cracking petroleum
**PROPENES** > PROPENE
**PROPENOIC** as in *propenoic acid* systematic name of acrylic acid
**PROPENOL** *n* liquid used to make allylic alcohol
**PROPENOLS** > PROPENOL
**PROPENSE** *adj* inclining forward
**PROPENYL** *n* three-carbon radical
**PROPER** *adj* real or genuine ▷ *n* service or psalm regarded as appropriate to a specific day, season, etc
**PROPERDIN** *n* protein present in blood serum that, acting with complement, is involved in the destruction of alien cells, such as bacteria
**PROPERER** > PROPER
**PROPEREST** > PROPER
**PROPERLY** > PROPER
**PROPERS** > PROPER
**PROPERTY** *same as* > PROPRIUM
**PROPHAGE** *n* virus that exists in a bacterial cell and undergoes division with its host without destroying it
**PROPHAGES** > PROPHAGE
**PROPHASE** *n* first stage of mitosis, during which the nuclear membrane disappears and the nuclear material resolves itself into chromosomes
**PROPHASES** > PROPHASE
**PROPHASIC** > PROPHASE
**PROPHECY** *n* prediction
**PROPHESY** *vb* foretell
**PROPHET** *n* person supposedly chosen by God to spread His word
**PROPHETIC** *adj* foretelling what will happen
**PROPHETS** > PROPHET
**PROPHYLL** *n* leaf-shaped plant structure
**PROPHYLLS** > PROPHYLL
**PROPIONIC** as in *propionic acid* former name for propanoic acid
**PROPJET** *another name for* > TURBOPROP

**PROPJETS** > PROPJET
**PROPMAN** *n* member of the stage crew in charge of the stage props
**PROPMEN** > PROPMAN
**PROPODEON** *n* part of an insect's thorax
**PROPODEUM** *variant of* > PROPODEON
**PROPOLIS** *n* greenish-brown resinous aromatic substance collected by bees from the buds of trees for use in the construction of hives
**PROPONE** *vb* propose or put forward, esp before a court
**PROPONED** > PROPONE
**PROPONENT** *n* person who argues in favour of something
**PROPONES** > PROPONE
**PROPONING** > PROPONE
**PROPOSAL** *n* act of proposing
**PROPOSALS** > PROPOSAL
**PROPOSE** *vb* put forward for consideration
**PROPOSED** > PROPOSE
**PROPOSER** > PROPOSE
**PROPOSERS** > PROPOSE
**PROPOSES** > PROPOSE
**PROPOSING** > PROPOSE
**PROPOSITA** *n* woman from whom a line of descent is traced
**PROPOSITI** *n* people from whom lines of descent are traced
**PROPOUND** *vb* put forward for consideration
**PROPOUNDS** > PROPOUND
**PROPPANT** *n* material used in the oil extraction process
**PROPPANTS** > PROPPANT
**PROPPED** > PROP
**PROPPING** > PROP
**PROPRETOR** *n* (in ancient Rome) citizen, esp an ex-praetor, granted a praetor's imperium, to be exercised outside Rome
**PROPRIA** > PROPRIUM
**PROPRIETY** *n* quality of being appropriate or fitting
**PROPRIUM** *n* attribute that is not essential to a species but is common and peculiar to it
**PROPS** > PROP
**PROPTOSES** > PROPTOSIS
**PROPTOSIS** *n* forward displacement of an organ or part, such as the eyeball
**PROPULSOR** *n* propeller
**PROPYL** *n* of, consisting of, or containing the monovalent group of atoms $C_3H_7$-
**PROPYLA** > PROPYLON
**PROPYLAEA** *n* porticos, esp those that form the

entrances to temples
**PROPYLENE** n gas found in petroleum and used to produce many organic compounds
**PROPYLIC** > PROPYL
**PROPYLITE** n altered andesite or similar rock containing calcite, chlorite, etc, produced by the action of hot water
**PROPYLON** n portico, esp one that forms the entrance to a temple
**PROPYLONS** > PROPYLON
**PROPYLS** > PROPYL
**PRORATE** vb divide, assess, or distribute (something) proportionately
**PRORATED** > PRORATE
**PRORATES** > PRORATE
**PRORATING** > PRORATE
**PRORATION** > PRORATE
**PRORE** n forward part of ship
**PRORECTOR** n official in German academia
**PROREFORM** adj in favour of or supporting reform, esp within politics
**PRORES** > PRORE
**PROROGATE** vb discontinue legislative meetings
**PROROGUE** vb suspend (parliament) without dissolving it
**PROROGUED** > PROROGUE
**PROROGUES** > PROROGUE
**PROS** > PRO
**PROSAIC** adj lacking imagination, dull
**PROSAICAL** same as > PROSAIC
**PROSAISM** n prosaic quality or style
**PROSAISMS** > PROSAISM
**PROSAIST** > PROSAISM
**PROSAISTS** > PROSAISM
**PROSATEUR** n writer of prose
**PROSCENIA** n arches or openings separating stages from auditoria together with the areas immediately in front of the arches
**PROSCRIBE** vb prohibit, outlaw
**PROSCRIPT** n proscription or prohibition
**PROSE** n ordinary speech or writing in contrast to poetry ▷ vb speak or write in a tedious style
**PROSECT** vb dissect a cadaver for a public demonstration
**PROSECTED** > PROSECT
**PROSECTOR** n person who prepares or dissects anatomical subjects for demonstration
**PROSECTS** > PROSECT
**PROSECUTE** vb bring a

criminal charge against
**PROSED** > PROSE
**PROSELIKE** > PROSE
**PROSELYTE** n recent convert
**PROSEMAN** n writer of prose
**PROSEMEN** > PROSEMAN
**PROSER** n writer of prose
**PROSERS** > PROSER
**PROSES** > PROSE
**PROSEUCHA** n place of prayer
**PROSEUCHE** n prayer
**PROSIER** > PROSY
**PROSIEST** > PROSY
**PROSIFIED** > PROSIFY
**PROSIFIES** > PROSIFY
**PROSIFY** vb write prose
**PROSILY** > PROSY
**PROSIMIAN** n any primate of the primitive suborder Prosimii, including lemurs, lorises, and tarsiers ▷ adj of, relating to, or belonging to the Prosimii
**PROSINESS** > PROSY
**PROSING** > PROSE
**PROSINGS** > PROSE
**PROSIT** interj good health! cheers!
**PROSO** n millet
**PROSODIAL** adj of prosody
**PROSODIAN** n writer of prose
**PROSODIC** > PROSODY
**PROSODIES** > PROSODY
**PROSODIST** > PROSODY
**PROSODY** n study of poetic metre and structure
**PROSOMA** n head and thorax of an arachnid
**PROSOMAL** > PROSOMA
**PROSOMAS** > PROSOMA
**PROSOMATA** > PROSOMA
**PROSOPON** n (in Christianity) manifestation of any of the persons of the Trinity
**PROSOPONS** > PROSOPON
**PROSOS** > PROSO
**PROSPECT** n something anticipated ▷ vb explore, esp for gold
**PROSPECTS** > PROSPECT
**PROSPER** vb be successful
**PROSPERED** > PROSPER
**PROSPERS** > PROSPER
**PROSS** n prostitute
**PROSSES** > PROSS
**PROSSIE** n prostitute
**PROSSIES** > PROSSIE
**PROST** same as > PROSIT
**PROSTATE** n gland in male mammals that surrounds the neck of the bladder ▷ adj of or relating to the prostate gland
**PROSTATES** > PROSTATE
**PROSTATIC** same as > PROSTATE
**PROSTERNA** n sternums or thoraces of insects
**PROSTIE** n prostitute
**PROSTIES** > PROSTIE

**PROSTOMIA** n lobes at the head ends of earthworms and other annelids
**PROSTRATE** adj lying face downwards ▷ vb lie face downwards
**PROSTYLE** adj (of a building) having a row of columns in front, esp as in the portico of a Greek temple ▷ n prostyle building, portico, etc
**PROSTYLES** > PROSTYLE
**PROSUMER** n amateur user of electronic equipment suitable for professionals
**PROSUMERS** > PROSUMER
**PROSY** adj dull and long-winded
**PROTAMIN** same as > PROTAMINE
**PROTAMINE** n any of a group of basic simple proteins that occur, in association with nucleic acids, in the sperm of some fish
**PROTAMINS** > PROTAMIN
**PROTANDRY** n condition (in hermaphrodite plants) of maturing the anthers before the stigma
**PROTANOPE** n person with type of colour blindness
**PROTASES** > PROTASIS
**PROTASIS** n antecedent of a conditional statement
**PROTATIC** > PROTASIS
**PROTEA** n African shrub with showy flowers
**PROTEAN** adj constantly changing ▷ n creature that can change shape
**PROTEANS** > PROTEAN
**PROTEAS** > PROTEA
**PROTEASE** n any enzyme involved in proteolysis
**PROTEASES** > PROTEASE
**PROTECT** vb defend from trouble, harm, or loss
**PROTECTED** > PROTECT
**PROTECTER** same as > PROTECTOR
**PROTECTOR** n person or thing that protects
**PROTECTS** > PROTECT
**PROTEGE** n person who is protected and helped by another
**PROTEGEE** n woman or girl who is protected and helped by another
**PROTEGEES** > PROTEGEE
**PROTEGES** > PROTEGE
**PROTEI** > PROTEUS
**PROTEID** n protein
**PROTEIDE** variant of > PROTEID
**PROTEIDES** > PROTEIDE
**PROTEIDS** > PROTEID
**PROTEIN** n any of a group of complex organic compounds that are essential for life

**PROTEINIC** > PROTEIN
**PROTEINS** > PROTEIN
**PROTEND** vb hold out or stretch
**PROTENDED** > PROTEND
**PROTENDS** > PROTEND
**PROTENSE** n extension
**PROTENSES** > PROTENSE
**PROTEOME** n full complement of proteins that occur within a cell, tissue, or organism
**PROTEOMES** > PROTEOME
**PROTEOMIC** > PROTEOME
**PROTEOSE** n compounds formed during proteolysis that is less complex than metaproteins but more so than peptones
**PROTEOSES** > PROTEOSE
**PROTEST** n declaration or demonstration of objection ▷ vb object, disagree
**PROTESTED** > PROTEST
**PROTESTER** > PROTEST
**PROTESTOR** > PROTEST
**PROTESTS** > PROTEST
**PROTEUS** n aerobic bacterium
**PROTEUSES** > PROTEUS
**PROTHALLI** n small flat free-living gametophtyes in ferns, club mosses etc
**PROTHESES** > PROTHESIS
**PROTHESIS** n process in the development of a language by which a phoneme or syllable is prefixed to a word to facilitate pronunciation
**PROTHETIC** > PROTHESIS
**PROTHORAX** n first segment of the thorax of an insect, which bears the first pair of walking legs
**PROTHYL** variant of > PROTYLE
**PROTHYLS** > PROTHYL
**PROTIST** n (in some classification systems) any organism belonging to the kingdom Protista
**PROTISTAN** > PROTIST
**PROTISTIC** > PROTIST
**PROTISTS** > PROTIST
**PROTIUM** n most common isotope of hydrogen
**PROTIUMS** > PROTIUM
**PROTOAVIS** n bird-like fossil
**PROTOCOL** n rules of behaviour for formal occasions
**PROTOCOLS** > PROTOCOL
**PROTODERM** n outer primary meristem of a plant
**PROTOGINE** n type of granite
**PROTOGYNY** n (in hermaphrodite plants and animals) condition of producing female gametes

before male ones
**PROTON** n positively
charged particle in the
nucleus of an atom
**PROTONATE** vb provide
atom with proton
**PROTONEMA** n branched
threadlike structure that
grows from a moss spore
and eventually develops
into the moss plant
**PROTONIC** adj (of a solvent,
such as water) able to
donate hydrogen ions to
solute molecules
**PROTONS** > PROTON
**PROTOPOD** n part of
crustacean's leg
**PROTOPODS** > PROTOPOD
**PROTORE** n primary mineral
deposit
**PROTORES** > PROTORE
**PROTOSTAR** n cloud of
interstellar gas and dust
that gradually collapses,
forming a hot dense core,
and evolves into a star
once nuclear fusion can
occur in the core
**PROTOTYPE** n original or
model to be copied or
developed
**PROTOXID** variant
of > PROTOXIDE
**PROTOXIDE** n oxide of an
element that contains the
smallest amount of oxygen
of any of its oxides
**PROTOXIDS** > PROTOXID
**PROTOZOA** > PROTOZOAN
**PROTOZOAL** > PROTOZOAN
**PROTOZOAN** n microscopic
one-celled creature
▷ adj of or relating to
protozoans
**PROTOZOIC** > PROTOZOAN
**PROTOZOON** same
as > PROTOZOAN
**PROTRACT** vb lengthen or
extend (a situation etc)
**PROTRACTS** > PROTRACT
**PROTRADE** adj in favour of
trade
**PROTRUDE** vb stick out,
project
**PROTRUDED** > PROTRUDE
**PROTRUDES** > PROTRUDE
**PROTYL** same as > PROTYLE
**PROTYLE** n hypothetical
primitive substance
from which the chemical
elements were supposed
to have been formed
**PROTYLES** > PROTYLE
**PROTYLS** > PROTYL
**PROUD** adj feeling pleasure
and satisfaction
**PROUDER** > PROUD
**PROUDEST** > PROUD
**PROUDFUL** adj full of pride
**PROUDISH** adj rather proud
**PROUDLY** > PROUD
**PROUDNESS** > PROUD
**PROUL** variant of > PROWL

**PROULED** > PROUL
**PROULER** Scots variant
of > PROWLER
**PROULERS** > PROULER
**PROULING** > PROUL
**PROULS** > PROUL
**PROUNION** adj in favour
of or supporting the
constitutional union
between two or more
countries
**PROUSTITE** n red mineral
consisting of silver arsenic
sulphide in hexagonal
crystalline form
**PROVABLE** > PROVE
**PROVABLY** > PROVE
**PROVAND** n food
**PROVANDS** > PROVAND
**PROVANT** vb supply with
provisions
**PROVANTED** > PROVANT
**PROVANTS** > PROVANT
**PROVE** vb establish the
validity of
**PROVEABLE** > PROVE
**PROVEABLY** > PROVEABLE
**PROVED** > PROVE
**PROVEDOR** variant
of > PROVEDORE
**PROVEDORE** n purveyor
**PROVEDORS** > PROVEDOR
**PROVEN** > PROVE
**PROVEND** same as > PROVAND
**PROVENDER** n fodder
**PROVENDS** > PROVEND
**PROVENLY** > PROVE
**PROVER** > PROVE
**PROVERB** n short saying
that expresses a truth or
gives a warning ▷ vb utter
or describe (something) in
the form of a proverb
**PROVERBED** > PROVERB
**PROVERBS** > PROVERB
**PROVERS** > PROVE
**PROVES** > PROVE
**PROVIANT** variant
of > PROVAND
**PROVIANTS** > PROVIANT
**PROVIDE** vb make available
**PROVIDED** > PROVIDE
**PROVIDENT** adj thrifty
**PROVIDER** > PROVIDE
**PROVIDERS** > PROVIDE
**PROVIDES** > PROVIDE
**PROVIDING** > PROVIDE
**PROVIDOR** variant
of > PROVEDORE
**PROVIDORS** > PROVIDOR
**PROVINCE** n area governed
as a unit of a country or
empire
**PROVINCES** > PROVINCE
**PROVINE** vb plant branch
of vine in ground for
propagation
**PROVINED** > PROVINE
**PROVINES** > PROVINE
**PROVING** > PROVE
**PROVINGS** > PROVE
**PROVINING** > PROVINE
**PROVIRAL** > PROVIRUS
**PROVIRUS** n inactive form

of a virus in a host cell
**PROVISION** n act of
supplying something ▷ vb
supply with food
**PROVISO** n condition,
stipulation
**PROVISOES** > PROVISO
**PROVISOR** n person who
receives provision
**PROVISORS** > PROVISOR
**PROVISORY** adj containing
a proviso
**PROVISOS** > PROVISO
**PROVOCANT** n provocateur;
one who deliberately
behaves controversially
to provoke argument or
other strong reactions
**PROVOKE** vb deliberately
anger
**PROVOKED** > PROVOKE
**PROVOKER** > PROVOKE
**PROVOKERS** > PROVOKE
**PROVOKES** > PROVOKE
**PROVOKING** > PROVOKE
**PROVOLONE** n mellow,
pale yellow, soft, and
sometimes smoked
cheese, made of cow's
milk: usually moulded in
the shape of a pear
**PROVOST** n head of certain
university colleges in
Britain
**PROVOSTRY** n office of
provost
**PROVOSTS** > PROVOST
**PROW** n bow of a vessel
▷ adj gallant
**PROWAR** adj in favour of or
supporting war
**PROWER** > PROW
**PROWESS** n superior skill or
ability
**PROWESSES** > PROWESS
**PROWEST** > PROW
**PROWL** vb move stealthily
around a place as if in
search of prey or plunder
▷ n prowling
**PROWLED** > PROWL
**PROWLER** > PROWL
**PROWLERS** > PROWL
**PROWLING** > PROWL
**PROWLINGS** > PROWL
**PROWLS** > PROWL
**PROWS** > PROW
**PROXEMIC** > PROXEMICS
**PROXEMICS** n study of
spatial interrelationships
in humans or in
populations of animals of
the same species
**PROXIES** > PROXY
**PROXIMAL** same
as > PROXIMATE
**PROXIMATE** adj next or
nearest in space or time
**PROXIMITY** n nearness in
space or time
**PROXIMO** adv in or during
the next or coming month
**PROXY** n person authorized
to act on behalf of

someone else
**PROYN** obsolete spelling
of > PRUNE
**PROYNE** obsolete spelling
of > PRUNE
**PROYNES** > PROYNE
**PROYNS** > PROYNE
**PROZYMITE** n Christian
using leavened bread for
the Eucharist
**PRUDE** n person who is
excessively modest, prim,
or proper
**PRUDENCE** n caution in
practical affairs
**PRUDENCES** > PRUDENCE
**PRUDENT** adj cautious,
discreet, and sensible
**PRUDENTLY** > PRUDENT
**PRUDERIES** > PRUDE
**PRUDERY** > PRUDE
**PRUDES** > PRUDE
**PRUDISH** > PRUDE
**PRUDISHLY** > PRUDE
**PRUH** variant of > PROO
**PRUINA** n woolly white
covering on some lichens
**PRUINAS** > PRUINA
**PRUINE** obsolete spelling
of > PRUNE
**PRUINES** > PRUNE
**PRUINOSE** adj coated with
a powdery or waxy bloom
**PRUNABLE** > PRUNE
**PRUNE** n dried plum ▷ vb
cut off dead parts or
excessive branches from (a
tree or plant)
**PRUNED** > PRUNE
**PRUNELLA** n strong fabric,
esp a twill-weave worsted,
used for gowns and the
uppers of some shoes
**PRUNELLAS** > PRUNELLA
**PRUNELLE** same
as > PRUNELLA
**PRUNELLES** > PRUNELLE
**PRUNELLO** same
as > PRUNELLA
**PRUNELLOS** > PRUNELLO
**PRUNER** > PRUNE
**PRUNERS** > PRUNE
**PRUNES** > PRUNE
**PRUNING** > PRUNE
**PRUNINGS** > PRUNE
**PRUNT** n glass
ornamentation
**PRUNTED** > PRUNT
**PRUNTS** > PRUNT
**PRUNUS** n type of
ornamental tree or shrub
**PRUNUSES** > PRUNUS
**PRURIENCE** > PRURIENT
**PRURIENCY** n sexual desire
**PRURIENT** adj excessively
interested in sexual
matters
**PRURIGO** n chronic
inflammatory disease of
the skin characterized by
the formation of papules
and intense itching
**PRURIGOS** > PRURIGO
**PRURITIC** > PRURITUS

PRURITUS *n* any intense sensation of itching

PRUSIK *n* sliding knot that locks under pressure and can be used to form a loop in which a climber can place his or her foot in order to stand or ascend a rope ▷ *vb* climb (up a standing rope) using prusiks

PRUSIKED > PRUSIK

PRUSIKING > PRUSIK

PRUSIKS > PRUSIK

PRUSSIATE *n* any cyanide, ferrocyanide, or ferricyanide

PRUSSIC as in *prussic acid* weakly acidic extremely poisonous aqueous solution of hydrogen cyanide

PRUTA *same as* > PRUTAH

PRUTAH *n* former Israeli coin

PRUTOT > PRUTAH

PRUTOTH > PRUTAH

PRY *vb* make an impertinent or uninvited inquiry into a private matter ▷ *n* act of prying

PRYER *same as* > PRIER

PRYERS > PRYER

PRYING > PRY

PRYINGLY > PRY

PRYINGS > PRY

PRYS *old variant of* > PRICE

PRYSE *old variant of* > PRICE

PRYTANEA > PRYTANEUM

PRYTANEUM *n* public hall of a city in ancient Greece

PRYTHEE *same as* > PRITHEE

PSALM *n* sacred song ▷ *vb* sing a psalm

PSALMBOOK *n* book of psalms

PSALMED > PSALM

PSALMIC > PSALM

PSALMING > PSALM

PSALMIST *n* writer of psalms

PSALMISTS > PSALMIST

PSALMODIC > PSALMODY

PSALMODY *n* singing of sacred music

PSALMS > PSALM

PSALTER *n* devotional or liturgical book containing a version of Psalms

PSALTERIA *n* omasums

PSALTERS > PSALTER

PSALTERY *n* ancient instrument played by plucking strings

PSALTRESS *n* woman who sings psalms

PSALTRIES > PSALTRY

PSALTRY *same as* > PSALTERY

PSAMMITE *rare name for* > SANDSTONE

PSAMMITES > PSAMMITE

PSAMMITIC > PSAMMITE

PSAMMON *n* community

of microscopic life forms living between grains of sand on shores

PSAMMONS > PSAMMON

PSCHENT *n* ancient Egyptian crown

PSCHENTS > PSCHENT

PSELLISM *n* stammering

PSELLISMS > PSELLISM

PSEPHISM *n* proposition adopted by a majority vote

PSEPHISMS > PSEPHISM

PSEPHITE *n* any rock, such as a breccia, that consists of large fragments embedded in a finer matrix

PSEPHITES > PSEPHITE

PSEPHITIC > PSEPHITE

PSEUD *n* pretentious person

PSEUDAXES > PSEUDAXIS

PSEUDAXIS *another name for* > SYMPODIUM

PSEUDERY *n* pretentious talk

PSEUDISH > PSEUD

PSEUDO *n* pretentious person

PSEUDONYM *n* fictitious name adopted esp by an author

PSEUDOPOD *n* temporary projection from the body of a single-celled animal

PSEUDOS > PSEUDO

PSEUDS > PSEUD

PSHAW *n* exclamation of disgust, impatience, disbelief, etc

PSHAWS > PSHAW

PSI *n* 23rd letter of the Greek alphabet

PSILOCIN *n* hallucinogenic substance

PSILOCINS > PSILOCIN

PSILOSES > PSILOSIS

PSILOSIS *n* disease of the small intestine

PSILOTIC > PSILOSIS

PSION *n* type of elementary particle

PSIONIC > PSIONICS

PSIONICS *n* study of the practical use of psychic powers

PSIONS > PSION

PSIS > PSI

PSOAE > PSOAS

PSOAI > PSOAS

PSOAS *n* either of two muscles of the loins that aid in flexing and rotating the thigh

PSOATIC > PSOAS

PSOCID *n* tiny wingless insect

PSOCIDS > PSOCID

PSORA *n* itching skin complaint

PSORALEA *n* any plant of the tropical and subtropical leguminous genus *Psoralea*, having curly leaves, white or

purple flowers, and short one-seeded pods

PSORALEAS > PSORALEA

PSORALEN *n* treatment for some skin diseases

PSORALENS > PSORALEN

PSORAS > PSORA

PSORIASES > PSORIASIS

PSORIASIS *n* skin disease with reddish spots and patches covered with silvery scales

PSORIATIC > PSORIASIS

PSORIC > PSORA

PSST *interj* sound made to attract someone's attention, esp without others noticing

PST *interj* sound made to attract someone's attention

PSYCH *vb* psychoanalyse

PSYCHE *same as* > PSYCH

PSYCHED > PSYCH

PSYCHES > PSYCH

PSYCHIC *adj* having mental powers which cannot be explained by natural laws ▷ *n* person with psychic powers

PSYCHICAL > PSYCHIC

PSYCHICS > PSYCHIC

PSYCHING > PSYCH

PSYCHISM *n* belief in a universal soul

PSYCHISMS > PSYCHISM

PSYCHIST > PSYCHISM

PSYCHISTS > PSYCHISM

PSYCHO *n* psychopath

PSYCHOGAS *n* gas with a mind-altering effect

PSYCHOID *n* name for an animal's innate impetus to perform actions

PSYCHOIDS > PSYCHOID

PSYCHOS > PSYCHO

PSYCHOSES > PSYCHOSIS

PSYCHOSIS *n* severe mental disorder in which the sufferer's contact with reality becomes distorted

PSYCHOTIC *adj* of, relating to, or characterized by psychosis ▷ *n* person suffering from psychosis

PSYCHS > PSYCH

PSYLLA *same as* > PSYLLID

PSYLLAS > PSYLLA

PSYLLID *n* any homopterous insect of the family *Psyllidae*, which comprises the jumping plant lice

PSYLLIDS > PSYLLID

PSYLLIUM *n* grain, the husks of which are used medicinally as a laxative and to reduce blood cholesterol levels

PSYLLIUMS > PSYLLIUM

PSYOP *n* psychological operation

PSYOPS > PSYOP

PSYWAR *n* psychological

warfare

PSYWARS > PSYWAR

PTARMIC *n* material that causes sneezing

PTARMICS > PTARMIC

PTARMIGAN *n* bird of the grouse family which turns white in winter

PTERIA > PTERION

PTERIDINE *n* yellow crystalline base

PTERIN *n* compound such as folic acid

PTERINS > PTERIN

PTERION *n* point on the side of the skull where a number of bones meet

PTEROPOD *n* small marine gastropod mollusc in which the foot is expanded into two winglike lobes for swimming and the shell is absent or thin-walled

PTEROPODS > PTEROPOD

PTEROSAUR *n* extinct flying reptile

PTERYGIA > PTERYGIUM

PTERYGIAL *adj* of or relating to a fin or wing

PTERYGIUM *n* abnormal tissue over corner of eye

PTERYGOID *n* either of two long bony plates extending downwards from each side of the sphenoid bone within the skull

PTERYLA *n* any of the tracts of skin that bear contour feathers, arranged in lines along the body of a bird

PTERYLAE > PTERYLA

PTILOSES > PTILOSIS

PTILOSIS *n* falling out of eye lashes

PTISAN *n* grape juice drained off without pressure

PTISANS > PTISAN

PTOMAIN *same as* > PTOMAINE

PTOMAINE *n* any of a group of poisonous alkaloids found in decaying matter

PTOMAINES > PTOMAINE

PTOMAINIC > PTOMAINE

PTOMAINS > PTOMAIN

PTOOEY *interj* imitation of the sound of spitting

PTOSES > PTOSIS

PTOSIS *n* prolapse or drooping of a part, esp the eyelid

PTOTIC > PTOSIS

PTUI *same as* > PTOOEY

PTYALIN *n* amylase secreted in the saliva of man and other animals

PTYALINS > PTYALIN

PTYALISE *same as* > PTYALIZE

PTYALISED > PTYALISE

PTYALISES > PTYALISE

PTYALISM *n* excessive

secretion of saliva
**PTYALISMS** > PTYALISM
**PTYALIZE** *vb* expel saliva from the mouth
**PTYALIZED** > PTYALIZE
**PTYALIZES** > PTYALIZE
**PTYXES** > PTYXIS
**PTYXIS** *n* folding of a leaf in a bud
**PUB** *n* building with a bar licensed to sell alcoholic drinks ▷ *vb* visit a pub or pubs
**PUBBED** > PUB
**PUBBING** > PUB
**PUBE** *n* pubic hair
**PUBERAL** *adj* relating to puberty
**PUBERTAL** > PUBERTY
**PUBERTIES** > PUBERTY
**PUBERTY** *n* beginning of sexual maturity
**PUBES** > PUBE
**PUBESCENT** *adj* reaching or having reached puberty
**PUBIC** *adj* of the lower abdomen
**PUBIS** *n* one of the three sections of the hipbone that forms part of the pelvis
**PUBLIC** *adj* of or concerning the people as a whole ▷ *n* community, people in general
**PUBLICAN** *n* person who owns or runs a pub
**PUBLICANS** > PUBLICAN
**PUBLICISE** *same as* > PUBLICIZE
**PUBLICIST** *n* person, esp a press agent or journalist, who publicizes something
**PUBLICITY** *n* process or information used to arouse public attention
**PUBLICIZE** *vb* bring to public attention
**PUBLICLY** *adv* in a public manner
**PUBLICS** > PUBLIC
**PUBLISH** *vb* produce and issue (printed matter) for sale
**PUBLISHED** > PUBLISH
**PUBLISHER** *n* company or person that publishes books, periodicals, music, etc
**PUBLISHES** > PUBLISH
**PUBS** > PUB
**PUCAN** *n* traditional Connemara open sailing boat
**PUCANS** > PUCAN
**PUCCOON** *n* any of several North American boraginaceous plants of the genus *Lithospermum*, esp *L. canescens*, that yield a red dye
**PUCCOONS** > PUCCOON
**PUCE** *adj* purplish-brown ▷ *n* colour varying from

deep red to dark purplish-brown
**PUCELAGE** *n* virginity
**PUCELAGES** > PUCELAGE
**PUCELLE** *n* maid or virgin
**PUCELLES** > PUCELLE
**PUCER** > PUCE
**PUCES** > PUCE
**PUCEST** > PUCE
**PUCK** *n* mischievous or evil spirit ▷ *vb* strike (the ball) in hurling
**PUCKA** *same as* > PUKKA
**PUCKED** > PUCK
**PUCKER** *vb* gather into wrinkles ▷ *n* wrinkle or crease
**PUCKERED** > PUCKER
**PUCKERER** > PUCKER
**PUCKERERS** > PUCKER
**PUCKERIER** > PUCKERY
**PUCKERING** > PUCKER
**PUCKEROOD** *adj* ruined
**PUCKERS** > PUCKER
**PUCKERY** *adj* (of wine) high in tannins
**PUCKFIST** *n* puffball
**PUCKFISTS** > PUCKFIST
**PUCKING** > PUCK
**PUCKISH** > PUCK
**PUCKISHLY** > PUCK
**PUCKLE** *n* early type of machine gun
**PUCKLES** > PUCKLE
**PUCKS** > PUCK
**PUD** *short for* > PUDDING
**PUDDEN** *dialect spelling of* > PUDDING
**PUDDENS** > PUDDEN
**PUDDER** *vb* make bother or fuss
**PUDDERED** > PUDDER
**PUDDERING** > PUDDER
**PUDDERS** > PUDDER
**PUDDIES** > PUDDY
**PUDDING** *n* dessert, esp a cooked one served hot
**PUDDINGS** > PUDDING
**PUDDINGY** > PUDDING
**PUDDLE** *n* small pool of water, esp of rain ▷ *vb* make (clay etc) into puddle
**PUDDLED** > PUDDLE
**PUDDLER** > PUDDLE
**PUDDLERS** > PUDDLE
**PUDDLES** > PUDDLE
**PUDDLIER** > PUDDLE
**PUDDLIEST** > PUDDLE
**PUDDLING** *n* process for converting pig iron into wrought iron by heating it with ferric oxide in a furnace to oxidize the carbon
**PUDDLINGS** > PUDDLING
**PUDDLY** > PUDDLE
**PUDDOCK** *same as* > PADDOCK
**PUDDOCKS** > PUDDOCK
**PUDDY** *n* paw
**PUDENCIES** > PUDENCY
**PUDENCY** *n* modesty, shame, or prudishness
**PUDENDA** > PUDENDUM
**PUDENDAL** > PUDENDUM

**PUDENDOUS** *adj* shameful
**PUDENDUM** *n* human external genital organs collectively, esp of a female
**PUDENT** *adj* lacking in ostentation; humble
**PUDGE** *same as* > PODGE
**PUDGES** > PUDGE
**PUDGIER** > PUDGY
**PUDGIEST** > PUDGY
**PUDGILY** > PUDGY
**PUDGINESS** > PUDGY
**PUDGY** *adj* podgy
**PUDIBUND** *adj* prudish
**PUDIC** > PUDENDUM
**PUDICITY** *n* modesty
**PUDOR** *n* sense of shame
**PUDORS** > PUDOR
**PUDS** > PUD
**PUDSEY** *variant of* > PUDSY
**PUDSIER** > PUDSY
**PUDSIEST** > PUDSY
**PUDSY** *adj* plump
**PUDU** *n* diminutive Andean antelope with short straight horns and reddish-brown spotted coat
**PUDUS** > PUDU
**PUEBLO** *n* communal village, built by certain Indians of the southwestern US and parts of Latin America, consisting of one or more flat-roofed stone or adobe houses
**PUEBLOS** > PUEBLO
**PUER** *vb* steep hides in an alkaline substance from the dung of dogs
**PUERED** > PUER
**PUERILE** *adj* silly and childish
**PUERILELY** > PUERILE
**PUERILISM** *n* immature or childish behaviour by an adult
**PUERILITY** > PUERILE
**PUERING** > PUER
**PUERPERA** *n* woman who has recently given birth
**PUERPERAE** > PUERPERA
**PUERPERAL** *adj* concerning the period following childbirth
**PUERPERIA** *n* periods of around six weeks following childbirths when uteruses return to their normal size and shape
**PUERS** > PUER
**PUFF** *n* (sound of) short blast of breath, wind, etc ▷ *vb* blow or breathe in short quick draughts
**PUFFBALL** *n* ball-shaped fungus
**PUFFBALLS** > PUFFBALL
**PUFFBIRD** *n* brownish tropical American bird with a large head
**PUFFBIRDS** > PUFFBIRD

**PUFFED** > PUFF
**PUFFER** *n* person or thing that puffs
**PUFFERIES** > PUFFERY
**PUFFERS** > PUFFER
**PUFFERY** *n* exaggerated praise, esp in publicity or advertising
**PUFFIER** > PUFFY
**PUFFIEST** > PUFFY
**PUFFILY** > PUFFY
**PUFFIN** *n* black-and-white sea bird with a brightly-coloured beak
**PUFFINESS** > PUFFY
**PUFFING** > PUFF
**PUFFINGLY** > PUFF
**PUFFINGS** > PUFF
**PUFFINS** > PUFFIN
**PUFFS** > PUFF
**PUFFY** *adj* short of breath
**PUFTALOON** *n* Australian fried scone
**PUG** *n* small snub-nosed dog ▷ *vb* mix or knead (clay) with water to form a malleable mass or paste
**PUGAREE** *same as* > PUGGREE
**PUGAREES** > PUGAREE
**PUGGAREE** *same as* > PUGGREE
**PUGGAREES** > PUGGAREE
**PUGGED** > PUG
**PUGGERIES** > PUGGERY
**PUGGERY** *same as* > PUGGREE
**PUGGIE** *n* Scottish word for fruit machine
**PUGGIER** > PUGGY
**PUGGIES** > PUGGIE
**PUGGIEST** > PUGGY
**PUGGINESS** > PUGGY
**PUGGING** > PUG
**PUGGINGS** > PUG
**PUGGISH** > PUG
**PUGGLE** *vb* stir up by poking
**PUGGLED** > PUGGLE
**PUGGLES** > PUGGLE
**PUGGLING** > PUGGLE
**PUGGREE** *n* scarf, usually pleated, around the crown of some hats, esp sun helmets
**PUGGREES** > PUGGREE
**PUGGRIES** > PUGGRY
**PUGGRY** *same as* > PUGGREE
**PUGGY** *adj* sticky, claylike ▷ *n* term of endearment
**PUGH** *n* exclamation of disgust
**PUGHS** > PUGH
**PUGIL** *n* pinch or small handful
**PUGILISM** *n* art, practice, or profession of fighting with the fists
**PUGILISMS** > PUGILISM
**PUGILIST** > PUGILISM
**PUGILISTS** > PUGILISM
**PUGILS** > PUGIL
**PUGMARK** *n* trail of an animal
**PUGMARKS** > PUGMARK
**PUGNACITY** *n* readiness to fight

**PUGREE** *same as* > PUGGREE

**PUGREES** > PUGREE

**PUGS** > PUG

**PUH** *interj* exclamation expressing contempt or disgust

**PUHA** *n* sow thistle

**PUHAS** > PUHA

**PUIR** *Scottish word for* > POOR

**PUIRER** > PUIR

**PUIREST** > PUIR

**PUIRTITH** *n* poverty

**PUIRTITHS** > PUIRTITH

**PUISNE** *adj* (esp of a subordinate judge) of lower rank ▷ *n* judge of lower rank

**PUISNES** > PUISNE

**PUISNY** *adj* younger or inferior

**PUISSANCE** *n* showjumping competition that tests a horse's ability to jump large obstacles

**PUISSANT** *adj* powerful

**PUISSAUNT** *same as* > PUISSANT

**PUJA** *n* ritual in honour of the gods, performed either at home or in the mandir (temple)

**PUJAH** *same as* > PUJA

**PUJAHS** > PUJAH

**PUJAS** > PUJA

**PUKA** *in New Zealand English, same as* > BROADLEAF

**PUKATEA** *n* aromatic New Zealand tree, valued for its high-quality timber

**PUKATEAS** > PUKATEA

**PUKE** *vb* vomit ▷ *n* act of vomiting

**PUKED** > PUKE

**PUKEKO** *n* brightly coloured New Zealand wading bird

**PUKEKOS** > PUKEKO

**PUKER** *n* person who vomits

**PUKERS** > PUKER

**PUKES** > PUKE

**PUKING** > PUKE

**PUKKA** *adj* properly done, constructed, etc

**PUKU** *n* belly or stomach

**PUKUS** > PUKU

**PUL** *n* Afghan monetary unit worth one hundredth of an afghani

**PULA** *n* standard monetary unit of Botswana, divided into 100 thebe

**PULAO** *same as* > PILAU

**PULAOS** > PULAO

**PULAS** > PULA

**PULDRON** *same as* > PAULDRON

**PULDRONS** > PULDRON

**PULE** *vb* whine or whimper

**PULED** > PULE

**PULER** > PULE

**PULERS** > PULE

**PULES** > PULE

**PULI** > PUL

**PULICENE** *adj* flea-ridden

**PULICIDE** *n* flea-killing substance

**PULICIDES** > PULICIDE

**PULIER** > PULY

**PULIEST** > PULY

**PULIK** > PUL

**PULING** > PULE

**PULINGLY** > PULE

**PULINGS** > PULE

**PULIS** > PUL

**PULK** *same as* > PULKA

**PULKA** *n* reindeer-drawn sleigh

**PULKAS** > PULKA

**PULKHA** *same as* > PULKA

**PULKHAS** > PULKHA

**PULKS** > PULK

**PULL** *vb* exert force on (an object) to move it towards the source of the force ▷ *n* act of pulling

**PULLBACK** *n* act of pulling back

**PULLBACKS** > PULLBACK

**PULLED** > PULL

**PULLER** > PULL

**PULLERS** > PULL

**PULLET** *n* young hen

**PULLETS** > PULLET

**PULLEY** *n* wheel with a grooved rim in which a belt, chain, or piece of rope runs in order to lift weights by a downward pull

**PULLEYS** > PULLEY

**PULLI** > PULLUS

**PULLING** > PULL

**PULLMAN** *n* luxurious railway coach, esp a sleeping car

**PULLMANS** > PULLMAN

**PULLORUM** *as in pullorum disease* acute serious bacterial disease of very young birds

**PULLOUT** *n* removable section of a magazine, etc

**PULLOUTS** > PULLOUT

**PULLOVER** *n* sweater that is pulled on over the head

**PULLOVERS** > PULLOVER

**PULLS** > PULL

**PULLULATE** *vb* (of animals, etc) breed rapidly or abundantly

**PULLUP** *n* exercise in which the body is raised up by the arms pulling on a horizontal bar fixed above the head

**PULLUPS** > PULLUP

**PULLUS** *n* technical term for a chick or young bird

**PULMO** *n* lung

**PULMONARY** *adj* of the lungs

**PULMONATE** *adj* having lungs or lung-like organs ▷ *n* any pulmonate mollusc

**PULMONES** > PULMO

**PULMONIC** *adj* of or relating

to the lungs ▷ *n* person with lung disease

**PULMONICS** > PULMONIC

**PULMOTOR** *n* apparatus for pumping oxygen into the lungs during artificial respiration

**PULMOTORS** > PULMOTOR

**PULP** *n* soft wet substance made from crushed or beaten matter ▷ *vb* reduce to pulp

**PULPAL** > PULP

**PULPALLY** > PULP

**PULPBOARD** *n* board made from wood pulp

**PULPED** > PULP

**PULPER** > PULP

**PULPERS** > PULP

**PULPIER** > PULPY

**PULPIEST** > PULPY

**PULPIFIED** > PULPIFY

**PULPIFIES** > PULPIFY

**PULPIFY** *vb* reduce to pulp

**PULPILY** > PULPY

**PULPINESS** > PULPY

**PULPING** > PULP

**PULPIT** *n* raised platform for a preacher ▷ *vb* give a sermon

**PULPITAL** > PULPIT

**PULPITED** > PULPIT

**PULPITEER** *n* deliverer of sermon

**PULPITER** *n* preacher

**PULPITERS** > PULPITER

**PULPITING** > PULPIT

**PULPITRY** *n* art of delivering sermons

**PULPITS** > PULPIT

**PULPITUM** *n* stone screen dividing nave and choir

**PULPITUMS** > PULPITUM

**PULPLESS** > PULP

**PULPMILL** *n* mill making raw material for paper

**PULPMILLS** > PULPMILL

**PULPOUS** *n* soft and yielding

**PULPS** > PULP

**PULPSTONE** *n* calcified mass in a tooth cavity

**PULPWOOD** *n* pine, spruce, or any other soft wood used to make paper

**PULPWOODS** > PULPWOOD

**PULPY** *adj* having a soft or soggy consistency

**PULQUE** *n* light alcoholic drink from Mexico made from the juice of various agave plants, esp the maguey

**PULQUES** > PULQUE

**PULS** > PUL

**PULSANT** *adj* vibrant

**PULSAR** *n* small dense star which emits regular bursts of radio waves

**PULSARS** > PULSAR

**PULSATE** *vb* throb, quiver

**PULSATED** > PULSATE

**PULSATES** > PULSATE

**PULSATILE** *adj* beating

rhythmically

**PULSATING** > PULSATE

**PULSATION** *n* act of pulsating

**PULSATIVE** > PULSATE

**PULSATOR** *n* device that stimulates rhythmic motion of a body

**PULSATORS** > PULSATOR

**PULSATORY** *adj* of or relating to pulsation

**PULSE** *n* regular beating of blood through the arteries at each heartbeat ▷ *vb* beat, throb, or vibrate

**PULSED** > PULSE

**PULSEJET** *n* type of ramjet engine

**PULSEJETS** > PULSEJET

**PULSELESS** > PULSE

**PULSER** *n* thing that pulses

**PULSERS** > PULSER

**PULSES** > PULSE

**PULSIDGE** *archaic word for* > PULSE

**PULSIDGES** > PULSIDGE

**PULSIFIC** *adj* causing the pulse to increase

**PULSING** > PULSE

**PULSION** *n* act of driving forward

**PULSIONS** > PULSION

**PULSOJET** *same as* > PULSEJET

**PULSOJETS** > PULSOJET

**PULTAN** *n* native Indian regiment

**PULTANS** > PULTAN

**PULTON** *same as* > PULTAN

**PULTONS** > PULTON

**PULTOON** *same as* > PULTAN

**PULTOONS** > PULTOON

**PULTUN** *same as* > PULTAN

**PULTUNS** > PULTUN

**PULTURE** *n* food and drink claimed by foresters as their right from anyone within the limits of a given forest

**PULTURES** > PULTURE

**PULU** *n* substance from Hawaiian ferns, used for stuffing cushions, etc

**PULUS** > PULU

**PULVER** *vb* make into powder

**PULVERED** > PULVER

**PULVERINE** *n* ashes of the barilla plant

**PULVERING** > PULVER

**PULVERISE** *same as* > PULVERIZE

**PULVERIZE** *vb* reduce to fine pieces

**PULVEROUS** *adj* consisting of tiny particles

**PULVERS** > PULVER

**PULVIL** *vb* apply perfumed powder

**PULVILIO** *same as* > PULVILLO

**PULVILIOS** > PULVILIO

**PULVILLAR** *adj* like cushion

**PULVILLE** *same as* > PULVIL

PULVILLED > PULVIL
PULVILLES > PULVILLE
PULVILLI > PULVILLUS
PULVILLIO *same as* > PULVILLO
PULVILLO *n* perfume in the form of a powder
PULVILLOS > PULVILLO
PULVILLUS *n* small pad between the claws at the end of an insect's leg
PULVILS > PULVIL
PULVINAR *n* part of the thalamus
PULVINARS > PULVINAR
PULVINATE *adj* (of a frieze) curved convexly
PULVINI > PULVINUS
PULVINUS *n* swelling at the base of a leafstalk
PULWAR *n* light Indian river boat
PULWARS > PULWAR
PULY *adj* whiny
PUMA *n* large American wild cat with a greyish-brown coat
PUMAS > PUMA
PUMELO *same as* > POMELO
PUMELOS > PUMELO
PUMICATE *vb* pound fruit with pumice to make juice
PUMICATED > PUMICATE
PUMICATES > PUMICATE
PUMICE *n* light porous stone used for scouring ▷ *vb* rub or polish with pumice
PUMICED > PUMICE
PUMICEOUS > PUMICE
PUMICER > PUMICE
PUMICERS > PUMICE
PUMICES > PUMICE
PUMICING > PUMICE
PUMICITE *n* fine-grained variety of pumice
PUMICITES > PUMICITE
PUMIE *n* small stone
PUMIES > PUMIE
PUMMEL *vb* strike repeatedly with or as if with the fists
PUMMELED > PUMMEL
PUMMELING > PUMMEL
PUMMELLED > PUMMEL
PUMMELO *same as* > POMELO
PUMMELOS > PUMMELO
PUMMELS > PUMMEL
PUMP *n* machine used to force a liquid or gas to move in a particular direction ▷ *vb* raise or drive with a pump
PUMPED > PUMP
PUMPER > PUMP
PUMPERS > PUMP
PUMPHOOD *n* cover for the upper wheel of a chain pump
PUMPHOODS > PUMPHOOD
PUMPING > PUMP
PUMPION *archaic word for* > PUMPKIN
PUMPIONS > PUMPION

PUMPKIN *n* large round fruit with an orange rind, soft flesh, and many seeds
PUMPKING *n* person involved in a web-based project who has temporary but exclusive authority to make changes to the master source code
PUMPKINGS > PUMPKING
PUMPKINS > PUMPKIN
PUMPLESS > PUMP
PUMPLIKE > PUMP
PUMPS > PUMP
PUMY *adj* large and round
PUN *n* use of words to exploit double meanings for humorous effect ▷ *vb* make puns
PUNA *n* high cold dry plateau, esp in the Andes
PUNALUA *n* marriage between the sisters of one family to the brothers of another
PUNALUAN > PUNALUA
PUNALUAS > PUNALUA
PUNAS > PUNA
PUNCE *n* kick ▷ *vb* kick
PUNCED > PUNCE
PUNCES > PUNCE
PUNCH *vb* strike at with a clenched fist ▷ *n* blow with a clenched fist
PUNCHBAG *n* stuffed or inflated bag suspended by a flexible rod, that is punched for exercise, esp boxing training
PUNCHBAGS > PUNCHBAG
PUNCHBALL *n* stuffed or inflated ball supported by a flexible rod, that is punched for exercise, esp boxing training
PUNCHBOWL *n* large bowl for serving punch
PUNCHED > PUNCH
PUNCHEON *n* large cask of variable capacity, usually between 70 and 120 gallons
PUNCHEONS > PUNCHEON
PUNCHER > PUNCH
PUNCHERS > PUNCH
PUNCHES > PUNCH
PUNCHIER > PUNCHY
PUNCHIEST > PUNCHY
PUNCHILY > PUNCHY
PUNCHING > PUNCH
PUNCHLESS > PUNCH
PUNCHY *adj* forceful
PUNCING > PUNCE
PUNCTA > PUNCTUM
PUNCTATE *adj* having or marked with minute spots, holes, or depressions
PUNCTATED *same as* > PUNCTATE
PUNCTATOR *n* marker of points
PUNCTILIO *n* strict attention to minute

points of etiquette
PUNCTO *n* tip of a fencing sword
PUNCTOS > PUNCTO
PUNCTUAL *adj* arriving or taking place at the correct time
PUNCTUATE *vb* put punctuation marks in
PUNCTULE *n* very small opening
PUNCTULES > PUNCTULE
PUNCTUM *n* tip or small point
PUNCTURE *n* small hole made by a sharp object, esp in a tyre ▷ *vb* pierce a hole in
PUNCTURED > PUNCTURE
PUNCTURER > PUNCTURE
PUNCTURES > PUNCTURE
PUNDIT *n* expert who speaks publicly on a subject
PUNDITIC *adj* of or relating to pundits
PUNDITRY *n* expressing of expert opinions
PUNDITS > PUNDIT
PUNDONOR *n* point of honour
PUNG *n* horse-drawn sleigh with a boxlike body on runners
PUNGA *variant spelling of* > PONGA
PUNGAS > PUNGA
PUNGENCE *n* pungency
PUNGENCES > PUNGENCE
PUNGENCY > PUNGENT
PUNGENT *adj* having a strong sharp bitter flavour
PUNGENTLY > PUNGENT
PUNGLE *vb* make payment
PUNGLED > PUNGLE
PUNGLES > PUNGLE
PUNGLING > PUNGLE
PUNGS > PUNG
PUNIER > PUNY
PUNIEST > PUNY
PUNILY > PUNY
PUNINESS > PUNY
PUNISH *vb* cause (someone) to suffer or undergo a penalty for some wrongdoing
PUNISHED > PUNISH
PUNISHER > PUNISH
PUNISHERS > PUNISH
PUNISHES > PUNISH
PUNISHING > PUNISH
PUNITION *n* punishment
PUNITIONS > PUNITION
PUNITIVE *adj* relating to punishment
PUNITORY *same as* > PUNITIVE
PUNJI *n* sharpened bamboo stick
PUNJIS > PUNJI
PUNK *n* anti-Establishment youth movement and style of rock music of the late 1970s ▷ *adj* relating to the

punk youth movement of the late 1970s
PUNKA *n* fan made of a palm leaf or leaves
PUNKAH *same as* > PUNKA
PUNKAHS > PUNKAH
PUNKAS > PUNKA
PUNKER > PUNK
PUNKERS > PUNK
PUNKEST > PUNK
PUNKEY *n* small winged insect
PUNKEYS > PUNKEY
PUNKIE *same as* > PUNKEY
PUNKIER > PUNKY
PUNKIES > PUNKIE
PUNKIEST > PUNKY
PUNKIN *same as* > PUMPKIN
PUNKINESS > PUNKY
PUNKINS > PUNKIN
PUNKISH > PUNK
PUNKS > PUNK
PUNKY *adj* of punk music
PUNNED > PUN
PUNNER > PUN
PUNNERS > PUN
PUNNET *n* small basket for fruit
PUNNETS > PUNNET
PUNNIER > PUNNY
PUNNIEST > PUNNY
PUNNING > PUN
PUNNINGLY > PUN
PUNNINGS > PUN
PUNNY *adj* of puns
PUNS > PUN
PUNSTER *n* person who is fond of making puns
PUNSTERS > PUNSTER
PUNT *n* open flat-bottomed boat propelled by a pole ▷ *vb* travel in a punt
PUNTED > PUNT
PUNTEE *same as* > PUNTY
PUNTEES > PUNTEE
PUNTER *n* person who bets
PUNTERS > PUNTER
PUNTIES > PUNTY
PUNTING > PUNT
PUNTO *n* hit in fencing
PUNTOS > PUNTO
PUNTS > PUNT
PUNTSMAN *n* man in charge of a river punt
PUNTSMEN > PUNTSMAN
PUNTY *n* long iron rod used in the finishing process of glass-blowing
PUNY *adj* small and feeble
PUP *n* young of certain animals, such as dogs and seals ▷ *vb* (of dogs, seals, etc) to give birth to pups
PUPA *n* insect at the stage of development between a larva and an adult
PUPAE > PUPA
PUPAL > PUPA
PUPARIA > PUPARIUM
PUPARIAL > PUPARIUM
PUPARIUM *n* hard barrel-shaped case enclosing the pupae of the housefly and other dipterous insects

**PUPAS** > PUPA
**PUPATE** vb (of an insect larva) to develop into a pupa
**PUPATED** > PUPATE
**PUPATES** > PUPATE
**PUPATING** > PUPATE
**PUPATION** > PUPATE
**PUPATIONS** > PUPATE
**PUPFISH** n type of small fish
**PUPFISHES** > PUPFISH
**PUPIL** n person who is taught by a teacher
**PUPILAGE** same as > PUPILLAGE
**PUPILAGES** > PUPILAGE
**PUPILAR** > PUPIL
**PUPILARY** same as > PUPILLARY
**PUPILLAGE** n condition of being a pupil or duration for which one is a pupil
**PUPILLAR** > PUPIL
**PUPILLARY** adj of or relating to a pupil or a legal ward
**PUPILLATE** vb cry like a peacock
**PUPILS** > PUPIL
**PUPILSHIP** n state of being a pupil
**PUPPED** > PUP
**PUPPET** n small doll or figure moved by strings or by the operator's hand
**PUPPETEER** n person who operates puppets
**PUPPETRY** n art of making and manipulating puppets and presenting puppet shows
**PUPPETS** > PUPPET
**PUPPIED** > PUPPY
**PUPPIES** > PUPPY
**PUPPING** > PUP
**PUPPODUM** same as > POPPADOM
**PUPPODUMS** > PUPPODUM
**PUPPY** n young dog ▷ vb have puppies
**PUPPYDOM** n state of being a puppy
**PUPPYDOMS** > PUPPYDOM
**PUPPYHOOD** > PUPPY
**PUPPYING** > PUPPY
**PUPPYISH** > PUPPY
**PUPPYISM** n impudence
**PUPPYISMS** > PUPPYISM
**PUPPYLIKE** > PUPPY
**PUPS** > PUP
**PUPU** n Hawaiian dish
**PUPUNHA** n fruit of a type of palm tree
**PUPUNHAS** > PUPUNHA
**PUPUS** > PUPU
**PUR** same as > PURR
**PURANA** n any of a class of Sanskrit writings not included in the Vedas, characteristically recounting the birth and deeds of Hindu gods and the creation, destruction,

or recreation of the universe
**PURANAS** > PURANA
**PURANIC** > PURANA
**PURBLIND** adj partly or nearly blind
**PURCHASE** vb obtain by payment ▷ n thing that is bought
**PURCHASED** > PURCHASE
**PURCHASER** > PURCHASE
**PURCHASES** > PURCHASE
**PURDA** same as > PURDAH
**PURDAH** n Muslim and Hindu custom of keeping women in seclusion, with clothing that conceals them completely when they go out
**PURDAHED** > PURDAH
**PURDAHS** > PURDAH
**PURDAS** > PURDA
**PURDONIUM** n type of coal scuttle having a slanted cover that is raised to open it, and an inner removable metal container for the coal
**PURE** adj unmixed, untainted ▷ vb make pure
**PUREBLOOD** n purebred animal
**PUREBRED** adj denoting a pure strain obtained through many generations of controlled breeding ▷ n purebred animal
**PUREBREDS** > PUREBRED
**PUREED** > PUREE
**PUREE** n smooth thick pulp of cooked and sieved fruit, vegetables, meat, or fish ▷ vb make (cooked foods) into a puree
**PUREED** > PUREE
**PUREEING** > PUREE
**PUREES** > PUREE
**PURELY** adv in a pure manner
**PURENESS** > PURE
**PURER** > PURE
**PURES** > PURE
**PUREST** > PURE
**PURFLE** n ruffled or curved ornamental band, as on clothing, furniture, etc ▷ vb decorate with such a band or bands
**PURFLED** > PURFLE
**PURFLER** > PURFLE
**PURFLERS** > PURFLE
**PURFLES** > PURFLE
**PURFLING** same as > PURFLE
**PURFLINGS** > PURFLING
**PURFLY** > PURFLE
**PURGATION** n act of purging or state of being purged
**PURGATIVE** adj (medicine) designed to cause defecation ▷ n medicine for emptying the bowels
**PURGATORY** n place or state of temporary suffering

**PURGE** vb rid (a thing or place) of (unwanted things or people) ▷ n purging
**PURGEABLE** > PURGE
**PURGED** > PURGE
**PURGER** > PURGE
**PURGERS** > PURGE
**PURGES** > PURGE
**PURGING** > PURGE
**PURGINGS** > PURGE
**PURI** n unleavened flaky Indian bread, that is deep-fried in ghee and served hot
**PURIFIED** > PURIFY
**PURIFIER** n device or substance that frees something of extraneous, contaminating, or debasing matter
**PURIFIERS** > PURIFIER
**PURIFIES** > PURIFY
**PURIFY** vb make or become pure
**PURIFYING** > PURIFY
**PURIM** n Jewish holiday
**PURIMS** > PURIM
**PURIN** same as > PURINE
**PURINE** n colourless crystalline solid that can be prepared from uric acid
**PURINES** > PURINE
**PURING** > PURE
**PURINS** > PURIN
**PURIRI** n forest tree of New Zealand
**PURIRIS** > PURIRI
**PURIS** > PURI
**PURISM** n strict insistence on the correct usage or style, such as in grammar or art
**PURISMS** > PURISM
**PURIST** > PURISM
**PURISTIC** > PURISM
**PURISTS** > PURISM
**PURITAN** n person who follows strict moral or religious principles ▷ adj of or like a puritan
**PURITANIC** > PURITAN
**PURITANS** > PURITAN
**PURITIES** > PURITY
**PURITY** n state or quality of being pure
**PURL** n stitch made by knitting a plain stitch backwards ▷ vb knit in purl
**PURLED** > PURL
**PURLER** n headlong or spectacular fall
**PURLERS** > PURLER
**PURLICUE** vb finish a pen stroke with a flourish
**PURLICUED** > PURLICUE
**PURLICUES** > PURLICUE
**PURLIEU** n land on the edge of a royal forest
**PURLIEUS** > PURLIEU
**PURLIN** n horizontal beam that supports the rafters of a roof
**PURLINE** same as > PURLIN

**PURLINES** > PURLINE
**PURLING** > PURL
**PURLINGS** > PURL
**PURLINS** > PURLIN
**PURLOIN** vb steal
**PURLOINED** > PURLOIN
**PURLOINER** > PURLOIN
**PURLOINS** > PURLOIN
**PURLS** > PURL
**PUROMYCIN** n type of antibiotic
**PURPIE** old Scots word for > PURSLANE
**PURPIES** > PURPIE
**PURPLE** n colour between red and blue ▷ adj of a colour between red and blue ▷ vb make purple
**PURPLED** > PURPLE
**PURPLER** > PURPLE
**PURPLES** > PURPLE
**PURPLEST** > PURPLE
**PURPLIER** > PURPLE
**PURPLIEST** > PURPLE
**PURPLING** > PURPLE
**PURPLISH** > PURPLE
**PURPLY** > PURPLE
**PURPORT** vb claim (to be or do something) ▷ n apparent meaning, significance
**PURPORTED** adj alleged
**PURPORTS** > PURPORT
**PURPOSE** n reason for which something is done or exists
**PURPOSED** > PURPOSE
**PURPOSELY** adv intentionally
**PURPOSES** > PURPOSE
**PURPOSING** > PURPOSE
**PURPOSIVE** adj having or showing a definite intention
**PURPURA** n any of several blood diseases causing purplish spots or patches on the skin due to subcutaneous bleeding
**PURPURAS** > PURPURA
**PURPURE** n purple
**PURPUREAL** adj having a purple colour
**PURPURES** > PURPURE
**PURPURIC** > PURPURA
**PURPURIN** n red crystalline compound used as a stain for biological specimens
**PURPURINS** > PURPURIN
**PURPY** variant of > PURPIE
**PURR** vb (of cats) make low vibrant sound, usu when pleased ▷ n this sound
**PURRED** > PURR
**PURRING** > PURR
**PURRINGLY** > PURR
**PURRINGS** > PURR
**PURRS** > PURR
**PURS** > PUR
**PURSE** n small bag for money ▷ vb draw (one's lips) together into a small round shape
**PURSED** > PURSE

PURSEFUL n that which can be contained in purse
PURSEFULS > PURSEFUL
PURSELIKE > PURSE
PURSER n ship's officer who keeps the accounts
PURSERS > PURSER
PURSES > PURSE
PURSEW archaic spelling of > PURSUE
PURSEWED > PURSEW
PURSEWING > PURSEW
PURSEWS > PURSEW
PURSIER > PURSY
PURSIEST > PURSY
PURSILY > PURSY
PURSINESS > PURSY
PURSING > PURSE
PURSLAIN same as > PURSLANE
PURSLAINS > PURSLAIN
PURSLANE n weedy portulacaceous plant, Portulaca oleracea, with small yellow flowers and fleshy leaves, which are used in salads and as a potherb
PURSLANES > PURSLANE
PURSUABLE > PURSUE
PURSUAL n act of pursuit
PURSUALS > PURSUAL
PURSUANCE n carrying out of an action or plan
PURSUANT adj in agreement or conformity
PURSUE vb chase
PURSUED > PURSUE
PURSUER > PURSUE
PURSUERS > PURSUE
PURSUES > PURSUE
PURSUING > PURSUE
PURSUINGS > PURSUE
PURSUIT n pursuing
PURSUITS > PURSUIT
PURSY adj short-winded
PURTIER > PURTY
PURTIEST > PURTY
PURTRAID > PURTRAY
PURTRAY archaic spelling of > PORTRAY
PURTRAYD > PURTRAY
PURTRAYS > PURTRAY
PURTY adj pretty
PURULENCE > PURULENT
PURULENCY > PURULENT
PURULENT adj of or containing pus
PURVEY vb supply (provisions) ▷ n food and drink laid on at a wedding reception, etc
PURVEYED > PURVEY
PURVEYING > PURVEY
PURVEYOR n person, organization, etc, that supplies food and provisions
PURVEYORS > PURVEYOR
PURVEYS > PURVEY
PURVIEW n scope or range of activity or outlook
PURVIEWS > PURVIEW
PUS n yellowish matter

produced by infected tissue
PUSES > PUS
PUSH vb move or try to move by steady force ▷ n act of pushing
PUSHBALL n game in which two teams try to push a heavy ball towards opposite goals
PUSHBALLS > PUSHBALL
PUSHCART n handcart, typically having two wheels and a canvas roof, used esp by street vendors
PUSHCARTS > PUSHCART
PUSHCHAIR n folding chair on wheels for a baby
PUSHDOWN n list in which the last item added is at the top
PUSHDOWNS > PUSHDOWN
PUSHED adj short of
PUSHER n person who sells illegal drugs
PUSHERS > PUSHER
PUSHES > PUSH
PUSHFUL > PUSH
PUSHFULLY > PUSH
PUSHIER > PUSHY
PUSHIEST > PUSHY
PUSHILY > PUSHY
PUSHINESS > PUSHY
PUSHING prep almost or nearly (a certain age, speed, etc) ▷ adj aggressively ambitious ▷ adv almost or nearly (a certain age, speed, etc)
PUSHINGLY > PUSHING
PUSHOVER n something easily achieved
PUSHOVERS > PUSHOVER
PUSHPIN n pin with a small ball-shaped head
PUSHPINS > PUSHPIN
PUSHROD n metal rod transmitting the reciprocating motion that operates the valves of an internal-combustion engine having the camshaft in the crankcase
PUSHRODS > PUSHROD
PUSHUP n exercise in which the body is alternately raised from and lowered to the floor by the arms only, the trunk being kept straight with the toes and hands resting on the floor
PUSHUPS > PUSHUP
PUSHY adj too assertive or ambitious
PUSLE old spelling of > PUZZLE
PUSLED > PUSLE
PUSLES > PUSLE
PUSLEY same as > PURSLANE
PUSLEYS > PUSLEY
PUSLIKE > PUS
PUSLING > PUSLE
PUSS same as > PUSSY
PUSSEL n slatternly

woman
PUSSELS > PUSSEL
PUSSER n naval purser
PUSSERS > PUSSER
PUSSES > PUSS
PUSSIER > PUSSY
PUSSIES > PUSSY
PUSSIEST > PUSSY
PUSSLEY n weedy trailing herb
PUSSLEYS > PUSSLEY
PUSSLIES > PUSSLY
PUSSLIKE > PUSS
PUSSLY variant of > PUSSLEY
PUSSY n cat ▷ adj containing or full of pus
PUSSYCAT same as > PUSSY
PUSSYCATS > PUSSYCAT
PUSSYFOOT vb behave too cautiously ▷ n person who pussyfoots
PUSSYTOES n type of low-growing plant
PUSTULANT adj causing the formation of pustules ▷ n agent causing such formation
PUSTULAR > PUSTULE
PUSTULATE vb form into pustules ▷ adj covered with pustules
PUSTULE n pimple containing pus
PUSTULED > PUSTULE
PUSTULES > PUSTULE
PUSTULOUS > PUSTULE
PUT vb cause to be (in a position, state, or place) ▷ n throw in putting the shot
PUTAMEN n hard endocarp or stone of fruits such as the peach, plum, and cherry
PUTAMINA > PUTAMEN
PUTATIVE adj reputed, supposed
PUTCHEON n trap for catching salmon
PUTCHEONS > PUTCHEON
PUTCHER n trap for catching salmon
PUTCHERS > PUTCHER
PUTCHOCK same as > PACHAK
PUTCHOCKS > PUTCHOCK
PUTCHUK same as > PACHAK
PUTCHUKS > PUTCHUK
PUTDOWN n snub or insult
PUTDOWNS > PUTDOWN
PUTEAL n enclosure around a well
PUTEALS > PUTEAL
PUTELI same as > PATELA
PUTELIS > PUTELI
PUTID adj having an unpleasant odour
PUTLOCK same as > PUTLOG
PUTLOCKS > PUTLOCK
PUTLOG n short horizontal beam that with others supports the floor planks of a scaffold
PUTLOGS > PUTLOG
PUTOFF n pretext or delay

PUTOFFS > PUTOFF
PUTOIS n brush to paint pottery
PUTOISES > PUTOIS
PUTON n hoax or piece of mockery
PUTONGHUA n Chinese language
PUTONS > PUTON
PUTOUT n baseball play in which the batter or runner is put out
PUTOUTS > PUTOUT
PUTREFIED > PUTREFY
PUTREFIER > PUTREFY
PUTREFIES > PUTREFY
PUTREFY vb rot and produce an offensive smell
PUTRID adj rotten and foul-smelling
PUTRIDER > PUTRID
PUTRIDEST > PUTRID
PUTRIDITY > PUTRID
PUTRIDLY > PUTRID
PUTS > PUT
PUTSCH n sudden violent attempt to remove a government from power
PUTSCHES > PUTSCH
PUTSCHIST n person taking part in putsch
PUTT n stroke on the putting green to roll the ball into or near the hole ▷ vb strike (the ball) in this way
PUTTED > PUTT
PUTTEE n (esp as part of a military uniform) strip of cloth worn wound around the leg from the ankle to the knee
PUTTEES > PUTTEE
PUTTEN old Scots past participle of > PUT
PUTTER n golf club for putting ▷ vb busy oneself in a desultory though agreeable manner
PUTTERED > PUTTER
PUTTERER > PUTTER
PUTTERERS > PUTTER
PUTTERING > PUTTER
PUTTERS > PUTTER
PUTTI > PUTTO
PUTTIE same as > PUTTEE
PUTTIED > PUTTY
PUTTIER n glazier
PUTTIERS > PUTTIER
PUTTIES > PUTTY
PUTTING > PUT
PUTTINGS > PUT
PUTTO n representation of a small boy, a cherub or cupid, esp in baroque painting or sculpture
PUTTOCK n type of bird of prey
PUTTOCKS > PUTTOCK
PUTTS > PUTT
PUTTY n stiff paste of whiting and linseed oil ▷ vb fill, fix, or coat with putty

PUTTYING > PUTTY
PUTTYLESS > PUTTY
PUTTYLIKE > PUTTY
PUTTYROOT n North American orchid
PUTURE n claim of foresters for food for men, horses, hawks, and hounds, within the bounds of the forest
PUTURES > PUTURE
PUTZ n despicable or stupid person ▷ vb waste time
PUTZED > PUTZ
PUTZES > PUTZ
PUTZING > PUTZ
PUY n small volcanic cone
PUYS > PUY
PUZZEL n prostitute
PUZZELS > PUZZEL
PUZZLE vb perplex and confuse or be perplexed or confused ▷ n problem that cannot be easily solved
PUZZLED > PUZZLE
PUZZLEDLY > PUZZLE
PUZZLEDOM > PUZZLE
PUZZLER n person or thing that puzzles
PUZZLERS > PUZZLER
PUZZLES > PUZZLE
PUZZLING > PUZZLE
PUZZOLANA same as > POZZOLANA
PYA n monetary unit of Myanmar worth one hundredth of a kyat
PYAEMIA n blood poisoning with pus-forming microorganisms in the blood
PYAEMIAS > PYAEMIA
PYAEMIC > PYAEMIA
PYAS > PYA
PYAT n magpie ▷ adj pied
PYATS > PYAT
PYCNIC same as > PYKNIC
PYCNICS > PYCNIC
PYCNIDIA > PYCNIDIUM
PYCNIDIAL > PYCNIDIUM
PYCNIDIUM n small flask-shaped structure containing spores that occurs in ascomycetes and certain other fungi
PYCNITE n variety of topaz
PYCNITES > PYCNITE
PYCNON old word for > SEMITONE
PYCNONS > PYCNON
PYCNOSES > PYCNOSIS
PYCNOSIS n process of shrinking in a cell nucleus
PYCNOTIC > PYCNOSIS
PYE same as > PIE
PYEBALD same as > PIEBALD
PYEBALDS > PYEBALD
PYELITIC > PYELITIS
PYELITIS n inflammation of the pelvis of the kidney
PYELOGRAM n film produced by pyelography
PYEMIA same as > PYAEMIA

PYEMIAS > PYEMIA
PYEMIC > PYAEMIA
PYENGADU variant of > PYINKADO
PYENGADUS > PYENGADU
PYES > PYE
PYET same as > PYAT
PYETS > PYET
PYGAL n relating to the buttocks
PYGARG n type of horned mammal
PYGARGS > PYGARG
PYGIDIA > PYGIDIUM
PYGIDIAL > PYGIDIUM
PYGIDIUM n terminal segment, division, or other structure in certain annelids, arthropods, and other invertebrates
PYGIDIUMS > PYGIDIUM
PYGMAEAN > PYGMY
PYGMEAN > PYGMY
PYGMIES > PYGMY
PYGMOID adj of or like pygmies
PYGMY n something that is a very small example of its type ▷ adj very small
PYGMYISH > PYGMY
PYGMYISM > PYGMY
PYGMYISMS > PYGMY
PYGOSTYLE n vertebral bone in birds
PYIC adj relating to pus
PYIN n constituent of pus
PYINKADO n leguminous tree native to India and Myanmar
PYINKADOS > PYINKADO
PYINS > PYIN
PYJAMA same as > PYJAMAS
PYJAMAED > PYJAMAS
PYJAMAS pl n loose-fitting trousers and top worn in bed
PYKNIC adj (of a physical type) characterized by a broad squat fleshy physique with a large chest and abdomen ▷ n person with squat physique
PYKNICS > PYKNIC
PYKNOSES > PYKNOSIS
PYKNOSIS n thickening of a cell
PYKNOSOME n stocky body type
PYKNOTIC > PYKNOSIS
PYLON n steel tower-like structure supporting electrical cables
PYLONS > PYLON
PYLORI > PYLORUS
PYLORIC > PYLORUS
PYLORUS n small circular opening at the base of the stomach through which partially digested food (chyme) passes to the duodenum
PYLORUSES > PYLORUS
PYNE archaic variant

of > PINE
PYNED > PYNE
PYNES > PYNE
PYNING > PYNE
PYODERMA n any skin eruption characterized by pustules or the formation of pus
PYODERMAS > PYODERMA
PYODERMIC > PYODERMA
PYOGENIC adj of or relating to the formation of pus
PYOID adj resembling pus
PYONER old variant of > PIONEER
PYORRHEA same as > PYORRHOEA
PYORRHEAL > PYORRHOEA
PYORRHEAS > PYORRHEA
PYORRHEIC > PYORRHOEA
PYORRHOEA n disease of the gums and tooth sockets which causes bleeding of the gums and the formation of pus
PYOSES > PYOSIS
PYOSIS n formation of pus
PYOT same as > PYAT
PYOTS > PYOT
PYRACANTH n type of thorny shrub
PYRAL > PYRE
PYRALID n tropical moth
PYRALIDID same as > PYRALID
PYRALIDS > PYRALID
PYRALIS same as > PYRALID
PYRALISES > PYRALIS
PYRAMID n solid figure with a flat base and triangular sides sloping upwards to a point ▷ vb build up or be arranged in the form of a pyramid
PYRAMIDAL > PYRAMID
PYRAMIDED > PYRAMID
PYRAMIDES > PYRAMIS
PYRAMIDIA n pyramidal apices of obelisks
PYRAMIDIC > PYRAMID
PYRAMIDON n type of pipe for an organ
PYRAMIDS > PYRAMID
PYRAMIS n pyramid-shaped structure
PYRAMISES > PYRAMIS
PYRAN n unsaturated heterocyclic compound having a ring containing five carbon atoms and one oxygen atom and two double bonds
PYRANOID > PYRAN
PYRANOSE n structure in many sugars
PYRANOSES > PYRANOSE
PYRANS > PYRAN
PYRAZOLE n crystalline soluble basic heterocyclic compound
PYRAZOLES > PYRAZOLE
PYRE n pile of wood for burning a corpse on
PYRENE n solid polynuclear

aromatic hydrocarbon extracted from coal tar
PYRENEITE n dark mineral found in the Pyrenees
PYRENES > PYRENE
PYRENOID n any of various small protein granules that occur in certain algae, mosses, and protozoans and are involved in the synthesis of starch
PYRENOIDS > PYRENOID
PYRES > PYRE
PYRETHRIN n oily water-insoluble compound used as an insecticide
PYRETHRUM n Eurasian chrysanthemum with white, pink, red, or purple flowers
PYRETIC adj of, relating to, or characterized by fever
PYREX n tradename for any of a variety of borosilicate glasses that have low coefficients of expansion, making them suitable for heat-resistant glassware used in cookery and chemical apparatus
PYREXES > PYREX
PYREXIA technical name for > FEVER
PYREXIAL > PYREXIA
PYREXIAS > PYREXIA
PYREXIC > PYREXIA
PYRIC adj of or relating to burning
PYRIDIC > PYRIDINE
PYRIDINE n colourless hygroscopic liquid with a characteristic odour
PYRIDINES > PYRIDINE
PYRIDOXAL n naturally occurring derivative of pyridoxine that is a precursor of a coenzyme involved in several enzymic reactions
PYRIDOXIN n derivative of pyridine
PYRIFORM adj (esp of organs of the body) pear-shaped
PYRITE n yellow mineral consisting of iron sulphide in cubic crystalline form
PYRITES same as > PYRITE
PYRITIC > PYRITE
PYRITICAL > PYRITE
PYRITISE same as > PYRITIZE
PYRITISED > PYRITISE
PYRITISES > PYRITISE
PYRITIZE vb convert into pyrites
PYRITIZED > PYRITIZE
PYRITIZES > PYRITIZE
PYRITOUS > PYRITE
PYRO n pyromaniac
PYROCERAM n transparent ceramic material
PYROCLAST n piece of lava ejected from a volcano

**PYROGEN** *n* any of a group of substances that cause a rise in temperature in an animal body

**PYROGENIC** *adj* produced by or producing heat

**PYROGENS** > PYROGEN

**PYROLA** *n* evergreen perennial

**PYROLAS** > PYROLA

**PYROLATER** *n* worshipper of fire

**PYROLATRY** > PYROLATER

**PYROLISE** *same as* > PYROLIZE

**PYROLISED** > PYROLISE

**PYROLISES** > PYROLISE

**PYROLIZE** *vb* subject to pyrolysis

**PYROLIZED** > PYROLIZE

**PYROLIZES** > PYROLIZE

**PYROLOGY** *n* study of heat

**PYROLYSE** *vb* subject to pyrolysis

**PYROLYSED** > PYROLYSE

**PYROLYSER** > PYROLYSE

**PYROLYSES** > PYROLYSE

**PYROLYSIS** *n* application of heat to chemical compounds in order to cause decomposition

**PYROLYTIC** > PYROLYSIS

**PYROLYZE** *same as* > PYROLYSE

**PYROLYZED** > PYROLYZE

**PYROLYZER** > PYROLYZE

**PYROLYZES** > PYROLYZE

**PYROMANCY** *n* divination by fire or flames

**PYROMANIA** *n* uncontrollable urge to set things on fire

**PYROMETER** *n* instrument for measuring high temperatures

**PYROMETRY** > PYROMETER

**PYRONE** *n* type of heterocyclic compound

**PYRONES** > PYRONE

**PYRONINE** *n* red dye used as biological stain

**PYRONINES** > PYRONINE

**PYROPE** *n* deep yellowish-red garnet that consists of magnesium aluminium silicate and is used as a gemstone

**PYROPES** > PYROPE

**PYROPHONE** *n* musical instrument using hydrogen flames

**PYROPUS** *variant of* > PYROPE

**PYROPUSES** > PYROPUS

**PYROS** > PYRO

**PYROSCOPE** *n* instrument for measuring intensity of heat

**PYROSES** > PYROSIS

**PYROSIS** *technical name for* > HEARTBURN

**PYROSOME** *n* tube-shaped glowing marine creature

**PYROSOMES** > PYROSOME

**PYROSTAT** *n* device that

activates an alarm or extinguisher in the event of a fire

**PYROSTATS** > PYROSTAT

**PYROXENE** *n* silicate mineral

**PYROXENES** > PYROXENE

**PYROXENIC** > PYROXENE

**PYROXYLE** *same as* > PYROXYLIN

**PYROXYLES** > PYROXYLE

**PYROXYLIC** > PYROXYLIN

**PYROXYLIN** *n* yellow substance obtained by nitrating cellulose with a mixture of nitric and sulphuric acids

**PYRRHIC** *n* metrical foot of two short or unstressed syllables ▷ *adj* of or relating to such a metrical foot

**PYRRHICS** > PYRRHIC

**PYRRHOUS** *adj* ruddy or reddish

**PYRROL** *same as* > PYRROLE

**PYRROLE** *n* colourless insoluble toxic liquid with a five-membered ring containing one nitrogen atom

**PYRROLES** > PYRROLE

**PYRROLIC** > PYRROLE

**PYRROLS** > PYRROL

**PYRUVATE** *n* ester or salt of pyruvic acid

**PYRUVATES** > PYRUVATE

**PYRUVIC** as in *pyruvic acid* colourless pleasant-smelling liquid

**PYTHIUM** *n* type of fungi

**PYTHIUMS** > PYTHIUM

**PYTHON** *n* large nonpoisonous snake that crushes its prey

**PYTHONESS** *n* woman, such as Apollo's priestess at Delphi, believed to be possessed by an oracular spirit

**PYTHONIC** > PYTHON

**PYTHONS** > PYTHON

**PYURIA** *n* any condition characterized by the presence of pus in the urine

**PYURIAS** > PYURIA

**PYX** *n* any receptacle for the Eucharistic Host ▷ *vb* put (something) in a pyx

**PYXED** > PYX

**PYXES** > PYX

**PYXIDES** > PYXIS

**PYXIDIA** > PYXIDIUM

**PYXIDIUM** *n* dry fruit of such plants as the plantain

**PYXIE** *n* creeping evergreen shrub of the eastern US with small white or pink star-shaped flowers

**PYXIES** > PYXIE

**PYXING** > PYX

**PYXIS** *same as* > PYXIDIUM

**PZAZZ** *same as* > PIZZAZZ

**PZAZZES** > PZAZZ

# Qq

QABALA *same as* >KABBALAH
QABALAH *same
  as* >KABBALAH
QABALAHS >QABALAH
QABALAS >QABALA
QABALISM >QABALAH
QABALISMS >QABALAH
QABALIST >QABALAH
QABALISTS >QABALAH
QADI *variant spelling
  of* >CADI
QADIS >QADI
QAID *n* chief
QAIDS >QAID
QAIMAQAM *n* Turkish officer
  or official
QAIMAQAMS >QAIMAQAM
QALAMDAN *n* writing case
QALAMDANS >QALAMDAN
QANAT *n* underground
  irrigation channel
QANATS >QANAT
QASIDA *n* Arabic verse form
QASIDAS >QASIDA
QAT *variant spelling of* >KHAT
QATS >QAT
QAWWAL *n* qawwali singer
QAWWALI *n* Islamic
  religious song, esp in Asia
QAWWALIS >QAWWALI
QAWWALS >QAWWAL
QI *variant of* >CHI
QIBLA *variant of* >KIBLAH
QIBLAS >QIBLA
QIGONG *n* system of
  breathing and exercise
  designed to benefit both
  physical and mental health
QIGONGS >QIGONG
QINDAR *n* Albanian
  monetary unit worth one
  hundredth of a lek
QINDARKA >QINDAR

QINDARS >QINDAR
QINGHAOSU *n* Chinese herb
QINTAR *same as* >QINDAR
QINTARS >QINTAR
QIS >QI
QIVIUT *n* soft muskox wool
QIVIUTS >QIVIUT
QOPH *variant of* >KOPH
QOPHS >QOPH
QORMA *variant spelling
  of* >KORMA
QORMAS >QORMA
QUA *prep* in the capacity of
QUAALUDE *n* methaqualone
QUAALUDES >QUAALUDE
QUACK *vb* (of a duck) utter a
  harsh guttural sound ▷ *n*
  an unqualified person who
  claims medical knowledge
QUACKED >QUACK
QUACKER >QUACK
QUACKERS >QUACK
QUACKERY *n* activities or
  methods of a quack
QUACKIER >QUACK
QUACKIEST >QUACK
QUACKING >QUACK
QUACKISH >QUACK
QUACKISM *same
  as* >QUACKERY
QUACKISMS >QUACKISM
QUACKLE *same as* >QUACK
QUACKLED >QUACKLE
QUACKLES >QUACKLE
QUACKLING >QUACKLE
QUACKS >QUACK
QUACKY >QUACK
QUAD *n* quadrangle
QUADDED *adj* formed of
  multiple quads
QUADDING *n* birdwatching
  in a specified area
QUADPLEX *n* apartment on

four floors
QUADRANS *n* Roman coin
QUADRANT *n* quarter of a
  circle
QUADRANTS >QUADRANT
QUADRAT *n* area of
  vegetation, often one
  square metre, marked out
  for study of the plants in
  the surrounding area
QUADRATE *n* cube or
  square, or a square or
  cubelike object ▷ *vb* make
  square or rectangular
  ▷ *adj* of or relating to this
  bone
QUADRATED >QUADRATE
QUADRATES >QUADRATE
QUADRATIC *n* equation
  in which the variable is
  raised to the power of two,
  but nowhere raised to a
  higher power ▷ *adj* of the
  second power
QUADRATS >QUADRAT
QUADRATUS *n* type of
  muscle
QUADRELLA *n* four
  nominated horse races in
  which the punter bets on
  selecting the four winners
QUADRIC *adj* having or
  characterized by an
  equation of the second
  degree, usually in two
  or three variables ▷ *n*
  quadric curve, surface, or
  function
QUADRICEP *n* muscle in
  thigh
QUADRICS >QUADRIC
QUADRIFID *adj* divided
  into four lobes or other

parts
QUADRIGA *n* (in the
  classical world) a two-
  wheeled chariot drawn by
  four horses abreast
QUADRIGAE >QUADRIGA
QUADRIGAS >QUADRIGA
QUADRILLE *n* square dance
  for four couples
QUADRIVIA *n* higher
  divisions of the seven
  liberal arts
QUADROON *n* an offensive
  term for the offspring of
  a mulatto and a white
  person
QUADROONS >QUADROON
QUADRUMAN *n* nonhuman
  primate
QUADRUPED *n* any animal
  with four legs ▷ *adj*
  having four feet
QUADRUPLE *vb* multiply
  by four ▷ *adj* four times
  as much or as many ▷ *n*
  quantity or number four
  times as great as another
QUADRUPLY >QUADRUPLE
QUADS >QUAD
QUAERE *n* query or question
  ▷ *interj* ask or inquire:
  used esp to introduce a
  question ▷ *vb* ask
QUAERED >QUAERE
QUAEREING >QUAERE
QUAERES >QUAERE
QUAERITUR *sentence
  substitute* question is
  asked
QUAESITUM *n* object
  sought
QUAESTOR *n* any of several
  magistrates of ancient

Rome, usually a financial administrator

**QUAESTORS** > QUAESTOR
**QUAFF** *vb* drink heartily or in one draught
**QUAFFABLE** > QUAFF
**QUAFFED** > QUAFF
**QUAFFER** > QUAFF
**QUAFFERS** > QUAFF
**QUAFFING** > QUAFF
**QUAFFS** > QUAFF
**QUAG** *another word for* > QUAGMIRE
**QUAGGA** *n* recently extinct zebra, striped only on the head and shoulders
**QUAGGAS** > QUAGGA
**QUAGGIER** > QUAGGY
**QUAGGIEST** > QUAGGY
**QUAGGY** *adj* resembling a marsh or quagmire
**QUAGMIRE** *n* soft wet area of land ▷ *vb* bog down
**QUAGMIRED** > QUAGMIRE
**QUAGMIRES** > QUAGMIRE
**QUAGMIRY** > QUAGMIRE
**QUAGS** > QUAG
**QUAHAUG** *same as* > QUAHOG
**QUAHAUGS** > QUAHAUG
**QUAHOG** *n* edible clam
**QUAHOGS** > QUAHOG
**QUAI** *same as* > QUAY
**QUAICH** *n* small shallow drinking cup, usually with two handles
**QUAICHES** > QUAICH
**QUAICHS** > QUAICH
**QUAIGH** *same as* > QUAICH
**QUAIGHS** > QUAIGH
**QUAIL** *n* small game bird of the partridge family ▷ *vb* shrink back with fear
**QUAILED** > QUAIL
**QUAILING** > QUAIL
**QUAILINGS** > QUAIL
**QUAILS** > QUAIL
**QUAINT** *adj* attractively unusual, esp in an old-fashioned style
**QUAINTER** > QUAINT
**QUAINTEST** > QUAINT
**QUAINTLY** > QUAINT
**QUAIR** *n* book
**QUAIRS** > QUAIR
**QUAIS** > QUAI
**QUAKE** *vb* shake or tremble with or as if with fear ▷ *n* earthquake
**QUAKED** > QUAKE
**QUAKER** > QUAKE
**QUAKERS** > QUAKE
**QUAKES** > QUAKE
**QUAKIER** > QUAKY
**QUAKIEST** > QUAKY
**QUAKILY** > QUAKY
**QUAKINESS** > QUAKY
**QUAKING** > QUAKE
**QUAKINGLY** > QUAKE
**QUAKINGS** > QUAKE
**QUAKY** *adj* inclined to quake
**QUALE** *n* essential property or quality
**QUALIA** > QUALE
**QUALIFIED** > QUALIFY

**QUALIFIER** *n* person or thing that qualifies, esp a contestant in a competition who wins a preliminary heat or contest and so earns the right to take part in the next round
**QUALIFIES** > QUALIFY
**QUALIFY** *vb* provide or be provided with the abilities necessary for a task, office, or duty
**QUALITIED** *adj* possessing qualities
**QUALITIES** > QUALITY
**QUALITY** *n* degree or standard of excellence ▷ *adj* excellent or superior
**QUALM** *n* pang of conscience
**QUALMIER** > QUALM
**QUALMIEST** > QUALM
**QUALMING** *adj* having a qualm
**QUALMISH** > QUALM
**QUALMLESS** > QUALM
**QUALMS** > QUALM
**QUALMY** > QUALM
**QUAMASH** *another name for* > CAMASS
**QUAMASHES** > QUAMASH
**QUANDANG** *same as* > QUANDONG
**QUANDANGS** > QUANDANG
**QUANDARY** *n* difficult situation or dilemma
**QUANDONG** *n* small Australian tree with edible fruit and nuts used in preserves
**QUANDONGS** > QUANDONG
**QUANGO** *n* quasi-autonomous nongovernmental organization: any partly independent official body set up by a government
**QUANGOS** > QUANGO
**QUANNET** *n* flat file with handle at one end
**QUANNETS** > QUANNET
**QUANT** *n* long pole for propelling a boat, esp a punt, by pushing on the bottom of a river or lake ▷ *vb* propel (a boat) with a quant
**QUANTA** > QUANTUM
**QUANTAL** *adj* of or relating to a quantum or an entity that is quantized
**QUANTALLY** > QUANTAL
**QUANTED** > QUANT
**QUANTIC** *n* mathematical function
**QUANTICAL** > QUANTIC
**QUANTICS** > QUANTIC
**QUANTIFY** *vb* discover or express the quantity of
**QUANTILE** *n* element of a division
**QUANTILES** > QUANTILE
**QUANTING** > QUANT

**QUANTISE** *same as* > QUANTIZE
**QUANTISED** > QUANTISE
**QUANTISER** > QUANTISE
**QUANTISES** > QUANTISE
**QUANTITY** *n* specified or definite amount or number
**QUANTIZE** *vb* restrict (a physical quantity) to one of a set of values characterized by quantum numbers
**QUANTIZED** > QUANTIZE
**QUANTIZER** > QUANTIZE
**QUANTIZES** > QUANTIZE
**QUANTONG** *same as* > QUANDONG
**QUANTONGS** > QUANTONG
**QUANTS** > QUANT
**QUANTUM** *n* desired or required amount, esp a very small one ▷ *adj* of or designating a major breakthrough or sudden advance
**QUARE** *adj* remarkable or strange
**QUARENDEN** *n* dark-red apple
**QUARENDER** *same as* > QUARENDEN
**QUARER** > QUARE
**QUAREST** > QUARE
**QUARK** *n* subatomic particle thought to be the fundamental unit of matter
**QUARKS** > QUARK
**QUARREL** *n* angry disagreement ▷ *vb* have a disagreement or dispute
**QUARRELED** > QUARREL
**QUARRELER** > QUARREL
**QUARRELS** > QUARREL
**QUARRIAN** *n* cockatiel of scrub and woodland regions of inland Australia
**QUARRIANS** > QUARRIAN
**QUARRIED** > QUARRY
**QUARRIER** *another word for* > QUARRYMAN
**QUARRIERS** > QUARRIER
**QUARRIES** > QUARRY
**QUARRION** *same as* > QUARRIAN
**QUARRIONS** > QUARRION
**QUARRY** *n* place where stone is dug from the surface of the earth ▷ *vb* extract (stone) from a quarry
**QUARRYING** > QUARRY
**QUARRYMAN** *n* man who works in or manages a quarry
**QUARRYMEN** > QUARRYMAN
**QUART** *n* unit of liquid measure equal to two pints (1.136 litres)
**QUARTAN** *adj* (esp of a malarial fever) occurring every third day ▷ *n* quartan malaria

**QUARTANS** > QUARTAN
**QUARTE** *n* fourth of eight basic positions from which a parry or attack can be made in fencing
**QUARTER** *n* one of four equal parts of something ▷ *vb* divide into four equal parts ▷ *adj* being or consisting of one of four equal parts
**QUARTERED** *adj* (of a shield) divided into four sections, each having contrasting arms or having two sets of arms, each repeated in diagonally opposite corners
**QUARTERER** > QUARTER
**QUARTERLY** *adj* occurring, due, or issued at intervals of three months ▷ *n* magazine issued every three months ▷ *adv* once every three months
**QUARTERN** *n* fourth part of certain weights or measures, such as a peck or a pound
**QUARTERNS** > QUARTERN
**QUARTERS** *pl n* accommodation, esp as provided for military personnel
**QUARTES** > QUARTE
**QUARTET** *n* group of four performers
**QUARTETS** > QUARTET
**QUARTETT** *same as* > QUARTET
**QUARTETTE** *same as* > QUARTET
**QUARTETTI** > QUARTETTO
**QUARTETTO** *same as* > QUARTET
**QUARTETTS** > QUARTETT
**QUARTIC** *n* biquadratic equation
**QUARTICS** > QUARTIC
**QUARTIER** *n* city district
**QUARTIERS** > QUARTIER
**QUARTILE** *n* one of three values of a variable dividing its distribution into four groups with equal frequencies ▷ *adj* of a quartile
**QUARTILES** > QUARTILE
**QUARTO** *n* book size in which the sheets are folded into four leaves
**QUARTOS** > QUARTO
**QUARTS** > QUART
**QUARTZ** *n* hard glossy mineral
**QUARTZES** > QUARTZ
**QUARTZIER** > QUARTZ
**QUARTZITE** *n* very hard metamorphic rock consisting of a mosaic of intergrown quartz crystals
**QUARTZOSE** > QUARTZ
**QUARTZOUS** > QUARTZ
**QUARTZY** > QUARTZ

QUASAR *n* extremely distant starlike object that emits powerful radio waves

QUASARS > QUASAR

QUASH *vb* annul or make void

QUASHED > QUASH

QUASHEE *same as* > QUASHIE

QUASHEES > QUASHEE

QUASHER > QUASH

QUASHERS > QUASH

QUASHES > QUASH

QUASHIE *n* in the Caribbean, an unsophisticated or gullible male Black peasant

QUASHIES > QUASHIE

QUASHING > QUASH

QUASI *adv* as if

QUASS *variant of* > KVASS

QUASSES > QUASS

QUASSIA *n* tropical American tree, the wood of which yields a substance used in insecticides

QUASSIAS > QUASSIA

QUASSIN *n* bitter crystalline substance

QUASSINS > QUASSIN

QUAT *n* spot

QUATCH *vb* move

QUATCHED > QUATCH

QUATCHES > QUATCH

QUATCHING > QUATCH

QUATE *n* fortune

QUATORZE *n* cards worth 14 points in piquet

QUATORZES > QUATORZE

QUATRAIN *n* stanza or poem of four lines

QUATRAINS > QUATRAIN

QUATRE *n* playing card with four pips

QUATRES > QUATRE

QUATS > QUAT

QUAVER *vb* (of a voice) quiver or tremble ▷ *n* note half the length of a crotchet

QUAVERED > QUAVER

QUAVERER > QUAVER

QUAVERERS > QUAVER

QUAVERIER > QUAVER

QUAVERING > QUAVER

QUAVERS > QUAVER

QUAVERY > QUAVER

QUAY *n* wharf built parallel to the shore

QUAYAGE *n* system of quays

QUAYAGES > QUAYAGE

QUAYD *archaic past participle of* > QUAIL

QUAYLIKE > QUAY

QUAYS > QUAY

QUAYSIDE *n* edge of a quay along the water

QUAYSIDES > QUAYSIDE

QUAZZIER > QUAZZY

QUAZZIEST > QUAZZY

QUAZZY *adj* unwell

QUBIT *n* quantum bit

QUBITS > QUBIT

QUBYTE *n* unit of eight

qubits

QUBYTES > QUBYTE

QUEACH *n* thicket

QUEACHES > QUEACH

QUEACHIER > QUEACHY

QUEACHY *adj* unwell

QUEAN *n* boisterous, impudent, or disreputable woman

QUEANS > QUEAN

QUEASIER > QUEASY

QUEASIEST > QUEASY

QUEASILY > QUEASY

QUEASY *adj* having the feeling that one is about to vomit

QUEAZIER > QUEAZY

QUEAZIEST > QUEAZY

QUEAZY *same as* > QUEASY

QUEBRACHO *n* anacardiaceous South American tree

QUEECHIER > QUEECHY

QUEECHY *same as* > QUEACHY

QUEEN *n* female sovereign who is the official ruler or head of state ▷ *vb* flaunt one's homosexuality

QUEENCAKE *n* small light cake containing currants

QUEENDOM *n* territory, state, people, or community ruled over by a queen

QUEENDOMS > QUEENDOM

QUEENED > QUEEN

QUEENHOOD > QUEEN

QUEENIE *n* scallop

QUEENIER > QUEENY

QUEENIES > QUEENIE

QUEENIEST > QUEENY

QUEENING > QUEEN

QUEENINGS > QUEEN

QUEENITE *n* supporter of a queen

QUEENITES > QUEENITE

QUEENLESS > QUEEN

QUEENLET *n* queen of a small realm

QUEENLETS > QUEENLET

QUEENLIER > QUEENLY

QUEENLY *adj* resembling or appropriate to a queen ▷ *adv* in a manner appropriate to a queen

QUEENS > QUEEN

QUEENSHIP > QUEEN

QUEENSIDE *n* half of a chessboard in which the queen starts

QUEENY *adj* effeminate

QUEER *adj* not normal or usual ▷ *n* derogatory name for a homosexual person ▷ *vb* spoil or thwart

QUEERCORE *n* gay-oriented punk music

QUEERDOM *n* gay culture

QUEERDOMS > QUEERDOM

QUEERED > QUEER

QUEERER > QUEER

QUEEREST > QUEER

QUEERING > QUEER

QUEERISH > QUEER

QUEERITY > QUEER

QUEERLY > QUEER

QUEERNESS > QUEER

QUEERS > QUEER

QUEEST *n* wood pigeon

QUEESTS > QUEEST

QUEINT *same as* > QUAINT

QUELCH *same as* > SQUELCH

QUELCHED > QUELCH

QUELCHES > QUELCH

QUELCHING > QUELCH

QUELEA *n* East African weaver bird

QUELEAS > QUELEA

QUELL *vb* suppress

QUELLABLE > QUELL

QUELLED > QUELL

QUELLER > QUELL

QUELLERS > QUELL

QUELLING > QUELL

QUELLS > QUELL

QUEME *vb* please

QUEMED > QUEME

QUEMES > QUEME

QUEMING > QUEME

QUENA *n* Andean flute

QUENAS > QUENA

QUENCH *vb* satisfy (one's thirst)

QUENCHED > QUENCH

QUENCHER > QUENCH

QUENCHERS > QUENCH

QUENCHES > QUENCH

QUENCHING > QUENCH

QUENELLE *n* finely sieved mixture of cooked meat or fish, shaped into various forms and cooked in stock or fried as croquettes

QUENELLES > QUENELLE

QUEP *interj* expression of derision

QUERCETIC > QUERCETIN

QUERCETIN *n* yellow crystalline pigment found naturally in the rind and bark of many plants

QUERCETUM *n* group of oak trees

QUERCINE *adj* of or relating to oak trees

QUERCITIN *same as* > QUERCETIN

QUERIDA *n* sweetheart

QUERIDAS > QUERIDA

QUERIED > QUERY

QUERIER > QUERY

QUERIERS > QUERY

QUERIES > QUERY

QUERIMONY *n* complaint

QUERIST *n* person who makes inquiries or queries

QUERISTS > QUERIST

QUERN *n* stone hand mill for grinding corn

QUERNS > QUERN

QUERULOUS *adj* complaining or whining

QUERY *n* question, esp one raising doubt ▷ *vb* express uncertainty, doubt, or an objection concerning

(something)

QUERYING > QUERY

QUERYINGS > QUERY

QUEST *n* long and difficult search ▷ *vb* go in search of

QUESTANT *n* one who quests

QUESTANTS > QUEST

QUESTED > QUEST

QUESTER > QUEST

QUESTERS > QUEST

QUESTING > QUEST

QUESTINGS > QUEST

QUESTION *n* form of words addressed to a person in order to obtain an answer ▷ *vb* put a question or questions to (a person)

QUESTIONS > QUESTION

QUESTOR *same as* > QUAESTOR

QUESTORS > QUESTOR

QUESTRIST *n* one who quests

QUESTS > QUEST

QUETCH *vb* move

QUETCHED > QUETCH

QUETCHES > QUETCH

QUETCHING > QUETCH

QUETHE *vb* say

QUETHES > QUETHE

QUETHING > QUETHE

QUETSCH *n* plum brandy

QUETSCHES > QUETSCH

QUETZAL *n* crested bird of Central and N South America

QUETZALES > QUETZAL

QUETZALS > QUETZAL

QUEUE *n* line of people or vehicles waiting for something ▷ *vb* form or remain in a line while waiting

QUEUED > QUEUE

QUEUEING > QUEUE

QUEUEINGS > QUEUE

QUEUER > QUEUE

QUEUERS > QUEUE

QUEUES > QUEUE

QUEUING > QUEUE

QUEUINGS > QUEUE

QUEY *n* young cow

QUEYN *n* girl

QUEYNIE *same as* > QUEYN

QUEYNIES > QUEYNIE

QUEYNS > QUEYN

QUEYS > QUEY

QUEZAL *same as* > QUETZAL

QUEZALES > QUEZAL

QUEZALS > QUEZAL

QUIBBLE *vb* make trivial objections ▷ *n* trivial objection

QUIBBLED > QUIBBLE

QUIBBLER > QUIBBLE

QUIBBLERS > QUIBBLE

QUIBBLES > QUIBBLE

QUIBBLING > QUIBBLE

QUIBLIN *same as* > QUIBBLE

QUIBLINS > QUIBLIN

QUICH *vb* move

QUICHE *n* savoury flan with an egg custard filling to

which vegetables etc are added
QUICHED > QUICH
QUICHES > QUICHE
QUICHING > QUICH
QUICK adj speedy, fast ▷ n area of sensitive flesh under a nail ▷ adv in a rapid manner
QUICKBEAM n rowan tree
QUICKEN vb make or become faster ▷ n rowan tree
QUICKENED > QUICKEN
QUICKENER > QUICKEN
QUICKENS > QUICKEN
QUICKER > QUICK
QUICKEST > QUICK
QUICKIE n anything done or made hurriedly ▷ adj made or done rapidly
QUICKIES > QUICKIE
QUICKLIME n white solid used in the manufacture of glass and steel
QUICKLY > QUICK
QUICKNESS > QUICK
QUICKS > QUICK
QUICKSAND n deep mass of loose wet sand that sucks anything on top of it into it
QUICKSET adj (of plants or cuttings) planted so as to form a hedge ▷ n hedge composed of such plants
QUICKSETS > QUICKSET
QUICKSTEP n fast modern ballroom dance ▷ vb perform this dance
QUID n pound (sterling)
QUIDAM n specified person
QUIDAMS > QUIDAM
QUIDDANY n quince jelly
QUIDDIT same as > QUIDDITY
QUIDDITCH n imaginary game in which players fly on broomsticks
QUIDDITS > QUIDDIT
QUIDDITY n essential nature of something
QUIDDLE vb waste time
QUIDDLED > QUIDDLE
QUIDDLER > QUIDDLE
QUIDDLERS > QUIDDLE
QUIDDLES > QUIDDLE
QUIDDLING > QUIDDLE
QUIDNUNC n person eager to learn news and scandal
QUIDNUNCS > QUIDNUNC
QUIDS > QUID
QUIESCE vb quieten
QUIESCED > QUIETEN
QUIESCENT adj quiet, inactive, or dormant
QUIESCES > QUIESCE
QUIESCING > QUIESCE
QUIET adj with little noise ▷ n quietness ▷ vb make or become quiet
QUIETED > QUIET
QUIETEN vb make or become quiet
QUIETENED > QUIETEN

QUIETENER > QUIETEN
QUIETENS > QUIETEN
QUIETER > QUIET
QUIETERS > QUIET
QUIETEST > QUIET
QUIETING > QUIET
QUIETINGS > QUIET
QUIETISM n passivity and calmness of mind towards external events
QUIETISMS > QUIETISM
QUIETIST > QUIETISM
QUIETISTS > QUIETISM
QUIETIVE n sedative drug
QUIETIVES > QUIETIVE
QUIETLY > QUIET
QUIETNESS > QUIET
QUIETS > QUIET
QUIETSOME > QUIET
QUIETUDE n quietness, peace, or tranquillity
QUIETUDES > QUIETUDE
QUIETUS n release from life
QUIETUSES > QUIETUS
QUIFF n tuft of hair brushed up above the forehead
QUIFFS > QUIFF
QUIGHT vb quit
QUIGHTED > QUIGHT
QUIGHTING > QUIGHT
QUIGHTS > QUIGHT
QUILL n pen made from the feather of a bird's wing or tail ▷ vb wind (thread, yarn, etc) onto a spool or bobbin
QUILLAI another name for > SOAPBARK
QUILLAIA same as > QUILLAI
QUILLAIAS > QUILLAIA
QUILLAIS > QUILLAI
QUILLAJA same as > QUILLAI
QUILLAJAS > QUILLAJA
QUILLBACK n freshwater fish
QUILLED > QUILL
QUILLET n quibble or subtlety
QUILLETS > QUILLET
QUILLING n decorative craftwork in which material such as glass, fabric or paper is formed into small bands or rolls that form the basis of a design
QUILLINGS > QUILLING
QUILLMAN n clerk
QUILLMEN > QUILLMAN
QUILLON n either half of the extended crosspiece of a sword or dagger
QUILLONS > QUILLON
QUILLS > QUILL
QUILLWORK n embroidery using porcupine quills
QUILLWORT n aquatic tracheophyte plant with quill-like leaves
QUILT n padded covering for a bed ▷ vb stitch together two layers of (fabric) with padding

between them
QUILTED > QUILT
QUILTER > QUILT
QUILTERS > QUILT
QUILTING n material used for making a quilt
QUILTINGS > QUILTING
QUILTS > QUILT
QUIM n taboo word for the female genitals
QUIMS > QUIM
QUIN same as > QUINT
QUINA n quinine
QUINARIES > QUINARY
QUINARY adj consisting of fives or by fives ▷ n set of five
QUINAS > QUINA
QUINATE adj arranged in or composed of five parts
QUINCE n acid-tasting pear-shaped fruit
QUINCES > QUINCE
QUINCHE vb move
QUINCHED > QUINCHE
QUINCHES > QUINCHE
QUINCHING > QUINCHE
QUINCUNX n group of five objects arranged in the shape of a rectangle with one at each corner and the fifth in the centre
QUINE variant of > QUEAN
QUINELA same as > QUINELLA
QUINELAS > QUINELA
QUINELLA n form of betting on a horse race in which the punter bets on selecting the first and second place-winners in any order
QUINELLAS > QUINELLA
QUINES > QUINE
QUINIC as in quinic acid white crystalline soluble optically active carboxylic acid
QUINIDINE n crystalline alkaloid drug
QUINIE n girl
QUINIELA same as > QUINELLA
QUINIELAS > QUINIELA
QUINIES > QUINIE
QUININ same as > QUININE
QUININA same as > QUININE
QUININAS > QUININA
QUININE n bitter drug used as a tonic and formerly to treat malaria
QUININES > QUININE
QUININS > QUININ
QUINNAT n Pacific salmon
QUINNATS > QUINNAT
QUINO same as > KENO
QUINOA n type of grain high in nutrients
QUINOAS > QUINOA
QUINOID same as > QUINONOID
QUINOIDAL > QUINOID
QUINOIDS > QUINOID
QUINOL n white crystalline

soluble phenol used as a photographic developer
QUINOLIN same as > QUINOLINE
QUINOLINE n oily colourless insoluble basic heterocyclic compound
QUINOLINS > QUINOLIN
QUINOLONE n any of a group of synthetic antibiotics
QUINOLS > QUINOL
QUINONE n yellow crystalline water-soluble unsaturated ketone
QUINONES > QUINONE
QUINONOID adj of, resembling, or derived from quinone
QUINOS > QUINO
QUINQUINA same as > QUININE
QUINS > QUIN
QUINSIED > QUINSY
QUINSIES > QUINSY
QUINSY n inflammation of the throat or tonsils
QUINT same as > QUIN
QUINTA n Portuguese vineyard where grapes for wine or port are grown
QUINTAIN n post or target set up for tilting exercises for mounted knights or foot soldiers
QUINTAINS > QUINTAIN
QUINTAL n unit of weight equal to (esp in Britain) 112 pounds (50.85 kg) or (esp in US) 100 pounds (45.36 kg)
QUINTALS > QUINTAL
QUINTAN adj (of a fever) occurring every fourth day ▷ n quintan fever
QUINTANS > QUINTAN
QUINTAR n Albanian unit of currency
QUINTARS > QUINTAR
QUINTAS > QUINTA
QUINTE n fifth of eight basic positions from which a parry or attack can be made in fencing
QUINTES > QUINTE
QUINTET n group of five performers
QUINTETS > QUINTET
QUINTETT same as > QUINTET
QUINTETTE same as > QUINTET
QUINTETTI > QUINTETTO
QUINTETTO same as > QUINTET
QUINTETTS > QUINTETT
QUINTIC adj of or relating to the fifth degree ▷ n mathematical function
QUINTICS > QUINTIC
QUINTILE n aspect of 72° between two heavenly bodies
QUINTILES > QUINTILE

QUINTIN *same as* > QUINTAIN

QUINTINS > QUINTIN

QUINTROON *n* person with one Black great-great-grandparent

QUINTS > QUINT

QUINTUPLE *vb* multiply by five ▷ *adj* five times as much or as many ▷ *n* quantity or number five times as great as another

QUINTUPLY > QUINTUPLE

QUINZE *n* card game with rules similar to those of vingt-et-un, except that the score aimed at is 15 rather than 21

QUINZES > QUINZE

QUIP *n* witty saying ▷ *vb* make a quip

QUIPO *same as* > QUIPU

QUIPOS > QUIPO

QUIPPED > QUIP

QUIPPER > QUIP

QUIPPERS > QUIP

QUIPPIER > QUIP

QUIPPIEST > QUIP

QUIPPING > QUIP

QUIPPISH > QUIP

QUIPPU *same as* > QUIPU

QUIPPUS > QUIPPU

QUIPPY > QUIP

QUIPS > QUIP

QUIPSTER *n* person inclined to make sarcastic or witty remarks

QUIPSTERS > QUIPSTER

QUIPU *n* device of the Incas of Peru used to record information, consisting of an arrangement of variously coloured and knotted cords attached to a base cord

QUIPUS > QUIPU

QUIRE *n* set of 24 or 25 sheets of paper ▷ *vb* arrange in quires

QUIRED > QUIRE

QUIRES > QUIRE

QUIRING > QUIRE

QUIRISTER *same as* > CHORISTER

QUIRK *n* peculiarity of character ▷ *vb* quip

QUIRKED > QUIRK

QUIRKIER > QUIRK

QUIRKIEST > QUIRK

QUIRKILY > QUIRK

QUIRKING > QUIRK

QUIRKISH > QUIRK

QUIRKS > QUIRK

QUIRKY > QUIRK

QUIRT *n* whip with a leather thong at one end ▷ *vb* strike with a quirt

QUIRTED > QUIRT

QUIRTING > QUIRT

QUIRTS > QUIRT

QUISLING *n* traitor who aids an occupying enemy force

QUISLINGS > QUISLING

QUIST *n* wood pigeon

QUISTS > QUIST

QUIT *vb* stop (doing something) ▷ *adj* free (from)

QUITCH *vb* move

QUITCHED > QUITCH

QUITCHES > QUITCH

QUITCHING > QUITCH

QUITCLAIM *n* formal renunciation of any claim against a person or of a right to land ▷ *vb* renounce (a claim) formally

QUITE *archaic form of* > QUIT

QUITED > QUITE

QUITES > QUITE

QUITING > QUITE

QUITRENT *n* (formerly) a rent payable by a freeholder or copyholder to his lord that released him from liability to perform services

QUITRENTS > QUITRENT

QUITS > QUIT

QUITTAL *n* repayment of an action with a similar action

QUITTALS > QUITTAL

QUITTANCE *n* release from debt or other obligation

QUITTED > QUIT

QUITTER *n* person who lacks perseverance

QUITTERS > QUITTER

QUITTING > QUIT

QUITTOR *n* infection of the cartilages on the side of a horse's foot, characterized by inflammation and the formation of pus

QUITTORS > QUITTOR

QUIVER *vb* shake with a tremulous movement ▷ *n* shaking or trembling

QUIVERED > QUIVER

QUIVERER > QUIVER

QUIVERERS > QUIVER

QUIVERFUL *n* amount that a quiver can hold

QUIVERIER > QUIVER

QUIVERING > QUIVER

QUIVERISH > QUIVER

QUIVERS > QUIVER

QUIVERY > QUIVER

QUIXOTE *n* impractical idealist

QUIXOTES > QUIXOTE

QUIXOTIC *adj* romantic and unrealistic

QUIXOTISM > QUIXOTIC

QUIXOTRY > QUIXOTIC

QUIZ *n* entertainment in which the knowledge of the players is tested by a series of questions ▷ *vb* investigate by close questioning

QUIZZED > QUIZ

QUIZZER > QUIZ

QUIZZERS > QUIZ

QUIZZERY > QUIZ

QUIZZES > QUIZ

QUIZZICAL *adj* questioning and mocking

QUIZZIFY > QUIZ

QUIZZING > QUIZ

QUIZZINGS > QUIZ

QUOAD *adv* as far as

QUOD *n* jail ▷ *vb* say

QUODDED > QUOD

QUODDING > QUOD

QUODLIBET *n* light piece of music based on two or more popular tunes

QUODLIN *n* cooking apple

QUODLINS > QUODLIN

QUODS > QUOD

QUOHOG *n* edible clam

QUOHOGS > QUOHOG

QUOIF *vb* arrange (the hair)

QUOIFED > QUOIF

QUOIFING > QUOIF

QUOIFS > QUOIF

QUOIN *n* external corner of a building ▷ *vb* wedge

QUOINED > QUOIN

QUOINING > QUOIN

QUOINS > QUOIN

QUOIST *n* wood pigeon

QUOISTS > QUOIST

QUOIT *n* large ring used in the game of quoits ▷ *vb* throw as a quoit

QUOITED > QUOIT

QUOITER > QUOIT

QUOITERS > QUOIT

QUOITING > QUOIT

QUOITS *n* game in which quoits are tossed at a stake in the ground in attempts to encircle it

QUOKKA *n* small Australian wallaby

QUOKKAS > QUOKKA

QUOLL *n* Australian catlike carnivorous marsupial

QUOLLS > QUOLL

QUOMODO *n* manner

QUOMODOS > QUOMODO

QUONDAM *adj* of an earlier time

QUONK *vb* make an accidental noise while broadcasting

QUONKED > QUONK

QUONKING > QUONK

QUONKS > QUONK

QUOOKE *archaic past participle of* > QUAKE

QUOP *vb* pulsate or throb

QUOPPED > QUOP

QUOPPING > QUOP

QUOPS > QUOP

QUORATE *adj* having or being a quorum

QUORUM *n* minimum number of people required to be present at a meeting before any transactions can take place

QUORUMS > QUORUM

QUOTA *n* share that is due from, due to, or allocated to a group or person

QUOTABLE *adj* apt or suitable for quotation

QUOTABLY > QUOTABLE

QUOTAS > QUOTA

QUOTATION *n* written or spoken passage repeated exactly in a later work, speech, or conversation

QUOTATIVE *n* word indicating quotation

QUOTE *vb* repeat (words) exactly from (an earlier work, speech, or conversation) ▷ *n* quotation ▷ *interj* expression used parenthetically to indicate that the words that follow it form a quotation

QUOTED > QUOTE

QUOTER > QUOTE

QUOTERS > QUOTE

QUOTES > QUOTE

QUOTH *vb* said

QUOTHA *interj* expression of mild sarcasm, used in picking up a word or phrase used by someone else

QUOTIDIAN *adj* daily ▷ *n* malarial fever characterized by attacks that recur daily

QUOTIENT *n* result of the division of one number or quantity by another

QUOTIENTS > QUOTIENT

QUOTING > QUOTE

QUOTITION *n* division by repeated subtraction

QUOTUM *same as* > QUOTA

QUOTUMS > QUOTUM

QURSH *same as* > QURUSH

QURSHES > QURUSH

QURUSH *n* Saudi Arabian currency unit

QURUSHES > QURUSH

QUYTE *same as* > QUIT

QUYTED > QUYTE

QUYTES > QUYTE

QUYTING > QUYTE

QWERTIES > QWERTY

QWERTY *n* standard English-language typewriter or computer keyboard

QWERTYS > QWERTY

# Rr

RABANNA n Madagascan woven raffia

RABANNAS > RABANNA

RABAT vb rotate so that the plane rotated coincides with another

RABATINE n type of collar

RABATINES > RABATINE

RABATMENT > RABAT

RABATO n wired or starched collar, often of intricate lace, that stood up at the back and sides: worn in the 17th century

RABATOES > RABATO

RABATOS > RABATO

RABATS > RABAT

RABATTE same as > RABAT

RABATTED > RABAT

RABATTES > RABATTE

RABATTING > RABAT

RABBET n recess, groove, or step, usually of rectangular section, cut into a surface or along the edge of a piece of timber to receive a mating piece ▷ vb cut or form a rabbet in (timber)

RABBETED > RABBET

RABBETING > RABBET

RABBETS > RABBET

RABBI n Jewish spiritual leader

RABBIES > RABBI

RABBIN same as > RABBI

RABBINATE n position, function, or tenure of office of a rabbi

RABBINIC adj of or relating to the rabbis, their teachings, writings, views, language, etc

RABBINICS n study of rabbinic literature of the post-Talmudic period

RABBINISM n teachings and traditions of the rabbis of the Talmudic period

RABBINIST > RABBINISM

RABBINITE > RABBINISM

RABBINS > RABBIN

RABBIS > RABBI

RABBIT n small burrowing mammal with long ears ▷ vb talk too much

RABBITED > RABBIT

RABBITER n person who traps and sells rabbits

RABBITERS > RABBITER

RABBITING n activity of hunting rabbits

RABBITO same as > RABBITOH

RABBITOH n (formerly) an itinerant seller of rabbits for eating

RABBITOHS > RABBITOH

RABBITOS > RABBITO

RABBITRY n place where tame rabbits are kept and bred

RABBITS > RABBIT

RABBITY adj rabbitlike

RABBLE n disorderly crowd of noisy people ▷ vb stir, mix, or skim (the molten charge) in a roasting furnace

RABBLED > RABBLE

RABBLER n iron tool or device for stirring, mixing, or skimming a molten charge in a roasting furnace

RABBLERS > RABBLER

RABBLES > RABBLE

RABBLING > RABBLE

RABBLINGS > RABBLE

RABBONI n very respectful Jewish title or form of address meaning my great master

RABBONIS > RABBONI

RABI n (in Pakistan, India, etc) a crop that is harvested at the end of winter

RABIC > RABIES

RABID adj fanatical

RABIDER > RABID

RABIDEST > RABID

RABIDITY > RABID

RABIDLY > RABID

RABIDNESS > RABID

RABIES n usu fatal viral disease transmitted by dogs and certain other animals

RABIETIC > RABIES

RABIS > RABI

RACA adj biblical word meaning worthless or empty-headed

RACAHOUT n acorn flour or drink made from it

RACAHOUTS > RACAHOUT

RACCAHOUT same as > RACAHOUT

RACCOON n small N American mammal with a long striped tail

RACCOONS > RACCOON

RACE n contest of speed ▷ vb compete with in a race

RACECARD n card or booklet at a race meeting with the times of the races, names

of the runners, etc, printed on it

RACECARDS > RACECARD

RACED > RACE

RACEGOER n one who attends a race meeting, esp a habitual frequenter of race meetings

RACEGOERS > RACEGOER

RACEGOING > RACEGOER

RACEHORSE n horse specially bred for racing

RACEMATE n racemic compound

RACEMATES > RACEMATE

RACEME n cluster of flowers along a central stem, as in the foxglove

RACEMED adj with or in racemes

RACEMES > RACEME

RACEMIC adj of, concerned with, or being a mixture of equal amounts of enantiomers and consequently having no optical activity

RACEMISE same as > RACEMIZE

RACEMISED > RACEMISE

RACEMISES > RACEMISE

RACEMISM > RACEMIC

RACEMISMS > RACEMIC

RACEMIZE vb change or cause to change into a racemic mixture

RACEMIZED > RACEMIZE

RACEMIZES > RACEMIZE

RACEMOID adj resembling a raceme

RACEMOSE adj being or resembling a raceme

RACEMOUS same

_as_ > RACEMOSE
RACEPATH _same_
_as_ > RACETRACK
RACEPATHS > RACEPATH
RACER _n_ person, animal, or machine that races
RACERS > RACER
RACES _pl n the._ a series of contests of speed between horses (or sometimes greyhounds) over a set course at prearranged times
RACETRACK _n_ track for racing
RACEWALK _vb_ race by walking fast rather than running
RACEWALKS > RACEWALK
RACEWAY _n_ racetrack, esp one for banger racing
RACEWAYS > RACEWAY
RACH _n_ scent hound
RACHE _same as_ > RACH
RACHES > RACH
RACHET _same as_ > RATCHET
RACHETED > RACHET
RACHETING > RACHET
RACHETS > RACHET
RACHIAL > RACHIS
RACHIDES > RACHIS
RACHIDIAL > RACHIS
RACHIDIAN > RACHIS
RACHILLA _n_ (in grasses) the short stem of a spikelet that bears the florets
RACHILLAE > RACHILLA
RACHILLAS > RACHILLA
RACHIS _n_ main axis or stem of an inflorescence or compound leaf
RACHISES > RACHIS
RACHITIC > RACHITIS
RACHITIS _another name for_ > RICKETS
RACIAL _adj_ relating to the division of the human species into races
RACIALISE _same as_ > RACIALIZE
RACIALISM _same as_ > RACISM
RACIALIST > RACIALISM
RACIALIZE _vb_ render racial in tone or content
RACIALLY > RACIAL
RACIATION _n_ evolutionary development of races
RACIER > RACY
RACIEST > RACY
RACILY > RACY
RACINESS > RACY
RACING _adj_ denoting or associated with horse races ▷ _n_ practice of engaging horses (or sometimes greyhounds) in contests of speed
RACINGS > RACING
RACISM _n_ hostile attitude or behaviour to members of other races, based on a belief in the innate superiority of one's own

race
RACISMS > RACISM
RACIST > RACISM
RACISTS > RACISM
RACK _n_ framework for holding particular articles, such as coats or luggage ▷ _vb_ cause great suffering to
RACKED > RACK
RACKER > RACK
RACKERS > RACK
RACKET _n_ noisy disturbance ▷ _vb_ make a commotion
RACKETED > RACKET
RACKETEER _n_ person making illegal profits ▷ _vb_ operate a racket
RACKETER _n_ someone making a racket
RACKETERS > RACKETER
RACKETIER > RACKETY
RACKETING > RACKET
RACKETRY _n_ noise and commotion
RACKETS _n_ ball game played in a paved walled court
RACKETT _n_ early double-reeded wind instrument
RACKETTS > RACKETT
RACKETY _adj_ involving noise, commotion and excitement
RACKFUL > RACK
RACKFULS > RACK
RACKING > RACK
RACKINGLY > RACK
RACKINGS > RACK
RACKLE _adj_ dialect word meaning rash
RACKS > RACK
RACKWORK _n_ mechanism with a rack and pinion
RACKWORKS > RACKWORK
RACLETTE _n_ Swiss dish of melted cheese served on boiled potatoes
RACLETTES > RACLETTE
RACLOIR _n_ scraper
RACLOIRS > RACLOIR
RACON _n_ radar beacon
RACONS > RACON
RACONTEUR _n_ skilled storyteller
RACOON _same as_ > RACCOON
RACOONS > RACOON
RACQUET _same as_ > RACKET
RACQUETED > RACQUET
RACQUETS > RACQUET
RACY _adj_ slightly shocking
RAD _n_ former unit of absorbed ionizing radiation dose equivalent to an energy absorption per unit mass of 0.01 joule per kilogram of irradiated material. 1 rad is equivalent to 0.01 gray ▷ _vb_ fear ▷ _adj_ slang term for great
RADAR _n_ device for tracking distant objects by

bouncing high-frequency radio pulses off them
RADARS > RADAR
RADDED > RAD
RADDER > RAD
RADDEST > RAD
RADDING > RAD
RADDLE _same as_ > RUDDLE
RADDLED _adj_ (of a person) unkempt or run-down in appearance
RADDLEMAN _same as_ > RUDDLEMAN
RADDLEMEN > RADDLEMAN
RADDLES > RADDLE
RADDLING > RADDLE
RADDOCKE _same as_ > RUDDOCK
RADDOCKES > RADDOCKE
RADE _(in Scots dialect) past tense of_ > RIDE
RADGE _adj_ angry or uncontrollable ▷ _n_ person acting in such a way
RADGER > RADGE
RADGES > RADGE
RADGEST > RADGE
RADIABLE _adj_ able to be x-rayed
RADIAL _adj_ spreading out from a common central point ▷ _n_ radial-ply tyre
RADIALE _n_ bone in the wrist
RADIALIA > RADIALE
RADIALISE _same as_ > RADIALIZE
RADIALITY > RADIAL
RADIALIZE _vb_ arrange in a pattern of radii
RADIALLY > RADIAL
RADIALS > RADIAL
RADIAN _n_ unit for measuring angles, equal to 57.296°
RADIANCE _n_ quality or state of being radiant
RADIANCES > RADIANCE
RADIANCY _same as_ > RADIANCE
RADIANS > RADIAN
RADIANT _adj_ looking happy ▷ _n_ point or object that emits radiation, esp the part of a heater that gives out heat
RADIANTLY > RADIANT
RADIANTS > RADIANT
RADIATA _as in radiata pine_ type of pine tree
RADIATAS > RADIATA
RADIATE _vb_ spread out from a centre ▷ _adj_ having rays or a radial structure
RADIATED > RADIATE
RADIATELY > RADIATE
RADIATES > RADIATE
RADIATING > RADIATE
RADIATION _n_ transmission of energy from one body to another
RADIATIVE _adj_ emitting or causing the emission of radiation

RADIATOR _n_ arrangement of pipes containing hot water or steam to heat a room
RADIATORS > RADIATOR
RADIATORY _same as_ > RADIATIVE
RADICAL _adj_ fundamental ▷ _n_ person advocating fundamental (political) change
RADICALLY _adv_ thoroughly
RADICALS > RADICAL
RADICAND _n_ number or quantity from which a root is to be extracted, usually preceded by a radical sign
RADICANDS > RADICAND
RADICANT _adj_ forming roots from the stem
RADICATE _vb_ root or cause to take root
RADICATED > RADICATE
RADICATES > RADICATE
RADICCHIO _n_ Italian variety of chicory, with purple leaves streaked with white that are eaten raw in salads
RADICEL _n_ very small root
RADICELS > RADICEL
RADICES > RADIX
RADICLE _n_ small or developing root
RADICLES > RADICLE
RADICULAR _adj_ root-related
RADICULE _same as_ > RADICLE
RADICULES > RADICULE
RADII > RADIUS
RADIO _n_ use of electromagnetic waves for broadcasting, communication, etc ▷ _vb_ transmit (a message) by radio ▷ _adj_ of, relating to, or using radio
RADIOED > RADIO
RADIOGRAM _n_ image produced on a specially sensitized photographic film or plate by radiation, usually by X-rays or gamma rays
RADIOING > RADIO
RADIOLOGY _n_ science of using x-rays in medicine
RADIOMAN _n_ radio operator
RADIOMEN > RADIOMAN
RADIONICS _n_ dowsing technique using a pendulum to detect the energy fields that are emitted by all forms of matter
RADIOS > RADIO
RADIOTHON _n_ lengthy radio programme to raise charity funds, etc
RADISH _n_ small hot-flavoured root vegetable eaten raw in salads
RADISHES > RADISH

**RADIUM** *n* radioactive metallic element
**RADIUMS** > RADIUM
**RADIUS** *n* (length of) a straight line from the centre to the circumference of a circle
**RADIUSES** > RADIUS
**RADIX** *n* any number that is the base of a number system or of a system of logarithms
**RADIXES** > RADIX
**RADOME** *n* protective housing for a radar antenna made from a material that is transparent to radio waves
**RADOMES** > RADOME
**RADON** *n* radioactive gaseous element
**RADONS** > RADON
**RADS** > RAD
**RADULA** *n* horny tooth-bearing strip on the tongue of molluscs that is used for rasping food
**RADULAE** > RADULA
**RADULAR** > RADULA
**RADULAS** > RADULA
**RADULATE** > RADULA
**RADWASTE** *n* radioactive wast
**RADWASTES** > RADWASTE
**RAFALE** *n* burst of artillery fire
**RAFALES** > RAFALE
**RAFF** *n* rubbish
**RAFFIA** *n* prepared palm fibre for weaving mats etc
**RAFFIAS** > RAFFIA
**RAFFINATE** *n* liquid left after a solute has been extracted by solvent extraction
**RAFFINOSE** *n* trisaccharide of fructose, glucose, and galactose that occurs in sugar beet, cotton seed, certain cereals, etc
**RAFFISH** *adj* slightly disreputable
**RAFFISHLY** > RAFFISH
**RAFFLE** *n* lottery with goods as prizes ▷ *vb* offer as a prize in a raffle
**RAFFLED** > RAFFLE
**RAFFLER** > RAFFLE
**RAFFLERS** > RAFFLE
**RAFFLES** > RAFFLE
**RAFFLESIA** *n* any of various tropical Asian parasitic leafless plants whose flowers smell of putrid meat and are pollinated by carrion flies
**RAFFLING** > RAFFLE
**RAFFS** > RAFF
**RAFT** *n* floating platform of logs, planks, etc ▷ *vb* convey on or travel by raft, or make a raft from
**RAFTED** > RAFT
**RAFTER** *n* one of the main

beams of a roof ▷ *vb* to fit with rafters
**RAFTERED** > RAFTER
**RAFTERING** > RAFTER
**RAFTERS** > RAFTER
**RAFTING** > RAFT
**RAFTINGS** > RAFT
**RAFTMAN** *same as* > RAFTSMAN
**RAFTMEN** > RAFTMAN
**RAFTS** > RAFT
**RAFTSMAN** *n* someone who does rafting
**RAFTSMEN** > RAFTSMAN
**RAG** *n* fragment of cloth ▷ *vb* tease ▷ *adj* (in British universities and colleges) of various events organized to raise money for charity
**RAGA** *n* any of several conventional patterns of melody and rhythm that form the basis for freely interpreted compositions. Each pattern is associated with different aspects of religious devotion
**RAGAS** > RAGA
**RAGBAG** *n* confused assortment, jumble
**RAGBAGS** > RAGBAG
**RAGBOLT** *n* bolt that has angled projections on it to prevent it working loose once it has been driven home
**RAGBOLTS** > RAGBOLT
**RAGDE** *archaic past form of* > RAGE
**RAGE** *n* violent anger or passion ▷ *vb* speak or act with fury
**RAGED** > RAGE
**RAGEE** *same as* > RAGI
**RAGEES** > RAGEE
**RAGEFUL** > RAGE
**RAGER** > RAGE
**RAGERS** > RAGE
**RAGES** > RAGE
**RAGG** *same as* > RAGSTONE
**RAGGA** *n* dance-oriented style of reggae
**RAGGAS** > RAGGA
**RAGGED** > RAG
**RAGGEDER** > RAG
**RAGGEDEST** > RAG
**RAGGEDIER** > RAGGEDY
**RAGGEDLY** > RAG
**RAGGEDY** *adj* somewhat ragged
**RAGGEE** *same as* > RAGI
**RAGGEES** > RAGGEE
**RAGGERIES** > RAGGERY
**RAGGERY** *n* rags
**RAGGIER** > RAGGY
**RAGGIES** > RAGGY
**RAGGIEST** > RAGGY
**RAGGING** > RAG
**RAGGINGS** > RAG
**RAGGLE** *n* thin groove cut in stone or brickwork, esp to hold the edge of a roof ▷ *vb* cut a raggle in

**RAGGLED** > RAGGLE
**RAGGLES** > RAGGLE
**RAGGLING** > RAGGLE
**RAGGS** > RAGG
**RAGGY** *adj* raglike ▷ *n* cereal grass cultivated in Africa and Asia for its edible grain
**RAGHEAD** *n* offensive term for an Arab person
**RAGHEADS** > RAGHEAD
**RAGI** *n* cereal grass cultivated in Africa and Asia for its edible grain
**RAGING** > RAGE
**RAGINGLY** > RAGE
**RAGINGS** > RAGE
**RAGINI** *n* Indian musical form related to a raga
**RAGINIS** > RAGINI
**RAGIS** > RAGI
**RAGLAN** *adj* (of a sleeve) joined to a garment by diagonal seams from the neck to the underarm ▷ *n* coat with sleeves that continue to the collar instead of having armhole seams
**RAGLANS** > RAGLAN
**RAGMAN** *n* rag-and-bone man
**RAGMANS** > RAGMAN
**RAGMEN** > RAGMAN
**RAGMENT** *n* statute, roll, or list
**RAGMENTS** > RAGMENT
**RAGOUT** *n* richly seasoned stew of meat and vegetables ▷ *vb* make into a ragout
**RAGOUTED** > RAGOUT
**RAGOUTING** > RAGOUT
**RAGOUTS** > RAGOUT
**RAGPICKER** *n* rag-and-bone man
**RAGS** > RAG
**RAGSTONE** *n* hard sandstone or limestone, esp when used for building
**RAGSTONES** > RAGSTONE
**RAGTAG** *n* disparaging term for common people
**RAGTAGS** > RAGTAG
**RAGTIME** *n* style of jazz piano music
**RAGTIMER** > RAGTIME
**RAGTIMERS** > RAGTIME
**RAGTIMES** > RAGTIME
**RAGTOP** *n* informal word for a car with a folding or removable roof
**RAGTOPS** > RAGTOP
**RAGULED** *same as* > RAGULY
**RAGULY** *adj* (in heraldry) having toothlike or stublike projections
**RAGWEED** *n* any of several plants regarded as weeds, some of which produce a large amount of hay-fever-causing pollen
**RAGWEEDS** > RAGWEED
**RAGWHEEL** *n* toothed wheel

**RAGWHEELS** > RAGWHEEL
**RAGWORK** *n* weaving or needlework using rags
**RAGWORKS** > RAGWORK
**RAGWORM** *n* type of worm that lives chiefly in burrows in sand or mud
**RAGWORMS** > RAGWORM
**RAGWORT** *n* plant with ragged leaves and yellow flowers
**RAGWORTS** > RAGWORT
**RAH** *informal US word for* > CHEER
**RAHED** > RAH
**RAHING** > RAH
**RAHS** > RAH
**RAHUI** *n* Māori prohibition
**RAHUIS** > RAHUI
**RAI** *n* type of Algerian popular music based on traditional Algerian music influenced by modern Western pop
**RAIA** *same as* > RAYAH
**RAIAS** > RAIA
**RAID** *n* sudden surprise attack or search ▷ *vb* make a raid on
**RAIDED** > RAID
**RAIDER** > RAID
**RAIDERS** > RAID
**RAIDING** > RAID
**RAIDINGS** > RAID
**RAIDS** > RAID
**RAIK** *n* wander ▷ *vb* wander
**RAIKED** > RAIK
**RAIKING** > RAIK
**RAIKS** > RAIK
**RAIL** *n* horizontal bar, esp as part of a fence or track ▷ *vb* complain bitterly or loudly
**RAILBED** *n* ballast layer supporting the sleepers of a railway track
**RAILBEDS** > RAILBED
**RAILBIRD** *n* racing aficionado
**RAILBIRDS** > RAILBIRD
**RAILBUS** *n* buslike vehicle for use on railway lines
**RAILBUSES** > RAILBUS
**RAILCAR** *n* passenger-carrying railway vehicle consisting of a single coach with its own power unit
**RAILCARD** *n* card which pensioners, young people, etc can buy, entitling them to cheaper rail travel
**RAILCARDS** > RAILCARD
**RAILCARS** > RAILCAR
**RAILE** *archaic spelling of* > RAIL
**RAILED** > RAIL
**RAILER** > RAIL
**RAILERS** > RAIL
**RAILES** > RAILE
**RAILHEAD** *n* terminal of a railway
**RAILHEADS** > RAILHEAD

**RAILING** *n* fence made of rails supported by posts
**RAILINGLY** > RAIL
**RAILINGS** > RAILING
**RAILLERY** *n* teasing or joking
**RAILLESS** > RAIL
**RAILLIES** > RAILLY
**RAILLY** *old word for* > MOCK
**RAILMAN** *n* railway employee
**RAILMEN** > RAILMAN
**RAILROAD** *same as* > RAILWAY
**RAILROADS** > RAILROAD
**RAILS** > RAIL
**RAILWAY** *n* track of iron rails on which trains run
**RAILWAYS** > RAILWAY
**RAILWOMAN** *n* female railway employee
**RAILWOMEN** > RAILWOMAN
**RAIMENT** *n* clothing
**RAIMENTS** > RAIMENT
**RAIN** *n* water falling in drops from the clouds ▷ *vb* fall or pour down as rain
**RAINBAND** *n* dark band in the solar spectrum caused by water in the atmosphere
**RAINBANDS** > RAINBAND
**RAINBIRD** *n* a bird whose call is believed to be a sign of impending rain
**RAINBIRDS** > RAINBIRD
**RAINBOW** *n* arch of colours in the sky
**RAINBOWED** *adj* resembling or involving a rainbow
**RAINBOWS** > RAINBOW
**RAINBOWY** > RAINBOW
**RAINCHECK** *n* ticket stub allowing readmission to a game on a later date should bad weather prevent play
**RAINCOAT** *n* water-resistant overcoat
**RAINCOATS** > RAINCOAT
**RAINDATE** *n* US term for an alternative date in case of rain
**RAINDATES** > RAINDATE
**RAINDROP** *n* water droplet that falls from the sky when it is raining
**RAINDROPS** > RAINDROP
**RAINE** *archaic spelling of* > REIGN
**RAINED** > RAIN
**RAINES** > RAINE
**RAINFALL** *n* amount of rain
**RAINFALLS** > RAINFALL
**RAINIER** > RAINY
**RAINIEST** > RAINY
**RAINILY** > RAINY
**RAININESS** > RAINY
**RAINING** > RAIN
**RAINLESS** > RAIN
**RAINMAKER** *n* (among American Indians) a professional practitioner of ritual incantations or

other actions intended to cause rain to fall
**RAINOUT** *n* radioactive fallout or atmospheric pollution carried to the earth by rain
**RAINOUTS** > RAINOUT
**RAINPROOF** *adj* (of garments, materials, buildings, etc) impermeable to rainwater ▷ *vb* make rainproof
**RAINS** *pl n the.* the season of heavy rainfall, esp in the tropics
**RAINSPOUT** *n* waterspout
**RAINSTORM** *n* storm with heavy rain
**RAINTIGHT** *same as* > RAINPROOF
**RAINWASH** *n* action of rain ▷ *vb* erode or wet as a result of rain
**RAINWATER** *n* water from rain
**RAINWEAR** *n* protective garments intended for use in wet weather
**RAINWEARS** > RAINWEAR
**RAINY** *adj* characterized by a large rainfall
**RAIRD** *same as* > REIRD
**RAIRDS** > RAIRD
**RAIS** > RAI
**RAISABLE** > RAISE
**RAISE** *vb* lift up ▷ *n* increase in pay
**RAISEABLE** > RAISE
**RAISED** > RAISE
**RAISER** > RAISE
**RAISERS** > RAISE
**RAISES** > RAISE
**RAISIN** *n* dried grape
**RAISING** *n* rule that moves a constituent from an embedded clause into the main clause
**RAISINGS** > RAISING
**RAISINS** > RAISIN
**RAISINY** > RAISIN
**RAISONNE** *adj* carefully thought out
**RAIT** *same as* > RET
**RAITA** *n* Indian dish of chopped cucumber, mint, etc, in yogurt, served with curries
**RAITAS** > RAITA
**RAITED** > RAIT
**RAITING** > RAIT
**RAITS** > RAIT
**RAIYAT** *same as* > RYOT
**RAIYATS** > RAIYAT
**RAJ** *n* (in India) government
**RAJA** *same as* > RAJAH
**RAJAH** *n* (in India, formerly) a ruler or landlord: sometimes used as a form of address or as a title preceding a name
**RAJAHS** > RAJAH
**RAJAHSHIP** > RAJAH
**RAJAS** > RAJA

**RAJASHIP** > RAJA
**RAJASHIPS** > RAJA
**RAJES** > RAJ
**RAKE** *n* tool with a long handle and a crosspiece with teeth, used for smoothing earth or gathering leaves, hay, etc ▷ *vb* gather or smooth with a rake
**RAKED** > RAKE
**RAKEE** *same as* > RAKI
**RAKEES** > RAKEE
**RAKEHELL** *n* dissolute man ▷ *adj* profligate
**RAKEHELLS** > RAKEHELL
**RAKEHELLY** *adj* profligate
**RAKEOFF** *n* share of profits, esp one that is illegal or given as a bribe
**RAKEOFFS** > RAKEOFF
**RAKER** *n* person who rakes
**RAKERIES** > RAKERY
**RAKERS** > RAKER
**RAKERY** *n* rakish behaviour
**RAKES** > RAKE
**RAKESHAME** *n* old word for someone shamefully dissolute
**RAKI** *n* strong spirit distilled in Turkey, the former Yugoslavia, etc, from grain, usually flavoured with aniseed or other aromatics
**RAKING** *n* offence committed when a player deliberately scrapes an opponent's leg, arm, etc with the studs of his or her boots
**RAKINGS** > RAKING
**RAKIS** > RAKI
**RAKISH** *adj* dashing or jaunty
**RAKISHLY** > RAKISH
**RAKSHAS** *same as* > RAKSHASA
**RAKSHASA** *n* Hindu demon
**RAKSHASAS** > RAKSHASA
**RAKSHASES** > RAKSHAS
**RAKU** *n* type of Japanese pottery
**RAKUS** > RAKU
**RALE** *n* abnormal coarse crackling sound heard on auscultation of the chest, usually caused by the accumulation of fluid in the lungs
**RALES** > RALE
**RALLIED** > RALLY
**RALLIER** > RALLY
**RALLIERS** > RALLY
**RALLIES** > RALLY
**RALLIFORM** *adj* of rail family of birds
**RALLINE** *adj* of, relating to, or belonging to the *Rallidae*, a family of birds that includes the rails, crakes, and coots
**RALLY** *n* large gathering of people for a meeting ▷ *vb*

bring or come together after dispersal or for a common cause
**RALLYE** *US variant of* > RALLY
**RALLYES** > RALLYE
**RALLYING** > RALLY
**RALLYINGS** > RALLY
**RALLYIST** > RALLY
**RALLYISTS** > RALLY
**RALPH** *vb* slang word meaning vomit
**RALPHED** > RALPH
**RALPHING** > RALPH
**RALPHS** > RALPH
**RAM** *n* male sheep ▷ *vb* strike against with force
**RAMADA** *n* outdoor eating area with roof but open sides
**RAMADAS** > RAMADA
**RAMAKIN** *same as* > RAMEKIN
**RAMAKINS** > RAMAKIN
**RAMAL** *adj* relating to a branch or branches
**RAMATE** *adj* with branches
**RAMBLA** *n* dried-up riverbed
**RAMBLAS** > RAMBLA
**RAMBLE** *vb* walk without a definite route ▷ *n* walk, esp in the country
**RAMBLED** > RAMBLE
**RAMBLER** *n* person who rambles
**RAMBLERS** > RAMBLER
**RAMBLES** > RAMBLE
**RAMBLING** *adj* large and irregularly shaped ▷ *n* activity of going for long walks in the country
**RAMBLINGS** > RAMBLING
**RAMBUTAN** *n* SE Asian tree that has bright red edible fruit
**RAMBUTANS** > RAMBUTAN
**RAMCAT** *n* dialect word for a male cat
**RAMCATS** > RAMCAT
**RAMEAL** *same as* > RAMAL
**RAMEE** *same as* > RAMIE
**RAMEES** > RAMEE
**RAMEKIN** *n* small ovenproof dish for a single serving of food
**RAMEKINS** > RAMEKIN
**RAMEN** *n* Japanese dish consisting of a clear broth containing thin white noodles and sometimes vegetables, meat, etc
**RAMENS** > RAMEN
**RAMENTA** > RAMENTUM
**RAMENTUM** *n* any of the thin brown scales that cover the stems and leaves of young ferns
**RAMEOUS** *same as* > RAMAL
**RAMEQUIN** *same as* > RAMEKIN
**RAMEQUINS** > RAMEQUIN
**RAMET** *n* any of the individuals in a group of clones

RAMETS > RAMET
RAMI *same as* > RAMIE
RAMIE *n* woody Asian shrub with broad leaves and a stem that yields a flaxlike fibre
RAMIES > RAMIE
RAMIFIED > RAMIFY
RAMIFIES > RAMIFY
RAMIFORM *adj* having a branchlike shape
RAMIFY *vb* become complex
RAMIFYING > RAMIFY
RAMILIE *same as* > RAMILLIE
RAMILIES > RAMILIE
RAMILLIE *n* wig with a plait at the back fashionable in the 18th century
RAMILLIES > RAMILLIE
RAMIN *n* swamp-growing tree found in Malaysia and Indonesia
RAMINS > RAMIN
RAMIS > RAMI
RAMJET *n* type of jet engine in which fuel is burned in a duct using air compressed by the forward speed of the aircraft
RAMJETS > RAMJET
RAMMED > RAM
RAMMEL *n* discarded or waste matter
RAMMELS > RAMMEL
RAMMER > RAM
RAMMERS > RAM
RAMMIER > RAMMISH
RAMMIES > RAMMISH
RAMMIEST > RAMMISH
RAMMING > RAM
RAMMISH *adj* like a ram, esp in being lustful or foul-smelling
RAMMISHLY > RAMMISH
RAMMLE *n* collection of items saved in case they become useful
RAMMLES > RAMMLE
RAMMY *n* noisy disturbance or free-for-all *▷ vb* make a rammy
RAMONA *same as* > SAGEBRUSH
RAMONAS > RAMONA
RAMOSE *adj* having branches
RAMOSELY > RAMOSE
RAMOSITY > RAMOSE
RAMOUS *same as* > RAMOSE
RAMOUSLY > RAMOSE
RAMP *n* slope joining two level surfaces *▷ vb* (esp of animals) to rush around in a wild excited manner
RAMPAGE *vb* dash about violently
RAMPAGED > RAMPAGE
RAMPAGER > RAMPAGE
RAMPAGERS > RAMPAGE
RAMPAGES > RAMPAGE
RAMPAGING > RAMPAGE

RAMPANCY > RAMPANT
RAMPANT *adj* growing or spreading uncontrollably
RAMPANTLY > RAMPANT
RAMPART *n* mound or wall for defence *▷ vb* provide with a rampart
RAMPARTED > RAMPART
RAMPARTS > RAMPART
RAMPAUGE *Scots variant of* > RAMPAGE
RAMPAUGED > RAMPAUGE
RAMPAUGES > RAMPAUGE
RAMPED > RAMP
RAMPER > RAMP
RAMPERS > RAMP
RAMPICK *same as* > RAMPIKE
RAMPICKED > RAMPICK
RAMPICKS > RAMPICK
RAMPIKE *n* US or dialect word for a dead tree
RAMPIKES > RAMPIKE
RAMPING > RAMP
RAMPINGS > RAMP
RAMPION *n* European and Asian plant that has clusters of bluish flowers and an edible white tuberous root used in salads
RAMPIONS > RAMPION
RAMPIRE *archaic variant of* > RAMPART
RAMPIRED > RAMPIRE
RAMPIRES > RAMPIRE
RAMPOLE *same as* > RAMPIKE
RAMPOLES > RAMPOLE
RAMPS > RAMP
RAMPSMAN *n* mugger
RAMPSMEN > RAMPSMAN
RAMROD *n* long thin rod used for cleaning the barrel of a gun or forcing gunpowder into an old-fashioned gun *▷ adj* (of someone's posture) very straight and upright *▷ vb* drive
RAMRODDED > RAMROD
RAMRODS > RAMROD
RAMS > RAM
RAMSHORN as in *ramshorn snail* any of various freshwater snails
RAMSHORNS > RAMSHORN
RAMSON *n* type of garlic
RAMSONS > RAMSON
RAMSTAM *adv* headlong *▷ adj* headlong
RAMTIL *n* African plant grown in India esp for its oil
RAMTILLA *same as* > RAMTIL
RAMTILLAS > RAMTILLA
RAMTILS > RAMTIL
RAMULAR *adj* relating to a branch or branches
RAMULI > RAMULUS
RAMULOSE *adj* (of the parts or organs of animals and plants) having many small branches
RAMULOUS *same as* > RAMULOSE

RAMULUS *n* small branch
RAMUS *n* barb of a bird's feather
RAN > RUN
RANA *n* genus of frogs
RANARIAN *adj* of or relating to frogs
RANARIUM *n* place for keeping frogs
RANARIUMS > RANARIUM
RANAS > RANA
RANCE *Scots word for* > PROP
RANCED > RANCE
RANCEL *vb* (in Shetland and Orkney) carry out a search
RANCELS > RANCEL
RANCES > RANCE
RANCH *n* large cattle farm in the American West *▷ vb* run a ranch
RANCHED > RANCH
RANCHER *n* person who owns, manages, or works on a ranch
RANCHERIA *n* native American settlement or home of a rancher
RANCHERIE *n* (in British Columbia, Canada) a settlement of North American Indians, esp on a reserve
RANCHERO *another word for* > RANCHER
RANCHEROS > RANCHERO
RANCHERS > RANCHER
RANCHES > RANCH
RANCHING > RANCH
RANCHINGS > RANCH
RANCHLESS > RANCH
RANCHLIKE > RANCH
RANCHMAN *n* man who owns, manages, or works on a ranch
RANCHMEN > RANCHMAN
RANCHO *n* hut or group of huts for housing ranch workers
RANCHOS > RANCHO
RANCID *adj* (of butter, bacon, etc) stale and having an offensive smell
RANCIDER > RANCID
RANCIDEST > RANCID
RANCIDITY > RANCID
RANCIDLY > RANCID
RANCING > RANCE
RANCOR *same as* > RANCOUR
RANCORED > RANCOR
RANCOROUS > RANCOUR
RANCORS > RANCOR
RANCOUR *n* deep bitter hate
RANCOURS > RANCOUR
RAND *n* monetary unit of S Africa; leather strip on the heel of a shoe *▷ vb* cut into rands
RANDAN *n* boat rowed by three people, in which the person in the middle uses two oars and the people fore and aft use one oar each
RANDANS > RANDAN

RANDED > RAND
RANDEM *adv* with three horses harnessed together as a team *▷ n* carriage or team of horses so driven
RANDEMS > RANDEM
RANDIE *same as* > RANDY
RANDIER > RANDY
RANDIES > RANDY
RANDIEST > RANDY
RANDILY > RANDY
RANDINESS > RANDY
RANDING > RAND
RANDLORD *n* mining magnate during the 19th-century gold boom in Johannesburg
RANDLORDS > RANDLORD
RANDOM *adj* made or done by chance or without plan *▷ n* (in mining) the course of a vein of ore
RANDOMISE *same as* > RANDOMIZE
RANDOMIZE *vb* set up (a selection process, sample, etc) in a deliberately random way in order to enhance the statistical validity of any results obtained
RANDOMLY > RANDOM
RANDOMS > RANDOM
RANDON *old variant of* > RANDOM
RANDONS > RANDON
RANDS > RAND
RANDY *adj* sexually aroused *▷ n* rude or reckless person
RANEE *same as* > RANI
RANEES > RANEE
RANG > RING
RANGATIRA *n* Māori chief of either sex
RANGE *n* limits of effectiveness or variation *▷ vb* vary between one point and another
RANGED > RANGE
RANGELAND *n* land that naturally produces forage plants suitable for grazing but where rainfall is too low or erratic for growing crops
RANGER *n* official in charge of a nature reserve etc
RANGERS > RANGER
RANGES > RANGE
RANGI *n* sky
RANGIER > RANGY
RANGIEST > RANGY
RANGILY > RANGY
RANGINESS > RANGY
RANGING > RANGE
RANGINGS > RANGE
RANGIORA *n* evergreen New Zealand shrub or small tree with large ovate leaves and small greenish-white flowers
RANGIORAS > RANGIORA
RANGIS > RANGI
RANGOLI *n* traditional

Indian ground decoration
using coloured sand or
chalks

**RANGOLIS** > RANGOLI

**RANGY** adj having long
slender limbs

**RANI** n wife or widow of a
rajah

**RANID** n frog

**RANIDS** > RANID

**RANIFORM** n froglike

**RANINE** adj relating to frogs

**RANIS** > RANI

**RANK** n relative place or
position ▷ vb have a
specific rank or position
▷ adj complete or absolute

**RANKE** archaic variant
of > RANK

**RANKED** > RANK

**RANKER** n soldier in the
ranks

**RANKERS** > RANKER

**RANKES** > RANKE

**RANKEST** > RANK

**RANKING** adj prominent
▷ n position on a scale

**RANKINGS** > RANKING

**RANKISH** adj old word
meaning rather rank

**RANKISM** n discrimination
against people on the
grounds of rank

**RANKISMS** > RANKISM

**RANKLE** vb continue to
cause resentment or
bitterness

**RANKLED** > RANKLE

**RANKLES** > RANKLE

**RANKLESS** > RANK

**RANKLING** > RANKLE

**RANKLY** > RANK

**RANKNESS** > RANK

**RANKS** > RANK

**RANKSHIFT** n phenomenon
in which a unit at one
rank in the grammar has
the function of a unit at a
lower rank, as for example
in the phrase the house on
the corner, where the words
on the corner shift down
from the rank of group to
the rank of word ▷ vb
shift or be shifted from
one linguistic rank to
another

**RANPIKE** same as > RAMPIKE

**RANPIKES** > RANPIKE

**RANSACK** vb search
thoroughly

**RANSACKED** > RANSACK

**RANSACKER** > RANSACK

**RANSACKS** > RANSACK

**RANSEL** same as > RANCEL

**RANSELS** > RANSEL

**RANSHAKLE** Scots word
for > RANSACK

**RANSOM** n money
demanded in return for the
release of someone who
has been kidnapped ▷ vb
pay money to obtain the
release of a captive

**RANSOMED** > RANSOM

**RANSOMER** > RANSOM

**RANSOMERS** > RANSOM

**RANSOMING** > RANSOM

**RANSOMS** > RANSOM

**RANT** vb talk in a loud and
excited way ▷ n loud
excited speech

**RANTED** > RANT

**RANTER** > RANT

**RANTERISM** > RANT

**RANTERS** > RANT

**RANTING** > RANT

**RANTINGLY** > RANT

**RANTINGS** > RANT

**RANTIPOLE** n reckless
person ▷ vb behave like a
rantipole

**RANTS** > RANT

**RANULA** n saliva-filled cyst
that develops under the
tongue

**RANULAR** n cyst of lower
surface of tongue

**RANULAS** > RANULA

**RANUNCULI** pl n plants of
the genus that includes
the buttercup, crowfoot,
spearwort, and lesser
celandine

**RANZEL** same as > RANCEL

**RANZELMAN** n (in Shetland
and Orkney) type of
constable

**RANZELMEN** > RANZELMAN

**RANZELS** > RANZEL

**RAOULIA** n flowering plant
of New Zealand

**RAOULIAS** > RAOULIA

**RAP** vb hit with a sharp
quick blow ▷ n quick
sharp blow

**RAPACIOUS** adj greedy or
grasping

**RAPACITY** > RAPACIOUS

**RAPE** vb force to submit to
sexual intercourse ▷ n act
of raping

**RAPED** > RAPE

**RAPER** > RAPE

**RAPERS** > RAPE

**RAPES** > RAPE

**RAPESEED** n seed of the
oilseed rape plant

**RAPESEEDS** > RAPESEED

**RAPHAE** > RAPHE

**RAPHANIA** n type of
ergotism possibly
resulting from
consumption of radish
seeds

**RAPHANIAS** > RAPHANIA

**RAPHE** n elongated ridge of
conducting tissue along
the side of certain seeds

**RAPHES** > RAPHE

**RAPHIA** same as > RAFFIA

**RAPHIAS** > RAPHIA

**RAPHIDE** n any of
numerous needle-shaped
crystals, usually of calcium
oxalate, that occur in
many plant cells as a
metabolic product

**RAPHIDES** > RAPHIDE

**RAPHIS** same as > RAPHIDE

**RAPID** adj quick, swift

**RAPIDER** > RAPID

**RAPIDEST** > RAPID

**RAPIDITY** > RAPID

**RAPIDLY** > RAPID

**RAPIDNESS** > RAPID

**RAPIDS** pl n part of a river
with a fast turbulent
current

**RAPIER** n fine-bladed
sword

**RAPIERED** adj carrying a
rapier

**RAPIERS** > RAPIER

**RAPINE** n pillage or
plundering

**RAPINES** > RAPINE

**RAPING** > RAPE

**RAPINI** pl n type of leafy
vegetable

**RAPIST** n person who
commits rape

**RAPISTS** > RAPIST

**RAPLOCH** n Scots word
for homespun woollen
material ▷ adj Scots
word meaning coarse or
homemade

**RAPLOCHS** > RAPLOCH

**RAPPAREE** n Irish irregular
soldier of the late 17th
century

**RAPPAREES** > RAPPAREE

**RAPPE** n Arcadian dish of
grated potatoes and pork
or chicken

**RAPPED** > RAP

**RAPPEE** n moist English
snuff of the 18th and 19th
centuries

**RAPPEES** > RAPPEE

**RAPPEL** n (formerly) a
drumbeat to call soldiers
to arms ▷ vb abseil

**RAPPELED** > RAPPEL

**RAPPELING** > RAPPEL

**RAPPELLED** > RAPPEL

**RAPPELS** > RAPPEL

**RAPPEN** n Swiss coin equal
to one hundredth of a franc

**RAPPER** n something used
for rapping, such as a
knocker on a door

**RAPPERS** > RAPPER

**RAPPES** > RAPPE

**RAPPING** > RAP

**RAPPINGS** > RAP

**RAPPINI** same as > RAPINI

**RAPPORT** n harmony or
agreement

**RAPPORTS** > RAPPORT

**RAPS** > RAP

**RAPT** adj engrossed or
spellbound

**RAPTLY** > RAPT

**RAPTNESS** > RAPT

**RAPTOR** n any bird of prey

**RAPTORIAL** adj (of the
feet of birds) adapted for
seizing prey

**RAPTORS** > RAPTOR

**RAPTURE** n ecstasy ▷ vb

entrance

**RAPTURED** > RAPTURE

**RAPTURES** > RAPTURE

**RAPTURING** > RAPTURE

**RAPTURISE** same
as > RAPTURIZE

**RAPTURIST** > RAPTURE

**RAPTURIZE** vb go into
ecstasies

**RAPTUROUS** adj
experiencing or
manifesting ecstatic joy or
delight

**RARE** adj uncommon
▷ archaic spelling of > REAR

**RAREBIT** as in Welsh rarebit
dish made from melted
cheese and sometimes
milk and seasonings and
served on toast

**RAREBITS** > RAREBIT

**RARED** > RARE

**RAREE** as in raree show
street show or carnival

**RAREFIED** adj highly
specialized, exalted

**RAREFIER** > RAREFY

**RAREFIERS** > RAREFY

**RAREFIES** > RAREFY

**RAREFY** vb make or become
rarer or less dense

**RAREFYING** > RAREFY

**RARELY** adv seldom

**RARENESS** > RARE

**RARER** > RARE

**RARERIPE** adj ripening
early ▷ n fruit or vegetable
that ripens early

**RARERIPES** > RARERIPE

**RARES** > RARE

**RAREST** > RARE

**RARIFIED** same
as > RAREFIED

**RARIFIES** > RARIFY

**RARIFY** same as > RAREFY

**RARIFYING** > RARIFY

**RARING** adj ready

**RARITIES** > RARITY

**RARITY** n something that
is valuable because it is
unusual

**RARK** as in rark up informal
New Zealand expression
meaning reprimand
severely

**RARKED** > RARK

**RARKING** > RARK

**RARKS** > RARK

**RAS** n headland

**RASBORA** n often brightly
coloured tropical fish

**RASBORAS** > RASBORA

**RASCAILLE** n rabble

**RASCAL** n rogue ▷ adj
belonging to the mob or
rabble

**RASCALDOM** > RASCAL

**RASCALISM** > RASCAL

**RASCALITY** n mischievous,
disreputable, or dishonest
character, behaviour, or
action

**RASCALLY** adj dishonest or
mean ▷ adv in a dishonest

or mean fashion
**RASCALS** > RASCAL
**RASCASSE** n any of various fishes with venomous spines on the dorsal and anal fins
**RASCASSES** > RASCASSE
**RASCHEL** n type of loosely knitted fabric
**RASCHELS** > RASCHEL
**RASE** same as > RAZE
**RASED** > RASE
**RASER** > RASE
**RASERS** > RASE
**RASES** > RASE
**RASH** adj hasty, reckless, or incautious ▷ n eruption of spots or patches on the skin ▷ vb (in old usage) cut
**RASHED** > RASH
**RASHER** n thin slice of bacon
**RASHERS** > RASHER
**RASHES** > RASH
**RASHEST** > RASH
**RASHIE** n Australian word for a shirt worn by surfers as protection against sunburn, heat rash, etc
**RASHIES** > RASHIE
**RASHING** > RASH
**RASHLIKE** > RASH
**RASHLY** > RASH
**RASHNESS** > RASH
**RASING** > RASE
**RASMALAI** n Indian dessert made from cheese, milk, and almonds
**RASMALAIS** > RASMALAI
**RASORIAL** adj (of birds such as domestic poultry) adapted for scratching the ground for food
**RASP** n harsh grating noise ▷ vb speak in a grating voice
**RASPATORY** n surgical instrument for abrading
**RASPBERRY** n red juicy edible berry
**RASPED** > RASP
**RASPER** > RASP
**RASPERS** > RASP
**RASPIER** > RASPY
**RASPIEST** > RASPY
**RASPINESS** > RASPY
**RASPING** adj (esp of a noise) harsh or grating
**RASPINGLY** > RASPING
**RASPINGS** pl n browned breadcrumbs for coating fish and other foods before frying, baking, etc
**RASPISH** > RASP
**RASPS** > RASP
**RASPY** same as > RASPING
**RASSE** n small S Asian civet
**RASSES** > RASSE
**RASSLE** dialect variant of > WRESTLE
**RASSLED** > RASSLE
**RASSLES** > RASSLE
**RASSLING** > RASSLE

**RAST** archaic past form of > RACE
**RASTA** n member of a particular Black religious movement
**RASTAFARI** n Black religious movement
**RASTER** n image consisting of rows of pixel information, such as a JPEG, GIF etc ▷ vb use web-based technology to turn a digital image into a large picture composed of a grid of black and white dots
**RASTERED** > RASTER
**RASTERING** > RASTER
**RASTERISE** same as > RASTERIZE
**RASTERIZE** vb (in computing) convert into pixels for screen output
**RASTERS** > RASTER
**RASTRUM** n pen for drawing the five lines of a musical stave simultaneously
**RASTRUMS** > RASTRUM
**RASURE** n scraping
**RASURES** > RASURE
**RAT** n small rodent ▷ vb inform (on)
**RATA** n New Zealand hard-wood forest tree with crimson flowers
**RATABLE** adj able to be rated or evaluated
**RATABLES** pl n property that is liable to rates
**RATABLY** > RATABLE
**RATAFEE** same as > RATAFIA
**RATAFEES** > RATAFEE
**RATAFIA** n liqueur made from fruit
**RATAFIAS** > RATAFIA
**RATAL** n amount on which rates are assessed ▷ adj of or relating to rates (local taxation)
**RATALS** > RATAL
**RATAN** same as > RATTAN
**RATANIES** > RATANY
**RATANS** > RATAN
**RATANY** n flowering desert shrub
**RATAPLAN** n drumming sound ▷ vb drum
**RATAPLANS** > RATAPLAN
**RATAS** > RATA
**RATATAT** n sound of knocking on a door
**RATATATS** > RATATAT
**RATBAG** n eccentric, stupid, or unreliable person
**RATBAGS** > RATBAG
**RATBITE** as in ratbite fever acute infectious disease that can be caught from the bite of an infected rat
**RATCH** same as > RATCHET
**RATCHED** > RATCH
**RATCHES** > RATCH
**RATCHET** n set of teeth on a bar or wheel allowing

motion in one direction only ▷ vb move using or as if using a ratchet system
**RATCHETED** > RATCHET
**RATCHETS** > RATCHET
**RATCHING** > RATCH
**RATE** n degree of speed or progress ▷ vb consider or value
**RATEABLE** same as > RATABLE
**RATEABLY** > RATEABLE
**RATED** > RATE
**RATEEN** same as > RATINE
**RATEENS** > RATEEN
**RATEL** n large African and S Asian musteline mammal
**RATELS** > RATEL
**RATEMETER** n device for counting and averaging the number of events in a given time
**RATEPAYER** n person who pays local rates on a building
**RATER** > RATE
**RATERS** > RATE
**RATES** pl n (in some countries) a tax on property levied by a local authority
**RATFINK** n contemptible or undesirable person
**RATFINKS** > RATFINK
**RATFISH** n deep-sea fish with a whiplike tail
**RATFISHES** > RATFISH
**RATH** same as > RATHE
**RATHA** n (in India) a four-wheeled carriage drawn by horses or bullocks
**RATHAS** > RATHA
**RATHE** adj blossoming or ripening early in the season
**RATHER** adv some extent ▷ interj expression of strong affirmation ▷ sentence substitute expression of strong affirmation, often in answer to a question
**RATHEREST** adv archaic word equivalent to soonest
**RATHERIPE** same as > RATHRIPE
**RATHERISH** adv (in informal English) quite or fairly
**RATHEST** adv dialect or archaic word meaning soonest
**RATHOLE** n rat's hiding place or burrow
**RATHOLES** > RATHOLE
**RATHOUSE** n psychiatric hospital or asylum
**RATHOUSES** > RATHOUSE
**RATHRIPE** adj dialect word meaning mature or ripe ahead of time ▷ n variety of apple or other fruit that is quick to ripen

**RATHRIPES** > RATHRIPE
**RATHS** > RATH
**RATICIDE** n rat poison
**RATICIDES** > RATICIDE
**RATIFIED** > RATIFY
**RATIFIER** > RATIFY
**RATIFIERS** > RATIFY
**RATIFIES** > RATIFY
**RATIFY** vb give formal approval to
**RATIFYING** > RATIFY
**RATINE** n coarse loosely woven cloth
**RATINES** > RATINE
**RATING** n valuation or assessment
**RATINGS** > RATING
**RATIO** n relationship between two numbers or amounts expressed as a proportion
**RATION** n fixed allowance of food etc ▷ vb limit to a certain amount per person
**RATIONAL** adj reasonable, sensible ▷ n rational number
**RATIONALE** n reason for an action or decision
**RATIONALS** > RATIONAL
**RATIONED** > RATION
**RATIONING** > RATION
**RATIONS** pl n fixed daily allowance of food, esp to military personnel or when supplies are limited
**RATIOS** > RATIO
**RATITE** adj (of flightless birds) having a breastbone that lacks a keel for the attachment of flight muscles ▷ n bird, such as an ostrich, kiwi, or rhea, that belongs to this group
**RATITES** > RATITE
**RATLIKE** > RAT
**RATLIN** same as > RATLINE
**RATLINE** n any of a series of light lines tied across the shrouds of a sailing vessel for climbing aloft
**RATLINES** > RATLINE
**RATLING** n young rat
**RATLINGS** > RATLING
**RATLINS** > RATLIN
**RATO** n rocket-assisted take-off
**RATOO** same as > RATU
**RATOON** n new shoot that grows from near the root or crown of crop plants, esp the sugar cane, after the old growth has been cut back ▷ vb propagate or cause to propagate by such a growth
**RATOONED** > RATOON
**RATOONER** n plant that spreads by ratooning
**RATOONERS** > RATOONER
**RATOONING** > RATOON
**RATOONS** > RATOON
**RATOOS** > RATOO
**RATOS** > RATO

**RATPACK** *n* members of the press who pursue celebrities and give wide coverage of their private lives

**RATPACKS** > RATPACK

**RATPROOF** *adj* impenetrable by rats

**RATS** > RAT

**RATSBANE** *n* rat poison, esp arsenic oxide

**RATSBANES** > RATSBANE

**RATTAIL** *n* type of fish

**RATTAILED** *adj* having tail like rat

**RATTAILS** > RATTAIL

**RATTAN** *n* climbing palm with jointed stems used for canes

**RATTANS** > RATTAN

**RATTED** > RAT

**RATTEEN** *same as* > RATINE

**RATTEENS** > RATTEEN

**RATTEN** *vb* sabotage or steal tools in order to disrupt the work of

**RATTENED** > RATTEN

**RATTENER** > RATTEN

**RATTENERS** > RATTEN

**RATTENING** > RATTEN

**RATTENS** > RATTEN

**RATTER** *n* dog or cat that catches and kills rats

**RATTERIES** > RATTERY

**RATTERS** > RATTER

**RATTERY** *n* rats' dwelling area

**RATTIER** > RATTY

**RATTIEST** > RATTY

**RATTILY** > RATTY

**RATTINESS** > RATTY

**RATTING** > RAT

**RATTINGS** > RAT

**RATTISH** *adj* of, resembling, or infested with rats

**RATTLE** *vb* give out a succession of short sharp sounds ▷ *n* short sharp sound

**RATTLEBAG** *n* rattle made out of a bag containing a variety of different things

**RATTLEBOX** *n* any of various tropical and subtropical leguminous plants that have inflated pods within which the seeds rattle

**RATTLED** > RATTLE

**RATTLER** *n* something that rattles

**RATTLERS** > RATTLER

**RATTLES** > RATTLE

**RATTLIER** > RATTLY

**RATTLIEST** > RATTLY

**RATTLIN** *same as* > RATLINE

**RATTLINE** *same as* > RATLINE

**RATTLINES** > RATTLINE

**RATTLING** *adv* exceptionally, very ▷ *n* succession of short sharp sounds

**RATTLINGS** > RATTLING

**RATTLINS** > RATTLIN

**RATTLY** *adj* having a rattle

**RATTON** *n* dialect word for a little rat

**RATTONS** > RATTON

**RATTOON** *same as* > RATOON

**RATTOONED** > RATTOON

**RATTOONS** > RATTOON

**RATTRAP** *n* device for catching rats

**RATTRAPS** > RATTRAP

**RATTY** *adj* bad-tempered, irritable

**RATU** *n* title used by Fijian chiefs or nobles

**RATUS** > RATU

**RAUCID** *adj* raucous

**RAUCITIES** > RAUCOUS

**RAUCITY** > RAUCOUS

**RAUCLE** *adj* Scots word for rough or tough

**RAUCLER** > RAUCLE

**RAUCLEST** > RAUCLE

**RAUCOUS** *adj* hoarse or harsh

**RAUCOUSLY** > RAUCOUS

**RAUGHT** *archaic past form of* > REACH

**RAUN** *n* fish roe or spawn

**RAUNCH** *n* lack of polish or refinement ▷ *vb* behave in a raunchy manner

**RAUNCHED** > RAUNCH

**RAUNCHES** > RAUNCH

**RAUNCHIER** > RAUNCHY

**RAUNCHILY** > RAUNCHY

**RAUNCHING** > RAUNCH

**RAUNCHY** *adj* earthy, sexy

**RAUNGE** *archaic word for* > RANGE

**RAUNGED** > RAUNGE

**RAUNGES** > RAUNGE

**RAUNGING** > RAUNGE

**RAUNS** > RAUN

**RAUPATU** *n* confiscation or seizure of land

**RAUPATUS** > RAUPATU

**RAUPO** *n* New Zealand bulrush

**RAURIKI** *n* sow thistle, any of various plants with prickly leaves, milky juice and yellow heads

**RAURIKIS** > RAURIKI

**RAUWOLFIA** *n* tropical tree or shrub

**RAVAGE** *vb* cause extensive damage to ▷ *n* destructive action

**RAVAGED** > RAVAGE

**RAVAGER** > RAVAGE

**RAVAGERS** > RAVAGE

**RAVAGES** > RAVAGE

**RAVAGING** > RAVAGE

**RAVE** *vb* talk wildly or with enthusiasm ▷ *n* enthusiastically good review

**RAVED** > RAVE

**RAVEL** *vb* tangle or become entangled ▷ *n* tangle or complication

**RAVELED** > RAVEL

**RAVELER** > RAVEL

**RAVELERS** > RAVEL

**RAVELIN** *n* outwork having two embankments at a salient angle

**RAVELING** > RAVEL

**RAVELINGS** > RAVEL

**RAVELINS** > RAVELIN

**RAVELLED** > RAVEL

**RAVELLER** > RAVEL

**RAVELLERS** > RAVEL

**RAVELLING** > RAVEL

**RAVELLY** > RAVEL

**RAVELMENT** *n* ravel or tangle

**RAVELS** > RAVEL

**RAVEN** *n* black bird like a large crow ▷ *adj* (of hair) shiny black ▷ *vb* seize or seek (plunder, prey, etc)

**RAVENED** > RAVEN

**RAVENER** > RAVEN

**RAVENERS** > RAVEN

**RAVENING** *adj* (of animals) hungrily searching for prey

**RAVENINGS** *pl n* rapacious behaviour and activities

**RAVENLIKE** > RAVEN

**RAVENOUS** *adj* very hungry

**RAVENS** > RAVEN

**RAVER** *n* person who leads a wild or uninhibited social life

**RAVERS** > RAVER

**RAVES** > RAVE

**RAVIGOTE** *n* rich white sauce with herbs and shallots

**RAVIGOTES** > RAVIGOTE

**RAVIGOTTE** *n* French salad sauce

**RAVIN** *archaic spelling of* > RAVEN

**RAVINE** *n* narrow steep-sided valley worn by a stream

**RAVINED** > RAVIN

**RAVINES** > RAVINE

**RAVING** *adj* delirious ▷ *n* frenzied, irrational, or wildly extravagant talk or utterances

**RAVINGLY** > RAVING

**RAVINGS** > RAVING

**RAVINING** > RAVIN

**RAVINS** > RAVIN

**RAVIOLI** *n* small squares of pasta with a savoury filling

**RAVIOLIS** > RAVIOLI

**RAVISH** *vb* enrapture

**RAVISHED** > RAVISH

**RAVISHER** > RAVISH

**RAVISHERS** > RAVISH

**RAVISHES** > RAVISH

**RAVISHING** *adj* lovely or entrancing

**RAW** *adj* uncooked ▷ *as in* *in the raw* without clothes

**RAWARU** *n* New Zealand name for blue cod

**RAWBONE** *archaic variant of* > RAWBONED

**RAWBONED** *adj* having a lean bony physique

**RAWER** > RAW

**RAWEST** > RAW

**RAWHEAD** *n* bogeyman

**RAWHEADS** > RAWHEAD

**RAWHIDE** *n* untanned hide ▷ *vb* whip

**RAWHIDED** > RAWHIDE

**RAWHIDES** > RAWHIDE

**RAWHIDING** > RAWHIDE

**RAWIN** *n* monitoring of winds in the upper atmosphere using radar and a balloon

**RAWING** *(in dialect) same as* > ROWEN

**RAWINGS** > RAWING

**RAWINS** > RAWIN

**RAWISH** > RAW

**RAWLY** > RAW

**RAWMAISH** *n* Irish word for foolish or exaggerated talk

**RAWN** *(in dialect) same as* > ROWEN

**RAWNESS** > RAW

**RAWNESSES** > RAW

**RAWNS** > RAWN

**RAWS** > RAW

**RAX** *vb* stretch or extend ▷ *n* act of stretching or straining

**RAXED** > RAX

**RAXES** > RAX

**RAXING** > RAX

**RAY** *n* single line or narrow beam of light ▷ *vb* (of an object) to emit (light) in rays or (of light) to issue in the form of rays

**RAYA** *same as* > RAYAH

**RAYAH** *n* (formerly) a non-Muslim subject of the Ottoman Empire

**RAYAHS** > RAYAH

**RAYAS** > RAYA

**RAYED** > RAY

**RAYGRASS** *same as* > RYEGRASS

**RAYING** > RAY

**RAYLE** *archaic spelling of* > RAIL

**RAYLED** > RAYLE

**RAYLES** > RAYLE

**RAYLESS** *adj* dark

**RAYLESSLY** > RAYLESS

**RAYLET** *n* small ray

**RAYLETS** > RAYLET

**RAYLIKE** *adj* resembling a ray

**RAYLING** > RAYLE

**RAYNE** *archaic spelling of* > REIGN

**RAYNES** > RAYNE

**RAYON** *n* (fabric made of) a synthetic fibre

**RAYONS** > RAYON

**RAYS** > RAY

**RAZE** *vb* destroy (buildings or a town) completely

**RAZED** > RAZE

**RAZEE** *n* sailing ship that has had its upper deck or decks removed ▷ *vb* remove the upper deck or decks of (a sailing ship)

RAZEED > RAZEE
RAZEEING > RAZEE
RAZEES > RAZEE
RAZER > RAZE
RAZERS > RAZE
RAZES > RAZE
RAZING > RAZE
RAZMATAZ *n* noisy or showy fuss or activity
RAZOO *n* imaginary coin
RAZOOS > RAZOO
RAZOR *n* sharp instrument for shaving ▷ *vb* cut or shave with a razor
RAZORABLE *adj* able to be shaved
RAZORBACK *n* another name for the common rorqual
RAZORBILL *n* sea bird of the North Atlantic with a stout sideways flattened bill
RAZORED > RAZOR
RAZORING > RAZOR
RAZORS > RAZOR
RAZURE *same as* > RASURE
RAZURES > RAZURE
RAZZ *vb* make fun of
RAZZBERRY *US variant of* > RASPBERRY
RAZZED > RAZZ
RAZZES > RAZZ
RAZZIA *n* raid for plunder or slaves, esp one carried out by Moors in North Africa
RAZZIAS > RAZZIA
RAZZING > RAZZ
RAZZLE as in *on the razzle* celebration
RAZZLES > RAZZLE
RE *prep* concerning
REABSORB *vb* absorb again
REABSORBS > REABSORB
REACCEDE *vb* accede again
REACCEDED > REACCEDE
REACCEDES > REACCEDE
REACCENT *vb* accent again
REACCENTS > REACCENT
REACCEPT *vb* accept again
REACCEPTS > REACCEPT
REACCLAIM *vb* acclaim again
REACCUSE *vb* accuse again
REACCUSED > REACCUSE
REACCUSES > REACCUSE
REACH *vb* arrive at ▷ *n* distance that one can reach
REACHABLE > REACH
REACHED > REACH
REACHER > REACH
REACHERS > REACH
REACHES > REACH
REACHING > REACH
REACHLESS *adj* unreachable or unattainable
REACQUIRE *vb* get or gain (something) again which one has owned
REACT *vb* act in response (to)

REACTANCE *n* resistance to the flow of an alternating current caused by the inductance or capacitance of the circuit
REACTANT *n* substance that participates in a chemical reaction
REACTANTS > REACTANT
REACTED > REACT
REACTING > REACT
REACTION *n* physical or emotional response to a stimulus
REACTIONS > REACTION
REACTIVE *adj* chemically active
REACTOR *n* apparatus in which a nuclear reaction is maintained and controlled to produce nuclear energy
REACTORS > REACTOR
REACTS > REACT
REACTUATE *vb* activate again
READ *vb* look at and understand or take in (written or printed matter) ▷ *n* matter suitable for reading
READABLE *adj* enjoyable to read
READABLY > READABLE
READAPT *vb* adapt again
READAPTED > READAPT
READAPTS > READAPT
READD *vb* add again
READDED > READD
READDICT *vb* cause to become addicted again
READDICTS > READDICT
READDING > READD
READDRESS *vb* look at or discuss (an issue, situation, etc) from a new or different point of view
READDS > READD
READER *n* person who reads
READERLY *adj* pertaining to or suitable for a reader
READERS > READER
READIED > READY
READIER > READY
READIES *pl n* ready money
READIEST > READY
READILY *adv* promptly
READINESS *n* state of being ready or prepared
READING > READ
READINGS > READ
READJUST *vb* adapt to a new situation
READJUSTS > READJUST
READMIT *vb* let (a person, country, etc) back in to a place or organization
READMITS > READMIT
READOPT *vb* adopt again
READOPTED > READOPT
READOPTS > READOPT
READORN *vb* adorn again
READORNED > READORN
READORNS > READORN
READOUT *n* act of retrieving

information from a computer memory or storage device
READOUTS > READOUT
READS > READ
READVANCE *vb* advance again
READVISE *vb* advise again
READVISED > READVISE
READVISES > READVISE
READY *adj* prepared for use or action ▷ *vb* prepare
READYING > READY
READYMADE *adj* made for purchase and immediate use by any customer
REAEDIFY *vb* rebuild
REAEDIFYE *same as* > REAEDIFY
REAFFIRM *vb* state again, confirm
REAFFIRMS > REAFFIRM
REAFFIX *vb* affix again
REAFFIXED > REAFFIX
REAFFIXES > REAFFIX
REAGENCY > REAGENT
REAGENT *n* chemical substance that reacts with another, used to detect the presence of the other
REAGENTS > REAGENT
REAGIN *n* type of antibody that is formed against an allergen and is attached to the cells of a tissue. The antigen–antibody reaction that occurs on subsequent contact with the allergen causes tissue damage, leading to the release of histamine and other substances responsible for an allergic reaction
REAGINIC > REAGIN
REAGINS > REAGIN
REAK *same as* > RECK
REAKED > REAK
REAKING > REAK
REAKS > REAK
REAL *adj* existing in fact ▷ *n* name of a former small Spanish or Spanish-American silver coin as well as of the standard monetary unit of Brazil
REALER > REAL
REALES > REAL
REALEST > REAL
REALGAR *n* rare orange-red soft mineral consisting of arsenic sulphide in monoclinic crystalline form
REALGARS > REALGAR
REALIA *pl n* real-life facts and material used in teaching
REALIGN *vb* change or put back to a new or former place or position
REALIGNED > REALIGN
REALIGNS > REALIGN
REALISE *same as* > REALIZE

REALISED > REALISE
REALISER > REALISE
REALISERS > REALISE
REALISES > REALISE
REALISING > REALISE
REALISM *n* awareness or acceptance of things as they are
REALISMS > REALISM
REALIST *n* person who is aware of and accepts the physical universe, events, etc, as they are
REALISTIC *adj* seeing and accepting things as they really are, practical
REALISTS > REALIST
REALITIES > REALITY
REALITY *n* state of things as they are
REALIZE *vb* become aware or grasp the significance of
REALIZED > REALIZE
REALIZER > REALIZE
REALIZERS > REALIZE
REALIZES > REALIZE
REALIZING > REALIZE
REALLIE *old or dialect variant of* > REALLY
REALLIED > REALLY
REALLIES > REALLY
REALLOT *vb* allot again
REALLOTS > REALLOT
REALLY *adv* very ▷ *interj* exclamation of dismay, doubt, or surprise ▷ *vb* (in archaic usage) rally
REALLYING > REALLY
REALM *n* kingdom
REALMLESS > REALM
REALMS > REALM
REALNESS > REAL
REALO *n* member of the German Green party with moderate views
REALOS > REALO
REALS > REAL
REALTER *vb* alter again
REALTERED > REALTER
REALTERS > REALTER
REALTIE *n* archaic word meaning sincerity
REALTIES > REALTY
REALTIME *adj* (of a data-processing system) constantly updating to reflect the latest changes in data
REALTOR *n* estate agent
REALTORS > REALTOR
REALTY *n* immovable property
REAM *n* twenty quires of paper, generally 500 sheets ▷ *vb* enlarge (a hole) by use of a reamer
REAME *archaic variant of* > REALM
REAMED > REAM
REAMEND *vb* amend again
REAMENDED > REAMEND
REAMENDS > REAMEND
REAMER *n* steel tool with a cylindrical or tapered

shank around which
longitudinal teeth
are ground, used for
smoothing the bores of
holes accurately to size
**REAMERS** > REAMER
**REAMES** > REAME
**REAMIER** > REAMY
**REAMIEST** > REAMY
**REAMING** > REAM
**REAMS** > REAM
**REAMY** *Scots for* > CREAMY
**REAN** *same as* > REEN
**REANALYSE** *vb* analyse
again
**REANALYZE** *US spelling
of* > REANALYSE
**REANIMATE** *vb* refresh or
enliven (something) again
**REANNEX** *vb* annex again
**REANNEXED** > REANNEX
**REANNEXES** > REANNEX
**REANOINT** *vb* anoint again
**REANOINTS** > REANOINT
**REANS** > REAN
**REANSWER** *vb* answer again
**REANSWERS** > REANSWER
**REAP** *vb* cut and gather (a
harvest)
**REAPABLE** > REAP
**REAPED** > REAP
**REAPER** *n* person who reaps
or machine for reaping
**REAPERS** > REAPER
**REAPHOOK** *n* sickle
**REAPHOOKS** > REAPHOOK
**REAPING** > REAP
**REAPPAREL** *vb* clothe again
**REAPPEAR** *vb* appear again
**REAPPEARS** > REAPPEAR
**REAPPLIED** > REAPPLY
**REAPPLIES** > REAPPLY
**REAPPLY** *vb* put or spread
(something) on again
**REAPPOINT** *vb* assign (a
person, committee, etc) to
a post or role again
**REAPPROVE** *vb* approve
again
**REAPS** > REAP
**REAR** *n* back part ▷ *vb* care
for and educate (children)
**REARED** > REAR
**REARER** > REAR
**REARERS** > REAR
**REARGUARD** *n* troops
protecting the rear of an
army
**REARGUE** *vb* argue again
**REARGUED** > REARGUE
**REARGUES** > REARGUE
**REARGUING** > REARGUE
**REARHORSE** *n* mantis
**REARING** > REAR
**REARISE** *vb* arise again
**REARISEN** > REARISE
**REARISES** > REARISE
**REARISING** > REARISE
**REARLY** *old word for* > EARLY
**REARM** *vb* arm again
**REARMED** > REARM
**REARMICE** > REARMOUSE
**REARMING** > REARM
**REARMOST** *adj* nearest the

back
**REARMOUSE** *same
as* > REREMOUSE
**REARMS** > REARM
**REAROSE** > REARISE
**REAROUSAL** > REAROUSE
**REAROUSE** *vb* arouse again
**REAROUSED** > REAROUSE
**REAROUSES** > REAROUSE
**REARRANGE** *vb* organize
differently, alter
**REARREST** *vb* arrest again
**REARRESTS** > REARREST
**REARS** > REAR
**REARWARD** *adj* in the rear
▷ *adv* towards the rear
▷ *n* position in the rear,
esp the rear division of a
military formation
**REARWARDS** *same
as* > REARWARD
**REASCEND** *vb* ascend again
**REASCENDS** > REASCEND
**REASCENT** *n* new ascent
**REASCENTS** > REASCENT
**REASON** *n* cause or motive
▷ *vb* think logically in
forming conclusions
**REASONED** *adj* well thought
out or well presented
**REASONER** > REASON
**REASONERS** > REASON
**REASONING** *n* process of
drawing conclusions from
facts or evidence
**REASONS** > REASON
**REASSAIL** *vb* assail again
**REASSAILS** > REASSAIL
**REASSERT** *vb* assert (rights,
claims, etc) again
**REASSERTS** > REASSERT
**REASSESS** *vb* reconsider
the value or importance of
**REASSIGN** *vb* move
(personnel, resources,
etc) to a new post,
department, location, etc
**REASSIGNS** > REASSIGN
**REASSORT** *vb* assort again
**REASSORTS** > REASSORT
**REASSUME** *vb* assume again
**REASSUMED** > REASSUME
**REASSUMES** > REASSUME
**REASSURE** *vb* restore
confidence to
**REASSURED** > REASSURE
**REASSURER** > REASSURE
**REASSURES** > REASSURE
**REAST** *same as* > REEST
**REASTED** > REAST
**REASTIER** > REASTY
**REASTIEST** > REASTY
**REASTING** > REAST
**REASTS** > REAST
**REASTY** *adj* (in dialect)
rancid
**REATA** *n* lasso
**REATAS** > REATA
**REATE** *n* type of crowfoot
**REATES** > REATE
**REATTACH** *vb* attach again
**REATTACK** *vb* attack again
**REATTACKS** > REATTACK
**REATTAIN** *vb* attain again

**REATTAINS** > REATTAIN
**REATTEMPT** *vb* attempt
again
**REAVAIL** *vb* avail again
**REAVAILED** > REAVAIL
**REAVAILS** > REAVAIL
**REAVE** *vb* carry off
(property, prisoners, etc)
by force
**REAVED** > REAVE
**REAVER** > REAVE
**REAVERS** > REAVE
**REAVES** > REAVE
**REAVING** > REAVE
**REAVOW** *vb* avow again
**REAVOWED** > REAVOW
**REAVOWING** > REAVOW
**REAVOWS** > REAVOW
**REAWAKE** *vb* awake again
**REAWAKED** > REAWAKE
**REAWAKEN** *vb* emerge or
rouse from sleep
**REAWAKENS** > REAWAKEN
**REAWAKES** > REAWAKE
**REAWAKING** > REAWAKE
**REAWOKE** > REAWAKE
**REAWOKEN** > REAWAKE
**REB** *n* Confederate soldier
in the American Civil War
(1861–65)
**REBACK** *vb* provide with
a new back, backing, or
lining
**REBACKED** > REBACK
**REBACKING** > REBACK
**REBACKS** > REBACK
**REBADGE** *vb* relaunch (a
product) under a new
name, brand, or logo
**REBADGED** > REBADGE
**REBADGES** > REBADGE
**REBADGING** > REBADGE
**REBAIT** *vb* bait again
**REBAITED** > REBAIT
**REBAITING** > REBAIT
**REBAITS** > REBAIT
**REBALANCE** *vb* balance
again
**REBAPTISE** *same
as* > REBAPTIZE
**REBAPTISM** *n* new baptism
**REBAPTIZE** *vb* baptize
again
**REBAR** *n* rod providing
reinforcement in concrete
structures
**REBARS** > REBAR
**REBATABLE** > REBATE
**REBATE** *n* discount or
refund ▷ *vb* cut a rabbet in
**REBATED** > REBATE
**REBATER** > REBATE
**REBATERS** > REBATE
**REBATES** > REBATE
**REBATING** > REBATE
**REBATO** *same as* > RABATO
**REBATOES** > REBATO
**REBATOS** > REBATO
**REBBE** *n* individual's
chosen spiritual mentor
**REBBES** > REBBE
**REBBETZIN** *n* wife of a
rabbi
**REBEC** *n* medieval stringed

instrument resembling
the violin but having a
lute-shaped body
**REBECK** *same as* > REBEC
**REBECKS** > REBECK
**REBECS** > REBEC
**REBEGAN** > REBEGIN
**REBEGIN** *vb* begin again
**REBEGINS** > REBEGIN
**REBEGUN** > REBEGIN
**REBEL** *vb* revolt against the
ruling power ▷ *n* person
who rebels ▷ *adj* rebelling
**REBELDOM** > REBEL
**REBELDOMS** > REBEL
**REBELLED** > REBEL
**REBELLER** > REBEL
**REBELLERS** > REBEL
**REBELLING** > REBEL
**REBELLION** *n* organized
open resistance to
authority
**REBELLOW** *vb* re-echo
loudly
**REBELLOWS** > REBELLOW
**REBELS** > REBEL
**REBID** *vb* bid again
**REBIDDEN** > REBID
**REBIDDING** > REBID
**REBIDS** > REBID
**REBILL** *vb* bill again
**REBILLED** > REBILL
**REBILLING** > REBILL
**REBILLS** > REBILL
**REBIND** *vb* bind again
**REBINDING** > REBIND
**REBINDS** > REBIND
**REBIRTH** *n* revival or
renaissance
**REBIRTHS** > REBIRTH
**REBIT** > REBITE
**REBITE** *vb* (in printing) to
give another application
of acid in order to cause
further cutting of a plate
**REBITES** > REBITE
**REBITING** > REBITE
**REBITTEN** > REBITE
**REBLEND** *vb* blend again
**REBLENDED** > REBLEND
**REBLENDS** > REBLEND
**REBLENT** *same as* > REBLEND
**REBLOOM** *vb* bloom again
**REBLOOMED** > REBLOOM
**REBLOOMS** > REBLOOM
**REBLOSSOM** *vb* blossom
again
**REBOANT** *adj* resounding or
reverberating
**REBOARD** *vb* board again
**REBOARDED** > REBOARD
**REBOARDS** > REBOARD
**REBOATION** *n* repeated
bellow
**REBODIED** > REBODY
**REBODIES** > REBODY
**REBODY** *vb* give a new body
to
**REBODYING** > REBODY
**REBOIL** *vb* boil again
**REBOILED** > REBOIL
**REBOILING** > REBOIL
**REBOILS** > REBOIL
**REBOOK** *vb* book again

REBOOKED > REBOOK
REBOOKING > REBOOK
REBOOKS > REBOOK
REBOOT vb shut down and then restart (a computer system)
REBOOTED > REBOOT
REBOOTING > REBOOT
REBOOTS > REBOOT
REBOP same as > BEBOP
REBOPS > REBOP
REBORE n boring of a cylinder to restore its true shape ▷ vb carry out this process
REBORED > REBORE
REBORES > REBORE
REBORING > REBORE
REBORN adj active again after a period of inactivity
REBORROW vb borrow again
REBORROWS > REBORROW
REBOTTLE vb bottle again
REBOTTLED > REBOTTLE
REBOTTLES > REBOTTLE
REBOUGHT > REBUY
REBOUND vb spring back ▷ n act of rebounding
REBOUNDED > REBOUND
REBOUNDER > REBOUND
REBOUNDS > REBOUND
REBOZO n long wool or linen scarf covering the shoulders and head, worn by Latin American women
REBOZOS > REBOZO
REBRACE vb brace again
REBRACED > REBRACE
REBRACES > REBRACE
REBRACING > REBRACE
REBRANCH vb branch again
REBRAND vb change or update the image of (an organization or product)
REBRANDED > REBRAND
REBRED > REBREED
REBREED vb breed again
REBREEDS > REBREED
REBS > REB
REBUFF vb reject or snub ▷ n blunt refusal, snub
REBUFFED > REBUFF
REBUFFING > REBUFF
REBUFFS > REBUFF
REBUILD vb build (a building or town) again, after severe damage
REBUILDED archaic past form of > REBUILD
REBUILDS > REBUILD
REBUILT > REBUILD
REBUKABLE > REBUKE
REBUKE vb scold sternly ▷ n stern scolding
REBUKED > REBUKE
REBUKEFUL > REBUKE
REBUKER > REBUKE
REBUKERS > REBUKE
REBUKES > REBUKE
REBUKING > REBUKE
REBURIAL > REBURY
REBURIALS > REBURY
REBURIED > REBURY
REBURIES > REBURY

REBURY vb bury again
REBURYING > REBURY
REBUS n puzzle consisting of pictures and symbols representing words or syllables
REBUSES > REBUS
REBUT vb prove that (a claim) is untrue
REBUTMENT > REBUT
REBUTS > REBUT
REBUTTAL > REBUT
REBUTTALS > REBUT
REBUTTED > REBUT
REBUTTER n defendant's pleading in reply to a claimant's surrejoinder
REBUTTERS > REBUTTER
REBUTTING > REBUT
REBUTTON vb button again
REBUTTONS > REBUTTON
REBUY vb buy again
REBUYING > REBUY
REBUYS > REBUY
REC n short for recreation
RECAL same as > RECALL
RECALESCE vb glow again
RECALL vb recollect or remember ▷ n ability to remember
RECALLED > RECALL
RECALLER > RECALL
RECALLERS > RECALL
RECALLING > RECALL
RECALLS > RECALL
RECALMENT > RECAL
RECALS > RECALL
RECAMIER n shade of pink
RECAMIERS > RECAMIER
RECANE vb cane again
RECANED > RECANE
RECANES > RECANE
RECANING > RECANE
RECANT vb withdraw (a statement or belief) publicly
RECANTED > RECANT
RECANTER > RECANT
RECANTERS > RECANT
RECANTING > RECANT
RECANTS > RECANT
RECAP vb recapitulate ▷ n recapitulation
RECAPPED > RECAP
RECAPPING > RECAP
RECAPS > RECAP
RECAPTION n process of taking back one's own wife, child, property, etc, without causing a breach of the peace
RECAPTOR > RECAPTURE
RECAPTORS > RECAPTURE
RECAPTURE vb experience again ▷ n act of recapturing
RECARPET vb replace one carpet with another
RECARPETS > RECARPET
RECARRIED > RECARRY
RECARRIES > RECARRY
RECARRY vb carry again
RECAST vb organize or set out in a different way

RECASTING > RECAST
RECASTS > RECAST
RECATALOG vb catalogue again
RECATCH vb catch again
RECATCHES > RECATCH
RECAUGHT > RECATCH
RECAUTION vb caution again
RECCE vb reconnoitre ▷ n reconnaissance
RECCED > RECCE
RECCEED > RECCE
RECCEING > RECCE
RECCES > RECCE
RECCIED > RECCY
RECCIES > RECCY
RECCO same as > RECCE
RECCOS > RECCO
RECCY same as > RECCE
RECCYING > RECCY
RECEDE vb move to a more distant place
RECEDED > RECEDE
RECEDES > RECEDE
RECEDING > RECEDE
RECEIPT n written acknowledgment of money or goods received ▷ vb acknowledge payment of (a bill), as by marking it
RECEIPTED > RECEIPT
RECEIPTOR n person who receipts
RECEIPTS > RECEIPT
RECEIVAL n act of receiving or state of being received
RECEIVALS > RECEIVAL
RECEIVE vb take, accept, or get
RECEIVED adj generally accepted
RECEIVER n part of telephone that is held to the ear
RECEIVERS > RECEIVER
RECEIVES > RECEIVE
RECEIVING > RECEIVE
RECEMENT vb cement again
RECEMENTS > RECEMENT
RECENCIES > RECENT
RECENCY > RECENT
RECENSE vb revise
RECENSED > RECENSE
RECENSES > RECENSE
RECENSING > RECENSE
RECENSION n critical revision of a literary work
RECENSOR vb censor again
RECENSORS > RECENSOR
RECENT adj having happened lately
RECENTER > RECENT
RECENTEST > RECENT
RECENTLY > RECENT
RECENTRE vb centre again
RECENTRED > RECENTRE
RECENTRES > RECENTRE
RECEPT n idea or image formed in the mind by repeated experience of a particular pattern of

sensory stimulation
RECEPTION n area for receiving guests, clients, etc
RECEPTIVE adj willing to accept new ideas, suggestions, etc
RECEPTOR n sensory nerve ending that changes specific stimuli into nerve impulses
RECEPTORS > RECEPTOR
RECEPTS > RECEPT
RECERTIFY vb certify again
RECESS n niche or alcove ▷ vb place or set (something) in a recess
RECESSED > RECESS
RECESSES > RECESS
RECESSING > RECESS
RECESSION n period of economic difficulty when little is being bought or sold
RECESSIVE adj receding ▷ n recessive gene or character
RECHANGE vb change again
RECHANGED > RECHANGE
RECHANGES > RECHANGE
RECHANNEL vb channel again
RECHARGE vb cause (a battery etc) to take in and store electricity again
RECHARGED > RECHARGE
RECHARGER > RECHARGE
RECHARGES > RECHARGE
RECHART vb chart again
RECHARTED > RECHART
RECHARTER vb charter again
RECHARTS > RECHART
RECHATE same as > RECHEAT
RECHATES > RECHATE
RECHAUFFE n warmed-up leftover food
RECHEAT n (in a hunt) sounding of the horn to call back the hounds ▷ vb sound the horn to call back the hounds
RECHEATED > RECHEAT
RECHEATS > RECHEAT
RECHECK vb check again
RECHECKED > RECHECK
RECHECKS > RECHECK
RECHERCHE adj refined or elegant
RECHEW vb chew again
RECHEWED > RECHEW
RECHEWING > RECHEW
RECHEWS > RECHEW
RECHIE adj smoky
RECHLESSE archaic form of > RECKLESS
RECHOOSE vb choose again
RECHOOSES > RECHOOSE
RECHOSE > RECHOOSE
RECHOSEN > RECHOOSE
RECIPE n directions for cooking a dish
RECIPES > RECIPE
RECIPIENT n person who

receives something
**RECIRCLE** vb circle again
**RECIRCLED** > RECIRCLE
**RECIRCLES** > RECIRCLE
**RECISION** n act of
cancelling or rescinding
**RECISIONS** > RECISION
**RECIT** n narrative
**RECITABLE** > RECITE
**RECITAL** n musical
performance by a soloist
or soloists
**RECITALS** > RECITAL
**RECITE** vb repeat (a poem,
story, etc) aloud to an
audience
**RECITED** > RECITE
**RECITER** > RECITE
**RECITERS** > RECITE
**RECITES** > RECITE
**RECITING** > RECITE
**RECITS** > RECIT
**RECK** vb mind or care about
(something)
**RECKAN** adj strained,
tormented, or twisted
**RECKED** > RECK
**RECKING** > RECK
**RECKLESS** adj heedless of
danger
**RECKLING** dialect word
for > RUNT
**RECKLINGS** > RECKLING
**RECKON** vb consider or
think
**RECKONED** > RECKON
**RECKONER** n any of various
devices or tables used to
facilitate reckoning, esp a
ready reckoner
**RECKONERS** > RECKONER
**RECKONING** n counting or
calculating
**RECKONS** > RECKON
**RECKS** > RECK
**RECLAD** > RECLOTHE
**RECLAIM** vb regain
possession of ▷ n act
of reclaiming or state of
being reclaimed
**RECLAIMED** > RECLAIM
**RECLAIMER** > RECLAIM
**RECLAIMS** > RECLAIM
**RECLAME** n public acclaim
or attention
**RECLAMES** > RECLAME
**RECLASP** vb clasp again
**RECLASPED** > RECLASP
**RECLASPS** > RECLASP
**RECLEAN** vb clean again
**RECLEANED** > RECLEAN
**RECLEANS** > RECLEAN
**RECLIMB** vb climb again
**RECLIMBED** > RECLIMB
**RECLIMBS** > RECLIMB
**RECLINATE** adj (esp of a
leaf or stem) naturally
curved or bent backwards
so that the upper part rests
on the ground
**RECLINE** vb rest in a
leaning position
**RECLINED** > RECLINE
**RECLINER** n type of

armchair having a back
that can be adjusted to
slope at various angles
and, usually, a leg rest
**RECLINERS** > RECLINER
**RECLINES** > RECLINE
**RECLINING** > RECLINE
**RECLOSE** vb close again
**RECLOSED** > RECLOSE
**RECLOSES** > RECLOSE
**RECLOSING** > RECLOSE
**RECLOTHE** vb clothe again
**RECLOTHED** > RECLOTHE
**RECLOTHES** > RECLOTHE
**RECLUSE** n person who
avoids other people ▷ adj
solitary
**RECLUSELY** > RECLUSE
**RECLUSES** > RECLUSE
**RECLUSION** > RECLUSE
**RECLUSIVE** > RECLUSE
**RECLUSORY** n recluse's
dwelling or cell
**RECOAL** vb supply or be
supplied with fresh coal
**RECOALED** > RECOAL
**RECOALING** > RECOAL
**RECOALS** > RECOAL
**RECOAT** vb coat again
**RECOATED** > RECOAT
**RECOATING** > RECOAT
**RECOATS** > RECOAT
**RECOCK** vb cock again
**RECOCKED** > RECOCK
**RECOCKING** > RECOCK
**RECOCKS** > RECOCK
**RECODE** vb put into a new
code
**RECODED** > RECODE
**RECODES** > RECODE
**RECODIFY** vb codify again
**RECODING** > RECODE
**RECOGNISE** same
as > RECOGNIZE
**RECOGNIZE** vb identify as
(a person or thing) already
known
**RECOIL** vb jerk or spring
back ▷ n backward jerk
**RECOILED** > RECOIL
**RECOILER** > RECOIL
**RECOILERS** > RECOIL
**RECOILING** > RECOIL
**RECOILS** > RECOIL
**RECOIN** vb coin again
**RECOINAGE** n new coinage
**RECOINED** > RECOIN
**RECOINING** > RECOIN
**RECOINS** > RECOIN
**RECOLLECT** vb call back to
mind, remember
**RECOLLET** n member of
a particular Franciscan
order
**RECOLLETS** > RECOLLET
**RECOLOR** vb give a new
colour to
**RECOLORED** > RECOLOR
**RECOLORS** > RECOLOR
**RECOMB** vb comb again
**RECOMBED** > RECOMB
**RECOMBINE** vb join
together again
**RECOMBING** > RECOMB

**RECOMBS** > RECOMB
**RECOMFORT** archaic word
for > COMFORT
**RECOMMEND** vb advise or
counsel
**RECOMMIT** vb send (a bill)
back to a committee for
further consideration
**RECOMMITS** > RECOMMIT
**RECOMPACT** vb compact
again
**RECOMPILE** vb compile
again
**RECOMPOSE** vb restore to
composure or calmness
**RECOMPUTE** vb compute
again
**RECON** n smallest
genetic unit capable of
recombining
**RECONCILE** vb harmonize
(conflicting beliefs etc)
**RECONDITE** adj difficult to
understand
**RECONDUCT** vb conduct
again
**RECONFER** vb confer again
**RECONFERS** > RECONFER
**RECONFINE** vb confine
again
**RECONFIRM** vb confirm (an
arrangement, agreement,
etc) again
**RECONNECT** vb link or be
linked together again
**RECONNED** > RECON
**RECONNING** > RECON
**RECONQUER** vb conquer
again
**RECONS** > RECON
**RECONSIGN** vb consign
again
**RECONSOLE** vb console
again
**RECONSULT** vb consult
again
**RECONTACT** vb contact
again
**RECONTOUR** vb contour
again
**RECONVENE** vb gather
together again after an
interval
**RECONVERT** vb change
(something) back to a
previous state or form
**RECONVEY** vb convey again
**RECONVEYS** > RECONVEY
**RECONVICT** vb convict
again
**RECOOK** vb cook again
**RECOOKED** > RECOOK
**RECOOKING** > RECOOK
**RECOOKS** > RECOOK
**RECOPIED** > RECOPY
**RECOPIES** > RECOPY
**RECOPY** vb copy again
**RECOPYING** > RECOPY
**RECORD** n document or
other thing that preserves
information ▷ vb put in
writing
**RECORDED** > RECORD
**RECORDER** n person or

machine that records, esp
a video, cassette, or tape
recorder
**RECORDERS** > RECORDER
**RECORDING** n something,
esp music, that has been
recorded
**RECORDIST** n person that
records
**RECORDS** > RECORD
**RECORK** vb cork again
**RECORKED** > RECORK
**RECORKING** > RECORK
**RECORKS** > RECORK
**RECOUNT** vb tell in detail
**RECOUNTAL** > RECOUNT
**RECOUNTED** > RECOUNT
**RECOUNTER** n narrator of
a story
**RECOUNTS** > RECOUNT
**RECOUP** vb regain or make
good (a loss)
**RECOUPE** vb (in law) keep
back or withhold
**RECOUPED** > RECOUP
**RECOUPING** > RECOUP
**RECOUPLE** vb couple again
**RECOUPLED** > RECOUPLE
**RECOUPLES** > RECOUPLE
**RECOUPS** > RECOUP
**RECOURE** archaic variant
of > RECOVER
**RECOURED** > RECOURE
**RECOURES** > RECOURE
**RECOURING** > RECOURE
**RECOURSE** archaic word
for > RETURN
**RECOURSED** > RECOURSE
**RECOURSES** > RECOURSE
**RECOVER** vb become
healthy again
**RECOVERED** > RECOVER
**RECOVEREE** n (in law)
person found against in a
recovery case
**RECOVERER** > RECOVER
**RECOVEROR** n (in law)
person successfully
demanding a right in a
recovery case
**RECOVERS** > RECOVER
**RECOVERY** n act of
recovering from sickness,
a shock, or a setback
**RECOWER** archaic variant
of > RECOVER
**RECOWERED** > RECOWER
**RECOWERS** > RECOWER
**RECOYLE** archaic spelling
of > RECOIL
**RECOYLED** > RECOYLE
**RECOYLES** > RECOYLE
**RECOYLING** > RECOYLE
**RECRATE** vb crate again
**RECRATED** > RECRATE
**RECRATES** > RECRATE
**RECRATING** > RECRATE
**RECREANCE** > RECREANT
**RECREANCY** > RECREANT
**RECREANT** n disloyal or
cowardly person ▷ adj
cowardly
**RECREANTS** > RECREANT
**RECREATE** vb amuse

(oneself or someone else)
**RECREATED** > RECREATE
**RECREATES** > RECREATE
**RECREATOR** > RECREATE
**RECREMENT** n any substance, such as bile, that is secreted from a part of the body and later reabsorbed instead of being excreted
**RECROSS** vb move or go across (something) again
**RECROSSED** > RECROSS
**RECROSSES** > RECROSS
**RECROWN** vb crown again
**RECROWNED** > RECROWN
**RECROWNS** > RECROWN
**RECRUIT** vb enlist (new soldiers, members, etc) ▷ n newly enlisted soldier
**RECRUITAL** n act of recruiting
**RECRUITED** > RECRUIT
**RECRUITER** > RECRUIT
**RECRUITS** > RECRUIT
**RECS** > REC
**RECTA** > RECTUM
**RECTAL** adj of the rectum
**RECTALLY** > RECTAL
**RECTANGLE** n oblong four-sided figure with four right angles
**RECTI** > RECTUS
**RECTIFIED** > RECTIFY
**RECTIFIER** n electronic device, such as a semiconductor diode or valve, that converts an alternating current to a direct current by suppression or inversion of alternate half cycles
**RECTIFIES** > RECTIFY
**RECTIFY** vb put right, correct
**RECTION** n (in grammar) the determination of the form of one word by another word
**RECTIONS** > RECTION
**RECTITIC** > RECTITIS
**RECTITIS** n inflammation of the rectum
**RECTITUDE** n moral correctness
**RECTO** n right-hand page of a book
**RECTOCELE** n protrusion or herniation of the rectum into the vagina
**RECTOR** n clergyman in charge of a parish
**RECTORAL** adj of or relating to God's rule or to a rector
**RECTORATE** > RECTOR
**RECTORESS** n female rector or the wife or widow of a rector
**RECTORIAL** adj of or relating to a rector ▷ n election of a rector
**RECTORIES** > RECTORY
**RECTORS** > RECTOR
**RECTORY** n rector's house

**RECTOS** > RECTO
**RECTRESS** same as > RECTORESS
**RECTRICES** > RECTRIX
**RECTRIX** n any of the large stiff feathers of a bird's tail, used in controlling the direction of flight
**RECTUM** n final section of the large intestine
**RECTUMS** > RECTUM
**RECTUS** n straight muscle, esp either of two muscles of the anterior abdominal wall
**RECUILE** archaic variant of > RECOIL
**RECUILED** > RECUILE
**RECUILES** > RECUILE
**RECUILING** > RECUILE
**RECULE** archaic variant of > RECOIL
**RECULED** > RECULE
**RECULES** > RECULE
**RECULING** > RECULE
**RECUMBENT** adj lying down
**RECUR** vb happen again
**RECURE** vb archaic word for cure or recover
**RECURED** > RECURE
**RECURES** > RECURE
**RECURING** > RECURE
**RECURRED** > RECUR
**RECURRENT** adj happening or tending to happen again or repeatedly
**RECURRING** > RECUR
**RECURS** > RECUR
**RECURSION** n act or process of returning or running back
**RECURSIVE** > RECURSION
**RECURVATE** adj bent back
**RECURVE** vb curve or bend (something) back or down or (of something) to be so curved or bent
**RECURVED** > RECURVE
**RECURVES** > RECURVE
**RECURVING** > RECURVE
**RECUSAL** n withdrawal of a judge from a case
**RECUSALS** > RECUSAL
**RECUSANCE** > RECUSANT
**RECUSANCY** > RECUSANT
**RECUSANT** n Roman Catholic who did not attend the services of the Church of England ▷ adj (formerly, of Catholics) refusing to attend services of the Church of England
**RECUSANTS** > RECUSANT
**RECUSE** vb (in law) object to or withdraw (a judge)
**RECUSED** > RECUSE
**RECUSES** > RECUSE
**RECUSING** > RECUSE
**RECUT** vb cut again
**RECUTS** > RECUT
**RECUTTING** > RECUT
**RECYCLATE** n recyclable material
**RECYCLE** vb reprocess

(used materials) for further use ▷ n repetition of a fixed sequence of events
**RECYCLED** > RECYCLE
**RECYCLER** > RECYCLE
**RECYCLERS** > RECYCLE
**RECYCLES** > RECYCLE
**RECYCLING** > RECYCLE
**RECYCLIST** > RECYCLE
**RED** adj of a colour varying from crimson to orange and seen in blood, fire, etc ▷ n red colour
**REDACT** vb compose or draft (an edict, proclamation, etc)
**REDACTED** > REDACT
**REDACTING** > REDACT
**REDACTION** > REDACT
**REDACTOR** > REDACT
**REDACTORS** > REDACT
**REDACTS** > REDACT
**REDAMAGE** vb damage again
**REDAMAGED** > REDAMAGE
**REDAMAGES** > REDAMAGE
**REDAN** n fortification of two parapets at a salient angle
**REDANS** > REDAN
**REDARGUE** vb archaic word for disprove or refute
**REDARGUED** > REDARGUE
**REDARGUES** > REDARGUE
**REDATE** vb change date of
**REDATED** > REDATE
**REDATES** > REDATE
**REDATING** > REDATE
**REDBACK** n small venomous Australian spider
**REDBACKS** > REDBACK
**REDBAIT** vb harass those with leftwing leanings
**REDBAITED** > REDBAIT
**REDBAITER** n person who deliberately antagonizes communists
**REDBAITS** > REDBAIT
**REDBAY** n type of tree
**REDBAYS** > REDBAY
**REDBELLY** n any of various animals having red underparts, especially the char or the redbelly turtle
**REDBIRD** n type of bird, the male of which is distinguished by its bright red plumage and black wings
**REDBIRDS** > REDBIRD
**REDBONE** n type of American dog
**REDBONES** > REDBONE
**REDBREAST** n robin
**REDBRICK** adj (of a university in Britain) founded in the late 19th or early 20th century ▷ n denoting, relating to, or characteristic of a provincial British university of relatively recent foundation, esp as

distinguished from Oxford and Cambridge
**REDBRICKS** > REDBRICK
**REDBUD** n American leguminous tree with heart-shaped leaves and small budlike pink flowers
**REDBUDS** > REDBUD
**REDBUG** another name for > CHIGGER
**REDBUGS** > REDBUG
**REDCAP** n military policeman
**REDCAPS** > REDCAP
**REDCOAT** n British soldier
**REDCOATS** > REDCOAT
**REDD** vb bring order to ▷ n act or an instance of redding
**REDDED** > REDD
**REDDEN** vb make or become red
**REDDENDA** > REDDENDUM
**REDDENDO** n (in Scotland) legal clause specifying what payment or duties are required in exchange for something
**REDDENDOS** > REDDENDO
**REDDENDUM** n legal clause specifying what shall be given in return for the granting of a lease
**REDDENED** > REDDEN
**REDDENING** > REDDEN
**REDDENS** > REDDEN
**REDDER** > REDD
**REDDERS** > REDD
**REDDEST** > RED
**REDDIER** > REDDY
**REDDIEST** > REDDY
**REDDING** > REDD
**REDDINGS** > REDD
**REDDISH** adj somewhat red
**REDDISHLY** > REDDISH
**REDDLE** same as > RUDDLE
**REDDLED** > REDDLE
**REDDLEMAN** same as > RUDDLEMAN
**REDDLEMEN** > REDDLEMAN
**REDDLES** > REDDLE
**REDDLING** > REDDLE
**REDDS** > REDD
**REDDY** adj reddish
**REDE** n advice or counsel ▷ vb advise
**REDEAL** vb deal again
**REDEALING** > REDEAL
**REDEALS** > REDEAL
**REDEALT** > REDEAL
**REDEAR** n variety of sunfish with a red flash above the gills
**REDEARS** > REDEAR
**REDECIDE** vb decide again
**REDECIDED** > REDECIDE
**REDECIDES** > REDECIDE
**REDECRAFT** n logic
**REDED** > REDE
**REDEEM** vb make up for
**REDEEMED** > REDEEM
**REDEEMER** > REDEEM
**REDEEMERS** > REDEEM
**REDEEMING** adj making up

for faults or deficiencies
**REDEEMS** > REDEEM
**REDEFEAT** vb defeat again
**REDEFEATS** > REDEFEAT
**REDEFECT** vb defect back
or again
**REDEFECTS** > REDEFECT
**REDEFIED** > REDEFY
**REDEFIES** > REDEFY
**REDEFINE** vb define
(something) again or
differently
**REDEFINED** > REDEFINE
**REDEFINES** > REDEFINE
**REDEFY** vb defy again
**REDEFYING** > REDEFY
**REDELESS** > REDE
**REDELIVER** vb deliver
again
**REDEMAND** vb demand
again
**REDEMANDS** > REDEMAND
**REDENIED** > REDENY
**REDENIES** > REDENY
**REDENY** vb deny again
**REDENYING** > REDENY
**REDEPLOY** vb assign to a
new position or task
**REDEPLOYS** > REDEPLOY
**REDEPOSIT** vb deposit
again
**REDES** > REDE
**REDESCEND** vb descend
again
**REDESIGN** vb change the
design of (something) ▷ n
something that has been
redesigned
**REDESIGNS** > REDESIGN
**REDEVELOP** vb rebuild
or renovate (an area or
building)
**REDEYE** n inferior whiskey
**REDEYES** > REDEYE
**REDFIN** n any of various
small fishes with reddish
fins that are popular
aquarium fishes
**REDFINS** > REDFIN
**REDFISH** n male salmon
that has recently spawned
**REDFISHES** > REDFISH
**REDFOOT** n fatal disease
of newborn lambs of
unknown cause in which
the horny layers of the
feet become separated,
exposing the red laminae
below
**REDFOOTS** > REDFOOT
**REDHANDED** adj in the act of
doing something criminal,
wrong, or shameful
**REDHEAD** n person with
reddish hair
**REDHEADED** > REDHEAD
**REDHEADS** > REDHEAD
**REDHORSE** n type of fish
**REDHORSES** > REDHORSE
**REDIA** n parasitic larva
of flukes that has simple
locomotory organs,
pharynx, and intestine and
gives rise either to other

rediae or to a different
larva (the cercaria)
**REDIAE** > REDIA
**REDIAL** vb dial (a telephone
number) again
**REDIALED** > REDIAL
**REDIALING** > REDIAL
**REDIALLED** > REDIAL
**REDIALS** > REDIAL
**REDIAS** > REDIA
**REDICTATE** vb dictate
again
**REDID** > REDO
**REDIGEST** vb digest again
**REDIGESTS** > REDIGEST
**REDIGRESS** vb digress
again
**REDING** > REDE
**REDINGOTE** n woman's
coat with a close-fitting
top and a full skirt
**REDIP** vb dip again
**REDIPPED** > REDIP
**REDIPPING** > REDIP
**REDIPS** > REDIP
**REDIPT** archaic past form
of > REDIP
**REDIRECT** vb send in a new
direction or course
**REDIRECTS** > REDIRECT
**REDISCUSS** vb discuss
again
**REDISPLAY** vb display
again
**REDISPOSE** vb dispose
again
**REDISTIL** vb distil again
**REDISTILL** US spelling
of > REDISTIL
**REDISTILS** > REDISTIL
**REDIVIDE** vb divide again
**REDIVIDED** > REDIVIDE
**REDIVIDES** > REDIVIDE
**REDIVIVUS** adj returned
to life
**REDIVORCE** vb divorce
again
**REDLEG** n derogatory term
for poor White
**REDLEGS** > REDLEG
**REDLINE** vb (esp of a bank
or group of banks) to
refuse a loan to (a person
or country) because of the
presumed risks involved
**REDLINED** > REDLINE
**REDLINER** > REDLINE
**REDLINERS** > REDLINE
**REDLINES** > REDLINE
**REDLINING** > REDLINE
**REDLY** > RED
**REDNECK** n (in the
southwestern US)
derogatory term for a poor
uneducated White farm
worker ▷ adj reactionary
and bigoted
**REDNECKED** adj with a red
neck
**REDNECKS** > REDNECK
**REDNESS** > RED
**REDNESSES** > RED
**REDO** vb do over again
in order to improve ▷ n

instance of redoing
something
**REDOCK** vb dock again
**REDOCKED** > REDOCK
**REDOCKING** > REDOCK
**REDOCKS** > REDOCK
**REDOES** > REDO
**REDOING** > REDO
**REDOLENCE** > REDOLENT
**REDOLENCY** > REDOLENT
**REDOLENT** adj reminiscent
(of)
**REDON** vb don again
**REDONE** > REDO
**REDONNED** > REDON
**REDONNING** > REDON
**REDONS** > REDON
**REDOS** > REDO
**REDOUBLE** vb increase,
multiply, or intensify ▷ n
act of redoubling
**REDOUBLED** > REDOUBLE
**REDOUBLER** > REDOUBLE
**REDOUBLES** > REDOUBLE
**REDOUBT** n small fort
defending a hilltop or pass
▷ vb fear
**REDOUBTED** > REDOUBT
**REDOUBTS** > REDOUBT
**REDOUND** vb cause
advantage or
disadvantage (to)
**REDOUNDED** > REDOUND
**REDOUNDS** > REDOUND
**REDOUT** n reddened vision
and other symptoms
caused by a rush of blood
to the head in response
to negative gravitational
stresses
**REDOUTS** > REDOUT
**REDOWA** n Bohemian folk
dance similar to the waltz
**REDOWAS** > REDOWA
**REDOX** n chemical reaction
in which one substance is
reduced and the other is
oxidized
**REDOXES** > REDOX
**REDPOLL** n mostly grey-
brown finch with a red
crown and pink breast
**REDPOLLS** > REDPOLL
**REDRAFT** vb write a second
copy of (a letter, proposal,
essay, etc) ▷ n second
draft
**REDRAFTED** > REDRAFT
**REDRAFTS** > REDRAFT
**REDRAW** vb draw or draw
up (something) again or
differently
**REDRAWER** > REDRAW
**REDRAWERS** > REDRAW
**REDRAWING** > REDRAW
**REDRAWN** > REDRAW
**REDRAWS** > REDRAW
**REDREAM** vb dream again
**REDREAMED** > REDREAM
**REDREAMS** > REDREAM
**REDREAMT** > REDREAM
**REDRESS** vb make amends
for ▷ n compensation or
amends

**REDRESSED** > REDRESS
**REDRESSER** > REDRESS
**REDRESSES** > REDRESS
**REDRESSOR** > REDRESS
**REDREW** > REDRAW
**REDRIED** > REDRY
**REDRIES** > REDRY
**REDRILL** vb drill again
**REDRILLED** > REDRILL
**REDRILLS** > REDRILL
**REDRIVE** vb drive again
**REDRIVEN** > REDRIVE
**REDRIVES** > REDRIVE
**REDRIVING** > REDRIVE
**REDROOT** n yellow-flowered
bog plant of E North
America whose roots yield
a red dye
**REDROOTS** > REDROOT
**REDROVE** > REDRIVE
**REDRY** vb dry again
**REDRYING** > REDRY
**REDS** > RED
**REDSEAR** same
as > REDSHORT
**REDSHANK** n large Eurasian
sandpiper with red legs
**REDSHANKS** > REDSHANK
**REDSHARE** n red algae
**REDSHIFT** n shift in the
lines of the spectrum of an
astronomical object
**REDSHIFTS** > REDSHIFT
**REDSHIRE** same
as > REDSHARE
**REDSHIRT** vb take a year
out of a sports team
**REDSHIRTS** > REDSHIRT
**REDSHORT** vb become
brittle at red-hot
temperatures
**REDSKIN** n offensive term
for Native American
**REDSKINS** > REDSKIN
**REDSTART** n European
bird of the thrush family,
the male of which has an
orange-brown tail and
breast
**REDSTARTS** > REDSTART
**REDSTREAK** n variety of
apple
**REDTAIL** n variety of bird
with red colouring on its
tail
**REDTAILS** > REDTAIL
**REDTOP** n sensationalist
tabloid newspaper
**REDTOPS** > REDTOP
**REDUB** vb fix or repair
**REDUBBED** > REDUB
**REDUBBING** > REDUB
**REDUBS** > REDUB
**REDUCE** vb bring down,
lower
**REDUCED** > REDUCE
**REDUCER** n chemical
solution used to lessen
the density of a negative
or print by oxidizing some
of the blackened silver to
soluble silver compounds
**REDUCERS** > REDUCER
**REDUCES** > REDUCE

REDUCIBLE > REDUCE
REDUCIBLY > REDUCE
REDUCING > REDUCE .
REDUCTANT n reducing agent
REDUCTASE n any enzyme that catalyses a biochemical reduction reaction
REDUCTION n act of reducing
REDUCTIVE > REDUCTION
REDUCTOR n apparatus in which substances can be reduced
REDUCTORS > REDUCTOR
REDUIT n fortified part from which a garrison may fight on once an enemy has taken outworks
REDUITS > REDUIT
REDUNDANT adj (of a worker) no longer needed
REDUVIID n any hemipterous bug of the family Reduviidae, which includes the assassin bugs and the wheel bug ▷ adj of, relating to, or belonging to the family Reduviidae
REDUVIIDS > REDUVIID
REDUX adj brought back or returned
REDWARE another name for > KELP
REDWARES > REDWARE
REDWATER n tick-borne disease of cattle
REDWATERS > REDWATER
REDWING n small European thrush
REDWINGS > REDWING
REDWOOD n giant Californian conifer with reddish bark
REDWOODS > REDWOOD
REDYE vb dye again
REDYED > REDYE
REDYEING > REDYE
REDYES > REDYE
REE n Scots word for walled enclosure
REEARN vb earn again
REEARNED > REEARN
REEARNING > REEARN
REEARNS > REEARN
REEBOK same as > RHEBOK
REEBOKS > REEBOK
REECH vb (in dialect) smoke
REECHED > REECH
REECHES > REECH
REECHIE same as > REECHY
REECHIER > REECHY
REECHIEST > REECHY
REECHING > REECH
REECHO vb echo again
REECHOED > REECHO
REECHOES > REECHO
REECHOING > REECHO
REECHY adj (in dialect) smoky
REED n tall grass that grows in swamps and shallow

water
REEDBED n area of wetland with reeds growing in it
REEDBEDS > REEDBED
REEDBIRD n any of several birds that frequent reed beds, esp (in the US and Canada) the bobolink
REEDBIRDS > REEDBIRD
REEDBUCK n buff-coloured African antelope with inward-curving horns
REEDBUCKS > REEDBUCK
REEDE obsolete variant of > RED
REEDED > REED
REEDEN adj of or consisting of reeds
REEDER n thatcher
REEDERS > REEDER
REEDES > REEDE
REEDIER > REEDY
REEDIEST > REEDY
REEDIFIED > REEDIFY
REEDIFIES > REEDIFY
REEDIFY vb edify again or rebuild
REEDILY > REEDY
REEDINESS > REEDY
REEDING n set of small semicircular architectural mouldings
REEDINGS > REEDING
REEDIT vb edit again
REEDITED > REEDIT
REEDITING > REEDIT
REEDITION n new edition
REEDITS > REEDIT
REEDLIKE adj resembling a reed
REEDLING n tawny titlike Eurasian songbird common in reed beds
REEDLINGS > REEDLING
REEDMACE n tall reedlike marsh plant
REEDMACES > REEDMACE
REEDMAN n musician who plays a wind instrument that has a reed
REEDMEN > REEDMAN
REEDS > REED
REEDSTOP n organ stop controlling a rank of reed pipes
REEDSTOPS > REEDSTOP
REEDUCATE vb educate again
REEDY adj harsh and thin in tone
REEF n ridge of rock or coral near the surface of the sea ▷ vb roll up part of a sail
REEFABLE > REEF
REEFED > REEF
REEFER n short thick jacket worn esp by sailors
REEFERS > REEFER
REEFIER > REEFY
REEFIEST > REEFY
REEFING > REEF
REEFINGS > REEF
REEFS > REEF
REEFY adj with reefs

REEJECT vb eject again
REEJECTED > REEJECT
REEJECTS > REEJECT
REEK vb smell strongly ▷ n strong unpleasant smell
REEKED > REEK
REEKER > REEK
REEKERS > REEK
REEKIE same as > REEKY
REEKIER > REEK
REEKIEST > REEK
REEKING > REEK
REEKINGLY > REEK
REEKS > REEK
REEKY adj steamy or smoky
REEL n cylindrical object on which film, tape, thread, or wire is wound ▷ vb stagger, sway, or whirl
REELABLE > REEL
REELECT vb elect again
REELECTED > REELECT
REELECTS > REELECT
REELED > REEL
REELER > REEL
REELERS > REEL
REELEVATE vb elevate again
REELING > REEL
REELINGLY > REEL
REELINGS > REEL
REELMAN n (formerly) member of a beach life-saving team operating a winch
REELMEN > REELMAN
REELS > REEL
REEMBARK vb embark again
REEMBARKS > REEMBARK
REEMBODY vb embody again
REEMBRACE vb embrace again
REEMERGE vb emerge again
REEMERGED > REEMERGE
REEMERGES > REEMERGE
REEMIT vb emit again
REEMITS > REEMIT
REEMITTED > REEMIT
REEMPLOY vb employ again
REEMPLOYS > REEMPLOY
REEN n ditch, esp a drainage channel
REENACT vb enact again
REENACTED > REENACT
REENACTOR > REENACT
REENACTS > REENACT
REENDOW vb endow again
REENDOWED > REENDOW
REENDOWS > REENDOW
REENFORCE vb enforce again
REENGAGE vb engage again
REENGAGED > REENGAGE
REENGAGES > REENGAGE
REENGRAVE vb engrave again
REENJOY vb enjoy again
REENJOYED > REENJOY
REENJOYS > REENJOY
REENLARGE vb enlarge again
REENLIST vb enlist again
REENLISTS > REENLIST

REENROLL vb enrol again
REENROLLS > REENROLL
REENS > REEN
REENSLAVE vb enslave again
REENTER vb enter again
REENTERED > REENTER
REENTERS > REENTER
REENTRANT n reentering angle ▷ adj (of an angle) pointing inwards
REENTRIES > REENTRY
REENTRY n return of a spacecraft into the earth's atmosphere
REEQUIP vb equip again
REEQUIPS > REEQUIP
REERECT vb erect again
REERECTED > REERECT
REERECTS > REERECT
REES > REE
REEST vb (esp of horses) to be noisily uncooperative
REESTED > REEST
REESTIER > REESTY
REESTIEST > REESTY
REESTING > REEST
REESTS > REEST
REESTY same as > REASTY
REEVE n local representative of the king in a shire until the early 11th century ▷ vb pass (a rope or cable) through an eye or other narrow opening
REEVED > REEVE
REEVES > REEVE
REEVING > REEVE
REEVOKE vb evoke again
REEVOKED > REEVOKE
REEVOKES > REEVOKE
REEVOKING > REEVOKE
REEXAMINE vb examine again
REEXECUTE vb execute again
REEXHIBIT vb exhibit again
REEXPEL vb expel again
REEXPELS > REEXPEL
REEXPLAIN vb explain again
REEXPLORE vb explore again
REEXPORT vb export again
REEXPORTS > REEXPORT
REEXPOSE vb expose again
REEXPOSED > REEXPOSE
REEXPOSES > REEXPOSE
REEXPRESS vb express
REF n referee in sport ▷ vb referee
REFACE vb repair or renew the facing of (a wall)
REFACED > REFACE
REFACES > REFACE
REFACING > REFACE
REFALL vb fall again
REFALLEN > REFALL
REFALLING > REFALL
REFALLS > REFALL
REFASHION vb give a new

form to (something)
**REFASTEN** *vb* fasten again
**REFASTENS** > REFASTEN
**REFECT** *vb* archaic word
for restore or refresh with
food and drink
**REFECTED** > REFECT
**REFECTING** > REFECT
**REFECTION** *n* refreshment
with food and drink
**REFECTIVE** > REFECT
**REFECTORY** *n* room for
meals in a college etc
**REFECTS** > REFECT
**REFED** > REFEED
**REFEED** *vb* feed again
**REFEEDING** > REFEED
**REFEEDS** > REFEED
**REFEEL** *vb* feel again
**REFEELING** > REFEEL
**REFEELS** > REFEEL
**REFEL** *vb* refute
**REFELL** > REFALL
**REFELLED** > REFEL
**REFELLING** > REFEL
**REFELS** > REFEL
**REFELT** > REFEEL
**REFENCE** *vb* fence again
**REFENCED** > REFENCE
**REFENCES** > REFENCE
**REFENCING** > REFENCE
**REFER** *vb* allude (to)
**REFERABLE** > REFER
**REFEREE** *n* umpire in
sports, esp soccer or
boxing ▷ *vb* act as referee
of
**REFEREED** > REFEREE
**REFEREES** > REFEREE
**REFERENCE** *n* act of
referring
**REFERENDA** *pl n* polls to
determine the view of the
electorate on something;
referendums
**REFERENT** *n* object or idea
to which a word or phrase
refers
**REFERENTS** > REFERENT
**REFERRAL** > REFER
**REFERRALS** > REFER
**REFERRED** > REFER
**REFERRERS** > REFER
**REFERRING** > REFER
**REFERS** > REFER
**REFFED** > REF
**REFFING** > REF
**REFFO** *n* offensive name for
a European refugee after
World War II
**REFFOS** > REFFO
**REFIGHT** *vb* fight again ▷ *n*
second or new fight
**REFIGHTS** > REFIGHT
**REFIGURE** *vb* figure again
**REFIGURED** > REFIGURE
**REFIGURES** > REFIGURE
**REFILE** *vb* file again
**REFILED** > REFILE
**REFILES** > REFILE
**REFILING** > REFILE
**REFILL** *vb* fill again ▷ *n*
second or subsequent

filling
**REFILLED** > REFILL
**REFILLING** > REFILL
**REFILLS** > REFILL
**REFILM** *vb* film again
**REFILMED** > REFILM
**REFILMING** > REFILM
**REFILMS** > REFILM
**REFILTER** *vb* filter again
**REFILTERS** > REFILTER
**REFINABLE** > REFINE
**REFINANCE** *vb* finance
again
**REFIND** *vb* find again
**REFINDING** > REFIND
**REFINDS** > REFIND
**REFINE** *vb* purify
**REFINED** *adj* cultured or
polite
**REFINEDLY** > REFINED
**REFINER** *n* person, device,
or substance that removes
impurities, sediment, or
other unwanted matter
from something
**REFINERS** > REFINER
**REFINERY** *n* place where
sugar, oil, etc is refined
**REFINES** > REFINE
**REFINING** > REFINE
**REFININGS** > REFINE
**REFINISH** *vb* finish again
**REFIRE** *vb* fire again
**REFIRED** > REFIRE
**REFIRES** > REFIRE
**REFIRING** > REFIRE
**REFIT** *vb* make ready for
use again by repairing or
re-equipping ▷ *n* repair
or re-equipping for further
use
**REFITMENT** > REFIT
**REFITS** > REFIT
**REFITTED** > REFIT
**REFITTING** > REFIT
**REFIX** *vb* fix again
**REFIXED** > REFIX
**REFIXES** > REFIX
**REFIXING** > REFIX
**REFLAG** *vb* flag again
**REFLAGGED** > REFLAG
**REFLAGS** > REFLAG
**REFLATE** *vb* inflate or be
inflated again
**REFLATED** > REFLATE
**REFLATES** > REFLATE
**REFLATING** > REFLATE
**REFLATION** *n* increase
in the supply of money
and credit designed to
encourage economic
activity
**REFLECT** *vb* throw back,
esp rays of light, heat, etc
**REFLECTED** > REFLECT
**REFLECTER** *n* archaic word
for a critic
**REFLECTOR** *n* polished
surface for reflecting light
etc
**REFLECTS** > REFLECT
**REFLET** *n* iridescent glow
or lustre, as on ceramic
ware

**REFLETS** > REFLET
**REFLEW** > REFLY
**REFLEX** *n* involuntary
response to a stimulus
or situation ▷ *adj* (of
a muscular action)
involuntary ▷ *vb* bend,
turn, or reflect backwards
**REFLEXED** > REFLEX
**REFLEXES** > REFLEX
**REFLEXING** > REFLEX
**REFLEXION** *n* act of
reflecting or the state of
being reflected
**REFLEXIVE** *adj* denoting
a pronoun that refers
back to the subject of a
sentence or clause ▷ *n*
reflexive pronoun or verb
**REFLEXLY** > REFLEX
**REFLIES** > REFLY
**REFLOAT** *vb* float again
**REFLOATED** > REFLOAT
**REFLOATS** > REFLOAT
**REFLOOD** *vb* flood again
**REFLOODED** > REFLOOD
**REFLOODS** > REFLOOD
**REFLOW** *vb* flow again
**REFLOWED** > REFLOW
**REFLOWER** *vb* flower again
**REFLOWERS** > REFLOWER
**REFLOWING** > REFLOW
**REFLOWN** > REFLY
**REFLOWS** > REFLOW
**REFLUENCE** > REFLUENT
**REFLUENT** *adj* flowing back
**REFLUX** *vb* boil or be boiled
in a vessel attached to a
condenser, so that the
vapour condenses and
flows back into the vessel
▷ *n* act of refluxing
**REFLUXED** > REFLUX
**REFLUXES** > REFLUX
**REFLUXING** > REFLUX
**REFLY** *vb* fly again
**REFLYING** > REFLY
**REFOCUS** *vb* focus again or
anew
**REFOCUSED** > REFOCUS
**REFOCUSES** > REFOCUS
**REFOLD** *vb* fold again
**REFOLDED** > REFOLD
**REFOLDING** > REFOLD
**REFOLDS** > REFOLD
**REFOOT** *vb* foot again
**REFOOTED** > REFOOT
**REFOOTING** > REFOOT
**REFOOTS** > REFOOT
**REFOREST** *vb* replant (an
area that was formerly
forested) with trees
**REFORESTS** > REFOREST
**REFORGE** *vb* forge again
**REFORGED** > REFORGE
**REFORGES** > REFORGE
**REFORGING** > REFORGE
**REFORM** *n* improvement
▷ *vb* improve
**REFORMADE** *archaic variant
of* > REFORMADO
**REFORMADO** *n* formerly, an
officer whose men have
been disbanded

**REFORMAT** *vb* format again
**REFORMATE** *n* gas formed in
certain processes
**REFORMATS** > REFORMAT
**REFORMED** > REFORM
**REFORMER** > REFORM
**REFORMERS** > REFORM
**REFORMING** > REFORM
**REFORMISM** *n* doctrine or
movement advocating
reform, esp political or
religious reform, rather
than abolition
**REFORMIST** > REFORMISM
**REFORMS** > REFORM
**REFORTIFY** *vb* fortify again
or further
**REFOUGHT** > REFIGHT
**REFOUND** *vb* found again
**REFOUNDED** > REFOUND
**REFOUNDER** > REFOUND
**REFOUNDS** > REFOUND
**REFRACT** *vb* change the
course of (light etc)
passing from one medium
to another
**REFRACTED** > REFRACT
**REFRACTOR** *n* object or
material that refracts
**REFRACTS** > REFRACT
**REFRAIN** *n* frequently
repeated part of a song
▷ *vb* abstain (from action)
**REFRAINED** > REFRAIN
**REFRAINER** > REFRAIN
**REFRAINS** > REFRAIN
**REFRAME** *vb* support
or enclose (a picture,
photograph, etc) in a new
or different frame
**REFRAMED** > REFRAME
**REFRAMES** > REFRAME
**REFRAMING** > REFRAME
**REFREEZE** *vb* freeze or be
frozen again after having
defrosted
**REFREEZES** > REFREEZE
**REFRESH** *vb* revive or
reinvigorate, as through
food, drink, or rest
**REFRESHED** > REFRESH
**REFRESHEN** *vb* freshen
again
**REFRESHER** *n* something
that refreshes, such as a
cold drink
**REFRESHES** > REFRESH
**REFRIED** > REFRY
**REFRIES** > REFRY
**REFRINGE** *formerly used to
mean* > REFRACT
**REFRINGED** > REFRINGE
**REFRINGES** > REFRINGE
**REFRONT** *vb* put a new
front on
**REFRONTED** > REFRONT
**REFRONTS** > REFRONT
**REFROZE** > REFREEZE
**REFROZEN** > REFREEZE
**REFRY** *vb* fry again
**REFRYING** > REFRY
**REFS** > REF
**REFT** > REAVE
**REFUEL** *vb* supply or be

supplied with fresh fuel

**REFUELED** > REFUEL

**REFUELING** > REFUEL

**REFUELLED** > REFUEL

**REFUELS** > REFUEL

**REFUGE** *n* (source of) shelter or protection ▷ *vb* take refuge or give refuge to

**REFUGED** > REFUGE

**REFUGEE** *n* person who seeks refuge, esp in a foreign country

**REFUGEES** > REFUGEE

**REFUGES** > REFUGE

**REFUGIA** > REFUGIUM

**REFUGING** > REFUGE

**REFUGIUM** *n* geographical region that has remained unaltered by a climatic change affecting surrounding regions and that therefore forms a haven for relict fauna and flora

**REFULGENT** *adj* shining, radiant

**REFUND** *vb* pay back ▷ *n* return of money

**REFUNDED** > REFUND

**REFUNDER** > REFUND

**REFUNDERS** > REFUND

**REFUNDING** > REFUND

**REFUNDS** > REFUND

**REFURBISH** *vb* renovate and brighten up

**REFURNISH** *vb* furnish again

**REFUSABLE** > REFUSE

**REFUSAL** *n* denial of anything demanded or offered

**REFUSALS** > REFUSAL

**REFUSE** *vb* decline, deny, or reject ▷ *n* rubbish or useless matter

**REFUSED** > REFUSE

**REFUSENIK** *n* person who refuses to obey a law or cooperate with the government because of strong beliefs

**REFUSER** > REFUSE

**REFUSERS** > REFUSE

**REFUSES** > REFUSE

**REFUSING** > REFUSE

**REFUSION** *n* new or further fusion

**REFUSIONS** > REFUSION

**REFUSNIK** *same as* > REFUSENIK

**REFUSNIKS** > REFUSNIK

**REFUTABLE** > REFUTE

**REFUTABLY** > REFUTE

**REFUTAL** *n* act or process of refuting

**REFUTALS** > REFUTAL

**REFUTE** *vb* disprove

**REFUTED** > REFUTE

**REFUTER** > REFUTE

**REFUTERS** > REFUTE

**REFUTES** > REFUTE

**REFUTING** > REFUTE

**REG** *n* large expanse of

stony desert terrain

**REGAIN** *vb* get back or recover ▷ *n* process of getting something back, esp lost weight

**REGAINED** > REGAIN

**REGAINER** > REGAIN

**REGAINERS** > REGAIN

**REGAINING** > REGAIN

**REGAINS** > REGAIN

**REGAL** *adj* of or like a king or queen ▷ *n* portable organ equipped only with small reed pipes, popular from the 15th century and recently revived for modern performance

**REGALE** *vb* entertain (someone) with stories etc ▷ *n* feast

**REGALED** > REGALE

**REGALER** > REGALE

**REGALERS** > REGALE

**REGALES** > REGALE

**REGALIA** *pl n* ceremonial emblems of royalty or high office

**REGALIAN** *adj* royal

**REGALIAS** > REGALIA

**REGALING** > REGALE

**REGALISM** *n* principle that the sovereign has supremacy in church affairs

**REGALISMS** > REGALISM

**REGALIST** > REGALISM

**REGALISTS** > REGALISM

**REGALITY** *n* state or condition of being royal

**REGALLY** > REGAL

**REGALNESS** > REGAL

**REGALS** > REGAL

**REGAR** *same as* > REGUR

**REGARD** *vb* consider ▷ *n* respect or esteem

**REGARDANT** *adj* (of a beast) shown looking backwards over its shoulder

**REGARDED** > REGARD

**REGARDER** > REGARD

**REGARDERS** > REGARD

**REGARDFUL** *adj* showing regard (for)

**REGARDING** *prep* on the subject of

**REGARDS** > REGARD

**REGARS** > REGAR

**REGATHER** *vb* gather again

**REGATHERS** > REGATHER

**REGATTA** *n* meeting for yacht or boat races

**REGATTAS** > REGATTA

**REGAUGE** *vb* gauge again

**REGAUGED** > REGAUGE

**REGAUGES** > REGAUGE

**REGAUGING** > REGAUGE

**REGAVE** > REGIVE

**REGEAR** *vb* readjust

**REGEARED** > REGEAR

**REGEARING** > REGEAR

**REGEARS** > REGEAR

**REGELATE** *vb* undergo or cause to undergo regelation

**REGELATED** > REGELATE

**REGELATES** > REGELATE

**REGENCE** *old variant of* > REGENCY

**REGENCES** > REGENCE

**REGENCIES** > REGENCY

**REGENCY** *n* status or period of office of a regent

**REGENT** *n* ruler of a kingdom during the absence, childhood, or illness of its monarch ▷ *adj* ruling as a regent

**REGENTAL** > REGENT

**REGENTS** > REGENT

**REGES** > REX

**REGEST** *n* archaic word for register

**REGESTS** > REGEST

**REGGAE** *n* style of Jamaican popular music with a strong beat

**REGGAES** > REGGAE

**REGGO** *same as* > REGO

**REGGOS** > REGGO

**REGICIDAL** > REGICIDE

**REGICIDE** *n* killing of a king

**REGICIDES** > REGICIDE

**REGIE** *n* government-directed management or government monopoly

**REGIES** > REGIE

**REGILD** *vb* gild again

**REGILDED** > REGILD

**REGILDING** > REGILD

**REGILDS** > REGILD

**REGILT** *archaic past form of* > REGILD

**REGIME** *n* system of government

**REGIMEN** *n* prescribed system of diet etc

**REGIMENS** > REGIMEN

**REGIMENT** *n* organized body of troops as a unit of the army ▷ *vb* force discipline or order on, esp in a domineering manner

**REGIMENTS** > REGIMENT

**REGIMES** > REGIME

**REGIMINAL** *adj* regimen-related

**REGINA** *n* queen

**REGINAE** > REGINA

**REGINAL** *adj* queenly

**REGINAS** > REGINA

**REGION** *n* administrative division of a country

**REGIONAL** *adj* of, characteristic of, or limited to a region ▷ *n* regional heat of a competition

**REGIONALS** > REGIONAL

**REGIONARY** *same as* > REGIONAL

**REGIONS** > REGION

**REGISSEUR** *n* official in a dance company with varying duties, usually including directing productions

**REGISTER** *n* (book

containing) an official list or record of things ▷ *vb* enter in a register or set down in writing

**REGISTERS** > REGISTER

**REGISTRAR** *n* keeper of official records

**REGISTRY** *n* place where official records are kept

**REGIUS** as in *regius professor* Crown-appointed holder of a university chair

**REGIVE** *vb* give again or back

**REGIVEN** > REGIVE

**REGIVES** > REGIVE

**REGIVING** > REGIVE

**REGLAZE** *vb* glaze again

**REGLAZED** > REGLAZE

**REGLAZES** > REGLAZE

**REGLAZING** > REGLAZE

**REGLET** *n* flat narrow architectural moulding

**REGLETS** > REGLET

**REGLORIFY** *vb* glorify again

**REGLOSS** *vb* gloss again or give a new gloss to

**REGLOSSED** > REGLOSS

**REGLOSSES** > REGLOSS

**REGLOW** *vb* glow again

**REGLOWED** > REGLOW

**REGLOWING** > REGLOW

**REGLOWS** > REGLOW

**REGLUE** *vb* glue again

**REGLUED** > REGLUE

**REGLUES** > REGLUE

**REGLUING** > REGLUE

**REGMA** *n* type of fruit with cells that break open and break away when ripe

**REGMAKER** *n* drink taken to relieve the symptoms of a hangover

**REGMAKERS** > REGMAKER

**REGMATA** > REGMA

**REGNA** > REGNUM

**REGNAL** *adj* of a sovereign, reign, or kingdom

**REGNANCY** > REGNANT

**REGNANT** *adj* reigning

**REGNUM** *n* reign or rule

**REGO** *n* registration of a motor vehicle

**REGOLITH** *n* layer of loose material covering the bedrock of the earth and moon, etc, comprising soil, sand, rock fragments, volcanic ash, glacial drift, etc

**REGOLITHS** > REGOLITH

**REGORGE** *vb* vomit up

**REGORGED** > REGORGE

**REGORGES** > REGORGE

**REGORGING** > REGORGE

**REGOS** > REGO

**REGOSOL** *n* type of azonal soil consisting of unconsolidated material derived from freshly deposited alluvium or sands

**REGOSOLS** > REGOSOL

**REGRADE** *vb* grade again

REGRADED > REGRADE
REGRADES > REGRADE
REGRADING > REGRADE
REGRAFT vb graft again
REGRAFTED > REGRAFT
REGRAFTS > REGRAFT
REGRANT vb grant again
REGRANTED > REGRANT
REGRANTS > REGRANT
REGRATE vb buy up
(commodities) in advance
so as to raise their price for
profitable resale
REGRATED > REGRATE
REGRATER > REGRATE
REGRATERS > REGRATE
REGRATES > REGRATE
REGRATING > REGRATE
REGRATOR > REGRATE
REGRATORS > REGRATE
REGREDE vb go back
REGREDED > REGREDE
REGREDES > REGREDE
REGREDING > REGREDE
REGREEN vb green again
REGREENED > REGREEN
REGREENS > REGREEN
REGREET vb greet again or
return greetings of
REGREETED > REGREET
REGREETS > REGREET
REGRESS vb revert to a
former worse condition
▷ n return to a former and
worse condition
REGRESSED > REGRESS
REGRESSES > REGRESS
REGRESSOR > REGRESS
REGRET vb feel sorry about
▷ n feeling of repentance,
guilt, or sorrow
REGRETFUL > REGRET
REGRETS > REGRET
REGRETTED > REGRET
REGRETTER > REGRET
REGREW > REGROW
REGRIND vb grind again
REGRINDS > REGRIND
REGROOM vb groom again
REGROOMED > REGROOM
REGROOMS > REGROOM
REGROOVE vb groove again
REGROOVED > REGROOVE
REGROOVES > REGROOVE
REGROUND > REGRIND
REGROUP vb reorganize
(military forces) after an
attack or a defeat
REGROUPED > REGROUP
REGROUPS > REGROUP
REGROW vb grow or be
grown again after having
been cut or having died or
withered
REGROWING > REGROW
REGROWN > REGROW
REGROWS > REGROW
REGROWTH n growing back
of hair, plants, etc
REGROWTHS > REGROWTH
REGS > REG
REGUERDON vb reward
REGULA n rule
REGULABLE adj able to be

regulated
REGULAE > REGULA
REGULAR adj normal,
customary, or usual ▷ n
regular soldier
REGULARLY > REGULAR
REGULARS > REGULAR
REGULATE vb control, esp
by rules
REGULATED > REGULATE
REGULATES > REGULATE
REGULATOR n device that
automatically controls
pressure, temperature, etc
REGULI > REGULUS
REGULINE > REGULUS
REGULISE variant spelling
of > REGULIZE
REGULISED > REGULISE
REGULISES > REGULISE
REGULIZE vb turn into
regulus
REGULIZED > REGULIZE
REGULIZES > REGULIZE
REGULO n any of a number
of temperatures to which
a gas oven may be set
REGULOS > REGULO
REGULUS n impure metal
forming beneath the slag
during the smelting of ores
REGULUSES > REGULUS
REGUR n black loamy Indian
soil
REGURS > REGUR
REH n (in India) salty
surface crust on the soil
REHAB vb help (addict,
disabled person, prisoner,
etc) to readapt to
society or a new job ▷ n
treatment or help given to
an addict, disabled person,
or prisoner, etc
REHABBED > REHAB
REHABBER > REHAB
REHABBERS > REHAB
REHABBING > REHAB
REHABS > REHAB
REHAMMER vb hammer
again
REHAMMERS > REHAMMER
REHANDLE vb handle again
REHANDLED > REHANDLE
REHANDLES > REHANDLE
REHANG vb hang again
REHANGED > REHANG
REHANGING > REHANG
REHANGS > REHANG
REHARDEN vb harden again
REHARDENS > REHARDEN
REHASH vb rework or reuse
▷ n old ideas presented in
a new form
REHASHED > REHASH
REHASHES > REHASH
REHASHING > REHASH
REHEAR vb hear again
REHEARD > REHEAR
REHEARING > REHEAR
REHEARS > REHEAR
REHEARSAL n preparatory
practice session
REHEARSE vb practise (a

play, concert, etc)
REHEARSED > REHEARSE
REHEARSER > REHEARSE
REHEARSES > REHEARSE
REHEAT vb heat or be
heated again
REHEATED > REHEAT
REHEATER > REHEAT
REHEATERS > REHEAT
REHEATING > REHEAT
REHEATS > REHEAT
REHEEL vb put a new heel
or new heels on
REHEELED > REHEEL
REHEELING > REHEEL
REHEELS > REHEEL
REHEM vb hem again
REHEMMED > REHEM
REHEMMING > REHEM
REHEMS > REHEM
REHINGE vb put a new hing
or new hinges on
REHINGED > REHINGE
REHINGES > REHINGE
REHINGING > REHINGE
REHIRE vb hire again
REHIRED > REHIRE
REHIRES > REHIRE
REHIRING > REHIRE
REHOBOAM n wine bottle
holding the equivalent
of six normal bottles
(approximately 156
ounces)
REHOBOAMS > REHOBOAM
REHOUSE vb provide with a
new (and better) home
REHOUSED > REHOUSE
REHOUSES > REHOUSE
REHOUSING > REHOUSE
REHS > REH
REHUNG > REHANG
REHYDRATE vb hydrate
again
REI n name for a former
Portuguese coin, more
properly called a real
REIF n Scots word
meaning robbery or
plunder
REIFIED > REIFY
REIFIER > REIFY
REIFIERS > REIFY
REIFIES > REIFY
REIFS > REIF
REIFY vb consider or
make (an abstract idea or
concept) real or concrete
REIFYING > REIFY
REIGN n period of a
sovereign's rule ▷ vb rule
(a country)
REIGNED > REIGN
REIGNING > REIGN
REIGNITE vb catch fire or
cause to catch fire again
REIGNITED > REIGNITE
REIGNITES > REIGNITE
REIGNS > REIGN
REIK Scots word for > SMOKE
REIKI n form of therapy in
which the practitioner is
believed to channel energy
into the patient in order

to encourage healing or
restore wellbeing
REIKIS > REIKI
REIKS > REIK
REILLUME vb relight
REILLUMED > REILLUME
REILLUMES > REILLUME
REIMAGE vb image again
REIMAGED > REIMAGE
REIMAGES > REIMAGE
REIMAGINE vb imagine
again
REIMAGING > REIMAGE
REIMBURSE vb refund, pay
back
REIMMERSE vb immerse
again
REIMPLANT vb implant
again
REIMPORT vb import
(goods manufactured from
exported raw materials)
▷ n act of reimporting
REIMPORTS > REIMPORT
REIMPOSE vb establish
previously imposed laws,
controls, etc, again
REIMPOSED > REIMPOSE
REIMPOSES > REIMPOSE
REIN vb check or manage
with reins
REINCITE vb incite again
REINCITED > REINCITE
REINCITES > REINCITE
REINCUR vb incur again
REINCURS > REINCUR
REINDEER n deer of
arctic regions with large
branched antlers
REINDEERS > REINDEER
REINDEX vb index again
REINDEXED > REINDEX
REINDEXES > REINDEX
REINDICT vb indict again
REINDICTS > REINDICT
REINDUCE vb induce again
REINDUCED > REINDUCE
REINDUCES > REINDUCE
REINDUCT vb induct again
REINDUCTS > REINDUCT
REINED > REIN
REINETTE n variety of
apple
REINETTES > REINETTE
REINFECT vb infect or
contaminate again
REINFECTS > REINFECT
REINFLAME vb inflame
again
REINFLATE vb inflate again
REINFORCE vb give added
emphasis to
REINFORM vb inform again
REINFORMS > REINFORM
REINFUND vb archaic word
for pour in again
REINFUNDS > REINFUND
REINFUSE vb infuse again
REINFUSED > REINFUSE
REINFUSES > REINFUSE
REINHABIT vb inhabit
again
REINING > REIN
REINJECT vb inject again

REINJECTS > REINJECT
REINJURE *vb* injure again
REINJURED > REINJURE
REINJURES > REINJURE
REINJURY *n* further injury
REINK *vb* ink again
REINKED > REINK
REINKING > REINK
REINKS > REINK
REINLESS > REIN
REINS *pl n* narrow straps attached to a bit to guide a horse
REINSERT *vb* insert again
REINSERTS > REINSERT
REINSMAN *n* driver in a trotting race
REINSMEN > REINSMAN
REINSPECT *vb* inspect again
REINSPIRE *vb* inspire again
REINSTAL *same as* > REINSTALL
REINSTALL *vb* put in place and connect (machinery, equipment, etc) again
REINSTALS > REINSTAL
REINSTATE *vb* restore to a former position
REINSURE *vb* insure again
REINSURED > REINSURE
REINSURER > REINSURE
REINSURES > REINSURE
REINTER *vb* inter again
REINTERS > REINTER
REINVADE *vb* invade again
REINVADED > REINVADE
REINVADES > REINVADE
REINVENT *vb* replace (a product, etc) with an entirely new version
REINVENTS > REINVENT
REINVEST *vb* put back profits from a previous investment into the same enterprise
REINVESTS > REINVEST
REINVITE *vb* invite again
REINVITED > REINVITE
REINVITES > REINVITE
REINVOKE *vb* invoke again
REINVOKED > REINVOKE
REINVOKES > REINVOKE
REINVOLVE *vb* involve again
REIRD *Scots word for* > DIN
REIRDS > REIRD
REIS > REI
REISES > REI
REISSUE *n* book, record, etc, that is published or released again after being unavailable for a time ▷ *vb* publish or release (a book, record, etc) again after a period of unavailability
REISSUED > REISSUE
REISSUER > REISSUE
REISSUERS > REISSUE
REISSUES > REISSUE
REISSUING > REISSUE
REIST *same as* > REEST
REISTAFEL *same*

*as* > RIJSTAFEL
REISTED > REIST
REISTING > REIST
REISTS > REIST
REITBOK *same*
*as* > REEDBUCK
REITBOKS > REITBOK
REITER *n* soldier in the German cavalry
REITERANT > REITERATE
REITERATE *vb* repeat again and again
REITERS > REITER
REIVE *vb* go on a plundering raid
REIVED > REIVE
REIVER > REIVE
REIVERS > REIVE
REIVES > REIVE
REIVING > REIVE
REJACKET *n* put a new jacket on
REJACKETS > REJACKET
REJECT *vb* refuse to accept or believe ▷ *n* person or thing rejected as not up to standard
REJECTED > REJECT
REJECTEE *n* someone who has been rejected
REJECTEES > REJECTEE
REJECTER > REJECT
REJECTERS > REJECT
REJECTING > REJECT
REJECTION > REJECT
REJECTIVE > REJECT
REJECTOR > REJECT
REJECTORS > REJECT
REJECTS > REJECT
REJIG *vb* re-equip (a factory or plant) ▷ *n* act or process of rejigging
REJIGGED > REJIG
REJIGGER > REJIG
REJIGGERS > REJIG
REJIGGING > REJIG
REJIGS > REJIG
REJOICE *vb* feel or express great happiness
REJOICED > REJOICE
REJOICER > REJOICE
REJOICERS > REJOICE
REJOICES > REJOICE
REJOICING > REJOICE
REJOIN *vb* join again
REJOINDER *n* answer, retort
REJOINED > REJOIN
REJOINING > REJOIN
REJOINS > REJOIN
REJON *n* bullfighting lance
REJONEO *n* bullfighting activity in which a mounted bullfighter spears the bull with lances
REJONEOS > REJONEO
REJONES > REJON
REJOURN *vb* archaic word meaning postpone or adjourn
REJOURNED > REJOURN
REJOURNS > REJOURN
REJUDGE *vb* judge again
REJUDGED > REJUDGE

REJUDGES > REJUDGE
REJUDGING > REJUDGE
REJUGGLE *vb* juggle again
REJUGGLED > REJUGGLE
REJUGGLES > REJUGGLE
REJUSTIFY *vb* justify again
REKE *same as* > RECK
REKED > REKE
REKES > REKE
REKEY *vb* key again
REKEYED > REKEY
REKEYING > REKEY
REKEYS > REKEY
REKINDLE *vb* arouse former emotions or interests
REKINDLED > REKINDLE
REKINDLES > REKINDLE
REKING > REKE
REKNIT *vb* knit again
REKNITS > REKNIT
REKNITTED > REKNIT
REKNOT *vb* knot again
REKNOTS > REKNOT
REKNOTTED > REKNOT
RELABEL *vb* label again
RELABELED > RELABEL
RELABELS > RELABEL
RELACE *vb* lace again
RELACED > RELACE
RELACES > RELACE
RELACHE *n* break
RELACHES > RELACHE
RELACING > RELACE
RELACQUER *vb* apply a new coat of lacquer to
RELAID > RELAY
RELAND *vb* land again
RELANDED > RELAND
RELANDING > RELAND
RELANDS > RELAND
RELAPSE *vb* fall back into bad habits, illness, etc ▷ *n* return of bad habits, illness, etc
RELAPSED > RELAPSE
RELAPSER > RELAPSE
RELAPSERS > RELAPSE
RELAPSES > RELAPSE
RELAPSING > RELAPSE
RELATA > RELATUM
RELATABLE > RELATE
RELATE *vb* establish a relation between
RELATED *adj* linked by kinship or marriage
RELATEDLY > RELATED
RELATER > RELATE
RELATERS > RELATE
RELATES > RELATE
RELATING > RELATE
RELATION *n* connection between things
RELATIONS *pl n* social or political dealings between individuals or groups
RELATIVAL *adj* of or relating to a relative
RELATIVE *adj* true to a certain degree or extent ▷ *n* person connected by blood or marriage
RELATIVES > RELATIVE
RELATOR *n* person who relates a story

RELATORS > RELATOR
RELATUM *n* one of the objects between which a relation is said to hold
RELAUNCH *vb* launch again ▷ *n* another launching, or something that is relaunched
RELAUNDER *vb* launder again
RELAX *vb* make or become looser, less tense, or less rigid
RELAXABLE > RELAX
RELAXANT *n* drug or agent that relaxes, esp one that relaxes tense muscles ▷ *adj* of, relating to, or tending to produce relaxation
RELAXANTS > RELAXANT
RELAXED > RELAX
RELAXEDLY > RELAX
RELAXER *n* person or thing that relaxes, esp a substance used to straighten curly hair
RELAXERS > RELAXER
RELAXES > RELAX
RELAXIN *n* mammalian polypeptide hormone secreted by the corpus luteum during pregnancy, which relaxes the pelvic ligaments
RELAXING > RELAX
RELAXINS > RELAXIN
RELAY *n* fresh set of people or animals relieving others ▷ *vb* pass on (a message)
RELAYED > RELAY
RELAYING > RELAY
RELAYS > RELAY
RELEARN *vb* learn (something previously known) again
RELEARNED > RELEARN
RELEARNS > RELEARN
RELEARNT > RELEARN
RELEASE *vb* set free ▷ *n* setting free
RELEASED > RELEASE
RELEASEE *n* someone to whom an estate is released or someone released from captivity
RELEASEES > RELEASEE
RELEASER > RELEASE
RELEASERS > RELEASE
RELEASES > RELEASE
RELEASING > RELEASE
RELEASOR *n* someone releasing an estate to someone else
RELEASORS > RELEASOR
RELEGABLE *adj* able to be relegated
RELEGATE *vb* put in a less important position
RELEGATED > RELEGATE
RELEGATES > RELEGATE
RELEND *vb* lend again
RELENDING > RELEND
RELENDS > RELEND

**RELENT** vb give up a harsh intention, become less severe
**RELENTED** > RELENT
**RELENTING** > RELENT
**RELENTS** > RELENT
**RELET** vb let again
**RELETS** > RELET
**RELETTER** vb redo lettering of
**RELETTERS** > RELETTER
**RELETTING** > RELET
**RELEVANCE** > RELEVANT
**RELEVANCY** > RELEVANT
**RELEVANT** adj do with the matter in hand
**RELEVE** n dance move in which heels are off the ground
**RELEVES** > RELEVE
**RELIABLE** adj able to be trusted, dependable ▷ n something or someone believed to be reliable
**RELIABLES** > RELIABLE
**RELIABLY** > RELIABLE
**RELIANCE** n dependence, confidence, or trust
**RELIANCES** > RELIANCE
**RELIANT** > RELIANCE
**RELIANTLY** > RELIANCE
**RELIC** n something that has survived from the past
**RELICENSE** vb license again
**RELICS** > RELIC
**RELICT** n relic
**RELICTION** n process by which sea water or fresh water recedes over time, changing the waterline and leaving land exposed
**RELICTS** > RELICT
**RELIDE** archaic past form of > RELY
**RELIE** archaic spelling of > RELY
**RELIED** > RELY
**RELIEF** n gladness at the end or removal of pain, distress, etc
**RELIEFS** > RELIEF
**RELIER** > RELY
**RELIERS** > RELY
**RELIES** > RELY
**RELIEVE** vb bring relief to
**RELIEVED** adj experiencing relief, esp from worry or anxiety
**RELIEVER** n person or thing that relieves
**RELIEVERS** > RELIEVER
**RELIEVES** > RELIEVE
**RELIEVING** > RELIEVE
**RELIEVO** same as > RELIEF
**RELIEVOS** > RELIEVO
**RELIGHT** vb ignite or cause to ignite again
**RELIGHTED** > RELIGHT
**RELIGHTS** > RELIGHT
**RELIGIEUX** n member of a monastic order or clerical body
**RELIGION** n system of

belief in and worship of a supernatural power or god
**RELIGIONS** > RELIGION
**RELIGIOSE** adj affectedly or extremely pious
**RELIGIOSO** adj religious ▷ adv in a religious manner
**RELIGIOUS** adj of religion ▷ n monk or nun
**RELINE** vb line again or anew
**RELINED** > RELINE
**RELINES** > RELINE
**RELINING** > RELINE
**RELINK** vb link again
**RELINKED** > RELINK
**RELINKING** > RELINK
**RELINKS** > RELINK
**RELIQUARY** n case or shrine for holy relics
**RELIQUE** archaic spelling of > RELIC
**RELIQUEFY** vb liquefy again
**RELIQUES** > RELIQUE
**RELIQUIAE** pl n fossil remains of animals or plants
**RELISH** vb enjoy, like very much ▷ n liking or enjoyment
**RELISHED** > RELISH
**RELISHES** > RELISH
**RELISHING** > RELISH
**RELIST** vb list again
**RELISTED** > RELIST
**RELISTING** > RELIST
**RELISTS** > RELIST
**RELIT** > RELIGHT
**RELIVABLE** > RELIVE
**RELIVE** vb experience (a sensation etc) again, esp in the imagination
**RELIVED** > RELIVE
**RELIVER** vb deliver up again
**RELIVERED** > RELIVER
**RELIVERS** > RELIVER
**RELIVES** > RELIVE
**RELIVING** > RELIVE
**RELLENO** n Mexican dish of stuffed vegetable
**RELLENOS** > RELLENO
**RELLIES** pl n relatives or relations
**RELLISH** (in music) variant of > RELISH
**RELLISHED** > RELLISH
**RELLISHES** > RELLISH
**RELOAD** vb put fresh ammunition into (a firearm)
**RELOADED** > RELOAD
**RELOADER** > RELOAD
**RELOADERS** > RELOAD
**RELOADING** > RELOAD
**RELOADS** > RELOAD
**RELOAN** vb loan again
**RELOANED** > RELOAN
**RELOANING** > RELOAN
**RELOANS** > RELOAN
**RELOCATE** vb move to a new place to live or work

**RELOCATED** > RELOCATE
**RELOCATEE** n someone who is relocated
**RELOCATES** > RELOCATE
**RELOCATOR** n program designed to transfer files from one computer to another
**RELOCK** vb lock again
**RELOCKED** > RELOCK
**RELOCKING** > RELOCK
**RELOCKS** > RELOCK
**RELOOK** vb look again
**RELOOKED** > RELOOK
**RELOOKING** > RELOOK
**RELOOKS** > RELOOK
**RELUCENT** adj bright
**RELUCT** vb struggle or rebel
**RELUCTANT** adj unwilling or disinclined
**RELUCTATE** vb be or appear reluctant
**RELUCTED** > RELUCT
**RELUCTING** > RELUCT
**RELUCTS** > RELUCT
**RELUME** vb light or brighten again
**RELUMED** > RELUME
**RELUMES** > RELUME
**RELUMINE** same as > RELUME
**RELUMINED** > RELUMINE
**RELUMINES** > RELUMINE
**RELUMING** > RELUME
**RELY** vb depend (on)
**RELYING** > RELY
**REM** n dose of ionizing radiation that produces the same effect in man as one roentgen of x- or gamma-radiation
**REMADE** n object that has been reconstructed from original materials
**REMADES** > REMADE
**REMAIL** vb mail again
**REMAILED** > REMAIL
**REMAILING** > REMAIL
**REMAILS** > REMAIL
**REMAIN** vb continue
**REMAINDER** n part which is left ▷ vb offer (copies of a poorly selling book) at reduced prices
**REMAINED** > REMAIN
**REMAINING** > REMAIN
**REMAINS** pl n relics, esp of ancient buildings
**REMAKE** vb make again in a different way ▷ n new version of an old film
**REMAKER** > REMAKE
**REMAKERS** > REMAKE
**REMAKES** > REMAKE
**REMAKING** > REMAKE
**REMAN** vb man again or afresh
**REMAND** vb send back into custody or put on bail before trial
**REMANDED** > REMAND
**REMANDING** > REMAND
**REMANDS** > REMAND
**REMANENCE** n ability

of a material to retain magnetization, equal to the magnetic flux density of the material after the removal of the magnetizing field
**REMANENCY** archaic variant of > REMANENCE
**REMANENT** adj remaining or left over ▷ n archaic word meaning remainder
**REMANENTS** > REMANENT
**REMANET** n something left over
**REMANETS** > REMANET
**REMANIE** n fragments and fossils of older origin found in a more recent deposit
**REMANIES** > REMANIE
**REMANNED** > REMAN
**REMANNING** > REMAN
**REMANS** > REMAN
**REMAP** vb map again
**REMAPPED** > REMAP
**REMAPPING** > REMAP
**REMAPS** > REMAP
**REMARK** vb make a casual comment (on) ▷ n observation or comment
**REMARKED** > REMARK
**REMARKER** > REMARK
**REMARKERS** > REMARK
**REMARKET** vb market again
**REMARKETS** > REMARKET
**REMARKING** > REMARK
**REMARKS** > REMARK
**REMARQUE** n printing mark in the margin of a plate
**REMARQUED** adj having had a remarque put on
**REMARQUES** > REMARQUE
**REMARRIED** > REMARRY
**REMARRIES** > REMARRY
**REMARRY** vb marry again following a divorce or the death of one's previous husband or wife
**REMASTER** vb make a new master audio recording, now usually digital, from (an earlier recording), to produce compact discs or stereo records with improved sound reproduction
**REMASTERS** > REMASTER
**REMATCH** n second or return game or contest between two players ▷ vb match (two contestants) again
**REMATCHED** > REMATCH
**REMATCHES** > REMATCH
**REMATE** vb mate again ▷ n finishing pass in bullfighting
**REMATED** > REMATE
**REMATES** > REMATE
**REMATING** > REMATE
**REMBLAI** n earth used for an embankment or rampart
**REMBLAIS** > REMBLAI

**REMBLE** *dialect word for* > REMOVE
**REMBLED** > REMBLE
**REMBLES** > REMBLE
**REMBLING** > REMBLE
**REMEAD** *archaic or dialect word for* > REMEDY
**REMEADED** > REMEAD
**REMEADING** > REMEAD
**REMEADS** > REMEAD
**REMEASURE** *vb* measure again
**REMEDE** *archaic or dialect word for* > REMEDY
**REMEDED** > REMEDE
**REMEDES** > REMEDE
**REMEDIAL** *adj* intended to correct a specific disability, handicap, etc
**REMEDIAT** *archaic word for* > REMEDIAL
**REMEDIATE** *archaic word for* > REMEDIAL
**REMEDIED** > REMEDY
**REMEDIES** > REMEDY
**REMEDING** > REMEDE
**REMEDY** *n* means of curing pain or disease ▷ *vb* put right
**REMEDYING** > REMEDY
**REMEET** *vb* meet again
**REMEETING** > REMEET
**REMEETS** > REMEET
**REMEID** *archaic or dialect word for* > REMEDY
**REMEIDED** > REMEID
**REMEIDING** > REMEID
**REMEIDS** > REMEID
**REMELT** *vb* melt again
**REMELTED** > REMELT
**REMELTING** > REMELT
**REMELTS** > REMELT
**REMEMBER** *vb* retain in or recall to one's memory
**REMEMBERS** > REMEMBER
**REMEN** *n* ancient Egyptian measurement unit
**REMEND** *vb* mend again
**REMENDED** > REMEND
**REMENDING** > REMEND
**REMENDS** > REMEND
**REMENS** > REMEN
**REMERCIED** > REMERCY
**REMERCIES** > REMERCY
**REMERCY** *vb* archaic word for thank
**REMERGE** *vb* merge again
**REMERGED** > REMERGE
**REMERGES** > REMERGE
**REMERGING** > REMERGE
**REMET** > REMEET
**REMEX** *n* any of the large flight feathers of a bird's wing
**REMIGATE** *vb* row
**REMIGATED** > REMIGATE
**REMIGATES** > REMIGATE
**REMIGES** > REMEX
**REMIGIAL** > REMEX
**REMIGRATE** *vb* migrate again
**REMIND** *vb* cause to remember
**REMINDED** > REMIND

**REMINDER** *n* something that recalls the past
**REMINDERS** > REMINDER
**REMINDFUL** *adj* serving to remind
**REMINDING** > REMIND
**REMINDS** > REMIND
**REMINISCE** *vb* talk or write of past times, experiences, etc
**REMINT** *vb* mint again
**REMINTED** > REMINT
**REMINTING** > REMINT
**REMINTS** > REMINT
**REMISE** *vb* give up or relinquish (a right, claim, etc) ▷ *n* second thrust made on the same lunge after the first has missed
**REMISED** > REMISE
**REMISES** > REMISE
**REMISING** > REMISE
**REMISS** *adj* negligent or careless
**REMISSION** *n* reduction in the length of a prison term
**REMISSIVE** > REMISSION
**REMISSLY** > REMISS
**REMISSORY** *adj* liable to or intended to gain remission
**REMIT** *vb* send (money) for goods, services, etc, esp by post ▷ *n* area of competence or authority
**REMITMENT** *n* archaic word for remittance or remission
**REMITS** > REMIT
**REMITTAL** > REMIT
**REMITTALS** > REMIT
**REMITTED** > REMIT
**REMITTEE** *n* recipient of a remittance
**REMITTEES** > REMITTEE
**REMITTENT** *adj* (of a disease) periodically less severe
**REMITTER** *n* person who remits
**REMITTERS** > REMITTER
**REMITTING** > REMIT
**REMITTOR** *same as* > REMITTER
**REMITTORS** > REMITTOR
**REMIX** *vb* change the relative prominence of each performer's part of (a recording) ▷ *n* remixed version of a recording
**REMIXED** > REMIX
**REMIXES** > REMIX
**REMIXING** > REMIX
**REMIXT** *informal past form of* > REMIX
**REMIXTURE** > REMIX
**REMNANT** *n* small piece, esp of fabric, left over ▷ *adj* remaining
**REMNANTAL** *adj* existing as remnant
**REMNANTS** > REMNANT
**REMODEL** *vb* give a different shape or form to ▷ *n*

something that has been remodelled
**REMODELED** > REMODEL
**REMODELER** > REMODEL
**REMODELS** > REMODEL
**REMODIFY** *vb* modify again
**REMOISTEN** *vb* moisten again
**REMOLADE** *same as* > REMOULADE
**REMOLADES** > REMOLADE
**REMOLD** *US spelling of* > REMOULD
**REMOLDED** > REMOLD
**REMOLDING** > REMOLD
**REMOLDS** > REMOLD
**REMONTANT** *adj* (esp of cultivated roses) flowering more than once in a single season ▷ *n* rose having such a growth
**REMONTOIR** *n* any of various devices used in watches, clocks, etc, to compensate for errors arising from the changes in the force driving the escapement
**REMORA** *n* spiny-finned fish
**REMORAS** > REMORA
**REMORID** > REMORA
**REMORSE** *n* feeling of sorrow and regret for something one did
**REMORSES** > REMORSE
**REMOTE** *adj* far away, distant ▷ *n* (in informal usage) remote control
**REMOTELY** > REMOTE
**REMOTER** > REMOTE
**REMOTES** > REMOTE
**REMOTEST** > REMOTE
**REMOTION** *n* removal
**REMOTIONS** > REMOTION
**REMOUD** *Spenserian variant of* > REMOVED
**REMOULADE** *n* mayonnaise sauce flavoured with herbs, mustard, and capers, served with salads, cold meat, etc
**REMOULD** *vb* change completely ▷ *n* renovated tyre
**REMOULDED** > REMOULD
**REMOULDS** > REMOULD
**REMOUNT** *vb* get on (a horse, bicycle, etc) again ▷ *n* fresh horse, esp (formerly) to replace one killed or injured in battle
**REMOUNTED** > REMOUNT
**REMOUNTS** > REMOUNT
**REMOVABLE** > REMOVE
**REMOVABLY** > REMOVE
**REMOVAL** *n* removing, esp changing residence
**REMOVALS** > REMOVAL
**REMOVE** *vb* take away or off ▷ *n* degree of difference
**REMOVED** *adj* very different or distant
**REMOVEDLY** *adv* at a distance

**REMOVER** > REMOVE
**REMOVERS** > REMOVE
**REMOVES** > REMOVE
**REMOVING** > REMOVE
**REMS** > REM
**REMUAGE** *n* (in the making of sparkling wine) process of turning the bottles to let the sediment out
**REMUAGES** > REMUAGE
**REMUDA** *n* stock of horses enabling riders to change mounts
**REMUDAS** > REMUDA
**REMUEUR** *n* (in the making of sparkling wine) person carrying out remuage, or the turning of bottles
**REMUEURS** > REMUEUR
**REMURMUR** *vb* murmur again or murmur in reply
**REMURMURS** > REMURMUR
**REN** *archaic variant of* > RUN
**RENAGUE** *same as* > RENEGE
**RENAGUED** > RENAGUE
**RENAGUES** > RENAGUE
**RENAGUING** > RENAGUE
**RENAIL** *vb* nail again
**RENAILED** > RENAIL
**RENAILING** > RENAIL
**RENAILS** > RENAIL
**RENAL** *adj* of the kidneys
**RENAME** *vb* change the name of (someone or something)
**RENAMED** > RENAME
**RENAMES** > RENAME
**RENAMING** > RENAME
**RENASCENT** *adj* becoming active or vigorous again
**RENATURE** *vb* return to natural state
**RENATURED** > RENATURE
**RENATURES** > RENATURE
**RENAY** *vb* archaic word meaning renounce
**RENAYED** > RENAY
**RENAYING** > RENAY
**RENAYS** > RENAY
**RENCONTRE** *n* unexpected meeting
**REND** *vb* tear or wrench apart
**RENDED** > REND
**RENDER** *vb* cause to become ▷ *n* first thin coat of plaster applied to a surface
**RENDERED** > RENDER
**RENDERER** > RENDER
**RENDERERS** > RENDER
**RENDERING** *n* act or an instance of performing a play, piece of music, etc
**RENDERS** > RENDER
**RENDIBLE** > REND
**RENDING** > REND
**RENDITION** *n* performance
**RENDS** > REND
**RENDZINA** *n* dark interzonal type of soil found in grassy or formerly grassy areas of moderate rainfall, esp on chalklands

RENDZINAS > RENDZINA
RENEGADE n person who
 deserts a cause ▷ vb
 become a renegade
RENEGADED > RENEGADE
RENEGADES > RENEGADE
RENEGADO archaic word
 for > RENEGADE
RENEGADOS > RENEGADO
RENEGATE old variant
 of > RENEGATE
RENEGATES > RENEGATE
RENEGE vb go back (on a
 promise etc)
RENEGED > RENEGE
RENEGER > RENEGE
RENEGERS > RENEGE
RENEGES > RENEGE
RENEGING > RENEGE
RENEGUE same as > RENEGE
RENEGUED > RENEGUE
RENEGUER > RENEGUE
RENEGUERS > RENEGE
RENEGUES > RENEGUE
RENEGUING > RENEGUE
RENEST vb nest again or
 form a new nest
RENESTED > RENEST
RENESTING > RENEST
RENESTS > RENEST
RENEW vb begin again
RENEWABLE > RENEW
RENEWABLY > RENEW
RENEWAL n act of renewing
 or state of being renewed
RENEWALS > RENEWAL
RENEWED > RENEW
RENEWEDLY > RENEW
RENEWER > RENEW
RENEWERS > RENEW
RENEWING > RENEW
RENEWINGS > RENEW
RENEWS > RENEW
RENEY same as > RENAY
RENEYED > RENEY
RENEYING > RENEY
RENEYS > RENEY
RENFIERST adj archaic
 word for turned fierce
RENFORCE vb archaic word
 for reinforce
RENFORCED > RENFORCE
RENFORCES > RENFORCE
RENFORST > RENFORCE
RENGA n type of
 collaborative poetry found
 in Japan
RENGAS > RENGA
RENIED > RENY
RENIES > RENY
RENIFORM adj having the
 shape or profile of a kidney
RENIG same as > RENEGE
RENIGGED > RENIG
RENIGGING > RENIG
RENIGS > RENIG
RENIN n proteolytic
 enzyme secreted by the
 kidneys, which plays an
 important part in the
 maintenance of blood
 pressure
RENINS > RENIN
RENITENCE > RENITENT

RENITENCY > RENITENT
RENITENT adj reluctant
RENK adj unpleasant
RENKER > RENK
RENKEST > RENK
RENMINBI same as > YUAN
RENMINBIS > RENMINBI
RENNASE same as > RENNIN
RENNASES > RENNASE
RENNE archaic variant
 of > RUN
RENNED > REN
RENNES > RENNE
RENNET n substance for
 curdling milk to make
 cheese
RENNETS > RENNET
RENNIN n enzyme that
 occurs in gastric juice and
 is a constituent of rennet.
 It coagulates milk by
 converting caseinogen to
 casein
RENNING > REN
RENNINGS > REN
RENNINS > RENNIN
RENOGRAM n X-ray kidney
 image
RENOGRAMS > RENOGRAM
RENOTIFY vb notify again
RENOUNCE vb give up
 (a belief, habit, etc)
 voluntarily ▷ n failure to
 follow suit in a card game
RENOUNCED > RENOUNCE
RENOUNCER > RENOUNCE
RENOUNCES > RENOUNCE
RENOVATE vb restore to
 good condition
RENOVATED > RENOVATE
RENOVATES > RENOVATE
RENOVATOR > RENOVATE
RENOWN n widespread good
 reputation ▷ vb make
 famous
RENOWNED adj famous
RENOWNER n renown giver
RENOWNERS > RENOWNER
RENOWNING > RENOWN
RENOWNS > RENOWN
RENS > REN
RENT n payment made by
 a tenant to a landlord or
 owner of a property ▷ vb
 grant the right to use one's
 property for payment
RENTABLE > REND
RENTAL n sum payable as
 rent ▷ adj of or relating
 to rent
RENTALLER n (in Scots
 law) tenant with very
 favourable terms
RENTALS > RENTAL
RENTE n annual income
 from capital investment
RENTED > RENT
RENTER n person who lets
 his property in return for
 rent, esp a landlord
RENTERS > RENTER
RENTES > RENTE
RENTIER n person who
 lives off unearned income

 such as rents or interest
RENTIERS > RENTIER
RENTING > RENT
RENTINGS > RENT
RENTS > RENT
RENUMBER vb number
 again or afresh
RENUMBERS > RENUMBER
RENVERSE vb archaic word
 meaning overturn
RENVERSED > RENVERSE
RENVERSES > RENVERSE
RENVERST > RENVERSE
RENVOI n referring of a
 dispute or other legal
 question to a jurisdiction
 other than that in which
 it arose
RENVOIS > RENVOI
RENVOY old variant
 of > RENVOI
RENVOYS > RENVOY
RENY same as > RENAY
RENYING > RENY
REO n language
REOBJECT vb object again
REOBJECTS > REOBJECT
REOBSERVE vb observe
 again
REOBTAIN vb obtain again
REOBTAINS > REOBTAIN
REOCCUPY vb occupy (a
 building, area, etc) again
REOCCUR vb happen, take
 place, or come about again
REOCCURS > REOCCUR
REOFFEND vb commit
 another offence
REOFFENDS > REOFFEND
REOFFER vb offer again
REOFFERED > REOFFER
REOFFERS > REOFFER
REOIL vb oil again
REOILED > REOIL
REOILING > REOIL
REOILS > REOIL
REOPEN vb open again after
 a period of being closed or
 suspended
REOPENED > REOPEN
REOPENER n clause in a
 legal document allowing
 for an issue to be revisited
 at a subsequent date
REOPENERS > REOPENER
REOPENING > REOPEN
REOPENS > REOPEN
REOPERATE vb operate
 again
REOPPOSE vb oppose again
REOPPOSED > REOPPOSE
REOPPOSES > REOPPOSE
REORDAIN vb ordain again
REORDAINS > REORDAIN
REORDER vb change the
 order of
REORDERED > REORDER
REORDERS > REORDER
REORIENT vb adjust or
 align (something) in a new
 or different way
REORIENTS > REORIENT
REOS > REO
REOUTFIT vb outfit again

REOUTFITS > REOUTFIT
REOVIRUS n type of virus
REOXIDISE same
 as > REOXIDIZE
REOXIDIZE vb oxidize
 again
REP n sales representative
 ▷ vb work as a
 representative
REPACIFY vb pacify again
REPACK vb place or arrange
 (articles) in (a container)
 again or in a different way
REPACKAGE vb wrap or put
 (something) in a package
 again
REPACKED > REPACK
REPACKING > REPACK
REPACKS > REPACK
REPAID > REPAY
REPAINT vb apply a new or
 fresh coat of paint
REPAINTED > REPAINT
REPAINTS > REPAINT
REPAIR vb restore to good
 condition, mend ▷ n act
 of repairing
REPAIRED > REPAIR
REPAIRER > REPAIR
REPAIRERS > REPAIR
REPAIRING > REPAIR
REPAIRMAN n man
 whose job it is to repair
 machines, appliances, etc
REPAIRMEN > REPAIRMAN
REPAIRS > REPAIR
REPAND adj having a wavy
 margin
REPANDLY > REPAND
REPANEL vb panel again or
 anew
REPANELED > REPANEL
REPANELS > REPANEL
REPAPER vb paper again or
 afresh
REPAPERED > REPAPER
REPAPERS > REPAPER
REPARABLE adj able to be
 repaired or remedied
REPARABLY > REPARABLE
REPARK vb park again
REPARKED > REPARK
REPARKING > REPARK
REPARKS > REPARK
REPARTEE n interchange of
 witty retorts ▷ vb retort
REPARTEED > REPARTEE
REPARTEES ▻ REPARTEE
REPASS vb pass again
REPASSAGE n passage back
 or return
REPASSED > REPASS
REPASSES > REPASS
REPASSING > REPASS
REPAST n meal ▷ vb feed
 (on)
REPASTED > REPAST
REPASTING > REPAST
REPASTS > REPAST
REPASTURE old word
 for > FOOD
REPATCH vb patch again
REPATCHED > REPATCH
REPATCHES > REPATCH

**REPATTERN** vb pattern again
**REPAVE** vb pave again
**REPAVED** > REPAVE
**REPAVES** > REPAVE
**REPAVING** > REPAVE
**REPAY** vb pay back, refund
**REPAYABLE** > REPAY
**REPAYING** > REPAY
**REPAYMENT** > REPAY
**REPAYS** > REPAY
**REPEAL** vb cancel (a law) officially ▷ n act of repealing
**REPEALED** > REPEAL
**REPEALER** > REPEAL
**REPEALERS** > REPEAL
**REPEALING** > REPEAL
**REPEALS** > REPEAL
**REPEAT** vb say or do again ▷ n act or instance of repeating
**REPEATED** adj done, made, or said again and again
**REPEATER** n firearm that may be discharged many times without reloading
**REPEATERS** > REPEATER
**REPEATING** > REPEAT
**REPEATS** > REPEAT
**REPECHAGE** n extra heat or test providing second chance to previous losers or failing candidates
**REPEG** vb peg again
**REPEGGED** > REPEG
**REPEGGING** > REPEG
**REPEGS** > REPEG
**REPEL** vb be disgusting to
**REPELLANT** same as > REPELLENT
**REPELLED** > REPEL
**REPELLENT** adj distasteful ▷ n something that repels, esp a chemical to repel insects
**REPELLER** > REPEL
**REPELLERS** > REPEL
**REPELLING** > REPEL
**REPELS** > REPEL
**REPENT** vb feel regret for (a deed or omission) ▷ adj lying or creeping along the ground
**REPENTANT** adj reproaching oneself for one's past actions or sins
**REPENTED** > REPENT
**REPENTER** > REPENT
**REPENTERS** > REPENT
**REPENTING** > REPENT
**REPENTS** > REPENT
**REPEOPLE** vb people again
**REPEOPLED** > REPEOPLE
**REPEOPLES** > REPEOPLE
**REPERCUSS** vb have repercussions
**REPEREPE** n New Zealand word for the elephant fish, a large fish of the southwest Pacific with a trunk-like snout
**REPERK** vb perk again
**REPERKED** > REPERK

**REPERKING** > REPERK
**REPERKS** > REPERK
**REPERTORY** n repertoire
**REPERUSAL** n fresh perusal
**REPERUSE** vb peruse again
**REPERUSED** > REPERUSE
**REPERUSES** > REPERUSE
**REPETEND** n digit or series of digits in a recurring decimal that repeats itself
**REPETENDS** > REPETEND
**REPHRASE** vb express in different words
**REPHRASED** > REPHRASE
**REPHRASES** > REPHRASE
**REPIGMENT** vb pigment again
**REPIN** vb pin again
**REPINE** vb fret or complain
**REPINED** > REPINE
**REPINER** > REPINE
**REPINERS** > REPINE
**REPINES** > REPINE
**REPINING** > REPINE
**REPININGS** > REPINE
**REPINNED** > REPIN
**REPINNING** > REPIN
**REPINS** > REPIN
**REPIQUE** n score of 30 points made from the cards held by a player before play begins ▷ vb score a repique against (someone)
**REPIQUED** > REPIQUE
**REPIQUES** > REPIQUE
**REPIQUING** > REPIQUE
**REPLA** > REPLUM
**REPLACE** vb substitute for
**REPLACED** > REPLACE
**REPLACER** > REPLACE
**REPLACERS** > REPLACE
**REPLACES** > REPLACE
**REPLACING** > REPLACE
**REPLAN** vb plan again
**REPLANNED** > REPLAN
**REPLANS** > REPLAN
**REPLANT** vb plant again
**REPLANTED** > REPLANT
**REPLANTS** > REPLANT
**REPLASTER** vb plaster again
**REPLATE** vb plate again
**REPLATED** > REPLATE
**REPLATES** > REPLATE
**REPLATING** > REPLATE
**REPLAY** n immediate reshowing on TV of an incident in sport, esp in slow motion ▷ vb play (a match, recording, etc) again
**REPLAYED** > REPLAY
**REPLAYING** > REPLAY
**REPLAYS** > REPLAY
**REPLEAD** vb plead again
**REPLEADED** > REPLEAD
**REPLEADER** n right to plead again
**REPLEADS** > REPLEAD
**REPLED** > REPLEAD
**REPLEDGE** vb pledge again
**REPLEDGED** > REPLEDGE
**REPLEDGES** > REPLEDGE

**REPLENISH** vb fill up again, resupply
**REPLETE** adj filled or gorged ▷ vb fill again
**REPLETED** > REPLETE
**REPLETELY** > REPLETE
**REPLETES** > REPLETE
**REPLETING** > REPLETE
**REPLETION** n state or condition of being replete
**REPLEVIED** > REPLEVY
**REPLEVIES** > REPLEVY
**REPLEVIN** n recovery of goods unlawfully taken, made subject to establishing the validity of the recovery in a legal action and returning the goods if the decision is adverse
**REPLEVINS** > REPLEVIN
**REPLEVY** vb recover possession of (goods) by replevin
**REPLICA** n exact copy
**REPLICAS** > REPLICA
**REPLICASE** n type of enzyme
**REPLICATE** vb make or be a copy of ▷ adj folded back on itself
**REPLICON** n region of a DNA molecule that is replicated from a single origin
**REPLICONS** > REPLICON
**REPLIED** > REPLY
**REPLIER** > REPLY
**REPLIERS** > REPLY
**REPLIES** > REPLY
**REPLOT** vb plot again
**REPLOTS** > REPLOT
**REPLOTTED** > REPLOT
**REPLOW** vb plow again
**REPLOWED** > REPLOW
**REPLOWING** > REPLOW
**REPLOWS** > REPLOW
**REPLUM** n internal separating wall in some fruits
**REPLUMB** vb plumb again
**REPLUMBED** > REPLUMB
**REPLUMBS** > REPLUMB
**REPLUNGE** vb plunge again
**REPLUNGED** > REPLUNGE
**REPLUNGES** > REPLUNGE
**REPLY** vb answer or respond ▷ n answer or response
**REPLYING** > REPLY
**REPO** n act of repossessing
**REPOINT** vb repair the joints of (brickwork, masonry, etc) with mortar or cement
**REPOINTED** > REPOINT
**REPOINTS** > REPOINT
**REPOLISH** vb polish again
**REPOLL** vb poll again
**REPOLLED** > REPOLL
**REPOLLING** > REPOLL
**REPOLLS** > REPOLL
**REPOMAN** n informal word for a man employed to

repossess goods in cases of non-payment
**REPOMEN** > REPOMAN
**REPONE** vb restore (someone) to his former status, office, etc
**REPONED** > REPONE
**REPONES** > REPONE
**REPONING** > REPONE
**REPORT** vb give an account of ▷ n account or statement
**REPORTAGE** n act or process of reporting news or other events of general interest
**REPORTED** > REPORT
**REPORTER** n person who gathers news for a newspaper, TV, etc
**REPORTERS** > REPORTER
**REPORTING** > REPORT
**REPORTS** > REPORT
**REPOS** > REPO
**REPOSAL** n repose
**REPOSALL** archaic spelling of > REPOSAL
**REPOSALLS** > REPOSALL
**REPOSALS** > REPOSE
**REPOSE** n peace ▷ vb lie or lay at rest
**REPOSED** > REPOSE
**REPOSEDLY** > REPOSE
**REPOSEFUL** > REPOSE
**REPOSER** > REPOSE
**REPOSERS** > REPOSE
**REPOSES** > REPOSE
**REPOSING** > REPOSE
**REPOSIT** vb put away, deposit, or store up
**REPOSITED** > REPOSIT
**REPOSITOR** n any instrument used for correcting the position of displaced organs or bones
**REPOSITS** > REPOSIT
**REPOSSESS** vb (of a lender) take back property from a customer who is behind with payments
**REPOST** vb post again
**REPOSTED** > REPOST
**REPOSTING** > REPOST
**REPOSTS** > REPOST
**REPOSURE** old word for > REPOSE
**REPOSURES** > REPOSURE
**REPOT** vb put (a house plant) into a new usually larger pot
**REPOTS** > REPOT
**REPOTTED** > REPOT
**REPOTTING** > REPOT
**REPOUR** vb pour back or again
**REPOURED** > REPOUR
**REPOURING** > REPOUR
**REPOURS** > REPOUR
**REPOUSSE** adj raised in relief, as a design on a thin piece of metal hammered through from the underside ▷ n design or surface made in this way
**REPOUSSES** > REPOUSSE

REPOWER *vb* put new engine in
REPOWERED > REPOWER
REPOWERS > REPOWER
REPP *same as* > REP
REPPED > REP
REPPING > REP
REPPINGS > REP
REPPS > REPP
REPREEVE *archaic spelling of* > REPRIEVE
REPREEVED > REPREEVE
REPREEVES > REPREEVE
REPREHEND *vb* find fault with
REPRESENT *vb* act as a delegate or substitute for
REPRESS *vb* keep (feelings) in check
REPRESSED *adj* (of a person) repressing feelings, instincts, desires, etc
REPRESSER > REPRESS
REPRESSES > REPRESS
REPRESSOR *n* protein synthesized under the control of a repressor gene, which has the capacity to bind to the operator gene and thereby shut off the expression of the structural genes of an operon
REPRICE *vb* price again
REPRICED > REPRICE
REPRICES > REPRICE
REPRICING > REPRICE
REPRIEFE *n* (in archaic usage) reproof
REPRIEFES > REPRIEFE
REPRIEVAL *old word for* > REPRIEVE
REPRIEVE *vb* postpone the execution of (a condemned person) ▷ *n* (document granting) postponement or cancellation of a punishment
REPRIEVED > REPRIEVE
REPRIEVER > REPRIEVE
REPRIEVES > REPRIEVE
REPRIMAND *vb* blame (someone) officially for a fault ▷ *n* official blame
REPRIME *vb* prime again
REPRIMED > REPRIME
REPRIMES > REPRIME
REPRIMING > REPRIME
REPRINT *vb* print further copies of (a book) ▷ *n* reprinted copy
REPRINTED > REPRINT
REPRINTER > REPRINT
REPRINTS > REPRINT
REPRISAL *n* retaliation
REPRISALS > REPRISAL
REPRISE *n* repeating of an earlier theme ▷ *vb* repeat an earlier theme
REPRISED > REPRISE
REPRISES > REPRISE
REPRISING > REPRISE

REPRIVE *archaic spelling of* > REPRIEVE
REPRIVED > REPRIVE
REPRIVES > REPRIVE
REPRIVING > REPRIVE
REPRIZE *archaic spelling of* > REPRISE
REPRIZED > REPRIZE
REPRIZES > REPRIZE
REPRIZING > REPRIZE
REPRO *n* imitation or facsimile of a work of art; reproduction
REPROACH *vb* blame, rebuke
REPROBACY > REPROBATE
REPROBATE *n* depraved or disreputable (person) ▷ *adj* morally unprincipled ▷ *vb* disapprove of
REPROBE *vb* probe again
REPROBED > REPROBE
REPROBES > REPROBE
REPROBING > REPROBE
REPROCESS *vb* treat or prepare (something) by a special method again
REPRODUCE *vb* produce a copy of
REPROGRAM *vb* program again
REPROOF *n* severe blaming of someone for a fault ▷ *vb* treat (a coat, jacket, etc) so as to renew its texture, waterproof qualities, etc
REPROOFED > REPROOF
REPROOFS > REPROOF
REPROS > REPRO
REPROVAL *same as* > REPROOF
REPROVALS > REPROVAL
REPROVE *vb* speak severely to (someone) about a fault
REPROVED > REPROVE
REPROVER > REPROVE
REPROVERS > REPROVE
REPROVES > REPROVE
REPROVING > REPROVE
REPRYVE *archaic spelling of* > REPRIEVE
REPRYVED > REPRYVE
REPRYVES > REPRYVE
REPRYVING > REPRYVE
REPS > REP
REPTANT *adj* creeping, crawling, or lying along the ground
REPTATION *n* creeping action
REPTILE *n* cold-blooded egg-laying vertebrate with horny scales or plates, such as a snake or tortoise ▷ *adj* creeping, crawling, or squirming
REPTILES > REPTILE
REPTILIA > REPTILIUM
REPTILIAN *adj* of, relating to, resembling, or characteristic of reptiles
REPTILIUM *n* place where live reptiles are kept for show

REPTILOID *adj* resembling a reptile
REPUBLIC *n* form of government in which the people or their elected representatives possess the supreme power
REPUBLICS > REPUBLIC
REPUBLISH *vb* publish again
REPUDIATE *vb* reject the authority or validity of
REPUGN *vb* oppose or conflict (with)
REPUGNANT *adj* offensive or distasteful
REPUGNED > REPUGN
REPUGNING > REPUGN
REPUGNS > REPUGN
REPULP *vb* pulp again
REPULPED > REPULP
REPULPING > REPULP
REPULPS > REPULP
REPULSE *vb* be disgusting to ▷ *n* driving back
REPULSED > REPULSE
REPULSER > REPULSE
REPULSERS > REPULSE
REPULSES > REPULSE
REPULSING > REPULSE
REPULSION *n* distaste or aversion
REPULSIVE *adj* loathsome, disgusting
REPUMP *vb* pump again
REPUMPED > REPUMP
REPUMPING > REPUMP
REPUMPS > REPUMP
REPUNIT *n* any number that consists entirely of the same repeated digits, such as 111 or 55,555
REPUNITS > REPUNIT
REPURE *vb* archaic word meaning make pure again
REPURED > REPURE
REPURES > REPURE
REPURIFY *vb* purify again
REPURING > REPURE
REPURPOSE *vb* find new purpose for
REPURSUE *vb* pursue again
REPURSUED > REPURSUE
REPURSUES > REPURSUE
REPUTABLE *adj* of good reputation, respectable
REPUTABLY > REPUTABLE
REPUTE *n* reputation ▷ *vb* consider (a person or thing) to be as specified
REPUTED *adj* supposed
REPUTEDLY *adv* according to general belief or supposition
REPUTES > REPUTE
REPUTING > REPUTE
REPUTINGS > REPUTE
REQUALIFY *vb* qualify again
REQUERE *archaic variant of* > REQUIRE
REQUERED > REQUERE
REQUERES > REQUERE
REQUERING > REQUERE

REQUEST *vb* ask ▷ *n* asking
REQUESTED > REQUEST
REQUESTER > REQUEST
REQUESTOR > REQUEST
REQUESTS > REQUEST
REQUICKEN *vb* quicken again
REQUIEM *n* Mass celebrated for the dead
REQUIEMS > REQUIEM
REQUIGHT *archaic spelling of* > REQUITE
REQUIGHTS > REQUIGHT
REQUIN *vb* type of shark
REQUINS > REQUIN
REQUIRE *vb* want or need
REQUIRED > REQUIRE
REQUIRER > REQUIRE
REQUIRERS > REQUIRE
REQUIRES > REQUIRE
REQUIRING > REQUIRE
REQUISITE *adj* necessary, essential ▷ *n* essential thing
REQUIT *vb* quit again
REQUITAL *n* act or an instance of requiting
REQUITALS > REQUITAL
REQUITE *vb* return to someone (the same treatment or feeling as received)
REQUITED > REQUITE
REQUITER > REQUITE
REQUITERS > REQUITE
REQUITES > REQUITE
REQUITING > REQUITE
REQUITS > REQUIT
REQUITTED > REQUIT
REQUOTE *vb* quote again
REQUOTED > REQUOTE
REQUOTES > REQUOTE
REQUOTING > REQUOTE
REQUOYLE *archaic spelling of* > RECOIL
REQUOYLED > REQUOYLE
REQUOYLES > REQUOYLE
RERACK *vb* rack again
RERACKED > RERACK
RERACKING > RERACK
RERACKS > RERACK
RERADIATE *vb* radiate again
RERAIL *vb* put back on a railway line
RERAILED > RERAIL
RERAILING *n* replacement of existing rails on a railway line
RERAILS > RERAIL
RERAISE *vb* raise again
RERAISED > RERAISE
RERAISES > RERAISE
RERAISING > RERAISE
RERAN > RERUN
REREAD *vb* read (something) again
REREADING > REREAD
REREADS > REREAD
REREBRACE *n* armour worn on the upper arm
RERECORD *vb* record again
RERECORDS > RERECORD
REREDOS *n* ornamental

screen behind an altar
REREDOSES > REREDOS
REREDOSSE same
as > REREDOS
RERELEASE vb release
again
REREMAI n New Zealand
word for the basking shark
REREMICE > REREMOUSE
REREMIND vb remind again
REREMINDS > REREMIND
REREMOUSE n archaic or
dialect word for BAT (the
animal)
RERENT vb rent again
RERENTED > RERENT
RERENTING > RERENT
RERENTS > RERENT
REREPEAT vb repeat again
REREPEATS > REREPEAT
REREVIEW vb review again
REREVIEWS > REREVIEW
REREVISE vb revise again
REREVISED > REREVISE
REREVISES > REREVISE
REREWARD archaic spelling
of > REARWARD
REREWARDS archaic spelling
of > REARWARDS
RERIG vb rig again
RERIGGED > RERIG
RERIGGING > RERIG
RERIGS > RERIG
RERISE vb rise again
RERISEN > RERISE
RERISES > RERISE
RERISING > RERISE
REROLL vb roll again
REROLLED > REROLL
REROLLER > REROLL
REROLLERS > REROLL
REROLLING > REROLL
REROLLS > REROLL
REROOF vb put a new roof
or roofs on
REROOFED > REROOF
REROOFING > REROOF
REROOFS > REROOF
REROSE > RERISE
REROUTE vb send or direct
by a different route
REROUTED > REROUTE
REROUTES > REROUTE
REROUTING > REROUTE
RERUN n film or programme
that is broadcast again,
repeat ▷ vb put on (a film
or programme) again
RERUNNING > RERUN
RERUNS > RERUN
RES informal word
for > RESIDENCE
RESADDLE vb saddle again
RESADDLED > RESADDLE
RESADDLES > RESADDLE
RESAID > RESAY
RESAIL vb sail again
RESAILED > RESAIL
RESAILING > RESAIL
RESAILS > RESAIL
RESALABLE > RESALE
RESALE n selling of
something purchased
earlier

RESALES > RESALE
RESALGAR archaic variant
of > REALGAR
RESALGARS > RESALGAR
RESALUTE vb salute back
or again
RESALUTED > RESALUTE
RESALUTES > RESALUTE
RESAMPLE vb (in graphics
or digital photography)
change the size or
resolution of
RESAMPLED > RESAMPLE
RESAMPLES > RESAMPLE
RESAT > RESIT
RESAW vb saw again
RESAWED > RESAW
RESAWING > RESAW
RESAWN > RESAW
RESAWS > RESAW
RESAY vb say again or in
response
RESAYING > RESAY
RESAYS > RESAY
RESCALE vb resize
RESCALED > RESCALE
RESCALES > RESCALE
RESCALING > RESCALE
RESCHOOL vb retrain
RESCHOOLS > RESCHOOL
RESCIND vb annul or repeal
RESCINDED > RESCIND
RESCINDER > RESCIND
RESCINDS > RESCIND
RESCORE vb score afresh
RESCORED > RESCORE
RESCORES > RESCORE
RESCORING > RESCORE
RESCREEN vb screen again
RESCREENS > RESCREEN
RESCRIPT n (in ancient
Rome) an ordinance
taking the form of a
reply by the emperor to a
question on a point of law
RESCRIPTS > RESCRIPT
RESCUABLE > RESCUE
RESCUE vb deliver from
danger or trouble, save ▷ n
rescuing
RESCUED > RESCUE
RESCUER > RESCUE
RESCUERS > RESCUE
RESCUES > RESCUE
RESCUING > RESCUE
RESCULPT vb sculpt again
RESCULPTS > RESCULPT
RESEAL vb close or secure
tightly again
RESEALED > RESEAL
RESEALING > RESEAL
RESEALS > RESEAL
RESEARCH n systematic
investigation to
discover facts or collect
information ▷ vb carry
out investigations
RESEASON vb season again
RESEASONS > RESEASON
RESEAT vb show (a person)
to a new seat
RESEATED > RESEAT
RESEATING > RESEAT
RESEATS > RESEAT

RESEAU n mesh
background to a lace or
other pattern
RESEAUS > RESEAU
RESEAUX > RESEAU
RESECT vb cut out part of
(a bone, an organ, or other
structure or part)
RESECTED > RESECT
RESECTING > RESECT
RESECTION n excision of
part of a bone, organ, or
other part
RESECTS > RESECT
RESECURE vb secure again
RESECURED > RESECURE
RESECURES > RESECURE
RESEDA n plant that has
small spikes of grey-green
flowers ▷ adj of a greyish-
green colour
RESEDAS > RESEDA
RESEE vb see again
RESEED vb form seed and
reproduce naturally,
forming a constant plant
population
RESEEDED > RESEED
RESEEDING > RESEED
RESEEDS > RESEED
RESEEING > RESEE
RESEEK vb seek again
RESEEKING > RESEEK
RESEEKS > RESEEK
RESEEN > RESEE
RESEES > RESEE
RESEIZE vb seize again
RESEIZED > RESEIZE
RESEIZES > RESEIZE
RESEIZING > RESEIZE
RESEIZURE > RESEIZE
RESELECT vb choose
(someone or something)
again, esp to choose an
existing office-holder as
candidate for re-election
RESELECTS > RESELECT
RESELL vb sell (something)
one has previously bought
RESELLER > RESELL
RESELLERS > RESELL
RESELLING > RESELL
RESELLS > RESELL
RESEMBLE vb be or look like
RESEMBLED > RESEMBLE
RESEMBLER > RESEMBLE
RESEMBLES > RESEMBLE
RESEND vb send again
RESENDING > RESEND
RESENDS > RESEND
RESENT vb feel bitter about
RESENTED > RESENT
RESENTER > RESENT
RESENTERS > RESENT
RESENTFUL adj feeling
or characterized by
resentment
RESENTING > RESENT
RESENTIVE archaic word
for > RESENTFUL
RESENTS > RESENT
RESERPINE n insoluble
alkaloid, extracted from
the roots of the plant

Rauwolfia serpentina, used
medicinally to lower blood
pressure and as a sedative
RESERVE vb set aside,
keep for future use ▷ n
something, esp money
or troops, kept for
emergencies
RESERVED adj not showing
one's feelings, lacking
friendliness
RESERVER > RESERVE
RESERVERS > RESERVE
RESERVES > RESERVE
RESERVICE vb service
again
RESERVING > RESERVE
RESERVIST n member of a
military reserve
RESERVOIR n natural or
artificial lake storing
water for community
supplies
RESES > RES
RESET vb set again (a
broken bone, matter in
type, a gemstone, etc)
▷ n act or an instance of
setting again
RESETS > RESET
RESETTED > RESET
RESETTER > RESET
RESETTERS > RESET
RESETTING > RESET
RESETTLE vb settle to live
in a different place
RESETTLED > RESETTLE
RESETTLES > RESETTLE
RESEW vb sew again
RESEWED > RESEW
RESEWING > RESEW
RESEWN > RESEW
RESEWS > RESEW
RESH n 20th letter of the
Hebrew alphabet
RESHAPE vb shape
(something) again or
differently
RESHAPED > RESHAPE
RESHAPER > RESHAPE
RESHAPERS > RESHAPE
RESHAPES > RESHAPE
RESHAPING > RESHAPE
RESHARPEN vb sharpen
again
RESHAVE vb shave again
RESHAVED > RESHAVE
RESHAVEN > RESHAVE
RESHAVES > RESHAVE
RESHAVING > RESHAVE
RESHES > RESH
RESHINE vb shine again
RESHINED > RESHINE
RESHINES > RESHINE
RESHINGLE vb put new
shingles on
RESHINING > RESHINE
RESHIP vb ship again
RESHIPPED > RESHIP
RESHIPPER > RESHIP
RESHIPS > RESHIP
RESHOD > RESHOE
RESHOE vb put a new shoe or
shoes on

**RESHOED** > RESHOE
**RESHOEING** > RESHOE
**RESHOES** > RESHOE
**RESHONE** > RESHINE
**RESHOOT** *vb* shoot again
**RESHOOTS** > RESHOOT
**RESHOT** > RESHOOT
**RESHOW** *vb* show again
**RESHOWED** > RESHOW
**RESHOWER** *vb* have another shower
**RESHOWERS** > RESHOWER
**RESHOWING** > RESHOW
**RESHOWN** > RESHOW
**RESHOWS** > RESHOW
**RESHUFFLE** *n* reorganization ▷ *vb* reorganize
**RESIANCE** *archaic word for* > RESIDENCE
**RESIANCES** > RESIANCE
**RESIANT** *archaic word for* > RESIDENT
**RESIANTS** > RESIANT
**RESID** *n* residual oil left over from the petroleum distillation process
**RESIDE** *vb* dwell permanently
**RESIDED** > RESIDE
**RESIDENCE** *n* home or house
**RESIDENCY** *n* regular series of concerts by a band or singer at one venue
**RESIDENT** *n* person who lives in a place ▷ *adj* living in a place
**RESIDENTS** > RESIDENT
**RESIDER** > RESIDE
**RESIDERS** > RESIDE
**RESIDES** > RESIDE
**RESIDING** > RESIDE
**RESIDS** > RESID
**RESIDUA** > RESIDUUM
**RESIDUAL** *adj* of or being a remainder ▷ *n* something left over as a residue
**RESIDUALS** > RESIDUAL
**RESIDUARY** *adj* of, relating to, or constituting a residue
**RESIDUE** *n* what is left, remainder
**RESIDUES** > RESIDUE
**RESIDUOUS** *adj* residual
**RESIDUUM** *n* residue
**RESIDUUMS** > RESIDUUM
**RESIFT** *vb* sift again
**RESIFTED** > RESIFT
**RESIFTING** > RESIFT
**RESIFTS** > RESIFT
**RESIGHT** *vb* sight again
**RESIGHTED** > RESIGHT
**RESIGHTS** > RESIGHT
**RESIGN** *vb* give up office, a job, etc
**RESIGNED** *adj* content to endure
**RESIGNER** > RESIGN
**RESIGNERS** > RESIGN
**RESIGNING** > RESIGN
**RESIGNS** > RESIGN
**RESILE** *vb* spring or shrink

back
**RESILED** > RESILE
**RESILES** > RESILE
**RESILIENT** *adj* (of a person) recovering quickly from a shock etc
**RESILIN** *n* substance found in insect bodies
**RESILING** > RESILE
**RESILINS** > RESILIN
**RESILVER** *vb* silver again
**RESILVERS** > RESILVER
**RESIN** *n* sticky substance from plants, esp pines ▷ *vb* treat or coat with resin
**RESINATA** *n* type of wine
**RESINATAS** > RESINATA
**RESINATE** *vb* impregnate with resin
**RESINATED** > RESINATE
**RESINATES** > RESINATE
**RESINED** > RESIN
**RESINER** *n* applier or collector of resin
**RESINERS** > RESINER
**RESINIFY** *vb* become or cause to be resinous
**RESINING** > RESIN
**RESINISE** *variant spelling of* > RESINIZE
**RESINISED** > RESINISE
**RESINISES** > RESINISE
**RESINIZE** *vb* apply resin to
**RESINIZED** > RESINIZE
**RESINIZES** > RESINIZE
**RESINLIKE** > RESIN
**RESINOID** *adj* resembling, characteristic of, or containing resin ▷ *n* any resinoid substance, esp a synthetic compound
**RESINOIDS** > RESINOID
**RESINOSES** > RESINOSIS
**RESINOSIS** *n* excessive resin loss in diseased or damaged conifers
**RESINOUS** > RESIN
**RESINS** > RESIN
**RESINY** *adj* resembling, containing or covered with resin
**RESIST** *vb* withstand or oppose ▷ *n* substance used to protect something, esp a coating that prevents corrosion
**RESISTANT** *adj* characterized by or showing resistance ▷ *n* person or thing that resists
**RESISTED** > RESIST
**RESISTENT** *same as* > RESISTANT
**RESISTER** > RESIST
**RESISTERS** > RESIST
**RESISTING** > RESIST
**RESISTIVE** *adj* exhibiting electrical resistance
**RESISTOR** *n* component of an electrical circuit producing resistance
**RESISTORS** > RESISTOR
**RESISTS** > RESIST

**RESIT** *vb* take (an exam) again ▷ *n* exam that has to be taken again
**RESITE** *vb* move to a different site
**RESITED** > RESITE
**RESITES** > RESITE
**RESITING** > RESITE
**RESITS** > RESIT
**RESITTING** > RESIT
**RESITUATE** *vb* situate elsewhere
**RESIZE** *vb* change size of
**RESIZED** > RESIZE
**RESIZES** > RESIZE
**RESIZING** > RESIZE
**RESKETCH** *vb* sketch again
**RESKEW** *archaic spelling of* > RESCUE
**RESKEWED** > RESKEW
**RESKEWING** > RESKEW
**RESKEWS** > RESKEW
**RESKILL** *vb* train (workers) to acquire new skills
**RESKILLED** > RESKILL
**RESKILLS** > RESKILL
**RESKUE** *archaic spelling of* > RESCUE
**RESKUED** > RESKUE
**RESKUES** > RESKUE
**RESKUING** > RESKUE
**RESLATE** *vb* slate again
**RESLATED** > RESLATE
**RESLATES** > RESLATE
**RESLATING** > RESLATE
**RESMELT** *vb* smelt again
**RESMELTED** > RESMELT
**RESMELTS** > RESMELT
**RESMOOTH** *vb* smooth again
**RESMOOTHS** > RESMOOTH
**RESNATRON** *n* tetrode used to generate high power at high frequencies
**RESOAK** *vb* soak again
**RESOAKED** > RESOAK
**RESOAKING** > RESOAK
**RESOAKS** > RESOAK
**RESOD** *vb* returf
**RESODDED** > RESOD
**RESODDING** > RESOD
**RESODS** > RESOD
**RESOFTEN** *vb* soften again
**RESOFTENS** > RESOFTEN
**RESOJET** *n* type of jet engine
**RESOJETS** > RESOJET
**RESOLD** > RESELL
**RESOLDER** *vb* solder again
**RESOLDERS** > RESOLDER
**RESOLE** *vb* put a new sole or new soles on
**RESOLED** > RESOLE
**RESOLES** > RESOLE
**RESOLING** > RESOLE
**RESOLUBLE** *adj* able to be resolved
**RESOLUTE** *adj* firm in purpose ▷ *n* someone resolute
**RESOLUTER** > RESOLUTE
**RESOLUTES** > RESOLUTE
**RESOLVE** *vb* decide with an effort of will ▷ *n* absolute determination

**RESOLVED** *adj* determined
**RESOLVENT** *adj* serving to dissolve or separate something into its elements ▷ *n* something that resolves
**RESOLVER** > RESOLVE
**RESOLVERS** > RESOLVE
**RESOLVES** > RESOLVE
**RESOLVING** > RESOLVE
**RESONANCE** *n* echoing, esp with a deep sound
**RESONANT** *adj* resounding or re-echoing ▷ *n* type of unobstructed speech sound
**RESONANTS** > RESONANT
**RESONATE** *vb* resound or cause to resound
**RESONATED** > RESONATE
**RESONATES** > RESONATE
**RESONATOR** *n* any body or system that displays resonance, esp a tuned electrical circuit or a conducting cavity in which microwaves are generated by a resonant current
**RESORB** *vb* absorb again
**RESORBED** > RESORB
**RESORBENT** > RESORB
**RESORBING** > RESORB
**RESORBS** > RESORB
**RESORCIN** *n* substance used principally in dyeing
**RESORCINS** > RESORCIN
**RESORT** *vb* have recourse (to) for help etc ▷ *n* place for holidays
**RESORTED** > RESORT
**RESORTER** > RESORT
**RESORTERS** > RESORT
**RESORTING** > RESORT
**RESORTS** > RESORT
**RESOUGHT** > RESEEK
**RESOUND** *vb* echo or ring with sound
**RESOUNDED** > RESOUND
**RESOUNDS** > RESOUND
**RESOURCE** *n* thing resorted to for support ▷ *vb* provide funding or other resources for
**RESOURCED** > RESOURCE
**RESOURCES** > RESOURCE
**RESOW** *vb* sow again
**RESOWED** > RESOW
**RESOWING** > RESOW
**RESOWN** > RESOW
**RESOWS** > RESOW
**RESPACE** *vb* change the spacing of
**RESPACED** > RESPACE
**RESPACES** > RESPACE
**RESPACING** > RESPACE
**RESPADE** *vb* dig over
**RESPADED** > RESPADE
**RESPADES** > RESPADE
**RESPADING** > RESPADE
**RESPEAK** *vb* speak further
**RESPEAKS** > RESPEAK
**RESPECIFY** *vb* specify again

RESPECT n consideration ▷ vb treat with esteem
RESPECTED > RESPECT
RESPECTER n person who respects someone or something
RESPECTS > RESPECT
RESPELL vb spell again
RESPELLED > RESPELL
RESPELLS > RESPELL
RESPELT > RESPELL
RESPIRE vb breathe
RESPIRED > RESPIRE
RESPIRES > RESPIRE
RESPIRING > RESPIRE
RESPITE n pause, interval of rest ▷ vb grant a respite to
RESPITED > RESPITE
RESPITES > RESPITE
RESPITING > RESPITE
RESPLEND vb be resplendent
RESPLENDS > RESPLEND
RESPLICE vb splice again
RESPLICED > RESPLICE
RESPLICES > RESPLICE
RESPLIT vb split again
RESPLITS > RESPLIT
RESPOKE > RESPEAK
RESPOKEN > RESPEAK
RESPOND vb answer ▷ n pilaster or an engaged column that supports an arch or a lintel
RESPONDED > RESPOND
RESPONDER > RESPOND
RESPONDS > RESPOND
RESPONSA n that part of rabbinic literature concerned with written rulings in answer to questions
RESPONSE n answer
RESPONSER n radio or radar receiver used in conjunction with an interrogator to receive and display signals from a transponder
RESPONSES > RESPONSE
RESPONSOR same as > RESPONSER
RESPONSUM n written answer from a rabbinic authority to a question submitted
RESPOOL vb rewind onto spool
RESPOOLED > RESPOOL
RESPOOLS > RESPOOL
RESPOT vb (in billiards) replace on one of the spots
RESPOTS > RESPOT
RESPOTTED > RESPOT
RESPRANG > RESPRING
RESPRAY n new coat of paint applied to a car, van, etc ▷ vb spray (a car, wheels, etc) with a new coat of paint
RESPRAYED > RESPRAY
RESPRAYS > RESPRAY
RESPREAD vb spread again

RESPREADS > RESPREAD
RESPRING vb put new springs in
RESPRINGS > RESPRING
RESPROUT vb sprout again
RESPROUTS > RESPROUT
RESPRUNG > RESPRING
RESSALDAR n native cavalry commander in mixed Anglo-Indian army
REST n freedom from exertion etc ▷ vb take a rest
RESTABLE vb put in stable again or elsewhere
RESTABLED > RESTABLE
RESTABLES > RESTABLE
RESTACK vb stack again
RESTACKED > RESTACK
RESTACKS > RESTACK
RESTAFF vb staff again
RESTAFFED > RESTAFF
RESTAFFS > RESTAFF
RESTAGE vb produce or perform a new production of (a play)
RESTAGED > RESTAGE
RESTAGES > RESTAGE
RESTAGING > RESTAGE
RESTAMP vb stamp again
RESTAMPED > RESTAMP
RESTAMPS > RESTAMP
RESTART vb commence (something) or set (something) in motion again ▷ n act or an instance of starting again
RESTARTED > RESTART
RESTARTER > RESTART
RESTARTS > RESTART
RESTATE vb state or affirm (something) again or in a different way
RESTATED > RESTATE
RESTATES > RESTATE
RESTATING > RESTATE
RESTATION vb station elsewhere
RESTED > REST
RESTEM vb stem again
RESTEMMED > RESTEM
RESTEMS > RESTEM
RESTER > REST
RESTERS > REST
RESTFUL adj relaxing or soothing
RESTFULLY > RESTFUL
RESTIER > RESTY
RESTIEST > RESTY
RESTIFF same as > RESTIVE
RESTIFORM adj (esp of bundles of nerve fibres) shaped like a cord or rope
RESTING > REST
RESTINGS > REST
RESTITCH vb stitch again
RESTITUTE vb restore
RESTIVE adj restless or impatient
RESTIVELY > RESTIVE
RESTLESS adj bored or dissatisfied
RESTO n restored antique, vintage car, etc

RESTOCK vb replenish stores or supplies
RESTOCKED > RESTOCK
RESTOCKS > RESTOCK
RESTOKE vb stoke again
RESTOKED > RESTOKE
RESTOKES > RESTOKE
RESTOKING > RESTOKE
RESTORAL n restoration
RESTORALS > RESTORAL
RESTORE vb return (a building, painting, etc) to its original condition
RESTORED > RESTORE
RESTORER > RESTORE
RESTORERS > RESTORE
RESTORES > RESTORE
RESTORING > RESTORE
RESTOS > RESTO
RESTRAIN vb hold (someone) back from action
RESTRAINS > RESTRAIN
RESTRAINT n something that restrains
RESTRESS vb stress again or differently
RESTRETCH vb stretch again
RESTRICT vb confine to certain limits
RESTRICTS > RESTRICT
RESTRIKE vb strike again
RESTRIKES > RESTRIKE
RESTRING vb string again or anew
RESTRINGE vb restrict
RESTRINGS > RESTRING
RESTRIVE vb strive again
RESTRIVEN > RESTRIVE
RESTRIVES > RESTRIVE
RESTROOM n room in a public building having lavatories, washing facilities, and sometimes couches
RESTROOMS > RESTROOM
RESTROVE > RESTRIVE
RESTRUCK > RESTRIKE
RESTRUNG > RESTRING
RESTS > REST
RESTUDIED > RESTUDY
RESTUDIES > RESTUDY
RESTUDY vb study again
RESTUFF vb put new stuffing in
RESTUFFED > RESTUFF
RESTUFFS > RESTUFF
RESTUMP vb Australian building term for provide with new stumps
RESTUMPED > RESTUMP
RESTUMPS > RESTUMP
RESTY adj restive
RESTYLE vb style again
RESTYLED > RESTYLE
RESTYLES > RESTYLE
RESTYLING > RESTYLE
RESUBJECT vb subject again
RESUBMIT vb submit again
RESUBMITS > RESUBMIT
RESULT n outcome or consequence ▷ vb be the

outcome or consequence (of)
RESULTANT adj arising as a result ▷ n sum of two or more vectors, such as the force resulting from two or more forces acting on a single point
RESULTED > RESULT
RESULTFUL > RESULT
RESULTING > RESULT
RESULTS > RESULT
RESUMABLE > RESUME
RESUME vb begin again ▷ n summary
RESUMED > RESUME
RESUMER > RESUME
RESUMERS > RESUME
RESUMES > RESUME
RESUMING > RESUME
RESUMMON vb summon again
RESUMMONS > RESUMMON
RESUPINE adj lying on the back
RESUPPLY vb provide (with something) again
RESURFACE vb arise or occur again
RESURGE vb rise again from or as if from the dead
RESURGED > RESURGE
RESURGENT adj rising again, as to new life, vigour, etc
RESURGES > RESURGE
RESURGING > RESURGE
RESURRECT vb restore to life
RESURVEY vb survey again
RESURVEYS > RESURVEY
RESUSPEND vb put back into suspension
RESWALLOW vb swallow again
RET vb moisten or soak (flax, hemp, jute, etc) to promote bacterial action in order to facilitate separation of the fibres from the woody tissue by beating
RETABLE n ornamental screenlike structure above and behind an altar, esp one used as a setting for a religious picture or carving
RETABLES > RETABLE
RETACK vb tack again
RETACKED > RETACK
RETACKING > RETACK
RETACKLE vb tackle again
RETACKLED > RETACKLE
RETACKLES > RETACKLE
RETACKS > RETACK
RETAG vb tag again
RETAGGED > RETAG
RETAGGING > RETAG
RETAGS > RETAG
RETAIL n selling of goods individually or in small amounts to the public ▷ adj of or engaged in such

selling ▷ *adv* by retail ▷ *vb*
sell or be sold retail
**RETAILED** > RETAIL
**RETAILER** *n* > RETAIL
**RETAILERS** > RETAIL
**RETAILING** > RETAIL
**RETAILOR** *vb* tailor afresh
**RETAILORS** > RETAILOR
**RETAILS** > RETAIL
**RETAIN** *vb* keep in one's
possession
**RETAINED** > RETAIN
**RETAINER** *n* fee to retain
someone's services
**RETAINERS** > RETAINER
**RETAINING** > RETAIN
**RETAINS** > RETAIN
**RETAKE** *vb* recapture ▷ *n*
act of rephotographing a
scene
**RETAKEN** > RETAKE
**RETAKER** > RETAKE
**RETAKERS** > RETAKE
**RETAKES** > RETAKE
**RETAKING** > RETAKE
**RETAKINGS** > RETAKE
**RETALIATE** *vb* repay an
injury or wrong in kind
**RETALLIED** > RETALLY
**RETALLIES** > RETALLY
**RETALLY** *vb* count up again
**RETAMA** *n* type of shrub
**RETAMAS** > RETAMA
**RETAPE** *vb* tape again
**RETAPED** > RETAPE
**RETAPES** > RETAPE
**RETAPING** > RETAPE
**RETARD** *vb* delay or slow
(progress or development)
▷ *n* offensive term for a
retarded person
**RETARDANT** *n* substance
that reduces the rate of a
chemical reaction ▷ *adj*
having a slowing effect
**RETARDATE** *n* person who
is retarded
**RETARDED** *adj*
underdeveloped, esp
mentally
**RETARDER** *n* person or
thing that retards
**RETARDERS** > RETARDER
**RETARDING** > RETARD
**RETARDS** > RETARD
**RETARGET** *vb* target afresh
or differently
**RETARGETS** > RETARGET
**RETASTE** *vb* taste again
**RETASTED** > RETASTE
**RETASTES** > RETASTE
**RETASTING** > RETASTE
**RETAUGHT** > RETEACH
**RETAX** *vb* tax again
**RETAXED** > RETAX
**RETAXES** > RETAX
**RETAXING** > RETAX
**RETCH** *vb* try to vomit ▷ *n*
involuntary spasm of the
stomach
**RETCHED** > RETCH
**RETCHES** > RETCH
**RETCHING** > RETCH
**RETCHLESS** *archaic variant*

*of* > RECKLESS
**RETE** *n* any network of
nerves or blood vessels
**RETEACH** *vb* teach again
**RETEACHES** > RETEACH
**RETEAM** *vb* team up again
**RETEAMED** > RETEAM
**RETEAMING** > RETEAM
**RETEAMS** > RETEAM
**RETEAR** *vb* tear again
**RETEARING** > RETEAR
**RETEARS** > RETEAR
**RETELL** *vb* relate (a story,
etc) again or differently
**RETELLER** > RETELL
**RETELLERS** > RETELL
**RETELLING** > RETELL
**RETELLS** > RETELL
**RETEM** *n* type of shrub
**RETEMPER** *vb* temper again
**RETEMPERS** > RETEMPER
**RETEMS** > RETEM
**RETENE** *n* yellow crystalline
hydrocarbon found in tar
oils from pine wood and in
certain fossil resins
**RETENES** > RETENE
**RETENTION** *n* retaining
**RETENTIVE** *adj* capable of
retaining or remembering
**RETES** > RETE
**RETEST** *vb* test
(something) again or
differently
**RETESTED** > RETEST
**RETESTIFY** *vb* testify again
**RETESTING** > RETEST
**RETESTS** > RETEST
**RETEXTURE** *vb* restore
natural texture to
**RETHINK** *vb* consider
again, esp with a view to
changing one's tactics
▷ *n* act or an instance of
thinking again
**RETHINKER** > RETHINK
**RETHINKS** > RETHINK
**RETHOUGHT** > RETHINK
**RETHREAD** *vb* thread again
**RETHREADS** > RETHREAD
**RETIA** > RETE
**RETIAL** > RETE
**RETIARII** > RETIARIUS
**RETIARIUS** *n* (in ancient
Rome) a gladiator armed
with a net and trident
**RETIARY** *adj* of, relating to,
or resembling a net or web
**RETICELLA** *n* form of lace
**RETICENCE** > RETICENT
**RETICENCY** > RETICENT
**RETICENT** *adj*
uncommunicative,
reserved
**RETICLE** *n* network of fine
lines, wires, etc, placed
in the focal plane of an
optical instrument to
assist measurement of the
size or position of objects
under observation
**RETICLES** > RETICLE
**RETICULA** > RETICULUM
**RETICULAR** *adj* in the form

of a network or having a
network of parts
**RETICULE** *same as* > RETICLE
**RETICULES** > RETICULE
**RETICULUM** *n* any fine
network, esp one in the
body composed of cells,
fibres, etc
**RETIE** *vb* tie again
**RETIED** > RETIE
**RETIEING** > RETIE
**RETIES** > RETIE
**RETIFORM** *adj* netlike
**RETIGHTEN** *vb* tighten
again
**RETILE** *vb* put new tiles in
or on
**RETILED** > RETILE
**RETILES** > RETILE
**RETILING** > RETILE
**RETIME** *vb* time again or
alter time of
**RETIMED** > RETIME
**RETIMES** > RETIME
**RETIMING** > RETIME
**RETINA** *n* light-sensitive
membrane at the back of
the eye
**RETINAE** > RETINA
**RETINAL** *adj* of or relating
to the retina ▷ *n* aldehyde
form of the polyene retinol
(vitamin A) that associates
with the protein opsin
to form the visual purple
pigment rhodopsin
**RETINALS** > RETINAL
**RETINAS** > RETINA
**RETINE** *n* chemical found
in body cells that slows cell
growth and division
**RETINENE** *n* aldehyde form
of the polyene retinol
(vitamin A) that associates
with the protein opsin
to form the visual purple
pigment rhodopsin
**RETINENES** > RETINENE
**RETINES** > RETINE
**RETINITE** *n* any of various
resins of fossil origin, esp
one derived from lignite
**RETINITES** > RETINITE
**RETINITIS** *n*
inflammation of the retina
**RETINOID** *adj* resinlike ▷ *n*
derivative of vitamin A
**RETINOIDS** > RETINOID
**RETINOL** *n* another name
for vitamin A and rosin oil
**RETINOLS** > RETINOL
**RETINT** *vb* tint again or
change tint of
**RETINTED** > RETINT
**RETINTING** > RETINT
**RETINTS** > RETINT
**RETINUE** *n* band of
attendants
**RETINUED** > RETINUE
**RETINUES** > RETINUE
**RETINULA** *n* part of the
compound eye in certain
arthropods
**RETINULAE** > RETINULA

**RETINULAR** > RETINULA
**RETINULAS** > RETINULA
**RETIRACY** *n* (in US English)
retirement
**RETIRAL** *n* act of retiring
from office, one's work, etc
**RETIRALS** > RETIRAL
**RETIRANT** *n* (in US English)
retired person
**RETIRANTS** > RETIRANT
**RETIRE** *vb* (cause to) give
up office or work, esp
through age
**RETIRED** *adj* having retired
from work etc
**RETIREDLY** > RETIRED
**RETIREE** *n* person who has
retired from work
**RETIREES** > RETIREE
**RETIRER** > RETIRE
**RETIRERS** > RETIRE
**RETIRES** > RETIRE
**RETIRING** *adj* shy
**RETITLE** *vb* give a new
title to
**RETITLED** > RETITLE
**RETITLES** > RETITLE
**RETITLING** > RETITLE
**RETOLD** > RETELL
**RETOOK** > RETAKE
**RETOOL** *vb* replace, re-
equip, or rearrange the
tools in (a factory, etc)
**RETOOLED** > RETOOL
**RETOOLING** > RETOOL
**RETOOLS** > RETOOL
**RETORE** > RETEAR
**RETORN** > RETEAR
**RETORSION** *n* retaliatory
action taken by a state
whose citizens have been
mistreated by a foreign
power by treating the
subjects of that power
similarly
**RETORT** *vb* reply quickly,
wittily, or angrily ▷ *n*
quick, witty, or angry reply
**RETORTED** > RETORT
**RETORTER** > RETORT
**RETORTERS** > RETORT
**RETORTING** > RETORT
**RETORTION** *n* act of
retorting
**RETORTIVE** > RETORT
**RETORTS** > RETORT
**RETOTAL** *vb* add up again
**RETOTALED** > RETOTAL
**RETOTALS** > RETOTAL
**RETOUCH** *vb* restore or
improve by new touches,
esp of paint ▷ *n* art or
practice of retouching
**RETOUCHED** > RETOUCH
**RETOUCHER** > RETOUCH
**RETOUCHES** > RETOUCH
**RETOUR** *vb* (in Scottish law)
to return as heir
**RETOURED** > RETOUR
**RETOURING** > RETOUR
**RETOURS** > RETOUR
**RETRACE** *vb* go back over (a
route etc) again
**RETRACED** > RETRACE

RETRACER > RETRACE
RETRACERS > RETRACE
RETRACES > RETRACE
RETRACING > RETRACE
RETRACK vb track again
RETRACKED > RETRACK
RETRACKS > RETRACK
RETRACT vb withdraw (a statement etc)
RETRACTED > RETRACT
RETRACTOR n any of various muscles that retract an organ or part
RETRACTS > RETRACT
RETRAICT archaic form of > RETREAT
RETRAICTS > RETRAICT
RETRAIN vb train to do a new or different job
RETRAINED > RETRAIN
RETRAINEE > RETRAIN
RETRAINS > RETRAIN
RETRAIT archaic form of > RETREAT
RETRAITE archaic form of > RETREAT
RETRAITES > RETRAITE
RETRAITS > RETRAIT
RETRAITT n archaic word meaning portrait
RETRAITTS > RETRAITT
RETRAL adj at, near, or towards the back
RETRALLY > RETRAL
RETRATE archaic form of > RETREAT
RETRATED > RETRATE
RETRATES > RETRATE
RETRATING > RETRATE
RETREAD n remould ▷ vb remould tread again
RETREADED > RETREAD
RETREADS > RETREAD
RETREAT vb move back from a position, withdraw ▷ n act of or military signal for retiring or withdrawal
RETREATED > RETREAT
RETREATER > RETREAT
RETREATS > RETREAT
RETREE n imperfectly made paper
RETREES > RETREE
RETRENCH vb reduce expenditure, cut back
RETRIAL n second trial of a case or defendant in a court of law
RETRIALS > RETRIAL
RETRIBUTE vb give back
RETRIED > RETRY
RETRIES > RETRY
RETRIEVAL n act or process of retrieving
RETRIEVE vb fetch back again ▷ n chance of being retrieved
RETRIEVED > RETRIEVE
RETRIEVER n dog trained to retrieve shot game
RETRIEVES > RETRIEVE
RETRIM vb trim again
RETRIMMED > RETRIM
RETRIMS > RETRIM

RETRO adj associated with or revived from the past
RETROACT vb act in opposition
RETROACTS > RETROACT
RETROCEDE vb give back
RETROD > RETREAD
RETRODDEN > RETREAD
RETRODICT vb make surmises about the past using information from the present
RETROFIRE n act of firing a retrorocket
RETROFIT vb equip (a vehicle, piece of equipment, etc) with new parts, safety devices, etc, after manufacture
RETROFITS > RETROFIT
RETROFLEX adj bent or curved backwards
RETROJECT vb throw backwards (opposed to project)
RETRONYM n word coined for existing thing to distinguish it from new thing
RETRONYMS > RETRONYM
RETROPACK n system of retrorockets on a spacecraft
RETRORSE adj (esp of plant parts) pointing backwards or in a direction opposite to normal
RETROS > RETRO
RETROUSSE adj (of a nose) turned upwards
RETROVERT vb turn back
RETRY vb try again (a case already determined)
RETRYING > RETRY
RETS > RET
RETSINA n Greek wine flavoured with resin
RETSINAS > RETSINA
RETTED > RET
RETTERIES > RETTERY
RETTERY n flax-retting place
RETTING > RET
RETUND vb weaken or blunt
RETUNDED > RETUND
RETUNDING > RETUND
RETUNDS > RETUND
RETUNE vb tune (a musical instrument) differently or again
RETUNED > RETUNE
RETUNES > RETUNE
RETUNING > RETUNE
RETURF vb turf again
RETURFED > RETURF
RETURFING > RETURF
RETURFS > RETURF
RETURN vb go or come back ▷ n returning ▷ adj of or being a return
RETURNED > RETURN
RETURNEE n person who returns to his native country, esp after war

service
RETURNEES > RETURNEE
RETURNER n person or thing that returns
RETURNERS > RETURNER
RETURNIK n someone returning or intending to return to their native land, especially when this is in the former Soviet Union
RETURNIKS > RETURNIK
RETURNING > RETURN
RETURNS > RETURN
RETUSE adj having a rounded apex and a central depression
RETWIST vb twist again
RETWISTED > RETWIST
RETWISTS > RETWIST
RETYING > RETIE
RETYPE vb type again
RETYPED > RETYPE
RETYPES > RETYPE
RETYPING > RETYPE
REUNIFIED > REUNIFY
REUNIFIES > REUNIFY
REUNIFY vb bring together again something previously divided
REUNION n meeting of people who have been apart
REUNIONS > REUNION
REUNITE vb bring or come together again after a separation
REUNITED > REUNITE
REUNITER > REUNITE
REUNITERS > REUNITE
REUNITES > REUNITE
REUNITING > REUNITE
REUPTAKE vb absorb again
REUPTAKES > REUPTAKE
REURGE vb urge again
REURGED > REURGE
REURGES > REURGE
REURGING > REURGE
REUSABLE adj able to be used more than once
REUSABLES pl n products which can be used more than once
REUSE vb use again ▷ n act of using something again
REUSED > REUSE
REUSES > REUSE
REUSING > REUSE
REUTILISE same as > REUTILIZE
REUTILIZE vb utilize again
REUTTER vb utter again
REUTTERED > REUTTER
REUTTERS > REUTTER
REV n revolution (of an engine) ▷ vb increase the speed of revolution of (an engine)
REVALENTA n lentil flour
REVALUATE same as > REVALUE
REVALUE vb adjust the exchange value of (a currency) upwards
REVALUED > REVALUE

REVALUES > REVALUE
REVALUING > REVALUE
REVAMP vb renovate or restore ▷ n something that has been renovated or revamped
REVAMPED > REVAMP
REVAMPER > REVAMP
REVAMPERS > REVAMP
REVAMPING > REVAMP
REVAMPS > REVAMP
REVANCHE n revenge
REVANCHES > REVANCHE
REVARNISH vb varnish again
REVEAL vb make known ▷ n vertical side of an opening in a wall, esp the side of a window or door between the frame and the front of the wall
REVEALED > REVEAL
REVEALER > REVEAL
REVEALERS > REVEAL
REVEALING adj disclosing information that one did not know
REVEALS > REVEAL
REVEHENT adj (in anatomy) carrying back
REVEILLE n morning bugle call to waken soldiers
REVEILLES > REVEILLE
REVEL vb take pleasure (in) ▷ n occasion of noisy merrymaking
REVELATOR n revealer
REVELED > REVEL
REVELER > REVEL
REVELERS > REVEL
REVELING > REVEL
REVELLED > REVEL
REVELLER > REVEL
REVELLERS > REVEL
REVELLING > REVEL
REVELMENT > REVEL
REVELRIES > REVELRY
REVELROUS > REVELRY
REVELRY n festivity
REVELS > REVEL
REVENANT n something, esp a ghost, that returns
REVENANTS > REVENANT
REVENGE n retaliation for wrong done ▷ vb make retaliation for
REVENGED > REVENGE
REVENGER > REVENGE
REVENGERS > REVENGE
REVENGES > REVENGE
REVENGING > REVENGE
REVENGIVE > REVENGE
REVENUAL > REVENUE
REVENUE n income, esp of a state
REVENUED > REVENUE
REVENUER n revenue officer or cutter
REVENUERS > REVENUER
REVENUES > REVENUE
REVERABLE > REVERE
REVERB n electronic device that creates artificial acoustics ▷ vb

reverberate
**REVERBED** > REVERB
**REVERBING** > REVERB
**REVERBS** > REVERB
**REVERE** *vb* be in awe of and respect greatly
**REVERED** > REVERE
**REVERENCE** *n* awe mingled with respect and esteem
**REVEREND** *adj* worthy of reverence ▷ *n* clergyman
**REVERENDS** > REVEREND
**REVERENT** *adj* showing reverence
**REVERER** > REVERE
**REVERERS** > REVERE
**REVERES** > REVERE
**REVERIE** *n* absent-minded daydream
**REVERIES** > REVERIE
**REVERIFY** *vb* verify again
**REVERING** > REVERE
**REVERIST** *n* someone given to reveries
**REVERISTS** > REVERIST
**REVERS** *n* turned back part of a garment, such as the lapel
**REVERSAL** *n* act or an instance of reversing
**REVERSALS** > REVERSAL
**REVERSE** *vb* turn upside down or the other way round ▷ *n* opposite ▷ *adj* opposite or contrary
**REVERSED** > REVERSE
**REVERSELY** > REVERSE
**REVERSER** > REVERSE
**REVERSERS** > REVERSE
**REVERSES** > REVERSE
**REVERSI** *n* game played on a draughtsboard with 64 pieces, black on one side and white on the other. When pieces are captured they are turned over to join the capturing player's forces
**REVERSING** > REVERSE
**REVERSION** *n* return to a former state, practice, or belief
**REVERSIS** *n* type of card game
**REVERSO** *another name for* > VERSO
**REVERSOS** > REVERSO
**REVERT** *vb* return to a former state
**REVERTANT** *n* mutant that has reverted to an earlier form ▷ *adj* having mutated to an earlier form
**REVERTED** > REVERT
**REVERTER** > REVERT
**REVERTERS** > REVERT
**REVERTING** > REVERT
**REVERTIVE** > REVERT
**REVERTS** > REVERT
**REVERY** *same as* > REVERIE
**REVEST** *vb* restore (former power, authority, status, etc, to a person) or (of power, authority, etc) to be

restored
**REVESTED** > REVEST
**REVESTING** > REVEST
**REVESTRY** *same as* > VESTRY
**REVESTS** > REVEST
**REVET** *vb* face (a wall or embankment) with stones
**REVETMENT** *n* facing of stones, sandbags, etc, to protect a wall, embankment, or earthworks
**REVETS** > REVET
**REVETTED** > REVET
**REVETTING** > REVET
**REVEUR** *n* daydreamer
**REVEURS** > REVEUR
**REVEUSE** *n* female daydreamer
**REVEUSES** > REVEUSE
**REVIBRATE** *vb* vibrate again
**REVICTUAL** *vb* victual again
**REVIE** *vb* archaic cards term meaning challenge by placing a larger stake
**REVIED** > REVIE
**REVIES** > REVIE
**REVIEW** *n* critical assessment of a book, concert, etc ▷ *vb* hold or write a review of
**REVIEWAL** *same as* > REVIEW
**REVIEWALS** > REVIEWAL
**REVIEWED** > REVIEW
**REVIEWER** > REVIEW
**REVIEWERS** > REVIEW
**REVIEWING** > REVIEW
**REVIEWS** > REVIEW
**REVILE** *vb* be abusively scornful of
**REVILED** > REVILE
**REVILER** > REVILE
**REVILERS** > REVILE
**REVILES** > REVILE
**REVILING** > REVILE
**REVILINGS** > REVILE
**REVIOLATE** *vb* violate again
**REVISABLE** > REVISE
**REVISAL** > REVISE
**REVISALS** > REVISE
**REVISE** *vb* change or alter ▷ *n* act, process, or result of revising
**REVISED** > REVISE
**REVISER** > REVISE
**REVISERS** > REVISE
**REVISES** > REVISE
**REVISING** > REVISE
**REVISION** *n* act of revising
**REVISIONS** > REVISION
**REVISIT** *vb* visit again
**REVISITED** > REVISIT
**REVISITS** > REVISIT
**REVISOR** > REVISE
**REVISORS** > REVISE
**REVISORY** *adj* of or having the power of revision
**REVIVABLE** > REVIVE
**REVIVABLY** > REVIVE
**REVIVAL** *n* reviving or renewal

**REVIVALS** > REVIVAL
**REVIVE** *vb* bring or come back to life, vigour, use, etc
**REVIVED** > REVIVE
**REVIVER** > REVIVE
**REVIVERS** > REVIVE
**REVIVES** > REVIVE
**REVIVIFY** *vb* give new life to
**REVIVING** > REVIVE
**REVIVINGS** > REVIVE
**REVIVOR** *n* means of reviving a lawsuit that has been suspended owing to the death or marriage of one of the parties
**REVIVORS** > REVIVOR
**REVOCABLE** *adj* capable of being revoked
**REVOCABLY** > REVOCABLE
**REVOICE** *vb* utter again
**REVOICED** > REVOICE
**REVOICES** > REVOICE
**REVOICING** > REVOICE
**REVOKABLE** *same as* > REVOCABLE
**REVOKABLY** > REVOCABLE
**REVOKE** *vb* cancel (a will, agreement, etc) ▷ *n* act of revoking
**REVOKED** > REVOKE
**REVOKER** > REVOKE
**REVOKERS** > REVOKE
**REVOKES** > REVOKE
**REVOKING** > REVOKE
**REVOLT** *n* uprising against authority ▷ *vb* rise in rebellion
**REVOLTED** > REVOLT
**REVOLTER** > REVOLT
**REVOLTERS** > REVOLT
**REVOLTING** *adj* disgusting, horrible
**REVOLTS** > REVOLT
**REVOLUTE** *adj* (esp of the margins of a leaf) rolled backwards and downwards
**REVOLVE** *vb* turn round, rotate ▷ *n* circular section of a stage that can be rotated by electric power to provide a scene change
**REVOLVED** > REVOLVE
**REVOLVER** *n* repeating pistol
**REVOLVERS** > REVOLVER
**REVOLVES** > REVOLVE
**REVOLVING** *adj* denoting or relating to an engine, such as a radial aero engine, in which the cylinders revolve about a fixed shaft
**REVOTE** *vb* decide or grant again by a new vote
**REVOTED** > REVOTE
**REVOTES** > REVOTE
**REVOTING** > REVOTE
**REVS** > REV
**REVUE** *n* theatrical entertainment with topical sketches and songs
**REVUES** > REVUE
**REVUIST** > REVUE

**REVUISTS** > REVUE
**REVULSED** *adj* filled with disgust
**REVULSION** *n* strong disgust
**REVULSIVE** *adj* of or causing revulsion ▷ *n* counterirritant
**REVVED** > REV
**REVVING** > REV
**REVYING** > REVIE
**REW** *archaic spelling of* > RUE
**REWAKE** *vb* awaken again
**REWAKED** > REWAKE
**REWAKEN** *vb* awaken again
**REWAKENED** > REWAKEN
**REWAKENS** > REWAKEN
**REWAKES** > REWAKE
**REWAKING** > REWAKE
**REWAN** *archaic past form of* > REWIN
**REWARD** *n* something given in return for a service ▷ *vb* pay or give something to (someone) for a service, information, etc
**REWARDED** > REWARD
**REWARDER** > REWARD
**REWARDERS** > REWARD
**REWARDFUL** > REWARD
**REWARDING** *adj* giving personal satisfaction, worthwhile
**REWARDS** > REWARD
**REWAREWA** *n* New Zealand tree
**REWAREWAS** > REWAREWA
**REWARM** *vb* warm again
**REWARMED** > REWARM
**REWARMING** > REWARM
**REWARMS** > REWARM
**REWASH** *vb* wash again
**REWASHED** > REWASH
**REWASHES** > REWASH
**REWASHING** > REWASH
**REWAX** *vb* wax again
**REWAXED** > REWAX
**REWAXES** > REWAX
**REWAXING** > REWAX
**REWEAR** *vb* wear again
**REWEARING** > REWEAR
**REWEARS** > REWEAR
**REWEAVE** *vb* weave again
**REWEAVED** > REWEAVE
**REWEAVES** > REWEAVE
**REWEAVING** > REWEAVE
**REWED** *vb* wed again
**REWEDDED** > REWED
**REWEDDING** > REWED
**REWEDS** > REWED
**REWEIGH** *vb* weigh again
**REWEIGHED** > REWEIGH
**REWEIGHS** > REWEIGH
**REWELD** *vb* weld again
**REWELDED** > REWELD
**REWELDING** > REWELD
**REWELDS** > REWELD
**REWET** *vb* wet again
**REWETS** > REWET
**REWETTED** > REWET
**REWETTING** > REWET
**REWIDEN** *vb* widen again
**REWIDENED** > REWIDEN
**REWIDENS** > REWIDEN

REWIN vb win again
REWIND vb wind again
REWINDED > REWIND
REWINDER > REWIND
REWINDERS > REWIND
REWINDING > REWIND
REWINDS > REWIND
REWINNING > REWIN
REWINS > REWIN
REWIRABLE > REWIRE
REWIRE vb provide (a house, engine, etc) with new wiring
REWIRED > REWIRE
REWIRES > REWIRE
REWIRING > REWIRE
REWOKE > REWAKE
REWOKEN > REWAKE
REWON > REWIN
REWORD vb alter the wording of
REWORDED > REWORD
REWORDING > REWORD
REWORDS > REWORD
REWORE > REWEAR
REWORK vb improve or bring up to date
REWORKED > REWORK
REWORKING > REWORK
REWORKS > REWORK
REWORN > REWEAR
REWOUND > REWIND
REWOVE > REWEAVE
REWOVEN > REWEAVE
REWRAP vb wrap again
REWRAPPED > REWRAP
REWRAPS > REWRAP
REWRAPT > REWRAP
REWRITE vb write again in a different way ▷ n something rewritten
REWRITER > REWRITE
REWRITERS > REWRITE
REWRITES > REWRITE
REWRITING > REWRITE
REWRITTEN > REWRITE
REWROTE > REWRITE
REWROUGHT > REWORK
REWS > REW
REWTH archaic variant of > RUTH
REWTHS > REWTH
REX n king
REXES > REX
REXINE n tradename for a form of artificial leather
REXINES > REXINE
REYNARD n fox
REYNARDS > REYNARD
REZ n informal word for an instance of reserving; reservation
REZERO vb reset to zero
REZEROED > REZERO
REZEROES > REZERO
REZEROING > REZERO
REZEROS > REZERO
REZONE vb zone again
REZONED > REZONE
REZONES > REZONE
REZONING > REZONE
REZZES > REZ
RHABDOID adj rod-shaped ▷ n rod-shaped structure

found in cells of some plants and animals
RHABDOIDS > RHABDOID
RHABDOM n (in insect anatomy) any of many similar rodlike structures found in the eye
RHABDOMAL > RHABDOM
RHABDOME same as > RHABDOM
RHABDOMES > RHABDOME
RHABDOMS > RHABDOM
RHABDUS n sponge spicule
RHABDUSES > RHABDUS
RHACHIAL > RACHIS
RHACHIDES > RHACHIS
RHACHILLA same as > RACHILLA
RHACHIS same as > RACHIS
RHACHISES > RHACHIS
RHACHITIS same as > RACHITIS
RHAGADES pl n cracks found in the skin
RHAMNOSE n type of plant sugar
RHAMNOSES > RHAMNOSE
RHAMNUS n buckthorn
RHAMNUSES > RHAMNUS
RHAMPHOID adj beaklike
RHANJA n Indian English word for a male lover
RHANJAS > RHANJA
RHAPHAE > RHAPHE
RHAPHE same as > RAPHE
RHAPHES > RHAPHE
RHAPHIDE same as > RAPHIDE
RHAPHIDES > RHAPHIDE
RHAPHIS same as > RAPHIDE
RHAPONTIC n rhubarb
RHAPSODE n (in ancient Greece) professional reciter of poetry
RHAPSODES > RHAPSODE
RHAPSODIC adj of or like a rhapsody
RHAPSODY n freely structured emotional piece of music
RHATANIES > RHATANY
RHATANY n South American leguminous shrub
RHEA n S American three-toed ostrich
RHEAS > RHEA
RHEBOK n woolly brownish-grey southern African antelope
RHEBOKS > RHEBOK
RHEMATIC adj of or relating to word formation
RHEME n constituent of a sentence that adds most new information, in addition to what has already been said in the discourse. The rheme is usually, but not always, associated with the subject
RHEMES > RHEME
RHENIUM n silvery-white metallic element with a

high melting point
RHENIUMS > RHENIUM
RHEOBASE n minimum nerve impulse required to elicit a response from a tissue
RHEOBASES > RHEOBASE
RHEOBASIC > RHEOBASE
RHEOCHORD n wire inserted into an electrical circuit to vary or regulate the current
RHEOCORD same as > RHEOCHORD
RHEOCORDS > RHEOCORD
RHEOLOGIC > RHEOLOGY
RHEOLOGY n branch of physics concerned with the flow and change of shape of matter
RHEOMETER n instrument for measuring the velocity of the blood flow
RHEOMETRY > RHEOMETER
RHEOPHIL adj liking flowing water
RHEOSTAT n instrument for varying the resistance of an electrical circuit
RHEOSTATS > RHEOSTAT
RHEOTAXES > RHEOTAXIS
RHEOTAXIS n movement of an organism towards or away from a current of water
RHEOTOME n interrupter
RHEOTOMES > RHEOTOME
RHEOTROPE n electric-current-reversing device
RHESUS n macaque monkey
RHESUSES > RHESUS
RHETOR n teacher of rhetoric
RHETORIC n art of effective speaking or writing
RHETORICS > RHETORIC
RHETORISE same as > RHETORIZE
RHETORIZE vb make use of rhetoric
RHETORS > RHETOR
RHEUM n watery discharge from the eyes or nose
RHEUMATIC adj (person) affected by rheumatism ▷ n person suffering from rheumatism
RHEUMATIZ n dialect word meaning rheumatism, any painful disorder of joints, muscles, or connective tissue
RHEUMED adj rheumy
RHEUMIC adj of or relating to rheum
RHEUMIER > RHEUMY
RHEUMIEST > RHEUMY
RHEUMS > RHEUM
RHEUMY adj of the nature of rheum
RHEXES > RHEXIS
RHEXIS n rupture
RHEXISES > RHEXIS

RHIES > RHY
RHIGOLENE n volatile liquid obtained from petroleum and used as a local anaesthetic
RHIME old spelling of > RHYME
RHIMES > RHIME
RHINAL adj of or relating to the nose
RHINE n dialect word for a ditch
RHINES > RHINE
RHINITIC > RHINITIS
RHINITIS n inflammation of the mucous membrane that lines the nose
RHINO n rhinoceros
RHINOCERI n rhinoceroses
RHINOLITH n calculus formed in the nose
RHINOLOGY n branch of medical science concerned with the nose and its diseases
RHINOS > RHINO
RHIPIDATE adj shaped like a fan
RHIPIDION n fan found in Greek Orthodox churches
RHIPIDIUM n on a plant, a fan-shaped arrangement of flowers
RHIZIC adj of or relating to the root of an equation
RHIZINE same as > RHIZOID
RHIZINES > RHIZINE
RHIZOBIA > RHIZOBIUM
RHIZOBIAL > RHIZOBIUM
RHIZOBIUM n any rod-shaped bacterium of the genus Rhizobium, typically occurring in the root nodules of leguminous plants
RHIZOCARP n plant that fruits underground or whose root remains intact while the leaves die off annually
RHIZOCAUL n rootlike stem
RHIZOID n any of various slender hairlike structures that function as roots in the gametophyte generation of mosses, ferns, and related plants
RHIZOIDAL > RHIZOID
RHIZOIDS > RHIZOID
RHIZOMA same as > RHIZOME
RHIZOMATA > RHIZOMA
RHIZOME n thick underground stem producing new plants
RHIZOMES > RHIZOME
RHIZOMIC > RHIZOME
RHIZOPI > RHIZOPUS
RHIZOPOD n any protozoan of the phylum Rhizopoda, characterized by naked protoplasmic processes (pseudopodia). The group includes the amoebas

▷ *adj* of, relating to, or belonging to the *Rhizopoda*

**RHIZOPODS** > RHIZOPOD

**RHIZOPUS** *n* any zygomycetous fungus of the genus *Rhizopus*, esp *R. nigricans*, a bread mould

**RHIZOTOMY** *n* surgical incision into the roots of spinal nerves, esp for the relief of pain

**RHO** *n* 17th letter in the Greek alphabet, a consonant transliterated as r or rh

**RHODAMIN** *same as* > RHODAMINE

**RHODAMINE** *n* any one of a group of synthetic red or pink basic dyestuffs used for wool and silk. They are made from phthalic anhydride and aminophenols

**RHODAMINS** > RHODAMIN

**RHODANATE** *n* sulphocyanate

**RHODANIC** *adj* of or relating to sulphocyanic acid

**RHODANISE** *same as* > RHODANIZE

**RHODANIZE** *vb* plate with rhodium

**RHODIC** *adj* of or containing rhodium, esp in the tetravalent state

**RHODIE** *same as* > RHODY

**RHODIES** > RHODY

**RHODINAL** *n* substance with a lemon-like smell found esp in citronella and certain eucalyptus oils

**RHODINALS** > RHODINAL

**RHODIUM** *n* hard metallic element

**RHODIUMS** > RHODIUM

**RHODOLITE** *n* pale violet or red variety of garnet, used as a gemstone

**RHODONITE** *n* brownish translucent mineral

**RHODOPSIN** *n* red pigment in the rods of the retina in vertebrates. It is dissociated by light into retinene, the light energy being converted into nerve signals, and is re-formed in the dark

**RHODORA** *n* type of shrub

**RHODORAS** > RHODORA

**RHODOUS** *adj* of or containing rhodium (but proportionally more than a rhodic compound)

**RHODY** *n* rhododendron

**RHOEADINE** *n* alkaloid found in the poppy

**RHOMB** *same as* > RHOMBUS

**RHOMBI** > RHOMBUS

**RHOMBIC** *adj* relating to or having the shape of a rhombus

**RHOMBICAL** *same*

*as* > RHOMBIC

**RHOMBOI** > RHOMBOS

**RHOMBOID** *n* parallelogram with adjacent sides of unequal length ▷ *adj* having such a shape

**RHOMBOIDS** > RHOMBOID

**RHOMBOS** *n* wooden slat attached to a thong that makes a roaring sound when the thong is whirled

**RHOMBS** > RHOMB

**RHOMBUS** *n* parallelogram with sides of equal length but no right angles, diamond-shaped figure

**RHOMBUSES** > RHOMBUS

**RHONCHAL** > RHONCHUS

**RHONCHI** > RHONCHUS

**RHONCHIAL** > RHONCHUS

**RHONCHUS** *n* rattling or whistling respiratory sound resembling snoring, caused by secretions in the trachea or bronchi

**RHONE** *same as* > RONE

**RHONES** > RHONE

**RHOPALIC** *adj* describes verse in which each successive word has one more syllable than the word before

**RHOPALISM** > RHOPALIC

**RHOS** > RHO

**RHOTACISE** *same*

*as* > RHOTACIZE

**RHOTACISM** *n* excessive use or idiosyncratic pronunciation of r

**RHOTACIST** > RHOTACISM

**RHOTACIZE** *vb* pronounce r excessively or idiosyncratically

**RHOTIC** *adj* denoting or speaking a dialect of English in which postvocalic rs are pronounced

**RHOTICITY** > RHOTIC

**RHUBARB** *n* garden plant of which the fleshy stalks are cooked as fruit ▷ *interj* noise made by actors to simulate conversation, esp by repeating the word *rhubarb* ▷ *vb* simulate conversation in this way

**RHUBARBED** > RHUBARB

**RHUBARBS** > RHUBARB

**RHUBARBY** > RHUBARB

**RHUMB** as in *rhumb line* imaginary line on the surface of a sphere, such as the earth, that intersects all meridians at the same angle

**RHUMBA** *same as* > RUMBA

**RHUMBAED** > RHUMBA

**RHUMBAING** > RHUMBA

**RHUMBAS** > RHUMBA

**RHUMBS** > RHUMB

**RHUS** *n* genus of shrubs and small trees, several species of which are cultivated

as ornamentals for their colourful autumn foliage

**RHUSES** > RHUS

**RHY** *archaic spelling of* > RYE

**RHYME** *n* sameness of the final sounds at the ends of lines of verse, or in words ▷ *vb* make a rhyme

**RHYMED** > RHYME

**RHYMELESS** > RHYME

**RHYMER** *same*

*as* > RHYMESTER

**RHYMERS** > RHYMER

**RHYMES** > RHYME

**RHYMESTER** *n* mediocre poet

**RHYMING** > RHYME

**RHYMIST** > RHYME

**RHYMISTS** > RHYME

**RHYNE** *same as* > RHINE

**RHYNES** > RHYNE

**RHYOLITE** *n* fine-grained igneous rock consisting of quartz, feldspars, and mica or amphibole. It is the volcanic equivalent of granite

**RHYOLITES** > RHYOLITE

**RHYOLITIC** > RHYOLITE

**RHYTA** > RHYTON

**RHYTHM** *n* any regular movement or beat

**RHYTHMAL** *adj* rhythmic

**RHYTHMED** > RHYTHM

**RHYTHMI** > RHYTHMUS

**RHYTHMIC** *adj* of, relating to, or characterized by rhythm, as in movement or sound

**RHYTHMICS** *n* study of rhythmic movement

**RHYTHMISE** *same*

*as* > RHYTHMIZE

**RHYTHMIST** *n* person who has a good sense of rhythm

**RHYTHMIZE** *vb* make rhythmic

**RHYTHMS** > RHYTHM

**RHYTHMUS** *n* rhythm

**RHYTIDOME** *n* bark

**RHYTINA** *n* type of sea cow

**RHYTINAS** > RHYTINA

**RHYTON** *n* (in ancient Greece) a horn-shaped drinking vessel with a hole in the pointed end through which to drink

**RHYTONS** > RHYTON

**RIA** *n* long narrow inlet of the seacoast, being a former valley that was submerged by a rise in the level of the sea. Rias are found esp on the coasts of SW Ireland and NW Spain

**RIAL** *n* standard monetary unit of Iran

**RIALS** > RIAL

**RIALTO** *n* market or exchange

**RIALTOS** > RIALTO

**RIANCIES** > RIANT

**RIANCY** > RIANT

**RIANT** *adj* laughing

**RIANTLY** > RIANT

**RIAS** > RIA

**RIATA** *same as* > REATA

**RIATAS** > RIATA

**RIB** *n* one of the curved bones forming the framework of the upper part of the body ▷ *vb* provide or mark with ribs

**RIBA** *n* (in Islam) interest or usury, as forbidden by the Koran

**RIBALD** *adj* humorously or mockingly rude or obscene ▷ *n* ribald person

**RIBALDLY** > RIBALD

**RIBALDRY** *n* ribald language or behaviour

**RIBALDS** > RIBALD

**RIBAND** *n* ribbon awarded for some achievement

**RIBANDS** > RIBAND

**RIBAS** > RIBA

**RIBATTUTA** *n* (in music) type of trill

**RIBAUD** *archaic variant of* > RIBALD

**RIBAUDRED** *archaic variant of* > RIBALD

**RIBAUDRY** *archaic variant of* > RIBALDRY

**RIBAUDS** > RIBAUD

**RIBAVIRIN** *n* type of antiviral drug

**RIBBAND** *same as* > RIBAND

**RIBBANDS** > RIBBAND

**RIBBED** > RIB

**RIBBER** *n* someone who ribs

**RIBBERS** > RIBBER

**RIBBIER** > RIBBY

**RIBBIEST** > RIBBY

**RIBBING** > RIB

**RIBBINGS** > RIB

**RIBBON** *n* narrow band of fabric used for trimming, tying, etc ▷ *vb* adorn with a ribbon or ribbons

**RIBBONED** > RIBBON

**RIBBONING** > RIBBON

**RIBBONRY** *n* ribbons or ribbon work

**RIBBONS** > RIBBON

**RIBBONY** > RIBBON

**RIBBY** *adj* with noticeable ribs

**RIBCAGE** *n* bony structure of ribs enclosing the lungs

**RIBCAGES** > RIBCAGE

**RIBES** *n* genus of shrubs that includes currants

**RIBGRASS** *same*

*as* > RIBWORT

**RIBIBE** *n* rebeck

**RIBIBES** > RIBIBE

**RIBIBLE** *same as* > RIBIBE

**RIBIBLES** > RIBIBLE

**RIBIER** *n* variety of grape

**RIBIERS** > RIBIER

**RIBLESS** > RIB

**RIBLET** *n* small rib

**RIBLETS** > RIBLET

**RIBLIKE** > RIB

**RIBOSE** *n* pentose sugar

that is an isomeric form of arabinose and that occurs in RNA and riboflavin
**RIBOSES** > RIBOSE
**RIBOSOMAL** > RIBOSOME
**RIBOSOME** *n* any of numerous minute particles in the cytoplasm of cells, either free or attached to the endoplasmic reticulum, that contain RNA and protein and are the site of protein synthesis
**RIBOSOMES** > RIBOSOME
**RIBOZYMAL** > RIBOZYME
**RIBOZYME** *n* RNA molecule capable of catalysing a chemical reaction, usually the cleavage of another RNA molecule
**RIBOZYMES** > RIBOZYME
**RIBS** > RIB
**RIBSTON** *n* variety of apple
**RIBSTONE** *same as* > RIBSTON
**RIBSTONES** > RIBSTONE
**RIBSTONS** > RIBSTON
**RIBWORK** *n* work or structure involving ribs
**RIBWORKS** > RIBWORK
**RIBWORT** *n* Eurasian plant with lancelike ribbed leaves and a dense spike of small white flowers
**RIBWORTS** > RIBWORT
**RICE** *n* cereal plant grown on wet ground in warm countries ▷ *vb* sieve (potatoes or other vegetables) to a coarse mashed consistency
**RICEBIRD** *n* any of various birds frequenting rice fields, esp the Java sparrow
**RICEBIRDS** > RICEBIRD
**RICED** > RICE
**RICER** *n* kitchen utensil with small holes through which cooked potatoes and similar soft foods are pressed to form a coarse mash
**RICERCAR** *same as* > RICERCARE
**RICERCARE** *n* elaborate polyphonic composition making extensive use of contrapuntal imitation and usually very slow in tempo
**RICERCARI** > RICERCARE
**RICERCARS** > RICERCAR
**RICERCATA** *same as* > RICERCARE
**RICERS** > RICER
**RICES** > RICE
**RICEY** *adj* resembling or containing rice
**RICH** *adj* owning a lot of money or property, wealthy ▷ *vb* (in archaic usage) enrich
**RICHED** > RICH

**RICHEN** *vb* enrich
**RICHENED** > RICHEN
**RICHENING** > RICHEN
**RICHENS** > RICHEN
**RICHER** > RICH
**RICHES** *pl n* wealth
**RICHESSE** *n* wealth or richness
**RICHESSES** > RICHESSE
**RICHEST** > RICH
**RICHING** > RICH
**RICHLY** *adv* elaborately
**RICHNESS** *n* state or quality of being rich
**RICHT** *adj, adv, n, vb* right
**RICHTED** > RICHT
**RICHTER** > RICHT
**RICHTEST** > RICHT
**RICHTING** > RICHT
**RICHTS** > RICHT
**RICHWEED** *n* type of plant
**RICHWEEDS** > RICHWEED
**RICIER** > RICY
**RICIEST** > RICY
**RICIN** *n* highly toxic protein, a lectin, derived from castor-oil seeds: used in experimental cancer therapy
**RICING** > RICE
**RICINS** > RICIN
**RICINUS** *n* genus of plants
**RICINUSES** > RICINUS
**RICK** *n* stack of hay etc ▷ *vb* wrench or sprain (a joint)
**RICKED** > RICK
**RICKER** *n* young kauri tree of New Zealand
**RICKERS** > RICKER
**RICKETIER** > RICKETY
**RICKETILY** > RICKETY
**RICKETS** *n* disease of children marked by softening of the bones, bow legs, etc, caused by vitamin D deficiency
**RICKETTY** *same as* > RICKETY
**RICKETY** *adj* shaky or unstable
**RICKEY** *n* cocktail consisting of gin or vodka, lime juice, and soda water, served iced
**RICKEYS** > RICKEY
**RICKING** > RICK
**RICKLE** *n* unsteady or shaky structure, esp a dilapidated building
**RICKLES** > RICKLE
**RICKLY** *adj* archaic word for run-down or rickety
**RICKRACK** *n* zigzag braid used for trimming
**RICKRACKS** > RICKRACK
**RICKS** > RICK
**RICKSHA** *same as* > RICKSHAW
**RICKSHAS** > RICKSHA
**RICKSHAW** *n* light two-wheeled man-drawn Asian vehicle
**RICKSHAWS** > RICKSHAW
**RICKSTAND** *n* platform on

which to put a rick
**RICKSTICK** *n* tool used when making hayricks
**RICKYARD** *n* place where hayricks are put
**RICKYARDS** > RICKYARD
**RICOCHET** *vb* (of a bullet) rebound from a solid surface ▷ *n* such a rebound
**RICOCHETS** > RICOCHET
**RICOTTA** *n* soft white unsalted Italian cheese made from sheep's milk
**RICOTTAS** > RICOTTA
**RICRAC** *same as* > RICKRACK
**RICRACS** > RICRAC
**RICTAL** > RICTUS
**RICTUS** *n* gape or cleft of an open mouth or beak
**RICTUSES** > RICTUS
**RICY** *same as* > RICE Y
**RID** *vb* clear or relieve (of)
**RIDABLE** > RIDE
**RIDDANCE** *n* act of getting rid of something undesirable or unpleasant
**RIDDANCES** > RIDDANCE
**RIDDED** > RID
**RIDDEN** > RIDE
**RIDDER** > RID
**RIDDERS** > RID
**RIDDING** > RID
**RIDDLE** *n* question made puzzling to test one's ingenuity ▷ *vb* speak in riddles
**RIDDLED** > RIDDLE
**RIDDLER** > RIDDLE
**RIDDLERS** > RIDDLE
**RIDDLES** > RIDDLE
**RIDDLING** > RIDDLE
**RIDDLINGS** > RIDDLE
**RIDE** *vb* sit on and control or propel (a horse, bicycle, etc) ▷ *n* journey on a horse etc, or in a vehicle
**RIDEABLE** > RIDE
**RIDENT** *adj* laughing, smiling, or gay
**RIDER** *n* person who rides
**RIDERED** > RIDER
**RIDERLESS** > RIDER
**RIDERS** > RIDER
**RIDERSHIP** > RIDER
**RIDES** > RIDE
**RIDGE** *n* long narrow hill ▷ *vb* form into a ridge or ridges
**RIDGEBACK** as in *Rhodesian ridgeback* large short-haired breed of dog characterized by a ridge of hair growing along the back in the opposite direction to the rest of the coat
**RIDGED** > RIDGE
**RIDGEL** *same as* > RIDGELING
**RIDGELIKE** > RIDGE
**RIDGELINE** *n* ridge
**RIDGELING** *n* domestic male animal with one or both testicles

undescended, esp a horse
**RIDGELS** > RIDGEL
**RIDGEPOLE** *n* timber along the ridge of a roof, to which the rafters are attached
**RIDGER** *n* plough used to form furrows and ridges
**RIDGERS** > RIDGER
**RIDGES** > RIDGE
**RIDGETOP** *n* summit of ridge
**RIDGETOPS** > RIDGETOP
**RIDGETREE** *another name for* > RIDGEPOLE
**RIDGEWAY** *n* road or track along a ridge, esp one of great antiquity
**RIDGEWAYS** > RIDGEWAY
**RIDGIER** > RIDGE
**RIDGIEST** > RIDGE
**RIDGIL** *same as* > RIDGELING
**RIDGILS** > RIDGIL
**RIDGING** > RIDGE
**RIDGINGS** > RIDGE
**RIDGLING** *same as* > RIDGELING
**RIDGLINGS** > RIDGLING
**RIDGY** > RIDGE
**RIDICULE** *n* treatment of a person or thing as ridiculous ▷ *vb* laugh at, make fun of
**RIDICULED** > RIDICULE
**RIDICULER** > RIDICULE
**RIDICULES** > RIDICULE
**RIDING** > RIDE
**RIDINGS** > RIDE
**RIDLEY** *n* marine turtle
**RIDLEYS** > RIDLEV
**RIDOTTO** *n* entertainment with music and dancing, often in masquerade: popular in 18th-century England
**RIDOTTOS** > RIDOTTO
**RIDS** > RID
**RIEL** *n* standard monetary unit of Cambodia, divided into 100 sen
**RIELS** > RIEL
**RIEM** *n* strip of hide
**RIEMPIE** *n* leather thong or lace used mainly to make chair seats
**RIEMPIES** > RIEMPIE
**RIEMS** > RIEM
**RIESLING** *n* type of white wine
**RIESLINGS** > RIESLING
**RIEVE** *n* archaic word for rob or plunder
**RIEVER** *n* archaic word for robber or plunderer
**RIEVERS** > RIEVER
**RIEVES** > RIEVE
**RIEVING** > RIEVE
**RIF** *vb* lay off
**RIFAMPIN** *n* drug used in the treatment of tuberculosis, meningitis, and leprosy
**RIFAMPINS** > RIFAMPIN

RIFAMYCIN n antibiotic
RIFE adj widespread or common
RIFELY > RIFE
RIFENESS > RIFE
RIFER > RIFE
RIFEST > RIFE
RIFF n short repeated melodic figure ▷ vb play or perform riffs in jazz or rock music
RIFFAGE n (in jazz or rock music) act or an instance of playing a short series of chords
RIFFAGES > RIFFAGE
RIFFED > RIFF
RIFFING > RIFF
RIFFLE vb flick through (pages etc) quickly ▷ n rapid in a stream
RIFFLED > RIFFLE
RIFFLER n file with a curved face for filing concave surfaces
RIFFLERS > RIFFLER
RIFFLES > RIFFLE
RIFFLING > RIFFLE
RIFFOLA n use of an abundance of dominant riffs
RIFFOLAS > RIFFOLA
RIFFRAFF n rabble, disreputable people
RIFFRAFFS > RIFFRAFF
RIFFS > RIFF
RIFLE n firearm with a long barrel ▷ vb cut spiral grooves inside the barrel of a gun
RIFLEBIRD n any of various birds of paradise
RIFLED > RIFLE
RIFLEMAN n person skilled in the use of a rifle, esp a soldier
RIFLEMEN > RIFLEMAN
RIFLER > RIFLE
RIFLERIES > RIFLERY
RIFLERS > RIFLE
RIFLERY n rifle shots
RIFLES > RIFLE
RIFLING n cutting of spiral grooves on the inside of a firearm's barrel
RIFLINGS > RIFLING
RIFLIP n genetic difference between two individuals
RIFLIPS > RIFLIP
RIFS > RIF
RIFT n break in friendly relations ▷ vb burst or cause to burst open
RIFTE archaic word for > RIFT
RIFTED > RIFT
RIFTIER > RIFT
RIFTIEST > RIFT
RIFTING > RIFT
RIFTLESS > RIFT
RIFTS > RIFT
RIFTY > RIFT
RIG vb arrange in a

dishonest way ▷ n apparatus for drilling for oil and gas
RIGADOON n old Provençal couple dance, light and graceful, in lively duple time
RIGADOONS > RIGADOON
RIGATONI n macaroni in the form of short ridged often slightly curved pieces
RIGATONIS > RIGATONI
RIGAUDON same as > RIGADOON
RIGAUDONS > RIGAUDON
RIGG n type of fish
RIGGALD same as > RIDGELING
RIGGALDS > RIGGALD
RIGGED > RIG
RIGGER n workman who rigs vessels, etc
RIGGERS > RIGGER
RIGGING > RIG
RIGGINGS > RIG
RIGGISH adj dialect word meaning wanton
RIGGS > RIGG
RIGHT adj just ▷ adv correctly ▷ n claim, title, etc allowed or due ▷ vb bring or come back to a normal or correct state
RIGHTABLE adj capable of being righted
RIGHTABLY > RIGHTABLE
RIGHTED > RIGHT
RIGHTEN vb set right
RIGHTENED > RIGHTEN
RIGHTENS > RIGHTEN
RIGHTEOUS adj upright, godly, or virtuous
RIGHTER > RIGHT
RIGHTERS > RIGHT
RIGHTEST > RIGHT
RIGHTFUL adj in accordance with what is right
RIGHTIES > RIGHTY
RIGHTING > RIGHT
RIGHTINGS > RIGHT
RIGHTISH adj somewhat right, esp politically
RIGHTISM > RIGHTIST
RIGHTISMS > RIGHTIST
RIGHTIST adj (person) on the political right ▷ n supporter of the political right
RIGHTISTS > RIGHTIST
RIGHTLESS > RIGHT
RIGHTLY adv in accordance with the true facts or justice
RIGHTMOST > RIGHT
RIGHTNESS n state or quality of being right
RIGHTO n expression of agreement or compliance
RIGHTOS > RIGHTO
RIGHTS > RIGHT
RIGHTSIZE vb restructure (an organization) to

cut costs and improve effectiveness without ruthlessly downsizing
RIGHTWARD adj situated on or directed towards the right ▷ adv towards or on the right
RIGHTY n informal word for a right-winger
RIGID adj inflexible or strict ▷ adv completely or excessively ▷ n strict and unbending person
RIGIDER > RIGID
RIGIDEST > RIGID
RIGIDIFY vb make or become rigid
RIGIDISE same as > RIGIDIZE
RIGIDISED > RIGIDISE
RIGIDISES > RIGIDISE
RIGIDITY > RIGID
RIGIDIZE vb make or become rigid
RIGIDIZED > RIGIDIZE
RIGIDIZES > RIGIDIZE
RIGIDLY > RIGID
RIGIDNESS > RIGID
RIGIDS > RIGID
RIGLIN same as > RIDGELING
RIGLING same as > RIDGELING
RIGLINGS > RIGLING
RIGLINS > RIGLIN
RIGMAROLE n long complicated procedure
RIGOL n (in dialect) ditch or gutter
RIGOLL same as > RIGOL
RIGOLLS > RIGOLL
RIGOLS > RIGOL
RIGOR same as > RIGOUR
RIGORISM n strictness in judgment or conduct
RIGORISMS > RIGORISM
RIGORIST > RIGORISM
RIGORISTS > RIGORISM
RIGOROUS adj harsh, severe, or stern
RIGORS > RIGOR
RIGOUR n harshness, severity, or strictness
RIGOURS > RIGOUR
RIGOUT n person's clothing
RIGOUTS > RIGOUT
RIGS > RIG
RIGSDALER n any of various former Scandinavian or Dutch small silver coins
RIGWIDDIE n part of the carthorse's harness to which the shafts of the cart attach
RIGWOODIE same as > RIGWIDDIE
RIJSTAFEL n assortment of Indonesian rice dishes
RIKISHA same as > RICKSHAW
RIKISHAS > RIKISHA
RIKISHI n sumo wrestler
RIKSHAW same

as > RICKSHAW
RIKSHAWS > RIKSHAW
RILE vb anger or annoy
RILED > RILE
RILES > RILE
RILEY adj cross or irritable
RILIER > RILEY
RILIEST > RILEY
RILIEVI > RILIEVO
RILIEVO same as > RELIEF
RILING > RILE
RILL n small stream ▷ vb trickle
RILLE same as > RILL
RILLED > RILL
RILLES > RILLE
RILLET n little rill
RILLETS > RILLET
RILLETTES pl n potted meat
RILLING > RILL
RILLMARK n mark left by the trickle of a rill
RILLMARKS > RILLMARK
RILLS > RILL
RIM n edge or border ▷ vb put a rim on (a pot, cup, wheel, etc)
RIMA n long narrow opening
RIMAE > RIMA
RIMAYE n crevasse at the head of a glacier
RIMAYES > RIMAYE
RIME same as > RHYME
RIMED > RIME
RIMELESS > RHYME
RIMER same as > RHYMESTER
RIMERS > RIMER
RIMES > RIME
RIMESTER same as > RHYMESTER
RIMESTERS > RIMESTER
RIMFIRE adj (of a cartridge) having the primer in the rim of the base ▷ n cartridge of this type
RIMFIRES > RIMFIRE
RIMIER > RIMY
RIMIEST > RIMY
RIMINESS > RIMY
RIMING > RIME
RIMLAND n area situated on the outer edges of a region
RIMLANDS > RIMLAND
RIMLESS > RIM
RIMMED > RIM
RIMMER n tool for shaping the edge of something
RIMMERS > RIMMER
RIMMING > RIM
RIMMINGS > RIM
RIMOSE adj (esp of plant parts) having the surface marked by a network of intersecting cracks
RIMOSELY > RIMOSE
RIMOSITY > RIMOSE
RIMOUS same as > RIMOSE
RIMPLE vb crease or wrinkle
RIMPLED > RIMPLE
RIMPLES > RIMPLE
RIMPLING > RIMPLE

**RIMROCK** n rock forming the boundaries of a sandy or gravelly alluvial deposit
**RIMROCKS** > RIMROCK
**RIMS** > RIM
**RIMSHOT** n deliberate simultaneous striking of skin and rim of drum
**RIMSHOTS** > RIMSHOT
**RIMU** n New Zealand tree whose wood is used for building and furniture
**RIMUS** > RIMU
**RIMY** adj coated with rime
**RIN** Scots variant of > RUN
**RIND** n tough outer coating of fruits, cheese, or bacon ▷ vb take the bark off
**RINDED** > RIND
**RINDIER** > RINDY
**RINDIEST** > RINDY
**RINDING** > RIND
**RINDLESS** > RIND
**RINDS** > RIND
**RINDY** adj with a rind or rindlike skin
**RINE** archaic variant of > RIND
**RINES** > RINE
**RING** vb give out a clear resonant sound, as a bell ▷ n ringing
**RINGBARK** same as > RING
**RINGBARKS** > RINGBARK
**RINGBIT** n type of bit worn by a horse
**RINGBITS** > RINGBIT
**RINGBOLT** n bolt with a ring fitted through an eye attached to the bolt head
**RINGBOLTS** > RINGBOLT
**RINGBONE** n abnormal bony growth affecting the pastern of a horse, often causing lameness
**RINGBONES** > RINGBONE
**RINGDOVE** n large Eurasian pigeon with white patches on the wings and neck
**RINGDOVES** > RINGDOVE
**RINGED** > RING
**RINGENT** adj (of the corolla of plants such as the snapdragon) consisting of two distinct gaping lips
**RINGER** n person or thing apparently identical to another
**RINGERS** > RINGER
**RINGGIT** n standard monetary unit of Malaysia, divided into 100 sen
**RINGGITS** > RINGGIT
**RINGHALS** n variety of cobra
**RINGING** > RING
**RINGINGLY** > RING
**RINGINGS** > RING
**RINGLESS** > RING
**RINGLET** n curly lock of hair
**RINGLETED** > RINGLET
**RINGLETS** > RINGLET
**RINGLIKE** > RING
**RINGMAN** n (in dialect) ring finger

**RINGMEN** > RINGMAN
**RINGNECK** n any bird that has ringlike markings round its neck
**RINGNECKS** > RINGNECK
**RINGS** > RING
**RINGSIDE** n row of seats nearest a boxing or circus ring ▷ adj providing a close uninterrupted view
**RINGSIDER** n someone with a ringside seat or position
**RINGSIDES** > RINGSIDE
**RINGSTAND** n stand for laboratory equipment
**RINGSTER** n member of a ring controlling a market in antiques, art treasures, etc
**RINGSTERS** > RINGSTER
**RINGTAIL** n possum with a curling tail used to grip branches while climbing
**RINGTAILS** > RINGTAIL
**RINGTAW** n game of marbles in which the aim is to knock other players' marbles out of a ring
**RINGTAWS** > RINGTAW
**RINGTONE** n musical tune played by a mobile phone when a call is received
**RINGTONES** > RINGTONE
**RINGTOSS** n game in which participants try to throw hoops onto an upright stick
**RINGWAY** n bypass
**RINGWAYS** > RINGWAY
**RINGWISE** adj used to being in the ring and able to respond appropriately
**RINGWOMB** n complication at lambing resulting from failure of the cervix to open
**RINGWOMBS** > RINGWOMB
**RINGWORK** n circular earthwork
**RINGWORKS** > RINGWORK
**RINGWORM** n fungal skin disease in circular patches
**RINGWORMS** > RINGWORM
**RINK** n sheet of ice for skating or curling ▷ vb skate on a rink
**RINKED** > RINK
**RINKHALS** n S African cobra that can spit venom
**RINKING** > RINK
**RINKS** > RINK
**RINNING** > RIN
**RINS** > RIN
**RINSABLE** > RINSE
**RINSE** vb remove soap from (washed clothes, hair, etc) by applying clean water ▷ n rinsing
**RINSEABLE** > RINSE
**RINSED** > RINSE
**RINSER** > RINSE
**RINSERS** > RINSE

**RINSES** > RINSE
**RINSIBLE** > RINSE
**RINSING** > RINSE
**RINSINGS** > RINSE
**RIOJA** n red or white Spanish wine with a vanilla bouquet and flavour
**RIOJAS** > RIOJA
**RIOT** n disorderly unruly disturbance ▷ vb take part in a riot
**RIOTED** > RIOT
**RIOTER** > RIOT
**RIOTERS** > RIOT
**RIOTING** > RIOT
**RIOTINGS** > RIOT
**RIOTISE** n archaic word for riotous behaviour and excess
**RIOTISES** > RIOTISE
**RIOTIZE** same as > RIOTISE
**RIOTIZES** > RIOTIZE
**RIOTOUS** adj unrestrained
**RIOTOUSLY** > RIOTOUS
**RIOTRIES** > RIOTRY
**RIOTRY** n riotous behaviour
**RIOTS** > RIOT
**RIP** vb tear violently ▷ n split or tear
**RIPARIAL** adj riparian
**RIPARIAN** adj of or on the banks of a river ▷ n person who owns land on a river bank
**RIPARIANS** > RIPARIAN
**RIPCORD** n cord pulled to open a parachute
**RIPCORDS** > RIPCORD
**RIPE** adj ready to be reaped, eaten, etc ▷ vb ripen
**RIPECK** same as > RYEPECK
**RIPECKS** > RIPECK
**RIPED** > RIPE
**RIPELY** > RIPE
**RIPEN** vb grow ripe
**RIPENED** > RIPEN
**RIPENER** > RIPEN
**RIPENERS** > RIPEN
**RIPENESS** > RIPE
**RIPENING** > RIPEN
**RIPENS** > RIPEN
**RIPER** adj more ripe ▷ n old Scots word meaning plunderer
**RIPERS** > RIPER
**RIPES** > RIPE
**RIPEST** > RIPE
**RIPIENI** > RIPIENO
**RIPIENIST** n orchestral member who is there to swell the sound rather than play solo
**RIPIENO** n (in baroque concertos and concerti grossi) the full orchestra, as opposed to the instrumental soloists
**RIPIENOS** > RIPIENO
**RIPING** > RIPE
**RIPOFF** n grossly overpriced article

**RIPOFFS** > RIPOFF
**RIPOST** same as > RIPOSTE
**RIPOSTE** n verbal retort ▷ vb make a riposte
**RIPOSTED** > RIPOSTE
**RIPOSTES** > RIPOSTE
**RIPOSTING** > RIPOSTE
**RIPOSTS** > RIPOST
**RIPP** n old Scots word for a handful of grain
**RIPPABLE** > RIP
**RIPPED** > RIP
**RIPPER** n person who rips
**RIPPERS** > RIPPER
**RIPPIER** n archaic word for fish seller
**RIPPIERS** > RIPPIER
**RIPPING** > RIP
**RIPPINGLY** > RIP
**RIPPLE** n slight wave or ruffling of a surface ▷ vb flow or form into little waves (on)
**RIPPLED** > RIPPLE
**RIPPLER** > RIPPLE
**RIPPLERS** > RIPPLE
**RIPPLES** > RIPPLE
**RIPPLET** n tiny ripple
**RIPPLETS** > RIPPLET
**RIPPLIER** > RIPPLE
**RIPPLIEST** > RIPPLE
**RIPPLING** > RIPPLE
**RIPPLINGS** > RIPPLE
**RIPPLY** > RIPPLE
**RIPPS** > RIPP
**RIPRAP** vb deposit broken stones in or on
**RIPRAPPED** > RIPRAP
**RIPRAPS** > RIPRAP
**RIPS** > RIP
**RIPSAW** n handsaw for cutting along the grain of timber ▷ vb saw with a ripsaw
**RIPSAWED** > RIPSAW
**RIPSAWING** > RIPSAW
**RIPSAWN** > RIPSAW
**RIPSAWS** > RIPSAW
**RIPSTOP** n tear-resistant cloth
**RIPSTOPS** > RIPSTOP
**RIPT** archaic past form of > RIP
**RIPTIDE** n stretch of turbulent water in the sea, caused by the meeting of currents or abrupt changes in depth
**RIPTIDES** > RIPTIDE
**RIRORIRO** n small NZ bush bird that hatches the eggs of the shining cuckoo
**RIRORIROS** > RIRORIRO
**RISALDAR** n Indian cavalry officer
**RISALDARS** > RISALDAR
**RISE** vb get up from a lying, sitting, or kneeling position ▷ n rising
**RISEN** > RISE
**RISER** n person who rises, esp from bed
**RISERS** > RISER
**RISES** > RISE

RISHI *n* Indian seer or sage
RISHIS > RISHI
RISIBLE *adj* causing laughter, ridiculous
RISIBLES *pl n* sense of humour
RISIBLY > RISIBLE
RISING > RISE
RISINGS > RISE
RISK *n* chance of disaster or loss ▷ *vb* act in spite of the possibility of (injury or loss)
RISKED > RISK
RISKER > RISK
RISKERS > RISK
RISKFUL > RISK
RISKIER > RISKY
RISKIEST > RISKY
RISKILY > RISKY
RISKINESS > RISKY
RISKING > RISK
RISKLESS > RISK
RISKS > RISK
RISKY *adj* full of risk, dangerous
RISOLUTO *adj* musical term meaning firm and decisive ▷ *adv* firmly and decisively
RISOTTO *n* dish of rice cooked in stock with vegetables, meat, etc
RISOTTOS > RISOTTO
RISP *vb* Scots word meaning rasp
RISPED > RISP
RISPETTI > RISPETTO
RISPETTO *n* kind of folk song
RISPING > RISP
RISPINGS > RISP
RISPS > RISP
RISQUE *n* risk
RISQUES > RISQUE
RISSOLE *n* cake of minced meat, coated with breadcrumbs and fried
RISSOLES > RISSOLE
RISTRA *n* string of dried chilli peppers
RISTRAS > RISTRA
RISUS *n* involuntary grinning expression
RISUSES > RISUS
RIT *vb* Scots word for cut or slit
RITARD *n* (in music) a slowing down
RITARDS > RITARD
RITE *n* formal practice or custom, esp religious
RITELESS > RITE
RITENUTO *adv* held back momentarily ▷ *n* (in music) a slowing down
RITENUTOS > RITENUTO
RITES > RITE
RITONAVIR *n* drug used to treat HIV
RITORNEL *n* (in music) orchestral passage
RITORNELL *same as* > RITORNEL
RITORNELS > RITORNEL

RITS > RIT
RITT *same as* > RIT
RITTED > RIT
RITTER *n* knight or horseman
RITTERS > RITTER
RITTING > RIT
RITTS > RITT
RITUAL *n* prescribed order of rites ▷ *adj* concerning rites
RITUALISE *same as* > RITUALIZE
RITUALISM *n* exaggerated emphasis on the importance of rites and ceremonies
RITUALIST > RITUALISM
RITUALIZE *vb* engage in ritualism or devise rituals
RITUALLY > RITUAL
RITUALS > RITUAL
RITZ *as in* put on the ritz assume a superior air or make an ostentatious display
RITZES > RITZ
RITZIER > RITZY
RITZIEST > RITZY
RITZILY > RITZY
RITZINESS > RITZY
RITZY *adj* luxurious or elegant
RIVA *n* rock cleft
RIVAGE *n* bank, shore, or coast
RIVAGES > RIVAGE
RIVAL *n* person or thing that competes with or equals another for favour, success, etc ▷ *adj* in the position of a rival ▷ *vb* (try to) equal
RIVALED > RIVAL
RIVALESS *n* female rival
RIVALING > RIVAL
RIVALISE *same as* > RIVALIZE
RIVALISED > RIVALISE
RIVALISES > RIVALISE
RIVALITY > RIVAL
RIVALIZE *vb* become a rival
RIVALIZED > RIVALIZE
RIVALIZES > RIVALIZE
RIVALLED > RIVAL
RIVALLESS > RIVAL
RIVALLING > RIVAL
RIVALRIES > RIVALRY
RIVALROUS > RIVALRY
RIVALRY *n* keen competition
RIVALS > RIVAL
RIVALSHIP > RIVAL
RIVAS > RIVA
RIVE *vb* split asunder
RIVED > RIVE
RIVEL *vb* archaic word meaning wrinkle
RIVELLED > RIVEL
RIVELLING > RIVEL
RIVELS > RIVEL
RIVEN > RIVE
RIVER *n* large natural

stream of water
RIVERAIN *same as* > RIPARIAN
RIVERAINS > RIVERAIN
RIVERBANK *n* bank of a river
RIVERBED *n* bed of a river
RIVERBEDS > RIVERBOAT
RIVERBOAT *n* boat, especially a barge, designed for use on rivers
RIVERED *adj* with a river or rivers
RIVERET *n* archaic word for rivulet or stream
RIVERETS > RIVERET
RIVERHEAD *n* source of river
RIVERINE *same as* > RIPARIAN
RIVERLESS > RIVER
RIVERLIKE *adj* resembling a river
RIVERMAN *n* boatman or man earning his living working on a river
RIVERMEN > RIVERMAN
RIVERS > RIVER
RIVERSIDE *n* area beside a river
RIVERWARD *adj* towards the river ▷ *adv* towards the river
RIVERWAY *n* river serving as a waterway
RIVERWAYS > RIVERWAY
RIVERWEED *n* type of plant found growing near rivers
RIVERY *adj* riverlike
RIVES > RIVE
RIVET *n* bolt for fastening metal plates, the end being put through holes and then beaten flat ▷ *vb* fasten with rivets
RIVETED > RIVET
RIVETER > RIVET
RIVETERS > RIVET
RIVETING > RIVET
RIVETINGS > RIVET
RIVETS > RIVET
RIVETTED > RIVET
RIVETTING > RIVET
RIVIERA *n* coastline resembling the Mediterranean Riviera
RIVIERAS > RIVIERA
RIVIERE *n* necklace the diamonds or other precious stones of which gradually increase in size up to a large centre stone
RIVIERES > RIVIERE
RIVING > RIVE
RIVLIN *n* Scots word for rawhide shoe
RIVLINS > RIVLIN
RIVO *interj* (in the past) an informal toast
RIVOS > RIVO
RIVULET *n* small stream
RIVULETS > RIVULET
RIVULOSE *adj* having meandering lines

RIYAL *n* standard monetary unit of Qatar, divided into 100 dirhams
RIYALS > RIYAL
RIZ *(in some dialects)* past form of > RISE
RIZA *n* partial icon cover made from precious metal
RIZARD *n* redcurrant
RIZARDS > RIZARD
RIZAS > RIZA
RIZZAR *n* Scots word for red currant ▷ *vb* Scots word for sun-dry
RIZZARED > RIZZAR
RIZZARING > RIZZAR
RIZZARS > RIZZAR
RIZZART *n* Scots word for red currant
RIZZARTS > RIZZART
RIZZER *same as* > RIZZAR
RIZZERED > RIZZER
RIZZERING > RIZZER
RIZZERS > RIZZER
RIZZOR *vb* dry
RIZZORED > RIZZOR
RIZZORING > RIZZOR
RIZZORS > RIZZOR
ROACH *n* Eurasian freshwater fish ▷ *vb* clip (mane) short so that it stands upright
ROACHED *adj* arched convexly, as the back of certain breeds of dog, such as the whippet
ROACHES > ROACH
ROACHING > ROACH
ROAD *n* way prepared for passengers, vehicles, etc
ROADBED *n* material used to make a road
ROADBEDS > ROADBED
ROADBLOCK *n* barricade across a road to stop traffic for inspection etc
ROADCRAFT *n* skills and knowledge of a road user
ROADEO *n* competition in which drivers or other road users put their skills on the road to the test
ROADEOS > ROADEO
ROADHOUSE *n* pub or restaurant on a country road
ROADIE *n* person who transports and sets up equipment for a band
ROADIES > ROADIE
ROADING *n* road building
ROADINGS > ROADING
ROADKILL *n* remains of an animal or animals killed on the road by motor vehicles
ROADKILLS > ROADKILL
ROADLESS > ROAD
ROADMAN *n* someone involved in road repair or construction
ROADMEN > ROADMAN
ROADS > ROAD
ROADSHOW *n* radio show broadcast live from one of

a number of places being visited by a touring disc jockey
ROADSHOWS > ROADSHOW
ROADSIDE n side of a road ▷ adj situated beside a road
ROADSIDES > ROADSIDE
ROADSMAN same as > ROADMAN
ROADSMEN > ROADSMAN
ROADSTEAD same as > ROAD
ROADSTER n open car with only two seats
ROADSTERS > ROADSTER
ROADWAY n part of a road used by vehicles
ROADWAYS > ROADWAY
ROADWORK n sports training by running along roads
ROADWORKS pl n repairs to a road, esp blocking part of the road
ROAM vb wander about ▷ n act of roaming
ROAMED > ROAM
ROAMER > ROAM
ROAMERS > ROAM
ROAMING > ROAM
ROAMINGS > ROAM
ROAMS > ROAM
ROAN adj (of a horse) having a brown or black coat sprinkled with white hairs ▷ n roan horse
ROANS > ROAN
ROAR vb make or utter a loud deep hoarse sound like that of a lion ▷ n such a sound
ROARED > ROAR
ROARER > ROAR
ROARERS > ROAR
ROARIE Scots word for > NOISY
ROARIER > ROARY
ROARIEST > ROARY
ROARING > ROAR
ROARINGLY > ROARING
ROARINGS > ROAR
ROARMING adj severe
ROARS > ROAR
ROARY adj roarlike or tending to roar
ROAST vb cook by dry heat, as in an oven ▷ n roasted joint of meat ▷ adj roasted
ROASTED > ROAST
ROASTER n person or thing that roasts
ROASTERS > ROASTER
ROASTING adj extremely hot ▷ n severe criticism or scolding
ROASTINGS > ROASTING
ROASTS > ROAST
ROATE archaic form of > ROTE
ROATED > ROATE
ROATES > ROATE
ROATING > ROATE
ROB vb steal from
ROBALO n tropical fish

ROBALOS > ROBALO
ROBAND n piece of marline used for fastening a sail to a spar
ROBANDS > ROBAND
ROBBED > ROB
ROBBER > ROB
ROBBERIES > ROBBERY
ROBBERS > ROB
ROBBERY n stealing of property from a person by using or threatening to use force
ROBBIN same as > ROBAND
ROBBING > ROB
ROBBINS > ROBBIN
ROBE n long loose outer garment ▷ vb put a robe on
ROBED > ROBE
ROBES > ROBE
ROBIN n small brown bird with a red breast
ROBING > ROBE
ROBINGS > ROBE
ROBINIA n type of leguminous tree
ROBINIAS > ROBINIA
ROBINS > ROBIN
ROBLE n oak tree
ROBLES > ROBLE
ROBORANT adj tending to fortify or increase strength ▷ n drug or agent that increases strength
ROBORANTS > ROBORANT
ROBOT n automated machine, esp one performing functions in a human manner
ROBOTIC > ROBOT
ROBOTICS n science of designing and using robots
ROBOTISE same as > ROBOTIZE
ROBOTISED > ROBOTISE
ROBOTISES > ROBOTISE
ROBOTISM > ROBOT
ROBOTISMS > ROBOT
ROBOTIZE vb automate
ROBOTIZED > ROBOTIZE
ROBOTIZES > ROBOTIZE
ROBOTRIES > ROBOT
ROBOTRY > ROBOT
ROBOTS > ROBOT
ROBS > ROB
ROBURITE n flameless explosive
ROBURITES > ROBURITE
ROBUST adj very strong and healthy
ROBUSTA n species of coffee tree
ROBUSTAS > ROBUSTA
ROBUSTER > ROBUST
ROBUSTEST > ROBUST
ROBUSTLY > ROBUST
ROC n monstrous bird of Arabian mythology
ROCAILLE n decorative rock or shell work, esp as ornamentation in a rococo fountain, grotto, or

interior
ROCAILLES > ROCAILLE
ROCAMBOLE n variety of sand leek whose garlic-like bulb is used for seasoning
ROCH same as > ROTCH
ROCHES > ROTCH
ROCHET n white surplice with tight sleeves, worn by bishops, abbots, and certain other Church dignitaries
ROCHETS > ROCHET
ROCK n hard mineral substance that makes up part of the earth's crust, stone ▷ vb (cause to) sway to and fro ▷ adj of or relating to rock music
ROCKABIES > ROCKABY
ROCKABLE > ROCK
ROCKABY same as > ROCKABYE
ROCKABYE n lullaby or rocking motion used with a baby during lullabies
ROCKABYES > ROCKABYE
ROCKAWAY n four-wheeled horse-drawn carriage, usually with two seats and a hard top
ROCKAWAYS > ROCKAWAY
ROCKBOUND adj hemmed in or encircled by rocks
ROCKCRESS n low-growing plant with white flowers
ROCKED > ROCK
ROCKER n rocking chair
ROCKERIES > ROCKERY
ROCKERS > ROCKER
ROCKERY n mound of stones in a garden for rock plants
ROCKET n self-propelling device powered by the burning of explosive contents (used as a firework, weapon, etc) ▷ vb move fast, esp upwards, like a rocket
ROCKETED > ROCKET
ROCKETEER n engineer or scientist concerned with the design, operation, or launching of rockets
ROCKETER n bird that launches itself into the air like a rocket when flushed
ROCKETERS > ROCKETER
ROCKETING > ROCKET
ROCKETRY n science and technology of the design and operation of rockets
ROCKETS > ROCKET
ROCKFALL n instance of rocks breaking away and falling from an outcrop
ROCKFALLS > ROCKFALL
ROCKFISH n any of various fishes that live among rocks
ROCKHOUND n person interested in rocks and minerals

ROCKIER > ROCKY n archaic or dialect word for rock pigeon
ROCKIERS > ROCKY
ROCKIEST > ROCKY
ROCKILY > ROCKY
ROCKINESS > ROCKY
ROCKING > ROCK
ROCKINGLY > ROCKING
ROCKINGS > ROCK
ROCKLAY same as > ROKELAY
ROCKLAYS > ROCKLAY
ROCKLESS > ROCK
ROCKLIKE > ROCK
ROCKLING n any of various small sea fishes having an elongated body and barbels around the mouth
ROCKLINGS > ROCKLING
ROCKOON n rocket carrying scientific equipment for studying the upper atmosphere, fired from a balloon at high altitude
ROCKOONS > ROCKOON
ROCKROSE n any of various shrubs or herbaceous plants cultivated for their roselike flowers
ROCKROSES > ROCKROSE
ROCKS > ROCK
ROCKSHAFT n shaft that rotates backwards and forwards rather than continuously, esp one used in the valve gear of a steam engine
ROCKSLIDE n fall of rocks down hillside
ROCKWATER n water that comes out of rock
ROCKWEED n any of various seaweeds that grow on rocks exposed at low tide
ROCKWEEDS > ROCKWEED
ROCKWORK n structure made of rock
ROCKWORKS > ROCKWORK
ROCKY adj having many rocks
ROCOCO adj (of furniture, architecture, etc) having much elaborate decoration in an early 18th-century style ▷ n style of architecture and decoration that originated in France in the early 18th century, characterized by elaborate but graceful, light, ornamentation, often containing asymmetrical motifs
ROCOCOS > ROCOCO
ROCQUET n another name for the salad plant rocket
ROCQUETS > ROCQUET
ROCS > ROC
ROD n slender straight bar, stick ▷ vb clear with a rod
RODDED > ROD
RODDING > ROD
RODDINGS > ROD
RODE vb (of the male

649

woodcock) to perform a display flight at dusk during the breeding season

**RODED** > RODE

**RODENT** n animal with teeth specialized for gnawing, such as a rat, mouse, or squirrel

**RODENTS** > RODENT

**RODEO** n display of skill by cowboys, such as bareback riding ▷ vb take part in a rodeo

**RODEOED** > RODEO

**RODEOING** > RODEO

**RODEOS** > RODEO

**RODES** > RODE

**RODEWAY** archaic spelling of > ROADWAY

**RODEWAYS** > RODEWAY

**RODFISHER** n angler

**RODGERSIA** n flowering plant

**RODING** > RODE

**RODINGS** > RODE

**RODLESS** > ROD

**RODLIKE** > ROD

**RODMAN** n someone who uses or fishes with a rod

**RODMEN** > RODMAN

**RODS** > ROD

**RODSMAN** same as > RODMAN

**RODSMEN** > RODSMAN

**RODSTER** n angler

**RODSTERS** > RODSTER

**ROE** n mass of eggs in a fish, sometimes eaten as food

**ROEBUCK** n male of the roe deer

**ROEBUCKS** > ROEBUCK

**ROED** adj with roe inside

**ROEMER** n drinking glass, typically having an ovoid bowl on a short stem

**ROEMERS** > ROEMER

**ROENTGEN** n unit measuring a radiation dose

**ROENTGENS** > ROENTGEN

**ROES** > ROE

**ROESTONE** same as > OOLITE

**ROESTONES** > ROESTONE

**ROGALLO** n flexible fabric delta wing, originally designed as a possible satellite retrieval vehicle but actually developed in the 1960s as the first successful hang-glider

**ROGALLOS** > ROGALLO

**ROGATION** n solemn supplication, esp in a form of ceremony prescribed by the Church

**ROGATIONS** > ROGATION

**ROGATORY** adj (esp in legal contexts) seeking or authorized to seek information

**ROGER** interj (used in signalling) message received ▷ vb (of a man) to copulate (with)

**ROGERED** > ROGER

**ROGERING** > ROGER

**ROGERINGS** > ROGER

**ROGERS** > ROGER

**ROGNON** n isolated rock outcrop on a glacier

**ROGNONS** > ROGNON

**ROGUE** n dishonest or unprincipled person ▷ adj (of a wild beast) having a savage temper and living apart from the herd ▷ vb rid (a field or crop) of plants that are inferior, diseased, or of an unwanted variety

**ROGUED** > ROGUE

**ROGUEING** > ROGUE

**ROGUERIES** > ROGUERY

**ROGUERY** n dishonest or immoral behaviour

**ROGUES** > ROGUE

**ROGUESHIP** n being a rogue

**ROGUING** > ROGUE

**ROGUISH** adj dishonest or unprincipled

**ROGUISHLY** > ROGUISH

**ROGUY** same as > ROGUISH

**ROIL** vb make (a liquid) cloudy or turbid by stirring up dregs or sediment

**ROILED** > ROIL

**ROILIER** > ROILY

**ROILIEST** > ROILY

**ROILING** > ROIL

**ROILS** > ROIL

**ROILY** adj cloudy or muddy

**ROIN** same as > ROYNE

**ROINED** > ROIN

**ROINING** > ROIN

**ROINISH** same as > ROYNISH

**ROINS** > ROIN

**ROIST** archaic variant of > ROISTER

**ROISTED** > ROIST

**ROISTER** vb make merry noisily or boisterously

**ROISTERED** > ROISTER

**ROISTERER** > ROISTER

**ROISTERS** > ROISTER

**ROISTING** > ROIST

**ROISTS** > ROIST

**ROJAK** n (in Malaysia) a salad dish served in chilli sauce

**ROJAKS** > ROJAK

**ROJI** n Japanese tea garden or its path of stones

**ROJIS** > ROJI

**ROK** same as > ROC

**ROKE** vb (in dialect) steam or smoke

**ROKED** > ROKE

**ROKELAY** n type of cloak

**ROKELAYS** > ROKELAY

**ROKER** n variety of ray

**ROKERS** > ROKER

**ROKES** > ROKE

**ROKIER** > ROKY

**ROKIEST** > ROKY

**ROKING** > ROKE

**ROKKAKU** n hexagonal Japanese kite

**ROKS** > ROK

**ROKY** adj (in dialect) steamy or smoky

**ROLAG** n roll of carded wool ready for spinning

**ROLAGS** > ROLAG

**ROLAMITE** n type of bearing using two rollers and a moving flexible band

**ROLAMITES** > ROLAMITE

**ROLE** n task or function

**ROLES** > ROLE

**ROLF** vb massage following a particular technique

**ROLFED** > ROLF

**ROLFER** > ROLF

**ROLFERS** > ROLF

**ROLFING** > ROLF

**ROLFINGS** > ROLF

**ROLFS** > ROLF

**ROLL** vb move by turning over and over ▷ n act of rolling over or from side to side

**ROLLABLE** > ROLL

**ROLLAWAY** n mounted on rollers so as to be easily moved, esp to be stored away after use

**ROLLAWAYS** > ROLLAWAY

**ROLLBACK** n reduction to a previous price

**ROLLBACKS** > ROLLBACK

**ROLLBAR** n bar that reinforces the frame of a car, esp one used for racing, rallying, etc, to protect the driver if the car should turn over

**ROLLBARS** > ROLLBAR

**ROLLED** > ROLL

**ROLLER** n rotating cylinder used for smoothing or supporting a thing to be moved, spreading paint, etc

**ROLLERS** > ROLLER

**ROLLICK** vb behave in a carefree, frolicsome, or boisterous manner ▷ n boisterous or carefree escapade or event

**ROLLICKED** > ROLLICK

**ROLLICKS** > ROLLICK

**ROLLICKY** adj rollicking

**ROLLING** > ROLL

**ROLLINGS** > ROLL

**ROLLMOP** n herring fillet rolled round onion slices and pickled

**ROLLMOPS** > ROLLMOP

**ROLLNECK** adj (of a garment) having a high neck that is worn rolled over ▷ n rollneck sweater or other garment

**ROLLNECKS** > ROLLNECK

**ROLLOCK** same as > ROWLOCK

**ROLLOCKS** > ROLLOCK

**ROLLOUT** n presentation to the public of a new aircraft, product, etc; launch

**ROLLOUTS** > ROLLOUT

**ROLLOVER** n instance of a

prize continuing in force for an additional period

**ROLLOVERS** > ROLLOVER

**ROLLS** > ROLL

**ROLLTOP** as in rolltop desk desk having a slatted wooden panel that can be pulled down over the writing surface when not in use

**ROLLWAY** n incline down which logs are rolled

**ROLLWAYS** > ROLLWAY

**ROM** n male gypsy

**ROMA** n gypsy

**ROMAGE** archaic variant of > RUMMAGE

**ROMAGES** > ROMAGE

**ROMAIKA** n Greek dance

**ROMAIKAS** > ROMAIKA

**ROMAINE** n usual US and Canadian name for cos (lettuce)

**ROMAINES** > ROMAINE

**ROMAJI** n Roman alphabet as used to write Japanese

**ROMAJIS** > ROMAJI

**ROMAL** same as > RUMAL

**ROMALS** > ROMAL

**ROMAN** adj in or relating to the vertical style of printing type used for most printed matter ▷ n roman type

**ROMANCE** n love affair ▷ vb exaggerate or fantasize

**ROMANCED** > ROMANCE

**ROMANCER** > ROMANCE

**ROMANCERS** > ROMANCE

**ROMANCES** > ROMANCE

**ROMANCING** > ROMANCE

**ROMANISE** same as > ROMANIZE

**ROMANISED** > ROMANISE

**ROMANISES** > ROMANISE

**ROMANIZE** vb impart a Roman Catholic character to (a ceremony, practice, etc)

**ROMANIZED** > ROMANIZE

**ROMANIZES** > ROMANIZE

**ROMANO** n hard light-coloured sharp-tasting cheese

**ROMANOS** > ROMANO

**ROMANS** > ROMAN

**ROMANTIC** adj of or dealing with love ▷ n romantic person or artist

**ROMANTICS** > ROMANTIC

**ROMANZA** n short instrumental piece of song-like character

**ROMANZAS** > ROMANZA

**ROMAS** > ROMA

**ROMAUNT** n verse romance

**ROMAUNTS** > ROMAUNT

**ROMCOM** n film or television comedy based around the romantic relationships of the characters

**ROMCOMS** > ROMCOM

**ROMELDALE** n type of sheep

**ROMEO** n ardent male lover

ROMEOS > ROMEO
ROMNEYA n bushy type of poppy
ROMNEYAS > ROMNEYA
ROMP vb play wildly and joyfully ▷ n boisterous activity
ROMPED > ROMP
ROMPER n playful or boisterous child
ROMPERS pl n child's overalls
ROMPING > ROMP
ROMPINGLY > ROMP
ROMPISH > ROMP
ROMPISHLY > ROMP
ROMPS > ROMP
ROMS > ROM
RONCADOR n any of several types of fish
RONCADORS > RONCADOR
RONDACHE n round shield
RONDACHES > RONDACHE
RONDAVEL n circular building, often thatched
RONDAVELS > RONDAVEL
RONDE n round dance
RONDEAU n poem consisting of 13 or 10 lines with the opening words of the first line used as a refrain
RONDEAUX > RONDEAU
RONDEL n rondeau consisting of three stanzas of 13 or 14 lines with a two-line refrain appearing twice or three times
RONDELET n brief rondeau, having five or seven lines and a refrain taken from the first line
RONDELETS > RONDELET
RONDELLE n type of bead
RONDELLES > RONDELLE
RONDELS > RONDEL
RONDES > RONDE
RONDINO n short rondo
RONDINOS > RONDINO
RONDO n piece of music with a leading theme continually returned to
RONDOS > RONDO
RONDURE n circle or curve
RONDURES > RONDURE
RONE n drainpipe or gutter for carrying rainwater from a roof
RONEO vb duplicate (a document) from a stencil ▷ n document reproduced by this process
RONEOED > RONEO
RONEOING > RONEO
RONEOS > RONEO
RONEPIPE same as > RONE
RONEPIPES > RONEPIPE
RONES > RONE
RONG archaic past participle of > RING
RONGGENG n Malay traditional dance
RONGGENGS > RONGGENG
RONIN n lordless samurai,

esp one whose feudal lord had been deprived of his territory
RONINS > RONIN
RONION same as > RUNNION
RONIONS > RONION
RONNE archaic form of > RUN
RONNEL n type of pesticide
RONNELS > RONNEL
RONNIE n Dublin slang word for moustache
RONNIES > RONNIE
RONNING > RONNE
RONT archaic variant of > RUNT
RONTE archaic variant of > RUNT
RONTES > RONTE
RONTGEN variant spelling of > ROENTGEN
RONTGENS > RONTGEN
RONTS > RONT
RONYON same as > RUNNION
RONYONS > RONYON
RONZER n New Zealand word for a New Zealander not from Auckland
RONZERS > RONZER
ROO n kangaroo
ROOD n Cross
ROODS > ROOD
ROOF n outside upper covering of a building, car, etc ▷ vb put a roof on
ROOFED > ROOF
ROOFER > ROOF
ROOFERS > ROOF
ROOFIE n tablet of sedative drug
ROOFIER > ROOFY
ROOFIES > ROOFIE
ROOFIEST > ROOFY
ROOFING n material used to build a roof
ROOFINGS > ROOFING
ROOFLESS > ROOF
ROOFLIKE > ROOF
ROOFLINE n uppermost edge of a roof
ROOFLINES > ROOFLINE
ROOFS > ROOF
ROOFSCAPE n view of the rooftops of a town, city, etc
ROOFTOP n outside part of the roof of a building
ROOFTOPS > ROOFTOP
ROOFTREE same as > RIDGEPOLE
ROOFTREES > ROOFTREE
ROOFY adj with roofs
ROOIBOS n tea prepared from the dried leaves of an African plant
ROOIKAT n South African lynx
ROOIKATS > ROOIKAT
ROOINEK n contemptuous name for an Englishman
ROOINEKS > ROOINEK
ROOK n Eurasian bird of the crow family ▷ vb swindle
ROOKED > ROOK
ROOKERIES > ROOKERY
ROOKERY n colony of rooks,

penguins, or seals
ROOKIE n new recruit
ROOKIER > ROOKY
ROOKIES > ROOKIE
ROOKIEST > ROOKY
ROOKING > ROOK
ROOKISH > ROOK
ROOKS > ROOK
ROOKY adj abounding in rooks
ROOM n enclosed area in a building ▷ vb occupy or share a room
ROOMED > ROOM
ROOMER > ROOM
ROOMERS > ROOM
ROOMETTE n self-contained compartment in a railway sleeping car
ROOMETTES > ROOMETTE
ROOMFUL n number or quantity sufficient to fill a room
ROOMFULS > ROOMFUL
ROOMIE n roommate
ROOMIER > ROOMY
ROOMIES > ROOMIE
ROOMIEST > ROOMY
ROOMILY > ROOMY
ROOMINESS > ROOMY
ROOMING > ROOM
ROOMMATE n person with whom one shares a room or apartment
ROOMMATES > ROOMMATE
ROOMS > ROOM
ROOMSOME adj archaic word meaning roomy
ROOMY adj spacious
ROON n Scots word for shred or strip
ROONS > ROON
ROOP same as > ROUP
ROOPED > ROOP
ROOPIER > ROOPY
ROOPIEST > ROOPY
ROOPING > ROOP
ROOPIT same as > ROOPY
ROOPS > ROOP
ROOPY adj (in dialect) hoarse
ROORBACH same as > ROORBACK
ROORBACHS > ROORBACH
ROORBACK n false or distorted report or account, used to obtain political advantage
ROORBACKS > ROORBACK
ROOS > ROO
ROOSA n type of grass
ROOSAS > ROOSA
ROOSE vb flatter
ROOSED > ROOSE
ROOSER > ROOSE
ROOSERS > ROOSE
ROOSES > ROOSE
ROOSING > ROOSE
ROOST n perch for fowls ▷ vb perch
ROOSTED > ROOST
ROOSTER n domestic cock
ROOSTERS > ROOSTER
ROOSTING > ROOST

ROOSTS > ROOST
ROOT n part of a plant that grows down into the earth obtaining nourishment ▷ vb establish a root and start to grow
ROOTAGE n root system
ROOTAGES > ROOTAGE
ROOTCAP n layer of cells at root tip
ROOTCAPS > ROOTCAP
ROOTED > ROOT
ROOTEDLY > ROOT
ROOTER > ROOT
ROOTERS > ROOT
ROOTHOLD > ROOT
ROOTHOLDS > ROOT
ROOTIER > ROOT
ROOTIES > ROOTY
ROOTIEST > ROOT
ROOTINESS > ROOT
ROOTING > ROOT
ROOTINGS > ROOT
ROOTLE same as > ROOT
ROOTLED > ROOTLE
ROOTLES > ROOTLE
ROOTLESS adj having no sense of belonging
ROOTLET n small root or branch of a root
ROOTLETS > ROOTLET
ROOTLIKE > ROOT
ROOTLING > ROOTLE
ROOTS adj (of popular music) going back to the origins of a style, esp in being unpretentious
ROOTSIER > ROOTS
ROOTSIEST > ROOTS
ROOTSTALK same as > RHIZOME
ROOTSTOCK same as > RHIZOME
ROOTSY > ROOTS
ROOTWORM n beetle larvae feeding on roots
ROOTWORMS > ROOTWORM
ROOTY adj rootlike ▷ n (in military slang) bread
ROPABLE adj capable of being roped
ROPE n thick cord
ROPEABLE same as > ROPABLE
ROPED > ROPE
ROPELIKE > ROPE
ROPER n someone who makes ropes
ROPERIES > ROPERY
ROPERS > ROPER
ROPERY n place where ropes are made
ROPES > ROPE
ROPEWALK n long narrow usually covered path or shed where ropes are made
ROPEWALKS > ROPEWALK
ROPEWAY n type of aerial lift
ROPEWAYS > ROPEWAY
ROPEWORK n making, mending, or tying ropes
ROPEWORKS > ROPEWORK
ROPEY adj inferior or

inadequate
ROPIER > ROPY
ROPIEST > ROPY
ROPILY > ROPEY
ROPINESS > ROPEY
ROPING > ROPE
ROPINGS > ROPE
ROPY same as > ROPEY
ROQUE n game developed from croquet, played on a hard surface with a resilient surrounding border from which the ball can rebound
ROQUES > ROQUE
ROQUET vb drive one's ball against (another person's ball) in order to be allowed to croquet ▷ n act of roqueting
ROQUETED > ROQUET
ROQUETING > ROQUET
ROQUETS > ROQUET
ROQUETTE n another name for the salad plant rocket
ROQUETTES > ROQUETTE
RORAL archaic word for > DEWY
RORE archaic spelling of > ROAR
RORES > RORE
RORIC same as > RORAL
RORID same as > RORAL
RORIE same as > RORARY
RORIER > RORY
RORIEST > RORY
RORQUAL n toothless whale with a dorsal fin
RORQUALS > RORQUAL
RORT n dishonest scheme ▷ vb take unfair advantage of something
RORTED > RORT
RORTER n small-scale confidence trickster
RORTERS > RORTER
RORTIER > RORT
RORTIEST > RORT
RORTING > RORT
RORTS > RORT
RORTY > RORT
RORY adj dewy
ROSACE another name for > ROSETTE
ROSACEA n chronic inflammatory disease causing the skin of the face to become abnormally flushed and sometimes pustular
ROSACEAS > ROSACEA
ROSACEOUS adj of or belonging to a family of plants typically having five-petalled flowers, which includes the rose, strawberry, and many fruit trees
ROSACES > ROSACE
ROSAKER archaic word for > REALGAR
ROSAKERS > ROSAKER
ROSALIA n melody which is repeated but at a higher

pitch each time
ROSALIAS > ROSALIA
ROSANILIN n reddish-brown crystalline insoluble derivative of aniline used as a red dye
ROSARIA > ROSARIUM
ROSARIAN n person who cultivates roses, esp professionally
ROSARIANS > ROSARIAN
ROSARIES > ROSARY
ROSARIUM n rose garden
ROSARIUMS > ROSARIUM
ROSARY n series of prayers
ROSBIF n term used in France for an English person
ROSBIFS > ROSBIF
ROSCID adj dewy
ROSCOE slang word for > GUN
ROSCOES > ROSCOE
ROSE > RISE
ROSEAL adj rosy or roselike
ROSEATE adj rose-coloured
ROSEATELY > ROSEATE
ROSEBAY as in rosebay willowherb perennial plant with spikes of deep pink flowers
ROSEBAYS > ROSEBAY
ROSEBOWL n bowl for displaying roses or other flowers
ROSEBOWLS > ROSEBOWL
ROSEBUD n rose which has not yet fully opened
ROSEBUDS > ROSEBUD
ROSEBUSH n flowering shrub
ROSED > RISE
ROSEFINCH n any of various finches with pink patches
ROSEFISH n red food fish of North Atlantic coastal waters
ROSEHIP n berry-like fruit of a rose plant
ROSEHIPS > ROSEHIP
ROSELESS > RISE
ROSELIKE > RISE
ROSELLA n type of Australian parrot
ROSELLAS > ROSELLA
ROSELLE n Indian flowering plant
ROSELLES > ROSELLE
ROSEMARY n fragrant flowering shrub
ROSEOLA n feverish condition of young children that lasts for some five days during the last two of which the patient has a rose-coloured rash. It is caused by the human herpes virus
ROSEOLAR > ROSEOLA
ROSEOLAS > ROSEOLA
ROSERIES > ROSERY
ROSEROOT n Eurasian mountain plant
ROSEROOTS > ROSEROOT

ROSERY n bed or garden of roses
ROSES > RISE
ROSESLUG n one of various types of pest that feed on roses
ROSESLUGS > ROSESLUG
ROSET n Scots word meaning rosin ▷ vb rub rosin on
ROSETED > ROSET
ROSETING > ROSET
ROSETS > ROSET
ROSETTE n rose-shaped ornament, esp a circular bunch of ribbons
ROSETTED > ROSET
ROSETTES > ROSETTE
ROSETTY > ROSET
ROSETY > ROSET
ROSEWATER n scented water used as a perfume and in cooking, made by the distillation of rose petals or by impregnation with oil of roses
ROSEWOOD n fragrant wood used to make furniture
ROSEWOODS > ROSEWOOD
ROSHI n teacher of Zen Buddhism
ROSHIS > ROSHI
ROSIED > ROSY
ROSIER archaic word for > ROSEBUSH
ROSIERE archaic word for > ROSEBUSH
ROSIERES > ROSIERE
ROSIERS > ROSIER
ROSIES > ROSY
ROSIEST > ROSY
ROSILY > ROSY
ROSIN n resin used for treating the bows of violins etc ▷ vb apply rosin to
ROSINATE n chemical compound
ROSINATES > ROSINATE
ROSINED > ROSIN
ROSINER n strong alcoholic drink
ROSINERS > ROSINER
ROSINESS > ROSY
ROSING > RISE
ROSINING > ROSIN
ROSINOL n yellowish fluorescent oily liquid obtained from certain resins, used in the manufacture of carbon black, varnishes, and lacquers
ROSINOLS > ROSINOL
ROSINOUS adj rosiny
ROSINS > ROSIN
ROSINWEED n any of several North American plants of the genus Silphium and related genera, having resinous juice, sticky foliage, and a strong smell
ROSINY > ROSIN
ROSIT same as > ROSET

ROSITED > ROSIT
ROSITING > ROSIT
ROSITS > ROSIT
ROSMARINE archaic form of > ROSEMARY
ROSOGLIO same as > ROSOLIO
ROSOGLIOS > ROSOGLIO
ROSOLIO n type of cordial
ROSOLIOS > ROSOLIO
ROSSER n bark-removing machine
ROSSERS > ROSSER
ROST archaic spelling of > ROAST
ROSTED > ROST
ROSTELLA > ROSTELLUM
ROSTELLAR > ROSTELLUM
ROSTELLUM n small beaklike process, such as the hooked projection from the top of the head in tapeworms or the outgrowth from the stigma of an orchid
ROSTER n list of people and their turns of duty ▷ vb place on a roster
ROSTERED > ROSTER
ROSTERING > ROSTER
ROSTERS > ROSTER
ROSTI n cheese-topped fried Swiss dish consisting of grated potato and, optionally, onion
ROSTING > ROST
ROSTIS > ROSTI
ROSTRA > ROSTRUM
ROSTRAL adj of or like a beak or snout
ROSTRALLY > ROSTRAL
ROSTRATE adj having a beak or beaklike process
ROSTRATED same as > ROSTRATE
ROSTRUM n platform or stage
ROSTRUMS > ROSTRUM
ROSTS > ROST
ROSULA n rosette
ROSULAS > ROSULA
ROSULATE adj in the form of a rose
ROSY adj pink-coloured ▷ vb redden or make pink
ROSYING > ROSY
ROT vb decompose or decay ▷ n decay
ROTA n list of people who take it in turn to do a particular task
ROTACHUTE n device serving the same purpose as a parachute, in which the canopy is replaced by freely revolving rotor blades, used for the delivery of stores or recovery of missiles
ROTAL adj of or relating to wheels or rotation
ROTAMETER n device for measuring the flow of a liquid

**ROTAN** *another name for* > RATTAN

**ROTANS** > ROTAN

**ROTAPLANE** *n* aircraft that derives its lift from freely revolving rotor blades

**ROTARIES** > ROTARY

**ROTARY** *adj* revolving ▷ *n* traffic roundabout

**ROTAS** > ROTA

**ROTATABLE** > ROTATE

**ROTATE** *vb* (cause to) move round a centre or on a pivot ▷ *adj* designating a corolla the united petals of which radiate from a central point like the spokes of a wheel

**ROTATED** > ROTATE

**ROTATES** > ROTATE

**ROTATING** *adj* revolving around a central axis, line, or point

**ROTATION** *n* act of rotating

**ROTATIONS** > ROTATION

**ROTATIVE** *same as* > ROTATORY

**ROTATOR** *n* person, device, or part that rotates or causes rotation

**ROTATORES** > ROTATOR

**ROTATORS** > ROTATOR

**ROTATORY** *adj* of, relating to, possessing, or causing rotation

**ROTAVATE** *same as* > ROTAVATE

**ROTAVATED** > ROTAVATE

**ROTAVATES** > ROTAVATE

**ROTAVATOR** *n* type of machine with rotating blades that will break up soil

**ROTAVIRUS** *n* any member of a genus of viruses that cause worldwide endemic infections. They occur in birds and mammals, cause diarrhoea in children, and are usually transmitted in food prepared with unwashed hands

**ROTCH** *n* little auk

**ROTCHE** *same as* > ROTCH

**ROTCHES** > ROTCH

**ROTCHIE** *same as* > ROTCH

**ROTCHIES** > ROTCHIE

**ROTE** *n* mechanical repetition ▷ *vb* learn by rote

**ROTED** > ROTE

**ROTENONE** *n* white odourless crystalline substance extracted from the roots of derris: a powerful insecticide

**ROTENONES** > ROTENONE

**ROTES** > ROTE

**ROTGRASS** *n* type of grass blamed for sheeprot

**ROTGUT** *n* alcoholic drink of inferior quality

**ROTGUTS** > ROTGUT

**ROTHER** *dialect word for* > OX

**ROTHERS** > ROTHER

**ROTI** *n* (in India and the Caribbean) a type of unleavened bread

**ROTIFER** *n* minute aquatic multicellular invertebrate

**ROTIFERAL** > ROTIFER

**ROTIFERAN** > ROTIFER

**ROTIFERS** > ROTIFER

**ROTIFORM** *adj* in the shape of a wheel

**ROTING** > ROTE

**ROTIS** > ROTI

**ROTL** *n* unit of weight used in Muslim countries, varying in value between about one and five pounds

**ROTLS** > ROTL

**ROTO** *n* printing process using a cylinder etched with many small recesses, from which ink is transferred to a moving web of paper, plastic, etc, in a rotary press

**ROTOGRAPH** *n* photograph made using a particular method ▷ *vb* photograph using this method

**ROTOLO** *n* (in Italian cuisine) a roll

**ROTOLOS** > ROTOLO

**ROTON** *n* quantum of vortex motion

**ROTONS** > ROTON

**ROTOR** *n* revolving portion of a dynamo, motor, or turbine

**ROTORS** > ROTOR

**ROTOS** > ROTO

**ROTOTILL** *vb* break up the soil using a rototiller

**ROTOTILLS** > ROTOTILL

**ROTOVATE** *vb* break up (the surface of the earth, or an area of ground) using a rotavator

**ROTOVATED** > ROTOVATE

**ROTOVATES** > ROTOVATE

**ROTOVATOR** *same as* > ROTAVATOR

**ROTS** > ROT

**ROTTAN** *n* (in dialect) a rat

**ROTTANS** > ROTTAN

**ROTTE** *n* ancient stringed instrument

**ROTTED** > ROT

**ROTTEN** *adj* decaying ▷ *adv* extremely ▷ *n* (in dialect) a rat

**ROTTENER** > ROTTEN

**ROTTENEST** > ROTTEN

**ROTTENLY** > ROTTEN

**ROTTENS** > ROTTEN

**ROTTER** *n* despicable person

**ROTTERS** > ROTTER

**ROTTES** > ROTTE

**ROTTING** > ROT

**ROTULA** *n* kneecap

**ROTULAE** > ROTULA

**ROTULAS** > ROTULA

**ROTUND** *adj* round and plump ▷ *vb* make round

**ROTUNDA** *n* circular building or room, esp with a dome

**ROTUNDAS** > ROTUNDA

**ROTUNDATE** *adj* rounded

**ROTUNDED** > ROTUND

**ROTUNDER** > ROTUND

**ROTUNDEST** > ROTUND

**ROTUNDING** > ROTUND

**ROTUNDITY** > ROTUND

**ROTUNDLY** > ROTUND

**ROTUNDS** > ROTUND

**ROTURIER** *n* freeholder or ordinary person

**ROTURIERS** > ROTURIER

**ROUBLE** *n* monetary unit of Russia, Belarus, and Tajikistan

**ROUBLES** > ROUBLE

**ROUCHE** *same as* > RUCHE

**ROUCHES** > ROUCHE

**ROUCOU** *another name for* > ANNATTO

**ROUCOUS** > ROUCOU

**ROUE** *n* man given to immoral living

**ROUEN** *n* breed of duck

**ROUENS** > ROUEN

**ROUES** > ROUE

**ROUGE** *n* red cosmetic used to colour the cheeks ▷ *vb* apply rouge to

**ROUGED** > ROUGE

**ROUGES** > ROUGE

**ROUGH** *adj* uneven or irregular ▷ *vb* make rough ▷ *n* rough state or area

**ROUGHAGE** *n* indigestible constituents of food which aid digestion

**ROUGHAGES** > ROUGHAGE

**ROUGHBACK** *n* rough-skinned flatfish

**ROUGHCAST** *n* mixture of plaster and small stones for outside walls ▷ *vb* coat with this ▷ *adj* covered with or denoting roughcast

**ROUGHDRY** *vb* dry (clothes or linen) without smoothing

**ROUGHED** > ROUGH

**ROUGHEN** *vb* make or become rough

**ROUGHENED** > ROUGHEN

**ROUGHENS** > ROUGHEN

**ROUGHER** *n* person that does the rough preparatory work on something ▷ *adj* more rough

**ROUGHERS** > ROUGHER

**ROUGHEST** > ROUGH

**ROUGHHEW** *vb* cut or hew (timber, stone, etc) roughly without finishing the surfac

**ROUGHHEWN** > ROUGHHEW

**ROUGHHEWS** > ROUGHHEW

**ROUGHIE** *n* small food fish found in southern and western Australian waters

**ROUGHIES** > ROUGHIE

**ROUGHING** > ROUGH

**ROUGHISH** *adj* somewhat rough

**ROUGHLEG** *n* any of several kinds of large hawk with feathered legs

**ROUGHLEGS** > ROUGHLEG

**ROUGHLY** *adv* without being exact or fully authenticated

**ROUGHNECK** *n* violent person

**ROUGHNESS** > ROUGH

**ROUGHS** > ROUGH

**ROUGHSHOD** *adj* (of a horse) shod with rough-bottomed shoes to prevent slidi

**ROUGHT** *archaic past form of* > REACH

**ROUGHY** *spelling variant of* > ROUGHIE

**ROUGING** > ROUGE

**ROUILLE** *n* kind of sauce

**ROUILLES** > ROUILLE

**ROUL** *archaic form of* > ROLL

**ROULADE** *n* slice of meat rolled, esp around a stuffing, and cooked

**ROULADES** > ROULADE

**ROULE** *archaic form of* > ROLL

**ROULEAU** *n* roll of paper containing coins

**ROULEAUS** > ROULEAU

**ROULEAUX** > ROULEAU

**ROULES** > ROULE

**ROULETTE** *n* gambling game played with a revolving wheel and a ball ▷ *vb* use a toothed wheel on (something), as in engraving, making stationery, etc

**ROULETTED** > ROULETTE

**ROULETTES** > ROULETTE

**ROULS** > ROUL

**ROUM** *archaic spelling of* > ROOM

**ROUMING** *n* pasture given for an animal

**ROUMINGS** > ROUMING

**ROUMS** > ROUM

**ROUNCE** *n* handle that is turned to move paper and plates on a printing press

**ROUNCES** > ROUNCE

**ROUNCEVAL** *n* giant or monster

**ROUNCIES** > ROUNCY

**ROUNCY** *archaic word for* > HORSE

**ROUND** *adj* spherical, cylindrical, circular, or curved ▷ *prep* indicating an encircling movement, presence on all sides, etc ▷ *vb* move round ▷ *n* round shape

**ROUNDARCH** *adj* with rounded arches

**ROUNDBALL** *n* form of basketball

**ROUNDED** *adj* round or curved

**ROUNDEDLY** >ROUNDED

**ROUNDEL** same as >ROUNDELAY

**ROUNDELAY** n simple song with a refrain

**ROUNDELS** >ROUNDEL

**ROUNDER** n run round all four bases after one hit in rounders

**ROUNDERS** n bat-and-ball team game

**ROUNDEST** >ROUND

**ROUNDHAND** n style of handwriting with large rounded curves

**ROUNDHEEL** n immoral woman

**ROUNDING** n process in which a number is approximated as the closest number that can be expressed using the number of bits or digits available

**ROUNDINGS** >ROUNDING

**ROUNDISH** adj somewhat round

**ROUNDLE** same as >ROUNDEL

**ROUNDLES** >ROUNDLE

**ROUNDLET** n small circle

**ROUNDLETS** >ROUNDLET

**ROUNDLY** adv thoroughly

**ROUNDNESS** >ROUND

**ROUNDS** >ROUND

**ROUNDSMAN** n person who makes rounds, as for inspection or to deliver goods

**ROUNDSMEN** >ROUNDSMAN

**ROUNDTRIP** n US term for return trip

**ROUNDUP** n act of gathering together livestock, people, facts, etc

**ROUNDUPS** >ROUNDUP

**ROUNDURE** n archaic word meaning roundness

**ROUNDURES** >ROUNDURE

**ROUNDWOOD** n small pieces of timber (about 5–15 cm, or 2–6 in.) in diameter

**ROUNDWORM** n worm that is a common intestinal parasite of man

**ROUP** n any of various chronic respiratory diseases of birds, esp poultry ▷ vb sell by auction

**ROUPED** >ROUP

**ROUPET** adj Scots word meaning hoarse or croaky

**ROUPIER** >ROUP

**ROUPIEST** >ROUP

**ROUPILY** >ROUP

**ROUPING** >ROUP

**ROUPIT** same as >ROUPET

**ROUPS** >ROUP

**ROUPY** >ROUP

**ROUSANT** adj (in heraldry) rising

**ROUSE** same as >REVEILLE

**ROUSED** >ROUSE

**ROUSEMENT** n stirring up

**ROUSER** n person or thing that rouses people, such as a stirring speech or compelling rock song

**ROUSERS** >ROUSER

**ROUSES** >ROUSE

**ROUSING** adj lively, vigorous

**ROUSINGLY** >ROUSING

**ROUSSEAU** n pemmican fried in its own fat

**ROUSSEAUS** >ROUSSEAU

**ROUSSETTE** n dogfish

**ROUST** vb rout or stir, as out of bed

**ROUSTED** >ROUST

**ROUSTER** n unskilled labourer on an oil rig

**ROUSTERS** >ROUSTER

**ROUSTING** >ROUST

**ROUSTS** >ROUST

**ROUT** n overwhelming defeat ▷ vb defeat and put to flight

**ROUTE** n roads taken to reach a destination ▷ vb send by a particular route

**ROUTED** >ROUTE

**ROUTEING** >ROUTE

**ROUTEMAN** n (in US English) delivery man or salesman doing a particular round

**ROUTEMEN** >ROUTEMAN

**ROUTER** n device that allows data to be moved efficiently between two points on a network

**ROUTERS** >ROUTER

**ROUTES** >ROUTE

**ROUTEWAY** n track, road, or waterway, etc, used as a route to somewhere

**ROUTEWAYS** >ROUTEWAY

**ROUTH** n abundance ▷ adj abundant

**ROUTHIE** adj abundant, plentiful, or well filled

**ROUTHIER** >ROUTHIE

**ROUTHIEST** >ROUTHIE

**ROUTHS** >ROUTH

**ROUTINE** n usual or regular method of procedure ▷ adj ordinary or regular

**ROUTINEER** n someone who believes in routine

**ROUTINELY** >ROUTINE

**ROUTINES** >ROUTINE

**ROUTING** >ROUT

**ROUTINGS** >ROUT

**ROUTINISE** same as >ROUTINIZE

**ROUTINISM** >ROUTINE

**ROUTINIST** >ROUTINE

**ROUTINIZE** vb make routine

**ROUTOUS** >ROUT

**ROUTOUSLY** >ROUT

**ROUTS** >ROUT

**ROUX** n fat and flour cooked together as a basis for sauces

**ROVE** >REEVE

**ROVED** >REEVE

**ROVEN** >REEVE

**ROVER** n wanderer, traveller

**ROVERS** >ROVER

**ROVES** >REEVE

**ROVING** >ROVE

**ROVINGLY** >ROVING

**ROVINGS** >ROVE

**ROW** n straight line of people or things ▷ vb propel (a boat) by oars

**ROWABLE** >ROW

**ROWAN** n tree producing bright red berries, mountain ash

**ROWANS** >ROWAN

**ROWBOAT** n small boat propelled by one or more pairs of oars

**ROWBOATS** >ROWBOAT

**ROWDEDOW** same as >ROWDYDOW

**ROWDEDOWS** >ROWDEDOW

**ROWDIER** >ROWDY

**ROWDIES** >ROWDY

**ROWDIEST** >ROWDY

**ROWDILY** >ROWDY

**ROWDINESS** >ROWDY

**ROWDY** adj disorderly, noisy, and rough ▷ n person like this

**ROWDYDOW** n hullabaloo

**ROWDYDOWS** >ROWDYDOW

**ROWDYISH** >ROWDY

**ROWDYISM** n rowdy behaviour or tendencies or a habitual pattern of rowdy behaviour

**ROWDYISMS** >ROWDYISM

**ROWED** >ROW

**ROWEL** n small spiked wheel on a spur ▷ vb goad (a horse) using a rowel

**ROWELED** >ROWEL

**ROWELING** >ROWEL

**ROWELLED** >ROWEL

**ROWELLING** >ROWEL

**ROWELS** >ROWEL

**ROWEN** another word for >AFTERMATH

**ROWENS** >ROWEN

**ROWER** >ROW

**ROWERS** >ROW

**ROWING** >ROW

**ROWINGS** >ROW

**ROWLOCK** n device on a boat that holds an oar in place

**ROWLOCKS** >ROWLOCK

**ROWME** archaic variant of >ROOM

**ROWMES** >ROWME

**ROWND** archaic variant of >ROUND

**ROWNDED** >ROWND

**ROWNDELL** archaic variant of >ROUNDEL

**ROWNDELLS** >ROWNDELL

**ROWNDING** >ROWND

**ROWNDS** >ROWND

**ROWOVER** n act of winning a rowing race unopposed, by rowing the course

**ROWOVERS** >ROWOVER

**ROWS** >ROW

**ROWT** archaic variant of >ROUT

**ROWTED** >ROWT

**ROWTH** same as >ROUTH

**ROWTHS** >ROWTH

**ROWTING** >ROWT

**ROWTS** >ROWT

**ROYAL** adj of, befitting, or supported by a king or queen ▷ n member of a royal family

**ROYALET** n minor king

**ROYALETS** >ROYALET

**ROYALISE** same as >ROYALIZE

**ROYALISED** >ROYALISE

**ROYALISES** >ROYALISE

**ROYALISM** >ROYALIST

**ROYALISMS** >ROYALIST

**ROYALIST** n supporter of monarchy ▷ adj of or relating to royalists

**ROYALISTS** >ROYALIST

**ROYALIZE** vb make royal

**ROYALIZED** >ROYALIZE

**ROYALIZES** >ROYALIZE

**ROYALLER** >ROYAL

**ROYALLEST** >ROYAL

**ROYALLY** >ROYAL

**ROYALMAST** n highest part of mast

**ROYALS** >ROYAL

**ROYALTIES** >ROYALTY

**ROYALTY** n royal people

**ROYNE** archaic word for >GNAW

**ROYNED** >ROYNE

**ROYNES** >ROYNE

**ROYNING** >ROYNE

**ROYNISH** archaic word for >MANGY

**ROYST** same as >ROIST

**ROYSTED** >ROYST

**ROYSTER** same as >ROISTER

**ROYSTERED** >ROYSTER

**ROYSTERER** >ROYSTER

**ROYSTERS** >ROISTER

**ROYSTING** >ROYST

**ROYSTS** >ROYST

**ROZELLE** same as >ROSELLE

**ROZELLES** >ROZELLE

**ROZET** same as >ROSET

**ROZETED** >ROZET

**ROZETING** >ROZET

**ROZETS** >ROZET

**ROZIT** same as >ROSET

**ROZITED** >ROZIT

**ROZITING** >ROZIT

**ROZITS** >ROZIT

**ROZZER** n policeman

**ROZZERS** >ROZZER

**RUANA** n woollen wrap resembling a poncho

**RUANAS** >RUANA

**RUB** vb apply pressure and friction to (something) with a circular or backwards-and-forwards movement ▷ n act of rubbing

**RUBABOO** n soup or stew made by boiling pemmican with, if available, flour and vegetables

RUBABOOS > RUBABOO
RUBACE *same as* > RUBASSE
RUBACES > RUBACE
RUBAI *n* verse form of
Persian origin consisting
of four-line stanzas
RUBAIYAT *n* (in Persian
poetry) a verse form
consisting of four-line
stanzas
RUBASSE *n* type of quartz
containing red haematite
RUBASSES > RUBASSE
RUBATI > RUBATO
RUBATO *n* (with) expressive
flexibility of tempo ▷ *adv*
be played with a flexible
tempo
RUBATOS > RUBATO
RUBBABOO *same*
*as* > RUBABOO
RUBBABOOS > RUBABOO
RUBBED > RUB
RUBBER *n* strong
waterproof elastic
material, orig. made from
the dried sap of a tropical
tree, now usu synthetic
▷ *adj* made of or producing
rubber ▷ *vb* provide with
rubber coating
RUBBERED > RUBBER
RUBBERIER > RUBBERY
RUBBERING > RUBBER
RUBBERISE *same*
*as* > RUBBERIZE
RUBBERIZE *vb* coat or treat
with rubber
RUBBERS > RUBBER
RUBBERY *adj* having the
texture of or resembling
rubber, esp in flexibility or
toughness
RUBBET *old Scots past form*
*of* > ROB
RUBBIDIES > RUBBIDY
RUBBIDY *same as* > RUBBITY
RUBBIES > RUBBY
RUBBING > RUB
RUBBINGS > RUB
RUBBISH *n* waste matter
▷ *vb* criticize
RUBBISHED > RUBBISH
RUBBISHES > RUBBISH
RUBBISHLY *variant*
*of* > RUBBISHY
RUBBISHY *adj* worthless, of
poor quality, or useless
RUBBIT *old Scots past form*
*of* > ROB
RUBBITIES > RUBBITY
RUBBITY *n* pub
RUBBLE *n* fragments of
broken stone, brick, etc
▷ *vb* turn into rubble
RUBBLED > RUBBLE
RUBBLES > RUBBLE
RUBBLIER > RUBBLE
RUBBLIEST > RUBBLE
RUBBLING > RUBBLE
RUBBLY > RUBBLE
RUBBOARD *n* board for
scrubbing clothes on
RUBBOARDS > RUBBOARD

RUBBY *n* rubbing alcohol,
esp when mixed with
cheap wine for drinking
RUBDOWN *n* act of drying or
cleaning vigorously
RUBDOWNS > RUBDOWN
RUBE *n* unsophisticated
countryman
RUBEFIED > RUBEFY
RUBEFIES > RUBEFY
RUBEFY *vb* make red, esp (of
a counterirritant) to make
the skin go red
RUBEFYING > RUBEFY
RUBEL *n* currency unit of
Belarus
RUBELLA *n* mild
contagious viral disease
characterized by cough,
sore throat, and skin rash
RUBELLAN *n* red-coloured
mineral
RUBELLANS > RUBELLAN
RUBELLAS > RUBELLA
RUBELLITE *n* red
transparent variety of
tourmaline, used as a
gemstone
RUBELS > RUBEL
RUBEOLA *technical name*
*for* > MEASLES
RUBEOLAR > RUBEOLA
RUBEOLAS > RUBEOLA
RUBES > RUBE
RUBESCENT *adj* reddening
RUBICELLE *n* variety of
spinel that is orange or
yellow in colour
RUBICON *n* point of no
return ▷ *vb* (in bezique) to
beat before the loser has
managed to gain as many
as 1000 points
RUBICONED > RUBICON
RUBICONS > RUBICON
RUBICUND *adj* ruddy
RUBIDIC > RUBIDIUM
RUBIDIUM *n* soft highly
reactive radioactive
element
RUBIDIUMS > RUBIDIUM
RUBIED > RUBY
RUBIER > RUBY
RUBIES > RUBY
RUBIEST > RUBY
RUBIFIED > RUBIFY
RUBIFIES > RUBIFY
RUBIFY *same as* > RUBEFY
RUBIFYING > RUBIFY
RUBIGO *old Scots word*
*for* > PENIS
RUBIGOS > RUBIGO
RUBIN *archaic word*
*for* > RUBY
RUBINE *archaic word*
*for* > RUBY
RUBINEOUS *same*
*as* > RUBIOUS
RUBINES > RUBINE
RUBINS > RUBIN
RUBIOUS *adj* of the colour
ruby
RUBLE *same as* > ROUBLE
RUBLES > RUBLE

RUBOFF *n* resulting effect
on something else;
consequences
RUBOFFS > RUBOFF
RUBOUT *n* killing or
elimination
RUBOUTS > RUBOUT
RUBRIC *n* set of rules for
behaviour ▷ *adj* written,
printed, or marked in red
RUBRICAL > RUBRIC
RUBRICATE *vb* print (a
book or manuscript) with
red titles, headings, etc
RUBRICIAN *n* authority on
liturgical rubrics
RUBRICS > RUBRIC
RUBS > RUB
RUBSTONE *n* stone used for
sharpening or smoothing,
esp a whetstone
RUBSTONES > RUBSTONE
RUBUS *n* fruit-bearing
genus of shrubs
RUBY *n* red precious
gemstone ▷ *adj* deep red
▷ *vb* redden
RUBYING > RUBY
RUBYLIKE > RUBY
RUC *same as* > ROC
RUCHE *n* pleat or frill of lace
etc as a decoration ▷ *vb*
put a ruche on
RUCHED > RUCHE
RUCHES > RUCHE
RUCHING *n* material used
for a ruche
RUCHINGS > RUCHING
RUCK *n* rough crowd of
common people ▷ *vb*
wrinkle or crease
RUCKED > RUCK
RUCKING > RUCK
RUCKLE *another word*
*for* > RUCK
RUCKLED > RUCKLE
RUCKLES > RUCKLE
RUCKLING > RUCKLE
RUCKMAN *n* person who
plays in the ruck
RUCKMEN > RUCKMAN
RUCKS > RUCK
RUCKSACK *n* large pack
carried on the back
RUCKSACKS > RUCKSACK
RUCKSEAT *n* seat fixed to or
forming part of a rucksack
RUCKSEATS > RUCKSEAT
RUCKUS *n* uproar
RUCKUSES > RUCKUS
RUCOLA *n* another name for
the salad plant rocket
RUCOLAS > RUCOLA
RUCS > RUC
RUCTATION *n* archaic word
meaning eructation or
belch
RUCTION *n* uproar
RUCTIONS > RUCTION
RUCTIOUS *adj* tending or
likely to cause ructions
RUD *n* red or redness ▷ *vb*
redden
RUDACEOUS *adj* (of

conglomerate, breccia,
and similar rocks)
composed of coarse-
grained material
RUDAS *n* Scots word for a
coarse, rude old woman
RUDASES > RUDAS
RUDBECKIA *n* any plant of
the North American genus
*Rudbeckia*, cultivated for
their showy flowers
RUDD *n* European
freshwater fish
RUDDED > RUD
RUDDER *n* vertical hinged
piece at the stern of a boat
or at the rear of an aircraft,
for steering
RUDDERS > RUDDER
RUDDIED > RUDDY
RUDDIER > RUDDY
RUDDIES > RUDDY
RUDDIEST > RUDDY
RUDDILY > RUDDY
RUDDINESS > RUDDY
RUDDING > RUD
RUDDLE *n* red ochre, used
esp to mark sheep ▷ *vb*
mark (sheep) with ruddle
RUDDLED > RUDDLE
RUDDLEMAN *n* ruddle dealer
RUDDLEMEN > RUDDLEMAN
RUDDLES > RUDDLE
RUDDLING > RUDDLE
RUDDOCK *dialect name for*
*the* > ROBIN
RUDDOCKS > RUDDOCK
RUDDS > RUDD
RUDDY *adj* of a fresh healthy
red colour ▷ *adv* bloody
▷ *vb* redden
RUDDYING > RUDDY
RUDE *archaic spelling*
*of* > ROOD
RUDELY > RUDE
RUDENESS > RUDE
RUDER > RUDE
RUDERAL *n* plant that
grows on waste ground
▷ *adj* growing in waste
places
RUDERALS > RUDERAL
RUDERIES > RUDE
RUDERY > RUDE
RUDES > RUDE
RUDESBIES > RUDESBY
RUDESBY *n* archaic word for
rude person
RUDEST > RUDE
RUDIE *n* member of a youth
movement originating in
the 1960s
RUDIES > RUDIE
RUDIMENT *n* first principles
or elementary stages of a
subject
RUDIMENTS > RUDIMENT
RUDISH *adj* somewhat rude
RUDS > RUD
RUE *vb* feel regret for ▷ *n*
plant with evergreen
bitter leaves
RUED > RUE
RUEFUL *adj* regretful or

sorry
RUEFULLY > RUEFUL
RUEING > RUE
RUEINGS > RUE
RUELLE n area between bed and wall, at one time used by French ladies of standing for receiving visitors
RUELLES > RUELLE
RUELLIA n genus of plants
RUELLIAS > RUELLIA
RUER > RUE
RUERS > RUE
RUES > RUE
RUFESCENT adj tinged with red or becoming red
RUFF n circular pleated, gathered, or fluted collar of lawn, muslin, etc, often starched or wired, worn by both men and women in the 16th and 17th centuries ▷ vb trump
RUFFE n European freshwater fish
RUFFED > RUFF
RUFFES > RUFFE
RUFFIAN n violent lawless person ▷ vb act like a ruffian
RUFFIANED > RUFFIAN
RUFFIANLY > RUFFIAN
RUFFIANS > RUFFIAN
RUFFIN archaic name for > RUFFE
RUFFING > RUFF
RUFFINS > RUFFIN
RUFFLE vb disturb the calm of ▷ n frill or pleat
RUFFLED > RUFFLE
RUFFLER n person or thing that ruffles
RUFFLERS > RUFFLER
RUFFLES > RUFFLE
RUFFLIER > RUFFLY
RUFFLIEST > RUFFLY
RUFFLIKE > RUFF
RUFFLING > RUFFLE
RUFFLINGS > RUFFLE
RUFFLY adj ruffled
RUFFS > RUFF
RUFIYAA n standard monetary unit of the Maldives, divided into 100 laari
RUFIYAAS > RUFIYAA
RUFOUS adj reddish-brown
RUG n small carpet ▷ vb (in dialect) tug
RUGA n fold, wrinkle, or crease
RUGAE > RUGA
RUGAL adj (in anatomy) with ridges or folds
RUGALACH same as > RUGELACH
RUGBIES > RUGBY
RUGBY n form of football played with an oval ball which may be handled by the players
RUGELACH n fruit and

nut pastry shaped like a croissant
RUGGED adj rocky or steep
RUGGEDER > RUGGED
RUGGEDEST > RUGGED
RUGGEDISE same as > RUGGEDIZE
RUGGEDIZE vb make durable, as for military use
RUGGEDLY > RUGGED
RUGGELACH same as > RUGELACH
RUGGER same as > RUGBY
RUGGERS > RUGGER
RUGGIER > RUGGY
RUGGIEST > RUGGY
RUGGING > RUG
RUGGINGS > RUG
RUGGY adj (in dialect) rough or rugged
RUGLIKE > RUG
RUGOLA n another name for the salad plant rocket
RUGOLAS > RUGOLA
RUGOSA n any of various shrubs descended from a particular type of wild rose
RUGOSAS > RUGOSA
RUGOSE adj wrinkled
RUGOSELY > RUGOSE
RUGOSITY > RUGOSE
RUGOUS same as > RUGOSE
RUGS > RUG
RUGULOSE adj with little wrinkles
RUIN vb destroy or spoil completely ▷ n destruction or decay
RUINABLE > RUIN
RUINATE vb archaic word for bring or come to ruin
RUINATED > RUINATE
RUINATES > RUINATE
RUINATING > RUINATE
RUINATION n act of ruining
RUINED > RUIN
RUINER > RUIN
RUINERS > RUIN
RUING > RUE
RUINGS > RUE
RUINING > RUIN
RUININGS > RUIN
RUINOUS adj causing ruin
RUINOUSLY > RUINOUS
RUINS > RUIN
RUKH same as > ROC
RUKHS > RUKH
RULABLE > RULE
RULE n statement of what is allowed, for example in a game or procedure ▷ vb govern
RULED > RULE
RULELESS > RULE
RULER n person who governs ▷ vb punish by hitting with a ruler
RULERED > RULER
RULERING > RULER
RULERS > RULER
RULERSHIP > RULER
RULES > RULE
RULESSE adj archaic word meaning ruleless or

without rules
RULIER > RULY
RULIEST > RULY
RULING n formal decision ▷ adj controlling or exercising authority
RULINGS > RULING
RULLION n Scots word for rawhide shoe
RULLIONS > RULLION
RULLOCK same as > ROWLOCK
RULLOCKS > RULLOCK
RULY adj orderly
RUM n alcoholic drink distilled from sugar cane ▷ adj odd, strange
RUMAKI n savoury of chicken liver and sliced water chestnut wrapped in bacon
RUMAKIS > RUMAKI
RUMAL n handkerchief or type of cloth
RUMALS > RUMAL
RUMBA n lively ballroom dance of Cuban origin ▷ vb dance the rumba
RUMBAED > RUMBA
RUMBAING > RUMBA
RUMBAS > RUMBA
RUMBELOW n nonsense word used in the refrain of certain sea shanties
RUMBELOWS > RUMBELOW
RUMBLE vb make a low continuous noise ▷ n deep resonant sound
RUMBLED > RUMBLE
RUMBLER > RUMBLE
RUMBLERS > RUMBLE
RUMBLES > RUMBLE
RUMBLIER > RUMBLY
RUMBLIEST > RUMBLY
RUMBLING > RUMBLE
RUMBLINGS > RUMBLE
RUMBLY adj rumbling or liable to rumble
RUMBO n rum-based cocktail
RUMBOS > RUMBO
RUME archaic form of > RHEUM
RUMEN n first compartment of the stomach of ruminants, behind the reticulum, in which food is partly digested before being regurgitated as cud
RUMENS > RUMEN
RUMES > RUME
RUMINA > RUMEN
RUMINAL > RUMEN
RUMINANT n cud-chewing (animal, such as a cow, sheep, or deer) ▷ adj of ruminants
RUMINANTS > RUMINANT
RUMINATE vb chew the cud
RUMINATED > RUMINATE
RUMINATES > RUMINATE
RUMINATOR > RUMINATE
RUMKIN n archaic term for a drinking vessel

RUMKINS > RUMKIN
RUMLY > RUM
RUMMAGE vb search untidily and at length ▷ n untidy search through a collection of things
RUMMAGED > RUMMAGE
RUMMAGER > RUMMAGE
RUMMAGERS > RUMMAGE
RUMMAGES > RUMMAGE
RUMMAGING > RUMMAGE
RUMMER > RUM
RUMMERS > RUM
RUMMEST > RUM
RUMMIER > RUMMY
RUMMIES > RUMMY
RUMMIEST > RUMMY
RUMMILY > RUMMY
RUMMINESS > RUMMY
RUMMISH adj rather strange, peculiar or odd
RUMMY n card game in which players try to collect sets or sequences ▷ adj of or like rum in taste or smell
RUMNESS > RUM
RUMNESSES > RUM
RUMOR same as > RUMOUR
RUMORED > RUMOR
RUMORING > RUMOR
RUMOROUS adj involving or containing rumours
RUMORS > RUMOR
RUMOUR n unproved statement ▷ vb pass around or circulate in the form of a rumour
RUMOURED > RUMOUR
RUMOURER n someone given to spreading rumours
RUMOURERS > RUMOURER
RUMOURING > RUMOUR
RUMOURS > RUMOUR
RUMP n buttocks ▷ vb turn back on
RUMPED > RUMP
RUMPIES > RUMPY
RUMPING > RUMP
RUMPLE vb make untidy, crumpled, or dishevelled ▷ n wrinkle, fold, or crease
RUMPLED > RUMPLE
RUMPLES > RUMPLE
RUMPLESS > RUMP
RUMPLIER > RUMPLE
RUMPLIEST > RUMPLE
RUMPLING > RUMPLE
RUMPLY > RUMPLE
RUMPO n slang word for sexual intercourse
RUMPOS > RUMPO
RUMPS > RUMP
RUMPUS n noisy commotion
RUMPUSES > RUMPUS
RUMPY n tailless Manx cat ▷ adj with a large or noticeable rump
RUMRUNNER n alcohol smuggler
RUMS > RUM
RUN vb move with a more rapid gait than walking

▷ *n* act or spell of running
**RUNABOUT** *n* small car used
for short journeys ▷ *vb*
move busily from place to
place
**RUNABOUTS** > RUNABOUT
**RUNAGATE** *n* vagabond,
fugitive, or renegade
**RUNAGATES** > RUNAGATE
**RUNANGA** *n* Māori assembly
or council
**RUNAROUND** *n* deceitful
or evasive treatment of a
person
**RUNAWAY** *n* person or
animal that runs away
**RUNAWAYS** > RUNAWAY
**RUNBACK** *n* (in tennis) the
areas behind the baselines
of the court
**RUNBACKS** > RUNBACK
**RUNCH** *n* another name for
white charlock
**RUNCHES** > RUNCH
**RUNCIBLE** as in *runcible
spoon* forklike utensil with
two prongs and one sharp
curved prong
**RUNCINATE** *adj* (of a leaf)
having a saw-toothed
margin with the teeth or
lobes pointing backwards
**RUND** *same as* > ROON
**RUNDALE** *n* (formerly) the
name given, esp in Ireland
and earlier in Scotland, to
the system of land tenure
in which each land-holder
had several strips of land
that were not contiguous
**RUNDALES** > RUNDALE
**RUNDLE** *n* rung of a ladder
**RUNDLED** *adj* rounded
**RUNDLES** > RUNDLE
**RUNDLET** *n* liquid measure,
generally about 15 gallons
**RUNDLETS** > RUNDLET
**RUNDOWN** *adj* tired;
exhausted ▷ *n* brief
review, résumé, or
summary
**RUNDOWNS** > RUNDOWN
**RUNDS** > RUND
**RUNE** *n* any character of
the earliest Germanic
alphabet
**RUNECRAFT** *n*
understanding of and skill
working with runes
**RUNED** *n* with runes on
**RUNELIKE** *adj* resembling a
rune or runes
**RUNES** > RUNE
**RUNFLAT** *adj* having
a safety feature that
prevents tyres becoming
dangerous or liable to
damage when flat
**RUNG** > RING
**RUNGLESS** > RING
**RUNGS** > RING
**RUNIC** > RUNE
**RUNKLE** *vb* (in dialect)
crease or wrinkle

**RUNKLED** > RUNKLE
**RUNKLES** > RUNKLE
**RUNKLING** > RUNKLE
**RUNLESS** > RUN
**RUNLET** *n* cask for wine,
beer, etc
**RUNLETS** > RUNLET
**RUNNABLE** > RUN
**RUNNEL** *n* small brook
**RUNNELS** > RUNNEL
**RUNNER** *n* competitor in
a race
**RUNNERS** > RUNNER
**RUNNET** *dialect word
for* > RENNET
**RUNNETS** > RUNNET
**RUNNIER** > RUNNY
**RUNNIEST** > RUNNY
**RUNNINESS** > RUNNY
**RUNNING** > RUN
**RUNNINGLY** > RUN
**RUNNINGS** > RUN
**RUNNION** *n* archaic
pejorative term for a
woman
**RUNNIONS** > RUNNION
**RUNNY** *adj* tending to flow
**RUNOFF** *n* extra race to
decide the winner after
a tie
**RUNOFFS** > RUNOFF
**RUNOUT** *n* dismissal of a
batsman by running him
out
**RUNOUTS** > RUNOUT
**RUNOVER** *n* incident in
which someone is run over
by a vehicle
**RUNOVERS** > RUNOVER
**RUNRIG** *same as* > RUNDALE
**RUNRIGS** > RUNRIG
**RUNROUND** *same
as* > RUNAROUND
**RUNROUNDS** > RUNROUND
**RUNS** > RUN
**RUNT** *n* smallest animal in
a litter
**RUNTED** *adj* stunted
**RUNTIER** > RUNT
**RUNTIEST** > RUNT
**RUNTINESS** > RUNT
**RUNTISH** > RUNT
**RUNTISHLY** > RUNT
**RUNTS** > RUNT
**RUNTY** > RUNT
**RUNWAY** *n* hard level
roadway where aircraft
take off and land
**RUNWAYS** > RUNWAY
**RUPEE** *n* monetary unit of
India and Pakistan
**RUPEES** > RUPEE
**RUPIA** *n* type of skin
eruption
**RUPIAH** *n* standard
monetary unit of
Indonesia, divided into
100 sen
**RUPIAHS** > RUPIAH
**RUPIAS** > RUPIA
**RUPTURE** *n* breaking,
breach ▷ *vb* break, burst,
or sever
**RUPTURED** > RUPTURE

**RUPTURES** > RUPTURE
**RUPTURING** > RUPTURE
**RURAL** *adj* in or of the
countryside ▷ *n* country
dweller
**RURALISE** *same
as* > RURALIZE
**RURALISED** > RURALISE
**RURALISES** > RURALISE
**RURALISM** > RURAL
**RURALISMS** > RURAL
**RURALIST** > RURAL
**RURALISTS** > RURAL
**RURALITE** > RURAL
**RURALITES** > RURAL
**RURALITY** > RURAL
**RURALIZE** *vb* make rural in
character, appearance, etc
**RURALIZED** > RURALIZE
**RURALIZES** > RURALIZE
**RURALLY** > RURAL
**RURALNESS** > RURAL
**RURALS** > RURAL
**RURBAN** *adj* part country,
part urban
**RURP** *n* very small piton
**RURPS** > RURP
**RURU** *another name
for* > MOPOKE
**RURUS** > RURU
**RUSA** *n* type of deer with a
mane
**RUSALKA** *n* water nymph
or spirit
**RUSALKAS** > RUSALKA
**RUSAS** > RUSA
**RUSCUS** *n* type of shrub
**RUSCUSES** > RUSCUS
**RUSE** *n* stratagem or trick
**RUSES** > RUSE
**RUSH** *vb* move or do very
quickly ▷ *n* sudden quick
or violent movement ▷ *adj*
done with speed, hasty
**RUSHED** > RUSH
**RUSHEE** *n* someone
interested in gaining
fraternity or sorority
membership
**RUSHEES** > RUSHEE
**RUSHEN** *adj* made of rushes
**RUSHER** > RUSH
**RUSHERS** > RUSH
**RUSHES** *pl n* (in film-
making) the initial prints
of a scene or scenes before
editing, usually prepared
daily
**RUSHIER** > RUSHY
**RUSHIEST** > RUSHY
**RUSHINESS** > RUSHY
**RUSHING** > RUSH
**RUSHINGS** > RUSH
**RUSHLIGHT** *n* narrow
candle, formerly in use,
made of the pith of various
types of rush dipped in
tallow
**RUSHLIKE** > RUSH
**RUSHY** *adj* full of rushes
**RUSINE** *adj* of or relating to
rusa deer
**RUSK** *n* hard brown crisp
biscuit, used esp for

feeding babies
**RUSKS** > RUSK
**RUSMA** *n* Turkish depilatory
**RUSMAS** > RUSMA
**RUSSE** as in *charlotte russe*
cold dessert made from
whipped cream, custard,
etc, surrounded by sponge
fingers
**RUSSEL** *n* type of woollen
fabric
**RUSSELS** > RUSSEL
**RUSSET** *adj* reddish-brown
▷ *n* apple with rough
reddish-brown skin ▷ *vb*
become russet-coloured
**RUSSETED** > RUSSET
**RUSSETING** > RUSSET
**RUSSETS** > RUSSET
**RUSSETY** > RUSSET
**RUSSIA** *n* Russia leather
**RUSSIAS** > RUSSIA
**RUSSIFIED** > RUSSIFY
**RUSSIFIES** > RUSSIFY
**RUSSIFY** *vb* cause to
become Russian in
character
**RUSSULA** *n* any fungus of
the large basidiomycetous
genus *Russula*, of typical
toadstool shape and often
brightly coloured
**RUSSULAE** > RUSSULA
**RUSSULAS** > RUSSULA
**RUST** *n* reddish-brown
coating formed on iron etc
that has been exposed to
moisture ▷ *adj* reddish-
brown ▷ *vb* become
coated with rust
**RUSTABLE** *adj* liable to rust
**RUSTED** > RUST
**RUSTIC** *adj* of or
resembling country people
▷ *n* person from the
country
**RUSTICAL** *n* rustic
**RUSTICALS** > RUSTICAL
**RUSTICANA** *pl n* objects,
such as agricultural
implements, garden
furniture, etc, relating to
the countryside or made in
imitation of rustic styles
**RUSTICATE** *vb* banish
temporarily from
university as a
punishment
**RUSTICIAL** *made-up variant
of* > RUSTIC
**RUSTICISE** *same
as* > RUSTICIZE
**RUSTICISM** > RUSTIC
**RUSTICITY** > RUSTIC
**RUSTICIZE** *vb* make rustic
**RUSTICLY** > RUSTIC
**RUSTICS** > RUSTIC
**RUSTIER** > RUSTY
**RUSTIEST** > RUSTY
**RUSTILY** > RUSTY
**RUSTINESS** > RUSTY
**RUSTING** > RUST
**RUSTINGS** > RUST
**RUSTLE** *n* (make) a low

whispering sound ▷ *vb*
steal (cattle)
**RUSTLED** > RUSTLE
**RUSTLER** *n* cattle thief
**RUSTLERS** > RUSTLER
**RUSTLES** > RUSTLE
**RUSTLESS** > RUST
**RUSTLING** > RUSTLE
**RUSTLINGS** > RUSTLE
**RUSTPROOF** *adj* treated
against rusting
**RUSTRE** *n* (in heraldry)
lozenge with a round hole
in the middle showing the
background colour
**RUSTRED** > RUSTRE
**RUSTRES** > RUSTRE
**RUSTS** > RUST
**RUSTY** *adj* coated with rust
**RUT** *n* furrow made by
wheels ▷ *vb* be in a period
of sexual excitability
**RUTABAGA** *n* Eurasian plant
with a bulbous edible
root which is used as a
vegetable and as cattle
fodder
**RUTABAGAS** > RUTABAGA
**RUTACEOUS** *adj* of, relating
to, or belonging to the
*Rutaceae*, a family of
tropical and temperate
flowering plants many
of which have aromatic
leaves. The family includes
rue and citrus trees
**RUTH** *n* pity
**RUTHENIC** *adj* of or
containing ruthenium,
esp in a high valency state
**RUTHENIUM** *n* rare hard
brittle white element
**RUTHFUL** *adj* full of or
causing sorrow or pity
**RUTHFULLY** > RUTHFUL
**RUTHLESS** *adj* pitiless,
merciless
**RUTHS** > RUTH
**RUTILANT** *adj* of a reddish
colour or glow
**RUTILATED** *adj* (of
minerals, esp quartz)
containing needles of
rutile
**RUTILE** *n* black, yellowish,
or reddish-brown mineral
**RUTILES** > RUTILE
**RUTIN** *n* bioflavonoid
found in various plants
including rue
**RUTINS** > RUTIN
**RUTS** > RUT
**RUTTED** > RUT
**RUTTER** *n* (in history) type
of cavalry soldier
**RUTTERS** > RUTTER
**RUTTIER** > RUTTY
**RUTTIEST** > RUTTY
**RUTTILY** > RUTTY
**RUTTINESS** > RUTTY
**RUTTING** > RUT
**RUTTINGS** > RUT
**RUTTISH** *adj* (of an animal)
in a condition of rut

**RUTTISHLY** > RUTTISH
**RUTTY** *adj* full of ruts or
holes
**RYA** *n* type of rug
originating in Scandinavia
**RYAL** *n* one of several old
coins
**RYALS** > RYAL
**RYAS** > RYA
**RYBAT** *n* polished stone
piece forming the side of a
window or door
**RYBATS** > RYBAT
**RYBAUDRYE** *archaic variant
of* > RIBALDRY
**RYE** *n* kind of grain used for
fodder and bread
**RYEBREAD** *n* any of various
breads made entirely or
partly from rye flour, often
with caraway seeds
**RYEBREADS** > RYEBREAD
**RYEFLOUR** *n* flour made
from rye
**RYEFLOURS** > RYEFLOUR
**RYEGRASS** *n* any of various
grasses of the genus
*Lolium* native to Europe, N
Africa, and Asia and widely
cultivated as forage crops
**RYEPECK** *n* punt-mooring
pole
**RYEPECKS** > RYEPECK
**RYES** > RYE
**RYFE** *archaic variant
of* > RIFE
**RYKE** *Scots variant
of* > REACH
**RYKED** > RYKE
**RYKES** > RYKE
**RYKING** > RYKE
**RYMME** *same as* > RIM
**RYMMED** > RYMME
**RYMMES** > RYMME
**RYMMING** > RYMME
**RYND** *n* (in milling) crossbar
piece forming part of the
support structure of the
upper millstone
**RYNDS** > RYND
**RYOKAN** *n* traditional
Japanese inn
**RYOKANS** > RYOKAN
**RYOT** *n* (in India) a peasant
or tenant farmer
**RYOTS** > RYOT
**RYOTWARI** *n* (in India)
system of land tenure in
which land taxes are paid
to the state
**RYOTWARIS** > RYOTWARI
**RYPE** *n* ptarmigan
**RYPECK** *same as* > RYEPECK
**RYPECKS** > RYPECK
**RYPER** > RYPE

# Ss

**SAB** *n* person engaged in direct action to prevent a targeted activity taking place ▷ *vb* take part in such action

**SABADILLA** *n* tropical American liliaceous plant

**SABAL** *n* variety of palm tree

**SABALS** > SABAL

**SABATON** *n* foot covering in suit of armour

**SABATONS** > SABATON

**SABAYON** *n* dessert or sweet sauce made with egg yolks, sugar, and wine beaten together over heat till thick

**SABAYONS** > SABAYON

**SABBAT** *n* midnight meeting of witches

**SABBATH** *n* period of rest

**SABBATHS** > SABBATH

**SABBATIC** *n* period of leave granted to university staff

**SABBATICS** > SABBATIC

**SABBATINE** *adj* of Saturday

**SABBATISE** *same as* > SABBATIZE

**SABBATISM** *n* sabbath observance

**SABBATIZE** *vb* observe as sabbath

**SABBATS** > SABBAT

**SABBED** > SAB

**SABBING** > SAB

**SABE** *n* very informal word meaning sense or savvy ▷ *vb* very informal word meaning know or savvy

**SABED** > SABE

**SABEING** > SABE

**SABELLA** *n* marine worm

**SABELLAS** > SABELLA

**SABER** *same as* > SABRE

**SABERED** > SABER

**SABERING** > SABER

**SABERLIKE** > SABER

**SABERS** > SABER

**SABES** > SABE

**SABIN** *n* unit of acoustic absorption equal to the absorption resulting from one square foot of a perfectly absorbing surface

**SABINE** *variant of* > SAVIN

**SABINES** > SABINE

**SABINS** > SABIN

**SABIR** *n* member of ancient Turkic people

**SABIRS** > SABIR

**SABKHA** *n* flat coastal plain with a salt crust, common in Arabia

**SABKHAH** *n* sabkha

**SABKHAHS** > SABKHAH

**SABKHAS** > SABKHA

**SABKHAT** *n* sabkha

**SABKHATS** > SABKHAT

**SABLE** *n* dark fur from a small weasel-like Arctic animal ▷ *adj* black

**SABLED** > SABLE

**SABLEFISH** *n* North American fish

**SABLES** > SABLE

**SABLING** > SABLE

**SABOT** *n* wooden shoe traditionally worn by peasants in France

**SABOTAGE** *n* intentional damage done to machinery, systems, etc ▷ *vb* damage intentionally

**SABOTAGED** > SABOTAGE

**SABOTAGES** > SABOTAGE

**SABOTEUR** *n* person who commits sabotage

**SABOTEURS** > SABOTEUR

**SABOTIER** *n* wearer of wooden clogs

**SABOTIERS** > SABOTIER

**SABOTS** > SABOT

**SABRA** *n* native-born Israeli Jew

**SABRAS** > SABRA

**SABRE** *n* curved cavalry sword ▷ *vb* injure or kill with a sabre

**SABRED** > SABRE

**SABRES** > SABRE

**SABREUR** *n* person wielding sabre

**SABREURS** > SABREUR

**SABRING** > SABRE

**SABS** > SAB

**SABULINE** *same as* > SABULOUS

**SABULOSE** *same as* > SABULOUS

**SABULOUS** *adj* like sand in texture

**SABURRA** *n* granular deposit

**SABURRAL** > SABURRA

**SABURRAS** > SABURRA

**SAC** *n* pouchlike structure in an animal or plant

**SACATON** *n* coarse grass of the southwestern US and Mexico, grown for hay and pasture

**SACATONS** > SACATON

**SACBUT** *n* medieval trombone

**SACBUTS** > SACBUT

**SACCADE** *n* movement of the eye when it makes a

sudden change of fixation, as in reading

**SACCADES** > SACCADE

**SACCADIC** > SACCADE

**SACCATE** *adj* in the form of a sac

**SACCHARIC** *as in saccharic acid* white soluble solid acid

**SACCHARIN** *n* artificial sweetener

**SACCHARUM** *n* cane sugar

**SACCIFORM** *adj* like a sac

**SACCOI** > SACCOS

**SACCOS** *n* bishop's garment in the Orthodox Church

**SACCOSES** > SACCOS

**SACCULAR** *adj* of or resembling a sac

**SACCULATE** *adj* of, relating to, or possessing a saccule, saccules, or a sacculus

**SACCULE** *n* small sac

**SACCULES** > SACCULE

**SACCULI** > SACCULUS

**SACCULUS** *same as* > SACCULE

**SACELLA** > SACELLUM

**SACELLUM** *n* tomb within a church

**SACHEM** *same as* > SAGAMORE

**SACHEMDOM** > SACHEM

**SACHEMIC** > SACHEM

**SACHEMS** > SACHEM

**SACHET** *n* small envelope or bag containing a single portion

**SACHETED** *adj* contained in a sachet

**SACHETS** > SACHET

**SACK** *n* large bag made of coarse material ▷ *vb* dismiss

SACKABLE *adj* of or denoting an offence, infraction of rules, etc, that is sufficiently serious to warrant dismissal from an employment

SACKAGE *n* act of sacking a place

SACKAGES > SACKAGE

SACKBUT *n* medieval form of trombone

SACKBUTS > SACKBUT

SACKCLOTH *n* coarse fabric used for sacks, formerly worn as a penance

SACKED > SACK

SACKER > SACK

SACKERS > SACK

SACKFUL > SACK

SACKFULS > SACKFUL

SACKING *n* rough woven material used for sacks

SACKINGS > SACKING

SACKLESS *adj* old word meaning innocent

SACKLIKE > SACK

SACKS > SACK

SACKSFUL > SACKFUL

SACLESS *adj* old word meaning unchallengeable

SACLIKE > SAC

SACQUE *same as* > SACK

SACQUES > SACQUE

SACRA > SACRUM

SACRAL *adj* of or associated with sacred rites ▷ *n* sacral vertebra

SACRALGIA *n* pain in sacrum

SACRALISE *same as* > SACRALIZE

SACRALIZE *vb* make sacred

SACRALS > SACRAL

SACRAMENT *n* ceremony of the Christian Church, esp Communion

SACRARIA > SACRARIUM

SACRARIAL > SACRARIUM

SACRARIUM *n* sanctuary of a church

SACRED *adj* holy

SACREDLY > SACRED

SACRIFICE *n* giving something up ▷ *vb* offer as a sacrifice

SACRIFIDE *vb* old form of sacrifice

SACRIFIED > SACRIFY

SACRIFIES > SACRIFY

SACRIFY *vb* old form of sacrifice

SACRILEGE *n* misuse or desecration of something sacred

SACRING *n* act or ritual of consecration, esp of the Eucharist or of a bishop

SACRINGS > SACRING

SACRIST *same as* > SACRISTAN

SACRISTAN *n* person in charge of the contents of a church

SACRISTS > SACRIST

SACRISTY *n* room in a church where sacred objects are kept

SACRUM *n* wedge-shaped bone at the base of the spine

SACRUMS > SACRUM

SACS > SAC

SAD *adj* sorrowful, unhappy ▷ *vb* New Zealand word meaning express sadness or displeasure strongly

SADDEN *vb* make (someone) sad

SADDENED > SADDEN

SADDENING > SADDEN

SADDENS > SADDEN

SADDER > SAD

SADDEST > SAD

SADDHU *same as* > SADHU

SADDHUS > SADDHU

SADDISH > SAD

SADDLE *n* rider's seat on a horse or bicycle ▷ *vb* put a saddle on (a horse)

SADDLEBAG *n* pouch or small bag attached to the saddle of a horse, bicycle, or motorcycle

SADDLEBOW *n* pommel of a saddle

SADDLED > SADDLE

SADDLER *n* maker or seller of saddles

SADDLERS > SADDLER

SADDLERY *n* saddles and harness for horses collectively

SADDLES > SADDLE

SADDLING > SADDLE

SADDO *vb* make sad ▷ *n* socially inadequate or pathetic person

SADDOS > SADDO

SADE *same as* > SADHE

SADES > SADE

SADHANA *n* one of a number of spiritual practices or disciplines which lead to perfection, these being contemplation, asceticism, worship of a god, and correct living

SADHANAS > SADHANA

SADHE *n* 18th letter in the Hebrew alphabet

SADHES > SADHE

SADHU *n* Hindu wandering holy man

SADHUS > SADHU

SADI *variant of* > SADHE

SADIRON *n* heavy iron pointed at both ends, for pressing clothes

SADIRONS > SADIRON

SADIS > SADI

SADISM *n* gaining of (sexual) pleasure from inflicting pain

SADISMS > SADISM

SADIST > SADISM

SADISTIC > SADISM

SADISTS > SADISM

SADLY > SAD

SADNESS > SAD

SADNESSES > SAD

SADO *variant of* > CHADO

SADOS > SADO

SADZA *n* southern African porridge

SADZAS > SADZA

SAE *Scot word for* > SO

SAECULUM *n* age in astronomy

SAECULUMS > SAECULUM

SAETER *n* upland pasture in Norway

SAETERS > SAETER

SAFARI *n* expedition to hunt or observe wild animals, esp in Africa ▷ *vb* go on safari

SAFARIED > SAFARI

SAFARIING > SAFARI

SAFARIS > SAFARI

SAFARIST *n* person on safari

SAFARISTS > SAFARIST

SAFE *adj* secure, protected ▷ *n* strong lockable container ▷ *vb* make safe

SAFED > SAFE

SAFEGUARD *vb* protect ▷ *n* protection

SAFELIGHT *n* light that can be used in a room in which photographic material is handled, transmitting only those colours to which a particular type of film, plate, or paper is relatively insensitive

SAFELY > SAFE

SAFENESS > SAFE

SAFER > SAFE

SAFES > SAFE

SAFEST > SAFE

SAFETIED > SAFETY

SAFETIES > SAFETY

SAFETY *n* state of being safe ▷ *vb* make safe

SAFETYING > SAFETY

SAFETYMAN *n* defensive player in American football

SAFETYMEN > SAFETYMAN

SAFFIAN *n* leather tanned with sumach and usually dyed a bright colour

SAFFIANS > SAFFIAN

SAFFLOWER *n* thistle-like plant with flowers used for dye and oil

SAFFRON *n* orange-coloured flavouring obtained from a crocus ▷ *adj* orange

SAFFRONED *adj* containing saffron

SAFFRONS > SAFFRON

SAFFRONY *adj* like saffron

SAFING > SAFE

SAFRANIN *same as* > SAFRANINE

SAFRANINE *n* any of a class of azine dyes, used for textiles and biological stains

SAFRANINS > SAFRANIN

SAFROL *n* oily liquid obtained from sassafras

SAFROLE *n* colourless or yellowish oily water-insoluble liquid

SAFROLES > SAFROLE

SAFROLS > SAFROL

SAFRONAL *n* oily liquid derived from saffron

SAFRONALS > SAFRONAL

SAFT *Scot word for* > SOFT

SAFTER > SAFT

SAFTEST > SAFT

SAG *vb* sink in the middle ▷ *n* droop

SAGA *n* legend of Norse heroes

SAGACIOUS *adj* wise

SAGACITY *n* foresight, discernment, or keen perception

SAGAMAN *n* person reciting Norse sagas

SAGAMEN > SAGAMAN

SAGAMORE *n* (among some Native Americans) a chief or eminent man

SAGAMORES > SAGAMORE

SAGANASH *n* Algonquian term for an Englishman

SAGAPENUM *n* resin formerly used as drug

SAGAS > SAGA

SAGATHIES > SAGATHY

SAGATHY *n* type of light fabric

SAGBUT *n* medieval trombone

SAGBUTS > SAGBUT

SAGE *n* very wise man ▷ *adj* wise

SAGEBRUSH *n* aromatic plant of West N America

SAGELY > SAGE

SAGENE *n* fishing net

SAGENES > SAGENE

SAGENESS > SAGE

SAGENITE *n* mineral found in crystal form

SAGENITES > SAGENITE

SAGENITIC > SAGENITE

SAGER > SAGE

SAGES > SAGE

SAGEST > SAGE

SAGGAR *n* clay box in which fragile ceramic wares are placed for protection during firing ▷ *vb* put in a saggar

SAGGARD *n* saggar

SAGGARDS > SAGGARD

SAGGARED > SAGGAR

SAGGARING > SAGGAR

SAGGARS > SAGGAR

SAGGED > SAG

SAGGER *same as* > SAGGAR

SAGGERED > SAGGER

SAGGERING > SAGGER

SAGGERS > SAGGER

SAGGIER > SAGGY

SAGGIEST > SAGGY

SAGGING > SAG

SAGGINGS > SAG

SAGGY *adj* tending to sag

**SAGIER** > SAGY
**SAGIEST** > SAGY
**SAGINATE** *vb* fatten livestock
**SAGINATED** > SAGINATE
**SAGINATES** > SAGINATE
**SAGITTA** *n* sine of an arc
**SAGITTAL** *adj* resembling an arrow
**SAGITTARY** *n* centaur
**SAGITTAS** > SAGITTA
**SAGITTATE** *adj* (esp of leaves) shaped like the head of an arrow
**SAGO** *n* starchy cereal from the powdered pith of the sago palm tree
**SAGOIN** *n* South American monkey
**SAGOINS** > SAGOIN
**SAGOS** > SAGO
**SAGOUIN** *n* South American monkey
**SAGOUINS** > SAGOUIN
**SAGRADA** as in *cascara sagrada* dried bark of the cascara buckthorn, used as a stimulant and laxative
**SAGS** > SAG
**SAGUARO** *n* giant cactus of desert regions of Arizona, S California, and Mexico
**SAGUAROS** > SAGUARO
**SAGUIN** *n* South American monkey
**SAGUINS** > SAGUIN
**SAGUM** *n* Roman soldier's cloak
**SAGY** *adj* like or containing sage
**SAHEB** *same as* > SAHIB
**SAHEBS** > SAHEB
**SAHIB** *n* Indian term of address placed after a man's name as a mark of respect
**SAHIBA** *n* respectful Indian term of address for woman
**SAHIBAH** *n* sahiba
**SAHIBAHS** > SAHIBAH
**SAHIBAS** > SAHIBA
**SAHIBS** > SAHIB
**SAHIWAL** *n* breed of cattle in India
**SAHIWALS** > SAHIWAL
**SAHUARO** *same as* > SAGUARO
**SAHUAROS** > SAHUARO
**SAI** *n* South American monkey
**SAIBLING** *n* freshwater fish
**SAIBLINGS** > SAIBLING
**SAIC** *n* boat of eastern Mediterranean
**SAICE** *same as* > SYCE
**SAICES** > SAICE
**SAICK** *n* boat of eastern Mediterranean
**SAICKS** > SAICK
**SAICS** > SAIC
**SAID** *same as* > SAYYID
**SAIDEST** > SAY
**SAIDS** > SAID
**SAIDST** > SAY

**SAIGA** *n* either of two antelopes of the plains of central Asia
**SAIGAS** > SAIGA
**SAIKEI** *n* Japanese ornamental miniature landscape
**SAIKEIS** > SAIKEI
**SAIKLESS** *old Scots word for* > INNOCENT
**SAIL** *n* sheet of fabric stretched to catch the wind for propelling a sailing boat ▷ *vb* travel by water
**SAILABLE** > SAIL
**SAILBOARD** *n* board with a mast and single sail, used for windsurfing
**SAILBOAT** *n* boat propelled chiefly by sail
**SAILBOATS** > SAILBOAT
**SAILCLOTH** *n* fabric for making sails
**SAILED** > SAIL
**SAILER** *n* vessel, esp one equipped with sails, with specified sailing characteristics
**SAILERS** > SAILER
**SAILFISH** *n* large tropical game fish, with a long sail-like fin on its back
**SAILING** *n* practice, art, or technique of sailing a vessel
**SAILINGS** > SAILING
**SAILLESS** > SAIL
**SAILMAKER** *n* person who makes sails
**SAILOR** *n* member of a ship's crew
**SAILORING** *n* activity of working as sailor
**SAILORLY** > SAILOR
**SAILORS** > SAILOR
**SAILPLANE** *n* high-performance glider
**SAILROOM** *n* space on ship for storing sails
**SAILROOMS** > SAILROOM
**SAILS** > SAIL
**SAIM** *Scots word for* > LARD
**SAIMIN** *n* Hawaiian dish of noodles
**SAIMINS** > SAIMIN
**SAIMIRI** *n* South American monkey
**SAIMIRIS** > SAIMIRI
**SAIMS** > SAIM
**SAIN** *vb* make the sign of the cross over so as to bless or protect from evil or sin
**SAINE** *vb* old form of say
**SAINED** > SAIN
**SAINFOIN** *n* Eurasian plant with pink flowers, widely grown as feed for grazing farm animals
**SAINFOINS** > SAINFOIN
**SAINING** > SAIN
**SAINS** > SAIN
**SAINT** *n* person venerated after death as specially

holy ▷ *vb* canonize
**SAINTDOM** > SAINT
**SAINTDOMS** > SAINT
**SAINTED** *adj* formally recognized by a Christian Church as a saint
**SAINTESS** *n* female saint
**SAINTFOIN** *n* sainfoin
**SAINTHOOD** *n* state or character of being a saint
**SAINTING** > SAINT
**SAINTISH** > SAINT
**SAINTISM** *n* quality of being saint
**SAINTISMS** > SAINTISM
**SAINTLESS** > SAINT
**SAINTLIER** > SAINTLY
**SAINTLIKE** > SAINT
**SAINTLILY** > SAINTLY
**SAINTLING** *n* little saint
**SAINTLY** *adj* behaving in a very good, patient, or holy way
**SAINTS** > SAINT
**SAINTSHIP** > SAINT
**SAIQUE** *n* boat in eastern Mediterranean
**SAIQUES** > SAIQUE
**SAIR** *Scot word for* > SORE
**SAIRED** > SAIR
**SAIRER** > SAIR
**SAIREST** > SAIR
**SAIRING** > SAIR
**SAIRS** > SAIR
**SAIS** > SAI
**SAIST** > SAY
**SAITH** *form of the present tense (indicative mood) of* > SAY
**SAITHE** *n* dark-coloured food fish found in northern seas
**SAITHES** > SAITHE
**SAITHS** > SAITH
**SAIYID** *n* Muslim descended from Mohammed's grandson
**SAIYIDS** > SAIYID
**SAJOU** *n* South American monkey
**SAJOUS** > SAJOU
**SAKAI** *n* Malaysian aborigine
**SAKAIS** > SAKAI
**SAKE** *n* benefit
**SAKER** *n* large falcon of E Europe and central Asia
**SAKERET** *n* male saker
**SAKERETS** > SAKERET
**SAKERS** > SAKER
**SAKES** > SAKE
**SAKI** *same as* > SAKE
**SAKIA** *n* water wheel in Middle East
**SAKIAS** > SAKIA
**SAKIEH** *n* water wheel in Middle East
**SAKIEHS** > SAKIEH
**SAKIS** > SAKI
**SAKIYEH** *n* water wheel in Middle East
**SAKIYEHS** > SAKIYEH
**SAKKOI** > SAKKOS
**SAKKOS** *n* bishop's garment

in Orthodox Church
**SAKKOSES** > SAKKOS
**SAKSAUL** *n* Asian tree
**SAKSAULS** > SAKSAUL
**SAL** *pharmacological term for* > SALT
**SALAAM** *n* low bow of greeting among Muslims ▷ *vb* make a salaam
**SALAAMED** > SALAAM
**SALAAMING** > SALAAM
**SALAAMS** > SALAAM
**SALABLE** *same as* > SALEABLE
**SALABLY** > SALEABLY
**SALACIOUS** *adj* excessively concerned with sex
**SALACITY** *n* excessive interest in sex
**SALAD** *n* dish of raw vegetables, eaten as a meal or part of a meal
**SALADANG** *n* variety of ox
**SALADANGS** > SALADANG
**SALADE** *same as* > SALLET
**SALADES** > SALADE
**SALADING** *n* ingredients for salad
**SALADINGS** > SALADING
**SALADS** > SALAD
**SALAL** *n* North American shrub
**SALALS** > SALAL
**SALAMI** *n* highly spiced sausage
**SALAMIS** > SALAMI
**SALAMON** *n* word used in old oaths
**SALAMONS** > SALAMON
**SALANGANE** *n* Asian swift
**SALARIAT** *n* salary-earning class
**SALARIATS** > SALARIAT
**SALARIED** *adj* earning or providing a salary
**SALARIES** > SALARY
**SALARY** *n* fixed regular payment, usu monthly, to an employee ▷ *vb* pay a salary to
**SALARYING** > SALARY
**SALARYMAN** *n* (in Japan) an office worker
**SALARYMEN** > SALARYMAN
**SALBAND** *n* coating of mineral
**SALBANDS** > SALBAND
**SALCHOW** *n* type of figure-skating jump
**SALCHOWS** > SALCHOW
**SALE** *n* exchange of goods for money
**SALEABLE** *adj* fit or likely to be sold
**SALEABLY** > SALEABLE
**SALEP** *n* dried ground starchy tubers of various orchids, used for food and formerly as drugs
**SALEPS** > SALEP
**SALERATUS** *n* sodium bicarbonate when used in baking powder
**SALERING** *n* enclosed area

for livestock at market
**SALERINGS** > SALERING
**SALEROOM** *n* place where
goods are sold by auction
**SALEROOMS** > SALEROOM
**SALES** > SALE
**SALESGIRL** *n* person who
sells goods
**SALESLADY** *n* person who
sells goods
**SALESMAN** *n* person who
sells goods
**SALESMEN** > SALESMAN
**SALESROOM** *n* room in
which merchandise on
sale is displayed
**SALET** *same as* > SALLET
**SALETS** > SALET
**SALEWD** > SALUE
**SALEYARD** *n* area with pens
for holding animals before
auction
**SALEYARDS** > SALEYARD
**SALFERN** *n* plant of borage
family
**SALFERNS** > SALFERN
**SALIAUNCE** *n* old word
meaning onslaught
**SALIC** *adj* (of rocks and
minerals) having a high
content of silica and
alumina
**SALICES** > SALIX
**SALICET** *n* soft-toned
organ stop
**SALICETA** > SALICETUM
**SALICETS** > SALICET
**SALICETUM** *n* plantation of
willows
**SALICIN** *n* colourless or
white crystalline water-
soluble glucoside
**SALICINE** *same as* > SALICIN
**SALICINES** > SALICINE
**SALICINS** > SALICIN
**SALICYLIC** as in *salicylic
acid* white crystalline
substance with a
sweet taste and a bitter
aftertaste
**SALIENCE** > SALIENT
**SALIENCES** > SALIENT
**SALIENCY** *n* quality of
being prominent
**SALIENT** *adj* prominent,
noticeable ⊳ *n* projecting
part of a front line
**SALIENTLY** > SALIENT
**SALIENTS** > SALIENT
**SALIFIED** > SALIFY
**SALIFIES** > SALIFY
**SALIFY** *vb* treat, mix with,
or cause to combine with
a salt
**SALIFYING** > SALIFY
**SALIGOT** *n* water chestnut
**SALIGOTS** > SALIGOT
**SALIMETER** *n* hydrometer
for measuring salt in a
solution
**SALIMETRY** > SALIMETER
**SALINA** *n* salt marsh, lake,
or spring
**SALINAS** > SALINA

**SALINE** *adj* containing salt
⊳ *n* solution of sodium
chloride and water
**SALINES** > SALINE
**SALINISE** *same
as* > SALINIZE
**SALINISED** > SALINISE
**SALINISES** > SALINISE
**SALINITY** > SALINE
**SALINIZE** *vb* treat with
salt
**SALINIZED** > SALINIZE
**SALINIZES** > SALINIZE
**SALIVA** *n* liquid that forms
in the mouth, spittle
**SALIVAL** > SALIVA
**SALIVARY** > SALIVA
**SALIVAS** > SALIVA
**SALIVATE** *vb* produce
saliva
**SALIVATED** > SALIVATE
**SALIVATES** > SALIVATE
**SALIVATOR** > SALIVATE
**SALIX** *n* plant or tree of
willow family
**SALL** *archaic form of* > SHALL
**SALLAD** *old spelling
of* > SALAD
**SALLADS** > SALLAD
**SALLAL** *n* North American
shrub
**SALLALS** > SALLAL
**SALLE** *n* hall
**SALLEE** *n* SE Australian
eucalyptus with a pale
grey bark
**SALLEES** > SALLEE
**SALLES** > SALLE
**SALLET** *n* light round
helmet extending over the
back of the neck
**SALLETS** > SALLET
**SALLIED** > SALLY
**SALLIER** > SALLY
**SALLIERS** > SALLY
**SALLIES** > SALLY
**SALLOW** *adj* of an unhealthy
pale or yellowish colour
⊳ *vb* make sallow ⊳ *n* any
of several small willow
trees
**SALLOWED** > SALLOW
**SALLOWER** > SALLOW
**SALLOWEST** > SALLOW
**SALLOWING** > SALLOW
**SALLOWISH** > SALLOW
**SALLOWLY** > SALLOW
**SALLOWS** > SALLOW
**SALLOWY** > SALLOW
**SALLY** *n* violent excursion
⊳ *vb* set or rush out
**SALLYING** > SALLY
**SALLYPORT** *n* opening in a
fortified place from which
troops may make a sally
**SALMI** *n* ragout of game
stewed in a rich brown
sauce
**SALMIS** *same as* > SALMI
**SALMON** *n* large fish with
orange-pink flesh valued
as food ⊳ *adj* orange-pink
**SALMONET** *n* young salmon
**SALMONETS** > SALMONET

**SALMONID** *n* any fish of the
family *Salmonidae*
**SALMONIDS** > SALMONID
**SALMONOID** *adj* belonging
to the order of soft-finned
teleost fishes that includes
the salmon, whitefish,
grayling, and char ⊳ *n* any
of these fish
**SALMONS** > SALMON
**SALOL** *n* white sparingly
soluble crystalline
compound with a slight
aromatic odour, used as a
preservative and to absorb
light in sun-tan lotions,
plastics, etc
**SALOLS** > SALOL
**SALOMETER** *n* instrument
for measuring salt in
solution
**SALON** *n* commercial
premises of a hairdresser,
beautician, etc
**SALONS** > SALON
**SALOON** *n* closed car with
four or more seats
**SALOONS** > SALOON
**SALOOP** *n* infusion of
aromatic herbs or other
plant parts formerly used
as a tonic or cure
**SALOOPS** > SALOOP
**SALOP** *variant of* > SALOOP
**SALOPIAN** > SALOOP
**SALOPS** > SALOP
**SALP** *n* minute animal
floating in sea
**SALPA** *n* any of various
minute floating animals of
warm oceans
**SALPAE** > SALPA
**SALPAS** > SALPA
**SALPIAN** *n* minute animal
floating in sea
**SALPIANS** > SALPIAN
**SALPICON** *n* mixture of
chopped fish, meat, or
vegetables in a sauce
**SALPICONS** > SALPICON
**SALPID** *n* minute animal
floating in sea
**SALPIDS** > SALPID
**SALPIFORM** > SALPA
**SALPINGES** > SALPINX
**SALPINX** *n* Fallopian tube
or Eustachian tube
**SALPINXES** > SALPINX
**SALPS** > SALP
**SALS** > SAL
**SALSA** *n* lively Puerto Rican
dance ⊳ *vb* dance the
salsa
**SALSAED** > SALSA
**SALSAING** > SALSA
**SALSAS** > SALSA
**SALSE** *n* volcano expelling
mud
**SALSES** > SALSE
**SALSIFIES** > SALSIFY
**SALSIFY** *n* Mediterranean
plant with a long white
edible root
**SALSILLA** *n* tropical

American vine
**SALSILLAS** > SALSILLA
**SALT** *n* white crystalline
substance used to season
food ⊳ *vb* season or
preserve with salt
**SALTANDO** *n* staccato piece
of violin playing
**SALTANT** *adj* (of an
organism) differing from
others of its species
because of a saltation ⊳ *n*
saltant organism
**SALTANTS** > SALTANT
**SALTATE** *vb* go through
saltation
**SALTATED** > SALTATE
**SALTATES** > SALTATE
**SALTATING** > SALTATE
**SALTATION** *n* abrupt
variation in the
appearance of an
organism, usu caused by
genetic mutation
**SALTATO** *n* saltando
**SALTATORY** *adj* specialized
for jumping
**SALTBOX** *n* box for salt with
a sloping lid
**SALTBOXES** > SALTBOX
**SALTBUSH** *n* shrub that
grows in alkaline desert
regions
**SALTCAT** *n* salty medicine
for pigeons
**SALTCATS** > SALTCAT
**SALTCHUCK** *n* any body of
salt water
**SALTED** *adj* seasoned,
preserved, or treated with
salt
**SALTER** *n* person who deals
in or manufactures salt
**SALTERN** *n* place where salt
is obtained from pools of
evaporated sea water
**SALTERNS** > SALTERN
**SALTERS** > SALTER
**SALTEST** > SALT
**SALTFISH** *n* salted cod
**SALTIE** *n* saltwater
crocodile
**SALTIER** *variant
of* > SALTIRE
**SALTIERS** > SALTIER
**SALTIES** > SALTIE
**SALTIEST** > SALTY
**SALTILY** > SALTY
**SALTINE** *n* salty biscuit
**SALTINES** > SALTINE
**SALTINESS** > SALTY
**SALTING** *n* area of
low ground regularly
inundated with salt water
**SALTINGS** > SALTING
**SALTIRE** *n* diagonal cross
on a shield
**SALTIRES** > SALTIRE
**SALTISH** > SALT
**SALTISHLY** > SALT
**SALTLESS** > SALT
**SALTLIKE** > SALT
**SALTLY** > SALT
**SALTNESS** > SALT

**SALTO** n daring jump ▷ vb perform a daring jump
**SALTOED** > SALTO
**SALTOING** > SALTO
**SALTOS** > SALTO
**SALTPAN** n shallow basin containing salt, gypsum, etc, that was deposited from an evaporated salt lake
**SALTPANS** > SALTPAN
**SALTPETER** same as > SALTPETRE
**SALTPETRE** n compound used in gunpowder and as a preservative
**SALTS** > SALT
**SALTUS** n break in the continuity of a sequence, esp the omission of a necessary step in a logical argument
**SALTUSES** > SALTUS
**SALTWATER** adj living in the sea
**SALTWORK** n place where salt is refined
**SALTWORKS** n place, building, or factory where salt is produced
**SALTWORT** n any of several chenopodiaceous plants with prickly leaves, striped stems, and small green flowers
**SALTWORTS** > SALTWORT
**SALTY** adj of, tasting of, or containing salt
**SALUBRITY** n quality of being favourable to health or wholesome
**SALUE** vb old word meaning salute
**SALUED** > SALUE
**SALUES** > SALUE
**SALUING** > SALUE
**SALUKI** n type of tall hound with a smooth coat
**SALUKIS** > SALUKI
**SALURETIC** n drug that increases secretion of salt in urine
**SALUTARY** adj producing a beneficial result
**SALUTE** n motion of the arm as a formal military sign of respect ▷ vb greet with a salute
**SALUTED** > SALUTE
**SALUTER** > SALUTE
**SALUTERS** > SALUTE
**SALUTES** > SALUTE
**SALUTING** > SALUTE
**SALVABLE** adj capable of or suitable for being saved or salvaged
**SALVABLY** > SALVABLE
**SALVAGE** n saving of a ship or other property from destruction ▷ vb save from destruction or waste
**SALVAGED** > SALVAGE
**SALVAGEE** n rope on sailing ship

**SALVAGEES** > SALVAGEE
**SALVAGER** > SALVAGE
**SALVAGERS** > SALVAGE
**SALVAGES** > SALVAGE
**SALVAGING** > SALVAGE
**SALVARSAN** n old medicine containing arsenic
**SALVATION** n fact or state of being saved from harm or the consequences of sin
**SALVATORY** n place for storing something safely
**SALVE** n healing or soothing ointment ▷ vb soothe or appease
**SALVED** > SALVE
**SALVER** same as > SALVOR
**SALVERS** > SALVER
**SALVES** > SALVE
**SALVETE** n Latin greeting
**SALVETES** > SALVETE
**SALVIA** n plant with blue or red flowers
**SALVIAS** > SALVIA
**SALVIFIC** adj acting to salve
**SALVING** > SALVE
**SALVINGS** > SALVE
**SALVO** n simultaneous discharge of guns etc ▷ vb attack with a salvo
**SALVOED** > SALVO
**SALVOES** > SALVO
**SALVOING** > SALVO
**SALVOR** n person instrumental in salvaging a vessel or its cargo
**SALVORS** > SALVOR
**SALVOS** > SALVO
**SALWAR** as in salwar kameez long tunic worn over a pair of baggy trousers, usually worn by women, esp in Pakistan
**SAM** vb collect
**SAMA** n Japanese title of respect
**SAMAAN** n South American tree
**SAMAANS** > SAMAAN
**SAMADHI** n state of deep meditative contemplation which leads to higher consciousness
**SAMADHIS** > SAMADHI
**SAMAN** n South American tree
**SAMANS** > SAMAN
**SAMARA** n dry indehiscent one-seeded fruit with a winglike extension to aid dispersal
**SAMARAS** > SAMARA
**SAMARITAN** n kindly person who helps another in distress
**SAMARIUM** n silvery metallic element
**SAMARIUMS** > SAMARIUM
**SAMAS** > SAMA
**SAMBA** n lively Brazilian dance ▷ vb perform such a dance
**SAMBAED** > SAMBA

**SAMBAING** > SAMBA
**SAMBAL** n Malaysian dish
**SAMBALS** > SAMBAL
**SAMBAR** n S Asian deer with three-tined antlers
**SAMBARS** > SAMBAR
**SAMBAS** > SAMBA
**SAMBHAR** n Indian dish
**SAMBHARS** > SAMBHAR
**SAMBHUR** n Asian deer
**SAMBHURS** > SAMBHUR
**SAMBO** n offensive word for a Black person
**SAMBOS** > SAMBO
**SAMBUCA** n Italian liqueur
**SAMBUCAS** > SAMBUCA
**SAMBUKE** n ancient Greek stringed instrument
**SAMBUKES** > SAMBUKE
**SAMBUR** same as > SAMBAR
**SAMBURS** > SAMBUR
**SAME** adj identical, not different, unchanged ▷ n something identical
**SAMECH** n letter in Hebrew alphabet
**SAMECHS** > SAMECH
**SAMEK** variant of > SAMEKH
**SAMEKH** n 15th letter in the Hebrew alphabet transliterated as s
**SAMEKHS** > SAMEKH
**SAMEKS** > SAMEK
**SAMEL** adj of brick, not sufficiently fired
**SAMELY** adj the same
**SAMEN** old Scots form of > SAME
**SAMENESS** n state or quality of being the same
**SAMES** > SAME
**SAMEY** adj monotonous
**SAMFOO** n style of casual dress worn by Chinese women, consisting of a waisted blouse and trousers
**SAMFOOS** > SAMFOO
**SAMFU** n Chinese female outfit
**SAMFUS** > SAMFU
**SAMIEL** same as > SIMOOM
**SAMIELS** > SAMIEL
**SAMIER** > SAMEY
**SAMIEST** > SAMEY
**SAMISEN** n Japanese plucked stringed instrument with a long neck, an unfretted fingerboard, and a rectangular soundbox
**SAMISENS** > SAMISEN
**SAMITE** n heavy fabric of silk, often woven with gold or silver threads, used in the Middle Ages for clothing
**SAMITES** > SAMITE
**SAMITHI** same as > SAMITI
**SAMITHIS** > SAMITHI
**SAMITI** n (in India) an association, esp one formed to organize political activity

**SAMITIS** > SAMITI
**SAMIZDAT** n (in the former Soviet Union) a system of secret printing and distribution of banned literature
**SAMIZDATS** > SAMIZDAT
**SAMLET** n young salmon
**SAMLETS** > SAMLET
**SAMLOR** n motor vehicle in Thailand
**SAMLORS** > SAMLOR
**SAMMED** > SAM
**SAMMIES** > SAMMY
**SAMMING** > SAM
**SAMMY** n (in South Africa) an Indian fruit and vegetable vendor who goes from house to house
**SAMNITIS** n poisonous plant mentioned by Spenser
**SAMOSA** n (in Indian cookery) a small fried triangular spiced meat or vegetable pasty
**SAMOSAS** > SAMOSA
**SAMOVAR** n Russian tea urn
**SAMOVARS** > SAMOVAR
**SAMOYED** n Siberian breed of dog of the spitz type, having a dense white or cream coat with a distinct ruff, and a tightly curled tail
**SAMOYEDS** > SAMOYED
**SAMP** n crushed maize used for porridge
**SAMPAN** n small boat with oars used in China
**SAMPANS** > SAMPAN
**SAMPHIRE** n plant found on rocks by the seashore
**SAMPHIRES** > SAMPHIRE
**SAMPI** n old Greek number character
**SAMPIRE** n samphire
**SAMPIRES** > SAMPIRE
**SAMPIS** > SAMPI
**SAMPLE** n part taken as representative of a whole ▷ vb take and test a sample of
**SAMPLED** > SAMPLE
**SAMPLER** n piece of embroidery showing the embroiderer's skill
**SAMPLERS** > SAMPLER
**SAMPLERY** n making of samplers
**SAMPLES** > SAMPLE
**SAMPLING** n process of selecting a random sample
**SAMPLINGS** > SAMPLING
**SAMPS** > SAMP
**SAMS** > SAM
**SAMSARA** n endless cycle of birth, death, and rebirth
**SAMSARAS** > SAMSARA
**SAMSHOO** n Chinese alcoholic drink
**SAMSHOOS** > SAMSHOO
**SAMSHU** n alcoholic drink from China that is made

from fermented rice and resembles sake

**SAMSHUS** > SAMSHU

**SAMURAI** n member of an ancient Japanese warrior caste

**SAMURAIS** > SAMURAI

**SAN** n sanatorium

**SANATIVE** less common word for > CURATIVE

**SANATORIA** pl n institutions for the care of chronically ill people

**SANATORY** adj healing

**SANBENITO** n yellow garment bearing a red cross, worn by penitent heretics in the Inquisition

**SANCAI** n glaze in Chinese pottery

**SANCAIS** > SANCAI

**SANCHO** n African stringed instrument

**SANCHOS** > SANCHO

**SANCTA** > SANCTUM

**SANCTIFY** vb make holy

**SANCTION** n permission, authorization ▷ vb allow, authorize

**SANCTIONS** > SANCTION

**SANCTITY** n sacredness, inviolability

**SANCTUARY** n holy place

**SANCTUM** n sacred place

**SANCTUMS** > SANCTUM

**SAND** n substance consisting of small grains of rock, esp on a beach or in a desert ▷ vb smooth with sandpaper

**SANDABLE** > SAND

**SANDAL** n light shoe consisting of a sole attached by straps ▷ vb put sandals on

**SANDALED** > SANDAL

**SANDALING** > SANDAL

**SANDALLED** > SANDAL

**SANDALS** > SANDAL

**SANDARAC** n either of two coniferous trees having hard fragrant dark wood

**SANDARACH** same as > SANDARAC

**SANDARACS** > SANDARAC

**SANDBAG** n bag filled with sand, used as protection against gunfire or flood water ▷ vb protect with sandbags

**SANDBAGS** > SANDBAG

**SANDBANK** n bank of sand below the surface of a river or sea

**SANDBANKS** > SANDBANK

**SANDBAR** n ridge of sand in a river or sea, often exposed at low tide

**SANDBARS** > SANDBAR

**SANDBLAST** n (clean with) a jet of sand blown from a nozzle under pressure ▷ vb clean or decorate (a surface) with a sandblast

**SANDBOX** n container on a railway locomotive from which sand is released onto the rails to assist the traction

**SANDBOXES** > SANDBOX

**SANDBOY** as in happy as a sandboy very happy or high-spirited

**SANDBOYS** > SANDBOY

**SANDBUR** n variety of wild grass

**SANDBURR** n variety of wild grass

**SANDBURRS** > SANDBURR

**SANDBURS** > SANDBUR

**SANDCRACK** n crack in horse's hoof

**SANDDAB** n type of small Pacific flatfish

**SANDDABS** > SANDDAB

**SANDED** > SAND

**SANDEK** n man who holds a baby being circumcised

**SANDEKS** > SANDEK

**SANDER** n power tool for smoothing surfaces

**SANDERS** > SANDER

**SANDERSES** > SANDER

**SANDFISH** n burrowing Pacific fish

**SANDFLIES** > SANDFLY

**SANDFLY** n any of various small mothlike dipterous flies: the bloodsucking females transmit diseases including leishmaniasis

**SANDGLASS** less common word for > HOURGLASS

**SANDHEAP** n heap of sand

**SANDHEAPS** > SANDHEAP

**SANDHI** n modification of the form or sound of a word under the influence of an adjacent word

**SANDHILL** n hill of sand

**SANDHILLS** > SANDHILL

**SANDHIS** > SANDHI

**SANDHOG** n person who works in underground or underwater construction projects

**SANDHOGS** > SANDHOG

**SANDIER** > SANDY

**SANDIEST** > SANDY

**SANDINESS** > SANDY

**SANDING** > SAND

**SANDINGS** > SAND

**SANDIVER** n scum forming on molten glass

**SANDIVERS** > SANDIVER

**SANDLESS** > SAND

**SANDLIKE** > SAND

**SANDLING** n sand eel

**SANDLINGS** > SANDLING

**SANDLOT** n area of vacant ground used by children for playing baseball and other games

**SANDLOTS** > SANDLOT

**SANDMAN** n (in folklore) a magical person supposed to put children to sleep by sprinkling sand in their

eyes

**SANDMEN** > SANDMAN

**SANDPAPER** n paper coated with sand for smoothing a surface ▷ vb smooth with sandpaper

**SANDPEEP** n small sandpiper

**SANDPEEPS** > SANDPEEP

**SANDPILE** n pile of sand

**SANDPILES** > SANDPILE

**SANDPIPER** n shore bird with a long bill and slender legs

**SANDPIT** n shallow pit or container holding sand for children to play in

**SANDPITS** > SANDPIT

**SANDPUMP** n pump for wet sand

**SANDPUMPS** > SANDPUMP

**SANDS** > SAND

**SANDSHOE** n light canvas shoe with a rubber sole

**SANDSHOES** > SANDSHOE

**SANDSOAP** n gritty general-purpose soap

**SANDSOAPS** > SANDSOAP

**SANDSPOUT** n sand sucked into air by whirlwind

**SANDSPUR** n American wild grass

**SANDSPURS** > SANDSPUR

**SANDSTONE** n rock composed of sand

**SANDSTORM** n desert wind that whips up clouds of sand

**SANDWICH** n two slices of bread with a layer of food between ▷ vb insert between two other things

**SANDWORM** n any of various polychaete worms that live in burrows on sandy shores, esp the lugworm

**SANDWORMS** > SANDWORM

**SANDWORT** n any of numerous caryophyllaceous plants which grow in dense tufts on sandy soil and have white or pink solitary flowers

**SANDWORTS** > SANDWORT

**SANDY** adj covered with sand

**SANE** adj of sound mind ▷ vb heal

**SANED** > SANE

**SANELY** > SANE

**SANENESS** > SANE

**SANER** > SANE

**SANES** > SANE

**SANEST** > SANE

**SANG** Scots word for > SONG

**SANGA** n Ethiopian ox

**SANGAR** n breastwork of stone or sods

**SANGAREE** n spiced drink similar to sangria

**SANGAREES** > SANGAREE

**SANGARS** > SANGAR

**SANGAS** > SANGA

**SANGER** n sandwich

**SANGERS** > SANGER

**SANGFROID** n composure or self-possession

**SANGH** n Indian union or association

**SANGHAT** n fellowship or assembly, esp a local Sikh community or congregation

**SANGHATS** > SANGHAT

**SANGHS** > SANGH

**SANGLIER** n wild boar

**SANGLIERS** > SANGLIER

**SANGO** same as > SANGER

**SANGOMA** n witch doctor or herbalist

**SANGOMAS** > SANGOMA

**SANGOS** > SANGO

**SANGRIA** n Spanish drink of red wine and fruit

**SANGRIAS** > SANGRIA

**SANGS** > SANG

**SANGUIFY** vb turn into blood

**SANGUINE** adj cheerful, optimistic ▷ n red pencil containing ferric oxide, used in drawing

**SANGUINED** > SANGUINE

**SANGUINES** > SANGUINE

**SANICLE** n type of plant with clusters of small white flowers and oval fruits with hooked bristles

**SANICLES** > SANICLE

**SANIDINE** n alkali feldspar that is found in lavas

**SANIDINES** > SANIDINE

**SANIES** n thin greenish foul-smelling discharge from a wound, etc, containing pus and blood

**SANIFIED** > SANIFY

**SANIFIES** > SANIFY

**SANIFY** vb make healthy

**SANIFYING** > SANIFY

**SANING** > SANE

**SANIOUS** > SANIES

**SANITARIA** variant of > SANATORIA

**SANITARY** adj promoting health by getting rid of dirt and germs

**SANITATE** vb make sanitary

**SANITATED** > SANITATE

**SANITATES** > SANITATE

**SANITIES** > SANITY

**SANITISE** same as > SANITIZE

**SANITISED** > SANITISE

**SANITISER** > SANITISE

**SANITISES** > SANITISE

**SANITIZE** vb omit unpleasant details to make (news) more acceptable

**SANITIZED** > SANITIZE

**SANITIZER** > SANITIZE

**SANITIZES** > SANITIZE

**SANITORIA** variant of > SANATORIA

**SANITY** n state of having a

normal healthy mind
**SANJAK** n (in the Turkish Empire) a subdivision of a vilayet
**SANJAKS** > SANJAK
**SANK** > SINK
**SANKO** n African stringed instrument
**SANKOS** > SANKO
**SANNIE** Scots word for > SANDSHOE
**SANNIES** > SANNIE
**SANNOP** n Native American married man
**SANNOPS** > SANNOP
**SANNUP** n Native American married man
**SANNUPS** > SANNUP
**SANNYASI** n Brahman who having attained the fourth and last stage of life as a beggar will not be reborn, but will instead be absorbed into the Universal Soul
**SANNYASIN** same as > SANNYASI
**SANNYASIS** > SANNYASI
**SANPAN** n sampan
**SANPANS** > SANPAN
**SANPRO** n sanitary-protection products, collectively
**SANPROS** > SANPRO
**SANS** archaic word for > WITHOUT
**SANSA** n African musical instrument
**SANSAR** n name of a wind that blows in Iran
**SANSARS** > SANSAR
**SANSAS** > SANSA
**SANSEI** n American whose parents were Japanese immigrants
**SANSEIS** > SANSEI
**SANSERIF** n style of printer's typeface
**SANSERIFS** > SANSERIF
**SANT** n devout person in India
**SANTAL** n sandalwood
**SANTALIC** adj of sandalwood
**SANTALIN** n substance giving sandalwood its colour
**SANTALINS** > SANTALIN
**SANTALOL** n liquid from sandalwood used in perfume
**SANTALOLS** > SANTALOL
**SANTALS** > SANTAL
**SANTERA** n priestess of santeria
**SANTERAS** > SANTERA
**SANTERIA** n Caribbean religious cult
**SANTERIAS** > SANTERIA
**SANTERO** n priest of santeria
**SANTEROS** > SANTERO
**SANTIMI** > SANTIMS
**SANTIMS** n money unit in

Latvia
**SANTIMU** same as > SANTIMS
**SANTIR** n Middle Eastern stringed instrument
**SANTIRS** > SANTIR
**SANTO** n saint or representation of one
**SANTOL** n fruit from Southeast Asia
**SANTOLINA** n any plant of an evergreen Mediterranean genus grown for its silvery-grey felted foliage
**SANTOLS** > SANTOL
**SANTON** n French figurine
**SANTONICA** n oriental wormwood plant
**SANTONIN** n white crystalline soluble substance extracted from the dried flower heads of santonica
**SANTONINS** > SANTONIN
**SANTONS** > SANTON
**SANTOOR** same as > SANTIR
**SANTOORS** > SANTOOR
**SANTOS** > SANTO
**SANTOUR** n Middle Eastern stringed instrument
**SANTOURS** > SANTOUR
**SANTS** > SANT
**SANTUR** n Middle Eastern stringed instrument
**SANTURS** > SANTUR
**SANYASI** same as > SANNYASI
**SANYASIS** > SANNYASI
**SAOUARI** n tropical American tree
**SAOUARIS** > SAOUARI
**SAP** n moisture that circulates in plants ▷ vb undermine
**SAPAJOU** n capuchin monkey
**SAPAJOUS** > SAPAJOU
**SAPAN** n tropical tree
**SAPANS** > SAPAN
**SAPANWOOD** n small S Asian tree
**SAPEGO** n skin disease
**SAPEGOES** > SAPEGO
**SAPELE** n type of W African tree
**SAPELES** > SAPELE
**SAPFUL** adj full of sap
**SAPHEAD** n simpleton, idiot, or fool
**SAPHEADED** > SAPHEAD
**SAPHEADS** > SAPHEAD
**SAPHENA** n either of two large superficial veins of the legs
**SAPHENAE** > SAPHENA
**SAPHENAS** > SAPHENA
**SAPHENOUS** > SAPHENA
**SAPID** adj having a pleasant taste
**SAPIDITY** > SAPID
**SAPIDLESS** adj lacking flavour
**SAPIDNESS** > SAPID
**SAPIENCE** > SAPIENT

**SAPIENCES** > SAPIENT
**SAPIENCY** > SAPIENT
**SAPIENS** adj relating to or like modern human beings
**SAPIENT** adj wise, shrewd ▷ n wise person
**SAPIENTLY** > SAPIENT
**SAPIENTS** > SAPIENT
**SAPLESS** > SAP
**SAPLING** n young tree
**SAPLINGS** > SAPLING
**SAPODILLA** n large tropical American evergreen tree
**SAPOGENIN** n substance derived from saponin
**SAPONARIA** See > SOAPWORT
**SAPONATED** adj treated or combined with soap
**SAPONIFY** vb convert (a fat) into a soap by treatment with alkali
**SAPONIN** n any of a group of plant glycosides
**SAPONINE** n saponin
**SAPONINES** > SAPONINE
**SAPONINS** > SAPONIN
**SAPONITE** n type of clay mineral
**SAPONITES** > SAPONITE
**SAPOR** n quality in a substance that is perceived by the sense of taste
**SAPORIFIC** > SAPOR
**SAPOROUS** > SAPOR
**SAPORS** > SAPOR
**SAPOTA** same as > SAPODILLA
**SAPOTAS** > SAPOTA
**SAPOTE** n Central American tree
**SAPOTES** > SAPOTE
**SAPOUR** variant of > SAPOR
**SAPOURS** > SAPOUR
**SAPPAN** n tropical tree
**SAPPANS** > SAPPAN
**SAPPED** > SAP
**SAPPER** n soldier in an engineering unit
**SAPPERS** > SAPPER
**SAPPHIC** adj lesbian ▷ n verse written in a particular form
**SAPPHICS** > SAPPHIC
**SAPPHIRE** n blue precious stone ▷ adj deep blue
**SAPPHIRED** adj blue-coloured
**SAPPHIRES** > SAPPHIRE
**SAPPHISM** n lesbianism
**SAPPHISMS** > SAPPHISM
**SAPPHIST** n lesbian
**SAPPHISTS** > SAPPHIST
**SAPPIER** > SAPPY
**SAPPIEST** > SAPPY
**SAPPILY** > SAPPY
**SAPPINESS** > SAPPY
**SAPPING** > SAP
**SAPPLE** vb Scots word meaning wash in water
**SAPPLED** > SAPPLE
**SAPPLES** > SAPPLE
**SAPPLING** > SAPPLE
**SAPPY** adj (of plants) full of sap

**SAPRAEMIA** n blood poisoning caused by toxins of putrefactive bacteria
**SAPRAEMIC** > SAPRAEMIA
**SAPREMIA** American spelling of > SAPRAEMIA
**SAPREMIAS** > SAPREMIA
**SAPREMIC** > SAPREMIA
**SAPROBE** n organism that lives on decaying organisms
**SAPROBES** > SAPROBE
**SAPROBIAL** > SAPROBE
**SAPROBIC** > SAPROBE
**SAPROLITE** n deposit of earth, etc, formed by decomposition of rocks that has remained in its original site
**SAPROPEL** n unconsolidated sludge consisting of the decomposed remains of aquatic organisms at the bottoms of lakes and oceans
**SAPROPELS** > SAPROPEL
**SAPROZOIC** adj (of animals or plants) feeding on dead organic matter
**SAPS** > SAP
**SAPSAGO** n hard greenish Swiss cheese made with sour skimmed milk and coloured and flavoured with clover
**SAPSAGOS** > SAPSAGO
**SAPSUCKER** n either of two North American woodpeckers
**SAPUCAIA** n Brazilian tree
**SAPUCAIAS** > SAPUCAIA
**SAPWOOD** n soft wood, just beneath the bark in tree trunks, that consists of living tissue
**SAPWOODS** > SAPWOOD
**SAR** n marine fish ▷ vb Scots word meaning savour
**SARABAND** same as > SARABANDE
**SARABANDE** n slow stately Spanish dance
**SARABANDS** > SARABAND
**SARAFAN** n Russian woman's cloak
**SARAFANS** > SARAFAN
**SARAN** n any one of a class of thermoplastic resins
**SARANGI** n stringed instrument of India played with a bow
**SARANGIS** > SARANGI
**SARANS** > SARAN
**SARAPE** n serape
**SARAPES** > SARAPE
**SARBACANE** n type of blowpipe
**SARCASM** n (use of) bitter or wounding ironic language
**SARCASMS** > SARCASM
**SARCASTIC** adj full of or

showing sarcasm

**SARCENET** _n_ fine soft silk fabric formerly from Italy and used for clothing, ribbons, etc

**SARCENETS** > SARCENET

**SARCINA** _n_ type of bacterium

**SARCINAE** > SARCINA

**SARCINAS** > SARCINA

**SARCOCARP** _n_ fleshy mesocarp of such fruits as the peach or plum

**SARCODE** _n_ material making up living cell

**SARCODES** > SARCODE

**SARCODIC** > SARCODE

**SARCOID** _adj_ of, relating to, or resembling flesh ▷ _n_ tumour resembling a sarcoma

**SARCOIDS** > SARCOID

**SARCOLOGY** _n_ study of flesh

**SARCOMA** _n_ malignant tumour beginning in connective tissue

**SARCOMAS** > SARCOMA

**SARCOMATA** > SARCOMA

**SARCOMERE** _n_ any of the units that together comprise skeletal muscle

**SARCONET** _n_ type of silk

**SARCONETS** > SARCONET

**SARCOPTIC** _adj_ relating to mange

**SARCOSOME** _n_ energy-producing tissue in muscle

**SARCOUS** _adj_ (of tissue) muscular or fleshy

**SARD** _n_ orange, red, or brown variety of chalcedony, used as a gemstone

**SARDANA** _n_ Catalan dance

**SARDANAS** > SARDANA

**SARDAR** _n_ title used before the name of Sikh men

**SARDARS** > SARDAR

**SARDEL** _n_ small fish

**SARDELLE** _n_ small fish

**SARDELLES** > SARDELLE

**SARDELS** > SARDEL

**SARDINE** _n_ small fish of the herring family, usu preserved tightly packed in tins ▷ _vb_ cram together

**SARDINED** > SARDINE

**SARDINES** > SARDINE

**SARDINING** > SARDINE

**SARDIUS** _same as_ > SARD

**SARDIUSES** > SARDIUS

**SARDONIAN** _adj_ sardonic

**SARDONIC** _adj_ mocking or scornful

**SARDONYX** _n_ brown-and-white gemstone

**SARDS** > SARD

**SARED** > SAR

**SAREE** _same as_ > SARI

**SAREES** > SAREE

**SARGASSO** _same as_ > SARGASSUM

**SARGASSOS** > SARGASSO

**SARGASSUM** _n_ type of floating seaweed

**SARGE** _n_ sergeant

**SARGES** > SARGE

**SARGO** _same as_ > SARGUS

**SARGOS** _variant of_ > SARGUS

**SARGOSES** > SARGOS

**SARGUS** _n_ species of sea fish

**SARGUSES** > SARGUS

**SARI** _n_ long piece of cloth draped around the body and over one shoulder, worn by Hindu women

**SARIN** _n_ chemical used in warfare as a lethal nerve gas producing asphyxia

**SARING** > SAR

**SARINS** > SARIN

**SARIS** > SARI

**SARK** _n_ shirt or (formerly) chemise

**SARKIER** > SARKY

**SARKIEST** > SARKY

**SARKING** _n_ flat planking supporting the roof cladding of a building

**SARKINGS** > SARKING

**SARKS** > SARK

**SARKY** _adj_ sarcastic

**SARMENT** _n_ thin twig

**SARMENTA** > SARMENTUM

**SARMENTS** > SARMENT

**SARMENTUM** _n_ runner on plant

**SARMIE** _n_ sandwich

**SARMIES** > SARMIE

**SARNEY** _n_ sandwich

**SARNEYS** > SARNEY

**SARNIE** _n_ sandwich

**SARNIES** > SARNIE

**SAROD** _n_ Indian stringed musical instrument that may be played with a bow or plucked

**SARODE** _n_ Indian stringed instrument

**SARODES** > SARODE

**SARODIST** _n_ sarod player

**SARODISTS** > SARODIST

**SARODS** > SAROD

**SARONG** _n_ long piece of cloth tucked around the waist or under the armpits, worn esp in Malaysia

**SARONGS** > SARONG

**SARONIC** > SAROS

**SAROS** _n_ cycle of about 18 years 11 days in which eclipses of the sun and moon occur in the same sequence

**SAROSES** > SAROS

**SARPANCH** _n_ head of a panchayat

**SARRASIN** _n_ buckwheat

**SARRASINS** > SARRASIN

**SARRAZIN** _n_ buckwheat

**SARRAZINS** > SARRAZIN

**SARS** > SAR

**SARSAR** _same as_ > SANSAR

**SARSARS** > SARSAR

**SARSDEN** _n_ sarsen

**SARSDENS** > SARSDEN

**SARSEN** _n_ boulder of silicified sandstone found in large numbers in S England

**SARSENET** _same as_ > SARCENET

**SARSENETS** > SARSENET

**SARSENS** > SARSEN

**SARSNET** _n_ type of silk

**SARSNETS** > SARSNET

**SARTOR** _humorous or literary word for_ > TAILOR

**SARTORIAL** _adj_ of men's clothes or tailoring

**SARTORIAN** _adj_ of tailoring

**SARTORII** > SARTORIUS

**SARTORIUS** _n_ long ribbon-shaped muscle that aids in flexing the knee

**SARTORS** > SARTOR

**SARUS** _n_ Indian bird of crane family

**SARUSES** > SARUS

**SASARARA** _n_ scolding

**SASARARAS** > SASARARA

**SASER** _n_ device for amplifying ultrasound, working on a similar principle to a laser

**SASERS** > SASER

**SASH** _n_ decorative strip of cloth worn round the waist or over one shoulder ▷ _vb_ furnish with a sash, sashes, or sash windows

**SASHAY** _vb_ move or walk in a casual or a showy manner

**SASHAYED** > SASHAY

**SASHAYING** > SASHAY

**SASHAYS** > SASHAY

**SASHED** > SASH

**SASHES** > SASH

**SASHIMI** _n_ Japanese dish of thin fillets of raw fish

**SASHIMIS** > SASHIMI

**SASHING** > SASH

**SASHLESS** > SASH

**SASIN** _another name for_ > BLACKBUCK

**SASINE** _n_ granting of legal possession of feudal property

**SASINES** > SASINE

**SASINS** > SASIN

**SASKATOON** _n_ species of serviceberry of W Canada

**SASQUATCH** _n_ (in Canadian folklore) hairy beast or manlike monster said to leave huge footprints

**SASS** _n_ insolent or impudent talk or behaviour ▷ _vb_ talk or answer back in such a way

**SASSABIES** > SASSABY

**SASSABY** _n_ African antelope of grasslands and semideserts

**SASSAFRAS** _n_ American tree with aromatic bark used medicinally

**SASSARARA** _n_ scolding

**SASSE** _n_ old word meaning canal lock

**SASSED** > SASS

**SASSES** > SASS

**SASSIER** > SASSY

**SASSIES** > SASSY

**SASSIEST** > SASSY

**SASSILY** > SASSY

**SASSINESS** > SASSY

**SASSING** > SASS

**SASSOLIN** _n_ boric acid

**SASSOLINS** > SASSOLIN

**SASSOLITE** _n_ boric acid

**SASSWOOD** _same as_ > SASSY

**SASSWOODS** > SASSWOOD

**SASSY** _adj_ insolent, impertinent ▷ _n_ W African leguminous tree with poisonous bark

**SASSYWOOD** _n_ trial by ordeal in Liberia

**SASTRA** _same as_ > SHASTRA

**SASTRAS** > SASTRA

**SASTRUGA** _n_ one of a series of ridges on snow-covered plains, caused by the action of wind laden with ice particles

**SASTRUGI** > SASTRUGA

**SAT** > SIT

**SATAI** _same as_ > SATAY

**SATAIS** > SATAI

**SATANG** _n_ monetary unit of Thailand worth one hundredth of a baht

**SATANGS** > SATANG

**SATANIC** _adj_ of Satan

**SATANICAL** _same as_ > SATANIC

**SATANISM** _n_ worship of the devil

**SATANISMS** > SATANISM

**SATANIST** > SATANISM

**SATANISTS** > SATANISM

**SATANITY** _n_ quality of being satanic

**SATARA** _n_ type of cloth

**SATARAS** > SATARA

**SATAY** _n_ Indonesian and Malaysian dish consisting of pieces of chicken, pork, etc, grilled on skewers and served with peanut sauce

**SATAYS** > SATAY

**SATCHEL** _n_ bag, usu with a shoulder strap, for carrying books

**SATCHELED** _adj_ carrying a satchel

**SATCHELS** > SATCHEL

**SATE** _vb_ satisfy (a desire or appetite) fully

**SATED** > SATE

**SATEDNESS** > SATE

**SATEEN** _n_ glossy linen or cotton fabric, woven in such a way that it resembles satin

**SATEENS** > SATEEN

**SATELESS** _adj_ old word meaning insatiable

**SATELLITE** _n_ species of bacteria

**SATELLITE** _n_ man-made device orbiting in space ▷ _adj_ of or used in the

transmission of television signals from a satellite to the home ▷ *vb* transmit by communications satellite
**SATEM** *adj* denoting or belonging to a particular group of Indo-European languages
**SATES** > SATE
**SATI** *n* Indian widow suicide
**SATIABLE** *adj* capable of being satiated
**SATIABLY** > SATIABLE
**SATIATE** *vb* provide with more than enough, so as to disgust
**SATIATED** > SATIATE
**SATIATES** > SATIATE
**SATIATING** > SATIATE
**SATIATION** > SATIATE
**SATIETIES** > SATIETY
**SATIETY** *n* feeling of having had too much
**SATIN** *n* silky fabric with a glossy surface on one side ▷ *adj* like satin in texture ▷ *vb* cover with satin
**SATINED** > SATIN
**SATINET** *n* thin or imitation satin
**SATINETS** > SATINET
**SATINETTA** *n* thin satin
**SATINETTE** *same as* > SATINET
**SATING** > SATE
**SATINING** > SATIN
**SATINPOD** *n* honesty (the plant)
**SATINPODS** > SATINPOD
**SATINS** > SATIN
**SATINWOOD** *n* tropical tree yielding hard wood
**SATINY** > SATIN
**SATIRE** *n* use of ridicule to expose vice or folly
**SATIRES** > SATIRE
**SATIRIC** *same as* > SATIRICAL
**SATIRICAL** *adj* of, relating to, or containing satire
**SATIRISE** *same as* > SATIRIZE
**SATIRISED** > SATIRISE
**SATIRISER** > SATIRIZE
**SATIRISES** > SATIRISE
**SATIRIST** *n* writer of satire
**SATIRISTS** > SATIRIST
**SATIRIZE** *vb* ridicule by means of satire
**SATIRIZED** > SATIRIZE
**SATIRIZER** > SATIRIZE
**SATIRIZES** > SATIRIZE
**SATIS** > SATI
**SATISFICE** *vb* act in such a way as to satisfy the minimum requirements for achieving a particular result
**SATISFIED** > SATISFY
**SATISFIER** > SATISFY
**SATISFIES** > SATISFY
**SATISFY** *vb* please, content
**SATIVE** *adj* old word meaning cultivated
**SATORI** *n* state of sudden indescribable intuitive enlightenment
**SATORIS** > SATORI
**SATRAP** *n* (in ancient Persia) a provincial governor or subordinate ruler
**SATRAPAL** > SATRAP
**SATRAPIES** > SATRAPY
**SATRAPS** > SATRAP
**SATRAPY** *n* province, office, or period of rule of a satrap
**SATSUMA** *n* kind of small orange
**SATSUMAS** > SATSUMA
**SATURABLE** *adj* capable of being saturated
**SATURANT** *n* substance that causes a solution, etc, to be saturated ▷ *adj* (of a substance) causing saturation
**SATURANTS** > SATURANT
**SATURATE** *vb* soak thoroughly
**SATURATED** *adj* (of a solution or solvent) containing the maximum amount of solute that can normally be dissolved at a given temperature and pressure
**SATURATER** > SATURATE
**SATURATES** > SATURATE
**SATURATOR** > SATURATE
**SATURNIC** *adj* poisoned by lead
**SATURNIID** *n* any moth of the mainly tropical family *Saturniidae*, typically having large brightly coloured wings ▷ *adj* of, relating to, or belonging to the *Saturniidae*
**SATURNINE** *adj* gloomy in temperament or appearance
**SATURNISM** *n* lead poisoning
**SATURNIST** *n* old word meaning glum person
**SATYR** *n* woodland god, part man, part goat
**SATYRA** *n* female satyr
**SATYRAL** *n* mythical beast in heraldry
**SATYRALS** > SATYRAL
**SATYRAS** > SATYRA
**SATYRESS** *n* female satyr
**SATYRIC** > SATYR
**SATYRICAL** > SATYR
**SATYRID** *n* butterfly with typically brown or dark wings with paler markings
**SATYRIDS** > SATYRID
**SATYRISK** *n* small satyr
**SATYRISKS** > SATYRISK
**SATYRLIKE** > SATYR
**SATYRS** > SATYR
**SAU** *archaic past tense of* > SEE
**SAUBA** *n* South American ant
**SAUBAS** > SAUBA
**SAUCE** *n* liquid added to food to enhance flavour ▷ *vb* prepare (food) with sauce
**SAUCEBOAT** *n* gravy boat
**SAUCEBOX** *n* saucy person
**SAUCED** > SAUCE
**SAUCELESS** > SAUCE
**SAUCEPAN** *n* cooking pot with a long handle
**SAUCEPANS** > SAUCEPAN
**SAUCEPOT** *n* cooking pot with lid
**SAUCEPOTS** > SAUCEPOT
**SAUCER** *n* small round dish put under a cup
**SAUCERFUL** > SAUCER
**SAUCERS** > SAUCER
**SAUCES** > SAUCE
**SAUCH** *n* sallow or willow
**SAUCHS** > SAUCH
**SAUCIER** *n* chef who makes sauces
**SAUCIERS** > SAUCIER
**SAUCIEST** > SAUCY
**SAUCILY** > SAUCY
**SAUCINESS** > SAUCY
**SAUCING** > SAUCE
**SAUCISSE** *n* type of explosive fuse
**SAUCISSES** > SAUCISSE
**SAUCISSON** *n* type of explosive fuse
**SAUCY** *adj* impudent
**SAUFGARD** *old form of* > SAFEGUARD
**SAUFGARDS** > SAUFGARD
**SAUGER** *n* small North American pikeperch
**SAUGERS** > SAUGER
**SAUGH** *same as* > SAUCH
**SAUGHS** > SAUGH
**SAUGHY** *adj* Scots word meaning made of willow
**SAUL** *Scots word for* > SOUL
**SAULGE** *n* old word for sage plant
**SAULGES** > SAULGE
**SAULIE** *n* Scots word meaning professional mourner
**SAULIES** > SAULIE
**SAULS** > SAUL
**SAULT** *n* waterfall in Canada
**SAULTS** > SAULT
**SAUNA** *n* Finnish-style steam bath ▷ *vb* have a sauna
**SAUNAED** > SAUNA
**SAUNAING** > SAUNA
**SAUNAS** > SAUNA
**SAUNT** *Scots form of* > SAINT
**SAUNTED** > SAUNT
**SAUNTER** *vb* walk in a leisurely manner, stroll ▷ *n* leisurely walk
**SAUNTERED** > SAUNTER
**SAUNTERER** > SAUNTER
**SAUNTERS** > SAUNTER
**SAUNTING** > SAUNT
**SAUNTS** > SAUNT
**SAUREL** *n* type of mackerel
**SAURELS** > SAUREL
**SAURIAN** *adj* of or like a lizard ▷ *n* former name for > LIZARD
**SAURIANS** > SAURIAN
**SAURIES** > SAURY
**SAUROID** *adj* like a lizard
**SAUROPOD** *n* type of herbivorous dinosaur including the brontosaurus and the diplodocus
**SAUROPODS** > SAUROPOD
**SAURY** *n* type of fish of tropical and temperate seas, having an elongated body and long toothed jaws
**SAUSAGE** *n* minced meat in an edible tube-shaped skin
**SAUSAGES** > SAUSAGE
**SAUT** *Scot word for* > SALT
**SAUTE** *vb* fry quickly in a little fat ▷ *n* dish of sautéed food ▷ *adj* sautéed until lightly brown
**SAUTED** > SAUT
**SAUTEED** > SAUTE
**SAUTEEING** > SAUTE
**SAUTEES** > SAUTE
**SAUTEING** > SAUTE
**SAUTERNE** *n* sauternes
**SAUTERNES** *n* sweet white French wine
**SAUTES** > SAUTE
**SAUTING** > SAUT
**SAUTOIR** *n* long necklace or pendant
**SAUTOIRE** *variant of* > SAUTOIR
**SAUTOIRES** > SAUTOIRE
**SAUTOIRS** > SAUTOIR
**SAUTS** > SAUT
**SAV** *short for* > SAVELOY
**SAVABLE** > SAVE
**SAVAGE** *adj* wild, untamed ▷ *n* uncivilized person ▷ *vb* attack ferociously
**SAVAGED** > SAVAGE
**SAVAGEDOM** > SAVAGE
**SAVAGELY** > SAVAGE
**SAVAGER** > SAVAGE
**SAVAGERY** *n* viciousness and cruelty
**SAVAGES** > SAVAGE
**SAVAGEST** > SAVAGE
**SAVAGING** > SAVAGE
**SAVAGISM** > SAVAGE
**SAVAGISMS** > SAVAGE
**SAVANNA** *n* open grasslands, usually with scattered bushes or trees, characteristic of much of tropical Africa
**SAVANNAH** *same as* > SAVANNA
**SAVANNAHS** > SAVANNAH
**SAVANNAS** > SAVANNA
**SAVANT** *n* learned person
**SAVANTE** > SAVANT
**SAVANTES** > SAVANT

**SAVANTS** > SAVANT
**SAVARIN** n type of cake
**SAVARINS** > SAVARIN
**SAVATE** n form of boxing in which blows may be delivered with the feet as well as the hands
**SAVATES** > SAVATE
**SAVE** vb rescue or preserve from harm, protect ▷ n act of preventing a goal ▷ prep except
**SAVEABLE** > SAVE
**SAVED** > SAVE
**SAVEGARD** vb old word meaning protect
**SAVEGARDS** > SAVEGARD
**SAVELOY** n spicy smoked sausage
**SAVELOYS** > SAVELOY
**SAVER** > SAVE
**SAVERS** > SAVE
**SAVES** > SAVE
**SAVEY** vb understand
**SAVEYED** > SAVEY
**SAVEYING** > SAVEY
**SAVEYS** > SAVEY
**SAVIN** n small spreading juniper bush of Europe, N Asia, and North America
**SAVINE** same as > SAVIN
**SAVINES** > SAVINE
**SAVING** n economy ▷ prep except ▷ adj tending to save or preserve
**SAVINGLY** > SAVING
**SAVINGS** > SAVING
**SAVINS** > SAVIN
**SAVIOR** same as > SAVIOUR
**SAVIORS** > SAVIOR
**SAVIOUR** n person who rescues another
**SAVIOURS** > SAVIOUR
**SAVOR** same as > SAVOUR
**SAVORED** > SAVOR
**SAVORER** > SAVOR
**SAVORERS** > SAVOR
**SAVORIER** > SAVORY
**SAVORIES** > SAVORY
**SAVORIEST** > SAVORY
**SAVORILY** > SAVOUR
**SAVORING** > SAVOR
**SAVORLESS** > SAVOUR
**SAVOROUS** > SAVOUR
**SAVORS** > SAVOR
**SAVORY** same as > SAVOURY
**SAVOUR** vb enjoy, relish ▷ n characteristic taste or odour
**SAVOURED** > SAVOUR
**SAVOURER** > SAVOUR
**SAVOURERS** > SAVOUR
**SAVOURIER** > SAVOURY
**SAVOURIES** > SAVOURY
**SAVOURILY** > SAVOURY
**SAVOURING** > SAVOURY
**SAVOURLY** adv old word meaning refeshingly
**SAVOURS** > SAVOUR
**SAVOURY** adj salty or spicy ▷ n savoury dish served before or after a meal
**SAVOY** n variety of cabbage
**SAVOYARD** n person keenly

interested in the operettas of Gilbert and Sullivan
**SAVOYARDS** > SAVOYARD
**SAVOYS** > SAVOY
**SAVS** > SAV
**SAVVEY** vb understand
**SAVVEYED** > SAVVEY
**SAVVEYING** > SAVVEY
**SAVVEYS** > SAVVEY
**SAVVIED** > SAVVY
**SAVVIER** > SAVVY
**SAVVIES** > SAVVY
**SAVVIEST** > SAVVY
**SAVVILY** > SAVVY
**SAVVINESS** > SAVVY
**SAVVY** vb understand ▷ n understanding, intelligence ▷ adj shrewd
**SAVVYING** > SAVVY
**SAW** n hand tool for cutting wood and metal ▷ vb cut with a saw
**SAWAH** n paddyfield
**SAWAHS** > SAWAH
**SAWBILL** n any of various hummingbirds of the genus Ramphodon
**SAWBILLS** > SAWBILL
**SAWBLADE** n blade of a saw
**SAWBLADES** > SAWBLADE
**SAWBONES** n surgeon or doctor
**SAWBUCK** n sawhorse, esp one having an X-shaped supporting structure
**SAWBUCKS** > SAWBUCK
**SAWDER** n flattery ▷ vb flatter
**SANDERED** > SAWDER
**SANDERING** > SAWDER
**SANDERS** > SAWDER
**SAWDUST** n fine wood fragments made in sawing ▷ vb cover with sawdust
**SAWDUSTED** > SAWDUST
**SAWDUSTS** > SAWDUST
**SAWDUSTY** > SAWDUST
**SAWED** > SAW
**SAWER** > SAW
**SAWERS** > SAW
**SAWFISH** n fish with a long toothed snout
**SAWFISHES** > SAWFISH
**SAWFLIES** > SAWFLY
**SAWFLY** n any of various hymenopterous insects
**SAWHORSE** n structure for supporting wood that is being sawn
**SAWHORSES** > SAWHORSE
**SAWING** > SAW
**SAWINGS** > SAW
**SAWLIKE** > SAW
**SAWLOG** n log suitable for sawing
**SAWLOGS** > SAWLOG
**SAWMILL** n mill where timber is sawn into planks
**SAWMILLS** > SAWMILL
**SAWN** past participle of > SAW
**SAWNEY** n derogatory word for a fool
**SAWNEYS** > SAWNEY
**SAWPIT** n pit above which a

log is sawn into planks
**SAWPITS** > SAWPIT
**SAWS** > SAW
**SAWSHARK** n shark with long sawlike snout
**SAWSHARKS** > SAWSHARK
**SAWTEETH** > SAWTOOTH
**SAWTIMBER** n wood for sawing
**SAWTOOTH** adj (of a waveform) having an amplitude that varies linearly with time between two values
**SAWYER** n person who saws timber for a living
**SAWYERS** > SAWYER
**SAX** same as > SAXOPHONE
**SAXATILE** adj living among rocks
**SAXAUL** n Asian tree
**SAXAULS** > SAXAUL
**SAXE** as in saxe blue light greyish-blue colour
**SAXES** > SAX
**SAXHORN** n valved brass instrument used chiefly in brass and military bands
**SAXHORNS** > SAXHORN
**SAXICOLE** variant of > SAXATILE
**SAXIFRAGE** n alpine rock plant with small flowers
**SAXITOXIN** n poison extracted from mollusc
**SAXONIES** > SAXONY
**SAXONITE** n igneous rock
**SAXONITES** > SAXONITE
**SAXONY** n fine 3-ply yarn used for knitting and weaving
**SAXOPHONE** n brass wind instrument with keys and a curved body
**SAXTUBA** n bass saxhorn
**SAXTUBAS** > SAXTUBA
**SAY** vb speak or utter ▷ n right or chance to speak
**SAYABLE** > SAY
**SAYED** same as > SAYYID
**SAYEDS** > SAYED
**SAYER** > SAY
**SAYERS** > SAY
**SAYEST** > SAY
**SAYID** same as > SAYYID
**SAYIDS** > SAYID
**SAYING** > SAY
**SAYINGS** > SAY
**SAYNE** > SAY
**SAYON** n type of tunic
**SAYONARA** n Japanese farewell
**SAYONARAS** > SAYONARA
**SAYONS** > SAYON
**SAYS** > SAY
**SAYST** > SAY
**SAYYID** n Muslim claiming descent from Mohammed's grandson Husain
**SAYYIDS** > SAYYID
**SAZ** n Middle Eastern stringed instrument
**SAZERAC** n mixed drink

of whisky, Pernod, syrup, bitters, and lemon
**SAZERACS** > SAZERAC
**SAZES** > SAZ
**SAZHEN** n Russian measure of length
**SAZHENS** > SAZHEN
**SAZZES** > SAZ
**SBIRRI** > SBIRRO
**SBIRRO** n Italian police officer
**SCAB** n crust formed over a wound ▷ vb become covered with a scab
**SCABBARD** n sheath for a sword or dagger
**SCABBARDS** > SCABBARD
**SCABBED** > SCAB
**SCABBIER** > SCABBY
**SCABBIEST** > SCABBY
**SCABBILY** > SCABBY
**SCABBING** > SCAB
**SCABBLE** vb shape (stone) roughly
**SCABBLED** > SCABBLE
**SCABBLES** > SCABBLE
**SCABBLING** > SCABBLE
**SCABBY** adj covered with scabs
**SCABIES** n itchy skin disease
**SCABIETIC** > SCABIES
**SCABIOSA** n flowering plant
**SCABIOSAS** > SCABIOSA
**SCABIOUS** n plant with showy blue, red, or whitish dome-shaped flower heads ▷ adj having or covered with scabs
**SCABLAND** n barren rocky land
**SCABLANDS** pl n type of terrain consisting of bare rock surfaces, with little or no soil cover and scanty vegetation
**SCABLIKE** > SCAB
**SCABRID** adj having a rough or scaly surface
**SCABROUS** adj rough and scaly
**SCABS** > SCAB
**SCAD** n any of various carangid fishes
**SCADS** pl n large amount or number
**SCAFF** n Scots word meaning food
**SCAFFIE** n Scots word meaning street cleaner
**SCAFFIES** > SCAFFIE
**SCAFFOLD** n temporary platform for workmen ▷ vb provide with a scaffold
**SCAFFOLDS** > SCAFFOLD
**SCAFFS** > SCAFF
**SCAG** n tear in a garment or piece of cloth ▷ vb make a tear in (cloth)
**SCAGGED** > SCAG
**SCAGGING** > SCAG
**SCAGLIA** n type of

limestone
**SCAGLIAS** > SCAGLIA
**SCAGLIOLA** *n* type of
imitation marble made of
glued gypsum
**SCAGS** > SCAG
**SCAIL** *vb* Scots word
meaning disperse
**SCAILED** > SCAIL
**SCAILING** > SCAIL
**SCAILS** > SCAIL
**SCAITH** *vb* old word
meaning injure
**SCAITHED** > SCAITH
**SCAITHING** > SCAITH
**SCAITHS** > SCAITH
**SCALA** *n* passage inside the
cochlea
**SCALABLE** *adj* capable of
being scaled or climbed
**SCALABLY** > SCALABLE
**SCALADE** *short*
*for* > ESCALADE
**SCALADES** > SCALADE
**SCALADO** *same as* > SCALADE
**SCALADOS** > SCALADO
**SCALAE** > SCALA
**SCALAGE** *n* percentage
deducted from the price
of goods liable to shrink
or leak
**SCALAGES** > SCALAGE
**SCALAR** *adj* (variable
quantity) having
magnitude but no
direction ▷ *n* quantity,
such as time or
temperature, that has
magnitude but not
direction
**SCALARE** *another name*
*for* > ANGELFISH
**SCALARES** > SCALARE
**SCALARS** > SCALAR
**SCALATION** *n* way scales
are arranged
**SCALAWAG** *same*
*as* > SCALLYWAG
**SCALAWAGS** > SCALAWAG
**SCALD** *same as* > SKALD
**SCALDED** > SCALD
**SCALDER** > SCALD
**SCALDERS** > SCALD
**SCALDFISH** *n* small
European flatfish
**SCALDHEAD** *n* diseased
scalp
**SCALDIC** > SKALD
**SCALDING** > SCALD
**SCALDINGS** > SCALD
**SCALDINI** > SCALDINO
**SCALDINO** *n* Italian brazier
**SCALDS** > SCALD
**SCALDSHIP** *n* position of
being Scandinavian poet
**SCALE** *n* one of the thin
overlapping plates
covering fishes and
reptiles ▷ *vb* remove
scales from
**SCALED** > SCALE
**SCALELESS** > SCALE
**SCALELIKE** > SCALE
**SCALENE** *adj* (of a triangle)

with three unequal sides
**SCALENI** > SCALENUS
**SCALENUS** *n* any one of the
three muscles situated on
each side of the neck
**SCALEPAN** *n* part of scales
holding weighed object
**SCALEPANS** > SCALEPAN
**SCALER** *n* person or thing
that scales
**SCALERS** > SCALER
**SCALES** > SCALE
**SCALETAIL** *n* type of
squirrel
**SCALEUP** *n* increase
**SCALEUPS** > SCALEUP
**SCALEWORK** *n* artistic
representation of scales
**SCALIER** > SCALY
**SCALIEST** > SCALY
**SCALINESS** > SCALY
**SCALING** > SCALING
**SCALINGS** > SCALE
**SCALL** *n* disease of the
scalp characterized
by itching and scab
formation
**SCALLAWAG** *same*
*as* > SCALLYWAG
**SCALLED** > SCALL
**SCALLIES** > SCALLY
**SCALLION** *same*
*as* > SHALLOT
**SCALLIONS** > SCALLION
**SCALLOP** *n* edible shellfish
with two fan-shaped
shells ▷ *vb* decorate (an
edge) with scallops
**SCALLOPED** > SCALLOP
**SCALLOPER** > SCALLOP
**SCALLOPS** > SCALLOP
**SCALLS** > SCALL
**SCALLY** *n* rascal
**SCALLYWAG** *n* scamp, rascal
**SCALOGRAM** *n* scale for
measuring opinion
**SCALP** *n* skin and hair on
top of the head ▷ *vb* cut
off the scalp of
**SCALPED** > SCALP
**SCALPEL** *n* small surgical
knife
**SCALPELS** > SCALPEL
**SCALPER** > SCALP
**SCALPERS** > SCALP
**SCALPING** *n* process in
which the top portion of
a metal ingot is machined
away before use
**SCALPINGS** > SCALPING
**SCALPINS** *n* small stones
**SCALPLESS** > SCALP
**SCALPRUM** *n* large scalpel
**SCALPRUMS** > SCALPRUM
**SCALPS** > SCALP
**SCALY** *adj* resembling or
covered in scales
**SCAM** *n* dishonest scheme
▷ *vb* swindle (someone) by
means of a trick
**SCAMBLE** *vb* scramble
**SCAMBLED** > SCAMBLE
**SCAMBLER** > SCAMBLE
**SCAMBLERS** > SCAMBLE

**SCAMBLES** > SCAMBLE
**SCAMBLING** > SCAMBLE
**SCAMEL** *n* Shakespearian
word of uncertain
meaning
**SCAMELS** > SCAMEL
**SCAMMED** > SCAM
**SCAMMER** *n* person who
perpetrates a scam
**SCAMMERS** > SCAMMER
**SCAMMING** > SCAM
**SCAMMONY** *n* twining Asian
convolvulus plant
**SCAMP** *n* mischievous child
▷ *vb* perform without care
**SCAMPED** > SCAMP
**SCAMPER** *vb* run about
hurriedly or in play ▷ *n*
scampering
**SCAMPERED** > SCAMP
**SCAMPERER** > SCAMPER
**SCAMPERS** > SCAMP
**SCAMPI** *pl n* large prawns
**SCAMPIES** > SCAMPI
**SCAMPING** > SCAMP
**SCAMPINGS** > SCAMP
**SCAMPIS** > SCAMPI
**SCAMPISH** > SCAMP
**SCAMPS** > SCAMP
**SCAMS** > SCAM
**SCAMSTER** *same*
*as* > SCAMMER
**SCAMSTERS** > SCAMSTER
**SCAMTO** *n* argot of urban
South African Blacks
**SCAMTOS** > SCAMTO
**SCAN** *vb* scrutinize carefully
▷ *n* scanning
**SCAND** > SCAN
**SCANDAL** *n* disgraceful
action or event ▷ *vb*
disgrace
**SCANDALED** > SCANDAL
**SCANDALS** > SCANDAL
**SCANDENT** *adj* (of plants)
having a climbing habit
**SCANDIA** *n* scandium oxide
**SCANDIAS** > SCANDIA
**SCANDIC** *adj* of or
containing scandium
**SCANDIUM** *n* rare silvery-
white metallic element
**SCANDIUMS** > SCANDIUM
**SCANNABLE** > SCAN
**SCANNED** > SCAN
**SCANNER** *n* electronic
device used for scanning
**SCANNERS** > SCANNER
**SCANNING** > SCAN
**SCANNINGS** > SCAN
**SCANS** > SCAN
**SCANSION** *n* metrical
scanning of verse
**SCANSIONS** > SCANSION
**SCANT** *adj* barely sufficient,
meagre ▷ *vb* limit in size
or quantity ▷ *adv* scarcely
**SCANTED** > SCANT
**SCANTER** > SCANT
**SCANTEST** > SCANT
**SCANTIER** > SCANTY
**SCANTIES** *n* women's
underwear
**SCANTIEST** > SCANTY

**SCANTILY** > SCANTY
**SCANTING** > SCANT
**SCANTITY** *n* quality of
being scant
**SCANTLE** *vb* stint
**SCANTLED** > SCANTLE
**SCANTLES** > SCANTLE
**SCANTLING** *n* piece of sawn
timber, such as a rafter,
that has a small cross
section
**SCANTLY** > SCANT
**SCANTNESS** > SCANT
**SCANTS** > SCANT
**SCANTY** *adj* barely
sufficient or not sufficient
**SCAPA** *variant of* > SCARPER
**SCAPAED** > SCAPA
**SCAPAING** > SCAPA
**SCAPAS** > SCAPA
**SCAPE** *n* leafless stalk in
plants that arises from a
rosette of leaves and bears
one or more flowers ▷ *vb*
archaic word for escape
**SCAPED** > SCAPE
**SCAPEGOAT** *n* person
made to bear the blame
for others ▷ *vb* make a
scapegoat of
**SCAPELESS** *adj* allowing no
escape
**SCAPEMENT** *n* escapement
**SCAPES** > SCAPE
**SCAPHOID** *obsolete word*
*for* > NAVICULAR
**SCAPHOIDS** > SCAPHOID
**SCAPHOPOD** *n* any marine
mollusc of the class
*Scaphopoda*
**SCAPI** > SCAPUS
**SCAPING** > SCAPE
**SCAPOLITE** *n* any of a
group of colourless, white,
grey, or violet fluorescent
minerals
**SCAPOSE** > SCAPE
**SCAPPLE** *vb* shape roughly
**SCAPPLED** > SCAPPLE
**SCAPPLES** > SCAPPLE
**SCAPPLING** > SCAPPLE
**SCAPULA** *n* shoulder blade
**SCAPULAE** > SCAPULA
**SCAPULAR** *adj* of the
scapula ▷ *n* loose
sleeveless garment worn
by monks over their habits
**SCAPULARS** > SCAPULAR
**SCAPULARY** *same*
*as* > SCAPULAR
**SCAPULAS** > SCAPULA
**SCAPUS** *n* flower stalk
**SCAR** *n* mark left by a
healed wound ▷ *vb* mark
or become marked with
a scar
**SCARAB** *n* sacred beetle of
ancient Egypt
**SCARABAEI** *pl n* scarabs
**SCARABEE** *n* old word for
scarab beetle
**SCARABEES** > SCARABEE
**SCARABOID** *adj* resembling
a scarab beetle ▷ *n* beetle

that resembles a scarab
**SCARABS** > SCARAB
**SCARCE** adj insufficient to meet demand
**SCARCELY** adv hardly at all
**SCARCER** > SCARCE
**SCARCEST** > SCARCE
**SCARCITY** n inadequate supply
**SCARE** vb frighten or be frightened ▷ n fright, sudden panic ▷ adj causing (needless) fear or alarm
**SCARECROW** n figure dressed in old clothes, set up to scare birds away from crops
**SCARED** > SCARE
**SCAREDER** > SCARE
**SCAREDEST** > SCARE
**SCAREHEAD** n newspaper headline intended to shock
**SCARER** > SCARE
**SCARERS** > SCARE
**SCARES** > SCARE
**SCAREY** adj frightening
**SCARF** n piece of material worn round the neck, head, or shoulders ▷ vb join in this way
**SCARFED** > SCARF
**SCARFER** > SCARF
**SCARFING** > SCARF
**SCARFINGS** > SCARF
**SCARFISH** n type of fish
**SCARFPIN** n decorative pin securing scarf
**SCARFPINS** > SCARFPIN
**SCARFS** > SCARF
**SCARFSKIN** n outermost layer of the skin
**SCARFWISE** adv like scarf
**SCARIER** > SCARY
**SCARIEST** > SCARY
**SCARIFIED** > SCARIFY
**SCARIFIER** > SCARIFY
**SCARIFIES** > SCARIFY
**SCARIFY** vb scratch or cut slightly all over
**SCARILY** > SCARY
**SCARINESS** > SCARY
**SCARING** > SCARE
**SCARIOSE** same as > SCARIOUS
**SCARIOUS** adj (of plant parts) membranous, dry, and brownish in colour
**SCARLESS** > SCAR
**SCARLET** n brilliant red ▷ adj bright red ▷ vb make scarlet
**SCARLETED** > SCARLET
**SCARLETS** > SCARLET
**SCARMOGE** n old form of skirmish
**SCARMOGES** > SCARMOGE
**SCARP** n steep slope ▷ vb wear or cut so as to form a steep slope
**SCARPA** vb run away
**SCARPAED** > SCARPA

**SCARPAING** > SCARPA
**SCARPAS** > SCARPA
**SCARPED** > SCARP
**SCARPER** vb run away ▷ n hasty departure
**SCARPERED** > SCARPER
**SCARPERS** > SCARPER
**SCARPETTI** > SCARPETTO
**SCARPETTO** n type of shoe
**SCARPH** vb join with scarf joint
**SCARPHED** > SCARPH
**SCARPHING** > SCARPH
**SCARPHS** > SCARPH
**SCARPINES** n device for torturing feet
**SCARPING** > SCARP
**SCARPINGS** > SCARP
**SCARPS** > SCARP
**SCARRE** n Shakespearian word of unknown meaning
**SCARRED** > SCAR
**SCARRES** > SCARRE
**SCARRIER** > SCAR
**SCARRIEST** > SCAR
**SCARRING** > SCAR
**SCARRINGS** > SCAR
**SCARRY** > SCAR
**SCARS** > SCAR
**SCART** vb scratch or scrape ▷ n scratch or scrape
**SCARTED** > SCART
**SCARTH** Scots word for > CORMORANT
**SCARTHS** > SCARTH
**SCARTING** > SCART
**SCARTS** > SCART
**SCARVES** > SCARF
**SCARY** adj frightening
**SCAT** vb go away ▷ n jazz singing using improvised vocal sounds instead of words
**SCATBACK** n American football player
**SCATBACKS** > SCATBACK
**SCATCH** same as > STILT
**SCATCHES** > SCATCH
**SCATH** vb old word meaning injure
**SCATHE** vb attack with severe criticism ▷ n harm
**SCATHED** > SCATHE
**SCATHEFUL** adj old word meaning harmful
**SCATHES** > SCATHE
**SCATHING** adj harshly critical
**SCATHS** > SCATH
**SCATOLE** n substance found in coal
**SCATOLES** > SCATOLE
**SCATOLOGY** n preoccupation with obscenity, esp with references to excrement
**SCATS** > SCAT
**SCATT** n old word meaning tax ▷ vb tax
**SCATTED** > SCAT
**SCATTER** vb throw about in various directions ▷ n scattering

**SCATTERED** > SCATTER
**SCATTERER** > SCATTER
**SCATTERS** > SCATTER
**SCATTERY** adj dispersed
**SCATTIER** > SCATTY
**SCATTIEST** > SCATTY
**SCATTILY** > SCATTY
**SCATTING** > SCAT
**SCATTINGS** > SCAT
**SCATTS** > SCATT
**SCATTY** adj empty-headed
**SCAUD** Scot word for > SCALD
**SCAUDED** > SCAUD
**SCAUDING** > SCAUD
**SCAUDS** > SCAUD
**SCAUP** variant of > SCALP
**SCAUPED** > SCAUP
**SCAUPER** same as > SCORPER
**SCAUPERS** > SCAUPER
**SCAUPING** > SCAUP
**SCAUPS** > SCAUP
**SCAUR** same as > SCAR
**SCAURED** > SCAUR
**SCAURIES** > SCAURY
**SCAURING** > SCAUR
**SCAURS** > SCAUR
**SCAURY** n young seagull
**SCAVAGE** n old word meaning toll
**SCAVAGER** > SCAVAGE
**SCAVAGERS** > SCAVAGE
**SCAVAGES** > SCAVAGE
**SCAVENGE** vb search for (anything usable) among discarded material
**SCAVENGED** > SCAVENGE
**SCAVENGER** n person who scavenges
**SCAVENGES** > SCAVENGE
**SCAW** n headland
**SCAWS** > SCAW
**SCAWTITE** n mineral containing calcium
**SCAWTITES** > SCAWTITE
**SCAZON** n metre in poetry
**SCAZONS** > SCAZON
**SCAZONTES** > SCAZON
**SCAZONTIC** > SCAZON
**SCEAT** n Anglo-Saxon coin
**SCEATT** n Anglo-Saxon coin
**SCEATTAS** > SCEAT
**SCEDULE** old spelling of > SCHEDULE
**SCEDULED** > SCEDULE
**SCEDULES** > SCEDULE
**SCEDULING** > SCEDULE
**SCELERAT** n villain
**SCELERATE** n villain
**SCELERATS** > SCELERAT
**SCENA** n scene in an opera, usually longer than a single aria
**SCENARIES** > SCENARY
**SCENARIO** n summary of the plot of a play or film
**SCENARIOS** > SCENARIO
**SCENARISE** same as > SCENARIZE
**SCENARIST** > SCENARIO
**SCENARIZE** vb create scenario
**SCENARY** n scenery
**SCENAS** > SCENA
**SCEND** vb (of a vessel) to

surge upwards in a heavy sea ▷ n upward heaving of a vessel pitching
**SCENDED** > SCEND
**SCENDING** > SCEND
**SCENDS** > SCEND
**SCENE** n place of action of a real or imaginary event ▷ vb set in a scene
**SCENED** > SCENE
**SCENEMAN** n person shifting stage scenery
**SCENEMEN** > SCENEMAN
**SCENERIES** > SCENERY
**SCENERY** n natural features of a landscape
**SCENES** > SCENE
**SCENIC** adj picturesque ▷ n something scenic
**SCENICAL** > SCENE
**SCENICS** > SCENIC
**SCENING** > SCENE
**SCENT** n pleasant smell ▷ vb detect by smell
**SCENTED** > SCENT
**SCENTFUL** adj old word meaning having scent
**SCENTING** > SCENT
**SCENTINGS** > SCENT
**SCENTLESS** > SCENT
**SCENTS** > SCENT
**SCEPSIS** n doubt
**SCEPSISES** > SCEPSIS
**SCEPTER** same as > SCEPTRE
**SCEPTERED** > SCEPTER
**SCEPTERS** > SCEPTER
**SCEPTIC** n person who habitually doubts generally accepted beliefs ▷ adj of or relating to sceptics
**SCEPTICAL** adj not convinced that something is true
**SCEPTICS** > SCEPTIC
**SCEPTRAL** adj royal
**SCEPTRE** n ornamental rod symbolizing royal power ▷ vb invest with authority
**SCEPTRED** > SCEPTRE
**SCEPTRES** > SCEPTRE
**SCEPTRING** > SCEPTRE
**SCEPTRY** adj having sceptre
**SCERNE** vb old word meaning discern
**SCERNED** > SCERNE
**SCERNES** > SCERNE
**SCERNING** > SCERNE
**SCHANSE** n stones heaped to shelter soldier in battle
**SCHANSES** > SCHANSE
**SCHANTZE** n stones heaped to shelter soldier in battle
**SCHANTZES** > SCHANTZE
**SCHANZE** n stones heaped to shelter soldier in battle
**SCHANZES** > SCHANZE
**SCHAPPE** n yarn or fabric made from waste silk
**SCHAPPED** > SCHAPPE
**SCHAPPES** > SCHAPPE
**SCHAPSKA** n cap worn by lancer
**SCHAPSKAS** > SCHAPSKA

SCHATCHEN same
as >SHADCHAN
SCHAV n Polish soup
SCHAVS >SCHAV
SCHECHITA n slaughter
of animals according to
Jewish law
SCHEDULAR >SCHEDULE
SCHEDULE n plan of
procedure for a project
▷ vb plan to occur at a
certain time
SCHEDULED adj arranged
or planned according to
a programme, timetable,
etc
SCHEDULER >SCHEDULE
SCHEDULES >SCHEDULE
SCHEELITE n white,
brownish, or greenish
mineral
SCHELLUM n Scots word
meaning rascal
SCHELLUMS >SCHELLUM
SCHELM n South African
word meaning rascal
SCHELMS >SCHELM
SCHEMA n overall plan or
diagram
SCHEMAS >SCHEMA
SCHEMATA >SCHEMA
SCHEMATIC adj presented
as a plan or diagram ▷ n
schematic diagram, esp of
an electrical circuit
SCHEME n systematic plan
▷ vb plan in an underhand
manner
SCHEMED >SCHEME
SCHEMER >SCHEME
SCHEMERS >SCHEME
SCHEMES >SCHEME
SCHEMIE n Scots
derogatory word for a
resident of a housing
scheme
SCHEMIES >SCHEMIE
SCHEMING adj given
to making plots ▷ n
intrigues
SCHEMINGS >SCHEMING
SCHERZI >SCHERZO
SCHERZO n brisk lively
piece of music
SCHERZOS >SCHERZO
SCHIAVONE n type of sword
SCHIEDAM n type of
gin produced in the
Netherlands
SCHIEDAMS >SCHIEDAM
SCHILLER n unusual
iridescent or metallic
lustre in some minerals
SCHILLERS >SCHILLER
SCHILLING n former
monetary unit of Austria
SCHIMMEL n roan horse
SCHIMMELS >SCHIMMEL
SCHISM n (group resulting
from) division in an
organization
SCHISMA n musical term
SCHISMAS >SCHISMA
SCHISMS >SCHISM

SCHIST n crystalline rock
which splits into layers
SCHISTOSE >SCHIST
SCHISTOUS >SCHIST
SCHISTS >SCHIST
SCHIZIER >SCHIZY
SCHIZIEST >SCHIZY
SCHIZO n derogatory
term for a schizophrenic
(person) ▷ adj
schizophrenic
SCHIZOID adj abnormally
introverted ▷ n schizoid
person
SCHIZOIDS >SCHIZOID
SCHIZONT n cell formed
from a trophozoite during
the asexual stage of the
life cycle of sporozoan
protozoans
SCHIZONTS >SCHIZONT
SCHIZOPOD n any of
various shrimplike
crustaceans
SCHIZOS >SCHIZO
SCHIZY adj slang term
meaning schizophrenic
SCHIZZIER >SCHIZZY
SCHIZZY adj slang term
meaning schizophrenic
SCHLAGER n German
duelling sword
SCHLAGERS >SCHLAGER
SCHLEMIEL n awkward
or unlucky person whose
endeavours usually fail
SCHLEMIHL same
as >SCHLEMIEL
SCHLEP vb drag or lug
(oneself or an object) with
difficulty ▷ n stupid or
clumsy person
SCHLEPP vb schlep
SCHLEPPED >SCHLEP
SCHLEPPER n incompetent
person
SCHLEPPS >SCHLEPP
SCHLEPPY >SCHLEPP
SCHLEPS >SCHLEP
SCHLICH n finely crushed
ore
SCHLICHS >SCHLICH
SCHLIERE n (in physics or
geology) streak of different
density or composition
from surroundings
SCHLIEREN >SCHLIERE
SCHLIERIC >SCHLIERE
SCHLOCK n goods or
produce of cheap or
inferior quality ▷ adj
cheap, inferior, or trashy
SCHLOCKER n thing of poor
quality
SCHLOCKS >SCHLOCK
SCHLOCKY adj of poor
quality
SCHLONG slang word
for >PENIS
SCHLONGS >SCHLONG
SCHLOSS n castle
SCHLOSSES >SCHLOSS
SCHLUB n coarse or
contemptible person

SCHLUBS >SCHLUB
SCHLUMP vb move in lazy
way
SCHLUMPED >SCHLUMP
SCHLUMPS >SCHLUMP
SCHLUMPY >SCHLUMP
SCHMALTZ n excessive
sentimentality
SCHMALTZY adj excessively
sentimental
SCHMALZ same
as >SCHMALTZ
SCHMALZES >SCHMALZ
SCHMALZY adj schmaltzy
SCHMATTE same
as >SCHMUTTER
SCHMATTES >SCHMATTE
SCHMEAR n situation,
matter, or affair ▷ vb
spread or smear
SCHMEARED >SCHMEAR
SCHMEARS >SCHMEAR
SCHMECK n taste
SCHMECKS >SCHMECK
SCHMEER same
as >SCHMEAR
SCHMEERED >SCHMEER
SCHMEERS >SCHMEER
SCHMELZ n ornamental
glass
SCHMELZE variant
of >SCHMELZ
SCHMELZES >SCHMELZ
SCHMICK n informal
Australian word for
excellent, elegant, or
stylish
SCHMO n dull, stupid, or
boring person
SCHMOCK n stupid person
SCHMOCKS >SCHMOCK
SCHMOE n stupid person
SCHMOES >SCHMO
SCHMOOS variant
of >SCHMOOSE
SCHMOOSE vb chat
SCHMOOSED >SCHMOOSE
SCHMOOSES >SCHMOOSE
SCHMOOZ n chat
SCHMOOZE vb chat or gossip
▷ n trivial conversation
SCHMOOZED >SCHMOOZE
SCHMOOZER >SCHMOOZE
SCHMOOZES >SCHMOOZE
SCHMOOZY >SCHMOOZE
SCHMOS >SCHMO
SCHMUCK n stupid or
contemptible person
SCHMUCKS >SCHMUCK
SCHMUTTER n cloth or
clothing
SCHNAPPER same
as >SNAPPER
SCHNAPPS n strong
alcoholic spirit
SCHNAPS same
as >SCHNAPPS
SCHNAPSES >SCHNAPS
SCHNAUZER n wire-haired
breed of dog of the terrier
type, originally from
Germany
SCHNECKE >SCHNECKEN
SCHNECKEN pl n sweet

spiral-shaped bread roll
flavoured with cinnamon
and nuts
SCHNELL adj German word
meaning quick
SCHNITZEL n thin slice of
meat, esp veal
SCHNOOK n stupid or
gullible person
SCHNOOKS >SCHNOOK
SCHNORKEL less common
variant of >SNORKEL
SCHNORR vb beg
SCHNORRED >SCHNORR
SCHNORRER n person who
lives off the charity of
others
SCHNORRS >SCHNORR
SCHNOZ n nose
SCHNOZES >SCHNOZ
SCHNOZZ n nose
SCHNOZZES >SCHNOZZ
SCHNOZZLE slang word
for >NOSE
SCHOLAR n learned person
SCHOLARCH n head of
school
SCHOLARLY >SCHOLAR
SCHOLARS >SCHOLAR
SCHOLIA >SCHOLIUM
SCHOLIAST n medieval
annotator, esp of classical
texts
SCHOLION n scholarly
annotation
SCHOLIUM n commentary
or annotation, esp on a
classical text
SCHOLIUMS >SCHOLIUM
SCHOOL n place where
children are taught or
instruction is given in a
subject ▷ vb educate or
train
SCHOOLBAG n school pupil's
bag
SCHOOLBOY n child
attending school
SCHOOLDAY n day for going
to school
SCHOOLE n old form of
shoal
SCHOOLED >SCHOOL
SCHOOLERY n old word
meaning something
taught
SCHOOLES >SCHOOLE
SCHOOLIE n schoolteacher
or a high-school student
SCHOOLIES >SCHOOLIE
SCHOOLING n education
SCHOOLKID n child who
goes to school
SCHOOLMAN n scholar
versed in the learning of
the Schoolmen
SCHOOLMEN >SCHOOLMAN
SCHOOLS >SCHOOL
SCHOONER n sailing ship
rigged fore-and-aft
SCHOONERS >SCHOONER
SCHORL n type of black
tourmaline
SCHORLS >SCHORL

SCHOUT n council officer in Netherlands
SCHOUTS > SCHOUT
SCHRIK variant of > SKRIK
SCHRIKS > SCHRIK
SCHROD n young cod
SCHRODS > SCHROD
SCHTICK same as > SHTICK
SCHTICKS > SCHTICK
SCHTIK n schtick
SCHTIKS > SCHTIK
SCHTOOK n trouble
SCHTOOKS > SCHTOOK
SCHTOOM adj silent
SCHTUCK n trouble
SCHTUCKS > SCHTUCK
SCHUIT n Dutch boat with flat bottom
SCHUITS > SCHUIT
SCHUL same as > SHUL
SCHULN > SCHUL
SCHULS > SCHUL
SCHUSS n straight high-speed downhill run ▷ vb perform a schuss
SCHUSSED > SCHUSS
SCHUSSER > SCHUSS
SCHUSSERS > SCHUSS
SCHUSSES > SCHUSS
SCHUSSING > SCHUSS
SCHUYT n Dutch boat with flat bottom
SCHUYTS > SCHUYT
SCHVARTZE n Yiddish word for black person
SCHWA n central vowel representing the sound that occurs in unstressed syllables in English
SCHWARTZE same as > SCHVARTZE
SCHWAS > SCHWA
SCIAENID adj of or relating to a family of mainly tropical and subtropical marine percoid fishes ▷ n any of these fish
SCIAENIDS > SCIAENID
SCIAENOID same as > SCIAENID
SCIAMACHY n fight with an imaginary enemy
SCIARID n small fly
SCIARIDS > SCIARID
SCIATIC adj of the hip ▷ n sciatic part of the body
SCIATICA n severe pain in the large nerve in the back of the leg
SCIATICAL > SCIATICA
SCIATICAS > SCIATICA
SCIATICS > SCIATIC
SCIENCE n systematic study and knowledge of natural or physical phenomena
SCIENCED adj old word meaning learned
SCIENCES > SCIENCE
SCIENT adj old word meaning scientific
SCIENTER adv knowingly
SCIENTIAL adj of or relating to science

SCIENTISE same as > SCIENTIZE
SCIENTISM n application of, or belief in, the scientific method
SCIENTIST n person who studies or practises a science
SCIENTIZE vb treat scientifically
SCILICET adv namely
SCILLA n a plant with small bell-shaped flowers
SCILLAS > SCILLA
SCIMETAR n scimitar
SCIMETARS > SCIMETAR
SCIMITAR n curved oriental sword
SCIMITARS > SCIMITAR
SCIMITER n scimitar
SCIMITERS > SCIMITER
SCINCOID adj of, relating to, or resembling a skink ▷ n any animal, esp a lizard, resembling a skink
SCINCOIDS > SCINCOID
SCINTILLA n very small amount
SCIOLISM n practice of opinionating on subjects of which one has only superficial knowledge
SCIOLISMS > SCIOLISM
SCIOLIST > SCIOLISM
SCIOLISTS > SCIOLISM
SCIOLOUS > SCIOLISM
SCIOLTO adv musical direction meaning freely
SCIOMACHY same as > SCIAMACHY
SCIOMANCY n divination with the help of ghosts
SCION n descendant or heir
SCIONS > SCION
SCIOPHYTE n any plant that grows best in the shade
SCIOSOPHY n unscientific system of knowledge
SCIROC n hot Mediterranean wind
SCIROCCO n hot Mediterranean wind
SCIROCCOS > SCIROCCO
SCIROCS > SCIROC
SCIRRHI > SCIRRHUS
SCIRRHOID > SCIRRHUS
SCIRRHOUS adj of or resembling a scirrhus
SCIRRHUS n hard cancerous growth composed of fibrous tissues
SCISSEL n waste metal left over from sheet metal after discs have been punched out of it
SCISSELS > SCISSEL
SCISSIL n scissel
SCISSILE adj capable of being cut or divided
SCISSILS > SCISSIL
SCISSION n act or an instance of cutting,

splitting, or dividing
SCISSIONS > SCISSION
SCISSOR vb cut (an object) with scissors
SCISSORED > SCISSOR
SCISSORER > SCISSOR
SCISSORS pl n cutting instrument with two crossed pivoted blades
SCISSURE n longitudinal cleft
SCISSURES > SCISSURE
SCIURID n squirrel or related rodent
SCIURIDS > SCIURID
SCIURINE adj relating to a family of rodents that includes squirrels, marmots, and chipmunks ▷ n any sciurine animal
SCIURINES > SCIURINE
SCIUROID adj (of an animal) resembling a squirrel
SCLAFF vb cause (the club) to hit (the ground behind the ball) when making a stroke ▷ n sclaffing stroke or shot
SCLAFFED > SCLAFF
SCLAFFER > SCLAFF
SCLAFFERS > SCLAFF
SCLAFFING > SCLAFF
SCLAFFS > SCLAFF
SCLATE vb Scots word meaning slate
SCLATED > SCLATE
SCLATES > SCLATE
SCLATING > SCLATE
SCLAUNDER n old form of slander
SCLAVE n old form of slave
SCLAVES > SCLAVE
SCLERA n tough white substance that forms the outer covering of the eyeball
SCLERAE > SCLERA
SCLERAL > SCLERA
SCLERAS > SCLERA
SCLERE n supporting anatomical structure, esp a sponge spicule
SCLEREID n type of biological cell
SCLEREIDE n type of biological cell
SCLEREIDS > SCLEREID
SCLEREMA n condition in which body tissues harden
SCLEREMAS > SCLEREMA
SCLERES > SCLERE
SCLERITE n any of the hard chitinous plates that make up the exoskeleton of an arthropod
SCLERITES > SCLERITE
SCLERITIC > SCLERITE
SCLERITIS n inflammation of the sclera
SCLEROID adj (of organisms and their parts) hard or hardened
SCLEROMA n any small

area of abnormally hard tissue, esp in a mucous membrane
SCLEROMAS > SCLEROMA
SCLEROSAL > SCLEROSIS
SCLEROSE vb affect with sclerosis
SCLEROSED adj hardened
SCLEROSES > SCLEROSIS
SCLEROSIS n abnormal hardening of body tissues
SCLEROTAL n bony area in sclerotic
SCLEROTIA pl n masses of hyphae formed in certain fungi
SCLEROTIC same as > SCLERA
SCLEROTIN n protein in the cuticle of insects that becomes hard and dark
SCLEROUS adj hard
SCLIFF n Scots word for small piece
SCLIFFS > SCLIFF
SCLIM vb Scots word meaning climb
SCLIMMED > SCLIM
SCLIMMING > SCLIM
SCLIMS > SCLIM
SCODIER > SCODY
SCODIEST > SCODY
SCODY adj unkempt
SCOFF vb express derision ▷ n mocking expression
SCOFFED > SCOFF
SCOFFER > SCOFF
SCOFFERS > SCOFF
SCOFFING > SCOFF
SCOFFINGS > SCOFF
SCOFFLAW n person who habitually flouts or violates the law
SCOFFLAWS > SCOFFLAW
SCOFFS > SCOFF
SCOG vb shelter
SCOGGED > SCOG
SCOGGING > SCOG
SCOGS > SCOG
SCOINSON n part of door or window frame
SCOINSONS > SCOINSON
SCOLD vb find fault with, reprimand ▷ n person who scolds
SCOLDABLE > SCOLD
SCOLDED > SCOLD
SCOLDER > SCOLD
SCOLDERS > SCOLD
SCOLDING > SCOLD
SCOLDINGS > SCOLD
SCOLDS > SCOLD
SCOLECES > SCOLEX
SCOLECID n variety of worm
SCOLECIDS > SCOLECID
SCOLECITE n white zeolite mineral
SCOLECOID adj like scolex
SCOLEX n headlike part of a tapeworm
SCOLIA > SCOLION
SCOLICES > SCOLEX
SCOLIOMA n condition

with abnormal curvature
of spine
**SCOLIOMAS** > SCOLIOMA
**SCOLION** n ancient Greek
drinking song
**SCOLIOSES** > SCOLIOSIS
**SCOLIOSIS** n abnormal
lateral curvature of the
spine
**SCOLIOTIC** > SCOLIOSIS
**SCOLLOP** variant
of > SCALLOP
**SCOLLOPED** > SCOLLOP
**SCOLLOPS** > SCOLLOP
**SCOLYTID** n type of beetle
**SCOLYTIDS** > SCOLYTID
**SCOLYTOID** n type of beetle
**SCOMBRID** n fish of
mackerel family
**SCOMBRIDS** > SCOMBRID
**SCOMBROID** adj relating
to a suborder of marine
spiny-finned fishes ▷ n
any fish belonging to this
suborder
**SCOMFISH** vb Scots word
meaning stifle
**SCONCE** n bracket on a
wall for holding candles
or lights ▷ vb challenge
(a fellow student) on
the grounds of a social
misdemeanour to drink
a large quantity of beer
without stopping
**SCONCED** > SCONCE
**SCONCES** > SCONCE
**SCONCHEON** n part of door
or window frame
**SCONCING** > SCONCE
**SCONE** n small plain cake
baked in an oven or on a
griddle
**SCONES** > SCONE
**SCONTION** n part of door or
window frame
**SCONTIONS** > SCONTION
**SCOOBIES** > SCOOBY
**SCOOBY** n clue; notion
**SCOOCH** vb compress one's
body into smaller space
**SCOOCHED** > SCOOCH
**SCOOCHES** > SCOOCH
**SCOOCHING** > SCOOCH
**SCOOG** vb shelter
**SCOOGED** > SCOOG
**SCOOGING** > SCOOG
**SCOOGS** > SCOOG
**SCOOP** n shovel-like tool for
ladling or hollowing out
▷ vb take up or hollow out
with or as if with a scoop
**SCOOPABLE** > SCOOP
**SCOOPED** > SCOOP
**SCOOPER** > SCOOP
**SCOOPERS** > SCOOP
**SCOOPFUL** > SCOOP
**SCOOPFULS** > SCOOP
**SCOOPING** > SCOOP
**SCOOPINGS** > SCOOP
**SCOOPS** > SCOOP
**SCOOPSFUL** > SCOOP
**SCOOSH** vb squirt ▷ n
squirt or rush of liquid

**SCOOSHED** > SCOOSH
**SCOOSHES** > SCOOSH
**SCOOSHING** > SCOOSH
**SCOOT** vb leave or move
quickly ▷ n act of scooting
**SCOOTCH** same as > SCOOCH
**SCOOTCHED** > SCOOTCH
**SCOOTCHES** > SCOOTCH
**SCOOTED** > SCOOT
**SCOOTER** n child's vehicle
propelled by pushing on
the ground with one foot
**SCOOTERS** > SCOOTER
**SCOOTING** > SCOOT
**SCOOTS** > SCOOT
**SCOP** n (in Anglo-Saxon
England) a bard or minstrel
**SCOPA** n tuft of hairs on the
abdomen or hind legs of
bees, used for collecting
pollen
**SCOPAE** > SCOPA
**SCOPAS** > SCOPA
**SCOPATE** adj having tuft
**SCOPE** n opportunity for
using abilities ▷ vb look
at or examine carefully
**SCOPED** > SCOPE
**SCOPELID** n deep-sea fish
**SCOPELIDS** > SCOPELID
**SCOPELOID** n deep-sea fish
**SCOPES** > SCOPE
**SCOPING** > SCOPE
**SCOPOLINE** n soluble
crystalline alkaloid
**SCOPS** > SCOP
**SCOPULA** n small tuft of
dense hairs on the legs and
chelicerae of some spiders
**SCOPULAE** > SCOPULA
**SCOPULAS** > SCOPULA
**SCOPULATE** > SCOPULA
**SCORBUTIC** adj of or having
scurvy
**SCORCH** vb burn on the
surface ▷ n slight burn
**SCORCHED** > SCORCH
**SCORCHER** n very hot day
**SCORCHERS** > SCORCHER
**SCORCHES** > SCORCH
**SCORCHING** > SCORCH
**SCORDATO** adj musical term
meaning out of tune
**SCORE** n points gained in a
game or competition ▷ vb
gain (points) in a game
**SCORECARD** n card on
which scores are recorded
in games such as golf
**SCORED** > SCORE
**SCORELESS** adj without
anyone scoring
**SCORELINE** n final score in
game
**SCOREPAD** n pad for
recording score in game
**SCOREPADS** > SCOREPAD
**SCORER** > SCORE
**SCORERS** > SCORE
**SCORES** > SCORE
**SCORIA** n mass of solidified
lava containing many
cavities
**SCORIAC** > SCORIA

**SCORIAE** > SCORIA
**SCORIFIED** > SCORIFY
**SCORIFIER** > SCORIFY
**SCORIFIES** > SCORIFY
**SCORIFY** vb remove
(impurities) from metals
by forming scoria
**SCORING** n act or practice
of scoring
**SCORINGS** > SCORING
**SCORIOUS** > SCORIA
**SCORN** n open contempt
▷ vb despise
**SCORNED** > SCORN
**SCORNER** > SCORN
**SCORNERS** > SCORN
**SCORNFUL** > SCORN
**SCORNING** > SCORN
**SCORNINGS** > SCORN
**SCORNS** > SCORN
**SCORODITE** n mineral
containing iron and
aluminium
**SCORPER** n kind of fine
chisel with a square or
curved tip
**SCORPERS** > SCORPER
**SCORPIOID** adj of,
relating to, or resembling
scorpions
**SCORPION** n small lobster-
shaped animal with
a sting at the end of a
jointed tail
**SCORPIONS** > SCORPION
**SCORRENDO** adj musical
term meaning gliding
**SCORSE** vb exchange
**SCORSED** > SCORSE
**SCORSER** > SCORSE
**SCORSERS** > SCORSE
**SCORSES** > SCORSE
**SCORSING** > SCORSE
**SCOT** n payment or tax
**SCOTCH** vb put an end to
▷ n gash
**SCOTCHED** > SCOTCH
**SCOTCHES** > SCOTCH
**SCOTCHING** > SCOTCH
**SCOTER** n type of sea duck
**SCOTERS** > SCOTER
**SCOTIA** n deep concave
moulding
**SCOTIAS** > SCOTIA
**SCOTOMA** n blind spot
**SCOTOMAS** > SCOTOMA
**SCOTOMATA** > SCOTOMA
**SCOTOMIA** n dizziness
**SCOTOMIAS** > SCOTOMIA
**SCOTOMIES** > SCOTOMY
**SCOTOMY** n dizziness
**SCOTOPHIL** adj liking
darkness
**SCOTOPIA** n ability of the
eye to adjust for night
vision
**SCOTOPIAS** > SCOTOPIA
**SCOTOPIC** > SCOTOPIA
**SCOTS** > SCOT
**SCOTTIE** n type of small
sturdy terrier
**SCOTTIES** > SCOTTIE
**SCOUG** vb shelter
**SCOUGED** > SCOUG

**SCOUGING** > SCOUG
**SCOUGS** > SCOUG
**SCOUNDREL** n cheat or
deceiver
**SCOUP** vb Scots word
meaning jump
**SCOUPED** > SCOUP
**SCOUPING** > SCOUP
**SCOUPS** > SCOUP
**SCOUR** vb clean or polish by
rubbing with something
rough ▷ n scouring
**SCOURED** > SCOUR
**SCOURER** > SCOUR
**SCOURERS** > SCOUR
**SCOURGE** n person or thing
causing severe suffering
▷ vb cause severe suffering
to
**SCOURGED** > SCOURGE
**SCOURGER** > SCOURGE
**SCOURGERS** > SCOURGE
**SCOURGES** > SCOURGE
**SCOURGING** > SCOURGE
**SCOURIE** n young seagull
**SCOURIES** > SCOURIE
**SCOURING** > SCOUR
**SCOURINGS** pl n residue left
after cleaning grain
**SCOURS** > SCOUR
**SCOURSE** vb exchange
**SCOURSED** > SCOURSE
**SCOURSES** > SCOURSE
**SCOURSING** > SCOURSE
**SCOUSE** n stew made from
left-over meat
**SCOUSER** n inhabitant of
Liverpool
**SCOUSERS** > SCOUSER
**SCOUSES** > SCOUSE
**SCOUT** n person sent out to
reconnoitre ▷ vb act as a
scout
**SCOUTED** > SCOUT
**SCOUTER** > SCOUT
**SCOUTERS** > SCOUT
**SCOUTH** n Scots word
meaning plenty of scope
**SCOUTHER** vb Scots word
meaning scorch
**SCOUTHERS** > SCOUTHER
**SCOUTHERY** > SCOUTHER
**SCOUTHS** > SCOUTH
**SCOUTING** > SCOUT
**SCOUTINGS** > SCOUT
**SCOUTS** > SCOUT
**SCOW** n unpowered barge
used for carrying freight
▷ vb transport by scow
**SCOWDER** vb Scots word
meaning scorch
**SCOWDERED** > SCOWDER
**SCOWDERS** > SCOWDER
**SCOWED** > SCOW
**SCOWING** > SCOW
**SCOWL** n (have) an angry
or sullen expression ▷ vb
have an angry or bad-
tempered facial expression
**SCOWLED** > SCOWL
**SCOWLER** n person who
scowls
**SCOWLERS** > SCOWLER
**SCOWLING** > SCOWL

**SCOWLS** > SCOWL
**SCOWP** vb Scots word meaning jump
**SCOWPED** > SCOWP
**SCOWPING** > SCOWP
**SCOWPS** > SCOWP
**SCOWRER** n old word meaning hooligan
**SCOWRERS** > SCOWRER
**SCOWRIE** n young seagull
**SCOWRIES** > SCOWRIE
**SCOWS** > SCOW
**SCOWTH** n Scots word meaning plenty of scope
**SCOWTHER** vb Scots word meaning scorch
**SCOWTHERS** > SCOWTHER
**SCOWTHS** > SCOWTH
**SCOZZA** n rowdy person, esp one who drinks a lot of alcohol
**SCOZZAS** > SCOZZA
**SCRAB** vb scratch
**SCRABBED** > SCRAB
**SCRABBING** > SCRAB
**SCRABBLE** vb scrape at with the hands, feet, or claws ▷ n board game in which words are formed by letter tiles
**SCRABBLED** > SCRABBLE
**SCRABBLER** > SCRABBLE
**SCRABBLES** > SCRABBLE
**SCRABBLY** adj covered with stunted trees
**SCRABS** > SCRAB
**SCRAE** Scots word for > SCREE
**SCRAES** > SCRAE
**SCRAG** n thin end of a neck of mutton ▷ vb wring the neck of
**SCRAGGED** > SCRAG
**SCRAGGIER** > SCRAGGY
**SCRAGGILY** > SCRAGGY
**SCRAGGING** > SCRAG
**SCRAGGLY** adj untidy or irregular
**SCRAGGY** adj thin, bony
**SCRAGS** > SCRAG
**SCRAICH** vb Scots word meaning scream
**SCRAICHED** > SCRAICH
**SCRAICHS** > SCRAICH
**SCRAIGH** vb Scots word meaning scream
**SCRAIGHED** > SCRAIGH
**SCRAIGHS** > SCRAIGH
**SCRAM** vb go away quickly ▷ n emergency shutdown of a nuclear reactor
**SCRAMB** vb scratch with nails or claws
**SCRAMBED** > SCRAMB
**SCRAMBING** > SCRAMB
**SCRAMBLE** vb climb or crawl hastily or awkwardly ▷ n scrambling
**SCRAMBLED** > SCRAMBLE
**SCRAMBLER** n electronic device that makes transmitted speech unintelligible
**SCRAMBLES** > SCRAMBLE
**SCRAMBS** > SCRAMB

**SCRAMJET** n type of jet engine
**SCRAMJETS** > SCRAMJET
**SCRAMMED** > SCRAM
**SCRAMMING** > SCRAM
**SCRAMS** > SCRAM
**SCRAN** n food
**SCRANCH** vb crunch
**SCRANCHED** > SCRANCH
**SCRANCHES** > SCRANCH
**SCRANNEL** adj thin ▷ n thin person or thing
**SCRANNELS** > SCRANNEL
**SCRANNIER** > SCRANNY
**SCRANNY** adj scrawny
**SCRANS** > SCRAN
**SCRAP** n small piece ▷ vb discard as useless
**SCRAPABLE** > SCRAPE
**SCRAPBOOK** n book with blank pages in which newspaper cuttings or pictures are stuck
**SCRAPE** vb rub with something rough or sharp ▷ n act or sound of scraping
**SCRAPED** > SCRAPE
**SCRAPEGUT** n old word for fiddle player
**SCRAPER** > SCRAPE
**SCRAPERS** > SCRAPE
**SCRAPES** > SCRAPE
**SCRAPHEAP** n pile of discarded material
**SCRAPIE** n disease of sheep and goats
**SCRAPIES** > SCRAPIE
**SCRAPING** n act of scraping
**SCRAPINGS** > SCRAPING
**SCRAPPAGE** n act of scrapping
**SCRAPPED** > SCRAP
**SCRAPPER** n person who scraps
**SCRAPPERS** > SCRAPPER
**SCRAPPIER** > SCRAPPY
**SCRAPPILY** > SCRAPPY
**SCRAPPING** > SCRAP
**SCRAPPLE** n scraps of pork cooked with cornmeal and formed into a loaf
**SCRAPPLES** > SCRAPPLE
**SCRAPPY** adj fragmentary, disjointed
**SCRAPS** > SCRAP
**SCRAPYARD** n place for scrap metal
**SCRAT** vb scratch
**SCRATCH** vb mark or cut with claws, nails, or anything rough or sharp ▷ n wound, mark, or sound made by scratching ▷ adj put together at short notice
**SCRATCHED** > SCRATCH
**SCRATCHER** n person, animal, or thing that scratches
**SCRATCHES** n disease of horses characterized by dermatitis in the region of the fetlock

**SCRATCHIE** n scratchcard
**SCRATCHY** > SCRATCH
**SCRATS** > SCRAT
**SCRATTED** > SCRAT
**SCRATTING** > SCRAT
**SCRATTLE** vb dialect word meaning scratch
**SCRATTLED** > SCRATTLE
**SCRATTLES** > SCRATTLE
**SCRAUCH** vb squawk
**SCRAUCHED** > SCRAUCH
**SCRAUCHS** > SCRAUCH
**SCRAUGH** vb squawk
**SCRAUGHED** > SCRAUGH
**SCRAUGHS** > SCRAUGH
**SCRAW** n sod from the surface of a peat bog or from a field
**SCRAWL** vb write carelessly or hastily ▷ n scribbled writing
**SCRAWLED** > SCRAWL
**SCRAWLER** > SCRAWL
**SCRAWLERS** > SCRAWL
**SCRAWLIER** > SCRAWL
**SCRAWLING** > SCRAWL
**SCRAWLS** > SCRAWL
**SCRAWLY** > SCRAWL
**SCRAWM** vb dialect word meaning scratch
**SCRAWMED** > SCRAWM
**SCRAWMING** > SCRAWM
**SCRAWMS** > SCRAWM
**SCRAWNIER** > SCRAWNY
**SCRAWNILY** > SCRAWNY
**SCRAWNY** adj thin and bony
**SCRAWP** vb scratch (the skin) to relieve itching
**SCRAWPED** > SCRAWP
**SCRAWPING** > SCRAWP
**SCRAWPS** > SCRAWP
**SCRAWS** > SCRAW
**SCRAY** n tern
**SCRAYE** n tern
**SCRAYES** > SCRAYE
**SCRAYS** > SCRAY
**SCREAK** vb screech or creak ▷ n screech or creak
**SCREAKED** > SCREAK
**SCREAKIER** > SCREAK
**SCREAKING** > SCREAK
**SCREAKS** > SCREAK
**SCREAKY** > SCREAK
**SCREAM** vb utter a piercing cry, esp of fear or pain ▷ n shrill piercing cry
**SCREAMED** > SCREAM
**SCREAMER** n person or thing that screams
**SCREAMERS** > SCREAMER
**SCREAMING** > SCREAM
**SCREAMS** > SCREAM
**SCREE** n slope of loose shifting stones
**SCREECH** n (utter) a shrill cry ▷ vb utter a shrill cry
**SCREECHED** > SCREECH
**SCREECHER** > SCREECH
**SCREECHES** > SCREECH
**SCREECHY** adj loud and shrill
**SCREED** n long tedious piece of writing ▷ vb rip
**SCREEDED** > SCREED

**SCREEDER** > SCREED
**SCREEDERS** > SCREED
**SCREEDING** > SCREED
**SCREEDS** > SCREED
**SCREEN** n surface of a television set, VDU, etc, on which an image is formed ▷ vb shelter or conceal with or as if with a screen
**SCREENED** > SCREEN
**SCREENER** > SCREEN
**SCREENERS** > SCREEN
**SCREENFUL** > SCREEN
**SCREENIE** n informal Australian word for screensaver
**SCREENIES** > SCREENIE
**SCREENING** > SCREEN
**SCREENS** > SCREEN
**SCREES** > SCREE
**SCREET** vb shed tears ▷ n act or sound of crying
**SCREETED** > SCREET
**SCREETING** > SCREET
**SCREETS** > SCREET
**SCREEVE** vb write
**SCREEVED** > SCREEVE
**SCREEVER** > SCREEVE
**SCREEVERS** > SCREEVE
**SCREEVES** > SCREEVE
**SCREEVING** > SCREEVE
**SCREICH** same as > SCREIGH
**SCREICHED** > SCREICH
**SCREICHES** > SCREICH
**SCREICHS** > SCREICH
**SCREIGH** Scot word for > SCREECH
**SCREIGHED** > SCREIGH
**SCREIGHS** > SCREIGH
**SCREW** n metal pin with a spiral ridge along its length, twisted into materials to fasten them together ▷ vb turn (a screw)
**SCREWABLE** > SCREW
**SCREWBALL** n odd or eccentric person ▷ adj crazy or eccentric
**SCREWBEAN** n variety of mesquite
**SCREWED** adj fastened by a screw or screws
**SCREWER** > SCREW
**SCREWERS** > SCREW
**SCREWIER** > SCREWY
**SCREWIEST** > SCREWY
**SCREWING** > SCREW
**SCREWINGS** > SCREW
**SCREWLIKE** > SCREW
**SCREWS** > SCREW
**SCREWTOP** n lid with a threaded rim that is turned to close it securely
**SCREWTOPS** > SCREWTOP
**SCREWUP** n something done badly
**SCREWUPS** > SCREWUP
**SCREWWORM** n larva of a fly that develops beneath the skin of living mammals often causing illness or death
**SCREWY** adj crazy or

eccentric

**SCRIBABLE** > SCRIBE

**SCRIBAL** > SCRIBE

**SCRIBBLE** vb write hastily or illegibly ▷ n something scribbled

**SCRIBBLED** > SCRIBBLE

**SCRIBBLER** n often derogatory term for a writer of poetry, novels, journalism, etc

**SCRIBBLES** > SCRIBBLE

**SCRIBBLY** > SCRIBBLE

**SCRIBE** n person who copies documents ▷ vb to score a line with a pointed instrument

**SCRIBED** > SCRIBE

**SCRIBER** n pointed steel tool used to score materials as a guide to cutting, etc

**SCRIBERS** > SCRIBER

**SCRIBES** > SCRIBE

**SCRIBING** > SCRIBE

**SCRIBINGS** > SCRIBE

**SCRIBISM** > SCRIBE

**SCRIBISMS** > SCRIBE

**SCRIECH** vb Scots word meaning screech

**SCRIECHED** > SCRIECH

**SCRIECHS** > SCRIECH

**SCRIED** > SCRY

**SCRIENE** n old form of screen

**SCRIENES** > SCRIENE

**SCRIES** > SCRY

**SCRIEVE** vb Scots word meaning write

**SCRIEVED** > SCRIEVE

**SCRIEVES** > SCRIEVE

**SCRIEVING** > SCRIEVE

**SCRIGGLE** vb wriggle

**SCRIGGLED** > SCRIGGLE

**SCRIGGLES** > SCRIGGLE

**SCRIGGLY** > SCRIGGLE

**SCRIKE** vb old word meaning shriek

**SCRIKED** > SCRIKE

**SCRIKES** > SCRIKE

**SCRIKING** > SCRIKE

**SCRIM** n open-weave muslin or hessian fabric, used in upholstery, lining, building

**SCRIMMAGE** n rough or disorderly struggle ▷ vb engage in a scrimmage

**SCRIMP** vb be very economical

**SCRIMPED** > SCRIMP

**SCRIMPER** > SCRIMP

**SCRIMPERS** > SCRIMP

**SCRIMPIER** > SCRIMP

**SCRIMPILY** > SCRIMP

**SCRIMPING** > SCRIMP

**SCRIMPIT** adj Scots word meaning ungenerous

**SCRIMPLY** adv sparingly

**SCRIMPS** > SCRIMP

**SCRIMPY** > SCRIMP

**SCRIMS** > SCRIM

**SCRIMSHAW** n art of decorating or carving

shells, etc, done by sailors as a leisure activity ▷ vb produce scrimshaw (from)

**SCRIMURE** old word for > FENCER

**SCRIMURES** > SCRIMURE

**SCRINE** n old form of shrine

**SCRINES** > SCRINE

**SCRIP** n certificate representing a claim to stocks or shares

**SCRIPPAGE** n contents of scrip

**SCRIPS** > SCRIP

**SCRIPT** n text of a film, play, or TV programme ▷ vb write a script for

**SCRIPTED** > SCRIPT

**SCRIPTER** n person who writes scripts for films, play, or television dramas

**SCRIPTERS** > SCRIPTER

**SCRIPTING** > SCRIPT

**SCRIPTORY** adj of writing

**SCRIPTS** > SCRIPT

**SCRIPTURE** n sacred writings of a religion

**SCRITCH** vb screech

**SCRITCHED** > SCRITCH

**SCRITCHES** > SCRITCH

**SCRIVE** Scots word for > WRITE

**SCRIVED** > SCRIVE

**SCRIVENER** n person who writes out deeds, letters, etc

**SCRIVES** > SCRIVE

**SCRIVING** > SCRIVE

**SCROBE** n groove

**SCROBES** > SCROBE

**SCROD** n young cod or haddock, esp one split and prepared for cooking

**SCRODDLED** adj made of scraps of pottery

**SCRODS** > SCROD

**SCROFULA** n tuberculosis of the lymphatic glands

**SCROFULAS** > SCROFULA

**SCROG** n Scots word meaning small tree

**SCROGGIE** adj having scrogs upon it

**SCROGGIER** > SCROGGIE

**SCROGGIN** n mixture of nuts and dried fruits

**SCROGGINS** > SCROGGIN

**SCROGGY** variant of > SCROGGIE

**SCROGS** > SCROG

**SCROLL** n roll of parchment or paper ▷ vb move (text) up or down on a VDU screen

**SCROLLED** > SCROLL

**SCROLLING** > SCROLL

**SCROLLS** > SCROLL

**SCROME** vb crawl or climb, esp using the hands to aid movement

**SCROMED** > SCROME

**SCROMES** > SCROME

**SCROMING** > SCROME

**SCROOCH** vb scratch (the

skin) to relieve itching

**SCROOCHED** > SCROOCH

**SCROOCHES** > SCROOCH

**SCROOGE** variant of > SCROUGE

**SCROOGED** > SCROOGE

**SCROOGES** > SCROOGE

**SCROOGING** > SCROOGE

**SCROOP** vb emit a grating or creaking sound ▷ n such a sound

**SCROOPED** > SCROOP

**SCROOPING** > SCROOP

**SCROOPS** > SCROOP

**SCROOTCH** vb hunch up

**SCRORP** n deep scratch or weal

**SCRORPS** > SCRORP

**SCROTA** > SCROTUM

**SCROTAL** > SCROTUM

**SCROTE** n slang derogatory word meaning a worthless fellow

**SCROTES** > SCROTE

**SCROTUM** n pouch of skin containing the testicles

**SCROTUMS** > SCROTUM

**SCROUGE** vb crowd or press

**SCROUGED** > SCROUGE

**SCROUGER** n American word meaning whopper

**SCROUGERS** > SCROUGER

**SCROUGES** > SCROUGE

**SCROUGING** > SCROUGE

**SCROUNGE** vb get by cadging or begging

**SCROUNGED** > SCROUNGE

**SCROUNGER** > SCROUNGE

**SCROUNGES** > SCROUNGE

**SCROUNGY** adj shabby

**SCROW** n scroll

**SCROWDGE** vb squeeze

**SCROWDGED** > SCROWDGE

**SCROWDGES** > SCROWDGE

**SCROWL** vb old form of scroll

**SCROWLE** vb old form of scroll

**SCROWLED** > SCROWL

**SCROWLES** > SCROWLE

**SCROWLING** > SCROWL

**SCROWLS** > SCROWL

**SCROWS** > SCROW

**SCROYLE** n old word meaning wretch

**SCROYLES** > SCROYLE

**SCRUB** vb clean by rubbing, often with a hard brush and water ▷ n scrubbing ▷ adj stunted or inferior

**SCRUBBED** > SCRUB

**SCRUBBER** n woman who has many sexual partners

**SCRUBBERS** > SCRUBBER

**SCRUBBIER** > SCRUBBY

**SCRUBBILY** > SCRUBBY

**SCRUBBING** > SCRUB

**SCRUBBY** adj covered with scrub

**SCRUBLAND** n area of scrub vegetation

**SCRUBS** > SCRUB

**SCRUFF** same as > SCUM

**SCRUFFIER** > SCRUFFY

**SCRUFFILY** > SCRUFFY

**SCRUFFS** > SCRUFF

**SCRUFFY** adj unkempt or shabby

**SCRUM** n restarting of play in which opposing packs of forwards push against each other to gain possession of the ball ▷ vb form a scrum

**SCRUMDOWN** n forming of scrum in rugby

**SCRUMMAGE** same as > SCRUM

**SCRUMMED** > SCRUM

**SCRUMMIE** n informal word for a scrum half

**SCRUMMIER** > SCRUMMY

**SCRUMMIES** > SCRUMMIE

**SCRUMMING** > SCRUM

**SCRUMMY** adj delicious

**SCRUMP** vb steal (apples) from an orchard or garden

**SCRUMPED** > SCRUMP

**SCRUMPIES** > SCRUMPY

**SCRUMPING** > SCRUMP

**SCRUMPLE** vb crumple or crush

**SCRUMPLED** > SCRUMPLE

**SCRUMPLES** > SCRUMPLE

**SCRUMPOX** n skin infection spread among players in scrum

**SCRUMPS** > SCRUMP

**SCRUMPY** n rough dry cider

**SCRUMS** > SCRUM

**SCRUNCH** vb crumple or crunch or be crumpled or crunched ▷ n act or sound of scrunching

**SCRUNCHED** > SCRUNCH

**SCRUNCHES** > SCRUNCH

**SCRUNCHIE** n loop of elastic covered loosely with fabric, used to hold the hair in a ponytail

**SCRUNCHY** adj crunchy

**SCRUNT** n Scots word meaning stunted thing

**SCRUNTIER** > SCRUNT

**SCRUNTS** > SCRUNT

**SCRUNTY** > SCRUNT

**SCRUPLE** n doubt produced by one's conscience or morals ▷ vb have doubts on moral grounds

**SCRUPLED** > SCRUPLE

**SCRUPLER** > SCRUPLE

**SCRUPLERS** > SCRUPLE

**SCRUPLES** > SCRUPLE

**SCRUPLING** > SCRUPLE

**SCRUTABLE** adj open to or able to be understood by scrutiny

**SCRUTATOR** n person who examines or scrutinizes

**SCRUTINY** n close examination

**SCRUTO** n trapdoor on stage

**SCRUTOIRE** n writing desk

**SCRUTOS** > SCRUTO

**SCRUZE** vb old word meaning squeeze

**SCRUZED** > SCRUZE

SCRUZES > SCRUZE
SCRUZING > SCRUZE
SCRY *vb* divine, esp by crystal gazing
SCRYDE > SCRY
SCRYER > SCRY
SCRYERS > SCRY
SCRYING > SCRY
SCRYINGS > SCRY
SCRYNE *n* old form of shrine
SCRYNES > SCRYNE
SCUBA *n* apparatus used in skin diving, consisting of cylinders containing compressed air attached to a breathing apparatus ▷ *vb* dive using scuba equipment
SCUBAED > SCUBA
SCUBAING > SCUBA
SCUBAS > SCUBA
SCUCHIN *n* old form of scutcheon
SCUCHINS > SCUCHIN
SCUD *vb* move along swiftly ▷ *n* act of scudding
SCUDDALER *n* Scots word meaning leader of festivities
SCUDDED > SCUD
SCUDDER > SCUD
SCUDDERS > SCUD
SCUDDING > SCUD
SCUDDLE *vb* scuttle
SCUDDLED > SCUDDLE
SCUDDLES > SCUDDLE
SCUDDLING > SCUDDLE
SCUDI > SCUDO
SCUDLER *n* Scots word meaning leader of festivities
SCUDLERS > SCUDLER
SCUDO *n* any of several former Italian coins
SCUDS > SCUD
SCUFF *vb* drag (the feet) while walking ▷ *n* mark caused by scuffing
SCUFFED > SCUFF
SCUFFER *n* type of sandal
SCUFFERS > SCUFFER
SCUFFING > SCUFF
SCUFFLE *vb* fight in a disorderly manner ▷ *n* disorderly struggle
SCUFFLED > SCUFFLE
SCUFFLER > SCUFFLE
SCUFFLERS > SCUFFLE
SCUFFLES > SCUFFLE
SCUFFLING > SCUFFLE
SCUFFS > SCUFF
SCUFT *n* dialect word meaning nape of neck
SCUFTS > SCUFT
SCUG *vb* shelter
SCUGGED > SCUG
SCUGGING > SCUG
SCUGS > SCUG
SCUL *n* old form of school
SCULCH *n* rubbish
SCULCHES > SCULCH
SCULK *vb* old form of skulk
SCULKED > SCULK
SCULKER > SCULK

SCULKERS > SCULK
SCULKING > SCULK
SCULKS > SCULK
SCULL *n* small oar ▷ *vb* row (a boat) using sculls
SCULLE *n* old form of school
SCULLED > SCULL
SCULLER > SCULL
SCULLERS > SCULL
SCULLERY *n* small room where washing-up and other kitchen work is done
SCULLES > SCULLE
SCULLING > SCULL
SCULLINGS > SCULL
SCULLION *n* servant employed to do the hard work in a kitchen
SCULLIONS > SCULLION
SCULLS > SCULL
SCULP *variant of* > SCULPTURE
SCULPED > SCULP
SCULPIN *n* any of various fishes of the family *Cottidae*
SCULPING > SCULP
SCULPINS > SCULPIN
SCULPS > SCULP
SCULPSIT (he or she) sculptured it: used formerly on sculptures next to a sculptor's name
SCULPT *same as* > SCULPTURE
SCULPTED > SCULPT
SCULPTING > SCULPT
SCULPTOR *n* person who makes sculptures
SCULPTORS > SCULPTOR
SCULPTS > SCULPT
SCULPTURE *n* art of making figures or designs in wood, stone, etc ▷ *vb* represent in sculpture
SCULS > SCUL
SCULTCH *same as* > SCULCH
SCULTCHES > SCULTCH
SCUM *n* impure or waste matter on the surface of a liquid ▷ *vb* remove scum from
SCUMBAG *n* offensive or despicable person
SCUMBAGS > SCUMBAG
SCUMBER *vb* old word meaning defecate
SCUMBERED > SCUMBER
SCUMBERS > SCUMBER
SCUMBLE *vb* soften or blend (an outline or colour) with a thin upper coat of opaque colour ▷ *n* upper layer of colour applied in this way
SCUMBLED > SCUMBLE
SCUMBLES > SCUMBLE
SCUMBLING > SCUMBLE
SCUMFISH *vb* Scots word meaning disgust
SCUMLESS > SCUM
SCUMLIKE > SCUM
SCUMMED > SCUM
SCUMMER > SCUM

SCUMMERS > SCUM
SCUMMIER > SCUMMY
SCUMMIEST > SCUMMY
SCUMMILY > SCUMMY
SCUMMING > SCUM
SCUMMINGS > SCUM
SCUMMY *adj* of, resembling, consisting of, or covered with scum
SCUMS > SCUM
SCUNCHEON *n* inner part of a door jamb or window frame
SCUNDERED *adj* Irish dialect word for embarrassed
SCUNGE *vb* borrow ▷ *n* dirty or worthless person
SCUNGED > SCUNGE
SCUNGES > SCUNGE
SCUNGIER > SCUNGY
SCUNGIEST > SCUNGY
SCUNGILLI *n* seafood dish of conch
SCUNGING > SCUNGE
SCUNGY *adj* sordid or dirty
SCUNNER *vb* feel aversion ▷ *n* strong aversion
SCUNNERED *adj* annoyed, discontented, or bored
SCUNNERS > SCUNNER
SCUP *n* common sparid fish of American coastal regions of the Atlantic
SCUPPAUG *n* sea fish
SCUPPAUGS > SCUPPAUG
SCUPPER *vb* defeat or ruin ▷ *n* drain in the side of a ship
SCUPPERED > SCUPPER
SCUPPERS > SCUPPER
SCUPS > SCUP
SCUR *n* small unattached growth of horn at the site of a normal horn in cattle
SCURF *n* flaky skin on the scalp
SCURFIER > SCURF
SCURFIEST > SCURF
SCURFS > SCURF
SCURFY > SCURF
SCURRED > SCUR
SCURRIED > SCURRY
SCURRIER *n* old word meaning scout
SCURRIERS > SCURRIER
SCURRIES > SCURRY
SCURRIL *adj* old word meaning vulgar
SCURRILE *adj* old word meaning vulgar
SCURRING > SCUR
SCURRIOUR *n* old word meaning scout
SCURRY *vb* move hastily ▷ *n* act or sound of scurrying
SCURRYING > SCURRY
SCURS > SCUR
SCURVIER > SCURVY
SCURVIES > SCURVY
SCURVIEST > SCURVY
SCURVILY > SCURVY
SCURVY *n* disease caused by lack of vitamin C ▷ *adj* mean and despicable

SCUSE *shortened form of* > EXCUSE
SCUSED > SCUSE
SCUSES > SCUSE
SCUSING > SCUSE
SCUT *n* short tail of the hare, rabbit, or deer
SCUTA > SCUTUM
SCUTAGE *n* payment sometimes exacted by a lord from his vassal in lieu of military service
SCUTAGES > SCUTAGE
SCUTAL > SCUTE
SCUTATE *adj* (of animals) having or covered with large bony or horny plates
SCUTATION > SCUTATE
SCUTCH *vb* separate the fibres from the woody part of (flax) by pounding ▷ *n* tool used for this
SCUTCHED > SCUTCH
SCUTCHEON *same as* > SHIELD
SCUTCHER *same as* > SCUTCH
SCUTCHERS > SCUTCHER
SCUTCHES > SCUTCH
SCUTCHING > SCUTCH
SCUTE *n* horny or chitinous plate that makes up part of the exoskeleton in armadillos, etc
SCUTELLA > SCUTELLUM
SCUTELLAR > SCUTELLUM
SCUTELLUM *n* last of three plates into which the notum of an insect's thorax is divided
SCUTES > SCUTE
SCUTIFORM *adj* (esp of plant parts) shaped like a shield
SCUTIGER *n* species of centipede
SCUTIGERS > SCUTIGER
SCUTS > SCUT
SCUTTER *informal word for* > SCURRY
SCUTTERED > SCUTTER
SCUTTERS > SCUTTER
SCUTTLE *n* fireside container for coal ▷ *vb* run with short quick steps
SCUTTLED > SCUTTLE
SCUTTLER > SCUTTLE
SCUTTLERS > SCUTTLE
SCUTTLES > SCUTTLE
SCUTTLING > SCUTTLE
SCUTUM *n* middle of three plates into which the notum of an insect's thorax is divided
SCUTWORK *n* menial or dull work
SCUTWORKS > SCUTWORK
SCUZZ *n* dirt
SCUZZBALL *n* despicable person
SCUZZES > SCUZZ
SCUZZIER > SCUZZY
SCUZZIEST > SCUZZY
SCUZZY *adj* unkempt, dirty, or squalid

SCYBALA > SCYBALUM
SCYBALOUS > SCYBALUM
SCYBALUM *n* hard faeces in stomach
SCYE *n* Scots word meaning sleeve-hole
SCYES > SCYE
SCYPHATE *adj* shaped like cup
SCYPHI > SCYPHUS
SCYPHUS *n* ancient Greek two-handled drinking cup without a footed base
SCYTALE *n* coded message in ancient Sparta
SCYTALES > SCYTALE
SCYTHE *n* long-handled tool with a curved blade for cutting grass ▷ *vb* cut with a scythe
SCYTHED > SCYTHE
SCYTHEMAN *n* scythe user
SCYTHEMEN > SCYTHEMAN
SCYTHER > SCYTHE
SCYTHERS > SCYTHE
SCYTHES > SCYTHE
SCYTHING > SCYTHE
SDAINE *vb* old form of disdain
SDAINED > SDAINE
SDAINES > SDAINE
SDAINING > SDAINE
SDAYN *vb* old form of disdain
SDAYNED > SDAYN
SDAYNING > SDAYN
SDAYNS > SDAYN
SDEIGN *vb* old form of disdain
SDEIGNE *vb* old form of disdain
SDEIGNED > SDEIGN
SDEIGNES > SDEIGNE
SDEIGNING > SDEIGN
SDEIGNS > SDEIGN
SDEIN *vb* old form of disdain
SDEINED > SDEIN
SDEINING > SDEIN
SDEINS > SDEIN
SEA *n* mass of salt water covering three quarters of the earth's surface
SEABAG *n* canvas bag for holding a sailor's belongings
SEABAGS > SEABAG
SEABANK *n* sea shore
SEABANKS > SEABANK
SEABEACH *n* beach at seaside
SEABED *n* bottom of sea
SEABEDS > SEABED
SEABIRD *n* bird that lives on the sea
SEABIRDS > SEABIRD
SEABLITE *n* prostrate annual plant of the goosefoot family
SEABLITES > SEABLITE
SEABOARD *n* coast
SEABOARDS > SEABOARD
SEABOOT *n* sailor's waterproof boot

SEABOOTS > SEABOOT
SEABORNE *adj* carried on or by the sea
SEABOTTLE *n* type of seaweed
SEACOAST *n* land bordering on the sea
SEACOASTS > SEACOAST
SEACOCK *n* valve in the hull of a vessel below the water line for admitting sea water or for pumping out bilge water
SEACOCKS > SEACOCK
SEACRAFT *n* skill as sailor
SEACRAFTS > SEACRAFT
SEACUNNY *n* quartermaster on Indian ship
SEADOG *another word for* > FOGBOW
SEADOGS > SEADOG
SEADROME *n* aerodrome floating on sea
SEADROMES > SEADROME
SEAFARER *n* traveller who goes by sea
SEAFARERS > SEAFARER
SEAFARING *adj* working or travelling by sea ▷ *n* act of travelling by sea
SEAFLOOR *n* bottom of the sea
SEAFLOORS > SEAFLOOR
SEAFOLK *n* people who sail sea
SEAFOLKS > SEAFOLK
SEAFOOD *n* edible saltwater fish or shellfish
SEAFOODS > SEAFOOD
SEAFOWL *n* seabird
SEAFOWLS > SEAFOWL
SEAFRONT *n* built-up area facing the sea
SEAFRONTS > SEAFRONT
SEAGIRT *adj* surrounded by the sea
SEAGOING *adj* built for travelling on the sea
SEAGULL *n* gull
SEAGULLS > SEAGULL
SEAHAWK *n* skua
SEAHAWKS > SEAHAWK
SEAHOG *n* porpoise
SEAHOGS > SEAHOG
SEAHORSE *n* marine fish with a horselike head that swims upright
SEAHORSES > SEAHORSE
SEAHOUND *n* dogfish
SEAHOUNDS > SEAHOUND
SEAKALE *n* European coastal plant
SEAKALES > SEAKALE
SEAL *n* piece of wax, lead, etc with a special design impressed upon it, attached to a letter or document as a mark of authentication ▷ *vb* close with or as if with a seal
SEALABLE > SEAL
SEALANT *n* any substance used for sealing
SEALANTS > SEALANT

SEALCH *Scots word for* > SEAL
SEALCHS > SEALCH
SEALED *adj* (of a road) having a hard surface
SEALER *n* person or thing that seals
SEALERIES > SEALERY
SEALERS > SEALER
SEALERY *n* occupation of hunting seals
SEALGH *Scots word for* > SEAL
SEALGHS > SEALGH
SEALIFT *vb* transport by ship
SEALIFTED > SEALIFT
SEALIFTS > SEALIFT
SEALINE *n* company running regular sailings
SEALINES > SEALINE
SEALING > SEAL
SEALINGS > SEAL
SEALLIKE *adj* resembling a seal
SEALPOINT *n* popular variety of Siamese cat
SEALS > SEAL
SEALSKIN *n* skin or prepared fur of a seal, used to make coats
SEALSKINS > SEALSKIN
SEALWAX *n* sealing wax
SEALWAXES > SEALWAX
SEALYHAM *n* type of short-legged terrier
SEALYHAMS > SEALYHAM
SEAM *n* line where two edges are joined, as by stitching ▷ *vb* mark with furrows or wrinkles
SEAMAID *n* mermaid
SEAMAIDS > SEAMAID
SEAMAN *n* sailor
SEAMANLY > SEAMAN
SEAMARK *n* aid to navigation, such as a conspicuous object on a shore used as a guide
SEAMARKS > SEAMARK
SEAME *n* old word meaning grease
SEAMED > SEAM
SEAMEN > SEAMAN
SEAMER *n* fast bowler who makes the ball bounce on its seam so that it will change direction
SEAMERS > SEAMER
SEAMES > SEAME
SEAMIER > SEAMY
SEAMIEST > SEAMY
SEAMINESS > SEAMY
SEAMING > SEAM
SEAMLESS *adj* (of a garment) without seams
SEAMLIKE > SEAM
SEAMOUNT *n* submarine mountain rising more than 1000 metres above the surrounding ocean floor
SEAMOUNTS > SEAMOUNT
SEAMS > SEAM
SEAMSET *n* tool for flattening seams in metal

SEAMSETS > SEAMSET
SEAMSTER *n* person who sews
SEAMSTERS > SEAMSTER
SEAMY *adj* sordid
SEAN *vb* fish with seine net
SEANCE *n* meeting at which spiritualists attempt to communicate with the dead
SEANCES > SEANCE
SEANED > SEAN
SEANING > SEAN
SEANS > SEAN
SEAPIECE *n* artwork depicting sea
SEAPIECES > SEAPIECE
SEAPLANE *n* aircraft designed to take off from and land on water
SEAPLANES > SEAPLANE
SEAPORT *n* town or city with a harbour for boats and ships
SEAPORTS > SEAPORT
SEAQUAKE *n* agitation and disturbance of the sea caused by an earthquake at the sea bed
SEAQUAKES > SEAQUAKE
SEAQUARIA *pl n* areas of salt water where sea animals are kept
SEAR *vb* scorch, burn the surface of ▷ *n* mark caused by searing ▷ *adj* dried up
SEARAT *n* pirate
SEARATS > SEARAT
SEARCE *vb* sift
SEARCED > SEARCE
SEARCES > SEARCE
SEARCH *vb* examine closely in order to find something ▷ *n* searching
SEARCHED > SEARCH
SEARCHER > SEARCH
SEARCHERS > SEARCH
SEARCHES > SEARCH
SEARCHING *adj* keen or thorough
SEARCING > SEARCE
SEARE *adj* old word meaning dry and withered
SEARED > SEAR
SEARER > SEAR
SEAREST > SEAR
SEARING > SEAR
SEARINGLY > SEAR
SEARINGS > SEAR
SEARNESS > SEAR
SEAROBIN *n* type of American gurnard
SEAROBINS > SEAROBIN
SEARS > SEAR
SEAS > SEA
SEASCAPE *n* picture of a scene at sea
SEASCAPES > SEASCAPE
SEASCOUT *n* member of seagoing scouts
SEASCOUTS > SEASCOUT
SEASE *vb* old form of seize
SEASED > SEASE

SEASES > SEASE

SEASHELL n empty shell of a mollusc

SEASHELLS > SEASHELL

SEASHORE n land bordering on the sea

SEASHORES > SEASHORE

SEASICK adj suffering from nausea caused by the motion of a ship

SEASICKER > SEASICK

SEASIDE n area, esp a holiday resort, on the coast

SEASIDES > SEASIDE

SEASING > SEASE

SEASON n one of four divisions of the year, each of which has characteristic weather conditions ▷ vb flavour with salt, herbs, etc

SEASONAL adj depending on or varying with the seasons ▷ n seasonal thing

SEASONALS > SEASONAL

SEASONED > SEASON

SEASONER > SEASON

SEASONERS > SEASON

SEASONING n salt, herbs, etc added to food to enhance flavour

SEASONS > SEASON

SEASPEAK n language used by sailors

SEASPEAKS > SEASPEAK

SEASTRAND n seashore

SEASURE n old form of seizure

SEASURES > SEASURE

SEAT n thing designed or used for sitting on ▷ vb cause to sit

SEATBACK n back of seat

SEATBACKS > SEATBACK

SEATBELT n safety belt in vehicle

SEATBELTS > SEATBELT

SEATED > SEAT

SEATER n person or thing that seats

SEATERS > SEATER

SEATING n supply or arrangement of seats ▷ adj of or relating to the provision of places to sit

SEATINGS > SEATING

SEATLESS > SEAT

SEATMATE n person sitting in next seat

SEATMATES > SEATMATE

SEATRAIN n ship that can carry train

SEATRAINS > SEATRAIN

SEATROUT n trout living in the sea

SEATROUTS > SEATROUT

SEATS > SEAT

SEATWORK n schoolwork done at pupils' desks

SEATWORKS > SEATWORK

SEAWALL n wall built to prevent encroachment or erosion by the sea

SEAWALLS > SEAWALL

SEAWAN n shell beads, usually unstrung, used by certain North American Indians as money

SEAWANS > SEAWAN

SEAWANT n Native American name for silver coins

SEAWANTS > SEAWANT

SEAWARD same as > SEAWARDS

SEAWARDLY > SEAWARD

SEAWARDS adv towards the sea

SEAWARE n any of numerous large coarse seaweeds

SEAWARES > SEAWARE

SEAWATER n water from sea

SEAWATERS > SEAWATER

SEAWAY n waterway giving access to an inland port, navigable by ocean-going ships

SEAWAYS > SEAWAY

SEAWEED n plant growing in the sea

SEAWEEDS > SEAWEED

SEAWIFE n variety of sea fish

SEAWIVES > SEAWIFE

SEAWOMAN n mermaid

SEAWOMEN > SEAWOMAN

SEAWORM n marine worm

SEAWORMS > SEAWORM

SEAWORTHY adj (of a ship) in fit condition for a sea voyage

SEAZE vb old form of seize

SEAZED > SEAZE

SEAZES > SEAZE

SEAZING > SEAZE

SEBACEOUS adj of, like, or secreting fat or oil

SEBACIC adj derived from sebacic acid, a white crystalline acid

SEBASIC same as > SEBACIC

SEBATE n salt of sebacic acid

SEBATES > SEBATE

SEBESTEN n Asian tree

SEBESTENS > SEBESTEN

SEBIFIC adj producing fat

SEBORRHEA n skin disease in which excessive oil is secreted

SEBUM n oily substance secreted by the sebaceous glands

SEBUMS > SEBUM

SEBUNDIES > SEBUNDY

SEBUNDY n irregular soldier in India

SEC same as > SECANT

SECALOSE n type of sugar

SECALOSES > SECALOSE

SECANT n (in trigonometry) the ratio of the length of the hypotenuse to the length of the adjacent side in a right-angled triangle

SECANTLY > SECANT

SECANTS > SECANT

SECATEUR n secateurs

SECATEURS pl n small pruning shears

SECCO n wall painting done on dried plaster with tempera or pigments ground in limewater

SECCOS > SECCO

SECEDE vb withdraw formally from a political alliance or federation

SECEDED > SECEDE

SECEDER > SECEDE

SECEDERS > SECEDE

SECEDES > SECEDE

SECEDING > SECEDE

SECERN vb (of a gland or follicle) to secrete

SECERNED > SECERN

SECERNENT > SECERN

SECERNING > SECERN

SECERNS > SECERN

SECESH n secessionist in US Civil War

SECESHER n secessionist in US Civil War

SECESHERS > SECESHER

SECESHES > SECESH

SECESSION n act of seceding

SECH n hyperbolic secant

SECHS > SECH

SECKEL variant of > SECKLE

SECKELS > SECKEL

SECKLE n type of pear

SECKLES > SECKLE

SECLUDE vb keep (a person) from contact with others

SECLUDED adj private, sheltered

SECLUDES > SECLUDE

SECLUDING > SECLUDE

SECLUSION n state of being secluded

SECLUSIVE adj tending to seclude

SECO adj (of wine) dry

SECODONT n animal with cutting back teeth

SECODONTS > SECODONT

SECONAL n tradename for secobarbitol

SECONALS > SECONAL

SECOND adj coming directly after the first ▷ n person or thing coming second ▷ vb express formal support for (a motion proposed in a meeting)

SECONDARY adj of less importance ▷ n person or thing that is secondary

SECONDE n second of eight positions from which a parry or attack can be made in fencing

SECONDED > SECOND

SECONDEE n person who is seconded

SECONDEES > SECONDEE

SECONDER > SECOND

SECONDERS > SECOND

SECONDES > SECONDE

SECONDI > SECONDO

SECONDING > SECOND

SECONDLY same as > SECOND

SECONDO n left-hand part in a piano duet

SECONDS > SECOND

SECPAR n distance unit in astronomy

SECPARS > SECPAR

SECRECIES > SECRECY

SECRECY n state of being secret

SECRET adj kept from the knowledge of others ▷ n something kept secret

SECRETA n secretions

SECRETAGE n use of mercury in treating furs

SECRETARY n person who deals with correspondence and general clerical work

SECRETE vb (of an organ, gland, etc) produce and release (a substance)

SECRETED > SECRETE

SECRETER > SECRET

SECRETES > SECRET

SECRETEST > SECRET

SECRETIN n peptic hormone secreted by the mucosae of the duodenum and jejunum

SECRETING > SECRETE

SECRETINS > SECRETIN

SECRETION n substance that is released from a cell, organ, or gland

SECRETIVE adj inclined to keep things secret

SECRETLY > SECRET

SECRETOR > SECRETE

SECRETORS > SECRETE

SECRETORY adj of, relating to, or producing a secretion

SECRETS > SECRET

SECS > SEC

SECT n often disparaging term for a subdivision of a religious or political group, esp one with extreme beliefs

SECTARIAL > SECT

SECTARIAN adj of a sect ▷ n member of a sect

SECTARIES > SECTARY

SECTARY n member of a sect

SECTATOR n member of sect

SECTATORS > SECTATOR

SECTILE adj able to be cut smoothly

SECTILITY > SECTILE

SECTION n part cut off ▷ vb cut or divide into sections

SECTIONAL adj concerned with a particular area or group within a country or community

SECTIONED > SECTION

SECTIONS > SECTION

SECTOR n part or subdivision ▷ vb divide

into sectors
SECTORAL > SECTOR
SECTORED > SECTOR
SECTORIAL adj of or
relating to a sector
SECTORING > SECTOR
SECTORISE same
as > SECTORIZE
SECTORIZE vb split into
sectors
SECTORS > SECTOR
SECTS > SECT
SECULAR adj worldly, as
opposed to sacred ▷ n
member of the secular
clergy
SECULARLY > SECULAR
SECULARS > SECULAR
SECULUM n age in
astronomy
SECULUMS > SECULUM
SECUND adj having or
designating parts
arranged on or turned to
one side of the axis
SECUNDINE n one of
the two integuments
surrounding the ovule of
a plant
SECUNDLY > SECUND
SECUNDUM adj according to
SECURABLE > SECURE
SECURANCE > SECURE
SECURE adj free from
danger ▷ vb obtain
SECURED > SECURE
SECURELY > SECURE
SECURER > SECURE
SECURERS > SECURE
SECURES > SECURE
SECUREST > SECURE
SECURING > SECURE
SECURITAN n person
believing they are secure
SECURITY n precautions
against theft, espionage,
or other danger
SED old spelling of > SAID
SEDAN same as > SALOON
SEDANS > SEDAN
SEDARIM > SEDER
SEDATE adj calm and
dignified ▷ vb give a
sedative drug to
SEDATED > SEDATE
SEDATELY > SEDATE
SEDATER > SEDATE
SEDATES > SEDATE
SEDATEST > SEDATE
SEDATING > SEDATE
SEDATION n state of calm,
esp when brought about
by sedatives
SEDATIONS > SEDATION
SEDATIVE adj having a
soothing or calming effect
▷ n sedative drug
SEDATIVES > SEDATIVE
SEDENT adj seated
SEDENTARY adj done
sitting down, involving
little exercise
SEDER n Jewish ceremonial
meal held on the first

night or first two nights of
Passover
SEDERS > SEDER
SEDERUNT n sitting of an
ecclesiastical assembly,
court, etc
SEDERUNTS > SEDERUNT
SEDES Latin word for > SEAT
SEDGE n coarse grasslike
plant growing on wet
ground
SEDGED adj having sedge
SEDGELAND n land covered
with sedge
SEDGES > SEDGE
SEDGIER > SEDGE
SEDGIEST > SEDGE
SEDGY > SEDGE
SEDILE n seat for clergy in
church
SEDILIA n group of three
seats where the celebrant
and ministers sit at certain
points during High Mass
SEDILIUM n seat for clergy
in church
SEDIMENT n matter which
settles to the bottom of a
liquid
SEDIMENTS > SEDIMENT
SEDITION n speech or
action encouraging
rebellion against the
government
SEDITIONS > SEDITION
SEDITIOUS adj of, like, or
causing sedition
SEDUCE vb persuade into
sexual intercourse
SEDUCED > SEDUCE
SEDUCER n person who
entices, allures, or seduces
SEDUCERS > SEDUCER
SEDUCES > SEDUCE
SEDUCIBLE > SEDUCE
SEDUCING > SEDUCE
SEDUCINGS > SEDUCE
SEDUCIVE adj seductive
SEDUCTION n act of
seducing or the state of
being seduced
SEDUCTIVE adj (of
a woman) sexually
attractive
SEDUCTOR n person who
seduces
SEDUCTORS > SEDUCTOR
SEDULITY > SEDULOUS
SEDULOUS adj diligent or
persevering
SEDUM n rock plant
SEDUMS > SEDUM
SEE vb perceive with the
eyes or mind ▷ n diocese
of a bishop
SEEABLE > SEE
SEECATCH n male seal in
Aleutians
SEED n mature fertilized
grain of a plant ▷ vb sow
with seed
SEEDBED n area of soil
prepared for the growing
of seedlings before they

are transplanted
SEEDBEDS > SEEDBED
SEEDBOX n part of plant
that contains seeds
SEEDBOXES > SEEDBED
SEEDCAKE n sweet cake
flavoured with caraway
seeds and lemon rind or
essence
SEEDCAKES > SEEDCAKE
SEEDCASE n part of a fruit
enclosing the seeds
SEEDCASES > SEEDCASE
SEEDEATER n bird feeding
on seeds
SEEDED > SEED
SEEDER n person or thing
that seeds
SEEDERS > SEEDER
SEEDIER > SEEDY
SEEDIEST > SEEDY
SEEDILY > SEEDY
SEEDINESS > SEEDY
SEEDING > SEED
SEEDINGS > SEED
SEEDLESS > SEED
SEEDLIKE > SEED
SEEDLING n young plant
raised from a seed
SEEDLINGS > SEEDLING
SEEDLIP n basket holding
seeds to be sown
SEEDLIPS > SEEDLIP
SEEDMAN n seller of seeds
SEEDMEN > SEEDMAN
SEEDNESS n old word
meaning sowing of seeds
SEEDPOD n carpel enclosing
the seeds of a flowering
plant
SEEDPODS > SEEDPOD
SEEDS > SEED
SEEDSMAN n seller of seeds
SEEDSMEN > SEEDSMAN
SEEDSTOCK n livestock
used for breeding
SEEDTIME n season when
seeds are sown
SEEDTIMES > SEEDTIME
SEEDY adj shabby
SEEING > SEE
SEEINGS > SEE
SEEK vb try to find or
obtain
SEEKER > SEEK
SEEKERS > SEEK
SEEKING > SEEK
SEEKS > SEEK
SEEL vb sew up the eyelids
of (a hawk or falcon) so as
to render it quiet and tame
SEELD adj old word
meaning rare
SEELED > SEEL
SEELIE pl n good
benevolent fairies
SEELIER > SEELY
SEELIEST > SEELY
SEELING > SEEL
SEELINGS > SEEL
SEELS > SEEL
SEELY adj old word
meaning happy
SEEM vb appear to be

SEEMED > SEEM
SEEMER > SEEM
SEEMERS > SEEM
SEEMING adj apparent but
not real ▷ n outward or
false appearance
SEEMINGLY adv in
appearance but not
necessarily in actuality
SEEMINGS > SEEMING
SEEMLESS adj old word
meaning unseemly
SEEMLIER > SEEMLY
SEEMLIEST > SEEMLY
SEEMLIHED n old word
meaning seemliness
SEEMLY adj proper or
fitting ▷ adv properly or
decorously
SEEMLYHED n old word
meaning seemliness
SEEMS > SEEM
SEEN > SEE
SEEP vb trickle through
slowly, ooze ▷ n small
spring or place where
water, oil, etc, has oozed
through the ground
SEEPAGE n act or process of
seeping
SEEPAGES > SEEPAGE
SEEPED > SEEP
SEEPIER > SEEPY
SEEPIEST > SEEPY
SEEPING > SEEP
SEEPS > SEEP
SEEPY adj tending to seep
SEER n person who sees
SEERESS > SEER
SEERESSES > SEER
SEERS > SEER
SEES > SEE
SEESAW n plank balanced
in the middle so that two
people seated on either
end ride up and down
alternately ▷ vb move up
and down
SEESAWED > SEESAW
SEESAWING > SEESAW
SEESAWS > SEESAW
SEETHE vb be very agitated
▷ n act or state of seething
SEETHED > SEETHE
SEETHER > SEETHE
SEETHERS > SEETHE
SEETHES > SEETHE
SEETHING adj boiling or
foaming as if boiling
SEETHINGS > SEETHING
SEEWING n suing
SEFER n scrolls of the Law
SEG n metal stud on shoe
sole
SEGAR n cigar
SEGARS > SEGAR
SEGETAL adj (of weeds)
growing amongst crops
SEGGAR n box in which
pottery is baked
SEGGARS > SEGGAR
SEGHOL n pronunciation
mark in Hebrew
SEGHOLATE n vowel sound

in Hebrew
**SEGHOLS** > SEGHOL
**SEGMENT** n one of several sections into which something may be divided ▷ vb divide into segments
**SEGMENTAL** adj of, like, or having the form of a segment
**SEGMENTED** > SEGMENT
**SEGMENTS** > SEGMENT
**SEGNI** > SEGNO
**SEGNO** n sign at the beginning or end of a section directed to be repeated
**SEGNOS** > SEGNO
**SEGO** n American variety of lily
**SEGOL** variant of > SEGHOL
**SEGOLATE** variant of > SEGHOLATE
**SEGOLATES** > SEGOLATE
**SEGOLS** > SEGOL
**SEGOS** > SEGO
**SEGREANT** adj having raised wings in heraldry
**SEGREGANT** n organism different because of segregation
**SEGREGATE** vb set apart
**SEGS** > SEG
**SEGUE** vb proceed from one section or piece of music to another without a break ▷ n practice or an instance of playing music in this way
**SEGUED** > SEGUE
**SEGUEING** > SEGUE
**SEGUES** > SEGUE
**SEI** n type of rorqual
**SEICENTO** n 17th century with reference to Italian art and literature
**SEICENTOS** > SEICENTO
**SEICHE** n periodic oscillation of the surface of an enclosed or semienclosed body of water
**SEICHES** > SEICHE
**SEIDEL** n vessel for drinking beer
**SEIDELS** > SEIDEL
**SEIF** n long ridge of blown sand in a desert
**SEIFS** > SEIF
**SEIGNEUR** n feudal lord
**SEIGNEURS** > SEIGNEUR
**SEIGNEURY** n estate of a seigneur
**SEIGNIOR** n (in England) the lord of a seigniory
**SEIGNIORS** > SEIGNIOR
**SEIGNIORY** n (in England) the fee or manor of a seignior
**SEIGNORAL** adj relating to the quality of being a lord
**SEIGNORY** n lordship
**SEIK** Scot word for > SICK
**SEIKER** > SEIK
**SEIKEST** > SEIK

**SEIL** vb dialect word meaning strain
**SEILED** > SEIL
**SEILING** > SEIL
**SEILS** > SEIL
**SEINE** n large fishing net that hangs vertically from floats ▷ vb catch (fish) using this net
**SEINED** > SEINE
**SEINER** > SEINE
**SEINERS** > SEINE
**SEINES** > SEINE
**SEINING** > SEINE
**SEININGS** > SEINE
**SEIR** n fish of Indian seas
**SEIRS** > SEIR
**SEIS** > SEI
**SEISABLE** > SEISE
**SEISE** vb put into legal possession of (property, etc)
**SEISED** > SEISE
**SEISER** > SEISE
**SEISERS** > SEISE
**SEISES** > SEISE
**SEISIN** n feudal possession of an estate in land
**SEISING** > SEISE
**SEISINGS** > SEISE
**SEISINS** > SEISIN
**SEISM** n earthquake
**SEISMAL** adj of earthquakes
**SEISMIC** adj relating to earthquakes
**SEISMICAL** same as > SEISMIC
**SEISMISM** n occurrence of earthquakes
**SEISMISMS** > SEISMISM
**SEISMS** > SEISM
**SEISOR** n person who takes seisin
**SEISORS** > SEISOR
**SEISURE** n act of seisin
**SEISURES** > SEISURE
**SEITAN** same as > SEITEN
**SEITANS** > SEITAN
**SEITEN** n gluten from wheat
**SEITENS** > SEITEN
**SEITIES** > SEITY
**SEITY** n selfhood
**SEIZABLE** > SEIZE
**SEIZE** vb take hold of forcibly or quickly
**SEIZED** > SEIZE
**SEIZER** > SEIZE
**SEIZERS** > SEIZE
**SEIZES** > SEIZE
**SEIZIN** same as > SEISIN
**SEIZING** n binding used for holding together two ropes, two spars, etc, esp by lashing with a separate rope
**SEIZINGS** > SEIZING
**SEIZINS** > SEIZIN
**SEIZOR** n person who takes seisin
**SEIZORS** > SEIZOR
**SEIZURE** n sudden violent

attack of an illness
**SEIZURES** > SEIZURE
**SEJANT** adj (of a beast) shown seated
**SEJEANT** same as > SEJANT
**SEKOS** n holy place
**SEKOSES** > SEKOS
**SEKT** n German sparkling wine
**SEKTS** > SEKT
**SEL** Scot word for > SELF
**SELACHIAN** adj relating to a large subclass of cartilaginous fishes including the sharks, rays, dogfish, and skates ▷ n any fish belonging to this subclass
**SELADANG** n Malaysian tapir
**SELADANGS** > SELADANG
**SELAH** n Hebrew word of unknown meaning occurring in the Old Testament psalms, and thought to be a musical direction
**SELAHS** > SELAH
**SELAMLIK** n men's quarters in Turkish house
**SELAMLIKS** > SELAMLIK
**SELCOUTH** adj old word meaning strange
**SELD** adj old word meaning rare
**SELDOM** adv not often, rarely
**SELDOMLY** > SELDOM
**SELDSEEN** adj old word meaning seldom seen
**SELDSHOWN** adj old word meaning seldom shown
**SELE** n old word meaning happiness
**SELECT** vb pick out or choose ▷ adj chosen in preference to others
**SELECTA** n disc jockey
**SELECTAS** > SELECTA
**SELECTED** > SELECT
**SELECTEE** n person who is selected, esp for military service
**SELECTEES** > SELECTEE
**SELECTING** > SELECT
**SELECTION** n selecting
**SELECTIVE** adj chosen or choosing carefully
**SELECTLY** > SELECT
**SELECTMAN** n any of the members of the local boards of most New England towns
**SELECTMEN** > SELECTMAN
**SELECTOR** n person or thing that selects
**SELECTORS** > SELECTOR
**SELECTS** > SELECT
**SELENATE** n any salt or ester formed by replacing one or both of the hydrogens of selenic acid with metal ions or organic groups

**SELENATES** > SELENATE
**SELENIAN** adj of the moon
**SELENIC** adj of or containing selenium, esp in the hexavalent state
**SELENIDE** n compound containing selenium
**SELENIDES** > SELENIDE
**SELENIOUS** adj of or containing selenium in the divalent or tetravalent state
**SELENITE** n colourless glassy variety of gypsum
**SELENITES** > SELENITE
**SELENITIC** > SELENITE
**SELENIUM** n nonmetallic element with photoelectric properties
**SELENIUMS** > SELENIUM
**SELENOSES** > SELENOSIS
**SELENOSIS** n poisoned condition caused by selenium
**SELENOUS** same as > SELENIOUS
**SELES** > SELE
**SELF** n distinct individuality or identity of a person or thing ▷ pron myself, yourself, himself, or herself ▷ vb reproduce by oneself
**SELFDOM** n selfhood
**SELFDOMS** > SELFDOM
**SELFED** > SELF
**SELFHEAL** n low-growing European herbaceous plant
**SELFHEALS** > SELFHEAL
**SELFHOOD** n state of having a distinct identity
**SELFHOODS** > SELFHOOD
**SELFING** > SELF
**SELFINGS** > SELF
**SELFISH** adj caring too much about oneself and not enough about others
**SELFISHLY** > SELFISH
**SELFISM** n emphasis on self
**SELFISMS** > SELFISM
**SELFIST** > SELFISM
**SELFISTS** > SELFISM
**SELFLESS** adj unselfish
**SELFNESS** n egotism
**SELFS** > SELF
**SELFSAME** adj very same
**SELFWARD** adj toward self
**SELFWARDS** adv towards self
**SELICTAR** n Turkish sword-bearer
**SELICTARS** > SELICTAR
**SELKIE** same as > SILKIE
**SELKIES** > SELKIE
**SELL** vb exchange (something) for money ▷ n manner of selling
**SELLA** n area of bone in body
**SELLABLE** > SELL
**SELLAE** > SELLA
**SELLAS** > SELLA

**SELLE** n old word meaning seat

**SELLER** n person who sells

**SELLERS** > SELLER

**SELLES** > SELLE

**SELLING** > SELL

**SELLOFF** n act of selling cheaply

**SELLOFFS** > SELLOFF

**SELLOTAPE** n tradename for a type of transparent adhesive tape

**SELLOUT** n performance of a show etc for which all the tickets are sold

**SELLOUTS** > SELLOUT

**SELLS** > SELL

**SELS** > SEL

**SELSYN** same as > SYNCHRO

**SELSYNS** > SELSYN

**SELTZER** n natural effervescent water containing minerals

**SELTZERS** > SELTZER

**SELVA** n dense equatorial forest characterized by tall broad-leaved evergreen trees, lianas, etc

**SELVAGE** n edge of cloth, woven so as to prevent unravelling ▷ vb edge or border

**SELVAGED** > SELVAGE

**SELVAGEE** n rope used as strap

**SELVAGEES** > SELVAGEE

**SELVAGES** > SELVAGE

**SELVAGING** > SELVAGE

**SELVAS** > SELVA

**SELVEDGE** same as > SELVAGE

**SELVEDGED** > SELVEDGE

**SELVEDGES** > SELVEDGE

**SELVES** > SELF

**SEMAINIER** n chest of drawers

**SEMANTEME** same as > SEMEME

**SEMANTIC** adj relating to the meaning of words

**SEMANTICS** n study of linguistic meaning

**SEMANTIDE** n type of molecule

**SEMANTRA** > SEMANTRON

**SEMANTRON** n bar struck instead of bell in Orthodox church

**SEMAPHORE** n system of signalling by holding two flags in different positions to represent letters of the alphabet ▷ vb signal (information) by semaphore

**SEMATIC** adj (of the conspicuous coloration of certain animals) acting as a warning, esp to potential predators

**SEMBLABLE** adj resembling or similar ▷ n something that resembles another thing

**SEMBLABLY** > SEMBLABLE

**SEMBLANCE** n outward or superficial appearance

**SEMBLANT** n semblance

**SEMBLANTS** > SEMBLANT

**SEMBLE** vb seem

**SEMBLED** > SEMBLE

**SEMBLES** > SEMBLE

**SEMBLING** > SEMBLE

**SEME** adj dotted (with)

**SEMEE** variant of > SEME

**SEMEED** adj seme

**SEMEIA** > SEMEION

**SEMEION** n unit of metre in ancient poetry

**SEMEIOTIC** same as > SEMIOTIC

**SEMEME** n meaning of a morpheme

**SEMEMES** > SEMEME

**SEMEMIC** > SEMEME

**SEMEN** n sperm-carrying fluid produced by male animals

**SEMENS** > SEMEN

**SEMES** > SEME

**SEMESTER** n either of two divisions of the academic year

**SEMESTERS** > SEMESTER

**SEMESTRAL** > SEMESTER

**SEMI** n semidetached house

**SEMIANGLE** n half angle

**SEMIARID** adj denoting land that lies on the edges of a desert but has a slightly higher rainfall

**SEMIBALD** adj partly bald

**SEMIBOLD** adj denoting a weight of typeface between medium and bold face ▷ n semibold type

**SEMIBOLDS** > SEMIBOLD

**SEMIBREVE** n musical note four beats long

**SEMIBULL** n papal bull issued before coronation

**SEMIBULLS** > SEMIBULL

**SEMICOLON** n punctuation mark (;)

**SEMICOMA** n condition similar to a coma

**SEMICOMAS** > SEMICOMA

**SEMICURED** adj partly cured

**SEMIDEAF** adj partly deaf

**SEMIDEIFY** vb treat almost as god

**SEMIDOME** n half-dome, esp one used to cover a semicircular apse

**SEMIDOMED** adj having semidome

**SEMIDOMES** > SEMIDOME

**SEMIDRY** adj partly dry

**SEMIDWARF** adj smaller than standard variety

**SEMIE** n historical name for a student in second year at a Scottish university

**SEMIERECT** adj partly erect

**SEMIES** > SEMIE

**SEMIFINAL** n match or round before the final

**SEMIFIT** adj not fully fit

**SEMIFLUID** adj having properties between those of a liquid and those of a solid ▷ n substance that has such properties because of high viscosity

**SEMIGALA** adj characterized by quite a lot of celebration and fun

**SEMIGLOSS** adj (of paint) giving finish between matt and gloss

**SEMIGROUP** n type of set in mathematics

**SEMIHARD** adj partly hard

**SEMIHIGH** adj moderately high

**SEMIHOBO** n person looking almost like hobo

**SEMIHOBOS** > SEMIHOBO

**SEMILLON** n grape used to make wine

**SEMILLONS** > SEMILLON

**SEMILOG** adj semilogarithmic

**SEMILUNAR** adj shaped like a crescent or half-moon

**SEMILUNE** n half-moon shape

**SEMILUNES** > SEMILUNE

**SEMIMAT** adj semimatt

**SEMIMATT** adj with surface midway between matt and gloss

**SEMIMATTE** adj semimatt

**SEMIMETAL** n metal not fully malleable

**SEMIMICRO** adj using microwaves

**SEMIMILD** adj somewhat mild

**SEMIMOIST** adj slightly wet

**SEMIMUTE** adj having speech impairment through hearing loss

**SEMINA** > SEMEN

**SEMINAL** adj original and influential

**SEMINALLY** > SEMINAL

**SEMINAR** n meeting of a group of students for discussion

**SEMINARS** > SEMINAR

**SEMINARY** n college for priests

**SEMINATE** vb sow

**SEMINATED** > SEMINATE

**SEMINATES** > SEMINATE

**SEMINOMA** n malignant tumour of the testicle

**SEMINOMAD** n person living partly nomadic life

**SEMINOMAS** > SEMINOMA

**SEMINUDE** adj partly nude

**SEMIOLOGY** same as > SEMIOTICS

**SEMIOPEN** adj half-open

**SEMIOSES** > SEMIOSIS

**SEMIOSIS** n action involving establishing relationship between signs

**SEMIOTIC** adj relating to

signs and symbols, esp spoken or written signs

**SEMIOTICS** n study of human communications, esp signs and symbols

**SEMIOVAL** adj shaped like half of oval

**SEMIPED** n measure in poetic metre

**SEMIPEDS** > SEMIPED

**SEMIPIOUS** adj quite pious

**SEMIPLUME** n type of bird feather

**SEMIPOLAR** as in semipolar bond type of chemical bond

**SEMIPRO** n semiprofessional

**SEMIPROS** > SEMIPRO

**SEMIRAW** adj not fully cooked or processed

**SEMIRIGID** adj (of an airship) maintaining shape by means of a main supporting keel and internal gas pressure

**SEMIROUND** adj with one flat side and one round side

**SEMIRURAL** adj partly rural

**SEMIS** > SEMI

**SEMISES** > SEMI

**SEMISOFT** adj partly soft

**SEMISOLID** adj having a viscosity and rigidity intermediate between that of a solid and a liquid ▷ n substance in this state

**SEMISOLUS** n advertisement that appears on the same page as another advertisement but not adjacent to it

**SEMISTIFF** adj partly stiff

**SEMISWEET** adj partly sweet

**SEMITAR** old spelling of > SCIMITAR

**SEMITARS** > SEMITAR

**SEMITAUR** old spelling of > SCIMITAR

**SEMITAURS** > SEMITAR

**SEMITIST** n student of Semitic languages and culture

**SEMITISTS** > SEMITIST

**SEMITONAL** > SEMITONE

**SEMITONE** n smallest interval between two notes in Western music

**SEMITONES** > SEMITONE

**SEMITONIC** > SEMITONE

**SEMITRUCK** n articulated lorry

**SEMIURBAN** adj suburban

**SEMIVOCAL** adj of or relating to a semivowel

**SEMIVOWEL** n vowel-like sound that acts like a consonant, such as the sound w in well

**SEMIWILD** adj not fully domesticated

**SEMIWORKS** adj equipped

SEMMIT *n* vest

SEMMITS > SEMMIT

SEMOLINA *n* hard grains of wheat left after the milling of flour, used to make puddings and pasta

SEMOLINAS > SEMOLINA

SEMPER *adv* Latin word meaning always

SEMPLE *adj* Scots word meaning simple

SEMPLER > SEMPLE

SEMPLEST > SEMPLE

SEMPLICE *adv* be performed in a simple manner

SEMPRE *adv* (preceding a tempo or dynamic marking) always

SEMPSTER *n* person who sews

SEMPSTERS > SEMPSTER

SEMSEM *n* sesame

SEMSEMS > SEMSEM

SEMUNCIA *n* ancient Roman coin

SEMUNCIAE > SEMUNCIA

SEMUNCIAL > SEMUNCIA

SEMUNCIAS > SEMUNCIA

SEN *n* monetary unit of Brunei, Cambodia, Indonesia, Malaysia, and formerly of Japan

SENA *n* (in India) the army: used in the names of certain paramilitary political organizations

SENARIES > SENARY

SENARII > SENARIUS

SENARIUS *n* type of poem

SENARY *adj* of or relating to the number six

SENAS > SENA

SENATE *n* main governing body at some universities

SENATES > SENATE

SENATOR *n* member of a senate

SENATORS > SENATOR

SEND *vb* cause (a person or thing) to go to or be taken or transmitted to a place

SENDABLE > SEND

SENDAL *n* fine silk fabric used, esp in the Middle Ages, for ceremonial clothing, etc

SENDALS > SENDAL

SENDED *vb* old word meaning sent

SENDER > SEND

SENDERS > SEND

SENDING > SEND

SENDINGS > SEND

SENDOFF *n* demonstration of good wishes at a person's departure ▷ *vb* dispatch (something, such as a letter)

SENDOFFS > SENDOFF

SENDS > SEND

SENDUP *n* parody or imitation

SENDUPS > SENDUP

SENE *n* money unit in Samoa

SENECA *variant of* > SENEGA

SENECAS > SENECA

SENECIO *n* any plant of the genus *Senecio*

SENECIOS > SENECIO

SENEGA *n* milkwort plant of the eastern US, with small white flowers

SENEGAS > SENEGA

SENESCENT *adj* growing old

SENESCHAL *n* steward of the household of a medieval prince or nobleman

SENGI *n* African shrew

SENGREEN *n* house leek

SENGREENS > SENGREEN

SENHOR *n* Portuguese term of address for man

SENHORA *n* Portuguese term of address for woman

SENHORAS > SENHORA

SENHORES > SENHOR

SENHORITA *n* Portuguese term of address for girl

SENHORS > SENHOR

SENILE *adj* mentally or physically weak because of old age ▷ *n* senile person

SENILELY > SENILE

SENILES > SENILE

SENILITY > SENILE

SENIOR *adj* superior in rank or standing ▷ *n* senior person

SENIORITY *n* state of being senior

SENIORS > SENIOR

SENITI *n* money unit in Tonga

SENNA *n* tropical plant

SENNACHIE *n* Gaelic storyteller

SENNAS > SENNA

SENNET *n* fanfare: used as a stage direction in Elizabethan drama

SENNETS > SENNET

SENNIGHT *archaic word for* > WEEK

SENNIGHTS > SENNIGHT

SENNIT *n* flat braided cordage used on ships

SENNITS > SENNIT

SENOPIA *n* short-sightedness in old age

SENOPIAS > SENOPIA

SENOR *n* Spanish term of address equivalent to *sir* or *Mr*

SENORA *n* Spanish term of address equivalent to *madam* or *Mrs*

SENORAS > SENORA

SENORES > SENOR

SENORITA *n* Spanish term of address equivalent to *madam* or *Miss*

SENORITAS > SENORITA

SENORS > SENOR

SENRYU *n* Japanese short poem

SENS > SEN

SENSA > SENSUM

SENSATE *adj* perceived by the senses ▷ *vb* make sensate

SENSATED > SENSATE

SENSATELY > SENSATE

SENSATES > SENSATE

SENSATING > SENSATE

SENSATION *n* ability to feel things physically

SENSE *n* any of the faculties of perception or feeling ▷ *vb* perceive

SENSED > SENSE

SENSEFUL *adj* full of sense

SENSEI *n* martial arts teacher

SENSEIS > SENSEI

SENSELESS *adj* foolish

SENSES > SENSE

SENSIBLE *adj* having or showing good sense ▷ *n* sensible thing or person

SENSIBLER > SENSIBLE

SENSIBLES > SENSIBLE

SENSIBLY > SENSIBLE

SENSILE *adj* capable of feeling

SENSILLA > SENSILLUM

SENSILLAE > SENSILLUM

SENSILLUM *n* sense organ in insects

SENSING > SENSE

SENSINGS > SENSE

SENSISM *n* theory that ideas spring from senses

SENSISMS > SENSISM

SENSIST > SENSISM

SENSISTS > SENSISM

SENSITISE *same as* > SENSITIZE

SENSITIVE *adj* easily hurt or offended

SENSITIZE *vb* make sensitive

SENSOR *n* device that detects or measures the presence of something, such as radiation

SENSORIA > SENSORIUM

SENSORIAL *same as* > SENSORY

SENSORILY > SENSORY

SENSORIUM *n* area of the brain considered responsible for receiving and integrating sensations from the outside world

SENSORS > SENSOR

SENSORY *adj* of the senses or sensation

SENSUAL *adj* giving pleasure to the body and senses rather than the mind

SENSUALLY > SENSUAL

SENSUM *n* sensation detached from the information it conveys and also from its source in the external world

SENSUOUS *adj* pleasing to the senses

SENT *n* former monetary unit of Estonia

SENTE *n* money unit in Lesotho

SENTED > SEND

SENTENCE *n* sequence of words capable of standing alone as a statement, question, or command ▷ *vb* pass sentence on (a convicted person)

SENTENCED > SENTENCE

SENTENCER > SENTENCE

SENTENCES > SENTENCE

SENTENTIA *n* opinion

SENTI > SENT

SENTIENCE *n* state or quality of being sentient

SENTIENCY *same as* > SENTIENCE

SENTIENT *adj* capable of feeling ▷ *n* sentient person or thing

SENTIENTS > SENTIENT

SENTIMENT *n* thought, opinion, or attitude

SENTIMO *n* money unit in Philippines

SENTIMOS > SENTIMO

SENTINEL *n* sentry ▷ *vb* guard as a sentinel

SENTINELS > SENTINEL

SENTING > SEND

SENTRIES > SENTRY

SENTRY *n* soldier on watch

SENTS > SENT

SENVIES > SENVY

SENVY *n* mustard

SENZA *prep* without

SEPAD *vb* suppose

SEPADDED > SEPAD

SEPADDING > SEPAD

SEPADS > SEPAD

SEPAL *n* leaflike division of the calyx of a flower

SEPALED > SEPAL

SEPALINE *same as* > SEPALOID

SEPALLED > SEPAL

SEPALODY *n* changing of flower part into sepal

SEPALOID *adj* (esp of petals) resembling a sepal in structure and function

SEPALOUS *adj* with sepals

SEPALS > SEPAL

SEPARABLE *adj* able to be separated

SEPARABLY > SEPARABLE

SEPARATA > SEPARATUM

SEPARATE *vb* act as a barrier between ▷ *adj* not the same, different ▷ *n* item of clothing that only covers half the body

SEPARATED > SEPARATE

SEPARATES > SEPARATE

SEPARATOR *n* person or thing that separates

SEPARATUM *n* separate

printing of article from magazine

**SEPHEN** n stingray

**SEPHENS** > SEPHEN

**SEPIA** n reddish-brown pigment ▷ adj dark reddish-brown, like the colour of very old photographs

**SEPIAS** > SEPIA

**SEPIC** adj of sepia

**SEPIMENT** n hedge

**SEPIMENTS** > SEPIMENT

**SEPIOLITE** n meerschaum

**SEPIOST** n cuttlefish bone

**SEPIOSTS** > SEPIOST

**SEPIUM** n cuttlefish bone

**SEPIUMS** > SEPIUM

**SEPMAG** adj designating a film or television programme for which the sound is recorded on separate magnetic material and run in synchronism with the picture

**SEPOY** n (formerly) Indian soldier in the service of the British

**SEPOYS** > SEPOY

**SEPPUKU** n Japanese ritual suicide

**SEPPUKUS** > SEPPUKU

**SEPS** n species of lizard

**SEPSES** > SEPSIS

**SEPSIS** n poisoning caused by pus-forming bacteria

**SEPT** n clan, esp in Ireland or Scotland

**SEPTA** > SEPTUM

**SEPTAGE** n waste removed from septic tank

**SEPTAGES** > SEPTAGE

**SEPTAL** adj of or relating to a septum

**SEPTARIA** > SEPTARIUM

**SEPTARIAN** > SEPTARIUM

**SEPTARIUM** n mass of mineral substance having cracks filled with another mineral

**SEPTATE** adj divided by septa

**SEPTATION** n division by partitions

**SEPTEMFID** adj divided into seven

**SEPTEMVIR** n member of government of seven men

**SEPTENARY** adj of or relating to the number seven ▷ n number seven

**SEPTENNIA** pl n cycles of seven years

**SEPTET** n group of seven performers

**SEPTETS** > SEPTET

**SEPTETTE** same as > SEPTET

**SEPTETTES** > SEPTETTE

**SEPTIC** adj (of a wound) infected ▷ n infected wound

**SEPTICAL** > SEPTIC

**SEPTICITY** > SEPTIC

**SEPTICS** > SEPTIC

**SEPTIFORM** adj acting as partition

**SEPTIMAL** adj of number seven

**SEPTIME** n seventh of eight basic positions from which a parry can be made in fencing

**SEPTIMES** > SEPTIME

**SEPTIMOLE** n group of seven musical notes

**SEPTLEVA** n gambling term from old card game

**SEPTLEVAS** > SEPTLEVA

**SEPTS** > SEPT

**SEPTUM** n dividing partition between two cavities in the body

**SEPTUMS** > SEPTUM

**SEPTUOR** n group of seven musicians

**SEPTUORS** > SEPTUOR

**SEPTUPLE** vb multiply by seven ▷ adj seven times as much or as many ▷ n quantity or number seven times as great as another

**SEPTUPLED** > SEPTUPLE

**SEPTUPLES** > SEPTUPLE

**SEPTUPLET** n group of seven notes played in a time value of six, eight, etc

**SEPULCHER** same as > SEPULCHRE

**SEPULCHRE** n tomb or burial vault ▷ vb bury in a sepulchre

**SEPULTURE** n act of placing in a sepulchre

**SEQUACITY** quality of being pliant or controllable

**SEQUEL** n novel, play, or film that continues the story of an earlier one

**SEQUELA** n any abnormal bodily condition or disease related to or arising from a pre-existing disease

**SEQUELAE** > SEQUELA

**SEQUELISE** same as > SEQUELIZE

**SEQUELIZE** vb create sequel to

**SEQUELS** > SEQUEL

**SEQUENCE** n arrangement of two or more things in successive order ▷ vb arrange in a sequence

**SEQUENCED** > SEQUENCE

**SEQUENCER** n electronic device that determines the order in which a number of operations occur

**SEQUENCES** > SEQUENCE

**SEQUENCY** n number of changes in mathematical list

**SEQUENT** adj following in order or succession ▷ n something that follows

**SEQUENTLY** > SEQUENT

**SEQUENTS** > SEQUENT

**SEQUESTER** vb seclude

**SEQUESTRA** pl n detached pieces of necrotic bone that often migrate to wounds

**SEQUIN** n small ornamental metal disc on a garment ▷ vb apply sequins

**SEQUINED** > SEQUIN

**SEQUINING** > SEQUIN

**SEQUINNED** > SEQUIN

**SEQUINS** > SEQUIN

**SEQUITUR** n conclusion that follows from the premises

**SEQUITURS** > SEQUITUR

**SEQUOIA** n giant Californian coniferous tree

**SEQUOIAS** > SEQUOIA

**SER** n unit of weight used in India, usually taken as one fortieth of a maund

**SERA** > SERUM

**SERAC** n pinnacle of ice among crevasses on a glacier, usually on a steep slope

**SERACS** > SERAC

**SERAFILE** n line of soldiers

**SERAFILES** > SERAFILE

**SERAFIN** n old silver coin of Goa

**SERAFINS** > SERAFIN

**SERAGLIO** n harem of a Muslim palace

**SERAGLIOS** > SERAGLIO

**SERAI** n (in the East) a caravanserai or inn

**SERAIL** same as > SERAGLIO

**SERAILS** > SERAIL

**SERAIS** > SERAI

**SERAL** > SERE

**SERANG** n native captain of a crew of sailors in the East Indies

**SERANGS** > SERANG

**SERAPE** n blanket-like shawl often of brightly-coloured wool worn by men in Latin America

**SERAPES** > SERAPE

**SERAPH** n member of the highest order of angels

**SERAPHIC** adj of or resembling a seraph

**SERAPHIM** > SERAPH

**SERAPHIMS** > SERAPH

**SERAPHIN** n angel

**SERAPHINE** n old keyboard instrument

**SERAPHINS** > SERAPHIN

**SERAPHS** > SERAPH

**SERASKIER** n Turkish military leader

**SERDAB** n secret chamber in an ancient Egyptian tomb

**SERDABS** > SERDAB

**SERE** adj dried up or withered ▷ n series of changes occurring in the ecological succession of a particular community

▷ vb sear

**SERED** > SERE

**SEREIN** n fine rain falling from a clear sky after sunset, esp in the tropics

**SEREINS** > SEREIN

**SERENADE** n music played or sung to a woman by a lover ▷ vb sing or play a serenade to (someone)

**SERENADED** > SERENADE

**SERENADER** > SERENADE

**SERENADES** > SERENADE

**SERENATA** n 18th-century cantata, often dramatic in form

**SERENATAS** > SERENATA

**SERENATE** n old form of serenade

**SERENATES** > SERENATE

**SERENE** adj calm, peaceful ▷ vb make serene

**SERENED** > SERENE

**SERENELY** > SERENE

**SERENER** > SERENE

**SERENES** > SERENE

**SERENEST** > SERENE

**SERENING** > SERENE

**SERENITY** n state or quality of being serene

**SERER** > SERE

**SERES** > SERE

**SEREST** > SERE

**SERF** n medieval farm labourer who could not leave the land he worked on

**SERFAGE** > SERF

**SERFAGES** > SERF

**SERFDOM** > SERF

**SERFDOMS** > SERF

**SERFHOOD** > SERF

**SERFHOODS** > SERF

**SERFISH** > SERF

**SERFLIKE** > SERF

**SERFS** > SERF

**SERFSHIP** > SERF

**SERFSHIPS** > SERF

**SERGE** n strong woollen fabric

**SERGEANCY** > SERGEANT

**SERGEANT** n noncommissioned officer in the army

**SERGEANTS** > SERGEANT

**SERGEANTY** n form of feudal tenure

**SERGED** adj with sewn seam

**SERGER** n sewing machine attachment for finishing seams

**SERGERS** > SERGER

**SERGES** > SERGE

**SERGING** n type of sewing

**SERGINGS** > SERGING

**SERIAL** n story or play produced in successive instalments ▷ adj of or forming a series

**SERIALISE** same as > SERIALIZE

**SERIALISM** n musical technique using a

sequence of notes in a definite order

**SERIALIST** *n* writer of serials

**SERIALITY** > SERIAL

**SERIALIZE** *vb* publish or present as a serial

**SERIALLY** > SERIAL

**SERIALS** > SERIAL

**SERIATE** *adj* forming a series ▷ *vb* form into a series

**SERIATED** > SERIATE

**SERIATELY** > SERIATE

**SERIATES** > SERIATE

**SERIATIM** *adv* in a series

**SERIATING** > SERIATE

**SERIATION** > SERIATE

**SERIC** *adj* of silk

**SERICEOUS** *adj* covered with a layer of small silky hairs

**SERICIN** *n* gelatinous protein found on the fibres of raw silk

**SERICINS** > SERICIN

**SERICITE** *n* type of mica

**SERICITES** > SERICITE

**SERICITIC** > SERICITE

**SERICON** *n* solution used in alchemy

**SERICONS** > SERICON

**SERIEMA** *n* either of two cranelike South American birds

**SERIEMAS** > SERIEMA

**SERIES** *n* group or succession of related things, usu arranged in order

**SERIF** *n* small line at the extremities of a main stroke in a type character

**SERIFED** *adj* having serifs

**SERIFFED** *adj* having serifs

**SERIFS** > SERIF

**SERIGRAPH** *n* colour print made by an adaptation of the silk-screen process

**SERIN** *n* any of various small yellow-and-brown finches

**SERINE** *n* sweet-tasting amino acid

**SERINES** > SERINE

**SERINETTE** *n* barrel organ

**SERING** > SERE

**SERINGA** *n* any of several trees that yield rubber

**SERINGAS** > SERINGA

**SERINS** > SERIN

**SERIOUS** *adj* giving cause for concern

**SERIOUSLY** *adv* in a serious manner or to a serious degree

**SERIPH** *same as* > SERIF

**SERIPHS** > SERIPH

**SERJEANCY** *n* rank of sergeant

**SERJEANT** *same as* > SERGEANT

**SERJEANTS** > SERJEANT

**SERJEANTY** *n* type of feudal tenure

**SERK** *Scots word for* > SHIRT

**SERKALI** *n* government in Africa

**SERKALIS** > SERKALI

**SERKS** > SERK

**SERMON** *n* speech on a religious or moral subject by a clergyman in a church service ▷ *vb* deliver a sermon

**SERMONED** > SERMON

**SERMONEER** *n* preacher

**SERMONER** *variant of* > SERMONEER

**SERMONERS** > SERMONER

**SERMONET** *n* short sermon

**SERMONETS** > SERMONET

**SERMONIC** > SERMON

**SERMONING** > SERMON

**SERMONISE** *same as* > SERMONIZE

**SERMONIZE** *vb* make a long moralizing speech

**SERMONS** > SERMON

**SEROLOGIC** > SEROLOGY

**SEROLOGY** *n* science concerned with serums

**SERON** *n* crate

**SERONS** > SERON

**SEROON** *n* crate

**SEROONS** > SEROON

**SEROPUS** *n* liquid consisting of serum and pus

**SEROPUSES** > SEROPUS

**SEROSA** *n* one of the thin membranes surrounding the embryo in an insect's egg

**SEROSAE** > SEROSA

**SEROSAL** > SEROSA

**SEROSAS** > SEROSA

**SEROSITY** > SEROUS

**SEROTINAL** *same as* > SEROTINE

**SEROTINE** *adj* produced, flowering, or developing late in the season ▷ *n* either of two insectivorous bats

**SEROTINES** > SEROTINE

**SEROTINY** *n* state of being serotinous

**SEROTONIN** *n* compound that occurs in the brain, intestines, and blood platelets and acts as a neurotransmitter

**SEROTYPE** *n* category into which material, usually a bacterium, is placed based on its serological activity ▷ *vb* class according to serotype

**SEROTYPED** > SEROTYPE

**SEROTYPES** > SEROTYPE

**SEROUS** *adj* of, containing, or like serum

**SEROVAR** *n* subdivision of species

**SEROVARS** > SEROVAR

**SEROW** *n* either of two antelopes of mountainous regions of S and SE Asia

**SEROWS** > SEROW

**SERPENT** *n* snake

**SERPENTRY** *n* serpents

**SERPENTS** > SERPENT

**SERPIGO** *n* any progressive skin eruption, such as ringworm or herpes

**SERPIGOES** > SERPIGO

**SERPIGOS** > SERPIGO

**SERPULA** *n* marine worm

**SERPULAE** > SERPULA

**SERPULID** *n* marine polychaete worm

**SERPULIDS** > SERPULID

**SERPULITE** *n* variety of fossil

**SERR** *vb* press close together

**SERRA** *n* sawlike part or organ

**SERRAE** > SERRA

**SERRAN** *n* species of fish

**SERRANID** *n* any of numerous marine fishes including the sea basses, and sea perches ▷ *adj* of or belonging to the family *Serranidae*

**SERRANIDS** > SERRANID

**SERRANO** *n* type of Spanish ham

**SERRANOID** *same as* > SERRANID

**SERRANOS** > SERRANO

**SERRANS** > SERRAN

**SERRAS** > SERRA

**SERRATE** *adj* (of leaves) having a margin of forward pointing teeth ▷ *vb* make serrate

**SERRATED** *adj* having a notched or sawlike edge

**SERRATES** > SERRATE

**SERRATI** > SERRATUS

**SERRATING** > SERRATE

**SERRATION** *n* state or condition of being serrated

**SERRATURE** *same as* > SERRATION

**SERRATUS** *n* muscle in thorax

**SERRE** *vb* press close together

**SERRED** > SERRE

**SERREFILE** *n* file of soldiers

**SERRES** > SERRE

**SERRICORN** *n* with serrate antennae

**SERRIED** *adj* in close formation

**SERRIEDLY** > SERRIED

**SERRIES** > SERRY

**SERRIFORM** *adj* resembling a notched or sawlike edge

**SERRING** > SERRE

**SERRS** > SERR

**SERRULATE** *adj* (esp of leaves) minutely serrate

**SERRY** *vb* close together

**SERRYING** > SERRY

**SERS** > SER

**SERUEWE** *vb* old word meaning survey

**SERUEWED** > SERUEWE

**SERUEWES** > SERUEWE

**SERUEWING** > SERUEWE

**SERUM** *n* watery fluid left after blood has clotted

**SERUMAL** > SERUM

**SERUMS** > SERUM

**SERVABLE** > SERVE

**SERVAL** *n* feline African mammal

**SERVALS** > SERVAL

**SERVANT** *n* person employed to do household work for another ▷ *vb* work as a servant

**SERVANTED** > SERVANT

**SERVANTRY** *n* servants

**SERVANTS** > SERVANT

**SERVE** *vb* work for (a person, community, or cause) ▷ *n* act of serving the ball

**SERVEABLE** > SERVE

**SERVED** > SERVE

**SERVER** *n* player who serves in racket games

**SERVERIES** > SERVERY

**SERVERS** > SERVER

**SERVERY** *n* room from which food is served

**SERVES** > SERVE

**SERVEWE** *vb* old word meaning survey

**SERVEWED** > SERVEWE

**SERVEWES** > SERVEWE

**SERVEWING** > SERVEWE

**SERVICE** *n* serving ▷ *adj* serving the public rather than producing goods ▷ *vb* provide a service or services to

**SERVICED** > SERVICE

**SERVICER** > SERVICE

**SERVICERS** > SERVICE

**SERVICES** > SERVICE

**SERVICING** > SERVICE

**SERVIENT** *adj* subordinate

**SERVIETTE** *n* table napkin

**SERVILE** *adj* too eager to obey people, fawning ▷ *n* servile person

**SERVILELY** > SERVILE

**SERVILES** > SERVILE

**SERVILISM** *n* condition of being servile

**SERVILITY** > SERVILE

**SERVING** *n* portion of food

**SERVINGS** > SERVING

**SERVITOR** *n* servant or attendant

**SERVITORS** > SERVITOR

**SERVITUDE** *n* bondage or slavery

**SERVLET** *n* small program that runs on a web server often accessing databases in response to client input

**SERVLETS** > SERVLET

**SERVO** *n* servomechanism ▷ *adj* of a servomechanism

**SERVOS** > SERVO

**SERVQUAL** *n* provision of

high-quality products by an organization backed by a high level of service for consumers

**SERVQUALS** > SERVQUAL

**SESAME** n plant cultivated for its seeds and oil, which are used in cooking

**SESAMES** > SESAME

**SESAMOID** adj of or relating to various small bones formed in tendons ▷ n sesamoid bone

**SESAMOIDS** > SESAMOID

**SESE** interj exclamation found in Shakespeare

**SESELI** n garden plant

**SESELIS** > SESELI

**SESEY** interj exclamation found in Shakespeare

**SESH** short for > SESSION

**SESHES** > SESH

**SESS** n old word meaning tax

**SESSA** interj exclamation found in Shakespeare

**SESSES** > SESS

**SESSILE** adj (of flowers or leaves) having no stalk

**SESSILITY** > SESSILE

**SESSION** n period spent in an activity

**SESSIONAL** > SESSION

**SESSIONS** pl n sittings or a sitting of justice in court

**SESSPOOL** n cesspool

**SESSPOOLS** > SESSPOOL

**SESTERCE** n silver or, later, bronze coin of ancient Rome worth a quarter of a denarius

**SESTERCES** > SESTERCE

**SESTERTIA** pl n ancient Roman money accounts

**SESTERTII** pl n sesterces

**SESTET** n last six lines of a sonnet

**SESTETS** > SESTET

**SESTETT** n group of six

**SESTETTE** n group of six

**SESTETTES** > SESTETTE

**SESTETTO** n composition for six musicians

**SESTETTOS** > SESTETTO

**SESTETTS** > SESTETT

**SESTINA** n elaborate verse form of Italian origin

**SESTINAS** > SESTINA

**SESTINE** n poem of six lines

**SESTINES** > SESTINE

**SESTON** n type of plankton

**SESTONS** > SESTON

**SET** vb put in a specified position or state ▷ n setting or being set ▷ adj fixed or established beforehand

**SETA** n (in invertebrates and some plants) any bristle or bristle-like appendage

**SETACEOUS** > SETA

**SETAE** > SETA

**SETAL** > SETA

**SETBACK** n anything that delays progress

**SETBACKS** > SETBACK

**SETENANT** n pair of postage stamps of different values joined together

**SETENANTS** > SETENANT

**SETIFORM** adj shaped like a seta

**SETLINE** n any of various types of fishing line

**SETLINES** > SETLINE

**SETNESS** > SET

**SETNESSES** > SET

**SETOFF** n counterbalance

**SETOFFS** > SETOFF

**SETON** n surgical thread inserted below the skin

**SETONS** > SETON

**SETOSE** adj covered with setae

**SETOUS** > SETA

**SETOUT** n beginning or outset

**SETOUTS** > SETOUT

**SETS** > SET

**SETSCREW** n screw that fits into the boss or hub of a wheel, and prevents motion of the part relative to the shaft on which it is mounted

**SETSCREWS** > SETSCREW

**SETT** n badger's burrow

**SETTEE** n couch

**SETTEES** > SETTEE

**SETTER** n long-haired gun dog ▷ vb treat with a piece of setterwort

**SETTERED** > SETTER

**SETTERING** > SETTER

**SETTERS** > SETTER

**SETTING** > SET

**SETTINGS** > SET

**SETTLE** vb arrange or put in order ▷ n long wooden bench with high back and arms

**SETTLED** > SETTLE

**SETTLER** n colonist

**SETTLERS** > SETTLER

**SETTLES** > SETTLE

**SETTLING** > SETTLE

**SETTLINGS** pl n any matter or substance that has settled at the bottom of a liquid

**SETTLOR** n person who settles property on someone

**SETTLORS** > SETTLOR

**SETTS** > SETT

**SETUALE** n valerian

**SETUALES** > SETUALE

**SETULE** n small bristle

**SETULES** > SETULE

**SETULOSE** > SETULE

**SETULOUS** > SETULE

**SETUP** n way in which anything is organized or arranged

**SETUPS** > SETUP

**SETWALL** n valerian

**SETWALLS** > SETWALL

**SEVEN** n one more than six ▷ adj amounting to seven ▷ determiner amounting to seven

**SEVENFOLD** adj having seven times as many or as much ▷ adv by seven times as many or as much

**SEVENS** n Rugby Union match or series of matches played with seven players on each side

**SEVENTEEN** n ten and seven ▷ adj amounting to seventeen ▷ determiner amounting to seventeen

**SEVENTH** n (of) number seven in a series ▷ adj coming after the sixth and before the eighth ▷ adv after the sixth person, position, event, etc

**SEVENTHLY** same as > SEVENTH

**SEVENTHS** > SEVENTH

**SEVENTIES** > SEVENTY

**SEVENTY** n ten times seven ▷ adj amounting to seventy ▷ determiner amounting to seventy

**SEVER** vb cut through or off

**SEVERABLE** adj able to be severed

**SEVERAL** adj some, a few ▷ n individual person

**SEVERALLY** adv separately

**SEVERALS** > SEVERAL

**SEVERALTY** n state of being several or separate

**SEVERANCE** n act of severing or state of being severed

**SEVERE** adj strict or harsh

**SEVERED** > SEVER

**SEVERELY** > SEVERE

**SEVERER** > SEVERE

**SEVEREST** > SEVERE

**SEVERIES** > SEVERY

**SEVERING** > SEVER

**SEVERITY** > SEVERE

**SEVERS** > SEVER

**SEVERY** n part of vaulted ceiling

**SEVICHE** n Mexican fish dish

**SEVICHES** > SEVICHE

**SEVRUGA** n species of sturgeon

**SEVRUGAS** > SEVRUGA

**SEW** vb join with thread repeatedly passed through with a needle

**SEWABLE** > SEW

**SEWAGE** n waste matter or excrement carried away in sewers

**SEWAGES** > SEWAGE

**SEWAN** same as > SEAWAN

**SEWANS** > SEWAN

**SEWAR** n Asian dagger

**SEWARS** > SEWAR

**SEWED** > SEW

**SEWEL** n scarecrow

**SEWELLEL** n mountain beaver

**SEWELLELS** > SEWELLEL

**SEWELS** > SEWEL

**SEWEN** same as > SEWIN

**SEWENS** > SEWEN

**SEWER** n drain to remove waste water and sewage ▷ vb provide with sewers

**SEWERAGE** n system of sewers

**SEWERAGES** > SEWERAGE

**SEWERED** > SEWER

**SEWERING** > SEWER

**SEWERINGS** > SEWER

**SEWERLESS** > SEWER

**SEWERLIKE** > SEWER

**SEWERS** > SEWER

**SEWIN** n sea trout

**SEWING** > SEW

**SEWINGS** > SEW

**SEWINS** > SEWIN

**SEWN** > SEW

**SEWS** > SEW

**SEX** n state of being male or female ▷ vb find out the sex of ▷ adj of sexual matters

**SEXAHOLIC** n person who is addicted to sex

**SEXED** adj having a specified degree of sexuality

**SEXENNIAL** adj occurring once every six years or over a period of six years ▷ n sixth anniversary

**SEXER** n person checking sex of chickens

**SEXERCISE** n sexual activity, regarded as a way of keeping fit

**SEXERS** > SEXER

**SEXES** > SEX

**SEXFID** adj split into six

**SEXFOIL** n flower with six petals or leaves

**SEXFOILS** > SEXFOIL

**SEXIER** > SEXY

**SEXIEST** > SEXY

**SEXILY** > SEXY

**SEXINESS** > SEXY

**SEXING** > SEX

**SEXISM** n discrimination on the basis of a person's sex

**SEXISMS** > SEXISM

**SEXIST** > SEXISM

**SEXISTS** > SEXISM

**SEXLESS** adj neither male nor female

**SEXLESSLY** > SEXLESS

**SEXLINKED** adj (of a gene) found on a sex chromosome

**SEXOLOGIC** > SEXOLOGY

**SEXOLOGY** n study of sexual behaviour in human beings

**SEXPERT** n person who professes a knowledge of sexual matters

**SEXPERTS** > SEXPERT

**SEXPOT** n person, esp a

young woman, considered as being sexually very attractive

**SEXPOTS** > SEXPOT

**SEXT** n fourth of the seven canonical hours of the divine office or the prayers prescribed for it: originally the sixth hour of the day (noon)

**SEXTAIN** same as > SESTINA

**SEXTAINS** > SEXTAIN

**SEXTAN** adj (of a fever) marked by paroxysms that recur after an interval of five days

**SEXTANS** n Roman coin

**SEXTANSES** > SEXTANS

**SEXTANT** n navigator's instrument for measuring angles to calculate one's position

**SEXTANTAL** > SEXTANT

**SEXTANTS** > SEXTANT

**SEXTARII** > SEXTARIUS

**SEXTARIUS** n ancient Roman quantity measure

**SEXTET** n group of six performers

**SEXTETS** > SEXTET

**SEXTETT** n sextet

**SEXTETTE** same as > SEXTET

**SEXTETTES** > SEXTETTE

**SEXTETTS** > SEXTETT

**SEXTILE** n one of five values of a variable dividing its distribution into six groups with equal frequencies

**SEXTILES** > SEXTILE

**SEXTO** same as > SIXMO

**SEXTOLET** n group of six musical notes

**SEXTOLETS** > SEXTOLET

**SEXTON** n official in charge of a church and churchyard

**SEXTONESS** n female sexton

**SEXTONS** > SEXTON

**SEXTOS** > SEXTO

**SEXTS** > SEXT

**SEXTUOR** n sextet

**SEXTUORS** > SEXTUOR

**SEXTUPLE** vb multiply by six ▷ adj six times as much or as many ▷ n quantity or number six times as great as another

**SEXTUPLES** > SEXTUPLE

**SEXTUPLES** > SEXTUPLE

**SEXTUPLET** n one of six children born at one birth

**SEXTUPLY** > SEXTUPLE

**SEXUAL** adj of or characterized by sex

**SEXUALISE** same as > SEXUALIZE

**SEXUALISM** n emphasising of sexuality

**SEXUALIST** > SEXUALISM

**SEXUALITY** n state or quality of being sexual

**SEXUALIZE** vb make or become sexual or sexually

aware

**SEXUALLY** > SEXUAL

**SEXVALENT** adj with valency of six

**SEXY** adj sexually exciting or attractive

**SEY** n Scots word meaning part of cow carcase

**SEYEN** n old form of scion

**SEYENS** > SEYEN

**SEYS** > SEY

**SEYSURE** n old form of seizure

**SEYSURES** > SEYSURE

**SEZ** vb informal spelling of 'says'

**SFERICS** same as > SPHERICS

**SFORZANDI** > SFORZANDO

**SFORZANDO** adv be played with strong initial attack ▷ n symbol written above a note, indicating this

**SFORZATI** > SFORZATO

**SFORZANDO** same as > SFORZANDO

**SFORZATOS** > SFORZATO

**SFUMATO** n gradual transition between areas of different colour in painting

**SFUMATOS** > SFUMATO

**SGRAFFITI** > SGRAFFITO

**SGRAFFITO** n technique in mural or ceramic decoration in which the top layer of glaze is incised with a design to reveal parts of the ground

**SH** same as > SHILLING

**SHA** interj be quiet

**SHABASH** interj (in Indian English) bravo or well done

**SHABBATOT** pl n Jewish sabbaths

**SHABBIER** > SHABBY

**SHABBIEST** > SHABBY

**SHABBILY** > SHABBY

**SHABBLE** n Scots word meaning old sword

**SHABBLES** > SHABBLE

**SHABBY** adj worn or dilapidated in appearance

**SHABRACK** n cavalryman's saddle cloth

**SHABRACKS** > SHABRACK

**SHACK** n rough hut ▷ vb evade (work or responsibility)

**SHACKED** > SHACK

**SHACKING** > SHACK

**SHACKLE** n metal ring for securing a person's wrists or ankles ▷ vb fasten with shackles

**SHACKLED** > SHACKLE

**SHACKLER** > SHACKLE

**SHACKLERS** > SHACKLE

**SHACKLES** > SHACKLE

**SHACKLING** > SHACKLE

**SHACKO** same as > SHAKO

**SHACKOES** > SHACKO

**SHACKOS** > SHACKO

**SHACKS** > SHACK

**SHAD** n herring-like fish

**SHADBERRY** n edible purplish berry of the shadbush

**SHADBLOW** n type of shrub

**SHADBLOWS** > SHADBLOW

**SHADBUSH** n type of N American tree or shrub

**SHADCHAN** n Jewish marriage broker

**SHADCHANS** > SHADCHAN

**SHADDOCK** another name for > POMELO

**SHADDOCKS** > SHADDOCK

**SHADE** n relative darkness ▷ vb screen from light

**SHADED** > SHADE

**SHADELESS** > SHADE

**SHADER** > SHADE

**SHADERS** > SHADE

**SHADES** pl n gathering darkness at nightfall

**SHADFLIES** > SHADFLY

**SHADFLY** American name for > MAYFLY

**SHADIER** > SHADY

**SHADIEST** > SHADY

**SHADILY** > SHADY

**SHADINESS** > SHADY

**SHADING** n graded areas of tone indicating light and dark in a painting or drawing

**SHADINGS** > SHADING

**SHADKHAN** same as > SHADCHAN

**SHADKHANS** > SHADKHAN

**SHADOOF** n mechanism for raising water, esp as used in Egypt and the Near East

**SHADOOFS** > SHADOOF

**SHADOW** n dark shape cast on a surface when something stands between a light and the surface ▷ vb cast a shadow over

**SHADOWBOX** vb practise boxing against an imaginary opponent

**SHADOWED** > SHADOW

**SHADOWER** > SHADOW

**SHADOWERS** > SHADOW

**SHADOWIER** > SHADOWY

**SHADOWILY** > SHADOWY

**SHADOWING** > SHADOW

**SHADOWS** > SHADOW

**SHADOWY** adj (of a place) full of shadows

**SHADRACH** n lump of iron that has not been melted in the furnace

**SHADRACHS** > SHADRACH

**SHADS** > SHAD

**SHADUF** same as > SHADOOF

**SHADUFS** > SHADUF

**SHADY** adj situated in or giving shade

**SHAFT** n long narrow straight handle of a tool or weapon ▷ vb treat badly

**SHAFTED** > SHAFT

**SHAFTER** > SHAFT

**SHAFTERS** > SHAFT

**SHAFTING** n assembly

of rotating shafts for transmitting power

**SHAFTINGS** > SHAFTING

**SHAFTLESS** > SHAFT

**SHAFTS** > SHAFT

**SHAG** n coarse shredded tobacco ▷ adj (of a carpet) having a long pile ▷ vb have sexual intercourse with (a person)

**SHAGBARK** n North American hickory tree

**SHAGBARKS** > SHAGBARK

**SHAGGABLE** adj sexually attractive

**SHAGGED** > SHAG

**SHAGGIER** > SHAGGY

**SHAGGIEST** > SHAGGY

**SHAGGILY** > SHAGGY

**SHAGGING** > SHAG

**SHAGGY** adj covered with rough hair or wool

**SHAGPILE** adj (of carpet) having long fibres

**SHAGREEN** n sharkskin

**SHAGREENS** > SHAGREEN

**SHAGROON** n nineteenth-century Australian settler in Canterbury

**SHAGROONS** > SHAGROON

**SHAGS** > SHAG

**SHAH** n formerly, ruler of Iran

**SHAHADA** n Islamic declaration of faith, repeated daily by Muslims

**SHAHADAS** > SHAHADA

**SHAHDOM** > SHAH

**SHAHDOMS** > SHAH

**SHAHS** > SHAH

**SHAHTOOSH** n soft wool that comes from the protected Tibetan antelope

**SHAIKH** n sheikh

**SHAIKHS** > SHAIKH

**SHAIRD** n Scots word meaning shred

**SHAIRDS** > SHAIRD

**SHAIRN** Scots word for > DUNG

**SHAIRNS** > SHAIRN

**SHAITAN** n (in Muslim countries) an evil spirit

**SHAITANS** > SHAITAN

**SHAKABLE** > SHAKE

**SHAKE** vb move quickly up and down or back and forth ▷ n shaking

**SHAKEABLE** > SHAKE

**SHAKED** vb old form of shook

**SHAKEDOWN** n act of extortion

**SHAKEN** > SHAKE

**SHAKEOUT** n process of reducing the number of people in a workforce

**SHAKEOUTS** > SHAKEOUT

**SHAKER** n container in which drinks are mixed or from which powder is shaken

**SHAKERS** > SHAKER

**SHAKES** >SHAKE
**SHAKEUP** n radical reorganization
**SHAKEUPS** >SHAKEUP
**SHAKIER** >SHAKY
**SHAKIEST** >SHAKY
**SHAKILY** >SHAKY
**SHAKINESS** >SHAKY
**SHAKING** >SHAKE
**SHAKINGS** >SHAKE
**SHAKO** n tall cylindrical peaked military hat with a plume
**SHAKOES** >SHAKO
**SHAKOS** >SHAKO
**SHAKT** vb old form of shook
**SHAKUDO** n Japanese alloy of copper and gold
**SHAKUDOS** >SHAKUDO
**SHAKY** adj unsteady
**SHALE** n flaky sedimentary rock
**SHALED** >SHALE
**SHALELIKE** >SHALE
**SHALES** >SHALE
**SHALEY** >SHALE
**SHALIER** >SHALE
**SHALIEST** >SHALE
**SHALING** >SHALE
**SHALL** vb used as an auxiliary to make the future tense
**SHALLI** n type of fabric
**SHALLIS** >SHALLI
**SHALLON** n American shrub
**SHALLONS** >SHALLON
**SHALLOON** n light twill-weave woollen fabric used chiefly for coat linings, etc
**SHALLOONS** >SHALLOON
**SHALLOP** n light boat used for rowing in shallow water
**SHALLOPS** >SHALLOP
**SHALLOT** n kind of small onion
**SHALLOTS** >SHALLOT
**SHALLOW** adj not deep ▷ n shallow place in a body of water ▷ vb make or become shallow
**SHALLOWED** >SHALLOW
**SHALLOWER** >SHALLOW
**SHALLOWLY** >SHALLOW
**SHALLOWS** >SHALLOW
**SHALM** n old woodwind instrument
**SHALMS** >SHALM
**SHALOM** n Jewish greeting meaning 'peace be with you'
**SHALOMS** >SHALOM
**SHALOT** n shallot
**SHALOTS** >SHALOT
**SHALT** singular form of the present tense (indicative mood) of >SHALL
**SHALWAR** n pair of loose-fitting trousers tapering to a narrow fit around the ankles, worn in the Indian subcontinent, often with a kameez
**SHALWARS** >SHALWAR

**SHALY** >SHALE
**SHAM** n thing or person that is not genuine ▷ adj not genuine ▷ vb fake, feign
**SHAMA** n Indian songbird
**SHAMABLE** >SHAME
**SHAMABLY** >SHAME
**SHAMAN** n priest of shamanism
**SHAMANIC** >SHAMAN
**SHAMANISM** n religion of northern Asia, based on a belief in good and evil spirits
**SHAMANIST** >SHAMANISM
**SHAMANS** >SHAMAN
**SHAMAS** >SHAMA
**SHAMATEUR** n sportsperson who is officially an amateur but accepts payment
**SHAMBA** n (in E Africa) any field used for growing crops
**SHAMBAS** >SHAMBA
**SHAMBLE** vb walk in a shuffling awkward way ▷ n awkward or shuffling walk
**SHAMBLED** >SHAMBLE
**SHAMBLES** n disorderly event or place
**SHAMBLIER** >SHAMBLE
**SHAMBLING** >SHAMBLE
**SHAMBLY** >SHAMBLE
**SHAMBOLIC** adj completely disorganized
**SHAME** n painful emotion caused by awareness of having done something dishonourable or foolish ▷ vb cause to feel shame
**SHAMEABLE** >SHAME
**SHAMEABLY** >SHAME
**SHAMED** >SHAME
**SHAMEFAST** adj old form of shamefaced
**SHAMEFUL** adj causing or deserving shame
**SHAMELESS** adj with no sense of shame
**SHAMER** n cause of shame
**SHAMERS** >SHAME
**SHAMES** >SHAME
**SHAMIANA** n tent in India
**SHAMIANAH** n tent in India
**SHAMIANAS** >SHAMIANA
**SHAMINA** n wool blend of pashm and shahtoosh
**SHAMINAS** >SHAMINA
**SHAMING** >SHAME
**SHAMISEN** n Japanese stringed instrument
**SHAMISENS** >SHAMISEN
**SHAMMAS** same as >SHAMMES
**SHAMMASH** same as >SHAMMES
**SHAMMASIM** >SHAMMES
**SHAMMED** >SHAM
**SHAMMER** >SHAM
**SHAMMERS** >SHAM
**SHAMMES** n official acting as the beadle, sexton, and

caretaker of a synagogue
**SHAMMIED** >SHAMMY
**SHAMMIES** >SHAMMY
**SHAMMING** >SHAM
**SHAMMOS** same as >SHAMMES
**SHAMMOSIM** >SHAMMES
**SHAMMY** n piece of chamois leather ▷ vb rub with a shammy
**SHAMMYING** >SHAMMY
**SHAMOIS** n chamois
**SHAMOS** same as >SHAMMES
**SHAMOSIM** >SHAMMES
**SHAMOY** n chamois ▷ vb rub with a shamoy
**SHAMOYED** >SHAMOY
**SHAMOYING** >SHAMOY
**SHAMOYS** >SHAMOY
**SHAMPOO** n liquid soap for washing hair, carpets, or upholstery ▷ vb wash with shampoo
**SHAMPOOED** >SHAMPOO
**SHAMPOOER** >SHAMPOO
**SHAMPOOS** >SHAMPOO
**SHAMROCK** n clover leaf, esp as the Irish emblem
**SHAMROCKS** >SHAMROCK
**SHAMS** >SHAM
**SHAMUS** n police or private detective
**SHAMUSES** >SHAMUS
**SHAN** variant of >SHAND
**SHANACHIE** n Gaelic storyteller
**SHAND** n old word meaning fake coin
**SHANDIES** >SHANDY
**SHANDRIES** >SHANDRY
**SHANDRY** n light horse-drawn cart
**SHANDS** >SHAND
**SHANDY** n drink made of beer and lemonade
**SHANGHAI** vb force or trick (someone) into doing something ▷ n catapult
**SHANGHAIS** >SHANGHAI
**SHANK** n lower leg ▷ vb (of fruits, roots, etc) to show disease symptoms, esp discoloration
**SHANKBONE** n bone in lower leg
**SHANKED** >SHANK
**SHANKING** >SHANK
**SHANKS** >SHANK
**SHANNIES** >SHANNY
**SHANNY** n European blenny of rocky coastal waters
**SHANS** >SHAN
**SHANTEY** same as >SHANTY
**SHANTEYS** >SHANTEY
**SHANTI** n peace
**SHANTIES** >SHANTY
**SHANTIH** same as >SHANTI
**SHANTIHS** >SHANTIH
**SHANTIS** >SHANTI
**SHANTUNG** n soft Chinese silk with a knobbly surface
**SHANTUNGS** >SHANTUNG
**SHANTY** n shack or crude dwelling

**SHANTYMAN** n man living in shanty
**SHANTYMEN** >SHANTYMAN
**SHAPABLE** >SHAPE
**SHAPE** n outward form of an object ▷ vb form or mould
**SHAPEABLE** >SHAPE
**SHAPED** >SHAPE
**SHAPELESS** adj (of a person or object) lacking a pleasing shape
**SHAPELIER** >SHAPELY
**SHAPELY** adj having an attractive shape
**SHAPEN** vb old form of shaped
**SHAPER** >SHAPE
**SHAPERS** >SHAPE
**SHAPES** >SHAPE
**SHAPEUP** n system of hiring dockers for a day's work
**SHAPEUPS** >SHAPEUP
**SHAPEWEAR** n underwear that shapes body
**SHAPING** >SHAPE
**SHAPINGS** >SHAPE
**SHAPS** n leather over-trousers worn by cowboys
**SHARABLE** >SHARE
**SHARD** n broken piece of pottery or glass
**SHARDED** adj old word meaning hidden under dung
**SHARDS** >SHARD
**SHARE** n part of something that belongs to or is contributed by a person ▷ vb give or take a share of (something)
**SHAREABLE** >SHARE
**SHARECROP** vb cultivate (farmland) as a sharecropper
**SHARED** >SHARE
**SHAREMAN** n member of fishing-boat crew who shares profits
**SHAREMEN** >SHAREMAN
**SHARER** >SHARE
**SHARERS** >SHARE
**SHARES** >SHARE
**SHARESMAN** n member of fishing-boat crew who shares profits
**SHARESMEN** >SHARESMAN
**SHAREWARE** n software available to all users without the need for a licence
**SHARIA** n body of doctrines that regulate the lives of Muslims
**SHARIAH** same as >SHARIA
**SHARIAHS** >SHARIAH
**SHARIAS** >SHARIA
**SHARIAT** n Islamic religious law
**SHARIATS** >SHARIAT
**SHARIF** same as >SHERIF
**SHARIFIAN** >SHARIF
**SHARIFS** >SHARIF
**SHARING** >SHARE

**SHARINGS** > SHARE
**SHARK** n large usu predatory sea fish ▷ vb obtain (something) by cheating or deception
**SHARKED** > SHARK
**SHARKER** n shark hunter
**SHARKERS** > SHARKER
**SHARKING** > SHARK
**SHARKINGS** > SHARK
**SHARKLIKE** > SHARK
**SHARKS** > SHARK
**SHARKSKIN** n stiff glossy fabric
**SHARN** Scots word for > DUNG
**SHARNIER** > SHARN
**SHARNIEST** > SHARN
**SHARNS** > SHARN
**SHARNY** > SHARN
**SHARON** as in sharon fruit persimmon
**SHARP** adj having a keen cutting edge or fine point ▷ adv promptly ▷ n symbol raising a note one semitone above natural pitch ▷ vb make sharp
**SHARPED** > SHARP
**SHARPEN** vb make or become sharp or sharper
**SHARPENED** > SHARPEN
**SHARPENER** > SHARPEN
**SHARPENS** > SHARPEN
**SHARPER** n person who cheats
**SHARPERS** > SHARPER
**SHARPEST** > SHARP
**SHARPIE** n member of a teenage group having short hair and distinctive clothes
**SHARPIES** > SHARPIE
**SHARPING** > SHARP
**SHARPINGS** > SHARP
**SHARPISH** adj fairly sharp ▷ adv promptly
**SHARPLY** > SHARP
**SHARPNESS** > SHARP
**SHARPS** > SHARP
**SHARPY** n swindler
**SHASH** vb old form of sash
**SHASHED** > SHASH
**SHASHES** > SHASH
**SHASHING** > SHASH
**SHASHLICK** same as > SHASHLIK
**SHASHLIK** n type of kebab
**SHASHLIKS** > SHASHLIK
**SHASLIK** n type of kebab
**SHASLIKS** > SHASLIK
**SHASTER** same as > SHASTRA
**SHASTERS** > SHASTER
**SHASTRA** n any of the sacred writings of Hinduism
**SHASTRAS** > SHASTRA
**SHAT** past tense and past participle of > SHIT
**SHATTER** vb break into pieces ▷ n fragment
**SHATTERED** adj completely exhausted
**SHATTERER** > SHATTER
**SHATTERS** > SHATTER

**SHATTERY** adj liable to shatter
**SHAUCHLE** vb Scots word meaning shuffle
**SHAUCHLED** > SHAUCHLE
**SHAUCHLES** > SHAUCHLE
**SHAUCHLY** > SHAUCHLE
**SHAUGH** n old word meaning small wood
**SHAUGHS** > SHAUGH
**SHAUL** vb old form of shawl
**SHAULED** > SHAUL
**SHAULING** > SHAUL
**SHAULS** > SHAUL
**SHAVABLE** > SHAVE
**SHAVE** vb remove (hair) from (the face, head, or body) with a razor or shaver ▷ n shaving
**SHAVEABLE** > SHAVE
**SHAVED** > SHAVE
**SHAVELING** n derogatory term for a priest or clergyman with a shaven head
**SHAVEN** adj closely shaved or tonsured
**SHAVER** n electric razor
**SHAVERS** > SHAVER
**SHAVES** > SHAUL
**SHAVETAIL** n American slang for second lieutenant
**SHAVIE** n Scots word meaning trick
**SHAVIES** > SHAVIE
**SHAVING** > SHAVE
**SHAVINGS** > SHAVE
**SHAW** n small wood ▷ vb show
**SHAWED** > SHAW
**SHAWING** > SHAW
**SHAWL** n piece of cloth worn over a woman's shoulders or wrapped around a baby ▷ vb cover with a shawl
**SHAWLED** > SHAWL
**SHAWLEY** n Irish word for woman wearing shawl
**SHAWLEYS** > SHAWLEY
**SHAWLIE** n disparaging term for a working-class woman who wears a shawl
**SHAWLIES** > SHAWLIE
**SHAWLING** > SHAWL
**SHAWLINGS** > SHAWL
**SHAWLLESS** > SHAWL
**SHAWLS** > SHAWL
**SHAWM** n medieval form of the oboe with a conical bore and flaring bell
**SHAWMS** > SHAWM
**SHAWN** variant of > SHAWM
**SHAWS** > SHAW
**SHAY** dialect word for > CHAISE
**SHAYA** n Indian plant
**SHAYAS** > SHAYA
**SHAYS** > SHAY
**SHAZAM** interj magic slogan
**SHCHI** n Russian cabbage soup
**SHCHIS** > SHCHI

**SHE** pron female person or animal previously mentioned ▷ n female person or animal
**SHEA** n tropical African tree
**SHEADING** n any of the six subdivisions of the Isle of Man
**SHEADINGS** > SHEADING
**SHEAF** n bundle of papers ▷ vb tie into a sheaf
**SHEAFED** > SHEAF
**SHEAFIER** > SHEAF
**SHEAFIEST** > SHEAF
**SHEAFING** > SHEAF
**SHEAFLIKE** > SHEAF
**SHEAFS** > SHEAF
**SHEAFY** > SHEAF
**SHEAL** vb old word meaning shell
**SHEALED** > SHEAL
**SHEALING** > SHEAL
**SHEALINGS** > SHEAL
**SHEALS** > SHEAL
**SHEAR** vb clip hair or wool from ▷ n breakage caused through strain or twisting
**SHEARED** > SHEAR
**SHEARER** > SHEAR
**SHEARERS** > SHEAR
**SHEARING** > SHEAR
**SHEARINGS** > SHEAR
**SHEARLEG** n one spar of shearlegs
**SHEARLEGS** same as > SHEERLEGS
**SHEARLING** n young sheep after its first shearing
**SHEARMAN** n person who trims cloth
**SHEARMEN** > SHEARMAN
**SHEARS** > SHEAR
**SHEAS** > SHEA
**SHEATFISH** n European catfish
**SHEATH** n close-fitting cover, esp for a knife or sword
**SHEATHE** vb put into a sheath
**SHEATHED** > SHEATHE
**SHEATHER** > SHEATHE
**SHEATHERS** > SHEATHE
**SHEATHES** > SHEATHE
**SHEATHIER** > SHEATHE
**SHEATHING** n any material used as an outer layer
**SHEATHS** > SHEATH
**SHEATHY** > SHEATHE
**SHEAVE** vb gather or bind into sheaves ▷ n wheel with a grooved rim, esp one used as a pulley
**SHEAVED** > SHEAVE
**SHEAVES** > SHEAF
**SHEAVING** > SHEAVE
**SHEBANG** n situation, matter, or affair
**SHEBANGS** > SHEBANG
**SHEBEAN** same as > SHEBEEN
**SHEBEANS** > SHEBEAN
**SHEBEEN** n place where alcohol is sold illegally ▷ vb run a shebeen

**SHEBEENED** > SHEBEEN
**SHEBEENER** > SHEBEEN
**SHEBEENS** > SHEBEEN
**SHECHITA** n Jewish method of killing animals for food
**SHECHITAH** same as > SHECHITA
**SHECHITAS** > SHECHITA
**SHED** n building used for storage or shelter or as a workshop ▷ vb get rid of
**SHEDABLE** > SHED
**SHEDDABLE** > SHED
**SHEDDED** > SHED
**SHEDDER** n person or thing that sheds
**SHEDDERS** > SHEDDER
**SHEDDING** > SHED
**SHEDDINGS** > SHED
**SHEDFUL** n quantity or amount contained in a shed
**SHEDFULS** > SHEDFUL
**SHEDLIKE** > SHED
**SHEDLOAD** n very large amount or number
**SHEDLOADS** > SHEDLOAD
**SHEDS** > SHED
**SHEEL** vb old word meaning shell
**SHEELED** > SHEEL
**SHEELING** > SHEEL
**SHEELS** > SHEEL
**SHEEN** n glistening brightness on the surface of something ▷ adj shining and beautiful ▷ vb give a sheen to
**SHEENED** > SHEEN
**SHEENEY** n offensive word for Jew
**SHEENEYS** > SHEENEY
**SHEENFUL** > SHEEN
**SHEENIE** n offensive word for Jew
**SHEENIER** > SHEEN
**SHEENIES** > SHEENIE
**SHEENIEST** > SHEEN
**SHEENING** > SHEEN
**SHEENS** > SHEEN
**SHEENY** > SHEEN
**SHEEP** n ruminant animal bred for wool and meat
**SHEEPCOT** n sheepcote
**SHEEPCOTE** another word for > SHEEPFOLD
**SHEEPCOTS** > SHEEPCOT
**SHEEPDOG** n dog used for herding sheep
**SHEEPDOGS** > SHEEPDOG
**SHEEPFOLD** n pen or enclosure for sheep
**SHEEPHEAD** n species of fish
**SHEEPIER** > SHEEP
**SHEEPIEST** > SHEEP
**SHEEPISH** adj embarrassed because of feeling foolish
**SHEEPLE** pl n informal derogatory word for people who follow the majority in matters of opinion, taste, etc

SHEEPLIKE > SHEEP
SHEEPMAN n person who keeps sheep
SHEEPMEN > SHEEPMAN
SHEEPO n person employed to bring sheep to the catching pen in a shearing shed
SHEEPOS > SHEEPO
SHEEPSKIN n skin of a sheep with the fleece still on, used for clothing or rugs
SHEEPWALK n tract of land for grazing sheep
SHEEPY > SHEEP
SHEER adj absolute, complete ▷ adv steeply ▷ vb change course suddenly ▷ n any transparent fabric used for making garments
SHEERED > SHEER
SHEERER > SHEER
SHEEREST > SHEER
SHEERING > SHEER
SHEERLEG n one spar of sheerlegs
SHEERLEGS n device for lifting heavy weights
SHEERLY > SHEER
SHEERNESS > SHEER
SHEERS > SHEER
SHEESH interj exclamation of surprise or annoyance
SHEET n large piece of cloth used as an inner bed cover ▷ vb provide with, cover, or wrap in a sheet
SHEETED > SHEET
SHEETER > SHEET
SHEETERS > SHEET
SHEETFED adj printing on separate sheets of paper
SHEETIER > SHEET
SHEETIEST > SHEET
SHEETING n material from which sheets are made
SHEETINGS > SHEETING
SHEETLESS > SHEET
SHEETLIKE > SHEET
SHEETROCK n brand name for plasterboard
SHEETS > SHEET
SHEETY > SHEET
SHEEVE n part of mine winding gear
SHEEVES > SHEEVE
SHEGETZ n offensive word for non-Jew
SHEHITA n slaughter of animal according to Jewish religious law
SHEHITAH n slaughter of animal according to Jewish religious law
SHEHITAHS > SHEHITAH
SHEHITAS > SHEHITA
SHEIK same as > SHEIKH
SHEIKDOM same as > SHEIKHDOM
SHEIKDOMS > SHEIKDOM
SHEIKH n Arab chief
SHEIKHA n chief wife of

sheikh
SHEIKHAS > SHEIKHA
SHEIKHDOM n territory ruled by a sheikh
SHEIKHS > SHEIKH
SHEIKS > SHEIK
SHEILA n girl or woman
SHEILAS > SHEILA
SHEILING n hut used by shepherds
SHEILINGS > SHEILING
SHEITAN n Muslim demon
SHEITANS > SHEITAN
SHEKALIM > SHEKEL
SHEKEL n monetary unit of Israel
SHEKELIM > SHEKEL
SHEKELS > SHEKEL
SHELDDUCK n species of large duck
SHELDRAKE same as > SHELDUCK
SHELDUCK n large brightly coloured wild duck of Europe and Asia
SHELDUCKS > SHELDUCK
SHELF n board fixed horizontally for holding things ▷ vb put on a shelf
SHELFED > SHELF
SHELFFUL > SHELF
SHELFFULS > SHELF
SHELFIER > SHELF
SHELFIEST > SHELF
SHELFING > SHELF
SHELFLIKE > SHELF
SHELFROOM n space on shelf
SHELFS > SHELF
SHELFY > SHELF
SHELL n hard outer covering of an egg, nut, or certain animals ▷ vb take the shell from
SHELLAC n resin used in varnishes ▷ vb coat with shellac
SHELLACK vb shellac
SHELLACKS > SHELLAC
SHELLACS > SHELLAC
SHELLBACK n sailor who has crossed the equator
SHELLBARK same as > SHAGBARK
SHELLDUCK n shelduck
SHELLED > SHELL
SHELLER > SHELL
SHELLERS > SHELL
SHELLFIRE n firing of artillery shells
SHELLFISH n sea-living animal, esp one that can be eaten, with a shell
SHELLFUL > SHELL
SHELLFULS > SHELL
SHELLIER > SHELL
SHELLIEST > SHELL
SHELLING > SHELL
SHELLINGS > SHELL
SHELLS > SHELL
SHELLWORK n decoration with shells
SHELLY > SHELL
SHELTA n secret language

used by some traveling people in Britain and Ireland
SHELTAS > SHELTA
SHELTER n structure providing protection from danger or the weather ▷ vb give shelter to
SHELTERED adj protected from wind and rain
SHELTERER > SHELTER
SHELTERS > SHELTER
SHELTERY > SHELTER
SHELTIE n small dog similar to a collie
SHELTIES > SHELTY
SHELTY same as > SHELTIE
SHELVE vb put aside or postpone
SHELVED > SHELVE
SHELVER > SHELVE
SHELVERS > SHELVE
SHELVES > SHELF
SHELVIER > SHELVY
SHELVIEST > SHELVY
SHELVING n (material for) shelves
SHELVINGS > SHELVING
SHELVY adj having shelves
SHEMOZZLE n noisy confusion or dispute
SHEND vb put to shame
SHENDING > SHEND
SHENDS > SHEND
SHENT > SHEND
SHEOL n hell
SHEOLS > SHEOL
SHEPHERD n person who tends sheep ▷ vb guide or watch over (people)
SHEPHERDS > SHEPHERD
SHEQALIM n plural of sheqel
SHEQEL same as > SHEKEL
SHEQELS > SHEQEL
SHERANG n person in charge
SHERANGS > SHERANG
SHERBERT same as > SHERBET
SHERBERTS > SHERBET
SHERBET n fruit-flavoured fizzy powder
SHERBETS > SHERBET
SHERD same as > SHARD
SHERDS > SHERD
SHERE old spelling of > SHEER
SHEREEF same as > SHERIF
SHEREEFS > SHEREEF
SHERIA same as > SHARIA
SHERIAS > SHERIA
SHERIAT n Muslim religious law
SHERIATS > SHERIAT
SHERIF n descendant of Mohammed through his daughter Fatima
SHERIFF n (in the US) chief law enforcement officer of a county
SHERIFFS > SHERIFF
SHERIFIAN > SHERIF
SHERIFS > SHERIF
SHERLOCK n detective

SHERLOCKS > SHERLOCK
SHEROOT n cheroot
SHEROOTS > SHEROOT
SHERPA n official who assists at a summit meeting
SHERPAS > SHERPA
SHERRIES > SHERRY
SHERRIS n old form of sherry
SHERRISES > SHERRIS
SHERRY n pale or dark brown fortified wine
SHERWANI n long coat closed up to the neck, worn by men in India
SHERWANIS > SHERWANI
SHES > SHE
SHET vb old form of shut
SHETLAND n type of wool spun in the Shetland islands
SHETLANDS > SHETLAND
SHETS > SHET
SHETTING > SHET
SHEUCH n ditch or trough ▷ vb dig
SHEUCHED > SHEUCH
SHEUCHING > SHEUCH
SHEUCHS > SHEUCH
SHEUGH same as > SHEUCH
SHEUGHED > SHEUGH
SHEUGHING > SHEUGH
SHEUGHS > SHEUGH
SHEVA n mark in Hebrew writing
SHEVAS > SHEVA
SHEW archaic spelling of > SHOW
SHEWBREAD n loaves of bread placed every Sabbath on the table beside the altar of incense in the tabernacle of ancient Israel
SHEWED > SHEW
SHEWEL n old word meaning scarecrow
SHEWELS > SHEWEL
SHEWER > SHEW
SHEWERS > SHEW
SHEWING > SHEW
SHEWN > SHEW
SHEWS > SHEW
SHH interj sound made to ask for silence
SHIAI n judo contest
SHIAIS > SHIAI
SHIATSU n massage in which pressure is applied to the same points of the body as in acupuncture
SHIATSUS > SHIATSU
SHIATZU n shiatzu
SHIATZUS > SHIATZU
SHIBAH n Jewish period of mourning
SHIBAHS > SHIBAH
SHIBUICHI n Japanese alloy of copper and silver
SHICKER n alcoholic drink
SHICKERED adj drunk
SHICKERS > SHICKER
SHICKSA n non-Jewish girl

SHICKSAS > SHICKSA

SHIDDER n old word meaning female animal

SHIDDERS > SHIDDER

SHIDDUCH n arranged marriage

SHIED > SHY

SHIEL vb sheal

SHIELD n piece of armour carried on the arm to protect the body from blows or missiles ▷ vb protect

SHIELDED > SHIELD

SHIELDER > SHIELD

SHIELDERS > SHIELD

SHIELDING > SHIELD

SHIELDS > SHIELD

SHIELED > SHIEL

SHIELING n rough hut or shelter used by people tending cattle on high or remote ground

SHIELINGS > SHIELING

SHIELS > SHIEL

SHIER n horse that shies habitually

SHIERS > SHIER

SHIES > SHY

SHIEST > SHY

SHIFT vb move ▷ n shifting

SHIFTABLE > SHIFT

SHIFTED > SHIFT

SHIFTER > SHIFT

SHIFTERS > SHIFT

SHIFTIER > SHIFTY

SHIFTIEST > SHIFTY

SHIFTILY > SHIFTY

SHIFTING > SHIFT

SHIFTINGS > SHIFT

SHIFTLESS adj lacking in ambition or initiative

SHIFTS > SHIFT

SHIFTWORK n system of employment where an individual's normal hours of work are outside the period of normal day working

SHIFTY adj evasive or untrustworthy

SHIGELLA n any rod-shaped Gram-negative bacterium of the genus Shigella

SHIGELLAE > SHIGELLA

SHIGELLAS > SHIGELLA

SHIITAKE n kind of mushroom widely used in Oriental cookery

SHIITAKES > SHIITAKE

SHIKAR n hunting, esp big-game hunting ▷ vb hunt (game, esp big game)

SHIKAREE same as > SHIKARI

SHIKAREES > SHIKAREE

SHIKARI n (in India) a hunter

SHIKARIS > SHIKARI

SHIKARRED > SHIKAR

SHIKARS > SHIKAR

SHIKKER n Yiddish term for drunk person

SHIKKERS > SHIKKER

SHIKSA n often derogatory term for a non-Jewish girl

SHIKSAS > SHIKSA

SHIKSE n non-Jewish girl

SHIKSEH same as > SHIKSE

SHIKSEHS > SHIKSEH

SHIKSES > SHIKSE

SHILINGI n money unit in Tanzania

SHILL n confidence trickster's assistant ▷ vb act as a shill

SHILLABER n keen customer

SHILLALA n short Irish clud or cudgel

SHILLALAH same as > SHILLALA

SHILLALAS > SHILLALA

SHILLED > SHILL

SHILLELAH same as > SHILLALA

SHILLING n former British coin

SHILLINGS > SHILLING

SHILLS > SHILL

SHILPIT adj puny

SHILY > SHY

SHIM n thin strip of material placed between two close surfaces to fill a gap ▷ vb fit or fill up with a shim

SHIMAAL n hot Middle Eastern wind

SHIMAALS > SHIMAAL

SHIMMED > SHIM

SHIMMER n (shine with) a faint unsteady light ▷ vb shine with a faint unsteady light

SHIMMERED > SHIMMER

SHIMMERS > SHIMMER

SHIMMERY adj shining with a glistening or tremulous light

SHIMMEY n chemise

SHIMMEYS > SHIMMEY

SHIMMIED > SHIMMY

SHIMMIES > SHIMMY

SHIMMING > SHIM

SHIMMY n American ragtime dance with much shaking of the hips and shoulders ▷ vb dance the shimmy

SHIMMYING > SHIMMY

SHIMOZZLE n predicament

SHIMS > SHIM

SHIN n front of the lower leg ▷ vb climb by using the hands or arms and legs

SHINBONE n tibia

SHINBONES > SHINBONE

SHINDIES > SHINDY

SHINDIG n noisy party

SHINDIGS > SHINDIG

SHINDY n quarrel or commotion

SHINDYS > SHINDY

SHINE vb give out or reflect light; cause to gleam ▷ n brightness or lustre

SHINED > SHINE

SHINELESS > SHINE

SHINER n black eye

SHINERS > SHINER

SHINES > SHINE

SHINESS > SHY

SHINESSES > SHY

SHINGLE n wooden roof tile ▷ vb cover (a roof) with shingles

SHINGLED > SHINGLE

SHINGLER > SHINGLE

SHINGLERS > SHINGLE

SHINGLES n disease causing a rash of small blisters along a nerve

SHINGLIER > SHINGLE

SHINGLING > SHINGLE

SHINGLY > SHINGLE

SHINGUARD n rigid piece of plastic to protect footballer's shin

SHINIER > SHINY

SHINIES > SHINY

SHINIEST > SHINY

SHINILY > SHINY

SHININESS > SHINY

SHINING > SHINE

SHININGLY > SHINE

SHINJU n (formerly, in Japan) a ritual double suicide of lovers

SHINJUS > SHINJU

SHINKIN n worthless person

SHINKINS > SHINKIN

SHINLEAF n wintergreen

SHINLEAFS > SHINLEAF

SHINNE n old form of chin

SHINNED > SHIN

SHINNERY n American oak tree

SHINNES > SHINNE

SHINNEY vb climb with hands and legs

SHINNEYED > SHINNEY

SHINNEYS > SHINNEY

SHINNIED > SHINNY

SHINNIES > SHINNY

SHINNING > SHIN

SHINNY same as > SHINTY

SHINNYING > SHINNY

SHINS > SHIN

SHINTIED > SHINTY

SHINTIES > SHINTY

SHINTY n game like hockey ▷ vb play shinty

SHINTYING > SHINTY

SHINY adj bright and polished

SHIP n large seagoing vessel ▷ vb send or transport by carrier, esp a ship

SHIPBOARD adj taking place or used aboard a ship

SHIPBORNE adj carried on ship

SHIPFUL n amount carried by ship

SHIPFULS > SHIPFUL

SHIPLAP n method of constructing ship hull

SHIPLAPS > SHIPLAP

SHIPLESS > SHIP

SHIPLOAD n quantity carried by a ship

SHIPLOADS > SHIPLOAD

SHIPMAN n master or captain of a ship

SHIPMATE n sailor serving on the same ship as another

SHIPMATES > SHIPMATE

SHIPMEN > SHIPMAN

SHIPMENT n act of shipping cargo

SHIPMENTS > SHIPMENT

SHIPOWNER n person who owns or has shares in a ship or ships

SHIPPABLE > SHIP

SHIPPED > SHIP

SHIPPEN n dialect word for cattle shed

SHIPPENS > SHIPPEN

SHIPPER n person or company that ships

SHIPPERS > SHIPPER

SHIPPIE n prostitute who solicits at a port

SHIPPIES > SHIPPIE

SHIPPING > SHIP

SHIPPINGS > SHIP

SHIPPO n Japanese enamel work

SHIPPON n dialect word for cattle shed

SHIPPONS > SHIPPON

SHIPPOS > SHIPPO

SHIPPOUND n Baltic weight measure

SHIPS > SHIP

SHIPSHAPE adj orderly or neat ▷ adv in a neat and orderly manner

SHIPSIDE n part of wharf next to ship

SHIPSIDES > SHIPSIDE

SHIPWAY n structure on which a vessel is built, then launched

SHIPWAYS > SHIPWAY

SHIPWORM n any wormlike marine bivalve mollusc of the genus Teredo

SHIPWORMS > SHIPWORM

SHIPWRECK n destruction of a ship through storm or collision ▷ vb cause to undergo shipwreck

SHIPYARD n place where ships are built

SHIPYARDS > SHIPYARD

SHIR n gathering in material

SHIRALEE n swag

SHIRALEES > SHIRALEE

SHIRE n county ▷ vb refresh or rest

SHIRED > SHIRE

SHIREMAN n sheriff

SHIREMEN > SHIREMAN

SHIRES > SHIRE

SHIRING > SHIRE

SHIRK vb avoid (duty or work) ▷ n person who shirks

SHIRKED > SHIRK
SHIRKER > SHIRK
SHIRKERS > SHIRK
SHIRKING > SHIRK
SHIRKS > SHIRK
SHIRR vb gather (fabric) into two or more parallel rows to decorate a dress, etc ▷ n series of gathered rows decorating a dress, blouse, etc
SHIRRA old Scots word for > SHERIFF
SHIRRALEE n swagman's bundle of possessions
SHIRRAS > SHIRRA
SHIRRED > SHIRR
SHIRRING > SHIRR
SHIRRINGS > SHIRR
SHIRRS > SHIRR
SHIRS > SHIR
SHIRT n garment for the upper part of the body ▷ vb put a shirt on
SHIRTBAND n neckband on shirt
SHIRTED > SHIRT
SHIRTIER > SHIRTY
SHIRTIEST > SHIRTY
SHIRTILY > SHIRTY
SHIRTING n fabric used in making men's shirts
SHIRTINGS > SHIRTING
SHIRTLESS > SHIRT
SHIRTS > SHIRT
SHIRTTAIL n part of a shirt that extends below the waist
SHIRTY adj bad-tempered or annoyed
SHISH as in shish kebab dish of meat and vegetables threaded onto skewers and grilled
SHISHA same as > HOOKAH
SHISHAS > SHISHA
SHISO n Asian plant with aromatic leaves that are used in cooking
SHISOS > SHISO
SHIST n schist
SHISTS > SHIST
SHIT taboo vb defecate ▷ n excrement ▷ interj exclamation of anger or disgust
SHIITAKE same as > SHIITAKE
SHITAKES > SHITAKE
SHITE same as > SHIT
SHITED > SHITE
SHITES > SHITE
SHITFACED adj drunk
SHITHEAD n taboo slang fool
SHITHEADS > SHITHEAD
SHITHOLE n dirty place
SHITHOLES > SHITHOLE
SHITING > SHITE
SHITLESS adj very frightened
SHITLIST n list of hated things
SHITLISTS > SHITLIST
SHITLOAD n taboo slang

for a lot
SHITLOADS > SHITLOAD
SHITS > SHIT
SHITTAH n tree mentioned in the Old Testament
SHITTAHS > SHITTAH
SHITTED > SHIT
SHITTIER > SHIT
SHITTIEST > SHIT
SHITTILY > SHIT
SHITTIM > SHITTAH
SHITTIMS > SHITTAH
SHITTING > SHIT
SHITTY > SHIT
SHIUR n lesson in which a passage of the Talmud is studied together by a group of people
SHIURIM > SHIUR
SHIV variant spelling of > CHIV
SHIVA variant of > SHIVAH
SHIVAH n Jewish period of formal mourning
SHIVAHS > SHIVAH
SHIVAREE n discordant mock serenade to newlyweds, made with pans, kettles, etc
SHIVAREED > SHIVAREE
SHIVAREES > SHIVAREE
SHIVAS > SHIVA
SHIVE n flat cork or bung for wide-mouthed bottles
SHIVER vb tremble, as from cold or fear ▷ n shivering
SHIVERED > SHIVER
SHIVERER > SHIVER
SHIVERERS > SHIVER
SHIVERIER > SHIVERY
SHIVERING > SHIVER
SHIVERS > SHIVER
SHIVERY adj inclined to shiver or tremble
SHIVES > SHIVE
SHIVITI n Jewish decorative plaque with religious message
SHIVITIS > SHIVITI
SHIVOO n Australian word meaning rowdy party
SHIVOOS > SHIVOO
SHIVS > SHIV
SHIVVED > SHIV
SHIVVING > SHIV
SHKOTZIM n plural of shegetz
SHLEMIEHL Yiddish word for > FOOL
SHLEMIEL same as > SCHLEMIEL
SHLEMIELS > SHLEMIEL
SHLEP vb schlep
SHLEPP vb schlep
SHLEPPED > SHLEP
SHLEPPER > SHLEP
SHLEPPERS > SHLEP
SHLEPPING > SHLEP
SHLEPPS > SHLEPP
SHLEPS > SHLEP
SHLIMAZEL n unlucky person
SHLOCK n something of poor quality

SHLOCKIER > SHLOCK
SHLOCKS > SHLOCK
SHLOCKY > SHLOCK
SHLOSHIM n period of thirty days' deep mourning following a death
SHLOSHIMS > SHLOSHIM
SHLUB same as > SCHLUB
SHLUBS > SHLUB
SHLUMP vb move in lazy way
SHLUMPED > SHLUMP
SHLUMPING > SHLUMP
SHLUMPS > SHLUMP
SHLUMPY > SHLUMP
SHMALTZ n schmaltz
SHMALTZES > SHMALTZ
SHMALTZY > SHMALTZ
SHMATTE n rag
SHMATTES > SHMATTE
SHMEAR n set of things
SHMEARS > SHMEAR
SHMEK n smell
SHMEKS > SHMEK
SHMO same as > SCHMO
SHMOCK n despicable person
SHMOCKS > SHMOCK
SHMOES > SHMO
SHMOOSE variant of > SCHMOOZE
SHMOOSED > SHMOOSE
SHMOOSES > SHMOOSE
SHMOOSING > SHMOOSE
SHMOOZE variant of > SCHMOOZE
SHMOOZED > SHMOOZE
SHMOOZES > SHMOOZE
SHMOOZING > SHMOOZE
SHMUCK n despicable person
SHMUCKS > SCHMUCK
SHNAPPS same as > SCHNAPPS
SHNAPS n schnaps
SHNOOK n stupid person
SHNOOKS > SHNOOK
SHNORRER same as > SCHNORRER
SHNORRERS > SHNORRER
SHOAL n large number of fish swimming together ▷ vb make or become shallow ▷ adj (of the draught of a vessel) drawing little water
SHOALED > SHOAL
SHOALER > SHOAL
SHOALEST > SHOAL
SHOALIER > SHOALY
SHOALIEST > SHOALY
SHOALING > SHOAL
SHOALINGS > SHOAL
SHOALNESS > SHOAL
SHOALS > SHOAL
SHOALWISE adv in a large group or in large groups
SHOALY adj shallow
SHOAT n piglet that has recently been weaned
SHOATS > SHOAT
SHOCHET n (in Judaism) a person who has been specially trained and

licensed to slaughter animals and birds in accordance with the laws of shechita
SHOCHETIM > SHOCHET
SHOCHETS > SHOCHET
SHOCK vb horrify, disgust, or astonish ▷ n sudden violent emotional disturbance ▷ adj bushy
SHOCKABLE > SHOCK
SHOCKED > SHOCK
SHOCKER n person or thing that shocks or horrifies
SHOCKERS > SHOCKER
SHOCKING adj causing horror, disgust, or astonishment
SHOCKS > SHOCK
SHOD > SHOE
SHODDEN vb old form of shod
SHODDIER > SHODDY
SHODDIES > SHODDY
SHODDIEST > SHODDY
SHODDILY > SHODDY
SHODDY adj made or done badly ▷ n yarn or fabric made from wool waste or clippings
SHODER n skins used in making gold leaf
SHODERS > SHODER
SHOE n outer covering for the foot, ending below the ankle ▷ vb fit with a shoe or shoes
SHOEBILL n large wading bird of tropical E African swamps
SHOEBILLS > SHOEBILL
SHOEBLACK n (esp formerly) a person who shines boots and shoes
SHOEBOX n cardboard box for shoes
SHOEBOXES > SHOEBOX
SHOED > SHOE
SHOEHORN n smooth curved implement inserted at the heel of a shoe to ease the foot into it ▷ vb cram (people or things) into a very small space
SHOEHORNS > SHOEHORN
SHOEING > SHOE
SHOEINGS > SHOE
SHOELACE n cord for fastening shoes
SHOELACES > SHOELACE
SHOELESS > SHOE
SHOEMAKER n person who makes or repairs shoes or boots
SHOEPAC n waterproof boot
SHOEPACK n waterproof boot
SHOEPACKS > SHOEPACK
SHOEPACS > SHOEPAC
SHOER n person who shoes horses
SHOERS > SHOER
SHOES > SHOE

**SHOESHINE** *n* act or an instance of polishing a pair of shoes

**SHOETREE** *n* piece of metal, wood, or plastic inserted in a shoe to keep its shape

**SHOETREES** > SHOETREE

**SHOFAR** *n* ram's horn sounded in the synagogue daily during the month of Elul and repeatedly on Rosh Hashanah

**SHOFARS** > SHOFAR

**SHOFROTH** > SHOFAR

**SHOG** *vb* shake

**SHOGGED** > SHOG

**SHOGGING** > SHOG

**SHOGGLE** *vb* shake

**SHOGGLED** > SHOGGLE

**SHOGGLES** > SHOGGLE

**SHOGGLIER** > SHOGGLE

**SHOGGLING** > SHOGGLE

**SHOGGLY** > SHOGGLE

**SHOGI** *n* Japanese chess

**SHOGIS** > SHOGI

**SHOGS** > SHOG

**SHOGUN** *n* Japanese chief military commander

**SHOGUNAL** > SHOGUN

**SHOGUNATE** *n* office or rule of a shogun

**SHOGUNS** > SHOGUN

**SHOJI** *n* Japanese rice-paper screen in a sliding wooden frame

**SHOJIS** > SHOJI

**SHOLA** *n* Indian plant

**SHOLAS** > SHOLA

**SHOLOM** *n* Hebrew greeting

**SHOLOMS** > SHOLOM

**SHONE** > SHINE

**SHONEEN** *n* Irishman who imitates English ways

**SHONEENS** > SHONEEN

**SHONKIER** > SHONKY

**SHONKIEST** > SHONKY

**SHONKY** *adj* unreliable or unsound

**SHOO** *interj* go away! ▷ *vb* drive away as by saying 'shoo'

**SHOOED** > SHOO

**SHOOFLIES** > SHOOFLY

**SHOOFLY** as in *shoofly pie* US dessert similar to treacle tart

**SHOOGIE** *vb* Scots word meaning swing

**SHOOGIED** > SHOOGIE

**SHOOGIES** > SHOOGIE

**SHOOGLE** *vb* shake, sway, or rock back and forth ▷ *n* rocking motion

**SHOOGLED** > SHOOGLE

**SHOOGLES** > SHOOGLE

**SHOOGLIER** > SHOOGLE

**SHOOGLING** > SHOOGLE

**SHOOGLY** > SHOOGLE

**SHOOING** > SHOO

**SHOOK** *n* set of parts ready for assembly

**SHOOKS** > SHOOK

**SHOOL** *dialect word for* > SHOVEL

**SHOOLE** *dialect word for* > SHOVEL

**SHOOLED** > SHOOL

**SHOOLES** > SHOOLE

**SHOOLING** > SHOOL

**SHOOLS** > SHOOL

**SHOON** *plural of* > SHOE

**SHOORA** *same as* > SHURA

**SHOORAS** > SHOORA

**SHOOS** > SHOO

**SHOOT** *vb* hit, wound, or kill with a missile fired from a weapon ▷ *n* new branch or sprout of a plant

**SHOOTABLE** > SHOOT

**SHOOTDOWN** *n* act of shooting down aircraft

**SHOOTER** *n* person or thing that shoots

**SHOOTERS** > SHOOTER

**SHOOTING** > SHOOT

**SHOOTINGS** > SHOOT

**SHOOTIST** *n* person who shoots

**SHOOTISTS** > SHOOTIST

**SHOOTOUT** *n* conclusive gunfight

**SHOOTOUTS** > SHOOTOUT

**SHOOTS** > SHOOT

**SHOP** *n* place for sale of goods and services ▷ *vb* visit a shop or shops to buy goods

**SHOPBOARD** *n* shop counter

**SHOPBOY** *n* boy working in shop

**SHOPBOYS** > SHOPBOY

**SHOPE** *n* old form of shape

**SHOPFRONT** *n* area of shop facing street

**SHOPFUL** *n* amount stored in shop

**SHOPFULS** > SHOPFUL

**SHOPGIRL** *n* girl working in shop

**SHOPGIRLS** > SHOPGIRL

**SHOPHAR** *same as* > SHOFAR

**SHOPHARS** > SHOPHAR

**SHOPHROTH** > SHOPHAR

**SHOPLIFT** *vb* steal from shop

**SHOPLIFTS** > SHOPLIFT

**SHOPMAN** *n* man working in shop

**SHOPMEN** > SHOPMAN

**SHOPPE** *old-fashioned spelling of* > SHOP

**SHOPPED** > SHOP

**SHOPPER** *n* person who buys goods in a shop

**SHOPPERS** > SHOPPER

**SHOPPES** > SHOPPE

**SHOPPIER** > SHOPPY

**SHOPPIEST** > SHOPPY

**SHOPPING** > SHOP

**SHOPPINGS** > SHOP

**SHOPPY** *adj* of a shop

**SHOPS** > SHOP

**SHOPTALK** *n* conversation about one's work, carried on outside working hours

**SHOPTALKS** > SHOPTALK

**SHOPWORN** *adj* worn or faded from being displayed in a shop

**SHORAN** *n* short-range radar system

**SHORANS** > SHORAN

**SHORE** *n* edge of a sea or lake ▷ *vb* prop or support

**SHOREBIRD** *n* bird that lives close to the water

**SHORED** > SHORE

**SHORELESS** *adj* without a shore suitable for landing

**SHORELINE** *n* edge of a sea, lake, or wide river

**SHOREMAN** *n* person who lives on shore

**SHOREMEN** > SHOREMAN

**SHORER** > SHORE

**SHORERS** > SHORE

**SHORES** > SHORE

**SHORESIDE** *n* area at shore

**SHORESMAN** *n* fishing industry worker on shore

**SHORESMEN** > SHORESMAN

**SHOREWARD** *adj* near or facing the shore ▷ *adv* towards the shore

**SHOREWEED** *n* tufty aquatic perennial plant

**SHORING** > SHORE

**SHORINGS** > SHORE

**SHORL** *n* black mineral

**SHORLS** > SHORL

**SHORN** *past participle of* > SHEAR

**SHORT** *adj* not long ▷ *adv* abruptly ▷ *n* drink of spirits ▷ *vb* short-circuit

**SHORTAGE** *n* deficiency

**SHORTAGES** > SHORTAGE

**SHORTARM** *adj* (of a punch) with the arm bent

**SHORTCAKE** *n* shortbread

**SHORTCUT** *n* route that is shorter than the usual one

**SHORTCUTS** > SHORTCUT

**SHORTED** > SHORT

**SHORTEN** *vb* make or become shorter

**SHORTENED** > SHORTEN

**SHORTENER** > SHORTEN

**SHORTENS** > SHORTEN

**SHORTER** > SHORT

**SHORTEST** > SHORT

**SHORTFALL** *n* deficit

**SHORTGOWN** *n* old Scots word meaning woman's jacket

**SHORTHAIR** *n* cat with short fur

**SHORTHAND** *n* system of rapid writing using symbols to represent words

**SHORTHEAD** *n* species of fish

**SHORTHOLD** *n* as in *shorthold tenancy* letting of a dwelling for between one and five years at a fair rent

**SHORTHORN** *n* member of a breed of cattle with short horns

**SHORTIA** *n* American flowering plant

**SHORTIAS** > SHORTIA

**SHORTIE** *n* person or thing that is extremely short

**SHORTIES** > SHORTY

**SHORTING** > SHORT

**SHORTISH** > SHORT

**SHORTLIST** *n* list of suitable applicants for a job, etc

**SHORTLY** *adv* soon

**SHORTNESS** > SHORT

**SHORTS** *pl n* trousers reaching the top of the thigh or partway to the knee

**SHORTSTOP** *n* fielding position to the left of second base viewed from home plate

**SHORTWAVE** *n* radio wave with a wavelength in the range 10–100 metres

**SHORTY** *same as* > SHORTIE

**SHOT** *vb* load with shot

**SHOTE** *same as* > SHOAT

**SHOTES** > SHOTE

**SHOTFIRER** *n* person detonating blasting charge

**SHOTGUN** *n* gun for firing a charge of shot at short range ▷ *adj* involving coercion or duress ▷ *vb* shoot or threaten with or as if with a shotgun

**SHOTGUNS** > SHOTGUN

**SHOTHOLE** *n* drilled hole in to which explosive is put for blasting

**SHOTHOLES** > SHOTHOLE

**SHOTMAKER** *n* sport player making good shots

**SHOTPROOF** *adj* able to withstand shot

**SHOTPUT** *n* athletic event in which a heavy metal ball is thrown

**SHOTPUTS** > SHOTPUT

**SHOTS** > SHOT

**SHOTT** *n* shallow temporary salt lake or marsh in the North African desert

**SHOTTE** *n* old form of shoat

**SHOTTED** > SHOT

**SHOTTEN** *adj* (of fish, esp herring) having recently spawned

**SHOTTES** > SHOTTE

**SHOTTING** > SHOT

**SHOTTLE** *n* small drawer

**SHOTTLES** > SHOTTLE

**SHOTTS** > SHOTT

**SHOUGH** *n* old word meaning lapdog

**SHOUGHS** > SHOUGH

**SHOULD** > SHALL

**SHOULDER** *n* part of the body to which an arm, foreleg, or wing is attached ▷ *vb* bear (a burden or responsibility)

**SHOULDERS** > SHOULDER

**SHOULDEST** *same as* > SHOULDST

**SHOULDST** *form of the past tense of* > SHALL
**SHOUSE** *n* toilet ▷ *adj* unwell or in poor spirits
**SHOUSES** > SHOUSE
**SHOUT** *n* loud cry ▷ *vb* cry out loudly
**SHOUTED** > SHOUT
**SHOUTER** > SHOUT
**SHOUTERS** > SHOUT
**SHOUTHER** *Scots form of* > SHOULDER
**SHOUTHERS** > SHOUTHER
**SHOUTIER** > SHOUTY
**SHOUTIEST** > SHOUTY
**SHOUTING** > SHOUT
**SHOUTINGS** > SHOUT
**SHOUTLINE** *n* line in advertisement made prominent to catch attention
**SHOUTS** > SHOUT
**SHOUTY** *adj* characterized by or involving shouting
**SHOVE** *vb* push roughly ▷ *n* rough push
**SHOVED** > SHOVE
**SHOVEL** *n* tool for lifting or moving loose material ▷ *vb* lift or move as with a shovel
**SHOVELED** > SHOVEL
**SHOVELER** *n* type of duck
**SHOVELERS** > SHOVELER
**SHOVELFUL** > SHOVEL
**SHOVELING** > SHOVEL
**SHOVELLED** > SHOVEL
**SHOVELLER** > SHOVEL
**SHOVELS** > SHOVEL
**SHOVER** > SHOVE
**SHOVERS** > SHOVE
**SHOVES** > SHOVE
**SHOVING** *n* act of pushing hard
**SHOVINGS** > SHOVING
**SHOW** *vb* make, be, or become noticeable or visible ▷ *n* public exhibition
**SHOWABLE** > SHOW
**SHOWBIZ** *n* entertainment industry including theatre, films, and TV
**SHOWBIZZY** > SHOWBIZ
**SHOWBOAT** *n* paddle-wheel river steamer with a theatre and a repertory company ▷ *vb* perform or behave in a showy and flamboyant way
**SHOWBOATS** > SHOWBOAT
**SHOWBOX** *n* box containing showman's material
**SHOWBOXES** > SHOWBOX
**SHOWBREAD** *same as* > SHEWBREAD
**SHOWCASE** *n* situation in which something is displayed to best advantage ▷ *vb* exhibit or display ▷ *adj* displayed or meriting display as in a showcase
**SHOWCASED** > SHOWCASE

**SHOWCASES** > SHOWCASE
**SHOWD** *vb* rock or sway to and fro ▷ *n* rocking motion
**SHOWDED** > SHOWD
**SHOWDING** > SHOWD
**SHOWDOWN** *n* confrontation that settles a dispute
**SHOWDOWNS** > SHOWDOWN
**SHOWDS** > SHOWD
**SHOWED** > SHOW
**SHOWER** *n* kind of bath in which a person stands while being sprayed with water ▷ *vb* wash in a shower
**SHOWERED** > SHOWER
**SHOWERER** > SHOWER
**SHOWERERS** > SHOWER
**SHOWERFUL** > SHOWER
**SHOWERIER** > SHOWER
**SHOWERING** > SHOWER
**SHOWERS** > SHOWER
**SHOWERY** > SHOWER
**SHOWGHE** *n* old word meaning lapdog
**SHOWGHES** > SHOWGHE
**SHOWGIRL** *n* girl who appears in shows, etc, esp as a singer or dancer
**SHOWGIRLS** > SHOWGIRL
**SHOWIER** > SHOWY
**SHOWIEST** > SHOWY
**SHOWILY** > SHOWY
**SHOWINESS** > SHOWY
**SHOWING** > SHOW
**SHOWINGS** > SHOW
**SHOWMAN** *n* man skilled at presenting anything spectacularly
**SHOWMANLY** > SHOWMAN
**SHOWMEN** > SHOWMAN
**SHOWN** > SHOW
**SHOWOFF** *n* person who makes a vain display of himself or herself
**SHOWOFFS** > SHOWOFF
**SHOWPIECE** *n* excellent specimen shown for display or as an example
**SHOWPLACE** *n* place visited for its beauty or interest
**SHOWRING** *n* area where animals are displayed for sale or competition
**SHOWRINGS** > SHOWRING
**SHOWROOM** *n* room in which goods for sale are on display
**SHOWROOMS** > SHOWROOM
**SHOWS** > SHOW
**SHOWTIME** *n* time when show begins
**SHOWTIMES** > SHOWTIME
**SHOWY** *adj* gaudy
**SHOWYARD** *n* yard where cattle are displayed
**SHOWYARDS** > SHOWYARD
**SHOYU** *n* Japanese variety of soy sauce
**SHOYUS** > SHOYU
**SHRADDHA** *n* Hindu offering to an ancestor
**SHRADDHAS** > SHRADDHA

**SHRANK** > SHRINK
**SHRAPNEL** *n* artillery shell filled with pellets which scatter on explosion
**SHRAPNELS** > SHRAPNEL
**SHRED** *n* long narrow strip torn from something ▷ *vb* tear to shreds
**SHREDDED** > SHRED
**SHREDDER** > SHRED
**SHREDDERS** > SHRED
**SHREDDIER** > SHRED
**SHREDDING** > SHRED
**SHREDDY** > SHRED
**SHREDLESS** > SHRED
**SHREDS** > SHRED
**SHREEK** *old spelling of* > SHRIEK
**SHREEKED** > SHREEK
**SHREEKING** > SHREEK
**SHREEKS** > SHREEK
**SHREIK** *old spelling of* > SHRIEK
**SHREIKED** > SHREIK
**SHREIKING** > SHREIK
**SHREIKS** > SHREIK
**SHREW** *n* small mouselike animal ▷ *vb* curse or damn
**SHREWD** *adj* clever and perceptive
**SHREWDER** > SHREWD
**SHREWDEST** > SHREWD
**SHREWDIE** *n* shrewd person
**SHREWDIES** > SHREWDIE
**SHREWDLY** > SHREWD
**SHREWED** > SHREW
**SHREWING** > SHREW
**SHREWISH** *adj* (esp of a woman) bad-tempered and nagging
**SHREWLIKE** > SHREW
**SHREWMICE** *pl n* shrews
**SHREWS** > SHREW
**SHRI** *n* Indian title of respect
**SHRIECH** *old spelling of* > SHRIEK
**SHRIECHED** > SHRIECH
**SHRIECHES** > SHRIECH
**SHRIEK** *n* shrill cry ▷ *vb* utter (with) a shriek
**SHRIEKED** > SHRIEK
**SHRIEKER** > SHRIEK
**SHRIEKERS** > SHRIEK
**SHRIEKIER** > SHRIEK
**SHRIEKING** > SHRIEK
**SHRIEKS** > SHRIEK
**SHRIEKY** > SHRIEK
**SHRIEVAL** *adj* of or relating to a sheriff
**SHRIEVE** *archaic word for* > SHERIFF
**SHRIEVED** > SHRIEVE
**SHRIEVES** > SHRIEVE
**SHRIEVING** > SHRIEVE
**SHRIFT** *n* act or an instance of shriving or being shriven
**SHRIFTS** > SHRIFT
**SHRIGHT** *n* old word meaning shriek
**SHRIGHTS** > SHRIGHT
**SHRIKE** *n* songbird with

a heavy hooked bill ▷ *vb* archaic word for shriek
**SHRIKED** > SHRIKE
**SHRIKES** > SHRIKE
**SHRIKING** > SHRIKE
**SHRILL** *adj* (of a sound) sharp and high-pitched ▷ *vb* utter shrilly
**SHRILLED** > SHRILL
**SHRILLER** > SHRILL
**SHRILLEST** > SHRILL
**SHRILLIER** > SHRILL
**SHRILLING** > SHRILL
**SHRILLS** > SHRILL
**SHRILLY** > SHRILL
**SHRIMP** *n* small edible shellfish ▷ *vb* fish for shrimps
**SHRIMPED** > SHRIMP
**SHRIMPER** > SHRIMP
**SHRIMPERS** > SHRIMP
**SHRIMPIER** > SHRIMP
**SHRIMPING** > SHRIMP
**SHRIMPS** > SHRIMP
**SHRIMPY** > SHRIMP
**SHRINAL** > SHRINE
**SHRINE** *n* place of worship associated with a sacred person or object ▷ *vb* enshrine
**SHRINED** > SHRINE
**SHRINES** > SHRINE
**SHRINING** > SHRINE
**SHRINK** *vb* become or make smaller ▷ *n* psychiatrist
**SHRINKAGE** *n* decrease in size, value, or weight
**SHRINKER** > SHRINK
**SHRINKERS** > SHRINK
**SHRINKING** > SHRINK
**SHRINKS** > SHRINK
**SHRIS** > SHRI
**SHRITCH** *vb* old word meaning shriek
**SHRITCHED** > SHRITCH
**SHRITCHES** > SHRITCH
**SHRIVE** *vb* hear the confession of (a penitent)
**SHRIVED** > SHRIVE
**SHRIVEL** *vb* shrink and wither
**SHRIVELED** > SHRIVEL
**SHRIVELS** > SHRIVEL
**SHRIVEN** > SHRIVE
**SHRIVER** > SHRIVE
**SHRIVERS** > SHRIVE
**SHRIVES** > SHRIVE
**SHRIVING** > SHRIVE
**SHRIVINGS** > SHRIVE
**SHROFF** *n* (in China and Japan) expert employed to separate counterfeit money from the genuine ▷ *vb* test (money) and separate out the counterfeit and base
**SHROFFAGE** > SHROFF
**SHROFFED** > SHROFF
**SHROFFING** > SHROFF
**SHROFFS** > SHROFF
**SHROOM** *n* slang for magic mushroom ▷ *vb* take magic mushrooms
**SHROOMED** > SHROOM

SHROOMER > SHROOM
SHROOMERS > SHROOM
SHROOMING > SHROOM
SHROOMS > SHROOM
SHROUD n piece of cloth used to wrap a dead body ▷ vb conceal
SHROUDED > SHROUD
SHROUDIER > SHROUD
SHROUDING > SHROUD
SHROUDS > SHROUD
SHROUDY > SHROUD
SHROVE vb dialect word meaning to observe Shrove-tide
SHROVED > SHROVE
SHROVES > SHROVE
SHROVING > SHROVE
SHROW vb old form of shrew
SHROWD adj old form of shrewd
SHROWED > SHROW
SHROWING > SHROW
SHROWS > SHROW
SHRUB n woody plant smaller than a tree ▷ vb plant shrubs
SHRUBBED > SHRUB
SHRUBBERY n area planted with shrubs
SHRUBBIER > SHRUBBY
SHRUBBING > SHRUB
SHRUBBY adj consisting of, planted with, or abounding in shrubs
SHRUBLAND n land covered by shrubs
SHRUBLESS > SHRUB
SHRUBLIKE > SHRUB
SHRUBS > SHRUB
SHRUG vb raise and then drop (the shoulders) as a sign of indifference or doubt ▷ n shrugging
SHRUGGED > SHRUG
SHRUGGING > SHRUG
SHRUGS > SHRUG
SHRUNK > SHRINK
SHRUNKEN adj reduced in size
SHTCHI n Russian cabbage soup
SHTCHIS > SHTCHI
SHTETEL n Jewish community in Eastern Europe
SHTETELS > SHTETEL
SHTETL n (formerly) a small Jewish community in Eastern Europe
SHTETLACH > SHTETL
SHTETLS > SHTETL
SHTICK n comedian's routine
SHTICKIER > SHTICK
SHTICKS > SHTICK
SHTICKY > SHTICK
SHTIK n shtick
SHTIKS > SHTIK
SHTOOK n trouble
SHTOOKS > SHTOOK
SHTOOM adj silent
SHTUCK n trouble
SHTUCKS > SHTUCK

SHTUM adj silent
SHTUMM adj silent
SHTUP vb have sex (with)
SHTUPPED > SHTUP
SHTUPPING > SHTUP
SHTUPS > SHTUP
SHUBUNKIN n type of goldfish
SHUCK n outer covering of something ▷ vb remove the shucks from
SHUCKED > SHUCK
SHUCKER > SHUCK
SHUCKERS > SHUCK
SHUCKING > SHUCK
SHUCKINGS > SHUCK
SHUCKS pl n something of little value ▷ interj exclamation of disappointment, annoyance, etc
SHUDDER vb shake or tremble violently, esp with horror ▷ n shaking or trembling
SHUDDERED > SHUDDER
SHUDDERS > SHUDDER
SHUDDERY > SHUDDER
SHUFFLE vb walk without lifting the feet ▷ n shuffling
SHUFFLED > SHUFFLE
SHUFFLER > SHUFFLE
SHUFFLERS > SHUFFLE
SHUFFLES > SHUFFLE
SHUFFLING > SHUFFLE
SHUFTI same as > SHUFTY
SHUFTIES > SHUFTY
SHUFTIS > SHUFTI
SHUFTY n look
SHUGGIES > SHUGGY
SHUGGY n swing, as at a fairground
SHUL Yiddish word for > SYNAGOGUE
SHULE vb saunter
SHULED > SHULE
SHULES > SHULE
SHULING > SHULE
SHULN > SHUL
SHULS > SHUL
SHUN vb avoid
SHUNLESS adj old word meaning not to be shunned
SHUNNABLE > SHUN
SHUNNED > SHUN
SHUNNER > SHUN
SHUNNERS > SHUN
SHUNNING > SHUN
SHUNPIKE vb take side road to avoid toll at turnpike
SHUNPIKED > SHUNPIKE
SHUNPIKER > SHUNPIKE
SHUNPIKES > SHUNPIKE
SHUNS > SHUN
SHUNT vb move (objects or people) to a different position ▷ n shunting
SHUNTED > SHUNT
SHUNTER n small railway locomotive used for manoeuvring coaches
SHUNTERS > SHUNTER

SHUNTING > SHUNT
SHUNTINGS > SHUNT
SHUNTS > SHUNT
SHURA n consultative council or assembly
SHURAS > SHURA
SHUSH interj be quiet! ▷ vb quiet by saying 'shush'
SHUSHED > SHUSH
SHUSHER > SHUSH
SHUSHERS > SHUSH
SHUSHES > SHUSH
SHUSHING > SHUSH
SHUT vb bring together or fold, close
SHUTDOWN n closing of a factory, shop, or other business ▷ vb discontinue operations permanently
SHUTDOWNS > SHUTDOWN
SHUTE variant of > CHUTE
SHUTED > SHUTE
SHUTES > SHUTE
SHUTEYE n sleep
SHUTEYES > SHUTEYE
SHUTING > SHUTE
SHUTOFF n device that shuts something off, esp a machine control
SHUTOFFS > SHUTOFF
SHUTOUT n game in which the opposing team does not score ▷ vb keep out or exclude
SHUTOUTS > SHUTOUT
SHUTS > SHUT
SHUTTER n hinged doorlike cover for closing off a window ▷ vb close or equip with a shutter
SHUTTERED > SHUTTER
SHUTTERS > SHUTTER
SHUTTING > SHUT
SHUTTLE n bobbin-like device used in weaving ▷ vb move by or as if by a shuttle
SHUTTLED > SHUTTLE
SHUTTLER > SHUTTLE
SHUTTLERS > SHUTTLE
SHUTTLES > SHUTTLE
SHUTTLING > SHUTTLE
SHVARTZE same as > SCHVARTZE
SHVARTZES > SHVARTZE
SHWA same as > SCHWA
SHWANPAN same as > SWANPAN
SHWANPANS > SHWANPAN
SHWAS > SHWA
SHWESHWE n African cotton print fabric
SHWESHWES > SHWESHWE
SHY adj not at ease in company ▷ vb start back in fear ▷ n throw
SHYER > SHY
SHYERS > SHY
SHYEST > SHY
SHYING > SHY
SHYISH > SHY
SHYLOCK vb lend money at an exorbitant rate of interest

SHYLOCKED > SHYLOCK
SHYLOCKS > SHYLOCK
SHYLY > SHY
SHYNESS > SHY
SHYNESSES > SHY
SHYPOO n liquor of poor quality
SHYPOOS > SHYPOO
SHYSTER n person, esp a lawyer or politician, who uses discreditable or unethical methods
SHYSTERS > SHYSTER
SI same as > TE
SIAL n silicon-rich and aluminium-rich rocks of the earth's continental upper crust
SIALIC > SIAL
SIALID n species of fly
SIALIDAN > SIALID
SIALIDANS > SIALID
SIALIDS > SIALID
SIALOGRAM n X-ray of salivary gland
SIALOID adj resembling saliva
SIALOLITH n hard deposit formed in salivary gland
SIALON n type of ceramic
SIALONS > SIALON
SIALS > SIAL
SIAMANG n large black gibbon
SIAMANGS > SIAMANG
SIAMESE variant of > SIAMEZE
SIAMESED > SIAMESE
SIAMESES > SIAMESE
SIAMESING > SIAMESE
SIAMEZE vb join together
SIAMEZED > SIAMEZE
SIAMEZES > SIAMEZE
SIAMEZING > SIAMEZE
SIB n blood relative
SIBB n sib
SIBBS > SIBB
SIBILANCE > SIBILANT
SIBILANCY > SIBILANT
SIBILANT adj hissing ▷ n consonant pronounced with a hissing sound
SIBILANTS > SIBILANT
SIBILATE vb pronounce or utter (words or speech) with a hissing sound
SIBILATED > SIBILATE
SIBILATES > SIBILATE
SIBILATOR > SIBILATE
SIBILOUS > SIBILANT
SIBLING n brother or sister
SIBLINGS > SIBLING
SIBS > SIB
SIBSHIP n group of children of the same parents
SIBSHIPS > SIBSHIP
SIBYL n (in ancient Greece and Rome) prophetess
SIBYLIC > SIBYL
SIBYLLIC > SIBYL
SIBYLLINE > SIBYL
SIBYLS > SIBYL
SIC adv thus ▷ vb attack

SICCAN adj Scots word meaning such

SICCAR adj sure

SICCATIVE n substance added to a liquid to promote drying

SICCED > SIC

SICCING > SIC

SICCITIES > SICCITY

SICCITY n dryness

SICE same as > SYCE

SICES > SICE

SICH adj old form of such

SICHT Scot word for > SIGHT

SICHTED > SICHT

SICHTING > SICHT

SICHTS > SICHT

SICILIANA n Sicilian dance

SICILIANE > SICILIANA

SICILIANO n old dance in six-beat or twelve-beat time

SICK adj vomiting or likely to vomit ▷ n vomit ▷ vb vomit

SICKBAY n room for the treatment of sick people, for example on a ship

SICKBAYS > SICKBAY

SICKBED n bed where sick person lies

SICKBEDS > SICKBED

SICKED > SICK

SICKEE n person off work through illness

SICKEES > SICKEE

SICKEN vb make nauseated or disgusted

SICKENED > SICKEN

SICKENER n something that induces sickness or nausea

SICKENERS > SICKENER

SICKENING adj causing horror or disgust

SICKENS > SICKEN

SICKER > SICK

SICKERLY adv Scots word meaning surely

SICKEST > SICK

SICKIE n day of sick leave from work

SICKIES > SICKIE

SICKING > SICK

SICKISH > SICK

SICKISHLY > SICK

SICKLE n tool with a curved blade for cutting grass or grain ▷ vb cut with a sickle

SICKLED > SICKLE

SICKLEMAN n person reaping with sickle

SICKLEMEN > SICKLEMAN

SICKLEMIA n form of anaemia

SICKLEMIC > SICKLEMIA

SICKLES > SICKLE

SICKLIED > SICKLY

SICKLIER > SICKLY

SICKLIES > SICKLY

SICKLIEST > SICKLY

SICKLILY > SICKLY

SICKLING > SICKLE

SICKLY adj unhealthy, weak ▷ adv suggesting sickness ▷ vb make sickly

SICKLYING > SICKLY

SICKNESS n particular illness or disease

SICKNURSE n person nursing sick person

SICKO n person who is mentally disturbed or perverted ▷ adj perverted or in bad taste

SICKOS > SICKO

SICKOUT n form of industrial action in which all workers in a workplace report sick simultaneously

SICKOUTS > SICKOUT

SICKROOM n room to which a person who is ill is confined

SICKROOMS > SICKROOM

SICKS > SICK

SICLIKE adj Scots word meaning suchlike

SICS > SIC

SIDA n Australian hemp plant

SIDALCEA n type of perennial N American plant

SIDALCEAS > SIDALCEA

SIDAS > SIDA

SIDDHA n (in Hinduism) person who has achieved perfection

SIDDHAS > SIDDHA

SIDDHI n (in Hinduism) power attained with perfection

SIDDHIS > SIDDHI

SIDDHUISM n (in Indian English) any contrived metaphor or simile

SIDDUR n Jewish prayer book

SIDDURIM > SIDDUR

SIDDURS > SIDDUR

SIDE n line or surface that borders anything ▷ adj at or on the side

SIDEARM n weapon worn on belt

SIDEARMS > SIDEARM

SIDEBAND n frequency band either above or below the carrier frequency

SIDEBANDS > SIDEBAND

SIDEBAR n small newspaper article beside larger one

SIDEBARS > SIDEBAR

SIDEBOARD n piece of furniture for holding plates, cutlery, etc in a dining room

SIDEBONES n part of horse's hoof

SIDEBURNS pl n man's side whiskers

SIDECAR n small passenger car on the side of a motorcycle

SIDECARS > SIDECAR

SIDECHECK n part of horse's harness

SIDED > SIDE

SIDEDNESS > SIDE

SIDEDRESS vb place fertilizer in the soil near the roots of a plant

SIDEHILL n side of hill

SIDEHILLS > SIDEHILL

SIDEKICK n close friend or associate

SIDEKICKS > SIDEKICK

SIDELIGHT n either of two small lights on the front of a vehicle

SIDELINE n subsidiary interest or source of income ▷ vb prevent (a player) from taking part in a game

SIDELINED > SIDELINE

SIDELINER > SIDELINE

SIDELINES pl n area immediately outside the playing area, where substitute players sit

SIDELING adj to one side

SIDELOCK n long lock of hair on side of head

SIDELOCKS > SIDELOCK

SIDELONG adj sideways ▷ adv obliquely

SIDEMAN n member of a dance band or a jazz group other than the leader

SIDEMEN > SIDEMAN

SIDENOTE n note written in margin

SIDENOTES > SIDENOTE

SIDEPATH n minor path

SIDEPATHS > SIDEPATH

SIDEPIECE n part forming side of something

SIDER n one who sides with another

SIDERAL adj from the stars

SIDERATE vb strike violently

SIDERATED > SIDERATE

SIDERATES > SIDERATE

SIDEREAL adj of or determined with reference to the stars

SIDERITE n pale yellow to brownish-black mineral

SIDERITES > SIDERITE

SIDERITIC > SIDERITE

SIDEROAD n (esp in Ontario) a road going at right angles to concession roads

SIDEROADS > SIDEROAD

SIDEROSES > SIDEROSIS

SIDEROSIS n lung disease caused by breathing in fine particles of iron or other metallic dust

SIDEROTIC > SIDEROSIS

SIDERS > SIDER

SIDES > SIDE

SIDESHOOT n minor shoot growing on plant

SIDESHOW n entertainment offered along with the main show

SIDESHOWS > SIDESHOW

SIDESLIP same as > SLIP

SIDESLIPS > SIDESLIP

SIDESMAN n man elected to help the parish church warden

SIDESMEN > SIDESMAN

SIDESPIN n horizontal spin put on ball

SIDESPINS > SIDESPIN

SIDESTEP vb dodge (an issue) ▷ n movement to one side, such as in dancing or boxing

SIDESTEPS > SIDESTEP

SIDESWIPE n unexpected criticism of someone or something while discussing another subject ▷ vb make a sideswipe

SIDETRACK vb divert from the main topic ▷ n railway siding

SIDEWALK n paved path for pedestrians, at the side of a road

SIDEWALKS > SIDEWALK

SIDEWALL n either of the sides of a pneumatic tyre between the tread and the rim

SIDEWALLS > SIDEWALL

SIDEWARD adj directed or moving towards one side ▷ adv towards one side

SIDEWARDS adv towards one side

SIDEWAY variant of > SIDEWAYS

SIDEWAYS adv or from the side ▷ adj moving or directed to or from one side

SIDEWHEEL n one of the paddle wheels of a sidewheeler

SIDEWISE adv sideways

SIDH pl n fairy people

SIDHA n (in Hinduism) person who has achieved perfection

SIDHAS > SIDHA

SIDHE pl n inhabitants of fairyland

SIDING n short stretch of railway track on which trains are shunted from the main line

SIDINGS > SIDING

SIDLE vb walk in a furtive manner ▷ n sideways movement

SIDLED > SIDLE

SIDLER > SIDLE

SIDLERS > SIDLE

SIDLES > SIDLE

SIDLING > SIDLE

SIDLINGLY > SIDLE

SIECLE n century, period, or era

SIECLES >SIECLE
SIEGE n surrounding and blockading of a place ▷ vb lay siege to
SIEGED >SIEGE
SIEGER n person who besieges
SIEGERS >SIEGER
SIEGES >SIEGE
SIEGING >SIEGE
SIELD vb old word meaning given a ceiling
SIEMENS n SI unit of electrical conductance
SIEN n old word meaning scion
SIENITE n type of igneous rock
SIENITES >SIENITE
SIENNA n reddish- or yellowish-brown pigment made from natural earth
SIENNAS >SIENNA
SIENS >SIEN
SIENT n old word meaning scion
SIENTS >SIENT
SIEROZEM n type of soil
SIEROZEMS >SIEROZEM
SIERRA n range of mountains in Spain or America with jagged peaks
SIERRAN >SIERRA
SIERRAS >SIERRA
SIES same as >SIS
SIESTA n afternoon nap, taken in hot countries
SIESTAS >SIESTA
SIETH n old form of scythe
SIETHS >SIETH
SIEUR n French word meaning lord
SIEURS >SIEUR
SIEVE n utensil with mesh through which a substance is sifted or strained ▷ vb sift or strain through a sieve
SIEVED >SIEVE
SIEVELIKE >SIEVE
SIEVERT n derived SI unit of dose equivalent, equal to 1 joule per kilogram
SIEVERTS >SIEVERT
SIEVES >SIEVE
SIEVING >SIEVE
SIF adj South African slang for disgusting
SIFAKA n either of two large rare arboreal lemuroid primates
SIFAKAS >SIFAKA
SIFFLE vb whistle
SIFFLED >SIFFLE
SIFFLES >SIFFLE
SIFFLEUR n male professional whistler
SIFFLEURS >SIFFLEUR
SIFFLEUSE n female professional whistler
SIFFLING >SIFFLE
SIFREI >SEFER
SIFT vb remove the coarser

particles from a substance with a sieve
SIFTED >SIFT
SIFTER >SIFT
SIFTERS >SIFT
SIFTING >SIFT
SIFTINGLY >SIFT
SIFTINGS pl n material or particles separated out by or as if by a sieve
SIFTS >SIFT
SIGANID n tropical fish
SIGANIDS >SIGANID
SIGH n long audible breath expressing sadness, tiredness, relief, or longing ▷ vb utter a sigh
SIGHED >SIGH
SIGHER >SIGH
SIGHERS >SIGH
SIGHFUL >SIGH
SIGHING >SIGH
SIGHINGLY >SIGH
SIGHLESS >SIGH
SIGHLIKE >SIGH
SIGHS >SIGH
SIGHT n ability to see ▷ vb catch sight of
SIGHTABLE >SIGHT
SIGHTED adj not blind
SIGHTER n any of six practice shots allowed to each competitor in a tournament
SIGHTERS >SIGHTER
SIGHTING >SIGHT
SIGHTINGS >SIGHT
SIGHTLESS adj blind
SIGHTLIER >SIGHTLY
SIGHTLINE n uninterrupted line of vision
SIGHTLY adj pleasing or attractive to see
SIGHTS >SIGHT
SIGHTSAW >SIGHTSEE
SIGHTSEE vb visit the famous or interesting sights of (a place)
SIGHTSEEN >SIGHTSEE
SIGHTSEER >SIGHTSEE
SIGHTSEES >SIGHTSEE
SIGHTSMAN n tourist guide
SIGHTSMEN >SIGHTSMAN
SIGIL n seal or signet
SIGILLARY >SIGIL
SIGILLATE adj closed with seal
SIGILS >SIGIL
SIGISBEI >SIGISBEO
SIGISBEO n male escort for a married woman
SIGLA n list of symbols used in a book
SIGLAS >SIGLA
SIGLOI >SIGLOS
SIGLOS n silver coin of ancient Persia worth one twentieth of a daric
SIGLUM n symbol used in book
SIGMA n 18th letter in the Greek alphabet
SIGMAS >SIGMA

SIGMATE adj shaped like the Greek letter sigma or the Roman S ▷ n sigmate thing ▷ vb add a sigma
SIGMATED >SIGMATE
SIGMATES >SIGMATE
SIGMATIC >SIGMATE
SIGMATING >SIGMATE
SIGMATION >SIGMATE
SIGMATISM n repetition of letter s
SIGMATRON n machine for generating X-rays
SIGMOID adj shaped like the letter S ▷ n S-shaped bend in the final portion of the large intestine
SIGMOIDAL variant of >SIGMOID
SIGMOIDS >SIGMOID
SIGN n indication of something not immediately or outwardly observable ▷ vb write (one's name) on (a document or letter) to show its authenticity or one's agreement
SIGNA pl n symbols
SIGNABLE >SIGN
SIGNAGE n signs collectively, esp street signs or signs giving directions
SIGNAGES >SIGNAGE
SIGNAL n sign or gesture to convey information ▷ adj very important ▷ vb convey (information) by signal
SIGNALED >SIGNAL
SIGNALER >SIGNAL
SIGNALERS >SIGNAL
SIGNALING >SIGNAL
SIGNALISE same as >SIGNALIZE
SIGNALIZE vb make noteworthy or conspicuous
SIGNALLED >SIGNAL
SIGNALLER >SIGNAL
SIGNALLY adv conspicuously or especially
SIGNALMAN n railwayman in charge of signals and points
SIGNALMEN >SIGNALMAN
SIGNALS >SIGNAL
SIGNARIES >SIGNARY
SIGNARY n set of symbols
SIGNATORY n one of the parties who sign a document ▷ adj having signed a document or treaty
SIGNATURE n person's name written by himself or herself in signing something
SIGNBOARD n board carrying a sign or notice, often to advertise a business or product

SIGNED >SIGN
SIGNEE n person signing document
SIGNEES >SIGNEE
SIGNER n person who signs something
SIGNERS >SIGNER
SIGNET n small seal used to authenticate documents ▷ vb stamp or authenticate with a signet
SIGNETED >SIGNET
SIGNETING >SIGNET
SIGNETS >SIGNET
SIGNEUR old spelling of >SENIOR
SIGNEURIE n old word meaning seniority
SIGNIEUR n old word meaning lord
SIGNIEURS >SIGNIEUR
SIGNIFICS n study of meaning
SIGNIFIED >SIGNIFY
SIGNIFIER >SIGNIFY
SIGNIFIES >SIGNIFY
SIGNIFY vb indicate or suggest
SIGNING n system of communication using hand and arm movements, such as one used by deaf people
SIGNINGS >SIGNING
SIGNIOR same as >SIGNOR
SIGNIORI >SIGNIOR
SIGNIORS >SIGNIOR
SIGNIORY n old word meaning lordship
SIGNLESS >SIGN
SIGNOR n Italian term of address equivalent to sir or Mr
SIGNORA n Italian term of address equivalent to madam or Mrs
SIGNORAS >SIGNORA
SIGNORE n Italian man: a title of respect equivalent to sir
SIGNORES >SIGNORE
SIGNORI >SIGNORE
SIGNORIA n government of Italian city
SIGNORIAL >SIGNORIA
SIGNORIAS >SIGNORIA
SIGNORIES >SIGNORY
SIGNORINA n Italian term of address equivalent to madam or Miss
SIGNORINE >SIGNORINA
SIGNORINI >SIGNORINO
SIGNORINO n young gentleman
SIGNORS >SIGNOR
SIGNORY same as >SEIGNIORY
SIGNPOST n post bearing a sign that shows the way ▷ vb mark with signposts
SIGNPOSTS >SIGNPOST
SIGNS >SIGN
SIJO n Korean poem
SIJOS >SIJO

**SIK** adj excellent
**SIKA** n Japanese forest-dwelling deer
**SIKAS** > SIKA
**SIKE** n small stream
**SIKER** adj old spelling of sicker
**SIKES** > SIKE
**SIKORSKY** n type of helicopter
**SILAGE** n fodder crop harvested while green and partially fermented in a silo ▷ vb make silage
**SILAGED** > SILAGE
**SILAGEING** > SILAGE
**SILAGES** > SILAGE
**SILAGING** > SILAGE
**SILANE** n gas containing silicon
**SILANES** > SILANE
**SILASTIC** n tradename for a type of flexible silicone rubber
**SILASTICS** > SILASTIC
**SILD** n any of various small young herrings, esp when prepared and canned in Norway
**SILDS** > SILD
**SILE** vb pour with rain
**SILED** > SILE
**SILEN** n god of woodland
**SILENCE** n absence of noise or speech ▷ vb make silent
**SILENCED** adj (of a clergyman) forbidden to preach or perform his clerical functions
**SILENCER** n device to reduce the noise of an engine exhaust or gun
**SILENCERS** > SILENCER
**SILENCES** > SILENCE
**SILENCING** > SILENCE
**SILENE** n any plant of the large perennial genus Silene
**SILENES** > SILENE
**SILENI** > SILENUS
**SILENS** > SILEN
**SILENT** adj tending to speak very little ▷ n silent film
**SILENTER** > SILENT
**SILENTEST** > SILENT
**SILENTLY** > SILENT
**SILENTS** > SILENT
**SILENUS** n woodland deity
**SILER** n strainer
**SILERS** > SILER
**SILES** > SILE
**SILESIA** n twill-weave fabric of cotton or other fibre
**SILESIAS** > SILESIA
**SILEX** n type of heat-resistant glass made from fused quartz
**SILEXES** > SILEX
**SILICA** n hard glossy mineral found as quartz and in sandstone

**SILICAS** > SILICA
**SILICATE** n compound of silicon, oxygen, and a metal
**SILICATED** > SILICATE
**SILICATES** > SILICATE
**SILICEOUS** adj of, relating to, or containing abundant silica
**SILICIC** adj of, concerned with, or containing silicon or an acid obtained from silicon
**SILICIDE** n any one of a class of binary compounds formed between silicon and certain metals
**SILICIDES** > SILICIDE
**SILICIFY** vb convert or be converted into silica
**SILICIOUS** same as > SILICEOUS
**SILICIUM** rare name for > SILICON
**SILICIUMS** > SILICIUM
**SILICLE** same as > SILICULA
**SILICLES** > SILICLE
**SILICON** n brittle nonmetallic element widely used in chemistry and industry ▷ adj denoting an area of a country that contains much high-technology industry
**SILICONE** n tough synthetic substance made from silicon and used in lubricants
**SILICONES** > SILICONE
**SILICONS** > SILICON
**SILICOSES** > SILICOSIS
**SILICOSIS** n lung disease caused by inhaling silica dust
**SILICOTIC** n person suffering from silicosis
**SILICULA** n short broad siliqua, occurring in such cruciferous plants as honesty and shepherd's-purse
**SILICULAE** > SILICULA
**SILICULAS** > SILICULA
**SILICULE** same as > SILICULA
**SILICULES** > SILICULE
**SILING** > SILE
**SILIQUA** n long dry dehiscent fruit of cruciferous plants such as the wallflower
**SILIQUAE** > SILIQUA
**SILIQUAS** > SILIQUA
**SILIQUE** same as > SILIQUA
**SILIQUES** > SILIQUE
**SILIQUOSE** > SILIQUA
**SILIQUOUS** > SILIQUA
**SILK** n fibre made by the larva of a certain moth ▷ vb (of maize) develop long hairlike styles
**SILKALENE** same as > SILKALINE

**SILKALINE** n fine smooth cotton fabric used for linings, etc
**SILKED** > SILK
**SILKEN** adj made of silk ▷ vb make like silk
**SILKENED** > SILKEN
**SILKENING** > SILKEN
**SILKENS** > SILKEN
**SILKIE** n Scots word for a seal
**SILKIER** > SILKY
**SILKIES** > SILKIE
**SILKIEST** > SILKY
**SILKILY** > SILKY
**SILKINESS** > SILKY
**SILKING** > SILK
**SILKLIKE** > SILK
**SILKOLINE** n material like silk
**SILKS** > SILK
**SILKTAIL** n waxwing
**SILKTAILS** > SILKTAIL
**SILKWEED** another name for > MILKWEED
**SILKWEEDS** > SILKWEED
**SILKWORM** n caterpillar that spins a cocoon of silk
**SILKWORMS** > SILKWORM
**SILKY** adj of or like silk
**SILL** n ledge at the bottom of a window or door
**SILLABUB** same as > SYLLABUB
**SILLABUBS** > SILLABUB
**SILLADAR** n Indian irregular cavalryman
**SILLADARS** > SILLADAR
**SILLER** n silver ▷ adj silver
**SILLERS** > SILLER
**SILLIBUB** n syllabub
**SILLIBUBS** > SILLIBUB
**SILLIER** > SILLY
**SILLIES** > SILLY
**SILLIEST** > SILLY
**SILLILY** > SILLY
**SILLINESS** > SILLY
**SILLOCK** n young coalfish
**SILLOCKS** > SILLOCK
**SILLS** > SILL
**SILLY** adj foolish ▷ n foolish person
**SILO** n pit or airtight tower for storing silage or grains ▷ vb put in a silo
**SILOED** > SILO
**SILOING** > SILO
**SILOS** > SILO
**SILOXANE** n any of a class of compounds containing alternate silicon and oxygen atoms
**SILOXANES** > SILOXANE
**SILPHIA** > SILPHIUM
**SILPHIUM** n American flowering wild plant
**SILPHIUMS** > SILPHIUM
**SILT** n mud deposited by moving water ▷ vb fill or be choked with silt
**SILTATION** > SILT
**SILTED** > SILT
**SILTIER** > SILT
**SILTIEST** > SILT

**SILTING** > SILT
**SILTS** > SILT
**SILTSTONE** n variety of fine sandstone formed from consolidated silt
**SILTY** > SILT
**SILURIAN** n formed in the third period of the Palaeozoic
**SILURID** n any freshwater fish of the family Siluridae including catfish ▷ adj of, relating to, or belonging to the family Siluridae
**SILURIDS** > SILURID
**SILURIST** n member of ancient Silurian tribe
**SILURISTS** > SILURIST
**SILUROID** n freshwater fish
**SILUROIDS** > SILUROID
**SILVA** same as > SYLVA
**SILVAE** > SILVA
**SILVAN** same as > SYLVAN
**SILVANS** > SILVAN
**SILVAS** > SILVA
**SILVATIC** adj wild, not domestic
**SILVER** n white precious metal ▷ adj made of or of the colour of silver ▷ vb coat with silver
**SILVERED** > SILVER
**SILVERER** > SILVER
**SILVERERS** > SILVER
**SILVEREYE** n greenish-coloured songbird of Africa, Australia, New Zealand, and Asia
**SILVERIER** > SILVERY
**SILVERING** > SILVER
**SILVERISE** same as > SILVERIZE
**SILVERIZE** vb coat with silver
**SILVERLY** adv like silver
**SILVERN** adj silver
**SILVERS** > SILVER
**SILVERY** adj like silver
**SILVEX** n type of weedkiller
**SILVEXES** > SILVEX
**SILVICAL** adj of trees
**SILVICS** n study of trees
**SIM** n computer game that simulates an activity such as flying or playing a sport
**SIMA** n silicon-rich and magnesium-rich rocks of the earth's oceanic crust
**SIMAR** variant spelling of > CYMAR
**SIMAROUBA** n any tropical American tree of the genus Simarouba
**SIMARRE** n woman's loose gown
**SIMARRES** > SIMARRE
**SIMARS** > SIMAR
**SIMARUBA** same as > SIMAROUBA
**SIMARUBAS** > SIMARUBA
**SIMAS** > SIMA
**SIMATIC** > SIMA

SIMAZINE *n* organic weedkiller

SIMAZINES > SIMAZINE

SIMBA *E African word for* > LION

SIMBAS > SIMBA

SIMI *n* East African sword

SIMIAL *adj* of apes

SIMIAN *n* a monkey or ape ▷ *adj* of or resembling a monkey or ape

SIMIANS > SIMIAN

SIMILAR *adj* alike but not identical

SIMILARLY > SIMILAR

SIMILE *n* figure of speech comparing one thing to another, using 'as' or 'like'

SIMILES > SIMILE

SIMILISE *same as* > SIMILIZE

SIMILISED > SIMILISE

SIMILISES > SIMILISE

SIMILIZE *vb* use similes

SIMILIZED > SIMILIZE

SIMILIZES > SIMILIZE

SIMILOR *n* alloy used in cheap jewellery

SIMILORS > SIMILOR

SIMIOID *adj* of apes

SIMIOUS *adj* of apes

SIMIS > SIMI

SIMITAR *same as* > SCIMITAR

SIMITARS > SIMITAR

SIMKIN *word used in India for* > CHAMPAGNE

SIMKINS > SIMKIN

SIMLIN *n* American variety of squash plant

SIMLINS > SIMLIN

SIMMER *vb* cook gently at just below boiling point ▷ *n* state of simmering

SIMMERED > SIMMER

SIMMERING > SIMMER

SIMMERS > SIMMER

SIMNEL *as in simnel cake* fruit cake with marzipan eaten at Easter

SIMNELS > SIMNEL

SIMOLEON *n* American slang for dollar

SIMOLEONS > SIMOLEON

SIMONIAC *n* person who is guilty of practising simony

SIMONIACS > SIMONIAC

SIMONIES > SIMONY

SIMONIOUS > SIMONY

SIMONISE *same as* > SIMONIZE

SIMONISED > SIMONISE

SIMONISES > SIMONISE

SIMONIST > SIMONY

SIMONISTS > SIMONY

SIMONIZE *vb* polish with wax

SIMONIZED > SIMONIZE

SIMONIZES > SIMONIZE

SIMONY *n* practice of buying or selling Church benefits such as pardons

SIMOOM *n* hot suffocating sand-laden desert wind

SIMOOMS > SIMOOM

SIMOON *same as* > SIMOOM

SIMOONS > SIMOON

SIMORG *n* bird in Persian myth

SIMORGS > SIMORG

SIMP *short for* > SIMPLETON

SIMPAI *n* Indonesian monkey

SIMPAIS > SIMPAI

SIMPATICO *adj* pleasant or congenial

SIMPER *vb* smile in a silly or affected way ▷ *n* simpering smile

SIMPERED > SIMPER

SIMPERER > SIMPER

SIMPERERS > SIMPER

SIMPERING > SIMPER

SIMPERS > SIMPER

SIMPKIN *word used in India for* > CHAMPAGNE

SIMPKINS > SIMPKIN

SIMPLE *adj* easy to understand or do ▷ *n* simpleton ▷ *vb* archaic word meaning to look for medicinal herbs

SIMPLED > SIMPLE

SIMPLER > SIMPLE

SIMPLERS > SIMPLE

SIMPLES > SIMPLE

SIMPLESSE *n* old word meaning simplicity

SIMPLEST > SIMPLE

SIMPLETON *n* foolish or half-witted person

SIMPLEX *adj* permitting the transmission of signals in only one direction in a radio circuit ▷ *n* simple not a compound word

SIMPLEXES > SIMPLEX

SIMPLICES > SIMPLEX

SIMPLICIA *n* species of moth

SIMPLIFY *vb* make less complicated

SIMPLING > SIMPLE

SIMPLINGS > SIMPLE

SIMPLISM *n* quality of being extremely naive

SIMPLISMS > SIMPLISM

SIMPLIST *n* old word meaning expert in herbal medicine

SIMPLISTE *adj* simplistic

SIMPLISTS > SIMPLIST

SIMPLY *adv* in a simple manner

SIMPS > SIMP

SIMS > SIM

SIMUL *adj* simultaneous ▷ *n* simultaneous broadcast

SIMULACRA *pl n* representations of things

SIMULACRE *n* resemblance

SIMULANT *adj* simulating ▷ *n* simulant thing

SIMULANTS > SIMULANT

SIMULAR *n* person or thing that simulates or imitates ▷ *adj* fake

SIMULARS > SIMULAR

SIMULATE *vb* make a pretence of ▷ *adj* assumed or simulated

SIMULATED *adj* being an imitation of the genuine article, usually made from cheaper material

SIMULATES > SIMULATE

SIMULATOR *n* device that simulates specific conditions for the purposes of research or training

SIMULCAST *vb* broadcast (a programme) simultaneously on radio and television ▷ *n* programme broadcast in this way

SIMULIUM *n* tropical fly

SIMULIUMS > SIMULIUM

SIMULS > SIMUL

SIMURG *n* bird in Persian myth

SIMURGH *n* bird in Persian myth

SIMURGHS > SIMURGH

SIMURGS > SIMURG

SIN *n* offence or transgression ▷ *vb* commit a sin

SINAPISM *n* mixture of black mustard seeds and an adhesive, applied to the skin

SINAPISMS > SINAPISM

SINCE *prep* during the period of time after ▷ *adv* from that time

SINCERE *adj* without pretence or deceit

SINCERELY > SINCERE

SINCERER > SINCERE

SINCEREST > SINCERE

SINCERITY > SINCERE

SINCIPITA > SINCIPUT

SINCIPUT *n* forward upper part of the skull

SINCIPUTS > SINCIPUT

SIND *variant of* > SYNE

SINDED > SIND

SINDING > SIND

SINDINGS > SIND

SINDON *n* type of cloth

SINDONS > SINDON

SINDS > SIND

SINE *n* ratio of the length of the opposite side to that of the hypotenuse in a right-angled triangle ▷ *vb* variant of > SYNE

SINECURE *n* paid job with minimal duties

SINECURES > SINECURE

SINED > SINE

SINES > SINE

SINEW *n* tough fibrous tissue joining muscle to bone ▷ *vb* make strong

SINEWED *adj* having sinews

SINEWIER > SINEWY

SINEWIEST > SINEWY

SINEWING > SINEW

SINEWLESS > SINEW

SINEWS > SINEW

SINEWY *adj* lean and muscular

SINFONIA *n* symphony orchestra

SINFONIAS > SINFONIA

SINFONIE > SINFONIA

SINFUL *adj* guilty of sin

SINFULLY > SINFUL

SING *vb* make musical sounds with the voice ▷ *n* act or performance of singing

SINGABLE > SING

SINGALONG *n* act of singing along with a performer

SINGE *vb* burn the surface of ▷ *n* superficial burn

SINGED > SINGE

SINGEING > SINGE

SINGER *n* person who sings, esp professionally

SINGERS > SINGER

SINGES > SINGE

SINGING > SING

SINGINGLY > SING

SINGINGS > SING

SINGLE *adj* one only ▷ *n* single thing ▷ *vb* pick out from others

SINGLED > SINGLE

SINGLEDOM *n* state of being unmarried or not involved in a long-term relationship

SINGLES *pl n* match played with one person on each side

SINGLET *n* sleeveless vest

SINGLETON *n* only card of a particular suit held by a player

SINGLETS > SINGLET

SINGLING > SINGLE

SINGLINGS > SINGLE

SINGLY *adv* one at a time

SINGS > SING

SINGSONG *n* informal singing session ▷ *adj* (of the voice) repeatedly rising and falling in pitch

SINGSONGS > SINGSONG

SINGSONGY > SINGSONG

SINGSPIEL *n* type of German comic opera with spoken dialogue

SINGULAR *adj* (of a word or form) denoting one person or thing ▷ *n* singular form of a word

SINGULARS > SINGULAR

SINGULARY *adj* (of an operator) monadic

SINGULT *n* old word meaning sob

SINGULTS > SINGULT

SINGULTUS *technical name for* > HICCUP

SINH *n* hyperbolic sine

SINHS > SINH

SINICAL > SINE

SINICISE *same as* > SINICIZE

SINICISED > SINICISE

SINICISES > SINICISE

SINICIZE *vb* make Chinese
SINICIZED >SINICIZE
SINICIZES >SINICIZE
SINING >SINE
SINISTER *adj* threatening or suggesting evil or harm
SINISTRAL *adj* of, relating to, or located on the left side, esp the left side of the body
SINK *vb* submerge (in liquid) ▷ *n* fixed basin with a water supply and drainage pipe
SINKABLE >SINK
SINKAGE *n* act of sinking or degree to which something sinks or has sunk
SINKAGES >SINKAGE
SINKER *n* weight for a fishing line
SINKERS >SINKER
SINKHOLE *n* depression in the ground surface, esp in limestone, where a surface stream disappears underground
SINKHOLES >SINKHOLE
SINKIER >SINKY
SINKIEST >SINKY
SINKING >SINK
SINKINGS >SINK
SINKS >SINK
SINKY *adj* giving underfoot
SINLESS *adj* free from sin or guilt
SINLESSLY >SINLESS
SINNED >SIN
SINNER *n* person that sins ▷ *vb* behave like a sinner
SINNERED >SINNER
SINNERING >SINNER
SINNERS >SIN
SINNET *n* braided rope
SINNETS >SINNET
SINNING >SIN
SINNINGIA *n* tropical flowering plant
SINOLOGUE >SINOLOGY
SINOLOGY *n* study of Chinese culture, etc
SINOPIA *n* pigment made from iron ore
SINOPIAS >SINOPIA
SINOPIE >SINOPIA
SINOPIS *n* pigment made from iron ore
SINOPISES >SINOPIS
SINOPITE *n* iron ore
SINOPITES >SINOPITE
SINS >SIN
SINSYNE *adv* Scots word meaning since
SINTER *n* whitish porous incrustation that is deposited from hot springs ▷ *vb* form large particles from (metal powders or powdery ores) by heating or pressure
SINTERED >SINTER
SINTERING >SINTER
SINTERS >SINTER

SINTERY >SINTER
SINUATE *vb* wind
SINUATED *same as* >SINUATE
SINUATELY >SINUATE
SINUATES >SINUATE
SINUATING >SINUATE
SINUATION *same as* >SINUOSITY
SINUITIS *variant of* >SINUSITIS
SINUOSE *adj* sinuous
SINUOSITY *n* quality of being sinuous
SINUOUS *adj* full of turns or curves
SINUOUSLY >SINUOUS
SINUS *n* hollow space in a bone, esp an air passage opening into the nose
SINUSES >SINUS
SINUSITIS *n* inflammation of a sinus membrane
SINUSLIKE >SINUS
SINUSOID *n* any of the irregular terminal blood vessels that replace capillaries in certain organs ▷ *adj* resembling a sinus
SINUSOIDS >SINUSOID
SIP *vb* drink in small mouthfuls ▷ *n* amount sipped
SIPE *vb* soak
SIPED >SIPE
SIPES >SIPE
SIPHON *n* bent tube which uses air pressure to draw liquid from a container ▷ *vb* draw off thus
SIPHONAGE >SIPHON
SIPHONAL >SIPHON
SIPHONATE *adj* having a syphon
SIPHONED >SIPHON
SIPHONET *n* sucking tube on an aphid
SIPHONETS >SIPHONET
SIPHONIC >SIPHON
SIPHONING >SIPHON
SIPHONS >SIPHON
SIPHUNCLE *n* tube inside shellfish
SIPING >SIPE
SIPPED >SIP
SIPPER >SIP
SIPPERS >SIP
SIPPET *n* small piece of toast eaten with soup or gravy
SIPPETS >SIPPET
SIPPING >SIP
SIPPLE *vb* sip
SIPPLED >SIPPLE
SIPPLES >SIPPLE
SIPPLING >SIPPLE
SIPPY *as in* sippy cup infant's drinking cup with a tight-fitting lid and perforated spout
SIPS >SIP
SIR *n* polite term of

address for a man ▷ *vb* call someone 'sir'
SIRCAR *n* government in India
SIRCARS >SIRCAR
SIRDAR *same as* >SARDAR
SIRDARS >SIRDAR
SIRE *n* male parent of a horse or other domestic animal ▷ *vb* father
SIRED >SIRE
SIREE *emphasized form of* >SIR
SIREES >SIREE
SIREN *n* device making a loud wailing noise as a warning
SIRENIAN *adj* belonging to the *Sirenia*, an order of aquatic herbivorous placental mammals that contains the dugong and manatee ▷ *n* any animal belonging to the order *Sirenia*
SIRENIANS >SIRENIAN
SIRENIC >SIREN
SIRENISE *variant of* >SIRENIZE
SIRENISED >SIRENISE
SIRENISES >SIRENISE
SIRENIZE *vb* bewitch
SIRENIZED >SIRENIZE
SIRENIZES >SIRENIZE
SIRENS >SIREN
SIRES >SIRE
SIRGANG *n* Asian bird
SIRGANGS >SIRGANG
SIRI *n* betel
SIRIASES >SIRIASIS
SIRIASIS *n* sunstroke
SIRIH *n* betel
SIRIHS >SIRIH
SIRING >SIRE
SIRIS >SIRI
SIRKAR *n* government in India
SIRKARS >SIRKAR
SIRLOIN *n* prime cut of loin of beef
SIRLOINS >SIRLOIN
SIRNAME *vb* old form of surname
SIRNAMED >SIRNAME
SIRNAMES >SIRNAME
SIRNAMING >SIRNAME
SIROC *n* sirocco
SIROCCO *n* hot wind blowing from N Africa into S Europe
SIROCCOS >SIROCCO
SIROCS >SIROC
SIRONISE *same as* >SIRONIZE
SIRONISED >SIRONISE
SIRONISES >SIRONISE
SIRONIZE *vb* treat (a woollen fabric) chemically to prevent it wrinkling after being washed
SIRONIZED >SIRONIZE
SIRONIZES >SIRONIZE
SIROSET *adj* of the chemical treatment of

woollen fabrics to give a permanent-press effect
SIRRA *disrespectful form of* >SIR
SIRRAH *n* contemptuous term used in addressing a man or boy
SIRRAHS >SIRRAH
SIRRAS >SIRRA
SIRRED >SIR
SIRREE *n* form of 'sir' used for emphasis
SIRREES >SIRREE
SIRRING >SIR
SIRS >SIR
SIRUP *same as* >SYRUP
SIRUPED >SIRUP
SIRUPIER >SIRUP
SIRUPIEST >SIRUP
SIRUPING >SIRUP
SIRUPS >SIRUP
SIRUPY >SIRUP
SIRVENTE *n* verse form employed by the troubadours of Provence to satirize political themes
SIRVENTES >SIRVENTE
SIS *n* sister
SISAL *n* (fibre of) plant used in making ropes
SISALS >SISAL
SISERARY *n* scolding
SISES >SIS
SISKIN *n* yellow-and-black finch
SISKINS >SISKIN
SISS *shortening of* >SISTER
SISSES >SISS
SISSIER >SISSY
SISSIES >SISSY
SISSIEST >SISSY
SISSIFIED >SISSY
SISSINESS >SISSY
SISSOO *n* Indian tree
SISSOOS >SISSOO
SISSY *n* weak or cowardly (person) ▷ *adj* effeminate, weak, or cowardly
SISSYISH >SISSY
SISSYNESS >SISSY
SIST *vb* Scottish law term meaning stop
SISTED >SIST
SISTER *n* girl or woman with the same parents as another person ▷ *adj* closely related, similar ▷ *vb* be or be like a sister
SISTERED >SISTER
SISTERING >SISTER
SISTERLY *adj* of or like a sister
SISTERS >SISTER
SISTING >SIST
SISTRA >SISTRUM
SISTROID *adj* contained between the convex sides of two intersecting curves
SISTRUM *n* musical instrument of ancient Egypt consisting of a metal rattle
SISTRUMS >SISTRUM
SISTS >SIST

**SIT** *vb* rest one's body upright on the buttocks

**SITAR** *n* Indian stringed musical instrument

**SITARIST** > SITAR

**SITARISTS** > SITAR

**SITARS** > SITAR

**SITATUNGA** *another name for* > MARSHBUCK

**SITCOM** *n* situation comedy

**SITCOMS** > SITCOM

**SITE** *n* place where something is, was, or is intended to be located ▷ *vb* provide with a site

**SITED** > SITE

**SITELLA** *n* type of small generally black-and-white bird

**SITELLAS** > SITELLA

**SITES** > SITE

**SITFAST** *n* sore on a horse's back caused by rubbing of the saddle

**SITFASTS** > SITFAST

**SITH** *archaic word for* > SINCE

**SITHE** *vb* old form of scythe

**SITHED** > SITHE

**SITHEE** *interj* look here! listen!

**SITHEN** *adv* old word meaning since

**SITHENCE** *adv* old word meaning since

**SITHENS** *adv* old word meaning since

**SITHES** > SITHE

**SITHING** > SITHE

**SITING** > SITE

**SITIOLOGY** *n* study of diet and nutrition

**SITKA** *as in sitka spruce* tall North American spruce tree

**SITKAMER** *n* sitting room

**SITKAMERS** > SITKAMER

**SITOLOGY** *n* scientific study of food, diet, and nutrition

**SITREP** *n* military situation report

**SITREPS** > SITREP

**SITS** > SIT

**SITTAR** *n* sitar

**SITTARS** > SITTAR

**SITTELLA** *variant spelling of* > SITELLA

**SITTELLAS** > SITTELLA

**SITTEN** *adj* dialect word for in the saddle

**SITTER** *n* baby-sitter

**SITTERS** > SITTER

**SITTINE** *adj* of nuthatch bird family

**SITTING** > SIT

**SITTINGS** > SIT

**SITUATE** *vb* place ▷ *adj* (now used esp in legal contexts) situated

**SITUATED** > SITUATE

**SITUATES** > SITUATE

**SITUATING** > SITUATE

**SITUATION** *n* state of affairs

**SITULA** *n* bucket-shaped container, usually of metal or pottery and often richly decorated

**SITULAE** > SITULA

**SITUP** *n* exercise in which the body is brought into a sitting position from one lying on the back

**SITUPS** > SITUP

**SITUS** *n* position or location, esp the usual or right position of an organ or part of the body

**SITUSES** > SITUS

**SITUTUNGA** *n* African antelope

**SITZ** *as in sitz bath* bath in which the buttocks and hips are immersed in hot water

**SITZKRIEG** *n* period during a war in which both sides change positions very slowly or not at all

**SITZMARK** *n* depression in the snow where a skier has fallen

**SITZMARKS** > SITZMARK

**SIVER** *same as* > SYVER

**SIVERS** > SIVER

**SIWASH** *vb* (in the Pacific Northwest) to camp out with only natural shelter

**SIWASHED** > SIWASH

**SIWASHES** > SIWASH

**SIWASHING** > SIWASH

**SIX** *n* one more than five

**SIXAIN** *n* stanza or poem of six lines

**SIXAINE** *n* six-line stanza of poetry

**SIXAINES** > SIXAINE

**SIXAINS** > SIXAIN

**SIXER** *same as* > SIX

**SIXERS** > SIXER

**SIXES** > SIX

**SIXFOLD** *adj* having six times as many or as much ▷ *adv* by six times as many or as much

**SIXMO** *n* book size resulting from folding a sheet of paper into six leaves or twelve pages, each one sixth the size of the sheet

**SIXMOS** > SIXMO

**SIXPENCE** *n* former British and Australian coin worth six pennies

**SIXPENCES** > SIXPENCE

**SIXPENNY** *adj* (of a nail) two inches in length

**SIXSCORE** *n* hundred and twenty

**SIXSCORES** > SIXSCORE

**SIXTE** *n* sixth of eight basic positions from which a parry or attack can be made in fencing

**SIXTEEN** *n* six and ten ▷ *adj* amounting to sixteen

▷ *determiner* amounting to sixteen

**SIXTEENER** *n* poem verse with sixteen syllables

**SIXTEENMO** *n* book size resulting from folding a sheet of paper into 16 leaves or 32 pages

**SIXTEENS** > SIXTEEN

**SIXTEENTH** *adj* coming after the fifteenth in numbering order ▷ *n* one of 16 equal or nearly equal parts of something

**SIXTES** > SIXTE

**SIXTH** *n* (of) number six in a series ▷ *adj* coming after the fifth and before the seventh in numbering order ▷ *adv* after the fifth person, position, etc

**SIXTHLY** *same as* > SIXTH

**SIXTHS** > SIXTH

**SIXTIES** > SIXTY

**SIXTIETH** *adj* being the ordinal number of sixty in numbering order ▷ *n* one of 60 approximately equal parts of something

**SIXTIETHS** > SIXTIETH

**SIXTY** *n* six times ten ▷ *adj* amounting to sixty

**SIXTYISH** > SIXTY

**SIZABLE** *adj* quite large

**SIZABLY** > SIZABLE

**SIZAR** *n* (at certain universities) an undergraduate receiving a maintenance grant from the college

**SIZARS** > SIZAR

**SIZARSHIP** > SIZAR

**SIZE** *n* dimensions, bigness ▷ *vb* arrange according to size

**SIZEABLE** *same as* > SIZABLE

**SIZEABLY** > SIZABLE

**SIZED** *adj* of a specified size

**SIZEISM** *n* discrimination on the basis of a person's size, esp against people considered to be overweight

**SIZEISMS** > SIZEISM

**SIZEIST** > SIZEISM

**SIZEISTS** > SIZEISM

**SIZEL** *n* scrap metal clippings

**SIZELS** > SIZEL

**SIZER** > SIZE

**SIZERS** > SIZE

**SIZES** > SIZE

**SIZIER** > SIZE

**SIZIEST** > SIZE

**SIZINESS** > SIZE

**SIZING** > SIZE

**SIZINGS** > SIZE

**SIZISM** *n* discrimination against people because of weight

**SIZISMS** > SIZISM

**SIZIST** > SIZISM

**SIZISTS** > SIZISM

**SIZY** > SIZE

**SIZZLE** *vb* make a hissing sound like frying fat ▷ *n* hissing sound

**SIZZLED** > SIZZLE

**SIZZLER** *n* something that sizzles

**SIZZLERS** > SIZZLER

**SIZZLES** > SIZZLE

**SIZZLING** *adj* extremely hot

**SIZZLINGS** > SIZZLING

**SJAMBOK** *n* whip or riding crop made of hide ▷ *vb* beat with a sjambok

**SJAMBOKED** > SJAMBOK

**SJAMBOKS** > SJAMBOK

**SJOE** *interj* South African exclamation of surprise, admiration, exhaustion, etc

**SKA** *n* type of West Indian pop music of the 1960s

**SKAG** *same as* > SCAG

**SKAGS** > SKAG

**SKAIL** *vb* Scots word meaning disperse

**SKAILED** > SKAIL

**SKAILING** > SKAIL

**SKAILS** > SKAIL

**SKAITH** *vb* Scots word meaning injure

**SKAITHED** > SKAITH

**SKAITHING** > SKAITH

**SKAITHS** > SKAITH

**SKALD** *n* (in ancient Scandinavia) a bard or minstrel

**SKALDIC** > SKALD

**SKALDS** > SKALD

**SKALDSHIP** > SKALD

**SKANGER** *n* Irish derogatory slang for a young working-class person who wears casual sports clothes

**SKANGERS** > SKANGER

**SKANK** *n* fast dance to reggae music ▷ *vb* perform this dance

**SKANKED** > SKANK

**SKANKER** > SKANK

**SKANKERS** > SKANK

**SKANKIER** > SKANKY

**SKANKIEST** > SKANKY

**SKANKING** > SKANK

**SKANKINGS** > SKANK

**SKANKS** > SKANK

**SKANKY** *adj* dirty or unattractive

**SKART** *Scots word for* > CORMORANT

**SKARTH** *Scots word for* > CORMORANT

**SKARTHS** > SKARTH

**SKARTS** > SKART

**SKAS** > SKA

**SKAT** *n* three-handed card game using 32 cards, popular in German-speaking communities

**SKATE** *n* boot with a steel blade or sets of wheels attached to the sole for gliding over ice or a hard surface ▷ *vb* glide on or as

if on skates
**SKATED** > SKATE
**SKATEPARK** *n* place for skateboarding
**SKATER** *n* person who skates
**SKATERS** > SKATER
**SKATES** > SKATE
**SKATING** > SKATE
**SKATINGS** > SKATE
**SKATOL** *n* skatole
**SKATOLE** *n* white or brownish crystalline solid
**SKATOLES** > SKATOLE
**SKATOLS** > SKATOL
**SKATS** > SKAT
**SKATT** *n* dialect word meaning throw
**SKATTS** > SKATT
**SKAW** *variant of* > SCAW
**SKAWS** > SKAW
**SKEAN** *n* kind of double-edged dagger formerly used in Ireland and Scotland
**SKEANE** *same as* > SKEIN
**SKEANES** > SKEANE
**SKEANS** > SKEAN
**SKEAR** *dialect form of* > SCARE
**SKEARED** > SKEAR
**SKEARIER** > SKEARY
**SKEARIEST** > SKEARY
**SKEARING** > SKEAR
**SKEARS** > SKEAR
**SKEARY** *dialect form of* > SCARY
**SKEDADDLE** *vb* run off ▷ *n* hasty retreat
**SKEE** *variant spelling of* > SKI
**SKEECHAN** *n* old Scots type of beer
**SKEECHANS** > SKEECHAN
**SKEED** > SKEE
**SKEEF** *adj, adv* South African slang for at an oblique angle
**SKEEING** > SKEE
**SKEELIER** > SKEELY
**SKEELIEST** > SKEELY
**SKEELY** *adj* Scots word meaning skilful
**SKEEN** *n* type of ibex
**SKEENS** > SKEEN
**SKEER** *dialect form of* > SCARE
**SKEERED** > SKEER
**SKEERIER** > SKEERY
**SKEERIEST** > SKEERY
**SKEERING** > SKEER
**SKEERS** > SKEER
**SKEERY** *dialect form of* > SCARY
**SKEES** > SKEE
**SKEESICKS** *American word meaning* > ROGUE
**SKEET** *n* form of clay-pigeon shooting
**SKEETER** *informal word for* > MOSQUITO
**SKEETERS** > SKEETER
**SKEETS** > SKEET
**SKEG** *n* reinforcing brace between the after end of a

keel and the rudderpost
**SKEGG** *n* skeg
**SKEGGER** *n* young salmon
**SKEGGERS** > SKEGGER
**SKEGGS** > SKEGG
**SKEGS** > SKEG
**SKEIGH** *adj* Scots word meaning shy
**SKEIGHER** > SKEIGH
**SKEIGHEST** > SKEIGH
**SKEIN** *n* yarn wound in a loose coil ▷ *vb* wind into a skein
**SKEINED** > SKEIN
**SKEINING** > SKEIN
**SKEINS** > SKEIN
**SKELDER** *vb* beg
**SKELDERED** > SKELDER
**SKELDERS** > SKELDER
**SKELETAL** > SKELETON
**SKELETON** *n* framework of bones inside a person's or animal's body ▷ *adj* reduced to a minimum
**SKELETONS** > SKELETON
**SKELF** *n* splinter of wood, esp when embedded accidentally in the skin
**SKELFS** > SKELF
**SKELL** *n* homeless person
**SKELLIE** *adj* skelly
**SKELLIED** > SKELLY
**SKELLIER** > SKELLY
**SKELLIES** > SKELLY
**SKELLIEST** > SKELLY
**SKELLOCH** *n* Scots word meaning scream
**SKELLOCHS** > SKELLOCH
**SKELLS** > SKELL
**SKELLUM** *n* rogue
**SKELLUMS** > SKELLUM
**SKELLY** *n* whitefish of certain lakes in the Lake District ▷ *vb* look sideways or squint ▷ *adj* cross-eyed
**SKELLYING** > SKELLY
**SKELM** *n* villain or crook
**SKELMS** > SKELM
**SKELP** *vb* slap ▷ *n* slap
**SKELPED** > SKELP
**SKELPING** > SKELP
**SKELPINGS** > SKELP
**SKELPIT** *vb* Scots word meaning skelped
**SKELPS** > SKELP
**SKELTER** *vb* scurry
**SKELTERED** > SKELTER
**SKELTERS** > SKELTER
**SKELUM** *n* Scots word meaning rascal
**SKELUMS** > SKELUM
**SKEN** *vb* squint or stare
**SKENE** *n* Scots word meaning dagger
**SKENES** > SKENE
**SKENNED** > SKEN
**SKENNING** > SKEN
**SKENS** > SKEN
**SKEO** *n* Scots dialect word meaning hut
**SKEOS** > SKEO
**SKEP** *n* beehive, esp one constructed of straw ▷ *vb*

gather into a hive
**SKEPFUL** *n* amount skep will hold
**SKEPFULS** > SKEP
**SKEPPED** > SKEP
**SKEPPING** > SKEP
**SKEPS** > SKEP
**SKEPSIS** *n* doubt
**SKEPSISES** > SKEPSIS
**SKEPTIC** *same as* > SCEPTIC
**SKEPTICAL** > SKEPTIC
**SKEPTICS** > SKEPTIC
**SKER** *vb* scour
**SKERRED** > SKER
**SKERRICK** *n* small fragment or amount
**SKERRICKS** > SKERRICK
**SKERRIES** > SKERRY
**SKERRING** > SKER
**SKERRY** *n* rocky island or reef
**SKERS** > SKER
**SKET** *vb* splash (water)
**SKETCH** *n* rough drawing ▷ *vb* make a sketch (of)
**SKETCHED** > SKETCH
**SKETCHER** > SKETCH
**SKETCHERS** > SKETCH
**SKETCHES** > SKETCH
**SKETCHIER** > SKETCHY
**SKETCHILY** > SKETCHY
**SKETCHING** > SKETCH
**SKETCHPAD** *n* pad of paper for sketching
**SKETCHY** *adj* incomplete or inadequate
**SKETS** > SKET
**SKETTED** > SKET
**SKETTING** > SKET
**SKEW** *vb* make slanting or crooked ▷ *adj* slanting or crooked ▷ *n* slanting position
**SKEWBACK** *n* sloping surface on both sides of a segmental arch that takes the thrust
**SKEWBACKS** > SKEWBACK
**SKEWBALD** *adj* (horse) marked with patches of white and another colour ▷ *n* horse with this marking
**SKEWBALDS** > SKEWBALD
**SKEWED** > SKEW
**SKEWER** *n* pin to hold meat together during cooking ▷ *vb* fasten with a skewer
**SKEWERED** > SKEWER
**SKEWERING** > SKEWER
**SKEWERS** > SKEWER
**SKEWEST** > SKEW
**SKEWING** > SKEW
**SKEWNESS** *n* quality or condition of being skew
**SKEWS** > SKEW
**SKEWWHIFF** *adj* crooked or slanting
**SKI** *n* one of a pair of long runners fastened to boots for gliding over snow or water ▷ *vb* travel on skis
**SKIABLE** > SKI
**SKIAGRAM** *n* picture made

from shadows
**SKIAGRAMS** > SKIAGRAM
**SKIAGRAPH** *n* skiagram
**SKIAMACHY** *same as* > SCIAMACHY
**SKIASCOPE** *n* medical instrument for examining the eye to detect errors of refraction
**SKIASCOPY** *n* retinoscopy
**SKIATRON** *n* type of cathode ray tube
**SKIATRONS** > SKIATRON
**SKIBOB** *n* vehicle made of two short skis for gliding down snow slopes
**SKIBOBBED** > SKIBOB
**SKIBOBBER** > SKIBOB
**SKIBOBS** > SKIBOB
**SKID** *vb* (of a moving vehicle) slide sideways uncontrollably ▷ *n* skidding
**SKIDDED** > SKID
**SKIDDER** > SKID
**SKIDDERS** > SKID
**SKIDDIER** > SKID
**SKIDDIEST** > SKID
**SKIDDING** > SKID
**SKIDDOO** *vb* go away quickly
**SKIDDOOED** > SKIDDOO
**SKIDDOOS** > SKIDDOO
**SKIDDY** > SKID
**SKIDLID** *n* crash helmet
**SKIDLIDS** > SKIDLID
**SKIDOO** *n* snowmobile ▷ *vb* travel on a skidoo
**SKIDOOED** > SKIDOO
**SKIDOOING** > SKIDOO
**SKIDOOS** > SKIDOO
**SKIDPAN** *n* area made slippery so that vehicle drivers can practise controlling skids
**SKIDPANS** > SKIDPAN
**SKIDPROOF** *adj* (of a road surface, tyre, etc) preventing or resistant to skidding
**SKIDS** > SKID
**SKIDWAY** *n* platform on which logs ready for sawing are piled
**SKIDWAYS** > SKIDWAY
**SKIED** > SKY
**SKIER** > SKI
**SKIERS** > SKI
**SKIES** > SKY
**SKIEY** *adj* of the sky
**SKIEYER** > SKIEY
**SKIEYEST** > SKIEY
**SKIFF** *n* small boat ▷ *vb* travel in a skiff
**SKIFFED** > SKIFF
**SKIFFING** > SKIFF
**SKIFFLE** *n* style of popular music of the 1950s, played chiefly on guitars and improvised percussion instruments ▷ *vb* play this style of music
**SKIFFLED** > SKIFFLE
**SKIFFLES** > SKIFFLE

**SKIFFLESS** > SKIFF
**SKIFFLING** > SKIFFLE
**SKIFFS** > SKIFF
**SKIING** > SKI
**SKIINGS** > SKI
**SKIJORER** > SKIJORING
**SKIJORERS** > SKIJORING
**SKIJORING** n sport in which a skier is pulled over snow or ice, usually by a horse
**SKILFUL** adj having or showing skill
**SKILFULLY** > SKILFUL
**SKILL** n special ability or expertise
**SKILLED** adj possessing or demonstrating accomplishment, skill, or special training
**SKILLESS** > SKILL
**SKILLET** n small frying pan or shallow cooking pot
**SKILLETS** > SKILLET
**SKILLFUL** same as > SKILFUL
**SKILLIER** > SKILLY
**SKILLIES** > SKILLY
**SKILLIEST** > SKILLY
**SKILLING** n former Scandinavian coin of low denomination
**SKILLINGS** > SKILLING
**SKILLION** n part of a building having a lower, esp sloping, roof
**SKILLIONS** > SKILLION
**SKILLS** > SKILL
**SKILLY** n thin soup or gruel ▷ adj skilled
**SKIM** vb remove floating matter from the surface of (a liquid) ▷ n act or process of skimming
**SKIMBOARD** n type of surfboard, shorter than standard and rounded at both ends ▷ vb surf on a skimboard
**SKIMMED** > SKIM
**SKIMMER** n person or thing that skims
**SKIMMERS** > SKIMMER
**SKIMMIA** n shrub of S and SE Asia grown for its ornamental red berries and evergreen foliage
**SKIMMIAS** > SKIMMIA
**SKIMMING** > SKIM
**SKIMMINGS** pl n material that is skimmed off a liquid
**SKIMO** n informal and offensive word for an Inuit
**SKIMOBILE** n motor vehicle with skis for travelling on snow
**SKIMOS** > SKIMO
**SKIMP** vb not invest enough time, money, material, etc
**SKIMPED** > SKIMP
**SKIMPIER** > SKIMPY
**SKIMPIEST** > SKIMPY
**SKIMPILY** > SKIMPY

**SKIMPING** > SKIMP
**SKIMPS** > SKIMP
**SKIMPY** adj scanty or insufficient
**SKIMS** > SKIM
**SKIN** n outer covering of the body ▷ vb remove the skin of
**SKINCARE** n use of cosmetics in taking care of skin
**SKINCARES** > SKINCARE
**SKINFLICK** n film containing much nudity and sex
**SKINFLINT** n miser
**SKINFOOD** n cosmetic cream for the skin
**SKINFOODS** > SKINFOOD
**SKINFUL** n sufficient alcoholic drink to make one drunk
**SKINFULS** > SKINFUL
**SKINHEAD** n youth with very short hair
**SKINHEADS** > SKINHEAD
**SKINK** n any lizard of the family Scincidae ▷ vb serve a drink
**SKINKED** > SKINK
**SKINKER** > SKINK
**SKINKERS** > SKINK
**SKINKING** > SKINK
**SKINKS** > SKINK
**SKINLESS** > SKIN
**SKINLIKE** > SKIN
**SKINNED** > SKIN
**SKINNER** n person who prepares or deals in animal skins
**SKINNERS** > SKINNER
**SKINNIER** > SKINNY
**SKINNIEST** > SKINNY
**SKINNING** > SKIN
**SKINNY** adj thin
**SKINS** > SKIN
**SKINT** adj having no money
**SKINTER** > SKINT
**SKINTEST** > SKINT
**SKINTIGHT** adj fitting tightly over the body
**SKIO** n Scots dialect word meaning hut
**SKIORING** n sport of being towed on skis by horse
**SKIORINGS** > SKIORING
**SKIOS** > SKIO
**SKIP** vb leap lightly from one foot to the other ▷ n skipping
**SKIPJACK** n important food fish of tropical seas
**SKIPJACKS** > SKIPJACK
**SKIPLANE** n aircraft fitted with skis to enable it to land on and take off from snow
**SKIPLANES** > SKIPLANE
**SKIPPABLE** > SKIP
**SKIPPED** > SKIP
**SKIPPER** vb captain ▷ n captain of a ship or aircraft
**SKIPPERED** > SKIPPER
**SKIPPERS** > SKIPPER

**SKIPPET** n small round box for preserving a document or seal
**SKIPPETS** > SKIPPET
**SKIPPIER** > SKIPPY
**SKIPPIEST** > SKIPPY
**SKIPPING** > SKIP
**SKIPPINGS** > SKIP
**SKIPPY** adj in high spirits
**SKIPS** > SKIP
**SKIRL** n sound of bagpipes ▷ vb (of bagpipes) to give out a shrill sound
**SKIRLED** > SKIRL
**SKIRLING** > SKIRL
**SKIRLINGS** > SKIRL
**SKIRLS** > SKIRL
**SKIRMISH** n brief or minor fight or argument ▷ vb take part in a skirmish
**SKIRR** vb move, run, or fly rapidly ▷ n whirring or grating sound, as of the wings of birds in flight
**SKIRRED** > SKIRR
**SKIRRET** n umbelliferous Old World plant
**SKIRRETS** > SKIRRET
**SKIRRING** > SKIRR
**SKIRRS** > SKIRR
**SKIRT** n woman's garment hanging from the waist ▷ vb border
**SKIRTED** > SKIRT
**SKIRTER** n man who skirts fleeces
**SKIRTERS** > SKIRTER
**SKIRTING** n border fixed round the base of an interior wall to protect it from kicks, dirt, etc
**SKIRTINGS** pl n ragged edges trimmed from the fleece of a sheep
**SKIRTLESS** > SKIRT
**SKIRTLIKE** > SKIRT
**SKIRTS** > SKIRT
**SKIS** > SKI
**SKIT** n brief satirical sketch
**SKITCH** vb (of a dog) to attack
**SKITCHED** > SKITCH
**SKITCHES** > SKITCH
**SKITCHING** > SKITCH
**SKITE** n boast ▷ vb boast
**SKITED** > SKITE
**SKITES** > SKITE
**SKITING** > SKITE
**SKITS** > SKIT
**SKITTER** vb move or run rapidly or lightly
**SKITTERED** > SKITTER
**SKITTERS** > SKITTER
**SKITTERY** adj moving lightly and rapidly
**SKITTISH** adj playful or lively
**SKITTLE** n bottle-shaped object used as a target in some games ▷ vb play skittles
**SKITTLED** > SKITTLE
**SKITTLES** > SKITTLE

**SKITTLING** > SKITTLE
**SKIVE** vb evade work or responsibility
**SKIVED** > SKIVE
**SKIVER** n tanned outer layer split from a skin ▷ vb cut leather
**SKIVERED** > SKIVER
**SKIVERING** > SKIVER
**SKIVERS** > SKIVER
**SKIVES** > SKIVE
**SKIVIE** adj old Scots word meaning disarranged
**SKIVIER** > SKIVIE
**SKIVIEST** > SKIVIE
**SKIVING** > SKIVE
**SKIVINGS** > SKIVE
**SKIVVIED** > SKIVVY
**SKIVVIES** > SKIVVY
**SKIVVY** n female servant who does menial work ▷ vb work as a skivvy
**SKIVVYING** > SKIVVY
**SKIVY** > SKIVE
**SKIWEAR** n clothes for skiing in
**SKLATE** Scots word for > SLATE
**SKLATED** > SKLATE
**SKLATES** > SKLATE
**SKLATING** > SKLATE
**SKLENT** Scots word for > SLANT
**SKLENTED** > SKLENT
**SKLENTING** > SKLENT
**SKLENTS** > SKLENT
**SKLIFF** n Scots word meaning little piece
**SKLIFFS** > SKLIFF
**SKLIM** vb Scots word meaning climb
**SKLIMMED** > SKLIM
**SKLIMMING** > SKLIM
**SKLIMS** > SKLIM
**SKOAL** same as > SKOL
**SKOALED** > SKOAL
**SKOALING** > SKOAL
**SKOALS** > SKOAL
**SKOFF** vb eat greedily
**SKOFFED** > SKOFF
**SKOFFING** > SKOFF
**SKOFFS** > SKOFF
**SKOKIAAN** n (in South Africa) a potent alcoholic beverage
**SKOKIAANS** > SKOKIAAN
**SKOL** sentence substitute good health! (a drinking toast) ▷ vb down (an alcoholic drink) in one go
**SKOLIA** > SKOLION
**SKOLION** n ancient Greek drinking song
**SKOLLED** > SKOL
**SKOLLIE** same as > SKOLLY
**SKOLLIES** > SKOLLY
**SKOLLING** > SKOL
**SKOLLY** n hooligan, usually one of a gang
**SKOLS** > SKOL
**SKOOKUM** adj strong or brave
**SKOOL** ironically illiterate or childish spelling of > SCHOOL

SKOOLS > SKOOL
SKOOSH *vb* Scots word meaning squirt
SKOOSHED > SKOOSH
SKOOSHES > SKOOSH
SKOOSHING > SKOOSH
SKORT *n* pair of shorts with a front panel which gives the appearance of a skirt
SKORTS > SKORT
SKOSH *n* little bit
SKOSHES > SKOSH
SKRAN *n* food
SKRANS > SKRAN
SKREEGH *vb* Scots word meaning screech
SKREEGHED > SKREEGH
SKREEGHS > SKREEGH
SKREEN *n* screen
SKREENS > SKREEN
SKREIGH *vb* Scots word meaning screech
SKREIGHED > SKREIGH
SKREIGHS > SKREIGH
SKRIECH *vb* Scots word meaning screech
SKRIECHED > SKRIECH
SKRIECHS > SKRIECH
SKRIED > SKRY
SKRIEGH *vb* Scots word meaning screech
SKRIEGHED > SKRIEGH
SKRIEGHS > SKRIEGH
SKRIES > SKRY
SKRIK *n* South African word meaning fright
SKRIKE *vb* cry
SKRIKED > SKRIKE
SKRIKES > SKRIKE
SKRIKING > SKRIKE
SKRIKS > SKRIK
SKRIMMAGE *vb* scrimmage
SKRIMP *vb* steal apples
SKRIMPED > SKRIMP
SKRIMPING > SKRIMP
SKRIMPS > SKRIMP
SKRUMP *vb* steal apples
SKRUMPED > SKRUMP
SKRUMPING > SKRUMP
SKRUMPS > SKRUMP
SKRY *vb* try to tell future
SKRYER > SKRY
SKRYERS > SKRY
SKRYING > SKRY
SKUA *n* large predatory gull
SKUAS > SKUA
SKUDLER *n* Scots word meaning leader of festivities
SKUDLERS > SKUDLER
SKUG *vb* shelter
SKUGGED > SKUG
SKUGGING > SKUG
SKUGS > SKUG
SKULK *vb* move stealthily ▷ *n* person who skulks
SKULKED > SKULK
SKULKER > SKULK
SKULKERS > SKULK
SKULKING > SKULK
SKULKINGS > SKULK
SKULKS > SKULK
SKULL *n* bony framework of the head ▷ *vb* strike on

the head
SKULLCAP *n* close-fitting brimless cap
SKULLCAPS > SKULLCAP
SKULLED > SKULL
SKULLING > SKULL
SKULLS > SKULL
SKULPIN *n* North American fish
SKULPINS > SKULPIN
SKUMMER *vb* defecate
SKUMMERED > SKUMMER
SKUMMERS > SKUMMER
SKUNK *n* small black-and-white N American mammal which emits a foul-smelling fluid when attacked ▷ *vb* defeat overwhelmingly in a game
SKUNKBIRD *n* North American songbird
SKUNKED > SKUNK
SKUNKIER > SKUNK
SKUNKIEST > SKUNK
SKUNKING > SKUNK
SKUNKS > SKUNK
SKUNKWEED *n* low-growing fetid swamp plant of N America
SKUNKY > SKUNK
SKURRIED > SKURRY
SKURRIES > SKURRY
SKURRY *vb* scurry
SKURRYING > SKURRY
SKUTTLE *vb* scuttle
SKUTTLED > SKUTTLE
SKUTTLES > SKUTTLE
SKUTTLING > SKUTTLE
SKY *n* upper atmosphere as seen from the earth ▷ *vb* hit high in the air
SKYBOARD *n* small board used for skysurfing
SKYBOARDS > SKYBOARD
SKYBORN *adj* born in heaven
SKYBORNE *adj* flying through sky
SKYBOX *n* luxurious suite high up in the stand of a sports stadium
SKYBOXES > SKYBOX
SKYBRIDGE *n* covered, elevated bridge connecting two buildings
SKYCAP *n* luggage porter at American airport
SKYCAPS > SKYCAP
SKYCLAD *adj* naked
SKYDIVE *vb* take part in skydiving
SKYDIVED > SKYDIVE
SKYDIVER > SKYDIVE
SKYDIVERS > SKYDIVE
SKYDIVES > SKYDIVE
SKYDIVING *n* sport of jumping from an aircraft and performing manoeuvres before opening one's parachute
SKYDOVE > SKYDIVE
SKYED > SKY
SKYER *n* cricket ball hit up into air

SKYERS > SKYER
SKYEY *adj* of the sky
SKYF *n* South African slang for a cigarette or substance for smoking ▷ *vb* smoke a cigarette
SKYFED > SKYF
SKYFING > SKYF
SKYFS > SKYF
SKYHOME *n* Australian slang for a sub-penthouse flat in a tall building
SKYHOMES > SKYHOME
SKYHOOK *n* hook hung from helicopter
SKYHOOKS > SKYHOOK
SKYIER > SKYEY
SKYIEST > SKYEY
SKYING > SKY
SKYISH > SKY
SKYJACK *vb* hijack (an aircraft)
SKYJACKED > SKYJACK
SKYJACKER > SKYJACK
SKYJACKS > SKYJACK
SKYLAB *n* orbiting space station
SKYLABS > SKYLAB
SKYLARK *n* lark that sings while soaring at a great height ▷ *vb* play or frolic
SKYLARKED > SKYLARK
SKYLARKER > SKYLARK
SKYLARKS > SKYLARK
SKYLIGHT *n* window in a roof or ceiling
SKYLIGHTS > SKYLIGHT
SKYLIKE > SKY
SKYLINE *n* outline of buildings, trees, etc against the sky
SKYLINES > SKYLINE
SKYLIT *adj* having skylight
SKYMAN *n* paratrooper
SKYMEN > SKYMAN
SKYPHOI > SKYPHOS
SKYPHOS *n* ancient Greek drinking cup
SKYR *n* Scandinavian cheese
SKYRE *vb* Scots word meaning shine
SKYRED > SKYRE
SKYRES > SKYRE
SKYRING > SKYRE
SKYROCKET *vb* rise very quickly
SKYRS > SKYR
SKYSAIL *n* square sail set above the royal on a square-rigger
SKYSAILS > SKYSAIL
SKYSCAPE *n* painting, drawing, photograph, etc, representing or depicting the sky
SKYSCAPES > SKYSCAPE
SKYSURF *vb* perform freefall aerobatics
SKYSURFED > SKYSURF
SKYSURFER *n* someone who performs stunts with a small board attached to his or her feet while in

free fall
SKYSURFS > SKYSURF
SKYTE *vb* Scots word meaning slide
SKYTED > SKYTE
SKYTES > SKYTE
SKYTING > SKYTE
SKYWALK *n* tightrope walk at great height
SKYWALKS > SKYWALK
SKYWARD *adj* towards the sky ▷ *adv* towards the sky
SKYWARDS *same as* > SKYWARD
SKYWAY *n* air route
SKYWAYS > SKYWAY
SKYWRITE *vb* write message in sky with smoke from aircraft
SKYWRITER > SKYWRITE
SKYWRITES > SKYWRITE
SKYWROTE > SKYWRITE
SLAB *n* broad flat piece ▷ *vb* cut or make into a slab or slabs
SLABBED > SLAB
SLABBER *vb* dribble from the mouth
SLABBERED > SLABBER
SLABBERER > SLABBER
SLABBERS > SLABBER
SLABBERY > SLABBER
SLABBIER > SLAB
SLABBIEST > SLAB
SLABBING > SLAB
SLABBY > SLAB
SLABLIKE > SLAB
SLABS > SLAB
SLABSTONE *n* flagstone
SLACK *same as* > SLAKE
SLACKED > SLACK
SLACKEN *vb* make or become slack
SLACKENED > SLACKEN
SLACKENER > SLACKEN
SLACKENS > SLACKEN
SLACKER *n* person who evades work or duty
SLACKERS > SLACKER
SLACKEST > SLACK
SLACKING > SLACK
SLACKLY > SLACK
SLACKNESS > SLACK
SLACKS *pl n* casual trousers
SLADANG *n* Malayan tapir
SLADANGS > SLADANG
SLADE *n* little valley
SLADES > SLADE
SLAE *Scots word for* > SLOE
SLAES > SLAE
SLAG *n* waste left after metal is smelted ▷ *vb* criticize
SLAGGED > SLAG
SLAGGIER > SLAG
SLAGGIEST > SLAG
SLAGGING > SLAG
SLAGGINGS > SLAG
SLAGGY > SLAG
SLAGS > SLAG
SLAID *vb* Scots word for 'slid'
SLAIN > SLAY
SLAINTE *interj* cheers!

**SLAIRG** Scots word for > SPREAD
**SLAIRGED** > SLAIRG
**SLAIRGING** > SLAIRG
**SLAIRGS** > SLAIRG
**SLAISTER** vb cover with a sloppy mess ▷ n sloppy mess
**SLAISTERS** > SLAISTER
**SLAISTERY** > SLAISTER
**SLAKABLE** > SLAKE
**SLAKE** vb satisfy (thirst or desire)
**SLAKEABLE** > SLAKE
**SLAKED** > SLAKE
**SLAKELESS** adj impossible to slake
**SLAKER** > SLAKE
**SLAKERS** > SLAKE
**SLAKES** > SLAKE
**SLAKING** > SLAKE
**SLALOM** n skiing or canoeing race over a winding course ▷ vb take part in a slalom
**SLALOMED** > SLALOM
**SLALOMER** > SLALOM
**SLALOMERS** > SLALOM
**SLALOMING** > SLALOM
**SLALOMIST** > SLALOM
**SLALOMS** > SLALOM
**SLAM** vb shut, put down, or hit violently and noisily ▷ n act or sound of slamming
**SLAMDANCE** vb dance aggressively, bumping into others
**SLAMMAKIN** n woman's loose dress
**SLAMMED** > SLAM
**SLAMMER** n prison
**SLAMMERS** > SLAMMER
**SLAMMING** > SLAM
**SLAMMINGS** > SLAM
**SLAMS** > SLAM
**SLANDER** n false and malicious statement about a person ▷ vb utter slander about
**SLANDERED** > SLANDER
**SLANDERER** > SLANDER
**SLANDERS** > SLANDER
**SLANE** n spade for cutting turf
**SLANES** > SLANE
**SLANG** n very informal language ▷ vb use insulting language to (someone)
**SLANGED** > SLANG
**SLANGER** n street vendor
**SLANGERS** > SLANGER
**SLANGIER** > SLANG
**SLANGIEST** > SLANG
**SLANGILY** > SLANG
**SLANGING** > SLANG
**SLANGINGS** > SLANG
**SLANGISH** > SLANG
**SLANGS** > SLANG
**SLANGUAGE** n language using slang
**SLANGULAR** adj of or using slang

**SLANGY** > SLANG
**SLANK** dialect word for > LANK
**SLANT** vb lean at an angle, slope ▷ n slope
**SLANTED** > SLANT
**SLANTER** same as > SLINTER
**SLANTERS** > SLANTER
**SLANTING** > SLANT
**SLANTLY** > SLANT
**SLANTS** > SLANT
**SLANTWAYS** same as > SLANTWISE
**SLANTWISE** adj in a slanting or oblique direction
**SLANTY** adj slanting
**SLAP** n blow with the open hand or a flat object ▷ vb strike with the open hand or a flat object
**SLAPDASH** adj careless and hasty ▷ adv carelessly or hastily ▷ n slapdash activity or work
**SLAPHAPPY** adj cheerfully irresponsible or careless
**SLAPHEAD** n derogatory term for a bald person
**SLAPHEADS** > SLAPHEAD
**SLAPJACK** n simple card game
**SLAPJACKS** > SLAPJACK
**SLAPPED** > SLAP
**SLAPPER** > SLAP
**SLAPPERS** > SLAP
**SLAPPING** > SLAP
**SLAPS** > SLAP
**SLAPSHOT** n hard, fast, often wild, shot executed with a powerful downward swing
**SLAPSHOTS** > SLAPSHOT
**SLAPSTICK** n boisterous knockabout comedy
**SLART** vb spill (something)
**SLARTED** > SLART
**SLARTING** > SLART
**SLARTS** > SLART
**SLASH** vb cut with a sweeping stroke ▷ n sweeping stroke
**SLASHED** > SLASH
**SLASHER** n tool or tractor-drawn machine used for cutting scrub or undergrowth in the bush
**SLASHERS** > SLASHER
**SLASHES** > SLASH
**SLASHFEST** n film or computer game that features bloody killings involving blades
**SLASHING** adj aggressively critical ▷ n act of slashing
**SLASHINGS** > SLASHING
**SLAT** n narrow strip of wood or metal ▷ vb provide with slats
**SLATCH** n slack part of rope
**SLATCHES** > SLATCH
**SLATE** n rock which splits easily into thin layers ▷ vb cover with slates ▷ adj

dark grey
**SLATED** > SLATE
**SLATELIKE** > SLATE
**SLATER** n person trained in laying roof slates
**SLATERS** > SLATER
**SLATES** > SLATE
**SLATEY** adj slightly mad
**SLATHER** vb spread quickly or lavishly
**SLATHERED** > SLATHER
**SLATHERS** > SLATHER
**SLATIER** > SLATY
**SLATIEST** > SLATY
**SLATINESS** > SLATY
**SLATING** n act or process of laying slates
**SLATINGS** > SLATING
**SLATS** > SLAT
**SLATTED** > SLAT
**SLATTER** vb be slovenly
**SLATTERED** > SLATTER
**SLATTERN** n slovenly woman
**SLATTERNS** > SLATTERN
**SLATTERS** > SLATTER
**SLATTERY** adj slovenly
**SLATTING** > SLAT
**SLATTINGS** > SLAT
**SLATY** adj consisting of or resembling slate
**SLAUGHTER** vb kill (animals) for food ▷ n slaughtering
**SLAVE** n person owned by another for whom he or she has to work ▷ vb work like a slave
**SLAVED** > SLAVE
**SLAVER** n person or ship engaged in the slave trade ▷ vb dribble saliva from the mouth
**SLAVERED** > SLAVER
**SLAVERER** > SLAVER
**SLAVERERS** > SLAVER
**SLAVERIES** > SLAVERY
**SLAVERING** > SLAVER
**SLAVERS** > SLAVER
**SLAVERY** n state or condition of being a slave
**SLAVES** > SLAVE
**SLAVEY** n female general servant
**SLAVEYS** > SLAVEY
**SLAVING** > SLAVE
**SLAVISH** adj of or like a slave
**SLAVISHLY** > SLAVISH
**SLAVOCRAT** n US slaveholder before the Civil War
**SLAVOPHIL** n person who admires the Slavs or their cultures
**SLAW** short for > COLESLAW
**SLAWS** > SLAW
**SLAY** vb kill
**SLAYABLE** > SLAY
**SLAYED** > SLAY
**SLAYER** > SLAY
**SLAYERS** > SLAY
**SLAYING** > SLAY
**SLAYS** > SLAY

**SLEAVE** n tangled thread ▷ vb disentangle (twisted thread, etc)
**SLEAVED** > SLEAVE
**SLEAVES** > SLEAVE
**SLEAVING** > SLEAVE
**SLEAZE** n behaviour in public life considered immoral, dishonest, or disreputable
**SLEAZEBAG** n disgusting person
**SLEAZES** > SLEAZE
**SLEAZIER** > SLEAZY
**SLEAZIEST** > SLEAZY
**SLEAZILY** > SLEAZY
**SLEAZO** n sleazy person
**SLEAZOID** n sleazy person
**SLEAZOIDS** > SLEAZOID
**SLEAZY** adj run-down or sordid
**SLED** same as > SLEDGE
**SLEDDED** > SLED
**SLEDDER** > SLED
**SLEDDERS** > SLED
**SLEDDING** > SLED
**SLEDDINGS** > SLED
**SLEDED** > SLED
**SLEDGE** n carriage on runners for sliding on snow ▷ vb travel by sledge
**SLEDGED** > SLEDGE
**SLEDGER** > SLEDGE
**SLEDGERS** > SLEDGE
**SLEDGES** > SLEDGE
**SLEDGING** > SLEDGE
**SLEDGINGS** > SLEDGE
**SLEDS** > SLED
**SLEE** Scots word for > SLY
**SLEECH** n slippery mud
**SLEECHES** > SLEECH
**SLEECHIER** > SLEECH
**SLEECHY** > SLEECH
**SLEEK** adj glossy, smooth, and shiny ▷ vb make smooth and glossy, as by grooming, etc
**SLEEKED** > SLEEK
**SLEEKEN** vb make sleek
**SLEEKENED** > SLEEKEN
**SLEEKENS** > SLEEKEN
**SLEEKER** > SLEEK
**SLEEKERS** > SLEEK
**SLEEKEST** > SLEEK
**SLEEKIER** > SLEEK
**SLEEKIEST** > SLEEK
**SLEEKING** > SLEEK
**SLEEKINGS** > SLEEK
**SLEEKIT** adj smooth
**SLEEKLY** > SLEEK
**SLEEKNESS** > SLEEK
**SLEEKS** > SLEEK
**SLEEKY** > SLEEK
**SLEEP** n state of rest characterized by unconsciousness ▷ vb be in or as if in a state of sleep
**SLEEPAWAY** n camp for teenagers
**SLEEPER** n railway car fitted for sleeping in
**SLEEPERS** > SLEEPER
**SLEEPERY** Scots word for > SLEEPY

**SLEEPIER** > SLEEPY

**SLEEPIEST** > SLEEPY

**SLEEPILY** > SLEEPY

**SLEEPING** > SLEEP

**SLEEPINGS** > SLEEP

**SLEEPLESS** *adj* (of a night) one during which one does not sleep

**SLEEPLIKE** > SLEEP

**SLEEPOUT** *n* small building for sleeping in

**SLEEPOUTS** > SLEEPOUT

**SLEEPOVER** *n* occasion when a person stays overnight at a friend's house

**SLEEPRY** *Scots word for* > SLEEPY

**SLEEPS** > SLEEP

**SLEEPSUIT** *n* baby's sleeping garment

**SLEEPWALK** *vb* walk while asleep

**SLEEPWEAR** *n* clothes for sleeping in

**SLEEPY** *adj* needing sleep

**SLEER** > SLEE

**SLEEST** > SLEE

**SLEET** *n* rain and snow or hail falling together ▷ *vb* fall as sleet

**SLEETED** > SLEET

**SLEETIER** > SLEET

**SLEETIEST** > SLEET

**SLEETING** > SLEET

**SLEETS** > SLEET

**SLEETY** > SLEET

**SLEEVE** *n* part of a garment which covers the arm

**SLEEVED** > SLEEVE

**SLEEVEEN** *n* sly obsequious smooth-tongued person

**SLEEVEENS** > SLEEVEEN

**SLEEVELET** *n* protective covering for forearm

**SLEEVER** *n* old beer measure

**SLEEVERS** > SLEEVER

**SLEEVES** > SLEEVE

**SLEEVING** *n* tubular flexible insulation into which bare wire can be inserted

**SLEEVINGS** > SLEEVING

**SLEEZIER** > SLEEZY

**SLEEZIEST** > SLEEZY

**SLEEZY** *adj* sleazy

**SLEIDED** *adj* old word meaning separated

**SLEIGH** *same as* > SLEDGE

**SLEIGHED** > SLEIGH

**SLEIGHER** > SLEIGH

**SLEIGHERS** > SLEIGH

**SLEIGHING** > SLEIGH

**SLEIGHS** > SLEIGH

**SLEIGHT** *n* skill or cunning

**SLEIGHTS** > SLEIGHT

**SLENDER** *adj* slim

**SLENDERER** > SLENDER

**SLENDERLY** > SLENDER

**SLENTER** *same as* > SLINTER

**SLENTERS** > SLINTER

**SLEPT** > SLEEP

**SLEUTH** *n* detective ▷ *vb*

track or follow

**SLEUTHED** > SLEUTH

**SLEUTHING** > SLEUTH

**SLEUTHS** > SLEUTH

**SLEW** *vb* twist sideways, esp awkwardly

**SLEWED** > SLEW

**SLEWING** > SLEW

**SLEWS** > SLEW

**SLEY** *n* weaver's tool for separating threads

**SLEYS** > SLEY

**SLICE** *n* thin flat piece cut from something ▷ *vb* cut into slices

**SLICEABLE** > SLICE

**SLICED** > SLICE

**SLICER** > SLICE

**SLICERS** > SLICE

**SLICES** > SLICE

**SLICING** > SLICE

**SLICINGS** > SLICE

**SLICK** *adj* persuasive and glib ▷ *n* patch of oil on water ▷ *vb* make smooth or sleek

**SLICKED** > SLICK

**SLICKEN** *vb* make smooth

**SLICKENED** > SLICKEN

**SLICKENER** > SLICKEN

**SLICKENS** > SLICKEN

**SLICKER** *n* sly or untrustworthy person

**SLICKERED** *adj* wearing a waterproof jacket

**SLICKERS** > SLICKER

**SLICKEST** > SLICK

**SLICKING** > SLICK

**SLICKINGS** > SLICK

**SLICKLY** > SLICK

**SLICKNESS** > SLICK

**SLICKROCK** *n* weathered and smooth sandstone or other rock

**SLICKS** > SLICK

**SLICKSTER** *n* dishonest person

**SLID** > SLIDE

**SLIDABLE** > SLIDE

**SLIDDEN** > SLIDE

**SLIDDER** *vb* slip

**SLIDDERED** > SLIDDER

**SLIDDERS** > SLIDDER

**SLIDDERY** *adj* slippery

**SLIDE** *vb* slip smoothly along (a surface) ▷ *n* sliding

**SLIDED** > SLIDE

**SLIDER** > SLIDE

**SLIDERS** > SLIDE

**SLIDES** > SLIDE

**SLIDEWAY** *n* sloping channel down which things are slid

**SLIDEWAYS** > SLIDEWAY

**SLIDING** > SLIDE

**SLIDINGLY** > SLIDE

**SLIDINGS** > SLIDE

**SLIER** > SLY

**SLIEST** > SLY

**SLIEVE** *n* Irish mountain

**SLIEVES** > SLIEVE

**SLIGHT** *adj* small in quantity or extent

▷ *n* snub ▷ *vb* insult (someone) by behaving rudely

**SLIGHTED** > SLIGHT

**SLIGHTER** > SLIGHT

**SLIGHTERS** > SLIGHT

**SLIGHTEST** > SLIGHT

**SLIGHTING** *adj* characteristic of a slight

**SLIGHTISH** > SLIGHT

**SLIGHTLY** *adv* in small measure or degree

**SLIGHTS** > SLIGHT

**SLILY** > SLY

**SLIM** *adj* not heavy or stout, thin ▷ *vb* make or become slim by diet and exercise

**SLIMDOWN** *n* instance of an organization cutting staff

**SLIMDOWNS** > SLIMDOWN

**SLIME** *n* unpleasant thick slippery substance ▷ *vb* cover with slime

**SLIMEBALL** *n* odious and contemptible person

**SLIMED** > SLIME

**SLIMES** > SLIME

**SLIMIER** > SLIMY

**SLIMIEST** > SLIMY

**SLIMILY** > SLIMY

**SLIMINESS** > SLIMY

**SLIMING** > SLIME

**SLIMLINE** *adj* slim

**SLIMLY** > SLIM

**SLIMMED** > SLIM

**SLIMMER** > SLIM

**SLIMMERS** > SLIM

**SLIMMEST** > SLIM

**SLIMMING** > SLIM

**SLIMMINGS** > SLIM

**SLIMMISH** > SLIM

**SLIMNESS** > SLIM

**SLIMPSIER** > SLIMPSY

**SLIMPSY** *adj* thin and flimsy

**SLIMS** > SLIM

**SLIMSIER** > SLIMSY

**SLIMSIEST** > SLIMSY

**SLIMSY** *adj* frail

**SLIMY** *adj* of, like, or covered with slime

**SLING** *n* bandage hung from the neck to support an injured hand or arm ▷ *vb* throw

**SLINGBACK** *n* shoe with a strap that goes around the back of the heel

**SLINGER** > SLING

**SLINGERS** > SLING

**SLINGING** > SLING

**SLINGS** > SLING

**SLINGSHOT** *n* Y-shaped implement with a loop of elastic fastened to the ends of the two prongs, used for shooting small stones, etc

**SLINK** *vb* move furtively or guiltily ▷ *n* animal, esp a calf, born prematurely

**SLINKED** > SLINK

**SLINKER** > SLINK

**SLINKERS** > SLINK

**SLINKIER** > SLINKY

**SLINKIEST** > SLINKY

**SLINKILY** > SLINKY

**SLINKING** > SLINK

**SLINKS** > SLINK

**SLINKSKIN** *n* skin of premature calf

**SLINKWEED** *n* plant believed to make cow give birth prematurely

**SLINKY** *adj* (of clothes) figure-hugging

**SLINTER** *n* dodge, trick, or stratagem

**SLINTERS** > SLINTER

**SLIOTAR** *n* ball used in hurling

**SLIOTARS** > SLIOTAR

**SLIP** *vb* lose balance by sliding ▷ *n* slipping

**SLIPCASE** *n* protective case for a book that is open at one end so that only the spine of the book is visible

**SLIPCASED** *adj* having a slipcase

**SLIPCASES** > SLIPCASE

**SLIPCOVER** *n* fitted but easily removable cloth cover for a chair, sofa, etc

**SLIPDRESS** *n* silky sleeveless dress

**SLIPE** *n* wool removed from the pelt of a slaughtered sheep by immersion in a chemical bath ▷ *vb* remove skin

**SLIPED** > SLIPE

**SLIPES** > SLIPE

**SLIPFORM** *n* mould used in building

**SLIPFORMS** > SLIPFORM

**SLIPING** > SLIPE

**SLIPKNOT** *n* knot tied so that it will slip along the rope round which it is made

**SLIPKNOTS** > SLIPKNOT

**SLIPLESS** > SLIP

**SLIPNOOSE** *n* noose made with a slipknot, so that it tightens when pulled

**SLIPOUT** *n* instance of slipping out

**SLIPOUTS** > SLIPOUT

**SLIPOVER** *adj* of or denoting a garment that can be put on easily over the head ▷ *n* such a garment, esp a sleeveless pullover

**SLIPOVERS** > SLIPOVER

**SLIPPAGE** *n* act or an instance of slipping

**SLIPPAGES** > SLIPPAGE

**SLIPPED** > SLIP

**SLIPPER** *n* light shoe for indoor wear ▷ *vb* hit or beat with a slipper

**SLIPPERED** > SLIPPER

**SLIPPERS** > SLIPPER

**SLIPPERY** *adj* so smooth or wet as to cause slipping or be difficult to hold

**SLIPPIER** >SLIPPY
**SLIPPIEST** >SLIPPY
**SLIPPILY** >SLIPPY
**SLIPPING** >SLIP
**SLIPPY** *adj* slippery
**SLIPRAIL** *n* rail in a fence that can be slipped out of place to make an opening
**SLIPRAILS** >SLIPRAIL
**SLIPS** >SLIP
**SLIPSHEET** *n* sheet of paper that is interleaved between freshly printed sheets
**SLIPSHOD** *adj* (of an action) careless
**SLIPSLOP** *n* weak or unappetizing food or drink
**SLIPSLOPS** >SLIPSLOP
**SLIPSOLE** *n* separate sole on shoe
**SLIPSOLES** >SLIPSOLE
**SLIPT** *vb* old form of slipped
**SLIPUP** *n* mistake or mishap
**SLIPUPS** >SLIPUP
**SLIPWARE** *n* pottery that has been decorated with slip
**SLIPWARES** >SLIPWARE
**SLIPWAY** *n* launching slope on which ships are built or repaired
**SLIPWAYS** >SLIPWAY
**SLISH** *n* old word meaning cut
**SLISHES** >SLISH
**SLIT** *n* long narrow cut or opening ▷ *vb* make a long straight cut in
**SLITHER** *vb* slide unsteadily ▷ *n* slithering movement
**SLITHERED** >SLITHER
**SLITHERS** >SLITHER
**SLITHERY** *adj* moving with a slithering motion
**SLITLESS** >SLIT
**SLITLIKE** >SLIT
**SLITS** >SLIT
**SLITTED** >SLIT
**SLITTER** >SLIT
**SLITTERS** >SLIT
**SLITTIER** >SLIT
**SLITTIEST** >SLIT
**SLITTING** >SLIT
**SLITTY** >SLIT
**SLIVE** *vb* slip
**SLIVED** >SLIVE
**SLIVEN** >SLIVE
**SLIVER** *n* small thin piece ▷ *vb* cut into slivers
**SLIVERED** >SLIVER
**SLIVERER** >SLIVER
**SLIVERERS** >SLIVER
**SLIVERING** >SLIVER
**SLIVERS** >SLIVER
**SLIVES** >SLIVE
**SLIVING** >SLIVE
**SLIVOVIC** *n* plum brandy
**SLIVOVICA** *n* plum brandy
**SLIVOVITZ** *n* plum brandy from E Europe

**SLIVOWITZ** *n* plum brandy
**SLOAN** *n* severe telling-off
**SLOANS** >SLOAN
**SLOB** *n* lazy and untidy person
**SLOBBER** *vb* dribble or drool ▷ *n* liquid or saliva spilt from the mouth
**SLOBBERED** >SLOBBER
**SLOBBERER** >SLOBBER
**SLOBBERS** >SLOBBER
**SLOBBERY** >SLOBBER
**SLOBBIER** >SLOB
**SLOBBIEST** >SLOB
**SLOBBISH** >SLOB
**SLOBBY** >SLOB
**SLOBLAND** *n* muddy ground
**SLOBLANDS** >SLOBLAND
**SLOBS** >SLOB
**SLOCKEN** *vb* Scots word meaning slake
**SLOCKENED** >SLOCKEN
**SLOCKENS** >SLOCKEN
**SLOE** *n* sour blue-black fruit
**SLOEBUSH** *n* bush on which sloes grow
**SLOES** >SLOE
**SLOETHORN** *n* sloe plant
**SLOETREE** *n* sloe plant
**SLOETREES** >SLOETREE
**SLOG** *vb* work hard and steadily ▷ *n* long and exhausting work or walk
**SLOGAN** *n* catchword or phrase used in politics or advertising
**SLOGANEER** *n* person who coins or employs slogans frequently ▷ *vb* coin or employ slogans so as to sway opinion
**SLOGANISE** *same as* >SLOGANIZE
**SLOGANIZE** *vb* use slogans
**SLOGANS** >SLOGAN
**SLOGGED** >SLOG
**SLOGGER** >SLOG
**SLOGGERS** >SLOG
**SLOGGING** >SLOG
**SLOGS** >SLOG
**SLOID** *n* Swedish woodwork
**SLOIDS** >SLOID
**SLOJD** *n* Swedish woodwork
**SLOJDS** >SLOJD
**SLOKEN** *vb* Scots word meaning slake
**SLOKENED** >SLOKEN
**SLOKENING** >SLOKEN
**SLOKENS** >SLOKEN
**SLOMMOCK** *vb* walk assertively with a hip-rolling gait
**SLOMMOCKS** >SLOMMOCK
**SLOOM** *vb* slumber
**SLOOMED** >SLOOM
**SLOOMIER** >SLOOM
**SLOOMIEST** >SLOOM
**SLOOMING** >SLOOM
**SLOOMS** >SLOOM
**SLOOMY** >SLOOM
**SLOOP** *n* small single-masted ship

**SLOOPS** >SLOOP
**SLOOSH** *vb* wash with water
**SLOOSHED** >SLOOSH
**SLOOSHES** >SLOOSH
**SLOOSHING** >SLOOSH
**SLOOT** *n* ditch for irrigation or drainage
**SLOOTS** >SLOOT
**SLOP** *vb* splash or spill ▷ *n* spilt liquid
**SLOPE** *vb* slant ▷ *n* sloping surface
**SLOPED** >SLOPE
**SLOPER** >SLOPE
**SLOPERS** >SLOPE
**SLOPES** >SLOPE
**SLOPEWISE** >SLOPE
**SLOPIER** >SLOPE
**SLOPIEST** >SLOPE
**SLOPING** >SLOPE
**SLOPINGLY** >SLOPE
**SLOPPED** >SLOP
**SLOPPIER** >SLOPPY
**SLOPPIEST** >SLOPPY
**SLOPPILY** >SLOPPY
**SLOPPING** >SLOP
**SLOPPY** *adj* careless or untidy
**SLOPS** >SLOP
**SLOPWORK** *n* manufacture of cheap shoddy clothing or the clothes so produced
**SLOPWORKS** >SLOPWORK
**SLOPY** >SLOPE
**SLORM** *vb* wipe carelessly
**SLORMED** >SLORM
**SLORMING** >SLORM
**SLORMS** >SLORM
**SLOSH** *vb* pour carelessly ▷ *n* splashing sound
**SLOSHED** >SLOSH
**SLOSHES** >SLOSH
**SLOSHIER** >SLOSH
**SLOSHIEST** >SLOSH
**SLOSHING** >SLOSH
**SLOSHINGS** >SLOSH
**SLOSHY** >SLOSH
**SLOT** *n* narrow opening for inserting something ▷ *vb* make a slot or slots in
**SLOTBACK** *n* American football player
**SLOTBACKS** >SLOTBACK
**SLOTH** *n* slow-moving animal of tropical America ▷ *vb* be lazy
**SLOTHED** >SLOTH
**SLOTHFUL** *adj* lazy or idle
**SLOTHING** >SLOTH
**SLOTHS** >SLOTH
**SLOTS** >SLOT
**SLOTTED** >SLOT
**SLOTTER** >SLOT
**SLOTTERS** >SLOT
**SLOTTING** >SLOT
**SLOUCH** *vb* sit, stand, or move with a drooping posture ▷ *n* drooping posture
**SLOUCHED** >SLOUCH
**SLOUCHER** >SLOUCH
**SLOUCHERS** >SLOUCH
**SLOUCHES** >SLOUCH

**SLOUCHIER** >SLOUCHY
**SLOUCHILY** >SLOUCHY
**SLOUCHING** >SLOUCH
**SLOUCHY** *adj* slouching
**SLOUGH** *n* bog ▷ *vb* (of a snake) shed (its skin)
**SLOUGHED** >SLOUGH
**SLOUGHIER** >SLOUGH
**SLOUGHING** >SLOUGH
**SLOUGHS** >SLOUGH
**SLOUGHY** >SLOUGH
**SLOVE** >SLIVE
**SLOVEN** *n* habitually dirty or untidy person
**SLOVENLY** *adj* dirty or untidy ▷ *adv* in a slovenly manner
**SLOVENRY** *n* quality of being slovenly
**SLOVENS** >SLOVEN
**SLOW** *adj* taking a longer time than is usual or expected ▷ *adv* slowly ▷ *vb* reduce the speed (of)
**SLOWBACK** *n* lazy person
**SLOWBACKS** >SLOWBACK
**SLOWCOACH** *n* person who moves or works slowly
**SLOWDOWN** *n* any slackening of pace
**SLOWDOWNS** >SLOWDOWN
**SLOWED** >SLOW
**SLOWER** >SLOW
**SLOWEST** >SLOW
**SLOWING** >SLOW
**SLOWINGS** >SLOW
**SLOWISH** >SLOW
**SLOWLY** >SLOW
**SLOWNESS** >SLOW
**SLOWPOKE** *same as* >SLOWCOACH
**SLOWPOKES** >SLOWPOKE
**SLOWS** >SLOW
**SLOWWORM** *n* small legless lizard
**SLOWWORMS** >SLOWWORM
**SLOYD** *n* Swedish woodwork
**SLOYDS** >SLOYD
**SLUB** *n* lump in yarn or fabric, often made intentionally to give a knobbly effect ▷ *vb* draw out and twist (a sliver of fibre) preparatory to spinning ▷ *adj* (of material) having an irregular appearance
**SLUBB** *same as* >SLUB
**SLUBBED** >SLUB
**SLUBBER** *vb* smear
**SLUBBERED** >SLUBBER
**SLUBBERS** >SLUBBER
**SLUBBIER** >SLUB
**SLUBBIEST** >SLUB
**SLUBBING** >SLUB
**SLUBBINGS** >SLUB
**SLUBBS** >SLUBB
**SLUBBY** >SLUB
**SLUBS** >SLUB
**SLUDGE** *n* thick mud
**SLUDGED** >SLUDGE
**SLUDGES** >SLUDGE
**SLUDGIER** >SLUDGY

SLUDGIEST > SLUDGY
SLUDGING > SLUDGE
SLUDGY *adj* consisting of, containing, or like sludge
SLUE *same as* > SLEW
SLUED > SLUE
SLUEING > SLUE
SLUES > SLUE
SLUFF *same as* > SLOUGH
SLUFFED > SLUFF
SLUFFING > SLUFF
SLUFFS > SLUFF
SLUG *n* land snail with no shell ▷ *vb* hit hard
SLUGABED *n* person who remains in bed through laziness
SLUGABEDS > SLUGABED
SLUGFEST *n* fist fight
SLUGFESTS > SLUGFEST
SLUGGABED *same as* > SLUGABED
SLUGGARD *n* lazy person ▷ *adj* lazy
SLUGGARDS > SLUGGARD
SLUGGED > SLUG
SLUGGER *n* (esp in boxing, baseball, etc) a person who strikes hard
SLUGGERS > SLUGGER
SLUGGING > SLUG
SLUGGISH *adj* slow-moving, lacking energy
SLUGHORN *same as* > SLOGAN
SLUGHORNE *same as* > SLOGAN
SLUGHORNS > SLUGHORN
SLUGS > SLUG
SLUICE *n* channel that carries a rapid current of water ▷ *vb* drain water by means of a sluice
SLUICED > SLUICE
SLUICES > SLUICE
SLUICEWAY *same as* > SLUICE
SLUICIER > SLUICE
SLUICIEST > SLUICE
SLUICING > SLUICE
SLUICY > SLUICE
SLUING > SLUE
SLUIT *n* water channel in South Africa
SLUITS > SLUIT
SLUM *n* squalid overcrowded house or area ▷ *vb* temporarily and deliberately experience poorer places or conditions than usual
SLUMBER *n* sleep ▷ *vb* sleep
SLUMBERED > SLUMBER
SLUMBERER > SLUMBER
SLUMBERERS > SLUMBERER
SLUMBERS > SLUMBER
SLUMBERY *adj* sleepy
SLUMBROUS *adj* sleepy
SLUMBRY *same as* > SLUMBERY
SLUMGUM *n* material left after wax is extracted from honeycomb
SLUMGUMS > SLUMGUM
SLUMISM *n* existence of slums

SLUMISMS > SLUMISM
SLUMLORD *n* absentee landlord of slum property, esp one who profiteers
SLUMLORDS > SLUMLORD
SLUMMED > SLUM
SLUMMER > SLUM
SLUMMERS > SLUM
SLUMMIER > SLUM
SLUMMIEST > SLUM
SLUMMING > SLUM
SLUMMINGS > SLUM
SLUMMOCK *vb* move slowly and heavily
SLUMMOCKS > SLUMMOCK
SLUMMY > SLUM
SLUMP *vb* (of prices or demand) decline suddenly ▷ *n* sudden decline in prices or demand
SLUMPED > SLUMP
SLUMPIER > SLUMPY
SLUMPIEST > SLUMPY
SLUMPING > SLUMP
SLUMPS > SLUMP
SLUMPY *adj* boggy
SLUMS > SLUM
SLUNG > SLING
SLUNGSHOT *n* weight attached to the end of a cord and used as a weapon
SLUNK > SLINK
SLUR *vb* pronounce or utter (words) indistinctly ▷ *n* slurring of words
SLURB *n* suburban slum
SLURBAN > SLURB
SLURBS > SLURB
SLURP *vb* eat or drink noisily ▷ *n* slurping sound
SLURPED > SLURP
SLURPER > SLURP
SLURPERS > SLURP
SLURPING > SLURP
SLURPS > SLURP
SLURRED > SLUR
SLURRIED > SLURRY
SLURRIES > SLURRY
SLURRING > SLUR
SLURRY *n* muddy liquid mixture ▷ *vb* spread slurry
SLURRYING > SLURRY
SLURS > SLUR
SLUSE *same as* > SLUICE
SLUSES > SLUICE
SLUSH *n* watery muddy substance ▷ *vb* make one's way through or as if through slush
SLUSHED > SLUSH
SLUSHES > SLUSH
SLUSHIER > SLUSHY
SLUSHIES > SLUSHY
SLUSHIEST > SLUSHY
SLUSHILY > SLUSHY
SLUSHING > SLUSH
SLUSHY *adj* of, resembling, or consisting of slush ▷ *n* unskilled kitchen assistant
SLUT *n* derogatory term for a dirty or immoral woman
SLUTCH *n* mud
SLUTCHES > SLUTCH
SLUTCHIER > SLUTCH

SLUTCHY > SLUTCH
SLUTS > SLUT
SLUTTERY *n* state of being slut
SLUTTIER > SLUT
SLUTTIEST > SLUT
SLUTTISH > SLUT
SLUTTY > SLUT
SLY *adj* crafty
SLYBOOTS *pl n* person who is sly
SLYER > SLY
SLYEST > SLY
SLYISH > SLY
SLYLY > SLY
SLYNESS > SLY
SLYNESSES > SLY
SLYPE *n* covered passageway in a church that connects the transept to the chapterhouse
SLYPES > SLYPE
SMA *Scots word for* > SMALL
SMAAK *vb* South African slang for like or love
SMAAKED > SMAAK
SMAAKING > SMAAK
SMAAKS > SMAAK
SMACK *vb* slap sharply ▷ *n* sharp slap ▷ *adv* squarely or directly
SMACKED > SMACK
SMACKER *n* loud kiss
SMACKERS > SMACKER
SMACKHEAD *n* person who is addicted to heroin
SMACKING *adj* brisk
SMACKINGS > SMACKING
SMACKS > SMACK
SMAIK *n* Scots word meaning rascal
SMAIKS > SMAIK
SMALL *adj* not large in size, number, or amount ▷ *n* narrow part of the lower back ▷ *adv* into small pieces ▷ *vb* make small
SMALLAGE *n* wild celery
SMALLAGES > SMALLAGE
SMALLBOY *n* steward's assistant or deputy steward in European households in W Africa
SMALLBOYS > SMALLBOY
SMALLED > SMALL
SMALLER > SMALL
SMALLEST > SMALL
SMALLING > SMALL
SMALLISH > SMALL
SMALLNESS > SMALL
SMALLPOX *n* contagious disease with blisters that leave scars
SMALLS > SMALL
SMALLSAT *n* small communications satellite
SMALLSATS > SMALLSAT
SMALLTIME *adj* unimportant
SMALM *same as* > SMARM
SMALMED > SMALM
SMALMILY > SMALMY
SMALMING > SMALM
SMALMS > SMALM

SMALMY *same as* > SMARMY
SMALT *n* type of silica glass coloured deep blue with cobalt oxide
SMALTI > SMALTO
SMALTINE *n* mineral containing cobalt
SMALTINES > SMALTINE
SMALTITE *n* silver-white to greyish mineral
SMALTITES > SMALTITE
SMALTO *n* coloured glass, etc, used in mosaics
SMALTOS > SMALTO
SMALTS > SMALT
SMARAGD *n* any green gemstone, such as the emerald
SMARAGDE *same as* > SMARAGD
SMARAGDES > SMARAGDE
SMARAGDS > SMARAGD
SMARM *vb* bring (oneself) into favour (with) ▷ *n* obsequious flattery
SMARMED > SMARM
SMARMIER > SMARMY
SMARMIEST > SMARMY
SMARMILY > SMARMY
SMARMING > SMARM
SMARMS > SMARM
SMARMY *adj* unpleasantly suave or flattering
SMART *adj* well-kept and neat ▷ *vb* feel or cause stinging pain ▷ *n* stinging pain ▷ *adv* in a smart manner
SMARTARSE *n* derogatory term for a clever person, esp one who parades his knowledge offensively
SMARTARSE *same as* > SMARTARSE
SMARTED > SMART
SMARTEN *vb* make or become smart
SMARTENED > SMARTEN
SMARTENS > SMARTEN
SMARTER > SMART
SMARTEST > SMART
SMARTIE *same as* > SMARTY
SMARTIES > SMARTY
SMARTING > SMART
SMARTISH > SMART
SMARTLY > SMART
SMARTNESS > SMART
SMARTS *pl n* know-how, intelligence, or wits
SMARTWEED *n* grass with acrid smell
SMARTY *n* would-be clever person
SMASH *vb* break violently and noisily ▷ *n* act or sound of smashing ▷ *adv* with a smash
SMASHABLE > SMASH
SMASHED *adj* completely intoxicated with alcohol
SMASHER *n* attractive person or thing
SMASHEROO *n* excellent person or thing

SMASHERS > SMASHER
SMASHES > SMASH
SMASHING adj excellent
SMASHINGS > SMASHING
SMASHUP n bad collision of cars
SMASHUPS > SMASHUP
SMATCH less common word for > SMACK
SMATCHED > SMATCH
SMATCHES > SMATCH
SMATCHING > SMATCH
SMATTER n smattering ▷ vb prattle
SMATTERED > SMATTER
SMATTERER > SMATTER
SMATTERS > SMATTER
SMAZE n smoky haze, less damp than fog
SMAZES > SMAZE
SMEAR vb spread with a greasy or sticky substance ▷ n dirty mark or smudge
SMEARCASE n American type of cottage cheese
SMEARED > SMEAR
SMEARER > SMEAR
SMEARERS > SMEAR
SMEARIER > SMEARY
SMEARIEST > SMEARY
SMEARILY > SMEARY
SMEARING > SMEAR
SMEARS > SMEAR
SMEARY adj smeared, dirty
SMEATH n duck
SMEATHS > SMEATH
SMECTIC adj (of a substance) existing in state in which the molecules are oriented in layers
SMECTITE n type of clay mineral
SMECTITES > SMECTITE
SMECTITIC > SMECTITE
SMEDDUM n any fine powder
SMEDDUMS > SMEDDUM
SMEE n duck
SMEECH Southwest English dialect form of > SMOKE
SMEECHED > SMEECH
SMEECHES > SMEECH
SMEECHING > SMEECH
SMEEK vb smoke
SMEEKED > SMEEK
SMEEKING > SMEEK
SMEEKS > SMEEK
SMEES > SMEE
SMEETH n duck
SMEETHS > SMEETH
SMEGMA n whitish sebaceous secretion that accumulates beneath the prepuce
SMEGMAS > SMEGMA
SMELL vb perceive (a scent or odour) by means of the nose ▷ n ability to perceive odours by the nose
SMELLED > SMELL
SMELLER > SMELL
SMELLERS > SMELL
SMELLIER > SMELLY

SMELLIES pl n pleasant-smelling products such as perfumes, body lotions, bath salts, etc
SMELLIEST > SMELLY
SMELLING > SMELL
SMELLINGS > SMELL
SMELLS > SMELL
SMELLY adj having a nasty smell
SMELT vb extract metal from an ore
SMELTED > SMELL
SMELTER n industrial plant where smelting is carried out
SMELTERS > SMELTER
SMELTERY variant of > SMELTER
SMELTING > SMELL
SMELTINGS > SMELL
SMELTS > SMELL
SMERK same as > SMIRK
SMERKED > SMERK
SMERKING > SMERK
SMERKS > SMERK
SMEUSE n way through hedge
SMEUSES > SMEUSE
SMEW n duck of N Europe and Asia
SMEWS > SMEW
SMICKER vb look at someone amorously
SMICKERED > SMICKER
SMICKERS > SMICKER
SMICKET n smock
SMICKETS > SMICKET
SMICKLY adv amorously
SMIDDIED > SMIDDY
SMIDDIES > SMIDDY
SMIDDY Scots word for > SMITHY
SMIDDYING > SMIDDY
SMIDGE n very small amount or part
SMIDGEN n very small amount or part
SMIDGENS > SMIDGEN
SMIDGEON same as > SMIDGEN
SMIDGEONS > SMIDGEON
SMIDGES > SMIDGE
SMIDGIN same as > SMIDGEN
SMIDGINS > SMIDGIN
SMIERCASE same as > SMEARCASE
SMIGHT same as > SMITE
SMIGHTING > SMIGHT
SMIGHTS > SMIGHT
SMILAX n type of climbing shrub
SMILAXES > SMILAX
SMILE n turning up of the corners of the mouth to show pleasure or friendliness ▷ vb give a smile
SMILED > SMILE
SMILEFUL adj full of smiles
SMILELESS > SMILE
SMILER > SMILE
SMILERS > SMILE
SMILES > SMILE

SMILET n little smile
SMILETS > SMILET
SMILEY n symbol depicting a smile or other facial expression, used in e-mail ▷ adj cheerful
SMILEYS > SMILEY
SMILING > SMILE
SMILINGLY > SMILE
SMILINGS > SMILE
SMILODON n extinct sabre-toothed tiger
SMILODONS > SMILODON
SMIR n drizzly rain ▷ vb drizzle lightly
SMIRCH n stain ▷ vb disgrace
SMIRCHED > SMIRCH
SMIRCHER > SMIRCH
SMIRCHERS > SMIRCH
SMIRCHES > SMIRCH
SMIRCHING > SMIRCH
SMIRK n smug smile ▷ vb give a smirk
SMIRKED > SMIRK
SMIRKER > SMIRK
SMIRKERS > SMIRK
SMIRKIER > SMIRK
SMIRKIEST > SMIRK
SMIRKILY > SMIRK
SMIRKING > SMIRK
SMIRKS > SMIRK
SMIRKY > SMIRK
SMIRR same as > SMIR
SMIRRED > SMIRR
SMIRRIER > SMIRR
SMIRRIEST > SMIRR
SMIRRING > SMIRR
SMIRRS > SMIRR
SMIRRY > SMIRR
SMIRS > SMIR
SMIRTING n flirting amongst those smoking outside a non-smoking office, pub, etc
SMIRTINGS > SMIRTING
SMIT > SMITE
SMITE vb strike hard
SMITER > SMITE
SMITERS > SMITE
SMITES > SMITE
SMITH n worker in metal ▷ vb work in metal
SMITHED > SMITH
SMITHERS pl n little shattered pieces
SMITHERY n trade or craft of a blacksmith
SMITHIED > SMITHY
SMITHIES > SMITHY
SMITHING > SMITH
SMITHS > SMITH
SMITHY n blacksmith's workshop ▷ vb work as a smith
SMITHYING > SMITHY
SMITING > SMITE
SMITS > SMIT
SMITTED > SMIT
SMITTEN > SMITE
SMITTING > SMIT
SMITTLE adj infectious
SMOCK n loose overall ▷ vb gather (material) by

sewing in a honeycomb pattern
SMOCKED > SMOCK
SMOCKING n ornamental needlework used to gather material
SMOCKINGS > SMOCKING
SMOCKLIKE > SMOCK
SMOCKS > SMOCK
SMOG n mixture of smoke and fog
SMOGGIER > SMOG
SMOGGIEST > SMOG
SMOGGY > SMOG
SMOGLESS > SMOG
SMOGS > SMOG
SMOILE same as > SMILE
SMOILED > SMOILE
SMOILES > SMOILE
SMOILING > SMOILE
SMOKABLE > SMOKE
SMOKE n cloudy mass that rises from something burning ▷ vb give off smoke or treat with smoke
SMOKEABLE > SMOKE
SMOKEBUSH n plant with small light flowers
SMOKED > SMOKE
SMOKEHO same as > SMOKO
SMOKEHOOD n hood worn to keep out smoke
SMOKEHOS > SMOKEHO
SMOKEJACK n device formerly used for turning a roasting spit, operated by the movement of ascending gases in a chimney
SMOKELESS adj having or producing little or no smoke
SMOKELIKE > SMOKE
SMOKEPOT n device for producing smoke
SMOKEPOTS > SMOKEPOT
SMOKER n person who habitually smokes tobacco
SMOKERS > SMOKER
SMOKES > SMOKE
SMOKETREE n shrub with clusters of yellowish flowers
SMOKEY same as > SMOKY
SMOKIER > SMOKY
SMOKIES > SMOKY
SMOKIEST > SMOKY
SMOKILY > SMOKY
SMOKINESS > SMOKY
SMOKING > SMOKE
SMOKINGS > SMOKING
SMOKO n short break from work for tea or a cigarette
SMOKOS > SMOKO
SMOKY adj filled with or giving off smoke, sometimes excessively ▷ n haddock that has been smoked
SMOLDER same as > SMOULDER
SMOLDERED > SMOLDER
SMOLDERS > SMOLDER
SMOLT n young salmon at

the stage when it migrates to the sea
**SMOLTS** > SMOLT
**SMOOCH** *vb* kiss and cuddle ▷ *n* smooching
**SMOOCHED** > SMOOCH
**SMOOCHER** > SMOOCH
**SMOOCHERS** > SMOOCH
**SMOOCHES** > SMOOCH
**SMOOCHING** > SMOOCH
**SMOOCHY** *adj* romantic
**SMOODGE** *same as* > SMOOCH
**SMOODGED** > SMOODGE
**SMOODGES** > SMOODGE
**SMOODGING** > SMOODGE
**SMOOGE** *same as* > SMOOCH
**SMOOGED** > SMOOGE
**SMOOGES** > SMOOGE
**SMOOGING** > SMOOGE
**SMOOR** *vb* Scots word meaning put out fire
**SMOORED** > SMOOR
**SMOORING** > SMOOR
**SMOORS** > SMOOR
**SMOOSH** *vb* paint to give softened look
**SMOOSHED** > SMOOSH
**SMOOSHES** > SMOOSH
**SMOOSHING** > SMOOSH
**SMOOT** *vb* work as printer
**SMOOTED** > SMOOT
**SMOOTH** *adj* even in surface, texture, or consistency ▷ *vb* make smooth ▷ *adv* in a smooth manner ▷ *n* smooth part of something
**SMOOTHED** > SMOOTH
**SMOOTHEN** *vb* make or become smooth
**SMOOTHENS** > SMOOTHEN
**SMOOTHER** > SMOOTH
**SMOOTHERS** > SMOOTH
**SMOOTHES** > SMOOTH
**SMOOTHEST** > SMOOTH
**SMOOTHIE** *n* slang, usu derogatory term for a charming but possibly insincere man
**SMOOTHIES** > SMOOTHY
**SMOOTHING** > SMOOTH
**SMOOTHISH** > SMOOTH
**SMOOTHLY** > SMOOTH
**SMOOTHS** > SMOOTH
**SMOOTHY** *same as* > SMOOTHIE
**SMOOTING** > SMOOT
**SMOOTS** > SMOOT
**SMORBROD** *n* Danish hors d'oeuvre
**SMORBRODS** > SMORBROD
**SMORE** *same as* > SMOOR
**SMORED** > SMORE
**SMORES** > SMORE
**SMORING** > SMORE
**SMORZANDO** *adv* musical instruction meaning fading away gradually
**SMORZATO** *same as* > SMORZANDO
**SMOTE** > SMITE
**SMOTHER** *vb* suffocate or stifle ▷ *n* anything, such as a cloud of smoke, that stifles

**SMOTHERED** > SMOTHER
**SMOTHERER** > SMOTHER
**SMOTHERS** > SMOTHER
**SMOTHERY** > SMOTHER
**SMOUCH** *vb* kiss
**SMOUCHED** > SMOUCH
**SMOUCHES** > SMOUCH
**SMOUCHING** > SMOUCH
**SMOULDER** *vb* burn slowly with smoke but no flame ▷ *n* dense smoke, as from a smouldering fire
**SMOULDERS** > SMOULDER
**SMOULDRY** *adj* smouldering
**SMOUSE** *vb* South African word meaning peddle
**SMOUSED** > SMOUSE
**SMOUSER** > SMOUSE
**SMOUSERS** > SMOUSE
**SMOUSES** > SMOUSE
**SMOUSING** > SMOUSE
**SMOUT** *n* child or undersized person ▷ *vb* creep or sneak
**SMOUTED** > SMOUT
**SMOUTING** > SMOUT
**SMOUTS** > SMOUT
**SMOWT** *same as* > SMOUT
**SMOWTS** > SMOWT
**SMOYLE** *same as* > SMILE
**SMOYLED** > SMOYLE
**SMOYLES** > SMOYLE
**SMOYLING** > SMOYLE
**SMRITI** *n* class of Hindu sacred literature derived from the Vedas
**SMRITIS** > SMRITI
**SMUDGE** *vb* make or become smeared or soiled ▷ *n* dirty mark
**SMUDGED** > SMUDGE
**SMUDGEDLY** > SMUDGE
**SMUDGER** > SMUDGE
**SMUDGERS** > SMUDGE
**SMUDGES** > SMUDGE
**SMUDGIER** > SMUDGY
**SMUDGIEST** > SMUDGY
**SMUDGILY** > SMUDGY
**SMUDGING** > SMUDGE
**SMUDGY** *adj* smeared, blurred, or soiled, or likely to become so
**SMUG** *adj* self-satisfied ▷ *vb* make neat
**SMUGGED** > SMUG
**SMUGGER** > SMUG
**SMUGGERY** *n* condition or an instance of being smug
**SMUGGEST** > SMUG
**SMUGGING** > SMUG
**SMUGGLE** *vb* import or export (goods) secretly and illegally
**SMUGGLED** > SMUGGLE
**SMUGGLER** > SMUGGLE
**SMUGGLERS** > SMUGGLE
**SMUGGLES** > SMUGGLE
**SMUGGLING** > SMUGGLE
**SMUGLY** > SMUG
**SMUGNESS** > SMUG
**SMUGS** > SMUG
**SMUR** *same as* > SMIR
**SMURFING** *n* intentionally flooding and

overwhelming a computer network with messages by means of a program
**SMURFINGS** > SMURFING
**SMURRED** > SMUR
**SMURRIER** > SMUR
**SMURRIEST** > SMUR
**SMURRING** > SMUR
**SMURRY** > SMUR
**SMURS** > SMUR
**SMUSH** *vb* crush
**SMUSHED** > SMUSH
**SMUSHES** > SMUSH
**SMUSHING** > SMUSH
**SMUT** *n* obscene jokes, pictures, etc ▷ *vb* mark or become marked or smudged, as with soot
**SMUTCH** *vb* smudge ▷ *n* mark
**SMUTCHED** > SMUTCH
**SMUTCHES** > SMUTCH
**SMUTCHIER** > SMUTCH
**SMUTCHING** > SMUTCH
**SMUTCHY** > SMUTCH
**SMUTS** > SMUT
**SMUTTED** > SMUT
**SMUTTIER** > SMUT
**SMUTTIEST** > SMUT
**SMUTTILY** > SMUT
**SMUTTING** > SMUT
**SMUTTY** > SMUT
**SMYTRIE** *n* Scots word meaning collection
**SMYTRIES** > SMYTRIE
**SNAB** *same as* > SNOB
**SNABBLE** *same as* > SNAFFLE
**SNABBLED** > SNABBLE
**SNABBLES** > SNABBLE
**SNABBLING** > SNABBLE
**SNABS** > SNAB
**SNACK** *n* light quick meal ▷ *vb* eat a snack
**SNACKED** > SNACK
**SNACKER** > SNACK
**SNACKERS** > SNACK
**SNACKETTE** *n* snack bar
**SNACKING** > SNACK
**SNACKS** > SNACK
**SNAFFLE** *n* jointed bit for a horse ▷ *vb* steal
**SNAFFLED** > SNAFFLE
**SNAFFLES** > SNAFFLE
**SNAFFLING** > SNAFFLE
**SNAFU** *n* confusion or chaos regarded as the normal state ▷ *adj* confused or muddled up, as usual ▷ *vb* throw into chaos
**SNAFUED** > SNAFU
**SNAFUING** > SNAFU
**SNAFUS** > SNAFU
**SNAG** *n* difficulty or disadvantage ▷ *vb* catch or tear on a point
**SNAGGED** > SNAG
**SNAGGIER** > SNAGGY
**SNAGGIEST** > SNAGGY
**SNAGGING** > SNAG
**SNAGGY** *adj* having sharp protuberances
**SNAGLIKE** > SNAG
**SNAGS** > SNAG
**SNAIL** *n* slow-moving

mollusc with a spiral shell ▷ *vb* move slowly
**SNAILED** > SNAIL
**SNAILERY** *n* place where snails are bred
**SNAILFISH** *n* sea snail
**SNAILIER** > SNAIL
**SNAILIEST** > SNAIL
**SNAILING** > SNAIL
**SNAILLIKE** *adj* resembling a snail
**SNAILS** > SNAIL
**SNAILY** > SNAIL
**SNAKE** *n* long thin scaly limbless reptile ▷ *vb* move in a winding course like a snake
**SNAKEBIRD** *n* darter bird
**SNAKEBIT** *adj* bitten by snake
**SNAKEBITE** *n* bite of a snake
**SNAKED** > SNAKE
**SNAKEFISH** *n* fish resembling snake
**SNAKEHEAD** *n* Chinese criminal involved in the illegal transport of Chinese citizens to other parts of the world
**SNAKELIKE** > SNAKE
**SNAKEPIT** *n* pit filled with snakes
**SNAKEPITS** > SNAKEPIT
**SNAKEROOT** *n* any of various North American plants
**SNAKES** > SNAKE
**SNAKESKIN** *n* skin of a snake, esp when made into a leather valued for handbags, shoes, etc
**SNAKEWEED** *same as* > SNAKEROOT
**SNAKEWISE** *adv* in snakelike way
**SNAKEWOOD** *n* South American tree
**SNAKEY** *same as* > SNAKY
**SNAKIER** > SNAKY
**SNAKIEST** > SNAKY
**SNAKILY** > SNAKY
**SNAKINESS** > SNAKY
**SNAKING** > SNAKE
**SNAKISH** > SNAKE
**SNAKY** *adj* twisted or winding
**SNAP** *vb* break suddenly ▷ *n* act or sound of snapping ▷ *adj* made on the spur of the moment ▷ *adv* with a snap
**SNAPBACK** *n* sudden rebound or change in direction
**SNAPBACKS** > SNAPBACK
**SNAPHANCE** *n* flintlock gun
**SNAPLESS** > SNAP
**SNAPLINK** *n* metal link used in mountaineering
**SNAPLINKS** > SNAPLINK
**SNAPPABLE** > SNAP
**SNAPPED** > SNAP
**SNAPPER** *n* food fish of

Australia and New Zealand
▷ vb stumble
**SNAPPERED** > SNAPPER
**SNAPPERS** > SNAPPER
**SNAPPIER** > SNAPPY
**SNAPPIEST** > SNAPPY
**SNAPPILY** > SNAPPY
**SNAPPING** > SNAP
**SNAPPINGS** > SNAP
**SNAPPISH** *same as* > SNAPPY
**SNAPPY** *adj* irritable
**SNAPS** > SNAP
**SNAPSHOT** *n* informal
photograph
**SNAPSHOTS** > SNAPSHOT
**SNAPTIN** *n* container for
food
**SNAPTINS** > SNAPTIN
**SNAPWEED** *n* impatiens
**SNAPWEEDS** > SNAPWEED
**SNAR** *same as* > SNARL
**SNARE** *n* trap with a noose
▷ vb catch in or as if in a
snare
**SNARED** > SNARE
**SNARELESS** > SNARE
**SNARER** > SNARE
**SNARERS** > SNARE
**SNARES** > SNARE
**SNARF** *vb* eat or drink
greedily
**SNARFED** > SNARF
**SNARFING** > SNARF
**SNARFS** > SNARF
**SNARIER** > SNARE
**SNARIEST** > SNARE
**SNARING** > SNARE
**SNARINGS** > SNARE
**SNARK** *n* imaginary
creature in Lewis Carroll's
poetry
**SNARKIER** > SNARKY
**SNARKIEST** > SNARKY
**SNARKILY** > SNARKY
**SNARKS** > SNARK
**SNARKY** *adj* unpleasant and
scornful
**SNARL** *vb* (of an animal)
growl with bared teeth ▷ n
act or sound of snarling
**SNARLED** > SNARL
**SNARLER** > SNARL
**SNARLERS** > SNARL
**SNARLIER** > SNARL
**SNARLIEST** > SNARL
**SNARLING** > SNARL
**SNARLINGS** > SNARL
**SNARLS** > SNARL
**SNARLY** > SNARL
**SNARRED** > SNAR
**SNARRING** > SNAR
**SNARS** > SNAR
**SNARY** > SNARE
**SNASH** *vb* Scots word
meaning speak cheekily
**SNASHED** > SNASH
**SNASHES** > SNASH
**SNASHING** > SNASH
**SNASTE** *n* candle wick
**SNASTES** > SNASTE
**SNATCH** *vb* seize or try
to seize suddenly ▷ n
snatching
**SNATCHED** > SNATCH

**SNATCHER** > SNATCH
**SNATCHERS** > SNATCH
**SNATCHES** > SNATCH
**SNATCHIER** > SNATCHY
**SNATCHILY** > SNATCHY
**SNATCHING** > SNATCH
**SNATCHY** *adj* disconnected
or spasmodic
**SNATH** *n* handle of a scythe
**SNATHE** *same as* > SNATH
**SNATHES** > SNATHE
**SNATHS** > SNATH
**SNAW** *Scots variant of* > SNOW
**SNAWED** > SNAW
**SNAWING** > SNAW
**SNAWS** > SNAW
**SNAZZIER** > SNAZZY
**SNAZZIEST** > SNAZZY
**SNAZZILY** > SNAZZY
**SNAZZY** *adj* stylish and
flashy
**SNEAD** *n* scythe handle
**SNEADS** > SNEAD
**SNEAK** *vb* move furtively
▷ n cowardly or
underhand person ▷ adj
without warning
**SNEAKED** > SNEAK
**SNEAKER** *n* soft shoe
**SNEAKERED** *adj* wearing
sneakers
**SNEAKERS** *pl n* canvas
shoes with rubber soles
**SNEAKUP** *n* sneaky person
**SNEAKUPS** > SNEAKUP
**SNEAKIER** > SNEAK
**SNEAKIEST** > SNEAK
**SNEAKILY** > SNEAK
**SNEAKING** *adj* slight but
persistent
**SNEAKISH** *adj* typical of
sneak
**SNEAKS** > SNEAK
**SNEAKSBY** *n* sneak
**SNEAKY** > SNEAK
**SNEAP** *vb* nip
**SNEAPED** > SNEAP
**SNEAPING** > SNEAP
**SNEAPS** > SNEAP
**SNEATH** *same as* > SNATH
**SNEATHS** > SNEATH
**SNEB** *same as* > SNIB
**SNEBBE** *same as* > SNUB
**SNEBBED** > SNEB
**SNEBBES** > SNEBBE
**SNEBBING** > SNEB
**SNEBS** > SNEB
**SNECK** *n* small squared
stone used in a rubble
wall to fill spaces between
stones ▷ vb fasten (a
latch)
**SNECKED** > SNECK
**SNECKING** > SNECK
**SNECKS** > SNECK
**SNED** *vb* prune or trim
**SNEDDED** > SNED
**SNEDDING** > SNED
**SNEDS** > SNED
**SNEE** *vb* cut
**SNEED** > SNEE
**SNEEING** > SNEE
**SNEER** *n* contemptuous
expression or remark ▷ vb

show contempt by a sneer
**SNEERED** > SNEER
**SNEERER** > SNEER
**SNEERERS** > SNEER
**SNEERFUL** > SNEER
**SNEERIER** > SNEERY
**SNEERIEST** > SNEERY
**SNEERING** > SNEER
**SNEERINGS** > SNEER
**SNEERS** > SNEER
**SNEERY** *adj* contemptuous
or scornful
**SNEES** > SNEE
**SNEESH** *n* Scots word
meaning pinch of snuff
**SNEESHAN** *n* Scots word
meaning pinch of snuff
**SNEESHANS** > SNEESHAN
**SNEESHES** > SNEESH
**SNEESHIN** *same
as* > SNEESHAN
**SNEESHING** *same
as* > SNEESHAN
**SNEESHINS** > SNEESHIN
**SNEEZE** *vb* expel air
from the nose suddenly,
involuntarily, and noisily
▷ n act or sound of
sneezing
**SNEEZED** > SNEEZE
**SNEEZER** > SNEEZE
**SNEEZERS** > SNEEZE
**SNEEZES** > SNEEZE
**SNEEZIER** > SNEEZE
**SNEEZIEST** > SNEEZE
**SNEEZING** > SNEEZE
**SNEEZINGS** > SNEEZE
**SNEEZY** > SNEEZE
**SNELL** *adj* biting ▷ vb
attach hook to fishing line
**SNELLED** > SNELL
**SNELLER** > SNELL
**SNELLEST** > SNELL
**SNELLING** > SNELL
**SNELLS** > SNELL
**SNELLY** > SNELL
**SNIB** *n* catch of a door
or window ▷ vb bolt or
fasten (a door)
**SNIBBED** > SNIB
**SNIBBING** > SNIB
**SNIBS** > SNIB
**SNICK** *n* (make) a small
cut or notch ▷ vb make
a small cut or notch in
(something)
**SNICKED** > SNICK
**SNICKER** *same as* > SNIGGER
**SNICKERED** > SNICKER
**SNICKERER** > SNICKER
**SNICKERS** > SNICKER
**SNICKERY** > SNICKER
**SNICKET** *n* passageway
between walls or fences
**SNICKETS** > SNICKET
**SNICKING** > SNICK
**SNICKS** > SNICK
**SNIDE** *adj* critical in an
unfair and nasty way ▷ n
sham jewellery ▷ vb fill
or load
**SNIDELY** > SNIDE
**SNIDENESS** > SNIDE
**SNIDER** > SNIDE

**SNIDES** > SNIDE
**SNIDEST** > SNIDE
**SNIDEY** *same as* > SNIDE
**SNIDIER** > SNIDEY
**SNIDIEST** > SNIDEY
**SNIES** > SNY
**SNIFF** *vb* inhale through
the nose in short audible
breaths ▷ n act or sound
of sniffing
**SNIFFABLE** > SNIFF
**SNIFFED** > SNIFF
**SNIFFER** *n* device for
detecting hidden
substances such as drugs
or explosives, esp by their
odour
**SNIFFERS** > SNIFFER
**SNIFFIER** > SNIFFY
**SNIFFIEST** > SNIFFY
**SNIFFILY** > SNIFFY
**SNIFFING** > SNIFF
**SNIFFINGS** > SNIFF
**SNIFFISH** *adj* disdainful
**SNIFFLE** *vb* sniff
repeatedly, as when
suffering from a cold ▷ n
slight cold
**SNIFFLED** > SNIFFLE
**SNIFFLER** > SNIFFLE
**SNIFFLERS** > SNIFFLE
**SNIFFLES** *pl n the.* a cold in
the head
**SNIFFLIER** > SNIFFLE
**SNIFFLING** > SNIFFLE
**SNIFFLY** > SNIFFLE
**SNIFFS** > SNIFF
**SNIFFY** *adj* contemptuous
or scornful
**SNIFT** *same as* > SNIFF
**SNIFTED** > SNIFT
**SNIFTER** *n* small quantity
of alcoholic drink ▷ vb
sniff
**SNIFTERED** > SNIFTER
**SNIFTERS** > SNIFTER
**SNIFTIER** > SNIFTY
**SNIFTIEST** > SNIFTY
**SNIFTING** > SNIFT
**SNIFTS** > SNIFT
**SNIFTY** *adj* slang word
meaning excellent
**SNIG** *vb* drag (a felled log)
by a chain or cable
**SNIGGED** > SNIG
**SNIGGER** *n* a sly laugh ▷ vb
laugh slyly
**SNIGGERED** > SNIGGER
**SNIGGERER** > SNIGGER
**SNIGGERS** > SNIGGER
**SNIGGING** > SNIG
**SNIGGLE** *vb* fish for eels by
dangling or thrusting a
baited hook into cavities
▷ n baited hook used for
sniggling eels
**SNIGGLED** > SNIGGLE
**SNIGGLER** > SNIGGLE
**SNIGGLERS** > SNIGGLE
**SNIGGLES** > SNIGGLE
**SNIGGLING** > SNIGGLE
**SNIGLET** *n* invented word
**SNIGLETS** > SNIGLET
**SNIGS** > SNIG

**SNIP** *vb* cut in small quick strokes with scissors or shears ▷ *n* bargain ▷ *interj* representation of the sound of scissors or shears closing
**SNIPE** *n* wading bird with a long straight bill ▷ *vb* shoot at (a person) from cover
**SNIPED** > SNIPE
**SNIPEFISH** *n* any teleost fish of the family *Macrorhamphosidae*
**SNIPELIKE** > SNIPE
**SNIPER** *n* person who shoots at someone from cover
**SNIPERS** > SNIPER
**SNIPES** > SNIPE
**SNIPIER** > SNIPY
**SNIPIEST** > SNIPY
**SNIPING** > SNIPE
**SNIPINGS** > SNIPE
**SNIPPED** > SNIP
**SNIPPER** > SNIP
**SNIPPERS** > SNIP
**SNIPPET** *n* small piece
**SNIPPETS** > SNIPPET
**SNIPPETY** > SNIPPET
**SNIPPIER** > SNIPPY
**SNIPPIEST** > SNIPPY
**SNIPPILY** > SNIPPY
**SNIPPING** > SNIP
**SNIPPINGS** > SNIP
**SNIPPY** *adj* scrappy
**SNIPS** > SNIP
**SNIPY** *adj* like a snipe
**SNIRT** *n* Scots word meaning suppressed laugh
**SNIRTLE** *vb* Scots word meaning snicker
**SNIRTLED** > SNIRTLE
**SNIRTLES** > SNIRTLE
**SNIRTLING** > SNIRTLE
**SNIRTS** > SNIRT
**SNIT** *n* fit of temper
**SNITCH** *vb* act as an informer ▷ *n* informer
**SNITCHED** > SNITCH
**SNITCHER** > SNITCH
**SNITCHERS** > SNITCH
**SNITCHES** > SNITCH
**SNITCHIER** > SNITCHY
**SNITCHING** > SNITCH
**SNITCHY** *adj* bad-tempered or irritable
**SNITS** > SNIT
**SNIVEL** *vb* cry in a whining way ▷ *n* act of snivelling
**SNIVELED** > SNIVEL
**SNIVELER** > SNIVEL
**SNIVELERS** > SNIVEL
**SNIVELING** > SNIVEL
**SNIVELLED** > SNIVEL
**SNIVELLER** > SNIVEL
**SNIVELLY** > SNIVEL
**SNIVELS** > SNIVEL
**SNOB** *n* person who judges others by social rank
**SNOBBERY** > SNOB
**SNOBBIER** > SNOB
**SNOBBIEST** > SNOB
**SNOBBILY** > SNOB

**SNOBBISH** > SNOB
**SNOBBISM** > SNOB
**SNOBBISMS** > SNOB
**SNOBBY** > SNOB
**SNOBLING** *n* little snob
**SNOBLINGS** > SNOBLING
**SNOBS** > SNOB
**SNOD** *vb* Scots word meaning make tidy
**SNODDED** > SNOD
**SNODDER** > SNOD
**SNODDEST** > SNOD
**SNODDING** > SNOD
**SNODDIT** > SNOD
**SNODS** > SNOD
**SNOEK** *n* edible marine fish
**SNOEKS** > SNOEK
**SNOEP** *adj* mean or tight-fisted
**SNOG** *vb* kiss and cuddle ▷ *n* act of kissing and cuddling
**SNOGGED** > SNOG
**SNOGGING** > SNOG
**SNOGS** > SNOG
**SNOKE** *same as* > SNOOK
**SNOKED** > SNOKE
**SNOKES** > SNOKE
**SNOKING** > SNOKE
**SNOOD** *n* pouch, often of net, loosely holding a woman's hair at the back ▷ *vb* hold (the hair) in a snood
**SNOODED** > SNOOD
**SNOODING** > SNOOD
**SNOODS** > SNOOD
**SNOOK** *n* any of several large game fishes ▷ *vb* lurk
**SNOOKED** > SNOOK
**SNOOKER** *n* game played on a billiard table ▷ *vb* leave (a snooker opponent) in a position such that another ball blocks the target ball
**SNOOKERED** > SNOOKER
**SNOOKERS** > SNOOKER
**SNOOKING** > SNOOK
**SNOOKS** > SNOOK
**SNOOL** *vb* Scots word meaning dominate
**SNOOLED** > SNOOL
**SNOOLING** > SNOOL
**SNOOLS** > SNOOL
**SNOOP** *vb* pry ▷ *n* snooping
**SNOOPED** > SNOOP
**SNOOPER** *n* person who snoops
**SNOOPERS** > SNOOPER
**SNOOPIER** > SNOOP
**SNOOPIEST** > SNOOP
**SNOOPILY** > SNOOP
**SNOOPING** > SNOOP
**SNOOPS** > SNOOP
**SNOOPY** > SNOOP
**SNOOT** *n* nose ▷ *vb* look contemptuously at
**SNOOTED** > SNOOT
**SNOOTFUL** *n* enough alcohol to make someone drunk
**SNOOTFULS** > SNOOTFUL
**SNOOTIER** > SNOOTY
**SNOOTIEST** > SNOOTY
**SNOOTILY** > SNOOTY

**SNOOTING** > SNOOT
**SNOOTS** > SNOOT
**SNOOTY** *adj* haughty
**SNOOZE** *vb* take a brief light sleep ▷ *n* brief light sleep
**SNOOZED** > SNOOZE
**SNOOZER** > SNOOZE
**SNOOZERS** > SNOOZE
**SNOOZES** > SNOOZE
**SNOOZIER** > SNOOZE
**SNOOZIEST** > SNOOZE
**SNOOZING** > SNOOZE
**SNOOZLE** *vb* cuddle and sleep
**SNOOZLED** > SNOOZLE
**SNOOZLES** > SNOOZLE
**SNOOZLING** > SNOOZLE
**SNOOZY** > SNOOZE
**SNORE** *vb* make snorting sounds while sleeping ▷ *n* sound of snoring
**SNORED** > SNORE
**SNORER** > SNORE
**SNORERS** > SNORE
**SNORES** > SNORE
**SNORING** > SNORE
**SNORINGS** > SNORE
**SNORKEL** *n* tube allowing a swimmer to breathe while face down on the surface of the water ▷ *vb* swim using a snorkel
**SNORKELED** > SNORKEL
**SNORKELER** > SNORKEL
**SNORKELS** > SNORKEL
**SNORT** *vb* exhale noisily through the nostrils ▷ *n* act or sound of snorting
**SNORTED** > SNORT
**SNORTER** *n* person or animal that snorts
**SNORTERS** > SNORTER
**SNORTIER** > SNORT
**SNORTIEST** > SNORT
**SNORTING** > SNORT
**SNORTINGS** > SNORT
**SNORTS** > SNORT
**SNORTY** > SNORT
**SNOT** *n* mucus from the nose ▷ *vb* blow one's nose
**SNOTS** > SNOT
**SNOTTED** > SNOT
**SNOTTER** *vb* breathe through obstructed nostrils
**SNOTTERED** > SNOTTER
**SNOTTERS** > SNOTTER
**SNOTTERY** *n* snot
**SNOTTIE** *n* midshipman
**SNOTTIER** > SNOTTY
**SNOTTIES** > SNOTTY
**SNOTTIEST** > SNOTTY
**SNOTTILY** > SNOTTY
**SNOTTING** > SNOT
**SNOTTY** *adj* covered with mucus from the nose
**SNOUT** *n* animal's projecting nose and jaws ▷ *vb* have or give a snout
**SNOUTED** > SNOUT
**SNOUTIER** > SNOUT
**SNOUTIEST** > SNOUT
**SNOUTING** > SNOUT
**SNOUTISH** > SNOUT

**SNOUTLESS** > SNOUT
**SNOUTLIKE** > SNOUT
**SNOUTS** > SNOUT
**SNOUTY** > SNOUT
**SNOW** *n* frozen vapour falling from the sky in flakes ▷ *vb* fall as or like snow
**SNOWBALL** *n* snow pressed into a ball for throwing ▷ *vb* increase rapidly
**SNOWBALLS** > SNOWBALL
**SNOWBANK** *n* bank of snow
**SNOWBANKS** > SNOWBANK
**SNOWBELL** *n* Asian shrub
**SNOWBELLS** > SNOWBELL
**SNOWBELT** *n* northern states of USA
**SNOWBELTS** > SNOWBELT
**SNOWBERRY** *n* shrub grown for its white berries
**SNOWBIRD** *n* person addicted to cocaine, or sometimes heroin
**SNOWBIRDS** > SNOWBIRD
**SNOWBLINK** *n* whitish glare in the sky reflected from snow
**SNOWBOARD** *n* board on which a person stands to slide across the snow
**SNOWBOOT** *n* boot for walking in snow
**SNOWBOOTS** > SNOWBOOT
**SNOWBOUND** *adj* shut in by snow
**SNOWBRUSH** *n* brush for clearing snow
**SNOWBUSH** *n* North American plant
**SNOWCAP** *n* cap of snow on top of a mountain
**SNOWCAPS** > SNOWCAP
**SNOWCAT** *n* tracked vehicle for travelling over snow
**SNOWCATS** > SNOWCAT
**SNOWDRIFT** *n* bank of deep snow
**SNOWDROP** *n* small white bell-shaped spring flower
**SNOWDROPS** > SNOWDROP
**SNOWED** *adj* under the influence of narcotic drugs
**SNOWFALL** *n* fall of snow
**SNOWFALLS** > SNOWFALL
**SNOWFIELD** *n* large area of permanent snow
**SNOWFLAKE** *n* single crystal of snow
**SNOWFLECK** *n* snow bunting
**SNOWFLICK** *same as* > SNOWFLECK
**SNOWIER** > SNOWY
**SNOWIEST** > SNOWY
**SNOWILY** > SNOWY
**SNOWINESS** > SNOWY
**SNOWING** > SNOW
**SNOWISH** *adj* like snow
**SNOWK** *same as* > SNOOK
**SNOWKED** > SNOWK
**SNOWKING** > SNOWK
**SNOWKS** > SNOWK
**SNOWLAND** *n* area where

snow lies
**SNOWLANDS** >SNOWLAND
**SNOWLESS** >SNOW
**SNOWLIKE** >SNOW
**SNOWLINE** *n* limit of
permanent snow
**SNOWLINES** >SNOWLINE
**SNOWMAKER** *n* machine
making artificial snow
**SNOWMAN** *n* figure shaped
out of snow
**SNOWMELT** *n* melting of
snow in spring
**SNOWMELTS** >SNOWMELT
**SNOWMEN** >SNOWMAN
**SNOWMOLD** *n* fungus
growing on grass under
snow
**SNOWMOLDS** >SNOWMOLD
**SNOWPACK** *n* body of hard-
packed snow
**SNOWPACKS** >SNOWPACK
**SNOWPLOW** *n* implement or
vehicle for clearing snow
away
**SNOWPLOWS** >SNOWPLOW
**SNOWS** >SNOW
**SNOWSCAPE** *n* snow-
covered landscape
**SNOWSHED** *n* shelter built
over an exposed section of
railway line to prevent its
blockage by snow
**SNOWSHEDS** >SNOWSHED
**SNOWSHOE** *n* racket-shaped
frame with a network of
thongs stretched across it,
worn on the feet to make
walking on snow less
difficult ▷ *vb* walk or go
using snowshoes
**SNOWSHOED** >SNOWSHOE
**SNOWSHOER** >SNOWSHOE
**SNOWSHOES** >SNOWSHOE
**SNOWSLIDE** *n* snow
avalanche
**SNOWSLIP** *n* small snow
avalanche
**SNOWSLIPS** >SNOWSLIP
**SNOWSTORM** *n* storm with
heavy snow
**SNOWSUIT** *n* one-piece
winter outer garment for
child
**SNOWSUITS** >SNOWSUIT
**SNOWY** *adj* covered with or
abounding in snow
**SNUB** *vb* insult deliberately
▷ *n* deliberate insult ▷ *adj*
(of a nose) short and blunt
**SNUBBE** *n* stub
**SNUBBED** >SNUB
**SNUBBER** >SNUB
**SNUBBERS** >SNUB
**SNUBBES** >SNUBBE
**SNUBBIER** >SNUB
**SNUBBIEST** >SNUB
**SNUBBING** >SNUB
**SNUBBINGS** >SNUB
**SNUBBISH** >SNUB
**SNUBBY** >SNUB
**SNUBNESS** >SNUB
**SNUBS** >SNUB
**SNUCK** *past tense and past*

*participle of* >SNEAK
**SNUDGE** *vb* be miserly
**SNUDGED** >SNUDGE
**SNUDGES** >SNUDGE
**SNUDGING** >SNUDGE
**SNUFF** *n* powdered tobacco
for sniffing up the nostrils
▷ *vb* extinguish (a candle)
**SNUFFBOX** *n* small
container for holding snuff
**SNUFFED** >SNUFF
**SNUFFER** >SNUFF
**SNUFFERS** >SNUFF
**SNUFFIER** >SNUFFY
**SNUFFIEST** >SNUFFY
**SNUFFILY** >SNUFFY
**SNUFFING** >SNUFF
**SNUFFINGS** >SNUFF
**SNUFFLE** *vb* breathe noisily
or with difficulty ▷ *n* act
or the sound of snuffling
**SNUFFLED** >SNUFFLE
**SNUFFLER** >SNUFFLE
**SNUFFLERS** >SNUFFLE
**SNUFFLES** *same*
*as* >SNIFFLES
**SNUFFLIER** >SNUFFLE
**SNUFFLING** >SNUFFLE
**SNUFFLY** >SNUFFLE
**SNUFFS** >SNUFF
**SNUFFY** *adj* of, relating to,
or resembling snuff
**SNUG** *adj* warm and
comfortable ▷ *n* (in
Britain and Ireland) small
room in a pub ▷ *vb* make
or become comfortable
and warm
**SNUGGED** >SNUG
**SNUGGER** >SNUG
**SNUGGERIE** *n* small bar in
pub
**SNUGGERY** *n* cosy and
comfortable place or room
**SNUGGEST** >SNUG
**SNUGGIES** *pl n* specially
warm underwear
**SNUGGING** >SNUG
**SNUGGLE** *vb* nestle into
a person or thing for
warmth or from affection
▷ *n* act of snuggling
**SNUGGLED** >SNUGGLE
**SNUGGLES** >SNUGGLE
**SNUGGLING** >SNUGGLE
**SNUGLY** >SNUG
**SNUGNESS** >SNUG
**SNUGS** >SNUG
**SNUSH** *vb* take snuff
**SNUSHED** >SNUSH
**SNUSHES** >SNUSH
**SNUSHING** >SNUSH
**SNUZZLE** *vb* root in ground
**SNUZZLED** >SNUZZLE
**SNUZZLES** >SNUZZLE
**SNUZZLING** >SNUZZLE
**SNY** *same as* >SNYE
**SNYE** *n* side channel of a
river
**SNYES** >SNYE
**SO** *adv* such an extent
▷ *interj* exclamation of
surprise, triumph, or
realization

**SOAK** *vb* make wet ▷ *n*
soaking
**SOAKAGE** *n* process or
a period in which a
permeable substance is
soaked in a liquid
**SOAKAGES** >SOAKAGE
**SOAKAWAY** *n* pit filled with
rubble, etc, into which rain
or waste water drains
**SOAKAWAYS** >SOAKAWAY
**SOAKED** >SOAK
**SOAKEN** >SOAK
**SOAKER** >SOAK
**SOAKERS** >SOAK
**SOAKING** >SOAK
**SOAKINGLY** >SOAK
**SOAKINGS** >SOAK
**SOAKS** >SOAK
**SOAP** *n* compound of alkali
and fat, used with water
as a cleaning agent ▷ *vb*
apply soap to
**SOAPBARK** *n* W South
American rosaceous tree
**SOAPBARKS** >SOAPBARK
**SOAPBERRY** *n* any of
various chiefly tropical
American sapindaceous
trees
**SOAPBOX** *n* crate used as
a platform for speech-
making ▷ *vb* deliver a
speech from a soapbox
**SOAPBOXED** >SOAPBOX
**SOAPBOXES** >SOAPBOX
**SOAPED** >SOAP
**SOAPER** *n* soap opera
**SOAPERS** >SOAPER
**SOAPIE** *n* soap opera
**SOAPIER** >SOAPY
**SOAPIES** >SOAPIE
**SOAPIEST** >SOAPY
**SOAPILY** >SOAPY
**SOAPINESS** >SOAPY
**SOAPING** >SOAP
**SOAPLAND** *n* Japanese
massage parlour and
brothel
**SOAPLANDS** >SOAPLAND
**SOAPLESS** >SOAP
**SOAPLIKE** >SOAP
**SOAPROOT** *n* plant with
roots used as soap
substitute
**SOAPROOTS** >SOAPROOT
**SOAPS** >SOAP
**SOAPSTONE** *n* soft mineral
used for making table tops
and ornaments
**SOAPSUDS** *pl n* foam or
lather produced when
soap is mixed with water
**SOAPSUDSY** >SOAPSUDS
**SOAPWORT** *n* Eurasian plant
with clusters of fragrant
pink or white flowers
**SOAPWORTS** >SOAPWORT
**SOAPY** *adj* covered with
soap
**SOAR** *vb* rise or fly upwards
▷ *n* act of soaring
**SOARAWAY** *adj* exceedingly
successful

**SOARE** *n* young hawk
**SOARED** >SOAR
**SOARER** >SOAR
**SOARERS** >SOAR
**SOARES** >SOARE
**SOARING** >SOAR
**SOARINGLY** >SOAR
**SOARINGS** >SOAR
**SOARS** >SOAR
**SOAVE** *n* dry white Italian
wine
**SOAVES** >SOAVE
**SOB** *vb* weep with
convulsive gasps ▷ *n* act
or sound of sobbing
**SOBA** *n* (in Japanese
cookery) noodles made
from buckwheat flour
**SOBAS** >SOBA
**SOBBED** >SOB
**SOBBER** >SOB
**SOBBERS** >SOB
**SOBBING** >SOB
**SOBBINGLY** >SOB
**SOBBINGS** >SOB
**SOBEIT** *conj* provided that
**SOBER** *adj* not drunk ▷ *vb*
make or become sober
**SOBERED** >SOBER
**SOBERER** >SOBER
**SOBEREST** >SOBER
**SOBERING** >SOBER
**SOBERISE** *same*
*as* >SOBERIZE
**SOBERISED** >SOBERISE
**SOBERISES** >SOBERISE
**SOBERIZE** *vb* make sober
**SOBERIZED** >SOBERIZE
**SOBERIZES** >SOBERIZE
**SOBERLY** >SOBER
**SOBERNESS** >SOBER
**SOBERS** >SOBER
**SOBFUL** *adj* tearful
**SOBOLE** *n* creeping
underground stem that
produces roots and buds
**SOBOLES** >SOBOLE
**SOBRIETY** *n* state of being
sober
**SOBRIQUET** *n* nickname
**SOBS** >SOB
**SOC** *n* feudal right to hold
court
**SOCA** *n* mixture of soul and
calypso music popular in
the E Caribbean
**SOCAGE** *n* tenure of land by
certain services, esp of an
agricultural nature
**SOCAGER** >SOCAGE
**SOCAGERS** >SOCAGE
**SOCAGES** >SOCAGE
**SOCAS** >SOCA
**SOCCAGE** *same as* >SOCAGE
**SOCCAGES** >SOCCAGE
**SOCCER** *n* football played
by two teams of eleven
kicking a spherical ball
**SOCCERS** >SOCCER
**SOCIABLE** *adj* friendly or
companionable ▷ *n* type
of open carriage with two
seats facing each other
**SOCIABLES** >SOCIABLE

SOCIABLY > SOCIABLE
SOCIAL adj living in a community ▷ n informal gathering
SOCIALISE same as > SOCIALIZE
SOCIALISM n political system which advocates public ownership of industries, resources, and transport
SOCIALIST n supporter or advocate of socialism ▷ adj of or relating to socialism
SOCIALITE n member of fashionable society
SOCIALITY n tendency of groups and persons to develop social links and live in communities
SOCIALIZE vb meet others socially
SOCIALLY > SOCIAL
SOCIALS > SOCIAL
SOCIATE n associate
SOCIATES > SOCIATE
SOCIATION n plant community
SOCIATIVE adj of association
SOCIETAL adj of or relating to society, esp human society or social relations
SOCIETIES > SOCIETY
SOCIETY n human beings considered as a group
SOCIOGRAM n chart showing social relationships
SOCIOLECT n language spoken by particular social class
SOCIOLOGY n study of human societies
SOCIOPATH n person with a personality disorder characterized by a tendency to commit antisocial acts without any feelings of guilt
SOCK n knitted covering for the foot ▷ vb hit hard
SOCKED > SOCK
SOCKET n hole or recess into which something fits ▷ vb furnish with or place into a socket
SOCKETED > SOCKET
SOCKETING > SOCKET
SOCKETS > SOCKET
SOCKETTE n sock not covering ankle
SOCKETTES > SOCKETTE
SOCKEYE n Pacific salmon with red flesh
SOCKEYES > SOCKEYE
SOCKING > SOCK
SOCKLESS > SOCK
SOCKMAN same as > SOCMAN
SOCKMEN > SOCKMAN
SOCKO adj excellent
SOCKS > SOCK
SOCLE another name

for > PLINTH
SOCLES > SOCLE
SOCMAN n tenant holding land by socage
SOCMEN > SOCMAN
SOCS > SOC
SOD n (piece of) turf ▷ vb cover with sods
SODA n compound of sodium
SODAIC adj containing soda
SODAIN same as > SUDDEN
SODAINE same as > SUDDEN
SODALESS > SODA
SODALIST n member of sodality
SODALISTS > SODALIST
SODALITE n blue, grey, yellow, or colourless mineral
SODALITES > SODALITE
SODALITY n religious or charitable society
SODAMIDE n white crystalline compound used as a dehydrating agent
SODAMIDES > SODAMIDE
SODAS > SODA
SODBUSTER n farmer who grows crops
SODDED > SOD
SODDEN adj soaked ▷ vb make or become sodden
SODDENED > SODDEN
SODDENING > SODDEN
SODDENLY > SODDEN
SODDENS > SODDEN
SODDIER > SODDY
SODDIES > SODDY
SODDIEST > SODDY
SODDING > SOD
SODDY adj covered with turf
SODGER dialect variant of > SOLDIER
SODGERED > SODGER
SODGERING > SODGER
SODGERS > SODGER
SODIC adj containing sodium
SODICITY > SODIC
SODIUM n silvery-white metallic element
SODIUMS > SODIUM
SODOM n person who performs sodomy
SODOMIES > SODOMY
SODOMISE same as > SODOMIZE
SODOMISED > SODOMISE
SODOMISES > SODOMISE
SODOMIST > SODOMY
SODOMISTS > SODOMY
SODOMITE n person who practises sodomy
SODOMITES > SODOMITE
SODOMITIC > SODOMY
SODOMIZE vb be the active partner in anal intercourse
SODOMIZED > SODOMIZE
SODOMIZES > SODOMIZE
SODOMS > SODOM
SODOMY n anal intercourse

SODS > SOD
SOEVER adv in any way at all
SOFA n couch
SOFABED n sofa that converts into a bed
SOFABEDS > SOFABED
SOFAR n system for determining a position at sea
SOFARS > SOFAR
SOFAS > SOFA
SOFFIONI n holes in volcano that emit steam
SOFFIT n underside of a part of a building or a structural component
SOFFITS > SOFFIT
SOFT adj easy to shape or cut ▷ adv softly ▷ vb soften
SOFTA n Muslim student of divinity and jurisprudence, esp in Turkey
SOFTAS > SOFTA
SOFTBACK n paperback
SOFTBACKS > SOFTBACK
SOFTBALL n game similar to baseball, played using a larger softer ball
SOFTBALLS > SOFTBALL
SOFTBOUND adj having paperback binding
SOFTCORE adj not explicit
SOFTCOVER n book with paper covers
SOFTED > SOFT
SOFTEN vb make or become soft or softer
SOFTENED > SOFTEN
SOFTENER n substance added to another substance to increase its softness
SOFTENERS > SOFTENER
SOFTENING > SOFTEN
SOFTENS > SOFTEN
SOFTER > SOFT
SOFTEST > SOFT
SOFTGOODS n clothing and soft furniture
SOFTHEAD n half-witted person
SOFTHEADS > SOFTHEAD
SOFTIE n person who is easily upset
SOFTIES > SOFTY
SOFTING > SOFT
SOFTISH > SOFT
SOFTLING n weakling
SOFTLINGS > SOFTLING
SOFTLY > SOFT
SOFTNESS n quality or an instance of being soft
SOFTPASTE artifical porcelain made from clay
SOFTS > SOFT
SOFTSHELL n crab or turtle with a soft shell
SOFTWARE n computer programs
SOFTWARES > SOFTWARE
SOFTWOOD n wood of a

coniferous tree
SOFTWOODS > SOFTWOOD
SOFTY same as > SOFTIE
SOG vb soak
SOGER same as > SODGER
SOGERS > SOGER
SOGGED > SOG
SOGGIER > SOGGY
SOGGIEST > SOGGY
SOGGILY > SOGGY
SOGGINESS > SOGGY
SOGGING > SOG
SOGGINGS > SOG
SOGGY adj soaked
SOGS > SOG
SOH n (in tonic sol-fa) fifth degree of any major scale
SOHO interj exclamation announcing the sighting of a hare
SOHS > SOH
SOIGNE adj well-groomed, elegant
SOIGNEE variant of > SOIGNE
SOIL n top layer of earth ▷ vb make or become dirty
SOILAGE n green fodder, esp when freshly cut and fed to livestock in a confined area
SOILAGES > SOILAGE
SOILBORNE adj carried in soil
SOILED > SOIL
SOILIER > SOIL
SOILIEST > SOIL
SOILINESS > SOIL
SOILING > SOIL
SOILINGS > SOIL
SOILLESS > SOIL
SOILS > SOIL
SOILURE n act of soiling or the state of being soiled
SOILURES > SOILURE
SOILY > SOIL
SOIREE n evening party or gathering
SOIREES > SOIREE
SOJA same as > SOYA
SOJAS > SOJA
SOJOURN n temporary stay ▷ vb stay temporarily
SOJOURNED > SOJOURN
SOJOURNER > SOJOURN
SOJOURNS > SOJOURN
SOKAH same as > SOCA
SOKAHS > SOKAH
SOKAIYA n Japanese extortionist
SOKE n right to hold a local court
SOKEMAN same as > SOCMAN
SOKEMANRY n feudal tenure by socage
SOKEMEN > SOKEMAN
SOKEN n feudal district
SOKENS > SOKEN
SOKES > SOKE
SOKOL n Czech gymnastic association
SOKOLS > SOKOL
SOL n liquid colloidal solution
SOLA > SOLUM

**SOLACE** vb comfort in distress ▷ n comfort in misery or disappointment
**SOLACED** > SOLACE
**SOLACER** > SOLACE
**SOLACERS** > SOLACE
**SOLACES** > SOLACE
**SOLACING** > SOLACE
**SOLACIOUS** adj providing solace
**SOLAH** n Indian plant
**SOLAHS** > SOLAH
**SOLAN** archaic name for > GANNET
**SOLAND** n solan goose
**SOLANDER** n box for botanical specimens, maps, etc, made in the form of a book, the front cover being the lid
**SOLANDERS** > SOLANDER
**SOLANDS** > SOLAND
**SOLANIN** same as > SOLANINE
**SOLANINE** n poisonous alkaloid found in various solanaceous plants
**SOLANINES** > SOLANINE
**SOLANINS** > SOLANIN
**SOLANO** n hot wind in Spain
**SOLANOS** > SOLANO
**SOLANS** > SOLAN
**SOLANUM** n any plant of the mainly tropical genus that includes the potato, aubergine, and certain nightshades
**SOLANUMS** > SOLANUM
**SOLAR** adj of the sun
**SOLARIA** > SOLARIUM
**SOLARISE** same as > SOLARIZE
**SOLARISED** > SOLARISE
**SOLARISES** > SOLARISE
**SOLARISM** n explanation of myths in terms of the movements and influence of the sun
**SOLARISMS** > SOLARISM
**SOLARIST** > SOLARISM
**SOLARISTS** > SOLARISM
**SOLARIUM** n place with beds and ultraviolet lights used for acquiring an artificial suntan
**SOLARIUMS** > SOLARIUM
**SOLARIZE** vb treat by exposure to the sun's rays
**SOLARIZED** > SOLARIZE
**SOLARIZES** > SOLARIZE
**SOLARS** > SOLUM
**SOLAS** > SOLUM
**SOLATE** vb change from gel to liquid
**SOLATED** > SOLATE
**SOLATES** > SOLATE
**SOLATIA** > SOLATIUM
**SOLATING** > SOLATE
**SOLATION** n liquefaction of a gel
**SOLATIONS** > SOLATION
**SOLATIUM** n compensation awarded for injury to the feelings

**SOLD** n obsolete word for salary
**SOLDADO** n soldier
**SOLDADOS** > SOLDADO
**SOLDAN** archaic word for > SULTAN
**SOLDANS** > SOLDAN
**SOLDE** n wages
**SOLDER** n soft alloy used to join two metal surfaces ▷ vb join with solder
**SOLDERED** > SOLDER
**SOLDERER** > SOLDER
**SOLDERERS** > SOLDER
**SOLDERING** > SOLDER
**SOLDERS** > SOLDER
**SOLDES** > SOLDE
**SOLDI** > SOLDO
**SOLDIER** n member of an army ▷ vb serve in an army
**SOLDIERED** > SOLDIER
**SOLDIERLY** adj of or befitting a good soldier
**SOLDIERS** > SOLDIER
**SOLDIERY** n soldiers collectively
**SOLDO** n former Italian copper coin worth one twentieth of a lira
**SOLDS** > SOLD
**SOLE** adj one and only ▷ n underside of the foot ▷ vb provide (a shoe) with a sole
**SOLECISE** variant of > SOLECIZE
**SOLECISED** > SOLECISE
**SOLECISES** > SOLECISE
**SOLECISM** n minor grammatical mistake
**SOLECISMS** > SOLECISM
**SOLECIST** > SOLECISM
**SOLECISTS** > SOLECISM
**SOLECIZE** vb commit a solecism
**SOLECIZED** same as > SOLECIZE
**SOLECIZES** > SOLECIZE
**SOLED** > SOLE
**SOLEI** > SOLEUS
**SOLEIN** same as > SULLEN
**SOLELESS** > SOLE
**SOLELY** adv only, completely
**SOLEMN** adj serious, deeply sincere
**SOLEMNER** > SOLEMN
**SOLEMNESS** > SOLEMN
**SOLEMNEST** > SOLEMN
**SOLEMNIFY** vb make serious or grave
**SOLEMNISE** same as > SOLEMNIZE
**SOLEMNITY** n state or quality of being solemn
**SOLEMNIZE** vb celebrate or perform (a ceremony)
**SOLEMNLY** > SOLEMN
**SOLENESS** > SOLE
**SOLENETTE** n small European sole
**SOLENODON** n either of two rare shrewlike

nocturnal mammals of the Caribbean
**SOLENOID** n coil of wire magnetized by passing a current through it
**SOLENOIDS** > SOLENOID
**SOLEPLATE** n joist forming the lowest member of a timber frame
**SOLEPRINT** n print of sole of foot
**SOLER** > SOLE
**SOLERA** n system for aging sherry and other fortified wines
**SOLERAS** > SOLERA
**SOLERET** n armour for foot
**SOLERETS** > SOLERET
**SOLERS** > SOLER
**SOLES** > SOLE
**SOLEUS** n muscle in calf of leg
**SOLEUSES** > SOLEUS
**SOLFATARA** n volcanic vent emitting only sulphurous gases and water vapour or sometimes hot mud
**SOLFEGE** variant of > SOLFEGGIO
**SOLFEGES** > SOLFEGE
**SOLFEGGI** > SOLFEGGIO
**SOLFEGGIO** n voice exercise in which runs, scales, etc, are sung to the same syllable or syllables
**SOLFERINO** n moderate purplish-red colour
**SOLGEL** adj changing between sol and gel
**SOLI** adv (of a piece or passage) to be performed by or with soloists
**SOLICIT** vb request
**SOLICITED** > SOLICIT
**SOLICITOR** n lawyer who advises clients and prepares documents and cases
**SOLICITS** > SOLICIT
**SOLICITY** n act of making a request
**SOLID** adj (of a substance) keeping its shape ▷ n three-dimensional shape
**SOLIDAGO** n any plant of the chiefly American genus Solidago
**SOLIDAGOS** > SOLIDAGO
**SOLIDARE** n old coin
**SOLIDARES** > SOLIDARE
**SOLIDARY** adj marked by unity of interests, responsibilities, etc
**SOLIDATE** vb consolidate
**SOLIDATED** > SOLIDATE
**SOLIDATES** > SOLIDATE
**SOLIDER** > SOLID
**SOLIDEST** > SOLID
**SOLIDI** > SOLIDUS
**SOLIDIFY** vb make or become solid or firm
**SOLIDISH** > SOLID
**SOLIDISM** n belief that diseases spring from

damage to solid parts of body
**SOLIDISMS** > SOLIDISM
**SOLIDIST** > SOLIDISM
**SOLIDISTS** > SOLIDISM
**SOLIDITY** > SOLID
**SOLIDLY** > SOLID
**SOLIDNESS** > SOLID
**SOLIDS** > SOLID
**SOLIDUM** n part of pedestal
**SOLIDUMS** > SOLIDUM
**SOLIDUS** same as > SLASH
**SOLILOQUY** n speech made by a person while alone, esp in a play
**SOLING** > SOLE
**SOLION** n amplifier used in chemistry
**SOLIONS** > SOLION
**SOLIPED** n animal whose hooves are not cloven
**SOLIPEDS** > SOLIPED
**SOLIPSISM** n doctrine that the self is the only thing known to exist
**SOLIPSIST** > SOLIPSISM
**SOLIQUID** n semi-solid, semi-liquid solution
**SOLIQUIDS** > SOLIQUID
**SOLITAIRE** n game for one person played with pegs set in a board
**SOLITARY** adj alone, single ▷ n hermit
**SOLITO** adv musical instruction meaning play in usual manner
**SOLITON** n type of isolated particle-like wave
**SOLITONS** > SOLITON
**SOLITUDE** n state of being alone
**SOLITUDES** > SOLITUDE
**SOLIVE** n type of joist
**SOLIVES** > SOLIVE
**SOLLAR** n archaic word meaning attic
**SOLLARS** > SOLLAR
**SOLLER** same as > SOLLAR
**SOLLERET** n protective covering for the foot consisting of riveted plates of armour
**SOLLERETS** > SOLLERET
**SOLLERS** > SOLLER
**SOLLICKER** n something very large
**SOLO** n music for one performer ▷ adj done alone ▷ adv by oneself, alone ▷ vb undertake a venture alone, esp to operate an aircraft alone or climb alone
**SOLOED** > SOLO
**SOLOING** > SOLO
**SOLOIST** n person who performs a solo
**SOLOISTIC** > SOLOIST
**SOLOISTS** > SOLOIST
**SOLON** n US congressman
**SOLONCHAK** n type of intrazonal soil of arid regions with a greyish

surface crust
**SOLONETS** *same*
*as* > SOLONETZ
**SOLONETZ** *n* type of
intrazonal soil with
a high saline content
characterized by leaching
**SOLONS** > SOLON
**SOLOS** > SOLO
**SOLPUGID** *n* venomous
arachnid
**SOLPUGIDS** > SOLPUGID
**SOLS** > SOL
**SOLSTICE** *n* either the
shortest (in winter) or
longest (in summer) day of
the year
**SOLSTICES** > SOLSTICE
**SOLUBLE** *adj* able to be
dissolved ▷ *n* soluble
substance
**SOLUBLES** > SOLUBLE
**SOLUBLY** > SOLUBLE
**SOLUM** *n* upper layers of
the soil profile, affected by
climate and vegetation
**SOLUMS** > SOLUM
**SOLUNAR** *adj* relating to sun
and moon
**SOLUS** *adj* alone
**SOLUTE** *n* substance in a
solution that is dissolved
▷ *adj* loose or unattached
**SOLUTES** > SOLUTE
**SOLUTION** *n* answer to a
problem
**SOLUTIONS** > SOLUTION
**SOLUTIVE** *adj* dissolving
**SOLVABLE** *adj* capable of
being solved
**SOLVATE** *vb* undergo, cause
to undergo, or partake in
solvation
**SOLVATED** > SOLVATE
**SOLVATES** > SOLVATE
**SOLVATING** > SOLVATE
**SOLVATION** *n* type of
chemical process
**SOLVE** *vb* find the answer
to (a problem)
**SOLVED** > SOLVE
**SOLVENCY** *n* ability to pay
all debts
**SOLVENT** *adj* having
enough money to pay
one's debts ▷ *n* liquid
capable of dissolving other
substances
**SOLVENTLY** > SOLVENT
**SOLVENTS** > SOLVENT
**SOLVER** > SOLVE
**SOLVERS** > SOLVE
**SOLVES** > SOLVE
**SOLVING** > SOLVE
**SOM** *n* currency of
Kyrgyzstan and
Uzbekistan
**SOMA** *n* body of an
organism, esp an animal,
as distinct from the germ
cells
**SOMAN** *n*
organophosphorus
compound developed as

a nerve gas in Germany
during World War II
**SOMANS** > SOMAN
**SOMAS** > SOMA
**SOMASCOPE** *n* instrument
for inspecting internal
organs
**SOMATA** > SOMA
**SOMATIC** *adj* of the body, as
distinct from the mind
**SOMATISM** *n* materialism
**SOMATISMS** > SOMATISM
**SOMATIST** > SOMATISM
**SOMATISTS** > SOMATISM
**SOMBER** *adj* (in the US)
sombre ▷ *vb* (in the US)
make sombre
**SOMBERED** > SOMBER
**SOMBERER** > SOMBER
**SOMBEREST** > SOMBER
**SOMBERING** > SOMBER
**SOMBERLY** > SOMBER
**SOMBERS** > SOMBER
**SOMBRE** *adj* dark, gloomy
▷ *vb* make sombre
**SOMBRED** > SOMBRE
**SOMBRELY** > SOMBRE
**SOMBRER** > SOMBRE
**SOMBRERO** *n* wide-
brimmed Mexican hat
**SOMBREROS** > SOMBRERO
**SOMBRES** > SOMBRE
**SOMBREST** > SOMBRE
**SOMBRING** > SOMBRE
**SOMBROUS** > SOMBRE
**SOME** *adj* unknown or
unspecified ▷ *pron* certain
unknown or unspecified
people or things
▷ *adv* approximately
▷ *determiner* (a) certain
unknown or unspecified
**SOMEBODY** *pron* some
person ▷ *n* important
person
**SOMEDAY** *adv* at some
unspecified time in the
future
**SOMEDEAL** *adv* to some
extent
**SOMEDELE** *same*
*as* > SOMEDEAL
**SOMEGATE** *adv* Scots word
meaning somehow
**SOMEHOW** *adv* in some
unspecified way
**SOMEONE** *pron* somebody
▷ *n* significant or
important person
**SOMEONES** > SOMEONE
**SOMEPLACE** *adv* in, at, or to
some unspecified place or
region
**SOMERSET** *variant*
*of* > SOMERSAULT
**SOMERSETS** > SOMERSET
**SOMETHING** *pron* unknown
or unspecified thing or
amount ▷ *n* impressive or
important person or thing
**SOMETIME** *adv* at some
unspecified time ▷ *adj*
former
**SOMETIMES** *adv* from time

to time, now and then
**SOMEWAY** *adv* in some
unspecified manner
**SOMEWAYS** *same*
*as* > SOMEWAY
**SOMEWHAT** *adv* some
extent, rather ▷ *n* vague
amount
**SOMEWHATS** > SOMEWHAT
**SOMEWHEN** *adv* at some
time
**SOMEWHERE** *adv* in, to, or
at some unspecified or
unknown place
**SOMEWHILE** *adv* sometimes
**SOMEWHY** *adv* for some
reason
**SOMEWISE** *adv* in some way
or to some degree
**SOMITAL** > SOMITE
**SOMITE** *n* any of a series of
dorsal paired segments
of mesoderm occurring
along the notochord in
vertebrate embryos
**SOMITES** > SOMITE
**SOMITIC** > SOMITE
**SOMMELIER** *n* wine steward
in a restaurant or hotel
**SOMNIAL** *adj* of dreams
**SOMNIATE** *vb* dream
**SOMNIATED** > SOMNIATE
**SOMNIATES** > SOMNIATE
**SOMNIFIC** *adj* inducing
sleep
**SOMNOLENT** *adj* drowsy
**SOMONI** *n* monetary unit of
Tajikistan
**SOMS** > SOM
**SOMY** > SOM
**SON** *n* male offspring
**SONANCE** > SONANT
**SONANCES** > SONANT
**SONANCIES** > SONANT
**SONANCY** > SONANT
**SONANT** *n* voiced sound
able to form a syllable
or syllable nucleus ▷ *adj*
denoting a voiced sound
like this
**SONANTAL** > SONANT
**SONANTIC** > SONANT
**SONANTS** > SONANT
**SONAR** *n* device for
detecting underwater
objects by the reflection of
sound waves
**SONARMAN** *n* sonar operator
**SONARMEN** > SONARMAN
**SONARS** > SONAR
**SONATA** *n* piece of music
in several movements for
one instrument with or
without piano
**SONATAS** > SONATA
**SONATINA** *n* short sonata
**SONATINAS** > SONATINA
**SONATINE** *same*
*as* > SONATINA
**SONCE** *n* Scots word
meaning good luck
**SONCES** > SONCE
**SONDAGE** *n* deep trial
trench for inspecting

stratigraphy
**SONDAGES** > SONDAGE
**SONDE** *n* rocket, balloon, or
probe used for observing
in the upper atmosphere
**SONDELI** *n* Indian shrew
**SONDELIS** > SONDELI
**SONDER** *n* yacht category
**SONDERS** > SONDER
**SONDES** > SONDE
**SONE** *n* subjective unit of
loudness
**SONERI** *n* Indian cloth of
gold
**SONERIS** > SONERI
**SONES** > SONE
**SONG** *n* music for the voice
**SONGBIRD** *n* any bird with a
musical call
**SONGBIRDS** > SONGBIRD
**SONGBOOK** *n* book of songs
**SONGBOOKS** > SONGBOOK
**SONGCRAFT** *n* art of
songwriting
**SONGFEST** *n* event with
many songs
**SONGFESTS** > SONGFEST
**SONGFUL** *adj* tuneful
**SONGFULLY** > SONGFUL
**SONGKOK** *n* (in Malaysia
and Indonesia) a kind
of oval brimless hat,
resembling a skull
**SONGKOKS** > SONGKOK
**SONGLESS** > SONG
**SONGLIKE** > SONG
**SONGMAN** *n* singer
**SONGMEN** > SONGMAN
**SONGOLOLO** *n* kind of
millipede
**SONGS** > SONG
**SONGSMITH** *n* person who
writes songs
**SONGSTER** *n* singer
**SONGSTERS** > SONGSTER
**SONHOOD** > SON
**SONHOODS** > SON
**SONIC** *adj* of or producing
sound
**SONICALLY** > SONIC
**SONICATE** *vb* subject to
sound waves
**SONICATED** > SONICATE
**SONICATES** > SONICATE
**SONICATOR** > SONICATE
**SONICS** *n* study of
mechanical vibrations in
matter
**SONLESS** > SON
**SONLIKE** > SON
**SONLY** *adj* like a son
**SONNE** *same as* > SON
**SONNES** > SONNE
**SONNET** *n* fourteen-line
poem with a fixed rhyme
scheme ▷ *vb* compose
sonnets
**SONNETARY** > SONNET
**SONNETED** > SONNET
**SONNETEER** *n* writer of
sonnets
**SONNETING** > SONNET
**SONNETISE** *same*
*as* > SONNETIZE

**SONNETIZE** vb write sonnets

**SONNETS** >SONNET

**SONNETTED** >SONNET

**SONNIES** >SONNY

**SONNY** n term of address to a boy

**SONOBUOY** n buoy equipped to detect underwater noises and transmit them by radio

**SONOBUOYS** >SONOBUOY

**SONOGRAM** n three-dimensional representation of a sound signal

**SONOGRAMS** >SONOGRAM

**SONOGRAPH** n device for scanning sound

**SONOMETER** same as >MONOCHORD

**SONORANT** n type of frictionless continuant or nasal

**SONORANTS** >SONORANT

**SONORITY** >SONOROUS

**SONOROUS** adj (of sound) deep or resonant

**SONOVOX** n device used to alter sound of human voice in music recordings

**SONOVOXES** >SONOVOX

**SONS** >SON

**SONSE** same as >SONCE

**SONSES** >SONSE

**SONSHIP** >SON

**SONSHIPS** >SON

**SONSIE** same as >SONSY

**SONSIER** >SONSY

**SONSIEST** >SONSY

**SONSY** adj plump

**SONTAG** n type of knitted women's cape

**SONTAGS** >SONTAG

**SONTIES** n Shakespearian oath

**SOOCHONG** same as >SOUCHONG

**SOOCHONGS** >SOOCHONG

**SOOEY** interj call used to summon pigs

**SOOGEE** vb clean ship using a special solution

**SOOGEED** >SOOGEE

**SOOGEEING** >SOOGEE

**SOOGEES** >SOOGEE

**SOOGIE** same as >SOUGEE

**SOOGIED** >SOOGIE

**SOOGIEING** >SOOGIE

**SOOGIES** >SOOGIE

**SOOJEY** same as >SOOGEE

**SOOJEYS** >SOOJEY

**SOOK** n baby ▷ vb suck

**SOOKED** >SOOK

**SOOKING** >SOOK

**SOOKS** >SOOK

**SOOL** vb incite (a dog) to attack

**SOOLE** same as >SOOL

**SOOLED** >SOOL

**SOOLES** >SOOLE

**SOOLING** >SOOL

**SOOLS** >SOOL

**SOOM** Scots word for >SWIM

**SOOMED** >SOOM

**SOOMING** >SOOM

**SOOMS** >SOOM

**SOON** adv in a short time

**SOONER** adv rather ▷ n native of Oklahoma

**SOONERS** >SOONER

**SOONEST** adv as soon as possible

**SOOP** Scots word for >SWEEP

**SOOPED** >SOOP

**SOOPING** >SOOP

**SOOPINGS** >SOOP

**SOOPS** >SOOP

**SOOPSTAKE** adv sweeping up all stakes

**SOOT** n black powder formed by the incomplete burning of an organic substance ▷ vb cover with soot

**SOOTE** n sweet

**SOOTED** >SOOT

**SOOTERKIN** n mythical black afterbirth of Dutch women that was believed to result from their warming themselves on stoves

**SOOTES** >SOOT

**SOOTFLAKE** n speck of soot

**SOOTH** n truth or reality ▷ adj true or real

**SOOTHE** vb make calm

**SOOTHED** >SOOTHE

**SOOTHER** >SOOTHE vb flatter

**SOOTHERED** >SOOTHE

**SOOTHERS** >SOOTHE

**SOOTHES** >SOOTHE

**SOOTHEST** >SOOTH

**SOOTHFAST** adj truthful

**SOOTHFUL** adj truthful

**SOOTHING** adj having a calming, assuaging, or relieving effect

**SOOTHINGS** >SOOTHING

**SOOTHLICH** adv truly

**SOOTHLY** >SOOTH

**SOOTHS** >SOOTH

**SOOTHSAID** >SOOTHSAY

**SOOTHSAY** vb predict the future

**SOOTHSAYS** >SOOTHSAY

**SOOTIER** >SOOTY

**SOOTIEST** >SOOTY

**SOOTILY** >SOOTY

**SOOTINESS** >SOOTY

**SOOTING** >SOOT

**SOOTLESS** >SOOT

**SOOTS** >SOOT

**SOOTY** adj covered with soot

**SOP** n concession to pacify someone ▷ vb mop up or absorb (liquid)

**SOPAPILLA** n Mexican deep-fried pastry

**SOPH** shortened form of >SOPHOMORE

**SOPHERIC** >SOPHERIM

**SOPHERIM** n Jewish scribes

**SOPHIES** >SOPHY

**SOPHISM** n argument that seems reasonable but is actually false and misleading

**SOPHISMS** >SOPHISM

**SOPHIST** n person who uses clever but invalid arguments

**SOPHISTER** n (esp formerly) a second-year undergraduate at certain British universities

**SOPHISTIC** adj of or relating to sophists or sophistry

**SOPHISTRY** n clever but invalid argument

**SOPHISTS** >SOPHIST

**SOPHOMORE** n student in second year at college

**SOPHS** >SOPH

**SOPHY** n title of the Persian monarchs

**SOPITE** vb lull to sleep

**SOPITED** >SOPITE

**SOPITES** >SOPITE

**SOPITING** >SOPITE

**SOPOR** n abnormally deep sleep

**SOPORIFIC** adj causing sleep ▷ n drug that causes sleep

**SOPOROSE** adj sleepy

**SOPOROUS** same as >SOPOROSE

**SOPORS** >SOPOR

**SOPPED** >SOP

**SOPPIER** >SOPPY

**SOPPIEST** >SOPPY

**SOPPILY** >SOPPY

**SOPPINESS** >SOPPY

**SOPPING** >SOP

**SOPPINGS** >SOP

**SOPPY** adj oversentimental

**SOPRA** adv musical instruction meaning above

**SOPRANI** >SOPRANO

**SOPRANINI** >SOPRANINO

**SOPRANINO** n instrument with the highest possible pitch in a family of instruments

**SOPRANIST** n soprano

**SOPRANO** n singer with the highest female or boy's voice ▷ adj of a musical instrument that is the highest or second highest pitched in its family

**SOPRANOS** >SOPRANO

**SOPS** >SOP

**SORA** n North American rail with a yellow bill

**SORAGE** n first year in hawk's life

**SORAGES** >SORAGE

**SORAL** >SORUS

**SORAS** >SORA

**SORB** n any of various related trees, esp the mountain ash ▷ vb absorb or adsorb

**SORBABLE** >SORB

**SORBARIA** n Asian shrub

**SORBARIAS** >SORBARIA

**SORBATE** n salt of sorbic acid

**SORBATES** >SORBATE

**SORBED** >SORB

**SORBENT** >SORB

**SORBENTS** >SORB

**SORBET** same as >SHERBET

**SORBETS** >SORBET

**SORBIC** >SORB

**SORBING** >SORB

**SORBITE** n mineral found in steel

**SORBITES** >SORBITE

**SORBITIC** >SORBITE

**SORBITISE** same as >SORBITIZE

**SORBITIZE** vb turn metal into form containing sorbite

**SORBITOL** n white water-soluble crystalline alcohol with a sweet taste

**SORBITOLS** >SORBITOL

**SORBO** as in sorbo rubber spongy form of rubber

**SORBOSE** n sweet-tasting hexose sugar derived from the berries of the mountain ash

**SORBOSES** >SORBOSE

**SORBS** >SORB

**SORBUS** n rowan or related tree

**SORBUSES** >SORBUS

**SORCERER** n magician

**SORCERERS** >SORCERER

**SORCERESS** same as >SORCERER

**SORCERIES** >SORCERY

**SORCEROUS** >SORCERY

**SORCERY** n witchcraft or magic

**SORD** n flock of mallard ducks

**SORDA** n deaf woman

**SORDES** pl n dark incrustations on the lips and teeth of patients with prolonged fever

**SORDID** adj dirty, squalid

**SORDIDER** >SORDID

**SORDIDEST** >SORDID

**SORDIDLY** >SORDID

**SORDINE** same as >SORDINO

**SORDINES** >SORDINE

**SORDINI** >SORDINO

**SORDINO** n mute for a stringed or brass musical instrument

**SORDO** n deaf man

**SORDOR** n sordidness

**SORDORS** >SORDOR

**SORDS** >SORD

**SORE** adj painful ▷ n painful area on the body ▷ adv greatly ▷ vb make sore

**SORED** >SORE

**SOREDIA** >SOREDIUM

**SOREDIAL** >SOREDIUM

**SOREDIATE** >SOREDIUM

**SOREDIUM** n organ of vegetative reproduction in lichens

**SOREE** same as >SORA

SOREES > SOREE
SOREHEAD n peevish or disgruntled person
SOREHEADS > SOREHEAD
SOREHON n old Irish feudal right
SOREHONS > SOREHON
SOREL variant of > SORREL
SORELL same as > SORREL
SORELLS > SORELL
SORELS > SOREL
SORELY adv greatly
SORENESS > SORE
SORER > SORE
SORES > SORE
SOREST > SORE
SOREX n shrew or related animal
SOREXES > SOREX
SORGHO same as > SORGO
SORGHOS > SORGHO
SORGHUM n kind of grass cultivated for grain
SORGHUMS > SORGHUM
SORGO n any of several varieties of sorghum that have watery sweet juice
SORGOS > SORGO
SORI > SORUS
SORICINE adj of or resembling a shrew
SORICOID same as > SORICINE
SORING > SORE
SORINGS > SORE
SORITES n polysyllogism in which the premises are arranged so that intermediate conclusions are omitted, being understood, and only the final conclusion is stated
SORITIC > SORITES
SORITICAL > SORITES
SORN vb obtain food, lodging, etc, from another person by presuming on his or her generosity
SORNED > SORN
SORNER > SORN
SORNERS > SORE
SORNING > SORN
SORNINGS > SORN
SORNS > SORN
SOROBAN n Japanese abacus
SOROBANS > SOROBAN
SOROCHE n altitude sickness
SOROCHES > SOROCHE
SORORAL adj of sister
SORORALLY > SORORAL
SORORATE n custom in some societies of a widower marrying his deceased wife's younger sister
SORORATES > SORORATE
SORORIAL same as > SORORAL
SORORISE same as > SORORIZE
SORORISED > SORORISE
SORORISES > SORORISE

SORORITY n society for female students
SORORIZE vb socialize in sisterly way
SORORIZED > SORORIZE
SORORIZES > SORORIZE
SOROSES > SOROSIS
SOROSIS n fleshy multiple fruit
SOROSISES > SOROSIS
SORPTION n process in which one substance takes up or holds another
SORPTIONS > SORPTION
SORPTIVE > SORPTION
SORRA Irish word for > SORROW
SORRAS > SORRA
SORREL n bitter-tasting plant
SORRELS > SORREL
SORRIER > SORRY
SORRIEST > SORRY
SORRILY > SORRY
SORRINESS > SORRY
SORROW n grief or sadness ▷ vb grieve
SORROWED > SORROW
SORROWER > SORROW
SORROWERS > SORROW
SORROWFUL > SORROW
SORROWING > SORROW
SORROWS > SORROW
SORRY adj feeling pity or regret ▷ interj exclamation expressing apology or asking someone to repeat what he or she has said
SORRYISH > SORRY
SORT n group all sharing certain qualities or characteristics ▷ vb arrange according to kind
SORTA adv phonetic representation of 'sort of'
SORTABLE > SORT
SORTABLY > SORT
SORTAL n type of logical or linguistic concept
SORTALS > SORTAL
SORTANCE n suitableness
SORTANCES > SORTANCE
SORTATION n act of sorting
SORTED interj exclamation of satisfaction, approval, etc ▷ adj possessing the desired recreational drugs
SORTER > SORT
SORTERS > SORT
SORTES n divination by opening book at random
SORTIE n relatively short return trip ▷ vb make a sortie
SORTIED > SORTIE
SORTIEING > SORTIE
SORTIES > SORTIE
SORTILEGE n act or practice of divination by drawing lots
SORTILEGY same as > SORTILEGE
SORTING > SORT

SORTINGS > SORT
SORTITION n act of casting lots
SORTMENT n assortment
SORTMENTS > SORTMENT
SORTS > SORT
SORUS n cluster of sporangia on the undersurface of certain fern leaves
SOS > SO
SOSATIE n skewer of curried meat pieces
SOSATIES > SOSATIE
SOSS vb make dirty or muddy
SOSSED > SOSS
SOSSES > SOSS
SOSSING > SOSS
SOSSINGS > SOSS
SOSTENUTI > SOSTENUTO
SOSTENUTO adv to be performed in a smooth sustained manner
SOT n habitual drunkard ▷ adv indeed: used to contradict a negative statement ▷ vb be a drunkard
SOTERIAL adj of salvation
SOTH archaic variant of > SOOTH
SOTHS > SOTH
SOTOL n American plant related to agave
SOTOLS > SOTOL
SOTS > SOT
SOTTED > SOT
SOTTEDLY > SOT
SOTTING > SOT
SOTTINGS > SOT
SOTTISH > SOT
SOTTISHLY > SOT
SOTTISIER n collection of jokes
SOU n former French coin
SOUARI n tree of tropical America
SOUARIS > SOUARI
SOUBISE n purée of onions mixed into a thick white sauce and served over eggs, fish, etc
SOUBISES > SOUBISE
SOUBRETTE n minor female role in comedy, often that of a pert maid
SOUCAR n Indian banker
SOUCARS > SOUCAR
SOUCE same as > SOUSE
SOUCED > SOUCE
SOUCES > SOUCE
SOUCHONG n black tea with large leaves
SOUCHONGS > SOUCHONG
SOUCING > SOUCE
SOUCT > SOUCE
SOUDAN obsolete variant of > SULTAN
SOUDANS > SOUDAN
SOUFFLE n light fluffy dish made with beaten egg whites and other ingredients ▷ adj made

light and puffy, as by beating and cooking
SOUFFLED > SOUFFLE
SOUFFLEED > SOUFFLE
SOUFFLES > SOUFFLE
SOUGH vb (of the wind) make a sighing sound ▷ n soft continuous murmuring sound
SOUGHED > SOUGH
SOUGHING > SOUGH
SOUGHS > SOUGH
SOUGHT > SEEK
SOUK same as > SOOK
SOUKED > SOUK
SOUKING > SOUK
SOUKOUS n style of African popular music characterized by syncopated rhythms and intricate contrasting guitar melodies
SOUKOUSES > SOUKOUS
SOUKS > SOUK
SOUL n spiritual and immortal part of a human being
SOULDAN same as > SOLDAN
SOULDANS > SOULDAN
SOULDIER same as > SOLDIER
SOULDIERS > SOULDIER
SOULED adj having soul
SOULFUL adj full of emotion
SOULFULLY > SOULFUL
SOULLESS adj lacking human qualities, mechanical
SOULLIKE adj resembling a soul
SOULMATE n person with whom one has most affinity
SOULMATES > SOULMATE
SOULS > SOUL
SOUM vb decide how many animals can graze particular pasture
SOUMED > SOUM
SOUMING > SOUM
SOUMINGS > SOUM
SOUMS > SOUM
SOUND n something heard, noise ▷ vb make or cause to make a sound ▷ adj in good condition ▷ adv soundly
SOUNDABLE > SOUND
SOUNDBITE n short pithy sentence or phrase extracted from a longer speech
SOUNDBOX n resonating chamber of the hollow body of a violin, guitar, etc
SOUNDCARD n component giving computer sound effects
SOUNDED > SOUND
SOUNDER n electromagnetic device formerly used in telegraphy to convert electric signals into

audible sounds
**SOUNDERS** > SOUNDER
**SOUNDEST** > SOUND
**SOUNDING** *adj* resounding
**SOUNDINGS** > SOUNDING
**SOUNDLESS** *adj* extremely
still or silent
**SOUNDLY** > SOUND
**SOUNDMAN** *n* sound recorder
in television crew
**SOUNDMEN** > SOUNDMAN
**SOUNDNESS** > SOUND
**SOUNDPOST** *n* small post
on guitars, violins, etc,
that joins the front surface
to the back and allows
the whole body of the
instrument to vibrate
**SOUNDS** > SOUND
**SOUP** *n* liquid food made
from meat, vegetables, etc
▷ *vb* give soup to
**SOUPCON** *n* small amount
**SOUPCONS** > SOUPCON
**SOUPED** > SOUP
**SOUPER** *n* person
dispensing soup
**SOUPERS** > SOUPER
**SOUPFIN** *n* Pacific requiem
shark valued for its fins
**SOUPFINS** > SOUPFIN
**SOUPIER** > SOUPY
**SOUPIEST** > SOUPY
**SOUPING** > SOUP
**SOUPLE** *same as* > SUPPLE
**SOUPLED** > SOUPLE
**SOUPLES** > SOUPLE
**SOUPLESS** > SOUP
**SOUPLIKE** > SOUP
**SOUPLING** > SOUPLE
**SOUPS** > SOUP
**SOUPSPOON** *n* spoon for
eating soup
**SOUPY** *adj* having the
appearance or consistency
of soup
**SOUR** *adj* sharp-tasting
▷ *vb* make or become sour
**SOURBALL** *n* tart-flavoured
boiled sweet
**SOURBALLS** > SOURBALL
**SOURCE** *n* origin or starting
point ▷ *vb* establish a
supplier of (a product, etc)
**SOURCED** > SOURCE
**SOURCEFUL** *adj* offering
useful things
**SOURCES** > SOURCE
**SOURCING** > SOURCE
**SOURCINGS** > SOURCE
**SOURDINE** *n* soft stop on an
organ or harmonium
**SOURDINES** > SOURDINE
**SOURDOUGH** *adj* (of bread)
made with fermented
dough used as a leaven ▷ *n*
(in Western US, Canada,
and Alaska) an old-time
prospector or pioneer
**SOURED** > SOUR
**SOURER** > SOUR
**SOUREST** > SOUR
**SOURING** > SOUR
**SOURINGS** > SOUR

**SOURISH** > SOUR
**SOURISHLY** > SOUR
**SOURLY** > SOUR
**SOURNESS** > SOUR
**SOUROCK** *n* Scots word for
sorrel plant
**SOUROCKS** > SOUROCK
**SOURPUSS** *n* person
who is always gloomy,
pessimistic, or bitter
**SOURS** > SOUR
**SOURSE** *same as* > SOURCE
**SOURSES** > SOURSE
**SOURSOP** *n* small West
Indian tree
**SOURSOPS** > SOURSOP
**SOURWOOD** *n* sorrel tree
**SOURWOODS** > SOURWOOD
**SOUS** > SOU
**SOUSE** *vb* plunge
(something) into liquid
▷ *n* liquid used in pickling
**SOUSED** > SOUSE
**SOUSES** > SOUSE
**SOUSING** > SOUSE
**SOUSINGS** > SOUSE
**SOUSLIK** *same as* > SUSLIK
**SOUSLIKS** > SOUSLIK
**SOUT** *same as* > SOOT
**SOUTACHE** *n* narrow braid
used as a decorative
trimming
**SOUTACHES** > SOUTACHE
**SOUTANE** *n* Roman Catholic
priest's cassock
**SOUTANES** > SOUTANE
**SOUTAR** *same as* > SOUTER
**SOUTARS** > SOUTAR
**SOUTENEUR** *n* pimp
**SOUTER** *n* shoemaker or
cobbler
**SOUTERLY** > SOUTER
**SOUTERS** > SOUTER
**SOUTH** *n* direction towards
the South Pole, opposite
north ▷ *adj* or in the south
▷ *adv* in, to, or towards the
south ▷ *vb* turn south
**SOUTHEAST** *adv* (in or to)
direction between south
and east ▷ *n* point of the
compass or the direction
midway between south
and east ▷ *adj* of or
denoting the southeastern
part of a specified country,
area, etc
**SOUTHED** > SOUTH
**SOUTHER** *n* strong wind or
storm from the south ▷ *vb*
turn south
**SOUTHERED** > SOUTHER
**SOUTHERLY** *adj* of or in the
south ▷ *adv* towards the
south ▷ *n* wind from the
south
**SOUTHERN** *adj* situated in
or towards the south ▷ *n*
southerner
**SOUTHERNS** > SOUTHERN
**SOUTHERS** > SOUTHER
**SOUTHING** *n* movement,
deviation, or distance
covered in a southerly

direction
**SOUTHINGS** > SOUTHING
**SOUTHLAND** *n* southern
part of country
**SOUTHMOST** *adj* situated or
occurring farthest south
**SOUTHPAW** *n* left-handed
person, esp a boxer ▷ *adj*
left-handed
**SOUTHPAWS** > SOUTHPAW
**SOUTHRON** *n* southerner
**SOUTHRONS** > SOUTHRON
**SOUTHS** > SOUTH
**SOUTHSAID** > SOUTHSAY
**SOUTHSAY** *same*
*as* > SOOTHSAY
**SOUTHSAYS** > SOUTHSAY
**SOUTHWARD** *adv* towards
the south
**SOUTHWEST** *adv* (in or to)
direction between south
and west ▷ *n* point of the
compass or the direction
midway between west and
south ▷ *adj* of or denoting
the southwestern part of a
specified country, area, etc
**SOUTIE** *same as* > SOUTPIEL
**SOUTIES** > SOUTIE
**SOUTPIEL** *n* South African
derogatory slang for an
English-speaking South
African
**SOUTPIELS** > SOUTPIEL
**SOUTS** > SOUT
**SOUVENIR** *n* keepsake,
memento ▷ *vb* steal or
keep (something, esp a
small article) for one's own
use
**SOUVENIRS** > SOUVENIR
**SOUVLAKI** *same*
*as* > SOUVLAKIA
**SOUVLAKIA** *n* Greek dish
of kebabs, esp made with
lamb
**SOUVLAKIS** > SOUVLAKI
**SOV** *shortening*
*of* > SOVEREIGN
**SOVENANCE** *n* memory
**SOVEREIGN** *n* king or
queen ▷ *adj* (of a state)
independent
**SOVIET** *n* formerly, elected
council at various levels of
government in the USSR
▷ *adj* of the former USSR
**SOVIETIC** > SOVIET
**SOVIETISE** *same*
*as* > SOVIETIZE
**SOVIETISM** *n* principle or
practice of government
through soviets
**SOVIETIST** > SOVIETISM
**SOVIETIZE** *vb* bring (a
country, person, etc) under
Soviet control or influence
**SOVIETS** > SOVIET
**SOVKHOZ** *n* (in the former
Soviet Union) a large
mechanized farm owned
by the state
**SOVKHOZES** > SOVKHOZ
**SOVKHOZY** > SOVKHOZ

**SOVRAN** *literary word*
*for* > SOVEREIGN
**SOVRANLY** > SOVRAN
**SOVRANS** > SOVRAN
**SOVRANTY** > SOVRAN
**SOVS** > SOV
**SOW** *vb* scatter or plant
(seed) in or on (the ground)
▷ *n* female adult pig
**SOWABLE** > SOW
**SOWANS** *same as* > SOWENS
**SOWAR** *n* Indian cavalryman
**SOWARREE** *n* Indian
mounted escort
**SOWARREES** > SOWARREE
**SOWARRIES** > SOWARRY
**SOWARRY** *same*
*as* > SOWARREE
**SOWARS** > SOWAR
**SOWBACK** *another name*
*for* > HOGBACK
**SOWBACKS** > SOWBACK
**SOWBELLY** *n* salt pork from
pig's belly
**SOWBREAD** *n* S European
primulaceous plant
**SOWBREADS** > SOWBREAD
**SOWCAR** *same as* > SOUCAR
**SOWCARS** > SOWCAR
**SOWCE** *same as* > SOUSE
**SOWCED** > SOWCE
**SOWCES** > SOWCE
**SOWCING** > SOWCE
**SOWED** > SOW
**SOWENS** *n* pudding made
from oatmeal husks
steeped and boiled
**SOWER** > SOW
**SOWERS** > SOW
**SOWF** *same as* > SOWTH
**SOWFED** > SOWF
**SOWFF** *same as* > SOWTH
**SOWFFED** > SOWFF
**SOWFFING** > SOWFF
**SOWFFS** > SOWFF
**SOWFING** > SOWF
**SOWFS** > SOWF
**SOWING** > SOW
**SOWINGS** > SOW
**SOWL** *same as* > SOLE
**SOWLE** *same as* > SOLE
**SOWLED** > SOWL
**SOWLES** > SOWLE
**SOWLING** > SOWL
**SOWLS** > SOWL
**SOWM** *same as* > SOUM
**SOWMED** > SOWM
**SOWMING** > SOWM
**SOWMS** > SOWM
**SOWN** > SOW
**SOWND** *vb* wield
**SOWNDED** > SOWND
**SOWNDING** > SOWND
**SOWNDS** > SOWND
**SOWNE** *same as* > SOUND
**SOWNES** > SOWNE
**SOWP** *n* spoonful
**SOWPS** > SOWP
**SOWS** > SOW
**SOWSE** *same as* > SOUSE
**SOWSED** > SOWSE
**SOWSES** > SOWSE
**SOWSING** > SOWSE
**SOWSSE** *same as* > SOUSE

SOWSSED > SOWSSE
SOWSSES > SOWSSE
SOWSSING > SOWSSE
SOWTER same as > SOUTER
SOWTERS > SOWTER
SOWTH vb Scots word meaning whistle
SOWTHED > SOWTH
SOWTHING > SOWTH
SOWTHS > SOWTH
SOX pl n informal spelling of 'socks'
SOY as in soy sauce salty dark brown sauce made from soya beans, used in Chinese and Japanese cookery
SOYA n plant whose edible bean is used for food and as a source of oil
SOYAS > SOYA
SOYBEAN n soya bean
SOYBEANS > SOYBEAN
SOYLE n body
SOYLES > SOYLE
SOYMILK n milk substitute made from soya
SOYMILKS > SOYMILK
SOYS > SOY
SOYUZ n Russian spacecraft used to ferry crew to and from space stations
SOYUZES > SOYUZ
SOZIN n form of protein
SOZINE same as > SOZIN
SOZINES > SOZIN
SOZINS > SOZIN
SOZZLE vb make wet
SOZZLED adj drunk
SOZZLES > SOZZLE
SOZZLIER > SOZZLY
SOZZLIEST > SOZZLY
SOZZLING > SOZZLE
SOZZLY adj wet
SPA n resort with a mineral-water spring ▷ vb visit a spa
SPACE n unlimited expanse in which all objects exist and move ▷ vb place at intervals
SPACEBAND n device on a linecaster for evening up the spaces between words
SPACED > SPACE
SPACELAB n laboratory in space where scientific experiments are performed
SPACELABS > SPACELAB
SPACELESS adj having no limits in space
SPACEMAN n person who travels in space
SPACEMEN > SPACEMAN
SPACEPORT n base equipped to launch, maintain, and test spacecraft
SPACER n piece of material used to create or maintain a space between two things
SPACERS > SPACER

SPACES > SPACE
SPACESHIP n (in science fiction) a spacecraft used for travel between planets and galaxies
SPACESUIT n sealed pressurized suit worn by an astronaut
SPACEWALK n instance of floating and manoeuvring in space, outside but attached by a lifeline to a spacecraft ▷ vb float and manoeuvre in space while outside but attached to a spacecraft
SPACEWARD adv into space
SPACEY adj vague and dreamy, as if under the influence of drugs
SPACIAL same as > SPATIAL
SPACIALLY > SPACIAL
SPACIER > SPACEY
SPACIEST > SPACEY
SPACINESS > SPACEY
SPACING n arrangement of letters, words, etc, on a page in order to achieve legibility
SPACINGS > SPACING
SPACIOUS adj having a large capacity or area
SPACKLE vb fill holes in plaster
SPACKLED > SPACKLE
SPACKLES > SPACKLE
SPACKLING > SPACKLE
SPACY same as > SPACEY
SPADASSIN n swordsman
SPADE n tool for digging
SPADED > SPADE
SPADEFISH n type of spiny-finned food fish
SPADEFUL n amount spade will hold
SPADEFULS > SPADEFUL
SPADELIKE > SPADE
SPADEMAN n man who works with spade
SPADEMEN > SPADEMAN
SPADER > SPADE
SPADERS > SPADE
SPADES > SPADE
SPADESMAN same as > SPADEMAN
SPADESMEN > SPADEMAN
SPADEWORK n hard preparatory work
SPADGER n sparrow
SPADGERS > SPADGER
SPADICES > SPADIX
SPADILLE n (in ombre and quadrille) the ace of spades
SPADILLES > SPADILLE
SPADILLIO same as > SPADILLE
SPADILLO same as > SPADILLE
SPADILLOS > SPADILLO
SPADING > SPADE
SPADIX n spike of small flowers on a fleshy stem
SPADIXES > SPADIX

SPADO n neutered animal
SPADOES > SPADO
SPADONES > SPADO
SPADOS > SPADO
SPADROON n type of sword
SPADROONS > SPADROON
SPAE vb foretell (the future)
SPAED > SPAE
SPAEING > SPAE
SPAEINGS > SPAE
SPAEMAN n man who foretells future
SPAEMEN > SPAEMAN
SPAER > SPAE
SPAERS > SPAE
SPAES > SPAE
SPAETZLE n German noodle dish
SPAETZLES > SPAETZLE
SPAEWIFE n woman who can supposedly foretell the future
SPAEWIVES > SPAEWIFE
SPAG vb (of a cat) to scratch (a person) with the claws ▷ n Australian offensive slang for an Italian
SPAGERIC same as > SPAGYRIC
SPAGERICS > SPAGERIC
SPAGERIST > SPAGERIC
SPAGGED > SPAG
SPAGGING > SPAG
SPAGHETTI n pasta in the form of long strings
SPAGIRIC same as > SPAGYRIC
SPAGIRICS > SPAGIRIC
SPAGIRIST > SPAGIRIC
SPAGS > SPAG
SPAGYRIC adj of or relating to alchemy ▷ n alchemist
SPAGYRICS > SPAGYRIC
SPAGYRIST > SPAGYRIC
SPAHEE same as > SPAHI
SPAHEES > SPAHEE
SPAHI n (formerly) an irregular cavalryman in the Turkish armed forces
SPAHIS > SPAHI
SPAIL Scots word for > SPALL
SPAILS > SPAIL
SPAIN variant of > SPANE
SPAINED > SPAIN
SPAING > SPA
SPAINGS > SPA
SPAINING > SPAIN
SPAINS > SPAIN
SPAIRGE Scots word for > SPARGE
SPAIRGED > SPAIRGE
SPAIRGES > SPAIRGE
SPAIRGING > SPAIRGE
SPAIT same as > SPATE
SPAITS > SPAIT
SPAKE past tense of > SPEAK
SPALD same as > SPAULD
SPALDEEN n ball used in street game
SPALDEENS > SPALDEEN
SPALDS > SPALD
SPALE Scots word for > SPALL
SPALES > SPALE
SPALL n splinter or chip

of ore, rock, or stone ▷ vb split or cause to split into such fragments
SPALLABLE > SPALL
SPALLE same as > SPAULD
SPALLED > SPALL
SPALLER > SPALL
SPALLERS > SPALL
SPALLES > SPALLE
SPALLING > SPALL
SPALLINGS > SPALL
SPALLS > SPALL
SPALPEEN n itinerant seasonal labourer
SPALPEENS > SPALPEEN
SPALT vb split
SPALTED > SPALT
SPALTING > SPALT
SPALTS > SPALT
SPAM vb send unsolicited e-mail simultaneously to a number of newsgroups on the internet ▷ n unsolicited electronic mail or text messages sent in this way
SPAMBOT n computer programme that identifies email addresses to send spam to
SPAMBOTS > SPAMBOT
SPAMMED > SPAM
SPAMMER > SPAM
SPAMMERS > SPAM
SPAMMIE n love bite
SPAMMIER > SPAMMY
SPAMMIES > SPAMMIE
SPAMMIEST > SPAMMY
SPAMMING > SPAM
SPAMMINGS > SPAM
SPAMMY adj bland
SPAMS > SPAM
SPAN n space between two points ▷ vb stretch or extend across
SPANAEMIA n lack of red corpuscles in blood
SPANAEMIC > SPANAEMIA
SPANCEL n length of rope for hobbling an animal, esp a horse or cow ▷ vb hobble (an animal) with a loose rope
SPANCELED > SPANCEL
SPANCELS > SPANCEL
SPANDEX n type of synthetic stretch fabric made from polyurethane fibre
SPANDEXES > SPANDEX
SPANDREL n triangular surface bounded by the outer curve of an arch and the adjacent wall
SPANDRELS > SPANDREL
SPANDRIL same as > SPANDREL
SPANDRILS > SPANDRIL
SPANE vb Scots word meaning wean
SPANED > SPANE
SPANES > SPANE
SPANG adv exactly, firmly, or straight ▷ vb dash

SPANGED > SPANG
SPANGHEW *vb* throw in air
SPANGHEWS > SPANGHEW
SPANGING > SPANG
SPANGLE *n* small shiny metallic ornament ▷ *vb* decorate with spangles
SPANGLED > SPANGLE
SPANGLER > SPANGLE
SPANGLERS > SPANGLE
SPANGLES > SPANGLE
SPANGLET *n* little spangle
SPANGLETS > SPANGLET
SPANGLIER > SPANGLE
SPANGLING > SPANGLE
SPANGLY > SPANGLE
SPANGS > SPANG
SPANIEL *n* dog with long ears and silky hair
SPANIELS > SPANIEL
SPANING > SPANE
SPANK *vb* slap with the open hand, on the buttocks or legs ▷ *n* such a slap
SPANKED > SPANK
SPANKER *n* fore-and-aft sail or a mast that is aftermost in a sailing vessel
SPANKERS > SPANKER
SPANKING *adj* outstandingly fine or smart ▷ *n* series of spanks, usually as a punishment for children
SPANKINGS > SPANKING
SPANKS > SPANK
SPANLESS *adj* impossible to span
SPANNED > SPAN
SPANNER *n* tool for gripping and turning a nut or bolt
SPANNERS > SPANNER
SPANNING > SPAN
SPANS > SPAN
SPANSPEK *n* cantaloupe melon
SPANSPEKS > SPANSPEK
SPANSULE *n* modified-release capsule of a drug
SPANSULES > SPANSULE
SPANWORM *n* larva of a type of moth
SPANWORMS > SPANWORM
SPAR *n* pole used as a ship's mast, boom, or yard ▷ *vb* box or fight using light blows for practice
SPARABLE *n* small nail with no head, used for fixing the soles and heels of shoes
SPARABLES > SPARABLE
SPARAXIS *n* type of plant with dainty spikes of star-shaped purple, red, or orange flowers
SPARD > SPARE
SPARE *adj* extra ▷ *n* duplicate kept in case of damage or loss ▷ *vb* refrain from punishing or harming
SPAREABLE > SPARE
SPARED > SPARE

SPARELESS *adj* merciless
SPARELY > SPARE
SPARENESS > SPARE
SPARER > SPARE
SPARERIB *n* cut of pork ribs with most of the meat trimmed off
SPARERIBS > SPARERIB
SPARERS > SPARE
SPARES > SPARE
SPAREST > SPARE
SPARGE *vb* sprinkle or scatter (something)
SPARGED > SPARGE
SPARGER > SPARGE
SPARGERS > SPARGE
SPARGES > SPARGE
SPARGING > SPARGE
SPARID *n* type of marine percoid fish ▷ *adj* of or belonging to this family of fish
SPARIDS > SPARID
SPARING *adj* economical
SPARINGLY > SPARING
SPARK *n* fiery particle thrown out from a fire or caused by friction ▷ *vb* give off sparks
SPARKE *n* weapon
SPARKED > SPARK
SPARKER > SPARK
SPARKERS > SPARK
SPARKES > SPARKE
SPARKIE *n* electrician
SPARKIER > SPARKY
SPARKIES > SPARKIE
SPARKIEST > SPARKY
SPARKILY > SPARKY
SPARKING > SPARK
SPARKISH > SPARK
SPARKLE *vb* glitter with many points of light ▷ *n* sparkling points of light
SPARKLED > SPARKLE
SPARKLER *n* hand-held firework that emits sparks
SPARKLERS > SPARKLER
SPARKLES > SPARKLE
SPARKLESS > SPARK
SPARKLET *n* little spark
SPARKLETS > SPARKLET
SPARKLIER > SPARKLY
SPARKLIES > SPARKLY
SPARKLING *adj* (of wine or mineral water) slightly fizzy
SPARKLY *adj* sparkling ▷ *n* sparkling thing
SPARKPLUG *n* device in an engine that ignites the fuel
SPARKS *n* electrician
SPARKY *adj* lively
SPARLIKE > SPAR
SPARLING *n* European smelt
SPARLINGS > SPARLING
SPAROID *same as* > SPARID
SPAROIDS > SPAROID
SPARRE *same as* > SPAR
SPARRED > SPAR
SPARRER > SPAR
SPARRERS > SPAR

SPARRES > SPARRE
SPARRIER > SPARRY
SPARRIEST > SPARRY
SPARRING > SPAR
SPARRINGS > SPAR
SPARROW *n* small brownish bird
SPARROWS > SPARROW
SPARRY *adj* (of minerals) containing, relating to, or resembling spar
SPARS > SPAR
SPARSE *adj* thinly scattered
SPARSEDLY > SPARSE
SPARSELY > SPARSE
SPARSER > SPARSE
SPARSEST > SPARSE
SPARSITY > SPARSE
SPART *n* esparto
SPARTAN *adj* strict and austere ▷ *n* disciplined or brave person
SPARTANS > SPARTAN
SPARTEINE *n* viscous oily alkaloid extracted from the broom plant and lupin seeds
SPARTERIE *n* things made from esparto
SPARTH *n* type of battle-axe
SPARTHE *same as* > SPARTH
SPARTHES > SPARTHE
SPARTHS > SPARTH
SPARTINA *n* grass growing in salt marshes
SPARTINAS > SPARTINA
SPARTS > SPART
SPAS > SPA
SPASM *n* involuntary muscular contraction ▷ *vb* go into spasm
SPASMATIC > SPASM
SPASMED > SPASM
SPASMIC > SPASM
SPASMING > SPASM
SPASMODIC *adj* occurring in spasms
SPASMS > SPASM
SPASTIC *n* offensive slang for a person with cerebral palsy ▷ *adj* suffering from cerebral palsy
SPASTICS > SPASTIC
SPAT *vb* have a quarrel
SPATE *n* large number of things happening within a period of time
SPATES > SPATE
SPATFALL *n* mass of larvae on sea bed
SPATFALLS > SPATFALL
SPATHAL > SPATHE
SPATHE *n* large sheathlike leaf enclosing a flower cluster
SPATHED > SPATHE
SPATHES > SPATHE
SPATHIC *adj* (of minerals) resembling spar, esp in having good cleavage
SPATHOSE *same as* > SPATHIC
SPATIAL *adj* of or in space
SPATIALLY > SPATIAL
SPATLESE *n* type of

German wine, usu white
SPATLESEN > SPATLESE
SPATLESES > SPATLESE
SPATS > SPAT
SPATTED > SPAT
SPATTEE *n* type of gaiter
SPATTEES > SPATTEE
SPATTER *vb* scatter or be scattered in drops over (something) ▷ *n* spattering sound
SPATTERED > SPATTER
SPATTERS > SPATTER
SPATTING > SPIT
SPATULA *n* utensil with a broad flat blade for spreading or stirring
SPATULAR > SPATULA
SPATULAS > SPATULA
SPATULATE *adj* shaped like a spatula
SPATULE *n* spatula
SPATULES > SPATULE
SPATZLE *same as* > SPAETZLE
SPATZLES > SPATZLE
SPAUL *same as* > SPAULD
SPAULD *n* shoulder
SPAULDS > SPAULD
SPAULS > SPAUL
SPAVIE *Scots variant of* > SPAVIN
SPAVIES > SPAVIE
SPAVIET *adj* Scots word meaning spavined
SPAVIN *n* enlargement of the hock of a horse by a bony growth
SPAVINED *adj* affected with spavin
SPAVINS > SPAVIN
SPAW *same as* > SPA
SPAWL *vb* spit
SPAWLED > SPAWL
SPAWLING > SPAWL
SPAWLS > SPAWL
SPAWN *n* jelly-like mass of eggs of fish, frogs, or molluscs ▷ *vb* (of fish, frogs, or molluscs) lay eggs
SPAWNED > SPAWN
SPAWNER > SPAWN
SPAWNERS > SPAWN
SPAWNIER > SPAWNY
SPAWNIEST > SPAWNY
SPAWNING > SPAWN
SPAWNINGS > SPAWN
SPAWNS > SPAWN
SPAWNY *adj* like spawn
SPAWS > SPAW
SPAY *vb* remove the ovaries from (a female animal)
SPAYAD *n* male deer
SPAYADS > SPAYAD
SPAYD *same as* > SPAYAD
SPAYDS > SPAYD
SPAYED > SPAY
SPAYING > SPAY
SPAYS > SPAY
SPAZ *vb* offensive slang meaning lose self-control
SPAZA *as in spaza shop* South African slang for a small shop in a township
SPAZZ *same as* > SPAZ

SPAZZED > SPAZ
SPAZZES > SPAZ
SPAZZING > SPAZ
SPEAK *vb* say words, talk
SPEAKABLE > SPEAK
SPEAKEASY *n* place where alcoholic drink was sold illegally during Prohibition
SPEAKER *n* person who speaks, esp at a formal occasion
SPEAKERS > SPEAKER
SPEAKING > SPEAK
SPEAKINGS > SPEAK
SPEAKOUT *n* firm or brave statement of one's beliefs
SPEAKOUTS > SPEAKOUT
SPEAKS > SPEAK
SPEAL *same as* > SPULE
SPEALS > SPEAL
SPEAN *same as* > SPANE
SPEANED > SPEAN
SPEANING > SPEAN
SPEANS > SPEAN
SPEAR *n* weapon consisting of a long shaft with a sharp point ▷ *vb* pierce with or as if with a spear
SPEARED > SPEAR
SPEARER > SPEAR
SPEARERS > SPEAR
SPEARFISH *n* another name for > MARLIN
SPEARGUN *n* device for shooting spears underwater
SPEARGUNS > SPEARGUN
SPEARHEAD *vb* lead (an attack or campaign) ▷ *n* leading force in an attack or campaign
SPEARIER > SPEAR
SPEARIEST > SPEAR
SPEARING > SPEAR
SPEARLIKE > SPEAR
SPEARMAN *n* soldier armed with a spear
SPEARMEN > SPEARMAN
SPEARMINT *n* type of mint
SPEARS > SPEAR
SPEARWORT *n* any of several Eurasian ranunculaceous plants
SPEARY > SPEAR
SPEAT *same as* > SPATE
SPEATS > SPEAT
SPEC *vb* set specifications
SPECCED > SPEC
SPECCIES > SPECCY
SPECCING > SPEC
SPECCY *n* person wearing spectacles
SPECIAL *adj* distinguished from others of its kind ▷ *n* product, programme, etc which is only available at a certain time ▷ *vb* advertise and sell (an item) at a reduced price
SPECIALER > SPECIAL
SPECIALLY > SPECIAL
SPECIALS > SPECIAL
SPECIALTY *n* special

interest or skill
SPECIATE *vb* form or develop into a new biological species
SPECIATED > SPECIATE
SPECIATES > SPECIATE
SPECIE *n* coins as distinct from paper money
SPECIES *n* group of plants or animals that are related closely enough to interbreed naturally
SPECIFIC *adj* particular, definite ▷ *n* drug used to treat a particular disease
SPECIFICS > SPECIFIC
SPECIFIED > SPECIFY
SPECIFIER > SPECIFY
SPECIFIES > SPECIFY
SPECIFY *vb* refer to or state specifically
SPECIMEN *n* individual or part typifying a whole
SPECIMENS > SPECIMEN
SPECIOUS *adj* apparently true, but actually false
SPECK *n* small spot or particle ▷ *vb* mark with specks or spots
SPECKED > SPECK
SPECKIER > SPECKY
SPECKIEST > SPECKY
SPECKING > SPECK
SPECKLE *n* small spot ▷ *vb* mark with speckles
SPECKLED > SPECKLE
SPECKLES > SPECKLE
SPECKLESS > SPECK
SPECKLING > SPECKLE
SPECKS > SPECK
SPECKY *same as* > SPECCY
SPECS *pl n* spectacles
SPECTACLE *n* strange, interesting, or ridiculous sight
SPECTATE *vb* watch
SPECTATED > SPECTATE
SPECTATES > SPECTATE
SPECTATOR *n* person viewing anything, onlooker
SPECTER *same as* > SPECTRE
SPECTERS > SPECTER
SPECTRA > SPECTRUM
SPECTRAL *adj* of or like a spectre
SPECTRE *n* ghost
SPECTRES > SPECTRE
SPECTRIN *n* any one of a class of fibrous proteins found in the membranes of red blood cells
SPECTRINS > SPECTRIN
SPECTRUM *n* range of different colours, radio waves, etc in order of their wavelengths
SPECTRUMS > SPECTRUM
SPECULA > SPECULUM
SPECULAR *adj* of, relating to, or having the properties of a mirror
SPECULATE *vb* guess, conjecture

SPECULUM *n* medical instrument for examining body cavities
SPECULUMS > SPECULUM
SPED > SPEED
SPEECH *n* act, power, or manner of speaking ▷ *vb* make a speech
SPEECHED > SPEECH
SPEECHES > SPEECH
SPEECHFUL > SPEECH
SPEECHIFY *vb* make speeches, esp boringly
SPEECHING > SPEECH
SPEED *n* swiftness ▷ *vb* go quickly
SPEEDBALL *n* mixture of heroin with amphetamine or cocaine
SPEEDBOAT *n* light fast motorboat
SPEEDED > SPEED
SPEEDER > SPEED
SPEEDERS > SPEED
SPEEDFUL > SPEED
SPEEDIER > SPEEDY
SPEEDIEST > SPEEDY
SPEEDILY > SPEEDY
SPEEDING > SPEED
SPEEDINGS > SPEED
SPEEDLESS > SPEED
SPEEDO *n* speedometer
SPEEDOS > SPEEDO
SPEEDREAD *vb* read very quickly
SPEEDS > SPEED
SPEEDSTER *n* fast car, esp a sports model
SPEEDUP *n* acceleration
SPEEDUPS > SPEEDUP
SPEEDWAY *n* track for motorcycle racing
SPEEDWAYS > SPEEDWAY
SPEEDWELL *n* plant with small blue flowers
SPEEDY *adj* prompt
SPEEL *n* splinter of wood ▷ *vb* Scots word meaning climb
SPEELED > SPEEL
SPEELER > SPEEL
SPEELERS > SPEEL
SPEELING > SPEEL
SPEELS > SPEEL
SPEER *same as* > SPEIR
SPEERED > SPEER
SPEERING > SPEER
SPEERINGS > SPEER
SPEERS > SPEER
SPEIL *dialect word for* > CLIMB
SPEILED > SPEIL
SPEILING > SPEIL
SPEILS > SPEIL
SPEIR *vb* ask
SPEIRED > SPEIR
SPEIRING > SPEIR
SPEIRINGS > SPEIR
SPEIRS > SPEIR
SPEISE *same as* > SPEISS
SPEISES > SPEISE
SPEISS *n* arsenides and antimonides that form when ores containing

arsenic or antimony are smelted
SPEISSES > SPEISS
SPEK *n* bacon, fat, or fatty pork used for larding venison or other game
SPEKBOOM *n* South African shrub
SPEKBOOMS > SPEKBOOM
SPEKS > SPEK
SPELAEAN *adj* of, found in, or inhabiting caves
SPELD *vb* Scots word meaning spread
SPELDED > SPELD
SPELDER *same as* > SPELD
SPELDERED > SPELDER
SPELDERS > SPELDER
SPELDIN *n* fish split and dried
SPELDING *same as* > SPELDIN
SPELDINGS > SPELDING
SPELDINS > SPELDIN
SPELDRIN > VARIANT OF > SPELDIN
SPELDRING *same as* > SPELDIN
SPELDRINS > SPELDRIN
SPELDS > SPELD
SPELEAN *same as* > SPELAEAN
SPELK *n* splinter of wood
SPELKS > SPELK
SPELL *vb* give in correct order the letters that form (a word) ▷ *n* formula of words supposed to have magic power
SPELLABLE > SPELL
SPELLBIND *vb* cause to be spellbound
SPELLDOWN *n* spelling competition
SPELLED > SPELL
SPELLER *n* person who spells words in the manner specified
SPELLERS > SPELLER
SPELLFUL *adj* magical
SPELLICAN *same as* > SPILLIKIN
SPELLING > SPELL
SPELLINGS > SPELL
SPELLS > SPELL
SPELT > SPELL
SPELTER *n* impure zinc, usually containing about 3 per cent of lead and other impurities
SPELTERS > SPELTER
SPELTS > SPELL
SPELTZ *n* wheat variety
SPELTZES > SPELTZ
SPELUNK *vb* explore caves
SPELUNKED > SPELUNK
SPELUNKER *n* person whose hobby is the exploration and study of caves
SPELUNKS > SPELUNK
SPENCE *n* larder or pantry
SPENCER *n* short fitted coat or jacket

SPENCERS > SPENCER
SPENCES > SPENCE
SPEND vb pay out (money)
SPENDABLE > SPEND
SPENDALL n spendthrift
SPENDALLS > SPENDALL
SPENDER n person who spends money in a manner specified
SPENDERS > SPENDER
SPENDIER > SPENDY
SPENDIEST > SPENDY
SPENDING > SPEND
SPENDINGS > SPEND
SPENDS > SPEND
SPENDY adj expensive
SPENSE same as > SPENCE
SPENSES > SPENSE
SPENT > SPEND
SPEOS n (esp in ancient Egypt) a temple or tomb cut into a rock face
SPEOSES > SPEOS
SPERLING same as > SPARLING
SPERLINGS > SPERLING
SPERM n male reproductive cell released in semen during ejaculation
SPERMARIA pl n spermaries
SPERMARY n any organ in which spermatozoa are produced, esp a testis
SPERMATIA pl n male reproductive cells in red algae and some fungi
SPERMATIC adj of or relating to spermatozoa
SPERMATID n any of four immature male gametes that are formed from a spermatocyte
SPERMIC same as > SPERMATIC
SPERMINE n colourless basic water-soluble amine that is found in semen, sputum, and animal tissues
SPERMINES > SPERMINE
SPERMOUS same as > SPERMATIC
SPERMS > SPERM
SPERRE vb bolt
SPERRED > SPERRE
SPERRES > SPERRE
SPERRING > SPERRE
SPERSE vb disperse
SPERSED > SPERSE
SPERSES > SPERSE
SPERSING > SPERSE
SPERST > SPERSE
SPERTHE same as > SPARTH
SPERTHES > SPERTHE
SPET same as > SPIT
SPETCH n piece of animal skin
SPETCHES > SPETCH
SPETS > SPET
SPETSNAZ n Soviet intelligence force
SPETTING > SPET
SPETZNAZ same as > SPETSNAZ

SPEUG n sparrow
SPEUGS > SPEUG
SPEW vb vomit ▷ n something ejected from the mouth
SPEWED > SPEW
SPEWER > SPEW
SPEWERS > SPEW
SPEWIER > SPEWY
SPEWIEST > SPEWY
SPEWINESS > SPEWY
SPEWING > SPEW
SPEWS > SPEW
SPEWY adj marshy
SPHACELUS n death of living tissue
SPHAER same as > SPHERE
SPHAERE same as > SPHERE
SPHAERES > SPHAERE
SPHAERITE n aluminium phosphate
SPHAERS > SPHAERE
SPHAGNOUS > SPHAGNUM
SPHAGNUM n moss found in bogs
SPHAGNUMS > SPHAGNUM
SPHAIREE n game resembling tennis played with wooden bats and a perforated plastic ball
SPHAIREES > SPHAIREE
SPHEAR same as > SPHERE
SPHEARE same as > SPHERE
SPHEARES > SPHEARE
SPHEARS > SPHEAR
SPHENDONE n ancient Greek headband
SPHENE n brown, yellow, green, or grey lustrous mineral
SPHENES > SPHENE
SPHENIC adj having the shape of a wedge
SPHENODON technical name for the > TUATARA
SPHENOID adj wedge-shaped ▷ n wedge-shaped thing
SPHENOIDS > SPHENOID
SPHERAL adj of or shaped like a sphere
SPHERE n perfectly round solid object ▷ vb surround or encircle
SPHERED > SPHERE
SPHERES > SPHERE
SPHERIC same as > SPHERICAL
SPHERICAL adj shaped like a sphere
SPHERICS n geometry and trigonometry of figures on the surface of a sphere
SPHERIER > SPHERY
SPHERIEST > SPHERY
SPHERING > SPHERE
SPHEROID n solid figure that is almost but not exactly a sphere
SPHEROIDS > SPHEROID
SPHERULAR > SPHERULE
SPHERULE n very small sphere or globule
SPHERULES > SPHERULE

SPHERY adj resembling a sphere
SPHINCTER n ring of muscle which controls the opening and closing of a hollow organ
SPHINGES > SPHINX
SPHINGID n hawk moth
SPHINGIDS > SPHINGID
SPHINX n one of the huge statues built by the ancient Egyptians, with the body of a lion and the head of a man
SPHINXES > SPHINX
SPHYGMIC adj of or relating to the pulse
SPHYGMOID adj resembling the pulse
SPHYGMUS n person's pulse
SPHYNX n breed of cat
SPHYNXES > SPHYNX
SPIAL n observation
SPIALS > SPIAL
SPIC n derogatory word for a Spanish-speaking person
SPICA n spiral bandage formed by a series of overlapping figure-of-eight turns
SPICAE > SPICA
SPICAS > SPICA
SPICATE adj having, arranged in, or relating to spikes
SPICATED same as > SPICATE
SPICCATO n style of playing a bowed stringed instrument in which the bow bounces lightly off the strings ▷ adv be played in this manner
SPICCATOS > SPICCATO
SPICE n aromatic substance used as flavouring ▷ vb flavour with spices
SPICEBUSH n North American lauraceous shrub
SPICED > SPICE
SPICELESS > SPICE
SPICER > SPICE
SPICERIES > SPICERY
SPICERS > SPICE
SPICERY n spices collectively
SPICES > SPICE
SPICEY same as > SPICY
SPICIER > SPICY
SPICIEST > SPICY
SPICILEGE n anthology
SPICILY > SPICY
SPICINESS > SPICY
SPICING > SPICE
SPICK adj neat and clean ▷ n spic
SPICKER > SPICK
SPICKEST > SPICK
SPICKNEL same as > SPIGNEL
SPICKNELS > SPICKNEL
SPICKS > SPICK
SPICS > SPIC

SPICULA > SPICULUM
SPICULAE > SPICULUM
SPICULAR > SPICULUM
SPICULATE > SPICULE
SPICULE n small slender pointed structure or crystal
SPICULES > SPICULE
SPICULUM same as > SPICULE
SPICY adj flavoured with spices
SPIDE n Irish derogatory slang for a young working-class man who dresses in casual sports clothes
SPIDER n small eight-legged creature which spins a web to catch insects for food
SPIDERIER > SPIDERY
SPIDERISH > SPIDER
SPIDERMAN n person who erects the steel structure of a building
SPIDERMEN > SPIDERMAN
SPIDERS > SPIDER
SPIDERWEB n spider's web
SPIDERY adj thin and angular like a spider's legs
SPIDES > SPIDE
SPIE same as > SPY
SPIED > SPY
SPIEGEL n manganese-rich pig iron
SPIEGELS > SPIEGEL
SPIEL n speech made to persuade someone to do something ▷ vb deliver a prepared spiel
SPIELED > SPIEL
SPIELER > SPIEL
SPIELERS > SPIEL
SPIELING > SPIEL
SPIELS > SPIEL
SPIER variant of > SPEIR
SPIERED > SPIER
SPIERING > SPIER
SPIERS > SPIER
SPIES > SPY
SPIF n postage stamp perforated with the initials of a firm to avoid theft by employees
SPIFF vb make smart
SPIFFED > SPIFF
SPIFFIED > SPIFFY
SPIFFIER > SPIFFY
SPIFFIES > SPIFFY
SPIFFIEST > SPIFFY
SPIFFILY > SPIFFY
SPIFFING adj excellent
SPIFFS > SPIFF
SPIFFY adj smart ▷ n smart thing or person
SPIFFYING > SPIFFY
SPIFS > SPIF
SPIGHT same as > SPITE
SPIGHTED > SPIGHT
SPIGHTING > SPIGHT
SPIGHTS > SPIGHT
SPIGNEL n European umbelliferous plant
SPIGNELS > SPIGNEL
SPIGOT n stopper for, or tap

fitted to, a cask
**SPIGOTS** >SPIGOT
**SPIK** same as >SPIC
**SPIKE** n sharp point ▷ vb
put spikes on
**SPIKED** >SPIKE
**SPIKEFISH** n large sea fish
**SPIKELET** n unit of a grass
inflorescence
**SPIKELETS** >SPIKELET
**SPIKELIKE** >SPIKE
**SPIKENARD** n fragrant
Indian plant with rose-
purple flowers
**SPIKER** >SPIKE
**SPIKERIES** >SPIKERY
**SPIKERS** >SPIKE
**SPIKERY** n High-Church
Anglicanism
**SPIKES** >SPIKE
**SPIKEY** same as >SPIKY
**SPIKIER** >SPIKY
**SPIKIEST** >SPIKY
**SPIKILY** >SPIKY
**SPIKINESS** >SPIKY
**SPIKING** >SPIK
**SPIKS** >SPIK
**SPIKY** adj resembling a
spike
**SPILE** n heavy timber
stake or pile ▷ vb provide
or support with a spile
**SPILED** >SPILE
**SPILES** >SPILE
**SPILIKIN** same
as >SPILLIKIN
**SPILIKINS** >SPILIKIN
**SPILING** >SPILE
**SPILINGS** >SPILE
**SPILITE** n type of igneous
rock
**SPILITES** >SPILITE
**SPILITIC** >SPILITE
**SPILL** vb pour from or as if
from a container ▷ n fall
**SPILLABLE** >SPILL
**SPILLAGE** n instance or the
process of spilling
**SPILLAGES** >SPILLAGE
**SPILLED** >SPILL
**SPILLER** >SPILL
**SPILLERS** >SPILL
**SPILLIKIN** n thin strip
of wood, cardboard, or
plastic used in spillikins
**SPILLING** >SPILL
**SPILLINGS** >SPILL
**SPILLOVER** n act of spilling
over
**SPILLS** >SPILL
**SPILLWAY** n channel that
carries away surplus
water, as from a dam
**SPILLWAYS** >SPILLWAY
**SPILOSITE** n form of slate
**SPILT** >SPILL
**SPILTH** n something
spilled
**SPILTHS** >SPILTH
**SPIM** n unsolicited
commercial
communications received
on a computer via an
instant-messaging system

**SPIMS** >SPIM
**SPIN** vb revolve or cause
to revolve rapidly ▷ n
revolving motion
**SPINA** n spine
**SPINACENE** n type of
vaccine
**SPINACH** n dark green leafy
vegetable
**SPINACHES** >SPINACH
**SPINACHY** >SPINACH
**SPINAE** >SPINA
**SPINAGE** same as >SPINACH
**SPINAGES** >SPINAGE
**SPINAL** adj of the spine ▷ n
anaesthetic administered
in the spine
**SPINALLY** >SPINAL
**SPINALS** >SPINAL
**SPINAR** n fast-spinning
star
**SPINARS** >SPINAR
**SPINAS** >SPINA
**SPINATE** adj having a spine
**SPINDLE** n rotating rod
that acts as an axle ▷ vb
form into a spindle or
equip with spindles
**SPINDLED** >SPINDLE
**SPINDLER** >SPINDLE
**SPINDLERS** >SPINDLE
**SPINDLES** >SPINDLE
**SPINDLIER** >SPINDLY
**SPINDLING** adj long
and slender, esp
disproportionately so ▷ n
spindling person or thing
**SPINDLY** adj long, slender,
and frail
**SPINDRIFT** n spray blown
up from the sea
**SPINE** n backbone
**SPINED** >SPINE
**SPINEL** n any of a group
of hard glassy minerals of
variable colour
**SPINELESS** adj lacking
courage
**SPINELIKE** >SPINE
**SPINELLE** same as >SPINEL
**SPINELLES** >SPINELLE
**SPINELS** >SPINEL
**SPINES** >SPINE
**SPINET** n small
harpsichord
**SPINETS** >SPINET
**SPINETTE** same as >SPINET
**SPINETTES** >SPINETTE
**SPINIER** >SPINY
**SPINIEST** >SPINY
**SPINIFEX** n coarse spiny
Australian grass
**SPINIFORM** adj like a thorn
**SPININESS** >SPINY
**SPINK** n finch
**SPINKS** >SPINK
**SPINLESS** >SPIN
**SPINNAKER** n large sail on a
racing yacht
**SPINNER** n bowler who
specializes in spinning
the ball to make it change
direction when it bounces
or strikes the bat

**SPINNERET** n organ
through which silk threads
come out of a spider
**SPINNERS** >SPINNER
**SPINNERY** n spinning mill
**SPINNET** same as >SPINET
**SPINNETS** >SPINNET
**SPINNEY** n small wood
**SPINNEYS** >SPINNEY
**SPINNIES** >SPINNY
**SPINNING** >SPIN
**SPINNINGS** >SPIN
**SPINNY** same as >SPINNEY
**SPINODE** another name
for >CUSP
**SPINODES** >SPINODE
**SPINOFF** n development
derived incidentally from
an existing enterprise
**SPINOFFS** >SPINOFF
**SPINONE** as in Italian
spinone wiry-coated gun
dog
**SPINONI** >SPINONE
**SPINOR** n type of
mathematical object
**SPINORS** >SPINOR
**SPINOSE** adj (esp of plants)
bearing many spines
**SPINOSELY** >SPINOSE
**SPINOSITY** >SPINOSE
**SPINOUS** adj resembling a
spine or thorn
**SPINOUT** n spinning skid
that causes a car to run off
the road
**SPINOUTS** >SPINOUT
**SPINS** >SPIN
**SPINSTER** n unmarried
woman
**SPINSTERS** >SPINSTER
**SPINTEXT** n preacher
**SPINTEXTS** >SPINTEXT
**SPINTO** n lyrical singing
voice
**SPINTOS** >SPINTO
**SPINULA** n small spine
**SPINULAE** >SPINULA
**SPINULATE** adj like a spine
**SPINULE** n very small
spine, thorn, or prickle
**SPINULES** >SPINULE
**SPINULOSE** >SPINULE
**SPINULOUS** >SPINULE
**SPINY** adj covered with
spines
**SPIRACLE** n small
blowhole for breathing
through, such as that of a
whale
**SPIRACLES** >SPIRACLE
**SPIRACULA** pl n spiracles
**SPIRAEA** n plant with small
white or pink flowers
**SPIRAEAS** >SPIRAEA
**SPIRAL** n continuous curve
formed by a point winding
about a central axis at an
ever-increasing distance
from it ▷ vb move in a
spiral ▷ adj having the
form of a spiral
**SPIRALED** >SPIRAL
**SPIRALING** >SPIRAL

**SPIRALISM** n ascent in
spiral structure
**SPIRALIST** >SPIRALISM
**SPIRALITY** >SPIRAL
**SPIRALLED** >SPIRAL
**SPIRALLY** >SPIRAL
**SPIRALS** >SPIRAL
**SPIRANT** n fricative
consonant
**SPIRANTS** >SPIRANT
**SPIRASTER** n part of living
sponge
**SPIRATED** adj twisted in
spiral
**SPIRATION** n breathing
**SPIRE** n pointed part of a
steeple ▷ vb assume the
shape of a spire
**SPIREA** same as >SPIRAEA
**SPIREAS** >SPIREA
**SPIRED** >SPIRE
**SPIRELESS** >SPIRE
**SPIRELET** another name
for >FLECHE
**SPIRELETS** >SPIRELET
**SPIREM** same as >SPIREME
**SPIREME** n tangled mass
of chromatin threads into
which the nucleus of a cell
is resolved at the start of
mitosis
**SPIREMES** >SPIREME
**SPIREMS** >SPIREM
**SPIRES** >SPIRE
**SPIREWISE** >SPIRE
**SPIRIC** n type of curve
**SPIRICS** >SPIRIC
**SPIRIER** >SPIRE
**SPIRIEST** >SPIRE
**SPIRILLA** >SPIRILLUM
**SPIRILLAR** >SPIRILLUM
**SPIRILLUM** n any
bacterium having a curved
or spirally twisted rodlike
body
**SPIRING** >SPIRE
**SPIRIT** n nonphysical
aspect of a person
concerned with profound
thoughts ▷ vb carry away
mysteriously
**SPIRITED** adj lively
**SPIRITFUL** >SPIRIT
**SPIRITING** >SPIRIT
**SPIRITISM** n belief that
the spirits of the dead can
communicate with the
living
**SPIRITIST** >SPIRITISM
**SPIRITOSO** adv to be
played in a spirited or
animated manner
**SPIRITOUS** adj high-
spirited
**SPIRITS** >SPIRIT
**SPIRITUAL** adj relating
to the spirit ▷ n type
of religious folk song
originating among Black
slaves in America
**SPIRITUEL** adj having a
refined and lively mind
or wit
**SPIRITUS** n spirit

**SPIRITY** _adj_ spirited
**SPIRLING** same as > SPARLING
**SPIRLINGS** > SPIRLING
**SPIROGRAM** _n_ record made by spirograph
**SPIROGYRA** _n_ green freshwater plant that floats on the surface of ponds and ditches
**SPIROID** _adj_ resembling a spiral or displaying a spiral form
**SPIRT** same as > SPURT
**SPIRTED** > SPIRT
**SPIRTING** > SPIRT
**SPIRTLE** same as > SPURTLE
**SPIRTLES** > SPIRTLE
**SPIRTS** > SPIRT
**SPIRULA** _n_ tropical cephalopod mollusc
**SPIRULAE** > SPIRULA
**SPIRULAS** > SPIRULA
**SPIRULINA** _n_ any filamentous cyanobacterium of the genus _Spirulina_
**SPIRY** > SPIRE
**SPIT** _vb_ eject (saliva or food) from the mouth ⊳ _n_ saliva
**SPITAL** _n_ hospital, esp for the needy sick
**SPITALS** > SPITAL
**SPITBALL** _n_ small missile made from chewed paper
**SPITBALLS** > SPITBALL
**SPITCHER** _adj_ doomed
**SPITE** _n_ deliberate nastiness ⊳ _vb_ annoy or hurt from spite
**SPITED** > SPITE
**SPITEFUL** _adj_ full of or motivated by spite
**SPITES** > SPITE
**SPITFIRE** _n_ person with a fiery temper
**SPITFIRES** > SPITFIRE
**SPITING** > SPITE
**SPITS** > SPIT
**SPITTED** > SPIT
**SPITTEN** > SPIT
**SPITTER** > SPIT
**SPITTERS** > SPIT
**SPITTING** > SPIT
**SPITTINGS** > SPIT
**SPITTLE** _n_ fluid produced in the mouth, saliva
**SPITTLES** > SPITTLE
**SPITTOON** _n_ bowl to spit into
**SPITTOONS** > SPITTOON
**SPITZ** _n_ stockily built dog with a pointed face, erect ears, and a tightly curled tail
**SPITZES** > SPITZ
**SPIV** _n_ smartly dressed man who makes a living by shady dealings
**SPIVS** > SPIV
**SPIVVERY** _n_ behaviour of spivs
**SPIVVIER** > SPIV

**SPIVVIEST** > SPIV
**SPIVVY** > SPIV
**SPLAKE** _n_ type of hybrid trout bred by Canadian zoologists
**SPLAKES** > SPLAKE
**SPLASH** _vb_ scatter liquid on (something) ⊳ _n_ splashing sound
**SPLASHED** > SPLASH
**SPLASHER** _n_ anything used for protection against splashes
**SPLASHERS** > SPLASHER
**SPLASHES** > SPLASH
**SPLASHIER** > SPLASHY
**SPLASHILY** > SPLASHY
**SPLASHING** > SPLASH
**SPLASHY** _adj_ having irregular marks
**SPLAT** _n_ wet slapping sound ⊳ _vb_ make wet slapping sound
**SPLATCH** _vb_ splash
**SPLATCHED** > SPLATCH
**SPLATCHES** > SPLATCH
**SPLATS** > SPLAT
**SPLATTED** > SPLAT
**SPLATTER** _n_ splash ⊳ _vb_ splash (something or someone) with small blobs
**SPLATTERS** > SPLATTER
**SPLATTING** > SPLAT
**SPLAY** _vb_ spread out, with ends spreading in different directions ⊳ _adj_ spread out ⊳ _n_ surface of a wall that forms an oblique angle to the main flat surfaces
**SPLAYED** > SPLAY
**SPLAYFEET** > SPLAYFOOT
**SPLAYFOOT** _n_ foot of which the toes are spread out
**SPLAYING** > SPLAY
**SPLAYS** > SPLAY
**SPLEEN** _n_ abdominal organ which filters bacteria from the blood
**SPLEENFUL** _adj_ bad-tempered or irritable
**SPLEENIER** > SPLEEN
**SPLEENISH** > SPLEEN
**SPLEENS** > SPLEEN
**SPLEENY** > SPLEEN
**SPLENDENT** _adj_ shining brightly
**SPLENDID** _adj_ excellent
**SPLENDOR** same as > SPLENDOUR
**SPLENDORS** > SPLENDOR
**SPLENDOUR** _n_ state or quality of being splendid
**SPLENETIC** _adj_ spiteful or irritable ⊳ _n_ spiteful or irritable person
**SPLENIA** > SPLENIUM
**SPLENIAL** > SPLENIUS
**SPLENIC** _adj_ of, relating to, or in the spleen
**SPLENII** > SPLENIUS
**SPLENITIS** _n_ inflammation of the spleen

**SPLENIUM** _n_ structure in brain
**SPLENIUMS** > SPLENIUM
**SPLENIUS** _n_ either of two flat muscles situated at the back of the neck
**SPLENT** same as > SPLINT
**SPLENTS** > SPLENT
**SPLEUCHAN** _n_ pouch for tobacco
**SPLICE** _vb_ join by interweaving or overlapping ends
**SPLICED** > SPLICE
**SPLICER** > SPLICE
**SPLICERS** > SPLICE
**SPLICES** > SPLICE
**SPLICING** > SPLICE
**SPLIFF** _n_ cannabis, used as a drug
**SPLIFFS** > SPLIFF
**SPLINE** _n_ type of narrow key around a shaft that fits into a corresponding groove ⊳ _vb_ provide (a shaft, part, etc) with splines
**SPLINED** > SPLINE
**SPLINES** > SPLINE
**SPLINING** > SPLINE
**SPLINT** _n_ rigid support for a broken bone ⊳ _vb_ apply a splint to (a broken arm, etc)
**SPLINTED** > SPLINT
**SPLINTER** _n_ thin sharp piece broken off, esp from wood ⊳ _vb_ break into fragments
**SPLINTERS** > SPLINTER
**SPLINTERY** _adj_ liable to produce or break into splinters
**SPLINTING** > SPLINT
**SPLINTS** > SPLINT
**SPLIT** _vb_ break into separate pieces ⊳ _n_ splitting
**SPLITS** > SPLIT
**SPLITTED** > SPLIT
**SPLITTER** > SPLIT
**SPLITTERS** > SPLIT
**SPLITTING** > SPLIT
**SPLODGE** _n_ large uneven spot or stain ⊳ _vb_ mark (something) with a splodge or splodges
**SPLODGED** > SPLODGE
**SPLODGES** > SPLODGE
**SPLODGIER** > SPLODGE
**SPLODGILY** > SPLODGE
**SPLODGING** > SPLODGE
**SPLODGY** > SPLODGE
**SPLOOSH** _vb_ splash or cause to splash about uncontrollably ⊳ _n_ instance or sound of splooshing
**SPLOOSHED** > SPLOOSH
**SPLOOSHES** > SPLOOSH
**SPLORE** _n_ revel
**SPLORES** > SPLORE
**SPLOSH** _vb_ scatter (liquid) vigorously about in blobs

⊳ _n_ instance or sound of sploshing
**SPLOSHED** > SPLOSH
**SPLOSHES** > SPLOSH
**SPLOSHING** > SPLOSH
**SPLOTCH** _vb_ splash, daub
**SPLOTCHED** > SPLOTCH
**SPLOTCHES** > SPLOTCH
**SPLOTCHY** > SPLOTCH
**SPLURGE** _vb_ spend money extravagantly ⊳ _n_ bout of extravagance
**SPLURGED** > SPLURGE
**SPLURGER** > SPLURGE
**SPLURGERS** > SPLURGE
**SPLURGES** > SPLURGE
**SPLURGIER** > SPLURGE
**SPLURGING** > SPLURGE
**SPLURGY** > SPLURGE
**SPLUTTER** _vb_ utter with spitting or choking sounds ⊳ _n_ spluttering
**SPLUTTERS** > SPLUTTER
**SPLUTTERY** > SPLUTTER
**SPOD** _n_ boring, unattractive, or overstudious person
**SPODDIER** > SPOD
**SPODDIEST** > SPOD
**SPODDY** > SPOD
**SPODE** _n_ type of English china or porcelain
**SPODES** > SPODE
**SPODIUM** _n_ black powder
**SPODIUMS** > SPODIUM
**SPODOGRAM** _n_ ash from plant used in studying it
**SPODOSOL** _n_ ashy soil
**SPODOSOLS** > SPODOSOL
**SPODS** > SPOD
**SPODUMENE** _n_ greyish-white, green, or lilac pyroxene mineral
**SPOFFISH** _adj_ officious
**SPOFFY** same as > SPOFFISH
**SPOIL** _vb_ damage
**SPOILABLE** > SPOIL
**SPOILAGE** _n_ amount of material that has been spoilt
**SPOILAGES** > SPOILAGE
**SPOILED** > SPOIL
**SPOILER** _n_ device on an aircraft or car to increase drag
**SPOILERS** > SPOILER
**SPOILFIVE** _n_ card game for two or more players with five cards each
**SPOILFUL** _adj_ taking spoils
**SPOILING** > SPOIL
**SPOILS** > SPOIL
**SPOILSMAN** _n_ person who shares in the spoils of office or advocates the spoils system
**SPOILSMEN** > SPOILSMAN
**SPOILT** > SPOIL
**SPOKE** _n_ radial member of a wheel ⊳ _vb_ equip with spokes
**SPOKED** > SPOKE
**SPOKEN** > SPEAK
**SPOKES** > SPOKE

SPOKESMAN n person chosen to speak on behalf of a group
SPOKESMEN > SPOKESMAN
SPOKEWISE > SPEAK
SPOKING > SPOKE
SPOLIATE less common word for > DESPOIL
SPOLIATED > SPOLIATE
SPOLIATES > SPOLIATE
SPOLIATOR > SPOLIATE
SPONDAIC adj of, relating to, or consisting of spondees ▷ n spondaic line
SPONDAICS > SPONDAIC
SPONDEE n metrical foot of two long syllables
SPONDEES > SPONDEE
SPONDULIX n money
SPONDYL n vertebra
SPONDYLS > SPONDYL
SPONGE n sea animal with a porous absorbent skeleton ▷ vb wipe with a sponge
SPONGEBAG n small bag for holding toiletries when travelling
SPONGED > SPONGE
SPONGEOUS adj spongy
SPONGER n person who sponges on others
SPONGERS > SPONGER
SPONGES > SPONGE
SPONGIER > SPONGY
SPONGIEST > SPONGY
SPONGILY > SPONGY
SPONGIN n fibrous horny protein that forms the skeletal framework of the bath sponge and related sponges
SPONGING > SPONGE
SPONGINS > SPONGIN
SPONGIOSE > SPONGE
SPONGIOUS > SPONGE
SPONGOID > SPONGE
SPONGY adj of or resembling a sponge
SPONSAL n marriage
SPONSALIA n marriage ceremony
SPONSIBLE adj responsible
SPONSING same as > SPONSON
SPONSINGS > SPONSING
SPONSION n act or process of becoming surety
SPONSIONS > SPONSION
SPONSON n outboard support for a gun enabling it to fire fore and aft
SPONSONS > SPONSON
SPONSOR n person who promotes something ▷ vb act as a sponsor for
SPONSORED > SPONSOR
SPONSORS > SPONSOR
SPONTOON n form of halberd carried by some junior infantry officers in the 18th and 19th centuries
SPONTOONS > SPONTOON
SPOOF n mildly satirical

parody ▷ vb fool (a person) with a trick or deception
SPOOFED > SPOOF
SPOOFER > SPOOF
SPOOFERS > SPOOF
SPOOFERY > SPOOF
SPOOFING > SPOOF
SPOOFS > SPOOF
SPOOFY > SPOOF
SPOOK n ghost ▷ vb frighten
SPOOKED > SPOOK
SPOOKERY n spooky events
SPOOKIER > SPOOKY
SPOOKIEST > SPOOKY
SPOOKILY > SPOOKY
SPOOKING > SPOOK
SPOOKISH > SPOOK
SPOOKS > SPOOK
SPOOKY adj ghostly or eerie
SPOOL n cylinder round which something can be wound ▷ vb wind or be wound onto a spool or reel
SPOOLED > SPOOL
SPOOLER > SPOOL
SPOOLERS > SPOOL
SPOOLING > SPOOL
SPOOLINGS > SPOOL
SPOOLS > SPOOL
SPOOM vb sail fast before wind
SPOOMED > SPOOM
SPOOMING > SPOOM
SPOOMS > SPOOM
SPOON n shallow bowl attached to a handle for eating, stirring, or serving food ▷ vb lift with a spoon
SPOONBAIT n type of lure used in angling
SPOONBILL n wading bird of warm regions with a long flat bill
SPOONED > SPOON
SPOONEY same as > SPOONY
SPOONEYS > SPOONEY
SPOONFED adj having been given someone else's opinions
SPOONFUL n amount that a spoon is able to hold
SPOONFULS > SPOONFUL
SPOONIER > SPOONY
SPOONIES > SPOONY
SPOONIEST > SPOONY
SPOONILY > SPOONY
SPOONING > SPOON
SPOONS > SPOON
SPOONSFUL > SPOONFUL
SPOONWAYS adv like spoons
SPOONWISE same as > SPOONWAYS
SPOONY adj foolishly or stupidly amorous ▷ n fool or silly person, esp one in love
SPOOR n trail of an animal ▷ vb track (an animal) by following its trail
SPOORED > SPOOR
SPOORER > SPOOR
SPOORERS > SPOOR

SPOORING > SPOOR
SPOORS > SPOOR
SPOOT n razor shell
SPOOTS > SPOOT
SPORADIC adj intermittent, scattered
SPORAL > SPORE
SPORANGIA pl n organs in fungi in which asexual spores are produced
SPORE n minute reproductive body of some plants ▷ vb produce, carry, or release spores
SPORED > SPORE
SPORES > SPORE
SPORICIDE n substance killing spores
SPORIDESM n group of spores
SPORIDIA > SPORIDIUM
SPORIDIAL > SPORIDIUM
SPORIDIUM n type of spore
SPORING > SPORE
SPOROCARP n specialized leaf branch in certain aquatic ferns that encloses the sori
SPOROCYST n thick-walled rounded structure produced by sporozoan protozoans
SPOROCYTE n diploid cell that divides by meiosis to produce four haploid spores
SPOROGENY n process of spore formation in plants and animals
SPOROGONY n process in sporozoans by which sporozoites are formed
SPOROID adj of or like a spore
SPOROPHYL n leaf in ferns that bears the sporangia
SPOROZOA n class of microscopic creature
SPOROZOAL > SPOROZOA
SPOROZOAN n any parasitic protozoan of the phylum Apicomplexa ▷ adj of or relating to sporozoans
SPOROZOIC > SPOROZOA
SPOROZOON same as > SPOROZOAN
SPORRAN n pouch worn in front of a kilt
SPORRANS > SPORRAN
SPORT n activity for pleasure, competition, or exercise ▷ vb wear proudly
SPORTABLE adj playful
SPORTANCE n playing
SPORTED > SPORT
SPORTER > SPORT
SPORTERS > SPORT
SPORTFUL > SPORT
SPORTIER > SPORTY
SPORTIES > SPORTY
SPORTIEST > SPORTY
SPORTIF adj sporty
SPORTILY > SPORTY

SPORTING adj of sport
SPORTIVE adj playful
SPORTLESS > SPORT
SPORTS adj of or used in sports ▷ n meeting held at a school or college for competitions in athletic events
SPORTSMAN n person who plays sports
SPORTSMEN > SPORTSMAN
SPORTY adj (of a person) interested in sport ▷ n young person who typically wears sportswear, is competitive about sport, and takes an interest in his or her fitness
SPORULAR > SPORULE
SPORULATE vb produce spores, esp by multiple fission
SPORULE n spore, esp a very small spore
SPORULES > SPORULE
SPOSH n slush
SPOSHES > SPOSH
SPOSHIER > SPOSH
SPOSHIEST > SPOSH
SPOSHY > SPOSH
SPOT n small mark on a surface ▷ vb notice
SPOTLESS adj absolutely clean
SPOTLIGHT n powerful light illuminating a small area ▷ vb draw attention to
SPOTLIT > SPOTLIGHT
SPOTS > SPOT
SPOTTABLE > SPOT
SPOTTED > SPOT
SPOTTER n person whose hobby is watching for and noting numbers or types of trains or planes
SPOTTERS > SPOTTER
SPOTTIE n young deer of up to three months of age
SPOTTIER > SPOTTY
SPOTTIES > SPOTTIE
SPOTTIEST > SPOTTY
SPOTTILY > SPOTTY
SPOTTING > SPOT
SPOTTINGS > SPOT
SPOTTY adj with spots
SPOUSAGE n marriage
SPOUSAGES > SPOUSAGE
SPOUSAL n marriage ceremony ▷ adj of or relating to marriage
SPOUSALLY > SPOUSAL
SPOUSALS > SPOUSAL
SPOUSE n husband or wife ▷ vb marry
SPOUSED > SPOUSE
SPOUSES > SPOUSE
SPOUSING > SPOUSE
SPOUT vb pour out in a stream or jet ▷ n projecting tube or lip for pouring liquids
SPOUTED > SPOUT

SPOUTER > SPOUT
SPOUTERS > SPOUT
SPOUTIER > SPOUT
SPOUTIEST > SPOUT
SPOUTING n rainwater downpipe on the outside of a building
SPOUTINGS > SPOUTING
SPOUTLESS > SPOUT
SPOUTS > SPOUT
SPOUTY > SPOUT
SPRACK adj vigorous
SPRACKLE vb clamber
SPRACKLED > SPRACKLE
SPRACKLES > SPRACKLE
SPRAD > SPREAD
SPRADDLE n disease of fowl preventing them from standing
SPRADDLED adj affected by spraddle
SPRADDLES > SPRADDLE
SPRAG n chock or steel bar used to prevent a vehicle from running backwards on an incline ▷ vb use sprag to prevent vehicle from moving
SPRAGGED > SPRAG
SPRAGGING > SPRAG
SPRAGS > SPRAG
SPRAID vb chapped
SPRAIN vb injure (a joint) by a sudden twist ▷ n such an injury
SPRAINED > SPRAIN
SPRAINING > SPRAIN
SPRAINS > SPRAIN
SPRAINT n piece of otter's dung
SPRAINTS > SPRAINT
SPRANG n branch
SPRANGLE vb sprawl
SPRANGLED > SPRANGLE
SPRANGLES > SPRANGLE
SPRANGS > SPRANG
SPRAT n small sea fish
SPRATS > SPRAT
SPRATTLE vb scramble
SPRATTLED > SPRATTLE
SPRATTLES > SPRATTLE
SPRAUCHLE same as > SPRACKLE
SPRAUNCY adj smart
SPRAWL vb lie or sit with the limbs spread out ▷ n part of a city that has spread untidily over a large area
SPRAWLED > SPRAWL
SPRAWLER > SPRAWL
SPRAWLERS > SPRAWL
SPRAWLIER > SPRAWL
SPRAWLING > SPRAWL
SPRAWLS > SPRAWL
SPRAWLY > SPRAWL
SPRAY n (device for producing) fine drops of liquid ▷ vb scatter in fine drops
SPRAYED > SPRAY
SPRAYER > SPRAY
SPRAYERS > SPRAY
SPRAYEY > SPRAY

SPRAYIER > SPRAY
SPRAYIEST > SPRAY
SPRAYING > SPRAY
SPRAYINGS > SPRAY
SPRAYS > SPRAY
SPREAD vb open out or be displayed to the fullest extent ▷ n spreading ▷ adj extended or stretched out, esp to the fullest extent
SPREADER n machine or device used for scattering bulk materials over a relatively wide area
SPREADERS > SPREADER
SPREADING > SPREAD
SPREADS > SPREAD
SPREAGH n cattle raid
SPREAGHS > SPREAGH
SPREATHE vb chap
SPREATHED adj sore
SPREATHES > SPREATHE
SPREAZE same as > SPREATHE
SPREAZED same as > SPREATHED
SPREAZES > SPREAZE
SPREAZING > SPREAZE
SPRECHERY n theft of cattle
SPRECKLED adj speckled
SPRED same as > SPREAD
SPREDD same as > SPREAD
SPREDDE same as > SPREAD
SPREDDEN > SPREDDE
SPREDDES > SPREDDE
SPREDDING > SPREDDE
SPREDDS > SPREDD
SPREDS > SPRED
SPREE n session of overindulgence, usu in drinking or spending money ▷ vb go on a spree
SPREED > SPREE
SPREEING > SPREE
SPREES > SPREE
SPREETHE same as > SPREATHE
SPREETHED > SPREETHE
SPREETHES > SPREETHE
SPREEZE same as > SPREATHE
SPREEZED > SPREEZE
SPREEZES > SPREEZE
SPREEZING > SPREEZE
SPREKELIA n bulbous plant grown for its striking crimson or white pendent flowers
SPRENT > SPRINKLE
SPREW same as > SPRUE
SPREWS > SPREW
SPRIER > SPRY
SPRIEST > SPRY
SPRIG n twig or shoot ▷ vb fasten or secure with sprigs
SPRIGGED > SPRIG
SPRIGGER > SPRIG
SPRIGGERS > SPRIG
SPRIGGIER > SPRIG
SPRIGGING > SPRIG
SPRIGGY > SPRIG
SPRIGHT same as > SPRITE

SPRIGHTED > SPRIGHT
SPRIGHTLY adj lively and brisk ▷ adv in a lively manner
SPRIGHTS > SPRIGHT
SPRIGS > SPRIG
SPRIGTAIL n species of duck
SPRING vb move suddenly upwards or forwards in a single motion, jump ▷ n season between winter and summer
SPRINGAL n young man
SPRINGALD same as > SPRINGAL
SPRINGALS > SPRINGAL
SPRINGBOK n S African antelope
SPRINGE n type of snare for catching small wild animals or birds ▷ vb set such a snare
SPRINGED > SPRINGE
SPRINGER n small spaniel
SPRINGERS > SPRINGER
SPRINGES > SPRINGE
SPRINGIER > SPRINGY
SPRINGILY > SPRINGY
SPRINGING > SPRING
SPRINGLE same as > SPRINGE
SPRINGLES > SPRINGE
SPRINGLET n small spring
SPRINGS > SPRING
SPRINGY adj elastic
SPRINKLE vb scatter (liquid or powder) in tiny drops or particles over (something) ▷ n act or an instance of sprinkling or a quantity that is sprinkled
SPRINKLED > SPRINKLE
SPRINKLER n device with small holes that is attached to a garden hose or watering can and used to spray water
SPRINKLES > SPRINKLE
SPRINT n short race run at top speed ▷ vb run a short distance at top speed
SPRINTED > SPRINT
SPRINTER > SPRINT
SPRINTERS > SPRINT
SPRINTING > SPRINT
SPRINTS > SPRINT
SPRIT n small spar set diagonally across a sail to extend it
SPRITE n elf
SPRITEFUL > SPRITE
SPRITELY same as > SPRIGHTLY
SPRITES > SPRITE
SPRITS > SPRIT
SPRITSAIL n sail extended by a sprit
SPRITZ vb spray liquid
SPRITZED > SPRITZ
SPRITZER n tall drink of wine and soda water
SPRITZERS > SPRITZER
SPRITZES > SPRITZ

SPRITZIG adj (of wine) sparkling ▷ n sparkling wine
SPRITZIGS > SPRITZIG
SPRITZING > SPRITZ
SPROCKET n wheel with teeth on the rim, that drives or is driven by a chain
SPROCKETS > SPROCKET
SPROD n young salmon
SPRODS > SPROD
SPROG n child
SPROGS > SPROG
SPRONG > SPRING
SPROUT vb put forth shoots ▷ n shoot
SPROUTED > SPROUT
SPROUTING > SPROUT
SPROUTS > SPROUT
SPRUCE n kind of fir ▷ adj neat and smart
SPRUCED > SPRUCE
SPRUCELY > SPRUCE
SPRUCER > SPRUCE
SPRUCES > SPRUCE
SPRUCEST > SPRUCE
SPRUCIER > SPRUCE
SPRUCIEST > SPRUCE
SPRUCING > SPRUCE
SPRUCY > SPRUCE
SPRUE n vertical channel in a mould through which plastic or molten metal is poured
SPRUES > SPRUE
SPRUG n sparrow
SPRUGS > SPRUG
SPRUIK vb speak in public (used esp of a showman or salesman)
SPRUIKED > SPRUIK
SPRUIKER > SPRUIK
SPRUIKERS > SPRUIK
SPRUIKING > SPRUIK
SPRUIKS > SPRUIK
SPRUIT n small tributary stream or watercourse
SPRUITS > SPRUIT
SPRUNG > SPRING
SPRUSH Scots form of > SPRUCE
SPRUSHED > SPRUSH
SPRUSHES > SPRUSH
SPRUSHING > SPRUSH
SPRY adj active or nimble
SPRYER > SPRY
SPRYEST > SPRY
SPRYLY > SPRY
SPRYNESS > SPRY
SPUD n potato ▷ vb remove (bark) or eradicate (weeds) with a spud
SPUDDED > SPUD
SPUDDER same as > SPUD
SPUDDERS > SPUDDER
SPUDDIER > SPUDDY
SPUDDIEST > SPUDDY
SPUDDING > SPUD
SPUDDINGS > SPUD
SPUDDLE n feeble movement
SPUDDLES > SPUDDLE
SPUDDY adj short and fat

SPUDS > SPUD
SPUE same as > SPEW
SPUED > SPUE
SPUEING > SPUE
SPUER > SPUE
SPUERS > SPUE
SPUES > SPUE
SPUG same as > SPUGGY
SPUGGIES > SPUGGY
SPUGGY n house sparrow
SPUGS > SPUG
SPUILZIE vb plunder
SPUILZIED > SPUILZIE
SPUILZIES > SPUILZIE
SPUING > SPUE
SPULE Scots word
for > SHOULDER
SPULES > SPULE
SPULYE same as > SPUILZIE
SPULYED > SPULYE
SPULYEING > SPULYE
SPULYES > SPULYE
SPULYIE same as > SPUILZIE
SPULYIED > SPULYIE
SPULYIES > SPULYIE
SPULZIE same as > SPUILZIE
SPULZIED > SPULZIE
SPULZIES > SPULZIE
SPUMANTE n Italian
sparkling wine
SPUMANTES > SPUMANTE
SPUME vb froth ▷ n foam or
froth on the sea
SPUMED > SPUME
SPUMES > SPUME
SPUMIER > SPUM
SPUMIEST > SPUM
SPUMING > SPUME
SPUMONE n creamy Italian
ice cream
SPUMONES > SPUMONE
SPUMONI same
as > SPUMONE
SPUMONIS > SPUMONI
SPUMOUS > SPUME
SPUMY > SPUME
SPUN > SPIN
SPUNGE same as > SPONGE
SPUNGES > SPUNGE
SPUNK n courage, spirit
▷ vb catch fire
SPUNKED > SPUNK
SPUNKIE n will-o'-the-wisp
SPUNKIER > SPUNK
SPUNKIES > SPUNKIE
SPUNKIEST > SPUNK
SPUNKILY > SPUNK
SPUNKING > SPUNK
SPUNKS > SPUNK
SPUNKY > SPUNK
SPUNYARN n small stuff
made from rope yarns
twisted together
SPUNYARNS > SPUNYARN
SPUR n stimulus or
incentive ▷ vb urge on,
incite (someone)
SPURGALL vb prod with
spur
SPURGALLS > SPURGALL
SPURGE n plant with milky
sap
SPURGES > SPURGE
SPURIAE n type of bird

feathers
SPURIOUS adj not genuine
SPURLESS > SPUR
SPURLING same
as > SPARLING
SPURLINGS > SPURLING
SPURN vb reject with scorn
▷ n instance of spurning
SPURNE vb spur
SPURNED > SPURN
SPURNER > SPURN
SPURNERS > SPURN
SPURNES > SPURNE
SPURNING > SPURN
SPURNINGS > SPURN
SPURNS > SPURN
SPURRED > SPUR
SPURRER > SPUR
SPURRERS > SPUR
SPURREY n any of several
low-growing European
plants
SPURREYS > SPURREY
SPURRIER n maker of spurs
SPURRIERS > SPURRIER
SPURRIES > SPURRY
SPURRIEST > SPURRY
SPURRING > SPUR
SPURRINGS > SPUR
SPURRY n spurrey ▷ adj
resembling a spur
SPURS > SPUR
SPURT vb gush or cause to
gush out in a jet ▷ n short
sudden burst of activity or
speed
SPURTED > SPURT
SPURTER > SPURT
SPURTING > SPURT
SPURTLE n wooden spoon
for stirring porridge
SPURTLES > SPURTLE
SPURTS > SPURT
SPURWAY n path used by
riders
SPURWAYS > SPURWAY
SPUTA > SPUTUM
SPUTNIK n early Soviet
artificial satellite
SPUTNIKS > SPUTNIK
SPUTTER n splutter ▷ vb
splutter
SPUTTERED > SPUTTER
SPUTTERER > SPUTTER
SPUTTERS > SPUTTER
SPUTTERY > SPUTTER
SPUTUM n spittle, usu
mixed with mucus
SPY n person employed to
obtain secret information
▷ vb act as a spy
SPYAL n spy
SPYALS > SPYAL
SPYGLASS n small
telescope
SPYHOLE n small hole in a
door, etc through which
one may watch secretly
SPYHOLES > SPYHOLE
SPYING > SPY
SPYINGS > SPY
SPYMASTER n person who
controls spy network

SPYPLANE n military
aeroplane used to spy on
enemy
SPYPLANES > SPYPLANE
SPYRE same as > SPIRE
SPYRES > SPYRE
SPYWARE n software
installed via the internet
on a computer without
the user's knowledge and
used to gain information
about the user
SPYWARES > SPYWARE
SQUAB n young bird yet to
leave the nest ▷ adj (of
birds) recently hatched
and still unfledged ▷ vb
fall
SQUABASH vb crush
SQUABBED > SQUAB
SQUABBER > SQUAB
SQUABBEST > SQUAB
SQUABBIER > SQUAB
SQUABBING > SQUAB
SQUABBISH > SQUAB
SQUABBLE n (engage in a)
petty or noisy quarrel ▷ vb
quarrel over a small matter
SQUABBLED > SQUABBLE
SQUABBLER > SQUABBLE
SQUABBLES > SQUABBLE
SQUABBY > SQUAB
SQUABS > SQUAB
SQUACCO n S European
heron
SQUACCOS > SQUACCO
SQUAD n small group of
people working or training
together ▷ vb set up
squads
SQUADDED > SQUAD
SQUADDIE n private soldier
SQUADDIES > SQUADDIE
SQUADDING > SQUAD
SQUADDY same
as > SQUADDIE
SQUADRON n division of an
air force, fleet, or cavalry
regiment ▷ vb assign to
squadrons
SQUADRONE n former
Scottish political party
SQUADRONS > SQUADRON
SQUADS > SQUAD
SQUAIL vb throw sticks at
SQUAILED > SQUAIL
SQUAILER > SQUAIL
SQUAILERS > SQUAIL
SQUAILING > SQUAIL
SQUAILS > SQUAIL
SQUALENE n terpene first
found in the liver of sharks
SQUALENES > SQUALENE
SQUALID adj dirty and
unpleasant
SQUALIDER > SQUALID
SQUALIDLY > SQUALID
SQUALL n sudden strong
wind ▷ vb cry noisily, yell
SQUALLED > SQUALL
SQUALLER > SQUALL
SQUALLERS > SQUALL
SQUALLIER > SQUALL
SQUALLING > SQUALL

SQUALLISH > SQUALL
SQUALLS > SQUALL
SQUALLY > SQUALL
SQUALOID adj of or like a
shark
SQUALOR n disgusting dirt
and filth
SQUALORS > SQUALOR
SQUAMA n scale or scalelike
structure
SQUAMAE > SQUAMA
SQUAMATE > SQUAMA
SQUAMATES > SQUAMA
SQUAME same as > SQUAMA
SQUAMELLA n small scale
SQUAMES > SQUAME
SQUAMOSAL n thin platelike
paired bone in the skull
of vertebrates ▷ adj of or
relating to this bone
SQUAMOSE same
as > SQUAMOUS
SQUAMOUS adj (of
epithelium) consisting of
one or more layers of flat
platelike cells
SQUAMULA same
as > SQUAMELLA
SQUAMULAS > SQUAMULA
SQUAMULE same
as > SQUAMELLA
SQUAMULES > SQUAMULE
SQUANDER vb waste
(money or resources)
▷ n extravagance or
dissipation
SQUANDERS > SQUANDER
SQUARE n geometric figure
with four equal sides and
four right angles ▷ adj
square in shape ▷ vb
multiply (a number) by
itself ▷ adv squarely,
directly
SQUARED > SQUARE
SQUARELY adv in a direct
way
SQUARER > SQUARE
SQUARERS > SQUARE
SQUARES > SQUARE
SQUAREST > SQUARE
SQUARIAL n type of square
dish for receiving satellite
television
SQUARIALS > SQUARIAL
SQUARING > SQUARE
SQUARINGS > SQUARE
SQUARISH > SQUARE
SQUARK n hypothetical
boson partner of a quark
SQUARKS > SQUARK
SQUARROSE adj having a
rough surface
SQUARSON n clergyman
who is also landowner
SQUARSONS > SQUARSON
SQUASH vb crush flat ▷ n
sweet fruit drink diluted
with water
SQUASHED > SQUASH
SQUASHER > SQUASH
SQUASHERS > SQUASH
SQUASHES > SQUASH
SQUASHIER > SQUASHY

SQUASHILY > SQUASHY
SQUASHING > SQUASH
SQUASHY *adj* soft and easily squashed
SQUAT *vb* crouch with the knees bent and the weight on the feet ▷ *n* place where squatters live ▷ *adj* short and broad
SQUATLY > SQUAT
SQUATNESS > SQUAT
SQUATS > SQUAT
SQUATTED > SQUAT
SQUATTER *n* illegal occupier of unused premises
SQUATTERS > SQUATTER
SQUATTEST > SQUAT
SQUATTIER > SQUATTY
SQUATTILY > SQUATTY
SQUATTING > SQUAT
SQUATTLE *vb* squat
SQUATTLED > SQUATTLE
SQUATTLES > SQUATTLE
SQUATTY *adj* short and broad
SQUAW *n* offensive term for a Native American woman
SQUAWBUSH *n* American shrub
SQUAWFISH *n* North American minnow
SQUAWK *n* loud harsh cry ▷ *vb* utter a squawk
SQUAWKED > SQUAWK
SQUAWKER > SQUAWK
SQUAWKERS > SQUAWK
SQUAWKIER > SQUAWK
SQUAWKING > SQUAWK
SQUAWKS > SQUAWK
SQUAWKY > SQUAWK
SQUAWMAN *n* offensive term for a White man married to a Native American woman
SQUAWMEN > SQUAWMAN
SQUAWROOT *n* North American parasitic plant
SQUAWS > SQUAW
SQUEAK *n* short shrill cry or sound ▷ *vb* make or utter a squeak
SQUEAKED > SQUEAK
SQUEAKER > SQUEAK
SQUEAKERS > SQUEAK
SQUEAKERY > SQUEAK
SQUEAKIER > SQUEAK
SQUEAKILY > SQUEAK
SQUEAKING > SQUEAK
SQUEAKS > SQUEAK
SQUEAKY > SQUEAK
SQUEAL *n* long shrill cry or sound ▷ *vb* make or utter a squeal
SQUEALED > SQUEAL
SQUEALER > SQUEAL
SQUEALERS > SQUEAL
SQUEALING > SQUEAL
SQUEALS > SQUEAL
SQUEAMISH *adj* easily sickened or shocked
SQUEEGEE *n* tool with a rubber blade for clearing water from a surface ▷ *vb* remove (water or other

liquid) from (something) by use of a squeegee
SQUEEGEED > SQUEEGEE
SQUEEGEES > SQUEEGEE
SQUEEZE *vb* grip or press firmly ▷ *n* squeezing
SQUEEZED > SQUEEZE
SQUEEZER > SQUEEZE
SQUEEZERS > SQUEEZE
SQUEEZES > SQUEEZE
SQUEEZIER > SQUEEZE
SQUEEZING > SQUEEZE
SQUEEZY > SQUEEZE
SQUEG *vb* oscillate
SQUEGGED > SQUEG
SQUEGGER > SQUEG
SQUEGGERS > SQUEG
SQUEGGING > SQUEG
SQUEGS > SQUEG
SQUELCH *vb* make a wet sucking sound, as by walking through mud ▷ *n* squelching sound
SQUELCHED > SQUELCH
SQUELCHER > SQUELCH
SQUELCHES > SQUELCH
SQUELCHY > SQUELCH
SQUIB *n* small firework that hisses before exploding
SQUIBBED > SQUIB
SQUIBBING > SQUIB
SQUIBS > SQUIB
SQUID *n* sea creature with a long soft body and ten tentacles ▷ *vb* (of a parachute) to assume an elongated squidlike shape owing to excess air pressure
SQUIDDED > SQUID
SQUIDDING > SQUID
SQUIDGE *vb* squash
SQUIDGED > SQUIDGE
SQUIDGES > SQUIDGE
SQUIDGIER > SQUIDGY
SQUIDGING > SQUIDGE
SQUIDGY *adj* soft, moist, and squashy
SQUIDS > SQUID
SQUIER *same as* > SQUIRE
SQUIERS > SQUIER
SQUIFF *same as* > SQUIFFY
SQUIFFED *same as* > SQUIFFY
SQUIFFER *n* concertina
SQUIFFERS > SQUIFFER
SQUIFFIER > SQUIFFY
SQUIFFY *adj* slightly drunk
SQUIGGLE *n* wavy line ▷ *vb* wriggle
SQUIGGLED > SQUIGGLE
SQUIGGLER > SQUIGGLE
SQUIGGLES > SQUIGGLE
SQUIGGLY > SQUIGGLE
SQUILGEE *same as* > SQUEEGEE
SQUILGEED > SQUILGEE
SQUILGEES > SQUILGEE
SQUILL *n* Mediterranean plant of the lily family
SQUILLA *n* any mantis shrimp of the genus *Squilla*
SQUILLAE > SQUILLA

SQUILLAS > SQUILLA
SQUILLION *n* extremely large but unspecified number, quantity, or amount
SQUILLS > SQUILL
SQUINANCY *same as* > QUINSY
SQUINCH *n* small arch across an internal corner of a tower, used to support a superstructure such as a spire ▷ *vb* squeeze
SQUINCHED > SQUINCH
SQUINCHES > SQUINCH
SQUINIED > SQUINY
SQUINIES > SQUINY
SQUINNIED > SQUINNY
SQUINNIER > SQUINNY
SQUINNIES > SQUINNY
SQUINNY *vb* squint ▷ *adj* squint
SQUINT *vb* have eyes which face in different directions ▷ *n* squinting condition of the eye ▷ *adj* crooked
SQUINTED > SQUINT
SQUINTER > SQUINT
SQUINTERS > SQUINT
SQUINTEST > SQUINT
SQUINTIER > SQUINT
SQUINTING > SQUINT
SQUINTS > SQUINT
SQUINTY > SQUINT
SQUINY *same as* > SQUINNY
SQUINYING > SQUINY
SQUIRAGE *n* body of squires
SQUIRAGES > SQUIRAGE
SQUIRALTY *same as* > SQUIRAGE
SQUIRARCH *n* person who believes in government by squires
SQUIRE *n* country gentleman, usu the main landowner in a community ▷ *vb* (of a man) escort (a woman)
SQUIREAGE *same as* > SQUIRAGE
SQUIRED > SQUIRE
SQUIREDOM > SQUIRE
SQUIREEN *n* petty squire
SQUIREENS > SQUIREEN
SQUIRELY > SQUIRE
SQUIRES > SQUIRE
SQUIRESS *n* wife of squire
SQUIRING > SQUIRE
SQUIRISH > SQUIRE
SQUIRM *vb* wriggle, writhe ▷ *n* wriggling movement
SQUIRMED > SQUIRM
SQUIRMER > SQUIRM
SQUIRMERS > SQUIRM
SQUIRMIER > SQUIRMY
SQUIRMING > SQUIRM
SQUIRMS > SQUIRM
SQUIRMY *adj* moving with a wriggling motion
SQUIRR *same as* > SKIRR
SQUIRRED > SQUIRR
SQUIRREL *n* small bushy-tailed tree-living animal ▷ *vb* store for future use

SQUIRRELS > SQUIRREL
SQUIRRELY > SQUIRREL
SQUIRRING > SQUIRR
SQUIRRS > SQUIRR
SQUIRT *vb* force (a liquid) or (of a liquid) be forced out of a narrow opening ▷ *n* jet of liquid
SQUIRTED > SQUIRT
SQUIRTER > SQUIRT
SQUIRTERS > SQUIRT
SQUIRTING > SQUIRT
SQUIRTS > SQUIRT
SQUISH *n* (make) a soft squelching sound ▷ *vb* crush (something) with a soft squelching sound
SQUISHED > SQUISH
SQUISHES > SQUISH
SQUISHIER > SQUISHY
SQUISHING > SQUISH
SQUISHY *adj* soft and yielding to the touch
SQUIT *n* insignificant person
SQUITCH *n* couch grass
SQUITCHES > SQUITCH
SQUITS > SQUIT
SQUIZ *n* look or glance, esp an inquisitive one
SQUIZZES > SQUIZ
SQUOOSH *vb* squash
SQUOOSHED > SQUOOSH
SQUOOSHES > SQUOOSH
SQUOOSHY > SQUOOSH
SQUUSH *same as* > SQUOOSH
SQUUSHED > SQUUSH
SQUUSHES > SQUUSH
SQUUSHING > SQUUSH
SRADDHA *n* Hindu offering to ancestor
SRADDHAS > SRADDHA
SRADHA *same as* > SRADHA
SRADHAS > SRADHA
SRI *n* title of respect used when addressing a Hindu
SRIS > SRI
ST *interj* exclamation to attract attention
STAB *vb* pierce with something pointed ▷ *n* stabbing
STABBED > STAB
STABBER > STAB
STABBERS > STAB
STABBING > STAB
STABBINGS > STAB
STABILATE *n* preserved collection of tiny animals
STABILE *n* stationary abstract construction, usually of wire, metal, wood, etc ▷ *adj* fixed
STABILES > STABILE
STABILISE *same as* > STABILIZE
STABILITY *n* quality of being stable
STABILIZE *vb* make or become stable
STABLE *n* building in which horses are kept ▷ *vb* put or keep (a horse) in a stable ▷ *adj* firmly fixed or

established

**STABLEBOY** *n* boy or man who works in a stable

**STABLED** >STABLE

**STABLEMAN** *same as* >STABLEBOY

**STABLEMEN** >STABLEMAN

**STABLER** *n* stable owner

**STABLERS** >STABLER

**STABLES** >STABLE

**STABLEST** >STABLE

**STABLING** *n* stable buildings or accommodation

**STABLINGS** >STABLING

**STABLISH** *archaic variant of* >ESTABLISH

**STABLY** >STABLE

**STABS** >STAB

**STACCATI** >STACCATO

**STACCATO** *adv* with the notes sharply separated ▷ *adj* consisting of short abrupt sounds ▷ *n* staccato note

**STACCATOS** >STACCATO

**STACHYS** *n* any plant of the genus *Stachys*

**STACHYSES** >STACHYS

**STACK** *n* ordered pile ▷ *vb* pile in a stack

**STACKABLE** >STACK

**STACKED** >STACK

**STACKER** >STACK

**STACKERS** >STACK

**STACKET** *n* fence of wooden posts

**STACKETS** >STACKET

**STACKING** *n* arrangement of aircraft traffic in busy flight lanes

**STACKINGS** >STACKING

**STACKLESS** >STACK

**STACKROOM** *n* area of library where books are not on open shelves

**STACKS** >STACK

**STACKUP** *n* number of aircraft waiting to land

**STACKUPS** >STACKUP

**STACKYARD** *n* place where livestock are kept

**STACTE** *n* one of several sweet-smelling spices used in incense

**STACTES** >STACTE

**STADDA** *n* type of saw

**STADDAS** >STADDA

**STADDLE** *n* type of support or prop

**STADDLES** >STADDLE

**STADE** *same as* >STADIUM

**STADES** >STADE

**STADIA** *n* instrument used in surveying

**STADIAL** *n* stage in development of glacier

**STADIALS** >STADIAL

**STADIAS** >STADIA

**STADIUM** *n* sports arena with tiered seats for spectators

**STADIUMS** >STADIUM

**STAFF** *n* people employed

in an organization ▷ *vb* supply with personnel

**STAFFAGE** *n* ornamentation in work of art

**STAFFAGES** >STAFFAGE

**STAFFED** >STAFF

**STAFFER** *n* member of staff, esp, in journalism, of editorial staff

**STAFFERS** >STAFFER

**STAFFING** >STAFF

**STAFFMAN** *n* person who holds the levelling staff when a survey is being made

**STAFFMEN** >STAFFMAN

**STAFFROOM** *n* common room for teachers

**STAFFS** >STAFF

**STAG** *n* adult male deer ▷ *adv* without a female escort ▷ *vb* apply for (shares in a new issue) with the intention of selling them for a quick profit

**STAGE** *n* step or period of development ▷ *vb* put (a play) on stage

**STAGEABLE** >STAGE

**STAGED** >STAGE

**STAGEFUL** *n* amount that can appear on stage

**STAGEFULS** >STAGEFUL

**STAGEHAND** *n* person who moves props and scenery on a stage

**STAGELIKE** >STAGE

**STAGER** *n* person of experience

**STAGERIES** >STAGERY

**STAGERS** >STAGER

**STAGERY** *n* theatrical effects or techniques

**STAGES** >STAGE

**STAGEY** *same as* >STAGY

**STAGGARD** *n* male red deer in the fourth year of life

**STAGGARDS** >STAGGARD

**STAGGART** *same as* >STAGGARD

**STAGGARTS** >STAGGART

**STAGGED** >STAG

**STAGGER** *vb* walk unsteadily ▷ *n* staggering

**STAGGERED** >STAGGER

**STAGGERER** >STAGGER

**STAGGERS** *n* disease of horses and other domestic animals that causes staggering

**STAGGERY** >STAGGER

**STAGGIE** *n* little stag

**STAGGIER** >STAG

**STAGGIES** >STAGGIE

**STAGGIEST** >STAG

**STAGGING** >STAG

**STAGGY** >STAG

**STAGHORN** *n as in staghorn fern* type of fern with fronds that resemble antlers

**STAGHORNS** >STAGHORN

**STAGHOUND** *n* breed of hound similar in appearance to the foxhound but larger

**STAGIER** >STAGY

**STAGIEST** >STAGY

**STAGILY** >STAGY

**STAGINESS** >STAGY

**STAGING** *n* temporary support used in building

**STAGINGS** >STAGING

**STAGNANCE** >STAGNANT

**STAGNANCY** >STAGNANT

**STAGNANT** *adj* (of water or air) stale from not moving

**STAGNATE** *vb* be stagnant

**STAGNATED** >STAGNATE

**STAGNATES** >STAGNATE

**STAGS** >STAG

**STAGY** *adj* too theatrical or dramatic

**STAID** *adj* sedate, serious, and rather dull

**STAIDER** >STAID

**STAIDEST** >STAID

**STAIDLY** >STAID

**STAIDNESS** >STAID

**STAIG** *Scots variant of* >STAG

**STAIGS** >STAIG

**STAIN** *vb* discolour, mark ▷ *n* discoloration or mark

**STAINABLE** >STAIN

**STAINED** >STAIN

**STAINER** >STAIN

**STAINERS** >STAIN

**STAINING** >STAIN

**STAININGS** >STAIN

**STAINLESS** *adj* resistant to discoloration, esp discoloration resulting from corrosion ▷ *n* stainless steel

**STAINS** >STAIN

**STAIR** *n* one step in a flight of stairs

**STAIRCASE** *n* flight of stairs with a handrail or banisters ▷ *vb* buy other houses in same building

**STAIRED** *adj* having stairs

**STAIRFOOT** *n* place at foot of stairs

**STAIRHEAD** *n* top of a flight of stairs

**STAIRLESS** >STAIR

**STAIRLIFT** *n* wall-mounted lifting device to carry person up stairs

**STAIRLIKE** >STAIR

**STAIRS** *pl n* flight of steps between floors, usu indoors

**STAIRSTEP** *n* one of the steps in a staircase

**STAIRWAY** *n* staircase

**STAIRWAYS** >STAIRWAY

**STAIRWELL** *n* vertical shaft in a building that contains a staircase

**STAIRWISE** *adv* by steps

**STAIRWORK** *n* unseen plotting

**STAITH** *same as* >STAITHE

**STAITHE** *n* wharf

**STAITHES** >STAITHE

**STAITHS** >STAITH

**STAKE** *n* pointed stick or post driven into the ground as a support or marker ▷ *vb* support or mark out with stakes

**STAKED** >STAKE

**STAKEOUT** *n* police surveillance of an area or house ▷ *vb* keep an area or house under surveillance

**STAKEOUTS** >STAKEOUT

**STAKES** >STAKE

**STAKING** >STAKE

**STALACTIC** *adj* relating to the masses of calcium carbonate hanging from the roofs of limestone caves

**STALAG** *n* German prisoner-of-war camp in World War II

**STALAGS** >STALAG

**STALE** *adj* not fresh ▷ *vb* make or become stale ▷ *n* urine of horses or cattle

**STALED** >STALE

**STALELY** >STALE

**STALEMATE** *n* (in chess) position in which any of a player's moves would put his king in check, resulting in a draw ▷ *vb* subject to a stalemate

**STALENESS** >STALE

**STALER** >STALE

**STALES** >STALE

**STALEST** >STALE

**STALING** >STALE

**STALK** *n* plant's stem ▷ *vb* follow or approach stealthily

**STALKED** >STALK

**STALKER** >STALK

**STALKERS** >STALK

**STALKIER** >STALKY

**STALKIEST** >STALKY

**STALKILY** >STALKY

**STALKING** >STALK

**STALKINGS** >STALK

**STALKLESS** >STALK

**STALKLIKE** >STALK

**STALKO** *n* idle gentleman

**STALKOES** >STALKO

**STALKS** >STALK

**STALKY** *adj* like a stalk

**STALL** *n* small stand for the display and sale of goods ▷ *vb* stop (a motor vehicle or engine) or (of a motor vehicle or engine) stop accidentally

**STALLAGE** *n* rent paid for market stall

**STALLAGES** >STALLAGE

**STALLED** >STALL

**STALLING** >STALL

**STALLINGS** >STALL

**STALLION** *n* uncastrated male horse

**STALLIONS** >STALLION

**STALLMAN** *n* keeper of a stall

STALLMEN > STALLMAN

STALLS > STALL

STALWART *adj* strong and sturdy ▷ *n* stalwart person

STALWARTS > STALWART

STALWORTH *n* stalwart person

STAMEN *n* pollen-producing part of a flower

STAMENED *adj* having stamen

STAMENS > STAMEN

STAMINA *n* enduring energy and strength

STAMINAL > STAMINA

STAMINAS > STAMINA

STAMINATE *adj* (of plants) having stamens, esp having stamens but no carpels

STAMINEAL *adj* having a stamen

STAMINODE *n* stamen that produces no pollen

STAMINODY *n* development of any of various plant organs into stamens

STAMINOID *adj* like a stamen

STAMMEL *n* coarse woollen cloth in former use for undergarments

STAMMELS > STAMMEL

STAMMER *vb* speak or say with involuntary pauses or repetition of syllables ▷ *n* tendency to stammer

STAMMERED > STAMMER

STAMMERER > STAMMER

STAMMERS > STAMMER

STAMNOI > STAMNOS

STAMNOS *n* ancient Greek jar

STAMP *n* piece of gummed paper stuck to an envelope or parcel to show that the postage has been paid ▷ *vb* bring (one's foot) down forcefully

STAMPED > STAMP

STAMPEDE *n* sudden rush of frightened animals or of a crowd ▷ *vb* (cause to) take part in a stampede

STAMPEDED > STAMPEDE

STAMPEDER > STAMPEDE

STAMPEDES > STAMPEDE

STAMPEDO *same as* > STAMPEDE

STAMPEDOS > STAMPEDO

STAMPER > STAMP

STAMPERS > STAMP

STAMPING > STAMP

STAMPINGS > STAMP

STAMPLESS > STAMP

STAMPS > STAMP

STANCE *n* attitude

STANCES > STANCE

STANCH *vb* stem the flow of (a liquid, esp blood) ▷ *adj* loyal and dependable

STANCHED > STANCH

STANCHEL *same*

*as* > STANCHION

STANCHELS > STANCHEL

STANCHER > STANCH

STANCHERS > STANCH

STANCHES > STANCH

STANCHEST > STANCH

STANCHING > STANCH

STANCHION *n* upright bar used as a support ▷ *vb* provide or support with a stanchion or stanchions

STANCHLY > STANCH

STANCK *adj* faint

STAND *vb* be in, rise to, or place in an upright position ▷ *n* stall for the sale of goods

STANDARD *n* level of quality ▷ *adj* usual, regular, or average

STANDARDS > STANDARD

STANDAWAY *adj* erect

STANDBY *n* person or thing that is ready for use

STANDBYS > STANDBY

STANDDOWN *n* return to normal after alert

STANDEE *n* person who stands, esp when there are no vacant seats

STANDEES > STANDEE

STANDEN > STAND

STANDER > STAND

STANDERS > STAND

STANDFAST *n* reliable person or thing

STANDGALE *same*

*as* > STANIEL

STANDING > STAND

STANDINGS > STAND

STANDISH *n* stand, usually of metal, for pens, ink bottles, etc

STANDOFF *n* act or an instance of standing off or apart ▷ *vb* stay at a distance

STANDOFFS > STANDOFF

STANDOUT *n* distinctive or outstanding person or thing

STANDOUTS > STANDOUT

STANDOVER *n* threatening or intimidating act

STANDPAT *n* (in poker) refusal to change one's card

STANDPIPE *n* tap attached to a water main to provide a public water supply

STANDS > STAND

STANDUP *n* comedian who performs solo

STANDUPS > STANDUP

STANE *Scot word for* > STONE

STANED > STANE

STANES > STANE

STANG *vb* sting

STANGED > STANG

STANGING > STANG

STANGS > STANG

STANHOPE *n* light one-seater carriage with two or four wheels

STANHOPES > STANHOPE

STANIEL *n* kestrel

STANIELS > STANIEL

STANINE *n* scale of nine levels

STANINES > STANINE

STANING > STANE

STANK *vb* dam

STANKED > STINK

STANKING > STINK

STANKS > STINK

STANNARY *n* place or region where tin is mined or worked

STANNATE *n* salt of stannic acid

STANNATES > STANNATE

STANNATOR *n* member of old Cornish parliament

STANNEL *same as* > STANIEL

STANNELS > STANNEL

STANNIC *adj* of or containing tin, esp in the tetravalent state

STANNITE *n* grey metallic mineral

STANNITES > STANNITE

STANNOUS *adj* of or containing tin, esp in the divalent state

STANNUM *n* tin (the metal)

STANNUMS > STANNUM

STANOL *n* drug taken to prevent heart disease

STANOLS > STANOL

STANYEL *same as* > STANIEL

STANYELS > STANYEL

STANZA *n* verse of a poem

STANZAED > STANZA

STANZAIC > STANZA

STANZAS > STANZA

STANZE *same as* > STANZA

STANZES > STANZE

STANZO *same as* > STANZA

STANZOES > STANZO

STANZOS > STANZO

STAP *same as* > STOP

STAPEDES > STAPES

STAPEDIAL > STAPES

STAPEDII > STAPEDIUS

STAPEDIUS *n* muscle in stapes

STAPELIA *n* fleshy cactus-like leafless African plant

STAPELIAS > STAPELIA

STAPES *n* stirrup-shaped bone that is the innermost of three small bones in the middle ear of mammals

STAPH *n* staphylococcus

STAPHS > STAPH

STAPLE *n* U-shaped piece of metal used to fasten papers or secure things ▷ *vb* fasten with staples ▷ *adj* of prime importance, principal

STAPLED > STAPLE

STAPLER *n* small device for fastening papers together

STAPLERS > STAPLER

STAPLES > STAPLE

STAPLING > STAPLE

STAPPED > STAP

STAPPING > STAP

STAPPLE *same as* > STOPPLE

STAPPLES > STAPPLE

STAPS > STAP

STAR *n* hot gaseous mass in space, visible in the night sky as a point of light ▷ *vb* feature or be featured as a star ▷ *adj* leading, famous

STARAGEN *n* tarragon

STARAGENS > STARAGEN

STARBOARD *n* right-hand side of a ship, when facing forward ▷ *adj* of or on this side ▷ *vb* turn or be turned towards the starboard

STARBURST *n* pattern of rays or lines radiating from a light source

STARCH *n* carbohydrate forming the main food element in bread, potatoes, etc, and used mixed with water for stiffening fabric ▷ *vb* stiffen (fabric) with starch ▷ *adj* (of a person) formal

STARCHED > STARCH

STARCHER > STARCH

STARCHERS > STARCH

STARCHES > STARCH

STARCHIER > STARCHY

STARCHILY > STARCHY

STARCHING > STARCH

STARCHY *adj* containing starch

STARDOM *n* status of a star in the entertainment or sports world

STARDOMS > STARDOM

STARDRIFT *n* regular movement of stars

STARDUST *n* dusty material found between the stars

STARDUSTS > STARDUST

STARE *vb* look or gaze fixedly (at) ▷ *n* fixed gaze

STARED > STARE

STARER > STARE

STARERS > STARE

STARES > STARE

STARETS *n* Russian holy man

STARETSES > STARETS

STARETZ *same as* > STARETZ

STARETZES > STARETZ

STARFISH *n* star-shaped sea creature

STARFRUIT *n* tree with edible yellow fruit which is star-shaped on cross section

STARGAZE *vb* observe the stars

STARGAZED > STARGAZE

STARGAZER > STARGAZE

STARGAZES > STARGAZE

STARING > STARE

STARINGLY > STARE

STARINGS > STARE

STARK *adj* harsh, unpleasant, and plain ▷ *adv* completely ▷ *vb* stiffen

STARKED > STARK

STARKEN vb become or make stark

STARKENED > STARKEN

STARKENS > STARKEN

STARKER > STARK

STARKERS adj completely naked

STARKEST > STARK

STARKING > STARK

STARKLY > STARK

STARKNESS > STARK

STARKS > STARK

STARLESS > STAR

STARLET n young actress presented as a future star

STARLETS > STARLET

STARLIGHT n light that comes from the stars ▷ adj of or like starlight

STARLIKE > STAR

STARLING n songbird with glossy black speckled feathers

STARLINGS > STARLING

STARLIT same as > STARLIGHT

STARN same as > STERN

STARNED > STARN

STARNIE n Scots word for little star

STARNIES > STARNIE

STARNING > STARN

STARNOSE n American mole with starlike nose

STARNOSES > STARNOSE

STARNS > STARN

STAROSTA n headman of Russian village

STAROSTAS > STAROSTA

STAROSTY n estate of Polish nobleman

STARR n (in Judaism) release from a debt

STARRED > STAR

STARRIER > STARRY

STARRIEST > STARRY

STARRILY > STARRY

STARRING > STAR

STARRINGS > STARE

STARRS > STARR

STARRY adj full of or like stars

STARS > STAR

STARSHINE n starlight

STARSHIP n spacecraft in science fiction

STARSHIPS > STARSHIP

STARSPOT n dark patch on surface of star

STARSPOTS > STARSPOT

STARSTONE n precious stone reflecting light in starlike pattern

START vb take the first step, begin ▷ n first part of something

STARTED > START

STARTER n first course of a meal

STARTERS > STARTER

STARTFUL adj tending to start

STARTING > START

STARTINGS > START

STARTISH same as > STARTFUL

STARTLE vb slightly surprise or frighten

STARTLED > STARTLE

STARTLER > STARTLE

STARTLERS > STARTLE

STARTLES > STARTLE

STARTLING adj causing surprise or fear

STARTLISH adj easily startled

STARTLY same as > STARTLISH

STARTS > START

STARTSY > STARETS

STARTUP n business enterprise that has been launched recently

STARTUPS > STARTUP

STARVE vb die or suffer or cause to die or suffer from hunger

STARVED > STARVE

STARVER > STARVE

STARVERS > STARVE

STARVES > STARVE

STARVING > STARVE

STARVINGS > STARVE

STARWORT n plant with star-shaped flowers

STARWORTS > STARWORT

STASES > STASIS

STASH vb store in a secret place ▷ n secret store

STASHED > STASH

STASHES > STASH

STASHIE same as > STUSHIE

STASHIES > STASHIE

STASHING > STASH

STASIDION n stall in Greek church

STASIMA > STASIMON

STASIMON n ode sung in Greek tragedy

STASIS n stagnation in the normal flow of bodily fluids, such as the blood or urine

STAT n statistic

STATABLE > STATE

STATAL adj of a federal state

STATANT adj (of an animal) in profile with all four feet on the ground

STATE n condition of a person or thing ▷ adj of or concerning the State ▷ vb express in words

STATEABLE > STATE

STATED adj (esp of a sum) determined by agreement

STATEDLY > STATED

STATEHOOD > STATE

STATELESS adj not belonging to any country

STATELET n small state

STATELETS > STATELET

STATELIER > STATELY

STATELILY > STATELY

STATELY adj dignified or grand ▷ adv in a stately manner

STATEMENT n something stated ▷ vb assess (a pupil) with regard to his or her special educational needs

STATER n any of various usually silver coins of ancient Greece

STATEROOM n private cabin on a ship

STATERS > STATER

STATES > STATE

STATESIDE adv of, in, to, or towards the US

STATESMAN n experienced and respected political leader

STATESMEN > STATESMAN

STATEWIDE adj throughout a state

STATIC adj stationary or inactive ▷ n crackling sound or speckled picture caused by interference in radio or television reception

STATICAL > STATIC

STATICE n plant name formerly used for both thrift and sea lavender

STATICES > STATICE

STATICKY > STATIC

STATICS n branch of mechanics dealing with the forces producing a state of equilibrium

STATIM adv right away

STATIN n type of drug that lowers the levels of low-density lipoproteins in the blood

STATING > STATE

STATINS > STATIN

STATION n place where trains stop for passengers ▷ vb assign (someone) to a particular place

STATIONAL > STATION

STATIONED > STATION

STATIONER n dealer in stationery

STATIONS > STATION

STATISM n theory or practice of concentrating economic and political power in the state

STATISMS > STATISM

STATIST n advocate of statism ▷ adj of, characteristic of, advocating, or relating to statism

STATISTIC n numerical fact collected and classified systematically

STATISTS > STATIST

STATIVE adj denoting a verb describing a state rather than an activity, act, or event ▷ n stative verb

STATIVES > STATIVE

STATOCYST n organ of balance in some invertebrates

STATOLITH n any of the granules of calcium carbonate occurring in a statocyst

STATOR n stationary part of a rotary machine or device, esp of a motor or generator

STATORS > STATOR

STATS > STAT

STATUA same as > STATUE

STATUARY n statues collectively ▷ adj of, relating to, or suitable for statues

STATUAS > STATUA

STATUE n large sculpture of a human or animal figure

STATUED adj decorated with or portrayed in a statue or statues

STATUES > STATUE

STATUETTE n small statue

STATURE n person's height

STATURED adj having stature

STATURES > STATURE

STATUS n social position

STATUSES > STATUS

STATUSY adj conferring or having status

STATUTE n written law

STATUTES > STATUTE

STATUTORY adj required or authorized by law

STAUMREL n stupid person

STAUMRELS > STAUMREL

STAUN Scot word for > STAND

STAUNCH same as > STANCH

STAUNCHED > STAUNCH

STAUNCHER > STAUNCH

STAUNCHES > STAUNCH

STAUNCHLY > STAUNCH

STAUNING > STAUN

STAUNS > STAUN

STAVE same as > STAFF

STAVED > STAVE

STAVES > STAVE

STAVING > STAVE

STAVUDINE n drug used to treat HIV

STAW Scots form of > STALL

STAWED > STAW

STAWING > STAW

STAWS > STAW

STAY vb remain in a place or condition ▷ n period of staying in a place

STAYAWAY n strike in South Africa

STAYAWAYS > STAYAWAY

STAYED > STAY

STAYER n person or thing that stays

STAYERS > STAYER

STAYING > STAY

STAYLESS adj with no stays or support

STAYMAKER n corset maker

STAYNE same as > STAIN

STAYNED > STAYNE

STAYNES > STAYNE

STAYNING > STAYNE

STAYRE *same as* > STAIR

STAYRES > STAYRE

STAYS *pl n* old-fashioned corsets with bones in them

STAYSAIL *n* sail fastened on a stay

STAYSAILS > STAYSAIL

STEAD *n* place or function that should be taken by another ▷ *vb* help or benefit

STEADED > STEAD

STEADFAST *adj* firm, determined

STEADICAM *n* tradename for a mechanism for steadying a hand-held camera

STEADIED > STEADY

STEADIER > STEADY

STEADIERS > STEADY

STEADIES > STEADY

STEADIEST > STEADY

STEADILY > STEADY

STEADING *n* farmstead

STEADINGS > STEADING

STEADS > STEAD

STEADY *adj* not shaky or wavering ▷ *vb* make steady ▷ *adv* in a steady manner

STEADYING > STEADY

STEAK *n* thick slice of meat, esp beef

STEAKS > STEAK

STEAL *vb* take unlawfully or without permission

STEALABLE > STEAL

STEALAGE *n* theft

STEALAGES > STEALAGE

STEALE *n* handle

STEALED > STEAL

STEALER *n* person who steals something

STEALERS > STEALER

STEALES > STEALE

STEALING > STEAL

STEALINGS > STEAL

STEALS > STEAL

STEALT > STEAL

STEALTH *n* moving carefully and quietly ▷ *adj* (of technology) able to render an aircraft almost invisible to radar ▷ *vb* approach undetected

STEALTHED > STEALTH

STEALTHS > STEALTH

STEALTHY *adj* characterized by great caution, secrecy, etc

STEAM *n* vapour into which water changes when boiled ▷ *vb* give off steam

STEAMBOAT *n* boat powered by a steam engine

STEAMED > STEAM

STEAMER *n* steam-propelled ship ▷ *vb* travel by steamer

STEAMERED > STEAMER

STEAMERS > STEAMER

STEAMIE *n* public wash house

STEAMIER > STEAMY

STEAMIES > STEAMIE

STEAMIEST > STEAMY

STEAMILY > STEAMY

STEAMING *adj* very hot ▷ *n* robbery, esp of passengers in a railway carriage or bus, by a large gang of armed youths

STEAMINGS > STEAMING

STEAMROLL *vb* crush (opposition) by overpowering force

STEAMS > STEAM

STEAMSHIP *n* ship powered by steam engines

STEAMY *adj* full of steam

STEAN *n* earthenware vessel

STEANE *same as* > STEEN

STEANED > STEANE

STEANES > STEANE

STEANING > STEANE

STEANINGS > STEANE

STEANS > STEAN

STEAPSIN *n* pancreatic lipase

STEAPSINS > STEAPSIN

STEAR *same as* > STEER

STEARAGE *same as* > STEERAGE

STEARAGES > STEARAGE

STEARATE *n* any salt or ester of stearic acid

STEARATES > STEARATE

STEARD > STEAR

STEARE *same as* > STEER

STEARED > STEARE

STEARES > STEARE

STEARIC *adj* of or relating to suet or fat

STEARIN *n* colourless crystalline ester of glycerol and stearic acid

STEARINE *same as* > STEARIN

STEARINES > STEARINE

STEARING > STEAR

STEARINS > STEARIN

STEARS > STEAR

STEARSMAN *same as* > STEERSMAN

STEARSMEN > STEARSMAN

STEATITE *same as* > SOAPSTONE

STEATITES > STEATITE

STEATITIC > STEATITE

STEATOMA *n* tumour of sebaceous gland

STEATOMAS > STEATOMA

STEATOSES > STEATOSIS

STEATOSIS *n* abnormal accumulation of fat

STED *same as* > STEAD

STEDD *same as* > STEAD

STEDDE *same as* > STEAD

STEDDED > STED

STEDDES > STEDDE

STEDDIED > STEDDY

STEDDIES > STEDDY

STEDDING > STED

STEDDS > STEDD

STEDDY *same as* > STEADY

STEDDYING > STEDDY

STEDE *same as* > STEAD

STEDED > STEDE

STEDES > STEDE

STEDFAST *same as* > STEADFAST

STEDING > STEDE

STEDS > STED

STEED *same as* > STEAD

STEEDED > STEED

STEEDIED > STEEDY

STEEDIES > STEEDY

STEEDING > STEED

STEEDLIKE > STEED

STEEDS > STEED

STEEDY *same as* > STEEDY

STEEDYING > STEEDY

STEEK *vb* Scots word meaning shut

STEEKED > STEEK

STEEKING > STEEK

STEEKIT > STEEK

STEEKS > STEEK

STEEL *n* hard malleable alloy of iron and carbon ▷ *vb* prepare (oneself) for something unpleasant

STEELBOW *n* material lent to tenant by landlord

STEELBOWS > STEELBOW

STEELD > STEEL

STEELED > STEEL

STEELHEAD *n* silvery North Pacific variety of the rainbow trout

STEELIE *n* steel ball bearing used as marble

STEELIER > STEELIE

STEELIES > STEELIE

STEELIEST > STEELIE

STEELING > STEEL

STEELINGS > STEEL

STEELMAN *n* person working in steel industry

STEELMEN > STEELMAN

STEELS *pl n* shares and bonds of steel companies

STEELWARE *n* things made of steel

STEELWORK *n* frame, foundation, building, or article made of steel

STEELY > STEEL

STEELYARD *n* portable balance consisting of a pivoted bar with two unequal arms

STEEM *variant of* > ESTEEM

STEEMED > STEEM

STEEMING > STEEM

STEEMS > STEEM

STEEN *vb* line with stone

STEENBOK *n* small antelope of central and southern Africa

STEENBOKS > STEENBOK

STEENBRAS *n* variety of sea bream

STEENBUCK *same as* > STEENBOK

STEENED > STEEN

STEENING > STEEN

STEENINGS > STEEN

STEENKIRK *n* type of cravat

STEENS > STEEN

STEEP *adj* sloping sharply ▷ *vb* soak or be soaked in liquid ▷ *n* instance or the process of steeping or the condition of being steeped

STEEPED > STEEP

STEEPEN *vb* become or cause (something) to become steep or steeper

STEEPENED > STEEPEN

STEEPENS > STEEPEN

STEEPER > STEEP

STEEPERS > STEEP

STEEPEST > STEEP

STEEPEUP *adj* very steep

STEEPIER > STEEPY

STEEPIEST > STEEPY

STEEPING > STEEP

STEEPISH > STEEP

STEEPLE *same as* > SPIRE

STEEPLED > STEEPLE

STEEPLES > STEEPLE

STEEPLY > STEEP

STEEPNESS > STEEP

STEEPS > STEEP

STEEPUP *adj* very steep

STEEPY *same as* > STEEP

STEER *vb* direct the course of (a vehicle or ship) ▷ *n* castrated male ox

STEERABLE > STEER

STEERAGE *n* cheapest accommodation on a passenger ship

STEERAGES > STEERAGE

STEERED > STEER

STEERER > STEER

STEERERS > STEER

STEERIES > STEERY

STEERING > STEER

STEERINGS > STEER

STEERLING *n* young steer

STEERS > STEER

STEERSMAN *n* person who steers a vessel

STEERSMEN > STEERSMAN

STEERY *n* commotion

STEEVE *n* spar having a pulley block at one end, used for stowing cargo on a ship ▷ *vb* stow (cargo) securely in the hold of a ship

STEEVED > STEEVE

STEEVELY > STEEVE

STEEVER > STEEVE

STEEVES > STEEVE

STEEVEST > STEEVE

STEEVING > STEEVE

STEEVINGS > STEEVE

STEGNOSES > STEGNOSIS

STEGNOSIS *n* constriction of bodily pores

STEGNOTIC > STEGNOSIS

STEGODON *n* mammal of Pliocene to Pleistocene times, similar to the mastodon

STEGODONS > STEGODON

STEGODONT *same as* > STEGODON

STEGOMYIA *former name*

for > AEDES
**STEGOSAUR** *n* quadrupedal herbivorous dinosaur
**STEIL** *same as* > STEAL
**STEILS** > STEIL
**STEIN** *same as* > STEEN
**STEINBOCK** *another name for* > IBEX
**STEINBOK** *same as* > STEENBOK
**STEINBOKS** > STEINBOK
**STEINED** > STEIN
**STEINING** > STEIN
**STEININGS** > STEIN
**STEINKIRK** *same as* > STEENKIRK
**STEINS** > STEIN
**STELA** *same as* > STELE
**STELAE** > STELE
**STELAI** > STELE
**STELAR** > STELE
**STELE** *n* upright stone slab or column decorated with figures or inscriptions
**STELENE** > STELE
**STELES** > STELE
**STELIC** > STELE
**STELL** *n* shelter for cattle or sheep built on moorland or hillsides ▷ *vb* position or place
**STELLA** *n* star or something star-shaped
**STELLAR** *adj* of stars
**STELLAS** > STELLA
**STELLATE** *adj* resembling a star in shape
**STELLATED** *same as* > STELLATE
**STELLED** > STELL
**STELLERID** *n* starfish
**STELLIFY** *vb* change or be changed into a star
**STELLING** > STELL
**STELLION** *n* Mediterranean lizard
**STELLIONS** > STELLION
**STELLITE** *n* tradename for any of various alloys containing cobalt, chromium, carbon, tungsten, and molybdenum
**STELLITES** > STELLITE
**STELLS** > STELL
**STELLULAR** *adj* displaying or abounding in small stars
**STEM** *vb* stop (the flow of something) ▷ *n* main axis of a plant, which bears the leaves, axillary buds, and flowers
**STEMBOK** *same as* > STEENBOK
**STEMBOKS** > STEMBOK
**STEMBUCK** *same as* > STEENBOK
**STEMBUCKS** > STEMBUCK
**STEME** *same as* > STEAM
**STEMED** > STEME
**STEMES** > STEME
**STEMHEAD** *n* head of the stem of a vessel

**STEMHEADS** > STEMHEAD
**STEMING** > STEME
**STEMLESS** > STEM
**STEMLET** *n* little stem
**STEMLETS** > STEMLET
**STEMLIKE** > STEM
**STEMMA** *n* family tree
**STEMMAS** > STEMMA
**STEMMATA** > STEMMA
**STEMMATIC** > STEMMA
**STEMME** *archaic variant of* > STEM
**STEMMED** > STEM
**STEMMER** > STEM
**STEMMERS** > STEM
**STEMMERY** *n* tobacco factory
**STEMMES** > STEMME
**STEMMIER** > STEMMY
**STEMMIEST** > STEMMY
**STEMMING** > STEM
**STEMMINGS** > STEM
**STEMMY** *adj* (of wine) young and raw
**STEMPEL** *n* timber support
**STEMPELS** > STEMPEL
**STEMPLE** *same as* > STEMPEL
**STEMPLES** > STEMPLE
**STEMS** > STEM
**STEMSON** *n* curved timber scarfed into or bolted to the stem and keelson at the bow of a wooden vessel
**STEMSONS** > STEMSON
**STEMWARE** *n* collective term for glasses, goblets, etc, with stems
**STEMWARES** > STEMWARE
**STEN** *vb* stride
**STENCH** *n* foul smell ▷ *vb* cause to smell
**STENCHED** > STENCH
**STENCHES** > STENCH
**STENCHFUL** > STENCH
**STENCHIER** > STENCH
**STENCHING** > STENCH
**STENCHY** > STENCH
**STENCIL** *n* thin sheet with cut-out pattern through which ink or paint passes to form the pattern on the surface below ▷ *vb* make (a pattern) with a stencil
**STENCILED** > STENCIL
**STENCILER** > STENCIL
**STENCILS** > STENCIL
**STEND** *vb* Scots word meaning bound
**STENDED** > STEND
**STENDING** > STEND
**STENDS** > STEND
**STENGAH** *same as* > STINGER
**STENGAHS** > STENGAH
**STENLOCK** *n* fish of northern seas
**STENLOCKS** > STENLOCK
**STENNED** > STEN
**STENNING** > STEN
**STENO** *n* stenographer
**STENOBATH** *n* stenobathic organism
**STENOKIES** > STENOKY
**STENOKOUS** *adj* able to

live in narrow range of environments
**STENOKY** *n* life and survival that is dependent on conditions remaining within a narrow range of variables
**STENOPAIC** *adj* having narrow opening
**STENOS** > STENO
**STENOSED** *adj* abnormally contracted
**STENOSES** > STENOSIS
**STENOSIS** *n* abnormal narrowing of a bodily canal or passage
**STENOTIC** > STENOSIS
**STENOTYPE** *n* machine with a keyboard for recording speeches in a phonetic shorthand
**STENOTYPY** *n* form of shorthand in which alphabetic combinations are used to represent groups of sounds or short common words
**STENS** > STEN
**STENT** *n* surgical implant used to keep an artery open ▷ *vb* assess
**STENTED** > STENT
**STENTING** > STENT
**STENTOR** *n* person with an unusually loud voice
**STENTORS** > STENTOR
**STENTOUR** *n* tax assessor
**STENTOURS** > STENTOUR
**STENTS** > STENT
**STEP** *vb* move and set down the foot, as when walking ▷ *n* stepping
**STEPBAIRN** *Scots word for* > STEPCHILD
**STEPCHILD** *n* stepson or stepdaughter
**STEPDAME** *n* woman married to one's father
**STEPDAMES** > STEPDAME
**STEPHANE** *n* ancient Greek headdress
**STEPHANES** > STEPHANE
**STEPLIKE** > STEP
**STEPNEY** *n* spare wheel
**STEPNEYS** > STEPNEY
**STEPPE** *n* extensive grassy plain usually without trees
**STEPPED** > STEP
**STEPPER** *n* person who or animal that steps, esp a horse or a dancer
**STEPPERS** > STEPPER
**STEPPES** > STEPPE
**STEPPING** > STEP
**STEPS** > STEP
**STEPSON** *n* son of one's husband or wife by an earlier relationship
**STEPSONS** > STEPSON
**STEPSTOOL** *n* stool able to be used as step
**STEPT** > STEP
**STEPWISE** *adj* arranged in the manner of or

resembling steps
▷ *adv* with the form or appearance of steps
**STERADIAN** *n* SI unit of solid angle
**STERCORAL** *adj* relating to excrement
**STERCULIA** *n* dietary fibre used as a food stabilizer and denture adhesive
**STERE** *n* unit used to measure volumes of stacked timber
**STEREO** *n* stereophonic record player ▷ *adj* (of a sound system) using two or more separate microphones to feed two or more loudspeakers through separate channels ▷ *vb* make stereophonic
**STEREOED** > STEREO
**STEREOING** > STEREO
**STEREOME** *n* tissue of a plant that provides mechanical support
**STEREOMES** > STEREOME
**STEREOS** > STEREO
**STERES** > STERE
**STERIC** *adj* of or caused by the spatial arrangement of atoms in a molecule
**STERICAL** *same as* > STERIC
**STERIGMA** *n* minute stalk bearing a spore or chain of spores in certain fungi
**STERIGMAS** > STERIGMA
**STERILANT** *n* any substance or agent used in sterilization
**STERILE** *adj* free from germs
**STERILELY** > STERILE
**STERILISE** *same as* > STERILIZE
**STERILITY** > STERILE
**STERILIZE** *vb* make sterile
**STERLET** *n* small sturgeon of seas and rivers in N Asia and E Europe
**STERLETS** > STERLET
**STERLING** *n* British money system ▷ *adj* genuine and reliable
**STERLINGS** > STERLING
**STERN** *adj* severe, strict ▷ *n* rear part of a ship ▷ *vb* row boat backward
**STERNA** > STERNUM
**STERNAGE** *n* sterns
**STERNAGES** > STERNAGE
**STERNAL** > STERNUM
**STERNEBRA** *n* part of breastbone
**STERNED** > STERN
**STERNER** > STERN
**STERNEST** > STERN
**STERNFAST** *n* rope for securing boat at stern
**STERNING** > STERN
**STERNITE** *n* part of arthropod
**STERNITES** > STERNITE
**STERNITIC** > STERNITE

STERNLY > STERN

STERNMOST adj farthest to the stern

STERNNESS > STERN

STERNPORT n opening in stern of ship

STERNPOST n main upright timber or structure at the stern of a vessel

STERNS > STERN

STERNSON n timber scarfed into or bolted to the sternpost and keelson at the stern of a wooden vessel

STERNSONS > STERNSON

STERNUM n long flat bone in the front of the body, to which the collarbone and most of the ribs are attached

STERNUMS > STERNUM

STERNWARD adv towards the stern

STERNWAY n movement of a vessel sternforemost

STERNWAYS > STERNWAY

STEROID n organic compound containing a carbon ring system, such as many hormones

STEROIDAL > STEROID

STEROIDS > STEROID

STEROL n natural insoluble alcohol such as cholesterol and ergosterol

STEROLS > STEROL

STERTOR n laborious or noisy breathing caused by obstructed air passages

STERTORS > STERTOR

STERVE same as > STARVE

STERVED > STERVE

STERVES > STERVE

STERVING > STERVE

STET interj instruction to ignore an alteration previously made by a proofreader ▷ vb indicate to a printer that certain deleted matter is to be kept ▷ n word or mark indicating that certain deleted written matter is to be retained

STETS > STET

STETTED > STET

STETTING > STET

STEVEDORE n person who loads and unloads ships ▷ vb load or unload (a ship, ship's cargo, etc)

STEVEN n voice

STEVENS > STEVEN

STEW n food cooked slowly in a closed pot ▷ vb cook slowly in a closed pot

STEWABLE > STEW

STEWARD n person who looks after passengers on a ship or aircraft ▷ vb act as a steward (of)

STEWARDED > STEWARD

STEWARDRY n office of steward

STEWARDS > STEWARD

STEWARTRY variant of > STEWARDRY

STEWBUM n drunkard

STEWBUMS > STEWBUM

STEWED adj (of food) cooked by stewing

STEWER > STEW

STEWERS > STEW

STEWIER > STEW

STEWIEST > STEW

STEWING > STEW

STEWINGS > STEW

STEWPAN n pan used for making stew

STEWPANS > STEWPAN

STEWPOND n fishpond

STEWPONDS > STEWPOND

STEWPOT n pot used for making stew

STEWPOTS > STEWPOT

STEWS > STEW

STEWY > STEW

STEY adj Scots word meaning steep

STEYER > STEY

STEYEST > STEY

STHENIA n abnormal strength

STHENIAS > STHENIA

STHENIC adj abounding in energy or bodily strength

STIBBLE Scots form of > STUBBLE

STIBBLER n horse allowed to eat stubble

STIBBLERS > STIBBLE

STIBBLES > STIBBLE

STIBIAL > STIBIUM

STIBINE n colourless slightly soluble poisonous gas

STIBINES > STIBINE

STIBIUM obsolete name for > ANTIMONY

STIBIUMS > STIBIUM

STIBNITE n soft greyish mineral

STIBNITES > STIBNITE

STICCADO n type of xylophone

STICCADOS > STICCADO

STICCATO same as > STICCADO

STICCATOS > STICCATO

STICH n line of poetry

STICHARIA pl n priest's robes of the Greek Church

STICHERA > STICHERON

STICHERON n short hymn in Greek Church

STICHIC > STICH

STICHIDIA pl n seaweed branches

STICHOI > STICHOS

STICHOS n line of poem

STICHS > STICH

STICK n long thin piece of wood ▷ vb push (a pointed object) into (something)

STICKABLE > STICK

STICKBALL n form of baseball played in street

STICKED > STICK

STICKER n adhesive label or sign ▷ vb put stickers on

STICKERED > STICKER

STICKERS > STICKER

STICKFUL > STICK

STICKFULS > STICK

STICKIED > STICKY

STICKIER > STICKY

STICKIES > STICKY

STICKIEST > STICKY

STICKILY > STICKY

STICKING > STICK

STICKINGS > STICK

STICKIT Scots form of > STUCK

STICKJAW n stodgy food

STICKJAWS > STICKJAW

STICKLE vb dispute stubbornly, esp about minor points

STICKLED > STICKLE

STICKLER n person who insists on something

STICKLERS > STICKLER

STICKLES > STICKLE

STICKLIKE > STICK

STICKLING > STICKLE

STICKMAN n human figure drawn in thin strokes

STICKMEN > STICKMAN

STICKOUT n conspicuous person or thing

STICKOUTS > STICKOUT

STICKPIN n tiepin

STICKPINS > STICKPIN

STICKS > STICK

STICKSEED n type of Eurasian and North American plant

STICKUM n adhesive

STICKUMS > STICKUM

STICKUP n robbery at gun-point

STICKUPS > STICKUP

STICKWEED n any of several plants that have clinging fruits or seeds, esp the ragweed

STICKWORK n use of stick in hockey

STICKY adj covered with an adhesive substance ▷ vb make sticky ▷ n inquisitive look or stare

STICKYING > STICKY

STICTION n frictional force to be overcome to set one object in motion when it is in contact with another

STICTIONS > STICTION

STIDDIE same as > STITHY

STIDDIED > STIDDIE

STIDDIES > STIDDIE

STIE same as > STY

STIED same as > STY

STIES > STY

STIEVE same as > STEEVE

STIEVELY > STIEVE

STIEVER > STIEVE

STIEVEST > STIEVE

STIFF adj not easily bent or moved ▷ n corpse ▷ adv completely or utterly ▷ vb fail completely

STIFFED > STIFF

STIFFEN vb make or become stiff

STIFFENED > STIFFEN

STIFFENER > STIFFEN

STIFFENS > STIFFEN

STIFFER > STIFF

STIFFEST > STIFF

STIFFIE n erection of the penis

STIFFIES > STIFFIE

STIFFING > STIFF

STIFFISH > STIFF

STIFFLY > STIFF

STIFFNESS > STIFF

STIFFS > STIFF

STIFFWARE n computer software that is hard to modify

STIFFY n erection of the penis

STIFLE vb suppress ▷ n joint in the hind leg of a horse, dog, etc, between the femur and tibia

STIFLED > STIFLE

STIFLER > STIFLE

STIFLERS > STIFLE

STIFLES > STIFLE

STIFLING adj uncomfortably hot and stuffy

STIFLINGS > STIFLING

STIGMA n mark of social disgrace

STIGMAL adj of part of insect wing

STIGMAS > STIGMA

STIGMATA > STIGMA

STIGMATIC adj relating to or having a stigma or stigmata ▷ n person marked with the stigmata

STIGME n dot in Greek punctuation

STIGMES > STIGME

STILB n unit of luminance equal to 1 candela per square centimetre.

STILBENE n colourless or slightly yellow crystalline hydrocarbon used in the manufacture of dyes

STILBENES > STILBENE

STILBITE n white or yellow zeolite mineral

STILBITES > STILBITE

STILBS > STILB

STILE same as > STYLE

STILED > STILE

STILES > STILE

STILET same as > STYLET

STILETS > STILET

STILETTO n high narrow heel on a woman's shoe ▷ vb stab with a stiletto

STILETTOS > STILETTO

STILING > STILE

STILL adv now or in the future as before ▷ adj motionless ▷ n calmness;

apparatus for distillation
▷ *vb* make still

**STILLAGE** *n* frame or stand for keeping things off the ground, such as casks in a brewery

**STILLAGES** >STILLAGE

**STILLBORN** *adj* born dead ▷ *n* stillborn fetus or baby

**STILLED** >STILL

**STILLER** >STILL

**STILLERS** >STILL

**STILLEST** >STILL

**STILLIER** >STILLY

**STILLIEST** >STILLY

**STILLING** >STILL

**STILLINGS** >STILL

**STILLION** *n* stand for cask

**STILLIONS** >STILLION

**STILLMAN** *n* someone involved in the operation of a still

**STILLMEN** >STILLMAN

**STILLNESS** >STILL

**STILLROOM** *n* room in which distilling is carried out

**STILLS** >STILL

**STILLY** *adv* quietly or calmly ▷ *adj* still, quiet, or calm

**STILT** *n* either of a pair of long poles with footrests for walking raised from the ground ▷ *vb* raise or place on or as if on stilts

**STILTBIRD** *n* long-legged wading bird

**STILTED** *adj* stiff and formal in manner

**STILTEDLY** >STILTED

**STILTER** >STILT

**STILTERS** >STILT

**STILTIER** >STILT

**STILTIEST** >STILT

**STILTING** >STILT

**STILTINGS** >STILT

**STILTISH** >STILT

**STILTS** >STILT

**STILTY** >STILT

**STIM** *n* very small amount

**STIME** *same as* >STYME

**STIMED** >STIME

**STIMES** >STIME

**STIMIE** *same as* >STYMIE

**STIMIED** >STIMIE

**STIMIES** >STIMIE

**STIMING** >STIME

**STIMS** >STIM

**STIMULANT** *n* something, such as a drug, that acts as a stimulus ▷ *adj* stimulating

**STIMULATE** *vb* act as a stimulus (on)

**STIMULI** >STIMULUS

**STIMULUS** *n* something that rouses a person or thing to activity

**STIMY** *same as* >STYMIE

**STIMYING** >STIMY

**STING** *vb* (of certain animals or plants) wound by injecting with poison

▷ *n* wound or pain caused by or as if by stinging

**STINGAREE** *popular name for* >STINGRAY

**STINGBULL** *n* spiny fish

**STINGED** >STING

**STINGER** *n* person, plant, animal, etc, that stings or hurts

**STINGERS** >STINGER

**STINGFISH** *same as* >STINGBULL

**STINGIER** >STINGY

**STINGIES** >STINGY

**STINGIEST** >STINGY

**STINGILY** >STINGY

**STINGING** >STING

**STINGINGS** >STING

**STINGLESS** >STING

**STINGO** *n* strong alcohol

**STINGOS** >STINGO

**STINGRAY** *n* flatfish capable of inflicting painful wounds

**STINGRAYS** >STINGRAY

**STINGS** >STING

**STINGY** *adj* mean or miserly ▷ *n* stinging nettle

**STINK** *n* strong unpleasant smell ▷ *vb* give off a strong unpleasant smell

**STINKARD** *n* smelly person

**STINKARDS** >STINKARD

**STINKBUG** *n* type of insect that releases an unpleasant odour

**STINKBUGS** >STINKBUG

**STINKER** *n* difficult or unpleasant person or thing

**STINKEROO** *n* bad or contemptible person or thing

**STINKERS** >STINKER

**STINKHORN** *n* type of fungus with an offensive odour

**STINKIER** >STINKY

**STINKIEST** >STINKY

**STINKING** >STINK

**STINKINGS** >STINK

**STINKO** *adj* drunk

**STINKPOT** *n* person or thing that stinks

**STINKPOTS** >STINKPOT

**STINKS** >STINK

**STINKWEED** *n* plant that has a disagreeable smell when bruised

**STINKWOOD** *n* any of various trees having offensive-smelling wood

**STINKY** *adj* having a foul smell

**STINT** *vb* be miserly with (something) ▷ *n* allotted amount of work

**STINTED** >STINT

**STINTEDLY** >STINT

**STINTER** >STINT

**STINTERS** >STINT

**STINTIER** >STINT

**STINTIEST** >STINT

**STINTING** >STINT

**STINTINGS** >STINT

**STINTLESS** >STINT

**STINTS** >STINT

**STINTY** >STINT

**STIPA** *n* variety of grass

**STIPAS** >STIPA

**STIPE** *n* stalk in plants that bears reproductive structures

**STIPED** *same as* >STIPITATE

**STIPEL** *n* small paired leaflike structure at the base of certain leaflets

**STIPELS** >STIPEL

**STIPEND** *n* regular allowance or salary, esp that paid to a clergyman

**STIPENDS** >STIPEND

**STIPES** *n* second maxillary segment in insects and crustaceans

**STIPIFORM** >STIPES

**STIPITATE** *adj* possessing or borne on the end of a stipe

**STIPITES** >STIPES

**STIPPLE** *vb* paint, draw, or engrave using dots ▷ *n* technique of stippling or a picture produced by or using stippling

**STIPPLED** >STIPPLE

**STIPPLER** >STIPPLE

**STIPPLERS** >STIPPLE

**STIPPLES** >STIPPLE

**STIPPLING** >STIPPLE

**STIPULAR** >STIPULE

**STIPULARY** >STIPULE

**STIPULATE** *vb* specify as a condition of an agreement ▷ *adj* (of a plant) having stipules

**STIPULE** *n* small paired usually leaflike outgrowth occurring at the base of a leaf or its stalk

**STIPULED** >STIPULE

**STIPULES** >STIPULE

**STIR** *vb* mix up (a liquid) by moving a spoon etc around in it ▷ *n* stirring

**STIRABOUT** *n* kind of porridge orginally made in Ireland

**STIRE** *same as* >STEER

**STIRED** >STIRE

**STIRES** >STIRE

**STIRING** >STIRE

**STIRK** *n* heifer of 6 to 12 months old

**STIRKS** >STIRK

**STIRLESS** >STIR

**STIRP** *same as* >STIRPS

**STIRPES** >STIRPS

**STIRPS** *n* line of descendants from an ancestor

**STIRRA** *same as* >SIRRA

**STIRRABLE** >STIR

**STIRRAH** *same as* >SIRRAH

**STIRRAHS** >STIRRAH

**STIRRAS** >STIRRA

**STIRRE** *obsolete form of* >STEER

**STIRRED** >STIR

**STIRRER** *n* person who deliberately causes trouble

**STIRRERS** >STIRRER

**STIRRES** >STIRRE

**STIRRING** >STIR

**STIRRINGS** >STIR

**STIRRUP** *n* metal loop attached to a saddle for supporting a rider's foot

**STIRRUPS** >STIRRUP

**STIRS** >STIR

**STISHIE** *same as* >STUSHIE

**STISHIES** >STISHIE

**STITCH** *n* link made by drawing thread through material with a needle ▷ *vb* sew

**STITCHED** >STITCH

**STITCHER** >STITCH

**STITCHERS** >STITCH

**STITCHERY** *n* needlework, esp modern embroidery

**STITCHES** >STITCH

**STITCHING** >STITCH

**STITHIED** >STITHY

**STITHIES** >STITHY

**STITHY** *n* forge or anvil ▷ *vb* forge on an anvil

**STITHYING** >STITHY

**STIVE** *vb* stifle

**STIVED** >STIVE

**STIVER** *n* former Dutch coin worth one twentieth of a guilder

**STIVERS** >STIVER

**STIVES** >STIVE

**STIVIER** >STIVY

**STIVIEST** >STIVY

**STIVING** >STIVE

**STIVY** *adj* stuffy

**STOA** *n* covered walk that has a colonnade on one or both sides, esp as used in ancient Greece

**STOAE** >STOA

**STOAI** >STOA

**STOAS** >STOA

**STOAT** *n* small mammal of the weasel family, with brown fur that turns white in winter

**STOATS** >STOAT

**STOB** *same as* >STAB

**STOBBED** >STOB

**STOBBING** >STOB

**STOBS** >STOB

**STOCCADO** *n* fencing thrust

**STOCCADOS** >STOCCADO

**STOCCATA** *same as* >STOCCADO

**STOCCATAS** >STOCCATA

**STOCIOUS** *same as* >STOTIOUS

**STOCK** *n* total amount of goods available for sale in a shop ▷ *adj* kept in stock, standard ▷ *vb* keep for sale or future use

**STOCKADE** *n* enclosure or barrier made of stakes ▷ *vb* surround with a stockade

**STOCKADED** >STOCKADE

**STOCKADES** > STOCKADE

**STOCKAGE** n livestock put to graze on crops

**STOCKAGES** > STOCKAGE

**STOCKCAR** n car that has been strengthened for a form of racing in which the cars often collide

**STOCKCARS** > STOCKCAR

**STOCKED** > STOCK

**STOCKER** > STOCK

**STOCKERS** > STOCK

**STOCKFISH** n fish, such as cod or haddock, cured by splitting and drying in the air

**STOCKHORN** n instrument made from animal horn

**STOCKIER** > STOCKY

**STOCKIEST** > STOCKY

**STOCKILY** > STOCKY

**STOCKINET** n machine-knitted elastic fabric

**STOCKING** n close-fitting covering for the foot and leg

**STOCKINGS** > STOCKING

**STOCKISH** adj stupid or dull

**STOCKIST** n dealer who stocks a particular product

**STOCKISTS** > STOCKIST

**STOCKLESS** > STOCK

**STOCKLIST** n list of items in stock

**STOCKLOCK** n lock that is enclosed in a wooden case

**STOCKMAN** n man engaged in the rearing or care of farm livestock, esp cattle

**STOCKMEN** > STOCKMAN

**STOCKPILE** vb store a large quantity of (something) for future use ▷ n accumulated store

**STOCKPOT** n pot in which stock for soup is made

**STOCKPOTS** > STOCKPOT

**STOCKROOM** n room in which a stock of goods is kept in a shop or factory

**STOCKS** pl n instrument of punishment consisting of a heavy wooden frame with holes in which the feet, hands, or head of an offender were locked

**STOCKTAKE** vb take stock

**STOCKTOOK** > STOCKTAKE

**STOCKWORK** n group of veins in mine

**STOCKY** adj (of a person) broad and sturdy

**STOCKYARD** n yard where farm animals are sold

**STODGE** n heavy starchy food ▷ vb stuff (oneself or another) with food

**STODGED** > STODGE

**STODGER** n dull person

**STODGERS** > STODGER

**STODGES** > STODGE

**STODGIER** > STODGY

**STODGIEST** > STODGY

**STODGILY** > STODGY

**STODGING** > STODGE

**STODGY** adj (of food) heavy and starchy

**STOEP** n verandah

**STOEPS** > STOEP

**STOGEY** same as > STOGY

**STOGEYS** > STOGEY

**STOGIE** same as > STOGY

**STOGIES** > STOGY

**STOGY** n any long cylindrical inexpensive cigar

**STOIC** n person who suffers hardship without showing his or her feelings ▷ adj suffering hardship without showing one's feelings

**STOICAL** adj suffering great difficulties without showing one's feelings

**STOICALLY** > STOICAL

**STOICISM** n indifference to pleasure and pain

**STOICISMS** > STOICISM

**STOICS** > STOIC

**STOIT** vb bounce

**STOITED** > STOIT

**STOITER** vb stagger

**STOITERED** > STOITER

**STOITERS** > STOITER

**STOITING** > STOIT

**STOITS** > STOIT

**STOKE** vb feed and tend (a fire or furnace)

**STOKED** adj very pleased

**STOKEHOLD** n hold for a ship's boilers

**STOKEHOLE** n hole in a furnace through which it is stoked

**STOKER** n person employed to tend a furnace on a ship or train powered by steam

**STOKERS** > STOKER

**STOKES** n cgs unit of kinematic viscosity

**STOKESIA** n American flowering plant

**STOKESIAS** > STOKESIA

**STOKING** > STOKE

**STOKVEL** n (in S Africa) informal savings pool or syndicate

**STOKVELS** > STOKVEL

**STOLE** n long scarf or shawl

**STOLED** adj wearing a stole

**STOLEN** > STEAL

**STOLES** > STOLE

**STOLID** adj showing little emotion or interest

**STOLIDER** > STOLID

**STOLIDEST** > STOLID

**STOLIDITY** > STOLID

**STOLIDLY** > STOLID

**STOLLEN** n rich sweet bread containing nuts, raisins, etc

**STOLLENS** > STOLLEN

**STOLN** > STEAL

**STOLON** n long horizontal stem that grows along the surface of the soil and propagates by producing

roots and shoots at the nodes or tip

**STOLONATE** adj having a stolon

**STOLONIC** > STOLON

**STOLONS** > STOLON

**STOLPORT** n airport for short take-off aircraft

**STOLPORTS** > STOLPORT

**STOMA** n pore in a plant leaf that controls the passage of gases into and out of the plant

**STOMACH** n organ in the body which digests food ▷ vb put up with

**STOMACHAL** > STOMACH

**STOMACHED** > STOMACH

**STOMACHER** n decorative V-shaped panel of stiff material worn over the chest and stomach

**STOMACHIC** adj stimulating gastric activity ▷ n stomachic medicine

**STOMACHS** > STOMACH

**STOMACHY** adj having a large belly

**STOMACK** as in have a stomack (in E Africa) be pregnant

**STOMACKS** > STOMACK

**STOMAL** > STOMA

**STOMAS** > STOMA

**STOMATA** > STOMA

**STOMATAL** adj of, relating to, or possessing stomata or a stoma

**STOMATE** n opening on leaf through which water evaporates

**STOMATES** > STOMATE

**STOMATIC** adj of or relating to a mouth or mouthlike part

**STOMATOUS** same as > STOMATAL

**STOMIA** > STOMIUM

**STOMIUM** n part of the sporangium of ferns that ruptures to release the spores

**STOMIUMS** > STOMIUM

**STOMODAEA** > STOMODEUM

**STOMODEA** > STOMODEUM

**STOMODEAL** > STOMODEUM

**STOMODEUM** n oral cavity of a vertebrate embryo

**STOMP** vb tread heavily ▷ n rhythmic stamping jazz dance

**STOMPED** > STOMP

**STOMPER** n rock or jazz song with a particularly strong and danceable beat

**STOMPERS** > STOMPER

**STOMPIE** n cigarette butt

**STOMPIES** > STOMPIE

**STOMPING** > STOMP

**STOMPS** > STOMP

**STONABLE** > STONE

**STOND** same as > STAND

**STONDS** > STOND

**STONE** n material of which

rocks are made ▷ vb throw stones at

**STONEABLE** > STONE

**STONEBOAT** n type of sleigh used for moving rocks from fields

**STONECAST** n short distance

**STONECHAT** n songbird that has black feathers and a reddish-brown breast

**STONECROP** n type of plant with fleshy leaves and red, yellow, or white flowers

**STONED** adj under the influence of alcohol or drugs

**STONEFISH** n venomous tropical marine scorpaenid fish

**STONEFLY** n any insect of the order Plecoptera, in which the larvae are aquatic

**STONEHAND** n type of compositor

**STONELESS** > STONE

**STONELIKE** > STONE

**STONEN** adj of stone

**STONER** n device for removing stones from fruit

**STONERAG** n type of lichen

**STONERAGS** > STONERAG

**STONERAW** same as > STONERAG

**STONERAWS** > STONERAW

**STONERN** same as > STONEN

**STONERS** > STONER

**STONES** > STONE

**STONESHOT** n stone's throw

**STONEWALL** vb obstruct or hinder discussion

**STONEWARE** n hard kind of pottery fired at a very high temperature ▷ adj made of stoneware

**STONEWASH** vb wash with stones to give worn appearance

**STONEWORK** n part of a building made of stone

**STONEWORT** n any of various green algae which grow in brackish or fresh water

**STONEY** same as > STONY

**STONG** > STING

**STONIED** > STONY

**STONIER** > STONY

**STONIES** > STONY

**STONIEST** > STONY

**STONILY** > STONY

**STONINESS** > STONY

**STONING** > STONE

**STONINGS** > STONE

**STONISH** same as > ASTONISH

**STONISHED** > STONISH

**STONISHES** > STONISH

**STONK** vb bombard (soldiers, buildings, etc) with artillery ▷ n concentrated bombardment by artillery

STONKED > STONK
STONKER vb destroy
STONKERED adj completely exhausted or beaten
STONKERS > STONKER
STONKING > STONK
STONKS > STONK
STONN same as > STUN
STONNE same as > STUN
STONNED > STONNE
STONNES > STONNE
STONNING > STONN
STONNS > STONN
STONY adj of or like stone ▷ vb astonish
STONYING > STONY
STOOD > STAND
STOODEN > STAND
STOOGE n actor who feeds lines to a comedian or acts as the butt of his jokes ▷ vb act as a stooge
STOOGED > STOOGE
STOOGES > STOOGE
STOOGING > STOOGE
STOOK n number of sheaves set upright in a field to dry with their heads together ▷ vb set up (sheaves) in stooks
STOOKED > STOOK
STOOKER > STOOK
STOOKERS > STOOK
STOOKIE n stucco
STOOKIES > STOOKIE
STOOKING > STOOK
STOOKS > STOOK
STOOL n chair without arms or back ▷ vb (of a plant) send up shoots from the base of the stem
STOOLBALL n game resembling cricket played by girls
STOOLED > STOOL
STOOLIE n police informer
STOOLIES > STOOLIE
STOOLING > STOOL
STOOLS > STOOL
STOOP vb bend forward and downward
STOOPBALL n American street game
STOOPE same as > STOUP
STOOPED > STOOP
STOOPER > STOOP
STOOPERS > STOOP
STOOPES > STOOPE
STOOPING > STOOP
STOOPS > STOOP
STOOR same as > STOUR
STOORS > STOOR
STOOSHIE same as > STUSHIE
STOOSHIES > STOOSHIE
STOP vb cease or cause to cease from doing (something) ▷ n stopping or being stopped
STOPBANK n embankment to prevent flooding
STOPBANKS > STOPBANK
STOPCOCK n valve to control or stop the flow of

fluid in a pipe
STOPCOCKS > STOPCOCK
STOPE n steplike excavation made in a mine to extract ore ▷ vb mine (ore, etc) by cutting stopes
STOPED > STOPE
STOPER n drill used in mining
STOPERS > STOPER
STOPES > STOPE
STOPGAP n temporary substitute
STOPGAPS > STOPGAP
STOPING n process by which country rock is broken up and engulfed by the upward movement of magma
STOPINGS > STOPING
STOPLESS > STOP
STOPLIGHT n red light on a traffic signal indicating that vehicles coming towards it should stop
STOPOFF n break in a journey
STOPOFFS > STOPOFF
STOPOVER n short break in a journey ▷ vb make a stopover
STOPOVERS > STOPOVER
STOPPABLE > STOP
STOPPAGE n act of stopping something or the state of being stopped
STOPPAGES > STOPPAGE
STOPPED > STOP
STOPPER n plug for closing a bottle etc ▷ vb close or fit with a stopper
STOPPERED > STOPPER
STOPPERS > STOPPER
STOPPING > STOP
STOPPINGS > STOP
STOPPLE same as > STOPPER
STOPPLED > STOPPLE
STOPPLES > STOPPLE
STOPPLING > STOPPLE
STOPS > STOP
STOPT > STOP
STOPWATCH n watch which can be stopped instantly for exact timing of a sporting event
STOPWORD n common word not used in computer search engines
STOPWORDS > STOPWORD
STORABLE > STORE
STORABLES > STORE
STORAGE n storing
STORAGES > STORAGE
STORAX n type of tree or shrub with drooping showy white flowers
STORAXES > STORAX
STORE vb collect and keep (things) for future use ▷ n shop
STORED > STORE
STOREMAN n man looking after storeroom
STOREMEN > STOREMAN

STORER > STORE
STOREROOM n room in which things are stored
STORERS > STORE
STORES pl n supply or stock of food and other essentials for a journey
STORESHIP n ship carrying naval stores
STOREWIDE adj throughout stores
STOREY n floor or level of a building
STOREYED adj having a storey or storeys
STOREYS > STOREY
STORGE n affection
STORGES > STORGE
STORIATED adj decorated with flowers or animals
STORIED > STORY
STORIES > STORY
STORIETTE n short story
STORING > STORE
STORK n large wading bird
STORKS > STORK
STORM n violent weather with wind, rain, or snow ▷ vb attack or capture (a place) suddenly
STORMBIRD n petrel
STORMED > STORM
STORMER n outstanding example of its kind
STORMERS > STORMER
STORMFUL > STORM
STORMIER > STORMY
STORMIEST > STORMY
STORMILY > STORMY
STORMING adj characterized by or displaying dynamism, speed, and energy
STORMINGS > STORM
STORMLESS > STORM
STORMLIKE > STORM
STORMS > STORM
STORMY adj characterized by storms
STORNELLI > STORNELLO
STORNELLO n type of Italian poem
STORY n narration of a chain of events ▷ vb decorate with scenes from history
STORYBOOK n book containing stories for children ▷ adj better or happier than in real life
STORYETTE n short story
STORYING > STORY
STORYINGS > STORY
STORYLINE n plot of a book, film, play, etc
STOSS adj (of the side of a hill) facing the onward flow of a glacier ▷ n hillside facing glacier flow
STOSSES > STOSS
STOT n bullock ▷ vb bounce or cause to bounce
STOTIN n monetary unit of Slovenia, worth one

hundredth of a tolar
STOTINKA n monetary unit of Bulgaria, worth one hundredth of a lev
STOTINKI > STOTINKA
STOTINOV > STOTIN
STOTINS > STOTIN
STOTIOUS adj drunk
STOTS > STOT
STOTT same as > STOT
STOTTED > STOT
STOTTER same as > STOT
STOTTERED > STOTTER
STOTTERS > STOTTER
STOTTIE n wedge of bread cut from a flat round loaf that has been split and filled with meat, cheese, etc
STOTTIES > STOTTIE
STOTTING > STOT
STOTTS > STOTT
STOUN same as > STUN
STOUND n short while ▷ vb ache
STOUNDED > STOUND
STOUNDING > STOUND
STOUNDS > STOUND
STOUNING > STOUN
STOUNS > STOUN
STOUP n small basin for holy water
STOUPS > STOUP
STOUR n turmoil or conflict
STOURE same as > STOUR
STOURES > STOURE
STOURIE same as > STOURY
STOURIER > STOURY
STOURIEST > STOURY
STOURS > STOUR
STOURY adj dusty
STOUSH vb hit or punch (someone) ▷ n fighting or violence
STOUSHED > STOUSH
STOUSHES > STOUSH
STOUSHIE same as > STUSHIE
STOUSHIES > STOUSHIE
STOUSHING > STOUSH
STOUT adj fat ▷ n strong dark beer
STOUTEN vb make or become stout
STOUTENED > STOUTEN
STOUTENS > STOUTEN
STOUTER > STOUT
STOUTEST > STOUT
STOUTH n Scots word meaning theft
STOUTHS > STOUTH
STOUTISH > STOUT
STOUTLY > STOUT
STOUTNESS > STOUT
STOUTS > STOUT
STOVAINE n anaesthetic drug
STOVAINES > STOVAINE
STOVE n apparatus for cooking or heating ▷ vb process (ceramics, metalwork, etc) by heating in a stove
STOVED > STOVE

**STOVEPIPE** *n* pipe that takes fumes and smoke away from a stove

**STOVER** *n* fodder

**STOVERS** >STOVER

**STOVES** >STOVE

**STOVETOP** *US word for* >HOB

**STOVETOPS** >STOVETOP

**STOVIES** *pl n* potatoes stewed with onions

**STOVING** >STOVE

**STOVINGS** >STOVE

**STOW** *vb* pack or store

**STOWABLE** >STOW

**STOWAGE** *n* space or charge for stowing goods

**STOWAGES** >STOWAGE

**STOWAWAY** *n* person who hides on a ship or aircraft in order to travel free ▷ *vb* travel in such a way

**STOWAWAYS** >STOWAWAY

**STOWDOWN** *n* packing of ship's hold

**STOWDOWNS** >STOWDOWN

**STOWED** >STOW

**STOWER** >STOW

**STOWERS** >STOW

**STOWING** >STOW

**STOWINGS** >STOW

**STOWLINS** *adv* stealthily

**STOWN** >STEAL

**STOWND** *same as* >STOUND

**STOWNDED** >STOWND

**STOWNDING** >STOWND

**STOWNDS** >STOWND

**STOWLINS** *same as* >STOWLINS

**STOWP** *same as* >STOUP

**STOWPS** >STOWP

**STOWRE** *same as* >STOUR

**STOWRES** >STOWRE

**STOWS** >STOW

**STRABISM** *n* abnormal alignment of one or both eyes

**STRABISMS** >STRABISM

**STRAD** *n* violin made by Stradivarius

**STRADDLE** *vb* have one leg or part on each side of (something) ▷ *n* act or position of straddling

**STRADDLED** >STRADDLE

**STRADDLER** >STRADDLE

**STRADDLES** >STRADDLE

**STRADIOT** *n* Venetian cavalryman

**STRADIOTS** >STRADIOT

**STRADS** >STRAD

**STRAE** *Scots form of* >STRAW

**STRAES** >STRAE

**STRAFE** *vb* attack (an enemy) with machine guns from the air ▷ *n* act or instance of strafing

**STRAFED** >STRAFE

**STRAFER** >STRAFE

**STRAFERS** >STRAFE

**STRAFES** >STRAFE

**STRAFF** *same as* >STRAFE

**STRAFFED** >STRAFF

**STRAFFING** >STRAFF

**STRAFFS** >STRAFF

**STRAFING** >STRAFE

**STRAG** *n* straggler

**STRAGGLE** *vb* go or spread in a rambling or irregular way

**STRAGGLED** >STRAGGLE

**STRAGGLER** >STRAGGLE

**STRAGGLES** >STRAGGLE

**STRAGGLY** >STRAGGLE

**STRAGS** >STRAG

**STRAICHT** *Scots word for* >STRAIGHT

**STRAIGHT** *adj* not curved or crooked ▷ *adv* in a straight line ▷ *n* straight part, esp of a racetrack ▷ *vb* tighten

**STRAIGHTS** >STRAIGHT

**STRAIK** *Scots word for* >STROKE

**STRAIKED** >STRAIK

**STRAIKING** >STRAIK

**STRAIKS** >STRAIK

**STRAIN** *vb* subject to mental tension ▷ *n* tension or tiredness

**STRAINED** *adj* not natural, forced

**STRAINER** *n* sieve

**STRAINERS** >STRAINER

**STRAINING** >STRAIN

**STRAINS** >STRAIN

**STRAINT** *n* pressure

**STRAINTS** >STRAINT

**STRAIT** *n* narrow channel connecting two areas of sea ▷ *adj* (of spaces, etc) affording little room ▷ *vb* tighten

**STRAITED** >STRAIT

**STRAITEN** *vb* embarrass or distress, esp financially

**STRAITENS** >STRAITEN

**STRAITER** >STRAIT

**STRAITEST** >STRAIT

**STRAITING** >STRAIT

**STRAITLY** >STRAIT

**STRAITS** >STRAIT

**STRAKE** *n* curved metal plate forming part of the metal rim on a wooden wheel

**STRAKED** *adj* having a strake

**STRAKES** >STRAKE

**STRAMACON** *same as* >STRAMAZON

**STRAMASH** *n* uproar ▷ *vb* destroy

**STRAMAZON** *n* downward fencing stroke

**STRAMMEL** *same as* >STRUMMEL

**STRAMMELS** >STRAMMEL

**STRAMONY** *n* former asthma medicine made from the dried leaves and flowers of the thorn apple

**STRAMP** *Scots variant of* >TRAMP

**STRAMPED** >STRAMP

**STRAMPING** >STRAMP

**STRAMPS** >STRAMP

**STRAND** *vb* run aground ▷ *n* shore

**STRANDED** >STRAND

**STRANDER** >STRAND

**STRANDERS** >STRAND

**STRANDING** >STRAND

**STRANDS** >STRAND

**STRANG** *dialect variant of* >STRONG

**STRANGE** *adj* odd or unusual ▷ *n* odd or unfamiliar person or thing

**STRANGELY** >STRANGE

**STRANGER** *n* person who is not known or is new to a place or experience

**STRANGERS** >STRANGER

**STRANGES** >STRANGE

**STRANGEST** >STRANGE

**STRANGLE** *vb* kill by squeezing the throat

**STRANGLED** >STRANGLE

**STRANGLER** *n* person or thing that strangles

**STRANGLES** *n* acute bacterial disease of horses

**STRANGURY** *n* painful excretion of urine caused by muscular spasms of the urinary tract

**STRAP** *n* strip of flexible material for lifting or holding in place ▷ *vb* fasten with a strap or straps

**STRAPHANG** *vb* travel standing on public transport

**STRAPHUNG** >STRAPHANG

**STRAPLESS** *adj* (of women's clothes) without straps over the shoulders

**STRAPLINE** *n* subheading in a newspaper or magazine article or in any advertisement

**STRAPPADO** *n* system of torture in which a victim was hoisted by a rope tied to his wrists and then allowed to drop until his fall was suddenly checked by the rope ▷ *vb* subject to strappado

**STRAPPED** >STRAP

**STRAPPER** *n* strapping person

**STRAPPERS** >STRAPPER

**STRAPPIER** >STRAPPY

**STRAPPING** >STRAP

**STRAPPY** *adj* having straps

**STRAPS** >STRAP

**STRAPWORT** *n* plant with leaves like straps

**STRASS** *another word for* >PASTE

**STRASSES** >STRASS

**STRATA** >STRATUM

**STRATAGEM** *n* clever plan, trick

**STRATAL** >STRATUM

**STRATAS** >STRATUM

**STRATEGIC** *adj* advantageous

**STRATEGY** *n* overall plan

**STRATH** *n* flat river valley

**STRATHS** >STRATH

**STRATI** >STRATUS

**STRATIFY** *vb* form or be formed in layers or strata

**STRATONIC** *adj* of army

**STRATOSE** *adj* formed in strata

**STRATOUS** *adj* of stratus

**STRATUM** *n* layer, esp of rock

**STRATUMS** >STRATUM

**STRATUS** *n* grey layer cloud

**STRAUCHT** *Scots word for* >STRETCH

**STRAUCHTS** >STRAUCHT

**STRAUGHT** *same as* >STRAUCHT

**STRAUGHTS** >STRAUGHT

**STRAUNGE** *same as* >STRANGE

**STRAVAGE** *same as* >STRAVAIG

**STRAVAGED** >STRAVAGE

**STRAVAGES** >STRAVAGE

**STRAVAIG** *vb* wander aimlessly

**STRAVAIGS** >STRAVAIG

**STRAW** *n* dried stalks of grain ▷ *vb* spread around

**STRAWED** >STRAW

**STRAWEN** *adj* of straw

**STRAWHAT** *adj* of summer dramatic performance

**STRAWIER** >STRAWY

**STRAWIEST** >STRAWY

**STRAWING** >STRAW

**STRAWLESS** >STRAW

**STRAWLIKE** >STRAW

**STRAWN** >STREW

**STRAWS** >STRAW

**STRAWWORM** *n* aquatic larva of a caddis fly

**STRAWY** *adj* containing straw, or like straw in colour or texture

**STRAY** *vb* wander ▷ *adj* having strayed ▷ *n* stray animal

**STRAYED** >STRAY

**STRAYER** >STRAY

**STRAYERS** >STRAY

**STRAYING** >STRAY

**STRAYINGS** >STRAY

**STRAYLING** *n* stray

**STRAYS** >STRAY

**STRAYVE** *vb* wander aimlessly

**STRAYVED** >STRAYVE

**STRAYVES** >STRAYVE

**STRAYVING** >STRAYVE

**STREAK** *n* long band of contrasting colour or substance ▷ *vb* mark with streaks

**STREAKED** >STREAK

**STREAKER** >STREAK

**STREAKERS** >STREAK

**STREAKIER** >STREAKY

**STREAKILY** >STREAKY

**STREAKING** >STREAK

**STREAKS** >STREAK

**STREAKY** *adj* marked with streaks

**STREAM** *n* small river ▷ *vb*

flow steadily

**STREAMBED** *n* bottom of stream

**STREAMED** > STREAM

**STREAMER** *n* strip of coloured paper that unrolls when tossed

**STREAMERS** > STREAMER

**STREAMIER** > STREAMY

**STREAMING** > STREAM

**STREAMLET** > STREAM

**STREAMS** > STREAM

**STREAMY** *adj* (of an area, land, etc) having many streams

**STREEK** *Scots word for* > STRETCH

**STREEKED** > STREEK

**STREEKER** > STREEK

**STREEKERS** > STREEK

**STREEKING** > STREEK

**STREEKS** > STREEK

**STREEL** *n* slovenly woman ▷ *vb* trail

**STREELED** > STREEL

**STREELING** > STREEL

**STREELS** > STREEL

**STREET** *n* public road, usu lined with buildings ▷ *vb* lay out a street or streets

**STREETAGE** *n* toll charged for using a street

**STREETBOY** *n* boy living on the street

**STREETCAR** *n* tram

**STREETED** > STREET

**STREETFUL** *n* amount of people or things street can hold

**STREETIER** > STREETY

**STREETING** > STREET

**STREETS** > STREET

**STREETY** *adj* of streets

**STREIGHT** *same as* > STRAIT

**STREIGHTS** > STREIGHT

**STREIGNE** *same as* > STRAIN

**STREIGNED** > STREIGNE

**STREIGNES** > STREIGNE

**STRELITZ** *n* former Russian soldier

**STRELITZI** > STRELITZ

**STRENE** *same as* > STRAIN

**STRENES** > STRENE

**STRENGTH** *n* quality of being strong

**STRENGTHS** > STRENGTH

**STRENUITY** > STRENUOUS

**STRENUOUS** *adj* requiring great energy or effort

**STREP** *n* streptococcus

**STREPENT** *adj* noisy

**STREPS** > STREP

**STRESS** *n* tension or strain ▷ *vb* emphasize

**STRESSED** > STRESS

**STRESSES** > STRESS

**STRESSFUL** > STRESS

**STRESSING** > STRESS

**STRESSOR** *n* event, experience, etc, that causes stress

**STRESSORS** > STRESSOR

**STRETCH** *vb* extend or be extended ▷ *n* stretching

**STRETCHED** > STRETCH

**STRETCHER** *n* frame covered with canvas, on which an injured person is carried ▷ *vb* transport (a sick or injured person) on a stretcher

**STRETCHES** > STRETCH

**STRETCHY** *adj* characterized by elasticity

**STRETTA** *same as* > STRETTO

**STRETTAS** > STRETTA

**STRETTE** > STRETTA

**STRETTI** > STRETTO

**STRETTO** *n* (in a fugue) the close overlapping of two parts or voices

**STRETTOS** > STRETTO

**STREUSEL** *n* crumbly topping for rich pastries

**STREUSELS** > STREUSEL

**STREW** *vb* scatter (things) over a surface

**STREWAGE** > STREW

**STREWAGES** > STREW

**STREWED** > STREW

**STREWER** > STREW

**STREWERS** > STREW

**STREWING** > STREW

**STREWINGS** > STREW

**STREWMENT** *n* strewing

**STREWN** > STREW

**STREWS** > STREW

**STREWTH** *interj* expression of surprise or alarm

**STRIA** *n* scratch or groove on the surface of a rock crystal

**STRIAE** > STRIA

**STRIATA** > STRIATUM

**STRIATE** *adj* marked with striae ▷ *vb* mark with striae

**STRIATED** *adj* having a pattern of scratches or grooves

**STRIATES** > STRIATE

**STRIATING** > STRIATE

**STRIATION** *same as* > STRIA

**STRIATUM** *n* part of brain

**STRIATUMS** > STRIATUM

**STRIATURE** *n* way something is striated

**STRICH** *n* screech owl

**STRICHES** > STRICH

**STRICK** *n* any bast fibres preparatory to being made into slivers

**STRICKEN** *adj* seriously affected by disease, grief, pain, etc

**STRICKLE** *n* board used for sweeping off excess material in a container ▷ *vb* level, form, or sharpen with a strickle

**STRICKLED** > STRICKLE

**STRICKLES** > STRICKLE

**STRICKS** > STRICK

**STRICT** *adj* stern or severe

**STRICTER** > STRICT

**STRICTEST** > STRICT

**STRICTION** *n* act of restricting

**STRICTISH** > STRICT

**STRICTLY** > STRICT

**STRICTURE** *n* severe criticism

**STRIDDEN** > STRIDE

**STRIDDLE** *same as* > STRADDLE

**STRIDDLED** > STRIDDLE

**STRIDDLES** > STRIDDLE

**STRIDE** *vb* walk with long steps ▷ *n* long step

**STRIDENCE** > STRIDENT

**STRIDENCY** > STRIDENT

**STRIDENT** *adj* loud and harsh

**STRIDER** > STRIDE

**STRIDERS** > STRIDE

**STRIDES** > STRIDE

**STRIDING** > STRIDE

**STRIDLING** *adv* astride

**STRIDOR** *n* high-pitched whistling sound made during respiration

**STRIDORS** > STRIDOR

**STRIFE** *n* conflict, quarrelling

**STRIFEFUL** > STRIFE

**STRIFES** > STRIFE

**STRIFT** *n* struggle

**STRIFTS** > STRIFT

**STRIG** *vb* remove stalk from

**STRIGA** *same as* > STRIA

**STRIGAE** > STRIGA

**STRIGATE** *adj* streaked

**STRIGGED** > STRIG

**STRIGGING** > STRIG

**STRIGIL** *n* curved blade used by the ancient Romans and Greeks to scrape the body after bathing

**STRIGILS** > STRIGIL

**STRIGINE** *adj* of or like owl

**STRIGOSE** *adj* bearing stiff hairs or bristles

**STRIGS** > STRIG

**STRIKE** *vb* cease work as a protest ▷ *n* stoppage of work as a protest

**STRIKEOUT** *n* dismissal in baseball due to three successive failures to hit the ball

**STRIKER** *n* striking worker

**STRIKERS** > STRIKER

**STRIKES** > STRIKE

**STRIKING** > STRIKE

**STRIKINGS** > STRIKE

**STRING** *n* thin cord used for tying ▷ *vb* provide with a string or strings

**STRINGED** *adj* (of a musical instrument) having strings that are plucked or played with a bow

**STRINGENT** *adj* strictly controlled or enforced

**STRINGER** *n* journalist retained by a newspaper to cover a particular town or area

**STRINGERS** > STRINGER

**STRINGIER** > STRINGY

**STRINGILY** > STRINGY

**STRINGING** > STRING

**STRINGS** > STRING

**STRINGY** *adj* like string

**STRINKLE** *Scots variant of* > SPRINKLE

**STRINKLED** > STRINKLE

**STRINKLES** > STRINKLE

**STRIP** *vb* take (the covering or clothes) off ▷ *n* act of stripping

**STRIPE** *n* long narrow band of contrasting colour or substance ▷ *vb* mark (something) with stripes

**STRIPED** *adj* marked or decorated with stripes

**STRIPER** *n* officer who has a stripe or stripes on his uniform, esp in the navy

**STRIPERS** > STRIPER

**STRIPES** > STRIPE

**STRIPEY** *same as* > STRIPY

**STRIPIER** > STRIPY

**STRIPIEST** > STRIPY

**STRIPING** > STRIPE

**STRIPINGS** > STRIPE

**STRIPLING** *n* youth

**STRIPPED** > STRIP

**STRIPPER** *n* person who performs a striptease

**STRIPPERS** > STRIPPER

**STRIPPING** > STRIP

**STRIPS** > STRIP

**STRIPT** > STRIP

**STRIPY** *adj* marked by or with stripes

**STRIVE** *vb* make a great effort

**STRIVED** > STRIVE

**STRIVEN** > STRIVE

**STRIVER** > STRIVE

**STRIVERS** > STRIVE

**STRIVES** > STRIVE

**STRIVING** > STRIVE

**STRIVINGS** > STRIVE

**STROAM** *vb* wander

**STROAMED** > STROAM

**STROAMING** > STROAM

**STROAMS** > STROAM

**STROBE** *n* high intensity flashing beam of light ▷ *vb* give the appearance of slow motion by using a strobe

**STROBED** > STROBE

**STROBES** > STROBE

**STROBIC** *adj* spinning or appearing to spin

**STROBIL** *n* scaly multiple fruit

**STROBILA** *n* body of a tapeworm, consisting of a string of similar segments

**STROBILAE** > STROBILA

**STROBILAR** > STROBILA

**STROBILE** *same as* > STROBILUS

**STROBILES** > STROBILE

**STROBILI** > STROBILUS

**STROBILS** > STROBIL

**STROBILUS** *technical name for* > CONE

**STROBING** > STROBE

**STROBINGS** >STROBE
**STRODDLE** *same*
*as* >STRADDLE
**STRODDLED** >STRODDLE
**STRODDLES** >STRODDLE
**STRODE** >STRIDE
**STRODLE** *same*
*as* >STRADDLE
**STRODLED** >STRODLE
**STRODLES** >STRODLE
**STRODLING** >STRODLE
**STROKE** *vb* touch or caress lightly with the hand ▷ *n* light touch or caress with the hand
**STROKED** >STROKE
**STROKEN** >STRIKE
**STROKER** >STROKE
**STROKERS** >STROKE
**STROKES** >STROKE
**STROKING** >STROKE
**STROKINGS** >STROKE
**STROLL** *vb* walk in a leisurely manner ▷ *n* leisurely walk
**STROLLED** >STROLL
**STROLLER** *n* chair-shaped carriage for a baby
**STROLLERS** >STROLLER
**STROLLING** >STROLL
**STROLLS** >STROLL
**STROMA** *n* gel-like matrix of chloroplasts and certain cells
**STROMAL** >STROMA
**STROMATA** >STROMA
**STROMATIC** >STROMA
**STROMB** *n* shellfish like a whelk
**STROMBS** >STROMB
**STROMBUS** *same*
*as* >STROMB
**STROND** *same as* >STRAND
**STRONDS** >STROND
**STRONG** *adj* having physical power
**STRONGARM** *adj* involving physical force
**STRONGBOX** *n* box in which valuables are locked for safety
**STRONGER** >STRONG
**STRONGEST** >STRONG
**STRONGISH** >STRONG
**STRONGLY** >STRONG
**STRONGMAN** *n* performer, esp one in a circus, who performs feats of strength
**STRONGMEN** >STRONGMAN
**STRONGYL** *same*
*as* >STRONGYLE
**STRONGYLE** *n* type of parasitic worm chiefly occurring in the intestines of horses
**STRONGYLS** >STRONGYL
**STRONTIA** >STRONTIUM
**STRONTIAN** *n* type of white mineral
**STRONTIAS** >STRONTIA
**STRONTIC** >STRONTIUM
**STRONTIUM** *n* silvery-white metallic element
**STROOK** >STRIKE

**STROOKE** *n* stroke
**STROOKEN** *same*
*as* >STRICKEN
**STROOKES** >STROOKE
**STROP** *n* leather strap for sharpening razors ▷ *vb* sharpen (a razor, etc) on a strop
**STROPHE** *n* first of two movements made by a chorus during the performance of a choral ode
**STROPHES** >STROPHE
**STROPHIC** *adj* of, relating to, or employing a strophe or strophes
**STROPHOID** *n* type of curve on graph
**STROPHULI** *pl n* skin inflammations seen primarily on small children
**STROPPED** >STROP
**STROPPER** >STROP
**STROPPERS** >STROP
**STROPPIER** >STROPPY
**STROPPILY** >STROPPY
**STROPPING** >STROP
**STROPPY** *adj* angry or awkward
**STROPS** >STROP
**STROSSERS** *same*
*as* >TROUSERS
**STROUD** *n* coarse woollen fabric
**STROUDING** *n* woolly material for making strouds
**STROUDS** >STROUD
**STROUP** *Scots word*
*for* >SPOUT
**STROUPACH** *n* cup of tea
**STROUPAN** *same*
*as* >STROUPACH
**STROUPANS** >STROUPAN
**STROUPS** >STROUP
**STROUT** *vb* bulge
**STROUTED** >STROUT
**STROUTING** >STROUT
**STROUTS** >STROUT
**STROVE** >STRIVE
**STROW** *archaic variant*
*of* >STREW
**STROWED** >STROW
**STROWER** >STROW
**STROWERS** >STROW
**STROWING** >STROW
**STROWINGS** >STROW
**STROWN** >STROW
**STROWS** >STROW
**STROY** *archaic variant*
*of* >DESTROY
**STROYED** >STROY
**STROYER** >STROY
**STROYERS** >STROY
**STROYING** >STROY
**STROYS** >STROY
**STRUCK** >STRIKE
**STRUCKEN** *same*
*as* >STRICKEN
**STRUCTURE** *n* complex construction ▷ *vb* give a structure to
**STRUDEL** *n* thin sheet of

filled dough rolled up and baked, usu with an apple filling
**STRUDELS** >STRUDEL
**STRUGGLE** *vb* work, strive, or make one's way with difficulty ▷ *n* striving
**STRUGGLED** >STRUGGLE
**STRUGGLER** >STRUGGLE
**STRUGGLES** >STRUGGLE
**STRUM** *vb* play (a guitar or banjo) by sweeping the thumb or a plectrum across the strings
**STRUMA** *n* abnormal enlargement of the thyroid gland
**STRUMAE** >STRUMA
**STRUMAS** >STRUMA
**STRUMATIC** >STRUMA
**STRUMITIS** *n* inflammation of thyroid gland
**STRUMMED** >STRUM
**STRUMMEL** *n* straw
**STRUMMELS** >STRUMMEL
**STRUMMER** >STRUM
**STRUMMERS** >STRUM
**STRUMMING** >STRUM
**STRUMOSE** >STRUMA
**STRUMOUS** >STRUMA
**STRUMPET** *n* prostitute ▷ *vb* turn into a strumpet
**STRUMPETS** >STRUMPET
**STRUMS** >STRUM
**STRUNG** >STRING
**STRUNT** *Scots word*
*for* >STRUT
**STRUNTED** >STRUNT
**STRUNTING** >STRUNT
**STRUNTS** >STRUNT
**STRUT** *vb* walk pompously, swagger ▷ *n* bar supporting a structure
**STRUTS** >STRUT
**STRUTTED** >STRUT
**STRUTTER** >STRUT
**STRUTTERS** >STRUT
**STRUTTING** >STRUT
**STRYCHNIA** *n* strychnine
**STRYCHNIC** *adj* of, relating to, or derived from strychnine
**STUB** *n* short piece left after use ▷ *vb* strike (the toe) painfully against an object
**STUBBED** >STUB
**STUBBIE** *same as* >STUBBY
**STUBBIER** >STUBBY
**STUBBIES** >STUBBY
**STUBBIEST** >STUBBY
**STUBBILY** >STUBBY
**STUBBING** >STUB
**STUBBLE** *n* short stalks of grain left in a field after reaping
**STUBBLED** *adj* having the stubs of stalks left after a crop has been cut and harvested
**STUBBLES** >STUBBLE
**STUBBLIER** >STUBBLE
**STUBBLY** >STUBBLE
**STUBBORN** *adj* refusing to

agree or give in ▷ *vb* make stubborn
**STUBBORNS** >STUBBORN
**STUBBY** *adj* short and broad ▷ *n* small bottle of beer
**STUBS** >STUB
**STUCCO** *n* plaster used for coating or decorating walls ▷ *vb* apply stucco to (a building)
**STUCCOED** >STUCCO
**STUCCOER** >STUCCO
**STUCCOERS** >STUCCO
**STUCCOES** >STUCCO
**STUCCOING** >STUCCO
**STUCCOS** >STUCCO
**STUCK** *n* thrust
**STUCKS** >STUCK
**STUD** *n* small piece of metal attached to a surface for decoration ▷ *vb* set with studs
**STUDBOOK** *n* written record of the pedigree of a purebred stock, esp of racehorses
**STUDBOOKS** >STUDBOOK
**STUDDED** >STUD
**STUDDEN** >STAND
**STUDDIE** *Scots word*
*for* >ANVIL
**STUDDIES** >STUDDIE
**STUDDING** >STUD
**STUDDINGS** >STUD
**STUDDLE** *n* post
**STUDDLES** >STUDDLE
**STUDENT** *n* person who studies a subject, esp at university
**STUDENTRY** *n* body of students
**STUDENTS** >STUDENT
**STUDENTY** *adj* informal, sometimes derogatory term denoting the characteristics believed typical of an undergraduate student
**STUDFARM** *n* farm where horses are bred
**STUDFARMS** >STUDFARM
**STUDFISH** *n* American minnow
**STUDHORSE** *another word*
*for* >STALLION
**STUDIED** *adj* carefully practised
**STUDIEDLY** >STUDIED
**STUDIER** >STUDY
**STUDIERS** >STUDY
**STUDIES** >STUDY
**STUDIO** *n* workroom of an artist or photographer
**STUDIOS** >STUDIO
**STUDIOUS** *adj* fond of study
**STUDLIER** >STUDLY
**STUDLIEST** >STUDLY
**STUDLY** *adj* strong and virile
**STUDS** >STUD
**STUDWORK** *n* work decorated with studs
**STUDWORKS** >STUDWORK
**STUDY** *vb* be engaged in

learning (a subject) ▷ *n* act or process of studying
**STUDYING** >STUDY
**STUFF** *n* substance or material ▷ *vb* pack, cram, or fill completely
**STUFFED** >STUFF
**STUFFER** >STUFF
**STUFFERS** >STUFF
**STUFFIER** >STUFFY
**STUFFIEST** >STUFFY
**STUFFILY** >STUFFY
**STUFFING** *n* seasoned mixture with which food is stuffed
**STUFFINGS** >STUFFING
**STUFFLESS** >STUFF
**STUFFS** >STUFF
**STUFFY** *adj* lacking fresh air
**STUGGIER** >STUGGY
**STUGGIEST** >STUGGY
**STUGGY** *adj* stout
**STUIVER** *same as* >STIVER
**STUIVERS** >STUIVER
**STUKKEND** *adj* South African slang for broken or wrecked
**STULL** *n* timber prop or platform in a stope
**STULLS** >STULL
**STULM** *n* shaft
**STULMS** >STULM
**STULTIFY** *vb* dull (the mind) by boring routine
**STUM** *n* partly fermented wine added to fermented wine as a preservative ▷ *vb* preserve (wine) by adding stum
**STUMBLE** *vb* trip and nearly fall ▷ *n* stumbling
**STUMBLED** >STUMBLE
**STUMBLER** >STUMBLE
**STUMBLERS** >STUMBLE
**STUMBLES** >STUMBLE
**STUMBLIER** >STUMBLY
**STUMBLING** >STUMBLE
**STUMBLY** *adj* tending to stumble
**STUMER** *n* forgery or cheat
**STUMERS** >STUMER
**STUMM** *same as* >SHTOOM
**STUMMED** >STUM
**STUMMEL** *n* bowl of pipe
**STUMMELS** >STUMMEL
**STUMMING** >STUM
**STUMP** *n* base of a tree left when the main trunk has been cut away ▷ *vb* baffle
**STUMPAGE** *n* standing timber or its value
**STUMPAGES** >STUMPAGE
**STUMPED** >STUMP
**STUMPER** >STUMP
**STUMPERS** >STUMP
**STUMPIER** >STUMPY
**STUMPIES** >STUMPY
**STUMPIEST** >STUMPY
**STUMPILY** >STUMPY
**STUMPING** >STUMP
**STUMPS** >STUMP
**STUMPWORK** *n* type of embroidery featuring raised figures, padded

with cotton wool or hair
**STUMPY** *adj* short and thick ▷ *n* stumpy thing
**STUMS** >STUM
**STUN** *vb* shock or overwhelm ▷ *n* state or effect of being stunned
**STUNG** >STING
**STUNK** >STINK
**STUNKARD** *adj* sulky
**STUNNED** >STUN
**STUNNER** *n* beautiful person or thing
**STUNNERS** >STUNNER
**STUNNING** >STUN
**STUNNINGS** >STUN
**STUNS** >STUN
**STUNSAIL** *n* type of light auxiliary sail
**STUNSAILS** >STUNSAIL
**STUNT** *vb* prevent or impede the growth of ▷ *n* acrobatic or dangerous action
**STUNTED** >STUNT
**STUNTING** >STUNT
**STUNTMAN** *n* person who performs dangerous acts in a film, etc in place of an actor
**STUNTMEN** >STUNTMAN
**STUNTS** >STUNT
**STUPA** *n* domed edifice housing Buddhist or Jain relics
**STUPAS** >STUPA
**STUPE** *n* hot damp cloth applied to the body to relieve pain ▷ *vb* treat with a stupe
**STUPED** >STUPE
**STUPEFIED** >STUPEFY
**STUPEFIER** >STUPEFY
**STUPEFIES** >STUPEFY
**STUPEFY** *vb* make insensitive or lethargic
**STUPENT** *adj* astonished
**STUPES** >STUPE
**STUPID** *adj* lacking intelligence ▷ *n* stupid person
**STUPIDER** >STUPID
**STUPIDEST** >STUPID
**STUPIDITY** *n* quality or state of being stupid
**STUPIDLY** >STUPID
**STUPIDS** >STUPID
**STUPING** >STUPE
**STUPOR** *n* dazed or unconscious state
**STUPOROUS** >STUPOR
**STUPORS** >STUPOR
**STUPRATE** *vb* ravish
**STUPRATED** >STUPRATE
**STUPRATES** >STUPRATE
**STURDIED** >STURDY
**STURDIER** >STURDY
**STURDIES** >STURDY
**STURDIEST** >STURDY
**STURDILY** >STURDY
**STURDY** *adj* healthy and robust ▷ *n* disease of sheep
**STURE** *same as* >STOOR

**STURGEON** *n* fish from which caviar is obtained
**STURGEONS** >STURGEON
**STURMER** *n* type of eating apple with pale green skin
**STURMERS** >STURMER
**STURNINE** >STURNUS
**STURNOID** >STURNUS
**STURNUS** *n* bird of starling family
**STURNUSES** >STURNUS
**STURT** *vb* bother
**STURTED** >STURT
**STURTING** >STURT
**STURTS** >STURT
**STUSHIE** *n* commotion, rumpus, or row
**STUSHIES** >STUSHIE
**STUTTER** *vb* speak with repetition of initial consonants ▷ *n* tendency to stutter
**STUTTERED** >STUTTER
**STUTTERER** >STUTTER
**STUTTERS** >STUTTER
**STY** *vb* climb
**STYE** *n* inflammation at the base of an eyelash
**STYED** >STYE
**STYES** >STYE
**STYGIAN** *adj* dark, gloomy, or hellish
**STYING** >STY
**STYLAR** >STYLUS
**STYLATE** *adj* having style
**STYLE** *n* shape or design ▷ *vb* shape or design
**STYLEBOOK** *n* book containing rules of punctuation, etc, for the use of writers, editors, and printers
**STYLED** >STYLE
**STYLELESS** >STYLE
**STYLER** >STYLE
**STYLERS** >STYLE
**STYLES** >STYLE
**STYLET** *n* wire for insertion into a flexible cannula or catheter to maintain its rigidity during passage
**STYLETS** >STYLET
**STYLI** >STYLUS
**STYLIE** *adj* fashion-conscious
**STYLIER** >STYLIE
**STYLIEST** >STYLIE
**STYLIFORM** *adj* shaped like a stylus or bristle
**STYLING** >STYLE
**STYLINGS** >STYLE
**STYLISE** *same as* >STYLIZE
**STYLISED** >STYLISE
**STYLISER** >STYLISE
**STYLISERS** >STYLISE
**STYLISES** >STYLISE
**STYLISH** *adj* smart, elegant, and fashionable
**STYLISHLY** >STYLISH
**STYLISING** >STYLISE
**STYLIST** *n* hairdresser
**STYLISTIC** *adj* of literary or artistic style
**STYLISTS** >STYLIST

**STYLITE** *n* one of a class of recluses who in ancient times lived on the top of high pillars
**STYLITES** >STYLITE
**STYLITIC** >STYLITE
**STYLITISM** >STYLITE
**STYLIZE** *vb* cause to conform to an established stylistic form
**STYLIZED** >STYLIZE
**STYLIZER** >STYLIZE
**STYLIZERS** >STYLIZE
**STYLIZES** >STYLIZE
**STYLIZING** >STYLIZE
**STYLO** *n* type of fountain pen
**STYLOBATE** *n* continuous horizontal course of masonry that supports a colonnade
**STYLOID** *adj* resembling a stylus ▷ *n* spiny growth
**STYLOIDS** >STYLOID
**STYLOLITE** *n* any of the small striated columnar or irregular structures within the strata of some limestones
**STYLOPES** >STYLOPS
**STYLOPISE** *same as* >STYLOPIZE
**STYLOPIZE** *vb* (of a stylops) to parasitize (a host)
**STYLOPS** *n* type of insect that lives as a parasite in other insects
**STYLOS** >STYLO
**STYLUS** *n* needle-like device on a record player that rests in the groove of the record and picks up the sound signals
**STYLUSES** >STYLUS
**STYME** *vb* peer
**STYMED** >STYME
**STYMES** >STYME
**STYMIE** *vb* hinder or thwart
**STYMIED** >STYMY
**STYMIEING** >STYMIE
**STYMIES** >STYMY
**STYMING** >STYME
**STYMY** *same as* >STYMIE
**STYMYING** >STYMY
**STYPSIS** *n* action, application, or use of a styptic
**STYPSISES** >STYPSIS
**STYPTIC** *adj* (drug) used to stop bleeding ▷ *n* styptic drug
**STYPTICAL** >STYPTIC
**STYPTICS** >STYPTIC
**STYRAX** *n* type of tropical or subtropical tree
**STYRAXES** >STYRAX
**STYRE** *same as* >STIR
**STYRED** >STYRE
**STYRENE** *n* colourless oily volatile flammable water-insoluble liquid
**STYRENES** >STYRENE
**STYRES** >STYRE
**STYRING** >STYRE

STYROFOAM n tradename for a light expanded polystyrene plastic

STYTE vb bounce

STYTED >STYTE

STYTES >STYTE

STYTING >STYTE

SUABILITY >SUABLE

SUABLE adj liable to be sued in a court

SUABLY >SUABLE

SUASIBLE >SUASION

SUASION n persuasion

SUASIONS >SUASION

SUASIVE >SUASION

SUASIVELY >SUASION

SUASORY >SUASION

SUAVE adj smooth and sophisticated in manner

SUAVELY >SUAVE

SUAVENESS >SUAVE

SUAVER >SUAVE

SUAVEST >SUAVE

SUAVITIES >SUAVE

SUAVITY >SUAVE

SUB n subeditor ▷ vb act as a substitute

SUBA n shepherd's cloak

SUBABBOT n abbot who is subordinate to another abbot

SUBABBOTS >SUBABBOT

SUBACID adj (esp of some fruits) moderately acid or sour

SUBACIDLY >SUBACID

SUBACRID adj slightly acrid

SUBACT vb subdue

SUBACTED >SUBACT

SUBACTING >SUBACT

SUBACTION >SUBACT

SUBACTS >SUBACT

SUBACUTE adj intermediate between acute and chronic

SUBADAR n (formerly) the chief native officer of a company of Indian soldiers in the British service

SUBADARS >SUBADAR

SUBADULT n animal not quite at adult stage

SUBADULTS >SUBADULT

SUBAERIAL adj in open air

SUBAGENCY n agency employed by larger agency

SUBAGENT n agent who is subordinate to another agent

SUBAGENTS >SUBAGENT

SUBAH same as >SUBADAR

SUBAHDAR same as >SUBADAR

SUBAHDARS >SUBAHDAR

SUBAHDARY n office of subahdar

SUBAHS >SUBAH

SUBAHSHIP >SUBAH

SUBALAR adj below a wing

SUBALPINE adj situated in or relating to the regions at the foot of mountains

SUBALTERN n British army officer below the rank of captain ▷ adj of inferior position or rank

SUBAPICAL adj below an apex

SUBAQUA adj of or relating to underwater sport

SUBARCTIC adj of or relating to latitudes immediately south of the Arctic Circle

SUBAREA n area within a larger area

SUBAREAS >SUBAREA

SUBARID adj receiving slightly more rainfall than arid regions

SUBAS >SUBA

SUBASTRAL adj terrestrial

SUBATOM n part of an atom

SUBATOMIC adj of or being one of the particles which make up an atom

SUBATOMS >SUBATOM

SUBAUDIO adj (of sound) low frequency

SUBAURAL adj below the ear

SUBAXIAL adj below an axis of the body

SUBBASAL >SUBBASE

SUBBASE same as >SUBBASS

SUBBASES >SUBBASE

SUBBASIN n geographical basin within larger basin

SUBBASINS >SUBBASIN

SUBBASS another name for >BOURDON

SUBBASSES >SUBBASS

SUBBED >SUB

SUBBIE n subcontractor

SUBBIES >SUBBIE

SUBBING >SUB

SUBBINGS >SUB

SUBBLOCK n part of mathematical matrix

SUBBLOCKS >SUBBLOCK

SUBBRANCH n branch within another branch

SUBBREED n breed within a larger breed

SUBBREEDS >SUBBREED

SUBBUREAU n bureau subordinate to the main bureau

SUBBY same as >SUBBIE

SUBCANTOR n deputy to a cantor

SUBCASTE n subdivision of a caste

SUBCASTES >SUBCASTE

SUBCAUDAL adj below a tail

SUBCAUSE n factor less important than a cause

SUBCAUSES >SUBCAUSE

SUBCAVITY n cavity within a larger cavity

SUBCELL n cell within a larger cell

SUBCELLAR n cellar below another cellar

SUBCELLS >SUBCELL

SUBCENTER n secondary center

SUBCHASER n anti-submarine warship

SUBCHIEF n chief below the main chief

SUBCHIEFS >SUBCHIEF

SUBCHORD n part of a curve

SUBCHORDS >SUBCHORD

SUBCLAIM n claim that is part of a larger claim

SUBCLAIMS >SUBCLAIM

SUBCLAN n clan within a larger clan

SUBCLANS >SUBCLAN

SUBCLASS n principal subdivision of a class ▷ vb assign to a subclass

SUBCLAUSE n subordinate section of a larger clause in a document

SUBCLERK n clerk who is subordinate to another clerk

SUBCLERKS >SUBCLERK

SUBCLIMAX n community in which development has been arrested before climax has been attained

SUBCODE n computer tag identifying data

SUBCODES >SUBCODE

SUBCOLONY n colony established by existing colony

SUBCONSUL n assistant to a consul

SUBCOOL vb make colder

SUBCOOLED >SUBCOOL

SUBCOOLS >SUBCOOL

SUBCORTEX n matter of the brain situated beneath the cerebral cortex

SUBCOSTA n vein in insect wing

SUBCOSTAE >SUBCOSTA

SUBCOSTAL adj below the rib

SUBCOUNTY n division of a county

SUBCRUST n secondary crust below main crust

SUBCRUSTS >SUBCRUST

SUBCULT n cult within larger cult

SUBCULTS >SUBCULT

SUBCUTES >SUBCUTIS

SUBCUTIS n layer of tissue beneath outer skin

SUBDEACON n cleric who assists at High Mass

SUBDEALER n dealer who buys from other dealer

SUBDEAN n deputy of dean

SUBDEANS >SUBDEAN

SUBDEB n young woman who is not yet a debutante

SUBDEBS >SUBDEB

SUBDEPOT n depot within a larger depot

SUBDEPOTS >SUBDEPOT

SUBDEPUTY n assistant to a deputy

SUBDERMAL adj below the skin

SUBDEW same as >SUBDUE

SUBDEWED >SUBDEW

SUBDEWING >SUBDEW

SUBDEWS >SUBDEW

SUBDIVIDE vb divide (a part of something) into smaller parts

SUBDOLOUS adj clever

SUBDORSAL adj situated close to the back

SUBDUABLE >SUBDUE

SUBDUABLY >SUBDUE

SUBDUAL >SUBDUE

SUBDUALS >SUBDUE

SUBDUCE vb withdraw

SUBDUCED >SUBDUCE

SUBDUCES >SUBDUCE

SUBDUCING >SUBDUCE

SUBDUCT vb draw or turn (the eye, etc) downwards

SUBDUCTED >SUBDUCT

SUBDUCTS >SUBDUCT

SUBDUE vb overcome

SUBDUED adj cowed, passive, or shy

SUBDUEDLY >SUBDUED

SUBDUER >SUBDUE

SUBDUERS >SUBDUE

SUBDUES >SUBDUE

SUBDUING >SUBDUE

SUBDUPLE adj in proportion of one to two

SUBDURAL adj between the dura mater and the arachnoid

SUBDWARF n star smaller than a dwarf star

SUBDWARFS >SUBDWARF

SUBECHO n echo resonating more quietly than another echo

SUBECHOES >SUBECHO

SUBEDAR same as >SUBADAR

SUBEDARS >SUBEDAR

SUBEDIT vb edit and correct (written or printed material)

SUBEDITED >SUBEDIT

SUBEDITOR n person who checks and edits text for a newspaper or magazine

SUBEDITS >SUBEDIT

SUBENTIRE adj slightly indented

SUBENTRY n entry within another entry

SUBEPOCH n epoch within another epoch

SUBEPOCHS >SUBEPOCH

SUBEQUAL adj not quite equal

SUBER n cork

SUBERATE n salt of suberic acid

SUBERATES >SUBERATE

SUBERECT adj not quite erect

SUBEREOUS same as >SUBEROSE

SUBERIC same as >SUBEROSE

SUBERIN n fatty or waxy substance that is present in the walls of cork cells

SUBERINS >SUBERIN

SUBERISE same

*as* >SUBERIZE
SUBERISED >SUBERISE
SUBERISES >SUBERISE
SUBERIZE *vb* impregnate
(cell walls) with suberin
during the formation of
corky tissue
SUBERIZED >SUBERIZE
SUBERIZES >SUBERIZE
SUBEROSE *adj* relating to,
resembling, or consisting
of cork
SUBEROUS *same*
*as* >SUBEROSE
SUBERS >SUBER
SUBFAMILY *n* taxonomic
group that is a subdivision
of a family
SUBFEU *vb* grant feu to
vassal
SUBFEUED >SUBFEU
SUBFEUING >SUBFEU
SUBFEUS >SUBFEU
SUBFIELD *n* subdivision of
a field
SUBFIELDS >SUBFIELD
SUBFILE *n* file within
another file
SUBFILES >SUBFILE
SUBFIX *n* suffix
SUBFIXES >SUBFIX
SUBFLOOR *n* rough floor
that forms a base for a
finished floor
SUBFLOORS >SUBFLOOR
SUBFLUID *adj* viscous
SUBFOSSIL *n* something
partly fossilized
SUBFRAME *n* frame on
which car body is built
SUBFRAMES >SUBFRAME
SUBFUSC *adj* devoid of
brightness or appeal ▷ *n*
(at Oxford University)
formal academic dress
SUBFUSCS >SUBFUSC
SUBFUSK *same as* >SUBFUSC
SUBFUSKS >SUBFUSK
SUBGENERA >SUBGENUS
SUBGENRE *n* genre within a
larger genre
SUBGENRES >SUBGENRE
SUBGENUS *n* taxonomic
group that is a subdivision
of a genus but of higher
rank than a species
SUBGOAL *n* secondary goal
SUBGOALS >SUBGOAL
SUBGRADE *n* ground
beneath a roadway or
pavement
SUBGRADES >SUBGRADE
SUBGRAPH *n* graph sharing
vertices of other graph
SUBGRAPHS >SUBGRAPH
SUBGROUP *n* small group
that is part of a larger
group
SUBGROUPS >SUBGROUP
SUBGUM *n* Chinese dish
SUBGUMS >SUBGUM
SUBHA *n* string of beads
used in praying and
meditating

SUBHAS >SUBHA
SUBHEAD *n* heading of a
subsection in a printed
work
SUBHEADS >SUBHEAD
SUBHEDRAL *adj* with some
characteristics of crystal
SUBHUMAN *adj* less than
human
SUBHUMANS >SUBHUMAN
SUBHUMID *adj* not wet
enough for trees to grow
SUBIDEA *n* secondary idea
SUBIDEAS >SUBIDEA
SUBIMAGO *n* first winged
stage of the mayfly
SUBIMAGOS >SUBIMAGO
SUBINCISE *vb* perform
subincision
SUBINDEX *same*
*as* >SUBSCRIPT
SUBINFEUD *vb* grant by
feudal tenant to further
tenant
SUBITEM *n* item that is less
important than another
item
SUBITEMS >SUBITEM
SUBITISE *same*
*as* >SUBITIZE
SUBITISED >SUBITISE
SUBITISES >SUBITISE
SUBITIZE *vb* perceive
the number of (a group
of items) at a glance and
without counting
SUBITIZED >SUBITIZE
SUBITIZES >SUBITIZE
SUBITO *adv* (preceding
or following a dynamic
marking, etc) suddenly
SUBJACENT *adj* forming a
foundation
SUBJECT *n* person or
thing being dealt with or
studied ▷ *adj* being under
the rule of a monarch or
government ▷ *vb* cause to
undergo
SUBJECTED >SUBJECT
SUBJECTS >SUBJECT
SUBJOIN *vb* add or attach
at the end of something
spoken, written, etc
SUBJOINED >SUBJOIN
SUBJOINS >SUBJOIN
SUBJUGATE *vb* bring (a
group of people) under
one's control
SUBLATE *vb* deny
SUBLATED >SUBLATE
SUBLATES >SUBLATE
SUBLATING >SUBLATE
SUBLATION >SUBLATE
SUBLEASE *n* lease of
property made by a person
who is himself or herself
a lessee or tenant of that
property ▷ *vb* grant a
sublease of (property)
SUBLEASED >SUBLEASE
SUBLEASES >SUBLEASE
SUBLESSEE >SUBLEASE
SUBLESSOR >SUBLEASE

SUBLET *vb* rent out
(property rented from
someone else) ▷ *n*
sublease
SUBLETHAL *adj* not strong
enough to kill
SUBLETS >SUBLET
SUBLETTER >SUBLET
SUBLEVEL *n* subdivision of
a level
SUBLEVELS >SUBLEVEL
SUBLIMATE *vb* direct
the energy of (a strong
desire, esp a sexual one)
into socially acceptable
activities ▷ *n* material
obtained when a
substance is sublimed
▷ *adj* exalted or purified
SUBLIME *adj* of high moral,
intellectual, or spiritual
value ▷ *vb* change from a
solid to a vapour without
first melting
SUBLIMED >SUBLIME
SUBLIMELY >SUBLIME
SUBLIMER >SUBLIME
SUBLIMERS >SUBLIME
SUBLIMES >SUBLIME
SUBLIMEST >SUBLIME
SUBLIMING >SUBLIME
SUBLIMISE *same*
*as* >SUBLIMIZE
SUBLIMIT *n* limit on a
subcategory
SUBLIMITS >SUBLIMIT
SUBLIMITY >SUBLIME
SUBLIMIZE *vb* make
sublime
SUBLINE *n* secondary
headline
SUBLINEAR *adj* beneath
a line
SUBLINES >SUBLINE
SUBLOT *n* subdivision of
a lot
SUBLOTS >SUBLOT
SUBLUNAR *same*
*as* >SUBLUNARY
SUBLUNARY *adj* situated
between the moon and the
earth
SUBLUNATE *adj* almost
crescent-shaped
SUBLUXATE *vb* partially
dislocate
SUBMAN *n* primitive form of
human
SUBMARINE *n* vessel which
can operate below the
surface of the sea ▷ *adj*
below the surface of the
sea ▷ *vb* slide beneath
seatbelt in car crash
SUBMARKET *n* specialized
market within larger
market
SUBMATRIX *n* part of
matrix
SUBMEN >SUBMAN
SUBMENTA >SUBMENTUM
SUBMENTAL *adj* situated
beneath the chin
SUBMENTUM *n* base of insect

lip
SUBMENU *n* further list of
options within computer
menu
SUBMENUS >SUBMENU
SUBMERGE *vb* put or go
below the surface of water
or other liquid
SUBMERGED *adj* (of plants
or plant parts) growing
beneath the surface of the
water
SUBMERGES >SUBMERGE
SUBMERSE *same*
*as* >SUBMERGE
SUBMERSED *same*
*as* >SUBMERGED
SUBMERSES >SUBMERGE
SUBMICRON *n* object only
visible through powerful
microscope
SUBMISS *adj* docile
SUBMISSLY *adv*
submissively
SUBMIT *vb* surrender
SUBMITS >SUBMIT
SUBMITTAL >SUBMIT
SUBMITTED >SUBMIT
SUBMITTER >SUBMIT
SUBMUCOSA *n* connective
tissue beneath a mucous
membrane
SUBMUCOUS >SUBMUCOSA
SUBNASAL *adj* beneath
nose
SUBNET *n* part of network
SUBNETS >SUBNET
SUBNEURAL *adj* beneath a
nerve centre
SUBNICHE *n* subdivision of
a niche
SUBNICHES >SUBNICHE
SUBNIVEAL *adj* beneath
the snow
SUBNIVEAN *same*
*as* >SUBNIVEAL
SUBNODAL *adj* below the
level of a node
SUBNORMAL *adj* less than
normal, esp in intelligence
▷ *n* subnormal person
SUBNUCLEI *pl n* plural of
subnucleus, secondary
nucleus
SUBOCEAN *adj* beneath the
ocean
SUBOCTAVE *n* octave below
another
SUBOCULAR *adj* below the
eye
SUBOFFICE *n* office that
is subordinate to another
office
SUBOPTIC *adj* below the
eye
SUBORAL *adj* not quite oral
SUBORDER *n* taxonomic
group that is a subdivision
of an order
SUBORDERS >SUBORDER
SUBORN *vb* bribe or incite
(a person) to commit a
wrongful act
SUBORNED >SUBORN

**SUBORNER** > SUBORN
**SUBORNERS** > SUBORN
**SUBORNING** > SUBORN
**SUBORNS** > SUBORN
**SUBOSCINE** adj belonging to a subfamily of birds
**SUBOVAL** adj not quite oval
**SUBOVATE** adj almost egg-shaped
**SUBOXIDE** n oxide of an element containing less oxygen than the common oxide formed by the element
**SUBOXIDES** > SUBOXIDE
**SUBPANEL** n panel that is part of larger panel
**SUBPANELS** > SUBPANEL
**SUBPAR** adj not up to standard
**SUBPART** n part within another part
**SUBPARTS** > SUBPART
**SUBPENA** same as > SUBPOENA
**SUBPENAED** > SUBPENA
**SUBPENAS** > SUBPENA
**SUBPERIOD** n subdivision of time period
**SUBPHASE** n subdivision of phase
**SUBPHASES** > SUBPHASE
**SUBPHYLA** > SUBPHYLUM
**SUBPHYLAR** > SUBPHYLUM
**SUBPHYLUM** n taxonomic group that is a subdivision of a phylum
**SUBPLOT** n secondary plot in a novel, play, or film
**SUBPLOTS** > SUBPLOT
**SUBPOENA** n writ requiring a person to appear before a law court ▷ vb summon (someone) with a subpoena
**SUBPOENAS** > SUBPOENA
**SUBPOLAR** adj not quite polar
**SUBPOTENT** adj not at full strength
**SUBPRIOR** n monk junior to a prior
**SUBPRIORS** > SUBPRIOR
**SUBPUBIC** adj beneath the pubic bone
**SUBRACE** n race of people considered to be inferior
**SUBRACES** > SUBRACE
**SUBREGION** n subdivision of a region, esp a zoogeographical or ecological region
**SUBRENT** n rent paid to renter who rents to another
**SUBRENTS** > SUBRENT
**SUBRING** n mathematical ring that is a subset of another ring
**SUBRINGS** > SUBRING
**SUBROGATE** vb put (one person or thing) in the place of another in respect of a right or claim

**SUBRULE** n rule within another rule
**SUBRULES** > SUBRULE
**SUBS** > SUB
**SUBSACRAL** adj below the sacrum
**SUBSALE** n sale carried out within the process of a larger sale
**SUBSALES** > SUBSALE
**SUBSAMPLE** vb take further sample from existing sample
**SUBSCALE** n scale within a scale
**SUBSCALES** > SUBSCALE
**SUBSCHEMA** n part of computer database used by an individual
**SUBSCRIBE** vb pay (a subscription)
**SUBSCRIPT** adj (character) printed below the line ▷ n subscript character
**SUBSEA** adj undersea
**SUBSECIVE** adj left over
**SUBSECT** n sect within a larger sect
**SUBSECTOR** n subdivision of sector
**SUBSECTS** > SUBSECT
**SUBSELLIA** pl n ledges underneath the hinged seats in a church
**SUBSENSE** n definition that is division of wider definition
**SUBSENSES** > SUBSENSE
**SUBSERE** n secondary sere arising when the progress of a sere towards its climax has been interrupted
**SUBSERES** > SUBSERE
**SUBSERIES** n series within a larger series
**SUBSERVE** vb be helpful or useful to
**SUBSERVED** > SUBSERVE
**SUBSERVES** > SUBSERVE
**SUBSET** n mathematical set contained within a larger set
**SUBSETS** > SUBSET
**SUBSHAFT** n secondary shaft in mine
**SUBSHAFTS** > SUBSHAFT
**SUBSHELL** n part of a shell of an atom
**SUBSHELLS** > SUBSHELL
**SUBSHRUB** n small bushy plant that is woody except for the tips of the branches
**SUBSHRUBS** > SUBSHRUB
**SUBSIDE** vb become less intense
**SUBSIDED** > SUBSIDE
**SUBSIDER** > SUBSIDE
**SUBSIDERS** > SUBSIDE
**SUBSIDES** > SUBSIDE
**SUBSIDIES** > SUBSIDY
**SUBSIDING** > SUBSIDE
**SUBSIDISE** same as > SUBSIDIZE
**SUBSIDIZE** vb help

financially
**SUBSIDY** n financial aid
**SUBSIST** vb manage to live
**SUBSISTED** > SUBSIST
**SUBSISTER** > SUBSIST
**SUBSISTS** > SUBSIST
**SUBSITE** n location within a website
**SUBSITES** > SUBSITE
**SUBSIZAR** n type of undergraduate at Cambridge
**SUBSIZARS** > SUBSIZAR
**SUBSKILL** n element of a wider skill
**SUBSKILLS** > SUBSKILL
**SUBSOCIAL** adj lacking a complex or definite social structure
**SUBSOIL** n earth just below the surface soil ▷ vb plough (land) to a depth below the normal ploughing level
**SUBSOILED** > SUBSOIL
**SUBSOILER** > SUBSOIL
**SUBSOILS** > SUBSOIL
**SUBSOLAR** adj (of a point on the earth) directly below the sun
**SUBSONG** n subdued form of birdsong modified from the full territorial song
**SUBSONGS** > SUBSONG
**SUBSONIC** adj moving at a speed less than that of sound
**SUBSPACE** n part of a mathematical matrix
**SUBSPACES** > SUBSPACE
**SUBSTAGE** n part of a microscope below the stage
**SUBSTAGES** > SUBSTAGE
**SUBSTANCE** n physical composition of something
**SUBSTATE** n subdivision of state
**SUBSTATES** > SUBSTATE
**SUBSTRACT** same as > SUBTRACT
**SUBSTRATA** pl n layers lying underneath other layers
**SUBSTRATE** n substance upon which an enzyme acts
**SUBSTRUCT** vb build as a foundation
**SUBSTYLAR** > SUBSTYLE
**SUBSTYLE** n line on a dial
**SUBSTYLES** > SUBSTYLE
**SUBSULTUS** n abnormal twitching
**SUBSUME** vb include (an idea, case, etc) under a larger classification or group
**SUBSUMED** > SUBSUME
**SUBSUMES** > SUBSUME
**SUBSUMING** > SUBSUME
**SUBSYSTEM** n system operating within a larger system
**SUBTACK** Scots word

for > SUBLEASE
**SUBTACKS** > SUBTACK
**SUBTASK** n task that is part of a larger task
**SUBTASKS** > SUBTASK
**SUBTAXA** > SUBTAXON
**SUBTAXON** n supplementary piece of identifying information in plant or animal scientific name
**SUBTAXONS** > SUBTAXON
**SUBTEEN** n young person who has not yet become a teenager
**SUBTEENS** > SUBTEEN
**SUBTENANT** n person who rents property from a tenant
**SUBTEND** vb be opposite (an angle or side)
**SUBTENDED** > SUBTEND
**SUBTENDS** > SUBTEND
**SUBTENSE** n line that subtends
**SUBTENSES** > SUBTENSE
**SUBTENURE** n tenancy given by other tenant
**SUBTEST** n test that is part of larger test
**SUBTESTS** > SUBTEST
**SUBTEXT** n underlying theme in a piece of writing
**SUBTEXTS** > SUBTEXT
**SUBTHEME** n secondary theme
**SUBTHEMES** > SUBTHEME
**SUBTIDAL** adj below the level of low tide
**SUBTIL** same as > SUBTLE
**SUBTILE** rare spelling of > SUBTLE
**SUBTILELY** > SUBTILE
**SUBTILER** > SUBTILE
**SUBTILEST** > SUBTILE
**SUBTILIN** n antibiotic drug
**SUBTILINS** > SUBTILIN
**SUBTILISE** same as > SUBTILIZE
**SUBTILITY** > SUBTILE
**SUBTILIZE** vb bring to a purer state
**SUBTILTY** > SUBTILE
**SUBTITLE** n secondary title of a book ▷ vb provide with a subtitle or subtitles
**SUBTITLED** > SUBTITLE
**SUBTITLES** > SUBTITLE
**SUBTLE** adj not immediately obvious
**SUBTLER** > SUBTLE
**SUBTLEST** > SUBTLE
**SUBTLETY** n fine distinction
**SUBTLY** > SUBTLE
**SUBTONE** n subdivision of a tone
**SUBTONES** > SUBTONE
**SUBTONIC** n seventh degree of a major or minor scale
**SUBTONICS** > SUBTONIC
**SUBTOPIA** n suburban

development that
encroaches on rural areas
yet appears to offer the
attractions of country life
to suburban dwellers
**SUBTOPIAN** > SUBTOPIA
**SUBTOPIAS** > SUBTOPIA
**SUBTOPIC** *n* topic within a
larger topic
**SUBTOPICS** > SUBTOPIC
**SUBTORRID** *same
as* > SUBTROPIC
**SUBTOTAL** *n* total made
up by a column of figures,
forming part of the total
made up by a larger
column or group ▷ *vb*
establish or work out a
subtotal for (a column,
group, etc)
**SUBTOTALS** > SUBTOTAL
**SUBTRACT** *vb* take (one
number or quantity) from
another
**SUBTRACTS** > SUBTRACT
**SUBTREND** *n* minor trend
**SUBTRENDS** > SUBTREND
**SUBTRIBE** *n* tribe within a
larger tribe
**SUBTRIBES** > SUBTRIBE
**SUBTRIST** *adj* slightly sad
**SUBTROPIC** *adj* relating to
the region lying between
the tropics and the
temperate lands
**SUBTRUDE** *vb* intrude
stealthily
**SUBTRUDED** > SUBTRUDE
**SUBTRUDES** > SUBTRUDE
**SUBTUNIC** *adj* below
membrane ▷ *n* garment
worn under a tunic
**SUBTUNICS** > SUBTUNIC
**SUBTYPE** *n* secondary or
subordinate type or genre
**SUBTYPES** > SUBTYPE
**SUBUCULA** *n* ancient
Roman man's
undergarment
**SUBUCULAS** > SUBUCULA
**SUBULATE** *adj* (esp of plant
parts) tapering to a point
**SUBUNIT** *n* distinct part or
component of something
larger
**SUBUNITS** > SUBUNIT
**SUBURB** *n* residential area
on the outskirts of a city
**SUBURBAN** *adj* mildly
derogatory term for
inhabiting a suburb ▷ *n*
mildly derogatory term
for a person who lives in a
suburb
**SUBURBANS** > SUBURBAN
**SUBURBED** > SUBURB
**SUBURBIA** *n* suburbs and
their inhabitants
**SUBURBIAS** > SUBURBIA
**SUBURBS** > SUBURB
**SUBURSINE** *adj* of a bear
subspecies
**SUBVASSAL** *n* vassal of a
vassal

**SUBVENE** *vb* happen
in such a way as to be
of assistance, esp in
preventing something
**SUBVENED** > SUBVENE
**SUBVENES** > SUBVENE
**SUBVENING** > SUBVENE
**SUBVERSAL** > SUBVERT
**SUBVERSE** *same
as* > SUBVERT
**SUBVERSED** > SUBVERSE
**SUBVERSES** > SUBVERSE
**SUBVERST** > SUBVERSE
**SUBVERT** *vb* overthrow the
authority of
**SUBVERTED** > SUBVERT
**SUBVERTER** > SUBVERT
**SUBVERTS** > SUBVERT
**SUBVICAR** *n* assistant to
a vicar
**SUBVICARS** > SUBVICAR
**SUBVIRAL** *adj* of, caused by,
or denoting a part of the
structure of a virus
**SUBVIRUS** *n* organism
smaller than a virus
**SUBVISUAL** *adj* not visible
to the naked eye
**SUBVOCAL** *adj* formed
in mind without being
spoken aloud
**SUBWARDEN** *n* assistant to
a warden
**SUBWAY** *n* passage under a
road or railway ▷ *vb* travel
by subway
**SUBWAYED** > SUBWAY
**SUBWAYING** > SUBWAY
**SUBWAYS** > SUBWAY
**SUBWOOFER** *n* loudspeaker
for very low tones
**SUBWORLD** *n* underworld
**SUBWORLDS** > SUBWORLD
**SUBWRITER** *n* person
carrying out writing tasks
for other writer
**SUBZERO** *adj* lower than
zero
**SUBZONAL** > SUBZONE
**SUBZONE** *n* subdivision of
a zone
**SUBZONES** > SUBZONE
**SUCCADE** *n* piece of candied
fruit
**SUCCADES** > SUCCADE
**SUCCAH** *same as* > SUKKAH
**SUCCAHS** > SUCCAH
**SUCCEDENT** *adj* following
**SUCCEED** *vb* accomplish
an aim
**SUCCEEDED** > SUCCEED
**SUCCEEDER** > SUCCEED
**SUCCEEDS** > SUCCEED
**SUCCENTOR** *n* deputy of the
precentor of a cathedral
that has retained its
statutes from pre-
Reformation days
**SUCCES** *French word
for* > SUCCESS
**SUCCESS** *n* achievement of
something attempted
**SUCCESSES** > SUCCESS
**SUCCESSOR** *n* person who

succeeds someone in a
position
**SUCCI** > SUCCUS
**SUCCINATE** *n* any salt or
ester of succinic acid
**SUCCINCT** *adj* brief and
clear
**SUCCINIC** *adj* of, relating
to, or obtained from amber
**SUCCINITE** *n* type of amber
**SUCCINYL** *n* constituent of
succinic acid
**SUCCINYLS** > SUCCINYL
**SUCCISE** *adj* ending
abruptly, as if cut off
**SUCCOR** *same as* > SUCCOUR
**SUCCORED** > SUCCOR
**SUCCORER** > SUCCOR
**SUCCORERS** > SUCCOR
**SUCCORIES** > SUCCORY
**SUCCORING** > SUCCOR
**SUCCORS** > SUCCOR
**SUCCORY** *another name
for* > CHICORY
**SUCCOS** *same as* > SUCCOTH
**SUCCOSE** > SUCCUS
**SUCCOT** *same as* > SUKKOTH
**SUCCOTASH** *n* mixture of
cooked sweet corn kernels
and lima beans, served as a
vegetable
**SUCCOTH** *variant
of* > SUKKOTH
**SUCCOUR** *n* help in distress
▷ *vb* give aid to (someone
in time of difficulty)
**SUCCOURED** > SUCCOUR
**SUCCOURER** > SUCCOUR
**SUCCOURS** > SUCCOUR
**SUCCOUS** > SUCCUS
**SUCCUBA** *same
as* > SUCCUBUS
**SUCCUBAE** > SUCCUBA
**SUCCUBAS** > SUCCUBA
**SUCCUBI** > SUCCUBUS
**SUCCUBINE** > SUCCUBUS
**SUCCUBOUS** *adj* having the
leaves arranged so that
the upper margin of each
leaf is covered by the lower
margin of the next leaf
along
**SUCCUBUS** *n* female demon
believed to have sex with
sleeping men
**SUCCULENT** *adj* juicy and
delicious ▷ *n* succulent
plant
**SUCCUMB** *vb* give way (to
something overpowering)
**SUCCUMBED** > SUCCUMB
**SUCCUMBER** > SUCCUMB
**SUCCUMBS** > SUCCUMB
**SUCCURSAL** *adj* (esp of a
religious establishment)
subsidiary ▷ *n* subsidiary
establishment
**SUCCUS** *n* fluid
**SUCCUSS** *vb* shake (a
patient) to detect the
sound of fluid in the
thoracic or another bodily
cavity
**SUCCUSSED** > SUCCUSS

**SUCCUSSES** > SUCCUSS
**SUCH** *adj* of the kind
specified ▷ *pron* such
things
**SUCHLIKE** *pron* such or
similar things ▷ *n* such
or similar things ▷ *adj* of
such a kind
**SUCHNESS** > SUCH
**SUCHWISE** > SUCH
**SUCK** *vb* draw (liquid or
air) into the mouth ▷ *n*
sucking
**SUCKED** > SUCK
**SUCKEN** *Scots word
for* > DISTRICT
**SUCKENER** *n* tenant
**SUCKENERS** > SUCKENER
**SUCKENS** > SUCKEN
**SUCKER** *n* person who
is easily deceived or
swindled ▷ *vb* strip off the
suckers from (a plant)
**SUCKERED** > SUCKER
**SUCKERING** > SUCKER
**SUCKERS** > SUCKER
**SUCKET** *same as* > SUCCADE
**SUCKETS** > SUCKET
**SUCKFISH** *n* type of spiny-
finned marine fish
**SUCKIER** > SUCKY
**SUCKIEST** > SUCKY
**SUCKING** *adj* not yet
weaned
**SUCKINGS** > SUCKING
**SUCKLE** *vb* feed at the
breast
**SUCKLED** > SUCKLE
**SUCKLER** > SUCKLE
**SUCKLERS** > SUCKLE
**SUCKLES** > SUCKLE
**SUCKLESS** > SUCK
**SUCKLING** *n* unweaned
baby or young animal
**SUCKLINGS** > SUCKLING
**SUCKS** *interj* expression of
disappointment
**SUCKY** *adj* despicable
**SUCRALOSE** *n* artificial
sweetener
**SUCRASE** *another name
for* > INVERTASE
**SUCRASES** > SUCRASE
**SUCRE** *n* former standard
monetary unit of Ecuador
**SUCRES** > SUCRE
**SUCRIER** *n* small container
for sugar at table
**SUCRIERS** > SUCRIER
**SUCROSE** *same as* > SUGAR
**SUCROSES** > SUCROSE
**SUCTION** *n* sucking ▷ *vb*
subject to suction
**SUCTIONAL** > SUCTION
**SUCTIONED** > SUCTION
**SUCTIONS** > SUCTION
**SUCTORIAL** *adj* specialized
for sucking or adhering
**SUCTORIAN** *n* microscopic
creature
**SUCURUJU** *n* anaconda
**SUCURUJUS** > SUCURUJU
**SUD** *singular of* > SUDS
**SUDAMEN** *n* small cavity in

745

the skin
**SUDAMINA** >SUDAMEN
**SUDAMINAL** >SUDAMEN
**SUDARIA** >SUDARIUM
**SUDARIES** >SUDARY
**SUDARIUM** n room in a
Roman bathhouse where
sweating is induced by
heat
**SUDARY** same as >SUDARIUM
**SUDATE** vb sweat
**SUDATED** >SUDATE
**SUDATES** >SUDATE
**SUDATING** >SUDATE
**SUDATION** >SUDATE
**SUDATIONS** >SUDATE
**SUDATORIA** same
as >SUDARIA
**SUDATORY** >SUDORIUM
**SUDD** n floating masses
of reeds and weeds that
occur on the White Nile
**SUDDEN** adj done or
occurring quickly and
unexpectedly
**SUDDENLY** adv quickly and
without warning
**SUDDENS** >SUDDEN
**SUDDENTY** n suddenness
**SUDDER** n supreme court
in India
**SUDDERS** >SUDDER
**SUDDS** >SUDD
**SUDOR** technical name
for >SWEAT
**SUDORAL** >SUDOR
**SUDORIFIC** adj (drug)
causing sweating ▷ n
drug that causes sweating
**SUDOROUS** >SUDOR
**SUDORS** >SUDOR
**SUDS** pl n froth of soap and
water, lather ▷ vb wash
in suds
**SUDSED** >SUDS
**SUDSER** n soap opera
**SUDSERS** >SUDSER
**SUDSES** >SUDS
**SUDSIER** >SUDS
**SUDSIEST** >SUDS
**SUDSING** >SUDS
**SUDSLESS** >SUDS
**SUDSY** >SUDS
**SUE** vb start legal
proceedings against
**SUEABLE** >SUE
**SUED** >SUE
**SUEDE** n leather with a
velvety finish on one side
▷ vb give a suede finish to
**SUEDED** >SUEDE
**SUEDES** >SUEDE
**SUEDETTE** n imitation
suede fabric
**SUEDETTES** >SUEDETTE
**SUEDING** >SUEDE
**SUENT** adj smooth
**SUER** >SUE
**SUERS** >SUE
**SUES** >SUE
**SUET** n hard fat obtained
from sheep and cattle,
used in cooking
**SUETIER** >SUET

**SUETIEST** >SUET
**SUETS** >SUET
**SUETTIER** >SUET
**SUETTIEST** >SUET
**SUETTY** >SUET
**SUETY** >SUET
**SUFFARI** same as >SAFARI
**SUFFARIS** >SUFFARI
**SUFFECT** adj additional
**SUFFER** vb undergo or be
subjected to
**SUFFERED** >SUFFER
**SUFFERER** >SUFFER
**SUFFERERS** >SUFFER
**SUFFERING** n pain, misery,
or loss experienced by a
person who suffers
**SUFFERS** >SUFFER
**SUFFETE** n official in
ancient Carthage
**SUFFETES** >SUFFETE
**SUFFICE** vb be enough for
a purpose
**SUFFICED** >SUFFICE
**SUFFICER** >SUFFICE
**SUFFICERS** >SUFFICE
**SUFFICES** >SUFFICE
**SUFFICING** >SUFFICE
**SUFFIX** n letter or letters
added to the end of a word
to form another word ▷ vb
add (a letter or letters) to
the end of a word to form
another word
**SUFFIXAL** >SUFFIX
**SUFFIXED** >SUFFIX
**SUFFIXES** >SUFFIX
**SUFFIXING** >SUFFIX
**SUFFIXION** >SUFFIX
**SUFFLATE** archaic word
for >INFLATE
**SUFFLATED** >SUFFLATE
**SUFFLATES** >SUFFLATE
**SUFFOCATE** vb kill or be
killed by deprivation of
oxygen
**SUFFRAGAN** n bishop
appointed to assist an
archbishop ▷ adj (of
any bishop of a diocese)
subordinate to and
assisting his superior
archbishop
**SUFFRAGE** n right to vote in
public elections
**SUFFRAGES** >SUFFRAGE
**SUFFUSE** vb spread through
or over (something)
**SUFFUSED** >SUFFUSE
**SUFFUSES** >SUFFUSE
**SUFFUSING** >SUFFUSE
**SUFFUSION** >SUFFUSE
**SUFFUSIVE** >SUFFUSE
**SUGAN** n straw rope
**SUGANS** >SUGAN
**SUGAR** n sweet crystalline
carbohydrate used to
sweeten food and drinks
▷ vb sweeten or cover
with sugar
**SUGARALLY** n liquorice
**SUGARBUSH** n area covered
in sugar maple trees
**SUGARCANE** n coarse grass

that yields sugar
**SUGARCOAT** vb cover with
sugar
**SUGARED** adj made sweeter
or more appealing with or
as with sugar
**SUGARER** >SUGAR
**SUGARERS** >SUGAR
**SUGARIER** >SUGARY
**SUGARIEST** >SUGARY
**SUGARING** n method of
removing unwanted body
hair
**SUGARINGS** >SUGARING
**SUGARLESS** >SUGAR
**SUGARLIKE** >SUGAR
**SUGARLOAF** n large conical
mass of unrefined sugar
**SUGARPLUM** n crystallized
plum
**SUGARS** >SUGAR
**SUGARY** adj of, like, or
containing sugar
**SUGGEST** vb put forward
(an idea) for consideration
**SUGGESTED** >SUGGEST
**SUGGESTER** >SUGGEST
**SUGGESTS** >SUGGEST
**SUGGING** n practice of
selling products under the
pretence of conducting
market research
**SUGGINGS** >SUGGING
**SUGH** same as >SOUGH
**SUGHED** >SUGH
**SUGHING** >SUGH
**SUGHS** >SUGH
**SUI** adj of itself
**SUICIDAL** adj liable to
commit suicide
**SUICIDE** n killing oneself
intentionally ▷ vb
commit suicide
**SUICIDED** >SUICIDE
**SUICIDES** >SUICIDE
**SUICIDING** >SUICIDE
**SUID** n pig or related
animal
**SUIDIAN** >SUID
**SUIDIANS** >SUID
**SUIDS** >SUID
**SUILLINE** adj of or like a
pig
**SUING** >SUE
**SUINGS** >SUE
**SUINT** n water-soluble
substance found in the
fleece of sheep
**SUINTS** >SUINT
**SUIPLAP** n South African
slang for a drunkard
**SUIPLAPS** >SUIPLAP
**SUIT** n set of clothes
designed to be worn
together ▷ vb be
appropriate for
**SUITABLE** adj appropriate
or proper
**SUITABLY** >SUITABLE
**SUITCASE** n portable
travelling case for clothing
**SUITCASES** >SUITCASE
**SUITE** n set of connected
rooms in a hotel

**SUITED** >SUIT
**SUITER** n piece of luggage
for carrying suits and
dresses
**SUITERS** >SUITER
**SUITES** >SUITE
**SUITING** n fabric used for
suits
**SUITINGS** >SUITING
**SUITLIKE** >SUIT
**SUITOR** n man who is
courting a woman ▷ vb
act as a suitor
**SUITORED** >SUITOR
**SUITORING** >SUITOR
**SUITORS** >SUITOR
**SUITRESS** n female suitor
**SUITS** >SUIT
**SUIVANTE** n lady's maid
**SUIVANTES** >SUIVANTE
**SUIVEZ** vb musical
direction meaning follow
**SUJEE** same as >SOOGEE
**SUJEES** >SUJEE
**SUK** same as >SOUK
**SUKH** same as >SOUK
**SUKHS** >SUKH
**SUKIYAKI** n Japanese dish
consisting of very thinly
sliced beef, vegetables,
and seasonings cooked
together quickly
**SUKIYAKIS** >SUKIYAKI
**SUKKAH** n temporary
structure with a roof
of branches in which
orthodox Jews eat and, if
possible, sleep during the
festival of Sukkoth
**SUKKAHS** >SUKKAH
**SUKKOS** same as >SUKKOTH
**SUKKOT** same as >SUKKOTH
**SUKKOTH** n eight-day
Jewish harvest festival
**SUKS** >SUK
**SULCAL** >SULCUS
**SULCALISE** same
as >SULCALIZE
**SULCALIZE** vb furrow
**SULCATE** adj marked with
longitudinal parallel
grooves
**SULCATED** same
as >SULCATE
**SULCATION** >SULCATE
**SULCI** >SULCUS
**SULCUS** n linear groove,
furrow, or slight
depression
**SULDAN** same as >SULTAN
**SULDANS** >SULDAN
**SULFA** same as >SULPHA
**SULFAS** >SULFA
**SULFATASE** n type of
enzyme
**SULFATE** same
as >SULPHATE
**SULFATED** >SULFATE
**SULFATES** >SULFATE
**SULFATIC** adj relating to
sulphate
**SULFATING** >SULFATE
**SULFATION** >SULFATE
**SULFID** same as >SULPHIDE

**SULFIDE** same
as >SULPHIDE
**SULFIDES** >SULFIDE
**SULFIDS** >SULFID
**SULFINYL** same
as >SULPHINYL
**SULFINYLS** >SULFINYL
**SULFITE** same
as >SULPHITE
**SULFITES** >SULFITE
**SULFITIC** >SULFITE
**SULFO** same as >SULPHONIC
**SULFONATE** n salt or ester
of sulphonic acid
**SULFONE** same
as >SULPHONE
**SULFONES** >SULFONE
**SULFONIC** >SULFONE
**SULFONIUM** n one of a type
of salts
**SULFONYL** same
as >SULPHURYL
**SULFONYLS** >SULFONYL
**SULFOXIDE** n compound
containing sulphur
**SULFUR** variant
of >SULPHUR
**SULFURATE** vb treat with
sulphur
**SULFURED** >SULFUR
**SULFURET** same
as >SULPHURET
**SULFURETS** >SULFURET
**SULFURIC** >SULFUR
**SULFURING** >SULFUR
**SULFURISE** variant
of >SULFURIZE
**SULFURIZE** vb combine or
treat with sulphur
**SULFUROUS** adj resembling
sulphur
**SULFURS** >SULFUR
**SULFURY** >SULFUR
**SULFURYL** same
as >SULPHURYL
**SULFURYLS** >SULFURYL
**SULK** vb be silent and sullen
because of resentment or
bad temper ▷ n resentful
or sullen mood
**SULKED** >SULK
**SULKER** same as >SULK
**SULKERS** >SULKER
**SULKIER** >SULKY
**SULKIES** >SULKY
**SULKIEST** >SULKY
**SULKILY** >SULKY
**SULKINESS** >SULKY
**SULKING** >SULK
**SULKS** >SULK
**SULKY** adj moody or
silent because of anger
or resentment ▷ n light
two-wheeled vehicle for
one person, usually drawn
by one horse
**SULLAGE** n filth or waste,
esp sewage
**SULLAGES** >SULLAGE
**SULLEN** adj unwilling to
talk or be sociable ▷ n
sullen mood
**SULLENER** >SULLEN
**SULLENEST** >SULLEN

**SULLENLY** >SULLEN
**SULLENS** >SULLEN
**SULLIABLE** >SULLY
**SULLIED** >SULLY
**SULLIES** >SULLY
**SULLY** vb ruin (someone's
reputation) ▷ n stain
**SULLYING** >SULLY
**SULPHA** n any of a group
of sulphonamides that
prevent the growth of
bacteria
**SULPHAS** >SULPHA
**SULPHATE** n salt or ester of
sulphuric acid ▷ vb treat
with a sulphate or convert
into a sulphate
**SULPHATED** >SULPHATE
**SULPHATES** >SULPHATE
**SULPHATIC** >SULPHATE
**SULPHID** same
as >SULPHIDE
**SULPHIDE** n compound
of sulphur with another
element
**SULPHIDES** >SULPHIDE
**SULPHIDS** >SULPHID
**SULPHINYL** another term
for >THIONYL
**SULPHITE** n salt or ester of
sulphurous acid
**SULPHITES** >SULPHITE
**SULPHITIC** >SULPHITE
**SULPHONE** n type of organic
compound
**SULPHONES** >SULPHONE
**SULPHONIC** as in sulphonic
acid type of strong organic
acid
**SULPHONYL** same
as >SULPHURYL
**SULPHUR** n pale yellow
nonmetallic element ▷ vb
treat with sulphur
**SULPHURED** >SULPHUR
**SULPHURET** vb treat or
combine with sulphur
**SULPHURIC** >SULPHUR
**SULPHURS** >SULPHUR
**SULPHURY** >SULPHUR
**SULPHURYL** n particular
chemical divalent group
**SULTAN** n sovereign of a
Muslim country
**SULTANA** n kind of raisin
**SULTANAS** >SULTANA
**SULTANATE** n territory of
a sultan
**SULTANESS** same
as >SULTANA
**SULTANIC** >SULTAN
**SULTANS** >SULTAN
**SULTRIER** >SULTRY
**SULTRIEST** >SULTRY
**SULTRILY** >SULTRY
**SULTRY** adj (of weather or
climate) hot and humid
**SULU** n type of sarong worn
in Fiji
**SULUS** >SULU
**SUM** n result of addition,
total ▷ vb add or form a
total of (something)
**SUMAC** same as >SUMACH

**SUMACH** n type of
temperate or subtropical
shrub or small tree
**SUMACHS** >SUMACH
**SUMACS** >SUMAC
**SUMATRA** n violent storm
blowing from the direction
of Sumatra
**SUMATRAS** >SUMATRA
**SUMLESS** adj uncountable
**SUMMA** n compendium of
theology, philosophy, or
canon law, or sometimes
of all three together
**SUMMABLE** >SUM
**SUMMAE** >SUMMA
**SUMMAND** n number or
quantity forming part of
a sum
**SUMMANDS** >SUMMAND
**SUMMAR** Scots variant
of >SUMMER
**SUMMARIES** >SUMMARY
**SUMMARILY** >SUMMARY
**SUMMARISE** same
as >SUMMARIZE
**SUMMARIST** >SUMMARIZE
**SUMMARIZE** vb make or be a
summary of (something)
**SUMMARY** n brief account
giving the main points
of something ▷ adj
done quickly, without
formalities
**SUMMAS** >SUMMA
**SUMMAT** pron something
▷ n impressive or
important person or thing
**SUMMATE** vb add up
**SUMMATED** >SUMMATE
**SUMMATES** >SUMMATE
**SUMMATING** >SUMMATE
**SUMMATION** n summary
**SUMMATIVE** >SUMMATION
**SUMMATS** >SUMMAT
**SUMMED** >SUM
**SUMMER** n warmest season
of the year, between spring
and autumn ▷ vb spend
the summer (at a place)
**SUMMERED** >SUMMER
**SUMMERIER** >SUMMER
**SUMMERING** >SUMMER
**SUMMERLY** >SUMMER
**SUMMERS** >SUMMER
**SUMMERSET** n somersault
**SUMMERY** >SUMMER
**SUMMING** >SUM
**SUMMINGS** >SUM
**SUMMIST** n writer of
summae
**SUMMISTS** >SUMMIST
**SUMMIT** n top of a
mountain or hill ▷ vb
reach summit
**SUMMITAL** >SUMMIT
**SUMMITED** >SUMMIT
**SUMMITEER** n person who
participates in a summit
conference
**SUMMITING** >SUMMIT
**SUMMITRY** n practice of
conducting international
negotiations by summit

conferences
**SUMMITS** >SUMMIT
**SUMMON** vb order (someone)
to come
**SUMMONED** >SUMMON
**SUMMONER** >SUMMON
**SUMMONERS** >SUMMON
**SUMMONING** >SUMMON
**SUMMONS** n command
summoning someone
▷ vb order (someone) to
appear in court
**SUMMONSED** >SUMMONS
**SUMMONSES** >SUMMONS
**SUMO** n Japanese style of
wrestling
**SUMOIST** >SUMO
**SUMOISTS** >SUMO
**SUMOS** >SUMO
**SUMOTORI** n sumo wrestler
**SUMOTORIS** >SUMOTORI
**SUMP** n container in an
internal-combustion
engine into which oil can
drain
**SUMPH** n stupid person
**SUMPHISH** >SUMPH
**SUMPHS** >SUMPH
**SUMPIT** n Malay blowpipe
**SUMPITAN** same as >SUMPIT
**SUMPITANS** >SUMPITAN
**SUMPITS** >SUMPIT
**SUMPS** >SUMP
**SUMPSIMUS** n correct form
of expression
**SUMPTER** n packhorse,
mule, or other beast of
burden
**SUMPTERS** >SUMPTER
**SUMPTUARY** adj
controlling expenditure
or extravagant use of
resources
**SUMPTUOUS** adj lavish,
magnificent
**SUMPWEED** n American
weed
**SUMPWEEDS** >SUMPWEED
**SUMS** >SUM
**SUN** n star around which
the earth and other
planets revolve ▷ vb
expose (oneself) to the
sun's rays
**SUNBACK** adj (of dress) cut
low at back
**SUNBAKE** vb sunbathe, esp
in order to become tanned
▷ n period of sunbaking
**SUNBAKED** adj (esp of roads,
etc) dried or cracked by the
sun's heat
**SUNBAKES** >SUNBAKE
**SUNBAKING** >SUNBAKE
**SUNBATH** n exposure of the
body to the sun to get a
suntan
**SUNBATHE** vb lie in the
sunshine in order to get a
suntan
**SUNBATHED** >SUNBATHE
**SUNBATHER** >SUNBATHE
**SUNBATHES** >SUNBATHE
**SUNBATHS** >SUNBATH

**SUNBEAM** n ray of sun
**SUNBEAMED** >SUNBEAM
**SUNBEAMS** >SUNBEAM
**SUNBEAMY** >SUNBEAM
**SUNBEAT** adj exposed to sun
**SUNBEATEN** same as >SUNBEAT
**SUNBED** n machine for giving an artificial tan
**SUNBEDS** >SUNBED
**SUNBELT** n southern states of the US
**SUNBELTS** >SUNBELT
**SUNBERRY** n red fruit like the blackberry
**SUNBIRD** n any small songbird of the family Nectariniidae
**SUNBIRDS** >SUNBIRD
**SUNBLIND** n blind that shades a room from the sun's glare
**SUNBLINDS** >SUNBLIND
**SUNBLOCK** n cream applied to the skin to protect it from the sun's rays
**SUNBLOCKS** >SUNBLOCK
**SUNBONNET** n hat that shades the face and neck from the sun
**SUNBOW** n bow of prismatic colours similar to a rainbow, produced when sunlight shines through spray
**SUNBOWS** >SUNBOW
**SUNBRIGHT** adj bright as the sun
**SUNBURN** n painful reddening of the skin caused by overexposure to the sun ▷ vb become sunburnt
**SUNBURNED** >SUNBURN
**SUNBURNS** >SUNBURN
**SUNBURNT** >SUNBURN
**SUNBURST** n burst of sunshine, as through a break in the clouds
**SUNBURSTS** >SUNBURST
**SUNCHOKE** n Jerusalem artichoke
**SUNCHOKES** >SUNCHOKE
**SUNDAE** n ice cream topped with fruit etc
**SUNDAES** >SUNDAE
**SUNDARI** n Indian tree
**SUNDARIS** >SUNDARI
**SUNDECK** n upper open deck on a passenger ship
**SUNDECKS** >SUNDECK
**SUNDER** vb break apart
**SUNDERED** >SUNDER
**SUNDERER** >SUNDER
**SUNDERERS** >SUNDER
**SUNDERING** >SUNDER
**SUNDERS** >SUNDER
**SUNDEW** n any of several bog plants of the genus Drosera
**SUNDEWS** >SUNDEW
**SUNDIAL** n device showing the time by means of a pointer that casts a

shadow on a marked dial
**SUNDIALS** >SUNDIAL
**SUNDOG** n small rainbow or halo near the horizon
**SUNDOGS** >SUNDOG
**SUNDOWN** same as >SUNSET
**SUNDOWNED** >SUNDOWN
**SUNDOWNER** n tramp, esp one who seeks food and lodging at sundown when it is too late to work
**SUNDOWNS** >SUNDOWN
**SUNDRA** same as >SUNDARI
**SUNDRAS** >SUNDRA
**SUNDRESS** n dress for hot weather that exposes the shoulders, arms, and back, esp one with straps over the shoulders
**SUNDRI** same as >SUNDARI
**SUNDRIES** >SUNDRY
**SUNDRILY** >SUNDRY
**SUNDRIS** >SUNDRI
**SUNDROPS** n American primrose
**SUNDRY** adj several, various
**SUNFAST** adj not fading in sunlight
**SUNFISH** n large sea fish with a rounded body
**SUNFISHES** >SUNFISH
**SUNFLOWER** n tall plant with large golden flowers
**SUNG** >SING
**SUNGAR** same as >SANGAR
**SUNGARS** >SUNGAR
**SUNGLASS** n convex lens used to focus the sun's rays and thus produce heat or ignition
**SUNGLOW** n pinkish glow often seen in the sky before sunrise or after sunset
**SUNGLOWS** >SUNGLOW
**SUNGREBE** another name for >FINFOOT
**SUNGREBES** >SUNGREBE
**SUNHAT** n hat that shades the face and neck from the sun
**SUNHATS** >SUNHAT
**SUNK** n bank or pad
**SUNKEN** adj unhealthily hollow
**SUNKET** n something good to eat
**SUNKETS** >SUNKET
**SUNKIE** n little stool
**SUNKIES** >SUNKIE
**SUNKS** >SUNK
**SUNLAMP** n lamp that generates ultraviolet rays
**SUNLAMPS** >SUNLAMP
**SUNLAND** n sunny area
**SUNLANDS** >SUNLAND
**SUNLESS** adj without sun or sunshine
**SUNLESSLY** >SUNLESS
**SUNLIGHT** n light that comes from the sun
**SUNLIGHTS** >SUNLIGHT
**SUNLIKE** >SUN
**SUNLIT** >SUNLIGHT

**SUNN** n leguminous plant of the East Indies, having yellow flowers
**SUNNA** n body of traditional Islamic law
**SUNNAH** same as >SUNNA
**SUNNAHS** >SUNNAH
**SUNNAS** >SUNNA
**SUNNED** >SUN
**SUNNIER** >SUNNY
**SUNNIES** pl n pair of sunglasses
**SUNNIEST** >SUNNY
**SUNNILY** >SUNNY
**SUNNINESS** >SUNNY
**SUNNING** >SUN
**SUNNS** >SUNN
**SUNNY** adj full of or exposed to sunlight
**SUNPORCH** n porch for sunbathing on
**SUNPROOF** >SUN
**SUNRAY** n ray of light from the sun
**SUNRAYS** >SUNRAY
**SUNRISE** n daily appearance of the sun above the horizon
**SUNRISES** >SUNRISE
**SUNRISING** same as >SUNRISE
**SUNROOF** n panel in the roof of a car that opens to let in air
**SUNROOFS** >SUNROOF
**SUNROOM** n room or glass-enclosed porch designed to display beautiful views
**SUNROOMS** >SUNROOM
**SUNS** >SUN
**SUNSCALD** n sun damage on tomato plants
**SUNSCALDS** >SUNSCALD
**SUNSCREEN** n cream or lotion applied to exposed skin to protect it from the ultraviolet rays of the sun
**SUNSEEKER** n person looking for sunny weather
**SUNSET** n daily disappearance of the sun below the horizon
**SUNSETS** >SUNSET
**SUNSHADE** n anything used to shade people from the sun, such as a parasol or awning
**SUNSHADES** >SUNSHADE
**SUNSHINE** n light and warmth from the sun
**SUNSHINES** >SUNSHINE
**SUNSHINY** >SUNSHINE
**SUNSPOT** n dark patch appearing temporarily on the sun's surface
**SUNSPOTS** >SUNSPOT
**SUNSTAR** n any starfish of the genus Solaster, having up to 13 arms radiating from a central disc
**SUNSTARS** >SUNSTAR
**SUNSTONE** n type of translucent feldspar with reddish-gold speckles

**SUNSTONES** >SUNSTONE
**SUNSTROKE** n illness caused by prolonged exposure to intensely hot sunlight
**SUNSTRUCK** adj suffering from sunstroke
**SUNSUIT** n child's outfit consisting of a brief top and shorts or a short skirt
**SUNSUITS** >SUNSUIT
**SUNTAN** n browning of the skin caused by exposure to the sun
**SUNTANNED** >SUNTAN
**SUNTANS** >SUNTAN
**SUNTRAP** n very sunny sheltered place
**SUNTRAPS** >SUNTRAP
**SUNUP** same as >SUNRISE
**SUNUPS** >SUNUP
**SUNWARD** same as >SUNWARDS
**SUNWARDS** adv towards the sun
**SUNWISE** adv moving in the same direction as the sun
**SUP** same as >SUPINE
**SUPAWN** same as >SUPPAWN
**SUPAWNS** >SUPAWN
**SUPE** n superintendent
**SUPER** adj excellent ▷ n superannuation ▷ interj enthusiastic expression of approval or assent ▷ vb work as superintendent
**SUPERABLE** adj able to be surmounted or overcome
**SUPERABLY** >SUPERABLE
**SUPERADD** vb add (something) to something that has already been added
**SUPERADDS** >SUPERADD
**SUPERATE** vb overcome
**SUPERATED** >SUPERATE
**SUPERATES** >SUPERATE
**SUPERATOM** n cluster of atoms behaving like a single atom
**SUPERB** adj excellent, impressive, or splendid
**SUPERBAD** adj exceptionally bold
**SUPERBANK** n bank that owns other banks
**SUPERBER** >SUPERB
**SUPERBEST** >SUPERB
**SUPERBIKE** n high-performance motorcycle
**SUPERBITY** >SUPERB
**SUPERBLY** >SUPERB
**SUPERBOLD** adj exceptionally bold
**SUPERBOMB** n large bomb
**SUPERBRAT** n exceptionally unpleasant child
**SUPERBUG** n bacterium resistant to antibiotics
**SUPERBUGS** >SUPERBUG
**SUPERCAR** n very expensive fast or powerful car with a centrally located engine
**SUPERCARS** >SUPERCAR

SUPERCEDE *former variant of* >SUPERSEDE

SUPERCHIC *adj* highly chic

SUPERCITY *n* very large city

SUPERCLUB *n* large and important club

SUPERCOIL *vb* form a complex coil

SUPERCOLD *adj* very cold

SUPERCOOL *vb* cool or be cooled to a temperature below that at which freezing or crystallization should occur

SUPERCOP *n* high-ranking police officer

SUPERCOPS >SUPERCOP

SUPERCOW *n* dairy cow that produces a very high milk yield

SUPERCOWS >SUPERCOW

SUPERCUTE *adj* very cute

SUPERED >SUPER

SUPEREGO *n* that part of the unconscious mind that governs ideas about what is right and wrong

SUPEREGOS >SUPEREGO

SUPERETTE *n* small store or dairy laid out along the lines of a supermarket

SUPERFAN *n* very devoted fan

SUPERFANS >SUPERFAN

SUPERFARM *n* very large farm

SUPERFAST *adj* very fast

SUPERFINE *adj* of exceptional fineness or quality

SUPERFIRM *adj* very firm

SUPERFIT *adj* highly fit

SUPERFIX *n* linguistic feature distinguishing the meaning of one word that of another

SUPERFLUX *n* superfluity

SUPERFUND *n* large fund

SUPERFUSE *vb* pour or be poured so as to cover something

SUPERGENE *n* cluster of genes

SUPERGLUE *n* extremely strong and quick-drying glue ▷ *vb* fix with superglue

SUPERGOOD *adj* very good

SUPERGUN *n* large powerful gun

SUPERGUNS >SUPERGUN

SUPERHEAT *vb* heat (a vapour, esp steam) to a temperature above its saturation point for a given pressure

SUPERHERO *n* any of various comic-strip characters with superhuman abilities or magical powers

SUPERHET *n* type of radio receiver

SUPERHETS >SUPERHET

SUPERHIGH *adj* extremely high

SUPERHIT *n* very popular hit

SUPERHITS >SUPERHIT

SUPERHIVE *n* upper part of beehive

SUPERHOT *adj* very hot

SUPERHYPE *n* exaggerated hype

SUPERING >SUPER

SUPERIOR *adj* greater in quality, quantity, or merit ▷ *n* person of greater rank or status

SUPERIORS >SUPERIOR

SUPERJET *n* supersonic aircraft

SUPERJETS >SUPERJET

SUPERJOCK *n* very athletic person

SUPERLAIN >SUPERLIE

SUPERLAY >SUPERLIE

SUPERLIE *vb* lie above

SUPERLIES >SUPERLIE

SUPERLOAD *n* variable weight on a structure

SUPERLONG *adj* very long

SUPERLOO *n* automated public toilet

SUPERLOOS >SUPERLOO

SUPERMALE *former name for* >METAMALE

SUPERMAN *n* man with great physical or mental powers

SUPERMART *n* large self-service store selling food and household supplies

SUPERMAX *n* having or relating to the very highest levels of security

SUPERMEN >SUPERMAN

SUPERMIND *n* very powerful brain

SUPERMINI *n* small car, usually a hatchback, that is economical to run but has a high level of performance

SUPERMOM *n* very capable and busy mother

SUPERMOMS >SUPERMOM

SUPERMOTO *n* form of motorcycle racing over part-tarmac and part-dirt circuits

SUPERNAL *adj* of or from the world of the divine

SUPERNATE *n* liquid lying above a sediment

SUPERNOVA *n* star that explodes and briefly becomes exceptionally bright

SUPERPIMP *n* pimp controlling many prostitutes

SUPERPLUS *n* surplus

SUPERPORT *n* large port

SUPERPOSE *vb* transpose (the coordinates of one geometric figure) to

coincide with those of another

SUPERPRO *n* person regarded as a real professional

SUPERPROS >SUPERPRO

SUPERRACE *n* important race

SUPERREAL *adj* surreal

SUPERRICH *adj* exceptionally wealthy

SUPERROAD *n* very large road

SUPERS >SUPER

SUPERSAFE *adj* very safe

SUPERSALE *n* large sale

SUPERSALT *n* acid salt

SUPERSAUR *n* very large dinosaur

SUPERSEDE *vb* replace, supplant

SUPERSELL *vb* sell in very large numbers

SUPERSEX *n* sterile organism in which the ratio between the sex chromosomes is disturbed

SUPERSHOW *n* very impressive show

SUPERSIZE *vb* make larger

SUPERSOFT *adj* very soft

SUPERSOLD >SUPERSELL

SUPERSPY *n* highly accomplished spy

SUPERSTAR *n* very famous entertainer or sportsperson

SUPERSTUD *n* highly virile man

SUPERTAX *n* extra tax on incomes above a certain level

SUPERTHIN *adj* very thin

SUPERVENE *vb* occur as an unexpected development

SUPERVISE *vb* watch over to direct or check

SUPERWAIF *n* very young and very thin supermodel

SUPERWAVE *n* large wave

SUPERWEED *n* hybrid plant that contains genes for herbicide resistance

SUPERWIDE *n* very wide lens

SUPERWIFE *n* highly accomplished wife

SUPES >SUPE

SUPINATE *vb* turn (the hand and forearm) so that the palm faces up or forwards

SUPINATED >SUPINATE

SUPINATES >SUPINATE

SUPINATOR *n* muscle of the forearm that can produce the motion of supination

SUPINE *adj* lying flat on one's back ▷ *n* noun form derived from a verb in Latin

SUPINELY >SUPINE

SUPINES >SUPINE

SUPLEX *n* wrestling hold

in which a wrestler grasps his opponent round the waist from behind and carries him backwards

SUPLEXES >SUPLEX

SUPPAWN *n* kind of porridge

SUPPAWNS >SUPPAWN

SUPPEAGO *same as* >SERPIGO

SUPPED >SUP

SUPPER *n* light evening meal ▷ *vb* eat supper

SUPPERED >SUPPER

SUPPERING >SUPPER

SUPPERS >SUPPER

SUPPING >SUP

SUPPLANT *vb* take the place of, oust

SUPPLANTS >SUPPLANT

SUPPLE *adj* (of a person) moving and bending easily and gracefully ▷ *vb* make or become supple

SUPPLED >SUPPLE

SUPPLELY *same as* >SUPPLY

SUPPLER >SUPPLE

SUPPLES >SUPPLE

SUPPLEST >SUPPLE

SUPPLIAL *n* instance of supplying

SUPPLIALS >SUPPLIAL

SUPPLIANT *n* person who requests humbly

SUPPLICAT *n* university petition

SUPPLIED >SUPPLY

SUPPLIER >SUPPLY

SUPPLIERS >SUPPLY

SUPPLIES >SUPPLY

SUPPLING >SUPPLE

SUPPLY *vb* provide with something required ▷ *n* supplying ▷ *adj* acting as a temporary substitute ▷ *adv* in a supple manner

SUPPLYING >SUPPLY

SUPPORT *vb* bear the weight of ▷ *n* supporting

SUPPORTED >SUPPORT

SUPPORTER *n* person who supports a team, principle, etc

SUPPORTS >SUPPORT

SUPPOSAL *n* supposition

SUPPOSALS >SUPPOSAL

SUPPOSE *vb* presume to be true

SUPPOSED *adj* presumed to be true without proof, doubtful

SUPPOSER >SUPPOSE

SUPPOSERS >SUPPOSE

SUPPOSES >SUPPOSE

SUPPOSING >SUPPOSE

SUPPRESS *vb* put an end to

SUPPURATE *vb* (of a wound etc) produce pus

SUPRA *adv* above, esp referring to earlier parts of a book etc

SUPREMACY *n* supreme power

SUPREME *adj* highest in authority, rank, or degree

▷ *n* rich velouté sauce made with a base of veal or chicken stock, with cream or egg yolks added

**SUPREMELY** > SUPREME

**SUPREMER** > SUPREME

**SUPREMES** > SUPREME

**SUPREMEST** > SUPREME

**SUPREMITY** *n* supremeness

**SUPREMO** *n* person in overall authority

**SUPREMOS** > SUPREMO

**SUPS** > SUP

**SUQ** *same as* > SOUK

**SUQS** > SUQ

**SUR** *prep* above

**SURA** *n* any of the 114 chapters of the Koran

**SURAH** *n* twill-weave fabric of silk or rayon, used for dresses, blouses, etc

**SURAHS** > SURAH

**SURAL** *adj* of or relating to the calf of the leg

**SURAMIN** *n* drug used in treating sleeping sickness

**SURAMINS** > SURAMIN

**SURANCE** *same as* > ASSURANCE

**SURANCES** > SURANCE

**SURAS** > SURA

**SURAT** *n* (formerly) a cotton fabric from the Surat area of India

**SURATS** > SURAT

**SURBAHAR** *n* Indian string instrument

**SURBAHARS** > SURBAHAR

**SURBASE** *n* uppermost part, such as a moulding, of a pedestal, base, or skirting

**SURBASED** *adj* having a surbase

**SURBASES** > SURBASE

**SURBATE** *vb* make feet sore through walking

**SURBATED** > SURBATE

**SURBATES** > SURBATE

**SURBATING** > SURBATE

**SURBED** *vb* put something on its edge

**SURBEDDED** > SURBED

**SURBEDS** > SURBED

**SURBET** > SURBATE

**SURCEASE** *n* cessation or intermission ▷ *vb* desist from (some action)

**SURCEASED** > SURCEASE

**SURCEASES** > SURCEASE

**SURCHARGE** *n* additional charge ▷ *vb* charge (someone) an additional sum or tax

**SURCINGLE** *n* girth for a horse which goes around the body, used esp with a racing saddle ▷ *vb* put a surcingle on or over (a horse)

**SURCOAT** *n* tunic worn by a knight over his armour during the Middle Ages

**SURCOATS** > SURCOAT

**SURCULI** > SURCULUS

**SURCULOSE** *adj* (of a plant) bearing suckers

**SURCULUS** *n* sucker on plant

**SURD** *n* number that cannot be expressed in whole numbers ▷ *adj* of or relating to a surd

**SURDITIES** > SURDITY

**SURDITY** *n* deafness

**SURDS** > SURD

**SURE** *adj* free from uncertainty or doubt ▷ *interj* certainly ▷ *vb* archaic form of sewer

**SURED** > SURE

**SUREFIRE** *adj* certain to succeed

**SURELY** *adv* it must be true that

**SURENESS** > SURE

**SURER** > SURE

**SURES** > SURE

**SUREST** > SURE

**SURETIED** > SURETY

**SURETIES** > SURETY

**SURETY** *n* person who takes responsibility for the fulfilment of another's obligation ▷ *vb* be surety for

**SURETYING** > SURETY

**SURF** *n* foam caused by waves breaking on the shore ▷ *vb* take part in surfing

**SURFABLE** > SURF

**SURFACE** *n* outside or top of an object ▷ *vb* become apparent

**SURFACED** > SURFACE

**SURFACER** > SURFACE

**SURFACERS** > SURFACE

**SURFACES** > SURFACE

**SURFACING** > SURFACE

**SURFBIRD** *n* American shore bird

**SURFBIRDS** > SURFBIRD

**SURFBOARD** *n* long smooth board used in surfing

**SURFBOAT** *n* boat with a high bow and stern and flotation chambers

**SURFBOATS** > SURFBOAT

**SURFED** > SURF

**SURFEIT** *n* excessive amount ▷ *vb* supply or feed excessively

**SURFEITED** > SURFEIT

**SURFEITER** > SURFEIT

**SURFEITS** > SURFEIT

**SURFER** > SURFING

**SURFERS** > SURFING

**SURFFISH** *n* fish of American coastal seas

**SURFICIAL** *adj* superficial

**SURFIE** *n* young person whose main interest is in surfing

**SURFIER** > SURF

**SURFIES** > SURFIE

**SURFIEST** > SURF

**SURFING** *n* sport of riding

towards the shore on a surfboard on the crest of a wave

**SURFINGS** > SURFING

**SURFLIKE** > SURF

**SURFMAN** *n* sailor skilled in sailing through surf

**SURFMEN** > SURFMAN

**SURFPERCH** *n* type of marine fish of North American Pacific coastal waters

**SURFRIDER** > SURFING

**SURFS** > SURF

**SURFSIDE** *adj* next to the sea

**SURFY** > SURF

**SURGE** *n* sudden powerful increase ▷ *vb* increase suddenly

**SURGED** > SURGE

**SURGEFUL** > SURGE

**SURGELESS** > SURGE

**SURGENT** > SURGE

**SURGEON** *n* doctor who specializes in surgery

**SURGEONCY** *n* office, duties, or position of a surgeon, esp in the army or navy

**SURGEONS** > SURGEON

**SURGER** > SURGE

**SURGERIES** > SURGERY

**SURGERS** > SURGE

**SURGERY** *n* treatment in which the patient's body is cut open in order to treat the affected part

**SURGES** > SURGE

**SURGICAL** *adj* involving or used in surgery

**SURGIER** > SURGE

**SURGIEST** > SURGE

**SURGING** > SURGE

**SURGINGS** > SURGE

**SURGY** > SURGE

**SURICATE** *n* type of meerkat

**SURICATES** > SURICATE

**SURIMI** *n* blended seafood product made from precooked fish, restructured into stick shapes

**SURIMIS** > SURIMI

**SURING** > SURE

**SURLIER** > SURLY

**SURLIEST** > SURLY

**SURLILY** > SURLY

**SURLINESS** > SURLY

**SURLOIN** *same as* > SIRLOIN

**SURLOINS** > SURLOIN

**SURLY** *adj* ill-tempered and rude

**SURMASTER** *n* deputy headmaster

**SURMISAL** > SURMISE

**SURMISALS** > SURMISE

**SURMISE** *n* guess, conjecture ▷ *vb* guess (something) from incomplete or uncertain evidence

**SURMISED** > SURMISE

**SURMISER** > SURMISE

**SURMISERS** > SURMISE

**SURMISES** > SURMISE

**SURMISING** > SURMISE

**SURMOUNT** *vb* overcome (a problem)

**SURMOUNTS** > SURMOUNT

**SURMULLET** *n* red mullet

**SURNAME** *n* family name ▷ *vb* furnish with or call by a surname

**SURNAMED** > SURNAME

**SURNAMER** > SURNAME

**SURNAMERS** > SURNAME

**SURNAMES** > SURNAME

**SURNAMING** > SURNAME

**SURPASS** *vb* be greater than or superior to

**SURPASSED** > SURPASS

**SURPASSER** > SURPASS

**SURPASSES** > SURPASS

**SURPLICE** *n* loose white robe worn by clergymen and choristers

**SURPLICED** > SURPLICE

**SURPLICES** > SURPLICE

**SURPLUS** *n* amount left over in excess of what is required ▷ *adj* extra ▷ *vb* be left over in excess of what is required

**SURPLUSED** > SURPLUS

**SURPLUSES** > SURPLUS

**SURPRINT** *vb* print (additional matter) over something already printed ▷ *n* marks, printed matter, etc, that have been surprinted

**SURPRINTS** > SURPRINT

**SURPRISAL** > SURPRISE

**SURPRISE** *n* unexpected event ▷ *vb* cause to feel amazement or wonder

**SURPRISED** > SURPRISE

**SURPRISER** > SURPRISE

**SURPRISES** > SURPRISE

**SURPRIZE** *same as* > SURPRISE

**SURPRIZED** > SURPRIZE

**SURPRIZES** > SURPRIZE

**SURQUEDRY** *n* arrogance

**SURQUEDY** *same as* > SURQUEDRY

**SURRA** *n* tropical febrile disease of animals

**SURRAS** > SURRA

**SURREAL** *adj* bizarre ▷ *n* atmosphere or qualities evoked by surrealism

**SURREALLY** > SURREAL

**SURREBUT** *vb* give evidence to support the surrebutter

**SURREBUTS** > SURREBUT

**SURREINED** *adj* (of horse) ridden too much

**SURREJOIN** *vb* reply to legal rejoinder

**SURRENDER** *vb* give oneself up ▷ *n* surrendering

**SURRENDRY** *same as* > SURRENDER

**SURREY** *n* light four-wheeled horse-drawn carriage having two or

four seats
**SURREYS** > SURREY
**SURROGACY** > SURROGATE
**SURROGATE** *n* substitute
▷ *adj* acting as a
substitute ▷ *vb* put in
another's position as a
deputy, substitute, etc
**SURROUND** *vb* be, come, or
place all around (a person
or thing) ▷ *n* border or
edging
**SURROUNDS** > SURROUND
**SURROYAL** *n* high point on
stag's horns
**SURROYALS** > SURROYAL
**SURTAX** *n* extra tax on
incomes above a certain
level ▷ *vb* assess for
liability to surtax
**SURTAXED** > SURTAX
**SURTAXES** > SURTAX
**SURTAXING** > SURTAX
**SURTITLE** *singular
of* > SURTITLE
**SURTITLES** *pl n* brief
translations of the text of
an opera or play projected
above the stage
**SURTOUT** *n* man's overcoat
resembling a frock coat,
popular in the late 19th
century
**SURTOUTS** > SURTOUT
**SURUCUCU** *n* South
American snake
**SURUCUCUS** > SURUCUCU
**SURVEIL** *same
as* > SURVEILLE
**SURVEILED** > SURVEIL
**SURVEILLE** *vb* observe
closely
**SURVEILS** > SURVEIL
**SURVEY** *vb* view or consider
in a general way ▷ *n*
surveying
**SURVEYAL** > SURVEY
**SURVEYALS** > SURVEY
**SURVEYED** > SURVEY
**SURVEYING** *n* practice
of measuring altitudes,
angles, and distances on
the land surface so that
they can be accurately
plotted on a map
**SURVEYOR** *n* person whose
occupation is to survey
land or buildings
**SURVEYORS** > SURVEYOR
**SURVEYS** > SURVEY
**SURVIEW** *vb* survey
**SURVIEWED** > SURVIEW
**SURVIEWS** > SURVIEW
**SURVIVAL** *n* condition of
having survived ▷ *adj* of,
relating to, or assisting the
act of surviving
**SURVIVALS** > SURVIVAL
**SURVIVE** *vb* continue
to live or exist after (a
difficult experience)
**SURVIVED** > SURVIVE
**SURVIVER** *same
as* > SURVIVOR

**SURVIVERS** > SURVIVER
**SURVIVES** > SURVIVE
**SURVIVING** > SURVIVE
**SURVIVOR** *n* person or
thing that survives
**SURVIVORS** > SURVIVOR
**SUS** *same as* > SUSS
**SUSCEPTOR** *n* sponsor
**SUSCITATE** *vb* excite
**SUSES** > SUS
**SUSHI** *n* Japanese dish of
small cakes of cold rice
with a topping of raw fish
**SUSHIS** > SUSHI
**SUSLIK** *n* central Eurasian
ground squirrel
**SUSLIKS** > SUSLIK
**SUSPECT** *vb* believe
(someone) to be guilty
without having any proof
▷ *adj* not to be trusted ▷ *n*
person who is suspected
**SUSPECTED** > SUSPECT
**SUSPECTER** > SUSPECT
**SUSPECTS** > SUSPECT
**SUSPENCE** *same
as* > SUSPENSE
**SUSPEND** *vb* hang from a
high place
**SUSPENDED** > SUSPEND
**SUSPENDER** *n* elastic strap
for holding up women's
stockings
**SUSPENDS** > SUSPEND
**SUSPENS** *same
as* > SUSPENSE
**SUSPENSE** *n* state of
uncertainty while
awaiting news, an event,
etc
**SUSPENSER** *n* film that
creates a feeling of
suspense
**SUSPENSES** > SUSPENSE
**SUSPENSOR** *n* ligament or
muscle that holds a part in
position
**SUSPICION** *n* feeling of not
trusting a person or thing
**SUSPIRE** *vb* sigh or utter
with a sigh
**SUSPIRED** > SUSPIRE
**SUSPIRES** > SUSPIRE
**SUSPIRING** > SUSPIRE
**SUSS** *vb* attempt to work
out (a situation, etc),
using one's intuition ▷ *n*
sharpness of mind
**SUSSED** > SUSS
**SUSSES** > SUSS
**SUSSING** > SUSS
**SUSTAIN** *vb* maintain or
prolong ▷ *n* prolongation
of a note, by playing
technique or electronics
**SUSTAINED** > SUSTAIN
**SUSTAINER** *n* rocket
engine that maintains the
velocity of a space vehicle
after the booster has been
jettisoned
**SUSTAINS** > SUSTAIN
**SUSTINENT** *adj* sustaining
**SUSU** *n* (in the Caribbean)

savings fund shared by
friends
**SUSURRANT** > SUSURRATE
**SUSURRATE** *vb* make a soft
rustling sound
**SUSURROUS** *adj* full of
murmuring sounds
**SUSURRUS** > SUSURRATE
**SUSUS** > SUSU
**SUTILE** *adj* involving
sewing
**SUTLER** *n* (formerly)
a merchant who
accompanied an army in
order to sell provisions to
the soldiers
**SUTLERIES** > SUTLER
**SUTLERS** > SUTLER
**SUTLERY** > SUTLER
**SUTOR** *n* cobbler
**SUTORIAL** > SUTOR
**SUTORIAN** > SUTOR
**SUTORS** > SUTOR
**SUTRA** *n* Sanskrit sayings or
collections of sayings
**SUTRAS** > SUTRA
**SUTTA** *n* Buddhist scripture
**SUTTAS** > SUTTA
**SUTTEE** *n* former Hindu
custom whereby a widow
burnt herself to death on
her husband's funeral pyre
**SUTTEEISM** > SUTTEE
**SUTTEES** > SUTTEE
**SUTTLE** *vb* work as sutler
**SUTTLED** > SUTTLE
**SUTTLES** > SUTTLE
**SUTTLETIE** *same
as* > SUBTLETY
**SUTTLING** > SUTTLE
**SUTTLY** > SUBTLE
**SUTURAL** > SUTURE
**SUTURALLY** > SUTURE
**SUTURE** *n* stitch joining
the edges of a wound ▷ *vb*
join (the edges of a wound,
etc) by means of sutures
**SUTURED** > SUTURE
**SUTURES** > SUTURE
**SUTURING** > SUTURE
**SUZERAIN** *n* state or
sovereign with limited
authority over another
self-governing state
**SUZERAINS** > SUZERAIN
**SVARAJ** *same as* > SWARAJ
**SVARAJES** > SVARAJ
**SVASTIKA** *same
as* > SWASTIKA
**SVASTIKAS** > SVASTIKA
**SVEDBERG** *n* unit used in
physics
**SVEDBERGS** > SVEDBERG
**SVELTE** *adj* attractively or
gracefully slim
**SVELTELY** > SVELTE
**SVELTER** > SVELTE
**SVELTEST** > SVELTE
**SWAB** *n* small piece of
cotton wool used to
apply medication, clean a
wound, etc ▷ *vb* clean (a
wound) with a swab
**SWABBED** > SWAB

**SWABBER** *n* person who
uses a swab
**SWABBERS** > SWABBER
**SWABBIE** *same as* > SWABBY
**SWABBIES** > SWABBY
**SWABBING** > SWAB
**SWABBY** *n* seaman
**SWABS** > SWAB
**SWACK** *adj* flexible
**SWACKED** *adj* in a state of
intoxication, stupor, or
euphoria induced by drugs
or alcohol
**SWAD** *n* loutish person
**SWADDIE** *same as* > SWADDY
**SWADDIES** > SWADDY
**SWADDLE** *vb* wrap (a baby)
in swaddling clothes ▷ *n*
swaddling clothes
**SWADDLED** > SWADDLE
**SWADDLER** > SWADDLE
**SWADDLERS** > SWADDLE
**SWADDLES** > SWADDLE
**SWADDLING** > SWADDLE
**SWADDY** *n* private soldier
**SWADS** > SWADDLE
**SWAG** *n* stolen property
▷ *vb* sway from side to side
**SWAGE** *n* shaped tool or die
used in forming cold metal
by hammering ▷ *vb* form
(metal) with a swage
**SWAGED** > SWAGE
**SWAGER** > SWAGE
**SWAGERS** > SWAGE
**SWAGES** > SWAGE
**SWAGGED** > SWAG
**SWAGGER** *vb* walk or behave
arrogantly ▷ *n* arrogant
walk or manner ▷ *adj*
elegantly fashionable
**SWAGGERED** > SWAGGER
**SWAGGERER** > SWAGGER
**SWAGGERS** > SWAGGER
**SWAGGIE** *same as* > SWAGGER
**SWAGGIES** > SWAGGIE
**SWAGGING** > SWAG
**SWAGING** > SWAGE
**SWAGMAN** *n* tramp who
carries his belongings in a
bundle on his back
**SWAGMEN** > SWAGMAN
**SWAGS** > SWAG
**SWAGSHOP** *n* shop selling
cheap goods
**SWAGSHOPS** > SWAGSHOP
**SWAGSMAN** *same
as* > SWAGMAN
**SWAGSMEN** > SWAGSMAN
**SWAIL** *same as* > SWALE
**SWAILS** > SWAIL
**SWAIN** *n* suitor
**SWAINING** *n* acting as
suitor
**SWAININGS** > SWAINING
**SWAINISH** > SWAIN
**SWAINS** > SWAIN
**SWALE** *n* moist depression
in a tract of land, usually
with rank vegetation ▷ *vb*
sway
**SWALED** > SWALE
**SWALES** > SWALE
**SWALIER** > SWALE

**SWALIEST** > SWALE
**SWALING** > SWALE
**SWALINGS** > SWALE
**SWALLET** *n* hole where water goes underground
**SWALLETS** > SWALLET
**SWALLOW** *vb* cause to pass down one's throat ⊳ *n* swallowing
**SWALLOWED** > SWALLOW
**SWALLOWER** > SWALLOW
**SWALLOWS** > SWALLOW
**SWALY** > SWALE
**SWAM** > SWIM
**SWAMI** *n* Hindu religious teacher
**SWAMIES** > SWAMI
**SWAMIS** > SWAMI
**SWAMP** *n* watery area of land, bog ⊳ *vb* cause (a boat) to fill with water and sink
**SWAMPED** > SWAMP
**SWAMPER** *n* person who lives or works in a swampy region, esp in the southern US
**SWAMPERS** > SWAMPER
**SWAMPIER** > SWAMP
**SWAMPIEST** > SWAMP
**SWAMPING** > SWAMP
**SWAMPISH** > SWAMP
**SWAMPLAND** *n* permanently waterlogged area
**SWAMPLESS** > SWAMP
**SWAMPS** > SWAMP
**SWAMPY** > SWAMP
**SWAMY** *same as* > SWAMI
**SWAN** *n* large usu white water bird with a long graceful neck ⊳ *vb* wander about idly
**SWANG** > SWING
**SWANHERD** *n* person who herds swans
**SWANHERDS** > SWANHERD
**SWANK** *vb* show off or boast ⊳ *n* showing off or boasting
**SWANKED** > SWANK
**SWANKER** > SWANK
**SWANKERS** > SWANK
**SWANKEST** > SWANK
**SWANKEY** *same as* > SWANKY
**SWANKEYS** > SWANKY
**SWANKIE** *same as* > SWANKY
**SWANKIER** > SWANKY
**SWANKIES** > SWANKY
**SWANKIEST** > SWANKY
**SWANKILY** > SWANKY
**SWANKING** > SWANK
**SWANKPOT** *same as* > SWANK
**SWANKPOTS** > SWANKPOT
**SWANKS** > SWANK
**SWANKY** *adj* expensive and showy, stylish ⊳ *n* lively person
**SWANLIKE** > SWAN
**SWANNED** > SWAN
**SWANNERY** *n* place where swans are kept and bred
**SWANNIE** *n* (in NZ) type of all-weather heavy woollen shirt

**SWANNIER** > SWANNY
**SWANNIES** > SWANNIE
**SWANNIEST** > SWANNY
**SWANNING** > SWAN
**SWANNINGS** > SWAN
**SWANNY** *adj* swanlike
**SWANPAN** *n* Chinese abacus
**SWANPANS** > SWANPAN
**SWANS** > SWAN
**SWANSDOWN** *n* fine soft feathers of a swan
**SWANSKIN** *n* skin of a swan with the feathers attached
**SWANSKINS** > SWANSKIN
**SWAP** *vb* exchange (something) for something else ⊳ *n* exchange
**SWAPPED** > SWAP
**SWAPPER** > SWAP
**SWAPPERS** > SWAP
**SWAPPING** > SWAP
**SWAPPINGS** > SWAP
**SWAPS** > SWAP
**SWAPT** > SWAP
**SWAPTION** *another name for* > SWAP
**SWAPTIONS** > SWAPTION
**SWARAJ** *n* (in British India) self-government
**SWARAJES** > SWARAJ
**SWARAJISM** > SWARAJ
**SWARAJIST** > SWARAJ
**SWARD** *n* stretch of short grass ⊳ *vb* cover or become covered with grass
**SWARDED** > SWARD
**SWARDIER** > SWARDY
**SWARDIEST** > SWARDY
**SWARDING** > SWARD
**SWARDS** > SWARD
**SWARDY** *adj* covered with sward
**SWARE** > SWEAR
**SWARF** *n* material removed by cutting tools in the machining of metals, stone, etc ⊳ *vb* faint
**SWARFED** > SWARF
**SWARFING** > SWARF
**SWARFS** > SWARF
**SWARM** *n* large group of bees or other insects ⊳ *vb* move in a swarm
**SWARMED** > SWARM
**SWARMER** > SWARM
**SWARMERS** > SWARM
**SWARMING** > SWARM
**SWARMINGS** > SWARM
**SWARMS** > SWARM
**SWART** *adj* swarthy
**SWARTH** *same as* > SWART
**SWARTHIER** > SWARTHY
**SWARTHILY** > SWARTHY
**SWARTHS** > SWARTH
**SWARTHY** *adj* dark-complexioned
**SWARTNESS** > SWART
**SWARTY** > SWART
**SWARVE** *same as* > SWARF
**SWARVED** > SWARF
**SWARVES** > SWARF
**SWARVING** > SWARF

**SWASH** *n* rush of water up a beach following each break of the waves ⊳ *vb* (esp of water or things in water) to wash or move with noisy splashing
**SWASHED** > SWASH
**SWASHER** *n* braggart
**SWASHERS** > SWASHER
**SWASHES** > SWASH
**SWASHIER** > SWASHY
**SWASHIEST** > SWASHY
**SWASHING** > SWASH
**SWASHINGS** > SWASH
**SWASHWORK** *n* type of work done on lathe
**SWASHY** *adj* slushy
**SWASTICA** *same as* > SWASTIKA
**SWASTICAS** > SWASTICA
**SWASTIKA** *n* symbol in the shape of a cross with the arms bent at right angles, used as the emblem of Nazi Germany
**SWASTIKAS** > SWASTIKA
**SWAT** *vb* strike or hit sharply ⊳ *n* swatter
**SWATCH** *n* sample of cloth
**SWATCHES** > SWATCH
**SWATH** *n* width of one sweep of a scythe or of the blade of a mowing machine
**SWATHABLE** > SWATHE
**SWATHE** *vb* bandage or wrap completely ⊳ *n* bandage or wrapping
**SWATHED** > SWATHE
**SWATHER** > SWATHE
**SWATHERS** > SWATHE
**SWATHES** > SWATHE
**SWATHIER** > SWATH
**SWATHIEST** > SWATH
**SWATHING** > SWATHE
**SWATHS** > SWATH
**SWATHY** > SWATH
**SWATS** > SWAT
**SWATTED** > SWAT
**SWATTER** *n* device for killing insects, esp a meshed flat attached to a handle ⊳ *vb* splash
**SWATTERED** > SWATTER
**SWATTERS** > SWATTER
**SWATTING** > SWAT
**SWATTINGS** > SWAT
**SWAY** *vb* swing to and fro or from side to side ⊳ *n* power or influence
**SWAYABLE** > SWAY
**SWAYBACK** *n* abnormal sagging in the spine of older horses
**SWAYBACKS** > SWAYBACK
**SWAYED** > SWAY
**SWAYER** > SWAY
**SWAYERS** > SWAY
**SWAYFUL** > SWAY
**SWAYING** > SWAY
**SWAYINGS** > SWAY
**SWAYL** *same as* > SWEAL
**SWAYLED** > SWAYL
**SWAYLING** > SWAYL

**SWAYLINGS** > SWAYL
**SWAYLS** > SWAYL
**SWAYS** > SWAY
**SWAZZLE** *n* small metal instrument used to produce a shrill voice
**SWAZZLES** > SWAZZLE
**SWEAL** *vb* scorch
**SWEALED** > SWEAL
**SWEALING** > SWEAL
**SWEALINGS** > SWEAL
**SWEALS** > SWEAL
**SWEAR** *vb* use obscene or blasphemous language
**SWEARD** *same as* > SWORD
**SWEARDS** > SWEARD
**SWEARER** > SWEAR
**SWEARERS** > SWEAR
**SWEARING** > SWEAR
**SWEARINGS** > SWEAR
**SWEARS** > SWEAR
**SWEARWORD** *n* word considered obscene or blasphemous
**SWEAT** *n* salty liquid given off through the pores of the skin ⊳ *vb* have sweat coming through the pores
**SWEATBAND** *n* strip of cloth tied around the forehead or wrist to absorb sweat
**SWEATBOX** *n* device for causing tobacco leaves, fruit, or hides to sweat
**SWEATED** *adj* made by exploited labour
**SWEATER** *n* (woollen) garment for the upper part of the body
**SWEATERS** > SWEATER
**SWEATIER** > SWEATY
**SWEATIEST** > SWEATY
**SWEATILY** > SWEATY
**SWEATING** > SWEAT
**SWEATINGS** > SWEAT
**SWEATLESS** > SWEAT
**SWEATS** > SWEAT
**SWEATSHOP** *n* place where employees work long hours in poor conditions for low pay
**SWEATSUIT** *n* knitted suit worn by athletes for training
**SWEATY** *adj* covered with sweat
**SWEDE** *n* kind of turnip
**SWEDES** > SWEDE
**SWEDGER** *n* Scots dialect word for sweet
**SWEDGERS** > SWEDGER
**SWEE** *vb* sway
**SWEED** > SWEE
**SWEEING** > SWEE
**SWEEL** *same as* > SWEAL
**SWEELED** > SWEEL
**SWEELING** > SWEEL
**SWEELS** > SWEEL
**SWEENEY** *n* police flying squad
**SWEENEYS** > SWEENEY
**SWEENIES** > SWEENY
**SWEENY** *n* wasting of the shoulder muscles of a

horse

**SWEEP** vb remove dirt from (a floor) with a broom ▷ n sweeping

**SWEEPBACK** n rearward inclination of a component or surface

**SWEEPER** n device used to sweep carpets, consisting of a long handle attached to a revolving brush

**SWEEPERS** > SWEEPER

**SWEEPIER** > SWEEP

**SWEEPIEST** > SWEEP

**SWEEPING** > SWEEP

**SWEEPINGS** pl n debris, litter, or refuse

**SWEEPS** > SWEEP

**SWEEPY** > SWEEP

**SWEER** variant of > SWEIR

**SWEERED** > SWEER

**SWEERER** > SWEER

**SWEEREST** > SWEER

**SWEERING** > SWEER

**SWEERS** > SWEER

**SWEERT** > SWEER

**SWEES** > SWEE

**SWEET** adj tasting of or like sugar ▷ n shaped piece of food consisting mainly of sugar ▷ vb sweeten

**SWEETCORN** n variety of maize, the kernels of which are eaten when young

**SWEETED** > SWEET

**SWEETEN** vb make (food or drink) sweet or sweeter

**SWEETENED** > SWEETEN

**SWEETENER** n sweetening agent that does not contain sugar

**SWEETENS** > SWEETEN

**SWEETER** > SWEET

**SWEETEST** > SWEET

**SWEETFISH** n small Japanese fish

**SWEETIE** n lovable person

**SWEETIES** > SWEETIE

**SWEETING** n variety of sweet apple

**SWEETINGS** > SWEETING

**SWEETISH** > SWEET

**SWEETLY** > SWEET

**SWEETMAN** n (in the Caribbean) a man kept by a woman

**SWEETMEAL** adj (of biscuits) sweet and wholemeal

**SWEETMEAT** n sweet delicacy such as a small cake

**SWEETMEN** > SWEETMAN

**SWEETNESS** > SWEET

**SWEETPEA** n climbing plant with fragrant flowers of delicate pastel colours

**SWEETPEAS** > SWEETPEA

**SWEETS** > SWEET

**SWEETSHOP** n shop selling confectionery

**SWEETSOP** n small West Indian tree

**SWEETSOPS** > SWEETSOP

**SWEETWOOD** n tropical tree

**SWEETY** same as > SWEETIE

**SWEIR** vb swear ▷ adj lazy

**SWEIRED** > SWEIR

**SWEIRER** > SWEIR

**SWEIREST** > SWEIR

**SWEIRING** > SWEIR

**SWEIRNESS** > SWEIR

**SWEIRS** > SWEIR

**SWEIRT** > SWEIR

**SWELCHIE** n whirlpool in Orkney

**SWELCHIES** > SWELCHIE

**SWELL** vb expand or increase ▷ n swelling or being swollen ▷ adj excellent or fine

**SWELLDOM** n fashionable society

**SWELLDOMS** > SWELLDOM

**SWELLED** > SWELL

**SWELLER** > SWELL

**SWELLERS** > SWELL

**SWELLEST** > SWELL

**SWELLFISH** popular name for > PUFFER

**SWELLHEAD** n conceited person

**SWELLING** > SWELL

**SWELLINGS** > SWELL

**SWELLISH** > SWELL

**SWELLS** > SWELL

**SWELT** vb die

**SWELTED** > SWELT

**SWELTER** vb feel uncomfortably hot ▷ n hot and uncomfortable condition

**SWELTERED** > SWELTER

**SWELTERS** > SWELTER

**SWELTING** > SWELT

**SWELTRIER** > SWELTRY

**SWELTRY** adj sultry

**SWELTS** > SWELT

**SWEPT** > SWEEP

**SWEPTBACK** adj (of an aircraft wing) having the leading edge inclined backwards towards the rear

**SWEPTWING** adj (of an aircraft) having wings swept backwards

**SWERF** same as > SWARF

**SWERFED** > SWERF

**SWERFING** > SWERF

**SWERFS** > SWERF

**SWERVABLE** > SWERVE

**SWERVE** vb turn aside from a course sharply or suddenly ▷ n swerving

**SWERVED** > SWERVE

**SWERVER** > SWERVE

**SWERVERS** > SWERVE

**SWERVES** > SWERVE

**SWERVING** > SWERVE

**SWERVINGS** > SWERVE

**SWEVEN** n vision or dream

**SWEVENS** > SWEVEN

**SWEY** same as > SWEE

**SWEYED** > SWEY

**SWEYING** > SWEY

**SWEYS** > SWEY

**SWIDDEN** n area of land

where slash-and-burn techniques have been used to prepare it for cultivation

**SWIDDENS** > SWIDDEN

**SWIES** > SWY

**SWIFT** adj moving or able to move quickly ▷ n fast-flying bird with pointed wings ▷ adv swiftly or quickly ▷ vb make tight

**SWIFTED** > SWIFT

**SWIFTER** n line run around the ends of capstan bars to prevent their falling out of their sockets

**SWIFTERS** > SWIFTER

**SWIFTEST** > SWIFT

**SWIFTIE** n trick, ruse, or deception

**SWIFTIES** > SWIFTY

**SWIFTING** > SWIFT

**SWIFTLET** n type of small Asian swift

**SWIFTLETS** > SWIFTLET

**SWIFTLY** > SWIFT

**SWIFTNESS** > SWIFT

**SWIFTS** > SWIFT

**SWIFTY** same as > SWIFTIE

**SWIG** n large mouthful of drink ▷ vb drink in large mouthfuls

**SWIGGED** > SWIG

**SWIGGER** > SWIG

**SWIGGERS** > SWIG

**SWIGGING** > SWIG

**SWIGS** > SWIG

**SWILER** n (in Newfoundland) a seal hunter

**SWILERS** > SWILER

**SWILL** vb drink greedily ▷ n sloppy mixture containing waste food, fed to pigs

**SWILLED** > SWILL

**SWILLER** > SWILL

**SWILLERS** > SWILL

**SWILLING** > SWILL

**SWILLINGS** > SWILL

**SWILLS** > SWILL

**SWIM** vb move along in water by movements of the limbs ▷ n act or period of swimming

**SWIMMABLE** > SWIM

**SWIMMER** > SWIM

**SWIMMERET** n any of the small paired appendages on the abdomen of crustaceans

**SWIMMERS** pl n swimming costume

**SWIMMIER** > SWIMMY

**SWIMMIEST** > SWIMMY

**SWIMMILY** > SWIMMY

**SWIMMING** > SWIM

**SWIMMINGS** > SWIM

**SWIMMY** adj dizzy

**SWIMS** > SWIM

**SWIMSUIT** n woman's swimming garment that leaves the arms and legs bare

**SWIMSUITS** > SWIMSUIT

**SWIMWEAR** n swimming

costumes

**SWIMWEARS** > SWIMWEAR

**SWINDGE** same as > SWINGE

**SWINDGED** > SWINDGE

**SWINDGES** > SWINDGE

**SWINDGING** > SWINDGE

**SWINDLE** vb cheat (someone) out of money ▷ n instance of swindling

**SWINDLED** > SWINDLE

**SWINDLER** > SWINDLE

**SWINDLERS** > SWINDLE

**SWINDLES** > SWINDLE

**SWINDLING** > SWINDLE

**SWINE** n contemptible person

**SWINEHERD** n person who looks after pigs

**SWINEHOOD** > SWINE

**SWINELIKE** > SWINE

**SWINEPOX** n acute infectious viral disease of pigs

**SWINERIES** > SWINERY

**SWINERY** n pig farm

**SWINES** > SWINE

**SWING** vb move to and fro, sway ▷ n swinging

**SWINGBEAT** n type of modern dance music that combines soul, rhythm and blues, and hip-hop

**SWINGBOAT** n piece of fairground equipment consisting of a boat-shaped carriage for swinging in

**SWINGBY** n act of spacecraft passing close to planet

**SWINGBYS** > SWINGBY

**SWINGE** vb beat, flog, or punish

**SWINGED** > SWINGE

**SWINGEING** > SWINGE

**SWINGER** n person regarded as being modern and lively

**SWINGERS** > SWINGER

**SWINGES** > SWINGE

**SWINGIER** > SWINGY

**SWINGIEST** > SWINGY

**SWINGING** > SWING

**SWINGINGS** > SWING

**SWINGISM** n former resistance to use of agricultural machines

**SWINGISMS** > SWINGISM

**SWINGLE** n flat-bladed wooden instrument used for beating and scraping flax ▷ vb use a swingle on

**SWINGLED** > SWINGLE

**SWINGLES** > SWINGLE

**SWINGLING** > SWINGLE

**SWINGMAN** n musician specializing in swing music

**SWINGMEN** > SWINGMAN

**SWINGS** > SWING

**SWINGTREE** n crossbar in a horse's harness

**SWINGY** adj lively and modern

**SWINISH** > SWINE

**SWINISHLY** > SWINE

**SWINK** vb toil or drudge ▷ n toil or drudgery
**SWINKED** > SWINK
**SWINKER** > SWINK
**SWINKERS** > SWINK
**SWINKING** > SWINK
**SWINKS** > SWINK
**SWINNEY** variant of > SWEENY
**SWINNEYS** > SWINNEY
**SWIPE** vb strike (at) with a sweeping blow ▷ n hard blow
**SWIPED** > SWIPE
**SWIPER** > SWIPE
**SWIPERS** > SWIPE
**SWIPES** pl n beer, esp when poor or weak
**SWIPEY** adj drunk
**SWIPIER** > SWIPEY
**SWIPIEST** > SWIPEY
**SWIPING** > SWIPE
**SWIPLE** same as > SWIPPLE
**SWIPLES** > SWIPLE
**SWIPPLE** n part of a flail that strikes the grain
**SWIPPLES** > SWIPPLE
**SWIRE** n neck
**SWIRES** > SWIRE
**SWIRL** vb turn with a whirling motion ▷ n whirling motion
**SWIRLED** > SWIRL
**SWIRLIER** > SWIRL
**SWIRLIEST** > SWIRL
**SWIRLING** > SWIRL
**SWIRLS** > SWIRL
**SWIRLY** > SWIRL
**SWISH** vb move with a whistling or hissing sound ▷ n whistling or hissing sound ▷ adj fashionable, smart
**SWISHED** > SWISH
**SWISHER** > SWISH
**SWISHERS** > SWISH
**SWISHES** > SWISH
**SWISHEST** > SWISH
**SWISHIER** > SWISHY
**SWISHIEST** > SWISHY
**SWISHING** > SWISH
**SWISHINGS** > SWISH
**SWISHY** adj moving with a swishing sound
**SWISS** n type of muslin
**SWISSES** > SWISS
**SWISSING** n method of treating cloth
**SWISSINGS** > SWISSING
**SWITCH** n device for opening and closing an electric circuit ▷ vb change abruptly
**SWITCHED** > SWITCH
**SWITCHEL** n type of beer
**SWITCHELS** > SWITCHEL
**SWITCHER** > SWITCH
**SWITCHERS** > SWITCH
**SWITCHES** > SWITCH
**SWITCHIER** > SWITCH
**SWITCHING** > SWITCH
**SWITCHMAN** n person who operates railway points
**SWITCHMEN** > SWITCHMAN

**SWITCHY** > SWITCH
**SWITH** adv swiftly
**SWITHE** same as > SWITH
**SWITHER** vb hesitate or be indecisive ▷ n state of hesitation or uncertainty
**SWITHERED** > SWITHER
**SWITHERS** > SWITHER
**SWITHLY** > SWITH
**SWITS** same as > SWITCH
**SWITSES** > SWITS
**SWIVE** vb have sexual intercourse with (a person)
**SWIVED** > SWIVE
**SWIVEL** vb turn on a central point ▷ n coupling device that allows an attached object to turn freely
**SWIVELED** > SWIVEL
**SWIVELING** > SWIVEL
**SWIVELLED** > SWIVEL
**SWIVELS** > SWIVEL
**SWIVES** > SWIVE
**SWIVET** n nervous state
**SWIVETS** > SWIVET
**SWIVING** > SWIVE
**SWIZ** n swindle or disappointment
**SWIZZ** same as > SWIZ
**SWIZZED** > SWIZZ
**SWIZZES** > SWIZZ
**SWIZZING** > SWIZZ
**SWIZZLE** n unshaken cocktail ▷ vb stir a swizzle stick in (a drink)
**SWIZZLED** > SWIZZLE
**SWIZZLER** > SWIZZLE
**SWIZZLERS** > SWIZZLE
**SWIZZLES** > SWIZZLE
**SWIZZLING** > SWIZZLE
**SWOB** less common word for > SWAB
**SWOBBED** > SWOB
**SWOBBER** > SWOB
**SWOBBERS** > SWOB
**SWOBBING** > SWOB
**SWOBS** > SWOB
**SWOFFER** > SWOFFING
**SWOFFERS** > SWOFFING
**SWOFFING** n sport of saltwater fly-fishing
**SWOFFINGS** > SWOFFING
**SWOLLEN** > SWELL
**SWOLLENLY** > SWELL
**SWOLN** > SWELL
**SWONE** archaic variant of > SWOON
**SWONES** > SWONE
**SWOON** n faint ▷ vb faint because of shock or strong emotion
**SWOONED** > SWOON
**SWOONER** > SWOON
**SWOONERS** > SWOON
**SWOONIER** > SWOONY
**SWOONIEST** > SWOONY
**SWOONING** > SWOON
**SWOONINGS** > SWOON
**SWOONS** > SWOON
**SWOONY** adj romantic or sexy
**SWOOP** vb sweep down or pounce on suddenly ▷ n

swooping
**SWOOPED** > SWOOP
**SWOOPER** > SWOOP
**SWOOPERS** > SWOOP
**SWOOPIER** > SWOOP
**SWOOPIEST** > SWOOP
**SWOOPING** > SWOOP
**SWOOPS** > SWOOP
**SWOOPY** > SWOOP
**SWOOSH** vb make a swirling or rustling sound when moving or pouring out ▷ n swirling or rustling sound or movement
**SWOOSHED** > SWOOSH
**SWOOSHES** > SWOOSH
**SWOOSHING** > SWOOSH
**SWOP** same as > SWAP
**SWOPPED** > SWOP
**SWOPPER** > SWOP
**SWOPPERS** > SWOP
**SWOPPING** > SWOP
**SWOPPINGS** > SWOP
**SWOPS** > SWOP
**SWOPT** > SWOP
**SWORD** n weapon with a long sharp blade ▷ vb bear a sword
**SWORDBILL** n South American hummingbird
**SWORDED** > SWORD
**SWORDER** n fighter with sword
**SWORDERS** > SWORDER
**SWORDFISH** n large fish with a very long upper jaw
**SWORDING** > SWORD
**SWORDLESS** > SWORD
**SWORDLIKE** > SWORD
**SWORDMAN** same as > SWORDSMAN
**SWORDMEN** > SWORDMAN
**SWORDPLAY** n action or art of fighting with a sword
**SWORDS** > SWORD
**SWORDSMAN** n person skilled in the use of a sword
**SWORDSMEN** > SWORDSMAN
**SWORDTAIL** n type of small freshwater fish of Central America
**SWORE** > SWEAR
**SWORN** > SWEAR
**SWOT** vb study (a subject) intensively ▷ n person who studies hard
**SWOTS** > SWOT
**SWOTTED** > SWOT
**SWOTTER** > SWOT
**SWOTTERS** > SWOT
**SWOTTIER** > SWOTTY
**SWOTTIEST** > SWOTTY
**SWOTTING** > SWOT
**SWOTTINGS** > SWOT
**SWOTTY** adj given to studying hard, esp to the exclusion of other activities
**SWOUN** same as > SWOON
**SWOUND** same as > SWOON
**SWOUNDED** > SWOUND
**SWOUNDING** > SWOUND
**SWOUNDS** less common

spellings of > ZOUNDS
**SWOUNE** same as > SWOON
**SWOUNED** > SWOUNE
**SWOUNES** > SWOUNE
**SWOUNING** > SWOUNE
**SWOUNS** > SWOUN
**SWOWND** same as > SWOON
**SWOWNDS** > SWOWND
**SWOWNE** same as > SWOON
**SWOWNES** > SWOWNE
**SWOZZLE** same as > SWAZZLE
**SWOZZLES** > SWOZZLE
**SWUM** > SWIM
**SWUNG** > SWING
**SWY** n Australian gambling game involving two coins
**SYBARITE** n lover of luxury ▷ adj luxurious or sensuous
**SYBARITES** > SYBARITE
**SYBARITIC** > SYBARITE
**SYBBE** same as > SIB
**SYBBES** > SYBBE
**SYBIL** same as > SIBYL
**SYBILS** > SYBIL
**SYBO** n spring onion
**SYBOE** same as > SYBO
**SYBOES** > SYBOE
**SYBOTIC** adj of a swineherd
**SYBOTISM** > SYBOTIC
**SYBOTISMS** > SYBOTIC
**SYBOW** same as > SYBO
**SYBOWS** > SYBOW
**SYCAMINE** n mulberry tree mentioned in the Bible, thought to be the black mulberry
**SYCAMINES** > SYCAMINE
**SYCAMORE** n tree with five-pointed leaves and two-winged fruits
**SYCAMORES** > SYCAMORE
**SYCE** n (formerly, in India) a servant employed to look after horses, etc
**SYCEE** n silver ingots formerly used as a medium of exchange in China
**SYCEES** > SYCEE
**SYCES** > SYCE
**SYCOMORE** same as > SYCAMORE
**SYCOMORES** > SYCOMORE
**SYCONIA** > SYCONIUM
**SYCONIUM** n fleshy fruit of the fig
**SYCOPHANT** n person who uses flattery to win favour from people with power or influence
**SYCOSES** > SYCOSIS
**SYCOSIS** n chronic inflammation of the hair follicles
**SYE** vb strain
**SYED** > SYE
**SYEING** > SYE
**SYEN** same as > SCION
**SYENITE** n light-coloured coarse-grained plutonic igneous rock
**SYENITES** > SYENITE
**SYENITIC** > SYENITE
**SYENS** > SYEN

SYES > SYE
SYKE *same as* > SIKE
SYKER *adv* surely
SYKES > SYKE
SYLI *n* Finnish unit of volume
SYLIS > SYLI
SYLLABARY *n* table or list of syllables
SYLLABI > SYLLABUS
SYLLABIC *adj* of or relating to syllables ▷ *n* syllabic consonant
SYLLABICS > SYLLABIC
SYLLABIFY *vb* divide (a word) into syllables
SYLLABISE *same as* > SYLLABIZE
SYLLABISM *n* use of a writing system consisting of characters for syllables
SYLLABIZE *vb* divide into syllables
SYLLABLE *n* part of a word pronounced as a unit
SYLLABLED > SYLLABLE
SYLLABLES > SYLLABLE
SYLLABUB *n* dessert of beaten cream, sugar, and wine
SYLLABUBS > SYLLABUB
SYLLABUS *n* list of subjects for a course of study
SYLLEPSES > SYLLEPSIS
SYLLEPSIS *n* (in grammar or rhetoric) the use of a single sentence construction in which a verb, adjective, etc is made to cover two syntactical functions
SYLLEPTIC > SYLLEPSIS
SYLLOGISE *same as* > SYLLOGIZE
SYLLOGISM *n* form of logical reasoning consisting of two premises and a conclusion
SYLLOGIST > SYLLOGISM
SYLLOGIZE *vb* reason or infer by using syllogisms
SYLPH *n* slender graceful girl or woman
SYLPHIC *sylph*
SYLPHID *n* little sylph
SYLPHIDE *same as* > SYLPHID
SYLPHIDES > SYLPHIDE
SYLPHIDS > SYLPHID
SYLPHIER > SYLPH
SYLPHIEST > SYLPH
SYLPHINE > SYLPH
SYLPHISH > SYLPH
SYLPHLIKE > SYLPH
SYLPHS > SYLPH
SYLPHY > SYLPH
SYLVA *n* trees growing in a particular region
SYLVAE > SYLVA
SYLVAN *adj* relating to woods and trees ▷ *n* inhabitant of the woods, esp a spirit
SYLVANER *n* German

variety of grape
SYLVANERS > SYLVANER
SYLVANITE *n* silver-white mineral
SYLVANS > SYLVAN
SYLVAS > SYLVA
SYLVATIC *adj* growing, living, or occurring in a wood or beneath a tree
SYLVIA *n* songbird
SYLVIAS > SYLVIA
SYLVIINE > SYLVIA
SYLVIN *same as* > SYLVITE
SYLVINE *same as* > SYLVITE
SYLVINES > SYLVINE
SYLVINITE *n* rock containing sylvine
SYLVINS > SYLVIN
SYLVITE *n* soluble colourless, white, or coloured mineral
SYLVITES > SYLVITE
SYMAR *same as* > CYMAR
SYMARS > SYMAR
SYMBION *same as* > SYMBIONT
SYMBIONS > SYMBION
SYMBIONT *n* organism living in a state of symbiosis
SYMBIONTS > SYMBIONT
SYMBIOSES > SYMBIOSIS
SYMBIOSIS *n* close association of two species living together to their mutual benefit
SYMBIOT *same as* > SYMBIONT
SYMBIOTE *same as* > SYMBIONT
SYMBIOTES > SYMBIOTE
SYMBIOTIC > SYMBIOSIS
SYMBIOTS > SYMBIOT
SYMBOL *n* sign or thing that stands for something else ▷ *vb* be a symbol
SYMBOLE *same as* > CYMBAL
SYMBOLED > SYMBOL
SYMBOLES > SYMBOLE
SYMBOLIC *adj* of or relating to a symbol or symbols
SYMBOLICS *n* study of beliefs
SYMBOLING > SYMBOL
SYMBOLISE *same as* > SYMBOLIZE
SYMBOLISM *n* representation of something by symbols
SYMBOLIST *n* person who uses or can interpret symbols ▷ *adj* of, relating to, or characterizing symbolism or symbolists
SYMBOLIZE *vb* be a symbol of
SYMBOLLED > SYMBOL
SYMBOLOGY *n* use, study, or interpretation of symbols
SYMBOLS > SYMBOL
SYMITAR *same as* > SCIMITAR
SYMITARE *same as* > SCIMITAR
SYMITARES > SYMITARE

SYMITARS > SYMITAR
SYMMETRAL > SYMMETRY
SYMMETRIC *adj* (of a disease) affecting both sides of the body
SYMMETRY *n* state of having two halves that are mirror images of each other
SYMPATHIN *n* substance released at certain sympathetic nerve endings
SYMPATHY *n* compassion for someone's pain or distress
SYMPATICO *adj* nice
SYMPATRIC *adj* (of biological speciation or species) existing in the same geographical areas
SYMPATRY *n* existing of organisms together without interbreeding
SYMPETALY *n* quality of having petals that are united
SYMPHILE *n* insect that lives in the nests of social insects and is fed and reared by the inmates
SYMPHILES > SYMPHILE
SYMPHILY *n* presence of different kinds of animal in ants' nests
SYMPHONIC > SYMPHONY
SYMPHONY *n* composition for orchestra, with several movements
SYMPHYSES > SYMPHYSIS
SYMPHYSIS *n* growing together of parts or structures
SYMPHYTIC > SYMPHYSIS
SYMPLAST *n* continuous system of protoplasts, linked by plasmodesmata and bounded by the cell wall
SYMPLASTS > SYMPLAST
SYMPLOCE *n* word repetition in successive clauses
SYMPLOCES > SYMPLOCE
SYMPODIA > SYMPODIUM
SYMPODIAL > SYMPODIUM
SYMPODIUM *n* main axis of growth in the grapevine and similar plants
SYMPOSIA > SYMPOSIUM
SYMPOSIAC *adj* of, suitable for, or occurring at a symposium
SYMPOSIAL > SYMPOSIUM
SYMPOSIUM *n* conference for discussion of a particular topic
SYMPTOM *n* sign indicating the presence of an illness
SYMPTOMS > SYMPTOM
SYMPTOSES > SYMPTOSIS
SYMPTOSIS *n* wasting condition
SYMPTOTIC > SYMPTOSIS
SYN *adv* Scots word

for > SINCE
SYNAGOG *same as* > SYNAGOGUE
SYNAGOGAL > SYNAGOGUE
SYNAGOGS > SYNAGOG
SYNAGOGUE *n* Jewish place of worship and religious instruction
SYNALEPHA *n* elision of vowels in speech
SYNANDRIA *pl n* peculiar bunchings of stamens
SYNANGIA > SYNANGIUM
SYNANGIUM *n* junction between arteries
SYNANON *n* type of therapy given to drug addicts
SYNANONS > SYNANON
SYNANTHIC > SYNANTHY
SYNANTHY *n* abnormal joining between flowers
SYNAPHEA *n* continuity in metre of verses of poem
SYNAPHEAS > SYNAPHEA
SYNAPHEIA *same as* > SYNAPHEA
SYNAPSE *n* gap where nerve impulses pass between two nerve cells ▷ *vb* create a synapse
SYNAPSED > SYNAPSE
SYNAPSES > SYNAPSIS
SYNAPSID *n* prehistoric mammal-like reptile
SYNAPSIDS > SYNAPSID
SYNAPSING > SYNAPSE
SYNAPSIS *n* association in pairs of homologous chromosomes at the start of meiosis
SYNAPTASE *n* type of enzyme
SYNAPTE *n* litany in Greek Orthodox Church
SYNAPTES > SYNAPTE
SYNAPTIC *adj* of or relating to a synapse
SYNARCHY *n* joint rule
SYNASTRY *n* coincidence of astrological influences
SYNAXARIA *pl n* readings in the Greek Orthodox Church
SYNAXES > SYNAXIS
SYNAXIS *n* early Christian meeting
SYNC *n* synchronization ▷ *vb* synchronize
SYNCARP *n* fleshy multiple fruit
SYNCARPS > SYNCARP
SYNCARPY *n* quality of consisting of united carpels
SYNCED > SYNC
SYNCH *same as* > SYNC
SYNCHED > SYNCH
SYNCHING > SYNCH
SYNCHRO *n* type of electrical device
SYNCHRONY *n* state of being synchronous
SYNCHROS > SYNCHRO
SYNCHS > SYNCH

SYNCHYSES > SYNCHYSIS
SYNCHYSIS n muddled meaning
SYNCING > SYNC
SYNCLINAL > SYNCLINE
SYNCLINE n downward slope of stratified rock in which the layers dip towards each other from either side
SYNCLINES > SYNCLINE
SYNCOM n communications satellite in stationary orbit
SYNCOMS > SYNCOM
SYNCOPAL > SYNCOPE
SYNCOPATE vb stress the weak beats in (a rhythm) instead of the strong ones
SYNCOPE n omission of one or more sounds or letters from the middle of a word
SYNCOPES > SYNCOPE
SYNCOPIC > SYNCOPE
SYNCOPTIC > SYNCOPE
SYNCRETIC adj of the tendency of languages to reduce their use of inflection
SYNCS > SYNC
SYNCYTIA > SYNCYTIUM
SYNCYTIAL > SYNCYTIUM
SYNCYTIUM n mass of cytoplasm containing many nuclei and enclosed in a cell membrane
SYND same as > SYNE
SYNDACTYL adj (of certain animals) having two or more digits growing fused together ▷ n animal with this arrangement of digits
SYNDED > SYND
SYNDESES > SYNDESIS
SYNDESIS n use of syndetic constructions
SYNDET n synthetic detergent
SYNDETIC adj denoting a grammatical construction in which two clauses are connected by a conjunction
SYNDETON n syndetic construction
SYNDETONS > SYNDETON
SYNDETS > SYNDET
SYNDIC n business or legal agent of some universities or other institutions
SYNDICAL adj relating to the theory that syndicates of workers should seize the means of production
SYNDICATE n group of people or firms undertaking a joint business project ▷ vb publish (material) in several newspapers
SYNDICS > SYNDIC
SYNDING > SYND
SYNDINGS > SYND
SYNDROME n combination of symptoms indicating a

particular disease
SYNDROMES > SYNDROME
SYNDROMIC > SYNDROME
SYNDS > SYND
SYNE vb rinse ▷ n rinse ▷ adv since
SYNECHIA n abnormality of the eye
SYNECHIAS > SYNECHIA
SYNECIOUS adj having male and female organs together on a branch
SYNECTIC > SYNECTICS
SYNECTICS n method of identifying and solving problems that depends on creative thinking
SYNED > SYNE
SYNEDRIA > SYNEDRION
SYNEDRIAL > SYNEDRION
SYNEDRION n assembly of judges
SYNEDRIUM same as > SYNEDRION
SYNERESES > SYNERESIS
SYNERESIS n process in which a gel contracts on standing and exudes liquid
SYNERGIA same as > SYNERGY
SYNERGIAS > SYNERGIA
SYNERGIC > SYNERGY
SYNERGID n type of cell in embryo
SYNERGIDS > SYNERGID
SYNERGIES > SYNERGY
SYNERGISE same as > SYNERGIZE
SYNERGISM same as > SYNERGY
SYNERGIST n drug, muscle, etc, that increases the action of another ▷ adj of or relating to synergism
SYNERGIZE vb act in synergy
SYNERGY n working together of two or more people, substances, or things to produce an effect greater than the sum of their individual effects
SYNES > SYNE
SYNESES > SYNESIS
SYNESIS n grammatical construction in which the inflection or form of a word is conditioned by the meaning rather than the syntax
SYNESISES > SYNESIS
SYNFUEL n synthetic fuel
SYNFUELS > SYNFUEL
SYNGAMIC > SYNGAMY
SYNGAMIES > SYNGAMY
SYNGAMOUS > SYNGAMY
SYNGAMY n sexual reproduction
SYNGAS n mixture of carbon monoxide and hydrogen
SYNGASES > SYNGAS
SYNGASSES > SYNGAS
SYNGENEIC adj with

identical genes
SYNGENIC adj with the same genetic makeup
SYNGRAPH n document signed by several parties
SYNGRAPHS > SYNGRAPH
SYNING > SYNE
SYNIZESES > SYNIZESIS
SYNIZESIS n contraction of two vowels originally belonging to separate syllables into a single syllable
SYNKARYA > SYNKARYON
SYNKARYON n nucleus of a fertilized egg
SYNOD n church council
SYNODAL adj of or relating to a synod ▷ n money paid to a bishop by less senior members of the clergy at a synod
SYNODALS > SYNOD
SYNODIC adj relating to or involving a conjunction or two successive conjunctions of the same star, planet, or satellite
SYNODICAL > SYNOD
SYNODS > SYNOD
SYNODSMAN n layman at synod
SYNODSMEN > SYNODSMAN
SYNOECETE same as > SYNOEKETE
SYNOECISE same as > SYNOECIZE
SYNOECISM n union
SYNOECIZE vb unite
SYNOEKETE n insect that lives in the nests of social insects without receiving any attentions from the inmates
SYNOICOUS variant of > SYNECIOUS
SYNONYM n word with the same meaning as another
SYNONYME same as > SYNONYM
SYNONYMES > SYNONYME
SYNONYMIC > SYNONYM
SYNONYMS > SYNONYM
SYNONYMY n study of synonyms
SYNOPSES > SYNOPSIS
SYNOPSIS n summary or outline
SYNOPSISE same as > SYNOPSIZE
SYNOPSIZE vb make a synopsis of
SYNOPTIC adj of or relating to a synopsis ▷ n any of the three synoptic Gospels
SYNOPTICS > SYNOPTIC
SYNOPTIST > SYNOPTIC
SYNOVIA n clear thick fluid that lubricates the body joints
SYNOVIAL adj of or relating to the synovia
SYNOVIAS > SYNOVIA
SYNOVITIC > SYNOVITIS

SYNOVITIS n inflammation of the membrane surrounding a joint
SYNROC n titanium-ceramic substance that can incorporate nuclear waste in its crystals
SYNROCS > SYNROC
SYNTACTIC adj relating to or determined by syntax
SYNTAGM same as > SYNTAGMA
SYNTAGMA n syntactic unit or a word or phrase forming a syntactic unit
SYNTAGMAS > SYNTAGMA
SYNTAGMIC > SYNTAGMA
SYNTAGMS > SYNTAGM
SYNTAN n synthetic tanning substance
SYNTANS > SYNTAN
SYNTAX n way in which words are arranged to form phrases and sentences
SYNTAXES > SYNTAX
SYNTECTIC > SYNTEXIS
SYNTENIC > SYNTENY
SYNTENIES > SYNTENY
SYNTENY n presence of two or more genes on the same chromosome
SYNTEXIS n liquefaction
SYNTH n type of electrophonic musical instrument operated by a keyboard and pedals
SYNTHESES > SYNTHESIS
SYNTHESIS n combination of objects or ideas into a whole
SYNTHETIC adj (of a substance) made artificially ▷ n synthetic substance or material
SYNTHON n molecule used in synthesis
SYNTHONS > SYNTHON
SYNTHPOP n pop music using synthesizers
SYNTHPOPS > SYNTHPOP
SYNTHRONI pl n combined thrones for bishops and their subordinates
SYNTHS > SYNTH
SYNTONIC adj emotionally in harmony with one's environment
SYNTONIES > SYNTONY
SYNTONIN n substance in muscle
SYNTONINS > SYNTONIN
SYNTONISE same as > SYNTONIZE
SYNTONIZE vb make frequencies match
SYNTONOUS same as > SYNTONIC
SYNTONY n matching of frequencies
SYNURA n variety of microbe
SYNURAE > SYNURA

SYPE *same as* > SIPE
SYPED > SYPE
SYPES > SYPE
SYPH *shortening of* > SYPHILIS
SYPHER *vb* lap (a chamfered edge of one plank over that of another) in order to form a flush surface
SYPHERED > SYPHER
SYPHERING > SYPHER
SYPHERS > SYPHER
SYPHILIS *n* serious sexually transmitted disease
SYPHILISE *same as* > SYPHILIZE
SYPHILIZE *vb* infect with syphilis
SYPHILOID > SYPHILIS
SYPHILOMA *n* tumour or gumma caused by infection with syphilis
SYPHON *same as* > SIPHON
SYPHONED > SYPHON
SYPHONING > SYPHON
SYPHONS > SYPHON
SYPHS > SYPH
SYPING > SYPE
SYRAH *n* type of French red wine
SYRAHS > SYRAH
SYREN *same as* > SIREN
SYRENS > SYREN
SYRETTE *n* small disposable syringe
SYRETTES > SYRETTE
SYRINGA *n* mock orange or lilac
SYRINGAS > SYRINGA
SYRINGE *n* device for withdrawing or injecting fluids, consisting of a hollow cylinder, a piston, and a hollow needle ▷ *vb* wash out or inject with a syringe
SYRINGEAL > SYRINX
SYRINGED > SYRINGE
SYRINGES > SYRINX
SYRINGING > SYRINGE
SYRINX *n* vocal organ of a bird, which is situated in the lower part of the trachea
SYRINXES > SYRINX
SYRPHIAN *same as* > SYRPHID
SYRPHIANS > SYRPHIAN
SYRPHID *n* type of fly
SYRPHIDS > SYRPHID
SYRTES > SYRTIS
SYRTIS *n* area of quicksand
SYRUP *n* solution of sugar in water ▷ *vb* bring to the consistency of syrup
SYRUPED > SYRUP
SYRUPIER > SYRUPY
SYRUPIEST > SYRUPY
SYRUPING > SYRUP
SYRUPLIKE > SYRUP
SYRUPS > SYRUP
SYRUPY *adj* thick and sweet
SYSADMIN *n* computer system administrator
SYSADMINS > SYSADMIN
SYSOP *n* person who runs a system or network
SYSOPS > SYSOP
SYSSITIA *n* ancient Spartan communal meal
SYSSITIAS > SYSSITIA
SYSTALTIC *adj* (esp of the action of the heart) characterized by alternate contractions and dilations
SYSTEM *n* method or set of methods
SYSTEMED *adj* having system
SYSTEMIC *adj* affecting the entire animal or body ▷ *n* systemic pesticide, fungicide, etc
SYSTEMICS > SYSTEMIC
SYSTEMISE *same as* > SYSTEMIZE
SYSTEMIZE *vb* give a system to
SYSTEMS > SYSTEM
SYSTOLE *n* regular contraction of the heart as it pumps blood
SYSTOLES > SYSTOLE
SYSTOLIC > SYSTOLE
SYSTYLE *n* building with different types of columns
SYSTYLES > SYSTYLE
SYTHE *same as* > SITH
SYTHES > SYTHE
SYVER *n* street drain or the grating over it
SYVERS > SYVER
SYZYGAL > SYZYGY
SYZYGETIC > SYZYGY
SYZYGIAL > SYZYGY
SYZYGIES > SYZYGY
SYZYGY *n* either of the two positions of a celestial body when sun, earth, and the body lie in a straight line

# Tt

TA *interj* thank you

TAAL *n* language: usually, by implication, Afrikaans

TAALS > TAAL

TAATA *child's word for* > FATHER

TAATAS > TAATA

TAB *n* small flap or projecting label ▷ *vb* supply with a tab

TABANID *n* stout-bodied fly, the females of which have mouthparts specialized for sucking blood

TABANIDS > TABANID

TABARD *n* short sleeveless tunic decorated with a coat of arms, worn in medieval times

TABARDED *adj* wearing a tabard

TABARDS > TABARD

TABARET *n* hard-wearing fabric of silk or similar cloth with stripes of satin or moire, used esp for upholstery

TABARETS > TABARET

TABASHEER *n* dried bamboo sap, used medicinally

TABASHIR *same as* > TABASHEER

TABASHIRS > TABASHIR

TABBED > TAB

TABBIED > TABBY

TABBIES > TABBY

TABBINET *same as* > TABINET

TABBINETS > TABBINET

TABBING > TAB

TABBIS *n* silken cloth

TABBISES > TABBIS

TABBOULEH *n* kind of Middle Eastern salad made with cracked wheat, mint, parsley, and usually cucumber

TABBOULI *same as* > TABBOULEH

TABBOULIS > TABBOULI

TABBY *vb* make (eg a material) appear wavy ▷ *n* female domestic cat

TABBYHOOD *n* spinsterhood

TABBYING > TABBY

TABEFIED > TABEFY

TABEFIES > TABEFY

TABEFY *vb* emaciate or become emaciated

TABEFYING > TABEFY

TABELLION *n* scribe or notary authorized by the Roman Empire

TABER *old variant of* > TABOR

TABERD *same as* > TABARD

TABERDAR *n* holder of a scholarship at Queen's College, Oxford

TABERDARS > TABERDAR

TABERDS > TABERD

TABERED > TABER

TABERING > TABER

TABERS > TABER

TABES *n* wasting of a bodily organ or part

TABESCENT *adj* progressively emaciating

TABETIC > TABES

TABETICS > TABES

TABI *n* thick-soled Japanese sock, worn with sandals

TABID *adj* emaciated

TABINET *n* type of tabbied fabric

TABINETS > TABINET

TABIS > TABI

TABLA *n* one of a pair of Indian drums played with the hands

TABLAS > TABLA

TABLATURE *n* any of a number of forms of musical notation, esp for playing the lute, consisting of letters and signs indicating rhythm and fingering

TABLE *n* piece of furniture with a flat top supported by legs ▷ *vb* submit (a motion) for discussion by a meeting

TABLEAU *n* silent motionless group arranged to represent some scene

TABLEAUS > TABLEAU

TABLEAUX > TABLEAU

TABLED > TABLE

TABLEFUL > TABLE

TABLEFULS > TABLE

TABLELAND *n* high plateau

TABLELESS > TABLE

TABLEMATE *n* someone with whom one shares a table

TABLES > TABLE

TABLESFUL > TABLE

TABLET *n* medicinal pill ▷ *vb* make (something) into a tablet

TABLETED > TABLET

TABLETING > TABLET

TABLETOP *n* upper surface of a table

TABLETOPS > TABLETOP

TABLETS > TABLET

TABLETTED > TABLET

TABLEWARE *n* articles such as dishes, plates, knives, forks, etc, used at meals

TABLEWISE *adv* in the form of a table

TABLIER *n* (formerly) part of a dress resembling an apron

TABLIERS > TABLIER

TABLING > TABLE

TABLINGS > TABLE

TABLOID *n* small-sized newspaper with many photographs and a concise, usu sensational style

TABLOIDS > TABLOID

TABLOIDY *adj* characteristic of a tabloid newspaper; trashy

TABOGGAN *same as* > TOBOGGAN

TABOGGANS > TABOGGAN

TABOO *n* prohibition resulting from religious or social conventions ▷ *adj* forbidden by a taboo ▷ *vb* place under a taboo

TABOOED > TABOO

TABOOING > TABOO

TABOOLEY *variant of* > TABBOULEH

TABOOLEYS > TABOOLEY

TABOOS > TABOO

TABOR *vb* play the tabor

TABORED > TABOR

TABORER > TABOR

TABORERS > TABOR

TABORET *n* low stool, originally in the shape of a drum

**TABORETS** >TABORET
**TABORIN** *same as* >TABORET
**TABORINE** *same as* >TABOURIN
**TABORINES** >TABORINE
**TABORING** >TABOR
**TABORINS** >TABORIN
**TABORS** >TABOR
**TABOULEH** *variant of* >TABBOULEH
**TABOULEHS** >TABOULEH
**TABOULI** *same as* >TABBOULEH
**TABOULIS** >TABOULI
**TABOUR** *same as* >TABOR
**TABOURED** >TABOUR
**TABOURER** >TABOUR
**TABOURERS** >TABOUR
**TABOURET** *same as* >TABORET
**TABOURETS** >TABOURET
**TABOURIN** *same as* >TABORET
**TABOURING** >TABOUR
**TABOURINS** >TABOURIN
**TABOURS** >TABOUR
**TABRERE** *same as* >TABOR
**TABRERES** >TABRERE
**TABRET** *n* smaller version of a tabor
**TABRETS** >TABRET
**TABS** >TAB
**TABU** *same as* >TABOO
**TABUED** >TABU
**TABUING** >TABU
**TABULA** *n* tablet for writing on
**TABULABLE** >TABULATE
**TABULAE** >TABULA
**TABULAR** *adj* arranged in a table
**TABULARLY** >TABULAR
**TABULATE** *vb* arrange (information) in a table ▷ *adj* having a flat surface
**TABULATED** >TABULATE
**TABULATES** >TABULATE
**TABULATOR** *n* key on a typewriter or word processor that sets stops so that data can be arranged and presented in columns
**TABULI** *variant of* >TABBOULEH
**TABULIS** >TABULI
**TABUN** *n* organic compound used in chemical warfare as a lethal nerve gas
**TABUNS** >TABUN
**TABUS** >TABU
**TACAHOUT** *n* abnormal outgrowth on the tamarisk plant
**TACAHOUTS** >TACAHOUT
**TACAMAHAC** *n* any of several strong-smelling resinous gums obtained from certain trees, used in making ointments, incense, etc
**TACAN** *n* electronic ultrahigh-frequency navigation system for

aircraft which gives a continuous indication of bearing and distance from a transmitting station
**TACANS** >TACAN
**TACE** *same as* >TASSET
**TACES** >TACE
**TACET** *vb* (on a musical score) a direction indicating that a particular instrument or singer does not take part in a movement or part of a movement
**TACETED** >TACET
**TACETING** >TACET
**TACETS** >TACET
**TACH** *n* device for measuring speed
**TACHE** *n* buckle, clasp, or hook
**TACHES** >TACHE
**TACHINA** as in *tachina fly* bristly fly
**TACHINID** *n* type of fly
**TACHINIDS** >TACHINID
**TACHISM** *same as* >TACHISME
**TACHISME** *n* type of action painting evolved in France in which haphazard dabs and blots of colour are treated as a means of instinctive or unconscious expression
**TACHISMES** >TACHISME
**TACHISMS** >TACHISM
**TACHIST** >TACHISM
**TACHISTE** >TACHISME
**TACHISTES** >TACHISME
**TACHISTS** >TACHIST
**TACHO** *same as* >TACHOGRAM
**TACHOGRAM** *n* graphical record of readings
**TACHOS** >TACHO
**TACHS** >TACH
**TACHYLITE** *same as* >TACHYLYTE
**TACHYLYTE** *n* black basaltic glass often found on the edges of intrusions of basalt
**TACHYON** *n* hypothetical elementary particle capable of travelling faster than the velocity of light
**TACHYONIC** >TACHYON
**TACHYONS** >TACHYON
**TACHYPNEA** *n* abnormally rapid breathing
**TACIT** *adj* implied but not spoken
**TACITLY** >TACIT
**TACITNESS** >TACIT
**TACITURN** *adj* habitually uncommunicative
**TACK** *n* short nail with a large head ▷ *vb* fasten with tacks
**TACKBOARD** *n* noticeboard
**TACKED** >TACK
**TACKER** >TACK
**TACKERS** >TACK

**TACKET** *n* nail, esp a hobnail
**TACKETS** >TACKET
**TACKETY** >TACKET
**TACKEY** *same as* >TACKY
**TACKIER** >TACKY
**TACKIES** *pl n* tennis shoes or plimsolls
**TACKIEST** >TACKY
**TACKIFIED** >TACKIFY
**TACKIFIER** >TACKIFY
**TACKIFIES** >TACKIFY
**TACKIFY** *vb* give (eg rubber) a sticky feel
**TACKILY** >TACKY
**TACKINESS** >TACKY
**TACKING** >TACK
**TACKINGS** >TACK
**TACKLE** *vb* deal with (a task) ▷ *n* act of tackling an opposing player
**TACKLED** >TACKLE
**TACKLER** >TACKLE
**TACKLERS** >TACKLE
**TACKLES** >TACKLE
**TACKLESS** >TACK
**TACKLING** >TACKLE
**TACKLINGS** >TACKLE
**TACKS** >TACK
**TACKSMAN** *n* leaseholder, esp a tenant in the Highlands who sublets
**TACKSMEN** >TACKSMAN
**TACKY** *adj* slightly sticky
**TACMAHACK** *same as* >TACAMAHAC
**TACNODE** *n* in maths, point at which two branches of a curve have a common tangent, each branch extending in both directions of the tangent
**TACNODES** >TACNODE
**TACO** *n* tortilla fried until crisp, served with a filling
**TACONITE** *n* fine-grained sedimentary rock containing magnetite, haematite, and silica, which occurs in the Lake Superior region: a low-grade iron ore
**TACONITES** >TACONITE
**TACOS** >TACO
**TACRINE** *n* drug used to treat Alzheimer's disease
**TACRINES** >TACRINE
**TACT** *n* skill in avoiding giving offence
**TACTFUL** >TACT
**TACTFULLY** >TACT
**TACTIC** *n* method or plan to achieve an end
**TACTICAL** *adj* of or employing tactics
**TACTICIAN** >TACTICS
**TACTICITY** *n* quality of regularity in the arrangement of repeated units within a polymer chain
**TACTICS** *n* art of directing military forces in battle
**TACTILE** *adj* of or having

the sense of touch
**TACTILELY** >TACTILE
**TACTILIST** *n* artist whose work strives to appeal to the sense of touch
**TACTILITY** >TACTILE
**TACTION** *n* act of touching
**TACTIONS** >TACTION
**TACTISM** *another word for* >TAXIS
**TACTISMS** >TACTISM
**TACTLESS** >TACT
**TACTS** >TACT
**TACTUAL** *adj* caused by touch
**TACTUALLY** >TACTUAL
**TAD** *n* small bit or piece
**TADDIE** *short for* >TADPOLE
**TADDIES** >TADDIE
**TADPOLE** *n* limbless tailed larva of a frog or toad
**TADPOLES** >TADPOLE
**TADS** >TAD
**TADVANCE** *vb* Spenserian form of advance
**TAE** *Scots form of the verb* >TOE
**TAED** >TAE
**TAEDIUM** *archaic spelling of* >TEDIUM
**TAEDIUMS** >TAEDIUM
**TAEING** >TAE
**TAEKWONDO** *n* Korean martial art
**TAEL** *n* unit of weight, used in the Far East, having various values between one to two and a half ounces
**TAELS** >TAEL
**TAENIA** *n* (in ancient Greece) a narrow fillet or headband for the hair
**TAENIAE** >TAENIA
**TAENIAS** >TAENIA
**TAENIASES** >TAENIASIS
**TAENIASIS** *n* infestation with tapeworms
**TAENIATE** *adj* ribbon-like
**TAENIOID** *adj* ribbon-like
**TAES** >TAE
**TAFFAREL** *same as* >TAFFRAIL
**TAFFARELS** >TAFFAREL
**TAFFEREL** *same as* >TAFFRAIL
**TAFFERELS** >TAFFEREL
**TAFFETA** *n* shiny silk or rayon fabric
**TAFFETAS** *same as* >TAFFETA
**TAFFETIES** >TAFFETY
**TAFFETY** *same as* >TAFFETA
**TAFFIA** *same as* >TAFIA
**TAFFIAS** >TAFFIA
**TAFFIES** >TAFFY
**TAFFRAIL** *n* rail at the back of a ship or boat
**TAFFRAILS** >TAFFRAIL
**TAFFY** *same as* >TOFFEE
**TAFIA** *n* type of rum, esp from Guyana or the Caribbean
**TAFIAS** >TAFIA

**TAG** *n* label bearing information ▷ *vb* attach a tag to

**TAGALONG** *n* one who trails behind, esp uninvited; a hanger-on

**TAGALONGS** > TAGALONG

**TAGAREEN** *n* junk shop

**TAGAREENS** > TAGAREEN

**TAGBOARD** *n* sturdy form of cardboard

**TAGBOARDS** > TAGBOARD

**TAGETES** *n* any of a genus of plants with yellow or orange flowers, including the French and African marigolds

**TAGGANT** *n* microscopic material added to substance to identify it

**TAGGANTS** > TAGGANT

**TAGGED** > TAG

**TAGGEE** *n* one who has been made to wear a tag

**TAGGEES** > TAGGEE

**TAGGER** *n* one who marks with a tag

**TAGGERS** > TAGGER

**TAGGIER** > TAGGY

**TAGGIEST** > TAGGY

**TAGGING** > TAG

**TAGGINGS** > TAG

**TAGGY** *adj* (of wool, hair, etc) matted

**TAGHAIRM** *n* form of divination once practised in the Highlands of Scotland

**TAGHAIRMS** > TAGHAIRM

**TAGINE** *n* large, heavy N African cooking pot with a conical lid

**TAGINES** > TAGINE

**TAGLIKE** *adj* resembling a tag

**TAGLINE** *n* funny line of joke

**TAGLINES** > TAGLINE

**TAGLIONI** *n* type of coat

**TAGLIONIS** > TAGLIONI

**TAGMA** *n* distinct region of the body of an arthropod, such as the head, thorax, or abdomen of an insect

**TAGMATA** > TAGMA

**TAGMEME** *n* class of speech elements all of which may fulfil the same grammatical role in a sentence

**TAGMEMES** > TAGMEME

**TAGMEMIC** > TAGMEME

**TAGMEMICS** > TAGMEME

**TAGRAG** *same as* > RAGTAG

**TAGRAGS** > TAGRAG

**TAGS** > TAG

**TAGUAN** *n* large nocturnal flying squirrel of high forests in the East Indies that uses its long tail as a rudder

**TAGUANS** > TAGUAN

**TAHA** *n* type of South African bird

**TAHAS** > TAHA

**TAHINA** *same as* > TAHINI

**TAHINAS** > TAHINA

**TAHINI** *n* paste made from ground sesame seeds, used esp in Middle Eastern cookery

**TAHINIS** > TAHINI

**TAHOU** *same as* > SILVEREYE

**TAHOUS** > TAHOU

**TAHR** *n* goatlike bovid mammal of mountainous regions of S and SW Asia, having a shaggy coat and curved horns

**TAHRS** > TAHR

**TAHSIL** *n* administrative division of a zila in certain states in India

**TAHSILDAR** *n* officer in charge of the collection of revenues, etc, in a tahsil

**TAHSILS** > TAHSIL

**TAI** as in *tai chi chuan* Chinese system of callisthenics characterized by coordinated and rhythmic movements

**TAIAHA** *n* carved weapon in the form of a staff, now used in Māori ceremonial oratory

**TAIAHAS** > TAIAHA

**TAIG** *n* often derogatory term for Roman Catholic

**TAIGA** *n* belt of coniferous forest extending across much of subarctic North America, Europe, and Asia

**TAIGAS** > TAIGA

**TAIGLACH** *same as* > TEIGLACH

**TAIGLE** *vb* entangle or impede

**TAIGLED** > TAIGLE

**TAIGLES** > TAIGLE

**TAIGLING** > TAIGLE

**TAIGS** > TAIG

**TAIHOA** *interj* hold on! no hurry!

**TAIKONAUT** *n* astronaut from the People's Republic of China

**TAIL** *n* rear part of an animal's body, usu forming a flexible appendage ▷ *adj* at the rear ▷ *vb* follow (someone) secretly

**TAILARD** *n* one having a tail

**TAILARDS** > TAILARD

**TAILBACK** *n* queue of traffic stretching back from an obstruction

**TAILBACKS** > TAILBACK

**TAILBOARD** *n* removable or hinged rear board on a truck etc

**TAILBONE** *nontechnical name for* > COCCYX

**TAILBONES** > TAILBONE

**TAILCOAT** *n* man's black coat having a horizontal cut over the hips and a tapering tail with a vertical slit up to the waist

**TAILCOATS** > TAILCOAT

**TAILED** > TAIL

**TAILENDER** *n* (in cricket) the batter last in the batting order

**TAILER** *n* one that tails

**TAILERON** *n* aileron located on the tailplane of an aircraft

**TAILERONS** > TAILERON

**TAILERS** > TAILER

**TAILFAN** *n* fanned structure at the hind end of a lobster or related crustacean, formed from the telson and uropods

**TAILFANS** > TAILFAN

**TAILFIN** *n* decorative projection at back of car

**TAILFINS** > TAILFIN

**TAILFLIES** > TAILFLY

**TAILFLY** *n* in angling, the lowest fly on a wet-fly cast

**TAILGATE** *n* door at the rear of a hatchback vehicle ▷ *vb* drive very close behind (a vehicle)

**TAILGATED** > TAILGATE

**TAILGATER** > TAILGATE

**TAILGATES** > TAILGATE

**TAILING** *n* part of a beam, rafter, projecting brick or stone, etc, embedded in a wall

**TAILINGS** *pl n* waste left over after certain processes, such as from an ore-crushing plant or in milling grain

**TAILLAMP** *n* rear light

**TAILLAMPS** > TAILLAMP

**TAILLE** *n* (in France before 1789) a tax levied by a king or overlord on his subjects

**TAILLES** > TAILLE

**TAILLESS** > TAIL

**TAILLEUR** *n* woman's suit

**TAILLEURS** > TAILLEUR

**TAILLIE** *n* (in law) the limitation of an estate or interest to a person and the heirs of his body

**TAILLIES** > TAILLIE

**TAILLIGHT** *same as* > TAILLAMP

**TAILLIKE** *adj* resembling a tail

**TAILOR** *n* person who makes men's clothes ▷ *vb* cut or style (a garment) to specific requirements

**TAILORED** > TAILOR

**TAILORESS** *n* female tailor

**TAILORING** > TAILOR

**TAILORS** > TAILOR

**TAILPIECE** *n* piece added at the end of something, for example a report

**TAILPIPE** *vb* attach an object, esp a tin can, to the tail of an animal

**TAILPIPED** > TAILPIPE

**TAILPIPES** > TAILPIPE

**TAILPLANE** *n* small stabilizing wing at the rear of an aircraft

**TAILRACE** *n* channel that carries water away from a water wheel, turbine, etc

**TAILRACES** > TAILRACE

**TAILS** *adv* with the side of a coin that does not have a portrait of a head on it uppermost

**TAILSKID** *n* runner under the tail of an aircraft

**TAILSKIDS** > TAILSKID

**TAILSLIDE** *n* backwards descent of an aeroplane after stalling while in an upward trajectory

**TAILSPIN** *n* uncontrolled spinning dive of an aircraft

**TAILSPINS** > TAILSPIN

**TAILSTOCK** *n* casting that slides on the bed of a lathe in alignment with the headstock and is locked in position to support the free end of a workpiece

**TAILWATER** *n* water flowing in a tailrace

**TAILWHEEL** *n* wheel fitted to the rear of a vehicle, esp the landing wheel under the tail of an aircraft

**TAILWIND** *n* wind coming from the rear

**TAILWINDS** > TAILWIND

**TAILYE** *same as* > TAILLIE

**TAILYES** > TAILYE

**TAILZIE** *same as* > TAILLIE

**TAILZIES** > TAILZIE

**TAIN** *n* tinfoil used in backing mirrors

**TAINS** > TAIN

**TAINT** *vb* spoil with a small amount of decay, contamination, or other bad quality ▷ *n* something that taints

**TAINTED** > TAINT

**TAINTING** > TAINT

**TAINTLESS** > TAINT

**TAINTS** > TAINT

**TAINTURE** *n* contamination; staining

**TAINTURES** > TAINTURE

**TAIPAN** *n* large poisonous Australian snake

**TAIPANS** > TAIPAN

**TAIRA** *same as* > TAYRA

**TAIRAS** > TAIRA

**TAIS** > TAI

**TAISCH** *n* (in Scotland) apparition of a person whose death is imminent

**TAISCHES** > TAISCH

**TAISH** *same as* > TAISCH

**TAISHES** > TAISH

**TAIT** *same as* > TATE

**TAITS** > TAIT

**TAIVER** *same as* > TAVER

**TAIVERED** > TAIVER

**TAIVERING** > TAIVER

**TAIVERS** > TAIVER

**TAIVERT** *adj* Scots word meaning confused or bewildered

**TAJ** *n* tall conical cap worn as a mark of distinction by Muslims

**TAJES** > TAJ

**TAJINE** *same as* > TAGINE

**TAJINES** > TAJINE

**TAK** *Scots variant spelling of* > TAKE

**TAKA** *n* standard monetary unit of Bangladesh, divided into 100 paise

**TAKABLE** > TAKE

**TAKAHE** *n* very rare flightless New Zealand bird

**TAKAHES** > TAKAHE

**TAKAMAKA** *same as* > TACAMAHAC

**TAKAMAKAS** > TAKAMAKA

**TAKAS** > TAKA

**TAKE** *vb* remove from a place ▷ *n* one of a series of recordings from which the best will be used

**TAKEABLE** > TAKE

**TAKEAWAY** *adj* (of food) sold for consumption away from the premises ▷ *n* shop or restaurant selling meals for eating elsewhere

**TAKEAWAYS** > TAKEAWAY

**TAKEDOWN** *n* disassembly

**TAKEDOWNS** > TAKEDOWN

**TAKEN** > TAKE

**TAKEOFF** *n* act or process of making an aircraft airborne

**TAKEOFFS** > TAKEOFF

**TAKEOUT** *n* shop or restaurant that sells such food

**TAKEOUTS** > TAKEOUT

**TAKEOVER** *n* act of taking control of a company by buying a large number of its shares

**TAKEOVERS** > TAKEOVER

**TAKER** *n* person who agrees to take something that is offered

**TAKERS** > TAKER

**TAKES** > TAKE

**TAKEUP** *n* the claiming or acceptance of something, esp a state benefit, that is due or available

**TAKEUPS** > TAKEUP

**TAKHI** *n* type of wild Mongolian horse

**TAKHIS** > TAKHI

**TAKI** *same as* > TAKHIW

**TAKIER** > TAKY

**TAKIEST** > TAKY

**TAKIN** *n* massive bovid mammal of mountainous regions of S Asia, having a shaggy coat, short legs, and horns that point backwards and upwards

**TAKING** > TAKE

**TAKINGLY** > TAKE

**TAKINGS** > TAKE

**TAKINS** > TAKIN

**TAKIS** > TAKI

**TAKKIES** *same as* > TACKIES

**TAKS** > TAK

**TAKY** *adj* appealing

**TALA** *n* standard monetary unit of Samoa, divided into 100 sene

**TALAK** *same as* > TALAQ

**TALAKS** > TALAK

**TALANT** *old variant of* > TALON

**TALANTS** > TALANT

**TALAPOIN** *n* smallest of the guenon monkeys of swampy central W African forests, having olive-green fur and slightly webbed digits

**TALAPOINS** > TALAPOIN

**TALAQ** *n* Muslim form of divorce

**TALAQS** > TALAQ

**TALAR** *n* ankle-length robe

**TALARIA** *pl n* winged sandals, such as those worn by Hermes

**TALARS** > TALAR

**TALAS** > TALA

**TALAUNT** *old variant of* > TALON

**TALAUNTS** > TALAUNT

**TALAYOT** *n* ancient Balearic stone tower

**TALAYOTS** > TALAYOT

**TALBOT** *n* (formerly) an ancient breed of large hound, usually white or light-coloured, having pendulous ears and strong powers of scent

**TALBOTS** > TALBOT

**TALBOTYPE** *n* early type of photographic process (invented by W H Fox Talbot) or a photograph produced using it

**TALC** *n* talcum powder ▷ *vb* apply talc to ▷ *adj* of, or relating to, talc

**TALCED** > TALC

**TALCIER** > TALCY

**TALCIEST** > TALCY

**TALCING** > TALC

**TALCKED** > TALCKY

**TALCKIER** > TALCKY

**TALCKIEST** > TALCKY

**TALCKING** > TALCKY

**TALCKY** *same as* > TALCY

**TALCOSE** > TALC

**TALCOUS** > TALC

**TALCS** > TALC

**TALCUM** *n* white, grey, brown, or pale green mineral, found in metamorphic rocks. It is used in the manufacture of talcum powder and electrical insulatorsr

**TALCUMS** > TALCUM

**TALCY** *adj* like, containing, or covered in talc

**TALE** *n* story

**TALEA** *n* rhythmic pattern in certain mediaeval choral compositions

**TALEAE** > TALEA

**TALEFUL** *adj* having many tales

**TALEGALLA** *n* brush turkey, of New Guinea and Australia

**TALEGGIO** *n* Italian cheese

**TALEGGIOS** > TALEGGIO

**TALENT** *n* natural ability

**TALENTED** > TALENT

**TALENTS** > TALENT

**TALER** *same as* > THALER

**TALERS** > TALER

**TALES** *n* group of persons summoned from among those present in court or from bystanders to fill vacancies on a jury panel

**TALESMAN** > TALES

**TALESMEN** > TALES

**TALEYSIM** > TALLITH

**TALI** > TALUS

**TALIGRADE** *adj* (of mammals) walking on the outer side of the foot

**TALION** *n* system or legal principle of making the punishment correspond to the crime

**TALIONIC** *adj* of or relating to talion

**TALIONS** > TALION

**TALIPAT** *same as* > TALIPOT

**TALIPATS** > TALIPAT

**TALIPED** *adj* having a club foot ▷ *n* club-footed person

**TALIPEDS** > TALIPED

**TALIPES** *n* congenital deformity of the foot by which it is twisted in any of various positions

**TALIPOT** *n* palm tree of the East Indies, having large leaves that are used for fans, thatching houses, etc

**TALIPOTS** > TALIPOT

**TALISMAN** *n* object believed to have magic power

**TALISMANS** > TALISMAN

**TALK** *vb* express ideas or feelings by means of speech ▷ *n* speech or lecture

**TALKABLE** > TALK

**TALKATHON** *n* epic bout of discussion or speechifying

**TALKATIVE** *adj* fond of talking

**TALKBACK** *n* broadcast in which telephone comments or questions from the public are transmitted live

**TALKBACKS** > TALKBACK

**TALKBOX** *n* voice box

**TALKBOXES** > TALKBOX

**TALKED** > TALK

**TALKER** > TALK

**TALKERS** > TALK

**TALKFEST** *n* lengthy discussion

**TALKFESTS** > TALKFEST

**TALKIE** *n* early film with a soundtrack

**TALKIER** > TALKY

**TALKIES** > TALKIE

**TALKIEST** > TALKY

**TALKINESS** *n* quality or condition of being talky

**TALKING** *n* speech; the act of speaking

**TALKINGS** > TALKING

**TALKS** > TALK

**TALKY** *adj* containing too much dialogue or inconsequential talk

**TALL** *adj* higher than average

**TALLAGE** *n* tax levied by the Norman and early Angevin kings on their Crown lands and royal towns ▷ *vb* levy a tax (upon)

**TALLAGED** > TALLAGE

**TALLAGES** > TALLAGE

**TALLAGING** > TALLAGE

**TALLAISIM** > TALLITH

**TALLAT** *same as* > TALLET

**TALLATS** > TALLAT

**TALLBOY** *n* high chest of drawers

**TALLBOYS** > TALLBOY

**TALLENT** *n* plenty

**TALLENTS** > TALLENT

**TALLER** > TALL

**TALLET** *n* loft

**TALLETS** > TALLET

**TALLGRASS** *n* long grass in North American prairie

**TALLIABLE** *adj* taxable

**TALLIATE** *vb* levy a tax

**TALLIATED** > TALLIATE

**TALLIATES** > TALLIATE

**TALLIED** > TALLY

**TALLIER** > TALLY

**TALLIERS** > TALLY

**TALLIES** > TALLY

**TALLIS** *variant of* > TALLITH

**TALLISES** > TALLIS

**TALLISH** *adj* quite tall

**TALLISIM** > TALLITH

**TALLIT** *variant of* > TALLITH

**TALLITES** > TALLIT

**TALLITH** *n* white shawl with fringed corners worn over the head and shoulders by Jewish males during religious services

**TALLITHES** > TALLITH

**TALLITHIM** > TALLITH

**TALLITHS** > TALLITH

**TALLITIM** > TALLIT

**TALLITOT** > TALLIT

**TALLITOTH** > TALLITH

**TALLITS** > TALLIT

**TALLNESS** > TALL

**TALLOL** *n* oily liquid used for making soaps, lubricants, etc

**TALLOLS** > TALLOL

**TALLOT** *same as* > TALLET

**TALLOTS** > TALLOT

**TALLOW** *n* hard animal fat

used to make candles ▷ *vb* cover or smear with tallow

**TALLOWED** > TALLOW

**TALLOWING** > TALLOW

**TALLOWISH** > TALLOW

**TALLOWS** > TALLOW

**TALLOWY** > TALLOW

**TALLS** > TALL

**TALLY** *vb* (of two things) correspond ▷ *n* record of a debt or score

**TALLYHO** *n* cry of a participant at a hunt to encourage the hounds when the quarry is sighted ▷ *vb* to make the cry of tallyho

**TALLYHOED** > TALLYHO

**TALLYHOS** > TALLYHO

**TALLYING** > TALLY

**TALLYMAN** *n* scorekeeper or recorder

**TALLYMEN** > TALLYMAN

**TALLYSHOP** *n* shop that allows customers to pay in instalments

**TALMA** *n* short cloak

**TALMAS** > TALMA

**TALMUD** *n* primary source of Jewish religious law, consisting of the Mishnah and the Gemara

**TALMUDIC** > TALMUD

**TALMUDISM** > TALMUD

**TALMUDS** > TALMUD

**TALON** *n* bird's hooked claw

**TALONED** > TALON

**TALONS** > TALON

**TALOOKA** *same as* > TALUK

**TALOOKAS** > TALOOKA

**TALPA** *n* sebaceous cyst

**TALPAE** > TALPA

**TALPAS** > TALPA

**TALUK** *n* subdivision of a district

**TALUKA** *same as* > TALUK

**TALUKAS** > TALUKA

**TALUKDAR** *n* person in charge of a taluk

**TALUKDARS** > TALUKDAR

**TALUKS** > TALUK

**TALUS** *n* bone of the ankle that articulates with the leg bones to form the ankle joint

**TALUSES** > TALUS

**TALWEG** *same as* > THALWEG

**TALWEGS** > TALWEG

**TAM** *n* tam-o'-shanter

**TAMABLE** > TAME

**TAMAL** *same as* > TAMALE

**TAMALE** *n* Mexican dish made of minced meat mixed with crushed maize and seasonings, wrapped in maize husks and steamed

**TAMALES** > TAMALE

**TAMALS** > TAMAL

**TAMANDU** *same as* > TAMANDUA

**TAMANDUA** *n* small arboreal edentate mammal

**TAMANDUAS** > TAMANDUA

**TAMANDUS** > TAMANDU

**TAMANOIR** *n* anteater

**TAMANOIRS** > TAMANOIR

**TAMANU** *n* poon tree

**TAMANUS** > TAMANU

**TAMARA** *n* powder consisting of cloves, cinnamon, fennel, coriander, etc, used in certain cuisines

**TAMARACK** *n* North American larch, with reddish-brown bark, bluish-green needle-like leaves, and shiny oval cones

**TAMARACKS** > TAMARACK

**TAMARAO** *same as* > TAMARAU

**TAMARAOS** > TAMARAO

**TAMARAS** > TAMARA

**TAMARAU** *n* small rare member of the cattle tribe of lowland areas of Mindoro in the Philippines

**TAMARAUS** > TAMARAU

**TAMARI** *n* Japanese variety of soy sauce

**TAMARILLO** *n* shrub with a red oval edible fruit

**TAMARIN** *n* small monkey of South and Central American forests

**TAMARIND** *n* tropical tree

**TAMARINDS** > TAMARIND

**TAMARINS** > TAMARIN

**TAMARIS** > TAMARI

**TAMARISK** *n* evergreen shrub with slender branches and feathery flower clusters

**TAMARISKS** > TAMARISK

**TAMASHA** *n* (in India) a show

**TAMASHAS** > TAMASHA

**TAMBAC** *same as* > TOMBAC

**TAMBACS** > TAMBAC

**TAMBAK** *same as* > TOMBAC

**TAMBAKS** > TAMBAK

**TAMBALA** *n* unit of Malawian currency

**TAMBALAS** > TAMBALA

**TAMBER** *same as* > TIMBRE

**TAMBERS** > TAMBER

**TAMBOUR** *n* embroidery frame, consisting of two hoops over which the fabric is stretched while being worked ▷ *vb* embroider (fabric or a design) on a tambour

**TAMBOURAS** > TAMBOURA

**TAMBOURED** > TAMBOUR

**TAMBOURER** *n* one who embroiders on a tambour

**TAMBOURIN** *n* 18th-century Provençal folk dance

**TAMBOURS** > TAMBOUR

**TAMBUR** *n* old Turkish stringed instrument

**TAMBURA** *n* Middle-Eastern stringed instrument with a long neck, related to the tambur

**TAMBURAS** > TAMBURA

**TAMBURIN** *same as* > TAMBURIN

**TAMBURINS** > TAMBURIN

**TAMBURS** > TAMBUR

**TAME** *adj* (of animals) brought under human control ▷ *vb* make tame

**TAMEABLE** > TAME

**TAMED** > TAME

**TAMEIN** *n* Burmese skirt

**TAMEINS** > TAMEIN

**TAMELESS** > TAME

**TAMELY** > TAME

**TAMENESS** > TAME

**TAMER** > TAME

**TAMERS** > TAME

**TAMES** > TAME

**TAMEST** > TAME

**TAMIN** *n* thin woollen fabric

**TAMINE** *same as* > TAMIN

**TAMINES** > TAMINE

**TAMING** *n* act of making (something) tame

**TAMINGS** > TAMING

**TAMINS** > TAMIN

**TAMIS** *same as* > TAMMY

**TAMISE** *n* type of thin cloth

**TAMISES** > TAMIS

**TAMMAR** *n* small scrub wallaby of Australia, with a thick dark-coloured coat

**TAMMARS** > TAMMAR

**TAMMIE** *n* short for tam-o'shanter, a traditional Scottish hat

**TAMMIED** > TAMMY

**TAMMIES** > TAMMY

**TAMMY** *n* glazed woollen or mixed fabric, used for linings, undergarments, etc ▷ *vb* (esp formerly) to strain (sauce, soup, etc) through a tammy

**TAMMYING** > TAMMY

**TAMOXIFEN** *n* drug that antagonizes the action of oestrogen and is used to treat breast cancer and some types of infertility in women

**TAMP** *vb* pack down by repeated taps

**TAMPALA** *n* Asian plant (Amaranthus tricolor), eaten as food

**TAMPALAS** > TAMPALA

**TAMPAN** *n* biting mite

**TAMPANS** > TAMPAN

**TAMPED** > TAMP

**TAMPER** *vb* interfere ▷ *n* person or thing that tamps, esp an instrument for packing down tobacco in a pipe

**TAMPERED** > TAMPER

**TAMPERER** > TAMPER

**TAMPERERS** > TAMPER

**TAMPERING** > TAMPER

**TAMPERS** > TAMPER

**TAMPING** *adj* very angry ▷ *n* act or instance of tamping

**TAMPINGS** > TAMPING

**TAMPION** *n* plug placed in a gun's muzzle when the gun is not in use to keep out moisture and dust

**TAMPIONS** > TAMPION

**TAMPON** *n* absorbent plug of cotton wool inserted into the vagina during menstruation ▷ *vb* use a tampon

**TAMPONADE** > TAMPON

**TAMPONAGE** > TAMPON

**TAMPONED** > TAMPON

**TAMPONING** > TAMPON

**TAMPONS** > TAMPON

**TAMPS** > TAMP

**TAMS** > TAM

**TAMWORTH** *n* any of a hardy rare breed of long-bodied reddish pigs

**TAMWORTHS** > TAMWORTH

**TAN** *n* brown coloration of the skin from exposure to sunlight ▷ *vb* (of skin) go brown from exposure to sunlight ▷ *adj* yellowish-brown

**TANA** *n* small Madagascan lemur

**TANADAR** *n* commanding officer of an Indian police station

**TANADARS** > TANADAR

**TANAGER** *n* any American songbird of the family *Thraupidae*, having a short thick bill and a brilliantly coloured male plumage

**TANAGERS** > TANAGER

**TANAGRA** *n* type of tanager

**TANAGRAS** > TANAGRA

**TANAGRINE** *adj* of or relating to the tanager

**TANAISTE** *n* prime minister of the Republic of Ireland

**TANAISTES** > TANAISTE

**TANALISED** *adj* having been treated with the trademarked timber preservative Tanalith

**TANALIZED** *same as* > TANALISED

**TANAS** > TANA

**TANBARK** *n* bark of certain trees, esp the oak and hemlock, used as a source of tannin

**TANBARKS** > TANBARK

**TANDEM** *n* bicycle for two riders, one behind the other

**TANDEMS** > TANDEM

**TANDOOR** *n* type of Indian clay oven

**TANDOORI** *adj* (of food) cooked in an Indian clay oven ▷ *n* Indian method of cooking meat or vegetables on a spit in a clay oven

TANDOORIS > TANDOORI
TANDOORS > TANDOOR
TANE old Scottish variant of > TAKEN
TANG n strong taste or smell ▷ vb cause to ring
TANGA n triangular loincloth worn by indigenous peoples in tropical America
TANGAS > TANGA
TANGED > TANG
TANGELO n hybrid produced by crossing a tangerine tree with a grapefruit tree
TANGELOS > TANGELO
TANGENCE n touching
TANGENCES > TANGENCE
TANGENCY > TANGENT
TANGENT n line that touches a curve without intersecting it
TANGENTAL > TANGENT
TANGENTS > TANGENT
TANGERINE n small orange-like fruit of an Asian citrus tree ▷ adj reddish-orange
TANGHIN n strong poison formerly used in Madagascar to determine the guilt or otherwise of crime suspects
TANGHININ n active ingredient in tanghin
TANGHINS > TANGHIN
TANGI n Māori funeral ceremony
TANGIBLE adj able to be touched ▷ n tangible thing or asset
TANGIBLES > TANGIBLE
TANGIBLY > TANGIBLE
TANGIE n water spirit of Orkney, appearing as a figure draped in seaweed, or as a seahorse
TANGIER > TANGY
TANGIES > TANGIE
TANGIEST > TANGY
TANGINESS > TANGY
TANGING > TANG
TANGIS > TANGI
TANGLE n confused mass or situation ▷ vb twist together in a tangle
TANGLED > TANGLE
TANGLER > TANGLE
TANGLERS > TANGLE
TANGLES > TANGLE
TANGLIER > TANGLE
TANGLIEST > TANGLE
TANGLING n act or condition of tangling
TANGLINGS > TANGLING
TANGLY > TANGLE
TANGO n S American dance ▷ vb dance a tango
TANGOED > TANGO
TANGOES > TANGO
TANGOING > TANGO
TANGOIST > TANGO
TANGOISTS > TANGO

TANGOLIKE > TANGO
TANGOS > TANGO
TANGRAM n Chinese puzzle in which a square, cut into a parallelogram, a square, and five triangles, is formed into figures
TANGRAMS > TANGRAM
TANGS > TANG
TANGUN n small and sturdy Tibetan pony
TANGUNS > TANGUN
TANGY adj having a pungent, fresh, or briny flavour or aroma
TANH n hyperbolic tangent
TANHS > TANH
TANIST n heir apparent of a Celtic chieftain chosen by election during the chief's lifetime: usually the worthiest of his kin
TANISTRY > TANIST
TANISTS > TANIST
TANIWHA n mythical Māori monster that lives in water
TANIWHAS > TANIWHA
TANK n container for liquids or gases ▷ vb put or keep in a tank
TANKA n Japanese verse form consisting of five lines, the first and third having five syllables, the others seven
TANKAGE n capacity or contents of a tank or tanks
TANKAGES > TANKAGE
TANKARD n large beer-mug, often with a hinged lid
TANKARDS > TANKARD
TANKAS > TANKA
TANKED > TANK
TANKER n ship or truck for carrying liquid in bulk
TANKERS > TANKER
TANKFUL n quantity contained in a tank
TANKFULS > TANKFUL
TANKIA n type of boat used in Canton
TANKIAS > TANKIA
TANKIES > TANKY
TANKING n heavy defeat
TANKINGS > TANKING
TANKINI n woman's two-piece swimming costume consisting of a vest or camisole top and bikini briefs
TANKINIS > TANKINI
TANKLESS > TANK
TANKLIKE > TANK
TANKS > TANK
TANKSHIP same as > TANKER
TANKSHIPS > TANKSHIP
TANKY n die-hard communist
TANLING n suntanned person
TANLINGS > TANLING
TANNA n Indian police station or army base
TANNABLE > TAN

TANNAGE n act or process of tanning
TANNAGES > TANNAGE
TANNAH same as > TANNA
TANNAHS > TANNAH
TANNAS > TANNA
TANNATE n any salt or ester of tannic acid
TANNATES > TANNATE
TANNED > TAN
TANNER > TAN
TANNERIES > TANNERY
TANNERS > TAN
TANNERY n place where hides are tanned
TANNEST > TAN
TANNIC adj of, containing, or produced from tannin or tannic acid
TANNIE n in S Africa, title of respect used to refer to an elderly woman
TANNIES > TANNIE
TANNIN n vegetable substance used in tanning
TANNING > TAN
TANNINGS > TAN
TANNINS > TANNIN
TANNISH > TAN
TANNOY n sound-amplifying apparatus used as a public-address system esp in a large building, such as a university ▷ vb announce (something) using a Tannoy system
TANNOYED > TANNOY
TANNOYING > TANNOY
TANNOYS > TANNOY
TANREC same as > TENREC
TANRECS > TANREC
TANS > TAN
TANSIES > TANSY
TANSY n yellow-flowered plant
TANTALATE n any of various salts of tantalic acid formed when the pentoxide of tantalum dissolves in an alkali
TANTALIC adj of or containing tantalum, esp in the pentavalent state
TANTALISE same as > TANTALIZE
TANTALISM > TANTALISE
TANTALITE n heavy brownish mineral consisting of a tantalum oxide of iron and manganese in orthorhombic crystalline form
TANTALIZE vb torment by showing but withholding something desired
TANTALOUS adj of or containing tantalum in the trivalent state
TANTALUM n hard greyish-white metallic element
TANTALUMS > TANTALUM
TANTALUS n case in which bottles of wine and spirits

may be locked with their contents tantalizingly visible
TANTARA n blast, as on a trumpet or horn
TANTARARA same as > TANTARA
TANTARAS > TANTARA
TANTI adj old word for worthwhile
TANTIVIES > TANTIVY
TANTIVY adv at full speed ▷ interj hunting cry, esp at full gallop
TANTO adv too much
TANTONIES > TANTONY
TANTONY n runt
TANTRA n sacred books of Tantrism, written between the 7th and 17th centuries AD, mainly in the form of a dialogue between Siva and his wife
TANTRAS > TANTRA
TANTRIC > TANTRA
TANTRISM n teaching of tantra
TANTRISMS > TANTRISM
TANTRUM n childish outburst of temper
TANTRUMS > TANTRUM
TANUKI n animal similar to a raccoon, found in Japan
TANUKIS > TANUKI
TANYARD n part of a tannery
TANYARDS > TANYARD
TANZANITE n blue gemstone
TAO n (in Confucian philosophy) the correct course of action
TAOISEACH n prime minister of the Republic of Ireland
TAONGA n treasure
TAONGAS > TAONGA
TAOS > TAO
TAP vb knock lightly and usu repeatedly ▷ n light knock
TAPA n inner bark of the paper mulberry
TAPACOLO n small bird of Chile and Argentina
TAPACOLOS > TAPACOLO
TAPACULO same as > TAPACOLO
TAPACULOS > TAPACULO
TAPADERA n leather covering for the stirrup on an American saddle
TAPADERAS > TAPADERA
TAPADERO same as > TAPADERA
TAPADEROS > TAPADERO
TAPALO n Latin American scarf, often patterned and brightly coloured
TAPALOS > TAPALO
TAPAS pl n (in Spanish cookery) light snacks or appetizers, usually eaten with drinks

**TAPE** *n* narrow long strip of material ▷ *vb* record on magnetic tape
**TAPEABLE** > TAPE
**TAPED** > TAPE
**TAPELESS** > TAPE
**TAPELIKE** > TAPE
**TAPELINE** *n* tape or length of metal marked off in inches, centimetres, etc, used principally for measuring and fitting garments
**TAPELINES** > TAPELINE
**TAPEN** *adj* made of tape
**TAPENADE** *n* savoury paste made from capers, olives, and anchovies, with olive oil and lemon juice
**TAPENADES** > TAPENADE
**TAPER** > TAPE
**TAPERED** > TAPE
**TAPERER** > TAPE
**TAPERERS** > TAPE
**TAPERING** > TAPE
**TAPERINGS** > TAPE
**TAPERNESS** *n* state or quality of being tapered
**TAPERS** > TAPE
**TAPERWISE** *adv* in the manner of a taper
**TAPES** > TAPE
**TAPESTRY** *n* fabric decorated with coloured woven designs ▷ *vb* portray in tapestry
**TAPET** *n* example of tapestry
**TAPETA** > TAPETUM
**TAPETAL** > TAPETUM
**TAPETI** *n* forest rabbit of Brazil
**TAPETIS** > TAPETI
**TAPETS** > TAPET
**TAPETUM** *n* layer of nutritive cells in the sporangia of ferns and anthers of flowering plants that surrounds developing spore cells
**TAPEWORM** *n* long flat parasitic worm living in the intestines of vertebrates
**TAPEWORMS** > TAPEWORM
**TAPHOLE** *n* hole in a furnace for running off molten metal or slag
**TAPHOLES** > TAPHOLE
**TAPHONOMY** *n* study of the processes affecting an organism after death that result in its fossilization
**TAPHOUSE** *n* inn or bar
**TAPHOUSES** > TAPHOUSE
**TAPING** > TAPE
**TAPIOCA** *n* beadlike starch made from cassava root, used in puddings
**TAPIOCAS** > TAPIOCA
**TAPIR** *n* piglike mammal of tropical America and SE Asia, with a long snout
**TAPIROID** > TAPIR

**TAPIRS** > TAPIR
**TAPIS** *n* tapestry or carpeting, esp as formerly used to cover a table in a council chamber
**TAPISES** > TAPIS
**TAPIST** *n* person who records (read out) printed matter in an audio format for the benefit of visually impaired people
**TAPISTS** > TAPIST
**TAPLASH** *n* dregs of beer
**TAPLASHES** > TAPLASH
**TAPPA** *same as* > TAPA
**TAPPABLE** > TAP
**TAPPAS** > TAPPA
**TAPPED** > TAP
**TAPPER** *n* person who taps
**TAPPERS** > TAPPER
**TAPPET** *n* short steel rod in an engine, transferring motion from one part to another
**TAPPETS** > TAPPET
**TAPPICE** *vb* hide
**TAPPICED** > TAPPICE
**TAPPICES** > TAPPICE
**TAPPICING** > TAPPICE
**TAPPING** > TAP
**TAPPINGS** > TAP
**TAPPIT** *adj* crested; topped
**TAPROOM** *n* public bar in a hotel or pub
**TAPROOMS** > TAPROOM
**TAPROOT** *n* main root of a plant, growing straight down
**TAPROOTED** > TAPROOT
**TAPROOTS** > TAPROOT
**TAPS** > TAP
**TAPSMAN** *n* old word for a barman
**TAPSMEN** > TAPSMAN
**TAPSTER** *n* barman
**TAPSTERS** > TAPSTER
**TAPSTRESS** > TAPSTER
**TAPSTRY** *adj* relating to tapestry
**TAPU** *adj* sacred ▷ *n* Māori religious or superstitious restriction on something
**TAPUS** > TAPU
**TAQUERIA** *n* restaurant specializing in tacos
**TAQUERIAS** > TAQUERIA
**TAR** *n* thick black liquid distilled from coal etc ▷ *vb* coat with tar
**TARA** *same as* > TARO
**TARAIRE** *n* type of New Zealand tree
**TARAKIHI** *n* common edible sea fish of New Zealand waters
**TARAKIHIS** > TARAKIHI
**TARAMA** *n* cod roe
**TARAMAS** > TARAMA
**TARAMEA** *n* variety of New Zealand speargrass
**TARAMEAS** > TARAMEA
**TARAND** *n* northern animal of legend, now supposed to have been the reindeer

**TARANDS** > TARAND
**TARANTARA** *same as* > TANTARA
**TARANTAS** *same as* > TARANTASS
**TARANTASS** *n* large horse-drawn four-wheeled Russian carriage without springs
**TARANTISM** *n* nervous disorder marked by uncontrollable bodily movement, widespread in S Italy during the 15th to 17th centuries: popularly thought to be caused by the bite of a tarantula
**TARANTIST** > TARANTISM
**TARANTULA** *n* large hairy spider with a poisonous bite
**TARAS** > TARA
**TARAXACUM** *n* perennial plant with dense heads of small yellow flowers and seeds with a feathery attachment
**TARBOGGIN** *same as* > TOBOGGAN
**TARBOOSH** *n* felt or cloth brimless cap, usually red and often with a silk tassel, formerly worn by Muslim men
**TARBOUCHE** *same as* > TARBOOSH
**TARBOUSH** *same as* > TARBOOSH
**TARBOY** *n* boy who applies tar to the skin of sheep cut during shearing
**TARBOYS** > TARBOY
**TARBUSH** *same as* > TARBOOSH
**TARBUSHES** > TARBUSH
**TARCEL** *same as* > TARCEL
**TARCELS** > TARCEL
**TARDIED** > TARDY
**TARDIER** > TARDY
**TARDIES** > TARDY
**TARDIEST** > TARDY
**TARDILY** > TARDY
**TARDINESS** > TARDY
**TARDIVE** *adj* tending to develop late
**TARDO** *adj* (of music) slow; to be played slowly
**TARDY** *adj* slow or late ▷ *vb* delay or impede (something or someone)
**TARDYING** > TARDY
**TARDYON** *n* particle travelling slower than the speed of light
**TARDYONS** > TARDYON
**TARE** *n* weight of the wrapping or container of goods ▷ *vb* weigh (a package, etc) in order to calculate the amount of tare
**TARED** > TARE
**TARES** > TARE
**TARGE** *vb* interrogate

**TARGED** > TARGE
**TARGES** > TARGE
**TARGET** *n* object or person a missile is aimed at ▷ *vb* aim or direct
**TARGETED** > TARGET
**TARGETEER** *n* soldier armed with a small round shield
**TARGETING** > TARGET
**TARGETS** > TARGET
**TARGING** > TARGE
**TARIFF** *n* tax levied on imports ▷ *vb* impose punishment for a criminal offence
**TARIFFED** > TARIFF
**TARIFFING** > TARIFF
**TARIFFS** > TARIFF
**TARING** > TARE
**TARINGS** > TARE
**TARLATAN** *n* open-weave cotton fabric, used for stiffening garments
**TARLATANS** > TARLATAN
**TARLETAN** *same as* > TARLATAN
**TARLETANS** > TARLETAN
**TARMAC** *See also* > MACADAM
**TARMACKED** > TARMAC
**TARMACS** > TARMAC
**TARN** *n* small mountain lake
**TARNAL** *adj* damned ▷ *adv* extremely
**TARNALLY** > TARNAL
**TARNATION** *euphemism for* > DAMNATION
**TARNISH** *vb* make or become stained or less bright ▷ *n* discoloration or blemish
**TARNISHED** > TARNISH
**TARNISHER** > TARNISH
**TARNISHES** > TARNISH
**TARNS** > TARN
**TARO** *n* plant with a large edible rootstock
**TAROC** *old variant of* > TAROT
**TAROCS** > TAROC
**TAROK** *old variant of* > TAROT
**TAROKS** > TAROK
**TAROS** > TARO
**TAROT** *n* special pack of cards used mainly in fortune-telling ▷ *adj* relating to tarot cards
**TAROTS** > TAROT
**TARP** *informal word for* > TARPAULIN
**TARPAN** *n* European wild horse common in prehistoric times but now extinct
**TARPANS** > TARPAN
**TARPAPER** *n* paper coated or impregnated with tar
**TARPAPERS** > TARPAPER
**TARPAULIN** *n* (sheet of) heavy waterproof fabric
**TARPON** *n* large silvery clupeoid game fish found in warm Atlantic waters
**TARPONS** > TARPON

TARPS > TARP

TARRAGON n aromatic herb

TARRAGONS > TARRAGON

TARRAS same as > TRASS

TARRASES > TARRAS

TARRE old word meaning to provoke or goad

TARRED > TAR

TARRES > TARRE

TARRIANCE archaic word for > DELAY

TARRIED > TARRY

TARRIER > TARRY

TARRIERS > TARRY

TARRIES > TARRY

TARRIEST > TARRY

TARRINESS > TARRY

TARRING > TAR

TARRINGS > TAR

TARROCK n seabird

TARROCKS > TARROCK

TARROW vb exhibit reluctance

TARROWED > TARROW

TARROWING > TARROW

TARROWS > TARROW

TARRY vb linger or delay ▷ n stay ▷ adj covered in or resembling tar

TARRYING > TARRY

TARS > TAR

TARSAL adj of the tarsus or tarsi ▷ n tarsal bone

TARSALGIA n pain in the tarsus

TARSALS > TARSAL

TARSEAL n bitumen surface of a road

TARSEALS > TARSEAL

TARSEL same as > TERCEL

TARSELS > TARSEL

TARSI > TARSUS

TARSIA another term for > INTARSIA

TARSIAS > TARSIA

TARSIER n small nocturnal primate of the E Indies, which has very large eyes

TARSIERS > TARSIER

TARSIOID adj resembling a tarsier

TARSIPED n generic term for a number of marsupials

TARSIPEDS > TARSIPED

TARSUS n bones of the heel and ankle collectively

TART n pie or flan with a sweet filling ▷ adj sharp or bitter ▷ adj (of a flavour, food, etc) sour, acid, or astringent ▷ vb (of food, drink, etc) become tart (sour)

TARTAN n design of straight lines crossing at right angles, esp one associated with a Scottish clan

TARTANA n small Mediterranean sailing boat

TARTANAS > TARTANA

TARTANE same as > TARTANA

TARTANED > TARTAN

TARTANES > TARTANE

TARTANRY n derogatory term for excessive use of tartan and other Scottish imagery to produce a distorted sentimental view of Scotland and its history

TARTANS > TARTAN

TARTAR n hard deposit on the teeth

TARTARE n mayonnaise sauce mixed with hard-boiled egg yolks, chopped herbs, capers, and gherkins

TARTARES > TARTARE

TARTARIC adj of or derived from tartar or tartaric acid

TARTARISE same as > TARTARIZE

TARTARIZE vb impregnate or treat with tartar or tartar emetic

TARTARLY adj resembling a tartar

TARTAROUS adj consisting of, containing, or resembling tartar

TARTARS > TARTAR

TARTED > TART

TARTER > TART

TARTEST > TART

TARTIER > TARTY

TARTIEST > TARTY

TARTILY > TARTY

TARTINE n slice of bread with butter or jam spread on it

TARTINES > TARTINE

TARTINESS > TARTY

TARTING > TART

TARTISH > TART

TARTISHLY > TART

TARTLET n individual pastry case with a filling of fruit or other sweet or savoury mixture

TARTLETS > TARTLET

TARTLY > TART

TARTNESS > TART

TARTRATE n any salt or ester of tartaric acid

TARTRATED adj being in the form of a tartrate

TARTRATES > TARTRATE

TARTS > TART

TARTUFE same as > TARTUFFE

TARTUFES > TARTUFE

TARTUFFE n person who hypocritically pretends to be deeply pious

TARTUFFES > TARTUFFE

TARTY adj resembling a promiscuous woman; provocative in a cheap and bawdy way

TARWEED n resinous Californian plant with a pungent scent

TARWEEDS > TARWEED

TARWHINE n bream of E Australia, silver in colour with gold streaks

TARWHINES > TARWHINE

TARZAN n man with great physical strength, agility, and virility

TARZANS > TARZAN

TAS old form of > TASS

TASAR same as > TUSSORE

TASARS > TASAR

TASER vb use a Taser (trademark) stun gun on (someone)

TASERED > TASER

TASERING > TASER

TASERS > TASER

TASH vb stain or besmirch

TASHED > TASH

TASHES > TASH

TASHING > TASH

TASIMETER n device for measuring small temperature changes. It depends on the changes of pressure resulting from expanding or contracting solids

TASIMETRY > TASIMETER

TASK n piece of work to be done ▷ vb give someone a task to do

TASKBAR n area of computer screen showing what programs are running

TASKBARS > TASKBAR

TASKED > TASK

TASKER > TASK

TASKERS > TASK

TASKING > TASK

TASKINGS > TASK

TASKLESS > TASK

TASKS > TASK

TASKWORK n hard or unpleasant work

TASKWORKS > TASKWORK

TASLET same as > TASSET

TASLETS > TASLET

TASS n cup, goblet, or glass

TASSE same as > TASSET

TASSEL n decorative fringed knot of threads ▷ vb adorn with a tassel or tassels

TASSELED > TASSEL

TASSELING > TASSEL

TASSELL same as > TASSEL

TASSELLED > TASSEL

TASSELLS > TASSELL

TASSELLY > TASSEL

TASSELS > TASSEL

TASSES > TASSE

TASSET n piece of armour consisting of one or more plates fastened on to the bottom of a cuirass to protect the thigh

TASSETS > TASSET

TASSIE same as > TASS

TASSIES > TASSIE

TASSWAGE vb old poetic contraction of "to assuage"

TASTABLE > TASTE

TASTE n sense by which the flavour of a substance is distinguished in the mouth ▷ vb distinguish the taste of (a substance)

TASTEABLE > TASTE

TASTED > TASTE

TASTEFUL adj having or showing good taste

TASTELESS adj bland or insipid

TASTER n person employed to test the quality of food or drink by tasting it

TASTERS > TASTER

TASTES > TASTE

TASTEVIN n small shallow cup for wine tasting

TASTEVINS > TASTEVIN

TASTIER > TASTY

TASTIEST > TASTY

TASTILY > TASTY

TASTINESS > TASTY

TASTING > TASTE

TASTINGS > TASTE

TASTY adj pleasantly flavoured

TAT n tatty or tasteless article(s) ▷ vb make (something) by tatting

TATAHASH n stew containing potatoes and cheap cuts of meat

TATAMI n thick rectangular mat of woven straw, used as a standard to measure a Japanese room

TATAMIS > TATAMI

TATAR n brutal person

TATARS > TATAR

TATE n small tuft of fibre

TATER n potato

TATERS > TATER

TATES > TATE

TATH vb (of cattle) to defecate

TATHED > TATH

TATHING > TATH

TATHS > TATH

TATIE same as > TATTIE

TATIES > TATIE

TATLER old variant of > TATTLER

TATLERS > TATLER

TATOU n armadillo

TATOUAY n large armadillo of South America

TATOUAYS > TATOUAY

TATOUS > TATOU

TATS > TAT

TATSOI n variety of Chinese cabbage

TATSOIS > TATSOI

TATT same as > TAT

TATTED > TAT

TATTER vb make or become torn

TATTERED > TATTER

TATTERING > TATTER

TATTERS > TATTER

TATTERY same as > TATTERED

TATTIE Scot or dialect word for > POTATO

TATTIER > TATTY

TATTIES > TATTIE

**TATTIEST** > TATTY
**TATTILY** > TATTY
**TATTINESS** > TATTY
**TATTING** > TAT
**TATTINGS** > TAT
**TATTLE** n gossip or chatter
▷ vb gossip or chatter
**TATTLED** > TATTLE
**TATTLER** n person who
tattles
**TATTLERS** > TATTLER
**TATTLES** > TATTLE
**TATTLING** > TATTLE
**TATTLINGS** > TATTLE
**TATTOO** n pattern made on
the body by pricking the
skin and staining it with
indelible inks ▷ vb make
such a pattern on the skin
**TATTOOED** > TATTOO
**TATTOOER** > TATTOO
**TATTOOERS** > TATTOO
**TATTOOING** > TATTOO
**TATTOOIST** > TATTOO
**TATTOOS** > TATTOO
**TATTOW** old variant
of > TATTOO
**TATTOWED** > TATTOW
**TATTOWING** > TATTOW
**TATTOWS** > TATTOW
**TATTS** > TATT
**TATTY** adj worn out,
shabby, tawdry, or
unkempt
**TATU** old variant of > TATTOO
**TATUED** > TATU
**TATUING** > TATU
**TATUS** > TATU
**TAU** n 19th letter in the
Greek alphabet
**TAUBE** n type of German
aeroplane
**TAUBES** > TAUBE
**TAUGHT** > TEACH
**TAUHINU** New Zealand name
for > POPLAR
**TAUHINUS** > TAUHINU
**TAUHOU** same as > SILVEREYE
**TAUIWI** n Māori term for
the non-Māori people of
New Zealand
**TAUIWIS** > TAUIWI
**TAULD** vb old Scots variant
of told
**TAUNT** vb tease with jeers
▷ n jeering remark ▷ adj
(of the mast or masts of a
sailing vessel) unusually
tall
**TAUNTED** > TAUNT
**TAUNTER** > TAUNT
**TAUNTERS** > TAUNT
**TAUNTING** > TAUNT
**TAUNTINGS** > TAUNT
**TAUNTS** > TAUNT
**TAUON** n negatively
charged elementary
particle
**TAUONS** > TAUON
**TAUPATA** n New Zealand
shrub or tree, with shiny
dark green leaves
**TAUPE** adj brownish-grey
▷ n brownish-grey colour

**TAUPES** > TAUPE
**TAUPIE** same as > TAWPIE
**TAUPIES** > TAUPIE
**TAUREAN** adj born under or
characteristic of Taurus
**TAURIC** same as > TAUREAN
**TAURIFORM** adj in the form
of a bull
**TAURINE** adj of, relating to,
or resembling a bull ▷ n
derivative of the amino
acid, cysteine, obtained
from the bile of animals
**TAURINES** > TAURINE
**TAUS** > TAU
**TAUT** adj drawn tight ▷ vb
Scots word meaning to
tangle
**TAUTAUG** same as > TAUTOG
**TAUTAUGS** > TAUTAUG
**TAUTED** > TAUT
**TAUTEN** vb make or become
taut
**TAUTENED** > TAUTEN
**TAUTENING** > TAUTEN
**TAUTENS** > TAUTEN
**TAUTER** > TAUT
**TAUTEST** > TAUT
**TAUTING** > TAUT
**TAUTIT** adj Scots word
meaning tangled
**TAUTLY** > TAUT
**TAUTNESS** > TAUT
**TAUTOG** n large dark-
coloured wrasse, used as a
food fish
**TAUTOGS** > TAUTOG
**TAUTOLOGY** n use of words
which merely repeat
something already stated
**TAUTOMER** n either of the
two forms of a chemical
compound that exhibits
tautomerism
**TAUTOMERS** > TAUTOMER
**TAUTONYM** n taxonomic
name in which the generic
and specific components
are the same
**TAUTONYMS** > TAUTONYM
**TAUTONYMY** > TAUTONYM
**TAUTS** > TAUT
**TAV** n 23rd and last letter in
the Hebrew alphabet
**TAVA** n thick Indian frying
pan
**TAVAH** variant of > TAVA
**TAVAHS** > TAVAH
**TAVAS** > TAVA
**TAVER** vb wander about
**TAVERED** > TAVER
**TAVERING** > TAVER
**TAVERN** n pub
**TAVERNA** n (in Greece) a
guesthouse that has its
own bar
**TAVERNAS** > TAVERNA
**TAVERNER** n keeper of a
tavern
**TAVERNERS** > TAVERNER
**TAVERNS** > TAVERN
**TAVERS** > TAVER
**TAVERT** adj bewildered or
confused

**TAVS** > TAV
**TAW** vb convert skins into
leather
**TAWA** n tall timber tree from
New Zealand, with edible
purple berries
**TAWAI** n any of various
species of beech of the
genus Nothofagus of New
Zealand, originally called
"birches" by the settlers
**TAWAIS** > TAWAI
**TAWAS** > TAWA
**TAWDRIER** > TAWDRY
**TAWDRIES** > TAWDRY
**TAWDRIEST** > TAWDRY
**TAWDRILY** > TAWDRY
**TAWDRY** adj cheap, showy,
and of poor quality ▷ n
gaudy finery of poor
quality
**TAWED** > TAW
**TAWER** > TAW
**TAWERIES** > TAWERY
**TAWERS** > TAW
**TAWERY** n place where
tawing is carried out
**TAWHAI** same as > TAWAI
**TAWHAIS** > TAWHAI
**TAWHIRI** n small New
Zealand tree with wavy
green glossy leaves
**TAWIE** adj easily persuaded
or managed
**TAWIER** > TAWIE
**TAWIEST** > TAWIE
**TAWING** > TAW
**TAWINGS** > TAW
**TAWNEY** same as > TAWNY
**TAWNEYS** > TAWNEY
**TAWNIER** > TAWNY
**TAWNIES** > TAWNY
**TAWNIEST** > TAWNY
**TAWNILY** > TAWNY
**TAWNINESS** > TAWNY
**TAWNY** adj yellowish-
brown ▷ n light brown to
brownish-orange colour
**TAWPIE** n foolish or
maladroit girl
**TAWPIES** > TAWPIE
**TAWS** same as > TAWSE
**TAWSE** n leather strap
with one end cut into
thongs, formerly used
by schoolteachers to
hit children who had
misbehaved ▷ vb punish
(someone) with or as if
with a tawse
**TAWSED** > TAWSE
**TAWSES** > TAWSE
**TAWSING** > TAWSE
**TAWT** same as > TAUT
**TAWTED** > TAWT
**TAWTIE** > TAWT
**TAWTIER** > TAWT
**TAWTIEST** > TAWT
**TAWTING** > TAWT
**TAWTS** > TAWT
**TAX** n compulsory payment
levied by a government on
income, property, etc to
raise revenue ▷ vb levy a

tax on
**TAXA** > TAXON
**TAXABLE** adj capable of
being taxed ▷ n person,
income, property, etc, that
is subject to tax
**TAXABLES** > TAXABLE
**TAXABLY** > TAXABLE
**TAXACEOUS** adj of, relating
to, or belonging to the
Taxaceae, a family of
coniferous trees that
includes the yews
**TAXAMETER** old variant
of > TAXIMETER
**TAXATION** n levying of
taxes
**TAXATIONS** > TAXATION
**TAXATIVE** > TAXATION
**TAXED** > TAX
**TAXEME** n any element
of speech that may
differentiate one
utterance from another
with a different meaning
**TAXEMES** > TAXEME
**TAXEMIC** > TAXEME
**TAXER** > TAX
**TAXERS** > TAX
**TAXES** > TAX
**TAXI** n car with a driver
that may be hired to take
people to any specified
destination ▷ vb (of an
aircraft) run along the
ground before taking off or
after landing
**TAXIARCH** n soldier in
charge of a Greek taxis
**TAXIARCHS** > TAXIARCH
**TAXICAB** same as > TAXI
**TAXICABS** > TAXICAB
**TAXIDERMY** n art of
stuffing and mounting
animal skins to give them
a lifelike appearance
**TAXIED** > TAXI
**TAXIES** > TAXIS
**TAXIING** > TAXI
**TAXIMAN** n taxi driver
**TAXIMEN** > TAXIMAN
**TAXIMETER** n meter fitted
to a taxi to register the
fare, based on the length of
the journey
**TAXING** adj demanding,
onerous
**TAXINGLY** > TAXING
**TAXINGS** > TAX
**TAXIPLANE** n aircraft that
is available for hire
**TAXIS** n movement of a cell
or organism in a particular
direction in response to an
external stimulus ancient
Greek army unit
**TAXITE** n type of volcanic
rock
**TAXITES** > TAXITE
**TAXITIC** > TAXITE
**TAXIWAY** n marked path
along which aircraft
taxi to or from a runway,
parking area, etc

TAXIWAYS >TAXIWAY
TAXLESS >TAX
TAXMAN n collector of taxes
TAXMEN >TAXMAN
TAXOL n trademarked anti-cancer drug
TAXOLS >TAXOL
TAXON n any taxonomic group or rank
TAXONOMER >TAXONOMY
TAXONOMIC >TAXONOMY
TAXONOMY n classification of plants and animals into groups
TAXONS >TAXON
TAXOR >TAX
TAXORS >TAX
TAXPAID adj (of taxable products, esp wine) having had the applicable tax paid already
TAXPAYER n person or organization that pays taxes
TAXPAYERS >TAXPAYER
TAXPAYING >TAXPAYER
TAXUS n genus of conifers
TAXWISE adv regarding tax
TAXYING >TAXI
TAY Irish dialect word for >TEA
TAYASSUID n peccary
TAYBERRY n hybrid shrub produced by crossing a blackberry, raspberry, and loganberry
TAYRA n large arboreal musteline mammal, of Central and South America, with a dark brown body and paler head
TAYRAS >TAYRA
TAYS >TAY
TAZZA n wine cup with a shallow bowl and a circular foot
TAZZAS >TAZZA
TAZZE >TAZZA
TCHICK vb make a click by creating a vacuum in the mouth with the tongue pressed againt the palate then suddenly breaking the seal by withdrawing part of the tongue from the palate
TCHICKED >TCHICK
TCHICKING >TCHICK
TCHICKS >TCHICK
TCHOTCHKE n trinket
TE n (in tonic sol-fa) seventh degree of any major scale
TEA n drink made from infusing the dried leaves of an Asian bush in boiling water ▷ vb take tea
TEABERRY n berry of the wintergreen
TEABOARD n tea tray
TEABOARDS >TEABOARD
TEABOWL n small bowl used (instead of a teacup) for serving tea

TEABOWLS >TEABOWL
TEABOX n box for storing tea
TEABOXES >TEABOX
TEABREAD n loaf-shaped cake that contains dried fruit which has been steeped in cold tea before baking: served sliced and buttered
TEABREADS >TEABREAD
TEACAKE n flat bun, usually eaten toasted and buttered
TEACAKES >TEACAKE
TEACART n trolley from which tea is served
TEACARTS >TEACART
TEACH vb tell or show (someone) how to do something
TEACHABLE >TEACH
TEACHABLY >TEACH
TEACHER n person who teaches, esp in a school
TEACHERLY >TEACHER
TEACHERS >TEACHER
TEACHES >TEACH
TEACHIE old form of >TETCHY
TEACHING >TEACH
TEACHINGS >TEACH
TEACHLESS adj unable to be taught
TEACUP n cup out of which tea may be drunk
TEACUPFUL n amount a teacup will hold, about four fluid ounces
TEACUPS >TEACUP
TEAD old word for >TORCH
TEADE same as >TEAD
TEADES >TEADE
TEADS >TEAD
TEAED >TEA
TEAGLE vb raise or hoist using a tackle
TEAGLED >TEAGLE
TEAGLES >TEAGLE
TEAGLING >TEAGLE
TEAHOUSE n restaurant, esp in Japan or China, where tea and light refreshments are served
TEAHOUSES >TEAHOUSE
TEAING >TEA
TEAK n very hard wood of an E Indian tree
TEAKS >TEAK
TEAKWOOD another word for >TEAK
TEAKWOODS >TEAKWOOD
TEAL n kind of small duck
TEALIKE adj resembling tea
TEALS >TEAL
TEAM n group of people forming one side in a game ▷ vb make or cause to make a team
TEAMAKER n person or thing that makes tea

TEAMAKERS >TEAMAKER
TEAMED >TEAM
TEAMER >TEAM
TEAMERS >TEAM
TEAMING >TEAM
TEAMINGS >TEAM
TEAMMATE n fellow member of a team
TEAMMATES >TEAMMATE
TEAMS >TEAM
TEAMSTER n commercial vehicle driver
TEAMSTERS >TEAMSTER
TEAMWISE adv in respect of a team; in the manner of a team
TEAMWORK n cooperative work by a team
TEAMWORKS >TEAMWORK
TEAPOT n container with a lid, spout, and handle for making and serving tea
TEAPOTS >TEAPOT
TEAPOY n small table or stand with a tripod base
TEAPOYS >TEAPOY
TEAR n drop of fluid appearing in and falling from the eye ▷ vb rip a hole in ▷ vb shed tears
TEARABLE >TEAR
TEARAWAY n wild or unruly person
TEARAWAYS >TEARAWAY
TEARDOWN n demolition; disassembly
TEARDOWNS >TEARDOWN
TEARDROP same as >TEAR
TEARDROPS >TEARDROP
TEARED >TEAR
TEARER >TEAR
TEARERS >TEAR
TEARFUL adj weeping or about to weep
TEARFULLY >TEARFUL
TEARGAS n gas or vaopr that makes the eyes smart and water ▷ vb deploy teargas against
TEARGASES >TEARGAS
TEARIER >TEARY
TEARIEST >TEARY
TEARILY >TEARY
TEARINESS >TEARY
TEARING >TEAR
TEARLESS >TEAR
TEAROOM same as >TEASHOP
TEAROOMS >TEAROOM
TEARS >TEAR
TEARSHEET n page in a newspaper or periodical that is cut or perforated so that it can be easily torn out
TEARSTAIN n stain or streak left by tears
TEARSTRIP n part of packaging torn to open it
TEARY adj characterized by, covered with, or secreting tears
TEAS >TEA
TEASABLE >TEASE
TEASE vb make fun of

(someone) in a provoking or playful way ▷ n person who teases
TEASED >TEASE
TEASEL n plant with prickly leaves and flowers ▷ vb tease (a fabric)
TEASELED >TEASEL
TEASELER >TEASEL
TEASELERS >TEASEL
TEASELING >TEASEL
TEASELLED >TEASEL
TEASELLER >TEASEL
TEASELS >TEASEL
TEASER n annoying or difficult problem
TEASERS >TEASER
TEASES >TEASE
TEASHOP n restaurant where tea and light refreshments are served
TEASHOPS >TEASHOP
TEASING >TEASE
TEASINGLY >TEASE
TEASINGS >TEASE
TEASPOON n small spoon for stirring tea
TEASPOONS >TEASPOON
TEAT n nipple of a breast or udder
TEATASTER n person assessing teas by tasting them
TEATED >TEAT
TEATIME n late afternoon
TEATIMES >TEATIME
TEATS >TEAT
TEAWARE n implements and vessels for brewing and serving tea
TEAWARES >TEAWARE
TEAZE old variant of >TEASE
TEAZED >TEAZE
TEAZEL same as >TEASEL
TEAZELED >TEAZEL
TEAZELING >TEAZEL
TEAZELLED >TEAZEL
TEAZELS >TEAZEL
TEAZES >TEAZE
TEAZING >TEAZE
TEAZLE same as >TEASEL
TEAZLED >TEAZLE
TEAZLES >TEAZLE
TEAZLING >TEAZLE
TEBBAD n sandstorm
TEBBADS >TEBBAD
TEC short for >DETECTIVE
TECH n technical college
TECHED adj showing slight insanity
TECHIE n person who is skilled in the use of technology ▷ adj relating to or skilled in the use of technology
TECHIER >TECHY
TECHIES >TECHIE
TECHIEST >TECHY
TECHILY >TECHY
TECHINESS >TECHY
TECHNIC another word for >TECHNIQUE
TECHNICAL adj of or specializing in industrial,

practical, or mechanical arts and applied sciences ▷ *n* small armed military truck

**TECHNICS** *n* study or theory of industry and industrial arts

**TECHNIKON** *n* technical college

**TECHNIQUE** *n* method or skill used for a particular task

**TECHNO** *n* type of electronic dance music with a very fast beat

**TECHNOPOP** *n* pop music sharing certain features with techno

**TECHNOS** >TECHNO

**TECHS** >TECH

**TECHY** *same as* >TECHIE

**TECKEL** *n* dachshund

**TECKELS** >TECKEL

**TECS** >TEC

**TECTA** >TECTUM

**TECTAL** >TECTUM

**TECTIFORM** *adj* in the form of a roof

**TECTITE** *same as* >TEKTITE

**TECTITES** >TECTITE

**TECTONIC** *adj* denoting or relating to construction or building

**TECTONICS** *n* study of the earth's crust and the forces affecting it

**TECTONISM** >TECTONIC

**TECTORIAL** *as in tectorial membrane* membrane in the inner ear that covers the organ of Corti

**TECTRICES** >TECTRIX

**TECTRIX** *another name for* >COVERT

**TECTUM** *n* any roof-like structure in the body, esp the dorsal area of the midbrain

**TECTUMS** >TECTUM

**TED** *vb* shake out (hay), so as to dry it

**TEDDED** >TED

**TEDDER** *n* machine equipped with a series of small rotating forks for tedding hay

**TEDDERED** >TEDDER

**TEDDERING** >TEDDER

**TEDDERS** >TEDDER

**TEDDIE** *same as* >TEDDY

**TEDDIES** >TEDDY

**TEDDING** >TED

**TEDDY** *n* teddy bear

**TEDESCA** *adj* (of a piece of music) in German style

**TEDESCHE** >TEDESCA

**TEDESCHI** >TEDESCO

**TEDESCO** *adj* German

**TEDIER** >TEDY

**TEDIEST** >TEDY

**TEDIOSITY** >TEDIOUS

**TEDIOUS** *adj* causing fatigue or boredom

**TEDIOUSLY** >TEDIOUS

**TEDISOME** *old Scottish variant of* >TEDIOUS

**TEDIUM** *n* monotony

**TEDIUMS** >TEDIUM

**TEDS** >TED

**TEDY** *same as* >TEDIOUS

**TEE** *n* small peg from which a golf ball can be played at the start of each hole ▷ *vb* position (the ball) ready for striking, on or as if on a tee

**TEED** >TEE

**TEEING** >TEE

**TEEK** *adj* in Indian English, well

**TEEL** *same as* >SESAME

**TEELS** >TEEL

**TEEM** *vb* be full of

**TEEMED** >TEEM

**TEEMER** >TEEM

**TEEMERS** >TEEM

**TEEMFUL** >TEEM

**TEEMING** >TEEM

**TEEMINGLY** >TEEM

**TEEMLESS** >TEEM

**TEEMS** >TEEM

**TEEN** *n* affliction or woe ▷ *n* teenager ▷ *vb* set alight

**TEENAGE** *adj* (of a person) aged between 13 and 19 ▷ *n* this period of time

**TEENAGED** *adj* (of a person) aged between 13 and 19

**TEENAGER** *n* person aged between 13 and 19

**TEENAGERS** >TEENAGER

**TEEND** *same as* >TIND

**TEENDED** >TEEND

**TEENDING** >TEEND

**TEENDS** >TEEND

**TEENE** *same as* >TEEN

**TEENED** >TEEN

**TEENER** >TEEN

**TEENERS** >TEEN

**TEENES** >TEENE

**TEENFUL** >TEEN

**TEENIER** >TEENY

**TEENIEST** >TEENY

**TEENING** >TEEN

**TEENS** >TEEN

**TEENSIER** >TEENSY

**TEENSIEST** >TEENSY

**TEENSY** *same as* >TEENY

**TEENTIER** >TEENTY

**TEENTIEST** >TEENTY

**TEENTSIER** >TEENTSY

**TEENTSY** *same as* >TEENY

**TEENTY** *same as* >TEENY

**TEENY** *adj* extremely small

**TEENYBOP** *adj* of, or relating to, a young teenager who avidly follows fashions in music and clothes

**TEEPEE** *same as* >TEPEE

**TEEPEES** >TEEPEE

**TEER** *vb* smear; daub

**TEERED** >TEER

**TEERING** >TEER

**TEERS** >TEER

**TEES** >TEE

**TEETER** *vb* wobble or move unsteadily

**TEETERED** >TEETER

**TEETERING** >TEETER

**TEETERS** >TEETER

**TEETH** >TOOTH

**TEETHE** *vb* (of a baby) grow his or her first teeth

**TEETHED** >TEETHE

**TEETHER** *n* object for an infant to bite on during teething

**TEETHERS** >TEETHER

**TEETHES** >TEETHE

**TEETHING** >TEETHE

**TEETHINGS** >TEETHING

**TEETHLESS** >TEETH

**TEETOTAL** *adj* drinking no alcohol ▷ *vb* advocate total abstinence from alcohol

**TEETOTALS** >TEETOTAL

**TEETOTUM** *n* spinning top bearing letters of the alphabet on its four sides

**TEETOTUMS** >TEETOTUM

**TEF** *n* annual grass, of NE Africa, grown for its grain

**TEFF** *same as* >TEF

**TEFFS** >TEFF

**TEFILLAH** *n* either of the pair of blackened square cases containing parchments inscribed with biblical passages, bound by leather thongs to the head and left arm, and worn by Jewish men during weekday morning prayers

**TEFILLIN** >TEFILLAH

**TEFLON** *n* a trademark for polytetrafluoroethylene when used in nonstick cooking vessels

**TEFLONS** >TEFLON

**TEFS** >TEF

**TEG** *n* two-year-old sheep

**TEGG** *same as* >TEG

**TEGGS** >TEGG

**TEGMEN** *n* either of the leathery forewings of the cockroach and related insects

**TEGMENTA** >TEGMENTUM

**TEGMENTAL** >TEGMENTUM

**TEGMENTUM** *n* one of the hard protective sometimes hairy or resinous specialized leaves surrounding the buds of certain plants

**TEGMINA** >TEGMEN

**TEGMINAL** >TEGMEN

**TEGS** >TEG

**TEGU** *n* large South American lizard

**TEGUA** *n* type of moccasin

**TEGUAS** >TEGUA

**TEGUEXIN** *same as* >TEGU

**TEGUEXINS** >TEGUEXIN

**TEGULA** *n* one of a pair of coverings of the forewings of certain insects

**TEGULAE** >TEGULA

**TEGULAR** *adj* of, relating to, or resembling a tile or tiles

**TEGULARLY** >TEGULAR

**TEGULATED** *adj* overlapping in the manner of roof tiles

**TEGUMEN** *same as* >TEGMEN

**TEGUMENT** *n* protective layer around an ovule

**TEGUMENTS** >TEGUMENT

**TEGUMINA** >TEGUMEN

**TEGUS** >TEGU

**TEHR** *same as* >TAHR

**TEHRS** >TEHR

**TEIGLACH** *n* dish consisting of morsels of dough boiled in honey

**TEIID** *n* member of the Teiidae family of lizards

**TEIIDS** >TEIID

**TEIL** *n* lime tree

**TEILS** >TEIL

**TEIND** *Scot and northern English word for* >TITHE

**TEINDED** >TEIND

**TEINDING** >TEIND

**TEINDS** >TEIND

**TEKKIE** *variant of* >TECHIE

**TEKKIES** >TEKKIE

**TEKNONYMY** *n* practice of naming a child after his or her parent

**TEKTITE** *n* small dark glassy object found in several areas around the world, thought to be a product of meteorite impact

**TEKTITES** >TEKTITE

**TEKTITIC** >TEKTITE

**TEL** *same as* >TELL

**TELA** *n* any delicate tissue or weblike structure

**TELAE** >TELA

**TELAMON** *n* column in the form of a male figure, used to support an entablature

**TELAMONES** >TELAMON

**TELAMONS** >TELAMON

**TELARY** *adj* capable of spinning a web

**TELCO** *n* telecommunications company

**TELCOS** >TELCO

**TELD** *same as* >TAULD

**TELE** *same as* >TELLY

**TELECAST** *vb* broadcast by television ▷ *n* television broadcast

**TELECASTS** >TELECAST

**TELECHIR** *n* robot arm controlled by a human operator

**TELECHIRS** >TELECHIR

**TELECINE** *n* apparatus for producing a television signal from cinematograph film

**TELECINES** >TELECINE

**TELECOM** *n* telecommunications

**TELECOMS** *same as* >TELECOM

**TELEDU** *n* badger of SE Asia and Indonesia, having dark brown hair with a

white stripe along the back and producing a fetid secretion from the anal glands when attacked
**TELEDUS** > TELEDU
**TELEFAX** *another word for* > FAX
**TELEFAXED** > TELEFAX
**TELEFAXES** > TELEFAX
**TELEFILM** *n* TV movie
**TELEFILMS** > TELEFILM
**TELEGA** *n* rough four-wheeled cart used in Russia
**TELEGAS** > TELEGA
**TELEGENIC** *adj* having or showing a pleasant television image
**TELEGONIC** > TELEGONY
**TELEGONY** *n* supposed influence of a previous sire on offspring borne by a female to other sires
**TELEGRAM** *n* formerly, a message sent by telegraph ▷ *vb* send a telegram
**TELEGRAMS** > TELEGRAM
**TELEGRAPH** *n* formerly, a system for sending messages over a distance along a cable ▷ *vb* communicate by telegraph
**TELEMAN** *n* noncommissioned officer in the US navy, usually charged with communications duties
**TELEMARK** *n* turn in which one ski is placed far forward of the other and turned gradually inwards ▷ *vb* perform a telemark turn
**TELEMARKS** > TELEMARK
**TELEMATIC** *adj* of, or relating to, the branch of science concerned with the use of technological devices to transmit information over long distances
**TELEMEN** > TELEMAN
**TELEMETER** *n* any device for recording or measuring a distant event and transmitting the data to a receiver or observer ▷ *vb* obtain and transmit (data) from a distant source, esp from a spacecraft
**TELEMETRY** *n* use of electronic devices to record or measure a distant event and transmit the data to a receiver
**TELEOLOGY** *n* belief that all things have a predetermined purpose
**TELEONOMY** *n* condition of having a fundamental purpose
**TELEOSAUR** *n* type of crocodile from the Jurassic

period
**TELEOST** *n* bony fish with rayed fins and a swim bladder ▷ *adj* of, relating to, or belonging to this type of fish
**TELEOSTS** > TELEOST
**TELEPATH** *n* person who is telepathic ▷ *vb* practise telepathy
**TELEPATHS** > TELEPATH
**TELEPATHY** *n* direct communication between minds
**TELEPHEME** *n* any message sent by telephone
**TELEPHONE** *n* device for transmitting sound over a distance along wires ▷ *vb* call or talk to (a person) by telephone ▷ *adj* of or using a telephone
**TELEPHONY** *n* system of telecommunications for the transmission of speech or other sounds
**TELEPHOTO** *n* short for telephoto lens: a compound camera lens that produces a magnified image of distant objects
**TELEPLAY** *n* play written for television
**TELEPLAYS** > TELEPLAY
**TELEPOINT** *n* system providing a place where a cordless telephone can be connected to a telephone network
**TELEPORT** *vb* (in science fiction) to transport (a person or object) across a distance instantaneously
**TELEPORTS** > TELEPORT
**TELERAN** *n* electronic navigational aid in which the image of a ground-based radar system is televised to aircraft in flight so that a pilot can see the position of his aircraft in relation to others
**TELERANS** > TELERAN
**TELERGIC** > TELERGY
**TELERGIES** > TELERGY
**TELERGY** *n* name for the form of energy supposedly transferred during telepathy
**TELES** > TELE
**TELESALE** > TELESALES
**TELESALES** *n* selling of a product or service by telephone
**TELESCOPE** *n* optical instrument for magnifying distant objects ▷ *vb* shorten
**TELESCOPY** *n* branch of astronomy concerned with the use and design of telescopes
**TELESEME** *n* old-fashioned

electric signalling system
**TELESEMES** > TELESEME
**TELESES** > TELESIS
**TELESHOP** *vb* buy goods by telephone or Internet
**TELESHOPS** > TELESHOP
**TELESIS** *n* purposeful use of natural and social processes to obtain specific social goals
**TELESM** *n* talisman
**TELESMS** > TELESM
**TELESTIC** *adj* relating to a hierophant
**TELESTICH** *n* short poem in which the last letters of each successive line form a word
**TELESTICS** *n* ancient pseudoscientific art of animating statues, idols, etc, or causing them to be inhabited by a diety
**TELETEX** *n* international means of communicating text between a variety of terminals
**TELETEXES** > TELETEX
**TELETEXT** *n* system which shows information and news on television screens
**TELETEXTS** > TELETEXT
**TELETHON** *n* lengthy television programme to raise charity funds, etc
**TELETHONS** > TELETHON
**TELETRON** *n* system for showing enlarged televisual images in eg sports stadiums
**TELETRONS** > TELETRON
**TELETYPE** *vb* send typed message by telegraph
**TELETYPED** > TELETYPE
**TELETYPES** > TELETYPE > TELETYPESETTING
**TELEVIEW** *vb* watch television
**TELEVIEWS** > TELEVIEW
**TELEVISE** *vb* broadcast on television
**TELEVISED** > TELEVISE
**TELEVISER** > TELEVISE
**TELEVISES** > TELEVISE
**TELEVISOR** *n* apparatus through which one transmits or receives televisual images
**TELEX** *n* international communication service using teleprinters ▷ *vb* transmit by telex
**TELEXED** > TELEX
**TELEXES** > TELEX
**TELEXING** > TELEX
**TELFER** *same as* > TELPHERAGE
**TELFERAGE** *n* overhead transport system in which an electrically driven truck runs along a single rail or cable, the load being suspended in a separate car beneath

**TELFERED** > TELFER
**TELFERIC** > TELFER
**TELFERING** > TELFER
**TELFERS** > TELFER
**TELFORD** *n* road built using a method favoured by Thomas Telford (1757-1834)
**TELFORDS** > TELFORD
**TELIA** > TELIUM
**TELIAL** > TELIUM
**TELIC** *adj* directed or moving towards some goal
**TELICALLY** > TELIC
**TELIUM** *n* spore-producing body of some rust fungi in which the teliospores are formed
**TELL** *vb* make known in words ▷ *n* large mound resulting from the accumulation of rubbish on a long-settled site, esp one with mudbrick buildings, particularly in the Middle East
**TELLABLE** > TELL
**TELLAR** *same as* > TILLER
**TELLARED** > TELLAR
**TELLARING** > TELLAR
**TELLARS** > TELLAR
**TELLEN** *same as* > TELLIN
**TELLENS** > TELLEN
**TELLER** *n* narrator ▷ *vb* (of a plant) to produce tillers
**TELLERED** > TELLER
**TELLERING** > TELLER
**TELLERS** > TELLER
**TELLIES** > TELLY
**TELLIN** *n* slim marine bivalve molluscs that live in intertidal sand
**TELLING** > TELL
**TELLINGLY** > TELL
**TELLINGS** > TELL
**TELLINOID** > TELLIN
**TELLINS** > TELLIN
**TELLS** > TELL
**TELLTALE** *n* person who reveals secrets ▷ *adj* revealing
**TELLTALES** > TELLTALE
**TELLURAL** *adj* tellurial; of or relating to the earth
**TELLURATE** *n* any salt or ester of telluric acid
**TELLURIAN** *same as* > TELLURION
**TELLURIC** *adj* of, relating to, or originating on or in the earth or soil
**TELLURIDE** *n* any compound of tellurium, esp one formed between tellurium and a more electropositive element or group
**TELLURION** *n* instrument that shows how day and night and the seasons result from the tilt of the earth, its rotation on its axis, and its revolution around the sun

**TELLURISE** same
as > TELLURIZE
**TELLURITE** n any salt or
ester of tellurous acid
**TELLURIUM** n brittle
silvery-white nonmetallic
element
**TELLURIZE** vb mix or
combine with tellurium
**TELLUROUS** adj of or
containing tellurium, esp
in a low valence state
**TELLUS** n earth
**TELLUSES** > TELLUS
**TELLY** n television
**TELLYS** > TELLY
**TELNET** n computer
system allowing one user
to access remotely other
computers on the same
network ▷ vb use a telnet
system
**TELNETED** > TELNET
**TELNETING** > TELNET
**TELNETS** > TELNET
**TELNETTED** > TELNET
**TELOI** > TELOS
**TELOME** n fundamental
unit of a plant's structure
**TELOMERE** n either of the
ends of a chromosome
**TELOMERES** > TELOMERE
**TELOMES** > TELOME
**TELOMIC** > TELOME
**TELOPHASE** n final stage
of mitosis, during which
a set of chromosomes
is present at each end
of the cell and a nuclear
membrane forms around
each, producing two new
nuclei
**TELOS** n objective;
ultimate purpose
**TELOSES** > TELOS
**TELOTAXES** > TELOTAXIS
**TELOTAXIS** n movement of
an organism in response
to one particular stimulus,
overriding any response to
other stimuli present
**TELPHER** same
as > TELFERAGE
**TELPHERED** > TELPHER
**TELPHERIC** > TELPHER
**TELPHERS** > TELPHER
**TELS** > TEL
**TELSON** n last segment or
an appendage on the last
segment of the body of
crustaceans and arachnids
**TELSONIC** > TELSON
**TELSONS** > TELSON
**TELT** same as > TAULD
**TEMAZEPAM** n sedative
in the form of a gel-like
capsule, which is taken
orally or melted and
injected by drug users
**TEMBLOR** n earthquake or
earth tremor
**TEMBLORES** > TEMBLOR
**TEMBLORS** > TEMBLOR
**TEME** old variant of > TEAM

**TEMED** > TEME
**TEMENE** > TEMENOS
**TEMENOS** n sacred area, esp
one surrounding a temple
**TEMERITY** n boldness or
audacity
**TEMEROUS** > TEMERITY
**TEMES** > TEME
**TEMP** same as > TEMPORARY
**TEMPED** > TEMP
**TEMPEH** n fermented soya
beans
**TEMPEHS** > TEMPEH
**TEMPER** n outburst of anger
▷ vb make less extreme
**TEMPERA** n painting
medium for powdered
pigments
**TEMPERAS** > TEMPERA
**TEMPERATE** adj (of climate)
not extreme ▷ vb temper
**TEMPERED** adj (of a scale)
having the frequency
differences between notes
adjusted in accordance
with the system of equal
temperament
**TEMPERER** > TEMPER
**TEMPERERS** > TEMPER
**TEMPERING** > TEMPER
**TEMPERS** > TEMPER
**TEMPEST** n violent storm
▷ vb agitate or disturb
violently
**TEMPESTED** > TEMPEST
**TEMPESTS** > TEMPEST
**TEMPI** > TEMPO
**TEMPING** > TEMP
**TEMPLAR** n lawyer, esp a
barrister, who lives or has
chambers in the Inner or
Middle Temple in London
**TEMPLARS** > TEMPLAR
**TEMPLATE** n pattern
used to cut out shapes
accurately
**TEMPLATES** > TEMPLATE
**TEMPLE** n building for
worship
**TEMPLED** > TEMPLE
**TEMPLES** > TEMPLE
**TEMPLET** same
as > TEMPLATE
**TEMPLETS** > TEMPLET
**TEMPO** n rate or pace
**TEMPORAL** adj of time ▷ n
any body part relating
to or near the temple or
temples
**TEMPORALS** > TEMPORAL
**TEMPORARY** adj lasting
only for a short time ▷ n
person, esp a secretary
or other office worker,
employed on a temporary
basis
**TEMPORE** adv in the time of
**TEMPORISE** same
as > TEMPORIZE
**TEMPORIZE** vb gain time by
negotiation or evasiveness
**TEMPOS** > TEMPO
**TEMPS** > TEMP
**TEMPT** vb entice (a person)

to do something wrong
**TEMPTABLE** > TEMPT
**TEMPTED** > TEMPT
**TEMPTER** > TEMPT
**TEMPTERS** > TEMPT
**TEMPTING** adj attractive or
inviting
**TEMPTINGS** > TEMPTING
**TEMPTRESS** n woman who
sets out to allure or seduce
a man or men
**TEMPTS** > TEMPT
**TEMPURA** n Japanese dish
of seafood or vegetables
dipped in batter and deep-
fried, often at the table
**TEMPURAS** > TEMPURA
**TEMS** same as > TEMSE
**TEMSE** vb sieve
**TEMSED** > TEMSE
**TEMSES** > TEMSE
**TEMSING** > TEMSE
**TEMULENCE** n drunkenness
**TEMULENCY** same
as > TEMULENCE
**TEMULENT** > TEMULENCE
**TEN** n one more than nine
▷ adj amounting to ten
**TENABLE** adj able to be
upheld or maintained
**TENABLY** > TENABLE
**TENACE** n holding of two
nonconsecutive high cards
of a suit, such as the ace
and queen
**TENACES** > TENACE
**TENACIOUS** adj holding fast
**TENACITY** > TENACIOUS
**TENACULA** > TENACULUM
**TENACULUM** n surgical or
dissecting instrument
for grasping and holding
parts, consisting of a
slender hook mounted in
a handle
**TENAIL** same as > TENAILLE
**TENAILLE** n low outwork
in the main ditch between
two bastions
**TENAILLES** > TENAILLE
**TENAILLON** n outwork
shoring up a ravelin
**TENAILS** > TENAIL
**TENANCIES** > TENANCY
**TENANCY** n temporary
possession or use of lands
or property owned by
somebody else, in return
for payment
**TENANT** n person who rents
land or a building ▷ vb
hold (land or property) as
a tenant
**TENANTED** > TENANT
**TENANTING** > TENANT
**TENANTRY** n tenants
collectively
**TENANTS** > TENANT
**TENCH** n freshwater game
fish of the carp family
**TENCHES** > TENCH
**TEND** vb be inclined
**TENDANCE** n care and
attention

**TENDANCES** > TENDANCE
**TENDED** > TEND
**TENDENCE** same
as > TENDENCY
**TENDENCES** > TENDENCE
> TENDENCIOUSNESS
**TENDENCY** n inclination to
act in a certain way
**TENDENZ** same
as > TENDENCY
**TENDENZEN** > TENDENZ
**TENDER** adj not tough ▷ vb
offer ▷ n such an offer
**TENDERED** > TENDER
**TENDERER** > TENDER
**TENDERERS** > TENDER
**TENDEREST** > TENDER
**TENDERING** > TENDER
**TENDERISE** same
as > TENDERIZE
**TENDERIZE** vb soften
(meat) by pounding or
treatment with a special
substance
**TENDERLY** > TENDER
**TENDERS** > TENDER
**TENDING** > TEND
**TENDINOUS** adj of,
relating to, possessing, or
resembling tendons
**TENDON** n strong tissue
attaching a muscle to a
bone
**TENDONS** > TENDON
**TENDRE** n care
**TENDRES** > TENDRE
**TENDRESSE** n feeling of
love; tenderness
**TENDRIL** n slender stem
by which a climbing plant
clings
**TENDRILED** > TENDRIL
**TENDRILS** > TENDRIL
**TENDRON** n shoot
**TENDRONS** > TENDRON
**TENDS** > TEND
**TENDU** n position in ballet
**TENDUS** > TENDU
**TENE** same as > TEEN
**TENEBRAE** n darkness
**TENEBRIO** n type of small
mealworm
**TENEBRIOS** > TENEBRIO
> TENEBRIOUSNESS
**TENEBRISM** n school, style,
or method of painting,
adopted chiefly by 17th-
century Spanish and
Neapolitan painters, esp
Caravaggio, characterized
by large areas of dark
colours, usually relieved
with a shaft of light
**TENEBRIST** > TENEBRISM
**TENEBRITY** n darkness;
gloominess
**TENEBROSE** same
as > TENEBROUS
**TENEBROUS** adj gloomy,
shadowy, or dark
**TENEMENT** n (esp in
Scotland or the US)
building divided into
several flats

**TENEMENTS** >TENEMENT
**TENENDUM** n part of a deed that specifies the terms of tenure
**TENENDUMS** >TENENDUM
**TENES** >TENE
**TENESMIC** >TENESMUS
**TENESMUS** n bowel disorder
**TENET** n doctrine or belief
**TENETS** >TENET
**TENFOLD** n one tenth
**TENFOLDS** >TENFOLD
**TENGE** n standard monetary unit of Kazakhstan, divided into 100 tiyn
**TENGES** >TENGE
**TENIA** same as >TAENIA
**TENIAFUGE** same as >TENIACIDE
**TENIACIDE** n substance, esp a drug, that kills tapeworms
**TENIAE** >TENIA
**TENIAFUGE** same as >TENIACIDE
**TENIAS** >TENIA
**TENIASES** >TENIASIS
**TENIASIS** same as >TAENIASIS
**TENIOID** >TENIA
**TENNE** n tawny colour
**TENNER** n ten-pound note
**TENNERS** >TENNER
**TENNES** >TENNE
**TENNIES** >TENNY
**TENNIS** n game in which players use rackets to hit a ball back and forth over a net
**TENNISES** >TENNIS
**TENNIST** n tennis player
**TENNISTS** >TENNIST
**TENNO** n formal title of the Japanese emperor, esp when regarded as a divine religious leader
**TENNOS** >TENNO
**TENNY** same as >TENNE
**TENON** n projecting end on a piece of wood fitting into a slot in another ▷ vb form a tenon on (a piece of wood)
**TENONED** >TENON
**TENONER** >TENON
**TENONERS** >TENON
**TENONING** >TENON
**TENONS** >TENON
**TENOR** n (singer with) the second highest male voice ▷ adj (of a voice or instrument) between alto and baritone
**TENORIST** n musician playing any tenor instrument
**TENORISTS** >TENORIST
**TENORITE** n black mineral found in copper deposits and consisting of copper oxide in the form of either metallic scales or earthy masses. Formula: CuO
**TENORITES** >TENORITE
**TENORLESS** >TENOR

**TENOROON** n tenor bassoon
**TENOROONS** >TENOROON
**TENORS** >TENOR
**TENOTOMY** n surgical division of a tendon
**TENOUR** old variant of >TENOR
**TENOURS** >TENOUR
**TENPENCE** n sum of money equivalent to ten pennies
**TENPENCES** >TENPENCE
**TENPENNY** adj (of a nail) three inches in length
**TENPIN** n one of the pins used in tenpin bowling
**TENPINS** >TENPIN
**TENREC** n small mammal resembling hedgehogs or shrews
**TENRECS** >TENREC
**TENS** >TEN
**TENSE** adj emotionally strained ▷ vb make or become tense ▷ n form of a verb showing the time of action
**TENSED** >TENSE
**TENSELESS** >TENSE
**TENSELY** >TENSE
**TENSENESS** >TENSE
**TENSER** >TENSE
**TENSES** >TENSE
**TENSEST** >TENSE
**TENSIBLE** adj capable of being stretched
**TENSIBLY** >TENSIBLE
**TENSILE** adj of tension
**TENSILELY** >TENSILE
**TENSILITY** >TENSILE
**TENSING** >TENSE
**TENSION** n hostility or suspense ▷ vb tighten
**TENSIONAL** >TENSION
**TENSIONED** >TENSION
**TENSIONER** >TENSION
**TENSIONS** >TENSION
**TENSITIES** >TENSITY
**TENSITY** rare word for >TENSION
**TENSIVE** adj of or causing tension or strain
**TENSON** n type of French lyric poem
**TENSONS** >TENSON
**TENSOR** n any muscle that can cause a part to become firm or tense
**TENSORIAL** >TENSOR
**TENSORS** >TENSOR
**TENT** n portable canvas shelter ▷ vb camp in a tent
**TENTACLE** n flexible organ of many invertebrates, used for grasping, feeding, etc
**TENTACLED** >TENTACLE
**TENTACLES** >TENTACLE
**TENTACULA** >TENTACLE
**TENTAGE** n tents collectively
**TENTAGES** >TENTAGE
**TENTATION** n method of achieving the

correct adjustment of a mechanical device by a series of trials
**TENTATIVE** adj provisional or experimental ▷ n investigative attempt
**TENTED** >TENT
**TENTER** >TENT
**TENTERED** >TENT
**TENTERING** >TENT
**TENTERS** >TENT
**TENTFUL** n number of people or objects that can fit in a tent
**TENTFULS** >TENTFUL
**TENTH** n (of) number ten in a series ▷ adj coming after the ninth in numbering or counting order, position, time, etc ▷ adv after the ninth person, position, event, etc
**TENTHLY** same as >TENTH
**TENTHS** >TENTH
**TENTIE** adj wary
**TENTIER** >TENTIE
**TENTIEST** >TENTIE
**TENTIGO** n morbid preoccupation with sex
**TENTIGOS** >TENTIGO
**TENTING** >TENT
**TENTINGS** >TENT
**TENTLESS** >TENT
**TENTLIKE** >TENT
**TENTMAKER** n maker of tents
**TENTORIA** >TENTORIUM
**TENTORIAL** >TENTORIUM
**TENTORIUM** n tough membrane covering the upper part of the cerebellum
**TENTS** >TENT
**TENTWISE** adv in the manner of a tent
**TENTY** same as >TENTIE
**TENUE** n deportment
**TENUES** >TENUIS
**TENUIOUS** same as >TENUOUS
**TENUIS** n (in the grammar of classical Greek) any of the voiceless stops as represented by kappa, pi, or tau (k, p, t)
**TENUITIES** >TENUOUS
**TENUITY** >TENUOUS
**TENUOUS** adj slight or flimsy
**TENUOUSLY** >TENUOUS
**TENURABLE** >TENURE
**TENURE** n (period of) the holding of an office or position
**TENURED** adj having tenure of office
**TENURES** >TENURE
**TENURIAL** >TENURE
**TENURING** n process of making tenured
**TENUTI** >TENUTO
**TENUTO** adv (of a note) to be held for or beyond its full time value ▷ vb note

sustained thus
**TENUTOS** >TENUTO
**TENZON** same as >TENSON
**TENZONS** >TENZON
**TEOCALLI** n any of various truncated pyramids built by the Aztecs as bases for their temples
**TEOCALLIS** >TEOCALLI
**TEOPAN** n enclosure surrounding a teocalli
**TEOPANS** >TEOPAN
**TEOSINTE** n tall Central American annual grass, related to maize and grown for forage in the southern US
**TEOSINTES** >TEOSINTE
**TEPA** n type of tree native to South America
**TEPAL** n any of the subdivisions of a perianth that is not clearly differentiated into calyx and corolla
**TEPALS** >TEPAL
**TEPAS** >TEPA
**TEPEE** n cone-shaped tent, formerly used by Native Americans
**TEPEES** >TEPEE
**TEPEFIED** >TEPEFY
**TEPEFIES** >TEPEFY
**TEPEFY** vb make or become tepid
**TEPEFYING** >TEPEFY
**TEPHIGRAM** n chart depicting variations in atmospheric conditions relative to altitude
**TEPHILLAH** same as >TEFILLAH
**TEPHILLIN** >TEPHILLAH
**TEPHRA** n solid matter ejected during a volcanic eruption
**TEPHRAS** >TEPHRA
**TEPHRITE** n variety of basalt
**TEPHRITES** >TEPHRITE
**TEPHRITIC** >TEPHRITE
**TEPHROITE** n manganese silicate
**TEPID** adj slightly warm
**TEPIDARIA** pl n in Ancient Rome, the warm rooms of the baths
**TEPIDER** >TEPID
**TEPIDEST** >TEPID
**TEPIDITY** >TEPID
**TEPIDLY** >TEPID
**TEPIDNESS** >TEPID
**TEPOY** same as >TEAPOY
**TEPOYS** >TEPOY
**TEQUILA** n Mexican alcoholic drink
**TEQUILAS** >TEQUILA
**TEQUILLA** same as >TEQUILA
**TEQUILLAS** >TEQUILLA
**TERABYTE** n large unit of computer memory
**TERABYTES** >TERABYTE
**TERAFLOP** n measure

of processing speed, consisting of a thousand billion floating-point operations a second

**TERAFLOPS** > TERAFLOP

**TERAGLIN** n edible marine fish of Australia which has fine scales and is blue in colour

**TERAGLINS** > TERAGLIN

**TERAHERTZ** n large unit of electrical frequency

**TERAI** n felt hat with a wide brim worn in subtropical regions

**TERAIS** > TERAI

**TERAKIHI** same as > TARAKIHI

**TERAKIHIS** > TERAKIHI

**TERAOHM** n unit of resistance equal to $10^{12}$ ohms

**TERAOHMS** > TERAOHM

**TERAPH** n any of various small household gods or images venerated by ancient Semitic peoples

**TERAPHIM** > TERAPH

**TERAPHIMS** > TERAPH

**TERAS** n monstrosity; teratism

**TERATA** > TERAS

**TERATISM** n malformed animal or human, esp in the fetal stage

**TERATISMS** > TERATISM

**TERATOGEN** n any substance, organism, or process that causes malformations in a fetus

**TERATOID** adj resembling a monster

**TERATOMA** n tumour or group of tumours composed of tissue foreign to the site of growth

**TERATOMAS** > TERATOMA

**TERAWATT** n unit of power equal to one million megawatts

**TERAWATTS** > TERAWATT

**TERBIA** n amorphous white insoluble powder

**TERBIAS** > TERBIA

**TERBIC** > TERBIUM

**TERBIUM** n rare metallic element

**TERBIUMS** > TERBIUM

**TERCE** n third of the seven canonical hours of the divine office, originally fixed at the third hour of the day, about 9 am

**TERCEL** n male falcon or hawk, esp as used in falconry

**TERCELET** same as > TERCEL

**TERCELETS** > TERCELET

**TERCELS** > TERCEL

**TERCES** > TERCE

**TERCET** n group of three lines of verse that rhyme together or are connected by rhyme with adjacent

groups of three lines

**TERCETS** > TERCET

**TERCIO** n regiment of Spanish or Italian infantry

**TERCIOS** > TERCIO

**TEREBENE** n mixture of hydrocarbons prepared from oil of turpentine and sulphuric acid, used to make paints and varnishes and medicinally as an expectorant and antiseptic

**TEREBENES** > TEREBENE

**TEREBIC** as in terebic acid white crystalline carboxylic acid produced by the action of nitric acid on turpentin

**TEREBINTH** n small anacardiaceous tree with winged leafstalks and clusters of small flowers, and yielding a turpentine

**TEREBRA** n ancient Roman device used for boring holes in defensive walls

**TEREBRAE** > TEREBRA

**TEREBRANT** n type of hymenopterous insect

**TEREBRAS** > TEREBRA

**TEREBRATE** adj (of animals, esp insects) having a boring or penetrating organ, such as a sting ▷ vb bore

**TEREDINES** > TEREDO

**TEREDO** n marine mollusc that bores into and destroys submerged timber

**TEREDOS** > TEREDO

**TEREFA** same as > TREF

**TEREFAH** same as > TREF

**TEREK** n type of sandpiper

**TEREKS** > TEREK

**TERES** n shoulder muscle

**TERETE** adj (esp of plant parts) smooth and usually cylindrical and tapering

**TERETES** > TERETE

**TERF** old variant of > TURF

**TERFE** old variant of > TURF

**TERFES** > TERFE

**TERFS** > TERF

**TERGA** > TERGUM

**TERGAL** > TERGUM

**TERGITE** n constituent part of a tergum

**TERGITES** > TERGITE

**TERGUM** n cuticular plate covering the dorsal surface of a body segment of an arthropod

**TERIYAKI** adj basted with soy sauce and rice wine and broiled over an open fire ▷ n dish prepared in this way

**TERIYAKIS** > TERIYAKI

**TERM** n word or expression ▷ vb name or designate

**TERMAGANT** n unpleasant and bad-tempered woman

**TERMED** > TERM

**TERMER** same as > TERMOR

**TERMERS** > TERMER

**TERMINAL** adj (of an illness) ending in death ▷ n place where people or vehicles begin or end a journey

**TERMINALS** > TERMINAL

**TERMINATE** vb bring or come to an end

**TERMINER** n person or thing that limits or determines

**TERMINERS** > TERMINER

**TERMING** > TERM

**TERMINI** > TERMINUS

**TERMINISM** n philosophical theory

**TERMINIST** > TERMINISM

**TERMINUS** n railway or bus station at the end of a line

**TERMITARY** n termite nest

**TERMITE** n white antlike insect that destroys timber

**TERMITES** > TERMITE

**TERMITIC** > TERMITE

**TERMLESS** adj without limit or boundary

**TERMLIES** > TERMLY

**TERMLY** n publication issued once a term

**TERMOR** n person who holds an estate for a term of years or until he dies

**TERMORS** > TERMOR

**TERMS** > TERM

**TERMTIME** n time during a term, esp a school or university term

**TERMTIMES** > TERMTIME

**TERN** n gull-like sea bird with a forked tail and pointed wings

**TERNAL** > TERN

**TERNARIES** > TERNARY

**TERNARY** adj consisting of three parts ▷ n group of three

**TERNATE** adj (esp of a leaf) consisting of three leaflets or other parts

**TERNATELY** > TERNATE

**TERNE** n alloy of lead containing tin (10–20 per cent) and antimony (1.5–2 per cent) ▷ vb coat with this alloy

**TERNED** > TERNE

**TERNES** > TERNE

**TERNING** > TERNE

**TERNION** n group of three

**TERNIONS** > TERNION

**TERNS** > TERN

**TERPENE** n any one of a class of unsaturated hydrocarbons, such as the carotenes, that are found in the essential oils of many plants

**TERPENES** > TERPENE

**TERPENIC** > TERPENE

**TERPENOID** > TERPENE

**TERPINEOL** n terpene

alcohol with an odour of lilac, present in several essential oils

**TERPINOL** same as > TERPINEOL

**TERPINOLS** > TERPINOL

**TERRA** n (in legal contexts) earth or land

**TERRACE** n row of houses built as one block ▷ vb form into or provide with a terrace

**TERRACED** > TERRACE

**TERRACES** > TERRACE

**TERRACING** n series of terraces, esp one dividing a slope into a steplike system of flat narrow fields

**TERRAE** > TERRA

**TERRAFORM** vb engage in planetary engineering to enhance the capacity of an extraterrestrial planetary environment to sustain life

**TERRAIN** same as > TERRANE

**TERRAINS** > TERRAIN

**TERRAMARA** n neolithic Italian pile-dwelling

**TERRAMARE** > TERRAMARA

**TERRANE** n series of rock formations, esp one having a prevalent type of rock

**TERRANES** > TERRANE

**TERRAPIN** n small turtle-like reptile

**TERRAPINS** > TERRAPIN

**TERRARIA** > TERRARIUM

**TERRARIUM** n enclosed container for small plants or animals

**TERRAS** same as > TRASS

**TERRASES** > TERRAS

**TERRAZZO** n floor of marble chips set in mortar and polished

**TERRAZZOS** > TERRAZZO

**TERREEN** old variant of > TUREEN

**TERREENS** > TERREEN

**TERRELLA** n magnetic globe designed to simulate and demonstrate the earth's magnetic fields

**TERRELLAS** > TERRELLA

**TERRENE** adj of or relating to the earth ▷ n land

**TERRENELY** > TERRENE

**TERRENES** > TERRENE > TERRESTRIAL

**TERRET** n either of the two metal rings on a harness saddle through which the reins are passed

**TERRETS** > TERRET

**TERRIBLE** adj very serious ▷ n something terrible

**TERRIBLES** > TERRIBLE

**TERRIBLY** adv in a terrible manner

**TERRICOLE** n plant or animal living on land

**TERRIER** n any of various

breeds of small active dog
**TERRIERS** >TERRIER
**TERRIES** >TERRY
**TERRIFIC** adj great or intense
**TERRIFIED** >TERRIFY
**TERRIFIER** >TERRIFY
**TERRIFIES** >TERRIFY
**TERRIFY** vb fill with fear
**TERRINE** n earthenware dish with a lid
**TERRINES** >TERRINE
**TERRIT** same as >TERRET
**TERRITORY** n district
**TERRITS** >TERRIT
**TERROIR** n combination of factors, including soil, climate, and environment, that gives a wine its distinctive character
**TERROIRS** >TERROIR
**TERROR** n great fear
**TERRORFUL** >TERROR
**TERRORISE** same as >TERRORIZE
**TERRORISM** n use of violence and intimidation to achieve political ends
**TERRORIST** n person who employs terror or terrorism, esp as a political weapon
**TERRORIZE** vb force or oppress by fear or violence
**TERRORS** >TERROR
**TERRY** n fabric with small loops covering both sides, used esp for making towels
**TERSE** adj neat and concise
**TERSELY** >TERSE
**TERSENESS** >TERSE
**TERSER** >TERSE
**TERSEST** >TERSE
**TERSION** n action of rubbing off or wiping
**TERSIONS** >TERSION
**TERTIA** same as >TERCIO
**TERTIAL** same as >TERTIARY
**TERTIALS** >TERTIAL
**TERTIAN** adj (of a fever or the symptoms of a disease, esp malaria) occurring every other day ▷ n tertian fever or symptoms
**TERTIANS** >TERTIAN
**TERTIARY** adj third in degree, order, etc ▷ n any of the tertiary feathers
**TERTIAS** >TERTIA
**TERTIUM** as in tertium quid unknown or indefinite thing related in some way to two known or definite things, but distinct from both
**TERTIUS** n third (in a group)
**TERTIUSES** >TERTIUS
**TERTS** n card game using 32 cards
**TERVALENT** same as >TRIVALENT
**TERYLENE** n tradename

for a synthetic polyester fibre or fabric based on terephthalic acid, characterized by lightness and crease resistance and used for clothing, sheets, ropes, sails, etc
**TERYLENES** >TERYLENE
**TERZETTA** n tercet
**TERZETTAS** >TERZETTA
**TERZETTI** >TERZETTO
**TERZETTO** n trio, esp a vocal one
**TERZETTOS** >TERZETTO
**TES** >TE
**TESLA** n derived SI unit of magnetic flux density equal to a flux of 1 weber in an area of 1 square metre.
**TESLAS** >TESLA
**TESSELATE** vb cover with small tiles
**TESSELLA** n little tessera
**TESSELLAE** >TESSELLA
**TESSELLAR** adj of or relating to tessellae
**TESSERA** n small square tile used in mosaics
**TESSERACT** n cube inside another cube
**TESSERAE** >TESSERA
**TESSERAL** >TESSERA
**TESSITURA** n general pitch level of a piece of vocal music
**TESSITURE** >TESSITURA
**TEST** vb try out to ascertain the worth, capability, or endurance of ▷ n critical examination
**TESTA** n hard outer layer of a seed
**TESTABLE** >TEST
**TESTACEAN** n microscopic animal with hard shell
**TESTACIES** >TESTATE
**TESTACY** >TESTATE
**TESTAE** >TESTA
**TESTAMENT** n proof or tribute
**TESTAMUR** n certificate proving an examination has been passed
**TESTAMURS** >TESTAMUR
**TESTATE** adj having left a valid will ▷ n person who dies and leaves a legally valid will
**TESTATES** >TESTATE
**TESTATION** >TESTATOR
**TESTATOR** n maker of a will
**TESTATORS** >TESTATOR
**TESTATRIX** same as >TESTATOR
**TESTATUM** n part of a purchase deed
**TESTATUMS** >TESTATUM
**TESTCROSS** vb subject to a testcross, a genetic test for ascertaining whether an individual is homozygous or heterozygous
**TESTE** n witness
**TESTED** >TEST

**TESTEE** n person subjected to a test
**TESTEES** >TESTEE
**TESTER** n person or thing that tests or is used for testing
**TESTERN** vb give (someone) a teston
**TESTERNED** >TESTERN
**TESTERNS** >TESTERN
**TESTERS** >TESTER
**TESTES** >TESTIS
**TESTICLE** n either of the two male reproductive glands
**TESTICLES** >TESTICLE
**TESTIER** >TESTY
**TESTIEST** >TESTY
**TESTIFIED** >TESTIFY
**TESTIFIER** >TESTIFY
**TESTIFIES** >TESTIFY
**TESTIFY** vb give evidence under oath
**TESTILY** >TESTY
**TESTIMONY** n declaration of truth or fact ▷ vb testify
**TESTINESS** >TESTY
**TESTING** >TEST
**TESTINGS** >TEST
**TESTIS** same as >TESTICLE
**TESTON** n French silver coin of the 16th century
**TESTONS** >TESTON
**TESTOON** same as >TESTON
**TESTOONS** >TESTOON
**TESTRIL** same as >TESTRILL
**TESTRILL** n sixpence
**TESTRILLS** >TESTRILL
**TESTRILS** >TESTRIL
**TESTS** >TEST
**TESTUDO** n form of shelter used by the ancient Roman Army for protection against attack from above, consisting either of a mobile arched structure or of overlapping shields held by the soldiers over their heads
**TESTUDOS** >TESTUDO
**TESTY** adj irritable or touchy
**TET** same as >TETH
**TETANAL** >TETANUS
**TETANIC** adj of, relating to, or producing tetanus or the spasms of tetanus ▷ n tetanic drug or agent
**TETANICAL** >TETANUS
**TETANICS** >TETANIC
**TETANIES** >TETANY
**TETANISE** same as >TETANIZE
**TETANISED** >TETANISE
**TETANISES** >TETANISE
**TETANIZE** vb induce tetanus in (a muscle)
**TETANIZED** >TETANIZE
**TETANIZES** >TETANIZE
**TETANOID** >TETANUS
**TETANUS** n acute infectious disease producing muscular spasms and convulsions

**TETANUSES** >TETANUS
**TETANY** n abnormal increase in the excitability of nerves and muscles resulting in spasms of the arms and legs, caused by a deficiency of parathyroid secretion
**TETCHED** same as >TECHED
**TETCHIER** >TETCHY
**TETCHIEST** >TETCHY
**TETCHILY** >TETCHY
**TETCHY** adj cross and irritable
**TETE** n elaborate hairstyle
**TETES** >TETE
**TETH** n ninth letter of the Hebrew alphabet transliterated as t and pronounced more or less like English t with pharyngeal articulation
**TETHER** n rope or chain for tying an animal to a spot ▷ vb tie up with rope
**TETHERED** >TETHER
**TETHERING** >TETHER
**TETHERS** >TETHER
**TETHS** >TETH
**TETOTUM** same as >TEETOTUM
**TETOTUMS** >TETOTUM
**TETRA** n brightly coloured tropical freshwater fish
**TETRACID** adj (of a base) capable of reacting with four molecules of a monobasic acid
**TETRACIDS** >TETRACID
**TETRACT** n sponge spicule with four rays
**TETRACTS** >TETRACT
**TETRAD** n group or series of four
**TETRADIC** >TETRAD
**TETRADITE** n person who believes that the number four has supernatural significance
**TETRADS** >TETRAD
**TETRAGON** n figure with four angles and four sides >TETRAGONAL
**TETRAGONS** >TETRAGON
**TETRAGRAM** n any word of four letters
**TETRALOGY** n series of four related works
**TETRAMER** n four-molecule polymer
**TETRAMERS** >TETRAMER
**TETRAPLA** n book containing versions of the same text in four languages
**TETRAPLAS** >TETRAPLA
**TETRAPOD** n any vertebrate that has four limbs
**TETRAPODS** >TETRAPOD
**TETRAPODY** n metrical unit consisting of four feet
**TETRARCH** n ruler of one fourth of a country
**TETRARCHS** >TETRARCH

**TETRARCHY** > TETRARCH
**TETRAS** > TETRA
**TETRAXON** n four-pointed spicule
**TETRAXONS** > TETRAXON
**TETRI** n currency unit of Georgia
**TETRIS** > TETRI
**TETRODE** n electronic valve having four electrodes, namely a cathode, control grid, screen grid, and anode
**TETRODES** > TETRODE
**TETRONAL** n sedative drug
**TETRONALS** > TETRONAL
**TETROXID** same as > TETROXIDE
**TETROXIDE** n any oxide that contains four oxygen atoms per molecule
**TETROXIDS** > TETROXID
**TETRYL** n yellow crystalline explosive solid used in detonators
**TETRYLS** > TETRYL
**TETS** > TET
**TETTER** n blister or pimple ▷ vb cause a tetter to erupt (on)
**TETTERED** > TETTER
**TETTERING** > TETTER
**TETTEROUS** > TETTER
**TETTERS** > TETTER
**TETTIX** n cicada
**TETTIXES** > TETTIX
**TEUCH** Scots variant of > TOUGH
**TEUCHAT** Scots variant of > TEWIT
**TEUCHATS** > TEUCHAT
**TEUCHER** > TEUCH
**TEUCHEST** > TEUCH
**TEUCHTER** n in Scotland, derogatory word used by Lowlanders for a Highlander
**TEUCHTERS** > TEUCHTER
**TEUGH** same as > TEUCH
**TEUGHER** > TEUGH
**TEUGHEST** > TEUGH
**TEUGHLY** > TEUGH
**TEUTONISE** same as > TEUTONIZE
**TEUTONIZE** vb make or become German or Germanic
**TEVATRON** n machine used in nuclear research
**TEVATRONS** > TEVATRON
**TEW** vb work hard
**TEWART** same as > TUART
**TEWARTS** > TEWART
**TEWED** > TEW
**TEWEL** n horse's rectum
**TEWELS** > TEWEL
**TEWHIT** same as > TEWIT
**TEWHITS** > TEWHIT
**TEWING** > TEW
**TEWIT** n lapwing
**TEWITS** > TEWIT
**TEWS** > TEW
**TEX** n unit of weight used to measure yarn density

**TEXAS** n structure on the upper deck of a paddle-steamer containing the officers' quarters and the wheelhouse
**TEXASES** > TEXAS
**TEXES** > TEX
**TEXT** n main body of a book as distinct from illustrations etc ▷ vb send a text message to (someone)
**TEXTBOOK** n standard book on a particular subject ▷ adj perfect
**TEXTBOOKS** > TEXTBOOK
**TEXTER** n person who communicates by text messaging
**TEXTERS** > TEXTER
**TEXTILE** n fabric or cloth, esp woven ▷ adj of (the making of) fabrics
**TEXTILES** > TEXTILE
**TEXTLESS** > TEXT
**TEXTORIAL** adj of or relating to weaving or weavers
**TEXTPHONE** n phone designed to translate speech into text and vice versa
**TEXTS** > TEXT
**TEXTUAL** adj of, based on, or relating to, a text or texts
**TEXTUALLY** > TEXTUAL
**TEXTUARY** adj of, relating to, or contained in a text ▷ n textual critic
**TEXTURAL** > TEXTURE
**TEXTURE** n structure, feel, or consistency ▷ vb give a distinctive texture to (something)
**TEXTURED** > TEXTURE
**TEXTURES** > TEXTURE
**TEXTURING** > TEXTURE
**TEXTURISE** same as > TEXTURIZE
**TEXTURIZE** vb texture
**THACK** Scots word for > THATCH
**THACKED** > THACK
**THACKING** > THACK
**THACKS** > THACK
**THAE** Scots word for > THOSE
**THAGI** same as > THUGGEE
**THAGIS** > THAGI
**THAIM** Scots variant of > THEM
**THAIRM** n catgut
**THAIRMS** > THAIRM
**THALAMI** > THALAMUS
**THALAMIC** > THALAMUS
**THALAMUS** n either of the two contiguous egg-shaped masses of grey matter at the base of the brain
**THALASSIC** adj of or relating to the sea
**THALER** n former German, Austrian, or Swiss silver

coin
**THALERS** > THALER
**THALI** n meal consisting of several small meat or vegetable dishes accompanied by rice, bread, etc, and sometimes by a starter or a sweet
**THALIAN** adj of or relating to comedy
**THALIS** > THALI
**THALLI** > THALLUS
**THALLIC** adj of or containing thallium, esp in the trivalent state
**THALLINE** > THALLUS
**THALLIOUS** > THALLIUM
**THALLIUM** n highly toxic metallic element
**THALLIUMS** > THALLIUM
**THALLOID** > THALLUS
**THALLOUS** adj of or containing thallium, esp in the monovalent state
**THALLUS** n undifferentiated vegetative body of algae, fungi, and lichens
**THALLUSES** > THALLUS
**THALWEG** n longitudinal outline of a riverbed from source to mouth
**THALWEGS** > THALWEG
**THAN** prep used to introduce the second element of a comparison ▷ n old variant of "then" (that time)
**THANA** same as > TANA
**THANADAR** same as > TANADAR
**THANADARS** > THANADAR
**THANAGE** n state of being a thane
**THANAGES** > THANAGE
**THANAH** same as > TANA
**THANAHS** > THANAH
**THANAS** > THANA
**THANATISM** n belief that the soul ceases to exist when the body dies
**THANATIST** > THANATISM
**THANATOID** adj like death
**THANATOS** n Greek personification of death
**THANE** n Anglo-Saxon or medieval Scottish nobleman
**THANEDOM** > THANE
**THANEDOMS** > THANE
**THANEHOOD** > THANE
**THANES** > THANE
**THANESHIP** > THANE
**THANGKA** n (in Tibetan Buddhism) a religious painting on a scroll
**THANGKAS** > THANGKA
**THANK** vb express gratitude to
**THANKED** > THANK
**THANKEE** interj thank you
**THANKER** > THANK
**THANKERS** > THANK
**THANKFUL** adj grateful

**THANKING** > THANK
**THANKINGS** > THANK
**THANKLESS** adj unrewarding or unappreciated
**THANKS** pl n words of gratitude ▷ interj polite expression of gratitude
**THANKYOU** n conventional expression of gratitude
**THANKYOUS** > THANKYOU
**THANNA** same as > TANA
**THANNAH** same as > TANA
**THANNAHS** > THANNAH
**THANNAS** > THANNA
**THANS** > THAN
**THAR** same as > TAHR
**THARM** n stomach
**THARMS** > THARM
**THARS** > THAR
**THAT** pron used to refer to something already mentioned or familiar, or further away
**THATAWAY** adv that way
**THATCH** n roofing material of reeds or straw ▷ vb roof (a house) with reeds or straw
**THATCHED** > THATCH
**THATCHER** > THATCH
**THATCHERS** > THATCH
**THATCHES** > THATCH
**THATCHIER** > THATCH
**THATCHING** > THATCH
**THATCHT** old variant of > THATCHED
**THATCHY** > THATCH
**THATNESS** n state or quality of being 'that'
**THAUMATIN** n type of natural sweetener
**THAW** vb make or become unfrozen ▷ n thawing
**THAWED** > THAW
**THAWER** > THAW
**THAWERS** > THAW
**THAWIER** > THAWY
**THAWIEST** > THAWY
**THAWING** > THAW
**THAWINGS** > THAW
**THAWLESS** > THAW
**THAWS** > THAW
**THAWY** adj tending to thaw
**THE** determiner definite article, used before a noun
**THEACEOUS** adj of, relating to, or belonging to the Theaceae, a family of evergreen trees and shrubs of tropical and warm regions: includes the tea plant
**THEANDRIC** adj both divine and human
**THEARCHIC** > THEARCHY
**THEARCHY** n rule or government by God or gods
**THEATER** same as > THEATRE
**THEATERS** > THEATER
**THEATRAL** adj of or relating to the theatre
**THEATRE** n place where

plays etc are performed
**THEATRES** >THEATRE
**THEATRIC** *adj* of or relating to the theatre
**THEATRICS** *n* art of staging plays
**THEAVE** *n* young ewe
**THEAVES** >THEAVE
**THEBAINE** *n* poisonous white crystalline alkaloid, found in opium but without opioid actions
**THEBAINES** >THEBAINE
**THEBE** *n* inner satellite of Jupiter discovered in 1979
**THEBES** >THEBE
**THECA** *n* enclosing organ, cell, or spore case, esp the capsule of a moss
**THECAE** >THECA
**THECAL** >THECA
**THECATE** >THECA
**THECODONT** *adj* (of mammals and certain reptiles) having teeth that grow in sockets ▷ *n* extinct reptile
**THEE** *pron* refers to the person addressed: used mainly by members of the Society of Friends ▷ *vb* use the word "thee"
**THEED** >THEE
**THEEING** >THEE
**THEEK** *Scots variant of* >THATCH
**THEEKED** >THEEK
**THEEKING** >THEEK
**THEEKS** >THEEK
**THEELIN** *trade name for* >ESTRONE
**THEELINS** >THEELIN
**THEELOL** *n* estriol
**THEELOLS** >THEELOL
**THEES** >THEE
**THEFT** *n* act or an instance of stealing
**THEFTLESS** >THEFT
**THEFTS** >THEFT
**THEFTUOUS** *adj* tending to commit theft
**THEGITHER** *Scots variant of* >TOGETHER
**THEGN** *same as* >THANE
**THEGNLY** >THEGN
**THEGNS** >THEGN
**THEIC** *n* person who drinks excessive amounts of tea
**THEICS** >THEIC
**THEIN** *old variant of* >THANE
**THEINE** *another name for* >CAFFEINE
**THEINES** >THEINE
**THEINS** >THEIN
**THEIR** *determiner* of, belonging to, or associated in some way with them
**THEIRS** *pron* (thing or person) belonging to them
**THEIRSELF** *pron* dialect form of themselves: reflexive form of they or them

**THEISM** *n* belief in a God or gods
**THEISMS** >THEISM
**THEIST** >THEISM
**THEISTIC** >THEISM
**THEISTS** >THEISM
**THELEMENT** *n* old contraction of "the element"
**THELF** *n* old contraction of "the element"
**THELITIS** *n* inflammation of the nipple
**THELVES** >THELF
**THELYTOKY** *n* type of reproduction resulting in female offspring only
**THEM** *pron* refers to people or things other than the speaker or those addressed
**THEMA** *n* theme
**THEMATA** >THEMA
**THEMATIC** *adj* of, relating to, or consisting of a theme or themes ▷ *n* thematic vowel
**THEMATICS** >THEMATIC
**THEME** *n* main idea or subject being discussed ▷ *vb* design, decorate, arrange, etc, in accordance with a theme
**THEMED** >THEME
**THEMELESS** >THEME
**THEMES** >THEME
**THEMING** >THEME
**THEMSELF** *pron* reflexive form of one, whoever, anybody
**THEN** *adv* at that time ▷ *pron* that time ▷ *adj* existing or functioning at that time ▷ *n* that time
**THENABOUT** *adv* around then
**THENAGE** *old variant of* >THANAGE
**THENAGES** >THENAGE
**THENAL** *adj* of or relating to the thenar
**THENAR** *n* palm of the hand ▷ *adj* of or relating to the palm or the region at the base of the thumb
**THENARS** >THENAR
**THENCE** *adv* from that place or time
**THENS** >THEN
**THEOCRACY** *n* government by a god or priests
**THEOCRASY** *n* mingling into one of deities or divine attributes previously regarded as distinct
**THEOCRAT** >THEOCRACY
**THEOCRATS** >THEOCRACY
**THEODICY** *n* branch of theology concerned with defending the attributes of God against objections resulting from physical and moral evil

**THEOGONIC** >THEOGONY
**THEOGONY** *n* origin and descent of the gods
**THEOLOG** *same as* >THEOLOGUE
**THEOLOGER** *n* theologian
**THEOLOGIC** >THEOLOGY
**THEOLOGS** >THEOLOG
**THEOLOGUE** *n* theologian
**THEOLOGY** *n* study of religions and religious beliefs
**THEOMACHY** *n* battle among the gods or against them
**THEOMANCY** *n* divination or prophecy by an oracle or by people directly inspired by a god
**THEOMANIA** *n* religious madness, esp when it takes the form of believing oneself to be a god
**THEONOMY** *n* state of being governed by God
**THEOPATHY** *n* religious emotion engendered by the contemplation of or meditation upon God
**THEOPHAGY** *n* sacramental eating of a god
**THEOPHANY** *n* manifestation of a deity to man in a form that, though visible, is not necessarily material
**THEORBIST** >THEORBO
**THEORBO** *n* obsolete form of the lute, having two necks, one above the other, the second neck carrying a set of unstopped sympathetic bass strings
**THEORBOS** >THEORBO
**THEOREM** *n* proposition that can be proved by reasoning
**THEOREMIC** >THEOREM
**THEOREMS** >THEOREM
**THEORETIC** *adj* of, or based on, a theory
**THEORIC** *n* theory; conjecture
**THEORICS** >THEORIC
**THEORIES** >THEORY
**THEORIQUE** *same as* >THEORIC
**THEORISE** *same as* >THEORIZE
**THEORISED** >THEORISE
**THEORISER** >THEORISE
**THEORISES** >THEORISE
**THEORIST** *n* originator of a theory
**THEORISTS** >THEORIST
**THEORIZE** *vb* form theories, speculate
**THEORIZED** >THEORIZE
**THEORIZER** >THEORIZE
**THEORIZES** >THEORIZE
**THEORY** *n* set of ideas to explain something
**THEOSOPH** *n* proponent of theosophy
**THEOSOPHS** >THEOSOPH

**THEOSOPHY** *n* religious or philosophical system claiming to be based on intuitive insight into the divine nature
**THEOTOKOI** >THEOTOKOS
**THEOTOKOS** *n* mother of God
**THEOW** *n* slave in Anglo-Saxon Britain
**THEOWS** >THEOW
**THERALITE** *n* type of igneous rock
**THERAPIES** >THERAPY
**THERAPIST** *n* person skilled in a particular type of therapy
**THERAPSID** *n* extinct reptile: considered to be the ancestors of mammals
**THERAPY** *n* curing treatment
**THERBLIG** *n* basic unit of work in an industrial process
**THERBLIGS** >THERBLIG
**THERE** *adv* in or to that place ▷ *n* that place
**THEREAT** *adv* at that point or time
**THEREAWAY** *adv* in that direction
**THEREBY** *adv* by that means
**THEREFOR** *adv* for this, that, or it
**THEREFORE** *adv* consequently, that being so
**THEREFROM** *adv* from that or there
**THEREIN** *adv* in or into that place or thing
**THEREINTO** *adv* into that place, circumstance, etc
**THEREMIN** *n* electronic musical instrument, played by moving the hands through electromagnetic fields created by two metal rods
**THEREMINS** >THEREMIN
**THERENESS** *n* quality of having existence
**THEREOF** *adv* of or concerning that or it
**THEREON** *archaic word for* >THEREUPON
**THEREOUT** *another word for* >THEREFROM
**THERES** >THERE
**THERETO** *adv* that or it
**THEREUNTO** *adv* to that
**THEREUPON** *adv* immediately after that
**THEREWITH** *adv* with or in addition to that
**THERIAC** *n* ointment or potion of varying composition, used as an antidote to a poison
**THERIACA** *same as* >THERIAC
**THERIACAL** >THERIAC
**THERIACAS** >THERIACA

**THERIACS** >THERIAC
**THERIAN** n animal of the class Theria, a subclass of mammals
**THERIANS** >THERIAN
**THERM** n unit of measurement of heat public bath
**THERMAE** pl n public baths or hot springs, esp in ancient Greece or Rome
**THERMAL** adj of heat ▷ n rising current of warm air
**THERMALLY** >THERMAL
**THERMALS** >THERMAL
**THERME** old variant of >THERM
**THERMEL** n type of thermometer measuring temperature by means of thermoelectric current
**THERMELS** >THERMEL
**THERMES** >THERME
**THERMETTE** n device, used outdoors, for boiling water rapidly
**THERMIC** same as >THERMAL
**THERMICAL** same as >THERMAL
**THERMIDOR** as in lobster thermidor dish of cooked lobster
**THERMION** n electron or ion emitted by a body at high temperature
**THERMIONS** >THERMION
**THERMIT** variant of >THERMITE
**THERMITE** as in thermite process process for reducing metallic oxides
**THERMITES** >THERMITE
**THERMITS** >THERMIT
**THERMOS** n trademark term for a type of stoppered vacuum flask used to preserve the temperature of its contents
**THERMOSES** >THERMOS
**THERMOSET** n material (esp a synthetic plastic or resin) that hardens permanently after one application of heat and pressure
**THERMOTIC** adj of or because of heat
**THERMS** >THERM
**THEROID** adj of, relating to, or resembling a beast
**THEROLOGY** n study of mammals
**THEROPOD** n bipedal carnivorous saurischian dinosaur with strong hind legs and grasping hands
**THEROPODS** >THEROPOD
**THESAURAL** >THESAURUS
**THESAURI** >THESAURUS
**THESAURUS** n book containing lists of synonyms and related words
**THESE** determiner form of

this used before a plural noun
**THESES** >THESIS
**THESIS** n written work submitted for a degree
**THESP** short for >THESPIAN
**THESPIAN** adj of or relating to drama and the theatre ▷ n actor or actress
**THESPIANS** >THESPIAN
**THESPS** >THESP
**THETA** n eighth letter of the Greek alphabet
**THETAS** >THETA
**THETCH** old variant spelling of >THATCH
**THETCHED** >THETCH
**THETCHES** >THETCH
**THETCHING** >THETCH
**THETE** n member of the lowest order of freeman in ancient Athens
**THETES** >THETE
**THETHER** old variant of >THITHER
**THETIC** adj (in classical prosody) of, bearing, or relating to a metrical stress
**THETICAL** another word for >THETIC
**THEURGIC** >THEURGY
**THEURGIES** >THEURGY
**THEURGIST** >THEURGY
**THEURGY** n intervention of a divine or supernatural agency in the affairs of man
**THEW** n muscle, esp if strong or well-developed
**THEWED** adj strong; muscular
**THEWES** >THEW
**THEWIER** >THEW
**THEWIEST** >THEW
**THEWLESS** >THEW
**THEWS** >THEW
**THEWY** >THEW
**THEY** pron people or things other than the speaker or people addressed
**THIAMIN** same as >THIAMINE
**THIAMINE** n vitamin found in the outer coat of rice and other grains
**THIAMINES** >THIAMINE
**THIAMINS** >THIAMIN
**THIASUS** n congregation of people who have gathered to sing and dance in honour of a god
**THIASUSES** >THIASUS
**THIAZIDE** n diuretic drug
**THIAZIDES** >THIAZIDE
**THIAZIN** same as >THIAZINE
**THIAZINE** n any of a group of organic compounds containing a ring system composed of four carbon atoms, a sulphur atom, and a nitrogen atom
**THIAZINES** >THIAZINE
**THIAZINS** >THIAZIN

**THIAZOL** same as >THIAZOLE
**THIAZOLE** n colourless liquid with a pungent smell that contains a ring system composed of three carbon atoms, a sulphur atom, and a nitrogen atom
**THIAZOLES** >THIAZOLE
**THIAZOLS** >THIAZOL
**THIBET** n coloured woollen cloth
**THIBETS** >THIBET
**THIBLE** n stick for stirring porridge
**THIBLES** >THIBLE
**THICK** adj of great or specified extent from one side to the other ▷ vb thicken
**THICKED** >THICK
**THICKEN** vb make or become thick or thicker
**THICKENED** >THICKEN
**THICKENER** >THICKEN
**THICKENS** >THICKEN
**THICKER** >THICK
**THICKEST** >THICK
**THICKET** n dense growth of small trees
**THICKETED** adj covered in thicket
**THICKETS** >THICKET
**THICKETY** >THICKET
**THICKHEAD** n stupid or ignorant person
**THICKIE** same as >THICKO
**THICKIES** >THICKY
**THICKING** >THICK
**THICKISH** >THICK
**THICKLEAF** n succulent plant with sessile or short-stalked fleshy leaves
**THICKLY** >THICK
**THICKNESS** n state of being thick
**THICKO** n slow-witted unintelligent person
**THICKOES** >THICKO
**THICKOS** >THICKO
**THICKS** >THICK
**THICKSET** adj stocky in build
**THICKSETS** >THICKSET
**THICKSKIN** n insensitive person
**THICKY** same as >THICKO
**THIEF** n person who steals
**THIEVE** vb steal
**THIEVED** >THIEVE
**THIEVERY** >THIEVE
**THIEVES** >THIEVE
**THIEVING** adj given to stealing other people's possessions
**THIEVINGS** >THIEVING
**THIEVISH** >THIEF
**THIG** vb beg
**THIGGER** >THIG
**THIGGERS** >THIG
**THIGGING** >THIG
**THIGGINGS** >THIG
**THIGGIT** Scots inflection of >THIG

**THIGH** n upper part of the human leg
**THIGHBONE** same as >FEMUR
**THIGHED** adj having thighs
**THIGHS** >THIGH
**THIGS** >THIG
**THILK** pron that same
**THILL** another word for >SHAFT
**THILLER** n horse that goes between the thills of a cart
**THILLERS** >THILLER
**THILLS** >THILL
**THIMBLE** n cap protecting the end of the finger when sewing ▷ vb use a thimble
**THIMBLED** >THIMBLE
**THIMBLES** >THIMBLE
**THIMBLING** >THIMBLE
**THIN** adj not thick ▷ vb make or become thin ▷ adv in order to produce something thin
**THINCLAD** n track-and-field athlete
**THINCLADS** >THINCLAD
**THINDOWN** n reduction in the amount of particles, esp protons, of very high energy reaching and penetrating the earth's atmosphere from outer space
**THINDOWNS** >THINDOWN
**THINE** adj (something) of or associated with you (thou) ▷ pron something belonging to you (thou) ▷ determiner of, belonging to, or associated in some way with you (thou)
**THING** n material object
**THINGAMY** n person or thing the name of which is unknown
**THINGHOOD** n existence; state or condition of being a thing
**THINGIER** >THINGY
**THINGIES** >THINGY
**THINGIEST** >THINGY
**THINGNESS** n state of being a thing
**THINGS** >THING
**THINGUMMY** n person or thing the name of which is unknown, temporarily forgotten, or deliberately overlooked
**THINGY** adj existing in reality; actual
**THINK** vb consider, judge, or believe
**THINKABLE** adj able to be conceived or considered
**THINKABLY** >THINKABLE
**THINKER** >THINK
**THINKERS** >THINK
**THINKING** >THINK
**THINKINGS** >THINK
**THINKS** >THINK

THINLY >THIN
THINNED >THIN
THINNER >THIN
THINNERS >THIN
THINNESS >THIN
THINNEST >THIN
THINNING >THIN
THINNINGS >THIN
THINNISH >THIN
THINS >THIN
THIO adj of, or relating to, sulphur
THIOFURAN another name for >THIOPHEN
THIOL n any of a class of sulphur-containing organic compounds with the formula RSH, where R is an organic group
THIOLIC >THIOL
THIOLS >THIOL
THIONATE n any salt or ester of thionic acid
THIONATES >THIONATE
THIONIC adj of, relating to, or containing sulphur
THIONIN same as >THIONINE
THIONINE n crystalline derivative of thiazine used as a violet dye to stain microscope specimens
THIONINES >THIONINE
THIONINS >THIONIN
THIONYL n of, consisting of, or containing the divalent group SO
THIONYLS >THIONYL
THIOPHEN n colourless liquid heterocyclic compound found in the benzene fraction of coal tar and manufactured from butane and sulphur
THIOPHENE same as >THIOPHEN
THIOPHENS >THIOPHEN
THIOPHIL adj having an attraction to sulphur
THIOTEPA n drug used in chemotherapy
THIOTEPAS >THIOTEPA
THIOUREA n white water-soluble crystalline substance with a bitter taste
THIOUREAS >THIOUREA
THIR Scots word for >THESE
THIRAM n antifungal agent
THIRAMS >THIRAM
THIRD adj of number three in a series ▷ n one of three equal parts ▷ adv in the third place ▷ vb divide (something) by three
THIRDED >THIRD
THIRDHAND adv from the second of two intermediaries
THIRDING >THIRD
THIRDINGS >THIRD
THIRDLY >THIRD
THIRDS >THIRD
THIRDSMAN n intermediary

THIRDSMEN >THIRDSMAN
THIRL vb bore or drill
THIRLAGE n obligation imposed upon tenants of certain lands requiring them to have their grain ground at a specified mill
THIRLAGES >THIRLAGE
THIRLED >THIRL
THIRLING >THIRL
THIRLS >THIRL
THIRST n desire to drink ▷ vb feel thirst
THIRSTED >THIRST
THIRSTER >THIRST
THIRSTERS >THIRSTER
THIRSTFUL >THIRST
THIRSTIER >THIRSTY
THIRSTILY >THIRSTY
THIRSTING >THIRST
THIRSTS >THIRST
THIRSTY adj feeling a desire to drink
THIRTEEN n three plus ten ▷ adj amounting to thirteen ▷ determiner amounting to thirteen
THIRTEENS >THIRTEEN
THIRTIES >THIRTY
THIRTIETH adj being the ordinal number of thirty in counting order, position, time, etc: often written 30th ▷ n one of 30 approximately equal parts of something
THIRTY n three times ten ▷ adj amounting to thirty ▷ determiner amounting to thirty
THIRTYISH adj around thirty years of age
THIS pron used to refer to a thing or person nearby, just mentioned, or about to be mentioned ▷ adj used to refer to the present time
THISAWAY adv this way
THISNESS n state or quality of being this
THISTLE n prickly plant with dense flower heads
THISTLES >THISTLE
THISTLIER >THISTLE
THISTLY >THISTLE
THITHER adv or towards that place
THITHERTO adv until that time
THIVEL same as >THIBLE
THIVELS >THIVEL
THLIPSES >THLIPSIS
THLIPSIS n compression, esp of part of the body
THO short for >THOUGH
THOFT n bench (in a boat) upon which a rower sits
THOFTS >THOFT
THOLE n wooden pin set in the side of a rowing boat to serve as a fulcrum for rowing ▷ vb bear or put up with

THOLED >THOLE
THOLEIITE n type of volcanic rock
THOLEPIN same as >THOLE
THOLEPINS >THOLEPIN
THOLES >THOLE
THOLI >THOLUS
THOLING >THOLE
THOLOBATE n structure supporting a dome
THOLOI >THOLOS
THOLOS n dry-stone beehive-shaped tomb associated with the Mycenaean culture of Greece in the 16th to the 12th century BC
THOLUS n domed tomb
THON Scot word for >YON
THONDER Scot word for >YONDER
THONG n thin strip of leather etc
THONGED adj fastened with a thong
THONGS >THONG
THORACAL another word for >THORACIC
THORACES >THORAX
THORACIC adj of, near, or relating to the thorax
THORAX n part of the body between the neck and the abdomen
THORAXES >THORAX
THORIA >THORIUM
THORIAS >THORIUM
THORIC >THORIUM
THORITE n yellow, brownish, or black radioactive mineral consisting of tetragonal thorium silicate. It occurs in coarse granite and is a source of thorium
THORITES >THORITE
THORIUM n radioactive metallic element
THORIUMS >THORIUM
THORN n prickle on a plant ▷ vb jag or prick (something) as if with a thorn
THORNBACK n European ray with a row of spines along the back and tail
THORNBILL n South American hummingbirds
THORNBUSH n tree, shrub, or bush with thorns
THORNED >THORN
THORNIER >THORNY
THORNIEST >THORNY
THORNILY >THORNY
THORNING >THORN
THORNLESS >THORN
THORNLIKE >THORN
THORNS >THORN
THORNSET adj set with thorns
THORNTREE n tree with thorns
THORNY adj covered with thorns

THORO (nonstandard) variant spelling of >THOROUGH
THORON n radioisotope of radon that is a decay product of thorium
THORONS >THORON
THOROUGH adj complete ▷ n passage
THOROUGHS >THOROUGH
THORP n small village
THORPE same as >THORP
THORPES >THORPE
THORPS >THORP
THOSE determiner form of that used before a plural noun
THOTHER pron old contraction of the other
THOU pron used when talking to one person ▷ n one thousandth of an inch ▷ vb use the word thou
THOUED >THOU
THOUGH adv nevertheless
THOUGHT >THINK
THOUGHTED adj with thoughts
THOUGHTEN adj convinced
THOUGHTS >THINK
THOUING >THOU
THOUS >THOU
THOUSAND n ten hundred ▷ adj amounting to a thousand ▷ determiner amounting to a thousand
THOUSANDS >THOUSAND
THOWEL old variant of >THOLE
THOWELS >THOWEL
THOWL old variant of >THOLE
THOWLESS adj lacking in vigour
THOWLS >THOWEL
THRAE same as >FRAE
THRAIPING n thrashing
THRALDOM same as >THRALL
THRALDOMS >THRALDOM
THRALL n state of being in the power of another person ▷ vb enslave or dominate
THRALLDOM same as >THRALL
THRALLED >THRALL
THRALLING >THRALL
THRALLS >THRALL
THRANG n throng ▷ vb throng ▷ adj crowded
THRANGED >THRANG
THRANGING >THRANG
THRANGS >THRANG
THRAPPLE n throat or windpipe ▷ vb throttle
THRAPPLED >THRAPPLE
THRAPPLES >THRAPPLE
THRASH vb beat, esp with a stick or whip ▷ n party
THRASHED >THRASH
THRASHER same as >THRESHER
THRASHERS >THRASHER
THRASHES >THRASH
THRASHING n severe beating

**THRASONIC** *adj* bragging or boastful

**THRAVE** *n* twenty-four sheaves of corn

**THRAVES** >THRAVE

**THRAW** *vb* twist (something); make something thrawn

**THRAWARD** *adj* contrary or stubborn

**THRAWART** *same as* >THRAWARD

**THRAWED** >THRAW

**THRAWING** >THRAW

**THRAWN** *adj* crooked or twisted

**THRAWNLY** >THRAWN

**THRAWS** >THRAW

**THREAD** *n* fine strand or yarn ▷ *vb* pass thread through

**THREADED** >THREAD

**THREADEN** *adj* made of thread

**THREADER** >THREAD

**THREADERS** >THREAD

**THREADFIN** *n* spiny-finned tropical marine fish

**THREADIER** >THREADY

**THREADING** >THREAD

**THREADS** *slang word for* >CLOTHES

**THREADY** *adj* of, relating to, or resembling a thread or threads

**THREAP** *vb* scold

**THREAPED** >THREAP

**THREAPER** >THREAP

**THREAPERS** >THREAP

**THREAPING** >THREAP

**THREAPIT** *variant past participle of* >THREAP

**THREAPS** >THREAP

**THREAT** *n* declaration of intent to harm

**THREATED** >THREAT

**THREATEN** *vb* make or be a threat to

**THREATENS** >THREATEN

**THREATFUL** >THREAT

**THREATING** >THREAT

**THREATS** >THREAT

**THREAVE** *same as* >THRAVE

**THREAVES** >THREAVE

**THREE** *n* one more than two ▷ *adj* amounting to three ▷ *determiner* amounting to three

**THREEFOLD** *adv* (having) three times as many or as much ▷ *adj* having three times as many or as much

**THREENESS** *n* state or quality of being three

**THREEP** *same as* >THREAP

**THREEPED** >THREEP

**THREEPER** >THREAP

**THREEPERS** >THREAP

**THREEPING** >THREEP

**THREEPIT** *variant past participle of* >THREEP

**THREEPS** >THREEP

**THREES** >THREE

**THREESOME** *n* group of three

**THRENE** *n* dirge; threnody

**THRENES** >THRENE

**THRENETIC** >THRENE

**THRENODE** *same as* >THRENODY

**THRENODES** >THRENODE

**THRENODIC** >THRENODY

**THRENODY** *n* lament for the dead

**THRENOS** *n* threnody; lamentation

**THRENOSES** >THRENOS

**THREONINE** *n* essential amino acid that occurs in certain proteins

**THRESH** *vb* beat (wheat etc) to separate the grain from the husks and straw ▷ *n* act of threshing

**THRESHED** >THRESH

**THRESHEL** *n* flail

**THRESHELS** >THRESHEL

**THRESHER** *n* any of a genus of large sharks occurring in tropical and temperate seas. They have a very long whiplike tail

**THRESHERS** >THRESHER

**THRESHES** >THRESH

**THRESHING** >THRESH

**THRESHOLD** *n* bar forming the bottom of a doorway

**THRETTIES** >THRETTY

**THRETTY** *nonstandard variant of* >THIRTY

**THREW** >THROW

**THRICE** *adv* three times

**THRID** *old variant of* >THREAD

**THRIDACE** *n* sedative made from lettuce juice

**THRIDACES** >THRIDACE

**THRIDDED** >THRID

**THRIDDING** >THRID

**THRIDS** >THRID

**THRIFT** *n* wisdom and caution with money

**THRIFTIER** >THRIFTY

**THRIFTILY** >THRIFTY

**THRIFTS** >THRIFT

**THRIFTY** *adj* not wasteful with money

**THRILL** *n* sudden feeling of excitement ▷ *vb* (cause to) feel a thrill

**THRILLANT** *another word for* >THRILLING

**THRILLED** >THRILL

**THRILLER** *n* book, film, etc with an atmosphere of mystery or suspense

**THRILLERS** >THRILLER

**THRILLIER** >THRILLY

**THRILLING** *adj* very exciting or stimulating

**THRILLS** >THRILL

**THRILLY** *adj* causing thrills

**THRIMSA** *same as* >THRYMSA

**THRIMSAS** >THRIMSA

**THRIP** *same as* >THRIPS

**THRIPS** *n* small slender-bodied insect with piercing mouthparts that feeds on plant sap

**THRIPSES** >THRIPS

**THRISSEL** *Scots variant of* >THISTLE

**THRISSELS** >THRISSEL

**THRIST** *old variant of* >THIRST

**THRISTED** >THRIST

**THRISTING** >THRIST

**THRISTLE** *Scots variant of* >THISTLE

**THRISTLES** >THRISTLE

**THRISTS** >THRIST

**THRISTY** >THRIST

**THRIVE** *vb* flourish or prosper

**THRIVED** >THRIVE

**THRIVEN** >THRIVE

**THRIVER** >THRIVE

**THRIVERS** >THRIVE

**THRIVES** >THRIVE

**THRIVING** >THRIVE

**THRIVINGS** >THRIVE

**THRO** *same as* >THROUGH

**THROAT** *n* passage from the mouth and nose to the stomach and lungs ▷ *vb* vocalize in the throat

**THROATED** >THROAT

**THROATIER** >THROATY

**THROATILY** >THROATY

**THROATING** >THROAT

**THROATS** >THROAT

**THROATY** *adj* (of the voice) hoarse

**THROB** *vb* pulsate repeatedly ▷ *n* throbbing

**THROBBED** >THROB

**THROBBER** >THROB

**THROBBERS** >THROB

**THROBBING** >THROB

**THROBLESS** >THROB

**THROBS** >THROB

**THROE** *n* pang or pain ▷ *n* endure throes

**THROED** >THROE

**THROEING** >THROE

**THROES** *pl n* violent pangs or pains

**THROMBI** >THROMBUS

**THROMBIN** *n* enzyme that acts on fibrinogen in blood causing it to clot

**THROMBINS** >THROMBIN

**THROMBOSE** *vb* become or affect with a thrombus

**THROMBUS** *n* clot of coagulated blood that forms within a blood vessel or inside the heart and remains at the site of its formation, often impeding the flow of blood

**THRONE** *n* ceremonial seat of a monarch or bishop ▷ *vb* place or be placed on a throne

**THRONED** >THRONE

**THRONES** >THRONE

**THRONG** *vb* crowd ▷ *n* great number of people or things crowded together ▷ *adj* busy

**THRONGED** >THRONG

**THRONGFUL** >THRONG

**THRONGING** >THRONG

**THRONGS** >THRONG

**THRONING** >THRONE

**THRONNER** *n* person who is good at doing odd jobs

**THRONNERS** >THRONNER

**THROPPLE** *vb* strangle or choke

**THROPPLED** >THROPPLE

**THROPPLES** >THROPPLE

**THROSTLE** *n* song thrush

**THROSTLES** >THROSTLE

**THROTTLE** *n* device controlling the amount of fuel entering an engine ▷ *vb* strangle

**THROTTLED** >THROTTLE

**THROTTLER** >THROTTLE

**THROTTLES** >THROTTLE

**THROUGH** *prep* from end to end or side to side of ▷ *adj* finished

**THROUGHLY** *adv* thoroughly

**THROVE** >THRIVE

**THROW** *vb* hurl through the air ▷ *n* throwing

**THROWAWAY** *adj* done or said casually ▷ *vb* get rid of or discard ▷ *n* handbill or advertisement distributed in a public place

**THROWBACK** *n* person or thing that reverts to an earlier type ▷ *vb* remind someone of (something he or she said or did previously) in order to upset him or her

**THROWE** *old variant of* >THROE

**THROWER** >THROW

**THROWERS** >THROW

**THROWES** >THROWE

**THROWING** >THROW

**THROWINGS** >THROW

**THROWN** >THROW

**THROWS** >THROW

**THROWSTER** *n* person who twists silk or other fibres into yarn

**THRU** *same as* >THROUGH

**THRUM** *vb* strum rhythmically but without expression on (a musical instrument) ▷ *n* in textiles, unwoven ends of warp thread

**THRUMMED** >THRUM

**THRUMMER** >THRUM

**THRUMMERS** >THRUM

**THRUMMIER** >THRUMMY

**THRUMMING** >THRUM

**THRUMMY** *adj* made of thrums

**THRUMS** >THRUM

**THRUPENNY** as in *thrupenny bit* twelve-sided British coin of nickel-brass, valued at three old pence, obsolete since 1971

**THRUPUT** *n* quantity of raw material or information processed in a given period

**THRUPUTS** >THRUPUT
**THRUSH** n brown songbird
**THRUSHES** >THRUSH
**THRUST** vb push forcefully ▷ n forceful stab
**THRUSTED** >THRUST
**THRUSTER** n person or thing that thrusts
**THRUSTERS** >THRUSTER
**THRUSTFUL** >THRUST
**THRUSTING** >THRUST
**THRUSTOR** variant of >THRUSTER
**THRUSTORS** >THRUSTOR
**THRUSTS** >THRUST
**THRUTCH** n narrow, fast-moving stream ▷ vb thrust
**THRUTCHED** >THRUTCH
**THRUTCHES** >THRUTCH
**THRUWAY** n thoroughfare
**THRUWAYS** >THRUWAY
**THRYMSA** n gold coin used in Anglo-Saxon England
**THRYMSAS** >THRYMSA
**THUD** n dull heavy sound ▷ vb make such a sound
**THUDDED** >THUD
**THUDDING** >THUD
**THUDS** >THUD
**THUG** n violent man, esp a criminal
**THUGGEE** n methods and practices of the thugs of India
**THUGGEES** >THUGGEE
**THUGGERY** >THUG
**THUGGISH** >THUG
**THUGGISM** >THUG
**THUGGISMS** >THUG
**THUGGO** n tough and violent person
**THUGGOS** >THUGGO
**THUGS** >THUG
**THUJA** n coniferous tree of North America and East Asia, with scalelike leaves, small cones, and an aromatic wood
**THUJAS** >THUJA
**THULIA** n oxide of thulium
**THULIAS** >THULIA
**THULITE** n rose-coloured zoisite sometimes incorporated into jewellery
**THULITES** >THULITE
**THULIUM** n malleable ductile silvery-grey element
**THULIUMS** >THULIUM
**THUMB** n short thick finger set apart from the others ▷ vb touch or handle with the thumb
**THUMBED** >THUMB
**THUMBHOLE** n hole for putting the thumb into
**THUMBIER** >THUMBY
**THUMBIEST** >THUMBY
**THUMBING** >THUMB
**THUMBKIN** same as >THUMBKIN
**THUMBKINS** n thumbscrew

**THUMBLESS** >THUMB
**THUMBLIKE** >THUMB
**THUMBLING** n extremely small person
**THUMBNAIL** n nail of the thumb ▷ adj concise and brief
**THUMBNUT** n nut with projections enabling it to be turned by the thumb and forefinger
**THUMBNUTS** >THUMBNUT
**THUMBPOT** n tiny flowerpot
**THUMBPOTS** >THUMBPOT
**THUMBS** >THUMB
**THUMBTACK** n short tack with a broad smooth head for fastening papers to a drawing board, etc
**THUMBY** adj clumsy; uncoordinated
**THUMP** n (sound of) a dull heavy blow ▷ vb strike heavily
**THUMPED** >THUMP
**THUMPER** >THUMP
**THUMPERS** >THUMP
**THUMPING** adj huge or excessive
**THUMPS** >THUMP
**THUNDER** n loud noise accompanying lightning ▷ vb rumble with thunder
**THUNDERED** >THUNDER
**THUNDERER** >THUNDER
**THUNDERS** >THUNDER
**THUNDERY** >THUNDER
**THUNDROUS** >THUNDER
**THUNK** another word for >THUD
**THUNKED** >THUNK
**THUNKING** >THUNK
**THUNKS** >THUNK
**THURIBLE** same as >CENSER
**THURIBLES** >THURIBLE
**THURIFER** n person appointed to carry the censer at religious ceremonies
**THURIFERS** >THURIFER
**THURIFIED** >THURIFY
**THURIFIES** >THURIFY
**THURIFY** vb burn incense near or before an altar, shrine, etc
**THURL** same as >THIRL
**THURLS** >THURL
**THUS** adv in this manner ▷ n aromatic gum resin
**THUSES** >THUS
**THUSLY** adv in such a way; thus
**THUSNESS** n state or quality of being thus
**THUSWISE** adj in this way; thus
**THUYA** same as >THUJA
**THUYAS** >THUYA
**THWACK** n whack ▷ vb beat with something flat ▷ interj exclamation imitative of this sound
**THWACKED** >THWACK
**THWACKER** >THWACK

**THWACKERS** >THWACK
**THWACKING** >THWACK
**THWACKS** >THWACK
**THWAITE** n piece of land cleared from forest or reclaimed from wasteland
**THWAITES** >THWAITE
**THWART** vb foil or frustrate ▷ n seat across a boat ▷ adj passing or being situated across ▷ adv across
**THWARTED** >THWART
**THWARTER** >THWART
**THWARTERS** >THWART
**THWARTING** >THWART
**THWARTLY** >THWART
**THWARTS** >THWART
**THY** adj of or associated with you (thou) ▷ determiner belonging to or associated in some way with you (thou)
**THYINE** adj of relating to the sandarac tree
**THYLACINE** n extinct doglike Tasmanian marsupial
**THYLAKOID** n small membranous sac within a chloroplast
**THYLOSE** old variant of >TYLOSIS
**THYLOSES** >THYLOSIS
**THYLOSIS** same as >TYLOSIS
**THYME** n aromatic herb
**THYMES** >THYME
**THYMEY** >THYME
**THYMI** >THYMUS
**THYMIC** adj of or relating to the thymus
**THYMIDINE** n crystalline nucleoside of thymine, found in DNA
**THYMIER** >THYME
**THYMIEST** >THYME
**THYMINE** n white crystalline pyrimidine base found in DNA
**THYMINES** >THYMINE
**THYMOCYTE** n lymphocyte found in the thymus
**THYMOL** n substance obtained from thyme, used as an antiseptic
**THYMOLS** >THYMOL
**THYMOSIN** n hormone secreted by the thymus
**THYMOSINS** >THYMOSIN
**THYMUS** n small gland at the base of the neck
**THYMUSES** >THYMUS
**THYMY** >THYME
**THYRATRON** n gas-filled tube that has three electrodes and can be switched between an 'off' state and an 'on' state. It has been superseded, except for application involving high-power switching, by the thyristor
**THYREOID** same as >THYROID

**THYREOIDS** >THYREOID
**THYRISTOR** n any of a group of semiconductor devices, such as the silicon-controlled rectifier, that can be switched between two states
**THYROID** n (of) a gland in the neck controlling body growth ▷ adj of or relating to the thyroid gland
**THYROIDAL** >THYROID
**THYROIDS** >THYROID
**THYROXIN** same as >THYROXINE
**THYROXINE** n principal hormone produced by the thyroid gland
**THYROXINS** >THYROXIN
**THYRSE** n type of inflorescence, occurring in the lilac and grape, in which the main branch is racemose and the lateral branches cymose
**THYRSES** >THYRSE
**THYRSI** >THYRSUS
**THYRSOID** >THYRSE
**THYRSUS** same as >THYRSE
**THYSELF** pron reflexive form of thou
**TI** same as >TE
**TIAR** same as >TIARA
**TIARA** n semicircular jewelled headdress
**TIARAED** >TIARA
**TIARAS** >TIARA
**TIARS** >TIAR
**TIBIA** n inner bone of the lower leg
**TIBIAE** >TIBIA
**TIBIAL** >TIBIA
**TIBIAS** >TIBIA
**TIC** n spasmodic muscular twitch
**TICAL** n former standard monetary unit of Thailand, replaced by the baht in 1928
**TICALS** >TICAL
**TICCA** adj (of a thing or the services of a person) having been acquired for temporary use in exchange for payment
**TICCED** >TIC
**TICCING** >TIC
**TICE** vb tempt or allure; entice
**TICED** >TICE
**TICES** >TICE
**TICH** same as >TITCH
**TICHES** >TICH
**TICHIER** >TICHY
**TICHIEST** >TICHY
**TICHY** same as >TITCHY
**TICK** n mark (✓) used to check off or indicate the correctness of something ▷ vb mark with a tick
**TICKED** >TICK
**TICKEN** same as >TICKING
**TICKENS** >TICKEN

TICKER n heart

TICKERS > TICKER

TICKET n card or paper entitling the holder to admission, travel, etc ▷ vb attach or issue a ticket to

TICKETED > TICKET

TICKETING > TICKET

TICKETS pl n death or ruin

TICKEY n South African threepenny piece, which was replaced by the five-cent coin in 1961

TICKEYS > TICKEY

TICKIES > TICKY

TICKING n strong material for mattress covers

TICKINGS > TICKING

TICKLACE n (in Newfoundland) a kittiwake

TICKLACES > TICKLACE

TICKLE vb touch or stroke (a person) to produce laughter ▷ n tickling

TICKLED > TICKLE

TICKLER n difficult or delicate problem

TICKLERS > TICKLER

TICKLES > TICKLE

TICKLIER > TICKLE

TICKLIEST > TICKLE

TICKLING > TICKLE

TICKLINGS > TICKLE

TICKLISH adj sensitive to tickling

TICKLY > TICKLE

TICKS > TICK

TICKSEED another name for > COREOPSIS

TICKSEEDS > TICKSEED

TICKTACK n bookmakers' sign language ▷ vb make a ticking sound

TICKTACKS > TICKTACK

TICKTOCK n ticking sound made by a clock ▷ vb make a ticking sound

TICKTOCKS > TICKTOCK

TICKY same as > TICKEY

TICS > TIC

TICTAC same as > TICKTACK

TICTACKED > TICTAC

TICTACS > TICTAC

TICTOC same as > TICKTOCK

TICTOCKED > TICTOC

TICTOCS > TICTOC

TID n girl

TIDAL adj (of a river, lake, or sea) having tides

TIDALLY > TIDAL

TIDBIT same as > TITBIT

TIDBITS > TIDBIT

TIDDIER > TIDDY

TIDDIES > TIDDY

TIDDIEST > TIDDY

TIDDLE vb busy oneself with inconsequential tasks

TIDDLED > TIDDLE

TIDDLER n very small fish

TIDDLERS > TIDDLER

TIDDLES > TIDDLE

TIDDLEY same as > TIDDLY

TIDDLEYS > TIDDLEY

TIDDLIER > TIDDLY

TIDDLIES > TIDDLY

TIDDLIEST > TIDDLY

TIDDLING > TIDDLE

TIDDLY adj tiny ▷ n alcoholic beverage

TIDDY n four of trumps in the card game gleek

TIDE n rise and fall of the sea caused by the gravitational pull of the sun and moon ▷ vb carry or be carried with or as if with the tide

TIDED > TIDE

TIDELAND n land between high-water and low-water marks

TIDELANDS > TIDELAND

TIDELESS > TIDE

TIDELIKE > TIDE

TIDEMARK n mark left by the highest or lowest point of a tide

TIDEMARKS > TIDEMARK

TIDEMILL n watermill powered by the force of the tide

TIDEMILLS > TIDEMILL

TIDERIP same as > RIPTIDE

TIDERIPS > TIDERIP

TIDES > TIDE

TIDESMAN n customs official at a port

TIDESMEN > TIDESMAN

TIDEWATER n water that advances and recedes with the tide

TIDEWAVE n undulation of the earth's water levels as the tide moves around it

TIDEWAVES > TIDEWAVE

TIDEWAY n strong tidal current or its channel, esp the tidal part of a river

TIDEWAYS > TIDEWAY

TIDIED > TIDY

TIDIER > TIDY

TIDIERS > TIDY

TIDIES > TIDY

TIDIEST > TIDY

TIDILY > TIDY

TIDINESS > TIDY

TIDING > TIDE

TIDINGS pl n news

TIDIVATE same as > TITIVATE

TIDIVATED > TITIVATE

TIDIVATES > TITIVATE

TIDS > TID

TIDY adj neat and orderly ▷ vb put in order ▷ n small container for odds and ends

TIDYING > TIDY

TIDYTIPS n herb with flowers resembling those of the daisy

TIE vb fasten or be fastened with string, rope, etc ▷ n long narrow piece of material worn knotted round the neck

TIEBACK n length of cord, ribbon, or other fabric used for tying a curtain to one side

TIEBACKS > TIEBACK

TIEBREAK n deciding game in drawn match

TIEBREAKS > TIEBREAK

TIECLASP n clip, often ornamental, which holds a tie in place against a shirt

TIECLASPS > TIECLASP

TIED > TIE

TIEING > TIE

TIELESS > TIE

TIEPIN n ornamental pin used to pin the two ends of a tie to a shirt

TIEPINS > TIEPIN

TIER n one of a set of rows placed one above and behind the other ▷ vb be or arrange in tiers

TIERCE same as > TERCE

TIERCED adj (of a shield) divided into three sections of similar size but different colour

TIERCEL same as > TERCEL

TIERCELET another name for > TERCEL

TIERCELS > TIERCEL

TIERCERON n (in Gothic architecture) a type of rib on a vault

TIERCES > TIERCE

TIERCET same as > TERCET

TIERCETS > TIERCET

TIERED > TIER

TIERING > TIER

TIEROD n any rod- or bar-shaped structural member designed to prevent the separation of two parts, as in a vehicle

TIERODS > TIEROD

TIERS > TIER

TIES > TIE

TIETAC n fastener for holding a tie in place

TIETACK same as > TIETAC

TIETACKS > TIETACK

TIETACS > TIETAC

TIFF n petty quarrel ▷ vb have or be in a tiff

TIFFANIES > TIFFANY

TIFFANY n sheer fine gauzy fabric

TIFFED > TIFF

TIFFIN n (in India) a light meal, esp at midday ▷ vb take tiffin

TIFFINED > TIFFIN

TIFFING > TIFF

TIFFINGS > TIFF

TIFFINING > TIFFIN

TIFFINS > TIFFIN

TIFFS > TIFF

TIFOSI > TIFOSO

TIFOSO n fanatical fan (esp an Italian F1 fan)

TIFT (Scots) variant of > TIFF

TIFTED > TIFT

TIFTING > TIFT

TIFTS > TIFT

TIG n child's game

TIGE n trunk of an architectural column

TIGER n large yellow-and-black striped Asian cat

TIGEREYE n golden brown silicified variety of crocidolite, used as an ornamental stone

TIGEREYES > TIGEREYE

TIGERISH > TIGER

TIGERISM n arrogant and showy manner

TIGERISMS > TIGERISM

TIGERLIKE adj resembling a tiger

TIGERLY adj of or like a tiger

TIGERS > TIGER

TIGERY > TIGER

TIGES > TIGE

TIGGED > TIG

TIGGING > TIG

TIGHT adj stretched or drawn taut ▷ adv in a close, firm, or secure way

TIGHTASS n inhibited or excessively self-controlled person

TIGHTEN vb make or become tight or tighter

TIGHTENED > TIGHTEN

TIGHTENER > TIGHTEN

TIGHTENS > TIGHTEN

TIGHTER > TIGHT

TIGHTEST > TIGHT

TIGHTISH > TIGHT

TIGHTKNIT adj closely integrated

TIGHTLY > TIGHT

TIGHTNESS > TIGHT

TIGHTROPE n rope stretched taut on which acrobats perform

TIGHTS pl n one-piece clinging garment covering the body from the waist to the feet

TIGHTWAD n stingy person

TIGHTWADS > TIGHTWAD

TIGHTWIRE n wire tightrope

TIGLIC as in tiglic acid syrupy liquid or crystalline colourless unsaturated carboxylic acid

TIGLON same as > TIGON

TIGLONS > TIGLON

TIGON n hybrid offspring of a male tiger and a female lion

TIGONS > TIGON

TIGRESS n female tiger

TIGRESSES > TIGRESS

TIGRIDIA n type of tropical American plant

TIGRIDIAS > TIGRIDIA

TIGRINE adj of, characteristic of, or resembling a tiger

TIGRISH > TIGER

TIGRISHLY > TIGER

TIGROID adj resembling

a tiger
**TIGS** >TIG
**TIKA** same as >TIKKA
**TIKANGA** n Māori ways or customs
**TIKANGAS** >TIKANGA
**TIKAS** >TIKA
**TIKE** same as >TYKE
**TIKES** >TIKE
**TIKI** n small carving of a grotesque person worn as a pendant ▷ vb take a scenic tour around an area
**TIKIED** >TIKI
**TIKIING** >TIKI
**TIKIS** >TIKI
**TIKKA** adj marinated in spices and dry-roasted ▷ n act of marking a tikka on the forehead
**TIKKAS** >TIKKA
**TIKOLOSHE** same as >TOKOLOSHE
**TIL** another name for >SESAME
**TILAK** n coloured spot or mark worn by Hindus, esp on the forehead, often indicating membership of a religious sect, caste, etc, or (in the case of a woman) marital status
**TILAKS** >TILAK
**TILAPIA** n type of fish
**TILAPIAS** >TILAPIA
**TILBURIES** >TILBURY
**TILBURY** n light two-wheeled horse-drawn open carriage, seating two people
**TILDE** n mark (~) used in Spanish to indicate that the letter 'n' is to be pronounced in a particular way
**TILDES** >TILDE
**TILE** n flat piece of ceramic, plastic, etc used to cover a roof, floor, or wall ▷ vb cover with tiles
**TILED** >TILE
**TILEFISH** n large brightly coloured deep-sea percoid food fish
**TILELIKE** adj like a tile
**TILER** >TILE
**TILERIES** >TILERY
**TILERS** >TILE
**TILERY** n place where tiles are produced
**TILES** >TILE
**TILING** n tiles collectively
**TILINGS** >TILING
**TILL** prep until ▷ vb cultivate (land) ▷ n drawer for money, usu in a cash register ▷ n unstratified glacial deposit consisting of rock fragments of various sizes
**TILLABLE** >TILL
**TILLAGE** n act, process, or art of tilling
**TILLAGES** >TILLAGE

**TILLED** >TILL
**TILLER** n on boats, a handle fixed to the top of a rudderpost to serve as a lever in steering ▷ vb use a tiller
**TILLERED** >TILLER
**TILLERING** >TILLER
**TILLERMAN** n one working a tiller
**TILLERMEN** >TILLERMAN
**TILLERS** >TILL
**TILLICUM** n (in the Pacific Northwest) a friend
**TILLICUMS** >TILLICUM
**TILLIER** >TILL
**TILLIEST** >TILL
**TILLING** >TILL
**TILLINGS** >TILL
**TILLITE** n rock formed from hardened till
**TILLITES** >TILLITE
**TILLS** >TILL
**TILLY** >TILL
**TILS** >TIL
**TILT** vb slant at an angle ▷ n slope
**TILTABLE** >TILT
**TILTED** >TILT
**TILTER** >TILT
**TILTERS** >TILT
**TILTH** n (condition of) land that has been tilled
**TILTHS** >TILTH
**TILTING** >TILT
**TILTINGS** >TILT
**TILTMETER** n instrument for measuring the tilt of the earth's surface
**TILTROTOR** n aircraft with rotors that can be tilted
**TILTS** >TILT
**TILTYARD** n (formerly) an enclosed area for tilting
**TILTYARDS** >TILTYARD
**TIMARAU** same as >TAMARAU
**TIMARAUS** >TIMARAU
**TIMARIOT** n one holding a fief in feudal Turkey
**TIMARIOTS** >TIMARIOT
**TIMBAL** n type of kettledrum
**TIMBALE** n mixture of meat, fish, etc, in a rich sauce, cooked in a mould lined with potato or pastry
**TIMBALES** >TIMBALE
**TIMBALS** >TIMBAL
**TIMBER** n wood as a building material ▷ adj made out of timber ▷ vb provide with timbers ▷ interj lumberjack's shouted warning when a tree is about to fall
**TIMBERED** adj made of or containing timber or timbers
**TIMBERING** n timbers collectively
**TIMBERMAN** n any of various longicorn beetles that have destructive wood-eating larvae

**TIMBERMEN** >TIMBERMAN
**TIMBERS** >TIMBER
**TIMBERY** >TIMBER
**TIMBO** n Amazonian vine from which a useful insecticide can be derived
**TIMBOS** >TIMBO
**TIMBRAL** adj relating to timbre
**TIMBRE** n distinctive quality of sound of a voice or instrument
**TIMBREL** n tambourine
**TIMBRELS** >TIMBREL
**TIMBRES** >TIMBRE
**TIME** n past, present, and future as a continuous whole ▷ vb note the time taken by
**TIMEBOMB** n bomb containing a timing mechanism that determines the time it will detonate
**TIMEBOMBS** >TIMEBOMB
**TIMECARD** n card used with a time clock
**TIMECARDS** >TIMECARD
**TIMED** >TIME
**TIMEFRAME** n period of time within which certain events are scheduled to occur
**TIMELESS** adj unaffected by time
**TIMELIER** >TIMELY
**TIMELIEST** >TIMELY
**TIMELINE** n graphic representation showing the passage of time as a line
**TIMELINES** >TIMELINE
**TIMELY** adj at the appropriate time ▷ adv at the right or an appropriate time
**TIMENOGUY** n taut rope on a ship
**TIMEOUS** adj in good time
**TIMEOUSLY** >TIMEOUS
**TIMEOUT** n in sport, interruption in play during which players rest, discuss tactics, or make substitutions
**TIMEOUTS** >TIMEOUT
**TIMEPASS** n way of passing the time ▷ vb pass the time
**TIMEPIECE** n watch or clock
**TIMER** n device for measuring time, esp a switch or regulator that causes a mechanism to operate at a specific time
**TIMERS** >TIMER
**TIMES** >TIME
**TIMESAVER** n something that saves time
**TIMESCALE** n period of time within which events occur or are due to occur
**TIMETABLE** n plan

showing the times when something takes place, the departure and arrival times of trains or buses, etc ▷ vb set a time when a particular thing should be done
**TIMEWORK** n work paid for by the length of time taken, esp by the hour or the day
**TIMEWORKS** >TIMEWORK
**TIMEWORN** adj showing the adverse effects of overlong use or of old age
**TIMID** adj easily frightened
**TIMIDER** >TIMID
**TIMIDEST** >TIMID
**TIMIDITY** >TIMID
**TIMIDLY** >TIMID
**TIMIDNESS** >TIMID
**TIMING** n ability to judge when to do or say something so as to make the best effect
**TIMINGS** >TIMING
**TIMIST** n one concerned with time
**TIMISTS** >TIMIST
**TIMOCRACY** n political unit or system in which possession of property serves as the first requirement for participation in government
**TIMOLOL** n relaxant medicine used for (example) to reduce blood pressure
**TIMOLOLS** >TIMOLOL
**TIMON** n apparatus by which a vessel is steered
**TIMONEER** n helmsman; tillerman
**TIMONEERS** >TIMONEER
**TIMONS** >TIMON
**TIMOROUS** adj timid
**TIMORSOME** adj timorous; timid
**TIMOTHIES** >TIMOTHY
**TIMOTHY** as in timothy grass perennial grass of temperate regions, having erect stiff stems and cylindrical flower spikes: grown for hay and pasture
**TIMOUS** same as >TIMEOUS
**TIMOUSLY** >TIMOUS
**TIMPANA** n traditional Maltese baked pasta and pastry dish
**TIMPANI** pl n set of kettledrums
**TIMPANIST** >TIMPANI
**TIMPANO** n kettledrum
**TIMPANUM** same as >TYMPANUM
**TIMPANUMS** >TIMPANUM
**TIMPS** same as >TIMPANI
**TIN** n soft metallic element ▷ vb put (food) into tins
**TINAJA** n large jar for cooling water

**TINAJAS** >TINAJA
**TINAMOU** *n* any bird of the order *Tinamiformes* of Central and South America, having small wings, a heavy body, and an inconspicuous plumage
**TINAMOUS** >TINAMOU
**TINCAL** another name for >BORAX
**TINCALS** >TINCAL
**TINCHEL** *n* in Scotland, a circle of deer hunters who gradually close in on their quarry
**TINCHELS** >TINCHEL
**TINCT** *vb* tint ▷ *adj* tinted or coloured
**TINCTED** >TINCT
**TINCTING** >TINCT
**TINCTS** >TINCT
**TINCTURE** *n* medicinal extract in a solution of alcohol ▷ *vb* give a tint or colour to
**TINCTURED** >TINCTURE
**TINCTURES** >TINCTURE
**TIND** *vb* set alight
**TINDAL** *n* petty officer
**TINDALS** >TINDAL
**TINDED** >TIND
**TINDER** *n* dry easily-burning material used to start a fire
**TINDERBOX** *n* formerly, small box for tinder, esp one fitted with a flint and steel
**TINDERS** >TINDER
**TINDERY** >TINDER
**TINDING** >TIND
**TINDS** >TIND
**TINE** *n* prong of a fork or antler ▷ *vb* lose
**TINEA** *n* any fungal skin disease, esp ringworm
**TINEAL** >TINEA
**TINEAS** >TINEA
**TINED** >TINE
**TINEID** *n* any moth of the family *Tineidae*, which includes the clothes moths ▷ *adj* of, relating to, or belonging to the family *Tineidae*
**TINEIDS** >TINEID
**TINES** >TINE
**TINFOIL** *n* paper-thin sheet of metal, used for wrapping foodstuffs
**TINFOILS** >TINFOIL
**TINFUL** *n* contents of a tin or the amount a tin will hold
**TINFULS** >TINFUL
**TING** same as >THING
**TINGE** *n* slight tint ▷ *vb* give a slight tint or trace to
**TINGED** >TINGE
**TINGEING** >TINGE
**TINGES** >TINGE
**TINGING** >TINGE
**TINGLE** *n* (feel) a prickling

or stinging sensation ▷ *vb* feel a mild prickling or stinging sensation, as from cold or excitement
**TINGLED** >TINGLE
**TINGLER** >TINGLE
**TINGLERS** >TINGLE
**TINGLES** >TINGLE
**TINGLIER** >TINGLE
**TINGLIEST** >TINGLE
**TINGLING** >TINGLE
**TINGLINGS** >TINGLE
**TINGLISH** *adj* exciting
**TINGLY** >TINGLE
**TINGS** >TING
**TINGUAITE** *n* type of igneous rock
**TINHORN** *n* cheap pretentious person, esp a gambler with extravagant claims ▷ *adj* cheap and showy
**TINHORNS** >TINHORN
**TINIER** >TINY
**TINIES** *pl n* small children
**TINIEST** >TINY
**TINILY** >TINY
**TININESS** >TINY
**TINING** >TINE
**TINK** shortened form of >TINKER
**TINKED** >TINK
**TINKER** *n* derogatory term for travelling mender of pots and pans ▷ *vb* fiddle with (an engine etc) in an attempt to repair it
**TINKERED** >TINKER
**TINKERER** >TINKER
**TINKERERS** >TINKER
**TINKERING** >TINKER
**TINKERS** >TINKER
**TINKERTOY** *n* children's construction set
**TINKING** >TINK
**TINKLE** *vb* ring with a high tinny sound like a small bell ▷ *n* this sound or action
**TINKLED** >TINKLE
**TINKLER** same as >TINKER
**TINKLERS** >TINKLER
**TINKLES** >TINKLE
**TINKLIER** >TINKLE
**TINKLIEST** >TINKLE
**TINKLING** >TINKLE
**TINKLINGS** >TINKLE
**TINKLY** >TINKLE
**TINKS** >TINK
**TINLIKE** >TIN
**TINMAN** *n* one who works with tin or tin plate
**TINMEN** >TINMAN
**TINNED** >TIN
**TINNER** *n* tin miner
**TINNERS** >TINNER
**TINNIE** same as >TINNY
**TINNIER** >TINNY
**TINNIES** >TINNY
**TINNIEST** >TINNY
**TINNILY** >TINNY
**TINNINESS** >TINNY
**TINNING** >TIN
**TINNINGS** >TIN

**TINNITUS** *n* ringing, hissing, or booming sensation in one or both ears, caused by infection of the middle or inner ear, a side effect of certain drugs, etc
**TINNY** *adj* (of sound) thin and metallic ▷ *n* can of beer
**TINPLATE** *n* thin steel sheet coated with a layer of tin that protects the steel from corrosion ▷ *vb* coat (a metal or object) with a layer of tin, usually either by electroplating or by dipping in a bath of molten tin
**TINPLATED** >TINPLATE
**TINPLATES** >TINPLATE
**TINPOT** *adj* worthless or unimportant ▷ *n* pot made of tin
**TINPOTS** >TINPOT
**TINS** >TIN
**TINSEL** *n* decorative metallic strips or threads ▷ *adj* made of or decorated with tinsel ▷ *vb* decorate with or as if with tinsel
**TINSELED** >TINSEL
**TINSELING** >TINSEL
**TINSELLED** >TINSEL
**TINSELLY** >TINSEL
**TINSELRY** *n* tinsel-like material
**TINSELS** >TINSEL
**TINSEY** old variant of >TINSEL
**TINSEYS** >TINSEY
**TINSMITH** *n* person who works with tin or tin plate
**TINSMITHS** >TINSMITH
**TINSNIPS** *n* metal cutters
**TINSTONE** *n* black or brown stone
**TINSTONES** >TINSTONE
**TINT** *n* (pale) shade of a colour ▷ *vb* give a tint to
**TINTACK** *n* tin-plated tack
**TINTACKS** >TINTACK
**TINTED** >TINT
**TINTER** >TINT
**TINTERS** >TINT
**TINTIER** >TINTY
**TINTIEST** >TINTY
**TINTINESS** >TINTY
**TINTING** >TINT
**TINTINGS** >TINT
**TINTLESS** >TINT
**TINTOOKIE** *n* in informal Australian English, fawning or servile person
**TINTS** >TINT
**TINTY** *adj* having many tints
**TINTYPE** another name for >FERROTYPE
**TINTYPES** >TINTYPE
**TINWARE** *n* objects made of tin plate
**TINWARES** >TINWARE
**TINWORK** *n* objects made

of tin
**TINWORKS** *n* place where tin is mined, smelted, or rolled
**TINY** *adj* very small
**TIP** *n* narrow or pointed end of anything ▷ *vb* put a tip on
**TIPCART** *n* cart that can be tipped to empty out its contents
**TIPCARTS** >TIPCART
**TIPCAT** *n* game in which a short sharp-ended piece of wood (the cat) is tipped in the air with a stick
**TIPCATS** >TIPCAT
**TIPI** variant spelling of >TEPEE
**TIPIS** >TIPI
**TIPLESS** >TIP
**TIPOFF** *n* warning or hint, esp given confidentially and based on inside information
**TIPOFFS** >TIPOFF
**TIPPABLE** >TIP
**TIPPED** >TIP
**TIPPEE** *n* person who receives a tip, esp regarding share prices
**TIPPEES** >TIPPEE
**TIPPER** *n* person who gives or leaves a tip
**TIPPERS** >TIPPER
**TIPPET** *n* scarflike piece of fur, often made from a whole animal skin, worn, esp formerly, round a woman's shoulders
**TIPPETS** >TIPPET
**TIPPIER** >TIPPY
**TIPPIEST** >TIPPY
**TIPPING** >TIP
**TIPPINGS** >TIP
**TIPPLE** *vb* drink alcohol habitually, esp in small quantities ▷ *n* alcoholic drink
**TIPPLED** >TIPPLE
**TIPPLER** >TIPPLE
**TIPPLERS** >TIPPLE
**TIPPLES** >TIPPLE
**TIPPLING** >TIPPLE
**TIPPY** *adj* extremely fashionable or stylish
**TIPPYTOE** same as >TIPTOE
**TIPPYTOED** >TIPPYTOE
**TIPPYTOES** >TIPPYTOE
**TIPS** >TIP
**TIPSHEET** *n* list of advice or instructions
**TIPSHEETS** >TIPSHEET
**TIPSIER** >TIPSY
**TIPSIEST** >TIPSY
**TIPSIFIED** >TIPSIFY
**TIPSIFIES** >TIPSIFY
**TIPSIFY** *vb* make tipsy
**TIPSILY** >TIPSY
**TIPSINESS** >TIPSY
**TIPSTAFF** *n* court official
**TIPSTAFFS** >TIPSTAFF
**TIPSTAVES** >TIPSTAFF
**TIPSTER** *n* person who

sells tips about races
**TIPSTERS** >TIPSTER
**TIPSTOCK** *n* detachable section of a gunstock, usually gripped by the left hand of the user
**TIPSTOCKS** >TIPSTOCK
**TIPSY** *adj* slightly drunk
**TIPT** >TIP
**TIPTOE** *vb* walk quietly with the heels off the ground
**TIPTOED** >TIPTOE
**TIPTOEING** >TIPTOE
**TIPTOES** >TIPTOE
**TIPTOP** *adj* of the highest quality or condition ▷ *adv* of the highest quality or condition ▷ *n* best in quality ▷ *n* very top; pinnacle
**TIPTOPS** >TIPTOP
**TIPTRONIC** *n* type of gearbox that has both automatic and manual options
**TIPULA** *n* crane fly
**TIPULAS** >TIPULA
**TIPUNA** *n* ancestor
**TIPUNAS** >TIPUNA
**TIRADE** *n* long angry speech
**TIRADES** >TIRADE
**TIRAGE** *n* drawing of wine from a barrel prior to bottling
**TIRAGES** >TIRAGE
**TIRAMISU** *n* Italian dessert made with sponge soaked in coffee and Marsala, topped with soft cheese and powdered chocolate
**TIRAMISUS** >TIRAMISU
**TIRASSE** *n* mechanism in an organ connecting two pedals, so that both may be depressed at once
**TIRASSES** >TIRASSE
**TIRE** *vb* reduce the energy of, as by exertion
**TIRED** *adj* exhausted
**TIREDER** >TIRED
**TIREDEST** >TIRED
**TIREDLY** >TIRED
**TIREDNESS** >TIRED
**TIRELESS** *adj* energetic and determined
**TIRELING** *n* fatigued person or animal
**TIRELINGS** >TIRELING
**TIRES** >TIRE
**TIRESOME** *adj* boring and irritating
**TIREWOMAN** *n* an obsolete term for lady's maid
**TIREWOMEN** >TIREWOMAN
**TIRING** >TIRE
**TIRINGS** >TIRE
**TIRITI** *n* another name for the Treaty of Waitangi
**TIRITIS** >TIRITI
**TIRL** *vb* turn
**TIRLED** >TIRL
**TIRLING** >TIRL

**TIRLS** >TIRL
**TIRO** *same as* >TYRO
**TIROES** >TIRO
**TIRONIC** *variant of* >TYRONIC
**TIROS** >TIRO
**TIRR** *vb* strip or denude
**TIRRED** >TIRR
**TIRRING** >TIRR
**TIRRIT** *n* panic; scare
**TIRRITS** >TIRRIT
**TIRRIVEE** *n* outburst of bad temper; rumpus
**TIRRIVEES** >TIRRIVEE
**TIRRIVIE** *same as* >TIRRIVEE
**TIRRIVIES** >TIRRIVIE
**TIRRS** >TIRR
**TIS** >TI
**TISANE** *n* infusion of dried or fresh leaves or flowers, as camomile
**TISANES** >TISANE
**TISICK** *n* splutter; cough
**TISICKS** >TISICK
**TISSUAL** *adj* relating to tissue
**TISSUE** *n* substance of an animal body or plant ▷ *vb* weave into tissue
**TISSUED** >TISSUE
**TISSUES** >TISSUE
**TISSUEY** >TISSUE
**TISSUING** >TISSUE
**TISSULAR** *adj* relating to tissue
**TISWAS** *n* state of anxiety or excitement
**TISWASES** >TISWAS
**TIT** *n* any of various small songbirds; informal term for a female breast ▷ *vb* jerk or tug
**TITAN** *n* person who is huge, strong, or very important
**TITANATE** *n* any salt or ester of titanic acid
**TITANATES** >TITANATE
**TITANESS** *n* person who is huge, strong, or very important
**TITANIA** >TITANIUM
**TITANIAS** >TITANIA
**TITANIC** *adj* huge or very important
**TITANIS** *n* large predatory flightless prehistoric bird
**TITANISES** >TITANIS
**TITANISM** *n* titanic power
**TITANISMS** >TITANISM
**TITANITE** *another name for* >SPHENE
**TITANITES** >TITANITE
**TITANIUM** *n* strong light metallic element used to make alloys
**TITANIUMS** >TITANIUM
**TITANOUS** *adj* of or containing titanium, esp in the trivalent state
**TITANS** >TITAN
**TITBIT** *n* tasty piece of food

**TITBITS** >TITBIT
**TITCH** *n* small person
**TITCHES** >TITCH
**TITCHIER** >TITCHY
**TITCHIEST** >TITCHY
**TITCHY** *adj* very small
**TITE** *adj* immediately
**TITELY** *adv* immediately
**TITER** *same as* >TITRE
**TITERS** >TITER
**TITFER** *n* hat
**TITFERS** >TITFER
**TITHABLE** *adj* (until 1936) liable to pay tithes
**TITHE** *n* esp formerly, one tenth of one's income or produce paid to the church as a tax ▷ *vb* charge or pay a tithe
**TITHED** >TITHE
**TITHER** >TITHE
**TITHERS** >TITHE
**TITHES** >TITHE
**TITHING** >TITHE
**TITHINGS** >TITHING
**TITHONIA** *n* Central American herb with flowers resembling sunflowers
**TITHONIAS** >TITHONIA
**TITI** *n* small omnivorous New World monkey of South America, with long beautifully coloured fur and a long nonprehensile tail
**TITIAN** *n* reddish gold colour
**TITIANS** >TITIAN
**TITILLATE** *vb* excite or stimulate pleasurably
**TITIS** >TITI
**TITIVATE** *vb* smarten up
**TITIVATED** >TITIVATE
**TITIVATES** >TITIVATE
**TITIVATOR** >TITIVATE
**TITLARK** *another name for* >PIPIT
**TITLARKS** >TITLARK
**TITLE** *n* name of a book, film, etc ▷ *vb* give a title to
**TITLED** *adj* aristocratic
**TITLELESS** >TITLE
**TITLER** *n* one who writes titles
**TITLERS** >TITLE
**TITLES** >TITLE
**TITLING** >TITLE
**TITLINGS** >TITLE
**TITLIST** *n* titleholder
**TITLISTS** >TITLIST
**TITMAN** *n* (of pigs) the runt of a litter
**TITMEN** >TITMAN
**TITMICE** >TITMOUSE
**TITMOSE** *old spelling of* >TITMOUSE
**TITMOUSE** *n* any small active songbird
**TITOKI** *n* New Zealand evergreen tree with a spreading crown and glossy green leaves
**TITOKIS** >TITOKI

**TITRABLE** >TITRATE
**TITRANT** *n* solution in a titration that is added from a burette to a measured quantity of another solution
**TITRANTS** >TITRANT
**TITRATE** *vb* measure the volume or concentration of (a solution) by titration
**TITRATED** >TITRATE
**TITRATES** >TITRATE
**TITRATING** >TITRATE
**TITRATION** *n* operation in which a measured amount of one solution is added to a known quantity of another solution until the reaction between the two is complete
**TITRATOR** *n* device used to perform titration
**TITRATORS** >TITRATOR
**TITRE** *n* concentration of a solution as determined by titration
**TITRES** >TITRE
**TITS** >TIT
**TITTED** >TIT
**TITTER** *vb* laugh in a suppressed way ▷ *n* suppressed laugh
**TITTERED** >TITTER
**TITTERER** >TITTER
**TITTERERS** >TITTER
**TITTERING** >TITTER
**TITTERS** >TITTER
**TITTIE** *n* sister; young woman
**TITTIES** >TITTIE
**TITTING** >TIT
**TITTISH** *adj* testy
**TITTIVATE** *same as* >TITIVATE
**TITTLE** *n* very small amount ▷ *vb* chatter; tattle
**TITTLEBAT** *n* child's name for the stickleback fish
**TITTLED** >TITTLE
**TITTLES** >TITTLE
**TITTLING** >TITTLE
**TITTUP** *vb* prance or frolic ▷ *n* caper
**TITTUPED** >TITTUP
**TITTUPING** >TITTUP
**TITTUPPED** >TITTUP
**TITTUPPY** *same as* >TITTUPY
**TITTUPS** >TITTUP
**TITTUPY** *adj* spritely; lively
**TITTY** *same as* >TITTIE
**TITUBANCY** *n* staggering or stumbling
**TITUBANT** *adj* staggering
**TITUBATE** *vb* stagger
**TITUBATED** >TITUBATE
**TITUBATES** >TITUBATE
**TITULAR** *adj* in name only ▷ *n* bearer of a title
**TITULARLY** >TITULAR
**TITULARS** >TITULAR
**TITULARY** *same as* >TITULAR
**TITULE** *same as* >TITLE

**TITULED** >TITULE

**TITULES** >TITULE

**TITULI** >TITULUS

**TITULING** >TITULE

**TITULUS** n (in crucifixion) a sign attached to the top of the cross on which were written the condemned man's name and crime

**TITUP** same as >TITTUP

**TITUPED** >TITUP

**TITUPING** >TITUP

**TITUPPED** >TITUP

**TITUPPING** >TITUP

**TITUPS** >TITUP

**TITUPY** same as >TITTUPY

**TIVY** same as >TANTIVY

**TIX** pl n tickets

**TIZWAS** same as >TISWAS

**TIZWASES** >TIZWAS

**TIZZ** same as >TIZZY

**TIZZES** >TIZZ

**TIZZIES** >TIZZY

**TIZZY** n confused or agitated state

**TJANTING** n pen-like tool used in batik for applying molten wax to fabric

**TJANTINGS** >TJANTING

**TMESES** >TMESIS

**TMESIS** n interpolation of a word or group of words between the parts of a compound word

**TO** prep indicating movement towards, equality or comparison, etc ▷ adv a closed position

**TOAD** n animal like a large frog

**TOADEATER** rare word for >TOADY

**TOADFISH** n spiny-finned bottom-dwelling marine fish of tropical and temperate seas, with a flattened tapering body and a wide mouth

**TOADFLAX** n plant with narrow leaves and yellow-orange flowers

**TOADGRASS** another name for >TOADRUSH

**TOADIED** >TOADY

**TOADIES** >TOADY

**TOADISH** >TOAD

**TOADLESS** adj having no toads

**TOADLIKE** >TOAD

**TOADRUSH** n annual rush growing in damp lowlands

**TOADS** >TOAD

**TOADSTONE** n amygdaloidal basalt occurring in the limestone regions of Derbyshire

**TOADSTOOL** n poisonous fungus like a mushroom

**TOADY** n ingratiating person ▷ vb be ingratiating

**TOADYING** >TOADY

**TOADYISH** >TOADY

**TOADYISM** >TOADY

**TOADYISMS** >TOADY

**TOAST** n sliced bread browned by heat ▷ vb brown (bread) by heat

**TOASTED** >TOAST

**TOASTER** >TOAST

**TOASTERS** >TOAST

**TOASTIE** same as >TOASTY

**TOASTIER** >TOASTY

**TOASTIES** >TOASTY

**TOASTIEST** >TOASTY

**TOASTING** >TOAST

**TOASTINGS** >TOAST

**TOASTS** >TOAST

**TOASTY** n toasted sandwich ▷ adj tasting or smelling like toast

**TOAZE** variant spelling of >TOZE

**TOAZED** >TOAZE

**TOAZES** >TOAZE

**TOAZING** >TOAZE

**TOBACCO** n plant with large leaves dried for smoking

**TOBACCOES** >TOBACCO

**TOBACCOS** >TOBACCO

**TOBIES** >TOBY

**TOBOGGAN** n narrow sledge for sliding over snow ▷ vb ride a toboggan

**TOBOGGANS** >TOBOGGAN

**TOBOGGIN** variant spelling of >TOBOGGAN

**TOBOGGINS** >TOBOGGIN

**TOBY** n water stopcock at the boundary of a street and house section

**TOC** n in communications code, signal for letter t

**TOCCATA** n rapid piece of music for a keyboard instrument

**TOCCATAS** >TOCCATA

**TOCCATE** >TOCCATA

**TOCCATINA** n short toccata

**TOCHER** n dowry ▷ vb give a dowry to

**TOCHERED** >TOCHER

**TOCHERING** >TOCHER

**TOCHERS** >TOCHER

**TOCK** n sound made by a clock ▷ vb (of a clock) make such a sound

**TOCKED** >TOCK

**TOCKIER** >TOCKY

**TOCKIEST** >TOCKY

**TOCKING** >TOCK

**TOCKLEY** slang word for >PENIS

**TOCKLEYS** >TOCKLEY

**TOCKS** >TOCK

**TOCKY** adj muddy

**TOCO** n punishment

**TOCOLOGY** n branch of medicine concerned with childbirth

**TOCOS** >TOCO

**TOCS** >TOC

**TOCSIN** n warning signal

**TOCSINS** >TOCSIN

**TOD** n unit of weight, used for wool, etc, usually equal to 28 pounds ▷ vb produce a tod

**TODAY** n this day ▷ adv on this day

**TODAYS** >TODAY

**TODDE** same as >TOD

**TODDED** >TOD

**TODDES** >TODDE

**TODDIES** >TODDY

**TODDING** >TOD

**TODDLE** vb walk with short unsteady steps ▷ n act or an instance of toddling

**TODDLED** >TODDLE

**TODDLER** n child beginning to walk

**TODDLERS** >TODDLER

**TODDLES** >TODDLE

**TODDLING** >TODDLE

**TODDY** n sweetened drink of spirits and hot water

**TODIES** >TODY

**TODS** >TOD

**TODY** n small bird of the Caribbean, with a red-and-green plumage and long straight bill

**TOE** n digit of the foot ▷ vb touch or kick with the toe

**TOEA** n monetary unit of Papua New Guinea, worth one-hundredth of a kina

**TOEAS** >TOEA

**TOEBIE** n South African slang for sandwich

**TOEBIES** >TOEBIE

**TOECAP** n strengthened covering for the toe of a shoe

**TOECAPS** >TOECAP

**TOECLIP** n clip on a bicycle pedal into which the toes are inserted to prevent the foot from slipping

**TOECLIPS** >TOECLIP

**TOED** >TOE

**TOEHOLD** n small space on a mountain for supporting the toe of the foot in climbing

**TOEHOLDS** >TOEHOLD

**TOEIER** >TOEY

**TOEIEST** >TOEY

**TOEING** >TOE

**TOELESS** adj not having toes

**TOELIKE** >TOE

**TOENAIL** n thin hard clear plate covering part of the upper surface of the end of each toe ▷ vb join (beams) by driving nails obliquely

**TOENAILED** >TOENAIL

**TOENAILS** >TOENAIL

**TOEPIECE** n part of a shoe that covers the toes

**TOEPIECES** >TOEPIECE

**TOEPLATE** n metal reinforcement of the part of the sole of a shoe or boot underneath the toes

**TOEPLATES** >TOEPLATE

**TOERAG** n contemptible person

**TOERAGGER** same as >TOERAG

**TOERAGS** >TOERAG

**TOES** >TOE

**TOESHOE** n ballet pump with padded toes

**TOESHOES** >TOESHOE

**TOETOE** same as >TOITOI

**TOETOES** >TOETOE

**TOEY** adj (of a person) nervous or anxious

**TOFF** n well-dressed or upper-class person

**TOFFEE** n chewy sweet made of boiled sugar

**TOFFEES** >TOFFEE

**TOFFIER** >TOFFY

**TOFFIES** >TOFFY

**TOFFIEST** >TOFFY

**TOFFISH** adj belonging to or characteristic of the upper class

**TOFFS** adj like a toff

**TOFFY** same as >TOFFEE

**TOFORE** prep before

**TOFT** n homestead

**TOFTS** >TOFT

**TOFU** n soft food made from soya-bean curd

**TOFUS** >TOFU

**TOFUTTI** n tradename for any of a variety of nondairy, soya-based food products, esp frozen desserts

**TOFUTTIS** >TOFUTTI

**TOG** n unit for measuring the insulating power of duvets ▷ vb dress oneself, esp in smart clothes

**TOGA** n garment worn by citizens of ancient Rome ▷ vb wear a toga

**TOGAE** >TOGA

**TOGAED** >TOGA

**TOGAS** >TOGA

**TOGATE** adj clad in a toga

**TOGATED** same as >TOGATE

**TOGAVIRUS** n one of family of viruses

**TOGE** old variant of >TOGA

**TOGED** >TOGE

**TOGES** >TOGE

**TOGETHER** adv in company ▷ adj organized

**TOGGED** >TOG

**TOGGER** vb play football ▷ n football player

**TOGGERIES** >TOGGERY

**TOGGERS** >TOGGER

**TOGGERY** n clothes

**TOGGING** >TOG

**TOGGLE** n small bar-shaped button inserted through a loop for fastening ▷ vb supply or fasten with a toggle or toggles

**TOGGLED** >TOGGLE

**TOGGLER** >TOGGLE

**TOGGLERS** >TOGGLE

**TOGGLES** >TOGGLE

**TOGGLING** >TOGGLE

**TOGS** >TOG

**TOGUE** n large North American freshwater game fish

TOGUES >TOGUE
TOHEROA n large edible mollusc of New Zealand with a distinctive flavour
TOHEROAS >TOHEROA
TOHO n (to a hunting dog) an instruction to stop
TOHOS >TOHO
TOHUNGA n Māori priest
TOHUNGAS >TOHUNGA
TOIL n hard work ▷ vb work hard
TOILE n transparent linen or cotton fabric
TOILED >TOIL
TOILER >TOIL
TOILERS >TOIL
TOILES >TOILE
TOILET n a bowl connected to a drain for receiving and disposing of urine and faeces ▷ vb go to the toilet
TOILETED >TOILET
TOILETING >TOILET
TOILETRY n object or cosmetic used to clean or groom oneself
TOILETS >TOILET
TOILETTE same as >TOILET
TOILETTES >TOILETTE
TOILFUL same as >TOILSOME
TOILFULLY >TOILFUL
TOILINET n type of fabric with a woollen weft and a cotton or silk warp
TOILINETS >TOILINET
TOILING >TOIL
TOILINGS >TOIL
TOILLESS >TOIL
TOILS >TOIL
TOILSOME adj requiring hard work
TOILWORN adj fatigued, wearied by work
TOING as in toing and froing state of going back and forth
TOINGS >TOING
TOISE n obsolete French unit of length roughly equal to 2m
TOISEACH n ancient Celtic nobleman
TOISEACHS >TOISEACH
TOISECH same as >TOISEACH
TOISECHS >TOISECH
TOISES >TOISE
TOISON n fleece
TOISONS >TOISON
TOIT vb walk or move in an unsteady manner, as from old age
TOITED >TOIT
TOITING >TOIT
TOITOI n tall grasses with feathery fronds
TOITOIS >TOITOI
TOITS >TOIT
TOKAMAK n reactor used in thermonuclear experiments
TOKAMAKS >TOKAMAK

TOKAY n small gecko of S and SE Asia, having a retractile claw at the tip of each digit
TOKAYS >TOKAY
TOKE n draw on a cannabis cigarette ▷ vb take a draw on a cannabis cigarette
TOKED >TOKE
TOKEN n sign or symbol ▷ adj nominal or slight
TOKENED >TOKEN
TOKENING >TOKEN
TOKENISM n policy of making only a token effort, esp to comply with a law
TOKENISMS >TOKENISM
TOKENS >TOKEN
TOKER >TOKE
TOKERS >TOKE
TOKES >TOKE
TOKING >TOKE
TOKO same as >TOCO
TOKOLOGY same as >TOCOLOGY
TOKOLOSHE n (in Bantu folklore) a malevolent mythical manlike animal of short stature
TOKOLOSHI variant of >TOKOLOSHE
TOKOMAK variant spelling of >TOKAMAK
TOKOMAKS >TOKOMAK
TOKONOMA n recess off a living room
TOKONOMAS >TOKONOMA
TOKOS >TOKO
TOKOTOKO n ceremonial carved Māori walking stick
TOKOTOKOS >TOKOTOKO
TOKTOKKIE n large South African beetle
TOLA n unit of weight, used in India, equal to 180 ser or 180 grains
TOLAN n white crystalline derivative of acetylene
TOLANE same as >TOLAN
TOLANES >TOLANE
TOLANS >TOLAN
TOLAR n standard monetary unit of Slovenia, divided into 100 stotin
TOLARJEV >TOLAR
TOLARJI >TOLAR
TOLARS >TOLAR
TOLAS >TOLA
TOLBOOTH same as >TOLLBOOTH
TOLBOOTHS >TOLBOOTH
TOLD >TELL
TOLE same as >TOLL
TOLED >TOLE
TOLEDO n type of sword originally made in Toledo
TOLEDOS >TOLEDO
TOLERABLE adj bearable
TOLERABLY >TOLERABLE
TOLERANCE n acceptance of other people's rights to their own opinions or actions

TOLERANT adj able to tolerate the beliefs, actions, opinions, etc, of others
TOLERATE vb allow to exist or happen
TOLERATED >TOLERATE
TOLERATES >TOLERATE
TOLERATOR >TOLERATE
TOLES >TOLE
TOLEWARE n enamelled or lacquered metal ware, usually gilded
TOLEWARES >TOLEWARE
TOLIDIN same as >TOLIDINE
TOLIDINE n compound used in dying and in chemical analysis, esp as an indicator of the presence of free chlorine in water
TOLIDINES >TOLIDINE
TOLIDINS >TOLIDIN
TOLING >TOLE
TOLINGS >TOLE
TOLL vb ring (a bell) slowly and regularly, esp to announce a death ▷ n tolling
TOLLABLE >TOLL
TOLLAGE same as >TOLL
TOLLAGES >TOLLAGE
TOLLBAR n bar blocking passage of a thoroughfare, raised on payment of a toll
TOLLBARS >TOLLBAR
TOLLBOOTH n booth or kiosk at which a toll is collected
TOLLDISH n dish used to measure out the portion of grain given to a miller as payment for his or her work
TOLLED >TOLL
TOLLER >TOLL
TOLLERS >TOLLER
TOLLGATE n gate across a toll road or bridge at which travellers must pay
TOLLGATES >TOLLGATE
TOLLHOUSE n small house at a tollgate occupied by a toll collector
TOLLIE same as >TOLLY
TOLLIES >TOLLY
TOLLING >TOLL
TOLLINGS >TOLL
TOLLMAN n man who collects tolls
TOLLMEN >TOLLMAN
TOLLS >TOLL
TOLLWAY n road on which users must pay tolls to travel
TOLLWAYS >TOLLWAY
TOLLY n castrated calf
TOLSEL n tolbooth
TOLSELS >TOLSEL
TOLSEY n tolbooth
TOLSEYS >TOLBOOTH
TOLT n type of obsolete English writ
TOLTER vb struggle or

move with difficulty, as in mud
TOLTERED >TOLTER
TOLTERING >TOLTER
TOLTERS >TOLTER
TOLTS >TOLT
TOLU n sweet-smelling balsam obtained from a South American tree, used in medicine and perfume
TOLUATE n any salt or ester of any of the three isomeric forms of toluic acid
TOLUATES >TOLUATE
TOLUENE n colourless volatile flammable liquid obtained from petroleum and coal tar
TOLUENES >TOLUENE
TOLUIC as in toluic acid white crystalline derivative of toluene existing in three isomeric forms
TOLUID n white crystalline derivative of glycocoll
TOLUIDE variant of >TOLUID
TOLUIDES >TOLUIDE
TOLUIDIDE n chemical deriving from toluene
TOLUIDIN n type of dye
TOLUIDINE n compound used in dye production
TOLUIDINS >TOLUIDIN
TOLUIDS >TOLUID
TOLUOL another name for >TOLUENE
TOLUOLE another name for >TOLUENE
TOLUOLES >TOLUOLE
TOLUOLS >TOLUOL
TOLUS >TOLU
TOLUYL n of, consisting of, or containing any of three isomeric groups $CH_3C_6H_4CO-$, derived from a toluic acid by removal of the hydroxyl group
TOLUYLS >TOLUYL
TOLYL n of, consisting of, or containing any of three isomeric groups, $CH_3C_6H_4-$, derived from toluene
TOLYLS >TOLYL
TOLZEY n tolbooth
TOLZEYS >TOLZEY
TOM n male cat ▷ adj (of an animal) male ▷ vb prostitute oneself
TOMAHAWK n fighting axe of the Native Americans
TOMAHAWKS >TOMAHAWK
TOMALLEY n fat from a lobster, called "liver", and eaten as a delicacy
TOMALLEYS >TOMALLEY
TOMAN n gold coin formerly issued in Persia
TOMANS >TOMAN
TOMATILLO n Mexican plant bearing edible berries of the same name
TOMATO n red fruit used in

salads and as a vegetable
**TOMATOES** >TOMATO
**TOMATOEY** >TOMATO
**TOMB** n grave
**TOMBAC** n any of various
brittle alloys containing
copper and zinc and
sometimes tin and
arsenic: used for making
cheap jewellery, etc
**TOMBACK** variant spelling
of >TOMBAC
**TOMBACKS** >TOMBAC
**TOMBACS** >TOMBAC
**TOMBAK** same as >TOMBAC
**TOMBAKS** >TOMBAK
**TOMBAL** adj like or relating
to a tomb
**TOMBED** >TOMB
**TOMBIC** adj of or relating to
tombs
**TOMBING** >TOMB
**TOMBLESS** >TOMB
**TOMBLIKE** >TOMB
**TOMBOC** n weapon
**TOMBOCS** >TOMBOC
**TOMBOLA** n lottery with
tickets drawn from a
revolving drum
**TOMBOLAS** >TOMBOLA
**TOMBOLO** n narrow sand or
shingle bar linking a small
island with another island
or the mainland
**TOMBOLOS** >TOMBOLO
**TOMBOY** n girl who acts or
dresses like a boy
**TOMBOYISH** >TOMBOY
**TOMBOYS** >TOMBOY
**TOMBS** >TOMB
**TOMBSTONE** n gravestone
**TOMCAT** vb (of a man) to be
promiscuous
**TOMCATS** >TOMCAT
**TOMCATTED** >TOMCAT
**TOMCOD** n small fish
resembling the cod
**TOMCODS** >TOMCOD
**TOME** n large heavy book
**TOMENTA** >TOMENTUM
**TOMENTOSE** >TOMENTUM
**TOMENTOUS** >TOMENTUM
**TOMENTUM** n feltlike
covering of downy hairs
on leaves and other plant
parts
**TOMES** >TOME
**TOMFOOL** n fool ▷ vb act
the fool
**TOMFOOLED** >TOMFOOL
**TOMFOOLS** >TOMFOOL
**TOMIA** >TOMIUM
**TOMIAL** >TOMIUM
**TOMIUM** n sharp edge of a
bird's beak
**TOMMED** >TOM
**TOMMIED** >TOMMY
**TOMMIES** >TOMMY
**TOMMING** >TOM
**TOMMY** n private in
the British Army ▷ vb
(formerly) to exploit
workers by paying them
in goods rather than in

money
**TOMMYING** >TOMMY
**TOMMYROT** n utter nonsense
**TOMMYROTS** >TOMMYROT
**TOMO** n shaft formed by
the action of water on
limestone or volcanic rock
**TOMOGRAM** n x-ray
photograph of a selected
plane section of the
human body or some other
solid object
**TOMOGRAMS** >TOMOGRAM
**TOMOGRAPH** n device for
making tomograms
**TOMORROW** n (on) the day
after today ▷ adv on the
day after today
**TOMORROWS** >TOMORROW
**TOMOS** >TOMO
**TOMPION** same as >TAMPION
**TOMPIONS** >TOMPION
**TOMPON** same as >TAMPON
**TOMPONED** >TOMPON
**TOMPONING** >TOMPON
**TOMPONS** >TOMPON
**TOMS** >TOM
**TOMTIT** n small European
bird that eats insects and
seeds
**TOMTITS** >TOMTIT
**TON** n unit of weight equal
to 2240 pounds or 1016
kilograms (long ton) or, in
the US, 2000 pounds or
907 kilograms (short ton);
style, distinction
**TONAL** adj written in a key
**TONALITE** n igneous rock
found in the Italian Alps
**TONALITES** >TONALITE
**TONALITY** n presence
of a musical key in a
composition
**TONALLY** >TONAL
**TONANT** adj very loud
**TONDI** >TONDO
**TONDINI** >TONDINO
**TONDINO** n small tondo
**TONDINOS** >TONDINO
**TONDO** n circular easel
painting or relief carving
**TONDOS** >TONDO
**TONE** n sound with
reference to its pitch,
volume, etc ▷ vb
harmonize (with)
**TONEARM** same as >PICKUP
**TONEARMS** >TONEARM
**TONED** >TONE
**TONELESS** adj having no
tone
**TONEME** n phoneme that
is distinguished from
another phoneme only by
its tone
**TONEMES** >TONEME
**TONEMIC** >TONEME
**TONEPAD** n keypad used to
transmit information by
generating tones that can
be recognised by a central
system as corresponding
to particular digits

**TONEPADS** >TONEPAD
**TONER** n cosmetic applied
to the skin to reduce
oiliness
**TONERS** >TONER
**TONES** >TONE
**TONETIC** adj (of a
language) distinguishing
words semantically by
distinction of tone as well
as by other sounds
**TONETICS** pl n area of
linguistics concentrating
on the use of tone to
distinguish words
semantically
**TONETTE** n small musical
instrument resembling a
recorder
**TONETTES** >TONETTE
**TONEY** variant spelling
of >TONY
**TONG** n (formerly) a
secret society of Chinese
Americans ▷ vb gather
or seize with tongs ▷ n
(formerly) a Chinese secret
society
**TONGA** n light two-wheeled
vehicle used in rural areas
of India
**TONGAS** >TONGA
**TONGED** >TONG
**TONGER** n one who uses
tongs to gather oysters
**TONGERS** >TONGER
**TONGING** >TONG
**TONGMAN** another word
for >TONGER
**TONGMEN** >TONGMAN
**TONGS** pl n large pincers for
grasping and lifting
**TONGSTER** n tong member
**TONGSTERS** >TONGSTER
**TONGUE** n muscular organ
in the mouth, used in
speaking and tasting ▷ vb
use the tongue
**TONGUED** >TONGUE
**TONGUELET** n small tongue
**TONGUES** >TONGUE
**TONGUING** >TONGUE
**TONGUINGS** >TONGUE
**TONIC** n medicine to
improve body tone ▷ adj
invigorating
**TONICALLY** >TONIC
**TONICITY** n state,
condition, or quality of
being tonic
**TONICS** >TONIC
**TONIER** >TONY
**TONIES** >TONY
**TONIEST** >TONY
**TONIGHT** n (in or during)
the night or evening of
this day ▷ adv in or during
the night or evening of
this day
**TONIGHTS** >TONIGHT
**TONING** >TONE
**TONINGS** >TONE
**TONISH** >TON
**TONISHLY** >TON

**TONITE** n explosive used in
quarrying
**TONITES** >TONITE
**TONK** vb strike with a
heavy blow ▷ n effete or
effeminate man
**TONKA** as in tonka bean
tall leguminous tree of
tropical America, having
fragrant black almond-
shaped seeds
**TONKED** >TONK
**TONKER** >TONK
**TONKERS** >TONK
**TONKING** >TONK
**TONKS** >TONK
**TONLET** n skirt of a suit
of armour, consisting of
overlapping metal bands
**TONLETS** >TONLET
**TONNAG** n type of (usually
tartan) shawl
**TONNAGE** n weight capacity
of a ship
**TONNAGES** >TONNAGE
**TONNAGS** >TONNAG
**TONNE** same as >TON
**TONNEAU** n detachable
cover to protect the rear
part of an open car when it
is not carrying passengers
**TONNEAUS** >TONNEAU
**TONNEAUX** >TONNEAU
**TONNELL** old spelling
of >TUNNEL
**TONNELLS** >TONNELL
**TONNER** n something, for
example a vehicle, that
weighs one ton
**TONNERS** >TONNE
**TONNES** >TONNE
**TONNISH** >TON
**TONNISHLY** >TON
**TONOMETER** n instrument
for measuring the pitch
of a sound, esp one
consisting of a set of
tuning forks
**TONOMETRY** >TONOMETER
**TONOPLAST** n membrane
enclosing a vacuole in a
plant cell
**TONS** >TON
**TONSIL** n small gland in the
throat
**TONSILAR** >TONSIL
**TONSILLAR** >TONSIL
**TONSILS** >TONSIL
**TONSOR** n barber
**TONSORIAL** adj of a barber
or his trade
**TONSORS** >TONSOR
**TONSURE** n shaving of all
or the top of the head as
a religious or monastic
practice ▷ vb shave the
head of
**TONSURED** >TONSURE
**TONSURES** >TONSURE
**TONSURING** >TONSURE
**TONTINE** n annuity
scheme by which several
subscribers accumulate
and invest a common fund

out of which they receive an annuity that increases as subscribers die until the last survivor takes the whole

**TONTINER** n subscriber to a tontine

**TONTINERS** > TONTINER

**TONTINES** > TONTINE

**TONUS** n normal tension of a muscle at rest

**TONUSES** > TONUS

**TONY** adj stylish or distinctive ▷ n stylish or distinctive person

**TOO** adv also, as well

**TOOART** variant spelling of > TUART

**TOOARTS** > TOOART

**TOOK** > TAKE

**TOOL** n implement used by hand ▷ vb work on with a tool

**TOOLBAG** n bag for storing or carrying tools

**TOOLBAGS** > TOOLBAG

**TOOLBAR** n horizontal row or vertical column of selectable buttons displayed on a computer screen, allowing the user to select a variety of functions

**TOOLBARS** > TOOLBAR

**TOOLBOX** n box for storing or carrying tools

**TOOLBOXES** > TOOLBOX

**TOOLED** > TOOL

**TOOLER** > TOOL

**TOOLERS** > TOOL

**TOOLHEAD** n adjustable attachment for a machine tool that holds the tool in position

**TOOLHEADS** > TOOLHEAD

**TOOLHOUSE** another word for > TOOLSHED

**TOOLING** n any decorative work done with a tool, esp a design stamped onto a book cover, piece of leatherwork, etc

**TOOLINGS** > TOOLING

**TOOLKIT** n set of tools designed to be used together or for a particular purpose

**TOOLKITS** > TOOLKIT

**TOOLLESS** adj having no tools

**TOOLMAKER** n person who makes tools

**TOOLMAN** n person who works with tools

**TOOLMEN** > TOOLMAN

**TOOLROOM** n room, as in a machine shop, where tools are made or stored

**TOOLROOMS** > TOOLROOM

**TOOLS** > TOOL

**TOOLSET** n set of predefined tools associated with a particular computer

application

**TOOLSETS** > TOOLSET

**TOOLSHED** n small shed in the garden or yard of a house used for storing tools, esp those for gardening

**TOOLSHEDS** > TOOLSHED

**TOOM** vb empty (something) ▷ adj empty

**TOOMED** > TOOM

**TOOMER** > TOOM

**TOOMEST** > TOOM

**TOOMING** > TOOM

**TOOMS** > TOOM

**TOON** n large meliaceous tree of the East Indies and Australia, having clusters of flowers from which a dye is obtained

**TOONIE** n Canadian two-dollar coin

**TOONIES** > TOONIE

**TOONS** > TOON

**TOORIE** n tassel or bobble on a bonnet

**TOORIES** > TOORIE

**TOOSHIE** adj angry

**TOOT** n short hooting sound ▷ vb (cause to) make such a sound

**TOOTED** > TOOT

**TOOTER** > TOOT

**TOOTERS** > TOOT

**TOOTH** n bonelike projection in the jaws of most vertebrates for biting and chewing

**TOOTHACHE** n pain in or near a tooth

**TOOTHCOMB** n comb with fine teeth set closely together

**TOOTHED** adj having a tooth or teeth

**TOOTHFISH** as in Patagonian toothfish Chilean sea bass

**TOOTHFUL** n little (esp alcoholic) drink

**TOOTHFULS** > TOOTHFUL

**TOOTHIER** > TOOTHY

**TOOTHIEST** > TOOTHY

**TOOTHILY** > TOOTHY

**TOOTHING** > TOOTH

**TOOTHINGS** > TOOTH

**TOOTHLESS** > TOOTH

**TOOTHLIKE** > TOOTH

**TOOTHPICK** n small stick for removing scraps of food from between the teeth

**TOOTHS** > TOOTH

**TOOTHSOME** adj delicious or appetizing in appearance, flavour, or smell

**TOOTHWASH** n tooth-cleaning liquid

**TOOTHWORT** n parasitic plant

**TOOTHY** adj having or showing numerous, large, or prominent teeth

**TOOTING** > TOOT

**TOOTLE** vb hoot softly or repeatedly ▷ n soft hoot or series of hoots

**TOOTLED** > TOOTLE

**TOOTLER** > TOOTLE

**TOOTLERS** > TOOTLE

**TOOTLES** > TOOTLE

**TOOTLING** > TOOTLE

**TOOTS** Scots version of > TUT

**TOOTSED** > TOOTS

**TOOTSES** > TOOTS

**TOOTSIE** same as > TOOTSY

**TOOTSIES** > TOOTSY

**TOOTSING** > TOOTS

**TOOTSY** same as > TOOTS

**TOP** n highest point or part ▷ adj at or of the top ▷ vb form a top on

**TOPALGIA** n pain restricted to a particular spot: a neurotic or hysterical symptom

**TOPALGIAS** > TOPALGIA

**TOPARCH** n ruler of a small state or realm

**TOPARCHS** > TOPARCH

**TOPARCHY** > TOPARCH

**TOPAZ** n semiprecious stone in various colours

**TOPAZES** > TOPAZ

**TOPAZINE** adj like topaz

**TOPCOAT** n overcoat

**TOPCOATS** > TOPCOAT

**TOPCROSS** n class of hybrid

**TOPE** vb drink alcohol regularly ▷ n small European shark

**TOPECTOMY** n (formerly) the surgical removal of part of the cerebral cortex to relieve certain psychiatric disorders

**TOPED** > TOPE

**TOPEE** n lightweight hat worn in tropical countries

**TOPEES** > TOPE

**TOPEK** same as > TUPIK

**TOPEKS** > TOPEK

**TOPER** > TOPE

**TOPERS** > TOPE

**TOPES** > TOPE

**TOPFLIGHT** adj superior or excellent quality; outstanding

**TOPFUL** variant spelling of > TOPFULL

**TOPFULL** adj full to the top

**TOPH** n variety of sandstone

**TOPHE** variant spelling of > TOPH

**TOPHES** > TOPHE

**TOPHI** > TOPHUS

**TOPHS** > TOPH

**TOPHUS** n deposit of sodium urate in the helix of the ear or surrounding a joint

**TOPI** same as > TOPEE

**TOPIARIAN** > TOPIARY

**TOPIARIES** > TOPIARY

**TOPIARIST** > TOPIARY

**TOPIARY** n art of trimming trees and bushes into decorative shapes ▷ adj of

or relating to topiary

**TOPIC** n subject of a conversation, book, etc

**TOPICAL** adj relating to current events

**TOPICALLY** > TOPICAL

**TOPICS** > TOPIC

**TOPING** > TOPE

**TOPIS** > TOPI

**TOPKICK** n (formerly) sergeant

**TOPKICKS** > TOPKICK

**TOPKNOT** n crest, tuft, decorative bow, etc, on the top of the head

**TOPKNOTS** > TOPKNOT

**TOPLESS** adj (of a costume or woman) with no covering for the breasts

**TOPLINE** vb headline; be the main focus of a newspaper story

**TOPLINED** > TOPLINE

**TOPLINER** > TOPLINE

**TOPLINERS** > TOPLINE

**TOPLINES** > TOPLINE

**TOPLINING** > TOPLINE

**TOPLOFTY** adj haughty or pretentious

**TOPMAKER** n wool dealer

**TOPMAKERS** > TOPMAKER

**TOPMAKING** > TOPMAKER

**TOPMAN** n sailor positioned in the rigging of the topsail

**TOPMAST** n mast next above a lower mast on a sailing vessel

**TOPMASTS** > TOPMAST

**TOPMEN** > TOPMAN

**TOPMINNOW** n small American freshwater cyprinodont fish

**TOPMOST** adj highest or best

**TOPNOTCH** adj excellent

**TOPO** n picture of a mountain with details of climbing routes superimposed on it

**TOPOGRAPH** n type of x-ray photograph

**TOPOI** > TOPO

**TOPOLOGIC** > TOPOLOGY

**TOPOLOGY** n geometry of the properties of a shape which are unaffected by continuous distortion

**TOPONYM** n name of a place

**TOPONYMAL** > TOPONYMY

**TOPONYMIC** > TOPONYMY

**TOPONYMS** > TOPONYM

**TOPONYMY** n study of place names

**TOPOS** > TOPO

**TOPOTYPE** n specimen plant or animal taken from an area regarded as the typical habitat

**TOPOTYPES** > TOPOTYPE

**TOPPED** > TOP

**TOPPER** n top hat

**TOPPERS** > TOPPER

**TOPPING** > TOP

**TOPPINGLY** > TOP
**TOPPINGS** > TOP
**TOPPLE** *vb* (cause to) fall over
**TOPPLED** > TOPPLE
**TOPPLES** > TOPPLE
**TOPPLING** > TOPPLE
**TOPS** > TOP
**TOPSAIL** *n* square sail carried on a yard set on a topmast
**TOPSAILS** > TOPSAIL
**TOPSIDE** *n* lean cut of beef from the thigh containing no bone
**TOPSIDER** *n* person in charge
**TOPSIDERS** > TOPSIDER
**TOPSIDES** > TOPSIDE
**TOPSMAN** *n* chief drover
**TOPSMEN** > TOPSMAN
**TOPSOIL** *n* surface layer of soil ▷ *vb* spread topsoil on (land)
**TOPSOILED** > TOPSOIL
**TOPSOILS** > TOPSOIL
**TOPSPIN** *n* spin imparted to make a ball bounce or travel exceptionally far, high, or quickly, as by hitting it with a sharp forward and upward stroke
**TOPSPINS** > TOPSPIN
**TOPSTITCH** *vb* stitch a line the outside of a garment, running close to a seam
**TOPSTONE** *n* stone forming the top of something
**TOPSTONES** > TOPSTONE
**TOPWORK** *vb* graft shoots or twigs onto the main branches of (for example, a fruit tree) to modify its yield
**TOPWORKED** > TOPWORK
**TOPWORKS** > TOPWORK
**TOQUE** *same as* > TUQUE
**TOQUES** > TOQUE
**TOQUET** *same as* > TOQUE
**TOQUETS** > TOQUET
**TOQUILLA** *another name for* > JIPIJAPA
**TOQUILLAS** > TOQUILLA
**TOR** *n* high rocky hill
**TORA** *variant spelling of* > TORAH
**TORAH** *n* whole body of traditional Jewish teaching, including the Oral Law
**TORAHS** > TORAH
**TORAN** *n* (in Indian architecture) an archway, usually wooden and often ornately carved
**TORANA** *same as* > TORAN
**TORANAS** > TORANA
**TORANS** > TORAN
**TORAS** > TORA
**TORBANITE** *n* type of oil shale
**TORC** *same as* > TORQUE
**TORCH** *n* small portable

battery-powered lamp ▷ *vb* deliberately set (a building) on fire
**TORCHABLE** > TORCH
**TORCHED** > TORCH
**TORCHER** > TORCH
**TORCHERE** *n* tall narrow stand for holding a candelabrum
**TORCHERES** > TORCHERE
**TORCHERS** > TORCH
**TORCHES** > TORCH
**TORCHIER** *n* standing lamp with a bowl for casting light upwards and so giving all-round indirect illumination
**TORCHIERE** *same as* > TORCHIER
**TORCHIERS** > TORCHIER
**TORCHIEST** > TORCHY
**TORCHING** > TORCH
**TORCHINGS** > TORCH
**TORCHLIKE** > TORCH
**TORCHON** as in *torchon lace* coarse linen or cotton lace with a simple openwork pattern
**TORCHONS** > TORCHON
**TORCHWOOD** *n* rutaceous tree or shrub of Florida and the Caribbean, with hard resinous wood used for torches
**TORCHY** *adj* sentimental; maudlin; characteristic of a torch song
**TORCS** > TORC
**TORCULAR** *n* tourniquet
**TORCULARS** > TORCULAR
**TORDION** *n* old triple-time dance for two people
**TORDIONS** > TORDION
**TORE** *same as* > TORUS
**TOREADOR** *n* bullfighter
**TOREADORS** > TOREADOR
**TORERO** *n* bullfighter, esp one on foot
**TOREROS** > TORERO
**TORES** > TORE
**TOREUTIC** > TOREUTICS
**TOREUTICS** *n* art of making detailed ornamental reliefs, esp in metal, by embossing and chasing
**TORGOCH** *n* type of char
**TORGOCHS** > TORGOCH
**TORI** > TORUS
**TORIC** *adj* of, relating to, or having the form of a torus
**TORICS** > TORIC
**TORIES** > TORY
**TORII** *n* gateway, esp one at the entrance to a Japanese Shinto temple
**TORMENT** *vb* cause (someone) great suffering ▷ *n* great suffering
**TORMENTA** > TORMENTUM
**TORMENTED** > TORMENT
**TORMENTER** *same as* > TORMENTOR
**TORMENTIL** *n* creeping plant with yellow four-

petalled flowers
**TORMENTOR** *n* person or thing that torments
**TORMENTS** > TORMENT
**TORMENTUM** *n* type of Roman catapult
**TORMINA** *n* complaints
**TORMINAL** > TORMINA
**TORMINOUS** > TORMINA
**TORN** > TEAR
**TORNADE** *same as* > TORNADO
**TORNADES** > TORNADE
**TORNADIC** > TORNADO
**TORNADO** *n* violent whirlwind
**TORNADOES** > TORNADO
**TORNADOS** > TORNADO
**TORNILLO** *n* shrub found in Mexico and some southwestern states of the US
**TORNILLOS** > TORNILLO
**TORO** *n* bull
**TOROID** *n* surface generated by rotating a closed plane curve about a coplanar line that does not intersect the curve
**TOROIDAL** > TOROID
**TOROIDS** > TOROID
**TOROS** > TORO
**TOROSE** *adj* (of a cylindrical part) having irregular swellings
**TOROSITY** > TOROSE
**TOROT** > TORAH
**TOROTH** > TORAH
**TOROUS** *same as* > TOROSE
**TORPEDO** *n* self-propelled underwater missile ▷ *vb* attack or destroy with or as if with torpedoes
**TORPEDOED** > TORPEDO
**TORPEDOER** > TORPEDO
**TORPEDOES** > TORPEDO
**TORPEDOS** > TORPEDO
**TORPEFIED** > TORPEFY
**TORPEFIES** > TORPEFY
**TORPEFY** *n* make torpid
**TORPID** *adj* sluggish and inactive
**TORPIDITY** > TORPID
**TORPIDLY** > TORPID
**TORPIDS** *n* series of boat races held at Oxford University during Lent
**TORPITUDE** *another word for* > TORPOR
**TORPOR** *n* torpid state
**TORPORS** > TORPOR
**TORQUATE** > TORQUES
**TORQUATED** > TORQUES
**TORQUE** *n* force causing rotation ▷ *vb* apply torque to (something)
**TORQUED** > TORQUE
**TORQUER** > TORQUE
**TORQUERS** > TORQUE
**TORQUES** *n* distinctive band of hair, feathers, skin, or colour around the neck of an animal
**TORQUESES** > TORQUES

**TORQUING** > TORQUE
**TORR** *n* unit of pressure equal to one millimetre of mercury (133.3 newtons per square metre)
**TORREFIED** > TORREFY
**TORREFIES** > TORREFY
**TORREFY** *vb* dry (drugs, ores, etc) by subjection to intense heat
**TORRENT** *n* rushing stream ▷ *adj* like or relating to a torrent
**TORRENTS** > TORRENT
**TORRET** *same as* > TERRET
**TORRETS** > TORRET
**TORRID** *adj* very hot and dry
**TORRIDER** > TORRID
**TORRIDEST** > TORRID
**TORRIDITY** > TORRID
**TORRIDLY** > TORRID
**TORRIFIED** > TORRIEFY
**TORRIFIES** > TORRIFY
**TORRIFY** *same as* > TORREFY
**TORRS** > TORR
**TORS** > TOR
**TORSADE** *n* ornamental twist or twisted cord, as on hats
**TORSADES** > TORSADE
**TORSE** *same as* > TORSO
**TORSEL** *n* wooden beam along the top of a wall for distributing the weight of something laid upon it
**TORSELS** > TORSEL
**TORSES** > TORSE
**TORSI** > TORSO
**TORSION** *n* twisting of a part by equal forces being applied at both ends but in opposite directions
**TORSIONAL** > TORSION
**TORSIONS** > TORSION
**TORSIVE** *adj* twisted
**TORSK** *n* fish with a single long dorsal fin
**TORSKS** > TORSK
**TORSO** *n* trunk of the human body
**TORSOS** > TORSO
**TORT** *n* civil wrong or injury for which damages may be claimed
**TORTA** *n* (in mining) a flat circular pile of silver ore
**TORTAS** > TORTA
**TORTE** *n* rich cake, originating in Austria, usually decorated or filled with cream, fruit, nuts, and jam
**TORTEN** > TORTE
**TORTES** > TORTE
**TORTILE** *adj* twisted or coiled
**TORTILITY** > TORTILE
**TORTILLA** *n* thin Mexican pancake
**TORTILLAS** > TORTILLA
**TORTILLON** *another word for* > STUMP
**TORTIOUS** *adj* having the nature of or involving a

tort
**TORTIVE** adj twisted
**TORTOISE** n slow-moving land reptile with a dome-shaped shell
**TORTOISES** > TORTOISE
**TORTONI** n rich ice cream often flavoured with sherry
**TORTONIS** > TORTONI
**TORTRICES** > TORTRIX
**TORTRICID** n small moth of the chiefly temperate family Tortricidae, ▷ adj of, relating to, or belonging to the family Tortricidae
**TORTRIX** n type of moth
**TORTRIXES** > TORTRIX
**TORTS** > TORT
**TORTUOUS** adj winding or twisting
**TORTURE** vb cause (someone) severe pain or mental anguish ▷ n severe physical or mental pain
**TORTURED** > TORTURE
**TORTURER** > TORTURE
**TORTURERS** > TORTURE
**TORTURES** > TORTURE
**TORTURING** > TORTURE
**TORTUROUS** > TORTURE
**TORULA** n species of fungal microorganisms
**TORULAE** > TORULA
**TORULAS** > TORULA
**TORULI** > TORULUS
**TORULIN** n vitamin found in yeast
**TORULINS** > TORULIN
**TORULOSE** adj (of something cylindrical) alternately swollen and pinched along its length
**TORULOSES** > TORULOSIS
**TORULOSIS** n infection by one of the torula
**TORULUS** n socket in an insect's head in which its antenna is attached
**TORUS** n large convex moulding approximately semicircular in cross section, esp one used on the base of a classical column
**TORY** n ultraconservative or reactionary person ▷ adj ultraconservative or reactionary
**TOSA** n large reddish dog, originally bred for fighting
**TOSAS** > TOSA
**TOSE** same as > TOZE
**TOSED** > TOSE
**TOSES** > TOSE
**TOSH** n nonsense ▷ vb tidy or trim
**TOSHACH** n military leader of a clan
**TOSHACHS** > TOSHACH
**TOSHED** > TOSH
**TOSHER** > TOSH
**TOSHERS** > TOSH

**TOSHES** > TOSH
**TOSHIER** > TOSHY
**TOSHIEST** > TOSHY
**TOSHING** > TOSH
**TOSHY** adj neat; trim
**TOSING** > TOSE
**TOSS** vb throw lightly ▷ n tossing
**TOSSED** > TOSS
**TOSSEN** old past participle of > TOSS
**TOSSER** n stupid or despicable person
**TOSSERS** > TOSSER
**TOSSES** > TOSS
**TOSSIER** > TOSSY
**TOSSIEST** > TOSSY
**TOSSILY** > TOSSY
**TOSSING** > TOSS
**TOSSINGS** > TOSS
**TOSSPOT** n habitual drinker
**TOSSPOTS** > TOSSPOT
**TOSSUP** n an instance of tossing up a coin
**TOSSUPS** > TOSSUP
**TOSSY** adj impudent
**TOST** old past participle of > TOSS
**TOSTADA** n crispy deep-fried tortilla topped with meat, cheese, and refried beans
**TOSTADAS** > TOSTADA
**TOSTADO** same as > TOSTADA
**TOSTADOS** > TOSTADO
**TOT** n small child ▷ vb total
**TOTABLE** > TOTE
**TOTAL** n whole, esp a sum of parts ▷ adj complete ▷ vb amount to
**TOTALED** > TOTAL
**TOTALING** > TOTAL
**TOTALISE** same as > TOTALIZE
**TOTALISED** > TOTALISE
**TOTALISER** > TOTALISE
**TOTALISES** > TOTALISE
**TOTALISM** n practice of a dictatorial one party state that regulates every form of life
**TOTALISMS** > TOTALISM
**TOTALIST** > TOTALISM
**TOTALISTS** > TOTALISM
**TOTALITY** n whole amount
**TOTALIZE** vb combine or make into a total
**TOTALIZED** > TOTALIZE
**TOTALIZER** > TOTALIZE
**TOTALIZES** > TOTALIZE
**TOTALLED** > TOTAL
**TOTALLING** > TOTAL
**TOTALLY** > TOTAL
**TOTALS** > TOTAL
**TOTANUS** another name for > REDSHANK
**TOTANUSES** > TOTANUS
**TOTAQUINE** n mixture of quinine and other alkaloids derived from cinchona bark, used as a substitute for quinine in treating malaria
**TOTARA** n tall coniferous

forest tree of New Zealand, with a hard durable wood
**TOTARAS** > TOTARA
**TOTE** vb carry (a gun etc) ▷ n act of or an instance of toting
**TOTEABLE** > TOTE
**TOTED** > TOTE
**TOTEM** n tribal badge or emblem
**TOTEMIC** > TOTEM
**TOTEMISM** n belief in kinship of groups or individuals having a common totem
**TOTEMISMS** > TOTEMISM
**TOTEMIST** > TOTEMISM
**TOTEMISTS** > TOTEMISM
**TOTEMITE** > TOTEMISM
**TOTEMITES** > TOTEMITE
**TOTEMS** > TOTEM
**TOTER** > TOTE
**TOTERS** > TOTE
**TOTES** > TOTE
**TOTHER** n other
**TOTIENT** n quantity of numbers less than, and sharing no common factors with, a given number
**TOTIENTS** > TOTIENT
**TOTING** > TOTE
**TOTITIVE** n number less than, and having no common factors with, a given number
**TOTITIVES** > TOTITIVE
**TOTS** > TOT
**TOTTED** > TOT
**TOTTER** vb move unsteadily ▷ n act or an instance of tottering
**TOTTERED** > TOTTER
**TOTTERER** > TOTTER
**TOTTERERS** > TOTTER
**TOTTERING** > TOTTER
**TOTTERS** > TOTTER
**TOTTERY** > TOTTER
**TOTTIE** adj very small
**TOTTIER** > TOTTY
**TOTTIES** > TOTTY
**TOTTIEST** > TOTTY
**TOTTING** > TOT
**TOTTINGS** > TOT
**TOTTY** n people, esp women, collectively considered as sexual objects ▷ adj very small
**TOUCAN** n tropical American bird with a large bill
**TOUCANET** n type of small toucan
**TOUCANETS** > TOUCAN
**TOUCANS** > TOUCAN
**TOUCH** vb come into contact with ▷ n sense by which an object's qualities are perceived when they come into contact with part of the body ▷ adj of a non-contact version of particular sport
**TOUCHABLE** > TOUCH

**TOUCHBACK** n play in which the ball is put down by a player behind his own goal line when the ball has been put across the goal line by an opponent
**TOUCHDOWN** n moment at which a landing aircraft or spacecraft comes into contact with the landing surface ▷ vb (of an aircraft or spacecraft) to land
**TOUCHE** interj acknowledgment of the striking home of a remark or witty reply
**TOUCHED** adj emotionally moved
**TOUCHER** > TOUCH
**TOUCHERS** > TOUCH
**TOUCHES** > TOUCH
**TOUCHHOLE** n hole in the breech of early cannon and firearms through which the charge was ignited
**TOUCHIER** > TOUCHY
**TOUCHIEST** > TOUCHY
**TOUCHILY** > TOUCHY
**TOUCHING** adj emotionally moving ▷ prep relating to or concerning
**TOUCHINGS** > TOUCH
**TOUCHLESS** > TOUCH
**TOUCHLINE** n side line of the pitch in some games
**TOUCHMARK** n maker's mark stamped on pewter objects
**TOUCHPAD** n part of laptop computer functioning like mouse
**TOUCHPADS** > TOUCHPAD
**TOUCHTONE** adj of or relating to a telephone dialling system in which each of the buttons pressed generates a tone of a different pitch, which is transmitted to the exchange
**TOUCHUP** n renovation or retouching, as of a painting
**TOUCHUPS** > TOUCHUP
**TOUCHWOOD** n something, esp dry wood, used as tinder
**TOUCHY** adj easily offended
**TOUGH** adj strong or resilient ▷ n rough violent person
**TOUGHED** > TOUGH
**TOUGHEN** vb make or become tough or tougher
**TOUGHENED** > TOUGHEN
**TOUGHENER** > TOUGHEN
**TOUGHENS** > TOUGHEN
**TOUGHER** > TOUGH
**TOUGHEST** > TOUGH
**TOUGHIE** n person who is tough
**TOUGHIES** > TOUGHIE
**TOUGHING** > TOUGH
**TOUGHISH** > TOUGH

TOUGHLY >TOUGH
TOUGHNESS n quality or an instance of being tough
TOUGHS >TOUGH
TOUGHY same as >TOUGHIE
TOUK same as >TUCK
TOUKED >TOUK
TOUKING >TOUK
TOUKS >TOUK
TOUN n town
TOUNS >TOUN
TOUPEE n small wig
TOUPEES >TOUPEE
TOUPET same as >TOUPEE
TOUPETS >TOUPET
TOUR n journey visiting places of interest along the way ▷ vb make a tour (of)
TOURACO n any brightly coloured crested arboreal African bird of the family Musophagidae: order Cuculiformes (cuckoos, etc)
TOURACOS >TOURACO
TOURED >TOUR
TOURER n large open car with a folding top, usually seating a driver and four passengers
TOURERS >TOURER
TOURIE same as >TOORIE
TOURIES >TOURIE
TOURING >TOUR
TOURINGS >TOUR
TOURISM n tourist travel as an industry
TOURISMS >TOURISM
TOURIST n person travelling for pleasure ▷ adj of or relating to tourists or tourism
TOURISTA variant of >TOURIST
TOURISTAS >TOURISTA
TOURISTED adj busy with tourists
TOURISTIC >TOURIST
TOURISTS >TOURIST
TOURISTY adj informal term for full of tourists or tourist attractions
TOURNEDOS n thick round steak of beef
TOURNEY n knightly tournament ▷ vb engage in a tourney
TOURNEYED >TOURNEY
TOURNEYER >TOURNEY
TOURNEYS >TOURNEY
TOURNURE n outline or contour
TOURNURES >TOURNURE
TOURS >TOUR
TOURTIERE n type of meat pie
TOUSE vb tangle, ruffle, or disarrange; treat roughly
TOUSED >TOUSE
TOUSER >TOUSE
TOUSERS >TOUSE
TOUSES >TOUSE
TOUSIER >TOUSY
TOUSIEST >TOUSY
TOUSING >TOUSE

TOUSINGS >TOUSE
TOUSLE vb make (hair or clothes) ruffled and untidy ▷ n disorderly, tangled, or rumpled state
TOUSLED >TOUSLE
TOUSLES >TOUSLE
TOUSLING >TOUSLE
TOUSTIE adj irritable; testy
TOUSTIER >TOUSTIE
TOUSTIEST >TOUSTIE
TOUSY adj tousled
TOUT vb seek business in a persistent manner ▷ n person who sells tickets for a popular event at inflated prices
TOUTED >TOUT
TOUTER >TOUT
TOUTERS >TOUT
TOUTIE childishly irritable or sullen
TOUTIER >TOUTIE
TOUTIEST >TOUTIE
TOUTING >TOUT
TOUTS >TOUT
TOUZE variant spelling of >TOUSE
TOUZED >TOUZE
TOUZES >TOUZE
TOUZIER >TOUZY
TOUZIEST >TOUZY
TOUZING >TOUZE
TOUZLE rare spelling of >TOUSLE
TOUZLED >TOUZLE
TOUZLES >TOUZLE
TOUZLING >TOUZLE
TOUZY variant spelling of >TOUSY
TOVARICH same as >TOVARISCH
TOVARISCH n comrade: a term of address
TOVARISH same as >TOVARISCH
TOW vb drag, esp by means of a rope ▷ n towing
TOWABLE >TOW
TOWAGE n charge made for towing
TOWAGES >TOWAGE
TOWARD same as >TOWARDS
TOWARDLY adj compliant
TOWARDS prep in the direction of
TOWAWAY n vehicle which has been towed away (because, for example, it was illegally parked)
TOWAWAYS >TOWAWAY
TOWBAR n metal bar on a car for towing vehicles
TOWBARS >TOWBAR
TOWBOAT n another word for tug (the boat)
TOWBOATS >TOWBOAT
TOWED >TOW
TOWEL n cloth for drying things ▷ vb dry or wipe with a towel
TOWELED >TOWEL
TOWELETTE n paper towel
TOWELHEAD n offensive

term for someone who wears a turban
TOWELING >TOWEL
TOWELINGS >TOWEL
TOWELLED >TOWEL
TOWELLING n material used for making towels
TOWELS >TOWEL
TOWER n tall structure, often forming part of a larger building
TOWERED adj having a tower or towers
TOWERIER >TOWERY
TOWERIEST >TOWERY
TOWERING adj very tall or impressive
TOWERLESS adj not having a tower
TOWERLIKE adj like a tower
TOWERS >TOWER
TOWERY adj with towers
TOWHEAD n often disparaging term for a person with blond or yellowish hair
TOWHEADED adj having blonde or yellowish hair
TOWHEADS >TOWHEAD
TOWHEE n any of various North American brownish-coloured sparrows of the genera Pipilo and Chlorura
TOWHEES >TOWHEE
TOWIE n truck used for towing
TOWIER >TOW
TOWIES >TOWIE
TOWIEST >TOW
TOWING >TOW
TOWINGS >TOW
TOWKAY n sir
TOWKAYS >TOWKAY
TOWLINE same as >TOWROPE
TOWLINES >TOWLINE
TOWMON same as >TOWMOND
TOWMOND n old word for year
TOWMONDS >TOWMOND
TOWMONS >TOWMON
TOWMONT same as >TOWMOND
TOWMONTS >TOWMONT
TOWN n group of buildings larger than a village
TOWNEE same as >TOWNIE
TOWNEES >TOWNEE
TOWNFOLK same as >TOWNSFOLK
TOWNHALL n chief building in which municipal business is transacted, often with a hall for public meetings
TOWNHOME another word for >TOWNHOUSE
TOWNHOMES >TOWNHOME
TOWNHOUSE n terraced house in an urban area, esp a fashionable one, often having the main living room on the first floor with an integral garage on

the ground floor
TOWNIE n often disparaging term for a resident in a town, esp as distinct from country dwellers
TOWNIER >TOWNY
TOWNIES >TOWNY
TOWNIEST >TOWNY
TOWNISH >TOWN
TOWNLAND n division of land of various sizes
TOWNLANDS >TOWNLAND
TOWNLESS >TOWN
TOWNLET n small town
TOWNLETS >TOWNLET
TOWNLIER >TOWNLY
TOWNLIEST >TOWNLY
TOWNLING n person who lives in a town
TOWNLINGS >TOWNLING
TOWNLY adj characteristic of a town
TOWNS >TOWN
TOWNSCAPE n view of an urban scene
TOWNSFOLK n people of a town
TOWNSHIP n small town
TOWNSHIPS >TOWNSHIP
TOWNSKIP n old term for a mischievous and roguish child who frequents city streets
TOWNSKIPS >TOWNSKIP
TOWNSMAN n inhabitant of a town
TOWNSMEN >TOWNSMAN
TOWNWEAR n clothes suitable for wearing while persuing activities usually associated with towns
TOWNY adj characteristic of a town
TOWPATH n path beside a canal or river, originally for horses towing boats
TOWPATHS >TOWPATH
TOWPLANE n aeroplane that tows gliders
TOWPLANES >TOWPLANE
TOWROPE n rope or cable used for towing a vehicle or vessel
TOWROPES >TOWROPE
TOWS >TOW
TOWSACK n sack made from tow
TOWSACKS >TOWSACK
TOWSE same as >TOUSE
TOWSED >TOWSE
TOWSER >TOWSE
TOWSERS >TOWSE
TOWSES >TOWSE
TOWSIER >TOWSY
TOWSIEST >TOWSY
TOWSING >TOWSE
TOWSY same as >TOUSY
TOWT vb sulk
TOWTED >TOWT
TOWTING >TOWT
TOWTS >TOWT
TOWY >TOW
TOWZE same as >TOUSE

TOWZED >TOWZE
TOWZES >TOWZE
TOWZIER >TOWZY
TOWZIEST >TOWZY
TOWZING >TOWZE
TOWZY same as >TOUSY
TOXAEMIA n blood poisoning
TOXAEMIAS >TOXAEMIA
TOXAEMIC >TOXAEMIA
TOXAPHENE n amber waxy solid with a pleasant pine odour, consisting of chlorinated terpenes, esp chlorinated camphene: used as an insecticide
TOXEMIA same as >TOXAEMIA
TOXEMIAS >TOXEMIA
TOXEMIC >TOXAEMIA
TOXIC adj poisonous ▷ n toxic substance
TOXICAL adj toxic
TOXICALLY >TOXIC
TOXICANT n toxic substance ▷ adj poisonous
TOXICANTS >TOXICANT
TOXICITY n degree of strength of a poison
TOXICOSES >TOXICOSIS
TOXICOSIS n any disease or condition caused by poisoning
TOXICS >TOXIC
TOXIGENIC adj producing poison
TOXIN n poison of bacterial origin
TOXINE nonstandard variant spelling of >TOXIN
TOXINES >TOXINE
TOXINS >TOXIN
TOXOCARA n parasitic worm infesting the intestines of cats and dogs
TOXOCARAS >TOXOCARA
TOXOID n toxin that has been treated to reduce its toxicity and is used in immunization to stimulate production of antitoxins
TOXOIDS >TOXOID
TOXOPHILY n archer
TOY n something designed to be played with ▷ adj designed to be played with ▷ vb play, fiddle, or flirt
TOYED >TOY
TOYER >TOY
TOYERS >TOY
TOYING >TOY
TOYINGS >TOY
TOYISH adj resembling a toy
TOYISHLY >TOYISH
TOYLESOME old spelling of >TOILSOME
TOYLESS >TOY
TOYLIKE >TOY
TOYLSOM old spelling of >TOILSOME
TOYMAN n man who sells toys

TOYMEN >TOYMAN
TOYO n Japanese straw-like material made out of rice paper and used to make hats
TOYON n shrub related to the rose
TOYONS >TOYON
TOYOS >TOYO
TOYS >TOY
TOYSHOP n shop selling toys
TOYSHOPS >TOYSHOP
TOYSOME adj playful
TOYTOWN adj having an unreal and picturesque appearance
TOYWOMAN n woman who sells toys
TOYWOMEN >TOYWOMAN
TOZE vb tease out; (of wool, etc) card
TOZED >TOZE
TOZES >TOZE
TOZIE n type of shawl
TOZIES >TOZIE
TOZING >TOZE
TRABEATE same as >TRABEATED
TRABEATED adj constructed with horizontal beams as opposed to arches
TRABECULA n any of various rod-shaped structures that divide organs into separate chambers
TRABS pl n training shoes
TRACE vb locate or work out (the cause of something) ▷ n track left by something
TRACEABLE >TRACE
TRACEABLY >TRACE
TRACED >TRACE
TRACELESS >TRACE
TRACER n projectile which leaves a visible trail
TRACERIED >TRACERY
TRACERIES >TRACERY
TRACERS >TRACER
TRACERY n pattern of interlacing lines
TRACES >TRACE
TRACEUR n parkour participant
TRACEURS >TRACEUR
TRACHEA n windpipe
TRACHEAE >TRACHEA
TRACHEAL >TRACHEA
TRACHEARY adj using tracheae to breathe
TRACHEAS >TRACHEA
TRACHEATE >TRACHEA
TRACHEID n element of xylem tissue consisting of an elongated lignified cell with tapering ends and large pits
TRACHEIDE same as >TRACHEID
TRACHEIDS >TRACHEID

TRACHEOLE n small trachea found in some insects
TRACHINUS n weever fish
TRACHITIS n another spelling of tracheitis (inflammation of the trachea)
TRACHLE vb (of hair, clothing, etc) make untidy; dishevel; rumple
TRACHLED >TRACHLE
TRACHLES >TRACHLE
TRACHLING >TRACHLE
TRACHOMA n chronic contagious disease of the eye characterized by inflammation of the inner surface of the lids and the formation of scar tissue
TRACHOMAS >TRACHOMA
TRACHYTE n light-coloured fine-grained volcanic rock
TRACHYTES >TRACHYTE
TRACHYTIC adj (of the texture of certain igneous rocks) characterized by a parallel arrangement of crystals, which mark the flow of the lava when still molten
TRACING n traced copy
TRACINGS >TRACING
TRACK n rough road or path ▷ vb follow the trail or path of
TRACKABLE >TRACK
TRACKAGE n collective term for the railway tracks in general, or those in a given area or belonging to a particular company, etc
TRACKAGES >TRACKAGE
TRACKBALL n device consisting of a small ball, mounted in a cup, which can be rotated to move the cursor around the screen
TRACKED >TRACK
TRACKER >TRACK
TRACKERS >TRACK
TRACKING n act or process of following something or someone
TRACKINGS >TRACKING
TRACKLESS adj having or leaving no trace or trail
TRACKMAN n workman who lays and maintains railway track
TRACKMEN >TRACKMAN
TRACKPAD same as >TOUCHPAD
TRACKPADS >TRACKPAD
TRACKROAD another word for >TOWPATH
TRACKS >TRACK
TRACKSIDE n area alongside a track
TRACKSUIT n warm loose-fitting suit worn by athletes etc, esp during training
TRACKWAY n path or track
TRACKWAYS >TRACKWAY

TRACT n wide area ▷ vb track
TRACTABLE adj easy to manage or control
TRACTABLY >TRACTABLE
TRACTATE n short tract
TRACTATES >TRACTATE
TRACTATOR n person who writes tracts
TRACTED >TRACT
TRACTILE adj capable of being drawn out
TRACTING >TRACT
TRACTION n pulling, esp by engine power
TRACTIONS >TRACTION
TRACTIVE >TRACTION
TRACTOR n motor vehicle with large rear wheels for pulling farm machinery
TRACTORS >TRACTOR
TRACTRIX n (in geometry) type of curve
TRACTS >TRACT
TRACTUS n anthem sung in some RC masses
TRACTUSES >TRACTUS
TRAD n traditional jazz, as revived in the 1950s
TRADABLE >TRADE
TRADE n buying, selling, or exchange of goods ▷ vb buy and sell ▷ adj intended for or available only to people in industry or business
TRADEABLE >TRADE
TRADED >TRADE
TRADEFUL adj (of shops, for example) full of trade
TRADELESS >TRADE
TRADEMARK n (legally registered) name or symbol used by a firm to distinguish its goods ▷ vb label with a trademark
TRADENAME n name used by a trade to refer to a commodity, service, etc
TRADEOFF n exchange, esp as a compromise
TRADEOFFS >TRADEOFF
TRADER n person who engages in trade
TRADERS >TRADER
TRADES >TRADE
TRADESMAN n skilled worker
TRADESMEN >TRADESMAN
TRADING >TRADE
TRADINGS >TRADE
TRADITION n handing down from generation to generation of customs and beliefs
TRADITIVE adj traditional
TRADITOR n Christian who betrayed his fellow Christians at the time of the Roman persecutions
TRADITORS >TRADITOR
TRADS >TRAD
TRADUCE vb slander
TRADUCED >TRADUCE

**TRADUCER** >TRADUCE
**TRADUCERS** >TRADUCE
**TRADUCES** >TRADUCE
**TRADUCIAN** >TRADUCE
**TRADUCING** >TRADUCE
**TRAFFIC** n vehicles coming and going on a road ▷ vb trade, usu illicitly
**TRAFFICKY** adj (of a street, area, town, etc) busy with motor vehicles
**TRAFFICS** >TRAFFIC
**TRAGAL** >TRAGUS
**TRAGEDIAN** n person who acts in or writes tragedies
**TRAGEDIES** >TRAGEDY
**TRAGEDY** n shocking or sad event
**TRAGELAPH** n mythical animal: a cross between a goat and a stag
**TRAGI** >TRAGUS
**TRAGIC** adj of or like a tragedy ▷ n tragedian
**TRAGICAL** same as >TRAGIC
**TRAGICS** >TRAGIC
**TRAGOPAN** n pheasant of S and SE Asia, with a brilliant plumage and brightly coloured fleshy processes on the head
**TRAGOPANS** >TRAGOPAN
**TRAGULE** n mouse deer
**TRAGULES** >TRAGULE
**TRAGULINE** adj like or characteristic of a tragule
**TRAGUS** n cartilaginous fleshy projection that partially covers the entrance to the external ear
**TRAHISON** n treason
**TRAHISONS** >TRAHISON
**TRAIK** vb trudge; trek with difficulty
**TRAIKED** >TRAIK
**TRAIKING** >TRAIK
**TRAIKIT** >TRAIK
**TRAIKS** >TRAIK
**TRAIL** n path, track, or road ▷ vb drag along the ground
**TRAILABLE** adj capable of being trailed
**TRAILED** >TRAIL
**TRAILER** n vehicle designed to be towed by another vehicle ▷ vb use a trailer to advertise (something)
**TRAILERED** >TRAILER
**TRAILERS** >TRAILER
**TRAILHEAD** n place where a trail begins
**TRAILING** adj (of a plant) having a long stem which spreads over the ground or hangs loosely
**TRAILLESS** adj without trail
**TRAILS** >TRAIL
**TRAILSIDE** adj beside a trail
**TRAIN** vb instruct in a skill

▷ n line of railway coaches or wagons drawn by an engine
**TRAINABLE** >TRAIN
**TRAINBAND** n company of English militia from the 16th to the 18th century
**TRAINED** >TRAIN
**TRAINEE** n person being trained ▷ adj (of a person) undergoing training
**TRAINEES** >TRAINEE
**TRAINER** n person who trains an athlete or sportsman
**TRAINERS** pl n shoes in the style of those used for sports training
**TRAINFUL** n quantity of people or cargo that would be capable of filling a train
**TRAINFULS** >TRAINFUL
**TRAINING** n process of bringing a person to an agreed standard of proficiency by practice and instruction
**TRAININGS** >TRAINING
**TRAINLESS** >TRAIN
**TRAINLOAD** n quantity of people or cargo sufficient to fill a train
**TRAINMAN** n man who works on a train
**TRAINMEN** >TRAINMAN
**TRAINS** >TRAIN
**TRAINWAY** n railway track; channel in a built-up area through which a train passes
**TRAINWAYS** >TRAINWAY
**TRAIPSE** vb walk wearily ▷ n long or tiring walk
**TRAIPSED** >TRAIPSE
**TRAIPSES** >TRAIPSE
**TRAIPSING** >TRAIPSE
**TRAIT** n characteristic feature
**TRAITOR** n person guilty of treason or treachery
**TRAITORLY** adj of or characteristic of a traitor
**TRAITORS** >TRAITOR
**TRAITRESS** >TRAITOR
**TRAITS** >TRAIT
**TRAJECT** vb transport or transmit
**TRAJECTED** >TRAJECT
**TRAJECTS** >TRAJECT
**TRAM** same as >TRAMMEL
**TRAMCAR** same as >TRAM
**TRAMCARS** >TRAMCAR
**TRAMEL** variant spelling of >TRAMMEL
**TRAMELED** >TRAMEL
**TRAMELING** >TRAMEL
**TRAMELL** variant spelling of >TRAMMEL
**TRAMELLED** >TRAMELL
**TRAMELLS** >TRAMELL
**TRAMELS** >TRAMEL
**TRAMLESS** >TRAM
**TRAMLINE** n tracks on which a tram runs

**TRAMLINED** adj having tramlines
**TRAMLINES** >TRAMLINE
**TRAMMED** >TRAM
**TRAMMEL** n hindrance to free action or movement ▷ vb hinder or restrain
**TRAMMELED** >TRAMMEL
**TRAMMELER** >TRAMMEL
**TRAMMELS** >TRAMMEL
**TRAMMIE** n conductor or driver of a tram
**TRAMMIES** >TRAMMIE
**TRAMMING** >TRAM
**TRAMP** vb travel on foot, hike ▷ n homeless person who travels on foot
**TRAMPED** >TRAMP
**TRAMPER** n person who tramps
**TRAMPERS** >TRAMPER
**TRAMPET** variant spelling of >TRAMPETTE
**TRAMPETS** >TRAMPET
**TRAMPETTE** n small trampoline
**TRAMPIER** >TRAMPY
**TRAMPIEST** >TRAMPY
**TRAMPING** >TRAMP
**TRAMPINGS** >TRAMP
**TRAMPISH** >TRAMP
**TRAMPLE** vb tread on and crush ▷ n action or sound of trampling
**TRAMPLED** >TRAMPLE
**TRAMPLER** >TRAMPLE
**TRAMPLERS** >TRAMPLE
**TRAMPLES** >TRAMPLE
**TRAMPLING** >TRAMPLE
**TRAMPOLIN** n variant of trampoline: a tough canvass sheet suspended by springs from a frame, used by acrobats, gymnasts, etc
**TRAMPS** >TRAMP
**TRAMPY** adj (of woman) disreputable
**TRAMROAD** same as >TRAMWAY
**TRAMROADS** >TRAMROAD
**TRAMS** >TRAM
**TRAMWAY** same as >TRAMLINE
**TRAMWAYS** >TRAMWAY
**TRANCE** n unconscious or dazed state ▷ vb put into or as into a trance
**TRANCED** >TRANCE
**TRANCEDLY** >TRANCE
**TRANCES** >TRANCE
**TRANCHE** n portion of something large, esp a sum of money
**TRANCHES** >TRANCHE
**TRANCHET** n stoneage cutting tool
**TRANCHETS** >TRANCHET
**TRANCING** >TRANCE
**TRANECT** n ferry
**TRANECTS** >TRANECT
**TRANGAM** n bauble or trinket
**TRANGAMS** >TRANGAM

**TRANGLE** n (in heraldry) a small fesse
**TRANGLES** >TRANGLE
**TRANK** n short form of tranquillizer: drug that calms a person
**TRANKS** >TRANK
**TRANKUM** same as >TRANGAM
**TRANKUMS** >TRANKUM
**TRANNIE** n transistor radio
**TRANNIES** >TRANNY
**TRANNY** same as >TRANNIE
**TRANQ** same as >TRANK
**TRANQS** >TRANQ
**TRANQUIL** adj calm and quiet
**TRANS** n short from of translation
**TRANSACT** vb conduct or negotiate (a business deal)
**TRANSACTS** >TRANSACT
**TRANSAXLE** n combined axle and gearbox
**TRANSCEND** vb rise above
**TRANSDUCE** vb change one form of energy to another
**TRANSE** n way through; passage
**TRANSECT** n sample strip of land used to monitor plant distribution and animal populations within a given area ▷ vb cut or divide crossways
**TRANSECTS** >TRANSECT
**TRANSENNA** n screen around a shrine
**TRANSEPT** n either of the two shorter wings of a cross-shaped church
**TRANSEPTS** >TRANSEPT
**TRANSES** >TRANSE
**TRANSEUNT** adj (of a mental act) causing effects outside the mind
**TRANSFARD** old past participle of >TRANSFER
**TRANSFECT** vb transfer genetic material isolated from a cell or virus into another cell
**TRANSFER** vb move or send from one person or place to another ▷ n transferring
**TRANSFERS** >TRANSFER
**TRANSFIX** vb astound or stun
**TRANSFIXT** >TRANSFIX
**TRANSFORM** vb change the shape or character of ▷ n result of a mathematical transformation
**TRANSFUSE** vb give a transfusion to
**TRANSGENE** n gene that is transferred from an organism of one species to an organism of another species by genetic engineering
**TRANSHIP** same as >TRANSSHIP

TRANSHIPS > TRANSHIP

TRANSHUME vb (of livestock) move to suitable grazing grounds according to the season

TRANSIENT same as > TRANSEUNT

TRANSIRE n document allowing goods to pass through customs

TRANSIRES > TRANSIRE

TRANSIT n passage or conveyance of goods or people ▷ vb make transit

TRANSITED > TRANSIT

TRANSITS > TRANSIT

TRANSLATE vb turn from one language into another

TRANSMEW old variant of > TRANSMUTE

TRANSMEWS > TRANSMEW

TRANSMIT vb pass (something) from one person or place to another

TRANSMITS > TRANSMIT > TRANSMITTIVITY

TRANSMOVE vb change the form, character, or substance of

TRANSMUTE vb change the form or nature of

TRANSOM n horizontal bar across a window

TRANSOMED > TRANSOM

TRANSOMS > TRANSOM

TRANSONIC adj of or relating to conditions when travelling at or near the speed of sound

TRANSPIRE vb become known

TRANSPORT vb convey from one place to another ▷ n business or system of transporting

TRANSPOSE vb interchange two things ▷ n matrix resulting from interchanging the rows and columns of a given matrix

TRANSSHIP vb transfer or be transferred from one ship or vehicle to another

TRANSUDE vb (of a fluid) ooze or pass through interstices, pores, or small holes

TRANSUDED > TRANSUDE

TRANSUDES > TRANSUDE

TRANSUME vb make an official transcription of

TRANSUMED > TRANSUME

TRANSUMES > TRANSUME

TRANSUMPT n official transcription

TRANSVEST vb wear clothes traditionally associated with the opposite sex

TRANT vb travel from place to place selling goods

TRANTED > TRANT

TRANTER > TRANT

TRANTERS > TRANT

TRANTING > TRANT

TRANTS > TRANT

TRAP n device for catching animals ▷ vb catch

TRAPAN same as > TREPAN

TRAPANNED > TRAPAN

TRAPANNER > TRAPAN

TRAPANS > TRAPAN

TRAPBALL n old ball game in which a ball is placed in a see-saw device called a trap, flicked up by a batsman hitting one end of the trap, and then hit with a bat

TRAPBALLS > TRAPBALL

TRAPDOOR n door in floor or roof

TRAPDOORS > TRAPDOOR

TRAPE same as > TRAIPSE

TRAPED > TRAPE

TRAPES same as > TRAIPSE

TRAPESED > TRAPES

TRAPESES > TRAPES

TRAPESING > TRAPES

TRAPEZE n horizontal bar suspended from two ropes, used by circus acrobats ▷ vb swing on a trapeze

TRAPEZED > TRAPEZE

TRAPEZES > TRAPEZE

TRAPEZIA > TRAPEZIUM

TRAPEZIAL > TRAPEZIUM

TRAPEZII > TRAPEZIUS

TRAPEZING > TRAPEZE

TRAPEZIST n trapeze artist

TRAPEZIUM same as > TRAPEZOID

TRAPEZIUS n either of two flat triangular muscles, one covering each side of the back and shoulders, that rotate the shoulder blades

TRAPEZOID same as > TRAPEZIUM

TRAPING > TRAPE

TRAPLIKE > TRAP

TRAPLINE n line of traps

TRAPLINES > TRAPLINE

TRAPNEST n nest that holds a hen in place so that the number of eggs it alone produces can be counted

TRAPNESTS > TRAPNEST

TRAPPEAN adj of, relating to, or consisting of igneous rock, esp a basalt

TRAPPED > TRAP

TRAPPER n person who traps animals for their fur

TRAPPERS > TRAPPER

TRAPPIER > TRAPPY

TRAPPIEST > TRAPPY

TRAPPING > TRAP

TRAPPINGS pl n accessories that symbolize an office or position

TRAPPOSE adj of or relating to traprock

TRAPPOUS same as > TRAPPOSE

TRAPPY adj having many traps

TRAPROCK another name for > TRAP

TRAPROCKS > TRAPROCK

TRAPS > TRAP

TRAPT old past participle of > TRAP

TRAPUNTO n type of quilting that is only partly padded in a design

TRAPUNTOS > TRAPUNTO

TRASH n anything worthless ▷ vb attack or destroy maliciously

TRASHCAN n dustbin

TRASHCANS > TRASHCAN

TRASHED adj drunk

TRASHER > TRASH

TRASHERS > TRASH

TRASHERY > TRASH

TRASHES > TRASH

TRASHIER > TRASHY

TRASHIEST > TRASHY

TRASHILY > TRASHY

TRASHING > TRASH

TRASHMAN another name for > BINMAN

TRASHMEN > TRASHMAN

TRASHTRIE n trash

TRASHY adj cheap, worthless, or badly made

TRASS n variety of the volcanic rock tuff, used to make a hydraulic cement

TRASSES > TRASS

TRAT n type of fishing line holding a series of baited hooks

TRATS > TRAT

TRATT short for > TRATTORIA

TRATTORIA n Italian restaurant

TRATTORIE > TRATTORIA

TRATTS > TRATT

TRAUCHLE n work or a task that is tiring, monotonous, and lengthy ▷ vb walk or work slowly and wearily

TRAUCHLED adj exhausted by long hard work or concern

TRAUCHLES > TRAUCHLE

TRAUMA n emotional shock

TRAUMAS > TRAUMA

TRAUMATA > TRAUMA

TRAUMATIC > TRAUMA

TRAVAIL n labour or toil ▷ vb suffer or labour painfully, esp in childbirth

TRAVAILED > TRAVAIL

TRAVAILS > TRAVAIL

TRAVE n stout wooden cage in which difficult horses are shod

TRAVEL vb go from one place to another, through an area, or for a specified distance ▷ n travelling, esp as a tourist

TRAVELED same as > TRAVELLED

TRAVELER same as > TRAVELLER

TRAVELERS > TRAVELER

TRAVELING > TRAVEL

TRAVELLED adj having experienced or undergone much travelling

TRAVELLER n person who makes a journey or travels a lot

TRAVELOG n film, lecture, or brochure on travel

TRAVELOGS > TRAVELOG

TRAVELS > TRAVEL

TRAVERSAL > TRAVERSE

TRAVERSE vb pass or go over

TRAVERSED > TRAVERSE

TRAVERSER > TRAVERSE

TRAVERSES > TRAVERSE

TRAVERTIN n porous rock

TRAVES > TRAVE

TRAVESTY n grotesque imitation or mockery ▷ vb make or be a travesty of

TRAVIS same as > TREVISS

TRAVISES > TRAVIS

TRAVOIS n sled used for dragging logs

TRAVOISE same as > TRAVOIS

TRAVOISES > TRAVOISE

TRAWL n net dragged at deep levels behind a fishing boat ▷ vb fish with such a net

TRAWLED > TRAWL

TRAWLER n trawling boat

TRAWLERS > TRAWLER

TRAWLEY same as > TROLLEY

TRAWLEYS > TRAWLEY

TRAWLING > TRAWL

TRAWLINGS > TRAWL

TRAWLNET n large net, usually in the shape of a sock or bag, drawn at deep levels behind special boats (trawlers)

TRAWLNETS > TRAWLNET

TRAWLS > TRAWL

TRAY n flat board, usu with a rim, for carrying things

TRAYBIT n threepenny bit

TRAYBITS > TRAYBIT

TRAYFUL n as many or as much as will fit on a tray

TRAYFULS > TRAYFUL

TRAYNE old spelling of > TRAIN

TRAYNED > TRAYNE

TRAYNES > TRAYNE

TRAYNING > TRAYNE

TRAYS > TRAY

TRAZODONE n drug used to treat depression

TREACHER n traitor; treacherous person

TREACHERS > TREACHER

TREACHERY n wilful betrayal

TREACHOUR same as > TREACHER

TREACLE n thick dark syrup produced when sugar is refined ▷ vb add treacle to

TREACLED > TREACLE

**TREACLES** > TREACLE
**TREACLIER** > TREACLE
**TREACLING** > TREACLE
**TREACLY** > TREACLE
**TREAD** vb set one's foot on ▷ n way of walking or dancing
**TREADED** > TREAD
**TREADER** > TREAD
**TREADERS** > TREAD
**TREADING** > TREAD
**TREADINGS** > TREAD
**TREADLE** n lever worked by the foot to turn a wheel ▷ vb work (a machine) with a treadle
**TREADLED** > TREADLE
**TREADLER** > TREADLE
**TREADLERS** > TREADLE
**TREADLES** > TREADLE
**TREADLESS** adj (of a tyre, for example) having no tread
**TREADLING** > TREADLE
**TREADMILL** n cylinder turned by treading on steps projecting from it
**TREADS** > TREAD
**TREAGUE** n agreement to stop fighting
**TREAGUES** > TREAGUE
**TREASON** n betrayal of one's sovereign or country
**TREASONS** > TREASON
**TREASURE** n collection of wealth, esp gold or jewels ▷ vb prize or cherish
**TREASURED** > TREASURE
**TREASURER** n official in charge of funds
**TREASURES** > TREASURE
**TREASURY** n storage place for treasure
**TREAT** vb deal with or regard in a certain manner ▷ n pleasure, entertainment, etc given or paid for by someone else
**TREATABLE** > TREAT
**TREATED** > TREAT
**TREATER** > TREAT
**TREATERS** > TREAT
**TREATIES** > TREATY
**TREATING** > TREAT
**TREATINGS** > TREAT
**TREATISE** n formal piece of writing on a particular subject
**TREATISES** > TREATISE
**TREATMENT** n medical care
**TREATS** > TREAT
**TREATY** n signed contract between states
**TREBBIANO** n grape used to make wine
**TREBLE** adj triple ▷ n (singer with or part for) a soprano voice ▷ vb increase three times
**TREBLED** > TREBLE
**TREBLES** > TREBLE
**TREBLING** > TREBLE
**TREBLY** > TREBLE
**TREBUCHET** n large

medieval siege engine for hurling missiles consisting of a sling on a pivoted wooden arm set in motion by the fall of a weight
**TREBUCKET** same as > TREBUCHET
**TRECENTO** n 14th century, esp with reference to Italian art and literature
**TRECENTOS** > TRECENTO
**TRECK** same as > TREK
**TRECKED** > TRECK
**TRECKING** > TRECK
**TRECKS** > TRECK
**TREDDLE** variant spelling of > TREADLE
**TREDDLED** > TREDDLE
**TREDDLES** > TREDDLE
**TREDDLING** > TREDDLE
**TREDILLE** same as > TREDRILLE
**TREDILLES** > TREDILLE
**TREDRILLE** n card game for three players
**TREE** n large perennial plant with a woody trunk
**TREED** > TREE
**TREEHOUSE** n house built in tree
**TREEING** > TREE
**TREELAWN** n narrow band of grass between a road and a pavement, usually planted with trees
**TREELAWNS** > TREELAWN
**TREELESS** > TREE
**TREELIKE** > TREE
**TREEN** adj made of wood ▷ n art of making treenware
**TREENAIL** n dowel used for pinning planks or timbers together
**TREENAILS** > TREENAIL
**TREENS** > TREEN
**TREENWARE** n dishes and other household utensils made of wood, as by pioneers in North America
**TREES** > TREE
**TREESHIP** n state of being a tree
**TREESHIPS** > TREESHIP
**TREETOP** n top of a tree
**TREETOPS** > TREETOP
**TREEWARE** n books, magazines, or other reading materials that are printed on paper made from wood pulp as opposed to texts in the form of computer software, CD-ROM, audio books, etc
**TREEWARES** > TREEWARE
**TREEWAX** n yellowish wax secreted by an oriental scale insect
**TREEWAXES** > TREEWAX
**TREF** adj in Judaism, ritually unfit to be eaten
**TREFA** same as > TREF

**TREFAH** same as > TREF
**TREFOIL** n plant, such as clover, with a three-lobed leaf
**TREFOILED** > TREFOIL
**TREFOILS** > TREFOIL
**TREGETOUR** n juggler
**TREHALA** n edible sugary substance obtained from the pupal cocoon of an Asian weevil
**TREHALAS** > TREHALA
**TREHALOSE** n white crystalline disaccharide that occurs in yeast and certain fungi
**TREIF** same as > TREF
**TREIFA** same as > TREF
**TREILLAGE** n latticework
**TREILLE** another word for > TRELLIS
**TREILLES** > TREILLE
**TREK** n long difficult journey, esp on foot ▷ vb make such a journey
**TREKKED** > TREK
**TREKKER** > TREK
**TREKKERS** > TREK
**TREKKING** > TREK
**TREKS** > TREK
**TRELLIS** n framework of horizontal and vertical strips of wood ▷ vb interweave (strips of wood, etc) to make a trellis
**TRELLISED** > TRELLIS
**TRELLISES** > TRELLIS
**TREMA** n mark consisting of two dots placed over the second of two adjacent vowels to indicate it is to be pronounced separately rather than forming a diphthong with the first
**TREMAS** > TREMA
**TREMATIC** adj relating to the gills
**TREMATODE** n parasitic flatworm
**TREMATOID** > TREMATODE
**TREMBLANT** adj (of jewels) set in such a way that they shake when the wearer moves
**TREMBLE** vb shake or quiver ▷ n trembling
**TREMBLED** > TREMBLE
**TREMBLER** n device that vibrates to make or break an electrical circuit
**TREMBLERS** > TREMBLER
**TREMBLES** n disease of cattle and sheep characterized by muscular incoordination and tremor, caused by ingestion of white snakeroot or rayless goldenrod
**TREMBLIER** > TREMBLE
**TREMBLING** > TREMBLE
**TREMBLY** > TREMBLE
**TREMIE** n large metal hopper and pipe used

to distribute freshly mixed concrete over an underwater site.
**TREMIES** > TREMIE
**TREMOLANT** another word for > TREMOLO
**TREMOLITE** n white or pale green mineral of the amphibole group consisting of calcium magnesium silicate
**TREMOLO** n quivering effect in singing or playing
**TREMOLOS** > TREMOLO
**TREMOR** n involuntary shaking ▷ vb tremble
**TREMORED** > TREMOR
**TREMORING** > TREMOR
**TREMOROUS** > TREMOR
**TREMORS** > TREMOR
**TREMULANT** n device on an organ by which the wind stream is made to fluctuate in intensity producing a tremolo effect
**TREMULATE** vb produce a tremulous sound
**TREMULOUS** adj trembling, as from fear or excitement
**TRENAIL** same as > TREENAIL
**TRENAILS** > TRENAIL
**TRENCH** n long narrow ditch, esp one used as a shelter in war ▷ adj of or involving military trenches ▷ vb make a trench in (a place)
**TRENCHAND** old variant of > TRENCHANT
**TRENCHANT** adj incisive
**TRENCHARD** same as > TRENCHER
**TRENCHED** > TRENCH
**TRENCHER** n wooden plate for serving food
**TRENCHERS** > TRENCHER
**TRENCHES** > TRENCH
**TRENCHING** > TRENCH
**TREND** n general tendency or direction ▷ vb take a certain trend
**TRENDED** > TREND
**TRENDIER** > TRENDY
**TRENDIES** > TRENDY
**TRENDIEST** > TRENDY
**TRENDIFY** vb render fashionable
**TRENDILY** > TRENDY
**TRENDING** > TREND
**TRENDOID** n follower of trends
**TRENDOIDS** > TRENDOID
**TRENDS** > TREND
**TRENDY** adj consciously fashionable (person) ▷ adj consciously fashionable
**TRENDYISM** > TRENDY
**TRENISE** n one of the figures in a quadrille
**TRENISES** > TRENISE
**TRENTAL** n mass said in remembrance of a person 30 days after his or her

death
**TRENTALS** >TRENTAL
**TREPAN** *same as* >TREPHINE
**TREPANG** *n* any of various large sea cucumbers of tropical Oriental seas, the body walls of which are used as food by the Japanese and Chinese
**TREPANGS** >TREPANG
**TREPANNED** >TREPAN
**TREPANNER** >TREPAN
**TREPANS** >TREPAN
**TREPHINE** *n* surgical sawlike instrument for removing circular sections of bone, esp from the skull ▷ *vb* remove a circular section of bone from (esp the skull)
**TREPHINED** >TREPHINE
**TREPHINER** >TREPHINE
**TREPHINES** >TREPHINE
**TREPID** *adj* trembling
**TREPIDANT** *adj* trembling
**TREPONEMA** *n* anaerobic spirochaete bacterium that causes syphilis
**TREPONEME** *same as* >TREPONEMA
**TRES** *adj* very
**TRESPASS** *vb* go onto another's property without permission ▷ *n* trespassing
**TRESS** *n* lock of hair, esp a long lock of woman's hair ▷ *vb* arrange in tresses
**TRESSED** *adj* having a tress or tresses as specified
**TRESSEL** *variant spelling of* >TRESTLE
**TRESSELS** >TRESSEL
**TRESSES** >TRESS
**TRESSIER** >TRESS
**TRESSIEST** >TRESS
**TRESSING** >TRESS
**TRESSOUR** *same as* >TRESSURE
**TRESSOURS** >TRESSOUR
**TRESSURE** *n* narrow inner border on a shield, usually decorated with fleurs-de-lys
**TRESSURED** >TRESSURE
**TRESSURES** >TRESSURE
**TRESSY** >TRESS
**TREST** *old variant of* >TRESTLE
**TRESTLE** *n* board fixed on pairs of spreading legs, used as a support
**TRESTLES** >TRESTLE
**TRESTS** >TREST
**TRET** *n* (formerly) an allowance according to weight granted to purchasers for waste due to transportation
**TRETINOIN** *n* retinoid drug used to treat certain skin conditions
**TRETS** >TRET
**TREVALLY** *n* any of various

food and game fishes
**TREVALLYS** >TREVALLY
**TREVET** *same as* >TRIVET
**TREVETS** >TREVET
**TREVIS** *variant spelling of* >TREVISS
**TREVISES** >TREVIS
**TREVISS** *n* partition in a stable for keeping animals apart
**TREVISSES** >TREVISS
**TREW** *old variant spelling of* >TRUE
**TREWS** *pl n* close-fitting tartan trousers
**TREWSMAN** *n* Highlander
**TREWSMEN** >TREWSMAN
**TREY** *n* any card or dice throw with three spots
**TREYBIT** *same as* >TRAYBIT
**TREYBITS** >TREYBIT
**TREYS** >TREY
**TREZ** *same as* >TREY
**TREZES** >TREZ
**TRIABLE** *adj* liable to be tried judicially
**TRIAC** *n* device for regulating the amount of electric current allowed to reach a circuit
**TRIACID** *adj* (of a base) capable of reacting with three molecules of a monobasic acid
**TRIACIDS** >TRIACID
**TRIACS** >TRIAC
**TRIACT** *adj* having three rays
**TRIACTINE** *same as* >TRIACT
**TRIAD** *n* group of three
**TRIADIC** *n* something that has the characteristics of a triad
**TRIADICS** >TRIADIC
**TRIADISM** >TRIAD
**TRIADISMS** >TRIAD
**TRIADIST** >TRIAD
**TRIADISTS** >TRIAD
**TRIADS** >TRIAD
**TRIAGE** *n* (in a hospital) the principle or practice of sorting emergency patients into categories of priority for treatment ▷ *vb* sort (patients) into categories of priority for treatment
**TRIAGED** >TRIAGE
**TRIAGES** >TRIAGE
**TRIAGING** >TRIAGE
**TRIAL** *n* investigation of a case before a judge
**TRIALISM** *n* belief that man consists of body, soul, and spirit
**TRIALISMS** >TRIALISM
**TRIALIST** *same as* >TRIALLIST
**TRIALISTS** >TRIALIST
**TRIALITY** >TRIALISM
**TRIALLED** >TRIAL
**TRIALLING** >TRIAL
**TRIALLIST** *n* person

who takes part in a competition
**TRIALOGUE** *n* dialogue between three people
**TRIALS** >TRIAL
**TRIALWARE** *n* computer software that can be used without charge for a limited evaluation period
**TRIANGLE** *n* geometric figure with three sides
**TRIANGLED** >TRIANGLE
**TRIANGLES** >TRIANGLE
**TRIAPSAL** *adj* (of a church) having three apses
**TRIARCH** *n* one of three rulers of a triarchy
**TRIARCHS** >TRIARCH
**TRIARCHY** *n* government by three people
**TRIASSIC** *adj* of, denoting, or formed in the first period of the Mesozoic era
**TRIATHLON** *n* athletic contest in which each athlete competes in three different events: swimming, cycling, and running
**TRIATIC** *n* rope between a ship's mastheads
**TRIATICS** >TRIATIC
**TRIATOMIC** *adj* a molecule having three atoms
**TRIAXIAL** *adj* having three axes ▷ *n* sponge spicule with three axes
**TRIAXIALS** >TRIAXIAL
**TRIAXON** *another name for* >TRIAXIAL
**TRIAXONS** >TRIAXON
**TRIAZIN** *same as* >TRIAZINE
**TRIAZINE** *n* any of three azines that contain three nitrogen atoms in their molecules
**TRIAZINES** >TRIAZINE
**TRIAZINS** >TRIAZIN
**TRIAZOLE** *n* heterocyclic compound
**TRIAZOLES** >TRIAZOLE
**TRIAZOLIC** >TRIAZOLE
**TRIBADE** *n* lesbian, esp one who practises tribadism
**TRIBADES** >TRIBADE
**TRIBADIC** >TRIBADE
**TRIBADIES** >TRIBADY
**TRIBADISM** *n* lesbian practice in which one partner lies on top of the other and simulates the male role in heterosexual intercourse
**TRIBADY** *another word for* >TRIBADISM
**TRIBAL** *adj* of or denoting a tribe or tribes
**TRIBALISM** *n* loyalty to a tribe
**TRIBALIST** >TRIBALISM
**TRIBALLY** >TRIBAL
**TRIBALS** >TRIBAL
**TRIBASIC** *adj* (of an acid) containing three

replaceable hydrogen atoms in the molecule
**TRIBBLE** *n* frame for drying paper
**TRIBBLES** >TRIBBLE
**TRIBE** *n* group of clans or families believed to have a common ancestor
**TRIBELESS** >TRIBE
**TRIBES** >TRIBE
**TRIBESMAN** *n* member of a tribe
**TRIBESMEN** >TRIBESMAN
**TRIBLET** *n* spindle or mandrel used in making rings, tubes, etc
**TRIBLETS** >TRIBLET
**TRIBOLOGY** *n* study of friction, lubrication, and wear between moving surfaces
**TRIBRACH** *n* metrical foot of three short syllables
**TRIBRACHS** >TRIBRACH
**TRIBULATE** *vb* trouble
**TRIBUNAL** *n* board appointed to inquire into a specific matter
**TRIBUNALS** >TRIBUNAL
**TRIBUNARY** >TRIBUNE
**TRIBUNATE** *n* office or rank of a tribune
**TRIBUNE** *n* people's representative, esp in ancient Rome
**TRIBUNES** >TRIBUNE
**TRIBUTARY** *n* stream or river flowing into a larger one ▷ *adj* (of a stream or river) flowing into a larger one
**TRIBUTE** *n* sign of respect or admiration
**TRIBUTER** *n* miner
**TRIBUTERS** >TRIBUTER
**TRIBUTES** >TRIBUTE
**TRICAR** *n* car with three wheels
**TRICARS** >TRICAR
**TRICE** *n* moment ▷ *vb* haul up or secure
**TRICED** >TRICE
**TRICEP** *same as* >TRICEPS
**TRICEPS** *n* muscle at the back of the upper arm
**TRICEPSES** >TRICEPS
**TRICERION** *n* candlestick with three arms
**TRICES** >TRICE
**TRICHINA** *n* parasitic nematode worm, occurring in the intestines of pigs, rats, and man and producing larvae that form cysts in skeletal muscle
**TRICHINAE** >TRICHINA
**TRICHINAL** >TRICHINA
**TRICHINAS** >TRICHINA
**TRICHITE** *n* any of various needle-shaped crystals that occur in some glassy volcanic rocks
**TRICHITES** >TRICHITE
**TRICHITIC** >TRICHITE

**TRICHOID** adj resembling a hair

**TRICHOME** n any hairlike outgrowth from the surface of a plant

**TRICHOMES** >TRICHOME

**TRICHOMIC** >TRICHOME

**TRICHORD** n musical instrument with three strings

**TRICHORDS** >TRICHORD

**TRICHOSES** >TRICHOSIS

**TRICHOSIS** n any abnormal condition or disease of the hair

**TRICHROIC** n state of having three colours

**TRICHROME** adj three-coloured

**TRICING** >TRICE

**TRICK** n deceitful or cunning action or plan ▷ vb cheat or deceive

**TRICKED** >TRICK

**TRICKER** >TRICK

**TRICKERS** >TRICK

**TRICKERY** n practice or an instance of using tricks

**TRICKIE** Scots form of >TRICKY

**TRICKIER** >TRICKY

**TRICKIEST** >TRICKY

**TRICKILY** >TRICKY

**TRICKING** >TRICK

**TRICKINGS** >TRICK

**TRICKISH** same as >TRICKY

**TRICKLE** vb (cause to) flow in a thin stream or drops ▷ n gradual flow

**TRICKLED** >TRICKLE

**TRICKLES** >TRICKLE

**TRICKLESS** >TRICKLE

**TRICKLET** n tiny trickle

**TRICKLETS** >TRICKLET

**TRICKLIER** >TRICKLE

**TRICKLING** >TRICKLE

**TRICKLY** >TRICKLE

**TRICKS** >TRICK

**TRICKSIER** >TRICKSY

**TRICKSOME** adj full of tricks

**TRICKSTER** n person who deceives or plays tricks

**TRICKSY** adj playing tricks habitually

**TRICKY** adj difficult, needing careful handling

**TRICLAD** n type of worm having a tripartite intestine

**TRICLADS** >TRICLAD

**TRICLINIA** n plural of triclinium: in Ancient Rome, reclining couch

**TRICLINIC** adj relating to or belonging to the crystal system characterized by three unequal axes, no pair of which are perpendicular

**TRICLOSAN** n drug used to treat skin infections

**TRICOLOR** same as >TRICOLOUR

**TRICOLORS** >TRICOLOR

**TRICOLOUR** n three-coloured striped flag ▷ adj having or involving three colours

**TRICORN** n cocked hat with opposing brims turned back and caught in three places ▷ adj having three horns or corners

**TRICORNE** same as >TRICORN

**TRICORNES** >TRICORNE

**TRICORNS** >TRICORN

**TRICOT** n thin rayon or nylon fabric knitted or resembling knitting, used for dresses, etc

**TRICOTINE** n twill-weave woollen fabric resembling gabardine

**TRICOTS** >TRICOT

**TRICROTIC** adj (of the pulse) having a tracing characterized by three elevations with each beat

**TRICTRAC** n game similar to backgammon

**TRICTRACS** >TRICTRAC

**TRICUSPID** adj having three points, cusps, or segments ▷ n tooth having three cusps

**TRICYCLE** n three-wheeled cycle ▷ vb ride a tricycle

**TRICYCLED** >TRICYCLE

**TRICYCLER** >TRICYCLE

**TRICYCLES** >TRICYCLE

**TRICYCLIC** adj (of a chemical compound) containing three rings in the molecular structure ▷ n antidepressant drug having a tricyclic molecular structure

**TRIDACNA** n giant clam

**TRIDACNAS** >TRIDACNA

**TRIDACTYL** adj having three digits on one hand or foot

**TRIDARN** n sideboard with three levels

**TRIDARNS** >TRIDARN

**TRIDE** old spelling of the past tense of >TRY

**TRIDENT** n three-pronged spear ▷ adj having three prongs

**TRIDENTAL** adj having three prongs, teeth, etc

**TRIDENTED** adj having three prongs

**TRIDENTS** >TRIDENT

**TRIDUAN** adj three days long

**TRIDUUM** n period of three days for prayer before a feast

**TRIDUUMS** >TRIDUUM

**TRIDYMITE** n form of silica

**TRIE** old spelling of >TRY

**TRIECIOUS** adj (of a plant) having male, female, and hermaphroditic flowers

**TRIED** >TRY

**TRIELLA** n three

nominated horse races in which the punter bets on selecting the three winners

**TRIELLAS** >TRIELLA

**TRIENE** n chemical compound containing three double bonds

**TRIENES** >TRIENE

**TRIENNIA** >TRIENNIUM

**TRIENNIAL** adj happening every three years ▷ n relating to, lasting for, or occurring every three years

**TRIENNIUM** n period or cycle of three years

**TRIENS** n Byzantine gold goin worth one third of a solidus

**TRIENTES** >TRIENS

**TRIER** n person or thing that tries

**TRIERARCH** n citizen responsible for fitting out a state trireme, esp in Athens

**TRIERS** >TRIER

**TRIES** >TRY

**TRIETERIC** adj occurring once every two years

**TRIETHYL** adj consisting of three groups of ethyls

**TRIFACIAL** adj relating to the trigeminal nerve

**TRIFECTA** n form of betting in which the punter selects the first three place-winners in a horse race in the correct order

**TRIFECTAS** >TRIFECTA

**TRIFF** adj terrific; very good indeed

**TRIFFER** >TRIFF

**TRIFFEST** >TRIFF

**TRIFFIC** adj terrific; very good indeed

**TRIFFID** n any of a species of fictional plants that supposedly grew to a gigantic size, were capable of moving about, and could kill humans

**TRIFFIDS** >TRIFFID

**TRIFFIDY** adj resembling a triffid

**TRIFID** adj divided or split into three parts or lobes

**TRIFLE** n insignificant thing or amount ▷ vb deal (with) as if worthless

**TRIFLED** >TRIFLE

**TRIFLER** >TRIFLE

**TRIFLERS** >TRIFLE

**TRIFLES** >TRIFLE

**TRIFLING** adj insignificant

**TRIFLINGS** >TRIFLE

**TRIFOCAL** adj having three focuses ▷ n glasses that have trifocal lenses

**TRIFOCALS** >TRIFOCAL

**TRIFOLD** less common word for >TRIPLE

**TRIFOLIES** >TRIFOLY

**TRIFOLIUM** n leguminous plant with leaves divided into three leaflets and dense heads of small white, yellow, red, or purple flowers

**TRIFOLY** same as >TREFOIL

**TRIFORIA** >TRIFORIUM

**TRIFORIAL** >TRIFORIUM

**TRIFORIUM** n arcade above the arches of the nave, choir, or transept of a church

**TRIFORM** adj having three parts

**TRIFORMED** same as >TRIFORM

**TRIG** adj neat or spruce ▷ vb make or become spruce

**TRIGAMIES** >TRIGAMY

**TRIGAMIST** >TRIGAMY

**TRIGAMOUS** >TRIGAMY

**TRIGAMY** n condition of having three spouses

**TRIGGED** >TRIG

**TRIGGER** n small lever releasing a catch on a gun or machine ▷ vb set (an action or process) in motion

**TRIGGERED** >TRIGGER

**TRIGGERS** >TRIGGER

**TRIGGEST** >TRIG

**TRIGGING** >TRIG

**TRIGLOT** n person who can speak three languages

**TRIGLOTS** >TRIGLOT

**TRIGLY** >TRIG

**TRIGLYPH** n stone block in a Doric frieze, having three vertical channels

**TRIGLYPHS** >TRIGLYPH

**TRIGNESS** >TRIG

**TRIGO** n wheat field

**TRIGON** n (in classical Greece or Rome) a triangular harp or lyre

**TRIGONAL** adj triangular

**TRIGONIC** >TRIGON

**TRIGONOUS** adj (of stems, seeds, and similar parts) having a triangular cross section

**TRIGONS** >TRIGON

**TRIGOS** >TRIGO

**TRIGRAM** n three-letter inscription

**TRIGRAMS** >TRIGRAM

**TRIGRAPH** n combination of three letters used to represent a single speech sound or phoneme, such as eau in French beau

**TRIGRAPHS** >TRIGRAPH

**TRIGS** >TRIG

**TRIGYNIAN** adj relating to the Trigynia order of plants

**TRIGYNOUS** adj (of a plant) having three pistils

**TRIHEDRA** >TRIHEDRON

**TRIHEDRAL** adj having or formed by three plane

faces meeting at a point
▷ *n* figure formed by the
intersection of three lines
in different planes
**TRIHEDRON** *n* figure
determined by the
intersection of three
planes
**TRIHYBRID** *n* hybrid that
differs from its parents in
three genetic traits
**TRIHYDRIC** *adj* (of
an alcohol or similar
compound) containing
three hydroxyl groups
**TRIJET** *n* jet with three
engines
**TRIJETS** > TRIJET
**TRIJUGATE** *adj* in three
pairs
**TRIJUGOUS** *same*
*as* > TRIJUGATE
**TRIKE** *n* tricycle
**TRIKES** > TRIKE
**TRILBIES** > TRILBY
**TRILBY** *n* man's soft felt hat
**TRILBYS** > TRILBY
**TRILD** *old past tense*
*of* > TRILL
**TRILEMMA** *n* quandary
posed by three alternative
courses of action
**TRILEMMAS** > TRILEMMA
**TRILINEAR** *adj* consisting
of, bounded by, or relating
to three lines
**TRILITH** *same*
*as* > TRILITHON
**TRILITHIC** > TRILITHON
**TRILITHON** *n* structure
consisting of two upright
stones with a third placed
across the top, such as
those of Stonehenge
**TRILITHS** > TRILITH
**TRILL** *n* rapid alternation
between two notes ▷ *vb*
play or sing a trill
**TRILLED** > TRILL
**TRILLER** > TRILL
**TRILLERS** > TRILL
**TRILLING** > TRILL
**TRILLINGS** > TRILL
**TRILLION** *n* one million
million ▷ *adj* amounting
to a trillion
**TRILLIONS** > TRILLION
**TRILLIUM** *n* plant of Asia
and North America that
has three leaves at the top
of the stem with a single
white, pink, or purple
three-petalled flower
**TRILLIUMS** > TRILLIUM
**TRILLO** *n* (in music) a trill
**TRILLOES** > TRILL
**TRILLS** > TRILL
**TRILOBAL** > TRILOBE
**TRILOBATE** *adj* (esp of
a leaf) consisting of or
having three lobes or parts
**TRILOBE** *n* three-lobed
thing
**TRILOBED** *adj* having three

lobes
**TRILOBES** > TRILOBE
**TRILOBITE** *n* small
prehistoric sea animal
**TRILOGIES** > TRILOGY
**TRILOGY** *n* series of three
related books, plays, etc
**TRIM** *adj* neat and
smart ▷ *vb* cut or prune
into good shape ▷ *n*
decoration
**TRIMARAN** *n* three-hulled
boat
**TRIMARANS** > TRIMARAN
**TRIMER** *n* polymer or a
molecule of a polymer
consisting of three
identical monomers
**TRIMERIC** > TRIMER
**TRIMERISM** > TRIMER
**TRIMEROUS** *adj* (of plants)
having parts arranged in
groups of three
**TRIMERS** > TRIMER
**TRIMESTER** *n* period of
three months
**TRIMETER** *n* verse line
consisting of three
metrical feet ▷ *adj*
designating such a line
**TRIMETERS** > TRIMETER
**TRIMETHYL** *adj* having
three methyl groups
**TRIMETRIC** *adj* of, relating
to, or consisting of a
trimeter or trimeters
**TRIMLY** > TRIM
**TRIMMED** > TRIM
**TRIMMER** > TRIM
**TRIMMERS** > TRIM
**TRIMMEST** > TRIM
**TRIMMING** > TRIM
**TRIMMINGS** > TRIM
**TRIMNESS** > TRIM
**TRIMORPH** *n* substance, esp
a mineral, that exists in
three distinct forms
**TRIMORPHS** > TRIMORPH
**TRIMOTOR** *n* vehicle with
three motors
**TRIMOTORS** > TRIMOTOR
**TRIMS** > TRIM
**TRIMTAB** *n* small control
surface attached to the
trailing edge of a main
control surface to enable
the pilot to balance an
aircraft
**TRIMTABS** > TRIMTAB
**TRIN** *n* triplet
**TRINAL** > TRINE
**TRINARY** *adj* made up of
three parts
**TRINDLE** *vb* move heavily
on (or as if on) wheels
**TRINDLED** > TRINDLE
**TRINDLES** > TRINDLE
**TRINDLING** > TRINDLE
**TRINE** *n* aspect of 120°
between two planets, an
orb of 8° being allowed
▷ *adj* of or relating to a
trine ▷ *vb* put in a trine
aspect

**TRINED** > TRINE
**TRINES** > TRINE
**TRINGLE** *n* slim rod
**TRINGLES** > TRINGLE
**TRINING** > TRINE
**TRINITIES** > TRINITY
**TRINITRIN** *n* pale yellow
viscous explosive liquid
substance made from
glycerol and nitric and
sulphuric acids
**TRINITY** *n* group of three
**TRINKET** *n* small or
worthless ornament or
piece of jewellery ▷ *vb*
ornament with trinkets
**TRINKETED** > TRINKET
**TRINKETER** > TRINKET
**TRINKETRY** > TRINKET
**TRINKETS** > TRINKET
**TRINKUM** *n* trinket or
bauble
**TRINKUMS** > TRINKUM
**TRINODAL** *adj* having three
nodes
**TRINOMIAL** *adj* consisting
of or relating to three
terms ▷ *n* polynomial
consisting of three terms,
such as $ax^2 + bx + c$
**TRINS** > TRIN
**TRIO** *n* group of three
**TRIODE** *n* electronic valve
having three electrodes,
a cathode, an anode, and
a grid
**TRIODES** > TRIODE
**TRIOL** *n* any of a class of
alcohols that have three
hydroxyl groups per
molecule
**TRIOLEIN** *n* naturally
occurring glyceride of oleic
acid, found in fats and oils
**TRIOLEINS** > TRIOLEIN
**TRIOLET** *n* verse form of
eight lines
**TRIOLETS** > TRIOLET
**TRIOLS** > TRIOL
**TRIONES** *n* seven stars of
the constellation Ursa
Major
**TRIONYM** another name
*for* > TRINOMIAL
**TRIONYMAL** > TRIONYM
**TRIONYMS** > TRIONYM
**TRIOR** old form of > TRIER
**TRIORS** > TRIOR
**TRIOS** > TRIO
**TRIOSE** *n* simple
monosaccharide produced
by the oxidation of glycerol
**TRIOSES** > TRIOSE
**TRIOXID** *same as* > TRIOXIDE
**TRIOXIDE** *n* any oxide that
contains three oxygen
atoms per molecule
**TRIOXIDES** > TRIOXIDE
**TRIOXIDS** > TRIOXIDE
**TRIOXYGEN** technical name
*for* > OXYGEN
**TRIP** *n* journey to a place
and back, esp for pleasure
▷ *vb* (cause to) stumble

**TRIPACK** *n* pack of three
**TRIPACKS** > TRIPACK
**TRIPART** *adj* composed of
three parts
**TRIPE** *n* stomach of a cow
used as food
**TRIPEDAL** *adj* having three
feet
**TRIPERIES** > TRIPERY
**TRIPERY** *n* place where
tripe is prepared
**TRIPES** > TRIPE
**TRIPEY** > TRIPE
**TRIPHASE** *adj* having three
phases
**TRIPHONE** *n* group of three
phonemes
**TRIPHONES** > TRIPHONE
**TRIPIER** > TRIPE
**TRIPIEST** > TRIPE
**TRIPITAKA** *n* three
collections of books
making up the Buddhist
canon of scriptures
**TRIPLANE** *n* aeroplane
having three wings
arranged one above the
other
**TRIPLANES** > TRIPLANE
**TRIPLE** *adj* having three
parts ▷ *vb* increase three
times ▷ *n* something that
is, or contains, three times
as much as normal
**TRIPLED** > TRIPLE
**TRIPLES** > TRIPLE
**TRIPLET** *n* one of three
babies born at one birth
**TRIPLETS** > TRIPLET
**TRIPLEX** *n* building
divided into three separate
dwellings
**TRIPLEXES** > TRIPLEX
**TRIPLIED** > TRIPLY
**TRIPLIES** > TRIPLY
**TRIPLING** > TRIPLE
**TRIPLINGS** > TRIPLE
**TRIPLITE** *n* brownish-red
phosphate
**TRIPLITES** > TRIPLITE
**TRIPLOID** *adj* having or
relating to three times
the haploid number of
chromosomes ▷ *n* triploid
organism
**TRIPLOIDS** > TRIPLOID
**TRIPLOIDY** *n* triploid state
**TRIPLY** *vb* give a reply to
a duply
**TRIPLYING** > TRIPLY
**TRIPOD** *n* three-legged
stand, stool, etc
**TRIPODAL** > TRIPOD
**TRIPODIC** > TRIPOD
**TRIPODIES** > TRIPODY
**TRIPODS** > TRIPOD
**TRIPODY** *n* metrical unit
consisting of three feet
**TRIPOLI** *n* lightweight
porous siliceous rock
derived by weathering and
used in a powdered form
as a polish, filter, etc
**TRIPOLIS** > TRIPOLI

**TRIPOS** n final
examinations for an
honours degree at
Cambridge University
**TRIPOSES** > TRIPOS
**TRIPPANT** adj (in heraldry)
in the process of tripping
**TRIPPED** > TRIP
**TRIPPER** n tourist
**TRIPPERS** > TRIPPER
**TRIPPERY** adj like a tripper
**TRIPPET** n any mechanism
that strikes or is struck at
regular intervals, as by a
cam
**TRIPPETS** > TRIPPET
**TRIPPIER** > TRIPPY
**TRIPPIEST** > TRIPPY
**TRIPPING** > TRIP
**TRIPPINGS** > TRIP
**TRIPPLE** vb canter
**TRIPPLED** > TRIPPLE
**TRIPPLER** > TRIPPLE
**TRIPPLERS** > TRIPPLE
**TRIPPLES** > TRIPPLE
**TRIPPLING** > TRIPPLE
**TRIPPY** adj suggestive
of or resembling the
effect produced by a
hallucinogenic drug
**TRIPS** > TRIP
**TRIPSES** > TRIPSIS
**TRIPSIS** n act of kneading
the body to promote
circulation, suppleness,
etc
**TRIPTAN** n drug used to
treat migraine
**TRIPTANE** n colourless
highly flammable liquid
**TRIPTANES** > TRIPTANE
**TRIPTANS** > TRIPTAN
**TRIPTOTE** n word that has
only three cases
**TRIPTOTES** > TRIPTOTE
**TRIPTYCA** variant
of > TRIPTYCH
**TRIPTYCAS** > TRIPTYCA
**TRIPTYCH** n painting or
carving on three hinged
panels, often forming an
altarpiece
**TRIPTYCHS** > TRIPTYCH
**TRIPTYQUE** n customs
permit for the temporary
importation of a motor
vehicle
**TRIPUDIA** > TRIPUDIUM
**TRIPUDIUM** n ancient
religious dance
**TRIPWIRE** n wire that
activates a trap, mine, etc,
when tripped over
**TRIPWIRES** > TRIPWIRE
**TRIPY** > TRIPE
**TRIQUETRA** n ornament
in the shape of three
intersecting ellipses
roughly forming a triangle
**TRIRADIAL** adj having or
consisting of three rays or
radiating branches
**TRIREME** n ancient Greek
warship with three rows of

oars on each side
**TRIREMES** > TRIREME
**TRISAGION** n old hymn
**TRISCELE** variant spelling
of > TRISKELE
**TRISCELES** > TRISCELE
**TRISECT** vb divide into
three parts, esp three
equal parts
**TRISECTED** > TRISECT
**TRISECTOR** > TRISECT
**TRISECTS** > TRISECT
**TRISEME** n metrical foot
of a length equal to three
short syllables
**TRISEMES** > TRISEME
**TRISEMIC** > TRISEME
**TRISERIAL** adj arranged in
three rows or series
**TRISHAW** another name
for > RICKSHAW
**TRISHAWS** > TRISHAW
**TRISKELE** n three-limbed
symbol
**TRISKELES** > TRISKELE
**TRISKELIA** n plural of
singular triskelion: three-
limbed symbol
**TRISMIC** > TRISMUS
**TRISMUS** n state of being
unable to open the mouth
because of sustained
contractions of the
jaw muscles, caused by
tetanus
**TRISMUSES** > TRISMUS
**TRISODIUM** adj containing
three sodium atoms
**TRISOME** n chromosome
occurring three times
(rather than twice) in a cell
**TRISOMES** > TRISOME
**TRISOMIC** > TRISOMY
**TRISOMICS** n study of
trisomy
**TRISOMIES** > TRISOMY
**TRISOMY** n condition of
having one chromosome
of the set represented
three times in an
otherwise diploid
organism, cell, etc
**TRIST** variant spelling
of > TRISTE
**TRISTATE** adj (of a digital
computer chip) having
high, low, and floating
output states
**TRISTE** adj sad
**TRISTESSE** n sadness
**TRISTEZA** n disease
affecting citrus trees
**TRISTEZAS** > TRISTEZA
**TRISTFUL** same as > TRISTE
**TRISTICH** n poem, stanza,
or strophe that consists of
three lines
**TRISTICHS** > TRISTICH
**TRISUL** n trident symbol
of Siva
**TRISULA** same as > TRISUL
**TRISULAS** > TRISULA
**TRISULS** > TRISUL
**TRITE** adj (of a remark or

idea) commonplace and
unoriginal ▷ n (on a lyre)
the third string from the
highest in pitch
**TRITELY** > TRITE
**TRITENESS** > TRITE
**TRITER** > TRITE
**TRITES** > TRITE
**TRITEST** > TRITE
**TRITHEISM** n belief in
three gods, esp in the
Trinity as consisting of
three distinct gods
**TRITHEIST** > TRITHEISM
**TRITHING** n tripartition
**TRITHINGS** > TRITHING
**TRITIATE** vb replace
normal hydrogen atoms in
(a compound) by those of
tritium
**TRITIATED** > TRITIATE
**TRITIATES** > TRITIATE
**TRITICAL** n trite;
hackneyed
**TRITICALE** n fertile hybrid
cereal
**TRITICISM** n something
trite
**TRITICUM** n any annual
cereal grass of the genus
Triticum, which includes
the wheats
**TRITICUMS** > TRITICUM
**TRITIDE** n tritium
compound
**TRITIDES** > TRITIDE
**TRITIUM** n radioactive
isotope of hydrogen
**TRITIUMS** > TRITIUM
**TRITOMA** another name
for > KNIPHOFIA
**TRITOMAS** > TRITOMA
**TRITON** n any of various
chiefly tropical marine
gastropod molluscs,
having large beautifully-
coloured spiral shells
**TRITONE** n musical interval
consisting of three whole
tones
**TRITONES** > TRITONE
**TRITONIA** n any plant of
the perennial cormous
S. African genus Tritonia,
with typically scarlet or
orange flowers
**TRITONIAS** > TRITONIA
**TRITONS** > TRITON
**TRITURATE** vb grind or
rub into a fine powder
or pulp ▷ n powder or
pulp resulting from this
grinding
**TRIUMPH** n (happiness
caused by) victory or
success ▷ vb be victorious
or successful
**TRIUMPHAL** adj celebrating
a triumph
**TRIUMPHED** > TRIUMPH
**TRIUMPHER** > TRIUMPH
**TRIUMPHS** > TRIUMPH
**TRIUMVIR** n (esp in ancient
Rome) a member of a

triumvirate
**TRIUMVIRI** > TRIUMVIR
**TRIUMVIRS** > TRIUMVIR
**TRIUMVIRY** n triumvirate
**TRIUNE** adj constituting
three in one, esp the three
persons in one God of the
Trinity ▷ n group of three
**TRIUNES** > TRIUNE
**TRIUNITY** > TRIUNE
**TRIVALENT** adj having a
valency of three
**TRIVALVE** n animal having
three valves
**TRIVALVED** adj having
three valves
**TRIVALVES** > TRIVALVE
**TRIVET** n metal stand for a
pot or kettle
**TRIVETS** > TRIVET
**TRIVIA** pl n trivial things
or details
**TRIVIAL** adj of little
importance
**TRIVIALLY** > TRIVIAL
**TRIVIUM** n (in medieval
learning) the lower
division of the seven
liberal arts, consisting of
grammar, rhetoric, and
logic
**TRIVIUMS** > TRIVIUM
**TRIWEEKLY** adv every three
weeks ▷ n triweekly
publication
**TRIZONAL** > TRIZONE
**TRIZONE** n area comprising
three zones
**TRIZONES** > TRIZONE
**TROAD** same as > TROD
**TROADE** same as > TROD
**TROADES** > TROADE
**TROADS** > TROAD
**TROAK** old form of > TRUCK
**TROAKED** > TROAK
**TROAKING** > TROAK
**TROAKS** > TROAK
**TROAT** vb (of a rutting buck)
to call or bellow
**TROATED** > TROAT
**TROATING** > TROAT
**TROATS** > TROAT
**TROCAR** n surgical
instrument for removing
fluid from bodily cavities,
consisting of a puncturing
device situated inside a
tube
**TROCARS** > TROCAR
**TROCHAIC** adj of, relating
to, or consisting of
trochees ▷ n verse
composed of trochees
**TROCHAICS** > TROCHAIC
**TROCHAL** adj shaped like a
wheel
**TROCHAR** old variant spelling
of > TROCAR
**TROCHARS** > TROCHAR
**TROCHE** another name
for > LOZENGE
**TROCHEE** n metrical foot
of one long and one short
syllable

TROCHEES >TROCHEE
TROCHES >TROCHE
TROCHI >TROCHUS
TROCHIL same
  as >TROCHILUS
TROCHILI >TROCHILUS
TROCHILIC adj relating
  to the movement of a
  hummingbird's wings
TROCHILS >TROCHIL
TROCHILUS n any of several
  Old World warblers
TROCHISK another word
  for >TROCHE
TROCHISKS >TROCHISK
TROCHITE n joint of a
  crinoid
TROCHITES >TROCHITE
TROCHLEA n any bony or
  cartilaginous part with
  a grooved surface over
  which a bone, tendon, etc,
  may slide or articulate
TROCHLEAE >TROCHLEA
TROCHLEAR as in trochlear
  nerve either one of the
  fourth pair of cranial
  nerves, which supply the
  superior oblique muscle of
  the eye
TROCHLEAS >TROCHLEA
TROCHOID n curve
  described by a fixed point
  on the radius or extended
  radius of a circle as the
  circle rolls along a straight
  line ▷ adj rotating or
  capable of rotating about
  a central axis
TROCHOIDS >TROCHOID
TROCHUS n hoop (used in
  exercise)
TROCHUSES >TROCHUS
TROCK same as >TRUCK
TROCKED >TROCK
TROCKEN adj dry (used of
  wine, esp German wine)
TROCKING >TROCK
TROCKS >TROCK
TROD vb past participle of
  tread ▷ n path
TRODDEN >TREAD
TRODE same as >TROD
TRODES >TRODE
TRODS >TROD
TROELIE same as >TROOLIE
TROELIES >TROELIE
TROELY same as >TROOLIE
TROFFER n trough-like
  fixture for holding in place
  and reflecting light from a
  fluorescent tube
TROFFERS >TROFFER
TROG vb walk, esp aimlessly
  or heavily
TROGGED >TROG
TROGGING >TROG
TROGGS n loyalty; fidelity
TROGON n bird of tropical
  and subtropical regions
  of America, Africa, and
  Asia. They have a brilliant
  plumage, short hooked
  bill, and long tail

TROGONS >TROGON
TROGS >TROG
TROIKA n Russian vehicle
  drawn by three horses
  abreast
TROIKAS >TROIKA
TROILISM n sexual activity
  involving three people
TROILISMS >TROILISM
TROILIST >TROILISM
TROILISTS >TROILISM
TROILITE n iron
  sulphide present in most
  meteorites
TROILITES >TROILITE
TROILUS n type of large
  butterfly
TROILUSES >TROILUS
TROIS Scots form of >TROY
TROKE same as >TRUCK
TROKED >TROKE
TROKES >TROKE
TROKING >TROKE
TROLAND n unit of light
  intensity in the eye
TROLANDS >TROLAND
TROLL n giant or dwarf
  in Scandinavian folklore
  ▷ vb fish by dragging a lure
  through the water
TROLLED >TROLL
TROLLER >TROLL
TROLLERS >TROLL
TROLLEY n small wheeled
  table for food and drink
TROLLEYED >TROLLEY
TROLLEYS pl n men's
  underpants
TROLLIED >TROLLY
TROLLIES >TROLLY
TROLLING >TROLL
TROLLINGS >TROLL
TROLLIUS n plant with
  globe-shaped flowers
TROLLOP n promiscuous
  or slovenly woman ▷ vb
  behave like a trollop
TROLLOPED >TROLLOP
TROLLOPEE n loose dress
  or gown
TROLLOPS >TROLLOP
TROLLOPY >TROLLOP
TROLLS >TROLL
TROLLY same as >TROLLEY
TROLLYING >TROLLY
TROMBONE n brass musical
  instrument with a sliding
  tube
TROMBONES >TROMBONE
TROMINO n shape made
  from three squares, each
  joined to the next along
  one full side
TROMINOES >TROMINO
TROMINOS >TROMINO
TROMMEL n revolving
  cylindrical sieve used to
  screen crushed ore
TROMMELS >TROMMEL
TROMP vb trample
TROMPE n apparatus for
  supplying the blast of air
  in a forge, consisting of a
  thin column down which

water falls, drawing in air
  through side openings
TROMPED >TROMP
TROMPES >TROMPE
TROMPING >TROMP
TROMPS >TROMP
TRON n public weighing
  machine
TRONA n greyish mineral
  that consists of hydrated
  sodium carbonate and
  occurs in salt deposits
TRONAS >TRONA
TRONC n pool into which
  waiters, waitresses, hotel
  workers, etc, pay their tips
TRONCS >TRONC
TRONE same as >TRON
TRONES >TRONE
TRONK n jail
TRONKS >TRONK
TRONS >TRON
TROOLIE n large palm leaf
TROOLIES >TROOLIE
TROOP n large group ▷ vb
  move in a crowd
TROOPED >TROOP
TROOPER n cavalry soldier
TROOPERS >TROOPER
TROOPIAL same
  as >TROUPIAL
TROOPIALS >TROOPIAL
TROOPING >TROOP
TROOPS >TROOP
TROOPSHIP n ship used
  to transport military
  personnel
TROOSTITE n reddish or
  greyish mineral that is
  a variety of willemite in
  which some of the zinc is
  replaced by manganese
TROOZ same as >TREWS
TROP adv too, too much
TROPAEOLA n plural of
  singular tropaeolum (a
  garden plant)
TROPARIA >TROPARION
TROPARION n short hymn
TROPE n figure of speech
  ▷ vb use tropes (in speech
  or writing)
TROPED >TROPE
TROPEOLIN n type of dye
TROPES >TROPE
TROPHESY n disorder of
  the nerves relating to
  nutrition
TROPHI n collective term
  for the mandibles other
  parts of an insect's mouth
TROPHIC adj of or relating
  to nutrition
TROPHIED >TROPHY
TROPHIES >TROPHY
TROPHY n cup, shield, etc
  given as a prize ▷ adj
  regraded as a highly
  desirable symbol of wealth
  or success ▷ vb award a
  trophy to (someone)
TROPHYING >TROPHY
TROPIC n either of two
  lines of latitude at 23½°N

(tropic of Cancer) or 23½°S
  (tropic of Capricorn)
TROPICAL adj of or in the
  tropics ▷ n tropical thing
  or place
TROPICALS >TROPICAL
TROPICS >TROPIC
TROPIN n andrenal
  androgen
TROPINE n white
  crystalline poisonous
  hygroscopic alkaloid
  obtained by heating
  atropine or hyoscyamine
  with barium hydroxide
TROPINES >TROPINE
TROPING >TROPE
TROPINS >TROPIN
TROPISM n tendency of a
  plant or animal to turn or
  curve in response to an
  external stimulus
TROPISMS >TROPISM
TROPIST >TROPISM
TROPISTIC >TROPISM
TROPISTS >TROPISM
TROPOLOGY n use of
  figurative language in
  speech or writing
TROPONIN n muscle-tissue
  protein involved in the
  controlling of muscle
  contraction
TROPONINS >TROPONIN
TROPPO adv too much ▷ adj
  mentally affected by a
  tropical climate
TROSSERS old form
  of >TROUSERS
TROT vb (of a horse) move
  at a medium pace, lifting
  the feet in diagonal pairs
  ▷ n trotting
TROTH n pledge of
  devotion, esp a betrothal
  ▷ vb promise to marry
  (someone)
TROTHED >TROTH
TROTHFUL >TROTH
TROTHING >TROTH
TROTHLESS >TROTH
TROTHS >TROTH
TROTLINE n long line
  suspended across a
  stream, river, etc, to which
  shorter hooked and baited
  lines are attached
TROTLINES >TROTLINE
TROTS >TROT
TROTTED >TROT
TROTTER n pig's foot
TROTTERS >TROTTER
TROTTING >TROT
TROTTINGS >TROT
TROTTOIR n pavement
TROTTOIRS >TROTTOIR
TROTYL n trinitrotoluene;
  a yellow solid: used chiefly
  as a high explosive and is
  also an intermediate in the
  manufacture of dyestuffs
TROTYLS >TROTYL
TROUBLE n (cause of)
  distress or anxiety ▷ vb

(cause to) worry
**TROUBLED** > TROUBLE
**TROUBLER** > TROUBLE
**TROUBLERS** > TROUBLE
**TROUBLES** > TROUBLE
**TROUBLING** > TROUBLE
**TROUBLOUS** *adj* unsettled or agitated
**TROUCH** *n* rubbish
**TROUCHES** > TROUCH
**TROUGH** *n* long open container, esp for animals' food or water ▷ *vb* eat, consume, or take greedily
**TROUGHS** > TROUGH
**TROULE** *old variant of* > TROLL
**TROULED** > TROULE
**TROULES** > TROULE
**TROULING** > TROULE
**TROUNCE** *vb* defeat utterly
**TROUNCED** > TROUNCE
**TROUNCER** > TROUNCE
**TROUNCERS** > TROUNCE
**TROUNCES** > TROUNCE
**TROUNCING** > TROUNCE
**TROUPE** *n* company of performers ▷ *vb* (esp of actors) to move or travel in a group
**TROUPED** > TROUPE
**TROUPER** *n* member of a troupe
**TROUPERS** > TROUPER
**TROUPES** > TROUPE
**TROUPIAL** *n* any of various American orioles
**TROUPIALS** > TROUPIAL
**TROUPING** > TROUPE
**TROUSE** *pl n* close-fitting breeches worn in Ireland
**TROUSER** *adj* of trousers ▷ *vb* take (something, esp money), often surreptitiously or unlawfully ▷ *n* of or relating to trousers
**TROUSERED** > TROUSERS
**TROUSERS** *pl n* two-legged outer garment with legs reaching usu to the ankles
**TROUSES** > TROUSE
**TROUSSEAU** *n* bride's collection of clothing etc for her marriage
**TROUT** *n* game fish related to the salmon ▷ *vb* fish for trout
**TROUTER** > TROUT
**TROUTERS** > TROUT
**TROUTFUL** *adj* (of a body of water) full of trout
**TROUTIER** > TROUT
**TROUTIEST** > TROUT
**TROUTING** > TROUT
**TROUTINGS** > TROUT
**TROUTLESS** > TROUT
**TROUTLET** *n* small trout
**TROUTLETS** > TROUTLET
**TROUTLING** *n* small trout
**TROUTS** > TROUT
**TROUTY** > TROUT
**TROUVERE** *n* any of a group of poets of N France during

the 12th and 13th centuries who composed chiefly narrative works
**TROUVERES** > TROUVERE
**TROUVEUR** *same as* > TROUVERE
**TROUVEURS** > TROUVEUR
**TROVE** as in *treasure-trove* valuable articles, such as coins, bullion, etc, found hidden in the earth or elsewhere and of unknown ownership
**TROVER** *n* (formerly) the act of wrongfully assuming proprietary rights over personal goods or property belonging to another
**TROVERS** > TROVER
**TROVES** > TROVE
**TROW** *vb* think, believe, or trust
**TROWED** > TROW
**TROWEL** *n* hand tool with a wide blade for spreading mortar, lifting plants, etc ▷ *vb* use a trowel on (plaster, soil, etc)
**TROWELED** > TROWEL
**TROWELER** > TROWEL
**TROWELERS** > TROWEL
**TROWELING** > TROWEL
**TROWELLED** > TROWEL
**TROWELLER** > TROWEL
**TROWELS** > TROWEL
**TROWING** > TROW
**TROWS** > TROW
**TROWSERS** *old spelling of* > TROUSERS
**TROWTH** *variant spelling of* > TROTH
**TROWTHS** > TROWTH
**TROY** as in *troy weight* system of weights used for precious metals and gemstones, based on the grain, which is identical to the avoirdupois grain
**TROYS** > TROY
**TRUANCIES** > TRUANT
**TRUANCY** > TRUANT
**TRUANT** *n* pupil who stays away from school without permission ▷ *adj* being or relating to a truant ▷ *vb* play truant
**TRUANTED** > TRUANT
**TRUANTING** > TRUANT
**TRUANTLY** > TRUANT
**TRUANTRY** > TRUANT
**TRUANTS** > TRUANT
**TRUCAGE** *n* art forgery
**TRUCAGES** > TRUCAGE
**TRUCE** *n* temporary agreement to stop fighting ▷ *vb* make a truce
**TRUCED** > TRUCE
**TRUCELESS** > TRUCE
**TRUCES** > TRUCE
**TRUCHMAN** *n* interpreter; translator
**TRUCHMANS** > TRUCHMAN
**TRUCHMEN** > TRUCHMAN
**TRUCIAL** > TRUCE

**TRUCING** > TRUCE
**TRUCK** *n* railway goods wagon ▷ *vb* exchange (goods); barter
**TRUCKABLE** > TRUCK
**TRUCKAGE** *n* conveyance of cargo by truck
**TRUCKAGES** > TRUCKAGE
**TRUCKED** > TRUCK
**TRUCKER** *n* truck driver
**TRUCKERS** > TRUCKER
**TRUCKFUL** *n* amount of something that can be conveyed in a truck
**TRUCKFULS** > TRUCKFUL
**TRUCKIE** *n* truck driver
**TRUCKIES** > TRUCKIE
**TRUCKING** *n* transportation of goods by lorry
**TRUCKINGS** > TRUCKING
**TRUCKLE** *vb* yield weakly or give in ▷ *n* small wheel
**TRUCKLED** > TRUCKLE
**TRUCKLER** > TRUCKLE
**TRUCKLERS** > TRUCKLE
**TRUCKLES** > TRUCKLE
**TRUCKLINE** *n* organisation that conveys freight by truck
**TRUCKLING** > TRUCKLE
**TRUCKLOAD** *n* amount carried by a truck
**TRUCKMAN** *n* truck driver
**TRUCKMEN** > TRUCKMAN
**TRUCKS** > TRUCK
**TRUCKSTOP** *n* place providing fuel, oil, and often service facilities for truck drivers
**TRUCULENT** *adj* aggressively defiant
**TRUDGE** *vb* walk heavily or wearily ▷ *n* long tiring walk
**TRUDGED** > TRUDGE
**TRUDGEN** *n* type of swimming stroke that uses overarm action, as in the crawl, and a scissors kick
**TRUDGENS** > TRUDGEN
**TRUDGEON** *nonstandard variant of* > TRUDGEN
**TRUDGEONS** > TRUDGEON
**TRUDGER** > TRUDGE
**TRUDGERS** > TRUDGE
**TRUDGES** > TRUDGE
**TRUDGING** > TRUDGE
**TRUDGINGS** > TRUDGE
**TRUE** *adj* in accordance with facts
**TRUEBLUE** *n* staunch royalist or Conservative
**TRUEBLUES** > TRUEBLUE
**TRUEBORN** *adj* being such by birth
**TRUEBRED** *adj* thoroughbred
**TRUED** > TRUE
**TRUEING** > TRUE
**TRUELOVE** *n* person that one loves
**TRUELOVES** > TRUELOVE

**TRUEMAN** *n* honest person
**TRUEMEN** > TRUEMAN
**TRUENESS** > TRUE
**TRUEPENNY** *n* truthful person
**TRUER** > TRUE
**TRUES** > TRUE
**TRUEST** > TRUE
**TRUFFE** *rare word for* > TRUFFLE
**TRUFFES** > TRUFFE
**TRUFFLE** *n* edible underground fungus ▷ *vb* hunt for truffles
**TRUFFLED** > TRUFFLE
**TRUFFLES** > TRUFFLE
**TRUFFLING** > TRUFFLE
**TRUG** *n* long shallow basket used by gardeners
**TRUGO** *n* game similar to croquet, originally improvised in Victoria from the rubber discs used as buffers on railway carriages
**TRUGOS** > TRUGO
**TRUGS** > TRUG
**TRUING** > TRUE
**TRUISM** *n* self-evident truth
**TRUISMS** > TRUISM
**TRUISTIC** > TRUISM
**TRULL** *n* prostitute
**TRULLS** > TRULL
**TRULY** *adv* in a true manner
**TRUMEAU** *n* section of a wall or pillar between two openings
**TRUMEAUX** > TRUMEAU
**TRUMP** *adj* (card) of the suit outranking the others ▷ *vb* play a trump card on (another card) ▷ *pl n* suit outranking the others
**TRUMPED** > TRUMP
**TRUMPERY** *n* something useless or worthless ▷ *adj* useless or worthless
**TRUMPET** *n* valved brass instrument with a flared tube ▷ *vb* proclaim loudly
**TRUMPETED** > TRUMPET
**TRUMPETER** *n* person who plays the trumpet, esp one whose duty it is to play fanfares, signals, etc
**TRUMPETS** > TRUMPET
**TRUMPING** > TRUMP
**TRUMPINGS** > TRUMP
**TRUMPLESS** > TRUMP
**TRUMPS** > TRUMP
**TRUNCAL** *adj* of or relating to the trunk
**TRUNCATE** *vb* cut short ▷ *adj* cut short
**TRUNCATED** *adj* (of a cone, pyramid, prism, etc) having an apex or end removed by a plane intersection that is usually nonparallel to the base
**TRUNCATES** > TRUNCATE
**TRUNCHEON** *n* club formerly carried by a policeman ▷ *vb* beat with

a truncheon

**TRUNDLE** *vb* move heavily on wheels ▷ *n* act or an instance of trundling

**TRUNDLED** >TRUNDLE

**TRUNDLER** *n* golf or shopping trolley

**TRUNDLERS** >TRUNDLER

**TRUNDLES** >TRUNDLE

**TRUNDLING** >TRUNDLE

**TRUNK** *n* main stem of a tree ▷ *vb* lop or truncate

**TRUNKED** >TRUNK

**TRUNKFISH** *n* tropical fish, having the body encased in bony plates with openings for the fins, eyes, mouth, etc

**JRUNKFUL** >TRUNK

**TRUNKFULS** >TRUNK

**TRUNKING** *n* cables that take a common route through an exchange building linking ranks of selectors

**TRUNKINGS** >TRUNKING

**TRUNKLESS** >TRUNK

**TRUNKS** *pl n* shorts worn by a man for swimming

**TRUNNEL** *same as* >TREENAIL

**TRUNNELS** >TRUNNEL

**TRUNNION** *n* one of a pair of coaxial projections attached to opposite sides of a container, cannon, etc, to provide a support about which it can turn in a vertical

**TRUNNIONS** >TRUNNION

**TRUQUAGE** *variant of* >TRUCAGE

**TRUQUAGES** >TRUQUAGE

**TRUQUEUR** *n* art forger

**TRUQUEURS** >TRUQUEUR

**TRUSS** *vb* tie or bind up ▷ *n* device for holding a hernia, etc in place

**TRUSSED** >TRUSS

**TRUSSER** >TRUSS

**TRUSSERS** >TRUSS

**TRUSSES** >TRUSS

**TRUSSING** *n* system of trusses, esp for strengthening or reinforcing a structure

**TRUSSINGS** >TRUSSING

**TRUST** *vb* believe in and rely on ▷ *n* confidence in the truth, reliability, etc of a person or thing ▷ *adj* of or relating to a trust or trusts

**TRUSTABLE** >TRUST

**TRUSTED** >TRUST

**TRUSTEE** *n* person holding property on another's behalf ▷ *vb* act as a trustee

**TRUSTEED** >TRUSTEE

**TRUSTEES** >TRUSTEE

**TRUSTER** >TRUST

**TRUSTERS** >TRUST

**TRUSTFUL** *adj* inclined to trust others

**TRUSTIER** >TRUSTY

**TRUSTIES** >TRUSTY

**TRUSTIEST** >TRUSTY

**TRUSTILY** >TRUSTY

**TRUSTING** *same as* >TRUSTFUL

**TRUSTLESS** *adj* untrustworthy

**TRUSTOR** *n* person who sets up a trust

**TRUSTORS** >TRUSTOR

**TRUSTS** >TRUST

**TRUSTY** *adj* faithful or reliable ▷ *n* trustworthy convict to whom special privileges are granted

**TRUTH** *n* state of being true

**TRUTHFUL** *adj* honest

**TRUTHIER** >TRUTHY

**TRUTHIEST** >TRUTHY

**TRUTHLESS** >TRUTH

**TRUTHLIKE** *n* truthful

**TRUTHS** >TRUTH

**TRUTHY** *adj* truthful

**TRY** *vb* make an effort or attempt ▷ *n* attempt or effort

**TRYE** *adj* very good; select

**TRYER** *variant of* >TRIER

**TRYERS** >TRYER

**TRYING** >TRY

**TRYINGLY** >TRY

**TRYINGS** >TRY

**TRYKE** *variant spelling of* >TRIKE

**TRYKES** >TRYKE

**TRYMA** *n* drupe produced by the walnut and similar plants, in which the endocarp is a hard shell and the epicarp is dehiscent

**TRYMATA** >TRYMA

**TRYOUT** *n* a trial or test, as of an athlete or actor

**TRYOUTS** >TRYOUT

**TRYP** *n* parasitic protozoan

**TRYPAN** as in *trypan blue* dye obtained from tolidine that is absorbed by the macrophages of the reticuloendothelial system and is therefore used for staining cells in biological research

**TRYPS** >TRYP

**TRYPSIN** *n* enzyme occurring in pancreatic juice

**TRYPSINS** >TRYPSIN

**TRYPTIC** >TRYPSIN

**TRYSAIL** *n* small fore-and-aft sail set on a sailing vessel to help keep her head to the wind in a storm

**TRYSAILS** >TRYSAIL

**TRYST** *n* arrangement to meet ▷ *vb* meet at or arrange a tryst

**TRYSTE** *variant spelling of* >TRYST

**TRYSTED** >TRYST

**TRYSTER** >TRYST

**TRYSTERS** >TRYST

**TRYSTES** >TRYSTE

**TRYSTING** >TRYST

**TRYSTS** >TRYST

**TRYWORKS** *n* furnace for rendering blubber

**TSADDIK** *variant of* >ZADDIK

**TSADDIKIM** >TSADDIK

**TSADDIKS** >TSADDIK

**TSADDIQ** *variant of* >ZADDIK

**TSADDIQIM** >TSADDIQ

**TSADDIQS** >TSADDIQ

**TSADE** *variant spelling of* >SADHE

**TSADES** >TSADE

**TSADI** *variant of* >SADHE

**TSADIS** >TSADI

**TSAMBA** *n* Tibetan dish made from roasted barley and tea

**TSAMBAS** >TSAMBA

**TSANTSA** *n* (among the Shuar subgroup of the Jivaro people of Ecuador) shrunken head of an enemy kept as a trophy

**TSANTSAS** >TSANTSA

**TSAR** *n* Russian emperor

**TSARDOM** >TSAR

**TSARDOMS** >TSAR

**TSAREVICH** *n* tsar's son

**TSAREVNA** *n* daughter of a Russian tsar

**TSAREVNAS** >TSAREVNA

**TSARINA** *n* wife of a Russian tsar

**TSARINAS** >TSARINA

**TSARISM** *n* system of government by a tsar, esp in Russia until 1917

**TSARISMS** >TSARISM

**TSARIST** >TSARISM

**TSARISTS** >TSARISM

**TSARITSA** *same as* >TSARINA

**TSARITSAS** >TSARITSA

**TSARITZA** *variant spelling of* >TSARITSA

**TSARITZAS** >TSARITZA

**TSARS** >TSAR

**TSATSKE** *variant of* >TCHOTCHKE

**TSATSKES** >TSATSKE

**TSESSEBE** *South African variant of* >SASSABY

**TSESSEBES** >TSESSEBE

**TSETSE** *n* any of various bloodsucking African dipterous flies which transmit the pathogens of various diseases

**TSETSES** >TSETSE

**TSIGANE** *variant of* >TZIGANE

**TSIGANES** >TSIGANE

**TSIMMES** *variant spelling of* >TZIMMES

**TSITSITH** *n* tassels or fringes of thread attached to the four corners of the tallith

**TSK** *vb* utter the sound "tsk", usu in disapproval

**TSKED** >TSK

**TSKING** >TSK

**TSKS** >TSK

**TSKTSK** *same as* >TSK

**TSKTSKED** >TSKTSK

**TSKTSKING** >TSKTSK

**TSKTSKS** >TSKTSK

**TSOORIS** *variant of* >TSURIS

**TSORES** *variant of* >TSURIS

**TSORIS** *variant of* >TSURIS

**TSORRISS** *variant of* >TSURIS

**TSOTSI** *n* Black street thug or gang member

**TSOTSIS** >TSOTSI

**TSOURIS** *variant of* >TSURIS

**TSOURISES** >TSOURIS

**TSUBA** *n* sword guard of a Japanese sword

**TSUBAS** >TSUBA

**TSUNAMI** *n* tidal wave, usu caused by an earthquake under the sea

**TSUNAMIC** >TSUNAMI

**TSUNAMIS** >TSUNAMI

**TSURIS** *n* grief or strife

**TSURISES** >TSURIS

**TSUTSUMU** *n* Japanese art of wrapping gifts

**TSUTSUMUS** >TSUTSUMU

**TUAN** *n* lord

**TUANS** >TUAN

**TUART** *n* eucalyptus tree of Australia, yielding a very durable light-coloured timber

**TUARTS** >TUART

**TUATARA** *n* large lizard-like New Zealand reptile

**TUATARAS** >TUATARA

**TUATERA** *variant spelling of* >TUATARA

**TUATERAS** >TUATERA

**TUATH** *n* territory of an ancient Irish tribe

**TUATHS** >TUATH

**TUATUA** *n* edible marine bivalve of New Zealand waters

**TUB** *n* open, usu round container ▷ *vb* wash (oneself or another) in a tub

**TUBA** *n* valved low-pitched brass instrument

**TUBAE** >TUBA

**TUBAGE** *n* insertion of a tube

**TUBAGES** >TUBAGE

**TUBAIST** >TUBA

**TUBAISTS** >TUBA

**TUBAL** *adj* of or relating to a tube

**TUBAR** *another word for* >TUBULAR

**TUBAS** >TUBA

**TUBATE** *less common word for* >TUBULAR

**TUBBABLE** >TUB

**TUBBED** >TUB

**TUBBER** >TUB

**TUBBERS** >TUB

**TUBBIER** >TUBBY

**TUBBIEST** >TUBBY

**TUBBINESS** >TUBBY

**TUBBING** >TUB

**TUBBINGS** >TUB

**TUBBISH** adj fat

**TUBBY** adj (of a person) short and fat

**TUBE** n hollow cylinder

**TUBECTOMY** n excision of the Fallopian tubes

**TUBED** >TUBE

**TUBEFUL** n quantity (of something) that a tube can hold

**TUBEFULS** >TUBEFUL

**TUBELESS** adj without a tube

**TUBELIKE** adj resembling a tube

**TUBENOSE** n seabird with tubular nostrils on its beak

**TUBENOSES** >TUBENOSE

**TUBER** n fleshy underground root of a plant such as a potato

**TUBERCLE** n small rounded swelling

**TUBERCLED** adj having tubercles

**TUBERCLES** >TUBERCLE

**TUBERCULA** n plural of tuberculum (another name for "tubercle")

**TUBERCULE** variant of >TUBERCLE

**TUBEROID** adj resembling a tuber

**TUBEROSE** same as >TUBEROUS

**TUBEROSES** >TUBEROSE

**TUBEROUS** adj (of plants) forming, bearing, or resembling a tuber or tubers

**TUBERS** >TUBER

**TUBES** >TUBE

**TUBEWORK** n collective term for tubes or tubing

**TUBEWORKS** >TUBEWORK

**TUBEWORM** n undersea worm

**TUBEWORMS** >TUBEWORM

**TUBFAST** n period of fasting and sweating in a tub, intended as a cure for disease

**TUBFASTS** >TUBFAST

**TUBFISH** another name for >GURNARD

**TUBFISHES** >TUBFISH

**TUBFUL** n amount a tub will hold

**TUBFULS** >TUBFUL

**TUBICOLAR** adj tube-dwelling

**TUBICOLE** n tube-dwelling creature

**TUBICOLES** >TUBICOLE

**TUBIFEX** n any small reddish freshwater oligochaete worm of the genus *Tubifex*

**TUBIFEXES** >TUBIFEX

**TUBIFICID** n type of threadlike annelid worm

**TUBIFORM** same as >TUBULAR

**TUBING** n length of tube

**TUBINGS** >TUBING

**TUBIST** >TUBA

**TUBISTS** >TUBA

**TUBLIKE** >TUB

**TUBS** >TUB

**TUBULAR** adj of or shaped like a tube

**TUBULARLY** >TUBULAR

**TUBULATE** vb form or shape into a tube

**TUBULATED** >TUBULATE

**TUBULATES** >TUBULATE

**TUBULATOR** >TUBULATE

**TUBULE** n any small tubular structure, esp in an animal or plant

**TUBULES** >TUBULE

**TUBULIN** n protein forming the basis of microtubules

**TUBULINS** >TUBULIN

**TUBULOSE** adj tube-shaped; consisting of tubes

**TUBULOUS** adj tube-shaped

**TUBULURE** n tube leading into a retort or other receptacle

**TUBULURES** >TUBULURE

**TUCHUN** n (formerly) a Chinese military governor or warlord

**TUCHUNS** >TUCHUN

**TUCK** vb push or fold into a small space ▷ n stitched fold ▷ vb touch or strike

**TUCKAHOE** n type of edible root

**TUCKAHOES** >TUCKAHOE

**TUCKED** >TUCK

**TUCKER** n food ▷ vb weary or tire completely

**TUCKERBAG** n in Australia, bag or box used for carrying food

**TUCKERBOX** same as >TUCKERBAG

**TUCKERED** >TUCKER

**TUCKERING** >TUCKER

**TUCKERS** >TUCKER

**TUCKET** n flourish on a trumpet

**TUCKETS** >TUCKET

**TUCKING** >TUCK

**TUCKS** >TUCK

**TUCKSHOP** n shop, esp one in or near a school, where food such as cakes and sweets are sold

**TUCKSHOPS** >TUCKSHOP

**TUCOTUCO** n colonial burrowing South American rodent

**TUCOTUCOS** >TUCOTUCO

**TUCUTUCO** variant spelling of >TUCOTUCO

**TUCUTUCOS** >TUCUTUCO

**TUCUTUCU** same as >TUCOTUCO

**TUCUTUCUS** >TUCUTUCU

**TUFA** n porous rock formed as a deposit from springs

**TUFACEOUS** >TUFA

**TUFAS** >TUFA

**TUFF** n porous rock formed from volcanic dust or ash

**TUFFE** old form of >TUFT

**TUFFES** >TUFFE

**TUFFET** n small mound or seat

**TUFFETS** >TUFFET

**TUFFS** >TUFF

**TUFOLI** n type of tubular pasta

**TUFT** n bunch of feathers, grass, hair, etc held or growing together at the base ▷ vb provide or decorate with a tuft or tufts

**TUFTED** adj having a tuft or tufts

**TUFTER** >TUFT

**TUFTERS** >TUFT

**TUFTIER** >TUFT

**TUFTIEST** >TUFT

**TUFTILY** >TUFT

**TUFTING** >TUFT

**TUFTINGS** >TUFT

**TUFTS** >TUFT

**TUFTY** >TUFT

**TUG** vb pull hard ▷ n hard pull

**TUGBOAT** same as >TUG

**TUGBOATS** >TUGBOAT

**TUGGED** >TUG

**TUGGER** >TUG

**TUGGERS** >TUG

**TUGGING** >TUG

**TUGGINGLY** >TUG

**TUGGINGS** >TUG

**TUGHRA** n Turkish Sultan's official emblem

**TUGHRAS** >TUGHRA

**TUGHRIK** same as >TUGRIK

**TUGHRIKS** >TUGHRIK

**TUGLESS** >TUG

**TUGRA** variant of >TUGHRA

**TUGRAS** >TUGRA

**TUGRIK** n standard monetary unit of Mongolia, divided into 100 möngös

**TUGRIKS** >TUGRIK

**TUGS** >TUG

**TUI** n New Zealand honeyeater that mimics human speech and the songs of other birds

**TUILLE** n (in a suit of armour) hanging plate protecting the thighs

**TUILLES** >TUILLE

**TUILLETTE** n little tuille

**TUILYIE** vb fight

**TUILYIED** >TUILYIE

**TUILYIES** >TUILYIE

**TUILZIE** variant form of >TUILYIE

**TUILZIED** >TUILZIE

**TUILZIES** >TUILZIE

**TUINA** n form of massage originating in China

**TUINAS** >TUINA

**TUIS** >TUI

**TUISM** n practice of putting the interests of another

before one's own

**TUISMS** >TUISM

**TUITION** n instruction, esp received individually or in a small group

**TUITIONAL** >TUITION

**TUITIONS** >TUITION

**TUKTOO** same as >TUKTU

**TUKTOOS** >TUKTOO

**TUKTU** (in Canada) another name for >CARIBOU

**TUKTUS** >TUKTU

**TULADI** n large trout found in Canada and northern areas of the US

**TULADIS** >TULADI

**TULAREMIA** n infectious disease of rodents

**TULAREMIC** >TULAREMIA

**TULBAN** old form of >TURBAN

**TULBANS** >TULBAN

**TULCHAN** n skin of a calf placed next to a cow to induce it to give milk

**TULCHANS** >TULCHAN

**TULE** n type of bulrush found in California

**TULES** >TULE

**TULIP** n plant with bright cup-shaped flowers

**TULIPANT** n turban

**TULIPANTS** >TULIPANT

**TULIPLIKE** >TULIP

**TULIPS** >TULIP

**TULIPWOOD** n light soft wood of the tulip tree, used in making furniture and veneer

**TULLE** n fine net fabric of silk etc

**TULLES** >TULLE

**TULLIBEE** n cisco of the Great Lakes of Canada

**TULLIBEES** >TULLIBEE

**TULPA** n being or object created through willpower and visualization techniques

**TULPAS** >TULPA

**TULWAR** n Indian sabre

**TULWARS** >TULWAR

**TUM** informal or childish word for >STOMACH

**TUMBLE** vb (cause to) fall, esp awkwardly or violently ▷ n fall

**TUMBLEBUG** n type of dung beetle

**TUMBLED** >TUMBLE

**TUMBLER** n stemless drinking glass

**TUMBLERS** >TUMBLER

**TUMBLES** >TUMBLE

**TUMBLESET** n somersault

**TUMBLING** >TUMBLE

**TUMBLINGS** >TUMBLING

**TUMBREL** n farm cart for carrying dung, esp one that tilts backwards to deposit its load

**TUMBRELS** >TUMBREL

**TUMBRIL** same as >TUMBREL

TUMBRILS >TUMBRIL
TUMEFIED >TUMEFY
TUMEFIES >TUMEFY
TUMEFY vb make or become tumid
TUMEFYING >TUMEFY
TUMESCE vb swell
TUMESCED >TUMESCE
TUMESCENT adj swollen or becoming swollen
TUMESCES >TUMESCE
TUMESCING >TUMESCE
TUMID adj (of an organ or part of the body) enlarged or swollen
TUMIDITY >TUMID
TUMIDLY >TUMID
TUMIDNESS >TUMID
TUMMIES >TUMMY
TUMMLER n comedian or other entertainer employed to encourage audience participation or to persuade guests at a resort to take part in communal activities
TUMMLERS >TUMMLER
TUMMY n stomach
TUMOR same as >TUMOUR
TUMORAL >TUMOUR
TUMORLIKE >TUMOUR
TUMOROUS >TUMOUR
TUMORS >TUMOR
TUMOUR n abnormal growth in or on the body
TUMOURS >TUMOUR
TUMP n small mound or clump ▷ vb make a tump around
TUMPED >TUMP
TUMPHIES >TUMPHY
TUMPHY n dolt; fool
TUMPIER >TUMP
TUMPIEST >TUMP
TUMPING >TUMP
TUMPLINE n (in the US and Canada, esp formerly) leather or cloth band strung across the forehead or chest and attached to a pack or load in order to support it
TUMPLINES >TUMPLINE
TUMPS >TUMP
TUMPY >TUMP
TUMS >TUM
TUMSHIE n turnip
TUMSHIES >TUMSHIE
TUMULAR adj of, relating to, or like a mound
TUMULARY same as >TUMULAR
TUMULI >TUMULUS
TUMULOSE adj abounding in small hills or mounds
TUMULOUS same as >TUMULOSE
TUMULT n uproar or commotion ▷ vb stir up a commotion
TUMULTED >TUMULT
TUMULTING >TUMULT
TUMULTS >TUMULT
TUMULUS n burial mound

TUMULUSES >TUMULUS
TUN n large beer cask ▷ vb put into or keep in tuns
TUNA n large marine food fish
TUNABLE adj able to be tuned
TUNABLY >TUNABLE
TUNAS >TUNA
TUNBELLY n large round belly
TUND vb beat; strike
TUNDED >TUND
TUNDING >TUND
TUNDISH n type of funnel
TUNDISHES >TUNDISH
TUNDRA n vast treeless Arctic region with permanently frozen subsoil
TUNDRAS >TUNDRA
TUNDS >TUND
TUNDUN n wooden instrument used by Native Australians in religious rites
TUNDUNS >TUNDUN
TUNE n (pleasing) sequence of musical notes ▷ vb adjust (a musical instrument) so that it is in tune
TUNEABLE same as >TUNABLE
TUNEABLY >TUNEABLE
TUNED >TUNE
TUNEFUL adj having a pleasant tune
TUNEFULLY >TUNEFUL
TUNELESS adj having no melody or tune
TUNER n part of a radio or television receiver for selecting channels
TUNERS >TUNER
TUNES >TUNE
TUNESMITH n composer of light or popular music and songs
TUNEUP n adjustments made to an engine to improve its performance
TUNEUPS >TUNEUP
TUNG as in tung oil fast-drying oil obtained from the seeds of a central Asian euphorbiaceous tree, used in paints, varnishes, etc, as a drying agent and to give a water-resistant finish
TUNGS >TUNG
TUNGSTATE n salt of tungstic acid
TUNGSTEN n greyish-white metal
TUNGSTENS >TUNGSTEN
TUNGSTIC adj of or containing tungsten, esp in a high valence state
TUNGSTITE n yellow earthy rare secondary mineral that consists of tungsten oxide and occurs with tungsten ores

TUNGSTOUS adj of or containing tungsten in a low valence state
TUNIC n close-fitting jacket forming part of some uniforms
TUNICA n tissue forming a layer or covering of an organ or part, such as any of the tissue layers of a blood vessel wall
TUNICAE >TUNICA
TUNICATE n minute primitive marine chordate animal ▷ adj of, relating to this animal ▷ vb wear a tunic
TUNICATED >TUNICATE
TUNICATES >TUNICATE
TUNICIN n cellulose-like substance found in tunicates
TUNICINS >TUNICIN
TUNICKED adj wearing a tunic
TUNICLE n liturgical vestment worn by the subdeacon and bishops at High Mass and other religious ceremonies
TUNICLES >TUNICLE
TUNICS >TUNIC
TUNIER >TUNY
TUNIEST >TUNY
TUNING n set of pitches to which the open strings of a guitar, violin, etc, are tuned
TUNINGS >TUNING
TUNNAGE same as >TONNAGE
TUNNAGES >TUNNAGE
TUNNED >TUN
TUNNEL n underground passage ▷ vb make a tunnel (through)
TUNNELED >TUNNEL
TUNNELER >TUNNEL
TUNNELERS >TUNNEL
TUNNELING >TUNNEL
TUNNELLED >TUNNEL
TUNNELLER >TUNNEL
TUNNELS >TUNNEL
TUNNIES >TUNNY
TUNNING >TUN
TUNNINGS >TUN
TUNNY same as >TUNA
TUNS >TUN
TUNY adj having an easily discernable melody
TUP n male sheep ▷ vb cause (a ram) to mate with a ewe, or (of a ram) to mate with (a ewe)
TUPEK same as >TUPIK
TUPEKS >TUPEK
TUPELO n large tree of deep swamps and rivers of the southern US
TUPELOS >TUPELO
TUPIK n tent of seal or caribou skin used for shelter by the Inuit in summer

TUPIKS >TUPIK
TUPLE n row of values in a relational database
TUPLES >TUPLE
TUPPED >TUP
TUPPENCE same as >TWOPENCE
TUPPENCES >TUPPENCE
TUPPENNY same as >TWOPENNY
TUPPING >TUP
TUPS >TUP
TUPTOWING n study of Greek grammar
TUPUNA same as >TIPUNA
TUPUNAS >TUPUNA
TUQUE n knitted cap with a long tapering end
TUQUES >TUQUE
TURACIN n red pigment found in touraco feathers
TURACINS >TURACIN
TURACO same as >TOURACO
TURACOS >TURACO
TURACOU variant of >TOURACO
TURACOUS >TURACOU
TURBAN n Muslim, Hindu, or Sikh man's head covering, made by winding cloth round the head
TURBAND old variant of >TURBAN
TURBANDS >TURBAND
TURBANED >TURBAN
TURBANNED >TURBAN
TURBANS >TURBAN
TURBANT old variant of >TURBAN
TURBANTS >TURBANT
TURBARIES >TURBARY
TURBARY n land where peat or turf is cut or has been cut
TURBETH variant of >TURPETH
TURBETHS >TURBETH
TURBID adj muddy, not clear
TURBIDITE n sediment deposited by a turbidity current
TURBIDITY >TURBID
TURBIDLY >TURBID
TURBINAL same as >TURBINATE
TURBINALS >TURBINAL
TURBINATE adj of or relating to any of the thin scroll-shaped bones situated on the walls of the nasal passages ▷ n turbinate bone
TURBINE n machine or generator driven by gas, water, etc turning blades
TURBINED adj having a turbine
TURBINES >TURBINE
TURBIT n crested breed of domestic pigeon
TURBITH variant of >TURPETH

**TURBITHS** >TURBITH
**TURBITS** >TURBIT
**TURBO** *n* compressor in an engine
**TURBOCAR** *n* car driven by a gas turbine
**TURBOCARS** >TURBOCAR
**TURBOFAN** *n* engine in which a large fan driven by a turbine forces air rearwards to increase the thrust
**TURBOFANS** >TURBOFAN
**TURBOJET** *n* gas turbine in which the exhaust gases provide the propulsive thrust to drive an aircraft
**TURBOJETS** >TURBOJET
**TURBOND** *old variant of* >TURBAN
**TURBONDS** >TURBOND
**TURBOPROP** *n* gas turbine for driving an aircraft propeller
**TURBOS** >TURBO
**TURBOT** *n* large European edible flatfish
**TURBOTS** >TURBOT
**TURBULENT** *adj* involving a lot of sudden changes and conflicting elements
**TURCOPOLE** *n* lightly armed and highly mobile class of Crusader
**TURD** *n* piece of excrement
**TURDINE** *adj* of, relating to, or characteristic of thrushes
**TURDION** *variant of* >TORDION
**TURDIONS** >TURDION
**TURDOID** *same as* >TURDINE
**TURDS** >TURD
**TUREEN** *n* serving dish for soup
**TUREENS** >TUREEN
**TURF** *n* short thick even grass ▷ *vb* cover with turf
**TURFED** >TURF
**TURFEN** *adj* made of turf
**TURFGRASS** *n* grass grown for lawns
**TURFIER** >TURFY
**TURFIEST** >TURFY
**TURFINESS** >TURFY
**TURFING** >TURF
**TURFINGS** >TURF
**TURFITE** *same as* >TURFMAN
**TURFITES** >TURFITE
**TURFLESS** >TURF
**TURFLIKE** >TURF
**TURFMAN** *n* person devoted to horse racing
**TURFMEN** >TURFMAN
**TURFS** >TURF
**TURFSKI** *n* ski down a grassy hill on skis modified with integral wheels
**TURFSKIS** >TURFSKI
**TURFY** *adj* of, covered with, or resembling turf
**TURGENCY** >TURGENT
**TURGENT** *obsolete word for* >TURGID
**TURGENTLY** >TURGENT
**TURGID** *adj* (of language) pompous
**TURGIDER** >TURGID
**TURGIDEST** >TURGID
**TURGIDITY** >TURGID
**TURGIDLY** >TURGID
**TURGITE** *n* red or black mineral consisting of hydrated ferric oxide
**TURGITES** >TURGITE
**TURGOR** *n* normal rigid state of a cell, caused by pressure of the cell contents against the cell wall or membrane
**TURGORS** >TURGOR
**TURION** *n* perennating bud produced by many aquatic plants
**TURIONS** >TURION
**TURISTA** *n* traveller's diarrhoea
**TURISTAS** >TURISTA
**TURK** *n* obsolete derogatory term for a violent, brutal, or domineering person
**TURKEY** *n* large bird bred for food
**TURKEYS** >TURKEY
**TURKIES** *old form of* >TURQUOISE
**TURKIESES** >TURKIES
**TURKIS** *old form of* >TURQUOISE
**TURKISES** >TURKIS
**TURKOIS** *old form of* >TURQUOISE
**TURKOISES** >TURKOIS
**TURKS** >TURK
**TURLOUGH** *n* seasonal lake or pond
**TURLOUGHS** >TURLOUGH
**TURM** *n* troop of horsemen
**TURME** *variant of* >TURM
**TURMERIC** *n* yellow spice obtained from the root of an Asian plant
**TURMERICS** >TURMERIC
**TURMES** >TURME
**TURMOIL** *n* agitation or confusion ▷ *vb* make or become turbulent
**TURMOILED** >TURMOIL
**TURMOILS** >TURMOIL
**TURMS** >TURM
**TURN** *vb* change the position or direction (of) ▷ *n* turning
**TURNABLE** >TURN
**TURNABOUT** *n* act of turning so as to face a different direction
**TURNAGAIN** *n* revolution
**TURNBACK** *n* one who turns back (from a challenge, for example)
**TURNBACKS** >TURNBACK
**TURNCOAT** *n* person who deserts one party or cause to join another
**TURNCOATS** >TURNCOAT
**TURNCOCK** *n* (formerly) official employed to turn on the water for the mains supply
**TURNCOCKS** >TURNCOCK
**TURNDOWN** *vb, adj*
**TURNDOWN** capable of being or designed to be folded or doubled down *n* instance of turning down
**TURNDOWNS** >TURNDOWN
**TURNDUN** *another name for* >TUNDUN
**TURNDUNS** >TURNDUN
**TURNED** >TURN
**TURNER** *n* person or thing that turns, esp a person who operates a lathe
**TURNERIES** >TURNERY
**TURNERS** >TURNER
**TURNERY** *n* objects made on a lathe
**TURNHALL** *n* building in which gymnastics is taught and practised
**TURNHALLS** >TURNHALL
**TURNING** *n* road or path leading off a main route
**TURNINGS** >TURNING
**TURNIP** *n* root vegetable with orange or white flesh ▷ *vb* sow (a field) with turnips
**TURNIPED** >TURNIP
**TURNIPING** >TURNIP
**TURNIPS** >TURNIP
**TURNKEY** *n* jailer ▷ *adj* denoting a project, as in civil engineering, in which a single contractor has responsibility for the complete job from the start to the time of installation or occupancy
**TURNKEYS** >TURNKEY
**TURNOFF** *n*
**TURN OFF** *n* a road or other way branching off from the main
**TURNOFFS** >TURNOFF
**TURNON** *n* something sexually exciting
**TURNONS** >TURNON
**TURNOUT** *n* number of people appearing at a gathering
**TURNOUTS** >TURNOUT
**TURNOVER** *n* total sales made by a business over a certain period
**TURNOVERS** >TURNOVER
**TURNPIKE** *n* road where a toll is collected at barriers
**TURNPIKES** >TURNPIKE
**TURNROUND** *n* act or process in which a ship, aircraft, etc, unloads passengers and freight at end of a trip and reloads for next trip
**TURNS** >TURN
**TURNSKIN** *n* old name for a werewolf
**TURNSKINS** >TURNSKIN
**TURNSOLE** *n* any of various plants having flowers that are said to turn towards the sun
**TURNSOLES** >TURNSOLE
**TURNSPIT** *n* (formerly) a servant or small dog whose job was to turn the spit on which meat, poultry, etc, was roasting
**TURNSPITS** >TURNSPIT
**TURNSTILE** *n* revolving gate for admitting one person at a time
**TURNSTONE** *n* shore bird
**TURNTABLE** *n* revolving platform
**TURNUP** *n* the turned-up fold at the bottom of some trouser legs
**TURNUPS** >TURNUP
**TUROPHILE** *n* person who loves cheese
**TURPETH** *n* convolvulaceous plant of the East Indies, having roots with purgative properties
**TURPETHS** >TURPETH
**TURPITUDE** *n* wickedness
**TURPS** *n* colourless, flammable liquid
**TURQUOIS** *variant of* >TURQUOISE
**TURQUOISE** *adj* blue-green ▷ *n* blue-green precious stone
**TURRET** *n* small tower
**TURRETED** *adj* having or resembling a turret or turrets
**TURRETS** >TURRET
**TURRIBANT** *old variant of* >TURBAN
**TURRICAL** *adj* of, relating to, or resembling a turret
**TURTLE** *n* sea tortoise
**TURTLED** >TURTLE
**TURTLER** >TURTLE
**TURTLERS** >TURTLE
**TURTLES** >TURTLE
**TURTLING** >TURTLE
**TURTLINGS** >TURTLE
**TURVES** >TURF
**TUSCHE** *n* substance used in lithography for drawing the design and as a resist in silk-screen printing and lithography
**TUSCHES** >TUSCHE
**TUSH** *interj* exclamation of disapproval or contempt ▷ *n* small tusk ▷ *vb* utter the interjection "tush"
**TUSHED** >TUSH
**TUSHERIES** >TUSHERY
**TUSHERY** *n* use of affectedly archaic language in novels, etc
**TUSHES** >TUSH
**TUSHIE** *n* pair of buttocks
**TUSHIES** >TUSHIE
**TUSHING** >TUSH
**TUSHKAR** *variant of* >TUSKAR
**TUSHKARS** >TUSHKAR
**TUSHKER** *variant of* >TUSKAR

TUSHKERS >TUSHKER
TUSHY *variant of* >TUSHIE
TUSK *n* long pointed tooth of an elephant, walrus, etc ▷ *vb* stab, tear, or gore with the tusks
TUSKAR *n* peat-cutting spade
TUSKARS >TUSKAR
TUSKED >TUSK
TUSKER *n* any animal with prominent tusks, esp a wild boar or elephant
TUSKERS >TUSKER
TUSKIER >TUSK
TUSKIEST >TUSK
TUSKING >TUSK
TUSKINGS >TUSK
TUSKLESS >TUSK
TUSKLIKE >TUSK
TUSKS >TUSK
TUSKY >TUSK
TUSSAH *same as* >TUSSORE
TUSSAHS >TUSSAH
TUSSAL >TUSSIS
TUSSAR *variant of* >TUSSORE
TUSSARS >TUSSAR
TUSSEH *variant of* >TUSSORE
TUSSEHS >TUSSEH
TUSSER *same as* >TUSSORE
TUSSERS >TUSSER
TUSSES >TUSSIS
TUSSIS *technical name for* *a* >COUGH
TUSSISES >TUSSIS
TUSSIVE >TUSSIS
TUSSLE *vb* fight or scuffle ▷ *n* energetic fight, struggle, or argument
TUSSLED >TUSSLE
TUSSLES >TUSSLE
TUSSLING >TUSSLE
TUSSOCK *n* tuft of grass
TUSSOCKED *adj* having tussocks
TUSSOCKS >TUSSOCK
TUSSOCKY >TUSSOCK
TUSSOR *variant of* >TUSSORE
TUSSORE *n* strong coarse brownish Indian silk obtained from the cocoons of an Oriental saturniid silkworm
TUSSORES >TUSSORE
TUSSORS >TUSSOR
TUSSUCK *variant of* >TUSSOCK
TUSSUCKS >TUSSUCK
TUSSUR *variant of* >TUSSORE
TUSSURS >TUSSUR
TUT *interj* an exclamation of mild reprimand, disapproval, or surprise ▷ *vb* express disapproval by the exclamation of "tut-tut." ▷ *n* payment system based on measurable work done rather that time spent doing it
TUTANIA *n* alloy of low melting point containing tin, antimony, copper and used mostly for decorative purposes

TUTANIAS >TUTANIA
TUTEE *n* one who is tutored, esp in a university
TUTEES >TUTEE
TUTELAGE *n* instruction or guidance, esp by a tutor
TUTELAGES >TUTELAGE
TUTELAR *same as* >TUTELARY
TUTELARS >TUTELAR
TUTELARY *adj* having the role of guardian or protector ▷ *n* tutelary person, deity, or saint
TUTENAG *n* zinc alloy
TUTENAGS >TUTENAG
TUTIORISM *n* (in Roman Catholic moral theology) the doctrine that in cases of moral doubt it is best to follow the safer course or that in agreement with the law
TUTIORIST >TUTIORISM
TUTMAN *n* one who does tutwork
TUTMEN >TUTMAN
TUTOR *n* person teaching individuals or small groups ▷ *vb* act as a tutor to
TUTORAGE >TUTOR
TUTORAGES >TUTOR
TUTORED >TUTOR
TUTORESS *n* female tutor
TUTORIAL *n* period of instruction with a tutor ▷ *adj* of or relating to a tutor
TUTORIALS >TUTORIAL
TUTORING >TUTOR
TUTORINGS >TUTOR
TUTORISE *variant spelling of* >TUTORIZE
TUTORISED >TUTORISE
TUTORISES >TUTORISE
TUTORISM >TUTOR
TUTORISMS >TUTOR
TUTORIZE *vb* tutor
TUTORIZED >TUTOR
TUTORIZES >TUTORIZE
TUTORS >TUTOR
TUTORSHIP >TUTOR
TUTOYED >TUTOY
TUTOYER *vb* speak to someone on familiar terms
TUTOYERED >TUTOYER
TUTOYERS >TUTOYER
TUTRESS *same as* >TUTORESS
TUTRESSES >TUTRESS
TUTRICES >TUTRIX
TUTRIX *n* female tutor; tutoress
TUTRIXES >TUTRIX
TUTS *Scots version of* >TUT
TUTSAN *n* woodland shrub of Europe and W Asia
TUTSANS >TUTSAN
TUTSED >TUTS
TUTSES >TUTS
TUTSING >TUTS
TUTTED >TUT
TUTTI *adv* be performed

by the whole orchestra or choir ▷ *n* piece of tutti music
TUTTIES >TUTTY
TUTTING >TUT
TUTTINGS >TUT
TUTTIS >TUTTI
TUTTY *n* finely powdered impure zinc oxide obtained from the flues of zinc-smelting furnaces and used as a polishing powder
TUTU *n* short stiff skirt worn by ballerinas
TUTUED *adj* wearing tutu
TUTUS >TUTU
TUTWORK *n* work paid using a tut system
TUTWORKER >TUTWORK
TUTWORKS >TUTWORK
TUX *short for* >TUXEDO
TUXEDO *n* dinner jacket
TUXEDOED *adj* wearing a tuxedo
TUXEDOES >TUXEDO
TUXEDOS >TUXEDO
TUXES >TUX
TUYER *variant of* >TUYERE
TUYERE *n* water-cooled nozzle through which air is blown into a cupola, blast furnace, or forge
TUYERES >TUYERE
TUYERS >TUYER
TUZZ *n* tuft or clump of hair
TUZZES >TUZZ
TWA *Scots word for* >TWO
TWADDLE *n* silly or pretentious talk or writing ▷ *vb* talk or write in a silly or pretentious way
TWADDLED >TWADDLE
TWADDLER >TWADDLE
TWADDLERS >TWADDLE
TWADDLES >TWADDLE
TWADDLIER >TWADDLE
TWADDLING >TWADDLE
TWADDLY >TWADDLE
TWAE *same as* >TWA
TWAES >TWAE
TWAFALD *Scots variant of* >TWOFOLD
TWAIN *n* two
TWAINS >TWAIN
TWAITE *n* herring-like food fish
TWAITES >TWAITE
TWAL *n* twelve
TWALPENNY *n* shilling
TWALS >TWAL
TWANG *n* sharp ringing sound ▷ *vb* (cause to) make a twang
TWANGED >TWANG
TWANGER >TWANG
TWANGERS >TWANG
TWANGIER >TWANG
TWANGIEST >TWANG
TWANGING >TWANG
TWANGINGS >TWANG
TWANGLE *vb* make a continuous loose twanging sound (on a

musical instrument, for example)
TWANGLED >TWANGLE
TWANGLER >TWANGLE
TWANGLERS >TWANGLE
TWANGLES >TWANGLE
TWANGLING >TWANGLE
TWANGS >TWANG
TWANGY >TWANG
TWANK *vb* make an sharply curtailed twang
TWANKAY *n* variety of Chinese green tea
TWANKAYS >TWANKAY
TWANKIES >TWANKY
TWANKS >TWANK
TWANKY *same as* >TWANKAY
TWAS >TWA
TWASOME *same as* >TWOSOME
TWASOMES >TWASOME
TWAT *n* taboo term for female genitals
TWATS >TWAT
TWATTLE *rare word for* >TWADDLE
TWATTLED >TWATTLE
TWATTLER >TWATTLE
TWATTLERS >TWATTLE
TWATTLES >TWATTLE
TWATTLING >TWATTLE
TWAY *old variant of* >TWAIN
TWAYBLADE *n* type of orchid
TWAYS >TWAY
TWEAK *vb* pinch or twist sharply ▷ *n* tweaking
TWEAKED >TWEAK
TWEAKER *n* engineer's small screwdriver, used for fine adjustments
TWEAKERS >TWEAKER
TWEAKIER >TWEAK
TWEAKIEST >TWEAK
TWEAKING >TWEAK
TWEAKINGS >TWEAK
TWEAKS >TWEAK
TWEAKY >TWEAK
TWEE *adj* too sentimental, sweet, or pretty
TWEED *n* thick woollen cloth
TWEEDIER >TWEEDY
TWEEDIEST >TWEEDY
TWEEDLE *vb* improvise aimlessly on a musical instrument
TWEEDLED >TWEEDLE
TWEEDLER >TWEEDLE
TWEEDLERS >TWEEDLE
TWEEDLES >TWEEDLE
TWEEDLING >TWEEDLE
TWEEDS >TWEED
TWEEDY *adj* of or made of tweed
TWEEL *variant of* >TWILL
TWEELED >TWEEL
TWEELING >TWEEL
TWEELS >TWEEL
TWEELY >TWEE
TWEEN *same as* >BETWEEN
TWEENAGER *n* child of approximately eight to fourteen years of age
TWEENER *same*

*as* >TWEENAGER
THEENERS >TWEENER
THEENESS >TWEE
THEENIE *same as* >TWEENY
THEENIES >TWEENY
THEENS >TWEEN
THEENY *n* maid who assists both cook and housemaid
THEER *variant of* >TWIRE
THEERED >TWEER
THEERING >TWEER
THEERS >TWEER
THEEST >TWEE
TWEET *vb* chirp ▷ *interj* imitation of the thin chirping sound made by small birds
TWEETED >TWEET
TWEETER *n* loudspeaker reproducing high-frequency sounds
TWEETERS >TWEETER
TWEETING >TWEET
TWEETS >TWEET
TWEEZE *vb* take hold of or pluck (hair, small objects, etc) with or as if with tweezers
TWEEZED >TWEEZE
TWEEZER *same as* >TWEEZERS
TWEEZERS *pl n* small pincer-like tool
TWEEZES >TWEEZE
TWEEZING >TWEEZE
TWELFTH *n* (of) number twelve in a series ▷ *adj* of or being number twelve in a series
TWELFTHLY *adv* after the eleventh person, position, event, etc
TWELFTHS >TWELFTH
TWELVE *n* two more than ten ▷ *adj* amounting to twelve ▷ *determiner* amounting to twelve
TWELVEMO *another word for* >DUODECIMO
TWELVEMOS >TWELVEMO
TWELVES >TWELVE
TWENTIES >TWENTY
TWENTIETH *adj* coming after the nineteenth in numbering or counting order, position, time, etc ▷ *n* one of 20 approximately equal parts of something
TWENTY *n* two times ten ▷ *adj* amounting to twenty ▷ *determiner* amounting to twenty
TWENTYISH *adj* around 20
TWERP *n* silly person
TWERPIER >TWERP
TWERPIEST >TWERP
TWERPS >TWERP
TWERPY >TWERP
TWIBIL *same as* >TWIBILL
TWIBILL *n* mattock with a blade shaped like an adze at one end and like an axe at the other

TWIBILLS >TWIBILL
TWIBILS >TWIBIL
TWICE *adv* two times
TWICER *n* someone who does something twice
TWICERS >TWICER
TWICHILD *n* person in his or her dotage
TWIDDLE *vb* fiddle or twirl in an idle way ▷ *n* act or instance of twiddling
TWIDDLED >TWIDDLE
TWIDDLER >TWIDDLE
TWIDDLERS >TWIDDLE
TWIDDLES >TWIDDLE
TWIDDLIER >TWIDDLE
TWIDDLING >TWIDDLE
TWIDDLY >TWIDDLE
TWIER *variant of* >TUYERE
TWIERS >TWIER
TWIFOLD *variant of* >TWOFOLD
TWIFORKED *adj* having two forks; bifurcate
TWIFORMED *adj* having two forms
TWIG *n* small branch or shoot ▷ *vb* realize or understand
TWIGGED >TWIG
TWIGGEN *adj* made of twigs
TWIGGER >TWIG
TWIGGIER >TWIGGY
TWIGGIEST >TWIGGY
TWIGGING >TWIG
TWIGGY *adj* of or relating to a twig or twigs
TWIGHT *old variant of* >TWIT
TWIGHTED >TWIGHT
TWIGHTING >TWIGHT
TWIGHTS >TWIGHT
TWIGLESS >TWIG
TWIGLIKE >TWIG
TWIGLOO *n* temporary shelter made from twigs, branches, leaves, etc
TWIGLOOS >TWIGLOO
TWIGS >TWIG
TWIGSOME *adj* covered with twigs; twiggy
TWILIGHT *n* soft dim light just after sunset ▷ *adj* of or relating to the period towards the end of the day
TWILIGHTS >TWILIGHT
TWILIT >TWILIGHT
TWILL *n* fabric woven to produce parallel ridges ▷ *adj* (in textiles) of or designating a weave in which the weft yarns are worked around two or more warp yarns to produce an effect of parallel diagonal lines or ribs ▷ *vb* weave in this fashion
TWILLED >TWILL
TWILLIES >TWILLY
TWILLING >TWILL
TWILLINGS >TWILL
TWILLS >TWILL
TWILLY *n* machine having

a system of revolving spikes for opening and cleaning raw textile fibres
TWILT *variant of* >QUILT
TWILTED >TWILT
TWILTING >TWILT
TWILTS >TWILT
TWIN *n* one of a pair, esp of two children born at one birth ▷ *vb* pair or be paired
TWINBERRY *n* creeping wooden plant
TWINBORN *adj* born as a twin
TWINE *n* string or cord ▷ *vb* twist or coil round
TWINED >TWINE
TWINER >TWINE
TWINERS >TWINE
TWINES >TWINE
TWINGE *n* sudden sharp pain or emotional pang ▷ *vb* have or cause to have a twinge
TWINGED >TWINGE
TWINGEING >TWINGE
TWINGES >TWINGE
TWINGING >TWINGE
TWINIER >TWINE
TWINIEST >TWINE
TWINIGHT *adj* (of a baseball double-header) held in the late afternoon and evening
TWINING >TWINE
TWININGLY >TWINE
TWININGS >TWINE
TWINJET *n* jet aircraft with two engines
TWINJETS >TWINJET
TWINK *n* white correction fluid for deleting written text ▷ *vb* twinkle
TWINKED >TWINK
TWINKIE *n* stupid person
TWINKIES >TWINKIE
TWINKING >TWINK
TWINKLE *vb* shine brightly but intermittently ▷ *n* flickering brightness
TWINKLED >TWINKLE
TWINKLER >TWINKLE
TWINKLERS >TWINKLE
TWINKLES >TWINKLE
TWINKLING *n* very short time
TWINKLY >TWINKLE
TWINKS >TWINK
TWINLING *old name for* >TWIN
TWINLINGS >TWINLING
TWINNED >TWIN
TWINNING >TWIN
TWINNINGS >TWIN
TWINS >TWIN
TWINSET *n* matching jumper and cardigan
TWINSETS >TWINSET
TWINSHIP *n* condition of being a twin or twins
TWINSHIPS >TWIN
TWINTER *n* animal that is 2 years old
TWINTERS >TWINTER

TWINY >TWINE
TWIRE *vb* look intently at with (or as if with) difficulty
TWIRED >TWIRE
TWIRES >TWIRE
TWIRING >TWIRE
TWIRL *vb* turn or spin around quickly ▷ *n* whirl or twist
TWIRLED >TWIRL
TWIRLER >TWIRL
TWIRLERS >TWIRL
TWIRLIER >TWIRL
TWIRLIEST >TWIRL
TWIRLING >TWIRL
TWIRLS >TWIRL
TWIRLY >TWIRL
TWIRP *same as* >TWERP
TWIRPIER >TWIRP
TWIRPIEST >TWIRP
TWIRPS >TWIRP
TWIRPY >TWIRP
TWISCAR *variant of* >TUSKAR
TWISCARS >TWISCAR
TWIST *vb* turn out of the natural position ▷ *n* twisting
TWISTABLE >TWIST
TWISTED >TWIST
TWISTER *n* swindler
TWISTERS >TWISTER
TWISTIER >TWIST
TWISTIEST >TWIST
TWISTING >TWIST
TWISTINGS >TWIST
TWISTOR *n* variable corresponding to the coordinates of a point in space and time
TWISTORS >TWISTOR
TWISTS >TWIST
TWISTY >TWIST
TWIT *vb* poke fun at (someone) ▷ *n* foolish person
TWITCH *vb* move spasmodically ▷ *n* nervous muscular spasm
TWITCHED >TWITCH
TWITCHER *n* bird-watcher who tries to spot as many rare varieties as possible
TWITCHERS >TWITCHER
TWITCHES >TWITCH
TWITCHIER >TWITCHY
TWITCHILY >TWITCHY
TWITCHING >TWITCH
TWITCHY *adj* nervous, worried, and ill-at-ease
TWITE *n* N European finch with a brown streaked plumage
TWITES >TWITE
TWITS >TWIT
TWITTED >TWIT
TWITTEN *n* narrow alleyway
TWITTENS >TWITTEN
TWITTER *vb* (of birds) utter chirping sounds ▷ *n* act or sound of twittering
TWITTERED >TWITTER
TWITTERER >TWITTER

**TWITTERS** > TWITTER
**TWITTERY** > TWITTER
**TWITTING** > TWIT
**TWITTINGS** > TWIT
**TWIXT** same as > BETWIXT
**TWIZZLE** vb spin around
**TWIZZLED** > TWIZZLE
**TWIZZLES** > TWIZZLE
**TWIZZLING** > TWIZZLE
**TWO** n one more than one
**TWOCCER** > TWOCCING
**TWOCCERS** > TWOCCING
**TWOCCING** n act of breaking into a motor vehicle and driving it away
**TWOCCINGS** > TWOCCING
**TWOCKER** > TWOCCING
**TWOCKERS** > TWOCCING
**TWOCKING** same as > TWOCCING
**TWOCKINGS** > TWOCKING
**TWOER** n (in a game) something that scores two
**TWOERS** > TWOER
**TWOFER** n single ticket allowing the buyer entrance to two events, attractions, etc, for substantially less than the cost were he or she to pay for each individually
**TWOFERS** > TWOFER
**TWOFOLD** adj having twice as many or as much ▷ adv by twice as many or as much ▷ n folding piece of theatrical scenery
**TWOFOLDS** > TWOFOLD
**TWONESS** n state or condition of being two
**TWONESSES** > TWONESS
**TWONIE** same as > TOONIE
**TWONIES** > TWONIE
**TWOONIE** variant of > TOONIE
**TWOONIES** > TWOONIE
**TWOPENCE** n sum of two pennies
**TWOPENCES** > TWOPENCE
**TWOPENNY** adj cheap or tawdry
**TWOS** > TWO
**TWOSEATER** n vehicle providing seats for two people
**TWOSOME** n group of two people
**TWOSOMES** > TWOSOME
**TWOSTROKE** adj relating to or designating an internal-combustion engine whose piston makes two strokes for every explosion
**TWP** adj stupid
**TWYER** same as > TUYERE
**TWYERE** variant of > TUYERE
**TWYERES** > TWYERE
**TWYERS** > TWYER
**TWYFOLD** adj twofold
**TYCHISM** n theory that chance is an objective reality at work in the universe, esp in evolutionary adaptations

**TYCHISMS** > TYCHISM
**TYCOON** n powerful wealthy businessman; shogun
**TYCOONATE** n office or rule of a tycoon
**TYCOONERY** > TYCOON
**TYCOONS** > TYCOON
**TYDE** old variant of the past participle of > TIE
**TYE** n trough used in mining to separate valuable material from dross ▷ vb (in mining) isolate valuable material from dross using a tye
**TYED** > TYE
**TYEE** n large northern Pacific salmon
**TYEES** > TYEE
**TYEING** > TYE
**TYER** > TYE
**TYERS** > TYE
**TYES** > TYE
**TYG** n mug with two handles
**TYGS** > TYG
**TYIN** variant of > TYIYN
**TYING** > TIE
**TYIYN** n money unit of Kyrgyzstan
**TYKE** n often offensive term for small cheeky child
**TYKES** > TYKE
**TYKISH** > TYKE
**TYLECTOMY** n excision of a breast tumour
**TYLER** variant of > TILER
**TYLERS** > TYLER
**TYLOPOD** n mammal with padded feet, such as a camel or llama
**TYLOPODS** > TYLOPOD
**TYLOSES** > TYLOSIS
**TYLOSIN** n broad spectrum antibiotic
**TYLOSINS** > TYLOSIN
**TYLOSIS** n bladder-like outgrowth from certain cells in woody tissue that extends into and blocks adjacent conducting xylem cells
**TYLOTE** n knobbed sponge spicule
**TYLOTES** > TYLOTE
**TYMBAL** same as > TIMBAL
**TYMBALS** > TYMBAL
**TYMP** n blast furnace outlet through which molten metal flows
**TYMPAN** same as > TYMPANUM
**TYMPANA** > TYMPANUM
**TYMPANAL** adj relating to the tympanum
**TYMPANI** same as > TIMPANI
**TYMPANIC** adj of, relating to, or having a tympanum ▷ n part of the temporal bone in the mammalian skull that surrounds the auditory canal
**TYMPANICS** > TYMPANIC
**TYMPANIES** > TYMPANY

**TYMPANIST** > TIMPANI
**TYMPANO** > TYMPANI
**TYMPANS** > TYMPAN
**TYMPANUM** n cavity of the middle ear
**TYMPANUMS** > TYMPANUM
**TYMPANY** n distention of the abdomen
**TYMPS** > TYMP
**TYND** variant of > TIND
**TYNDE** variant of > TIND
**TYNE** variant of > TINE
**TYNED** variant of > TYNE
**TYNES** > TYNE
**TYNING** > TYNE
**TYPABLE** > TYPE
**TYPAL** rare word for > TYPICAL
**TYPE** n class or category ▷ vb print with a typewriter or word processor
**TYPEABLE** > TYPE
**TYPEBAR** n one of the bars in a typewriter that carry the type and are operated by keys
**TYPEBARS** > TYPEBAR
**TYPECASE** n compartmental tray for storing printer's type
**TYPECASES** > TYPECASE
**TYPECAST** vb continually cast (an actor or actress) in similar roles
**TYPECASTS** > TYPECAST
**TYPED** > TYPE
**TYPEFACE** n style of the type
**TYPEFACES** > TYPEFACE
**TYPES** > TYPE
**TYPESET** vb set (text for printing) in type
**TYPESETS** > TYPESET
**TYPESTYLE** another word for > TYPEFACE
**TYPEWRITE** vb write by means of a typewriter
**TYPEWROTE** > TYPEWRITE
**TYPEY** variant of > TYPY
**TYPHLITIC** > TYPHLITIS
**TYPHLITIS** n inflammation of the caecum
**TYPHOID** adj of or relating to typhoid fever
**TYPHOIDAL** > TYPHOID
**TYPHOIDIN** n culture of dead typhoid bacillus for injection into the skin to test for typhoid fever
**TYPHOIDS** > TYPHOID
**TYPHON** n whirlwind
**TYPHONIAN** > TYPHON
**TYPHONIC** > TYPHOON
**TYPHONS** > TYPHON
**TYPHOON** n violent tropical storm
**TYPHOONS** > TYPHOON
**TYPHOSE** adj relating to typhoid
**TYPHOUS** > TYPHUS
**TYPHUS** n infectious feverish disease

**TYPHUSES** > TYPHUS
**TYPIC** same as > TYPICAL
**TYPICAL** adj true to type, characteristic
**TYPICALLY** > TYPICAL
**TYPIER** > TYPY
**TYPIEST** > TYPY
**TYPIFIED** > TYPIFY
**TYPIFIER** > TYPIFY
**TYPIFIERS** > TYPIFY
**TYPIFIES** > TYPIFY
**TYPIFY** vb be typical of
**TYPIFYING** > TYPIFY
**TYPING** n work or activity of using a typewriter or word processor
**TYPINGS** > TYPING
**TYPIST** n person who types with a typewriter or word processor
**TYPISTS** > TYPIST
**TYPO** n typographical error
**TYPOGRAPH** n person skilled in the art of composing type and printing from it
**TYPOLOGIC** > TYPOLOGY
**TYPOLOGY** n doctrine or study of types or of the correspondence between them and the realities which they typify
**TYPOMANIA** n obsession with typology
**TYPOS** > TYPO
**TYPP** n unit of thickness of yarn
**TYPPS** > TYPP
**TYPTO** vb learn Greek conjugations
**TYPTOED** > TYPTO
**TYPTOING** > TYPTO
**TYPTOS** > TYPTO
**TYPY** adj (of an animal) typifying the breed
**TYRAMINE** n colourless crystalline amine derived from phenol
**TYRAMINES** > TYRAMINE
**TYRAN** vb act as a tyrant
**TYRANED** > TYRAN
**TYRANING** > TYRAN
**TYRANNE** variant of > TYRAN
**TYRANNED** > TYRANNE
**TYRANNES** > TYRANNE
**TYRANNESS** n female tyrant
**TYRANNIC** > TYRANNY
**TYRANNIES** > TYRANNY
**TYRANNING** > TYRANNE
**TYRANNIS** n tyrannical government
**TYRANNISE** same as > TYRANNIZE
**TYRANNIZE** vb exert power (over) oppressively or cruelly
**TYRANNOUS** > TYRANNY
**TYRANNY** n tyrannical rule
**TYRANS** > TYRAN
**TYRANT** n oppressive or cruel ruler ▷ vb act the tyrant
**TYRANTED** > TYRANT
**TYRANTING** > TYRANT

**TYRANTS** > TYRANT
**TYRE** *n* rubber ring, usu inflated, over the rim of a vehicle's wheel to grip the road ▷ *vb* fit a tyre or tyres to (a wheel, vehicle, etc)
**TYRED** > TYRE
**TYRELESS** > TYRE
**TYRES** > TYRE
**TYRING** > TYRE
**TYRO** *n* novice or beginner
**TYROCIDIN** *n* antibiotic
**TYROES** > TYRO
**TYRONES** > TYRO
**TYRONIC** > TYRO
**TYROPITTA** *n* Greek cheese pie
**TYROS** > TYRO
**TYROSINE** *n* aromatic nonessential amino acid
**TYROSINES** > TYROSINE
**TYSTIE** *n* black guillemot
**TYSTIES** > TYSTIE
**TYTE** *variant spelling of* > TITE
**TYTHE** *variant of* > TITHE
**TYTHED** > TYTHE
**TYTHES** > TYTHE
**TYTHING** > TYTHE
**TZADDIK** *variant of* > ZADDIK
**TZADDIKIM** > TZADDIK
**TZADDIKS** > TZADDIK
**TZADDIQ** *variant of* > ZADDIK
**TZADDIQIM** > TZADDIQ
**TZADDIQS** > TZADDIQ
**TZAR** *same as* > TSAR
**TZARDOM** > TZAR
**TZARDOMS** > TZAR
**TZAREVNA** *variant of* > TSAREVNA
**TZAREVNAS** > TZAREVNA
**TZARINA** *variant of* > TSARINA
**TZARINAS** > TZARINA
**TZARISM** *variant of* > TSARISM
**TZARISMS** > TZARISM
**TZARIST** > TZARISM
**TZARISTS** > TZARISM
**TZARITZA** *variant of* > TSARITSA
**TZARITZAS** > TZARITZA
**TZARS** > TZAR
**TZATZIKI** *n* Greek dip made from yogurt, chopped cucumber, and mint
**TZATZIKIS** > TZATZIKI
**TZETSE** *variant of* > TSETSE
**TZETSES** > TZETSE
**TZETZE** *variant of* > TSETSE
**TZETZES** > TZETZE
**TZIGANE** *n* type of Gypsy music
**TZIGANES** > TZIGANE
**TZIGANIES** > TZIGANY
**TZIGANY** *variant of* > TZIGANE
**TZIMMES** *n* traditional Jewish stew
**TZITZIS** *variant of* > TSITSITH
**TZITZIT** *variant of* > TZITZIT
**TZITZITH** *variant*

*of* > TSITSITH
**TZURIS** *variant of* > TSURIS

# Uu

UAKARI n type of monkey
UAKARIS > UAKARI
UBEROUS adj abundant
UBERTIES > UBERTY
UBERTY n abundance
UBIETIES > UBIETY
UBIETY n condition of
  being in a particular place
UBIQUE adv everywhere
UBIQUITIN n type of
  polypeptide
UBIQUITY n state
  of apparently being
  everywhere at once;
  omnipresence
UCKERS n type of naval
  game
UDAL n form of freehold
  possession of land existing
  in northern Europe
  before the introduction
  of the feudal system and
  still used in Orkney and
  Shetland
UDALLER n person
  possessing a udal
UDALLERS > UDALLER
UDALS > UDAL
UDDER n large baglike milk-
  producing gland of cows,
  sheep, or goats
UDDERED > UDDER
UDDERFUL > UDDER
UDDERLESS > UDDER
UDDERS > UDDER
UDO n stout perennial plant
  of Japan and China with
  berry-like black fruits and
  young shoots that are
  edible when blanched
UDOMETER n archaic term
  for an instrument for
  measuring rainfall or

snowfall
UDOMETERS > UDOMETER
UDOMETRIC > UDOMETER
UDOMETRY > UDOMETER
UDON n (in Japanese
  cookery) large noodles
  made of wheat flour
UDONS > UDON
UDOS > UDO
UDS interj God's or God save
UEY n u-turn
UEYS > UEY
UFO n flying saucer
UFOLOGIES > UFOLOGY
UFOLOGIST > UFOLOGY
UFOLOGY n study of UFOs
UFOS > UFO
UG vb hate
UGALI n type of stiff
  porridge made by mixing
  corn meal with boiling
  water: the basic starch
  constituent of a meal
UGALIS > UGALI
UGGED > UG
UGGING > UG
UGH interj exclamation of
  disgust ▷ n sound made
  to indicate disgust
UGHS > UGH
UGLIED > UGLY
UGLIER > UGLY
UGLIES > UGLY
UGLIEST > UGLY
UGLIFIED > UGLIFY
UGLIFIER > UGLIFY
UGLIFIERS > UGLIFY
UGLIFIES > UGLIFY
UGLIFY vb make or become
  ugly or more ugly
UGLIFYING > UGLIFY
UGLILY > UGLY
UGLINESS > UGLY

UGLY adj of unpleasant
  appearance ▷ vb make
  ugly
UGLYING > UGLY
UGS > UG
UGSOME adj loathsome
UH interj used to express
  hesitation
UHLAN n member of a body
  of lancers first employed in
  the Polish army and later
  in W European armies
UHLANS > UHLAN
UHURU n national
  independence
UHURUS > UHURU
UILLEAN as in uillean pipes
  bagpipes developed in
  Ireland and operated by
  squeezing bellows under
  the arm
UINTAHITE same
  as > UINTAITE
UINTAITE n variety of
  asphalt
UINTAITES > UINTAITE
UITLANDER n foreigner
UJAMAA as in ujamaa village
  communally organized
  village in Tanzania
UJAMAAS > UJAMAA
UKASE n (in imperial
  Russia) a decree from the
  tsar
UKASES > UKASE
UKE short form of > UKULELE
UKELELE same as > UKULELE
UKELELES > UKELELE
UKES > UKE
UKULELE n small guitar
  with four strings
UKULELES > UKULELE
ULAMA n body of Muslim

scholars or religious
  leaders
ULAMAS > ULAMA
ULAN same as > UHLAN
ULANS > ULAN
ULCER n open sore on
  the surface of the skin or
  mucous membrane. ▷ vb
  make or become ulcerous
ULCERATE vb make or
  become ulcerous
ULCERATED > ULCERATE
ULCERATES > ULCERATE
ULCERED > ULCER
ULCERING > ULCER
ULCEROUS adj of, like, or
  characterized by ulcers
ULCERS > ULCER
ULE n rubber tree
ULEMA same as > ULAMA
ULEMAS > ULEMA
ULES > ULE
ULEX n variety of shrub
ULEXES > ULEX
ULEXITE n type of mineral
ULEXITES > ULEXITE
ULICON same
  as > EULACHON
ULICONS > ULICON
ULIGINOSE same
  as > ULIGINOUS
ULIGINOUS adj marshy
ULIKON same
  as > EULACHON
ULIKONS > ULIKON
ULITIS n gingivitis
ULITISES > ULITIS
ULLAGE n volume by which
  a liquid container falls
  short of being full ▷ vb
  create ullage in
ULLAGED > ULLAGE
ULLAGES > ULLAGE

**ULLAGING** >ULLAGE
**ULLING** *n* process of filling
**ULLINGS** >ULLING
**ULMACEOUS** *adj* of, relating to, or belonging to the *Ulmaceae*, a temperate and tropical family of deciduous trees and shrubs having scaly buds, simple serrated leaves, and typically winged fruits: includes the elms
**ULMIN** *n* substance found in decaying vegetation
**ULMINS** >ULMIN
**ULNA** *n* inner and longer of the two bones of the human forearm
**ULNAD** *adv* towards the ulna
**ULNAE** >ULNA
**ULNAR** >ULNA
**ULNARE** *n* bone in the wrist
**ULNARIA** >ULNARE
**ULNAS** >ULNA
**ULOSES** >ULOSIS
**ULOSIS** *n* formation of a scar
**ULOTRICHY** *n* state of having woolly or curly hair
**ULPAN** *n* Israeli study centre
**ULPANIM** >ULPAN
**ULSTER** *n* man's heavy double-breasted overcoat
**ULSTERED** *adj* wearing an ulster
**ULSTERS** >ULSTER
**ULTERIOR** *adj* (of an aim, reason, etc) concealed or hidden
**ULTIMA** *n* final syllable of a word
**ULTIMACY** >ULTIMATE
**ULTIMAS** >ULTIMA
**ULTIMATA** >ULTIMATUM
**ULTIMATE** *adj* final in a series or process ▷ *n* most significant, highest, furthest, or greatest thing ▷ *vb* end
**ULTIMATED** >ULTIMATE
**ULTIMATES** >ULTIMATE
**ULTIMATUM** *n* final warning stating that action will be taken unless certain conditions are met
**ULTIMO** *adv* in or during the previous month
**ULTION** *n* vengeance
**ULTIONS** >ULTION
**ULTRA** *n* person who has extreme or immoderate beliefs or opinions ▷ *adj* extreme or immoderate, esp in beliefs or opinions
**ULTRACHIC** *adj* extremely chic
**ULTRACOLD** *adj* extremely cold
**ULTRACOOL** *adj* extremely cool
**ULTRADRY** *adj* extremely dry
**ULTRAFAST** *adj* extremely fast

**ULTRAFINE** *adj* extremely fine
**ULTRAHEAT** *vb* sterilize through extreme heat treatment
**ULTRAHIGH** as in *ultrahigh frequency* radio-frequency band or radio frequency lying between 3000 and 300 megahertz
**ULTRAHIP** *adj* extremely trendy
**ULTRAHOT** *adj* extremely hot
**ULTRAISM** *n* extreme philosophy, belief, or action
**ULTRAISMS** >ULTRAISM
**ULTRAIST** >ULTRAISM
**ULTRAISTS** >ULTRAISM
**ULTRALEFT** *adj* of the extreme political Left or extremely radical
**ULTRALOW** *adj* extremely low
**ULTRAPOSH** *adj* extremely posh
**ULTRAPURE** *adj* extremely pure
**ULTRARARE** *adj* extremely rare
**ULTRARED** *obsolete word for* >INFRARED
**ULTRAREDS** >ULTRARED
**ULTRARICH** *adj* extremely rich
**ULTRAS** >ULTRA
**ULTRASAFE** *adj* extremely safe
**ULTRASLOW** *adj* extremely slow
**ULTRASOFT** *adj* extremely soft
**ULTRATHIN** *adj* extremely thin
**ULTRATINY** *adj* extremely small
**ULTRAWIDE** *adj* extremely wide
**ULU** *n* type of knife
**ULULANT** >ULULATE
**ULULATE** *vb* howl or wail
**ULULATED** >ULULATE
**ULULATES** >ULULATE
**ULULATING** >ULULATE
**ULULATION** >ULULATE
**ULUS** >ULU
**ULVA** *n* genus of seaweed
**ULVAS** >ULVA
**ULYIE** *Scots variant of* >OIL
**ULYIES** >ULYIE
**ULZIE** *Scots variant of* >OIL
**ULZIES** >ULZIE
**UM** *interj* representation of a common sound made when hesitating in speech
**UMAMI** *n* savoury flavour
**UMAMIS** >UMAMI
**UMANGITE** *n* type of mineral
**UMANGITES** >UMANGITE
**UMBEL** *n* umbrella-like flower cluster with the stalks springing from the

central point
**UMBELED** *same as* >UMBELLED
**UMBELLAR** >UMBEL
**UMBELLATE** >UMBEL
**UMBELLED** *adj* having umbels
**UMBELLET** *same as* >UMBELLULE
**UMBELLETS** >UMBELLET
**UMBELLULE** *n* any of the small secondary umbels that make up a compound umbel
**UMBELS** >UMBEL
**UMBER** *adj* dark brown to reddish-brown ▷ *n* type of dark brown earth containing ferric oxide (rust) ▷ *vb* stain with umber
**UMBERED** >UMBER
**UMBERING** >UMBER
**UMBERS** >UMBER
**UMBERY** >UMBER
**UMBILICAL** *adj* of the navel
**UMBILICI** >UMBILICUS
**UMBILICUS** *n* navel
**UMBLE** as in *umble pie* (formerly) a pie made from the heart, entrails, etc, of a deer
**UMBLES** *another term for* >NUMBLES
**UMBO** *n* small hump projecting from the centre of the cap in certain mushrooms
**UMBONAL** >UMBO
**UMBONATE** >UMBO
**UMBONES** >UMBO
**UMBONIC** >UMBO
**UMBOS** >UMBO
**UMBRA** *n* shadow, esp the shadow cast by the moon onto the earth during a solar eclipse
**UMBRACULA** *pl n* umbrella-like structures
**UMBRAE** >UMBRA
**UMBRAGE** *n* displeasure or resentment ▷ *vb* shade
**UMBRAGED** >UMBRAGE
**UMBRAGES** >UMBRAGE
**UMBRAGING** >UMBRAGE
**UMBRAL** >UMBRA
**UMBRAS** >UMBRA
**UMBRATED** *adj* shown in a faint manner
**UMBRATIC** >UMBRA
**UMBRATILE** *adj* shadowy
**UMBRE** *same as* >UMBRETTE
**UMBREL** *n* umbrella
**UMBRELLA** *n* portable device used for protection against rain, consisting of a folding frame covered in material attached to a central rod ▷ *adj* containing or covering many different organizations, ideas, etc
**UMBRELLAS** >UMBRELLA
**UMBRELLO** *same*

*as* >UMBRELLA
**UMBRELLOS** >UMBRELLO
**UMBRELS** >UMBREL
**UMBRERE** *n* helmet visor
**UMBRERES** >UMBRERE
**UMBRES** >UMBRE
**UMBRETTE** *n* African wading bird
**UMBRETTES** >UMBRETTE
**UMBRIERE** *same as* >UMBRERE
**UMBRIERES** >UMBRIERE
**UMBRIL** *same as* >UMBRERE
**UMBRILS** >UMBRIL
**UMBROSE** *same as* >UMBROUS
**UMBROUS** *adj* shady
**UMFAZI** *n* African married woman
**UMFAZIS** >UMFAZI
**UMIAC** *variant of* >UMIAK
**UMIACK** *variant of* >UMIAK
**UMIACKS** >UMIACK
**UMIACS** >UMIAC
**UMIAK** *n* Inuit boat made of skins
**UMIAKS** >UMIAK
**UMIAQ** *same as* >UMIAK
**UMIAQS** >UMIAQ
**UMLAUT** *n* mark (¨) placed over a vowel, esp in German, to indicate a change in its sound ▷ *vb* modify by umlaut
**UMLAUTED** >UMLAUT
**UMLAUTING** >UMLAUT
**UMLAUTS** >UMLAUT
**UMLUNGU** *n* White man: used esp as a term of address
**UMLUNGUS** >UMLUNGU
**UMM** *same as* >UM
**UMP** *short for* >UMPIRE
**UMPED** >UMP
**UMPH** *same as* >HUMPH
**UMPIE** *informal word for* >UMPIRE
**UMPIES** >UMPY
**UMPING** >UMP
**UMPIRAGE** >UMPIRE
**UMPIRAGES** >UMPIRE
**UMPIRE** *n* official who rules on the playing of a game ▷ *vb* act as umpire in (a game)
**UMPIRED** >UMPIRE
**UMPIRES** >UMPIRE
**UMPIRING** >UMPIRE
**UMPS** >UMP
**UMPTEEN** *adj* very many ▷ *determiner* very many
**UMPTEENTH** *adj* latest in a tediously long series
**UMPTIETH** *same as* >UMPTEENTH
**UMPTY** *same as* >UMPTEEN
**UMPY** *same as* >UMPIE
**UMQUHILE** *adv* formerly
**UMTEENTH** *same as* >UMPTEENTH
**UMU** *n* type of oven
**UMWELT** *n* environmental factors, collectively, that are capable of affecting the

behaviour of an animal or individual

**UMWELTS** > UMWELT

**UMWHILE** same as > UMQUHILE

**UN** pron spelling of ONE intended to reflect a dialectal or informal pronunciation

**UNABASHED** adj not ashamed or embarrassed

**UNABATED** adv without any reduction in force ▷ adj without losing any original force or violence

**UNABATING** adj not growing less in strength

**UNABETTED** adj without assistance

**UNABIDING** adj not lasting

**UNABJURED** adj not denied

**UNABLE** adj lacking the necessary power, ability, or authority (to do something)

**UNABORTED** adj not aborted

**UNABRADED** adj not eroded

**UNABUSED** adj not abused

**UNABUSIVE** adj not abusive

**UNACCRUED** adj not accrued

**UNACCUSED** adj not charged with wrongdoing

**UNACERBIC** adj not acerbic

**UNACHING** adj not aching

**UNACIDIC** adj not acidic

**UNACTABLE** adj unable to be acted

**UNACTED** adj not acted or performed

**UNACTIVE** adj inactive

**UNADAPTED** adj not adapted

**UNADDED** adj not added

**UNADEPT** adj not adept

**UNADEPTLY** > UNADEPT

**UNADMIRED** adj not admired

**UNADOPTED** adj (of a road) not maintained by a local authority

**UNADORED** adj not adored

**UNADORNED** adj not decorated

**UNADULT** adj not mature

**UNADVISED** adj rash or unwise

**UNAFRAID** adj not frightened or nervous

**UNAGED** adj not old

**UNAGEING** adj not ageing

**UNAGILE** adj not agile

**UNAGING** same as > UNAGEING

**UNAGREED** adj not agreed

**UNAI** same as > UNAU

**UNAIDABLE** adj unable to be helped

**UNAIDED** adv without any help or assistance ▷ adj without having received any help

**UNAIDEDLY** > UNAIDED

**UNAIMED** adj not aimed or specifically targeted

**UNAIRED** adj not aired

**UNAIS** > UNAI

**UNAKIN** adj not related

**UNAKING** Shakespearean form of > UNACHING

**UNAKITE** n type of mineral

**UNAKITES** > UNAKITE

**UNALARMED** adj not alarmed

**UNALERTED** adj not alerted

**UNALIGNED** adj not aligned

**UNALIKE** adj not similar

**UNALIST** n priest holding only one benefice

**UNALISTS** > UNALIST

**UNALIVE** adj unaware

**UNALLAYED** adj not allayed

**UNALLEGED** adj not alleged

**UNALLIED** adj not allied

**UNALLOWED** adj not allowed

**UNALLOYED** adj not spoiled by being mixed with anything else

**UNALTERED** adj not altered

**UNAMASSED** adj not amassed

**UNAMAZED** adj not greatly surprised

**UNAMENDED** adj not amended

**UNAMERCED** adj not amerced

**UNAMIABLE** adj not amiable

**UNAMUSED** adj not entertained, diverted, or laughing

**UNAMUSING** adj not entertaining

**UNANCHOR** vb remove anchor

**UNANCHORS** > UNANCHOR

**UNANELED** adj not having received extreme unction

**UNANIMITY** > UNANIMOUS

**UNANIMOUS** adj in complete agreement

**UNANNEXED** adj not annexed

**UNANNOYED** adj not annoyed

**UNANXIOUS** adj not anxious

**UNAPPAREL** vb undress

**UNAPPLIED** adj not applied

**UNAPT** adj not suitable or qualified

**UNAPTLY** > UNAPT

**UNAPTNESS** > UNAPT

**UNARCHED** adj not arched

**UNARGUED** adj not debated

**UNARISEN** adj not having risen

**UNARM** less common word for > DISARM

**UNARMED** adj without weapons

**UNARMING** > UNARM

**UNARMORED** adj without armour

**UNARMS** > UNARM

**UNAROUSED** adj not aroused

**UNARRAYED** adj not arrayed

**UNARTFUL** adj not artful

**UNARY** adj consisting of, or affecting, a single element

or component

**UNASHAMED** adj not embarrassed, esp when doing something some people might find offensive

**UNASKED** adv without being asked to do something ▷ adj (of a question) not asked, although sometimes implied

**UNASSAYED** adj untried

**UNASSUMED** adj not assumed

**UNASSURED** adj insecure

**UNATONED** adj not atoned for

**UNATTIRED** adj unclothed

**UNATTUNED** adj unaccustomed

**UNAU** n two-toed sloth

**UNAUDITED** adj not having been audited

**UNAUS** > UNAU

**UNAVENGED** adj not avenged

**UNAVERAGE** adj not average

**UNAVERTED** adj not averted

**UNAVOIDED** adj not avoided

**UNAVOWED** adj not openly admitted

**UNAWAKE** adj not awake

**UNAWAKED** adj not aroused

**UNAWARDED** adj not awarded

**UNAWARE** adj not aware or conscious ▷ adv by surprise

**UNAWARELY** > UNAWARE

**UNAWARES** adv by surprise

**UNAWED** adj not awed

**UNAWESOME** adj not awesome

**UNAXED** adj not axed

**UNBACKED** adj (of a book, chair, etc) not having a back

**UNBAFFLED** adj not baffled

**UNBAG** vb take out of a bag

**UNBAGGED** > UNBAG

**UNBAGGING** > UNBAG

**UNBAGS** > UNBAG

**UNBAITED** adj not baited

**UNBAKED** adj not having been baked

**UNBALANCE** vb upset the equilibrium or balance of ▷ n imbalance or instability

**UNBALE** vb remove from bale

**UNBALED** > UNBALE

**UNBALES** > UNBALE

**UNBALING** > UNBALE

**UNBAN** vb stop banning or permit again

**UNBANDAGE** vb remove bandage from

**UNBANDED** adj not fastened with a band

**UNBANKED** adj not having been banked

**UNBANNED** > UNBAN

**UNBANNING** > UNBAN

**UNBANS** > UNBAN

**UNBAPTISE** same as > UNBAPTIZE

**UNBAPTIZE** vb remove the effect of baptism

**UNBAR** vb take away a bar or bars from

**UNBARBED** adj without barbs

**UNBARE** vb expose

**UNBARED** > UNBARE

**UNBARES** > UNBARE

**UNBARING** > UNBARE

**UNBARK** vb strip bark from

**UNBARKED** > UNBARK

**UNBARKING** > UNBARK

**UNBARKS** > UNBARK

**UNBARRED** > UNBAR

**UNBARRING** > UNBAR

**UNBARS** > UNBAR

**UNBASED** adj not having a base

**UNBASHFUL** adj not shy

**UNBASTED** adj not basted

**UNBATED** adj (of a sword, lance, etc) not covered with a protective button

**UNBATHED** adj unwashed

**UNBE** vb make non-existent

**UNBEAR** vb release (horse) from the bearing rein

**UNBEARDED** adj not having a beard

**UNBEARED** > UNBEAR

**UNBEARING** > UNBEAR

**UNBEARS** > UNBEAR

**UNBEATEN** adj having suffered no defeat

**UNBED** vb remove from bed

**UNBEDDED** > UNBED

**UNBEDDING** > UNBED

**UNBEDS** > UNBED

**UNBEEN** > UNBE

**UNBEGET** vb deprive of existence

**UNBEGETS** > UNBEGET

**UNBEGGED** adj not obtained by begging

**UNBEGOT** adj unbegotten

**UNBEGUILE** vb undeceive

**UNBEGUN** adj not commenced

**UNBEING** n non-existence

**UNBEINGS** > UNBEING

**UNBEKNOWN** adv without the knowledge (of a person) ▷ adj not known (to)

**UNBELIEF** n disbelief or rejection of belief

**UNBELIEFS** > UNBELIEF

**UNBELIEVE** vb disbelieve

**UNBELOVED** adj unhappy in love

**UNBELT** vb unbuckle the belt of (a garment)

**UNBELTED** > UNBELT

**UNBELTING** > UNBELT

**UNBELTS** > UNBELT

**UNBEMUSED** adj not bemused

**UNBEND** vb become less strict or more informal

in one's attitudes or behaviour

**UNBENDED** >UNBEND

**UNBENDING** *adj* rigid or inflexible

**UNBENDS** >UNBEND

**UNBENIGN** *adj* not benign

**UNBENT** *adj* not bent or bowed

**UNBEREFT** *adj* not bereft

**UNBERUFEN** *adj* not called for

**UNBESEEM** *vb* be unbefitting to

**UNBESEEMS** >UNBESEEM

**UNBESPEAK** *vb* annul

**UNBESPOKE** *adj* not bespoken

**UNBIAS** *vb* free from prejudice

**UNBIASED** *adj* not having or showing prejudice or favouritism

**UNBIASES** >UNBIAS

**UNBIASING** >UNBIAS

**UNBIASSED** *same as* >UNBIASED

**UNBIASSES** >UNBIAS

**UNBID** *same as* >UNBIDDEN

**UNBIDDEN** *adj* not ordered or asked

**UNBIGOTED** *adj* not bigoted

**UNBILLED** *adj* not having been billed

**UNBIND** *vb* set free from bonds or chains

**UNBINDING** >UNBIND

**UNBINDS** >UNBIND

**UNBISHOP** *vb* remove from the position of bishop

**UNBISHOPS** >UNBISHOP

**UNBITT** *vb* remove (cable) from the bitts

**UNBITTED** >UNBITT

**UNBITTEN** *adj* not having been bitten

**UNBITTER** *adj* not bitter

**UNBITTING** >UNBITT

**UNBITTS** >UNBITT

**UNBLAMED** *vb* not blamed

**UNBLENDED** *adj* not blended

**UNBLENT** *same as* >UNBLENDED

**UNBLESS** *vb* deprive of a blessing

**UNBLESSED** *adj* deprived of blessing

**UNBLESSES** >UNBLESS

**UNBLEST** *same as* >UNBLESSED

**UNBLIND** *vb* rid of blindness

**UNBLINDED** >UNBLIND

**UNBLINDS** >UNBLIND

**UNBLOCK** *vb* remove a blockage from

**UNBLOCKED** >UNBLOCK

**UNBLOCKS** >UNBLOCK

**UNBLOODED** *adj* not bloodied

**UNBLOODY** *adj* not covered with blood

**UNBLOTTED** *adj* not blotted

**UNBLOWED** *same as* >UNBLOWN

**UNBLOWN** *adj* (of a flower) still in the bud

**UNBLUNTED** *adj* not blunted

**UNBLURRED** *adj* not blurred

**UNBOARDED** *adj* not boarded

**UNBOBBED** *adj* not bobbed

**UNBODIED** *adj* having no body

**UNBODING** *adj* having no presentiment

**UNBOILED** *adj* not boiled

**UNBOLT** *vb* unfasten a bolt of (a door)

**UNBOLTED** *adj* (of grain, meal, or flour) not sifted

**UNBOLTING** >UNBOLT

**UNBOLTS** >UNBOLT

**UNBONDED** *adj* not bonded

**UNBONE** *vb* remove bone from

**UNBONED** *adj* (of meat, fish, etc) not having had the bones removed

**UNBONES** >UNBONE

**UNBONING** >UNBONE

**UNBONNET** *vb* remove the bonnet from

**UNBONNETS** >UNBONNET

**UNBOOKED** *adj* not reserved

**UNBOOKISH** *adj* not studious

**UNBOOT** *vb* remove boots from

**UNBOOTED** >UNBOOT

**UNBOOTING** >UNBOOT

**UNBOOTS** >UNBOOT

**UNBORE** *adj* unborn

**UNBORN** *adj* not yet born

**UNBORNE** *adj* not borne

**UNBOSOM** *vb* relieve (oneself) of (secrets or feelings) by telling someone

**UNBOSOMED** >UNBOSOM

**UNBOSOMER** >UNBOSOM

**UNBOSOMS** >UNBOSOM

**UNBOTTLE** *vb* allow out of bottle

**UNBOTTLED** >UNBOTTLE

**UNBOTTLES** >UNBOTTLE

**UNBOUGHT** *adj* not purchased

**UNBOUNCY** *adj* not bouncy

**UNBOUND** *adj* (of a book) not bound within a cover

**UNBOUNDED** *adj* having no boundaries or limits

**UNBOWED** *adj* not giving in or submitting

**UNBOWING** *adj* not bowing

**UNBOX** *vb* empty a box

**UNBOXED** >UNBOX

**UNBOXES** >UNBOX

**UNBOXING** >UNBOX

**UNBRACE** *vb* remove tension or strain from

**UNBRACED** >UNBRACE

**UNBRACES** >UNBRACE

**UNBRACING** >UNBRACE

**UNBRAID** *vb* remove braids from

**UNBRAIDED** >UNBRAID

**UNBRAIDS** >UNBRAID

**UNBRAKE** *vb* stop reducing speed by releasing brake

**UNBRAKED** >UNBRAKE

**UNBRAKES** >UNBRAKE

**UNBRAKING** >UNBRAKE

**UNBRANDED** *adj* not having a brand name

**UNBRASTE** *archaic past form of* >UNBRACE

**UNBRED** *adj* not taught or instructed

**UNBREECH** *vb* remove breech from

**UNBRIDGED** *adj* not spanned by a bridge

**UNBRIDLE** *vb* remove the bridle from (a horse)

**UNBRIDLED** *adj* (of feelings or behaviour) not controlled in any way

**UNBRIDLES** >UNBRIDLE

**UNBRIEFED** *adj* not instructed

**UNBRIGHT** *adj* not bright

**UNBRIZZED** *same as* >UNBRUISED

**UNBROILED** *adj* not broiled

**UNBROKE** *same as* >UNBROKEN

**UNBROKEN** *adj* complete or whole

**UNBROWNED** *adj* not browned

**UNBRUISED** *adj* not bruised

**UNBRUSED** *same as* >UNBRUISED

**UNBRUSHED** *adj* not brushed

**UNBUCKLE** *vb* undo the buckle or buckles of

**UNBUCKLED** >UNBUCKLE

**UNBUCKLES** >UNBUCKLE

**UNBUDDED** *adj* not having buds

**UNBUDGING** *adj* not moving

**UNBUILD** *vb* destroy

**UNBUILDS** >UNBUILD

**UNBUILT** >UNBUILD

**UNBULKY** *adj* not bulky

**UNBUNDLE** *vb* separate (hardware from software) for sales purposes

**UNBUNDLED** >UNBUNDLE

**UNBUNDLER** >UNBUNDLE

**UNBUNDLES** >UNBUNDLE

**UNBURDEN** *vb* relieve (one's mind or oneself) of a worry by confiding in someone

**UNBURDENS** >UNBURDEN

**UNBURIED** >UNBURY

**UNBURIES** >UNBURY

**UNBURNED** *same as* >UNBURNT

**UNBURNT** *adj* not burnt

**UNBURROW** *vb* remove from a burrow

**UNBURROWS** >UNBURROW

**UNBURTHEN** *same as* >UNBURDEN

**UNBURY** *vb* unearth

**UNBURYING** >UNBURY

**UNBUSTED** *adj* unbroken

**UNBUSY** *adj* not busy

**UNBUTTON** *vb* undo by

unfastening the buttons of (a garment)

**UNBUTTONS** >UNBUTTON

**UNCAGE** *vb* release from a cage

**UNCAGED** *adj* at liberty

**UNCAGES** >UNCAGE

**UNCAGING** >UNCAGE

**UNCAKE** *vb* remove compacted matter from

**UNCAKED** >UNCAKE

**UNCAKES** >UNCAKE

**UNCAKING** >UNCAKE

**UNCALLED** *adj* not called

**UNCANDID** *adj* not frank

**UNCANDLED** *adj* not illuminated by candle

**UNCANDOUR** *n* lack of candour

**UNCANNED** *adj* not canned

**UNCANNIER** >UNCANNY

**UNCANNILY** >UNCANNY

**UNCANNY** *adj* weird or mysterious

**UNCANONIC** *adj* unclerical

**UNCAP** *vb* remove a cap or top from (a container)

**UNCAPABLE** *same as* >INCAPABLE

**UNCAPE** *vb* remove the cape from

**UNCAPED** >UNCAPE

**UNCAPES** >UNCAPE

**UNCAPING** >UNCAPE

**UNCAPPED** >UNCAP

**UNCAPPING** >UNCAP

**UNCAPS** >UNCAP

**UNCARDED** *adj* not carded

**UNCAREFUL** *adj* careless

**UNCARING** *adj* thoughtless

**UNCART** *vb* remove from a cart

**UNCARTED** >UNCART

**UNCARTING** >UNCART

**UNCARTS** >UNCART

**UNCARVED** *adj* not carved

**UNCASE** *vb* display

**UNCASED** >UNCASE

**UNCASES** >UNCASE

**UNCASHED** *adj* not cashed

**UNCASING** >UNCASE

**UNCASKED** *adj* removed from a cask

**UNCAST** *adj* not cast

**UNCATCHY** *adj* not catchy

**UNCATE** *same as* >UNCINATE

**UNCATERED** *adj* not catered

**UNCAUGHT** *adj* not caught

**UNCAUSED** *adj* not brought into existence by any cause

**UNCE** *same as* >OUNCE

**UNCEASING** *adj* continuing without a break

**UNCEDED** *adj* not ceded

**UNCERTAIN** *adj* not able to be accurately known or predicted

**UNCES** >UNCE

**UNCESSANT** *same as* >INCESSANT

**UNCHAIN** *vb* remove a chain or chains from

**UNCHAINED** >UNCHAIN

UNCHAINS > UNCHAIN
UNCHAIR vb unseat from chair
UNCHAIRED > UNCHAIR
UNCHAIRS > UNCHAIR
UNCHANCY adj unlucky, ill-omened, or dangerous
UNCHANGED adj remaining the same
UNCHARGE vb unload
UNCHARGED adj (of land or other property) not subject to a charge
UNCHARGES > UNCHARGE
UNCHARITY n lack of charity
UNCHARM vb disenchant
UNCHARMED > UNCHARM
UNCHARMS > UNCHARM
UNCHARNEL vb exhume
UNCHARRED adj not charred
UNCHARTED adj (of an area of sea or land) not having had a map made of it, esp because it is unexplored
UNCHARY adj not cautious
UNCHASTE adj not chaste
UNCHASTER > UNCHASTE
UNCHECK vb remove check mark from
UNCHECKED adj not prevented from continuing or growing ▷ adv without being stopped or hindered
UNCHECKS > UNCHECK
UNCHEERED adj miserable
UNCHEWED adj not chewed
UNCHIC adj not chic
UNCHICLY > UNCHIC
UNCHILD vb deprive of children
UNCHILDED > UNCHILD
UNCHILDS > UNCHILD
UNCHILLED adj not chilled
UNCHOKE vb unblock
UNCHOKED > UNCHOKE
UNCHOKES > UNCHOKE
UNCHOKING > UNCHOKE
UNCHOSEN adj not chosen
UNCHRISOM adj unchristened
UNCHURCH vb excommunicate
UNCI > UNCUS
UNCIA n twelfth part
UNCIAE > UNCIA
UNCIAL adj of or written in letters that resemble modern capitals, as used in Greek and Latin manuscripts of the third to ninth centuries ▷ n uncial letter or manuscript
UNCIALLY > UNCIAL
UNCIALS > UNCIAL
UNCIFORM adj having the shape of a hook ▷ n any hook-shaped structure or part, esp a small bone of the wrist
UNCIFORMS > UNCIFORM
UNCINAL same as > UNCINATE

UNCINARIA same as > HOOKWORM
UNCINATE adj shaped like a hook
UNCINATED > UNCINATE
UNCINI > UNCINUS
UNCINUS n small hooked structure, such as one of the hooked chaetae of certain polychaete worms
UNCIPHER vb decode
UNCIPHERS > UNCIPHER
UNCITED adj not quoted
UNCIVIL adj impolite, rude or bad-mannered
UNCIVILLY > UNCIVIL
UNCLAD adj having no clothes on
UNCLAIMED adj not having been claimed
UNCLAMP vb remove clamp from
UNCLAMPED > UNCLAMP
UNCLAMPS > UNCLAMP
UNCLARITY adj lack of clarity
UNCLASP vb unfasten the clasp of (something)
UNCLASPED > UNCLASP
UNCLASPS > UNCLASP
UNCLASSED adj not divided into classes
UNCLASSY adj not classy
UNCLAWED adj not clawed
UNCLE n brother of one's father or mother ▷ vb refer to as uncle
UNCLEAN adj lacking moral, spiritual, or physical cleanliness
UNCLEANED adj not cleaned
UNCLEANER > UNCLEAN
UNCLEANLY adv in an unclean manner ▷ adj characterized by an absence of cleanliness
UNCLEAR adj confusing or hard to understand
UNCLEARED adj not cleared
UNCLEARER > UNCLEAR
UNCLEARLY > UNCLEAR
UNCLED > UNCLE
UNCLEFT adj not cleft
UNCLENCH vb relax from a clenched position
UNCLES > UNCLE
UNCLESHIP n position of an uncle
UNCLEW vb undo
UNCLEWED > UNCLEW
UNCLEWING > UNCLEW
UNCLEWS > UNCLEW
UNCLICHED adj not cliched
UNCLINCH same as > UNCLENCH
UNCLING > UNCLE
UNCLIP vb remove clip from
UNCLIPPED > UNCLIP
UNCLIPS > UNCLIP
UNCLIPT archaic past form of > UNCLIP
UNCLOAK vb remove cloak from

UNCLOAKED > UNCLOAK
UNCLOAKS > UNCLOAK
UNCLOG vb remove an obstruction from (a drain, etc)
UNCLOGGED > UNCLOG
UNCLOGS > UNCLOG
UNCLOSE vb open or cause to open
UNCLOSED > UNCLOSE
UNCLOSES > UNCLOSE
UNCLOSING > UNCLOSE
UNCLOTHE vb take off garments from
UNCLOTHED > UNCLOTHE
UNCLOTHES > UNCLOTHE
UNCLOUD vb clear clouds from
UNCLOUDED > UNCLOUD
UNCLOUDS > UNCLOUD
UNCLOUDY adj not cloudy
UNCLOVEN adj not cleaved
UNCLOYED adj not cloyed
UNCLOYING adj not cloying
UNCLUTCH vb open from tight grip
UNCLUTTER vb tidy and straighten up
UNCO adj awkward ▷ n awkward or clumsy person
UNCOATED adj not covered with a layer
UNCOATING n process whereby a virus exposes its genome in order to replicate
UNCOBBLED adj not cobbled
UNCOCK vb remove from a cocked position
UNCOCKED > UNCOCK
UNCOCKING > UNCOCK
UNCOCKS > UNCOCK
UNCODED adj not coded
UNCOER > UNCO
UNCOERCED adj unforced
UNCOEST > UNCO
UNCOFFIN vb take out of a coffin
UNCOFFINS > UNCOFFIN
UNCOIL vb unwind or untwist
UNCOILED > UNCOIL
UNCOILING > UNCOIL
UNCOILS > UNCOIL
UNCOINED adj (of a metal) not made into coin
UNCOLORED adj not coloured
UNCOLT vb divest of a horse
UNCOLTED > UNCOLT
UNCOLTING > UNCOLT
UNCOLTS > UNCOLT
UNCOMBED adj not combed
UNCOMBINE vb break apart
UNCOMELY adj not attractive
UNCOMIC adj not comical
UNCOMMON adj not happening or encountered often
UNCONCERN n apathy or indifference
UNCONFINE vb remove restrictions from

UNCONFORM adj dissimilar
UNCONFUSE vb remove confusion from
UNCONGEAL vb become liquid again
UNCOOKED adj raw
UNCOOL adj unsophisticated
UNCOOLED adj not cooled
UNCOPE vb unmuzzle
UNCOPED > UNCOPE
UNCOPES > UNCOPE
UNCOPING > UNCOPE
UNCORD vb release from cords
UNCORDED > UNCORD
UNCORDIAL adj unfriendly
UNCORDING > UNCORD
UNCORDS > UNCORD
UNCORK vb remove the cork from (a bottle)
UNCORKED > UNCORK
UNCORKING > UNCORK
UNCORKS > UNCORK
UNCORRUPT adj not corrupt
UNCOS > UNCO
UNCOSTLY adj inexpensive
UNCOUNTED adj unable to be counted
UNCOUPLE vb disconnect or become disconnected
UNCOUPLED > UNCOUPLE
UNCOUPLER > UNCOUPLE
UNCOUPLES > UNCOUPLE
UNCOURTLY adj not courtly
UNCOUTH adj lacking in good manners, refinement, or grace
UNCOUTHER > UNCOUTH
UNCOUTHLY > UNCOUTH
UNCOVER vb reveal or disclose
UNCOVERED adj not covered
UNCOVERS > UNCOVER
UNCOWL vb remove hood from
UNCOWLED > UNCOWL
UNCOWLING > UNCOWL
UNCOWLS > UNCOWL
UNCOY adj not modest
UNCOYNED same as > UNCOINED
UNCRACKED adj not cracked
UNCRATE vb remove from a crate
UNCRATED > UNCRATE
UNCRATES > UNCRATE
UNCRATING > UNCRATE
UNCRAZY adj not crazy
UNCREATE vb unmake
UNCREATED > UNCREATE
UNCREATES > UNCREATE
UNCREWED adj not crewed
UNCROPPED adj not cropped
UNCROSS vb cease to cross
UNCROSSED > UNCROSS
UNCROSSES > UNCROSS
UNCROWDED adj (of a confined space, area, etc) not containing too many people or things
UNCROWN vb take the crown from
UNCROWNED adj having the

813

powers, but not the title, of royalty

**UNCROWNS** > UNCROWN

**UNCRUDDED** *adj* uncurdled

**UNCRUMPLE** *vb* remove creases from

**UNCRUSHED** *adj* not crushed

**UNCTION** *n* act of anointing with oil in sacramental ceremonies

**UNCTIONS** > UNCTION

**UNCTUOUS** *adj* pretending to be kind and concerned

**UNCUFF** *vb* remove handcuffs from

**UNCUFFED** > UNCUFF

**UNCUFFING** > UNCUFF

**UNCUFFS** > UNCUFF

**UNCULLED** *adj* not culled

**UNCURABLE** *same as* > INCURABLE

**UNCURABLY** > UNCURABLE

**UNCURB** *vb* remove curbs from (a horse)

**UNCURBED** > UNCURB

**UNCURBING** > UNCURB

**UNCURBS** > UNCURB

**UNCURDLED** *adj* not curdled

**UNCURED** *adj* not cured

**UNCURIOUS** *adj* not curious

**UNCURL** *vb* move or cause to move out of a curled or rolled up position

**UNCURLED** > UNCURL

**UNCURLING** > UNCURL

**UNCURLS** > UNCURL

**UNCURRENT** *adj* not current

**UNCURSE** *vb* remove curse from

**UNCURSED** > UNCURSE

**UNCURSES** > UNCURSE

**UNCURSING** > UNCURSE

**UNCURTAIN** *vb* reveal

**UNCURVED** *adj* not curved

**UNCUS** *n* hooked part or process, as in the human cerebrum

**UNCUT** *adj* not shortened or censored

**UNCUTE** *adj* not cute

**UNCYNICAL** *adj* not cynical

**UNDAM** *vb* free from a dam

**UNDAMAGED** *adj* not spoilt or damaged

**UNDAMMED** > UNDAM

**UNDAMMING** > UNDAM

**UNDAMNED** *adj* not damned

**UNDAMPED** *adj* (of an oscillating system) having unrestricted motion

**UNDAMS** > UNDAM

**UNDARING** *adj* not daring

**UNDASHED** *adj* not dashed

**UNDATABLE** *adj* not able to be dated

**UNDATE** *vb* remove date from

**UNDATED** *adj* (of a manuscript, letter, etc) not having an identifying date

**UNDAUNTED** *adj* not put off, discouraged, or beaten

**UNDAWNING** *adj* not dawning

**UNDAZZLE** *vb* recover from a daze

**UNDAZZLED** > UNDAZZLE

**UNDAZZLES** > UNDAZZLE

**UNDE** *same as* > UNDEE

**UNDEAD** *adj* alive

**UNDEAF** *vb* restore hearing to

**UNDEAFED** > UNDEAF

**UNDEAFING** > UNDEAF

**UNDEAFS** > UNDEAF

**UNDEALT** *adj* not dealt (with)

**UNDEAR** *adj* not dear

**UNDEBASED** *adj* not debased

**UNDEBATED** *adj* not debated

**UNDECAGON** *n* polygon having eleven sides

**UNDECAYED** *adj* not rotten

**UNDECEIVE** *vb* reveal the truth to (someone previously misled or deceived)

**UNDECENT** *same as* > INDECENT

**UNDECIDED** *adj* not having made up one's mind

**UNDECIMAL** *adj* based on the number 11

**UNDECK** *vb* remove decorations from

**UNDECKED** > UNDECK

**UNDECKING** > UNDECK

**UNDECKS** > UNDECK

**UNDEE** *adj* wavy

**UNDEEDED** *adj* not transferred by deed

**UNDEFACED** *adj* not spoilt

**UNDEFIDE** *same as* > UNDEFIED

**UNDEFIED** *adj* not challenged

**UNDEFILED** *adj* not defiled

**UNDEFINED** *adj* not defined or made clear

**UNDEIFIED** > UNDEIFY

**UNDEIFIES** > UNDEIFY

**UNDEIFY** *vb* strip of the status of a deity

**UNDELAYED** *adj* not delayed

**UNDELETED** *adj* not deleted, or restored after being deleted

**UNDELIGHT** *n* absence of delight

**UNDELUDED** *adj* not deluded

**UNDENIED** *adj* not denied

**UNDENTED** *adj* not dented

**UNDER** *adv* indicating movement to or position beneath the underside or base ▷ *prep* less than

**UNDERACT** *vb* play (a role) without adequate emphasis

**UNDERACTS** > UNDERACT

**UNDERAGE** *adj* below the required or standard age ▷ *n* shortfall

**UNDERAGED** *adj* not old enough

**UNDERAGES** > UNDERAGE

**UNDERARM** *adj* denoting a style of throwing, bowling, or serving in which the hand is swung below shoulder level ▷ *adv* in an underarm style ▷ *n* armpit

**UNDERARMS** > UNDERARM

**UNDERATE** > UNDEREAT

**UNDERBAKE** *vb* bake insufficiently

**UNDERBEAR** *vb* endure

**UNDERBID** *vb* submit a bid lower than that of (others)

**UNDERBIDS** > UNDERBID

**UNDERBIT** > UNDERBITE

**UNDERBITE** *vb* use insufficient acid in etching

**UNDERBODY** *n* underpart of a body, as of an animal or motor vehicle

**UNDERBORE** > UNDERBEAR

**UNDERBOSS** *n* person who is second in command

**UNDERBRED** *adj* of impure stock

**UNDERBRIM** *n* part of a hat

**UNDERBUD** *vb* produce fewer buds than expected

**UNDERBUDS** > UNDERBUD

**UNDERBUSH** *n* undergrowth or underbrush

**UNDERBUY** *vb* buy (stock in trade) in amounts lower than required

**UNDERBUYS** > UNDERBUY

**UNDERCARD** *n* event supporting a main event

**UNDERCART** *n* aircraft undercarriage

**UNDERCAST** *vb* cast beneath

**UNDERCLAD** *adj* not wearing enough clothes

**UNDERCLAY** *n* grey or whitish clay rock containing fossilized plant roots and occurring beneath coal seams. When used as a refractory, it is known as fireclay

**UNDERCLUB** *vb* use a golf club that will not hit the ball as far as required

**UNDERCOAT** *n* coat of paint applied before the final coat ▷ *vb* apply an undercoat to a surface

**UNDERCOOK** *vb* cook for too short a time or at too low a temperature

**UNDERCOOL** *vb* cool insufficiently

**UNDERCUT** *vb* charge less than (a competitor) to obtain trade ▷ *n* act or an instance of cutting underneath

**UNDERCUTS** > UNDERCUT

**UNDERDAKS** *pl n* underpants

**UNDERDECK** *n* lower deck of a vessel

**UNDERDID** > UNDERDO

**UNDERDO** *vb* do (something) inadequately

**UNDERDOER** > UNDERDO

**UNDERDOES** > UNDERDO

**UNDERDOG** *n* person or team in a weak or underprivileged position

**UNDERDOGS** > UNDERDOG

**UNDERDONE** *adj* not cooked enough

**UNDERDOSE** *vb* give insufficient dose

**UNDERDRAW** *vb* sketch the subject before painting it on the same surface

**UNDERDREW** > UNDERDRAW

**UNDEREAT** *vb* not eat enough

**UNDEREATS** > UNDEREAT

**UNDERFED** > UNDERFEED

**UNDERFEED** *vb* give too little food to ▷ *n* apparatus by which fuel, etc, is supplied from below

**UNDERFELT** *n* thick felt laid under a carpet to increase insulation

**UNDERFIRE** *vb* bake insufficiently

**UNDERFISH** *vb* catch fewer fish than the permitted maximum amount

**UNDERFLOW** *n* undercurrent

**UNDERFONG** *vb* receive

**UNDERFOOT** *adv* under the feet

**UNDERFUND** *vb* provide insufficient funding

**UNDERFUR** *n* layer of dense soft fur occurring beneath the outer coarser fur in certain mammals, such as the otter and seal

**UNDERFURS** > UNDERFUR

**UNDERGIRD** *vb* strengthen or reinforce by passing a rope, cable, or chain around the underside of (an object, load, etc)

**UNDERGIRT** > UNDERGIRD

**UNDERGO** *vb* experience, endure, or sustain

**UNDERGOD** *n* subordinate god

**UNDERGODS** > UNDERGOD

**UNDERGOER** > UNDERGO

**UNDERGOES** > UNDERGO

**UNDERGONE** > UNDERGO

**UNDERGOWN** *n* gown worn under another article of clothing

**UNDERGRAD** *n* person studying for a first degree; undergraduate

**UNDERHAIR** *n* lower layer of animal's hair

**UNDERHAND** *adj* sly, deceitful, and secretive ▷ *adv* in an underhand manner or style

**UNDERHEAT** *vb* heat insufficiently

**UNDERHUNG** *adj* (of the lower jaw) projecting

beyond the upper jaw
**UNDERIVED** *adj* not derived
**UNDERJAW** *n* lower jaw
**UNDERJAWS** > UNDERJAW
**UNDERKEEP** *vb* suppress
**UNDERKEPT** > UNDERKEEP
**UNDERKILL** *n* less force
than is needed to defeat
enemy
**UNDERKING** *n* ruler
subordinate to a king
**UNDERLAID** *adj* laid
underneath
**UNDERLAIN** > UNDERLIE
**UNDERLAP** *vb* project under
the edge of
**UNDERLAPS** > UNDERLAP
**UNDERLAY** *n* felt or rubber
laid beneath a carpet to
increase insulation and
resilience ▷ *vb* place
(something) under or
beneath
**UNDERLAYS** > UNDERLAY
**UNDERLEAF** *n* (in
liverworts) any of the
leaves forming a row on
the underside of the stem:
usually smaller than the
two rows of lateral leaves
and sometimes absent.
**UNDERLET** *vb* let for a price
lower than expected or
justified
**UNDERLETS** > UNDERLET
**UNDERLIE** *vb* lie or be
placed under
**UNDERLIER** > UNDERLIE
**UNDERLIES** > UNDERLIE
**UNDERLINE** *vb* draw
a line under ▷ *n* line
underneath, esp under
written matter
**UNDERLING** *n* subordinate
**UNDERLIP** *n* lower lip
**UNDERLIPS** > UNDERLIP
**UNDERLIT** *adj* lit from
beneath
**UNDERLOAD** *vb* load
incompletely
**UNDERMAN** *vb* supply with
insufficient staff ▷ *n*
subordinate man
**UNDERMANS** > UNDERMAN
**UNDERMEN** > UNDERMAN
**UNDERMINE** *vb* weaken
gradually
**UNDERMOST** *adj* being the
furthest under ▷ *adv* in
the lowest place
**UNDERN** *n* time between
sunrise and noon
**UNDERNOTE** *n* undertone
**UNDERNS** > UNDERN
**UNDERPAID** *adj* not paid as
much as the job deserves
**UNDERPART** *n* lower part or
underside of something
such as an animal
**UNDERPASS** *n* section of
a road that passes under
another road or a railway
line
**UNDERPAY** *vb* pay someone

insufficiently
**UNDERPAYS** > UNDERPAY
**UNDERPEEP** *vb* peep under
**UNDERPIN** *vb* give strength
or support to
**UNDERPINS** > UNDERPIN
**UNDERPLAY** *vb* achieve (an
effect) by deliberate lack of
emphasis
**UNDERPLOT** *n* subsidiary
plot in a literary or
dramatic work
**UNDERPROP** *vb* prop up
from beneath
**UNDERRAN** > UNDERRUN
**UNDERRATE** *vb*
underestimate
**UNDERRIPE** *adj* not quite
ripe
**UNDERRUN** *vb* run beneath
**UNDERRUNS** > UNDERRUN
**UNDERSAID** > UNDERSAY
**UNDERSAY** *vb* say by way of
response
**UNDERSAYS** > UNDERSAY
**UNDERSEA** *adv* below the
surface of the sea
**UNDERSEAL** *n* coating
of tar etc applied to the
underside of a motor
vehicle to prevent
corrosion ▷ *vb* apply
such a coating to a motor
vehicle
**UNDERSEAS** *same*
*as* > UNDERSEA
**UNDERSELF** *n* subconscious
or person within
**UNDERSELL** *vb* sell at a
price lower than that of
another seller
**UNDERSET** *n* ocean
undercurrent ▷ *vb*
support from underneath
**UNDERSETS** > UNDERSET
**UNDERSHOT** *adj* (of the
lower jaw) projecting
beyond the upper jaw
**UNDERSIDE** *n* bottom or
lower surface
**UNDERSIGN** *vb* sign the
bottom (of a document)
**UNDERSIZE** *adj* smaller
than normal
**UNDERSKY** *n* lower sky
**UNDERSOIL** *another word*
*for* > SUBSOIL
**UNDERSOLD** > UNDERSELL
**UNDERSONG** *n*
accompanying secondary
melody
**UNDERSPIN** *n* backspin
**UNDERTAKE** *vb* agree
or commit oneself to
(something) or to do
(something)
**UNDERTANE** *Shakespearean*
*past participle*
*of* > UNDERTAKE
**UNDERTAX** *vb* tax
insufficiently
**UNDERTIME** *n* time
spent by an employee
at work in non-work-

related activities like
socializing, surfing the
internet, making personal
telephone calls, etc
**UNDERTINT** *n* slight,
subdued, or delicate tint
**UNDERTONE** *n* quiet tone
of voice
**UNDERTOOK** *past tense*
*of* > UNDERTAKE
**UNDERTOW** *n* strong
undercurrent flowing in
a different direction from
the surface current
**UNDERTOWS** > UNDERTOW
**UNDERUSE** *vb* use less than
normal
**UNDERUSED** > UNDERUSE
**UNDERUSES** > UNDERUSE
**UNDERVEST** *another name*
*for* > VEST
**UNDERVOTE** *n* vote cast but
invalid
**UNDERWAY** *adj* in progress
▷ *adv* in progress
**UNDERWEAR** *n* clothing
worn under the outer
garments and next to the
skin
**UNDERWENT** *past tense*
*of* > UNDERGO
**UNDERWING** *n* hind wing
of an insect, esp when
covered by the forewing
**UNDERWIRE** *vb* support
with wire underneath
**UNDERWIT** *n* half-wit
**UNDERWITS** > UNDERWIT
**UNDERWOOD** *n* small trees,
bushes, ferns, etc growing
beneath taller trees in a
wood or forest
**UNDERWOOL** *n* lower layer of
an animal's coat
**UNDERWORK** *vb* do less work
than expected
**UNDESERT** *n* lack of worth
**UNDESERTS** > UNDESERT
**UNDESERVE** *vb* fail to
deserve
**UNDESIRED** *adj* not desired
**UNDEVOUT** *adj* not devout
**UNDID** > UNDO
**UNDIES** *pl n* underwear, esp
women's
**UNDIGHT** *vb* remove
**UNDIGHTS** > UNDIGHT
**UNDIGNIFY** *vb* divest of
dignity
**UNDILUTED** *adj* (of a liquid)
not having any water
added to it
**UNDIMMED** *adj* (of eyes,
light, etc) still bright or
shining
**UNDINE** *n* female water
spirit
**UNDINES** > UNDINE
**UNDINISM** *n* obsession
with water
**UNDINISMS** > UNDINISM
**UNDINTED** *adj* not dinted
**UNDIPPED** *adj* not dipped
**UNDIVIDED** *adj* total and

whole-hearted
**UNDIVINE** *adj* not divine
**UNDO** *vb* open, unwrap
**UNDOABLE** *adj* impossible
**UNDOCILE** *adj* not docile
**UNDOCK** *vb* take out of a
dock
**UNDOCKED** > UNDOCK
**UNDOCKING** > UNDOCK
**UNDOCKS** > UNDOCK
**UNDOER** > UNDO
**UNDOERS** > UNDO
**UNDOES** > UNDO
**UNDOING** *n* cause of
someone's downfall
**UNDOINGS** > UNDOING
**UNDONE** *adj* not done or
completed
**UNDOOMED** *adj* not doomed
**UNDOTTED** *adj* not dotted
**UNDOUBLE** *vb* stretch out
**UNDOUBLED** > UNDOUBLE
**UNDOUBLES** > UNDOUBLE
**UNDOUBTED** *adj* certain or
indisputable
**UNDRAINED** *adj* not drained
**UNDRAPE** *vb* remove
drapery from
**UNDRAPED** > UNDRAPE
**UNDRAPES** > UNDRAPE
**UNDRAPING** > UNDRAPE
**UNDRAW** *vb* open (curtains)
**UNDRAWING** > UNDRAW
**UNDRAWN** > UNDRAW
**UNDRAWS** > UNDRAW
**UNDREADED** *adj* not feared
**UNDREAMED** *adj* not
thought of or imagined
**UNDREAMT** *same*
*as* > UNDREAMED
**UNDRESS** *vb* take off
clothes from (oneself
or another) ▷ *n* partial
or complete nakedness
▷ *adj* characterized by
or requiring informal or
normal working dress or
uniform
**UNDRESSED** *adj* partially or
completely naked
**UNDRESSES** > UNDRESS
**UNDREST** *same*
*as* > UNDRESSED
**UNDREW** > UNDRAW
**UNDRIED** *adj* not dried
**UNDRILLED** *adj* not drilled
**UNDRIVEN** *adj* not driven
**UNDROSSY** *adj* pure
**UNDROWNED** *adj* not
drowned
**UNDRUNK** *adj* not drunk
**UNDUBBED** *adj* (of a film,
etc) not dubbed
**UNDUE** *adj* greater than is
reasonable; excessive
**UNDUG** *adj* not having been
dug
**UNDULANCE** > UNDULANT
**UNDULANCY** > UNDULANT
**UNDULANT** *adj* resembling
waves
**UNDULAR** > UNDULATE
**UNDULATE** *vb* move in
waves ▷ *adj* having a wavy

or rippled appearance, margin, or form
UNDULATED >UNDULATE
UNDULATES >UNDULATE
UNDULATOR >UNDULATE
UNDULLED adj not dulled
UNDULOSE same
   as >UNDULOUS
UNDULOUS adj undulate
UNDULY adv excessively
UNDUTEOUS same
   as >UNDUTIFUL
UNDUTIFUL adj not dutiful
UNDY same as >UNDEE
UNDYED adj not dyed
UNDYING adj never ending, eternal
UNDYINGLY >UNDYING
UNDYNAMIC adj not dynamic
UNEAGER adj nonchalant
UNEAGERLY >UNEAGER
UNEARED adj not ploughed
UNEARNED adj not deserved
UNEARTH vb reveal or discover by searching
UNEARTHED >UNEARTH
UNEARTHLY adj ghostly or eerie
UNEARTHS >UNEARTH
UNEASE >UNEASY
UNEASES >UNEASY
UNEASIER >UNEASY
UNEASIEST >UNEASY
UNEASILY >UNEASY
UNEASY adj (of a person) anxious or apprehensive
UNEATABLE adj (of food) so rotten or unattractive as to be unfit to eat
UNEATEN adj (of food) not having been consumed
UNEATH adv not easily
UNEATHES same
   as >UNEATH
UNEDGE vb take the edge off
UNEDGED >UNEDGE
UNEDGES >UNEDGE
UNEDGING >UNEDGE
UNEDIBLE variant
   of >INEDIBLE
UNEDITED adj not edited
UNEFFACED adj not destroyed
UNELATED adj not elated
UNELECTED adj not elected
UNEMPTIED adj not emptied
UNENDED adj without end
UNENDING adj not showing any signs of ever stopping
UNENDOWED adj not endowed
UNENGAGED adj not engaged
UNENJOYED adj not enjoyed
UNENSURED adj not ensured
UNENTERED adj not having been entered previously
UNENVIED adj not envied
UNENVIOUS adj not envious
UNENVYING adj not envying
UNEQUABLE adj unstable
UNEQUAL adj not equal in

quantity, size, rank, value, etc ▷ n person who is not equal
UNEQUALED adj (in US English) not equalled
UNEQUALLY >UNEQUAL
UNEQUALS >UNEQUAL
UNERASED adj not rubbed out
UNEROTIC adj not erotic
UNERRING adj never mistaken, consistently accurate
UNESPIED adj unnoticed
UNESSAYED adj untried
UNESSENCE vb deprive of being
UNETH same as >UNEATH
UNETHICAL adj morally wrong
UNEVADED adj not evaded
UNEVEN adj not level or flat
UNEVENER >UNEVEN
UNEVENEST >UNEVEN
UNEVENLY >UNEVEN
UNEVOLVED adj not evolved
UNEXALTED adj not exalted
UNEXCITED adj not aroused to pleasure, interest, agitation, etc
UNEXCUSED adj not excused
UNEXOTIC adj not exotic
UNEXPERT same
   as >INEXPERT
UNEXPIRED adj not having expired
UNEXPOSED adj not having been exhibited or brought to public notice
UNEXTINCT adj not extinct
UNEXTREME adj not extreme
UNEYED adj unseen
UNFABLED adj not fictitious
UNFACT n event or thing not provable
UNFACTS >UNFACT
UNFADABLE adj incapable of fading
UNFADED adj not faded
UNFADING adj not fading
UNFAILING adj continuous or reliable
UNFAIR adj not right, fair, or just ▷ vb disfigure
UNFAIRED >UNFAIR
UNFAIRER >UNFAIR
UNFAIREST >UNFAIR
UNFAIRING >UNFAIR
UNFAIRLY >UNFAIR
UNFAIRS >UNFAIR
UNFAITH n lack of faith
UNFAITHS >UNFAITH
UNFAKED adj not faked
UNFALLEN adj not fallen
UNFAMED adj not famous
UNFAMOUS adj not famous
UNFANCY adj not fancy
UNFANNED adj not fanned
UNFASTEN vb undo, untie, or open or become undone, untied, or opened
UNFASTENS >UNFASTEN
UNFAULTY adj not faulty

UNFAVORED adj (in US English) not favoured
UNFAZED adj not disconcerted
UNFEARED adj unafraid
UNFEARFUL adj not scared
UNFEARING adj having no fear
UNFED adj not fed
UNFEED adj unpaid
UNFEELING adj without sympathy
UNFEIGNED adj not feigned
UNFELLED adj not cut down
UNFELT adj not felt
UNFELTED adj not felted
UNFENCE vb remove a fence from
UNFENCED adj not enclosed by a fence
UNFENCES >UNFENCE
UNFENCING >UNFENCE
UNFERTILE same
   as >INFERTILE
UNFETTER vb release from fetters, bonds, etc
UNFETTERS >UNFETTER
UNFEUDAL adj not feudal
UNFEUED adj not feued
UNFIGURED adj not numbered
UNFILDE archaic form
   of >UNFILED
UNFILED adj not filed
UNFILIAL adj not filial
UNFILLED adj (of a container, receptacle, etc) not having become or been made full
UNFILMED adj not filmed
UNFINE adj not fine
UNFIRED adj not fired
UNFIRM adj soft or unsteady
UNFISHED adj not used for fishing
UNFIT adj unqualified or unsuitable ▷ vb make unfit
UNFITLY adv in an unfit way
UNFITNESS >UNFIT
UNFITS >UNFIT
UNFITTED adj unsuitable
UNFITTER >UNFIT
UNFITTEST >UNFIT
UNFITTING adj not fitting
UNFIX vb unfasten, detach, or loosen
UNFIXED adj not fixed
UNFIXES >UNFIX
UNFIXING >UNFIX
UNFIXITY n instability
UNFIXT variant of >UNFIXED
UNFLAPPED adj not agitated or excited
UNFLASHY adj not flashy
UNFLAWED adj perfect
UNFLEDGED adj (of a young bird) not having developed adult feathers
UNFLESH vb remove flesh from
UNFLESHED >UNFLESH

UNFLESHES >UNFLESH
UNFLESHLY adj immaterial
UNFLEXED adj unbent
UNFLOORED adj without flooring
UNFLUSH vb lose the colour caused by flushing
UNFLUSHED >UNFLUSH
UNFLUSHES >UNFLUSH
UNFLUTED adj not fluted
UNFLYABLE adj unable to be flown
UNFOCUSED adj blurry
UNFOILED adj not thwarted
UNFOLD vb open or spread out from a folded state
UNFOLDED >UNFOLD
UNFOLDER >UNFOLD
UNFOLDERS >UNFOLD
UNFOLDING >UNFOLD
UNFOLDS >UNFOLD
UNFOND adj not fond
UNFOOL vb undeceive
UNFOOLED >UNFOOL
UNFOOLING >UNFOOL
UNFOOLS >UNFOOL
UNFOOTED adj untrodden
UNFORBID adj archaic word meaning unforbidden
UNFORCED adj not forced or having been forced
UNFORGED adj genuine
UNFORGOT adj archaic word meaning unforgotten
UNFORKED adj not forked
UNFORM vb make formless
UNFORMAL same
   as >INFORMAL
UNFORMED adj in an early stage of development
UNFORMING >UNFORM
UNFORMS >UNFORM
UNFORTUNE n misfortune
UNFOUGHT adj not fought
UNFOUND adj not found
UNFOUNDED adj not based on facts or evidence
UNFRAMED adj not framed
UNFRANKED adj not franked
UNFRAUGHT adj not fraught
UNFREE vb remove freedom from
UNFREED >UNFREE
UNFREEDOM n lack of freedom
UNFREEING >UNFREE
UNFREEMAN n person who is not a freeman
UNFREEMEN >UNFREEMAN
UNFREES >UNFREE
UNFREEZE vb thaw or cause to thaw
UNFREEZES >UNFREEZE
UNFRETTED adj not worried
UNFRIEND n enemy
UNFRIENDS >UNFRIEND
UNFROCK vb deprive (a priest in holy orders) of his or her priesthood
UNFROCKED >UNFROCK
UNFROCKS >UNFROCK
UNFROZE >UNFREEZE
UNFROZEN >UNFREEZE

UNFUELLED adj not fuelled
UNFUMED adj not fumigated
UNFUNDED adj not funded
UNFUNNY adj not funny
UNFURL vb unroll or unfold
UNFURLED > UNFURL
UNFURLING > UNFURL
UNFURLS > UNFURL
UNFURNISH vb clear
UNFURRED adj not adorned with fur
UNFUSED adj not fused
UNFUSSIER > UNFUSSY
UNFUSSILY > UNFUSSY
UNFUSSY adj not characterized by overelaborate detail
UNGAG vb restore freedom of speech to
UNGAGGED > UNGAG
UNGAGGING > UNGAG
UNGAGS > UNGAG
UNGAIN adj inconvenient
UNGAINFUL > UNGAIN
UNGAINLY adj lacking grace when moving ⊳ adv clumsily
UNGALLANT adj not gallant
UNGALLED adj not annoyed
UNGARBED adj undressed
UNGARBLED adj clear
UNGATED adj without gate
UNGAUGED adj not measured
UNGAZING adj not gazing
UNGEAR vb disengage
UNGEARED > UNGEAR
UNGEARING > UNGEAR
UNGEARS > UNGEAR
UNGELDED adj not gelded
UNGENIAL adj unfriendly
UNGENTEEL adj impolite
UNGENTLE adj not gentle
UNGENTLY > UNGENTLE
UNGENUINE adj false
UNGERMANE adj inappropriate
UNGET vb get rid of
UNGETS > UNGET
UNGETTING > UNGET
UNGHOSTLY adj not ghostly
UNGIFTED adj not talented
UNGILD vb remove gilding from
UNGILDED > UNGILD
UNGILDING > UNGILD
UNGILDS > UNGILD
UNGILT > UNGILD
UNGIRD vb remove belt from
UNGIRDED > UNGIRD
UNGIRDING > UNGIRD
UNGIRDS > UNGIRD
UNGIRT adj not belted
UNGIRTH vb release from a girth
UNGIRTHED > UNGIRTH
UNGIRTHS > UNGIRTH
UNGIVING adj inflexible
UNGLAD adj not glad
UNGLAZED adj not glazed
UNGLOSSED adj not glossed
UNGLOVE vb remove glove(s)

UNGLOVED > UNGLOVE
UNGLOVES > UNGLOVE
UNGLOVING > UNGLOVE
UNGLUE vb remove adhesive from
UNGLUED > UNGLUE
UNGLUES > UNGLUE
UNGLUING > UNGLUE
UNGOD vb remove status of being a god from
UNGODDED > UNGOD
UNGODDING > UNGOD
UNGODLIER > UNGODLY
UNGODLIKE adj not godlike
UNGODLILY > UNGODLY
UNGODLY adj unreasonable or outrageous
UNGODS > UNGOD
UNGORD same as > UNGORED
UNGORED adj not gored
UNGORGED same as > UNGORED
UNGOT same as > UNGOTTEN
UNGOTTEN adj not obtained or won
UNGOWN vb remove gown (from)
UNGOWNED > UNGOWN
UNGOWNING > UNGOWN
UNGOWNS > UNGOWN
UNGRACED adj not graced
UNGRADED adj not graded
UNGRASSED adj not covered with grass
UNGRAVELY adj in a light-hearted manner
UNGRAZED adj not grazed
UNGREASED adj not greased
UNGREEDY adj not greedy
UNGROOMED adj not groomed
UNGROUND adj not crushed
UNGROUPED adj not placed in a group
UNGROWN adj not fully developed
UNGRUDGED adj not grudged
UNGUAL adj of, relating to, or affecting the fingernails or toenails
UNGUARD vb expose (to attack)
UNGUARDED adj not protected
UNGUARDS > UNGUARD
UNGUENT n ointment
UNGUENTA > UNGUENTUM
UNGUENTS > UNGUENT
UNGUENTUM same as > UNGUENT
UNGUES > UNGUIS
UNGUESSED adj unexpected
UNGUIDED adj (of a missile, bomb, etc) not having a flight path controlled either by radio signals or internal preset or self-actuating homing devices
UNGUIFORM adj shaped like a nail or claw
UNGUILTY adj innocent
UNGUINOUS adj fatty
UNGUIS n nail, claw, or

hoof, or the part of the digit giving rise to it
UNGULA n truncated cone, cylinder, etc
UNGULAE > UNGULA
UNGULAR > UNGULA
UNGULATE n hoofed mammal
UNGULATES > UNGULATE
UNGULED adj hoofed
UNGUM vb remove adhesive from
UNGUMMED > UNGUM
UNGUMMING > UNGUM
UNGUMS > UNGUM
UNGYVE vb release from shackles
UNGYVED > UNGYVE
UNGYVES > UNGYVE
UNGYVING > UNGYVE
UNHABLE same as > UNABLE
UNHACKED adj not hacked
UNHAILED adj not hailed
UNHAIR vb remove the hair from (a hide)
UNHAIRED > UNHAIR
UNHAIRER > UNHAIR
UNHAIRERS > UNHAIR
UNHAIRING > UNHAIR
UNHAIRS > UNHAIR
UNHALLOW vb desecrate
UNHALLOWS > UNHALLOW
UNHALSED adj not hailed
UNHALVED adj not divided in half
UNHAND vb release from one's grasp
UNHANDED > UNHAND
UNHANDIER > UNHANDY
UNHANDILY > UNHANDY
UNHANDING > UNHAND
UNHANDLED adj not handled
UNHANDS > UNHAND
UNHANDY adj not skilful with one's hands
UNHANG vb take down from hanging position
UNHANGED adj not executed by hanging
UNHANGING > UNHANG
UNHANGS > UNHANG
UNHAPPIED > UNHAPPY
UNHAPPIER > UNHAPPY
UNHAPPIES > UNHAPPY
UNHAPPILY > UNHAPPY
UNHAPPY adj sad or depressed ⊳ vb make unhappy
UNHARBOUR vb force out of shelter
UNHARDY adj fragile
UNHARMED adj not hurt or damaged in any way
UNHARMFUL adj not harmful
UNHARMING adj not capable of harming
UNHARNESS vb remove the harness from (a horse, etc)
UNHARRIED adj not harried
UNHASP vb unfasten
UNHASPED > UNHASP
UNHASPING > UNHASP
UNHASPS > UNHASP
UNHASTING adj not rushing

UNHASTY adj not speedy
UNHAT vb doff one's hat
UNHATCHED adj (of an egg) not having broken to release the fully developed young
UNHATS > UNHAT
UNHATTED > UNHAT
UNHATTING > UNHAT
UNHAUNTED adj not haunted
UNHEAD vb remove the head from
UNHEADED adj not having a heading
UNHEADING > UNHEAD
UNHEADS > UNHEAD
UNHEAL vb expose
UNHEALED adj not having healed physically, mentally, or emotionally
UNHEALING adj not healing
UNHEALS > UNHEAL
UNHEALTH n illness
UNHEALTHS > UNHEALTH
UNHEALTHY adj likely to cause poor health
UNHEARD adj not listened to
UNHEARSE vb remove from a hearse
UNHEARSED > UNHEARSE
UNHEARSES > UNHEARSE
UNHEART vb discourage
UNHEARTED > UNHEART
UNHEARTS > UNHEART
UNHEATED adj not having been warmed up
UNHEDGED adj unprotected
UNHEEDED adj noticed but ignored
UNHEEDFUL adj not heedful
UNHEEDILY adv carelessly
UNHEEDING adj not heeding
UNHEEDY adj not heedful
UNHELE same as > UNHEAL
UNHELED > UNHELE
UNHELES > UNHELE
UNHELING > UNHELE
UNHELM vb remove the helmet of (oneself or another)
UNHELMED > UNHELM
UNHELMING > UNHELM
UNHELMS > UNHELM
UNHELPED adj without help
UNHELPFUL adj doing nothing to improve a situation
UNHEPPEN adj awkward
UNHEROIC adj not heroic
UNHERST archaic past form of > UNHEARSE
UNHEWN adj not hewn
UNHIDDEN adj not hidden
UNHINGE vb derange or unbalance (a person or his or her mind)
UNHINGED > UNHINGE
UNHINGES > UNHINGE
UNHINGING > UNHINGE
UNHIP adj not at all fashionable or up to date
UNHIPPER > UNHIP

**UNHIPPEST** > UNHIP
**UNHIRABLE** adj not fit to
be hired
**UNHIRED** adj not hired
**UNHITCH** vb unfasten or
detach
**UNHITCHED** > UNHITCH
**UNHITCHES** > UNHITCH
**UNHIVE** vb remove from
a hive
**UNHIVED** > UNHIVE
**UNHIVES** > UNHIVE
**UNHIVING** > UNHIVE
**UNHOARD** vb remove from
a hoard
**UNHOARDED** > UNHOARD
**UNHOARDS** > UNHOARD
**UNHOLIER** > UNHOLY
**UNHOLIEST** > UNHOLY
**UNHOLILY** > UNHOLY
**UNHOLPEN** same
as > UNHELPED
**UNHOLY** adj immoral or
wicked
**UNHOMELY** adj not homely
**UNHONEST** same
as > DISHONEST
**UNHONORED** adj not
honoured
**UNHOOD** vb remove hood
from
**UNHOODED** > UNHOOD
**UNHOODING** > UNHOOD
**UNHOODS** > UNHOOD
**UNHOOK** vb unfasten the
hooks of (a garment)
**UNHOOKED** > UNHOOK
**UNHOOKING** > UNHOOK
**UNHOOKS** > UNHOOK
**UNHOOP** vb remove hoop(s)
from
**UNHOOPED** > UNHOOP
**UNHOOPING** > UNHOOP
**UNHOOPS** > UNHOOP
**UNHOPED** adj unhoped-for
**UNHOPEFUL** adj not hopeful
**UNHORSE** vb knock or throw
from a horse
**UNHORSED** > UNHORSE
**UNHORSES** > UNHORSE
**UNHORSING** > UNHORSE
**UNHOSTILE** adj not hostile
**UNHOUSE** vb remove from
a house
**UNHOUSED** > UNHOUSE
**UNHOUSES** > UNHOUSE
**UNHOUSING** > UNHOUSE
**UNHUMAN** adj inhuman or
not human
**UNHUMANLY** > UNHUMAN
**UNHUMBLED** adj not
humbled
**UNHUNG** > UNHANG
**UNHUNTED** adj not hunted
**UNHURRIED** adj done at a
leisurely pace, without any
rush or anxiety
**UNHURT** adj not injured in
an accident, attack, etc
**UNHURTFUL** adj not hurtful
**UNHUSK** vb remove the husk
from
**UNHUSKED** > UNHUSK
**UNHUSKING** > UNHUSK

**UNHUSKS** > UNHUSK
**UNI** n (in informal English)
university
**UNIALGAL** adj
microbiological term
**UNIAXIAL** adj (esp
of plants) having an
unbranched main axis
**UNIBODY** n vehicle in which
frame and body are one
unit
**UNIBROW** n informal word
for eyebrows that meet
above the nose
**UNIBROWS** > UNIBROW
**UNICITIES** > UNICITY
**UNICITY** n oneness
**UNICOLOR** same
as > UNICOLOUR
**UNICOLOUR** adj of one
colour
**UNICORN** n imaginary
horselike creature with
one horn growing from its
forehead
**UNICORNS** > UNICORN
**UNICYCLE** n one-wheeled
vehicle driven by pedals,
used in a circus ▷ vb ride a
unicycle
**UNICYCLED** > UNICYCLE
**UNICYCLES** > UNICYCLE
**UNIDEAED** adj not having
ideas
**UNIDEAL** adj not ideal
**UNIFACE** n type of tool
**UNIFACES** > UNIFACE
**UNIFIABLE** > UNIFY
**UNIFIC** adj unifying
**UNIFIED** > UNIFY
**UNIFIER** > UNIFY
**UNIFIERS** > UNIFY
**UNIFIES** > UNIFY
**UNIFILAR** adj composed of,
having, or using only one
wire, thread, filament, etc
**UNIFORM** n special
identifying set of clothes
for the members of an
organization, such as
soldiers ▷ adj regular
and even throughout,
unvarying ▷ vb fit out (a
body of soldiers, etc) with
uniforms
**UNIFORMED** > UNIFORM
**UNIFORMER** > UNIFORM
**UNIFORMLY** > UNIFORM
**UNIFORMS** > UNIFORM
**UNIFY** vb make or become
one
**UNIFYING** > UNIFY
**UNIFYINGS** > UNIFY
**UNIJUGATE** adj (of a
compound leaf) having
only one pair of leaflets
**UNILINEAL** same
as > UNILINEAR
**UNILINEAR** adj developing
in a progressive sequence
**UNILLUMED** adj not
illuminated
**UNILOBAR** adj having one
lobe

**UNILOBED** same
as > UNILOBAR
**UNIMBUED** adj not imbued
**UNIMPEDED** adj not stopped
or disrupted by anything
**UNIMPOSED** adj not
imposed
**UNINCITED** adj unprovoked
**UNINDEXED** adj not indexed
**UNINJURED** adj not having
sustained any injury
**UNINSTALL** vb remove
from a computer system
**UNINSURED** adj not covered
by insurance
**UNINURED** adj
unaccustomed
**UNINVITED** adj not having
been asked ▷ adv without
having been asked
**UNINVOKED** adj not invoked
**UNION** n uniting or being
united ▷ adj of a trade
union
**UNIONISE** same
as > UNIONIZE
**UNIONISED** > UNIONISE
**UNIONISER** > UNIONISE
**UNIONISES** > UNIONISE
**UNIONISM** n principles of
trade unions
**UNIONISMS** > UNIONISM
**UNIONIST** n member or
supporter of a trade union
▷ adj of or relating to
union or unionism, esp
trade unionism
**UNIONISTS** > UNIONIST
**UNIONIZE** vb organize
(workers) into a trade
union
**UNIONIZED** > UNIONIZE
**UNIONIZER** > UNIONIZE
**UNIONIZES** > UNIONIZE
**UNIONS** > UNION
**UNIPAROUS** adj (of certain
animals) producing a
single offspring at each
birth
**UNIPED** n person or thing
with one foot
**UNIPEDS** > UNIPED
**UNIPLANAR** adj situated in
one plane
**UNIPOD** n one-legged
support, as for a camera
**UNIPODS** > UNIPOD
**UNIPOLAR** adj of, concerned
with, or having a single
magnetic or electric pole
**UNIPOTENT** adj able to form
only one type of cell
**UNIQUE** n person or thing
that is unique
**UNIQUELY** > UNIQUE
**UNIQUER** > UNIQUE
**UNIQUES** > UNIQUE
**UNIQUEST** > UNIQUE
**UNIRAMOSE** same
as > UNIRAMOUS
**UNIRAMOUS** adj (esp
of the appendages of
crustaceans) consisting of
a single branch

**UNIRONED** adj not ironed
**UNIRONIC** adj not ironic
**UNIS** > UNI
**UNISERIAL** adj in or
relating to a single series
**UNISEX** adj designed for
use by both sexes ▷ n
condition of seeming not
to belong obviously either
to one sex or the other
from the way one behaves
or dresses
**UNISEXES** > UNISEX
**UNISEXUAL** adj of one sex
only
**UNISIZE** adj in one size
only
**UNISON** n complete
agreement
**UNISONAL** > UNISON
**UNISONANT** > UNISON
**UNISONOUS** > UNISON
**UNISONS** > UNISON
**UNISSUED** adj not issued
**UNIT** n single undivided
entity or whole
**UNITAGE** > UNIT
**UNITAGES** > UNIT
**UNITAL** > UNIT
**UNITARD** n all-in-one
skintight suit
**UNITARDS** > UNITARD
**UNITARIAN** n supporter
of unity or centralization
▷ adj of or relating to unity
or centralization
**UNITARILY** > UNITARY
**UNITARY** adj consisting of a
single undivided whole
**UNITE** vb make or become
an integrated whole ▷ n
English gold coin minted
in the Stuart period,
originally worth 20
shillings
**UNITED** adj produced by
two or more people or
things in combination
**UNITEDLY** > UNITED
**UNITER** > UNITE
**UNITERS** > UNITE
**UNITES** > UNITE
**UNITIES** > UNITY
**UNITING** > UNITE
**UNITINGS** > UNITE
**UNITION** n joining
**UNITIONS** > UNITION
**UNITISE** same as > UNITIZE
**UNITISED** > UNITISE
**UNITISER** same
as > UNITIZER
**UNITISERS** > UNITISER
**UNITISES** > UNITISE
**UNITISING** > UNITISE
**UNITIVE** adj tending to
unite or capable of uniting
**UNITIVELY** > UNITIVE
**UNITIZE** vb convert (an
investment trust) into a
unit trust
**UNITIZED** > UNITIZE
**UNITIZER** n person or
thing that arranges units
into batches

UNITIZERS >UNITIZER
UNITIZES >UNITIZE
UNITIZING >UNITIZE
UNITRUST n type of income-producing trust fund
UNITRUSTS >UNITRUST
UNITS >UNIT
UNITY n state of being one
UNIVALENT adj (of a chromosome during meiosis) not paired with its homologue
UNIVALVE adj relating to, designating, or possessing a mollusc shell that consists of a single piece (valve) ▷ n gastropod mollusc or its shell
UNIVALVED >UNIVALVE
UNIVALVES >UNIVALVE
UNIVERSAL adj of or typical of the whole of mankind or of nature ▷ n something which exists or is true in all places and all situations
UNIVERSE n whole of all existing matter, energy, and space
UNIVERSES >UNIVERSE
UNIVOCAL adj unambiguous or unmistakable ▷ n word or term that has only one meaning
UNIVOCALS >UNIVOCAL
UNJADED adj not jaded
UNJAM vb remove blockage from
UNJAMMED >UNJAM
UNJAMMING >UNJAM
UNJAMS >UNJAM
UNJEALOUS adj not jealous
UNJOINED adj not joined
UNJOINT vb disjoint
UNJOINTED >UNJOINT
UNJOINTS >UNJOINT
UNJOYFUL adj not joyful
UNJOYOUS adj not joyous
UNJUDGED adj not judged
UNJUST adj not fair or just
UNJUSTER >UNJUST
UNJUSTEST >UNJUST
UNJUSTLY >UNJUST
UNKED adj alien
UNKEELED adj without a keel
UNKEMPT adj (of the hair) not combed
UNKEMPTLY >UNKEMPT
UNKEND same as >UNKENNED
UNKENNED adj unknown
UNKENNEL vb release from a kennel
UNKENNELS >UNKENNEL
UNKENT same as >UNKENNED
UNKEPT adj not kept
UNKET same as >UNKED
UNKID same as >UNKED
UNKIND adj unsympathetic or cruel
UNKINDER >UNKIND

UNKINDEST >UNKIND
UNKINDLED adj not kindled
UNKINDLY >UNKIND
UNKING vb strip of sovereignty
UNKINGED >UNKING
UNKINGING >UNKING
UNKINGLY adj not kingly
UNKINGS >UNKING
UNKINK vb straighten out
UNKINKED >UNKINK
UNKINKING >UNKINK
UNKINKS >UNKINK
UNKISS vb cancel (a previous action) with a kiss
UNKISSED adj not kissed
UNKISSES >UNKISS
UNKISSING >UNKISS
UNKNELLED adj not tolled
UNKNIGHT vb strip of knighthood
UNKNIGHTS >UNKNIGHT
UNKNIT vb make or become undone, untied, or unravelled
UNKNITS >UNKNIT
UNKNITTED >UNKNIT
UNKNOT vb disentangle or undo a knot or knots in
UNKNOTS >UNKNOT
UNKNOTTED >UNKNOT
UNKNOWING adj unaware or ignorant
UNKNOWN adj not known ▷ n unknown person, quantity, or thing
UNKNOWNS >UNKNOWN
UNKOSHER adj not conforming to Jewish religious law
UNLABELED adj not labelled
UNLABORED adj not laboured
UNLACE vb loosen or undo the lacing of (shoes, garments, etc)
UNLACED adj not laced
UNLACES >UNLACE
UNLACING >UNLACE
UNLADE less common word for >UNLOAD
UNLADED >UNLADE
UNLADEN adj not laden
UNLADES >UNLADE
UNLADING >UNLADE
UNLADINGS >UNLADE
UNLAID >UNLAY
UNLASH vb untie or unfasten
UNLASHED >UNLASH
UNLASHES >UNLASH
UNLASHING >UNLASH
UNLAST archaic variant of >UNLACED
UNLASTE archaic variant of >UNLACED
UNLATCH vb open or unfasten or come open or unfastened by the lifting or release of a latch
UNLATCHED >UNLATCH
UNLATCHES >UNLATCH
UNLAW vb penalize

UNLAWED >UNLAW
UNLAWFUL adj not permitted by law
UNLAWING >UNLAW
UNLAWS >UNLAW
UNLAY vb untwist (a rope or cable) to separate its strands
UNLAYING >UNLAY
UNLAYS >UNLAY
UNLEAD vb strip off lead
UNLEADED adj (of petrol) containing less tetraethyl lead, in order to reduce environmental pollution ▷ n petrol containing a reduced amount of tetraethyl lead
UNLEADEDS >UNLEADED
UNLEADING >UNLEAD
UNLEADS >UNLEAD
UNLEAL adj treacherous
UNLEARN vb try to forget something learnt or to discard accumulated knowledge
UNLEARNED same as >UNLEARNT
UNLEARNS >UNLEARN
UNLEARNT adj denoting knowledge or skills innately present rather than learnt
UNLEASED adj not leased
UNLEASH vb set loose or cause (something bad)
UNLEASHED >UNLEASH
UNLEASHES >UNLEASH
UNLED adj not led
UNLESS conj except under the circumstances that ▷ prep except
UNLET adj not rented
UNLETHAL adj not deadly
UNLETTED adj unimpeded
UNLEVEL adj not level ▷ vb make unbalanced
UNLEVELED >UNLEVEL
UNLEVELS >UNLEVEL
UNLEVIED adj not levied
UNLICH Spenserian form of >UNLIKE
UNLICKED adj not licked
UNLID vb remove lid from
UNLIDDED adj not lidded
UNLIDDING >UNLID
UNLIDS >UNLID
UNLIGHTED adj not lit
UNLIKABLE adj not likable
UNLIKE adj dissimilar or different ▷ prep not like or typical of ▷ n person or thing that is unlike another
UNLIKED adj not liked
UNLIKELY adj improbable
UNLIKES >UNLIKE
UNLIMBER vb disengage (a gun) from its limber
UNLIMBERS >UNLIMBER
UNLIME vb detach
UNLIMED >UNLIME
UNLIMES >UNLIME
UNLIMING >UNLIME

UNLIMITED adj apparently endless
UNLINE vb remove the lining from
UNLINEAL adj not lineal
UNLINED adj not having any lining
UNLINES >UNLINE
UNLINING >UNLINE
UNLINK vb undo the link or links between
UNLINKED >UNLINK
UNLINKING >UNLINK
UNLINKS >UNLINK
UNLISTED adj not entered on a list
UNLIT adj (of a fire, cigarette, etc) not lit and therefore not burning
UNLIVABLE adj not fit for living in
UNLIVE vb live so as to nullify, undo, or live down (past events or times)
UNLIVED >UNLIVE
UNLIVELY adj lifeless
UNLIVES >UNLIVE
UNLIVING >UNLIVE
UNLOAD vb remove (cargo) from (a ship, truck, or plane)
UNLOADED >UNLOAD
UNLOADER >UNLOAD
UNLOADERS >UNLOAD
UNLOADING >UNLOAD
UNLOADS >UNLOAD
UNLOBED adj without lobes
UNLOCATED adj not located
UNLOCK vb unfasten (a lock or door)
UNLOCKED adj not locked
UNLOCKING >UNLOCK
UNLOCKS >UNLOCK
UNLOGICAL same as >ILLOGICAL
UNLOOKED adj not looked (at)
UNLOOSE vb set free or release
UNLOOSED >UNLOOSE
UNLOOSEN same as >UNLOOSE
UNLOOSENS >UNLOOSEN
UNLOOSES >UNLOOSE
UNLOOSING >UNLOOSE
UNLOPPED adj not chopped off
UNLORD vb remove from position of being lord
UNLORDED >UNLORD
UNLORDING >UNLORD
UNLORDLY adv not in a lordlike manner
UNLORDS >UNLORD
UNLOSABLE adj unable to be lost
UNLOST adj not lost
UNLOVABLE adj too unpleasant or unattractive to be loved
UNLOVE vb stop loving
UNLOVED adj not loved by anyone
UNLOVELY adj unpleasant

in appearance or character
**UNLOVES** >UNLOVE
**UNLOVING** adj not feeling or showing love and affection
**UNLUCKIER** >UNLUCKY
**UNLUCKILY** >UNLUCKY
**UNLUCKY** adj having bad luck, unfortunate
**UNLYRICAL** adj not lyrical
**UNMACHO** adj not macho
**UNMADE** adj (of a bed) with the bedclothes not smoothed and tidied
**UNMAILED** adj not sent by post
**UNMAIMED** adj not injured
**UNMAKABLE** adj unable to be made
**UNMAKE** vb undo or destroy
**UNMAKER** >UNMAKE
**UNMAKERS** >UNMAKE
**UNMAKES** >UNMAKE
**UNMAKING** >UNMAKE
**UNMAKINGS** >UNMAKE
**UNMAN** vb cause to lose courage or nerve
**UNMANACLE** vb release from manacles
**UNMANAGED** adj not managed
**UNMANFUL** adj unmanly
**UNMANLIER** >UNMANLY
**UNMANLIKE** adj not worthy of a man
**UNMANLY** adj not masculine or virile
**UNMANNED** adj having no personnel or crew
**UNMANNING** >UNMAN
**UNMANNISH** adj not mannish
**UNMANS** >UNMAN
**UNMANTLE** vb remove mantle from
**UNMANTLED** >UNMANTLE
**UNMANTLES** >UNMANTLE
**UNMANURED** adj not treated with manure
**UNMAPPED** adj not charted
**UNMARD** same as >UNMARRED
**UNMARKED** adj having no signs of damage or injury
**UNMARRED** adj not marred
**UNMARRIED** adj not married
**UNMARRIES** >UNMARRY
**UNMARRY** vb divorce
**UNMASK** vb remove the mask or disguise from
**UNMASKED** >UNMASK
**UNMASKER** >UNMASK
**UNMASKERS** >UNMASK
**UNMASKING** >UNMASK
**UNMASKS** >UNMASK
**UNMATCHED** adj not equalled or surpassed
**UNMATED** adj not mated
**UNMATTED** adj not matted
**UNMATURED** adj not matured
**UNMEANING** adj having no meaning
**UNMEANT** adj unintentional

**UNMEEK** adj not submissive
**UNMEET** adj not meet
**UNMEETLY** >UNMEET
**UNMELLOW** adj not mellow
**UNMELTED** adj not melted
**UNMENDED** adj not mended
**UNMERITED** adj not merited or deserved
**UNMERRY** adj not merry
**UNMESH** vb release from mesh
**UNMESHED** >UNMESH
**UNMESHES** >UNMESH
**UNMESHING** >UNMESH
**UNMET** adj unfulfilled
**UNMETED** adj unmeasured
**UNMEW** vb release from confinement
**UNMEWED** >UNMEW
**UNMEWING** >UNMEW
**UNMEWS** >UNMEW
**UNMILKED** adj not milked
**UNMILLED** adj not milled
**UNMINDED** adj disregarded
**UNMINDFUL** adj careless, heedless, or forgetful
**UNMINED** adj not mined
**UNMINGLE** vb separate
**UNMINGLED** >UNMINGLE
**UNMINGLES** >UNMINGLE
**UNMIRY** adj not swampy
**UNMISSED** adj unnoticed
**UNMITER** same as >UNMITRE
**UNMITERED** >UNMITER
**UNMITERS** >UNMITER
**UNMITRE** vb divest of a mitre
**UNMITRED** >UNMITRE
**UNMITRES** >UNMITRE
**UNMITRING** >UNMITRE
**UNMIX** vb separate
**UNMIXABLE** adj incapable of being mixed
**UNMIXED** >UNMIX
**UNMIXEDLY** >UNMIXED
**UNMIXES** >UNMIX
**UNMIXING** >UNMIX
**UNMIXT** archaic past form of >UNMIX
**UNMOANED** adj unmourned
**UNMODISH** adj passé
**UNMOLD** same as >UNMOULD
**UNMOLDED** >UNMOLD
**UNMOLDING** >UNMOLD
**UNMOLDS** >UNMOLD
**UNMOLTEN** adj not molten
**UNMONEYED** adj poor
**UNMONIED** same as >UNMONEYED
**UNMOOR** vb weigh the anchor or drop the mooring of (a vessel)
**UNMOORED** >UNMOOR
**UNMOORING** >UNMOOR
**UNMOORS** >UNMOOR
**UNMORAL** adj outside morality
**UNMORALLY** >UNMORAL
**UNMORTISE** vb release from mortise
**UNMOTIVED** adj without motive
**UNMOULD** vb change shape of

**UNMOULDED** >UNMOULD
**UNMOULDS** >UNMOULD
**UNMOUNT** vb dismount
**UNMOUNTED** >UNMOUNT
**UNMOUNTS** >UNMOUNT
**UNMOURNED** adj not mourned
**UNMOVABLE** adj not movable
**UNMOVABLY** >UNMOVABLE
**UNMOVED** adj not affected by emotion, indifferent
**UNMOVEDLY** >UNMOVED
**UNMOVING** adj still and motionless
**UNMOWN** adj not mown
**UNMUFFLE** vb remove a muffle or muffles from
**UNMUFFLED** >UNMUFFLE
**UNMUFFLES** >UNMUFFLE
**UNMUSICAL** adj (of a person) unable to appreciate or play music
**UNMUZZLE** vb take the muzzle off (a dog, etc)
**UNMUZZLED** >UNMUZZLE
**UNMUZZLES** >UNMUZZLE
**UNNAIL** vb unfasten by removing nails
**UNNAILED** >UNNAIL
**UNNAILING** >UNNAIL
**UNNAILS** >UNNAIL
**UNNAMABLE** adj that cannot or must not be named
**UNNAMED** adj not mentioned by name
**UNNANELD** same as >UNANELED
**UNNATIVE** adj not native
**UNNATURAL** adj strange and frightening because not usual
**UNNEATH** adj archaic word for underneath
**UNNEEDED** adj not needed
**UNNEEDFUL** adj not needful
**UNNERVE** vb cause to lose courage, confidence, or self-control
**UNNERVED** >UNNERVE
**UNNERVES** >UNNERVE
**UNNERVING** >UNNERVE
**UNNEST** vb remove from a nest
**UNNESTED** >UNNEST
**UNNESTING** >UNNEST
**UNNESTS** >UNNEST
**UNNETHES** same as >UNNEATH
**UNNETTED** adj not having or not enclosed in a net
**UNNOBLE** vb strip of nobility
**UNNOBLED** >UNNOBLE
**UNNOBLES** >UNNOBLE
**UNNOBLING** >UNNOBLE
**UNNOISY** adj quiet
**UNNOTED** adj not noted
**UNNOTICED** adj without being seen or noticed
**UNNUANCED** adj without nuances
**UNOBEYED** adj not obeyed
**UNOBVIOUS** adj unapparent
**UNOFFERED** adj not offered

**UNOFTEN** adv infrequently
**UNOILED** adj not lubricated with oil
**UNOPEN** adj not open
**UNOPENED** adj closed, barred, or sealed
**UNOPPOSED** adj not opposed
**UNORDER** vb cancel an order
**UNORDERED** adj not ordered
**UNORDERLY** adj not orderly or disorderly
**UNORDERS** >UNORDER
**UNORNATE** same as >INORNATE
**UNOWED** same as >UNOWNED
**UNOWNED** adj not owned
**UNPACED** adj without the aid of a pacemaker
**UNPACK** vb remove the contents of (a suitcase, trunk, etc)
**UNPACKED** >UNPACK
**UNPACKER** >UNPACK
**UNPACKERS** >UNPACK
**UNPACKING** >UNPACK
**UNPACKS** >UNPACK
**UNPADDED** adj not padded
**UNPAGED** adj (of a book) having no page numbers
**UNPAID** adj without a salary or wage
**UNPAINED** adj not suffering pain
**UNPAINFUL** adj painless
**UNPAINT** vb remove paint from
**UNPAINTED** >UNPAINT
**UNPAINTS** >UNPAINT
**UNPAIRED** adj not paired up
**UNPALSIED** adj not affected with palsy
**UNPANEL** vb unsaddle
**UNPANELS** >UNPANEL
**UNPANGED** adj without pain or sadness
**UNPANNEL** same as >UNPANEL
**UNPANNELS** >UNPANNEL
**UNPAPER** vb remove paper from
**UNPAPERED** >UNPAPER
**UNPAPERS** >UNPAPER
**UNPARED** adj not pared
**UNPARTED** adj not parted
**UNPARTIAL** same as >IMPARTIAL
**UNPATCHED** adj not patched
**UNPATHED** adj not having a path
**UNPAVED** adj not covered in paving
**UNPAY** vb undo
**UNPAYABLE** adj incapable of being paid
**UNPAYING** >UNPAY
**UNPAYS** >UNPAY
**UNPEELED** adj not peeled
**UNPEERED** adj unparalleled
**UNPEG** vb remove the peg or pegs from, esp to unfasten
**UNPEGGED** >UNPEG
**UNPEGGING** >UNPEG

**UNPEGS** >UNPEG
**UNPEN** vb release from a pen
**UNPENNED** >UNPEN
**UNPENNIED** adj not having pennies
**UNPENNING** >UNPEN
**UNPENS** >UNPEN
**UNPENT** archaic past form of >UNPEN
**UNPEOPLE** vb empty of people
**UNPEOPLED** >UNPEOPLE
**UNPEOPLES** >UNPEOPLE
**UNPERCH** vb remove from a perch
**UNPERCHED** >UNPERCH
**UNPERCHES** >UNPERCH
**UNPERFECT** same as >IMPERFECT
**UNPERPLEX** vb remove confusion from
**UNPERSON** n person whose existence is officially denied or ignored
**UNPERSONS** >UNPERSON
**UNPERVERT** vb free (someone) from perversion
**UNPICK** vb undo (the stitches) of (a piece of sewing)
**UNPICKED** adj (of knitting, sewing, etc) having been unravelled or picked out
**UNPICKING** >UNPICK
**UNPICKS** >UNPICK
**UNPIERCED** adj not pierced
**UNPILE** vb remove from a pile
**UNPILED** >UNPILE
**UNPILES** >UNPILE
**UNPILING** >UNPILE
**UNPILOTED** adj unguided
**UNPIN** vb remove a pin or pins from
**UNPINKED** adj not decorated with a perforated pattern
**UNPINKT** same as >UNPINKED
**UNPINNED** >UNPIN
**UNPINNING** >UNPIN
**UNPINS** >UNPIN
**UNPITIED** adj not pitied
**UNPITIFUL** adj pitiless
**UNPITTED** adj not having had pits removed
**UNPITYING** adj not pitying
**UNPLACE** same as >DISPLACE
**UNPLACED** adj not given or put in a particular place
**UNPLACES** >UNPLACE
**UNPLACING** >UNPLACE
**UNPLAGUED** adj not plagued
**UNPLAINED** adj unmourned
**UNPLAIT** vb remove plaits from
**UNPLAITED** >UNPLAIT
**UNPLAITS** >UNPLAIT
**UNPLANKED** adj not planked
**UNPLANNED** adj not intentional or deliberate
**UNPLANTED** adj not planted
**UNPLAYED** adj not played

**UNPLEASED** adj not pleased or displeased
**UNPLEATED** adj not pleated
**UNPLEDGED** adj not pledged
**UNPLIABLE** adj not easily bent
**UNPLIABLY** >UNPLIABLE
**UNPLIANT** adj not pliant
**UNPLOWED** adj not ploughed
**UNPLUCKED** adj not plucked
**UNPLUG** vb disconnect (a piece of electrical equipment) by taking the plug out of the socket
**UNPLUGGED** adj using acoustic rather than electric instruments
**UNPLUGS** >UNPLUG
**UNPLUMB** vb remove lead from
**UNPLUMBED** adj not measured
**UNPLUMBS** >UNPLUMB
**UNPLUME** vb remove feathers from
**UNPLUMED** >UNPLUME
**UNPLUMES** >UNPLUME
**UNPLUMING** >UNPLUME
**UNPOETIC** adj not poetic
**UNPOINTED** adj not pointed
**UNPOISED** adj not poised
**UNPOISON** vb extract poison from
**UNPOISONS** >UNPOISON
**UNPOLICED** adj without police control
**UNPOLISH** vb remove polish from
**UNPOLITE** same as >IMPOLITE
**UNPOLITIC** another word for >IMPOLITIC
**UNPOLLED** adj not included in an opinion poll
**UNPOPE** vb strip of popedom
**UNPOPED** >UNPOPE
**UNPOPES** >UNPOPE
**UNPOPING** >UNPOPE
**UNPOPULAR** adj generally disliked or disapproved of
**UNPOSED** adj not posed
**UNPOSTED** adj not sent by post
**UNPOTABLE** adj undrinkable
**UNPOTTED** adj not planted in a pot
**UNPRAISE** vb withhold praise from
**UNPRAISED** >UNPRAISE
**UNPRAISES** >UNPRAISE
**UNPRAY** vb withdraw (a prayer)
**UNPRAYED** >UNPRAY
**UNPRAYING** >UNPRAY
**UNPRAYS** >UNPRAY
**UNPREACH** vb retract (a sermon)
**UNPRECISE** same as >IMPRECISE
**UNPREDICT** vb retract (a previous prediction)

**UNPREPARE** vb make unprepared
**UNPRESSED** adj not pressed
**UNPRETTY** adj unattractive
**UNPRICED** adj having no fixed or marked price
**UNPRIEST** vb strip of priesthood
**UNPRIESTS** >UNPRIEST
**UNPRIMED** adj not primed
**UNPRINTED** adj not printed
**UNPRISON** vb release from prison
**UNPRISONS** >UNPRISON
**UNPRIZED** adj not treasured
**UNPROBED** adj not examined
**UNPROP** vb remove support from
**UNPROPER** same as >IMPROPER
**UNPROPPED** >UNPROP
**UNPROPS** >UNPROP
**UNPROVED** adj not having been established as true, valid, or possible
**UNPROVEN** adj not established as true by evidence or demonstration
**UNPROVIDE** vb fail to supply requirements for
**UNPROVOKE** vb remove provocation from
**UNPRUNED** adj not pruned
**UNPUCKER** vb remove wrinkles from
**UNPUCKERS** >UNPUCKER
**UNPULLED** adj not pulled
**UNPURE** same as >IMPURE
**UNPURELY** >UNPURE
**UNPURGED** adj not purged
**UNPURSE** vb relax (lips) from pursed position
**UNPURSED** >UNPURSE
**UNPURSES** >UNPURSE
**UNPURSING** >UNPURSE
**UNPURSUED** adj not followed
**UNPUZZLE** vb figure out
**UNPUZZLED** >UNPUZZLE
**UNPUZZLES** >UNPUZZLE
**UNQUAKING** adj not quaking
**UNQUALIFY** vb disqualify
**UNQUEEN** vb depose from the position of queen
**UNQUEENED** >UNQUEEN
**UNQUEENLY** adv not in a queenlike manner
**UNQUEENS** >UNQUEEN
**UNQUELLED** adj not quelled
**UNQUIET** adj anxious or uneasy ▷ n state of unrest ▷ vb disquiet
**UNQUIETED** >UNQUIET
**UNQUIETER** >UNQUIET
**UNQUIETLY** >UNQUIET
**UNQUIETS** >UNQUIET
**UNQUOTE** interj expression used to indicate the end of a quotation that was introduced with the

word 'quote' ▷ vb close (a quotation), esp in printing
**UNQUOTED** >UNQUOTE
**UNQUOTES** >UNQUOTE
**UNQUOTING** >UNQUOTE
**UNRACED** adj not raced
**UNRACKED** adj not stretched
**UNRAISED** adj not raised
**UNRAKE** vb unearth through raking
**UNRAKED** adj not raked
**UNRAKES** >UNRAKE
**UNRAKING** >UNRAKE
**UNRANKED** adj not ranked
**UNRATED** adj not rated
**UNRAVAGED** adj not ravaged
**UNRAVEL** vb reduce (something knitted or woven) to separate strands
**UNRAVELED** >UNRAVEL
**UNRAVELS** >UNRAVEL
**UNRAZED** adj not razed
**UNRAZORED** adj unshaven
**UNREACHED** adj not reached
**UNREAD** adj (of a book or article) not yet read
**UNREADIER** >UNREADY
**UNREADILY** >UNREADY
**UNREADY** adj not ready or prepared
**UNREAL** adj (as if) existing only in the imagination
**UNREALISE** same as >UNREALIZE
**UNREALISM** n abstractionism
**UNREALITY** n quality or state of being unreal, fanciful, or impractical
**UNREALIZE** vb make unreal
**UNREALLY** >UNREAL
**UNREAPED** adj not reaped
**UNREASON** n irrationality or madness ▷ vb deprive of reason
**UNREASONS** >UNREASON
**UNREAVE** vb unwind
**UNREAVED** >UNREAVE
**UNREAVES** >UNREAVE
**UNREAVING** >UNREAVE
**UNREBATED** adj not refunded
**UNREBUKED** adj not rebuked
**UNRECKED** adj disregarded
**UNRED** same as >UNREAD
**UNREDREST** adj not redressed
**UNREDUCED** adj not reduced
**UNREDY** same as >UNREADY
**UNREEL** vb unwind from a reel
**UNREELED** >UNREEL
**UNREELER** n machine that unwinds something from a reel
**UNREELERS** >UNREELER
**UNREELING** >UNREEL
**UNREELS** >UNREEL
**UNREEVE** vb withdraw (a rope) from a block, thimble, etc

UNREEVED > UNREEVE
UNREEVES > UNREEVE
UNREEVING > UNREEVE
UNREFINED adj (of substances such as petroleum, ores, and sugar) not processed into a pure or usable form
UNREFUTED adj not refuted
UNREIN vb free from reins
UNREINED > UNREIN
UNREINING > UNREIN
UNREINS > UNREIN
UNRELATED adj not connected with each other
UNRELAXED adj not relaxed
UNREMOVED adj not removed
UNRENEWED adj not renewed
UNRENT adj not torn
UNRENTED adj not rented
UNREPAID adj not repaid
UNREPAIR less common word for > DISREPAIR
UNREPAIRS > UNREPAIR
UNRESERVE n candour
UNREST n rebellious state of discontent
UNRESTED adj not rested
UNRESTFUL adj restless
UNRESTING adj not resting
UNRESTS > UNREST
UNRETIRE vb resume work after retiring
UNRETIRED > UNRETIRE
UNRETIRES > UNRETIRE
UNREVISED adj not revised
UNREVOKED adj not revoked
UNRHYMED adj not rhymed
UNRIBBED adj not ribbed
UNRID adj unridden
UNRIDABLE adj not capable of being ridden
UNRIDDEN adj not or never ridden
UNRIDDLE vb solve or puzzle out
UNRIDDLED > UNRIDDLE
UNRIDDLER > UNRIDDLE
UNRIDDLES > UNRIDDLE
UNRIFLED adj (of a firearm or its bore) not rifled
UNRIG vb strip (a vessel) of standing and running rigging
UNRIGGED > UNRIG
UNRIGGING > UNRIG
UNRIGHT n wrong
UNRIGHTS > UNRIGHT
UNRIGS > UNRIG
UNRIMED same as > UNRHYMED
UNRINGED adj not having or wearing a ring
UNRINSED adj not rinsed
UNRIP vb rip open
UNRIPE adj not fully matured
UNRIPELY > UNRIPE
UNRIPENED same as > UNRIPE
UNRIPER > UNRIPE
UNRIPEST > UNRIPE

UNRIPPED > UNRIP
UNRIPPING > UNRIP
UNRIPS > UNRIP
UNRISEN adj not risen
UNRIVALED adj (in US English) matchless or unrivalled
UNRIVEN adj not torn apart
UNRIVET vb remove rivets from
UNRIVETED > UNRIVET
UNRIVETS > UNRIVET
UNROASTED adj not roasted
UNROBE same as > DISROBE
UNROBED > UNROBE
UNROBES > UNROBE
UNROBING > UNROBE
UNROLL vb open out or unwind (something rolled or coiled) or (of something rolled or coiled) become opened out or unwound
UNROLLED > UNROLL
UNROLLING > UNROLL
UNROLLS > UNROLL
UNROOF vb remove the roof from
UNROOFED > UNROOF
UNROOFING > UNROOF
UNROOFS > UNROOF
UNROOST vb remove from a perch
UNROOSTED > UNROOST
UNROOSTS > UNROOST
UNROOT less common word for > UPROOT
UNROOTED > UNROOT
UNROOTING > UNROOT
UNROOTS > UNROOT
UNROPE vb release from a rope
UNROPED > UNROPE
UNROPES > UNROPE
UNROPING > UNROPE
UNROSINED adj not coated with rosin
UNROTTED adj not rotted
UNROTTEN adj not rotten
UNROUGED adj not coloured with rouge
UNROUGH adj not rough
UNROUND vb release (lips) from a rounded position
UNROUNDED adj articulated with the lips spread
UNROUNDS > UNROUND
UNROUSED adj not roused
UNROVE > UNREEVE
UNROVEN > UNREEVE
UNROYAL adj not royal
UNROYALLY > UNROYAL
UNRUBBED adj not rubbed
UNRUDE adj not rude
UNRUFFE same as > UNROUGH
UNRUFFLE vb calm
UNRUFFLED adj calm and unperturbed
UNRUFFLES > UNRUFFLE
UNRULE n lack of authority
UNRULED adj not ruled
UNRULES > UNRULE
UNRULIER > UNRULY
UNRULIEST > UNRULY

UNRULY adj difficult to control or organize
UNRUMPLED adj neat
UNRUSHED adj unhurried
UNRUSTED adj not rusted
UNS > UN
UNSADDLE vb remove the saddle from (a horse)
UNSADDLED > UNSADDLE
UNSADDLES > UNSADDLE
UNSAFE adj dangerous
UNSAFELY > UNSAFE
UNSAFER > UNSAFE
UNSAFEST > UNSAFE
UNSAFETY n lack of safety
UNSAID adj not said or expressed
UNSAILED adj not sailed
UNSAINED adj not blessed
UNSAINT vb remove status of being a saint from
UNSAINTED > UNSAINT
UNSAINTLY adj not saintly
UNSAINTS > UNSAINT
UNSALABLE adj not capable of being sold
UNSALABLY > UNSALABLE
UNSALTED adj not seasoned, preserved, or treated with salt
UNSALUTED adj not saluted
UNSAMPLED adj not sampled
UNSAPPED adj not undermined
UNSASHED adj not furnished with a sash
UNSATABLE adj not able to be sated; insatiable
UNSATED adj not sated
UNSATIATE same as > INSATIABLE
UNSATING adj not satisfying
UNSAVED adj not saved
UNSAVORY same as > UNSAVOURY
UNSAVOURY adj distasteful or objectionable
UNSAWED same as > UNSAWN
UNSAWN adj not cut with a saw
UNSAY vb retract or withdraw (something said or written)
UNSAYABLE adj that cannot be said
UNSAYING > UNSAY
UNSAYS > UNSAY
UNSCALE same as > DESCALE
UNSCALED > UNSCALE
UNSCALES > UNSCALE
UNSCALING > UNSCALE
UNSCANNED adj not scanned
UNSCARRED adj not scarred
UNSCARY adj not scary
UNSCATHED adj not harmed or injured
UNSCENTED adj not filled or impregnated with odour or fragrance
UNSCOURED adj not scoured
UNSCREW vb loosen (a screw

or lid) by turning it
UNSCREWED > UNSCREW
UNSCREWS > UNSCREW
UNSCYTHED adj not cut with a scythe
UNSEAL vb remove or break the seal of
UNSEALED > UNSEAL
UNSEALING > UNSEAL
UNSEALS > UNSEAL
UNSEAM vb open or undo the seam of
UNSEAMED > UNSEAM
UNSEAMING > UNSEAM
UNSEAMS > UNSEAM
UNSEARED adj not seared
UNSEASON vb affect unfavourably
UNSEASONS > UNSEASON
UNSEAT vb throw or displace from a seat or saddle
UNSEATED > UNSEAT
UNSEATING > UNSEAT
UNSEATS > UNSEAT
UNSECRET adj not secret
UNSECULAR adj not secular
UNSECURED adj (of a loan, etc) secured only against general assets and not against a specific asset
UNSEDUCED adj not seduced
UNSEEABLE adj not able to be seen
UNSEEDED adj (of a player in a sport) not given a top player's position in the opening rounds of a tournament
UNSEEING adj not noticing or looking at anything
UNSEEL vb undo seeling
UNSEELED > UNSEEL
UNSEELIE pl n evil malevolent fairies ▷ adj of or belonging to the unseelie
UNSEELING > UNSEEL
UNSEELS > UNSEEL
UNSEEMING adj unseemly
UNSEEMLY adj not according to expected standards of behaviour ▷ adv in an unseemly manner
UNSEEN adj hidden or invisible ▷ adv without being seen ▷ n passage which is given to students for translation without them having seen it in advance
UNSEENS > UNSEEN
UNSEIZED adj not seized
UNSELDOM adv frequently
UNSELF vb remove self-centredness from ▷ n lack of self
UNSELFED > UNSELF
UNSELFING > UNSELF
UNSELFISH adj concerned about other people's wishes and needs rather

than one's own
**UNSELFS** > UNSELF
**UNSELL** vb speak unfavourably and off-puttingly of (something or someone)
**UNSELLING** > UNSELL
**UNSELLS** > UNSELL
**UNSELVES** > UNSELF
**UNSENSE** vb remove sense from
**UNSENSED** > UNSENSE
**UNSENSES** > UNSENSE
**UNSENSING** > UNSENSE
**UNSENT** adj not sent
**UNSERIOUS** adj not serious
**UNSERVED** adj not served
**UNSET** adj not yet solidified or firm ▷ vb displace
**UNSETS** > UNSET
**UNSETTING** > UNSET
**UNSETTLE** vb change or become changed from a fixed or settled condition
**UNSETTLED** adj lacking order or stability
**UNSETTLES** > UNSETTLE
**UNSEVERED** adj not severed
**UNSEW** vb undo stitching of
**UNSEWED** same as > UNSEW
**UNSEWING** > UNSEW
**UNSEWN** > UNSEW
**UNSEWS** > UNSEW
**UNSEX** vb deprive (a person) of the attributes of his or her sex, esp to make a woman more callous
**UNSEXED** > UNSEX
**UNSEXES** > UNSEX
**UNSEXING** > UNSEX
**UNSEXIST** adj not sexist
**UNSEXUAL** adj not sexual
**UNSEXY** adj not sexually attractive
**UNSHACKLE** vb release from shackles
**UNSHADED** adj not shaded
**UNSHADOW** vb remove shadow from
**UNSHADOWS** > UNSHADOW
**UNSHAKED** same as > UNSHAKEN
**UNSHAKEN** adj (of faith or feelings) not having been weakened
**UNSHALE** vb expose
**UNSHALED** > UNSHALE
**UNSHALES** > UNSHALE
**UNSHALING** > UNSHALE
**UNSHAMED** same as > UNASHAMED
**UNSHAPE** vb make shapeless
**UNSHAPED** > UNSHAPE
**UNSHAPELY** adj not shapely
**UNSHAPEN** adj having no definite shape
**UNSHAPES** > UNSHAPE
**UNSHAPING** > UNSHAPE
**UNSHARED** adj not shared
**UNSHARP** adj not sharp
**UNSHAVED** adj not shaved
**UNSHAVEN** adj (of a man who does not have a

beard) having stubble on his chin because he has not shaved recently
**UNSHEATHE** vb pull (a weapon) from a sheath
**UNSHED** adj not shed
**UNSHELL** vb remove from a shell
**UNSHELLED** > UNSHELL
**UNSHELLS** > UNSHELL
**UNSHENT** adj undamaged
**UNSHEWN** adj unshown
**UNSHIFT** vb release the shift key on a keyboard
**UNSHIFTED** > UNSHIFT
**UNSHIFTS** > UNSHIFT
**UNSHIP** vb be or cause to be unloaded, discharged, or disembarked from a ship
**UNSHIPPED** > UNSHIP
**UNSHIPS** > UNSHIP
**UNSHIRTED** adj not wearing a shirt
**UNSHOCKED** adj not shocked
**UNSHOD** adj not wearing shoes
**UNSHOE** vb remove shoes from
**UNSHOED** same as > UNSHOD
**UNSHOEING** > UNSHOE
**UNSHOES** > UNSHOE
**UNSHOOT** Shakespearean variant of > UNSHOUT
**UNSHOOTED** > UNSHOOT
**UNSHOOTS** > UNSHOOT
**UNSHORN** adj not cut
**UNSHOT** adj not shot
**UNSHOUT** vb revoke (an earlier statement) by shouting a contrary one
**UNSHOUTED** > UNSHOUT
**UNSHOUTS** > UNSHOUT
**UNSHOWN** adj not shown
**UNSHOWY** adj not showy
**UNSHRIVED** same as > UNSHRIVEN
**UNSHRIVEN** adj not shriven
**UNSHROUD** vb uncover
**UNSHROUDS** > UNSHROUD
**UNSHRUBD** adj not having shrubs
**UNSHRUNK** adj not shrunk
**UNSHUNNED** adj not shunned
**UNSHUT** vb open
**UNSHUTS** > UNSHUT
**UNSHUTTER** vb remove shutters from
**UNSICKER** adj unsettled
**UNSICKLED** adj not cut with a sickle
**UNSIFTED** adj not strained
**UNSIGHING** adj not lamented
**UNSIGHT** vb obstruct vision of
**UNSIGHTED** adj not sighted
**UNSIGHTLY** adj unpleasant to look at
**UNSIGHTS** > UNSIGHT
**UNSIGNED** adj (of a letter etc) anonymous
**UNSILENT** adj not silent

**UNSIMILAR** adj not similar
**UNSINEW** vb weaken
**UNSINEWED** > UNSINEW
**UNSINEWS** > UNSINEW
**UNSINFUL** adj without sin
**UNSISTING** adj Shakespearean term, possibly meaning insisting
**UNSIZABLE** adj of inadequate size
**UNSIZED** adj not made or sorted according to size
**UNSKILFUL** adj lacking dexterity or proficiency
**UNSKILLED** adj not having or requiring any special skill or training
**UNSKIMMED** adj not skimmed
**UNSKINNED** adj not skinned
**UNSLAIN** adj not killed
**UNSLAKED** adj not slaked
**UNSLICED** adj not sliced
**UNSLICK** adj not slick
**UNSLING** vb remove or release from a slung position
**UNSLINGS** > UNSLING
**UNSLUICE** vb let flow
**UNSLUICED** > UNSLUICE
**UNSLUICES** > UNSLUICE
**UNSLUNG** > UNSLING
**UNSMART** adj not smart
**UNSMILING** adj not wearing or assuming a smile
**UNSMITTEN** adj not smitten
**UNSMOKED** adj not smoked
**UNSMOOTH** vb roughen
**UNSMOOTHS** > UNSMOOTH
**UNSMOTE** same as > UNSMITTEN
**UNSNAG** vb remove snags from
**UNSNAGGED** > UNSNAG
**UNSNAGS** > UNSNAG
**UNSNAP** vb unfasten (the snap or catch) of (something)
**UNSNAPPED** > UNSNAP
**UNSNAPS** > UNSNAP
**UNSNARL** vb free from a snarl or tangle
**UNSNARLED** > UNSNARL
**UNSNARLS** > UNSNARL
**UNSNECK** vb unlatch
**UNSNECKED** > UNSNECK
**UNSNECKS** > UNSNECK
**UNSNUFFED** adj not snuffed
**UNSOAKED** adj not soaked
**UNSOAPED** adj not rubbed with soap
**UNSOBER** adj not sober
**UNSOBERLY** > UNSOBER
**UNSOCIAL** adj avoiding the company of other people
**UNSOCKET** vb remove from a socket
**UNSOCKETS** > UNSOCKET
**UNSOD** same as > UNSODDEN
**UNSODDEN** adj not soaked
**UNSOFT** adj hard
**UNSOILED** adj not soiled

**UNSOLACED** adj not comforted
**UNSOLD** adj not sold
**UNSOLDER** vb remove soldering from
**UNSOLDERS** > UNSOLDER
**UNSOLEMN** adj unceremonious
**UNSOLID** adj not solid
**UNSOLIDLY** > UNSOLID
**UNSOLVED** adj not having been solved or explained
**UNSONCY** same as > UNSONSY
**UNSONSIE** same as > UNSONSY
**UNSONSY** adj unfortunate
**UNSOOTE** adj not sweet
**UNSOOTHED** adj not soothed
**UNSORTED** adj not sorted
**UNSOUGHT** adj not sought after
**UNSOUL** vb cause to be soulless
**UNSOULED** > UNSOUL
**UNSOULING** > UNSOUL
**UNSOULS** > UNSOUL
**UNSOUND** adj unhealthy or unstable
**UNSOUNDED** adj not sounded
**UNSOUNDER** > UNSOUND
**UNSOUNDLY** > UNSOUND
**UNSOURCED** adj without a source
**UNSOURED** adj not soured
**UNSOWED** same as > UNSOWN
**UNSOWN** adj not sown
**UNSPAR** vb open
**UNSPARED** adj not spared
**UNSPARING** adj very generous
**UNSPARRED** > UNSPAR
**UNSPARS** > UNSPAR
**UNSPEAK** obsolete word for > UNSAY
**UNSPEAKS** > UNSPEAK
**UNSPED** adj not achieved
**UNSPELL** vb release from a spell
**UNSPELLED** > UNSPELL
**UNSPELLS** > UNSPELL
**UNSPENT** adj not spent
**UNSPHERE** vb remove from its, one's, etc, sphere or place
**UNSPHERED** > UNSPHERE
**UNSPHERES** > UNSPHERE
**UNSPIDE** same as > UNSPIED
**UNSPIED** adj unnoticed
**UNSPILLED** same as > UNSPILT
**UNSPILT** adj not spilt
**UNSPLIT** adj not split
**UNSPOILED** adj not damaged or harmed
**UNSPOILT** same as > UNSPOILED
**UNSPOKE** > UNSPEAK
**UNSPOKEN** adj not openly expressed
**UNSPOOL** vb unwind from spool
**UNSPOOLED** > UNSPOOL

**UNSPOOLS** > UNSPOOL
**UNSPOTTED** *adj* without spots or stains
**UNSPRAYED** *adj* not sprayed
**UNSPRUNG** *adj* without springs
**UNSPUN** *adj* not spun
**UNSQUARED** *adj* not made into a square shape
**UNSTABLE** *adj* lacking stability or firmness
**UNSTABLER** > UNSTABLE
**UNSTABLY** > UNSTABLE
**UNSTACK** *vb* remove from a stack
**UNSTACKED** > UNSTACK
**UNSTACKS** > UNSTACK
**UNSTAID** *adj* not staid
**UNSTAINED** *adj* not stained
**UNSTALKED** *adj* without a stalk
**UNSTAMPED** *adj* not stamped
**UNSTARCH** *vb* remove starch from
**UNSTARRED** *adj* not marked with a star
**UNSTARRY** *adj* not resembling or characteristic of a star from the entertainment world
**UNSTATE** *vb* deprive of state
**UNSTATED** *adj* not having been articulated or uttered
**UNSTATES** > UNSTATE
**UNSTATING** > UNSTATE
**UNSTAYED** *adj* unhindered
**UNSTAYING** *adj* nonstop
**UNSTEADY** *adj* not securely fixed ▷ *vb* make unsteady
**UNSTEEL** *vb* make (the heart, feelings, etc) more gentle or compassionate
**UNSTEELED** > UNSTEEL
**UNSTEELS** > UNSTEEL
**UNSTEMMED** *adj* without a stem
**UNSTEP** *vb* remove (a mast) from its step
**UNSTEPPED** > UNSTEP
**UNSTEPS** > UNSTEP
**UNSTERILE** *adj* not free from living, esp pathogenic, microorganisms
**UNSTICK** *vb* free or loosen (something stuck)
**UNSTICKS** > UNSTICK
**UNSTIFLED** *adj* not suppressed
**UNSTILLED** *adj* not reduced
**UNSTINTED** *adj* not stinted
**UNSTIRRED** *adj* not stirred
**UNSTITCH** *vb* remove stitching from
**UNSTOCK** *vb* remove stock from
**UNSTOCKED** *adj* without stock
**UNSTOCKS** > UNSTOCK
**UNSTONED** *adj* not stoned

**UNSTOP** *vb* remove the stop or stopper from
**UNSTOPPED** *adj* not obstructed or stopped up
**UNSTOPPER** *vb* unplug
**UNSTOPS** > UNSTOP
**UNSTOW** *vb* remove from storage
**UNSTOWED** > UNSTOW
**UNSTOWING** > UNSTOW
**UNSTOWS** > UNSTOW
**UNSTRAP** *vb* undo the straps fastening (something) in position
**UNSTRAPS** > UNSTRAP
**UNSTRESS** *n* absence of stress
**UNSTRING** *vb* remove the strings of
**UNSTRINGS** > UNSTRING
**UNSTRIP** *vb* strip
**UNSTRIPED** *adj* (esp of smooth muscle) not having stripes
**UNSTRIPS** > UNSTRIP
**UNSTRUCK** *adj* not struck
**UNSTRUNG** *adj* emotionally distressed
**UNSTUCK** *adj* freed from being stuck, glued, fastened, etc
**UNSTUDIED** *adj* natural or spontaneous
**UNSTUFFED** *adj* not stuffed
**UNSTUFFY** *adj* well-ventilated
**UNSTUFT** *same as* > UNSTUFFED
**UNSTUNG** *adj* not stung
**UNSTYLISH** *adj* unfashionable
**UNSUBDUED** *adj* not subdued
**UNSUBJECT** *adj* not subject
**UNSUBTLE** *adj* not subtle
**UNSUBTLY** > UNSUBTLE
**UNSUCCESS** *n* failure
**UNSUCKED** *adj* not sucked
**UNSUIT** *vb* make unsuitable
**UNSUITED** *adj* not appropriate for a particular task or situation
**UNSUITING** > UNSUIT
**UNSUITS** > UNSUIT
**UNSULLIED** *adj* (of a reputation, etc) not stained or tarnished
**UNSUMMED** *adj* not calculated
**UNSUNG** *adj* not acclaimed or honoured
**UNSUNK** *adj* not sunken
**UNSUNNED** *adj* not subjected to sunlight
**UNSUNNY** *adj* not sunny
**UNSUPPLE** *adj* rigid
**UNSURE** *adj* lacking assurance or self-confidence
**UNSURED** *adj* not assured
**UNSURELY** > UNSURE
**UNSURER** > UNSURE
**UNSUREST** > UNSURE
**UNSUSPECT** *adj* not open to

suspicion
**UNSWADDLE** *same as* > UNSWATHE
**UNSWATHE** *vb* unwrap
**UNSWATHED** > UNSWATHE
**UNSWATHES** > UNSWATHE
**UNSWAYED** *adj* not swayed
**UNSWEAR** *vb* retract or revoke (a sworn oath)
**UNSWEARS** > UNSWEAR
**UNSWEET** *adj* not sweet
**UNSWEPT** *adj* not swept
**UNSWOLLEN** *adj* not swollen
**UNSWORE** > UNSWEAR
**UNSWORN** > UNSWEAR
**UNTACK** *vb* remove saddle and harness, etc, from
**UNTACKED** > UNTACK
**UNTACKING** > UNTACK
**UNTACKLE** *vb* remove tackle from
**UNTACKLED** > UNTACKLE
**UNTACKLES** > UNTACKLE
**UNTACKS** > UNTACK
**UNTACTFUL** *adj* not tactful
**UNTAGGED** *adj* without a label
**UNTAILED** *adj* tailless
**UNTAINTED** *adj* not tarnished, contaminated, or polluted
**UNTAKEN** *adj* not taken
**UNTAMABLE** *adj* (of an animal or person) not capable of being tamed, subdued, or made obedient
**UNTAMABLY** > UNTAMABLE
**UNTAME** *vb* undo the taming of
**UNTAMED** *adj* not brought under human control
**UNTAMES** > UNTAME
**UNTAMING** > UNTAME
**UNTANGLE** *vb* free from tangles or confusion
**UNTANGLED** > UNTANGLE
**UNTANGLES** > UNTANGLE
**UNTANNED** *adj* not tanned
**UNTAPPED** *adj* not yet used
**UNTARRED** *adj* not coated with tar
**UNTASTED** *adj* not tasted
**UNTAUGHT** *adj* without training or education
**UNTAX** *vb* stop taxing
**UNTAXED** *adj* not subject to taxation
**UNTAXES** > UNTAX
**UNTAXING** > UNTAX
**UNTEACH** *vb* cause to disbelieve (teaching)
**UNTEACHES** > UNTEACH
**UNTEAM** *vb* disband a team
**UNTEAMED** > UNTEAM
**UNTEAMING** > UNTEAM
**UNTEAMS** > UNTEAM
**UNTEMPER** *vb* soften
**UNTEMPERS** > UNTEMPER
**UNTEMPTED** *adj* not tempted
**UNTENABLE** *adj* (of a theory, idea, etc) incapable of being defended

**UNTENABLY** > UNTENABLE
**UNTENANT** *vb* remove (a tenant)
**UNTENANTS** > UNTENANT
**UNTENDED** *adj* not cared for or attended to
**UNTENDER** *adj* not tender
**UNTENT** *vb* remove from a tent
**UNTENTED** > UNTENT
**UNTENTING** > UNTENT
**UNTENTS** > UNTENT
**UNTENTY** *adj* inattentive
**UNTENURED** *adj* not having tenure
**UNTESTED** *adj* not having been tested or examined
**UNTETHER** *vb* untie
**UNTETHERS** > UNTETHER
**UNTHANKED** *adj* not thanked
**UNTHATCH** *vb* remove the thatch from
**UNTHAW** *same as* > THAW
**UNTHAWED** *adj* not thawed
**UNTHAWING** > UNTHAW
**UNTHAWS** > UNTHAW
**UNTHINK** *vb* reverse one's opinion about
**UNTHINKS** > UNTHINK
**UNTHOUGHT** > UNTHINK
**UNTHREAD** *vb* draw out the thread or threads from (a needle, etc)
**UNTHREADS** > UNTHREAD
**UNTHRIFT** *n* unthrifty person
**UNTHRIFTS** > UNTHRIFT
**UNTHRIFTY** *adj* careless with money
**UNTHRONE** *less common word for* > DETHRONE
**UNTHRONED** > UNTHRONE
**UNTHRONES** > UNTHRONE
**UNTIDIED** > UNTIDY
**UNTIDIER** > UNTIDY
**UNTIDIES** > UNTIDY
**UNTIDIEST** > UNTIDY
**UNTIDILY** > UNTIDY
**UNTIDY** *adj* messy and disordered ▷ *vb* make untidy
**UNTIDYING** > UNTIDY
**UNTIE** *vb* open or free (something that is tied)
**UNTIED** > UNTIE
**UNTIEING** > UNTIE
**UNTIES** > UNTIE
**UNTIL** *prep* in or throughout the period before
**UNTILE** *vb* strip tiles from
**UNTILED** > UNTILE
**UNTILES** > UNTILE
**UNTILING** > UNTILE
**UNTILLED** *adj* not tilled
**UNTILTED** *adj* not tilted
**UNTIMED** *adj* not timed
**UNTIMELY** *adj* occurring before the expected or normal time ▷ *adv* prematurely or inopportunely
**UNTIMEOUS** *same*

*as* > UNTIMELY
UNTIN *vb* remove tin from
UNTINGED *adj* not tinged
UNTINNED > UNTIN
UNTINNING > UNTIN
UNTINS > UNTIN
UNTIPPED *adj* not tipped
UNTIRABLE *adj* not able to be fatigued
UNTIRED *adj* not tired
UNTIRING *adj* (of a person or their actions) continuing or persisting without declining in strength or vigour
UNTITLED *adj* without a title
UNTO *prep* to
UNTOILING *adj* not labouring
UNTOLD *adj* incapable of description
UNTOMB *vb* exhume
UNTOMBED > UNTOMB
UNTOMBING > UNTOMB
UNTOMBS > UNTOMB
UNTONED *adj* not toned
UNTORN *adj* not torn
UNTOUCHED *adj* not changed, moved, or affected
UNTOWARD *adj* causing misfortune or annoyance
UNTRACE *vb* remove traces from
UNTRACED *adj* not traced
UNTRACES > UNTRACE
UNTRACING > UNTRACE
UNTRACK *vb* remove from track
UNTRACKED *adj* not tracked
UNTRACKS > UNTRACK
UNTRADED *adj* not traded
UNTRAINED *adj* without formal or adequate training or education
UNTRAPPED *adj* not trapped
UNTREAD *vb* retrace (a course, path, etc)
UNTREADED > UNTREAD
UNTREADS > UNTREAD
UNTREATED *adj* (of an illness, etc) not having been dealt with
UNTRENDY *adj* not trendy
UNTRESSED *adj* not having a tress
UNTRIDE *same as* > UNTRIED
UNTRIED *adj* not yet used, done, or tested
UNTRIM *vb* deprive of elegance or adornment
UNTRIMMED > UNTRIM
UNTRIMS > UNTRIM
UNTROD > UNTREAD
UNTRODDEN > UNTREAD
UNTRUE *adj* incorrect or false
UNTRUER > UNTRUE
UNTRUEST > UNTRUE
UNTRUISM *n* something that is false
UNTRUISMS > UNTRUISM
UNTRULY > UNTRUE

UNTRUSS *vb* release from or as if from a truss
UNTRUSSED > UNTRUSS
UNTRUSSER *n* person who untrusses
UNTRUSSES > UNTRUSS
UNTRUST *n* mistrust
UNTRUSTS > UNTRUST
UNTRUSTY *adj* not trusty
UNTRUTH *n* statement that is not true, lie
UNTRUTHS > UNTRUTH
UNTUCK *vb* become or cause to become loose or not tucked in
UNTUCKED > UNTUCK
UNTUCKING > UNTUCK
UNTUCKS > UNTUCK
UNTUFTED *adj* not having tufts
UNTUMBLED *adj* not tumbled
UNTUNABLE *adj* not tuneful
UNTUNABLY > UNTUNABLE
UNTUNE *vb* make out of tune
UNTUNED > UNTUNE
UNTUNEFUL *adj* not tuneful
UNTUNES > UNTUNE
UNTUNING > UNTUNE
UNTURBID *adj* clear
UNTURF *vb* remove turf from
UNTURFED > UNTURF
UNTURFING > UNTURF
UNTURFS > UNTURF
UNTURN *vb* turn in a reverse direction
UNTURNED *adj* not turned
UNTURNING > UNTURN
UNTURNS > UNTURN
UNTUTORED *adj* without formal education
UNTWILLED *adj* not twilled
UNTWINE *vb* untwist, unravel, and separate
UNTWINED > UNTWINE
UNTWINES > UNTWINE
UNTWINING > UNTWINE
UNTWIST *vb* twist apart and loosen
UNTWISTED > UNTWIST
UNTWISTS > UNTWIST
UNTYING > UNTIE
UNTYINGS > UNTIE
UNTYPABLE *adj* incapable of being typed
UNTYPICAL *adj* not representative or characteristic of a particular type, person, etc
UNUNBIUM *n* chemical element
UNUNBIUMS > UNUNBIUM
UNUNITED *adj* separated
UNUNUNIUM *n* chemical element
UNURGED *adj* not urged
UNUSABLE *adj* not in good enough condition to be used
UNUSABLY > UNUSABLE
UNUSED *adj* not being or never having been used

UNUSEFUL *adj* useless
UNUSHERED *adj* not escorted
UNUSUAL *adj* uncommon or extraordinary
UNUSUALLY > UNUSUAL
UNUTTERED *adj* not uttered
UNVAIL *same as* > UNVEIL
UNVAILE *same as* > UNVEIL
UNVAILED > UNVAIL
UNVAILES > UNVAIL
UNVAILING > UNVAIL
UNVAILS > UNVAIL
UNVALUED *adj* not appreciated or valued
UNVARIED *adj* not varied
UNVARYING *adj* always staying the same
UNVEIL *vb* ceremonially remove the cover from (a new picture, plaque, etc)
UNVEILED > UNVEIL
UNVEILER *n* person who removes a veil
UNVEILERS > UNVEILER
UNVEILING *n* ceremony involving the removal of a veil covering a statue
UNVEILS > UNVEIL
UNVEINED *adj* without veins
UNVENTED *adj* not vented
UNVERSED *adj* not versed
UNVESTED *adj* not vested
UNVETTED *adj* not thoroughly examined
UNVEXED *adj* not annoyed
UNVEXT *same as* > UNVEXED
UNVIABLE *adj* not capable of succeeding, esp financially
UNVIEWED *adj* not viewed
UNVIRTUE *n* state of having no virtue
UNVIRTUES > UNVIRTUE
UNVISITED *adj* not visited
UNVISOR *vb* remove visor from
UNVISORED > UNVISOR
UNVISORS > UNVISOR
UNVITAL *adj* not vital
UNVIZARD *same as* > UNVIZARD
UNVIZARDS > UNVIZARD
UNVOCAL *adj* not vocal
UNVOICE *vb* pronounce without vibration of the vocal cords
UNVOICED *adj* not expressed or spoken
UNVOICES > UNVOICE
UNVOICING > UNVOICE
UNVULGAR *adj* not vulgar
UNWAGED *adj* (of a person) not having a paid job
UNWAKED *same as* > UNWAKENED
UNWAKENED *adj* not roused from sleep
UNWALLED *adj* not surrounded by walls
UNWANING *adj* not waning
UNWANTED *adj* not wanted or welcome

UNWARDED *adj* not warded
UNWARE *same as* > UNAWARE
UNWARELY > UNWARE
UNWARES *same as* > UNAWARES
UNWARIE *same as* > UNWARY
UNWARIER > UNWARY
UNWARIEST > UNWARY
UNWARILY > UNWARY
UNWARLIKE *adj* not warlike
UNWARMED *adj* not warmed
UNWARNED *adj* not warned
UNWARPED *adj* not warped
UNWARY *adj* not careful or cautious and therefore likely to be harmed
UNWASHED *adj* not washed ▷ *pl n* the masses
UNWASHEDS > UNWASHED
UNWASHEN *same as* > UNWASHED
UNWASTED *adj* not wasted
UNWASTING *adj* not wasting
UNWATCHED *adj* (of an automatic device, such as a beacon) not manned
UNWATER *vb* dry out
UNWATERED > UNWATER
UNWATERS > UNWATER
UNWATERY *adj* not watery
UNWAXED *adj* not treated with wax, esp of oranges or lemons, not sprayed with a protective coating of wax
UNWAYED *adj* having no routes
UNWEAL *n* ill or sorrow
UNWEALS > UNWEAL
UNWEANED *adj* not weaned
UNWEAPON *vb* disarm
UNWEAPONS > UNWEAPON
UNWEARIED *adj* not abating or tiring
UNWEARY *adj* not weary
UNWEAVE *vb* undo (weaving)
UNWEAVES > UNWEAVE
UNWEAVING > UNWEAVE
UNWEBBED *adj* not webbed
UNWED *adj* not wed
UNWEDDED *adj* not wedded
UNWEEDED *adj* not weeded
UNWEENED *adj* unknown
UNWEETING *same as* > UNWITTING
UNWEIGHED *adj* (of quantities purchased, etc) not measured for weight
UNWEIGHT *vb* remove weight from
UNWEIGHTS > UNWEIGHT
UNWELCOME *adj* unpleasant and unwanted
UNWELDED *adj* not welded
UNWELDY *same as* > UNWIELDY
UNWELL *adj* not healthy, ill
UNWEPT *adj* not wept for or lamented
UNWET *adj* not wet
UNWETTED *same as* > UNWET
UNWHIPPED *adj* not

whipped

**UNWHIPT** *same as* > UNWHIPPED

**UNWHITE** *adj* not white

**UNWIELDLY** *same as* > UNWIELDY

**UNWIELDY** *adj* too heavy, large, or awkward to be easily handled

**UNWIFELY** *adj* not like a wife

**UNWIGGED** *adj* without a wig

**UNWILFUL** *adj* complaisant

**UNWILL** *vb* will the reversal of (something that has already occurred)

**UNWILLED** *adj* not intentional

**UNWILLING** *adj* reluctant

**UNWILLS** > UNWILL

**UNWIND** *vb* relax after a busy or tense time

**UNWINDER** > UNWIND

**UNWINDERS** > UNWIND

**UNWINDING** > UNWIND

**UNWINDS** > UNWIND

**UNWINGED** *adj* without wings

**UNWINKING** *adj* vigilant

**UNWIPED** *adj* not wiped

**UNWIRE** *vb* remove wiring from

**UNWIRED** > UNWIRE

**UNWIRES** > UNWIRE

**UNWIRING** > UNWIRE

**UNWISDOM** *n* imprudence

**UNWISDOMS** > UNWISDOM

**UNWISE** *adj* foolish

**UNWISELY** > UNWISE

**UNWISER** > UNWISE

**UNWISEST** > UNWISE

**UNWISH** *vb* retract or revoke (a wish)

**UNWISHED** *adj* not desired

**UNWISHES** > UNWISH

**UNWISHFUL** *adj* not wishful

**UNWISHING** > UNWISH

**UNWIST** *adj* unknown

**UNWIT** *vb* divest of wit

**UNWITCH** *vb* release from witchcraft

**UNWITCHED** > UNWITCH

**UNWITCHES** > UNWITCH

**UNWITS** > UNWIT

**UNWITTED** > UNWIT

**UNWITTILY** > UNWITTY

**UNWITTING** *adj* not intentional

**UNWITTY** *adj* not clever and amusing

**UNWIVE** *vb* remove a wife from

**UNWIVED** > UNWIVE

**UNWIVES** > UNWIVE

**UNWIVING** > UNWIVE

**UNWOMAN** *vb* remove womanly qualities from

**UNWOMANED** > UNWOMAN

**UNWOMANLY** *adj* not womanly

**UNWOMANS** > UNWOMAN

**UNWON** *adj* not won

**UNWONT** *adj* unaccustomed

**UNWONTED** *adj* out of the ordinary

**UNWOODED** *adj* not wooded

**UNWOOED** *adj* not wooed

**UNWORDED** *adj* not expressed in words

**UNWORK** *vb* destroy (work previously done)

**UNWORKED** *adj* not worked

**UNWORKING** > UNWORK

**UNWORKS** > UNWORK

**UNWORLDLY** *adj* not concerned with material values or pursuits

**UNWORMED** *adj* not rid of worms

**UNWORN** *adj* not having deteriorated through use or age

**UNWORRIED** *adj* not bothered or perturbed

**UNWORTH** *n* lack of value

**UNWORTHS** > UNWORTH

**UNWORTHY** *adj* not deserving or worthy

**UNWOUND** *past tense and past participle of* > UNWIND

**UNWOUNDED** *adj* not wounded

**UNWOVE** > UNWEAVE

**UNWOVEN** > UNWEAVE

**UNWRAP** *vb* remove the wrapping from (something)

**UNWRAPPED** > UNWRAP

**UNWRAPS** > UNWRAP

**UNWREAKED** *adj* unavenged

**UNWREATHE** *vb* untwist from a wreathed shape

**UNWRINKLE** *vb* remove wrinkles from

**UNWRITE** *vb* cancel (what has been written)

**UNWRITES** > UNWRITE

**UNWRITING** > UNWRITE

**UNWRITTEN** *adj* not printed or in writing

**UNWROTE** > UNWRITE

**UNWROUGHT** *adj* not worked

**UNWRUNG** *adj* not twisted

**UNYEANED** *adj* not having given birth

**UNYOKE** *vb* release (an animal, etc) from a yoke

**UNYOKED** > UNYOKE

**UNYOKES** > UNYOKE

**UNYOKING** > UNYOKE

**UNYOUNG** *adj* not young

**UNZEALOUS** *adj* unenthusiastic

**UNZIP** *vb* unfasten the zip of (a garment) or (of a zip or a garment with a zip) to become unfastened

**UNZIPPED** > UNZIP

**UNZIPPING** > UNZIP

**UNZIPS** > UNZIP

**UNZONED** *adj* not divided into zones

**UP** *adv* indicating movement to or position at a higher place ▷ *adj* of a high or higher position ▷ *vb* increase or raise

**UPADAISY** *same as* > UPSADAISY

**UPAITHRIC** *adj* without a roof

**UPAS** *n* large Javan tree with whitish bark and poisonous milky sap

**UPASES** > UPAS

**UPBEAR** *vb* sustain

**UPBEARER** > UPBEAR

**UPBEARERS** > UPBEAR

**UPBEARING** > UPBEAR

**UPBEARS** > UPBEAR

**UPBEAT** *adj* cheerful and optimistic ▷ *n* unaccented beat

**UPBEATS** > UPBEAT

**UPBIND** *vb* bind up

**UPBINDING** > UPBIND

**UPBINDS** > UPBIND

**UPBLEW** > UPBLOW

**UPBLOW** *vb* inflate

**UPBLOWING** > UPBLOW

**UPBLOWN** > UPBLOW

**UPBLOWS** > UPBLOW

**UPBOIL** *vb* boil up

**UPBOILED** > UPBOIL

**UPBOILING** > UPBOIL

**UPBOILS** > UPBOIL

**UPBORE** > UPBEAR

**UPBORNE** *adj* held up

**UPBOUND** *adj* travelling upwards

**UPBOUNDEN** *same as* > UPBOUND

**UPBOW** *n* stroke of the bow from its tip to its nut on a stringed instrument

**UPBOWS** > UPBOW

**UPBRAID** *vb* scold or reproach

**UPBRAIDED** > UPBRAID

**UPBRAIDER** > UPBRAID

**UPBRAIDS** > UPBRAID

**UPBRAST** *same as* > UPBURST

**UPBRAY** *vb* shame

**UPBRAYED** > UPBRAY

**UPBRAYING** > UPBRAY

**UPBRAYS** > UPBRAY

**UPBREAK** *vb* escape upwards

**UPBREAKS** > UPBREAK

**UPBRING** *vb* rear

**UPBRINGS** > UPBRING

**UPBROKE** > UPBREAK

**UPBROKEN** > UPBREAK

**UPBROUGHT** > UPBRING

**UPBUILD** *vb* build up

**UPBUILDER** > UPBUILD

**UPBUILDS** > UPBUILD

**UPBUILT** > UPBUILD

**UPBURNING** *adj* burning upwards

**UPBURST** *vb* burst upwards

**UPBURSTS** > UPBURST

**UPBY** *same as* > UPBYE

**UPBYE** *adv* yonder

**UPCAST** *n* material cast or thrown up ▷ *adj* directed or thrown upwards ▷ *vb* throw or cast up

**UPCASTING** > UPCAST

**UPCASTS** > UPCAST

**UPCATCH** *vb* catch up

**UPCATCHES** > UPCATCH

**UPCAUGHT** > UPCATCH

**UPCHEER** *vb* cheer up

**UPCHEERED** > UPCHEER

**UPCHEERS** > UPCHEER

**UPCHUCK** *vb* vomit

**UPCHUCKED** > UPCHUCK

**UPCHUCKS** > UPCHUCK

**UPCLIMB** *vb* ascend

**UPCLIMBED** > UPCLIMB

**UPCLIMBS** > UPCLIMB

**UPCLOSE** *vb* close up

**UPCLOSED** > UPCLOSE

**UPCLOSES** > UPCLOSE

**UPCLOSING** > UPCLOSE

**UPCOAST** *adv* up the coast

**UPCOIL** *vb* make into a coil

**UPCOILED** > UPCOIL

**UPCOILING** > UPCOIL

**UPCOILS** > UPCOIL

**UPCOME** *vb* come up

**UPCOMES** > UPCOME

**UPCOMING** *adj* coming soon

**UPCOUNTRY** *adj* of or from the interior of a country ▷ *adv* towards or in the interior of a country ▷ *n* interior part of a region or country

**UPCOURT** *adv* up basketball court

**UPCURL** *vb* curl up

**UPCURLED** > UPCURL

**UPCURLING** > UPCURL

**UPCURLS** > UPCURL

**UPCURVE** *vb* curve upwards

**UPCURVED** > UPCURVE

**UPCURVES** > UPCURVE

**UPCURVING** > UPCURVE

**UPDART** *vb* dart upwards

**UPDARTED** > UPDART

**UPDARTING** > UPDART

**UPDARTS** > UPDART

**UPDATE** *vb* bring up to date ▷ *n* act of updating or something that is updated

**UPDATED** > UPDATE

**UPDATER** > UPDATE

**UPDATERS** > UPDATE

**UPDATES** > UPDATE

**UPDATING** > UPDATE

**UPDIVE** *vb* leap upwards

**UPDIVED** > UPDIVE

**UPDIVES** > UPDIVE

**UPDIVING** > UPDIVE

**UPDO** *n* type of hairstyle

**UPDOS** > UPDO

**UPDOVE** > UPDIVE

**UPDRAFT** *n* upwards air current

**UPDRAFTS** > UPDRAFT

**UPDRAG** *vb* drag up

**UPDRAGGED** > UPDRAG

**UPDRAGS** > UPDRAG

**UPDRAUGHT** *n* upward movement of air or other gas

**UPDRAW** *vb* draw up

**UPDRAWING** > UPDRAW

**UPDRAWN** > UPDRAW

**UPDRAWS** > UPDRAW

**UPDREW** > UPDRAW

**UPDRIED** > UPDRY

**UPDRIES** > UPDRY

UPDRY vb dry up
UPDRYING >UPDRY
UPEND vb turn or set (something) on its end
UPENDED >UPEND
UPENDING >UPEND
UPENDS >UPEND
UPFIELD adj in sport, away from the defending team's goal
UPFILL vb fill up
UPFILLED >UPFILL
UPFILLING >UPFILL
UPFILLS >UPFILL
UPFLING vb throw upwards
UPFLINGS >UPFLING
UPFLOW vb flow upwards
UPFLOWED >UPFLOW
UPFLOWING >UPFLOW
UPFLOWS >UPFLOW
UPFLUNG >UPFLING
UPFOLD vb fold up
UPFOLDED >UPFOLD
UPFOLDING >UPFOLD
UPFOLDS >UPFOLD
UPFOLLOW vb follow
UPFOLLOWS >UPFOLLOW
UPFRONT adj open and frank ▷ adv (of money) paid out at the beginning of a business arrangement
UPFURL vb roll up
UPFURLED >UPFURL
UPFURLING >UPFURL
UPFURLS >UPFURL
UPGANG n climb
UPGANGS >UPGANG
UPGATHER vb draw together
UPGATHERS >UPGATHER
UPGAZE vb gaze upwards
UPGAZED >UPGAZE
UPGAZES >UPGAZE
UPGAZING >UPGAZE
UPGIRD vb belt up
UPGIRDED >UPGIRD
UPGIRDING >UPGIRD
UPGIRDS >UPGIRD
UPGIRT >UPGIRD
UPGO vb ascend
UPGOES >UPGO
UPGOING >UPGO
UPGOINGS >UPGO
UPGONE >UPGO
UPGRADE vb promote (a person or job) to a higher rank
UPGRADED >UPGRADE
UPGRADER >UPGRADE
UPGRADERS >UPGRADE
UPGRADES >UPGRADE
UPGRADING >UPGRADE
UPGREW >UPGROW
UPGROW vb grow up
UPGROWING >UPGROW
UPGROWN >UPGROW
UPGROWS >UPGROW
UPGROWTH n process of developing or growing upwards
UPGROWTHS >UPGROWTH
UPGUSH vb flow upwards
UPGUSHED >UPGUSH
UPGUSHES >UPGUSH

UPGUSHING >UPGUSH
UPHAND adj lifted by hand
UPHANG vb hang up
UPHANGING >UPHANG
UPHANGS >UPHANG
UPHAUD Scots variant of >UPHOLD
UPHAUDING >UPHAUD
UPHAUDS >UPHAUD
UPHEAP vb computing term
UPHEAPED >UPHEAP
UPHEAPING >UPHEAP
UPHEAPS >UPHEAP
UPHEAVAL n strong, sudden, or violent disturbance
UPHEAVALS >UPHEAVAL
UPHEAVE vb heave or rise upwards
UPHEAVED >UPHEAVE
UPHEAVER >UPHEAVE
UPHEAVERS >UPHEAVE
UPHEAVES >UPHEAVE
UPHEAVING >UPHEAVE
UPHELD >UPHOLD
UPHILD archaic past form of >UPHOLD
UPHILL adj sloping or leading upwards ▷ adv up a slope ▷ n difficulty
UPHILLS >UPHILL
UPHOARD vb hoard up
UPHOARDED >UPHOARD
UPHOARDS >UPHOARD
UPHOIST vb raise
UPHOISTED >UPHOIST
UPHOISTS >UPHOIST
UPHOLD vb maintain or defend against opposition
UPHOLDER >UPHOLD
UPHOLDERS >UPHOLD
UPHOLDING >UPHOLD
UPHOLDS >UPHOLD
UPHOLSTER vb fit (a chair or sofa) with padding, springs, and covering
UPHOORD vb heap up
UPHOORDED >UPHOORD
UPHOORDS >UPHOORD
UPHOVE >UPHEAVE
UPHROE variant spelling of >EUPHROE
UPHROES >UPHROE
UPHUDDEN >UPHAUD
UPHUNG >UPHANG
UPHURL vb throw upwards
UPHURLED >UPHURL
UPHURLING >UPHURL
UPHURLS >UPHURL
UPJET vb stream upwards
UPJETS >UPJET
UPJETTED >UPJET
UPJETTING >UPJET
UPKEEP n act, process, or cost of keeping something in good repair
UPKEEPS >UPKEEP
UPKNIT vb bind
UPKNITS >UPKNIT
UPKNITTED >UPKNIT
UPLAID >UPLAY
UPLAND adj of or in an area of high or relatively high ground ▷ n area of high or

relatively high ground
UPLANDER n person hailing from the uplands
UPLANDERS >UPLANDER
UPLANDISH >UPLAND
UPLANDS >UPLAND
UPLAY vb stash
UPLAYING >UPLAY
UPLAYS >UPLAY
UPLEAD vb lead upwards
UPLEADING >UPLEAD
UPLEADS >UPLEAD
UPLEAN vb lean on something
UPLEANED >UPLEAN
UPLEANING >UPLEAN
UPLEANS >UPLEAN
UPLEANT >UPLEAN
UPLEAP vb jump upwards
UPLEAPED >UPLEAP
UPLEAPING >UPLEAP
UPLEAPS >UPLEAP
UPLEAPT >UPLEAP
UPLED >UPLEAD
UPLIFT vb raise or lift up ▷ n act or process of improving moral, social, or cultural conditions ▷ adj (of a bra) designed to lift and support the breasts
UPLIFTED >UPLIFT
UPLIFTER >UPLIFT
UPLIFTERS >UPLIFT
UPLIFTING adj acting to raise moral, spiritual, cultural, etc, levels
UPLIFTS >UPLIFT
UPLIGHT n lamp or wall light designed or positioned to cast its light upwards ▷ vb light in an upward direction
UPLIGHTED >UPLIGHT
UPLIGHTER n lamp or wall light designed or positioned to cast its light upwards
UPLIGHTS >UPLIGHT
UPLINK n transmitter on the ground that sends signals up to a communications satellite ▷ vb send (data) to a communications satellite
UPLINKED >UPLINK
UPLINKING >UPLINK
UPLINKS >UPLINK
UPLIT >UPLIGHT
UPLOAD vb transfer (data or a program) from one's own computer into the memory of another computer
UPLOADED >UPLOAD
UPLOADING >UPLOAD
UPLOADS >UPLOAD
UPLOCK vb lock up
UPLOCKED >UPLOCK
UPLOCKING >UPLOCK
UPLOCKS >UPLOCK
UPLOOK vb look up
UPLOOKED >UPLOOK
UPLOOKING >UPLOOK
UPLOOKS >UPLOOK

UPLYING adj raised
UPMAKE vb make up
UPMAKER >UPMAKE
UPMAKERS >UPMAKE
UPMAKES >UPMAKE
UPMAKING >UPMAKE
UPMAKINGS >UPMAKE
UPMANSHIP n one-upmanship
UPMARKET adj expensive and of superior quality
UPMOST another word for >UPPERMOST
UPO prep upon
UPON prep on
UPPED >UP
UPPER adj higher or highest in physical position, wealth, rank, or status ▷ n part of a shoe above the sole
UPPERCASE adj capitalized ▷ vb capitalize or print in capitals
UPPERCUT n short swinging upward punch delivered to the chin ▷ vb hit (an opponent) with an uppercut
UPPERCUTS >UPPERCUT
UPPERMOST adj highest in position, power, or importance ▷ adv in or into the highest place or position
UPPERPART n highest part
UPPERS >UPPER
UPPILE vb pile up
UPPILED >UPPILE
UPPILES >UPPILE
UPPILING >UPPILE
UPPING >UP
UPPINGS >UP
UPPISH adj snobbish, arrogant, or presumptuous
UPPISHLY >UPPISH
UPPITY adj snobbish, arrogant, or presumptuous
UPPROP vb support
UPPROPPED >UPPROP
UPPROPS >UPPROP
UPRAISE vb lift up
UPRAISED >UPRAISE
UPRAISER >UPRAISE
UPRAISERS >UPRAISE
UPRAISES >UPRAISE
UPRAISING >UPRAISE
UPRAN >UPRUN
UPRATE vb raise the value, rate, or size of, upgrade
UPRATED >UPRATE
UPRATES >UPRATE
UPRATING >UPRATE
UPREACH vb reach up
UPREACHED >UPREACH
UPREACHES >UPREACH
UPREAR vb lift up
UPREARED >UPREAR
UPREARING >UPREAR
UPREARS >UPREAR
UPREST n uprising
UPRESTS >UPREST

827

UPRIGHT *adj* vertical or erect ▷ *adv* vertically or in an erect position ▷ *n* vertical support, such as a post ▷ *vb* make upright
UPRIGHTED > UPRIGHT
UPRIGHTLY > UPRIGHT
UPRIGHTS > UPRIGHT
UPRISAL > UPRISE
UPRISALS > UPRISE
UPRISE *vb* rise up
UPRISEN > UPRISE
UPRISER > UPRISE
UPRISERS > UPRISE
UPRISES > UPRISE
UPRISING *n* rebellion or revolt
UPRISINGS > UPRISING
UPRIST *same as* > UPREST
UPRISTS > UPRIST
UPRIVER *adv* towards or near the source of a river ▷ *n* area located upstream
UPRIVERS > UPRIVER
UPROAR *n* disturbance characterized by loud noise and confusion ▷ *vb* cause an uproar
UPROARED > UPROAR
UPROARING > UPROAR
UPROARS > UPROAR
UPROLL *vb* roll up
UPROLLED > UPROLL
UPROLLING > UPROLL
UPROLLS > UPROLL
UPROOT *vb* pull up by or as if by the roots
UPROOTAL > UPROOT
UPROOTALS > UPROOT
UPROOTED > UPROOT
UPROOTER > UPROOT
UPROOTERS > UPROOT
UPROOTING > UPROOT
UPROOTS > UPROOT
UPROSE > UPRISE
UPROUSE *vb* rouse or stir up
UPROUSED > UPROUSE
UPROUSES > UPROUSE
UPROUSING > UPROUSE
UPRUN *vb* run up
UPRUNNING > UPRUN
UPRUNS > UPRUN
UPRUSH *n* upward rush, as of a consciousness ▷ *vb* rush upwards
UPRUSHED > UPRUSH
UPRUSHES > UPRUSH
UPRUSHING > UPRUSH
UPRYST *same as* > UPREST
UPS > UP
UPSADAISY *interj* expression of reassurance often uttered when someone stumbles or is lifted up
UPSCALE *adj* of or for the upper end of an economic or social scale ▷ *vb* upgrade
UPSCALED > UPSCALE
UPSCALES > UPSCALE
UPSCALING > UPSCALE
UPSEE *n* drunken revel
UPSEES > UPSEE

UPSEND *vb* send up
UPSENDING > UPSEND
UPSENDS > UPSEND
UPSENT > UPSEND
UPSET *adj* emotionally or physically disturbed or distressed ▷ *vb* tip over ▷ *n* unexpected defeat or reversal
UPSETS > UPSET
UPSETTER > UPSET
UPSETTERS > UPSET
UPSETTING > UPSET
UPSEY *same as* > UPSEE
UPSEYS > UPSEY
UPSHIFT *vb* move up (a gear)
UPSHIFTED > UPSHIFT
UPSHIFTS > UPSHIFT
UPSHOOT *vb* shoot upwards
UPSHOOTS > UPSHOOT
UPSHOT *n* final result or conclusion
UPSHOTS > UPSHOT
UPSIDE *n* upper surface or part
UPSIDES > UPSIDE
UPSIES > UPSY
UPSILON *n* 20th letter in the Greek alphabet
UPSILONS > UPSILON
UPSITTING *n* sitting up of a woman after childbirth
UPSIZE *vb* increase in size
UPSIZED > UPSIZE
UPSIZES > UPSIZE
UPSIZING > UPSIZE
UPSKILL *vb* improve the aptitude for work of (a person) by additional training
UPSKILLED > UPSKILL
UPSKILLS > UPSKILL
UPSLOPE *adv* up a or the slope
UPSOAR *vb* soar up
UPSOARED > UPSOAR
UPSOARING > UPSOAR
UPSOARS > UPSOAR
UPSPAKE > UPSPEAK
UPSPEAK *vb* speak with rising intonation
UPSPEAKS > UPSPEAK
UPSPEAR *vb* grow upwards in a spear-like manner
UPSPEARED > UPSPEAR
UPSPEARS > UPSPEAR
UPSPOKE > UPSPEAK
UPSPOKEN > UPSPEAK
UPSPRANG > UPSPRING
UPSPRING *vb* spring up or come into existence ▷ *vb* leap forwards or upwards
UPSPRINGS > UPSPRING
UPSPRUNG > UPSPRING
UPSTAGE *adj* at the back half of the stage ▷ *vb* draw attention to oneself from (someone else) ▷ *adv* on, at, or to the rear of the stage ▷ *n* back half of the stage
UPSTAGED > UPSTAGE
UPSTAGER > UPSTAGE

UPSTAGERS > UPSTAGE
UPSTAGES > UPSTAGE
UPSTAGING > UPSTAGE
UPSTAIR *same as* > UPSTAIRS
UPSTAIRS *adv* or on an upper floor of a building ▷ *n* upper floor ▷ *adj* situated on an upper floor
UPSTAND *vb* rise
UPSTANDS > UPSTAND
UPSTARE *vb* stare upwards
UPSTARED > UPSTARE
UPSTARES > UPSTARE
UPSTARING > UPSTARE
UPSTART *n* person who has risen suddenly to a position of power and behaves arrogantly ▷ *vb* start up, as in surprise, etc
UPSTARTED > UPSTART
UPSTARTS > UPSTART
UPSTATE *adv* towards, in, from, or relating to the outlying or northern sections of a state, esp of New York State ▷ *n* outlying, esp northern, sections of a state
UPSTATER > UPSTATE
UPSTATERS > UPSTATE
UPSTATES > UPSTATE
UPSTAY *vb* support
UPSTAYED > UPSTAY
UPSTAYING > UPSTAY
UPSTAYS > UPSTAY
UPSTEP *n* type of vocal intonation
UPSTEPPED > UPSTEP
UPSTEPS > UPSTEP
UPSTIR *vb* stir up ▷ *n* commotion
UPSTIRRED > UPSTIR
UPSTIRS > UPSTIR
UPSTOOD > UPSTAND
UPSTREAM *adj* in or towards the higher part of a stream ▷ *vb* stream upwards
UPSTREAMS > UPSTREAM
UPSTROKE *n* upward stroke or movement, as of a pen or brush
UPSTROKES > UPSTROKE
UPSURGE *n* rapid rise or swell ▷ *vb* surge up
UPSURGED > UPSURGE
UPSURGES > UPSURGE
UPSURGING > UPSURGE
UPSWARM *vb* rise in a swarm
UPSWARMED > UPSWARM
UPSWARMS > UPSWARM
UPSWAY *vb* swing in the air
UPSWAYED > UPSWAY
UPSWAYING > UPSWAY
UPSWAYS > UPSWAY
UPSWEEP *n* curve or sweep upwards ▷ *vb* sweep, curve, or brush or be swept, curved, or brushed upwards
UPSWEEPS > UPSWEEP
UPSWELL *vb* swell up or cause to swell up
UPSWELLED > UPSWELL
UPSWELLS > UPSWELL

UPSWEPT > UPSWEEP
UPSWING *n* recovery period in the trade cycle ▷ *vb* swing or move up
UPSWINGS > UPSWING
UPSWOLLEN > UPSWELL
UPSWUNG > UPSWING
UPSY *same as* > UPSEE
UPTA *same as* > UPTER
UPTAK *same as* > UPTAKE
UPTAKE *n* numbers taking up something such as an offer or the act of taking it up ▷ *vb* take up
UPTAKEN > UPTAKE
UPTAKES > UPTAKE
UPTAKING > UPTAKE
UPTAKS > UPTAK
UPTALK *n* style of speech in which every sentence ends with a rising tone, as if the speaker is always asking a question ▷ *vb* talk in this manner
UPTALKED > UPTALK
UPTALKING > UPTALK
UPTALKS > UPTALK
UPTEAR *vb* tear up
UPTEARING > UPTEAR
UPTEARS > UPTEAR
UPTEMPO *adj* fast ▷ *n* uptempo piece
UPTEMPOS > UPTEMPO
UPTER *adj* of poor quality
UPTHREW > UPTHROW
UPTHROW *n* upward movement of rocks on one side of a fault plane relative to rocks on the other side ▷ *vb* throw upwards
UPTHROWN > UPTHROW
UPTHROWS > UPTHROW
UPTHRUST *n* upward push
UPTHRUSTS > UPTHRUST
UPTHUNDER *vb* make a noise like thunder
UPTICK *n* rise or increase
UPTICKS > UPTICK
UPTIE *vb* tie up
UPTIED > UPTIE
UPTIES > UPTIE
UPTIGHT *adj* nervously tense, irritable, or angry
UPTIGHTER > UPTIGHT
UPTILT *vb* tilt up
UPTILTED > UPTILT
UPTILTING > UPTILT
UPTILTS > UPTILT
UPTIME *n* time during which a machine, such as a computer, actually operates
UPTIMES > UPTIME
UPTITLING *n* practice of conferring grandiose job titles to employees performing relatively menial jobs
UPTOOK > UPTAKE
UPTORE > UPTEAR
UPTORN > UPTEAR
UPTOSS *vb* throw upwards
UPTOSSED > UPTOSS

**UPTOSSES** >UPTOSS
**UPTOSSING** >UPTOSS
**UPTOWN** adv towards, in, or relating to some part of a town that is away from the centre ▷ n such a part of town, esp a residential part
**UPTOWNER** >UPTOWN
**UPTOWNERS** >UPTOWN
**UPTOWNS** >UPTOWN
**UPTRAIN** vb train up
**UPTRAINED** >UPTRAIN
**UPTRAINS** >UPTRAIN
**UPTREND** n upward trend
**UPTRENDS** >UPTREND
**UPTRILLED** adj trilled high
**UPTURN** n upward trend or improvement ▷ vb turn or cause to turn over or upside down
**UPTURNED** >UPTURN
**UPTURNING** >UPTURN
**UPTURNS** >UPTURN
**UPTYING** >UPTIE
**UPVALUE** vb raise the value of
**UPVALUED** >UPVALUE
**UPVALUES** >UPVALUE
**UPVALUING** >UPVALUE
**UPWAFT** vb waft upwards
**UPWAFTED** >UPWAFT
**UPWAFTING** >UPWAFT
**UPWAFTS** >UPWAFT
**UPWARD** same as >UPWARDS
**UPWARDLY** >UPWARD
**UPWARDS** adv from a lower to a higher place, level, condition, etc
**UPWELL** vb well up
**UPWELLED** >UPWELL
**UPWELLING** >UPWELL
**UPWELLS** >UPWELL
**UPWENT** >UPGO
**UPWHIRL** vb spin upwards
**UPWHIRLED** >UPWHIRL
**UPWHIRLS** >UPWHIRL
**UPWIND** adv into or against the wind ▷ adj going against the wind ▷ vb wind up
**UPWINDING** >UPWIND
**UPWINDS** >UPWIND
**UPWOUND** >UPWIND
**UPWRAP** vb wrap up
**UPWRAPS** >UPWRAP
**UPWROUGHT** adj wrought up
**UR** interj hesitant utterance used to fill gaps in talking
**URACHI** >URACHUS
**URACHUS** n cord of tissue connected to the bladder
**URACHUSES** >URACHUS
**URACIL** n pyrimidine present in all living cells, usually in a combined form, as in RNA
**URACILS** >URACIL
**URAEI** >URAEUS
**URAEMIA** n accumulation of waste products, normally excreted in the urine, in the blood: causes severe headaches,

vomiting, etc
**URAEMIAS** >URAEMIA
**URAEMIC** >URAEMIA
**URAEUS** n sacred serpent represented on the headdresses of ancient Egyptian kings and gods
**URAEUSES** >URAEUS
**URALI** n type of plant
**URALIS** >URALI
**URALITE** n amphibole mineral, similar to hornblende, that replaces pyroxene in some igneous and metamorphic rocks
**URALITES** >URALITE
**URALITIC** >URALITE
**URALITISE** same as >URALITIZE
**URALITIZE** vb turn into uralite
**URANIA** n uranium dioxide
**URANIAN** adj heavenly
**URANIAS** >URANIA
**URANIC** adj of or containing uranium, esp in a high valence state
**URANIDE** n any element having an atomic number greater than that of protactinium
**URANIDES** >URANIDE
**URANIN** n type of alkaline substance
**URANINITE** n blackish heavy radioactive mineral consisting of uranium oxide in cubic crystalline form together with radium, lead, helium, etc: occurs in coarse granite
**URANINS** >URANIN
**URANISCI** >URANISCUS
**URANISCUS** n palate
**URANISM** n homosexuality
**URANISMS** >URANISM
**URANITE** n any of various minerals containing uranium, esp torbernite or autunite
**URANITES** >URANITE
**URANITIC** >URANITE
**URANIUM** n radioactive silvery-white metallic element, used chiefly as a source of nuclear energy
**URANIUMS** >URANIUM
**URANOLOGY** n study of the universe and planets
**URANOUS** adj of or containing uranium, esp in a low valence state
**URANYL** n of, consisting of, or containing the divalent ion $UO_2^{2+}$ or the group $-UO_2$
**URANYLIC** >URANYL
**URANYLS** >URANYL
**URAO** n type of mineral
**URAOS** >URAO
**URARE** same as >URALI
**URARES** >URARE
**URARI** same as >URALI
**URARIS** >URARI

**URASE** same as >UREASE
**URASES** >URASE
**URATE** n any salt or ester of uric acid
**URATES** >URATE
**URATIC** >URATE
**URB** n urban area
**URBAN** adj of or living in a city or town
**URBANE** adj characterized by courtesy, elegance, and sophistication
**URBANELY** >URBANE
**URBANER** >URBANE
**URBANEST** >URBANE
**URBANISE** same as >URBANIZE
**URBANISED** >URBANISE
**URBANISES** >URBANISE
**URBANISM** n character of city life
**URBANISMS** >URBANISM
**URBANIST** n person who studies towns and cities
**URBANISTS** >URBANIST
**URBANITE** n resident of an urban community
**URBANITES** >URBANITE
**URBANITY** n quality of being urbane
**URBANIZE** vb make (a rural area) more industrialized and urban
**URBANIZED** >URBANIZE
**URBANIZES** >URBANIZE
**URBIA** n urban area
**URBIAS** >URBIA
**URBS** >URB
**URCEOLATE** adj shaped like an urn or pitcher
**URCEOLI** >URCEOLUS
**URCEOLUS** n organ of a plant
**URCHIN** n mischievous child
**URCHINS** >URCHIN
**URD** n type of plant with edible seeds
**URDE** adj (in heraldry) having points
**URDEE** same as >URDE
**URDS** >URD
**URDY** n heraldic line pattern
**URE** same as >AUROCHS
**UREA** n white soluble crystalline compound found in urine
**UREAL** >UREA
**UREAS** >UREA
**UREASE** n enzyme occurring in many plants, esp fungi, that converts urea to ammonium carbonate
**UREASES** >UREASE
**UREDIA** >UREDIUM
**UREDIAL** >UREDIUM
**UREDINE** >UREDO
**UREDINES** >UREDO
**UREDINIA** >UREDINIUM
**UREDINIAL** >UREDINIUM
**UREDINIUM** same as >UREDIUM

**UREDINOUS** >UREDO
**UREDIUM** n spore-producing body of some rust fungi in which uredospores are formed
**UREDO** less common name for >URTICARIA
**UREDOS** >UREDO
**UREDOSORI** pl n spore-producing bodies of some rust fungi in which uredospores are formed; uredia
**UREIC** >UREA
**UREIDE** n any of a class of organic compounds derived from urea by replacing one or more of its hydrogen atoms by organic groups
**UREIDES** >UREIDE
**UREMIA** same as >URAEMIA
**UREMIAS** >UREMIA
**UREMIC** >UREMIA
**URENA** n plant genus
**URENAS** >URENA
**URENT** adj burning
**UREOTELIC** adj excreting urea
**URES** >URE
**URESES** >URESIS
**URESIS** n urination
**URETER** n tube that conveys urine from the kidney to the bladder
**URETERAL** >URETER
**URETERIC** >URETER
**URETERS** >URETER
**URETHAN** same as >URETHANE
**URETHANE** n short for the synthetic material polyurethane
**URETHANES** >URETHANE
**URETHANS** >URETHAN
**URETHRA** n canal that carries urine from the bladder out of the body
**URETHRAE** >URETHRA
**URETHRAL** >URETHRA
**URETHRAS** >URETHRA
**URETIC** adj of or relating to the urine
**URGE** n strong impulse, inner drive, or yearning ▷ vb plead with or press (a person to do something)
**URGED** >URGE
**URGENCE** >URGENT
**URGENCES** >URGENT
**URGENCIES** >URGENT
**URGENCY** >URGENT
**URGENT** adj requiring speedy action or attention
**URGENTLY** >URGENT
**URGER** >URGE
**URGERS** >URGE
**URGES** >URGE
**URGING** >URGE
**URGINGLY** >URGE
**URGINGS** >URGE
**URIAL** n type of sheep
**URIALS** >URIAL
**URIC** adj of or derived from

urine
**URICASE** n type of enzyme
**URICASES** > URICASE
**URIDINE** n nucleoside present in all living cells in a combined form, esp in RNA
**URIDINES** > URIDINE
**URIDYLIC** as in *uridylic acid* nucleotide consisting of uracil, ribose, and a phosphate group. It is a constituent of RNA
**URINAL** n sanitary fitting used by men for urination
**URINALS** > URINAL
**URINANT** adj having the head downwards
**URINARIES** > URINARY
**URINARY** adj of urine or the organs that secrete and pass urine ▷ n reservoir for urine
**URINATE** vb discharge urine
**URINATED** > URINATE
**URINATES** > URINATE
**URINATING** > URINATE
**URINATION** > URINATE
**URINATIVE** > URINATE
**URINATOR** > URINATE
**URINATORS** > URINATE
**URINE** n pale yellow fluid excreted by the kidneys to the bladder and passed as waste from the body ▷ vb urinate
**URINED** > URINE
**URINEMIA** same as > UREMIA
**URINEMIAS** > URINEMIA
**URINEMIC** > URINEMIA
**URINES** > URINE
**URINING** > URINE
**URINOLOGY** same as > UROLOGY
**URINOSE** same as > URINOUS
**URINOUS** adj of, resembling, or containing urine
**URITE** n part of the abdomen
**URITES** > URITE
**URMAN** n forest
**URMANS** > URMAN
**URN** n vase used as a container for the ashes of the dead ▷ vb put in an urn
**URNAL** > URN
**URNED** > URN
**URNFIELD** n cemetery full of individual cremation urns ▷ adj (of a number of Bronze Age cultures) characterized by cremation in urns, which began in E Europe about the second millennium BC and by the seventh century BC had covered almost all of mainland Europe
**URNFIELDS** > URNFIELD
**URNFUL** n capacity of an

urn
**URNFULS** > URNFUL
**URNING** n homosexual man
**URNINGS** > URNING
**URNLIKE** > URN
**URNS** > URN
**UROBILIN** n brownish pigment found in faeces and sometimes in urine
**UROBILINS** > UROBILIN
**UROCHORD** n notochord of a larval tunicate, typically confined to the tail region
**UROCHORDS** > UROCHORD
**UROCHROME** n yellowish pigment that colours urine
**URODELAN** > URODELE
**URODELANS** > URODELAN
**URODELE** n any amphibian of the order *Urodela*, having a long body and tail and four short limbs: includes the salamanders and newts ▷ adj of, relating to, or belonging to the *Urodela*
**URODELES** > URODELE
**URODELOUS** > URODELE
**UROGENOUS** adj producing or derived from urine
**UROGRAPHY** n branch of radiology concerned with X-ray examination of the kidney and associated structures
**UROKINASE** n biochemical catalyst
**UROLAGNIA** n sexual arousal involving urination
**UROLITH** n calculus in the urinary tract
**UROLITHIC** > UROLITH
**UROLITHS** > UROLITH
**UROLOGIC** > UROLOGY
**UROLOGIES** > UROLOGY
**UROLOGIST** > UROLOGY
**UROLOGY** n branch of medicine concerned with the urinary system and its diseases
**UROMERE** n part of the abdomen
**UROMERES** > UROMERE
**UROPOD** n paired appendage that arises from the last segment of the body in lobsters and related crustaceans and forms part of the tail fan
**UROPODAL** > UROPOD
**UROPODOUS** > UROPOD
**UROPODS** > UROPOD
**UROPYGIA** > UROPYGIUM
**UROPYGIAL** > UROPYGIUM
**UROPYGIUM** n hindmost part of a bird's body, from which the tail feathers grow
**UROSCOPIC** > UROSCOPY
**UROSCOPY** n examination of the urine
**UROSES** > UROSIS
**UROSIS** n urinary disease
**UROSOME** n abdomen of

arthropods
**UROSOMES** > UROSOME
**UROSTEGE** n part of a serpent's tail
**UROSTEGES** > UROSTEGE
**UROSTOMY** n type of urinary surgery
**UROSTYLE** n bony rod forming the last segment of the vertebral column of frogs, toads, and related amphibians
**UROSTYLES** > UROSTYLE
**URP** dialect word for > VOMIT
**URPED** > URP
**URPING** > URP
**URPS** > URP
**URSA** n she-bear
**URSAE** > URSA
**URSID** n meteor
**URSIDS** > URSID
**URSIFORM** adj bear-shaped or bearlike in form
**URSINE** adj of or like a bear
**URSON** n type of porcupine
**URSONS** > URSON
**URTEXT** n earliest form of a text as established by linguistic scholars as a basis for variants in later texts still in existence
**URTEXTS** > URTEXT
**URTICA** n type of nettle
**URTICANT** n something that causes itchiness and irritation
**URTICANTS** > URTICANT
**URTICARIA** n skin condition characterized by the formation of itchy red or whitish raised patches, usually caused by an allergy
**URTICAS** > URTICA
**URTICATE** adj characterized by the presence of weals ▷ vb sting
**URTICATED** > URTICATE
**URTICATES** > URTICATE
**URUBU** n type of bird
**URUBUS** > URUBU
**URUS** another name for the > AUROCHS
**URUSES** > URUS
**URUSHIOL** n poisonous pale yellow liquid occurring in poison ivy and the lacquer tree
**URUSHIOLS** > URUSHIOL
**URVA** n Indian mongoose
**URVAS** > URVA
**US** pron refers to the speaker or writer and another person or other people
**USABILITY** > USABLE
**USABLE** adj able to be used
**USABLY** > USABLE
**USAGE** n regular or constant use
**USAGER** n person who has the use of something in trust

**USAGERS** > USAGER
**USAGES** > USAGE
**USANCE** n period of time permitted by commercial usage for the redemption of foreign bills of exchange
**USANCES** > USANCE
**USAUNCE** same as > USANCE
**USAUNCES** > USAUNCE
**USE** vb put into service or action ▷ n using or being used
**USEABLE** same as > USABLE
**USEABLY** > USABLE
**USED** adj second-hand
**USEFUL** adj able to be used advantageously or for several different purposes ▷ n odd-jobman or general factotum
**USEFULLY** > USEFUL
**USEFULS** > USEFUL
**USELESS** adj having no practical use
**USELESSLY** > USELESS
**USER** n continued exercise, use, or enjoyment of a right, esp in property
**USERNAME** n name given by computer user to gain access
**USERNAMES** > USERNAME
**USERS** > USER
**USES** > USE
**USHER** n official who shows people to their seats, as in a church ▷ vb conduct or escort
**USHERED** > USHER
**USHERESS** n female usher
**USHERETTE** n female assistant in a cinema who shows people to their seats
**USHERING** > USHER
**USHERINGS** > USHER
**USHERS** > USHER
**USHERSHIP** > USHER
**USING** > USE
**USNEA** n type of lichen
**USNEAS** > USNEA
**USQUABAE** n whisky
**USQUABAES** > USQUABAE
**USQUE** n whisky
**USQUEBAE** same as > USQUABAE
**USQUEBAES** > USQUABAE
**USQUES** > USQUE
**USTION** n burning
**USTIONS** > USTION
**USTULATE** adj charred
**USUAL** adj of the most normal, frequent, or regular type ▷ n ordinary or commonplace events
**USUALLY** adv most often, in most cases
**USUALNESS** > USUAL
**USUALS** > USUAL
**USUCAPION** n method of acquiring property
**USUCAPT** > USUCAPION
**USUCAPTED** > USUCAPION
**USUCAPTS** > USUCAPION

USUFRUCT n right to use and derive profit from a piece of property belonging to another, provided the property itself remains undiminished and uninjured in any way
USUFRUCTS > USUFRUCT
USURE vb be involved in usury
USURED > USURE
USURER n person who lends funds at an exorbitant rate of interest
USURERS > USURER
USURES > USURE
USURESS n female usurer
USURESSES > USURESS
USURIES > USURY
USURING > USURE
USURIOUS > USURY
USUROUS > USURY
USURP vb seize (a position or power) without authority
USURPED > USURP
USURPEDLY > USURP
USURPER > USURP
USURPERS > USURP
USURPING > USURP
USURPINGS > USURP
USURPS > USURP
USURY n practice of lending money at an extremely high rate of interest
USWARD adv towards us
USWARDS same as > USWARD
UT n syllable used in the fixed system of solmization for the note C
UTA n side-blotched lizard
UTAS n eighth day of a festival
UTASES > UTAS
UTE same as > UTILITY
UTENSIL n tool or container for practical use
UTENSILS > UTENSIL
UTERI > UTERUS
UTERINE adj of or affecting the womb
UTERITIS n inflammation of the womb
UTEROTOMY n surgery on the uterus
UTERUS n womb
UTERUSES > UTERUS
UTES > UTE
UTILE obsolete word for > USEFUL
UTILIDOR n above-ground insulated casing for pipes carrying water, sewerage and electricity in permafrost regions
UTILIDORS > UTILIDOR
UTILISE same as > UTILIZE
UTILISED > UTILISE
UTILISER > UTILISE
UTILISERS > UTILISE
UTILISES > UTILISE
UTILISING > UTILISE
UTILITIES > UTILITY

UTILITY n usefulness ▷ adj designed for use rather than beauty
UTILIZE vb make practical use of
UTILIZED > UTILIZE
UTILIZER > UTILIZE
UTILIZERS > UTILIZE
UTILIZES > UTILIZE
UTILIZING > UTILIZE
UTIS n uproar
UTISES > UTIS
UTMOST n the greatest possible degree or amount ▷ adj of the greatest possible degree or amount
UTMOSTS > UTMOST
UTOPIA n real or imaginary society, place, state, etc, considered to be perfect or ideal
UTOPIAN adj of or relating to a perfect or ideal existence ▷ n idealistic social reformer
UTOPIANS > UTOPIAN
UTOPIAS > UTOPIA
UTOPIAST > UTOPIA
UTOPIASTS > UTOPIA
UTOPISM > UTOPIA
UTOPISMS > UTOPIA
UTOPIST > UTOPIA
UTOPISTIC > UTOPIA
UTOPISTS > UTOPIA
UTRICLE n larger of the two parts of the membranous labyrinth of the internal ear
UTRICLES > UTRICLE
UTRICULAR > UTRICLE
UTRICULI > UTRICULUS
UTRICULUS same as > UTRICLE
UTS > UT
UTTER vb express (something) in sounds or words ▷ adj total or absolute
UTTERABLE > UTTER
UTTERANCE n something uttered
UTTERED > UTTER
UTTERER > UTTER
UTTERERS > UTTER
UTTEREST > UTTER
UTTERING > UTTER
UTTERINGS > UTTER
UTTERLESS > UTTER
UTTERLY adv extrremely
UTTERMOST same as > UTMOST
UTTERNESS > UTTER
UTTERS > UTTER
UTU n reward
UTUS > UTU
UVA n grape or fruit resembling this
UVAE > UVA
UVAROVITE n emerald-green garnet found in chromium deposits: consists of calcium chromium silicate
UVAS > UVA

UVEA n part of the eyeball consisting of the iris, ciliary body, and choroid
UVEAL > UVEA
UVEAS > UVEA
UVEITIC > UVEITIS
UVEITIS n inflammation of the uvea
UVEITISES > UVEITIS
UVEOUS > UVEA
UVULA n small fleshy part of the soft palate that hangs in the back of the throat
UVULAE > UVULA
UVULAR adj of or relating to the uvula ▷ n uvular consonant
UVULARLY > UVULAR
UVULARS > UVULAR
UVULAS > UVULA
UVULITIS n inflammation of the uvula
UXORIAL adj of or relating to a wife
UXORIALLY > UXORIAL
UXORICIDE n act of killing one's wife
UXORIOUS adj excessively fond of or dependent on one's wife

# Vv

**VAC** *vb* clean with a vacuum cleaner
**VACANCE** *n* vacant period
**VACANCES** >VACANCE
**VACANCIES** >VACANCY
**VACANCY** *n* unfilled job
**VACANT** *adj* (of a toilet, room, etc) unoccupied
**VACANTLY** >VACANT
**VACATABLE** >VACATE
**VACATE** *vb* cause (something) to be empty by leaving
**VACATED** >VACATE
**VACATES** >VACATE
**VACATING** >VACATE
**VACATION** *n* time when universities and law courts are closed ▷ *vb* take a vacation
**VACATIONS** >VACATION
**VACATUR** *n* annulment
**VACATURS** >VACATUR
**VACCINA** *same as* >VACCINIA
**VACCINAL** *adj* of or relating to vaccine or vaccination
**VACCINAS** >VACCINA
**VACCINATE** *vb* inject with a vaccine
**VACCINE** *n* substance designed to cause a mild form of a disease to make a person immune to the disease itself
**VACCINEE** *n* person who has been vaccinated
**VACCINEES** >VACCINEE
**VACCINES** >VACCINE
**VACCINIA** *technical name for* >COWPOX
**VACCINIAL** >VACCINIA
**VACCINIAS** >VACCINIA
**VACCINIUM** *n* shrub genus

**VACHERIN** *n* soft cheese made from cows' milk
**VACHERINS** >VACHERIN
**VACILLANT** *adj* indecisive
**VACILLATE** *vb* keep changing one's mind or opinions
**VACKED** >VAC
**VACKING** >VAC
**VACS** >VAC
**VACUA** >VACUUM
**VACUATE** *vb* empty
**VACUATED** >VACUATE
**VACUATES** >VACUATE
**VACUATING** >VACUATE
**VACUATION** >VACUATE
**VACUIST** *n* person believing in the existence of vacuums in nature
**VACUISTS** >VACUIST
**VACUITIES** >VACUITY
**VACUITY** *n* absence of intelligent thought or ideas
**VACUOLAR** >VACUOLE
**VACUOLATE** >VACUOLE
**VACUOLE** *n* fluid-filled cavity in the cytoplasm of a cell
**VACUOLES** >VACUOLE
**VACUOUS** *adj* not expressing intelligent thought
**VACUOUSLY** >VACUOUS
**VACUUM** *n* empty space from which all or most air or gas has been removed ▷ *vb* clean with a vacuum cleaner
**VACUUMED** >VACUUM
**VACUUMING** >VACUUM
**VACUUMS** >VACUUM
**VADE** *vb* fade
**VADED** >VADE

**VADES** >VADE
**VADING** >VADE
**VADOSE** *adj* of or derived from water occurring above the water table
**VAE** *same as* >VOE
**VAES** >VAE
**VAG** *n* vagrant
**VAGABOND** *n* person with no fixed home, esp a beggar
**VAGABONDS** >VAGABOND
**VAGAL** *adj* of, relating to, or affecting the vagus nerve
**VAGALLY** >VAGAL
**VAGARIES** >VAGARY
**VAGARIOUS** *adj* characterized or caused by vagaries
**VAGARISH** >VAGARY
**VAGARY** *n* unpredictable change
**VAGGED** >VAG
**VAGGING** >VAG
**VAGI** >VAGUS
**VAGILE** *adj* able to move freely
**VAGILITY** >VAGILE
**VAGINA** *n* (in female mammals) passage from the womb to the external genitals
**VAGINAE** >VAGINA
**VAGINAL** >VAGINA
**VAGINALLY** >VAGINA
**VAGINANT** *adj* sheathing
**VAGINAS** >VAGINA
**VAGINATE** *adj* (esp of plant parts) having a sheath
**VAGINATED** >VAGINATE
**VAGINITIS** *n* inflammation of the vagina

**VAGINOSES** >VAGINOSIS
**VAGINOSIS** *n* bacterial vaginal infection
**VAGINULA** *n* little sheath
**VAGINULAE** >VAGINULA
**VAGINULE** *same as* >VAGINULA
**VAGINULES** >VAGINULE
**VAGITUS** *n* new-born baby's cry
**VAGITUSES** >VAGITUS
**VAGOTOMY** *n* surgical division of the vagus nerve
**VAGOTONIA** *n* pathological overactivity of the vagus nerve
**VAGOTONIC** >VAGOTONIA
**VAGRANCY** *n* state or condition of being a vagrant
**VAGRANT** *n* person with no settled home ▷ *adj* wandering
**VAGRANTLY** >VAGRANT
**VAGRANTS** >VAGRANT
**VAGROM** *same as* >VAGRANT
**VAGROMS** >VAGROM
**VAGS** >VAG
**VAGUE** *adj* not clearly explained ▷ *vb* wander
**VAGUED** >VAGUE
**VAGUELY** >VAGUE
**VAGUENESS** >VAGUE
**VAGUER** >VAGUE
**VAGUES** >VAGUE
**VAGUEST** >VAGUE
**VAGUING** >VAGUE
**VAGUS** *n* tenth cranial nerve, which supplies the heart, lungs, and viscera
**VAHANA** *n* vehicle
**VAHANAS** >VAHANA
**VAHINE** *n* Polynesian

woman
**VAHINES** >VAHINE
**VAIL** vb lower (something, such as a weapon), esp as a sign of deference or submission
**VAILED** >VAIL
**VAILING** >VAIL
**VAILS** >VAIL
**VAIN** adj excessively proud, esp of one's appearance
**VAINER** >VAIN
**VAINESSE** n vainness
**VAINESSES** >VAINESSE
**VAINEST** >VAIN
**VAINGLORY** n boastfulness or vanity
**VAINLY** >VAIN
**VAINNESS** >VAIN
**VAIR** n fur, probably Russian squirrel, used to trim robes in the Middle Ages
**VAIRE** same as >VAIR
**VAIRIER** >VAIR
**VAIRIEST** >VAIR
**VAIRS** >VAIR
**VAIRY** >VAIR
**VAIVODE** n European ruler
**VAIVODES** >VAIVODE
**VAKASS** n type of cloak
**VAKASSES** >VAKASS
**VAKEEL** n ambassador
**VAKEELS** >VAKEEL
**VAKIL** same as >VAKEEL
**VAKILS** >VAKIL
**VALANCE** n piece of drapery round the edge of a bed ▷ vb provide with a valance
**VALANCED** >VALANCE
**VALANCES** >VALANCE
**VALANCING** >VALANCE
**VALE** n valley ▷ sentence substitute farewell
**VALENCE** same as >VALENCY
**VALENCES** >VALENCE
**VALENCIA** n type of fabric
**VALENCIAS** >VALENCIA
**VALENCIES** >VALENCY
**VALENCY** n power of an atom to make molecular bonds
**VALENTINE** n (person to whom one sends) a romantic card on Saint Valentine's Day, 14th February
**VALERATE** n salt of valeric acid
**VALERATES** >VALERATE
**VALERIAN** n herb used as a sedative
**VALERIANS** >VALERIAN
**VALERIC** adj of, relating to, or derived from valerian
**VALES** >VALE
**VALET** n man's personal male servant ▷ vb act as a valet (for)
**VALETA** n old-time dance in triple time
**VALETAS** >VALETA
**VALETE** n farewell

**VALETED** >VALET
**VALETES** >VALETE
**VALETING** >VALET
**VALETINGS** >VALET
**VALETS** >VALET
**VALGOID** >VALGUS
**VALGOUS** same as >VALGUS
**VALGUS** adj denoting a deformity of a limb ▷ n abnormal position of a limb
**VALGUSES** >VALGUS
**VALI** n Turkish civil governor
**VALIANCE** >VALIANT
**VALIANCES** >VALIANT
**VALIANCY** >VALIANT
**VALIANT** adj brave or courageous ▷ n brave person
**VALIANTLY** >VALIANT
**VALIANTS** >VALIANT
**VALID** adj soundly reasoned
**VALIDATE** vb make valid
**VALIDATED** >VALIDATE
**VALIDATES** >VALIDATE
**VALIDER** >VALID
**VALIDEST** >VALID
**VALIDITY** >VALID
**VALIDLY** >VALID
**VALIDNESS** >VALID
**VALINE** n essential amino acid
**VALINES** >VALINE
**VALIS** >VALI
**VALISE** n small suitcase
**VALISES** >VALISE
**VALKYR** variant of >VALKYRIE
**VALKYRIE** n (in Norse mythology) beatiful maiden who collects dead heroes on the battlefield to take to Valhalla
**VALKYRIES** >VALKYRIES
**VALKYRS** >VALKYR
**VALLAR** adj pertaining to a rampart
**VALLARY** >VALLAR
**VALLATE** adj surrounded with a wall
**VALLATION** n act or process of building fortifications
**VALLECULA** n any of various natural depressions or crevices
**VALLEY** n low area between hills, often with a river running through it
**VALLEYED** adj having a valley
**VALLEYS** >VALLEY
**VALLHUND** as in Swedish vallhund breed of dog
**VALLHUNDS** >VALLHUND
**VALLONIA** same as >VALONIA
**VALLONIAS** >VALLONIA
**VALLUM** n Roman rampart or earthwork
**VALLUMS** >VALLUM
**VALONEA** same as >VALONIA
**VALONEAS** >VALONEA

**VALONIA** n acorn cups and unripe acorns of a particular oak
**VALONIAS** >VALONIA
**VALOR** same as >VALOUR
**VALORISE** same as >VALORIZE
**VALORISED** >VALORISE
**VALORISES** >VALORISE
**VALORIZE** vb fix and maintain an artificial price for (a commodity) by governmental action
**VALORIZED** >VALORIZE
**VALORIZES** >VALORIZE
**VALOROUS** >VALOUR
**VALORS** >VALOR
**VALOUR** n bravery ▷ n courageous person
**VALOURS** >VALOUR
**VALPROATE** n medicament derived from valproic acid
**VALPROIC** as in valproic acid synthetic crystalline compound, used as an anticonvulsive
**VALSE** another word for >WALTZ
**VALSED** >VALSE
**VALSES** >VALSE
**VALSING** >VALSE
**VALUABLE** adj having great worth ▷ n valuable article of personal property, esp jewellery
**VALUABLES** >VALUABLE
**VALUABLY** >VALUABLE
**VALUATE** vb value or evaluate
**VALUATED** >VALUATE
**VALUATES** >VALUATE
**VALUATING** >VALUATE
**VALUATION** n assessment of worth
**VALUATOR** n person who estimates the value of objects, paintings, etc
**VALUATORS** >VALUATOR
**VALUE** n importance, usefulness ▷ vb assess the worth or desirability of
**VALUED** >VALUE
**VALUELESS** adj having or possessing no value
**VALUER** >VALUE
**VALUERS** >VALUE
**VALUES** >VALUE
**VALUING** >VALUE
**VALUTA** n value of one currency in terms of its exchange rate with another
**VALUTAS** >VALUTA
**VALVAL** same as >VALVULAR
**VALVAR** same as >VALVULAR
**VALVASSOR** same as >VAVASOR
**VALVATE** adj furnished with a valve or valves
**VALVE** n device to control the movement of fluid through a pipe ▷ vb provide with a valve
**VALVED** >VALVE

**VALVELESS** >VALVE
**VALVELET** same as >VALVULE
**VALVELETS** >VALVELET
**VALVELIKE** >VALVE
**VALVES** >VALVE
**VALVING** >VALVE
**VALVULA** same as >VALVULE
**VALVULAE** >VALVULA
**VALVULAR** adj of or having valves
**VALVULE** n small valve or a part resembling one
**VALVULES** >VALVULE
**VAMBRACE** n piece of armour used to protect the arm
**VAMBRACED** >VAMBRACE
**VAMBRACES** >VAMBRACE
**VAMOOSE** vb leave a place hurriedly
**VAMOOSED** >VAMOSE
**VAMOOSES** >VAMOSE
**VAMOOSING** >VAMOSE
**VAMOSE** same as >VAMOOSE
**VAMOSED** >VAMOSE
**VAMOSES** >VAMOSE
**VAMOSING** >VAMOSE
**VAMP** n sexually attractive woman who seduces men ▷ vb (of a woman) to seduce (a man)
**VAMPED** >VAMP
**VAMPER** >VAMP
**VAMPERS** >VAMP
**VAMPIER** >VAMP
**VAMPIEST** >VAMP
**VAMPING** >VAMP
**VAMPINGS** >VAMP
**VAMPIRE** n (in folklore) corpse that rises at night to drink the blood of the living ▷ vb assail
**VAMPIRED** >VAMPIRE
**VAMPIRES** >VAMPIRE
**VAMPIRIC** >VAMPIRE
**VAMPIRING** >VAMPIRE
**VAMPIRISE** same as >VAMPIRIZE
**VAMPIRISH** >VAMPIRE
**VAMPIRISM** n belief in the existence of vampires
**VAMPIRIZE** vb suck blood from
**VAMPISH** >VAMP
**VAMPISHLY** >VAMP
**VAMPLATE** n piece of metal mounted on a lance to protect the hand
**VAMPLATES** >VAMPLATE
**VAMPS** >VAMP
**VAMPY** >VAMP
**VAN** n motor vehicle for transporting goods ▷ vb send in a van
**VANADATE** n any salt or ester of a vanadic acid
**VANADATES** >VANADATE
**VANADIATE** same as >VANADATE
**VANADIC** adj of or containing vanadium, esp in a trivalent or pentavalent state

**VANADIUM** *n* metallic element, used in steel
**VANADIUMS** > VANADIUM
**VANADOUS** *adj* of or containing vanadium
**VANASPATI** *n* hydrogenated vegetable fat commonly used in India as a substitute for butter
**VANDA** *n* type of orchid
**VANDAL** *n* person who deliberately damages property
**VANDALIC** > VANDAL
**VANDALISE** *same as* > VANDALIZE
**VANDALISH** > VANDAL
**VANDALISM** *n* wanton or deliberate destruction caused by a vandal or an instance of such destruction
**VANDALIZE** *vb* cause damage to (personal or public property) deliberately
**VANDALS** > VANDAL
**VANDAS** > VANDA
**VANDYKE** *n* short pointed beard ▷ *vb* cut with deep zigzag indentations
**VANDYKED** > VANDYKE
**VANDYKES** > VANDYKE
**VANDYKING** > VANDYKE
**VANE** *n* flat blade on a rotary device such as a weathercock or propeller
**VANED** > VANE
**VANELESS** > VANE
**VANES** > VANE
**VANESSA** *n* type of butterfly
**VANESSAS** > VANESSA
**VANESSID** *n* type of butterfly ▷ *adj* relating to this butterfly
**VANESSIDS** > VANESSID
**VANG** *n* type of rope or tackle on a sailing ship
**VANGS** > VANG
**VANGUARD** *n* unit of soldiers leading an army
**VANGUARDS** > VANGUARD
**VANILLA** *n* seed pod of a tropical climbing orchid, used for flavouring ▷ *adj* flavoured with vanilla
**VANILLAS** > VANILLA
**VANILLIC** *adj* of, resembling, containing, or derived from vanilla or vanillin
**VANILLIN** *n* white crystalline aldehyde found in vanilla
**VANILLINS** > VANILLIN
**VANISH** *vb* disappear suddenly or mysteriously ▷ *n* second and weaker of the two vowels in a falling diphthong
**VANISHED** > VANISH
**VANISHER** > VANISH
**VANISHERS** > VANISH

**VANISHES** > VANISH
**VANISHING** > VANISH
**VANITAS** *n* type of Dutch painting
**VANITASES** > VANITAS
**VANITIED** *adj* with vanity units or mirrors
**VANITIES** > VANITY
**VANITORY** *n* vanity unit
**VANITY** *n* (display of) excessive pride
**VANLOAD** *n* amount van will carry
**VANLOADS** > VANLOAD
**VANMAN** *n* man in control of a van
**VANMEN** > VANMAN
**VANNED** > VAN
**VANNER** *n* horse used to pull delivery vehicles
**VANNERS** > VANNER
**VANNING** > VAN
**VANNINGS** > VAN
**VANPOOL** *n* van-sharing group
**VANPOOLS** > VANPOOL
**VANQUISH** *vb* defeat (someone) utterly
**VANS** > VAN
**VANT** *archaic word for* > VANGUARD
**VANTAGE** *n* state, position, or opportunity offering advantage ▷ *vb* benefit
**VANTAGED** > VANTAGE
**VANTAGES** > VANTAGE
**VANTAGING** > VANTAGE
**VANTBRACE** *n* armour for the arm
**VANTS** > VANT
**VANWARD** *adv* in or towards the front
**VAPID** *adj* lacking character, dull
**VAPIDER** > VAPID
**VAPIDEST** > VAPID
**VAPIDITY** > VAPID
**VAPIDLY** > VAPID
**VAPIDNESS** > VAPID
**VAPOR** *same as* > VAPOUR
**VAPORABLE** > VAPOR
**VAPORED** > VAPOR
**VAPORER** > VAPOR
**VAPORERS** > VAPOR
**VAPORETTI** > VAPORETTO
**VAPORETTO** *n* steam-powered passenger boat, as used on the canals in Venice
**VAPORIFIC** *adj* producing, causing, or tending to produce vapour
**VAPORING** > VAPOR
**VAPORINGS** > VAPOR
**VAPORISE** *same as* > VAPORIZE
**VAPORISED** > VAPORISE
**VAPORISER** *same as* > VAPORIZER
**VAPORISES** > VAPORISE
**VAPORISH** > VAPOR
**VAPORIZE** *vb* change into a vapour
**VAPORIZED** > VAPORIZE

**VAPORIZER** *n* substance that vaporizes or a device that causes vaporization
**VAPORIZES** > VAPORIZE
**VAPORLESS** > VAPOR
**VAPORLIKE** > VAPOR
**VAPOROUS** *same as* > VAPORIFIC
**VAPORS** > VAPOR
**VAPORWARE** *n* new software that has not yet been produced
**VAPORY** > VAPOUR
**VAPOUR** *n* moisture suspended in air as steam or mist ▷ *vb* evaporate
**VAPOURED** > VAPOUR
**VAPOURER** > VAPOUR
**VAPOURERS** > VAPOUR
**VAPOURING** > VAPOUR
**VAPOURISH** > VAPOUR
**VAPOURS** > VAPOUR
**VAPOURY** > VAPOUR
**VAPULATE** *vb* strike
**VAPULATED** > VAPULATE
**VAPULATES** > VAPULATE
**VAQUERO** *n* cattlehand
**VAQUEROS** > VAQUERO
**VAR** *n* unit of reactive power of an alternating current
**VARA** *n* unit of length used in Spain, Portugal, and South America
**VARACTOR** *n* semiconductor diode that acts as a voltage-dependent capacitor
**VARACTORS** > VARACTOR
**VARAN** *n* type of lizard
**VARANS** > VARAN
**VARAS** > VARA
**VARDIES** > VARDY
**VARDY** *n* verdict
**VARE** *n* rod
**VAREC** *n* ash obtained from kelp
**VARECH** *same as* > VAREC
**VARECHS** > VARECH
**VARECS** > VAREC
**VARES** > VARE
**VAREUSE** *n* type of coat
**VAREUSES** > VAREUSE
**VARGUENO** *n* type of Spanish cabinet
**VARGUENOS** > VARGUENO
**VARIA** *n* collection or miscellany, esp of literary works
**VARIABLE** *adj* not always the same, changeable ▷ *n* something that is subject to variation
**VARIABLES** > VARIABLE
**VARIABLY** > VARIABLE
**VARIANCE** *n* act of varying
**VARIANCES** > VARIANCE
**VARIANT** *adj* differing from a standard or type ▷ *n* something that differs from a standard or type
**VARIANTS** > VARIANT
**VARIAS** > VARIA
**VARIATE** *n* random

variable or a numerical value taken by it ▷ *vb* vary
**VARIATED** > VARIATE
**VARIATES** > VARIATE
**VARIATING** > VARIATE
**VARIATION** *n* something presented in a slightly different form
**VARIATIVE** > VARIATE
**VARICELLA** *n* chickenpox
**VARICES** > VARIX
**VARICOID** *same as* > CIRSOID
**VARICOSE** *adj* of or resulting from varicose veins
**VARICOSED** *same as* > VARICOSE
**VARICOSES** > VARICOSIS
**VARICOSIS** *n* any condition characterized by distension of the veins
**VARIED** > VARY
**VARIEDLY** > VARY
**VARIEGATE** *vb* alter the appearance of, esp by adding different colours
**VARIER** *n* person who varies
**VARIERS** > VARIER
**VARIES** > VARY
**VARIETAL** *adj* of or forming a variety, esp a biological variety ▷ *n* wine labelled with the name of the grape from which it is pressed
**VARIETALS** > VARIETAL
**VARIETIES** > VARIETY
**VARIETY** *n* state of being diverse or various
**VARIFOCAL** *adj* gradated to permit any length of vision between near and distant ▷ *n* lens of this type
**VARIFORM** *adj* varying in form or shape
**VARIOLA** *n* smallpox
**VARIOLAR** > VARIOLA
**VARIOLAS** > VARIOLA
**VARIOLATE** *vb* inoculate with the smallpox virus ▷ *adj* marked or pitted with or as if with the scars of smallpox
**VARIOLE** *n* any of the rounded masses that make up the rock variolite
**VARIOLES** > VARIOLE
**VARIOLITE** *n* type of basic igneous rock
**VARIOLOID** *adj* resembling smallpox ▷ *n* mild form of smallpox occurring in persons with partial immunity
**VARIOLOUS** *adj* relating to or resembling smallpox
**VARIORUM** *adj* containing notes by various scholars or critics or various versions of the text ▷ *n* edition or text of this kind
**VARIORUMS** > VARIORUM
**VARIOUS** *adj* of several

kinds
**VARIOUSLY** >VARIOUS
**VARISCITE** n green secondary mineral
**VARISIZED** adj of different sizes
**VARISTOR** n type of semiconductor device
**VARISTORS** >VARISTOR
**VARITYPE** vb produce (copy) on a Varityper ▷n copy produced on a Varityper
**VARITYPED** >VARITYPE
**VARITYPES** >VARITYPE
**VARIX** n tortuous dilated vein
**VARLET** n menial servant
**VARLETESS** n female varlet
**VARLETRY** n the rabble
**VARLETS** >VARLET
**VARLETTO** same as >VARLET
**VARLETTOS** >VARLETTO
**VARMENT** same as >VARMINT
**VARMENTS** >VARMENT
**VARMINT** n irritating or obnoxious person or animal
**VARMINTS** >VARMINT
**VARNA** n any of the four Hindu castes
**VARNAS** >VARNA
**VARNISH** n solution of oil and resin, put on a surface to make it hard and glossy ▷vb apply varnish to
**VARNISHED** >VARNISH
**VARNISHER** >VARNISH
**VARNISHES** >VARNISH
**VARNISHY** >VARNISH
**VAROOM** same as >VROOM
**VAROOMED** >VAROOM
**VAROOMING** >VAROOM
**VAROOMS** >VAROOM
**VARROA** n small parasite
**VARROAS** >VARROA
**VARS** >VAR
**VARSAL** adj universal
**VARSITIES** >VARSITY
**VARSITY** n university
**VARTABED** n position in the Armenian church
**VARTABEDS** >VARTABED
**VARUS** adj denoting a deformity of a limb ▷n abnormal position of a limb
**VARUSES** >VARUS
**VARVE** n typically thin band of sediment deposited annually in glacial lakes
**VARVED** adj having layers of sedimentary deposit
**VARVEL** n piece of falconry equipment
**VARVELLED** adj having varvels
**VARVELS** >VARVEL
**VARVES** >VARVE
**VARY** vb change
**VARYING** >VARY
**VARYINGLY** >VARY
**VARYINGS** >VARY
**VAS** n vessel or tube that

carries a fluid
**VASA** >VAS
**VASAL** >VAS
**VASCULA** >VASCULUM
**VASCULAR** adj relating to vessels
**VASCULUM** n metal box used by botanists in the field for carrying botanical specimens
**VASCULUMS** >VASCULUM
**VASE** n ornamental jar, esp for flowers
**VASECTOMY** n surgical removal of part of the vas deferens, as a contraceptive method
**VASELIKE** >VASE
**VASELINE** n translucent gelatinous substance obtained from petroleum
**VASELINES** >VASELINE
**VASES** >VASE
**VASIFORM** >VAS
**VASOMOTOR** adj (of a drug, agent, nerve, etc) affecting the diameter of blood vessels
**VASOSPASM** n sudden contraction of a blood vessel
**VASOTOCIN** n chemical found in birds, reptiles, and some amphibians
**VASOTOMY** n surgery on the vas deferens
**VASOVAGAL** adj relating to blood vessels and the vagus nerve
**VASSAIL** archaic variant of >VASSAL
**VASSAILS** >VASSAIL
**VASSAL** n man given land by a lord in return for military service ▷adj of or relating to a vassal ▷vb vassalize
**VASSALAGE** n condition of being a vassal or the obligations to which a vassal was liable
**VASSALESS** >VASSAL
**VASSALISE** same as >VASSALIZE
**VASSALIZE** vb make a vassal of
**VASSALLED** >VASSAL
**VASSALRY** n vassalage
**VASSALS** >VASSAL
**VAST** adj extremely large ▷n immense or boundless space
**VASTER** >VAST
**VASTEST** >VAST
**VASTIDITY** n vastness
**VASTIER** >VASTY
**VASTIEST** >VASTY
**VASTITIES** >VAST
**VASTITUDE** n condition or quality of being vast
**VASTITY** >VAST
**VASTLY** >VAST
**VASTNESS** >VAST
**VASTS** >VAST

**VASTY** archaic or poetic word for >VAST
**VAT** n large container for liquids ▷vb place, store, or treat in a vat
**VATABLE** adj subject to VAT
**VATFUL** n amount enough to fill a vat
**VATFULS** >VATFUL
**VATIC** adj of, relating to, or characteristic of a prophet
**VATICAL** same as >VATIC
**VATICIDE** n murder of a prophet
**VATICIDES** >VATICIDE
**VATICINAL** adj foretelling or prophesying
**VATMAN** n Customs and Excise employee
**VATMEN** >VATMAN
**VATS** >VAT
**VATTED** >VAT
**VATTER** n person who works with vats; blender
**VATTERS** >VATTER
**VATTING** >VAT
**VATU** n standard monetary unit of Vanuatu
**VATUS** >VATU
**VAU** same as >VAV
**VAUCH** vb move fast
**VAUCHED** >VAUCH
**VAUCHES** >VAUCH
**VAUCHING** >VAUCH
**VAUDOO** same as >VOODOO
**VAUDOOS** >VAUDOO
**VAUDOUX** same as >VOODOO
**VAULT** n secure room for storing valuables ▷vb jump over (something) by resting one's hand(s) on it.
**VAULTAGE** n group of vaults
**VAULTAGES** >VAULTAGE
**VAULTED** >VAULT
**VAULTER** >VAULT
**VAULTERS** >VAULT
**VAULTIER** >VAULTY
**VAULTIEST** >VAULTY
**VAULTING** n arrangement of ceiling vaults in a building ▷adj excessively confident
**VAULTINGS** >VAULTING
**VAULTLIKE** >VAULT
**VAULTS** >VAULT
**VAULTY** adj arched
**VAUNCE** >ADVANCE
**VAUNCED** >VAUNCE
**VAUNCES** >VAUNCE
**VAUNCING** >VAUNCE
**VAUNT** vb describe or display (success or possessions) boastfully ▷n boast
**VAUNTAGE** archaic variant of >VANTAGE
**VAUNTAGES** >VAUNTAGE
**VAUNTED** >VAUNT
**VAUNTER** >VAUNT
**VAUNTERS** >VAUNT
**VAUNTERY** n bravado
**VAUNTFUL** >VAUNT
**VAUNTIE** same as >VAUNTY
**VAUNTIER** >VAUNT

**VAUNTIEST** >VAUNT
**VAUNTING** >VAUNT
**VAUNTINGS** >VAUNT
**VAUNTS** >VAUNT
**VAUNTY** adj proud
**VAURIEN** n rascal
**VAURIENS** >VAURIEN
**VAUS** >VAU
**VAUT** same as >VAULT
**VAUTE** same as >VAULT
**VAUTED** >VAUTE
**VAUTES** >VAUTE
**VAUTING** >VAUT
**VAUTS** >VAUT
**VAV** n sixth letter of the Hebrew alphabet
**VAVASOR** n (in feudal society) vassal who also has vassals himself
**VAVASORS** >VAVASOR
**VAVASORY** n lands held by a vavasor
**VAVASOUR** same as >VAVASOR
**VAVASOURS** >VAVASOUR
**VAVASSOR** same as >VAVASOR
**VAVASSORS** >VAVASOR
**VAVS** >VAV
**VAW** n Hebrew letter
**VAWARD** n vanguard
**VAWARDS** >VAWARD
**VAWNTIE** same as >VAUNT
**VAWS** >VAW
**VAWTE** same as >VAULT
**VAWTED** >VAWTE
**VAWTES** >VAWTE
**VAWTING** >VAWTE
**VEAL** n calf meat ▷vb cover with a veil
**VEALE** same as >VEIL
**VEALED** >VEAL
**VEALER** n young bovine animal of up to 14 months old grown for veal
**VEALERS** >VEALER
**VEALES** >VEAL
**VEALIER** >VEAL
**VEALIEST** >VEAL
**VEALING** >VEAL
**VEALS** >VEAL
**VEALY** >VEAL
**VECTOR** n quantity that has size and direction, such as force ▷vb direct or guide (a pilot) by directions transmitted by radio
**VECTORED** >VECTOR
**VECTORIAL** >VECTOR
**VECTORING** >VECTOR
**VECTORISE** same as >VECTORIZE
**VECTORIZE** vb computing term
**VECTORS** >VECTOR
**VEDALIA** n Australian ladybird which is a pest of citrus fruits
**VEDALIAS** >VEDALIA
**VEDETTE** n small patrol vessel
**VEDETTES** >VEDETTE
**VEDUTA** n painting of a town or city

**VEDUTE** >VEDUTA
**VEDUTISTA** n artist who creates vedutas
**VEDUTISTI** >VEDUTISTA
**VEE** n letter 'v'
**VEEJAY** n video jockey
**VEEJAYS** >VEEJAY
**VEENA** same as >VINA
**VEENAS** >VEENA
**VEEP** n vice president
**VEEPEE** n vice president
**VEEPEES** >VEEPEE
**VEEPS** >VEEP
**VEER** vb change direction suddenly ▷ n change of course or direction
**VEERED** >VEER
**VEERIES** >VEERY
**VEERING** >VEER
**VEERINGLY** >VEER
**VEERINGS** >VEER
**VEERS** >VEER
**VEERY** n tawny brown North American thrush
**VEES** >VEE
**VEG** n vegetable or vegetables ▷ vb relax
**VEGA** n tobacco plantation
**VEGAN** n person who eats no meat, fish, eggs, or dairy products ▷ adj suitable for a vegan
**VEGANIC** adj farmed without the use of animal products or byproducts
**VEGANISM** >VEGAN
**VEGANISMS** >VEGAN
**VEGANS** >VEGAN
**VEGAS** >VEGA
**VEGELATE** n type of chocolate
**VEGELATES** >VEGELATE
**VEGEMITE** n informal word for a child
**VEGEMITES** >VEGEMITE
**VEGES** >VEG
**VEGETABLE** n edible plant ▷ adj of or like plants or vegetables
**VEGETABLY** >VEGETABLE
**VEGETAL** adj of or relating to plant life ▷ n vegetable
**VEGETALLY** >VEGETAL
**VEGETALS** >VEGETAL
**VEGETANT** adj causing growth or vegetation-like
**VEGETATE** vb live a dull boring life with no mental stimulation
**VEGETATED** >VEGETATE
**VEGETATES** >VEGETATE
**VEGETE** adj lively
**VEGETIST** n vegetable cultivator or enthusiast
**VEGETISTS** >VEGETIST
**VEGETIVE** adj dull or passive ▷ n vegetable
**VEGETIVES** >VEGETIVE
**VEGGED** >VEG
**VEGGES** >VEG
**VEGGIE** n vegetable ▷ adj vegetarian
**VEGGIES** >VEGGIE
**VEGGING** >VEG

**VEGIE** variant of >VEGGIE
**VEGIES** >VEGIE
**VEGO** adj vegetarian ▷ n vegetarian
**VEGOS** >VEGO
**VEHEMENCE** >VEHEMENT
**VEHEMENCY** >VEHEMENT
**VEHEMENT** adj expressing strong feelings
**VEHICLE** n machine for carrying people or objects
**VEHICLES** >VEHICLE
**VEHICULAR** >VEHICLE
**VEHM** n type of medieval German court
**VEHME** >VEHM
**VEHMIC** >VEHM
**VEHMIQUE** >VEHM
**VEIL** n piece of thin cloth covering the head or face ▷ vb cover with or as if with a veil
**VEILED** adj disguised
**VEILEDLY** >VEILED
**VEILER** >VEIL
**VEILERS** >VEIL
**VEILIER** >VEIL
**VEILIEST** >VEIL
**VEILING** n veil or the fabric used for veils
**VEILINGS** >VEILING
**VEILLESS** >VEIL
**VEILLEUSE** n small night-light
**VEILLIKE** >VEIL
**VEILS** >VEIL
**VEILY** >VEIL
**VEIN** n tube that takes blood to the heart ▷ vb diffuse over or cause to diffuse over in streaked patterns
**VEINAL** >VEIN
**VEINED** >VEIN
**VEINER** n wood-carving tool
**VEINERS** >VEINER
**VEINIER** >VEIN
**VEINIEST** >VEIN
**VEINING** n pattern or network of veins or streaks
**VEININGS** >VEINING
**VEINLESS** >VEIN
**VEINLET** n any small vein or venule
**VEINLETS** >VEINLET
**VEINLIKE** >VEIN
**VEINOUS** >VEIN
**VEINS** >VEIN
**VEINSTONE** another word for >GANGUE
**VEINSTUFF** another word for >GANGUE
**VEINULE** less common spelling of >VENULE
**VEINULES** >VEINULE
**VEINULET** same as >VEINLET
**VEINULETS** >VEINULET
**VEINY** >VEIN
**VELA** >VELUM
**VELAMEN** n thick layer of dead cells that covers the aerial roots of certain

orchids
**VELAMINA** >VELAMEN
**VELAR** adj of, relating to, or attached to a velum ▷ n velar sound
**VELARIA** >VELARIUM
**VELARIC** >VELAR
**VELARISE** same as >VELARIZE
**VELARISED** >VELARISE
**VELARISES** >VELARISE
**VELARIUM** n awning used to protect the audience in ancient Roman theatres and amphitheatres
**VELARIZE** vb pronounce or supplement the pronunciation of (a speech sound) with articulation at the soft palate
**VELARIZED** >VELARIZE
**VELARIZES** >VELARIZE
**VELARS** >VELAR
**VELATE** adj having or covered with velum
**VELATED** same as >VELATE
**VELATURA** n overglaze
**VELATURAS** >VELATURA
**VELCRO** n tradename for a fastening consisting of two strips of nylon fabric that form a strong bond when pressed together
**VELCROS** >VELCRO
**VELD** n high grassland in southern Africa
**VELDS** >VELD
**VELDSKOEN** n leather ankle boot
**VELDT** same as >VELD
**VELDTS** >VELDT
**VELE** same as >VEIL
**VELES** >VELE
**VELETA** same as >VALETA
**VELETAS** >VELETA
**VELIGER** n free-swimming larva of many molluscs
**VELIGERS** >VELIGER
**VELITES** pl n light-armed troops in ancient Rome, drawn from the poorer classes
**VELL** vb cut turf
**VELLEITY** n weakest level of desire or volition
**VELLENAGE** n (in Medieval Europe) status of being a villein
**VELLET** n velvet
**VELLETS** >VELLET
**VELLICATE** vb twitch, pluck, or pinch
**VELLON** n silver and copper alloy used in old Spanish coins
**VELLONS** >VELLON
**VELLS** >VELL
**VELLUM** n fine calfskin parchment ▷ adj made of or resembling vellum
**VELLUMS** >VELLUM
**VELOCE** adv be played rapidly
**VELOCITY** n speed of

movement in a given direction
**VELODROME** n arena with a banked track for cycle racing
**VELOUR** n fabric similar to velvet
**VELOURS** same as >VELOUR
**VELOUTE** n rich white sauce or soup made from stock, egg yolks, and cream
**VELOUTES** >VELOUTE
**VELOUTINE** n type of velvety fabric
**VELSKOEN** n type of shoe
**VELSKOENS** >VELSKOEN
**VELUM** n any of various membranous structures
**VELURE** n velvet or a similar fabric ▷ vb cover with velure
**VELURED** >VELURE
**VELURES** >VELURE
**VELURING** >VELURE
**VELVERET** n type of velvet-like fabric
**VELVERETS** >VELVERET
**VELVET** n fabric with a thick soft pile ▷ vb cover with velvet
**VELVETED** >VELVET
**VELVETEEN** n cotton velvet
**VELVETIER** >VELVET
**VELVETING** >VELVET
**VELVETS** >VELVET
**VELVETY** >VELVET
**VENA** n vein in the body
**VENAE** >VENA
**VENAL** adj easily bribed
**VENALITY** >VENAL
**VENALLY** >VENAL
**VENATIC** adj of, relating to, or used in hunting
**VENATICAL** same as >VENATIC
**VENATION** n arrangement of the veins in a leaf or in the wing of an insect
**VENATIONS** >VENATION
**VENATOR** n hunter
**VENATORS** >VENATOR
**VEND** vb sell
**VENDABLE** >VEND
**VENDABLES** >VEND
**VENDACE** n either of two small whitefish occurring in lakes in Scotland and NW England
**VENDACES** >VENDACE
**VENDAGE** n vintage
**VENDAGES** >VENDAGE
**VENDANGE** same as >VENDAGE
**VENDANGES** >VENDANGE
**VENDED** >VEND
**VENDEE** n person to whom something, esp real property, is sold
**VENDEES** >VENDEE
**VENDER** same as >VENDOR
**VENDERS** >VEND
**VENDETTA** n long-lasting quarrel between people

in which they attempt to harm each other
**VENDETTAS** >VENDETTA
**VENDEUSE** *n* female salesperson
**VENDEUSES** >VENDEUSE
**VENDIBLE** *adj* saleable or marketable ▷ *n* saleable object
**VENDIBLES** >VENDIBLE
**VENDIBLY** >VENDIBLE
**VENDING** >VEND
**VENDINGS** >VEND
**VENDIS** *same as* >VENDACE
**VENDISES** >VENDIS
**VENDISS** *same as* >VENDACE
**VENDISSES** >VENDIS
**VENDITION** >VEND
**VENDOR** *n* person who sells goods such as newspapers or hamburgers from a stall or cart
**VENDORS** >VENDOR
**VENDS** >VEND
**VENDUE** *n* public sale
**VENDUES** >VENDUE
**VENEER** *n* thin layer of wood etc covering a cheaper material ▷ *vb* cover (a surface) with a veneer
**VENEERED** >VENEER
**VENEERER** >VENEER
**VENEERERS** >VENEER
**VENEERING** *n* material used as veneer or a veneered surface
**VENEERS** >VENEER
**VENEFIC** *adj* having poisonous effects
**VENEFICAL** *same as* >VENEFIC
**VENENATE** *vb* poison
**VENENATED** >VENENATE
**VENENATES** >VENENATE
**VENENE** *n* medicine from snake venom
**VENENES** >VENENE
**VENENOSE** *adj* poisonous
**VENERABLE** *adj* worthy of deep respect
**VENERABLY** >VENERABLE
**VENERATE** *vb* hold (a person) in deep respect
**VENERATED** >VENERATE
**VENERATES** >VENERATE
**VENERATOR** >VENERATE
**VENEREAL** *adj* transmitted by sexual intercourse
**VENEREAN** *n* sex addict
**VENEREANS** >VENEREAN
**VENEREOUS** *adj* libidinous
**VENERER** *n* hunter
**VENERERS** >VENERER
**VENERIES** >VENERY
**VENERY** *n* pursuit of sexual gratification
**VENETIAN** *n* Venetian blind
**VENETIANS** >VENETIAN
**VENEWE** *same as* >VENUE
**VENEWES** >VENEWE
**VENEY** *n* thrust
**VENEYS** >VENEY
**VENGE** *vb* avenge

**VENGEABLE** >VENGE
**VENGEABLY** >VENGE
**VENGEANCE** *n* revenge
**VENGED** >VENGE
**VENGEFUL** *adj* wanting revenge
**VENGEMENT** >VENGE
**VENGER** >VENGE
**VENGERS** >VENGE
**VENGES** >VENGE
**VENGING** >VENGE
**VENIAL** *adj* (of a sin or fault) easily forgiven
**VENIALITY** >VENIAL
**VENIALLY** >VENIAL
**VENIDIUM** *n* genus of flowering plants
**VENIDIUMS** >VENIDIUM
**VENIN** *n* any of the poisonous constituents of animal venoms
**VENINE** *same as* >VENIN
**VENINES** >VENINE
**VENINS** >VENIN
**VENIRE** *n* list from which jurors are selected
**VENIREMAN** *n* person summoned for jury service
**VENIREMEN** >VENIREMAN
**VENIRES** >VENIRE
**VENISON** *n* deer meat
**VENISONS** >VENISON
**VENITE** *n* musical setting for the 95th psalm
**VENITES** >VENITE
**VENNEL** *n* lane
**VENNELS** >VENNEL
**VENOGRAM** *n* X-ray of a vein
**VENOGRAMS** >VENOGRAM
**VENOLOGY** *n* study of veins
**VENOM** *n* malice or spite ▷ *vb* poison
**VENOMED** >VENOM
**VENOMER** >VENOM
**VENOMERS** >VENOM
**VENOMING** >VENOM
**VENOMLESS** >VENOM
**VENOMOUS** >VENOM
**VENOMS** >VENOM
**VENOSE** *adj* having veins
**VENOSITY** *n* excessive quantity of blood in the venous system or in an organ or part
**VENOUS** *adj* of veins
**VENOUSLY** >VENOUS
**VENT** *n* outlet releasing fumes or fluid ▷ *vb* express (an emotion) freely
**VENTAGE** *n* small opening
**VENTAGES** >VENTAGE
**VENTAIL** *n* (in medieval armour) a covering for the lower part of the face
**VENTAILE** *same as* >VENTAIL
**VENTAILES** >VENTAILE
**VENTAILS** >VENTAIL
**VENTANA** *n* window
**VENTANAS** >VENTANA
**VENTAYLE** *same as* >VENTAIL
**VENTAYLES** >VENTAYLE
**VENTED** >VENT

**VENTER** >VENT
**VENTERS** >VENT
**VENTIDUCT** *n* air pipe
**VENTIFACT** *n* pebble that has been shaped by wind-blown sand
**VENTIGE** *same as* >VENTAGE
**VENTIGES** >VENTIGE
**VENTIL** *n* valve on a musical instrument
**VENTILATE** *vb* let fresh air into
**VENTILS** >VENTIL
**VENTING** >VENT
**VENTINGS** >VENT
**VENTLESS** >VENT
**VENTOSE** *adj* full of wind
**VENTOSITY** *n* flatulence
**VENTOUSE** *n* apparatus sometimes used to assist the delivery of a baby
**VENTOUSES** >VENTOUSE
**VENTRAL** *adj* relating to the front of the body ▷ *n* ventral fin
**VENTRALLY** >VENTRAL
**VENTRALS** >VENTRAL
**VENTRE** *same as* >VENTURE
**VENTRED** >VENTRE
**VENTRES** >VENTRE
**VENTRICLE** *n* cavity in an organ such as the heart
**VENTRING** >VENTRE
**VENTRINGS** >VENTRE
**VENTROUS** >VENTRE
**VENTS** >VENT
**VENTURE** *n* risky undertaking, esp in business ▷ *vb* do something risky
**VENTURED** >VENTURE
**VENTURER** >VENTURE
**VENTURERS** >VENTURE
**VENTURES** >VENTURE
**VENTURI** *n* tube used to control the flow of fluid
**VENTURING** >VENTURE
**VENTURIS** >VENTURI
**VENTUROUS** *adj* adventurous
**VENUE** *n* place where an organized gathering is held
**VENUES** >VENUE
**VENULAR** >VENULE
**VENULE** *n* any of the small branches of a vein
**VENULES** >VENULE
**VENULOSE** >VENULE
**VENULOUS** >VENULE
**VENUS** *n* type of marine bivalve mollusc
**VENUSES** >VENUS
**VENVILLE** *n* type of parish tenure
**VENVILLES** >VENVILLE
**VERA** as in *aloe vera* plant substance used in skin and hair preparations
**VERACIOUS** *adj* habitually truthful
**VERACITY** *n* truthfulness
**VERANDA** *n* porch or portico along the outside of a

building
**VERANDAED** >VERANDA
**VERANDAH** *same as* >VERANDA
**VERANDAHS** >VERANDAH
**VERANDAS** >VERANDA
**VERAPAMIL** *n* calcium-channel blocker used in the treatment of some types of irregular heart rhythm
**VERATRIA** *same as* >VERATRINE
**VERATRIAS** >VERATRIA
**VERATRIN** *same as* >VERATRINE
**VERATRINE** *n* white poisonous mixture obtained from the seeds of sabadilla
**VERATRINS** >VERATRIN
**VERATRUM** *n* genus of herbs
**VERATRUMS** >VERATRUM
**VERB** *n* word that expresses the idea of action, happening, or being
**VERBAL** *adj* spoken ▷ *n* abuse or invective ▷ *vb* implicate (someone) in a crime by quoting alleged admission of guilt in court
**VERBALISE** *same as* >VERBALIZE
**VERBALISM** *n* exaggerated emphasis on the importance of words
**VERBALIST** *n* person who deals with words alone, rather than facts, ideas, feeling, etc
**VERBALITY** >VERBAL
**VERBALIZE** *vb* express (something) in words
**VERBALLED** >VERBAL
**VERBALLY** >VERBAL
**VERBALS** >VERBAL
**VERBARIAN** *n* inventor of words
**VERBASCUM** *See* >MULLEIN
**VERBATIM** *adj* word for word ▷ *adv* using exactly the same words
**VERBENA** *n* plant with sweet-smelling flowers
**VERBENAS** >VERBENA
**VERBERATE** *vb* lash
**VERBIAGE** *n* excessive use of words
**VERBIAGES** >VERBIAGE
**VERBICIDE** *n* person who destroys a word
**VERBID** *n* any nonfinite form of a verb or any nonverbal word derived from a verb
**VERBIDS** >VERBID
**VERBIFIED** >VERBIFY
**VERBIFIES** >VERBIFY
**VERBIFY** *another word for* >VERBALIZE
**VERBILE** *n* person who is best stimulated by words
**VERBILES** >VERBILE
**VERBING** *n* use of nouns as

verbs

**VERBINGS** >VERBING
**VERBLESS** >VERB
**VERBOSE** *adj* speaking at tedious length
**VERBOSELY** >VERBOSE
**VERBOSER** >VERBOSE
**VERBOSEST** >VERBOSE
**VERBOSITY** >VERBOSE
**VERBOTEN** *adj* forbidden
**VERBS** >VERB
**VERD** as in *verd antique* dark green mottled impure variety of serpentine marble
**VERDANCY** >VERDANT
**VERDANT** *adj* covered in green vegetation
**VERDANTLY** >VERDANT
**VERDELHO** *n* type of grape
**VERDELHOS** >VERDELHO
**VERDERER** *n* judicial officer responsible for the maintenance of law and order in the royal forests
**VERDERERS** >VERDERER
**VERDEROR** *same as* >VERDERER
**VERDERORS** >VERDEROR
**VERDET** *n* type of verdigris
**VERDETS** >VERDET
**VERDICT** *n* decision of a jury
**VERDICTS** >VERDICT
**VERDIGRIS** *n* green film on copper, brass, or bronze
**VERDIN** *n* small W North American tit having grey plumage with a yellow head
**VERDINS** >VERDIN
**VERDIT** *same as* >VERDICT
**VERDITE** *n* type of rock used in jewellery
**VERDITER** *n* blue-green pigment made from copper
**VERDITERS** >VERDITER
**VERDITES** >VERDITE
**VERDITS** >VERDIT
**VERDOY** *n* floral or leafy shield decoration
**VERDURE** *n* flourishing green vegetation
**VERDURED** >VERDURE
**VERDURES** >VERDURE
**VERDUROUS** >VERDURE
**VERECUND** *adj* shy or modest
**VERGE** *n* grass border along a road ▷ *vb* move in a specified direction
**VERGED** >VERGE
**VERGENCE** *n* inward or outward turning movement of the eyes in convergence or divergence
**VERGENCES** >VERGENCE
**VERGENCY** *adj* inclination
**VERGER** *n* church caretaker
**VERGERS** >VERGER
**VERGES** >VERGE
**VERGING** >VERGE
**VERGLAS** *n* thin film of ice

on rock
**VERGLASES** >VERGLAS
**VERIDIC** *same as* >VERIDICAL
**VERIDICAL** *adj* truthful
**VERIER** >VERY
**VERIEST** >VERY
**VERIFIED** >VERIFY
**VERIFIER** >VERIFY
**VERIFIERS** >VERIFY
**VERIFIES** >VERIFY
**VERIFY** *vb* check the truth or accuracy of
**VERIFYING** >VERIFY
**VERILY** *adv* in truth
**VERISM** *n* extreme naturalism in art or literature
**VERISMO** *n* school of composition that originated in Italian opera
**VERISMOS** >VERISMO
**VERISMS** >VERISM
**VERIST** >VERISM
**VERISTIC** >VERISM
**VERISTS** >VERISM
**VERITABLE** *adj* rightly called, without exaggeration
**VERITABLY** >VERITABLE
**VERITAS** *n* truth
**VERITATES** >VERITAS
**VERITE** *adj* involving a high degree of realism or naturalism ▷ *n* this kind of realism in film
**VERITES** >VERITE
**VERITIES** >VERITY
**VERITY** *n* true statement or principle
**VERJUICE** *n* acid juice of unripe grapes, apples, or crab apples ▷ *vb* make sour
**VERJUICED** >VERJUICE
**VERJUICES** >VERJUICE
**VERKRAMP** *adj* bigoted or illiberal
**VERLAN** *n* variety of French slang in which the syllables are inverted
**VERLANS** >VERLAN
**VERLIG** *adj* enlightened
**VERLIGTE** *n* (during apartheid) a White political liberal
**VERLIGTES** >VERLIGTE
**VERMAL** >VERMIS
**VERMEIL** *n* gilded silver, bronze, or other metal, used esp in the 19th century ▷ *vb* decorate with vermeil ▷ *adj* vermilion
**VERMEILED** >VERMEIL
**VERMEILLE** *variant of* >VERMEIL
**VERMEILS** >VERMEIL
**VERMELL** *same as* >VERMEIL
**VERMELLS** >VERMELL
**VERMES** >VERMIS
**VERMIAN** >VERMIS
**VERMICIDE** *n* any substance used to kill

worms
**VERMICULE** *n* small worm
**VERMIFORM** *adj* shaped like a worm
**VERMIFUGE** *n* any drug or agent able to destroy or expel intestinal worms
**VERMIL** *same as* >VERMEIL
**VERMILIES** >VERMILY
**VERMILION** *adj* orange-red ▷ *n* mercuric sulphide, used as an orange-red pigment
**VERMILLED** >VERMIL
**VERMILS** >VERMIL
**VERMILY** *variant of* >VERMEIL
**VERMIN** *pl n* animals, esp insects and rodents, that spread disease or cause damage
**VERMINATE** *vb* breed vermin
**VERMINED** *adj* plagued with vermin
**VERMINOUS** *adj* relating to, infested with, or suggestive of vermin
**VERMINS** >VERMIN
**VERMINY** >VERMIN
**VERMIS** *n* middle lobe connecting the two halves of the cerebellum
**VERMOULU** *adj* worm-eaten
**VERMOUTH** *n* wine flavoured with herbs
**VERMOUTHS** >VERMOUTH
**VERMUTH** *same as* >VERMOUTH
**VERMUTHS** >VERMOUTH
**VERNACLE** *same as* >VERNICLE
**VERNACLES** >VERNACLE
**VERNAL** *adj* occurring in spring
**VERNALISE** *same as* >VERNALIZE
**VERNALITY** >VERNAL
**VERNALIZE** *vb* subject (ungerminated or germinating seeds) to low temperatures
**VERNALLY** >VERNAL
**VERNANT** >VERNAL
**VERNATION** *n* way in which leaves are arranged in the bud
**VERNICLE** *n* veronica
**VERNICLES** >VERNICLE
**VERNIER** *n* movable scale on a graduated measuring instrument for taking readings in fractions
**VERNIERS** >VERNIER
**VERNIX** *n* white substance covering the skin of a foetus
**VERNIXES** >VERNIX
**VERONAL** *n* a long-acting barbiturate used medicinally
**VERONALS** >VERONAL
**VERONICA** *n* plant with small blue, pink, or white

flowers
**VERONICAS** >VERONICA
**VERONIQUE** *adj* (of a dish) garnished with seedless white grapes
**VERQUERE** *n* type of backgammon game
**VERQUERES** >VERQUERE
**VERQUIRE** *variant of* >VERQUERE
**VERQUIRES** >VERQUIRE
**VERRA** *Scot word for* >VERY
**VERREL** *n* ferrule
**VERRELS** >VERREL
**VERREY** *same as* >VAIR
**VERRUCA** *n* wart, usu on the foot
**VERRUCAE** >VERRUCA
**VERRUCAS** >VERRUCA
**VERRUCOSE** *adj* covered with warts
**VERRUCOUS** *same as* >VERRUCOSE
**VERRUGA** *same as* >VERRUCA
**VERRUGAS** >VERRUGA
**VERRY** *same as* >VAIR
**VERS** *n* verse
**VERSAL** *n* embellished letter
**VERSALS** >VERSAL
**VERSANT** *n* side or slope of a mountain or mountain range
**VERSANTS** >VERSANT
**VERSATILE** *adj* having many skills or uses
**VERSE** *n* group of lines forming part of a song or poem ▷ *vb* write verse
**VERSED** *adj* thoroughly knowledgeable (about)
**VERSELET** *n* small verse
**VERSELETS** >VERSELET
**VERSEMAN** *n* man who writes verse
**VERSEMEN** >VERSEMAN
**VERSER** *n* versifier
**VERSERS** >VERSER
**VERSES** >VERSE
**VERSET** *n* short, often sacred, verse
**VERSETS** >VERSET
**VERSICLE** *n* short verse
**VERSICLES** >VERSICLE
**VERSIFIED** >VERSIFY
**VERSIFIER** >VERSIFY
**VERSIFIES** >VERSIFY
**VERSIFORM** *adj* changing in form
**VERSIFY** *vb* write in verse
**VERSIN** *same as* >VERSINE
**VERSINE** *n* mathematical term
**VERSINES** >VERSINE
**VERSING** >VERSE
**VERSINGS** >VERSE
**VERSINS** >VERSIN
**VERSION** *n* form of something, such as a piece of writing, with some differences from other forms
**VERSIONAL** >VERSION
**VERSIONER** *n* translator

VERSIONS >VERSION
VERSO n left-hand page of a book
VERSOS >VERSO
VERST n unit of length used in Russia
VERSTE same as >VERST
VERSTES >VERSTE
VERSTS >VERST
VERSUS prep in opposition to or in contrast with
VERSUTE adj cunning
VERT n right to cut green wood in a forest ▷ vb turn
VERTEBRA n one of the bones that form the spine
VERTEBRAE >VERTEBRA
VERTEBRAL >VERTEBRA
VERTEBRAS >VERTEBRA
VERTED >VERT
VERTEX n point on a geometric figure where the sides form an angle
VERTEXES >VERTEX
VERTICAL adj straight up and down ▷ n vertical direction
VERTICALS >VERTICAL
VERTICES >VERTEX
VERTICIL n circular arrangement of parts about an axis, esp leaves around a stem
VERTICILS >VERTICIL
VERTICITY n ability to turn
VERTIGO n dizziness, usu when looking down from a high place
VERTIGOES >VERTIGO
VERTIGOS >VERTIGO
VERTING >VERT
VERTIPORT n type of airport
VERTS >VERT
VERTU same as >VIRTU
VERTUE same as >VIRTU
VERTUES >VERTUE
VERTUOUS >VERTU
VERTUS >VERTU
VERVAIN n plant with spikes of blue, purple, or white flowers
VERVAINS >VERVAIN
VERVE n enthusiasm or liveliness
VERVEL same as >VARVEL
VERVELLED >VERVEL
VERVELS >VERVEL
VERVEN same as >VERVAIN
VERVENS >VERVEN
VERVES >VERVE
VERVET n variety of a South African guenon monkey
VERVETS >VERVET
VERY adv more than usually, extremely ▷ adj absolute, exact
VESICA n bladder
VESICAE >VESICA
VESICAL adj of or relating to a vesica, esp the urinary bladder
VESICANT n any substance

that causes blisters ▷ adj acting as a vesicant
VESICANTS >VESICANT
VESICATE vb blister
VESICATED >VESICATE
VESICATES >VESICATE
VESICLE n sac or small cavity, esp one containing fluid
VESICLES >VESICLE
VESICULA n vesicle
VESICULAE >VESICULA
VESICULAR >VESICLE
VESPA n type of wasp
VESPAS >VESPA
VESPER n evening prayer, service, or hymn
VESPERAL n liturgical book containing the prayers, psalms, and hymns used at vespers
VESPERALS >VESPERAL
VESPERS pl n service of evening prayer
VESPIARY n nest or colony of social wasps or hornets
VESPID n insect of the family that includes the common wasp and hornet ▷ adj of or belonging to this family
VESPIDS >VESPID
VESPINE adj of, relating to, or resembling a wasp or wasps
VESPOID adj like a wasp
VESSAIL archaic variant of >VESSEL
VESSAILS >VESSAIL
VESSEL n container or ship ▷ adj contained in a vessel
VESSELED >VESSEL
VESSELS >VESSEL
VEST n undergarment worn on the top half of the body ▷ vb give (authority) to (someone)
VESTA n short friction match, usually of wood
VESTAL adj pure, chaste ▷ n chaste woman
VESTALLY >VESTAL
VESTALS >VESTAL
VESTAS >VESTA
VESTED adj having an existing right to the immediate or future possession of property
VESTEE n person having a vested interest something
VESTEES >VESTEE
VESTIARY n room for storing clothes or dressing in, such as a vestry ▷ adj of or relating to clothes
VESTIBULA >VESTIBULE
VESTIBULE n small entrance hall
VESTIGE n small amount or trace
VESTIGES >VESTIGE
VESTIGIA >VESTIGIUM
VESTIGIAL adj remaining after a larger or more

important thing has gone
VESTIGIUM n trace
VESTIMENT same as >VESTMENT
VESTING >VEST
VESTINGS >VEST
VESTITURE n investiture
VESTLESS >VEST
VESTLIKE >VEST
VESTMENT n garment or robe, esp one denoting office, authority, or rank
VESTMENTS >VESTMENT
VESTRAL >VESTRY
VESTRIES >VESTRY
VESTRY n room in a church used as an office by the priest or minister
VESTRYMAN n member of a church vestry
VESTRYMEN >VESTRYMAN
VESTS >VEST
VESTURAL >VESTURE
VESTURE n garment or something that seems like a garment ▷ vb clothe
VESTURED >VESTURE
VESTURER n person in charge of church vestments
VESTURERS >VESTURER
VESTURES >VESTURE
VESTURING >VESTURE
VESUVIAN n match for lighting cigars
VESUVIANS >VESUVIAN
VET vb check the suitability of ▷ n military veteran
VETCH n climbing plant with a beanlike fruit used as fodder
VETCHES >VETCH
VETCHIER >VETCHY
VETCHIEST >VETCHY
VETCHLING n type of climbing plant
VETCHY adj consisting of vetches
VETERAN n person with long experience in a particular activity, esp military service ▷ adj long-serving
VETERANS >VETERAN
VETIVER n tall hairless grass of tropical and subtropical Asia
VETIVERS >VETIVER
VETIVERT n oil from the vetiver
VETIVERTS >VETIVERT
VETKOEK n South African cake
VETKOEKS >VETKOEK
VETO n official power to cancel a proposal ▷ vb enforce a veto against
VETOED >VETO
VETOER >VETO
VETOERS >VETO
VETOES >VETO
VETOING >VETO
VETOLESS >VETO
VETS >VET

VETTED >VET
VETTER >VET
VETTERS >VET
VETTING >VET
VETTURA n Italian mode of transport
VETTURAS >VETTURA
VETTURINI >VETTURINO
VETTURINO n person who drives a vettura
VEX vb frustrate, annoy
VEXATION n something annoying
VEXATIONS >VEXATION
VEXATIOUS adj vexing
VEXATORY >VEX
VEXED adj annoyed and puzzled
VEXEDLY >VEXED
VEXEDNESS >VEXED
VEXER >VEX
VEXERS >VEX
VEXES >VEX
VEXIL same as >VEXILLUM
VEXILLA >VEXILLUM
VEXILLAR >VEXILLUM
VEXILLARY >VEXILLUM
VEXILLATE >VEXILLUM
VEXILLUM n vane of a feather
VEXILS >VEXIL
VEXING >VEX
VEXINGLY >VEX
VEXINGS >VEX
VEXT same as >VEXED
VEZIR same as >VIZIER
VEZIRS >VEZIR
VIA prep by way of ▷ n road
VIABILITY >VIABLE
VIABLE adj able to be put into practice
VIABLY >VIABLE
VIADUCT n bridge over a valley
VIADUCTS >VIADUCT
VIAE >VIA
VIAL n small bottle for liquids ▷ vb put into a vial
VIALED >VIAL
VIALFUL >VIAL
VIALFULS >VIAL
VIALING >VIAL
VIALLED >VIAL
VIALLING >VIAL
VIALS >VIAL
VIAMETER n device to measure distance travelled
VIAMETERS >VIAMETER
VIAND n type of food, esp a delicacy
VIANDS >VIAND
VIAS >VIA
VIATIC same as >VIATICAL
VIATICA >VIATICUM
VIATICAL adj of or denoting a road or a journey ▷ n purchase of a terminal patient's life assurance policy so that he or she may make use of the proceeds
VIATICALS >VIATICAL
VIATICUM n Holy Communion given to a

person who is dying or in danger of death
**VIATICUMS** >VIATICUM
**VIATOR** *n* traveller
**VIATORES** >VIATOR
**VIATORIAL** *adj* pertaining to travelling
**VIATORS** >VIATOR
**VIBE** *n* feeling or flavour of the kind specified
**VIBES** *pl n* vibrations
**VIBEX** *n* mark under the skin
**VIBEY** *adj* lively and vibrant
**VIBICES** >VIBEX
**VIBIER** >VIBEY
**VIBIEST** >VIBEY
**VIBIST** *n* person who plays a vibraphone in a jazz band or group
**VIBISTS** >VIBIST
**VIBRACULA** *pl n* bristle-like polyps in certain bryozoans
**VIBRAHARP** *n* type of percussion instrument
**VIBRANCE** *n* vibrancy
**VIBRANCES** >VIBRANCE
**VIBRANCY** >VIBRANT
**VIBRANT** *adj* vigorous in appearance, energetic ▷ *n* trilled or rolled speech sound
**VIBRANTLY** >VIBRANT
**VIBRANTS** >VIBRANT
**VIBRATE** *vb* move back and forth rapidly
**VIBRATED** >VIBRATE
**VIBRATES** >VIBRATE
**VIBRATILE** >VIBRATE
**VIBRATING** >VIBRATE
**VIBRATION** *n* vibrating
**VIBRATIVE** >VIBRATE
**VIBRATO** *n* rapid fluctuation in the pitch of a note
**VIBRATOR** *n* device that produces vibratory motion
**VIBRATORS** >VIBRATOR
**VIBRATORY** >VIBRATE
**VIBRATOS** >VIBRATO
**VIBRIO** *n* curved or spiral rodlike bacterium
**VIBRIOID** >VIBRIO
**VIBRION** *same as* >VIBRIO
**VIBRIONIC** >VIBRIO
**VIBRIONS** >VIBRION
**VIBRIOS** >VIBRIO
**VIBRIOSES** >VIBRIOSIS
**VIBRIOSIS** *n* bacterial disease
**VIBRISSA** *n* any of the bristle-like sensitive hairs on the face of many mammals
**VIBRISSAE** >VIBRISSA
**VIBRISSAL** >VIBRISSA
**VIBRONIC** *adj* of, concerned with, or involving both electronic and vibrational energy levels of a molecule
**VIBS** *pl n* type of climbing shoes
**VIBURNUM** *n* subtropical

shrub with white flowers and berry-like fruits
**VIBURNUMS** >VIBURNUM
**VICAR** *n* member of the clergy in charge of a parish
**VICARAGE** *n* vicar's house
**VICARAGES** >VICARAGE
**VICARATE** *same as* >VICARIATE
**VICARATES** >VICARATE
**VICARESS** *n* rank of nun
**VICARIAL** *adj* of or relating to a vicar, vicars, or a vicariate
**VICARIANT** *n* any of several closely related species, etc, each of which exists in a separate geographical area
**VICARIATE** *n* office, rank, or authority of a vicar
**VICARIES** >VICARY
**VICARIOUS** *adj* felt indirectly by imagining what another person experiences
**VICARLY** >VICAR
**VICARS** >VICAR
**VICARSHIP** *same as* >VICARIATE
**VICARY** *n* office of a vicar
**VICE** *n* immoral or evil habit or action ▷ *adj* serving in place of ▷ *vb* grip (something) with or as if with a vice ▷ *prep* instead of
**VICED** >VICE
**VICEGERAL** *adj* of or relating to a person who deputizes for another
**VICELESS** >VICE
**VICELIKE** >VICE
**VICENARY** *adj* relating to or consisting of 20
**VICENNIAL** *adj* occurring every 20 years
**VICEREGAL** *adj* of a viceroy
**VICEREINE** *n* wife of a viceroy
**VICEROY** *n* governor of a colony who represents the monarch
**VICEROYS** >VICEROY
**VICES** >VICE
**VICESIMAL** *same as* >VIGESIMAL
**VICHIES** >VICHY
**VICHY** *n* French mineral water
**VICIATE** *same as* >VITIATE
**VICIATED** >VICIATE
**VICIATES** >VICIATE
**VICIATING** >VICIATE
**VICINAGE** *n* residents of a particular neighbourhood
**VICINAGES** >VICINAGE
**VICINAL** *adj* neighbouring
**VICING** >VICE
**VICINITY** *n* surrounding area
**VICIOSITY** *same as* >VITIOSITY
**VICIOUS** *adj* cruel and

violent
**VICIOUSLY** >VICIOUS
**VICOMTE** *n* French nobleman
**VICOMTES** >VICOMTE
**VICTIM** *n* person or thing harmed or killed
**VICTIMISE** *same as* >VICTIMIZE
**VICTIMIZE** *vb* punish unfairly
**VICTIMS** >VICTIM
**VICTOR** *n* person who has defeated an opponent, esp in war or in sport
**VICTORESS** *same as* >VICTRESS
**VICTORIA** *n* large sweet plum, red and yellow in colour
**VICTORIAS** >VICTORIA
**VICTORIES** >VICTORY
**VICTORINE** *n* woman's article of clothing
**VICTORS** >VICTOR
**VICTORY** *n* winning of a battle or contest
**VICTRESS** *n* female victor
**VICTRIX** *same as* >VICTRESS
**VICTRIXES** >VICTRIX
**VICTROLLA** *n* type of gramophone
**VICTUAL** *vb* supply with or obtain victuals
**VICTUALED** >VICTUAL
**VICTUALER** >VICTUAL
**VICTUALS** *pl n* food and drink
**VICUGNA** *same as* >VICUNA
**VICUGNAS** >VICUGNA
**VICUNA** *n* S American animal like the llama
**VICUNAS** >VICUNA
**VID** *informal word for* >VIDEO
**VIDAME** *n* French nobleman
**VIDAMES** >VIDAME
**VIDE** *interj* look
**VIDELICET** *adv* namely: used to specify items
**VIDENDA** >VIDENDUM
**VIDENDUM** *n* that which is to be seen
**VIDEO** *vb* record (a TV programme or event) on video ▷ *adj* relating to or used in producing television images ▷ *n* recording and showing of films and events using a television set, video tapes, and a video recorder
**VIDEODISC** *variant of* >VIDEODISK
**VIDEODISK** *n* disk on which information is stored in digital form
**VIDEOED** >VIDEO
**VIDEOFIT** *n* computer-generated picture of a person sought by the police
**VIDEOFITS** >VIDEOFIT
**VIDEOGRAM** *n* audiovisual recording

**VIDEOING** >VIDEO
**VIDEOLAND** *n* world of television and televised images
**VIDEOS** >VIDEO
**VIDEOTAPE** *vb* record (a TV programme) on video tape
**VIDEOTEX** *n* information system that displays data from a distant computer on a screen
**VIDEOTEXT** *n* means of representing on a TV screen information that is held in a computer
**VIDETTE** *same as* >VEDETTE
**VIDETTES** >VIDETTE
**VIDICON** *n* small television camera tube used in closed-circuit television
**VIDICONS** >VIDICON
**VIDIMUS** *n* inspection
**VIDIMUSES** >VIDIMUS
**VIDS** >VID
**VIDUAGE** *n* widows collectively
**VIDUAGES** >VIDUAGE
**VIDUAL** *adj* widowed
**VIDUITIES** >VIDUITY
**VIDUITY** *n* widowhood
**VIDUOUS** *adj* empty
**VIE** *vb* compete (with someone)
**VIED** >VIE
**VIELLE** *n* stringed musical instrument
**VIELLES** >VIELLE
**VIER** >VIE
**VIERS** >VIE
**VIES** >VIE
**VIEW** *n* opinion or belief ▷ *vb* think of (something) in a particular way
**VIEWABLE** >VIEW
**VIEWDATA** *n* interactive form of videotext
**VIEWDATAS** >VIEWDATA
**VIEWED** >VIEW
**VIEWER** *n* person who watches television
**VIEWERS** >VIEWER
**VIEWIER** >VIEWY
**VIEWIEST** >VIEWY
**VIEWINESS** >VIEWY
**VIEWING** *n* act of watching television
**VIEWINGS** >VIEWING
**VIEWLESS** *adj* (of windows, etc) not affording a view
**VIEWLY** *adj* pleasant on the eye
**VIEWPHONE** *n* videophone
**VIEWPOINT** *n* person's attitude towards something
**VIEWS** >VIEW
**VIEWY** *adj* having fanciful opinions or ideas
**VIFDA** *same as* >VIVDA
**VIFDAS** >VIFDA
**VIG** *n* interest on a loan that is paid to a moneylender
**VIGA** *n* rafter
**VIGAS** >VIGA

VIGESIMAL adj relating to or based upon the number 20
VIGIA n navigational hazard marked on a chart although its existence has not been confirmed
VIGIAS > VIGIA
VIGIL n night-time period of staying awake to look after a sick person, pray, etc
VIGILANCE n careful attention
VIGILANT adj watchful in case of danger
VIGILANTE n person who takes it upon himself or herself to enforce the law
VIGILS > VIGIL
VIGNERON n person who grows grapes for winemaking
VIGNERONS > VIGNERON
VIGNETTE n small illustration placed at the beginning or end of a chapter or book ▷ vb portray in a vignette
VIGNETTED > VIGNETTE
VIGNETTER n device used in printing vignettes
VIGNETTES > VIGNETTE
VIGOR same as > VIGOUR
VIGORISH n type of commission
VIGORO n women's game similar to cricket
VIGOROS > VIGORO
VIGOROSO adv in music, emphatically
VIGOROUS adj having physical or mental energy
VIGORS > VIGOR
VIGOUR n physical or mental energy
VIGOURS > VIGOUR
VIGS > VIG
VIHARA n type of Buddhist temple
VIHARAS > VIHARA
VIHUELA n obsolete plucked stringed instrument of Spain, related to the guitar
VIHUELAS > VIHUELA
VIKING n Dane, Norwegian, or Swede who raided by sea most of N and W Europe between the 8th and 11th centuries
VIKINGISM > VIKING
VIKINGS > VIKING
VILAYET n major administrative division of Turkey
VILAYETS > VILAYET
VILD same as > VILE
VILDE same as > VILE
VILDLY > VILD
VILDNESS > VILD
VILE adj very wicked
VILELY > VILE
VILENESS > VILE
VILER > VILE

VILEST > VILE
VILIACO n scoundrel
VILIACOES > VILIACO
VILIACOS > VILIACO
VILIAGO same as > VILIACO
VILIAGOES > VILIAGO
VILIAGOS > VILIAGO
VILIFIED > VILIFY
VILIFIER > VILIFY
VILIFIERS > VILIFY
VILIFIES > VILIFY
VILIFY vb attack the character of
VILIFYING > VILIFY
VILIPEND vb treat or regard with contempt
VILIPENDS > VILIPEND
VILL n township
VILLA n large house with gardens
VILLADOM > VILLA
VILLADOMS > VILLA
VILLAE > VILLA
VILLAGE n small group of houses in a country area
VILLAGER n inhabitant of a village ▷ adj backward, unsophisticated, or illiterate
VILLAGERS > VILLAGER
VILLAGERY n villages
VILLAGES > VILLAGE
VILLAGIO same as > VILIACO
VILLAGIOS > VILLAGIO
VILLAGREE variant of > VILLAGERY
VILLAIN n wicked person
VILLAINS > VILLAIN
VILLAINY n evil or vicious behaviour
VILLAN same as > VILLEIN
VILLANAGE > VILLAN
VILLANIES > VILLANY
VILLANOUS > VILLAIN
VILLANS > VILLAN
VILLANY same as > VILLAINY
VILLAR > VILL
VILLAS > VILLA
VILLATIC adj of or relating to a villa, village, or farm
VILLEIN n peasant bound in service to his lord
VILLEINS > VILLEIN
VILLENAGE n villein's status
VILLI > VILLUS
VILLIAGO same as > VILIACO
VILLIAGOS > VILLIAGO
VILLIFORM adj having the form of a villus or a series of villi
VILLOSE same as > VILLOUS
VILLOSITY n state of being villous
VILLOUS adj (of plant parts) covered with long hairs
VILLOUSLY > VILLOUS
VILLS > VILL
VILLUS n one of the finger-like projections in the small intestine of many vertebrates
VIM n force, energy

VIMANA n Indian mythological chariot of the gods
VIMANAS > VIMANA
VIMEN n long flexible shoot that occurs in certain plants
VIMINA > VIMEN
VIMINAL > VIMEN
VIMINEOUS adj having, producing, or resembling long flexible shoots
VIMS > VIM
VIN n French wine
VINA n stringed musical instrument related to the sitar
VINACEOUS adj of, relating to, or containing wine
VINAL n type of manmade fibre
VINALS > VINAL
VINAS > VINA
VINASSE n residue left in a still after distilling spirits, esp brandy
VINASSES > VINASSE
VINCA n type of trailing plant with blue flowers
VINCAS > VINCA
VINCIBLE adj capable of being defeated or overcome
VINCIBLY > VINCIBLE
VINCULA > VINCULUM
VINCULUM n horizontal line drawn above a group of mathematical terms
VINCULUMS > VINCULUM
VINDALOO n type of very hot Indian curry
VINDALOOS > VINDALOO
VINDEMIAL adj relating to a grape harvest
VINDICATE vb clear (someone) of guilt
VINE n climbing plant, esp one producing grapes ▷ vb form like a vine
VINEAL adj relating to wines
VINED > VINE
VINEGAR n acid liquid made from wine, beer, or cider ▷ vb apply vinegar to
VINEGARED > VINEGAR
VINEGARS > VINEGAR
VINEGARY adj containing vinegar
VINELESS > VINE
VINELIKE > VINE
VINER n vinedresser
VINERIES > VINERY
VINERS > VINER
VINERY n hothouse for growing grapes
VINES > VINE
VINEW vb become mouldy
VINEWED > VINEW
VINEWING > VINEW
VINEWS > VINEW
VINEYARD n plantation of grape vines, esp for making wine

VINEYARDS > VINEYARD
VINIC adj of, relating to, or contained in wine
VINIER > VINE
VINIEST > VINE
VINIFERA n species of vine
VINIFERAS > VINIFERA
VINIFIED > VINIFY
VINIFIES > VINIFY
VINIFY vb convert into wine
VINIFYING > VINIFY
VINING > VINE
VINO n wine
VINOLENT adj drunken
VINOLOGY n scientific study of vines
VINOS > VINO
VINOSITY n distinctive and essential quality and flavour of wine
VINOUS adj of or characteristic of wine
VINOUSLY > VINOUS
VINS > VIN
VINT vb sell (wine)
VINTAGE n wine from a particular harvest of grapes ▷ adj best and most typical ▷ vb gather (grapes) or make (wine)
VINTAGED > VINTAGE
VINTAGER n grape harvester
VINTAGERS > VINTAGER
VINTAGES > VINTAGE
VINTAGING > VINTAGE
VINTED > VINT
VINTING > VINT
VINTNER n dealer in wine
VINTNERS > VINTNER
VINTRIES > VINTRY
VINTRY n place where wine is sold
VINTS > VINT
VINY > VINE
VINYL n type of plastic, used in mock leather and records ▷ adj of or containing a particular group of atoms
VINYLIC > VINYL
VINYLS > VINYL
VIOL n early stringed instrument preceding the violin
VIOLA n stringed instrument lower in pitch than a violin
VIOLABLE > VIOLATE
VIOLABLY > VIOLATE
VIOLAS > VIOLA
VIOLATE vb break (a law or agreement) ▷ adj violated or dishonoured
VIOLATED > VIOLATE
VIOLATER > VIOLATE
VIOLATERS > VIOLATE
VIOLATES > VIOLATE
VIOLATING > VIOLATE
VIOLATION > VIOLATE
VIOLATIVE > VIOLATE
VIOLATOR > VIOLATE
VIOLATORS > VIOLATE

841

**VIOLD** *archaic or poetic past form of* >VIAL
**VIOLENCE** *n* use of physical force, usu intended to cause injury or destruction
**VIOLENCES** >VIOLENCE
**VIOLENT** *adj* using or involving physical force with the intention of causing injury or destruction ▷ *vb* coerce
**VIOLENTED** >VIOLENT
**VIOLENTLY** >VIOLENT
**VIOLENTS** >VIOLENT
**VIOLER** *n* person who plays the viol
**VIOLERS** >VIOLER
**VIOLET** *n* plant with bluish-purple flowers ▷ *adj* bluish-purple
**VIOLETS** >VIOLET
**VIOLIN** *n* small four-stringed musical instrument played with a bow.
**VIOLINIST** *n* person who plays the violin
**VIOLINS** >VIOLIN
**VIOLIST** *n* person who plays the viola
**VIOLISTS** >VIOLIST
**VIOLONE** *n* double-bass member of the viol family
**VIOLONES** >VIOLONE
**VIOLS** >VIOL
**VIOMYCIN** *n* type of antibiotic
**VIOMYCINS** >VIOMYCIN
**VIOSTEROL** *n* type of vitamin
**VIPER** *n* poisonous snake
**VIPERFISH** *n* predatory deep-sea fish
**VIPERINE** *same as* >VIPEROUS
**VIPERISH** *same as* >VIPEROUS
**VIPEROUS** *adj* of, relating to, or resembling a viper
**VIPERS** >VIPER
**VIRAEMIA** *n* condition in which virus particles circulate and reproduce in the bloodstream
**VIRAEMIAS** >VIRAEMIA
**VIRAEMIC** >VIRAEMIA
**VIRAGO** *n* aggressive woman
**VIRAGOES** >VIRAGO
**VIRAGOISH** >VIRAGO
**VIRAGOS** >VIRAGO
**VIRAL** *adj* of or caused by a virus
**VIRALLY** >VIRAL
**VIRANDA** *same as* >VERANDA
**VIRANDAS** >VIRANDA
**VIRANDO** *same as* >VERANDA
**VIRANDOS** >VIRANDA
**VIRE** *vb* turn
**VIRED** >VIRE
**VIRELAI** *same as* >VIRELAY
**VIRELAIS** >VIRELAI
**VIRELAY** *n* old French verse form

**VIRELAYS** >VIRELAY
**VIREMENT** *n* administrative transfer of funds from one part of a budget to another
**VIREMENTS** >VIREMENT
**VIREMIA** *same as* >VIRAEMIA
**VIREMIAS** >VIREMIA
**VIREMIC** >VIREMIA
**VIRENT** *adj* green
**VIREO** *n* American songbird
**VIREONINE** >VIREO
**VIREOS** >VIREO
**VIRES** >VIRE
**VIRESCENT** *adj* greenish or becoming green
**VIRETOT** *as in* on the viretot in a rush
**VIRETOTS** >VIRETOT
**VIRGA** *n* wisps of rain or snow that evaporate before reaching the earth
**VIRGAS** >VIRGA
**VIRGATE** *adj* long, straight, and thin ▷ *n* obsolete measure of land area, usually taken as equivalent to 30 acres
**VIRGATES** >VIRGATE
**VIRGE** *n* rod
**VIRGER** *n* rod-bearer
**VIRGERS** >VIRGER
**VIRGES** >VIRGE
**VIRGIN** *n* person, esp a woman, who has not had sexual intercourse ▷ *adj* not having had sexual intercourse ▷ *vb* behave like a virgin
**VIRGINAL** *adj* like a virgin ▷ *n* early keyboard instrument like a small harpsichord
**VIRGINALS** >VIRGINAL
**VIRGINED** >VIRGIN
**VIRGINIA** *n* type of flue-cured tobacco grown originally in Virginia
**VIRGINIAS** >VIRGINIA
**VIRGINING** >VIRGIN
**VIRGINITY** *n* condition or fact of being a virgin
**VIRGINIUM** *former name for* >FRANCIUM
**VIRGINLY** >VIRGIN
**VIRGINS** >VIRGIN
**VIRGULATE** *adj* rod-shaped or rodlike
**VIRGULE** *another name for* >SLASH
**VIRGULES** >VIRGULE
**VIRICIDAL** >VIRICIDE
**VIRICIDE** *n* substance that destroys viruses
**VIRICIDES** >VIRICIDE
**VIRID** *adj* verdant
**VIRIDIAN** *n* green pigment consisting of a hydrated form of chromic oxide
**VIRIDIANS** >VIRIDIAN
**VIRIDITE** *n* greenish mineral
**VIRIDITES** >VIRIDITE

**VIRIDITY** *n* quality or state of being green
**VIRILE** *adj* having the traditional male characteristics of physical strength and a high sex drive
**VIRILELY** >VIRILE
**VIRILISE** *same as* >VIRILIZE
**VIRILISED** >VIRILISE
**VIRILISES** >VIRILISE
**VIRILISM** *n* abnormal development in a woman of male secondary sex characteristics
**VIRILISMS** >VIRILISM
**VIRILITY** >VIRILE
**VIRILIZE** *vb* cause male characteristics to appear in female
**VIRILIZED** >VIRILIZE
**VIRILIZES** >VIRILIZE
**VIRILOCAL** *adj* living with husband's family
**VIRING** >VIRE
**VIRINO** *n* entity postulated to be the causative agent of BSE
**VIRINOS** >VIRINO
**VIRION** *n* virus in infective form, consisting of an RNA particle within a protein covering
**VIRIONS** >VIRION
**VIRL** *same as* >FERRULE
**VIRLS** >VIRL
**VIROGENE** *n* type of viral gene
**VIROGENES** >VIROGENE
**VIROID** *n* any of various infective RNA particles
**VIROIDS** >VIROID
**VIROLOGIC** >VIROLOGY
**VIROLOGY** *n* study of viruses
**VIROSE** *adj* poisonous
**VIROSES** >VIROSIS
**VIROSIS** *n* viral disease
**VIROUS** *same as* >VIROSE
**VIRTU** *n* taste or love for curios or works of fine art
**VIRTUAL** *adj* having the effect but not the form of
**VIRTUALLY** *adv* practically, almost
**VIRTUE** *n* moral goodness
**VIRTUES** >VIRTUE
**VIRTUOSA** *n* female virtuoso
**VIRTUOSAS** >VIRTUOSA
**VIRTUOSE** >VIRTUOSA
**VIRTUOSI** >VIRTUOSO
**VIRTUOSIC** >VIRTUOSO
**VIRTUOSO** *n* person with impressive esp musical skill ▷ *adj* showing exceptional skill or brilliance
**VIRTUOSOS** >VIRTUOSO
**VIRTUOUS** *adj* morally good
**VIRTUS** >VIRTU
**VIRUCIDAL** >VIRUCIDE
**VIRUCIDE** *same*

*as* >VIRICIDE
**VIRUCIDES** >VIRUCIDE
**VIRULENCE** *n* quality of being virulent
**VIRULENCY** *same as* >VIRULENCE
**VIRULENT** *adj* extremely bitter or hostile
**VIRUS** *n* microorganism that causes disease in humans, animals, and plants
**VIRUSES** >VIRUS
**VIRUSLIKE** >VIRUS
**VIRUSOID** *n* small plant virus
**VIRUSOIDS** >VIRUSOID
**VIS** *n* power, force, or strength
**VISA** *n* permission to enter a country, shown by a stamp on the passport ▷ *vb* enter a visa into (a passport)
**VISAED** >VISA
**VISAGE** *n* face
**VISAGED** >VISAGE
**VISAGES** >VISAGE
**VISAGIST** *same as* >VISAGISTE
**VISAGISTE** *n* person who designs and applies face make-up
**VISAGISTS** >VISAGIST
**VISAING** >VISA
**VISARD** *same as* >VIZARD
**VISARDS** >VISARD
**VISAS** >VISA
**VISCACHA** *n* South American rodent
**VISCACHAS** >VISCACHA
**VISCARIA** *n* type of perennial plant
**VISCARIAS** >VISCARIA
**VISCERA** *pl n* large abdominal organs
**VISCERAL** *adj* instinctive
**VISCERATE** *vb* disembowel
**VISCID** *adj* sticky
**VISCIDITY** >VISCID
**VISCIDLY** >VISCID
**VISCIN** *n* sticky substance found on plants
**VISCINS** >VISCIN
**VISCOID** *adj* (of a fluid) somewhat viscous
**VISCOIDAL** *same as* >VISCOID
**VISCOSE** *same as* >VISCOUS
**VISCOSES** >VISCOSE
**VISCOSITY** *n* state of being viscous
**VISCOUNT** *n* British nobleman ranking between an earl and a baron
**VISCOUNTS** >VISCOUNT
**VISCOUNTY** >VISCOUNT
**VISCOUS** *adj* thick and sticky
**VISCOUSLY** >VISCOUS
**VISCUM** *n* shrub genus
**VISCUMS** >VISCUM
**VISCUS** *n* internal organ

VISE vb advise or award a visa to ▷ n (in US English) vice

VISED >VISE

VISEED >VISE

VISEING >VISE

VISELIKE >VICE

VISES >VISE

VISIBLE adj able to be seen ▷ n visible item of trade

VISIBLES >VISIBLE

VISIBLY >VISIBLE

VISIE same as >VIZY

VISIED >VISIE

VISIEING >VISIE

VISIER >VISIE

VISIERS >VISIE

VISIES >VISIE

VISILE n person best stimulated by vision

VISILES >VISILE

VISING >VISE

VISION n ability to see ▷ vb see or show in or as if in a vision

VISIONAL adj of, relating to, or seen in a vision, apparition, etc

VISIONARY adj showing foresight ▷ n visionary person

VISIONED >VISION

VISIONER n visionary

VISIONERS >VISIONER

VISIONING >VISION

VISIONIST n type of visionary

VISIONS >VISION

VISIT vb go or come to see ▷ n instance of visiting

VISITABLE >VISIT

VISITANT n ghost or apparition ▷ adj paying a visit

VISITANTS >VISITANT

VISITATOR n official visitor

VISITE n type of cape

VISITED >VISIT

VISITEE n person who is visited

VISITEES >VISITEE

VISITER variant of >VISITOR

VISITERS >VISITER

VISITES >VISITE

VISITING >VISIT

VISITINGS >VISIT

VISITOR n person who visits a person or place

VISITORS >VISITOR

VISITRESS n female visitor

VISITS >VISIT

VISIVE adj visual

VISNE n neighbourhood

VISNES >VISNE

VISNOMIE same as >VISNOMY

VISNOMIES >VISNOMY

VISNOMY n method of judging character from facial features

VISON n type of mink

VISONS >VISON

VISOR n transparent part of a helmet that pulls down over the face ▷ vb cover, provide, or protect with a visor

VISORED >VISOR

VISORING >VISOR

VISORLESS >VISOR

VISORS >VISOR

VISTA n (beautiful) extensive view ▷ vb make into vistas

VISTAED >VISTA

VISTAING >VISTA

VISTAL >VISTA

VISTALESS >VISTA

VISTAS >VISTA

VISTO same as >VISTA

VISTOS >VISTO

VISUAL adj done by or used in seeing ▷ n sketch to show the proposed layout of an advertisement, as in a newspaper

VISUALISE same as >VISUALIZE

VISUALIST n visualiser

VISUALITY >VISUAL

VISUALIZE vb form a mental image of

VISUALLY >VISUAL

VISUALS >VISUAL

VITA n curriculum vitae

VITACEOUS adj of a family of flowering plants that includes the grapevine

VITAE >VITA

VITAL adj essential or highly important ▷ n bodily organs that are necessary to maintain life

VITALISE same as >VITALIZE

VITALISED >VITALISE

VITALISER >VITALISE

VITALISES >VITALISE

VITALISM n philosophical doctrine that the phenomena of life cannot be explained in purely mechanical terms

VITALISMS >VITALISM

VITALIST >VITALISM

VITALISTS >VITALISM

VITALITY n physical or mental energy

VITALIZE vb fill with life or vitality

VITALIZED >VITALIZE

VITALIZER >VITALIZE

VITALIZES >VITALIZE

VITALLY >VITAL

VITALNESS >VITAL

VITALS >VITAL

VITAMER n type of chemical

VITAMERS >VITAMER

VITAMIN n one of a group of substances that are essential in the diet for specific body processes

VITAMINE same as >VITAMIN

VITAMINES >VITAMINE

VITAMINIC >VITAMIN

VITAMINS >VITAMIN

VITAS >VITA

VITASCOPE n early type of film projector

VITATIVE adj fond of life

VITE adv musical direction

VITELLARY >VITELLUS

VITELLI >VITELLUS

VITELLIN n phosphoprotein that is the major protein in egg yolk

VITELLINE adj of or relating to the yolk of an egg

VITELLINS >VITELLIN

VITELLUS n yolk of an egg

VITESSE n speed

VITESSES >VITESSE

VITEX n type of herb

VITEXES >VITEX

VITIABLE >VITIATE

VITIATE vb spoil the effectiveness of

VITIATED >VITIATE

VITIATES >VITIATE

VITIATING >VITIATE

VITIATION >VITIATE

VITIATOR >VITIATE

VITIATORS >VITIATE

VITICETA >VITICETUM

VITICETUM n place where vines are cultivated

VITICIDE n vine killer

VITICIDES >VITICIDE

VITILIGO n area of skin that is white from albinism or loss of melanin pigmentation

VITILIGOS >VITILIGO

VITIOSITY n viciousness

VITRAGE n light fabric

VITRAGES >VITRAGE

VITRAIL n stained glass

VITRAIN n type of coal occurring as horizontal glassy bands of a nonsoiling friable material

VITRAINS >VITRAIN

VITRAUX >VITRAIL

VITREOUS adj like or made from glass

VITREUM n vitreous body

VITREUMS >VITREUM

VITRIC adj of, relating to, resembling, or having the nature of glass

VITRICS n glassware

VITRIFIED >VITRIFY

VITRIFIES >VITRIFY

VITRIFORM adj having the form or appearance of glass

VITRIFY vb change or be changed into glass or a glassy substance

VITRINE n glass display case or cabinet for works of art, curios, etc

VITRINES >VITRINE

VITRIOL n language expressing bitterness and hatred ▷ vb attack or injure with or as if with vitriol

VITRIOLED >VITRIOL

VITRIOLIC adj (of language) severely bitter or harsh

VITRIOLS >VITRIOL

VITTA n tubelike cavity containing oil that occurs in the fruits of certain plants

VITTAE >VITTA

VITTATE >VITTA

VITTLE obsolete or dialect spelling of >VICTUAL

VITTLED >VITTLE

VITTLES obsolete or dialect spelling of >VICTUALS

VITTLING >VITTLE

VITULAR same as >VITULINE

VITULINE adj of or resembling a calf or veal

VIVA interj long live (a person or thing) ▷ n examination in the form of an interview ▷ vb examine (a candidate) in a spoken interview

VIVACE adv in a lively manner ▷ adj be performed in a lively manner ▷ n piece of music to be performed in this way

VIVACES >VIVACE

VIVACIOUS adj full of energy and enthusiasm

VIVACITY n quality of being vivacious

VIVAED >VIVA

VIVAING >VIVA

VIVAMENTE adv in a lively manner

VIVANDIER n sutler

VIVARIA >VIVARIUM

VIVARIES >VIVARY

VIVARIUM n place where animals are kept in natural conditions

VIVARIUMS >VIVARIUM

VIVARY same as >VIVARIUM

VIVAS >VIVA

VIVAT interj long live ▷ n expression of acclamation

VIVATS >VIVAT

VIVDA n method of drying meat

VIVDAS >VIVDA

VIVE interj long live

VIVELY adv in a lively manner

VIVENCIES >VIVENCY

VIVENCY n physical or mental energy

VIVER n fish pond

VIVERRA n civet genus

VIVERRAS >VIVERRA

VIVERRID >VIVERRINE

VIVERRIDS >VIVERRINE

VIVERRINE n type of mammal of Eurasia and Africa ▷ adj of this family of mammals

VIVERS >VIVER

VIVES n disease found in

843

horses
**VIVIANITE** *n* type of mineral
**VIVID** *adj* very bright
**VIVIDER** >VIVID
**VIVIDEST** >VIVID
**VIVIDITY** >VIVID
**VIVIDLY** >VIVID
**VIVIDNESS** >VIVID
**VIVIFIC** *adj* giving life
**VIVIFIED** >VIVIFY
**VIVIFIER** >VIVIFY
**VIVIFIERS** >VIVIFY
**VIVIFIES** >VIVIFY
**VIVIFY** *vb* animate, inspire
**VIVIFYING** >VIVIFY
**VIVIPARA** *n* animal that produces offspring that develop as embryos within the female parent
**VIVIPARY** *n* act of giving birth producing offspring that have developed as embryos
**VIVISECT** *vb* subject (an animal) to vivisection
**VIVISECTS** >VIVISECT
**VIVO** *adv* with life and vigour
**VIVRES** *n* provisions
**VIXEN** *n* female fox
**VIXENISH** >VIXEN
**VIXENLY** >VIXEN
**VIXENS** >VIXEN
**VIZAMENT** *n* consultation
**VIZAMENTS** >VIZAMENT
**VIZARD** *n* means of disguise ▷ *vb* conceal by means of a disguise
**VIZARDED** >VIZARD
**VIZARDING** >VIZARD
**VIZARDS** >VIZARD
**VIZCACHA** *same as* >VISCACHA
**VIZCACHAS** >VIZCACHA
**VIZIED** >VIZY
**VIZIER** *n* high official in certain Muslim countries
**VIZIERATE** *n* position, rank, or authority of a vizier
**VIZIERIAL** >VIZIER
**VIZIERS** >VIZIER
**VIZIES** >VIZY
**VIZIR** *same as* >VIZIER
**VIZIRATE** >VIZIR
**VIZIRATES** >VIZIR
**VIZIRIAL** >VIZIR
**VIZIRS** >VIZIR
**VIZIRSHIP** >VIZIR
**VIZOR** *same as* >VISOR
**VIZORED** >VIZOR
**VIZORING** >VIZOR
**VIZORLESS** >VIZOR
**VIZORS** >VIZOR
**VIZSLA** *n* breed of Hungarian hunting dog with a smooth rusty-gold coat
**VIZSLAS** >VIZSLA
**VIZY** *vb* look
**VIZYING** >VIZY
**VIZZIE** *same as* >VIZY
**VIZZIED** >VIZZIE

**VIZZIEING** >VIZZIE
**VIZZIES** >VIZZIE
**VLEI** *n* area of low marshy ground, esp one that feeds a stream
**VLEIS** >VLEI
**VLIES** >VLY
**VLY** *same as* >VLEI
**VOAR** *n* spring
**VOARS** >VOAR
**VOCAB** *n* vocabulary
**VOCABLE** *n* word regarded simply as a sequence of letters or spoken sounds ▷ *adj* capable of being uttered
**VOCABLES** >VOCABLE
**VOCABLY** >VOCABLE
**VOCABS** >VOCAB
**VOCABULAR** >VOCABLE
**VOCAL** *adj* relating to the voice ▷ *n* piece of jazz or pop music that is sung
**VOCALESE** *n* style of jazz singing
**VOCALESES** >VOCALESE
**VOCALIC** *adj* of, relating to, or containing a vowel or vowels
**VOCALICS** *n* non-verbal aspects of voice
**VOCALION** *n* type of musical instrument
**VOCALIONS** >VOCALION
**VOCALISE** *same as* >VOCALIZE
**VOCALISED** >VOCALISE
**VOCALISER** >VOCALISE
**VOCALISES** >VOCALISE
**VOCALISM** *n* exercise of the voice, as in singing or speaking
**VOCALISMS** >VOCALISM
**VOCALIST** *n* singer
**VOCALISTS** >VOCALIST
**VOCALITY** >VOCAL
**VOCALIZE** *vb* express with the voice
**VOCALIZED** >VOCALIZE
**VOCALIZER** >VOCALIZE
**VOCALIZES** >VOCALIZE
**VOCALLY** >VOCAL
**VOCALNESS** >VOCAL
**VOCALS** >VOCAL
**VOCATION** *n* profession or trade
**VOCATIONS** >VOCATION
**VOCATIVE** *n* (in some languages) case of nouns used when addressing a person ▷ *adj* relating to, used in, or characterized by calling
**VOCATIVES** >VOCATIVE
**VOCES** >VOX
**VOCODER** *n* type of synthesizer that uses the human voice as an oscillator
**VOCODERS** >VOCODER
**VOCULAR** >VOCULE
**VOCULE** *n* faint noise made when articulating certain sounds

**VOCULES** >VOCULE
**VODKA** *n* (Russian) spirit distilled from potatoes or grain
**VODKAS** >VODKA
**VODOU** *variant of* >VOODOO
**VODUN** *same as* >VODUN
**VODOUNS** >VODOUN
**VODOUS** >VODOU
**VODUN** *n* voodoo
**VODUNS** >VODUN
**VOE** *n* (in Orkney and Shetland) a small bay or narrow creek
**VOEMA** *n* vigour or energy
**VOEMAS** >VOEMA
**VOERTSAK** *variant of* >VOETSEK
**VOERTSEK** *variant of* >VOETSEK
**VOES** >VOE
**VOETSAK** *same as* >VOETSEK
**VOETSEK** *interj* S African offensive expression of rejection
**VOGIE** *adj* conceited
**VOGIER** >VOGIE
**VOGIEST** >VOGIE
**VOGUE** *n* popular style ▷ *adj* popular or fashionable ▷ *vb* bring into vogue
**VOGUED** >VOGUE
**VOGUEING** *n* dance style of the late 1980s
**VOGUEINGS** >VOGUEING
**VOGUER** >VOGUE
**VOGUERS** >VOGUE
**VOGUES** >VOGUE
**VOGUEY** >VOGUE
**VOGUIER** >VOGUE
**VOGUIEST** >VOGUE
**VOGUING** *same as* >VOGUEING
**VOGUINGS** >VOGUING
**VOGUISH** >VOGUE
**VOGUISHLY** >VOGUE
**VOICE** *n* (quality of) sound made when speaking or singing ▷ *vb* express verbally
**VOICED** *adj* articulated with accompanying vibration of the vocal cords
**VOICEFUL** >VOICE
**VOICELESS** *adj* without a voice
**VOICEMAIL** *n* facility of leaving recorded message by telephone
**VOICEOVER** *n* spoken commentary by unseen narrator on film
**VOICER** >VOICE
**VOICERS** >VOICE
**VOICES** >VOICE
**VOICING** >VOICE
**VOICINGS** >VOICE
**VOID** *adj* not legally binding ▷ *n* feeling of deprivation ▷ *vb* make invalid
**VOIDABLE** *adj* capable of being voided
**VOIDANCE** *n* annulment, as of a contract

**VOIDANCES** >VOIDANCE
**VOIDED** *adj* (of a design) with a hole in the centre of the same shape as the design
**VOIDEE** *n* light meal eaten before bed
**VOIDEES** >VOIDEE
**VOIDER** >VOID
**VOIDERS** >VOID
**VOIDING** >VOID
**VOIDINGS** >VOID
**VOIDNESS** >VOID
**VOIDS** >VOID
**VOILA** *interj* word used to express satisfaction
**VOILE** *n* light semitransparent fabric
**VOILES** >VOILE
**VOISINAGE** *n* district or neighbourhood
**VOITURE** *n* type of vehicle
**VOITURES** >VOITURE
**VOITURIER** *n* driver of a voiture
**VOIVODE** *n* type of military leader
**VOIVODES** >VOIVODE
**VOL** *n* volume
**VOLA** *n* palm of hand or sole of foot
**VOLABLE** *adj* quick-witted
**VOLAE** >VOLA
**VOLAGE** *adj* changeable
**VOLANT** *adj* in a flying position
**VOLANTE** *n* Spanish horse carriage
**VOLANTES** >VOLANTE
**VOLAR** *adj* of or relating to the palm of the hand or the sole of the foot
**VOLARIES** >VOLARY
**VOLARY** *n* large bird enclosure
**VOLATIC** *adj* flying
**VOLATILE** *adj* liable to sudden change, esp in behaviour ▷ *n* volatile substance
**VOLATILES** >VOLATILE
**VOLCANIAN** *same as* >VOLCANIC
**VOLCANIC** *adj* of or relating to volcanoes
**VOLCANICS** *n* types of rock
**VOLCANISE** *same as* >VOLCANIZE
**VOLCANISM** *n* processes that result in the formation of volcanoes
**VOLCANIST** *n* person who studies volcanoes
**VOLCANIZE** *vb* subject to the effects of or change by volcanic heat
**VOLCANO** *n* mountain with a vent through which lava is ejected
**VOLCANOES** >VOLCANO
**VOLCANOS** >VOLCANO
**VOLE** *n* small rodent ▷ *vb* to win by taking all the tricks in a deal

VOLED >VOLE

VOLENS as in *nolens volens* whether willing or unwilling

VOLERIES >VOLERY

VOLERY *same as* >VOLARY

VOLES >VOLE

VOLET *n* type of veil

VOLETS >VOLET

VOLING >VOLE

VOLITANT *adj* flying or moving about rapidly

VOLITATE *vb* flutter

VOLITATED >VOLITATE

VOLITATES >VOLITATE

VOLITIENT >VOLITION

VOLITION *n* ability to decide things for oneself

VOLITIONS >VOLITION

VOLITIVE *adj* of, relating to, or emanating from the will ▷ *n* (in some languages) a verb form or mood used to express a wish or desire

VOLITIVES >VOLITIVE

VOLK *n* people or nation, esp the nation of Afrikaners

VOLKS >VOLK

VOLKSLIED *n* German folk song

VOLKSRAAD *n* Boer assembly in South Africa in the 19th century

VOLLEY *n* simultaneous discharge of ammunition ▷ *vb* discharge (ammunition) in a volley

VOLLEYED >VOLLEY

VOLLEYER >VOLLEY

VOLLEYERS >VOLLEY

VOLLEYING >VOLLEY

VOLLEYS >VOLLEY

VOLOST *n* (in the former Soviet Union) a rural soviet

VOLOSTS >VOLOST

VOLPINO *n* Italian breed of dog

VOLPINOS >VOLPINO

VOLPLANE *vb* glide in an aeroplane

VOLPLANED >VOLPLANE

VOLPLANES >VOLPLANE

VOLS >VOL

VOLT *n* unit of electric potential

VOLTA *n* quick-moving Italian dance popular during the 16th and 17th centuries

VOLTAGE *n* electric potential difference expressed in volts

VOLTAGES >VOLTAGE

VOLTAIC *adj* producing an electric current

VOLTAISM *another name for* >GALVANISM

VOLTAISMS >VOLTAISM

VOLTE *same as* >VOLT

VOLTES >VOLTE

VOLTI *adv* musical direction

VOLTIGEUR *n* French infantry member

VOLTINISM *n* number of annual broods of an animal

VOLTMETER *n* instrument for measuring voltage

VOLTS >VOLT

VOLUBIL *same as* >VOLUBLE

VOLUBLE *adj* talking easily and at length

VOLUBLY >VOLUBLE

VOLUCRINE *adj* relating to birds

VOLUME *n* size of the space occupied by something ▷ *vb* billow or surge in volume

VOLUMED >VOLUME

VOLUMES >VOLUME

VOLUMETER *n* any instrument for measuring the volume of a solid, liquid, or gas

VOLUMETRY *n* act of measuring by volume

VOLUMINAL >VOLUME

VOLUMING >VOLUME

VOLUMISE *same as* >VOLUMIZE

VOLUMISED >VOLUMISE

VOLUMISES >VOLUMISE

VOLUMIST *n* author

VOLUMISTS >VOLUMIST

VOLUMIZE *vb* create volume in something

VOLUMIZED >VOLUMIZE

VOLUMIZES >VOLUMIZE

VOLUNTARY *adj* done by choice ▷ *n* organ solo in a church service

VOLUNTEER *n* person who offers voluntarily to do something ▷ *vb* offer one's services

VOLUSPA *n* Icelandic mythological poem

VOLUSPAS >VOLUSPA

VOLUTE *n* spiral or twisting turn, form, or object ▷ *adj* having the form of a volute

VOLUTED >VOLUTE

VOLUTES >VOLUTE

VOLUTIN *n* granular substance found in cells

VOLUTINS >VOLUTIN

VOLUTION *n* rolling, revolving, or spiral form or motion

VOLUTIONS >VOLUTION

VOLUTOID >VOLUTE

VOLVA *n* cup-shaped structure that sheathes the base of the stalk of certain mushrooms

VOLVAE >VOLVA

VOLVAS >VOLVA

VOLVATE >VOLVA

VOLVE *vb* turn over

VOLVED >VOLVE

VOLVES >VOLVE

VOLVING >VOLVE

VOLVOX *n* freshwater protozoan

VOLVOXES >VOLVOX

VOLVULI >VOLVULUS

VOLVULUS *n* abnormal twisting of the intestines causing obstruction

VOMER *n* thin flat bone forming part of the separation between the nasal passages in mammals

VOMERINE >VOMER

VOMERS >VOMER

VOMICA *n* pus-containing cavity

VOMICAE >VOMICA

VOMICAS >VOMICA

VOMIT *vb* eject (the contents of the stomach) through the mouth ▷ *n* matter vomited

VOMITED >VOMIT

VOMITER >VOMIT

VOMITERS >VOMIT

VOMITING >VOMIT

VOMITINGS >VOMIT

VOMITIVE *same as* >VOMITORY

VOMITIVES >VOMITIVE

VOMITO *n* form of yellow fever

VOMITORIA *n* entrances in an amphitheatre

VOMITORY *adj* causing vomiting ▷ *n* vomitory agent

VOMITOS >VOMITO

VOMITOUS *adj* arousing feelings of disgust

VOMITS >VOMIT

VOMITUS *n* matter that has been vomited

VOMITUSES >VOMITUS

VOODOO *n* religion involving ancestor worship and witchcraft ▷ *adj* of or relating to voodoo ▷ *vb* affect by or as if by the power of voodoo

VOODOOED >VOODOO

VOODOOING >VOODOO

VOODOOISM *same as* >VOODOO

VOODOOIST >VOODOO

VOODOOS >VOODOO

VOORKAMER *n* front room of a house

VOORSKOT *n* advance payment made to a farmer for crops

VOORSKOTS >VOORSKOT

VOR *vb* (in dialect) warn

VORACIOUS *adj* craving great quantities of food

VORACITY >VORACIOUS

VORAGO *n* chasm

VORAGOES >VORAGO

VORANT *adj* devouring

VORLAGE *n* skiing position

VORLAGES >VORLAGE

VORPAL *adj* sharp

VORRED >VOR

VORRING >VOR

VORS >VOR

VORTEX *n* whirlpool

VORTEXES >VORTEX

VORTICAL >VORTEX

VORTICES >VORTEX

VORTICISM *n* art movement in 20th-century England

VORTICIST >VORTICISM

VORTICITY *n* rotational spin in a fluid

VORTICOSE *adj* rotating quickly

VOSTRO as in *vostro account* bank account held by a foreign bank with a British bank

VOTABLE >VOTE

VOTARESS *n* female votary

VOTARIES >VOTARY

VOTARIST *variant of* >VOTARY

VOTARISTS >VOTARIST

VOTARY *n* person dedicated to religion or to a cause ▷ *adj* ardently devoted to the services or worship of God

VOTE *n* choice made by a participant in a shared decision ▷ *vb* make a choice by a vote

VOTEABLE >VOTE

VOTED >VOTE

VOTEEN *n* devotee

VOTEENS >VOTEEN

VOTELESS >VOTE

VOTER *n* person who can or does vote

VOTERS >VOTER

VOTES >VOTE

VOTING >VOTE

VOTINGS >VOTE

VOTIVE *adj* done or given to fulfil a vow ▷ *n* votive offering

VOTIVELY >VOTIVE

VOTIVES >VOTIVE

VOTRESS >VOTARESS

VOTRESSES >VOTRESS

VOUCH *vb* give personal assurance ▷ *n* act of vouching

VOUCHED >VOUCH

VOUCHEE *n* person summoned to court to defend a title

VOUCHEES >VOUCHEE

VOUCHER *n* ticket used instead of money to buy specified goods ▷ *vb* summon someone to court as a vouchee

VOUCHERED >VOUCHER

VOUCHERS >VOUCHER

VOUCHES >VOUCH

VOUCHING >VOUCH

VOUCHSAFE *vb* give, entrust

VOUDON *variant of* >VOODOO

VOUDONS >VOUDON

VOUDOU *same as* >VOODOO

VOUDOUED >VOUDOU

VOUDOUING >VOUDOU

VOUDOUN *variant of* >VOODOO

**VOUDOUNS** >VOUDOUN
**VOUDOUS** >VOUDOU
**VOUGE** n form of pike used by foot soldiers in the 14th century and later
**VOUGES** >VOUGE
**VOULGE** n type of medieval weapon
**VOULGES** >VOULGE
**VOULU** adj deliberate
**VOUSSOIR** n wedge-shaped stone or brick that is used with others to construct an arch
**VOUSSOIRS** >VOUSSOIR
**VOUTSAFE** same as >VOUCHSAFE
**VOUTSAFED** >VOUTSAFE
**VOUTSAFES** >VOUTSAFE
**VOUVRAY** n dry white French wine
**VOUVRAYS** >VOUVRAY
**VOW** n solemn and binding promise ▷ vb promise solemnly
**VOWED** >VOW
**VOWEL** n speech sound made without obstructing the flow of breath ▷ vb say as a vowel
**VOWELISE** same as >VOWELIZE
**VOWELISED** >VOWELISE
**VOWELISES** >VOWELISE
**VOWELIZE** vb mark the vowel points in (a Hebrew word or text)
**VOWELIZED** >VOWELIZE
**VOWELIZES** >VOWELIZE
**VOWELLED** >VOWEL
**VOWELLESS** >VOWEL
**VOWELLING** >VOWEL
**VOWELLY** >VOWEL
**VOWELS** >VOWEL
**VOWER** >VOW
**VOWERS** >VOW
**VOWESS** n nun
**VOWESSES** >VOWESS
**VOWING** >VOW
**VOWLESS** >VOW
**VOWS** >VOW
**VOX** n voice or sound
**VOXEL** n term used in computing imaging
**VOXELS** >VOXEL
**VOYAGE** n long journey by sea or in space ▷ vb make a voyage
**VOYAGED** >VOYAGE
**VOYAGER** >VOYAGE
**VOYAGERS** >VOYAGE
**VOYAGES** >VOYAGE
**VOYAGEUR** n French canoeman who transported furs from trading posts in the North American interior
**VOYAGEURS** >VOYAGEUR
**VOYAGING** >VOYAGE
**VOYEUR** n person who obtains pleasure from watching people undressing or having sex
**VOYEURISM** >VOYEUR

**VOYEURS** >VOYEUR
**VOZHD** n Russian leader
**VOZHDS** >VOZHD
**VRAIC** n type of seaweed
**VRAICKER** n person who gathers vraic
**VRAICKERS** >VRAICKER
**VRAICKING** n act of gathering vraic
**VRAICS** >VRAIC
**VRIL** n life force
**VRILS** >VRIL
**VROOM** interj exclamation imitative of a car engine revving up ▷ vb move noisily and at high speed
**VROOMED** >VROOM
**VROOMING** >VROOM
**VROOMS** >VROOM
**VROT** adj South African slang for rotten
**VROU** n Afrikaner woman, esp a married woman
**VROUS** >VROU
**VROUW** n woman
**VROUWS** >VROUW
**VROW** same as >VROUW
**VROWS** >VROW
**VUG** n small cavity in a rock or vein, usually lined with crystals
**VUGG** same as >VUG
**VUGGIER** >VUG
**VUGGIEST** >VUG
**VUGGS** >VUGG
**VUGGY** >VUG
**VUGH** same as >VUG
**VUGHIER** >VUGH
**VUGHIEST** >VUGH
**VUGHS** >VUGH
**VUGHY** >VUG
**VUGS** >VUG
**VULCAN** n blacksmith
**VULCANIAN** adj of or relating to a volcanic eruption
**VULCANIC** same as >VOLCANIC
**VULCANISE** same as >VULCANIZE
**VULCANISM** same as >VOLCANISM
**VULCANIST** same as >VOLCANIST
**VULCANITE** n vulcanized rubber
**VULCANIZE** vb strengthen (rubber) by treating it with sulphur
**VULCANS** >VULCAN
**VULGAR** adj showing lack of good taste, decency, or refinement ▷ n common and ignorant person
**VULGARER** >VULGAR
**VULGAREST** >VULGAR
**VULGARIAN** n vulgar (rich) person
**VULGARISE** same as >VULGARIZE
**VULGARISM** n coarse word or phrase
**VULGARITY** n condition of being vulgar

**VULGARIZE** vb make vulgar or too common
**VULGARLY** >VULGAR
**VULGARS** >VULGAR
**VULGATE** n commonly recognized text or version ▷ adj generally accepted
**VULGATES** >VULGATE
**VULGO** adv generally
**VULGUS** n the common people
**VULGUSES** >VULGUS
**VULN** vb wound
**VULNED** >VULN
**VULNERARY** adj of, relating to, or used to heal a wound ▷ n vulnerary drug or agent
**VULNERATE** vb wound
**VULNING** >VULN
**VULNS** >VULN
**VULPICIDE** n person who kills foxes
**VULPINE** adj of or like a fox
**VULPINISM** >VULPINE
**VULPINITE** n type of granular anhydrite
**VULSELLA** n forceps
**VULSELLAE** >VULSELLA
**VULSELLUM** variant of >VULSELLA
**VULTURE** n large bird that feeds on the flesh of dead animals
**VULTURES** >VULTURE
**VULTURINE** adj of, relating to, or resembling a vulture
**VULTURISH** >VULTURE
**VULTURISM** n greed
**VULTURN** n type of turkey
**VULTURNS** >VULTURN
**VULTUROUS** same as >VULTURINE
**VULVA** n woman's external genitals
**VULVAE** >VULVA
**VULVAL** >VULVA
**VULVAR** >VULVA
**VULVAS** >VULVA
**VULVATE** >VULVA
**VULVIFORM** >VULVA
**VULVITIS** n inflammation of the vulva
**VUM** vb swear
**VUMMED** >VUM
**VUMMING** >VUM
**VUMS** >VUM
**VUTTIER** >VUTTY
**VUTTIEST** >VUTTY
**VUTTY** adj dirty
**VUVUZELA** n South African instrument blown by football fans
**VUVUZELAS** >VUVUZELA
**VYING** >VIE
**VYINGLY** >VIE

# Ww

**WAAC** _n_ (formerly) member of the Women's Auxiliary Army Corp

**WAACS** >WAAC

**WAB** _n_ offensive term for Mexican living in US

**WABAIN** _same as_ >OUABAIN

**WABAINS** >WABAIN

**WABBIT** _adj_ weary

**WABBLE** _same as_ >WOBBLE

**WABBLED** >WABBLE

**WABBLER** >WABBLE

**WABBLERS** >WABBLE

**WABBLES** >WABBLE

**WABBLIER** >WABBLE

**WABBLIEST** >WABBLE

**WABBLING** >WABBLE

**WABBLY** >WABBLE

**WABOOM** _another word_ _for_ >WAGENBOOM

**WABOOMS** >WABOOM

**WABS** >WAB

**WABSTER** _Scots form_ _of_ >WEBSTER

**WABSTERS** >WABSTER

**WACK** _n_ friend

**WACKE** _n_ any of various soft earthy rocks that resemble or are derived from basaltic rocks

**WACKER** _same as_ >WACK

**WACKERS** >WACKER

**WACKES** >WACKE

**WACKEST** >WACK

**WACKIER** >WACKY

**WACKIEST** >WACKY

**WACKILY** >WACKY

**WACKINESS** >WACKY

**WACKO** _adj_ mad or eccentric ▷ _n_ mad or eccentric person

**WACKOS** >WACKO

**WACKS** >WACK

**WACKY** _adj_ eccentric or funny

**WAD** _n_ black earthy ore of manganese ▷ _n_ small mass of soft material ▷ _vb_ form (something) into a wad

**WADABLE** >WADE

**WADD** _same as_ >WAD

**WADDED** >WAD

**WADDER** >WAD

**WADDERS** >WAD

**WADDIE** _same as_ >WADDY

**WADDIED** >WADDY

**WADDIES** >WADDY

**WADDING** >WAD

**WADDINGS** >WAD

**WADDLE** _vb_ walk with short swaying steps ▷ _n_ swaying walk

**WADDLED** >WADDLE

**WADDLER** >WADDLE

**WADDLERS** >WADDLE

**WADDLES** >WADDLE

**WADDLING** >WADDLE

**WADDLY** >WADDLE

**WADDS** >WAD

**WADDY** _n_ heavy wooden club used by Australian Aborigines ▷ _vb_ hit with a waddy

**WADDYING** >WADDY

**WADE** _vb_ walk with difficulty through water or mud ▷ _n_ act or an instance of wading

**WADEABLE** >WADE

**WADED** >WADE

**WADER** _n_ long-legged water bird

**WADERS** _pl n_ long waterproof boots which completely cover the legs, worn by anglers for standing in water

**WADES** >WADE

**WADI** _n_ (in N Africa and Arabia) river which is dry except in the wet season

**WADIES** >WADY

**WADING** >WADE

**WADINGS** >WADE

**WADIS** >WADI

**WADMAAL** _same as_ >WADMAL

**WADMAALS** >WADMAAL

**WADMAL** _n_ coarse thick woollen fabric, formerly woven esp in Orkney and Shetland, for outer garments

**WADMALS** >WADMAL

**WADMEL** _same as_ >WADMAL

**WADMELS** >WADMEL

**WADMOL** _same as_ >WADMAL

**WADMOLL** _same as_ >WADMAL

**WADMOLLS** >WADMOLL

**WADMOLS** >WADMOL

**WADS** >WAD

**WADSET** _vb_ pledge or mortgage

**WADSETS** >WADSET

**WADSETT** _same as_ >WADSET

**WADSETTED** >WADSET

**WADSETTER** >WADSET

**WADSETTS** >WADSETT

**WADT** _same as_ >WAD

**WADTS** >WADT

**WADY** _same as_ >WADI

**WAE** _old form of_ >WOE

**WAEFUL** _old form_ _of_ >WOEFUL

**WAENESS** _n_ sorrow

**WAENESSES** >WAENESS

**WAES** >WAE

**WAESOME** _adj_ sorrowful

**WAESUCK** _interj_ alas

**WAESUCKS** _interj_ alas

**WAFER** _n_ thin crisp biscuit ▷ _vb_ seal, fasten, or attach with a wafer

**WAFERED** >WAFER

**WAFERING** >WAFER

**WAFERS** >WAFER

**WAFERY** >WAFER

**WAFF** _n_ gust or puff of air ▷ _vb_ flutter or cause to flutter

**WAFFED** >WAFF

**WAFFIE** _n_ person regarded as having little worth to society

**WAFFIES** >WAFFIE

**WAFFING** >WAFF

**WAFFLE** _vb_ speak or write in a vague wordy way ▷ _n_ vague wordy talk or writing

**WAFFLED** >WAFFLE

**WAFFLER** >WAFFLE

**WAFFLERS** >WAFFLE

**WAFFLES** >WAFFLE

**WAFFLIER** >WAFFLE

**WAFFLIEST** >WAFFLE

**WAFFLING** >WAFFLE

**WAFFLINGS** >WAFFLE

**WAFFLY** >WAFFLE

**WAFFS** >WAFF

**WAFT** _vb_ drift or carry gently through the air ▷ _n_ something wafted

**WAFTAGE** >WAFT

**WAFTAGES** >WAFT

**WAFTED** >WAFT

**WAFTER** _n_ device that causes a draught

**WAFTERS** >WAFTER

**WAFTING** >WAFT

**WAFTINGS** >WAFT

**WAFTS** >WAFT

WAFTURE *n* act of wafting or waving

WAFTURES >WAFTURE

WAG *vb* move rapidly from side to side ▷ *n* wagging movement

WAGE *n* payment for work done, esp when paid weekly ▷ *vb* engage in (an activity)

WAGED >WAGE

WAGELESS >WAGE

WAGENBOOM *n* S African tree

WAGER *vb* bet on the outcome of something ▷ *n* bet on the outcome of an event or activity

WAGERED >WAGER

WAGERER >WAGER

WAGERERS >WAGER

WAGERING >WAGER

WAGERS >WAGER

WAGES >WAGE

WAGGA *n* blanket or bed covering made out of sacks stitched together

WAGGAS >WAGGA

WAGGED >WAG

WAGGER >WAG

WAGGERIES >WAGGERY

WAGGERS >WAG

WAGGERY *n* quality of being humorous

WAGGING >WAG

WAGGISH *adj* jocular or humorous

WAGGISHLY >WAGGISH

WAGGLE *vb* move with a rapid shaking or wobbling motion ▷ *n* rapid shaking or wobbling motion

WAGGLED >WAGGLE

WAGGLER *n* float only the bottom of which is attached to the fishing line

WAGGLERS >WAGGLER

WAGGLES >WAGGLE

WAGGLIER >WAGGLE

WAGGLIEST >WAGGLE

WAGGLING >WAGGLE

WAGGLY >WAGGLE

WAGGON *same as* >WAGON

WAGGONED >WAGGON

WAGGONER *same as* >WAGGONER

WAGGONERS >WAGGONER

WAGGONING >WAGGON

WAGGONS >WAGGON

WAGHALTER *n* person likely to be hanged

WAGING >WAGE

WAGMOIRE *obsolete word for* >QUAGMIRE

WAGMOIRES >WAGMOIRE

WAGON *n* four-wheeled vehicle for heavy loads ▷ *vb* transport by wagon

WAGONAGE *n* money paid for transport by wagon

WAGONAGES >WAGONAGE

WAGONED >WAGON

WAGONER *n* person who drives a wagon

WAGONERS >WAGONER

WAGONETTE *n* light four-wheeled horse-drawn vehicle with two lengthwise seats facing each other behind a crosswise driver's seat

WAGONFUL >WAGON

WAGONFULS >WAGON

WAGONING >WAGON

WAGONLESS >WAGON

WAGONLOAD *n* load that is or can be carried by a wagon

WAGONS >WAGON

WAGS >WAG

WAGSOME *another word for* >WAGGISH

WAGTAIL *n* small long-tailed bird

WAGTAILS >WAGTAIL

WAHCONDA *n* supreme being

WAHCONDAS >WAHCONDA

WAHINE *n* Māori woman, esp a wife

WAHINES >WAHINE

WAHOO *n* food and game fish of tropical seas

WAHOOS >WAHOO

WAI *n* in New Zealand, water

WAIATA *n* Māori song

WAIATAS >WAIATA

WAID >WEIGH

WAIDE >WEIGH

WAIF *n* young person who is, or seems, homeless or neglected ▷ *vb* treat as a waif

WAIFED >WAIF

WAIFING >WAIF

WAIFISH >WAIF

WAIFLIKE >WAIF

WAIFS >WAIF

WAIFT *n* piece of lost property found by someone other than the owner

WAIFTS >WAIFT

WAIL *vb* cry out in pain or misery ▷ *n* mournful cry

WAILED >WAIL

WAILER >WAIL

WAILERS >WAIL

WAILFUL >WAIL

WAILFULLY >WAIL

WAILING >WAIL

WAILINGLY >WAIL

WAILINGS >WAIL

WAILS >WAIL

WAILSOME >WAIL

WAIN *vb* transport ▷ *n* farm wagon

WAINAGE *n* carriages, etc, for transportation of goods

WAINAGES >WAINAGE

WAINED >WAIN

WAINING >WAIN

WAINS >WAIN

WAINSCOT *n* wooden lining of the lower part of the walls of a room ▷ *vb* line (a wall of a room) with a wainscot

WAINSCOTS >WAINSCOT

WAIR *vb* spend

WAIRED >WAIR

WAIRING >WAIR

WAIRS >WAIR

WAIRSH *variant spelling of* >WERSH

WAIRSHER >WAIRSH

WAIRSHEST >WAIRSH

WAIRUA *n* in New Zealand, spirit or soul

WAIRUAS >WAIRUA

WAIS >WAI

WAIST *n* part of the trunk between the ribs and the hips

WAISTBAND *n* band of material sewn on to the waist of a garment to strengthen it

WAISTBELT *n* belt

WAISTCOAT *n* sleeveless garment which buttons up the front, usu worn over a shirt and under a jacket

WAISTED *adj* having a waist or waistlike part

WAISTER *n* sailor performing menial duties

WAISTERS >WAISTER

WAISTING *n* act of wasting

WAISTINGS >WAISTING

WAISTLESS >WAIST

WAISTLINE *n* (size of) the waist of a person or garment

WAISTS >WAIST

WAIT *vb* remain inactive in expectation (of something) ▷ *n* act or period of waiting

WAITE *old form of* >WAIT

WAITED >WAIT

WAITER *n* man who serves in a restaurant etc ▷ *vb* serve at table

WAITERAGE *n* service

WAITERED >WAITER

WAITERING *n* act of serving at table

WAITERS >WAITER

WAITES >WAITE

WAITING >WAIT

WAITINGLY >WAIT

WAITINGS >WAIT

WAITLIST *n* waiting list

WAITLISTS >WAITLIST

WAITRESS *n* woman who serves people with food and drink in a restaurant ▷ *vb* work as a waitress

WAITRON *n* waiter or waitress

WAITRONS >WAITRON

WAITS >WAIT

WAITSTAFF *n* waiters and waitresses collectively

WAIVE *vb* refrain from enforcing (a law, right, etc)

WAIVED >WAIVE

WAIVER *n* act or instance of voluntarily giving up a claim, right, etc

WAIVERS >WAIVER

WAIVES >WAIVE

WAIVING >WAIVE

WAIVODE *same as* >VOIVODE

WAIVODES >WAIVODE

WAIWODE *same as* >VOIVODE

WAIWODES >WAIWODE

WAKA *n* Māori canoe

WAKAME *n* edible seaweed

WAKAMES >WAKAME

WAKANDA *n* supernatural quality said by Native American people to be held by natural objects

WAKANDAS >WAKANDA

WAKANE *n* type of seaweed

WAKANES >WAKANE

WAKAS >WAKA

WAKE *vb* rouse from sleep or inactivity ▷ *n* vigil beside a corpse the night before the funeral

WAKEBOARD *n* short surfboard for a rider towed behind a motorboat

WAKED >WAKE

WAKEFUL *adj* unable to sleep

WAKEFULLY >WAKEFUL

WAKELESS *adj* (of sleep) deep or unbroken

WAKEMAN *n* watchman

WAKEMEN >WAKEMAN

WAKEN *vb* wake

WAKENED >WAKEN

WAKENER >WAKEN

WAKENERS >WAKEN

WAKENING >WAKEN

WAKENINGS >WAKEN

WAKENS >WAKEN

WAKER >WAKE

WAKERIFE *adj* watchful

WAKERS >WAKE

WAKES >WAKE

WAKF *same as* >WAQF

WAKFS >WAKF

WAKIKI *n* Melanesian shell currency

WAKIKIS >WAKIKI

WAKING >WAKE

WAKINGS >WAKE

WALD *Scots form of* >WELD

WALDFLUTE *n* organ flute stop

WALDGRAVE *n* (in medieval Germany) an officer with jurisdiction over a royal forest

WALDHORN *n* organ reed stop

WALDHORNS >WALDHORN

WALDO *n* gadget for manipulating objects by remote control

WALDOES >WALDO

WALDOS >WALDO

WALDRAPP *n* type of ibis

WALDRAPPS >WALDRAPP

WALDS >WALD

WALE *same as* >WEAL

WALED >WALE

WALER *n* >WALE

WALERS >WALE

WALES >WALE

WALI *same as* >VALI

WALIER >WALY

**WALIES** >WALY

**WALIEST** >WALY

**WALING** >WALE

**WALIS** >WALI

**WALISE** *same as* >VALISE

**WALISES** >WALISE

**WALK** *vb* move on foot with at least one foot always on the ground ▷ *n* short journey on foot, usu for pleasure

**WALKABLE** >WALK

**WALKABOUT** *n* informal walk among the public by royalty etc

**WALKATHON** *n* long walk done, esp for charity

**WALKAWAY** *n* easily achieved victory

**WALKAWAYS** >WALKAWAY

**WALKED** >WALK

**WALKER** *n* person who walks

**WALKERS** >WALKER

**WALKING** *adj* (of a person) considered to possess the qualities of something inanimate as specified ▷ *n* act of walking

**WALKINGS** >WALKING

**WALKMILL** *same as* >WAULKMILL

**WALKMILLS** >WALKMILL

**WALKOUT** *n* strike

**WALKOUTS** >WALKOUT

**WALKOVER** *n* easy victory

**WALKOVERS** >WALKOVER

**WALKS** >WALK

**WALKUP** *n* building with stairs to upper floors

**WALKUPS** >WALKUP

**WALKWAY** *n* path designed for use by pedestrians

**WALKWAYS** >WALKWAY

**WALKYRIE** *variant of* >VALKYRIE

**WALKYRIES** >WALKYRIE

**WALL** *n* structure of brick, stone, etc used to enclose, divide, or support ▷ *vb* enclose or seal with a wall or walls

**WALLA** *same as* >WALLAH

**WALLABA** *n* type of S American tree

**WALLABAS** >WALLABA

**WALLABIES** >WALLABY

**WALLABY** *n* marsupial like a small kangaroo

**WALLAH** *n* person involved with or in charge of a specified thing

**WALLAHS** >WALLAH

**WALLAROO** *n* large stocky Australian kangaroo of rocky regions

**WALLAROOS** >WALLAROO

**WALLAS** >WALLA

**WALLBOARD** *n* thin board made of materials, such as compressed wood fibres or gypsum plaster, between stiff paper, and used to cover walls, partitions, etc

**WALLCHART** *n* chart on wall

**WALLED** >WALL

**WALLER** >WALL

**WALLERS** >WALL

**WALLET** *n* small folding case for paper money, documents, etc

**WALLETS** >WALLET

**WALLEYE** *n* fish with large staring eyes

**WALLEYED** >WALLEYE

**WALLEYES** >WALLEYE

**WALLFISH** *n* snail

**WALLIE** *same as* >WALLY

**WALLIER** >WALLY

**WALLIES** >WALLY

**WALLIEST** >WALLY

**WALLING** >WALL

**WALLINGS** >WALL

**WALLOP** *vb* hit hard ▷ *n* hard blow

**WALLOPED** >WALLOP

**WALLOPER** *n* person or thing that wallops

**WALLOPERS** >WALLOPER

**WALLOPING** *n* thrashing ▷ *adj* large or great

**WALLOPS** >WALLOP

**WALLOW** *vb* revel in an emotion ▷ *n* act or instance of wallowing

**WALLOWED** >WALLOW

**WALLOWER** >WALLOW

**WALLOWERS** >WALLOW

**WALLOWING** >WALLOW

**WALLOWS** >WALLOW

**WALLPAPER** *n* decorative paper to cover interior walls ▷ *vb* cover (walls) with wallpaper

**WALLS** >WALL

**WALLSEND** *n* type of coal

**WALLSENDS** >WALLSEND

**WALLWORT** *n* type of plant

**WALLWORTS** >WALLWORT

**WALLY** *n* stupid person ▷ *adj* fine, pleasing, or splendid

**WALLYBALL** *n* ball game played on court

**WALLYDRAG** *n* worthless person or animal

**WALNUT** *n* edible nut with a wrinkled shell ▷ *adj* made from the wood of a walnut tree

**WALNUTS** >WALNUT

**WALRUS** *n* large sea mammal with long tusks

**WALRUSES** >WALRUS

**WALTIER** >WALTY

**WALTIEST** >WALTY

**WALTY** *adj* (of a ship) likely to roll over

**WALTZ** *n* ballroom dance ▷ *vb* dance a waltz

**WALTZED** >WALTZ

**WALTZER** *n* person who waltzes

**WALTZERS** >WALTZER

**WALTZES** >WALTZ

**WALTZING** >WALTZ

**WALTZINGS** >WALTZ

**WALTZLIKE** >WALTZ

**WALY** *same as* >WALLY

**WAMBENGER** *another name for* >TUAN

**WAMBLE** *vb* move unsteadily ▷ *n* unsteady movement

**WAMBLED** >WAMBLE

**WAMBLES** >WAMBLE

**WAMBLIER** >WAMBLE

**WAMBLIEST** >WAMBLE

**WAMBLING** >WAMBLE

**WAMBLINGS** >WAMBLE

**WAMBLY** >WAMBLE

**WAME** *n* belly, abdomen, or womb

**WAMED** >WAME

**WAMEFOU** *Scots variant of* >WAMEFUL

**WAMEFOUS** >WAMEFOU

**WAMEFUL** *n* bellyful

**WAMEFULS** >WAMEFUL

**WAMES** >WAME

**WAMMUL** *n* dog

**WAMMULS** >WAMMUL

**WAMMUS** *same as* >WAMUS

**WAMMUSES** >WAMMUS

**WAMPEE** *n* type of Asian fruit tree

**WAMPEES** >WAMPEE

**WAMPISH** *vb* wave

**WAMPISHED** >WAMPISH

**WAMPISHES** >WAMPISH

**WAMPUM** *n* shells woven together, formerly used by Native Americans for money and ornament

**WAMPUMS** >WAMPUM

**WAMPUS** *same as* >WAMUS

**WAMPUSES** >WAMPUS

**WAMUS** *n* type of cardigan or jacket

**WAMUSES** >WAMUS

**WAN** *adj* pale and sickly looking ▷ *vb* make or become wan

**WANCHANCY** *adj* infelicitous

**WAND** *n* thin rod, esp one used in performing magic tricks

**WANDER** *vb* move about without a definite destination or aim ▷ *n* act or instance of wandering

**WANDERED** >WANDER

**WANDERER** >WANDER

**WANDERERS** >WANDER

**WANDERING** >WANDER

**WANDEROO** *n* macaque monkey of India and Sri Lanka, having black fur with a ruff of long greyish fur on each side of the face

**WANDEROOS** >WANDEROO

**WANDERS** >WANDER

**WANDLE** *adj* supple

**WANDLIKE** >WAND

**WANDOO** *n* eucalyptus tree of W Australia, having white bark and durable wood

**WANDOOS** >WANDOO

**WANDS** >WAND

**WANE** *vb* decrease gradually in size or strength

**WANED** >WANE

**WANES** >WANE

**WANEY** >WANE

**WANG** *n* cheekbone

**WANGAN** *same as* >WANIGAN

**WANGANS** >WANGAN

**WANGLE** *vb* get by devious methods ▷ *n* act or an instance of wangling

**WANGLED** >WANGLE

**WANGLER** >WANGLE

**WANGLERS** >WANGLE

**WANGLES** >WANGLE

**WANGLING** >WANGLE

**WANGLINGS** >WANGLE

**WANGS** >WANG

**WANGUN** *same as* >WANIGAN

**WANGUNS** >WANGUN

**WANHOPE** *n* delusion

**WANHOPES** >WANHOPE

**WANIER** >WANY

**WANIEST** >WANY

**WANIGAN** *n* provisions for camp

**WANIGANS** >WANIGAN

**WANING** >WANE

**WANINGS** >WANE

**WANION** *n* vehemence

**WANIONS** >WANION

**WANK** *vb* slang word for masturbate ▷ *n* instance of masturbating ▷ *adj* bad, useless, or worthless

**WANKED** >WANK

**WANKER** *n* slang word for worthless or stupid person

**WANKERS** >WANKER

**WANKIER** >WANKY

**WANKIEST** >WANKY

**WANKING** >WANK

**WANKLE** *adj* unstable

**WANKS** >WANK

**WANKSTA** *n* derogatory slang word for a person who acts or dresses like a gangster but who is not involved in crime

**WANKSTAS** >WANKSTA

**WANKY** *adj* slang word for pretentious

**WANLE** *same as* >WANDLE

**WANLY** >WAN

**WANNA** *vb* spelling of **want to** intended to reflect a dialectal or informal pronunciation

**WANNABE** *adj* wanting to be, or be like, a particular person or thing ▷ *n* person who wants to be, or be like, a particular person or thing

**WANNABEE** *same as* >WANNABE

**WANNABEES** >WANNABEE

**WANNABES** >WANNABE

**WANNED** >WAN

**WANNEL** *same as* >WANDLE

**WANNER** >WAN

**WANNESS** >WAN

**WANNESSES** >WAN

**WANNEST** >WAN

**WANNIGAN** *same as* >WANIGAN

**WANNIGANS** >WANNIGAN

**WANNING** > WAN
**WANNISH** *adj* rather wan
**WANS** > WAN
**WANT** *vb* need or long for
▷ *n* act or instance of
wanting
**WANTAGE** *n* shortage
**WANTAGES** > WANTAGE
**WANTED** > WANT
**WANTER** > WANT
**WANTERS** > WANT
**WANTHILL** *n* molehill
**WANTHILLS** > WANTHILL
**WANTIES** > WANTY
**WANTING** *adj* lacking ▷ *prep*
without
**WANTINGS** > WANT
**WANTON** *adj* without
motive, provocation, or
justification ▷ *n* sexually
unrestrained or immodest
woman ▷ *vb* behave in a
wanton manner
**WANTONED** > WANTON
**WANTONER** > WANTON
**WANTONERS** > WANTON
**WANTONEST** > WANTON
**WANTONING** > WANTON
**WANTONISE** *same*
*as* > WANTONIZE
**WANTONIZE** *vb* behave
wantonly
**WANTONLY** > WANTON
**WANTONS** > WANTON
**WANTS** > WANT
**WANTY** *adj* belt
**WANWORDY** *adj* without
merit
**WANWORTH** *n* inexpensive
purchase
**WANWORTHS** > WANWORTH
**WANY** > WANE
**WANZE** *vb* wane
**WANZED** > WANZE
**WANZES** > WANZE
**WANZING** > WANZE
**WAP** *vb* strike
**WAPENSHAW** *n* showing of
weapons
**WAPENTAKE** *n* subdivision
of certain shires or
counties, esp in the
Midlands and North of
England
**WAPINSHAW** *same*
*as* > WAPENSHAW
**WAPITI** *n* large N American
deer, now also common in
New Zealand
**WAPITIS** > WAPITI
**WAPPED** > WAP
**WAPPEND** *adj* tired
**WAPPER** *vb* blink
**WAPPERED** > WAPPER
**WAPPERING** > WAPPER
**WAPPERS** > WAPPER
**WAPPING** > WAP
**WAPS** > WAP
**WAQF** *n* endowment in
Muslim law
**WAQFS** > WAQF
**WAR** *n* fighting between
nations ▷ *adj* of, like,
or caused by war ▷ *vb*

conduct a war
**WARAGI** *n* Ugandan
alcoholic drink made from
bananas
**WARAGIS** > WARAGI
**WARATAH** *n* Australian
shrub with crimson
flowers
**WARATAHS** > WARATAH
**WARB** *n* dirty or
insignificant person
**WARBIER** > WARB
**WARBIEST** > WARB
**WARBLE** *vb* sing in a trilling
voice ▷ *n* act or an
instance of warbling
**WARBLED** > WARBLE
**WARBLER** *n* any of various
small songbirds
**WARBLERS** > WARBLER
**WARBLES** > WARBLE
**WARBLING** > WARBLE
**WARBLINGS** > WARBLE
**WARBONNET** *n* headband
with trailing feathers
worn by certain North
American Indian warriors
**WARBS** > WARB
**WARBY** > WARB
**WARCRAFT** *n* skill in warfare
**WARCRAFTS** > WARCRAFT
**WARD** *n* room in a hospital
for patients needing a
similar kind of care ▷ *vb*
guard or protect
**WARDCORN** *n* payment of
corn
**WARDCORNS** > WARDCORN
**WARDED** > WARD
**WARDEN** *n* person in charge
of a building and its
occupants ▷ *vb* act as a
warden
**WARDENED** > WARDEN
**WARDENING** > WARDEN
**WARDENRY** > WARDEN
**WARDENS** > WARDEN
**WARDER** *vb* guard ▷ *n*
prison officer
**WARDERED** > WARDER
**WARDERING** > WARDER
**WARDERS** > WARDER
**WARDIAN** as in *wardian case*
type of glass container for
housing delicate plants
**WARDING** > WARD
**WARDINGS** > WARD
**WARDLESS** > WARD
**WARDMOTE** *n* assembly of
the citizens or liverymen
of an area
**WARDMOTES** > WARDMOTE
**WARDOG** *n* veteran warrior
**WARDOGS** > WARDOG
**WARDRESS** *n* female officer
in charge of prisoners in
a jail
**WARDROBE** *n* cupboard for
hanging clothes in
**WARDROBED** > WARDROBE
**WARDROBER** *n* person in
charge of someone's
wardrobe
**WARDROBES** > WARDROBE

**WARDROOM** *n* officers'
quarters on a warship
**WARDROOMS** > WARDROOM
**WARDROP** *obsolete form
of* > WARDROBE
**WARDROPS** > WARDROP
**WARDS** > WARD
**WARDSHIP** *n* state of being
a ward
**WARDSHIPS** > WARDSHIP
**WARE** *n* articles of a
specified type or material
▷ *vb* spend or squander
**WARED** > WARE
**WAREHOU** *n* any of several
edible saltwater New
Zealand fish
**WAREHOUSE** *n* building for
storing goods prior to sale
or distribution ▷ *vb* store
or place in a warehouse,
esp a bonded warehouse
**WARELESS** *adj* careless
**WAREROOM** *n* store-room
**WAREROOMS** > WAREROOM
**WARES** *pl n* goods for sale
**WAREZ** *pl n* illegally copied
computer software which
has had its protection
codes de-activated
**WARFARE** *vb* engage in war
▷ *n* fighting or hostilities
**WARFARED** > WARFARE
**WARFARER** > WARFARE
**WARFARERS** > WARFARE
**WARFARES** > WARFARE
**WARFARIN** *n* crystalline
compound, used as a
medical anticoagulant
**WARFARING** > WARFARE
**WARFARINS** > WARFARIN
**WARHABLE** *adj* able to fight
in war
**WARHEAD** *n* explosive front
part of a missile
**WARHEADS** > WARHEAD
**WARHORSE** *n* (formerly) a
horse used in battle
**WARHORSES** > WARHORSE
**WARIBASHI** *n* disposable
chopsticks
**WARIER** > WARY
**WARIEST** > WARY
**WARILY** > WARY
**WARIMENT** *n* caution
**WARIMENTS** > WARIMENT
**WARINESS** > WARY
**WARING** > WARE
**WARISON** *n* (esp formerly)
a bugle note used as an
order to a military force to
attack
**WARISONS** > WARISON
**WARK** *Scots form of* > WORK
**WARKED** > WARK
**WARKING** > WARK
**WARKS** > WARK
**WARLESS** > WAR
**WARLIKE** *adj* of or relating
to war
**WARLING** *n* one who is not
liked
**WARLINGS** > WARLING
**WARLOCK** *n* man who

practises black magic
**WARLOCKRY** *n* witchcraft
**WARLOCKS** > WARLOCK
**WARLORD** *n* military leader
of a nation or part of a
nation
**WARLORDS** > WARLORD
**WARM** *adj* moderately hot
▷ *vb* make or become
warm ▷ *n* warm place or
area
**WARMAKER** *n* one who
wages war
**WARMAKERS** > WARMAKER
**WARMAN** *n* one experienced
in warfare
**WARMBLOOD** *n* type of horse
**WARMED** > WARM
**WARMEN** > WARMAN
**WARMER** > WARM
**WARMERS** > WARM
**WARMEST** > WARM
**WARMING** > WARM
**WARMINGS** > WARM
**WARMISH** > WARM
**WARMLY** > WARM
**WARMNESS** > WARM
**WARMONGER** *n* person who
encourages war
**WARMOUTH** *n* type of fish
**WARMOUTHS** > WARMOUTH
**WARMS** > WARM
**WARMTH** *n* mild heat
**WARMTHS** > WARMTH
**WARMUP** *n* preparatory
exercise routine
**WARMUPS** > WARMUP
**WARN** *vb* make aware of
possible danger or harm
**WARNED** > WARN
**WARNER** > WARN
**WARNERS** > WARN
**WARNING** *n* something
that warns ▷ *adj* giving or
serving as a warning
**WARNINGLY** > WARNING
**WARNINGS** > WARNING
**WARNS** > WARN
**WARP** *vb* twist out of shape
▷ *n* state of being warped
**WARPAGE** > WARP
**WARPAGES** > WARP
**WARPATH** *n* route taken by
Native Americans on a
warlike expedition
**WARPATHS** > WARPATH
**WARPED** > WARP
**WARPER** > WARP
**WARPERS** > WARP
**WARPING** > WARP
**WARPINGS** > WARP
**WARPLANE** *n* any aircraft
designed for and used in
warfare
**WARPLANES** > WARPLANE
**WARPOWER** *n* ability to wage
war
**WARPOWERS** > WARPOWER
**WARPS** > WARP
**WARPWISE** *adv* (weaving) in
the direction of the warp
**WARRAGAL** *same*
*as* > WARRIGAL
**WARRAGALS** > WARRAGAL

WARRAGLE same
as >WARRIGAL
WARRAGLES >WARRAGLE
WARRAGUL same
as >WARRIGAL
WARRAGULS >WARRAGUL
WARRAN same as >WARRANT
WARRAND same
as >WARRANT
WARRANDED >WARRAND
WARRANDS >WARRAND
WARRANED >WARRAN
WARRANING >WARRAN
WARRANS >WARRAN
WARRANT n (document
giving) official
authorization ▷ vb make
necessary
WARRANTED >WARRANT
WARRANTEE n person to
whom a warranty is given
WARRANTER >WARRANT
WARRANTOR n person or
company that provides a
warranty
WARRANTS >WARRANT
WARRANTY n (document
giving) a guarantee
WARRAY vb wage war on
WARRAYED >WARRAY
WARRAYING >WARRAY
WARRAYS >WARRAY
WARRE same as >WAR
WARRED >WAR
WARREN n series of burrows
in which rabbits live
WARRENER n gamekeeper
or keeper of a warren
WARRENERS >WARRENER
WARRENS >WARREN
WARREY same as >WARRAY
WARREYED >WARREY
WARREYING >WARREY
WARREYS >WARREY
WARRIGAL n dingo ▷ adj
wild
WARRIGALS >WARRIGAL
WARRING >WAR
WARRIOR n person who
fights in a war
WARRIORS >WARRIOR
WARRISON same
as >WARISON
WARRISONS >WARRISON
WARS n war
WARSAW n type of grouper
fish
WARSAWS >WARSAW
WARSHIP n ship designed
and equipped for naval
combat
WARSHIPS >WARSHIP
WARSLE dialect word
for >WRESTLE
WARSLED >WARSLE
WARSLER >WARSLE
WARSLERS >WARSLE
WARSLES >WARSLE
WARSLING >WARSLE
WARST obsolete form
of >WORST
WARSTLE dialect form
of >WRESTLE
WARSTLED >WARSTLE

WARSTLER >WARSTLE
WARSTLERS >WARSTLE
WARSTLES >WARSTLE
WARSTLING >WARSTLE
WART n small hard growth
on the skin
WARTED >WART
WARTHOG n wild African pig
with heavy tusks, wartlike
lumps on the face, and a
mane of coarse hair
WARTHOGS >WARTHOG
WARTIER >WART
WARTIEST >WART
WARTIME n time of war
▷ adj of or in a time of war
WARTIMES >WARTIME
WARTLESS >WART
WARTLIKE >WART
WARTS >WART
WARTWEED n type of plant
WARTWEEDS >WARTWEED
WARTWORT another word
for >WARTWEED
WARTWORTS >WARTWORT
WARTY >WART
WARWOLF n Roman engine
of war
WARWOLVES >WARWOLF
WARWORK n work
contributing to war effort
WARWORKS >WARWORK
WARWORN adj worn down
by war
WARY adj watchful or
cautious
WARZONE n area where
a war is taking place or
there is some other violent
conflict
WARZONES >WARZONE
WAS vb form of the
subjunctive mood used
in place of were, esp in
conditional sentences
WASABI n Japanese
cruciferous plant
cultivated for its thick
green pungent root
WASABIS >WASABI
WASE n pad to relieve
pressure of load carried
on head
WASES >WASE
WASH vb clean (oneself,
clothes, etc) with water
and usu soap ▷ n act or
process of washing
WASHABLE n thing that can
be washed ▷ adj (esp of
fabrics or clothes) capable
of being washed without
deteriorating
WASHABLES >WASHABLE
WASHAWAY another word
for >WASHOUT
WASHAWAYS >WASHAWAY
WASHBALL n ball of soap
WASHBALLS >WASHBALL
WASHBASIN n basin for
washing the face and
hands
WASHBOARD n board
having a surface, usually

of corrugated metal,
on which esp formerly,
clothes were scrubbed
WASHBOWL same
as >WASHBASIN
WASHBOWLS >WASHBOWL
WASHCLOTH n small piece of
cloth used to wash the face
and hands
WASHDAY n day on which
clothes and linen are
washed, often the same
day each week
WASHDAYS >WASHDAY
WASHED >WASH
WASHEN >WASH
WASHER n ring put under a
nut or bolt or in a tap as a
seal ▷ vb fit with a washer
WASHERED >WASHER
WASHERIES >WASHERY
WASHERING >WASHER
WASHERMAN n man who
washes clothes for a living
WASHERMEN >WASHERMAN
WASHERS >WASHER
WASHERY n plant at a mine
where water or other
liquid is used to remove
dirt from a mineral, esp
coal
WASHES >WASH
WASHHOUSE n (formerly)
building in which laundry
was done
WASHIER >WASHY
WASHIEST >WASHY
WASHILY >WASHY
WASHIN n increase in
the angle of attack of an
aircraft wing towards the
wing tip
WASHINESS >WASHY
WASHING n clothes to be
washed
WASHINGS >WASHING
WASHINS >WASHIN
WASHLAND n frequently-
flooded plain
WASHLANDS >WASHLAND
WASHOUT n complete
failure
WASHOUTS >WASHOUT
WASHPOT n pot for washing
things in
WASHPOTS >WASHPOT
WASHRAG same
as >WASHCLOTH
WASHRAGS >WASHRAG
WASHROOM n toilet
WASHROOMS >WASHROOM
WASHSTAND n piece of
furniture designed to hold
a basin for washing the
face and hands in
WASHTUB n tub or large
container used for
washing anything, esp
clothes
WASHTUBS >WASHTUB
WASHUP n outcome of a
process
WASHUPS >WASHUP
WASHWIPE n windscreen

spray-cleaning
mechanism
WASHWIPES >WASHWIPE
WASHWOMAN n woman who
washes clothes for a living
WASHWOMEN >WASHWOMAN
WASHY adj overdiluted or
weak
WASM n obsolete belief
WASMS >WASM
WASP n stinging insect with
a slender black-and-yellow
striped body
WASPIE n tight-waited
corset
WASPIER >WASP
WASPIES >WASPIE
WASPIEST >WASP
WASPILY >WASP
WASPINESS >WASP
WASPISH adj bad-tempered
WASPISHLY >WASPISH
WASPLIKE >WASP
WASPNEST n nest of wasp
WASPNESTS >WASPNEST
WASPS >WASP
WASPY >WASP
WASSAIL n formerly,
festivity when much
drinking took place ▷ vb
drink health of (a person)
at a wassail
WASSAILED >WASSAIL
WASSAILER >WASSAIL
WASSAILRY >WASSAIL
WASSAILS >WASSAIL
WASSERMAN n man-shaped
sea monster
WASSERMEN >WASSERMAN
WASSUP sentence substitute
what is happening?
WAST singular form of the past
tense of >BE
WASTABLE >WASTE
WASTAGE n loss by wear or
waste
WASTAGES >WASTAGE
WASTE vb use pointlessly or
thoughtlessly ▷ n act of
wasting or state of being
wasted ▷ adj rejected as
worthless or surplus to
requirements
WASTED >WASTE
WASTEFUL adj extravagant
WASTEL n fine bread or cake
WASTELAND n barren or
desolate area of land
WASTELOT n piece of waste
ground in a city
WASTELOTS >WASTELOT
WASTELS >WASTEL
WASTENESS >WASTE
WASTER vb waste ▷ n
layabout
WASTERED >WASTER
WASTERFUL Scots variant
of >WASTEFUL
WASTERIE same
as >WASTERY
WASTERIES >WASTERIE
WASTERING >WASTER
WASTERS >WASTER
WASTERY n extravagance

**WASTES** >WASTE
**WASTEWAY** *n* open ditch
**WASTEWAYS** >WASTEWAY
**WASTEWEIR** *another name for* >SPILLWAY
**WASTFULL** *obsolete form of* >WASTEFUL
**WASTING** *adj* reducing the vitality and strength of the body
**WASTINGLY** >WASTING
**WASTINGS** >WASTE
**WASTNESS** *n* obsolete form of wasteness
**WASTREL** *n* lazy or worthless person
**WASTRELS** >WASTREL
**WASTRIE** *same as* >WASTERY
**WASTRIES** >WASTRIE
**WASTRIFE** *n* wastefulness
**WASTRIFES** >WASTRIFE
**WASTRY** *n* wastefulness
**WASTS** >WAST
**WAT** *n* Thai Buddhist monastery or temple
**WATAP** *n* stringy thread made by Native Americans from the roots of conifers
**WATAPE** *same as* >WATAP
**WATAPES** >WATAPE
**WATAPS** >WATAP
**WATCH** *vb* look at closely ▷ *n* portable timepiece for the wrist or pocket
**WATCHABLE** *adj* interesting, enjoyable, or entertaining
**WATCHBAND** *n* watch strap
**WATCHBOX** *n* sentry's box
**WATCHCASE** *n* protective case for a watch, generally of metal such as gold, silver, brass, or gunmetal
**WATCHCRY** *n* slogan used to rally support
**WATCHDOG** *n* dog kept to guard property
**WATCHDOGS** >WATCHDOG
**WATCHED** >WATCH
**WATCHER** *n* person who watches
**WATCHERS** >WATCHER
**WATCHES** >WATCH
**WATCHET** *n* shade of blue
**WATCHETS** >WATCHET
**WATCHEYE** *n* eye with a light-coloured iris
**WATCHEYES** >WATCHEYE
**WATCHFUL** *adj* vigilant or alert
**WATCHING** >WATCH
**WATCHLIST** *n* list of things to be monitored
**WATCHMAN** *n* man employed to guard a building or property
**WATCHMEN** >WATCHMAN
**WATCHOUT** *n* lookout
**WATCHOUTS** >WATCHOUT
**WATCHWORD** *n* word or phrase that sums up the attitude of a particular group
**WATE** >WIT
**WATER** *n* clear colourless

tasteless liquid that falls as rain and forms rivers etc ▷ *vb* put water on or into
**WATERAGE** *n* transportation of cargo by means of ships, or the charges for such transportation
**WATERAGES** >WATERAGE
**WATERBED** *n* watertight mattress filled with water
**WATERBEDS** >WATERBED
**WATERBIRD** *n* any aquatic bird
**WATERBUCK** *n* any of various antelopes of the swampy areas of Africa, having long curved ridged horns
**WATERBUS** *n* boat offering regular transport service
**WATERDOG** *n* dog trained to hunt in water
**WATERDOGS** >WATERDOG
**WATERED** >WATER
**WATERER** >WATER
**WATERERS** >WATER
**WATERFALL** *n* place where the waters of a river drop vertically
**WATERFOWL** *n* bird that swims on water, such as a duck or swan
**WATERHEAD** *n* source of river
**WATERHEN** *another name for* >GALLINULE
**WATERHENS** >WATERHEN
**WATERIER** >WATERY
**WATERIEST** >WATERY
**WATERILY** >WATERY
**WATERING** >WATER
**WATERINGS** >WATER
**WATERISH** >WATER
**WATERJET** *n* jet of water
**WATERJETS** >WATERJET
**WATERLEAF** *n* carved column design
**WATERLESS** >WATER
**WATERLILY** *n* any of various aquatic plants having large leaves and showy flowers that float on the surface of the water
**WATERLINE** *n* level to which a ship's hull will be immersed when afloat
**WATERLOG** *vb* flood with water
**WATERLOGS** >WATERLOG
**WATERLOO** *n* total defeat
**WATERLOOS** >WATERLOO
**WATERMAN** *n* skilled boatman
**WATERMARK** *n* faint translucent design in a sheet of paper ▷ *vb* mark (paper) with a watermark
**WATERMEN** >WATERMAN
**WATERPOX** *n* chickenpox
**WATERS** >WATER
**WATERSHED** *n* important period or factor serving as a dividing line

**WATERSIDE** *n* area of land beside a river or lake
**WATERSKI** *vb* ski on water towed behind motorboat
**WATERSKIS** >WATERSKI
**WATERWAY** *n* river, canal, or other navigable channel used as a means of travel or transport
**WATERWAYS** >WATERWAY
**WATERWEED** *n* any of various weedy aquatic plants
**WATERWORK** *n* machinery, etc for storing, purifying, and distributing water
**WATERWORN** *adj* worn smooth by the action or passage of water
**WATERY** *adj* of, like, or containing water
**WATERZOOI** *n* type of Flemish stew
**WATS** >WAT
**WATT** *n* unit of power
**WATTAGE** *n* electrical power expressed in watts
**WATTAGES** >WATTAGE
**WATTAPE** *same as* >WATAP
**WATTAPES** >WATTAPE
**WATTER** >WAT
**WATTEST** >WAT
**WATTHOUR** *n* unit of energy equal to the power of one watt operating for an hour
**WATTHOURS** >WATTHOUR
**WATTLE** *n* branches woven over sticks to make a fence ▷ *adj* made of, formed by, or covered with wattle ▷ *vb* construct from wattle
**WATTLED** >WATTLE
**WATTLES** >WATTLE
**WATTLESS** >WATT
**WATTLING** >WATTLE
**WATTLINGS** >WATTLE
**WATTMETER** *n* meter for measuring electric power in watts
**WATTS** >WATT
**WAUCHT** *same as* >WAUGHT
**WAUCHTED** >WAUCHT
**WAUCHTING** >WAUCHT
**WAUCHTS** >WAUCHT
**WAUFF** *same as* >WAFF
**WAUFFED** >WAUFF
**WAUFFING** >WAUFF
**WAUFFS** >WAUFF
**WAUGH** *vb* bark
**WAUGHED** >WAUGH
**WAUGHING** >WAUGH
**WAUGHS** >WAUGH
**WAUGHT** *vb* drink in large amounts
**WAUGHTED** >WAUGHT
**WAUGHTING** >WAUGHT
**WAUGHTS** >WAUGHT
**WAUK** *vb* full (cloth)
**WAUKED** >WAUK
**WAUKER** >WAUK
**WAUKERS** >WAUK
**WAUKING** >WAUK
**WAUKMILL** *same as* >WAULKMILL

**WAUKMILLS** >WAUKMILL
**WAUKRIFE** *variant of* >WAKERIFE
**WAUKS** >WAUK
**WAUL** *vb* cry or wail plaintively like a cat
**WAULED** >WAUL
**WAULING** >WAUL
**WAULINGS** >WAUL
**WAULK** *same as* >WAUK
**WAULKED** >WAULK
**WAULKER** >WAULK
**WAULKERS** >WAULK
**WAULKING** >WAULK
**WAULKMILL** *n* cloth-fulling mill
**WAULKS** >WAULK
**WAULS** >WAUL
**WAUR** *obsolete form of* >WAR
**WAURED** >WAUR
**WAURING** >WAUR
**WAURS** >WAUR
**WAURST** >WAUR
**WAVE** *vb* move the hand to and fro as a greeting or signal ▷ *n* moving ridge on water
**WAVEBAND** *n* range of wavelengths or frequencies used for a particular type of radio transmission
**WAVEBANDS** >WAVEBAND
**WAVED** >WAVE
**WAVEFORM** *n* shape of the graph of a wave or oscillation obtained by plotting the value of some changing quantity against time
**WAVEFORMS** >WAVEFORM
**WAVEFRONT** *n* surface associated with a propagating wave and passing through all points in the wave that have the same phase
**WAVEGUIDE** *n* solid rod of dielectric or a hollow metal tube, usually of rectangular cross section, used as a path to guide microwaves
**WAVELESS** >WAVE
**WAVELET** *n* small wave
**WAVELETS** >WAVELET
**WAVELIKE** >WAVE
**WAVELLITE** *n* greyish-white, yellow, or brown mineral
**WAVEMETER** *n* instrument for measuring the frequency or wavelength of radio waves
**WAVEOFF** *n* signal or instruction to an aircraft not to land
**WAVEOFFS** >WAVEOFF
**WAVER** *vb* hesitate or be irresolute ▷ *n* act or an instance of wavering
**WAVERED** >WAVER
**WAVERER** >WAVER
**WAVERERS** >WAVER

WAVERIER > WAVERY
WAVERIEST > WAVERY
WAVERING > WAVER
WAVERINGS > WAVER
WAVEROUS *same as* > WAVERY
WAVERS > WAVER
WAVERY *adj* lacking firmness
WAVES > WAVE
WAVESHAPE *another word for* > WAVEFORM
WAVESON *n* goods floating on waves after shipwreck
WAVESONS > WAVESON
WAVEY *n* snow goose or other wild goose
WAVEYS > WAVEY
WAVICLE *n* origin of wave
WAVICLES > WAVICLE
WAVIER > WAVY
WAVIES > WAVY
WAVIEST > WAVY
WAVILY > WAVY
WAVINESS > WAVY
WAVING > WAVE
WAVINGS > WAVE
WAVY *adj* having curves ▷ *n* snow goose or other wild goose
WAW *another name for* > VAV
WAWA *n* speech ▷ *vb* speak
WAWAED > WAWA
WAWAING > WAWA
WAWAS > WAWA
WAWE *same as* > WAW
WAWES > WAWE
WAWL *same as* > WAUL
WAWLED > WAWL
WAWLING > WAWL
WAWLINGS > WAWL
WAWLS > WAWL
WAWS > WAW
WAX *n* solid shiny fatty or oily substance used for sealing, making candles, etc ▷ *vb* coat or polish with wax
WAXABLE > WAX
WAXBERRY *n* waxy fruit of the wax myrtle or the snowberry
WAXBILL *n* any of various chiefly African finchlike weaverbirds
WAXBILLS > WAXBILL
WAXCLOTH *another name for* > OILCLOTH
WAXCLOTHS > WAXCLOTH
WAXED > WAX
WAXEN *adj* made of or like wax
WAXER > WAX
WAXERS > WAX
WAXES > WAX
WAXEYE *n* small New Zealand bird with a white circle round its eye
WAXEYES > WAXEYE
WAXFLOWER *n* any of various plants with waxy flowers
WAXIER > WAXY
WAXIEST > WAXY
WAXILY > WAXY

WAXINESS > WAXY
WAXING > WAX
WAXINGS > WAX
WAXLIKE > WAX
WAXPLANT *n* climbing shrub of E Asia and Australia
WAXPLANTS > WAXPLANT
WAXWEED *n* type of wild flower
WAXWEEDS > WAXWEED
WAXWING *n* type of songbird
WAXWINGS > WAXWING
WAXWORK *n* lifelike wax model of a (famous) person
WAXWORKER > WAXWORK
WAXWORKS > WAXWORK
WAXWORM *n* waxmoth larva
WAXWORMS > WAXWORM
WAXY *adj* resembling wax in colour, appearance, or texture
WAY *n* manner or method ▷ *vb* travel
WAYBILL *n* document stating the nature, origin, and destination of goods being transported
WAYBILLS > WAYBILL
WAYBOARD *n* thin geological seam separating larger strata
WAYBOARDS > WAYBOARD
WAYBREAD *n* plantain
WAYBREADS > WAYBREAD
WAYED > WAY
WAYFARE *vb* travel
WAYFARED > WAYFARE
WAYFARER *n* traveller
WAYFARERS > WAYFARER
WAYFARES > WAYFARE
WAYFARING > WAYFARE
WAYGOING *n* leaving
WAYGOINGS > WAYGOING
WAYGONE *adj* travel-weary
WAYGOOSE *same as* > WAYZGOOSE
WAYGOOSES > WAYGOOSE
WAYING > WAY
WAYLAID > WAYLAY
WAYLAY *vb* lie in wait for and accost or attack
WAYLAYER > WAYLAY
WAYLAYERS > WAYLAY
WAYLAYING > WAYLAY
WAYLAYS > WAYLAY
WAYLEAVE *n* access to property granted by a landowner for payment
WAYLEAVES > WAYLEAVE
WAYLEGGO *interj* away here! let go!
WAYLESS > WAY
WAYMARK *n* symbol or signpost marking the route of a footpath ▷ *vb* mark out with waymarks
WAYMARKED > WAYMARK
WAYMARKS > WAYMARK
WAYMENT *vb* express grief
WAYMENTED > WAYMENT
WAYMENTS > WAYMENT
WAYPOINT *n* stopping point

on route
WAYPOINTS > WAYPOINT
WAYPOST *n* signpost
WAYPOSTS > WAYPOST
WAYS > WAY
WAYSIDE *n* side of a road
WAYSIDES > WAYSIDE
WAYWARD *adj* erratic, selfish, or stubborn
WAYWARDLY > WAYWARD
WAYWISER *n* device for measuring distance
WAYWISERS > WAYWISER
WAYWODE *n* Slavonic governor
WAYWODES > WAYWODE
WAYWORN *adj* worn or tired by travel
WAYZGOOSE *n* works outing made annually by a printing house
WAZIR *another word for* > VIZIER
WAZIRS > WAZIR
WAZOO *n* slang word for person's bottom
WAZOOS > WAZOO
WAZZOCK *n* foolish or annoying person
WAZZOCKS > WAZZOCK
WE *pron* speaker or writer and one or more others
WEAK *adj* lacking strength
WEAKEN *vb* make or become weak
WEAKENED > WEAKEN
WEAKENER > WEAKEN
WEAKENERS > WEAKEN
WEAKENING > WEAKEN
WEAKENS > WEAKEN
WEAKER > WEAK
WEAKEST > WEAK
WEAKFISH *n* any of several sea trouts
WEAKISH > WEAK
WEAKISHLY > WEAK
WEAKLIER > WEAKLY
WEAKLIEST > WEAKLY
WEAKLING *n* feeble person or animal
WEAKLINGS > WEAKLING
WEAKLY *adv* feebly ▷ *adj* weak or sickly
WEAKNESS *n* being weak
WEAKON *n* subatomic particle
WEAKONS > WEAKON
WEAKSIDE *n* (in basketball) side of court away from ball
WEAKSIDES > WEAKSIDE
WEAL *n* raised mark left on the skin by a blow
WEALD *n* open or forested country
WEALDS > WEALD
WEALS > WEAL
WEALSMAN *n* statesman
WEALSMEN > WEALSMAN
WEALTH *n* state of being rich
WEALTHIER > WEALTHY
WEALTHILY > WEALTHY
WEALTHS > WEALTH

WEALTHY *adj* possessing wealth
WEAMB *same as* > WAME
WEAMBS > WEAMB
WEAN *vb* accustom (a baby or young mammal) to food other than mother's milk
WEANED > WEAN
WEANEL *n* recently-weaned child or animal
WEANELS > WEANEL
WEANER *n* person or thing that weans
WEANERS > WEANER
WEANING > WEAN
WEANLING *n* child or young animal recently weaned
WEANLINGS > WEANLING
WEANS > WEAN
WEAPON *vb* arm ▷ *n* object used in fighting
WEAPONED > WEAPON
WEAPONEER *n* person associated with the use or maintenance of weapons, esp nuclear weapons
WEAPONING > WEAPON
WEAPONISE *same as* > WEAPONIZE
WEAPONIZE *vb* adapt (a chemical, bacillus, etc) in such a way that it can be used as a weapon
WEAPONRY *n* weapons collectively
WEAPONS > WEAPON
WEAR *vb* have on the body as clothing or ornament ▷ *n* clothes suitable for a particular time or purpose
WEARABLE *adj* suitable for wear or able to be worn ▷ *n* any garment that can be worn
WEARABLES > WEARABLE
WEARED > WEAR
WEARER > WEAR
WEARERS > WEAR
WEARIED > WEARY
WEARIER > WEARY
WEARIES > WEARY
WEARIEST > WEARY
WEARIFUL *same as* > WEARISOME
WEARILESS *adj* not wearied or able to be wearied
WEARILY > WEARY
WEARINESS > WEARY
WEARING *adj* tiring ▷ *n* act of wearing
WEARINGLY > WEARING
WEARINGS > WEAR
WEARISH *adj* withered
WEARISOME *adj* tedious
WEARPROOF *adj* resistant to damage from normal wear or usage
WEARS > WEAR
WEARY *adj* tired or exhausted ▷ *vb* make or become weary
WEARYING > WEARY
WEASAND *former name for the* > TRACHEA

**WEASANDS** >WEASAND
**WEASEL** n small carnivorous mammal with a long body and short legs ▷ vb use ambiguous language to avoid speaking directly or honestly
**WEASELED** >WEASEL
**WEASELER** >WEASEL
**WEASELERS** >WEASEL
**WEASELING** >WEASEL
**WEASELLED** >WEASEL
**WEASELLER** >WEASEL
**WEASELLY** >WEASEL
**WEASELS** >WEASEL
**WEASELY** >WEASEL
**WEASON** Scots form of >WEASAND
**WEASONS** >WEASON
**WEATHER** n day-to-day atmospheric conditions of a place ▷ vb (cause to) be affected by the weather
**WEATHERED** adj affected by exposure to the action of the weather
**WEATHERER** >WEATHER
**WEATHERLY** adj (of a sailing vessel) making very little leeway when close-hauled, even in a stiff breeze
**WEATHERS** >WEATHER
**WEAVE** vb make (fabric) by interlacing (yarn) on a loom
**WEAVED** >WEAVE
**WEAVER** n person who weaves, esp as a means of livelihood
**WEAVERS** >WEAVER
**WEAVES** >WEAVE
**WEAVING** >WEAVE
**WEAVINGS** >WEAVE
**WEAZAND** same as >WEASAND
**WEAZANDS** >WEAZAND
**WEAZEN** same as >WIZEN
**WEAZENED** >WEAZEN
**WEAZENING** >WEAZEN
**WEAZENS** >WEAZEN
**WEB** n net spun by a spider ▷ vb cover with or as if with a web
**WEBBED** >WEB
**WEBBIE** n person who is well versed in the use of the World Wide Web
**WEBBIER** >WEBBY
**WEBBIES** >WEBBIE
**WEBBIEST** >WEBBY
**WEBBING** n anything that forms a web
**WEBBINGS** >WEBBING
**WEBBY** adj of, relating to, resembling, or consisting of a web
**WEBCAM** n camera that transmits images over the internet
**WEBCAMS** >WEBCAM
**WEBCAST** n broadcast of an event over the internet ▷ vb make such a broadcast
**WEBCASTED** >WEBCAST
**WEBCASTER** >WEBCAST
**WEBCASTS** >WEBCAST
**WEBER** n SI unit of magnetic flux
**WEBERS** >WEBER
**WEBFED** adj (of printing press) printing from rolls of paper
**WEBFEET** >WEBFOOT
**WEBFOOT** n foot having the toes connected by folds of skin
**WEBFOOTED** >WEBFOOT
**WEBINAR** n interactive seminar conducted over the World Wide Web
**WEBINARS** >WEBINAR
**WEBLESS** >WEB
**WEBLIKE** >WEB
**WEBLISH** n shorthand form of English that is used in text messaging, chat rooms, etc
**WEBLISHES** >WEBLISH
**WEBLOG** n person's online journal
**WEBLOGGER** >WEBLOG
**WEBLOGS** >WEBLOG
**WEBMAIL** n system of electronic mail that allows account holders to access their mail via an internet site rather than downloading it
**WEBMAILS** >WEBMAIL
**WEBMASTER** n person responsible for the administration of a website on the World Wide Web
**WEBPAGE** n page on website
**WEBPAGES** >WEBPAGE
**WEBS** >WEB
**WEBSITE** n group of connected pages on the World Wide Web
**WEBSITES** >WEBSITE
**WEBSTER** archaic word for >WEAVER
**WEBSTERS** >WEBSTER
**WEBWHEEL** n wheel containing a plate or web instead of spokes
**WEBWHEELS** >WEBWHEEL
**WEBWORK** n work done using the World Wide Web
**WEBWORKS** >WEBWORK
**WEBWORM** n type of caterpillar
**WEBWORMS** >WEBWORM
**WECHT** n agricultural tool
**WECHTS** >WECHT
**WED** vb marry
**WEDDED** >WED
**WEDDER** dialect form of >WEATHER
**WEDDERED** >WEDDER
**WEDDERING** >WEDDER
**WEDDERS** >WEDDER
**WEDDING** >WED
**WEDDINGS** >WEDDING

**WEDEL** variant of >WEDELN
**WEDELED** >WEDEL
**WEDELING** >WEDEL
**WEDELN** n succession of high-speed turns performed in skiing ▷ vb perform a wedeln
**WEDELNED** >WEDELN
**WEDELNING** >WEDELN
**WEDELNS** >WEDELN
**WEDELS** >WEDEL
**WEDGE** n piece of material thick at one end and thin at the other ▷ vb fasten or split with a wedge
**WEDGED** >WEDGE
**WEDGELIKE** >WEDGE
**WEDGES** >WEDGE
**WEDGEWISE** adv in manner of a wedge
**WEDGIE** n wedge-heeled shoe
**WEDGIER** >WEDGE
**WEDGIES** >WEDGE
**WEDGIEST** >WEDGE
**WEDGING** >WEDGE
**WEDGINGS** >WEDGE
**WEDGY** >WEDGE
**WEDLOCK** n marriage
**WEDLOCKS** >WEDLOCK
**WEDS** >WED
**WEE** adj small or short ▷ n instance of urinating ▷ vb urinate
**WEED** n plant growing where undesired ▷ vb clear of weeds
**WEEDED** >WEED
**WEEDER** >WEED
**WEEDERIES** >WEEDERY
**WEEDERS** >WEED
**WEEDERY** n weed-ridden area
**WEEDICIDE** n weed-killer
**WEEDIER** >WEEDY
**WEEDIEST** >WEEDY
**WEEDILY** >WEEDY
**WEEDINESS** >WEEDY
**WEEDING** >WEED
**WEEDINGS** >WEED
**WEEDLESS** >WEED
**WEEDLIKE** >WEED
**WEEDS** pl n widow's mourning clothes
**WEEDY** adj (of a person) thin and weak
**WEEING** >WEE
**WEEK** n period of seven days, esp one beginning on a Sunday ▷ adv seven days before or after a specified day
**WEEKDAY** n any day of the week except Saturday or Sunday
**WEEKDAYS** >WEEKDAY
**WEEKE** same as >WICK
**WEEKEND** n Saturday and Sunday ▷ vb spend or pass a weekend
**WEEKENDED** >WEEKEND
**WEEKENDER** n person spending a weekend holiday in a place, esp

habitually
**WEEKENDS** adv at the weekend, esp regularly or during every weekend
**WEEKES** >WEEKE
**WEEKLIES** >WEEKLY
**WEEKLONG** adj lasting a week
**WEEKLY** adv happening, done, etc once a week ▷ n newspaper or magazine published once a week ▷ adj happening once a week or every week
**WEEKNIGHT** n evening or night of a weekday
**WEEKS** >WEEK
**WEEL** Scot word for >WELL
**WEELS** >WEEL
**WEEM** n underground home
**WEEMS** >WEEM
**WEEN** vb think or imagine (something)
**WEENED** >WEEN
**WEENIE** adj very small ▷ n wiener
**WEENIER** >WEENY
**WEENIES** >WEENIE
**WEENIEST** >WEENY
**WEENING** >WEEN
**WEENS** >WEEN
**WEENSIER** >WEENSY
**WEENSIEST** >WEENSY
**WEENSY** same as >WEENY
**WEENY** adj very small
**WEEP** vb shed tears ▷ n spell of weeping
**WEEPER** n person who weeps, esp a hired mourner
**WEEPERS** >WEEPER
**WEEPHOLE** n small drain hole in wall
**WEEPHOLES** >WEEPHOLE
**WEEPIE** same as >WEEPY
**WEEPIER** >WEEPY
**WEEPIES** >WEEPY
**WEEPIEST** >WEEPY
**WEEPILY** >WEEPY
**WEEPINESS** >WEEPY
**WEEPING** adj (of plants) having slender hanging branches
**WEEPINGLY** >WEEPING
**WEEPINGS** >WEEPING
**WEEPS** >WEEP
**WEEPY** adj liable to cry ▷ n sentimental film or book
**WEER** >WEE
**WEES** >WEE
**WEEST** >WEE
**WEET** dialect form of >WET
**WEETE** same as >WIT
**WEETED** >WEETE
**WEETEN** same as >WIT
**WEETER** >WEET
**WEETEST** >WEET
**WEETING** >WEET
**WEETINGLY** >WEET
**WEETLESS** obsolete variant of >WITLESS
**WEETS** >WEET
**WEEVER** n type of small fish
**WEEVERS** >WEEVER

**WEEVIL** n small beetle that eats grain etc
**WEEVILED** same as >WEEVILLED
**WEEVILLED** adj weevil-ridden
**WEEVILLY** another word for >WEEVILLED
**WEEVILS** >WEEVIL
**WEEVILY** another word for >WEEVILLED
**WEEWEE** vb urinate
**WEEWEED** >WEEWEE
**WEEWEEING** >WEEWEE
**WEEWEES** >WEEWEE
**WEFT** n cross threads in weaving ▷ vb form weft
**WEFTAGE** n texture
**WEFTAGES** >WEFTAGE
**WEFTE** n forsaken child
**WEFTED** >WEFT
**WEFTES** >WEFTE
**WEFTING** >WEFT
**WEFTS** >WEFT
**WEFTWISE** adv in the direction of the weft
**WEID** n sudden illness
**WEIDS** >WEID
**WEIGELA** n type of shrub
**WEIGELAS** >WEIGELA
**WEIGELIA** same as >WEIGELIA
**WEIGELIAS** >WEIGELIA
**WEIGH** vb have a specified weight
**WEIGHABLE** >WEIGH
**WEIGHAGE** n duty paid for weighing goods
**WEIGHAGES** >WEIGHAGE
**WEIGHED** >WEIGH
**WEIGHER** >WEIGH
**WEIGHERS** >WEIGH
**WEIGHING** >WEIGH
**WEIGHINGS** >WEIGH
**WEIGHMAN** n person responsible for weighing goods
**WEIGHMEN** >WEIGHMAN
**WEIGHS** >WEIGH
**WEIGHT** n heaviness of an object ▷ vb add weight to
**WEIGHTED** >WEIGHT
**WEIGHTER** >WEIGHT
**WEIGHTERS** >WEIGHT
**WEIGHTIER** >WEIGHTY
**WEIGHTILY** >WEIGHTY
**WEIGHTING** n extra allowance paid in special circumstances
**WEIGHTS** >WEIGHT
**WEIGHTY** adj important or serious
**WEIL** n whirlpool
**WEILS** >WEIL
**WEINER** same as >WIENER
**WEINERS** >WEINER
**WEIR** vb ward off ▷ n river dam
**WEIRD** adj strange or bizarre ▷ vb warn beforehand
**WEIRDED** >WEIRD
**WEIRDER** >WEIRD
**WEIRDEST** >WEIRD

**WEIRDIE** same as >WEIRDO
**WEIRDIES** >WEIRDIE
**WEIRDING** >WEIRD
**WEIRDLY** >WEIRD
**WEIRDNESS** >WEIRD
**WEIRDO** n peculiar person
**WEIRDOES** >WEIRDO
**WEIRDOS** >WEIRDO
**WEIRDS** >WEIRD
**WEIRDY** n weird person
**WEIRED** >WEIR
**WEIRING** >WEIR
**WEIRS** >WEIR
**WEISE** same as >WISE
**WEISED** >WEISE
**WEISES** >WEISE
**WEISING** >WEISE
**WEIZE** same as >WISE
**WEIZED** >WEIZE
**WEIZES** >WEIZE
**WEIZING** >WEIZE
**WEKA** n flightless New Zealand rail
**WEKAS** >WEKA
**WELAWAY** same as >WELLAWAY
**WELCH** same as >WELSH
**WELCHED** >WELCH
**WELCHER** >WELCH
**WELCHERS** >WELCH
**WELCHES** >WELCH
**WELCHING** >WELCH
**WELCOME** vb greet with pleasure ▷ n kindly greeting ▷ adj received gladly
**WELCOMED** >WELCOME
**WELCOMELY** >WELCOME
**WELCOMER** >WELCOME
**WELCOMERS** >WELCOME
**WELCOMES** >WELCOME
**WELCOMING** >WELCOME
**WELD** vb join (pieces of metal or plastic) by softening with heat ▷ n welded joint
**WELDABLE** >WELD
**WELDED** >WELD
**WELDER** >WELD
**WELDERS** >WELD
**WELDING** >WELD
**WELDINGS** >WELD
**WELDLESS** >WELD
**WELDMENT** n unit composed of welded pieces
**WELDMENTS** >WELDMENT
**WELDMESH** n type of metal fencing
**WELDOR** >WELD
**WELDORS** >WELDOR
**WELDS** >WELD
**WELFARE** n wellbeing
**WELFARES** >WELFARE
**WELFARISM** n policies or attitudes associated with a welfare state
**WELFARIST** >WELFARISM
**WELK** vb wither; dry up
**WELKE** obsolete form of >WELK
**WELKED** >WELK
**WELKES** >WELKE
**WELKIN** n sky, heavens, or upper air

**WELKING** >WELK
**WELKINS** >WELKIN
**WELKS** >WELK
**WELKT** adj twisted
**WELL** adv satisfactorily ▷ adj in good health ▷ interj exclamation of surprise, interrogation, etc ▷ n hole sunk into the earth to reach water, oil, or gas ▷ vb flow upwards or outwards
**WELLADAY** interj alas
**WELLADAYS** interj alas
**WELLANEAR** interj alas
**WELLAWAY** interj alas!
**WELLAWAYS** interj alas
**WELLBEING** n state of being well, happy, or prosperous
**WELLBORN** adj having been born into a wealthy family
**WELLCURB** n stone surround at top of well
**WELLCURBS** >WELLCURB
**WELLDOER** n moral person
**WELLDOERS** >WELLDOER
**WELLED** >WELL
**WELLHEAD** n source of a well or stream
**WELLHEADS** >WELLHEAD
**WELLHOLE** n well shaft
**WELLHOLES** >WELLHOLE
**WELLHOUSE** n housing for well
**WELLIE** n wellington boot
**WELLIES** >WELLY
**WELLING** >WELL
**WELLINGS** >WELL
**WELLNESS** n state of being in good physical and mental health
**WELLS** >WELL
**WELLSITE** n site of well
**WELLSITES** >WELLSITE
**WELLY** n energy or commitment
**WELSH** vb fail to pay a debt or fulfil an obligation
**WELSHED** >WELSH
**WELSHER** >WELSH
**WELSHERS** >WELSH
**WELSHES** >WELSH
**WELSHING** >WELSH
**WELT** same as >WEAL
**WELTED** >WELT
**WELTER** n jumbled mass ▷ vb roll about, writhe, or wallow
**WELTERED** >WELTER
**WELTERING** >WELTER
**WELTERS** >WELTER
**WELTING** >WELT
**WELTINGS** >WELT
**WELTS** >WELT
**WEM** same as >WAME
**WEMB** same as >WAME
**WEMBS** >WEMB
**WEMS** >WEM
**WEN** n cyst on the scalp
**WENA** n South African word for you
**WENCH** n young woman ▷ vb frequent the company of prostitutes

**WENCHED** >WENCH
**WENCHER** >WENCH
**WENCHERS** >WENCH
**WENCHES** >WENCH
**WENCHING** >WENCH
**WEND** vb go or travel
**WENDED** >WEND
**WENDIGO** n evil spirit or cannibal
**WENDIGOS** >WENDIGO
**WENDING** >WEND
**WENDS** >WEND
**WENGE** n type of tree found in central and West Africa
**WENGES** >WENGE
**WENNIER** >WEN
**WENNIEST** >WEN
**WENNISH** >WEN
**WENNY** >WEN
**WENS** >WEN
**WENT** n path
**WENTS** >WENT
**WEPT** >WEEP
**WERE** vb form of the past tense of be used after we, you, they, or a plural noun
**WEREGILD** same as >WERGILD
**WEREGILDS** >WEREGILD
**WEREWOLF** n (in folklore) person who can turn into a wolf
**WERGELD** same as >WERGILD
**WERGELDS** >WERGILD
**WERGELT** same as >WERGILD
**WERGELTS** >WERGILT
**WERGILD** n price set on a man's life in successive Anglo-Saxon and Germanic law codes, to be paid as compensation by his slayer
**WERGILDS** >WERGILD
**WERNERITE** another name for >SCAPOLITE
**WERO** n challenge made by an armed Māori warrior to a visitor to a marae
**WEROS** >WERO
**WERRIS** slang word for >URINATION
**WERRISES** >WERRIS
**WERSH** adj tasteless
**WERSHER** >WERSH
**WERSHEST** >WERSH
**WERT** singular form of the past tense of >BE
**WERWOLF** same as >WEREWOLF
**WERWOLVES** >WERWOLF
**WESAND** same as >WEASAND
**WESANDS** >WESAND
**WESKIT** informal word for >WAISTCOAT
**WESKITS** >WESKIT
**WESSAND** same as >WEASAND
**WESSANDS** >WESSAND
**WEST** n part of the horizon where the sun sets ▷ adj or in the west ▷ adv in, to, or towards the west ▷ vb move in westerly direction

**WESTBOUND** *adj* going towards the west
**WESTED** >WEST
**WESTER** *vb* move or appear to move towards the west ▷ *n* strong wind or storm from the west
**WESTERED** >WESTER
**WESTERING** >WESTER
**WESTERLY** *adj* of or in the west ▷ *adv* towards the west ▷ *n* wind blowing from the west
**WESTERN** *adj* of or in the west ▷ *n* film or story about cowboys in the western US
**WESTERNER** *n* person from the west of a country or area
**WESTERNS** >WESTERN
**WESTERS** >WESTER
**WESTIE** *n* informal word for a young working-class person from the western suburbs of Sydney
**WESTIES** >WESTIE
**WESTING** *n* movement, deviation, or distance covered in a westerly direction
**WESTINGS** >WESTING
**WESTLIN** *Scots word for* >WESTERN
**WESTLINS** *adv* to or in west
**WESTMOST** *adj* most western
**WESTS** >WEST
**WESTWARD** *adv* towards the west ▷ *n* westward part or direction ▷ *adj* moving, facing, or situated in the west
**WESTWARDS** *same as* >WESTWARD
**WET** *adj* covered or soaked with water or another liquid ▷ *n* moisture or rain ▷ *vb* make wet
**WETA** *n* type of wingless insect
**WETAS** >WETA
**WETBACK** *n* Mexican labourer who enters the US illegally
**WETBACKS** >WETBACK
**WETHER** *n* male sheep, esp a castrated one
**WETHERS** >WETHER
**WETLAND** *n* area of marshy land
**WETLANDS** >WETLAND
**WETLY** >WET
**WETNESS** >WET
**WETNESSES** >WET
**WETPROOF** *adj* waterproof
**WETS** >WET
**WETSUIT** *n* body suit for diving
**WETSUITS** >WETSUIT
**WETTABLE** >WET
**WETTED** >WET
**WETTER** >WET
**WETTERS** >WET

**WETTEST** >WET
**WETTIE** *n* wetsuit
**WETTIES** >WETTIE
**WETTING** >WET
**WETTINGS** >WET
**WETTISH** >WET
**WETWARE** *n* humorous term for the brain
**WETWARES** >WETWARE
**WEX** *obsolete form of* >WAX
**WEXE** *obsolete form of* >WAX
**WEXED** >WEX
**WEXES** >WEX
**WEXING** >WEX
**WEY** *n* measurement of weight
**WEYARD** *obsolete form of* >WEIRD
**WEYS** >WEY
**WEYWARD** *obsolete form of* >WEIRD
**WEZAND** *obsolete form of* >WEASAND
**WEZANDS** >WEZAND
**WHA** *Scot word for* >WHO
**WHACK** *vb* strike with a resounding blow ▷ *n* such a blow
**WHACKED** >WHACK
**WHACKER** >WHACK
**WHACKERS** >WHACK
**WHACKIER** >WHACKY
**WHACKIEST** >WHACKY
**WHACKING** *adj* huge ▷ *n* severe beating ▷ *adv* extremely
**WHACKINGS** >WHACKING
**WHACKO** *n* mad person
**WHACKOES** >WHACKO
**WHACKOS** >WHACKO
**WHACKS** >WHACK
**WHACKY** *variant spelling of* >WACKY
**WHAE** *same as* >WHA
**WHAISLE** *Scots form of* >WHEEZE
**WHAISLED** >WHAISLE
**WHAISLES** >WHAISLE
**WHAISLING** >WHAISLE
**WHAIZLE** *same as* >WHAISLE
**WHAIZLED** >WHAIZLE
**WHAIZLES** >WHAIZLE
**WHAIZLING** >WHAIZLE
**WHAKAIRO** *n* art of carving
**WHAKAIROS** >WHAKAIRO
**WHAKAPAPA** *n* genealogy
**WHALE** *n* large fish-shaped sea mammal ▷ *vb* hunt for whales
**WHALEBACK** *n* something shaped like the back of a whale
**WHALEBOAT** *n* narrow boat from 20 to 30 feet long having a sharp prow and stern, formerly used in whaling
**WHALEBONE** *n* horny substance hanging from the upper jaw of toothless whales
**WHALED** >WHALE
**WHALELIKE** >WHALE
**WHALEMAN** *n* person

employed in whaling
**WHALEMEN** >WHALEMAN
**WHALER** *n* ship or person involved in whaling
**WHALERIES** >WHALERY
**WHALERS** >WHALER
**WHALERY** *n* whaling
**WHALES** >WHALE
**WHALING** *n* hunting of whales for food and oil ▷ *adv* extremely
**WHALINGS** >WHALING
**WHALLY** *adj* (of eyes) with light-coloured irises
**WHAM** *interj* expression indicating suddenness or forcefulness ▷ *n* forceful blow or impact or the sound produced by such a blow or impact ▷ *vb* strike or cause to strike with great force
**WHAMMED** >WHAM
**WHAMMIES** >WHAMMY
**WHAMMING** >WHAM
**WHAMMO** *n* sound of a sudden collision
**WHAMMOS** >WHAMMO
**WHAMMY** *n* devastating setback
**WHAMO** *same as* >WHAMMO
**WHAMPLE** *n* strike
**WHAMPLES** >WHAMPLE
**WHAMS** >WHAM
**WHANAU** *n* (in Māori societies) a family, esp an extended family
**WHANAUS** >WHANAU
**WHANG** *vb* strike or be struck so as to cause a resounding noise ▷ *n* resounding noise produced by a heavy blow
**WHANGAM** *n* imaginary creature
**WHANGAMS** >WHANGAM
**WHANGED** >WHANG
**WHANGEE** *n* tall woody grass grown for its stems, which are used for bamboo canes
**WHANGEES** >WHANGEE
**WHANGING** >WHANG
**WHANGS** >WHANG
**WHAP** *same as* >WHOP
**WHAPPED** >WHAP
**WHAPPER** *same as* >WHOPPER
**WHAPPERS** >WHAPPER
**WHAPPING** >WHAP
**WHAPS** >WHAP
**WHARE** *n* Māori hut or dwelling place
**WHARENUI** *n* (in New Zealand) meeting house
**WHARENUIS** >WHARENUI
**WHAREPUNI** *n* (in a Māori community) a tall carved building used as a guesthouse
**WHARES** >WHARE
**WHARF** *n* platform at a harbour for loading and unloading ships ▷ *vb* put (goods, etc) on a wharf

**WHARFAGE** *n* accommodation for ships at wharves
**WHARFAGES** >WHARFAGE
**WHARFED** >WHARF
**WHARFIE** *n* person employed to load and unload ships
**WHARFIES** >WHARFIE
**WHARFING** >WHARF
**WHARFINGS** >WHARF
**WHARFS** >WHARF
**WHARVE** *n* wooden disc or wheel on a shaft serving as a flywheel or pulley
**WHARVES** >WHARVE
**WHAT** *pron* which thing ▷ *interj* exclamation of anger, surprise, etc ▷ *adv* in which way, how much ▷ *n* part; portion
**WHATA** *n* building on stilts or a raised platform for storing provisions
**WHATAS** >WHATA
**WHATEN** *adj* what; what kind of
**WHATEVER** *pron* everything or anything that ▷ *adj* intensive form of *what* ▷ *determiner* intensive form of *what* ▷ *interj* expression used to show indifference or dismissal
**WHATNA** *another word for* >WHATEN
**WHATNESS** *n* what something is
**WHATNOT** *n* similar unspecified thing
**WHATNOTS** >WHATNOT
**WHATS** >WHAT
**WHATSIS** *US form of* >WHATSIT
**WHATSISES** >WHATSIS
**WHATSIT** *n* person or thing the name of which is unknown, temporarily forgotten, or deliberately overlooked
**WHATSITS** >WHATSIT
**WHATSO** *n* of whatever kind
**WHATTEN** *same as* >WHATEN
**WHAUP** *n* curlew
**WHAUPS** >WHAUP
**WHAUR** *Scot word for* >WHERE
**WHAURS** >WHAUR
**WHEAL** *same as* >WEAL
**WHEALS** >WHEAL
**WHEAR** *obsolete variant of* >WHERE
**WHEARE** *obsolete variant of* >WHERE
**WHEAT** *n* grain used in making flour, bread, and pasta
**WHEATEAR** *n* small songbird
**WHEATEARS** >WHEATEAR
**WHEATEN** *n* type of dog ▷ *adj* made of the grain or flour of wheat
**WHEATENS** >WHEATEN
**WHEATIER** >WHEATY

**WHEATIEST** >WHEATY

**WHEATLAND** *n* region where wheat is grown

**WHEATLESS** >WHEAT

**WHEATMEAL** *n* brown, but not wholemeal, flour

**WHEATS** >WHEAT

**WHEATWORM** *n* parasitic nematode worm that forms galls in the seeds of wheat

**WHEATY** *adj* having a wheat-like taste

**WHEE** *interj* exclamation of joy, thrill, etc

**WHEECH** *vb* move quickly

**WHEECHED** >WHEECH

**WHEECHING** >WHEECH

**WHEECHS** >WHEECH

**WHEEDLE** *vb* coax or cajole

**WHEEDLED** >WHEEDLE

**WHEEDLER** >WHEEDLE

**WHEEDLERS** >WHEEDLE

**WHEEDLES** >WHEEDLE

**WHEEDLING** >WHEEDLE

**WHEEL** *n* disc that revolves on an axle ▷ *vb* push or pull (something with wheels)

**WHEELBASE** *n* distance between a vehicle's front and back axles

**WHEELED** *adj* having or equipped with a wheel or wheels

**WHEELER** *n* horse or other draught animal nearest the wheel

**WHEELERS** >WHEELER

**WHEELIE** *n* manoeuvre on a bike in which the front wheel is raised off the ground

**WHEELIER** >WHEELY

**WHEELIES** >WHEELIE

**WHEELIEST** >WHEELY

**WHEELING** >WHEEL

**WHEELINGS** >WHEEL

**WHEELLESS** *adj* having no wheels

**WHEELMAN** *n* helmsman

**WHEELMEN** >WHEELMAN

**WHEELS** >WHEEL

**WHEELSMAN** *same as* >WHEELMAN

**WHEELSMEN** >WHEELSMAN

**WHEELWORK** *n* arrangement of wheels in a machine, esp a train of gears

**WHEELY** *adj* resembling a wheel

**WHEEN** *n* few

**WHEENGE** *Scots form of* >WHINGE

**WHEENGED** >WHEENGE

**WHEENGES** >WHEENGE

**WHEENGING** >WHEENGE

**WHEENS** >WHEEN

**WHEEP** *vb* fly quickly and lightly

**WHEEPED** >WHEEP

**WHEEPING** >WHEEP

**WHEEPLE** *vb* whistle weakly

**WHEEPLED** >WHEEPLE

**WHEEPLES** >WHEEPLE

**WHEEPLING** >WHEEPLE

**WHEEPS** >WHEEP

**WHEESH** *vb* silence (a person, noise, etc) or be silenced

**WHEESHED** >WHEESH

**WHEESHES** >WHEESH

**WHEESHING** >WHEESH

**WHEESHT** *same as* >WHEESH

**WHEESHTED** >WHEESHT

**WHEESHTS** >WHEESHT

**WHEEZE** *vb* breathe with a hoarse whistling noise ▷ *n* wheezing sound

**WHEEZED** >WHEEZE

**WHEEZER** >WHEEZE

**WHEEZERS** >WHEEZE

**WHEEZES** >WHEEZE

**WHEEZIER** >WHEEZE

**WHEEZIEST** >WHEEZE

**WHEEZILY** >WHEEZE

**WHEEZING** >WHEEZE

**WHEEZINGS** >WHEEZE

**WHEEZLE** *vb* make hoarse breathing sound

**WHEEZLED** >WHEEZLE

**WHEEZLES** >WHEEZLE

**WHEEZLING** >WHEEZLE

**WHEEZY** >WHEEZE

**WHEFT** *same as* >WAFT

**WHEFTS** >WHEFT

**WHELK** *n* edible snail-like shellfish

**WHELKED** *adj* having or covered with whelks

**WHELKIER** >WHELK

**WHELKIEST** >WHELK

**WHELKS** >WHELK

**WHELKY** >WHELK

**WHELM** *vb* engulf entirely with or as if with water

**WHELMED** >WHELM

**WHELMING** >WHELM

**WHELMS** >WHELM

**WHELP** *n* pup or cub ▷ *vb* (of an animal) give birth

**WHELPED** >WHELP

**WHELPING** >WHELP

**WHELPLESS** >WHELP

**WHELPS** >WHELP

**WHEMMLE** *vb* overturn

**WHEMMLED** >WHEMMLE

**WHEMMLES** >WHEMMLE

**WHEMMLING** >WHEMMLE

**WHEN** *adv* at what time? ▷ *pron* at which time ▷ *n* question of when

**WHENAS** *conj* while; inasmuch as

**WHENCE** *n* point of origin ▷ *adv* from what place or source ▷ *pron* from what place, cause, or origin

**WHENCES** >WHENCE

**WHENCEVER** *adv* out of whatsoever place, cause or origin

**WHENEVER** *adv* at whatever time

**WHENS** >WHEN

**WHENUA** *n* land

**WHENUAS** >WHENUA

**WHENWE** *n* White

immigrant from Zimbabwe, caricatured as being tiresomely over-reminiscent of happier times

**WHENWES** >WHENWE

**WHERE** *adv* in, at, or to what place? ▷ *pron* in, at, or to which place ▷ *n* question as to the position, direction, or destination of something

**WHEREAS** *n* testimonial introduced by whereas

**WHEREASES** >WHEREAS

**WHEREAT** *adv* at or to which place

**WHEREBY** *pron* by which ▷ *adv* how? by what means?

**WHEREFOR** *adv* for which

**WHEREFORE** *adv* why ▷ *n* explanation or reason

**WHEREFROM** *adv* from what or where? whence? ▷ *pron* from which place

**WHEREIN** *adv* in what place or respect? ▷ *pron* in which place or thing

**WHEREINTO** *adv* into what place? ▷ *pron* into which place

**WHERENESS** *n* state of having a place

**WHEREOF** *adv* of what or which person or thing? ▷ *pron* of which person or thing

**WHEREON** *adv* on what thing or place? ▷ *pron* on which thing, place, etc

**WHEREOUT** *adv* out of which

**WHERES** >WHERE

**WHERESO** *adv* in or to unspecified place

**WHERETO** *adv* towards what (place, end, etc)? ▷ *pron* which

**WHEREUNTO** *same as* >WHERETO

**WHEREUPON** *adv* upon what?

**WHEREVER** *adv* at whatever place ▷ *pron* at, in, or to every place or point which

**WHEREWITH** *pron* with or by which ▷ *adv* with what?

**WHERRET** *vb* strike (someone) a blow ▷ *n* blow, esp a slap on the face

**WHERRETED** >WHERRET

**WHERRETS** >WHERRET

**WHERRIED** >WHERRY

**WHERRIES** >WHERRY

**WHERRIT** *vb* worry or cause to worry

**WHERRITED** >WHERRIT

**WHERRITS** >WHERRIT

**WHERRY** *n* any of certain kinds of half-decked commercial boats, such as barges, used in Britain ▷ *vb* travel in a wherry

**WHERRYING** >WHERRY

**WHERRYMAN** >WHERRY

**WHERRYMEN** >WHERRY

**WHERVE** *same as* >WHARVE

**WHERVES** >WHERVE

**WHET** *vb* sharpen (a tool) ▷ *n* act of whetting

**WHETHER** *conj* used to introduce any indirect question

**WHETS** >WHET

**WHETSTONE** *n* stone for sharpening tools

**WHETTED** >WHET

**WHETTER** >WHET

**WHETTERS** >WHET

**WHETTING** >WHET

**WHEUGH** *same as* >WHEW

**WHEUGHED** >WHEUGH

**WHEUGHING** >WHEUGH

**WHEUGHS** >WHEUGH

**WHEW** *interj* exclamation expressing relief, delight, etc ▷ *vb* express relief

**WHEWED** >WHEW

**WHEWING** >WHEW

**WHEWS** >WHEW

**WHEY** *n* watery liquid that separates from the curd when milk is clotted

**WHEYEY** >WHEY

**WHEYFACE** *n* pale bloodless face

**WHEYFACED** >WHEYFACE

**WHEYFACES** >WHEYFACE

**WHEYIER** >WHEY

**WHEYIEST** >WHEY

**WHEYISH** >WHEY

**WHEYLIKE** >WHEY

**WHEYS** >WHEY

**WHICH** *pron* used to request or refer to a choice from different possibilities ▷ *adj* used with a noun in requesting that the particular thing being referred to is further identified or distinguished

**WHICHEVER** *pron* any out of several ▷ *adj* any out of several ▷ *determiner* any (one, two, etc, out of several)

**WHICKER** *vb* (of a horse) to whinny or neigh

**WHICKERED** >WHICKER

**WHICKERS** >WHICKER

**WHID** *vb* move quickly

**WHIDAH** *same as* >WHYDAH

**WHIDAHS** >WHIDAH

**WHIDDED** >WHID

**WHIDDER** *vb* move with force

**WHIDDERED** >WHIDDER

**WHIDDERS** >WHIDDER

**WHIDDING** >WHID

**WHIDS** >WHID

**WHIFF** *n* puff of air or odour ▷ *vb* come, convey, or go in whiffs

**WHIFFED** >WHIFF

**WHIFFER** >WHIFF

**WHIFFERS** >WHIFF

**WHIFFET** *n* insignificant person

WHIFFETS >WHIFFET
WHIFFIER >WHIFFY
WHIFFIEST >WHIFFY
WHIFFING >WHIFF
WHIFFINGS >WHIFF
WHIFFLE vb think or
behave in an erratic or
unpredictable way
WHIFFLED >WHIFFLE
WHIFFLER n person who
whiffles
WHIFFLERS >WHIFFLER
WHIFFLERY n frivolity
WHIFFLES >WHIFFLE
WHIFFLING >WHIFFLE
WHIFFS >WHIFF
WHIFFY adj smelly
WHIFT n brief emission
of air
WHIFTS >WHIFT
WHIG vb go quickly
WHIGGED >WHIG
WHIGGING >WHIG
WHIGS >WHIG
WHILE n period of time
WHILED >WHILE
WHILERE adv a while ago
WHILES adv at times
WHILING >WHILE
WHILK archaic and dialect
word for >WHICH
WHILLIED >WHILLY
WHILLIES >WHILLY
WHILLY vb influence by
flattery
WHILLYING >WHILLY
WHILLYWHA variant
of >WHILLY
WHILOM adv formerly ▷ adj
one-time
WHILST same as >WHILE
WHIM n sudden fancy ▷ vb
have a whim
WHIMBERRY n whortleberry
WHIMBREL n small
European curlew with a
striped head
WHIMBRELS >WHIMBREL
WHIMMED >WHIM
WHIMMIER >WHIMMY
WHIMMIEST >WHIMMY
WHIMMING >WHIM
WHIMMY adj having whims
WHIMPER vb cry in a soft
whining way ▷ n soft
plaintive whine
WHIMPERED >WHIMPER
WHIMPERER >WHIMPER
WHIMPERS >WHIMPER
WHIMPLE same as >WIMPLE
WHIMPLED >WHIMPLE
WHIMPLES >WHIMPLE
WHIMPLING >WHIMPLE
WHIMS >WHIM
WHIMSEY same as >WHIMSY
WHIMSEYS >WHIMSEY
WHIMSICAL adj unusual,
playful, and fanciful
WHIMSIED >WHIMSY
WHIMSIER >WHIMSY
WHIMSIES >WHIMSY
WHIMSIEST >WHIMSY
WHIMSILY >WHIMSY
WHIMSY n capricious idea

▷ adj quaint, comical,
or unusual, often in a
tasteless way
WHIN n gorse
WHINBERRY same
as >WHIMBERRY
WHINCHAT n type of
songbird
WHINCHATS >WHINCHAT
WHINE n high-pitched
plaintive cry ▷ vb make
such a sound
WHINED >WHINE
WHINER >WHINE
WHINERS >WHINE
WHINES >WHINE
WHINEY same as >WHINY
WHINGDING same
as >WINGDING
WHINGE vb complain ▷ n
complaint
WHINGED >WHINGE
WHINGEING >WHINGE
WHINGER >WHINGE
WHINGERS >WHINGE
WHINGES >WHINGE
WHINGING >WHINGE
WHINIARD same
as >WHINYARD
WHINIARDS >WHINIARD
WHINIER >WHINY
WHINIEST >WHINY
WHININESS >WHINY
WHINING >WHINE
WHININGLY >WHINE
WHININGS >WHINE
WHINNIED >WHINNY
WHINNIER >WHINNY
WHINNIES >WHINNY
WHINNIEST >WHINNY
WHINNY vb neigh softly ▷ n
soft neigh ▷ adj covered
in whin
WHINNYING >WHINNY
WHINS >WHIN
WHINSTONE n any dark hard
fine-grained rock, such as
basalt
WHINY adj high-pitched
and plaintive
WHINYARD n sword
WHINYARDS >WHINYARD
WHIO n New Zealand
mountain duck with blue
plumage
WHIP n cord attached to a
handle, used for beating
animals or people ▷ vb
strike with a whip, strap,
or cane
WHIPBIRD n any of several
birds having a whistle
ending in a whipcrack
note
WHIPBIRDS >WHIPBIRD
WHIPCAT n tailor
WHIPCATS >WHIPCAT
WHIPCORD n strong
worsted or cotton fabric
with a diagonally ribbed
surface
WHIPCORDS >WHIPCORD
WHIPCORDY adj whipcord-
like

WHIPJACK n beggar
imitating a sailor
WHIPJACKS >WHIPJACK
WHIPLASH n quick lash of
a whip
WHIPLIKE >WHIP
WHIPPED >WHIP
WHIPPER >WHIP
WHIPPERS >WHIP
WHIPPET n racing dog like a
small greyhound
WHIPPETS >WHIPPET
WHIPPIER >WHIPPY
WHIPPIEST >WHIPPY
WHIPPING >WHIP
WHIPPINGS >WHIP
WHIPPY adj springy
WHIPRAY n stingray
WHIPRAYS >WHIPRAY
WHIPS >WHIP
WHIPSAW n any saw with
a flexible blade, such as a
bandsaw ▷ vb saw with a
whipsaw
WHIPSAWED >WHIPSAW
WHIPSAWN >WHIPSAW
WHIPSAWS >WHIPSAW
WHIPSNAKE n thin snake
like leather whip
WHIPSTAFF n ship's
steering bar
WHIPSTALL n stall in which
an aircraft goes into a
nearly vertical climb,
pauses, slips backwards
momentarily, and drops
suddenly with its nose
down
WHIPSTER n insignificant
but pretentious or cheeky
person, esp a young one
WHIPSTERS >WHIPSTER
WHIPSTOCK n handle of a
whip
WHIPT old past tense
of >WHIP
WHIPTAIL n type of lizard
WHIPTAILS >WHIPTAIL
WHIPWORM n parasitic
worm living in the
intestines of mammals
WHIPWORMS >WHIPWORM
WHIR n prolonged soft
swish or buzz, as of a
motor working or wings
flapping ▷ vb make or
cause to make a whir
WHIRL vb spin or revolve
▷ n whirling movement
WHIRLBAT n thing moved
with a whirl
WHIRLBATS >WHIRLBAT
WHIRLED >WHIRL
WHIRLER >WHIRL
WHIRLERS >WHIRL
WHIRLIER >WHIRLY
WHIRLIES n illness induced
by excessive use of alcohol
or drugs
WHIRLIEST >WHIRLY
WHIRLIGIG same
as >WINDMILL
WHIRLING >WHIRL
WHIRLINGS >WHIRL

WHIRLPOOL n strong
circular current of water
WHIRLS >WHIRL
WHIRLWIND n column of
air whirling violently
upwards in a spiral ▷ adj
much quicker than normal
WHIRLY adj characterized
by whirling
WHIRR same as >WHIR
WHIRRED >WHIR
WHIRRET vb strike with
sharp blow
WHIRRETED >WHIRRET
WHIRRETS >WHIRRET
WHIRRIED >WHIRRY
WHIRRIES >WHIRRY
WHIRRING >WHIR
WHIRRINGS >WHIR
WHIRRS >WHIRR
WHIRRY vb move quickly
WHIRRYING >WHIRRY
WHIRS >WHIR
WHIRTLE same as >WORTLE
WHIRTLES >WHIRTLE
WHISH less common word
for >SWISH
WHISHED >WHISH
WHISHES >WHISH
WHISHING >WHISH
WHISHT interj hush! be
quiet! ▷ adj silent or still
▷ vb make or become
silent
WHISHTED >WHISHT
WHISHTING >WHISHT
WHISHTS >WHISHT
WHISK vb move or remove
quickly ▷ n quick
movement
WHISKED >WHISK
WHISKER n any of the long
stiff hairs on the face of a
cat or other mammal
WHISKERED adj having
whiskers
WHISKERS >WHISKER
WHISKERY adj having
whiskers
WHISKET same as >WISKET
WHISKETS >WHISKET
WHISKEY n Irish or
American whisky
WHISKEYS >WHISKEY
WHISKIES >WHISKY
WHISKING >WHISK
WHISKS >WHISK
WHISKY n spirit distilled
from fermented cereals
WHISPER vb speak softly,
without vibration of the
vocal cords ▷ n soft voice
WHISPERED >WHISPER
WHISPERER n person or
thing that whispers
WHISPERS >WHISPER
WHISPERY >WHISPER
WHISS vb hiss
WHISSED >WHISS
WHISSES >WHISS
WHISSING >WHISS
WHIST same as >WHISHT
WHISTED >WHIST
WHISTING >WHIST

WHISTLE vb produce a shrill sound, esp by forcing the breath through pursed lips ▷ n whistling sound
WHISTLED >WHISTLE
WHISTLER n person or thing that whistles
WHISTLERS >WHISTLER
WHISTLES >WHISTLE
WHISTLING >WHISTLE
WHISTS >WHIST
WHIT n smallest particle
WHITE adj of the colour of snow ▷ n colour of snow
WHITEBAIT n small edible fish
WHITEBASS n type of fish
WHITEBEAM n type of tree
WHITECAP n wave with a white broken crest
WHITECAPS >WHITECAP
WHITECOAT n person who wears a white coat
WHITECOMB n fungal disease infecting the combs of certain fowls
WHITED as in whited sepulchre hypocrite
WHITEDAMP n mixture of poisonous gases, mainly carbon monoxide, occurring in coal mines
WHITEFACE n white stage make-up
WHITEFISH n type of fish
WHITEFLY n tiny whitish insect that is harmful to greenhouse plants
WHITEHEAD n type of pimple with a white head
WHITELY >WHITE
WHITEN vb make or become white or whiter
WHITENED >WHITEN
WHITENER n substance that makes something white or whiter
WHITENERS >WHITENER
WHITENESS >WHITE
WHITENING >WHITEN
WHITENS >WHITEN
WHITEOUT n atmospheric condition in which blizzards or low clouds make it very difficult to see
WHITEOUTS >WHITEOUT
WHITEPOT n custard or milk pudding
WHITEPOTS >WHITEPOT
WHITER >WHITE
WHITES pl n white clothes, as worn for playing cricket
WHITEST >WHITE
WHITETAIL n type of deer
WHITEWALL n pneumatic tyre having white sidewalls
WHITEWARE n white ceramics
WHITEWASH n substance for whitening walls ▷ vb cover with whitewash
WHITEWING n type of bird
WHITEWOOD n light-coloured wood often prepared for staining
WHITEY same as >WHITY
WHITEYS >WHITEY
WHITHER same as >WUTHER
WHITHERED >WHITHER
WHITHERS >WHITHER
WHITIER >WHITY
WHITIES >WHITY
WHITIEST >WHITY
WHITING n edible sea fish
WHITINGS >WHITING
WHITISH >WHITE
WHITLING n type of trout
WHITLINGS >WHITLING
WHITLOW n inflamed sore on a finger or toe, esp round a nail
WHITLOWS >WHITLOW
WHITRACK n weasel or stoat
WHITRACKS >WHITRACK
WHITRET n variant of whittret
WHITRETS >WHITRET
WHITRICK n dialect word for a male weasel
WHITRICKS >WHITRICK
WHITS >WHIT
WHITSTER n person who whitens clothes
WHITSTERS >WHITSTER
WHITTAW same as >WHITTAWER
WHITTAWER n person who treats leather
WHITTAWS >WHITTAW
WHITTER variant spelling of >WITTER
WHITTERED >WHITTER
WHITTERS >WHITTER
WHITTLE vb cut or carve (wood) with a knife ▷ n knife, esp a large one
WHITTLED >WHITTLE
WHITTLER >WHITTLE
WHITTLERS >WHITTLE
WHITTLES >WHITTLE
WHITTLING >WHITTLE
WHITTRET n male weasel
WHITTRETS >WHITTRET
WHITY adj of a white colour ▷ n derogatory term for a White person
WHIZ same as >WHIZZ
WHIZBANG n small-calibre shell
WHIZBANGS >WHIZBANG
WHIZZ vb make a loud buzzing sound ▷ n loud buzzing sound
WHIZZBANG same as >WHIZBANG
WHIZZED >WHIZZ
WHIZZER >WHIZZ
WHIZZERS >WHIZZ
WHIZZES >WHIZZ
WHIZZIER >WHIZZY
WHIZZIEST >WHIZZY
WHIZZING >WHIZZ
WHIZZINGS >WHIZZ
WHIZZY adj using sophisticated technology to produce vivid effects

WHO pron which person
WHOA interj command used, esp to horses, to stop or slow down
WHODUNIT same as >WHODUNNIT
WHODUNITS >WHODUNIT
WHODUNNIT n detective story, play, or film
WHOEVER pron any person who
WHOLE adj containing all the elements or parts ▷ n complete thing or system
WHOLEFOOD n food that has been processed as little as possible ▷ adj of or relating to wholefood
WHOLEMEAL adj (of flour) made from the whole wheat grain
WHOLENESS >WHOLE
WHOLES >WHOLE
WHOLESALE adv dealing by selling goods in large quantities to retailers ▷ n business of selling goods in large quantities and at lower prices to retailers for resale
WHOLESOME adj physically or morally beneficial
WHOLISM same as >HOLISM
WHOLISMS >WHOLISM
WHOLIST same as >HOLIST
WHOLISTIC same as >HOLISTIC
WHOLISTS >WHOLIST
WHOLLY adv completely or totally
WHOM pron objective form of who
WHOMBLE same as >WHEMMLE
WHOMBLED >WHOMBLE
WHOMBLES >WHOMBLE
WHOMBLING >WHOMBLE
WHOMEVER pron objective form of whoever
WHOMMLE same as >WHEMMLE
WHOMMLED >WHOMMLE
WHOMMLES >WHOMMLE
WHOMMLING >WHOMMLE
WHOMP vb strike; thump
WHOMPED >WHOMP
WHOMPING >WHOMP
WHOMPS >WHOMP
WHOMSO pron whom; whomever
WHOOBUB same as >HUBBUB
WHOOBUBS >WHOOBUB
WHOOF same as >WOOF
WHOOFED >WHOOF
WHOOFING >WHOOF
WHOOFS >WHOOF
WHOOP n shout or cry to express excitement ▷ vb emit a whoop
WHOOPED >WHOOP
WHOOPEE n cry of joy
WHOOPEES >WHOOPEE
WHOOPER n type of swan
WHOOPERS >WHOOPER

WHOOPIE same as >WHOOPEE
WHOOPIES >WHOOPIE
WHOOPING >WHOOP
WHOOPINGS >WHOOPING
WHOOPLA n commotion; fuss
WHOOPLAS >WHOOPLA
WHOOPS interj exclamation of surprise or of apology
WHOOPSIE n animal excrement
WHOOPSIES >WHOOPSIE
WHOOSH n hissing or rushing sound ▷ vb make or move with a hissing or rushing sound
WHOOSHED >WHOOSH
WHOOSHES >WHOOSH
WHOOSHING >WHOOSH
WHOOSIS n thingamajig
WHOOSISES >WHOOSIS
WHOOT obsolete variant of >HOOT
WHOOTED >WHOOT
WHOOTING >WHOOT
WHOOTS >WHOOT
WHOP vb strike, beat, or thrash ▷ n heavy blow or the sound made by such a blow
WHOPPED >WHOP
WHOPPER n anything unusually large
WHOPPERS >WHOPPER
WHOPPING n beating as punishment ▷ adj unusually large ▷ adv extremely
WHOPPINGS >WHOPPING
WHOPS >WHOP
WHORE n prostitute ▷ vb be or act as a prostitute
WHORED >WHORE
WHOREDOM n activity of whoring or state of being a whore
WHOREDOMS >WHOREDOM
WHORES >WHORE
WHORESON n bastard ▷ adj vile or hateful
WHORESONS >WHORESON
WHORING >WHORE
WHORISH >WHORE
WHORISHLY >WHORE
WHORL n ring of leaves or petals
WHORLBAT same as >WHIRLBAT
WHORLBATS >WHIRLBAT
WHORLED >WHORL
WHORLS >WHORL
WHORT n small shrub bearing blackish edible sweet berries
WHORTLE n whortleberry
WHORTLES >WHORTLE
WHORTS >WHORT
WHOSE pron of whom or of which ▷ determiner of whom? belonging to whom?
WHOSEVER pron belonging to whoever

**WHOSIS** *n* thingamajig
**WHOSISES** >WHOSIS
**WHOSO** *archaic word for* >WHOEVER
**WHOSOEVER** *same as* >WHOEVER
**WHOT** *obsolete variant of* >HOT
**WHOW** *interj* wow
**WHUMMLE** *vb* variant of whemmle
**WHUMMLED** >WHUMMLE
**WHUMMLES** >WHUMMLE
**WHUMMLING** >WHUMMLE
**WHUMP** *vb* make a dull thud ▷ *n* dull thud
**WHUMPED** >WHUMP
**WHUMPING** >WHUMP
**WHUMPS** >WHUMP
**WHUNSTANE** *Scots variant of* >WHINSTONE
**WHUP** *vb* defeat totally
**WHUPPED** >WHUP
**WHUPPING** >WHUP
**WHUPS** >WHUP
**WHY** *adv* for what reason ▷ *pron* because of which ▷ *n* reason, purpose, or cause of something
**WHYDAH** *n* type of black African bird
**WHYDAHS** >WHYDAH
**WHYDUNIT** *same as* >WHYDUNNIT
**WHYDUNITS** >WHYDUNIT
**WHYDUNNIT** *n* novel, film, etc, concerned with the motives of the criminal rather than his or her identity
**WHYEVER** *adv* for whatever reason
**WHYS** >WHY
**WIBBLE** *vb* wobble
**WIBBLED** >WIBBLE
**WIBBLES** >WIBBLE
**WIBBLING** >WIBBLE
**WICCA** *n* cult or practice of witchcraft
**WICCAN** *n* member of wicca
**WICCANS** >WICCAN
**WICCAS** >WICCA
**WICE** *Scots form of* >WISE
**WICH** *n* variant of wych
**WICHES** >WICH
**WICK** *n* cord through a lamp or candle which carries fuel to the flame ▷ *adj* lively or active ▷ *vb* (of a material) draw in (water, fuel, etc)
**WICKAPE** *same as* >WICOPY
**WICKAPES** >WICKAPE
**WICKED** *adj* morally bad ▷ *n* wicked person
**WICKEDER** >WICKED
**WICKEDEST** >WICKED
**WICKEDLY** >WICKED
**WICKEDS** >WICKED
**WICKEN** *variant of* >QUICKEN
**WICKENS** >WICKEN
**WICKER** *adj* made of woven cane ▷ *n* slender flexible twig or shoot, esp of

willow
**WICKERED** >WICKER
**WICKERS** >WICKER
**WICKET** *n* set of three cricket stumps and two bails
**WICKETS** >WICKET
**WICKIES** >WICKY
**WICKING** >WICK
**WICKINGS** >WICK
**WICKIUP** *n* crude shelter made of brushwood, mats, or grass and having an oval frame
**WICKIUPS** >WICKIUP
**WICKLESS** >WICK
**WICKS** >WICK
**WICKTHING** *n* creeping animal, such as a woodlouse
**WICKY** *same as* >QUICKEN
**WICKYUP** *same as* >WICKIUP
**WICKYUPS** >WICKYUP
**WICOPIES** >WICOPY
**WICOPY** *n* any of various N American trees, shrubs, or herbaceous plants
**WIDDER** *same as* >WIDOW
**WIDDERS** >WIDDER
**WIDDIE** *same as* >WIDDY
**WIDDIES** >WIDDY
**WIDDLE** *vb* urinate ▷ *n* urine
**WIDDLED** >WIDDLE
**WIDDLES** >WIDDLE
**WIDDLING** >WIDDLE
**WIDDY** *vb* rope made of twigs
**WIDE** *adj* large from side to side ▷ *adv* the full extent ▷ *n* (in cricket) a bowled ball ruled to be outside a batsman's reach
**WIDEAWAKE** *n* hat with a low crown and a very wide brim
**WIDEBAND** *n* wide bandwidth transmission medium
**WIDEBODY** *n* aircraft with a wide fuselage
**WIDELY** >WIDE
**WIDEN** *vb* make or become wider
**WIDENED** >WIDEN
**WIDENER** >WIDEN
**WIDENERS** >WIDEN
**WIDENESS** >WIDE
**WIDENING** >WIDEN
**WIDENS** >WIDEN
**WIDEOUT** *n* footballer who catches passes from the quarterback
**WIDEOUTS** >WIDEOUT
**WIDER** >WIDE
**WIDES** >WIDE
**WIDEST** >WIDE
**WIDGEON** *same as* >WIGEON
**WIDGEONS** >WIDGEON
**WIDGET** *n* any small device, the name of which is unknown or forgotten
**WIDGETS** >WIDGET
**WIDGIE** *n* female larrikin or

bodgie
**WIDGIES** >WIDGIE
**WIDISH** >WIDE
**WIDOW** *n* woman whose husband is dead and who has not remarried ▷ *vb* cause to become a widow
**WIDOWBIRD** *n* whydah
**WIDOWED** >WIDOW
**WIDOWER** *n* man whose wife is dead and who has not remarried
**WIDOWERED** >WIDOWER
**WIDOWERS** >WIDOWER
**WIDOWHOOD** >WIDOW
**WIDOWING** >WIDOW
**WIDOWMAN** *n* widower
**WIDOWMEN** >WIDOWMAN
**WIDOWS** >WIDOW
**WIDTH** *n* distance from side to side
**WIDTHS** >WIDTH
**WIDTHWAY** *adj* across the width
**WIDTHWAYS** *same as* >WIDTHWISE
**WIDTHWISE** *adv* in the direction of the width
**WIEL** *same as* >WEEL
**WIELD** *vb* hold and use (a weapon)
**WIELDABLE** >WIELD
**WIELDED** >WIELD
**WIELDER** >WIELD
**WIELDERS** >WIELD
**WIELDIER** >WIELDY
**WIELDIEST** >WIELDY
**WIELDING** >WIELD
**WIELDLESS** *adj* unwieldy
**WIELDS** >WIELD
**WIELDY** *adj* easily handled, used, or managed
**WIELS** >WIEL
**WIENER** *n* kind of smoked beef or pork sausage, similar to a frankfurter
**WIENERS** >WIENER
**WIENIE** *same as* >WIENER
**WIENIES** >WIENIE
**WIFE** *n* woman to whom a man is married ▷ *vb* marry
**WIFED** >WIFE
**WIFEDOM** *n* state of being a wife
**WIFEDOMS** >WIFEDOM
**WIFEHOOD** >WIFE
**WIFEHOODS** >WIFE
**WIFELESS** >WIFE
**WIFELIER** >WIFE
**WIFELIEST** >WIFE
**WIFELIKE** >WIFE
**WIFELY** >WIFE
**WIFES** >WIFE
**WIFEY** *n* wife
**WIFEYS** >WIFEY
**WIFIE** *n* woman
**WIFIES** >WIFIE
**WIFING** >WIFE
**WIFTIER** >WIFTY
**WIFTIEST** >WIFTY
**WIFTY** *adj* scatterbrained
**WIG** *n* artificial head of hair ▷ *vb* furnish with a wig

**WIGAN** *n* stiff fabric
**WIGANS** >WIGAN
**WIGEON** *n* duck found in marshland
**WIGEONS** >WIGEON
**WIGGA** *same as* >WIGGER
**WIGGAS** >WIGGA
**WIGGED** >WIG
**WIGGER** *n* white youth who adopts Black youth culture
**WIGGERIES** >WIGGERY
**WIGGERS** >WIGGER
**WIGGERY** *n* wigs
**WIGGIER** >WIGGY
**WIGGIEST** >WIGGY
**WIGGING** >WIG
**WIGGINGS** >WIG
**WIGGLE** *vb* move jerkily from side to side ▷ *n* wiggling movement
**WIGGLED** >WIGGLE
**WIGGLER** >WIGGLE
**WIGGLERS** >WIGGLE
**WIGGLES** >WIGGLE
**WIGGLIER** >WIGGLE
**WIGGLIEST** >WIGGLE
**WIGGLING** >WIGGLE
**WIGGLY** >WIGGLE
**WIGGY** *adj* eccentric
**WIGHT** *vb* blame ▷ *n* human being ▷ *adj* strong and brave
**WIGHTED** >WIGHT
**WIGHTING** >WIGHT
**WIGHTLY** *adv* swiftly
**WIGHTS** >WIGHT
**WIGLESS** >WIG
**WIGLET** *n* small wig
**WIGLETS** >WIGLET
**WIGLIKE** >WIG
**WIGMAKER** *n* person who makes wigs
**WIGMAKERS** >WIGMAKER
**WIGS** >WIG
**WIGWAG** *vb* move (something) back and forth ▷ *n* system of communication by flag semaphore
**WIGWAGGED** >WIGWAG
**WIGWAGGER** >WIGWAG
**WIGWAGS** >WIGWAG
**WIGWAM** *n* Native American's tent
**WIGWAMS** >WIGWAM
**WIKIUP** *same as* >WICKIUP
**WIKIUPS** >WIKIUP
**WILCO** *interj* expression in telecommunications etc, indicating that the message just received will be complied with
**WILD** *same as* >WIELD
**WILDCARD** *n* person given entry to competition without qualifying
**WILDCARDS** >WILDCARD
**WILDCAT** *n* European wild animal like a large domestic cat ▷ *adj* risky and financially unsound ▷ *vb* drill for petroleum or natural gas in an area having no known reserves

WILDCATS >WILDCAT
WILDED >WILD
WILDER vb lead or be led astray
WILDERED >WILDER
WILDERING >WILDER
WILDERS >WILDER
WILDEST >WILD
WILDFIRE n highly flammable material, such as Greek fire, formerly used in warfare
WILDFIRES >WILDFIRE
WILDFOWL n wild bird that is hunted for sport or food
WILDFOWLS >WILDFOWL
WILDGRAVE same as >WALDGRAVE
WILDING n uncultivated plant, esp the crab apple, or a cultivated plant that has become wild
WILDINGS >WILDING
WILDISH >WILD
WILDLAND n land which has not been cultivated
WILDLANDS >WILDLAND
WILDLIFE n wild animals and plants collectively
WILDLIFES >WILDLIFE
WILDLING same as >WILDING
WILDLINGS >WILDLING
WILDLY >WILD
WILDNESS >WILD
WILDS >WILD
WILDWOOD n wood or forest growing in a natural uncultivated state
WILDWOODS >WILDWOOD
WILE n trickery, cunning, or craftiness ▷ vb lure, beguile, or entice
WILED >WILE
WILEFUL adj deceitful
WILES >WILE
WILFUL adj headstrong or obstinate
WILFULLY >WILFUL
WILGA n small drought-resistant tree of Australia
WILGAS >WILGA
WILI n spirit
WILIER >WILY
WILIEST >WILY
WILILY >WILY
WILINESS >WILY
WILING >WILE
WILIS >WILI
WILJA n variety of potato
WILJAS >WILJA
WILL vb used as an auxiliary to form the future tense or to indicate intention, ability, or expectation ▷ n strong determination
WILLABLE adj able to be wished or determined by the will
WILLED adj having a will as specified
WILLEMITE n secondary mineral consisting of zinc

silicate
WILLER >WILL
WILLERS >WILL
WILLEST >WILL
WILLET n large American shore bird
WILLETS >WILLET
WILLEY same as >WILLY
WILLEYED >WILLEY
WILLEYING >WILLEY
WILLEYS >WILLEY
WILLFUL same as >WILFUL
WILLFULLY >WILLFUL
WILLIAM as in sweet william flowering plant
WILLIAMS >WILLIAM
WILLIE n informal word for a penis
WILLIED >WILLY
WILLIES >WILLY
WILLING adj ready or inclined (to do something)
WILLINGER >WILLING
WILLINGLY >WILLING
WILLIWAU same as >WILLIWAW
WILLIWAUS >WILLIWAU
WILLIWAW n sudden strong gust of cold wind blowing offshore from a mountainous coast
WILLIWAWS >WILLIWAW
WILLOW n tree with thin flexible branches ▷ vb (of raw textile fibres) to open and clean in a machine having a system of rotating spikes
WILLOWED >WILLOW
WILLOWER n willow
WILLOWERS >WILLOWER
WILLOWIER >WILLOWY
WILLOWING >WILLOW
WILLOWISH >WILLOW
WILLOWS >WILLOW
WILLOWY adj slender and graceful
WILLPOWER n ability to control oneself and one's actions
WILLS >WILL
WILLY vb clean in willowing-machine
WILLYARD adj timid
WILLYART same as >WILLYARD
WILLYING >WILLY
WILLYWAW same as >WILLIWAW
WILLYWAWS >WILLYWAW
WILT vb (cause to) become limp or lose strength ▷ n act of wilting or state of becoming wilted
WILTED >WILT
WILTING >WILT
WILTJA n Aboriginal shelter
WILTJAS >WILTJA
WILTS >WILT
WILY adj crafty or sly
WIMBLE n any of a number of hand tools, such as a brace and bit or a gimlet,

used for boring holes ▷ vb bore (a hole) with or as if with a wimble
WIMBLED >WIMBLE
WIMBLES >WIMBLE
WIMBLING >WIMBLE
WIMBREL same as >WHIMBREL
WIMBRELS >WIMBREL
WIMMIN n common intentional literary misspelling of 'women'
WIMP n feeble ineffectual person ▷ vb fail to complete something through fear
WIMPED >WIMP
WIMPIER >WIMP
WIMPIEST >WIMP
WIMPINESS >WIMP
WIMPING >WIMP
WIMPISH >WIMP
WIMPISHLY >WIMP
WIMPLE n garment framing the face, worn by medieval women and now by nuns ▷ vb ripple or cause to ripple or undulate
WIMPLED >WIMPLE
WIMPLES >WIMPLE
WIMPLING >WIMPLE
WIMPS >WIMP
WIMPY >WIMP
WIN vb come first in (a competition, fight, etc) ▷ n victory, esp in a game
WINCE vb draw back, as if in pain ▷ n wincing
WINCED >WINCE
WINCER >WINCE
WINCERS >WINCE
WINCES >WINCE
WINCEY n plain- or twill-weave cloth, usually having a cotton or linen warp and a wool filling
WINCEYS >WINCEY
WINCH n machine for lifting or hauling using a cable or chain wound round a drum ▷ vb lift or haul using a winch
WINCHED >WINCH
WINCHER >WINCH
WINCHERS >WINCH
WINCHES >WINCH
WINCHING >WINCH
WINCHMAN n man who operates winch
WINCHMEN >WINCHMAN
WINCING >WINCE
WINCINGS >WINCE
WINCOPIPE n type of plant
WIND n current of air ▷ vb render short of breath
WINDABLE n able to be wound
WINDAC same as >WINDAS
WINDACS >WINDAC
WINDAGE n deflection of a projectile as a result of the effect of the wind
WINDAGES >WINDAGE

WINDAS n windlass
WINDASES >WINDAS
WINDBAG n person who talks much but uninterestingly
WINDBAGS >WINDBAG
WINDBELL n light bell made to be sounded by wind
WINDBELLS >WINDBELL
WINDBILL n bill of exchange cosigned by a guarantor
WINDBILLS >WINDBILL
WINDBLAST n strong gust of wind
WINDBLOW n trees uprooted by wind
WINDBLOWN adj blown about by the wind
WINDBLOWS >WINDBLOW
WINDBORNE adj (of plant seeds, etc) borne on the wind
WINDBOUND adj (of a sailing vessel) prevented from sailing by an unfavourable wind
WINDBREAK n fence or line of trees providing shelter from the wind
WINDBURN n irritation and redness of the skin caused by prolonged exposure to winds of high velocity
WINDBURNS >WINDBURN
WINDBURNT >WINDBURN
WINDCHILL n chilling effect of wind and low temperature
WINDED >WIND
WINDER n person or device that winds, as an engine for hoisting the cages in a mine shaft
WINDERS >WINDER
WINDFALL n unexpected good luck
WINDFALLS >WINDFALL
WINDFLAW n squall
WINDFLAWS >WINDFLAW
WINDGALL n soft swelling in the area of the fetlock joint of a horse
WINDGALLS >WINDGALL
WINDGUN n air gun
WINDGUNS >WINDGUN
WINDHOVER dialect name for >KESTREL
WINDIER >WINDY
WINDIEST >WINDY
WINDIGO same as >WENDIGO
WINDIGOS >WINDIGO
WINDILY >WINDY
WINDINESS >WINDY
WINDING >WIND
WINDINGLY >WINDING
WINDINGS >WIND
WINDLASS n winch worked by a crank ▷ vb raise or haul (a weight, etc) by means of a windlass
WINDLE vb wind something round continuously

**WINDLED** >WINDLE
**WINDLES** >WINDLE
**WINDLESS** >WIND
**WINDLING** >WINDLE
**WINDLINGS** >WINDLE
**WINDMILL** n machine for grinding or pumping driven by sails turned by the wind ▷ vb move or cause to move like the arms of a windmill
**WINDMILLS** >WINDMILL
**WINDOCK** same as >WINNOCK
**WINDOCKS** >WINDOCK
**WINDORE** n window
**WINDORES** >WINDORE
**WINDOW** n opening in a wall to let in light or air ▷ vb furnish with windows
**WINDOWED** >WINDOW
**WINDOWING** >WINDOW
**WINDOWS** >WINDOW
**WINDOWY** >WINDOW
**WINDPIPE** n tube linking the throat and the lungs
**WINDPIPES** >WINDPIPE
**WINDPROOF** n windresistant
**WINDRING** adj winding
**WINDROSE** n diagram with radiating lines showing the strength and frequency of winds from each direction affecting a specific place
**WINDROSES** >WINDROSE
**WINDROW** n long low ridge or line of hay or a similar crop, designed to achieve the best conditions for drying or curing ▷ vb put (hay or a similar crop) into windrows
**WINDROWED** >WINDROW
**WINDROWER** >WINDROW
**WINDROWS** >WINDROW
**WINDS** >WIND
**WINDSAIL** n sail rigged as an air scoop over a hatch or companionway to catch breezes and divert them below
**WINDSAILS** >WINDSAIL
**WINDSES** pl n ventilation shafts within mines
**WINDSHAKE** n crack between the annual rings in wood
**WINDSHIP** n ship propelled by wind
**WINDSHIPS** >WINDSHIP
**WINDSOCK** n cloth cone on a mast at an airfield to indicate wind direction
**WINDSOCKS** >WINDSOCK
**WINDSTORM** n storm consisting of violent winds
**WINDSURF** vb sail standing on a board equipped with a mast, sail, and boom
**WINDSURFS** >WINDSURF
**WINDSWEPT** adj exposed to the wind

**WINDTHROW** n uprooting of trees by wind
**WINDTIGHT** adj impenetrable by wind
**WINDUP** n prank or hoax
**WINDUPS** >WINDUP
**WINDWARD** n direction from which the wind is blowing ▷ adj of or in the direction from which the wind blows ▷ adv towards the wind
**WINDWARDS** adv in the direction of the wind
**WINDWAY** n part of wind instrument
**WINDWAYS** >WINDWAY
**WINDY** adj denoting a time or conditions in which there is a strong wind
**WINE** n alcoholic drink made from fermented grapes ▷ adj of a dark purplish-red colour ▷ vb give wine to
**WINEBERRY** another name for >MAKO
**WINED** >WINE
**WINEGLASS** n glass for wine, usually with a small bowl on a stem with a flared base
**WINELESS** >WINE
**WINEMAKER** n maker of wine
**WINEPRESS** n any equipment used for squeezing the juice from grapes in order to make wine
**WINERIES** >WINERY
**WINERY** n place where wine is made
**WINES** >WINE
**WINESAP** n variety of apple
**WINESAPS** >WINESAP
**WINESHOP** n shop where wine is sold
**WINESHOPS** >WINESHOP
**WINESKIN** n skin of a sheep or goat sewn up and used as a holder for wine
**WINESKINS** >WINESKIN
**WINESOP** n old word for an alcoholic
**WINESOPS** >WINESOP
**WINEY** adj having the taste or qualities of wine
**WING** n one of the limbs or organs of a bird, insect, or bat that are used for flying ▷ vb fly
**WINGBACK** n football position
**WINGBACKS** >WINGBACK
**WINGBEAT** n complete cycle of moving the wing by a bird in flight
**WINGBEATS** >WINGBEAT
**WINGBOW** n distinctive band of colour marking the wing of a bird
**WINGBOWS** >WINGBOW

**WINGCHAIR** n chair with forward projections from back
**WINGDING** n noisy lively party or festivity
**WINGDINGS** >WINGDING
**WINGE** same as >WHINGE
**WINGED** adj furnished with wings
**WINGEDLY** >WINGED
**WINGEING** >WINGE
**WINGER** n player positioned on a wing
**WINGERS** >WINGER
**WINGES** >WINGE
**WINGIER** >WINGY
**WINGIEST** >WINGY
**WINGING** >WING
**WINGLESS** adj having no wings or vestigial wings
**WINGLET** n small wing
**WINGLETS** >WINGLET
**WINGLIKE** >WING
**WINGMAN** n player in the wing position in Australian Rules
**WINGMEN** >WINGMAN
**WINGOVER** n manoeuvre in which the direction of flight of an aircraft is reversed by putting it into a climbing turn until nearly stalled, the nose then being allowed to fall while continuing the turn
**WINGOVERS** >WINGOVER
**WINGS** >WING
**WINGSPAN** n distance between the wing tips of an aircraft, bird, or insect
**WINGSPANS** >WINGSPAN
**WINGSUIT** n type of skydiving suit
**WINGSUITS** >WINGSUIT
**WINGTIP** n outermost edge of a wing
**WINGTIPS** >WINGTIP
**WINGY** adj having wings
**WINIER** >WINY
**WINIEST** >WINY
**WINING** >WINE
**WINISH** >WINE
**WINK** vb close and open (an eye) quickly as a signal ▷ n winking
**WINKED** >WINK
**WINKER** n person or thing that winks
**WINKERS** >WINKER
**WINKING** >WINK
**WINKINGLY** >WINK
**WINKINGS** >WINK
**WINKLE** n shellfish with a spiral shell ▷ vb extract or prise out
**WINKLED** >WINKLE
**WINKLER** n one who forces person or thing out
**WINKLERS** >WINKLER
**WINKLES** >WINKLE
**WINKLING** >WINKLE
**WINKS** >WINK
**WINLESS** adj not having won anything

**WINN** n penny
**WINNA** vb will not
**WINNABLE** >WIN
**WINNARD** n heron
**WINNARDS** >WINNARD
**WINNED** >WIN
**WINNER** n person or thing that wins
**WINNERS** >WINNER
**WINNING** adj (of a person) charming, attractive, etc
**WINNINGLY** >WINNING
**WINNINGS** >WIN
**WINNLE** same as >WINNLE
**WINNLES** >WINNLE
**WINNOCK** n window
**WINNOCKS** >WINNOCK
**WINNOW** vb separate (chaff) from (grain) ▷ n device for winnowing
**WINNOWED** >WINNOW
**WINNOWER** >WINNOW
**WINNOWERS** >WINNOW
**WINNOWING** >WINNOW
**WINNOWS** >WINNOW
**WINNS** >WINN
**WINO** n destitute person who habitually drinks cheap wine
**WINOES** >WINO
**WINOS** >WINO
**WINS** >WIN
**WINSEY** same as >WINCEY
**WINSEYS** >WINSEY
**WINSOME** adj charming or winning
**WINSOMELY** >WINSOME
**WINSOMER** >WINSOME
**WINSOMEST** >WINSOME
**WINTER** n coldest season ▷ vb spend the winter
**WINTERED** >WINTER
**WINTERER** >WINTER
**WINTERERS** >WINTER
**WINTERFED** vb past tense of 'winterfeed' (to feed (livestock) in winter when the grazing is not rich enough)
**WINTERIER** >WINTERY
**WINTERING** >WINTER
**WINTERISE** same as >WINTERIZE
**WINTERISH** >WINTER
**WINTERIZE** vb prepare (a house, car, etc) to withstand winter conditions
**WINTERLY** same as >WINTRY
**WINTERS** >WINTER
**WINTERY** same as >WINTRY
**WINTLE** vb reel; stagger
**WINTLED** >WINTLE
**WINTLES** >WINTLE
**WINTLING** >WINTLE
**WINTRIER** >WINTRY
**WINTRIEST** >WINTRY
**WINTRILY** >WINTRY
**WINTRY** adj of or like winter
**WINY** same as >WINEY
**WINZE** n steeply inclined shaft, as for ventilation between levels
**WINZES** >WINZE

WIPE *vb* clean or dry by rubbing ▷ *n* wiping

WIPED >WIPE

WIPEOUT *n* instance of wiping out

WIPEOUTS >WIPEOUT

WIPER *n* any piece of cloth, such as a handkerchief, towel, etc, used for wiping

WIPERS >WIPER

WIPES >WIPE

WIPING >WIPE

WIPINGS >WIPE

WIPPEN *n* part of hammer action in piano

WIPPENS >WIPPEN

WIRABLE *adj* that can be wired

WIRE *n* thin flexible strand of metal ▷ *vb* fasten with wire

WIRED *adj* excited or nervous

WIREDRAW *vb* convert (metal) into wire by drawing through successively smaller dies

WIREDRAWN >WIREDRAW

WIREDRAWS >WIREDRAW

WIREDREW >WIREDRAW

WIREGRASS *n* fine variety of grass

WIREHAIR *n* type of terrier

WIREHAIRS >WIREHAIR

WIRELESS *adj* (of a computer network) connected by radio rather than by cables or fibre optics

WIRELIKE >WIRE

WIREMAN *n* person who installs and maintains electric wiring, cables, etc

WIREMEN >WIREMAN

WIREPHOTO *n* facsimile of a photograph transmitted electronically via a telephone system

WIRER *n* person who sets or uses wires to snare rabbits and similar animals

WIRERS >WIRER

WIRES >WIRE

WIRETAP *vb* make a connection to a telegraph or telephone wire in order to obtain information secretly

WIRETAPS >WIRETAP

WIREWAY *n* tube for electric wires

WIREWAYS >WIREWAY

WIREWORK *n* functional or decorative work made of wire

WIREWORKS *n* factory where wire or articles of wire are made

WIREWORM *n* destructive wormlike beetle larva

WIREWORMS >WIREWORM

WIREWOVE *adj* woven out of wire

WIRIER >WIRY

WIRIEST >WIRY

WIRILDA *n* acacia tree, *Acacia retinoides*, of SE Australia with edible seeds

WIRILDAS >WIRILDA

WIRILY >WIRY

WIRINESS >WIRY

WIRING *n* system of wires ▷ *adj* used in wiring

WIRINGS >WIRING

WIRRA *interj* exclamation of sorrow or deep concern

WIRRAH *n* saltwater fish, *Acanthistius serratus*, of Australia, with bright blue spots

WIRRAHS >WIRRAH

WIRRICOW *same as* >WORRICOW

WIRRICOWS >WIRRICOW

WIRY *adj* lean and tough

WIS *vb* know or suppose (something)

WISARD *obsolete spelling of* >WIZARD

WISARDS >WISARD

WISDOM *n* good sense and judgment

WISDOMS >WISDOM

WISE *vb* guide ▷ *adj* having wisdom ▷ *n* manner

WISEACRE *n* person who wishes to seem wise

WISEACRES >WISEACRE

WISEASS *n* person who thinks he or she is being witty or clever

WISEASSES >WISEASS

WISECRACK *n* clever, sometimes unkind, remark ▷ *vb* make a wisecrack

WISED >WISE

WISEGUY *n* person who wants to seem clever

WISEGUYS >WISEGUY

WISELIER >WISE

WISELIEST >WISE

WISELING *n* one who claims to be wise

WISELINGS >WISELING

WISELY >WISE

WISENESS >WISE

WISENT *n* European bison

WISENTS >WISENT

WISER >WISE

WISES >WISE

WISEST >WISE

WISEWOMAN *n* witch

WISEWOMEN >WISEWOMAN

WISH *vb* want or desire ▷ *n* expression of a desire

WISHA *interj* expression of surprise

WISHBONE *n* V-shaped bone above the breastbone of a fowl

WISHBONES >WISHBONE

WISHED >WISH

WISHER >WISH

WISHERS >WISH

WISHES >WISH

WISHFUL *adj* too optimistic

WISHFULLY >WISHFUL

WISHING >WISH

WISHINGS >WISH

WISHLESS >WISH

WISHT *variant of* >WHISHT

WISING >WISE

WISKET *n* basket

WISKETS >WISKET

WISP *n* light delicate streak ▷ *vb* move or act like a wisp

WISPED >WISP

WISPIER >WISPY

WISPIEST >WISPY

WISPILY >WISPY

WISPINESS >WISPY

WISPING >WISP

WISPISH >WISP

WISPLIKE >WISP

WISPS >WISP

WISPY *adj* thin, fine, or delicate

WISS *vb* urinate

WISSED >WIS

WISSES >WIS

WISSING >WIS

WIST *vb* know

WISTARIA *same as* >WISTERIA

WISTARIAS >WISTARIA

WISTED >WIST

WISTERIA *n* climbing shrub with blue or purple flowers

WISTERIAS >WISTERIA

WISTFUL *adj* sadly longing

WISTFULLY >WISTFUL

WISTING >WIST

WISTITI *n* marmoset

WISTITIS >WISTITI

WISTLY *adv* intently

WISTS >WIST

WIT *vb* detect ▷ *n* ability to use words or ideas in a clever and amusing way

WITAN *n* assembly of higher ecclesiastics and important laymen, including king's thegns, that met to counsel the king on matters such as judicial problems

WITANS >WITAN

WITBLITS *n* illegally distilled strong alcoholic drink

WITCH *n* person, usu female, who practises (black) magic ▷ *vb* cause or change by or as if by witchcraft

WITCHED >WITCH

WITCHEN *n* rowan tree

WITCHENS >WITCHEN

WITCHERY *n* practice of witchcraft

WITCHES >WITCH

WITCHETTY *n* edible larva of certain Australian moths and beetles

WITCHHOOD >WITCH

WITCHIER >WITCHY

WITCHIEST >WITCHY

WITCHING *adj* relating to or appropriate for witchcraft ▷ *n* witchcraft

WITCHINGS >WITCHING

WITCHKNOT *n* knot in hair

WITCHLIKE >WITCH

WITCHWEED *n* any of several scrophulariaceous plants of the genus *Striga*, esp *S. hermonthica*, that are serious pests of grain crops in parts of Africa and Asia

WITCHY *adj* like a witch

WITE *vb* blame

WITED >WITE

WITELESS *adj* witless

WITES >WITE

WITGAT *n* type of S African tree

WITGATS >WITGAT

WITH *prep* indicating presence alongside, possession, means of performance, characteristic manner, etc ▷ *n* division between flues in chimney

WITHAL *adv* as well

WITHDRAW *vb* take or move out or away

WITHDRAWN *adj* unsociable

WITHDRAWS >WITHDRAW

WITHDREW *past tense of* >WITHDRAW

WITHE *n* strong flexible twig, esp of willow, suitable for binding things together ▷ *vb* bind with withes

WITHED >WITHE

WITHER *vb* wilt or dry up

WITHERED >WITHER

WITHERER >WITHER

WITHERERS >WITHER

WITHERING >WITHER

WITHERITE *n* white, grey, or yellowish mineral

WITHEROD *n* American shrub

WITHERODS >WITHEROD

WITHERS *pl n* ridge between a horse's shoulder blades

WITHES >WITHE

WITHHAULT >WITHHOLD

WITHHELD >WITHHOLD

WITHHOLD *vb* refrain from giving

WITHHOLDS >WITHHOLD

WITHIER >WITHY

WITHIES >WITHY

WITHIEST >WITHY

WITHIN *adv* in or inside ▷ *prep* in or inside ▷ *n* something that is within

WITHING >WITHE

WITHINS >WITHIN

WITHOUT *prep* not accompanied by, using, or having ▷ *adv* outside ▷ *n* person who is without

WITHOUTEN *obsolete form of* >WITHOUT

WITHOUTS >WITHOUT

WITHS >WITH

WITHSTAND *vb* oppose or resist successfully

WITHSTOOD > WITHSTAND

WITHWIND *n* bindweed

WITHWINDS > WITHWIND

WITHY *n* willow tree, esp an osier ▷ *adj* (of people) tough and agile

WITHYWIND *same as* > WITHWIND

WITING > WITE

WITLESS *adj* foolish

WITLESSLY > WITLESS

WITLING *n* person who thinks himself witty

WITLINGS > WITLING

WITLOOF *n* chicory

WITLOOFS > WITLOOF

WITNESS *n* person who has seen something happen ▷ *vb* see at first hand

WITNESSED > WITNESS

WITNESSER > WITNESS

WITNESSES > WITNESS

WITNEY *n* type of blanket; heavy cloth

WITNEYS > WITNEY

WITS > WIT

WITTED *adj* having wit

WITTER *vb* chatter pointlessly or at unnecessary length ▷ *n* pointless chat

WITTERED > WITTER

WITTERING > WITTER

WITTERS > WITTER

WITTICISM *n* witty remark

WITTIER > WITTY

WITTIEST > WITTY

WITTILY > WITTY

WITTINESS > WITTY

WITTING *adj* deliberate

WITTINGLY > WITTING

WITTINGS > WIT

WITTOL *n* man who tolerates his wife's unfaithfulness

WITTOLLY > WITTOL

WITTOLS > WITTOL

WITTY *adj* clever and amusing

WITWALL *n* golden oriole

WITWALLS > WITWALL

WITWANTON *n* be disrespectfully witty

WIVE *vb* marry (a woman)

WIVED > WIVE

WIVEHOOD *obsolete variant of* > WIFEHOOD

WIVEHOODS > WIVEHOOD

WIVER *another word for* > WIVERN

WIVERN *same as* > WYVERN

WIVERNS > WIVERN

WIVERS > WIVER

WIVES > WIFE

WIVING > WIVE

WIZ *shortened form of* > WIZARD

WIZARD *n* magician ▷ *adj* superb

WIZARDLY > WIZARD

WIZARDRY *n* magic or sorcery

WIZARDS > WIZARD

WIZEN *vb* make or become shrivelled ▷ *n* archaic word for WEASAND (the gullet)

WIZENED *adj* shrivelled or wrinkled

WIZENING > WIZEN

WIZENS > WIZEN

WIZES > WIZ

WIZIER *same as* > VIZIER

WIZIERS > WIZIER

WIZZEN *same as* > WIZEN

WIZZENS > WIZZEN

WIZZES > WIZ

WO *archaic spelling of* > WOE

WOAD *n* blue dye obtained from a plant, used by the ancient Britons as a body dye

WOADED *adj* coloured blue with woad

WOADS > WOAD

WOADWAX *n* small Eurasian leguminous shrub

WOADWAXEN *n* small leguminous shrub with yellow flowers producing a yellow dye

WOADWAXES > WOADWAX

WOALD *same as* > WELD

WOALDS > WOALD

WOBBEGONG *n* Australian shark with brown-and-white skin

WOBBLE *vb* move unsteadily ▷ *n* wobbling movement or sound

WOBBLED > WOBBLE

WOBBLER > WOBBLE

WOBBLERS > WOBBLE

WOBBLES > WOBBLE

WOBBLIER > WOBBLY

WOBBLIES > WOBBLY

WOBBLIEST > WOBBLY

WOBBLING > WOBBLE

WOBBLINGS > WOBBLE

WOBBLY *adj* unsteady ▷ *n* temper tantrum

WOBEGONE *same as* > WOEBEGONE

WOCK *same as* > WOK

WOCKS > WOCK

WODGE *n* thick lump or chunk

WODGES > WODGE

WOE *n* grief

WOEBEGONE *adj* looking miserable

WOEFUL *adj* extremely sad

WOEFULLER > WOEFUL

WOEFULLY > WOEFUL

WOENESS > WOE

WOENESSES > WOE

WOES > WOE

WOESOME *adj* woeful

WOF *n* fool

WOFS > WOF

WOFUL *same as* > WOEFUL

WOFULLER > WOFUL

WOFULLEST > WOFUL

WOFULLY > WOFUL

WOFULNESS > WOFUL

WOG *n* derogatory word for a foreigner, esp one who is not White

WOGGISH > WOG

WOGGLE *n* ring of leather through which a Scout neckerchief is threaded

WOGGLES > WOGGLE

WOGS > WOG

WOIWODE *same as* > VOIVODE

WOIWODES > WOIWODE

WOK *n* bowl-shaped Chinese cooking pan, used for stir-frying

WOKE > WAKE

WOKEN > WAKE

WOKKA *as in* wokka board wobble board: a piece of fibreboard used as a musical instrument

WOKS > WOK

WOLD *same as* > WELD

WOLDS > WOLD

WOLF *n* wild predatory canine mammal ▷ *vb* eat ravenously

WOLFBERRY *n* type of shrub

WOLFED > WOLF

WOLFER *same as* > WOLVER

WOLFERS > WOLFER

WOLFFISH *n* any large northern deep-sea blennioid fish of the family Anarhichadidae with large sharp teeth and no pelvic fins

WOLFHOUND *n* very large breed of dog

WOLFING > WOLF

WOLFINGS > WOLF

WOLFISH > WOLF

WOLFISHLY > WOLF

WOLFKIN *n* young wolf

WOLFKINS > WOLFKIN

WOLFLIKE > WOLF

WOLFLING *n* young wolf

WOLFLINGS > WOLFLING

WOLFRAM *another name for* > TUNGSTEN

WOLFRAMS > WOLFRAM

WOLFS > WOLF

WOLFSBANE *n* any of several poisonous N temperate plants of the ranunculaceous genus *Aconitum*, esp *A. lycoctonum*, which has yellow hoodlike flowers

WOLFSKIN *n* skin of wolf used for clothing, etc

WOLFSKINS > WOLFSKIN

WOLLIES > WOLLY

WOLLY *n* pickled cucumber or olive

WOLVE *vb* hunt for wolves

WOLVED > WOLVE

WOLVER *n* person who hunts wolves

WOLVERENE *same as* > WOLVERINE

WOLVERINE *n* carnivorous mammal of Arctic regions

WOLVERS > WOLVER

WOLVES > WOLF

WOLVING > WOLVE

WOLVINGS > WOLVE

WOLVISH *same as* > WOLFISH

WOLVISHLY > WOLVISH

WOMAN *n* adult human female ▷ *adj* female ▷ *vb* provide with a woman or women

WOMANED > WOMAN

WOMANHOOD *n* state of being a woman

WOMANING > WOMAN

WOMANISE *same as* > WOMANIZE

WOMANISED > WOMANISE

WOMANISER > WOMANISE

WOMANISES > WOMANISE

WOMANISH *adj* effeminate

WOMANISM *n* feminism among black women

WOMANISMS > WOMANISM

WOMANIST > WOMANISM

WOMANISTS > WOMANISM

WOMANIZE *vb* (of a man) to indulge in many casual affairs with women

WOMANIZED > WOMANIZE

WOMANIZER > WOMANIZE

WOMANIZES > WOMANIZE

WOMANKIND *n* all women considered as a group

WOMANLESS > WOMAN

WOMANLIER > WOMANLY

WOMANLIKE *adj* like a woman

WOMANLY *adj* having qualities traditionally associated with a woman

WOMANNESS > WOMAN

WOMANS > WOMAN

WOMB *vb* enclose ▷ *n* hollow organ in female mammals where babies are conceived and develop

WOMBAT *n* small heavily-built burrowing Australian marsupial

WOMBATS > WOMBAT

WOMBED > WOMB

WOMBIER > WOMBY

WOMBIEST > WOMBY

WOMBING > WOMB

WOMBLIKE > WOMB

WOMBS > WOMB

WOMBY *adj* hollow; spacious

WOMEN > WOMAN

WOMENFOLK *pl n* women collectively

WOMENKIND *same as* > WOMANKIND

WOMERA *same as* > WOOMERA

WOMERAS > WOMERA

WOMMERA *same as* > WOOMERA

WOMMERAS > WOMMERA

WOMMIT *n* foolish person

WOMMITS > WOMMIT

WOMYN *same as* > WOMAN

WON *n* standard monetary unit of North Korea, divided into 100 chon ▷ *vb* live or dwell

WONDER *vb* be curious about ▷ *n* wonderful thing ▷ *adj* spectacularly

successful
**WONDERED** >WONDER
**WONDERER** >WONDER
**WONDERERS** >WONDER
**WONDERFUL** adj very fine
**WONDERING** >WONDER
**WONDERKID** n informal word for an exceptionally successful young person
**WONDEROUS** obsolete variant of >WONDROUS
**WONDERS** >WONDER
**WONDRED** adj splendid
**WONDROUS** adj wonderful ▷ adv (intensifier)
**WONGA** n money
**WONGAS** >WONGA
**WONGI** vb talk informally
**WONGIED** >WONGI
**WONGIING** >WONGI
**WONGIS** >WONGI
**WONING** >WON
**WONINGS** >WON
**WONK** n person who is obsessively interested in a specified subject
**WONKIER** >WONKY
**WONKIEST** >WONKY
**WONKS** >WONK
**WONKY** adj shaky or unsteady
**WONNED** >WON
**WONNER** >WON
**WONNERS** >WON
**WONNING** >WON
**WONNINGS** >WON
**WONS** >WON
**WONT** adj accustomed ▷ n custom ▷ vb become or cause to become accustomed
**WONTED** adj accustomed or habituated (to doing something)
**WONTEDLY** >WONTED
**WONTING** >WONT
**WONTLESS** >WONT
**WONTON** n dumpling filled with spiced minced pork
**WONTONS** >WONTON
**WONTS** >WONT
**WOO** vb seek the love or affection of (a woman)
**WOOBUT** same as >WOUBIT
**WOOBUTS** >WOOBUT
**WOOD** n substance trees are made of, used in carpentry and as fuel ▷ adj made of or using wood ▷ vb (of land) plant with trees
**WOODBIN** n box for firewood
**WOODBIND** same as >WOODBINE
**WOODBINDS** >WOODBIND
**WOODBINE** n honeysuckle
**WOODBINES** >WOODBINE
**WOODBINS** >WOODBIN
**WOODBLOCK** n hollow block of wood used as a percussion instrument
**WOODBORER** n any of various beetles of the families Anobiidae, Buprestidae, etc, the larvae

of which bore into and damage wood
**WOODBOX** n box for firewood
**WOODBOXES** >WOODBOX
**WOODCHAT** n songbird, Lanius senator, of Europe and N Africa, having a black-and-white plumage with a reddish-brown crown and a hooked bill
**WOODCHATS** >WOODCHAT
**WOODCHIP** n textured wallpaper
**WOODCHIPS** >WOODCHIP
**WOODCHOP** n wood-chopping competition, esp at a show
**WOODCHOPS** >WOODCHOP
**WOODCHUCK** n North American marmot, Marmota monax, having coarse reddish-brown fur
**WOODCOCK** n game bird
**WOODCOCKS** >WOODCOCK
**WOODCRAFT** n ability and experience in matters concerned with living in a wood or forest
**WOODCUT** n (print made from) an engraved block of wood
**WOODCUTS** >WOODCUT
**WOODED** adj covered with trees
**WOODEN** adj made of wood ▷ vb fell or kill (a person or animal)
**WOODENED** >WOODEN
**WOODENER** >WOODEN
**WOODENEST** >WOODEN
**WOODENING** >WOODEN
**WOODENLY** >WOODEN
**WOODENS** >WOODEN
**WOODENTOP** n dull, foolish, or unintelligent person
**WOODFREE** adj (of high-quality paper) made from pulp that has been treated chemically, removing impurities
**WOODGRAIN** n grain in wood
**WOODHEN** another name for >WEKA
**WOODHENS** >WOODHEN
**WOODHOLE** n store area for wood
**WOODHOLES** >WOODHOLE
**WOODHORSE** n frame for holding wood being sawn
**WOODHOUSE** n shed for firewood
**WOODIE** n gallows rope
**WOODIER** >WOODY
**WOODIES** >WOODIE
**WOODIEST** >WOODY
**WOODINESS** >WOODY
**WOODING** >WOOD
**WOODLAND** n forest ▷ adj living in woods
**WOODLANDS** >WOODLAND
**WOODLARK** n Old World lark, Lullula arborea, similar to but slightly smaller than

the skylark
**WOODLARKS** >WOODLARK
**WOODLESS** >WOOD
**WOODLICE** >WOODLOUSE
**WOODLORE** n woodcraft skills
**WOODLORES** >WOODLORE
**WOODLOT** n area restricted to the growing of trees
**WOODLOTS** >WOODLOT
**WOODLOUSE** n small insect-like creature with many legs
**WOODMAN** same as >WOODSMAN
**WOODMEAL** n sawdust powder
**WOODMEALS** >WOODMEAL
**WOODMEN** >WOODMAN
**WOODMICE** >WOODMOUSE
**WOODMOUSE** n field mouse
**WOODNESS** >WOOD
**WOODNOTE** n natural musical note or song, like that of a wild bird
**WOODNOTES** >WOODNOTE
**WOODPILE** n heap of firewood
**WOODPILES** >WOODPILE
**WOODPRINT** another name for >WOODCUT
**WOODREEVE** n steward responsible for wood
**WOODROOF** same as >WOODRUFF
**WOODROOFS** >WOODROOF
**WOODRUFF** n plant with small sweet-smelling white flowers and sweet-smelling leaves
**WOODRUFFS** >WOODRUFF
**WOODRUSH** n any of various juncaceous plants of the genus Luzula, chiefly of cold and temperate regions of the N hemisphere, having grasslike leaves and small brown flowers
**WOODS** pl n closely packed trees forming a forest or wood
**WOODSCREW** n metal screw that tapers to a point so that it can be driven into wood by a screwdriver
**WOODSHED** n small outbuilding where firewood, garden tools, etc, are stored
**WOODSHEDS** >WOODSHED
**WOODSHOCK** n type of bird
**WOODSIA** n any small fern of the genus Woodsia, of temperate and cold regions, having tufted rhizomes and numerous wiry fronds
**WOODSIAS** >WOODSIA
**WOODSIER** >WOODSY
**WOODSIEST** >WOODSY
**WOODSKIN** n canoe made of bark
**WOODSKINS** >WOODSKIN
**WOODSMAN** n person who

lives in a wood or who is skilled at woodwork or carving
**WOODSMEN** >WOODSMAN
**WOODSPITE** n green woodpecker
**WOODSTONE** n type of stone resembling wood
**WOODSTOVE** n wood-burning stove
**WOODSY** adj of, reminiscent of, or connected with woods
**WOODTONE** n colour matching that of wood
**WOODTONES** >WOODTONE
**WOODWALE** n green woodpecker
**WOODWALES** >WOODWALE
**WOODWARD** n person in charge of a forest or wood
**WOODWARDS** >WOODWARD
**WOODWAX** same as >WOODWAXEN
**WOODWAXEN** same as >WOADWAXEN
**WOODWAXES** >WOODWAX
**WOODWIND** n (of) a type of wind instrument made of wood ▷ adj of or denoting a type of wind instrument, such as the oboe
**WOODWINDS** >WOODWIND
**WOODWORK** n parts of a room or building made of wood
**WOODWORKS** >WOODWORK
**WOODWORM** n insect larva that bores into wood
**WOODWORMS** >WOODWORM
**WOODWOSE** n hairy wildman of the woods
**WOODWOSES** >WOODWOSE
**WOODY** adj (of a plant) having a very hard stem
**WOODYARD** n place where timber is cut and stored
**WOODYARDS** >WOODYARD
**WOOED** >WOO
**WOOER** >WOO
**WOOERS** >WOO
**WOOF** vb (of dogs) bark or growl
**WOOFED** >WOOF
**WOOFER** n loudspeaker reproducing low-frequency sounds
**WOOFERS** >WOOFER
**WOOFIER** >WOOFY
**WOOFIEST** >WOOFY
**WOOFING** >WOOF
**WOOFS** >WOOF
**WOOFTER** n derogatory term for a male homosexual
**WOOFTERS** >WOOFTER
**WOOFY** adj with close, dense texture
**WOOING** >WOO
**WOOINGLY** >WOO
**WOOINGS** >WOO
**WOOL** n soft hair of sheep, goats, etc
**WOOLD** vb wind (rope)

865

**WOOLDED** >WOOLD
**WOOLDER** n stick for winding rope
**WOOLDERS** >WOOLDER
**WOOLDING** >WOOLD
**WOOLDINGS** >WOOLD
**WOOLDS** >WOOLD
**WOOLED** same as >WOOLLED
**WOOLEN** same as >WOOLLEN
**WOOLENS** >WOOLEN
**WOOLER** same as >WOOLDER
**WOOLERS** >WOOLER
**WOOLFAT** same as >LANOLIN
**WOOLFATS** >WOOLFAT
**WOOLFELL** n skin of a sheep or similar animal with the fleece still attached
**WOOLFELLS** >WOOLFELL
**WOOLHAT** n poor white person in S States
**WOOLHATS** >WOOLHAT
**WOOLIE** n wool garment
**WOOLIER** >WOOLY
**WOOLIES** >WOOLY
**WOOLIEST** >WOOLY
**WOOLINESS** >WOOLY
**WOOLLED** adj (of animals) having wool
**WOOLLEN** adj relating to or consisting partly or wholly of wool ▷ n garment or piece of cloth made wholly or partly of wool, esp a knitted one
**WOOLLENS** >WOOLLEN
**WOOLLIER** >WOOLLY
**WOOLLIES** >WOOLLY
**WOOLLIEST** >WOOLLY
**WOOLLIKE** >WOOL
**WOOLLILY** >WOOLLY
**WOOLLY** adj of or like wool ▷ n knitted woollen garment
**WOOLMAN** n wool trader
**WOOLMEN** >WOOLMAN
**WOOLPACK** n cloth or canvas wrapping used to pack a bale of wool
**WOOLPACKS** >WOOLPACK
**WOOLS** >WOOL
**WOOLSACK** n sack containing or intended to contain wool
**WOOLSACKS** >WOOLSACK
**WOOLSEY** n cotton and wool blend
**WOOLSEYS** >WOOLSEY
**WOOLSHED** n large building in which sheep shearing takes place
**WOOLSHEDS** >WOOLSHED
**WOOLSKIN** n sheepskin with wool still on
**WOOLSKINS** >WOOLSKIN
**WOOLWARD** adv with woollen side touching the skin
**WOOLWORK** n embroidery with wool
**WOOLWORKS** >WOOLWORK
**WOOLY** same as >WOOLLY
**WOOMERA** n notched stick used by Australian Aborigines to aid the propulsion of a spear
**WOOMERANG** same as >WOOMERA
**WOOMERAS** >WOOMERA
**WOON** same as >WON
**WOONED** >WOON
**WOONING** >WOON
**WOONS** >WOON
**WOOPIE** n well-off older person
**WOOPIES** >WOOPIE
**WOOPS** vb (esp of small child) vomit
**WOOPSED** >WOOPS
**WOOPSES** >WOOPS
**WOOPSING** >WOOPS
**WOORALI** less common name for >CURARE
**WOORALIS** >WOORALI
**WOORARA** same as >WOURALI
**WOORARAS** >WOORARA
**WOORARI** same as >WOURALI
**WOORARIS** >WOORARI
**WOOS** >WOO
**WOOSE** same as >WUSS
**WOOSEL** same as >OUZEL
**WOOSELL** same as >OUZEL
**WOOSELLS** >WOOSELL
**WOOSELS** >WOOSEL
**WOOSES** >WOOSE
**WOOSH** same as >WHOOSH
**WOOSHED** >WOOSH
**WOOSHES** >WOOSH
**WOOSHING** >WOOSH
**WOOT** vb wilt thou?
**WOOTZ** n Middle-Eastern steel
**WOOTZES** >WOOTZ
**WOOZIER** >WOOZY
**WOOZIEST** >WOOZY
**WOOZILY** >WOOZY
**WOOZINESS** >WOOZY
**WOOZY** adj weak, dizzy, and confused
**WOP** same as >WHOP
**WOPPED** >WOP
**WOPPING** >WOP
**WOPS** >WOP
**WORCESTER** n type of woollen fabric
**WORD** n smallest single meaningful unit of speech or writing ▷ vb express in words
**WORDAGE** n words considered collectively, esp a quantity of words
**WORDAGES** >WORDAGE
**WORDBOOK** n book containing words, usually with their meanings
**WORDBOOKS** >WORDBOOK
**WORDBOUND** adj unable to find words to express sth
**WORDBREAK** n point at which a word is divided when it runs over from one line of print to the next
**WORDED** >WORD
**WORDGAME** n any game involving the formation, discovery, or alteration of a word or words
**WORDGAMES** >WORDGAME
**WORDIER** >WORDY
**WORDIEST** >WORDY
**WORDILY** >WORDY
**WORDINESS** >WORDY
**WORDING** n choice and arrangement of words
**WORDINGS** >WORDING
**WORDISH** adj talkative
**WORDLESS** adj inarticulate or silent
**WORDLORE** n knowledge about words
**WORDLORES** >WORDLORE
**WORDPLAY** n verbal wit based on the meanings and ambiguities of words
**WORDPLAYS** >WORDPLAY
**WORDS** >WORD
**WORDSMITH** n person skilled in using words
**WORDY** adj using too many words
**WORE** >WEAR
**WORK** n physical or mental effort directed to making or doing something ▷ adj of or for work ▷ vb (cause to) do work
**WORKABLE** adj able to operate efficiently
**WORKABLY** >WORKABLE
**WORKADAY** n working day ▷ adj ordinary
**WORKADAYS** >WORKADAY
**WORKBAG** n container for implements, tools, or materials, esp sewing equipment
**WORKBAGS** >WORKBAG
**WORKBENCH** n heavy table at which a craftsman or mechanic works
**WORKBOAT** n boat used for tasks
**WORKBOATS** >WORKBOAT
**WORKBOOK** n exercise book or textbook used for study, esp a textbook with spaces for answers
**WORKBOOKS** >WORKBOOK
**WORKBOX** same as >WORKBAG
**WORKBOXES** >WORKBOX
**WORKDAY** another word for >WORKADAY
**WORKDAYS** >WORKDAY
**WORKED** adj made or decorated with evidence of workmanship
**WORKER** n person who works in a specified way
**WORKERIST** n supporter of working-class politics
**WORKERS** >WORKER
**WORKFARE** n scheme under which the government of a country requires unemployed people to do community work or undergo job training in return for social-security payments
**WORKFARES** >WORKFARE
**WORKFLOW** n rate of progress of work
**WORKFLOWS** >WORKFLOW
**WORKFOLK** pl n working people, esp labourers on a farm
**WORKFOLKS** same as >WORKFOLK
**WORKFORCE** n total number of workers
**WORKFUL** adj hardworking
**WORKGIRL** n young female manual worker
**WORKGIRLS** >WORKGIRL
**WORKGROUP** n collection of networked computers
**WORKHORSE** n person or thing that does a lot of dull or routine work
**WORKHOUR** n time set aside for work
**WORKHOURS** >WORKHOUR
**WORKHOUSE** n (in England, formerly) institution where the poor were given food and lodgings in return for work
**WORKING** n operation or mode of operation of something ▷ adj relating to or concerned with a person or thing that works
**WORKINGS** >WORKING
**WORKLESS** >WORK
**WORKLOAD** n amount of work to be done, esp in a specified period
**WORKLOADS** >WORKLOAD
**WORKMAN** n manual worker
**WORKMANLY** adj appropriate to or befitting a good workman
**WORKMATE** n person who works with another person
**WORKMATES** >WORKMATE
**WORKMEN** >WORKMAN
**WORKOUT** n session of physical exercise for training or fitness
**WORKOUTS** >WORKOUT
**WORKPIECE** n piece of metal or other material that is in the process of being worked on or made or has actually been cut or shaped by a hand tool or machine
**WORKPLACE** n place, such as a factory or office, where people work
**WORKPRINT** n unfinished print of cinema film
**WORKROOM** n room in which work, usually manual labour, is done
**WORKROOMS** >WORKROOM
**WORKS** >WORK
**WORKSHEET** n sheet of paper containing exercises to be completed by a student
**WORKSHOP** n room or building for a manufacturing process

▷ *vb* perform (a play) with no costumes, set, or musical accompaniment
**WORKSHOPS** >WORKSHOP
**WORKSHY** *adj* not inclined to work
**WORKSOME** *adj* hardworking
**WORKSPACE** *n* area set aside for work
**WORKTABLE** *n* table at which writing, sewing, or other work may be done
**WORKTOP** *n* surface in a kitchen, used for food preparation
**WORKTOPS** >WORKTOP
**WORKUP** *n* medical examination
**WORKUPS** >WORKUP
**WORKWEAR** *n* clothes, such as overalls, as worn for work in a factory, shop, etc
**WORKWEARS** >WORKWEAR
**WORKWEEK** *n* number of hours or days in a week actually or officially allocated to work
**WORKWEEKS** >WORKWEEK
**WORKWOMAN** *n* female manual worker
**WORKWOMEN** >WORKWOMAN
**WORLD** *n* planet earth ▷ *adj* of the whole world
**WORLDBEAT** *n* popular music from outside western mainstream
**WORLDED** *adj* incorporating worlds
**WORLDLIER** >WORLDLY
**WORLDLING** *n* person who is primarily concerned with worldly matters or material things
**WORLDLY** *adj* not spiritual ▷ *adv* in a worldly manner
**WORLDS** >WORLD
**WORLDVIEW** *n* comprehensive view of human life and the universe
**WORLDWIDE** *adj* applying or extending throughout the world
**WORM** *n* small limbless invertebrate animal ▷ *vb* rid of worms
**WORMCAST** *n* coil of earth excreted by a burrowing worm
**WORMCASTS** >WORMCAST
**WORMED** >WORM
**WORMER** >WORM
**WORMERIES** >WORMERY
**WORMERS** >WORM
**WORMERY** *n* piece of apparatus, having a glass side or sides, in which worms are kept for study
**WORMFLIES** >WORMFLY
**WORMFLY** *n* type of lure dressed on a double hook, the barbs of which sit one above the other and back-to-back

**WORMGEAR** *n* gear with screw thread
**WORMGEARS** >WORMGEAR
**WORMHOLE** *n* hole made by a worm in timber, plants, or fruit
**WORMHOLED** >WORMHOLE
**WORMHOLES** >WORMHOLE
**WORMIER** >WORMY
**WORMIEST** >WORMY
**WORMIL** *n* burrowing larva of type of fly
**WORMILS** >WORMIL
**WORMINESS** >WORMY
**WORMING** >WORM
**WORMISH** >WORM
**WORMLIKE** >WORM
**WORMROOT** *n* plant used to cure worms
**WORMROOTS** >WORMROOT
**WORMS** *n* disease caused by parasitic worms living in the intestines
**WORMSEED** *n* any of various plants having seeds or other parts used in medicine to treat worm infestation
**WORMSEEDS** >WORMSEED
**WORMWOOD** *n* bitter plant
**WORMWOODS** >WORMWOOD
**WORMY** *adj* infested with or eaten by worms
**WORN** >WEAR
**WORNNESS** *n* quality or condition of being worn
**WORRAL** *n* type of lizard
**WORRALS** >WORRAL
**WORREL** *same as* >WORRAL
**WORRELS** >WORREL
**WORRICOW** *n* frightening creature
**WORRICOWS** >WORRICOW
**WORRIED** >WORRY
**WORRIEDLY** >WORRY
**WORRIER** >WORRY
**WORRIERS** >WORRY
**WORRIES** >WORRY
**WORRIMENT** *n* anxiety or the trouble that causes it
**WORRISOME** *adj* causing worry
**WORRIT** *vb* tease or worry
**WORRITED** >WORRIT
**WORRITING** >WORRIT
**WORRITS** >WORRIT
**WORRY** *vb* (cause to) be anxious or uneasy ▷ *n* (cause of) anxiety or concern
**WORRYCOW** *same as* >WORRICOW
**WORRYCOWS** >WORRYCOW
**WORRYGUTS** *n* person who tends to worry, esp about insignificant matters
**WORRYING** >WORRY
**WORRYINGS** >WORRY
**WORRYWART** *same as* >WORRYGUTS
**WORSE** *vb* defeat
**WORSED** >WORSE
**WORSEN** *vb* make or grow worse

**WORSENED** >WORSEN
**WORSENESS** *n* state or condition of being worse
**WORSENING** >WORSEN
**WORSENS** >WORSEN
**WORSER** *archaic or nonstandard word for* >WORSE
**WORSES** >WORSE
**WORSET** *n* worsted fabric
**WORSETS** >WORSET
**WORSHIP** *vb* show religious devotion to ▷ *n* act or instance of worshipping
**WORSHIPED** >WORSHIP
**WORSHIPER** *same as* >WORSHIPPER
**WORSHIPS** >WORSHIP
**WORSING** >WORSE
**WORST** *n* worst thing ▷ *vb* defeat
**WORSTED** *n* type of woollen yarn or fabric
**WORSTEDS** >WORSTED
**WORSTING** >WORST
**WORSTS** >WORST
**WORT** *n* any of various unrelated plants, esp formerly used to cure diseases
**WORTHED** >WORTH
**WORTHFUL** *adj* worthy
**WORTHIED** >WORTHY
**WORTHIER** >WORTHY
**WORTHIES** >WORTHY
**WORTHIEST** >WORTHY
**WORTHILY** >WORTHY
**WORTHING** >WORTH
**WORTHLESS** *adj* without value or usefulness
**WORTHS** >WORTH
**WORTHY** *adj* deserving admiration or respect ▷ *n* notable person ▷ *vb* make worthy
**WORTHYING** >WORTHY
**WORTLE** *n* plate with holes for drawing wire through
**WORTLES** >WORTLE
**WORTS** >WORT
**WOS** >WO
**WOSBIRD** *n* illegitimate child
**WOSBIRDS** >WOSBIRD
**WOST** *obsolete 2nd pers sing of* wit, to know
**WOT** *form of the present tense (indicative mood) of* wit, to know
**WOTCHER** *sentence substitute* slang term of greeting
**WOTS** >WOT
**WOTTED** >WOT
**WOTTEST** >WOT
**WOTTETH** >WOT
**WOTTING** >WOT
**WOUBIT** *n* type of caterpillar
**WOUBITS** >WOUBIT
**WOULD** >WILL
**WOULDEST** *same as* >WOULDST

**WOULDS** *same as* >WOULDST
**WOULDST** *singular form of the past tense of* >WILL
**WOUND** *vb* injure ▷ *n* injury
**WOUNDABLE** >WOUND
**WOUNDED** *adj* suffering from wounds
**WOUNDEDLY** >WOUNDED
**WOUNDER** >WOUND
**WOUNDERS** >WOUND
**WOUNDILY** >WOUNDY
**WOUNDING** >WOUND
**WOUNDINGS** >WOUND
**WOUNDLESS** >WOUND
**WOUNDS** >WOUND
**WOUNDWORT** *n* type of plant formerly used for dressing wounds
**WOUNDY** *adj* extreme
**WOURALI** *n* plant from which curare is obtained
**WOURALIS** >WOURALI
**WOVE** >WEAVE
**WOVEN** *n* article made from woven cloth
**WOVENS** >WOVEN
**WOW** *interj* exclamation of astonishment ▷ *n* astonishing person or thing ▷ *vb* be a great success with
**WOWED** >WOW
**WOWEE** *stronger form of* >WOW
**WOWF** *adj* mad
**WOWFER** >WOWF
**WOWFEST** >WOWF
**WOWING** >WOW
**WOWS** >WOW
**WOWSER** *n* puritanical person
**WOWSERS** >WOWSER
**WOX** >WAX
**WOXEN** >WAX
**WRACK** *n* seaweed ▷ *vb* strain or shake (something) violently
**WRACKED** >WRACK
**WRACKFUL** *n* ruinous
**WRACKING** >WRACK
**WRACKS** >WRACK
**WRAITH** *n* ghost
**WRAITHS** >WRAITH
**WRANG** *Scot word for* >WRONG
**WRANGED** >WRANG
**WRANGING** >WRANG
**WRANGLE** *vb* argue noisily ▷ *n* noisy argument
**WRANGLED** >WRANGLE
**WRANGLER** *n* one who wrangles
**WRANGLERS** >WRANGLER
**WRANGLES** >WRANGLE
**WRANGLING** >WRANGLE
**WRANGS** >WRANG
**WRAP** *vb* fold (something) round (a person or thing) so as to cover ▷ *n* garment wrapped round the shoulders
**WRAPOVER** *adj* (of a garment, esp a skirt) not sewn up at one side, but

worn wrapped round the body and fastened so that the open edges overlap ▷ *n* such a garment
**WRAPOVERS** >WRAPOVER
**WRAPPAGE** *n* material for wrapping
**WRAPPAGES** >WRAPPAGE
**WRAPPED** >WRAP
**WRAPPER** *vb* cover with wrapping ▷ *n* cover for a product
**WRAPPERED** >WRAPPER
**WRAPPERS** >WRAPPER
**WRAPPING** >WRAP
**WRAPPINGS** >WRAP
**WRAPROUND** *same as* >WRAPOVER
**WRAPS** >WRAP
**WRAPT** *same as* >RAPT
**WRASSE** *n* colourful sea fish
**WRASSES** >WRASSE
**WRASSLE** *same as* >WRESTLE
**WRASSLED** >WRASSLE
**WRASSLES** >WRASSLE
**WRASSLING** >WRASSLE
**WRAST** *same as* >WREST
**WRASTED** >WRAST
**WRASTING** >WRAST
**WRASTLE** *same as* >WRESTLE
**WRASTLED** >WRASTLE
**WRASTLES** >WRASTLE
**WRASTLING** >WRASTLE
**WRASTS** >WRAST
**WRATE** >WRITE
**WRATH** *n* intense anger ▷ *adj* incensed ▷ *vb* make angry
**WRATHED** >WRATH
**WRATHFUL** *adj* full of wrath
**WRATHIER** >WRATHY
**WRATHIEST** >WRATHY
**WRATHILY** >WRATHY
**WRATHING** >WRATH
**WRATHLESS** >WRATH
**WRATHS** >WRATH
**WRATHY** *same as* >WRATHFUL
**WRAWL** *vb* howl
**WRAWLED** >WRAWL
**WRAWLING** >WRAWL
**WRAWLS** >WRAWL
**WRAXLE** *vb* wrestle
**WRAXLED** >WRAXLE
**WRAXLES** >WRAXLE
**WRAXLING** >WRAXLE
**WRAXLINGS** >WRAXLE
**WREAK** *vb* inflict (vengeance, etc) or to cause (chaos, etc)
**WREAKED** >WREAK
**WREAKER** >WREAK
**WREAKERS** >WREAK
**WREAKFUL** *adj* seeking revenge
**WREAKING** >WREAK
**WREAKLESS** *adj* unrevengeful
**WREAKS** >WREAK
**WREATH** *n* twisted ring or band of flowers or leaves used as a memorial or tribute
**WREATHE** *vb* form into or take the form of a

wreath by intertwining or twisting together
**WREATHED** >WREATHE
**WREATHEN** *adj* twisted into wreath
**WREATHER** >WREATHE
**WREATHERS** >WREATHE
**WREATHES** >WREATHE
**WREATHIER** >WREATHY
**WREATHING** >WREATHE
**WREATHS** >WREATH
**WREATHY** *adj* twisted into wreath
**WRECK** *vb* destroy ▷ *n* remains of something that has been destroyed or badly damaged, esp a ship
**WRECKAGE** *n* wrecked remains
**WRECKAGES** >WRECKAGE
**WRECKED** *adj* in a state of intoxication, stupor, or euphoria, induced by drugs or alcohol
**WRECKER** *n* formerly, person who lured ships onto the rocks in order to plunder them
**WRECKERS** >WRECKER
**WRECKFISH** *n* large sea perch
**WRECKFUL** *adj* causing wreckage
**WRECKING** >WRECK
**WRECKINGS** >WRECK
**WRECKS** >WRECK
**WREN** *n* small brown songbird
**WRENCH** *vb* twist or pull violently ▷ *n* violent twist or pull
**WRENCHED** >WRENCH
**WRENCHER** >WRENCH
**WRENCHERS** >WRENCH
**WRENCHES** >WRENCH
**WRENCHING** >WRENCH
**WRENS** >WREN
**WREST** *vb* twist violently ▷ *n* act or an instance of wresting
**WRESTED** >WREST
**WRESTER** >WREST
**WRESTERS** >WREST
**WRESTING** >WREST
**WRESTLE** *vb* fight, esp as a sport, by grappling with and trying to throw down an opponent ▷ *n* act of wrestling
**WRESTLED** >WRESTLE
**WRESTLER** >WRESTLE
**WRESTLERS** >WRESTLE
**WRESTLES** >WRESTLE
**WRESTLING** *n* sport in which each contestant tries to overcome the other either by throwing or pinning him or her to the ground or by forcing a submission
**WRESTS** >WREST
**WRETCH** *n* despicable person
**WRETCHED** *adj* miserable or

unhappy
**WRETCHES** >WRETCH
**WRETHE** *same as* >WREATHE
**WRETHED** >WRETHE
**WRETHES** >WRETHE
**WRETHING** >WRETHE
**WRICK** *variant spelling (chiefly Brit) of* > RICK
**WRICKED** >WRICK
**WRICKING** >WRICK
**WRICKS** >WRICK
**WRIED** >WRY
**WRIER** >WRY
**WRIES** >WRY
**WRIEST** >WRY
**WRIGGLE** *vb* move with a twisting action ▷ *n* wriggling movement
**WRIGGLED** >WRIGGLE
**WRIGGLER** >WRIGGLE
**WRIGGLERS** >WRIGGLE
**WRIGGLES** >WRIGGLE
**WRIGGLIER** >WRIGGLE
**WRIGGLING** >WRIGGLE
**WRIGGLY** >WRIGGLE
**WRIGHT** *n* maker
**WRIGHTS** >WRIGHT
**WRING** *vb* twist, esp to squeeze liquid out of
**WRINGED** >WRING
**WRINGER** *same as* > MANGLE
**WRINGERS** >WRINGER
**WRINGING** >WRING
**WRINGINGS** >WRING
**WRINGS** >WRING
**WRINKLE** *n* slight crease, esp one in the skin due to age ▷ *vb* make or become slightly creased
**WRINKLED** >WRINKLE
**WRINKLES** >WRINKLE
**WRINKLIER** >WRINKLE
**WRINKLIES** *pl n* derogatory word for old people
**WRINKLING** >WRINKLE
**WRINKLY** >WRINKLE
**WRIST** *n* joint between the hand and the arm
**WRISTBAND** *n* band around the wrist, esp one attached to a watch or forming part of a long sleeve
**WRISTIER** >WRISTY
**WRISTIEST** >WRISTY
**WRISTLET** *n* band or bracelet worn around the wrist
**WRISTLETS** >WRISTLET
**WRISTLOCK** *n* wrestling hold in which a wrestler seizes his opponent's wrist and exerts pressure against the joints of his hand, arm, or shoulder
**WRISTS** >WRIST
**WRISTY** *adj* (of a player's style of hitting the ball in cricket, tennis, etc) characterized by considerable movement of the wrist
**WRIT** *n* written legal command

**WRITABLE** >WRITE
**WRITATIVE** *adj* inclined to write a lot
**WRITE** *vb* mark paper etc with symbols or words
**WRITEABLE** >WRITE
**WRITER** *n* author
**WRITERESS** *n* female writer
**WRITERLY** *adj* of or characteristic of a writer
**WRITERS** >WRITER
**WRITES** >WRITE
**WRITHE** *vb* twist or squirm in or as if in pain ▷ *n* act or an instance of writhing
**WRITHED** >WRITHE
**WRITHEN** *adj* twisted
**WRITHER** >WRITHE
**WRITHERS** >WRITHE
**WRITHES** >WRITHE
**WRITHING** >WRITHE
**WRITHINGS** >WRITHE
**WRITHLED** *adj* wrinkled
**WRITING** >WRITE
**WRITINGS** >WRITE
**WRITS** >WRIT
**WRITTEN** >WRITE
**WRIZLED** *adj* wrinkled
**WROATH** *n* unforeseen trouble
**WROATHS** >WROATH
**WROKE** >WREAK
**WROKEN** >WREAK
**WRONG** *adj* incorrect or mistaken ▷ *adv* in a wrong manner ▷ *n* something immoral or unjust ▷ *vb* treat unjustly
**WRONGDOER** *n* person who acts immorally or illegally
**WRONGED** >WRONG
**WRONGER** >WRONG
**WRONGERS** >WRONG
**WRONGEST** >WRONG
**WRONGFUL** *adj* unjust or illegal
**WRONGING** >WRONG
**WRONGLY** >WRONG
**WRONGNESS** >WRONG
**WRONGOUS** *adj* unfair
**WRONGS** >WRONG
**WROOT** *obsolete form of* > ROOT
**WROOTED** >WROOT
**WROOTING** >WROOT
**WROOTS** >WROOT
**WROTE** >WRITE
**WROTH** *adj* angry
**WROTHFUL** *same as* >WRATHFUL
**WROUGHT** *adj* (of metals) shaped by hammering or beating
**WRUNG** >WRING
**WRY** *adj* drily humorous ▷ *vb* twist or contort
**WRYBILL** *n* New Zealand plover whose bill is bent to one side enabling it to search for food beneath stones
**WRYBILLS** >WRYBILL
**WRYER** >WRY
**WRYEST** >WRY

WRYING >WRY
WRYLY >WRY
WRYNECK n woodpecker that has a habit of twisting its neck round
WRYNECKS >WRYNECK
WRYNESS >WRY
WRYNESSES >WRY
WRYTHEN adj twisted
WUD Scots form of >WOOD
WUDDED >WUD
WUDDING >WUD
WUDJULA n Australian word for a non-Aboriginal person
WUDJULAS >WUDJULA
WUDS >WUD
WUDU n practice of ritual washing before daily prayer
WUDUS >WUDU
WUKKAS pl n Australian taboo slang expression for no problems
WULFENITE n yellow, orange, red, or grey lustrous secondary mineral
WULL obsolete form of >WILL
WULLED >WILL
WULLING >WILL
WULLS >WILL
WUNNER same as >ONER
WUNNERS >WUNNER
WURLEY n Aboriginal hut
WURLEYS >WURLEY
WURLIE same as >WURLEY
WURLIES >WURLIE
WURST n large sausage, esp of a type made in Germany, Austria, etc
WURSTS >WURST
WURTZITE n zinc sulphide
WURTZITES >WURTZITE
WURZEL n root
WURZELS >WURZEL
WUS n casual term of address
WUSES >WUS
WUSHU n Chinese martial arts
WUSHUS >WUSHU
WUSS n feeble or effeminate person
WUSSES >WUSS
WUSSIER >WUSSY
WUSSIES >WUSSY
WUSSIEST >WUSSY
WUSSY adj feeble or effeminate ▷ n feeble person
WUTHER vb (of wind) blow and roar
WUTHERED >WUTHER
WUTHERING adj (of a wind) blowing strongly with a roaring sound
WUTHERS >WUTHER
WUXIA n genre of Chinese fiction and film, concerning the adventures of sword-wielding chivalrous heroes
WUXIAS >WUXIA

WUZZLE vb mix up
WUZZLED >WUZZLE
WUZZLES >WUZZLE
WUZZLING >WUZZLE
WYANDOTTE n heavy American breed of domestic fowl
WYCH n type of tree having flexible branches
WYCHES >WYCH
WYE n y-shaped pipe
WYES >WYE
WYLE vb entice
WYLED >WYLE
WYLES >WYLE
WYLIECOAT n petticoat
WYLING >WYLE
WYN n rune equivalent to English 'w'
WYND n narrow lane or alley
WYNDS >WYND
WYNN same as >WYN
WYNNS >WYNN
WYNS >WYN
WYSIWYG adj (of text and images displayed on a computer screen) being the same as what will be printed out
WYTE vb blame
WYTED >WYTE
WYTES >WYTE
WYTING >WYTE
WYVERN n heraldic beast having a serpent's tail and a dragon's head and a body with wings and two legs
WYVERNS >WYVERN

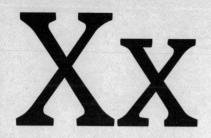

XANTHAM *n* acacia gum
XANTHAMS >XANTHAM
XANTHAN *same
as* >XANTHAM
XANTHANS >XANTHAN
XANTHATE *n* any salt or
ester of xanthic acid
XANTHATES >XANTHATE
XANTHEIN *n* soluble part of
the yellow pigment that
is found in the cell sap of
some flowers
XANTHEINS >XANTHEIN
XANTHENE *n* yellowish
crystalline heterocyclic
compound used as a
fungicide
XANTHENES >XANTHENE
XANTHIC *adj* of, containing,
or derived from xanthic
acid
XANTHIN *n* any of a group of
yellow or orange carotene
derivatives that occur in
the fruit and flowers of
certain plants
XANTHINE *n* crystalline
compound related in
structure to uric acid and
found in urine, blood,
certain plants, and certain
animal tissues
XANTHINES >XANTHINE
XANTHINS >XANTHIN
XANTHISM *n* condition of
skin, fur, or feathers in
which yellow coloration
predominates
XANTHISMS >XANTHISM
XANTHOMA *n* presence
in the skin of fatty
yellow or brownish
plaques or nodules, esp

on the eyelids, caused
by a disorder of lipid
metabolism
XANTHOMAS >XANTHOMA
XANTHONE *n* crystalline
compound
XANTHONES >XANTHONE
XANTHOUS *adj* of, relating
to, or designating races
with yellowish hair and a
light complexion
XANTHOXYL *n* South
American plant
XEBEC *n* small three-
masted Mediterranean
vessel with both square
and lateen sails, formerly
used by Algerian pirates
and later used for
commerce
XEBECS >XEBEC
XENIA *n* influence of
pollen upon the form of
the fruit developing after
pollination
XENIAL >XENIA
XENIAS >XENIA
XENIC *adj* denoting the
presence of bacteria
XENIUM *n* diplomatic gift
XENOBLAST *n* type of
mineral deposit
XENOCRYST *n* crystal
included within an
igneous rock as the
magma cooled but not
formed from it
XENOGAMY *n* fertilization
by the fusion of male and
female gametes from
different individuals of the
same species
XENOGENIC *adj* relating to

the supposed production
of offspring completely
unlike either parent
XENOGENY *n* offspring
unlike either parent
XENOGRAFT *n* tissue graft
obtained from a donor of a
different species from the
recipient
XENOLITH *n* fragment of
rock differing in origin,
composition, structure,
etc, from the igneous rock
enclosing it
XENOLITHS >XENOLITH
XENOMANIA *n* passion for
foreign things
XENOMENIA *n*
menstruation from
unusual orifices
XENON *n* colourless
odourless gas found in
very small quantities in
the air
XENONS >XENON
XENOPHILE *n* person who
likes foreigners or things
foreign
XENOPHOBE *n* person who
hates or fears foreigners or
strangers
XENOPHOBY *n* hatred or fear
of foreigners or strangers
XENOPHYA *n* parts of shell
or skeleton formed by
foreign bodies
XENOPUS *n* African frog
XENOPUSES >XENOPUS
XENOTIME *n* yellow-brown
mineral
XENOTIMES >XENOTIME
XENURINE *n* type of
armadillo

XENURINES >XENURINE
XERAFIN *n* Indian coin
XERAFINS >XERAFIN
XERANSES >XERANSIS
XERANSIS *n* gradual loss of
tissue moisture
XERANTIC >XERANSIS
XERAPHIM *same
as* >XERAFIN
XERAPHIMS >XERAPHIM
XERARCH *adj* (of a sere)
having its origin in a dry
habitat
XERASIA *n* dryness of the
hair
XERASIAS >XERASIA
XERIC *adj* of, relating to, or
growing in dry conditions
XERICALLY >XERIC
XERISCAPE *n* landscape
designed to conserve
water
XEROCHASY *n* release of
seeds or pollen on drying
XERODERMA *n* any
abnormal dryness of
the skin as the result of
diminished secretions
from the sweat or
sebaceous glands
XEROMA *n* excessive dryness
of the cornea
XEROMAS >XEROMA
XEROMATA >XEROMA
XEROMORPH *n* xerophilous
plant
XEROPHAGY *n* fasting by
eating only dry food
XEROPHILE *n* plant or
animal who likes living in
dry surroundings
XEROPHILY >XEROPHILE
XEROPHYTE *n* xerophilous

plant, such as a cactus
**XEROSERE** *n* sere that originates in dry surroundings
**XEROSERES** >XEROSERE
**XEROSES** >XEROSIS
**XEROSIS** *n* abnormal dryness of bodily tissues, esp the skin, eyes, or mucous membranes
**XEROSTOMA** *n* abnormal lack of saliva; dryness of the mouth
**XEROTES** *same as* >XEROSIS
**XEROTIC** >XEROSIS
**XEROX** *n* tradename for a machine employing a xerographic copying process ▷ *vb* produce a copy (of a document, etc) using such a machine
**XEROXED** >XEROX
**XEROXES** >XEROX
**XEROXING** >XEROX
**XERUS** *n* ground squirrel
**XERUSES** >XERUS
**XI** *n* 14th letter in the Greek alphabet
**XIPHOID** *adj* shaped like a sword ▷ *n* part of the sternum
**XIPHOIDAL** >XIPHOID
**XIPHOIDS** >XIPHOID
**XIPHOPAGI** *n* Siamese twins joined at the lower sternum
**XIS** >XI
**XOANA** >XOANON
**XOANON** *n* primitive image of a god, carved, esp originally, in wood, and supposed to have fallen from heaven
**XU** *n* Vietnamese currency unit
**XYLAN** *n* yellow polysaccharide consisting of xylose units: occurs in straw husks and other woody tissue
**XYLANS** >XYLAN
**XYLEM** *n* plant tissue that conducts water and minerals from the roots to all other parts
**XYLEMS** >XYLEM
**XYLENE** *n* type of hydrocarbon
**XYLENES** >XYLENE
**XYLENOL** *n* synthetic resin made from xylene
**XYLENOLS** >XYLENOL
**XYLIC** >XYLEM
**XYLIDIN** *same as* >XYLIDINE
**XYLIDINE** *n* mixture of six isomeric amines derived from xylene and used in dyes
**XYLIDINES** >XYLIDINE
**XYLIDINS** >XYLIDIN
**XYLITOL** *n* crystalline alcohol used as sweetener
**XYLITOLS** >XYLITOL
**XYLOCARP** *n* fruit, such as

a coconut, having a hard woody pericarp
**XYLOCARPS** >XYLOCARP
**XYLOGEN** *same as* >XYLEM
**XYLOGENS** >XYLOGEN
**XYLOGRAPH** *n* engraving in wood ▷ *vb* print (a design, illustration, etc) from a wood engraving
**XYLOID** *adj* of, relating to, or resembling wood
**XYLOIDIN** *n* type of explosive
**XYLOIDINE** *same as* >XYLOIDIN
**XYLOIDINS** >XYLOIDIN
**XYLOL** *another name (not in technical usage)* for >XYLENE
**XYLOLOGY** *n* study of the composition of wood
**XYLOLS** >XYLOL
**XYLOMA** *n* hard growth in fungi
**XYLOMAS** >XYLOMA
**XYLOMATA** >XYLOMA
**XYLOMETER** *n* device for measuring the specific gravity of wood
**XYLONIC** *adj* denoting an acid formed from xylose
**XYLONITE** *n* type of plastic
**XYLONITES** >XYLONITE
**XYLOPHAGE** *n* creature that eats wood
**XYLOPHONE** *n* musical instrument made of a row of wooden bars played with hammers
**XYLORIMBA** *n* large xylophone with an extended range of five octaves
**XYLOSE** *n* white crystalline dextrorotatory sugar found in the form of xylan in wood and straw
**XYLOSES** >XYLOSE
**XYLOTOMY** *n* preparation of sections of wood for examination by microscope
**XYLYL** *n* group of atoms
**XYLYLS** >XYLYL
**XYST** *n* long portico, esp one used in ancient Greece for athletics
**XYSTER** *n* surgical instrument for scraping bone
**XYSTERS** >XYSTER
**XYSTI** >XYSTUS
**XYSTOI** >XYSTOS
**XYSTOS** *same as* >XYST
**XYSTS** >XYST
**XYSTUS** *same as* >XYST

# Yy

YA *pron* you
YAAR *n* in informal Indian English, a friend
YAARS > YAAR
YABA *n* informal word for 'yet another bloody acronym'
YABBA *n* form of methamphetamine
YABBAS > YABBA
YABBER *vb* talk or jabber ▷ *n* talk or jabber
YABBERED > YABBER
YABBERING > YABBER
YABBERS > YABBER
YABBIE *same as* > YABBY
YABBIED > YABBY
YABBIES > YABBY
YABBY *n* small freshwater crayfish ▷ *vb* go out to catch yabbies
YABBYING > YABBY
YACCA *n* Australian plant with a woody stem, stiff grasslike leaves, and a spike of small white flowers
YACCAS > YACCA
YACHT *n* large boat with sails or an engine, used for racing or pleasure cruising ▷ *vb* sail in a yacht
YACHTED > YACHT
YACHTER > YACHT
YACHTERS > YACHT
YACHTIE *n* yachtsman
YACHTIES > YACHTIE
YACHTING *n* sport or practice of navigating a yacht
YACHTINGS > YACHTING
YACHTMAN *same as* > YACHTSMAN

YACHTMEN > YACHTMAN
YACHTS > YACHT
YACHTSMAN *n* person who sails a yacht
YACHTSMEN > YACHTSMAN
YACK *same as* > YAK
YACKA *same as* > YACCA
YACKAS > YACKA
YACKED > YACK
YACKER *same as* > YAKKA
YACKERS > YACKER
YACKING > YACK
YACKS > YACK
YAD *n* hand-held pointer used for reading the sefer torah
YADS > YAD
YAE *same as* > AE
YAFF *vb* bark
YAFFED > YAFF
YAFFING > YAFF
YAFFLE *n* woodpecker with a green back and wings, and a red crown
YAFFLES > YAFFLE
YAFFS > YAFF
YAG *n* artificial crystal
YAGER *same as* > JAEGER
YAGERS > YAGER
YAGGER *n* pedlar
YAGGERS > YAGGER
YAGI *n* type of highly directional aerial
YAGIS > YAGI
YAGS > YAG
YAH *interj* exclamation of derision or disgust ▷ *n* affected upper-class person
YAHOO *n* crude coarse person
YAHOOISM > YAHOO
YAHOOISMS > YAHOO

YAHOOS > YAHOO
YAHRZEIT *n* (in Judaism) the anniversary of the death of a close relative, on which it is customary to kindle a light and recite the Kaddish
YAHRZEITS > YAHRZEIT
YAHS > YAH
YAIRD *Scots form of* > YARD
YAIRDS > YAIRD
YAK *n* Tibetan ox with long shaggy hair ▷ *vb* talk continuously about unimportant matters
YAKHDAN *n* box for carrying ice on a pack animal
YAKHDANS > YAKHDAN
YAKIMONO *n* grilled food
YAKIMONOS > YAKIMONO
YAKITORI *n* Japanese dish consisting of small pieces of chicken skewered and grilled
YAKITORIS > YAKITORI
YAKKA *n* work
YAKKAS > YAKKA
YAKKED > YAK
YAKKER *same as* > YAKKA
YAKKERS > YAKKER
YAKKING > YAK
YAKOW *n* animal bred from a male yak and a domestic cow
YAKOWS > YAKOW
YAKS > YAK
YAKUZA *n* Japanese criminal organization involved in illegal gambling, extortion, gun-running, etc
YALD *adj* vigorous
YALE *n* mythical beast with

the body of an antelope (or similar animal) and swivelling horns
YALES > YALE
YAM *n* tropical root vegetable
YAMALKA *same as* > YARMULKE
YAMALKAS > YAMALKA
YAMEN *n* (in imperial China) the office or residence of a public official
YAMENS > YAMEN
YAMMER *vb* whine in a complaining manner ▷ *n* yammering sound
YAMMERED > YAMMER
YAMMERER > YAMMER
YAMMERERS > YAMMER
YAMMERS > YAMMER
YAMPIES > YAMPY
YAMPY *n* foolish person
YAMS > YAM
YAMULKA *same as* > YARMULKE
YAMULKAS > YAMULKA
YAMUN *same as* > YAMEN
YAMUNS > YAMUN
YANG *n* (in Chinese philosophy) one of two complementary principles maintaining harmony in the universe
YANGS > YANG
YANK *vb* pull or jerk suddenly ▷ *n* sudden pull or jerk
YANKED > YANK
YANKER > YANK
YANKERS > YANK
YANKIE *n* shrewish woman
YANKIES > YANKIE

YANKING >YANK
YANKS >YANK
YANQUI n slang word for American
YANQUIS >YANQUI
YANTRA n diagram used in meditation
YANTRAS >YANTRA
YAOURT n yoghurt
YAOURTS >YAOURT
YAP vb bark with a high-pitched sound ▷ n high-pitched bark ▷ interj imitation or representation of the sound of a dog yapping or people jabbering
YAPOCK same as >YAPOK
YAPOCKS >YAPOCK
YAPOK n type of opossum
YAPOKS >YAPOK
YAPON same as >YAUPON
YAPONS >YAPON
YAPP n type of book binding
YAPPED >YAP
YAPPER >YAP
YAPPERS >YAP
YAPPIE n young aspiring professional
YAPPIER >YAP
YAPPIES >YAPPIE
YAPPIEST >YAP
YAPPING >YAP
YAPPINGLY >YAP
YAPPS >YAPP
YAPPY >YAP
YAPS >YAP
YAPSTER >YAP
YAPSTERS >YAP
YAQONA n Polynesian shrub
YAQONAS >YAQONA
YAR adj nimble
YARCO n derogatory dialect word for a young working-class person who wears casual sports clothes
YARCOS >YARCO
YARD n unit of length equal to 36 inches or about 91.4 centimetres ▷ vb draft (animals), esp to a saleyard
YARDAGE n length measured in yards
YARDAGES >YARDAGE
YARDANG n ridge formed by wind erosion
YARDANGS >YARDANG
YARDARM n outer end of a ship's yard
YARDARMS >YARDARM
YARDBIRD n inexperienced, untrained, or clumsy soldier, esp one employed on menial duties
YARDBIRDS >YARDBIRD
YARDED >YARD
YARDER >YARD
YARDERS >YARD
YARDING n group of animals displayed for sale
YARDINGS >YARDING
YARDLAND n archaic unit of land

YARDLANDS >YARDLAND
YARDMAN n farm overseer
YARDMEN >YARDMAN
YARDS >YARD
YARDSTICK n standard against which to judge other people or things
YARDWAND same as >YARDSTICK
YARDWANDS >YARDWAND
YARDWORK n garden work
YARDWORKS >YARDWORK
YARE adj ready, brisk, or eager ▷ adv readily or eagerly
YARELY >YARE
YARER >YARE
YAREST >YARE
YARFA n peat
YARFAS >YARFA
YARK vb make ready
YARKED >YARK
YARKING >YARK
YARKS >YARK
YARMELKE same as >YARMULKE
YARMELKES >YARMELKE
YARMULKA same as >YARMULKE
YARMULKAS >YARMULKA
YARMULKE n skullcap worn by Jewish men
YARMULKES >YARMULKE
YARN n thread used for knitting or making cloth ▷ vb thread with yarn
YARNED >YARN
YARNER >YARN
YARNERS >YARN
YARNING >YARN
YARNS >YARN
YARPHA n peat
YARPHAS >YARPHA
YARR n wild white flower
YARRAMAN n horse
YARRAMANS >YARRAMAN
YARRAMEN >YARRAMAN
YARRAN n small hardy tree, Acacia homalophylla, of inland Australia
YARRANS >YARRAN
YARROW n wild plant with flat clusters of white flowers
YARROWS >YARROW
YARRS >YARR
YARTA Shetland word for >HEART
YARTAS >YARTA
YARTO same as >YARTA
YARTOS >YARTO
YASHMAC same as >YASHMAK
YASHMACS >YASHMAC
YASHMAK n veil worn by a Muslim woman to cover her face in public
YASHMAKS >YASHMAK
YASMAK same as >YASHMAK
YASMAKS >YASHMAK
YATAGAN same as >YATAGHAN
YATAGANS >YATAGAN
YATAGHAN n Turkish sword with a curved single-

edged blade
YATAGHANS >YATAGHAN
YATE n any of several small eucalyptus trees, esp Eucalyptus cornuta, yielding a very hard timber
YATES >YATE
YATTER vb talk at length ▷ n continuous chatter
YATTERED >YATTER
YATTERING >YATTER
YATTERS >YATTER
YAUD Scots word for >MARE
YAUDS >YAUD
YAULD adj alert, spritely, or nimble
YAUP variant spelling of >YAWP
YAUPED >YAUP
YAUPER >YAUP
YAUPERS >YAUP
YAUPING >YAUP
YAUPON n southern US evergreen holly shrub, Ilex vomitoria, with spreading branches, scarlet fruits, and oval leaves
YAUPONS >YAUPON
YAUPS >YAUP
YAUTIA n any of several Caribbean aroid plants of the genus Xanthosoma, cultivated for their edible leaves and underground stems
YAUTIAS >YAUTIA
YAW vb. (of an aircraft or ship) turn to one side or from side to side while moving ▷ n act or movement of yawing
YAWED >YAW
YAWEY >YAWS
YAWING >YAW
YAWL n two-masted sailing boat ▷ vb howl, weep, or scream harshly
YAWLED >YAWL
YAWLING >YAWL
YAWLS >YAWL
YAWMETER n instrument for measuring an aircraft's yaw
YAWMETERS >YAWMETER
YAWN vb open the mouth wide and take in air deeply, often when sleepy or bored ▷ n act of yawning
YAWNED >YAWN
YAWNER >YAWN
YAWNERS >YAWN
YAWNIER >YAWN
YAWNIEST >YAWN
YAWNING >YAWN
YAWNINGLY >YAWN
YAWNINGS >YAWN
YAWNS >YAWN
YAWNY >YAWN
YAWP vb gape or yawn, esp audibly ▷ n shout, bark, yelp, or cry
YAWPED >YAWP
YAWPER >YAWP
YAWPERS >YAWP

YAWPING >YAWP
YAWPINGS >YAWP
YAWPS >YAWP
YAWS n infectious tropical skin disease
YAWY >YAWS
YAY interj exclamation indicating approval, congratulation, or triumph ▷ n cry of approval
YAYS >YAY
YBET archaic past participle of >BEAT
YBLENT archaic past participle of >BLEND
YBORE archaic past participle of >BEAR
YBOUND archaic past participle of >BIND
YBOUNDEN archaic past participle of >BIND
YBRENT archaic past participle of >BURN
YCLAD archaic past participle of >CLOTHE
YCLED archaic past participle of >CLOTHE
YCLEEPE archaic form of >CLEPE
YCLEEPED >YCLEEPE
YCLEEPES >YCLEEPE
YCLEEPING >YCLEEPE
YCLEPED same as >YCLEPT
YCLEPT adj having the name of
YCOND archaic past participle of >CON
YDRAD archaic past participle of >DREAD
YDRED archaic past participle of >DREAD
YE pron you ▷ adj the
YEA interj yes ▷ adv indeed or truly ▷ sentence substitute >AYE ▷ n cry of agreement
YEAD vb proceed
YEADING >YEAD
YEADS >YEAD
YEAH n positive affirmation
YEAHS >YEAH
YEALDON n fuel
YEALDONS >YEALDON
YEALING n person of the same age as oneself
YEALINGS >YEALING
YEALM vb prepare for thatching
YEALMED >YEALM
YEALMING >YEALM
YEALMS >YEALM
YEAN vb (of a sheep or goat) to give birth to (offspring)
YEANED >YEAN
YEANING >YEAN
YEANLING n young of a goat or sheep
YEANLINGS >YEANLING
YEANS >YEAN
YEAR n time taken for the earth to make one revolution around the sun, about 365 days

YEARBOOK n reference book published annually containing details of the previous year's events
YEARBOOKS > YEARBOOK
YEARD vb bury
YEARDED > YEARD
YEARDING > YEARD
YEARDS > YEARD
YEAREND n end of the year
YEARENDS > YEAREND
YEARLIES > YEARLY
YEARLING n animal between one and two years old ▷ adj being a year old
YEARLINGS > YEARLING
YEARLONG adj throughout a whole year
YEARLY adv (happening) every year or once a year ▷ adj occurring, done, or appearing once a year or every year ▷ n publication, event, etc, that occurs once a year
YEARN vb want (something) very much
YEARNED > YEARN
YEARNER > YEARN
YEARNERS > YEARN
YEARNING n intense or overpowering longing, desire, or need
YEARNINGS > YEARNING
YEARNS > YEARN
YEARS > YEAR
YEAS > YEA
YEASAYER n person who usually agrees with proposals
YEASAYERS > YEASAYER
YEAST n fungus used to make bread rise and to ferment alcoholic drinks ▷ vb froth or foam
YEASTED > YEAST
YEASTIER > YEASTY
YEASTIEST > YEASTY
YEASTILY > YEASTY
YEASTING > YEAST
YEASTLESS > YEAST
YEASTLIKE > YEAST
YEASTS > YEAST
YEASTY adj of, resembling, or containing yeast
YEBO interj yes ▷ sentence substitute expression of affirmation
YECCH same as > YECH
YECCHS > YECCH
YECH n expression of disgust
YECHS > YECH
YECHY > YECH
YEDE same as > YEAD
YEDES > YEDE
YEDING > YEDE
YEED same as > YEAD
YEEDING > YEED
YEEDS > YEED
YEELIN n person of the same age as oneself
YEELINS > YEELIN

YEGG n burglar or safe-breaker
YEGGMAN same as > YEGG
YEGGMEN > YEGGMAN
YEGGS > YEGG
YEH same as > YEAH
YELD adj (of an animal) barren or too young to bear young
YELDRING n yellowhammer (bird)
YELDRINGS > YELDRING
YELDROCK same as > YELDRING
YELDROCKS > YELDROCK
YELK n yolk of an egg
YELKS > YELK
YELL vb shout or scream in a loud or piercing way ▷ n loud cry of pain, anger, or fear
YELLED > YELL
YELLER > YELL
YELLERS > YELL
YELLING > YELL
YELLINGS > YELL
YELLOCH vb yell
YELLOCHED > YELLOCH
YELLOCHS > YELLOCH
YELLOW n colour of gold, a lemon, etc ▷ adj of this colour ▷ vb make or become yellow
YELLOWED > YELLOW
YELLOWER > YELLOW
YELLOWEST > YELLOW
YELLOWFIN n type of tuna
YELLOWIER > YELLOW
YELLOWING > YELLOW
YELLOWISH > YELLOW
YELLOWLY > YELLOW
YELLOWS n any of various fungal or viral diseases of plants, characterized by yellowish discoloration and stunting
YELLOWY > YELLOW
YELLS > YELL
YELM same as > YEALM
YELMED > YELM
YELMING > YELM
YELMS > YELM
YELP n a short sudden cry ▷ vb utter a sharp or high-pitched cry of pain
YELPED > YELP
YELPER > YELP
YELPERS > YELP
YELPING > YELP
YELPINGS > YELP
YELPS > YELP
YELT n young sow
YELTS > YELT
YEMMER southwest English form of > EMBER
YEMMERS > YEMMER
YEN n monetary unit of Japan ▷ vb have a longing
YENNED > YEN
YENNING > YEN
YENS > YEN
YENTA n meddlesome woman
YENTAS > YENTA

YENTE same as > YENTA
YENTES > YENTE
YEOMAN n farmer owning and farming his own land
YEOMANLY adj of, relating to, or like a yeoman ▷ adv in a yeomanly manner, as in being brave, staunch, or loyal
YEOMANRY n yeomen
YEOMEN > YEOMAN
YEP n affirmative statement
YEPS > YEP
YERBA n stimulating South American drink made from dried leaves
YERBAS > YERBA
YERD vb bury
YERDED > YERD
YERDING > YERD
YERDS > YERD
YERK vb tighten stitches
YERKED > YERK
YERKING > YERK
YERKS > YERK
YERSINIA n plague bacterium
YERSINIAE > YERSINIA
YERSINIAS > YERSINIA
YES interj expresses consent, agreement, or approval ▷ n answer or vote of yes ▷ sentence substitute used to express acknowledgment, affirmation, consent, agreement, or approval or to answer when one is addressed ▷ vb reply in the affirmative
YESES > YES
YESHIVA n traditional Jewish school devoted chiefly to the study of rabbinic literature and the Talmud
YESHIVAH same as > YESHIVA
YESHIVAHS > YESHIVAH
YESHIVAS > YESHIVA
YESHIVOT > YESHIVA
YESHIVOTH > YESHIVA
YESK vb hiccup
YESKED > YESK
YESKING > YESK
YESKS > YESK
YESSED > YES
YESSES > YES
YESSING > YES
YEST archaic form of > YEAST
YESTER adj of or relating to yesterday
YESTERDAY n the day before today ▷ adv on or during the day before today
YESTEREVE n yesterday evening
YESTERN same as > YESTER
YESTREEN n yesterday evening
YESTREENS > YESTREEN
YESTS > YEST

YESTY archaic form of > YEASTY
YET adv up until then or now
YETI n large legendary manlike creature alleged to inhabit the Himalayan Mountains
YETIS > YETI
YETT n gate or door
YETTIE n young, entrepreneurial, and technology-based (person)
YETTIES > YETTIE
YETTS > YETT
YEUK vb itch
YEUKED > YEUK
YEUKING > YEUK
YEUKS > YEUK
YEUKY > YEUK
YEVE vb give
YEVEN > YEVE
YEVES > YEVE
YEVING > YEVE
YEW n evergreen tree with needle-like leaves and red berries
YEWEN adj made of yew
YEWS > YEW
YEX vb hiccup
YEXED > YEX
YEXES > YEX
YEXING > YEX
YFERE adv together
YGLAUNST archaic past participle of > GLANCE
YGO archaic past participle of > GO
YGOE archaic past participle of > GO
YIBBLES adv perhaps
YICKER vb squeal or squeak
YICKERED > YICKER
YICKERING > YICKER
YICKERS > YICKER
YID n offensive word for a Jew
YIDAKI n long wooden wind instrument played by the Aboriginal peoples of Arnhem Land
YIDAKIS > YIDAKI
YIDS > YID
YIELD vb produce or bear ▷ n amount produced
YIELDABLE > YIELD
YIELDED > YIELD
YIELDER > YIELD
YIELDERS > YIELD
YIELDING adj submissive
YIELDINGS > YIELD
YIELDS > YIELD
YIKE n argument, squabble, or fight ▷ vb argue, squabble, or fight
YIKED > YIKE
YIKES interj expression of surprise, fear, or alarm
YIKING > YIKE
YIKKER vb squeal or squeak
YIKKERED > YIKKER
YIKKERING > YIKKER
YIKKERS > YIKKER
YILL n ale

YILLS >YILL
YIN Scots word for >ONE
YINCE Scots form of >ONCE
YINS >YIN
YIP n emit a high-pitched bark
YIPE same as >YIPES
YIPES interj expression of surprise, fear, or alarm
YIPPED >YIP
YIPPEE interj exclamation of joy or pleasure
YIPPER n golfer who suffers from a failure of nerve
YIPPERS >YIPPER
YIPPIE n young person sharing hippy ideals
YIPPIES >YIPPIE
YIPPING >YIP
YIPPY same as >YIPPIE
YIPS >YIP
YIRD vb bury
YIRDED >YIRD
YIRDING >YIRD
YIRDS >YIRD
YIRK same as >YERK
YIRKED >YIRK
YIRKING >YIRK
YIRKS >YIRK
YIRR vb snarl, growl, or yell
YIRRED >YIRR
YIRRING >YIRR
YIRRS >YIRR
YIRTH n earth
YIRTHS >YIRTH
YITE n European bunting with a yellowish head and body and brown streaked wings and tail
YITES >YITE
YITIE same as >YITE
YITIES >YITIE
YITTEN adj frightened
YLEM n original matter from which the basic elements are said to have been formed following the explosion postulated in the big bang theory of cosmology
YLEMS >YLEM
YLIKE Spenserian form of >ALIKE
YLKE archaic spelling of >ILK
YLKES >YLKE
YMOLT Spenserian past participle of >MELT
YMOLTEN Spenserian past participle of >MELT
YMPE Spenserian form of >IMP
YMPES >YMPE
YMPING >YMPE
YMPT >YMPE
YNAMBU n South American bird
YNAMBUS >YNAMBU
YO interj expression used as a greeting or to attract someone's attention ▷ sentence substitute expression used as a greeting, to attract

someone's attention, etc ▷ n cry of greeting
YOB n bad-mannered aggressive youth
YOBBERIES >YOBBERY
YOBBERY n behaviour typical of aggressive surly youths
YOBBISH adj typical of aggressive surly youths
YOBBISHLY >YOBBISH
YOBBISM >YOB
YOBBISMS >YOB
YOBBO same as >YOB
YOBBOES >YOBBO
YOBBOS >YOBBO
YOBS >YOB
YOCK vb chuckle
YOCKED >YOCK
YOCKING >YOCK
YOCKS >YOCK
YOD n tenth letter in the Hebrew alphabet
YODE >YEAD
YODEL vb sing with abrupt changes between a normal and a falsetto voice ▷ n act or sound of yodelling
YODELED >YODEL
YODELER >YODEL
YODELERS >YODEL
YODELING >YODEL
YODELLED >YODEL
YODELLER >YODEL
YODELLERS >YODEL
YODELLING >YODEL
YODELS >YODEL
YODH same as >YOD
YODHS >YODH
YODLE variant spelling of >YODEL
YODLED >YODLE
YODLER >YODLE
YODLERS >YODLE
YODLES >YODLE
YODLING >YODLE
YODS >YOD
YOGA n Hindu method of exercise and discipline aiming at spiritual, mental, and physical wellbeing
YOGAS >YOGA
YOGEE same as >YOGI
YOGEES >YOGEE
YOGH n character used in Old and Middle English to represent a palatal fricative
YOGHOURT variant form of >YOGURT
YOGHOURTS >YOGHOURT
YOGHS >YOGH
YOGHURT same as >YOGURT
YOGHURTS >YOGHURT
YOGI n person who practises yoga
YOGIC >YOGA
YOGIN same as >YOGI
YOGINI >YOGI
YOGINIS >YOGI
YOGINS >YOGIN
YOGIS >YOGI
YOGISM >YOGI

YOGISMS >YOGI
YOGURT n slightly sour custard-like food made from milk that has had bacteria added to it, often sweetened and flavoured with fruit
YOGURTS >YOGURT
YOHIMBE n bark used in herbal medicine
YOHIMBES >YOHIMBE
YOHIMBINE n alkaloid found in the bark of the tree Corynanthe yohimbe
YOICK vb urge on foxhounds
YOICKED >YOICK
YOICKING >YOICK
YOICKS interj cry used by huntsmen to urge on the hounds to the fox ▷ vb urge on foxhounds
YOICKSED >YOICKS
YOICKSES >YOICKS
YOICKSING >YOICKS
YOJAN n Indian unit of distance
YOJANA same as >YOJAN
YOJANAS >YOJANA
YOJANS >YOJAN
YOK vb chuckle
YOKE n wooden bar put across the necks of two animals to hold them together ▷ vb put a yoke on
YOKED >YOKE
YOKEL n derogatory term for a person who lives in the country and is usu simple and old-fashioned
YOKELESS >YOKE
YOKELISH >YOKEL
YOKELS >YOKEL
YOKEMATE n colleague
YOKEMATES >YOKEMATE
YOKER >YOKE
YOKERS >YOKE
YOKES >YOKE
YOKING >YOKE
YOKINGS >YOKE
YOKKED >YOK
YOKKING >YOK
YOKOZUNA n grand champion sumo wrestler
YOKOZUNAS >YOKOZUNA
YOKS >YOK
YOKUL Shetland word for >YES
YOLD archaic past participle of >YIELD
YOLDRING n yellowhammer (bird)
YOLDRINGS >YOLDRING
YOLK n yellow part of an egg that provides food for the developing embryo
YOLKED >YOLK
YOLKIER >YOLK
YOLKIEST >YOLK
YOLKLESS >YOLK
YOLKS >YOLK
YOLKY >YOLK
YOM n day

YOMIM >YOM
YOMP vb walk or trek laboriously, esp heavily laden and over difficult terrain
YOMPED >YOMP
YOMPING >YOMP
YOMPS >YOMP
YON adj that or those over there ▷ adv yonder ▷ pron that person or thing
YOND same as >YON
YONDER adv over there ▷ adj situated over there ▷ determiner being at a distance, either within view or as if within view ▷ n person
YONDERLY >YONDER
YONDERS >YONDER
YONI n female genitalia, regarded as a divine symbol of sexual pleasure
YONIC adj resembling a vulva
YONIS >YONI
YONKER same as >YOUNKER
YONKERS >YONKER
YONKS pl n very long time
YONNIE n stone
YONNIES >YONNIE
YONT same as >YON
YOOF n non-standard spelling of youth, used humorously or facetiously
YOOFS >YOOF
YOOP n sob
YOOPS >YOOP
YOPPER n (formerly in Britain) a youth employed under the Youth Opportunities Programme)
YOPPERS >YOPPER
YORE n time long past ▷ adv in the past
YORES >YORE
YORK vb bowl or try to bowl (a batsman) by pitching the ball under or just beyond the bat
YORKED >YORK
YORKER n ball that pitches just under the bat
YORKERS >YORKER
YORKIE n Yorkshire terrier
YORKIES >YORKIE
YORKING >YORK
YORKS >YORK
YORP vb shout
YORPED >YORP
YORPING >YORP
YORPS >YORP
YOS >YO
YOTTABYTE n very large unit of computer memory
YOU pron person or people addressed ▷ n personality of the person being addressed
YOUK vb itch
YOUKED >YOUK
YOUKING >YOUK
YOUKS >YOUK

**YOUNG** *adj* in an early stage of life or growth ▷ *n* young people in general; offspring
**YOUNGER** > YOUNG
**YOUNGERS** *n* young people
**YOUNGEST** > YOUNG
**YOUNGISH** > YOUNG
**YOUNGLING** *n* young person, animal, or plant
**YOUNGLY** *adv* youthfully
**YOUNGNESS** > YOUNG
**YOUNGS** > YOUNG
**YOUNGSTER** *n* young person
**YOUNGTH** *n* youth
**YOUNGTHLY** *adj* youthful
**YOUNGTHS** > YOUNGTH
**YOUNKER** *n* young man
**YOUNKERS** > YOUNKER
**YOUPON** *same as* > YAUPON
**YOUPONS** > YOUPON
**YOUR** *adj* of, belonging to, or associated with you
**YOURN** *dialect form of* > YOURS
**YOURS** *pron* something belonging to you
**YOURSELF** *pron* reflexive form of you
**YOURT** *same as* > YURT
**YOURTS** > YOURT
**YOUS** *pron* refers to more than one person including the person or persons addressed but not including the speaker
**YOUSE** *same as* > YOUS
**YOUTH** *n* time of being young
**YOUTHEN** *vb* render more youthful-seeming
**YOUTHENED** > YOUTHEN
**YOUTHENS** > YOUTHEN
**YOUTHFUL** *adj* vigorous or active
**YOUTHHEAD** *same as* > YOUTHHOOD
**YOUTHHOOD** *n* youth
**YOUTHIER** > YOUTHY
**YOUTHIEST** > YOUTHY
**YOUTHLESS** > YOUTH
**YOUTHLY** *adv* young
**YOUTHS** > YOUTH
**YOUTHSOME** *archaic variant of* > YOUTHFUL
**YOUTHY** *Scots word for* > YOUNG
**YOW** *vb* howl
**YOWE** *Scot word for* > EWE
**YOWED** > YOW
**YOWES** > YOWE
**YOWIE** *n* legendary Australian apelike creature
**YOWIES** > YOWIE
**YOWING** > YOW
**YOWL** *n* loud mournful cry ▷ *vb* produce a loud mournful wail or cry
**YOWLED** > YOWL
**YOWLER** > YOWL
**YOWLERS** > YOWL
**YOWLEY** *n* yellowhammer (bird)

**YOWLEYS** > YOWLEY
**YOWLING** > YOWL
**YOWLINGS** > YOWL
**YOWLS** > YOWL
**YOWS** > YOW
**YPERITE** *n* mustard gas
**YPERITES** > YPERITE
**YPIGHT** *archaic past participle of* > PITCH
**YPLAST** *archaic past participle of* > PLACE
**YPLIGHT** *archaic past participle of* > PLIGHT
**YPSILOID** > YPSILON
**YPSILON** *same as* > UPSILON
**YPSILONS** > YPSILON
**YRAPT** *Spenserian form of* > RAPT
**YRAVISHED** *archaic past participle of* > RAVISH
**YRENT** *archaic past participle of* > REND
**YRIVD** *archaic past participle of* > RIVE
**YRNEH** *n* unit of reciprocal inductance
**YRNEHS** > YRNEH
**YSAME** *Spenserian word for* > TOGETHER
**YSHEND** *Spenserian form of* > SHEND
**YSHENDING** > YSHEND
**YSHENDS** > YSHEND
**YSHENT** > YSHEND
**YSLAKED** *archaic past participle of* > SLAKE
**YTOST** *archaic past participle of* > TOSS
**YTTERBIA** *n* colourless hygroscopic substance used in certain alloys and ceramics
**YTTERBIAS** > YTTERBIA
**YTTERBIC** > YTTERBIUM
**YTTERBITE** *n* rare mineral
**YTTERBIUM** *n* soft silvery element
**YTTERBOUS** > YTTERBIUM
**YTTRIA** *n* insoluble solid used mainly in incandescent mantles
**YTTRIAS** > YTTRIA
**YTTRIC** > YTTRIUM
**YTTRIOUS** > YTTRIUM
**YTTRIUM** *n* silvery metallic element used in various alloys
**YTTRIUMS** > YTTRIUM
**YU** *n* jade
**YUAN** *n* standard monetary unit of the People's Republic of China
**YUANS** > YUAN
**YUCA** *same as* > YUCCA
**YUCAS** > YUCA
**YUCCA** *n* tropical plant with spikes of white leaves
**YUCCAS** > YUCCA
**YUCCH** *interj* expression of disgust
**YUCH** *interj* expression of disgust
**YUCK** *interj* exclamation indicating contempt,

dislike, or disgust ▷ *vb* chuckle
**YUCKED** > YUCK
**YUCKER** > YUCK
**YUCKERS** > YUCK
**YUCKIER** > YUCKY
**YUCKIEST** > YUCKY
**YUCKINESS** > YUCKY
**YUCKING** > YUCK
**YUCKO** *adj* disgusting ▷ *interj* exclamation of disgust
**YUCKS** > YUCK
**YUCKY** *adj* disgusting, nasty
**YUFT** *n* Russia leather
**YUFTS** > YUFT
**YUG** *same as* > YUGA
**YUGA** *n* (in Hindu cosmology) one of the four ages of mankind
**YUGARIE** *variant spelling of* > EUGARIE
**YUGARIES** > YUGARIE
**YUGAS** > YUGA
**YUGS** > YUG
**YUK** *same as* > YUCK
**YUKATA** *n* light kimono
**YUKATAS** > YUKATA
**YUKE** *vb* itch
**YUKED** > YUKE
**YUKES** > YUKE
**YUKIER** > YUKY
**YUKIEST** > YUKY
**YUKING** > YUKE
**YUKKED** > YUK
**YUKKIER** > YUKKY
**YUKKIEST** > YUKKY
**YUKKING** > YUK
**YUKKY** *same as* > YUCKY
**YUKO** *n* score of five points in judo
**YUKOS** > YUKO
**YUKS** > YUK
**YUKY** *adj* itchy
**YULAN** *n* Chinese magnolia, *Magnolia denudata*, that is often cultivated for its showy white flowers
**YULANS** > YULAN
**YULE** *n* Christmas, the Christmas season, or Christmas festivities
**YULES** > YULE
**YULETIDE** *n* Christmas season
**YULETIDES** > YULETIDE
**YUM** *interj* expression of delight
**YUMMIER** > YUMMY
**YUMMIES** > YUMMY
**YUMMIEST** > YUMMY
**YUMMINESS** > YUMMY
**YUMMO** *adj* tasty ▷ *interj* exclamation of delight or approval
**YUMMY** *adj* delicious ▷ *interj* exclamation indicating pleasure or delight, as in anticipation of delicious food ▷ *n* delicious food item
**YUMP** *vb* leave the ground when driving over a ridge
**YUMPED** > YUMP

**YUMPIE** *n* young upwardly mobile person
**YUMPIES** > YUMPIE
**YUMPING** > YUMP
**YUMPS** > YUMP
**YUNX** *n* wryneck
**YUNXES** > YUNX
**YUP** *n* informal affirmative statement
**YUPON** *same as* > YAUPON
**YUPONS** > YUPON
**YUPPIE** *n* young highly-paid professional person, esp one who has a materialistic way of life ▷ *adj* typical of or reflecting the values of yuppies
**YUPPIEDOM** > YUPPIE
**YUPPIEISH** > YUPPIE
**YUPPIES** > YUPPY
**YUPPIFIED** > YUPPIFY
**YUPPIFIES** > YUPPIFY
**YUPPIFY** *vb* make yuppie in nature
**YUPPY** *same as* > YUPPIE
**YUPS** > YUP
**YURT** *n* circular tent consisting of a framework of poles covered with felt or skins, used by Mongolian and Turkic nomads of E and central Asia
**YURTA** *same as* > YURT
**YURTAS** > YURT
**YURTS** > YURT
**YUS** > YU
**YUTZ** *n* Yiddish word meaning fool
**YUTZES** > YUTZ
**YUZU** *n* type of citrus fruit
**YUZUS** > YUZU
**YWIS** *adv* certainly
**YWROKE** *archaic past participle of* > WREAK

# Zz

ZA n pizza
ZABAIONE n light foamy dessert
ZABAIONES > ZABAIONE
ZABAJONE same as > ZABAIONE
ZABAJONES > ZABAJONE
ZABETA n tariff
ZABETAS > ZACK
ZABRA n small sailing vessel
ZABRAS > ZABRA
ZABTIEH n Turkish police officer
ZABTIEHS > ZABTIEH
ZACATON n coarse grass
ZACATONS > ZACATON
ZACK n Australian five-cent piece
ZACKS > ZACK
ZADDICK adj righteous
ZADDIK n Hasidic Jewish leader
ZADDIKIM > ZADDIK
ZADDIKS > ZADDIK
ZAFFAR same as > ZAFFER
ZAFFARS > ZAFFAR
ZAFFER n impure cobalt oxide, used to impart a blue colour to enamels
ZAFFERS > ZAFFER
ZAFFIR same as > ZAFFER
ZAFFIRS > ZAFFIR
ZAFFRE same as > ZAFFER
ZAFFRES > ZAFFRE
ZAFTIG adj ripe or curvaceous
ZAG vb change direction sharply
ZAGGED > ZAG
ZAGGING > ZAG
ZAGS > ZAG
ZAIBATSU n group or combine comprising

a few wealthy families that controls industry, business, and finance in Japan
ZAIKAI n Japanese business community
ZAIKAIS > ZAIKAI
ZAIRE n currency used in the former Zaïre
ZAIRES > ZAIRE
ZAITECH n investment in financial markets by a company to supplement its main income
ZAITECHS > ZAITECH
ZAKAT n annual tax on Muslims to aid the poor in the Muslim community
ZAKATS > ZAKAT
ZAKOUSKA > ZAKOUSKI
ZAKOUSKI same as > ZAKUSKI
ZAKUSKA > ZAKUSKI
ZAKUSKI pl n hors d'œuvres, consisting of tiny open sandwiches spread with caviar, smoked sausage, etc
ZAMAN n tropical tree
ZAMANG same as > ZAMAN
ZAMANGS > ZAMANG
ZAMANS > ZAMAN
ZAMARRA n sheepskin coat
ZAMARRAS > ZAMARRA
ZAMARRO same as > ZAMARRA
ZAMARROS > ZAMARRO
ZAMBO n offensive word for a Black person
ZAMBOMBA n drum-like musical instrument
ZAMBOMBAS > ZAMBOMBA
ZAMBOORAK n small swivel-

mounted cannon
ZAMBOS > ZAMBO
ZAMBUCK n St John ambulance attendant, esp at a sports meeting
ZAMBUCKS > ZAMBUCK
ZAMBUK same as > ZAMBUCK
ZAMBUKS > ZAMBUK
ZAMIA n any cycadaceous plant of the genus Zamia, of tropical and subtropical America, having a short thick trunk, palmlike leaves, and short stout cones
ZAMIAS > ZAMIA
ZAMINDAR n (in India) the owner of an agricultural estate
ZAMINDARI n (in India) a large agricultural estate
ZAMINDARS > ZAMINDAR
ZAMINDARY same as > ZAMINDARI
ZAMOUSE n West African buffalo
ZAMOUSES > ZAMOUSE
ZAMPOGNA n Italian bagpipes
ZAMPOGNAS > ZAMPOGNA
ZAMPONE n sausage made from pig's trotters
ZAMPONI > ZAMPONE
ZAMZAWED adj (of tea) having been left in the pot to stew
ZANANA same as > ZENANA
ZANANAS > ZANANA
ZANDER n freshwater teleost pikeperch of Europe, Stizostedion lucioperca, valued as a food fish

ZANDERS > ZANDER
ZANELLA n twill fabric
ZANELLAS > ZANELLA
ZANIED > ZANY
ZANIER > ZANY
ZANIES > ZANY
ZANIEST > ZANY
ZANILY > ZANY
ZANINESS > ZANY
ZANJA n irrigation canal
ZANJAS > ZANJA
ZANJERO n irrigation supervisor
ZANJEROS > ZANJERO
ZANTE n type of wood
ZANTES > ZANTE
ZANTHOXYL variant spelling of > XANTHOXYL
ZANY adj comical in an endearing way ▷ n clown or buffoon, esp one in old comedies who imitated other performers with ludicrous effect ▷ vb clown
ZANYING > ZANY
ZANYISH > ZANY
ZANYISM > ZANY
ZANYISMS > ZANY
ZANZA same as > ZANZE
ZANZAS > ZANZA
ZANZE n African musical instrument
ZANZES > ZANZE
ZAP vb kill (by shooting) ▷ n energy, vigour, or pep ▷ interj exclamation used to express sudden or swift action
ZAPATA adj (of a moustache) drooping
ZAPATEADO n Spanish dance with stamping and

very fast footwork

**ZAPATEO** n Cuban folk dance

**ZAPATEOS** >ZAPATEO

**ZAPOTILLA** n shoe

**ZAPPED** >ZAP

**ZAPPER** n remote control for a television etc

**ZAPPERS** >ZAPPER

**ZAPPIER** >ZAPPY

**ZAPPIEST** >ZAPPY

**ZAPPING** >ZAP

**ZAPPY** adj energetic

**ZAPS** >ZAP

**ZAPTIAH** same as >ZAPTIEH

**ZAPTIAHS** >ZAPTIAH

**ZAPTIEH** n Turkish police officer

**ZAPTIEHS** >ZAPTIEH

**ZARAPE** n blanket-like shawl

**ZARAPES** >ZARAPE

**ZARATITE** n green amorphous mineral

**ZARATITES** >ZARATITE

**ZAREBA** n stockade or enclosure of thorn bushes around a village or campsite

**ZAREBAS** >ZAREBA

**ZAREEBA** same as >ZAREBA

**ZAREEBAS** >ZAREEBA

**ZARF** n (esp in the Middle East) a holder, usually ornamental, for a hot coffee cup

**ZARFS** >ZARF

**ZARIBA** same as >ZAREBA

**ZARIBAS** >ZARIBA

**ZARNEC** n sulphide of arsenic

**ZARNECS** >ZARNEC

**ZARNICH** same as >ZARNEC

**ZARNICHS** >ZARNICH

**ZARZUELA** n type of Spanish vaudeville or operetta, usually satirical in nature

**ZARZUELAS** >ZARZUELA

**ZAS** >ZA

**ZASTRUGA** variant spelling of >SASTRUGA

**ZASTRUGI** >ZASTRUGA

**ZATI** n type of macaque

**ZATIS** >ZATI

**ZAX** variant of >SAX

**ZAXES** >ZAX

**ZAYIN** n seventh letter of the Hebrew alphabet

**ZAYINS** >ZAYIN

**ZAZEN** n (in Zen Buddhism) deep meditation undertaken whilst sitting upright with legs crossed

**ZAZENS** >ZAZEN

**ZEA** n corn silk

**ZEAL** n great enthusiasm or eagerness

**ZEALANT** archaic variant of >ZEALOT

**ZEALANTS** >ZEALANT

**ZEALFUL** >ZEAL

**ZEALLESS** >ZEAL

**ZEALOT** n fanatic or

extreme enthusiast

**ZEALOTISM** >ZEALOT

**ZEALOTRY** n extreme or excessive zeal or devotion

**ZEALOTS** >ZEALOT

**ZEALOUS** adj extremely eager or enthusiastic

**ZEALOUSLY** >ZEALOUS

**ZEALS** >ZEAL

**ZEAS** >ZEAL

**ZEATIN** n cytokinin derived from corn

**ZEATINS** >ZEATIN

**ZEBEC** variant spelling of >XEBEC

**ZEBECK** same as >ZEBEC

**ZEBECKS** >ZEBECK

**ZEBECS** >ZEBEC

**ZEBRA** n black-and-white striped African animal of the horse family

**ZEBRAFISH** n striped tropical fish

**ZEBRAIC** adj like a zebra

**ZEBRANO** n type of striped wood

**ZEBRANOS** >ZEBRANO

**ZEBRAS** >ZEBRA

**ZEBRASS** n offspring of a male zebra and a female ass

**ZEBRASSES** >ZEBRASS

**ZEBRAWOOD** n tree yielding striped hardwood used in cabinetwork

**ZEBRINA** n trailing herbaceous plant

**ZEBRINAS** >ZEBRINA

**ZEBRINE** >ZEBRA

**ZEBRINES** >ZEBRA

**ZEBRINNY** n offspring of a male horse and a female zebra

**ZEBROID** >ZEBRA

**ZEBRULA** n offspring of a male zebra and a female horse

**ZEBRULAS** >ZEBRULA

**ZEBRULE** same as >ZEBRULA

**ZEBRULES** >ZEBRULE

**ZEBU** n Asian ox with a humped back and long horns

**ZEBUB** n large African fly

**ZEBUBS** >ZEBUB

**ZEBUS** >ZEBU

**ZECCHIN** same as >ZECCHINO

**ZECCHINE** same as >ZECCHINO

**ZECCHINES** >ZECCHINE

**ZECCHINI** >ZECCHINO

**ZECCHINO** n former gold coin

**ZECCHINOS** >ZECCHINO

**ZECCHINS** >ZECCHIN

**ZECHIN** same as >ZECCHINO

**ZECHINS** >ZECHIN

**ZED** n British and New Zealand spoken form of the letter z

**ZEDOARIES** >ZEDOARY

**ZEDOARY** n dried rhizome of the tropical Asian

plant Curcuma zedoaria, used as a stimulant and a condiment

**ZEDS** >ZED

**ZEE** same as >ZED

**ZEES** >ZEE

**ZEIN** n protein occurring in maize and used in the manufacture of plastics

**ZEINS** >ZEIN

**ZEITGEBER** n agent or event that sets or resets the biological clock

**ZEITGEIST** n spirit or attitude of a specific time or period

**ZEK** n Soviet prisoner

**ZEKS** >ZEK

**ZEL** n Turkish cymbal

**ZELANT** alternative form of >ZEALANT

**ZELANTS** >ZELANT

**ZELATOR** same as >ZELATRIX

**ZELATORS** >ZELATOR

**ZELATRICE** same as >ZELATRIX

**ZELATRIX** n nun who monitors the behaviour of younger nuns

**ZELKOVA** n type of elm tree

**ZELKOVAS** >ZELKOVA

**ZELOSO** adv with zeal

**ZELOTYPIA** n morbid zeal

**ZELS** >ZEL

**ZEMINDAR** same as >ZAMINDAR

**ZEMINDARI** >ZEMINDAR

**ZEMINDARS** >ZEMINDAR

**ZEMINDARY** n jurisdiction of a zemindar

**ZEMSTVA** >ZEMSTVO

**ZEMSTVO** n (in tsarist Russia) an elective provincial or district council established in most provinces of Russia by Alexander II in 1864 as part of his reform policy

**ZEMSTVOS** >ZEMSTVO

**ZENAIDA** n dove

**ZENAIDAS** >ZENAIDA

**ZENANA** n (in the East, esp in Muslim and Hindu homes) part of a house reserved for the women and girls of a household

**ZENANAS** >ZENANA

**ZENDIK** n unbeliever or heretic

**ZENDIKS** >ZENDIK

**ZENITH** n highest point of success or power

**ZENITHAL** >ZENITH

**ZENITHS** >ZENITH

**ZEOLITE** n any of a large group of glassy secondary minerals

**ZEOLITES** >ZEOLITE

**ZEOLITIC** >ZEOLITE

**ZEP** n type of long sandwich

**ZEPHYR** n soft gentle breeze

**ZEPHYRS** >ZEPHYR

**ZEPPELIN** n large cylindrical airship

**ZEPPELINS** >ZEPPELIN

**ZEPPOLE** n Italian fritter

**ZEPPOLES** >ZEPPOLE

**ZEPPOLI** >ZEPPOLE

**ZEPS** >ZEP

**ZERDA** n fennec

**ZERDAS** >ZERDA

**ZEREBA** same as >ZAREBA

**ZEREBAS** >ZEREBA

**ZERIBA** same as >ZAREBA

**ZERIBAS** >ZERIBA

**ZERK** n grease fitting

**ZERKS** >ZERK

**ZERO** n (symbol representing) the number 0 ▷ adj having no measurable quantity or size ▷ vb adjust (an instrument or scale) so as to read zero ▷ determiner no (thing) at all

**ZEROED** >ZERO

**ZEROES** >ZERO

**ZEROING** >ZERO

**ZEROS** >ZERO

**ZEROTH** adj denoting a term in a series that precedes the term otherwise regarded as the first term

**ZERUMBET** n plant stem used as stimulant and condiment

**ZERUMBETS** >ZERUMBET

**ZEST** n enjoyment or excitement ▷ vb give flavour, interest, or piquancy to

**ZESTED** >ZEST

**ZESTER** n kitchen utensil used to scrape fine shreds of peel from citrus fruits

**ZESTERS** >ZESTER

**ZESTFUL** >ZEST

**ZESTFULLY** >ZEST

**ZESTIER** >ZEST

**ZESTIEST** >ZEST

**ZESTILY** >ZEST

**ZESTING** >ZEST

**ZESTLESS** >ZEST

**ZESTS** >ZEST

**ZESTY** >ZEST

**ZETA** n sixth letter in the Greek alphabet, a consonant, transliterated as z

**ZETAS** >ZETA

**ZETETIC** adj proceeding by inquiry ▷ n investigation

**ZETETICS** >ZETETIC

**ZETTABYTE** n $10^{21}$ or $2^{70}$ bytes

**ZEUGMA** n figure of speech in which a word is used to modify or govern two or more words although appropriate to only one of them or making a different sense with each, as in the sentence Mr Pickwick took his hat and his leave (Charles Dickens)

ZEUGMAS >ZEUGMA
ZEUGMATIC >ZEUGMA
ZEUXITE n ferriferous mineral
ZEUXITES >ZEUXITE
ZEX n tool for cutting roofing slate
ZEXES >ZEX
ZEZE n stringed musical instrument
ZEZES >ZEZE
ZHO same as >ZO
ZHOMO n female zho
ZHOMOS >ZHOMO
ZHOS >ZHO
ZIBELINE n sable or the fur of this animal ▷ adj of, relating to, or resembling a sable
ZIBELINES >ZIBELINE
ZIBELLINE same as >ZIBELINE
ZIBET n large civet of S and SE Asia, having tawny fur marked with black spots and stripes
ZIBETH same as >ZIBET
ZIBETHS >ZIBETH
ZIFF n beard
ZIFFIUS n sea monster
ZIFFIUSES >ZIFFIUS
ZIFFS >ZIFF
ZIG same as >ZAG
ZIGAN n gypsy
ZIGANKA n Russian dance
ZIGANKAS >ZIGANKA
ZIGANS >ZIGAN
ZIGGED >ZIG
ZIGGING >ZIG
ZIGGURAT n (in ancient Mesopotamia) a temple in the shape of a pyramid
ZIGGURATS >ZIGGURAT
ZIGS >ZIG
ZIGZAG n line or course having sharp turns in alternating directions ▷ vb move in a zigzag ▷ adj formed in or proceeding in a zigzag ▷ adv in a zigzag manner
ZIGZAGGED >ZIGZAG
ZIGZAGGER >ZIGZAG
ZIGZAGGY >ZIGZAG
ZIGZAGS >ZIGZAG
ZIKKURAT same as >ZIGGURAT
ZIKKURATS >ZIKKURAT
ZIKURAT same as >ZIGGURAT
ZIKURATS >ZIKURAT
ZILA n administrative district in India
ZILAS >ZILA
ZILCH n nothing
ZILCHES >ZILCH
ZILL n finger cymbal
ZILLA same as >ZILA
ZILLAH same as >ZILA
ZILLAHS >ZILLAH
ZILLAS >ZILLA
ZILLION n extremely large but unspecified number

ZILLIONS >ZILLION
ZILLIONTH >ZILLION
ZILLS >ZILL
ZIMB same as >ZEBUB
ZIMBI n cowrie shell used as money
ZIMBIS >ZIMBI
ZIMBS >ZIMB
ZIMMER n tradename for a kind of walking frame
ZIMMERS >ZIMMER
ZIMOCCA n bath sponge
ZIMOCCAS >ZIMOCCA
ZIN short form of >ZINFANDEL
ZINC n bluish-white metallic element used in alloys and to coat metal ▷ vb coat with zinc
ZINCATE n any of a class of salts derived from the amphoteric hydroxide of zinc
ZINCATES >ZINCATE
ZINCED >ZINC
ZINCIC >ZINC
ZINCIER >ZINC
ZINCIEST >ZINC
ZINCIFIED >ZINCIFY
ZINCIFIES >ZINCIFY
ZINCIFY vb coat with zinc
ZINCING >ZINC
ZINCITE n red or yellow mineral consisting of zinc oxide in hexagonal crystalline form
ZINCITES >ZINCITE
ZINCKED >ZINC
ZINCKIER >ZINC
ZINCKIEST >ZINC
ZINCKIFY same as >ZINCIFY
ZINCKING >ZINC
ZINCKY >ZINC
ZINCO n printing plate made from zincography
ZINCODE n positive electrode
ZINCODES >ZINCODE
ZINCOID >ZINC
ZINCOS >ZINCO
ZINCOUS >ZINC
ZINCS >ZINC
ZINCY >ZINC
ZINDABAD vb long live: used as part of a slogan in India, Pakistan, etc
ZINE n magazine or fanzine
ZINEB n organic insecticide
ZINEBS >ZINEB
ZINES >ZINE
ZINFANDEL n type of Californian wine
ZING n quality in something that makes it lively or interesting ▷ vb make or move with or as if with a high-pitched buzzing sound
ZINGANI >ZINGANO
ZINGANO n gypsy
ZINGARA same as >ZINGARO
ZINGARE >ZINGARA

ZINGARI >ZINGARO
ZINGARO n Italian Gypsy
ZINGED >ZING
ZINGEL n small freshwater perch
ZINGELS >ZINGEL
ZINGER >ZING
ZINGERS >ZING
ZINGIBER n ginger plant
ZINGIBERS >ZINGIBER
ZINGIER >ZINGY
ZINGIEST >ZINGY
ZINGING >ZING
ZINGS >ZING
ZINGY adj vibrant
ZINKE n cornett
ZINKED >ZINC
ZINKENITE n steel-grey metallic mineral consisting of a sulphide of lead and antimony
ZINKES >ZINKE
ZINKIER >ZINC
ZINKIEST >ZINC
ZINKIFIED >ZINCIFY
ZINKIFIES >ZINKIFY
ZINKIFY vb coat with zinc
ZINKING >ZINC
ZINKY >ZINC
ZINNIA n plant of tropical and subtropical America, with solitary heads of brightly coloured flowers
ZINNIAS >ZINNIA
ZINS >ZIN
ZIP same as >ZIPPER
ZIPLESS >ZIP
ZIPLOCK adj fastened with interlocking plastic strips
ZIPPED >ZIP
ZIPPER n fastening device operating by means of two parallel rows of metal or plastic teeth on either side of a closure that are interlocked by a sliding tab ▷ vb fasten with a zipper
ZIPPERED adj provided or fastened with a zip
ZIPPERING >ZIPPER
ZIPPERS >ZIPPER
ZIPPIER >ZIPPY
ZIPPIEST >ZIPPY
ZIPPING >ZIP
ZIPPO n nothing
ZIPPOS >ZIPPO
ZIPPY adj full of energy
ZIPS >ZIP
ZIPTOP adj (of a bag) closed with a zip
ZIRAM n industrial fungicide
ZIRAMS >ZIRAM
ZIRCALLOY n alloy of zirconium containing small amounts of tin, chromium, and nickel. It is used in pressurized-water reactors
ZIRCALOY same as >ZIRCALLOY
ZIRCALOYS >ZIRCALOY
ZIRCON n mineral used as a gemstone and in industry

ZIRCONIA n white oxide of zirconium, used as a pigment for paints, a catalyst, and an abrasive
ZIRCONIAS >ZIRCONIA
ZIRCONIC >ZIRCONIUM
ZIRCONIUM n greyish-white metallic element that is resistant to corrosion
ZIRCONS >ZIRCON
ZIT n spot or pimple
ZITE same as >ZITI
ZITHER n musical instrument consisting of strings stretched over a flat box and plucked to produce musical notes
ZITHERIST >ZITHER
ZITHERN same as >ZITHER
ZITHERNS >ZITHER
ZITHERS >ZITHER
ZITI n type of pasta
ZITIS >ZITI
ZITS >ZIT
ZIZ same as >ZIZZ
ZIZANIA n aquatic grass
ZIZANIAS >ZIZANIA
ZIZEL n chipmunk
ZIZELS >ZIZEL
ZIZIT same as >ZIZITH
ZIZITH variant spelling of >TSITSITH
ZIZYPHUS n jujube tree
ZIZZ n short sleep ▷ vb take a short sleep, snooze
ZIZZED >ZIZZ
ZIZZES >ZIZZ
ZIZZING >ZIZZ
ZIZZLE vb sizzle
ZIZZLED >ZIZZLE
ZIZZLES >ZIZZLE
ZIZZLING >ZIZZLE
ZLOTE >ZLOTY
ZLOTIES >ZLOTY
ZLOTY n monetary unit of Poland
ZLOTYCH same as >ZLOTY
ZLOTYS >ZLOTY
ZO n Tibetan breed of cattle, developed by crossing the yak with common cattle
ZOA >ZOON
ZOAEA same as >ZOEA
ZOAEAE >ZOAEA
ZOAEAS >ZOAEA
ZOARIA >ZOARIUM
ZOARIAL >ZOARIUM
ZOARIUM n colony of zooids
ZOBO same as >ZO
ZOBOS >ZOBO
ZOBU same as >ZO
ZOBUS >ZOBU
ZOCALO n plaza in Mexico
ZOCALOS >ZOCALO
ZOCCO n plinth
ZOCCOLO same as >ZOCCO
ZOCCOLOS >ZOCCOLO
ZOCCOS >ZOCCO
ZODIAC n imaginary belt in the sky within which the sun, moon, and planets appear to move,

divided into twelve equal areas, called signs of the zodiac, each named after a constellation

**ZODIACAL** >ZODIAC

**ZODIACS** >ZODIAC

**ZOEA** n free-swimming larva of a crab or related crustacean, which has well-developed abdominal appendages and may bear one or more spines

**ZOEAE** >ZOEA

**ZOEAL** >ZOEA

**ZOEAS** >ZOAEA

**ZOECHROME** same as >ZOETROPE

**ZOECIA** >ZOECIUM

**ZOECIUM** same as >ZOOECIUM

**ZOEFORM** >ZOEA

**ZOETIC** adj pertaining to life

**ZOETROPE** n cylinder-shaped toy with a sequence of pictures on its inner surface which, when viewed through the vertical slits spaced regularly around it while the toy is rotated, produce an illusion of animation

**ZOETROPES** >ZOETROPE

**ZOETROPIC** >ZOETROPE

**ZOFTIG** adj ripe or curvaceous

**ZOIATRIA** n veterinary surgery

**ZOIATRIAS** >ZOIATRIA

**ZOIATRICS** n veterinary surgery

**ZOIC** adj relating to or having animal life

**ZOISITE** n grey, brown, or pink mineral

**ZOISITES** >ZOISITE

**ZOISM** n belief in magical animal powers

**ZOISMS** >ZOISM

**ZOIST** >ZOISM

**ZOISTS** >ZOISM

**ZOL** n South African slang for a cannabis cigarette

**ZOLS** >ZOL

**ZOMBI** same as >ZOMBIE

**ZOMBIE** n person who appears to be lifeless, apathetic, or totally lacking in independent judgment

**ZOMBIES** >ZOMBIE

**ZOMBIFIED** >ZOMBIFY

**ZOMBIFIES** >ZOMBIFY

**ZOMBIFY** vb turn into a zombie

**ZOMBIISM** >ZOMBIE

**ZOMBIISMS** >ZOMBIE

**ZOMBIS** >ZOMBI

**ZOMBORUK** n small swivel-mounted cannon

**ZOMBORUKS** >ZOMBORUK

**ZONA** n zone or belt

**ZONAE** >ZONA

**ZONAL** adj of, relating to, or of the nature of a zone

**ZONALLY** >ZONAL

**ZONARY** same as >ZONAL

**ZONATE** adj marked with, divided into, or arranged in zones

**ZONATED** same as >ZONATE

**ZONATION** n arrangement in zones

**ZONATIONS** >ZONATION

**ZONDA** n South American wind

**ZONDAS** >ZONDA

**ZONE** n area with particular features or properties ▷ vb divide into zones

**ZONED** >ZONE

**ZONELESS** >ZONE

**ZONER** n something which divides other things into zones

**ZONERS** >ZONER

**ZONES** >ZONE

**ZONETIME** n standard time of the time zone in which a ship is located at sea, each zone extending 7½° to each side of a meridian

**ZONETIMES** >ZONETIME

**ZONING** >ZONE

**ZONINGS** >ZONE

**ZONK** vb strike resoundingly

**ZONKED** adj highly intoxicated with drugs or alcohol

**ZONKING** >ZONK

**ZONKS** >ZONK

**ZONOID** adj resembling a zone

**ZONULA** n small zone or belt

**ZONULAE** >ZONULA

**ZONULAR** >ZONULA

**ZONULAS** >ZONULA

**ZONULE** n small zone, band, or area

**ZONULES** >ZONULE

**ZONULET** n small belt

**ZONULETS** >ZONULET

**ZONURE** n lizard with ringed tail

**ZONURES** >ZONURE

**ZOO** n place where live animals are kept for show

**ZOOBIOTIC** adj parasitic on or living in association with an animal

**ZOOBLAST** n animal cell

**ZOOBLASTS** >ZOOBLAST

**ZOOCHORE** n plant with the spores or seeds dispersed by animals

**ZOOCHORES** >ZOOCHORE

**ZOOCHORY** >ZOOCHORE

**ZOOCYTIA** >ZOOCYTIUM

**ZOOCYTIUM** n outer sheath of some social infusorians

**ZOOEA** same as >ZOEA

**ZOOEAE** >ZOOEA

**ZOOEAL** >ZOOEA

**ZOOEAS** >ZOOEA

**ZOOECIA** >ZOOECIUM

**ZOOECIUM** n part of a polyzoan colony that

houses the feeding zooids

**ZOOEY** >ZOO

**ZOOGAMETE** n gamete that can move independently

**ZOOGAMIES** >ZOOGAMY

**ZOOGAMOUS** >ZOOGAMY

**ZOOGAMY** n sexual reproduction in animals

**ZOOGENIC** adj produced from animals

**ZOOGENIES** >ZOOGENY

**ZOOGENOUS** same as >ZOOGENIC

**ZOOGENY** n doctrine of formation of animals

**ZOOGLEA** same as >ZOOGLOEA

**ZOOGLEAE** >ZOOGLEA

**ZOOGLEAL** >ZOOGLEA

**ZOOGLEAS** >ZOOGLEA

**ZOOGLOEA** n mass of bacteria adhering together by a jelly-like substance derived from their cell walls

**ZOOGLOEAE** >ZOOGLOEA

**ZOOGLOEAL** >ZOOGLOEA

**ZOOGLOEAS** >ZOOGLOEA

**ZOOGLOEIC** >ZOOGLOEA

**ZOOGONIES** >ZOOGONY

**ZOOGONOUS** >ZOOGONY

**ZOOGONY** same as >ZOOGENY

**ZOOGRAFT** n animal tissue grafted onto a human body

**ZOOGRAFTS** >ZOOGRAFT

**ZOOGRAPHY** n branch of zoology concerned with the description of animals

**ZOOID** n any independent animal body, such as an individual of a coral colony

**ZOOIDAL** >ZOOID

**ZOOIDS** >ZOOID

**ZOOIER** >ZOO

**ZOOIEST** >ZOO

**ZOOKEEPER** n person who cares for animals in a zoo

**ZOOKS** short form of >GADZOOKS

**ZOOLATER** >ZOOLATRY

**ZOOLATERS** >ZOOLATRY

**ZOOLATRIA** same as >ZOOLATRY

**ZOOLATRY** n (esp in ancient or primitive religions) the worship of animals as the incarnations of certain deities, symbols of particular qualities or natural forces, etc

**ZOOLITE** n fossilized animal

**ZOOLITES** >ZOOLITE

**ZOOLITH** n fossilized animal

**ZOOLITHIC** >ZOOLITH

**ZOOLITHS** >ZOOLITH

**ZOOLITIC** >ZOOLITE

**ZOOLOGIC** >ZOOLOGY

**ZOOLOGIES** >ZOOLOGY

**ZOOLOGIST** >ZOOLOGY

**ZOOLOGY** n study of

animals

**ZOOM** vb move or rise very rapidly ▷ n sound or act of zooming

**ZOOMANCY** n divination through observing the actions of animals

**ZOOMANIA** n extreme or excessive devotion to animals

**ZOOMANIAS** >ZOOMANIA

**ZOOMANTIC** >ZOOMANCY

**ZOOMED** >ZOOM

**ZOOMETRIC** >ZOOMETRY

**ZOOMETRY** n branch of zoology concerned with the relative length or size of the different parts of an animal or animals

**ZOOMING** >ZOOM

**ZOOMORPH** n representation of an animal form

**ZOOMORPHS** >ZOOMORPH

**ZOOMORPHY** >ZOOMORPH

**ZOOMS** >ZOOM

**ZOON** less common term for >ZOOID ▷ vb zoom

**ZOONAL** >ZOON

**ZOONED** >ZOON

**ZOONIC** adj concerning animals

**ZOONING** >ZOON

**ZOONITE** n segment of an articulated animal

**ZOONITES** >ZOONITE

**ZOONITIC** >ZOONITE

**ZOONOMIA** same as >ZOONOMY

**ZOONOMIAS** >ZOONOMIA

**ZOONOMIC** >ZOONOMY

**ZOONOMIES** >ZOONOMY

**ZOONOMIST** >ZOONOMY

**ZOONOMY** n science of animal life

**ZOONOSES** >ZOONOSIS

**ZOONOSIS** n any infection or disease that is transmitted to man from lower vertebrates

**ZOONOTIC** >ZOONOSIS

**ZOONS** >ZOON

**ZOOPATHY** n science of animal diseases

**ZOOPERAL** >ZOOPERY

**ZOOPERIES** >ZOOPERY

**ZOOPERIST** >ZOOPERY

**ZOOPERY** n experimentation on animals

**ZOOPHAGAN** n carnivore

**ZOOPHAGY** n eating other animals

**ZOOPHILE** n person who is devoted to animals and their protection from practices such as vivisection

**ZOOPHILES** >ZOOPHILE

**ZOOPHILIA** n morbid condition in which a person has a sexual attraction to animals

**ZOOPHILIC** >ZOOPHILE

**ZOOPHILY** same

*as* >ZOOPHILIA
**ZOOPHOBE** *n* >ZOOPHOBIA
**ZOOPHOBES** >ZOOPHOBIA
**ZOOPHOBIA** *n* unusual or morbid dread of animals
**ZOOPHORI** >ZOOPHORUS
**ZOOPHORIC** >ZOOPHORUS
**ZOOPHORUS** *n* frieze with animal figures
**ZOOPHYTE** *n* any animal resembling a plant, such as a sea anemone
**ZOOPHYTES** >ZOOPHYTE
**ZOOPHYTIC** >ZOOPHYTE
**ZOOPLASTY** *n* surgical transplantation to man of animal tissues
**ZOOS** >ZOO
**ZOOSCOPIC** >ZOOSCOPY
**ZOOSCOPY** *n* condition causing hallucinations of animals
**ZOOSPERM** *n* any of the male reproductive cells released in the semen during ejaculation
**ZOOSPERMS** >ZOOSPERM
**ZOOSPORE** *n* asexual spore of some algae and fungi that moves by means of flagella
**ZOOSPORES** >ZOOSPORE
**ZOOSPORIC** >ZOOSPORE
**ZOOSTEROL** *n* any of a group of animal sterols, such as cholesterol
**ZOOT** as in *zoot suit* man's suit consisting of baggy trousers with tapered bottoms and a long jacket with wide padded shoulders
**ZOOTAXIES** >ZOOTAXY
**ZOOTAXY** *n* science of the classification of animals
**ZOOTECHNY** *n* science of breeding animals
**ZOOTHECIA** *n* outer layers of certain protozoans
**ZOOTHEISM** *n* treatment of an animal as a god
**ZOOTHOME** *n* group of zooids
**ZOOTHOMES** >ZOOTHOME
**ZOOTIER** >ZOOTY
**ZOOTIEST** >ZOOTY
**ZOOTOMIC** >ZOOTOMY
**ZOOTOMIES** >ZOOTOMY
**ZOOTOMIST** >ZOOTOMY
**ZOOTOMY** *n* branch of zoology concerned with the dissection and anatomy of animals
**ZOOTOXIC** >ZOOTOXIN
**ZOOTOXIN** *n* toxin, such as snake venom, that is produced by an animal
**ZOOTOXINS** >ZOOTOXIN
**ZOOTROPE** *same as* >ZOETROPE
**ZOOTROPES** >ZOOTROPE
**ZOOTROPHY** *n* nourishment of animals
**ZOOTY** *adj* showy

**ZOOTYPE** *n* animal figure used as a symbol
**ZOOTYPES** >ZOOTYPE
**ZOOTYPIC** >ZOOTYPE
**ZOOZOO** *n* wood pigeon
**ZOOZOOS** >ZOOZOO
**ZOPILOTE** *n* small American vulture
**ZOPILOTES** >ZOPILOTE
**ZOPPA** *adj* syncopated
**ZOPPO** *same as* >ZOPPA
**ZORBING** *n* activity of travelling downhill inside a large air-cushioned hollow ball
**ZORBINGS** >ZORBING
**ZORBONAUT** *n* person who engages in the activity of zorbing
**ZORGITE** *n* copper-lead selenide
**ZORGITES** >ZORGITE
**ZORI** *n* Japanese sandal
**ZORIL** *same as* >ZORILLA
**ZORILLA** *n* skunk-like African musteline mammal having a long black-and-white coat
**ZORILLAS** >ZORILLA
**ZORILLE** *same as* >ZORILLA
**ZORILLES** >ZORILLE
**ZORILLO** *same as* >ZORILLE
**ZORILLOS** >ZORILLO
**ZORILS** >ZORIL
**ZORINO** *n* skunk fur
**ZORINOS** >ZORINO
**ZORIS** >ZORI
**ZORRO** *n* hoary fox
**ZORROS** >ZORRO
**ZOS** >ZO
**ZOSTER** *n* shingles; herpes zoster
**ZOSTERS** >ZOSTER
**ZOUAVE** *n* (formerly) member of a body of French infantry composed of Algerian recruits
**ZOUAVES** >ZOUAVE
**ZOUK** *n* style of dance music that combines African and Latin American rhythms and uses electronic instruments and modern studio technology
**ZOUKS** >ZOUK
**ZOUNDS** *interj* mild oath indicating surprise or indignation
**ZOWIE** *interj* expression of pleasurable surprise
**ZOYSIA** *n* any creeping perennial grass of the genus *Zoysia*, of warm dry regions, having short stiffly pointed leaves: often used for lawns
**ZOYSIAS** >ZOYSIA
**ZUCCHETTI** >ZUCCHETTO
**ZUCCHETTO** *n* small round skullcap worn by clergymen and varying in colour according to the rank of the wearer
**ZUCCHINI** *n* courgette

**ZUCCHINIS** >ZUCCHINI
**ZUCHETTA** *same*
*as* >ZUCCHETTO
**ZUCHETTAS** >ZUCHETTA
**ZUCHETTO** *same*
*as* >ZUCCHETTO
**ZUCHETTOS** >ZUCHETTO
**ZUFFOLI** >ZUFFOLO
**ZUFFOLO** *same as* >ZUFOLO
**ZUFOLI** >ZUFOLO
**ZUFOLO** *n* small flute
**ZUGZWANG** *n* (in chess) position in which one player can move only with loss or severe disadvantage ▷ *vb* manoeuvre (one's opponent) into a zugzwang
**ZUGZWANGS** >ZUGZWANG
**ZULU** *n* (in the NATO phonetic alphabet) used to represent z
**ZULUS** >ZULU
**ZUMBOORUK** *n* small swivel-mounted cannon
**ZUPA** *n* confederation of Serbian villages
**ZUPAN** *n* head of a zupa
**ZUPANS** >ZUPAN
**ZUPAS** >ZUPA
**ZURF** *same as* >ZARF
**ZURFS** >ZURF
**ZUZ** *n* ancient Hebrew silver coin
**ZUZIM** >ZUZ
**ZWIEBACK** *n* small type of rusk, which has been baked first as a loaf, then sliced and toasted, usually bought ready-made
**ZWIEBACKS** >ZWIEBACK
**ZYDECO** *n* type of Black Cajun music
**ZYDECOS** >ZYDECO
**ZYGA** >ZYGON
**ZYGAENID** *adj* of the burnet moth genus
**ZYGAENOID** *same as* >ZYGAENID
**ZYGAL** >ZYGON
**ZYGANTRA** >ZYGANTRUM
**ZYGANTRUM** *n* vertebral articulation in snakes and some lizards
**ZYGOCACTI** *n* branching cactuses
**ZYGODONT** *adj* possessing paired molar cusps
**ZYGOID** *same as* >DIPLOID
**ZYGOMA** *n* slender arch of bone that forms a bridge between the cheekbone and the temporal bone on each side of the skull of mammals
**ZYGOMAS** >ZYGOMA
**ZYGOMATA** >ZYGOMA
**ZYGOMATIC** *adj* of or relating to the zygoma
**ZYGON** *n* brain fissure
**ZYGOPHYTE** *n* plant that reproduces by means of zygospores

**ZYGOSE** >ZYGOSIS
**ZYGOSES** >ZYGOSIS
**ZYGOSIS** *n* (in bacteria) the direct transfer of DNA between two cells that are temporarily joined
**ZYGOSITY** >ZYGOSIS
**ZYGOSPERM** *same*
*as* >ZYGOSPORE
**ZYGOSPORE** *n* thick-walled sexual spore formed from the zygote of some fungi and algae
**ZYGOTE** *n* fertilized egg cell
**ZYGOTENE** *n* second stage of the prophase of meiosis, during which homologous chromosomes become associated in pairs (bivalents)
**ZYGOTENES** >ZYGOTENE
**ZYGOTES** >ZYGOTE
**ZYGOTIC** >ZYGOTE
**ZYLONITE** *variant spelling of* >XYLONITE
**ZYLONITES** >ZYLONITE
**ZYMASE** *n* mixture of enzymes that is obtained as an extract from yeast and ferments sugars
**ZYMASES** >ZYMASE
**ZYME** *n* ferment
**ZYMES** >ZYME
**ZYMIC** >ZYME
**ZYMITE** *n* priest who uses leavened bread during communion
**ZYMITES** >ZYMITE
**ZYMOGEN** *n* any of a group of compounds that are inactive precursors of enzymes and are activated by a kinase
**ZYMOGENE** *same*
*as* >ZYMOGEN
**ZYMOGENES** >ZYMOGENE
**ZYMOGENIC** *adj* of, or relating to a zymogen
**ZYMOGENS** >ZYMOGEN
**ZYMOGRAM** *n* band of electrophoretic medium showing a pattern of enzymes following electrophoresis
**ZYMOGRAMS** >ZYMOGRAM
**ZYMOID** *adj* relating to a ferment
**ZYMOLOGIC** >ZYMOLOGY
**ZYMOLOGY** *n* chemistry of fermentation
**ZYMOLYSES** >ZYMOLYSIS
**ZYMOLYSIS** *n* process of fermentation
**ZYMOLYTIC** >ZYMOLYSIS
**ZYMOME** *n* glutinous substance that is insoluble in alcohol
**ZYMOMES** >ZYMOME
**ZYMOMETER** *n* instrument for estimating the degree of fermentation
**ZYMOSAN** *n* insoluble carbohydrate found in yeast

**ZYMOSANS** > ZYMOSAN
**ZYMOSES** > ZYMOSIS
**ZYMOSIS** *same*
  *as* > ZYMOLYSIS
**ZYMOTIC** *adj* of, relating to,
  or causing fermentation
  ▷ *n* disease
**ZYMOTICS** > ZYMOTIC
**ZYMURGIES** > ZYMURGY
**ZYMURGY** *n* branch of
  chemistry concerned with
  fermentation processes in
  brewing, etc
**ZYTHUM** *n* Ancient Egyptian
  beer
**ZYTHUMS** > ZYTHUM
**ZYZZYVA** *n* American
  weevil
**ZYZZYVAS** > ZYZZYVA
**ZZZ** *n* informal word for
  sleep
**ZZZS** > ZZZ